KEY TO SPECIAL REFERENCE MATERIALS

abbreviations	Entered individually in alphabetical order beginning on page 1536.
alphabets	Comparative table at **alphabet.**
anatomy	Illustration at the relevant entry; for example, see **eye.**
biographical names	Entered in alphabetical order beginning on page 1409.
calendars	Comparative table at **calendar.**
chemical elements	Periodic table at **element.**
color	Diagrams and an explanation of the Dictionary's color system at **color.**
currency	Comparative table at **currency.**
geographic names	Entered individually in alphabetical order beginning on page 1466.
geologic time	Table at **geology.**
grammar	Refer to the relevant entry; for example, see **split infinitive.**
letter history	Full-page, illustrated orthographic history introducing each letter of the alphabet.
manual alphabet	Illustration at the entry.
maps	Locator maps at the geographic entries for most countries including **United States of America** and **Canada.**
Morse code	Table at the entry.
proofreaders' marks	Table at **proofread.**
Roman numerals	Table at **Roman numeral.**
signs and symbols	Table at **symbol.**
subatomic particles	Table at **particle.**
synonyms	Refer to the relevant entry; for example, see **flock**[1].
taxonomy	Taxonomic table of living organisms at **taxonomy.**
usage	Usage notes appear with the relevant entries; for example, **ain't, like**[2].
weights and measures	Table of common and scientific units at **measurement.**

Second College Edition

The American Heritage Dictionary

The Americar

Second College Edition

Heritage Dictionary

Houghton Mifflin Company BOSTON

Words that are believed to be registered trademarks have been checked with authoritative sources. No investigation has been made of common-law trademark rights in any word, because such investigation is impracticable. Words that are known to have current registrations are shown with an initial capital and are also identified as trademarks. The inclusion of any word in this Dictionary is not, however, an expression of the Publisher's opinion as to whether or not it is subject to proprietary rights. Indeed, no definition in this Dictionary is to be regarded as affecting the validity of any trademark.

All correspondence and inquiries should be directed to
Reference Division, Houghton Mifflin Company
One Beacon Street, Boston, MA 02108

Library of Congress Cataloging in Publication Data
Main entry under title:
American Heritage dictionary.
Rev. ed. of: American Heritage dictionary of the English language. New college ed. c1976.
1. English language—Dictionaries. I. Morris, William, 1913–
PE1625.A54 1982 423 82-9346
ISBN 0-395-32943-4
ISBN 0-395-32944-2 (thumb index)
ISBN 0-395-33959-6 (deluxe edition)

Manufactured in the United States of America

CONTENTS

INTRODUCTION

The publication of *The American Heritage Dictionary* in 1969 was a major event in the history of American lexicography. The goal of its editors, expressed by William Morris, was to create a new dictionary that would not only faithfully record our language but also add the sensible dimension of guidance toward grace and precision in the use of our language, which intelligent people seek in a dictionary. The overwhelming critical and popular success of the Dictionary has been testimony to the validity and achievement of that goal.

It is with pride in this tradition that we now offer the *Second College Edition,* the first complete revision of *The American Heritage Dictionary*. It is a book demanded by the profound changes and developments in language that have occurred in the last decade. A major concern has always been to provide users the information they need about language in an accessible and understandable way. This concern has guided the preparation of the new edition.

Like its predecessor, the *Second College Edition* covers the vocabulary ranging from the language of Shakespeare to the idiom of the present day. In order to present the vocabulary required by the well-informed, contemporary adult, the basic lexicon has been thoroughly reviewed, revised, and updated. Language is continually changing, continually being enriched from many sources. Dramatic sociological, cultural, and political developments have had a stunning impact on our language. Politics, business, various subcultures, and the media have contributed to a new general vocabulary. Thus, more than 10,000 new general vocabulary words and meanings have been carefully selected and meticulously defined by our permanent lexicographic staff and outside authorities from a variety of disciplines.

In recognition of the increased role played by technology and science in daily life, the *Second College Edition* also includes more than 5,000 new scientific and technical terms. The field of computer science exemplifies the unprecedented growth we have witnessed in technology and the sciences in recent years; growth that has produced vast stores of new words and meanings.

The soul of a dictionary, however, is the quality of its definitions. An objective of the *Second College Edition* is to provide the user with understanding, comprehension, and appreciation of the language in a readable manner. Therefore, we have endeavored to present the most prevalent, contemporary sense or meaning of a word first, with the other shades of meaning following logically from this current, central concept. This departure from traditional lexicography, wherein senses are presented chronologically with the oldest meaning first and the most current last, is unique to *The American Heritage Dictionary* and has been highly regarded by its users. Praised for their clarity and precision, the definitions are written in concise, lucid prose and avoid the dictionary shorthand that makes most dictionaries forbidding and confusing. With the exception of one abbreviation (*esp.* for *especially*) the new edition continues the policy of spelling out all words used in defining. The generous use of illustrative examples to clarify meanings and idiomatic usages has been expanded, drawing from the works of those contemporary writers who use the language in an intelligent, expressive, and effective way.

The appreciation of a word is not complete without an understanding of its history. The etymologies in the *Second College Edition* have all been reviewed by both special consultants and our etymological staff. Every effort has been made to provide a complete history of a word from earliest times. A few easily understood abbreviations have been introduced to allow for the inclusion of essential information, and the explanation of the obvious has been minimized in order to allow greater attention to the difficult and the obscure.

Certain changes have been made in the pronunciation system to improve the simplicity and clarity of the pronunciations. American speech takes many forms; the *Second College Edition* provides for each word one or more pronunciations expressed in symbols familiar to the reader untrained in phonetics.

In order to furnish the guidance regarded as an essential responsibility of a good dictionary, we have employed usage-context labels such as *Slang, Nonstandard,* and *Regional.* In addition, in an effort to provide practical solutions to usage questions, we have continued to call upon the widely celebrated *American Heritage Dictionary* Usage Panel. The Panel is composed of outstanding writers, speakers, and thinkers. After careful tabulation and analysis of the Panel's responses to usage questions, our special usage consultants and editors have prepared over 400 new usage notes for the *Second College Edition.* As a consequence, the *Second College Edition* can make the same claim as its predecessor: this Dictionary is "more precisely descriptive, in terms of current usage levels, than any heretofore published."

New features of the *Second College Edition* include separate biographical and geographical sections following the dictionary of general vocabulary. Coverage has been greatly expanded with the addition of approximately 5,000 new entries in each of these areas. The entries are presented in a new format that is liberally illustrated. Other new features include a section for abbreviations, current information on colleges and universities, and a concise style manual.

It will be obvious at a glance that the *Second College Edition* maintains the distinctive graphic design of the original edition. Using recent advances in typography and design, we have sought to produce a dictionary that is unmatched in attractiveness and ease of use. The page, with its readable type and comfortable margins, was designed to invite reading. The inclusion of several thousand illustrations, both line drawings and photographs, is intended to enhance understanding of the subjects they illustrate. The *Second College Edition* contains more than 3,000 new photographs, distinguishing it from any other college-level dictionary. Our aim has been to create a dictionary that engages the reader and provides more comprehensive information than would be possible through conventional design.

We have had the enthusiastic cooperation of many distinguished linguists and writers, several of whom have contributed articles on their areas of special interest. Professor Geoffrey Nunberg presents an insightful and witty perspective on the historical development of the controversy involving usage. In an effort to provide the contemporary views on both sides of this issue, articles by Professor Dwight Bolinger and Mr. William F. Buckley, Jr., are juxtaposed in the form of a debate. Professor Lee Pederson offers a fascinating and informative account of the many regional and social dialects that characterize American English as it is spoken today. Finally, Professor Henry Kučera discusses the mathematical properties and informational structure of language that facilitate its use as a communication code.

A work of the magnitude of the *Second College Edition* requires the cooperation of many hands and minds. We would like to thank the members of the Usage Panel for their generous contribution of time and informed opinions. Thanks, too, are due to our many consultants and advisers in the various scholarly, scientific, and technological disciplines. We also extend our gratitude and appreciation to the many editorial staff associates involved in the day-to-day tasks of revising the Dictionary. We are also grateful to the scores of readers who have forwarded their comments and suggestions, many of which have been incorporated into this new edition. Finally, we wish to acknowledge our debt to

William Morris and the other editors of the First Edition of this book. Without their pioneering work, this new edition clearly would not have been possible.

The editors of the *Second College Edition* have endeavored to produce the most useful, usable, and attractive dictionary currently available. It is our hope that readers will find this Dictionary a reliable and friendly guide to our language's treasury of words—the tools of communication and understanding.

STAFF

Margery S. Berube
DIRECTOR OF EDITORIAL OPERATIONS

Diane J. Neely
TRAFFIC COORDINATOR

Pamela B. DeVinne
PROJECT EDITOR

DEFINITIONS
Mark Boyer, *Editor*
Pamela B. DeVinne, *Editor*
Dolores R. Harris, *Editor*
Anne H. Soukhanov, *Editor*
Anne D. Steinhardt, *Editor*

Bruce Bohle
Lois P. Borup
Elaine H. Brix
Bruce L. Cohen
Eden Eskin
Walter M. Havighurst
Sally Hehir
Ernest S. Hildebrand, Jr.
Kerry W. Metz
David E. Milley
Trudy Nelson
Deborah Posner
James E. Shea
Andrea Denson Wechsler

PRONUNCIATIONS
Carol Chapin
Kathleen M. Kurowski
Rima McKinzey
Ramona Michaelis

SPECIAL CONSULTANTS
Fernando de Mello Vianna

Etymology
Stephen A. Bladey
George N. Clements
Thomas Creamer
John F. Eppling
Jay H. Jasanoff
Gregory Nagy
Richard F. Townsend

Usage
Dwight Bolinger
Geoffrey Nunberg
Nancy Wiegand

ETYMOLOGIES
Marion Severynse, *Associate Editor*

Colin A. M. Danby
Rachel Lucas
Lawrence O. Masland
Jacqueline H. Russom

BIOGRAPHICAL AND GEOGRAPHIC ENTRIES
Kaethe Ellis, *Editor*

Susan E. Berry
Bonnie Friedman
Kathleen Gerard
Deborah Karacozian
Allison McLean
Brett Milano
Edward Rader
Michael A. Seither
Faye Trachtenberg

COPY EDITING AND PROOFREADING
Caroline L. Becker
Susan L. Boulanger
Bruce Dale
Nancy Ann Etscovitz
Rhonda L. Holmes
Susan Innes
Susan Karp
Mary Mahoney Robson
Janet Meacham
Roberto Miranda
Mary Nadler
Laura Nell Provan
Katherine Schenck

PICTURE RESEARCH AND EDITING
Carole D. La Mond,
Picture and Research Editor
Sarah A. O'Reilly,
Assistant Picture Researcher
Donna L. Muise

EDITORIAL ASSISTANCE
Francine D. Figelman
Susan E. Sidd

COVER AND TEXT DESIGN AND LAYOUT
Irwin Glusker
Marsha Goldberg
James R. Hamilton
Richard Hannus
Geoffrey Hodgkinson

KEYBOARDING
Brenda Bregoli Sturtevant
Ronald M. Perkins
Celester Jackson
Caren L. Weisberg
Patricia A. Bates
David R. Pritchard
Joanne L. Nichols
Kelley P. Flynn
Steven McDonald

USAGE PANEL

Edwin Newman, Chairman
NBC news commentator; author of works on language and usage

Elie Abel
Reporter; broadcaster; educator; formerly Dean of the Graduate School of Journalism, Columbia University; recipient of George Foster Peabody Broadcasting Award for outstanding radio news (1968) and Overseas Press Club Award for best interpretation of foreign news (1969)

J. Donald Adams
Literary critic; formerly Editor, *The New York Times Book Review;* deceased

Shana Alexander
Writer and television commentator

Cleveland Amory
Columnist, *Saturday Review, TV Guide,* and *Holiday;* commentator, Group W Radio

Roger Angell
Writer; fiction editor, *The New Yorker;* formerly Editor, *Holiday*

Maya Angelou
Author; poet

Isaac Asimov
Writer; Professor of Biochemistry, Boston University School of Medicine

Ralph Backlund
Executive Editor, *Smithsonian;* formerly Producer and Executive Producer for news and public affairs, CBS; formerly Associate Editor and Managing Editor, *Horizon*

John Bainbridge
Staff writer, *The New Yorker*

Russell Baker
Columnist; writer; recipient of Frank Sullivan Memorial Award (1976), George Polk Memorial Award for commentary (1979), and Pulitzer Prize for distinguished commentary (1979)

Sheridan Baker
Professor of English, University of Michigan; formerly Editor, *The Michigan Quarterly Review*

Letitia Baldrige
Public relations consultant; author; syndicated columnist, *Los Angeles Times*

Lincoln Barnett
Writer; formerly Associate Editor, *Life*

Jacques Barzun
Writer; University Professor, Columbia University

Stewart Beach
Writer; formerly Executive Editor, *This Week;* deceased

Daniel Bell
Professor of Sociology, Harvard University; member of the editorial board, *Daedalus;* Co-editor, *The Public Interest*

Charles F. Berlitz
Author and editor of language instruction books; archaeologist; recipient of Dag Hammarskjöld International Prize for Literature (1976)

Theodore M. Bernstein
Editor; columnist; formerly Assistant Managing Editor, *The New York Times;* deceased

Pierre Berton
Columnist; news commentator; writer

Morris Bishop
Writer; Professor Emeritus of Romance Languages, Cornell University; past President, Modern Language Association; deceased

Alton Blakeslee
Science editor, The Associated Press; recipient of the Distinguished Journalism Award of the American Heart Association (1978)

Morton W. Bloomfield
Professor of English, Harvard University

Ben Zion Bokser
Rabbi, Forest Hills Jewish Center; Visiting Associate Professor, Jewish Theological Seminary

The Hon. Julian Bond
Legislator, civil-rights leader; author

Arna Bontemps
Writer; deceased

Daniel J. Boorstin
Historian; Librarian of Congress; recipient of Pulitzer Prize for history (1974)

Charles P. Boren
Associate Editor, *Lewiston* (Idaho) *Morning Tribune*

Catherine Drinker Bowen
Biographer; historian

The Hon. William W. Bradley
U.S. Senator from New Jersey; writer; formerly professional basketball player

Joseph A. Brandt
Professor Emeritus of Journalism, University of California, Los Angeles; formerly President, University of Oklahoma; formerly Director, University of Oklahoma Press, Princeton University Press, and University of Chicago Press

Paul Brooks
Writer; formerly Editor in Chief, General Books Department, Houghton Mifflin Company

Heywood Hale Broun
Actor; writer; television and radio commentator

Jeremy Brown
Writer; book reviewer; radio commentator; Publisher, Brownstone Press, Toronto, Canada

Herbert Brucker
Writer; formerly Editor, *Hartford Courant;* past President, American Society of Newspaper Editors; deceased

William F. Buckley, Jr.
Writer; columnist; Editor in Chief, *National Review;* recipient of Bellarmine Medal (1977)

Ed Bullins
Writer; playwright

Erwin D. Canham
Formerly Editor in Chief, *Christian Science Monitor;* past President, American Society of Newspaper Editors; past Chairman of the Board, United States Chamber of Commerce; deceased

Gerald Carson
Writer; member of Advisory Board, *American Heritage;* formerly Vice President, Benton & Bowles, Inc., and Director, Kenyon & Eckhardt, Inc.

Claudia Cassidy
Writer; formerly music and drama critic, *Chicago Tribune;* critic at large, *Chicago* magazine

Bruce Catton
Historian; Senior Editor, *American Heritage;* recipient of Pulitzer Prize for history (1954); deceased

Dick Cavett
Writer; entertainer; television talk-show host

John Ciardi
Poet; writer; Poetry Editor, *Saturday Review;* past President, National College English Association

Arthur A. Cohen
Writer; formerly Editor in Chief and Vice President, General Book Division, Holt, Rinehart and Winston, Inc.; co-founder, Meridian Books

Marc Connelly
Playwright; formerly Professor of Playwriting, Yale University; past President, Authors League of America and National Institute of Arts and Letters; deceased

Robin Cook, M.D.
Writer; Assistant in Ophthalmology, Honorary Staff, Massachusetts Eye and Ear Infirmary

Alistair Cooke
Chief American Correspondent, *The Guardian* (England); writer; commentator, British Broadcasting Corporation

Roy H. Copperud
Professor of Journalism, University of Southern California; columnist, *Editor & Publisher;* author of works on English usage

Robert Coughlan
Journalist; historian

Norman Cousins
Editor, *Saturday Review;* writer; recipient of Human Resources Award (1978)

Malcolm Cowley
Writer; literary adviser, Viking Press, Inc.; formerly Associate Editor, *The New Republic*

Robert W. Creamer
Senior Editor, *Sports Illustrated*

Charlotte Curtis
Associate Editor, *New York Times*

Marshall B. Davidson
Writer; Senior Editor, *Horizon*; formerly Editor of Publications, The Metropolitan Museum of Art, New York

Lois DeBakey
Educator; Professor of Scientific Communication, Baylor College of Medicine; Adjunct Professor of Scientific Communication, Tulane University School of Medicine; Recipient of Distinguished Service Award of the American Medical Writers Association (1970)

Vine Victor Deloria, Jr.
Attorney; writer

Peter De Vries
Writer; editorial staff, *The New Yorker*

Digby Diehl
Book Editor, *Los Angeles Herald Examiner;* formerly Book Editor, *Los Angeles Times;* formerly Vice President, National Book Critics' Circle

Annie Dillard
Writer; recipient of Pulitzer Prize for general nonfiction (1974)

René Dubos
Professor Emeritus, Rockefeller University; recipient of Pulitzer Prize for general nonfiction (1969); deceased

William K. Durr
Writer; educator; Professor of Education, Michigan State University; past President, International Reading Association

Freeman Dyson
Physicist; Professor of Physics, Institute of Advanced Study, Princeton University; formerly Professor of Physics, Cornell University

Ralph Ellison
Writer; educator

Frances FitzGerald
Writer; recipient of Overseas Press Club Award for interpretive reporting (1967), Pulitzer Prize for general nonfiction (1973), and Bancroft Award for history (1973)

John Fowles
Writer

Reuven Frank
Journalist; television producer

John Kenneth Galbraith
Economist; writer; formerly U.S. Ambassador to India; formerly Paul M. Warburg Professor of Economics, Harvard University

Michael G. Gartner
Editor and President, *Des Moines Register and Tribune*

J. Edward Gates
Lexicographer; editor; Professor of English, Indiana State University; author of works on lexicography

A. Bartlett Giamatti
President and formerly John Hay Whitney Professor of English, Yale University

Eric F. Goldman
Rollins Professor of History, Princeton University; formerly President, Society of American Historians; member of Advisory Board, *American Heritage;* formerly Special Consultant to the President of the United States

Sydney Harris
Drama critic and columnist, *Chicago Daily News*

The Hon. Mark O. Hatfield
U.S. Senator from Oregon

The Hon. S.I. Hayakawa
U.S. Senator from California; writer; educator; President Emeritus and formerly Professor of English, San Francisco State University

Nat Hentoff
Writer; columnist, *The Voice;* staff writer, *The New Yorker*

Gilbert Highet
Writer; Chairman of Advisory Board, *Horizon;* member of Editorial Board, Book-of-the-Month Club; formerly Anthon Professor of the Latin Language and Literature, Columbia University; deceased

Paul Horgan
Writer; Professor Emeritus and formerly Director, Center for Advanced Studies, Wesleyan University; recipient of Pulitzer (1975) and Bancroft (1954) prizes for history

Langston Hughes
Writer; poet; columnist; deceased

Charlayne Hunter-Gault
Journalist; correspondent, *The MacNeil-Lehrer Report*, PBS; formerly reporter, *New York Times* and *The New Yorker;* recipient of National Urban Coalition Award for urban reporting and Women at Work Award of the National Commission of Working Women

John K. Hutchens
Literary critic; member of Editorial Board, Book-of-the-Month Club; formerly book reviewer, *New York Herald Tribune*

William F. Johnston
Associate Professor and Newspaper Internship Coordinator, School of Communications, University of Washington

Alfred Kahn
Economist; educator; consultant; writer; Professor of Economics and formerly Dean of College of Arts and Sciences, Cornell University; formerly Chairman of Civil Aeronautics Board, Chairman of Council on Wage and Price Stability, and Special Adviser to the President of the United States

Roger Kahn
Writer; journalist

Justin Kaplan
Writer; winner of Pulitzer Prize for biography (1967)

Stanley Kauffmann
Editor; writer; film and theater critic, *The New Republic;* theater critic, *Saturday Review*

Alfred Kazin
Writer; Distinguished Professor of English, Graduate Center, City University of New York

Walter Kerr
Drama critic, *New York Times;* formerly drama critic, *New York Herald Tribune;* past President, New York Critics' Circle; recipient of Pulitzer Prize for criticism (1978)

John Kieran
Writer; naturalist; formerly member of Board of Experts, *Information Please* radio program; deceased

Maxine Kingston
Writer; recipient of National Book Critics' Circle Award for nonfiction (1976) and Anisfield-Wolf Race Relations Award (1978)

James Kraft
Program Officer, The National Endowment for the Humanities

Louis Kronenberger
Professor of Theatre Arts, Brandeis University; contributor, *Atlantic Monthly;* formerly drama critic, *Time*; deceased

Charles Kuralt
News correspondent, CBS

J.J. Lamberts
Professor of English, Arizona State University; author of works on English usage

Geoffrey Leech
Professor of Linguistics and Modern English Languages, University of Lancaster, England; author of works on linguistics and grammar

Milton I. Levine, M.D.
Professor of Clinical Pediatrics, New York Hospital-Cornell Medical Center; radio commentator, CBS; formerly syndicated newspaper columnist

Ralph F. Lewis
Editor and publisher, *Harvard Business Review;* deceased

Walter Lippmann
Syndicated newspaper columnist; recipient of Pulitzer Prize for international reporting (1962); deceased

Clare Boothe Luce
Playwright; formerly U.S. Representative from Connecticut; formerly U.S. Ambassador to Italy

Russell Lynes
Writer; Contributing Editor and formerly Managing Editor, *Harper's* magazine

Dwight Macdonald
Critic; deceased

William Manchester
Writer; correspondent; Adjunct Professor of History and Writer in Residence at Wesleyan University

Joan D. Manley
Publisher; Chairman of the Board, Time-Life Books, Inc.; Chairman of the Board, Book-of-the-Month Club, Inc.; member and past Chairman, Association of American Publishers

Robert Manning
Editor in Chief, *The Atlantic Monthly*

Alice Mayhew
Editor; Vice President, Simon and Shuster

Eugene McCarthy
Poet; educator; formerly U.S. Senator from Minnesota

David McCord
Poet; essayist; Honorary Curator of the Poetry and Farnsworth Rooms, Harvard College Library

Kenneth McCormick
Senior Consulting Editor, Doubleday & Company, Inc.; Consulting Editor, Franklin Library

Mary McGrory
Journalist; formerly political columnist, *Washington Star;* recipient of Pulitzer Prize for commentary (1975)

Margaret Mead
Writer; Curator Emeritus of Ethnology, American Museum of Natural History, New York; past President, American Association for the Advancement of Science; deceased

Ved Mehta
Editor, *The New Yorker*

Rhoda Métraux
Anthropologist; Research Associate, The American Museum of Natural History, New York

James Michener
Writer; recipient of Pulitzer Prize for fiction (1947)

Thomas Middleton
Columnist, *Saturday Review*

Richard Scott Mitchell
Mineralogist; educator; writer; Professor of Environmental Science, University of Virginia; Executive Editor, *Rocks and Minerals*

Richard S. Mitchell
Educator; founder, *Underground Grammarian*

Jessica Mitford
Writer

Marianne Moore
Writer; recipient of Pulitzer Prize for poetry (1952); deceased

Lance Morrow
Senior Writer, editor, columnist, *Time* magazine; recipient of National Magazine Award for essay and criticism (1981)

Bill Moyers
Journalist, editor, and correspondent, CBS; formerly Special Assistant and Press Secretary to the President of the United States; formerly Publisher, *Newsday*, and Contributing Editor, *Newsweek*

The Hon. Daniel P. Moynihan
U.S. Senator from New York; formerly Professor of Political Science, Harvard University

Lewis Mumford
Writer; past President, American Academy of Arts and Letters; formerly Professor of Humanities, Stanford University, and Professor of City and Regional Planning, University of Pennsylvania

Bess Myerson
Syndicated columnist, *New York Daily News;* consumer advocate; radio and television reporter; contributing editor, *Redbook*

Maurine Neuberger
Formerly U.S. Senator from Oregon

David Ogilvy
Creative Director, Ogilvy & Mather International

Robert S. Pirie
Attorney

Katherine Anne Porter
Writer; recipient of Pulitzer Prize for fiction (1966); deceased

Alvin F. Poussaint, M.D.
Psychiatrist; Associate Professor of Psychiatry, Harvard Medical School

Orville Prescott
Writer; formerly Co-editor, "Books of the Times," *New York Times*

Tony Randall
Actor

Ishmael Reed
Writer; publisher; teacher; recipient of National Institute of Arts and Letters Award (1975) and Michaux Award (1978)

Edward W. Rosenheim
Editor; author; Professor of English, University of Chicago; Director, National Humanities Institute

Leo Rosten
Author; social scientist

Berton Roueché
Staff writer, *The New Yorker*

Richard Rovere
Washington correspondent, *The New Yorker;* deceased

Vermont Royster
William Rand Kenan, Jr. Professor of Journalism and Mass Communication, University of North Carolina at Chapel Hill; formerly Editor, *Wall Street Journal;* recipient of Pulitzer Prize for editorial writing (1953)

Carl Sagan
Astronomer; writer; Professor of Astronomy and Space Sciences, Cornell University; recipient of Pulitzer Prize for general nonfiction (1978)

Winthrop Sargeant
Writer; translator; formerly music critic, *The New Yorker*

Robert Saudek
Television producer; Director, The Institute of Film and Television, New York University

Arthur Schlesinger, Jr.
Historian; recipient of Pulitzer Prize for history (1946) and biography (1966); Albert Schweitzer Professor of the Humanities, City University of New York

Glenn T. Seaborg
University Professor of Chemistry, University of California; formerly Chairman, U. S. Atomic Energy Commission; recipient of Nobel Prize for chemistry (1951)

Art Seidenbaum
Journalist; Editor, Book Review Section, *Los Angeles Times*

Harvey Shapiro
Poet; Editor, *New York Times Book Review*

John Simon
Writer; film critic, *New York* magazine and *National Review;* drama critic, *The Hudson Review*

Neil Simon
Playwright; screenwriter

Margaret Nicholson Smith
Writer; formerly Head of Contract and Copyright Department, Farrar, Straus & Giroux, Inc.; formerly Head of Publishing Department, Oxford University Press

Walter W. (Red) Smith
Sports columnist, *New York Times;* deceased

Theodore Sorensen
Attorney; writer, formerly Special Counsel to the President of the United States

Jean Stafford
Author; recipient of Pulitzer Prize for fiction (1970); deceased

Wallace Stegner
Writer; Professor Emeritus of English, Stanford University; recipient of Pulitzer Prize (1972) and National Book Award (1977) for fiction

Gloria Steinem
Writer; Editor, *Ms.* magazine

George R. Stewart
Writer; Professor Emeritus of English, University of California, Berkeley; deceased

Allen Tate
Poet; critic; Regents Professor of English, University of Minnesota; Editor, *The Sewanee Review;* recipient of National Institute of Arts and Letters National Medal for Literature (1976); deceased

Paul Theroux
Writer; recipient of Whitbread Prize for fiction (1978)

Henry F. Thoma
Formerly Editor in Chief and Head, College Department, Houghton Mifflin Company

The Hon. Stewart Udall
Chairman, Overview Corporation, formerly U.S. Secretary of the Interior and U.S. Representative from Arizona

Mark Van Doren
Writer; educator; recipient of Pulitzer Prize for poetry (1940); deceased

William Vaughan
Associate Editor, *Kansas City Star;* syndicated newspaper columnist; deceased

Douglas Turner Ward
Actor; playwright; recipient of Vernon Rice Award and Obie Award for acting (1966)

Calvert Watkins
Professor of Linguistics and the Classics, Harvard University

Richard Watts, Jr.
Drama critic, *New York Post;* deceased

Hobart G. Weekes
Associate Editor, *The New Yorker;* deceased

Anthony West
Writer; critic; formerly literary critic, *The New Yorker;* staff member, *The New Yorker*

Jacqueline Grennan Wexler
Writer; formerly President, Hunter College, City University of New York

Tom Wicker
Writer; journalist; Associate Editor, *New York Times*

Alden Wood
Vice President, American Mutual Insurance Companies; Professor of English, Simmons College; author of a column on English usage

Richard Young
Engineer; writer; editor; Chief Editor, *Pollution Engineering;* Vice President of Publishing, Pudvan Publishing Company

William Zinsser
Executive Editor, Book-of-the-Month Club; formerly Master of Branford College, Yale University; formerly columnist, *New York Herald Tribune* and *Life*

CONSULTANTS
TO THE AMERICAN HERITAGE DICTIONARY

ARTS AND HUMANITIES

Richard D. Altick
Regents' Professor of English, Ohio State University

Willi Apel
Professor Emeritus of Musicology, Indiana University

Charles F. Berlitz
Author and editor of language instruction books

James Marston Fitch
Professor of Architecture, Columbia University

Ignace J. Gelb
Frank P. Hixon Distinguished Service Professor of Assyriology, University of Chicago

Harold F. Harding
Benedict Professor of Speech, University of Texas, El Paso

James Humphry III
Vice President, The H. W. Wilson Company: formerly Chief Librarian, The Metropolitan Museum of Art, New York

Bernard M. W. Knox
Director, The Center for Hellenic Studies, Washington, D.C.

Burt Korall
Popular Music and Entertainment Critic, *Saturday Review*

Wayne C. Minnick
Professor of Speech and Associate Dean, College of Arts and Sciences, Florida State University

Beaumont Newhall
Director, George Eastman House, Rochester, N.Y.

Allardyce Nicoll
Formerly Chairman of Drama Department, Yale University; Professor Emeritus, English, The Shakespeare Institute, University of Birmingham (England)

George Kimball Plochmann
Professor of Philosophy, Southern Illinois University

Maurice F. Tauber
Melvil Dewey Professor of Library Service, Columbia University

Walter Terry
Dance critic, *Saturday Review*

John Walker
Director, The National Gallery of Art, Washington, D.C.

Calvert Watkins
Professor of Linguistics and the Classics, Harvard University

LIFE SCIENCES

Isaac Asimov
Associate Professor of Biochemistry, Boston University School of Medicine

Jesse F. Bone
Professor of Veterinary Medicine, Oregon State University

Ralph Buchsbaum
Professor of Biology, University of Pittsburgh

William H. Burt
Professor of Zoology and Curator of Mammals, University of Michigan

Spencer H. Davis, Jr.
Professor of Plant Pathology, Rutgers University

Frederick C. Fink
Manager, Microbiological Services, Pfizer Diagnostics Department, Chas. Pfizer & Co.; Inc.

Garrett Hardin
Professor of Biology, University of California, Santa Barbara

Adrian Lambert, M.D.
Associate Professor of Clinical Surgery, College of Physicians and Surgeons, Columbia University

Douglas A. Lancaster
Assistant Professor of Ecology and Systematics, Cornell University

R. H. Nelson
Executive Secretary, Entomological Society of America

James A. Peters
Curator, Reptiles and Amphibians, United States National Museum, Washington, D.C.

Joseph L. Peterson
Mycologist, Department of Plant Biology, Rutgers University

Olin Sewall Pettingill, Jr.
Director, Laboratory of Ornithology, Cornell University

Timothy Prout
Professor of Zoology, University of California, Riverside

Donn E. Rosen
Associate Curator, Department of Ichthyology, American Museum of Natural History, New York

Frederick E. Smith
Professor of Natural Resources, University of Michigan

William C. Steere
Director, The New York Botanical Garden; Professor of Botany, Columbia University

Norman Taylor
Formerly Curator of Plants, Brooklyn Botanic Garden, New York

Georg Zappler
Formerly Curator of Research, New Jersey State Museum, Trenton

PHYSICAL SCIENCES AND MATHEMATICS

Peter M. Bernays
Senior Associate Editor, Chemical Abstracts Service

Edward J. Cogan
Professor of Mathematics, Sarah Lawrence College

Richard Hanau
Professor of Physics, University of Kentucky

Paul J. Kliauga
Assistant to the Director of Publications, American Institute of Physics, New York

James E. Miller
Professor of Meteorology, New York University

Lloyd Motz
Professor of Astronomy, Columbia University

Frederick H. Pough
Contributing Editor, *Lapidary Journal;* formerly Director, Santa Barbara Museum of Natural History, Santa Barbara, Calif.

John A. Shimer
Professor of Geology, Brooklyn College

M. J. Sienko
Professor of Chemistry, Cornell University

Thaddeus L. Smith
Mathematical Statistician, National Insurance Actuarial and Statistical Association

George L. Trigg
Editor, *Physical Review Letters*

William C. Vergara
Director of Advanced Research, Bendix Corporation

PRACTICAL AND APPLIED SCIENCES

Frank O. Braynard
Editor, *Tow Line*

Col. Elbridge Colby, USA (retired)
Professor Emeritus of Journalism, George Washington University

Frederick C. Durant III
Assistant Director, National Air and Space Museum, Smithsonian Institution, Washington, D.C.

Dorothy Fey
Executive Director, The United States Trademark Association

Clayton Knight
Aviation historian

N. Dan Larsen
Staff architect, Rutgers University

Dorothy Nickerson
Past President, Inter-Society Color Council

Frank K. Perkins
Formerly bridge and games columnist, *The Boston Herald*

J. Lowell Pratt
Co-author, *The Official Encyclopedia of Sports*

Virginia L. Robertson
Home economics consultant, *Encyclopedia International*

Col. Milton Seaman, USAFR
Liaison Office Coordinator, U.S. Air Force Academy

Milton A. Sprague
Professor of Soils and Crops, Rutgers University

Victor Strauss
Printing consultant

RELIGION

Walter J. Burghardt, S.J.
Professor of Historical Theology, Woodstock College, Maryland; Editor, *Theological Studies*

Klaus J. Hansen
Associate Professor, Department of History, Queen's University, Kingston, Ont. (Canada)

Harry M. Orlinsky
Professor of Bible, Hebrew Union College-Jewish Institute of Religion, New York

Jaroslav Pelikan
Titus Street Professor of Ecclesiastical History, Yale University

Allison W. Phinney
Supervisor, Editorial Division, The First Church of Christ, Scientist, Boston, Mass.

The Rev. Canon Edward N. West
Sub-Dean of the Cathedral Church of St. John the Divine, New York

SOCIAL SCIENCES

Harold E. Driver
Professor of Anthropology, Indiana University

Thomas F. Dwyer, M.D.
Assistant Professor in Clinical Psychiatry, Harvard University; Associate in Psychiatry, Massachusetts General Hospital

John Flynn
Vice President, Perera Fifth Avenue, Inc.

Charles Fried
Professor of Law, Harvard Law School

Carl J. Friedrich
Eaton Professor of Government, Harvard University

N. L. Gage
Professor of Education and Psychology, Stanford University

John A. Garraty
Professor of History, Columbia University

William N. Kinnard, Jr.
Professor of Finance and Real Estate, University of Connecticut

Jesse William Markham
Professor of Business Administration, Harvard Graduate School of Business Administration

Wilbert E. Moore
Sociologist, Russell Sage Foundation

Hallam L. Movius, Jr.
Professor of Anthropology, Harvard University

Edwin B. Newman
Lecturer on Psychology, Harvard University; co-editor, *American Journal of Psychology*

J. H. Plumb
Professor of Modern English History, Christ's College, Cambridge University (England)

Norman J. G. Pounds
Professor of History and Geography, Indiana University

Bernard Wailes
Professor of Anthropology, University of Pennsylvania

Language, Culture, and the American Heritage

LEE PEDERSON
Emory University

American speech and writing record the transactions of nearly four hundred years of social history. Dialects embody patterns of sound, syntax, and meaning; literature documents those spoken forms in poetry and prose. Through the process of communication a native language becomes the social inheritance of all its speakers. In describing the linguistic resources of American English this Dictionary becomes a property book for the American people.

A century before Noah Webster organized his first American dictionary (1806), Jonathan Edwards defined the materials of inquiry in remarkably modern terms, in words that should appeal to every reader, whether layman, linguist, or lexicographer:

> By *conversation,* I mean intelligent beings expressing their minds one to another in words, or other signs intentionally directed to us for our notice, whose immediate and main design is to be signification of the mind of him who gives it.

Defining language as intelligent conversation, Edwards recognized the conceptual, symbolic, and functional aspects of human communication: the engagement of thought, the use of signs, and the transmission of ideas from one mind to another.

Today the English language makes conversation possible among three hundred million native speakers who share its system of symbolic behavior. This number includes speakers of American, Australian, British, Canadian, Irish, New Zealand, and Scottish English as members of the most influential speech community in the history of civilization. Their common cultural heritage makes possible the use of a single language by the members of these different groups, but each national variety with all its regional and social dialects reflects unique social experience.

Such experience makes a national vocabulary the most accessible and productive source of cultural information. Words are the complex linguistic structures that transmit the native lexicon through the systems of sound, grammar, and meaning. Words are also cultural emblems, symbols with social meaning that preserve the experience of human activity. Emerson said that words are signs of natural facts and wrote: "The etymologist finds the deadest word to have been once a brilliant picture. Language is fossil poetry." He demonstrated by his own example, moreover, that words are also signs of sociohistorical facts by giving the American meaning to *transcendentalism*. Roger Williams, America's first anthropologist, recorded an Algonquian dialect, provided us with the earliest occurrences in English of *birchen bark* and *squash,* and coined the phrase *Indian affairs*. George Washington furnished the earliest citations for *Democrat* and *Republican* and himself was the first to receive the designation *favorite son*. Noah Webster made the earliest use of the phrase *American English* with characteristic impatience but ultimate accuracy: "In fifty years from this time [1806], the American-English will be spoken by more people than all other dialects of the language." Such thought, conversation, and social interaction shaped the national character and gave substance to the lexicon. Contributions came from every sector of the American culture: education, religion, government, and even lexicography.

As the central component of American English culture the national language transmits the essential messages of all other cultural systems. All of these are inseparable from language: *family* (kinship and marriage), *training* (education and economics), *values* (morality, ethics, and religious rites), *government* (political and social control), *technology* (artifacts of survival), and *fine arts* (artifacts of the creative imagination and of spiritual expression). From the earliest days on its first frontiers American English carried forward the messages of the culture and the experience of the past. As it did its work the national language established an identity and expressed native ideas in an American voice. This dictionary records that American voice and gives substance to its underlying systems, *language* and *culture*.

Thoreau recognized a national dictionary as "a very concentrated and trustworthy natural history of the people":

> What they have a word for, they have a thing for. A traveller may tell us that he *thinks* they used a pavement, or built their cabins in a certain form, or soaked their seed corn in water . . .; but when one gives us the word for these things, the question is settled,—that is a clincher. Let us know what words they had and how they used them, and we can infer almost all the rest. The lexicographer not only *says* that a certain people have or do a certain thing, but, being evidently a disinterested party, it may be allowed that he brings sufficient evidence to prove it. He does not so much assert as exhibit. He has no transient or private purposes to serve.

HISTORICAL BACKGROUND OF ENGLISH

This natural history of the American people is the essential gift of the mother tongue. With all speakers of the English language Americans share the results of fifteen hundred years of linguistic development, and English had itself evolved for a full millennium before the first American words were spoken in Virginia. Furthermore, as a member of the Germanic language group of the Indo-European language family, English shares an ultimate heritage with most of the modern languages of Europe and Asia and with the official languages of every government in North and South America.

The essential features of the Germanic languages are these: (1) consonant modification, especially the First Germanic Consonant Shift, captured in Grimm's Law, that distinguishes the system from all other Indo-European consonant patterns, as illustrated by the correspondences between initial sounds in the Latin/English cognates *pater/father, tu/thou,* and *hortus/garden*; (2) vowel mutation in the specialization of Germanic vowels, diphthongs, and umlauted forms to give them values different from all other Indo-European vowel systems; (3) word stress on the first syllable; (4) seven classes of strong (irregular) verbs, such as *sing, sang, sung*; (5) three classes of weak (regular) verbs, such as *love, loved, loved*; (6) strong and weak adjectives that disappeared in Medieval English but endure elsewhere, as in the Modern German and Norwegian definite and indefinite articles; (7) a core vocabulary of common words. These shared characteristics define the thirteen modern Germanic languages: Danish, Faroese, Icelandic, Norwegian, Swedish, German, Yiddish, Low German, Dutch, Afrikaans, Flemish, Frisian, and English.

The history of the English language begins with the coming of invaders from the continent in A.D. 449, as reported in the Anglo-Saxon Chronicle. In the eighth century the Venerable Bede (A.D. 673–735) identified the Low Germans as Angles, Saxons, and Jutes. In Britain the Germans encountered their Indo-European relatives, the Celts, a Belgic tribe that had arrived some time after the advent of the Iron Age (700 B.C.) but before Caesar's invasions of 54 B.C. Like the Amerindians, the Celts left their greatest linguistic legacy in place names, such as *Avon, Bryn Mawr* (Welsh "great hill"), *Dover, Thames,* and probably *London*. Unlike the Amerindians, the Celts provided no vocabulary of flora, fauna, or cultural activities for the newcomers. This latter fact reflects differing geographical and cultural circumstances: the Celts and Germans were never separated by a distance greater than the narrow English Channel and shared a common Indo-European ancestry. Conversely, the Amerindians and English came from different environments thousands of miles apart, from homelands distinguished by their native forms of vegetation, animal life, and social behavior.

As the Low German dialects merged in England they gave rise to the Northumbrian, Mercian, and Saxon varieties of the language that is called Old English today. Three tenth-century texts show the close similarities of those dialects in their respective translations of Medieval Latin (Matthew 6:9) "Pater noster, qui est in caelis, sanctificetur nomen tuum . . .":

NORTHUMBRIAN

Fader urer ðu arð in heofnas, sie gehalgad
Father our thou art in heaven, be hallowed

noma ðin . . .
name thy . . .

MERCIAN

Fæder ure ðu ðe in heofunum earð,
Father our thou which in heaven art,

beo gehalgad ðin noma . . .
be hallowed thy name . . .

WEST SAXON

Fæder ure ðu ðe eart on heofonum, si
Father our thou which art in heaven, be

ðin nama gehalgod . . .
thy name hallowed . . .

Despite differences in pronunciation, word formation, and syntax, simple and effective conversation was surely possible among speakers of the different regional dialects of English. Conversation was also possible between the English and their Viking neighbors from the north. That cultural interaction extended throughout the Old English period (449–1066) is evidenced in the greatest literary monument of the Anglo-Saxons, their epic poem *Beowulf,* which has a thoroughly Scandinavian setting and cast.

Words shared by Anglo-Saxons and Vikings include *bring, can, come, father, folk, hear, house, life, mother, man, mine, ride, see, sit, smile, sorrow, summer, thine, wife, will, winter,* and *wise.* In addition to hundreds of such intimate correspondences, the Scandinavians gave English many other familiar words through cultural interaction: *anger, fellow, happy, husband, meek, root, rotten, skill, skin, sky,* and *ugly.* A second and much greater influence was brought to bear on the language and culture after the events of 1066, when the French-speaking descendants of the Vikings arrived from Normandy.

French Influences

The Norman-French presence marked the beginning of great changes in English social behavior, reflecting a gradual evolution of institutional and conversational forms. The chronicles and other writings show that Old English was in transition before the coming of the Normans, and later poetry and prose record unmodified Germanic forms deep into the Middle English period. In England, French became the official language of the dominant culture and spread its influence into every social system. Earlier, on the continent, the Normans had adopted Frankish laws, developed a system of knightly conduct, and perfected the skills of cavalry warfare. Through force and friendship they gave the English a chivalric code, a parliamentary system of government, and one of the most distinctive architectural styles in all of European civilization. During the period of Norman dominion the English dialects evolved without a native prestige form. The Scandinavian remnant of earlier times emerged in the speech of the northern counties, and the regional dialects were broadly reorganized. In the process Middlesex became the pre-eminent focal area, and from its center arose the London Standard, the most influential social variety the language has ever known.

The dialects of fourteenth-century England were the immediate ancestors of the London Standard, based on the speech of the Southeast Midland region. The recorded usage of that era illustrates great linguistic change, a process that began more than two hundred years earlier through the mingling of English and French. Causal relations for the change are hard to establish because phonological, grammatical, lexical, and cultural modifications were under way before the Battle of Hastings. Romance language words, such as *cheese, copper,* and *dish,* entered Low German dialects through Latin before the invasion of England in A.D. 449; from the same source came *cleric, psalm,* and *temple* with the Christianization of England in the seventh century. Late Romance loans in Old English include *pride* (French), *capon* and *castle* (French or Latin), and *apostle, epistle, lily,* and *peony* (Latin). Old English texts of the tenth century—the Vercelli Book, Exeter Book, Junius Codex, and *Beowulf* Codex—show the early simplification of weakly stressed vowels and inflectional patterns. During the reign of Edward the Confessor (1043–1066) a Norman association was firmly established between the king and his cousin, William the Conqueror, underscored by the installation of Robert of Jumièges as Archbishop of Canterbury in 1051.

During the next three hundred years the

French presence altered the development of English through direct contributions and reinforcement of linguistic trends already under way. Four fricative consonants emerged as distinctive elements of the sound system during this period, the initial sounds of *veal, zeal,* and *thee,* as well as the medial sound in *leisure.* None of these were distinctive in Old English, which had only the fricatives of modern *feel, seal, thing,* and *pressure,* respectively. The single outright contribution of Norman French to the sound system of English was the diphthong of *joy.* French usage did accelerate the leveling of weakly stressed vowels, the simplification of noun, pronoun, and adjective inflections, and the transfer of many strong (irregular) verbs to weak (regular) conjugations. For example, Old English forms of modern *doom* included *domes* (genitive singular), *domas* (nominative plural), and *domum* (dative plural); all became *doomes* in Middle English. Strong verbs such as *creopan, helpan,* and *slæpan* became the weak verbs *creep, help,* and *sleep,* although a residue of the old patterns endures in the past forms *crept* and *slept,* as well as *holp* (pronounced like *hope*) in several current American dialects.

More French loan-words entered English during the fourteenth century than during any comparable period before or since. As the French language fell into disuse in England many of its culturally useful words were borrowed. Here the relationship between speech and writing is an important consideration. The documented evidence of the written forms is conservative and lags behind current usage. After King John lost the province of Normandy in 1204, French influence on English society began to decline. Before the Hundred Years' War (1337–1453) began, English speech had already returned as the native tongue of the nobility, and before the century closed, had replaced French in the courts, Parliament, schools, and finally in the highly formal documents of titles, deeds, and wills.

Chaucer composed *The Canterbury Tales* in his native Southeast Midland dialect and so demonstrated the appropriateness of London speech as a literary medium, but this did not mark the triumph of a standard language within the culture at large. Just two years before he began his masterwork, Chaucer worried about the diversity of current speech in his envoy for *Troilus and Criseyde* (1385):

> And for ther is so gret diversite
> In Englissh and in writyng of oure tonge,
> So prey I god that non myswrite the(e),
> Ne the(e) mysmetre for defaute of tonge.
> And red wherso thow be, or elles songe,
> That thow be understonde, God I biseche!

He prayed that none miswrite, mismeter (wrongly scan the measures), or misunderstand the purpose of his earlier (*rather*) speech, his spoken words that became this "litel bok."

The Emergence of Modern English

Chaucer had good reason for concern. The Great Vowel Shift was beginning a modification in quality of all long vowels and diphthongs, and the inconsistent treatment of weakly stressed vowels placed many syllables in jeopardy. *The shift raised [a] to [æ] (and later [e]), [e] to [i], [ɔ] to [o], and [o] to [u]. The vowels formerly pronounced [i] and [u] became, respectively, [əi] (later [ai]) and [əu] (later [au]). Thus Chaucer's final vowels in *diversite* and *the(e)* rhyme with modern *they*; his pronoun *I* rhymes with modern *me*; his verb *write* rhymes with modern *feet; beseche* and *speche* rhyme with modern *aitch*; his pronoun *oure* rhymes with modern *boot.* Although metrical evidence is difficult to interpret, Chaucer quite possibly pronounced the weakly stressed *e* in *myswrite* and *elles* but ignored it in *tonge, understonde, speche,* and other words in this same stanza that comprise those seven iambic pentameter lines of rhyme royal.

At the outset of the early Modern English period (1500–1700) fewer than five million people in the world spoke English, as compared to twelve million speakers of French, ten million of German, nine million of Italian, and eight million of Spanish. During the next two centuries those "intelligent beings expressing their minds" in English included More, Tyndale, Milton, Newton, Locke, and Dryden. At its center was Elizabethan English, the language of Shakespeare, Marlowe, Bacon, Donne, Raleigh, Spenser, and the queen herself. From this stage of linguistic development came the earliest varieties of American

---

*All pronunciations in this article are in the notation of the International Phonetic Alphabet. The Pronunciation Key lists these symbols and their equivalents in the pronunciation system employed for this Dictionary.

English. By 1700 the number of English speakers had nearly doubled, while German, Italian, and Spanish had scarcely maintained their numbers of two centuries earlier, and only French surpassed the growth rate of English among the western European nations.

As an emergent world language English advanced with the spread of the London Standard and general education, with the loosening of class distinctions, and through the influence of what would today be called the mass media. By the year 1500 printed books in all of Europe included thirty-five thousand titles, most of which were in Latin. During the next hundred and forty years twenty thousand English titles appeared in print, and scribal composition of manuscripts became virtually a lost art. England regained its cultural self-reliance with those new sources of influence and the spread of empire. In 1579 E. K., the anonymous editor of Spenser's *The Shepheardes Calender,* commended his author and reflected the spirit of the age:

> For in my opinion it is one special prayse of many which are dew to this Poete, that he has labored to restore, as is their rightfull heritage, such good and naturall English words as have been long time out of use and almost cleane disherited. Which is the onely cause that our Mother tonge, which truely of it self is both ful enough for prose and stately enough for verse, hath long time ben counted more bare and barrein of both.

The English recognized the legitimacy of their native tongue for all modes of communication, including those technical fields formerly dominated by Latin and Greek. In his *Elementary* (1582) Richard Mulcaster defended the use of English and explained the implications of his work:

> For the account of our tongue, both in pen and speech, no man will doubt therof who is able to judge what those things be which any tongue be of account; which things I take to be three: the autority of the people which speak it, the matter and argument wherein the speech dealeth, the manifold use for which the speech serveth. For all which three our tongue needeth not give place to any of her peers.

Mulcaster and others wrote rules for pronunciation and grammar and tried to enrich the national word store. Earlier the Italians, Spanish, French, and Germans had done these same things for their own varieties of speech, as the transformation of local vernaculars into national languages characterized the Renaissance in every European country that it touched.

During the reign of Elizabeth (1558–1603) a language pattern developed that was to become the base form of early American English. London usage reflected the linguistic patriotism of the English Renaissance and accepted forms from a variety of regional and social dialects in the development of a spoken standard. Roger Ascham, Elizabeth's Latin tutor, was a Yorkshireman; Raleigh preserved his distinctive Devonshire speech throughout his life; Essex was from Hertfordshire; Sidney, from Kent; Shakespeare, from Warwickshire; of Welsh ancestry, John Donne emerged from the London merchant class. The language habits of all those speakers contributed to the shaping of the urban pattern and to the development of vigorous conversational speech.

THE BEGINNINGS OF AMERICAN ENGLISH

The fluid structure of Early Modern English underlies the formation of American English. Although the Great Vowel Shift had assigned new values to the long vowels, many British, Scottish, and Irish social dialects were slow to accept all of these emergent features. Morphology and syntax showed inventiveness and flexibility in word formation and adaptations, as with the free use of affixes in word building (*re-, de-, -ish, -ize*), functional shift of parts of speech (nouns used as verbs, verbs as nouns, and both as adjectival or adverbial modifiers), frequent parenthetical expression, and phrase structures of predication, complementation, and coordination that reflect the intonational contours of the spoken language.

Drawn from that rapidly flowing stream, American English shows a much greater uniformity than its origins might suggest. Einar Haugen has called this evolution of the national language in American "Babel in reverse." The concept of the American melting pot can be found in the writing of St. John de Crèvecoeur, a Norman-French immigrant and the eponym of St. Johnsbury, Vermont. In the *Letters of an American Farmer* (1782) he provided the logic for a unified American language and culture:

> What attachment can a poor European emigrant have for a country where he had nothing. The knowledge of the language, the love of a few kindred as poor as himself, were the only cords that tied him; his country is now that which gives him land, bread, protection, and consequence: *Ubi panis ibi*

> *patria* [where there is bread, there is one's fatherland] is the motto of all emigrants. What is an American, this new man? He is either a European, or the descendant of a European, hence that strange mixture of blood, which you will find in no other country. I could point out to you a family whose grandfather was an Englishman, whose wife was Dutch, whose son married a French woman, and whose present four sons have now four wives of different nations. *He* is an American, who, leaving behind him all of his ancient prejudices and manners, receives new ones from the new mode of life he has embraced, the new government he obeys, and the new rank he holds. He becomes an American by being received in the broad lap of our great *Alma Mater* [Dear Mother]. Here individuals of all nations are melted into a new race of men, whose labors and posterity will one day cause great changes in the world. Americans are the western pilgrims, who are carrying along with them that great mass of art, science, vigor, and industry which began long since in the east; they will finish the great circle. The Americans were once scattered all over Europe; here they are incorporated into one of the finest systems of population which has ever appeared, and which will hereafter become distinct by the power of the different climates they inhabit. The American ought therefore to love this country better than that wherein either he or his forefathers were born.

The first substantial collection of immigrant literature appeared in New England, where writers worked with Elizabethan patterns and recorded a variety of occasional spellings and distinctive forms. In *The History of Plimmoth Plantation* (1620–1647) William Bradford wrote *burthen, fadom, furder, gifen (given), gusle (guzzle), trible (triple), vacabund (vagabond),* and *woules (wolves).* Roger Williams rhymed *abode/God, blood/good,* and *America/away* in *A Key to the Language of America* (1643). Ann Bradstreet paired *conceit/great, stood/flood,* and *satisfy/reality* in *The Tenth Muse, Lately Sprung Up in America* (1650). Two generations later Edward Taylor alternated *spoil* and *spile,* as well as *soot* and *sut,* and rhymed *is/kiss, far/cur,* and *vile/soil.*

Early American grammar also showed a great variety of forms. In 1630, aboard the *Arabella* and westward-bound, John Winthrop preached "A Model of Christian Charity" with the line "We must love brotherly without dissimulation; we must love one another with a pure heart fervently." Bradford used *rid, runned* (and *ranne*), *drunk, writ,* and *shrunk* as past forms of *ride, run, drink, write,* and *shrink,* respectively. Williams declared, "My disease is I know not what" and offered the interrogative form "Sleep you?" Mary Rowlandson wrote, "It is not my tongue or pen can express the sorrow of my heart . . ." in her captive narrative of 1675.

During these same years cultural activity all along the Atlantic seaboard produced the first Americanisms. The following native words, among hundreds of others, originated, gained special meaning, or entered the English language through American speech in the seventeenth century: *creek* (stream), *fat pine, green corn,* and *papoose* from Massachusetts; *catfish, corn* (maize), *mock*[ing]*bird, polecat* (skunk), and *raccoon* from Virginia; *Chippewa, ground hog, Manhattan,* and *Podunk* from New York; *gang* [of birds], *hominy, snakeroot,* and *Virginian* from Maryland; *frontier people, oyster rake, samp,* and *wampum* from Rhode Island; *grocery* (store), *hot cakes* (corn cakes), *peavine* (a climbing plant similar to the pea), and *sunfish* from Pennsylvania; *settlement* and *swampland* from Connecticut; *Dutch grass* (any one of various grasses) and *hickory nut* from South Carolina; *frontier* from New Jersey. Beyond the frontiers *pilot* (a guide over a land route) appeared in what is now Colorado, and *Miami* from what is now Illinois.

Native American Influences

These words suggest the importance of Amerindian loans, especially for artifacts and places. From the Algonquian dialects alone English and French in the New World borrowed more than a hundred terms that remain current in American speech. In addition to *Chippewa, hominy, Manhattan, papoose, Podunk, samp, squash,* and *wampum,* the eastern tribes provided *caribou, mackinaw, pone, Tammany, terrapin,* and *toboggan.* These often suggest multiple language contacts; as *caribou* and *toboggan* entered through Canadian French in the north, *barbecue, canoe,* and *cushaw* came out of the West Indies through Spanish. Spanish later transmitted *anaqua* (the Texas "knockaway" tree), *coyote,* and *peyote* from the Nahuatl Indian language of Mexico. From Quechua, probably through the cooperative efforts of French and Spanish, New Orleans' *lagniappe* appeared somewhat later. The American place names comprise the greatest Amerindian contribution. From *Appalachia* and the *Alleghenies,* across all five Great Lakes (*Erie, Ontario, Huron, Michigan,* and *Superior*), from *Chicago* to *Sitka,* Indian words cover the continent. Emblematic of American language and culture are the blends, such as *Bayou La Batre,* Alabama (Choctaw *bayuk* = "creek" + French *de la Batre* = "of the [artillery] battery"), and *Minneapolis,* Minnesota (Dakota *minne* = "water" + Greek/English (a)*polis* = "city"), or the loan translations *Spearfish,* South Dakota, *Warroad,* Minnesota, and *Yellow Dirt Creek,* Georgia, besides the Indian loans of the state names *Alabama* (tribe), *Dakota* (tribe), and *Minnesota* (Dakota *minne* = "water" + *sota* = "white").

LOANS FROM THE EUROPEAN LANGUAGES

Early loans from European languages correspond with Dutch, French, and German settlements in the coastal colonies and along the first interior frontiers. During their New Amsterdam experience the Dutch added to American English the words *boss, Bowery, coleslaw, cookie, sleigh, stoop,* and *waffle*. Later they gave more place names, such as *Catskill, Kinderhook,* and *Schuyler.* Although Thoreau spoke of *Yankee ingenuity* in 1843, the durable nickname probably had its origin in the Dutch diminutive for *John (Johnny), Jan (Janke).* Saint Nicholas, clipped to *Sint Klaas* in a Dutch dialect, became *Santa Claus* before the Revolutionary War.

French loans contrast sharply with the Dutch and later German contributions. Although they also gave English such ordinary household words as *chowder, gopher, pumpkin, sashay, shanty,* and *shivaree,* the enterprising French illustrate their experience in a distinctive set of loans. Explorers, missionaries, and frontier warriors made American words of *bateau, coulee, crevasse, levee, portage, prairie,* and *voyageur.* As the English, Dutch, and Swedes struggled to control the seaboard the French ranged across the interior and left their mark with the names of places at *Bienville, Cape Girardeau, Prairie du Chien,* and *Sault Sainte Marie.*

Early German loans on the frontier are difficult to ascertain. Like the Scandinavians and Anglo-Saxons in England, the Germans and the English spoke languages with a common word stock that still endures in the basic vocabularies of both cultures. For the same reason it is impossible to determine whether *nosh* (snack) and *schlemiel* are of Yiddish or German origin and whether *spook* and *dumb* (stupid) are of Dutch or German origin, because in each case the words occur in both languages. Only when the Germans established discrete territories, as the Dutch had in New York, did the loans begin to appear in significant numbers from Pennsylvania, Cincinnati, Chicago, Milwaukee, St. Louis, and east-central Texas. From early Pennsylvania, American English probably received *smearcase, ponhaws* (*pannhass* = "pan" + *hare* = "scrapple"), *rainworm,* and possibly George Washington's most familiar title, *The Father of His Country,* which first appeared as *Des Landes Vater* on a *Nord Amerikanische Kalender* for 1779.

THE AMERICAN FRONTIER

The frontier contributions of the Swedes and folk speakers of British, Irish, and Scottish dialects are virtually impossible to identify because they were soon united in a common culture. As Crèvecoeur described the people at the outbreak of the Revolution:

> They are a mixture of English, Scotch, Irish, French, Dutch, Germans, and Swedes. From this promiscuous breed, that race now called Americans have risen. The eastern provinces [i.e., the coastal colonies] must needs be expected, as being unmixed descendants of Englishmen.

Early frontier speech probably included the pronouns *hit* (for *it*), *hisn, ourn, theirn,* and *yourn,* the inflected verb forms *clumb, drug, holp,* and *riz,* the auxiliary construction *mought could* (or *might could*), and a large number of folk pronunciations and lexical items. Scottish forms, also appearing in the poetry of Burns, include *duds* (clothes), *gumption, hunkers, mountain billy* (hillbilly), *tow* (cloth), and the distinctive pronunciations reflected in *chimla (chimney), het (heated),* and *southron (southern),* as well as the simplification of consonant clusters, as in *kin' (kind)* and *sin' (since),* and the total assimilation of *l* after back vowels, as in *ca' (call), fu' (full),* and *howe (hollow).* From Irish sources probably came *mammy, moonshine,* and *mountain dew.* General English folk forms also included *clean, flat,* and *plumb* (meaning "completely"), *passel* (from *parcel*), and *sass* (from *sauce*). Many of these forms appear in Middle English, and all survive in current American Midland and Southern dialects.

The Evolution of Dialects in American English

During the eighteenth century the principal dialect regions of American English developed. These are the historic cultural areas. Every major regional dialect area, past and present, corresponds almost perfectly with a cultural area delimited by other social systems. The presbyters of Appalachia mark the pattern of Scottish settlement, the Dutch and German barns show a Germanic presence in the eastern and east-central states, the methods of cooking cornmeal in *pones, dodgers,* and *hush puppies* reflect the settlement patterns of various groups, and the superstitions connected with chicken clavicles (*wishbone, pulley bone,* or *lucky bone*) identify social groups, as do the southern greetings *hey* (for *hi*) and *Christmas Gift!* The styles of folk, blues, jazz, and rock music also correspond with cultural areas, contrasting the perfected forms of the Carter Family in Appalachia and Huddie Ledbetter in the Upper Delta, the rural blues of Richard Amerson and the urban blues of Bill Broonzy, the Kansas City jazz of Count Basie and the Chicago jazz of Bud Freeman, or the middle Georgia rock of the Allman Brothers and the southern California rock of the Eagles. All of these are as regionally distinctive as the voices of the musicians are. Wherever clear-cut boundaries of culture can be reconstructed on the basis of historical information from archaeology, music, graphic arts, or the social sciences, dialect differences can be predicted, based on the most persuasive kind of circumstantial evidence: the recorded experience of the forebears of a speech community.

Modern American seaboard dialects preserve the early system from Maine to the Florida Keys and along the Gulf shores to Brownsville, Texas. The coastal communities shared the evolution of urban British pronunciation, grammar, and vocabulary, but very different speech forms developed throughout the interior along the old frontier. Neither of these regions is a uniform cultural area, but remarkable concordances of speech endure. Early centers at Boston, New York, and Philadelphia were quite different from their southern counterparts at Richmond, Charleston, and New Orleans. Along the Atlantic and Gulf coasts, however, the dialects shared important features: the loss of a constricted *r* after vowels (making *popper* homophonous with *Papa*); a contrast of stressed vowels in *Mary, merry,* and *marry*; a most distinctive diphthong in *dues, news,* and *shoes* that approaches that in *few, music,* and *pupil*; the loss of *h* in *whip, white, wheelbarrow,* and similar words; and even a "broad *a*" in *hammer, pasture,* and *Saturday.* Besides the familiar British past form *et* (of *eat*), the coastal dialects also shared lexical features, such as *hog's head cheese, haslets* (or *harslets*), and *piazza* (porch).

The coastal pattern divides near the Potomac. To the north the language and culture drifted away from British influence more quickly than they did in the South, where the early planters of Jefferson's agrarian democracy required close association with British commerce, education, and industry. Southern coastal dialects preserved several other British features: the "clear *l*" of *lean* in *Billy* and *Nelly* as opposed to the "dark *l*" of *load,* a flapped *r* in *three* and *thresh,* as heard in some current British pronunciations of *very* (written humorously as *veddy*), and even an occasional back vowel in *pot* and *crop.* Along the Gulf Coast these forms had mixed currency, largely because of the powerful influence of New Orleans, a cultural center that dominated the entire interior of the South until the Civil War. Basic Northern and Southern contrasts persist from the Potomac to the mouth of the Rio Grande: the Southern drawls (patterns of diphthongs, lengthening, and intonation), the vowel of *ride* [a] (which northerners confuse with *rod* [ɑ]), the vowel of *bird* [ɜɪ] (which northerners associate with Brooklynese), a positional variant [əu] in *house* and *mouse* but not in *rouse* and *cows,* the plural pronoun *you-all (y'all),* the past form *drug* (of *drag*), and a large set of vocabulary forms, such as *mosquito hawk* (dragonfly), *crocus sack* (burlap bag), *snap beans* (string beans), and *tote* (carry).

The New Orleans focal area interrupts this pattern, extending its influence from Mobile Bay to beyond the Sabine River. A General Coastal and New Orleans contrast is marked by *serenade, bateau, clabber cheese,* and *mush* along the Southern coast, except in the area of New Orleans dominion, where *shivaree (charivari), pirogue, cream cheese,* and *cush-cush* prevail. Although *cush* and *cush-cush* have currency throughout the South, nowhere else is there a double form to match the New Orleans usage. Other distinctive terms are *flambeau* (makeshift torch), *(h)armonica* (instead of Southern *harp*), *lagniappe* (something extra, instead of South Carolina *brawtus*, Texas-Spanish *pilon*, and Florida-Minorcan *countra*), *wishbone* (instead of South Midland and Southern *pulley bone*), and *creole tomatoes* (instead of Northern *cherry tomatoes* and Southern *tommytoes*).

Unlike coastal speech, the Midland dialects of that transition area between the North and South grew up in the interior. From Pennsylvania to Georgia the eastern boundary of the Midland dialect area coincides with the geography of the old frontier. Settlers took the land in the great migrations out of Pennsylvania, Maryland, and Virginia during the half century that preceded the Revolutionary War (1725–1775). Thomas' discovery of the Cumberland Gap in 1750 provided a southern gateway to the Middle West, that passage into Kentucky for the ancestors of both Jefferson Davis and Abraham Lincoln. Before the War of 1812 the frontier extended out of Pittsburgh and down the Ohio River in the north and out of the Yadkin Valley of North Carolina in the south, across Tennessee and Kentucky along the Wilderness Trail of Pennsylvania's Daniel Boone.

Like other American dialects, the Midland varieties rose from a British-English base, but on the frontier the social composition was different. Six of the seven ethnic groups mentioned by Crèvecoeur spoke no British English before they arrived in North America. Later those residents of the interior Midland dialect areas were landbound without ports of entry to receive the influence of English culture and to share in the development of the prestigious London forms. More important, the frontier people occupied themselves mainly with survival in a hostile region. Those factors influenced the disparate groups in a uniform way: Midland dialects resisted the phonological changes under way in England and in the coastal colonies to the north and south; English, Irish, and Scottish folk speech reinforced the regional grammar and vocabulary, giving these American dialects identities of their own.

The Midland pattern contrasts most sharply with the interior varieties of Northern and Southern speech. With a domain that in modern times extends from western New England and upstate New York, along the southern shores of the Great Lakes and then northwestward into the upper Middle West, the Inland Northern dialect spread from its eastern source after the War of 1812. With the construction of the Erie Canal, the watercourse from Albany to Buffalo gave upstate New York and New England access to the Great Lakes, as had the construction of the earlier and slower roadways and the later, more efficient railroads. As Northern speech extended out of upper New Jersey and northern Pennsylvania a major dialect boundary was established with the southern limit of *darning needle* (dragonfly), *pail*, and *whiffletree*, contrasting with North Midland *snake feeder, bucket*, and *singletree*. From upstate New York and across Ohio, Indiana, Illinois, and Iowa westward, the division of Northern and North Midland remains apparent in the pronunciation of *fog* and *hog*, which are pronounced with the vowel of *father* in the North and the vowel of *dog* in the North Midland, in the pronunciation of the diphthong of *cow, house*, and *towel*, which is [ɑu] in the North, beginning with a lower vowel that is closer to that of *father*, and [æu] in the North Midland, beginning with a higher vowel that is closer to that of *lather*, and the existence of an excrescent *r* in *"warsh"* and *"Warshington"* in some Midland speech. More clearly distinctive are the Northern terms *stone wall, pail, swill, teeter-totter, faucet, pit* [of a cherry or peach], and *fire-fly* contrasting with the Midland terms *stone fence, bucket, slops, seesaw, spicket* (spigot), *seed*, and *lightning bug*. In the West the Northern/Midland distinction is most clearly heard in the pronunciation of *car, yard*, and similar words: the Northern pronunciation is marked by a vowel closer to the vowel of *father*; the Midland pronunciation, by one closer to the vowel of *saw*.

Prior to the Civil War other interior forms spread from south of the Great Lakes to the fringes of the plantation cultures from Virginia to Texas and gave rise to the principal Midland varieties, North and South. Between those contrasting cultures the Midland area is perhaps best divided by a phonological Mason-Dixon Line established by the pronunciation of the medial consonant of *greasy*, with an [s] to the north and a [z] to the south. On the Atlantic Coast the boundary replicates the historic Mason-Dixon Line, the common border of Pennsylvania and Maryland. Philadelphia, with the pronunciation [s], must be considered a Northern territory. Westward, however, this difference in pronunciation marks the division within the Midland territory, from Ohio to Missouri. Heading south, a traveler encounters the line at approximately the same place where grits replace hash browns on the breakfast menu, where greens appear at dinner, and where nice, white rice served with Indiana- or Kentucky-fried chicken are all pronounced with a vowel that northerners confuse with the vowel common to *cat, hat,* and *sat.* With this feature comes the first suggestion of the drawl, indigenous bluegrass music, and stock-car, instead of Indy-type or midget-automobile, racing. Along that same line the northern extent of Southern cultural penetration appears in these contrasts: North Midland *bunk, wishbone, husks, headcheese, fritters, bag,* and *turtle* versus South Midland *pallet, pulley bone, shucks, souse* (or *pressed meat*), *flitters, sack,* and *terrapin.*

South Midland speech is a Southern dialect, formerly called Hill Southern in contrast with the Upcountry and Lower Southern patterns (Plantation Southern) to the south and east. The principal South Midland/Southern boundary follows the Blue Ridge Mountains across Virginia, the Carolinas, and Georgia. In South Carolina and Georgia the boundary coincides with the hundred-eighty-day growing season for cotton, the waterways, the soil types, and the cultural organizations inseparable from the plantation systems devoted to the cultivation of indigo, rice, and cane as well as cotton.

Those geographical features and cultural factors underlie the Midland enclaves, as far south as the Florida panhandle, and their Southern counterparts as far north as the St. Francis Basin of Arkansas and the boot heel of Missouri, the cotton country around New Madrid. South Midland is marked by the presence of a constricted *r* after a vowel in *bird, car,* and *horse* and identical vowels in *right* and *ride,* whereas Southern preserves a diphthong in *right* and similar words. Lexical contrasts include South Midland *green beans, red worm, fireboard, French harp* (for *harmonica*), and *tow sack* (for *burlap bag*), versus Southern *snap beans, earthworm, mantelpiece, harp,* and *crocus sack.* In the east South Midland contrasts with Virginia Piedmont Southern with *snake feeder, peanuts,* and *terrapin* versus *snake doctor, goobers,* and *cooter.* In the Mississippi Valley the South Midland dialect occupies the territory by-passed by the plantation cultures as unsuitable for the production of cotton, cane, and rice.

Where the planters extended their operations north and west, as in upper Louisiana, west Tennessee, Arkansas, and east Texas, Lower Southern features outline the area. The Coastal and Gulf Plains were settled from the east, but the deltas of the Mississippi, Atchafalaya, Yazoo, Red, and St. Francis rivers received their populations from the south. As a result interior Southern areas do not show the predictable gradations of uniformity from east to west that are found in the North and North Midland regions.

These Southern dialects are distinguished by coastal forms and by the distinctive contributions of the New Orleans focal area. Coastal Southern pronunciation includes the loss of constricted *r* after vowels, the contrast between the stressed vowels of *Mary, merry,* and *marry,* a "clear *l*" in *Billy* and *Nelly,* and vocabulary items such as *mosquito hawk, crocus sack, hoghead cheese* (or *hog's head cheese*), and *red bug* (instead of *chigger*). Besides *locker* (for *closet*) and *flambeau* (for *makeshift lamp*), the domain of New Orleans is marked by the pervasiveness of *lagniappe, pirogue* (a dugout canoe), *cream cheese* (cottage cheese), *wishbone* (instead of South Midland and Southern *pulley bone*), and *(h)armonica* (instead of South Midland *French harp* or Southern *harp*). Such forms appear as far north as Lake Providence and Monroe, Louisiana, Yazoo City, Mississippi, and along the Gulf Coast beyond the Sabine River into Texas and eastward to Mobile Bay.

The speech of the West is complicated by the blending of Northern, Midland, and Southern forms, as well as by a heavy Spanish influence from Texas to California. The Northern Midland boundary extends over Iowa and cuts across South Dakota in a northwesterly direction. In Montana and Idaho the presence of North and South Midland features reflects the history of the frontier and the enterprises of cattle, agriculture, and mining. Throughout the Rocky Mountains and the urban West Coast the dialects of the early settlers determined the pattern. Seattle and San Francisco speech grew from an Inland Northern base quite similar to old-fashioned Chicago speech. Denver and Los Angeles also developed from that same base, although the Hispanic influence in both places and the successive waves of newcomers from the East, especially in Los Angeles, have obscured the regional pattern that endures with greater stability in Seattle and San Francisco. The Midland influence is strongest west of the Rockies, from Idaho to Arizona, and especially in the conservative speech of Boise, Salt Lake City, and Phoenix. On a train near Yuma, Arizona, during the Great Depression, Woody Guthrie heard the complexity of American speech in the New West as he was going to California:

> There was a big mixture of people here. I could hear the fast accents from the big Eastern joints. You heard the slow, easy-going voices of Southern swamp dwellers, and the people from the Southern hills and mountains. Then another would talk up, and it would be the dry, nosy twang of the folks from the flat wheat plains; or the dialect of the people that come from other countries, whose parents talked another tongue. Then you would hear the slow, outdoor voices of the men from Arizona, riding a short hop to get a job, see a girl, or to throw a little celebration. There was the deep, thick voices of two or three Negroes. It sounded mighty good to me.

The Influence of Bilingualism

In just that way, moving across the country, the national idiom grew through languages and dialects in contact. Spanish, French, and German bilingualism marks the regional patterns of Florida, Louisiana, and Pennsylvania, as well as of south Texas. Gullah, an English-based pidgin, developed in the Sea Islands and low country of South Carolina and Georgia. From that source many varieties of American black folk speech are derived, reflecting various stages of creolization as the dialects merge with the dominant patterns. Social dialects grew through urban and rural experiences throughout the country, many of these related to the Americanization of European bilinguals in the urban North and the integration of blacks in all sectors of society. These dialects are further conditioned and refined by formal and situational styles, including slang, ethnic variation, and patterns of usage reflecting socioeconomic class.

Before urban American Spanish gained prominence in San Antonio, Los Angeles, and Miami, that language had already made large contributions to English in the West. Besides the place names, extending from the *Rio Grande* to *Montana,* the Spanish vocabulary marks the cattle country with Western words: *arroyo, bronc(o), chaparral, canyon, cinch, corral, frijoles, hoosegow, lasso, lariat, mesa, mustang, patio, pinto, pronto, ranch, remuda, rodeo, sombrero,* and *tortilla.*

In bilingual communities Spanish speakers of English tend to avoid regional dialect forms in favor of terms from the general vocabulary, despite the distinctive accent and syntax carried over from the parent language. The same tendency appears among the French in Louisiana, who freely use their native loans, such as *banquette* (sidewalk), *boudin* (blood sausage), *fais-dodo* (country dance), and *jambalaya,* as well as loan translations and adaptations, such as *coffee black, cream cheese* (cottage cheese), and *(h)armonica.* These same speakers resist the Southern regionalisms *pulley bone* and *snap beans.* German, Italian, Scandinavian, Slavic, Spanish, and Yiddish speakers reflect the same trend in the urban North, perhaps through learning from books rather than by simple oral acquisition, and perhaps through efforts to translate from their native tongues. In becoming Americans all of these people enriched the national language and culture. If examples are limited to food alone, Germans provided *bock beer* and *pretzels,* Italians brought *antipasto* and *pizza,* Scandinavians added *lingonberries* and *smorgasbord*; Slavs contributed *kolacky* and *kielbasa,* Yiddish-speaking Germans and Slavs gave *bagels* and *gefilte fish*; and Mexican Spanish provided the base for an endless variety of *enchiladas, burritos,* and *tacos* as its cooking entered the fast-food industry.

Contributions from the African Languages

The full impact of African languages through Gullah and Plantation Creole remains to be properly assessed, but evidence suggests the influence is significant. Among African loans these have gained currency in the national language: *chigger, goober, gumbo, jazz, juke (-box, -joint,* and *-step), okra, voodoo,* and *yam.* Some are regionally restricted to the South: *cooter* (turtle), *cush* and *cush-cush* (mush), and *pinder* (peanut). Others seem limited to the South Carolina and Georgia low country: *buckra* (white man), *det* (heavy), as in *det rain* and *det shower,* and *pinto* (coffin). In addition to the loan-words from Gullah (or "Geechee," the interior Georgia pattern), the creolization of that auxiliary language may have left its mark on American English phonology and grammar as well. As a contact vernacular or language of business (and the probable source of the word *pidgin*), Gullah provided a medium of communication for African slaves and their American supervisors. Thus the pidgin was a language native to neither group. In the development of Plantation Creole (from Portuguese *crioulo* = "white man") the language acquired the highly complex phonological and grammatical rules and complete vocabulary, features necessary in a self-reliant, independent language. General Southern features today include many correspondences with Plantation Creole, the creolized English black folk speech of the plantation cultures of cane, cotton, indigo, and rice. Southern vowel nasality often replaces nasal consonants in *am, been,* and *bacon,* but this feature occurs in Parisian and Louisiana French, as well as in Plantation Creole and West African languages. The simplification of consonant clusters, as in *des* (for *desk* and *desks*) or *tase* (for *taste* and *tastes*), is commonplace in all of those languages, as well as in the Scottish dialect of Robert Burns, who, like American southerners, black and white, often assimilated *l* after back vowels, as in *fa'* (fall) and *saut* (salt). Similarly, the pervasive deletion of articles, copulas, prepositions, and other function words, so characteristic of Gullah and its creolized extensions, is a feature regularly associated with the speech of French, German, and Spanish bilinguals. Nevertheless, this fact remains: large numbers of black and white speakers share those features across the lower South, especially in those areas dominated by the plantation cultures.

The Influence of Social Dialects

As creolization reflects the blending of languages and cultures, so slang, argot, and social dialects mark the activities of subcultures within the basic social structure. Although nothing as widespread as Cockney and Australian rhyming slang has developed in America, inventive usage here has steadily modified native speech. Most slang originates in the specialized conversations of particular groups, in which usage reinforces group identity and develops into private codes that may later gain wide acceptance. These include such now-familiar terms as *clout* and *gerrymander* from politics, *blues* and *jazz* from music, *headline* and *editorial* from journalism, and *by a nose, inside track, front-runner, shoo-in,* and *sure thing* from the vocabulary of horse racing. The distinctive words of other groups—pickpockets, CB operators, and computer specialists—suggest the ways in which the subcultures function and illustrate the ways in which language develops.

Social dialects also underlie the regional patterns of speech, reflecting absolute factors, such as age and ethnic origin, and relative factors, such as education and social position. As a healthy language is always changing, the age and experience of its speakers are recorded by incipient, dominant, and recessive forms, as demonstrated in the vocabulary of automobiles: the emergent *gas guzzler* and *pimpmobile,* the durable *sedan* and *limousine,* and the relic *tin lizzie* and *roadster*. Ethnic terms are the cultural birthrights of individual speakers and great linguistic resources for society at large. Yiddish *schlock, chutzpah, macher,* and *schmaltz* have moved from the Jewish communities to the national language, as have the specialized Sicilian terms *capo, Cosa Nostra,* and *Mafia* in urban American subcultures. Education reinforces language trends with the spread of generalized patterns of pronunciation, grammar, and vocabulary, but these are challenged by migrant accents in Chicago today just as they were in London four hundred years ago. As Latinos made *macho* an American word, blacks have put many Southern regionalisms, such as *funky, up-tight,* and *right on,* into common usage. The language reflects cultural patterns, refined and strengthened through association and social status.

Social dialects also mark the evolution of a language. In America the middle classes have generated great changes. These include the absorption of immigrant cultures at the lower level and influence upon the dominant culture at the higher level. As the linguistic and cultural forms are traditionally conservative in both aristocratic and folk groups, however different their social styles, middle-class society and speech alter those conventional patterns from below and from above. Just as members of the secular and regular clergy, educators, lawyers, politicians, and physicians helped shape the London Standard from the early Middle Ages through the English Renaissance because they were conversant with both the ruling class and the common people, so new patterns of American usage grow today through the influence of upper-middle-class dialects. Even stronger influences appear from the speech of the lower middle class, especially in urban centers, where clerks, cab drivers, and telephone operators come in contact with the entire community in their daily work.

Of these, ethnic dialects preserve the most complicated social varieties of language and reflect the essential spirit of American culture. As frontier societies developed distinctive regional patterns, Spanish, French, Dutch, Scandinavian, and German settlers used their native languages before adopting the dominant English dialect. English, Irish, and Scottish folk speech constituted probably the most influential ethnic varieties on the frontier, but these were modified by the language habits of their neighbors. In the process of Americanization, Europeans, Africans, and Asians gave the language some of its most familiar words: *chop suey, hamburger, hillbilly, juke box, pizza, prairie, rodeo, Santa Claus, smorgasbord,* and *tycoon.*

The national vocabulary reflects the intimacy of conversation and the evolution of democractic social forms. John Adams proposed that Congress establish an American Academy "for refining, correcting, improving, and ascertaining the English language." Later, when asked to preside over such activities, Thomas Jefferson responded:

> There are so many differences between us and England, of soil, climate, culture, productions, laws, religion, and government, that we must be left far behind the march of circumstances, were we to hold ourselves rigorously to their standard. If, like the French Academicians, it were proposed to *fix* our language, it would be fortunate that the step were not taken in the days of our Saxon ancestors, whose vocabulary would illy express the science of this day. Judicious neology can alone give strength and copiousness to language, and enable it to be the vehicle of new ideas.

Instead of rules from a National Academy of English, Americans accepted the common-law customs of intelligent conversation with all of its modifications through time and circumstance. Current usage, for example, may reject *illy express* and *judicious neology,* but history shows the correctness of Jefferson's message. He recognized the certainty of change, the function of language as a cultural tool, and the importance of thoughtful selection. Through common-law customs of speech and writing the national language develops words and records social facts. This Dictionary orders those materials of discourse and transmits the substance of the American heritage.

Usage and Acceptability in Language

In keeping with a tradition of providing balanced and accurate information on matters of usage, *The American Heritage Dictionary, Second College Edition* presents the following two essays. The opposing views set out in these essays will acquaint the reader with some of the issues that must be considered when a point of usage is in dispute.

Resolved: The prevailing usage of its speakers should be the chief determinant of acceptability in language.

Dwight Bolinger

For the affirmative:

To avoid the suggestion that prevailing usage in speech should determine acceptability in writing, let us assume that "speakers" includes "writers" and that "language" is both spoken and written.

Usage in the broad sense is always the determinant of correctness. The only way to falsify that assertion is to imagine that language somehow preceded its users in the form of a code that has been preserved through the ages with no intervening fall from grace and no need to reconstruct the rules from the ruins of surviving performance. From this standpoint the resolution is a truism.

From another standpoint it is a tautology. Usage should be the chief determinant because, chiefly, it has to be. A language is a universe of conventions that every child begins to learn at the moment of birth—some of them, such as rhythm, perhaps even in utero. The prevailing usage of the speakers within sight, touch, and hearing of the child determines how the sounds are formed, how words are crystallized out of an amorphous flow, how accents are imposed, how sequences are arranged, and all the other delicate and magical adjustments that compose the mechanism of every language on earth. By the age of ten and before any serious attention can be given to what "should be," the child has already learned ninety per cent of the structure required to communicate and is well along in the task of building a respectable vocabulary with meanings picked up in the same informal way. The rarity with which we need to consult a dictionary for our day-to-day words proves what "prevailing" means in this context.

It is only when usage is *in dispute* that one asks which way to go—and as such disputes are usually noisy, we exaggerate their frequency and importance. But here is where our leading statement makes the most sense.

The first question is, prevailing *where*? English is spoken as a native language on five continents. Even if it were possible to compute a statistic for "prevalence" in every usage over this domain, it would be impractical to enforce it; one has to recognize constituencies. Are they defined by region, social class, age, sex, voluntary association, setting, occasion, medium? Different usages prevail in each, and when they compete it is not easy to decide which should be preferred. Traditionally the rivalries have been between one regional usage and another or one class usage and another—or sometimes a bit of each, as regional and class lines tend to merge. In the United States the educational missionaries from New England took the authority of their speech and writing to the hinterland. In Britain the variety of English spoken by a class of speakers in England claimed precedence over other varieties in the rest of the United Kingdom as well as in England itself. But also, at various times and places, male speech has been regarded as superior to female, adult to juvenile, and formal to informal. This means, say, that the prevailing adult usage shall be the model for the child (all in good time, of course, for precocity may be offensive). The same need for continuity also demands that the speech of those steeped in the past shall be the model for everyone. Many believe that "the past" should mean "the literary past," and here is where the sticky choices are usually made.

Take Drew Pearson as he wrote the sentence "If the TV cameras were still in focus last week, the public would have seen the 27-year-old Roy still influencing almost every move the senator makes." Pearson did what many writers and speakers do nowadays: he chose "were" instead of the literary "had been." If he did it deliberately, perhaps he reasoned that "were" is more economical. The traditionalist retorts that until the whole sentence is read, "were" sounds as if it referred to a possible fact, not something contrary to fact, and this confuses the reader. Pearson counters that a reader who knows the chances will suspend judgment; as soon as "would have seen" is reached, everything comes clear; the trouble is the traditionalist's inflexibility. The traditionalist replies that Pearson could have done all his readers, flexible or inflexible, the courtesy of complete intelligibility at the price of one word. The argument goes on till dawn.

And brings us back to the question of constituencies. All our lives we shift from one to another. Each shift is a real or pretended claim of membership and imposes the obligation of conforming to the prevailing usage of the established members. Newcomers try but never fully succeed; nor do older members succeed in fending off all the mistakes from outside. The result is slow but constant change, accommodation, and reinterpretation. When all members "speak English" or "speak French" or any supposedly monolithic "language," there is little conscious attention to proper behavior. With one exception: when a new member tries to move not crosswise but *up* in society—and then is faced with a minefield of shibboleths whose chief purpose is to keep out the uncouth: "hopefully," "more perfect," "can't hardly," "he don't," "kind of a." Here the negative of our resolution appears to hold. More people say "I only wanted six" than say "I wanted only six." Therefore the prevailing usage is not a proper determinant of acceptability. But the ritual nature of the test is not avowed. Instead it is put as an impartial law, like the law that prohibits sleeping under bridges: one must not "misplace modifiers." But the logic is defective and the example is inconsistent: "I only wanted six" is clear from its intonation, and nobody objects to "I just wanted six." No matter; it still separates the chosen who make the rules from the outlanders who have only numbers on their side.

When well-meaning educators, hoping to boost learners up the social ladder, make a policy of such half-informed tinkering, the results they get too often exceed their hopes. Speakers overcompensate. Told not to split infinitives, they shy away from splitting any verbs at all and say "always have been" instead of "have always been." Warned against "like" as an adverb, they turn "as" into a preposition and write "As a baby, they babble." Taught never to say "It's me," they go the extra mile with "for we and they." Add to the targets that are overshot the ones that are not even aimed at: the illogical "I could care less" is stigmatized, but hardly anyone notices the equally illogical "to my knowledge" (replacing "to the best of my knowledge"), used to mean not certainty but uncertainty. Normative grammar is a hit-or-miss enterprise. Not that it needs to be—a more careful analysis and a heavier investment in teaching the language might make it an effective stabilizer. But there will be little enthusiasm for that as long as stigmatizing a few usages makes an effective test of social acceptability.

In this small corner of the language a minority of the highbrow and the well-born may succeed in conferring authority on a small number of usages. Meanwhile a hundred times as many others are fluctuating undetected, with their success or failure guaranteed by majority usage in their constituencies. And common to all constituencies is the great semi-inert mass of usage where no conflict arises because everyone already obeys the conventions unquestioningly and the rule is simply what people do—plurals in *-s,* "and" for conjunction, countless words with agreed-upon senses. The *Harper Dictionary of Contemporary Usage* contains a little over 2,700 entries. Make an outside guess and say that a given individual may be bothered by a third of those. Compare that figure with a working vocabulary and grammar of 30,000 words, collocations, idioms, clichés, and constructions about which there is no dispute, and the "chief" of "chief determinant" can be stamped in gold.

Does this self-contained universe of usage ultimately decide what is acceptable? When Margaret Fuller proclaimed in 1846, "I accept the universe," Thomas Carlyle delivered his now-famous retort, "She'd better."

WILLIAM F. BUCKLEY, JR.

For the negative:

What is it that brings verbal "acceptability"? It is suggested that usage should be the "chief" determinant. It occurs to me that the two sentences just now composed could not communicate what they now do save that precision in definition and inflection is still possible; and precision is still possible precisely because mere usage, however prolonged, does not baptize. Providence in due course sometimes accepts into its bosom sinners, but usually only after time served in the antechambers. And how will we know just when that dispensation is granted? Well, to answer that only in part in jest: by asking me.

Why me?

I had a colleague at *National Review,* a professor of political science at Yale University given to rather endearing narcissism, and another colleague, a lady of scrupulous editorial rigor, the kind who would write "If it be true that . . ." Suzanne La Follette was always approaching Willmoore Kendall, open dictionary in hand, spectacles perched over the end of her nose, to substantiate the illegitimacy of a particular usage by Kendall. After a half dozen of these encounters Kendall, exasperated, commented: "Don't you *see,* Suzanne, when people get around to writing dictionaries, they come to people like *me* to find out what to put *in* them."

I don't know a better penetration of the point. *"People like me."* At once, in Kendall's statement, one discerns the statesmanship of lexicography, which is on the one hand to authorize change, on the other to deny change's plebiscitary presumptions. Or, more exactly, to confine the constituency of change; to insist that only such as Kendall are consulted. It doesn't matter if 99 per cent of the American people say "spokesperson." Only if Kendall—and I—agree will it become "acceptable."

That word is in quotation marks to emphasize that it does not automatically convey exactly what it is that actually *happens* when acceptability is achieved. There is a sense in which a great many things become "acceptable" by the fact of their high incidence—for instance, lying and adultery. But the words manage to retain a pejorative impact because the deeds they denote are defined outside a purely democratic sociology. The *presumption* is against lying, as it is against adultery, which is less than to pronounce that lying and adultery are absolutely in all circumstances forbidden (though Immanuel Kant, for instance, always rejects the lie, and strict-constructionist Christianity, adultery). What is implied by the surviving pejorative is that *dispensations* are especially granted—ad hoc, ad personam. If the pejorative were bled out of the acts of lying and adultery, then the words would lose their moral dimension; the prevailing practices of society's citizens would determine the acceptability of the terms *lying* and *adultery*. That the pejorative survives surely tells us that intuitively people, recognizing their own weaknesses as such, do not wish the moral criteria to change. In short, acceptability is by no means routinely achieved merely by democratic affirmation.

And then I ask, What exactly is meant by the "chief" determinant of "acceptability"? What is it intended that the qualifier "chief" should convey? How is "chief" here defined? Is it intended to be conclusive? Or is it merely intended to invert the presumptions? Does it intend to convey that if the majority use "spokesperson," it becomes "acceptable" practice to do so? Or merely that if the majority indeed do so, objectors need to shoulder the burden of making a case for continuing illegitimacy? The resolution, we can see, hedges, both in the use of "acceptability" and in the use of the qualifier "chief." And understandably so, because although the Miss La Follettes of this world cannot be permitted to freeze a language in its tracks, when changes are authorized they must be authorized by the Kendalls of this world. The remaining question, then, is: Why?

Because, as is frequently pointed out by science, human progress is achieved by the taking of exact measurements. Language is inherently inexact, but even though the objective is asymptotically approached, it remains the objective; and such exactitude as language *is* capable of is a casualty of careless usage. But if carelessness is to be deplored, by whom will it be deplored? By those who judge it to be careless. And what are they to consult, in their anxiety, if not a dictionary? That dictionary may, in certain of its declarations, be held to be obsolete. But make sure that it is the Kendalls of this world who judge it so, because they are expertly trained and congenitally gifted. They know how to take careful measurements, and they use the language to do this.

How else?

Language is an aesthetic as well as an analytical tool. And to slur language is as painful to the well-tempered ear as to slur music. In music the individualist seeks to introduce a new modality. He may emerge as a great artist, or he may be held to be witless; juries will judge. Usually, in serious music, a genuinely new style requires fifty years to win acceptance. In language some words have been paying court to the admissions committee for centuries, while thousands upon thousands have simply given up. Some win almost immediate acceptance. But the question is always, acceptance by whom?

Vulgar, Slang, Regional, Nonstandard, Informal: most new meanings or uses need to work their way against that upstream drag; and resistance should be formal, i.e., embodied in a dictionary prepared to accept but also prepared to deny.

Lexicographers are sufficiently conversant with their craft to make judgments, yea, even unto designating a word, or a usage, *illiterate*. The other way is mobocratic, undifferentiated. And what is the purpose of a *guide* to usage if not—as required—to exclude? The negative function of a dictionary is a part of its function. It is not a sign of arrogance for the king to rule. That is what he is there for.

English and Good English

Geoffrey Nunberg
Stanford University

It is natural enough that the parties in the debate over what makes for "good English" should be preoccupied with their differences, but what tends to get overlooked in the process is that all sides share a great many common assumptions and that these assumptions are in fact every bit as particular and curious as the more notorious idiosyncracies of English spelling. It is not so much the linguistic virtues we recognize that are unusual. All of us admire language that is vivid, euphonious, rhythmic, and eloquent as well as clear, logical, and concise. But it is only these last that we elevate to the status of civic and moral responsibilities. We may pity the speaker with a tin ear, but so long as he expresses himself clearly and logically, we are not likely to hold him up as a horrible example of the failure of the educational system.

What is even more curious, we apply the canons of good usage only when we are considering the relatively restricted writing that we classify as expository prose. Essays on the sad state of the language seem invariably to begin with a ritual invocation to "the tongue of Shakespeare and Dickens," but the evidence of degeneration that they cite is never drawn from recent poetry or fiction. Instead examples of errors culled from advertisements, newspaper stories, and government reports are given, as if the fate of English lay entirely in the hands of its copywriters and bureaucrats rather than its artists.

All of this would have been puzzling to Dante or Cyrano—or to Shakespeare, for that matter. And others would find it odd, as well, that English grammarians made no effort to establish a single correct accent but rather allowed each nation—or, in America, each locality—to establish its own local standards of pronunciation. And finally, they would surely wonder why in centuries of bickering about usage the English-speaking world has never seriously tried to establish an academy to set things right once and for all. In short, asking a foreigner to understand our concept of good usage would be rather like asking a present-day banker to understand why Dante cast the usurers down to the seventh circle.

Our ideas of good usage were for the most part shaped in the eighteenth century. They owed something to the growth of literacy and the rise of the middle class, something to the replacement of the Stuart court by the German-speaking Hanovers, and something to a new perception of English as the language not just of England but also of the larger community of Great Britain and the colonies. The new attitudes were most closely associated with the rise of a new class of writers and intellectuals, freed for the first time from direct dependence on aristocratic patronage, who assumed cultural authority during the period. To a striking extent these men were outsiders: the Scotsmen Hume, Adam Smith, and Smollett, the Irishmen Burke, Steele, Swift, and Goldsmith, the Catholic Alexander Pope, and the middle-class provincials Gay, Sterne, and Dr. Johnson. Their object was to replace the social values of the declining aristocratic tradition with new values determined by a "natural" elite based on wit and learning, and they moved immediately to assume authority over the language, the only coin they had it in their power to mint. Never before or since have so many great minds occupied themselves with the problem of defining and rationalizing the English language—not just Johnson but Swift, Addison, Chesterfield, Priestley, Webster, and many more whose names are no longer familiar. If they did not succeed in "ascertaining" the language, as many had hoped, they did at least manage to fix the criteria by which language use would be judged for the next two hundred years.

The eighteenth-century grammarians never seriously questioned the doctrine that usage should be the "supreme arbiter" of linguistic correctness. As the great grammarian George Campbell observed in his 1776 *Philosophy of Rhetoric,* "Every tongue whatever is founded in use or custom." At stake was whose usage should rule and why. In earlier days English standards had been set in the relatively changeable speech of the aristocracy and its captive clergy, and a usage was justified largely according to the prestige of its users. The prescriptive grammarians, as they have come to be called, insisted instead that standards must be fixed and rational. To this end they argued the supremacy of literary precedents, in particular those of critical prose, as recorded and systematized in the comprehensive dictionaries and grammars that had begun to appear for the first time. Such models were more permanent and more democratic—for the great writers were selected, not by accidents of birth, but by natural talent and public approbation. More radical than their continental contemporaries, the grammarians argued that linguistic authority should be sharply separated from any national institutions. In 1712 Swift had been one of many to suggest the formation of an academy, to be composed partly of writers and partly of aristocrats, and one might actually have been constituted if the Tories had remained in power. But by mid-century the idea was universally rejected as inimical to what Johnson called the spirit of English liberty.

But the chief virtue of literary models of good usage, from the grammarians' point of view, was not in their fixity or their popular acceptance but in the fact that their merits could be explicitly justified by appeals to analogy, etymology, and logic; for the Age of Reason good usage had to be rationalized. Thus there began to appear such now-familiar dictates as the injunctions against usages like *It is me, more perfect, the tallest of the two,* and *as old, or older than,* among many others, all justified by reference to what logic should require. And a sharp distinction was drawn between those aspects of usage that allowed of rational justification and others, like pronunciation, that remained tied to social prestige.

In their zeal many of the grammarians—like their modern successors—seemed sometimes to want to make all usage subject to their idiosyncratic ideas of logic, without due respect for the idiomaticity of language. As modern linguists have been at pains to show, language has a logic of its own, which does not always reveal itself to casual reflection. To take just one example, linguists have noted that the rule requiring words like *everyone* and *each* to be followed by singular pronouns comes a cropper when the pronoun occurs outside of the clause that contains its antecedent. We simply cannot say, for example, *Everyone took his coat, and he left without saying good-bye*. But linguists err when they conclude that the "logical" justifications that the grammarians offered for good usage were really intended as excuses to justify the usage of the ruling classes. The specific rules that the grammarians insisted on may sometimes have been ill-considered, but that is less important than the general principle that the rules were intended to illustrate: good usage is determined in rational reflection on language.

What is more, while the literate middle class to which the prescriptive grammarians were speaking may have been by modern standards a small elite, it was much larger than the aristocracy whose linguistic standards it usurped, and in advancing the notion that linguistic values required an independent, rational justification the prescriptive grammarians set themselves squarely on the side of merit against hereditary privilege. Until recently, at least, English prescriptive grammar has been a doctrine closely associated with liberal ideals, as can be seen from the roster of its defenders, from Johnson to Matthew Arnold to George Orwell, W. H. Auden, and Lionel Trilling.

By the middle of the twentieth century, however, the social battle lines had been substantially redrawn. Earlier grammarians had given little time to inveighing against the speech of the provinces or the lower classes. It was simply understood that such models were unacceptable. But the twentieth century brought with it a new pluralistic idea of how cultural values should be determined, and prescriptive grammarians sometimes found themselves having to defend the very sorts of class values that had been attacked two hundred years before as they tried to show that middle-class language was superior in logic or clarity to the language of the lower classes or of ethnic minorities. At this point, moreover, the battle was joined by proponents of the new linguistics, who quite correctly pointed out that every language variety has its own internal logic and who questioned the authority of mere writers and critics to speak to matters that required considerable technical expertise. In the name of science the linguists insisted that there were no hard grounds for preferring the usage of one group over another and went on to argue that the entire notion of correctness rested on an ill-justified elitism.

By the time the controversy had reached its pitch, in the furor over the publication of more "permissive" dictionaries and grammar textbooks, there had been a curious ideological shift. Now the grammarians were attacked as apologists for the entrenched order, while the opponents of traditional doctrines of usage were branded mobocrats. As in other areas, the old liberals found themselves in alliance with the new right as writers like William F. Buckley, Jr. began to sound the same themes that George Orwell had insisted on a generation earlier.

At present we are at an impasse. Both sides fulgurate, while in the middle the lexicographers and educators often counsel an enlightened hypocrisy: even if the canons of good usage have no real justification, it is best that people be taught to conform to them so as not to give offense to traditionalists. And to be sure, there are no easy solutions, since each side has a part of the right in the matter. On the one hand, it is clear that there is no going back to the days of a homogeneous, literate elite whose linguistic authority is accepted unquestioningly. Nor can the technical authority of modern linguistics be repealed, any more than that of psychiatry, sociology, or the other sciences that have taken over a large part of the intellectual territory that used to belong to the critical public. The day is past when the dictates of any single lexicographer or grammarian could hope to command the attention, much less the deference, of the literate public.

At the same time, the linguists have not the fondest hope of convincing the public that all widely practiced forms of usage are equally acceptable; if anything, there is more support now for traditional standards than there was twenty years ago. And this is surely good, for if the idea that good usage has a rational justification is abandoned, people will return to the doctrine that the correctness of a usage is based entirely on the social prestige of the speaker—the very notion that both the eighteenth-century grammarians and the modern radicals have found intolerable. This has always been the English speaker's attitude toward pronunciation, which has been considered to lie outside the scope of rational justification; if the laissez-faire party had its way, all other aspects of usage would be reduced equally to matters of pure snobbery.

In an effort to steer a middle course various strategems have been tried. The *American Heritage Dictionary* has put together its Usage Panel, for example, on the assumption that the reader is best served by being told what practices a sample of educated, careful users of the language take to be correct. The solution is not perfect to be sure, in part because English speakers are no more willing now to submit to the rule of even an informally constituted academy than they were in Dr. Johnson's day, and in part because a panel of any kind is constrained to passing judgments and cannot collectively deliver itself of the sorts of reasoned justifications that underlie a genuine understanding of what makes good usage good. But by taking such judgments together with the great number of traditional principles that still appeal to our common good sense, and the many insights that modern linguistics provides, lexicographers can arrive at serviceable norms of usage of the sort that readers expect the Dictionary to provide. These norms must be guidelines, of course, not dictates, because the one thing that has not changed since the eighteenth century is the insistence of English speakers on the prerogative of making up their own minds about what is right. But in the end we must have faith in another virtue of English speakers, their willingness to listen to reason.

The Mathematics of Language

Henry Kučera
Brown University

Language is such a characteristically human activity and such a potentially exquisite transmitter of the literary imagination that many of us intuitively resent any suggestion that it may have prosaic, predictable, or even mathematical properties. And yet, over the last decade, we have seen much of our language communication recorded, processed, and transmitted by computers that are capable of reducing our written words to electronic signals, allowing us to search through them and organize them and then, if need be, transmit them electronically and almost instantaneously over long distances. Word processing, as we have rather unimaginatively named this computer manipulation of our linguistic records, is not only a billion-dollar industry but also a new information medium that may well revolutionize our world of communication as much as the invention of movable type did more than five hundred years ago. It still takes people to formulate ideas and to write the novels and the poems. But now the drudgery of having to retype entire pages of a manuscript in order to make a few corrections is gone. Word processing offers us the opportunity of easily shifting a sentence here and a paragraph there, the luxury of changing our mind about an awkward phrase or formulation while leaving the rest of our document intact, and even makes it possible to rely on the machine to find our misspellings and to correct them—until we end up with an elegant final version, with as many copies and variations as we wish to have. Once again in human history the machine offers us liberation from mechanical drudgery and the freedom to focus our imagination and energy on the substantive elements of language creativity and communication.

The fact that computers—these machines that many of us still think of as fast number crunchers—can encode, manipulate, process, and in a limited way understand language, is possible only because of the remarkable properties of natural language systems as they have evolved through a long history. In its essence language is a hierarchically organized structure of symbols, which allows us to express a potentially infinite number of ideas through finite means. The basic building blocks of the system are very few: the set of contrastive sounds—the phonemes of the language—which we represent by letters and letter combinations in our alphabetical writing systems. These elementary building blocks are combined in highly restricted ways into the basic meaningful units, the words of the language, which, again in accordance with systematic combinatory principles, form meaningful sequences of syntactically well-formed sentences. The entire system thus consists of the concatenation of a finite inventory of discrete units into a potentially infinite set of discourses, just as the ten numerals of our number system can be combined into an infinite set of different values and mathematical expressions. This analogous organization of language and numeric systems makes it possible to represent linguistic units by numbers and to manipulate them as if they were mathematical objects. That a computer can find a misspelled word in our document is no magic: if the machine has a dictionary available, with words coded in the internal computer representation as numbers, it can compare the numeric code of the words that we keyboard with the numerical value of the words in the dictionary in a simple arithmetical operation. If no match is found, our word is not in the dictionary and we have a good candidate for a misspelling.

EFFICIENCY AND REDUNDANCY

But languages—as they have evolved spontaneously in national communities over the ages—have much more complex mathematical properties than those resulting from a hierarchical structure of discrete units. Languages exhibit both efficiency and redundancy, two contradictory characteristics that linguistic systems balance against each other to achieve both communicational usefulness and reliability. Consider redundancy first: as limited as the repertory of the basic sounds (the set of phonemes) of a language is—thirty-three in English in the most common phonological analyses—only a small subset of their possible permutations can form actual words. An adult English speaker knows, for example, that *trip* is an English word. But he also knows that *tlip* is not an English word, and he does not have to go to a dictionary to discover that fact; no English word can begin with *tl-*. But when faced with *trin,* our English speaker—although not recognizing the word—may have to resort to a dictionary. It is at least theoretically a possible English word because it does not violate any of the general constraints on permissible sequences of English sounds.

Even on this elementary phonological level we thus find a substantial redundancy, the imposition of constraints on possible sequences and, consequently, the introduction of some information waste into the system, waste that is needed to enable us to communicate without an overwhelming number of errors and misunderstandings. If every possible permutation of sounds were an actual English word, our communication system would be very efficient indeed, and all our words could be very short; there would be no need for any word of more than four sounds, and we could have over a million of those. But communicating in such a system would become extremely difficult. Our physiological limitations in producing and perceiving sounds and sound sequences, and the properties of human memory, would make the learning and use of such a system practically impossible. But even if one could learn this distressingly efficient language, every noise, every imperfection or error that destroyed our perception of but a single sound, would disrupt our understanding, since the system's lack of redundancy would not allow us to guess what it was that we might have missed. Worse still, each time we heard one sound where another was intended, we would have heard a legitimate, albeit unintended, word. Thus redundancy, a universal property of all languages, is one of our great communicational friends, just as it is a friend of the computer designer, who utilizes the same principle to detect potentially damaging transmission errors. Of course, the constraints on permissible sequences of sounds that are utilized to achieve this redundancy may differ substantially from language to language; there are many languages in which a word can begin with an initial *tk-* cluster that English prohibits. The same is true on higher levels; English—a configurational language that relies on word order to signal many grammatical functions—imposes severe restrictions on possible sequences of words within a sentence, while languages with a "free" word order, such as Latin or Russian, allow seemingly endless permutations of items. But to make this possible these languages need an elaborate system of inflected forms and paradigms in which a small set of endings is combined in highly restricted ways with a word stem to signal the syntactic relations that are achieved through word order in English.

A branch of mathematics known as information theory provides a formal means of measuring the redundancy of a communication system. For natural languages these measurements are complex and difficult, but some overall estimates are possible. On the phonological level we have calculated for several languages (English, German, Russian, and Czech) that—taking only the constraints on sound sequences within syllables into account—redundancy reaches about 50 per cent. All languages, of course, have restrictions on which syllables may follow one another; the overall redundancy estimate thus must be put at least at the 80 per cent level. (For details see H. Kučera and G. K. Monroe, *A Comparative Quantitative Phonology of*

Russian, Czech and German, New York: American Elsevier, 1968.)

The other side of the coin in language design is efficiency. It has been known for a long time that words that are used very frequently tend to be short. We even abbreviate words as they become more common: *telephone* to *phone, airplane* to *plane, television* to *TV*—or *telly* if one lives in England—and so on. Computer analysis of large samples of language texts now provides us with accurate data to support this general conclusion. In the one-million-word Corpus of Present-Day American English, also known as the Brown Corpus, compiled from samples taken from 500 different sources of 15 different genres and styles of writing, words accounting for 57 per cent of the running texts (i.e., 57 per cent of the million word tokens) have four letters or fewer. But an entirely different situation comes to view if from the Brown Corpus we construct a dictionary, that is, a collection of different words, known in formal linguistics as types, with each word appearing only once in the list. Here words of four or fewer characters account for less than 9 per cent of the dictionary. This discrepancy in itself suggests the communication efficiency of language: the system is so designed that it is the short words that are repeated often in an average text and thus accumulate high frequency figures. The longer words are used sparingly; the repeat rate of the truly long words is negligible. For every occurrence of a ten-letter word there are eight occurrences of a three-letter word, and for every instance of a twenty-letter word there are 3,524 occurrences of a three-letter word. (For a description and various analyses of the Brown Corpus see H. Kučera and W. N. Francis, *Computational Analysis of Present-Day American English,* Providence: Brown University Press, 1967, and W. N. Francis and H. Kučera, *Frequency Analysis of English Usage: Lexicon and Grammar,* Boston: Houghton Mifflin Company, 1982.)

It is worthwhile to point out the similarity of this principle in human languages to the design of artificial communication systems. In the International Morse code the most frequent English letter, *e,* has the shortest symbol, one short signal, which requires minimum transmission time. The least frequent letters, *j, k,* and *y,* have the longest codes, each represented by one of various sequences of three long signals and one short. What Samuel Morse did by planning, languages have achieved in their natural evolution.

How Many Words?

Every linguist with an interest in the quantitative properties of language will on some occasion be faced with some form of the ultimate question in the word numbers game: "How many words did Shakespeare use?" "How many words are there in the English language?" "How many words should a dictionary have?"

The first question, at least, has a definite although not simple answer: Shakespeare's complete works consist of a total of 884,647 words of text containing a grand total of 29,066 different words, including proper names (see M. Spevack, *A Complete and Systematic Concordance to the Works of Shakespeare,* Hildesheim: Georg Olms Verlagsbuchhandlung, 1968–69). In order to understand the significance of these numbers, however, we have to be quite certain of what we mean by a word. What is it that we are counting? Even if we focus on written language only and define a word simply as a string of letters bounded by space on each side, our problem does not entirely disappear. We still have to decide whether to consider inflected forms, such as those formed from the verb *play* (*plays, playing, played*), to be words in their own right or simply members of a single class represented by the base form PLAY. If we take the first approach, we have four distinct words. If we take the second, we have only one, having created a set of grammatical forms, differing from one another and from the base form only in inflection, that linguists call a *lemma.* Even in English, where the inflectional system is quite limited, we thus have to exercise great terminological care when making statistical statements about the size of the vocabulary employed by a writer or used in a particular work. In a highly inflected language like Russian, where many nouns have ten different case and number forms, the difference between the number of word forms and the number of lemmas is large indeed.

If we compiled a good-sized English word list that listed all words, including regular inflections such as plurals or past tenses of verbs, and compared it to a list of exactly the same set of words represented just by a single base form, the ratio between the two lists would be about 1.6:1. (This ratio, too, is based on the analysis of the Brown Corpus.) We can then predict that a list of 100,000 word forms would contain about 62,500 lemmas and, conversely, that a 100,000-word dictionary giving base forms only could be expanded into about 160,000 word forms.

Conventional dictionaries are, by and large, collections of lemmas, represented by their base forms, which appear as boldface entries in alphabetical order; their inflected forms are given when their formation involves some irregularity or spelling change, but they are generally not listed when regular. The concept of a word, as we have become used to it from the structure of dictionaries, is thus closer to that of a lemma than to that of a word form. In frequency and vocabulary studies of the works of an author or of a collection of texts, however, it is usually the case that word forms are counted, not lemmas. There are several reasons for this: computers, not having linguistic skills, can detect as different words those strings of letters that are nonidentical, but they cannot easily recognize and put together those items that belong to a single lemma. Lemmatization involves a number of methodological linguistic decisions, some of them quite difficult. The figure of 29,066 different words used by Shakespeare thus refers to word forms, not to lemmas. Assuming that with the application of the same lemmatization principles the ratio of forms to lemmas that we discovered in the Brown Corpus, namely 1.6:1, also holds in Shakespeare's case, we can conclude that the total vocabulary of lemmas in the poet's work is approximately 18,000.

Given these rules of the game, how does the richness of Shakespeare's vocabulary compare to present-day English usage? In the analysis of the Brown Corpus word forms have been assigned to their lemma groups on the basis of well-defined principles, but the statistics for individual word forms have also been compiled. These two sets of results indicate that this million-word data base contains 61,805 word forms, which belong to 37,851 lemmas. The number of different words in the Brown Corpus is thus more than twice that of the complete works of Shakespeare, although the size of the two data bases is comparable. Does this mean that Shakespeare's vocabulary was modest and that English has over the last few hundred years evolved into a lexically much richer language? Not necessarily; many words have undoubtedly been added to our lexical store, but the main reason for the discrepancy is almost certainly the fact that the corpus of Shakespeare's writings is quite homogeneous in content and style, while the Brown Corpus is intentionally heterogeneous to make it representative of contemporary usage and was therefore selected from 500 different sources that range from newspapers to scientific writing to general fiction.

If all words were statistically equal, then each word form would occur about 16 times in the million-word text, and each lemma about 26 times. In actuality the rate of repetition of individual words, and thus their frequency, is extremely uneven. As already suggested in our discussion of the frequency of words of different length, word utilization in actual use varies enormously. The overall statistics are quite striking: the use rate of the first 100 most frequent words is so high that the first 100 word forms account for a full 47.4 per cent of all the text, that is, of all the running words (tokens) contained in the million; the 100 most frequent lemmas make up 49.6 per cent of all the text. To account for 80 per cent of the entire million-word text takes only 2,854 different word forms belonging to 2,124 distinct lemmas.

This highly skewed frequency distribution, exhibited by the words of any language, may lead to a false conclusion. The fact that one needs to know fewer than 3,000 words to understand 80 per cent of a reasonably representative modern English text does not mean that this kind of vocabulary could guarantee any of us cultural survival in a modern society. It must be realized, first of all, that many of the most frequent words in English are function words: articles, prepositions, and auxiliary verbal forms such as those of *be, have,* or *do*. The definite article *the* is by far the most frequent word in English, occurring 69,975 times in the million-word corpus. Although in the overall text the dominant parts of speech are nouns and verbs, accounting for about 26 per cent and 18 per cent, respectively, of all the word tokens, function words have by far the highest frequency of any category. The lemmas occupying frequency ranks from 1 through 32 are all function words or pronouns; the first content word, the verb *say,* appears only at rank 33, and the first noun, *man,* at rank 44. When we consider all distinct forms rather than just the lemmas, the dominance of function words and pronouns is even clearer; the first content form, the past tense *said,* is now only in rank 53, the adjective *new* occupies rank 64, and *man* has been relegated to rank 81. But it is precisely the function words—as essential as they may be for signaling the exact role of content words and their syntactic relation in a sentence—which are also the ones that because of their high predictability can be most easily guessed if they happen to be omitted from the text. Such omissions are precisely what characterizes newspaper headlines: *Actor Found in Critical Condition After Explosion* has been deprived of all articles and auxiliaries; in a full text the sentence would read something like *An actor has been found in critical condition after an explosion.* An eleven-word sentence has been reduced to a seven-word headline. From the point of view of transmitted information the function words are thus less crucial than the content words for the general understanding of a sentence. The less predictable a word is in a given context, the more its presence contributes to the "surprise value" of the sentence, to its informational role. In this sense the less frequent the word, the more important it will be—statistically speaking, at least—for understanding the communication. The 20 per cent of the text that is accounted for by the words of low frequency, none of which occurs more than 40 times in the million tokens, turns out to be crucial to the process of comprehension.

Over 22,000 of all the vocabulary items in the Brown Corpus are *hapax legomena,* words occurring only once in the entire million words of text. They thus constitute about 36 per cent of all distinct forms and a whopping 58 per cent of all lemmas. While the contribution of the *hapax legomena* to the vocabulary set is very substantial, they account for a minute proportion of the text itself—some 2.2 per cent, or about 22,000 occurrences per million. Nevertheless their communicational role is clearly important. High-frequency words, not only function words but common content words as well, are certain to occur in any text of reasonable length. The appearance of a particular low-frequency word, on the other hand, is quite unpredictable even in a long textual sample, because the choice of these words is necessarily tied to the subject matter and purpose of a given communication. While we can thus rely on the statistical fact that a large percentage of vocabulary items found in any reasonably representative English text, even one of sizable length, will appear only once, we cannot predict which particular words they will be for any particular textual body.

Using the Brown Corpus as the base of his calculations, John B. Carroll has hypothesized that if the same word-frequency distribution observed in the corpus were projected to a sample of infinite size, we would expect to find 340,193 different word forms (see John B. Carroll, "On Sampling from a Lognormal Model of Word-Frequency Distribution," in Kučera and Francis, cited above). One could interpret this figure somewhat loosely as approximating the union of the vocabulary sets of the authors of the 500 samples that constitute the Brown Corpus. It is important to remember again, however, that Carroll's calculations included proper names and were based on word forms, not on lemmas. Translated into base forms, the Carroll projection of the working vocabulary of today's printed English could then be estimated at around 210,000 lemmas, including proper names. Without proper names a cautious estimate of 170,000 lemmas could be made. Naturally if we wanted to include various highly specialized and technical terms, the total vocabulary of the language would increase, easily doubling these estimated lemma numbers.

If an understanding of 80 per cent of any text were sufficient for us to function as literate persons, we could manage with a vocabulary of less than 3,000 words and could dispense with dictionaries. Since it is not, dictionaries, which offer us the spelling, pronunciation, and definition of both the frequent and the rare, become our indispensable companions.

Guide to the Dictionary

The editors of *The American Heritage Dictionary, Second College Edition* have attempted to provide information to the user in such a way that no specialized knowledge of the organization of the Dictionary is necessary beyond a grasp of the principle of alphabetical order. This brief explanation of the conventions adopted in compiling this Dictionary is intended to assist in the location of the specific information within an entry that may be of greatest interest to the user.

Guide Words

As an aid to finding the page on which an entry appears, a pair of guide words, together with the page number, is printed at the top of each page:

makar | maladaptive 758

The word to the left of the vertical bar is the first of the sequence of entries on that page of the Dictionary. The word to the right of the bar is the last entry on the page. Thus *makar* and *maladaptive* and all entries that fall between them alphabetically are defined on page 758.

The Entry Words: Alphabetical Order

The entry word is printed in boldface type and set slightly to the left of the text column. As in most reference books, all entries—including compounds of two or more words—have been listed in strict alphabetical order, which takes account of each letter in turn through the full entry even if the entry consists of several words. Here is a typical alphabetical sequence: **car•bon, carbon 14, car•bon-14 dating, car•bo•na•ceous, car•bo•na•do¹, car•bo•na•do², car•bon•ate, carbonated water.**

Superscript Numbers

Words identical in spelling but with different etymologies are entered separately; the entries bear superscript numbers:

lime¹ (līm) *n.* **1.** A spiny tree, *Citrus aurantifolia,* native to Asia, having evergreen leaves, fragrant white flowers, and edible fruit. **2.** The egg-shaped fruit of the lime tree, having a green rind and acid juice used as flavoring. [Fr. < Prov. *limo* < Ar. *līmah.*]

lime² (līm) *n.* Any of several Old World linden trees. [Alteration of obs. *line,* linden < ME *lind* < OE.]

lime³ (līm) *n.* **1. a.** Calcium oxide. **b.** Any of various mineral and industrial forms of calcium oxide differing chiefly in water content and percentage of such constituents as silica, alumina, and iron. **2.** A sticky substance smeared on twigs and used to catch small birds; birdlime. —*tr.v.* **limed, lim•ing, limes. 1.** To treat with lime. **2.** To smear with birdlime. **3.** To catch or snare with or as if with birdlime. [ME < OE *līm.*] —**lim'y** *adj.*

Syllabication

An entry word and its inflected and derived forms, if any, are divided into syllables by means of centered dots:

ac•e•tate (ăs'ĭ-tāt') *n.* **1.** A salt or ester of acetic acid. **2.** Cellulose acetate or any of various products, esp. fibers, derived from it.

eth•yl (ĕth'əl) *n.* A univalent organic radical, C_2H_5. [ETHER + -YL.] —**eth•yl'ic** (ĕ-thĭl'ĭk) *adj.*

In entries consisting of more than one word whose terms are separated by a space, the words that appear elsewhere in this Dictionary as separate entries are not syllabicated:

ethyl acetate *n.* A colorless, volatile, flammable liquid, $CH_3COOC_2H_5$, used in perfumes, flavorings, lacquers, pharmaceuticals, and rayon, and as a general solvent.

Pronunciations are also syllabicated for the sake of clarity, although the syllabication of the phonetic form does not necessarily match the syllabication of the graphic form of the entry word. The former follows phonological rules; the latter represents the established practice of printers and editors in breaking words at the end of a line.

PRONUNCIATION

The pronunciation is enclosed in parentheses and appears immediately after the boldface entry word. Differing or variant pronunciations are given wherever necessary; these appear in parentheses following the forms to which they apply. The key to the use of the pronunciation symbols extends across the bottom of each pair of facing pages. A fuller key appears at the end of this subsection.

Pronunciation Symbols

The set of symbols used is designed to enable the reader to reproduce a satisfactory pronunciation with no more than a quick reference to the key. All pronunciations given are acceptable in all circumstances. When more than one is given, the first is assumed to be the most common, but the difference in frequency may be insignificant.

Americans do not all speak alike; nevertheless they can understand one another, at least on the level of speech sounds. For most words a single set of symbols can represent the pronunciation found in each regional variety of American English, provided the symbols are planned for the purpose stated above: to enable the reader to reproduce a satisfactory pronunciation. When a single pronunciation is offered in this Dictionary, the reader will supply those features of his own regional speech that are called forth by his reading of the key. Apart from regional variations in pronunciation, there are variations among social groups. The pronunciations recorded in this Dictionary are exclusively those of educated speech.

Explanatory Notes

ə: This nonalphabetical symbol is called a *schwa*. The symbol is used in the Dictionary to represent a reduced vowel, that is, a vowel that receives the weakest level of stress—which is unmarked—within a word and that therefore nearly always has a different quality than it would if it were stressed, as in **telegraph** (tĕl′ĭ-grăf′) and **telegraphy** (tə-lĕg′rə-fē). Vowels are never reduced to a single exact vowel; the schwa sound varies, sometimes according to the "full" vowel it is representing and often according to the sounds surrounding it.

âr: îr ûr These symbols represent vowels that have been altered by a following *r*. In some regional varieties of American English the words **Mary, merry,** and **marry** are pronounced alike: (mĕr′ē). However, in many individual American speech patterns the three words are distinguished. It is this pattern that the Dictionary represents: **Mary** (mâr′ē), **merry** (mĕr′ē), **marry** (măr′ē). Some words are heard in all three pronunciations, indistinctly grading one into another. For these words the Dictionary represents only (âr): **care** (kâr), **dairy** (dâr′ē).

In words such as **hear, beer,** and **dear** the vowel could be represented by (ē) were it not for the effect of the following *r*, which makes it approach (ĭ) in sound. In this Dictionary a special symbol, (îr), is used for this combination, as in **beer** (bîr).

The symbol (ûr) is used to represent the sound of the vowel in such words as **her** and **fur:** (hûr), (fûr).

ôr: ōr There are regional differences in the distinctions among various pronunciations of the syllable *-or-* . In pairs such as **for, four; horse, hoarse;** and **morning, mourning** the vowel varies between (ô) and (ō). In this Dictionary these vowels are represented as follows: **for** (fôr), **four** (fôr, fōr); **horse** (hôrs), **hoarse** (hôrs, hōrs); and **morning** (môr′nĭng), **mourning** (môr′nĭng, mōr′-). Other words for which both forms are shown include those such as **more** (môr, mōr) and **glory** (glôr′ē, glōr′ē).

Another group of words with variation in the pronunciation of the *-or-* syllable includes words such as **forest** and **horrid,** in which the pronunciation of *o* before *r* varies between (ô) and (ŏ). In these words the (ôr) pronunciation is given first: **forest** (fôr′ĭst, fŏr′-).

Syllabic Consonants. Two consonants often constitute complete syllables. These are *l* and *n,* called *syllabics* when they occur after stressed syllables ending in or followed by *d* or *t* in such words as **cradle** (krăd′l), **rattle** (răt′l), **redden** (rĕd′n), and **cotton** (kŏt′n). Both syllabic *l* and syllabic *n* also occur following *-rt-* and *-rd-* in such words as **myrtle** (mûr′tl), **hurdle** (hûr′dl), **certain** (sûr′tn), and **ardent** (är′dnt). Syllabic *n* is not shown following *-nd-* or *-nt-,* as in **abandon** (ə-băn′dən) and **mountain** (moun′tən); but syllabic *l* is shown in that position: **candle** (kăn′dl), **mantle** (măn′tl).

Stress. In this Dictionary stress, the relative degree of loudness with which the syllables of a word or phrase are spoken, is indicated in three different ways. An unmarked syllable has the weakest stress in the word. The strongest, or *primary,* stress is marked with a bold mark (′). An intermediate level of stress, here called *secondary,* is marked with a similar but lighter mark (′). Words of one syllable show no stress mark, since there is no other stress level to which the syllable is compared.

Sound-Spelling Correspondences

The following table is designed to aid the user in locating in the Dictionary words whose pronunciation is known but whose spelling presents difficulties. Such difficulties are caused by the fact that so many speech sounds can be spelled in more than one way, since the standard alphabet has twenty-six characters to represent the forty or more sounds used in the English language. If you are unable to find a word when you look it up, try another combination of letters that have the same sound.

Sound	Spelling	In These Sample Words
a (as in **pat**)	ai	**plaid**
	al	**calf, half, salve**
	au	**laugh**
a (as in **mane**)	ai	**aide, aigrette, maize, pain, plain, refrain, stain**
	ao	**gaol**
	au	**gauge**
	ay	**clay, day, payment, player, saying, tray**
	e	**bouquet, consomme, forte, sachet, suede**
	ea	**break, great**
	ei	**chow mein, reindeer, seine, veil, vein**
	eig	**deign, feign, reign**
	eigh	**eight, neighbor, sleigh, weigh**
	ey	**fey, obey, prey, they**
a (as in **care**)	ae	**aerate, aerial, aerobatics, aeronautics, aerosol**
	ai	**air, bairn, fair, hairdresser, lair, pair**
	ay	**prayer**
	e	**ere, there, where**
	ea	**bear, pear, tear, wear**
	ei	**Eire, heir, their**
a (as in **father**)	ah	**ah, mahjong, shah**
	al	**balm, calm, palm, psalm**
	e	**sergeant**
	ea	**hearken, heart, hearten, hearth, hearthstone**
b (as in **bib**)	bb	**blubber, cabbage, ebb, robber**
	bh	**bhang**
	pb	**cupboard, raspberry**

Sound	Spelling	In These Sample Words
ch (as in **church**)	c	**cello**
	cz	**Czech**
	tch	**batch, catch, latch, patch, stitch**
	ti	**bestial, question, suggestion**
	tu	**denture, naturalism, nature, pasture**
d (as in **deed**)	ed	**mailed, ringed, winged**
	dd	**bladder, gladden, ladder, saddle**
	dh	**dhow**
e (as in **pet**)	a	**any, many**
	ae	**aesthetic**
	ai	**again, said**
	ay	**says**
	ea	**cleanse, leaden, measure, measurement, thread**
	ei	**heifer, Seine**
	eo	**leopard**
	ie	**friend**
	oe	**Oedipus**
	u	**burial**
e (as in **be**)	ae	**Caesar, encyclopaedia, paean**
	ay	**quay**
	ea	**beach, each, leap, reach, reap, seaboard**
	ee	**beet, creep, meek**
	ei	**conceit, deceit, receive, receipt**
	eo	**people**
	ey	**covey, key, monkey**
	i	**miniskirt, piano, solarium, symposium**
	ie	**believe, fiend, siege**
	oe	**amoeba, phoenix**
	y	**comedy, quality, tracheotomy**

Sound	Spelling	In These Sample Words
f (as in **f**i**f**e)	ff	sti**ff**, sni**ff**le, whi**ff**
	gh	enou**gh**, rou**gh**, trou**gh**
	lf	ca**lf**, ha**lf**
	ph	al**ph**abet, gra**ph**, **ph**oto, s**ph**incter
g (as in **g**a**g**)	gg	bra**gg**ed, dru**gg**ed, slu**gg**ish
	gh	**gh**astly, **gh**erkin, **gh**etto, **gh**ost
	gu	**gu**errilla, **gu**ess, **gu**est
	gue	analo**gue**, catalo**gue**, epilo**gue**
h (as in **h**at)	wh	**wh**o, **wh**ose
	g	**G**ila monster
	j	**J**erez
i (as in p**i**t)	a	certific**a**te, clim**a**te, vill**a**ge
	e	**e**nough, r**e**buff, r**e**cite
	ee	b**ee**n
	ia	carr**ia**ge, marr**ia**ge
	ie	s**ie**ve
	o	w**o**men
	u	b**u**sy
	ui	b**ui**lt
	y	c**y**st, d**y**spepsia, n**y**mph, s**y**mbol
i (as in p**ie**)	ai	**ai**sle
	ay	**ay**e, b**ay**ou
	ei	**ei**derdown, h**ei**ght, s**ei**smograph, st**ei**n
	ey	**ey**e
	ie	d**ie**, l**ie**, t**ie**
	igh	r**igh**t, s**igh**, th**igh**
	is	**is**land
	uy	b**uy**
	y	l**y**re, m**y**opia, sk**y**
	ye	r**ye**
i (as in p**ier**)	e	c**e**real, h**e**re, s**e**ries
	ea	cl**ea**r, **ea**r, sm**ea**r
	ee	b**ee**r, st**ee**r, v**ee**r
	ei	w**ei**rd
j (as in **j**ar)	d	deci**d**uous, gra**d**uate, indivi**d**ual
	dg	ju**dg**ment, lo**dg**ing, tru**dg**ing
	di	sol**di**er
	dj	a**dj**ective
	g	a**g**itate, an**g**ina, **g**em, re**g**ister
	ge	diver**ge**, mer**ge**r, ven**ge**ance
	gg	exa**gg**erate
k (as in **k**ic**k**)	c	**c**all, e**c**stasy, e**c**zema
	cc	a**cc**ount, su**cc**otash, su**cc**ulent
	cch	sa**cch**arin
	ch	al**ch**emy, **ch**aos, s**ch**edule, s**ch**ool
	ck	a**ck**nowledge, cra**ck**, kna**ck**, pa**ck**age
	cqu	la**cqu**er
	cu	bis**cu**it, cir**cu**it
	lk	ba**lk**, ta**lk**, wa**lk**
	qu	**qu**ay
	que	pla**que**, tor**que**

Sound	Spelling	In These Sample Words
kw (as in **qu**ick)	ch	**ch**oir
	cqu	a**cqu**aint, a**cqu**ire, a**cqu**it
l (as in **l**id)	ll	**ll**ama, ta**ll**
	lh	**Lh**asa
m (as in **m**u**m**)	chm	dra**chm**
	gm	paradi**gm**, phle**gm**
	lm	ba**lm**, ca**lm**, psa**lm**
	mb	du**mb**, plu**mb**
	mm	ha**mm**er, ma**mm**oth, mu**mm**y
	mn	autu**mn**, hy**mn**, sole**mn**
n (as in **n**o)	gn	ali**gn**, **gn**at, **gn**arled
	kn	**kn**ee, **kn**ife, **kn**ow
	mn	**mn**emonic
	nn	ca**nn**y, i**nn**, ba**nn**er
	pn	**pn**eumonia
ng (as in thi**ng**)	n	a**n**chor, co**n**gress, i**n**k, u**n**cle
	ngue	to**ngue**
o (as in p**o**t)	a	w**a**ffle, w**a**tch, w**a**ter, wh**a**t
	ho	**ho**nest
	ou	tr**ou**gh
o (as in n**o**)	au	h**au**tboy, m**au**ve
	eau	b**eau**, bur**eau**, trouss**eau**
	eo	y**eo**man
	ew	s**ew**
	oa	cr**oa**k, f**oa**m, m**oa**n, r**oa**ch
	oe	f**oe**, J**oe**
	oh	**oh**, **oh**m
	oo	br**oo**ch
	ou	b**ou**lder, sh**ou**lder
	ough	bor**ough**, d**ough**, thor**ough**
	ow	cr**ow**, l**ow**
	owe	**owe**, Marl**owe**
o (as in p**aw** or f**o**r)	a	**a**ll, w**a**ter
	al	b**al**k, t**al**k, w**al**k
	ah	Ut**ah**
	ar	w**ar**m
	as	Arkans**as**
	au	c**au**ght, c**au**liflower, d**au**ghter, g**au**nt
	aw	**aw**e, **aw**ful, **aw**ning, br**aw**l
	oa	br**oa**d, **oa**r
	ough	b**ough**t, br**ough**t, th**ough**t, wr**ough**t
oi (as in n**oi**se)	oy	b**oy**, cl**oy**, r**oy**al
ou (as in **ou**t)	au	sauerkr**au**t
	aue	s**aue**rbraten
	hou	**hou**r
	ough	b**ough**
	ow	f**ow**l, sc**ow**l, s**ow**
oo (as in t**oo**k)	o	w**o**man, w**o**lf
	ou	c**ou**ld, sh**ou**ld, w**ou**ld
	u	b**u**sh, c**u**shion, f**u**ll

Sound	Spelling	In These Sample Words
oo (as in **boot**)	eu	l**eu**kemia, man**eu**ver, rh**eu**matic
	ew	dr**ew**, shr**ew**, fl**ew**
	ieu	l**ieu**, l**ieu**tenant
	o	d**o**, m**o**ve, tw**o**
	oe	can**oe**
	ou	gr**ou**p, s**ou**p, tr**ou**pe
	ough	thr**ough**
	u	pr**u**dent, r**u**de
	ue	ag**ue**, bl**ue**, fl**ue**
	ui	br**ui**se, fr**ui**t, j**ui**ce
p (as in **pop**)	pp	ha**pp**y, sna**pp**er, stri**pp**er
r (as in **roar**)	rh	**rh**apsody, **rh**eumatism, **rh**ythm
	rr	che**rr**y, ma**rr**iage, po**rr**idge
	rrh	ci**rrh**osis
	wr	**wr**ing, **wr**inkle, **wr**ite
s (as in **say**)	c	**c**ellar, **c**ent, **c**yst
	ce	ma**ce**, practi**ce**, sau**ce**
	ps	**ps**alm, **ps**eudonym, **ps**ychology
	sc	ab**sc**ess, adole**sc**ent, fa**sc**inate, **sc**ene
	sch	**sch**ism
	ss	la**ss**, pa**ss**, sa**ss**afras
	sth	i**sth**mus
sh (as in **ship**)	ce	o**ce**anic
	ch	**ch**ancre, **ch**andelier, mar**ch**ioness
	ci	defi**ci**ent, musi**ci**an, spe**ci**al
	psh	**psh**aw
	s	**s**ugar, **s**ure
	sc	con**sc**ience
	sch	**sch**ist, **sch**ottische
	se	nau**se**ous
	si	pen**si**on
	ss	mi**ss**ion, ti**ss**ue
	ti	elec**ti**on, na**ti**on, vibra**ti**on
t (as in **tie**)	ed	bump**ed**, crash**ed**, stopp**ed**
	ght	bou**ght**, cau**ght**, wrou**ght**
	pt	**pt**armigan, **pt**erodactyl

Sound	Spelling	In These Sample Words
	th	**Th**omas
	tt	be**tt**er, le**tt**uce, si**tt**er
	tw	**tw**o
th (as in **think**)	phth	**phth**isis
u (as in **cut**)	o	inc**o**me, s**o**me, s**o**n
	oe	d**oe**s
	oo	bl**oo**d, fl**oo**d
	ou	c**ou**ple, d**ou**blet, tr**ou**ble
yoo (as in **use**)	eau	b**eau**tiful
	eu	**eu**genic, **eu**phoria, f**eu**d
	eue	qu**eue**
	ew	f**ew**, p**ew**, p**ew**ter
	ieu	ad**ieu**
	iew	v**iew**
	u	p**u**berty, p**u**ce
	ue	c**ue**, p**ue**rile
	you	**you**
	yu	**yu**le
u (as in **fur**)	ear	**ear**n, l**ear**n, y**ear**n
	er	c**er**tain, f**er**n, h**er**d, t**er**m
	eur	restaurat**eur**
	ir	b**ir**d, f**ir**st, th**ir**ty
	or	w**or**d, w**or**k
	our	j**our**nal, j**our**ney, sc**our**ge
	yr	m**yr**tle
	yrrh	m**yrrh**
v (as in **valve**)	f	o**f**
	ph	Ste**ph**en
w (as in **with**)	o	**o**ne
	ou	**Ou**agadougou
	u	g**u**anine, g**u**ano, g**u**ava
y (as in **yes**)	i	min**i**on, on**i**on, opin**i**on
	j	hallelu**j**ah
z (as in **zebra**)	cz	**cz**ar
	s	her**s**, ri**s**e, your**s**
	ss	de**ss**ert, hu**ss**ar
	x	**x**erography, **x**ylophone
	zz	bu**zz**, fu**zz**
zh (as in **barrage**)	ge	gara**ge**, mira**ge**
	s	plea**s**ure, vi**s**ion

PART-OF-SPEECH LABELS

The following italicized labels, which come next in order after the pronunciation, are used to indicate parts of speech:

adj.	adjective	*indef.art.*	indefinite article
adv.	adverb	*interj.*	interjection
aux.	auxiliary	*n.*	noun
conj.	conjunction	*prep.*	preposition
def.art.	definite article	*pron.*	pronoun
		v.	verb

The italicized labels below are employed to indicate inflected forms:

pl. plural *sing.* singular

Words, such as **clothes** and **cattle**, that occur only in the plural are labeled as follows:

pl.n. plural noun

The following italicized labels are used for the traditional classification of verbs:

tr. transitive *intr.* intransitive

The labels for word elements are:

pref. prefix *suff.* suffix

Certain entries bear none of the labels given above; these include contractions, acronyms, symbols, trademarks, and word formatives or elements that never occur in initial or final position in a word. Examples:

can't (kănt, cänt). Cannot.

Ca The symbol for the element calcium.

Jaws of Life. A trademark for a pneumatic tool consisting of a pincerlike metal device that is inserted into the body of a severely damaged vehicle to provide access to persons trapped inside.

-o- Used as a connective to join word elements: *acidophilic.*

Combined Entries

Sometimes a term serves more than one grammatical function. For example, *effect* can be both a verb (as in *a leader who effected great changes*) and a noun (as in *the effects of a drug*). In such cases a *combined entry* will include all the parts of speech at one entry word; as an indication of the shift in function, a boldface dash introduces the new part-of-speech label. Next in order appear all the elements that apply to that part of speech, such as a differing syllabication or pronunciation, inflected forms, and definitions.

sus·pect (sə-spĕkt′) *v.* **-pect·ed, -pect·ing, -pects.** *—tr.* **1.** To surmise to be true or probable; imagine. **2.** To have doubts about; distrust: *suspected his motives.* **3.** To think (a person) guilty without proof: *suspect her of murder.* *—intr.* To have suspicion. *—n.* (sŭs′pĕkt′). A person who is suspected, esp. of committing a crime. *—adj.* (sŭs′pĕkt′, sə-spĕkt′). Open to or viewed with suspicion. [Lat. *suspectare,* freq. of *suspicere,* to watch : *sub-,* from below + *specere,* to look at.]

Inflected Forms

Inflected forms differ from the main-entry form by the addition of suffixes or by changes of the stem form. In this Dictionary the following inflected forms appear with the main entry:

1. Principal parts of all verbs, whether regular or irregular.
2. All degrees of adjectives and adverbs formed by inflection.
3. Irregular plurals of nouns.

Inflected forms, which are syllabicated and set in boldface type, always follow the part-of-speech label and are pronounced as necessary. When more than one inflected form is given, the forms are separated by commas. Inflected forms are normally shortened to the last syllable of the original entry word plus the inflected ending. Irregular inflected forms are spelled out to the extent that clarity requires. When inflected forms are shortened, each shortened form is preceded by a boldface hyphen:

en·ter (ĕn′tər) *v.* **-tered, -ter·ing, -ters.**

Note that a single letter at the beginning or at the end of an entry word never stands alone, nor is it ever dropped:

o·bey (ō-bā′) *v.* **o·beyed, o·bey·ing, o·beys.**

Inflected Forms: Principal Parts of Verbs

The principal parts of all verbs are entered in the following order: past tense, past participle, present participle, and third person singular present tense. When the past tense and past participle are identical, however, one form represents both:

sing (sĭng) *v.* **sang** (săng), **sung** (sŭng), **sing·ing, sings.**

pen·e·trate (pĕn′ĭ-trāt′) *v.* **-trat·ed, -trat·ing, -trates.**

Inflected Forms: Comparison of Adjectives and Adverbs

Adjectives and adverbs whose comparative and superlative degrees are formed by adding *-er* and *-est* to the unchanged entry word show these comparative and superlative suffixes immediately after the part-of-speech label:

high (hī) *adj.* **-er, -est. 1. a.** Having a relatively great elevation; extending far upward: *a high mountain; a high stool.*

Irregular forms are considered to be those terms whose form changes upon the addition of *-er* and *-est*. These forms follow the general rules of style and presentation for all inflected forms:

fuzz·y (fŭz′ē) *adj.* **-i·er, -i·est. 1.** Covered with fuzz.

Note that the existence of *-er* and *-est* forms does not preclude the use of *more* and *most* with a simple adjective or adverb to express the comparative and superlative degrees. Often the comparative and superlative can be expressed in either way, as in *fairer* or *more fair, fairest* or *most fair.*

Inflected Forms: Plurals of Nouns

Plurals of nouns other than those formed by suffixing *-s* or *-es* are shown and labeled *pl.* A regular plural is shown, however, for a noun that has both a regular and an irregular plural form as variants; both forms appear, and the convention for indicating primary and secondary variants applies to these plural forms as well:

a·moe·ba (ə-mē′bə) *n., pl.* **-bas** or **-bae** (-bē).

The regular plurals of nouns are also shown when the spelling might pose a problem for the user. Such nouns include those ending in *-o* and *-ey*:

po·ta·to (pə-tā′tō) *n., pl.* **-toes.**

tur·key (tûr′kē) *n., pl.* **-keys.**

A noun that is chiefly or exclusively plural in both form and meaning is so entered and defined:

cat·tle (kăt'l) *pl.n.* **1.** Various animals of the genus *Bos,* esp. those of the domesticated species *B. taurus,* raised in many breeds for meat and dairy products. **2.** Human beings, esp. when viewed as a mob.

A noun that is always plural in form but that is not always used with a plural verb is entered thus:

lin·guis·tics (lĭng-gwĭs'tĭks) *n. (used with a sing. verb).* The study of the nature and structure of human speech.

a·cous·tics (ə-ko͞o'stĭks) *n.* **1.** *(used with a sing. verb).* The scientific study of sound, esp. of its generation, transmission, and reception. **2.** *(used with a pl. verb).* The total effect of sound, esp. as produced in an enclosed space.

Separate Entries for Inflected Forms

Some verbs, such as **do, be,** and **have,** have archaic inflected forms, such as **dost, art,** and **hadst**, whose frequency of occurrence justifies their inclusion in the Dictionary. These forms are entered separately:

hath (hăth) *v. Archaic.* Third person singular present tense of **have.**

Also entered separately are the inflected forms of irregular verbs in which a vowel change signals a tense change. Such entries bear a part-of-speech label and are syllabicated and pronounced:

rid·den (rĭd'n) *v.* Past participle of **ride.**

Irregular plurals are entered separately in the Dictionary when such forms would occur more than one entry away from the main entry in alphabetical order. Example:

chil·dren (chĭl'drən) *n.* Plural of **child.**

LABELS

This Dictionary employs field and stylistic labels to provide the reader with specific subject orientation as well as guidance regarding the various levels of usage. The following paragraphs list and explain these labels.

Field Labels

A field label identifies the special area to which a definition applies. Such a label does not, however, restrict a definition to a particular field; it merely indicates that a definition has its primary application in the domain specified. Typical examples of the use of field labels are these:

jam[1] . . . *v.* . . . *—intr.* . . . **4.** *Mus.* To play jazz improvisations.

dump . . . *v.* . . . *—tr.* . . . **5.** *Computer Sci.* To reproduce (data stored internally in a computer) onto an external storage medium, as a printout.

or·i·gin . . . *n.* . . . **4.** *Anat.* The point of attachment of a muscle. **5.** *Math.* The point of intersection of coordinate axes, as in the Cartesian coordinate system.

Stylistic and Geographic Labels

Stylistic and geographic labels are restrictive in nature and limit a definition to a particular level or style of usage or to a particular region. All senses of a term that are not restricted by such a label are to be regarded as appropriate for use in all contexts. These labels are as follows:

Nonstandard. This label implies the existence of Standard American English. While it cannot be claimed that there is a uniform standard language throughout America, nevertheless there is widespread agreement as to those forms and usages that are not acceptable to educated speakers. Certain terms and expressions may have long existed in the language side by side with equivalent standard forms, but they have never been admitted to the standard language. Example:

no·wheres (nō'hwârz', -wârz') *adv. Nonstandard.* Nowhere.

Nonstandard is the most restrictive label in this Dictionary and supersedes all other labels such as *Regional.* Therefore, the word *like,* when used as an auxiliary, is simply labeled *Nonstandard.*

Informal. Among those whose speech is standard there are at least two levels of language, the language of formal discourse and the language of conversation. The great mass of words are the same in both, but many words that are perfectly acceptable in a conversation with friends or colleagues would be unsuitable in the formal prose, say, of an article written for publication in the journal of a learned society:

cut·up (kŭt'ŭp') *n. Informal.* A mischievous person; prankster.

Informal terms may, of course, appear in writing as a means of creating a particular effect.

Slang. This label indicates a style of language rather than a level of formality or cultivation. The distinguishing feature of slang is the striving for rhetorical effect through the use of extravagant and often facetious figures of speech. Slang is usually transitory and either dies out or is incorporated into the standard vocabulary as its rhetorical aspect is lost. Some forms of slang occur in the most cultivated speech but not in discourse that is intended to be formal. An example of slang is the adjectival use of the word *together*:

—*adj. Slang.* **1.** In tune with what is going on; hip. **2.** Unified and performing effectively.

Vulgar. The label *Vulgar* warns of social taboos attached to a word; the label may appear alone or in combination as *Vulgar Slang*.

Obscene. A term that is considered to violate accepted standards of decency is labeled *Obscene*.

Offensive. This label is reserved for terms such as racial slurs that are not only insulting and derogatory, but a discredit to the user as well.

Obsolete. The label *Obs.* is used for a term that is no longer in active use except in quotation or as an intentional archaism. That the object or situation to which a word refers may no longer exist or be in use does not make the word itself obsolete:

ha·rus·pex (hə-rŭs′pĕks′, hăr′ə-spĕks′) *n., pl.* **ha·rus·pi·ces** (hə-rŭs′pĭ-sēz′). A Roman priest who practiced divination by the inspection of the entrails of animals. [Lat.]

This entry is not labeled, since the term is in current use—even if only by historians—although the office and function it denotes are restricted to a particular period in the past. The label *Obs.* is applied only to words or senses that have disappeared from current use, as in sense **5**. of this example:

en·ter·tain·ment (ĕn′tər-tān′mənt) *n.* **1.** The act of entertaining. **2.** The art or field of entertaining. **3.** Something that entertains, esp. a performance or show. **4.** The pleasure afforded by being entertained; amusement. **5.** *Obs.* **a.** Maintenance; support. **b.** Employment.

Archaic. This label is applied to terms that once were common but are now rare, although they may be familiar because of their occurrence in certain contexts such as the literature of an earlier time. Example:

af·fray (ə-frā′) *n.* A noisy quarrel or brawl. —*tr.v* **-frayed, -fray·ing, -frays.** *Archaic.* To frighten.

Regional. When an expression is commonly used in one area and little used—even if known—in other areas, it bears in the Dictionary an area label, such as *Southwestern U.S.* and *New England*. Often an expression may be common to several areas and yet not be used in American speech in general. Such expressions are labeled *Regional;* for example, the use of **fair**[1] as a verb in *The weather will fair today*.

Chiefly British. The label *Chiefly Brit.* reflects the fact that the distinction between British and American vocabulary is seldom exclusive. In addition, British terms are often in use elsewhere in the world, as in Australia. An example of a usage that is labeled *Chiefly Brit.* is sense **5**. of **boot**[1], where the definition reads:

5. *Chiefly Brit.* An automobile trunk.

Other labels that restrict the usage of particular terms to specific areas of the English-speaking world are:

Austral.	Australian	*Scot.*	Scottish
Ir.	Irish	*So. Afr.*	South African

Cross-References

Cross-references are used to expand the information given at any one entry and at the same time avoid needless duplication. They are of two kinds. When two terms are synonymous, a full definition appears at the primary, or most frequently occurring term; the secondary term is entered at its own place in the alphabet and is defined by the primary term, set in lightface type, at which the user can find the full definition:

pek·an (pĕk′ən) *n.* The fisher (sense 2.a.). [Canadian Fr. *pékan,* of Algonquian orig.]

fish·er (fĭsh′ər) *n.* **1.** One that fishes. **2. a.** A carnivorous mammal, *Martes pennanti,* of northern North America, having thick, dark-brown fur. **b.** The fur of this animal.

In the second kind of cross-reference, which is used to enter variant and inflected forms, the primary entry to which the user is referred is set in boldface type:

flown[2] (flōn) *v.* Past participle of **fly**[1].

flied (flīd) *v.* Past tense and past participle of **fly**[1] (sense 7).

Order of Definitions

When a word has more than one sense, those senses are arranged in such a way that a complex word can to some extent be perceived as a structured unit. Senses are not arranged historically or by frequency of use. Rather, they are ordered analytically, according to central meaning clusters from which related subsenses and additional separate senses may evolve. Such a meaningful order is considered to be the most useful presentation for the general reader.

Sense Division: Numbers and Letters in Definitions

When an entry has more than one definition, these are numbered sequentially in boldface:

a·ban·doned (ə-băn′dənd) *adj.* **1.** Deserted or forsaken. **2.** Recklessly unrestrained; shameless.

When a numbered definition has two or more closely related subsenses, these are indicated by the boldface letters **a.**, **b.**, **c.**, and so on:

jag[1] (jăg) *n.* **1.** A sharp projection; barb. **2. a.** A hanging flap along the edge of a garment. **b.** A slash or slit in a garment exposing material of a different color.

In a combined entry the definitions are numbered in separate sequences that begin with **1.** after each part of speech; for instance:

lag[1] (lăg) *v.* **lagged, lag·ging, lags.** —*intr.* **1.** To fail to keep up a pace; straggle. **2.** To proceed or develop slowly or abnormally slowly. **3.** To fail, weaken, or slacken gradually; flag. **4.** To determine the order of play in billiards by successively hitting the cue ball against the end rail, the ball rebounding closest to the head rail indicating the player to shoot first. —*tr.* **1.** To cause to fail or lag behind. **2.** To shoot, throw, or pitch (a coin, for example) at a mark. —*n.* **1.** One that lags. **2.** The act, process, or condition of lagging. **3.** A condition of slowness or retardation. **4. a.** An extent or duration of lagging. **b.** An interval between events or phenomena.

Information applicable only to a particular sense of a word is entered at the appropriate sense number, as illustrated below:

Me·du·sa (mə-do͞o'sə, -zə, -dyo͞o'-) *n., pl.* **-sas** or **-sae** (-sē, -zē). **1.** *Gk. Myth.* One of the three Gorgons. **2. medusa.** The tentacled, usually bell-shaped, free-swimming sexual stage in the life cycle of a coelenterate of the class Scyphozoa or Hydrozoa. [Lat. < Gk. *Medousa.*]

At **Medusa 1.**, the label *Gk. Myth.* that appears after the boldface sense number applies only to that particular sense. At sense **2.**, the boldface lower-case form **medusa** indicates that the zoological sense of the word is always lower-cased in writing. Labels and other information applicable to all senses of an entry appear before all elements of the entry. Example:

zonk (zông*k*, zŏng*k*) *v.* **zonked, zonk·ing, zonks.** *Slang.* —*tr.* **1.** To stupefy; stun. **2.** To intoxicate with drugs or alcohol: *"zonk their patients with tranquilizers"* (Psychology Today). —*intr.* To be intoxicated with drugs or alcohol.

Here, the positioning of the *Slang* label before all transitive and intransitive senses of the word indicates that it applies to every one of those senses.

Explanatory Notes in Entries

Explanatory notes sometimes are used in lieu of definitions in certain entries such as those for function words, interjections, and intensives. Examples:

oh (ō) *interj.* **1.** Used to express strong emotion, such as surprise, fear, anger, or pain.

damned (dămd) *adj.* **-er, -est. 1.** Condemned, esp. to eternal punishment. **2.** *Informal.* Deserving condemnation; detestable: *this damned weather.* **3.** Used as an intensive: *a damned fool.*

Illustrative Examples

Thousands of illustrative examples—many of them attributed quotations—follow definitions. These italic examples, taken from the *American Heritage* citation files illustrating actual printed usage over a considerable period of time, show the defined terms in typical contexts. They are especially helpful in illustrating figurative senses, transitive and intransitive verbs, and shades of meaning. Examples:

sea change *n.* **1.** A change caused by the sea: *"Of his bones are coral made/ Those are pearls that were his eyes/ Nothing of him that doth fade/ But doth suffer a sea change"* (Shakespeare). **2.** A marked transformation: *"The script suffered considerable sea changes, particularly in structure"* (Harold Pinter).

lave (lāv) *v.* **laved, lav·ing, laves.** —*tr.* **1.** To wash; bathe. **2. a.** To lap or wash against. **b.** To flow along or against: *"The quiet and the cool laved her"* (Edna Ferber). —*intr. Archaic.* To wash oneself.

hands-on (hăndz'ŏn', -ôn') *adj.* Involving active participation; applied, as opposed to theoretical: *"We're involved in hands-on operations, pulling levers, pushing buttons"* (Arthur R. Taylor).

Variants

Standardization of American English is more nearly complete than at any earlier time, but the number of variant spellings in common use remains large. All variants presented in this Dictionary are acceptable in any context unless marked with a restrictive label, such as *Regional.* Variants are set in boldface type and are of two kinds.

Equal Variants

The word *or* between a main-entry term and a variant term indicates that the two forms are in almost equally frequent use in edited sources:

ax or **axe** (ăks) *n., pl.* **ax·es.**

Secondary Variants

When there is a distinct preference for one variant, the less preferred variant is introduced by the word *also*:

pat·i·na[2] (păt'ə-nə, pə-tē'nə) also **pa·tine** (pă-tēn') *n.*

All equal and secondary variants that are not adjacent to the main term in alphabetical order are entered as main entries in the appropriate place.

British Variants

A large class of variants consists of spellings that are preferred in British English and are sometimes used in American English. Variants such as **colour** and **centre** are labeled *Chiefly Brit.* The variant **-ise**, which occurs in many British sources and for which American English has **-ize** (for example, *realize, realise*), is not given unless it is also a common American variant. When a word that has a variant occurs in a compound, the variant is not repeated at the compound. For example, the *Chiefly Brit.* variant **colour** is given for **color** but is not repeated at **colorblind**, **color guard**, and other such compounds.

PHRASAL VERBS

A *phrasal verb* is an idiomatic expression consisting of a verb and an adverb or preposition with a unitary meaning that is equal to more than the sum of the separate meanings of its elements. Phrasal verbs are entered and defined as subentries following the last verb definitions, as in the following example at the main entry **come**:

—phrasal verbs. **come about. 1.** To take place; happen. **2.** To turn around. **3.** *Naut.* To change tack. **come across. 1.** To meet or find by chance: *came across his old roommate today.* **2.** *Slang.* To do or give what is wanted. **3.** To give an impression: *came across as an aggressive businessman.*

MODIFIERS

It has long been a characteristic feature of the English language that nouns may freely be used to modify other nouns, in the manner of an adjective. Like adjectives, these nouns may occupy the position preceding the noun; nevertheless they lack the freedom of occurrence of true adjectives in that they do not usually occur in the predicate after the verb *be*, nor do they occur with adverbial qualifiers such as *very*. Thus the use of the word *fruit* in such phrases as *fruit tree, fruit salad,* and *fruit juice* does not warrant the classification of *fruit* as an adjective. A construction with a noun modifier, when it is self-explanatory, is sometimes entered for the sake of illustration at the end of a noun entry and is introduced by the italic boldface subheading ***modifier***:

slang (slăng) *n.* **1.** The nonstandard vocabulary of a given culture or subculture, consisting typically of arbitrary and often ephemeral coinages and figures of speech characterized by spontaneity and sometimes by raciness. **2.** Language peculiar to a group; argot or jargon. ***—modifier:*** *a slang term.*

IDIOMS

Many entry words occur in phrases whose meanings cannot be derived from the meanings of the separate words making up the phrases. Such phrases, or idioms, are entered and defined in alphabetical order within the entry for the most significant word element in the idiom, as in the following example at the main entry **hand**:

—idioms. ... **hand over fist.** *Slang.* At a tremendous rate: *making money hand over fist.* **hands down.** With no trouble; easily.

The indefinite pronouns *one* and *someone*, when used in idioms, indicate that the object or the possessive pronoun used with a given idiom may vary according to context. The choice of *one* for the entry form means that the person referred to in the idiom can be identical to its subject; the pronoun *someone* means that the person referred to in the idiom cannot be identical to the subject. Thus, at the entry **mind**, the idiom **make up (one's) mind** appears and its form of entry indicates that the sentence *He made up his mind* is grammatical. At the entry **eye**, on the other hand, the idiom **give (someone) the eye** indicates that the sentence *She gave herself the eye* would be incorrect. Idioms appear as the last element of an entry after the last definition and immediately before the etymology if there is one.

ETYMOLOGIES

Etymologies appear in square brackets [ ] following the definitions. An etymology traces the history of a word from one language to another as far back in time as can be determined with reasonable certainty. The most recent known pre-Modern English stage is given first, with each earlier stage following in sequence:

cab•in ... [ME *caban* < OFr. *cabane* < LLat. *capanna.*]

A language name, linguistic form, and brief definition, or gloss, of that form are given for each stage of the derivation. In order to avoid redundancy, however, a language, form, or gloss is not repeated if it is identical to the corresponding item in the immediately preceding stage. In the example above, the different Middle English, Old French, and Late Latin forms have the same gloss, which is the same as the first definition of the Modern English word *cabin*: "a small, roughly built house." Sometimes the immediate ancestor of a Modern English word is not the usual citation form of a word, such as the infinitive or nominative singular, but an inflected form. In these cases the stem of the inflected form is given:

de•gen•er•ate ... [Lat. *degenerare, degenerat-* : *de-*, from + *genus*, race.]

Stems are given only for the form immediately preceding the Modern English form. The only exception is the inclusion of present-tense stems of Old French verbs when necessary to explain a Middle English form:

ban·ish . . . [ME *banishen* < OFr. *banir, baniss-,* of Germanic orig.]

Sometimes a stage in the history of a word is not attested although there is reasonable certainty from comparative evidence about what the missing linguistic form looked like and what language it belonged to. In such cases an asterisk (*) is placed before the form to indicate its hypothetical nature, and no gloss is assigned to it:

cab·e·zon ... [Sp. *cabezón,* aug. of *cabeza,* head < VLat. **capitia* < Lat. *caput,* head.]

At times it is necessary to cross-refer from one etymology to another, either to avoid repeating part of a lengthy and complex derivation or to indicate the close relationship between two different Modern English words:

bat³ . . . [Prob. a var. of BATE².]

ease . . . [ME *ese* < OFr. *aise* < Lat. *adjacens,* pr.part. of *adjacēre,* to lie near. —see ADJACENT.]

The entry at which more information can be found is printed in small capitals. A complete etymology of **bat³** will be found at **bate²**. A continuation of the etymology of **ease** starting with the Latin form *adjacēre* will be found at **adjacent**. In general, any word or word element in an etymology that is printed in small capitals is an entry in the Dictionary and should be referred to for more etymological information.

Some words are not given etymologies. These include interjections, trademarks, ethnic names that are Anglicizations of the group's own name for itself, words derived from names entered in the Geographic Entries section in the back of the Dictionary, and words derived from biographical names mentioned in the definition of the word itself. A large and important group of words that are not given explicit etymologies consists of those words that are compounds and derivatives formed in Modern English from morphemes entered in boldface in the Dictionary. Examples are **sodium chloride**, **emergence**, and **euploid**. If only a portion of a morpheme is used, an etymology is given and the unused portion of the morpheme is enclosed within parentheses:

bal·lis·to·car·di·o·gram . . . [BALLIST(IC) + CARDIOGRAM.]

The linking vowels **–o–** and **–i–** are defined in the Dictionary but are not shown in the etymologies. Compounds like **emergence** in which only the final vowel of one constituent has been deleted are considered self-evident enough not to need etymologies. Compounds that are not formed in Modern English are given full etymologies. A colon (:) is used to introduce the part of the etymology where the compound is analyzed into its component parts, which are joined by a plus sign (+):

de·pend . . . [ME *dependen,* to hang down < OFr. *dependre* < Lat. *dependēre* : *de-,* down + *pendēre,* to hang.]

The compound analyzed is the word immediately preceding the colon. Any linguistic form given after the colon is understood to belong to the same language as the compound unless it is explicitly assigned to another language:

pea·cock . . . [ME *pecok* : OE *pēa,* peafowl (< Lat. *pavo,* peacock) + *cok,* cock < OE *coc.*]

In this example the word *cok* is understood to be Middle English, whereas *pēa* is explicitly identified as an Old English form. Parentheses are used in etymologies to show the further history of one part of a compound, especially the part preceding the plus sign, as in **peacock**. They are also used when one part of a compound is itself a compound word; only one colon is used in any etymology:

pseud·e·pig·ra·pha . . . [Gk. : *pseudēs,* false (< *pseudein,* to lie) + *epigraphein,* to ascribe (*epi-,* upon + *graphein,* to write).]

The etymologies present a great deal of complex information in a small space, and for this reason certain typographic and styling conventions are used. Italics are used for non-Modern English linguistic forms, roman type for glosses and language names, and small capitals for cross-references to other etymologies in the Dictionary. All symbols and abbreviations are listed on a separate page in the front of the Dictionary, and all language names are entered and defined. The character *edh* (ð) is used to transliterate both the voiced and unvoiced *th* sound in Old English and Old Norse. Mandarin Chinese forms are given in the Pinyin system of transliteration. Transliterations of Greek, Hebrew, Arabic, and Russian letters are given in the alphabet table in the body of the book.

UNDEFINED FORMS

Additional words formed from the main-entry word by the addition of a suffix will be found at the end of many entries. These run-on entries are obviously related to the main-entry word and have the same essential meaning, but they have a different grammatical function, as indicated by the part-of-speech label. The use of run-on entries saves valuable space that would otherwise be used for definitions that would merely be repetitions of previous definitions or for a word formula that would give no more information than the part-of-speech label does. Run-on entries appear in boldface type, followed by a part-of-speech label. All run-ons are syllabicated; stress is indicated for all such undefined forms that have more than one syllable, and pronunciation is indicated as needed. For instance, at the main entry **sententious**, the undefined run-ons are:

—sen·ten′tious·ly *adv.* **—sen·ten′tious·ness** *n.*

When different run-on forms have the same grammatical function and the same meaning, they are separated by a comma and share a single part-of-speech label. For example, at **lucid**, these nouns have the same function and meaning and are run on together:

—lu·cid′i·ty, lu′cid·ness *n.* **—lu′cid·ly** *adv.*

In other instances, undefined run-ons have the same grammatical function but different meanings. These terms are run on separately, as shown at **pagan**:

—pa′gan·dom (-dəm) *n.* **—pa′gan·ish** *adj.* **—pa′gan·ism** *n.*

Sometimes the entry word appears unchanged at the end of the entry, with a different part-of-speech label. This indicates that the word is used in exactly the same senses as those defined above but with a different grammatical function. Again this eliminates definitions that would add no semantic information and would tell no more than is conveyed by the part-of-speech label.

Usage Notes

The Usage Notes are a significant aspect of the Dictionary and present information and guidance drawn from diverse sources. The members of the Usage Panel have made their contribution through their response to the periodic questionnaires developed by members of the editorial staff of the Dictionary. Linguists specializing in usage have played an invaluable role in assessing and evaluating the available evidence and in the selection and clarification of those points of usage considered to be of greatest interest to the user. It should be noted that all significant usages, regardless of their status, are recorded in the definitions. The Usage Notes, signaled by the italic boldface subheading ***Usage***, appear at the ends of some entries.

Synonyms

Paragraphs that provide discrimination of related words appear at the end of some entries and are headed ***Synonyms***. The terms treated together in such a paragraph should not be considered to have precisely the same meaning, however. The most valuable feature of these paragraphs is the discrimination of the different nuances and shades of meaning for the terms they include.

Biographical Entries, Geographic Entries, and Abbreviations

The reader will find separate A–Z listings in the back of this Dictionary for biographical names, geographic names, and abbreviations. The introductory matter heading each of these sections explains the coverage therein.

Abbreviations and Labels Used in this Dictionary

Field Labels

Label	Expansion of Abbreviation
Accounting.	
Acoustics.	
Aerospace.	
Anat.	Anatomy
Anthropol.	Anthropology
Archaeol.	Archaeology
Archit.	Architecture
Astron.	Astronomy
Astrophysics.	
Baseball.	
Basketball.	
Biochem.	Biochemistry
Biol.	Biology
Bot.	Botany
Chem.	Chemistry
Christian Science.	
Commerce.	
Computer Sci.	Computer Science
Eccles.	Ecclesiastical
Ecol.	Ecology
Econ.	Economics
Elect.	Electricity
Electronics.	
Engineering.	
Football.	
Games.	
Genetics.	
Geol.	Geology
Gram.	Grammar
Gk. Myth.	Greek Mythology
Gk. & Rom. Myth.	Greek and Roman Mythology
Heraldry.	
Hinduism.	
Islam.	

Label	Expansion of Abbreviation
Judaism.	
Law.	
Ling.	Linguistics
Logic.	
Math.	Mathematics
Med.	Medicine
Metallurgy.	
Meteorol.	Meteorology
Microbiol.	Microbiology
Mineral.	Mineralogy
Mormon Ch.	Mormon Church
Mus.	Music
Myth.	Mythology
Naut.	Nautical
Paleontol.	Paleontology
Pathol.	Pathology
Philos.	Philosophy
Physics.	
Physiol.	Physiology
Printing.	
Psychiat.	Psychiatry
Psychoanal.	Psychoanalysis
Psychol.	Psychology
Rom. Cath. Ch.	Roman Catholic Church
Rom. Myth.	Roman Mythology
Sports.	
Statistics.	
Theol.	Theology
WWI.	World War I
WWII.	World War II
Zool.	Zoology

Stylistic and Geographic Labels

Archaic.	
Austral.	Australian
Chiefly Brit.	Chiefly British
Informal.	
Ir.	Irish
Nonstandard.	
Obscene.	
Obs.	Obsolete
Offensive.	
Regional.	
Scot.	Scots
Slang.	
So. Afr.	South African
Vulgar.	

Abbreviations and Symbols Used in Etymologies

abbr.	abbreviation	p.	past
adj.	adjective	part.	participle, participial
adv.	adverb	p.part.	past participle
aug.	augmentative	p.t.	past tense
cent.	century	perh.	perhaps
comp.	comparative	pl.	plural
conj.	conjunction	poss.	possibly
dial.	dialectal	pr.	present
dim.	diminutive	pr.part.	present participle
ety.	etymology	prob.	probably
fem.	feminine	redup.	reduplication
freq.	frequentative	sing.	singular
fut.	future	St.	Saint
gerund.	gerundive	superl.	superlative
imit.	imitative	tr.	transitive
imper.	imperative	transl.	translation
intr.	intransitive	ult.	ultimately
M	Middle	usu.	usually
masc.	masculine	v.	verb
Med.	Medieval	var.	variant
Mod.	Modern		
n.	noun	*	unattested
naut.	nautical	<	derived from
O	Old	+	combined with
obs.	obsolete	ð	th in Old English and Old Norse
orig.	origin, originally		

Abbreviations of Languages Used in Etymologies

Abbreviation	Language
Afr.	Afrikaans
AFr.	Anglo-French
Am. E.	American English
Am. Sp.	American Spanish
AN	Anglo-Norman
Ar.	Arabic
Aram.	Aramaic
Balt.	Baltic
Brit.	British
Brit. E.	British English
Canadian Fr.	Canadian French
Celt.	Celtic
Chin.	Chinese
Dan.	Danish
Du.	Dutch
Egypt.	Egyptian
E.	English
Finn.	Finnish
Flem.	Flemish
Fr.	French
G.	German
Gael.	Gaelic
Gk.	Greek
Goth.	Gothic
Heb.	Hebrew
HG	High German
Hung.	Hungarian
Icel.	Icelandic
IE	Indo-European
Ir.	Irish
Iran.	Iranian
Ir. Gael.	Irish Gaelic
Ital.	Italian
J.	Japanese
Lat.	Latin
LGk.	Late Greek
Lith.	Lithuanian
Louisiana Fr.	Louisiana French
LG	Low German
MDu.	Middle Dutch
ME	Middle English
Med. Lat.	Medieval Latin
Mex. Sp.	Mexican Spanish
MHG	Middle High German
MLG	Middle Low German
Mod. E.	Modern English
NLat.	New Latin
Norman Fr.	Norman French
Norw.	Norwegian
ODan.	Old Danish
OE	Old English
OFr.	Old French
OHG	Old High German
OIr.	Old Irish
OItal.	Old Italian
ON	Old Norse
ONFr.	Old North French
OProv.	Old Provençal
OSp.	Old Spanish
Pers.	Persian
Pidgin E.	Pidgin English
Pol.	Polish
Port.	Portuguese
Prov.	Provençal
R.	Russian
Rum.	Rumanian
Sc.	Scottish
Scand.	Scandinavian
Sc. Gael.	Scottish Gaelic
Skt.	Sanskrit
Slav.	Slavic
Sp.	Spanish
Swed.	Swedish
Turk.	Turkish
VLat.	Vulgar Latin

STYLE MANUAL

This section of the Dictionary discusses and illustrates the basic, generally accepted stylistic conventions of American English. The more than 100 rules delineating the proper use of capital letters, italics, and punctuation marks are augmented and exemplified by over 300 verbal illustrations, many of which are quotations from the citation files of *The American Heritage Dictionary*. Following the Punctuation section, the reader will find a guide to the proper styling of footnotes and bibliographies. The 40 illustrative examples therein should prove useful to college and high-school students, professors and teachers, and general users of the language.

Unfortunately, the space constraints inherent in a college-level dictionary such as this one preclude discussion of all aspects of English grammar, stylistics, and diction. Hence, we recommend that readers seeking in-depth guidance to the use of graceful English prose consult one of the many books on the subject, such as the *Practical English Handbook*, 5th. ed., by Floyd C. Watkins, William B. Dillingham, and Edwin T. Martin (Boston: Houghton Mifflin, 1978).

CAPITALIZATION

The following should be capitalized:

beginnings

1. The first word of a sentence:

   Some diseases are acute; others are chronic.
   Aren't you my new neighbor?
   Great! Let's go!

2. The first word of a direct quotation, except when it is a split quotation closely woven into the sentence:

   Helen asked, "Do you think Satie was a serious composer?"

   "For me," I answered, "he was simply amusing."

   G. B. Shaw said that "assassination is the extreme form of censorship."

3. The first word of each line in a poem in traditional verse:

   Poets that lasting marble seek
   Must carve in Latin or in Greek.
   —Edmund Waller

proper names

4. The names of people, of organizations and their members, of councils and congresses, and of historical periods and events:

   Albert Einstein
   Marie Curie
   the Free and Accepted Masons
   a Mason
   Roman Catholic Church
   a Catholic
   the Republican Party
   a Democrat
   the Nuclear Regulatory Commission
   the Potsdam Conference
   the House of Representatives
   the Middle Ages
   World War II
   the Battle of the Bulge

5. The names of places and geographic divisions, districts, regions, and locales:

Boston	Middle East
Virginia	Far West
France	Mountain States
Fifth Avenue	Gulf Coast
Golden Gate Bridge	the North
Arctic Circle	the South
Western Hemisphere	the East
South Pole	the West
Torrid Zone	the Midwest
Continental Divide	the Southwest

   But do not capitalize words designating points of the compass unless a specific region is referred to:

   Turn south onto I-95.

6. The names of rivers, lakes, mountains, and oceans:

Connecticut River	Blue Ridge Mountains
Lake Geneva	Pacific Ocean

7. The names of ships, airplanes, and space vehicles:

U.S.S. *Kitty Hawk*
Lindbergh's *Spirit of St. Louis*
Voyager II

8. The names of nationalities, races, tribes, and languages:

Canadians	Bantu
Maori	German
Caucasian	Old High German

9. Words derived from proper names, when used in their primary senses:

Chinese emperors
Moroccan cities

But do not capitalize these derivations if they are used as integral elements of compound words having their own distinct meanings:

chinese red (i.e., a specific shade of red)
moroccan leather (i.e., a specific kind of leather)

titles of people

10. Words indicating familial relationships when preceding a person's name and forming a title:

Aunt Mary
Grandmother Walker

but

my aunt, Mary Smith
her grandmother, Mrs. Walker

11. Titles—civil, military, royal and noble, religious, and honorary—when preceding a name:

Justice Frankfurter	Lord Nelson
General Marshall	Pope John Paul II
Mayor White	Professor Malone
Queen Elizabeth II	

12. All references to the President and the Vice President of the United States:

President Truman	the President
Vice President Wallace	the Vice President

titles of publications and artistic works

13. All words except definite and indefinite articles, prepositions, and conjunctions within titles of literary, dramatic, artistic, and musical works:

the novel *All Quiet on the Western Front*
the short story "The Nose"
an article entitled "The Finiteness of Natural Lanuage"
Byron's poem "The Prisoner of Chillon"
the play *Cat on a Hot Tin Roof*
Van Gogh's *Wheat Field and Cypress Trees*
Bartok's *Concerto for Orchestra*

14. *The* in the title of a newspaper if it is considered an integral part of the publication's entire title:

The Wall Street Journal
the New York *Daily News*

salutations and complimentary closes

15. The first word of the salutation and of the complimentary close of a letter:

My dear Joyce	Sincerely yours
Dear Mr. Atkins	Yours sincerely

epithets

16. Epithets used as substitutes for the names of people or places:

the Iron Chancellor
the Big Apple

personifications

17. Words used in personification:

I met Murder in the way—/He had a mask like Castlereagh.

—Percy Bysshe Shelley

the pronoun I

18. The pronoun *I*:

"To whom am I speaking?"
"It is I."

names for the Deity and sacred works

19. Names for the Deity, for a Supreme Being, and for sacred books:

God and His blessings	Allah
the Almighty	the Messiah
the Savior	the Bible
the Holy Spirit	the Koran
Jehovah	the Talmud

days, months, and holidays

20. Days of the week, months of the year, holidays, and holy days:

Monday	Passover
January	Ramadan
Labor Day	Easter

courts

21. The names of specific judicial courts:

The Supreme Court of the United States
the United States Court of Appeals for the Fourth Circuit
Court of Justice of the European Communities

treaties and laws

22. The names of treaties, pacts, accords, acts, laws, and specific amendments:

Panama Canal Treaty
Treaty of Versailles
Warsaw Pact
Geneva Accords
the Labor Management Relations Act
the Sherman Antitrust Law
the First Amendment to the Constitution

trademarks and service marks

23. Registered trademarks and service marks:

Kleenex   Comsat
Xerox   Soap Box Derby

scientific terms

24. The names of geological eras, periods, epochs, and strata and the names of prehistoric divisions:

The Paleozoic era   Age of Reptiles
the Precambrian period   the Bronze Age
the Pleistocene epoch

25. The names of constellations, planets, and stars:

the Milky Way   Mars
the Southern Crown   Venus
Jupiter   Polaris

26. Genus—but not species—names in binomial nomenclature:

Chrysanthemum leucanthemum
Macaca mulatta
Rana pipiens

27. New Latin names of classes, families, and all groups higher than genera in botanical and zoological nomenclature:

Gastropoda
Nematoda

But do not capitalize adjectives and nouns derived from these New Latin names:

gastropod
a nematode

abbreviations and acronyms

28. Many abbreviations and acronyms (consult this Dictionary when in doubt about styling):

Nov.   M.B.A.
Tues.   UNESCO
Lt Col   MIRV
N.W.   OPEC

ITALICS

1. Indicate titles of books, plays, and very long poems:

For Whom the Bell Tolls
The Little Foxes
Paradise Lost

2. Indicate the titles of magazines and newspapers:

American Heritage magazine
The Wall Street Journal
the New York *Daily News*

Note that *The* is capitalized and italicized in publication titles only if it is considered an integral part of the entire title.

3. Set off the titles of motion pictures and radio and television series:

The French Lieutenant's Woman
All Things Considered
Masterpiece Theater

4. Indicate the titles of long musical compositions:

Messiah
Die Götterdämmerung
Bartok's *Concerto for Orchestra*
Elgar's *Enigma Variations*

5. Set off the names of paintings and sculpture:

Mona Lisa   *Pietà*
Guernica   *The Burghers of Calais*

6. Indicate words, letters, or numbers used as such:

The word *buzz* is onomatopoeic.
Can't means *won't* in his lexicon.
She formed her *n*'s like *u*'s.
A *6* looks like an inverted *9*.

7. Indicate foreign words and phrases not yet assimilated into English:

editors, machinists, *pâtissiers,* barbers, and hoboes

his *Sturm und Drang* period

8. Indicate the names of plaintiff and defendant in legal citations:

Madison v. *Kingsley*

9. Emphasize a word or phrase:

When you are quoted on the six o'clock news, you have *arrived.*

This device should be used sparingly.

10. Distinguish the New Latin names of genera, species, subspecies, and varieties in botanical and zoological nomenclature:

Homo sapiens
Sciurus carolinensis

Do not italicize phyla, classes, orders, and families in botanical and zoological nomenclature:

Gastropoda
Nematoda

11. Set off the names of ships, planes, and often spacecraft:

U.S.S. *Kitty Hawk*
Spirit of St. Louis
Voyager II

PUNCTUATION

Apostrophe ’

1. Indicates the possessive case of singular and plural nouns, indefinite pronouns, and surnames combined with designations such as *Jr., Sr.,* and *II*:

her aunt's house
their aunts' houses
the children's toys
Keats's "Ode to Psyche"
someone's bright idea
John Stone, Jr.'s car
the John Stone, Jrs.' car

2. Indicates joint possession when used with the last of two or more nouns in a series:

Smith and Roe's report

3. Indicates individual possession when used with each of two or more nouns in a series:

Smith's, Roe's, and Doe's reports

4. Indicates the plurals of figures, letters, or words used as such:

42's and 53's   *x*'s, *y*'s, and *z*'s
in the 1700's   an article with too many *also*'s

5. Indicates the omission of letters in contractions:

isn't   that's
couldn't   o'clock

6. Indicates the omission of figures in dates:

the class of '67

Brackets [ ]

1. Enclose words or passages in quotations to indicate the insertion of material written by someone other than the original writer:

. . . On these two commandments hang [are based] all the Law and the Prophets.

And summer's lease [allotted time] hath all too short a date [duration]. . . .

2. Enclose material inserted within matter already in parentheses:

(Washington [D.C.], January, 1983)

Colon :

1. Introduces words, phrases, or clauses that explain, amplify, or summarize what has preceded:

Suddenly I knew where we were: Paris.

The army was cut to pieces: more than fifty thousand men had been captured or killed.

The lasting influence of Greece's dramatic tradition is indicated by words still in our vocabulary: *chorus, comedy,* and *drama*.

She has three sources of income: stock dividends, interest from savings accounts, and salary.

2. Introduces a long quotation:

In his Gettysburg Address, Lincoln said: "Four score and seven years ago our fathers brought forth on this continent, a new nation, conceived in Liberty, and dedicated to the proposition that all men are created equal. . . ."

3. Introduces a list:

Among the conjunctive adverbs are the following: *so, therefore, hence, however, nevertheless, moreover, accordingly,* and *besides*.

4. Separates chapter and verse numbers in references to biblical quotations:

Esther 2:17

5. Separates city from publisher in footnotes and bibliographies:

Boston: Houghton Mifflin, 1982.

6. Separates hour and minute in time designations:

1:30 P.M.   a 9:15 class

7. Follows the salutation in a business letter:

Dear Sir or Madam:
Dear Mr. Johnson:
Gentlemen:

Comma ,

1. Separates the clauses of a compound sentence connected by a coordinating conjunction:

There is a difference between the musical works of Mozart and Haydn, and it is a difference worth discovering.

He didn't know where she got such an idea, but he didn't disagree.

The comma may be omitted in short compound sentences in which the connection between the clauses is close:

She understood the situation and she was furious.

He got in the car and he drove and drove.

2. Separates *and* or *or* from the final item in a series of three or more:

Lights of red, green, and blue wavelengths may be mixed to produce all colors.

The radio, television set, and stereo were arranged on one shelf.

Would you rather have ice cream, cake, or pie for dessert?

3. Separates two or more adjectives modifying the same noun if *and* could be used between them without changing the meaning:

a solid, heavy gait
a large, high-ceilinged room

but

a polished mahogany desk

4. Sets off a nonrestrictive clause or phrase (one that if eliminated would not change the meaning of the sentence):

The thief, who had entered through the window, went straight to the safe.

The comma should not be used when the clause is restrictive (essential to the meaning of the sentence):

The thief who had entered through the window went straight to the safe; the other burglar searched for the flat silver.

5. Sets off words or phrases in apposition to a noun or noun phrase:

   Plato, the famous Greek philosopher, was a pupil of Socrates.

   The composer of *Tristan and Isolde,* Richard Wagner, was a leading exponent of German romanticism.

   The comma should not be used if such words or phrases further specify the noun that precedes:

   The Greek philosopher Plato was a pupil of Socrates.

   The composer Richard Wagner was a leading exponent of German romanticism.

   The Dostoevsky novel *Crime and Punishment* was required reading.

6. Sets off transitional words and short expressions that require a pause in reading or speaking:

   Unfortunately, Mrs. Lee hadn't read many Russian novels.

   Did he, after all, look American?

   Peter lives with his family, of course.

   Indeed, the sight of him gave me quite a jolt.

7. Sets off words used to introduce a sentence:

   No, I haven't seen her.
   Well, why don't you do as I ask?

8. Sets off a subordinate clause or a long phrase that precedes a principal clause:

   By the time they finally found the restaurant, they were no longer hungry.

   After the army surrendered, the general was taken prisoner.

   Of all the illustrations in the book, the most striking are those that show the beauty of the mosaics.

9. Sets off short quotations and sayings:

   Jo told him, "Come tomorrow for dinner."

   The candidate said, "Actions speak louder than words."

   "I don't know if I can," he said, "but maybe I will."

10. Indicates the omission of a word or words:

    To err is human; to forgive, divine.

11. Sets off the year from the month in full dates:

    Louis XVI of France was guillotined on January 21, 1793.

    but also possible

    Louis XVI of France was guillotined in January 1793.

12. Sets off city and state in geographical names:

    Boston, Massachusetts, is the largest city in New England.

    512 Peaks Street
    Bedford, VA 24523

13. Separates series of four or more figures into thousands, millions, and so on:

    57,395 100,000

    The comma is not used in this way in dates or pagination:

    the year 1776 page 1100

14. Sets off words used in direct address:

    Ms. Stone, please submit your report as soon as possible.

    Thank you, Sandy, for your help.

    The forum is open to questions, ladies and gentlemen.

15. Separates a tag question from the rest of the sentence:

    You did say that you had the book, didn't you?

    Beethoven's "Eroica" is on the program, isn't it?

16. Sets off any sentence elements that might be misunderstood if the comma were not used:

    Some time after, the actual date was set.

    To Mary, Anne was just a nuisance.

    Whenever possible, friends provide moral support.

17. Follows the salutation in a personal letter and the complimentary close in a business or personal letter:

    Dear Patsy, Sincerely yours,

18. Sets off titles and degrees from surnames and from the rest of a sentence:

    John T. Brown, Jr.
    Michael A. Callahan, S.J.
    Maria I. Martin, M.D., presented the case.

Dash —

1. Indicates a sudden break or abrupt change in continuity:

   Well, you see, I—I've—I'm just not sure.

   He seemed very upset about—I never knew what.

   And then the problem—if it is a problem—can be solved.

2. Sets apart an explanatory or defining phrase:

   Foods high in protein—meats, fish, eggs, and cheese—should be a part of one's daily diet.

   We suddenly realized what the glittering gems were—emeralds.

3. Sets apart parenthetical material:

   He stares soulfully heavenward—to the great delight of the audience—when he plays Chopin.

   Allen—who had a lean face, a long nose, and cold blue eyes—was a stern, authoritarian man.

4. Marks an unfinished sentence:

   Well, then, I'll simply tell her that—

   "But if the plane is late—" he began.

5. Sets off a summarizing phrase or clause:

   Noam Chomsky, Morris Halle, Roman Jakobson—these are among America's most prominent linguists.

6. Sets off the name of an author or source, as at the end of a quotation:

   There never was a good war, or a bad peace.
   —Benjamin Franklin

Ellipses • • •

1. Indicate, by three spaced points, the omission of words or sentences within quoted matter:

   This ended, the power of the council . . . and the former regents were put on trial.

2. Indicate, by four spaced points, the omission of words at the end of a sentence:

   Nor have we been wanting in Attentions to our British Brethren. . . . They too have been deaf to the Voice of Justice. . . .

3. Indicate, when extended the length of a line, the omission of one or more lines of poetry:

   Come away, O human child!
   . . . .
   For the world's more full of weeping
   than you can understand.
   —William Butler Yeats

4. Are sometimes used as a device to catch and hold the reader's interest, especially in advertising copy:

   To help you Move and Grow
   with the Rigors of
   Business in the 1980's . . .
   and Beyond.
   —*The Journal of Business Strategy*

Exclamation Point !

1. Terminates an emphatic or exclamatory sentence:

   Go home immediately!
   You can't be serious!
   What a ball game that was!

2. Terminates an emphatic interjection:

   Bravo!

Hyphen -

1. Indicates that part of a word of more than one syllable has been carried over from one line to the next:

   Anatole France's actual name was Jacques Anatole Thibault.

2. Joins the elements of some compounds:

   great-grandfather
   cure-all
   ne'er-do-well

3. Joins the elements of compound modifiers preceding nouns:

   a well-dressed woman
   high-school athletics
   a fire-and-brimstone sermon
   a four-hour seminar
   a two-thirds share

4. Indicates that two or more compounds share a single base:

   three- and four-volume sets
   six- and seven-year-olds

5. Separates the prefix and root in some combinations:

prefix + proper noun or adjective	anti-Nazi pro-Nazi
some prefixes ending in a vowel + root beginning with a vowel	re-election co-author
stressed prefix + root word if absence of hyphen could cause misunderstanding of meanings	re-form/reform re-cover/recover re-creation/recreation

6. Substitutes for the word *to* between figures or words:

   pages 12-24
   the years 1790-1980
   the Boston-New York shuttle

7. Punctuates written-out compound numbers from 21 through 99:

   thirty-five years of age
   a man who is thirty-five
   two hundred thirty-one dollars

Parentheses ( )

1. Enclose material that is not an essential part of the sentence and that if not included would not alter its meaning:

   In an hour's time (some say less) the firefighters had extinguished the blaze.

   It was a dream (although a hazy one) of an ideal, poverty-free state.

   Susan doesn't feel (and why should she?) that she should pay higher rent.

2. Often enclose letters or figures to indicate subdivisions of a series:

   A movement in sonata form consists of the following sections: (a) the exposition; (b) the development; and (c) the recapitulation, which is often followed by a coda.

3. Enclose figures following and confirming written-out numbers, especially in legal and business documents:

   Delivery will be made in sixty (60) days.

4. Enclose abbreviations of written-out words when the abbreviations are used for the first time in a text and may be unfamiliar to the reader:

   The study regarding anti-ballistic missiles (ABM's) is classified.

Period •

1. Terminates a complete declarative or mild imperative sentence:

   The carved ornamentation of the façade dates back to the fourteenth century.

Come home when you can.

Would you please sign here.

2. Follows some abbreviations:

Jan.	Ave.
etc.	pp.
a.k.a.	Inc.
Rev.	Ltd.
St.	Op. cit.

Question Mark ?

1. Terminates a direct question:

What are your editorial skills?

Who is there?

but

I wonder who said "Speak softly and carry a big stick."

He asked when Harry planned to leave.

2. Indicates uncertainty:

Ferdinand Magellan (1480?–1521)

Quotation Marks " " ' '

double quotation marks

1. Enclose direct quotations:

"What was Berlin like during the war?" she asked.

"Ladies and gentlemen," the store manager said, "shoes are on sale today."

Arnold Toynbee wrote that "though not lovable, Caesar was and is attractive, indeed fascinating."

Will Rogers said: "Things in our country run in spite of goverment. Not by aid of it."

2. Enclose words or phrases to clarify their meaning or use or to indicate that they are being used in a special way:

"Dey" is a title formerly given to governors of Algiers.

By "brace" we mean the bracket and line joining two or more staves of music.

"The Big Apple" is a name for New York City.

3. Set off the translation of a foreign word or phrase:

déjà vu, "already seen"

Hakenkreuz means "hooked cross" or "swastika."

4. Set off the titles of series of books, of articles or chapters in publications, of essays, of short stories and poems, of individual television and radio programs, and of songs and short musical pieces:

"The Horizon Concise History" series
"Some Notes on Case Grammar in English"
Chapter 9, "Four in Freedom"
Gogol's "The Nose"
Shelley's "Ode to the West Wind"
"The Bob Hope Special"
Schubert's "Death and the Maiden"

single quotation marks

Enclose quotations within quotations:

"To me," he said, "the key word for modern business people is 'entrepreneurship.' "

Mary said, "I heard the thief yell, 'Quick! Let's get out of here!' "

Put commas and periods inside closing quotation marks; put semicolons and colons outside. Other punctuation, such as exclamation points and question marks, should be put inside the closing quotation marks only if it is part of the matter quoted.

Semicolon ;

1. Separates the clauses of a compound sentence having no coordinating conjunction:

The questions are provided by the analyst; the answers come from the data.

Many industries were paralyzed by the strike; factory owners left the district, taking their money with them.

2. Separates the clauses of a compound sentence in which the clauses contain internal punctuation, even when the clauses are joined by a conjunction:

Picnic baskets in hand, we walked to the beach, chose a sunny spot, and spread out the blankets; and the rest of the group followed us in a dune buggy.

3. Separates elements of a series in which items already contain commas:

Among the guests were Mary Adams; her daughter, Elaine; Henry Abrams, formerly of the Redding Institute; and two couples whom I had never met.

4. Separates clauses of a compound sentence joined by a conjunctive adverb, such as *nonetheless, however,* or *hence*:

We demanded a refund; however, the manufacturer refused to give us one.

5. May be used instead of a comma to signal longer pauses, for dramatic effect:

But I want you to know that when I cross the river my last conscious thoughts will be of the Corps; and the Corps; and the Corps.

—General Douglas MacArthur

Virgule /

1. Separates successive divisions in an extended date:

the fiscal year 1982/83

2. Represents the word *per*:

800 ft./sec.   4000 gal./min.

3. Means *or* between the words *and* and *or*:

matters of linguistic and/or sociological importance

Take skis and/or ice skates when you visit New England in the winter.

4. Separates two or more lines of poetry that are quoted and run in on successive lines of a text:

The actor had a memory lapse when he came to the lines "Why? all delights are vain, but that most vain/ Which, with pain purchas'd, doth inherit pain" and had to improvise.

FOOTNOTES AND BIBLIOGRAPHIES

Footnotes

Footnotes are used by writers to identify the sources of quotations, to acknowledge borrowed material, and to provide supplementary information in texts. They are indicated by superscript numbers ([1], [2], [3], etc.) placed immediately after the words or passages to be footnoted and following any terminal punctuation without intervening space. The footnotes proper are numerically ordered either at the bottom of each page on which references to them occur or at the end of the complete article, chapter, or book. The first line of a footnote is indented by five character spaces, and carried over lines are aligned flush with the left margin. The following typical examples are by no means exhaustive. For further information, readers may wish to consult the *MLA Handbook for Writers of Research Papers, Theses, and Dissertations* by Joseph Gibaldi and Walter S. Achtert (New York: Modern Language Association, 1980), *A Manual of Style,* 12th ed. (Chicago: University of Chicago Press, 1969), or *A Manual for Writers of Term Papers, Theses, and Dissertations,* 4th ed., by Kate L. Turabian (Chicago: University of Chicago Press, 1973).

Sample Footnotes

books

one author

[1]Edward Crankshaw, Bismarck (New York: The Viking Press, 1981), p. 19.

two or three authors

[2]David M. Robb and J. J. Garrison, Art in the Western World, 4th ed. (New York: Harper & Row, 1963), p. 119.

more than three authors

[3]Randolph Quirk, et al., A Grammar of Contemporary English (London: Longman Group Limited, 1979), pp. 231–233.

translation

[4]Aleksandr I. Solzhenitsyn, The Gulag Archipelago, trans. Thomas P. Whitney (New York: Harper & Row, 1973), p. 25.

edition

[5]The State of the Language, ed. Leonard Michaels and Christopher Ricks (Berkeley: University of California Press, 1980), p. 49.

later edition

[6]H. L. Mencken, The American Language, 4th ed. (New York: Alfred A. Knopf, 1980), p. 81.

translation and edition

[7]C. G. Jung, Memories, Dreams, Reflections, trans. Richard and Clara Winston, ed. Aniela Jaffé (New York: Vantage Books, 1963), pp. 373–377.

corporate author

[8]Report of the Commission on the Humanities (New York: American Council of Learned Societies, 1964), p. 120.

anonymous

[9]The Oxford Dictionary of Quotations, 3rd ed. (New York: Oxford University Press, 1979), p. 57.

work in a collection

[10]Lewis Mumford, ''What is a City?'' in City and Country in America, ed. David R. Weimer (New York: Appleton-Century-Crofts, 1962), p. 224.

a volume

[11]Randolph S. Churchill, Winston S. Churchill: Young Statesman 1901–1914, II (Boston: Houghton Mifflin Company, 1967), 87–88.

a book in a series

[12]Charles A. Moser, Antinihilism in the Russian Novel of the 1860's, Slavistic Printings and Reprintings, No. 42, ed. C. H. Van Schooneveld (The Hague: Mouton & Co., 1964), pp. 24–25.

articles

from a journal paged consecutively throughout its annual volume

[13]Martin Goldstein, ''The Debate in The Brothers Karamazov,'' Slavic and East European Journal, 14 (Fall 1970), 326–340.

from a journal paged separately for each of its issues

[14]R. C. Atkinson and R. M. Shiffrin, ''The Control of Short-term Memory,'' Scientific American, 225, No. 2 (1971), 82–90.

from a monthly magazine

[15]Russell Lynes, ''Usage: Precise and Otherwise,'' Harper's, Apr. 1970, p. 32.

from a weekly magazine

[16]William Safire, ''On Language: High Diver,'' The New York Times Magazine, 21 Feb. 1982, pp. 14, 16.

from a daily newspaper

[17]Neal Weinberg, ''What's that you didn't say you meant?'' Morning Union [Springfield, Mass.], 4 Jan. 1982, p. 15, cols. 1–4.

from a reference book

[18] ''Rome,'' The International Geographic Encyclopedia and Atlas (Boston: Houghton Mifflin Company, 1979).

a signed review

[19] Rex A. Wade, rev. of Revolutionary Russia, ed. Richard Pipes, Canadian Slavic Studies 3 (Winter 1969), 758–760.

letter to the editor

[20] Ralph E. Bailey, Letter, National Geographic 161 (March 1982), 272.

Bibliography

A bibliography is an alphabetical list of the works referred to in an article or book. Entries are alphabetized according to the authors' surnames; if anonymous, the entries are alphabetized by title. Unlike footnotes, bibliographic entries are not preceded by superscript numerals. The first line of each entry is aligned flush with the left margin, and carried over lines are indented by five character spaces.

Sample Bibliography

article from a journal paged separately for each of its issues

Atkinson, R. C., and R. M. Shiffrin. ''The Control of Short-term Memory.'' Scientific American, 225, No. 2 (1971), 82–90.

letter to the editor

Bailey, Ralph E. Letter, National Geographic 161 (1982), 272.

a volume

Churchill, Randolph S. Winston S. Churchill: Young Statesman 1901–1914. Vol. II. Boston: Houghton Mifflin, 1967.

book, one author

Crankshaw, Edward. Bismarck. New York: Viking, 1981.

article from a journal paged consecutively throughout its annual volume

Goldstein, Martin. ''The Debate in The Brothers Karamazov.'' Slavic and East European Journal 14 (1970), 326–340.

translation and edition

Jung, C. G. Memories, Dreams, Reflections. Trans. Richard and Clara Winston. Ed. Aniela Jaffé. New York: Vantage, 1963.

article, in a monthly magazine

Lynes, Russell. ''Usage, Precise and Otherwise.'' Harper's, Apr. 1970, pp. 32–36.

later edition

Mencken, H. L. The American Language. 4th ed. New York: Knopf, 1980.

edition

Michaels, Leonard, and Christopher Ricks, eds. The State of the Language. Berkeley: Univ. of California Press, 1980.

a book in a series

Moser, Charles A. Antinihilism in the Russian Novel of the 1860's. Slavistic Printings and Reprintings, No. 42. Ed. C. H. Van Schooneveld. The Hague: Mouton, 1964.

a work in a collection

Mumford, Lewis. ''What is a City?'' In City and Country in America. Ed. David R. Weimer. New York: Appleton-Century-Crofts, 1962, pp. 224–232.

book, anonymous

The Oxford Dictionary of Quotations. 3rd ed. New York: Oxford Univ. Press, 1979.

book, more than three authors

Quirk, Raldolph, et al. A Grammar of Contemporary English. London: Longman, 1979.

book, corporate author

Report of the Commission on the Humanities. New York: American Council of Learned Societies, 1964.

book, two or three authors

Robb, David M., and J. J. Garrison. Art in the Western World. 4th ed. New York: Harper & Row, 1963.

article, from a reference book

''Rome.'' The International Geographic Encyclopedia and Atlas. Boston: Houghton Mifflin Company, 1979.

article, from a weekly magazine

Safire, William. ''Oh Language: High Diver.'' The New York Times Magazine, 21 Feb. 1982, pp. 14, 16.

translation

Solzhenitsyn, Aleksandr I. The Gulag Archipelago. Trans. Thomas P. Whitney. New York: Harper & Row, 1973.

a signed review

Wade, Rex A. Rev. of Revolutionary Russia, ed. Richard Pipes. Canadian Slavic Studies 3 (1969), 758–760.

article, from a daily newspaper

Weinberg, Neal. ''What's that you didn't say you meant?'' Morning Union [Springfield, Mass.] 4 Jan. 1982, cols. 1–4.

PRONUNCIATION KEY

The system of indicating pronunciations in the Dictionary is explained in the section headed "Pronunciation" in the "Guide to the Dictionary." The column below headed AHD represents the pronunciation key used in the Dictionary. The right-hand column, labeled IPA, contains symbols from the International Phonetic Alphabet, widely used by scholars. The two systems do not precisely correspond, because they were differently conceived for somewhat different purposes.

spellings	AHD	IPA
pat	ă	æ
pay	ā	e
care	âr	ɛr, er
father	ä	ɑ:, ɑ
bib	b	b
church	ch	tʃ
deed, milled	d	d
pet	ĕ	ɛ
bee	ē	i
fife, phase, rough	f	f
gag	g	g
hat	h	h
which	hw	hw (also ʍ)
pit	ĭ	ɪ
pie, by	ī	aɪ
pier	îr	ɪr, ir
judge	j	dʒ
kick, cat, pique	k	k
lid, needle	l (nēd′l)	l, l̩ [ˈnidl̩]
mum	m	m
no, sudden	n (sŭd′n)	n, n̩ [ˈsʌdn̩]
thing	ng	ŋ
pot, horrid	ŏ	ɑ
toe, hoarse	ō	o
caught, paw, for	ô	ɔ
noise	oi	ɔɪ
took	o͝o	ʊ
boot	o͞o	u
out	ou	aʊ
pop	p	p
roar	r	r
sauce	s	s
ship, dish	sh	ʃ
tight, stopped	t	t
thin	th	θ
this	*th*	ð
cut	ŭ	ʌ
urge, term, firm, word, heard	ûr	ɝ, ɜr
valve	v	v
with	w	w
yes	y	j
zebra, xylem	z	z
vision, pleasure, garage	zh	ʒ
about, item, edible, gallop, circus	ə	ə
butter	ər	ɚ

FOREIGN

	AHD	IPA
French feu, *German* schön	œ	œ
French tu, *German* über	ü	y
German ich, *Scottish* loch	KH	x
French bon	N	õ, æ̃, ã, œ̃

STRESS

Primary stress	′	**bi·ol′o·gy** (bī-ŏl′ə-jē)
Secondary stress	′	**bi′o·log′i·cal** (bī′ə-lŏj′ĭ-kəl)

A

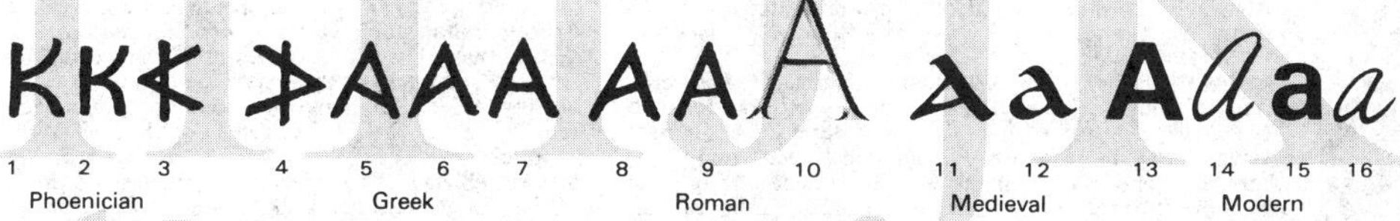

Around 1000 B.C. the Phoenicians and other Semitic peoples began to use graphic signs to represent individual speech sounds instead of syllables or words. They used a symbol in the forms (1,2,3) to represent a consonant, the glottal stop, and called it *'aleph,* their word for "ox," which begins with a glottal stop (represented in modern transliteration by '). Adapting the Phoenician alphabet, the Greeks, who did not have a glottal stop sound in their language, used *'aleph* to represent the sound of the vowel "a." They also changed its shape (4,5, 6,7) and altered its name to *alpha.* The Romans borrowed the alphabet from the Greeks via the Etruscans and adapted it for monumental inscriptions. Monumental script (10) is the prototype of modern capital letters (13,14). Medieval scribes adapted the Roman capitals to being quickly written on paper, parchment, and vellum. These uncial and cursive minuscules (11,12) are the prototypes of modern lower-case letters, both written and printed (16,15).

a

a or **A** (ā) *n., pl.* **a's** or **A's. 1.** The first letter of the modern English alphabet. **2.** Any of the speech sounds represented by the letter *a.* **3.** Something shaped like the letter A. **4.** The first in a series. **5.** The best or highest in quality or rank: *grade A milk.* **6. a.** The sixth tone in the scale of C major or the first note in the relative minor scale. **b.** The key or scale in which A is the tonic. **c.** A written or printed note representing this tone. **d.** A string, key, or pipe tuned to the pitch of this tone.

a[1] (ə; ā *when stressed) indef. art.* **1.** Used before nouns and noun phrases that denote a single, but unspecified, person or thing: *a region; a man.* **2.** Used before terms, such as *few* or *many,* denoting number: *a hundred men; only a few of the voters.* **3.** The same: *birds of a feather.* **4.** Any: *not a drop to drink.* **5. a.** Used before a proper name to denote a type or a member of a class: *the wisdom of a Socrates.* **b.** Used before a mass noun to indicate a single type or example: *a dry wine.* [ME < OE *an,* one.]

Usage: *A* is used before a word beginning with a consonant (*a frog*) or a consonant sound (*a university*); *an* is used before a word beginning with a vowel (*an egg*) or a vowel sound (*an hour*). *An* should not be used before words like *historical* and *hysterical* unless the *h* is not pronounced, a practice now uncommon in American speech.

aardvark

a[2] (ə) *prep.* In every; to each; per: *once a month; one dollar a pound.* [ME *a,* < OE *an* in.]

a[3] (ə; ā *when stressed) v. Regional.* Have: *He'd a come if he could.* [ME < *haven,* to have.]

a–[1] or **an–** *pref.* Without; not: *amoral.* [Gk.]

a–[2] *pref.* **1.** On; in: *abed.* **2.** In the act of: *aborning.* **3.** In the direction of: *astern.* **4.** In a specified state or condition: *abuzz.* [ME < OE < *an,* on.]

aard·vark (ärd′värk′) *n.* A burrowing mammal, *Orycteropus afer,* of southern Africa, having a stocky, hairy body, large ears, a long, tubular snout, and powerful digging claws. [Obs. Afr. : *aarde,* earth (< Du. < M. Du. *aerde*) + *vark,* pig (< M. Du. *varken*).]

aard·wolf (ärd′wo͝olf′) *n.* A hyenalike mammal, *Proteles cristatus,* of southern and eastern Africa, having gray fur with black stripes, and feeding mainly on termites and insect larvae. [Afr. : *aarde,* earth + *wolf,* wolf (< M. Du.).]

Aar·on (âr′ən, ăr′-) *n.* In the Old Testament, the original high priest of the Hebrew nation, the older brother of Moses. [LLat. < Gk. *Aarōn* < Heb. *'aharōn.*]

Aa·ron·ic (â-rŏn′ĭk, ă-rŏn′-) also **Aa·ron·i·cal** (-ĭ-kəl) *adj.* **1.** Of, pertaining to, or characteristic of Aaron. **2.** Of or pertaining to the lower order of priests in the Mormon Church.

Ab (äb, äv, ôv) *n.* Variant of **Av.**

AB (ā′bē′) *n.* A human blood type of the ABO group.

ab–[1] *pref.* Away from: *aboral.* [Lat. < *ab.*]

ab–[2] *pref.* Used to indicate a centimeter-gram-second system electromagnetic unit: *abcoulomb.* [< ABSOLUTE.]

a·ba (ə-bä′, ä-bä′) *n.* **1.** A light fabric woven of the hair of camels or goats. **2.** A loose-fitting sleeveless garment made of aba, worn by Arabs. [Ar. *'abā'.*]

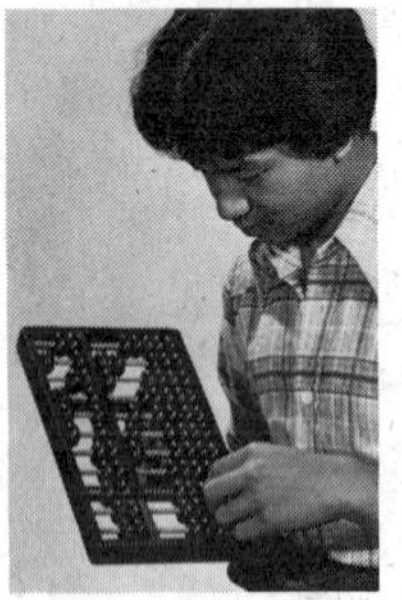

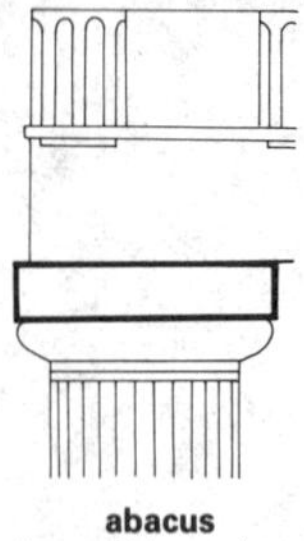

abacus
Above: Chinese abacus
Below: On a Doric column

ab·a·ca (ăb′ə-kä′) *n.* A Philippine plant, *Musa textilis,* related to the banana. Its leafstalks are the source of Manila hemp. [Sp. *abacá* < Tagolog *abaká.*]

a·back (ə-băk′) *adv. Archaic.* Back; backward. **—taken aback.** Dumbfounded; startled. [ME *abak* < OE *on bæc* : *on,* to + *bæc,* back.]

a·bac·te·ri·al (ā′băk-tîr′ē-əl) *adj.* Not caused by or identified with the presence of bacteria.

ab·a·cus (ăb′ə-kəs, ə-băk′əs) *n., pl.* **ab·a·cus·es** or **ab·a·ci** (ăb′ə-sī′, ə-băk′ī′). **1.** A manual computing device consisting of a frame holding parallel rods strung with movable counters. **2.** A slab on the top of the capital of a column. [Lat. < Gk. *abax,* counting board.]

a·baft (ə-băft′) *adv. Naut.* Toward the stern. *—prep.* Toward the stern from. [ME *on baft* : *on,* at + *baft,* rear < OE *beæftan,* behind (*be,* at + *æftan,* behind).]

ab·a·lo·ne (ăb′ə-lō′nē) *n.* Any of the various large, edible marine gastropods of the genus *Haliotis,* having an ear-shaped shell with a row of holes and a colorful, pearly interior, often used for making ornaments. [Am. Sp. *abulón.*]

ab·am·pere (ăb-ăm′pîr′) *n.* A centimeter-gram-second electromagnetic unit of current, equal to the current that produces a force of two dynes per centimeter of length on each of two infinitely long straight parallel wires one centimeter apart. It is equal to 10 amperes.

abbey
Westminster Abbey in London, England

a·ban·don (ə-băn′dən) *tr.v.* **-doned, -don·ing, -dons. 1.** To withdraw one's support or help from, esp. in spite of a duty, allegiance, or responsibility; desert: *abandon a friend in trouble.* **2.** To give up by leaving or ceasing to operate or inhabit, esp. as a result of danger or other impending threat: *abandon ship.* **3.** To surrender one's claim or right to; give up. **4.** To desist from; cease trying to continue. **5.** To yield (oneself) completely, as to emotion. *—n.* **1.** A complete surrender of inhibitions. **2.** Unbounded enthusiasm. [ME *abandounen* < OFr. *abandoner* < *á bandon* : *á,* at (< Lat. *ad*) + *bandon,* control.] **—a·ban′don·ment** *n.*

a·ban·doned (ə-băn′dənd) *adj.* **1.** Deserted or forsaken. **2.** Recklessly unrestrained; shameless.

ab·ap·i·cal (ăb-ăp′ĭ-kəl, -ā′pĭ-) *adj.* Being opposite to or directed away from the apex.

a·base (ə-bās′) *tr.v.* **a·based, a·bas·ing, a·bas·es.** To lower in rank, prestige, or esteem; humiliate. [ME *abassen* < OFr. *abaissir* : Lat. *ad-,* to + Med. Lat. *bassus,* low.] **—a·base′ment** *n.*

a·bash (ə-băsh′) *tr.v.* **a·bashed, a·bash·ing, a·bash·es.** To make ashamed or uneasy; disconcert. [ME *abaishen,* to lose one's composure < OFr. *esbahier* : *es-* (intensive) + *baer,* to gape.] **—a·bash′ment** *n.*

a·ba·sia (ə-bā′zhə) *n.* Dysfunction of muscular coordination in walking. [NLat. : A-[1] + Gk. *basis,* step < *bainein,* to go.]

a·bate (ə-bāt′) *v.* **a·bat·ed, a·bat·ing, a·bates.** *—tr.* **1.** To reduce in amount, degree, or intensity; lessen. **2.** To deduct from an amount; subtract. **3.** *Law.* **a.** To put an end to. **b.** To make void. *—intr.* **1.** To subside. **2.** *Law.* To become void. [ME *abaten* < OFr. *abattre,* to beat : *à-,* to (< Lat. *ad-*) + *batre,* to beat < Lat. *battuere.*]

a·bate·ment (ə-bāt′mənt) *n.* **1.** Diminution in degree or intensity; moderation. **2.** The amount abated; reduction. **3.** *Law.* The act of abating; elimination or annulment.

ab·at·toir (ăb′ə-twär′) *n.* A slaughterhouse. [Fr. < *abattre,* to strike down < OFr. —see ABATE.]

ab·ax·i·al (ă-băk′sē-əl) *adj.* Away from the axis.

ab·ba (ăb′ə, ä′bə) *n.* Father. Used as a title of honor in several Eastern churches. [ME < LLat. < Gk. < Aram. *abbā,* father.]

ab·ba·cy (ăb′ə-sē) *n., pl.* **-cies.** The office, term, or jurisdiction of an abbot. [ME *abbatie* < LLat. *abbatia* < *abba,* father. —see ABBA.]

ab·ba·tial (ə-bā′shəl) *adj.* Of or pertaining to an abbey, abbot, or abbess. [ME *abbacyal* < LLat. *abbatialis* < *abbas,* abbot.]

ab·bé (ăb′ā′, ă-bā′) *n.* A French title originally given to the superior of an abbey, now applied to any ecclesiastical figure. [Fr. < OFr. < LLat. *abbas,* abbot.]

ab·bess (ăb′ĭs) *n.* The female superior of a convent of nuns. [ME *abesse* < OFr. < LLat. *abbatissa* < *abbas,* abbot.]

Ab·be·vil·li·an (ăb′ə-vĭl′ē-ən) *adj.* Designating the earliest Paleolithic archaeological sites in Europe, characterized by bifacial stone hand axes. [After *Abbeville,* France.]

ab·bey (ăb′ē) *n., pl.* **-beys. 1.** A monastery or convent. **2.** An abbey church. [ME < OFr. *abaie* < LLat. *abbatia* < *abbas,* abbot.]

ab·bot (ăb′ət) *n.* The superior of a monastery. [ME *abbod* < OE < LLat. *abbas* < LGk. *abbas* < Aram. *abbā,* father.]

ab·bre·vi·ate (ə-brē′vē-āt′) *tr.v.* **-at·ed, -at·ing, -ates. 1.** To make shorter. **2.** To reduce (a word or phrase) to a shorter form intended to represent the full form. [ME *abbreviaten* < LLat. *abbreviare* : *ab-,* off + *breviare,* to shorten < *brevis,* short.] **—ab·bre′vi·a′tor** *n.*

ab·bre·vi·a·tion (ə-brē′vē-ā′shən) *n.* **1.** The act or product of abbreviating. **2.** A shortened form of a word or phrase used chiefly in writing to represent the complete form; for example, *Mass.* for *Massachusetts.*

ABC (ā′bē′-sē′) *n., pl.* **ABC's. 1.** Often **ABC's.** The alphabet. **2. ABC's.** The rudiments of reading and writing.

ABC art *n.* Minimal art.

ab·cou·lomb (ăb-ko͞o′-lŏm′, -lōm′) *n.* A centimeter-gram-second electromagnetic unit of charge, equal to the charge passing in one second through any cross section of a conductor carrying a steady current of one abampere. It is equal to ten coulombs.

Ab·di·as (ăb-dī′əs) *n.* Obadiah. [LLat. < Gk.]

ab·di·cate (ăb′dĭ-kāt′) *v.* **-cat·ed, -cat·ing, -cates.** *—tr.* To relinquish (power or responsibility) formally. *—intr.* To relinquish formally high office or responsibility. [Lat. *abdicare,* to disclaim : *ab-,* away + *dicare,* to proclaim.] **—ab′di·ca·ble** (-kə-bəl) *adj.* **—ab′di·ca′tion** *n.* **—ab′di·ca′tor** *n.*

ab·do·men (ăb′də-mən, ăb-dō′mən) *n.* **1.** The part of the body in mammals that lies between the thorax and the pelvis and encloses the viscera; belly. **2.** In arthropods, the major posterior part of the body. [Lat., belly.] **—ab·dom′i·nal** (ăb-dŏm′ə-nəl) *adj.* **—ab·dom′i·nal·ly** *adv.*

ab·dom·i·nous (ăb-dŏm′ə-nəs) *adj.* Potbellied.

ab·du·cens (ăb′-do͞o′sənz, -dyo͞o′-) *n., pl.* **ab·du·cen·tes** (ăb′-do͞o-sĕn′tēz′, -dyo͞o-). An abducens nerve. [Lat. *abducens,* pr.part. of *abducere,* to take away. —see ABDUCT.]

abducens nerve *n.* Either of the 6th pair of cranial nerves that convey the motor impulses to the eye muscles.

ab·duct (ăb-dŭkt′) *tr.v.* **-duct·ed, -duct·ing, -ducts. 1.** To carry off by force; kidnap. **2.** *Physiol.* To draw away from the median line of a bone or muscle or from an adjacent part or limb. [Lat. *abducere, abduct-* : *ab-,* away + *ducere,* to lead.] **—ab·duc′tion** *n.* **—ab·duc′tor** *n.*

a·beam (ə-bēm′) *adv.* At right angles to the keel of a ship.

a·be·ce·dar·i·an (ā′bē-sē-dâr′ē-ən) *n.* **1.** One who teaches or studies the alphabet. **2.** One who is just learning; beginner. *—adj.* **1.** Pertaining to the alphabet. **2.** Arranged alphabetically. **3.** Elementary; rudimentary. [ME < Med. Lat. *abecedarium,* alphabet < LLat. *abecedarius,* alphabetical < the names of the letters A B C D.]

a·bed (ə-bĕd′) *adv.* In bed.

A·bel (ā′bəl) *n.* In the Old Testament, the second son of Adam, slain by his elder brother, Cain. [ME < LLat. < Gk. < Heb. *Hebhel.*]

a·bele (ə-bēl′) *n.* The white poplar. [Du. *abeel* < OFr. *abel* < Med. Lat. *albellus,* dim. of Lat. *albus,* white.]

A·be·lian group (ə-bēl′yən, ə-bē′lē-ən) *n.* A commutative group. [After Niels Henrik *Abel* (1802–1829).]

a·bel·mosk (ā′bəl-mŏsk′) *n.* A hairy plant, *Hibiscus abelmoschus,* of tropical Asia, having large yellow flowers and musk-scented seeds that are used in perfumery. [NLat. *abelmoschus* < Ar. *ḥabbalmusk,* grain of musk : *ḥabb,* grain + *mosk,* musk < Pers. *mushk.*]

Ab·er·deen An·gus (ăb′ər-dēn ăng′gəs) *n.* Any of a breed of black, hornless beef cattle that originated in Scotland. [After *Aberdeen* and *Angus,* former counties of Scotland.]

ab·er·rant (ă-bĕr′ənt) *adj.* **1.** Deviating from the proper or expected course. **2.** Deviating from what is normal; untrue to type. **—ab·er′rance, ab·er′ran·cy** *n.*

ab·er·ra·tion (ăb′ə-rā′shən) *n.* **1.** A deviation from the proper or expected course. **2.** A departure from the normal or typical. **3.** A disorder or abnormal alteration in one's mental state. **4. a.** A defect of focus, such as blurring in an image. **b.** A physical defect in an optical element, as in a lens, that causes such an imperfection. **5.** *Astron.* The apparent displacement of the position of a celestial body in the direction of motion of an observer on earth, caused by the motion of the earth and the finiteness of the velocity of light. [Lat. *aberratio,* diversion < *aberrare,* to go astray : *ab-,* from + *errare,* to stray.]

a·bet (ə-bĕt′) *tr.v.* **a·bet·ted, a·bet·ting, a·bets.** To encourage, incite, or help, esp. in wrongdoing. [ME *abetten* < OFr. *abeter,* to entice : *a,* to (< Lat. *ad-*) + *beter,* to bait, of Germanic orig.] **—a·bet′ment** *n.* **—a·bet′tor, a·bet′ter** *n.*

a·bey·ance (ə-bā′əns) *n.* **1.** The condition of being temporarily set aside; suspension. **2.** *Law.* A condition of undetermined ownership, as of an estate that has not yet been assigned. [OFr. *abeance,* desire < *abaer,* to gape at : *a-,* at (< Lat. *ad-*) + *baer,* to gape.] **—a·bey′ant** *adj.*

ab·far·ad (ăb-făr′ăd′, -əd) *n.* A centimeter-gram-second electromagnetic unit of capacitance, equal to the capacitance of a capacitor having a charge of one abcoulomb and a potential difference of one abvolt. It is equal to one billion (10^9) farads.

ab·hen·ry (ăb-hĕn′rē) *n., pl.* **-ries.** A centimeter-gram-second electromagnetic unit of inductance, equal to the inductance resulting from a current variation of one abampere per second that produces an induced electromotive force of one abvolt. It is equal to one billionth (10^{-9}) henry.

ab·hor (ăb-hôr′) *tr.v.* **-horred, -hor·ring, -hors. 1.** To regard with horror or loathing; abominate. **2.** To reject vehemently; shun. [ME *abhorren* < Lat. *abhorrēre,* to shrink from : *ab-,* from + *horrēre,* to shudder.] **—ab·hor′rence** (-hôr′əns, -hŏr′-) *n.* **—ab·hor′rer** *n.*

ab·hor·rent (ăb-hôr′ənt, -hŏr′-) *adj.* **1.** Disgusting; loathsome; repellent. **2.** Feeling repugnance or loathing. **3.** In opposition. **—ab·hor′rent·ly** *adv.*

A·bib (ä-vēv′) *n.* In the ancient Hebrew calendar, an earlier name for the month of Nisan. [Heb. *'ābhībh,* (month of) fresh barley.]

a·bid·ance (ə-bīd′ns) *n.* **1.** An act or condition of abiding; continuance. **2.** Adherence; compliance: *abidance by parliamentary procedure.*

a·bide (ə-bīd′) *v.* **a·bode** (ə-bōd′) or **a·bid·ed, a·bid·ing, a·bides.** *—tr.* **1.** To wait patiently for. **2.** To be in store for; await. **3.** To withstand; persevere under. **4.** To accept the consequences of. **5.** To put up with; tolerate: *can't abide such incompetence.* *—intr.* **1.** To remain in one place or state. **2.** To continue; endure: "*Who can abide in the fierceness of his anger?*" (Cotton Mather). **3.** To dwell or sojourn. ***—phrasal verb.* abide by.** To conform to; comply with. [ME *abiden* < OE *ābīdan* : *a-* (intensive) + *bīdan,* to remain.] **—a·bid′er** *n.*

a·bid·ing (ə-bī′dĭng) *adj.* Long-lasting; enduring. **—a·bid′ing·ly** *adv.*

A·bies (ā′bēz, ä-bī′əs) *n.* A genus of firs in the pine family, with flattened, needlelike leaves and erect cones. [NLat. < Lat., silver fir.]

ab·i·et·ic acid (ăb′ē-ĕt′ĭk) *n.* A yellowish resinous powder, $C_{19}H_{29}COOH$, isolated from rosin and used in lacquers, varnishes, and soaps. [< Lat. *abies, abiet-,* silver fir.]

a·bil·i·ty (ə-bĭl′ĭ-tē) *n., pl.* **-ties. 1.** The quality of being able to do something; physical, mental, financial, or legal power to perform. **2.** A natural or acquired skill or talent. [ME *abilite* < OFr. *habilite* < Lat. *habilitas* < *habilis,* able.]

Synonyms: *ability, capacity, faculty, talent, skill, competence, aptitude.* These nouns name qualities that enable a person to accomplish something. *Ability* is the power, mental or physical, to do something, and usually implies doing it well. *Capacity* refers to the condition that permits one to acquire that power. *Faculty* denotes an ability, inherent or acquired, in one area of achievement: *a faculty for mathematics.* *Talent* emphasizes inborn ability in a particular field, especially the arts. *Skill* implies recognized ability acquired or developed through experience. *Competence* suggests ability to do something satisfactorily but not outstandingly. *Aptitude* usually implies inherent capacity for, and interest in, a particular activity.

-ability or **-ibility** *suff.* Ability, inclination, or suitability for a specified action or condition: *teachability.* [ME *-abilitie* < OFr. *-abilite* < Lat. *-abilitas.*]

ab in·i·ti·o (ăb′ ĭ-nĭsh′ē-ō′) *adv.* From the beginning. [Lat.]

a·bi·o·gen·e·sis (ā′bī-ō-jĕn′ĭ-sĭs) *n.* The hypothetical development of living organisms from nonliving matter. **—a′bi·o·ge·net′ic** (-jə-nĕt′ĭk), **a′bi·o·ge·net′i·cal** *adj.* **—a′bi·og′e·nist** (-ŏj′ə-nĭst) *n.*

a·bi·ot·ic (ā′bī-ŏt′ĭk) *adj.* Not biotic. **—a·bi·o′sis** (-ō′sĭs) *n.* **—a·bi·ot′ic·al·ly** *adv.*

ab·ject (ăb′jĕkt′, ăb-jĕkt′) *adj.* **1.** Of the most contemptible kind: *abject cowardice.* **2.** Of the most miserable kind; wretched: *abject poverty.* [ME, outcast < Lat. *abjectus,* p.part. of *abicere,* to cast away : *ab-,* from + *jacere,* to throw.] **—ab′ject′ly** *adv.* **—ab·ject′ness, ab·jec′tion** *n.*

ab·jure (ăb-jo͝or′) *tr.v.* **-jured, -jur·ing, -jures. 1.** To recant solemnly; repudiate: *abjure one's beliefs.* **2.** To renounce under oath; forswear. [ME *abjuren* < OFr. *abjurer* < Lat. *abjurare* : *ab-,* away + *jurare,* to swear.] **—ab′ju·ra′tion** (ăb′jo͝o-rā′shən) *n.* **—ab·jur′er** *n.*

ab·la·tion (ă-blā′shən) *n.* **1.** Surgical excision or amputation of any part of the body. **2.** The totality of erosive processes by which a glacier is reduced. **3.** *Aerospace.* The dissipation of heat generated by atmospheric friction, esp. in the atmospheric re-entry of a spacecraft or missile, by means of a melting heat shield. [LLat. *ablatio* < *ablatus,* p.part. of *auferre,* to carry away : *ab-,* away + *ferre,* to carry.]

ab·la·tive (ăb′lə-tĭv) *adj.* Designating a grammatical case indicating separation, direction away from, and sometimes manner or agency, found in some Indo-European languages. *—n.* **1.** The ablative case. **2.** A word in the ablative case. [ME < OFr. *ablatif* < Lat. *ablativus* < *ablatus,* p.part. of *auferre,* to carry away. —see ABLATION]

ablative absolute *n.* In Latin grammar, an adverbial phrase syntactically independent from the rest of the sentence and containing two main elements both in the ablative case.

ab·laut (äb′lout′, äp′-) *n.* A patterned change in root vowels of verb forms, characteristic of Indo-European languages, indicating alteration of tense, aspect, or function; for example, *ring, rang, rung.* [G. *Ablaut* : *ab,* off (< OHG *aba*) + *Laut,* sound < MHG *lūt* < OHG *hlūt.*]

Aberdeen Angus

a·blaze (ə-blāz′) *adj.* **1.** On fire. **2.** Radiant with bright color.

a·ble (ā′bəl) *adj.* **a·bler, a·blest. 1.** Having sufficient ability or resources. **2.** Especially capable or talented. [ME < OFr. < Lat. *habilis* < *habēre,* to hold.]

-able or **-ible** *suff.* **1.** Susceptible, capable, or worthy of a specified action: *debatable.* **2.** Inclined or given to a specified state or action: *blamable.* [ME < OFr. < Lat. *-abilis.*]

a·ble-bod·ied (ā′bəl-bŏd′ēd) *adj.* Physically strong and healthy.

able-bodied seaman *n.* A merchant seaman certified for all seaman's duties.

able seaman *n.* An able-bodied seaman.

a·bloom (ə-blo͞om′) *adj.* In bloom; flowering.

ab·lu·tion (ə-blo͞o′shən, ă-blo͞o′-) *n.* **1.** A washing or cleansing of the body, esp. as part of a religious rite. **2.** The liquid used in an ablution. [ME *ablucioun* < Lat. *ablutio* < *abluere,* to wash away : *ab,* away + *luere,* to wash.] **—ab·lu′tion·ar′y** (-shə-nĕr′ē) *adj.*

a·bly (ā′blē) *adv.* In an able manner; capably.

ABM (ā′bē-ĕm′) *n.* Antiballistic missile.

Ab·na·ki (ăb-nä′kē) *n., pl.* **Abnaki** or **-kis. 1.** A tribe of North American Indians of Maine, New Brunswick, and southern Quebec. **2.** A member of the Abnaki. **3.** The Algonquian language of the Abnaki.

ab·ne·gate (ăb′nĭ-gāt′) *tr.v.* **-gat·ed, -gat·ing, -gates.** To deny to oneself; renounce. [Lat. *abnegare, abnegat-,* to refuse : *ab-,* away + *negare,* to deny.]

ab·ne·ga·tion (ăb′nĭ-gā′shən) *n.* Self-denial.

ab·nor·mal (ăb-nôr′məl) *adj.* Not normal; deviant. [Lat. *abnormis* : *ab-,* away from + *norma,* rule.] **—ab·nor′mal·ly** *adv.*

ab·nor·mal·i·ty (ăb′nôr-măl′ĭ-tē) *n., pl.* **-ties. 1.** The condition of not being normal. **2.** An abnormal phenomenon.

abnormal psychology *n.* Psychopathology.

a·board (ə-bôrd′, ə-bōrd′) *adv.* On board a ship, train, airplane, or other passenger vehicle. *—prep.* On board of; on; in. [ME *abōrd* : *a-,* on + *bōrd,* ship.]

a·bode (ə-bōd′) *v.* Past tense and past participle of **abide.** *—n.* **1.** A dwelling place or home. **2.** The act of abiding; sojourn. [ME *abod* < *abiden,* to wait. —see ABIDE.]

ab·ohm (ă-bōm′) *n.* A centimeter-gram-second electromagnetic unit of resistance equal to one billionth (10^{-9}) of an ohm.

a·bol·ish (ə-bŏl′ĭsh) *tr.v.* **-ished, -ish·ing, -ish·es. 1.** To do away with; annul. **2.** To destroy completely. [ME *abolisshen* < OFr. *abolir, aboliss-* < Lat. *abolēre.*] **—a·bol′ish·a·ble** *adj.* **—a·bol′ish·er** *n.* **—a·bol′ish·ment** *n.*

Synonyms: *abolish, exterminate, extinguish, extirpate, eradicate, obliterate.* These verbs mean to get rid of. *Abolish* applies only to doing away with conditions or regulations, not material things or persons. *Exterminate* suggests destruction of living things by a deliberate, selective method. *Extinguish,* meaning to put out a flame or something likened to a flame, stresses the frailty of the object. *Extirpate* suggests effective destruction by getting at the roots or causes, while *eradicate* stresses the resistance to dislodgment posed by the object. *Obliterate* means to destroy so as to leave no trace, and applies principally to things.

ab·o·li·tion (ăb′ə-lĭsh′ən) *n.* **1.** An act of abolishing or the state of being abolished. **2.** The termination of slavery in the United States. [Fr. < Lat. *abolitio* < *abolitus,* p.part. of *abolēre,* to abolish.] **—ab′o·li′tion·ar′y** (-ə-nĕr′ē) *adj.*

ab·o·li·tion·ism (ăb′ə-lĭsh′ə-nĭz′əm) *n.* Advocacy of the abolition of slavery in the United States. **—ab′o·li′tion·ist** *n.*

ab·o·ma·sum (ăb′ō-mā′səm) *n., pl.* **-sa** (-sə). The fourth division of the stomach in ruminant animals, in which true digestion takes place. **—ab′o·ma′sal** (-səl) *adj.*

A-bomb (ā′bŏm′) *n.* An atomic bomb.

a·bom·i·na·ble (ə-bŏm′ə-nə-bəl) *adj.* **1.** Unequivocally detestable; loathsome. **2.** Thoroughly unpleasant or disagreeable: *abominable weather.* [ME *abhomināble* < OFr. < Lat. *abominabilis* < *abominari,* to abhor. —see ABOMINATE.] **—a·bom′i·na·bly** *adv.*

abominable snowman *n.* A hirsute manlike animal reportedly inhabiting the snows of the high Himalayas.

a·bom·i·nate (ə-bŏm′ə-nāt′) *tr.v.* **-nat·ed, -nat·ing, -nates. 1.** To detest thoroughly; abhor. **2.** *Informal.* To dislike intensely. [Lat. *abominari, abominat-,* to deprecate as a bad omen : *ab-,* away + *omen,* omen.] **—a·bom′i·na′tor** *n.*

a·bom·i·na·tion (ə-bŏm′ə-nā′shən) *n.* **1.** An abhorrence for someone or something; disgust. **2.** Something that elicits great dislike or abhorrence.

ab·o·ral (ă-bôr′əl, -bōr′-) *adj.* Opposite to or away from the mouth.

ab·o·rig·i·nal (ăb′ə-rĭj′ə-nəl) *adj.* **1.** Existing from the beginning or being the earliest of its type in an area; indigenous. **2.** Of or pertaining to aborigines. *—n.* An aborigine. **—ab′o·rig′i·nal·ly** *adv.*

A B R A C A D A B R A
A B R A C A D A B R
A B R A C A D A B
A B R A C A D A
A B R A C A D
A B R A C A
A B R A C
A B R A
A B R
A B
A

abracadabra
The letters of the word *abracadabra* arranged in an inverted pyramid to be worn as an amulet

ab·o·rig·i·ne (ăb′ə-rĭj′ə-nē) *n.* **1.** An autochthonous inhabitant of a region. **2. aborigines.** The flora and fauna native to a geographical area. [< Lat. *aborigines,* original inhabitants : *ab-,* from + *origine,* beginning.]

a·born·ing (ə-bôr′nĭng) *adv.* While coming into being or getting under way: *a revolution that almost died aborning.*

a·bort (ə-bôrt′) *v.* **a·bort·ed, a·bort·ing, a·borts.** *—intr.* **1.** To terminate pregnancy prematurely. **2.** To cease growth before full development or maturation. **3.** To terminate an operation or procedure with a missile or a space vehicle before completion, esp. because of equipment failure. *—tr.* **1.** To cause to terminate pregnancy prematurely. **2.** To interfere with the development of; conclude prematurely. **3.** To terminate before completion. *—n.* **1.** The act of terminating an operation or procedure with a missile or space vehicle before completion, esp. because of equipment failure. **2.** *Computer Sci.* A procedure to terminate execution of a program when an unrecoverable error or malfunction occurs. [Lat. *abortare,* freq. of *aboriri,* to disappear, miscarry : *ab-,* away + *oriri,* to appear.]

a·bor·ti·fa·cient (ə-bôr′tə-fā′shənt) *adj.* Causing abortion. *—n.* Anything used to induce abortion.

a·bor·tion (ə-bôr′shən) *n.* **1.** Induced termination of pregnancy before the fetus is capable of survival as an individual. **2.** A fatally premature expulsion of an embryo or fetus from the womb. **3.** Cessation of normal growth, esp. of an organ, prior to full development or maturation. **4.** An aborted organism. **5.** Something malformed or incompletely developed.

a·bor·tion·ist (ə-bôr′shə-nĭst) *n.* One who performs abortions.

a·bor·tive (ə-bôr′tĭv) *adj.* **1.** Failing to accomplish an intended objective; fruitless. **2.** Partially or imperfectly developed. **—a·bor′tive·ly** *adv.* **—a·bor′tive·ness** *n.*

ABO system (ā′bē′ō′) *n.* The antigenic system of human blood, which, by functioning genetically as an allelic unit, produces the four human blood groups or types, A, B, AB and O.

a·bou·li·a (ə-bo͞o′lē-ə) *n.* Variant of **abulia.**

a·bound (ə-bound′) *intr.v.* **a·bound·ed, a·bound·ing, a·bounds. 1.** To be great in number or amount. **2.** To be fully supplied or filled; teem. [ME *abounden* < OFr. *abonder* < Lat. *abundare,* to overflow : *ab-,* from + *undare,* to flow < *unda,* wave.]

a·bout (ə-bout′) *adv.* **1.** Approximately; nearly: *lasted about an hour.* **2.** Almost: *just about done.* **3.** To a reversed position or direction. **4.** In no particular direction: *wandering about town.* **5.** All around; on every side. **6.** In the area or vicinity; near. **7.** In succession; one after another: *Turn about is fair play.* *—prep.* **1.** On all sides of; surrounding. **2.** In the vicinity of; around. **3.** Almost the same as; close to; near. **4.** In reference to; relating to. **5.** In the possession of: *had his wits about him.* **6.** Ready or prepared to do something: *The chorus is about to sing.* **7.** Involved with or engaged in: *went about his business.* *—adj.* Moving here and there; astir: *be up and about.* [ME < OE *onbūtan* : *on,* in + *būtan,* outside.]

Synonyms: *about, around, round.* These terms are sometimes interchangeable, as adverbs and prepositions. However, *around* either specifies or suggests complete encirclement of something, whereas *about* and *round* are less exact and indicate, more or less, semiencirclement: *The children gathered about* (or *round*) *the fireplace; then they danced around the table.*

Usage: The construction *not about to* is often used to express determination: *We are not about to negotiate with terrorists.* A majority of the Usage Panel considers this usage acceptable in speech but not in formal writing.

a·bout-face (ə-bout′fās′) *n.* **1.** The act of pivoting to face in the opposite direction from the original, esp. in a military maneuver. **2.** A total change of attitude or standpoint. *—intr.v.* **-faced, -fac·ing, -fac·es.** To reverse direction.

a·bove (ə-bŭv′) *adv.* **1.** Overhead; on high: *the clouds above.* **2.** In heaven; heavenward. **3.** Upstairs: *a table in the dining room above.* **4.** In or to a higher place. **5.** In an earlier part of a given text: *figures quoted above.* **6.** In or to a higher rank or position: *the ranks of major and above.* *—prep.* **1.** Over or higher than: *a spring above the timberline.* **2.** Superior to in rank, position, or number; greater than: *principles above expediency.* **3.** Beyond the level or reach of: *a shot heard above the music.* **4.** In preference to. **5.** Too honorable to bend to: *above petty intrigue.* **6.** More than: *somewhat above normal temperature.* *—n.* Something that is above. *—adj.* Appearing earlier in the same text: *flaws in the above interpretation.* **—idiom. above all.** First of all; most important. [ME *aboven* < OE *abufan* : *a-,* on + *be,* by + *ufan,* up.]

Usage: The use of *above* as an adjective or noun in referring to a preceding text is most common in business and legal writing. In general writing its use as an adjective (*the above figures*) is accepted by a majority of the Usage Panel, but its use as a noun (*read the above*) is accepted by only a minority.

a·bove·board (ə-bŭv′bôrd′, -bōrd′) *adv. & adj.* Without deceit or trickery.

a·bove·ground (ə-bŭv′ground′) *adj.* **1.** Situated on or above the surface of the ground. **2.** Operating or existing within the establishment or in accordance with conventional standards: *journalistic practices unacceptable to the aboveground press.*

ab o·vo (ăb ō′vō) *adv.* From the beginning. [Lat., from the egg.]

ab·ra·ca·dab·ra (ăb′rə-kə-dăb′rə) *n.* **1.** A word once held to possess magical powers to ward off disease or disaster. **2.** Foolish or unintelligible talk. [LLat.]

a·bra·chi·a (ə-brā′kē-ə) *n.* Congenital absence of arms. [A-[1] + Gk. *brakhiōn,* arm.]

a·brad·ant (ə-brăd′nt) *n.* An abrasive. *—adj.* Abrasive.

a·brade (ə-brād′) *tr.v.* **a·brad·ed, a·brad·ing, a·brades.** To rub off or wear away by friction; erode. [Lat. *abradere,* to scrape off : *ab-,* off + *radere,* to scrape.]

A·bra·ham (ā′brə-hăm′) *n.* In the Old Testament, the first patriarch and progenitor of the Hebrew people; father of Isaac. [ME < LLat. < LGk. < Heb. *Abhrāhām.*]

a·bran·chi·ate (ā-brăng′kē-ĭt, -āt′) also **a·bran·chi·al** (-kē-əl) or **a·bran·chi·ous** (-kē-əs) *adj.* Having no gills. [Gk. *a-,* not + *brankhia,* gills.]

ab·ra·sion (ə-brā′zhən) *n.* **1.** The process of wearing down or rubbing away by means of friction. **2.** A scraped or worn area. [Med. Lat. *abrasio* < Lat. *abradere,* to scrape off. —see ABRADE.]

ab·ra·sive (ə-brā′sĭv, -zĭv) *adj.* Causing abrasion; harsh; rough. *—n.* A substance that abrades.

ab·re·act (ăb′rē-ăkt′) *tr.v.* **-act·ed, -act·ing, -acts.** To release (repressed emotions) by acting out, such as in words, action, or the imagination, the situation causing the conflict. [Transl. of G. *abreagieren* : *ab-,* away + *reagieren,* to react.] **—ab′re·ac′tion** *n.*

a·breast (ə-brĕst′) *adv.* **1.** Side by side. **2.** Up to date with: *keeping abreast of the latest developments.* [ME *abrest* < *on brest* : *on,* by + *brest,* breast.]

a·bridge (ə-brĭj′) *tr.v.* **a·bridged, a·bridg·ing, a·bridg·es. 1.** To reduce the length of (a written text); condense. **2.** To curtail; cut short. [ME *abregen* < OFr. *abregier* < LLat. *abbreviare,* to shorten. —see ABBREVIATE.] **—a·bridg′er** *n.*

a·bridg·ment also **a·bridge·ment** (ə-brĭj′mənt) *n.* **1. a.** The action of abridging. **b.** The state of being abridged. **2.** Condensation of a book.

a·broach (ə-brōch′) *adj.* **1.** Opened or positioned so that a liquid, such as wine, can be let out. **2.** Moving about; astir. [ME *abroche* < *a,* in + *broche,* a pointed object.]

a·broad (ə-brôd′) *adv.* **1.** Out of one's own country. **2.** In a foreign country or countries. **3.** Away from one's home. **4.** In circulation; at large. **5.** Covering a large area; widely. **6.** Not on target; in error. [ME *abrod,* wide < *on brod* : *on,* a‘ + *brod,* broad.]

ab·ro·gate (ăb′rə-gāt′) *tr.v.* **-gat·ed, -gat·ing, -gates.** To abolish or annul by authority. [Lat. *abrogare, abrogat-* : *ab-,* away + *rogare,* to propose.] **—ab′ro·ga′tion** *n.*

a·bro·sia (ə-brō′zhə) *n.* **1.** Abstinence from food; fasting. **2.** A wasting away. [Gk. *abrōsia,* fasting : *a-,* not + *brōsis,* eating.]

a·brupt (ə-brŭpt′) *adj.* **1.** Unexpectedly sudden. **2.** Suprisingly curt; brusque. **3.** Touching on one subject after another with sudden transitions: *abrupt, nervous prose.* **4.** Steeply inclined. **5.** *Biol.* Appearing to be cut or broken off short; truncate. [Lat. *abruptus,* p.part of *abrumpere,* to break off : *ab-,* off + *rumpere,* to break.] **—a·brupt′ly** *adv.* **—a·brupt′ness** *n.*

a·brup·tion (ə-brŭp′shən) *n.* An instance of suddenly breaking away or off.

ab·scess (ăb′sĕs′) *n.* A localized collection of pus in any part of the body, formed by tissue disintegration and surrounded by an inflamed area. —*intr.v.* **-scessed, -scess·ing, -scess·es.** To form an abscess. [Lat. *abscessus,* absence < *abscedere,* to go away : *ab-,* away + *cedere,* to go.]

ab·scise (ăb-sīz′) *v.* **-scised, -scis·ing, -scis·es.** —*tr.* To remove; cut off. —*intr.* To shed by abscission. [Lat. *abscindere, absciss-* : *ab-,* away + *caedere,* to cut.]

ab·scis·ic acid also **ab·scis·sic acid** (ăb-sĭz′ĭk) *n.* A common abscisin that inhibits plant growth.

ab·scis·in or **ab·scis·sin** (ăb-sĭs′ĭn) *n.* A group of plant hormones that may promote leaf abscission while inhibiting certain other growth mechanisms. [ABSCIS(SION) + -IN.]

ab·scis·sa (ăb-sĭs′ə) *n., pl.* **-scis·sas** or **-scis·sae** (-sĭs′ē). The coordinate representing the distance of a point from the *y*-axis in a plane Cartesian coordinate system, measured along a line parallel to the *x*-axis. [NLat. *(linea) abscissa,* (line) cut off < Lat. *abscissus,* p.part. of *abscindere,* to abscise.]

ab·scis·sion (ăb-sĭzh′ən) *n.* **1.** The act of cutting off. **2.** The process by which plant parts, such as leaves, are shed.

ab·scond (ăb-skŏnd′) *intr.v.* **-scond·ed, -scond·ing, -sconds.** To leave quickly and secretly and hide oneself, esp. to avoid arrest or prosecution. [Lat. *abscondere,* to hide : *ab-,* away + *condere,* to put.] —**ab·scond′er** *n.*

ab·sence (ăb′səns) *n.* **1.** The state of being away. **2.** The time during which one is away. **3.** The condition of not having something needed or desirable; lack.

ab·sent (ăb′sənt) *adj.* **1.** Missing or not present. **2.** Not existent; lacking. **3.** Feeling or exhibiting inattentiveness. —*tr.v.* (ăb-sĕnt′) **-sent·ed, -sent·ing, -sents.** To keep (oneself) away. [ME < OFr. < Lat. *absens,* p.part. of *abesse,* to be away : *ab-,* away + *esse,* to be.] —**ab′sent·ly** *adv.*

ab·sen·tee (ăb′sən-tē′) *n.* One who is absent. —*adj.* **1.** Of or pertaining to one that is absent. **2.** Not in residence. —See Usage note at **-ee**[1].

absentee ballot *n.* A ballot marked and mailed in advance by a voter away from the place where he is registered.

ab·sen·tee·ism (ăb′sən-tē′ĭz′əm) *n.* Habitual failure to appear, esp. for work or other regular duty.

ab·sent-mind·ed (ăb′sənt-mīn′dĭd) *adj.* Heedless of one's immediate surroundings or activity because of preoccupation with unrelated matters. —**ab′sent-mind′ed·ly** *adv.* —**ab′sent-mind′ed·ness** *n.*

absent without leave *adj.* Absent from one's assigned military post or duties without official permission but without the intention to desert.

ab·sinthe also **ab·sinth** (ăb′sĭnth′) *n.* **1.** A green liqueur having a bitter licorice flavor and a high alcoholic content, prepared from wormwood and other herbs. **2.** The wormwood. [Fr. < Lat. *absinthium,* wormwood.]

ab·so·lute (ăb′sə-lo͞ot′, ăb′sə-lo͞ot′) *adj.* **1.** Perfect in quality or nature; complete. **2.** Not mixed; pure: *absolute alcohol.* **3. a.** Not limited by restrictions or exceptions; unconditional: *absolute trust.* **b.** Unqualified in extent or degree; total: *absolute silence.* **4.** Not limited by constitutional provisions or other restraints. **5.** Unrelated to and independent of anything else. **6.** Not to be doubted or questioned; positive: *absolute proof.* **7.** *Gram.* **a.** Denoting a construction in a sentence that is syntactically independent of the main clause. For example, in *Their ship having sailed, we went home, Their ship having sailed* is an absolute phrase. **b.** Pertaining to a transitive verb when its object is implied but not stated. For example, *inspires* in *We have a teacher who inspires.* **c.** Pertaining to an adjective or pronoun that stands alone, the noun it modifies being implied but not stated. For example, *Theirs* and *best* in *Theirs were the best.* **8.** *Physics.* **a.** Pertaining to measurements or units of measurement derived from fundamental relationships of space, mass, and time. **b.** Pertaining to absolute temperature. **9.** *Law.* Complete and unconditional; final. —*n.* **1.** Something that is absolute. **2. the Absolute.** *Philos.* **a.** Something regarded as the ultimate basis of all thought and being. **b.** Something regarded as independent of and unrelated to anything else. [ME *absolut* < Lat. *absolutus,* ended < *absoluere,* to finish : *ab-* from + *solvere,* to loose.] —**ab′so·lute′ness** *n.*

absolute alcohol *n.* Ethyl alcohol containing no more than one per cent of water.

absolute ceiling *n.* The maximum altitude above sea level at which an aircraft or missile can maintain horizontal flight under standard atmospheric conditions.

ab·so·lute·ly (ăb′sə-lo͞ot′lē, ăb′sə-lo͞ot′lē) *adv.* **1.** Definitely and completely; unquestionably. **2.** *Gram.* In a manner that does not take an object.

Usage: *Absolutely* is often used informally to mean "quite," as in *an absolutely magnificent painting.* A majority of the Usage Panel disapproves of this use in formal writing.

absolute magnitude *n.* The intrinsic magnitude of a star computed as if viewed from a distance of 10 parsecs or 32.6 light-years.

absolute music *n.* Instrumental music that depends solely on its rhythmic, melodic, and contrapuntal structures.

absolute pitch *n.* **1.** The precise pitch of an isolated tone, as established by its rate of vibration measured on a standard scale. **2.** The ability to identify or sing any tone heard.

absolute scale *n.* A scale of temperature with absolute zero as the minimum and scale units equal in magnitude to centigrade degrees.

absolute temperature *n.* Temperature measured or calculated on the absolute scale.

absolute value *n.* **1.** The numerical value or magnitude of a quantity, as of a vector or of a negative integer, without regard to its sign. **2.** The modulus of a complex number, equal to the square root of the sum of the squares of the real and imaginary parts of the number.

absolute zero *n.* *Physics.* The temperature at which substances possess no thermal energy, equal to −273.15°C or −459.67°F.

ab·so·lu·tion (ăb′sə-lo͞o′shən) *n.* *Rom. Cath. Ch.* The formal remission of sin imparted by a priest as part of the sacrament of penance. [ME < OFr. < Lat. *absolutio,* acquittal < *absolvere,* to absolve.]

ab·so·lut·ism (ăb′sə-lo͞o′tĭz′əm) *n.* **1.** A form of government in which all power is vested in the monarch and his advisers. **2.** The political theory reflecting absolutism. **3.** An absolute doctrine, principle, or opinion. —**ab′so·lut′ist** *n.* —**ab′so·lu·tis′tic** (-lo͞o-tĭs′tĭk) *adj.*

ab·solve (əb-zŏlv′, -sŏlv′) *tr.v.* **-solved, -solv·ing, -solves.** **1.** To pronounce clear of blame or guilt. **2.** To relieve of a requirement or obligation. **3. a.** To grant a remission of sin to. **b.** To pardon or remit (a sin). [ME *absolven* < Lat. *absolvere.* —see ABSOLUTE.] —**ab·solv′a·ble** *adj.* —**ab·solv′er** *n.*

ab·sorb (əb-sôrb′, -zôrb′) *tr.v.* **-sorbed, -sorb·ing, -sorbs.** **1.** To take in through or as through pores or interstices; soak in or up. **2.** To occupy the full attention, interest, or time of; engross. **3.** *Chem. & Physics.* To retain wholly, without reflection or transmission, that which is taken in. **4.** To take in; assimilate: *immigrants absorbed into the mainstream of society.* **5.** To receive the impact of without recoil or echo. **6.** To defray (costs). **7.** To take in; accommodate: *couldn't absorb the additional expense.* [OFr. *absorber* < Lat. *absorbēre* : *ab-,* away + *sorbēre,* to suck.] —**ab·sorb′a·bil′i·ty** (əb-sôr′bə-bĭl′ĭ-tē, -zôr-) *n.* —**ab·sorb′a·ble** *adj.* —**ab·sorb′er** *n.* —**ab·sorb′ing·ly** *adv.*

ab·sorbed (əb-sôrbd′, -zôrbd′) *adj.* **1.** Engrossed. **2.** Sucked up or in. **3.** Assimilated. —**ab·sorb′ed·ly** (əb-sôr′bĭd-lē, -zôr′-) *adv.* —**ab·sorb′ed·ness** *n.*

ab·sor·be·fa·cient (əb-sôr′bə-fā′shənt, -zôr′-) *adj.* Inducing or causing absorption. —*n.* A medicine that induces absorption. [ABSORBE(NT) + -FACIENT.]

ab·sorb·ent (əb-sôr′bənt, -zôr′-) *adj.* Capable of absorbing something: *absorbent cotton.* —*n.* An absorbent substance. —**ab·sorb′en·cy** *n.*

ab·sorp·tance (əb-sôrp′təns, -zôrp′-) *n.* The ratio of absorbed to incident radiation. [ABSORPT(ION) + -ANCE.]

ab·sorp·tion (əb-sôrp′shən, -zôrp′-) *n.* **1.** The act or process of absorbing or the condition of being absorbed. **2.** A state of mental concentration. [Lat. *absorptio* < *absorbēre,* to absorb. —see ABSORB.] —**ab·sorp′tive** (-tĭv) *adj.*

absorption nebula *n.* A nebula that absorbs all incident radiation without re-emission.

absorption spectrum *n.* *Physics.* The spectrum of dark lines and bands observed when radiation traverses an absorbing medium.

ab·stain (ăb-stān′, əb-) *intr.v.* **-stained, -stain·ing, -stains.** To refrain from something by one's own choice. [ME *absteinen,* to avoid < OFr. *abstenir* < Lat. *abstinēre,* to hold back : *ab-,* away + *tenēre,* to hold.] —**ab·stain′er** *n.*

ab·ste·mi·ous (ăb-stē′mē-əs, əb-) *adj.* **1.** Eating and drinking in moderation. **2.** Restricted to bare necessities; sparing. [Lat. *abstemius* : *ab-,* away + *temetum,* liquor.] —**ab·ste′mi·ous·ly** *adv.* —**ab·ste′mi·ous·ness** *n.*

ab·sten·tion (ăb-stĕn′shən, əb-) *n.* The act or habit of abstaining. [LLat. *abstentio* < Lat. *abstinēre,* to hold back. —see ABSTAIN.]

ab·sti·nence (ăb′stə-nəns) *n.* **1.** Denial of the appetites, esp. denial of certain foods and drinks. **2.** Habitual abstention from alcoholic beverages. [ME < OFr. *abstenance* < Lat. *abstinentia* < *abstinēre,* to hold back. —see ABSTAIN.] —**ab′sti·nent** *adj.* —**ab′sti·nent·ly** *adv.*

Synonyms: *abstinence, self-denial, temperance, sobriety, continence.* These nouns express restraint of one's appetites or desires. *Abstinence* implies the willful avoidance of pleasures, especially of food and drink, thought to be harmful. *Self-denial* suggests resisting one's desires for some higher, moral goal. *Temperance* and *sobriety* both stress avoidance of alcohol, but *temperance* is more often associated with mere curtailment of drinking, while *sobriety* additionally suggests conservative action or manner. *Continence* specifically refers to restraint of sexual activity.

ab·stract (ăb-străkt′, ăb′străkt′) *adj.* **1.** Considered apart from concrete existence: *an abstract concept.* **2.** Not applied or practical; theoretical. **3.** Not easily understood; abstruse. **4.** Thought of or stated without reference to a specific instance: *abstract words like "truth" and "justice."* **5.** Designating a genre of painting or sculpture whose intellectual and affective content depends solely on intrinsic form. —*n.* (ăb′străkt′). **1.** A statement summarizing the important points of a given text. **2.** The concentrated essence of a larger whole. **3.** Something abstract, as a term. —*tr.v.* (ăb-străkt′) **-stract·ed, -stract·ing, -stracts. 1.** To take away; remove. **2.** To remove without permission; filch. **3.** To consider (a quality, for example) without reference to a particular example or object. **4.** (ăb′străkt′). To summarize. —***idiom.* in the abstract.** Apart from actual substance or experience. [ME < Lat. *abstractus,* p.part. of *abstrahere,* to draw away : *ab-,* away + *trahere,* to draw.] —**ab·stract′er** *n.* —**ab·stract′ly** *adv.* —**ab·stract′ness** *n.*

ab·stract·ed (ăb-străk′tĭd, ăb′străk′-) *adj.* **1.** Removed or separated. **2.** Deep in thought; preoccupied; meditative. —**ab·stract′ed·ly** *adv.* —**ab·stract′ed·ness** *n.*

Synonyms: *abstracted, absorbed, distraught, absent-minded.* These adjectives apply to absence of normal awareness of one's surroundings. *Abstracted* implies complete and pleasureable mental involvement in the object of thought. *Distraught* implies mental anxiety that makes concentration extremely difficult. *Absent-minded* suggests the making of trivial errors because the mind is straying from the matter at hand.

abstractionism
"The Great Sail" by Alexander Calder

abstract expressionism *n.* A school of painting that flourished after World War II until the early 1960's, characterized by the exclusion of representational content.

ab·strac·tion (ăb-străk′shən, əb-) *n.* **1.** The act or process of removing or separating: *the abstraction of metal from ore.* **2. a.** The act or process of separating the inherent qualities or properties of something from the actual physical object or concept to which they belong. **b.** A product of this process; a general idea or word representing a physical concept. **3.** Preoccupation; absent-mindedness. **4.** An abstract work of art.

ab·strac·tion·ism (ăb-străk′shə-nĭz′əm) *n.* The theory and practice of abstract art. —**ab·strac′tion·ist** *n.*

ab·strac·tive (ăb-străk′tĭv, əb-) *adj.* Of or derived by abstraction.

abstract of title *n.* A brief history of the transfers of a piece of land, including all claims that could be made against it.

Abyssinian cat

ab·struse (ăb-stro͞os′, əb-) *adj.* Difficult to understand; recondite. [Lat. *abstrusus,* hidden, p.part. of *abstrudere,* to hide : *ab-,* away + *trudere,* to push.] —**ab·struse′ly** *adv.* —**ab·struse′ness** *n.*

ab·surd (əb-sûrd′, -zûrd′) *adj.* **1.** Ridiculously incongruous or unreasonable. **2.** Of, pertaining to, or manifesting the view that there is no order or value in human life or in the universe; meaningless. **3.** Of or relating to absurdism or the absurd. —*n.* **1.** The quality or condition of existing in a meaningless and irrational universe in which an individual's life has no meaning or purpose. **2.** The literary genre that deals with the theme of an absurd universe. [Fr. *absurde* < Lat. *absurdus.*] —**ab·surd′i·ty** (-sûr′dĭ-tē, -zûr′-), **ab·surd′ness** *n.* —**ab·surd′ly** *adv.*

absurd theater *n.* Theater of the absurd.

a·bu·li·a also **a·bou·li·a** (ə-bo͞o′lē-ə, ə-byo͞o′-) *n.* Loss or impairment of the ability to decide or act independently. [NLat. < Gk. *aboulia,* indecision : *a-,* without + *boulē,* will.] —**a·bu′lic** (-lĭk) *adj.*

acacia

a·bun·dance (ə-bŭn′dəns) *n.* **1.** A great or plentiful amount. **2.** Fullness to overflowing: *"My thoughts . . . are from the abundance of my heart"* (De Quincey). **3.** Affluence; wealth.

a·bun·dant (ə-bŭn′dənt) *adj.* **1.** In plentiful supply; ample. **2.** Abounding with; rich: *a region abundant in wildlife.* [ME *abundant* < OFr. *abondant* < Lat. *abundans,* p.part. of *abundare,* to overflow. —see ABOUND.] —**a·bun′dant·ly** *adv.*

a·buse (ə-byo͞oz′) *tr.v.* **a·bused, a·bus·ing, a·bus·es. 1. a.** To use wrongly or improperly; misuse. **b.** *Obs.* To trick or deceive. **2.** To hurt or injure by maltreatment. **3.** To assail with contemptuous, coarse, or insulting words; revile. —*n.* (ə-byo͞os′). **1.** Improper use or handling; misuse. **2.** A corrupt practice or custom. **3.** Physical maltreatment. **4.** Insulting or coarse language. [ME *abusen* < OFr. *abuser* < *abus,* improper use < Lat. *abusus,* a using up, p.part. of *abuti,* to use up : *ab-,* away + *uti,* to use.] —**a·bus′er** *n.*

Synonyms: *abuse, misuse, mistreat, ill-treat, maltreat.* These verbs mean to treat a person or thing wrongfully or harmfully. *Abuse* applies to wrongful or unreasonable treatment by deed or word. *Misuse* stresses incorrect or unknowledgeable handling; it implies but does not emphasize harm. *Mistreat, ill-treat,* and *maltreat* all have the sense of inflicting injury, usually physical and often with intent to do harm. *Mistreat* may imply only negligence or lack of knowledge on the offender's part, but more often refers to harm inflicted deliberately. *Ill-treat* more specifically applies to harmful treatment of persons or animals. *Maltreat* implies rough handling.

acanthus
Above: Acanthus leaves
Below: Capital of a Corinthian column showing acanthus motif

a·bu·sive (ə-byo͞o′sĭv, -zĭv) *adj.* **1.** Of, pertaining to, or characterized by abuse. **2.** Wrongly or incorrectly used or treated. **3.** Serving to abuse; insulting. —**a·bu′sive·ly** *adv.*

a·but (ə-bŭt′) *v.* **a·but·ted, a·but·ting, a·buts.** —*intr.* To touch at one end or side of something; lie adjacent. —*tr.* To border upon; be next to. [ME *abutten* < OFr. *abouter,* to border on : *a-,* to + *bout,* end.] —**a·but′ter** *n.*

a·bu·ti·lon (ə-byo͞ot′l-ŏn′) *n.* Any of various shrubs or plants of the genus *Abutilon,* esp. the flowering maple. [NLat. *Abutilon,* genus name < Ar. *aubūṭīlūn.*]

a·but·ment (ə-bŭt′mənt) *n.* **1.** The act or process of abutting. **2. a.** Something that abuts. **b.** The point of contact of two abutting objects or parts. **3. a.** That part of a structure that bears the weight or pressure of an arch. **b.** A structure that supports the end of a bridge. **c.** A structure that anchors the cables of a suspension bridge.

a·but·tals (ə-bŭt′lz) *pl.n.* The parts of a piece of land that abut against other property; boundaries.

a·buzz (ə-bŭz′) *adj.* **1.** Filled with a buzzing sound. **2.** Filled or occupied with activity or talk.

ab·volt (ăb′vōlt′) *n.* A centimeter-gram-second electromagnetic unit of potential difference, equal to the potential difference between two points such that one erg of work must be performed to move a one-abcoulomb charge from one of the points to the other. It is equal to one hundred-millionth (10^{-8}) of a volt.

a·bysm (ə-bĭz′əm) *n.* An abyss. [ME *abīme* < OFr. < LLat. *abyssus.* —see ABYSS.]

a·bys·mal (ə-bĭz′məl) *adj.* **1.** Unfathomable; extreme. **2.** Of or resembling an abyss. —**a·bys′mal·ly** *adv.*

a·byss (ə-bĭs′) *n.* **1. a.** The primeval chaos. **b.** The bottomless pit; hell. **2.** An unfathomable chasm; a yawning gulf. **3.** An immeasurably profound depth or void: *the vast abysses of space and time.* [LLat. *abyssus* < Gk. *abussos,* bottomless : *a-,* without + *bussos,* bottom.]

a·bys·sal (ə-bĭs′əl) *adj.* **1.** Abysmal. **2.** Of or pertaining to the great depths of the oceans.

Ab·ys·sin·i·an cat (ăb′ĭ-sĭn′ē-ən) *n.* A short-haired cat of a breed developed from Near Eastern stocks, having a reddish-brown coat tipped with small black markings. [After *Abyssinia,* former name for Ethiopia.]

Ac The symbol for the element actinium.

ac– *pref.* Variant of **ad-** (sense 1). Used before *c, k,* and *q.*

–ac *suff.* Used to form adjectives from nouns: *ammoniac.* [NLat. *-acus,* adj. suffix < Gk. *-akos.*]

a·ca·cia (ə-kā′shə) *n.* **1.** Any of various chiefly tropical trees of the genus *Acacia,* having compound leaves and tight clusters of small yellow or white flowers. **2.** Gum arabic. [Lat. < Gk. *akakia.*]

ac·a·deme (ăk′ə-dēm′) *n.* **1.** The scholastic world or environment. **2.** A scholar, teacher, or pedant. **3.** A college or university. **4.** Academic life. [< Lat. *Academia,* the Academy.]

ac·a·de·mi·a (ăk′ə-dē′mē-ə) *n.* The academic world; academe. [NLat. < Lat. *Academia,* the Academy.]

ac·a·dem·ic (ăk′ə-dĕm′ĭk) *adj.* **1.** Of, pertaining to, or characteristic of a school. **2.** Relating to studies that are liberal or classical rather than technical or vocational. **3.** Pertaining or belonging to a scholarly organization. **4.** Scholarly to the point of being unaware of the outside world. **5.** Based on formal education. **6.** Formalistic or conventional. **7.** Theoretical or speculative without a practical purpose or intention. **8.** Without purpose or use because of being beyond the point of implementation. —*n.* A student or teacher. —**ac′a·dem′i·cal·ly** *adv.*

academic freedom *n.* Liberty to pursue and teach relevant knowledge and to discuss it freely without restriction from school or public officials or from other sources of influence.

ac·a·de·mi·cian (ăk′ə-də-mĭsh′ən, ə-kăd′ə-) *n.* A member of an art, literary, or scientific academy or society.

ac·a·dem·i·cism (ăk′ə-dĕm′ĭ-sĭz′əm) also **a·cad·e·mism** (ə-kăd′ə-mĭz′əm) *n.* Traditional formalism, esp. when reflected in art.

a·cad·e·my (ə-kăd′ə-mē) *n., pl.* **-mies. 1.** A school for special instruction. **2.** A secondary or college-preparatory school, esp. a private one. **3.** An association of scholars. **4. Academy.** A specified society of scholars or artists. **5. Academy. a.** Platonism. **b.** The disciples of Plato. [Lat. *Academia* < Gk. *Akadēmia,* the school where Plato taught.]

A·ca·di·an (ə-kā′dē-ən) *n.* **1.** One of the early French settlers of Acadia or their descendants. **2.** A dialect of French spoken by the Acadians. —**A·ca′di·an** *adj.*

a·ca·jou (ă-kə-zho͞o′) *n.* Mahogany, esp. when used for making furniture. [Fr., cashew < Port. *caju.*]

acantho– or **acanth–** *pref.* Thorn: *acanthoid.* [< Gk. *akanthos,* thorn plant < *akantha,* thorn.]

a·can·tho·ceph·a·lan (ə-kăn′thə-sĕf′ə-lən) also **a·can·tho·ceph·a·lid** (-lĭd) *n.* Any of various parasitic worms of the phylum Acanthocephala, having a proboscis armed with hooked spines. [< NLat. *Acanthocephala,* phylum name : ACANTHO- + Gk. *kephalē,* head.]

a·can·thoid (ə-kăn′thoid′) *adj.* Resembling a thorn or spine.

ac·an·thop·ter·yg·i·an (ăk′ən-thŏp′tə-rĭj′ē-ən) *n.* A fish of the superorder Acanthopterygii, which includes fishes having spiny fins, such as bass, perch, and mackerel. [< NLat. *Acanthopterygii,* superorder name : ACANTHO- + Gk. *pterugion,* dim. of *pterus,* wing < *pteron,* feather.] —**ac′an·thop′ter·yg′i·an** *adj.*

a·can·thus (ə-kăn′thəs) *n., pl.* **-thus·es** or **-thi** (-thī′). **1.** Any of various plants of the genus *Acanthus,* native to the Mediterranean region, having large, segmented, thistlelike leaves. **2.** *Archit.* An ornament patterned after the leaves of the acanthus, used esp. on capitals of Corinthian columns. [NLat. *Acanthus,* genus name < Gk. *akanthos,* thorn plant < *akantha,* thorn.]

a·cap·ni·a (ā-kăp′nē-ə) *n.* The absence of carbon dioxide in the blood and tissues. [NLat. < Lat. *acapnos,* without smoke (which contains carbon dioxide) < Gk. *akapnos* : *a-,* not + *kapnos,* smoke.]

a cap·pel·la (ä′ kə-pĕl′ə) *adv. Mus.* Without instrumental accompaniment. [Ital. : *a,* as + *capella,* chapel.]
ac·a·ri (ăk′ə-rī′) *n.* Plural of **acarus.**
ac·a·ri·a·sis (ăk′ə-rī′ə-sĭs) *n.* Infestation with mites. [ACAR(ID) + -IASIS.]
ac·a·rid (ăk′ə-rĭd) *n.* An arachnid of the order Acarina, which includes the mites and ticks. [NLat. *Acaridae,* family name < *Acarus,* genus name < Gk. *akari,* a kind of mite.] **—ac′a·rid** *adj.*
ac·a·roid resin (ăk′ə-roid′) *n.* A yellow or reddish gum obtained from various Australian grass trees, used in varnishes, lacquers, and the manufacture of paper. [NLat. *acaroides.*]
ac·a·rol·o·gy (ăk′ə-rŏl′ə-jē) *n.* The study of mites and ticks. [ACAR(ID) + -LOGY.]
ac·a·roph·i·ly (ăk′ə-rŏf′ə-lē) *n.* A symbiotic relationship to mites or ticks, usually in plants. [ACAR(ID) + -PHIL(O)- + -Y2.]
ac·a·ro·pho·bi·a (ăk′ə-rə-fō′bē-ə) *n.* An abnormal fear of mites or ticks. [ACAR(ID) + -PHOBIA.]
a·car·pous (ā-kär′pəs) *adj. Bot.* Producing no fruit; sterile.
ac·a·rus (ăk′ə-rəs) *n., pl.* **-ri** (-rī′). A mite, esp. one of the genus *Acarus.* [NLat. *Acarus,* genus name. —see ACARID.]
a·cat·a·lec·tic (ā-kăt′l-ĕk′tĭk) *adj.* Designating a line of verse having the required number of syllables in the last foot. *—n.* An acatalectic line. [LLat. *acatalecticus* < Gk. *akatalēktikos* : *a-,* not + *katalēktikos,* incomplete. —see CATALECTIC.]
a·cau·date (ā-kô′dāt′) also **a·cau·dal** (ā-kôd′l) *adj.* Having no tail.
a·cau·les·cent (ā′kô-lĕs′ənt) *adj.* Stemless or nearly so.
ac·cede (ăk-sēd′) *intr.v.* **-ced·ed, -ced·ing, -cedes. 1.** To give one's assent. **2.** To arrive at or come into an office or dignity. **3.** To become a party to an agreement or treaty. [ME *accēden,* to come near < Lat. *accedere,* to go near : *ad-,* to + *cedere,* to go.] **—ac·ced′ence** (-sēd′ns) *n.* **—ac·ced′er** *n.*
ac·cel·er·an·do (ä-chĕl′ə-rän′dō) *adj. Mus.* Gradually accelerating or quickening in time. Used as a direction. [Ital. < Lat. *accelerandum* < *accelerare,* to hasten. —see ACCELERATE.] **—ac·cel′er·an′do** *adv.*
ac·cel·er·ate (ăk-sĕl′ə-rāt′) *v.* **-at·ed, -at·ing, -ates.** *—tr.* **1.** To increase the speed of. **2.** To cause to occur sooner than expected. **3.** To cause to develop or progress more quickly. **4.** *Physics.* To cause a change of velocity. *—intr.* To move or act faster. [Lat. *accelerare* : *ad-* (intensive) + *celerare,* to quicken < *celer,* swift.] **—ac·cel′er·a′tive** (-rā′tĭv) *adj.*
ac·cel·er·a·tion (ăk-sĕl′ə-rā′shən) *n.* **1. a.** The act of accelerating. **b.** The process of being accelerated. **2.** *Physics.* The rate of change of velocity with respect to time.
acceleration of gravity *n.* The acceleration of freely falling bodies under the influence of terrestrial gravity, equal to 980.665 cm/sec^2 or approximately 32 ft/sec^2 at sea level.
ac·cel·er·a·tor (ăk-sĕl′ə-rā′tər) *n.* **1.** One that accelerates. **2.** A device, esp. the gas pedal of an automobile, for increasing the speed of a machine. **3.** *Chem.* A substance that increases the speed of a chemical reaction. **4.** *Physics.* A device, such as an electrostatic generator, cyclotron, or linear accelerator, that accelerates charged subatomic particles or nuclei to energies useful for research.
ac·cel·er·om·e·ter (ăk-sĕl′ə-rŏm′ĭ-tər) *n.* A device used to measure acceleration. [ACCELER(ATION) + -METER.]
ac·cent (ăk′sĕnt′) *n.* **1.** The relative prominence of a particular syllable of a word by greater intensity or by variation or modulation of pitch or tone. **2.** Vocal prominence or emphasis given to a particular syllable, word, or phrase. **3.** A characteristic pronunciation, esp.: **a.** One determined by the regional or social background of the speaker. **b.** One determined by the phonetic habits of the speaker's native language carried over to his use of another language. **4.** A mark or symbol used in the printing and writing of certain languages to indicate the vocal quality to be given to a particular letter: *an acute accent.* **5.** A mark or symbol used in printing and writing to indicate the stressed syllables of a spoken word. **6.** Rhythmically significant stress in a line of verse. **7. a.** Special stress given to a musical note within a phrase. **b.** A mark representing this stress. **8.** *Math.* **a.** A mark or one of several marks used as a superscript to distinguish among variables represented by the same symbol. **b.** A mark used as a superscript to indicate the first derivative of a variable. **9.** A mark or one of several marks used as a superscript to indicate a unit, such as feet (′) and inches (″) in linear measurement. **10.** A distinctive feature or quality. *—tr.v.* (ăk′sĕnt′, ăk-sĕnt′) **-cent·ed, -cent·ing, -cents. 1.** To stress or emphasize the pronunciation of. **2.** To mark with a printed accent. **3.** To call attention to; accentuate. [ME < OFr. < Lat. *accentus,* accentuation : *ad-,* to + *cantus,* song < *canere,* to sing (transl. of Gk. *prosōidia,* voice modulations).]
ac·cen·tu·al (ăk-sĕn′chōō-əl) *adj.* **1.** Of or pertaining to accent. **2.** Designating verse rhythm based on stress accents. **—ac·cen′tu·al·ly** *adv.*
ac·cen·tu·ate (ăk-sĕn′chōō-āt′) *tr.v.* **-at·ed, -at·ing, -ates. 1.** To pronounce with a stress or accent. **2.** To mark with an accent. **3.** To stress or emphasize. [Med. Lat. *accentuare, accentuat-* < Lat. *accentus,* accent.] **—ac·cen′tu·a′tion** *n.*
ac·cept (ăk-sĕpt′) *v.* **-cept·ed, -cept·ing, -cepts.** *—tr.* **1.** To receive (something offered), esp. gladly. **2.** To admit to a group or place. **3. a.** To regard as usual, proper, or right. **b.** To regard as true; believe in. **c.** To understand as having a specific meaning. **4.** To bear up under resignedly or patiently: *accept one's fate.* **5. a.** To answer affirmatively: *accept an invitation.* **b.** To take upon oneself the duties or responsibilities of. **6.** To be able to hold (something applied or inserted): *This wood will not accept oil paints.* **7.** To receive officially: *accept the committee's report.* **8.** To consent to pay, as by a signed agreement. *—intr.* To receive something, esp. willingly. [ME *accepten* < Lat. *acceptare,* freq. of *accipere,* to receive : *ad-,* to + *capere,* to take.]
ac·cept·a·ble (ăk-sĕp′tə-bəl) *adj.* **1.** Worthy of being accepted. **2.** Adequate enough to satisfy a need, requirement, or standard; satisfactory. **3.** Designating an amount or level that can be endured or allowed. **—ac·cept′a·bil′i·ty, ac·cept′a·ble·ness** *n.* **—ac·cept′a·bly** *adv.*
ac·cep·tance (ăk-sĕp′təns) *n.* **1.** The act or process of accepting. **2.** The state of being accepted or acceptable. **3.** Favorable reception; approval. **4.** Belief in something; agreement. **5. a.** A formal indication by a debtor of willingness to pay a time draft or bill of exchange. **b.** A written instrument so accepted. **6.** *Law.* Compliance by one party with the terms and conditions of another's offer so that a contract becomes legally binding between them.
ac·cep·tant (ăk-sĕp′tənt) *adj.* Accepting willingly.
ac·cep·ta·tion (ăk′sĕp-tā′shən) *n.* **1.** The usual or accepted meaning, as of a word or expression. **2.** Favorable reception. **3.** Ready belief.
ac·cept·ed (ăk-sĕp′tĭd) *adj.* Generally approved, believed, or recognized.
ac·cep·tor also **ac·cept·er** (ăk-sĕp′tər) *n.* **1.** One who signs a time draft or bill of exchange. **2.** *Chem.* **a.** The reactant in an induced reaction that has an increased rate of reaction in the presence of the inductor. **b.** The atom that contributes no atoms to a covalent bond.
ac·cess (ăk′sĕs′) *n.* **1.** A means of approaching or nearing; passage. **2.** The act of approaching. **3.** The right to enter or make use of: *has access to classified material.* **4.** The state or quality of being easy to approach or enter. **5.** An increase of growth. **6.** A sudden outburst: *an access of rage.* *—tr.v.* **-cessed, -cess·ing, -cess·es.** To gain access to: *accessed the information from the computer.* [ME *acces,* a coming to < OFr. < Lat. *accessus* < *accedere,* to arrive : *ad-,* to + *cedere,* to come.]
ac·ces·sa·ry (ăk-sĕs′ə-rē) *n.* Variant of **accessory.**
ac·ces·si·ble (ăk-sĕs′ə-bəl) *adj.* **1.** Easily approached or entered. **2.** Easily obtained. **3.** Easy to communicate or get along with. **4.** Open to: *accessible to flattery.* **—ac·ces′si·bil′i·ty, ac·ces′si·ble·ness** *n.* **—ac·ces′si·bly** *adv.*
ac·ces·sion (ăk-sĕsh′ən) *n.* **1.** The attainment of rank or dignity. **2. a.** An increase by means of something added: *an accession of property.* **b.** An addition. **3.** *Law.* **a.** The addition to or increase in value of property by means of improvements or natural growth. **b.** The right of a proprietor to ownership of such addition or increase. **4.** Agreement or assent. **5.** Access; admittance. **6.** A sudden outburst. *—tr.v.* **-sioned, -sion·ing, -sions.** To record as acquired. **—ac·ces′sion·al** *adj.*
ac·ces·so·ry also **ac·ces·sa·ry** (ăk-sĕs′ə-rē) *n., pl.* **-ries. 1.** Something subordinate or supplementary; adjunct. **2. a.** One who incites, aids, or abets a lawbreaker in the commission of a crime, but is not present at the time of the crime: *accessory before the fact.* **b.** One who aids a criminal after the commission of a crime, but was not present at the time of the crime: *accessory after the fact.* *—adj.* **1.** Having a secondary, supplementary, or subordinate function. **2.** Serving to aid or abet a lawbreaker, either before or after the commission of the crime, without being present at the time the crime was committed. [ME *accessorie* < Med. Lat. *accessorius* < *accessor,* helper < Lat. *accessus,* approach. —see ACCESS.] **—ac′ces·so′ri·al** (-sə-sôr′ē-əl, -sōr-) *adj.* **—ac·ces′so·ri·ly** *adv.* **—ac·ces′so·ri·ness** *n.*
accessory fruit *n.* A fruit, such as the pear, that contains fleshy tissue developed from floral parts as well as the ovary.
accessory nerve *n.* Either of the 11th pair of cranial nerves of higher vertebrate species that supply motor impulses to the upper thorax and pharynx.
access road *n.* A road that affords access to a certain area.
access time *n. Computer Sci.* The time lag between a request for information stored in a computer and its delivery.
ac·ciac·ca·tu·ra (ä-chä′kə-tōōr′ə) *n. Mus.* A short grace note one half step below a principal note, sounded immediately before or at the same time as the principal note to add sustained dissonance. [Ital. < *acciaccare,* to crush.]
ac·ci·dence (ăk′sĭ-dəns, -dĕns′) *n. Gram.* The section of morphology that deals with the inflections of words. [LLat. *accidentia* < Lat. *accidens,* accident.]
ac·ci·dent (ăk′sĭ-dənt, -dĕnt′) *n.* **1.** An unexpected and undesirable event. **2.** Something that occurs unexpectedly or unintentionally. **3.** A circumstance or attribute that is not essential to the nature of something. **4.** Fortune or chance: *rich by accident of birth.* **5.** *Geol.* An irregular or unusual natural formation or occurrence. [ME < OFr. < Lat. *accidens,* pr.part. of *accidere,* to happen : *ad-,* to + *cadere,* to fall.]

ac·ci·den·tal (ăk′sĭ-dĕn′tl) *adj.* **1.** Occurring unexpectedly and unintentionally; by chance. **2.** Not part of the real or essential nature of a thing. **3.** *Mus.* Of or denoting a sharp, flat, or natural not indicated in the key signature. —*n.* **1.** A factor or attribute that is not essential. **2.** *Mus.* A chromatically altered note not belonging to the key signature. **—ac′ci·den′tal·ly** *adv.*

Synonyms: *accidental, fortuitous, contingent, incidental, adventitious.* These adjectives are related in a general way but are not always interchangeable. *Accidental* primarily refers to what occurs by chance or unexpectedly; it can also mean subordinate or nonessential. *Fortuitous* stresses chance or accident even more strongly, and inferentially minimizes cause. *Contingent,* in this context, describes what is possible but uncertain because of chance or unforeseen or uncontrollable factors. *Incidental* refers to what is an adjunct to something else, and does not necessarily imply the operation of chance. *Adventitious* applies to what is not inherent in something but added extrinsically, sometimes by accident or chance.

accident insurance *n.* Insurance against injury or death because of accident.

ac·ci·dent-prone (ăk′sĭ-dənt-prōn′) *adj.* Having or susceptible to having a greater than average number of accidents or mishaps.

ac·cip·i·ter (ăk-sĭp′ĭ-tər) *n.* A hawk of the genus *Accipiter,* characterized by short wings and a long tail. [NLat. *Accipiter,* genus name < Lat., hawk.] **—ac·cip′i·trine′** (-trīn′, -trĭn) *adj.*

ac·claim (ə-klām′) *v.* **-claimed, -claim·ing, -claims.** —*tr.* To salute or hail; applaud. —*intr.* To shout approval. —*n.* Enthusiastic applause; acclamation. [Lat. *acclamare,* to shout at : *ad-,* at + *clamore,* to shout.] **—ac·claim′er** *n.*

ac·cla·ma·tion (ăk′lə-mā′shən) *n.* **1.** A shout or salute of enthusiastic approval. **2.** An oral vote, esp. an enthusiastic vote of approval taken without formal ballot: *a motion passed by acclamation.* [Lat. *acclamatio* < *acclamare,* to shout at. —see ACCLAIM.] **—ac·clam′a·to′ry** (ə-klăm′ə-tôr′ē, -tōr′ē) *adj.*

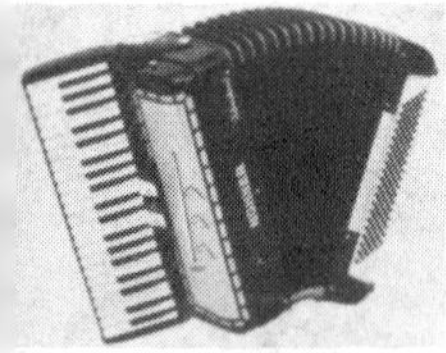
accordion

ac·cli·mate (ə-klī′mĭt, ăk′lə-māt′) *tr. & intr.v.* **-mat·ed, -mat·ing, -mates.** To accustom or become accustomed to a new environment or situation; adapt. [Fr. *acclimater* : *a-,* to (< Lat. *ad*) + *climat,* climate < OFr. —see CLIMATE.]

ac·cli·ma·tion (ăk′lə-mā′shən) *n.* **1.** The process of acclimating or of becoming acclimated. **2.** The adaptation of an organism to its natural climatic environment, as distinguished from acclimatization.

ac·cli·ma·ti·za·tion (ə-klī′mə-tĭ-zā′shən) *n.* **1.** The process of acclimatizing; acclimation. **2.** The climatic adaptation of an organism, esp. a plant, that has been moved to a new environment.

ac·cli·ma·tize (ə-klī′mə-tīz′) *tr. & intr.v.* **-tized, -tiz·ing, -tiz·es.** To acclimate. **—ac·cli′ma·tiz′er** *n.*

ac·cliv·i·ty (ə-klĭv′ĭ-tē) *n., pl.* **-ties.** An upward slope. [Lat. *acclivitas* < *acclivis,* uphill : *ad-,* to + *clivus,* slope.]

ac·co·lade (ăk′ə-lād′, -läd′) *n.* **1.** An embrace of greeting or salutation. **2.** An expression of approval; praise. **3.** The ceremonial bestowal of knighthood. [Fr. < Prov. *acolada* < *acolar,* to embrace : *a-,* to (< Lat. *ad*) + *col,* neck < Lat. *collum,* neck.]

ac·com·mo·date (ə-kŏm′ə-dāt′) *v.* **-dat·ed, -dat·ing, -dates.** —*tr.* **1.** To do a favor or service for; oblige. **2.** To provide for; supply with. **3.** To contain comfortably; have space for. **4.** To make suitable; adjust: *accommodates himself well to new surroundings.* **5.** To settle; reconcile. —*intr.* To become adjusted, as the eye to focusing on objects at a distance. [Lat. *accomodare, accomodat-,* to fit : *ad-,* to + *commodus,* suitable. —see COMMODIOUS.] **—ac·com′mo·da′tive** *adj.* **—ac·com′mo·da′tive·ness** *n.* **—ac·com′mo·da′tor** *n.*

ac·com·mo·dat·ing (ə-kŏm′ə-dā′tĭng) *adj.* Helpful and obliging. **—ac·com′mo·dat′ing·ly** *adv.*

ac·com·mo·da·tion (ə-kŏm′ə-dā′shən) *n.* **1.** The act of accommodating or state of being accommodated; adjustment. **2.** Something that meets a need; convenience. **3. accommodations. a.** Lodging; room and board. **b.** A seat, compartment, or room on a public vehicle. **4.** Reconciliation or settlement of opposing views; compromise. **5.** *Physiol.* Adaptation or adjustment in an organism, organ, or part, as in the lens of the eye to permit retinal focus of images of objects at different distances. **6.** A loan or other financial favor.

accommodation ladder *n.* A portable ladder or stairway hung from the side of a ship.

accommodation paper *n.* A note or bill drawn, accepted, or endorsed by one or more parties to enable another party to obtain credit or raise money without consideration or collateral.

ac·com·pa·ni·ment (ə-kŭm′pə-nē-mənt, ə-kŭmp′nē-) *n.* **1.** Something that accompanies; concomitant. **2.** Something added for embellishment, completeness, or symmetry; complement. **3.** A vocal or instrumental part that supports a solo part.

ac·com·pa·nist (ə-kŭm′pə-nĭst, ə-kŭmp′nĭst) *n.* A performer, such as a pianist, who plays an accompaniment.

ac·com·pa·ny (ə-kŭm′pə-nē, ə-kŭmp′nē) *v.* **-nied, -ny·ing, -nies.** —*tr.* **1.** To go along with; join in company. **2.** To supplement; add to. **3.** To coexist or occur with. **4.** To perform an accompaniment to. —*intr.* To play a musical accompaniment. [ME *accompanien* < OFr. *acompagnier* : *à,* to (< Lat. *ad*) + *compaignon,* companion. —see COMPANION.]

Synonyms: *accompany, conduct, escort, chaperon* (or *chaperone*). These verbs are compared as they mean to be with or to go with another person or persons. *Accompany* suggests going with another on an equal basis. *Conduct* implies guidance of others. *Escort* stresses protective guidance. *Chaperon* (or *chaperone*) specifies adult supervision of young persons.

ac·com·plice (ə-kŏm′plĭs) *n.* One who aids or abets a lawbreaker in a criminal act, either as a principal or an accessory. [< ME *a,* a + *complice,* companion. —see COMPLICE.]

ac·com·plish (ə-kŏm′plĭsh) *tr.v.* **-plished, -plish·ing, -plish·es.** **1.** To succeed in doing; bring to pass. **2.** To reach the end of; complete. [ME *accomplisshen* < OFr. *acomplir, accompliss-,* to complete : *a-,* to (< Lat. *ad*) + *complir,* to complete < Lat. *complere,* to fill out. —see COMPLETE.] **—ac·com′plish·a·ble** *adj.* **—ac·com′plish·er** *n.*

ac·com·plished (ə-kŏm′plĭsht) *adj.* **1.** Completed; finished. **2.** Skilled; expert: *an accomplished pianist.*

ac·com·plish·ment (ə-kŏm′plĭsh-mənt) *n.* **1.** The act of accomplishing or state of being accomplished; completion. **2.** Something completed successfully; achievement. **3.** Social poise.

ac·cord (ə-kôrd′) *tr.v.* **-cord·ed, -cord·ing, -cords.** **1.** To cause to conform or agree; bring into harmony. **2.** To grant; bestow upon: *I accord you my blessing.* —*intr.v.* To be in agreement, unity, or harmony. —*n.* **1.** Agreement; harmony. **2.** A settlement or compromise of conflicting opinions. **3.** A settlement of points at issue between nations. ***—idiom.* of (one's) own accord.** Voluntarily. [ME *accorden* < OFr. *acorder* < Med. Lat. *accordare* : Lat. *ad-,* to + Lat. *cor,* heart.]

ac·cor·dance (ə-kôr′dns) *n.* **1.** Agreement; conformity: *in accordance with your instructions.* **2.** The act of granting.

ac·cor·dant (ə-kôr′dnt) *adj.* In agreement or harmony; consonant. **—ac·cor′dant·ly** *adv.*

according as *conj.* **1.** Corresponding to the way in which; precisely as: *received the raise according as he was promised.* **2.** Depending on whether; if: *according as he accepts your suggestion.*

ac·cord·ing·ly (ə-kôr′dĭng-lē) *adv.* **1.** Correspondingly. **2.** Consequently.

according to *prep.* **1.** As stated or indicated by; on the authority of: *according to historians.* **2.** In keeping with; in agreement with: *according to instructions.* **3.** As determined by: *a list arranged according to the alphabet.*

ac·cor·di·on (ə-kôr′dē-ən) *n.* A portable musical instrument with a small keyboard and free metal reeds that sound when air is forced past them by pleated bellows operated by the player. —*adj.* Having folds or bends like the bellows of an accordion: *accordion pleats.* [G. *Akkordion* < *Akkord,* chord < Fr. *accord,* harmony < OFr. *acorder,* to accord.] **—ac·cor′di·on·ist** *n.*

ac·cost (ə-kôst′, ə-kŏst′) *tr.v.* **-cost·ed, -cost·ing, -costs.** **1.** To approach and speak to first. **2.** To solicit sexually. [OFr. *accoster* < Med. Lat. *acostare,* to adjoin : Lat. *ad-,* to + Lat. *costa,* side.]

ac·couche·ment (ä′-ko͞osh-mäɴ′) *n.* Parturition. [Fr. < *accoucher,* to assist in childbirth : *à,* to (< Lat. *ad*) + *coucher,* to put to bed < OFr., to lay down. —see COUCH.]

ac·count (ə-kount′) *n.* **1. a.** A narrative or record of events. **b.** A written or oral explanation, as of blame or cause. **2. a.** A precise list or enumeration of monetary transactions. **b.** A detailed list or enumeration. **3.** A business relationship involving the exchange of money or credit: *a charge account.* **4.** Worth, standing, or importance: *a man of some account.* **5.** Profit or advantage. —*tr.v.* **-count·ed, -count·ing, -counts.** To consider or esteem: *accounted him a merciful man.* ***—phrasal verb.* account for.** **1.** To make or render a reckoning, as of funds received and paid out or of persons or things: *survivors who have not been accounted for.* **2.** To be the explanation or cause of. **3.** To be answerable for. **4.** To kill, capture, or disable. ***—idioms.* call to account.** **1.** To challenge or contest. **2.** To hold answerable for. **give a good account of (oneself).** To act in a creditable manner. **on account.** **1.** On credit. **2.** In part payment of. **on account of.** **1.** Because of. **2.** *Regional.* Because. **on no account.** Under no circumstances. **on (one's) own account.** **1.** On one's own behalf. **2.** On one's own; by oneself: *wants to work on his own account.* **take into account.** To take into consideration; allow for. [ME < OFr. *acont* < *aconter,* to reckon : *a-,* to (< Lat. *ad*) + *cunter,* to count, ult. < Lat. *computare,* to sum up. —see COMPUTE.]

ac·count·a·ble (ə-koun′tə-bəl) *adj.* **1.** Answerable. **2.** Capable of being explained. **—ac·count′a·bil′i·ty, ac·count′a·ble·ness** *n.* **—ac·count′a·bly** *adv.*

ac·count·ant (ə-koun′tənt) *n.* One who keeps, audits, and inspects the financial records of individuals or business concerns and prepares financial and tax reports. **—ac·count′an·cy** (-tən-sē) *n.*

account executive *n.* An individual in an advertising firm who manages the account of one or more clients.

ac·count·ing (ə-koun′tĭng) *n.* The bookkeeping methods involved in making a financial record of business transactions and in the preparation of statements concerning the assets, liabilities, and operating results of a business.

ac·cou·ter (ə-ko͞o′tər) *tr.v.* **-tered, -ter·ing, -ters.** To outfit and equip, as for military duty. [Fr. *accoutrer* < OFr. *acoustrer.*]

ac·cou·ter·ment (ə-ko͞o′tər-mənt) *n.* **1.** The act of accoutering. **2.** Often **accouterments.** The equipment other than arms and dress issued to a soldier. **3. accouterments.** The outward forms whereby a thing may be recognized; trappings.

ac·cou·tre (ə-ko͞o′tər) *v. Chiefly Brit.* Variant of **accouter.**

ac·cou·tre·ment (ə-ko͞o′tər-mənt, -trə-mənt) *n. Chiefly Brit.* Variant of **accouterment.**

ac·cred·it (ə-krĕd′ĭt) *tr.v.* **-it·ed, -it·ing, -its. 1.** To ascribe or attribute to; credit with. **2. a.** To supply with credentials or authority; authorize. **b.** To appoint as an ambassador to a foreign government. **3.** To certify as meeting a prescribed standard. **4.** To believe. **5.** To enter on the credit side of an account book. [Fr. *accréditer* : *à,* to (< Lat. *ad*) + *credit,* credit < OFr. —see CREDIT.]

ac·cred·i·ta·tion (ə-krĕd′ĭ-tā′shən) *n.* The act of accrediting or the state of being accredited, esp. the granting of approval to an institution of learning by an official review board after the school has met specific requirements.

ac·crete (ə-krēt′) *v.* **-cret·ed, -cret·ing, -cretes.** —*tr.* To make larger or greater, as by increased growth. —*intr.* **1.** To grow together; fuse. **2.** To grow or increase gradually, as by addition. [Back-formation < ACCRETION.]

ac·cre·tion (ə-krē′shən) *n.* **1. a.** Growth or increase in size by gradual external addition, fusion, or inclusion. **b.** Something added externally to promote such growth or increase. **2.** *Biol.* The growing together of plant or animal tissues that are normally separate. **3.** *Geol.* Slow addition to land by deposition of water-borne sediment. **4.** *Law.* An increase of land along the shores of a body of water, as by alluvial deposit. **5.** *Astron.* An increase in the mass of a celestial object by the collection of surrounding interstellar gases and objects by gravity. [Lat. *accretio* < *accrescere,* to grow. —see ACCRUE.] **—ac·cre′tion·ar′y, ac·cre′tive** *adj.*

accretion disk *n.* A ring of interstellar material surrounding a celestial object with an intense gravitational field, as a black hole.

ac·cru·al (ə-kro͞o′əl) *n.* **1.** The act or process of accruing; increase. **2.** Something that increases or accrues.

ac·crue (ə-kro͞o′) *intr.v.* **-crued, -cru·ing, -crues. 1.** To come to someone or something as a gain, addition, or increment. **2.** To increase or accumulate, as by natural growth: *accruing interest on capital.* **3.** *Law.* To become an enforceable or permanent right. [ME *acreuen,* ult. < Lat. *accrescere,* to grow : *ad-,* to + *crescere,* to arise.] **—ac·crue′ment** *n.*

ac·cul·tur·ate (ə-kŭl′chə-rāt′) *v.* **-at·ed, -at·ing, -ates.** —*tr.* To cause (a society, for example) to change by the process of acculturation. —*intr.* To change or be modified by acculturation.

ac·cul·tur·a·tion (ə-kŭl′chə-rā′shən) *n.* **1. a.** The modification of the culture of a group or individual as a result of contact with a different culture. **b.** The modification of a primitive culture by means of such contact. **2.** The process by which the culture of a particular society is instilled in a human being from infancy onward.

ac·cum·bent (ə-kŭm′bənt) *adj.* **1.** Lying down; reclining. **2.** *Bot.* Resting against another part, as a cotyledon. [Lat. *accumbens, accumbent-,* pr.part. of *accumbere,* to recline at table : *ad-,* near to + *cumbere,* to recline.]

ac·cu·mu·late (ə-kyo͞om′yə-lāt′) *v.* **-lat·ed, -lat·ing, -lates.** —*tr.* To amass or gather; pile up; collect. —*intr.* To grow or increase; mount up. [Lat. *accumulare, accumulat-* : *ad-,* to + *cumulare,* to pile up < *cumulus,* heap.] **—ac·cu′mu·la·ble** (-lə-bəl) *adj.*

ac·cu·mu·la·tion (ə-kyo͞om′yə-lā′shən) *n.* **1.** The act of amassing or gathering, as into a heap or pile: *"Little things grew by continual accumulation"* (Samuel Johnson). **2.** The process of growing into a heap or large amount. **3.** A mass of something heaped up or collected: *an accumulation of rubbish.* **4. a.** The growth of a principal sum by retention of interest or profit. **b.** The gradual purchase of securities in a depressed market in anticipation of rising prices. **c.** In reckoning the yield on a bond, the difference between its face value and its cost if the bond is purchased at a discount.

ac·cu·mu·la·tive (ə-kyo͞om′yə-lā′tĭv, -lə-tĭv) *adj.* **1.** Characterized by or showing the effects of accumulation; cumulative. **2.** Having a propensity to amass; acquisitive. **—ac·cu′mu·la·tive·ly** *adv.* **—ac·cu′mu·la·tive·ness** *n.*

ac·cu·mu·la·tor (ə-kyo͞om′yə-lā′tər) *n.* **1.** One that accumulates. **2.** A register or electric circuit in a calculator or computer that stores figures for computation. **3.** *Chiefly Brit.* An automobile storage battery.

ac·cu·ra·cy (ăk′yər-ə-sē) *n.* The quality or state of being accurate; correctness.

ac·cu·rate (ăk′yər-ĭt) *adj.* **1.** In exact conformity to fact; errorless. **2.** Deviating only slightly or within acceptable limits from a standard. [Lat. *accuratus,* done with care, p.part. of *accurare,* to do with care : *ad-,* to + *curare,* to care for < *cura,* care.] **—ac′cu·rate·ly** *adv.* **—ac′cu·rate·ness** *n.*

ac·curs·ed (ə-kûr′sĭd, ə-kûrst′) also **ac·curst** (ə-kûrst′) *adj.* **1.** Under a curse; doomed. **2.** Abominable; hateful. [ME *acursed* < *acursen,* to put a curse on : *a-* (intensive) + OE *cursian,* to curse < *curs,* curse.] **—ac·curs′ed·ly** *adv.* **—ac·curs′ed·ness** *n.*

ac·cu·sa·tion (ăk′yo͞o-zā′shən) *n.* **1.** An act of accusing. **2.** An allegation. **3.** *Law.* A formal charge brought before a court against a person, stating that he is guilty of some punishable offense.

ac·cu·sa·tive (ə-kyo͞o′zə-tĭv) *adj.* Of or pertaining to the case of a noun, pronoun, adjective, or participle that is the direct object of a verb or the object of certain prepositions. —*n.* The accusative case. [ME *acusatif* < OFr. < Lat. *(casus) accusativus,* (case) of accusation < *accusare,* to accuse.] **—ac·cu′sa·tive·ly** *adv.*

ac·cu·sa·to·ri·al (ə-kyo͞o′zə-tôr′ē-əl, -tōr′-) also **ac·cu·sa·to·ry** (-tôr′ē, -tōr′ē) *adj.* Containing or implying accusation.

ac·cuse (ə-kyo͞oz′) *v.* **-cused, -cus·ing, -cus·es.** —*tr.* **1.** To charge with a shortcoming or error. **2.** To bring charges against (someone) for a misdeed: *two men accused of a crime.* —*intr.* To make an accusation against someone. [ME *acusen* < Lat. *accusare* : *ad-,* to + *causa,* lawsuit] **—ac·cus′er** *n.* **—ac·cus′ing·ly** *adv.*

ac·cused (ə-kyo͞ozd′) *n. Law.* The defendant or defendants in a criminal case: *one of the accused.*

ac·cus·tom (ə-kŭs′təm) *tr.v.* **-tomed, -tom·ing, -toms.** To familiarize, as by constant practice, use, or habit: *accustomed himself to working long hours.* [ME *accustomen* < OFr. *acostumer* : *a,* to + *costume,* custom. —see CUSTOM.]

ac·cus·tomed (ə-kŭs′təmd) *adj.* **1.** Usual, characteristic, or normal: *worked with her accustomed thoroughness.* **2.** In the habit of: *accustomed to sleeping late.*

AC/DC (ā′sē-dē′sē) *adj. Slang.* Bisexual (sense 3). [From the likening of a bisexual person to an appliance that works on either alternating or direct current.]

ace (ās) *n.* **1. a.** A single pip or spot on a playing card, die, or domino. **b.** A playing card, die, or domino having one spot or pip. **2.** In racket games: **a.** A serve which one's opponent fails to return. **b.** A point scored by serving an ace. **3.** The act of hitting a golf ball in the hole with one's first shot. **4.** *Informal.* A narrow margin. **5.** A military aircraft pilot who has destroyed five or more enemy aircraft. **6.** A person who is an expert in his field. —*adj. Informal.* Top-notch; first-rate. —*tr.v.* **aced, ac·ing, ac·es. 1.** To serve an ace against. **2.** To hit an ace in golf. **3.** To get the better of (someone). **4.** To receive a grade of A on: *she aced the exam.* **—idiom. ace in the hole. 1.** A hidden advantage. **2.** A hole in one in golf. **within an ace of.** On the verge of; very near to. [ME *as* < OFr. < Lat., unit.]

ace

-acean *suff.* **1.** -aceous. **2.** An organism belonging to a taxonomic group: *cetacean.* [< NLat *-acea,* neuter pl. of *-aceus,* -aceous.]

a·ce·di·a (ə-sē′dē-ə) *n.* Spiritual torpor; ennui. [LLat. < Gk. *akēdeia,* indifference : *a-,* without + *kēdos,* care.]

A·cel·da·ma (ə-sĕl′də-mə) *n.* A place with dreadful associations. [After *Aceldama,* a field bought with the money Judas received for betraying Jesus < Gk. *Akeldama* < Aram. *ḥăqēl dĕmā,* field of blood.]

a·cel·lu·lar (ā-sĕl′yə-lər) *adj.* Containing no cells.

-aceous *suff.* **1. a.** Of or relating to: *amylaceous.* **b.** Resembling or having the nature of: *amentaceous.* **2.** Belonging to a specified taxonomic category: *orchidaceous.* [NLat *-aceus* < Lat.]

a·ceph·a·lous (ā-sĕf′ə-ləs) *adj.* **1.** Headless or lacking a clearly defined head. **2.** Having no leader. [Med. Lat. *acephalus* < Gk. *akephalos* : *a-,* without + *kephalē,* head.]

a·ce·qui·a (ə-sā′kē-ə, ä-sä′-) *n. Southwestern U.S.* An irrigation canal. [Sp. < Ar. *assaqīyāh,* irrigation ditch.]

ac·er·ate (ăs′ə-rāt′) also **ac·er·at·ed** (-rā′tĭd) *adj. Biol.* Pointed at one end; needle-shaped. [< Lat. *acer,* sharp.]

a·cerb (ə-sûrb′) also **a·cer·bic** (ə-sûr′bĭk) *adj.* **1.** Sour or bitter in taste. **2.** Sharp or bitter in temper, mood, or expression. [Lat. *acerbus.*]

ac·er·bate (ăs′ər-bāt′) *tr.v.* **-bat·ed, -bat·ing, -bates.** To vex or annoy. [Lat. *acerbare, acerbat-,* to make harsh < *acerbus,* harsh.]

a·cer·bi·ty (ə-sûr′bĭ-tē) *n., pl.* **-ties. 1.** Sourness of taste. **2.** Sharpness or bitterness of temper, mood, or expression.

ac·er·ose (ăs′ə-rōs′) *adj.* Slender and sharp-pointed, as a pine needle. [NLat. *acerosus* < Lat. *acer,* sharp.]

a·cer·vate (ə-sûr′vĭt, ăs′ər-vāt′) *adj.* Growing in small heaps or compact clusters. [< Lat. *acervare, acervat-,* to heap up < *acervus,* heap.] **—a·cer′vate·ly** *adv.*

acet- *pref.* Variant of **aceto-.**

ac·e·tab·u·lum (ăs′ĭ-tăb′yə-ləm) *n., pl.* **-la** (-lə). **1.** *Anat.* The cup-shaped cavity in the hipbone into which the head of the thighbone fits. **2.** *Zool.* A sucker, such as that of an octopus or cuttlefish. [Lat., vinegar cup < *acetum,* vinegar.] **—ac′e·tab′u·lar** (-lər) *adj.*

ac·e·tal (ăs′ĭ-tăl′) *n.* **1.** A colorless, flammable, volatile liquid, $CH_3CH(OC_2H_5)_2$, used in cosmetics and as a solvent. **2.** Any of the class of compounds formed from aldehydes combined with alcohol. [G. *Azetal* : *acet-,* aceto- + *Alkohol,* alcohol.]

ac·et·al·de·hyde (ăs′ĭ-tăl′də-hīd′) *n.* A colorless, flammable liquid, C_2H_4O, used to manufacture acetic acid, perfumes, and drugs.

a·cet·a·mide (ə-sĕt′ə-mīd′, ăs′ĭt-ăm′īd′) also **a·cet·a·mid**

(-mĭd, -ĭd) *n.* The crystalline amide of acetic acid, CH_3CONH_2, used as a solvent and wetting agent and in lacquers and explosives.
a·cet·a·min·o·phen (ə-sē′tə-mĭn′ə-fən, ăs′ə-) *n.* A hydroxy derivative of acetanilide, $C_8H_9NO_2$, used in chemical synthesis and, in medicine, to reduce pain and fever. [ACET(O)- + AMIN(O)- + PHEN(OL).]
ac·et·an·i·lide (ăs′ĭt-ăn′l-ĭd′) also **ac·et·an·i·lid** (-ĭd) *n.* A white crystalline compound, $C_6H_5NH(COCH_3)$, used medicinally to relieve pain and reduce fever. [ACET(O)- + ANIL(INE) + -IDE.]
ac·e·tate (ăs′ĭ-tāt′) *n.* **1.** A salt or ester of acetic acid. **2.** Cellulose acetate or any of various products, esp. fibers, derived from it.
a·ce·tic (ə-sē′tĭk) *adj.* Of, pertaining to, or containing acetic acid or vinegar. [< Lat. *acetum,* vinegar. —see ACETUM]
acetic acid *n.* A clear, colorless organic acid, CH_3COOH, with a distinctive pungent odor, used as a solvent and in the manufacture of rubber, plastics, acetate fibers, pharmaceuticals, and photographic chemicals.
acetic anhydride *n.* An organic liquid, $(CH_3CO)_2O$, with a pungent odor, combining with water to produce acetic acid and used in the manufacture of various organic acetate derivatives.
a·ce·ti·fy (ə-sē′tə-fī′, ə-sĕt′ə-) *tr. & intr.v.* **-fied, -fy·ing, -fies.** To convert or become converted to acetic acid or vinegar. **—a·ce′ti·fi·ca′tion** *n.* **—a·ce′ti·fi·er** *n.*
aceto– or **acet–.** *pref.* **1.** Acetic acid: *acetify.* **2.** Acetyl: *acetanilide.* [< Lat. *acetum,* vinegar. —see ACETUM.]
ac·e·to·a·ce·tic acid (ăs′ĭ-tō-ə-sē′tĭk, ə-sē′tō-) *n.* A syrupy, colorless acid, CH_3COCH_2COOH, excreted in the urine and found in abnormal quantities in the urine of diabetics.
ac·e·tone (ăs′ĭ-tōn′) *n.* A colorless, volatile, extremely flammable liquid, CH_3COCH_3, widely used as an organic solvent. **—ac′e·ton′ic** (-tŏn′ĭk) *adj.*
acetone body *n.* A ketone body.
ac·e·to·phe·net·i·din (ăs′ĭ-tō-fə-nĕt′ĭ-dĭn, ə-sē′tō-) *n.* A white powder or crystalline solid, $CH_3CONHC_6H_4OC_2H_5$, used in medicine to reduce fever and relieve pain. [ACETO- + PHEN(O) + ET(HYL) + -ID(E) + -IN.]

achene
Dandelion achene

a·ce·tous (ə-sē′təs, ăs′ĭ-təs) *adj.* **1.** Of, pertaining to, or producing acetic acid or vinegar. **2.** Having an acetic taste; sour-tasting. [ME, sour < Med. Lat. *acetus* < Lat. *acetum,* vinegar. —see ACETUM.]
a·ce·tum (ə-sē′təm) *n.* **1.** Vinegar. **2.** An acetic acid solution of a drug. [Lat. *acetum* < *acēre,* to be sour < *acer,* sharp.]
a·ce·tyl (ə-sēt′l, ăs′ĭ-tl) *n.* The acetic acid radical CH_3CO. **—ac′e·tyl′ic** (ăs′ĭ-tĭl′ĭk) *adj.*
a·cet·y·late (ə-sĕt′l-āt′) *tr.v.* **-lat·ed, -lat·ing, -ates.** To bring an acetyl group into (an organic molecule), using a reagent such as acetic anhydride. **—a·cet′y·la′tion** *n.*
a·ce·tyl·cho·line (ə-sēt′l-kō′lēn′) *n.* A white crystalline compound, $C_7H_{17}NO_3$, that transmits nerve impulses across intercellular gaps and forms salts used to lower blood pressure and increase peristalsis.
a·ce·tyl·cho·lin·es·ter·ase (ə-sēt′l-kō′lə-nĕs′tə-rās′, -rāz′) *n.* Cholinesterase.
a·cet·y·lene (ə-sĕt′l-ēn′, -ən) *n.* A colorless, highly flammable or explosive gas, C_2H_2, used for metal welding and cutting and as an illuminant. **—a·cet′y·len′ic** *adj.*
acetylene series *n.* A series of unsaturated aliphatic hydrocarbons, each containing at least one triple carbon bond, having chemical properties resembling acetylene, and having the general formula C_nH_{2n-2} with acetylene being the simplest member.
a·ce·tyl·sal·i·cyl·ic acid (ə-sēt′l-săl′ĭ-sĭl′ĭk) *n.* Aspirin.
ace·y-deuc·y (ā′sē-do͞o′sē, -dyo͞o′-) *n.* A variation of backgammon. [ACE + DEUCE.]

Achilles
Achilles receiving armor

ach·a·la·sia (ăk′ə-lā′zhə) *n.* The inability of a ring muscle or sphincter to relax. [NLat. : A-[1] + Gk. *khalasis,* relaxation < *khalan,* to loosen.]
A·cha·tes (ə-kā′tēz) *n.* A loyal friend. [After *Achates,* the faithful companion of Aeneas, in the *Aeneid,* an epic poem by Virgil (70–19 B.C.).]
ache (āk) *intr.v.* **ached, ach·ing, aches. 1.** To suffer a dull, sustained pain. **2.** To feel sympathy or compassion. **3.** *Informal.* To yearn painfully. *—n.* **1.** A dull, steady pain. **2.** *Informal.* A longing or desire. [ME *aken* < OE *acan.*]
a·chene (ə-kēn′) *n.* A small, dry, thinwalled fruit, such as that of the buttercup and dandelion, that does not split open when ripe. [NLat. *achenium* : Gk. *a-,* not + Gk. *khainein,* to yawn.] **—a·che′ni·al** (ə-kē′nē-əl) *adj.*
A·cher·nar (ā′kər-när′) *n.* A star in the constellation Eridanus that is one of the brightest stars in the sky and is 114 light-years from Earth. [< Ar. *ākhīr alnahr,* the end of the river.]
Ach·er·on (ăk′ə-rŏn′, -rən) *n. Gk. Myth.* **1.** The river of woe over which Charon ferried the souls of the dead to Hades. **2.** Hades. [Gk. *Akherōn.*]
A·cheu·li·an also **A·cheu·le·an** (ə-sho͞o′lē-ən) *adj.* Designating a stage of culture of the European Lower Paleolithic Age between the second and third interglacial periods, characterized by symmetrical stone hand axes. [Fr. *acheuléen,* after St. *Acheul,* France.]
a·chieve (ə-chēv′) *v.* **a·chieved, a·chiev·ing, a·chieves.** *—tr.* **1.** To do or finish with success. **2.** To attain or get with effort: *finally achieved mastery of the piano.* *—intr.* To accomplish something successfully. [ME *acheven* < OFr. *achever* < *à chief (venir),* (to come) to a head.] **—a·chiev′a·ble** *adj.* **—a·chiev′er** *n.*
a·chieve·ment (ə-chēv′mənt) *n.* **1.** The act of accomplishing or finishing something. **2.** Something that has been accomplished successfully, esp. by means of exertion, skill, practice, or perseverance.
A·chil·les (ə-kĭl′ēz) *n. Gk. Myth.* The hero of Homer's *Iliad,* son of Peleus and Thetis. [Lat. < Gk. *Akhilleus.*]
Achilles' heel *n.* A small but mortal weakness. [From Achilles' being vulnerable only in the heel.]
Achilles jerk *n.* Reflex plantar flexian in response to a blow to the Achilles tendon.
Achilles tendon *n.* The large tendon running from the heel bone to the calf muscle of the leg.
ach·la·myd·e·ous (ăk′lə-mĭd′ē-əs, ā′klə-) *adj. Bot.* Having no calyx or corolla.
a·cho·li·a (ā-kō′lē-ə) *n.* A decrease or absence of bile secretion in the small intestine. [NLat. : A-[1] + Gk. *kholē,* bile.]
a·chon·drite (ā-kŏn′drīt′) *n.* A stony meteorite that contains no chondrules. **—a′chon·drit′ic** (-drĭt′ĭk) *adj.*
a·chon·dro·pla·sia (ā-kŏn′drō-plā′zhə, -zhē-ə) *n.* Improper development of cartilage at the ends of the long bones, resulting in congenital dwarfism. **—a·chon′dro·plas′tic** (-plăs′tĭk) *adj.*
ach·ro·mat·ic (ăk′rə-măt′ĭk) *adj.* **1.** Designating color perceived to have zero saturation and therefore no hue, such as neutral grays. **2.** Refracting light without spectral color separation. **3.** *Biol.* Staining poorly with standard dyes. **4.** *Mus.* Having only the diatonic tones of the scale. [Gk. *akhrōmatos* : *a-,* not + *khrōma,* color.] **—ach′ro·mat′i·cal·ly** *adv.* **—a·chro′ma·tism** (ā-krō′mə-tĭz′əm), **—ach′ro·ma·tic′i·ty** (ăk′rō-mə-tĭs′ĭ-tē) *n.*
achromatic lens *n.* A combination of lenses to produce images free of chromatic aberrations.
a·chro·ma·tin (ā-krō′mə-tĭn) *n.* The part of a cell nucleus that is relatively uncolored by stains or dyes. [ACHROMAT(IC) + -IN.] **—a·chro′ma·tin′ic** *adj.*
a·chro·ma·tize (ā-krō′mə-tīz′) *tr.v.* **-tized, -tiz·ing, -tiz·es.** To render achromatic; rid of color.
a·chro·mic (ā-krō′mĭk) *adj.* Having no color; colorless. [A-[1] + CHROMO- + -IC.]
ach·y (ā′kē) *adj.* **-i·er, -i·est.** Experiencing aches. **—ach′i·ness** *n.*
a·cic·u·la (ə-sĭk′yə-lə) *n., pl.* **-lae** (-lē′). A needlelike bristle, spine, or crystal. [NLat. < Lat., hairpin, dim. of *acus,* needle.] **—a·cic′u·lar, a·cic′u·late** (-lĭt, -lāt′), **a·cic′u·lat′ed** (-lā′tĭd) *adj.*
ac·id (ăs′ĭd) *n.* **1.** *Chem.* **a.** Any of a large class of substances the aqueous solutions of which are capable of turning litmus indicators red, of reacting with and dissolving certain metals to form salts, of reacting with bases or alkalis to form salts, or having a sour taste. **b.** A substance that ionizes in solution to give the positive ion of the solvent. **c.** A substance capable of giving up a proton. **d.** A molecule or ion that can combine with another by forming a covalent bond with two electrons of the other. **2.** A substance having a sour taste. **3.** The quality of being sarcastic, bitter, or scornful: *a letter oozing with acid.* **4.** *Slang.* LSD. *—adj.* **1.** *Chem.* **a.** Of or pertaining to an acid. **b.** Having a high concentration of acid. **2.** Having a sour taste. **3.** Biting; sarcastic, or scornful: *an acid wit.* [Lat. *acidus,* sour < *acēre,* to be sour < *acer,* sharp.] **—ac′id·ly** *adv.* **—ac′id·ness** *n.*
acid cell *n.* A parietal cell of the stomach.
ac·i·de·mi·a (ăs′ĭ-dē′mē-ə) *n.* A condition in which blood pH is below normal.
ac·id-fast (ăs′ĭd-făst′) *adj.* Not readily decolorized by acid. Used of bacteria. **—ac′id-fast′ness** *n.*
ac·id·head (ăs′ĭd-hĕd′) *n. Slang.* A person who uses LSD, esp. frequently.
a·cid·ic (ə-sĭd′ĭk) *adj.* **1.** Acid. **2.** Tending to form an acid.
a·cid·i·fy (ə-sĭd′ə-fī′) *tr. & intr.v.* **-fied, -fy·ing, -fies.** To make or become acid. **—a·cid′i·fi′a·ble** *adj.* **—a·cid′i·fi·ca′tion** *n.* **—a·cid′i·fi′er** *n.*
ac·i·dim·e·ter (ăs′ĭ-dĭm′ĭ-tər) *n.* A hydrometer used to determine the specific gravity of acid solutions. **—a·cid′i·met′ric** (ə-sĭd′ĭ-mĕt′rĭk) *adj.* **—ac′i·dim′e·try** *n.*
a·cid·i·ty (ə-sĭd′ĭ-tē) *n.* **1.** The state, quality, or degree of being acid. **2.** Hyperacidity.
ac·i·do·phil·ic (ăs′ĭ-dō-fĭl′ĭk) also **ac·i·doph·i·lus** (-dŏf′ə-ləs) *adj. Microbiol.* **1.** Growing well in an acid medium. **2.** Easily stained with acid dyes. **—a·cid′o·phil′** (ə-sĭd′ə-fĭl′), **a·cid′o·phile′** (-fīl′) *n.*
ac·i·doph·i·lus milk (ăs′ĭ-dŏf′ə-ləs) *n.* Milk containing bacterial cultures that thrive in dilute acid, often used in treating gastrointestinal disorders. [NLat. *acidophilus,* specific epithet of several species of bacteria : ACID + *-philus,* -philous.]
ac·i·do·sis (ăs′ĭ-dō′sĭs) *n.* An abnormal increase in the acidity of the body's fluids, due either to acid-accumulation or bicarbonate depletion. **—ac′i·dot′ic** (-dŏt′ĭk) *adj.*
acid precipitation *n.* Precipitation abnormally high in sulfuric and nitric acid content that is caused by industrial pollution.
acid rain *n.* Acid precipitation falling as rain.

acid rock *n.* Rock music with lyrics that suggest psychedelic experiences.

acid test *n.* A decisive or critical test of worth or quality. [From the testing of gold in nitric acid.]

a·cid·u·late (ə-sĭj′ə-lāt′) *tr. & intr.v.* **-lat·ed, -lat·ing, -lates.** To make or become slightly acid. [ACIDUL(OUS) + -ATE[1].] **—a·cid′u·la′tion** *n.*

a·cid·u·lous (ə-sĭj′ə-ləs) *adj.* Sour in feeling or manner; biting; caustic. [Lat. *acidulus,* sourish, dim. of *acidus,* sour. — see ACID.]

ac·i·dur·i·a (ăs′ĭ-dŏŏr′ē-ə, -dyŏŏr′-) *n.* A condition marked by excessive amounts of acid in the urine.

ac·i·nar (ăs′ĭ-nər, -när′) *adj.* Of or pertaining to an acinus.

ac·i·nus (ăs′ə-nəs) *n., pl.* **-ni** (-nī′). **1.** *Bot.* One of the small divisions or drupelets of an aggregate fruit such as the raspberry. **2.** A grape or a bunch of grapes. **3.** *Anat.* One of the small saclike dilations composing a compound gland. [Lat., berry.] **—a·cin′ic** (ə-sĭn′ĭk), **ac′i·nous** *adj.*

ack-ack (ăk′ăk′) *n. Slang.* **1.** An antiaircraft gun. **2.** Antiaircraft fire. [British telephone code for AA, abbreviation for ANTIAIRCRAFT.]

ac·knowl·edge (ăk-nŏl′ĭj) *tr.v.* **-edged, -edg·ing, -edg·es. 1. a.** To confess, avow, or admit the existence, reality, or truth of. **b.** To recognize as being valid or having force or power. **2. a.** To express recognition of. **b.** To express thanks or gratitude for. **3.** To report the receipt of. **4.** *Law.* To accept or certify as legally binding: *acknowledge a deed.* [Blend of ME *knowledgen,* to acknowledge (< *knowen,* to know) and ME *aknouen,* to recognize < OE *oncnāwan,* to know.] **—ac·knowl′edge·a·ble** *adj.*

Synonyms: *acknowledge, admit, own, avow, confess, concede.* These verbs mean to make a disclosure, sometimes with reluctance or under pressure. To *acknowledge* is to accept responsibility for something one makes known or to give recognition to someone. *Admit* usually implies marked reluctance in acknowledging one's acts or accepting a different point of view as a result of pressure. *Own* stresses personal acceptance of, and responsibility for, one's deeds. *Avow,* a strong term, means to assert openly and boldly and implies the likelihood of opposition. *Confess* usually emphasizes disclosure of wrongdoing. To *concede* is to yield to a claim or demand, often with some reluctance.

ac·knowl·edged (ăk-nŏl′ĭjd) *adj.* Commonly accepted or recognized.

ac·knowl·edg·ment also **ac·knowl·edge·ment** (ăk-nŏl′ĭj-mənt) *n.* **1.** The act of admitting or owning to something. **2.** Recognition of someone's or something's existence, validity, authority, or right. **3.** An answer or response in return for something done. **4.** An expression or token of appreciation or thanks. **5.** A formal declaration made to authoritative witnesses to ensure legal validity.

a·clin·ic line (ā-klĭn′ĭk) *n.* The magnetic equator.

ac·me (ăk′mē) *n.* The point of utmost attainment; peak. [Gk. *akmē.*]

ac·ne (ăk′nē) *n.* An inflammatory disease of the oil glands, characterized by pimples esp. on the face. [Poss. < Gk. *akmē,* point.] **—ac′ned** *adj.*

a·cock (ə-kŏk′) *adj. & adv.* In a cocked position.

ac·o·lyte (ăk′ə-līt′) *n.* **1.** One who assists a priest in the celebration of Mass. **2.** An attendant or follower. [ME *acolit* < OFr. < Med. Lat. *acolytus* < Gk. *akolouthos,* attendant < *akolouthein,* to follow.]

ac·o·nite (ăk′ə-nīt′) *n.* **1.** The monkshood. **2.** The dried, poisonous root of a species of monkshood, *A. napellus,* sometimes used in medicine to relieve pain or to reduce fever. [Fr. *aconit* < Lat. *aconitum* < Gk. *akoniton.*]

a·corn (ā′kôrn′, ā′kərn) *n.* The fruit of the oak tree, consisting of a thick-walled nut usually set in a woody, cuplike base. [ME *akorn* < OE *æcern.*]

acorn squash *n.* A type of squash shaped somewhat like an acorn and having a longitudinally ridged rind.

acorn tube *n.* A small, acorn-shaped vacuum tube used in very high frequency devices.

a·cot·y·le·don (ā-kŏt′l-ēd′n) *n.* A plant having no cotyledons, or seed leaves, such as a moss or fern. **—a·cot′y·le′don·ous** (-ēd′n-əs) *adj.*

a·cous·tic (ə-kōō′stĭk) also **a·cous·ti·cal** (-stĭ-kəl) *adj.* **1.** Of or pertaining to sound, the sense of hearing, or the science of sound. **2.** Designed to carry sound or to aid in hearing. **3. a.** Of, relating to, or being a musical instrument, as a guitar, that does not feature electronically modified sound. **b.** Being a musical performance that features acoustic instruments: *opened the show with an acoustic set.* —*n.* An acoustic musical instrument. [Gk. *akoustikos,* pertaining to hearing < *akouein,* to hear.] **—a·cous′ti·cal·ly** *adv.*

ac·ous·ti·cian (ăk′ōō-stĭsh′ən) *n.* A specialist in acoustics.

acoustic nerve *n.* The eighth cranial nerve, consisting of the *cochlear nerve,* which conducts acoustic stimuli to the brain, and the *vestibular nerve,* which conducts stimuli related to bodily equilibrium to the brain.

a·cous·tics (ə-kōō′stĭks) *n.* **1.** *(used with a sing. verb).* The scientific study of sound, esp. of its generation, transmission, and reception. **2.** *(used with a pl. verb).* The total effect of sound, esp. as produced in an enclosed space.

a·cous·to·e·lec·tric (ə-kōō′stō-ĭ-lĕk′trĭk) *adj.* Of or relating to electroacoustics. [ACOUST(IC) + ELECTRIC.] **—a·cous′to·e·lec′tric·al·ly** *adv.*

a·cous·to·op·tics (ə-kōō′stō-ŏp′tĭks) *n.* The science of the interaction of acoustic and optical phenomena. [ACOUST(IC) + OPTICS.] **—a·cous′to·op′ti·cal** *adj.* **—a·cous′to·op′ti·cal·ly** *adv.*

ac·quaint (ə-kwānt′) *tr.v.* **-quaint·ed, -quaint·ing, -quaints. 1.** To make familiar: *acquaint yourself with the controls.* **2.** To inform: *acquaint us with your plans.* [ME *aqueinten* < OFr. *acointier* < Med. Lat. *adcognitare* < Lat. *accognoscere,* to know perfectly : *ad-* (intensive) + *cognoscere,* to know. —see COGNITION.]

ac·quain·tance (ə-kwān′təns) *n.* **1.** Knowledge or information about someone or something. **2.** Knowledge of a person acquired by a relationship less intimate than friendship. **3.** A person or persons whom one knows. **—ac·quain′tance·ship′** *n.*

ac·quaint·ed (ə-kwān′tĭd) *adj.* **1.** Known by or familiar with another. **2.** Informed or familiar: *acquainted with the facts.*

ac·qui·esce (ăk′wē-ĕs′) *intr.v.* **-esced, -esc·ing, -esc·es.** To consent or comply passively or without protest. [Lat. *acquiescere* : *ad-,* to + *quiescere,* to rest < *quies,* rest.]

Usage: When *acquiesce* takes a preposition, it is usually used with *in* (*acquiesced in the ruling*) but sometimes with *to* (*acquiesced to her parents' wishes*). *Acquiesced with* is obsolete.

ac·qui·es·cence (ăk′wē-ĕs′əns) *n.* **1.** Passive assent or agreement without protest. **2.** The state of being acquiescent. **—ac′qui·es′cent** *adj.* **—ac′qui·es′cent·ly** *adv.*

ac·quire (ə-kwīr′) *tr.v.* **-quired, -quir·ing, -quires. 1.** To gain possession of. **2.** To get by one's own efforts. [ME *acquere* < OFr. *aquerre* < Lat. *acquirere,* to add to : *ad-,* to + *quaerere,* to get.] **—ac·quir′a·ble** *adj.*

acquired antibody *n.* An antibody produced by an immune response as compared with one occurring in the system naturally.

acquired immune deficiency syndrome *n.* AIDS.

acquired immunity *n.* Immunity developed in the physiology during a lifetime.

ac·quire·ment (ə-kwīr′mənt) *n.* **1.** The act of acquiring. **2.** An attainment, such as a skill or social accomplishment.

ac·qui·si·tion (ăk′wĭ-zĭsh′ən) *n.* **1.** The act of acquiring. **2.** Something acquired, esp. an addition to an established category or group. **3.** *Aerospace.* The process of locating a satellite, guided missile, or moving target so that its track or orbit can be determined. [ME *adquisicioun,* attainment < Lat. *acquisitio* < *acquirere,* to acquire : *ad-,* to + *quaerere,* to seek.]

ac·quis·i·tive (ə-kwĭz′ĭ-tĭv) *adj.* **1.** Characterized by a strong desire to gain and possess. **2.** Tending to acquire and retain ideas or information: *an acquisitive mind.* **—ac·quis′i·tive·ly** *adv.* **—ac·quis′i·tive·ness** *n.*

ac·quit (ə-kwĭt′) *tr.v.* **-quit·ted, -quit·ting, -quits. 1.** To free or clear from a charge or accusation. **2.** To release or discharge from a duty. **3.** To repay (an obligation). **4.** To conduct (oneself). [ME *aquiten* < OFr. *aquiter.*] **—ac·quit′ter** *n.*

ac·quit·tal (ə-kwĭt′l) *n. Law.* The judgment of a jury or judge that a person is not guilty of a crime as charged.

ac·quit·tance (ə-kwĭt′ns) *n.* A written release from an obligation.

a·cra·sia (ə-krā′zhə) *n.* Lack of self-control. [Gk. *akrasia,* incontinence < *akratēs,* powerless : *a-,* not + *kratos,* strength.]

a·cre (ā′kər) *n.* **1.** A unit of area in the U.S. Customary System, used in land measurement and equal to 160 square rods, 4,840 square yards, or 43,560 square feet. **2. acres.** Property in the form of land; estate. **3.** Often **acres.** A wide expanse of land. **4.** *Archaic.* A field or plot of land. [ME *aker* < OE *æcer.*]

acorn

a·cre·age (ā′kər-ĭj, ā′krĭj) *n.* Area of land in acres.

a·cre-foot (ā′kər-fŏŏt′) *n.* The volume of water, 43,560 cubic feet, that will cover an area of one acre to a depth of one foot.

a·cre-inch (ā′kər-ĭnch′) *n.* One-twelfth of an acre-foot, equal to 3,630 cubic feet.

ac·rid (ăk′rĭd) *adj.* **1.** Harsh to the taste or smell. **2.** Caustic in language or tone. [< Lat. *acer,* sharp.] **—a·crid′i·ty** (ə-krĭd′ĭ-tē), **ac′rid·ness** *n.* **—ac′rid·ly** *adv.*

ac·ri·dine (ăk′rĭ-dēn′) *n.* A coal tar derivative, $C_{13}H_9N$, that has a strongly irritating odor and is used in the manufacture of dyes and synthetics.

ac·ri·fla·vine (ăk′rə-flā′vēn′, -vĭn) *n.* A brown or orange powder, $C_{14}H_{14}N_3Cl$, derived from acridine and used as an antiseptic. [ACRI(DINE) + FLAVIN.]

ac·ri·mo·ni·ous (ăk′rə-mō′nē-əs) *adj.* Bitter in language or tone; rancorous. **—ac′ri·mo′ni·ous·ly** *adv.* **—ac′ri·mo′ni·ous·ness** *n.*

ac·ri·mo·ny (ăk′rə-mō′nē) *n.* Bitterness or ill-natured animosity, esp. in speech or manner. [Lat. *acrimonia,* sharpness < *acer,* sharp.]

acro– or **acr–** *pref.* **1. a.** Top; summit: *acropetal.* **b.** Height: *acrophobia.* **2. a.** Tip; beginning: *acronym.* **b.** Extremity of the body: *acromegaly.* [< Gk. *akros,* extreme.]

ac·ro·bat (ăk′rə-băt′) *n.* One skilled in feats of agility and balance. [Fr. *acrobate* < Gk. *akrobatēs* < *akrobatein,* to walk

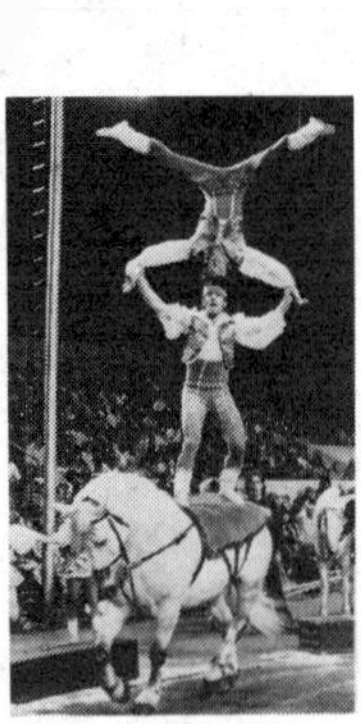

acrobatics

acropolis
The Acropolis, Athens, Greece

on tiptoe : *akros,* high + *batos,* walker < *bainein,* to walk.] **—ac'ro·bat'ic** *adj.* **—ac'ro·bat'i·cal·ly** *adv.*

ac·ro·bat·ics (ăk'rə-băt'ĭks) *n.* **1.** The actions of an acrobat. **2.** The art of an acrobat. **3.** A display of spectacular agility: *vocal acrobatics.*

ac·ro·car·pous (ăk'rō-kär'pəs) *adj.* Having the spore-bearing capsule at the end or top of a leafy stem or stalk, as in many mosses. [NLat. *acrocarpus* < Gk. *akrokarpos,* bearing fruit at the top : *akron,* top + *karpos,* fruit.]

ac·ro·ceph·a·ly (ăk'rə-sĕf'ə-lē) or **ac·ro·ce·phal·i·a** (-sə-fā'lē-ə) *n.* Oxycephaly. **—ac'ro·ce·phal'ic** (-făl'ĭk) *adj.*

ac·ro·drome (ăk'rə-drōm') also **a·crod·ro·mous** (ə-krŏd'rə-məs) *adj.* Coming to a point and having the veins terminate at the tip. Used of leaves.

ac·ro·gen (ăk'rə-jən) *n.* A flowerless plant, such as a fern or moss, having a stem from the tip of which all growth proceeds. **—ac'ro·gen'ic** (-jĕn'ĭk), **a·crog'e·nous** (ə-krŏj'ə-nəs) *adj.* **—a·crog'e·nous·ly** *adv.*

a·cro·le·in (ə-krō'lē-ĭn) *n.* A colorless, flammable, poisonous liquid, CH_2CHCHO, having an acrid odor and vapors dangerous to the eyes. [ACR(ID) + OLEIN.]

ac·ro·meg·a·ly (ăk'rō-mĕg'ə-lē) *n.* Pathological enlargement of the bones of the hands, feet, and face, resulting from chronic overactivity of the pituitary gland. [Fr. *acromégalie* : Gk. *akron,* extremity + Gk. *megas,* big.] **—ac'ro·me·gal'ic** (-mĭ-găl'ĭk) *adj. & n.*

ac·ro·mel·ic (ăk'rō-mĕl'ĭk) *adj.* Of, relating to, or pertinent to the end of the extremities. [ACRO- + Gk. *melos,* limb.]

a·cro·mi·on (ə-krō'mē-ən) *n.* The outer extremity of the scapula or shoulder blade. [NLat. < Gk. *akrōmion* : *akros,* extreme + *ōmion,* dim. of *ōmos,* shoulder.]

ac·ro·nym (ăk'rə-nĭm') *n.* A word formed from the initial letters of a name, as *WAC* for *W*omen's *A*rmy *C*orps, or by combining initial letters or parts of a series of words, as *radar* for *ra*dio *d*etecting *a*nd *r*anging. **—ac'ro·nym'ic, a·cron'y·mous** (ə-krŏn'ə-məs) *adj.*

a·crop·e·tal (ə-krŏp'ĭ-tl) *adj.* Developing upward toward the apex from the base, as do certain forms of inflorescence. **—a·crop'e·tal·ly** *adv.*

ac·ro·pho·bi·a (ăk'rə-fō'bē-ə) *n.* Abnormally intense fear of being in high places.

a·crop·o·lis (ə-krŏp'ə-lĭs) *n.* The fortified height or citadel of an ancient Greek city, esp. the citadel of Athens. [Gk. *akropolis* : *akron,* top + *polis,* city.]

ac·ro·spire (ăk'rə-spīr') *n.* The first sprout from a germinating grain seed. [Var. of dial. *akerspire* < ME : *acher,* ear of grain (< OE *æher*) + *spire,* shoot < OE *spīr.*]

a·cross (ə-krôs', ə-krŏs') *prep.* **1.** On, at, or from the other side of: *across the road.* **2.** So as to cross; over; through: *draw lines across the paper.* **3.** From one side of to the other: *a bridge across a river.* **4.** Into contact with: *came across her old roommate.* *—adv.* **1.** From one side to the other: *The bridge swayed when he ran across.* **2.** On or to the opposite side: *We came across by ferry.* **3.** Crossed; crosswise: *with arms across.* [ME *acrois* < AN *an croiz* : *an,* in + *croiz,* cross.]

a·cross-the-board (ə-krôs'*th*ə-bôrd', -bōrd', ə-krŏs'-) *adj.* **1.** Designating a racing wager whereby equal amounts are bet on the same contestant to win, place, or show. **2.** Including all categories or members, esp. in an occupation or industry: *an across-the-board wage increase.*

a·cros·tic (ə-krô'stĭk, ə-krŏs'tĭk) *n.* **1.** A poem or series of lines in which certain letters, usually the first in each line, form a name, motto, or message when read in sequence. **2.** A word square. [Fr. *acrostiche* < OFr. < Gk. *akrostikhis* : *akron,* end + *stikhos,* line.] **—a·cros'tic** *adj.* **—a·cros'ti·cal·ly** *adv.*

ac·ry·late resin also **acrylate** (ăk'rə-lāt') *n.* Any of a class of acrylic resins used in emulsion paints, adhesives, plastics, and textile and paper finishes.

a·cryl·ic (ə-krĭl'ĭk) *n.* **1.** Acrylic resin. **2.** Acrylic fiber. **3.** A paint containing acrylic resin. [ACR(OLEIN) + -YL + -IC.] **—a·cryl'ic** *adj.*

acrylic acid *n.* An easily polymerized, colorless, corrosive liquid, $H_2C{:}CHCOOH$, used as a monomer for acrylate resins.

acrylic fiber *n.* Any of numerous synthetic fibers polymerized from acrylonitrile.

acrylic resin *n.* Any of numerous thermoplastic or thermosetting polymers or copolymers of acrylic acid, methacrylic acid, esters of these acids, or acrylonitrile, used to produce synthetic rubbers and lightweight plastics.

ac·ry·lo·ni·trile (ăk'rə-lō-nī'trəl, -trēl', -trīl) *n.* A colorless, liquid organic compound, $H_2C{:}CHCN$, used in the manufacture of acrylic rubber and fibers. [ACRYL(IC RESIN) + NITRILE.]

act (ăkt) *n.* **1.** The process of doing or performing something; action: *the act of thinking.* **2.** Something that is done or performed; deed: *a charitable act.* **3.** An enactment, edict, or decree, as of a judicial or legislative body. **4.** A formal written record of proceedings or transactions. **5.** One of the major divisions or sections of a play or opera. **6.** A theatrical performance that forms part of a longer presentation: *a juggling act.* **7.** A manifestation of intentional or unintentional insincerity; pose: *put on an act.* *—v.* **act·ed, act·ing, acts.** *—tr.* **1.** To play the part of; assume the dramatic role of. **2.** To perform on the stage: *act a drama.* **3.** To behave like or pose as; impersonate: *act the fool.* **4.** To behave as suitable for: *Act your age.* *—intr.* **1.** To behave or comport oneself: *She acts like a lady.* **2. a.** To perform in a dramatic role or roles. **b.** To be suitable for theatrical performance: *This scene acts well.* **3.** To behave affectedly or unnaturally; pretend. **4.** To appear or seem to be: *The dog acted ferocious.* **5.** To carry out an action: *She acted immediately.* **6.** To operate or function in a specific way: *His mind acts quickly.* **7.** To serve or function as a substitute for someone or something: *A coin can act as a screwdriver.* **—phrasal verbs. act on** (or **upon**). **1.** To act according to: *He acted on my advice.* **2.** To produce an effect on. **act out. 1. a.** To perform in or as if in a play; dramatize: *act out a story.* **b.** To realize in action: *wanted to act out his theory.* **2.** *Psychoanal.* To express (unconscious impulses, for example) in an overt manner without awareness or understanding. **act up.** To misbehave or malfunction. [ME < OFr. *acte* < Lat. *actus,* a doing, and *actum,* a thing done, both < *agere,* to do.] **—ac'ta·bil'i·ty** *n.* **—act'a·ble** *adj.*

Usage: The nouns *act* and *action* are distinct in meaning. An *act* is the deed accomplished by means of an *action*; when Brutus killed Caesar, he committed the *act* of murder by means of the *action* of stabbing. We speak of a *stop-action movie camera* (i.e., one that can arrest physical motion), but a criminal is *caught in the act* (i.e., of committing a crime). A baseball pitcher may throw with an *unnatural action* (i.e., a physical movement difficult for the human arm); a parent who abandons a child performs an *unnatural act* (the deed is contrary to nature, not the series of activities with which it is performed).

Ac·tae·on (ăk-tē'ən) *n. Gk. Myth.* A young hunter who, having inadvertently observed Artemis while she was bathing, was turned by her into a stag and killed by his own dogs. [Lat. < Gk. *Aktaiōn.*]

ACTH (ā'sē'tē āch') *n.* A pituitary hormone synthesized or extracted from mammalian pituitaries for use in stimulating secretion of cortisone and other adrenal cortex hormones. [A(DRENO)C(ORTICO)T(ROPIC) H(ORMONE).]

ac·tin (ăk'tĭn) *n.* A muscle protein, active with myosin in muscular contraction. [Lat. *actus,* motion (< *agere,* to impel) + -IN.]

actin- *pref.* Variant of **actino-.**

ac·ti·nal (ăk'tĭ-nəl, ăk-tī'-) *adj.* Of or designating the part of a sea anemone or similar animal from which the tentacles or rays radiate. **—ac'ti·nal·ly** *adv.*

act·ing (ăk'tĭng) *adj.* **1.** Temporarily assuming the duties or authority of another. **2.** Containing directions for use in a dramatic performance. *—n.* **1.** The occupation of an actor. **2.** Performance as an actor. **3.** Simulated behavior; pretense.

ac·tin·i·a (ăk-tĭn'ē-ə) also **ac·tin·i·an** (-ən) *n., pl.* **-i·ae** (-ē-ē') also **-i·ans.** A sea anemone or a related animal. [NLat. *Actinia,* sea anemone genus < Gk. *aktis,* ray.]

ac·tin·ic (ăk-tĭn'ĭk) *adj.* Of or pertaining to actinism. **—ac·tin'i·cal·ly** *adv.*

actinic ray *n.* Photochemically active radiation, as of the sun.

ac·ti·nide (ăk'tə-nīd') *n.* Any of a series of chemically similar, mostly synthetic, radioactive elements with atomic numbers ranging from 89 (actinium) through 103 (lawrencium).

ac·ti·nism (ăk'tə-nĭz'əm) *n.* The intrinsic property in radiation that produces photochemical activity.

ac·tin·i·um (ăk-tĭn'ē-əm) *n. Symbol* **Ac** A radioactive element found in uranium ores, used in equilibrium with its decay products as a source of alpha rays. Its longest lived isotope is Ac 227 with a half-life of 21.7 years. Atomic number 89; melting point 1,050°C; boiling point (estimated) 3,200°C; specific gravity (calculated) 10.07; valence 3.

actino- or **actin-** *pref.* **1.** Radial in form: *actinoid.* **2.** Actinic radiation: *actinometer.* [< Gk. *aktis, aktin-,* ray.]

ac·ti·no·car·pous (ăk'tĭ-nō-kär'pəs) *adj.* Having fruit or flowers radiating from one point.

ac·tin·o·gen (ăk-tĭn'ə-jən) *n.* A radioactive element.

ac·ti·noid[1] (ăk'tə-noid') *adj.* Having a radial form, as a starfish.

ac·ti·noid[2] (ăk'tə-noid') *n.* An actinide.

ac·tin·o·lite (ăk-tĭn'ə-līt') *n.* A greenish variety of amphibole.

ac·ti·no·mere (ăk-tĭn'ə-mîr') *n.* A segment composing part of the body of a radially symmetrical animal.

ac·ti·nom·e·ter (ăk'tə-nŏm'ĭ-tər) *n.* Any of several radiometric instruments, such as a pyrheliometer, used chiefly for meteorological measurements of terrestrial and solar radiation. **—ac'ti·no·met'ric** (-nō-mĕt'rĭk), **ac'ti·no·met'ri·cal** *adj.* **—ac'ti·nom'e·try** *n.*

ac·ti·no·mor·phic (ăk'tə-nō-môr'fĭk) also **ac·ti·no·mor·phous** (-fəs) *adj.* Having radial symmetry; divisible vertically through two or more planes into similar halves.

ac·ti·no·my·cete (ăk'tə-nō-mī'sēt', -mī-sēt') *n.* Any of numerous generally filamentous and often pathogenic microorganisms of the family Actinomycetaceae, resembling both bacteria and fungi.

ac·ti·no·my·cin (ăk'tə-nō-mī'sĭn) *n.* Any of various often toxic antibiotic substances found in soil bacteria. [< NLat.

Antinomyces, a genus of soil bacteria : ACTINO- + Gk. *mukēs,* fungus.]

ac·ti·no·my·co·sis (ăk'tə-nō-mī-kō'sĭs) *n.* An inflammatory infection of cattle, hogs, and sometimes man, caused by microorganisms of the genus *Actinomyces,* and characterized by lumpy tumors of the neck, chest, and abdomen. **—ac'ti·no·my·cot'ic** (-kŏt'ĭk) *adj.*

ac·ti·non (ăk'tə-nŏn') *n.* A radioactive inert gaseous isotope of radon, with a half-life of 3.92 seconds.

ac·ti·no·u·ra·ni·um (ăk'tə-nō-yo͞o-rā'nē-əm) *n.* The isotope of uranium with mass number 235, fissionable with slow neutrons.

ac·ti·no·zo·an (ăk'tə-nō-zō'ən) *n.* An anthozoan.

ac·tion (ăk'shən) *n.* **1.** The state or process of acting or doing. **2.** An act or deed. **3.** A movement or a series of movements. **4.** The manner of movement: *a horse with good action.* **5.** Habitual or vigorous activity; energy: *a man of action.* **6.** Often **actions.** Behavior or conduct. **7. a.** The operating parts of a mechanism. **b.** The manner in which such parts operate. **8.** A change that occurs in the body or in a bodily organ as a result of its functioning. **9.** A physical change, as in position, mass, or energy, that an object or system undergoes. **10.** The series of events and episodes that form the plot of a story or play. **11.** The appearance of animation of a figure in painting or sculpture. **12.** *Law.* **a.** A judicial process; lawsuit. **b.** The right of an individual to exercise his privilege to legal process. **13.** Armed encounter; combat. **14.** The most important or exciting work or activity in a specific field or area: *always heads for where the action is.* —See Usage note at **act.**

ac·tion·a·ble (ăk'shə-nə-bəl) *adj.* Giving just cause for legal action. **—ac'tion·a·bly** *adv.*

action painting *n.* A style of abstract painting that uses techniques such as dribbling or splashing paint to achieve an effect of spontaneity.

action potential *n.* A recorded change in electrical potential of a cell or tissue when stimulated.

ac·ti·vate (ăk'tə-vāt') *tr.v.* **-vat·ed, -vat·ing, -vates. 1.** To set in motion; make active. **2.** To create or organize (a military unit, for example). **3.** To purify (sewage) by aeration. **4.** *Chem.* To accelerate a reaction in, as by heat. **5.** *Physics.* To make (a substance) radioactive. **—ac'ti·va'tion** *n.* **—ac'ti·va'tor** *n.*

activated carbon or **activated charcoal** *n.* Highly absorbent carbon obtained by heating granulated charcoal to exhaust contained gases, used in gas absorption, solvent recovery, or deodorization, and as an antidote to certain poisons.

activation analysis *n.* A method for analyzing a material for its component chemical elements by bombarding it with nuclear particles or gamma rays and identifying the resultant radiations.

ac·tive (ăk'tĭv) *adj.* **1.** In action; moving. **2.** Functioning or capable of functioning. **3.** Causing or initiating action or change. **4.** Engaged in activity; participating: *an active member of a club.* **5.** In a state of action; not passive or quiescent: *an active volcano.* **6.** Characterized by energetic action or activity; lively. **7.** *Gram.* **a.** Denoting a verb inflection or voice indicating that the subject of the sentence is performing or causing the action expressed by the verb. **b.** Expressing action rather than a state of being. Used of verbs such as *run, speak, move.* **8.** Producing profit, interest, or dividends: *active accounts.* **9.** On full military duty and full pay. **10.** *Mus.* Suggesting that something follows: *active tones.* —*n.* **1.** *Gram.* **a.** The active voice. **b.** A construction or form in the active voice. **2.** A participating member of an organization. [ME *actif* < OFr. < Lat. *activus* < *actus,* moving, p.part. of *agere,* to impel.] **—ac'tive·ly** *adv.* **—ac'tive·ness** *n.*

Synonyms: *active, energetic, dynamic, vigorous, lively.* These adjectives are compared as they qualify human activity. *Active* suggests a moving to and fro with little rest; *energetic,* sustained enthusiastic action with unflagging strength; and *dynamic,* exemplary forcefulness of activity inspiring to others. *Vigorous* implies manly capacity to act with healthy strength and firmness, while *lively* suggests brisk alertness and energy.

active immunity *n.* A long-lasting immunity to disease due to antibody production by an organism.

active transport *n.* The movement of a chemical substance through a gradient of concentration or electrical potential in the direction opposite to normal diffusion, requiring the expenditure of energy.

ac·tiv·ism (ăk'tə-vĭz'əm) *n.* A theory or practice based on militant action. **—ac'tiv·ist** *n.*

ac·tiv·i·ty (ăk-tĭv'ĭ-tē) *n., pl.* **-ties. 1.** The state of being active. **2.** Energetic action or movement. **3.** A specified form of supervised action or field of action. **4.** The intensity of a radioactive source.

act of God *n. Law.* An unforeseeable or inevitable occurrence, such as a tornado, caused by nature and not by man.

ac·to·my·o·sin (ăk'tə-mī'ə-sĭn) *n.* A system of actin and myosin that with other substances constitutes muscle fiber and is responsible for muscular contraction and expansion. [ACT(IN) + MYOSIN.]

ac·tor (ăk'tər) *n.* **1.** A male theatrical performer. **2.** One who takes part; participant. [ME *actour* < Lat. *actor,* doer < *agere,* to do.]

ac·tress (ăk'trĭs) *n.* A female theatrical performer.

Acts of the Apostles *n.* See table at **Bible.**

ac·tu·al (ăk'cho͞o-əl) *adj.* **1.** Existing in fact or reality: *questioned her actual intentions.* **2.** Being, existing, or acting at the present moment; current. **3.** Corresponding to all human facts. **4.** Based on fact: *an actual account.* [ME < OFr. *actuel* < Lat. *actualis* < *actus,* acting < *agere,* to do.] **—ac'tu·al·ly** *adv.*

ac·tu·al·i·ty (ăk'cho͞o-ăl'ĭ-tē) *n., pl.* **-ties. 1.** The state or fact of being actual; reality. **2. actualities.** Actual conditions or facts.

ac·tu·al·ize (ăk'cho͞o-ə-līz') *tr.v.* **-ized, -iz·ing, -iz·es. 1.** To realize in action. **2.** To describe or portray realistically. **—ac'tu·al·i·za'tion** *n.*

ac·tu·ar·y (ăk'cho͞o-ĕr'ē) *n., pl.* **-ies.** A statistician who computes insurance risks and premiums. [Lat. *actuarius,* secretary of accounts < *acta,* records < *actus,* p.part. of *agere,* to do.] **—ac'tu·ar'i·al** *adj.* **—ac'tu·ar'i·al·ly** *adv.*

ac·tu·ate (ăk'cho͞o-āt') *tr.v.* **-at·ed, -at·ing, -ates. 1.** To put into action or motion: *actuate a mechanism.* **2.** To move to action. [Med. Lat. *actuare, actuat-* < Lat. *actus,* act < *agere,* to do.] **—ac'tu·a'tion** *n.*

ac·tu·a·tor (ăk'cho͞o-ā'tər) *n.* One that activates, esp. a device responsible for actuating a mechanical device, as one connected to a computer by a sensor link.

ac·u·ate (ăk'yo͞o-āt') *adj.* Pointed at the end; sharpened. [ME *acuat* < Med. Lat. *acuatus* < Lat. *acus,* needle.]

a·cu·i·ty (ə-kyo͞o'ĭ-tē) *n.* Acuteness of perception; keenness. [ME *acuite* < OFr. < Lat. *acutus,* sharp. —see ACUTE.]

a·cu·le·ate (ə-kyo͞o'lē-ĭt, -āt') *adj. Biol.* Having a sting or prickles: *aculeate insects.* [Lat. *aculeatus* < *aculeus,* sting, dim. of *acus,* needle.]

a·cu·men (ə-kyo͞o'mən) *n.* Quickness and accuracy of judgment; keenness of insight. [Lat. *acumen* < *acuere,* to sharpen < *acus,* needle.]

a·cu·mi·nate (ə-kyo͞o'mə-nĭt, -nāt') *adj.* Tapering to a sharp point: *acuminate leaves.* —*tr.v.* (ə-kyo͞o'mə-nāt') **-nat·ed, -nat·ing, -nates.** To sharpen or taper. [Lat. *acuminatus,* p.part. of *acuminare,* to sharpen < *acumen,* acuteness. —see ACUMEN.] **—a·cu'mi·na'tion** *n.*

ac·u·punc·ture (ăk'yo͞o-pŭngk'chər) *n.* A traditional Chinese therapeutic technique whereby the body is punctured with fine needles. [Lat. *acus,* needle + PUNCTURE.] **—ac'u·punc'tur·ist** *n.*

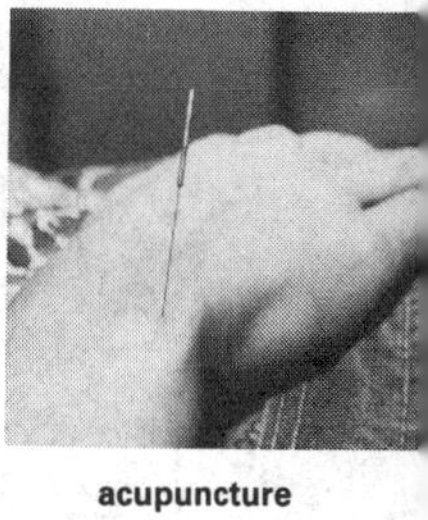

acupuncture

a·cute (ə-kyo͞ot') *adj.* **1.** Having a sharp point or tip; not blunt. **2.** Keenly perceptive or discerning; shrewd. **3.** Reacting readily to impressions; sensitive. **4.** Of great importance or consequence; crucial. **5.** Extremely severe or sharp; intense: *acute pain.* **6.** *Med.* Reaching a crisis rapidly. Used of a disease. **7.** *Mus.* High in pitch; shrill. **8.** *Geom.* Designating angles less than 90 degrees. [Lat. *acutus,* p.part. of *acuere,* to sharpen < *acus,* needle.] **—a·cute'ly** *adv.* **—a·cute'ness** *n.*

acute accent *n.* A mark (′) indicating: **a.** A raised pitch, in certain languages such as Chinese and Ancient Greek. **b.** Primary stress of a spoken sound or syllable. **c.** Metrical stress in poetry. **d.** Sound quality or vowel length.

a·cy·clic (ā-sī'klĭk, ā-sĭk'lĭk) *adj.* **1.** *Bot.* Not having or forming whorls; not cyclic. **2.** *Chem.* Having an open-chain molecular structure rather than a ring-shaped structure.

ac·yl (ăs'əl) *n. Chem.* A radical having the general formula RCO-, derived from an organic acid. [AC(ID) + -YL.]

ad[1] (ăd) *n. Informal.* An advertisement.

ad[2] (ăd) *n.* An advantage (sense 4).

ad– *pref.* **1.** or **ac-** or **af-** or **ag-** or **al-** or **ap-** or **as-** or **at-.** Toward; to: *adnoun.* **2.** Near; at: *adrenal.* **3.** In: *adumbrel.* [Lat. < *ad,* to.]

-ad *suff.* Toward; in the direction of: *cephalad.*

ad·age (ăd'ĭj) *n.* A short maxim or proverb. [Fr. < OFr. < Lat. *adagium,* proverb.]

a·da·gio (ə-dä'jō, -jē-ō', -zhō, -zhē-ō) *adv. Mus.* Slowly. Used as a direction. —*adj. Mus.* Slow in tempo; slower than andante. —*n., pl.* **-agios. 1.** *Mus.* A composition or movement played in an adagio tempo. **2.** A section of a pas de deux in which the ballerina and her partner perform steps requiring lyricism and great skill in lifting, balancing, and turning. [Ital. : *ad-,* at (< Lat.) + *agio,* ease < OProv. *aize* < Lat. *adjacens,* convenient. —see ADJACENT.]

Ad·am[1] (ăd'əm) *n.* **1.** In the Old Testament, the first man and progenitor of mankind. **2.** The unregenerate side of human nature: *the old Adam.* [LLat. < Heb. *'adhām,* man < *'adhāmāh,* earth.] **—A·dam'ic** (ə-dăm'ĭk) *adj.*

Ad·am[2] (ăd'əm) *adj.* Of or pertaining to the neoclassic style of furniture and architecture originated by Robert and James Adam.

Adam[1]
Early 16th-century illustration of Adam and Eve being tempted by the serpent

Ad·am-and-Eve (ăd'əm-ənd-ēv') *n.* The puttyroot. [From its human-shaped corms.]

ad·a·mant (ăd'ə-mənt, -mănt') *n.* **1.** A legendary stone believed to be impenetrable. **2.** An extremely hard substance. —*adj.* Firm in purpose or opinion; unyielding. [ME < OFr. *adamaunt* < Lat. *adamas* < Gk.]

ad·a·man·tine (ăd'ə-măn'tēn', -tīn', -tĭn') *adj.* **1.** Made of or resembling adamant. **2.** Having the hardness or luster of a diamond. **3.** Unyielding or inflexible.

addax

adder[2]

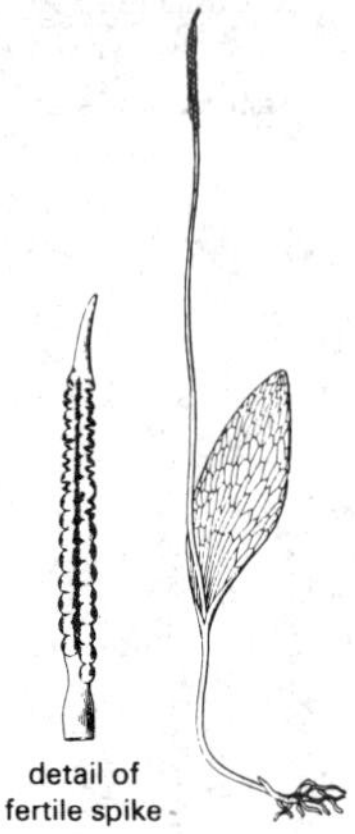

adder's-tongue

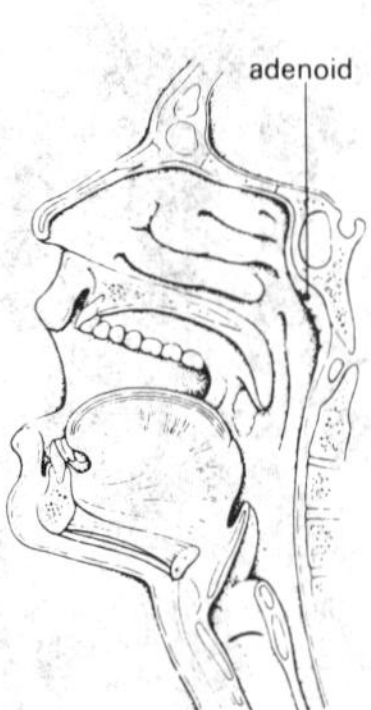

adenoid

Ad·am's apple (ăd′əmz) *n.* The projection of the largest laryngeal cartilage at the front of the throat, esp. in men. [Trans. of Heb. *tappūah hāādām.*]

Adam's needle *n.* The Spanish bayonet (sense 2). [From the spines on its leaves.]

a·dapt (ə-dăpt′) *v.* **a·dapt·ed, a·dapt·ing, a·dapts.** —*tr.* To adjust to a specified use or situation. —*intr.* To become adapted. [Lat. *adaptare* : *ad-*, to + *aptare,* to fit < *aptus,* fitting.]

a·dapt·a·ble (ə-dăp′tə-bəl) *adj.* Capable of adapting or of being adapted. **—a·dapt′a·bil′i·ty, a·dapt′a·ble·ness** *n.*

ad·ap·ta·tion (ăd′ăp-tā′shən) *n.* **1. a.** The state of being adapted. **b.** The act or process of adapting. **2.** Something that is changed or changes so as to become suitable to a new or special use or situation. **3.** An alteration or adjustment, often hereditary, by which a species or individual improves its condition in relationship to its environment. **4.** The responsive alteration of a sense organ to repeated stimuli. **5.** Change in behavior of an individual or group in adjustment to new or modified cultural surroundings. **—ad′ap·ta′tion·al** *adj.* **—ad′ap·ta′tion·al·ly** *adv.*

a·dapt·er also **a·dap·tor** (ə-dăp′tər) *n.* **1.** One that adapts. **2.** A device used to effect operative compatibility between different parts of one or more pieces of apparatus.

a·dap·tion (ə-dăp′shən) *n.* Adaptation.

a·dap·tive (ə-dăp′tĭv) *adj.* Tending toward, fit for, or having a capacity for adaptation. **—a·dap′tive·ly** *adv.* **—a·dap′tive·ness** *n.*

adaptive radiation *n.* The evolution of a relatively unspecialized species into several related species characterized by different specializations that fit them for life in various environments.

A·dar (ä-där′) *n.* The sixth month of the year in the Hebrew calendar. See table at **calendar**. [ME < Heb. *Adhār* < Akkadian *addaru* < *adāru,* to be dark.]

Adar She·ni (shā-nē′) *n.* Veadar. [Heb. *Adhār shēnī,* second Adar.]

ad·ax·i·al (ăd-ăk′sē-əl) *adj.* Of, relating to, or being on the side toward the stem or axis.

add (ăd) *v.* **add·ed, add·ing, adds.** —*tr.* **1.** To join or unite so as to increase in size, quantity, or scope. **2.** To combine (a column of figures, for example) to form a sum. **3.** To say or write further. —*intr.* **1.** To create or constitute an addition: *an exploit that will add to her reputation.* **2.** To find a sum in arithmetic. ***—phrasal verbs.* add up.** *Informal.* To be reasonable, plausible, or consistent; make sense. **add up to.** *Informal.* To mean; indicate. [ME *adden* < Lat. *addere* : *ad-*, to + *dare,* to give.] **—add′a·ble, add′i·ble** *adj.*

ad·dax (ăd′ăks′) *n.* An antelope, *Addax nasomaculatus,* of northern Africa having long, spirally twisted horns. [Lat., of African orig.]

add·ed-val·ue tax (ăd′ĭd-văl′yo͞o) *n.* Value-added tax.

ad·dend (ăd′ĕnd′, ə-dĕnd′) *n.* Any of a set of numbers to be added. [Short for ADDENDUM.]

ad·den·dum (ə-dĕn′dəm) *n., pl.* **-da** (-də). Something added or to be added, esp. a supplement to a book. [Lat. < *addere,* to add.]

add·er[1] (ăd′ər) *n.* One that adds, esp. a computer device that performs arithmetic addition.

ad·der[2] (ăd′ər) *n.* **1.** Any of various venomous Old World snakes of the family Viperidae, esp. the common viper, *Vipera berus,* of Eurasia. **2.** Any of several nonvenomous snakes popularly believed to be harmful. [ME < *an addre,* alteration of *a naddre* : *a,* a + *naddre,* snake < OE *nædre.*]

ad·der's-mouth (ăd′ərz-mouth′) *n.* Any of various orchids of the genus *Malaxis,* having clusters of small, usually greenish flowers. [From the resemblance of its flowers to the open mouths of snakes.]

ad·der's-tongue (ăd′ərz-tŭng′) *n.* **1.** Any of several ferns of the genus *Ophioglossum,* having a single sterile, leaflike frond, and a spore-bearing stalk. **2.** The dogtooth violet. [From the resemblance of the spike at the base of the frond to a snake's tongue.]

ad·dict (ə-dĭkt′) *tr.v.* **-dict·ed, -dict·ing, -dicts.** To devote or give (oneself) habitually or compulsively: *addicted to alcohol.* —*n.* (ăd′ĭkt). **1.** One who is addicted, esp. to narcotics. **2.** A devoted fan: *a soap opera addict.* [< Lat. *addictus,* bondsman, p.part of *addicere,* to sentence : *ad-*, to + *dicere,* to adjudge.] **—ad·dic′tion** *n.* **—ad·dic′tive** *adj.*

Ad·di·son's disease (ăd′ĭ-sənz) *n.* A disease caused by failure of the adrenal cortex to function, marked by a bronzelike skin pigmentation, anemia, and prostration. [After Thomas *Addison* (1793–1860), its discoverer.]

ad·di·tion (ə-dĭsh′ən) *n.* **1.** The act or process of adding. **2.** Something added, esp. a room or section added to a building. **3.** The process of computing with sets of numbers so as to find their sum. ***—idioms.* in addition.** Also; as well as. **in addition to.** Over and above; besides. [ME < OFr. < Lat. *additio* < *additus,* p.part. of *addere,* to add.] **—ad·di′tion·al** *adj.* **—ad·di′tion·al·ly** *adv.*

ad·di·tive (ăd′ĭ-tĭv) *adj.* Marked by, produced by, or involving addition. —*n.* A substance added in small amounts to something else to improve, strengthen, or otherwise alter it.

additive identity *n.* An identity element that in a given mathematical system leaves unchanged any element to which it is added.

additive identity element *n.* Zero.

additive inverse *n.* Inverse (sense 2.b.).

ad·dle (ăd′l) *v.* **-dled, -dling, -dles.** —*tr.* To muddle; confuse: *"My brain is a bit addled by whiskey"* (O'Neill). —*intr.* **1.** To become rotten; spoil. **2.** To become confused. —*adj.* **1.** Mixed up; confused: *addle-brained.* **2.** Spoiled or rotten. [< ME *adel,* muddled < OE, filth.]

ad·dress (ə-drĕs′) *tr.v.* **-dressed, -dress·ing, -dress·es. 1.** To speak to. **2.** To make a formal speech to. **3.** To direct (a spoken or written message) to the attention of: *address a protest to the Council.* **4.** To mark with a destination: *address a letter.* **5. a.** To direct (oneself) in speech to. **b.** To direct the efforts or attention of (oneself): *address oneself to a task.* **6.** To dispatch or consign (a ship, for example) to an agent or factor. **7.** To adjust and aim the club at (a golf ball) in preparing for a stroke. —*n.* (ə-drĕs′). **1.** A formal spoken or written communication: *polite forms of address.* **2.** A formal speech. **3.** *(also* ăd′rĕs′). The written or printed indication on mail or other deliverable items indicating destination. **4.** *(also* ăd′rĕs′).The location at which a particular organization or person may be found or reached. **5.** Often **addresses.** Courteous attentions; wooing. **6.** The manner or bearing of a person, esp. in conversation. **7.** Skillfulness or tact in handling a situation. **8.** The act of dispatching or consigning a ship, as to an agent or factor. **9.** *Computer Sci.* A number used in information storage or retrieval that is assigned to a specific memory location. [ME *adressen* < OFr. *adresser* : *a-*, to (< Lat. *ad-*) + *dresser,* to arrange. — see DRESS.]

ad·dress·a·ble (ə-drĕs′ə-bəl) *adj.* Accessible through an address, as in computer memory.

ad·dress·ee (ăd′rĕ-sē′, ə-drĕs′ē′) *n.* One to whom something is addressed.

ad·dress·er also **ad·dres·sor** (ə-drĕs′ər) *n.* A person who or a machine that addresses.

ad·duce (ə-do͞os′, ə-dyo͞os′) *tr.v.* **-duced, -duc·ing, -duc·es.** To cite as an example or means of proof in an argument; bring forward for consideration. [Lat. *adducere,* to bring to : *ad-*, to + *ducere,* to lead.] **—ad·duce′a·ble, ad·duc′i·ble** *adj.*

ad·duct (ə-dŭkt′, ă-) *tr.v.* **-duct·ed, -duct·ing, -ducts.** *Physiol.* To pull or draw toward the main axis. Used of muscles. [Back-formation from ADDUCTOR.] **—ad·duc′tion** *n.* **—ad·duc′tive** *adj.*

ad·duc·tor (ə-dŭk′tər) *n.* A muscle that adducts. [NLat. < Lat. *adducere,* to bring to. —see ADDUCE.]

-ade *suff.* A sweetened beverage of: *limeade.* [Fr., ult. < Lat. *-ata,* fem. of *-atus,* -ate.]

A·dé·lie penguin (ə-dā′lē) *n.* A common Antarctic penguin, *Pygoscelis adeliae,* of medium size, that has white underparts and a black back and head, and that lives and breeds in large exposed rookeries. [After the *Adélie* Coast, Antarctica.]

-adelphous *suff.* Having one or more groups of stamens: *diadelphous.* [NLat. *-adelphus* < Gk. *adelphos,* brother.]

a·demp·tion (ə-dĕmp′shən) *n. Law.* The disposal by a testator of specific property bequeathed in his will so as to invalidate the bequest. [Lat. *ademptio,* a taking away < *adimere,* to take away : *ad-*, to + *emere,* to take.]

aden- *pref.* Variant of **adeno-**.

ad·e·nec·to·my (ăd′n-ĕk′tə-mē) *n.* Surgical excision of a gland.

ad·e·nine (ăd′n-ēn′) *n.* A purine derivative, $C_5H_5N_5$, that is a constituent of nucleic acid in organs, as the pancreas and spleen.

ad·e·ni·tis (ăd′n-ī′tĭs) *n.* Inflammation of a lymph node or gland.

adeno- or **aden-** *pref.* Gland: *adenectomy.* [< Gk. *adēn.*]

ad·e·no·car·ci·no·ma (ăd′n-ō-kär′sə-nō′mə) *n.* A malignant tumor originating in glandular tissue. **—ad′e·no·car′ci·nom′a·tous** (-nŏm′ə-təs, -nō′mə-təs) *adj.*

ad·e·no·hy·poph·y·sis (ăd′n-ō-hī-pŏf′ĭ-sĭs) *n.* The anterior and intermediate glandular lobes of the pituitary gland. **—ad′e·no·hy·poph′y·se·al, ad′e·no·hy·poph′y·si·al** *adj.*

ad·e·noid (ăd′n-oid′) *n.* Lymphoid tissue growth in the nose above the throat that when swollen may obstruct nasal breathing, induce postnasal discharge, and make speech difficult.

ad·e·noi·dal (ăd′n-oid′l) *adj.* **1.** Glandlike; glandular. **2.** Of or pertaining to the adenoids. **3 a.** Having a nasal or constricted tone: *an adenoidal singer.* **b.** Mouth-breathing or gaping.

ad·e·no·ma (ăd′n-ō′mə) *n.* An epithelial tumor of glandular origin and structure that is usually benign or of low-grade malignancy. **—ad′e·nom′a·tous** (-ŏm′ə-təs) *adj.*

a·den·o·sine (ə-dĕn′ə-sēn′) *n.* An organic compound, $C_{10}H_{13}N_5O_4$, that is a structural component of nucleic acids. [Blend of ADENINE and RIBOSE.]

adenosine di·phos·phate (dī-fŏs′fāt′) *n.* ADP.

adenosine mon·o·phos·phate (mŏn′ō-fŏs′fāt′) *n.* **1.** Cyclic AMP. **2.** AMP.

adenosine triphosphate *n.* ATP.

ad·e·no·vi·rus (ăd′n-ō-vī′rəs) *n.* Any of various animal viruses that cause respiratory diseases, as catarrh, in humans. **—ad′e·no·vi′ral** *adj.*

a·den·yl·ate cy·clase (ə-dĕn′l-ĭt sī′klās, ăd′n-ĭl′ĭt) or **ad·e·nyl cyclase** (ăd′n-ĭl) *n.* The enzyme that catalyzes formation of cyclic AMP from ATP. [ADEN(INE) + -YL + -ATE[1] + CYCL- + -ASE.]

a·dept (ə-dĕpt′) *adj.* Highly skilled or proficient. —*n.* (ăd′ĕpt′). A highly skilled person; expert. [Lat. *adeptus,* p.part. of *adipisci,* to arrive at.] **—a·dept′ly** *adv.* **—a·dept′ness** *n.*

ad·e·quate (ăd′ĭ-kwĭt) *adj.* **1.** Able to satisfy a requirement; suitable. **2.** Barely satisfactory or sufficient. [Lat. *adaequatus,* p.part. of *adaequare,* to equalize : *ad-,* to + *aequare,* to make equal < *aequus,* equal.] **—ad′e·qua·cy** (-kwə-sē), **ad′e·quate·ness** *n.* **—ad′e·quate·ly** *adv.*

à deux (ä′ dœ′) *adj.* Of or involving two individuals, esp. when of a private or intimate nature. —*adv.* Privately with only two individuals involved: *dining à deux.* [Fr.]

ad·here (ăd-hîr′) *intr.v.* **-hered, -her·ing, -heres. 1.** To stick fast or together by or as if by grasping, suction, or being glued. **2.** To be devoted as a follower or supporter. **3.** To follow closely; carry out without deviation: *adhere to a plan.* [Fr. *adhérer* < Lat. *adhaerere,* to stick to : *ad-,* to + *haerere,* to stick.]

ad·her·ence (ăd-hîr′əns) *n.* **1.** The process or condition of adhering. **2.** Faithful attachment; devotion.

ad·her·ent (ăd-hîr′ənt) *adj.* **1.** Sticking or holding fast. **2.** *Bot.* Growing or fused together; adnate. —*n.* A supporter, as of a cause or individual. **—ad·her′ent·ly** *adv.*

ad·he·sion (ăd-hē′zhən) *n.* **1.** The act or state of adhering. **2.** Attachment or devotion; loyalty. **3.** Assent or agreement. **4.** A condition in which bodily tissues that are normally separate are joined together. **5.** The physical attraction or joining of two substances, esp. the macroscopically observable attraction of dissimilar substances. **6.** A fibrous band holding together normally separate anatomical structures. **7.** The pathological aggregation of dissimilar body materials to a visceral surface due to inflammation or trauma. [Fr. *adhésion* < Lat. *adhaesio* < *adhaerere,* to adhere.]

ad·he·si·o·to·my (ăd-hē′zē-ŏt′ə-mē) *n., pl.* **-mies.** The surgical division of adhesions.

ad·he·sive (ăd-hē′sĭv, -zĭv) *adj.* **1.** Tending to adhere; sticky. **2.** Gummed so as to adhere. —*n.* An adhesive substance, such as paste or cement. **—ad·he′sive·ly** *adv.* **—ad·he′sive·ness** *n.*

adhesive tape *n.* A tape lined on one side with an adhesive.

ad hoc (ăd hŏk′, hōk′) *adj. & adv.* For a specific purpose, case, or situation: *an ad hoc committee.* [Lat., to this.]

ad hom·i·nem (ăd hŏm′ə-nĕm′) *adj. & adv.* To the man; appealing to personal interests, prejudices, or emotions rather than to reason: *an ad hominem argument.* [Lat.]

ad·i·a·bat·ic (ăd′ē-ə-băt′ĭk, ā′dī-ə-) *adj.* Of, pertaining to, or designating a reversible thermodynamic process executed at constant entropy; loosely, occurring without gain or loss of heat. [Gk. *adiabatos,* impassable : *a-,* not + *diabatos,* passable (*dia,* through + *batos,* passable < *bainein,* to go).] **—ad′i·a·bat′i·cal·ly** *adv.*

a·dieu (ə-dyo͞o′, ə-do͞o′) *interj.* Good-by; farewell. —*n., pl.* **a·dieus** or **a·dieux** (ə-dyo͞oz′, ə-do͞oz′). A farewell. [ME < OFr. *a dieu,* (I commend you) to God : *a,* to (< Lat. *ad*) + *Dieu,* God < Lat. *deus.*]

ad in·fi·ni·tum (ăd ĭn′fə-nī′təm) *adj. & adv.* To infinity; without end; limitless. [Lat.]

ad in·ter·im (ăd ĭn′tər-əm) *adj. & adv.* In the meantime; meanwhile. [Lat.]

ad·i·os (ăd′ē-ōs′, ä′dē-) *interj.* Good-by; farewell. [Sp. *adiós* : *a,* to (< Lat. *ad*) + *Dios,* God < Lat. *deus.*]

ad·i·po·cere (ăd′ə-pō-sîr′) *n.* A brown, fatty, waxlike substance that forms on dead animal tissues in response to moisture. [ADIPO(SE) + Lat. *cera,* wax.]

ad·i·pose (ăd′ə-pōs′) *adj.* Of or related to animal fat; fatty. —*n.* The fat found in adipose tissue. [NLat. *adiposus* < Lat. *adeps,* lard.] **—ad′i·pose′ness, ad′i·pos′i·ty** (-pŏs′ĭ-tē) *n.*

adipose tissue *n.* Connective tissue in the body that contains stored cellular fat.

ad·it (ăd′ĭt) *n.* An almost horizontal entrance to a mine. [Lat. *aditus,* access < *adire,* to approach : *ad-,* toward + *ire,* to go.]

ad·ja·cen·cy (ə-jā′sən-sē) *n., pl.* **-cies. 1.** The state of being adjacent; contiguity. **2.** A thing that is adjacent.

ad·ja·cent (ə-jā′sənt) *adj.* **1.** Close to; lying near. **2.** Next to; adjoining. [ME < Lat. *adjacens,* pr.part. of *adjacēre,* to lie near : *ad-,* near to + *jacēre,* to lie.] **—ad·ja′cent·ly** *adv.*

adjacent angle *n.* Either of two angles having a common side and a common vertex.

ad·jec·ti·val (ăj′ĭk-tī′vəl) *adj.* Of, pertaining to, or functioning as an adjective. **—ad′jec·ti′val·ly** *adv.*

ad·jec·tive (ăj′ĭk-tĭv) *n.* **1.** *Gram.* Any of a class of words used to modify a noun or other substantive by limiting, qualifying, or specifying. **2.** *Ling.* Any of a form class distinguished in English morphologically by one of several suffixes, as *-able, -ous, -er,* and *-est,* or syntactically by position in a phrase or sentence, as *white* in *a white house.* **3.** A dependent or subordinate. [ME < OFr. *adjectif* < Lat. *adjectivus* < *adjicere,* to add to : *ad-,* to + *jacere,* to throw.] **—ad′jec·tive·ly** *adv.*

adjective pronoun *n. Gram.* A pronoun acting as an adjective, as *which* in *which dictionaries?* or *himself* in *He himself said so.*

ad·join (ə-join′) *v.* **-joined, -join·ing, -joins.** —*tr.* **1.** To be next to; be contiguous to. **2.** To attach to; unite. —*intr.* To be contiguous. [ME *ajoinen* < OFr. *ajoindre* < Lat. *adjungere,* to join to : *ad-,* to + *jungere,* to join.]

ad·join·ing (ə-joi′nĭng) *adj.* Neighboring; contiguous; next to.

ad·journ (ə-jûrn′) *v.* **-journed, -journ·ing, -journs.** —*tr.* To suspend until a later stated time. —*intr.* **1.** To suspend proceedings to another time or place. **2.** *Informal.* To move from one place to another: *adjourned to the living room.* [ME *ajournen* < OFr. *ajourner* : *a,* to (< Lat. *ad*) + *jour,* day < Lat. *diurnum.*] **—ad·journ′ment** *n.*

ad·judge (ə-jŭj′) *tr.v.* **-judged, -judg·ing, -judg·es. 1.** To determine or decide by judicial procedure; adjudicate. **2.** To order judicially; rule. **3.** To award (damages, for example) by law. **4.** To regard, consider, or deem. [ME *ajugen* < OFr. *ajuger* < Lat. *adjudicare.* —see ADJUDICATE.]

ad·ju·di·cate (ə-jo͞o′dĭ-kāt′) *tr.v.* **-cat·ed, -cat·ing, -cates.** To hear and settle (a case) by judicial procedure. [Lat. *adjudicare, adjudicat-,* to award to (judicially) : *ad-,* to + *judicare,* to judge < *judex,* judge.] **—ad·ju′di·ca′tion** *n.* **—ad·ju′di·ca′tive** *adj.* **—ad·ju′di·ca′tor** *n.*

ad·junct (ăj′ŭngkt′) *n.* **1.** Something attached to another thing but in a dependent or subordinate position. **2.** A person associated with another in some duty or service in a subordinate or auxiliary capacity. **3.** A word or words added in order to clarify, qualify, or modify other words. **4.** *Logic.* A nonessential attribute of a thing. —*adj.* **1.** Added or connected in a subordinate or auxiliary capacity: *an adjunct clause.* **2.** Attached to a faculty or staff in a temporary or auxiliary capacity. [Lat. *adjunctum* < *adjunctus,* p.part. of *adjungere,* to join to. —see ADJOIN.] **—ad·junc′tion** (ə-jŭngk′shən) *n.* **—ad·junc′tive** *adj.*

ad·ju·ra·tion (ăj′ə-rā′shən) *n.* An earnest or solemn appeal. **—ad·jur′a·to′ry** (ə-jo͝or′ə-tôr′ē, -tōr′ē) *adj.*

ad·jure (ə-jo͝or′) *tr.v.* **-jured, -jur·ing, -jures. 1.** To command or enjoin solemnly, as under oath. **2.** To appeal to or entreat earnestly. [ME *adjuren* < Lat. *adjurare,* to swear to : *ad-,* to + *jurare,* to swear.] **—ad·jur′er, ad·ju′ror** *n.*

ad·just (ə-jŭst′) *v.* **-just·ed, -just·ing, -justs.** —*tr.* **1.** To change so as to match or fit; cause to correspond. **2.** To bring into proper relationship. **3.** To adapt or conform, as to new conditions: *unable to adjust themselves to their environment.* **4.** To make accurate by regulation. **5.** To decide how much is to be paid on (an insurance claim). **6.** To correct (the range and direction of a gun) in firing. —*intr.* To adapt oneself; become suited or fit; conform. [Obs. Fr. *adjuster* < OFr. *ajoster* : Lat. *ad,* to + Lat. *juxta,* near.] **—ad·just′a·ble** *adj.* **—ad·just′a·bly** *adv.* **—ad·just′er, ad·jus′tor** *n.*

ad·just·ment (ə-jŭst′mənt) *n.* **1. a.** The act of making fit or conformable. **b.** The condition of being adjusted. **2.** A means for adjusting. **3.** The settlement of a debt or claim. **4.** A modification or correction: *an adjustment on a bill.*

ad·ju·tant (ăj′ə-tənt) *n.* **1.** A staff officer who helps a commanding officer with administrative affairs. **2.** An assistant. **3.** The marabou. [Lat. *adjutans, adjutant-,* pr.part. of *adjutare,* freq. of *adjuvare,* to help : *ad-,* to + *juvare,* to help.] **—ad′ju·tan·cy** (-tən-sē) *n.*

adjutant general *n., pl.* **adjutants general. 1.** An adjutant of a unit having a general staff. **2.** An officer in charge of the National Guard of one of the states of the United States. **3.** **Adjutant General.** The chief administrative officer, a major general, of the U.S. Army.

adjutant stork *n.* The marabou.

ad·ju·vant (ăj′ə-vənt) *n.* **1.** A pharmacological agent added to a drug to increase or aid its effect. **2.** An immunological agent that increases the antigenic response. [Lat. *adjuvans, adjuvant-,* pr.part. of *adjuvare,* to help. —see AID.]

Ad·le·ri·an (ăd-lîr′ē-ən) *adj.* Of or relating to a psychological school holding that behavior arises in subconscious efforts to compensate for inferiority or deficiency and that neurosis results from overcompensation. [After Alfred *Adler* (1870–1937).]

ad lib (ăd lĭb′) *adv.* In an unrestrained manner; freely; spontaneously. [Short for AD LIBITUM.]

ad-lib (ăd-lĭb′) *Informal.* —*v.* **-libbed, -lib·bing, -libs.** —*tr.* To improvise and deliver extemporaneously. —*intr.* To improvise, as a speech; extemporize. —*n.* Words, music, or actions ad-libbed. —*adj.* Spoken or performed spontaneously. **—ad-lib′ber** *n.*

ad lib·i·tum (ăd lĭb′ĭ-təm) *adj. Mus.* Performed with freedom. Used as a direction. [Lat. *ad,* to + *libitum,* pleasure.]

ad·man (ăd′măn′) *n. Informal.* A person employed in the advertising business.

ad·meas·ure (ăd-mĕzh′ər) *tr.v.* **-ured, -ur·ing, -ures.** To divide and distribute proportionally; apportion. [ME *amesuren* < OFr. *amesurer* : *a,* to (< Lat. *ad*) + *mesurer,* to measure.] **—ad·meas′ure·ment** *n.* **—ad·meas′ur·er** *n.*

Ad·me·tus (ăd-mē′təs) *n. Gk. Myth.* A king of Thessaly and husband of Alcestis. [Lat. < Gk. *Admētos.*]

ad·min·is·ter (ăd-mĭn′ĭ-stər) *v.* **-tered, -ter·ing, -ters.** —*tr.* **1.** To have charge of; manage. **2. a.** To give or apply in a formal way: *administer the last rites.* **b.** To apply as a remedy: *administer a sedative.* **3.** To mete out; dispense: *administer justice.* **4.** To manage or dispose of (a trust or estate) under a will or an official appointment. **5.** To impose, offer, or tender (an oath, for example). —*intr.* **1.** To manage as an administrator. **2.** To minister: *administering to their every*

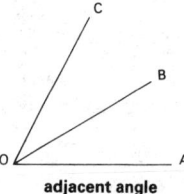

adjacent angle
AOB and BOC are adjacent angles

pleasure. [ME *administren* < OFr. *administrer* < Lat. *administrare* : *ad,* to + *ministrare,* to manage.] **—ad·min'is·tra·ble** *adj.* **—ad·min'is·trant** *adj. & n.*

ad·min·is·trate (ăd-mĭn'ĭ-strāt') *tr.v.* **-trat·ed, -trat·ing, -trates.** To administer.

ad·min·is·tra·tion (ăd-mĭn'ĭ-strā'shən) *n.* **1.** The management of affairs. **2.** The activity of a sovereign state in the exercise of its powers or duties. **3.** Often **Administration.** The persons collectively who make up the executive branch of a government. **4.** The management of an institution, public or private. **5.** The term of office of an executive officer or body. **6.** *Law.* The management and disposal of a trust or estate. **7.** The dispensing, applying, or tendering of something, such as an oath, sacrament, or medicine. **—ad·min'is·tra'tive** (-strā'tĭv, -strə-) *adj.* **—ad·min'is·tra'tive·ly** *adv.*

ad·min·is·tra·tor (ăd-mĭn'ĭ-strā'tər) *n.* **1.** One who administers, esp. business or public affairs; executive. **2.** A person appointed to administer an estate.

ad·mi·ra·ble (ăd'mər-ə-bəl) *adj.* Deserving admiration; excellent. **—ad'mi·ra·ble·ness** *n.* **—ad'mi·ra·bly** *adv.*

ad·mi·ral (ăd'mər-əl) *n.* **1.** The commander in chief of a navy or fleet. **2.** An Admiral of the Fleet. **3.** In the U.S. Navy, U.S. Coast Guard, and Royal Canadian Navy: **a.** An officer of the next-to-the-highest rank. **b.** A rear admiral. **c.** A vice admiral. **4.** The ship carrying an admiral; flagship. **5.** *Chiefly Brit.* The head of a fishing fleet. **6.** Any of various brightly colored butterflies of the genera *Limenitis* and *Vanessa.* [ME *amiral* < OFr. < Ar. *'amīr al-,* commander of.]

Admiral of the Fleet *n.* The highest rank in the U.S. Navy and Royal Canadian Navy, equivalent to General of the Army or field marshal.

ad·mi·ral·ty (ăd'mər-əl-tē) *n., pl.* **-ties. 1. a.** A court exercising jurisdiction over all maritime cases. **b.** Maritime law. **2. Admiralty.** The department of the British government (Board of Admiralty) having control over naval affairs.

ad·mi·ra·tion (ăd'mə-rā'shən) *n.* **1.** A feeling of pleasure, wonder, and approval. **2.** An object of wonder; marvel. **3.** *Archaic.* Wonder.

adobe
16th-century church near Albuquerque, New Mexico

ad·mire (ăd-mīr') *v.* **-mired, -mir·ing, -mires.** *—tr.* **1.** To regard with pleasure, wonder, and approval. **2.** To have a high opinion of; esteem or respect. **3.** *Archaic.* To marvel or wonder at. *—intr.* **1.** To feel or express admiration. **2.** *Regional.* To feel pleasure; be pleased. [Fr. *admirer* < OFr. *amirer* < Lat. *admirari,* to wonder at : *ad-,* at + *mirari,* to wonder < *mirus,* wonderful.] **—ad·mir'er** *n.* **—ad·mir'ing·ly** *adv.*

ad·mis·si·ble (ăd-mĭs'ə-bəl) *adj.* **1.** Capable of being accepted; allowable. **2.** Worthy of admission. **—ad·mis'si·bil'i·ty, ad·mis'si·ble·ness** *n.* **—ad·mis'si·bly** *adv.*

ad·mis·sion (ăd-mĭsh'ən) *n.* **1. a.** The act of admitting or allowing to enter. **b.** The state of being allowed to enter. **2.** The right to enter; access. **3.** The price required or paid for entering; entrance fee. **4.** The act or process of acceptance and entry into a position or situation; appointment. **5.** A confession of crime or wrongdoing. **6.** A voluntary acknowledgment that something is true. **7.** A fact or statement granted or admitted; concession. [ME < Lat. *admissio* < *admittere,* to admit.] **—ad·mis'sive** (-mĭs'ĭv) *adj.*

Usage: *Admission* has a more general meaning than *admittance,* which is used only to denote the obtaining of physical access to a place. To gain *admittance* to a club is to enter its facilities; to gain *admission* to a club is to become a member. One pays *admission* to a theater (i.e., the price of entering) in order to be allowed *admittance* (physical entry to the theater itself).

ad·mit (ăd-mĭt') *v.* **-mit·ted, -mit·ting, -mits.** *—tr.* **1.** To permit to enter. **2.** To serve as a means of entrance: *A ticket that admits the whole group.* **3.** To permit to join or exercise certain rights, functions, or privileges. **4.** To have room for; accommodate. **5.** To afford opportunity for; permit. **6.** To acknowledge; confess: *admit the truth.* **7.** To grant as true or valid, as for the sake of argument; concede. **8.** To accept or allow as true or valid. *—intr.* **1.** To afford possibility: *a problem admitting of no solution.* **2.** To allow entrance; afford access: *a door admitting to the hall.* [ME *admitten* < Lat. *admittere* : *ad,* to + *mittere,* to send.]

ad·mit·tance (ăd-mĭt'ns) *n.* **1.** The act of admitting or entering. **2.** Permission to enter; the power or right of entrance. **3.** *Elect.* The reciprocal of impedance. —See Usage note at **admission**

ad·mit·ted·ly (ăd-mĭt'ĭd-lē) *adv.* By general admission; confessedly.

ad·mix (ăd-mĭks') *tr. & intr.v.* **-mixed, -mix·ing, -mix·es.** To mix or blend. [Back-formation < obs. *admixt,* mixed into < Lat. *admixtus,* p.part. of *admiscēre,* to mix into : *ad,* to + *miscēre,* to mix.]

ad·mix·ture (ăd-mĭks'chər) *n.* **1. a.** The act of mingling or mixing. **b.** The state of being mingled or mixed. **2.** A combination, mixture, or blend. **3.** Something added in mixing.

ad·mon·ish (ăd-mŏn'ĭsh) *tr.v.* **-ished, -ish·ing, -ish·es. 1.** To reprove mildly or kindly but seriously. **2.** To counsel against something; caution. **3.** To point out something forgotten or disregarded, by means of a warning, reproof, or exhortation. [ME *admonishen,* alteration of *amonesten* < OFr. *amonester* < VLat. **admonestare,* var. of Lat. *admonēre* : *ad,* to + *monēre,* to warn.] **—ad·mon'ish·er** *n.* **—ad·mon'ish·ing·ly** *adv.* **—ad·mon'ish·ment** *n.*

Synonyms: *admonish, reprove, rebuke, reprimand, reproach.* These verbs refer to adverse criticism intended as a corrective. *Admonish* stresses the act of advising or warning so that a fault may be rectified or a danger avoided. *Reprove* usually implies gentle criticism and constructive intent. *Rebuke* refers to sharp, usually angry, criticism, as does *reprimand,* which often also implies an official or otherwise formal act. *Reproach* usually refers to sharp criticism made regretfully or unhappily out of a sense of disappointment.

ad·mo·ni·tion (ăd'mə-nĭsh'ən) *n.* **1.** Mild or kind reproof. **2.** Cautionary advice or warning. [ME *amonicioun* < OFr. *amonition* < Lat. *admonitio* < *admonēre,* to admonish.]

ad·mon·i·to·ry (ăd-mŏn'ĭ-tôr'ē, -tōr'ē) *adj.* Expressing admonition.

ad·nate (ăd'nāt') *adj. Biol.* Joined to or fused with another part or organ, as parts not usually united. [Lat. *adnatus,* var. of *agnatus,* connected by birth < *agnasci,* to be born in addition to. —see AGNATE.] **—ad·na'tion** (ăd-nā'shən) *n.*

ad nau·se·am (ăd nô'zē-əm) *adv.* To the point of nausea; to a disgusting or ridiculous degree. [Lat.]

ad·nex·a (ăd-nĕk'sə) *n.* Accessory or subordinate anatomical parts, as ovaries and oviducts. [NLat. < Lat. *adnexus, annexus,* p.part. of *annectere,* to bind to. —see ANNEX.] **—ad·nex'al** *adj.*

ad·noun (ăd'noun') *n. Gram.* An adjective, specifically when used as a noun, as in *the bold and the brave.* **—ad·nom'i·nal** (ăd-nŏm'ə-nəl) *adj.*

a·do (ə-dōō') *n.* Bustle; fuss; trouble; bother. [ME < the phrase *at do* : *at,* to + *do,* to do.]

a·do·be (ə-dō'bē) *n.* **1.** A sun-dried, unburned brick of clay and straw. **2.** Clay or soil from which adobe is made. **3.** A structure built with adobe. ***—modifier:*** *an adobe house.* [Sp. < Ar. *aṭṭoba* < *al- ṭoba,* the brick : *al,* the + *ṭōba,* brick.]

ad·o·les·cence (ăd'l-ĕs'əns) *n.* **1.** The period of physical and psychological development from the onset of puberty to maturity. **2.** A transitional period of development between youth and maturity: *the adolescence of a nation.*

ad·o·les·cent (ăd'l-ĕs'ənt) *adj.* Of, pertaining to, or undergoing adolescence. *—n.* An adolescent boy or girl, esp. a teen-ager. [ME < OFr. < Lat. *adolescens,* pr.part. of *adolescere,* to grow up : *ad,* toward + *alescere,* to grow, inchoative of *alere,* to nourish.]

Ad·o·nai (ăd'n-ī', ăd'n-oi') *n.* Lord. Used in Judaism as a spoken substitute for the ineffable name of God. [Heb. *adōnāi,* my lord < Phoenician *adōn,* lord.]

A·don·is (ə-dŏn'ĭs, ə-dō'nĭs) *n.* **1.** *Gk. Myth.* A youth loved by Aphrodite for his striking beauty. **2.** Often **adonis.** A young man of great physical beauty. [Gk. *Adōnis* < Phoenician *adōn,* lord.]

a·dopt (ə-dŏpt') *tr.v.* **a·dopt·ed, a·dopt·ing, a·dopts. 1.** To take into one's family through legal means and raise as one's own child. **2.** To take and follow (a course of action, for example) by choice or assent: *adopt a new technique.* **3.** To take up and make one's own, as an idea. **4.** To take on or assume: *adopted an air of importance.* **5.** To vote to accept: *adopt a resolution.* **6.** To choose as a standard or required textbook or reference book in a course. [ME *adopten* < OFr. *adopter* < Lat. *adoptare* : *ad,* to + *optare,* to choose.] **—a·dopt'a·ble** *adj.* **—a·dopt'er** *n.* **—a·dop'tion** *n.*

Usage: One refers to an *adopted* child but to *adoptive* parents.

a·dop·tee (ə-dŏp'tē) *n.* One that is adopted.

a·dop·tive (ə-dŏp'tĭv) *adj.* **1. a.** Tending to adopt. **b.** Characteristic of adoption. **2.** Related or acquired by adoption. —See Usage note at **adopt. —a·dop'tive·ly** *adv.*

a·dor·a·ble (ə-dôr'ə-bəl, ə-dōr'-) *adj.* **1.** *Informal.* Delightful; lovable; charming. **2.** *Archaic.* Worthy of worship or adoration. **—a·dor'a·bil'i·ty, a·dor'a·ble·ness** *n.* **—a·dor'a·bly** *adv.*

ad·o·ra·tion (ăd'ə-rā'shən) *n.* **1.** The act of worship. **2.** Profound love or regard.

a·dore (ə-dôr', ə-dōr') *v.* **a·dored, a·dor·ing, a·dores.** *—tr.* **1.** To worship as divine. **2.** To love deeply; revere. **3.** *Informal.* To like very much. *—intr.* To worship. [ME *adouren* < OFr. *adourer* < Lat. *adorare,* to pray to : *ad,* to + *orare,* to pray.] **—a·dor'er** *n.* **—a·dor'ing·ly** *adv.*

a·dorn (ə-dôrn') *tr.v.* **a·dorned, a·dorn·ing, a·dorns. 1.** To be a decoration to; lend beauty to. **2.** To fit out or decorate with or as if with ornaments. **3.** To enhance the distinction, beauty, splendor, or glory of; add luster to. [ME *adournen* < OFr. *adourner* < Lat. *adornare* : *ad,* to + *ornare,* to decorate.] **—a·dorn'er** *n.*

a·dorn·ment (ə-dôrn'mənt) *n.* **1.** The act of adorning. **2.** Something that adorns or beautifies; ornament.

ADP (ā'dē'pē') *n.* An ester, $C_{10}H_{15}N_5O_{10}P_2$, that is an adenosine derivative formed in cells and converted to ATP for the storage of energy.

ad rem (ăd rĕm') *adj. Law.* To the point; pertinent. [Lat.] **—ad rem** *adv.*

ad·re·nal (ə-drē'nəl) *adj.* **1.** At, near, or on the kidneys. **2.** Of or pertaining to the adrenal glands or their secretions. *—n.* An adrenal gland. **—ad·re'nal·ly** *adv.*

adrenal cortex *n.* The three-zoned center of the adrenal glands.

adrenal gland *n.* Either of two small dissimilarly shaped endocrine glands, one located above each kidney, consisting of the cortex, which secretes hormones, and the medulla, which secretes epinephrine.

A·dren·a·lin (ə-drĕn'ə-lĭn). A trademark for a preparation of adrenaline.

a·dren·a·line (ə-drĕn'ə-lĭn) *n.* A secretion of the adrenal glands; epinephrine.

ad·re·ner·gic (ăd'rə-nûr'jĭk) *adj.* Of, pertaining to, or having chemical activity like that of epinephrine, as certain nerve fibers. [ADREN(ALINE) + Gk. *ergon,* work.]

a·dre·no·chrome (ə-drē'nō-krōm', -nə-) *n.* A naturally occurring chemical formed during the oxidation of adrenaline. [ADREN(ALINE) + CHROME.]

ad·re·no·cor·ti·co·trop·ic (ə-drē'nō-kôr'tĭ-kō-trŏp'ĭk, -trō'pĭk) also **ad·re·no·cor·ti·co·troph·ic** (-trŏf'ĭk, -trō'fĭk) *adj.* Stimulating or otherwise acting upon the cortex of the adrenal gland. [ADREN(AL) + CORTICO- + -TROPIC.]

adrenocorticotropic hormone or **adrenocorticotroph** or **adrenocorticotrophin** *n.* ACTH.

a·drift (ə-drĭft') *adv. & adj.* **1.** Drifting or floating freely; not anchored. **2.** Without direction or purpose.

a·droit (ə-droit') *adj.* **1.** Dexterous; deft. **2.** Skillful and adept under pressing conditions. [Fr. < *a droit* : *a,* to (< Lat. *ad*) + *droit,* right < Lat. *directus.* —see DIRECT.] **—a·droit'ly** *adv.* **—a·droit'ness** *n.*

ad·sci·ti·tious (ăd'sĭ-tĭsh'əs) *adj.* Not inherent or essential; derived from something outside. [< Lat. *ascitus,* assumed, p.part. of *asciscere,* to assume : *ad,* to + *sciscere,* to accept, inchoative of *scire,* to know.]

ad·sorb (ăd-sôrb', -zôrb') *tr.v.* **-sorbed, -sorb·ing, -sorbs.** To take up by adsorption. [AD- + Lat. *sorbēre,* to suck.]

ad·sor·bate (ăd-sôr'bĭt, -bāt', ăd-zôr'-) *n.* An adsorbed substance.

ad·sor·bent (ăd-sôr'bənt, -zôr'-) *adj.* Capable of adsorption. *—n.* An adsorptive material, such as activated carbon.

ad·sorp·tion (ăd-sôrp'shən, -zôrp'-) *n.* The assimilation of gas, vapor, or dissolved matter by the surface of a solid or liquid. [ADSORB + -TION.] **—ad·sorp'tive** (-tĭv) *adj.*

ad·u·lar·i·a (ăj'ə-lâr'ē-ə, -lăr'-) *n.* A variety of orthoclase. [Ital. < Fr. *adulaire,* after *Adula,* a group of Swiss mountains.]

ad·u·late (ăj'ə-lāt') *tr.v.* **-lat·ed, -lat·ing, -lates.** To praise excessively or fawningly. [Back-formation < ADULATION.] **—ad'u·la'tor** *n.* **—ad'u·la·to'ry** (-lə-tôr'ē, -tōr'ē) *adj.*

ad·u·la·tion (ăj'ə-lā'shən) *n.* Excessive praise or flattery. [ME *adulacioun* < OFr. < Lat. *adulatio* < *adulari,* to flatter.]

a·dult (ə-dŭlt', ăd'ŭlt') *n.* **1.** One who has attained maturity or legal age. **2.** A fully grown, mature organism. *—adj.* **1.** Fully developed and mature. **2.** Pertaining to, befitting, or intended for mature persons: *adult education.* **3. a.** Restricted to adults: *adult movies.* **b.** Relating to or dealing with explicitly sexual or pornographic themes. [Lat. *adultus,* p.part. of *adolescere,* to grow up. —see ADOLESCENT.] **—a·dult'hood'** (-hŏŏd') *n.*

a·dul·ter·ant (ə-dŭl'tər-ənt) *n.* A substance that adulterates. *—adj.* Adulterating.

a·dul·ter·ate (ə-dŭl'tə-rāt') *tr.v.* **-at·ed, -at·ing, -ates.** To make impure, spurious, or inferior by adding extraneous or improper ingredients. *—adj.* (-tər-ĭt). **1.** Spurious; adulterated. **2.** Adulterous. [Lat. *adulterare, adulterat-,* to pollute.] **—a·dul'ter·a'tion** *n.* **—a·dul'ter·a'tor** *n.*

a·dul·ter·er (ə-dŭl'tər-ər) *n.* A man who commits adultery.

a·dul·ter·ess (ə-dŭl'trĭs, -tər-ĭs) *n.* A woman who commits adultery.

a·dul·ter·ine (ə-dŭl'tə-rīn', -rēn') *adj.* **1.** Characterized by adulteration; spurious. **2.** Unauthorized by law; illegal. **3.** Born of adultery: *adulterine offspring.* [Lat. *adulterinus* < *adulter,* adulterer < *adulterare,* to adulterate.]

a·dul·ter·ous (ə-dŭl'tər-əs, -trəs) *adj.* Relating to, inclined to, or marked by adultery. **—a·dul'ter·ous·ly** *adv.*

a·dul·ter·y (ə-dŭl'tə-rē, -trē) *n., pl.* **-ries.** Voluntary sexual intercourse between a married person and a partner other than the lawful spouse. [ME < OFr. *avouterie* < Lat. *adulterium* < *adulter,* adulterer < *adulterare,* to adulterate.]

ad·um·brate (ăd'əm-brāt', ə-dŭm'-) *tr.v.* **-brat·ed, -brat·ing, -brates. 1.** To give a sketchy outline of. **2.** To prefigure indistinctly; foreshadow. **3.** To disclose partially or guardedly. [Lat. *adumbrare, adumbrat-,* to overshadow : *ad,* to + *umbra,* shadow.] **—ad'um·bra'tion** *n.* **—ad·um'bra·tive** (ə-dŭm'brə-tĭv) *adj.* **—ad·um'bra·tive·ly** *adv.*

a·dust (ə-dŭst') *adj.* **1.** Burned; scorched. **2.** Melancholy; gloomy. [ME < Lat. *adustus,* p.part. of *adurere,* to set fire to : *ad,* to + *urere,* to burn.]

ad va·lo·rem (ăd' və-lôr'əm, -lōr'-) *adj.* In proportion to the value: *ad valorem duties on imported goods.* [Lat.]

ad·vance (ăd-văns') *v.* **-vanced, -vanc·ing, -vanc·es.** *—tr.* **1.** To move or cause to move forward. **2.** To put forward; propose; suggest. **3.** To aid the growth or progress of; further. **4.** To raise in rank; promote. **5.** To cause to occur sooner; hasten. **6.** To raise in amount or rate; increase. **7.** To pay (money or interest) before legally due. **8.** To supply or lend, esp. on credit. *—intr.* **1.** To go or move forward or onward. **2.** To make progress; improve. **3.** To rise in rank, position, or value. ***—phrasal verb.*** **advance on** (or **upon**). To move against, as when attacking. *—n.* **1.** The act or process of moving or going forward. **2.** Improvement; progress. **3.** A rise or increase of price or value. **4. advances.** Personal approaches made to secure acquaintance, favor, or an agreement; overtures. **5. a.** The furnishing of funds or goods on credit. **b.** The funds or goods so furnished; loan. **6.** Payment of money before legally or normally due. *—adj.* **1.** Made or given ahead of time; prior. **2.** Going before; in front; forward. ***—idiom.*** **in advance. 1.** In front. **2.** Ahead of time; beforehand. [ME *avauncen* < OFr. *avauncer* < VLat. **abantiare* < Lat. *abante,* from before : *ab,* from + *ante,* before.] **—ad·vanc'er** *n.*

Synonyms: *advance, progress, promote, forward, further.* These verbs all refer to movement forward or upward, literally or figuratively; they vary widely in application, however. *Advance* alone is both transitive and intransitive. Intransitively it applies to forward movement (literal) and to enlargement of scope or importance, rise in status, or the like (figurative). *Progress,* which is only intransitive, also has both these senses, and differs principally in stressing the idea of steady and orderly movement toward a goal. Transitively, *advance* alone applies to forward movement with reference to time *(advance a deadline, advance money)* and to causing to rise in value *(advance prices). Advance* and *promote* are generally interchangeable when they mean to raise a person in rank or grade. *Advance, promote, forward,* and *further* all have the transitive sense of making something (such as a cause, a career, or a business venture) go forward, figuratively, by providing assistance. *Advance* and *forward* are nonspecific in this sense; *promote* and *further* stress active support and encouragement. *Forward* alone has the transitive sense of sending something onward or ahead, especially mail.

Usage: *Advance,* as a noun, is used for forward movement (*the advance of the army*) or for progress or improvement in a figurative sense. *Advancement* is used mainly in the figurative sense: *career advancement.* In the figurative sense, moreover, there is a distinction between the two terms deriving from the transitive and intransitive forms of the verb *advance.* The noun *advancement* (unlike *advance*) often implies the existence of an agent or outside force. Thus, *the advance of science* means simply the progress of science, whereas *the advancement of science* implies progress resulting from the action of an agent or force: *The purpose of the legislation was the advancement of science.*

ad·vanced (ăd-vănst') *adj.* **1.** Highly developed or complex. **2.** At a higher level than others. **3.** Ahead of the times; progressive. **4. a.** Far along in course: *an advanced stage of illness.* **b.** Very old: *a man of advanced age.*

advanced degree *n.* A university degree higher than a bachelor's.

advanced standing *n.* The status of a college student granted credit, usually after passing a qualifying test, for courses omitted or taken elsewhere.

advance guard *n.* A detachment of troops sent ahead of the main force to reconnoiter and provide protection.

advance man *n.* **1.** An agent, as for a performing troupe, who makes business and publicity arrangements in advance. **2.** An assistant, as to a political candidate, who makes publicity arrangements and security checks in advance.

ad·vance·ment (ăd-văns'mənt) *n.* **1.** The act of advancing. **2.** A forward step; improvement. **3.** Development; progress: *the advancement of knowledge.* **4.** A promotion, as in rank. —See Usage note at **advance.**

ad·van·tage (ăd-văn'tĭj) *n.* **1.** A factor favorable or conducive to success. **2.** Benefit or profit; gain. **3.** A relatively favorable position; superiority of means. **4. a.** The first point scored in tennis after deuce. **b.** The resulting score. *—tr.v.* **-taged, -tag·ing, -tag·es.** To afford profit or gain to; benefit. ***—idioms.*** **take advantage of. 1.** To put to good use; avail oneself of. **2.** To profit selfishly by; exploit. **to advantage.** To good effect; profitably; favorably. [ME *avauntage* < OFr. < *avant,* before < Lat. *abante,* from before. —see ADVANCE.]

ad·van·ta·geous (ăd'văn-tā'jəs, -vən-) *adj.* Affording benefit or gain; useful. **—ad'van·ta'geous·ly** *adv.* **—ad'van·ta'geous·ness** *n.*

ad·vect (ăd-vĕkt') *tr.v.* **-vect·ed, -vect·ing, -vects. 1.** To convey horizontally by advection. **2.** To transport (a substance) by advection. [Back-formation < ADVECTION.]

ad·vec·tion (ăd-vĕk'shən) *n.* A local change in a property of a system, as of atmospheric temperature, caused by motion of the fluid in a gradient of the property. [Lat. *advectio,* conveyance < *advehere,* to carry to : *ad,* to + *vehere,* to carry.]

ad·vent (ăd'vĕnt') *n.* **1.** The coming or arrival, esp. of something momentous: *the advent of the computer.* **2. Advent. a.** The birth or coming of Christ. **b.** The period including four Sundays before Christmas. [ME, the Advent season < OFr. < Lat. *adventus,* arrival < *advenire,* to come to : *ad,* to + *venire,* to come.]

Ad·vent·ist (ăd'vĕn'-tĭst) *n.* A member of any of several Christian denominations that believe Christ's second coming and the end of the world are near at hand. **—Ad'vent'·ism** *n.*

ad·ven·ti·tia (ăd'vĕn-tĭsh'ə, -vən-) *n.* The outermost covering of an organ, as a blood vessel. [NLat. < Lat. *adventicius,* foreign. —see ADVENTITIOUS.]

ad·ven·ti·tious (ăd'vĕn-tĭsh'əs, -vən-) *adj.* **1.** Acquired by

Adonis
"Venus and Adonis" by Veronese

accident; added by chance. **2.** *Biol.* Appearing in an unusual place or in an irregular or sporadic manner: *adventitious shoots.* [Lat. *adventicious,* foreign < *adventus,* arrival. —see ADVENT.] **—ad'ven·ti'tious·ly** *adv.* **—ad'ven·ti'tious·ness** *n.*

ad·ven·tive (ăd-vĕn'tĭv) *Biol.* *—adj.* Not native to and not fully established in a new habitat or environment; locally or temporarily naturalized: *an adventive weed.* *—n.* An adventive organism. [< Lat. *adventus,* arrival. —see ADVENT.] **—ad·ven'tive·ly** *adv.*

Advent Sunday *n.* The first Sunday of Advent.

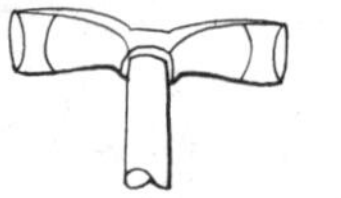
railroad adz

ad·ven·ture (ăd-vĕn'chər) *n.* **1.** An undertaking or enterprise of a hazardous nature. **2.** An unusual experience or course of events marked by excitement and suspense. **3.** Participation in hazardous or exciting experiences. **4.** A financial speculation or business venture. *—v.* **-tured, -tur·ing, -tures.** *—tr.* To venture; risk; dare. *—intr.* To take risks; engage in hazardous activities. [ME *aventure* < OFr. < Lat. *adventurus,* fut. part. of *advenire,* to arrive. —see ADVENT.] **—ad·ven'ture·some** (-səm) *adj.*

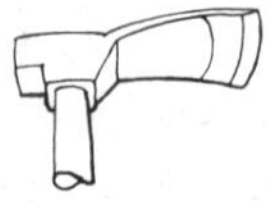
carpenter's adz

ad·ven·tur·er (ăd-vĕn'chər-ər) *n.* **1.** One who adventures. **2.** A soldier of fortune. **3.** A heavy speculator in business or trade. **4.** One who seeks wealth and social position by unscrupulous means.

ad·ven·tur·ess (ăd-vĕn'chər-ĭs) *n.* A woman who seeks social and financial advancement by unscrupulous means.

ad·ven·tur·ous (ăd-vĕn'chər-əs) *adj.* **1.** Inclined to undertake new and daring enterprises; bold. **2.** Hazardous; risky. **—ad·ven'tur·ous·ly** *adv.* **—ad·ven'tur·ous·ness** *n.*

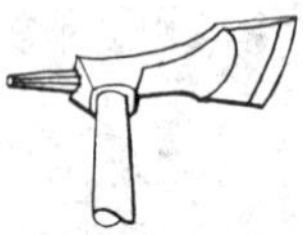
ship carpenter's adz

adz

ad·verb (ăd'vûrb') *n. Gram.* **1.** A part of speech comprising a class of words that modify a verb, adjective, or other adverb. **2.** A word belonging to this class, as *rapidly* in *He runs rapidly.* [ME *adverbe* < OFr. < Lat. *adverbium* : *ad,* to + *verbum,* word.]

ad·ver·bi·al (ăd-vûr'bē-əl) *adj.* Of, pertaining to, or used as an adverb. **—ad·ver'bi·al·ly** *adv.*

ad ver·bum (ăd vûr'bəm) *adv.* Word for word; verbatim. [Lat.]

ad·ver·sar·y (ăd'vər-sĕr'ē) *n., pl.* **-ies.** An opponent; enemy. [ME *adversarie* < Lat. *adversarius,* enemy < *adversus,* against. —see ADVERSE.]

ad·ver·sa·tive (ăd-vûr'sə-tĭv) *adj.* Expressing antithesis or opposition: *the adversative conjunction but.* *—n.* An adversative word. [Lat. *adversativus* < *adversari,* to oppose < *adversus,* against. —see ADVERSE.] **—ad·ver'sa·tive·ly** *adv.*

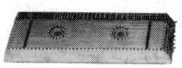

Aegisthus
Aegisthus slain by Orestes

ad·verse (ăd-vûrs', ăd'vûrs') *adj.* **1.** Antagonistic in design or effect; opposed: *adverse criticism.* **2.** Contrary to one's interests or welfare; unpropitious: *adverse circumstances.* **3.** In an opposite or opposing direction or position. **4.** *Bot.* Facing the axis or main stem. —See Usage note at **averse.** [ME < OFr. *advers* < Lat. *adversus,* p.part. of *advertere,* to turn toward : *ad-,* toward + *vertere,* to turn.] **—ad·verse'ly** *adv.* **—ad·verse'ness** *n.*

ad·ver·si·ty (ăd-vûr'sĭ-tē) *n., pl.* **-ties.** **1.** A state of hardship or affliction; misfortune. **2.** A calamitous event.

ad·vert[1] (ăd-vûrt') *intr.v.* **-vert·ed, -vert·ing, -verts.** To call attention; refer: *advert to a problem.* [ME *adverten* < OFr. *avertir,* to notice < Lat. *advertere,* to turn toward. —see ADVERSE.]

ad·vert[2] (ăd'vûrt') *n. Chiefly Brit.* An advertisement.

Aeolian harp

ad·ver·tise (ăd'vər-tīz') *v.* **-tised, -tis·ing, -tis·es.** *—tr.* **1.** To make public announcement of, esp. to proclaim the qualities or advantages of (a product or business) so as to increase sales. **2.** To make known; call attention to: *advertised her disappointment.* **3.** *Archaic.* To warn or notify: *"This event advertises me that there is such a fact as death"* (Thoreau). *—intr.* **1.** To call the attention of the public to a product or business. **2.** To inquire or seek in a public notice, as in a newspaper: *advertise for an apartment.* [ME *advertisen,* to notify < OFr. *avertir, avertiss-,* to notice. —see ADVERT.] **—ad'ver·tis'er** *n.*

ad·ver·tise·ment (ăd'vər-tīz'mənt, ăd-vûr'tĭs-, -tĭz-) *n.* A notice designed to attract public attention or patronage.

ad·ver·tis·ing (ăd'vər-tī'zĭng) *n.* **1.** The action of attracting public attention to a product or business. **2.** The business of preparing and distributing advertisements. **3.** Printed or spoken advertisements collectively.

Aeolus
Illumination on folio of a chorale, in Piccolimini Library, Siena, Italy

ad·vice (ăd-vīs') *n.* **1.** Opinion about what could or should be done about a problem; counsel. **2.** Often **advices.** Information or report, esp. when communicated from a distance: *advices from an ambassador.* [ME *avis* < OFr., view < Med. Lat. *advisum* : Lat. *ad-,* to + *visum,* something seen < *vidēre,* to see.]

ad·vis·a·ble (ăd-vī'zə-bəl) *adj.* Worthy of being recommended or suggested; prudent. **—ad·vis'a·bil'i·ty, ad·vis'a·ble·ness** *n.* **—ad·vis'a·bly** *adv.*

ad·vise (ăd-vīz') *v.* **-vised, -vis·ing, -vis·es.** *—tr.* **1.** To offer advice to; counsel. **2.** To recommend; suggest. **3.** To inform; notify: *advise a person of a decision.* *—intr.* **1.** To consult; take counsel: *advised with her associates.* **2.** To offer advice. [ME *avisen* < OFr. *aviser* < *avis,* view. —see ADVICE.]

Usage: *Advise* in the sense of "to inform" or "to notify" is acceptable to a majority of the Usage Panel, though many members would restrict this usage to business correspondence.

ad·vised (ăd-vīzd') *adj.* **1.** Considered; thought out: *well-advised; ill-advised.* **2.** Informed: *be kept advised.*

ad·vis·ed·ly (ăd-vī'zĭd-lē) *adv.* With careful consideration; deliberately.

ad·vi·see (ăd-vī'zē) *n.* One that is advised.

ad·vise·ment (ăd-vīz'mənt) *n.* Careful consideration.

ad·vis·er also **ad·vi·sor** (ăd-vī'zər) *n.* **1.** One who advises. **2.** A person who offers advice, esp. in an official or professional capacity. **3.** A teacher who advises students in academic and personal matters.

ad·vi·so·ry (ăd-vī'zə-rē) *adj.* **1.** Empowered to advise: *a student advisory committee.* **2.** Of, pertaining to, or containing advice: *an advisory memorandum.* *—n., pl.* **-ries.** A report giving information and esp. a warning: *a weather advisory.*

ad·vo·ca·cy (ăd'və-kə-sē) *n.* Active support, as of a cause, idea, or policy.

ad·vo·cate (ăd'və-kāt') *tr.v.* **-cat·ed, -cat·ing, -cates.** To speak in favor of; recommend. *—n.* (-kĭt, -kāt'). **1.** A person who argues for a cause; supporter or defender. **2.** A person who pleads in another's behalf; intercessor. [< ME *advocat,* lawyer < OFr. *avocat* < Lat. *advocatus,* p.part. of *advocare,* to summon for counsel : *ad-,* to + *vocare,* to call.] **—ad'vo·ca'tor** *n.*

ad·vow·son (ăd-vou'zən) *n.* In English ecclesiastical law, the right to present a vacant benefice. [ME *avouson* < OFr. *avoeson* < Med. Lat. *advocatia* < Lat. *advocatio,* a summoning < *advocare,* to summon. —see ADVOCATE.]

ad·y·tum (ăd'ĭ-təm) *n., pl.* **-ta** (-tə). The sanctum in an ancient temple. [Lat. < Gk. *aduton* < *adutos,* not to be entered : *a-,* not + *duein,* to enter.]

adz or **adze** (ădz) *n.* An axlike tool with a curved blade at right angles to the handle, used for dressing wood. [ME *adese* < OE *adesa.*]

ad·zu·ki bean (ăd-zo͞o'kē) *n.* A plant, *Phaseolus angularis,* having yellow flowers and pods bearing edible seeds, widely cultivated as a food crop in the Orient. [J. *azuki,* red bean.]

ae·ci·o·spore (ē'sē-ə-spôr', -spōr', -shē-) *n.* A rust spore, formed in a chainlike series in an aecium. [AECI(UM) + SPORE.]

ae·ci·um (ē'sē-əm, ē'shē-) *n., pl.* **-ci·a** (-sē-ə, -shē-ə). A cuplike structure in rust fungi containing chains of aeciospores. [NLat. < Gk. *aikia,* injury < *aeikēs,* injurious.] **—ae'ci·al** (ē'sē-əl, -shē-) *adj.*

a·e·des (ā-ē'dēz) *n., pl.* **aedes.** A mosquito of the genus *Aëdes,* such as *A. aegypti,* that transmits yellow fever and dengue. [NLat. *Aedes,* genus name < Gk. *aēdēs,* unpleasant : *a-,* not + *ēdos,* pleasant.]

ae·dile (ē'dīl') *n.* In ancient Rome, a magistrate who had charge of public works, police, and the grain supply. [Lat. *aedilis* < *aedes,* house.]

Ae·ge·an (ĭ-jē'ən) *adj.* Of, pertaining to, or designating the prehistoric civilization that flourished in the Aegean area in the Bronze Age.

Ae·geus (ē'jo͞os, ē'jē-əs) *n. Gk. Myth.* A king of Athens and the father of Theseus. [Lat. < Gk. *Aigeus.*]

Aeg·ir (ăg'ər) *n.* The god of the sea in Norse mythology. [ON.]

ae·gis (ē'jĭs) *n.* **1.** *Gk. Myth.* The shield of Zeus, lent by him to Athena. **2.** Protection. **3.** Sponsorship; patronage. [Lat. < Gk. *aigis.*]

Ae·gis·thus (ĭ-jĭs'thəs) *n. Gk. Myth.* The son of Thyestes and lover of Clytemnestra. [Lat. < Gk. *Aigisthos.*]

-aemia *suff.* Variant of **-emia.**

Ae·ne·as (ĭ-nē'əs) *n.* The Trojan hero of Virgil's *Aeneid,* son of Anchises and Aphrodite, who escaped the sack of Troy and wandered for seven years before settling in Italy. [Lat. < Gk. *Aineias.*]

a·e·ne·ous or **a·e·ne·us** (ā-ē'nē-əs) *adj.* Having a brassy or golden-green color. [Lat. *aeneus,* of bronze < *aes,* bronze.]

Ae·o·li·an (ē-ō'lē-ən, -ōl'yən) *adj.* **1.** Of or pertaining to Aeolis or its people. **2.** Of or pertaining to Aeolus, god of the winds. **3. aeolian.** Variant of **eolian.** *—n.* **1.** A member of one of the major Greek tribes that settled in central Greece, Lesbos, and Aeolis. **2.** Aeolic.

Aeolian harp *n.* A musical instrument consisting of an open box over which are stretched strings that sound when wind passes over them.

Ae·ol·ic (ē-ŏl'ĭk) *n.* A group of dialects of ancient Greek spoken by the Aeolians.

ae·ol·i·pile (ē-ŏl'ə-pīl') *n.* An ancient prototypal steam engine consisting of a spherical or cylindrical vessel fitted with circumferential exhaust jets and mounted to permit free rotation about the steam inlet axis. [< Lat. *Aeoli pylae,* gates of Aeolus : *Aeolus,* Aeolus + *pylae,* gates < Gk. *pulē,* gate.]

Ae·o·lus (ē'ə-ləs) *n. Gk. Myth.* **1.** The god of the winds. **2.** A king of Thessaly and ancestor of the Aeolians. [Lat. < Gk. *Aiolos* < *aiolos,* nimble.]

ae·on (ē'ŏn', ē'ən) *n.* Variant of **eon.**

ae·o·ni·an (ē-ō'nē-ən) *adj.* Variant of **eonian.**

ae·py·or·nis (ē'pē-ôr'nĭs) *n.* Any of an extinct genus of large, flightless birds of Madagascar. [NLat. *Aepyornis,* genus name : Gk. *aipys,* high + Gk. *ornis,* bird.]

ae·quor·in (ē-kwôr'ĭn, ē-kwŏr'-) *n.* A protein that is secreted by jellyfish and interacts with seawater to produce bioluminescent light. [NLat. *Aequorea,* jellyfish genus + -IN.]

aer- *pref.* Variant of **aero-.**

aer·ate (âr'āt') *tr.v.* **-at·ed, -at·ing, -ates.** **1.** To supply or charge (liquid) with a gas, esp. to charge with carbon dioxide. **2.** To expose to the circulation of air for purification. **3.** To supply (blood) with oxygen.

aer·a·tor (âr′ā′tər) *n.* **1.** One that aerates. **2.** A device for aerating liquids.

aer·i·al (âr′ē-əl, ā-îr′ē-əl) *adj.* **1.** Of, in, or caused by the air. **2.** Living in the air. **3.** Reaching high into the air; lofty. **4.** Suggestive of air, as in lightness; airy. **5.** Unsubstantial; imaginary. **6.** Of, for, or by aircraft. **7.** *Bot.* Borne in the air rather than underground or under water: *aerial roots.* —*n.* (âr′ē-əl). An antenna. [< Lat. *aerius* < Gk. *aerios* < *aēr,* air.]

aer·i·al·ist (âr′ē-ə-lĭst) *n.* An acrobat who performs on a tightrope, trapeze, or similar apparatus.

aerial ladder *n.* A ladder that can be extended to reach high places, esp. one mounted on a fire engine.

aer·ie also **aer·y** (âr′ē, ăr′ē, îr′ē) *n., pl.* **-ies.** **1.** The nest of an eagle or other predatory bird built on a crag or other high place. **2.** A house or stronghold built on a height. [Med. Lat. *aeria* < OFr. *aire.*]

aero– or **aer–** *pref.* **1. a.** Air; atmosphere: *aeroballistics.* **b.** Gas: *aerosol.* **2.** Aviation: *aeronautics.* [ME < OFr. < Lat. < Gk. < *aēr,* air.]

aer·o·bal·lis·tics (âr′ō-bə-lĭs′tĭks) *n. (used with a sing. verb).* Ballistics, esp. of missiles, in the atmosphere. —**aer′o·bal·lis′tic** *adj.*

aer·o·bat·ics (âr′ə-băt′ĭks) *n. (used with a sing. or pl. verb).* The performance of stunts, such as rolls and loops, with an airplane or glider. [AERO- + (ACRO)BATICS.]

aer·obe (âr′ōb′) *n.* An organism, such as a bacterium, requiring molecular oxygen or air to live. [Fr. *aérobie* : Gk. *aēr,* air + Gk. *bios,* life.]

aer·o·bic (â-rō′bĭk) *adj.* **1.** Living or occurring only in the presence of oxygen. **2.** Of or relating to aerobics. **3.** Of or relating to aerobes.

aer·o·bics (â-rō′bĭks) *n. (used with a sing. or pl. verb).* A system of physical conditioning that involves vigorous exercise, as calisthenics, combined with dance routines. [< AEROBIC.]

aer·o·bi·ol·o·gy (âr′ō-bī-ŏl′ə-jē) *n.* The branch of biology dealing with the atmospheric dispersion of materials of biologic significance, as pollen or microorganisms. —**aer′o·bi·o·log′i·cal** (-ə-lŏj′ĭ-kəl) *adj.* —**aer′o·bi·o·log′i·cal·ly** *adv.*

aer·o·bi·um (â-rō′bē-əm) *n.* An aerobe. [NLat. < AEROBE.]

aer·o·drome (âr′ə-drōm′) *n. Chiefly Brit.* Variant of **airdrome.**

aer·o·dy·nam·ics (âr′ō-dī-năm′ĭks) *n. (used with a sing. verb).* The dynamics of gases, esp. of atmospheric interactions with moving objects. —**aer′o·dy·nam′ic** *adj.*

aer·o·dyne (âr′ə-dīn′) *n.* A heavier-than-air aircraft deriving lift from motion. [AERO- + Gk. *dunamis,* power < *dunasthai,* to be able.]

aer·o·em·bo·lism (âr′ō-ĕm′bə-lĭz′əm) *n.* **1.** The presence of air bubbles in the heart or blood vessels, often resulting from a wound in one of the large veins of the neck. **2.** Caisson disease.

aer·o·foil (âr′ə-foil) *n. Chiefly Brit.* Variant of **airfoil.**

aer·o·gram also **aer·o·gramme** (âr′ə-grăm′) *n.* An air-mail letter written on a standard lightweight form that folds into the shape of an envelope and can be sent at a low postage rate.

aer·o·lite (âr′ə-līt′) also **aer·o·lith** (-lĭth′) *n.* A chiefly silicious meteorite. —**aer′o·lit′ic** (-lĭt′ĭk) *adj.*

aer·ol·o·gy (â-rŏl′ə-jē) *n.* Total atmospheric meteorology as opposed to surface-based study. —**aer′o·log′ic** (âr′ə-lŏj′ĭk), **aer′o·log′i·cal** *adj.* —**aer·ol′o·gist** *n.*

aer·o·mag·net·ics (âr′ō-măg-nĕt′ĭks) *n. (used with a sing. verb).* The science of magnetic characteristics associated with atmospheric conditions. —**aer′o·mag·net′ic** *adj.* —**aer′o·mag·net′i·cal·ly** *adv.*

aer·o·me·chan·ics (âr′ō-mə-kăn′ĭks) *n. (used with a sing. verb).* The science of the motion and equilibrium of air and other gases, comprising aerodynamics and aerostatics. —**aer′o·me·chan′i·cal** *adj.* —**aer′o·me·chan′i·cal·ly** *adv.*

aer·o·med·i·cine (âr′ō-mĕd′ĭ-sĭn) *n.* The medical study and treatment of disturbances, disorders, and diseases resulting from or associated with atmospheric flight. —**aer′o·med′i·cal** *adj.*

aer·o·me·te·or·o·graph (âr′ō-mē′tē-ôr′ə-grăf′, -ŏr′-) *n.* An aircraft instrument for simultaneously recording temperature, atmospheric pressure, and humidity.

aer·om·e·ter (â-rŏm′ĭ-tər) *n.* A device for determining the weight and density of air or other gas.

aer·o·naut (âr′ə-nôt′) *n.* A pilot or navigator of a balloon or lighter-than-air craft. [AERO- + Gk. *nautēs,* sailor.]

aer·o·nau·tic (âr′ə-nô′tĭk) also **aer·o·nau·ti·cal** (-tĭ-kəl) *adj.* Of or pertaining to aeronautics. —**aer′o·nau′ti·cal·ly** *adv.*

aer·o·nau·tics (âr′ə-nô′tĭks) *n. (used with a sing. verb).* **1.** The design and construction of aircraft. **2.** The theory and practice of aircraft navigation.

aer·o·neu·ro·sis (âr′ō-nŏŏ-rō′sĭs, -nyŏŏ-) *n.* A nervous exhaustion from prolonged piloting of aircraft.

aer·on·o·my (â-rŏn′ə-mē) *n.* The study of the upper atmosphere, esp. of regions of ionized gas.

aer·o·pause (âr′ō-pôz′) *n.* The region of the atmosphere above which aircraft cannot fly.

aer·o·pha·gia (âr′ə-fā′jə) *n.* The abnormal, spasmodic swallowing of air, esp. as a symptom of hysteria.

aer·o·pho·bi·a (âr′ə-fō′bē-ə) *n.* The abnormal fear of air, esp. drafts.

aer·o·phore (âr′ə-fôr′, -fōr′-) *n.* A device to supply air to a nonbreathing infant, or to a person in an anaerobic environment, such as a closed mine or an underwater area.

aer·o·phyte (âr′ə-fīt′) *n. Bot.* An epiphyte.

aer·o·plane (âr′ə-plān′) *n. Chiefly Brit.* Variant of **airplane.**

aer·o·shell (âr′ə-shĕl′) *n.* A protective, all-covering shell for a spacecraft entering an atmosphere from space at high speeds.

aer·o·sol (âr′ə-sôl′, -sōl′) *n.* **1.** A gaseous suspension of fine solid or liquid particles. **2. a.** A substance, such as a detergent, insecticide, or paint, packaged under pressure with a gaseous propellant for release as an aerosol. **b.** An aerosol bomb. [AERO- + SOL(UTION).]

aerosol bomb *n.* A usually hand-held container or dispenser from which an aerosol is released.

aer·o·space (âr′ō-spās′) *adj.* **1.** Of or designating the earth's atmosphere and the space beyond. **2.** Of or pertaining to the science or technology of flight. —**aer′o·space′** *n.*

aer·o·sphere (âr′ō-sfîr′) *n.* The lower portion of the atmosphere in which both unmanned and manned flight is possible.

aer·o·stat (âr′ō-stăt′) *n.* An aircraft, esp. a balloon or dirigible, deriving its lift from the buoyancy of surrounding air rather than from aerodynamic motion. [Fr. *aérostat* : Gk. *aēr,* air + Gk. *statos,* standing.] —**aer′o·stat′ic, aer′o·stat′i·cal** *adj.*

aer·o·stat·ics (âr′ō-stăt′ĭks) *n. (used with a sing. verb).* The science of gases in equilibrium and of the equilibrium of balloons or aircraft under changing atmospheric flight conditions.

aer·o·ther·mo·dy·nam·ics (âr′ō-thûr′mō-dī-năm′ĭks) *n. (used with a sing. verb).* The study of the thermodynamics of gases, esp. at high relative velocities.

aer·y[1] (âr′ē, ā′ə-rē) *adj.* **-i·er, -i·est.** Ethereal.

aer·y[2] (âr′ē, ăr′ē, îr′ē) *n.* Variant of **aerie.**

Aes·cu·la·pi·an (ĕs′kyə-lā′pē-ən) *adj.* Of or pertaining to the healing art; medical. [After AESCULAPIUS.]

Aes·cu·la·pi·us (ĕs′kyə-lā′pē-əs) *n. Rom. Myth.* The god of medicine and healing. [Lat. < Gk. *Asklēpios.*]

Ae·sir (â′sîr′) *pl.n.* The gods of Norse mythology. [ON, pl. of *āss,* god.]

Ae·so·pi·an (ē-sō′pē-ən) also **Ae·sop·ic** (ē-sŏp′ĭk) *adj.* **1.** In the manner of Aesop's animal fables. **2.** Veiled in allegorical suggestions, hints, and euphemisms so as to elude political censorship: *"they could express their views only in a diluted form, resorting to Aesopian hints and allusions"* (Isaac Deutscher).

aes·the·sia also **es·the·sia** (ĕs-thē′zhə) *n.* The ability to feel or perceive. [Back-formation < ANESTHESIA.]

aes·thete or **es·thete** (ĕs′thēt′) *n.* **1.** One who cultivates a superior appreciation of the beautiful. **2.** A person whose pursuit and admiration of beauty is thought to be excessive or affected. [Back-formation < AESTHETIC.]

aes·thet·ic or **es·thet·ic** (ĕs-thĕt′ĭk) *adj.* **1.** Of or pertaining to the criticism of taste. **2. a.** Of or pertaining to the sense of the beautiful: *the aesthetic faculties.* **b.** Artistic: *an aesthetic success.* **3. a.** Having a love of beauty. **b.** *Informal.* In accordance with accepted notions of good taste. [G. *ästhetisch* < NLat. *aestheticus* < Gk. *aisthētikos,* of sense perception < *aisthēta,* perceptible things < *aisthenasthai,* to perceive.] —**aes·thet′i·cal·ly** *adv.*

aes·the·ti·cian or **es·the·ti·cian** (ĕs′thĭ-tĭsh′ən) *n.* A critic concerned with the theory of beauty and the fine arts.

aes·thet·i·cism or **es·thet·i·cism** (ĕs-thĕt′ĭ-sĭz′əm) *n.* **1.** The pursuit of the beautiful; the cult of beauty and good taste. **2. a.** The belief that beauty is the basic principle from which all other principles are derived. **b.** A doctrine whereby art and artists are held to have no obligation or responsibility other than that of striving for beauty.

aes·thet·ics or **es·thet·ics** (ĕs-thĕt′ĭks) *n. (used with a sing. verb).* **1.** The branch of philosophy that provides a theory of the beautiful and of the fine arts. **2.** The theories and descriptions of the psychological response to beauty and artistic experiences. **3.** In the philosophy of Kant, the branch of metaphysics concerned with the laws of perception.

aes·ti·val (ĕs′tə-vəl) *adj.* Of, pertaining to, or appearing in summer. [ME *estival* < OFr. < Lat. *aestivalis* < *aestivus* < *aestas,* summer.]

aes·ti·vate (ĕs′tə-vāt′) *intr.v.* **-vat·ed, -vat·ing, -vates. 1.** *Zool.* To pass the summer, esp. in a state of dormancy. **2.** To spend the summer. [Lat. *aestivare* < *aestivus,* summery. —see AESTIVAL.]

aes·ti·va·tion (ĕs′tə-vā′shən) *n.* **1.** The act of spending or passing the summer. **2.** *Zool.* A state of dormancy or torpor during the summer or periods of drought. **3.** *Bot.* The arrangement of petals, sepals, and other floral organs in the unopened bud.

Ae·ther (ē′thər) *n. Gk. Myth.* The poetic personification of the clear upper air breathed by the Olympians. [Lat. < Gk. *aithēr,* upper air.]

ae·ti·ol·o·gy (ē′tē-ŏl′ə-jē) *n.* Variant of **etiology.**

af– *pref.* Variant of **ad-.** Used before *f.*

a·far (ə-făr′) *adv.* **1.** From a distance: *coming from afar.* **2.** At

aerialist

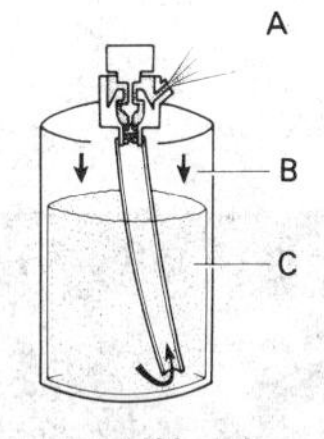

aerosol bomb
A. Aerosol spray
B. Gas under pressure
C. Solution of propellant and active ingredients

or to a distance; far away: *saw it afar off.* [ME *afer* < *on fer,* far and *of fer,* from afar < OE *feor,* far.]

a·feard also **a·feared** (ə-fîrd′) *adj. Regional & Archaic.* Afraid; frightened. [ME *afered* < OE *āfǣred,* p.part. of *āfǣran,* to frighten : *ā-* (intensive) + *fǣran,* to frighten < *fǣr,* fear.]

a·fe·brile (ā-fē′brəl, ā-fĕb′rəl) *adj.* Having no fever.

af·fa·ble (ăf′ə-bəl) *adj.* **1.** Easy to speak to; amiable. **2.** Mild; gentle; benign. [OFr. < Lat. *affabilis* < *affari,* to speak to : *ad-,* to + *fari,* to speak.] **—af′fa·bil′i·ty** *n.* **—af′fa·bly** *adv.*

af·fair (ə-fâr′) *n.* **1.** Something done or to be done; business. **2. affairs.** Transactions and other business matters: *a man of affairs.* **3. a.** An occurrence, event, or matter. **b.** An object or contrivance: *a first car that was a ramshackle affair.* **c. affairs.** Personal effects. **4.** A private matter; personal concern. **5.** A matter causing scandal and controversy: *the Dreyfus affair.* **6.** A love affair, esp. a brief one; liaison. [ME *afere* < OFr. *afaire* < *à faire,* to do.]

af·fect[1] (ə-fĕkt′) *tr.v.* **-fect·ed, -fect·ing, -fects. 1.** To have an influence on; bring about a change in. **2.** To touch or move the emotions of. **3.** To attack or infect, as a disease. *—n.* (ăf′ĕkt′). **1.** *Psychol.* **a.** A feeling or emotion as distinguished from cognition, thought, or action. **b.** A strong feeling having active consequences. **2.** *Obs.* A disposition, feeling, or tendency. [Lat. *afficere, affect-* : *ad-,* to + *facere,* to do.] **—af′fect′less** *adj.*

Synonyms: *affect, influence, impress, touch, move, strike.* These verbs can all mean to produce a mental or emotional effect. To *affect* is to change a person's emotions in some usually specified way. *Influence* implies a degree of control over the thinking and actions, as well as the emotions, of another. To *impress* is to produce a marked, usually favorable, effect on the mind. *Touch* usually means to arouse a brief sense of pathos, whereas *move* suggests profound emotional effect capable of inciting action. *Strike* implies instantaneous mental response to a stimulus such as a sight or an idea.

Usage: *Affect*[1] and *effect* have no senses in common. As a verb, *affect*[1] is most commonly used in the sense of "to influence" (*how smoking affects health*). *Effect* means "to bring about or execute": *layoffs designed to effect savings.*

af·fect[2] (ə-fĕkt′) *tr.v.* **-fect·ed, -fect·ing, -fects. 1.** To simulate or imitate in order to make some desired impression; assume; feign. **2. a.** To display a preference for. **b.** *Archaic.* To fancy; love. **c.** To tend to by nature; tend to assume: *affect crystalline form.* **3.** To imitate; copy: *"Spenser, in affecting the ancients, writ no language"* (Jonson). [ME *affecten* < Lat. *affectare,* to strive after, freq. of *afficere,* to affect, influence.] **—af·fect′er** *n.*

af·fec·ta·tion (ăf′ĕk-tā′shən) *n.* **1.** A show, pretense, or display. **2.** An artificial behavior or mannerism adopted to impress others; affectedness. [Lat. *affectatio* < *affectare,* to strive after. —see AFFECT[2].]

Synonyms: *affectation, pose, air* (and *airs*), *mannerism.* These nouns refer largely to personal attributes acquired as adornments to human character. An *affectation* is a little habit of speech or dress that the wearer has borrowed from his ideal, hoping to pass it off as genuinely his own. *Pose* denotes an attitude adopted with the aim of calling favorable attention to oneself. *Air,* meaning a distinctive but intangible quality, does not usually imply sham: *air of authority; air of a professor.* In the plural, however, it suggests affectation and snobbishness: *put on airs. Mannerism* denotes a peculiar trait or quirk that others find obtrusive and distracting.

af·fect·ed[1] (ə-fĕk′tĭd) *adj.* **1.** Acted upon, influenced, or changed. **2.** Emotionally stirred or moved. **3.** Infected or attacked, as by disease.

af·fect·ed[2] (ə-fĕk′tĭd) *adj.* **1.** Assumed or simulated to impress others. **2.** Speaking or behaving in an artificial way to make a particular impression. **3.** Disposed or inclined. **—af·fect′ed·ly** *adv.* **—af·fect′ed·ness** *n.*

af·fect·ing[1] (ə-fĕk′tĭng) *adj.* Evoking a usually strong emotional response; moving: *an affecting spectacle.* **—af·fect′ing·ly** *adv.*

af·fect·ing[2] (ə-fĕk′tĭng) *adj. Obs.* **1.** Displaying love. **2.** Feigning or pretending: *"I never heard such a drawling, affecting rogue"* (Shakespeare).

af·fec·tion (ə-fĕk′shən) *n.* **1.** A fond or tender feeling toward another. **2.** Often **affections.** Feeling or emotion: *an unbalanced state of affections.* **3.** Any pathological condition of the mind or body. **4.** The act of influencing, affecting, or acting upon. **5.** The state of being influenced or acted upon. **6.** An attribute. **7.** Mental disposition or tendency. [ME *affeccioun* < OFr. *affection* < Lat. *affectio* < *afficere,* to affect, influence.] **—af·fec′tion·al** *adj.* **—af·fec′tion·al·ly** *adv.*

af·fec·tion·ate (ə-fĕk′shə-nĭt) *adj.* **1.** Having or showing fond feelings or affection; loving; tender. **2.** *Obs.* Strongly or favorably disposed. **—af·fec′tion·ate·ly** *adv.* **—af·fec′tion·ate·ness** *n.*

af·fec·tive (ə-fĕk′tĭv) *adj.* **1.** *Psychol.* Pertaining to or resulting from emotions or feelings rather than from thought. **2.** Pertaining to or arousing affection or emotion; emotional.

af·fen·pin·scher (ăf′ən-pĭn′chər) *n.* Any of a breed of small dogs of European origin, having dark, wiry, shaggy hair and a tufted muzzle. [G. *Affe,* monkey + *Pinscher,* terrier.]

Afghan
A crocheted afghan

Afghan hound

af·fer·ent (ăf′ər-ənt) *adj.* Directed toward a central organ or section, as nerves that conduct impulses from the periphery of the body inward to the spinal cord. [Lat. *afferens, afferent-,* pr.part. of *afferre,* to bring toward : *ad-,* toward + *ferre,* to bring.]

af·fi·ance (ə-fī′əns) *tr.v.* **-anced, -anc·ing, -anc·es.** To bind in a pledge of marriage; betroth. [OFr. *afiancer* < *affier,* to trust to < Med. Lat. *affidare* : Lat. *ad-,* to + Lat. *fidus,* faithful.]

af·fi·ant (ə-fī′ənt) *n. Law.* One who makes an affidavit. [OFr. pr.part. of *affier,* to trust to. —see AFFIANCE.]

af·fi·da·vit (ăf′ĭ-dā′vĭt) *n. Law.* A written declaration made under oath before a notary public or other authorized officer. [Med. Lat. *affidavit,* he has pledged < *affidare,* to pledge. —see AFFIANCE.]

af·fil·i·ate (ə-fĭl′ē-āt′) *v.* **-at·ed, -at·ing, -ates.** *—tr.* **1.** To adopt or accept as a subordinate associate. **2.** To associate (oneself) as a subordinate, subsidiary, or member with. **3.** To admit as one's own child; adopt. **4.** *Law.* **a.** To determine the paternity of (an illegitimate child). **b.** To refer an illegitimate child to (its father). *—intr.* To associate or connect oneself: *a group that decided to affiliate.* *—n.* A person or organization associated with another in subordinate relationship. [Med. Lat. *affiliare, affiliat-,* to adopt : *ad-,* to + *filius,* son.] **—af·fil′i·a′tion** *n.*

af·fine (ə-fīn′) *adj.* **1.** Of or pertaining to a mathematical transformation of coordinates that is equivalent to a translation, contraction, or expansion with respect to a fixed origin and fixed coordinate system. **2.** Of or pertaining to the geometry of affine transformations. [OFr. *affin,* closely related. —see AFFINED.]

af·fined (ə-fīnd′) *adj. Archaic.* **1.** Joined by kinship or affinity. **2.** Beholden; bound. [Fr. *affiné* < OFr. *affin,* closely related < Lat. *affinis,* related by marriage : *ad-,* to + *finis,* boundary.]

af·fin·i·ty (ə-fĭn′ĭ-tē) *n., pl.* **-ties. 1.** A natural personal attraction. **2.** Relationship by marriage. **3.** An inherent similarity between things. **4.** A relationship or resemblance between biological species that implies a common origin. **5.** A chemical attraction or force that causes the atoms of certain elements to combine with atoms of another element and remain in the combined state. [ME *affinite* < OFr. *afinite* < Lat. *affinitas* < *affinis,* related by marriage. —see AFFINED.]

Usage: *Affinity* may be followed by *of, between,* or *with.* Thus, affinity *of* persons, *between* two persons, or *with* another person. In technical writing, *affinity* (meaning "a chemical or physical attraction") is followed by *for: a dye with an affinity for synthetic fabrics.* In general usage *affinity* retains some sense of a mutual relationship, and therefore its use with *for* is less widely accepted. A majority of the Usage Panel accept this example: *Even in school he showed an affinity for politics.* But a large majority reject this example: *Her affinity for living in California led her to reject a chance to return to New York.*

af·firm (ə-fûrm′) *v.* **-firmed, -firm·ing, -firms.** *—tr.* **1.** To declare positively or firmly; maintain to be true. **2.** To ratify or confirm. *—intr. Law.* To declare solemnly and formally but not under oath. [ME *affermen* < OFr. *afermer* < Lat. *affirmare* : *ad-,* to + *firmare,* to strengthen < *firmus,* strong.] **—af·firm′a·ble** *adj.* **—af·firm′a·bly** *adv.* **—af·fir′mant** *adj. & n.* **—af′fir·ma′tion** (ăf′ər-mā′shən) *n.* **—af·firm′er** *n.*

af·fir·ma·tive (ə-fûr′mə-tĭv) *adj.* **1.** Affirming or asserting that something is true or factual. **2.** *Logic.* Denoting a proposition in which the predicate states something about the subject to be true, as *apples have seeds.* *—n.* **1.** An affirmative word or phrase. **2.** The side in a debate that upholds a proposition. **—af·fir′ma·tive·ly** *adv.*

Usage: The expressions *in the affirmative* and *in the negative,* as in *she answered in the affirmative,* are generally regarded as pompous. *She answered yes* would be more acceptable even at the most formal levels of style.

affirmative action *n.* Action taken to provide equal opportunity, as in admissions or employment, for minority groups and women.

af·fix (ə-fĭks′) *tr.v.* **-fixed, -fix·ing, -fix·es. 1.** To secure (an object) to another; attach: *affix a label to a package.* **2.** To impute; attribute: *affix blame to him.* **3.** To place at the end; append: *affix a postscript.* *—n.* (ăf′ĭks′). **1.** Something that is attached, joined, or added. **2.** A word element, such as a prefix or suffix, that can only occur attached to a base, stem, or root. [Med. Lat. *affiare,* freq. of Lat. *affigere* : *ad-,* to + *figere,* to fasten.] **—af·fix′a·ble** *adj.* **—af·fix′er** *n.*

af·fla·tus (ə-flā′təs) *n.* A creative impulse; inspiration. [Lat., p.part. of *afflare,* to breathe on : *ad-,* toward + *flare,* to blow.]

af·flict (ə-flĭkt′) *tr.v.* **-flict·ed, -flict·ing, -flicts.** To inflict physical or mental suffering upon; cause grievous distress to: *"The second pain which will afflict the souls of the damned in hell is the pain of conscience"* (Joyce). [ME *afflighten* < Lat. *affligere,* to cast down : *ad-,* to + *fligere,* to strike.] **—af·flict′er** *n.* **—af·flic′tive** *adj.* **—af·flic′tive·ly** *adv.*

af·flic·tion (ə-flĭk′shən) *n.* **1.** A condition of pain, suffering, or distress. **2.** A cause of pain, suffering, or distress.

af·flu·ence (ăf′lo͞o-əns) *n.* **1.** A plentiful supply of material goods; wealth; riches. **2.** A plentiful supply; abundance. **3.** A flowing toward.

af·flu·en·cy (ăf'lo͞o'ən-sē, ə-flo͞o'-) *n.* Affluence.

af·flu·ent (ăf'lo͞o-ənt) *adj.* **1.** Rich; wealthy: *an affluent society.* **2.** Copious; abundant. **3.** Flowing freely. *—n.* A stream or river that flows into another or other body of water; tributary. [ME, abundant < OFr. < Lat. *affluens,* pr.part. of *affluere,* to abound in : *ad-,* to + *fluere,* to flow.] **—af'flu·ent·ly** *adv.*

af·flux (ăf'lŭks') *n.* A flowing to or toward a particular area: *an afflux of blood to the head.* [Lat. *affluxus,* p.part. of *affluere,* to flow to. —see AFFLUENT.]

af·ford (ə-fôrd', ə-fōrd') *tr.v.* **-ford·ed, -ford·ing, -fords. 1.** To have the financial means for; be able to meet the expense of. **2.** To be able to spare or give up: *could afford an hour for lunch.* **3.** To be able to do or perform (something) without incurring harm or criticism, or with benefit to oneself: *can afford to be tolerant.* **4.** To provide: *a sport affording good exercise.* [ME *aforthen* < OE *geforðian,* to carry out < *forðian,* to further < *forð,* forward.] **—af·ford'a·ble** *adj.*

af·for·est (ə-fôr'ĭst, ə-fŏr'-) *tr.v.* **-est·ed, -est·ing, -ests.** To convert (open land) into forest. [Med. Lat. *afforestare* : *ad-,* to + *forestare* < *foresta,* forest.] **—af·for'es·ta'tion** (ə-fôr'ĭ-stā'shən, ə-fŏr'-) *n.*

af·fran·chise (ə-frăn'chīz') *tr.v.* **-chised, -chis·ing, -chis·es.** To free from servitude; liberate from obligation or liabilities. [ME < OFr. *afranchir, afranchiss-* : *a-,* to (< Lat. *ad-*) + *franchir,* to free < *franc,* free. —see FRANK.]

af·fray (ə-frā') *n.* A noisy quarrel or brawl. *—tr.v.* **-frayed, -fray·ing, -frays.** *Archaic.* To frighten. [ME < OFr. *esfrei* < *esfreer,* to disturb.]

af·fri·cate (ăf'rĭ-kĭt) *n.* A speech sound produced when the breath stream is completely stopped and then released at articulation, the *t* plus *sh* sound in *clutch* or the *j* sound in *judge.* [Lat. *affricare, affricat-,* to rub against : *ad-,* to + *fricare,* to rub.]

af·fric·a·tive (ə-frĭk'ə-tĭv) *adj.* Of, pertaining to, or forming an affricate. *—n.* An affricate.

af·fright (ə-frīt') *Archaic. —tr.v.* **-fright·ed, -fright·ing, -frights.** To arouse fear in; terrify. *—n.* **1.** Terror. **2.** A cause of terror. **3.** The act of frightening. [ME *afrighten* < OE *afyrhtan.*] **—af·fright'ment** *n.*

af·front (ə-frŭnt') *tr.v.* **-front·ed, -front·ing, -fronts. 1.** To insult intentionally, esp. openly. **2.** To meet face to face defiantly; confront. *—n.* **1.** An open or intentional offense, slight, or insult. **2.** *Obs.* An encounter or meeting. [ME *afrounten* < OFr. *afronter* : Lat. *ad-,* to + Lat. *frons,* face.]

af·fu·sion (ə-fyo͞o'zhən) *n.* A pouring on of liquid, as in baptism. [LLat. *adfusio,* < *affundere,* to pour on : *ad-,* to + *fundere,* to pour.]

Af·ghan (ăf'găn', -gən) *n.* **1.** A native of Afghanistan. **2.** Pashto. **3. afghan.** A coverlet of wool, knitted or crocheted in colorful geometric designs. **4.** An Afghan hound. *—adj.* Of or pertaining to Afghanistan, its people, or their language. [Pashto *afghānī.*]

Afghan hound *n.* A large, slender dog of an ancient breed, having long, thick hair, a pointed muzzle, and drooping ears.

af·ghan·i (ăf-găn'ē, -gä'nē) *n.* See table at **currency.** [Pashto.]

a·fi·cio·na·do (ə-fĭsh'ē-ə-nä'dō, ə-fĭs'ē-, ə-fē'sē-) *n., pl.* **-dos.** An enthusiastic admirer or follower; devotee; fan. [Sp. < p.part. of *aficionar,* to induce a liking for < *afición,* liking < Lat. *affectio,* affection.]

a·field (ə-fēld') *adv.* **1.** Off the usual or desired track. **2.** Away from one's home or usual environment. **3.** To or on a field.

a·fire (ə-fīr') *adj. & adv.* **1.** On fire; burning. **2.** Intensely interested and involved.

a·flame (ə-flām') *adj. & adv.* **1.** On fire; flaming. **2.** Keenly excited and interested.

a·float (ə-flōt') *adj. & adv.* **1.** Floating. **2.** On a boat or ship away from the shore; at sea. **3.** In circulation; prevailing. **4.** Awash; flooded. **5.** Drifting about; moving without guidance. **6.** Free or out of difficulty, esp. financial difficulty: *couldn't keep the business afloat.*

a·flut·ter (ə-flŭt'ər) *adj.* In a flutter; nervous and excited.

a·foot (ə-fo͝ot') *adj. & adv.* **1.** Walking; on foot. **2.** In the process of being carried out; astir.

a·fore (ə-fôr', ə-fōr') *adv., prep., & conj. Archaic.* Before. [ME < OE *onforan* : *on,* at + *for,* fore.]

a·fore·men·tioned (ə-fôr'mĕn'shənd, ə-fōr'-) *adj.* Mentioned previously or before.

a·fore·said (ə-fôr'sĕd', ə-fōr'-) *adj.* Spoken of earlier.

a·fore·thought (ə-fôr'thôt', ə-fōr'-) *adj.* Planned or intended beforehand; premeditated: *malice aforethought.*

a·fore·time (ə-fôr'tīm', ə-fōr'-) *Archaic. —adv.* At a former or past time; previously. *—adj.* Earlier; former.

a for·ti·o·ri (ä fôr'tē-ôr'ē, ā fōr'tē-ō'rī') *adv.* For a stronger reason; all the more. Used of a conclusion arrived at with greater logical necessity than another. [Lat.]

a·foul of (ə-foul') *prep.* In or into a condition of collision, entanglement, or conflict. ***—idiom.* run (or fall) afoul of.** To become entangled or in conflict with.

a·fraid (ə-frād') *adj.* **1.** Filled with fear. **2.** Reluctant; averse: *not afraid of work.* **3.** Filled with regret: *I'm afraid you're wrong.* [ME *affraied,* p.part. of *affraien,* to frighten < OFr. *esfreer,* to disturb.]

A-frame (ā'frām) *n.* A structure, as a house, with steeply angled sides and a roof that reaches to the ground. [From its being shaped like a capital *A.*]

af·reet also **af·rit** (ăf'rēt', ə-frēt') *n. Arabic Myth.* A powerful evil spirit or gigantic and monstrous demon. [Ar. *'ifrīt.*]

a·fresh (ə-frĕsh') *adv.* Once more; anew; again.

Af·ri·can (ăf'rĭ-kən) *adj.* Of or pertaining to Africa or any of its peoples or languages. *—n.* **1.** A person born or living in Africa. **2.** A member of one of the indigenous peoples of Africa.

African lily *n.* A plant, *Agapanthus africanus,* native to southern Africa, having rounded clusters of blue, violet, or white flowers.

African mahogany *n.* **1. a.** Any of several African trees of the genus *Khaya,* esp. *K. ivorensis,* having wood similar to that of true mahogany. **b.** The wood of this tree, used for furniture, musical instruments, and boat interiors. **2.** Any of various other African woods resembling true mahogany.

African marigold *n.* A widely cultivated plant, *Tagetes erecta,* native to Mexico, having finely divided foliage and showy, rounded orange or yellow flowers.

African sleeping sickness *n.* Sleeping sickness.

African violet *n.* Any of several plants of the genus *Saintpaulia,* native to tropical Africa and widely cultivated as house plants, esp. *S. ionantha,* having violet, white, or pink flowers.

African violet

Af·ri·kaans (ăf'rĭ-käns', -känz') *n.* A language that developed from 17th-century Dutch and is an official language of the Republic of South Africa. [Afr. < Du. *Afrikaansch,* African.]

Af·ri·ka·ner (ăf'rĭ-kä'nər) *n.* An Afrikaans-speaking descendant of the Dutch settlers of South Africa. [Afr., African < Lat. *Africanus.*]

af·rit (ăf'rēt', ə-frēt') *n.* Variant of **afreet.**

Af·ro (ăf'rō) *n., pl.* **-ros.** A rounded, bushy hair style. *—adj.* **1.** Of or for an Afro: *an Afro comb.* **2.** Directly or indirectly African in style. [Perh. short for AFRO-AMERICAN.]

Afro– *pref.* African: *Afro-Asiatic.* [< Lat. *Afer,* an African.]

Af·ro-A·mer·i·can (ăf'rō-ə-mĕr'ĭ-kən) *adj.* Of or pertaining to American blacks of African ancestry, their history, or their culture. *—n.* An American black of African ancestry.

Af·ro-A·si·at·ic (ăf'rō-ā'zhē-ăt'ĭk, -zē-) *n.* A family of languages of southwestern Asia and northern Africa. **—Af'ro-A'si·at'ic** *adj.*

aft (aft) *adv. & adj. Naut.* At, in, toward, or close to the stern of a vessel. [Prob. shortening of ABAFT.]

af·ter (ăf'tər) *prep.* **1.** Behind in place or order. **2.** In quest or pursuit of: *seek after fame.* **3.** Concerning: *asked after you.* **4.** Subsequent in time to; at a later time than: *come after dinner.* **5.** Subsequent to and because of or regardless of: *friends after all their differences.* **6.** Following continually: *year after year.* **7.** Next to or lower than in order or importance. **8.** In the style of; in imitation of: *satires after Horace.* **9.** With the same or close to the same name as; in honor or commemoration of: *named after her mother.* **10.** According to the nature or desires of; in conformity to: *a man after my own heart.* **11.** Past the hour of: *five minutes after three.* *—adv.* **1.** Behind; in the rear. **2.** At a later or subsequent time; afterward. *—adj.* **1.** Subsequent in time or place; later; following: *in after years.* **2.** *Naut.* Nearer the stern of a vessel; *farther aft.* *—conj.* Following or subsequent to the time that: *I saw her after I arrived.* ***—idiom.* after all. 1.** When everything is considered. **2.** Eventually; ultimately. [ME < OE *æfter.*]

af·ter·birth (ăf'tər-bûrth') *n.* The placenta and fetal membranes expelled from the uterus after childbirth.

af·ter·burn·er (ăf'tər-bûr'nər) *n.* **1.** A device for augmenting the thrust of a jet engine by burning additional fuel with the uncombined oxygen in the hot exhaust gases. **2.** A device for burning or chemically altering unburned or partially burned carbon compounds in exhaust gases.

af·ter·care (ăf'tər-kâr') *n.* Treatment or special care given to convalescent patients, esp. after undergoing surgery.

af·ter·clap (ăf'tər-klăp') *n.* An unexpected, often unpleasant sequel to a matter that had been considered closed.

af·ter·damp (ăf'tər-dămp') *n.* An asphyxiating mixture of gases, primarily nitrogen and carbon dioxide, left in a mine after a fire or explosion.

af·ter·deck (ăf'tər-dĕk') *n. Naut.* The part of a ship's deck past amidships toward the stern.

af·ter·ef·fect (ăf'tĭr-ĭ-fĕkt') *n.* An effect following its cause after some delay, esp. a delayed or prolonged physiological or psychological response to a stimulus.

af·ter·glow (ăf'tər-glō') *n.* **1.** The light emitted or remaining after removal of a source of illumination, esp.: **a.** The atmospheric glow after sunset. **b.** The glow of an incandescent metal as it cools. **c.** Emission from a phosphor after removal of excitation. **2.** The comfortable feeling following a pleasant experience. **3.** A lingering impression of past brilliance.

af·ter-hours (ăf'tər-ourz') *adj.* **1.** Occurring after closing time: *after-hours drinking.* **2.** Open after a legal or established closing time: *an after-hours club.*

af·ter·im·age (ăf′tər-ĭm′ĭj) *n.* A visual image that persists after a visual stimulus ceases.
af·ter·life (ăf′tər-līf′) *n.* **1.** A life believed to follow death. **2.** The part of one's life that follows a particular event.
af·ter·mar·ket (ăf′tər-mär′kĭt) *n.* The demand for goods or services, such as repairs, associated with the upkeep of a previous purchase.
af·ter·math (ăf′tər-măth′) *n.* **1.** A consequence or result, esp. of a disaster or misfortune. **2.** A period of time following a disastrous event. **3.** A second crop of grass in the same season. [AFTER + obs. *math,* mowing, < OE *mǣð.*]
af·ter·most (ăf′tər-mōst′) *adj.* **1.** *Naut.* Nearest the stern; farthest aft. **2.** Nearest the end or rear; hindmost; last.
af·ter·noon (ăf′tər-no͞on′) *n.* **1.** The part of the day from noon until sunset. **2.** The closing part.
af·ter·pains (ăf′tər-pānz′) *pl.n.* The cramps or pains following childbirth, resulting from the contraction of the womb.
af·ter·piece (ăf′tər-pēs′) *n.* A short comic piece performed after a play.
af·ter·sen·sa·tion (ăf′tər-sĕn-sā′shən) *n.* A sensory impression, such as an afterimage or aftertaste, that persists or recurs after removal of a stimulus.
af·ter-shave (ăf′tər-shāv′) *n.* A usually fragrant lotion for use on the face after shaving.
af·ter·taste (ăf′tər-tāst′) *n.* **1.** A taste persisting in the mouth after the substance causing it is no longer present. **2.** A feeling that remains after an event or experience.
af·ter·thought (ăf′tər-thôt′) *n.* An idea, response, or explanation that occurs to one after an event or decision.
af·ter·time (ăf′tər-tīm′) *n.* The time to come; future.
af·ter·ward (ăf′tər-wərd) also **af·ter·wards** (-wərdz) *adv.* In or at a later time; subsequently.
af·ter·word (ăf′tər-wûrd′) *n.* An epilogue (sense 2).
af·ter·world (ăf′tər-wûrld′) *n.* A world thought to come after death.
aft·most (ăft′mōst′) *adj. Naut.* Farthest aft; aftermost.
Ag The symbol for the element silver. [Lat. *argentum.*]
ag– *pref.* Variant of **ad-**. Used before *g.*
a·ga also **a·gha** (ä′gə, ăg′a) *n.* A high official of the Ottoman Empire. [Turk. *ağa.*]
a·gain (ə-gĕn′) *adv.* **1.** Once more; another time; anew. **2.** To a previous place, position, or state: *left home but went back again.* **3.** Furthermore; moreover. **4.** On the other hand: *might go and again might not.* **5.** In return; in response; back. —*idioms.* **again and again.** Repeatedly; frequently. **as much again. 1.** The same amount. **2.** Twice as much. [ME < OE *ongeagn,* against.]
a·gainst (ə-gĕnst′) *prep.* **1.** In a direction or course opposite to: *row against the current.* **2.** So as to come into forcible contact with: *waves dashing against the shore.* **3.** In contact with so as to rest or press on: *leaned against the tree.* **4.** In hostile opposition or resistance to: *struggle against fate.* **5.** Contrary to; opposed to: *against my better judgment.* **6.** In contrast or comparison with the setting or background of: *dark colors against a fair skin.* **7.** In preparation for; in anticipation of: *food stored against winter.* **8.** As a defense or safeguard from: *protection against the cold.* **9.** To the account or debt of: *drew a check against her bank balance.* **10.** Directly opposite to; facing. [ME, alteration of *againes* < OE *ongeagn.*]
a·ga·lac·ti·a (ā-gə-lăk′tē-ə, -shē-ə, ăg′ə-) *n.* Nonsecretion or dysfunctional secretion of milk following childbirth. [NLat. < Gk. *agalaktia,* lack of milk : *a-,* not + *gala,* milk.]
a·ga·ma (ə-gä′mə, ăg′ə-) *n.* Any of various small, long-tailed, insect-eating lizards of the family Agamidae, found in Old World tropics. [Carib.]
Ag·a·mem·non (ăg′ə-mĕm′nŏn′, -nən) *n. Gk. Myth.* The king of Mycenae, leader of the Greeks against Troy, husband of Clytemnestra, and father of Orestes, Electra, and Iphigenia. [Gk. *Agamemnōn.*]
a·ga·mete (ā′gə-mēt′, ā-găm′ēt′) *n.* An asexual reproductive cell that progresses into an adult individual.
a·gam·ic (ā-găm′ĭk) *adj. Biol.* Occurring or reproducing without the union of male and female cells; asexual or parthenogenetic. [< LLat. *agamus,* unmarried < Gk. *agamos* : *a-,* not + *gamos,* marriage.] —**a·gam′i·cal·ly** *adv.*
a·gam·o·gen·e·sis (ā-găm′ə-jĕn′ĭ-sĭs, ăg′ə-mō-) *n.* Asexual reproduction, as by budding, cell division, or parthenogenesis. [AGAM(IC) + -GENESIS.]
ag·a·mous (ăg′ə-mas) *adj.* Agamic.
ag·a·pan·thus (ăg′ə-păn′thəs) *n.* Any plant of the genus *Agapanthus,* which includes the African lily. [NLat. *Agapanthus,* genus name : Gk. *agapē,* love + Gk. *anthos,* flower.]
a·gape¹ (ə-găp′, ə-găp′) *adv. & adj.* **1.** In a state of wonder or amazement. **2.** Wide open.
a·ga·pe² (ä-gä′pā, ä′gə-pā′) *n.* **1.** Christian love. **2.** Love that is spiritual, not sexual, in its nature. **3.** In the early Christian Church, the love feast accompanied by Eucharistic celebration. [Gk. *agapē,* love.]
a·gar (ā′gär′, ä′gär′) also **a·gar-a·gar** (ā′gär-ā′gär′, ä′gär-ä′-) *n.* A gelatinous material prepared from certain marine algae and used as a base for bacterial culture media, as a laxative, and for thickening certain foods. [Short for Malay *agar-agar.*]
ag·a·ric (ăg′-ər-ĭk, ə-găr′ĭk) *n.* **1.** Any fungus of the family Agaricaceae, including the common cultivated mushroom, *Agaricus campestris.* **2.** The dried fruiting body of the fungus *Fomes laricis,* formerly used in medicine. [Lat. *agaricum,* a kind of fungus < Gk. *agarikon.*]

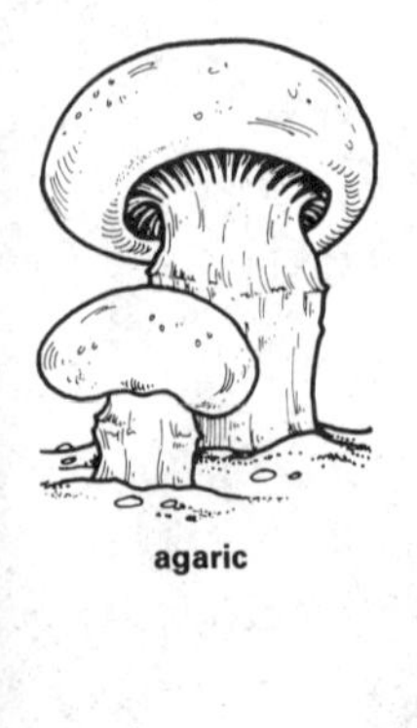

agaric

ag·ate (ăg′ĭt) *n.* **1.** A fine-grained, fibrous variety of chalcedony with color banding or irregular clouding. **2.** A child's marble made of agate or a glass imitation of it. **3.** A tool with agate parts, as a burnisher tipped with agate. **4.** A printer's type size, approximately $5\frac{1}{2}$ points. [ME *achate* < OFr. *acate* < Lat. *achates* < Gk. *akhatēs.*]
agate line *n.* A measure of space used in estimating printed advertising, usually one column wide and $\frac{1}{14}$ of an inch deep.
a·ga·ve (ə-gä′vē, ə-gā′-) *n.* Any of numerous fleshy-leaved tropical American plants of the genus *Agave,* which includes the century plant. Some species yield valuable fibers. [NLat. *Agave,* genus name < Gk. *agauē,* fem. of *agauos,* noble.]
age (āj) *n.* **1.** The period of time during which someone or something exists. **2.** A lifetime. **3.** The time in life when a person becomes qualified to assume certain civil and personal rights and responsibilities, usually at eighteen or twenty-one years; legal age: *under age.* **4.** A period of life denoted as differing from other periods; stage: *the age of adolescence.* **5.** The latter portion of life; the state of being old. **6.** Any period in history or geology designated by distinctive characteristics: *the age of enlightenment.* **7.** *Informal.* An extended period of time: *left ages ago.* **8.** *Psychol.* Mental age. —*v.* **aged, ag·ing, ag·es.** —*tr.* To cause to grow older or more mature. —*intr.* **1.** To become old. **2.** To manifest traits associated with old age. **3.** To develop a certain quality of ripeness; become mature: *cheese aging at room temperature.* [ME < OFr. *aage* < Lat. *aetas,* age.] —**ag′er** *n.*
-age *suff.* **1.** Collection; mass: *sewerage.* **2.** Relationship; connection: *parentage.* **3.** Condition; state: *vagabondage.* **4. a.** An action: *blockage.* **b.** Result of an action: *breakage.* **5.** Residence or place of: *vicarage.* **6.** Charge or fee: *cartage.* [ME < OFr. < Lat. *-aticum,* n. and adj. suffix.]
ag·ed (ā′jĭd) *adj.* **1.** Old; on in years. **2.** Of, pertaining to, or characteristic of old age. **3.** (ājd). Of the age of: *aged three.* **4.** *Geol.* Near the base level of erosion. —**ag′ed·ly** *adv.* —**ag′ed·ness** *n.*
age·ing (ā′jĭng) *n. Brit.* Variant of **aging.**
age·ism (ā′jĭz′əm) *n.* Discrimination based on age, esp. discrimination against middle-aged and elderly people. —**age′·ist** *n.*
age·less (āj′lĭs) *adj.* **1.** Never seeming to grow old. **2.** Existing forever; eternal. —**age′less·ly** *adv.* —**age′less·ness** *n.*
a·gen·cy (ā′jən-sē) *n., pl.* **-cies. 1.** Action; operation. **2.** A mode of action; means. **3.** A business or service authorized to act for others: *an employment agency.* **4.** A governmental department of administration or regulations. [Med. Lat. *agentia* < *agens,* effective. —see AGENT.]
a·gen·da (ə-jĕn′də) *n. (used with a sing. verb).* **1.** A list of things to be done, esp. the program for a meeting. **2.** Plural of **agendum.** [Lat. pl. of *agendum,* agendum.]
Usage: *Agenda,* meaning "list" or "program," is well established as a collective noun with singular verb; a great majority of the Usage Panel accepts such a combination.
a·gen·dum (ə-jĕn′dəm) *n., pl.* **-da** (-də) or **-das.** Something to be done, esp. an item on an agenda. [Lat., neuter gerund. of *agere,* to do.]
a·gen·e·sis (ā-jĕn′ĭ-sĭs) *n.* Failure of an organism, organ, or part to develop.
a·gent (ā′jənt) *n.* **1.** One that acts or has the power or authority to act. **2.** One that acts for or as the representative of another: *an insurance agent.* **3.** A means or mode by which something is done or caused; instrument. **4.** A force or substance that causes some change: *a chemical agent.* **5.** A representative of a government or administrative department of a government: *an FBI agent.* **6.** A spy. [ME < Lat. *agens,* effective, pr.part. of *agere,* to do.]
a·gen·tial (ā-jĕn′shəl) *adj.* Of, pertaining to, or acting as an agent or agency.
a·gent pro·vo·ca·teur (ä-zhäN′ prô-vô′kä-tœr′) *n., pl.* **a·gents pro·vo·ca·teurs** (ä-zhäN′ prô-vô′kä-tœr′). A secret agent who infiltrates an organization in order to incite trouble designed to make its members commit acts that will incur punishment. [Fr.]
age of consent *n. Law.* The age at which a female may legally choose to have sexual intercourse.
ag·er·a·tum (ăj′ə-rā′təm) *n.* **1.** Any of various plants of the genus *Ageratum,* esp. *A. houstonianum,* a commonly cultivated species having clusters of usually violet-blue flowers. **2.** Any of several other plants having flower clusters similar to the ageratum. [NLat. *Ageratum,* genus name < Gk. *agēratos,* ageless : *a-,* not + *gēras,* old age.]
ag·gie¹ (ăg′ē) *n.* A playing marble. [AG(ATE) + -IE.]
ag·gie² (ăg′ē) *n.* **1.** An agricultural college. **2.** A student enrolled at an agricultural college or in an agricultural program within a university. [AG(RICULTURAL) + -IE.]
ag·gior·na·men·to (ə-jôr′nə-mĕn′tō) *n., pl.* **-tos.** The process of bringing up to date an institution or organization. [Ital. < *aggiornare,* to update : *a-,* to (< Lat. *ad.*) + *giorno,* day < Lat. *diurnus,* daily < *dies,* day.]
ag·glom·er·ate (ə-glŏm′ə-rāt′) *tr. & intr.v.* **-at·ed, -at·ing, -ates.** To make or form into a rounded mass. —*adj.* (-ər-ĭt). Gathered into a rounded mass. —*n.* (-ər-ĭt). **1.** A confused

or jumbled mass of things clustered together; heap. **2.** A volcanic rock consisting of rounded and angular fragments fused together. [Lat. *agglomerare, agglomerat-,* to annex : *ad-,* to + *glomerare,* to form into a ball < *glomus,* ball.] **—ag·glom'er·a'tive** (-ə-rā'tĭv, -ər-ə-tĭv) *adj.* **—ag·glom'er·a'tor** *n.*

ag·glom·er·a·tion (ə-glŏm'ə-rā'shən) *n.* **1.** The act or process of agglomerating. **2.** The state of being agglomerated. **3.** A confused or jumbled mass; agglomerate.

ag·glu·ti·nate (ə-glo͞ot'n-āt') *v.* **-nat·ed, -nat·ing, -nates.** *—tr.* **1.** To join together by causing adhesion, as with glue. **2.** *Ling.* To form (words) by combining words or words and word elements. **3.** *Physiol.* To cause (red blood cells or microorganisms) to clump together. *—intr.* **1.** To join together into a group or mass. **2.** *Ling.* To form words by agglutination. **3.** To undergo agglutination. [Lat. *agglutinare, agglutinat* : *ad-,* to + *glutinare,* to glue < *gluten,* glue.] **—ag·glu'ti·nant** *adj. & n.*

ag·glu·ti·na·tion (ə-glo͞ot'n-ā'shən) *n.* **1.** The process of agglutinating; adhesion of distinct parts. **2.** A mass formed by agglutinating. **3.** *Ling.* The formation of words from morphemes that retain their original forms and meanings with little change during the combination process.

ag·glu·ti·na·tive (ə-glo͞ot'n-ā'tĭv) *adj.* **1.** Tending toward, concerning, or characteristic of agglutination. **2.** *Ling.* Designating a language in which words are formed primarily by means of agglutination.

ag·glu·ti·nin (ə-glo͞ot'n-ĭn) *n.* A substance that induces agglutination. [AGGLUTIN(ATION) + -IN.]

ag·glu·tin·o·gen (ăg'lo͞o-tĭn'ə-jən, ə-glo͞o'tn-) *n.* An antigen that stimulates the production of an agglutinin. [AGGLUTIN(IN) + -GEN.] **—ag'glu·tin'o·gen'ic** (ăg'lo͞o-tĭn'ə-jĕn'ĭk, ə-glo͞o'tn-) *adj.*

ag·grade (ə-grād') *tr.v.* **-grad·ed, -grad·ing, -grades.** To fill and raise the level of (the bed of a stream) by deposition of sediment. **—ag'gra·da'tion** (ăg'rə-dā'shən) *n.* **—ag'gra·da'tion·al** *adj.*

ag·gran·dize (ə-grăn'dīz', ăg'rən-) *tr.v.* **-dized, -diz·ing, -diz·es.** **1.** To increase the scope of; enlarge; extend. **2.** To make greater in power, influence, stature, or reputation. **3.** To make seem greater; exaggerate. [Fr. *aggrandir, aggrandiss-* : *a-,* to (< Lat. *ad-*) + *grandir,* to grow larger < Lat. *grandire* < *grandis,* large.] **—ag·gran'dize·ment** (ə-grăn'dĭz-mənt, -dīz'-) *n.* **—ag·gran'diz'er** *n.*

ag·gra·vate (ăg'rə-vāt') *tr.v.* **-vat·ed, -vat·ing, -vates.** **1.** To make worse or more troublesome; make more of a burden. **2.** *Informal.* To annoy or exasperate; provoke; irritate; vex. [Lat. *aggravare, aggravat-* : *ad,* to + *gravare,* to burden < *gravis,* heavy.] **—ag'gra·vat'ing·ly** *adv.* **—ag'gra·va'tive** *adj.* **—ag'gra·va'tor** *n.*

Usage: The word *aggravate* is widely used to mean "to irritate," as in *The mechanic's surliness aggravated me no end.* But many still insist that the word should be used only to mean "to make worse," in referring to a situation or condition, as in: *The plight of the small farmer has been aggravated by the drought. Kim's bad back was aggravated by his refusal to get sufficient rest.*

aggravated assault *n. Law.* Any of various assaults that are more serious than a common assault, esp. one performed with an intent to commit a crime.

ag·gra·va·tion (ăg'rə-vā'shən) *n.* **1.** The act of aggravating. **2.** The state of being aggravated. **3.** A thing that irritates or makes worse, more troublesome, or more irritated. **4.** *Informal.* Exasperation; bothersomeness.

ag·gre·gate (ăg'rĭ-gĭt) *adj.* **1.** Gathered together into a mass or sum so as to constitute a whole; total. **2.** *Bot.* Crowded or massed into a dense cluster. **3.** Composed of a mixture of minerals separable by mechanical means. *—n.* (-gĭt). **1.** Any total or whole considered with reference to its constituent parts; an assemblage or group of distinct particulars massed together; gross amount: "*An empire is the aggregate of many states under one common head*" (Burke). **2.** The mineral materials, such as sand or stone, used in making concrete. *—tr.v.* (-gāt') **-gat·ed, -gat·ing, -gates.** **1.** To gather into a mass, sum, or whole. **2.** To total up to; amount to. [ME *aggregat* < Lat. *aggregare,* to add to : *ad-,* to + *gregare,* to collect < *grex,* flock.] **—ag'gre·gate·ly** *adv.* **—ag'gre·ga'tion** *n.* **—ag'gre·ga'tive** *adj.* **—ag'gre·ga'tor** *n.*

aggregate fruit *n.* A fruit, such as the raspberry, developed from the pistils of a single flower and consisting of a coherent mass of drupelets.

ag·gress (ə-grĕs') *intr.v.* **-gressed, -gress·ing, -gress·es.** To start an attack or a quarrel. [Fr. *aggresser* < Lat. *aggredi* : *ad-,* toward + *gradi,* to go.]

Usage: Though the verb *aggress* has a long and honorable history, it has lately come to be associated primarily with the jargon of psychology and is often objected to.

ag·gres·sion (ə-grĕsh'ən) *n.* **1.** The act of commencing hostilities or invasion; assault. **2.** The habit or practice of launching attacks. **3.** *Psychoanal.* Hostile action or behavior.

ag·gres·sive (ə-grĕs'ĭv) *adj.* **1.** Inclined to move or act in a hostile fashion. **2.** Assertive; bold; enterprising. **—ag·gres'sive·ly** *adv.* **—ag·gres'sive·ness** *n.*

ag·gres·sor (ə-grĕs'ər) *n.* One that engages in aggression.

ag·grieve (ə-grēv') *tr.v.* **-grieved, -griev·ing, -grieves.** **1.** To distress or afflict. **2.** To injure unjustly; give reason for just complaint. [ME *agreven* < OFr. *agrever* < Lat. *aggravare,* to make worse. —see AGGRAVATE.]

ag·grieved (ə-grēvd') *adj.* **1.** Feeling distress or affliction. **2.** Treated wrongly; offended. **3.** *Law.* Treated unjustly by a decision of the court or other legal authority. **—ag·griev'ed·ly** (ə-grē'vĭd-lē) *adv.* **—ag·griev'ed·ness** *n.*

a·gha (ä'gə, ăg'ə) *n.* Variant of **aga.**

a·ghast (ə-găst') *adj.* Shocked, as by something horrible; terrified. [ME *agast,* p.part. of *agasten,* to frighten : *a-* (intensive) + *gasten,* to frighten < OE *gæstan* < *gāst,* ghost.]

ag·ile (ăj'əl, ăj'īl') *adj.* **1.** Able to move in a quick and easy fashion; active. **2.** Mentally alert. [OFr. < Lat. *agilis* < *agere,* to impel.] **—ag'ile·ly** *adv.* **—ag'ile·ness** *n.*

a·gil·i·ty (ə-jĭl'ĭ-tē) *n.* The state or quality of being agile; nimbleness; briskness.

a·gin (ə-gĭn') *prep. Regional.* Against.

ag·ing (ā'jĭng) *n.* **1.** The process of becoming old or mature. **2.** An artificial process for imparting the characteristics and properties of age.

ag·i·o (ăj'ē-ō') *n., pl.* **-os.** **1.** A premium paid for changing one kind of money to another. **2.** An allowance or premium for the difference in value between two currencies being exchanged. [Ital. < Med. Gk. *allagion,* exchange < *allagē,* change < *allos,* other.]

ag·i·tate (ăj'ĭ-tāt') *v.* **-tat·ed, -tat·ing, -tates.** *—tr.* **1.** To move with violence or sudden forcefulness; excite physically: *a storm agitating the ocean.* **2.** To upset; disturb: *agitated by grief.* **3.** To arouse interest in (a cause, for example) by the written or spoken word; discuss; debate. **4.** *Archaic.* To ponder over; plan. *—intr.* To stir up public interest in a cause. [Lat. *agitare, agitat-,* freq. of *agere,* to impel.] **—ag'i·tat'ed·ly** (-tā'tĭd-lē) *adv.* **—ag'i·ta'tive** *adj.*

ag·i·ta·tion (ăj'ĭ-tā'shən) *n.* **1.** The act of agitating. **2.** The state of being agitated; disturbance; commotion. **3.** Extreme emotional disturbance; perturbation. **4.** The stirring up of public interest in a matter of controversy, such as a political or social issue. **—ag'i·ta'tion·al** *adj.*

ag·i·ta·to (ăj'ĭ-tä'tō) *adj. Mus.* Agitated; fast and stirring. Used as a direction. [Ital. < Lat. *agitare,* to agitate.] **—ag'i·ta'to** *adv.*

ag·i·ta·tor (ăj'ĭ-tā'tər) *n.* **1.** A person who agitates, esp. one who engages in political agitation. **2.** A machine mechanism that stirs or shakes, as in a washing.

ag·it·prop (ăj'ĭt-prŏp') *n.* Communist-oriented political propaganda disseminated esp. through literature, drama, art, or music. [R., office of agitation and propaganda : *agitatsiya,* agitation + *propaganda,* propaganda.]

A·gla·ia (ə-glā'ə, ə-glī'ə) *n. Gk. Myth.* One of the three Graces. [Gk. < *aglaia,* splendor < *aglaos,* bright.]

a·gleam (ə-glēm') *adj. & adv.* Brightly shining.

ag·let (ăg'lĭt) *n.* **1.** A tag or metal sheath on the end of a lace, cord, or ribbon to facilitate its passing through eyelet holes. **2.** A device similar to the aglet used for an ornament. [ME < OFr. *aguillette,* dim. of *aguille,* needle < LLat. *acicula,* dim. of Lat. *acus,* needle.]

a·gley (ə-glī', ə-glā', ə-glē') *adv. Scot.* Off to one side; awry. [Scottish : *a-,* on + *gley,* to squint < ME *glien.*]

a·glim·mer (ə-glĭm'ər) *adj. & adv.* Lighting up faintly; glimmering.

a·glit·ter (ə-glĭt'ər) *adj.* Glittering; sparkling. **—a·glit'ter** *adv.*

a·glow (ə-glō') *adj. & adv.* In a glow; glowing.

a·gly·con (ə-glī'kŏn) or **a·gly·cone** (-kōn') *n.* A nonsugar component of a glycoside that is resolvable through hydrolysis.

ag·mi·nate (ăg'mə-nĭt, -nāt') also **ag·mi·nat·ed** (-nā'tĭd) *adj.* Gathered in clusters. [< Lat. *agmen, agmin-,* multitude.]

ag·nail (ăg'nāl') *n.* **1.** A hangnail. **2.** A painful sore or swelling around a fingernail or toenail. [ME *angnail,* corn < OE *angnægl,* a sore under the nail : *ang-,* tight + *nægel,* nail.]

ag·nate (ăg'nāt') *adj.* **1.** Related on or descended from the father's or male side. **2.** From a common source; akin. *—n.* A relative on the father's or male side only. [Lat. *agnatus,* a relation on the father's side < the p.part. of *agnasci,* to be born in addition to : *ad-,* to + *nasci,* to be born.] **—ag·nat'ic** (ăg-năt'ĭk) *adj.* **—ag·nat'i·cal·ly** *adv.* **—ag·na'tion** *n.*

Ag·ni (ŭg'nē) *n. Hinduism.* The Vedic god of fire and guardian of man. [Skt. *agniḥ,* fire.]

ag·no·men (ăg-nō'mən) *n., pl.* **-nom·i·na** (-nŏm'ə-nə). **1.** An additional cognomen given to a Roman citizen, often in honor of military victories. **2.** A nickname. [Lat. : *ad-,* to + *nomen,* name.]

ag·no·sia (ăg-nō'zhə) *n.* Pathologic loss of auditory, sensory, or visual comprehension. [NLat. < Gk. *agnōsia,* ignorance : *a-,* not + *gnōsis,* knowledge < *gignōskein,* to know.]

ag·nos·tic (ăg-nŏs'tĭk) *n.* Someone who believes that there can be no proof of the existence of God but does not deny the possibility that God exists. *—adj.* Pertaining to agnostics or their doctrines. [< Gk. *agnōstos,* unknown : *a-,* not + *gnōstos,* known < *gignōskein,* to know.] **—ag·nos'ti·cal·ly** *adv.*

ag·nos·ti·cism (ăg-nŏs'tĭ-sĭz'əm) *n.* **1.** *Philos.* The doctrines of the agnostics, holding that certainty, first or absolute truths, are unattainable and that only perceptual phenomena are objects of exact knowledge. **2.** *Theol.* A theory that

agave

Agnus Dei
On a casket

agouti

agrimony

does not deny God but denies the possibility of knowing Him.

Ag·nus De·i (ăg′nəs dē′ī′, än′yo͞os dā′ē, äg′no͞os′) *n.* **1.** The Lamb of God, an emblem of Christ. **2.** An iconographic representation of the Agnus Dei. **3.** A liturgical prayer to Christ. [Lat.]

a·go (ə-gō′) *adj.* Gone by; past: *two years ago.* —*adv.* In the past: *happened long ago.* [ME, p.part. of *agon,* to go away < OE *āgān* : *ā-* (intensive) + *gān,* to go.]

Usage: *Ago* may be followed by *that* or *when: It was a week ago that* (or *when*) *I saw him.* It may not be followed by *since: It was a week ago since I saw him. Since* is properly used without *ago,* as in *It has been a week since I saw him.*

a·gog (ə-gŏg′) *adv. & adj.* In a state of keen anticipation; highly excited; astir. [ME *agogge* < OFr. *en gogue,* in merriment.]

-agog *suff.* Variant of **-agogue.**

à go·go also **à-go-go** (ə-gō-gō′) *adv.* In a fast and lively manner; freely: *dancing à gogo.* [Fr., galore.]

-agogue or **-agog** *suff.* A substance that stimulates the flow of: *hemagogue.* [LLat. *-agogus* < Gk. *-agogos* < *agein,* to lead.]

a·gone (ə-gôn′, ə-gŏn′) *adj. & adv. Archaic.* Gone; gone by; past. [ME *agon,* p.part. of *agon,* to go away. —see AGO.]

a·gon·ic (ā-gŏn′ĭk, ə-gŏn′-) *adj.* Having no angle. [< Gk. *agōnos* : *a-,* not + *gōnia,* angle.]

agonic line *n.* An imaginary line on the earth's surface connecting points where the magnetic declination is zero.

ag·o·nist (ăg′ə-nĭst) *n.* **1.** *Physiol.* A muscle that contracts and is opposed by contraction in another muscle, the antagonist. **2.** One involved in a struggle or competition. [Back-formation < ANTAGONIST.]

ag·o·nis·tic (ăg′ə-nĭs′tĭk) also **ag·o·nis·ti·cal** (-tĭ-kəl) *adj.* **1.** Striving to overcome in argument; competitive; combative. **2.** Straining to achieve effect. **3.** Of or pertaining to contests, originally those of the ancient Greeks. [Gk. *agōnistikos* < *agōnistēs,* combatant < *agōn,* contest.] —**ag′o·nis′ti·cal·ly** *adv.*

ag·o·nize (ăg′ə-nīz′) *v.* **-nized, -niz·ing, -niz·es.** —*intr.* **1.** To be in extreme pain or suffer great anguish. **2.** To make a great effort; struggle. —*tr.* To cause great pain or anguish to. [OFr. *agoniser* < Med. Lat. *agonizare* < Gk. *agōnizesthai,* to struggle < *agōn,* contest.] —**ag′o·niz′ing·ly** *adv.*

ag·o·ny (ăg′ə-nē) *n., pl.* **-nies. 1.** The suffering of intense physical or mental pain. **2.** The struggle that precedes death. **3.** A sudden or intense emotion of a particular sort: *an agony of doubt.* **4.** A violent or intense struggle. [ME *agonie* < OFr. < Med. Lat. *agonia* < Gk. *agōnia* < *agōn,* struggle.]

agony column *n.* A newspaper column containing advertisements chiefly about missing relatives or friends.

ag·o·ra[1] (ăg′ə-rə) *n., pl.* **-rae** (-rē′) or **-ras.** A marketplace in ancient Greece, customarily used as a place of popular assembly. [Gk.]

a·go·ra[2] (ä′gə-rä′) *n., pl.* **-rot** (-rōt′) or **-roth** (-rōt′). See table at **currency.** [Heb. *'agōrāh* < *āgōr,* to collect.]

ag·o·ra·pho·bi·a (ăg′ə-rə-fō′bē-ə) *n.* Abnormal fear of open spaces. [Gk. *agora,* open space + -PHOBIA.] —**ag·o·ra·pho′bi·ac** *n.* —**ag′o·ra·pho′bic** (-fō′bĭk, -fŏb′ĭk) *adj.*

a·gou·ti (ə-go͞o′tē) *n., pl.* **-tis** or **-ties.** Any of several burrowing rodents of the genus *Dasyprocta,* of tropical America, having grizzled brownish or dark-gray fur. [Fr. < Sp. (South America) *agutí* < Guarani *acutí.*]

agr- *pref.* Variant of **agro-.**

a·graffe also **a·grafe** (ə-grăf′) *n.* **1.** A hook-and-loop arrangement used for a clasp on armor and clothing. **2.** A cramp iron for holding stones together in building. [Fr. *agrafe* < OFr. *agrafer,* to hook onto : *a-,* to (< Lat. *ad*) + *grafer,* to hook < *grafe,* hook, of Germanic orig.]

a·gran·u·lo·cy·to·sis (ā-grăn′yə-lō-sī-tō′sĭs) *n.* A drug-induced disease marked by high fever, lesions of the mucous membranes, and a decrease in granular white blood corpuscles.

ag·ra·pha also **Ag·ra·pha** (ăg′rə-fə) *pl.n.* The sayings of Jesus not in the Bible. [Gk. < *agraphos,* unwritten : *a-* not + *graphein,* to write.]

a·graph·i·a (ā-grăf′ē-ə) *n.* A disorder marked by the inability to write. [A-[1] + Gk. *graphein,* to write.] —**a·graph′ic** *adj.*

a·grar·i·an (ə-grâr′ē-ən) *adj.* **1.** Relating to or concerning the land and its ownership, cultivation, and tenure. **2.** Pertaining to agricultural or rural matters. —*n.* A person who favors equitable distribution of land. [< Lat. *agrarius* < *ager,* land.] —**a·grar′i·an·ly** *adv.*

a·grar·i·an·ism (ə-grâr′ē-ə-nĭz′əm) *n.* A movement for equitable distribution of land and for agrarian reform.

a·grav·ic (ā-grăv′ĭk) *adj.* Of or relating to a condition of no gravitation. [A-[1] + GRAV(ITY) + -IC.]

a·gree (ə-grē′) *v.* **a·greed, a·gree·ing, a·grees.** —*intr.* **1.** To grant consent; accede: *agreed to accompany us.* **2.** To come into or be in accord; match: *a copy that agrees with the original.* **3.** To be of one opinion: *didn't agree with me.* **4.** To come to an understanding or to terms: *finally agreed on the solution.* **5.** To be suitable or appropriate: *Spicy food does not agree with him.* **6.** *Gram.* To correspond in gender, number, case, or person. —*tr.* To grant or concede: *agreed that we should go.* [ME *agreen* < OFr. *agreer* < VLat. **aggratare* : Lat. *ad-,* to + Lat. *gratus,* pleasing.]

Synonyms: *agree, conform, harmonize, accord, correspond, coincide.* These verbs all indicate compatible relationship between people or things. *Agree* may indicate mere lack of incongruity or discord, but often it suggests acceptance of ideas or actions and thus accommodation. *Conform* stresses close resemblance in form, thought, or basic characteristics, sometimes the result of accommodation to established standards. *Harmonize* implies a relationship of unlike things combined or arranged to make a pleasing whole. *Accord* implies close similarity between things or harmonious relationship or both. *Correspond* refers either to actual similarity in form or nature or to similarity in function of unlike things. *Coincide* stresses exact agreement in space, time, or thought.

a·gree·a·ble (ə-grē′ə-bəl) *adj.* **1.** To one's liking; pleasing; pleasant. **2.** In accordance; suitable; conformable. **3.** Ready to consent or submit. —**a·gree′a·bil′i·ty, a·gree′a·ble·ness** *n.* —**a·gree′a·bly** *adv.*

a·greed (ə-grēd′) *adj.* **1.** Determined by common consent: *the agreed meeting place.* **2.** Of one opinion: *Both parties were agreed.* **3.** Allowed; granted: *Want to leave? Agreed.*

a·gree·ment (ə-grē′mənt) *n.* **1.** The act of agreeing. **2.** Harmony of opinion; accord. **3.** An arrangement between parties regarding a method of action; covenant. **4.** *Law.* **a.** A properly executed and legally binding compact. **b.** The writing or document embodying this. **5.** *Gram.* Correspondence in gender, number, case, or person between words.

a·gres·tal (ə-grĕs′təl) also **a·gres·tial** (-chəl) *adj.* Growing wild, esp. in cultivated areas, as weeds do. [Lat. *agrestis* < *ager,* land.]

a·gres·tic (ə-grĕs′tĭk) also **a·gres·ti·cal** (-tĭ-kəl) *adj.* **1.** Rural; rustic. **2.** Unpolished; crude.

ag·ri·a (ăg′rē-ə) *n.* Intense or extensive pustular eruption. [< Gk. *agria,* wild < *agros,* field.]

ag·ri·busi·ness (ăg′rə-bĭz′nĭs) *n.* Farming engaged in as big business, embracing the production, processing, and distribution of farm products and the manufacture of farm machinery, equipment, and supplies. [AGRI(CULTURE) + BUSINESS.]

ag·ri·cul·ture (ăg′rĭ-kŭl′chər) *n.* The science, art, and business of cultivating the soil, producing crops, and raising livestock; farming. [Lat. *agricultura* : *ager,* land + *cultura,* cultivation.] —**ag′ri·cul′tur·al** *adj.* —**ag′ri·cul′tur·al·ly** *adv.* —**ag′ri·cul′tur·ist, ag′ri·cul′tur·al·ist** *n.*

ag·ri·mo·ny (ăg′rə-mō′nē) *n., pl.* **-nies. 1.** Any of various plants of the genus *Agrimonia,* having compound leaves, long clusters of small yellow flowers, and bristly fruits. **2.** Any of several plants similar or related to the agrimony, such as the hemp agrimony. [ME *agrimonie* < OFr. *aigremoine* < Lat. *agrimonia,* alteration of *argemonia* < Gk. *argemōnē,* poppy.]

ag·ri·o·e·col·o·gy (ăg′rē-ō-ĭ-kŏl′ə-jē) *n.* The ecology of domestic or cultivated plants. [Gk. *agrios,* wild (< *agros,* field) + ECOLOGY.]

ag·ri·ol·o·gy (ăg′rē-ŏl′ə-jē) *n.* The study of peoples whose cultures are at an early stage of development. [Gk. *agrios,* wild (< *agros,* field) + -LOGY.] —**ag′ri·o·log′i·cal** (-ə-lŏj′ĭ-kəl) *adj.*

agro- or **agr-** *pref.* Field; soil: *agrology.* [< Gk. *agros,* field.]

ag·ro·bi·ol·o·gy (ăg′rō-bī-ŏl′ə-jē) *n.* The science of plant and animal growth and nutrition as related to soil variation and crop yield. —**ag′ro·bi′o·log′ic** (-ə-lŏj′ĭk), **ag′ro·bi′o·log′i·cal** *adj.* —**ag′ro·bi′o·log′i·cal·ly** *adv.* —**ag′ro·bi·ol′o·gist** *n.*

a·grol·o·gy (ə-grŏl′ə-jē) *n.* The applied science of soils in relation to crops. —**ag′ro·log′ic** (ăg′rə-lŏj′ĭk), **ag′ro·log′i·cal** *adj.* —**ag′ro·log′i·cal·ly** *adv.* —**a·grol′o·gist** *n.*

a·gron·o·my (ə-grŏn′ə-mē) also **ag·ro·nom·ics** (ăg′rə-nŏm′ĭks) *n.* The application of the various soil and plant sciences to soil management and the raising of crops; scientific agriculture. —**ag′ro·nom′ic** (ăg′rə-nŏm′ĭk), **ag′ro·nom′i·cal** *adj.* —**a·gron′o·mist** *n.*

ag·ros·tol·o·gy (ăg′rə-stŏl′ə-jē) *n.* The botanical study of grasses. [Gk. *agrōstis,* a kind of wild grass (< *agros,* field) + -LOGY.]

a·ground (ə-ground′) *adv. & adj.* Stranded in shallow water or on a reef or shoal: *a ship that ran aground.*

a·gryp·ni·a (ə-grĕp′nē-ə) *n.* Insomnia. [Gk. < *agrupnos,* wakeful.]

a·gue (ā′gyo͞o) *n.* **1.** A fever, like that of malaria, in which there are periods of chill, fever, and sweating. **2.** A chill or fit of shivering. [ME < OFr., short for *fievre ague,* sharp fever < Med. Lat. *febris acuta* : *febris,* fever + *acutus,* sharp.] —**a′gu·ish** (ā′gyo͞o-ĭsh) *adj.* —**a′gu·ish·ly** *adv.* —**a′gu·ish·ness** *n.*

a·gue·weed (ā′gyo͞o-wēd′) *n.* **1.** A plant, *Gentiana quinquefolia,* of eastern North America, having clusters of pale blue-violet or white flowers. **2.** Boneset.

ah (ä) *interj.* Used to express various emotions, such as surprise, delight, pain, satisfaction, or dislike.

a·ha (ä-hä′) *interj.* Used to express surprise, triumph, or pleasure.

a·head (ə-hĕd′) *adv.* **1.** At or to the front or head. **2.** In advance; before. **3.** Onward; forward. —***idioms.*** **ahead of.** In

front of. **be ahead.** *Informal.* To be gaining or winning. **get ahead.** To attain success.
a·hem (ə-hĕm′) *interj.* Used to attract attention or to express doubt or warning.
a·him·sa (ə-hĭm′sä′) *n.* A Buddhist and Hindu doctrine of nonviolence expressing belief in the sacredness of all living creatures. [Skt. *ahiṃsā* : *a-*, not + *hiṃsā*, injury < *hiṃsati*, he injures.]
a·hoy (ə-hoi′) *interj. Naut.* Used to hail a ship or person or to attract attention.
Ah·ri·man (ä′rĭ-mən) *n.* The spirit of evil in Zoroastrianism, understood by some as the arch rival of Ormazd. [Pers. *Ahrīman*, prob. < Avestan *aṅra mainyu* : *aṅra*, evil + *mainyu*, spirit.]
A·hu·ra Maz·da (ä-ho͝or′ə măz′də) *n.* Ormazd. [Avestan, wise god.]
ai (ī) *n.* A three-toed sloth of the genus *Bradypus.* [Port. < Tupi.]
aid (ād) *v.* **aid·ed, aid·ing, aids.** *—intr.* To help; assist. *—tr.* To give help or assistance to. *—n.* **1.** The act or result of helping; assistance. **2.** One that helps; an assistant or helper. **3.** An aide-de-camp or aide. **4.** In medieval England, a money payment to a feudal lord by a vassal. [ME *aiden* < OFr. *aider* < Lat. *adjutare*, freq. of *adjuvare*, to help : *ad-* (intensive) + *juvare*, to help.] **—aid′er** *n.*
aide (ād) *n.* **1.** An aide-de-camp. **2.** An assistant; helper: *a nurse's aide.* [Fr. < *aider*, to aid.]
aide-de-camp (ād′dĭ-kămp′) *n., pl.* **aides-de-camp.** A naval or military officer acting as secretary and confidential assistant to a superior officer of general or flag rank. [Fr.]
aide-mé·moire (ād′mām-wär′) *n.* **1.** Something that serves as an aid to memory, as a mnemonic device. **2.** An outline or memorandum setting forth the major points of a proposed agreement or discussion, used esp. in diplomatic communications. [Fr.]
AIDS (ādz) *n.* A disease caused by a virus that attacks the body's immunological system. AIDS is transmitted by venereal routes or blood products. [A(CQUIRED) I(MMUNE) D(EFICIENCY) S(YNDROME).]
ai·grette or **ai·gret** (ā-grĕt′, ā′grĕt′) *n.* **1.** An ornamental tuft of upright plumes, esp. the tail feathers of an egret. **2.** An ornament, such as a spray of gems, resembling an aigrette. [Fr., egret < OFr. —see EGRET.]
ai·guille (ā-gwēl′) *n.* **1.** A sharp, pointed mountain peak. **2.** A needle-shaped drill for boring holes in rock or masonry. [Fr., needle. —see AGLET.]
ai·guil·lette (ā′gwə-lĕt′) *n.* An ornamental cord or braid worn on the shoulder of a military uniform. [Fr. —see AGLET.]
ai·ki·do (ī′kē-dō′) *n.* A Japanese method of self-defense in which one's opponent's strength and weight are used against him. [J. *aikidō* : *ai*, mutual + *ki*, spirit + *dō*, art.]
ail (āl) *v.* **ailed, ail·ing, ails.** *—intr.* To feel ill or have pain; be unwell. *—tr.* To cause pain; make ill or uneasy; trouble. [ME *eilen* < OE *eglian* < *egle*, troublesome.]
ai·lan·thus (ā-lăn′thəs) *n.* A deciduous tree, *Ailanthus altissima*, native to China but naturalized in North America esp. in urban areas that has compound leaves and clusters of greenish flowers with an unpleasant odor. [NLat. *Ailanthus*, genus name < Amboinese *ai lanto*, tree of heaven.]
ai·le·ron (ā′lə-rŏn′) *n.* Either of two movable flaps on the wings of an airplane that can be used to control the plane's rolling and banking movements. [Fr., dim. of *aile*, wing < OFr. < Lat. *ala.*]
ail·ment (āl′mənt) *n.* A physical or mental disorder, esp. a mild illness.
ai·lu·ro·phile (ī-lo͝or′ə-fīl′, ā-lo͝or′-) *n.* One who loves cats. [Gk. *ailuros*, cat + -PHILE.]
ai·lu·ro·phobe (ī-lo͝or′ə-fōb′, ā-lo͝or′-) *n.* One who hates or fears cats. [Gk. *ailuros*, cat + -PHOBE.]
aim (ām) *v.* **aimed, aim·ing, aims.** *—tr.* To direct (a weapon, remark, or blow, for example) at someone or something. *—intr.* **1.** To direct a weapon: *a gunner aiming carefully.* **2.** To determine a course: *aim at better education.* **3.** To propose; intend: *aim to solve the problem.* *—n.* **1.** The act of aiming or pointing. **2.** The sighting or line of fire of something aimed. **3.** *Obs.* An object or point aimed at; target; mark. **4.** Purpose; intention; plan. **5.** *Obs.* A conjecture; guess. [ME *amen* < OFr. *aesmer*, to guess at : *a-*, at (< Lat. *ad*) + *esmer*, to guess < Lat. *aestimare*, to estimate.]
aim·less (ām′lĭs) *adj.* Without direction or purpose. **—aim′less·ly** *adv.* **—aim′less·ness** *n.*
ain (ān) *adj. Scot.* Own.
ain't (ānt). *Nonstandard.* **1.** Am not. **2.** Used also as a contraction for *are not, is not, has not,* and *have not.*
Usage: *Ain't* has acquired such a stigma over the years that it is beyond rehabilitation, even though it would serve a useful function as a contraction for *am not* and even though its use as an alternate form for *isn't, hasn't, aren't,* and *haven't* has a good historical justification. In questions, the variant *aren't I* is acceptable in speech to a majority of the Usage Panel, but in writing there is no generally acceptable substitute for the stilted *am I not.*
Ai·nu (ī′no͞o) *n., pl.* **Ainu** or **-nus. 1.** A member of an aboriginal Caucasian people inhabiting the northernmost islands of Japan. **2.** The language of the Ainus.
ai·o·li (ī-ō′lē) *n.* A rich garlic-flavored mayonnaise, used esp. on fish and vegetables. [Prov. : *ai*, garlic (< Lat. *allium*) + *oli*, oil (< Lat. *oleum*).]
air (âr) *n.* **1. a.** A colorless, odorless, tasteless gaseous mixture, mainly nitrogen (approximately 78 per cent) and oxygen (approximately 21 per cent) with lesser amounts of argon, carbon dioxide, neon, helium, and other gases. **b.** This mixture with varying amounts of moisture, low-altitude pollutants, and particulate matter, enveloping the earth; the atmosphere. **c.** The air or atmosphere in an enclosure. **2.** The sky; firmament. **3.** An atmospheric movement; breeze; wind. **4.** *Archaic.* Breath. **5.** Public utterance; circulation: *give air to one's grievances.* **6.** A peculiar or characteristic impression; aura: *a room with an air of loneliness.* **7.** Personal bearing, appearance, or manner; mien: *has an air of gentility.* **8. airs.** Affected manners; haughty pose: *gives herself aristocratic airs.* **9.** *Mus.* A melody or tune, esp.: **a.** The soprano or treble part in a harmonized composition. **b.** A solo with or without accompaniment. **10.** Air conditioning. *—tr.v.* **aired, air·ing, airs. 1.** To expose so that air can dry, cool, or freshen; ventilate. **2.** To give public utterance to; circulate. **—idioms. in the air. 1.** Abroad; prevalent. **2.** Uncertain; not settled; being thought out or formulated. **on (or off) the air.** Being (or not being) broadcast on radio or television. **take the air.** To go outdoors for fresh air; take a short walk or ride. **up in the air. 1.** Not decided; uncertain; in suspense. **2.** Agitated or excited; upset; angry. **walk on air.** To feel elated or extremely happy. [ME < OFr. < Lat. *aer* < Gk. *aēr.*]
air bag *n.* An automotive safety device consisting of a bag designed to inflate upon collision and prevent passengers from pitching forward.
air base *n.* A base for military aircraft.
air battery *n.* A rechargeable battery in which current is generated as a result of oxidation of metal.
air bladder *n. Biol.* **1.** An air-filled structure near the spinal column in many fishes that functions to maintain buoyancy or in some species as an aid in respiration or hearing. **2.** Any air-filled saclike structure, such as one of the dilated parts of the thallus in certain seaweeds.
air·boat (âr′bōt′) *n.* A swamp boat.
air·borne (âr′bôrn′, -bōrn′) *adj.* **1.** Carried by or through the air: *airborne pollen.* **2.** Transported in aircraft: *airborne troops.* **3.** In flight; flying.
air·brush also **air brush** (âr′brŭsh′) *n.* An atomizer using compressed air to spray paint or other liquids on a surface *—tr.v.* **-brushed, -brush·ing, -brush·es.** To spray with an airbrush.
air·burst (âr′bûrst′) *n.* An explosion of a bomb or shell in the atmosphere.
air chamber *n.* **1.** Any enclosure filled with air for a special purpose. **2.** An air chamber, esp. in a hydraulic system, in which air elastically compresses and expands to regulate the flow of a fluid.
air command *n.* A unit of the U.S. Air Force that is larger than an air force.
air-con·di·tion (âr′kən-dĭsh′ən) *tr.v.* **-tioned, -tion·ing, -tions.** To provide with or ventilate by air conditioning.
air conditioner *n.* Any apparatus for controlling, esp. lowering, the temperature and humidity of an enclosure.
air conditioning *n.* **1.** The state or condition produced by an air conditioner. **2.** A system of air conditioners.
air-cool (âr′ko͞ol′) *tr.v.* **-cooled, -cool·ing, -cools. 1.** To cool (an engine, for example) by a flow of air. **2.** To air-condition.
air corridor *n.* An air route established by international agreement.
air cover *n.* **1.** Protective use of military aircraft during ground operations. **2.** The aircraft used for air cover.
air·craft (âr′krăft′) *n., pl.* **aircraft.** A machine or device, including airplanes, helicopters, gliders, and dirigibles, capable of atmospheric flight.
aircraft carrier *n.* A large naval ship designed as a mobile air base at sea, having a long flat deck on which aircraft can take off and land.
air·crafts·man (âr′krăfts′mən) also **air·craft·man** (-krăft′mən) *n.* A noncommissioned member of the British Royal Air Force or the Royal Canadian Air Force.
air-cush·ion (âr′ko͝osh′ən) also **air-cush·ioned** (-ənd) *adj.* Of or relating to a vehicle that is supported a short distance above the surface of land or water by a cushion of forced air.
air division *n.* A unit of the U.S. Air Force larger than a wing and smaller than an air force.
air door *n.* A temperature-controlled, strong current of air, usually directed upward, that is used instead of a door.
air·drome (âr′drōm′) *n.* **1.** An airport. **2.** A landing field. **3.** An airplane hangar.
air·drop (âr′drŏp′) *n.* A delivery, as of supplies or troops, by parachute from aircraft in flight. *—tr. & intr.v.* **-dropped, -drop·ping, -drops.** To drop from an aircraft.
air-dry (âr′drī′) *tr.v.* **-dried, -dry·ing, -dries.** To dry by exposure to the air. *—adj.* Sufficiently dry so that further exposure to air will not evaporate moisture.
Aire·dale (âr′dāl′) *n.* A large terrier of a breed having rather

aigrette
Hat decorated with egret tail feathers

ailanthus

aileron

Airedale

long legs and a wiry tan coat marked with black. [After *Airedale,* a valley in Yorkshire, England.]
air embolism *n.* An aeroembolism.
air express *n.* A system of transportation of packages by air.
air·fare (âr′fâr′) *n.* Fare for travel by airplane.
air·field (âr′fēld′) *n.* **1.** An airport having hard-surfaced runways where aircraft can take off and land. **2.** A landing strip.
air·flow (âr′flō′) *n.* **1.** A flow of air. **2.** The air currents caused by the motion of an object such as an airplane or automobile.
air·foil (âr′foil′) *n.* An aircraft part or surface, such as a wing, propeller blade, or rudder, the shape and orientation of which control stability, direction, lift, thrust, or propulsion.
air force *n.* **1.** The aviation branch of a country's armed forces, as the United States Air Force. **2.** A unit of the U.S. Air Force larger than an air division and smaller than an air command.
air·frame (âr′frām′) *n.* An aircraft lacking only its power plant.
air freight *n.* **1.** A system of transporting freight by air. **2.** The amount charged for air freight.
air gas *n.* Producer gas.
air·glow (âr′glō′) *n.* A low- or middle-latitude, more or less steady, faint photochemical luminescence in the upper atmosphere.
air gun *n.* A gun discharged by compressed air.
air·head (âr′hĕd′) *n.* An area of hostile or enemy-controlled territory secured by paratroops.
air hole *n.* **1.** A hole or opening through which gas or air may pass. **2.** An opening in the frozen surface of a body of water. **3.** An air pocket.
air hunger *n.* The gasping, deep respiration symptomatic of coma and diabetic acidosis.
air·ing (âr′ĭng) *n.* **1.** Exposure to air for freshening or drying. **2.** Exposure to open air for exercise or health-promoting activity. **3.** Exposure to public notice or attention. **4.** A radio or television broadcast.
air lane *n.* A regular route of travel for aircraft; airway.
air layering *n.* A method of plant propagation in which a twig or shoot attached to the parent plant is wrapped in moist sphagnum moss or polyethylene plastic so that it will form roots and can later be removed and replanted.
air·less (âr′lĭs) *adj.* **1.** Without air. **2.** Lacking fresh air; stuffy. **3.** Without a breeze or wind; still. **—air′less·ness** *n.*
air letter *n.* **1.** An airmail letter. **2.** A sheet of airmail paper that can be folded as an envelope with a message inside.
air·lift (âr′lĭft′) *n.* A system of transporting troops or supplies by air when surface routes are blocked. *—v.* **-lift·ed, -lift·ing, -lifts.** *—tr.* To transport by air, as when ground routes are blocked. *—intr.* To transport supplies or troops by air.
air·line (âr′līn′) *n.* **1. a.** A system for scheduled transport of passengers and freight by air. **b.** A business organization providing such a system of air transport. **2.** An air route. **3.** The shortest distance between two geographical points; a direct line; beeline.
air·lin·er (âr′lī′nər) *n.* An airplane adapted for carrying passengers and operated by an airline.
air lock *n.* **1.** An airtight chamber, usually located between two regions of unequal pressure, in which air pressure can be regulated. **2.** A bubble or pocket of air or vapor, as in a pipe, that stops the normal flow of fluid through the conducting part.
air·mail (âr′māl′) *tr.v.* **-mailed, -mail·ing, -mails.** To send (a letter, for example) by air mail. *—adj.* Of, relating to, or for use with air mail: *an airmail stamp.*
air mail also **air·mail** (âr′māl′) *n.* **1.** The system of conveying mail by aircraft. **2.** Mail conveyed or to be conveyed by aircraft.
air·man (âr′mən) *n.* **1.** An enlisted man or woman in the U.S. Air Force. **2.** An enlisted man in the U.S. Navy working with aircraft. **3.** An aviator.
airman basic *n.* An enlisted man of the lowest rank in the U.S. Air Force.
airman first class *n.* An enlisted man in the U.S. Air Force ranking above an airman and below a sergeant.
air mass *n.* A large body of air with only small horizontal variations of temperature, pressure, and moisture.
air mattress *n.* An inflatable airtight sack used as a mattress.
Air Medal *n.* A decoration awarded by the U.S. Army, Air Force, or Navy for meritorious airborne conduct.
air mile *n.* A unit of distance in air navigation.
air piracy *n.* The hijacking of an airplane in flight; skyjacking. **—air pirate** *n.*
air·plane (âr′plān′) *n.* Any of various winged vehicles capable of flight, generally heavier than air and propelled by jet engines or propellers. [Alteration of *aeroplane,* prob. < Fr. *aéroplane* : *aéro-,* aero- + *planer,* to glide < *plan,* level < Lat. *planus,* flat.]
air plant *n.* An epiphyte.
air·play (âr′plā′) *n.* The broadcasting of a record on the air by a radio station.
air pocket *n.* A downward air current that causes an aircraft to lose altitude abruptly.

Ajax
Greek vase painting of Ajax, son of Telamon, playing a game with Achilles during the siege of Troy

air police *n.* Military police of an air force.
air·port (âr′pôrt′, -pōrt′) *n.* **1.** A tract of leveled land where aircraft can take off and land, usually equipped with hard-surfaced landing strips, a control tower, hangars, and accommodations for passengers and cargo. **2.** An installation similar to an airport in which the landing area is on water.
air·proof (âr′pro͞of′) *adj.* Impermeable to air. *—tr.v.* **-proofed, -proof·ing, -proofs.** To make impermeable to air.
air pump *n.* Equipment for compressing, removing, or forcing a flow of air.
air raid *n.* An attack by hostile military aircraft, esp. when armed with bombs.
air rifle *n.* A low-powered rifle, such as a BB gun, that uses manually compressed air to fire small pellets.
air sac *n.* An air-filled space, as one of the spaces in a bird's body that forms a connection between the lungs and the bone cavities.
air·screw (âr′skro͞o′) *n. Chiefly Brit.* The propeller of an airplane.
air·shed (âr′shĕd′) *n.* **1.** The air supply of a given region. **2.** The geographic area covered by an air supply. [AIR + (WATER)SHED.]
air·ship (âr′shĭp′) *n.* A self-propelled lighter-than-air craft with directional control surfaces; dirigible.
air·sick (âr′sĭk′) *adj.* Suffering from airsickness.
air·sick·ness (âr′sĭk′nĭs) *n.* Nausea and discomfort resulting from nervous tension or changes in pressure or motion in an aircraft.
air sock *n.* A windsock.
air·space (âr′spās′) *n.* **1.** The portion of the atmosphere above a particular land area, esp. a nation or other political subdivision. **2.** The space occupied by an aircraft formation or used in a maneuver.
air speed *n.* The speed, esp. of an aircraft, relative to the air.
air splint *n.* An inflatable cylinder used to immobilize fractures and sprains of extremities.
air spray *n.* **1.** A device for spraying liquids that uses compressed air. **2.** The liquid sprayed by an air spray.
air spring *n.* An enclosed volume of air that by its resilience acts as a spring or shock absorber.
air·strip (âr′strĭp′) *n.* A cleared area serving as an airfield, esp. in an emergency.
airt (ârt) *n. Scot.* One of the cardinal points on the compass; a direction. [ME *art* < Sc. Gael. *aird.*]
air taxi *n.* A small aircraft that makes short local flights to areas not serviced by regular airlines.
air·tight (âr′tīt′) *adj.* **1.** Impermeable by air or gas. **2.** Having no weak points; sound: *an airtight excuse.*
air·time (âr′tīm′) *n.* The time that a radio or television station is broadcasting.
air-to-air missile (âr′tə-âr′) *n.* A missile, usually guided, designed to be fired from aircraft at aircraft.
air-to-sur·face missile (âr′tə-sûr′fĭs) *n.* A missile, usually guided, designed to be fired from aircraft at targets on the ground.
air vesicle *n.* **1.** A terminal air sac in the lung, where gas exchange takes place in respiration. **2.** An air-filled space that aids in flotation of many water plants.
air·waves (âr′wāvz′) *pl.n.* The medium used for the transmission of radio and television signals.
air·way (âr′wā′) *n.* **1.** A passageway or shaft in which air circulates, as in ventilating a mine. **2.** A designated route of passage for an aircraft; air lane.
air·wor·thy (âr′wûr′*thē*) *adj.* **-thi·er, -thi·est.** In fit condition to fly: *an airworthy aircraft.* **—air′wor′thi·ness** *n.*
air·y (âr′ē) *adj.* **-i·er, -i·est. 1.** Having the constitution or nature of air. **2.** High in the air; lofty. **3.** Open to the air; breezy: *airy chambers.* **4.** Performed in the air; aerial. **5.** Resembling air; immaterial: *an airy apparition.* **6.** Impractical; insubstantial; unreal. **7.** Speculative; imaginative; visionary. **8.** Light as air; delicate: *an airy veil.* **9.** Displaying lofty nonchalance: *dismissing him in an airy manner.* **10.** Lighthearted; gay: *an airy mood.* **—air′i·ly** *adv.* **—air′i·ness** *n.*
aisle (īl) *n.* **1.** A part of a church divided laterally from the nave by a row of pillars or columns. **2.** A passageway between rows of seats, as in an auditorium. **3.** A passageway, as between counters in a department store. [ME *ele* < OFr., wing of a building < Lat. *ala.*]
aitch (āch) *n.* The letter *h.* [Fr. *hache.*]
aitch·bone (āch′bōn′) *n.* **1.** The rump bone in cattle. **2.** The cut of meat containing the aitchbone. [ME *hach-boon* < the phrase *an hach-boon,* an aitchbone, alteration of *a nachebon* : *nache,* buttock (< OFr. < Lat. *natis*) + *bon,* bone < OE *bān.*]
a·jar[1] (ə-jär′) *adv. & adj.* Partially opened: *left the door ajar.* [ME *on char* : *on,* in + *char,* turn < OE *cierr.*]
a·jar[2] (ə-jär′) *adv. & adj.* Not harmonious; jarring: *ajar with the times.*
A·jax (ā′jăks′) *n. Gk. Myth.* **1.** A warrior of great stature and prowess who fought against Troy; son of Telamon of Salamis. **2.** A warrior of small stature and arrogant character who fought against Troy; son of Ileus of Locris. [Lat. < Gk. *Aias.*]
a·kar·y·o·cyte (ā-kăr′ē-ō-sīt′) *n.* A cell that has no nucleus.
ak·ee (ăk′ē, ə-kē′) *n.* **1.** A tropical tree, *Blighia sapida,* native to Africa, having fragrant flowers and capsules containing

black seeds. **2.** The edible aril surrounding the seeds of the akee. [Native word in Liberia.]

a·kene (ā-kēn′) *n.* Variant of **achene**.

a·kim·bo (ə-kĭm′bō) *adj. & adv.* With the hands on the hips and the elbows bowed outward. [ME *in kenebowe.*]

a·kin (ə-kĭn′) *adj.* **1.** Of the same kin; related by blood. **2.** Having a similar quality or character; analogous. **3.** *Ling.* Cognate.

Ak·ka·di·an (ə-kā′dē-ən) *n.* **1.** A native or inhabitant of ancient Akkad. **2.** The Semitic language of the Akkadians. **—Ak·ka′di·an** *adj.*

Al The symbol for the element aluminum.

al– *pref.* Variant of **ad–**. Used before *l.*

-al[1] *suff.* Of, relating to, or characterized by: *parental.* [ME < OFr. < Lat. *-alis.*]

-al[2] *suff.* Action; process: *retrieval.* [ME *-aille* < OFr. < Lat. *-alia,* neuter pl. of *-alis,* adj. suffix.]

-al[3] *suff.* Aldehyde: *citronellal.* [< ALDEHYDE.]

a·la (ā′lə) *n., pl.* **a·lae** (ā′lē). A winglike structure or part, such as an ear lobe, the membranous border of some seeds, or one of the side petals of certain flowers, such as the sweet pea. [Lat., wing.]

à la also **a la** (ä′lä, ä′lə, ăl′ə) *prep.* In the style or manner of: *a poem à la Ogden Nash.* [Fr., short for *à la mode de,* in the manner of.]

al·a·bas·ter (ăl′ə-băs′tər) *n.* **1.** A dense translucent, white or tinted fine-grained gypsum. **2.** A variety of hard calcite, translucent and sometimes banded. **3.** A pale yellowish pink to yellowish gray. [ME *alabastre* < OFr. < Lat. *alabaster* < Gk. *alabastros,* poss. of Egypt. orig.]

à la carte (ä′lə kärt′, ăl′ə) *adv. & adj.* With a separate price for each item on the menu. [Fr., by the menu.]

a·lack (ə-lăk′) also **a·lack·a·day** (ə-lăk′ə-dā′) *interj. Archaic.* Used to express sorrow, regret, or alarm.

a·lac·ri·ty (ə-lăk′rĭ-tē) *n.* **1.** Cheerful willingness; eagerness. **2.** Speed or quickness; celerity. [Lat. *alacritas* < *alacer,* lively.] **—a·lac′ri·tous** (-təs) *adj.*

A·lad·din (ə-lăd′n) *n.* In the *Arabian Nights,* a boy who acquires a magic lamp and a magic ring with which he can summon two jinn to fulfill any desire.

a·lae (ā′lē) *n.* Plural of **ala**.

à la king (ä′lə kĭng′, ăl′ə) *adj.* Cooked in a cream sauce with green pepper or pimiento and mushrooms.

al·a·me·da (ăl′ə-mē′də, -mā′-) *n. Southwestern U.S.* A promenade or shaded walk, esp. one lined with poplars or other shade trees. [Sp. < *álamo,* poplar, alamo.]

al·a·mo (ăl′ə-mō′) *n., pl.* **-mos**. *Southwestern U.S.* A poplar tree, esp. a cottonwood. [Sp. *álamo* < Lat. *alnus,* alder and *ulmus,* elm.]

a·la·mode (ä′lə-mōd′, ăl′ə-) *n.* A lustrous plain-weave silk fabric for head coverings and scarfs. [< À LA MODE.]

à la mode (ä′lə mōd′, ăl′ə) *adj.* **1.** According to or in style or fashion. **2. a.** Served with ice cream, as certain desserts. **b.** Braised with vegetables and served in a rich, brown sauce, as meats. [Fr., in the fashion.]

al·a·nine (ăl′ə-nēn′) *n.* An amino acid, $C_3H_7NO_2$, that is a constituent of most proteins. [G. *Alanin,* ult. < *Aldehyd,* aldehyde.]

a·lar (ā′lər) *adj.* **1.** Of, pertaining to, or having wings or alae. **2.** Shaped like or resembling a wing. **3.** *Anat.* Pertaining to the armpit; axillary. [Lat. *alaris* < *ala,* wing.]

a·larm (ə-lärm′) *n.* **1.** A sudden fear caused by an apprehension or realization of danger; fright. **2.** A warning of approaching or existing danger. **3.** An electrical or mechanical device that serves to warn of danger by means of a sound or signal. **4.** The sounding mechanism of an alarm clock. **5.** A call to arms. *—tr.v.* **a·larmed, a·larm·ing, a·larms**. **1.** To frighten by a sudden revelation of danger. **2.** To warn of or indicate approaching or existing danger. [ME < OFr. *alarme* < OItal. *allarme* < *all' arme,* to arms : *alla,* to (< Lat. *ad illam,* to that) + *arme,* arms < Lat. *arma.*] **—a·larm′a·ble** *adj.* **—a·larm′ing·ly** *adv.*

alarm clock *n.* A clock that can be set to sound a bell or buzzer at any desired hour.

a·larm·ist (ə-lär′mĭst) *n.* A person who needlessly alarms or attempts to alarm others, as by inventing or spreading false or exaggerated rumors of impending danger or catastrophe. **—a·larm′ism** *n.*

alarm reaction *n.* An innate mechanism in animals and man providing a response to novel or threatening circumstances.

a·la·rum (ə-lăr′əm, ə-lär′-) *n. Archaic.* An alarm, esp. a call to arms. [ME *alarom,* var. of *alarm,* alarm.]

a·la·ry (ā′lə-rē) *adj.* **1.** Of or pertaining to wings. **2.** Resembling a wing; wing-shaped. [Lat. *alarius* < *ala,* wing.]

a·las (ə-lăs′) *interj.* Used to express sorrow, regret, grief, compassion, or apprehension of danger or evil.

a·las·ka (ə-lăs′kə) *n.* **1.** A kind of heavy-duty rubberized overshoe. **2. a.** A heavy dress and coat fabric of cotton and wool. **b.** A yarn made of cotton and wool. [After *Alaska.*]

Alaska cedar *n.* The Nootka cypress.

A·las·kan malamute (ə-lăs′kən) *n.* The malamute.

a·las·tor also **A·las·tor** (ə-lăs′tər, -tôr′) *n.* An avenging deity or spirit, the masculine personification of Nemesis, frequently evoked in Greek tragedy. [Gk. *alastōr* < *alastos,* unforgettable : *a-,* not + *lathein,* to forget.]

a·late (ā′lāt′) also **a·lat·ed** (ā′lā′tĭd) *adj. Biol.* Having thin, winglike extensions or parts; winged. [Lat. *alatus* < *ala,* wing.]

alb (ălb) *n.* A long white linen robe with tapered sleeves worn by a priest at Mass. [ME *albe* < OE < Med. Lat. *alba* < Lat. *albus,* white.]

al·ba·core (ăl′bə-kôr′, -kōr′) *n., pl.* **albacore** or **-cores**. A large marine fish, *Thunnus alalunga,* of warm seas, having edible flesh that is a major source of canned tuna. [Port. *albacor* < Ar. *al-bakrah* : *al,* the + *bakr,* young camel.]

Al·ba·ni·an (ăl-bā′nē-ən, -bān′yən, ôl-) *adj.* Of or pertaining to the People's Republic of Albania, its inhabitants, or their language. *—n.* **1.** A native or inhabitant of Albania. **2.** The Indo-European language of the Albanians.

al·ba·tross (ăl′bə-trôs′, -trŏs′) *n., pl.* **albatross** or **-tross·es**. **1.** Any of various large, web-footed birds of the family Diomedeidae, chiefly of the oceans of the Southern Hemisphere, having a hooked beak and long, narrow wings. **2.** An obvious handicap or constant burden. [Prob. alteration of *alcatras,* pelican < Port. or Sp. *alcatraz,* of Ar. orig. (Sense 2 after the *albatross* in *The Rime of the Ancient Mariner* by S. T. Coleridge, 1772–1834, which the mariner killed and had to wear around his neck as a penance).]

George Miksch Sutton

albatross
Above: Black-footed albatross
Below: Laysan albatross in flight

al·be·do (ăl-bē′dō) *n., pl.* **-dos**. The fraction of incident electromagnetic radiation reflected by a surface. [LLat., whiteness < Lat. *albus,* white.]

al·be·it (ôl-bē′ĭt, ăl-) *conj.* Although; even though; notwithstanding. [ME, although it be.]

al·bes·cent (ăl-bĕs′ənt) *adj.* Becoming white or moderately white; whitish. [Lat. *albescens, albescent-,* pr.part. of *albescere,* to become white < *albus,* white.]

Al·bi·gen·ses (ăl′bə-jĕn′sēz′) *pl.n.* The members of a Catharist religious sect of southern France in the 12th and 13th centuries, exterminated for heresy by the Inquisition. [Med. Lat., pl. of *Albigensis,* inhabitant of Albiga, a town in southern France where the sect was dominant.] **—Al′bi·gen′sian** (shən, sē-ən) *adj.* **—Al′bi·gen′sian·ism** *n.*

al·bi·nism (ăl′bə-nĭz′əm) *n.* **1.** The congenital absence of normal pigmentation in a person, animal, or plant. **2.** The condition of being an albino. [Fr. *albinisme* < G. *Albinismus* < *Albino,* albino.]

al·bi·no (ăl-bī′nō) *n., pl.* **-nos**. An organism lacking normal pigmentation, as a person having abnormally pale skin, very light hair, and lacking normal eye coloring, or an animal having white hair or fur and red eyes. [Port. < *albo,* white < Lat. *albus.*]

Al·bi·on (ăl′bē-ən) *n.* A literary name for Britain. [Lat.]

al·bite (ăl′bīt′) *n.* A widely distributed white feldspar, $NaAlSi_3O_8$, that is one of the common rock-forming plagioclase group. [Swed. *albit* < Lat. *albus,* white.] **—al·bit′ic** (-bĭt′ĭk), **al·bit′i·cal** (-ĭ-kəl) *adj.*

al·bum (ăl′bəm) *n.* **1.** A book or binder with blank pages for the insertion and preservation of collections, as of stamps, photographs, or autographs. **2. a.** A set of phonograph records stored together in jackets under one binding. **b.** The holder for such records. **c.** One or more 12-inch long-playing records in a slipcase. **d.** A phonograph record. **e.** A recording of different musical pieces. **3.** A printed collection of musical compositions, pictures, or literary selections. **4.** A tall, handsomely printed book, esp. popular in the 19th century, often having a profusion of illustrations and short, sentimental texts. [Lat., blank tablet < *albus,* white.]

al·bu·men (ăl-byo͞o′mən) *n.* **1.** A nutritive substance surrounding a developing embryo, such as the white of an egg or the material stored in a plant seed. **2.** Albumin. [Lat. < *albus,* white.]

al·bu·min (ăl-byo͞o′mĭn) *n.* Any of several simple, water-soluble proteins that are coagulated by heat and are found in egg white, blood serum, milk, various animal tissues, and many plant juices and tissues. [ALBUM(EN) + -IN.]

al·bu·mi·noid (ăl-byo͞o′mə-noid′) also **al·bu·mi·noi·dal** (-byo͞o′mə-noid′l) *adj.* Resembling albumin. *—n. Biochem.* Protein.

al·bu·mi·nous (ăl-byo͞o′mə-nəs) *adj.* Of, like, or pertaining to albumin or albumen.

al·bu·mi·nu·ri·a (ăl-byo͞o′mə-no͝or′ē-ə, -nyo͝or-) *n.* The presence of albumin in the urine, sometimes indicative of kidney disease. **—al·bu′mi·nu′ric** (-no͝or′ĭk, -nyo͝or′-) *adj.*

al·bu·mose (ăl′byə-mōs′, -mōz′) *n.* Any of a class of albuminous substances formed by enzymatic action on proteins during digestion. [Fr. : *albumine,* albumin + *-ose,* -ose.]

al·bur·num (ăl-bûr′nəm) *n.* Sapwood. [Lat. < *albus,* white.]

Al·ca·ic (ăl-kā′ĭk) *adj.* Of or designating a verse form used in Greek and Latin poetry, consisting of strophes having four tetrametric lines. *—n.* Verse composed in Alcaic strophes. [LLat. *Alcaicus,* of Alcaeus < Gk. *Alkaïkos* < *Alkaios,* a Greek lyric poet of the 7th cent. B.C.]

al·cai·de also **al·cay·de** (ăl-kī′dē) *n.* The commander or governor of a fortress in Spain or Portugal. [Sp. < Ar. *al-qā'id,* the commander < *qād,* to command.]

al·cal·de (ăl-kăl′dē) *n.* The mayor or chief judicial official of a Spanish or Spanish-American town. [Sp. < Ar. *al-qādī* : *al,* the + *qāda,* to judge.]

al·cay·de (ăl-kī′dē) *n.* Variant of **alcaide**.

al·caz·ar (ăl-kăz′ər, -kä′zər, ăl′kə-zär′) *n.* A Spanish palace or fortress, originally one built by the Moors. [Sp. *alcázar* < Ar. *alqaṣr* : *al,* the + *qaṣ,* camp.]

Al·ces·tis (ăl-sĕs'tĭs) *n. Gk. Myth.* The wife of King Admetus of Thessaly, who agreed to die in place of her husband and was later rescued from Hades by Hercules. [Lat. < Gk. *Alkēstis.*]

al·che·mist (ăl'kə-mĭst) *n.* A practitioner of alchemy. **—al'che·mis'tic, al'che·mis'ti·cal** *adj.*

al·che·mize (ăl'kə-mīz') *tr.v.* **-mized, -miz·ing, -miz·es.** To transform by or as if by alchemy.

al·che·my (ăl'kə-mē) *n.* **1.** A medieval chemical philosophy having as its asserted aims the transmutation of base metals into gold, the discovery of the panacea, and the preparation of the elixir of longevity. **2.** A seemingly magical power or process of transmuting: *"that alchemy . . . by which women can concoct a subtle poison from ordinary trifles"* (Hawthorne). [ME *alkamie* < OFr. *alquemie* < Med. Lat. *alchymia* < Ar. *al-kīmiyā* : *al,* the + *kīmiyā,* alchemy < LGk. *khēmeia,* perh. < Gk. *Khēmia,* Egypt, of Egypt. orig.] **—al·chem'i·cal** (ăl-kĕm'-ĭ-kəl), **al·chem'ic** *adj.* **—al·chem'i·cal·ly** *adv.*

Al·cin·o·us (ăl-sĭn'ō-əs) *n. Gk. Myth.* A king of Phaeacia, father of Nausicaa, who entertained Odysseus. [Lat. < Gk. *Alkinoos.*]

Alc·me·ne (ălk-mē'nē) *n. Gk. Myth.* Amphitryon's wife, who gave birth to Hercules after being seduced by Zeus. [Lat. < Gk. *Alkmēnē.*]

al·co·hol (ăl'kə-hôl') *n.* **1.** A colorless volatile flammable liquid, C_2H_5OH, synthesized or obtained by fermentation of sugars and starches and widely used, either pure or denatured, as a solvent, in drugs, cleaning solutions, explosives, and intoxicating beverages. **2.** Intoxicating liquor containing alcohol. **3.** Any of a series of hydroxyl compounds, the simplest of which are derived from saturated hydrocarbons, have the general formula $C_nH_{2n+1}OH$, and include ethanol and methanol. [Med. Lat., antimony < Ar. *al-kohl* : *al,* the + *kohl,* antimony.]

al·co·hol·ic (ăl'kə-hô'lĭk, -hŏl'ĭk) *adj.* **1.** Of, pertaining to, or resulting from alcohol. **2.** Containing or preserved in alcohol. **3.** Suffering from alcoholism. *—n.* A person who drinks alcoholic liquors habitually and to excess or who suffers from alcoholism.

al·co·hol·ic·i·ty (ăl'kə-hô-lĭs'ĭ-tē) *n.* Alcoholic content.

al·co·hol·ism (ăl'kə-hô-lĭz'əm) *n.* **1.** The compulsive consumption of and psycho-physiological dependence on alcoholic beverages. **2.** A chronic pathological condition, chiefly of the nervous and gastroenteric systems, caused by habitual excessive alcoholic consumption. **3.** Temporary mental disturbance, muscular incoordination, and paresis caused by excessive alcoholic consumption.

al·co·hol·ize (ăl'kə-hô-līz') *tr.v.* **-ized, -iz·ing, -iz·es.** To saturate, mix, or treat with alcohol. **—al'co·hol'i·za'tion** *n.*

al·co·hol·om·e·ter (ăl'kə-hô-lŏm'ĭ-tər) *n.* A hydrometer for determining the percentage of alcohol in liquids.

Al·co·ran (ăl'kə-răn') *n.* The Koran.

al·cove (ăl'kōv') *n.* **1.** A recess or partly enclosed extension connected to or forming part of a room. **2.** A secluded bower or similar enclosed structure in a garden. [Fr. *alcôve* < Sp. *alcoba* < Ar. *al-qubbah* : *al,* the + *qubbah,* vault.]

Al·cy·o·ne (ăl-sī'ə-nē) *n.* **1.** *Gk. Myth.* The daughter of Aeolus who, in grief over the death of her husband Ceyx, threw herself into the sea and was changed into a kingfisher. **2.** *Gk. Myth.* A nymph, one of the Pleiades. **3.** *Astron.* The brightest star in the Pleiades, in the constellation Taurus. [Lat. < Gk. *Alkuonē.*]

Al·deb·a·ran (ăl-dĕb'ər-ən) *n.* A double star in the constellation Taurus, one of the brightest stars in the sky, 68 light-years from Earth. [Med. Lat. < Ar. *al-dabarān* : *al,* the + *dabarān,* following < *dabar,* to follow.]

al·de·hyde (ăl'də-hīd') *n.* **1.** Any of a class of highly reactive organic chemical compounds obtained by oxidation of primary alcohols, characterized by the common group CHO, and used in the manufacture of resins, dyes, and organic acids. **2.** Acetaldehyde. [G. *Aldehyd* < NLat., short for *alcohol dehydrogenatum,* dehydrogenized alcohol.]

al den·te (ăl dĕn'tē) *adj. & adv.* Cooked enough to be firm but not soft: *pasta al dente.* [Ital.]

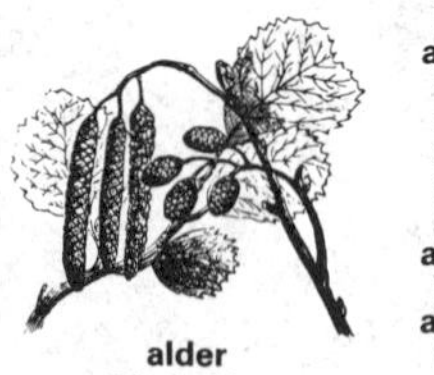

alder
Black alder

al·der (ôl'dər) *n.* Any of various deciduous shrubs or trees of the genus *Alnus,* growing in cool, moist places, and having reddish wood used in cabinet work. [ME < OE *alor.*]

al·der·man (ôl'dər-mən) *n.* **1.** In many town and city governments, a member of the municipal legislative body. **2.** In England and Ireland, a member of the higher branch of the municipal or borough council. **3.** In Anglo-Saxon England: **a.** A lord or prince. **b.** The chief officer of a shire. [ME, a person of high rank < OE *ealdorman* : *ealdor,* chief (< *eald,* old) + *man,* man.] **—al'der·man·cy** (-sē) *n.* **—al'der·man'ic** (-măn'ĭk) *adj.*

Al·der·ney (ôl'dər-nē) *n., pl.* **-neys.** One of a breed of small dairy cattle originally raised in the Channel Islands. [After *Alderney,* one of the Channel Islands.]

al·dol (ăl'dôl', -dōl') *n.* A thick colorless to pale-yellow liquid, $C_4H_8O_2$, obtained from acetaldehyde and used to make perfumes and in ore flotation. [ALD(EHYDE) + -OL[1].]

al·dol·ase (ăl'də-lās') *n.* An enzyme that catalyzes the breakdown of a fructose ester into triose sugars.

al·dose (ăl'dōs', -dōz') *n. Chem.* Any of a class of monosaccharide sugars containing an aldehyde group. [ALD(EHYDE) + -OSE[1].]

al·dos·ter·one (ăl-dŏs'tə-rōn') *n.* A steroid hormone that is secreted by the adrenal cortex and serves as a regulator of the salt and water balance in the body. [ALD(EHYDE) + STER(OL) + -ONE.]

al·drin (ôl'drĭn) *n.* An insecticide containing a naphthalene-derived compound, $C_{12}H_8Cl_6$. [After Kurt *Alder* (1902–1958).]

ale (āl) *n.* A fermented alcoholic beverage containing malt and hops, similar to but heavier than beer. [ME < OE *ealu.*]

a·le·a·to·ry (ā'lē-ə-tôr'ē, -tōr'ē) *adj.* **1.** Dependent upon chance, luck, or an uncertain outcome. **2.** Of or pertaining to gambling. **3.** Also **a·le·a·to·ric** (ā'lē-ə-tôr'ĭk, -tōr'-). *Mus.* Using or consisting of sound sequences played at random or arrived at by chance, as by throwing dice. [Lat. *aleatorius* < *aleator,* gambler < *alea,* dice.]

A·lec·to (ə-lĕk'tō) *n. Gk. Myth.* One of the Furies. [Lat. < Gk. *Alēktō.*]

a·lee (ə-lē') *adv. Naut.* At, on, or to the leeward side.

a·lef (ä'lĕf, -ləf) *n.* Variant of **aleph.**

al·e·gar (ăl'ĭ-gər, ā'lĭ-) *n.* Vinegar produced by the fermentation of ale. [ME : *ale,* ale + *egre,* sharp < OFr. < Lat. *acer.*]

ale·house (āl'hous') *n.* A place where ale is sold and served.

Al·e·man·ni (ăl'ə-măn'ī') *pl.n.* A group of Germanic tribes that settled in Alsace and nearby areas during the fourth century A.D. and were defeated by the Franks in 496. [Lat., of Germanic orig.]

Al·e·man·nic (ăl'ə-măn'ĭk) *n.* A group of High German dialects spoken in Alsace, Switzerland, and parts of southern Germany. *—adj.* Of or pertaining to the Alemanni or their language.

a·lem·bic (ə-lĕm'bĭk) *n.* **1.** An apparatus formerly used for distilling. **2.** Something that purifies, alters, or transforms by a process comparable to distillation. [ME *alambic* < OFr. < Med. Lat. *alembicus* < Ar. *al-anbīq* : *al,* the + *anbīq,* still < Gk. *ambix,* cup.]

a·leph also **a·lef** (ä'lĕf, -ləf) *n.* The 1st letter of the Hebrew alphabet. See table at **alphabet.** [Heb. *āleph* < *eleph,* ox.]

a·leph-null (ä'lĕf-nŭl', -ləf) *n.* The first transfinite number.

a·lert (ə-lûrt') *adj.* **1.** Vigilantly attentive; watchful: *alert to danger.* **2.** Mentally responsive and perceptive; quick. **3.** Brisk or lively in action. *—n.* **1.** A warning signal of attack or danger, esp. a siren warning of an air raid. **2.** The period of time during which an alert is in effect. *—tr.v.* **a·lert·ed, a·lert·ing, a·lerts.** To notify of approaching danger or action; warn. **—*idiom.* on the alert.** Watchful and prepared for danger or emergency. [Fr. *alerte* < Ital. *all'erta,* on the watch : *alla,* to (< Lat. *ad illam,* to that) + *erta,* watch, p.part. of *ergere,* to raise < Lat. *erigere.*]

al·eu·rone (ăl'yə-rōn') also **a·leu·ron** (-rŏn') *n.* Protein consisting of minute granules, forming the outermost layer of the endosperm in cereal grains. [G. *Aleuron* < Gk. *aleuron,* meal.] **—al'eu·ron'ic** (-rŏn'ĭk) *adj.*

A·leut (ə-lo͞ot', ăl'ē-o͞ot') *n., pl.* **Aleut** or **A·leuts. 1.** An Eskimo native of the Aleutian Islands. **2.** The language of the Aleuts. [R.]

A·leu·tian (ə-lo͞o'shən) *adj.* Of or pertaining to the Aleuts, their language, or their culture.

ale·wife[1] (āl'wīf') *n.* A fish, *Alosa pseudoharengus,* closely related to the herrings, of North American Atlantic waters and some inland lakes. [Perh. < ALEWIFE[2].]

ale·wife[2] (āl'wīf') *n.* A woman who keeps an alehouse.

al·ex·an·der also **Al·ex·an·der** (ăl'ĭg-zăn'dər) *n.* A cocktail made with crème de cacao, sweet cream, and brandy or gin. [From the name *Alexander.*]

Al·ex·an·dri·an (ăl'ĭg-zăn'drē-ən) *adj.* **1.** Of or pertaining to Alexander the Great. **2.** Of or pertaining to Alexandria, Egypt. **3.** Of, characteristic of, or designating a learned school of Hellenistic literature, science, and philosophy located at Alexandria in the last three centuries B.C.

al·ex·an·drine also **Al·ex·an·drine** (ăl'ĭg-zăn'drĭn) *n.* A line of English verse composed in iambic hexameter, usually with a caesura after the third foot, such as Pope's example: *"That like a wounded snake drags its slow length along."* *—adj.* Of, pertaining to, or composed in alexandrines. [Fr. *alexandrin* < OFr. < *Alexandre,* title of a romance about Alexander the Great (356–323 B.C.) that was written in this meter.]

al·ex·an·drite (ăl'ĭg-zăn'drīt') *n.* A greenish chrysoberyl that appears red in artificial light, used as a gemstone. [G. *Alexandrit,* after Alexander I (1777–1825), Czar of Russia.]

a·lex·i·a (ə-lĕk'sē-ə) *n.* A disorder in which cerebral lesions cause loss of the ability to read. [NLat. : A-[1] + Gk. *lexis,* speech < *legein,* to speak.]

a·lex·i·phar·mic (ə-lĕk'sə-fär'mĭk) *adj.* Preventing or resisting effects of poison or infection; antidotal; prophylactic. *—n.* An antidote. [< Gk. *alexipharmakos* : *alexein,* to ward off + *pharmakon,* poison.]

al·fal·fa (ăl-făl'fə) *n.* A plant, *Medicago sativa,* native to Eurasia, having compound leaves with three leaflets and clusters of small purple flowers, widely cultivated for forage and used as a commercial source of chlorophyll. [Sp. < Ar. *al-faṣfaṣah.*]

al·fil·a·ri·a or **al·fil·e·ri·a** (ăl-fĭl'ə-rē'ə) *n.* A plant, *Erodium* *cicutarium,* native to Europe but widely naturalized in North America, having finely divided leaves and small pink or purplish flowers. [Mex. Sp. *alfilerillo* < Sp., dim. of *alfiler,* pin < Ar. *al-khilāl,* the spine.]

al·for·ja (ăl-fôr′wä) *n. Western U.S.* A canvas or leather saddlebag. [Sp. < Ar. *al-khorj,* the supply.]

al·fres·co (ăl-frĕs′kō) *adv.* In the fresh air; outdoors. *—adj.* Taking place outdoors; outdoor. [Ital. *al fresco,* in the fresh (air) : *a il,* in the + *fresco,* fresh.]

al·ga (ăl′gə) *n., pl.* **-gae** (-jē). Any of various primitive, chiefly aquatic, one-celled or multicellular plants that lack true stems, roots, and leaves but usually contain chlorophyll. Included among the algae are kelps and other seaweeds, and the diatoms. [Lat., seaweed.] **—al′gal** (ăl′gəl) *adj.*

al·gar·ro·ba or **al·ga·ro·ba** (ăl′gə-rō′bə) *n.* **1.** The mesquite. **2.** The carob. **3.** The edible pod of either the mesquite or carob tree. [Sp. < Ar. *al-kharrūbah.*]

al·ge·bra (ăl′jə-brə) *n.* **1.** A generalization of arithmetic in which symbols, usually letters of the alphabet, represent numbers or members of a specified set of numbers and are related by operations that hold for all numbers in the set. **2.** A set together with operations defined in the set that obey specified laws. [ME < Med. Lat. < Ar. *al-jebr,* the (science of) reuniting : *al,* the + *jabr,* reunification.] **—al′ge·bra′ist** (-brā′ĭst) *n.*

al·ge·bra·ic (ăl′jə-brā′ĭk) *adj.* **1.** Of, pertaining to, or designating algebra. **2.** Designating an expression, equation, or function in which only numbers, letters, and arithmetic operations are contained or used. **3.** Indicating or restricted to a finite number of algebraic operations. **—al′ge·bra′i·cal·ly** *adv.*

algebraic language *n.* A computer language whose statements are designed to resemble algebraic expressions.

algebraic logic *n.* The sequence of operations wherein a problem is entered into a calculator or computer in the order in which it would be written by hand.

algebraic number *n.* A number that is a root of a polynomial equation with rational coefficients.

-algia *suff.* Pain: *neuralgia.* [Gk. < *algos,* pain.]

al·gi·cide (ăl′jə-sīd′) *n.* A chemical agent added to water to destroy algae. [ALG(A) + -CIDE.]

al·gid (ăl′jĭd) *adj.* Cold; chilly. [Fr. *algide* < Lat. *algidus* < *algēre,* to be cold.] **—al·gid′i·ty** (-jĭd′ĭ-tē) *n.*

al·gin (ăl′jĭn) *n.* A gelatinous substance obtained from certain algae, esp. the giant kelp, and used as a thickener and emulsifier. [ALG(A) + -IN.]

algo– *pref.* Pain: *algometer.* [Gk. < *algos,* pain.]

al·goid (ăl′goid′) *adj.* Of or resembling algae.

Al·gol (ăl′gŏl′, -gôl′) *n.* A double, eclipsing variable star in the constellation Perseus, almost as bright as Polaris. [Ar. *al-ghūl,* the ghoul. —see GHOUL.]

ALGOL (ăl′gŏl′, -gôl′) *n.* An arithmetic language by which numerical procedures may be precisely presented to a computer in a standard form. [ALG(ORITHMIC) O(RIENTED) L(ANGUAGE).]

al·go·lag·ni·a (ăl′gō-lăg′nē-ə) *n.* Sexual gratification derived from inflicting or experiencing pain. [NLat. : ALGO- + Gk. *lagneia,* lust.] **—al′go·lag′nic** *adj.* **—al′go·lag′nist** *n.*

al·gol·o·gy (ăl-gŏl′ə-jē) *n.* The study of algae. [ALG(A) + -LOGY.] **—al′go·log′i·cal** (ăl′gə-lŏj′ĭ-kəl) *adj.* **—al′go·log′i·cal·ly** *adv.* **—al·gol′o·gist** *n.*

al·gom·e·ter (ăl-gŏm′ĭ-tər) *n.* An apparatus for determining sensitivity to pain caused by pressure. **—al′go·met′ric** (-gə-mĕt′rĭk), **al′go·met′ri·cal** *adj.* **—al·gom′e·try** *n.*

Al·gon·ki·an (ăl-gŏng′kē-ən) *n., pl.* **Algonkian** or **-ans. 1.** *Geol.* Formerly, late Proterozoic. **2.** Variant of Algonquian. [After the *Algonkin* (Algonquin) Indians.]

Al·gon·kin (ăl-gŏng′kĭn) *n., pl.* **Algonkin** or **-kins.** Variant of **Algonquin.**

Al·gon·qui·an (ăl-gŏng′kwē-ən, -kē-ən) also **Al·gon·ki·an** (-kē-ən) *n., pl.* **Algonquian** or **-ans** also **Algonkian** or **-ans. 1.** A family of North American Indian languages spoken in an area from Labrador to the Carolinas between the Atlantic coast and the Rocky Mountains. **2.** A member of a tribe using an Algonquian language. **—Al·gon′quian** *adj.* [< ALGONQUIN.]

Al·gon·quin (ăl-gŏng′kwĭn, -kĭn) also **Al·gon·kin** (kĭn) *n., pl.* **Algonquin** or **-quins** also **Algonkin** or **-kins. 1.** Any of several North American Indian tribes formerly inhabiting the region along the Ottawa River and near the northern tributaries of the St. Lawrence River. **2.** The Algonquian language of the Algonquins. **3.** An Indian of the Algonquin tribes. [Canadian Fr.]

al·go·pho·bi·a (ăl′gə-fō′bē-ə) *n.* Abnormal fear of pain.

al·go·rism (ăl′gə-rĭz′əm) *n.* The Arabic system of numeration; the decimal system. [ME *algorisme* < OFr. < Med. Lat. *algorismus,* after Muhammad ibn-Musa *Al-Kharzimi* (780–850?).]

al·go·ris·tic (ăl′gə-rĭs′tĭk) *adj.* Yielding an exact answer, as a computational system guaranteeing accurate solution. [< ALGORISM.]

al·go·rithm (ăl′gə-rĭth′əm) *n. Math.* A mechanical or recursive computational procedure. [Var. of ALGORISM.] **—al′go·rith′mic** (-rĭth′mĭk) *adj.*

algorithmic language *n.* An arithmetic language presenting numerical procedures to a computer in standard form.

a·li·as (ā′lē-əs, āl′yəs) *n.* **1.** An assumed name. **2.** *Electronics.* A false signal in telecommunication links from beats between signal frequency and sampling frequency. *—adv.* Otherwise named: *Johnson, alias Rogers.* [Lat., otherwise < *alius,* other.]

A·li Ba·ba (ä′lē bä′bə, ăl′ē) *n.* In the *Arabian Nights,* a poor woodcutter who gains entrance to the treasure cave of the forty thieves by saying the magic words "Open, Sesame!"

al·i·bi (ăl′ə-bī′) *n., pl.* **-bis. 1.** *Law.* A form of defense whereby a defendant attempts to prove that he was elsewhere when the crime in question was committed. **2.** *Informal.* An excuse. *—intr.v.* **-bied, -bi·ing, -bis.** *Informal.* To make an excuse for oneself. [Lat., elsewhere : *alius,* other + *ubi,* where.]

Usage: *Alibi* (noun) in its nonlegal sense of "an excuse" is acceptable in written usage to almost half of the Usage Panel. As an intransitive verb (*they never alibi*), it is unacceptable in written usage to a large majority of the Panel.

al·i·ble (ăl′ə-bəl) *adj.* Having nutrients; nourishing. [Lat. *alibilis* < *alere,* to nourish.]

al·i·cy·clic (ăl′ĭ-sī′klĭk, -sĭk′lĭk) *adj. Chem.* Of, pertaining to, or designating chemical compounds having both aliphatic and cyclic characteristics or structures. [ALI(PHATIC) + CYCLIC.]

al·i·dade (ăl′ĭ-dād′) also **al·i·dad** (-dăd′) *n.* **1.** An indicator or sighting apparatus on a plane table, used in angular measurement. **2.** A topographic surveying and mapping instrument with a telescope and graduated vertical circle. [Fr. < Med. Lat. *allidada* < *al-'iḍāda,* revolving radius of a circle < *'aḍud,* upper arm.]

a·li·en (ā′lē-ən, āl′yən) *adj.* **1.** Owing political allegiance to another country or government; foreign. **2.** Belonging to, characteristic of, or derived from another country, place, society, or person; strange. **3.** Being inconsistent or opposed; repugnant: *Lying is alien to his nature.* *—n.* **1.** An unnaturalized foreign resident of a country. **2.** A member of another family, people, region, or country. **3.** An outsider. **4.** *Slang.* A creature from outer space. **5.** *Ecol.* A plant native to one region but naturalized in another. *—tr.v.* **-ened, -en·ing, -ens.** To transfer (property) to another. [ME < OFr. < Lat. *alienus* < *alius,* other.]

al·ien·a·ble (āl′yə-nə-bəl, ā′lē-ə-) *adj. Law.* Capable of being transferred to the ownership of another. **—al′ien·a·bil′i·ty** *n.*

al·ien·age (āl′yə-nĭj, ā′lē-ə-) *n.* The status of being an alien.

al·ien·ate (āl′yə-nāt′, ā′lē-ə-) *tr.v.* **-at·ed, -at·ing, -ates. 1.** To cause to become unfriendly or indifferent; estrange: *alienate a friend.* **2.** To remove or dissociate (oneself, for example): *"man cannot alienate himself from his own consciousness"* (Wylie Sypher). **3.** To cause to be transferred; turn away: *"he succeeded . . . in alienating the affections of my only ward"* (Oscar Wilde). **4.** *Law.* To transfer (property) to the ownership of another. [Lat. *alienare, alienat* < *alienus,* alien.] **—al′ien·a′tor** *n.*

al·ien·a·tion (āl′yə-nā′shən, ā′lē-ə-) *n.* **1.** The condition of being alienated; isolation. **2.** *Psychol.* A state of estrangement between the self and the objective world, or between different parts of the personality. **3.** *Law.* The act of transferring property or title to it to another.

al·ien·ee (āl′yə-nē′, ā′lē-ə-) *n. Law.* A person to whom ownership of property is transferred.

al·ien·ism (āl′yə-nĭz′əm, ā′lē-ə-) *n.* Alienage.

al·ien·ist (āl′yə-nĭst, ā′lē-ə-) *n. Law.* A physician who has been accepted by a court as an expert on the mental competence of principals or witnesses appearing before it. [Fr. *aliéniste* < *aliéné,* insane < Lat. *alienatus,* p.part. of *alienare,* to deprive of reason. —see ALIENATE.]

al·ien·or (āl′yə-nôr′, ā′lē-ə-) *n. Law.* A person who transfers ownership of property to another.

al·i·es·ter·ase (ăl′ĭ-ĕs′tər-ās′, -āz′) *n.* An esterase contributing to ester-link hydrolysis, particularly in aliphatic esters. [ALI(PHATIC) + ESTERASE.]

a·li·form (ā′lə-fôrm′, ăl′ə-) *adj.* Shaped like a wing; alar. [Lat. *ala,* wing + -FORM.]

a·light[1] (ə-līt′) *intr.v.* **a·light·ed** or **a·lit** (ə-lĭt′), **a·light·ing, a·lights. 1.** To come down and settle, as after flight. **2.** To dismount. **3.** *Archaic.* To come upon by chance. [ME *alighten* < OE *ālīhtan* : *ā-* (intensive) + *līhtan,* to relieve of a burden < *līht,* light.]

a·light[2] (ə-līt′) *adj.* **1.** Burning; lighted. **2.** Illuminated; lit up. [ME, p.part. of *alighten,* to set on fire < OE *alīhtan* : *a-* (intensive) + *līhtan,* to shine < *lēoht,* a light.] **—a·light′** *adv.*

a·lign also **a·line** (ə-līn′) *v.* **a·ligned, a·lign·ing, a·ligns** also **a·lined, a·lin·ing, a·lines.** *—tr.* **1.** To arrange in a line. **2.** To adjust (parts of a mechanism, for example) to produce a proper relationship or condition. **3.** To ally (oneself, for example) with one side of an argument or cause. *—intr.* To fall into line. [Fr. *aligner* < OFr. : *a-,* to (< Lat. *ad-*) + *ligne,* line < Lat. *linea.*] **—a·lign′er** *n.*

a·lign·ment also **a·line·ment** (ə-līn′mənt) *n.* **1.** Arrangement or position in a straight line. **2.** The process of aligning a device or mechanism or the condition of a device or mechanism being aligned. **3.** A ground plan. **4.** The act of aligning or the condition of being aligned.

a·like (ə-līk′) *adj.* Having close resemblance; similar: *"All good books are alike"* (Hemingway). *—adv.* In the same

alfalfa

p **pop** / r **roar** / s **sauce** / sh **ship, dish** / t **tight** / th **thin, path** / *th* **this, bathe** / ŭ **cut** / ûr **urge** / v **valve** / w **with** / y **yes** / z **zebra, size** / zh **vision** / ə **about, item, edible, gallop, circus** / œ *Fr.* **feu,** *Ger.* **schön** / ü *Fr.* **tu,** *Ger.* **über** / KH *Ger.* **ich,** *Scot.* **loch** / N *Fr.* **bon.**

manner or to the same degree: *They dress and walk alike.* [ME *ilike* < OE *gelīc*.] **—a·like'ness** *n.*

al·i·ment (ăl'ə-mənt) *n.* **1.** Food or nourishment. **2.** Something that supports or sustains. *—tr.v.* (ăl'ə-mĕnt') **-ment·ed, -ment·ing, -ments.** To supply with food or other sustenance. [ME < Lat. *alimentum* < *alere,* to nourish.] **—al'i·men'tal** (-mĕn'tl) *adj.* **—al'i·men'tal·ly** *adv.*

al·i·men·ta·ry (ăl'ə-mĕn'tə-rē, -trē) *adj.* **1.** Of or pertaining to food or nutrition. **2.** Providing nourishment.

alimentary canal *n.* The mucous-membrane-lined tube of the digestive system, extending from the mouth to the anus and including the pharynx, esophagus, stomach, and intestines.

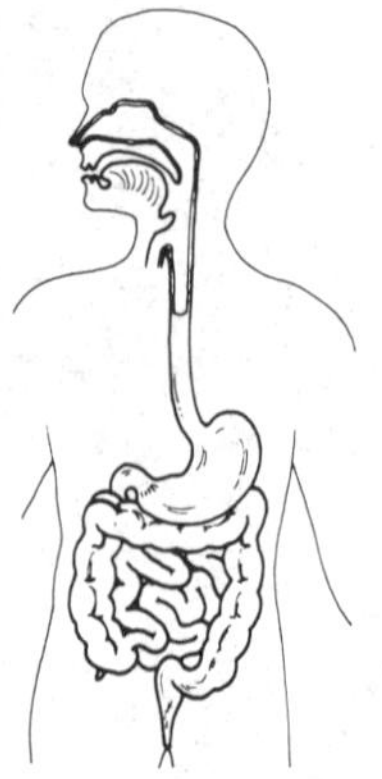

alimentary canal

al·i·men·ta·tion (ăl'ə-mĕn-tā'shən) *n.* **1.** The act or process of giving or receiving nourishment. **2.** Support; sustenance. **—al'i·men'ta·tive** (-tə-tĭv) *adj.*

al·i·mo·ny (ăl'ə-mō'nē) *n., pl.* **-nies. 1.** *Law.* An allowance for support made under court order and usually given by a man to his former wife after a divorce or legal separation. **2.** A means of livelihood maintenance. [Lat. *alimonia,* sustenance < *alere,* to nourish.]

a·line (ə-līn') *v.* Variant of **align.**

A-line (ā'līn') *adj.* Having a fitted top and a flared bottom: *an A-line dress.* [From garments being shaped like a capital *A.*]

a·line·ment (ə-līn'mənt) *n.* Variant of **alignment.**

al·i·phat·ic (ăl'ə-făt'ĭk) *adj.* Of, pertaining to, or designating organic chemical compounds in which the carbon atoms are linked in open chains rather than rings. [< Gk. *aleiphar, aleiphat-,* oil.]

al·i·quot (ăl'ĭ-kwŏt', -kwət) *adj.* **1.** *Math.* Of, pertaining to, or designating an exact divisor or factor of a quantity, esp. of an integer. **2.** Contained exactly or an exact number of times. [Fr. *aliquote* < Lat. *aliquot,* some number : *alius,* some + *quot,* how many.]

a·lit (ə-lĭt') *v.* A past tense and past participle of **alight**[1].

a·live (ə-līv') *adj.* **1.** Having life; living. **2.** In existence or operation; active: *keep your hopes alive.* **3.** Full of life; lively. **4.** Now living. Used as an intensive: *the strongest man alive.* **—idioms. alive to.** Aware of; sensitive to: *alive to the moods of others.* **alive with.** Swarming with: *a country alive with opportunity.* [ME < *on live* : *on,* in (< OE) + *live,* life < OE *līf.*] **—a·live'ness** *n.*

a·li·yah (ä-lē'yä, ə-lē'yə) *n.* Immigration of Jewish people into Israel. [Heb. *'alīyāh,* ascent.]

a·liz·a·rin (ə-lĭz'ər-ĭn) also **a·liz·a·rine** (-ĭn, -ə-rēn') *n.* An orange-red compound, $C_{14}H_8O_4$, used in dyes. [Fr. *alizarine* < *alizari,* madder root < Sp., prob. < Ar. *al-'aṣārah,* the juice pressed out.]

al·ka·hest (ăl'kə-hĕst') *n.* The hypothetical universal solvent once sought by alchemists. [Med. Lat. *alchahest.*]

al·ka·les·cent (ăl'kə-lĕs'ənt) *adj.* Becoming alkaline; slightly alkaline. [ALKAL(I) + -ESCENT.] **—al'ka·les'cence, al'ka·les'cen·cy** *n.*

al·ka·li (ăl'kə-lī') *n., pl.* **-lis** or **-lies. 1.** *Chem.* A carbonate or hydroxide of an alkali metal, the aqueous solution of which is bitter, slippery, caustic, and characteristically basic in reactions. **2.** Any of various soluble mineral salts found in natural water and arid soils. **3.** An alkali metal. [ME < Med. Lat. < Ar. *al-qalīy,* the ashes < *qalay,* to fry.]

al·ka·li·fy (ăl-kăl'ə-fī', ăl'kə-lə-fī') *tr. & intr.v.* **-fied, -fy·ing, -fies.** To make or become alkaline.

alkali metal *n.* Any of a group of soft, white, low-density, low-melting, highly reactive metallic elements, including lithium, sodium, potassium, rubidium, cesium, and francium.

al·ka·lim·e·ter (ăl'kə-lĭm'ĭ-tər) *n.* An apparatus for measuring alkalinity. **—al'ka·lim'e·try** *n.*

al·ka·line (ăl'kə-lĭn, -līn') *adj.* **1.** Of, relating to, or containing an alkali. **2.** Having a pH greater than 7.

alkaline earth *n.* **1.** An oxide of an alkaline-earth metal. **2.** An alkaline-earth metal.

alkaline-earth metal *n.* Any of a group of metallic elements, esp. calcium, strontium, and barium, but generally including beryllium, magnesium, and radium.

al·ka·lin·i·ty (ăl'kə-lĭn'ĭ-tē) *n.* The alkali concentration or alkaline quality of an alkali-containing substance.

al·ka·lize (ăl'kə-līz') also **al·ka·lin·ize** (-lə-nīz') *v.* **-lized, -liz·ing, -liz·es** also **-ized, -iz·ing, -iz·es.** *—tr.* To make alkaline. *—intr.* To become an alkali. **—al'ka·li·za'tion** *n.*

al·ka·loid (ăl'kə-loid') *n.* Any of various physiologically active, nitrogen-containing organic bases derived from plants, including nicotine, quinine, cocaine, atropine, and morphine. [ALKAL(I) + -OID.] **—al'ka·loid'al** (-loid'l) *adj.*

al·ka·lo·sis (ăl'kə-lō'sĭs) *n.* Pathologically high alkali content in the blood and tissues. [ALKAL(I) + -OSIS.]

al·kane (ăl'kān') *n.* A paraffin. [ALK(YL) + -ANE.]

al·ka·net (ăl'kə-nĕt') *n.* **1. a.** A European plant, *Alkanna tinctoria,* the roots of which yield a red dye. **b.** The root of this plant or a dye prepared from it. **2.** Any of several hairy plants of the genus *Anchusa,* native to the Old World, having clusters of blue flowers. **3.** The puccoon. [ME < Sp. *alcaneta,* dim. of *alcana,* henna < Med. Lat. *alchanna* < Ar. *al-hinnā',* the henna.]

al·kene (ăl'kēn') *n.* An olefin. [ALK(YL) + -ENE.]

al·kine (ăl'kīn') *n.* Variant of **alkyne.**

al·kyd or **alkyd resin** (ăl'kĭd) *n.* A widely used durable synthetic resin derived from glycerol and phthalic anhydride. [ALKY(L) + (ACI)D.]

al·kyl (ăl'kəl) *n. Chem.* A monovalent radical, such as ethyl or propyl, having the general formula C_nH_{2n+1}. [G. *Alkohol,* alcohol + -YL.]

al·kyl·a·tion (ăl'kə-lā'shən) *n. Chem.* A process in which an alkyl group is added to or substituted in a compound, as in the reaction of olefins with paraffin hydrocarbons to make high-octane fuels.

al·kyne also **al·kine** (ăl'kīn') *n.* Any of a group of open-chain hydrocarbons with a triple bond and the general formula C_nH_{2n-2}. [ALKY(L) + -(I)NE[2].]

all (ôl) *adj.* **1.** The total entity or extent of: *all Christendom.* **2.** The entire or total number, amount, or quantity of: *all the saints.* **3.** The utmost possible of: *in all truth.* **4.** Every: *all manner; all kinds.* **5.** Any whatsoever: *beyond all doubt.* **6.** Nothing but; only: *He was all skin and bones.* *—pron.* **1.** Each and every one: *All were drowned.* **2.** Each and every thing: *Ten ships sailed and all returned.* *—n.* **1.** Everything one has: *He gave his all.* **2.** The whole number; totality. *—adv.* **1.** Wholly; entirely; completely: *She is all wrong.* **2.** Each; apiece: *a score of five all.* **3.** Exclusively: *The cake is all for him.* **—idioms. all but.** Nearly; almost. **all in.** *Informal.* Tired; exhausted. **all in all.** Everything being taken into account. **at all. 1.** In any and every way. **2.** To any extent; whatever. **for all.** In spite of; despite. [ME *al* < OE *all.*]

Usage: Constructions like *all us students* are somewhat more informal than the corresponding *all of us students.* The construction *all that* is used informally in questions and negative sentences to mean "to the degree expected," as in *The film was not all that exciting.* A majority of the Usage Panel finds examples like these to be unacceptable in formal writing.

all– *pref.* Variant of **allo-.**

al·la breve (ăl'ə brĕv', ä'lə brĕv'ā) *adv. & adj. Mus.* In duple or quadruple meter with the half note being the unit of time. [Ital., according to the breve.]

Al·lah (ăl'ə, ä'lə) *n.* The supreme being in the Moslem religion. [Ar. *Allāh* : *al,* the + *Ilāh,* god.]

al·la·man·da also **al·la·man·de** (ăl'ə-măn'də) *n.* Any of several woody vines of the genus *Allamanda,* native to tropical America, having showy, funnel-shaped yellow flowers. [NLat. *Allamanda,* genus name, after Jean N. S. *Allamand* (1713–1787).]

all-A·mer·i·can (ôl'ə-mĕr'ĭ-kən) *adj.* **1. a.** Representative of the best of its kind in the United States. **b.** *Sports.* Chosen as the best amateur in the United States at a particular position or event. **2.** Composed of Americans or American materials exclusively. **3.** Entirely within the territorial limits of the United States. **4.** Of all the Americas. *—n.* Often **All-American.** An all-American athlete.

al·lan·toid (ə-lăn'toid') also **al·lan·toid·al** (ăl'ən-toid'l) *adj.* **1.** Of or having an allantois. **2.** Shaped like a sausage. *—n.* The allantois.

al·lan·to·is (ə-lăn'tō-ĭs) *n., pl.* **al·lan·to·i·des** (ăl'ən-tō'ĭ-dēz'). A membranous sac that develops from the hindgut in the embryos of mammals, birds, and reptiles. In mammals it takes part in the formation of the umbilical cord and the placenta. [NLat. < Gk. *allantoeidēs,* sausage-shaped : *allas,* sausage + *eidos,* shape.] **—al'lan·to'ic** (ăl'ən-tō'ĭk) *adj.*

all-a·round (ôl'ə-round') also **all-round** (ôl'round') *adj.* **1.** Comprehensive in extent or depth: *all-around vocational training.* **2.** Able to do many or all things well; versatile: *an all-around student.*

al·lay (ə-lā') *tr.v.* **-layed, -lay·ing, -lays. 1.** To lessen or relieve (pain or grief, for example); reduce the intensity of. **2.** To calm or pacify; set to rest. [ME *aleien* < OE *alecgan* : *a-* (intensive) + *lecgan,* to lay.] **—al·lay'er** *n.*

all clear *n.* **1.** A signal, usually by siren, that an air raid is over. **2.** An expression that signifies absence of immediate obstacles or impending danger.

al·le·ga·tion (ăl'ĭ-gā'shən) *n.* **1.** Something alleged. **2.** The act of alleging. **3.** A statement offered without proof, such as an excuse or plea. **4.** *Law.* An assertion made by a party that must be proved or supported with evidence. [Fr. *allégation* < Lat. *allegatio* < *allegare,* to adduce : *ad-,* to + *legare,* to depute.]

al·lege (ə-lĕj') *tr.v.* **-leged, -leg·ing, -leg·es. 1.** To assert to be true; affirm; declare. **2.** To assert without proof. **3.** To state (a plea or excuse, for example) in support or denial of a claim or accusation. **4.** *Archaic.* To cite or quote, as in confirmation. [ME *alleggen* < OFr. *alegier* < *esligier,* to disengage < LLat. **exlitigare* : Lat. *ex-,* out + Lat. *litigare,* to sue.] **—al·lege'a·ble** *adj.* **—al·leg'er** *n.*

al·leged (ə-lĕjd', ə-lĕj'ĭd) *adj.* Represented as existing or as being as described but not so proved; supposed: *an alleged infringement of regulations.* **—al·leg'ed·ly** (ə-lĕj'ĭd-lē) *adv.*

Usage: An *alleged* burglar is someone who is said to be a burglar but against whom no charges have yet been proved. An *alleged* incident is an event that is said to have taken place but which has not yet been verified. In their zeal to protect the rights of the accused, newspapers and law-enforcement officials sometimes misuse *alleged.* A man arrested for murder may be only an *alleged* murderer, for example, but he is a real, not an *alleged,* suspect in that his status as a suspect is not in doubt. Similarly, if a murder is known to have taken place, there is nothing alleged about the crime.

Al·le·ghe·ny spurge (ăl'ĭ-gā'nē) *n.* A low-growing, shrubby plant, *Pachysandra procumbens,* of the southeastern United States, having evergreen leaves and spikes of white or purplish flowers. [After the *Allegheny* Mountains.]

Allegheny vine *n.* The climbing fumitory.

al·le·giance (ə-lē'jəns) *n.* **1.** Loyalty or the obligation of loyalty, as to a nation, sovereign, or cause. **2.** The obligations of a vassal to his overlord. [ME *alligeaunce* < OFr. *ligeance* < *lige,* liege. —see LIEGE.] **—al·le'giant** *adj.*

al·le·gor·ic (ăl'ĭ-gôr'ĭk, -gŏr'-) also **al·le·gor·i·cal** (-ĭ-kəl) *adj.* Pertaining to, characteristic of, or containing allegory. **—al'le·gor'i·cal·ly** *adv.*

al·le·go·rize (ăl'ĭ-gô-rīz', -gō-, -gə-) *v.* **-rized, -riz·ing, -riz·es.** *—tr.* **1.** To express as or in the form of an allegory. **2.** To interpret allegorically. *—intr.* To use or make allegory. **—al'le·go'ri·za'tion** *n.* **—al'le·go·riz'er** *n.*

al·le·go·ry (ăl'ĭ-gôr'ē, -gōr'ē) *n., pl.* **-ries. 1. a.** A literary, dramatic, or pictorial device in which each literal character, object, and event represents a symbol illustrating an idea or moral or religious principle. **b.** An instance of such representation. **2.** A symbolic representation. [ME *allegorie* < Lat. *allegoria* < Gk. < *allēgorein,* to interpret allegorically : *allos,* other + *agoreuein,* to speak.] **—al'le·go'rist** *n.*

al·le·gret·to (ăl'ĭ-grĕt'ō, ä'lĭ-) *Mus. —adv.* In quick tempo; slower than allegro but faster than andante. Used as a direction. *—n., pl.* **-tos.** An allegretto movement or passage. [Ital., dim. of *allegro,* allegro.] **—al'le·gret'to** *adj.*

al·le·gro (ə-lĕg'rō, ə-lā'-) *Mus. —adv.* In rapid tempo; faster than allegretto but slower than presto. Used as a direction. *—n., pl.* **-gros.** An allegro movement or passage. [Ital., lively < Lat. *alacer.*] **—al·le'gro** *adj.*

al·lele (ə-lēl') *n.* Any of a group of possible mutational forms of a gene. [G. *Allel,* short for *Allelomorph,* allelomorph.] **—al·le'lic** (ə-lē'lĭk, ə-lĕl'ĭk) *adj.* **—al·le'lism** *n.*

al·le·lo·morph (ə-lē'lə-môrf', ə-lĕl'ə-) *n.* An allele. [Gk. *allēlōn,* mutually (< *allos,* other) + -MORPH.] **—al·le'lo·mor'phic** (-môr'fĭk) *adj.* **—al·le'lo·mor'phism'** (-môr'fĭz'əm) *n.*

al·le·lu·ia (ăl'ə-lo͞o'yə) *interj.* Hallelujah. [ME < Med. Lat. *alleluja* < LGk. *allelouia* < Heb. *hallelūyāh.*]

al·le·mande (ăl'ə-mănd', -mänd', ăl'ə-mănd', -mänd') *n.* **1. a.** A stately 16th-century dance in $^{2}/_{2}$ time. **b.** A musical composition written to or as if to accompany this dance, often used as the first movement of a suite. **2.** A lively, late 18th-century dance in $^{3}/_{4}$ time. [Fr., fem. of *allemand,* German < Lat. *Alemanni,* an ancient Germanic tribe.]

Al·len·ti·ac (ə-lĕn'tē-ăk') *n., pl.* **Allentiac** or **-acs. 1.** A tribe of South American Indians inhabiting west-central Argentina. **2.** A member of the Allentiac. **3.** The language of the Allentiac. [Sp.] **—Al·len'ti·ac'** *adj.*

al·ler·gen (ăl'ər-jən) *n.* A substance that causes an allergy. [G. *Allergen* : *Allergie,* allergy + *-gen,* -gen.] **—al'ler·gen'ic** (-jĕn'ĭk) *adj.*

al·ler·gic (ə-lûr'jĭk) *adj.* **1.** Characteristic of or concerning allergy. **2.** Having an allergy. **3.** *Informal.* Having a dislike; averse: *allergic to work.*

al·ler·gist (ăl'ər-jĭst) *n.* A physician specializing in allergies.

al·ler·gy (ăl'ər-jē) *n., pl.* **-gies. 1.** Hypersensitive or pathological reaction to environmental factors or substances, such as pollens, foods, dust, or microorganisms, in amounts that do not affect most people. **2.** Anaphylaxis. **3.** *Informal.* An adverse sentiment; antipathy. [G. *Allergie* : Gk. *allos,* other + Gk. *ergon,* effect.]

al·le·thrin (ăl'ə-thrĭn') *n.* A synthetic insecticide, $C_{19}H_{26}O_3$, similar to pyrethrin. [ALL(YL) + (PYR)ETHRIN.]

al·le·vi·ate (ə-lē'vē-āt') *tr.v.* **-at·ed, -at·ing, -ates.** To make more bearable; reduce: *taking drugs to alleviate the pain.* [LLat. *alleviare, alleviat-,* to lighten : Lat. *ad-,* to + *levis,* light.] **—al·le'vi·a'tion** *n.* **—al·le'vi·a'tor** *n.*

al·le·vi·a·tive (ə-lē'vē-ā'tĭv) also **al·le·vi·a·to·ry** (-ə-tôr'ē, -tōr'ē) *adj.* Promoting alleviation.

al·ley[1] (ăl'ē) *n., pl.* **-leys. 1.** A narrow street or passageway between or behind city buildings. **2.** A path between flowerbeds or trees in a garden or park. **3.** A bowling alley. **4.** The parallel lanes on either side of a tennis court reserved for use in doubles matches. **—idiom. up one's alley.** *Slang.* Compatible with one's interests or qualifications. [ME *alei* < OFr. *alée* < *aller,* to walk < Lat. *ambulare.*]

al·ley[2] (ăl'ē) *n., pl.* **-leys.** A large playing marble, often used as the shooter. [Short for ALABASTER.]

alley cat *n.* **1.** A homeless cat; stray. **2.** A domestic cat with no known ancestry.

al·ley·way (ăl'ē-wā') *n.* A narrow passage between buildings.

all-fired (ôl'fīrd') *adj. Slang.* Extreme; excessive. *—adv. Slang.* Extremely; excessively. [Alteration of *hell-fired.*]

All Fools' Day *n.* April Fools' Day.

all fours *n.* **1.** All four limbs of an animal or person: *A baby crawls on all fours.* **2.** Seven-up.

all hail *interj. Archaic.* All health.

All·hal·low·mas (ôl'hăl'ō-məs) also **All·hal·lows** (ôl'hăl'ōz) *n.* All Saints' Day.

all-heal (ôl'hēl') *n.* Any of several plants reputed to have healing powers, as the self-heal.

al·li·a·ceous (ăl'ē-ā'shəs) *adj.* Characteristic of onions or garlic, esp. in odor or taste. [Lat. *allium,* garlic + -ACEOUS.]

al·li·ance (ə-lī'əns) *n.* **1. a.** A formal pact of union or confederation between nations in a common cause. **b.** The nations so conjoined. **2.** A union, relationship, or connection by kinship, marriage, or common interest. **3.** A union or congruence of quality or type; affinity. **4.** The act of becoming or the state of being allied. [ME < OFr. *aliance* < *alier,* to ally.]

al·lied (ə-līd', ăl'īd') *adj.* **1.** Joined or united in a close relationship. **2.** Of a similar nature; related: *allied studies.* **3. Allied.** Of or pertaining to the Allies.

Al·lies (ăl'īz', ə-līz') *pl.n.* **1.** In World War I, the nations allied against the Central Powers of Europe. They were Russia, France, Great Britain, and later many others, including the United States. **2.** In World War II, the nations, primarily Great Britain, Russia, and the United States, allied against the Axis.

al·li·ga·tor (ăl'ĭ-gā'tər) *n.* **1.** Either of two large, amphibious reptiles, *Alligator mississipiensis,* of the southeastern United States, or *A. sinensis,* of China, having sharp teeth and powerful jaws, and differing from crocodiles in having a broader, shorter snout. **2.** Leather made from the hide of an alligator. **3.** A tool or fastener having strong, adjustable jaws often toothed. [< Sp. *el lagarto,* the lizard : *el,* the (< Lat. *ille,* that) + *lagarto,* lizard < Lat. *lacertus.*]

al·li·ga·tor·ing (ăl'ĭ-gā'tər-ĭng) *n.* The formation of cracks on the surface of paint layers. [From the resemblance of the cracks to the pattern of an alligator's scales.]

alligator pear *n.* The avocado.

alligator snapping turtle or **alligator snapper** *n.* A large freshwater turtle, *Macroclemys temmincki,* of the south-central United States, having a rough carapace and a hooked beak.

all-im·por·tant (ôl'ĭm-pôr'tnt) *adj.* Very important; crucial.

all-in·clu·sive (ôl'ĭn-klo͞o'sĭv) *adj.* Including everything; comprehensive.

al·lit·er·ate (ə-lĭt'ə-rāt') *v.* **-at·ed, -at·ing, -ates.** *—intr.* **1.** To use alliteration in speech or writing. **2.** To have or contain alliteration. *—tr.* To form or arrange with alliteration. [Back-formation < ALLITERATION.]

al·lit·er·a·tion (ə-lĭt'ə-rā'shən) *n.* The occurrence in a phrase or line of speech or writing of two or more words having the same initial sound, for example, *wailing in the winter wind.* [AD- + Lat. *littera,* letter.]

al·lit·er·a·tive (ə-lĭt'ə-rā'tĭv, -ər-ə-) *adj.* Of, manifesting, or characterized by alliteration. **—al·lit'er·a'tive·ly** *adv.* **—al·lit'er·a'tive·ness** *n.*

al·li·um (ăl'ē-əm) *n.* Any of various plants of the genus *Allium,* characterized by their pungent odor, and including the onion, leek, chive, garlic, and shallot. [NLat. *Allium,* genus name < Lat. *allium,* garlic.]

all-night (ôl'nīt') *adj.* **1.** Continuing all night: *an all-night party.* **2.** Open all night: *an all-night diner.*

all·night·er (ôl'nī'tər) *n. Slang.* The act or an instance of staying up all night to complete a project.

allo- or **all-** *pref.* **1.** Other; different: *allopatric.* **2.** Isomeric: *allocholesterol.* [Gk. < *allos,* other.]

al·lo·cate (ăl'ə-kāt') *tr.v.* **-cat·ed, -cat·ing, -cates. 1.** To designate for a special purpose; set apart. **2.** To distribute according to plan; allot. **3.** To determine the location of; locate. [Med. Lat. *allocare, allocat-* : Lat. *ad-,* to + Lat. *locare,* to place < *locus,* place.] **—al'lo·ca·ble** (-kə-bəl) *adj.* **—al'lo·ca'tion** *n.*

al·lo·cu·tion (ăl'ə-kyo͞o'shən) *n.* A formal and authoritative speech or address, esp. one that advises or informs. [Lat. *allocutio* < *alloqui,* to speak to : *ad-,* to + *loqui,* to speak.]

al·log·a·my (ə-lŏg'ə-mē) *n.* Cross-fertilization. **—al·log'a·mous** *adj.*

al·lo·graft (ăl'ə-grăft') *n.* A homograft.

al·lo·graph (ăl'ə-grăf') *n.* **1.** The form or shape of a letter of an alphabet or of any unit in a system of writing. **2.** A letter or combination of letters that can represent one phoneme. **3.** Writing, esp. a signature, made by one person for another.

al·lom·er·ism (ə-lŏm'ə-rĭz'əm) *n.* Consistency in crystalline form with variation in chemical composition. **—al·lom'er·ous** *adj.*

al·lom·e·try (ə-lŏm'ĭ-trē) *n. Biol.* The study of the change in proportion of various parts of an organism as a consequence of growth. **—al'lo·met'ric** (ăl'ə-mĕt'rĭk) *adj.*

al·lo·morph[1] (ăl'ə-môrf') *n.* A paramorph. **—al'lo·mor'phic** (-môr'fĭk) *adj.* **—al'lo·mor'phism** *n.*

al·lo·morph[2] (ăl'ə-môrf') *n.* Any of the variant forms of a morpheme. For example, the phonetic *s* of *cats, z* of *dogs,* and *iz* of *horses* are allomorphs of the English morpheme *s.* [ALLO- + MORPH(EME).] **—al'lo·mor'phic** (-môr'fĭk) *adj.* **—al'lo·mor'phism** *n.*

al·lo·nym (ăl'ə-nĭm') *n.* The name of a person, usually a historical person, assumed by a writer. [Fr. *allonyme* : Gk. *allos,* other + *onoma,* name.] **—al·lon'y·mous** (ə-lŏn'ə-məs) *adj.* **—al·lon'y·mous·ly** *adv.*

al·lo·path (ăl'ə-păth') also **al·lop·a·thist** (ə-lŏp'ə-thĭst) *n.* A person who practices or advocates allopathy.

al·lop·a·thy (ə-lŏp'ə-thē) *n.* Therapy with remedies that produce effects differing from those of the disease treated. [G.

allegory
Early 19th-century painting, "Washington and Miss Liberty" by an unknown artist

Allopathie : Gk. *allos,* other + *-pathie,* -pathy.] **—al'lo·path'ic** (ăl'ə-păth'ĭk) *adj.* **—al'lo·path'i·cal·ly** *adv.*

al·lo·pat·ric (ăl'ə-păt'rĭk) *adj. Ecol.* Occurring in separate, widely differing geographic areas. [ALLO- + Gk. *patra,* fatherland (< *patēr,* father) + -IC.] **—al'lo·pat'ri·cal·ly** *adv.*

al·lo·phane (ăl'ə-făn') *n.* An amorphous, translucent, variously colored mineral, essentially hydrous aluminum silicate. [Gk. *allophanēs,* appearing otherwise : *allos,* other + *phainein,* to appear.]

al·lo·phone (ăl'ə-fōn') *n.* Any of the variant forms of a phoneme. For example, the aspirated *p* of *pit* and the unaspirated *p* of *spit* are allophones of the English phoneme *p.* **—al'lo·phon'ic** (-fŏn'ĭk) *adj.*

al·lo·pu·ri·nol (ăl'ō-pyo͝or'ə-nôl') *n.* A drug, $C_5H_4N_4O_3$ used to treat gout by promoting uric acid excretion. [ALLO- + PURIN(E) + -OL[2].]

all-or-none (ôl'ər-nŭn') *adj.* Characterized by either complete response or total lack of response or effect, as in neurological action above a threshold.

al·lo·steric (ăl'ə-stĕr'ĭk) *adj.* Of or relating to molecular binding to an enzyme at a site other than the enzymatically active one.

allspice

al·lot (ə-lŏt') *tr.v.* **-lot·ted, -lot·ting, -lots. 1.** To distribute by lot; apportion. **2.** To give or assign as one's portion; allocate: *allot three weeks to a project.* [ME *alotten* < OFr. *aloter* : *a-,* to (< Lat. *ad-*) + *lot,* portion, of Germanic orig.] **—al·lot'ter** *n.*

al·lot·ment (ə-lŏt'mənt) *n.* **1.** The act of allotting. **2.** Something that is allotted. **3.** A portion of a serviceman's pay set aside for a member of his family or for insurance.

al·lo·trope (ăl'ə-trōp') *n.* A structurally differentiated form of an allotropic element. [Back-formation < ALLOTROPY.]

al·lot·ro·py (ə-lŏt'rə-pē) *n.* The existence, esp. in the solid state, of two or more crystalline or molecular structural forms of an element. **—al'lo·trop'ic** (ăl'ə-trŏp'ĭk), **al'lo·trop'i·cal** *adj.* **—al'lo·trop'i·cal·ly** *adv.*

all' ot·ta·va (ăl'ə-täv-ə, äl'ō-) *adv. Mus.* At an octave higher or lower than written. Used as a direction. [Ital., at the octave.]

al·lot·tee (ə-lŏt'ē') *n.* One to whom something is allotted.

all out *adv.* With every possible effort.

all-out (ôl'out') *adj.* Using all one's resources: *an all-out effort.*

all over *adv.* **1.** Over the whole area or extent: *embroidered all over with roses.* **2.** Everywhere: *searched all over for the money.* **3.** In all respects: *She's her grandmother all over.*

all-o·ver (ôl'ō'vər) *adj.* Covering an entire surface.

al·low (ə-lou') *tr.v.* **-lowed, -low·ing, -lows. 1.** To let do or happen; permit. **2.** To acknowledge or admit; concede: *allow the legality of a claim.* **3.** To permit to have: *allow oneself five dollars a day.* **4.** To make provision for: *allow time for a coffee break.* **5.** To permit the presence of: *No pets allowed.* **6.** To provide (the needed amount): *allow funds in case of emergency.* **7.** To admit; grant: *I allow that to be true.* **8.** To allow as a discount or in exchange: *allowed me twenty dollars on my old typewriter.* **—*phrasal verb.* allow of.** To permit: *a treatise allowing of several interpretations.* [ME *allouen,* to approve, permit < OFr. *alouer* < both Lat. *allaudare,* to praise, and Med. Lat. *allocare,* to allocate.] **—al·low'a·ble** *adj.* **—al·low'a·bly** *adv.*

al·low·ance (ə-lou'əns) *n.* **1.** The act of allowing. **2.** Something that is allowed. **3.** Something given, as money, at regular intervals or for a specific purpose: *a travel allowance.* **4.** A price reduction granted in exchange for used merchandise; discount. **5.** A consideration for possibilities or modifying circumstances: *an allowance for breakage.* **6.** An allowed difference in dimension of closely mating machine parts. *—tr.v.* **-anced, -anc·ing, -anc·es. 1.** To restrict to an allowance. **2.** To put on an allowance.

al·low·ed·ly (ə-lou'ĭd-lē) *adv.* By general admission; admittedly.

al·loy (ăl'oi', ə-loi') *n.* **1.** A homogeneous mixture or solid solution, usually of two or more metals, the atoms of one replacing or occupying interstitial positions between the atoms of the other. **2.** The relative degree of mixture with a base metal; fineness. **3.** Something added that lowers value or purity. *—tr.v.* (ə-loi', ăl'oi') **-loyed, -loy·ing, -loys. 1.** To combine (metals) to form an alloy. **2.** To lower purity or value of (a metal) by mixing with a cheaper metal. **3.** To debase by the addition of an inferior element. [OFr. *aloi* < *aloier,* to alloy < Lat. *alligare,* to bind to : *ad-,* to + *ligare,* to bind.]

all-pur·pose (ôl'pûr'pəs) *adj.* Useful in many ways.

all right *adv.* **1.** Satisfactory; average. **2.** Correct: *These figures are perfectly all right.* **3.** Uninjured. **4.** Very well; yes. **5.** Without a doubt: *He's a fool, all right.*

Usage: It is still not acceptable to write *all right* as a single word, *alright,* despite the parallel to words like *already* and *altogether* and despite the fact that in casual speech the expression is often pronounced as if it were one word.

almond

all-right (ôl'rīt') *adj. Slang.* **1.** Dependable; honorable: *an all-right fellow.* **2.** Good; excellent: *an all-right movie.*

all-round (ôl'round') *adj.* Variant of **all-around.**

All Saints' Day *n.* November 1, a church festival in honor of all saints.

all·seed (ôl'sēd') *n.* Any of several plants having many seeds, such as knotgrass.

All Souls' Day *n.* November 2, observed by the Roman Catholic Church as a day of prayer for souls in purgatory.

all·spice (ôl'spīs') *n.* **1.** A tropical American tree, *Pimenta officinalis,* having small white flowers and aromatic berries. **2.** The dried berries of the allspice, used whole or ground as a spice.

all-star (ôl'stär') *adj.* Made up wholly of star performers: *an all-star cast.* *—n. Sports.* A player chosen for an all-star team.

all-time (ôl'tīm') *adj. Informal.* Of all time: *an all-time attendance record.*

all told *adv.* With everything considered; in all.

al·lude (ə-lo͞od') *intr.v.* **-lud·ed, -lud·ing, -ludes.** To make an indirect reference to. [Lat. *alludere,* to play with : *ad-,* to + *ludere,* to play < *ludus,* game.]

Usage: *Allude* and *allusion* are often used where the more general terms *refer* and *reference* would be preferable. *Allude* and *allusion* apply to indirect reference that does not identify specifically. *Refer* and *reference,* unless qualified, usually imply direct, specific mention.

al·lure (ə-lo͝or') *v.* **-lured, -lur·ing, -lures.** *—tr.* To entice with something desirable; tempt. *—intr.* To tempt or fascinate. *—n.* The power to entice or tempt; fascination. [ME *aluren* < OFr. *alurer* : *a-,* to (< Lat. *ad-*) + *loirre,* bait, of Germanic orig.] **—al·lure'ment** *n.* **—al·lur'er** *n.* **—al·lur'ing·ly** *adv.*

al·lu·sion (ə-lo͞o'zhən) *n.* **1.** The act of alluding; indirect mention. **2.** An indirect, but pointed or meaningful reference. —See Usage note at **allude.** [LLat. *allusio,* a playing with < Lat. *alludere,* to play with. —see ALLUDE.]

al·lu·sive (ə-lo͞o'sĭv) *adj.* Containing or making allusions; suggestive. **—al·lu'sive·ly** *adv.* **—al·lu'sive·ness** *n.*

al·lu·vi·a (ə-lo͞o'vē-ə) *n.* A plural of **alluvium.**

al·lu·vi·al (ə-lo͞o'vē-əl) *adj.* Of, pertaining to, or composed of alluvium.

alluvial fan *n.* A fan-shaped accumulation of alluvium deposited at the mouth of a ravine.

al·lu·vi·on (ə-lo͞o'vē-ən) *n.* **1.** Alluvium. **2.** The flow of water against a shore or bank. **3.** Inundation by water; flood. **4.** *Law.* The increasing of land, esp. along a river bed, by deposited alluvium. [Lat. *alluvio* < *alluere,* to wash against : *ad-,* to + *luere,* to wash.]

al·lu·vi·um (ə-lo͞o'vē-əm) *n., pl.* **-vi·ums** or **-vi·a** (-vē-ə). Sediment deposited by flowing water, as in a river bed, flood plain, or delta. [Lat. < *alluvius,* alluvial < *alluere,* to wash against. —see ALLUVION.]

al·ly (ə-lī', ăl'ī') *v.* **-lied, -ly·ing, -lies.** *—tr.* **1.** To unite or connect in a formal relationship or bond, such as by treaty. **2.** To unite or connect in a personal relationship, such as friendship or marriage. *—intr.* To enter into an alliance. *—n.* (ăl'ī', ə-lī'), *pl.* **-lies. 1.** One that is united with another in some formal or personal relationship. **2.** A friend or close associate. [ME *allien* < OFr. *alier* < Lat. *alligare,* to bind to. —see ALLOY.]

al·lyl (ăl'əl) *n.* The univalent organic radical CH_2:$CHCH_2$. [Lat. *allium,* garlic + -YL (so called because it was first obtained from garlic).] **—al·lyl'ic** (ə-lĭl'ĭk) *adj.*

Al·ma·gest (ăl'mə-jĕst') *n.* **1.** An exhaustive chronicle on astronomy and geography compiled by Ptolemy about A.D. 150. **2. almagest.** Any of several medieval treatises concerned with astronomy or alchemy. [ME *almageste* < OFr. < Ar. *al-majisti* : *al,* the + Gk. *megistē* (*suntaxis*), greatest (composition), fem. of *megistos,* greatest, superl. of *megas,* great.]

al·ma ma·ter or **Al·ma Ma·ter** (ăl'mə mä'tər, äl'mə) *n.* **1.** The school, college, or university that one has attended. **2.** The anthem or school song of an institution of higher learning. [Lat., nourishing mother.]

al·ma·nac (ôl'mə-năk', ăl'-) *n.* **1.** An annual publication including calendars with weather forecasts, astronomical information, tide tables, and other related tabular information. **2.** An annual publication composed of various lists, charts, and tables of useful information in many unrelated fields. [ME *almenak* < Med. Lat. *almanach,* perh. < Gk. *almenikhiaka,* calendars.]

al·man·dine (ăl'mən-dēn') also **al·man·dite** (-dīt') *n.* A deep violet-red garnet, essentially $FeAl_2Si_3O_{12}$, found in metamorphic rocks and used as a gemstone. [ME *alabandine* < Lat. *alabandinus* < *Alabanda,* a town in ancient Asia Minor famous for its jewelry.]

al·might·y (ôl-mī'tē) *adj.* **1.** Having absolute power; all-powerful. **2.** *Informal.* Great or extreme: *an almighty din.* *—adv. Slang.* Extremely: *almighty scared.* *—n.* **the Almighty.** God. [ME *almighti* < OE *ealmihtig* : *eall,* all + *mihtig,* mighty < *miht,* might.] **—al·might'i·ly** *adv.*

al·mond (ä'mənd, ăm'ənd) *n.* **1.** A small tree, *Prunus amygdalus,* native to the Mediterranean region, having pink flowers and fruit containing an edible nut. **2.** The nut of the almond tree, ellipsoid in shape, and having a soft, yellowish-tan shell. **3.** Something having the oval, pointed form of an almond. **4.** A pale tan. [ME *almande* < OFr. < LLat. *amandula,* alteration of Lat. *amygdala* < Gk. *amugdalē.*]

al·mo·ner (ăl'mə-nər, ä'mə-) *n.* **1.** One who distributes alms. **2.** *Chiefly Brit.* A social worker in a hospital. [ME *aumener* < OFr. *aumonier,* ult. < Lat. *eleemosyna,* alms.]

al·most (ôl′mōst′, ôl-mōst′) *adv.* Slightly short of; very nearly. [ME < OE *ealmǣst* : *eall,* all + *mǣst,* most.]

alms (ämz) *pl.n.* Money or goods given to the poor in charity. [ME *almes* < OE *ælmesse* < LLat. *eleemosyna* < Gk. *eleēmosunē* < *eleēmōn,* pitiful < *eleos,* pity.]

alms·house (ämz′hous′) *n.* A poorhouse.

alms·man (ämz′mən) *n.* One dependent on alms for his support.

al·ni·co (ăl′nĭ-kō′) *n.* Any of several hard, strong alloys of aluminum, cobalt, copper, iron, nickel, and sometimes niobium or tantalum, used to make strong permanent magnets. [AL(UMINUM) + NI(CKEL) + CO(BALT).]

al·oe (ăl′ō) *n.* **1.** Any of various plants of the genus *Aloe,* mostly native to southern Africa, having fleshy, spiny-toothed leaves and red or yellow flowers. **2. aloes** *(used with a sing. verb).* A cathartic drug derived from *Aloe barbadensis.* **3. aloes** *(used with a sing. verb).* The fragrant wood of a tree, *Aquilaria agallocha,* of tropical Asia. [ME < OE *aluwe* < Lat. *aloe* < Gk. *aloē.*] **—al′o·et′ic** (ăl′ō-ĕt′ĭk) *adj.*

a·loft (ə-lôft′, ə-lŏft′) *adv.* **1.** In or into a high place; high or higher up. **2.** *Naut.* At or toward the upper rigging. *—prep.* On top of: *birds perching aloft telephone wires.* [ME < ON *ā lopt* : *ā,* in + *lopt,* air.]

a·log·i·cal (ā-lŏj′ĭ-kəl) *adj.* Beyond or not falling within the bounds of logic. **—a·log′i·cal·ly** *adv.* **—a·log′i·cal·ness** *n.*

a·lo·ha (ə-lō′ə, -hə, ä-lō′ä′, -hä′) *n.* Love. Used as an interjection to express greeting or farewell. [Hawaiian.]

al·o·in (ăl′ō-ĭn) *n.* A bitter crystalline compound obtained from the aloe and used as a laxative. [ALO(E) + -IN.]

a·lone (ə-lōn′) *adj.* **1.** Apart from anything or anyone else. **2.** Excluding anyone else; sole; only. **3.** With nothing further added: *The drive alone takes four days.* **4.** Without equal; unique: *alone in his ability to unite all factions of the party.* **—*idioms.* leave alone.** To refrain from interrupting or interfering with (someone). **let alone.** Not to speak of or think of: *I haven't a minute to spare, let alone an hour.* **let well enough alone.** To be satisfied with things as they are. **stand alone.** To be without equal. [ME < *al one,* all one.] **—a·lone′** *adv.* **—a·lone′ness** *n.*

Synonyms: *alone, lonely, lonesome, solitary.* These adjectives are compared as they describe lack of companionship. *Alone* emphasizes isolation from others and does not imply unhappiness. *Lonely* adds to isolation the painful consciousness of it. In *lonesome,* the desire for companionship is more plaintive, but less profound: *lonely for a lover; lonesome for a friend. Solitary* stresses physical isolation, sometimes self-imposed.

a·long (ə-lông′, ə-lŏng′) *adv.* **1.** In a line with; following the length or path of: *trees growing along by the river.* **2.** With a progressive onward motion; forward. **3.** In association; together: *one thing along with another.* **4.** As company; as a companion: *Bring your son along.* **5.** *Informal.* Advanced to some degree: *The evening was well along.* **6.** *Informal.* Approaching something, such as a time or an age: *along about midnight.* *—prep.* **1.** Over, through, or by the length of. **2.** In accordance with. **—*idioms.* all along.** From the very beginning; throughout. **be along.** *Informal.* To come to; arrive at a place: *They will be along soon.* **get along. 1.** To go onward. **2.** To manage successfully; survive. **3.** To be compatible; agree. **4.** *Slang.* To go away; get out. [ME < OE *andlang* : *and,* against + *lang,* long.]

a·long·shore (ə-lông′shôr′, -shōr′, ə-lŏng′-) *adv.* Along, near, or by the shore.

a·long·side (ə-lông′sīd′, ə-lŏng′-) *adv.* Along, near, at, or to the side of anything. *—prep.* By the side of; side by side with.

a·loof (ə-lo͞of′) *adj.* Distant, esp. in one's relations with other people; indifferent. *—adv.* At a distance, but within view; apart. [Obs. *aloof,* toward the wind : A-[2] + obs. *loof,* luff.] **—a·loof′ly** *adv.* **—a·loof′ness** *n.*

al·o·pe·cia (ăl′ə-pē′shə, -shē-ə) *n.* Loss of hair; baldness. [Lat. *alopecia,* fox-mange < Gk. *alōpekia* < *alōpēx,* fox.] **—al′o·pe′cic** (-pē′sĭk) *adj.*

a·loud (ə-loud′) *adv.* **1.** In a loud tone. **2.** With the voice; orally: *Read this passage aloud.*

alp (ălp) *n.* A high mountain. [Back-formation < the *Alps,* a group of mountains in Europe.]

al·pac·a (ăl-păk′ə) *n., pl.* **alpaca** or **-as. 1.** A domesticated South American mammal, *Lama pacos,* related to the llama, and having fine, long wool. **2. a.** The silky wool of the alpaca. **b.** Cloth made from alpaca. **3.** A glossy cotton or rayon and wool fabric, usually black. [Sp. < Aymara *allpaca.*]

al·pen·glow (ăl′pən-glō′) *n.* A rosy glow with which snow-covered mountain peaks are suffused at sunrise or dusk on a clear day. [Partial transl. of G. *Alpenglühen* : *Alpen,* Alps + *glühen,* to glow.]

al·pen·horn (ăl′pən-hôrn′) *n.* A curved wooden horn, sometimes as long as 20 feet, used by herdsmen in the Alps to call cows to pasture. [G. *Alpenhorn* : *Alpen,* Alps + *Horn,* horn.]

al·pen·stock (ăl′pən-stŏk′) *n.* A long staff with an iron point, used by mountain climbers. [G. *Alpenstock* : *Alpen,* Alps + *Stock,* staff.]

al·pes·trine (ăl-pĕs′trĭn) *adj.* Growing at high altitudes; alpine or subalpine. [< Med. Lat. *alpestris* < *Alpes,* the Alps.]

al·pha (ăl′fə) *n.* **1.** The 1st letter in the Greek alphabet. See table at **alphabet. 2.** The first of anything; beginning. **3.** *Astron.* The brightest or main star in a constellation. *—adj.* **1.** First in order of importance. **2.** *Chem.* Closest to the functional group of atoms in a molecule. **3.** Alphabetical. [Gk., of Phoenician orig.; akin to Heb. *āleph,* aleph.]

alpha and omega *n.* **1.** The first and the last: *"I am Alpha and Omega, the beginning and the ending, saith the Lord"* (Revelation 1:8). **2.** The most important part of something.

al·pha·bet (ăl′fə-bĕt′, -bĭt) *n.* **1.** The letters of a given language, arranged in the order fixed by custom. **2.** Any system of characters or symbols representing sounds or things. **3.** The basic or elementary principles of anything; rudiments. [Lat. *alphabetum* < Gk. *alphabētos* : *alpha,* alpha + *beta,* beta, the first two letters of the Greek alphabet.]

al·pha·bet·i·cal (ăl′fə-bĕt′ĭ-kəl) also **al·pha·bet·ic** (-bĕt′ĭk) *adj.* **1.** Arranged in the customary order of the letters of a language. **2.** Of, pertaining to, or expressed by an alphabet. **—al′pha·bet′i·cal·ly** *adv.*

al·pha·bet·ize (ăl′fə-bĭ-tīz′) *tr.v.* **-ized, -iz·ing, -iz·es. 1.** To arrange in alphabetical order. **2.** To supply with an alphabet. **—al′pha·bet′i·za′tion** (ăl′fə-bĕt′ĭ-zā′shən) *n.* **—al′pha·bet·iz′er** *n.*

Alpha Cen·tau·ri (sĕn-tôr′ē) *n.* A double star in Centaurus, the brightest in the constellation, 4.4 light-years from Earth.

Alpha Cru·cis (kro͞o′sĭs) *n.* A double star in the constellation Crux, approximately 230 light-years from Earth.

alpha decay *n.* The radioactive decay of an atomic nucleus by emission of an alpha particle.

alpha helix *n.* A common structure of proteins, characterized by a single chain of amino acids stabilized by hydrogen bonds. **—al′pha-hel′i·cal** *adj.*

al·pha·nu·mer·ic (ăl′fə-no͞o-mĕr′ĭk, -nyo͞o-) also **al·pha·mer·ic** (-fə-mĕr′ĭk) *adj.* **1.** Consisting of alphabetic and numerical symbols. **2.** Consisting of alphabetic and numerical symbols and of punctuation marks, mathematical symbols, and other conventional symbols used in computer work. [ALPHA(BETIC) + NUMERIC(AL).]

alpha particle *n.* A positively charged composite particle, indistinguishable from a helium atom nucleus and consisting of two protons and two neutrons.

alpha privative *n.* The Greek negative prefix *a-* (*an-* before vowels).

alpha ray *n.* A stream of alpha particles.

alpha rhythm also **alpha wave** *n.* The most common electroencephalographic waveform found in recordings of the electrical activity of the adult cerebral cortex, characteristically 8 to 12 smooth, regular oscillations per second in subjects at rest.

al·pho·sis (ăl-fō′sĭs) *n.* Lack of skin pigment, as in albinism. [Gk. *alphos,* leprosy + -OSIS.]

al·pine (ăl′pīn′) *adj.* **1. Alpine.** Of, pertaining to, or characteristic of the Alps or their inhabitants. **2.** Of or pertaining to high mountains. **3.** *Biol.* Living or growing on mountains above the timberline. **4.** Intended for or concerned with mountaineering. **5. Alpine.** Of or pertaining to competitive downhill racing and slalom skiing events. **6. Alpine.** Of or pertaining to a subdivision of the Caucasian race predominant around the Alps. [Lat. *Alpinus* < *Alpes,* the Alps.]

al·pin·ist also **Al·pin·ist** (ăl′pə-nĭst) *n.* A mountain climber. **—al′pin·ism** *n.*

al·read·y (ôl-rĕd′ē) *adv.* By this or a specified time; before; previously. [ME *alredi* : *al,* all + *redi,* ready.]

al·right (ôl-rīt′) *adv. Nonstandard.* All right.

Al·sa·tian (ăl-sā′shən) *adj.* Of or pertaining to Alsace, its inhabitants, or their culture. *—n.* **1.** A native or inhabitant of Alsace. **2.** *Chiefly Brit.* The German shepherd.

al·sike clover (ăl′sīk′) *n.* A plant, *Trifolium hybridum,* native to Eurasia and widely cultivated for forage, having compound leaves and pink or whitish flowers. [After *Alsike,* Sweden.]

al·so (ôl′sō) *adv.* Besides; in addition; likewise; too. *—conj.* And in addition. [ME < OE *ealswa* : *eall,* all + *swā,* so.]

Synonyms: *also, too, likewise, besides, moreover, furthermore.* These adverbs indicate the presence of, or introduce, something additional. The first three generally imply that the additional element or consideration is equal in weight to what precedes it. *Also* is more formal in sound than *too. Likewise* is very formal in tone, and may imply similarity between elements as well as equality. *Besides* often introduces an additional element that reinforces what has gone before. *Moreover* and *furthermore* frequently stress the importance of the additional element.

al·so-ran (ôl′sō-răn′) *n. Informal.* One that is defeated in a race, election, or other competition; loser.

alt (ălt) *adj. Mus.* Pitched in the first octave above the treble staff; high. *—n.* **1.** The first octave above the treble staff. **2.** A note or tone in the alt octave. [Lat. *altus,* high.]

Al·ta·ic (ăl-tā′ĭk) *n.* A language family of Europe and Asia that includes the Turkic, Tungusic, and Mongolic subfamilies. *—adj.* **1.** Of or pertaining to the Altai Mountains. **2.** Of or pertaining to Altaic. [After the *Altai* Mountains.]

Al·tair (ăl-tīr′, -târ′, ăl′tīr′, -târ′) *n.* A very bright, double, variable star in the constellation Aquila, approximately 15.7 light-years from Earth. [Ar. *al-ṭāir* < *al-nasr al-ṭāir,* the flying eagle.]

alpaca

alpenhorn
19th-century woodcut

alpenstock

alpine
Alpine skiing

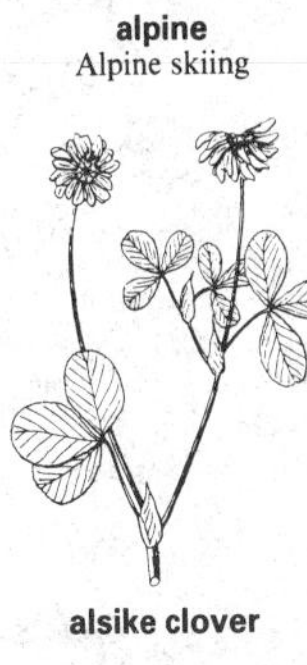
alsike clover

TABLE OF ALPHABETS

The transliterations shown are those used in the etymologies of this Dictionary. The names of the Hebrew and Greek letters are also entered and defined as English nouns. In some cases the English spelling is different from the transliterated spelling shown here, chiefly in the absence of diacritical marks. Thus the English word "omega" differs from the transliterated form *ōmega*. For individual histories of the English letters, see the opening page of each letter throughout the Dictionary.

HEBREW

Forms	Name	Sound
א	'aleph 'alef	'
ב	bēth	b (bh)
ג	gimel	g (gh)
ד	dāleth	d (dh)
ה	hē	h
ו	vav waw	w
ז	zayin	z
ח	ḥeth	ḥ
ט	ṭeth	ṭ
י	yod yodh	y
כ ך	kāph	k (kh)
ל	lāmedh	l
מ ם	mēm	m
נ ן	nūn	n
ס	samekh	s
ע	ʻayin	ʻ
פ ף	pē	p (ph)
צ ץ	sade ṣadhe	ṣ
ק	qōph	q
ר	rēsh	r
שׂ	sin	s
שׁ	shin	sh
ת	tāv tāw	t (th)

Vowels are not represented in normal Hebrew writing, but for educational purposes they are indicated by a system of subscript and superscript dots. The transliterations shown in parentheses are used when the letter falls at the end of a word. The transliterations with subscript dots are pharyngeal consonants as in Arabic. The second forms shown are used when the letter falls at the end of a word.

ARABIC

Forms 1	2	3	4	Name	Sound
ﺍ	ﺎ			'alif	'
ﺏ	ﺐ	ﺒ	ﺑ	bā	b
ﺕ	ﺖ	ﺘ	ﺗ	tā	t
ﺙ	ﺚ	ﺜ	ﺛ	thā	th
ﺝ	ﺞ	ﺠ	ﺟ	jīm	j
ﺡ	ﺢ	ﺤ	ﺣ	ḥā	ḥ
ﺥ	ﺦ	ﺨ	ﺧ	khā	kh
ﺩ	ﺪ			dāl	d
ﺫ	ﺬ			dhāl	dh
ﺭ	ﺮ			rā	r
ﺯ	ﺰ			zāy	z
ﺱ	ﺲ	ﺴ	ﺳ	sīn	s
ﺵ	ﺶ	ﺸ	ﺷ	shīn	sh
ﺹ	ﺺ	ﺼ	ﺻ	ṣād	ṣ
ﺽ	ﺾ	ﻀ	ﺿ	ḍād	ḍ
ﻁ	ﻂ	ﻄ	ﻃ	ṭā	ṭ
ﻅ	ﻆ	ﻈ	ﻇ	ẓā	ẓ
ﻉ	ﻊ	ﻌ	ﻋ	ʻayn	ʻ
ﻍ	ﻎ	ﻐ	ﻏ	ghayn	gh
ﻑ	ﻒ	ﻔ	ﻓ	fā	f
ﻕ	ﻖ	ﻘ	ﻗ	qāf	q
ﻙ	ﻚ	ﻜ	ﻛ	kāf	k
ﻝ	ﻞ	ﻠ	ﻟ	lām	l
ﻡ	ﻢ	ﻤ	ﻣ	mīm	m
ﻥ	ﻦ	ﻨ	ﻧ	nūn	n
ﻩ	ﻪ	ﻬ	ﻫ	hā	h
ﻭ	ﻮ			wāw	w
ﻱ	ﻲ	ﻴ	ﻳ	yā	y

The different forms in the four numbered columns are used when the letters are in: (1) isolation; (2) juncture with a previous letter; (3) juncture with the letters on both sides; (4) juncture with a following letter.

Long vowels are represented by the consonants *'alif* (for ā), *wāw* (for ū), and *yā* (for ī). Short vowels are not usually written; they can, however, be indicated by the following signs: ʹ*fatha* (for *a*), ˌ*kesra* (for *i*), and ʾ*damma* (for *u*).

Transliterations with subscript dots represent "emphatic" or pharyngeal consonants, which are pronounced in the usual way except that the pharynx is tightly narrowed during articulation. When two dots are placed over the *hā*, the new letter thus formed is called *tā marbūta*, and is pronounced (t).

There are several other diacritical marks indicating such situations as the doubling of a consonant or the elision of a vowel.

GREEK

Forms	Name	Sound
Α α	alpha	a
Β β	beta	b
Γ γ	gamma	g (n)
Δ δ	delta	d
Ε ε	epsilon	e
Ζ ζ	zēta	z
Η η	ēta	ē
Θ θ	thēta	th
Ι ι	iota	i
Κ κ	kappa	k
Λ λ	lambda	l
Μ μ	mu	m
Ν ν	nu	n
Ξ ξ	xi	x
Ο ο	omicron	o
Π π	pi	p
Ρ ρ	rhō	r (rh)
Σ σ ς	sigma	s
Τ τ	tau	t
Υ υ	upsilon	u
Φ φ	phi	ph
Χ χ	chi khi	kh
Ψ ψ	psi	ps
Ω ω	ōmega	ō

The superscript ʻ on an initial vowel or *rhō*, called the rough breathing, represents an aspirate. Lack of aspiration on an initial vowel is indicated by the superscript ʼ, called the smooth breathing. When *gamma* precedes *kappa*, *xi*, *khi*, or another *gamma*, it has the value *n* and is so transliterated. The second lowercase form of *sigma* is used only in final position.

RUSSIAN

Forms	Sound
А а	a
Б б	b
В в	v
Г г	g
Д д	d
Е е	e
Ж ж	zh
З з	z
И и Й й	i, ĭ
К к	k
Л л	l
М м	m
Н н	n
О о	o
П п	p
Р р	r
С с	s
Т т	t
У у	u
Ф ф	f
Х х	kh
Ц ц	ts
Ч ч	ch
Ш ш	sh
Щ щ	shch
Ъ ъ	''[1]
Ы ы	y
Ь ь	'[2]
Э э	e
Ю ю	yu
Я я	ya

[1]This letter, called the "hard sign," is very rare in modern Russian. It indicates that the previous consonant remains hard even when followed by a front vowel.

[2]This letter, called the "soft sign," indicates that the previous consonant is palatalized even when a front vowel does not follow.

al·tar (ôl'tər) *n.* **1.** Any elevated place or structure upon which sacrifices may be offered or before which religious ceremonies may be enacted. **2.** In Christian churches, a table or similar structure before which the divine offices are recited and upon which the Eucharist is celebrated. [ME *auter* < OE *altar* < Lat. *altare.*]
altar boy *n.* An attendant to an officiating clergyman in the performance of a liturgical service; acolyte.
al·tar·piece (ôl'tər-pēs') *n.* A painting, carving, or other artwork placed above and behind an altar.
altar rail *n.* A railing in front of the altar that separates the chancel from the rest of the church.
alt·az·i·muth (ăl-tăz'ə-məth) *n.* A mounting for astronomical telescopes that permits both horizontal and vertical rotation. [ALT(ITUDE) + AZIMUTH.]
al·ter (ôl'tər) *v.* **-tered, -ter·ing, -ters.** —*tr.* **1.** To change or make different; modify. **2.** To adjust (a garment) for a better fit. **3.** *Informal.* To castrate or spay. —*intr.* To change or become different. [ME *alteren* < Med. Lat. *alterare* < Lat. *alter,* other.]
al·ter·a·ble (ôl'tər-ə-bəl) *adj.* Capable of being altered. —**al'ter·a·bil'i·ty, al'ter·a·ble·ness** *n.* —**al'ter·a·bly** *adv.*
al·ter·a·tion (ôl'tə-rā'shən) *n.* **1.** The act or procedure of altering. **2.** The condition resulting from altering; modification; change.
al·ter·a·tive (ôl'tə-rā'tĭv, -tər-ə-tĭv) *adj.* **1.** Tending to alter or produce alteration. **2.** *Med.* Tending to restore normal health. —*n. Med.* An alterative treatment or medication.
al·ter·cate (ôl'tər-kāt') *intr.v.* **-cat·ed, -cat·ing, -cates.** To argue or dispute vehemently. [Lat. *altercari, altercat-,* to quarrel < *alter,* other.]
al·ter·ca·tion (ôl'tər-kā'shən) *n.* A heated and noisy quarrel.
al·ter e·go (ôl'tər ē'gō) *n.* **1.** Another side of oneself; second self. **2.** An intimate friend or constant companion. [Lat., other I.]
al·ter·nate (ôl'tər-nāt', ăl'-) *v.* **-nat·ed, -nat·ing, -nates.** —*intr.* **1.** To occur in successive turns: *The rainy season alternates with the dry season.* **2.** To pass from one state, action, or place to a second, back to the first, and so on indefinitely: *alternate between optimism and pessimism.* —*tr.* **1.** To do or execute by turns. **2.** To cause to follow in turns; interchange regularly. —*adj.* (-nĭt). **1.** Happening or following in turns; succeeding each other continuously. **2.** Designating or pertaining to every other one of a series: *alternate lines.* **3.** In place of another; substitute: *an alternate plan.* **4.** *Bot.* **a.** Growing at alternating intervals on either side of a stem: *alternate leaves.* **b.** Arranged alternately between other parts, as stamens between petals. —*n.* (-nĭt). A person acting in the place of another; substitute. [Lat. *alternare, alternat-* < *alternus,* by turns < *alter,* other.] —**al'ter·nate·ness** *n.* —**al'ter·nate·ly** *adv.*
alternate angle *n.* An angle on one side of a transversal that cuts two lines, having one of the intersected lines as a side.
alternating current *n.* An electric current that reverses direction in a circuit at regular intervals.
al·ter·na·tion (ôl'tər-nā'shən, ăl'-) *n.* Successive change from one thing to another and back again.
alternation of generations *n.* Metagenesis.
al·ter·na·tive (ôl-tûr'nə-tĭv, ăl-) *n.* **1. a.** The choice between two mutually exclusive possibilities. **b.** Either of these possibilities. **2.** One of a number of things from which one must be chosen: *a third alternative.* —*adj.* **1.** Allowing or necessitating a choice between two or more than two things. **2.** Existing outside traditional or conventional institutions or systems: *an alternative newspaper.* —**al·ter'na·tive·ly** *adv.*

Usage: *Alternative* is widely used to denote simply "one of a set of possible courses of action," but many traditionalists continue to insist that its use be restricted to situations in which only two possible choices present themselves. In this stricter sense, *alternative* is incompatible with all numerals (*there are three alternatives*), and the use of *two,* in particular, is held to be redundant (*the two alternatives are life and death* would be unacceptable to traditionalists). Similarly, traditionalists reject as unacceptable sentences like *there is no other alternative* on the grounds that it is equivalent to the simpler *there is no alternative.*

alternative box *n.* An element in a flow chart that signifies a decision to be made.
alternative school *n.* A school that is nontraditional, esp. in educational ideals or methods of teaching.
al·ter·na·tor (ôl'tər-nā'tər, ăl'-) *n.* An electric generator that produces alternating current.
al·the·a also **al·thae·a** (ăl-thē'ə) *n.* **1.** The rose of Sharon. **2.** Any plant of the genus *Althaea,* which includes the hollyhock. [Lat., mallows < Gk. *althaia* < *althein,* to heal.]
alt·horn (ălt'hôrn') *n.* A brass wind instrument that sometimes replaces the French horn. [G. : *alt,* alto + *Horn,* horn.]
al·though also **al·tho** (ôl-*th*ō') *conj.* Regardless of the fact that; even though. [ME : *al,* all + *though,* though.]

Usage: As conjunctions, *although* and *though* are generally interchangeable: *Although* (or *though*) *she smiled, she was angry. Although* is usually placed at the beginning of its clause (as in the preceding example), whereas *though* may occur placed elsewhere and is the more common term when used to link words or phrases: *wiser though poorer.*

al·tim·e·ter (ăl-tĭm'ĭ-tər) *n.* An instrument for determining elevation, esp. an aneroid barometer used in aircraft that senses pressure changes that accompany changes in altitude. [Lat. *altus,* high + -METER.] —**al·tim'e·try** *n.*
al·ti·pla·no (ăl'tĭ-plä'nō) *n.* A high plateau, as in the Andean regions of Bolivia, Peru, and Argentina. [Am. Sp. : Lat. *altus,* high + Lat. *planum,* plain.]
al·ti·tude (ăl'tĭ-to͞od', -tyo͞od') *n.* **1.** The height of a thing above a reference level, esp. above sea level or above the earth's surface. **2.** A high location or area. **3.** *Astron.* The angular distance of a celestial object above the horizon. **4.** The perpendicular distance from the base of a geometric figure to the opposite vertex, parallel side, or parallel surface. **5.** A high position or rank. [ME < Lat. *altitudo* < *altus,* high.] —**al'ti·tu'di·nal** (-to͞od'n-əl, -tyo͞od'-) *adj.*
altitude sickness *n.* Illness with symptoms such as nausea, breathlessness, and nosebleed, caused by an oxygen deficiency, such as that encountered at high altitudes.
al·to (ăl'tō) *n., pl.* **-tos.** *Mus.* **1.** A low, female singing voice; contralto. **2.** A countertenor. **3.** The range between soprano and tenor. **4.** A singer whose voice lies within the alto range. **5.** An instrument that sounds within the alto range. **6.** A vocal or instrumental part written for an alto voice or instrument. —***modifier:*** *an alto flute.* [Ital., high < Lat. *altus.*]
al·to·cu·mu·lus (ăl'tō-kyo͞o'myə-ləs) *n.* A cloud formation of rounded, fleecy, white or gray masses. [Lat. *altus,* high + CUMULUS.]
al·to·geth·er (ôl'tə-gĕ*th*'ər) *adv.* **1.** Entirely; completely; utterly: *lost the TV picture altogether.* **2.** With all included or counted; in all; all told: *Altogether 100 people were there.* **3.** On the whole; with everything considered: *Altogether, I'm sorry it happened.* —*n.* A whole. —***idiom.* in the altogether.** *Informal.* In the nude. [ME *al togeder* : *al,* all + *togeder,* together.]

Usage: *Altogether* should be distinguished from *all together. All together* is used of a group to indicate that its members performed or underwent an action collectively: *The nations stood all together. The prisoners were herded all together. All together* can be used only if it is possible to rephrase the sentence so that *all* and *together* may be separated by other words: *The books lay all together in a heap. All the books lay together in a heap.*

al·to-ri·lie·vo also **al·to-re·lie·vo** (ăl'tō-rĭ-lē'vō, ăl'tō-rĕl-yä'vō) *n., pl.* **al·to-re·lie·vos** also **al·to-ri·lie·vi** (ăl'tō-rĕl-yä'vē). High relief. [Ital. *alto rilievo.*]
al·to·stra·tus (ăl'tō-strā'təs, -străt'əs) *n.* An extended cloud formation of bluish or gray sheets or layers. [Lat. *altus,* high + STRATUS.]
al·tri·cial (ăl-trĭsh'əl) *adj.* Helpless and naked when hatched, as young pigeons. [< Lat. *altrix, altric-,* fem. of *altor,* nourisher < *alere,* to nourish.]
al·tru·ism (ăl'tro͞o-ĭz'əm) *n.* Concern for the welfare of others, as opposed to egoism; selflessness. [Fr. *altruisme,* prob. < Ital. *altrui,* someone else < Lat. *alter,* other.] —**al'tru·ist** (-ĭst) *n.* —**al'tru·is'tic** *adj.* —**al'tru·is'ti·cal·ly** *adv.*
al·u·la (ăl'yə-lə) *n., pl.* **-lae** (-lē'). The feathers attached to the part of a bird's wing corresponding to the thumb. [NLat., dim. of Lat. *ala,* wing.] —**al'u·lar** (-lər) *adj.*
al·um (ăl'əm) *n.* Any of various double sulfates of a trivalent metal such as aluminum, chromium, or iron and a univalent metal such as potassium or sodium, esp. aluminum potassium sulfate, $AlK(SO_4)_2 \cdot 12H_2O$, widely used in industry as clarifiers, hardeners, and purifiers, and medicinally as topical astringents and styptics. [ME < OFr. < Lat. *alumen.*]
a·lu·mi·na (ə-lo͞o'mə-nə) *n.* Any of several forms of aluminum oxide, Al_2O_3, occurring naturally as corundum, in a hydrated form in bauxite, and with various impurities as ruby, sapphire, and emery, used in aluminum production and in abrasives, refractories, ceramics, and electrical insulation. [NLat. < Lat. *alumen,* alum.]
a·lu·mi·nate (ə-lo͞o'mə-nāt', -nĭt) *n.* A chemical compound containing aluminum as part of a negative ion.
a·lu·mi·nif·er·ous (ə-lo͞o'mə-nĭf'ər-əs) *adj.* Containing or yielding aluminum, alumina, or alum. [Lat. *alumen, alumin-* + -FEROUS.]
al·u·min·i·um (ăl'yə-mĭn'ē-əm) *n. Chiefly Brit.* Variant of **aluminum.** [NLat. < *alumina,* alumina.]
a·lu·mi·nize (ə-lo͞o'mə-nīz') *tr.v.* **-nized, -niz·ing, -niz·es.** To coat or cover with aluminum or aluminum paint.
a·lu·mi·nous (ə-lo͞o'mə-nəs) *adj.* Of, pertaining to, or containing aluminum or alum.
a·lu·mi·num (ə-lo͞o'mə-nəm) *n. Symbol* **Al** A silvery-white, ductile metallic element, the most abundant in the earth's crust, but found only in combination, chiefly in bauxite. It is used to form many hard, light, corrosion-resistant alloys. Atomic number 13; atomic weight 26.98; melting point 660.2°C; boiling point 2,467°C; specific gravity 2.69; valence 3. [ALUMIN(A) + -IUM.]
aluminum oxide *n.* Alumina.
aluminum paste *n.* Aluminum powder ground in oil, used for aluminum paints.
aluminum sulfate *n.* A white crystalline compound, $Al_2(SO_4)_3$, used chiefly in papermaking, water purification, sanitation, and tanning.
a·lum·na (ə-lŭm'nə) *n., pl.* **-nae** (-nē'). A female graduate or

altar
Carmel Mission Basilica, Carmel, California

alternate
Alternate leaves of daisy fleabane

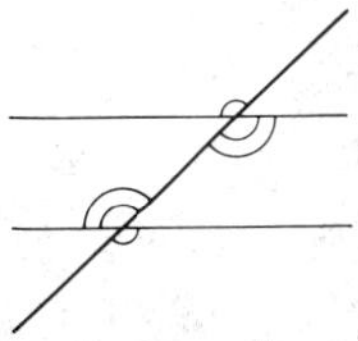
alternate angle
Alternate exterior angles shown by single arc; alternate interior angles shown by double arc

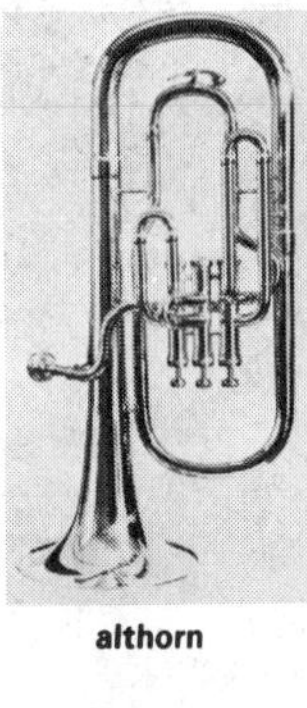
althorn

former student of a school, college, or university. —See Usage note at **alumnus**. [Lat., fem. of *alumnus*.]

a·lum·nus (ə-lŭm′nəs) *n., pl.* **-ni** (-nī′). A male graduate or former student of a school, college, or university. [Lat., pupil < *alere*, to nourish.]

Usage: *Alumni* is generally used to refer to both the alumni and alumnae of a coeducational institution.

al·um·root (ăl′əm-rōōt′, -rŏŏt′) *n.* **1.** Any of various North American plants of the genus *Heuchera*, having clusters of small white, reddish, or green flowers and astringent roots. **2.** The wild geranium.

A·lun·dum (ə-lŭn′dəm). A trademark for a hard, artificial abrasive of fused alumina, used in making oilstones and grinding wheels.

al·u·nite (ăl′yə-nīt′) *n.* A gray mineral, chiefly $K_2Al_3(OH)_6(SO_4)_3$, used in making alum and fertilizer. [Fr. < *alun*, alum < Lat. *alumen*.]

al·ve·o·lar (ăl-vē′ə-lər) *adj.* **1.** Of or pertaining to an alveolus. **2.** *Anat.* **a.** Pertaining to the jaw section containing the tooth sockets. **b.** Pertaining to the alveoli of the lungs. **3.** *Phonet.* Formed with the tip of the tongue touching or near the upper alveoli, as the English *t, d,* and *s.* —*n. Phonet.* A sound produced alveolarly. [Fr. *alvéolaire* < *alvéole*, alveolus < Lat. *alveolus*.] —**al·ve′o·lar·ly** *adv.*

al·ve·o·late (ăl-vē′ə-lĭt) *adj.* Having alveoli; deeply pitted; honeycombed. —**al·ve′o·la′tion** (-lā′shən) *n.*

al·ve·o·lus (ăl-vē′ə-ləs) *n., pl.* **-li** (-lī′). **1.** A small cavity or pit, such as a honeycomb cell. **2.** A tooth socket in the jawbone. **3.** An air sac of the lungs at the termination of a bronchiole. [Lat., small hollow, dim. of *alveus*, a hollow < *alvus*, belly.]

al·ways (ôl′wāz, -wĭz, -wēz) *adv.* **1.** At every time; invariably. **2.** For all time; continuously; forever: *They will be friends always.* **3.** At any time; in any event: *You can always quit if you're unhappy.* [ME *alwei* < OE *ealne weg*, all the way : *ealne*, accusative of *eall*, all + *weg*, way.]

a·lys·sum (ə-lĭs′əm) *n.* **1.** Any of various plants of the genus *Alyssum*, having dense clusters of yellow or white flowers. **2.** Sweet alyssum. [NLat. *Alyssum*, genus name < Gk. *alusson*, a plant believed to cure rabies : *a-*, not + *lussa*, rabies.]

Alz·heim·er's disease (älts′hī-mərz, ălts′-) *n.* A severe neurological disorder marked by progressive dementia and cerebral cortical atrophy. [After Alois *Alzheimer* (1864–1915).]

am (ăm; əm *when unstressed) v.* The first person singular, present indicative of **be**. [ME < OE *eom*.]

Am The symbol for the element americium.

a·mah also **a·ma** (ä′mə, ä′mä) *n.* In the Orient, a maidservant, esp. a wet nurse. [Port. *ama*, nurse < Med. Lat. *amma*, mother.]

Am·a·lek·ite (ăm′ə-lĕk′-īt′, ə-măl′ĭ-kīt′) *n.* In the Old Testament, a member of an ancient nomadic tribe reputedly descended from Esau's grandson Amalek. [Heb. *Amālēqī*, after *Amālēq*, Amalek.]

amaryllis

a·mal·gam (ə-măl′gəm) *n.* **1.** Any of various alloys of mercury with other metals, as with tin or silver. **2.** A combination of diverse elements. [ME < OFr. *amalgame* < Med. Lat. *amalgama*, prob. ult. < Gk. *malagma*, soft mass.]

a·mal·ga·mate (ə-măl′gə-māt′) *v.* **-mat·ed, -mat·ing, -mates.** —*tr.* **1.** To mix so as to make a unified whole; blend. **2.** To mix or alloy (a metal) with mercury. —*intr.* **1.** To combine, unite, or consolidate. **2.** To unite or blend with another metal. —**a·mal′ga·ma′tive** *adj.* —**a·mal′ga·ma′tor** *n.*

a·mal·ga·ma·tion (ə-măl′gə-mā′shən) *n.* **1.** The act of or condition resulting from amalgamating. **2.** A consolidation, as of several corporations. **3.** The dissolving of a metal in mercury to form an alloy.

a·man·dine (ä′mən-dēn′, ăm′ən-) *adj.* Prepared or garnished with almonds: *swordfish amandine.* [Fr. < *amande*, almond < OFr. *almande*. —see ALMOND.]

am·a·ni·ta (ăm′ə-nī′tə, -nē′-) *n.* Any of various mushrooms of the genus *Amanita*, most of which are extremely poisonous. [NLat. *Amanita*, genus name < Gk. *amanitai*, a fungus.]

a·man·ta·dine (ə-măn′tə-dēn′) *n.* An antiviral drug, $C_{10}H_{17}N.HCl$, also used to treat Parkinson's disease. [Alteration of E. *Adamantane*, a hydrocarbon + -INE[2].]

a·man·u·en·sis (ə-măn′yōō-ĕn′sĭs) *n., pl.* **-ses** (-sēz). One employed to take dictation or to copy manuscript. [Lat. *amanuensis* < the phrase *(servus) a manu*, (slave) at handwriting.]

am·a·ranth (ăm′ə-rănth′) *n.* **1.** Any of various, often weedy, plants of the genus *Amaranthus*, having clusters of small greenish or purplish flowers. **2.** An imaginary flower that never fades. **3.** A deep reddish purple to dark or grayish, purplish red. **4.** A dark red to purple azo dye. [NLat. *amaranthus*, genus name, alteration of Lat. *amarantus* < Gk. *amarantos*, unfading : *a-*, not + *marainein*, to wither.]

am·a·ran·thine (ăm′ə-răn′thĭn, -thīn′) *adj.* **1.** Of, pertaining to, or resembling the amaranth. **2.** Eternally beautiful; unfading; everlasting. **3.** Deep purple in color.

am·a·relle (ăm′ə-rĕl′) *n.* A variety of sour cherry having pale-red fruit. [G. < Med. Lat. *amarellum* < Lat. *amarus*, bitter.]

am·a·ret·to (ăm′ə-rĕt′ō) *n.* A liqueur flavored with almond. [Ital., dim. of *amaro*, bitter < Lat. *amarus*.]

am·a·ryl·lis (ăm′ə-rĭl′ĭs) *n.* **1.** A bulbous plant, *Amaryllis belladonna*, native to southern Africa, having large, lilylike reddish or white flowers. **2.** Any of several plants related or similar to the amaryllis. **3. Amaryllis.** In classical pastoral poetry, a conventional name for a shepherdess. [NLat. *Amaryllis*, genus name < Lat., name of a shepherdess < Gk. *Amarullis*.]

a·mass (ə-măs′) *tr.v.* **a·massed, a·mass·ing, a·mass·es.** **1.** To pile or gather up; collect. **2.** To accumulate, esp. for one's own pleasure or profit. [OFr. *amasser* : a-, to (< Lat. *ad-*) + *masse*, mass.] —**a·mass′a·ble** *adj.* —**a·mass′er** *n.* —**a·mass′ment** *n.*

am·a·teur (ăm′ə-tûr′, -tər, -ə-chŏŏr′, -chər, -tyŏŏr′) *n.* **1.** A person who engages in an art, science, study, or athletic activity as a pastime rather than as a profession. **2.** An athlete who has never participated in competition for money or a livelihood. **3.** One lacking professional skill or ease in a certain area, as in art. —*adj.* **1.** Of, pertaining to, or performed by an amateur. **2.** Made up of amateurs. **3.** Not professional; unskillful. [Fr. < Lat. *amator*, lover < *amare*, to love.] —**am′a·teur·ism** *n.*

am·a·teur·ish (ăm′ə-tûr′ĭsh, -chŏŏr′-, -tyŏŏr′-) *adj.* Characteristic of an amateur; not professional; unskillful. —**am′a·teur′ish·ly** *adv.* —**am′a·teur′ish·ness** *n.*

A·ma·ti (ä-mä′tē) *n.* A violin made by Nicolò Amati or the members of his family.

am·a·tive (ăm′ə-tĭv) *adj.* Amorous. [Lat. *amare, amat-*, to love + -IVE.] —**am′a·tive′·ly** *adv.* —**am′a·tive′·ness** *n.*

am·a·tol (ăm′ə-tôl′, -tŏl′) *n.* A highly explosive mixture of ammonium nitrate and trinitrotoluene. [< AM(MONIUM) + (TRINITRO)TOL(UENE).]

am·a·to·ry (ăm′ə-tôr′ē, -tōr′ē) *adj.* Of, pertaining to, or expressive of love, esp. sexual love. [Lat. *amatorius* < *amator*, lover < *amare*, to love.]

am·au·ro·sis (ăm′ô-rō′sĭs) *n.* Total loss of vision; blindness. [Gk. *amaurōsis* < *amauros*, dark.] —**am′au·rot′ic** (-rŏt′ĭk) *adj.*

a·maze (ə-māz′) *tr.v.* **a·mazed, a·maz·ing, a·maz·es.** **1.** To affect with surprise or great wonder; astonish. **2.** *Obs.* To bewilder. —*n. Archaic.* Amazement; wonder. [ME **amasen* < OE *āmasian*, to confound.] —**a·maz′ed·ly** (ə-mā′zĭd-lē) *adv.* —**a·maz′ed·ness** (-nĭs) *n.*

a·maze·ment (ə-māz′mənt) *n.* **1.** A state of extreme surprise or wonder; astonishment. **2.** *Obs.* Bewilderment; perplexity.

Am·a·zon (ăm′ə-zŏn′, -zən) *n.* **1.** *Gk. Myth.* A member of a nation of female warriors reputed to have lived in Scythia, near the Black Sea. **2.** Often **amazon.** A tall, vigorous, strong-willed woman. [ME < Lat. *Amazon* < Gk *Amazōn*.]

Am·a·zo·ni·an (ăm′ə-zō′nē-ən) *adj.* **1.** Characteristic of or resembling an Amazon. **2.** Often **amazonian.** Vigorous and strong-willed. Used of women.

am·a·zon·ite (ăm′ə-zə-nīt′) *n.* A green variety of microcline, often used as a semiprecious stone. [After the *Amazon* River.]

amazon stone *n.* Amazonite.

am·bage (ăm′bĭj) *n. Archaic.* **1.** A winding or indirect pathway. **2.** Often **ambages.** Roundabout ways. [Back-formation < ME *ambages*, equivocation < Lat. *ambages* : *ambi-*, around + *agere*, to drive.] —**am·ba′gious** (ăm-bā′jəs) *adj.*

am·bas·sa·dor (ăm-băs′ə-dər, -dôr′) *n.* **1.** A diplomatic official of the highest rank appointed and accredited as representative in residence by one government to another. **2.** Any of various diplomatic officials of the highest rank: **a. ambassador-at-large.** An ambassador not assigned to a particular country. **b. ambassador extraordinary.** An ambassador assigned to a specific mission. **c. ambassador plenipotentiary.** An ambassador empowered to negotiate treaties. **3.** A diplomatic official heading his country's permanent mission to certain international organizations, such as the United Nations. **4.** Any authorized messenger or representative. [ME *ambassadour* < OFr. *ambassadeur* < Med. Lat. *ambactia*, mission, of Germanic orig.] —**am·bas′sa·do′ri·al** (-dôr′ē-əl, -dōr′-) *adj.* —**am·bas′sa·dor·ship′** *n.*

am·ber (ăm′bər) *n.* **1.** A hard, translucent, yellow, orange, or brownish-yellow fossil resin, used for making jewelry and other ornamental objects. **2.** A brownish yellow. —***modifier:*** *an amber necklace.* —*adj.* Brownish yellow. [ME *ambre* < OFr. < Med. Lat. *ambra* < Ar. *ambar*, ambergris.]

am·ber·gris (ăm′bər-grĭs′, -grēs′) *n.* A waxy, grayish substance formed in the intestines of sperm whales and found floating at sea or washed ashore, used as a fixative in perfumes. [ME < OFr. *ambre gris* : *ambre*, amber + *gris*, gray.]

am·ber·jack (ăm′bər-jăk′) *n., pl.* **amberjack** or **-jacks.** Any of several food and game fishes of the genus *Seriola*, of temperate and tropical marine waters.

ambi– *pref.* Both: *ambiversion.* [Lat., around.]

am·bi·ance also **am·bi·ence** (ăm′bē-əns, äN-byäNs′) *n.* The special or distinctive atmosphere surrounding a person, place, or thing. [Fr. < *ambiant*, surrounding < Lat. *ambiens*. —see AMBIENT.]

am·bi·dex·ter·i·ty (ăm′bĭ-dĕk-stĕr′ĭ-tē) *n.* **1.** The state or quality of being ambidextrous. **2.** Deceit or hypocrisy.

am·bi·dex·trous (ăm′bĭ-dĕk′strəs) *adj.* **1.** Able to use both hands with equal facility. **2.** Unusually dexterous; adroit. **3.** Deceptive or hypocritical. [ME *ambidexter*, double dealing < Med. Lat. : Lat. *ambi-*, on both sides + Lat. *dexter*, right-handed.] —**am′bi·dex′trous·ly** *adv.*

am·bi·ence (ăm′bē-əns, äN-byäns′) *n.* Variant of **ambiance.**

ă **pat** / ā **pay** / âr **care** / ä **father** / b **bib** / ch **church** / d **deed** / ĕ **pet** / ē **be** / f **fife** / g **gag** / h **hat** / hw **which** / ĭ **pit** / ī **pie** / îr **pier** / j **judge** / k **kick** / l **lid, needle** / m **mum** / n **no, sudden** / ng **thing** / ŏ **pot** / ō **toe** / ô **paw, for** / oi **noise** / ou **out** / ŏŏ **took** / ōō **boot** /

am·bi·ent (ăm′bē-ənt) *adj.* Surrounding; encircling. [Lat. *ambiens, ambient-,* pr.part. of *ambire,* to surround : *ambi-,* around + *ire,* to go.]

am·bi·gu·i·ty (ăm′bĭ-gyo͞o′ĭ-tē) *n., pl.* **-ties. 1.** The state of being ambiguous. **2.** Something ambiguous.

ambiguity error *n.* A gross error, usually transient, in the readout of an electronic device that is caused by imprecise synchronism, as in analog-to-digital conversion.

am·big·u·ous (ăm-bĭg′yo͞o-əs) *adj.* **1.** Susceptible of multiple interpretation. **2.** Doubtful or uncertain. [Lat. *ambiguus,* uncertain < *ambigere,* to go about : *ambi-,* around + *agere,* to drive.]

Synonyms: *ambiguous, equivocal, obscure, recondite, abstruse, vague, cryptic, enigmatic.* These adjectives mean lacking clarity of meaning. *Ambiguous* indicates the presence of two or more possible meanings, usually because of faulty expression. An *equivocal* statement is deliberately unclear or misleading, suggesting a hedging to avoid exposure of one's position. *Obscure* suggests meaning hidden in difficult form, sometimes not worth digging out. *Recondite* and *abstruse,* less pejorative, connote the erudite obscurity of the scholar: *a recondite allusion missed by most readers; abstruse works of philosophy. Vague* primarily indicates a lack of definite form. *Cryptic* suggests a puzzling terseness intended to discourage understanding, and *enigmatic,* great significance hidden in mysterious and challenging form.

am·bi·po·lar (ăm′bĭ-pō′lər) *adj.* Applying equally to both positive ions and electrons in a plasma.

am·bit (ăm′bĭt) *n.* **1.** The external boundary of something; circuit. **2.** The sphere or scope of something. [Lat. *ambitus,* a going around < *ambire,* to go around. —see AMBIENT.]

am·bi·tion (ăm-bĭsh′ən) *n.* **1. a.** An eager or strong desire to achieve something. **b.** The object or goal desired. **2.** A desire for exertion or activity. [ME *ambicioun* < OFr. *ambition* < Lat. *ambitio* < *ambire,* to go around (for votes). —see AMBIENT.]

am·bi·tious (ăm-bĭsh′əs) *adj.* **1.** Full of, characterized by, or motivated by ambition. **2.** Greatly desirous; eager: *"I am not ambitious of ridicule"* (Burke). **3.** Showing or requiring much effort; challenging: *an ambitious plan.* **—am·bi′tious·ly** *adv.* **—am·bi′tious·ness** *n.*

am·biv·a·lence (ăm-bĭv′ə-ləns) *n.* **1.** The existence of mutually conflicting feelings or thoughts, such as love and hate, about some person, object, or idea. **2.** Uncertainty or indecisiveness as to what course to follow. [G. *Ambivalenz* : Lat. *ambi-,* on both sides + Lat. *valens,* being strong < *valēre,* to be strong.]

am·biv·a·lent (ăm-bĭv′ə-lənt) *adj.* Exhibiting ambivalence.

am·bi·ver·sion (ăm′bĭ-vûr′zhən, -shən) *n.* A personality trait showing both introversion and extroversion. [AMBI- + (IN-TRO)VERSION or (EXTRO)VERSION.] **—am′bi·vert′** (-vûrt′) *n.*

am·ble (ăm′bəl) *intr.v.* **-bled, -bling, -bles. 1.** To walk slowly or leisurely. **2.** To move along smoothly by lifting first both legs on one side and then both on the other, as do horses and other animals. *—n.* **1.** An ambling gait, esp. that of a horse. **2.** An unhurried or easy walk. [ME *amblen* < AN *aumbler* < Lat. *ambulare,* to walk.] **—am′bler** *n.*

am·blyg·o·nite (ăm-blĭg′ə-nīt′) *n.* A white or greenish mineral, $(Li,Na)Al(PO_4)(F,OH)$, that is an important source of lithium. [G. *Amblygonit* < Gk. *amblugōnios,* obtuse-angled : *amblus,* blunt + *gōnia,* angle.]

am·bly·o·pi·a (ăm′blē-ō′pē-ə) *n.* Dimness of vision without apparent physical defect or disease of the eye. [Gk. *ambluōpia* < *ambluōpos,* dim-sighted : *amblus,* dim. + *ōps, eye.*] **—am′bly·o′pic** (-ō′pĭk, -ŏp′ĭk) *adj.*

am·bo (ăm′bō′) *n., pl.* **am·bos** or **am·bo·nes** (ăm-bō′nēz). One of the two pulpits or raised stands in early Christian churches from which parts of the service were chanted or read. [Med. Lat. < Gk. *ambōn,* raised edge.]

Am·boi·nese (ăm′boi-nēz′, -nēs′) *n.* The language of Amboina.

am·boy·na also **am·boi·na** (ăm-boi′nə) *n.* The reddish-brown, curly-grained wood of a tree, *Pterocarpus indicus,* of southeastern Asia, used for decorative cabinetwork. [After *Amboina,* an island in the Moluccas, Indonesia.]

am·bro·sia (ăm-brō′zhə, -zhē-ə) *n.* **1.** *Gk. & Rom. Myth.* The food of the gods, thought to impart immortality. **2.** Something with an esp. delicious flavor or fragrance. [Lat. < Gk. < *ambrotos,* immortal, immortalizing : *a-,* not + *brotos,* mortal.]

am·bro·sial (ăm-brō′zhəl, -zhē-əl) also **am·bro·sian** (-zhən, -zhē-ən) *adj.* **1.** Suggestive of ambrosia; fragrant or delicious. **2.** Of or worthy of the gods; divine. **—am·bro′sial·ly** *adv.*

am·bro·type (ăm′brō-tīp) *n.* An early type of photograph made by imaging a negative on glass backed by a dark surface. [Gk. *ambrotos,* immortal + TYPE.]

am·bry (ăm′brē) *n., pl.* **-bries. 1.** A storeroom or cupboard; pantry. **2.** In churches, a niche near the altar for keeping sacred vessels and vestments. [ME *aumeneri,* place where alms are distributed < OFr. *aumonerie* < Lat. *armarium,* closet < *arma,* tools.]

ambs·ace (ām′zās′) *n.* **1.** Double aces, the lowest throw at dice. **2.** Misfortune; bad luck. **3.** The smallest amount or most worthless thing possible. [ME *ambes as* < OFr. < Lat. *ambas as,* : *ambo,* both + *as,* unit.]

am·bu·la·crum (ăm′byə-lā′krəm) *n., pl.* **-cra** (-krə). One of the five radial areas on the undersurface of the starfish and similar echinoderms, on which the tube feet are borne. [Lat., walk planted with trees < *ambulare,* to walk.]

am·bu·lance (ăm′byə-ləns) *n.* A vehicle specially equipped to transport the sick or wounded. [Fr. < *(hôpital) ambulant,* mobile (hospital) < Lat. *ambulans,* ambulant.]

ambulance chaser *n. Slang.* **1.** A lawyer or a lawyer's agent who obtains clients by persuading victims of accidents to sue for damages. **2.** A lawyer avid for clients.

am·bu·lant (ăm′byə-lənt) *adj.* Moving or walking about; shifting from place to place. [Fr. < Lat. *ambulans,* pr.part. of *ambulare,* to walk.]

am·bu·late (ăm′byə-lāt′) *intr.v.* **-lat·ed, -lat·ing, -lates.** To walk from place to place; move about. [Lat. *ambulare, ambulat-,* to walk.]

am·bu·la·to·ry (ăm′byə-lə-tôr′ē, -tōr′ē) *adj.* **1.** Of, pertaining to, or for walking. **2.** Capable of walking; not bedridden. **3.** Moving about; not stationary. **4.** *Law.* Capable of being changed or revoked, as a will during the life of the testator. *—n., pl.* **-ries.** A covered place for walking, as in a cloister.

am·bus·cade (ăm′bə-skād′, ăm′bə-skād′) *n.* An ambush. *—tr.v.* **-cad·ed, -cad·ing, -cades.** To ambush. [OFr. *embuscade* < Ital. *imboscata* < *imboscare,* to ambush < Med. Lat. **imbuscare* : Lat. *in-,* in + *buscus,* forest, of Germanic orig.] **—am′bus·cad′er** *n.*

am·bush (ăm′bo͝osh′) *n.* **1.** The act of lying in wait to attack by surprise. **2.** A surprise attack made from a concealed position. **3. a.** Those in hiding to make an ambush. **b.** Their hiding place. **4.** A hidden peril or trap. *—tr.v.* **-bushed, -bush·ing, -bush·es. 1.** To hide and wait in ambush. **2.** To attack from ambush. [ME *embushen,* to ambush < OFr. *embuschier* < Med. Lat. **imbuscare.* —see AMBUSCADE.] **—am′bush′er** *n.*

a·me·ba (ə-mē′bə) *n.* Variant of **amoeba.**

am·e·be·an (ăm′ē-bē′ən) *adj.* Variant of **amoebaean.**

am·e·bi·a·sis (ăm′ə-bī′ə-sĭs) *n.* An infection caused by amoebas, esp. *Entamoeba histolytica.* [AMEB(A) + -IASIS.]

amebic dysentery *n.* An acute, inflammatory amebiasis of the colon that is caused by the amoeba *Entamoeba histolytica* and results in severe pain and diarrhea.]

a·me·bo·cyte (ə-mē′bə-sīt′) *n.* Variant of **amoebocyte.**

a·meer (ī-mîr′, ă-mîr′) *n.* Variant of **emir.**

a·me·lio·rate (ə-mēl′yə-rāt′) *tr. & intr.v.* **-rat·ed, -rat·ing, -rates.** To make or become better; improve. [Alteration of MELIORATE.]

a·me·lio·ra·tion (ə-mēl′yə-rā′shən) *n.* **1.** The act of ameliorating. **2.** The state of being ameliorated; improvement.

a·men (ā-mĕn′, ä-mĕn′) *interj.* Used at the end of a prayer or a statement to express approval. *—adv.* Verily; truly. *—n.* **1.** An utterance of the interjection amen. **2.** An expression of conviction or assent. [ME < OE < LLat. *amen* < Gk. *amēn* < Heb. *āmēn,* certainly < *āman,* to strengthen.]

A·men also **A·mon** (ä′mən) *n.* The god of life and reproduction in Egyptian mythology, represented as a man with a ram's head.

a·me·na·ble (ə-mē′nə-bəl, ə-mĕn′ə-) *adj.* **1.** Willing to follow advice or suggestion. **2.** Responsible to authority; accountable. **3.** Open or liable to testing, criticism, or judgment. [Alteration of ME *menable* < OFr. < *mener,* to lead < Lat. *minare,* to drive < *minari,* to threaten < *minae,* threats.]

amen corner *n.* A church seat reserved for persons leading responsive amens.

a·mend (ə-mĕnd′) *v.* **a·mend·ed, a·mend·ing, a·mends.** *—tr.* **1.** To improve; better. **2.** To remove the faults or errors of; rectify. **3.** To alter (a legislative measure, for example) formally by adding, deleting, or rephrasing. *—intr.* To better one's conduct; reform. [ME *amenden* < OFr. < Lat. *emendare,* to correct : *ex-,* out of + *menda,* fault.]

a·men·da·to·ry (ə-mĕn′də-tôr′ē, -tōr′ē) *adj.* Serving or tending to amend; corrective.

a·mend·ment (ə-mĕnd′mənt) *n.* **1.** A change for the better; improvement. **2.** A correction. **3. a.** A revision or change. **b.** A formal statement of such a change.

a·mends (ə-mĕndz′) *pl.n.* Reparation or payment made as satisfaction for insult or injury. ***—idiom.* make amends.** To make up (to someone) for insult or injury. [ME *amendes* < OFr., pl. of *amende,* reparation < *amender,* to amend.]

a·men·i·ty (ə-mĕn′ĭ-tē, ə-mē′nĭ-) *n., pl.* **-ties. 1.** The quality of being pleasant or attractive; agreeableness. **2. a.** A feature that increases attractiveness or value, esp. of a piece of real estate or a geographical location. **b.** Something that increases physical or material comfort. **3. amenities.** Social courtesies; pleasantries; civilities. [ME *amenite* < OFr. < Lat. *amoenitas* < *amoenus,* pleasant.]

a·men·or·rhe·a or **a·men·or·rhoe·a** (ā-mĕn′ə-rē′ə) *n.* Abnormal suppression or absence of menstruation. [A-[1] + Gk. *mēn,* month + -RRHEA.] **—a·men′or·rhe′ic** *adj.*

am·ent[1] (ăm′ənt, ā′mənt) *n.* A catkin. [Lat. *amentum,* strap.]

a·ment[2] (ā′mĕnt′, ā′mənt) *n.* A mentally deficient or feeble-minded person. [< Lat. *amens, ament-,* insane : *a-,* out of + *mens,* mind.]

am·en·ta·ceous (ăm′ən-tā′shəs, ā′mən-) *adj.* **1.** Resembling or characteristic of an ament; catkinlike. **2.** Having aments or catkins.

Amazon
Amazon fighting Hercules

a·men·tia (ā-mĕn′shə, -shē-ə) *n.* Subnormal mental development; feeble-mindedness. [Lat. *amentia* < *amens,* insane. — see AMENT².]

am·en·tif·er·ous (ăm′ən-tĭf′ər-əs, ā′mən-) *adj. Bot.* Bearing aments or catkins.

Am·er·a·sian (ăm′ə-rā′zhən, -shən) *n.* An individual of mixed American and Asian descent. [AMER(ICAN) + ASIAN.] **—Am′er·a′sian** *adj.*

a·merce (ə-mûrs′) *tr.v.* **a·merced, a·merc·ing, a·merc·es.** **1.** To punish by a fine imposed arbitrarily at the discretion of the court. **2.** To punish by imposing an arbitrary penalty. [ME *amercen* < AN *amercier* < *à merci,* at the mercy of : *à,* to (< Lat. *ad*) + *merci,* mercy < Lat. *merces,* wages.]

A·mer·i·can (ə-mĕr′ĭ-kən) *adj.* **1.** Of, relating to, or characteristic of the United States of America, its people, culture, government, or history. **2.** Of, in, or pertaining to North or South America or the Western Hemisphere. **3.** Of or pertaining to the Indians inhabiting America. **4.** Indigenous to North or South America: *American elm; American elk.* —*n.* **1.** A native or inhabitant of America. **2.** A citizen of the United States. **—A·mer′i·can·ness** *n.*

A·mer·i·ca·na (ə-mĕr′ə-kä′nə, -kăn′ə, -kā′nə) *pl.n.* A collection of things relating to American history, folklore, or geography.

American Beauty *n.* A type of rose bearing large, long-stemmed purplish-red flowers.

American cheese *n.* A smooth, mild cheddar cheese, white to yellow in color.

American dream *n.* An American ideal of social equality and esp. material success.

American eagle *n.* The bald eagle, esp. as it appears on the Great Seal of the United States.

American elk *n.* The wapiti.

American English *n.* The English language as used in the United States.

American Indian *n.* A member of any of the aboriginal peoples of North America (except the Eskimos), South America, and the West Indies, considered to belong to the Mongoloid ethnic division of the human species.

A·mer·i·can·ism (ə-mĕr′ĭ-kə-nĭz′əm) *n.* **1.** A custom, trait, or tradition originating in the United States. **2.** A usage of language characteristic of American English. **3.** Allegiance to the United States and its customs and institutions.

A·mer·i·can·ist (ə-mĕr′ĭ-kə-nĭst) *n.* **1.** One who studies a facet of America, such as its history or geology. **2.** An anthropologist specializing in the study of American aboriginal culture. **3.** A person, other than a U.S. citizen, who is sympathetic to the United States and its policies.

American ivy *n.* The Virginia creeper.

A·mer·i·can·ize (ə-mĕr′ĭ-kə-nīz′) *v.* **-ized, -iz·ing, -iz·es.** —*tr.* To assimilate into American culture. —*intr.* To become American in spirit or methods. **—A·mer′i·can·i·za′tion** *n.*

American plan *n.* A system of hotel management in which a guest pays a fixed daily rate for room, meals, and service.

American saddle horse *n.* A three-gaited or five-gaited high-stepping saddle horse of a breed originating in Kentucky.

American sign language *n.* An American system of communication for the deaf that employs manual signs.

American Spanish *n.* The Spanish language as used in the Western Hemisphere.

American Standard Version *n.* A revised version of the King James Bible published in the United States in 1901.

am·er·i·ci·um (ăm′ə-rĭsh′ē-əm) *n.* A white metallic transuranic element of the actinide series, having isotopes with mass numbers from 237 to 246 and half-lives from 25 minutes to 7,950 years. Its longest-lived isotopes, Am 241 and Am 243, are alpha-ray emitters used as radiation sources in research. Atomic number 95; specific gravity 11.7; valences 3, 4, 5, 6. [After *America.*]

Am·er·ind (ăm′ə-rĭnd′) also **Am·er·in·di·an** (ăm′ə-rĭn′dē-ən) *n.* An American Indian or an Eskimo. [AMER(ICAN) + IND(IAN).] **—Am′er·in′di·an** *adj.* **—Am′er·in′dic** *adj.*

Am·es·lan (ăm′ə-slăn′) *n.* American sign language.

am·e·thop·ter·in (ăm′ə-thŏp′tə-rən′) *n.* Methotrexate. [A(MINO)- + METH- + *pter(oyl),* a chemical radical + -IN.]

am·e·thyst (ăm′ə-thĭst) *n.* **1.** A purple or violet form of transparent quartz used as a gemstone. **2.** A purple variety of corundum, used as a gemstone. **3.** A moderate purple to graying reddish purple. [ME *amatiste* < OFr. < Lat. *amethystus* < Gk. *amethustos* : *a-,* not + *methuein,* to be drunk (from the belief that it was a remedy for drunkenness).] **—am′e·thys′tine** *adj.*

am·e·tro·pi·a (ăm′ĭ-trō′pē-ə) *n.* An eye abnormality, such as nearsightedness, farsightedness, or astigmatism, resulting from faulty refraction. [Gk. *ametros,* without measure (*a-,* without + *metron,* measure) + -OPIA.]

Am·har·ic (ăm-hăr′ĭk) *n.* A Semitic language that is the official language in Ethiopia. —*adj.* Of or concerning Amhara. [After *Amhara,* a former province of Ethiopia.]

a·mi·a·ble (ā′mē-ə-bəl) *adj.* **1.** Having a pleasant disposition; good-natured. **2.** Cordial; sociable; congenial: *an amiable gathering.* [ME < OFr. < LLat. *amicabilis,* amicable.] **—a′mi·a·bil′i·ty, a′mi·a·ble·ness** *n.* **—a′mi·a·bly** *adv.*

Synonyms: *amiable, affable, good-natured, obliging, agreeable, pleasant.* These adjectives all refer to a tendency to please in social relations. *Amiable* implies friendliness and sweetness of disposition. *Affable* especially fits a person who is easy to approach and difficult to anger. *Good-natured* suggests a tolerant, easygoing disposition; sometimes it also implies a docile nature. *Obliging* specifies disposition to comply with the will of others; *agreeable* adds to this a sense of eagerness to please. *Pleasant* applies broadly to favorable manner or appearance.

am·i·an·thus (ăm′ē-ăn′thəs) also **am·i·an·tus** (-təs) *n.* An asbestos with fine, silky fibers. [Lat. *amiantus* < Gk. *amiantos,* undefiled : *a-,* not + *mianein,* to defile.]

am·i·ca·ble (ăm′ĭ-kə-bəl) *adj.* Characterized by or showing friendliness; friendly. [ME < LLat. *amicabilis* < Lat *amicus,* friend.] **—am′i·ca·bil′i·ty, am′i·ca·ble·ness** *n.* **—am′i·ca·bly** *adv.*

am·ice (ăm′ĭs) *n.* A liturgical vestment consisting of an oblong piece of white linen worn around the neck and shoulders and partly under the alb. [ME, alteration of *amit* < OFr. < Lat. *amictus,* mantle < *amicio,* to wrap around : *ambi-,* around + *jacere,* to throw.]

a·mi·cus cu·ri·ae (ə-mē′kəs kyo͝or′ē-ī′) *n., pl.* **a·mi·ci curiae** (ə-mē′kē). *Law.* A person invited to advise a court on a matter of law in a case to which he is not a party. [Lat., friend of the court.]

a·mid (ə-mĭd′) also **a·midst** (ə-mĭdst′) *prep.* Surrounded by; in the middle of. [ME < OE *onmiddan* : *on,* in + *midde,* middle.]

am·ide (ăm′īd′, -ĭd) *n.* **1.** An organic compound, such as acetamide, containing the $CONH_2$ group. **2.** A compound with a metal replacing hydrogen in ammonia, such as sodium amide, $NaNH_2$. [AM(MONIA) + -IDE.] **—a·mid′ic** (ə-mĭd′ĭk, ă-mĭd′-) *adj.*

am·i·dol (ăm′ĭ-dôl′, -dōl′) *n.* A colorless crystalline compound $(NH_2)_2C_6H_3OH{\cdot}2HCl$, used as a photographic developer. [G. *Amidol,* a trademark.]

a·mid·ships (ə-mĭd′shĭps′) also **a·mid·ship** (-shĭp′) *adv. Naut.* Midway between the bow and the stern.

a·midst (ə-mĭdst′) *prep.* Variant of **amid.**

a·mi·go (ə-mē′gō) *n., pl.* **-gos.** A friend. [Sp. < Lat. *amicus,* friend.]

a·mine (ə-mēn′, ăm′ēn′) *n.* Any of a group of organic compounds of nitrogen, such as ethylamine, $C_2H_5NH_2$, that may be considered ammonia derivatives in which one or more hydrogen atoms has been replaced by a hydrocarbon radical. [AM(MONIUM) + -INE².]

-amine *suff.* Amine: *diamine.* [< AMINE.]

a·mi·no (ə-mē′nō, ăm′ə-nō′) *adj.* Pertaining to an amine or other chemical compound containing NH_2 combined with a nonacid organic radical. [< AMINO-.]

amino- *pref.* Containing NH_2 combined with a nonacid organic radical: *aminopyrine.* [< AMINE.]

amino acid *n.* **1.** An organic compound containing both an amino group (NH_2) and a carboxylic acid group (COOH). **2.** A compound of the form $NH_2CHRCOOH$, found as essential components of the protein molecule.

a·mi·no·ac·i·de·mi·a (ə-mē′nō-ăs′ĭ-dē′mē-ə, ăm′ə-nō-) *n.* A condition marked by excess amino acids in the blood.

a·mi·no·ac·i·du·ri·a (ə-mē′nō-ăs′ĭ-do͝or′ē-ə, -dyo͝or′-, ăm′ə-nō-) *n.* A condition marked by excess amino acids in the urine.

a·mi·no·ben·zo·ic acid (ə-mē′nō-bĕn-zō′ĭk, ăm′ə-nō-) *n.* Any of three benzoic acid derivatives, $C_7H_7NO_2$, esp. the yellowish para form, which is part of the vitamin B complex.

a·mi·no·phe·nol (ə-mē′nō-fē′nōl′, -nôl′, ăm′ə-nō-) *n.* One of three organic compounds with composition $C_6H_4NH_2OH$, used as photographic developers and dye intermediates.

a·mi·no·py·rine (ə-mē′nō-pī′rēn′, ăm′ə-nō-) *n.* A colorless crystalline compound, $C_{13}H_{17}N_3O$, used to reduce fever and relieve pain. [AMINO- + (ANTI)PYRINE.]

a·mir (ĭ-mîr′, ā-mîr′) *n.* Variant of **emir.**

A·mish (ä′mĭsh, ăm′ĭsh, ā′mĭsh) *pl.n.* An orthodox Anabaptist sect that separated from the Mennonites in the late 17th century and exists today principally in southeastern Pennsylvania. —*adj.* Of or pertaining to this sect or its members. [G. *amisch,* after Jacob *Amman,* 17th-cent. Swiss Mennonite bishop.]

a·miss (ə-mĭs′) *adj.* Out of proper order: *What is amiss?* —*adv.* In an improper or defective way. **—idiom. take amiss.** To misunderstand; feel offended by. [ME *amis* < ON *a mis.*]

a·mi·to·sis (ā′mī-tō′sĭs) *n.* Cell division characterized by simple nuclear cleavage without the formation of chromosomes. **—a′mi·tot′ic** (-tŏt′ĭk) *adj.* **—a′mi·tot′i·cal·ly** *adv.*

am·i·trip·tyl·ine (ăm′ə-trĭp′tə-lēn′) *n.* An antidepressant drug, $C_{20}H_{23}N$. [AMI(NO)- + *tript-* (alteration and shortening of TRYPTOPHAN) + -YL + -INE².]

am·i·ty (ăm′ĭ-tē) *n., pl.* **-ties.** Peaceful relations, as between nations; friendship. [ME *amite* < OFr. < Med. Lat. **amicitas* < Lat. *amicus,* friend.]

am·me·ter (ăm′mē′tər) *n.* An instrument that measures electric current. [AM(PERE) + -METER.]

am·mine (ăm′ēn′, ă-mēn′) *n.* Any of a class of chemical compounds, such as aniline, derived from replacement of hydrogen atoms in ammonia by univalent hydrocarbon radicals.

[AMM(ONIA) + -INE².] **—am'mi·no'** (ăm'ə-nō', ə-mē'nō) *adj.*

am·mo (ăm'ō) *n.* Ammunition.

am·mo·nia (ə-mōn'yə) *n.* **1.** A colorless, pungent gas, NH_3, extensively used to manufacture fertilizers and a wide variety of nitrogen-containing organic and inorganic chemicals. **2.** Ammonium hydroxide. [NLat. < Lat. *(sal) ammoniacus,* (salt) of Amen < Gk. *Ammōniakos* < *Ammōn,* Amen (from its having been obtained from a region near the temple of Amen, in Libya).]

am·mo·ni·ac¹ (ə-mō'nē-ăk') also **am·mo·ni·a·cal** (ăm'ə-nī'ə-kəl). *adj.* Of, containing, or similar to ammonia.

am·mo·ni·ac² (ə-mō'nē-ăk') *n.* A strong-smelling gum resin from the stems of a plant, *Dorema ammoniacum,* of northern Asia, formerly used in medicine as an expectorant and stimulant. [ME *ammoniak* < *Ammōniacum* < Gk. *ammōniakon,* of Amen. —see AMMONIA.]

am·mo·ni·ate (ə-mō'nē-āt') *tr.v.* **-at·ed, -at·ing, -ates.** To treat or combine with ammonia. *—n.* A compound that contains ammonia. **—am·mo'ni·a'tion** *n.*

ammonia water *n.* Ammonium hydroxide.

am·mon·i·fi·ca·tion (ə-mŏn'ə-fĭ-kā'shən, ə-mō'nə-) *n.* **1.** Impregnation with ammonia or an ammonium compound. **2.** The generation of ammonia or ammonium compounds by the action of bacteria on nitrogenous organic matter in soil.

am·mon·i·fy (ə-mŏn'ə-fī', ə-mō'nə-) *tr. & intr.v.* **-fied, -fy·ing, -fies.** To subject or be subjected to ammonification. **—am·mon'i·fi'er** *n.*

am·mo·nite (ăm'ə-nīt') also **am·mo·noid** (-noid') *n.* The coiled, flat, chambered shell of any of various extinct mollusks of the class *Cephalopoda,* found as fossils in Mesozoic formations. [NLat. *Ammonites* < Lat. *(cornu) Ammonis,* (horn) of Amen.]

Am·mon·ite (ăm'ə-nīt') *n.* A member of a Semitic people living east of the Jordan River, mentioned frequently in the Old Testament. [LLat. *Ammonites,* the Ammonites < Heb. *'Ammōn,* city or people of Amman.]

am·mo·ni·um (ə-mō'nē-əm) *n.* The chemical ion NH_4^+. [AMMON(IA) + -IUM.]

ammonium carbonate *n.* A white powder with composition $(NH_4)HCO_3{\cdot}(NH_4)CO_2NH_2$, used in baking powders, smelling salts, and fire-extinguishing compounds.

ammonium chloride *n.* A slightly hygroscopic white crystalline compound, NH_4Cl, used in dry cells, as a soldering flux, as an expectorant, and in various industrial applications.

ammonium hydroxide *n.* A colorless basic aqueous solution of ammonia, NH_4OH, used as a household cleanser and to manufacture a wide variety of products including textiles, rayon, rubber, fertilizer, and plastic.

ammonium nitrate *n.* A colorless crystalline salt, NH_4NO_3, used in fertilizers, explosives, and solid rocket propellants.

ammonium sulfate *n.* A brownish-gray to white crystalline salt, $(NH_4)_2SO_4$, used in fertilizers and water purification.

am·mu·ni·tion (ăm'yə-nĭsh'ən) *n.* **1. a.** The projectiles, along with their fuses and primers, that can be fired from guns or otherwise propelled. **b.** A nuclear, biological, chemical, or explosive material used as a weapon. **2.** A means of offense or defense. [OFr. *amunition,* from the phrase *la munition,* the provisioning < Lat. *munitio,* fortification. —see MUNITION.]

am·ne·sia (ăm-nē'zhə) *n.* Partial or total loss of memory, esp. through shock, psychological disturbance, brain injury, or illness. [NLat. < Gk. *amnēsia,* forgetfulness.] **—am·ne'si·ac'** (-nē'zē-ăk', -zhē-ăk'), **am·ne'sic** (-nē'zĭk, -sĭk) *n. & adj.* **—am·nes'tic** (-nĕs'tĭk) *adj.*

am·nes·ty (ăm'nĭ-stē) *n., pl.* **-ties.** A general pardon for offenders by a government, esp. for political offenses. *—tr.v.* **-tied, -ty·ing, -ties.** To grant amnesty to. [Lat. *amnestia* < Gk. *amnēstos,* not remembered.]

am·ni·o·cen·te·sis (ăm'nē-ō-sĕn-tē'sĭs) *n., pl.* **-ses** (-sēz'). The surgical withdrawal of a sample of amniotic fluid from a pregnant female, esp. for use in the determination of sex or genetic disorder in the fetus. [NLat. : AMNION + Gk. *kentēsis,* act of pricking < *kentein,* to prick.]

am·ni·og·ra·phy (ăm'nē-ŏg'rə-fē) *n., pl.* **-phies.** Radiography of the uterine cavity following injection of a radiopaque substance. [AMNIO(N) + -GRAPHY.]

am·ni·on (ăm'nē-ən, -ŏn') *n., pl.* **-ni·ons** or **-ni·a** (-nē-ə). A thin, tough, membranous sac that contains a watery fluid in which the embryo of a mammal, bird, or reptile is suspended. [NLat. < Gk. *amniōn,* plate to hold a sacrificial victim's blood.] **—am'ni·ot'ic** (-ŏt'ĭk), **am'ni·on'ic** (-ŏn'ĭk) *adj.*

am·ni·os·co·py (ăm'nē-ŏs'kə-pē) *n., pl.* **-pies.** Endoscopic examination of the amniotic cavity. [AMNIO(N) + -SCOPY.] **—am'ni·o·scope'** (-ə-skōp') *n.*

a·moe·ba (ə-mē'bə) *n., pl.* **-bas** or **-bae** (-bē). Any of various protozoans of the genus *Amoeba* and related genera, occurring in water, soil, and as internal animal parasites, characteristically having an indefinite, changeable form and moving by means of pseudopodia. [NLat. < Gk. *amoibē,* change < *ameibein,* to change.] **—a·moe'bic** (-bĭk) *adj.*

am·oe·bae·an or **am·oe·be·an** (ăm'ē-bē'ən) *adj.* Alternately answering, as dialogue. [LLat. *amoebaeus* < Gk. *amoibaios* < *amoibē,* change. —see AMOEBA.]

am·oe·bi·a·sis (ăm'ə-bī'ə-sĭs) *n.* Variant of **amebiasis.**

amoebic dysentery *n.* Variant of **amebic dysentery.**

a·moe·bo·cyte (ə-mē'bə-sīt') *n.* A cell, such as a leucocyte, having amoebic form. [AMOEB(A) + -CYTE.]

a·moe·boid (ə-mē'boid') *adj.* Of or resembling an amoeba, esp. in changeability of form and means of locomotion.

a·mok (ə-mŭk', ə-mŏk') *adv. & adj.* Variant of **amuck.**

a·mo·le (ə-mō'lē) *n.* **1.** Any of several plants, chiefly of southwestern North America, having roots, bulbs, or other parts used as soap. **2.** The parts of the amole used as soap. [Mex. Sp. < Nahuatl *amolli.*]

a·mong (ə-mŭng') also **a·mongst** (ə-mŭngst') *prep.* **1.** In the midst of; surrounded by. **2.** In the group, number, or class of: *He is among the wealthy.* **3.** In the company of; in association with: *traveling among a group of tourists.* **4.** With many; by many or the entire number of: *a custom popular among the Greeks.* **5.** By the joint action of: *Among us, we will get the job done.* **6.** With portions to each of: *Distribute this among you.* **7.** Each with the other; between one another: *Don't fight among yourselves.* [ME < OE *on gemang* : *on,* in + *gemang,* throng.]

Synonyms: *among, amid, between.* These prepositions are compared as they pertain to positions in space or to their figurative equivalents. *Among* refers to being surrounded, or approximately so, by objects that are individual and separable: *living among the Indians. Amid* stresses being surrounded but not necessarily by separable things: *a house amid the trees; remain cool amid confusion. Between* refers to a location in space that separates two objects: *standing between two skyscrapers; caught between opposing viewpoints.*

a·mon·til·la·do (ə-mŏn'tl-ä'dō) *n., pl.* **-dos.** A pale dry sherry. [Sp. : *a-,* to (< Lat. *ad-*) + *Montilla,* a town in Spain.]

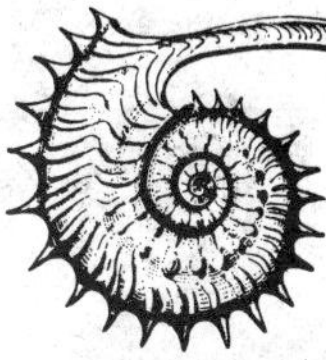

ammonite

a·mor·al (ā-môr'əl, ā-mŏr'-) *adj.* **1.** Not admitting of moral distinctions or judgments; neither moral nor immoral. **2.** Lacking moral sensibility; not caring about right and wrong. **—a'mo·ral'i·ty** (ā'mô-răl'ĭ-tē, -mə-), **a·mor'al·ism** *n.* **—a·mor'al·ly** *adv.*

am·o·ret·to (ăm'ə-rĕt'ō, ä'mə-) *n., pl.* **-ti** (-tē) or **-tos.** A cupid. [Ital., dim. of *Amore,* Cupid < Lat. *Amor* < *amor,* love < *amare,* to love.]

am·o·rist (ăm'ə-rĭst) *n.* One dedicated to love. [Lat. *amor,* love + -IST.]

Am·o·rite (ăm'ə-rīt') *n.* A member of a people inhabiting Canaan before the Israelites, mentioned frequently in the Old Testament. [< Heb. *Emōrī.*]

am·o·rous (ăm'ər-əs) *adj.* **1.** Strongly attracted to love, esp. sexual love. **2.** Indicative of love or sexual desire: *an amorous glance.* **3.** Of or associated with love: *an amorous poem.* **4.** In love; enamored: *amorous of her since the day they met.* [ME < OFr. *amoureus* < Med. Lat. *amorosus* < Lat. *amor,* love < *amare,* to love.] **—am'or·ous·ly** *adv.* **—am'or·ous·ness** *n.*

a·mor·phism (ə-môr'fĭz'əm) *n.* The state or quality of being amorphous.

a·mor·phous (ə-môr'fəs) *adj.* **1.** Without definite form; shapeless. **2.** Of no particular type; anomalous. **3.** Lacking organization; formless. **4.** Lacking distinct crystalline structure. [Gk. *amorphos* : *a-,* without + *morphē,* shape.] **—a·mor'phous·ly** *adv.* **—a·mor'phous·ness** *n.*

am·or·ti·za·tion (ăm'ər-tĭ-zā'shən, ə-môr'tĭ-) *n.* **1.** The act or process of amortizing. **2.** The money set aside for the purpose of amortization. **3.** In reckoning the yield of a bond bought at a premium, the periodic subtraction from its current yield of a proportionate share of the premium between the purchase date and the maturity date.

am·or·tize (ăm'ər-tīz', ə-môr'tīz') *tr.v.* **-tized, -tiz·ing, -tiz·es.** **1.** To liquidate (a debt) by installment payments or payment into a sinking fund. **2.** To write off (expenditures) by prorating over a certain period. **3.** *Law.* To sell or transfer (property) in mortmain. [ME *amortisen* < OFr. *amortir, amortiss-* < VLat. **admortire* : Lat. *ad-,* to + Lat. *mors,* death.] **—am'or·tiz'a·ble** *adj.*

a·mor·tize·ment (ə-môr'tĭz-mənt) *n.* Amortization.

A·mos (ā'məs) *n.* **1.** A Hebrew prophet of the eighth century B.C. **2.** See table at **Bible.** [Heb. *'Āmōs.*]

a·mount (ə-mount') *n.* **1.** The total of two or more quantities; aggregate. **2.** A number; sum. **3.** A principal plus its interest, as in a loan. **4.** The aggregate effect or meaning; import. **5.** Quantity: *a great amount of intelligence.* *—intr.v.* **a·mount·ed, a·mount·ing, a·mounts. 1.** To add up in number or quantity. **2.** To be equivalent or tantamount: *accusations amounting to an indictment.* [< ME *amounten,* to ascend < OFr. *amonter* < *amont,* upward < Lat. *ad montem,* to the hill < *mons,* hill.]

a·mour (ə-mŏŏr') *n.* A love affair, esp. an illicit one. [ME < OFr. < Lat. *amor,* love < *amare,* to love.]

a·mour-pro·pre (ə-mŏŏr'prôp'rə) *n.* Self-respect. [Fr.]

A·moy (ä-moi', ə-moi') *n.* The dialect of Chinese spoken in and around the city of Xiamen in Fujian Province in southeastern China. [After *Amoy,* former name for Xiamen.]

amp (ămp) *n.* An ampere.

AMP (ā'em-pē') *n.* A mononucleotide, $C_{10}H_{14}N_5O_7P$, found in animal cells, that is reversibly convertible to ADP and ATP. [A(DENOSINE) M(ONO)P(HOSPHATE).]

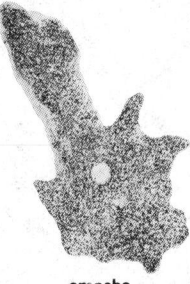

amoeba

am·pe·lop·sis (ăm'pə-lŏp'sĭs) *n.* Any of several woody vines of the genus *Ampelopsis,* having small greenish or yellowish flowers. [NLat. *Ampelopsis,* genus name : Gk. *ampelos,* grapevine + Gk. *opsis,* appearance.]

am·per·age (ăm′pər-ĭj, ăm′pîr′ĭj) *n.* The strength of an electric current expressed in amperes.

am·pere (ăm′pîr′) *n.* **1.** A unit of electric current in the meter-kilogram-second system. It is the steady current that when flowing in straight parallel wires of infinite length and negligible cross section, separated by a distance of one meter in free space, produces a force between the wires of 2 × 10^{-7} newtons per meter of length. **2.** A unit in the International System specified as one International coulomb per second and equal to 0.999835 ampere. [After André Marie *Ampère* (1775–1836).]

am·pere-hour (ăm′pîr-our′) *n.* The electric charge transferred past a specified circuit point by a current of one ampere in one hour.

amphitheater

am·pere-turn (ăm′pîr-tûrn′) *n.* A unit of magnetomotive force in the meter-kilogram-second system equal to the magnetomotive force around a path linking one turn of a conducting loop carrying a current of one ampere.

am·per·sand (ăm′pər-sănd′) *n.* The character or sign (&) representing *and.* [Alteration of *and per se and,* "& (the sign) by itself (is the word) and."]

am·phet·a·mine (ăm-fĕt′ə-mēn′, -mĭn) *n.* **1.** A colorless volatile liquid, $C_9H_{13}N$, used primarily as a central nervous system stimulant. **2.** A phosphate or sulfate of amphetamine, used as a central nervous system stimulant. [A(LPHA) + M(ETHYL) + PH(ENYL) + ET(HYL) + AMINE.]

amphi– *pref.* **1. a.** Both: *amphibiotic.* **b.** On both sides: *amphistylar.* **2.** Around: *amphithecium.* [Lat. < Gk. < *amphi,* on both sides.]

amphora

am·phi·ar·thro·sis (ăm′fē-är-thrō′sĭs) *n., pl.* **-ses** (-sēz′). A relatively immobile joint between bony surfaces connected by ligaments or elastic cartilage. [AMPHI- + ARTHROSIS.]

am·phib·i·an (ăm-fĭb′ē-ən) *n.* **1.** Any of various cold-blooded, smooth-skinned vertebrate organisms of the class Amphibia, such as a frog, that characteristically hatch as aquatic larvae that breathe by means of gills and that metamorphose to an adult form with air-breathing lungs. **2.** An amphibious organism. **3.** An aircraft that can take off and land either on land or on water. **4.** A vehicle that can move over land and on water. [< NLat. *Amphibia,* class name < Gk. *amphibion* < *amphibios,* amphibious.]

am·phi·bi·ot·ic (ăm′fə-bī-ŏt′ĭk) *adj.* Living in water during an early stage of development and on land during the adult stage.

am·phib·i·ous (ăm-fĭb′ē-əs) *adj.* **1.** Living or able to live both on land and in water. **2.** Able to operate on both land and water: *amphibious military vehicles.* **3.** Of a mixed or twofold nature. [Gk. *amphibios* : *amphi-,* on both sides + *bios,* life.] **—am·phib′i·ous·ly** *adv.* **—am·phib′i·ous·ness** *n.*

am·phi·bole (ăm′fə-bōl′) *n.* Any of a large group of structurally similar hydrated double silicate minerals, such as hornblende, containing various combinations of sodium, calcium, magnesium, iron, and aluminum. [Fr. < LLat. *amphibolus,* ambiguous < Gk. *amphibolos,* doubtful < *amphiballein,* to throw on either side : *amphi-,* on both sides + *ballein,* to throw.] **—am′phi·bol′ic** (-bŏl′ĭk) *adj.*

am·phib·o·lite (ăm-fĭb′ə-līt′) *n.* A chiefly amphibole rock with minor plagioclase and little quartz.

am·phib·o·lous (ăm-fĭb′ə-ləs) *adj.* Having two meanings; ambiguous; equivocal. [Gk. *amphibolos.* —see AMPHIBOLE.]

am·phi·brach (ăm′fə-brăk′) *n.* A trisyllabic metrical foot having one accented or long syllable between two unaccented or short syllables, as in the word *remember.* [Lat. *amphibrachys* < Gk. *amphibrakhus* : *amphi-,* on both sides + *brakhus,* short.]

am·phic·ty·o·ny (ăm-fĭk′tē-ə-nē) *n., pl.* **-nies.** In ancient Greece, a group of states sharing a common religious center or shrine, such as the one at Delphi. [Gk. *Amphiktonia* < *amphiktuones,* neighbors : *amphi-,* on the periphery + *ktizein,* to settle.] **—am·phic′ty·on′ic** (-ŏn′ĭk) *adj.*

am·phim·a·cer (ăm-fĭm′ə-sər) *n.* A trisyllabic foot having an unaccented or short syllable between two accented or long syllables, as in *prō domō.* [Lat. *amphimacrus* < Gk. *amphimakros* : *amphi-,* on both sides + *makros,* long.]

am·phi·mix·is (ăm′fə-mĭk′sĭs) *n., pl.* **-mix·es** (-mĭk′sēz′). True sexual reproduction, with fusion of sperm and egg nuclei. [NLat. : AMPHI- + Gk. *mixis,* a mingling < *mignunai,* to mingle.] **—am′phi·mic′tic** (-mĭk′tĭk) *adj.*

Am·phi·on (ăm-fī′ən) *n. Gk. Myth.* The son of Zeus and the twin brother of Zethus, with whom he conquered and fortified Thebes, building a wall around the city by charming the stones into place with the music of his magic lyre. [Gk. *Amphiōn.*]

am·phi·ox·us (ăm′fē-ŏk′səs) *n.* The lancelet. [NLat. : AMPHI- + Gk. *oxus,* sharp.]

am·phi·pod (ăm′fə-pŏd′) *n.* Any of numerous small crustaceans of the order Amphipoda, which includes the beach fleas. [< NLat. *Amphipoda,* order name : AMPHI- + Gk. *pous,* foot.]

am·phip·ro·style (ăm-fĭp′rō-stīl′, ăm′fĭ-prō′stīl′) *adj. Archit.* Having a prostyle or set of columns at each end, but none along the sides. [Lat. *amphiprostylos* < Gk. *amphiprostulos* : *amphi-,* on both sides + *prostulos,* with pillars in front. —see PROSTYLE.] **—am·phip′ro·style′** *n.*

am·phis·bae·na (ăm′fĭs-bē′nə) *n.* A mythological serpent having a head at each end of its body. [Lat. < Gk. *amphisbaina* : *amphis,* both ways (< *amphi-,* on both sides) + *bainein,* to go.] **—am′phis·bae′nic** *adj.*

am·phi·sty·lar (ăm′fĭ-stī′lər) *adj. Archit.* Having columns at both front and back or on each side. [AMPHI- + Gk. *stulos,* pillar.]

am·phi·the·a·ter (ăm′fə-thē′ə-tər) *n.* **1.** An oval or round structure having tiers of seats rising gradually outward from an open space or arena at the center. **2.** An arena where contests are held. **3.** A level area surrounded by upward sloping ground. **4.** An upper, sloping gallery in a theater. [Lat. *amphitheatrum* < Gk. *amphitheatron* : *amphi-,* around + *theatron,* theater. —see THEATER.] **—am′phi·the·at′ric** (-ăt′rĭk), **am′phi·the·at′ri·cal** *adj.* **—am′phi·the·at′ri·cal·ly** *adv.*

am·phi·the·a·tre (ăm′fə-thē′ə-tər) *n. Chiefly Brit.* Amphitheater.

am·phi·the·ci·um (ăm′fĭ-thē′shē-əm, -sē-əm) *n., pl.* **-ci·a** (-shē-ə, -sē-ə). The outer layer of cells of the spore-containing capsule of a moss. [NLat. : AMPHI- + Gk. *thēkion,* dim. of *thēkē,* case.]

Am·phi·tri·te (ăm′fĭ-trī′tē) *n. Gk. Myth.* The wife of Poseidon, goddess of the sea, and one of the Nereids. [Gk. *Amphitritē.*]

am·phit·ro·pous (ăm-fĭt′rə-pəs) *adj. Bot.* Partly inverted so that the point of attachment is near the middle. Used of an ovule or seed.

Am·phit·ry·on (ăm-fĭt′rē-ən) *n. Gk. Myth.* A king of Thebes and the husband of Alcmene. [Gk. *Amphitruōn.*]

am·pho·ra (ăm′fər-ə) *n., pl.* **-pho·rae** (-fə-rē′) or **-pho·ras.** A two-handled jar with a narrow neck, used by the ancient Greeks and Romans to carry wine or oil. [Lat. < Gk. *amphoreus,* short for *amphiphoreus* : *amphi-,* on both sides + *phoreus,* bearer < *pherein,* to bear.] **—am′pho·ral** (-rəl) *adj.*

am·pho·ter·ic (ăm′fə-tĕr′ĭk) *adj.* Capable of reacting either as an acid or a base. [< Gk. *amphoterus,* either of two < *amphō,* both.]

am·pi·cil·lin (ăm′pə-sĭl′ən) *n.* An antibiotic related to penicillin that is effective against gram-negative bacteria, used primarily to treat urinary, intestinal, and respiratory tract infections. [Blend of AMINO- and PENICILLIN.]

am·ple (ăm′pəl) *adj.* **-pler, -plest. 1.** Of large or great size, amount, extent, or capacity: *an ample living room.* **2. a.** Large in degree or kind; in abundant measure: *an ample reward.* **b.** More than enough: *ample evidence.* **3.** Sufficient for a particular need: *ample provisions for a week.* [ME < OFr. < Lat. *amplus.*] **—am′ple·ness** *n.* **—am′ply** (-plē) *adv.*

am·plex·i·caul (ăm-plĕk′sĭ-kôl′) *adj.* Having a base that clasps or encircles the stem, as some leaves do. [NLat. *amplexicaulis,* embracing stem : Lat. *amplexus,* an embracing < *amplector,* to embrace (*ambi-,* around + *plectere,* to twine) + Lat. *caulis,* stem.]

am·pli·fi·ca·tion (ăm′plə-fĭ-kā′shən) *n.* **1.** The act or result of amplifying. **2. a.** An addition to or expansion of a statement or idea. **b.** A statement with such an addition. **3.** *Physics.* **a.** The process of increasing the magnitude of a variable quantity, esp. the magnitude of a voltage or current, without altering any other quality. **b.** The result of such a process. **4.** *Electronics.* Gain (sense 3).

am·pli·fi·er (ăm′plə-fī′ər) *n.* **1.** One that amplifies, enlarges, or extends. **2.** *Electronics.* A device to produce amplification, esp. one using transistors or electron tubes of an electrical signal.

am·pli·fy (ăm′plə-fī′) *v.* **-fied, -fy·ing, -fies.** *—tr.* **1.** To make larger or more powerful; increase. **2.** To add to, as by illustrations; make complete. **3.** To exaggerate. **4.** *Electronics.* To produce amplification of. *—intr.v.* To write or discourse at length; expatiate. [ME *amplifien* < OFr. *amplifier* < Lat. *amplificare* : *amplus,* large + *facere,* to make.]

am·pli·tude (ăm′plĭ-to͞od′, -tyo͞od′) *n.* **1.** Greatness of size; magnitude. **2.** Fullness; copiousness. **3.** Breadth or range, as of intelligence. **4.** *Astron.* The angular distance along the horizon from true east or west to the intersection of the vertical circle of a celestial body with the horizon. **5.** *Physics.* The maximum value of a periodically varying quantity. **6.** *Math.* **a.** The maximum ordinate value of a periodic curve. **b.** The angle made with the positive horizontal axis by the vector representation of a complex number. **7.** *Electronics.* The magnitude of a voltage or current waveform. [Lat. *amplitudo* < *amplus,* large.]

amplitude modulation *n. Electronics.* **1.** The encoding of a carrier wave by variation of its amplitude in accordance with an input signal. **2.** A broadcast system that uses amplitude modulation.

am·poule also **am·pule** or **am·pul** (ăm′po͞ol, -pyo͞ol) *n.* A small glass vial, sealed after filling and used chiefly as a container for a hypodermic injection solution. [Fr. < OFr. < Lat. *ampulla.*]

am·pul·la (ăm-po͞ol′ə, -pŭl′ə) *n., pl.* **-pul·lae** (-po͞ol′ē, -pŭl′ē). **1.** A nearly round bottle with two handles used by the ancient Romans for wine, oil, or perfume. **2.** *Eccles.* A vessel for consecrated wine or holy oil. **3.** *Anat.* A small dilation in

a canal or duct, esp. one in the semicircular canal of the ear. [Lat.] **—am·pul'lar** (-ər) *adj.*
am·pu·tate (ăm'pyo͞o-tāt') *tr.v.* **-tat·ed, -tat·ing, -tates.** To cut off (a part of the body), esp. by surgery. [Lat. *amputare, amputat-,* to cut around : *ambi-,* around + *putare,* to cut.] **—am'pu·ta'tion** *n.* **—am'pu·ta'tor** *n.*
am·pu·tee (ăm'pyo͞o-tē') *n.* A person who has had one or more limbs removed by amputation. —See Usage note at **-ee[1]**.
am·ri·ta (ŭm-rē'tə) *n. Hindu Myth.* **1.** The ambrosia, prepared by the gods, that bestows immortality. **2.** The immortality achieved by drinking amrita. [Skt. *amṛtam* : *a-,* without + *mṛtam,* death.]
am·trac also **am·track** (ăm'trăk') *n.* A small, armed, amphibious vehicle first used in World War II to carry troops from ship to shore. [AM(PHIBIOUS) + TRAC(TOR).]
a·muck (ə-mŭk') also **a·mok** (ə-mŭk', ə-mŏk') *adv.* **1.** In a frenzy to do violence or kill: *rioters running amuck in the sreets.* **2.** In a jumbled or faulty manner. *—adj.* Crazed with murderous frenzy. [Malay *amok.*]
am·u·let (ăm'yə-lĭt) *n.* An object worn, esp. around the neck, as a charm against evil or injury. [Lat. *amuletum.*]
a·muse (ə-myo͞oz') *tr.v.* **a·mused, a·mus·ing, a·mus·es.** **1.** To occupy in an agreeable, pleasing, or entertaining fashion. **2.** To cause to laugh or smile by giving pleasure. **3.** *Archaic.* To delude or deceive; bemuse. [OFr. *amuser,* to stupefy : *a,* to (< Lat. *ad*)+ *muser,* to stare stupidly.] **—a·mus'a·ble** *adj.* **—a·mus'er** *n.*

Synonyms: *amuse, entertain, divert, regale.* These verbs refer to actions that provide pleasure, especially as a means of passing time. *Amuse* is the least specific. *Entertain* suggests more formal, deliberate acts of bringing about pleasure. *Divert* implies distraction from worrisome thought or care. *Regale* means to entertain lavishly.

a·muse·ment (ə-myo͞oz'mənt) *n.* **1.** The state of being amused, entertained, or pleased. **2.** Something that amuses.
amusement park *n.* A commercially operated enterprise that offers rides, games, and other forms of entertainment.
a·mus·ing (ə-myo͞o'zĭng) *adj.* **1.** Entertaining or pleasing. **2.** Arousing laughter. **—a·mus'ing·ly** *adv.*
a·mu·sive (ə-myo͞o'zĭv, -sĭv) *adj.* Providing amusement.
a·myg·da·la (ə-mĭg'də-lə) *n., pl.* **-lae** (-lē). *Anat.* An almond-shaped mass of gray matter in the anterior portion of the temporal lobe. [NLat. < Lat., almond < Gk. *amugdalē.*]
a·myg·dale (ə-mĭg'dāl) *n.* An amygdule. [Gk. *amygdalē,* almond.]
a·myg·da·lin (ə-mĭg'də-lĭn) *n.* A glycoside derived from the volatile essential oils of bitter almonds, peaches, and apricots, used to derive Laetrile. [Lat. *amygdala,* almond (< Gk. *amugdalē*) + -IN.]
a·myg·da·line (ə-mĭg'də-lĭn, -līn') *adj.* Of, pertaining to, or resembling an almond. [Lat. *amygdalinus* < Gk. *amugdalinos* < *amugdalē,* almond.]
a·myg·da·loid (ə-mĭg'də-loid') *n.* A volcanic rock containing many amygdules. *—adj.* Also **a·myg·da·loi·dal** (ə-mĭg'-də-loi'dl). **1.** Almond-shaped. **2.** Of or relating to the amygdala. **3.** *Geol.* Resembling amygdaloid. [Lat. *amygdala,* almond (< Gk. *amugdalē*) + -OID.]
a·myg·dule (ə-mĭg'dyo͞ol) *n.* A small gas bubble in lava or other igneous rock filled with secondary minerals such as zeolite, calcite, or quartz. [Lat. *amygdala,* almond (from its shape) + (NOD)ULE.]
am·yl (ăm'əl) *n.* **1.** The univalent organic radical C_5H_{11}, occurring in several isomeric forms in many organic compounds. **2.** *Slang.* Amyl nitrite. [Lat. *amylum,* starch. —see AMYLUM.]
amyl- *pref.* Variant of **amylo-.**
am·y·la·ceous (ăm'ə-lā'shəs) *adj.* Of, pertaining to, or resembling starch; starchy.
amyl acetate *n.* An organic compound, $CH_3COOC_5H_{11}$, used commercially in isomeric mixtures as a flavoring agent, as a paint and lacquer solvent, and in the preparation of penicillin.
amyl alcohol *n.* Any of eight isomers of the composition $C_5H_{11}OH$, one of which is the principal constituent of fusel oil.
am·y·lase (ăm'ə-lās', -lāz') *n.* Any of various enzymes that convert starch to sugar.
amyl nitrite *n.* The nitrous acid ester of isoamyl alcohol, used in medicine as a vasodilator.
amylo- or **amyl-** *pref.* Starch: *amylose.* [< Lat. *amylum,* starch.]
am·y·loid (ăm'ə-loid') *n.* **1.** A starchlike substance. **2.** *Pathol.* A hard protein deposit resulting from degeneration of tissue. *—adj.* Starchlike.
am·y·lol·y·sis (ăm'ə-lŏl'ə-sĭs) *n.* The enzymatic conversion of starch to sugars. **—am'y·lo·lyt'ic** (-lō-lĭt'ĭk) *adj.*
am·y·lop·sin (ăm'ə-lŏp'sĭn) *n.* The starch-digesting amylase produced by the pancreas. [AMYLO- + (TRY)PSIN.]
am·y·lose (ăm'ə-lōs', -lōz') *n.* The relatively soluble portion of starch.
am·y·lum (ăm'ə-ləm) *n.* Starch. [Lat. < Gk. *amulon,* starch < *amulos,* not ground at a mill : *a-,* not +*mulē,* mill.]
a·my·o·to·ni·a (ā'mī-ə-tō'nē-ə) *n.* Lack of muscle tone.
an[1] (ən; ăn *when stressed*) *indef. art.* A[1]. Used before words beginning with a vowel or with an unpronounced *h: an elephant; an hour.* —See Usage note at **a[1]**.[ME < OE *ān,* one.]
an[2] also **an'** (ən, ăn *when stressed*) *conj. Archaic.* And if; if: *"An I may hide my face, let me play Thisby too"* (Shakespeare). [ME, short for *and,* and < OE.]
an- *pref.* Variant of **a-[1]**. Used before vowels and frequently before h.
-an[1] *suff.* **1.** Of, relating to, or resembling: *brachyuran.* **2.** One relating to, belonging to, or resembling: *librarian.* [ME < OFr. < Lat. *-anus,* adj. and n. suffix.]
-an[2] *suff.* **1. a.** Unsaturated hydrocarbon: *urethan.* **b.** Heterocyclic compound: *furan.* **2.** Anhydride of a carbohydrate: *dextran.* [Alteration of -ANE.]
an·a[1] (ăn'ə, ä'nə) *n., pl.* **ana** or **-as.** **1.** A collection of various materials that reflect the character of a person or place. **2.** An item in such a collection. [< -ANA.]
an·a[2] (ăn'ə) *adv.* Both in the same quantity; of each. Used to refer to ingredients in prescriptions. [ME < Med. Lat. < Gk., at the rate of.]
ana- *pref.* **1.** Upward; up: *anabolism.* **2.** Backward; back: *anaplasia.* **3.** Again; anew: *anaphylaxis.* [Gk. < *ana,* up.]
-ana or **-iana** *suff.* A collection of items relating to a specified person or place: *Americana.* [NLat. < Lat. *-ana,* neuter pl. of *-anus,* -an.]
an·a·bae·na (ăn'ə-bē'nə) *n.* Any of various freshwater algae of the genus *Anabaena,* sometimes occurring in drinking water and causing a bad taste and odor. [NLat. *Anabaena,* genus name < Gk. *anabainein,* to go up : *ana-,* up + *bainein,* to go.]
An·a·bap·tist (ăn'ə-băp'tĭst) *n.* A member of one of the radical movements of the Reformation of the 16th century that insisted that only adult baptism was valid and held that true Christians should not bear arms, use force, or hold government office. [NLat. *anabaptista :* Gk. *ana-,* again + *baptizein,* to baptize < *baptein,* to dip.] **—An'a·bap'tism** *n.* **—An'a·bap'tist** *adj.*
an·a·bas (ăn'ə-băs) *n.* A member of the genus *Anabas,* which includes freshwater fishes of Africa and Asia. [NLat. *Anabas,* genus name < Gk. *anabas,* climbing, pr.part. of *anabainein,* to go up. —see ANABATIC.]
a·nab·a·sis (ə-năb'ĭ-sĭs) *n., pl.* **-ses** (-sēz'). A large-scale military advance, specifically, the Greek expedition across Asia Minor (401 B.C.) led by Cyrus the Younger of Persia, as described by Xenophon. [Gk. < *anabainein,* to go up. —see ANABATIC.]
an·a·bat·ic (ăn'ə-băt'ĭk) *adj.* Of or pertaining to rising wind currents. [Gk. *anabatikos* < *anabainein,* to rise: *ana,* up + *bainein,* to go.]
an·a·bi·o·sis (ăn'ə-bī-ō'sĭs) *n.* A restoring to life from a deathlike condition; resuscitation. [NLat. < Gk. *anabiōsis* < *anabioun,* to return to life : *ana-,* back + *bioun,* to live < *bios,* life.] **—an'a·bi·ot'ic** (-ŏt'ĭk) *adj.*
anabolic steroid *n.* Any of several synthetic hormones often used to increase muscle size and strength.
a·nab·o·lism (ə-năb'ə-lĭz'əm) *n.* The metabolic process by which simple substances are synthesized into the complex materials of living tissue. [ANA- + (META)BOLISM.] **—an'a·bol'ic** (ăn'ə-bŏl'ĭk) *adj.*
a·nach·ro·nism (ə-năk'rə-nĭz'əm) *n.* **1.** The representation of something as existing or happening at other than its proper or historical time. **2.** Something out of its proper time. [Fr. *anachronisme* < Gk. *anakhronismos* < *anakronizein,* to be an anachronism : *ana-,* backward + *khronizein,* to belong in time < *khronos,* time.] **—a·nach'ro·nis'tic, a·nach'ro·nous** (-nəs) *adj.* **—a·nach'ro·nis'ti·cal·ly, a·nach'ro·nous·ly** *adv.*
an·a·cli·sis (ăn'ə-klī'sĭs, ə-năk'lĭ-sĭs) *n.* Psychological dependence on others. [Gk. *anaklisis,* a leaning back < *anaklinein,* to lean on : *ana-,* on + *klinein,* to lean.] **—an'a·clit'ic** (-klĭt'-ĭk) *adj.*
an·a·co·lu·thon (ăn'ə-kə-lo͞o'thŏn') *n., pl.* **-thons** or **-tha** (-thə). An abrupt change within a sentence to a second grammatical construction inconsistent with the first, sometimes used for rhetorical effect, for example: *I warned him that if he continues to drink, what will become of him?* [LLat. < Gk. *anakolouthos,* inconsistent : *an-,* not + *akolouthos,* following.] **—an'a·co·lu'thic** *adj.*
an·a·con·da (ăn'ə-kŏn'də) *n.* **1.** A large, nonvenomous, arboreal snake, *Eunectes murinus,* of tropical South America, that constricts its prey in its coils. **2.** Any of several snakes similar or related to the anaconda. [Perh. alteration of Singhalese *henakandayā,* whip snake.]
A·nac·re·on·tic (ə-năk'rē-ŏn'tĭk) *adj.* In the manner of the poems of Anacreon, esp. in being convivial or amatory. *—n.* An Anacreontic poem.
an·a·cru·sis (ăn'ə-kro͞o'sĭs) *n.* **1.** One or more unstressed syllables at the beginning of a line of verse, before the reckoning of the normal meter begins. **2.** *Mus.* An upbeat. [NLat. < Gk. *anakrousis,* beginning of a tune < *anakrouein,* to begin : *ana-,* back + *krouein,* to push.]
an·a·dem (ăn'ə-dĕm') *n. Archaic.* A wreath or garland for the head. [Lat. *anadema* < Gk. *anadēma* < *anadein,* to bind up : *ana-,* up + *dein,* to bind.]
an·a·di·plo·sis (ăn'ə-də-plō'sĭs) *n.* Rhetorical repetition of the word or phrase that ends one phrase at the beginning of the next phrase. [Lat. *anadiplosis,* < Gk. *anadiplōsis* < *anadi-*

amulet
Pre-Columbian,
Peruvian

ploun, to redouble : *ana-,* again + *diploun,* to double < *diplous,* double.]

a·nad·ro·mous (ə-năd′rə-məs) *adj.* Migrating up rivers from the sea to breed in fresh water. [Gk. *anadromos,* a running up : *ana-,* up + *dromos,* race.]

a·nae·mi·a (ə-nē′mē-ə) *n.* Variant of **anemia.**

a·nae·mic (ə-nē′mĭk) *adj.* Variant of **anemic.**

an·aer·obe (ăn′ə-rōb′, ăn-âr′ōb′) *n.* A microorganism, as a bacterium, able to live in the absence of free oxygen. **—an′aer·o′bic** (ăn′ə-rō′bĭk, -âr-ō′bĭk) *adj.* **—an′aer·o′bic·al·ly** *adv.*

an·aes·the·sia (ăn′ĭs-thē′zhə) *n.* Variant of **anesthesia.**

an·aes·the·si·ol·o·gy (ăn′ĭs-thē′zē-ŏl′ə-jē) *n.* Variant of **anesthesiology.**

an·aes·thet·ic (ăn′ĭs-thĕt′ĭk) *adj. & n.* Variant of **anesthetic.**

a·naes·the·tist (ə-nĕs′thĭ-tĭst) *n.* Variant of **anesthetist.**

a·naes·the·tize (ənĕs′thĭ-tīz′) *v.* Variant of **anesthetize.**

an·a·glyph (ăn′ə-glĭf′) *n.* **1.** An ornament carved in low relief. **2.** A moving or still picture consisting of two slightly different perspectives of the same subject in contrasting colors that are superimposed on each other, and that produces a three-dimensional effect when viewed through two correspondingly colored filters. [Gk. *anagluphos,* carved in low relief : *ana-,* up + *gluphein,* to carve.] **—an′a·glyph′ic, an′a·glyp′tic** (-glĭp′tĭk) *adj.*

an·a·go·ge also **an·a·go·gy** (ăn′ə-gō′jē) *n.* A mystical interpretation of a word, passage, or text, esp. scriptural exegesis that detects allusions to heaven or the afterlife. [LLat. < LGk. *anagōgē* : *ana,* up + *agein,* to lead.] **—an′a·gog′ic** (-gŏj′ĭk), **an′a·gog′i·cal** *adj.* **—an′a·gog′i·cal·ly** *adv.*

an·a·gram (ăn′ə-grăm′) *n.* **1.** A word or phrase formed by reordering the letters of another word or phrase. **2. anagrams** *(used with a sing. verb).* A game whose object is to form words from a group of randomly picked letters. [Fr. *anagramme* : Gk. *ana-,* from bottom to top + Gk. *gramma,* letter < *graphein,* to write.] **—an′a·gram·mat′ic** (-grə-măt′ĭk) *adj.* **—an′a·gram·mat′i·cal·ly** *adv.*

an·a·gram·ma·tize (ăn′ə-grăm′ə-tīz′) *tr.v.* **-tized, -tiz·ing, -tizes.** To make an anagram of.

a·nal (ā′nəl) *adj.* **1.** Of, pertaining to, or near the anus. **2.** *Psychoanal.* **a.** Of, pertaining to, or denoting the stage of psychosexual development of the infant in which gratification is derived from sensations associated with the anus. **b.** Of, pertaining to, or denoting personality traits originating during toilet training and distinguished as anal-expulsive or anal-retentive. [NLat. *analis* < Lat. *anus,* anus.]

a·nal·cime (ə-năl′sēm′) also **a·nal·cite** (-sīt′) *n.* A white or light-colored zeolite, found in diabase and certain basalts. [Fr. < Gk. *analkimos,* weak (from its weak electric power) : *an-,* not + *alkimos,* brave < *alkē,* strength.]

an·a·lects (ăn′ə-lĕkts′) also **an·a·lec·ta** (ăn′ə-lĕk′tə) *pl.n.* Selections or parts of a literary work or group of works. [Lat. *analecta* < Gk. *analekta* < *analegein,* to gather : *ana-,* up + *legein,* to gather.] **—an′a·lec′tic** *adj.*

an·a·lem·ma (ăn′ə-lĕm′ə) *n.* A graduated scale, in the shape of a figure eight, indicating the sun's declination and the equation of time for every day of the year, usually found on sundials and globes. [Lat., sundial < Gk. *analēmma,* support < *analambanein,* to take up. —see ANALEPTIC.]

an·a·lep·tic (ăn′ə-lĕp′tĭk) *adj.* Restorative or stimulating. *—n.* An analeptic medication. [Gk. *analēptikos* < *analambanein,* to take up : *ana-,* up + *lambanein,* to take.]

a·nal-ex·pul·sive (ā′nəl-ĭk-spŭl′sĭv) *adj. Psychoanal.* Designating personality traits such as conceit, suspicion, ambition, and generosity, originating in habits, attitudes, or values associated with infantile pleasure in the expulsion of feces.

an·al·ge·si·a (ăn′əl-jē′zē-ə, -zhə) *n. Pathol.* Inability to feel pain while conscious. [NLat. < Gk. *analgēsia* : *an-,* without + *algos,* pain.] **—an′al·get′ic** *adj.*

an·al·ge·sic (ăn′əl-jē′zĭk, -sĭk) *n.* A medication that reduces or eliminates pain. *—adj.* Of or causing analgesia.

an·a·log (ăn′ə-lôg′, -lŏg′) *n.* Variant of **analogue.**

analog computer also **analogue computer** *n.* A computer in which numerical data are represented by analogous physical magnitudes or electrical signals.

analog data *pl.n. (used with a sing. or pl. verb).* Data presented or collected in continuous form, as temperature variation or voltage measurement.

an·a·log·i·cal (ăn′ə-lŏj′ĭ-kəl) *adj.* Of, pertaining to, composed of, or based upon an analogy. **—an′a·log′i·cal·ly** *adv.*

a·nal·o·gist (ə-năl′ə-jĭst) *n.* One who looks for or reasons from analogies.

a·nal·o·gize (ə-năl′ə-jīz′) *v.* **-gized, -giz·ing, -giz·es.** *—tr.* To make an analogy to. *—intr.* To think or reason by analogy.

a·nal·o·gous (ə-năl′ə-gəs) *adj.* **1.** Similar or alike in a way that permits the drawing of an analogy. **2.** *Biol.* Similar in function but not in evolutionary origin. [Lat. *analogus* < Gk. *analogos,* proportionate : *ana-,* according to + *logos,* proportion < *legein,* to speak.] **—a·nal′o·gous·ly** *adv.* **—a·nal′o·gous·ness** *n.*

an·a·logue also **an·a·log** (ăn′ə-lôg′, -lŏg′) *n.* **1.** Something that bears an analogy to something else. **2.** *Biol.* An organ or structure that is similar in function to one in another kind of organism, but is of dissimilar evolutionary origin. **3.** *Chem.* A structural derivative of a parent compound. [Fr. < Gk. *analogus,* proportionate —see ANALOGOUS.]

a·nal·o·gy (ə-năl′ə-jē) *n., pl.* **-gies. 1.** Correspondence in some respects between things otherwise dissimilar. **2.** *Biol.* Correspondence in function or position between organs of dissimilar evolutionary origin or structure. **3.** A form of logical inference, or an instance of it, based on the assumption that if two things are known to be alike in some respects, then they must be alike in other respects. **4.** *Ling.* The creation of forms on the basis of a proportion $a : b = c : x$. [Lat. *analogia* < Gk. < *analogos,* proportionate. —see ANALOGOUS.]

an·al·pha·bet·ic (ăn-ăl′fə-bĕt′ĭk) *adj.* **1.** Not alphabetical. **2.** Unable to read; illiterate. *—n.* An illiterate.

a·nal-re·ten·tive (ā′nəl-rĭ-tĕn′tĭv) *adj. Psychoanal.* Designating personality traits such as meticulousness, avarice, and obstinacy, originating in habits, attitudes, or values associated with infantile pleasure in retention of feces.

a·nal·y·sand (ə-năl′ĭ-sănd′) *n.* A person who is being psychoanalyzed. [< ANALYZE, by analogy with *multiplicand.*]

an·a·lyse (ăn′ə-līz′) *v. Chiefly Brit.* Variant of **analyze.**

a·nal·y·sis (ə-năl′ĭ-sĭs) *n., pl.* **-ses** (-sēz′). **1.** The separation of an intellectual or substantial whole into its constituent parts for individual study. **2.** *Chem.* **a.** Separation of a substance into its constituent elements to determine either their nature (qualitative analysis) or their proportions (quantitative analysis). **b.** The stated findings of such separation or determination. **3.** *Math.* **a.** Methodology principally involving algebra and calculus as opposed to synthetic geometry, group theory, and number theory. **b.** The method of proof in which a known truth is sought as a consequence of reasoning from the thing to be proved. **4.** *Ling.* The use of two or more words instead of an inflected form to express a grammatical category. **5.** Psychoanalysis. **6.** Systems analysis. [NLat. < Gk. *analusis,* a dissolving < *analuein,* to undo : *ana,* throughout + *luein,* to loosen.]

an·a·lyst (ăn′ə-lĭst) *n.* **1.** One who analyzes. **2.** A licensed practitioner of psychoanalysis. **3.** A systems analyst.

an·a·lyt·ic (ăn′ə-lĭt′ĭk) or **an·a·lyt·i·cal** (-ĭ-kəl) *adj.* **1.** Of or pertaining to analysis or analytics. **2.** Dividing into elemental parts or basic principles. **3.** Reasoning from a perception of the parts and interrelations of a subject. **4.** Expert in or using analysis, esp. in thinking: *an analytic mind; an analytic approach.* **5.** *Logic.* Following necessarily; tautologous: *an analytic truth.* **6.** *Math.* **a.** Using, subjected to, or capable of being subjected to a methodology involving algebra and calculus. **b.** Proving a known truth by reasoning from the thing to be proved. **7.** *Ling.* Expressing a grammatical category by using two or more words instead of an inflected form. **8.** Psychoanalytic. [LLat. *analyticus* < Gk. *analutikos* < *analuein,* to resolve. —see ANALYSIS.] **—an′a·lyt′i·cal·ly** *adv.*

analytical balance *n.* A balance for chemical analysis.

analytic geometry *n.* The analysis of geometric structures and properties principally by algebraic operations on variables defined in terms of position coordinates.

an·a·lyt·ics (ăn′ə-lĭt′ĭks) *n. (used with a sing. verb).* The branch of logic dealing with analysis.

an·a·lyze (ăn′ə-līz′) *tr.v.* **-lyzed, -lyz·ing, -lyz·es. 1.** To separate into parts or basic principles so as to determine the nature of the whole; examine methodically. **2.** To make a chemical analysis of. **3.** To make a mathematical analysis of. **4.** To psychoanalyze. [Prob. < Fr. *analyser* < *analyse,* analysis < Gk. *analusis.* —see ANALYSIS.] **—an′a·lyz′a·ble** *adj.* **—an′a·ly·za′tion** *n.* **—an′a·lyz′er** *n.*

an·am·ne·sis (ăn′ăm-nē′sĭs) *n., pl.* **-ses** (-sēz′). **1.** *Psychol.* A recalling to memory; recollection. **2.** *Med.* The complete case history of a patient. [NLat. < Gk. *anamnēsis* < *anamimnēskein,* to remind : *ana-,* again, *mimnēskein,* to recall.] **—an′am·nes′tic** (-nĕs′tĭk) *adj.* **—an′am·nes′ti·cal·ly** *adv.*

an·a·mor·phic (ăn′ə-môr′fĭk) *adj.* Having, producing, or designating different optical magnification along mutually perpendicular radii: *an anamorphic lens.*

an·a·mor·pho·sis (ăn′ə-môr′fə-sĭs) *n., pl.* **-ses** (-sēz′). An image distorted so that it can be viewed without distortion only from a special angle or with a special instrument. [Gk. *anamorphōsis,* re-formation : *ana-,* again + *morphē,* shape.]

an·an·drous (ăn-ăn′drəs) *adj. Bot.* Having no stamens.

An·a·ni·as (ăn′ə-nī′əs) *n.* In the New Testament, a liar who dropped dead when Peter rebuked him.

an·an·thous (ăn-ăn′thəs) *adj. Bot.* Lacking flowers.

an·a·pest also **an·a·paest** (ăn′ə-pĕst′) *n.* **1.** A metrical foot composed of two short syllables followed by one long one. **2.** A line of verse in anapest. [Lat. *anapestus* < Gk. *anapaistos* : *ana-,* back + *paiein,* to strike (so called because an anapest is a reversed dactyl).] **—an′a·pes′tic** *adj.*

an·a·phase (ăn′ə-fāz′) *n.* The stage of mitosis in which the daughter chromosomes move toward the poles of the nuclear spindle.

a·naph·o·ra (ə-năf′ə-rə) *n.* The deliberate repetition of a word or phrase at the beginning of several successive verses, clauses, or paragraphs. [LLat. < Gk. < *anapherein,* to repeat : *ana-,* again + *pherein,* to carry.]

an·aph·ro·dis·i·a (ăn-ăf′rə-dĭz′ē-ə, -dĭzh′ə) *n.* Absence or decline of sexual desire. [Gk. : *an,* without + *aphrodisia,* sexual desire. —see APHRODISIAC.] **—an·aph′ro·dis′i·ac** (ăn-ăf′rə-dĭz′ē-ăk′) *adj. & n.*

an·a·phy·lac·toid (ăn′ə-fə-lăk′toid) *adj. Pathol.* **1.** Of or pertaining to an anaphylactic reaction that occurs without causing antibodies. **2.** Of or pertaining to a toxic reaction caused in an unsensitized person by an excessive dose of a substance that causes anaphylaxis in a sensitized person.

an·a·phy·lax·is (ăn'ə-fə-lăk'sĭs) *n.* Hypersensitivity to a foreign substance, esp. in animals, induced by a small preliminary or sensitizing injection of the substance. [ANA- + (PRO)PHYLAXIS.] **—an'a·phy·lac'tic** (-lăk'tĭk) *adj.* **—an'a·phy·lac'ti·cal·ly** *adv.*

an·a·pla·sia (ăn'ə-plā'zhə) *n.* Reversion of cells to a more primitive or less differentiated form.

an·a·plas·tic (ăn'ə-plăs'tĭk) *adj.* **1.** *Med.* Pertaining to the surgical restoration of a lost or absent part. **2.** Of or pertaining to anaplasia of cells.

an·arch (ăn'ärk') *n.* A leader or adherent of anarchy. [Back-formation < ANARCHY.]

an·ar·chic (ăn-är'kĭk) or **an·ar·chi·cal** (-kĭ-kəl) *adj.* **1.** Of, like, or promoting anarchy. **2.** Lacking order or control; lawless. **—an·ar'chi·cal·ly** *adv.*

an·ar·chism (ăn'ər-kĭz'əm) *n.* **1.** The theory that all forms of government are oppressive and undesirable and should be abolished. **2.** Active resistance and terrorism against the state, as used by some anarchists. **3.** Rejection of all forms of coercive control and authority. **—an'ar·chis'tic** (ăn'-ər-kĭs'tĭk) *adj.*

an·ar·chist (ăn'ər-kĭst) *n.* A person who advocates or engages in anarchism.

an·ar·cho-syn·di·cal·ism (ăn-är'kō-sĭn'dĭ-kəl-ĭz'əm) *n.* Syndicalism. [ANARCH(Y) + SYNDICALISM.]

an·ar·chy (ăn'ər-kē) *n., pl.* **-chies. 1.** Absence of any form of political authority. **2.** Political disorder and confusion. **3.** Absence of any cohering principle, as a common standard or purpose. [Gk. *anarkhia* < *anarkhos,* without a ruler : *an-,* without + *arkhos,* ruler. —see -ARCH.]

an·ar·thri·a (ăn-är'thrē-ə) *n.* Loss of the ability to speak. [NLat. < Gk. *anarthros,* not articulated. —see ANARTHROUS.] **—an·ar'thric** (-thrĭk) *adj.*

an·ar·throus (ăn-är'thrəs) *adj.* **1.** *Gram.* Used without an article. **2.** *Zool.* Lacking joints; unjointed. [Gk. *anarthros,* not articulated : *an-,* without + *arthron,* joint.]

an·a·sar·ca (ăn'ə-sär'kə) *n.* A general accumulation of serum in various tissues and body cavities. [NLat. : Gk. *ana,* throughout + *sarx,* flesh.] **—an'a·sar'cous** (-sär'kəs) *adj.*

an·as·tig·mat (ăn-ăs'tĭg-măt') *n.* An anastigmatic lens.

an·as·tig·mat·ic (ăn-ăs'tĭg-măt'ĭk) *adj.* Not astigmatic. Used of a compound lens in which the separate components compensate for the astigmatism of each.

a·nas·to·mose (ə-năs'tə-mōz', -mōs') *v.* **-mosed, -mos·ing, -mos·es.** *—tr.* To join by anastomosis. *—intr.* To connect by anastomosis, as blood vessels. [Back-formation < ANASTOMOSIS.]

a·nas·to·mo·sis (ə-năs'tə-mō'sĭs) *n., pl.* **-ses** (-sēz'). **1.** The union or connection of branches, as of rivers, veins of leaves, or blood vessels. **2.** A surgical connection of separate or severed hollow organs to form a continuous channel. [NLat. < Gk. *anastomosis,* outlet < *anastomoun,* to furnish with a mouth : *ana-,* up + *stoma,* mouth.] **—a·nas'to·mot'ic** (-mŏt'ĭk) *adj.*

a·nas·tro·phe (ə-năs'trə-fē) *n.* Inversion of the normal syntactic order of words, for example: *To market went she.* [Gk. *anastrophē* < *anastrephein,* to turn upside down : *ana-,* back + *strephein,* to turn.]

an·a·tase (ăn'ə-tās', -tāz') *n.* A rare blue or light-yellow to brown mineral of titanium dioxide. [Fr. < Gk. *anatasis,* extension (from its long crystals) < *anateinein,* to extend : *ana-,* up + *teinein,* to stretch.]

a·nath·e·ma (ə-năth'ə-mə) *n., pl.* **-mas. 1.** A formal ecclesiastical ban, curse, or excommunication. **2.** A vehement denunciation; curse. **3.** One that is cursed or damned. **4.** One that is greatly reviled or loathed. [LLat., a person cursed < Gk. *anathema,* an accursed thing < *anatithenai,* to dedicate : *ana-,* up + *tithenai,* to put.]

a·nath·e·ma·tize (ə-năth'ə-mə-tīz') *tr.v.* **-tized, -tiz·ing, -tiz·es.** To proclaim an anathema on; curse. [Lat. *anathematizare* < Gk. *anathematizein* < *anathema,* anathema.]

An·a·to·li·an (ăn'ə-tō'lē-ən) *adj.* **1.** Of or pertaining to Anatolia or its inhabitants. **2.** Of or pertaining to a branch of the Indo-European language family that includes Hittite and other extinct languages of ancient Anatolia. *—n.* The Anatolian languages.

an·a·tom·i·cal (ăn'ə-tŏm'ĭ-kəl) also **an·a·tom·ic** (-tŏm'ĭk) *adj.* **1.** Of or pertaining to anatomy. **2.** Of or pertaining to dissection. **3.** Structural as opposed to functional. **—an'a·tom'i·cal·ly** *adv.*

a·nat·o·mist (ə-năt'ə-mĭst) *n.* An expert in or student of anatomy.

a·nat·o·mize (ə-năt'ə-mīz') *tr.v.* **-mized, -miz·ing, -miz·es. 1.** To dissect. **2.** To analyze in minute detail. **—a·nat'o·mi·za'tion** *n.*

a·nat·o·my (ə-năt'ə-mē) *n., pl.* **-mies. 1.** The structure of a plant or animal, or of any of its parts. **2.** The science of the shape and structure of organisms and their parts. **3.** A treatise on anatomic science. **4.** The dissection of a plant or animal to disclose the various parts, their positions, structure, and interrelation. **5.** A skeleton. **6.** A detailed examination or analysis. **7.** The human body. [ME *anatomie* < OFr. < LLat. *anatomia* < Gk. *anatomē,* dissection : *ana-,* up + *tomē,* a cutting < *temnein,* to cut.]

a·nat·ro·pous (ə-năt'rə-pəs) *adj.* Inverted, so that the micropyle is next to the hilum, and the embryonic root is at the other end. Used of an ovule.

a·nat·to (ə-nä'tō) *n.* Variant of **annatto.**

-ance *suff.* **1.** State or condition: *absorptance.* **2.** Action: *continuance.* [ME < OFr. < Lat. *-antia,* n. suffix < *-āns,* -ant.]

an·ces·tor (ăn'sĕs'tər) *n.* **1.** A person from whom one is descended, esp. if more remote than a grandparent; forefather. **2.** A forerunner or predecessor. **3.** *Law.* The person from whom an estate has been inherited. **4.** *Biol.* The actual or hypothetical organism or stock from which later kinds have evolved. [ME *auncestre* < OFr. < Lat. *antecessor* < *antecedere,* to precede : *ante-,* before + *cedere,* to go.]

an·ces·tral (ăn-sĕs'trəl) *adj.* Of, pertaining to, or evolved from an ancestor or ancestors. **—an·ces'tral·ly** *adv.*

an·ces·try (ăn'sĕs'trē) *n., pl.* **-tries. 1.** Ancestral descent or lineage. **2.** Ancestors collectively. [ME *auncestrie* < OFr. *ancesserie* < *ancessour,* ancestor < Lat. *antecessor.* —see ANCESTOR.]

An·chi·ses (ăn-kī'sēz') *n. Gk. & Rom. Myth.* The father of Aeneas, rescued by his son from fallen Troy. [Lat. < Gk. *Ankhisēs.*]

anchor

an·chor (ăng'kər) *n.* **1.** A heavy object attached to a vessel by a cable and cast overboard to keep the vessel in place either by its weight or by its flukes gripping the bottom. **2.** Something used to provide a rigid point of support, as for securing a rope. **3.** Something that provides security or stability. **4.** An anchorman or anchorwoman. *—v.* **-chored, -chor·ing, -chors.** *—tr.* **1.** To hold fast by or as if by an anchor. **2.** To narrate or coordinate (a newscast in which several correspondents give reports). *—intr.* To drop anchor; lie at anchor, as a ship. **—idiom. at anchor.** Anchored. [ME *anker* < OE *ancor* < Lat. *ancora* < Gk. *ankura.*]

an·chor·age (ăng'kər-ĭj) *n.* **1.** A place for anchoring. **2.** A fee charged for the privilege of anchoring. **3.** A means of securing or stabilizing: *Wall Street is the anchorage of the financial community.* **4. a.** The act of anchoring. **b.** The condition of being at anchor.

an·cho·ress (ăng'kə-rĭs) *n.* A woman who has retired into seclusion for religious reasons.

an·cho·rite (ăng'kə-rīt') also **an·cho·ret** (-rĕt') *n.* A person who has retired into seclusion for religious reasons. [ME < Med. Lat. *anchorita* < LLat. *anachoreta* < Gk. *anakhorētēs* < *anakōrein,* to retire : *ana-,* back + *khōrein,* to withdraw.] **—an'cho·rit'ic** (-rĭt'ĭk) *adj.*

an·chor·man (ăng'kər-măn') *n.* **1.** One heavily depended upon. **2.** *Sports.* The runner, usually the strongest on a team, who performs the last stage of a relay race. **3.** The narrator or coordinator of a newscast in which several correspondents give reports.

an·chor·wom·an (ăng'kər-wŏŏm'ən) *n.* A woman who narrates or coordinates a newscast in which several correspondents give reports.

an·cho·vy (ăn'chō'vē, ăn-chō'vē) *n., pl.* **anchovy** or **-vies.** Any of various small, herringlike marine fishes of the family Engraulidae. Several species are widely used as food fish. [Sp. *anchova.*]

an·chy·lose (ăng'kĭ-lōs', -lōz') *v.* Variant of **ankylose.**

an·chy·lo·sis (ăng'kĭ-lō'sĭs) *n.* Variant of **ankylosis.**

an·cien ré·gime (äɴ-syăɴ' rā-zhēm') *n.* **1.** The political and social system existing in France before the Revolution of 1789. **2.** Any former socio-political system. [Fr., old regime.]

an·cient[1] (ān'shənt) *adj.* **1.** Very old; aged. **2.** Of, existing, or occurring in times long past, esp. belonging to the historical period prior to the fall of the Western Roman Empire (A.D. 476). **3.** Old-fashioned or antiquated. **4.** Having the qualities associated with age, wisdom, or long use; venerable. *—n.* **1.** A very old person. **2.** A person who lived in ancient times. **3. ancients.** The peoples of the classical nations of antiquity. **4. ancients.** The ancient Greek and Roman authors. [ME *auncien* < OFr. < VLat. **anteanus* < Lat. *ante,* before.] **—an'cient·ly** *adv.* **—an'cient·ness** *n.*

an·cient[2] (ān'shənt) *n. Obs.* **1.** An ensign; flag. **2.** A flagbearer or lieutenant. [Var. of ENSIGN.]

Ancient Chinese *n.* The Chinese language as used until about the 13th century A.D.

ancient history *n.* **1.** The history of ancient times. **2.** *Informal.* Common knowledge, esp. of a recent event that has lost its original impact or importance.

an·cil·lar·y (ăn'sə-lĕr'ē) *adj.* **1.** Subordinate: *"For Degas, sculpture was never more than ancillary to his painting"* (Herbert Read). **2.** Helping; auxiliary. *—n., pl.* **-ies.** A servant. [Lat. *ancillaris,* pertaining to a maidservant < *ancilla,* maidservant, dim. of *ancula,* fem. of *anculus,* servant.]

an·cip·i·tal (ăn-sĭp'ĭ-təl) *adj.* Flattened and two-edged, as are certain plant stems. [< Lat. *anceps, ancipit-,* two-headed : ambi-, two + *caput,* head.]

an·con (ăng'kŏn') *n., pl.* **-con·es** (-kō'nēz). A projecting bracket used in classical architecture to carry the upper elements of a cornice; console. [Lat. *ancon* < Gk. *ankōn,* elbow.]

-ancy *suff.* -ance. [Lat. *-antia.* —see -ANCE.]

an·cy·lo·sto·mi·a·sis (ăn'sə-lō-stō-mī'ə-sĭs, ăng'kə-lō-) *n.* A disease caused by hookworm infestation and marked by progressive anemia. [NLat. *Ancylostoma,* hookworm genus (Gk. *ankulos,* curved + Gk. *stoma,* mouth) + -IASIS.]

and (ənd, ən; ănd *when stressed) conj.* **1.** Together with or along with; also; in addition; as well as. Used to connect words, phrases, or clauses that have the same grammatical function in a construction. **2.** Added to; plus: *Two and two makes four.* **3.** As a result; in consequence: *Seek, and ye shall find.* **4.** *Informal.* To. Used between finite verbs, such as *go, come, try, write,* or *see: try and find it; come and see.* **5.** *Archaic.* Then. Used to begin a sentence: *And he said unto her . . .* **6.** *Archaic.* If: *and it pleases you.* [ME < OE.]

Usage: Although frowned upon by some, the use of *and* to begin a sentence has a long and respectable history: *"And it came to pass in those days"* (Luke 2:1).

AND (ănd) *n. Computer Sci.* A logic operator equivalent to the sentential connective "and." [< AND.]

an·da·lu·site (ăn′də-lo͞o′sīt′) *n.* A mineral aluminum silicate, Al_2SiO_5, usually found in prisms of various colors. [Fr. *andalousite,* after *Andalusia,* where it was discovered.]

An·da·man·ese (ăn′də-mə-nēz′, -nēs′) *n., pl.* **Andamanese. 1.** Also **An·da·man** (ăn′də-mən). A member of a Negrito people native to the Andaman Islands. **2.** The language of the Andamanese, of no known linguistic affiliation. **—An′da·man·ese′** *adj.*

an·dan·te (än-dän′tā, ăn-dăn′tē) *Mus. —adv.* Moderate in tempo; faster than adagio, but slower than allegretto. Used as a direction. *—adj.* Moderately slow. *—n.* An andante movement or passage. [Ital., pr.part. of *andare,* to walk, ult. < Lat. *ambulare.*]

an·dan·ti·no (än′dän-tē′nō, ăn′dăn-tē′nō) *Mus. —adv.* Slightly faster than andante in tempo. Used as a direction. *—adj.* Slightly faster than andante. *—n., pl.* **-nos.** An andantino movement or passage. [Ital. dim. of *andante,* andante.]

an·de·site (ăn′dē-zīt′) *n.* A gray, fine-grained volcanic rock, chiefly plagioclase and feldspar. [G. *Andesit* : *Andes,* Andes (where it was found) + *-it,* -ite.]

andiron

AND gate *n. Computer Sci.* A signal circuit with two or more input wires that emits a signal only if all input wires receive coincident signals.

and·i·ron (ănd′ī′ərn) *n.* One of a pair of metal supports for holding up logs in a fireplace. [ME *aundiren,* alteration of OFr. *andier.*]

and/or (ănd′ôr) *conj.* Used to indicate that either *and* or *or* may be used to connect words, phrases, or clauses depending upon what meaning is intended.

Usage: *And/or* is widely used in legal and business writing. Its use in general writing to mean "one or the other or both" is acceptable but can appear stilted.

andr– *pref.* Variant of **andro-.**

an·dra·dite (ăn-drä′dīt′) *n.* A green to brown or black calcium-iron garnet, $Ca_3Fe_2(SiO_4)_3$. [After José B. de *Andrada* e Silva (d. 1838).]

An·drew (ăn′dro͞o) *n.* In the New Testament, one of the Apostles, the brother of Simon called Peter.

andro– or **andr–** *pref.* **1.** Male; masculine: *androgen.* **2.** Stamen or anther: *androecium.* [Gk. < *anēr, andr-,* man.]

An·dro·cles (ăn′drə-klēz′) *n.* A legendary Roman slave held to have been spared in the arena by a lion that remembered him as the man who had once removed a thorn from its paw. [Lat. < Gk. *Androklēs.*]

an·droe·ci·um (ăn-drē′shē-əm, -shəm) *n., pl.* **-ci·a** (-shē-ə, -shə). The stamens of a flower considered collectively. [NLat. : ANDR(O)- + Gk. *oikos,* house.] **—an·droe′cial** (-shəl) *adj.*

an·dro·gen (ăn′drə-jən) *n.* Any of the steroid hormones that develop and maintain masculine characteristics. **—an′dro·gen′ic** (-jĕn′ĭk) *adj.*

an·drog·e·nize (ăn-drŏj′ə-nīz′) *tr.v.* **-nized, -niz·ing, -niz·es.** To treat with usually large doses of male hormones. **—an·drog′e·ni·za′tion** *n.*

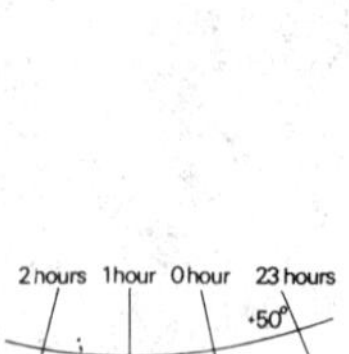

Andromeda

an·drog·e·nous (ăn-drŏj′ə-nəs) *adj.* Of or pertaining to production of male offspring.

an·drog·y·nous (ăn-drŏj′ə-nəs) *adj.* **1.** Having female and male characteristics in one; hermaphroditic. **2.** *Bot.* Composed of staminate and pistillate flowers. Used of the flower spikes of certain sedges. **3.** Being neither distinguishably masculine nor feminine, as in dress, appearance, or behavior; unisex. [Lat. *androgynus,* hermophrodite < Gk. *androgunos* : *anēr,* man + *gunē,* woman.] **—an·drog′y·ny** (-ə-nē) *n.*

an·droid (ăn′droid′) *adj.* Possessing human features. *—n.* A synthetic person created from biological materials.

An·drom·a·che (ăn-drŏm′ə-kē) *n. Gk. Myth.* The faithful wife of Hector, captured by the Greeks at the fall of Troy. [Lat. < Gk. *Andromakhē.*]

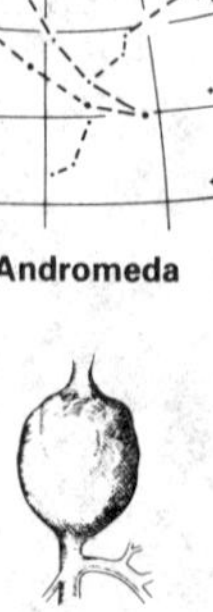

aneurysm

An·drom·e·da (ăn-drŏm′ə-də) *n.* **1.** *Gk. Myth.* The daughter of Cepheus and Cassiopeia and wife of Perseus, who had rescued her from a sea monster. **2.** A constellation in the Northern Hemisphere near Lacerta and Perseus. **3. andromeda.** Any of several shrubs of the genus *Andromeda* or of closely related genera. [Lat. < Gk. *Andromedē.*]

an·dros·ter·one (ăn-drŏs′tə-rōn′) *n.* A male sex hormone, excreted in urine and synthetically produced from cholesterol. [ANDRO- + STER(OL) + -ONE.]

–androus *suff.* Having a specified number or kind of stamens: *monandrous.* [NLat. *-andrus* < Gk. *-andros,* having men < *anēr, andr-,* man.]

–andry *suff.* **1.** The condition of having a specified kind or number of husbands: *monandry.* **2.** The condition of having a specified kind or number of stamens: *polyandry.* [< Gk. *anēr, andr-,* man.]

–ane *suff.* A saturated hydrocarbon: *hexane.* [Alteration of -ENE.]

an·ec·dot·age (ăn′ĭk-dō′tĭj) *n.* Anecdotes collectively.

an·ec·dot·al (ăn′ĭk-dōt′l) *adj.* Pertaining to, characterized by, or full of anecdotes.

an·ec·dote (ăn′ĭk-dōt′) *n.* **1.** A short account of some interesting or humorous incident. **2.** *pl.* **-dotes** or **-do·ta** (-dō′tə). Secret or hitherto undivulged particulars of history or biography. [Fr. < Gk. *anekdotos,* unpublished : *an-,* not + *ekdotos,* published < *ekdidonai,* to publish (*ek-,* out + *didonai,* to give).]

an·ec·dot·ic (ăn′ĭk-dŏt′ĭk) also **an·ec·dot·i·cal** (-ĭ-kəl) *adj.* **1.** Anecdotal. **2.** Full of or given to telling anecdotes.

an·ec·dot·ist (ăn′ĭk-dō′tĭst) *n.* A person who tells, collects, or publishes anecdotes.

an·e·cho·ic (ăn′ē-kō′ĭk) *adj.* Neither having nor producing echoes: *an anechoic chamber.*

a·nele (ə-nēl′) *tr.v.* **a·neled, a·nel·ing, a·neles.** *Archaic.* To anoint, esp. in administering extreme unction. [ME *anelen* : *an,* on (< OE) + *elen,* to anoint < *ele,* oil < OE < Lat. *oleum.* —see OIL.]

a·ne·mi·a also **a·nae·mi·a** (ə-nē′mē-ə) *n.* A pathological deficiency in the oxygen-carrying material of the blood, measured in unit volume concentrations of hemoglobin, red blood cell volume, and red blood cell number. [NLat. < Gk. *anaimia* : *an-,* without + *haima,* blood.]

a·ne·mic also **a·nae·mic** (ə-nē′mĭk) *adj.* **1.** Of, relating to, or suffering from anemia. **2.** Listless and weak; pallid. **—a·ne′mi·cal·ly** *adv.*

anemo– *pref.* Wind: *anemometer.* [< Gk. *anemos,* wind.]

a·nem·o·graph (ə-nĕm′ə-grăf′) *n.* A recording anemometer.

an·e·mog·ra·phy (ăn′ə-mŏg′rə-fē) *n.* The science of recording anemometrical measurements.

an·e·mom·e·ter (ăn′ə-mŏm′ĭ-tər) *n.* An instrument for indicating and measuring wind force and speed.

an·e·mom·e·try (ăn′ə-mŏm′ĭ-trē) *n.* The determination of wind force and velocity.

a·nem·o·ne (ə-nĕm′ə-nē) *n.* **1.** Any of various plants of the genus *Anemone,* of the North Temperate Zone, having white, purple, or red cup-shaped flowers. **2.** The sea anemone. [Lat. < Gk. *anemōnē.*]

anemone fish *n.* Any of various small, brightly colored marine fishes of the genus *Amphiprion,* that are found near sea anemones.

an·e·moph·i·lous (ăn′ə-mŏf′ə-ləs) *adj.* Pollinated by wind-dispersed pollen.

an·en·ceph·a·ly (ăn′ən-sĕf′ə-lē) *n., pl.* **-lies.** Congenital absence of the brain and spinal cord. **—an′en·ce·phal′ic** (-sə-făl′ĭk) *adj.*

a·nent (ə-nĕnt′) *prep.* **1.** Regarding; concerning. **2.** *Regional.* Opposite; close to. **3.** *Obs. & Chiefly Brit. Regional.* On a level with; in a line with. [ME < OE *onefn,* near : *on,* on + *efn,* even.]

an·er·oid (ăn′ə-roid′) *adj.* Not using fluid. [Fr. *anéroïde* : Gk. *a-,* not + Gk. *nēron,* water.]

aneroid barometer *n.* A barometer in which variations of atmospheric pressure are indicated by the relative bulges of a thin elastic metal disk covering a partially evacuated chamber.

an·es·the·sia also **an·aes·the·sia** (ăn′ĭs-thē′zhə) *n.* **1.** Total or partial loss of sensation, esp. tactile sensibility, induced by disease or an anesthetic. **2.** Artificially induced unconsciousness or local or general insensibility to pain. [NLat. < Gk. *anaisthēsia,* insensibilty : *an,* without + *aisthēsis,* feeling <*aisthanesthai,* to feel.]

an·es·the·si·ol·o·gy also **an·aes·the·si·ol·o·gy** (ăn′ĭs-thē′zē-ŏl′ə-jē) *n.* The medical study and application of anesthetics. **—an′es·the′si·ol′o·gist** *n.*

an·es·thet·ic also **an·aes·thet·ic** (ăn′ĭs-thĕt′ĭk) *adj.* **1.** Relating to or resembling anesthesia. **2.** Causing anesthesia. **3.** Insensitive. *—n.* An agent that causes unconsciousness or insensitivity to pain. [< Gk. *anaisthetos,* without feeling : *an-,* without + *aisthētos,* perceptible < *aisthanesthai,* to feel.]

a·nes·the·tist also **a·naes·the·tist** (ə-nĕs′thə-tĭst) *n.* A person, usually a physician, trained to administer anesthetics.

a·nes·the·tize also **a·naes·the·tize** (ə-nĕs′thə-tīz′) *tr.v.* **-tized, -tiz·ing, -tiz·es.** To induce anesthesia in. **—a·nes′the·ti·za′tion** *n.*

an·es·trus (ăn-ĕs′trəs) *n.* An interval of sexual dormancy between two periods of estrus.

an·eu·rysm also **an·eu·rism** (ăn′yə-rĭz′əm) *n.* **1.** A pathological blood-filled dilatation of a blood vessel. **2.** A dilatation of a cylindrical body in the manner of blood vessel aneurysm. [Gk. *aneurusma* < *aneurein,* to dilate : *ana-,* throughout + *eurus,* wide.]

a·new (ə-no͞o′, ə-nyo͞o′) *adv.* **1.** Once more; again. **2.** In a new and different way, form, or manner. [ME *a new* : *a,* of + *new,* new.]

an·frac·tu·os·i·ty (ăn-frăk′cho͞o-ŏs′ĭ-tē) *n., pl.* **-ties. 1.** The

condition or quality of being anfractuous. **2.** A winding channel, passage, or crevice. **3.** A complicated or involved process.
an·frac·tu·ous (ăn-frăk′cho͞o-əs) *adj.* Full of twists and turns; winding; tortuous. [Fr. *anfractueux* < LLat. *anfractuosus,* < Lat. *anfractus,* winding < *ambi-,* around + *fractus,* broken, p.part. of *frangere,* to break.]
an·ga·ry (ăng′gə-rē) also **an·gar·i·a** (ăng-gâr′ē-ə) *n.* The legal right of a belligerent state to seize, use, or destroy the property of a neutral, provided that full compensation is made. [Fr. *angarie* < LLat. *angaria,* service to a lord < Gk. *angareia,* impressment for public service < *angaros,* courier.]
an·gel (ān′jəl) *n.* **1. a.** *Theol.* An immortal, spiritual being attendant upon God. In medieval angelology, there are nine orders of spiritual beings (listed from the highest to lowest in rank): seraphim, cherubim, thrones, dominations or dominions, virtues, powers, principalities, archangels, and angels. **b.** The conventional representation of such a being in the image of a human figure with a halo and wings. **2.** A guardian spirit or guiding influence. **3. a.** A kind and lovable person. **b.** A person manifesting goodness, purity, and selflessness. **4.** *Christian Science.* God's thoughts passing to man. **5.** *Informal.* A financial backer of an enterprise, esp. of a dramatic production. **6. a.** Enemy aircraft. **b.** A radar echo of unknown origin. [ME < OE *engel* < LLat. *angelus* < LGk. *angelos,* < Gk. messenger.]
angel cake *n.* Angel food cake.
angel dust *n. Slang.* Phencyclidine.
An·ge·le·no (ăn′jə-lē′nō) *n.* A native or resident of Los Angeles. [Mex. Sp. *Angeleño,* after *Los Angeles,* California.]
an·gel·fish (ān′jəl-fĭsh′) *n., pl.* **angelfish** or **-fish·es. 1.** Any of several brightly colored fishes of the family Chaetodontidae, of warm seas, having laterally compressed bodies. **2.** A freshwater fish, *Pterophyllum scalare,* native to rivers of tropical South America, having a laterally compressed, usually striped body, and popular in aquariums.
angel food cake *n.* A white, almond-flavored sponge cake made of egg whites, sugar, and flour.
an·gel·ic (ăn-jĕl′ĭk) also **an·gel·i·cal** (-ĭ-kəl) *adj.* **1.** Of, pertaining to, consisting of, or belonging to angels: *angelic hosts.* **2. a.** Suggestive of or fit for an angel; pure and lovely. **b.** *Informal.* Kind and lovable. **—an·gel′i·cal·ly** *adv.*
an·gel·i·ca (ăn-jĕl′ĭ-kə) *n.* **1.** Any of various plants of the genus *Angelica,* having compound leaves and clusters of small white or greenish flowers, esp. *A. Archangelica,* whose aromatic seeds, leaves, stems, and roots are used in medicine and as flavoring. **2.** The candied stem of the angelica. **3.** Often **Angelica.** A sweet white wine or liqueur. [Med.Lat. *(herba) angelica,* angelic (herb) < LLat. < Gk. *angelikos* < *angelos,* messenger, angel.]
angelica tree *n.* Any of several spiny trees or shrubs, such as the Hercules'-club.
an·gel·ol·o·gy (ān′jəl-ŏl′ə-jē) *n.* The branch of theology having to do with angels.
angel shark *n.* Any of several raylike sharks of the genus *Squatina,* having a broad, flat head and body.
An·ge·lus also **an·ge·lus** (ăn′jə-ləs) *n. Rom. Cath. Ch.* **1.** A devotional prayer at morning, noon, and night to commemorate the Annunciation. **2.** A bell rung as a call to recite the Angelus. [Med. Lat., angel, first word of the prayer.]
an·ger (ăng′gər) *n.* **1.** A feeling of extreme displeasure, hostility, indignation, or exasperation toward someone or something; rage; wrath; ire. **2.** *Obs.* Trouble; pain; affliction. **3.** *Chiefly Brit. Regional.* An inflammation or sore. *—v.* **-gered, -ger·ing, -gers.** *—tr.* **1.** To make angry; enrage or provoke. **2.** *Chiefly Brit. Regional.* To make painful or inflamed. *—intr.* To become angry: *She angers too quickly.* [ME < ON *angr,* sorrow.]
Synonyms: *anger, rage, fury, ire, wrath, resentment, indignation.* These nouns denote varying degrees of marked displeasure. *Anger,* the most general, denotes strong, usually temporary displeasure without specifying manner of expression. *Rage* and *fury* are closely related in the sense of intense, uncontained, explosive emotion. *Fury* can be more destructive, *rage* more justified by circumstances. *Ire* is a poetic term for anger. *Wrath* applies especially to fervid anger that seeks vengeance or punishment on an epic scale. *Resentment* refers to ill will and suppressed anger generated by a sense of grievance. One feels *indignation* at seeing the mistreatment of someone or something dear and worthy.
an·ger·ly (ăng′gər-lē) *adv. Archaic.* Angrily: *"Again thou blushest angerly"* (Tennyson).
An·ge·vin (ăn′jə-vĭn) *adj.* **1.** Of or pertaining to the province of Anjou, France. **2.** Of or pertaining to the House of Anjou, esp. as represented by the Plantagenet kings of England descended from Geoffrey, Count of Anjou. [Fr. < OFr. < Med. Lat. *Andegavinus* < *Andegavia,* Anjou.]
an·gi·na (ăn-jī′nə, ăn′jə-) *n.* **1.** A disease, such as croup or diphtheria, in which spasmodic and painful suffocation or spasms occur. **2.** Angina pectoris. [Lat., quinsy < Gk. *ankonē,* a strangling.] **—an·gi′nal** *adj.* **—an′gi·nose′** (-jə-nōs′) *adj.*
angina pec·to·ris (pĕk′tə-rĭs) *n.* Severe paroxysmal pain in the chest associated with an insufficient supply of blood to the heart. [NLat. : Lat. *angina,* quinsy + *pectus,* chest.]
an·gi·og·raph·y (ăn′jē-ŏg′rə-fē) *n.* Roentgenography of the blood vessels following the injection of a radiopaque substance. [Gk. *angeion,* vessel + -GRAPHY.] **—an′gi·o·gram** (jē-ə-grăm′) *n.* **—an′gi·o·graph′ic** (ăn′jē-ə-grăf′ĭk) *adj.*
an·gi·ol·o·gy (ăn′jē-ŏl′ə-jē) *n.* The study of blood and lymph vessels. [Gk. *angeion,* vessel + -LOGY.]
an·gi·o·ma (ăn′jē-ō′mə) *n., pl.* **-mas** or **-ma·ta** (-mə-tə). A tumor composed of lymph and blood vessels. [Gk. *angeion,* vessel + -OMA.]
an·gi·op·a·thy (ăn′jē-op′ə-thē) *n., pl.* **-thies.** Any of several diseases of the blood or lymph vessels. [Gk. *angeion,* vessel + -PATHY.]
an·gi·o·sperm (ăn′jē-ə-spûrm′) *n.* A plant of the class Angiospermae, characterized by having seeds enclosed in an ovary; a flowering plant. [Gk. *angeion,* vessel + SPERM[1].]
an·gi·o·ten·sin (ăn′jē-ō-tĕn′sĭn) *n.* Either of two polypeptide hormones that are powerful vasoconstrictors. [Gk. *angeion,* vessel + TENS(ION) + -IN.]
an·gle[1] (ăng′gəl) *intr.v.* **-gled, -gling, -gles. 1.** To fish with a hook and line. **2.** To try to get something by using schemes, tricks, or other artful means: *angle for a promotion.* *—n. Obs.* A fishhook or fishing tackle. [ME *anglen* < *angel,* fishhook < OE.]
an·gle[2] (ăng′gəl) *n.* **1.** *Math.* **a.** The figure formed by two lines diverging from a common point. **b.** The figure formed by two planes diverging from a common line. **c.** The rotation required to superimpose either of two such lines or planes on the other. **d.** The space between such lines or surfaces. **e.** A solid angle. **2.** A sharp or projecting corner, as of a building. **3. a.** The place, position, or direction from which an object is presented to view: *a handsome building from any angle.* **b.** An aspect, as of a problem, seen from a specific point of view. **4.** *Slang.* A scheme; devious method. ***—modifier:*** *an angle bracket.* *—v.* **-gled, -gling, -gles.** *—tr.* **1.** To move or turn at an angle. **2.** To hit (a ball or puck, for example) at an angle. **3.** *Informal.* To impart a biased aspect or point of view to. *—intr.* To continue along or turn at angles or by angles: *The path angled through the woods.* [ME < OFr. < Lat. *angulus.*]
An·gle (ăng′gəl) *n.* A member of a Germanic people that migrated to England from southern Denmark in the 5th century A.D., founded the kingdoms of Northumbria, East Anglia, and Mercia, and together with the Jutes and Saxons formed the Anglo-Saxon peoples. [< Lat. *Angli,* the Angles, of Germanic orig.]
angle bracket *n.* A bracket (sense 4.b.).
an·gle·doz·er (ăng′gəl-dō′zər) *n.* A machine resembling a tractor, used to level or scrape ground, and constructed so that the dirt is pushed off to one side. [Orig. a trademark.]
angle iron *n.* A length of steel or iron bent at a right angle along its long dimension, used as a support or structural framework.
angle of attack *n.* The acute angle between the chord of an airfoil and a line representing the undisturbed relative airflow.
angle of incidence *n.* **1.** *Physics.* The angle formed by the path of a body or of radiation incident on a surface and a perpendicular to the surface at the point of impact. **2.** The angle of attack.
angle of reflection *n.* The acute angle formed by the path of a reflected body or reflected radiation with a perpendicular to the surface at the point of reflection.
angle of refraction *n.* The acute angle formed by the path of refracted radiation with a perpendicular to the refracting surface at the point of refraction.
angle of yaw *n.* The angle between an aircraft's longitudinal axis and its line of travel, as seen from above.
angle plate *n.* A right-angled metal bracket, used on the face plate of a lathe to hold pieces being worked.
an·gle·pod (ăng′gəl-pŏd′) *n.* Any of several plants of the genus *Gonolobus,* of the southern and central United States, having greenish or purple flowers and angular pods.
an·gler (ăng′glər) *n.* **1.** A fisherman who uses a hook. **2.** A scheming person. **3.** An anglerfish.
an·gler·fish (ăng′glər-fĭsh′) *n., pl.* **anglerfish** or **-fish·es.** Any of various marine fishes of the order Lophiiformes (or Pediculati), having a long dorsal fin ray that is suspended over the mouth and that serves as a lure to attract prey.
an·gle·site (ăng′glĭ-sīt′) *n.* A lead sulfate mineral, occurring in colorless or tinted crystals. [After *Anglesey,* Wales.]
an·gle·worm (ăng′gəl-wûrm′) *n.* A worm, such as an earthworm, used as bait in fishing.
An·gli·an (ăng′glē-ən) *adj.* Of or pertaining to the Angles. *—n.* **1.** An Angle. **2.** The Old English dialects of Mercian and Northumbrian.
An·gli·can (ăng′glĭ-kən) *adj.* **1.** Of, pertaining to, or characteristic of the Church of England or any of the churches related to it in origin and communion, such as the Protestant Episcopal Church. **2.** Of or pertaining to England or the English. *—n.* A member of the Church of England or of any of the churches related to it. [Med. Lat. *Anglicanus,* English < *Anglicus* < Lat. *Angli,* the Angles. —see ANGLE.]
Anglican Church *n.* The Church of England and the churches in other nations that are in complete agreement with it as to doctrine and discipline and are in communion with the Archbishop of Canterbury.

angel

angelfish

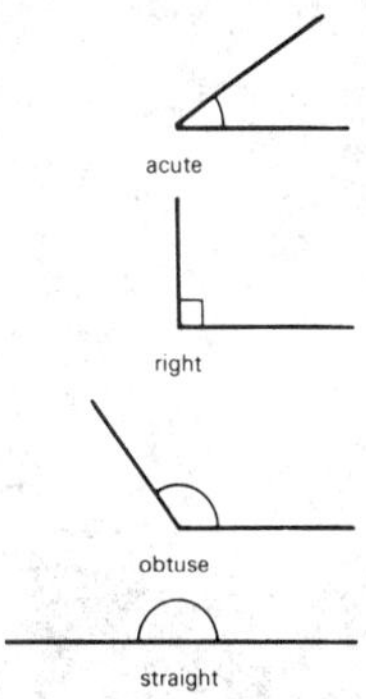

angle[2]

Anglican Communion *n.* The Anglican Church.
An·gli·can·ism (ăng'glĭ-kən-ĭz'əm) *n.* The doctrine, system, and practice of the Anglican Church.
An·gli·ce (ăng'glĭ-sē') *adv.* In the English form: *Firenze,* Anglice *Florence.* [Med. Lat. < *Anglicus,* English < Lat. *Angli,* the Angles. —see ANGLE.]
An·gli·cism also **an·gli·cism** (ăng'glə-sĭz'əm) *n.* **1.** A word, phrase, or idiom peculiar to the English language, esp. as spoken in England; Briticism. **2.** A typically English quality.
An·gli·cist (ăng'glĭ-sĭst) *n.* A specialist in English linguistics.
An·gli·cize also **an·gli·cize** (ăng'glə-sīz') *v.* **-cized, -ciz·ing, -ciz·es.** —*tr.* To make English or similar to English in form, idiom, style, or character. —*intr.* To become English in form or character. **—An'gli·ci·za'tion** *n.*
an·gling (ăng'glĭng) *n.* The act, process, or art of fishing with a hook and line and usually a rod.
An·glo (ăng'glō') *n., pl.* **-glos.** *Informal.* An Anglo-American, esp. a white resident of the United States who is not of Latin descent. [Short for ANGLO-AMERICAN.] **—An'glo'** *adj.*
Anglo– *pref.* England; English: *Anglo-Saxon.* [NLat. < Med. Lat. *Angli,* the English people < Lat., the Angles.]
An·glo-A·mer·i·can (ăng'glō-ə-mĕr'ĭ-kən) *adj.* **1.** Of, relating to, or between England and America, esp. the United States. **2.** Of or relating to Anglo-Americans. —*n.* An American, esp. a resident of the United States, whose language, ancestry, and culture are English.
An·glo-Cath·o·lic (ăng'glō-kăth'lĭk, -kăth'ə-lĭk) *n.* A member of the Anglican Communion whose religious convictions emphasize sacramental worship. **—An'glo-Cath'o·lic** *adj.*
An·glo-French (ăng'glō-frĕnch') *adj.* Of, relating to, or between England and France or their peoples; English and French. —*n.* Anglo-Norman (sense 2).
An·glo-In·di·an (ăng'glō-ĭn'dē-ən) *n.* A person of English and Indian descent. **—An'glo-In'di·an** *adj.*
An·glo-I·rish (ăng'glō-ī'rĭsh) *n.* **1.** A native of England living in Ireland. **2.** A native of Ireland living in England. **3.** A person of mixed Irish and English ancestry. **—An'glo-I'rish** *adj.*
An·glo-Nor·man (ăng'glō-nôr'mən) *n.* **1.** One of the Normans who lived in England after the Norman conquest of England in 1066, or a descendant of these settlers. **2. a.** The dialect of Old French derived chiefly from Norman French that was used by the Anglo-Normans. **b.** The form of this dialect used in English law until the 17th century. **—An'glo-Nor'man** *adj.*
An·glo·phile (ăng'glə-fīl') also **An·glo·phil** (-fĭl) *n.* An admirer of England and English things. —*adj.* Of or resembling Anglophiles. **—An'glo·phil'i·a** (-fĭl'ē-ə) *n.*
An·glo·phobe (ăng'glə-fōb') *n.* One who has an aversion to England or English things. —*adj.* Of or similar to Anglophobes. **—An'glo·pho'bi·a** *n.*
An·glo·phone (ăng'lə-fōn') *n.* An English-speaking individual, esp. in a country where two or more languages are spoken. **—An'glo·phon'ic** (-fŏn'ĭk) *adj.*
An·glo-Sax·on (ăng'glō-săk'sən) *n.* **1.** A member of one of the Germanic peoples (Angles, Saxons, and Jutes) who settled in Britain in the 5th and 6th centuries. **2.** Any of the descendants of the Anglo-Saxons who were dominant in England until the Norman Conquest of 1066. **3.** Old English (sense 1). **4.** A person of English ancestry. —*adj.* Of, pertaining to, or characteristic of Anglo-Saxons or their descendants, or their language or culture; English.
An·go·ra (ăng-gôr'ə, -gōr'ə) *n.* **1.** Often **angora. a.** The long, silky hair of the Angora goat. **b.** The fine, light hair of the Angora rabbit, sometimes blended with wool in fabrics. **c.** A yarn or fabric made from either of these fibers. **2.** An Angora cat. **3.** An Angora goat. **4.** An Angora rabbit. [After *Angora* (Ankara), Turkey.]

Angora goat

Angora cat *n.* A long-haired domestic cat.
Angora goat *n.* Any of a breed of domestic goats having long, silky hair.
Angora rabbit *n.* One of a breed of domestic rabbits having long, soft, usually white hair.
an·gos·tu·ra bark (ăng'gə-stŏŏr'ə, -tyŏŏr'ə) *n.* The bitter, aromatic bark of either of two Brazilian trees, *Galipea officinalis* or *Cusparia trifoliata,* used as a tonic. [After *Angostura,* former name of Ciudad Bolívar.]
an·gry (ăng'grē) *adj.* **-gri·er, -gri·est. 1.** Feeling or showing anger; incensed or enraged: *an angry customer.* **2.** Indicative of or resulting from anger: *an angry silence.* **3.** Having a menacing aspect; seeming to threaten: *angry clouds.* **4.** Inflamed: *an angry sore.* [ME *angri* < *anger,* anger.]
angry young man also **Angry Young Man** *n.* One of a group of English writers of the 1950's whose works are characterized by vigorous social protest.
angst (ängkst) *n.* A feeling of anxiety. [G.]
ang·strom or **ång·ström unit** (ăng'strəm) *n.* A unit of length equal to one hundred-millionth (10^{-8}) of a centimeter, used esp. to specify radiation wavelengths. [After Anders Jonas Ångström (1814–1874).]
an·guil·li·form (ăng-gwĭl'ə-fôrm') *adj.* Having the elongated shape of an eel. [Lat. *anguilla,* eel (dim. of *anguis,* snake) + -FORM.]
an·guine (ăng'gwĭn) *adj.* Of, pertaining to, or resembling a snake; snakelike. [Lat. *anguinus* < *anguis,* snake.]
an·guish (ăng'gwĭsh) *n.* An agonizing physical or mental pain; torment. —*v.* **-guished, -guish·ing, -guish·es.** —*tr.* To cause to suffer or feel anguish. —*intr.* To suffer or feel anguish. [ME *angwisshe,* < OFr. *anguisse* < Lat. *angustia,* narrowness < *angustus,* narrow.]
an·guished (ăng'gwĭsht) *adj.* Feeling, expressing, or caused by anguish.
an·gu·lar (ăng'gyə-lər) *adj.* **1.** Having, forming, or consisting of an angle or angles. **2.** Measured by an angle or degrees of an arc. **3.** Bony and lean; gaunt. **4.** Lacking grace or smoothness; awkward: *an angular gait.* **5.** Crotchety in manner or disposition; unyielding. [Lat. *angularis* < *angulus,* angle.] **—an'gu·lar·ly** *adv.* **—an'gu·lar·ness** *n.*
angular acceleration *n.* The rate of change of angular velocity with respect to time.
an·gu·lar·i·ty (ăng'gyə-lăr'ĭ-tē) *n., pl.* **-ties. 1.** The condition or quality of being angular. **2. angularities.** Angular forms, outlines, or corners.
angular momentum *n.* **1.** The vector product of the position vector and linear velocity of a particle in motion relative to an axis. **2.** The sum of such products, one for each component particle of an extended body, expressible as the product of the angular velocity and the moment of inertia of the body.
angular velocity *n.* A vector quantity describing rotational motion, the magnitude of which is the time rate of change of angle and the direction of which is along the axis of rotation.
an·gu·late (ăng'gyə-lĭt, -lāt') *adj.* Having angles or an angular shape. —*tr. & intr.v.* (-lāt') **-lat·ed, -lat·ing, -lates.** To make or become angular. **—an'gu·late·ly** *adv.*
an·gu·la·tion (ăng'gyə-lā'shən) *n.* **1.** The formation of angles. **2.** An angular part, position, or formation.
an·hin·ga (ăn-hĭng'gə) *n.* The water turkey. [Port. < Tupi.]
an·hy·dride (ăn-hī'drīd') *n.* A chemical compound formed from another by the removal of water. [ANHYDR(OUS) + -IDE.]
an·hy·drite (ăn-hī'drīt') *n.* A white to grayish or reddish mineral of anhydrous calcium sulfate, $CaSO_4$, occurring as layers in gypsum deposits. [ANHYDR(OUS) + -ITE[1].]
an·hy·drous (ăn-hī'drəs) *adj.* Without water, esp. water of crystallization. [Gk. *anudros* : *an-,* without + *hudōr,* water.]
a·ni (ä-nē') *n.* Any of several chiefly tropical American birds of the genus *Crotophaga,* having black plumage and a long tail. [Sp. (South America) *aní* < Tupi *ani.*]
an·il (ăn'ĭl) *n.* The indigo plant or the blue dye obtained from it. [Fr. < Port. < Ar. *an-nīl,* the indigo < Pers. *nīl,* indigo.]
an·ile (ăn'īl', ā'nīl') *adj.* Of or like an old woman. [Lat. *anilis* < *anus,* old woman.] **—a·nil'i·ty** (ə-nĭl'ĭ-tē) *n.*
an·i·line also **an·i·lin** (ăn'ə-lĭn) *n.* A colorless, oily, poisonous benzene derivative, $C_6H_5NH_2$, used in the manufacture of rubber, dyes, resins, pharmaceuticals, and varnishes. —*adj.* Derived from aniline. [G. *Anilin* : *Anil,* anil + *-in,* -ine.]
aniline dye *n.* Any of numerous synthetic dyes.
a·ni·lin·gus (ā'nə-lĭng'gəs) or **a·ni·linc·tus** (-lĭngk'təs) *n.* Oral stimulation of the anus for sexual stimulation. [NLat. : Lat. *anus,* anus + Lat. *lingere,* to lick.]
an·i·ma (ăn'ə-mə) *n.* The inner self; soul. [Lat.]
an·i·mad·ver·sion (ăn'ə-măd-vûr'zhən, -shən) *n.* **1.** Hostile criticism. **2.** A critical or censorious remark. [Lat. *animadversio* < *animadvertere,* to turn the mind toward —see ANIMADVERT.]
an·i·mad·vert (ăn'ə-măd-vûrt') *intr.v.* **-vert·ed, -vert·ing, -verts.** To remark or comment critically, usually with strong disapproval or censure: *felt impelled to animadvert on the wickedness of governments.* [Lat. *animadvertere,* to turn the mind toward : *animus,* mind + *vertere,* to turn.]
an·i·mal (ăn'ə-məl) *n.* **1.** An organism of the kingdom Animalia, distinguished from plants by certain typical characteristics such as the power of locomotion, fixed structure and limited growth, and nonphotosynthetic metabolism. **2.** An animal organism other than a human being, esp. a mammal. **3.** A person of inhuman character or bearing; someone who is bestial or brutish. **4.** Animality: *Drinking releases the animal in him.* —*adj.* **1.** Of, relating to, or characteristic of animals. **2.** Relating to the sensual or physical as distinct from the spiritual nature of people. [Lat. < *animalis,* living < *anima,* soul.]
animal crackers *pl.n.* Small cookies baked in various animal shapes.
an·i·mal·cule (ăn'ə-măl'kyōōl) also **an·i·mal·cu·lum** (-kyə-ləm) *n., pl.* **-cules** also **-cu·la** (-kyə-lə). **1.** A microscopic or minute organism, such as an amoeba or paramecium, usually thought of as an animal. **2.** *Archaic.* A tiny animal, such as a mosquito. [NLat. *animalculum,* dim. of Lat. *animal,* animal.]
animal heat *n.* The heat generated in an animal's body.
animal husbandry *n.* The care and breeding of domestic animals such as cattle, hogs, sheep, and horses.
an·i·mal·ism (ăn'ə-mə-lĭz'əm) *n.* **1.** A state of enjoying sound health and vigorous physical drives. **2.** A state of indifference to all but the physical appetites. **3.** The doctrine

that man is purely animal with no spiritual nature. **—an′i·mal·ist** *n.* **—an′i·mal·is′tic** (-ĭs′tĭk) *adj.*

an·i·mal·i·ty (ăn′ə-măl′ĭ-tē) *n.* **1.** The characteristics or nature of an animal. **2.** Animals collectively; the animal kingdom. **3.** The animal as distinct from the spiritual nature of man.

an·i·mal·ize (ăn′ə-mə-līz′) *tr.v.* **-ized, -iz·ing, -iz·es. 1.** To make coarse and brutal; sensualize. **2.** To endow (a deity) with the attributes of an animal. **—an′i·mal·i·za′tion** *n.*

animal kingdom *n.* The category of living organisms that includes all animals.

animal magnetism *n.* **1.** Hypnotism or mesmerism. **2.** Magnetic personal presence. **3.** Sensualism. **4.** *Christian Science.* "The voluntary or involuntary action of error in all its forms" (Mary Baker Eddy).

animal spirits *pl.n.* Vigorous buoyancy of good health.

animal starch *n.* Glycogen.

an·i·mate (ăn′ə-māt′) *tr.v.* **-mat·ed, -mat·ing, -mates. 1.** To give life to; fill with life. **2.** To impart interest or zest to; enliven: *"The party was animated by all kinds of men and women"* (René Dubos). **3.** To fill with spirit, courage, or resolution; encourage. **4.** To inspire to action; prompt. **5.** To impart motion or activity to. **6.** To make, design, or produce (a cartoon, for example) so as to create the illusion of motion. *—adj.* (ăn′ə-mĭt). **1.** Possessing life; living. **2.** Of or relating to animal life as distinct from plant life. **3.** Belonging to the class of nouns that stand for living things: *The word "dog" is animate, the word "car" inanimate.* [Lat. *animare, animat-* < *anima,* soul.]

an·i·mat·ed (ăn′ə-mā′tĭd) *adj.* **1.** Filled with life, activity, vigor, or spirit: *an animated discussion.* **2.** Made or designed so as to seem alive and moving: *an animated doll.* **3.** Containing or consisting of figures or objects that seem to move in a lifelike manner. **—an′i·mat′ed·ly** *adv.*

animated cartoon *n.* A motion picture consisting of a photographed series of drawings.

animated oat *n.* A grass, *Avena sterilis,* of the Mediterranean region, having spikelets that move or twist in response to changes in moisture.

an·i·mat·er (ăn′ə-mā′tər) *n.* Variant of **animator.**

an·i·ma·tion (ăn′ə-mā′shən) *n.* **1.** The act, process, or result of animating. **2.** The condition or quality of being animate. **3. a.** The art and process of preparing animated cartoons. **b.** An animated cartoon.

a·ni·ma·to (ä′nē-mä′tō) *adv. Mus.* In an animated or lively manner. Used as a direction. **—a′ni·ma′to** *adj.* [Ital. < Lat. *animatus,* p.part. of *animare,* to animate.]

an·i·ma·tor also **an·i·mat·er** (ăn′ə-mā′tər) *n.* **1.** One that animates. **2.** An artist or technician who prepares or produces an animated cartoon.

an·i·mism (ăn′ə-mĭz′əm) *n.* **1.** Any of various primitive beliefs whereby natural phenomena and things animate and inanimate are held to possess an innate soul. **2.** A theory of psychic concepts or of spiritual beings generally. **3.** The hypothesis, first advanced by Pythagoras and Plato, of an immaterial force animating the universe. **4.** An 18th-century doctrine that viewed the soul as the vital principle and source of both the normal and the abnormal phenomena of life. [G. *Animismus* : Lat. *anima,* soul + *-ismus,* -ism.]

an·i·mos·i·ty (ăn′ə-mŏs′ĭ-tē) *n., pl.* **-ties.** Bitter hostility or open enmity; active hatred. [ME *animosite* < OFr. < LLat. *animositas,* courage < Lat. *animosus,* bold < *animus,* soul.]

an·i·mus (ăn′ə-məs) *n.* **1.** An animating motive; intention or purpose. **2.** A feeling of animosity; bitter hostility or hatred. [Lat., soul, mind.]

an·i·on (ăn′ī′ən) *n.* A negatively charged ion that migrates to an anode, as in electrolysis. [Gk., (something) going up, pr.part. of *anienai,* to go up : *ana-,* up + *ienai,* to go.]

anis- *pref.* Variant of **aniso-.**

an·ise (ăn′ĭs) *n.* **1.** A plant, *Pimpinella anisum,* native to the Mediterranean region, having clusters of small yellowish-white flowers and licorice-flavored seeds. **2.** Aniseed. [ME *anis* < OFr. < Lat. *anisum* < Gk. *anison.*]

an·i·seed (ăn′ĭ-sēd′) *n.* The licorice-flavored seed of the anise plant, used in medicine and as flavoring. [ME *anis seed,* anise seed.]

an·i·sei·ko·ni·a (ăn-ī′sī-kō′nē-ə) *n.* An ocular defect in which image, shape, and size differ in each eye. [NLat. : ANIS(O)- + Gk. *eikōn,* image.]

an·i·sette (ăn′ə-sĕt′, -zĕt′) *n.* An anise-flavored liqueur. [Fr., dim. of *anis,* anise < OFr.]

aniso- or **anis-** *pref.* Unequal; dissimilar: *anisogamy.* [NLat. < Gk. *anisos,* unequal: *an-,* not + *isos,* equal.]

an·i·sog·a·my (ăn′ī-sŏg′ə-mē) *n.* A union between markedly different gametes. **—an′i·so·gam′ic** *adj.*

an·i·som·er·ous (ăn′ī-sŏm′ər-əs) *adj.* Having or designating floral whorls that have unequal numbers of parts.

an·i·so·met·ric (ăn-ī′sə-mĕt′rĭk) *adj.* Not isometric.

an·i·so·me·tro·pi·a (ăn-ī′sə-mĭ-trō′pē-ə) *n.* Difference in the refractive power of the eyes. [ANISO- + Gk. *metros,* measure + -OPIA.] **—an·i′so·me·trop′ic** *adj.*

an·i·so·trop·ic (ăn-ī′sə-trŏp′ĭk) *adj.* **1.** Not isotropic. **2.** *Physics.* Having properties that differ according to the direction of measurement. **—an·i′so·trop′i·cal·ly** *adv.* **—an′i·sot′ro·pism** (-sŏt′rə-pĭz′əm), **an′i·sot′ro·py** (-sŏt′rə-pē) *n.*

an·ker·ite (ăng′kə-rīt′) *n.* A dolomitelike mineral in which iron partially replaces magnesium. [G. *Ankerit,* after M.J. *Anker* (d. 1843).]

ankh (ăngk) *n.* An ansate cross. [Of Egypt. orig.]

an·kle (ăng′kəl) *n.* **1.** The joint, consisting of the bones and related structure, that connects the foot with the leg. **2.** The slender section of the leg immediately above the foot. [ME *ancle,* prob. of ON orig.]

an·kle·bone (ăng′kəl-bōn′) *n.* The talus.

an·klet (ăng′klĭt) *n.* **1.** An ornament worn around the ankle. **2.** A sock that reaches just above the ankle.

an·ky·lose also **an·chy·lose** (ăng′kə-lōs′, -lōz′) *v.* **-losed, -los·ing, -los·es.** *—tr.* To join or consolidate by ankylosis. *—intr.* To become joined or consolidated by ankylosis. [Back-formation < ANKYLOSIS.]

an·ky·lo·sis also **an·chy·lo·sis** (ăng′kə-lō′sĭs) *n.* **1.** *Anat.* The consolidation of bones or their parts forming a single unit. **2.** *Pathol.* The stiffening of a joint as the result of abnormal bone fusion. [NLat. < Gk. *ankulōsis,* stiffening of the joints < *ankulos,* bent.]

an·lace (ăn′lĭs) *n.* A two-edged medieval dagger. [ME *anelas.*]

anlace

an·la·ge also **An·la·ge** (än′lä′gə) *n., pl.* **-ges** or **-gen** (-gən). **1.** The initial cell structure from which an embryonic part or organ develops; primordium. **2.** A fundamental principle; foundation. [G., fundamental principle < MHG *anlāge,* request : *ane-,* on + *lāge,* act of laying.]

an·na (ä′nə) *n.* A former copper coin of India and Pakistan. [Hindi *ānā* < Skt. *aṇu-,* small.]

an·nal·ist (ăn′ə-lĭst) *n.* One who writes annals; chronicler.

an·nals (ăn′əlz) *pl.n.* **1.** A chronological record of the events of successive years. **2.** A descriptive account or record; history: *"The short and simple annals of the poor"* (Gray). **3.** A periodical journal compiling the records and reports of a particular learned field. [Lat. *(libri) annales,* yearly (books) < *annalis,* yearly < *annus,* year.]

An·na·mese (ăn′ə-mēz′, -mēs′) also **An·na·mite** (ăn′ə-mīt′). *—adj.* Of or pertaining to Annam, its inhabitants, their language, or their culture. *—n.* **1.** *pl.* **Annamese** also **-mites.** A native or inhabitant of Annam. **2.** Vietnamese (sense 2).

an·nat·to (ə-nä′tō) also **ar·nat·to** (är-nä′tō) *n., pl.* **-tos. 1.** A small tropical American tree, *Bixa orellana,* having red or pinkish flowers and seeds used in cooking. **2.** A yellowish-red dyestuff obtained from the pulp of annatto seeds. [Of Cariban orig.]

an·neal (ə-nēl′) *tr.v.* **-nealed, -neal·ing, -neals. 1.** To subject (glass or metal) to a process of heating and slow cooling in order to toughen and reduce brittleness. **2.** To temper. [ME *anelen* < OE *onǣlan,* to set fire to : *on,* on + *ǣlan,* to kindle < *āl,* fire.]

an·ne·lid (ăn′ə-lĭd) also **an·nel·i·dan** (ə-nĕl′ĭ-dən). *—adj.* Of or belonging to the phylum Annelida, which includes the earthworms, leeches, and other worms having cylindrical segmented bodies. *—n.* An annelid worm. [NLat. *Annelida,* phylum name < Fr. *annelé,* ringed < OFr. *annel,* ring < Lat. *anellus,* dim. of *anulus,* ring.]

an·nex (ə-nĕks′, ăn′ĕks′) *tr.v.* **-nexed, -nex·ing, -nex·es. 1.** To add or join to; append or attach, esp. to a larger or more significant thing. **2.** To incorporate (territory) into an existing country or state. **3.** To add or attach, as an attribute, condition, or consequence. *—n.* (ăn′ĕks′, ăn′ĭks). **1.** A building added on to a larger one, or an auxiliary building situated near the main one. **2.** An addition to a record or document. [ME *annexen* < OFr. *annexer* < Lat. *annexus,* p.part. of *annectere,* to connect : *ad-,* to + *nectere,* to bind.]

an·nex·a·tion (ăn′ĭk-sā′shən) *n.* **1.** The act or process of annexing. **2.** Something that has been annexed. **—an′nex·a′tion·al** *adj.* **—an′nex·a′tion·ism** *n.* **—an′nex·a′tion·ist** *n.*

an·nexe (ăn′ĭks′) *n. Chiefly Brit.* Variant of **annex.**

An·nie Oak·ley (ăn′ē ōk′lē) *n. Slang.* A complimentary ticket of admittance; a free ticket or pass. [After *Annie Oakley* (1860–1926).]

an·ni·hi·late (ə-nī′ə-lāt′) *v.* **-lat·ed, -lat·ing, -lates.** *—tr.* **1.** To destroy completely; reduce to nonexistence. **2.** To nullify or render void; abolish. **3.** *Informal.* To overwhelm completely; render helpless or ineffective. *—intr. Physics.* To participate in annihilation, as do an electron and a positron. [LLat. *annihilare, annihilat-* : Lat. *ad-,* to + Lat. *nihil,* nothing.] **—an·ni′hi·la·bil′i·ty** (-lə-bĭl′ĭ-tē) *n.* **—an·ni′hi·la·ble** (-lə-bəl) *adj.* **—an·ni′hi·la′tor** *n.*

an·ni·hi·la·tion (ə-nī′ə-lā′shən) *n.* **1.** The act or process of annihilating. **2.** The condition or result of having been annihilated; utter destruction. **3.** *Physics.* The phenomenon in which a particle and an antiparticle, such as an electron and a positron, disappear with a resultant release of energy approximately equivalent to the sum of their masses.

an·ni·ver·sa·ry (ăn′ə-vûr′sə-rē) *n., pl.* **-ries. 1.** The annual recurrence of an event that took place in some preceding year: *a wedding anniversary.* **2.** A commemorative celebration on the date of an anniversary. **—*modifier:*** *an anniversary party.* [ME *anniversarie* < Med. Lat. *anniversarium* < Lat. *anniversarius,* returning yearly : *annus,* year + *versus,* p.part. of *vertere,* to turn.]

an·no Dom·i·ni (ăn′ō dŏm′ə-nī′, dŏm′ə-nē) *adv.* In a specified year of the Christian era. Used chiefly in the abbreviated form: *A.D. 495.* [Lat., in the year of the Lord.]

an·no·tate (ăn′ō-tāt′) *v.* **-tat·ed, -tat·ing, -tates.** *—tr.* To furnish (a literary work) with critical commentary or explanatory notes; gloss. —*intr.* To gloss a text. [Lat. *annotare, annotat-*, to note down : *ad-*, to + *notāre*, to write < *nota*, note.]

an·no·ta·tion (ăn′ō-tā′shən) *n.* **1.** The act or process of annotating. **2.** A critical or explanatory note; commentary.

an·nounce (ə-nouns′) *tr.v.* **-nounced, -nounc·ing, -nounc·es. 1.** To bring to public notice; declare or proclaim officially or formally. **2.** To proclaim the presence or arrival of: *announce a caller.* **3.** To make aware or conscious of through the senses. **4.** To serve as an announcer. [ME *announcen* < OFr. *anoncier* < Lat. *annuntiare* : *ad-*, to + *nuntiare*, to report < *nuntius*, messenger.]

an·nounce·ment (ə-nouns′mənt) *n.* **1.** The act of announcing. **2.** Something that has been announced. **3.** A printed or published statement or notice.

an·nounc·er (ə-noun′sər) *n.* **1.** One that announces. **2.** A radio or television performer who provides program continuity and delivers commercial and other announcements.

an·noy (ə-noi′) *v.* **-noyed, -noy·ing, -noys.** —*tr.* **1.** To bother or irritate; disturb slightly. **2.** To harass or disturb by repeated attacks. —*intr.* To behave in an annoying manner. [ME *anoien* < OFr. *anoier* < LLat. *inodiare*, to make odious < Lat. *in odio*, odious : *in*, in + *odium*, hatred.]

Synonyms: *annoy, irritate, bother, irk, vex, provoke, aggravate, peeve, rile.* These verbs mean to disturb or disquiet a person and, usually, to stir anger. *Annoy* refers to mild disturbance caused by an act that tries one's patience. *Irritate* is closely related but somewhat stronger. *Bother* implies imposition that affects physical or mental composure. *Irk* stresses the wearisome quality of repeated disturbance. *Vex* applies to an act capable of bringing on anger or perplexity. *Provoke* implies strong and usually deliberate imposition and angry response, and *aggravate* is an approximate but informal equivalent. *Peeve,* also informal, suggests rather minor disturbance that produces a querulous, resentful response. *Rile* implies strong anger, openly displayed.

an·noy·ance (ə-noi′əns) *n.* **1.** Something that annoys; a nuisance. **2.** The act of annoying. **3.** Vexation; irritation.

an·noy·ing (ə-noi′ĭng) *adj.* Causing vexation or irritation; troublesome: *an annoying cough.* **—an·noy′ing·ly** *adv.*

an·nu·al (ăn′yo͞o-əl) *adj.* **1.** Recurring, done, or performed every year; yearly. **2.** Of or pertaining to a year; determined by a year's time: *an annual income.* **3.** *Bot.* Living and growing for only one year or season. —*n.* **1.** A periodical published yearly; yearbook. **2.** A plant that lives and grows for only one year or season, during which the life cycle is completed. [ME *annuel* < OFr. < LLat. *annualis* < Lat. *annus*, year.]

annual ring *n.* One of the concentric layers of wood, esp. in a tree trunk, indicating a year's growth in temperate climates and seasonal growth in regions of wet and dry seasons.

an·nu·i·tant (ə-no͞o′ĭ-tənt, ə-nyo͞o′-) *n.* A person who receives or is qualified to receive an annuity.

an·nu·i·ty (ə-no͞o′ĭ-tē, -nyo͞o′-) *n., pl.* **-ties. 1.** The annual payment of an allowance or income. **2.** The right to receive this payment or the obligation to make this payment. **3.** An investment on which a person receives fixed payments for a lifetime or a specified number of years. [ME *annuite* < ANFr. < Med. Lat. *annuitas* < Lat. *annuus*, yearly < *annus*, year.]

an·nul (ə-nŭl′) *tr.v.* **-nulled, -nul·ling, -nuls. 1.** To make or declare void or invalid, as a marriage or a law; nullify; cancel. **2.** To obliterate the existence or effect of. [ME *annullen* < OFr. *annuller* < LLat. *annullare* : Lat. *ad-*, to + Lat. *nullus*, none.]

an·nu·lar (ăn′yə-lər) *adj.* Forming or shaped like a ring. [OFr. *annulaire* < Lat. *anularis* < *anulus*, ring.]

annular eclipse *n.* A solar eclipse in which the moon covers all but a bright ring around the circumference of the sun.

annular ligament *n.* A ligament or fibrous band that rings the ankle joint or the wrist joint.

an·nu·late (ăn′yə-lĭt, -lāt′) also **an·nu·lat·ed** (-lā′tĭd) *adj.* Having or consisting of rings or ringlike segments. [Lat. *anulatus* < *anulus*, ring.]

an·nu·la·tion (ăn′yə-lā′shən) *n.* **1.** The act or process of forming rings. **2.** A ringlike structure or segment.

an·nu·let (ăn′yə-lĭt) *n. Archit.* A ringlike molding around the capital of a pillar. [Lat. *anulus*, ring + -ET.]

an·nu·li (ăn′yə-lī′) *n.* A plural of **annulus.**

an·nul·ment (ə-nŭl′mənt) *n.* **1.** The act of annulling. **2.** The retrospective as well as prospective invalidation of a marriage, as for nonconsummation, effected by means of a declaration stating that the marriage was never valid.

an·nu·lus (ăn′yə-ləs) *n., pl.* **-lus·es** or **-li** (-lī′). **1.** A ringlike figure, part, structure, or marking. **2.** *Math.* The figure bounded by and containing the area between two concentric circles. [Lat. *anulus*, ring.]

an·nun·ci·ate (ə-nŭn′sē-āt′) *tr.v.* **-at·ed, -at·ing, -ates.** To announce; proclaim: *"They do not so properly affirm, as annunciate it"* (Lamb). [Lat. *annuntiare.* —see ANNOUNCE.]

an·nun·ci·a·tion (ə-nŭn′sē-ā′shən) *n.* **1.** The act of announcing. **2.** An announcement; proclamation. **3. Annunciation. a.** The angel Gabriel's announcement of the Incarnation. **b.** The festival, on March 25, in celebration of this event.

Annunciation lily *n.* The Madonna lily.

an·nun·ci·a·tor (ə-nŭn′sē-ā′tər) *n.* **1.** One that announces. **2.** An electrical signaling device used in hotels or offices to indicate the source of calls on a switchboard.

an·nus mi·rab·i·lis (ăn′əs mĭ-răb′ə-lĭs) *n.* **1.** A year of wonders or disasters; fateful year: *"Hungary's blood bath was the saddest event in that annus mirabilis"* (C.L. Sulzberger). **2.** The year 1666, memorable for the great fire of London and the English victory over the Dutch. [NLat., wondrous year.]

a·no·a (ə-nō′ə) *n.* A small buffalo, *Anoa depressicornis,* of Celebes and the Philippines, having short, pointed horns. [Native word in Celebes.]

an·ode (ăn′ōd′) *n.* **1.** Any positively charged electrode, as of an electrolytic cell, storage battery, or electron tube. **2.** The negatively charged terminal of a primary cell or of a storage battery that is supplying current. [Gk. *anodos*, a way up : *ana-*, up + *hodos*, way.]

anode mud *n.* The residue of electrolytic refining, esp. of copper, high in concentrations of inert metals such as platinum, silver, and gold.

an·o·dize (ăn′ə-dīz′) *tr.v.* **-dized, -diz·ing, -diz·es.** To coat (a metallic surface) electrolytically with a protective oxide. [ANOD(E) + -IZE.] **—an′o·di·za′tion** *n.*

an·o·dyne (ăn′ə-dīn′) *adj.* **1.** Able to soothe or relieve pain. **2.** Relaxing: *anodyne novels about country life.* **3.** Watered-down; insipid: *anodyne references to progress and freedom.* —*n.* **1.** A medicine that relieves pain. **2.** Anything that soothes or comforts. [Lat. *anodynus* < Gk. *anōdunos*, free from pain : *an-*, without + *odunē*, pain.]

a·noint (ə-noint′) *tr.v.* **a·noint·ed, a·noint·ing, a·noints. 1.** To apply oil, ointment, or a similar substance to. **2.** To put oil on as a sign of sanctification or consecration in a religious ceremony. [ME *enointen* < OFr. *enoindre* < Lat. *inunguere* : *in-*, on + *ungere*, to smear.]

anointing of the sick *n. Rom.Cath.Ch.* The sacrament of anointing a critically ill person, praying for recovery, and asking for the absolution of sin.

a·no·le (ə-nō′lē) *n.* Any of various chiefly tropical New World lizards of the genus *Anolis,* characterized by a distensible throat flap and the ability to change color. [Fr. *anolis* < Cariban.]

a·nom·a·lous (ə-nŏm′ə-ləs) *adj.* Deviating from the normal or common order, form, or rule; abnormal; deviant. [LLat. *anomalos* < Gk., uneven : *an-*, not + *homalos*, even < *homos*, same.]

a·nom·a·ly (ə-nŏm′ə-lē) *n., pl.* **-lies. 1.** Deviation or departure from the normal or common order, form, or rule; abnormality. **2.** Anything anomalous, irregular, or abnormal. **3.** *Astron.* The angular deviation, as observed from the sun, of a planet from its perihelion. **—a·nom′a·lis′tic** (-lĭs′tĭk′), **a·nom′a·lis′ti·cal** *adj.* **—a·nom′a·lis′ti·cal·ly** *adv.*

an·o·mie or **an·o·my** (ăn′ə-mē) *n.* **1.** A collapse of the social structures governing a given society. **2.** The state of alienation experienced by an individual or class in such a situation. **3.** Personal disorganization resulting in unsocial behavior. [Gk. *anomia*, lawlessness < *anomos*, lawless : *a-*, without + *nomos*, law.]

a·non (ə-nŏn′) *adv.* **1.** At another time; again. **2.** *Archaic.* In a short time; soon: *"Such good men as he which is anon to be interred"* (Cotton Mather). **3.** *Archaic.* At once; immediately: *"The same is he that heareth the word, and anon with joy receiveth it"* (Matthew 13:20). **—*idiom.* ever** (or **now**) **and anon.** Time after time; now and then. [ME, at once < OE *onān* : *on*, in + *ān*, one.]

an·o·nym (ăn′ə-nĭm′) *n.* **1.** An anonymous person. **2.** A pseudonym. [Fr. *anonyme* < LLat. *anonymus*, anonymous.]

an·o·nym·i·ty (ăn′ə-nĭm′ĭ-tē) *n.* **1.** The quality or state of being anonymous. **2.** One that is anonymous.

a·non·y·mous (ə-nŏn′ə-məs) *adj.* **1.** Having an unknown or unacknowledged name. **2.** Having an unknown or withheld authorship or agency. [LLat. *anonymus* < Gk. *anōnumos*, nameless : *an-*, without + *onoma*, name.]

a·noph·e·les (ə-nŏf′ə-lēz′) *n.* Any of various mosquitoes of the genus *Anopheles,* many of which carry the malaria parasite and transmit the disease to man. [NLat. *Anopheles*, genus name < Gk. *anōphelēs*, useless : *an-*, without + *ophelos*, advantage.]

an·o·rak (ăn′ə-răk′) *n.* A heavy jacket with a hood, worn in polar regions; parka. [Eskimo (Greenland) *ánorâq.*]

an·o·rec·tic (ăn′ə-rĕk′tĭk) or **an·o·ret·ic** (-rĕt′ĭk) also **an·o·rex·ic** (-rĕk′sĭk) *adj.* **1.** Marked by loss of appetite. **2.** Suppressing or causing loss of appetite. —*n.* **1.** One that is anorectic. **2.** An anorectic drug. [Gk. *anorektos* : *an-*, without + *oregein*, to reach out for.]

an·o·rex·i·a (ăn′ə-rĕk′sē-ə) *n.* Loss of appetite, esp. as a result of disease. [Gk. : *an-*, without + *orexis*, appetite < *oregein*, to reach out for.]

anorexia nerv·o·sa (nûr-vō′sə) *n.* The pathological loss of appetite occurring chiefly in young women that is thought to be psychological in origin. [NLat., nervous anorexia.]

an·o·rex·ic (ăn′ə-rĕk′sĭk) *adj.* & *n.* Variant of **anorectic.**

an·or·thite (ăn-ôr′thīt′) *n.* A rare plagioclase feldspar with high calcium oxide content, occurring in igneous rocks. [Fr.

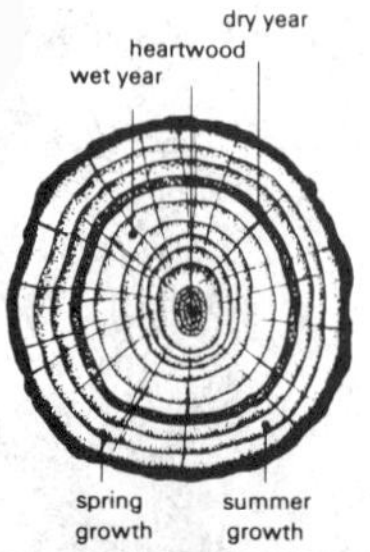

annual ring
Above: Cross section showing annual rings
Below: Cross section of a tree showing annual rings

annunciation
15th-century Flemish altarpiece depicting the Annunciation, by Robert Campin

anole

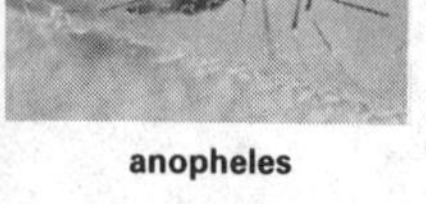

anopheles

: Gk. *an-*, not + Gk. *orthos,* straight (from its oblique crystals).]

an·or·tho·site (ăn-ôr′thə-sīt′) *n.* A plutonic rock, chiefly plagioclase. [Fr. *anorthose,* a kind of feldspar (Gk. *an-*, not + Gk. *orthos,* straight) + -ITE.]

an·os·mi·a (ăn-ŏz′mē-ə) *n.* Loss of the sense of smell. [NLat. : Gk. *an-*, without + Gk. *osmē,* odor.]

an·oth·er (ə-nŭ*th*′ər) *adj.* **1.** Additional; one more: *had another cup of coffee.* **2.** Distinctly different from the first: *took another route to town.* **3.** Some other: *put it off to another day.* —*pron.* **1.** An additional one. **2.** A different one. **3.** One of an undetermined number or group: *for one reason or another.*

an·ov·u·lant (ăn′ŏv′yə-lənt) *n.* An anovulatory drug. [AN- + OVUL(ATION) + -ANT.]

an·o·vu·la·tion (ăn-ō′vyə-lā′shən, -ŏv′yə-) *n.* The absence of ovulation.

an·o·vu·la·to·ry (ăn-ō′vyə-lə-tôr′ē, -tōr′ē, -ŏv′yə-) *adj.* Relating to the suppression of ovulation.

an·ox·e·mi·a (ăn′ŏk-sē′mē-ə) *n.* An abnormal decline in the oxygen content of the blood.

an·ox·i·a (ăn-ŏk′sē-ə) *n.* **1.** Absence of oxygen. **2.** A pathological deficiency of oxygen, esp. hypoxia. **—an·ox′ic** (-ŏk′sĭk) *adj.*

an·sate (ăn′sāt′) also **an·sat·ed** (-sā′tĭd) *adj.* Having a handle or a part resembling a handle. [Lat. *ansatus* < *ansa,* handle.]

ansate cross *n.* A cross shaped like a T with a loop at the top; ankh.

an·sat·ed (ăn′sā′tĭd) *adj.* Variant of **ansate.**

An·schluss (än′shlo͝os′) *n.* A union, esp. the political union of Nazi Germany and Austria in 1938. [G.]

an·ser·ine (ăn′sə-rīn′) *adj.* **1.** Of or belonging to the subfamily Anserinae, which includes the geese. **2.** Of or resembling a goose; gooselike. **3.** Also **an·ser·ous** (-sər-əs). Stupid; silly; foolish. [NLat. *Anserinae,* subfamily name < Lat. *anserinus,* pertaining to geese < *anser,* goose.]

an·swer (ăn′sər) *n.* **1.** A spoken or written reply, as to a question. **2. a.** A solution or result, as to a problem. **b.** The correct response or solution. **3.** An act in response or retaliation. **4.** *Law.* A defendant's defense against charges filed against him. —*v.* **-swered, -swer·ing, -swers.** —*intr.* **1.** To respond in words or action. **2.** To be liable or accountable: *answered for his actions.* **3.** To serve the purpose; suffice: *"often I do use three words where one would answer"* (Mark Twain). **4.** To correspond; match: *answering to the description.* —*tr.* **1.** To reply to. **2.** To respond correctly to. **3.** To fulfill the demands of; serve: *"my fortune has answered my desires"* (Walton). **4.** To conform or correspond to. **5.** To be responsible for; meet. [ME *answere* < OE *andswaru.*]

Synonyms: *answer, respond, reply, retort.* These verbs relate to action taken as the immediate result of a question or other stimulus. *Answer,* the most general, refers to any act that completes a process initiated by another. *Respond* suggests a physical act or change that follows a specific stimulus, but is now also used as a loose equivalent of *reply,* which means to answer in speech or writing to a direct question. *Retort* refers to a sharp, spoken remark of the same style or kind as that used by one's accuser or debating opponent.

an·swer·a·ble (ăn′sər-ə-bəl) *adj.* **1.** Required to render account; accountable. **2.** Capable of being answered. **3.** *Archaic.* Corresponding; suitable. **—an′swer·a·bil′i·ty, an′swer·a·ble·ness** *n.* **—an′swer·a·bly** *adv.*

ant (ănt) *n.* Any of various social insects of the family Formicidae, characteristically having wings only in the males and fertile females and living in colonies that have a complex social organization. [ME *amte* < OE *ǣmete.*]

ant– *pref.* Variant of **anti-.**

-ant *suff.* **1. a.** Performing, promoting, or causing a specified action: *acceptant.* **b.** Being in a specified state or condition: *flippant.* **2. a.** One that performs, promotes, or causes a specified action: *deodorant.* **b.** One that undergoes a specified action: *inhalant.* [ME < OFr. < Lat. *-ans, -ant-,* pr.part. suffix.]

an·ta (ăn′tə) *n., pl.* **-tae** (-tē). *Archit.* **1.** A thickening of the projecting end of the lateral wall of a Greek temple. **2.** A pier that constitutes one boundary of the porch. [Lat. *antae,* pilasters.]

ant·ac·id (ănt-ăs′ĭd) *adj.* Correcting acidity; neutralizing acids. —*n.* A substance, esp. a medicinal remedy, that neutralizes acid.

an·tae (ăn′tē) *n.* Plural of **anta.**

An·tae·us (ăn-tē′əs) *n. Gk. Myth.* A giant, invincible while touching the ground, who was lifted into the air by Hercules and crushed to death. [Lat. < Gk. *Antaios.*]

an·tag·o·nism (ăn-tăg′ə-nĭz′əm) *n.* **1.** Mutual resistance; opposition; hostility. **2.** The condition of being an opposing principle, force, or factor.

an·tag·o·nist (ăn-tăg′ə-nĭst) *n.* **1.** One who opposes and actively competes with another; adversary. **2.** *Anat.* A muscle that opposes another muscle. **3.** A drug that counteracts or neutralizes another drug. **—an·tag′o·nis′tic** *adj.* **—an·tag′o·nis′ti·cal·ly** *adv.*

an·tag·o·nize (ăn-tăg′ə-nīz′) *tr.v.* **-nized, -niz·ing, -niz·es.** **1.** To incur the dislike of. **2.** To counteract. [Gk. *antagōnizesthai,* to struggle against : *anti-,* against + *agōnizesthai,* to struggle < *agōn,* contest. —see AGONY.]

Ant·arc·tic (ănt-ärk′tĭk, -är′tĭk) *adj.* Of or pertaining to the regions surrounding the South Pole. [ME *Antartik* < OFr. *antartique* < Med. Lat. *antarcticus* < Lat., southern < Gk. *antarktikos* : *anti-,* opposite + *arktikos,* northern. —see ARCTIC.]

Antarctic Circle *n.* A parallel of latitude, 66 degrees, 33 minutes south, marking the limit of the South Frigid Zone.

An·tar·es (ăn-târ′ēz, -tăr′-) *n.* A double and variable star, the brightest in the southern sky, about 424 light-years from earth in the constellation Scorpius. [Gk. *antarēs* : *anti-,* opposite + *Ares,* Mars.]

ant cow *n.* An aphid that yields a honeylike substance on which ants feed.

an·te (ăn′tē) *n.* **1.** The stake that each poker player must put into the pool before receiving his hand or before receiving new cards. **2.** *Slang.* An amount to be paid, esp. as one's share: cost. —*tr.v.* **-ted** or **-teed, -te·ing, -tes.** **1.** To put (one's stake) into the pool in poker. **2.** *Slang.* To pay. [< Lat., before.]

ante– *pref.* **1.** Earlier; prior to: *antenatal.* **2.** Before; in front of: *anteroom.* [Lat. < *ante,* before.]

ant·eat·er (ănt′ē′tər) *n.* **1.** Any of several tropical American mammals of the family Myrmecophagidae, that lack teeth and feed on ants and termites, esp. *Myrmecophaga tridactyla,* having a long, narrow snout, a long, sticky tongue, and a long, shaggy-haired tail. **2.** Any of several other animals, such as the echidna, that feed on ants.

an·te·bel·lum (ăn′tē-bĕl′əm) *adj.* Belonging to the period prior to the Civil War. [Lat. *ante bellum,* before the war.]

an·te·cede (ăn′tĭ-sēd′) *tr.v.* **-ced·ed, -ced·ing, -cedes.** To go before in rank, place, or time; precede. [Lat. *antecedere* : *ante-,* before + *cedere,* to go.]

an·te·ce·dence (ăn′tĭ-sēd′ns) *n.* Precedence.

an·te·ce·dent (ăn′tĭ-sēd′nt) *adj.* Going before; preceding; prior. —*n.* **1.** One that precedes. **2.** Any occurrence or event prior to another. **3. antecedents.** One's ancestors or ancestry. **4.** *Gram.* The word, phrase, or clause to which a relative pronoun refers. **5.** *Math.* The first term of a ratio. **6.** *Logic.* The conditional member of a hypothetical proposition. **—an′te·ce′dent·ly** *adv.*

an·te·cham·ber (ăn′tē-chām′bər) *n.* A smaller room serving as an entryway into a larger room. [Fr. *antichambre* : *anti-,* before (< Lat. *ante-*) + *chambre,* chamber.]

an·te·choir (ăn′tĭ-kwīr′) *n.* A place in front of the choir reserved for the clergy and choir members.

an·te·date (ăn′tĭ-dāt′) *tr.v.* **-dat·ed, -dat·ing, -dates.** **1.** To be of an earlier date than; precede in time. **2.** To give a date earlier than the actual date; date back. —*n.* A date given to an event or a document that is earlier than the actual date.

an·te·di·lu·vi·an (ăn′tĭ-də-lo͞o′vē-ən) *adj.* **1.** Occurring or belonging to the era before the Flood written about in the Bible. **2.** Very old; antiquated: *an antediluvian refrigerator.* [ANTE- + Lat. *diluvium,* flood. —see DILUVIAL.] **—an′te·di·lu′vi·an** *n.*

an·te·fix (ăn′tē-fĭx′) *n., pl.* **-fix·es** or **-fix·a** (-fĭk′sə). *Archit.* An upright ornament along the eaves of a tiled roof designed to conceal the joints between the rows of tiles. [< Lat. *antefixus,* fastened in front : *ante-,* before + *fixus,* fastened, p. part. of *figere,* to fasten.] **—an′te·fix′al** *adj.*

an·te·lope (ăn′tl-ōp′) *n., pl.* **antelope** or **-lopes.** **1. a.** Any of various slender, swift-running, long-horned ruminants of the family Bovidae, of Africa and Asia. **b.** An animal that resembles a true antelope, as the pronghorn. **2.** Leather made from the hide of an antelope. [ME < Med. Lat. *anthalopus* < LGk. *antholops.*]

an·te·me·rid·i·an (ăn′tē-mə-rĭd′ē-ən) *adj.* Of, pertaining to, or taking place in the morning. [Lat. *antemeridianus* : *ante-,* before + *meridianus,* of noon. —see MERIDIAN.]

an·te me·rid·i·em (ăn′tē mə-rĭd′ē-əm) *adv. & adj.* Before noon. Used chiefly in the abbreviated form to specify the hour: *10:30* A.M.; *an* A.M. *appointment.* [Lat. : *ante,* before + *meridies,* noon.]

Usage: Strictly speaking, *12 A.M.* denotes midnight, and *12 P.M.* denotes noon, but there is sufficient confusion over these uses to make it advisable to use *12 noon* and *12 midnight* where clarity is required.

an·te mor·tem (ăn′tē môr′təm) *adj.* Before death. [Lat.]

an·te·na·tal (ăn′tē-nāt′l) *adj.* Before birth; prenatal.

an·ten·na (ăn-tĕn′ə) *n.* **1.** *pl.* **-ten·nae** (-tĕn′ē). One of the paired, flexible, jointed sensory appendages on the head of an insect, myriapod, or crustacean. **2.** *pl.* **-nas.** A metallic apparatus for sending and receiving electromagnetic waves; an aerial. [Med. Lat. < Lat., sail yard.] **—an·ten′nal** *adj.*

antenna loop *n.* A flat coil or wire serving both as antenna and as part of the internal circuitry of a receiver.

an·ten·nule (ăn-tĕn′yo͞ol′) *n. Zool.* A small antenna, esp. one of the first pair in crustaceans. [Fr., dim. of *antenne,* antenna < Lat. *antenna,* sail yard.]

an·te·pen·di·um (ăn′tē-pĕn′dē-əm) *n., pl.* **-di·a** (-dē-ə). **1.** A hanging for the front of an altar. **2.** A pulpit cloth. [Med. Lat. : Lat. *ante-,* before + *pendere,* to hang.]

an·te·pe·nult (ăn′tē-pē′nŭlt′, -pĭ-nŭlt′) *n.* The third syllable from the end in a word, as *te* in *antepenult.* [Short for LLat. *antepaenultima* < *antepaenultimus,* antepenultimate.]

ansate cross

anteater

antelope

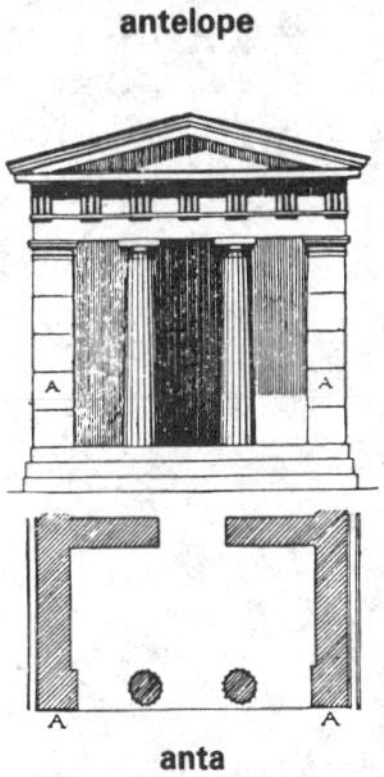

anta
Engraving and diagram of a temple, with antae indicated by A

an·te·pe·nul·ti·mate (ăn′tē-pĭ-nŭl′tə-mĭt) *adj.* Second from the last; third from the end in a series. —*n.* An antepenult. [LLat. *antepaenultimus* : Lat. *ante-*, before + Lat. *paenultimus,* next to last. —see PENULT.]

an·te·ri·or (ăn-tîr′ē-ər) *adj.* **1.** Placed in front; located forward. **2.** Prior in time; earlier. **3.** *Zool.* **a.** Located near the head in lower animals. **b.** Located on or near the front of the body in higher animals. **c.** Located on or near the front of an organ or on the ventral surface of the body in man. **4.** *Bot.* In front of and facing away from the axis or stem. [Lat., comp. of *ante,* before.] **—an·te′ri·or·ly** *adv.*

an·te·room (ăn′tē-ro͞om′, -ro͝om′) *n.* A waiting room.

ant·he·li·on (ănt-hē′lē-ən, ăn-thē′-) *n., pl.* **-li·a** (-lē-ə) or **-ons.** A luminous white, halolike area occasionally seen in the sky opposite the sun on the parhelic circle. [Gk. *anthēlion* < *anthēlios,* opposite the sun : *anti-,* opposite + *hēlios,* sun.]

ant·hel·min·tic (ănt′hĕl-mĭn′tĭk, ăn′thĕl-) also **ant·hel·min·thic** (-thĭk) *adj.* Acting to expel or destroy intestinal worms. —*n.* An anthelmintic remedy; a vermifuge. [ANTI- + Gk. *helmins, helminth-,* worm.]

an·them (ăn′thəm) *n.* **1.** A hymn of praise or loyalty. **2.** A sacred composition set to words from the Bible. [ME *anteme* < OE *antefn* < Med. Lat. *antiphona* < Gk. < *antiphōnos,* sounding in answer : *anti-,* in return + *phōnē,* voice.]

anthemion
Fragment of a frieze

an·the·mi·on (ăn-thē′mē-ən) *n., pl.* **-mi·a** (-mē-ə). A pattern of honeysuckle or palm leaves in a radiating cluster, used as a motif in Greek art. [Gk. < *anthos,* flower.]

an·ther (ăn′thər) *n. Bot.* The organ that is borne at the upper end of a stamen and that secretes and discharges pollen. [NLat. *anthera* < Med. Lat. *anthera,* pollen < Lat., a medicine extracted from flowers < Gk. *anthēros,* flowery < *anthos,* flower.]

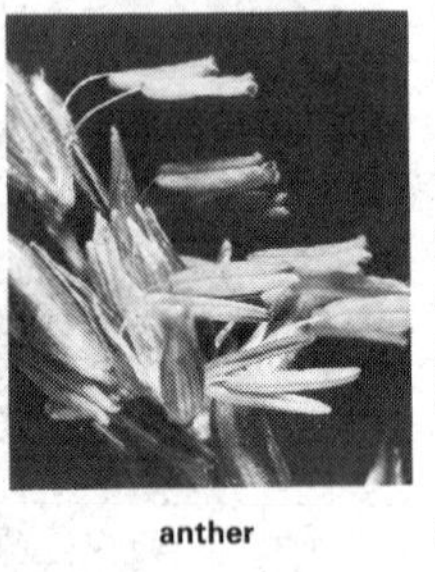

anther

an·ther·id·i·um (ăn′thə-rĭd′ē-əm) *n., pl.* **-i·a** (-ē-ə). *Bot.* An organ that produces male sex cells in the algae, fungi, mosses, and ferns. [NLat. : < *anthera,* anther.]

an·ther·o·zo·id (ăn′thər-ə-zō′ĭd) *n. Bot.* A male sex cell produced by an antheridium. [ANTHER + ZO(O)ID.]

an·the·sis (ăn-thē′sĭs) *n. Bot.* The blooming or time of full bloom of a flower. [Gk. *anthēsis,* flowering < *anthos,* flower.]

ant·hill (ănt′hĭl′) *n.* A mound formed by ants or termites in digging or building a nest.

antho– *pref.* Flower: *anthotaxy.* [< Gk. *anthos,* flower.]

an·tho·cy·a·nin (ăn′thō-sī′ə-nĭn) also **an·tho·cy·an** (-sī′ən, -ăn′) *n.* Any of a class of water-soluble pigments that impart to flowers and other plant parts any of the colors ranging from blue to most shades of red. [ANTHO- + CYANIN(E).]

an·tho·di·um (ăn-thō′dē-əm) *n., pl.* **-di·a** (-dē-ə). The flower head of composite plants, such as the aster, thistle, and goldenrod. [NLat. < Gk. *anthōdēs,* flowerlike : *anthos,* flower + *-eidēs,* -oid.]

an·thol·o·gize (ăn-thŏl′ə-jīz′) *tr.v.* **-gized, -giz·ing, -giz·es.** To compile or include in an anthology. **—an·thol′o·gist** *n.*

an·thol·o·gy (ăn-thŏl′ə-jē) *n., pl.* **-gies.** A collection of literary pieces, such as poems, short stories, or plays. [NLat. *anthologia* < Gk., flower gathering : *anthos,* flower + *logia,* collection < *legein,* to gather.] **—an′tho·log′i·cal** (ăn′thə-lŏj′ĭ-kəl) *adj.*

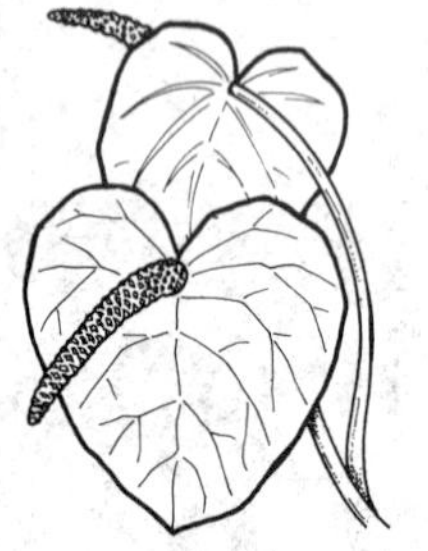

anthurium

an·tho·phore (ăn′thə-fôr′, -fōr′) *n. Bot.* A stalklike part in certain flowers, supporting the pistils and corolla.

an·tho·tax·y (ăn′thə-tăk′sē) also **an·tho·tax·is** (ăn′thə-tăk′sĭs) *n. Bot.* The arrangement of the parts of a flower.

-anthous *suff.* Having flowers: *ananthous.* [NLat. *-anthus* < Gk. *anthos,* flower.]

an·tho·zo·an (ăn′thə-zō′ən) *n.* Any of various marine organisms of the class Anthozoa, growing singly or in colonies and including the corals and sea anemones. **—an′tho·zo′an, an′tho·zo′ic** (-zō′ĭk) *adj.*

an·thra·cene (ăn′thrə-sēn′) *n.* A crystalline hydrocarbon, $C_6H_4(CH_2)C_6H_4$, extracted from coal tar and used in the manufacture of dyes and organic chemicals. [Gk. *anthrax, anthrak-,* charcoal + *-ene.*]

an·thra·cite (ăn′thrə-sīt′) *n.* A hard coal having a high carbon content and little volatile matter that burns with a clean flame. [Lat. *anthracites,* a kind of bloodstone < Gk. *anthrakitēs,* coal like < *anthrax,* charcoal.]

an·thrac·nose (ăn-thrăk′nōs′) *n.* Any of several diseases of plants caused by fungi and characterized by dead spots on the leaves, twigs, or fruit. [Fr. : Gk. *anthrax,* carbuncle + Gk. *nosos,* disease.]

an·thrax (ăn′thrăks′) *n. Pathol.* **1.** An infectious, usually fatal disease of warm-blooded animals, esp. of cattle and sheep, caused by *Bacillus anthracis* and transmissible to man, capable of affecting various organs, and esp. characterized by malignant ulcers. **2.** *pl.* **-thra·ces** (-thrə-sēz′). A lesion caused by anthrax. [ME *antrax,* malignant boil < Lat. *anthrax,* carbuncle < Gk.]

an·throp·ic (ăn-thrŏp′ĭk) also **an·throp·i·cal** (-ĭ-kəl) *adj.* Of or pertaining to man or the era of human life. [Gk. *anthrōpikos* < *anthropos,* human being.]

anthropo– *pref.* Human being: *anthropometry.* [Gk. < *anthropos,* human being.]

an·thro·po·cen·tric (ăn′thrə-pə-sĕn′trĭk) *adj.* **1.** Regarding man as the central fact or final aim of the universe. **2.** Interpreting reality exclusively in terms of human values and experience. **—an′thro·po·cen′tri·cal·ly** *adv.* **—an′thro·po·cen′trism** *n.*

an·thro·po·gen·e·sis (ăn′thrə-pə-jĕn′ĭ-sĭs) *n.* The scientific study of the origin of man. **—an′thro·po·gen′ic** (-jĕn′ĭk) *adj.*

an·thro·poid (ăn′thrə-poid′) *adj.* **1.** Resembling man, as the apes of the family Pongidae, which includes gorillas, chimpanzees, orang-utans, and gibbons. **2.** Resembling or characteristic of an ape; apelike. —*n.* Any member of the family Pongidae. **—an′thro·poid′al** *adj.*

anthropoid ape *n.* An anthropoid.

an·thro·pol·o·gy (ăn′thrə-pŏl′ə-jē) *n.* The scientific study of the origin and of the physical, social, and cultural development and behavior of man. **—an′thro·po·log′ic** (-pə-lŏj′ĭk), **an′thro·po·log′i·cal** (-ĭ-kəl) *adj.* **—an′thro·po·log′i·cal·ly** *adv.* **—an′thro·pol′o·gist** *n.*

an·thro·pom·e·try (ăn′thrə-pŏm′ĭ-trē) *n.* The study and technique of human body measurement for use in anthropological classification and comparison. **—an′thro·po·met′ric** (-pə-mĕt′rĭk), **an′thro·po·met′ri·cal** (-rĭ-kəl) *adj.* **—an′thro·po·met′ri·cal·ly** *adv.* **—an′thro·pom′e·trist** *n.*

an·thro·po·mor·phism (ăn′thrə-pə-môr′fĭz′əm) *n.* The attribution of human motivation, characteristics, or behavior to inanimate objects, animals, or natural phenomena. **—an′thro·po·mor′phic** *adj.* **—an′thro·po·mor′phi·cal·ly** *adv.*

an·thro·po·mor·phize (ăn′thrə-pə-môr′fīz′) *tr.v.* **-phized, -phiz·ing, -phiz·es.** To ascribe human characteristics to.

an·thro·po·mor·phous (ăn′thrə-pə-môr′fəs) *adj.* **1.** Having or suggesting human form and appearance. **2.** Ascribing human motivation, characteristics, or behavior to inanimate objects, animals, or natural phenomena. [Gk. *anthropomorphos* : *anthropos,* human being + *morphē,* shape.]

an·thro·pop·a·thism (ăn′thrə-pŏp′ə-thĭz′əm) *n.* The attribution of human feelings to nonhuman beings, objects, or natural phenomena. [Gk. *anthrōpopathēs,* with human feelings (*anthropos,* human being + *pathos,* feeling) + ISM.]

an·thro·poph·a·gus (ăn′thrə-pŏf′ə-gəs′) *n., pl.* **-gi** (-jī′). An eater of human flesh; cannibal. [Lat. *anthropophagus* < Gk. *anthrōpophagos,* maneating : *anthropos,* human being + *phagein,* to eat.] **—an′thro·po·phag′ic** (-pə-făj′ĭk), **an′thro·poph′a·gous** (-pŏf′ə-gəs) *adj.* **—an′thro·poph′a·gy** (-jē) *n.*

an·thur·i·um (ăn-tho͝or′ē-əm) *n.* Any of various tropical American plants of the genus *Anthurium,* many of which are cultivated for their showy flowers or foliage. [NLat. *Anthurium,* genus name : ANTH(O)- + Gk. *oura,* tail.]

an·ti (ăn′tī′, tē) *n., pl.* **-tis.** *Informal.* A person who is opposed to a group, policy, proposal, or practice. [< ANTI-.]

anti– or **ant–** *pref.* **1 a.** Opposite: *antimere.* **b.** Opposing; against: *anticlerical.* **c.** Counteracting; neutralizing: *antibody.* **2.** Reciprocal: *antilogarithm.* [Gk. < *anti,* opposite.]

an·ti·a·bor·tion (ăn′tē-ə-bôr′shən) *adj.* Opposed to abortion: *the antiabortion movement.* **—an′ti·a·bor′tion·ist** *n.*

an·ti·air·craft (ăn′tē-âr′krăft′) *adj.* Designed for defense, esp. from a surface position, against aircraft or missile attack. —*n.* An antiaircraft weapon.

an·ti·al·ler·gic (ăn′tē-ə-lûr′jĭk) also **an·ti·al·ler·gen·ic** (ăn′tē-ăl′ər-jĕn′ĭk) *adj.* Preventing or relieving allergies. **—an′ti·al′ler·gen′ic** *n.*

an·ti·an·xi·e·ty (ăn′tē-ăng-zī′ĭ-tē) *adj.* Preventing or relieving anxiety: *an antianxiety drug.*

an·ti·art (ăn′tē-ärt′) *n.* Art that rejects traditional art forms and theories.

an·ti·at·om (ăn′tē-ăt′əm) *n.* An atom composed of antiparticles.

an·ti·au·thor·i·tar·i·an (ăn′tē-ə-thôr′ĭ-târ′ē-ən, -thŏr′-) *adj.* Rejecting or hostile to authoritarians or authoritarianism. **—an′ti·au·thor·i·tar′i·an·ism** *n.*

an·ti·bac·ter·i·al (ăn′tē-băk-tîr′ē-əl) *adj.* Effective against bacteria.

an·ti·bal·lis·tic missile (ăn′tī-bə-lĭs′tĭk) *n.* A defensive missile designed to intercept and destroy a ballistic missile in flight.

an·ti·bar·y·on (ăn′tē-băr′ē-ŏn′) *n.* The antiparticle of the baryon.

an·ti·bi·o·sis (ăn′tē-bī-ō′sĭs) *n.* An association between two or more organisms that is injurious to one of them.

an·ti·bi·ot·ic (ăn′tē-bī-ŏt′ĭk) *n.* Any of various substances, such as penicillin and streptomycin, produced by certain fungi, bacteria, and other organisms, that are effective in inhibiting the growth of or destroying microorganisms and are widely used in the prevention and treatment of diseases. —*adj.* **1.** Of or pertaining to antibiotics. **2.** Of or pertaining to antibiosis. **—an′ti·bi·ot′i·cal·ly** *adv.*

an·ti·bod·y (ăn′tĭ-bŏd′ē) *n.* **1.** Any of various proteins in the blood that are generated in reaction to foreign proteins or polysaccharides, neutralize them, and thus produce immunity against certain microorganisms or their toxins. **2.** An object composed of antimatter.

an·ti·bus·ing (ăn′tē-bŭs′ĭng) *adj.* Opposed to the busing of students as a means of achieving racial balance in the public schools.

an·tic (ăn′tĭk) *n.* **1.** A ludicrous or extravagant act or gesture; caper; prank. **2.** *Archaic.* A clown; merry-andrew. —*adj.* Ludicrous; odd; fantastic. [Ital. *antico,* ancient < Lat. *antiquus,* old.] **—an′ti·cal·ly** *adv.*

an·ti·can·cer (ăn′tĭ-kăn′sər) also **an·ti·can·cer·ous** (-sər-əs) *adj.* Used against cancer: *anticancer drugs.*

an·ti·cat·a·lyst (ăn′tē-kăt′l-ĭst) *n.* **1.** A substance that retards or arrests a chemical reaction. **2.** A substance that reduces or destroys the effectiveness of a catalyst.

an·ti·cath·ode (ăn'tē-kăth'ōd') *n.* An electrode that is the target in a cathode ray tube, esp. in an x-ray tube.

an·ti·chlor (ăn'tĭ-klôr', -klōr') *n.* A substance, such as sodium thiosulfate, used to neutralize the excess chlorine or hypochlorite left after bleaching textiles, fiber, or paper pulp. [ANTI- + CHLOR(INE).] **—an'ti·chlo·ris'tic** (-klə-rĭs'tĭk) *adj.*

an·ti·cho·lin·er·gic (ăn'tē-kō'lə-nûr'jĭk) *adj.* Opposing or antagonistic to the physiological action of parasympathetic or other cholinergic nerve fibers. **—an'ti·cho'lin·er'gic** *n.*

an·ti·cho·lin·es·ter·ase (ăn'tē-kō'lə-nĕs'tə-rās', -rāz') *n.* Any substance that inhibits the activity of cholinesterase.

an·ti·christ (ăn'tĭ-krīst') *n.* **1.** An enemy of Christ. **2. Antichrist.** The epithet of the great antagonist who was expected by the early Church to set himself up against Christ in the last days before the Second Coming. [ME *Antecrist* < OFr. < Med. Lat. *Antichristus* < LLat. < Gk. *Antikhristos* : *anti-*, opposed to + *khristos,* anointed. —see CHRIST.]

an·tic·i·pant (ăn-tĭs'ə-pənt) *adj.* **1.** Coming or acting in advance. **2.** Expectant; anticipating. *—n.* One who anticipates.

an·tic·i·pate (ăn-tĭs'ə-pāt') *tr.v.* **-pat·ed, -pat·ing, -pates. 1.** To feel or realize beforehand; foresee. **2.** To look forward to, esp. with pleasure; expect. **3.** To act in advance so as to prevent; forestall. **4.** To foresee and fulfill in advance. **5.** To cause to happen in advance; accelerate. **6.** To use in advance, as income not yet available. **7.** To pay (a debt) before it is due. [Lat. *anticipare, anticipat-*, to take before : *ante-*, before + *capere,* to take.] **—an·tic'i·pat'a·ble** *adj.* **—an·tic'i·pa'tor** *n.* **—an·tic'i·pa·to'ry** (-pə-tôr'ē, -tōr'ē) *adj.*

Usage: Some traditionalists hold that *anticipate* should not be used simply as a synonym for *expect.* They would restrict its use to senses in which it suggests some advance action, either to fulfill (*anticipate my desires*) or to forestall (*anticipate her opponent's next move*). Others, including a majority of the Usage Panel, accept its use in the senses of "to feel or realize beforehand" and "to look forward to" (often with the implication of foretasting pleasure): *He is anticipating a visit with his son.*

an·tic·i·pa·tion (ăn-tĭs'ə-pā'shən) *n.* **1.** The act of anticipating. **2.** Something anticipated; expectation. **3.** Foreknowledge; intuition; presentiment. **4.** The use or assignment of funds, esp. from a trust fund, before legitimately available for use. **5.** *Mus.* The introduction of one note of a new chord before the previous chord is resolved.

an·tic·i·pa·tive (ăn-tĭs'ə-pā'tĭv, -pə-tĭv) *adj.* Inclined to or engaged in anticipation; expectant. **—an·tic'i·pa'tive·ly** *adv.*

an·ti·cler·i·cal (ăn'tē-klĕr'ĭ-kəl) *adj.* Opposed to the influence of the church or the clergy in political affairs. **—an'ti·cler'i·cal·ism** *n.*

an·ti·cli·max (ăn'tē-klī'măks') *n.* **1.** A decline viewed in disappointing contrast with a previous rise: *the anticlimax of a brilliant career.* **2.** Something trivial or commonplace that concludes a series of significant events. **3.** A sudden descent in speaking or writing from the impressive or significant to the ludicrous or inconsequential. **—an'ti·cli·mac'tic** (-klī-măk'tĭk) *adj.* **—an'ti·cli·mac'ti·cal·ly** *adv.*

an·ti·cli·nal (ăn'tē-klī'nəl) *adj.* Sloping downward in opposite directions, as an anticline.

an·ti·cline (ăn'tĭ-klīn') *n. Geol.* A fold with strata sloping downward on both sides from a common crest.

an·ti·clock·wise (ăn'tē-klŏk'wīz) *adv. & adj.* Counterclockwise.

an·ti·co·ag·u·lant (ăn'tē-kō-ăg'yə-lənt) *n.* A substance that suppresses or counteracts coagulation, esp. of the blood. *—adj.* Acting as an anticoagulant.

an·ti·co·in·ci·dence circuit (ăn'tē-kō-ĭn'sĭ-dəns) *n.* A specific binary logic element designed to provide input signals to a device according to fixed rules.

an·ti·con·vul·sant (ăn'tē-kən-vŭl'sənt) *n.* A drug used to prevent convulsions. **—an'ti·con·vul'sive** *adj.*

an·ti·cy·clone (ăn'tē-sī'klōn') *n.* An extensive system of winds spiraling outward from a high-pressure center, circling clockwise in the Northern Hemisphere and counterclockwise in the Southern Hemisphere. **—an'ti·cy·clon'ic** (-klŏn'ĭk) *adj.*

an·ti·de·pres·sant (ăn'tē-dĭ-prĕs'ənt) *n.* A drug used to prevent or treat depression. **—an'ti·de·pres'sive** *adj.*

an·ti·deu·ter·on (ăn'tē-do͞o'tə-rŏn', -dyo͞o'-) *n.* The antimatter equivalent of deuteron.

an·ti·dote (ăn'tĭ-dōt') *n.* **1.** A remedy or other agent to counteract the effects of a poison. **2.** Anything that relieves or counteracts an injurious effect. [Lat. *antidotum* < Gk. *antidoton* < *antididonai,* to give as a remedy against : *anti-*, against + *didonai,* to give.] **—an'ti·dot'al** (ăn'tĭ-dōt'l) *adj.* **—an'ti·dot'al·ly** *adv.*

Usage: *Antidote* may be followed by *to, for,* or *against: an antidote to boredom; an antidote for snakebite; an antidote against inflation.*

an·ti·e·lec·tron (ăn'tē-ĭ-lĕk'trŏn') *n.* A positron.

an·ti·en·zyme (ăn'tē-ĕn'zīm') *n.* A substance that neutralizes or counteracts an enzyme. **—an'ti·en'zy·mat'ic** (-zī-măt'ĭk, -zĭ-), **an'ti·en·zy'mic** (-zī'mĭk) *adj.*

an·ti·es·tab·lish·ment (ăn'tē-ĭ-stăb'lĭsh-mənt) *adj.* Marked by opposition or hostility to conventional social, political, or economic values or principles.

an·ti·feb·rile (ăn'tē-fĕb'rəl, -fē'brəl, -brīl') *adj.* Capable of reducing fever; antipyretic. *—n.* An antifebrile drug or agent.

an·ti·fed·er·al·ist also **An·ti·fed·er·al·ist** (ăn'tē-fĕd'ər-ə-lĭst, -fĕd'rə-lĭst) *n.* One who was opposed to the ratification of the U.S. Constitution. **—an'ti·fed'er·al·ism** *n.*

an·ti·fem·i·nist (ăn'tē-fĕm'ə-nĭst) *adj.* Opposed to feminism. **—an'ti·fem'i·nism** *n.* **—an'ti·fem'i·nist** *n.*

an·ti·fer·til·i·ty (ăn'tĭ-fər-tĭl'ĭ-tē, -tī) *adj.* Capable of reducing or destroying fertility; contraceptive.

an·ti·freeze (ăn'tĭ-frēz') *n.* A substance, often a liquid such as ethylene glycol or alcohol, mixed with another liquid to lower its freezing point.

an·ti·gal·ax·y (ăn'tē-găl'ək-sē) *n.* A galaxy comprised of antimatter.

an·ti·gen (ăn-'tĭ-jən) also **an·ti·gene** (-jēn') *n.* A substance that when introduced into the body stimulates the production of an antibody. **—an'ti·gen'ic** (-jĕn'ĭk) *adj.* **—an'ti·gen'i·cal·ly** *adv.* **—an'ti·ge·nic'i·ty** (-jə-nĭs'ĭ-tē) *n.*

An·tig·o·ne (ăn-tĭg'ə-nē) *n. Gk. Myth.* The daughter of Oedipus and Jocasta, who performed funeral rites over her brother's body in defiance of her uncle Creon. [Gk. *Antigonē.*]

an·ti·grav·i·ty (ăn'tē-grăv'ĭ-tē) *n.* The effect of reducing or canceling a gravitational field. *—adj.* Canceling or reducing gravity or protecting against its effect.

an·ti·he·li·um (ăn'tē-hē'lē-əm) *n.* The antimatter equivalent of helium.

an·ti·he·ro (ăn'tĭ-hîr'ō) *n.* A protagonist, as in a play, characterized by a lack of traditional heroic qualities, as courage.

an·ti·his·ta·mine (ăn'tē-hĭs'tə-mēn', -mĭn) *n.* Any of various drugs used to reduce physiological effects associated with histamine production in allergies and colds. **—an'ti·his'ta·min'ic** (-mĭn'ĭk) *adj.*

an·ti·hy·dro·gen (ăn'tē-hī'drə-jən) *n.* The antimatter equivalent of hydrogen.

an·ti-in·flam·ma·to·ry (ăn'tē-ĭn-flăm'ə-tôr'ē, -tōr'ē) *adj.* Acting against inflammation.

an·ti·knock (ăn'tĭ-nŏk') *n.* A substance, such as tetraethyl lead, added to gasoline to reduce engine knock.

an·ti·lep·ton (ăn'tē-lĕp'tŏn) *n.* The antiparticle of a lepton.

an·ti·log (ăn'tē-lôg', -lŏg') *n.* An antilogarithm.

an·ti·log·a·rithm (ăn'tē-lô'gə-rĭth'əm, -lŏg'ə-) *n.* The number for which a given logarithm stands; for example, where log *x* equals *y*, the *x* is the antilogarithm of *y*. **—an'ti·log'a·rith'mic** *adj.*

an·ti·ma·cas·sar (ăn'tē-mə-kăs'ər) *n.* A protective covering for the backs of chairs and sofas. [ANTI- + *Macassar,* a brand of hair oil.]

an·ti·mag·net·ic (ăn'tē-măg-nĕt'ĭk) *adj.* Impervious to the effect of a magnetic field; resistant to magnetization.

an·ti·ma·lar·i·al (ăn'tē-mə-lâr'ē-əl) *adj.* Effective against malaria. *—n.* An antimalarial drug.

an·ti·mat·ter (ăn'tĭ-măt'ər) *n.* Matter consisting of antiparticles and having positron-surrounded nuclei composed of antiprotons and antineutrons.

an·ti·mere (ăn'tĭ-mîr') *n. Biol.* A part or division corresponding to an opposite or similar part in an organism characterized by bilateral or radial symmetry. **—an'ti·mer'ic** (-mĕr'ĭk) *adj.*

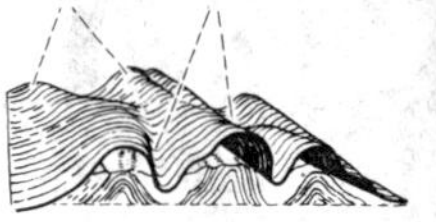

anticline
Sketch of a bed of limestone

an·ti·mi·cro·bi·al (ăn'tē-mī-krō'bē-əl) also **an·ti·mi·cro·bic** (-bĭk) *adj.* Capable of destroying or suppressing the growth of microorganisms. **—an'ti·mi·cro'bial** *n.*

an·ti·mis·sile missile (ăn'tē-mĭs'əl) *n.* A missile designed to intercept and destroy another missile in flight.

an·ti·mo·ni·al (ăn'tə-mō'nē-əl) *adj.* Of or containing antimony. *—n.* A medicine with antimony as an ingredient.

an·ti·mo·ny (ăn'tə-mō'nē) *n. Symbol* **Sb** A metallic element having four allotropic forms, the most common of which is a hard, extremely brittle, lustrous, silver-white, crystalline material. It is used in a wide variety of alloys, esp. with lead in battery plates, and in the manufacture of flame-proofing compounds, paints, semiconductor devices, and ceramic products. Atomic number 51; atomic weight 121.75; melting point 630.5°C; boiling point 1,380°C; specific gravity 6.691; valences 3, 5. [ME *antimonie* < Med. Lat. *antimonium.*]

antimony glance *n.* Stibnite.

an·ti·ne·o·plas·tic (ăn'tē-nē'ə-plăs'tĭk) *adj.* Inhibiting the growth or spread of neoplasms.

an·ti·neu·tri·no (ăn'tē-no͞o-trē'nō, -nyo͞o-) *n., pl.* **-nos.** The antiparticle of the neutrino.

an·ti·neu·tron (ăn'tē-no͞o'trŏn', -nyo͞o'-) *n.* The antiparticle of the neutron.

an·ti·node (ăn'tĭ-nōd') *n.* The region or point of maximum amplitude between adjacent nodes.

an·ti·no·mi·an (ăn'tĭ-nō'mē-ən) *n. Theol.* A member of a Christian sect holding that faith alone is necessary to salvation. [Med. Lat. *antinomus* : Gk. *anti-*, against + *nomos,* law.] **—an'ti·no'mi·an** *adj.* **—an'ti·no'mi·an·ism** *n.*

an·tin·o·my (ăn-tĭn'ə-mē) *n., pl.* **-mies. 1.** An apparent contradiction between valid principles or conclusions that seem equally necessary and reasonable. **2.** A conflict, opposition, or contradiction. [Lat. *antinomia* < Gk. : *anti-*, against + *nomos,* law.]

an·ti·nov·el (ăn′tē-nŏv′əl) *n.* A novel characterized by the absence of the traditional features of a work of fiction. **—an′ti·nov′el·ist** *n.*

an·ti·nu·cle·on (ăn′tē-nōō′klē-ŏn′, -nyōō′-) *n.* The antiparticle of a nucleon.

an·ti·ox·i·dant (ăn′tē-ŏk′sĭ-dənt) *n.* A chemical compound or substance that inhibits oxidation.

an·ti·par·ti·cle (ăn′tē-pär′tĭ-kəl) *n.* A subatomic particle, such as a positron, antiproton, or antineutron, having the same mass, average lifetime, spin, magnitude of magnetic moment, and magnitude of electric charge as the particle to which it corresponds but having the opposite sign of electric charge, opposite intrinsic parity, and opposite direction of magnetic moment.

an·ti·pas·to (ăn′tē-päs′tō) *n., pl.* **-tos** or **-ti** (-tē). An appetizer consisting of an assortment of smoked meats, fish, olives, tomatoes, hot peppers, cheese, and other ingredients, served with oil and vinegar. [Ital. : *anti-*, before (< Lat. *ante*) + *pasto,* food < Lat. *pastus* < *pascere,* to feed.]

reindeer

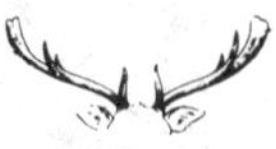

fallow deer

moose

antler

Anubis

an·tip·a·thet·ic (ăn-tĭp′ə-thĕt′ĭk) also **an·tip·a·thet·i·cal** (-ĭ-kəl) *adj.* **1.** Having an inherent feeling of aversion, repugnance, or opposition: *antipathetic to new ideas.* **2.** Causing a feeling of antipathy. **—an·tip′a·thet′i·cal·ly** *adv.*

an·tip·a·thy (ăn-tĭp′ə-thē) *n., pl.* **-thies. 1.** A strong feeling of aversion, repugnance, or opposition. **2.** An object of aversion. [Lat. *antipathia* < Gk. *antipatheia* : *anti-*, against + *pathos,* feeling.]

an·ti·pe·ri·od·ic (ăn′tē-pîr′ē-ŏd′ĭk) *adj.* Preventing regular recurrence of disease or fever. *—n.* An antiperiodic drug.

an·ti·per·son·nel (ăn′tē-pûr′sə-nĕl′) *adj.* Designed to inflict casualties on the military personnel or civilian population of an enemy country.

an·ti·per·spi·rant (ăn′tē-pûr′spər-ənt) *n.* A preparation applied to the skin to decrease or prevent excessive perspiration.

an·ti·phlo·gis·tic (ăn′tē-flə-jĭs′tĭk) *adj.* Reducing inflammation or fever. **—an′ti·phlo·gis′tic** *n.*

an·ti·phon (ăn′tə-fŏn′) *n.* **1.** A devotional composition sung responsively as part of a liturgy. **2.** A short liturgical text chanted responsively before a psalm or canticle. **3.** A response; answer: *a resounding antiphon of dissent.* [Fr. *antiphone* < Med. Lat. *antiphona,* sung responses. —see ANTHEM.]

an·tiph·o·nal (ăn-tĭf′ə-nəl) *adj.* **1.** Pertaining to or resembling an antiphon. **2.** Answering responsively, as in antiphony. **—an·tiph′o·nal·ly** *adv.*

an·tiph·o·nar·y (ăn-tĭf′ə-nĕr′ē) *n., pl.* **-ies.** A bound collection of antiphons, esp. of the responsive choral parts of the divine office.

an·tiph·o·ny (ăn-tĭf′ə-nē) *n., pl.* **-nies. 1.** Responsive or antiphonal singing or chanting. **2.** A composition that is sung responsively; antiphon. **3.** A sound or other effect that answers or echoes another.

an·tip·o·dal (ăn-tĭp′ə-dəl) *adj.* **1.** Of, pertaining to, or situated on the opposite side or sides of the earth. **2.** Diametrically opposed; exactly opposite.

an·ti·pode (ăn′tĭ-pōd′) *n.* A direct or diametrical opposite. [Back-formation from ANTIPODES.]

an·tip·o·des (ăn-tĭp′ə-dēz′) *pl.n.* **1.** Any two places or regions that are on opposite sides of the earth. **2.** *(used with a sing. or pl. verb).* Something that is the exact opposite or contrary of another. [ME < Lat. < Gk. < *antipous,* with the feet opposite : *anti-*, opposite + *pous,* foot.]

an·ti·pol·lu·tion (ăn′tē-pə-lōō′shən) *adj.* Intended to counteract or eliminate environmental pollution: *antipollution filters; antipollution laws.* **—an′ti·pol·lu′tion·ist** *n.*

an·ti·pope (ăn′tĭ-pōp′) *n.* A person claiming to be pope in opposition to the one chosen by church law. [ME < Med. Lat. *antipapa* : Lat. *anti-*, opposed to + *papa,* pope.]

an·ti·pov·er·ty (ăn′tē-pŏv′ər-tē) *adj.* Created or intended to alleviate poverty: *antipoverty programs.*

an·ti·pro·ton (ăn′tē-prō′tŏn′) *n.* The antiparticle of the proton.

an·ti·py·ret·ic (ăn′tē-pī-rĕt′ĭk) *adj.* Reducing or tending to reduce fever. *—n.* A medication that reduces fever. **—an′ti·py·re′sis** (-rē′sĭs) *n.*

an·ti·py·rine (ăn′tē-pī′rēn′) *n.* A white powder, $C_{11}H_{12}N_2O$, used to reduce fever and relieve pain. [Orig. a trademark.]

an·ti·quar·i·an (ăn′tĭ-kwâr′ē-ən) *adj.* **1.** Of or pertaining to antiquaries or the study of antiquities. **2.** Dealing in or having to do with old rare books. *—n.* An antiquary. **—an′ti·quar′i·an·ism** *n.*

an·ti·quark (ăn′tē-kwôrk) *n.* The antiparticle of a quark.

an·ti·quar·y (ăn′tĭ-kwĕr′ē) *n., pl.* **-ies.** A student of or dealer in antiquities. [Lat. *antiquarius* < *antiquus,* old.]

an·ti·quate (ăn′tĭ-kwāt′) *tr.v.* **-quat·ed, -quat·ing, -quates.** To make obsolete or old-fashioned. [Lat. *antiquare, antiquat-*, to leave in an old state < *antiquus,* old.] **—an′ti·qua′tion** *n.*

an·ti·quat·ed (ăn′tĭ-kwā′tĭd) *adj.* **1.** So old as to be no longer useful or suitable; obsolete: *antiquated laws.* **2.** Very old; aged. **—an′ti·quat′ed·ness** *n.*

an·tique (ăn-tēk′) *adj.* **1.** Of or belonging to ancient times, esp. of, from, or characteristic of ancient Greece or Rome. **2.** Belonging to, made in, or typical of an earlier period. **3.** Old-fashioned. *—n.* An object having special value because of its age, esp. a work of art or handicraft that is more than 100 years old. *—tr.v.* **-tiqued, -tiqu·ing, -tiques.** To give the appearance of an antique to. [Fr. < Lat. *antiquus,* old.] **—an·tique′ly** *adv.* **—an·tique′ness** *n.*

an·tiqu·er (ăn-tē′kər) *n.* One who treats or finishes new furniture so as to make it appear old or antique.

an·tiq·ui·ty (ăn-tĭk′wĭ-tē) *n., pl.* **-ties. 1.** Ancient times, esp. the times preceding the Middle Ages. **2.** The people, esp. the writers, of ancient times. **3.** The quality of being old or ancient; considerable age: *a carving of great antiquity.* **4.** Often **antiquities.** Something, as an object or relic, belonging to or dating from ancient times.

an·ti·ra·chit·ic (ăn′tē-rə-kĭt′ĭk) *adj.* Curing or preventing rickets. *—n.* An antirachitic drug or food.

an·tir·rhi·num (ăn′tə-rī′nəm) *n.* Any plant of the genus *Antirrhinum, as* a snapdragon. [NLat., genus name < Gk. *antirrhinon* : *anti-*, counterfeiting + *rhis,* nose.]

an·ti·scor·bu·tic (ăn′tē-skôr-byōō′tĭk) *adj.* Curing or preventing scurvy. *—n.* An antiscorbutic food or drug.

an·ti-Sem·ite (ăn′tē-sĕm′īt′) *n.* A person who is hostile toward or prejudiced against Jews. **—an′ti-Se·mit′ic** (-sə-mĭt′ĭk) *adj.* **—an′ti-Sem′i·tism** *n.*

an·ti·sep·sis (ăn′tĭ-sĕp′sĭs) *n.* The destruction of microorganisms that cause disease, fermentation, or putrefaction.

an·ti·sep·tic (ăn′tĭ-sĕp′tĭk) *adj.* **1.** Of, pertaining to, or designating antisepsis. **2.** Capable of producing antisepsis. **3.** Thoroughly clean. **4.** Devoid of enlivening or enriching qualities; austere. *—n.* An antiseptic drug or agent. **—an′ti·sep′ti·cal·ly** *adj.*

an·ti·se·rum (ăn′tĭ-sîr′əm) *n., pl.* **-rums** or **-ra** (-rə). Human or animal serum containing antibodies for at least one antigen.

an·ti·slav·er·y (ăn′tē-slā′və-rē, -slāv′rē) *adj.* Opposed to or against slavery. **—an′ti·slav′er·y** *n.*

an·ti·smog (ăn′tē-smŏg′, -smôg′) *adj.* Intended to counteract or eliminate smog: *antismog equipment for cars.*

an·ti·so·cial (ăn′tē-sō′shəl) *adj.* **1.** Shunning the society of others; not sociable. **2.** Opposed or hostile to the established social order; marked by or engaging in behavior that violates accepted mores: *drug abuse and other antisocial activity.* **—an′ti·so′cial·ly** *adv.*

an·ti·spas·mod·ic (ăn′tē-spăz-mŏd′ĭk) *adj.* Easing or preventing spasms. *—n.* An antispasmodic drug.

an·ti·stat·ic (ăn′tē-stăt′ĭk) also **an·ti·stat** (-tē-stăt′) *adj.* Preventing or inhibiting the buildup of static electricity.

an·tis·tro·phe (ăn-tĭs′trə-fē) *n.* **1.** In ancient Greek choral poetry or drama, the movement following and in the same meter as the strophe, sung while the chorus moves in the opposite direction from that of the strophe. **2.** The second stanza, and those like it, in a poem consisting of alternating stanzas in contrasting metric form. [LLat. < Gk. *antistrophē,* a turning back < *antistrephein,* to turn back : *anti-*, back + *strephein,* to turn.] **—an′ti·stroph′ic** (ăn′tĭ-strŏf′ĭk) *adj.* **—an′ti·stroph′i·cal·ly** *adv.*

an·ti·sub·ma·rine (ăn′tē-sŭb′mə-rēn′, -sŭb′mə-rēn′) *adj.* Designed to destroy enemy submarines.

an·ti·tank (ăn′tē-tăngk′) *adj.* Designed or used for combat against tanks or other armored vehicles.

an·tith·e·sis (ăn-tĭth′ĭ-sĭs) *n., pl.* **-ses** (-sēz′). **1.** Direct contrast; opposition. **2.** The direct or exact opposite. **3. a.** The juxtaposition of sharply contrasting ideas in balanced or parallel words, phrases, or grammatical structures, as *"He for God only, she for God in him"* (Milton). **b.** The second and contrasting part of such a juxtaposition. **4.** The second stage of the dialectic process. [LLat. < Gk., opposition < *antitithenai,* to oppose : *anti-*, against + *tithenai,* to set.]

an·ti·thet·i·cal (ăn′tĭ-thĕt′ĭ-kəl) also **an·ti·thet·ic** (-ĭk) *adj.* **1.** Pertaining to, of the nature of, or marked by antithesis. **2.** Directly opposed in every respect. [LLat. *antitheticus,* Gk. *antithetikos* < *antitethenai,* to oppose. —see ANTITHESIS.] **—an′ti·thet′i·cal·ly** *adv.*

an·ti·tox·ic (ăn′tē-tŏk′sĭk) *adj.* **1.** Counteracting a toxin or poison. **2.** Of or pertaining to an antitoxin.

an·ti·tox·in (ăn′tē-tŏk′sĭn) *n.* **1.** An antibody formed in response to and capable of neutralizing a poison of biological origin. **2.** An animal serum containing antitoxins.

an·ti·trades (ăn′tĭ-trādz′) *pl.n.* The westerly winds above the trade winds of the tropics, which become the westerly winds of the middle latitudes.

an·ti·trust (ăn′tē-trŭst′) *adj.* Opposing or concerned with the regulation of trusts, cartels, or similar business monopolies.

an·ti·tu·mor (ăn′tĭ-tōō′mər, -tyōō′-) also **an·ti·tu·mor·al** (-mər-əl) *adj.* Anticancer.

an·ti·tus·sive (ăn′tē-tŭs′ĭv) *adj.* Capable of relieving coughing. *—n.* An antitussive drug.

an·ti·type (ăn′tĭ-tīp′) *n.* **1.** One that is foreshadowed by or identified with an earlier symbol or type, as a figure in the New Testament who has a counterpart in the Old Testament. **2.** An opposite type. [Med. Lat. *antitypus* < Gk. *antitupos,* corresponding : *anti-*, opposite + *tupos,* impression.] **—an′ti·typ′i·cal** (-tĭp′ĭ-kəl) *adj.*

an·ti·ven·in (ăn′tē-vĕn′ĭn) *n.* **1.** An antitoxin active against venom. **2.** An antiserum containing an antivenin. [ANTI- + VEN(OM) + -IN.]

ant·ler (ănt′lər) *n.* One of a pair of hard, bony, deciduous growths, usually elongated and branched, that characteristically grow on the heads of male deer and related animals. [ME *aunteler* < OFr. *antoillier.*] —**ant'lered** (ănt'lərd) *adj.*

Ant·li·a (ănt'lē-ə) *n.* A constellation in the Southern Hemisphere near Hydra and Vela. [Lat. *antlia,* pump < Gk. *antlos,* bucket.]

ant lion *n.* **1.** Any insect of the family Myrmeleontidae, of which the adults resemble dragon flies. **2.** The larva of the ant lion, which digs holes to trap ants and other insects for food.

an·to·no·ma·sia (ăn'tə-nə-mā'zhə) *n.* **1.** The substitution of a title or epithet for a proper name, as in calling a king "His Majesty." **2.** The substitution of a personal name for a common noun to designate a member of a group or class, as in calling a libertine a "Don Juan." [Lat. < Gk. *antonomazein,* to name instead : *anti-,* instead of + *onomazein,* to name < *onoma,* name.]

an·to·nym (ăn'tə-nĭm') *n.* A word having a meaning opposite to a meaning of another word: *The word "light" is an antonym of "dark."* [ANT(I)- + -ONYM.] —**an'to·nym'ic** (-nĭm'ĭk) *adj.* —**an·ton'y·mous** (ăn-tŏn'ə-məs) *adj.* —**an·ton'y·my** *n.*

an·tre (ăn'tər) *n.* A cavern or cave. [Fr. < Lat. *antrum,* cave.]

an·trorse (ăn'trôrs') *adj. Biol.* Directed forward and upward. [NLat. *antrorsus,* perh. < Lat. *anterior,* before. —see ANTERIOR.] —**an'trorse'ly** *adv.*

an·trum (ăn'trəm) *n., pl.* **-tra** (-trə). A cavity, usually in bone, esp. either of the sinuses in the upper jaw opening into the nose. [LLat., cavity < Lat., cave < Gk. *antron.*] —**an'tral** *adj.*

A·nu·bis (ə-no͞o'bĭs, ə-nyo͞o'-) *n. Myth.* A jackal-headed Egyptian god who conducted the dead to judgment. [Lat. < Gk. *Anoubis,* of Egypt. orig.]

a·nu·ran (ə-no͝or'ən, ə-nyo͝or'-) *adj.* Of or pertaining to frogs and toads. —*n.* A frog or toad. [NLat. *Anura,* order of frogs and toads : AN- + Gk. *oura,* tail.]

an·u·re·sis (ăn'yə-rē'sĭs) *n.* **1.** Inability to urinate. **2.** Anuria. [AN- + Gk. *ourēsis,* urination < *ourein,* to urinate < *ouron,* urine.] —**an'u·ret'ic** (-rĕt'ĭk) *adj.*

a·nu·ri·a (ə-no͝or'ē-ə, ə-nyo͝or'-) *n.* **1.** The pathological condition characterized by failure to urinate. **2.** Anuresis. —**a·nu'ric** (ə-no͝or'ĭk, ə-nyo͝or'-) *adj.*

a·nu·rous (ə-no͝or'əs, ə-nyo͝or'-) *adj.* Having no tail; tailless.

a·nus (ā'nəs) *n., pl.* **a·nus·es.** The excretory opening of the alimentary canal. [Lat.]

an·vil (ăn'vĭl) *n.* **1.** A heavy block of iron or steel with a smooth, flat top on which metals are shaped by hammering. **2.** The fixed jaw in a set of calipers against which the object to be measured is placed. **3.** *Anat.* The incus. [ME *anvelt* < OE *anfilt.*]

anx·i·e·ty (ăng-zī'ĭ-tē) *n., pl.* **-ties.** **1 a.** A state of uneasiness and distress about future uncertainties; apprehension; worry. **b.** A cause of such uneasiness; worry. **2.** *Psychiat.* Intense fear or dread lacking an unambiguous cause or a specific threat. **3.** Eagerness or earnestness, often marked by uneasiness. [Lat. *anxietas* < *anxius,* anxious.]

Synonyms: *anxiety, worry, care, concern, solicitude.* These nouns express troubled states of mind. *Anxiety* suggests feelings of fear and concern detached from objective sources, feeding themselves, as it were. *Worry* implies persistent doubt or fear that produces strong mental agitation. *Care,* often in the plural, implies mental oppression of varying degree arising from heavy responsibilities. *Concern* has more to do with serious thought than with emotion, and stresses personal involvement in the source of mental unrest. *Solicitude* is active concern for the well-being of another person or persons.

anx·ious (ăngk'shəs, ăng'shəs) *adj.* **1 a.** Worried and distressed about some uncertain event or matter; uneasy. **b.** Attended with, showing, or causing such worry. **2.** Eagerly or earnestly desirous. [Lat. *anxius* < *angere,* to torment.] —**anx'ious·ly** *adv.* —**anx'ious·ness** *n.*

Usage: *Anxious* has a long history of use in America as a synonym for *eager,* but many insist that the distinction between the two words should be maintained and that *anxious* should be used only when its subject is apprehensive or concerned about the event anticipated. *I was anxious to get home before it rained,* but *I was eager* (not *anxious*) *to get home and have a nice dinner.*

an·y (ĕn'ē) *adj.* **1.** One or some, regardless of kind, quantity, or number: *Take any book you want. Are there any messages for me?* **2. a.** One or another selected at random: *Any child would do the same.* **b.** One or another without restriction or exception: *will accept any suggestion offered.* **3.** The whole amount of; all: *will turn over any profit to charity.* **4.** An indeterminate number or amount: *Is there any soda?* —*pron.* **1.** Any one or ones among three or more. **2.** Any quantity or part. —*adv.* To any degree or extent; at all: *didn't feel any better.* —See Usage note at **everyone.** [ME *ani* < OE *ænig.*]

Usage: The phrase *of any* is often used in informal contexts to mean "of all," as in *He is the best of any living authority on the subject.* A majority of the Usage Panel finds this construction unacceptable. *Any* is used to mean "at all" before a comparative adjective: *Is she any better? He is not any friendlier than before.* This use is entirely proper, but the related use of *any* all by itself to mean "at all" is considered informal. In writing, one should avoid sentences like *it didn't hurt any* or *if the child cries any, give her the bottle.*

an·y·bod·y (ĕn'ē-bŏd'ē, -bŭd'-ē) *pron.* Anyone. —*n.* A person of some consequence: *everybody who is anybody.* —See Usage note at **everyone.**

an·y·how (ĕn'ē-hou') *adv.* **1.** In any way or by any means whatever; at all. **2.** In any case. **3.** Carelessly; neglectfully.

an·y·more (ĕn'ē-môr', -mōr') *adv.* **1.** At the present; from now on: *mustn't talk anymore.* **2.** *Regional.* Nowadays.

Usage: In many dialects of American English, *anymore* is used to mean "nowadays," as in *the downtown garages are crowded anymore* or, sometimes, *anymore, she works a twelve-hour day.* This use is apt to confuse speakers who are not familiar with it and is not sufficiently well established to be acceptable in written prose.

an·y·one (ĕn'ē-wŭn', -wən) *pron.* Anybody; any person.

Usage: The one-word form *anyone* is used to mean "whatsoever person or persons." The two-word form *any one* is used to mean "whatever one (person or thing) of a group." *Anyone may join* means admission is open to everybody. *Any one may join* means admission is open to one person only. When followed by *of,* only *any one* can be used: *Any one* (not *anyone*) *of the boys could carry it by himself. Anyone* is often used in place of *everyone* in sentences like *She is the most thrifty person of anyone I know.* Such usage is unacceptable in formal writing to a majority of the Usage Panel.

an·y·place (ĕn'ē-plās') *adv.* To, in, or at any place; anywhere.

an·y·thing (ĕn'ē-thĭng') *pron.* Any object, occurrence, or matter whatever. —*adv.* To any degree or extent; at all. —***idiom.* anything but.** By no means; not at all.

an·y·time (ĕn'ē-tīm') *adv.* At any time.

an·y·way (ĕn'ē-wā') *adv.* Nevertheless; at any rate; anyhow.

an·y·ways (ĕn'ē-wāz') *adv. Nonstandard.* Anyway.

an·y·where (ĕn'ē-hwâr', -wâr') *adv.* **1.** To, in, or at any place. **2.** To any extent or degree; at all.

an·y·wise (ĕn'ē-wīz') *adv.* In any way or manner.

An·zac (ăn'zăk') *n.* A soldier who is from New Zealand or Australia. [A(USTRALIAN AND) N(EW) Z(EALAND) A(RMY) C(ORPS).]

A-O·K also **A-O·kay** (ā'ō-kā') *adj. & adv. Informal.* Perfectly OK.

A-one also **A-1** (ā'wŭn') *adj.* **1.** *Informal.* First-class; excellent; splendid. **2.** Having a hull and equipment in the best condition, as a ship.

a·o·rist (ā'ər-ĭst) *n. Gram.* A verb tense originally used in classical Greek that usually denotes past action without indicating completion, continuation, or repetition of this action. —*adj.* Of or in the aorist. [< Gk. *aoristos,* indefinite : *a-,* not + *horistos,* definable < *horizein,* to define < *horos,* boundary.] —**a'o·ris'tic** *adj.* —**a'o·ris'ti·cal·ly** *adv.*

a·or·ta (ā-ôr'tə) *n., pl.* **-tas** or **-tae** (-tē). *Anat.* The main trunk of the systemic arteries, carrying blood from the left side of the heart to the arteries of all limbs and organs except the lungs. [NLat. < Gk. *aortē* < *aeirein,* to lift.] —**a·or'tal, a·or'tic** *adj.*

a·ou·dad (ä'o͞o-dăd', ou'dăd') *n.* A wild sheep, *Ammotragus lervia,* of northern Africa, having long, curved horns and a beardlike growth of hair on the neck and chest. [Fr. < Berber *audad.*]

ap-¹ *pref.* Variant of **ad-.** Used before *p.*

ap-² *pref.* Variant of **apo-.**

a·pace (ə-pās') *adv.* At a rapid pace; swiftly. [ME *apas* < OFr. *à pas* : à, to (< Lat. *ad*) + *pas,* step. —see PACE.]

a·pache (ə-păsh') *n., pl.* **a·paches** (ə-păsh'). A member of the Parisian underworld. [Fr. < *Apache,* Apache Indian.]

A·pach·e (ə-păch'ē) *n., pl.* **Apache** or **-es.** **1.** A formerly nomadic tribe of North American Indians inhabiting the southwestern United States and northern Mexico. **2.** A member of the Apache. **3.** Any of the Athapascan languages of the Apache. [Mex. Sp., prob. < Zuñi *Apachu,* enemy.]

ap·a·nage (ăp'ə-nĭj) *n.* Variant of **appanage.**

ap·a·re·jo (ăp'ə-rā'hō, -rā'ō) *n., pl.* **-jos.** *Southwestern U.S.* A packsaddle made of a stuffed leather pad. [Mex. Sp. < Sp., equipment < *aparejar,* to prepare.]

a·part (ə-pärt') *adv.* **1. a.** In pieces. **b.** To pieces. **2. a.** Separately or at a distance in time, place, or position: *trees ten feet apart.* **b.** To one side; aside. **3.** One from another. **4.** Separately or aside for a particular function or purpose. **5.** Considered or viewed separately. **6.** Excepted or excluded from consideration; aside. —*adj.* Set apart; isolated. Used after a noun or in the predicate: *a race apart.* [ME < OFr. *à part,* to the side : *à,* to (< Lat. *ad*) + *part,* side < Lat. *pars.*]

apart from *prep.* With the exception of; besides.

a·part·heid (ə-pärt'hīt', -hāt') *n.* An official policy of racial segregation promulgated in the Republic of South Africa. [Afr. : Du. *apart,* separate < Fr. *à part,* apart + *-heid,* -hood.]

a·part·ment (ə-pärt'mənt) *n.* **1.** A room or suite of rooms designed for housekeeping and generally located in a building occupied by more than one household. **2.** A room. [Fr. *appartement* < Ital. *appartemento* < *appartare,* to separate < *a parte,* apart : *a,* to (< Lat. *ad*) + *parte,* side < Lat. *pars.*]

apartment house *n.* A building divided into apartments; apartment building.

anvil

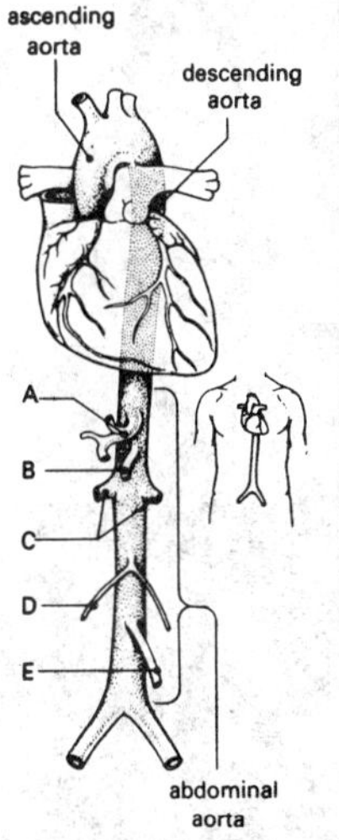

aorta
A. Celiac artery
B. Superior mesenteric artery
C. Renal arteries
D. Spermatic artery
E. Inferior mesenteric artery

aoudad

ape
Bornean orangutan

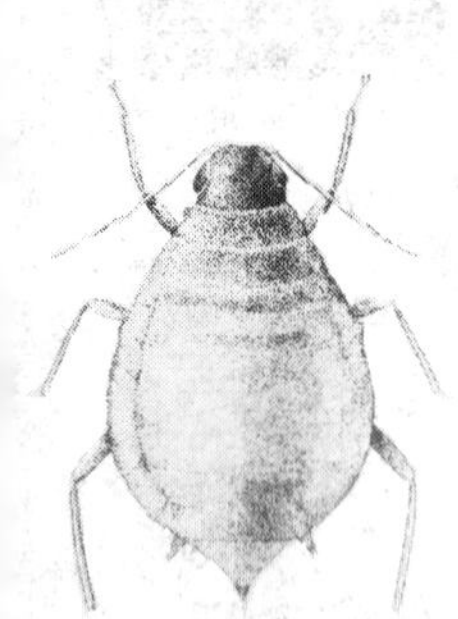
aphid

Aphrodite

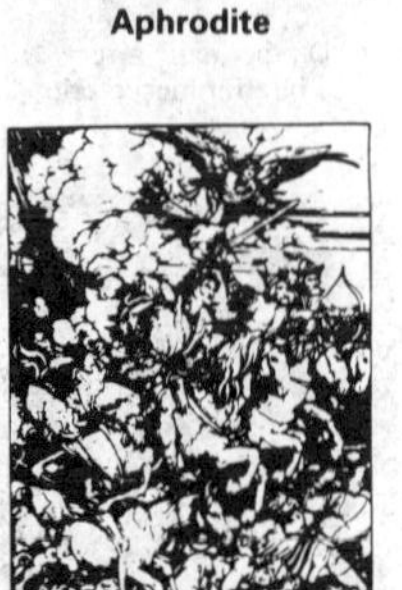
Apocalypse
"The Four Horsemen of the Apocalypse," woodcut by Albrecht Dürer

ap·a·tet·ic (ăp'ə-tĕt'ĭk) *adj.* Pertaining to or characteristic of coloration serving as natural camouflage. [Gk. *apatētikos,* deceptive < *apateuein,* to cheat < *apatē,* deceit.]

ap·a·thet·ic (ăp'ə-thĕt'ĭk) also **ap·a·thet·i·cal** (-ĭ-kəl) *adj.* **1.** Feeling or showing little or no emotion. **2.** Feeling or showing little or no interest; indifferent. [< APATHY.] **—ap'a·thet'i·cal·ly** *adv.*

ap·a·thy (ăp'ə-thē) *n.* **1.** Lack of emotion or feeling. **2.** Lack of interest in things generally found exciting, interesting, or moving; indifference. [Gk. *apatheia* < *apathēs,* without feeling : *a-,* without + *pathos,* feeling.]

ap·a·tite (ăp'ə-tīt') *n.* A natural, variously colored calcium fluoride phosphate, $Ca_5F(PO_4)_3$, with chlorine, hydroxyl, or carbonate sometimes replacing the fluoride. It is a source of phosphorus compounds and is used in the manufacture of fertilizers. [G. *Apatit* < Gk. *apatē,* deceit (from its often being mistaken for other minerals).]

ape (āp) *n.* **1. a.** Any of various large, tailless Old World primates of the family Pongidae, including the chimpanzee, gorilla, gibbon, and orangutan. **b.** Any monkey. **2.** A mimic or imitator. **3.** *Informal.* A clumsy, ill-bred, coarse person. *—tr.v.* **aped, ap·ing, apes.** To imitate the actions of; mimic. [ME < OE *apa.*] **—ap'er** *n.*

a·peak (ə-pēk') *adv.* & *adj. Naut.* In a vertical or almost vertical position or direction. [Fr. *à pic* : *à,* to (< Lat. *ad*) + *pic,* peak.]

ape-man (āp'măn') *n.* Any of several extinct primates considered intermediate between apes and modern man.

a·per·çu (ä'pĕr-sü') *n., pl.* **-çus** (-sü'). A short outline or summary. [Fr.]

a·pe·ri·ent (ə-pîr'ē-ənt) *adj.* Gently purgative; laxative. *—n.* A mild laxative. [Lat. *aperiens,* pr.part. of *aperire,* to open.]

a·pe·ri·od·ic (ā'pîr-ē-ŏd'ĭk) *adj.* Occurring without periodicity; irregular. **—a'pe·ri·od'i·cal·ly** *adv.* **—a·pe'ri·o·dic'i·ty** (-ə-dĭs'ĭ-tē) *n.*

a·pé·ri·tif (ä-pĕr'ĭ-tēf') *n.* A drink of alcoholic liquor or wine taken to stimulate the appetite before a meal. [Fr. < OFr. *aperitif,* purgative < Med. Lat. *aperitivus* < Lat. *aperire,* to open.]

ap·er·ture (ăp'ər-chər) *n.* **1.** A hole, gap, slit, or other opening; orifice. **2.** A usually adjustable opening in an optical instrument that limits the amount of light passing through a lens. [Lat. *apertura* < *apertus,* open, p.part. of *aperire,* to open.] **—ap'er·tur'al** *adj.*

aperture card *n.* A punched card upon which some portion of a microfilmed document is mounted.

a·pet·al·ous (ā-pĕt'l-əs) *adj. Bot.* Having no petals. **—a·pet'al·y** (ā-pĕt'l-ē) *n.*

a·pex (ā'pĕks') *n., pl.* **a·pex·es** or **a·pi·ces** (ā'pĭ-sēz', ăp'ĭ-). **1.** The highest point of something; vertex: *the apex of the hill.* **2.** The culmination, as of an activity or effort: *the apex of his career.* **3.** The pointed end of something; tip. [Lat.]

a·phaer·e·sis or **a·pher·e·sis** (ə-fĕr'ĭ-sĭs) *n., pl.* **-ses** (-sēz'). The loss of one or more letters or sounds from the beginning of a word, as in *most* for *almost.* [LLat. < Gk. *aphairesis,* removal < *aphairein,* to take away from : *apo-,* away from + *hairein,* to take.] **—aph'ae·ret'ic** (ăf'ə-rĕt'ĭk) *adj.*

a·pha·gi·a (ə-fā'jē-ə, -jə) *n.* Inability to swallow.

aph·a·nite (ăf'ə-nīt') *n.* Any dense, homogeneous rock with constituents so fine that they cannot be seen by the naked eye. [Fr. < Gk. *aphanēs,* unseen : *a-,* not + *phainesthai,* to appear < *phainein,* to show.] **—aph'a·nit'ic** (-nĭt'ĭk) *adj.*

a·pha·sia (ə-fā'zhə) *n.* Partial or total loss of the ability to articulate ideas in any form, resulting from brain damage. [Gk. < *aphatos,* speechless : *a-,* not + *phanai,* to speak.] **—a·pha'si·ac'** (-zē-ăk') *n.* **—a·pha'sic** (-zĭk, -sĭk) *adj.* & *n.*

a·phe·li·on (ə-fē'lē-ən, ə-fēl'yən) *n., pl.* **-li·a** (-lē-ə). The orbital point on a planetary orbit farthest from the sun. [NLat. : Gk. *apo-,* away from + Gk. *hēlios,* sun.]

a·phe·li·o·trop·ic (ə-fē'lē-ə-trŏp'ĭk) *adj.* Turning away from the sun or source of light, as roots do. **—a·phe'li·o·trop'i·cal·ly** *adv.* **—a·phe'li·ot'ro·pism** (-ŏt'rə-pĭz'əm) *n.*

a·pher·e·sis (ə-fĕr'ĭ-sĭs) *n.* Variant of **aphaeresis.**

aph·e·sis (ăf'ĭ-sĭs) *n., pl.* **-ses** (-sēz'). The loss of a short unstressed vowel from the beginning of a word, as in *squire* for *esquire.* [Gk., a release < *aphienai,* to let go : *apo-,* away + *hienai,* to send.] **—a·phet'ic** (ə-fĕt'ĭk) *adj.* **—a·phet'i·cal·ly** *adv.*

a·phid (ā'fĭd, ăf'ĭd) *n.* Any of various small, soft-bodied insects of the family Aphididae, which feed by sucking sap from plants. [< NLat. *Aphis, Aphid-,* type genus.] **—a·phid'i·an** (ə-fĭd'ē-ən) *adj.* & *n.*

a·phi·des (ā'fĭ-dēz', ăf'ĭ-) *n.* Plural of **aphis.**

aphid lion *n.* The larva of any of several insects of the family Chrysopidae, such as the lacewing, that feed on aphids.

a·phis (ā'fĭs, ăf'ĭs) *n., pl.* **a·phi·des** (ā'fĭ-dēz', ăf'ĭ-). An aphid, esp. one of the genus *Aphis.* [NLat. *Aphis,* genus name.]

a·pho·ni·a (ā-fō'nē-ə) *n.* Loss of speech or voicelessness caused by disease or injury to the organs of speech. [Gk. < *aphonos,* voiceless : *a-,* without + *phonē,* voice.] **—a·phon'ic** (ā-fŏn'ĭk, ā-fō'nĭk) *adj.*

aph·o·rism (ăf'ə-rĭz'əm) *n.* **1.** A brief statement of a principle. **2.** A tersely phrased statement of a truth or opinion; adage. [Fr. *aphorisme* < OFr. < Med. Lat. *aphorismus* < Gk. *aphorismos* < *aphorizein,* to distinguish : *apo-,* off + *horos,* boundary.] **—aph'o·ris'tic** (-rĭs'tĭk) *adj.* **—aph'o·ris'ti·cal·ly** *adv.*

aph·o·rize (ăf'ə-rīz') *intr.v.* **-rized, -riz·ing, -riz·es.** To express in or as if in aphorisms.

a·pho·tic (ā-fō'tĭk) *adj.* Without light.

aph·ro·dis·i·ac (ăf'rə-dĭz'ē-ăk') *adj.* Stimulating or intensifying sexual desire. *—n.* An aphrodisiac drug or food. [Gk. *aphrodisiakos* < *aphrodisia,* sexual pleasures < *Aphroditē,* Aphrodite.] **—aph'ro·di·si'a·cal** (ăf'rə-dĭ-zī'ə-kəl) *adj.*

Aph·ro·di·te (ăf'rə-dī'tē) *n.* **1.** *Gk. Myth.* The goddess of love and beauty. **2. aphrodite.** A brightly colored butterfly, *Argynnis aphrodite,* of North America. [Gk. *Aphroditē.*]

a·phyl·lous (ā-fĭl'əs) *adj. Bot.* Bearing no leaves. [Gk. *aphullos* : *a-,* without + *phullon,* leaf.] **—a'phyl'ly** (ā'fĭl'ē) *n.*

a·pi·an (ā'pē-ən) *adj.* Of or pertaining to bees. [Lat. *apianus* < *apis,* bee.]

a·pi·ar·i·an (ā'pē-âr'ē-ən) *adj.* Pertaining to bees or to the keeping and care of bees. *—n.* An apiarist.

a·pi·a·rist (ā'pē-ə-rĭst, ā'pē-ĕr'ĭst) *n.* A beekeeper.

a·pi·ar·y (ā'pē-ĕr'ē) *n., pl.* **-ies.** A place where bees and beehives are kept, esp. a place where bees are raised for their honey. [Lat. *apiarium,* beehive < *apis,* bee.]

ap·i·cal (ăp'ĭ-kəl, ā'pĭ-) *adj.* **1.** Of, pertaining to, located at, or constituting an apex. **2.** Pertaining to consonants articulated with the tip of the tongue, as *t, d,* and *s.* [NLat. *apicalis* < Lat. *apex,* top.] **—ap'i·cal·ly** *adv.*

a·pi·ces (ā'pĭ-sēz', ăp'ĭ-) *n.* A plural of **apex.**

a·pic·u·late (ə-pĭk'yə-lĭt) *adj.* Ending with a sharp, abrupt tip: *an apiculate leaf.* [< NLat. *apiculus,* sharp point, dim. of Lat. *apex,* point.]

a·pi·cul·ture (ā'pĭ-kŭl'chər) *n.* The raising and care of bees. [Lat. *apis,* bee + CULTURE.] **—a'pi·cul'tur·al** *adj.* **—a'pi·cul'tur·ist** *n.*

a·piece (ə-pēs') *adv.* To or for each one; each: *an apple apiece.* [ME *a pece* : *a,* by + *pece,* piece.]

A·pis (ā'pĭs) *n.* A sacred bull of the ancient Egyptians. [Lat. < Gk., of Egypt. orig.]

ap·ish (ā'pĭsh) *adj.* **1.** Resembling an ape. **2.** Slavishly or foolishly imitative. **3.** Silly; tricky; mischievous. **—ap'ish·ly** *adv.* **—ap'ish·ness** *n.*

a·piv·o·rous (ā-pĭv'ər-əs) *adj.* Feeding on bees. [Lat. *apis,* bee + -VOROUS.]

APL (ā'pē-ĕl') *n.* A computer programming language designed for use at remote terminals. [A + P(ROGRAMMING) + L(ANGUAGE).]

a·pla·cen·tal (ā'plə-sĕn'tl) *adj.* Having no placenta, as marsupials and monotremes.

ap·la·nat·ic (ăp'lə-năt'ĭk) *adj.* Of or pertaining to optical systems that correct for spherical aberration and coma. [< Gk. *aplanētos,* unable to go astray : *a-,* not + *planētos,* wandering < *planasthai,* to wander.]

a·pla·sia (ə-plā'zhə, -zhē-ə) *n.* Defective development or congenital absence of tissue, of an organ, or of an organic part.

a·plas·tic (ā-plăs'tĭk) *adj.* **1.** Lacking form. **2.** *Pathol.* Unable to form or regenerate tissue. **3.** *Pathol.* Of or relating to aplasia.

a·plen·ty (ə-plĕn'tē) *adj.* Being in abundance. *—adv.* **1.** In abundance. **2.** To an extreme degree.

ap·lite (ăp'līt') *n.* A fine-grained, light-colored granitic rock consisting primarily of orthoclase and quartz. [G. *Aplit* : Gk. *haplous,* single + *-it,* -ite.] **—ap·lit'ic** (ă-plĭt'ĭk) *adj.*

a·plomb (ə-plŏm', ə-plŭm') *n.* Self-confidence; poise; assurance. [Fr., balance < OFr. *à aplomb,* perpendicularly : *à,* according to (< Lat. *ad*) + *plomb,* lead weight < Lat. *plumbum,* lead.]

ap·ne·a also **ap·noe·a** (ăp-nē'ə, ăp'nē-ə) *n.* Transient suspension of respiration. [NLat. < Gk. *apnoia* : *a-,* without + *pnoē,* breathing < *pnein,* to breathe.] **—ap·ne'ic** *adj.*

apo– or **ap–** *pref.* **1. a.** Away from; off: *apheliotropic.* **b.** Separate: *apocarpous.* **2.** Without; not: *apogamy.* **3.** Related to; derived from: *apomorphine.* **4.** Metasomatic: *apophyllite.* [Gk. < *apo,* away from.]

A·poc·a·lypse (ə-pŏk'ə-lĭps') *n.* **1.** The last book of the New Testament, Revelation. See table at **Bible. 2. apocalypse.** A prophetic disclosure; revelation. [ME *Apocalipse* < LLat. *Apocalipsis* < Gk. *apokalupsis,* revelation < *apokaluptein,* to uncover : *apo-,* away + *kaluptein,* to cover.]

a·poc·a·lyp·tic (ə-pŏk'ə-lĭp'tĭk) also **a·poc·a·lyp·ti·cal** (-tĭ-kəl) *adj.* Of or pertaining to a prophetic disclosure or revelation. **—a·poc'a·lyp'ti·cal·ly** *adv.*

ap·o·carp (ăp'ə-kärp') *n.* An apocarpous fruit. [Back-formation < APOCARPOUS.]

ap·o·car·pous (ăp'ə-kär'pəs) *adj. Bot.* Having distinctly separated carpels. **—ap'o·car'py** (ăp'ə-kär'pē) *n.*

ap·o·chro·mat·ic (ăp'ə-krō-măt'ĭk) *adj.* Corrected for both chromatic and spherical aberration, as a lens.

a·poc·o·pe (ə-pŏk'ə-pē) *n.* The loss of one or more letters or sounds from the end of a word, as in *goin'* for *going.* [Lat. < Gk. *apokopē* < *apokoptein,* to cut off : *apo-,* off + *koptein,* to cut.]

ap·o·crine (ăp'ə-krĭn, -krīn', -krēn') *adj.* Of or pertaining to a gland that loses part of its cytoplasm in secretion. [< Gk. *apokrinein,* to set apart : *apo-,* away + *krinein,* to separate.]

A·poc·ry·pha (ə-pŏk'rə-fə) *n. (used with a sing. or pl. verb).* **1.** The 14 biblical books included in the Vulgate but considered uncanonical by Protestants because they are not part of the Hebrew Scriptures; 11 are accepted in the Roman Catholic canon. See table at **Bible**. **2.** Various early Christian writings proposed as additions to the New Testament but rejected by the major canons. **3. apocrypha.** Any writings of questionable authorship or authenticity. [ME *Apocripha* < LLat. *apocryphus,* spurious < Gk. *apokruphos,* hidden : *apo-,* away + *kruptein,* to hide.]

a·poc·ry·phal (ə-pŏk′rə-fəl) *adj.* **1.** Of questionable authorship or authenticity. **2.** False; counterfeit. **3. Apocryphal.** Of or having to do with the Apocrypha. **—a·poc′ry·phal·ly** *adv.*

ap·o·dal (ăp′ə-dəl) also **ap·o·dus** (-dəs) *adj.* Having no limbs, feet, or footlike appendages. [< Gk. *apous, apod-* : *a-,* without + *pous,* foot.]

ap·o·dic·tic (ăp′ə-dĭk′tĭk) *adj.* Clearly proven or demonstrated; incontestable. [Lat. *apodicticus* < Gk. *apodeiktikos* < *apodeiknunai,* to demonstrate : *apo,* away from + *deiknunai,* to show.] **—ap′o·dic′ti·cal·ly** *adv.*

a·pod·o·sis (ə-pŏd′ə-sĭs) *n., pl.* **-ses** (-sēz′). The clause stating the conclusion or consequence of a conditional sentence. [Gk. < *apodidonai,* to give back : *apo-,* away + *didonai,* to give.]

ap·o·dous (ăp′ə-dəs) *adj.* Apodal.

ap·o·en·zyme (ăp′ō-ĕn′zīm′) *n.* A protein requiring a coenzyme to function as an enzyme.

a·pog·a·my (ə-pŏg′ə-mē) *n.* The production of a new plant from a prothallus by budding, without sexual reproduction, as in ferns. **—ap′o·gam′ic** (ăp′ə-găm′ĭk), **a·pog′a·mous** (ə-pŏg′ə-məs) *adj.*

ap·o·gee (ăp′ə-jē) *n.* **1.** The point in the orbit of the moon or of an artificial satellite most distant from the earth. **2.** The farthest or highest point; apex. [Fr. *apogée* < NLat. *apogaeum* < Gk. *apogaion* < *apogaios,* far from the earth : *apo-,* away from + *gaia,* earth.] **—ap′o·ge′an** (-jē′ən) *adj.*

a·po·lit·i·cal (ā′pə-lĭt′ĭ-kəl) *adj.* **1.** Having no association with or interest in politics. **2.** Having no political importance. **—a′po·lit′i·cal·ly** *adv.*

A·pol·lo (ə-pŏl′ō) *n.* **1.** *Gk. Myth.* The god of the sun, prophecy, music, medicine, and poetry. **2. apollo.** Any young man of great physical beauty. [Lat. < Gk. *Apollōn.*]

Ap·ol·lo·ni·an (ăp′ə-lō′nē-ən) *adj.* **1.** Of or pertaining to Apollo. **2. apollonian.** Of a theoretical or rational nature; clearly defined and well-ordered; harmonious. **3. apollonian.** Noble; dignified; serene.

a·pol·o·get·ic (ə-pŏl′ə-jĕt′ĭk) *adj.* **1.** Making or expressing an apology. **2.** Explaining or defending in speech or writing. *—n.* A formal defense or apology. **—a·pol′o·get′i·cal·ly** *adv.*

a·pol·o·get·ics (ə-pŏl′ə-jĕt′ĭks) *n. (used with a sing. verb).* The branch of theology that deals with the defense and proof of Christianity.

ap·o·lo·gi·a (ăp′ə-lō′jē-ə, -jə) *n.* A formal defense or justification. [LLat., apology.]

a·pol·o·gist (ə-pŏl′ə-jĭst) *n.* A person who argues in defense or justification of another person or cause.

a·pol·o·gize (ə-pŏl′ə-jīz′) *intr.v.* **-gized, -giz·ing, -giz·es. 1.** To make excuse for or regretful acknowledgment of a fault or offense. **2.** To make a formal defense or justification in speech or writing. **—a·pol′o·giz′er** *n.*

ap·o·logue (ăp′ə-lôg′, -lŏg′) *n.* A moral fable. [Fr. < Lat. *apologus* < Gk. *apologos* : *apo-,* away + *logos,* speech.]

a·pol·o·gy (ə-pŏl′ə-jē) *n., pl.* **-gies. 1.** A statement of acknowledgment expressing regret or asking pardon for a fault or offense. **2.** A formal justification or defense. **3.** An inferior substitute. [OFr. *apologie* < LLat. *apologia* < Gk. : *apo-,* away + *logos,* speech.]

a·po·lune (ăp′ə-lo͞on′) *n.* The point of an orbit around the moon farthest from the moon's center. [APO- + Lat. *luna,* moon.]

ap·o·mict (ăp′ə-mĭkt′) *n.* An organism that is the result of apomixis. [Back-formation < E. *apomictic,* produced by apomixis.] **—ap′o·mic′tic** *adj.*

ap·o·mix·is (ăp′ə-mĭk′sĭs) *n.* A rare reproductive process in which a new individual is produced from a female cell or cells other than the egg cell, often in a manner that mimics sexual reproduction. [NLat. : APO- + Gk. *mixis,* sexual intercourse < *meignunai,* to have sexual intercourse.]

ap·o·mor·phine (ăp′ə-môr′fēn′) *n.* A poisonous white crystalline alkaloid, $C_{17}H_{17}NO_2$, derived from morphine and used medicinally as an expectorant, emetic, and hypnotic.

ap·o·neu·ro·sis (ăp′ə-no͝o-rō′sĭs, -nyo͝o-) *n., pl.* **-ses** (-sēz′). A sheetlike membrane, resembling a flattened tendon, that invests a muscle or connects it to its insertion. [Gk. *aponeurōsis* < *aponeurousthai,* to become tendinous : *apo-,* away + *neuron,* sinew.] **—ap′o·neu·rot′ic** (-rŏt′ĭk) *adj.*

ap·o·phthegm (ăp′ə-thĕm′) *n.* Variant of **apothegm.**

a·poph·y·ge (ə-pŏf′ə-jē) *n.* The curvature at the top and bottom of the shaft of a column. [Gk. *apophugē* : *apo-,* away + *phugē,* flight.]

a·poph·yl·lite (ə-pŏf′ə-līt′, ăp′ə-fĭl′īt′) *n.* A white, pale-pink, or pale-green crystalline mineral, essentially $KCa_4FSi_4O_{10}\cdot 8H_2O$.

a·poph·y·sis (ə-pŏf′ĭ-sĭs) *n., pl.* **-ses** (-sēz′). **1.** *Biol.* A swelling, projection, or outgrowth of an organ or part. **2.** *Geol.* A branch from a dike or vein. [NLat. < Gk. *apophusis* : *apo-,* off from + *phusis,* growth < *phuein,* to grow.] **—a·poph′y·sate′** (-sāt′), **a·poph′y·se′al** (ə-pŏf′ə-sē′əl) *adj.*

ap·o·plec·tic (ăp′ə-plĕk′tĭk) *adj.* **1.** Of, pertaining to, or causing apoplexy. **2.** Having or exhibiting symptoms of apoplexy. **3.** Such as can cause apoplexy: *an apoplectic fury.* **—ap′o·plec′ti·cal·ly** *adv.*

ap·o·plex·y (ăp′ə-plĕk′sē) *n.* Sudden loss of muscular control, with diminution or loss of sensation and consciousness, resulting from rupture or blocking of a blood vessel in the brain. [ME *apoplexie* < OFr. < LLat. *apoplexia* < Gk. < *apoplēssein,* to cripple by a stroke : *apo-* (intensive) + *plēssein,* to strike.]

a·port (ə-pôrt′, ə-pōrt′) *adv. Naut.* On or toward the port or left side.

ap·o·se·le·ne (ăp′ō-sə-lē′nē) *n.* Apolune. [APO- + Gk. *selene,* moon.]

ap·o·si·o·pe·sis (ăp′ə-sī′ə-pē′sĭs) *n., pl.* **-ses** (-sēz′). A sudden breaking off of a thought in the middle of a sentence, as though the speaker were unwilling or unable to continue. [LLat. < Gk. *aposiōpēsis* < *aposiōpan,* to become silent : *apo-* (intensive) + *siōpan,* to be silent < *siōpē,* silence.] **—ap′o·si′o·pet′ic** (-pĕt′ĭk) *adj.*

a·pos·ta·sy (ə-pŏs′tə-sē) *n., pl.* **-sies.** An abandonment of one's religious faith, political party, cause, or principles. [ME *apostasie* < LLat. *apostasia,* defection < Gk. *aphistanai,* to revolt : *apo-,* away from + *histanai,* to stand.]

a·pos·tate (ə-pŏs′tāt′, -tĭt) *n.* One who is guilty of apostasy. *—adj.* Guilty of apostasy. [ME *apostata* < LLat. < Gk. *apostatēs* < *aphistanai,* to revolt. —see APOSTASY.]

a·pos·ta·tize (ə-pŏs′tə-tīz′) *intr.v.* **-tized, -tiz·ing, -tiz·es.** To be guilty of apostasy.

a pos·te·ri·o·ri (ä′pō-stîr′ē-ôr′ē, -ôr′ī′, -ōr′ī′, ā′) *adj. Logic.* Denoting reasoning from facts or particulars to general principles or from effects to causes; inductive; empirical. [Lat., from the subsequent.]

a·pos·tle (ə-pŏs′əl) *n.* **1. Apostle.** One of a group made up esp. of the 12 disciples chosen by Christ to preach his gospel. **2.** A missionary of the early Christian Church. **3.** A leader of the first Christian mission to a country or region. **4.** One of the 12 members of the Mormon administrative council. **5.** One who leads or advocates a cause or movement: *an apostle of conservation.* [ME < OE *apostol* < LLat. *apostolus* < Gk. *apostulos,* messenger < *apostellein,* to send off : *apo-,* away from + *stellein,* to send.]

Apostles' Creed *n.* A Christian creed traditionally ascribed to the 12 Apostles.

a·pos·to·late (ə-pŏs′tə-lāt′, -lĭt) *n.* **1.** The office, duties, or mission of an apostle. **2.** An association of individuals for the dissemination of a religion or a doctrine. [LLat. *apostolatus* < *apostolus,* apostle.]

ap·os·tol·ic (ăp′ə-stŏl′ĭk) *adj.* **1.** Of, pertaining to, or contemporary with the 12 Apostles. **2.** Of or pertaining to the faith, teaching, or practice of the 12 Apostles. **3.** Of or pertaining to the pope as successor of Saint Peter.

Apostolic Father *n.* A church father who received personal instruction from the 12 Apostles or from their disciples.

a·pos·tro·phe¹ (ə-pŏs′trə-fē) *n.* The superscript sign (') used to indicate the omission of a letter or letters from a word, the possessive case, and certain plurals, esp. those of numbers and letters. [Fr. < LLat. *apostrophos* < Gk. < *apostrophein,* to turn away : *apo-,* away + *strephein,* to turn.] **—ap′os·troph′ic** (ăp′ə-strŏf′ĭk) *adj.*

a·pos·tro·phe² (ə-pŏs′trə-fē) *n.* A digression in discourse, esp. a turning away from an audience to address an absent or imaginary person. [Lat. < Gk. < *apostrephein,* to turn away. —see APOSTROPHE¹.] **—ap′os·troph′ic** (ăp′ə-strŏf′ĭk) *adj.*

a·pos·tro·phize (ə-pŏs′trə-fīz′) *tr. & intr.v.* **-phized, -phiz·ing, -phiz·es.** To address by or speak or write in apostrophe.

apothecaries' measure *n.* A system of liquid volume measure used in pharmacy.

apothecaries' weight *n.* A system of weights used in pharmacy and based on an ounce equal to 480 grains and a pound equal to 12 ounces.

a·poth·e·car·y (ə-pŏth′ĭ-kĕr′ē) *n., pl.* **-ries.** One who prepares and sells drugs and medicines; pharmacist. [ME *apotecarie* < Med. Lat. *apothecarius* < LLat., clerk < Lat. *apotheca,* storehouse < Gk. *apothēke* < *apotithenai,* to store : *apo-,* away + *tithenai,* to put.]

ap·o·the·ci·um (ăp′ə-thē′sē-əm, -shē-) *n., pl.* **-ci·a** (-sē-ə, -shē-ə). An open disk-shaped or cup-shaped fruiting body in certain fungi, lined with a spore-bearing layer. [NLat. < Lat. *apotheca,* storehouse. —see APOTHECARY.] **—ap′o·the′cial** (-shəl) *adj.*

ap·o·thegm also **ap·o·phthegm** (ăp′ə-thĕm′) *n.* A terse and witty instructive saying; maxim. [Gk. *apophegma* < *apophthengesthai,* to speak plainly : *apo-,* away + *phthengesthai,* to speak.] **—ap′o·theg·mat′ic** (-thĕg-măt′ĭk), **ap′o·theg·mat′i·cal** (-ĭ-kəl) *adj.* **—ap′o·theg·mat′i·cal·ly** *adv.*

ap·o·them (ăp′ə-thĕm′) *n.* The perpendicular distance from the center of a regular polygon to any of the sides. [APO- + Gk. *thema,* something laid down < *tithenai,* to put.]

a·poth·e·o·sis (ə-pŏth′ē-ō′sĭs, ăp′ə-thē′ə-sĭs) *n., pl.* **-ses** (-sēz′). **1.** Exaltation to divine rank or stature; deification. **2.** An exalted or glorified example: *He was the apotheosis of courage.* [LLat. < Gk. *apotheōsis* < *apotheoun,* to deify : *apo-,* from + *theos,* god.]

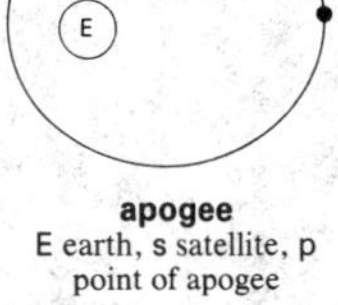

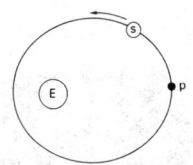

apogee
E earth, s satellite, p point of apogee

Apollo

apostle
12th-century illustration of the Last Supper

ap·o·the·o·size (ăp′ə-thē′ə-sīz′, ə-pŏth′ē-ə-sīz′) *tr.v.* **-sized, -siz·ing, -siz·es.** To glorify; exalt.

ap·o·tro·pa·ic (ăp′ə-trō-pā′ĭk) *adj.* Intended to ward off evil: *an apotropaic symbol.* [Gk. *apotropaios* < *apotrepein,* to ward off : *apo-,* from + *trepein,* to turn.] **—ap′o·tro·pa′i·cal·ly** *adv.*

Ap·pa·la·chian tea (ăp′ə-lā′chən, -lā′chē-ən, -lăch′ən) *n.* The withe rod. [After the *Appalachian* Mountains.]

ap·pall (ə-pôl′) *tr.v.* **-palled, -pall·ing, -palls.** To fill with consternation or dismay. [ME *apallen,* to grow faint < OFr. *apalir* : *à-,* to (< Lat. *ad*) + *palir,* to grow pale < Lat. *pallēre.*]

ap·pall·ing (ə-pô′lĭng) *adj.* Causing consternation or dismay; frightful: *appalling working conditions.* **—ap·pall′ing·ly** *adv.*

ap·pa·loo·sa (ăp′ə-lo͞o′sə) *n.* A horse of a breed developed in northwestern North America, characteristically having a spotted rump. [Prob. after the *Paloose* Indians, who bred the horse.]

ap·pa·nage also **ap·a·nage** (ăp′ə-nĭj) *n.* **1.** Land or another source of revenue given by a king for the maintenance of a member of the ruling family. **2.** Something extra offered to or claimed by a person as his due; perquisite. **3.** A natural accompaniment or adjunct. [Fr. *apanage* < OFr. < *apaner,* to make provisions for < Med. Lat. *appanare* : Lat. *ad-,* to + Lat. *panis,* bread.]

ap·pa·rat (ăp′ə-răt′, ä′pə-rät′) *n.* A political organization or an underground political movement. [R.]

ap·pa·ra·tchik (ä′pə-rä′chĭk) *n.* A member of a Communist apparat. [R. < *apparat,* apparat.]

apparatus

ap·pa·ra·tus (ăp′ə-rā′təs, -răt′əs) *n., pl.* **apparatus** or **-tus·es.** **1.** The totality of means by which a designated function is performed or a specific task executed. **2. a.** A machine. **b.** A group of machines used together or in succession to accomplish a task. **3.** *Physiol.* A group of organs having a collective function: *the respiratory apparatus.* **4.** A political organization. [Lat., preparation < *apparare,* to prepare : *ad-,* to + *parare,* to prepare.]

ap·par·el (ə-păr′əl) *n.* **1.** Clothing, esp. outer garments; attire. **2.** Something that covers or adorns: *trees with their apparel of foliage.* —*tr.v.* **-eled, -el·ing, -els** also **-elled, -el·ling, -els.** **1.** To clothe; dress. **2.** To adorn; embellish. [ME *appareil* < OFr. *apareil,* preparation < *apareillier,* to prepare < Lat. *apparare.* —see APPARATUS.]

ap·par·ent (ə-păr′ənt, ə-pâr′-) *adj.* **1.** Readily seen; open to view; visible. **2.** Readily understood or perceived; plain or obvious: *His anger was apparent to all.* **3.** Appearing as such but not necessarily so: *an apparent advantage.* [ME *apparaunt* < OFr. *aparant,* pr.part. of *aparoir,* to appear.] **—ap·par′ent·ly** *adv.* **—ap·par′ent·ness** *n.*

Usage: Used before a noun, *apparent* means "seeming": *For all his apparent wealth, Pat had no money to pay the rent.* Used after a form of the verb *be,* however, *apparent* can mean either "seeming" (as in *his virtues are only apparent*) or "obvious" (as in *the effects of the drought are apparent to anyone who sees the parched fields*). Writers should take care that the intended meaning is clear from the context.

apparent magnitude *n.* Magnitude (sense 2).

ap·pa·ri·tion (ăp′ə-rĭsh′ən) *n.* **1.** A ghostly figure; specter. **2.** A sudden or unusual sight. **3.** The act of appearing; appearance. [ME *apparicioun* < OFr. *apparition* < LLat. *apparitio,* an appearance < Lat. *apparēre,* to appear.] **—ap′pa·ri′tion·al** *adj.*

ap·par·i·tor (ə-păr′ĭ-tər) *n.* An official who was formerly sent to carry out the orders of a civil or ecclesiastical court. [Lat. < *apparēre,* to appear.]

ap·peal (ə-pēl′) *n.* **1.** An earnest or urgent request, entreaty, or supplication. **2.** A resort or application to a higher authority, as for sanction, corroboration, or a decision: *an appeal to reason.* **3.** The power of attracting or of arousing interest: *a city with appeal for tourists.* **4.** *Law.* **a.** The transfer of a case from a lower to a higher court for a new hearing. **b.** A request for a new hearing. **c.** A case so transferred. —*v.* **-pealed, -peal·ing, -peals.** —*intr.* **1.** To make an earnest or urgent request, as for help **2.** To have recourse, as for corroboration; resort. **3.** To be attractive or interesting. **4.** *Law.* To make or apply for an appeal. —*tr. Law.* To transfer or apply to transfer (a case) to a higher court for rehearing. [ME *apel* < OFr. < *apeler,* to appeal < Lat. *appellare,* to entreat.] **—ap·peal′a·ble** *adj.* **—ap·peal′er** *n.* **—ap·peal′ing·ly** *adv.*

ap·pear (ə-pîr′) *intr.v.* **-peared, -pear·ing, -pears.** **1.** To come into view; become visible: *a plane appearing in the sky.* **2.** To come into existence: *New strains of viruses appear periodically.* **3.** To seem or look to be: *appeared unhappy.* **4.** To seem likely: *It appears they will be late.* **5.** To come before the public; be presented or published: *has appeared in two plays.* **6.** *Law.* To present oneself formally before a court as defendant, plaintiff, or counsel. [ME *aperen* < OFr. *aparoir* < Lat. *apparēre* : *ad-,* to + *parēre,* to show.]

ap·pear·ance (ə-pîr′əns) *n.* **1.** The act or an instance of coming into sight. **2.** The act or an instance of coming into public view: *a rare personal appearance.* **3.** The outward aspect of someone or something: *a good appearance.* **4.** Something that appears; phenomenon. **5.** A superficial aspect; semblance: *keeping up an appearance of diligence.* **6. appearances.** Outward indications; circumstances: *a cheerful woman, to all appearances.*

ap·pease (ə-pēz′) *tr.v.* **-peased, -peas·ing, -peas·es.** **1.** To calm or pacify, esp. by giving what is demanded; placate. **2.** To satisfy or relieve: *appease thirst.* [ME *appesen* < OFr. *apaisier* : *à,* to (< Lat. *ad*) + *pais,* peace < Lat. *pax.*] **—ap·peas′a·ble** *adj.* **—ap·peas′a·bly** *adv.* **—ap·peas′er** *n.*

ap·pease·ment (ə-pēz′mənt) *n.* **1. a.** The act of appeasing. **b.** The condition of being appeased. **2.** The policy of granting concessions to potential enemies to maintain peace.

ap·pel (ə-pĕl′) *n.* A quick stamp of the foot used in fencing as a feint to produce an opening. [Fr., call < *appeler,* to call < OFr. *apeler,* to appeal.]

ap·pel·lant (ə-pĕl′ənt) *adj.* Of or pertaining to an appeal; appellate. —*n.* One who appeals a court decision.

ap·pel·late (ə-pĕl′ĭt) *adj.* Having the power to hear appeals and to review court decisions: *an appellate court.* [Lat. *appellatus,* p.part. of *appellare,* to entreat.]

ap·pel·la·tion (ăp′ə-lā′shən) *n.* **1.** A name or title. **2.** The act of naming. [ME *appelacion* < Lat. *appellatio* < *appellare,* to entreat.]

ap·pel·la·tive (ə-pĕl′ə-tĭv) *adj.* **1.** Of or relating to the assignment of names. **2.** *Gram.* Designating a class; common: *an appellative noun.* —*n.* A name or descriptive epithet. [ME < LLat. *appelativus* < *appellare,* to call upon, entreat.] **—ap·pel′la·tive·ly** *adv.*

ap·pel·lee (ăp′ə-lē′) *n.* One against whom an appeal is taken. [OFr. *apele* < *apeler,* to appeal.]

ap·pend (ə-pĕnd′) *tr.v.* **-pend·ed, -pend·ing, -pends.** **1.** To add as a supplement: *appended a list of errors to the report.* **2.** To fix to; attach. [Lat. *appendere,* to hang upon : *ad-,* to + *pendere,* to hang.]

ap·pend·age (ə-pĕn′dĭj) *n.* **1.** Something appended. **2.** *Biol.* A part or organ that is joined to an axis or trunk.

Synonyms: *appendage, appurtenance, adjunct, accessory, addition, attachment.* These nouns denote something added to a principal object. *Appendage* applies to what is likened to a limb in close but subordinate relation to the principal. An *appurtenance* is something, such as a president's limousine, that belongs to or goes with the principal without being essential to it. An *adjunct* is added to the principal but has its own function and is self-sustaining, like a tea room in the basement of a bookstore. *Accessory* denotes that which adds to the usefulness or appearance of something already complete in itself. *Addition* refers broadly to anything of the same nature or function added to the principal. An *attachment* usually contributes another function to the principal, to which it is physically linked.

ap·pen·dant (ə-pĕn′dənt) *adj.* **1.** Affixed as an appendage. **2.** Accompanying; attendant: *faith and its appendant hope.* **3.** *Law.* Belonging to a land grant as a subsidiary right. —*n.* **1.** Something appended. **2.** *Law.* A subsidiary right.

ap·pen·dec·to·my (ăp′ən-dĕk′tə-mē) *n., pl.* **-mies.** The surgical removal of the vermiform appendix. [APPEND(IX) + -ECTOMY.]

ap·pen·di·ci·tis (ə-pĕn′dĭ-sī′tĭs) *n.* Inflammation of the vermiform appendix. [APPENDIX + -ITIS.]

ap·pen·dic·u·lar (ăp′ən-dĭk′yə-lər) *adj.* Of, pertaining to, or consisting of an appendage or appendages. [< Lat. *appendicula,* dim. of *appendix,* appendix.]

ap·pen·dix (ə-pĕn′dĭks) *n., pl.* **-dix·es** or **-di·ces** (-dĭ-sēz′). **1. a.** An appendage. **b.** A collection of supplementary material, usually at the end of a book. **2.** The vermiform appendix. [Lat. < *appendere,* to hang upon. —see APPEND.]

ap·per·ceive (ăp′ər-sēv′) *tr.v.* **-ceived, -ceiv·ing, -ceives.** *Psychol.* To perceive in terms of past perceptions. [ME *apperceiven,* to notice < OFr. *apercevoir* : *à,* toward (< Lat. *ad*) + *perceivre,* to perceive. —see PERCEIVE.]

ap·per·cep·tion (ăp′ər-sĕp′shən) *n.* *Psychol.* **1.** Conscious perception with full awareness. **2.** The process of understanding by which newly observed qualities of an object are related to past experience. [Fr. *aperception* < *apercevoir,* to notice < OFr. —see APPERCEIVE.] **—ap′per·cep′tive** (-sĕp′tĭv) *adj.*

ap·per·tain (ăp′ər-tān′) *intr.v.* **-tained, -tain·ing, -tains.** To belong as a function or part; pertain properly: *problems appertaining to social reform.* [ME *appertenen* < OFr. *apartenir* < LLat. *appertinēre* : *ad-,* to + *pertinēre,* to belong. —see PERTAIN.]

ap·pe·stat (ăp′ĭ-stăt′) *n.* The mechanism in the central nervous system that controls food intake. [APPE(TITE) + -STAT.]

ap·pe·tence (ăp′ĭ-təns) *n.* **1.** A strong craving or desire. **2.** A tendency or proclivity; propensity. [Lat. *appetentia* < *appetere,* to strive after. —see APPETITE.]

ap·pe·ten·cy (ăp′ĭ-tən-sē) *n., pl.* **-cies.** Appetence.

ap·pe·tite (ăp′ĭ-tīt′) *n.* **1.** A desire for food or drink. **2.** A physical desire. **3.** A strong wish or urge: *an appetite for learning.* [ME *appetit* < OFr. < Lat. *appetitus,* strong desire < *appetere,* to strive after : *ad-,* toward + *petere,* to seek.] **—ap′pe·ti′tive** (ăp′ĭ-tī′tĭv, ə-pĕt′ĭ-tĭv) *adj.*

ap·pe·tiz·er (ăp′ĭ-tī′zər) *n.* A food or drink served usually before a meal to stimulate the appetite.

ap·pe·tiz·ing (ăp′ĭ-tī′zĭng) *adj.* Stimulating or appealing to the appetite. **—ap′pe·tiz′ing·ly** *adv.*

ap·plaud (ə-plôd′) *v.* **-plaud·ed, -plaud·ing, -plauds.** —*intr.*

To express approval, esp. by clapping the hands. —*tr.* **1.** To express approval of, esp. by clapping the hands. **2.** To praise; approve: *applauded his decision to complete his degree.* [Lat. *applaudere* : *ad-*, to + *plaudere,* to clap.] **—ap·plaud'er** *n.*

ap·plause (ə-plôz') *n.* **1.** Approval expressed esp. by the clapping of hands. **2.** Praise; commendation: *a scientific discovery that won critical applause.* [Med. Lat. *applausus* < Lat., p.part. of *applaudere,* to applaud.]

ap·ple (ăp'əl) *n.* **1. a.** A tree, *Pyrus malus,* of temperate regions, having fragrant pink or white flowers and edible fruit. **b.** The firm, rounded fruit of this tree or any of its varieties, having skin that is usually red but may be yellow or green. **2. a.** Any of several trees or plants having fruit resembling the apple, as the custard apple. **b.** The fruit of any of these trees or plants. **3.** The hard wood of an apple tree. [ME *appel* < OE *æppel.*]

apple green *n.* A moderate or vivid yellow green to light or strong yellowish green. **—ap'ple-green'** *adj.*

ap·ple·jack (ăp'əl-jăk') *n.* Brandy distilled from hard cider.

apple of Peru *n.* A plant, *Nicandra physalodes,* native to tropical America, having tubular blue or whitish flowers.

ap·ple-pol·ish (ăp'əl-pŏl'ĭsh) *intr.v.* **-ished, -ish·ing, -ish·es.** *Informal.* To seek favor by toadying. **—apple polisher** *n.*

ap·ple·sauce (ăp'əl-sôs') *n.* **1.** Apples stewed to a pulp, sweetened, and sometimes spiced. **2.** *Slang.* Foolishness; nonsense.

Ap·ple·ton layer (ăp'əl-tən) *n.* The F layer of the upper atmosphere. [After Sir Edward *Appleton* (1892–1965).]

ap·pli·ance (ə-plī'əns) *n.* A device or instrument, esp. one operated by electricity and designed for household use. [< APPLY.]

ap·pli·ca·ble (ăp'lĭ-kə-bəl, ə-plĭk'ə-) *adj.* Capable of being applied; appropriate. **—ap'pli·ca·bil'i·ty** *n.* **—ap'pli·ca·bly** *adv.*

ap·pli·cant (ăp'lĭ-kənt) *n.* A person who applies, as for a job. [Lat. *applicans,* pr.part. of *applicare,* to affix. —see APPLY.]

ap·pli·ca·tion (ăp'lĭ-kā'shən) *n.* **1.** The act of applying. **2.** Something that is applied, as a cosmetic or curative agent. **3. a.** The act of putting something to a special use or purpose: *an application of a new method.* **b.** A specific use to which something is put: *the application of science to industry.* **4.** The capacity of being usable; relevance: *Geometry has practical application.* **5.** Close attention; diligence: *shows application to her work.* **6. a.** A request, as for assistance, employment, or admission to a school. **b.** The form or document upon which such a request is made. [ME *applicacioun* < Med. Lat. *applicatio* < Lat. *applicare,* to affix. —see APPLY.]

ap·pli·ca·tive (ăp'lĭ-kā'tĭv, ə-plĭk'ə-) *adj.* **1.** Characterized by actual application; applied. **2.** Practical; applicatory. **—ap'pli·ca'tive·ly** *adv.*

ap·pli·ca·tor (ăp'lĭ-kā'tər) *n.* An instrument for applying something, such as medicine or glue.

ap·pli·ca·to·ry (ăp'lĭ-kə-tôr'ē, -tōr'ē, ə-plĭk'ə-) *adj.* Practical.

ap·plied (ə-plīd') *adj.* Put into practice or a particular use: *applied physics.*

ap·pli·qué (ăp'lĭ-kā') *n.* A decoration or ornament, as in needlework, made by cutting pieces of one material and applying them to the surface of another. —*adj.* Of or like appliqué. —*tr.v.* **-quéd, -qué·ing, -qués.** To decorate with appliqué. [Fr., p.part. of *appliquer,* to apply < Lat. *applicare,* to affix. —see APPLY.]

ap·ply (ə-plī') *v.* **-plied, -ply·ing, -plies.** —*tr.* **1.** To bring into nearness or contact with something; put on, upon, or to: *applied glue sparingly to the paper.* **2.** To put to or adapt for a special use: *applies all her money to her mortgage.* **3.** To put into action: *applied the brakes.* **4.** To devote (oneself or one's efforts) to something: *applied himself to his studies.* —*intr.* **1.** To be pertinent or relevant: *a rule that does not apply to me.* **2.** To request or seek assistance, employment, or admission: *will apply to college.* [ME *applien* < OFr. *aplier* < Lat. *applicare,* to affix : *ad-*, to + *plicare,* to fold together.]

ap·pog·gia·tu·ra (ə-pŏj'ə-to͝or'ə) *n.* *Mus.* An embellishing note, usually one step above or below the note it precedes and indicated by a small note or special sign. [Ital. < *appoggiare,* to lean on < VLat. **appodiare* : Lat. *ad-*, to + *podium,* support < Gk. *podion,* base < *pous,* foot.]

ap·point (ə-point') *tr.v.* **-point·ed, -point·ing, -points.** **1.** To select or designate to fill an office or position: *appointed her chief operating officer.* **2.** To fix or set by authority or by mutual agreement: *will appoint a date for the examination.* **3.** To furnish; equip: *a comfortably appointed house.* **4.** *Law.* To direct the disposition of (property) to a person or persons in exercise of a power granted for this purpose by a preceding deed. [ME *appointen,* to decide < OFr. *apointier,* to arrange < *à point,* to the point : *à*, to (< Lat. *ad*) + *point,* point < Lat. *punctum* < *pungere,* to prick.]

ap·point·ee (ə-poin'tē', ăp'oin-) *n.* **1.** A person who is appointed to an office or position. **2.** *Law.* One to whom a power of appointment of property is granted. —See Usage note at **-ee**[1].

ap·point·ive (ə-poin'tĭv) *adj.* Pertaining to or filled by appointment: *an appointive office.*

ap·point·ment (ə-point'mənt) *n.* **1.** The act of appointing or designating for an office or position. **2.** The office or position to which a person has been appointed. **3.** An arrangement to do something or meet someone at a particular time and place. **4. appointments.** Furnishings, fittings, or equipment. **5.** *Law.* The act of directing the disposition of property by virtue of a power granted for this purpose.

ap·poin·tor (ə-poin'tər, ə-poin'tôr') *n.* *Law.* One who executes a power of appointment of property.

ap·por·tion (ə-pôr'shən, ə-pōr'-) *tr.v.* **-tioned, -tion·ing, -tions.** To divide and assign according to a plan or proportion; allot. [OFr. *apportioner* : *à-* (< Lat. *ad*) + *portionner,* to divide into portions < *portion,* portion. —see PORTION.]

ap·por·tion·ment (ə-pôr'shən-mənt, ə-pōr'-) *n.* **1. a.** The act of apportioning. **b.** The condition of being apportioned. **2. a.** The proportional distribution of the number of members of the U.S. House of Representatives on the basis of the population of each state. **b.** The allotment of direct taxes on the basis of state population.

ap·pose (ă-pōz') *tr.v.* **-posed, -pos·ing, -pos·es.** To place (things) near to each other or side by side; juxtapose. [Back-formation < APPOSITION.]

ap·po·site (ăp'ə-zĭt) *adj.* Fitting; suitable; appropriate. [Lat. *appositus,* p.part. of *apponere,* to put near : *ad-*, to + *ponere,* to put.] **—ap'po·site·ly** *adv.* **—ap'po·site·ness** *n.*

ap·po·si·tion (ăp'ə-zĭsh'ən) *n.* **1.** *Gram.* **a.** A construction in which a noun or noun phrase is placed with another as an explanatory equivalent, both having the same syntactic relation to the other elements in the sentence, as *Copley* and *the painter* in *The painter Copley was born in Boston.* **b.** The relationship between such nouns or noun phrases. **2.** A placing side by side or next to each other. **3.** *Biol.* The growth of successive layers of a cell wall. [ME *apposicioun* < Med. Lat. *appositio* < Lat. *apponere,* to put near. —see APPOSITE.] **—ap'po·si'tion·al** *adj.* **—ap'po·si'tion·al·ly** *adv.*

ap·pos·i·tive (ə-pŏz'ĭ-tĭv) *adj.* Of, concerning, or being in apposition. —*n.* A word or phrase that is in apposition. **—ap·pos'i·tive·ly** *adv.*

ap·prais·al (ə-prā'zəl) *n.* **1.** The act of appraising. **2.** An expert or official valuation of something, as for taxation.

ap·praise (ə-prāz') *tr.v.* **-praised, -prais·ing, -prais·es.** **1.** To evaluate, esp. in an official capacity. **2.** To estimate the quality, amount, size, and other features of; judge. [ME *appreisen,* alteration of *apprisen* < OFr. *aprisier* < LLat. *appretiare* : Lat. *ad-*, to + Lat. *pretium,* price.] **—ap·prais'a·ble** *adj.* **—ap·praise'ment** *n.* **—ap·prais'er** *n.*

ap·pre·cia·ble (ə-prē'shə-bəl) *adj.* Capable of being noticed, estimated, or measured; noticeable. **—ap·pre'cia·bly** *adv.*

ap·pre·ci·ate (ə-prē'shē-āt') *v.* **-at·ed, -at·ing, -ates.** —*tr.* **1.** To recognize the quality, significance, or magnitude of; value: *appreciated their freedom.* **2.** To be fully aware of or sensitive to; realize: *I appreciate your problems.* **3.** To be thankful or show gratitude for: *really appreciate your help.* **4.** To enjoy and understand critically or emotionally: *appreciates literature and music.* **5.** To raise in value or price. —*intr.* To go up in value or price. [LLat. *appretiare, appretiat-*, to appraise.] **—ap·pre'ci·a'tor** *n.* **—ap·pre'cia·to'ry** (-shə-tôr'ē, -tōr'ē) *adj.*

Synonyms: *appreciate, value, prize, esteem, treasure, cherish.* These verbs express having a favorable opinion of someone or something. *Appreciate* applies especially to favor based on judgment and assessment. *Value* implies high regard for the importance of the object, while *prize* emphasizes its specialness. *Esteem* suggests respect of a formal sort; *treasure* and *cherish* suggest affectionate regard mixed with pride of possession.

appliqué
Floral design appliquéd to a quilted coverlet

ap·pre·ci·a·tion (ə-prē'shē-ā'shən) *n.* **1.** Recognition of the quality, value, significance, or magnitude of people and things. **2.** A judgment or opinion, esp. a favorable one. **3.** An expression of gratitude. **4.** Awareness or delicate perception, esp. of aesthetic qualities or values. **5.** A rise in value or price.

ap·pre·cia·tive (ə-prē'shə-tĭv, -shē-ā'tĭv) *adj.* Capable of or showing appreciation. **—ap·pre'cia·tive·ly** *adv.*

ap·pre·hend (ăp'rĭ-hĕnd') *v.* **-hend·ed, -hend·ing, -hends.** —*tr.* **1.** To take into custody; arrest: *apprehended the murderer.* **2.** To grasp mentally; understand. **3.** To look forward to fearfully; anticipate with anxiety. —*intr.* To understand. [ME *apprehenden* < Lat. *apprehendere,* to seize : *ad-*, to + *prehendere,* to grasp.]

Synonyms: *apprehend, comprehend, grasp, understand.* These verbs refer to varying degrees of mental perception. *Apprehend* is often limited to perception and does not imply full understanding. *Comprehend* stresses attainment of full understanding. *Grasp* suggests seizing an idea firmly. *Understand,* nearer in meaning to *comprehend,* can also suggest sympathy, compassion, or insight: *My parents don't understand me.*

ap·pre·hen·si·ble (ăp'rĭ-hĕn'sə-bəl) *adj.* Capable of being apprehended or understood. **—ap'pre·hen'si·bly** *adv.*

ap·pre·hen·sion (ăp'rĭ-hĕn'shən) *n.* **1.** A fearful or uneasy anticipation of the future; dread. **2.** The act of seizing or capturing; arrest. **3.** The ability to apprehend or understand; understanding. [LLat. *apprehensio,* understanding < *apprehendere,* to seize. —see APPREHEND.]

Synonyms: *apprehension, foreboding, presentiment, misgiving.* These nouns denote concern for something that

apricot

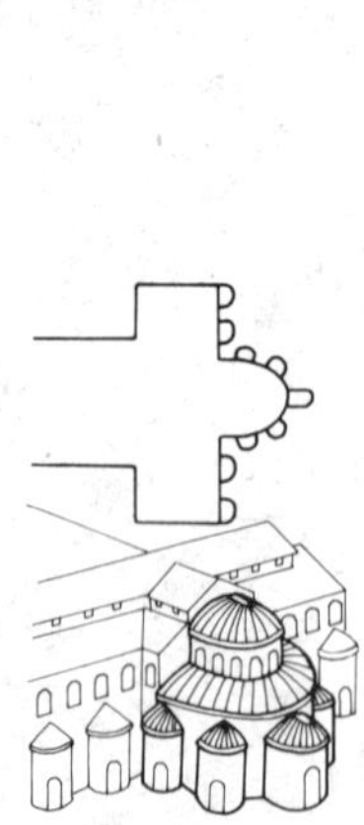
apse

impends. *Apprehension* refers broadly to anxiety about the future. *Foreboding* is a vague fear of the future, inferred irrationally from clues in the present. *Presentiment* denotes a less certain prophetic sense that something, not necessarily unpleasant, is imminent. *Misgiving,* usually used in the plural, applies to a specific instance of apprehension and stresses mistrust.

ap·pre·hen·sive (ăp′rĭ-hĕn′sĭv) *adj.* **1.** Anxious or fearful about the future; uneasy. **2.** Capable of understanding; quick to apprehend. **—ap′pre·hen′sive·ly** *adv.* **—ap′pre·hen′sive·ness** *n.*

ap·pren·tice (ə-prĕn′tĭs) *n.* **1.** One bound by legal agreement to work for another for a specific amount of time in return for instruction in a trade, art, or business. **2.** A person who is learning a trade or occupation, esp. as a member of a labor union. **3.** A beginner; learner. *—tr.v.* **-ticed, -tic·ing, -tic·es.** To place or take on as an apprentice. [ME *apprentis* < OFr. < *aprendre,* to learn < Lat. *apprehendere,* to seize. —see APPREHEND.] **—ap·pren′tice·ship′** *n.*

ap·pressed (ə-prĕst′) *adj.* Lying flat or pressed closely against something, as leaves on a stem. [< Lat. *appressus,* p.part. of *apprimere,* to press down : *ad-,* to + *premere,* to press.]

ap·prise (ə-prīz′) *tr.v.* **-prised, -pris·ing, -pris·es.** To give notice to; inform: *apprised him of his rights.* [Fr. *apprendre, appris-* < OFr. *aprendre,* to learn. —see APPRENTICE.]

ap·prize (ə-prīz′) *v. Chiefly Brit.* Variant of **apprise**.

ap·proach (ə-prōch′) *v.* **-proached, -proach·ing, -proach·es.** *—intr.* To come near or nearer, as in space or time. *—tr.* **1.** To come or go near or nearer to. **2.** To come close to in appearance, quality, condition, or other characteristics; approximate: *What approaches the joy of singing?* **3.** To make a proposal to; make overtures to: *approached the president for a promotion.* **4.** To begin to deal with or work on: *approaching a task.* *—n.* **1.** The act of approaching: *the approach of winter.* **2.** A fairly close resemblance; approximation. **3.** A way or means of reaching something; access: *an approach to the bridge.* **4.** The method used in dealing with or accomplishing something: *a logical approach to the problem.* **5.** An advance or overture made by one person to another. **6.** The golf stroke following the drive from the tee with which the player tries to get the ball onto the putting green. **7.** Works such as trenches or bulwarks for the protection of troops besieging a fortified position. [ME *approchen* < OFr. *aprochier* < LLat. *appropiare* : Lat. *ad-,* to + Lat. *propius,* nearer, comp. of *prope,* near.]

ap·proach·a·ble (ə-prō′chə-bəl) *adj.* **1.** Capable of being approached; accessible. **2.** Easily approached; receptive to overtures; friendly. **—ap·proach′a·bil′i·ty** *n.*

ap·pro·bate (ăp′rə-bāt′) *tr.v.* **-bat·ed, -bat·ing, -bates.** To sanction; authorize. [ME *approbaten* < Lat. *approbare,* to approve.] **—ap′pro·ba′tive, ap·pro′ba·to′ry** (ə-prō′bə-tôr′ē, -tōr′ē) *adj.*

ap·pro·ba·tion (ăp′rə-bā′shən) *n.* **1.** Praise; commendation. **2.** Official approval.

ap·pro·pri·a·ble (ə-prō′prē-ə-bəl) *adj.* Capable of being appropriated.

ap·pro·pri·ate (ə-prō′prē-ĭt) *adj.* Suitable for a particular person, condition, occasion, or place; proper; fitting. *—tr.v.* (-āt′) **-at·ed, -at·ing, -ates. 1.** To set apart for a specific use: *appropriating funds for education.* **2.** To take possession of or make use of exclusively for oneself, often without permission: *appropriated my unread newspaper and never returned it.* [ME *appropriat* < Med. Lat. *appropriatus,* p.part. of *appropriare,* to make one's own : Lat. *ad-,* to + Lat. *propius,* own.] **—ap·pro′pri·ate·ly** *adv.* **—ap·pro′pri·ate·ness** *n.* **—ap·pro′pri·a′tive** (-ā′tĭv) *adj.* **—ap·pro′pri·a′tor** *n.*

ap·pro·pri·a·tion (ə-prō′prē-ā′shən) *n.* **1.** The act of appropriating. **2.** Something appropriated, esp. public funds set aside for a specific purpose. **3.** A legislative act authorizing the expenditure of a designated amount of public funds for a specific purpose.

ap·prov·al (ə-prōō′vəl) *n.* **1.** The act of approving. **2.** An official approbation; sanction. **3.** Favorable regard; commendation. ***—idiom.* on approval.** For examination or trial by a potential customer without the obligation to buy.

ap·prove (ə-prōōv′) *v.* **-proved, -prov·ing, -proves.** *—tr.* **1.** To regard favorably; consider right or good: *approved his decision.* **2.** To confirm or consent to officially; sanction; ratify: *a treaty approved by the Senate.* **3.** *Obs.* To prove or demonstrate. *—intr.* To feel, voice, or demonstrate approval: *didn't approve of gambling.* [ME *approven* < OFr. *aprover* < Lat. *approbare* : *ad-,* to + *probare,* to test < *probus,* good.] **—ap·prov′a·ble** *adj.* **—ap·prov′ing·ly** *adv.*

Synonyms: *approve, endorse, sanction, certify, accredit, ratify.* These verbs all mean to express a favorable opinion of a person, thing, or action or to signify satisfaction or acceptance. *Approve* may indicate varying degrees of admiration. *Endorse* (or *indorse*), stronger than *approve,* implies expression of support, often by public statement. *Sanction* adds authorization, usually official, to approval. *Certify* and *accredit* imply official endorsement gained upon conforming to set standards. *Ratify* refers to making legal by formal official approval: *a treaty ratified by the legislatures of each of the countries involved.*

approved school *n. Chiefly Brit.* A reform school.

ap·prox·i·mate (ə-prŏk′sə-mĭt) *adj.* **1.** Almost exact, correct, complete, or perfect. **2.** Very similar; closely resembling. **3.** Close together; near. *—v.* (-māt′) **-mat·ed, -mat·ing, -mates.** *—tr.* **1.** To come close to; be nearly the same as. **2.** To cause to approach; bring near. *—intr.* To come near or close in degree, nature, quality, or other characteristics. [LLat. *approximatus,* p.part. of *approximare,* to approach : Lat. *ad-,* to + *proximare,* to come near < *proximus,* nearest.] **—ap·prox′i·mate·ly** *adv.*

ap·prox·i·ma·tion (ə-prŏk′sə-mā′shən) *n.* **1.** The act, process, or result of approximating. **2.** *Math.* An inexact result adequate for a given purpose. **—ap·prox′i·ma′tive** (-mā′tĭv) *adj.* **—ap·prox′i·ma′tive·ly** *adv.*

ap·pur·te·nance (ə-pûr′tn-əns) *n.* **1.** Something added to another, more important thing; accessory. **2. appurtenances.** Equipment, such as clothing, tools, or instruments, used for a specific purpose or task; gear. **3.** *Law.* A right, privilege, or property that is considered incident to the principal property for purposes such as passage of title, conveyance, or inheritance. [ME *appurtenaunce* < AN *apurtenance* < VLat. **appertinentia* < LLat. *appertinēre,* to appertain.] **—ap·pur′te·nant** *adj.*

a·prax·i·a (ā-prăk′sē-ə) *n.* The inability to perform coordinated movements as a result of lesions in the cerebral cortex. [Gk., inaction : *a-,* without + *praxis,* action < *prassein,* to do.] **—a·prac′tic** (ā-prăk′tĭk), **a·prax′ic** (ā-prăk′sĭk) *adj.*

a·près-ski (ä′prā-skē′, ăp′rā-) *n.* Social events or activities, as at a ski lodge, after skiing. [Fr. : *après,* after + *ski,* skiing.] **—a′près-ski′** *adj.*

a·pri·cot (ăp′rĭ-kŏt′, ā′prĭ-) *n.* **1.** A tree, *Prunus armeniaca,* native to western Asia and Africa, widely cultivated for its edible fruit. **2.** The juicy, yellow-orange peachlike fruit of the apricot. **3.** A moderate, light, or strong orange to strong orange yellow. [Alteration of earlier *abrecock* < Port. *albricoque* < Ar. *al-birqūq,* the apricot : *al,* the + LGk. *praikokion* < Lat. *praecoqquus,* ripe early (*prae-,* before + *coquere,* to ripen).]

A·pril (ā′prəl) *n.* The fourth month of the year according to the Gregorian calendar. See table at **calendar.** [ME < Lat. *aprilis.*]

April fool *n.* The victim of a trick played on April Fools' Day.

April Fools' Day *n.* April 1, marked as a day for playing practical jokes.

a pri·o·ri (ä′prē-ôr′ē, -ōr′ē, ā′prī-ôr′ī, -ōr′ī′) *adj.* **1.** Proceeding from a known or assumed cause to a necessarily related effect; deductive. **2.** Based on a hypothesis or theory rather than on experiment or experience. **3.** Made before or without examination; not supported by factual study. [Lat., from the former.] **—a′pri·o′ri** *adv.* **—a′pri·or′i·ty** (-ôr′ĭ-tē, -ōr′-) *n.*

a·pron (ā′prən) *n.* **1.** A garment, usually fastened in the back, worn over all or part of the front of the body to protect clothing. **2.** Something resembling an apron in appearance or function, as a protective shield for a machine. **3.** The paved strip in front of and around airport hangars and terminal buildings. **4.** The part of a stage in a theater extending in front of the curtain. **5. a.** A platform of planking or other material at the entrance to a dock. **b.** A covering or structure along a shoreline for protection against erosion. **c.** A platform serving a similar purpose below a dam or in a sluiceway. **6.** A continuous conveyor belt. **7.** An area covered by sand and gravel deposited at the front of a glacial moraine. *—tr.v.* **a·proned, a·pron·ing, a·prons.** To cover, protect, or provide with an apron. [ME < the phrase *a napron,* an apron < OFr. *naperon,* dim. of *nape,* tablecloth < Lat. *mappa,* napkin.]

apron string *n.* **1.** The string of an apron. **2.** Often **apron strings.** Complete control: *tied to his mother's apron strings.*

ap·ro·pos (ăp′rə-pō′) *adj.* Appropriate; pertinent. *—adv.* **1.** Appropriately; pertinently. **2.** By the way; incidentally: *Apropos, where were you yesterday?* *—prep.* Concerning; regarding: *apropos our date for lunch.* [Fr. *à propos,* to the purpose.]

apropos of *prep.* With reference to; speaking of: *a funny story apropos of politics.* [< APROPOS (adj.).]

apse (ăps) *n.* **1.** *Archit.* A semicircular or polygonal, usually domed projection of a building, esp. the altar or east end of a church. **2.** *Astron.* Apsis (sense 2). [LLat. *apsis.* —see APSIS.] **—ap′si·dal** (ăp′sĭ-dəl) *adj.*

ap·sis (ăp′sĭs) *n., pl.* **-si·des** (-sĭ-dēz′). **1.** *Archit.* An apse. **2.** *Astron.* The point of greatest or least distance of a celestial body from a center of attraction. [LLat. *apsis* < Lat., arch, vault < Gk. *hapsis* < *haptein,* to fasten.]

apt (ăpt) *adj.* **1.** Exactly suitable; appropriate: *an apt reply.* **2.** Likely: *apt to snow in January.* **3.** Having a tendency; inclined: *apt to take offense easily.* **4.** Quick to learn or understand: *an apt student.* [ME < Lat. *aptus,* p.part. of *apere,* to fasten.] **—apt′ly** *adv.* **—apt′ness** *n.*

Usage: *Apt* is more specific in meaning than *likely* and should be used only to indicate that its subject has a natural tendency to err or to do something undesirable. *He is apt to lose when he does not train hard,* but *He is likely* (not *apt*) *to win when he trains hard.*

APT (ā′pē-tē) *n.* A computer language designed for programming numerically controlled machine tools. [A(UTOMATICALLY) + P(ROGRAMMED) + T(OOL).]

ap·ter·al (ăp′tər-əl) *adj. Archit.* Having no columns along the sides. [< Gk. *apteros,* wingless : *a-,* without + *pteron,* wing.]

ap·ter·ous (ăp′tər-əs) *adj.* **1.** *Zool.* Having no wings: *an apterous insect.* **2.** *Bot.* Having no winglike parts or extensions.

ap·ter·yx (ăp′tə-rĭks′) *n.* The kiwi. [NLat. : A-[1] + Gk. *pterux,* wing.]

ap·ti·tude (ăp′tĭ-to͞od′, -tyo͞od′) *n.* **1.** A natural or acquired talent or ability; inclination. **2.** Quickness in learning and understanding; intelligence. **3.** The condition or quality of being fitting; appropriateness. [ME, tendency < Med. Lat. *aptitudo,* aptitude < *aptus,* apt.]

aptitude test *n.* A standardized test designed to measure the ability of an individual to develop skills or acquire knowledge.

A·pus (ā′pəs) *n.* A constellation in the Southern Hemisphere near Musca and Pavo. [Lat. *apus,* a kind of swallow < Gk. *apous,* sand martin < *apous,* without feet. —see APODAL.]

aq·ua (ăk′wə, ä′kwə) *n., pl.* **aq·uae** (ăk′wē, ä′kwī′) or **aq·uas.** **1.** Water. **2.** An aqueous solution. **3.** A light bluish green to light greenish blue. [Lat.] **—aq′ua** *adj.*

aq·ua·cade (ăk′wə-kād′, ä′kwə-) *n.* An entertainment spectacle of swimmers and divers, often performing in unison to the accompaniment of music. [AQUA + (CAVAL)CADE.]

aq·ua for·tis also **aq·ua·for·tis** (ăk′wə-fôr′tĭs, ä′kwə-) *n.* Nitric acid. [NLat., strong water.]

Aqua Lung. A trademark for an underwater breathing apparatus.

aq·ua·ma·rine (ăk′wə-mə-rēn′, ä′kwə-) *n.* **1.** A transparent blue-green variety of beryl, used as a gemstone. **2.** A pale blue to light greenish blue. [Lat. *aqua marina,* sea water.]

aq·ua·naut (ăk′wə-nôt′, ä′kwə-) *n.* A person trained to live in underwater installations and conduct, assist in, or be a subject of scientific research. [AQUA + Gk. *nautēs* sailor < *naus,* ship.]

aq·ua·plane (ăk′wə-plān′, ä′kwə-) *n.* A board on which a person rides in a standing position while it is pulled over the water by a motorboat. *—intr.v.* **-planed, -plan·ing, -planes.** To ride on an aquaplane. [AQUA + PLANE[1].]

aqua re·gi·a (rē′jē-ə, rē′jə) *n.* A corrosive, fuming, volatile mixture of hydrochloric and nitric acids, used for testing metals and dissolving platinum and gold. [Lat., royal water.]

aq·ua·relle (ăk′wə-rĕl′, ä′kwə-) *n.* A drawing done in transparent water colors. [Fr. < obs. Ital. *acquarella,* water color, dim. of *acqua,* water < Lat. *aqua.*] **—aq′ua·rel′list** *n.*

a·quar·i·a (ə-kwâr′ē-ə) *n.* A plural of **aquarium.**

a·quar·ist (ə-kwâr′ĭst) *n.* One who maintains an aquarium.

a·quar·i·um (ə-kwâr′ē-əm) *n., pl.* **-i·ums** or **-i·a** (-ē-ə). **1.** A tank, bowl, or other water-filled enclosure in which fish or other aquatic animals and, often, plants are kept. **2.** A place for the public exhibition of aquatic animals and plants. [< Lat. *aquarius,* of water < *aqua,* water.]

A·quar·i·us (ə-kwâr′ē-əs) *n.* **1.** A constellation in the equatorial region of the Southern Hemisphere near Pisces and Aquila. **2.** The 11th sign of the zodiac. [ME < Lat., water carrier < *aqua,* water.]

a·quat·ic (ə-kwŏt′ĭk, ə-kwăt′-) *adj.* **1.** Of or in water: *an aquatic environment.* **2.** Living or growing in or on the water. **3.** Taking place in or on the water. *—n.* **1.** An aquatic organism. **2. aquatics.** Sports performed in or on the water. [OFr. *aquatique* < Lat. *aquaticus* < *aqua,* water.]

aq·ua·tint (ăk′wə-tĭnt′, ä′kwə-) *n.* **1.** A process of etching capable of producing several tones by varying the etching time of different areas of a copper plate so that the resulting print resembles the flat tints of an ink or wash drawing. **2.** An etching made by aquatint. *—tr.v.* **-tint·ed, -tint·ing, -tints.** To etch in aquatint. [Fr. *aquatinte* < Ital. *acqua tinta,* dyed water : *acqua,* water (< Lat. *aqua*) + *tinta,* dyed < Lat. *tincta,* p.part. of *tingere,* to dye.]

a·qua·vit (ä′kwə-vēt′) *n.* A strong, clear Scandinavian liquor distilled from potato or grain mash and flavored with caraway seed. [Swed., Dan., and Norw. *akvavit* < Med. Lat. *aqua vitae,* water of life.]

aqua vi·tae (vī′tē) *n.* **1.** Alcohol. **2.** Whiskey, brandy, or other strong liquor. [ME *aquavite* < Med. Lat. *aqua vitae,* water of life.]

aq·ue·duct (ăk′wĭ-dŭkt′) *n.* **1.** A pipe or channel designed to transport water from a remote source, usually by gravity. **2.** A bridgelike structure supporting a conduit or canal passing over a river or low ground. **3.** *Anat.* A fluid channel or passage. [Lat. *aquaeductus* : *aqua,* water + *ductus,* p.part. of *ducere,* to lead.]

a·que·ous (ā′kwē-əs, ăk′wē-) *adj.* **1.** Pertaining to, similar to, containing, or dissolved in water; watery. **2.** *Geol.* Formed from matter deposited by water, as certain sedimentary rocks. [Med. Lat. *aqueus* < Lat. *aqua,* water.]

aqueous humor *n.* A clear, lymphlike fluid in the chamber of the eye between the cornea and the lens.

aqui– *pref.* Water: *aquiculture.* [Lat. < *aqua,* water.]

aq·ui·cul·ture (ăk′wĭ-kŭl′chər, ä′kwĭ-) *n.* Hydroponics. **—aq′ui·cul′tur·al** *adj.*

aq·ui·fer (ăk′wə-fər, ä′kwə-) *n.* A water-bearing rock, rock formation, or group of rock formations. **—a·quif′er·ous** (ə-kwĭf′ər-əs) *adj.*

Aq·ui·la (ăk′wə-lə) *n.* A constellation in the Northern Hemisphere and the Milky Way near Aquarius and Serpens Cauda. [Lat. *aquila,* eagle.]

aq·ui·le·gi·a (ăk′wə-lē′jē-ə, -lē′jə) *n.* A plant of the genus *Aquilegia;* columbine. [NLat. *Aquilegia,* genus name < Med. Lat. *aquilegia,* columbine.]

aq·ui·line (ăk′wə-līn′, -lĭn) *adj.* **1.** Of or similar to an eagle. **2.** Curved or hooked like an eagle's beak: *an aquiline nose.* [Lat. *aquilinus* < *aquila,* eagle.]

a·quiv·er (ə-kwĭv′ər) *adj.* Marked by quivering: *aquiver with anticipation.*

ar (är) *n.* Variant of **are**[2].

Ar The symbol for the element argon.

–ar *suff.* Of, relating to, or resembling: *polar.* [ME < OFr. *-er* < Lat. *-aris,* alteration of *-alis,* -al.]

A·ra (âr′ə) *n.* A constellation in the Southern Hemisphere near the constellations Norma and Telescopium. [Lat. *ara,* altar.]

Ar·ab (ăr′əb) *n.* **1.** A native or inhabitant of Arabia. **2.** Any of a Semitic people originally from Arabia but later widely scattered throughout the Near East, North Africa, and the Arabian Peninsula. **3.** Any of a nomadic people living in North African and Near Eastern desert regions. **4.** Any of a breed of swift, intelligent, graceful horses native to Arabia. **5.** A street Arab; waif. *—adj.* Arabian. [Fr. *Arabe* < Lat. *Arabs* < Gk. *Araps* < Ar. *'Arab.*]

ar·a·besque (ăr′ə-bĕsk′) *n.* **1.** A complex and ornate design of intertwined floral, foliate, and geometrical figures. **2.** A position in which a ballet dancer stands on one leg, the other leg extended backward with straight knee, and with the arms disposed in any of the various conventional positions. *—adj.* In the fashion of or formed as an arabesque. [Fr. < Ital. *arabesco,* in Arabian fashion < *Arab,* an Arab < Lat. *Arabs.*]

A·ra·bi·an (ə-rā′bē-ən) *adj.* Of or concerning Arabia or the Arabs; Arab. *—n.* **1.** A native or inhabitant of Arabia. **2.** A horse of a breed native to Arabia; Arab.

Arabian camel *n.* The dromedary.

Ar·a·bic (ăr′ə-bĭk) *adj.* Of or pertaining to Arabia, the Arabs, their language, or their culture. *—n.* A Semitic language consisting of numerous dialects that is the principal language of Arabia, Jordan, Syria, Iraq, Lebanon, Egypt, and parts of northern Africa.

Arabic numeral *n.* One of the numerical symbols 1, 2, 3, 4, 5, 6, 7, 8, 9, and 0.

Ar·ab·ist (ăr′ə-bĭst) *n.* A specialist in the Arabic language or culture.

ar·a·ble (ăr′ə-bəl) *adj.* Fit for cultivation. *—n.* Arable land. [ME < OFr. < Lat. *arabilis* < *arare,* to plow.]

A·rach·ne (ə-răk′nē) *n. Gk. Myth.* A maiden who was transformed into a spider by Athena for challenging her to a weaving contest. [Lat. < Gk. *Arakhnē* < *arakhnē,* spider.]

a·rach·nid (ə-răk′nĭd) *n.* Any of various arthropods of the class Arachnida, such as a spider, scorpion, mite, or tick, characteristically having four pairs of legs. [NLat. *Arachnida,* class name < Gk. *arakhnē,* spider.] **—a·rach′ni·dan** (-nĭ-dən) *adj. & n.*

a·rach·noid (ə-răk′noid′) *adj.* **1.** Resembling a spider's web. **2.** Of or relating to the arachnids. **3.** Covered with or consisting of thin, soft, entangled hairs like those of a cobweb. *—n.* **1.** An arachnid. **2.** A delicate membrane of the spinal cord and brain, lying between the pia mater and dura mater. [NLat. *arachnoides* < Gk. *arakhnoeidēs,* cobweblike : *arakhnē,* spider + *-eidēs,* -oid.]

Ar·a·go·nese (ăr′ə-gə-nēz′, -nēs′) *adj.* Of or pertaining to Aragon, its inhabitants, their language, or their culture. *—n., pl.* **Aragonese.** A native or inhabitant of Aragon.

a·rag·o·nite (ə-răg′ə-nīt′, ăr′ə-gə-) *n.* An orthorhombic mineral form of crystalline calcium carbonate, dimorphous with calcite. [After *Aragon,* a region of Spain.]

Ar·a·mae·an (ăr′ə-mē′ən) *n.* Variant of **Aramean.**

Ar·a·ma·ic (ăr′ə-mā′ĭk) *n.* The Semitic language originally of the ancient Arameans but widely used by non-Aramean peoples throughout southwest Asia from the 7th century B.C. to the 7th century A.D. **—Ar′a·ma′ic** *adj.*

Ar·a·me·an also **Ar·a·mae·an** (ăr′ə-mē′ən) *adj.* Of or pertaining to Aram, its inhabitants, their language, or their culture. *—n.* **1.** A native or inhabitant of Aram. **2.** Aramaic.

A·rap·a·ho also **A·rap·a·hoe** (ə-răp′ə-hō′) *n., pl.* **Arapaho** or **-hos** also **Arapahoe** or **-hoes.** **1.** A tribe of North American Indians formerly centered in the area of the Platte and Arkansas rivers, now settled in Oklahoma and Wyoming. **2.** A member of the Arapaho. **3.** The Algonquian language of the Arapaho. [Crow *aa-raxpé-ahu,* tattoo.]

ar·a·pai·ma (ăr′ə-pī′mə) *n.* A large South American freshwater food fish, *Arapaima gigas,* sometimes attaining a length of 15 feet. [Sp. (South America), prob. < Tupi.]

ar·a·ro·ba (ăr′ə-rō′bə) *n.* **1.** A Brazilian tree, *Andira araroba,* having yellowish wood from which a medicinal powder is obtained. **2.** The powder of the araroba. [Port., prob. of Tupian orig.]

Ar·au·ca·ni·an (ăr′ô-kā′nē-ən) also **A·rau·can** (ə-rô′kən) *n.* **1.** A member of a group of Indian peoples of south-central Chile and the western pampas of Argentina. **2.** The language of the Araucanians, which constitutes an independent

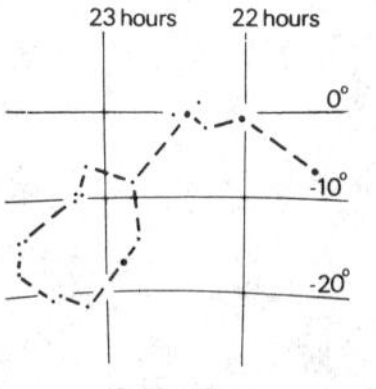

Aquarius

aqueduct
1st-century B.C. Roman aqueduct in Nîmes, France

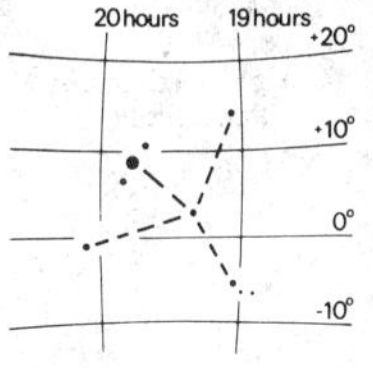

Aquila

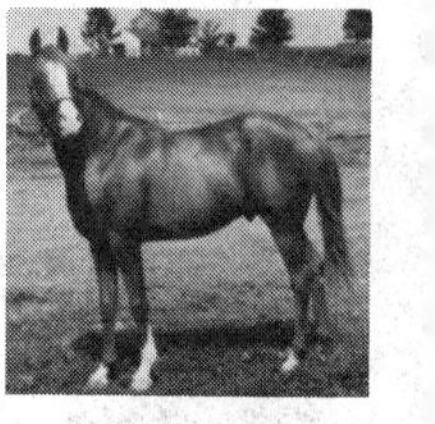
Arabian

language family. [Sp. *araucano,* after *Arauco,* a province in Chile.] **—Ar'au·ca'ni·an** *adj.*

ar·au·car·i·a (ăr'ô-kâr'ē-ə) *n.* Any of several evergreen trees of the genus *Araucaria,* as the monkey puzzle and Norfolk Island pine. [< Sp. *Araucaria,* (tree) of Arauco, a province in Chile.]

Ar·a·wak (ăr'ə-wäk') *n., pl.* **Arawak** or **-waks. 1.** An Indian people now living chiefly in certain regions of the Guianas. **2.** A member of the Arawak. **3.** The Arawakan language of the Arawak.

Ar·a·wa·kan (ăr'ə-wä'kən) *n., pl.* **Arawakan** or **-kans. 1.** A member of a group of Indian peoples living in a wide area of South America including Venezuela, Colombia, the Guianas, Peru, Bolivia, Paraguay, and the Amazon basin of Brazil. **2.** A language family that consists of the languages spoken by the Arawakan peoples. **—Ar'a·wa'kan** *adj.*

ar·ba·lest also **ar·be·lest** (är'bə-lĭst) *n.* A medieval missile launcher designed on the crossbow principle. [ME *arblast* < OFr. *arbaleste* < LLat. *arcuballista* : Lat. *arcus,* bow + Lat. *ballista,* ballista. —see BALLISTA.] **—ar'ba·lest'er** (-lĕs'tər) *n.*

ar·bi·ter (är'bĭ-tər) *n.* **1.** One chosen or appointed to judge or decide a disputed issue; arbitrator. **2.** One who has the power to judge or ordain at will: *an arbiter of fashion.* [ME *arbitour* < Lat. *arbiter.*]

ar·bi·tra·ble (är'bĭ-trə-bəl) *adj.* **1.** Subject to arbitration. **2.** Capable of being referred to an arbitrator.

ar·bi·trage (är'bĭ-träzh') *n.* The purchase of securities on one market for immediate resale on another in order to profit from a price discrepancy. [OFr., arbitration < *arbitrer,* to arbitrate < Lat. *arbitrari,* to give judgment. —see ARBITRATE.]

ar·bit·ra·ment (är-bĭt'rə-mənt) *n.* **1.** The act of arbitrating. **2.** The judgment or award of an arbitrator or arbiter. [ME *arbitrement* < OFr. < *arbitrer,* to judge < Lat. *arbitrari,* to give judgment. —see ARBITRATE.]

ar·bi·trar·y (är'bĭ-trĕr'ē) *adj.* **1.** Determined by whim or impulse, not by reason or law. **2.** Based on or subject to individual judgment or discretion. **3.** Established by a court or judge rather than by a specific law or statute. **4.** Not limited by law; despotic. [ME *arbitrarie* < Lat. *arbitrarius* < *arbiter,* arbiter.] **—ar'bi·trar'i·ly** (-trâr'-ə-lē) *adv.* **—ar'bi·trar'i·ness** *n.*

ar·bi·trate (är'bĭ-trāt') *v.* **-trat·ed, -trat·ing, -trates.** *—tr.* **1.** To judge or decide as or in the manner of an arbitrator. **2.** To submit to settlement or judgment by arbitration. *—intr.* **1.** To serve as an arbitrator or arbiter. **2.** To refer or submit a dispute to arbitration. [Lat. *arbitrari,* to give judgment < *arbiter,* arbiter.]

ar·bi·tra·tion (är'bĭ-trā'shən) *n.* The process by which the parties to a dispute submit their differences to the judgment of an impartial person or group appointed by mutual consent or statutory provision.

ar·bi·tra·tor (är'bĭ-trā'tər) *n.* **1.** A person chosen to settle the issue between parties engaged in a dispute or controversy. **2.** One having the ability or power to make authoritative decisions; arbiter.

arch[1]
Arch of Triumph, Paris, France

ar·bor[1] (är'bər) *n.* **1.** A shady garden shelter or bower, often made of rustic work or latticework on which vines, roses, or other climbing plants are grown. **2.** *Obs.* An orchard or garden. [ME *herber* < OFr. *herbier, erbier,* garden < *erbe,* herb. —see HERB.]

ar·bor[2] (är'bər) *n.* **1.** An axis or shaft supporting a rotating part on a lathe. **2.** A bar for supporting cutting tools. **3.** A spindle of a wheel, as in watches and clocks. **4.** *Archaic.* A tree. [Lat., tree.]

Arbor Day *n.* A day, usually in the spring, observed by many states of the United States for the community planting of trees.

ar·bo·re·al (är-bôr'ē-əl, -bōr'-) *adj.* **1.** Pertaining to or resembling a tree. **2.** Living in trees: *arboreal animals.* **—ar·bo're·al·ly** *adv.*

ar·bo·re·ous (är-bôr'ē-əs, -bōr'-) *adj.* **1.** Having many trees; wooded. **2.** Resembling or characteristic of a tree; treelike.

ar·bo·res·cent (är'bə-rĕs'ənt) *adj.* Having the form or characteristics of a tree; treelike. [Lat. *arborescens, arborescent-,* pr.part. of *arborescere,* to grow to be a tree < *arbor,* tree.] **—ar'bo·res'cence** *n.*

ar·bo·re·tum (är'bə-rē'təm) *n., pl.* **-tums** or **-ta** (-tə). A place for the scientific study and public exhibition of many species of trees and shrubs. [Lat., a place grown with trees < *arbor,* tree.]

ar·bo·ri·cul·ture (är'bə-rĭ-kŭl'chər, är-bôr'ĭ-, -bōr'-) *n.* The cultivation of trees for study or for the production of timber.

ar·bo·ri·za·tion (är'bər-ĭ-zā'shən) *n.* **1.** A treelike shape or arrangement, as that of certain minerals or fossils. **2.** The formation of an arborization.

ar·bo·rize (är'bə-rīz') *intr.v.* **-rized, -riz·ing, -riz·es.** To have or form many branches.

archaic smile

ar·bor·vi·tae also **ar·bor vi·tae** (är'bər-vī'tē) *n.* **1. a.** Any of several evergreen shrubs and trees of the genus *Thuja,* having tiny, scalelike leaves and egg-shaped cones. **b.** A similar tree of the genus *Thujopsis.* **2.** *Anat.* The white matter of the cerebellum, in cross section having the appearance of a tree. [NLat. *arbor vitae,* tree of life.]

ar·bour (är'bər) *n. Chiefly Brit.* Variant of **arbor[1]**.

ar·bo·vi·rus (är'bə-vī'rəs) *n.* Any of various arthropod-borne viruses that include the causative agent of encephalitis. [AR(THROPOD) + BO(RNE) + VIRUS.] **—ar'bo·vi'ral** *adj.* **—ar'bo·vi·rol'o·gy** (är'bō-vĭ-rŏl'ə-jē) *n.*

ar·bu·tus (är-byōō'təs) *n.* **1.** Any of several broad-leaved evergreen trees of the genus *Arbutus,* having clusters of white or pinkish flowers. **2.** The trailing arbutus. [NLat. *Arbutus,* genus name < Lat. *arbutus,* arbutus.]

arc (ärk) *n.* **1.** Something shaped like a bow, curve, or arch. **2.** *Math.* A segment of a curve. **3.** *Elect.* A luminous discharge of electric current crossing a gap between two electrodes. *—adj. Math.* Designating an inverse trigonometric function: *the arc sine of a quantity.* *—intr.v.* **arced** (ärkt) or **arcked, arc·ing** (är'kĭng) or **arck·ing, arcs.** To form an arc. [ME *ark* < OFr. *arc* < Lat. *arcus.*]

ar·cade (är-kād') *n.* **1.** *Archit.* **a.** A series of arches supported by columns, piers, or pillars. **b.** An arched, roofed building or part of a building. **2.** A roofed passageway or lane, esp. one with shops on either side. *—tr.v.* **-cad·ed, -cad·ing, -cades.** To provide with or form into an arcade: *an arcaded walk.* [Fr., archway < Ital. *arcata* < *arco,* arch < Lat. *arcus.*]

Ar·ca·di·a (är-kā'dē-ə) *n.* **1.** A region in ancient Greece regarded as an ideal of rural simplicity and contentment. **2.** Often **arcadia.** A region offering rural simplicity and contentment.

Ar·ca·di·an (är-kā'dē-ən) *adj.* **1.** Of, pertaining to, or characteristic of Arcadia. **2.** Often **arcadian.** Rustic, peaceful, and simple; pastoral. *—n.* **1.** A native of Arcadia. **2.** Often **arcadian.** A person who leads or prefers a simple, rural life. **3.** The dialect of ancient Greek used in Arcadia.

Ar·ca·dy (är'kə-dē) *n.* Arcadia.

ar·ca·na (är-kā'nə) *n.* A plural of **arcanum.**

ar·cane (är-kān') *adj.* Known or understood only by a few; esoteric. [Lat. *arcanus,* secret < *arcere,* to shut up < *arca,* chest.]

ar·ca·num (är-kā'nəm) *n., pl.* **-na** (-nə) or **-nums. 1.** A profound secret; mystery. **2.** The reputed great secret of nature that alchemists sought to find. **3.** An elixir. [Lat. < *arcanus,* secret. —see ARCANE.]

arc-bou·tant (är'bōō-täN') *n., pl.* **arcs-bou·tants** (är'bōō-täN'). A flying buttress. [Fr.]

arch[1] (ärch) *n.* **1.** A structural device, esp. of masonry, forming the curved, pointed, or flat upper edge of an opening or a support, as in a bridge or doorway. **2.** A structure similar to an arch, as a monument. **3.** Something curved like an arch: *the arch of a rainbow.* **4.** *Anat.* Any of various arch-shaped structures, esp. either of two such bony structures of the foot. *—v.* **arched, arch·ing, arch·es.** *—tr.* **1.** To supply with an arch. **2.** To cause to form an arch or similar curve: *arch one's eyebrows.* **3.** To span: *"the rude bridge that arched the flood"* (Emerson). *—intr.* To form an arch or archlike curve. [ME < OFr. *arche* < Lat. *arcus.*]

arch[2] (ärch) *adj.* **1.** Chief; principal: *an arch-thief.* **2.** Mischievous; roguish: *an arch glance.* [< ARCH-.] **—arch'ly** *adv.* **—arch'ness** *n.*

arch– *pref.* **1.** Variant of **archi-. 2.** The extreme or most characteristic example of its kind: *archconservative.* [ME. —see ARCHI-.]

–arch *suff.* Ruler; leader: *matriarch.* [ME *-arche* < OFr. < LLat. *-archa* < Lat. *-arches* < Gk. *-arkhēs* < *arkhos,* ruler < *arkhein,* to rule.]

Ar·chae·an (är-kē'ən) *adj.* Variant of **Archean.**

archaeo– or **archeo–** *pref.* Ancient; earlier; primitive: *archaeopteryx.* [NLat. < Gk. *arkhaio-* < *arkhaios,* ancient < *arkhē,* beginning.]

ar·chae·ol·o·gy or **ar·che·ol·o·gy** (är'kē-ŏl'ə-jē) *n.* The systematic recovery and study of material evidence, such as graves, buildings, tools, and pottery, remaining from past human life and culture. [Fr. *archéologie* < Gk. *arkhaiologia,* antiquarian lore : *arkhaios,* old + *-logia,* -logy.] **—ar'chae·o·log'i·cal** (-ə-lŏj'ĭ-kəl), **ar'chae·o·log'ic** *adj.* **—ar'chae·ol'o·gist** *n.*

ar·chae·op·ter·yx (är'kē-ŏp'tər-ĭks) *n.* An extinct primitive bird of the genus *Archaeopteryx,* of the Jurassic period, having lizardlike characteristics and representing a transitional form between reptiles and birds. [NLat. : ARCHAEO- + Gk. *pterux,* bird < *pteron,* wing.]

Ar·chae·o·zo·ic (är'kē-ə-zō'ĭk) *adj. & n.* Variant of **Archeozoic.**

ar·cha·ic (är-kā'ĭk) also **ar·cha·i·cal** (-ĭ-kəl) *adj.* **1.** Belonging to a much earlier time; ancient: *archaic sculpture.* **2.** No longer current or applicable; antiquated: *archaic laws.* **3.** Designating or characteristic of words and language that were once common but are now used chiefly to suggest an earlier style or period. [Fr. *archaïque* < Gk. *arkhaikos,* old-fashioned < *arkhaios,* old < *arkhē,* beginning < *arkhein,* to begin.] **—ar·cha'i·cal·ly** *adv.*

archaic smile *n.* A representation of the human mouth with slightly upturned corners, characteristic of early Greek sculpture produced before the 5th century B.C.

ar·cha·ism (är'kē-ĭz'əm, -kā-) *n.* **1.** An archaic word, phrase, idiom, or expression. **2.** An archaic style, quality, or usage. [NLat. *archaeismus* < Gk. *arkhaismos* < *arkhaios,* ancient. —see ARCHAIC.] **—ar'cha·ist** *n.* **—ar'cha·is'tic** (-ĭs'tĭk) *adj.*

ar·cha·ize (är'kē-īz', -kā-) *v.* **-ized, -iz·ing, -iz·es.** *—tr.* To give an archaic quality or character to; make archaic. —*intr.* To use archaisms. **—ar'cha·iz'er** *n.*

arch·an·gel (ärk'ān'jəl) *n. Theol.* **1.** A celestial being next in rank above an angel. **2. archangels.** The eighth of the nine orders of angels. [ME < OFr. < LLat. *archangelus* < LGk. *arkhangelos* : Gk. *arkh-*, archi- + *angelos*, angel.] **—arch'an·gel'ic** (-ăn-jĕl'ĭk) *adj.*

arch·bish·op (ärch-bĭsh'əp) *n.* A bishop of the highest rank, heading an archdiocese or province. [ME *arche-bishop* < OE *arce-bisceop* < LLat. *archiepiscopus* < LGk. *arkhiepiskopos* : Gk. *arkhi-*, archi- + *episkopos*, bishop. —see BISHOP.] **—arch·bish'op·ric** *n.*

arch·dea·con (ärch-dē'kən) *n.* A church official, chiefly in the Anglican Church, in charge of temporal and other affairs in a diocese, with powers delegated from the bishop. [ME *arche-deken* < OE *arcediakon* < LLat. *archidiăconus* < LGk. *arkhidiakonos* : Gk. *arkhi*, archi- + *diakonos*, deacon. —see DEACON.] **—arch·dea'con·ate** (-kə-nĭt) *n.* **—arch·dea'con·ship'** *n.*

arch·dea·con·ry (ärch-dē'kən-rē) *n., pl.* **-ries. 1.** The rank, office, or jurisdiction of an archdeacon. **2.** The residence or district of an archdeacon.

arch·di·o·cese (ärch-dī'ə-sĭs, -sēs', -sēz') *n.* A diocese under an archbishop's jurisdiction. **—arch'di·oc'e·san** (-ŏs'ĭ-sən) *adj.*

arch·du·cal (ärch-do͞o'kəl, -dyo͞o'-) *adj.* Of or pertaining to an archduke or an archduchy.

arch·duch·ess (ärch-dŭch'ĭs) *n.* **1.** The wife or widow of an archduke. **2.** A woman having a rank equivalent to that of an archduke, esp. an Austrian princess.

arch·duch·y (ärch-dŭch'ē) *n., pl.* **-ies.** The territory over which an archduke or an archduchess has authority.

arch·duke (ärch-do͞ok', -dyo͞ok') *n.* In certain royal families, esp. that of imperial Austria, a nobleman having a rank equivalent to that of a sovereign prince.

Ar·che·an also **Ar·chae·an** (är-kē'ən) *adj.* Of or pertaining to the oldest rocks of the Precambrian era, predominantly igneous in composition. [< Gk. *arkhaios*, ancient. —see ARCHAIC.]

arched (ärcht) *adj.* **1.** Forming an arch or a curve like that of an arch. **2.** Provided, made, or covered with an arch.

ar·che·go·ni·um (är'kĭ-gō'nē-əm) *n., pl.* **-ni·a** (-nē-ə). The multicellular female sex organ of mosses and related plants, producing a single egg. [NLat. < Gk. *arkhegonos*, original : *arkhe-*, archi- + *gonos*, race.] **—ar'che·go'ni·al** *adj.* **—ar'che·go'ni·ate** (-ĭt) *adj.*

arch·en·e·my (ärch-ĕn'ə-mē) *n.* **1.** A chief or principal enemy. **2.** Often **Archenemy.** The devil; Satan.

ar·chen·ter·on (är-kĕn'tə-rŏn', -rən) *n.* The embryonic digestive tract, essentially a cavity in the gastrula. **—ar'chen·ter'ic** (är'kĕn-tĕr'ĭk) *adj.*

archeo– *pref.* Variant of **archaeo-.**

ar·che·ol·o·gy (är'kē-ŏl'ə-jē) *n.* Variant of **archaeology.**

Ar·che·o·zo·ic also **Ar·chae·o·zo·ic** (är'kē-ə-zō'ĭk) *—adj.* Of, belonging to, or designating the earlier of two generally arbitrary divisions of the Precambrian era. *—n.* The Archeozoic era.

arch·er (är'chər) *n.* **1.** One who shoots with a bow and arrow. **2. Archer.** Sagittarius. [ME < OFr. *archier* < Med. Lat. *arcarius* < Lat. *arcus*, bow.]

arch·er·fish (är'chər-fĭsh') *n., pl.* **archerfish** or **-fish·es.** Any of several small Indo-Australian fishes of the family Toxotidae, capable of capturing insects by squirting water at them.

arch·er·y (är'chə-rē) *n.* **1.** The art, sport, or skill of shooting with a bow and arrow. **2.** The equipment of an archer. **3.** A troop or body of archers.

ar·che·spore (är'kĭ-spôr', -spōr') also **ar·che·spo·ri·um** (-spôr'ē-əm, -spōr'-) *n., pl.* **-spores** also **-spo·ri·a** (-spôr'ē-ə, -spōr'-). *Bot.* A spore-bearing cell or mass of cells. [NLat. *archesporium* : *arche(gonium)*, archegonium + *spora*, spore.] **—ar'che·spo'ri·al** *adj.*

ar·che·type (är'kĭ-tīp') *n.* An original model or type after which other similar things are patterned; prototype. [Lat. *archetypum* < Gk. *arkhetupon* : *arkhe-*, archi- + *tupos*, model.] **—ar'che·typ'al** (-tī'pəl), **ar'che·typ'ic** (-tĭp'ĭk), **ar'che·typ'i·cal** *adj.* **—ar'che·typ'i·cal·ly** *adv.*

arch·fiend (ärch-fēnd') *n.* **1.** A chief or foremost fiend. **2. the Archfiend.** The devil; Satan.

archi– or **arch–** *pref.* **1.** Chief; highest; most important: *archduke.* **2.** Earlier; primitive: *archenteron.* [ME *arche-*, arch- < OE *ærce-* and OFr. *arche-*, both < Lat. *archi-* < Gk. *arkhi-* < *arkhein*, to begin, rule.]

ar·chi·di·ac·o·nal (är'kĭ-dī-ăk'ə-nəl) *adj.* Of or pertaining to an archdeacon, his duties, or his office. [< LLat. *archidiaconus*, archdeacon.]

ar·chi·di·ac·o·nate (är'kĭ-dī-ăk'ə-nĭt) *n.* The office or status of an archdeacon. [Med. Lat. *archidiaconatus* < LLat. *archidiăconus*, archdeacon.]

ar·chi·e·pis·co·pal (är'kē-ĭ-pĭs'kə-pəl) *adj.* Of or pertaining to an archbishop or an archbishopric. [Med. Lat. *archiepiscopālis* < LLat. *archiepiscopus*, archbishop.] **—ar'chi·e·pis'co·pal'i·ty** (-păl'ĭ-tē) *n.* **—ar'chi·e·pis'co·pal·ly** *adv.* **—ar'chi·e·pis'co·pate** *n.*

archiepiscopal cross *n.* A processional crucifix mounted on a tall shaft and borne before an archbishop.

ar·chil (är'kĭl, -chĭl) *n.* Variant of **orchil.**

ar·chi·mage (är'kə-māj') *n.* A great magician or chief wizard. [LGk. *arkhimagos* : Gk. *arkhe-*, archi- + Gk. *Magos*, wizard < OPers. *Maguus*, one of a tribe of Medes.]

ar·chi·man·drite (är'kə-măn'drīt') *n. Gk. Orthodox Ch.* **1.** A cleric ranking below a bishop. **2.** The head of a monastery or group of monasteries. [LLat. *archimandrita* < LGk. *arkhimandritēs* : Gk. *arkhi-*, archi- + *mandra*, monastery < Gk., cattle pen.]

Ar·chi·me·de·an (är'kə-mē'dē-ən, -mĭ-dē'-) *adj.* Of or pertaining to the Greek mathematician Archimedes or his inventions.

Archimedean screw *n.* An ancient apparatus for raising water, consisting of either a spiral tube around an inclined axis or an inclined tube containing a tight-fitting, broad-threaded screw.

Ar·chi·me·des' screw (är'kə-mē'dēz') *n.* An Archimedean screw.

ar·chine also **ar·shin** (är-shēn') *n.* A Russian unit of linear measure equivalent to 28 inches. [R. *arshin*, of Turkic orig.]

ar·chi·pel·a·go (är'kə-pĕl'ə-gō') *n., pl.* **-goes** or **-gos. 1.** A large group of islands. **2.** A sea, as the Aegean, containing a large group of islands. [Ital. *Arcipelago*, the Aegean Sea : < Gk. *arkhi-*, archi- + Gk. *pelagos*, sea.] **—ar'chi·pe·lag'ic** (-pə-lăj'ĭk) *adj.*

ar·chi·tect (är'kĭ-tĕkt') *n.* **1.** One who designs and supervises the construction of buildings or other large structures. **2.** A planner or deviser: *the chief architect of their success.* [OFr. *architecte* < Lat. *architectus* < Gk. *arkhitektōn*, master builder : *arkhi-*, archi- + *tektōn*, builder.]

ar·chi·tec·ton·ic (är'kĭ-tĕk-tŏn'ĭk) also **ar·chi·tec·ton·i·cal** (-ĭ-kəl) *adj.* **1.** Of or pertaining to architecture or design. **2.** Having qualities characteristic of architecture; designed and structured. **3.** *Philos.* Relating to the scientific systematization of knowledge. [Lat. *architectonicus*, architectural < Gk. *arkhitektonikos* < *arkhitektōn*, architect.] **—ar'chi·tec·ton'i·cal·ly** *adv.*

ar·chi·tec·ton·ics (är'kĭ-tĕk-tŏn'ĭks) *n.* *(used with a sing. verb).* **1.** The science of architecture. **2.** Structural design, as in a musical work. **3.** *Philos.* The scientific systematization of knowledge.

ar·chi·tec·ture (är'kĭ-tĕk'chər) *n.* **1.** The art and science of designing and erecting buildings. **2.** Architectural structures collectively. **3.** A style and method of design and construction: *Byzantine architecture.* **4.** Design or orderly arrangement perceived by man: *the architecture of nature.* [OFr. < Lat. *architectura* < *architectus*, architect.] **—ar'chi·tec'tur·al** *adj.* **—ar'chi·tec'tur·al·ly** *adv.*

ar·chi·trave (är'kĭ-trāv') *n. Archit.* **1.** The lowermost part of an entablature, resting directly on top of a column in classical architecture. **2.** The molding around a door or window. [OFr. < OItal. : *archi*, archi- (< Lat.) + *trave*, beam < Lat. *trabs.*]

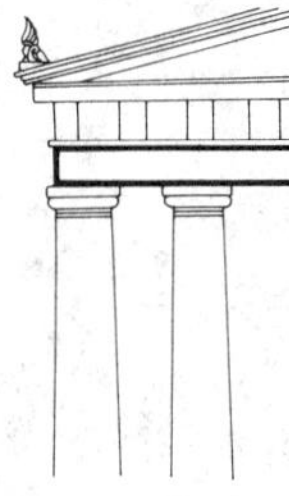
architrave

ar·chi·val (är-kī'vəl) *adj.* Of, pertaining to, or kept in archives.

archival standards *pl.n.* Standards set by the U.S. Bureau of Standards to assure permanence of microfilm images.

ar·chives (är'kīvz') *pl.n.* **1. a.** An organized body of records pertaining to an organization or institution. **b.** A place in which such records are preserved. **2.** A repository of evidence or information: *the archives of the mind.* [Fr. < LLat. *archium* < Gk. *arkheia* < *arkhē*, beginning < *arkhein*, to begin.]

ar·chi·vist (är'kə-vĭst, -kī'-) *n.* One who is in charge of archives.

ar·chi·volt (är'kə-vōlt') also **ar·chi·vault** (-vôlt') *n. Archit.* Decorative molding carried around an arched wall opening. [Ital. *archivolto* : *arco*, arch (< Lat. *arcus*) + *volta*, vault < Lat. *voluta*, fem. p.part. of *volvere*, to roll.]

ar·chon (är'kŏn', -kən) *n.* **1.** One of the nine principal magistrates of ancient Athens. **2.** Any of various officials of the Byzantine Empire. **3.** In certain Gnostic systems, one of several powers believed to be superior to the angels. [Gk. *arkhōn*, ruler, pr.part. of *arkhein*, to rule.] **—ar'chon·ship'** *n.*

arch·priest (ärch-prēst') *n.* **1.** Formerly, a priest holding first rank among the members of a cathedral chapter, acting as chief assistant to a bishop. **2.** A rural dean. Now used only as a title of honor. [ME *arche-prest* < OFr. *archeprestre* < LLat. *archipresbyter* < LGk. *arkhipresbuteros* : Gk. *arkhi-*, archi- + *presbuteros*, priest.]

arch·way (ärch'wā') *n.* **1.** A passageway under an arch. **2.** An arch covering or enclosing an entrance or passageway.

–archy *suff.* Rule; government: *oligarchy.* [ME *-archie* < OFr. < Lat. *-archia* < Gk. *-arkhia* < *-arkhēs*, ruler. —see -ARCH.]

ar·ci·form (är'sə-fôrm') *adj.* Formed like an arc.

arc jet *n.* An arc-jet engine.

arc-jet engine (ärk'jĕt') *n.* A rocket engine that operates by heating the propellant gas with an electric arc.

arcked (ärkt) *v.* A past tense and past participle of **arc.**

arck·ing (är'kĭng) *v.* A present participle of **arc.**

arc lamp also **arc light** *n.* An electric lamp in which a current traverses a gas between two incandescent electrodes.

arc·tic (ärk'tĭk, är'tĭk) *adj.* **1.** Extremely cold; frigid. **2. Arctic.** Of or relating to a geographic area extending from the North Pole to the northern timberline. *—n.* A warm, waterproof overshoe. [ME *artik* < Lat. *arcticus* < Gk. *arktikos* < *arktos,* bear, the northern constellation Ursa Major.]

Arctic Circle *n.* The parallel of latitude 66 degrees, 33 minutes north; the boundary between the North Temperate and North Frigid zones.

arctic fox *n.* A fox, *Alopex lagopus,* of arctic regions, having fur that is white or light-gray in winter and brown or blue-gray in summer.

Arc·tu·rus (ärk-to͝or′əs, -tyo͝or′-) *n. Astron.* The brightest star in the constellation Boötes, approximately 36 light-years from earth. [ME *Arctour* < Lat. *Arcturus* < Gk. *Arktouros* : *arktos,* bear + *ouros,* guard.]

ar·cu·ate (är′kyo͞o-ĭt, -āt′) also **ar·cu·at·ed** (-ā′tĭd) *adj.* Having the form of a bow; curved. [Lat. *arcuatus,* p.part. of *arcuare,* to bend like a bow < *arcus,* bow.]

ar·cu·a·tion (är′kyo͞o-ā′shən) *n.* **1.** The process of curving or the state of being curved. **2.** *Archit.* The use of arches or vaults in building.

-ard or **-art** *suff.* One that habitually or excessively is in a specified condition or performs a specified action: *drunkard.* [ME < OFr., of Germanic orig.]

ar·deb (är′dĕb′) *n.* A unit of dry measure of several countries of the Near East, usually equal to 5.6 U.S. bushels but with variations in different localities. [Ar. *ardabb* < Gk. *artabē.*]

ar·dent (är′dnt) *adj.* **1. a.** Expressing or characterized by warmth of passion, emotion, or desire: *an ardent lover.* **b.** Displaying or characterized by strong enthusiasm or devotion; fervent: *"an impassioned age, so ardent and serious in its pursuit of art"* (Walter Pater). **2.** Glowing; shining: *ardent eyes.* **3.** Hot as fire; burning: *"The temperate yet ardent climate"* (Winston Churchill). [ME *ardaunt* < OFr. < Lat. *ardens,* pr.part. of *ardēre,* to burn.] **—ar′den·cy** (-dn-sē) *n.* **—ar′dent·ly** *adv.* **—ar′dent·ness** *n.*

argali

ardent spirits *pl.n.* Strong alcoholic liquors, such as whiskey or gin.

ar·dor (är′dər) *n.* **1. a.** Great warmth or intensity, as of emotion, passion, or desire. **b.** Strong enthusiasm or devotion; zeal: *"the dazzling conquest of Mexico gave a new impulse to the ardor of discovery"* (William H. Prescott). **2.** Intense heat, as of fire. [ME *ardour* < OFr. < Lat. *ardor* < *ardēre,* to burn.]

ar·dour (är′dər) *n. Chiefly Brit.* Variant of **ardor.**

ar·du·ous (är′jo͞o-əs) *adj.* **1.** Demanding great care, effort, or labor; difficult: *"the arduous work of preparing a Dictionary of the English Language"* (Macaulay). **2.** Testing severely the powers of endurance; full of hardships: *a long, arduous, and exhausting war.* **3.** Hard to climb or surmount: *an arduous path; an arduous assignment.* [Lat. *arduus.*] **—ar′du·ous·ly** *adv.* **—ar′du·ous·ness** *n.*

are[1] (är) *v.* Present tense indicative plural and second person singular of **be.** [ME *aren* < OE *aron.*]

are[2] (âr, är) also **ar** (är) *n.* A metric unit of area equal to 100 square meters. [Fr. < Lat. *area,* open space.]

ar·e·a (âr′ē-ə) *n.* **1.** A section or region, as of land: *a farming area; the New York area.* **2.** A surface, esp. part of the earth's surface: *a landing area; mountainous areas.* **3.** A distinct part or section, as of a building, set aside for a specific function: *an area for business and an area for exercise.* **4.** The range or scope of something: *the area of finance.* **5.** The yard of a building; areaway. **6.** The measure of a planar region or of the surface of a solid. **7.** *Computer Sci.* A section of computer storage set aside for a particular purpose. [Lat. *area,* open space.]

Synonyms: *area, region, belt, zone, district, locality.* These nouns all mean a division of the space on a surface but differ in what is implied about the size and boundaries of the division. *Area,* the most inclusive term, means any particular portion of a surface and suggests a portion that spreads out in all directions from a center, with a vague periphery. If the area is a large geographical one, it is likely to be called a *region.* If the area is long and narrow, with fairly specific upper and lower limits, it may be called a *belt.* If the area has strictly defined boundaries, especially boundaries fixed arbitrarily so as to set the area apart from adjacent areas, it may be called a *zone: the temperate zone; a demilitarized zone.* If the area is one of human habitation and is regarded as a subdivision for administrative or jurisdictional purposes, it is a *district.* And if the area is simply a place where a thing in question is to be found, it is a *locality.*

Area Code also **area code** *n.* A number, often with three digits, assigned to a telephone area, as in the United States and Canada, used when placing a call to another area.

area rug *n.* A rug that covers a limited area of floor space in a room.

area search *n.* The systematic check of a large group of documents to select those belonging to a particular category.

ar·e·a·way (âr′ē-ə-wā′) *n.* **1.** A small sunken area allowing access or light and air to basement doors or windows. **2.** A passageway, often in close quarters between buildings.

a·re·ca (ə-rē′kə, ăr′ĭ-kə) *n.* Any of various tall palms of the genus *Areca,* of Southeast Asia, having white flowers and red or orange egg-shaped nuts. [Port. < Malayalam *aṭekka.*]

a·re·na (ə-rē′nə) *n.* **1.** The arca in the center of an ancient Roman amphitheater where contests and other spectacles were held. **2.** A modern auditorium for sports events. **3.** A sphere or field of conflict, interest, or activity: *the political arena.* [Lat. *harena.*]

ar·e·na·ceous (ăr′ə-nā′shəs) *adj.* **1.** Sandlike in appearance or qualities: *arenaceous limestone.* **2.** Growing in sandy areas. [Lat. *harenaceus* : *harena,* sand + *-aceus,* aceous.]

arena stage *n.* The stage of an arena theater.

arena theater *n.* A theater without a proscenium in which the stage is at the center of the auditorium, surrounded by seats.

ar·e·nic·o·lous (ăr′ə-nĭk′ə-ləs) *adj.* Growing or living in sand. [Lat. *harena,* sand + -COLOUS.]

aren't (ärnt, är′ənt). Are not.

a·re·o·la (ə-rē′ə-lə) also **ar·e·ole** (âr′ē-ōl′) *n., pl.* **-lae** (-lē′) or **-las** also **-oles** (-ōlz′). **1.** *Biol.* A small space or interstice, such as an area bounded by small veins in a leaf or an insect's wing. **2.** *Anat.* A small, dark-colored area around a center portion, as about a nipple or part of the iris of the eye. [Lat., small open space, dim. of *area,* open place.] **—a·re′o·lar, a·re′o·late** (-lĭt) *adj.* **—a·re′o·la′tion** *n.*

Ar·e·op·a·gite (ăr′ē-ŏp′ə-jīt′, -gīt′) *n.* A member of the council of the Areopagus in ancient Athens. **—Ar′e·op·a·git′ic** *adj.*

Ar·e·op·a·gus (ăr′ē-ŏp′ə-gəs) *n.* The highest council of ancient Athens.

Ar·es (âr′ēz′) *n. Gk. Myth.* The god of war. [Gk. *Arēs.*]

a·rête (ə-rāt′) *n.* A sharp, narrow mountain ridge or spur. [Fr., fishbone < OFr. *areste* < Lat. *arista.*]

Ar·e·thu·sa (ăr′ə-tho͞o′zə, -sə) *n.* **1.** *Gk. Myth.* A wood nymph who was changed into a fountain by Artemis. **2.** Any of several orchids of the genus *Arethusa,* esp. *A. bulbosa,* of eastern North America, having a solitary rose-purple flower fringed with yellow. [Lat. < Gk. *Arethousa.*]

ar·gal (är′gəl) *n.* Variant of **argol.**

ar·ga·li (är′gə-lē) *n., pl.* **argali** or **-lis.** A wild sheep, *Ovis ammon,* of the mountains of central and northern Asia, having large, spirally curved horns. [Mongolian.]

ar·gent (är′jənt) *n.* **1.** *Archaic.* Silver or something resembling it. **2.** *Heraldry.* The metal silver, represented by the color white. [ME < OFr. < Lat. *argentum,* silver.]

ar·gen·tic (är-jĕn′tĭk) *adj.* Of or containing silver.

ar·gen·tif·er·ous (är′jən-tĭf′ər-əs) *adj.* Bearing or producing silver.

ar·gen·tine (är′jən-tīn′, -tēn′) *adj.* Silvery. *—n.* **1.** Silver. **2.** Any of various silvery metals. [Fr. *argentin* < Lat. *argentinus* < *argentum,* silver.]

ar·gen·tite (är′jən-tīt′) *n.* A valuable silver ore, Ag_2S, with a lustrous, lead-gray color.

ar·gil (är′jĭl) *n.* Clay, esp. a white clay used by potters. [ME *argilla* < Lat. < Gk. *argillos.*]

ar·gil·la·ceous (är′jə-lā′shəs) *adj.* Of, containing, made of, or resembling clay; clayey.

ar·gil·lite (är′jə-līt′) *n.* A metamorphic rock, intermediate between shale and slate, that does not possess true slaty cleavage.

ar·gi·nine (är′jə-nēn′) *n.* An amino acid, $C_6H_{14}N_4O_2$, obtained from plant and animal protein or the digestive action of bacteria and necessary for nutrition. [G. *Arginin,* poss. < Gk. *arginoeis,* bright < *argos,* shining.]

Ar·give (är′jīv′, -gīv′) *adj.* **1.** Of or designating Argos or Argolis. **2.** Greek. *—n.* A Greek, esp. an inhabitant of Argos or Argolis.

Ar·go (är′gō′) *n.* **1.** *Gk. Myth.* The ship in which Jason sailed in search of the Golden Fleece. **2.** A constellation in the Southern Hemisphere, now known by the names of its four smaller parts, Carina, Puppis, Pyxis, and Vela.

ar·gol (är′gôl′) also **ar·gal** (-gəl) *n.* Crude potassium bitartrate, a by-product of winemaking. [ME *argoil* < AN.]

ar·gon (är′gŏn′) *n. Symbol* **Ar** A colorless, odorless, inert gaseous element constituting approximately one per cent of the earth's atmosphere, from which it is commercially obtained by fractionation for use in electric lamps, fluorescent tubes, and radio vacuum tubes and as an inert gas shield in arc welding. Atomic number 18; atomic weight 39.94; melting point −189.4°C; boiling point −185.9°C. [< Gk. *argos,* inert : *a-,* no + *ergon,* work.]

Ar·go·naut (är′gə-nôt′) *n.* **1.** *Gk. Myth.* One who sailed with Jason on the *Argo* in search of the Golden Fleece. **2.** One who went to California in 1849 in search of gold. **3. argonaut.** The paper nautilus. [Lat. *Argonauta* < Gk. *Argonautēs* : *Argō,* the ship Argo + *nautēs,* sailor < *naus,* ship.]

ar·go·sy (är′gə-sē) *n., pl.* **-sies. 1.** A large merchant ship. **2.** A fleet of ships. [Alteration of obs. *ragusye* < Ital. *ragusea,* vessel of *Ragusa,* former name of the port of Dubrovnik, Yugoslavia.]

ar·got (är′gō, -gət) *n.* A specialized vocabulary or set of idioms used by a particular class or group. [Fr.]

ar·gu·a·ble (är′gyo͞o-ə-bəl) *adj.* Open to argument. **—ar′gu·a·bly** *adv.*

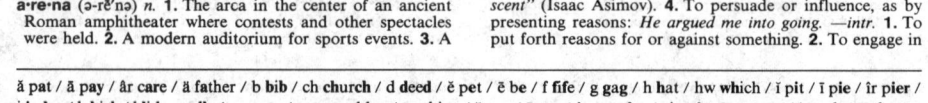

ar·gue (är′gyo͞o) *v.* **-gued, -gu·ing, -gues.** *—tr.* **1.** To put forth reasons for or against; debate. **2.** To prove or attempt to prove by reasoning; maintain. **3.** To give evidence of, indicate: *"similarities cannot always be used to argue descent"* (Isaac Asimov). **4.** To persuade or influence, as by presenting reasons: *He argued me into going.* *—intr.* **1.** To put forth reasons for or against something. **2.** To engage in a quarrel; dispute. [ME *arguen* < OFr. *arguer* < Lat. *arguere,* to make clear.] **—ar′gu·er** *n.*

Synonyms: *argue, quarrel, wrangle, squabble, haggle, bicker.* These verbs are compared as they mean to dispute. *Argue* implies intent to persuade an adversary in debate. *Quarrel* stresses animosity and estrangement. *Wrangle* refers to loud, contentious argument, and *squabble* to minor argument over a petty or trivial matter. *Haggle* specifies verbal bargaining, usually over a price, in a petty way. *Bicker* suggests sharp, recurrent exchange of remarks on a mean or petty level.

ar·gu·fy (är′gyə-fī′) *v.* **-fied, -fy·ing, -fies.** *Regional.* —*tr.* To argue over. —*intr.* To argue stubbornly; wrangle. **—ar′gu·fi′er** *n.*

ar·gu·ment (är′gyə-mənt) *n.* **1. a.** A discussion in which disagreement is expressed about some point; debate. **b.** A quarrel; contention. **c.** *Archaic.* A reason or matter for dispute or contention. **2. a.** A course of reasoning aimed at demonstrating the truth or falsehood of something. **b.** A fact or statement offered as proof or evidence. **3. a.** A summary or short statement of the plot or subject of a literary work. **b.** A topic; subject: "*You and love are still my argument*" (Shakespeare). **4.** *Logic.* The minor premise in a syllogism. **5.** *Math.* **a.** The independent variable of a function. **b.** The amplitude of a complex number. [ME < OFr. < Lat. *argumentum* < *arguere,* to make clear.]

Synonyms: *argument, dispute, controversy, wrangling.* These nouns denote discussions involving conflicting points of view. *Argument* is generally the least forceful. *Dispute* stresses division of opinion by its implication of contradictory points of view. Usually it also strongly implies animosity. *Controversy* is especially applicable to major differences over subjects involving many persons rather than two contending individuals. *Wrangling* is noisy, angry discussion.

ar·gu·men·ta (är′gyə-mĕn′tə) *n.* Plural of **argumentum.**

ar·gu·men·ta·tion (är′gyə-mĕn-tā′shən) *n.* **1.** The presentation and elaboration of an argument. **2.** Deductive reasoning in debate. **3.** A debate.

ar·gu·men·ta·tive (är′gyə-mĕn′tə-tĭv) *adj.* **1.** Given to arguing; disputatious. **2.** Of or characterized by argument: *an argumentative discourse.* **—ar′gu·men′ta·tive·ly** *adv.* **—ar′gu·men′ta·tive·ness** *n.*

ar·gu·men·tum (är′gyə-mĕn′təm) *n., pl.* **-ta** (-tə). *Logic.* An argument, demonstration, or appeal to reason. [Lat. —see ARGUMENT.]

argumentum ad hom·i·nem (ăd hŏm′ə-nĕm′) *n.* An argument appealing to personal prejudices and emotions rather than to logic or reason. [Lat., argument to the man.]

Ar·gus (är′gəs) *n.* **1.** *Gk. Myth.* A giant with a hundred eyes who was made guardian of Io and later slain by Hermes. **2.** An alert or watchful person; guardian. [Lat. < Gk. *Argos.*]

Ar·gus-eyed (är′gəs-īd′) *adj.* Extremely observant; vigilant.

argus pheasant *n.* A large bird, *Argusianus argus,* of southern Asia and the East Indies, having long tail feathers marked with brilliantly colored eyelike spots. [After *Argus,* whose hundred eyes were given to a peacock's tail.]

ar·gy-bar·gy (är′gē-bär′gē) *n. Chiefly Brit.* A lively or disputatious discussion; wrangling. [Sc., prob. var. of E. *argle-bargle,* redup. of *argle,* to argue obstinately, prob. < ARGUE. —see ARGUE.]

ar·gyle also **ar·gyll** (är′gīl′) *n.* **1.** A knitting pattern of varicolored, diamond-shaped areas on a solid color background. **2.** A sock knit in an argyle pattern. [After Campbell of *Argyle,* orig. from the pattern of their tartan.]

Ar·gy·rol (är′jə-rōl′, -rôl′). A trademark for a dark-brown silver-protein compound used as a local antiseptic.

ar·hat (är′hət) *n.* A Buddhist who has attained enlightenment. [Skt. < pr.part. of *arhati,* he deserves.] **—ar′hat·ship′** *n.*

a·ri·a (är′ē-ə) *n. Mus.* **1.** An air; melody. **2.** A solo vocal piece with instrumental accompaniment, as in an opera. [Ital., melody < Lat. *aer,* air.]

Ar·i·ad·ne (ăr′ē-ăd′nē) *n. Gk. Myth.* The daughter of Minos and Pasiphae who gave Theseus the thread with which to find his way out of the Minotaur's labyrinth. [Gk. *Ariadnē.*]

Ar·i·an (âr′ē-ən, ăr′-) *adj.* Pertaining to Arianism. —*n.* A believer in Arianism.

-arian *suff.* Believer in; advocate or promoter of: *utilitarian.* [Lat. *-arius,* -ary + -AN[1].]

Ar·i·an·ism (ăr′ē-ə-nĭz′əm, âr′-) *n. Theol.* The doctrines of Arius, denying that Jesus was of the same substance as God and holding instead that he was only the highest of created beings.

ar·id (ăr′ĭd) *adj.* **1.** Lacking moisture, esp. because of insufficient rainfall; dry. **2.** Lacking interest or feeling; lifeless; dull. [Lat. *aridus* < *arere,* to be dry.] **—a·rid′i·ty** (ə-rĭd′ĭ-tē), **ar′id·ness** *n.*

Ar·ies (âr′ēz′, âr′ē-ēz′) *n.* **1.** A constellation in the Northern Hemisphere near Taurus and Pisces. **2.** The first sign of the zodiac. [Lat. *aries,* ram.]

a·ri·et·ta (ä′rē-ĕt′ə) also **a·ri·ette** (-ĕt′) *n.* A short aria. [Ital., dim. of *aria,* aria.]

a·right (ə-rīt′) *adv.* Properly; correctly. [ME < OE *ariht* : *a-,* on + *riht,* right.]

ar·il (ăr′əl) *n.* An outer covering or appendage of some seeds, arising at or near the hilum. [Med. Lat. *arillus,* grape stone.] **—ar′iled** *adj.*

a·ri·o·so (ä′rē-ō′sō, -zō) *Mus.* —*adv.* In the style of an aria. Used as a direction to the performer. —*adj.* Resembling an aria. —*n., pl.* **-sos.** A passage or composition in arioso style. [Ital. < *aria,* aria.]

a·rise (ə-rīz′) *intr.v.* **a·rose** (ə-rōz′), **a·ris·en** (ə-rĭz′ən), **a·ris·ing, a·ris·es. 1.** To get up, as from a sitting or prone position. **2.** To move upward; ascend. **3.** To come into being; originate. **4.** To result, issue, or proceed: *new ideas arising from our discussion.* [ME *arisen* < OE *arīsan.*]

a·ris·ta (ə-rĭs′tə) *n., pl.* **-tae** (-tē) or **-tas.** A bristlelike part or process. [Lat., beard of grain.] **—a·ris′tate′** (-tāt′) *adj.*

ar·is·toc·ra·cy (ăr′ĭ-stŏk′rə-sē) *n., pl.* **-cies. 1.** A hereditary privileged ruling class or nobility. **2. a.** Government by the nobility or by a privileged minority or upper class. **b.** A state or country having this form of government. **3. a.** Government by the best citizens. **b.** A state having such government. **4.** A group or class considered to be superior. [OFr. *aristocratie,* government by the best < LLat. *aristocratia* < Gk. *aristokratia* : *aristos,* best + *kratos,* power.]

a·ris·to·crat (ə-rĭs′tə-krăt′, ăr′ĭs-) *n.* **1.** A member of the nobility or aristocracy. **2.** A person having the tastes, opinions, manners, and other characteristics of the aristocracy. **3.** A person who advocates government by an aristocracy. [Fr. *aristocrate* < *aristocratie,* aristocracy < OFr.] **—a·ris′to·crat′ic, a·ris′to·crat′i·cal** *adj.* **—a·ris′to·crat′i·cal·ly** *adv.*

Ar·is·to·te·li·an also **Ar·is·to·te·le·an** (ăr′ĭ-stə-tē′lē-ən, -tēl′yən) *adj.* Of or pertaining to the Greek philosopher Aristotle or his philosophy. —*n.* **1.** A follower of Aristotle or his teachings. **2.** A person who tends to be empirical or scientific in his methods or thought. **—Ar′is·to·te′li·an·ism** *n.*

Aristotelian logic *n.* **1.** Aristotle's deductive method of logic, esp. the theory of the syllogism. **2.** The formal logic based on Aristotle's and dealing with the relations between propositions in terms of their form instead of their content.

a·rith·me·tic (ə-rĭth′mĭ-tĭk) *n.* **1.** The mathematics of integers under addition, subtraction, multiplication, division, involution, and evolution. **2.** Computation or problem solving involving real numbers and the arithmetic operations. **3.** A book on arithmetic. —*adj.* **ar·ith·met·ic** (ăr′ĭth-mĕt′ĭk) or **ar·ith·met·i·cal** (-ĭ-kəl). Of or pertaining to arithmetic. [ME *arsmetrik,* alteration of OFr. *arismetique* < LLat. *arismetica,* alteration of Lat. *arithmetica* < Gk. *arithmētikē* (*tekhnē*), (the art) of counting < *arīthmein,* to count < *arithmos,* number.] **—ar′ith·met′i·cal·ly** *adv.* **—a·rith′me·ti′cian** (-tĭsh′ən) *n.*

ar·ith·met·ic mean (ăr′ĭth-mĕt′ĭk) *n.* The number obtained by dividing the sum of a set of quantities by the number of quantities in the set.

arithmetic progression *n.* A sequence, such as the odd integers 1, 3, 5, 7, . . . , in which each term after the first is formed by adding a constant to each preceding term.

-arium *suff.* A place or device containing or associated with: *planetarium.* [Lat., neuter of *-arius,* -ary.]

ark (ärk) *n.* **1.** In the Old Testament, the chest containing the Ten Commandments written on stone tablets, carried by the Hebrews during their desert wanderings. **2.** The Holy ark. **3.** In the Old Testament, the boat built by Noah for survival during the Flood. **4.** A large, commodious boat. **5.** A place of shelter or refuge. [ME < OE *arc* < Lat. *arca,* chest.]

arm[1] (ärm) *n.* **1.** An upper limb of the human body connecting the hand and wrist to the shoulder. **2.** A part similar to an arm, such as the forelimb of an animal or a long part projecting from a central support in a machine. **3.** Something designed to cover or support the human arm, as a sleeve on an article of clothing or a projecting support on a chair or sofa. **4.** Something branching out from a large mass: *an arm of the sea.* **5.** An administrative or functional branch, as of an organization. **6.** Power or authority: *the long arm of the law.* **—idioms. an arm and a leg.** An extravagant amount: *a cruise that cost an arm and a leg.* **with open arms.** Cordially; hospitably. [ME < OE *earm.*]

arm[2] (ärm) *n.* **1.** A weapon, esp. a firearm. **2.** A branch of a military force, such as the infantry. **3. arms.** Warfare. **4. arms. a.** Heraldic bearings. **b.** Insignia, as of a state, official, family, or organization. **—idiom. up in arms.** Aroused and ready to fight; indignant. —*v.* **armed, arm·ing, arms.** —*intr.* **1.** To supply or equip oneself with arms. **2.** To prepare oneself for or as if for warfare or conflict. —*tr.* **1.** To equip with weapons. **2.** To prepare for war; fortify. **3.** To provide with something that strengthens or increases efficiency. **4.** To prepare (a bomb, for example) for detonation, as by releasing a safety device. [ME *armes* < OFr. < Lat. *arma.*] **—arm′er** *n.*

ar·ma·da (är-mä′də, -mā′-) *n.* **1.** A fleet of warships. **2.** A large group of moving things: *an armada of ants crossing the lawn.* [Sp. < Med. Lat. *armata* < Lat. *armatus,* armed, p.part. of *armare,* to arm < *arma,* arms.]

ar·ma·dil·lo (är′mə-dĭl′ō) *n., pl.* **-los.** Any of several omnivorous, burrowing mammals of the family Dasypodidae, of southern North America and South America, having a covering of armorlike, jointed, bony plates. [Sp., dim. of *armado,* armored, p.part. of *armar,* to arm < Lat. *armare* < *arma,* arms.]

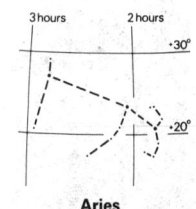

Ar·ma·ged·don (är′mə-gĕd′n) *n.* **1.** The scene of a final bat-

Argus

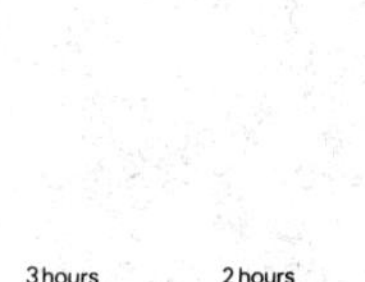

Aries

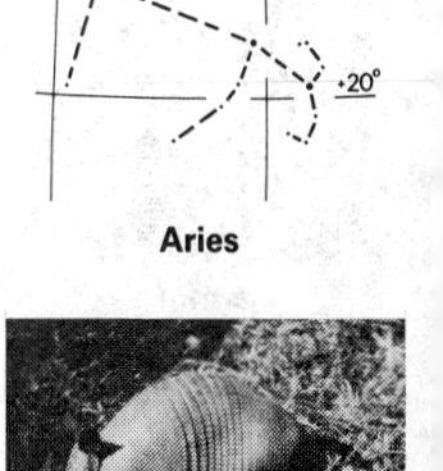

armadillo

p **pop** / r **roar** / s **sauce** / sh **ship, dish** / t **tight** / th **thin, path** / *th* **this, bathe** / ŭ **cut** / ûr **urge** / v **valve** / w **with** / y **yes** / z **zebra, size** / zh **vision** / ə **about, item, edible, gallop, circus** / œ *Fr.* **feu,** *Ger.* **schön** / ü *Fr.* **tu,** *Ger.* **über** / KH *Ger.* **ich,** *Scot.* **loch** / N *Fr.* **bon.**

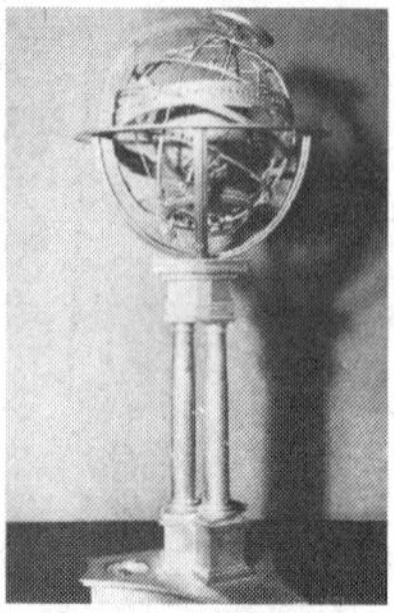

armillary sphere
15th-century armillary sphere

armoire
18th-century American Sheraton-style armoire

armor

arpeggio
Notation for a keyboard instrument

tle between the forces of good and evil, prophesied in the Bible to occur at the end of the world. **2.** A decisive conflict. [LLat. *Armagedon* < Gk. < Heb. *har megiddōn,* mountain district of Megiddo, the site of several great battles mentioned in the Bible.]

Ar·ma·gnac (är′mən-yăk′) *n.* A dry brandy. [Fr., after *Armagnac,* a region in southwest France.]

ar·ma·ment (är′mə-mənt) *n.* **1.** The weapons and supplies of war with which a military unit is equipped. **2.** Often **armaments.** All the military forces and war equipment of a country. **3.** A military force equipped for war. **4.** The process of arming for war. [Lat. *armamenta,* tools < *arma,* arms.]

ar·ma·men·tar·i·um (är′mə-mĕn-târ′ē-əm) *n., pl.* **-i·ums** or **-i·a** (-ē-ə). The complete equipment of a physician or medical institution, including books, supplies, and instruments. [Lat., arsenal < *armamenta,* tools, armaments.]

ar·ma·ture (är′mə-cho͝or′, -chər) *n.* **1.** *Elect.* **a.** The rotating part of a dynamo consisting essentially of copper wire wound around an iron core. **b.** The moving part of an electromagnetic device such as a relay, buzzer, or loud-speaker. **c.** A piece of soft iron connecting the poles of a magnet. **2.** *Biol.* The protective covering or structure of an animal or plant. **3.** A framework serving as a supporting core for clay sculpture. **4.** Armor. [Lat. *armatura,* equipment < *armare,* to arm < *arma,* arms.]

arm·chair (ärm′châr′) *n.* A chair with side structures to support the arms or elbows. *—adj.* Remote from active involvement: *an armchair warrior.*

armed (ärmd) *adj.* **1.** Equipped with weapons. **2.** Having or characterized by an arm or arms of a stated kind or number: *strong-armed.*

armed forces *pl.n.* The military forces of a country.

Ar·me·ni·an (är-mē′nē-ən, -mēn′yən) *n.* **1.** A native or inhabitant of Armenia. **2.** The Indo-European language of the Armenians. **—Ar·me′ni·an** *adj.*

ar·met (är′mĕt′) *n.* A medieval light helmet with a neck guard and movable visor. [OFr.]

arm·ful (ärm′fo͝ol′) *n.* As much as an arm can hold.

arm·hole (ärm′hōl′) *n.* An opening for the arm in a garment.

ar·mi·ger (är′mə-jər) *n.* **1.** An armorbearer for a knight; squire. **2.** A person entitled to heraldic arms. [Lat. : *arma,* arms + *gerere,* to carry.]

ar·mil·lar·y sphere (är′mə-lĕr′ē, är-mĭl′ə-rē) *n.* An astronomical model with solid rings, all circles of a single sphere, used to display relationships among the principal celestial circles. [Fr. *sphère armillaire* < Lat. *armilla,* bracelet < *armus,* shoulder.]

Ar·min·i·an·ism (är-mĭn′ē-ə-nĭz′əm) *n.* The doctrines of Jacobus Arminius and his followers, opposing the Calvinist doctrine of absolute predestination. **—Ar·min′i·an** *adj. & n.*

ar·mi·stice (är′mĭ-stĭs) *n.* A temporary cessation or suspension of hostilities by mutual consent; truce. [NLat. *armistitium* : Lat. *arma,* arms + Lat. *-stitium,* a stopping < *sistere,* to stop.]

Armistice Day *n.* November 11, celebrated as the anniversary of the armistice of World War I in 1918. It has been called Veterans' Day since 1954.

arm·let (ärm′lĭt) *n.* **1.** A band worn on the arm for ornament or identification. **2.** A small arm, as of the sea.

ar·moire (ärm-wär′, är′mər) *n.* A large ornate cabinet or wardrobe. [OFr., var. of *armaire* < Lat. *armarium,* closet < *arma,* tools.]

ar·mor (är′mər) *n.* **1.** A defensive covering, such as chain mail, worn to protect the body against weapons. **2.** A tough protective covering, such as the bony scales covering certain animals or metallic plates on tanks or warships. **3.** Something serving as a safeguard or protection. **4.** The armored vehicles of an army. *—tr.v.* **-mored, -mor·ing, -mors.** To cover with armor. [ME *armure* < OFr. *armëure* < Lat. *armatura* < *armare,* to arm < *arma,* arms.]

ar·mor·bear·er (är′mər-bâr′ər) *n.* One who carries the armor of a warrior.

ar·mor-clad (är′mər-klăd′) *adj.* Wearing or covered with armor.

ar·mored (är′mərd) *adj.* **1.** Clad or covered with armor. **2.** Equipped with armored vehicles, as a military unit.

ar·mor·er (är′mər-ər) *n.* **1.** One who makes or repairs armor. **2.** A manufacturer of weapons. **3.** An enlisted man in charge of maintenance and repair of the small arms of his unit.

ar·mo·ri·al (är-môr′ē-əl, -mōr′-) *adj.* Of or pertaining to heraldry or heraldic arms. *—n.* A book or treatise on heraldry.

Ar·mor·ic (är-môr′ĭk, -mōr′-) also **Ar·mor·i·can** (-ĭ-kən) *adj.* Of or pertaining to Armorica or the people or language of Armorica. *—n.* **1.** A native or inhabitant of Armorica. **2.** Breton (sense 2).

armor plate *n.* Specially formulated hard steel plate used to cover warships, vehicles, and fortifications. **—ar′mor-plat′ed** *adj.*

ar·mor·y (är′mə-rē) *n., pl.* **-ies. 1.** A storehouse for arms; arsenal. **2.** A building for storing arms and military equipment, esp. one serving as headquarters for military reserve personnel. **3.** An arms factory.

ar·mour (är′mər) *n. Chiefly Brit.* Variant of **armor.**

arm·pit (ärm′pĭt′) *n.* The hollow under the arm at the shoulder.

arm·rest (ärm′rĕst′) *n.* A support for the arm, as on a piece of furniture or the inner surface of the door of a vehicle.

arm-twist·ing (ärm′twĭs′tĭng) *n.* The use of esp. strong pressure to accomplish a goal: *"subjecting vulnerable congressmen to some political arm-twisting"* (James R. Gaines).

arm wrestling *n.* A form of wrestling in which two opponents sit facing each other with usually right hands interlocked and elbows firmly planted, as on a table surface, and attempt to force each other's arm down. **—arm′-wres′tle** *v.* **(-tled, -tling, -tles).**

ar·my (är′mē) *n., pl.* **-mies. 1.** A large body of men organized and trained for warfare on land. **2.** The entire military land forces of a country. **3.** A tactical and administrative military unit consisting of a headquarters, two or more army corps, and auxiliary forces. **4.** A large group of people organized for a specific cause. **5.** A large multitude, as of people or animals. [ME *armee* < OFr. < Med. Lat. *armata.* —see ARMADA.]

Army Air Forces *pl.n.* The aviation branch of the U.S. Army before the establishment of the U.S. Air Force.

army ant *n.* Any of various chiefly tropical New World ants of the subfamily Dorylinae, forming large colonies that move from place to place.

Army of the United States *n.* A temporary organization of all military forces during time of war, including the Army Reserves in the National Guard, and Selective Service personnel, as well as the regular U.S. Army.

ar·my·worm (är′mē-wûrm′) *n.* Any of various insect larvae that travel in large groups, destroying crops and other vegetation, esp. the caterpillar of a New World moth, *Leucania* (or *Pseudaletia*) *unipuncta.*

ar·nat·to (är-nä′tō) *n.* Variant of **annatto.**

ar·ni·ca (är′nĭ-kə) *n.* **1.** Any of various plants of the genus *Arnica,* having bright-yellow, rayed flowers. **2.** A tincture of the dried flower heads of *A. montana,* used for sprains and bruises. [NLat. *Arnica,* genus name.]

ar·oid (ăr′oid′, âr′-) *n.* Any of various plants of the family *Aracea,* which includes the arums. [AR(UM) + -OID.] **—ar′oid′** *adj.*

a·roint (ə-roint′) *tr.v.* **a·roint·ed, a·roint·ing, a·roints.** *Archaic.* Begone; avaunt: *"Aroint thee, witch!"* (Shakespeare). [Orig. unknown.]

a·ro·ma (ə-rō′mə) *n.* **1.** A pleasant, characteristic odor, as of a plant, spice, or food. **2.** A distinctive, intangible quality; aura. [Lat. < Gk., *arōma,* aromatic herb.]

ar·o·mat·ic (ăr′ə-măt′ĭk) *adj.* **1.** Having an aroma; fragrant, sweet-smelling, or spicy. **2.** *Chem.* Of, pertaining to, or containing the six-carbon ring characteristic of the benzene series and related organic groups. *—n.* An aromatic plant or substance. **—ar′o·mat′i·cal·ly** *adv.* **—ar′o·mat′ic·ness** *n.*

ar·o·ma·tic·i·ty (ăr′ə-mə-tĭs′ĭ-tē, ə-rō′mə-) *n.* Aromatic quality or character, esp. the distinctive structure or properties of the aromatic chemical compounds.

a·ro·ma·tize (ə-rō′mə-tīz′) *tr.v.* **-tized, -tiz·ing, -tiz·es. 1.** To make aromatic or fragrant. **2.** *Chem.* To subject to a reaction that results in an aromatic compound. **—a·ro′ma·ti·za′tion** *n.*

a·rose (ə-rōz′) *v.* Past tense of **arise.**

a·round (ə-round′) *adv.* **1.** On or to all sides or in all directions. **2.** In a circle or circular motion. **3.** To each member of a group: *enough to go around.* **4.** In or toward the opposite direction, position, or attitude. **5.** From one place to another; here and there: *wander around.* **6.** *Informal.* Close at hand; nearby: *He waited around all day.* **7.** *Informal.* To a specific place or area: *when you come around again.* **8.** *Informal.* To a normal or desired state. **9.** *Informal.* Approximately; about. *—prep.* **1.** On all sides of. **2.** So as to enclose, surround, or envelop. **3.** About the circumference or periphery of; encircling. **4.** About the central point of: *the earth's motion around the sun.* **5.** In or to various places within or near: *driving around the countryside.* **6.** On or to the farther side of: *the house around the corner.* **7.** *Informal.* Approximately at; near. **—*idioms.* get around.** *Informal.* **1.** To deal or cope with successfully. **2.** To succeed in evading or circumventing. **get around to.** *Informal.* To find time or occasion to give one's attention to. [ME, in the round, in circumference.]

a·round-the-clock (ə-round′*th*ə-klŏk′) *adj.* Variant of **round-the-clock.**

a·rouse (ə-rouz′) *v.* **a·roused, a·rous·ing, a·rous·es.** *—tr.* **1.** To awaken from or as if from sleep. **2.** To stir up; excite. *—intr.* To be or become aroused. [< ROUSE, on the model of such pairs as *rise, arise.*] **—a·rous′al** (ə-rou′zəl) *n.* **—a·rous′er** *n.*

ar·peg·gi·o (är-pĕj′ē-ō′, -pĕj′ō) *n., pl.* **-os.** *Mus.* **1.** The playing of the tones of a chord in rapid succession rather than simultaneously. **2.** A chord played or sung in arpeggio. [Ital. < *arpeggiare,* to play the harp < *arpa,* harp, of Germanic orig.] **—ar·peg′gi·oed′** *adj.*

ar·pent (är-pän′) *n.* An old French unit of land measurement approximately equivalent to an acre. [Fr. < OFr. < Lat. *arepennis,* half acre, of Gaulish orig.]

ar·que·bus (är′kə-bəs, -kwə-) *n.* Variant of **harquebus.**

ar·rack (ăr′ək, ə-răk′) *n.* A strong alcoholic drink of the Middle East and nearby regions of the Orient, usually distilled from rice or molasses. [Ar. *'araq,* fruit juice.]

ar·raign (ə-rān′) *tr.v.* **-raigned, -raign·ing, -raigns. 1.** *Law.* To call before a court to answer to an indictment. **2.** To call to account; charge: *"Johnson arraigned the modern politics of this country as entirely devoid of all principle"* (Boswell). [ME *arreinen* < OFr. *araisnier* < VLat. **adrationare* : Lat. *ad-*, to + Lat. *ratio*, account. —see REASON.] **—ar·raign′er** *n.* **—ar·raign′ment** *n.*

ar·range (ə-rānj′) *v.* **-ranged, -rang·ing, -rang·es.** —*tr.* **1.** To put into a specific order or relation; dispose. **2.** To plan or prepare for: *arrange a picnic.* **3.** To agree about; settle: *"It has been arranged for him by his family to marry a girl of his own class"* (Edmund Wilson). **4.** *Mus.* To reset (music) for other instruments or voices or for another style of performance. —*intr.* **1.** To come to an agreement. **2.** To make preparations; plan: *arrange for a sabbatical.* [ME *arengen* < OFr. *arengier* : *à-*, to (< Lat. *ad*) + *rengier*, to put in a line < *reng*, line, of Germanic orig.] **—ar·rang′er** *n.*

ar·range·ment (ə-rānj′mənt) *n.* **1.** The act or process of arranging. **2.** The condition, manner, or result of being arranged; disposal. **3.** A collection or set of things that have been arranged. **4.** Often **arrangements.** A provision or plan made in preparation for an undertaking. **5.** An agreement or settlement; disposition. **6.** *Mus.* **a.** An adaptation of a composition for other instruments or voices or to another style or level of difficulty. **b.** A composition so arranged.

ar·rant (ăr′ənt) *adj.* Being completely such; thoroughgoing: *an arrant knave.* [Var. of ERRANT.] **—ar′rant·ly** *adv.*

ar·ras (ăr′əs) *n.* **1.** A tapestry. **2.** A wall hanging, esp. of tapestry. [ME, after *Arras*, France.]

ar·ray (ə-rā′) *tr.v.* **-rayed, -ray·ing, -rays. 1.** To arrange or draw up, as troops in battle order. **2.** To deck in finery; adorn. —*n.* **1.** An orderly arrangement, esp. of troops. **2.** An impressive display of numerous persons or objects: *"a heathenish array of monstrous clubs and spears"* (Melville). **3.** Splendid attire; finery. **4.** *Math.* **a.** A rectangular arrangement of quantities in rows and columns, as in a matrix. **b.** Numerical data linearly ordered by magnitude. **5.** An arrangement of computer memory elements in one or several planes. [ME *arraien* < OFr. *areer* < VLat. **arredare*, of Germanic orig.]

ar·ray·al (ə-rā′əl) *n.* **1.** The act or process of arraying. **2.** Something arrayed; array.

ar·rear·age (ə-rîr′ĭj) *n.* **1.** The state of being in arrears. **2.** An amount owed in payment.

ar·rears (ə-rîrz′) *pl.n.* **1.** An unpaid and overdue debt or an unfulfilled obligation. **2.** The state of being behind in fulfilling contracted obligations or payments: *in arrears.* [< ME *arrere*, behind < OFr. *arere* < LLat. *ad retro*, backward : Lat. *ad*, to + Lat. *retro*, behind.]

ar·rest (ə-rĕst′) *tr.v.* **-rest·ed, -rest·ing, -rests. 1.** To stop or check the motion, progress, growth, or spread of. **2.** To seize and hold under authority of the law. **3.** To capture and hold briefly (the attention, for example); engage. —*n.* **1. a.** The act of arresting. **b.** The state of being arrested. **2.** A device for arresting motion, esp. of a moving part. —***idiom.* under arrest.** Detained in legal custody. [ME *aresten* < OFr. *arester* < VLat. **arrestare* : Lat. *ad-*, to + Lat. *restare*, to stand still (*re-*, back + *stare*, to stand).] **—ar·rest′er** *n.* **—ar·rest′ment** *n.*

ar·rest·ing (ə-rĕs′tĭng) *adj.* Attracting and holding the attention; striking. **—ar·rest′ing·ly** *adv.*

ar·rhyth·mi·a (ə-rĭth′mē-ə) *n.* Any irregularity in the force or rhythm of the heartbeat. [Gk. *arruthmia*, lack of rhythm < *arruthmos*, unrhythmical : *a-*, without + *rhuthmos*, rhythm.]

ar·rhyth·mic (ə-rĭth′mĭk) also **ar·rhyth·mi·cal** (-mĭ-kəl) *adj.* Lacking rhythm or regularity of rhythm. **—ar·rhyth′mi·cal·ly** *adv.*

ar·ri·ère-ban (ăr′ē-âr-băn′, -băn′) *n.* **1.** In medieval France, a royal proclamation by which vassals were summoned to military service. **2.** The vassals summoned by an arrière-ban. [Fr. < OFr. *ariere-ban*, alteration of *herban*, of Germanic orig.]

ar·ri·ère-pen·sée (ăr′ē-âr′päN-sā′) *n.* An ulterior motive. [Fr. : *arrière*, in back + *pensée*, thought.]

ar·ris (ăr′ĭs) *n., pl.* **arris** or **-ris·es.** *Archit.* The sharp edge or ridge formed by two surfaces meeting at an angle, as in a molding. [Alteration of OFr. *areste*, ridge. —see ARÊTE.]

ar·ri·val (ə-rī′vəl) *n.* **1.** The act of arriving. **2.** A person or thing that arrives or has arrived. **3.** The reaching of a goal or objective as a result of some process or effort.

ar·rive (ə-rīv′) *intr.v.* **-rived, -riv·ing, -rives. 1.** To reach a destination. **2.** To come at length; take place: *The day of crisis has arrived.* **3.** To achieve success or recognition. —***phrasal verb.* arrive at.** To reach through some process or effort: *arrive at a decision.* [ME *ariven* < OFr. *ariver* < VLat. **arripare* : Lat. *ad-*, to + Lat. *ripa*, shore.] **—ar·riv′er** *n.*

ar·ri·viste (ă-rē-vēst′) *n., pl.* **-vistes** (-vēst′). A social climber or opportunist; upstart. [Fr. < *arriver*, to arrive < OFr. *ariver.*]

ar·ro·ba (ə-rō′bə) *n. Archaic.* **1.** A unit of weight in Spanish-speaking countries equal to about 25 pounds. **2.** A unit of weight in Portuguese-speaking countries equal to about 32 pounds. **3.** A liquid measure used in Spanish-speaking countries, having varying value, but approximately equal to 17 quarts when used to measure wine. [Sp. and Port. < Ar. *ar-rub'*, the quarter (of a quintal).]

ar·ro·gance (ăr′ə-gəns) *n.* The state or quality of being arrogant.

ar·ro·gant (ăr′ə-gənt) *adj.* **1.** Overly convinced of one's own importance; overbearingly proud; haughty. **2.** Characterized by or arising from haughty self-importance. [ME *arrogaunt* < OFr. < Lat. *arrogans*, pr.part. of *arrogare*, to arrogate.] **—ar′ro·gant·ly** *adv.*

ar·ro·gate (ăr′ə-gāt′) *tr.v.* **-gat·ed, -gat·ing, -gates. 1.** To claim, take, or assume for oneself without right. **2.** To attribute to another unwarrantably. [Lat. *arrogare, arrogat-* : *ad-*, to + *rogare*, to ask.] **—ar′ro·ga′tion** *n.* **—ar′ro·ga′tive** *adj.* **—ar′ro·ga′tor** *n.*

ar·ron·disse·ment (ä-rôN′dēs-mäN′) *n.* **1.** The chief administrative subdivision of a department in France. **2.** A municipal subdivision of some large French cities. [Fr. < *arrondir*, to round out : *à*, to (< Lat. *ad*) + *rondir*, to make round.]

ar·row (ăr′ō) *n.* **1.** A straight, thin shaft that is shot from a bow and usually made of light wood with a pointed head at one end and flight-stabilizing feathers at the other. **2.** Something similar to an arrow in form, function, or speed. **3.** A sign or symbol shaped like an arrow and used to indicate direction. [ME *arwe* < OE *arewe.*]

ar·row·head (ăr′ō-hĕd′) *n.* **1.** The pointed, removable striking tip of an arrow. **2.** Something shaped like an arrowhead, such as a mark indicating a limit on a drawing. **3.** Any aquatic or marsh plant of the genus *Sagittaria*, having arrowhead-shaped leaves and white flowers.

ar·row·root (ăr′ō-ro͞ot′, -ro͝ot′) *n.* **1.** A tropical American plant, *Maranta arundinacea*, having roots that yield an edible starch. **2.** The starch from the arrowroot and from certain plants of the genera *Manihot, Curcuma*, and *Tacca.* [So called because it was used to draw poison from arrow wounds.]

ar·row-wood (ăr′ō-wo͝od′) *n.* Any of several small shrubs of the genus *Viburnum*, such as the dockmackie, having straight tough stems formerly used by the Indians to make arrows.

arrow worm *n.* Any of various small, slender marine worms of the phylum Chaetognatha, having prehensile bristles on each side of the mouth.

ar·roy·o (ə-roi′ō) *n., pl.* **-os. 1.** A deep gully cut by an intermittent stream; dry gulch. **2.** A brook or creek. [Sp., ult. < Lat. *arrugia*, mineshaft.]

arse (ärs) *n. Chiefly Brit.* Variant of **ass**[2].

ar·se·nal (är′sə-nəl) *n.* **1.** A governmental establishment for the storing, manufacturing, or repairing of arms, ammunition, and other war materiel. **2.** A stock of weapons. **3.** A store or supply: *She arrived with an arsenal of assistants.* [Ital. *arsenale* < Ar. *dār-aṣ-ṣinā′ah* : *dār*, house + *aṣ-*, the + *ṣinā′ah*, manufacture < *ṣana′a*, he made.]

ar·se·nate (är′sə-nĭt, -nāt′) *n.* A salt or ester of arsenic acid.

ar·se·nic (är′sə-nĭk) *n.* **1.** A highly poisonous metallic element having three allotropic forms, yellow, black, or gray, of which the brittle, crystalline gray is the most common. Arsenic and its compounds are used in insecticides, weed killers, solid-state doping agents, and various alloys. Atomic number 33; atomic weight 74.922; valence 3 or 5. Gray arsenic melts at 817°C (at 28 atm pressure), sublimes at 613°C, and has a specific gravity of 5.73. **2.** Arsenic trioxide. —*adj.* **ar·sen·ic** (är-sĕn′ĭk). Of or containing arsenic, esp. with valence 5. [ME *arsenik* < OFr. < Lat. *arrenicum* < Gk. *arsenikon*, yellow orpiment < Pers. *zarnīk* < *zar*, gold.]

ar·sen·ic acid (är-sĕn′ĭk) *n.* A poisonous white translucent crystalline compound, H_3AsO_4, used to manufacture arsenates.

ar·sen·i·cal (är-sĕn′ĭ-kəl) *adj.* Of or containing arsenic. —*n.* A drug or preparation containing arsenic.

ar·se·nic trioxide (är′sə-nĭk) *n.* A poisonous white amorphous powder, As_2O_3, used in insecticides, rat poison, and weed killers.

ar·se·nide (är′sə-nīd′) *n.* A compound of arsenic with a more electropositive element.

ar·se·ni·ous (är-sē′nē-əs) *adj.* Of or containing arsenic, esp. with valence 3.

ar·se·no·py·rite (är′sə-nō-pī′rīt′) *n.* A silver-white to gray arsenic ore, essentially $FeS_2 \cdot FeAs_2$.

ar·shin (är-shēn′) *n.* Variant of **archine.**

ar·sine (är-sēn′, är′sēn′) *n.* A colorless, flammable, very poisonous gas, AsH_3, used as a military poison gas, as a solid-state doping agent, and in organic synthesis. [ARS(ENIC) + -INE[2].]

ar·sis (är′sĭs) *n., pl.* **-ses** (-sēz′). **1.** Originally, the unaccented or shorter part of a foot of verse. **2.** In modern usage, the accented or longer part of a foot of verse. **3.** *Mus.* The upbeat or unaccented part of a measure. [LLat., raising of the voice < Gk., upward beat < *aeirein*, to lift.]

ar·son (är′sən) *n.* The crime of maliciously setting fire to the buildings or property of another or of burning one's own property for some improper purpose, as to collect insurance. [AN < OFr. *arçun* < Med. Lat. *arsio* < Lat. *ardēre*, to burn.] **—ar′son·ist** *n.*

ars·phen·a·mine (ärs-fĕn′ə-mēn′) *n.* A yellow hygroscopic powder, $C_{12}H_{12}N_2O_2As \cdot 2HCl \cdot 2H_2O$, formerly used to treat syphilis. [ARS(ENIC) + PHEN(YL) + AMINE.]

art[1] (ärt) *n.* **1.** Human effort to imitate, supplement, alter, or

arrowhead
Above: Tip of an arrow
Below: Sagittaria latifolia

counteract the work of nature. **2. a.** The conscious production or arrangement of sounds, colors, forms, movements, or other elements in a manner that affects the sense of beauty; specifically, the production of the beautiful in a graphic or plastic medium. **b.** The study of these activities. **c.** The product of these activities. **3.** High quality of conception or execution, as found in works of beauty; aesthetic value. **4.** Any field or category of art, such as music, ballet, or literature. **5.** A nonscientific branch of learning; one of the liberal arts. **6. a.** A system of principles and methods employed in the performance of a set of activities: *the art of building.* **b.** A trade or craft that applies such a system of principles and methods: *pursuing the baker's art.* **7.** A specific skill in adept performance, conceived as requiring the exercise of intuitive faculties that cannot be learned solely by study: *the art of writing letters.* **8. a. arts.** Artful devices; stratagems; tricks. **b.** Artfulness; contrivance; cunning. **9.** *Printing.* Illustrative material as distinguished from text. [ME < OFr. < Lat. *ars.*]

art² (ərt; ärt *when stressed*) *v. Archaic.* Second person singular, present indicative of **be.** [ME < OE *eart.*]

-art *suff.* Variant of **-ard.**

art dec·o (dĕk'ō) *n.* An early 20th-century style of decorative art featuring geometrical designs and bold colors. [Fr. *Art Déco,* from *Exposition Internationale des Arts Décoratifs et Industriels Moderns,* a 1925 exposition in Paris, France.]

ar·te·fact (är'tə-făkt') *n.* Variant of **artifact.**

ar·tel (är-tĕl') *n.* A cooperative enterprise of industrial or agricultural workers in the Soviet Union. [R. *artel'* < Ital. *artieri,* artisans < *arte,* work < Lat. *ars.*]

Ar·te·mis (är'tə-mĭs) *n. Gk. Myth.* The virgin goddess of the hunt and the moon, and twin sister of Apollo. [Gk.]

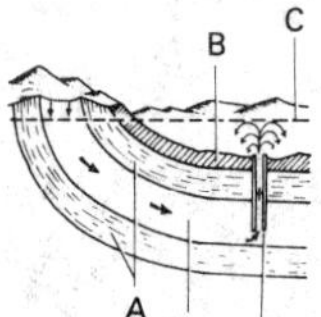

artesian well
A. Impervious stratum
B. Dry zone
C. Pressure gradient
D. Zone of saturation
E. Deep well

ar·te·mis·i·a (är'tə-mĭzh'ē-ə, -mĭzh'ə, -mĭz'ē-ə) *n.* Any of various plants of the genus *Artemisia,* which includes sagebrush and wormwood. [ME *artemesie,* mugwort < OFr. < Lat. *artemisia* < Gk., wormwood, after *Artemis,* to whom it was sacred.]

ar·te·ri·al (är-tîr'ē-əl) *adj.* **1.** Of, like, or in an artery or arteries. **2.** Of or designating the blood in the arteries that has absorbed oxygen in the lungs and is bright red. **3.** Of or designating a route of transportation carrying a main flow with many branches. —*n.* A through road or street. —**ar·te'ri·al·ly** *adv.*

ar·te·ri·al·ize (är-tîr'ē-əl-īz') *tr.v.* **-ized, -iz·ing, -iz·es.** To convert (venous blood) into arterial blood by absorption of oxygen in the lungs. —**ar·te'ri·al·i·za'tion** *n.*

arterio- *pref.* Artery: *arteriovenous.* [Gk. *artērio-* < *artēria,* artery.]

ar·te·ri·og·ra·phy (är-tîr'ē-ŏg'rə-fē) *n.* Roentgenography of the arteries following injection of a radiopaque dye. —**ar·te'ri·o·gram'** (är-tîr'ē-ə-grăm') *n.* —**ar·te'ri·o·graph'ic** *adj.*

ar·te·ri·ole (är-tîr'ē-ōl') *n.* One of the small terminal branches of an artery, esp. one that connects with a capillary. [NLat. *arteriola,* dim. of Lat. *arteria,* windpipe < Gk.] —**ar·te'ri·o'lar** (-ō'lər, -ə-lər) *adj.*

ar·te·ri·o·scle·ro·sis (är-tîr'ē-ō-sklə-rō'sĭs) *n.* A chronic disease in which thickening and hardening of arterial walls interferes with blood circulation. —**ar·te'ri·o·scle·rot'ic** (-rŏt'ĭk) *adj.*

ar·te·ri·o·ve·nous (är-tîr'ē-ō-vē'nəs) *adj.* Of, pertaining to, or connecting both arteries and veins.

ar·te·ri·tis (är'tə-rī'tĭs) *n.* Inflammation of an artery.

ar·ter·y (är'tə-rē) *n., pl.* **-ies. 1.** *Anat.* Any of a branching system of muscular tubes that carry blood away from the heart. **2.** A major route of transportation, into which local routes flow. [ME *arterie* < Lat. *arteria,* windpipe < Gk.]

artichoke

ar·te·sian well (är-tē'zhən) *n.* A well drilled through impermeable strata to reach water capable of rising to the surface by internal hydrostatic pressure. [Fr. *artésien,* of Artois, where such wells were first drilled.]

art film *n.* A motion picture intended to be a serious work of art, often experimental and not designed for mass appeal.

art·ful (ärt'fəl) *adj.* **1.** Exhibiting art or skill. **2.** Skillful, esp. in finding the means to an end; clever. **3.** Deceitful or tricky; crafty. **4.** Artificial; not genuine. —**art'ful·ly** *adv.* —**art'ful·ness** *n.*

arthr- *pref.* Variant of **arthro-.**

ar·thral·gia (är-thrăl'jə, -jē-ə) *n.* Neuralgic pain in a joint. —**ar·thral'gic** (-jĭk) *adj.*

ar·thri·tis (är-thrī'tĭs) *n.* Inflammation of a joint or joints. —**ar·thrit'ic** (-thrĭt'ĭk) *adj. & n.* —**ar·thrit'i·cal·ly** *adv.*

arthro- or **arthr-** *pref.* Joint: *arthropathy.* [< Gk. *arthron,* joint.]

ar·thro·mere (är'thrə-mîr') *n.* One of the typical body segments of an arthropod. —**ar'thro·mer'ic** (är'thrə-mĕr'ĭk, -mîr'ĭk) *adj.*

ar·throp·a·thy (är-thrŏp'ə-thē) *n.* Any disease of a joint.

ar·thro·pod (är'thrə-pŏd') *n.* Any of numerous invertebrate organisms of the phylum Arthropoda, which includes the insects, crustaceans, arachnids, and myriapods. Arthropods have a horny, segmented external covering and jointed limbs. [NLat. *Arthropoda,* phylum name : ARTHRO- + Gk. *pous,* foot.] —**ar·throp'o·dous** (är-thrŏp'ə-dəs), **ar·throp'o·dal** (-dəl) *adj.*

ar·thros·co·py (är-thrŏs'kə-pē) *n., pl.* **-pies.** The endoscopic examination of a joint, as the knee. —**ar'thro·scope'** (är'thrə-skōp') *n.* —**ar'thro·scop'ic** (är'thrə-skŏp'ĭk) *adj.*

ar·thro·sis (är-thrō'sĭs) *n., pl.* **-ses** (-sēz'). **1.** A connection or joint between bones. **2.** A degenerative process in a joint. [Gk. *arthrōsis* < *arthron,* joint.]

ar·thro·spore (är'thrə-spôr', -spōr') *n.* A sporelike cell characteristic of segmented filamentous fungi or certain algae. —**ar'thro·spor'ic, ar'thro·spor'ous** *adj.*

Ar·thur (är'thər) *n.* Legendary British hero, said to have been king of the Britons in the 6th century A.D. [ME *Artur* < Med. Lat. *Artorius,* prob. of Celtic orig.]

Ar·thu·ri·an (är-thŏŏr'ē-ən) *adj.* Of or pertaining to King Arthur and his Knights of the Round Table.

ar·ti·choke (är'tĭ-chōk') *n.* **1.** A thistlelike plant, *Cynara scolymus,* having a large flower head with numerous fleshy, scalelike bracts. **2.** The unopened flower head of an artichoke, cooked and eaten as a vegetable. **3.** The Jerusalem artichoke. [Dial. Ital. *articiocco,* alteration of *arcicioffo* < OSp. *alcarchofa* < Ar. *al-kharshūf.*]

ar·ti·cle (är'tĭ-kəl) *n.* **1.** An individual thing in a class; an item: *an article of clothing.* **2.** A small thing. **3.** A particular section or item of a series in a written document, such as a contract, constitution, or treaty. **4.** A nonfictional literary composition that forms an independent part of a publication; report or essay. **5.** *Gram.* Any of a class of words used to signal nouns and to specify their application. In English, the articles are *a* and *an* (indefinite articles) and *the* (definite article). **6.** A particular part or subject; a point or specific matter. —*tr.v.* **-cled, -cling, -cles. 1.** To set forth or state in articles. **2.** To make specific or formal charges against; accuse. **3.** To bind by articles set forth in a contract. [ME < OFr. < Lat. *articulus,* part, dim. of *artus,* joint.]

Articles of Confederation *pl.n.* The first constitution of the United States, adopted by the original 13 states in 1781 and lasting until 1788 when the present Constitution was ratified.

ar·tic·u·la·ble (är-tĭk'yə-lə-bəl) *adj.* Capable of being articulated.

ar·tic·u·lar (är-tĭk'yə-lər) *adj.* Of or pertaining to a joint or joints. [ME *articuler* < Lat. *articularis* < *articulus,* small joint. —see ARTICLE.] —**ar·tic'u·lar·ly** *adv.*

ar·tic·u·late (är-tĭk'yə-lĭt) *adj.* **1.** Endowed with the power of speech. **2.** Spoken in or divided into clear and distinct words or syllables. **3.** Capable of, speaking in, or characterized by clear, expressive language. **4.** *Biol.* Having joints or segments. —*v.* (är-tĭk'yə-lāt') **-lat·ed, -lat·ing, -lates.** —*tr.* **1.** To utter (a speech sound or sounds) by moving the necessary organs of speech. **2.** To pronounce distinctly and carefully; enunciate. **3.** To express in coherent verbal form; give words to: *couldn't articulate her fears.* **4.** To unite by forming a joint or joints. —*intr.* **1.** To utter a speech sound or sounds. **2.** To speak clearly and distinctly. **3.** To form a joint; be jointed. [Lat. *articulatus,* jointed, p.part. of *articulare,* to divide into joints < *articulus,* small joint. —see ARTICLE.] —**ar·tic'u·late·ly** *adv.* —**ar·tic'u·late·ness** *n.*

ar·tic·u·la·tion (är-tĭk'yə-lā'shən) *n.* **1.** The act or process of articulating; enunciation: *an articulation of the group's sentiments.* **2. a.** The movements of speech organs employed in producing a particular speech sound. **b.** A speech sound, esp. a consonant. **3. a.** A jointing together or being jointed together. **b.** The method or manner of jointing. **4.** *Zool.* A joint between bones or between movable parts of an outside shell. **5.** *Bot.* **a.** A joint between two separable parts, as a leaf and a stem. **b.** A node or a space on a stem between two nodes. —**ar·tic'u·la·tive** (-lə-tĭv, -lā'tĭv), **ar·tic'u·la·to'ry** (-lə-tôr'ē, -tōr'ē) *adj.* —**ar·tic'u·la'tor** *n.*

ar·ti·fact also **ar·te·fact** (är'tə-făkt') *n.* **1.** An object produced or shaped by human workmanship, esp., a tool, weapon, or ornament of archaeological or historical interest. **2.** *Biol.* A structure or substance not normally present but produced by some external agency or action. [Lat. *ars, art-* + *factum,* something made, p.part. of *facere,* to make.] —**ar'ti·fac'tu·al** (făk'chŏŏ-əl) *adj.*

ar·ti·fice (är'tə-fĭs) *n.* **1.** A crafty expedient; an artful device or stratagem. **2.** Subtle but base deception; trickery. **3.** Ingenuity; cleverness; skill. [Fr. < OFr., craftsmanship < Lat. *artificium* < *artifex,* craftsman : *ars,* art + *-fex,* maker < *facere,* to make.]

Synonyms: *artifice, trick, ruse, wile, feint, stratagem, maneuver, dodge, guile, finesse, subterfuge.* These nouns denote means for achieving an end by indirection. *Artifice* refers to something especially contrived to create a desired effect but not necessarily with intent to deceive. *Trick* often implies willful deception, but can also mean a playful, harmless act. *Ruse* stresses creation of a false impression with the intention of distracting. *Wile* suggests deceiving and trapping a victim by playing on his weak points. *Feint* denotes a deceptive act calculated to distract attention from a person's real end. *Stratagem* implies carefully planned deception. *Maneuver* usually applies more narrowly to a specific strategic move. *Dodge* stresses slyness and quickness in achieving deception. *Guile* refers to treachery, deceit, and cunning in general rather than to a specific application of them. *Finesse* is highly developed skill, often but not invariably associated with craftiness. *Subterfuge* applies to deception practiced especially to evade difficulty or unpleasantness.

ar·tif·i·cer (är-tĭf'ĭ-sər) *n.* **1.** A skilled worker; craftsman. **2.** A person adept at designing and constructing; inventor: *"The labyrinth...was built by Daedalus, a most skilful artificer"* (Thomas Bulfinch).

ar·ti·fi·cial (är'tə-fĭsh'əl) *adj.* **1.** Made by man rather than occurring in nature: *an artificial sweetener.* **2.** Made in imitation of something natural: *artificial flowers.* **3.** Not genuine or natural; feigned; pretended: *an artificial smile.* [ME < Lat. *artificialis* < *artificium,* craftsmanship. —see ARTIFICE.] **—ar'ti·fi'ci·al'i·ty** (-fĭsh'ē-ăl'ĭ-tē) *n.* **—ar'ti·fi'cial·ly** *adv.*

Synonyms: *artificial, synthetic, ersatz, simulated, spurious, specious, counterfeit, supposititious.* These adjectives mean not genuine. *Artificial,* broad in meaning and connotation, refers to things resulting from human effort, as distinguished from preexisting nature or character. *Synthetic* applies to a substance designed to appear or function like the original, often with certain advantages. An *ersatz* product is a transparently inferior, often pretentious, imitation. The remaining terms invariably imply fraud. *Simulated* refers to what is not real or true but is intentionally made to appear so. *Spurious* roughly means fraudulent, while *specious* adds the sense of attractiveness or seductiveness: *a spurious document; specious arguments of the Devil. Counterfeit* strongly implies imitation with intent to defraud; *supposititious* suggests the insertion of that which is fraudulent.

artificial horizon *n.* An instrument displaying a line on a flight indicator that lies within the horizontal plane and about which the pitching and banking movements of an airplane are shown.

artificial insemination *n.* The introduction of semen into the female reproductive organs without sexual contact.

artificial intelligence *n.* **1. a.** The characteristics of a machine programmed to imitate human intelligence functions. **b.** Research in methods of such programming. **2.** Research in methods of programming designed to supplement human intellectual abilities.

artificial language *n.* A language based on a set of prescribed rules established before the language is used.

artificial respiration *n.* Any of various methods used to restore normal breathing in an asphyxiated but living person, usually by rhythmic forcing of air into and out of the lungs.

ar·til·ler·ist (är-tĭl'ər-ĭst) *n.* An artilleryman; gunner.

ar·til·ler·y (är-tĭl'ə-rē) *n.* **1.** Large-caliber firing weapons, such as howitzers and cannons, that are mounted and manned by crews. **2.** Troops armed with artillery. **3.** The branch of an armed force that specializes in the use of artillery. **4.** The science of the use of guns; gunnery. **5.** Catapults, crossbows, slings, and similar devices for discharging missiles. [ME *artelrie* < OFr. *artillerie* < *artillier,* to fortify.]

ar·til·ler·y·man (är-tĭl'ə-rē-mən) *n.* A soldier in the artillery; artillerist.

artillery plant *n.* A tropical American plant, *Pilea muscosa,* that releases its pollen with an explosive discharge.

ar·ti·o·dac·tyl (är'tē-ō-dăk'təl) *n.* Any of various hoofed mammals of the order Artiodactyla, which includes cattle, deer, camels, hippopotamuses, and others, with an even number of toes, either two or four, on each foot. [< NLat. *Artiodactyla,* order name : Gk. *artios,* even + *dactulos,* toe.] **—ar'ti·o·dac'tyl, ar'ti·o·dac'ty·lous** (-tə-ləs) *adj.*

ar·ti·san (är'tĭ-zən, -sən) *n.* A person manually skilled in making a particular product; craftsman. [OFr. < OItal. *artigiano* < VLat. **artitianus* < Lat. *artitus,* skilled in the arts, p.part. of *artire,* to instruct in the arts < *ars,* art.]

art·ist (är'tĭst) *n.* **1.** One who creates works of art, esp. a painter, sculptor, or musician. **2.** Any person who performs his work as if it were an art. **3.** An artiste. [OFr. *artiste* < Ital. *artista* < *arte,* art < Lat. *ars.*]

ar·tiste (är-tēst') *n.* A public performer or entertainer, esp. a singer or dancer. [Fr. < OFr., artist.]

ar·tis·tic (är-tĭs'tĭk) *adj.* **1.** Of or relating to art or artists: *the artistic community.* **2.** Appreciative of or sensitive to art or beauty: *an artistic temperament.* **3.** Showing skill and artistry: *an artistic design.* **—ar·tis'ti·cal·ly** *adv.*

art·ist·ry (är'tĭ-strē) *n.* **1.** Artistic ability, quality, or workmanship. **2.** The practice or occupation of an artist.

art·less (ärt'lĭs) *adj.* **1.** Without guile, cunning, or deceit; ingenuous; naive: *an artless child.* **2.** Free of artificiality; natural; simple: *artless affection.* **3.** Lacking art or skill; crude. **4.** Uncultured; ignorant. **—art'less·ly** *adv.* **—art'less·ness** *n.*

art·mo·bile (ärt'mə-bēl') *n.* A trailer that serves as a traveling art exhibit.

art nou·veau (är' no͞o-vō', ärt') *n.* A style of decoration and architecture of the late 19th and early 20th century, characterized by the use of flowing, sinuous lines. [Fr., new art.]

art song *n.* A lyric song intended to be sung in recital and usually accompanied by a piano.

art·sy-craft·sy (ärt'sē-krăft'sē) *adj. Informal.* Showily or superficially artistic.

art·work (ärt'wûrk') *n.* **1.** Work in the graphic or plastic arts, esp. small, hand-made decorative or artistic objects. **2.** The illustrative and decorative elements of printed materials as distinguished from text.

art·y (är'tē) *adj.* **-i·er, -i·est.** *Informal.* Ostentatiously or affectedly artistic. **—art'i·ly** *adv.* **—art'i·ness** *n.*

ar·um (ăr'əm, âr'-) *n.* **1.** Any of various plants of the genus *Arum,* having arrow-shaped leaves and small flowers on a spadix surrounded by or enclosed within a spathe. **2.** Also **ar·um lily.** Any of several plants related to the arum, such as the calla. [NLat. *Arum,* genus name < Lat., wake-robin < Gk. *aron.*]

a·rus·pex (ə-rŭs'pĕks') *n.* Variant of **haruspex.**

-ary *suff.* **1.** Of or relating to: *bacillary.* **2.** One that pertains to or is connected with: *boundary.* [ME *-arie* < OFr. < Lat. *-arius,* adj. and n. suffix.]

Ar·y·an (âr'ē-ən, ăr'-) *n.* **1.** A member of an Indo-European-speaking people that invaded southwestern Asia and northwestern India in the second millennium B.C. **2.** A member of the people who spoke the parent language of the Indo-European languages. **3.** A member of any people speaking an Indo-European language. **4.** Indo-Iranian. —*adj.* **1.** Of or pertaining to the Indo-European languages or the hypothetical language from which they are derived. **2.** Of or pertaining to a speaker of an Indo-European language. **3.** Of or pertaining to Indo-Iranian. **4.** Of or pertaining to a presumed ethnic type exemplified by or descended from early speakers of Indo-European languages. [Skt. *ārya-,* noble.]

ar·y·te·noid (ăr'ĭ-tē'noid', ə-rĭt'n-oid') *adj. Anat.* **1.** Of or pertaining to either of two small cartilages attached to the back of the larynx and to the vocal cords. **2.** Of or pertaining to any of three small muscles of the larynx. —*n.* An arytenoid cartilage or muscle. [NLat. *arytaenoides* < Gk. *arutainoeidēs,* shaped like a ladle : *arutaina,* ladle (< *aruein,* to draw water) + *-eidēs,* shaped.] **—ar'y·te·noid'al** *adj.*

as[1] (ăz; əz *when unstressed*) *adv.* **1.** To the same extent or degree; equally. **2.** For instance: *large carnivores, as the bear or lion.* —*conj.* **1.** To the same degree or quantity that. Often used as a correlative after *so* or *as: as sweet as sugar; not so bad as you suggest.* **2.** In the same manner or way that: *Think as I think.* **3.** At the same time that; while. **4.** For the reason that; because. **5.** With the result that: *He was so foolish as to lie.* **6.** Though: *Great as Milton was, he proved a bad model.* **7.** *Informal.* That: *I don't know as I can.* —*pron.* **1.** That; which; who. Used after *same* or *such: I received the same grade as you.* **2.** A fact that: *The sun is hot, as everyone knows.* **3.** *Regional.* Who or which: *Those as want to can come with me.* —*prep.* **1.** In the role, capacity, or function of: *acting as a mediator.* **2.** In a manner similar to: *On this issue they thought as one.* **—*idiom.* as is.** *Informal.* Just the way it is; without making changes. [ME < OE *ealswā.*]

Usage: Traditionally, a distinction has been drawn between comparisons using *as. . .as* and comparisons using *so. . .as.* Comparisons with *as. . .as* may be used in any context, as in *Kim is as tall as Sandy; Pat is not as well shod as Jean.* The *so . . . as* construction is restricted to use in negative contexts (as in Mercutio's *'Tis not so deep as a well*), in questions (as in *Is it so bad as all that?*), and in clauses introduced by *if* or similar words (as in *If it is so bad as all that, why don't you leave?*). The distinction between the two types of comparison is fast disappearing in American usage, however, as the *so. . .as* construction becomes increasingly rare. The *as. . .as* comparison may be considered correct in any context. • In a comparison involving both *as. . .as* and *than,* the second *as* should be retained in written style. One writes *he is as bright as, or brighter than, his brother,* not *he is as bright or brighter than his brother,* which is unacceptable in formal style. • In many dialects, *as* is used instead of *that* in sentences like *we are not sure as we want to go* or *it's not certain as he left.* This construction is not sufficiently well established to be used in writing. • In comparisons, a pronoun following *as* may be either nominative *(I, he)* or objective *(me, him).* Traditionally, the nominative is used when the pronoun would be the subject of an "understood" verb that has been omitted; we should say *Pat is as happy as I* because the sentence has an equivalent version *Pat is as happy as I am.* By the same token,we should say *it surprised her as much as me,* using the objective pronoun, on the grounds that there is an equivalent sentence *it surprised her as much as it surprised me.* In sentences like these, the use of *me* where *I* would be considered correct is regarded as careless by traditionalists. The use of *I* where *me* would be correct, however, is likely to be regarded as a pretentious overcorrection. • *As* should be preceded by a comma when it expresses a causal relation, as in *He won't be coming, as we didn't invite him.* When used to express a time relation, *as* is not preceded by a comma: *He was finishing the painting as I walked into the room.* When a clause introduced by *as* begins a sentence, care should be taken that it is clear whether *as* is used to mean "because" or "at the same time as." The sentence *as they were leaving, I walked to the door* may mean either that I walked to the door because they left or at the same time that they were leaving. The connectives *since* and *while* can be ambiguous in the same way, as in examples like *since he has been living abroad, he has been speaking a lot of French* and *while your income is low, you should buy insurance.* When these clauses are moved to the end of the sentence, the proper placement of commas will serve to

art nouveau
Tiffany lamp

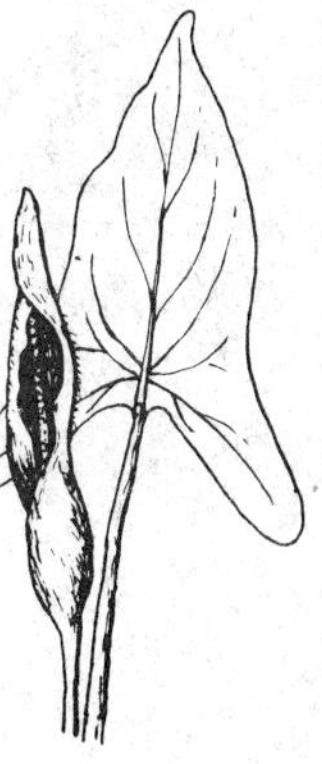

arum

distinguish the meanings. See also Usage notes at **because** and **than.**

as[2] (ăs) *n., pl.* **as·ses** (ăs'ĕz', ăs'ĭz). **1.** An ancient Roman coin of copper or copper alloy. **2.** A unit of weight in ancient Rome equal to about one troy pound. [Lat.]

As The symbol for the element arsenic.

as– *pref.* Variant of **ad-**. Used before *s.*

as·a·fet·i·da also **as·a·foet·i·da** (ăs'ə-fĕt'ĭ-də) *n.* A yellow-brown, bitter, offensive-smelling resinous material obtained from the roots of several plants of the genus *Ferula* and formerly used in medicine. [ME < Med. Lat. : *asa,* gum (< Pers. *azā*) + Lat. *fetida,* stinking. —see FETID.]

as·a·rum (ăs'ə-rəm) *n.* The dried, strong-scented roots of the wild ginger, *Asarum canadense,* formerly used in medicine and as a flavoring agent. [NLat. *Asarum,* genus name < Lat., wild spikenard < Gk. *asaron.*]

as·bes·tos also **as·bes·tus** (ăs-bĕs'təs, ăz-) *n.* Either of two incombustible, chemical-resistant, fibrous mineral forms of impure magnesium silicate, used for fireproofing, electrical insulation, building materials, brake linings, and chemical filters. *—adj.* Of, made of, or containing asbestos. [Lat. < Gk., unquenchable : *a-,* not + *sbennunai,* to quench.] **—as·bes'tine** (-tĭn), **as·bes'tic** (-tĭk) *adj.*

as·bes·to·sis (ăs'bĕs-tō'sĭs, ăz'-) *n.* Chronic lung inflammation caused by prolonged inhalation of asbestos particles. [ASBEST(OS) + -OSIS.] **—as'bes·tot'ic** (-tŏt'ĭk) *adj.*

as·bes·tus (ăs-bĕs'təs, ăz-) *n. & adj.* Variant of **asbestos.**

as·ca·ri·a·sis (ăs'kə-rī'ə-sĭs) *n.* Infestation with nematode worms of the species *Ascaris lumbricoides.* [ASCAR(ID) + -IASIS.]

as·ca·rid (ăs'kə-rĭd) *n.* Any of various nematode worms of the family Ascaridae, such as the common intestinal parasite *Ascaris lumbricoides.* [NLat. *Ascaridae,* family name < Gk. *askaris,* intestinal worm.]

as·cend (ə-sĕnd') *v.* **-cend·ed, -cend·ing, -cends.** *—intr.* **1.** To go or move upward; rise. **2.** To slope upward. *—tr.* **1.** To move upward upon or along; climb: *ascended the mountain.* **2.** To come to occupy: *a queen who ascended the throne years ago.* [ME *ascenden* < *Lat. ascendere* : *ad-,* toward + *scandere,* to climb.] **—as·cend'a·ble, as·cend'i·ble** *adj.*

as·cen·dance also **as·cen·dence** (ə-sĕn'dəns) *n.* Ascendancy.

as·cen·dan·cy also **as·cen·den·cy** (ə-sĕn'dən-sē) *n.* The state of being in the ascendant; domination: *"Germany only awaits trade revival to gain an immense mercantile ascendancy"* (Winston Churchill).

as·cen·dant also **as·cen·dent** (ə-sĕn'dənt) *adj.* **1.** Inclining or moving upward; ascending; rising. **2.** Dominant in position or influence; superior. *—n.* **1.** The position or state of being dominant or in power: *a conservative policy in the ascendant.* **2.** The section of the zodiac that rises in the east at the time of a particular event, as a person's birth. **3.** An ancestor.

ash[2]

as·cend·er (ə-sĕn'dər) *n.* **1.** One that ascends. **2. a.** The part of certain lower-case letters, as *d,* that extends above most other lower-case letters. **b.** A letter with such a part.

as·cend·ing (ə-sĕn'dĭng) *adj.* Going, growing, or moving upward: *a tree with ascending branches.* **—as·cend'ing·ly** *adv.*

as·cen·sion (ə-sĕn'shən) *n.* **1.** The act or process of ascending; ascent. **2.** *Astron.* The rising of a star above the horizon. [ME *ascensioun* < Lat. *ascensio* < *ascendere,* to ascend.] **—as·cen'sion·al** *adj.*

Ascension Day *n.* The 40th day after Easter observed in commemoration of Christ's ascension into heaven.

as·cent (ə-sĕnt') *n.* **1.** The act or process of ascending. **2.** An advancement, esp. in social status. **3.** An upward slope or incline. **4.** A going back in time or genealogical succession. [< ASCEND.]

as·cer·tain (ăs'ər-tān') *tr.v.* **-tained, -tain·ing, -tains. 1.** To discover through examination or experimentation. **2.** *Archaic.* To make certain and definite. [ME *acertainen,* to inform < OFr. *ascertener* : *a-,* to (< Lat. *ad-*) + *certain,* certain. —see CERTAIN.] **—as'cer·tain'a·ble** *adj.* **—as'cer·tain'a·ble·ness** *n.* **—as'cer·tain'a·bly** *adv.* **—as'cer·tain'ment** *n.*

as·cet·ic (ə-sĕt'ĭk) *n.* A person who renounces the comforts of society and leads a life of austere self-discipline, esp. as an act of religious devotion. *—adj.* Pertaining to or characteristic of an ascetic; self-denying; austere. [Gk. *askētēs,* hermit < *askein,* to work.]

as·ci (ăs'ī', -kī') *n.* Plural of **ascus.**

as·cid·i·an (ə-sĭd'ē-ən) *n.* Any of various saclike marine animals of the class Ascidiacea, which includes the sea squirts. [< NLat. *Ascidia,* genus name < Gk. *askidion,* dim. of *askos,* wineskin.]

as·cid·i·um (ə-sĭd'ē-əm) *n., pl.* **-i·a** (-ē-ə). *Bot.* A sac-shaped or bottle-shaped part or organ, such as a leaf of a pitcher plant. [NLat. < Gk. *askidion,* dim. of *askos,* wineskin.]

ASCII (ăs'kē) *n. Computer Sci.* **1.** A proposed standard for defining codes for information exchange between equipment produced by different manufacturers. **2.** A code that follows this proposed standard. [A(MERICAN) S(TANDARD) C(ODE FOR) I(NFORMATION) I(NTERCHANGE).]

as·ci·tes (ə-sī'tēz) *n., pl.* **ascites.** An abnormal accumulation of serous fluid in the abdominal cavity. [ME *aschites* < Med. Lat. *ascites* < Gk. *askitēs* < *askos,* belly.] **—as·cit'ic** (-sĭt'ĭk) *adj.*

As·cle·pi·us (ə-sklē'pē-əs) *n. Gk. Myth.* Apollo's son, the god of medicine.]Gk. *Asklēpios.*]

asco– *pref.* Ascus: *ascospore.* [NLat. < Gk. *askos,* bag.]

as·co·carp (ăs'kə-kärp') *n. Bot.* A globular structure containing the spore sacs of ascomycetous fungi.

as·co·go·ni·um (ăs'kə-gō'nē-əm) *n., pl.* **-ni·a** (-nē-ə). *Bot.* A female reproductive structure of certain fungi.

as·co·my·cete (ăs'kō-mī'sēt', -mī-sēt') *n. Bot.* Any of numerous fungi that produce spores in an ascus.

a·scor·bic acid (ə-skôr'bĭk) *n. Chem.* A white, crystalline vitamin, $C_6H_8O_6$, found in citrus fruits, tomatoes, potatoes, and leafy green vegetables and used to prevent scurvy. [A-[1] + SCORB(UT)IC.]

as·co·spore (ăs'kə-spôr', -spōr') *n.* A sexual spore formed in an ascus. **—as'co·spo'rous** (-spôr'əs, -spōr'-, ăs-kŏs'pər-əs), **as'co·spor'ic** (-spôr'ĭk, -spŏr'-) *adj.*

as·cot (ăs'kət, -kŏt') *n.* A scarf or necktie knotted so that its broad ends are laid flat upon each other. [After *Ascot,* England.]

as·cribe (ə-skrīb') *tr.v.* **-cribed, -crib·ing, -cribes. 1.** To attribute to a specified cause, source, or origin: *ascribed the poor harvest to drought.* **2.** To assign as an attribute. [ME *ascriben* < Lat. *ascribere : ad-,* to + *scribere,* to write.]

as·crip·tion (ə-skrĭp'shən) *n.* **1.** The act of ascribing. **2.** A statement that ascribes. [Lat. *ascriptio* < *ascribere,* to ascribe.]

as·cus (ăs'kəs) *n., pl.* **as·ci** (ăs'ī', -kī'). *Bot.* A membranous sac in certain fungi, containing ascospores. [NLat. < Gk. *askos,* bag.]

as·dic (ăz'dĭk) *n.* A sonar device used in antisubmarine warfare. [A(NTI)S(UBMARINE) + D(ETECTION) + I(NVESTIGATION) + C(OMMITTEE).]

-ase *suff.* Enzyme: *amylase.* [< DIASTASE.]

a·sea (ə-sē') *adv.* Toward or on the sea; at sea.

a·sep·sis (ə-sĕp'sĭs, ā-) *n.* The state of being free of pathogenic organisms.

a·sep·tic (ə-sĕp'tĭk, ā-) *adj.* **1.** Of or pertaining to asepsis. **2.** Lacking animation or emotion: *an aseptic smile.* **—a·sep'ti·cal·ly** *adv.*

a·sex·u·al (ā-sĕk'shōō-əl) *adj.* **1.** Having no evident sex or sex organs; sexless. **2.** Pertaining to or characterizing reproduction involving a single individual and without male or female gametes, as in binary fission or budding. **—a·sex'u·al'i·ty** (-ăl'ĭ-tē) *n.* **—a·sex'u·al·ly** *adv.*

as for *prep.* With regard to.

As·gard (ăs'gärd', äz'-) *n.Myth.* The heavenly residence of the Norse gods and slain heroes of war. [ON : *āss,* god + *garðr,* court.]

ash[1] (ăsh) *n.* **1.** The grayish-white to black soft solid residue of combustion. **2.** *Geol.* Pulverized particulate matter ejected by volcanic eruption. **3. ashes.** Ruins. **4. ashes.** Human remains, esp. after cremation. [ME *asshe* < OE *asce.*]

ash[2] (ăsh) *n.* **1.** Any of various trees of the genus *Fraxinus,* having compound leaves, clusters of small greenish flowers, and winged seeds. **2.** The durable, close-grained, elastic wood of an ash. [ME *asshe* < OE *æsc.*]

a·shamed (ə-shāmd') *adj.* **1.** Feeling shame or guilt. **2.** Reluctant through fear of shame: *ashamed to admit their error.* [ME < OE *āsceamod,* p.part. of *āsceamian,* to feel shame.]

A·shan·ti (ə-shăn'tē, ə-shän'-) *n., pl.* **Ashanti** or **-tis. 1.** An inhabitant of Ashanti. **2.** Twi.

ash can *n.* **1.** A large receptacle, usually of metal, for ashes or trash. **2.** *Slang.* A depth charge.

ash·en[1] (ăsh'ən) *adj.* **1.** Consisting of ashes. **2.** Resembling ashes, as in color: *an ashen complexion.*

ash·en[2] (ăsh'ən) *adj.* Of, pertaining to, or made from the wood of the ash tree.

Ash·er (ăsh'ər) *n.* **1.** In the Old Testament, a son of Jacob. **2.** The tribe of Israel descended from Asher. [Heb. *Ashēr.*]

Ash·ke·naz·i (ăsh'kə-năz'ē) *n., pl.* **-naz·im** (-năz'ĭm). A central or eastern European Jew, generally Yiddish-speaking. [Heb. *Ashkĕnāzi.*] **—Ash'ke·naz'ic** (-năz'ĭk) *adj.*

ash·lar (ăsh'lər) *n.* **1. a.** A squared block of building stone. **b.** Masonry of such stones. **2.** A thin, dressed rectangle of stone for facing walls. [ME *assheler* < OFr. *aisselier,* beam < Lat. *axilla,* dim. of *axis,* plank.]

a·shore (ə-shôr', ə-shōr') *adv.* **1.** Toward or on the shore. **2.** On land; aground.

ash·plant (ăsh'plănt') *n.* A staff or walking stick made from an ash sapling.

ash·ram (ăsh'rəm) *n.* **1.** *Hinduism.* A usually secluded residence of a Hindu philosopher or religious teacher. **2.** A religious retreat or commune. [Skt. *aśrama.*]

Ash·to·reth (ăsh'tə-rĕth') *n.* The ancient Syrian and Phoenician goddess of sexual love and fertility. [Heb. *'Ashtōreth.*]

ash·tray (ăsh'trā') *n.* A receptacle for tobacco ashes.

A·shur (ä'shōōr') *n.* The principal Assyrian deity and god of war and empire. [Assyrian *Ashūr.*]

Ash Wednesday *n.* The seventh Wednesday before Easter, and the first day of Lent.

ash·y (ăsh'ē) *adj.* **-i·er, -i·est. 1.** Pertaining to, resembling, or covered with ashes. **2.** Having the color of ashes; pallid; pale. **—ash'i·ness** *n.*

A·sian (ā′zhən, ā′shən) *adj.* Of or pertaining to Asia or its people. *—n.* A native or inhabitant of Asia.
A·si·at·ic (ā′zhē-ăt′ĭk, -shē-, -zē-) *adj.* Asian. *—n.* An Asian.
Asiatic cholera *n.* A form of cholera.
a·side (ə-sīd′) *adv.* **1.** On or to one side: *step aside.* **2.** Out of one's thoughts or mind: *put his doubts aside.* **3.** Apart: *a day set aside for rejoicing.* **4.** In reserve: *money put aside for gifts.* **5.** Dispensed with: *all joking aside.* *—n.* **1.** A line spoken by a character in a play that other actors on stage are supposed by dramatic convention not to hear. **2.** A parenthetical departure; digression.
aside from *prep.* Excluding; except for.
as if *conj.* In the same way that it would be if: *looked as if she were made of ice.*
as·i·nine (ăs′ə-nīn′) *adj.* **1.** Of, pertaining to, or like an ass. **2.** Stupid or silly; doltish: *asinine behavior.* [Lat. *asininus,* of an ass < *asinus,* ass.]
ask (ăsk, äsk) *v.* **asked, ask·ing, asks.** *—tr.* **1.** To put a question to. **2.** To seek information about; inquire about: *asked directions.* **3.** To request of or for; solicit: *asking a favor.* **4. a.** To require or call for. **b.** To expect or demand: *ask too much of a child.* **5.** To invite. **6.** *Archaic.* To publish, as marriage banns. *—intr.* **1.** To inquire: *asked about his mother.* **2.** To make a request: *asked for help.* [ME *asken* < OE *āscian.*]
Synonyms: *ask, question, inquire, query, interrogate, examine, quiz.* These verbs mean to seek information. *Ask* is the most widely applicable. *Question* implies continuous and careful asking during a given period. *Inquire* may refer to a simple act of asking, but often implies a comprehensive search for information. *Query* usually suggests questioning to settle a doubt. *Interrogate,* a more formal word, applies especially to official questioning. *Examine* refers to close and detailed questioning, and *quiz* to oral or written examination of students.
a·skance (ə-skăns′) also **a·skant** (ə-skănt′) *adv.* **1.** With a side or oblique glance; sidewise. **2.** With disapproval, suspicion, or distrust. [Orig. unknown.]
a·skew (ə-skyōō′) *adj. & adv.* To one side; awry: *rugs lying askew.* [Prob. A-[2] + SKEW.]
a·slant (ə-slănt′) *adj. & adv.* At a slant; obliquely. *—prep.* Obliquely over or across; athwart.
a·sleep (ə-slēp′) *adj.* **1.** In a condition of sleep. **2.** Inactive; dormant. **3.** Numb: *My leg is asleep.* **4.** Dead. *—adv.* Into a condition of sleep.
as long as *conj.* **1.** Since: *As long as you've offered, I accept.* **2.** On the condition that: *will cooperate as long as he's notified on time.*
a·slope (ə-slōp′) *adv. & adj.* At a slope or slant.
a·so·cial (ā-sō′shəl) *adj.* **1.** Avoiding the society of others; not gregarious. **2.** Marked by the incapacity to interact adequately with others.
as of *prep.* On; at: *terminated as of January 1.*
asp (ăsp) *n.* Any of several venomous Old World snakes, such as the small cobra, *Naja haje,* or the horned viper, *Cerastes cornutus,* both of Africa and Asia Minor. [ME *aspide* < Lat. *aspis* < Gk.]
as·par·a·gus (ə-spăr′ə-gəs) *n.* **1.** Any of several plants of the genus *Asparagus,* native to Eurasia, having small scales or needlelike branchlets rather than true leaves, esp. the widely cultivated species *A. officinalis.* **2.** The succulent, edible young shoots of the asparagus. [Lat. < Gk. *asparagos.*]
asparagus beetle *n.* A small, spotted beetle, *Crioceris asparagi,* that infests and damages asparagus plants.
asparagus fern *n.* A vine, *Asparagus plumosus,* native to southern Africa, having stems with a fernlike appearance.
as·par·tame (ăs′pər-tām′, ə-spär′-) *n.* An artificial sweetener, $C_{14}H_{18}N_2O_5$, formed from aspartic acid. [ASPART(IC ACID) + (PHENYL)A(LANINE) + M(ETHYL) + E(STER).]
as·par·tic acid (ə-spär′tĭk) *n.* A nonessential amino acid, $C_4H_7NO_4$, found esp. in young sugar cane and sugar-beet molasses. [< ASPARAGUS (from its being obtained from an amino acid found in asparagus).]
as·par·to·kin·ase (ə-spär′tō-kī′nās′) *n.* An enzyme that catalyzes aspartic acid phosphorylation by ATP. [ASPART(IC ACID) + KINASE.]
as·pect (ăs′pĕkt′) *n.* **1.** A particular facial expression; air: *a soldier of grim aspect.* **2.** Appearance to the eye, esp. when seen from a specific view. **3.** The way in which an idea, problem, or situation is viewed by the mind: *all aspects of the case.* **4.** A position facing or commanding a given direction; exposure. **5.** A side or surface facing in a particular direction: *the ventral aspect of the body.* **6.** The configuration of the stars or planets in relation to one another or to the subject, thought by astrologers to influence human affairs. **7.** *Gram.* A category of the verb denoting primarily the relation of the action to the passage of time, esp. in reference to completion, duration, or repetition. **8.** *Archaic.* A gaze; look. [ME < Lat. *aspectus,* a view, p.part. of *aspicere,* to look at : *ad-,* toward + *specere,* to look.]
aspect ratio *n.* The width-to-height ratio of a television image.
as·pen (ăs′pən) *n.* Any of several trees of the genus *Populus,* having leaves attached by flattened leafstalks so that they flutter readily in the wind. *—adj.* **1.** Of or relating to an aspen. **2.** Shivering or trembling like the leaves of an aspen. [ME *aspe* < OE *æsp.*]
as·per·ate (ăs′pə-rāt′) *tr.v.* **-at·ed, -at·ing, -ates.** To make uneven; roughen. [Lat. *asperare, asperat-* < *asper,* rough.]
as·per·ges (ə-spûr′jēz) *n. Rom. Cath. Ch.* A short rite, preceding the High Mass on Sundays, that consists of sprinkling the altar, clergy, and congregation with holy water. [Lat., from the phrase *asperges me,* you will sprinkle me, the first words of the rite.]
as·per·gill (ăs′pər-jĭl) also **as·per·gil·lum** (ăs′pər-jĭl′əm) *n., pl.* **-gills** also **-gil·la** (jĭl′ə). *Rom. Cath. Ch.* A brush, perforated container, or other instrument used for sprinkling holy water. [NLat. *aspergillum* < Lat. *aspergere,* to sprinkle. —see ASPERSE.]
as·per·gil·lo·sis (ăs′pər-jə-lō′sĭs) *n.* An infectious disease of the skin, lungs, and other parts of the body, caused by certain fungi of the genus *Aspergillus.* [ASPERGILL(US) + -OSIS.]
as·per·gil·lum (ăs′pər-jĭl′əm) *n.* Variant of **aspergill.**
as·per·gil·lus (ăs′pər-jĭl′əs) *n., pl.* **-gil·li** (-jĭl′ī′). Any of various fungi of the genus *Aspergillus,* which includes many common molds. [NLat. < *aspergillum,* aspergill, from its resemblance to an aspergill brush.]
as·per·i·ty (ă-spĕr′ĭ-tē) *n.* **1.** Roughness or harshness, as of surface, weather, or sound. **2.** Ill temper; irritability. [Lat. *asperitas* < *asper,* rough.]
as·perse (ə-spûrs′) *tr.v.* **-persed, -pers·ing, -pers·es.** **1.** To spread false charges or insinuations against; defame; slander. **2.** To sprinkle, as with water. [Lat. *aspergere, aspers-,* to sprinkle : *ad-,* toward + *spergere,* to strew.]
as·per·sion (ə-spûr′zhən, -shən) *n.* **1.** A calumnious report or remark; slander. **2.** The act of defaming or slandering. **3.** A sprinkling, esp. with holy water.
as·phalt (ăs′fôlt′) also **as·phal·tum** (ăs-fôl′təm) or **as·phal·tus** (-təs) *n.* **1.** A brownish-black solid or semisolid mixture of bitumens obtained from native deposits or as a petroleum by-product, used in paving, roofing, and waterproofing. **2.** Mixed asphalt and crushed stone gravel or sand, used for paving or roofing. *—tr.v.* **-phalt·ed, -phalt·ing, -phalts.** To pave or coat with asphalt. [ME *aspalt* < Med. Lat. *asphaltus* < Gk. *asphaltos.*]
as·phal·tite (ăs′fôl-tīt′) *n.* A solid, dark-colored complex of hydrocarbons, found in natural veins and deposits.
as·phal·tum (ăs-fôl′təm) or **as·phal·tus** (-təs) *n.* Variant of **asphalt.**
a·spher·ic (ā-sfîr′ĭk, ā-sfĕr′-) also **a·spher·i·cal** (-ĭ-kəl) *adj.* Varying slightly from sphericity and having only slight aberration, as a lens.
as·pho·del (ăs′fə-dĕl′) *n.* Any of several plants of the genera *Asphodeline* and *Asphodelus,* of the Mediterranean region, having clusters of white or yellow flowers. [Lat. *asphodelus* < Gk. *asphodelos.*]
as·phyx·i·a (ăs-fĭk′sē-ə) *n.* Unconsciousness or death caused by lack of oxygen. [Gk. *asphuxia,* stopping of the pulse : *a-,* without + *sphuxis,* heartbeat < *sphuzein,* to throb.]
as·phyx·i·ant (ăs-fĭk′sē-ənt) *adj.* Inducing or tending to induce asphyxia. *—n.* An asphyxiant substance or condition.
as·phyx·i·ate (ăs-fĭk′sē-āt′) *v.* **-at·ed, -at·ing, -ates.** *—tr.* To cause asphyxia in; smother. *—intr.* To undergo asphyxia; suffocate. **—as·phyx′i·a′tion** *n.* **—as·phyx′i·a′tor** *n.*
as·pic[1] (ăs′pĭk) *n.* **1.** A cold dish of meat, fish, vegetables, or fruit combined and set in a gelatin mold. **2.** A jellied garnish of meat or fish stock and gelatin. [Fr., asp (from the resemblance of the jelly's coloration to an asp's). —see ASPIC[2].]
as·pic[2] (ăs′pĭk) *n. Archaic.* An asp. [Fr. < OFr., alteration of *aspe* < Lat. *aspis* < Gk.]
as·pi·dis·tra (ăs′pĭ-dĭs′trə) *n.* Any of several Asian plants of the genus *Aspidistra,* esp. *A. lurida,* having long, tough, evergreen leaves and small brownish flowers, widely cultivated as a house plant. [NLat. *Aspidistra,* genus name < Gk. *aspis,* shield.]

aspidistra

as·pi·rant (ăs′pər-ənt, ə-spīr′-) *n.* A person who aspires, esp. for advancement, honors, or a high position. *—adj.* Aspiring for recognition or distinction.
as·pi·rate (ăs′pə-rāt′) *tr.v.* **-rat·ed, -rat·ing, -rates.** **1. a.** To pronounce (a vowel or word) with the initial release of breath associated with English *h,* as in *Hartford.* **b.** To follow (a consonant, esp. a stop consonant) with a puff of breath that is clearly audible before the next sound begins, as in English *p, t,* and *k* before vowels. **2.** *Med.* To remove (liquids or gases) by means of an aspirator. *—n.* (-pər-ĭt). **1.** The speech sound represented by English *h.* **2.** The puff of air accompanying the release of a stop consonant. **3.** Any speech sound followed by a puff of breath. [Lat. *aspirare, aspirat,* to breathe on : *ad-* to + *spirare,* to breathe.]
as·pi·ra·tion (ăs′pə-rā′shən) *n.* **1.** Expulsion of breath in speech. **2. a.** The pronunciation of a consonant with an aspirate. **b.** An aspirate. **3.** *Med.* Removal of liquids or gases with an aspirator. **4. a.** A strong desire for high achievement. **b.** An object of such desire; ambitious goal.
as·pi·ra·tor (ăs′pə-rā′tər) *n.* **1.** A device that removes liquids or gases from a space by suction, esp. one used medicinally to evacuate a bodily cavity. **2.** A suction pump used to create a partial vacuum.
as·pir·a·to·ry (ə-spīr′ə-tôr′ē, -tōr′ē) *adj.* Of, pertaining to, or suited for breathing or suction.
as·pire (ə-spīr′) *intr.v.* **-pired, -pir·ing, -pires.** **1.** To have a

great ambition; desire strongly: *aspired to be an actress.* **2.** To strive toward an end; aim at: *aspiring to great knowledge.* **3.** *Archaic.* To rise upward; soar. [ME *aspiren* < Lat. *aspirare,* to desire. —see ASPIRATE.] **—as·pir'er** *n.* **—as·pir'ing·ly** *adv.*

as·pi·rin (ăs'pə-rĭn, -prĭn) *n.* **1.** A white crystalline compound of acetylsalicylic acid, $CH_3COOC_6H_4COOH$, commonly used in tablet form as an antipyretic and analgesic. **2.** A tablet of aspirin. [Orig. a trademark.]

a·squint (ə-skwĭnt') *adv. & adj.* With a sidelong glance. [ME.]

ass[1] (ăs) *n., pl.* **ass·es** (ăs'ĭz). **1.** Any of several hoofed mammals of the genus *Equus,* resembling and closely related to the horses and zebras, and including the domesticated donkey. **2.** A vain, self-important, silly, or aggressively stupid person. [ME *asse* < OE *assa.*]

ass[2] (ăs) *n., pl.* **ass·es** (ăs'ĭz). **1.** *Vulgar Slang.* The buttocks. **2.** *Vulgar.* The anus. **3.** *Vulgar.* Coitus. [ME *ars* < OE *ears.*]

ass[1]
Sardinian ass

as·sa·gai or **as·se·gai** (ăs'ə-gī') *n.* **1.** A light spear or javelin, often with an iron tip, used by southern African tribesmen. **2.** A tree, *Curtisia faginea,* of southern Africa, having wood used for making assagais. [OFr. *azagaie,* prob. < OSp. *azagaya* < Ar. *az-zaghāyah* : *al,* the + Berber *zaghāyah,* spear.]

as·sai[1] (ä-sī') *n.* **1.** Any of several palm trees of the genus *Euterpe,* of tropical South America, having edible, fleshy purple fruit. **2.** A beverage made from the fruit of an assai. [Port. (Brazil) *assaí* < Tupi *assahi.*]

as·sai[2] (ä-sī') *adv. Mus.* Very. Used in tempo directions: *allegro assai.* [Ital. < VLat. **ad satis,* to sufficiency. —see ASSET.]

as·sail (ə-sāl') *tr.v.* **-sailed, -sail·ing, -sails. 1.** To attack with or as if with violent blows; assault. **2.** To attack verbally, as with ridicule or censure. [ME *assailen* < OFr. *assaillier* < VLat. **assalire,* var. of Lat. *assilire,* to jump on : *ad-,* onto + *salire,* to jump.] **—as·sail'a·ble** *adj.* **—as·sail'a·ble·ness** *n.* **—as·sail'er** *n.* **—as·sail'ment** *n.*

as·sail·ant (ə-sā'lənt) *n.* A person who assails another.

As·sam·ese (ăs'ə-mēz', -mēs') *adj.* Of or pertaining to Assam, its people, or their language. *—n., pl.* **Assamese. 1.** A native or inhabitant of Assam. **2.** The Indic language of the Assamese.

as·sas·sin (ə-săs'ĭn) *n.* **1.** A murderer, esp. one who carries out a plot to kill a public official or other prominent person. **2. Assassin.** A member of a secret order of Moslem fanatics who terrorized and killed Christian Crusaders. [Fr. < Med. Lat. *assassinus* < Ar. *ḥashshāshīn,* user of hashish < *ḥashīsh,* hashish.]

as·sas·si·nate (ə-săs'ə-nāt') *tr.v.* **-nat·ed, -nat·ing, -nates. 1.** To murder (a prominent person). **2.** To destroy or injure treacherously: *assassinate a rival's character.* **—as·sas'si·na'tion** *n.* **—as·sas'si·na'tive** *adj.* **—as·sas'si·na'tor** *n.*

assassin bug *n.* Any of various predatory insects of the large family Reduviidae, having short, curved, powerful beaks adapted for sucking blood and capable of inflicting a painful bite.

as·sault (ə-sôlt') *n.* **1.** A violent attack, either physical or verbal. **2. a.** A military attack upon a fortified area or place. **b.** The concluding stage of an attack in which there is close combat with the enemy. **3.** *Law.* An unlawful attempt or threat to injure another physically. **4.** Rape. *—v.* **-sault·ed, -sault·ing, -saults.** *—tr.* To attack or assail violently. *—intr.* To make an assault. [ME *assaut* < OFr. < VLat. **assaltus,* var. of Lat. *assultus,* p.part. of *assilire,* to jump on. —see ASSAIL.] **—as·sault'er** *n.*

assault and battery *n. Law.* The threat to use force upon another and the carrying out of the threat.

as·say (ăs'ā', ă-sā') *n.* **1. a.** The qualitative or quantitative analysis of a substance, esp. of an ore or drug. **b.** A substance to be so analyzed. **c.** The result of such an analysis. **2.** Any analysis or examination. **3.** *Obs.* An attempt; essay. *—v.* (ă-sā', ăs'ā') **-sayed, -say·ing, -says.** *—tr.* **1.** To subject to chemical analysis; make an assay of. **2.** To examine by trial or experiment; put to a test: *assay one's ability.* **3.** To evaluate; assess. **4.** To attempt; try. *—intr.* To be shown by analysis as having a certain proportion, usually of a precious metal. [ME *assai* < OFr. —see ESSAY.] **—as·say'a·ble** *adj.* **—as·say'er** *n.*

as·se·gai (ăs'ə-gī') *n.* Variant of **assagai.**

as·sem·blage (ə-sĕm'blĭj) *n.* **1. a.** The act of assembling. **b.** The state of being assembled. **2.** A collection of people or things. **3.** A fitting together of parts, as of a machine. **4.** A sculpture consisting of an arrangement of miscellaneous objects, such as scraps of metal, cloth, and string.

as·sem·ble (ə-sĕm'bəl) *v.* **-bled, -bling, -bles.** *—tr.* **1.** To bring or gather together into a group or whole. **2.** To fit or join together the parts of. *—intr.* To gather together; congregate. [ME *assemblen* < OFr. *assembler* < VLat. **assimulare* : Lat. *ad-,* to + Lat. *simul,* together.]

as·sem·bler (ə-sĕm'blər) *n.* **1.** One that assembles. **2.** *Computer Sci.* A computer program operating on symbolic input data to produce the equivalent machine code.

as·sem·bly (ə-sĕm'blē) *n., pl.* **-blies. 1. a.** The act of assembling. **b.** The state of being assembled. **2.** A group of persons gathered together for a common purpose. **3. Assembly.** In certain U.S. states, the lower house of the legislature. **4. a.** The putting together of manufactured parts to make a completed product, esp. a machine. **b.** A set of parts so assembled. **5.** The signal calling troops to form ranks.

assembly language *n. Computer Sci.* A programming language that is a close approximation of machine code.

assembly line *n.* A line of factory workers and equipment on which the product being assembled passes consecutively from operation to operation until completed.

as·sem·bly·man (ə-sĕm'blē-mən) *n.* A male member of a legislative assembly.

Assembly of God *n.* A Pentecostal congregation founded in the United States in 1914.

assembly time *n. Computer Sci.* The time required for an assembler to translate symbolic language into machine instructions.

as·sem·bly·wom·an (ə-sĕm'blē-wo͝om'ən) *n.* A female member of a legislative assembly.

as·sent (ə-sĕnt') *intr.v.* **-sent·ed, -sent·ing, -sents.** To express agreement; concur: *assented to his plan.* *—n.* **1.** Agreement, as to a proposal; compliance. **2.** Acquiescence; consent. [ME *assenten* < OFr. *assentir* < Lat. *assentari* : *ad-,* toward + *sentire,* to feel.] **—as·sent'er, as·sen'tor** *n.* **—as·sent'ing·ly** *adv.* **—as·sen'tive** *adj.* **—as·sen'tive·ness** *n.*

Synonyms: *assent, agree accede, acquiesce, accept, consent, concur, subscribe.* These verbs mean to go along with another's views, proposals, or actions. *Assent* implies saying "yes" in a formal, somewhat impersonal manner. *Agree* and *accede* are loosely related in the sense of assenting after discussion or persuasion. But *agree* suggests mutual accommodation in a meeting of minds, whereas *accede* implies yielding on the part of one person or group. *Acquiesce* suggests agreeing, despite reservations, because of unwillingness to oppose. *Accept* may indicate agreement with some reluctance. *Consent* indicates complete and voluntary personal commitment ot a proposal or desire. *Concur* refers to agreement with another's position, and may suggest that one has reached the same conclusion independently. *Subscribe* indicates hearty consent or approval.

as·sen·ta·tion (ăs'ĕn-tā'shən) *n.* Ill-considered or servile agreement with another's opinions.

as·sert (ə-sûrt') *tr.v.* **-sert·ed, -sert·ing, -serts. 1.** To state or express positively; affirm. **2.** To defend or maintain (one's rights, for example). **3. assert oneself.** To express oneself forcefully or boldly. [Lat. *asserere, assert-,* : *ad-,* to + *serere,* to join.] **—as·sert'a·ble, as·sert'i·ble** *adj.* **—as·sert'er, as·ser'tor** *n.*

Synonyms: *assert, asseverate, declare, affirm, aver, avow, allege.* These verbs all mean to state; they differ principally in emphasis. To *assert* is to state one's position boldly, and to *asseverate* is to add even greater emphasis to the position taken. *Declare* has the approximate force of *assert,* but may suggest formality of statement and authority in the speaker. *Affirm* and *aver* imply less forcefulness, but stress the speaker's confidence in the validity of his statement. *Avow* emphasizes moral commitment to the statement. *Allege* refers to making a controversial charge or statement without presentation of proof.

as·ser·tion (ə-sûr'shən) *n.* **1.** The act of asserting. **2.** Something asserted positively, often with no support or attempt at proof. **—as·ser'tion·al** *adj.*

as·ser·tive (ə-sûr'tĭv) *adj.* Inclined to bold assertion; confident. **—as·ser'tive·ly** *adv.* **—as·ser'tive·ness** *n.*

assertiveness training *n.* A method of training individuals to behave in a boldly self-confident manner.

as·ser·to·ry (ə-sûr'tə-rē) *adj.* Asserting or affirming.

as·ses[1] (ăs'ēz', ăs'ĭz) *n.* Plural of **as[2].**

ass·es[2] (ăs'ĭz) *n.* Plural of **ass[1]** and **ass[2].**

as·sess (ə-sĕs') *tr.v.* **-sessed, -sess·ing, -sess·es. 1.** To estimate the value of (property) for taxation. **2.** To set or determine the amount of (a tax, fine, or other payment). **3.** To charge (a person or property) with a tax, fine, or other special payment. **4.** To evaluate; appraise. [ME *assessen* < OFr. *assesser* < Lat. *assidēre,* to sit by (as an assistant judge) : *ad-,* near to + *sedēre,* to sit.] **—as·sess'a·ble** *adj.*

as·sess·ment (ə-sĕs'mənt) *n.* **1.** The act of assessing. **2.** An amount assessed.

as·ses·sor (ə-sĕs'ər) *n.* **1.** An official who makes assessments, as for taxation. **2.** An assistant to a judge, selected for his special knowledge of a particular area. **—as'ses·so'ri·al** (ăs'ə-sôr'ē-əl, -sōr'-) *adj.*

as·set (ăs'ĕt') *n.* **1.** A useful or valuable quality or thing; advantage: *An agreeable personality is a great asset.* **2.** A valuable item that is owned. **3. assets.** *Accounting.* The entries on a balance sheet showing all properties and claims against others that may be applied, directly or indirectly, to cover liabilities. [Back-formation < E. *assets* < AN *asetz,* sufficient goods to settle a testator's debts and legacies < OFr. *asez,* enough < VLat. **ad satis,* to sufficiency : Lat. *ad-,* to + *satis,* enough.]

Synonyms: *asset, possession, belongings, effects, property, resource.* These nouns refer to things a person owns, considered as components of wealth. *Asset* technically is used in the plural and refers to an item that can be turned into cash to cover liabilities. Less narrowly the term means any valuable thing or any personal quality or trait of practical value. *Possession* usually applies to any tangible item of

ă pat / ā pay / âr care / ä father / b **bib** / ch **church** / d **deed** / ĕ pet / ē be / f fife / g gag / h **hat** / hw **which** / ĭ pit / ī pie / îr **pier** / j **judge** / k **kick** / l lid, needle / m **mum** / n no, sudden / ng thing / ŏ pot / ō **toe** / ô paw, for / oi noise / ou **out** / o͝o **took** / o͞o **boot** /

value ranging from small to great. *Belongings* denotes the more personal items one owns, such as clothing and jewelry. *Effects* includes belongings and, sometimes, all other movable possessions. *Property* refers broadly to any real or tangible possession. *Resource* denotes any possession on hand or in reserve and available for use; the term thus includes actual and potential wealth.

as·sev·er·ate (ə-sĕv′ə-rāt′) *tr.v.* **-at·ed, -at·ing, -ates.** To declare seriously or positively; affirm. [Lat. *asseverare, asseverat-* : *ad-*, to + *severus,* serious.] **—as·sev′er·a′tion** *n.*

as·sib·i·late (ə-sĭb′ə-lāt′) *tr.v.* **-lat·ed, -lat·ing, -lates.** To pronounce with a hissing sound; make sibilant. [AD- + SIBILATE.] **—as·sib′i·la′tion** *n.*

as·si·du·i·ty (ăs′ĭ-dōō′ĭ-tē, -dyōō′-) *n., pl.* **-ties. 1.** The quality or condition of being assiduous; diligence. **2.** Often **assiduities.** Constant personal attention; solicitude.

as·sid·u·ous (ə-sĭj′ōō-əs) *adj.* **1.** Constant in application or attention; diligent: *an assiduous worker who strove for perfection.* **2.** Unceasing; persistent. [Lat. *assiduus* < *assidēre,* to attend to : *ad-*, near to + *sedēre,* to sit.] **—as·sid′u·ous·ly** *adv.* **—as·sid′u·ous·ness** *n.*

as·sign (ə-sīn′) *tr.v.* **-signed, -sign·ing, -signs. 1.** To set apart for a particular purpose; designate. **2.** To select for a duty or office; appoint. **3.** To give out as a task; allot. **4.** To ascribe; attribute. **5.** *Law.* To transfer (property, rights, or interests). **6.** To place (a unit or personnel) integrally into a particular military organization. *—n. Law.* An assignee. [ME *assignen* < OFr. *assignir* < Lat. *assignare* : *ad-*, to + *signare,* to mark < *signum,* sign.] **—as·sign′a·bil′i·ty** *n.* **—as·sign′a·ble** *adj.* **—as·sign′a·bly** *adv.* **—as·sign′er** *n.*

Synonyms: *assign, allot, apportion, allocate.* These verbs refer to distributing something. *Assign* applies to an authoritative act and makes no implication about equality of distribution: *assign a task. Allot* also refers to arbitrary distribution, as of money or time, usually for a specified purpose. *Apportion* refers to division according to prescribed rules, and implies fair distribution. *Allocate* usually means to set something aside from a larger quantity, particularly funds, for a specific purpose.

as·sig·nat (ăs′ĭg-năt′, ăs′ēn-yä′) *n.* One of the notes of the paper currency issued in France (1789–96) by the revolutionary government and backed by the security of confiscated lands. [Fr. < Lat. *assignatum,* to assign.]

as·sig·na·tion (ăs′ĭg-nā′shən) *n.* **1.** The act of assigning. **2.** Something assigned; assignment. **3.** An appointment for a meeting between lovers; tryst. **—as′sig·na′tion·al** *adj.*

as·sign·ee (ə-sī′nē′, ăs′ĭ-nē′) *n. Law.* **1.** A person to whom a transfer of property, rights, or interest is made. **2.** One appointed to act for another; deputy; agent.

as·sign·ment (ə-sīn′mənt) *n.* **1.** The act of assigning. **2.** Something assigned, as a task. **3.** A position or post of duty to which one is assigned. **4.** *Law.* **a.** The transfer of a claim, right, interest, or property. **b.** The document or deed by which this transfer is made.

as·sign·or (ə-sī′nôr′, ə-sī′nər, ăs′ə-nôr′) *n. Law.* A person who makes an assignment.

as·sim·i·la·ble (ə-sĭm′ə-lə-bəl) *adj.* Capable of being assimilated. **—as·sim′i·la·bil′i·ty** *n.*

as·sim·i·late (ə-sĭm′ə-lāt′) *v.* **-lat·ed, -lat·ing, -lates.** *—tr.* **1.** *Physiol.* **a.** To consume and incorporate into the body; digest. **b.** To transform (food) into living tissue; metabolize constructively. **2.** To absorb and incorporate (knowledge, for example) into the mind. **3.** To make similar; cause to assume a resemblance. **4.** *Ling.* To alter (a sound) by assimilation. **5.** To absorb (an immigrant or culturally distinct group) into the prevailing culture. *—intr.* To become assimilated. [ME *assimilaten* < Lat. *assimilare,* to make similar to : *ad-*, to + *similis,* like.] **—as·sim′i·la′tor** *n.*

as·sim·i·la·tion (ə-sĭm′ə-lā′shən) *n.* **1.** The act or process of assimilating. **2.** The condition or process of being assimilated. **3.** *Biol.* The process by which nourishment is changed into living tissue; constructive metabolism. **4.** *Ling.* The process by which a sound is modified to make it resemble an adjacent sound. For example, the prefix *in-* in *intolerable* becomes *im-* in *impossible* by assimilation. **5.** The process whereby a group, as a minority or immigrant group, gradually adopts the characteristics of another culture.

as·sim·i·la·tive (ə-sĭm′ə-lā′tĭv) also **as·sim·i·la·to·ry** (-lə-tôr′ē, -tōr′ē) *adj.* Marked by or causing assimilation.

As·sin·i·boin (ə-sĭn′ə-boin′) *n., pl.* **Assiniboin** or **-boins. 1.** A tribe of North American Indians of northeastern Montana and adjacent regions of Canada. **2.** A member of the Assiniboin. **3.** The Siouan language of the Assiniboin. [Fr. *Assiniboine,* of Ojibwa orig.] **—As·sin′i·boin′** *adj.*

as·sist (ə-sĭst′) *v.* **-sist·ed, -sist·ing, -sists.** *—tr.* **1.** To aid; help. **2.** To work with as an assistant. *—intr.* **1.** To give aid or support. **2.** To be present; attend. *—n.* **1.** An act of giving aid; help. **2. a.** *Baseball.* A fielding and throwing of the ball that enables a teammate to put out a runner. **b.** A pass of the ball or puck to the teammate scoring a goal, as in basketball or ice hockey. **3.** A machine or mechanical device providing aid. [ME *assisten* < OFr. *assister* < Lat. *assistere* : *ad-*, near to + *sistere,* to stand.] **—as·sist′er** *n.*

as·sis·tance (ə-sĭs′təns) *n.* **1.** The act of assisting. **2.** Aid; help: *financial assistance.*

as·sis·tant (ə-sĭs′tənt) *n.* One that assists; aide. *—adj.* **1.** Holding an auxiliary position; subordinate. **2.** Giving aid; auxiliary.

assistant professor *n.* A college teacher who ranks above an instructor and below an associate professor.

as·sis·tant·ship (ə-sĭs′tənt-shĭp′) *n.* An academic position that carries a stipend and usually involves part-time teaching or research, given to a qualified graduate student.

as·size (ə-sīz′) *n.* **1. a.** A session of a legislative body or court. **b.** A decree or edict rendered at such a session. **2. a.** An ordinance regulating weights and measures and the weights and prices of articles of consumption. **b.** The standards so set up. **3.** A judicial inquest, the writ by which it is instituted, or the verdict of the jurors. **4. assizes. a.** One of the periodic court sessions held in each of the counties of England and Wales for the trial of civil or criminal cases. **b.** The time or place of such sessions. [ME *assise* < OFr., act of sitting < p.part. of *asseior,* to seat < Lat. *assidēre,* to sit beside : *ad-*, at + *sedēre,* to sit.]

as·so·ci·a·ble (ə-sō′shē-ə-bəl, -shə-bəl) *adj.* Capable of being associated. **—as·so′ci·a·bil′i·ty** (-bĭl′ĭ-tē), **as·so′ci·a·ble·ness** *n.*

as·so·ci·ate (ə-sō′shē-āt′, -sē-) *v.* **-at·ed, -at·ing, -ates.** *—tr.* **1.** To bring into company with another; join in a relationship. **2.** To connect or join together; combine; link. **3.** To connect in the mind or imagination: *"I always somehow associate Chatterton with autumn"* (Keats). *—intr.* **1.** To join in or form a league, union, or association. **2.** To keep company. *—n.* (ə-sō′shē-ĭt, -āt′, -sē-). **1.** A person united with another or others in some action, enterprise, or business; partner; colleague. **2.** A companion; comrade. **3.** Anything that habitually accompanies or is associated with another; an attendant circumstance. **4.** A member of an institution or society who is granted only partial status or privileges. *—adj.* (ə-sō′shē-ĭt, -āt′, -sē-). **1.** Joined with another or others and having equal or nearly equal status: *an associate editor.* **2.** Having partial status or privileges: *an associate member of the club.* **3.** Following or accompanying; concomitant. [ME *associaten* < Lat. *associare,* to join to : *ad-*, to + *socius,* companion.]

associate professor *n.* A college or university teacher who ranks below a full professor and above an assistant professor.

as·so·ci·a·tion (ə-sō′sē-ā′shən, -shē-) *n.* **1.** The act of associating or the state of being associated. **2.** An organized body of people who have some interest, activity, or purpose in common; society; league. **3.** A mental connection or relation between thoughts, feelings, ideas, or sensations. **4.** *Chem.* Any of various processes of chemical combination, such as hydration, solvation, or complex-ion formation, depending on relatively weak chemical bonding. **5.** *Ecol.* A large number of organisms in a specific area with one or two dominant species. **—as·so′ci·a′tion·al** *adj.*

association football *n. Chiefly Brit.* Soccer.

as·so·ci·a·tive (ə-sō′shē-ā′tĭv, -sē-, -shə-tĭv) *adj.* **1.** Of, characterized by, resulting from, or causing association. **2.** *Math.* Independent of the grouping of elements. Used of mathematical operations: *If* $a + (b + c) = (a + b) + c$, *the operation indicated by* + *is associative.* **—as·so′ci·a′tive·ly** *adv.*

as·soil (ə-soil′) *tr.v.* **-soiled, -soil·ing, -soils.** *Archaic.* **1.** To absolve or pardon. **2.** To atone for. [ME *assoilen* < OFr. *assoldre, assoil-* < Lat. *absolvere,* to set free : *ab-*, away + *solvere,* to loosen.]

as·so·nance (ăs′ə-nəns) *n.* **1.** Resemblance in sound, esp. in the vowel sounds of words. **2.** A partial rhyme in which the accented vowel sounds correspond but the consonants differ, as in *brave* and *vain.* [Fr., < Lat. *assonans,* pr.part. of *assonare,* to respond to : *ad-*, to + *sonare,* to sound.] **—as′so·nant** *adj. & n.*

as·sort (ə-sôrt′) *v.* **-sort·ed, -sort·ing, -sorts.** *—tr.* **1.** To separate into groups according to kinds; classify. **2.** To supply with a variety of goods. *—intr.* **1.** To fall into a class; match. **2.** To associate; consort. [OFr. *assorter* : *a-*, to (< Lat. *ad-*) + *sorte,* kind < Lat. *sors,* chance, lot.] **—as·sort′a·tive** (ə-sôr′tə-tĭv) *adj.* **—as·sort′er** *n.*

as·sort·ed (ə-sôr′tĭd) *adj.* **1.** Consisting of a number of different kinds; various. **2.** Placed in classes; classified. **3.** Suited or matched.

as·sort·ment (ə-sôrt′mənt) *n.* **1.** The act of assorting; separation into classes. **2.** A collection of various things; variety.

as·suage (ə-swāj′) *tr.v.* **-suaged, -suag·ing, -suag·es. 1.** To make less burdensome or painful; ease: *"assuage the anguish of your bereavement"* (Lincoln). **2.** To satisfy or appease, as thirst. **3.** To pacify or calm. [ME *asswagen* < OFr. *assuagier* < VLat. **assuaviare* : Lat. *ad-*, to + *suavis,* sweet.] **—as·suage′ment** *n.*

as·sua·sive (ə-swā′sĭv, -zĭv) *adj.* Soothing.

as·sume (ə-sōōm′) *tr.v.* **-sumed, -sum·ing, -sumes. 1.** To put on; don (a garment, for example). **2.** To take upon oneself; undertake: *assuming the responsibility.* **3.** To invest oneself formally with: *assume the presidency.* **4.** To take on; adopt: *"The god assumes a human form"* (Ruskin). **5.** To feign; affect: *assumed an air of indifference.* **6.** To take for granted; suppose. **7.** *Theol.* To take up or receive, as into heaven. [ME *assumen* < Lat. *assumere,* to adopt : *ad-*, to +

sumere, to take.] **—as·sum′a·ble** *adj.* **—as·sum′a·bly** *adv.* **—as·sum′er** *n.*

as·sumed (ə-so͞omd′) *adj.* **1.** Pretended; adopted; fictitious: *an assumed name.* **2.** Taken for granted. **—as·sum′ed·ly** (ə-so͞o′mĭd-lē) *adv.*

as·sum·ing (ə-so͞o′mĭng) *adj.* Presumptuous; pretentious; arrogant. **—as·sum′ing·ly** *adv.*

as·sump·sit (ə-sŭmp′sĭt) *n. Law.* **1.** An agreement or promise not under seal; contract. **2.** A legal action to enforce or recover damages for a breach of such an agreement. [Lat., he undertook.]

as·sump·tion (ə-sŭmp′shən) *n.* **1.** The act of assuming. **2.** A statement accepted or supposed true without proof or demonstration. **3.** Presumption or arrogance. **4.** *Logic.* A minor premise. **5. Assumption. a.** *Theol.* The bodily taking up of the Virgin Mary into heaven after her death. **b.** A church feast on August 15 celebrating this event. [ME < Lat. *assumptio,* adoption < *assumere,* to adopt. —see ASSUME.]

as·sump·tive (ə-sŭmp′tĭv) *adj.* **1.** Of or characterized by assumption: *assumptive facts.* **2.** Taken for granted. **3.** Presumptuous; assuming. **—as·sump′tive·ly** *adv.*

as·sur·ance (ə-sho͝or′əns) *n.* **1.** The act of assuring or the state of being assured. **2.** A statement or indication that inspires confidence; guarantee. **3. a.** Freedom from doubt; certainty. **b.** Self-confidence. **4.** Boldness; audacity. **5.** *Chiefly Brit.* Insurance.

as·sure (ə-sho͝or′) *tr.v.* **-sured, -sur·ing, -sures. 1.** To inform confidently, with a view to removing doubt. **2.** To cause to feel sure; convince. **3.** To give confidence to; reassure. **4.** To make certain; ensure: *"Nothing in history assures the success of our civilization"* (Herbert J. Muller). **5.** To make safe or secure. **6.** *Chiefly Brit.* To insure, as against loss. [ME *assuren* < OFr. *assurer* < Med. Lat. *assecurare,* to make sure : Lat. *ad-,* to + *securus,* secure.] **—as·sur′a·ble** *adj.* **—as·sur′er** *n.*

Usage: *Assure, ensure,* and *insure* all mean "to make secure or certain." Only *assure* is used with reference to a person in the sense of "to set the mind at rest": *assured the leader of his loyalty.* Although *ensure* and *insure* are generally interchangeable, only *insure* is now widely used in the commercial sense of "to guarantee persons or property against risk."

as·sured (ə-sho͝ord′) *adj.* **1.** Made certain; guaranteed; undoubted. **2.** Confident; bold. **3.** Insured. **—as·sur′ed·ly** (-ĭd-lē) *adv.* **—as·sur′ed·ness** *n.*

as·sur·gent (ə-sûr′jənt) *adj.* **1.** Rising or tending to rise. **2.** *Bot.* Slanting or curving upward; ascending. [Lat. *assurgens, assurgent-,* pr.part. of *assurgere,* to rise up to : *ad-,* to + *surgere,* to rise. —see SURGE.] **—as·sur′gen·cy** *n.*

As·syr·i·an (ə-sîr′ē-ən) *adj.* Of or pertaining to Assyria, its people, language, or culture. *—n.* **1.** A native or inhabitant of Assyria. **2.** The Semitic language of the Assyrians.

As·syr·i·ol·o·gy (ə-sîr′ē-ŏl′ə-jē) *n.* The study of the ancient civilization of Assyria. **—As·syr′i·ol′o·gist** *n.*

-ast *suff.* One associated with: *ecdysiast.* [ME < Lat. *astes* < Gk. *-astēs,* n.suffix.]

a·sta·ble circuit (ā′stā′bəl) *n. Computer Sci.* A circuit that alternates continuously between two unstable states.

As·tar·te (ə-stär′tē) *n. Myth.* The Phoenician goddess of love and fertility. [Lat. *Astarte* < Gk., of Semitic orig.]

a·sta·sia (ə-stā′zhə) *n.* Inability to stand because of muscular incoordination. [Gk., unsteadiness < *astatos,* unsteady : *a-,* not + *statos,* standing.]

a·stat·ic (ā-stăt′ĭk) *adj.* **1.** Unsteady; unstable. **2.** *Computer Sci.* Having no particular directional characteristics. **—a·stat′i·cal·ly** *adv.* **—a·stat′i·cism** *n.*

as·ta·tine (ăs′tə-tēn′, -tĭn) *n. Symbol* **At** A highly unstable radioactive element that resembles iodine in solution and accumulates in the thyroid gland. Its longest lived isotope is At 210, having a half-life of 8.3 hours, and is used in medicine as a radioactive tracer. Atomic number 85; valences probably 1, 3, 5, or 7. [Gk. *astatos,* unstable + -INE².]

aster

as·ter (ăs′tər) *n.* **1.** Any of various plants of the genus *Aster,* having rayed, daisylike flowers ranging in color from white to bluish, purple, or pink. **2.** The China aster. **3.** *Biol.* A star-shaped structure appearing in the cytoplasm of the cell and associated with the centrosome during mitosis. [Lat., star < Gk. *astēr.*]

as·te·ri·at·ed (ă-stîr′ē-ā′tĭd) *adj. Mineral.* Exhibiting asterism. [< Gk. *asterios,* starry < *astēr,* star.]

as·ter·isk (ăs′tə-rĭsk′) *n.* **1.** A star-shaped figure (*) used in printing to indicate an omission or a reference to a footnote. **2.** *Ling.* An asterisk used to indicate an unattested form or entity. *—tr.v.* **-isked, -isk·ing, -isks.** To mark with an asterisk. [LLat. *asteriscus* < Gk. *asteriskos,* dim. of *astēr,* star.]

as·ter·ism (ăs′tə-rĭz′əm) *n.* **1.** *Printing.* Three asterisks in triangular form used to call attention to a following passage. **2.** *Astron.* **a.** A cluster of stars. **b.** A constellation. **3.** *Mineral.* A six-rayed starlike figure optically produced in some crystal structures by reflected or transmitted light. [Gk. *asterismos,* constellation < *astēr,* star.] **—as′ter·is′mal** *adj.*

a·stern (ə-stûrn′) *adv. Naut.* **1.** Behind a vessel. **2.** Toward the rear of a vessel. **3.** To the rear; backward. **—a·stern′** *adj.*

a·ster·nal (ā-stûr′nəl) *adj. Anat.* **1.** Not connected to the sternum. **2.** Lacking a sternum.

as·ter·oid (ăs′tə-roid′) *n.* **1.** *Astron.* Any of numerous celestial bodies with characteristic diameters between one and several hundred miles and orbits lying chiefly between Mars and Jupiter. **2.** *Zool.* A starfish. *—adj.* Also **as·ter·oid·al** (ăs′tə-roid′l). Star-shaped. [Gk. *asteroeidēs,* starlike : *astēr,* star + *-eidēs,* like.]

As·ter·o·pe (ă-stĕr′ə-pē) *n.* Variant of **Sterope.**

as·the·ni·a (ăs-thē′nē-ə) *n.* Loss or lack of bodily strength; weakness. [NLat. < Gk. *astheneia* < *asthenēs,* weak : *a-,* without + *sthenos,* strength.]

as·then·ic (ăs-thĕn′ĭk) *n.* A slender, lightly muscled human physique. **—as·then′ic, as·then′i·cal** *adj.*

as·the·no·pi·a (ăs′thə-nō′pē-ə) *n.* Eyestrain, esp. with headache and dimming of vision. [ASTHEN(IA) + -OPIA.] **—as′the·nop′ic** (-nŏp′ĭk) *adj.*

as·then·o·sphere (ăs-thĕn′ə-sfîr′) *n.* A zone of the earth's mantle that lies beneath the lithosphere and consists of several hundred kilometers of deformable rock. [Gk. *asthenēs,* weak (*a-,* not + *sthenos,* strength) + SPHERE.]

asth·ma (ăz′mə, ăs′-) *n.* A chronic respiratory disease, often arising from allergies, and accompanied by labored breathing, chest constriction, and coughing. [ME *asma* < Med. Lat. < Gk. *asthma.*] **—asth·mat′ic** (-măt′ĭk) *adj. & n.* **—asth·mat′i·cal·ly** *adv.*

as though *conj.* As if: *looked as though they had been quarreling.*

a·stig·ma·tism (ə-stĭg′mə-tĭz′əm) *n.* **1.** A refractive defect of a lens that prevents focusing of sharp, distinct images. **2.** Faulty vision caused by such defects in the lens of the eye. [A- (without) + Gk. *stigma,* point < *stizein,* to tattoo.] **—as′tig·mat′ic** (ăs′tĭg-măt′ĭk) *adj.* **—as′tig·mat′i·cal·ly** *adv.*

a·stir (ə-stûr′) *adj.* **1.** Moving about. **2.** Out of bed; awake. [Sc. *asteer* : *a,* on + *steer,* stir.]

as to *prep.* **1.** With regard to: *puzzled as to how it happened.* **2.** According to: *chosen as to ability.*

As·to·lat (ăs′tə-lŏt′, -lăt′) *n.* An English town in legends of King Arthur, possibly in modern Surrey.

a·stom·a·tous (ā-stŏm′ə-təs, ā-stō′mə-) also **as·tom·ous** (ăs′tə-məs) or **a·stom·a·tal** (ā-stŏm′ə-təl, -stō′mə-təl) *adj.* Having no mouth or stomata.

a·ston·ied (ə-stŏn′ēd) *adj. Archaic.* Bewildered; dazed. [ME *astonied,* p.part. of *astonen,* to amaze. —see ASTONISH.]

a·ston·ish (ə-stŏn′ĭsh) *tr.v.* **-ished, -ish·ing, -ish·es.** To fill with sudden wonder or amazement; confound. [Prob. alteration of obs. *astony,* to amaze < ME *astonen* < AN < VLat. **extonare* : Lat. *ex-,* out of + Lat. *tonare,* to thunder.] **—a·ston′ish·er** *n.* **—a·ston′ish·ing·ly** *adv.*

a·ston·ish·ment (ə-stŏn′ĭsh-mənt) *n.* **1.** Great surprise or amazement. **2.** A cause of amazement; marvel.

a·stound (ə-stound′) *tr.v.* **a·stound·ed, a·stound·ing, a·stounds.** To strike with sudden wonder. [< Obs. *astoned,* p.part. of obs. *astony,* to amaze. —see ASTONISH.] **—a·stound′ing·ly** *adv.*

astr– *pref.* Variant of **astro-.**

As·tra·chan (ăs′trə-kăn′, -kən) *n.* A tart red or yellow apple of Russian origin. [After *Astrakhan,* a city in the U.S.S.R.]

a·strad·dle (ə-străd′l) *adv.* In a straddling position; astride. *—prep.* So as to straddle; astride.

As·trae·a (ă-strē′ə) *n. Gk. Myth.* The goddess of justice. [NLat. < Gk. *astraios,* starry < *astron,* star.]

as·tra·gal (ăs′trə-gəl) *n. Archit.* A narrow, convex molding, often having the form of beading. [Lat. *astragalus* < Gk. *astragalos.*]

as·trag·a·lus (ə-străg′ə-ləs) *n., pl.* **-li** (-lī′). The talus. [NLat. < Gk. *astragalos,* vertebra.] **—as·trag′a·lar** *adj.*

as·tra·khan also **as·tra·chan** (ăs′trə-kăn′, -kən) *n.* **1.** The curly or wavy fur made from the skins of young lambs from the region of Astrakhan. **2.** A fabric with a curly, looped pile, made to resemble astrakhan.

as·tral (ăs′trəl) *adj.* **1.** Of, pertaining to, emanating from, or resembling the stars. **2.** *Biol.* Pertaining to or shaped like an aster; star-shaped. [LLat. *astralis* < Lat. *astrum,* star < Gk. *astron.*] **—as′tral·ly** *adv.*

as·tra·pho·bi·a (ăs′trə-fō′bē-ə) *n.* Abnormal fear of lightning and thunder. [Gk. *astrapē,* lightning + -PHOBIA.]

a·stray (ə-strā′) *adv.* **1.** Away from the correct path or direction. **2.** Away from the right or good; toward evil or wrong ways. [ME < OFr. *estraie,* p.part. of *estraier,* to stray. —see STRAY.] **—a·stray′** *adj.*

as·trict (ə-strĭkt′) *tr.v.* **-trict·ed, -trict·ing, -tricts.** To bind, esp. by moral or legal obligations. [Lat. *astrictus,* p.part. of *astringere,* to bind fast. —see ASTRINGE.] **—as·tric′tion** *n.*

as·tric·tive (ə-strĭk′tĭv) *adj.* Astringent. *—n.* An astringent. **—as·tric′tive·ly** *adv.* **—as·tric′tive·ness** *n.*

a·stride (ə-strīd′) *adv.* **1.** With a leg on each side of: *riding astride.* **2.** With the legs wide apart. *—prep.* **1.** Upon or over and with a leg on each side of. **2.** On both sides of; spanning or bridging.

astride of *prep.* Astride.

as·tringe (ə-strĭnj′) *tr.v.* **-tringed, -tring·ing, -tring·es.** To draw together; constrict. [Lat. *astringere,* to bind fast : *ad-,* to + *stringere,* to bind.]

as·trin·gent (ə-strĭn′jənt) *adj.* **1.** *Med.* Tending to draw together or constrict tissue; contracting; styptic. **2.** Harsh; severe. *—n.* An astringent substance or drug, such as alum. **—as·trin′gen·cy** *n.* **—as·trin′gent·ly** *adv.*

as·tri·on·ics (ăs′trē-ŏn′ĭks) *n. (used with a sing. verb).* Elec-

tronics used in astronautics. [ASTR(ONAUTIC) + (AV)IONICS.]
astro– or **astr–** *pref.* **1 a.** Star: *astrophysics.* **b.** Celestial body: *astrometry.* **c.** Outer space: *astronaut.* **2.** The aster of a cell: *astrosphere.* [ME < OFr. < Lat. < Gk. < *astron,* star.]
as·tro·bi·ol·o·gy (ăs'trō-bī-ŏl'ə-jē) *n.* Exobiology.
as·tro·bleme (ăs'trə-blĕm') *n.* A scar on the earth's surface left by meteorite impact. [ASTRO- + Gk. *blēma,* missile, wound < *ballein,* to throw.]
as·tro·chem·is·try (ăs'trō-kĕm'ĭ-strē) *n.* The chemistry of stars and interstellar space.
as·tro·cyte (ăs'trə-sīt') *n.* A star-shaped cell, esp. a neuroglial cell.
as·tro·cy·to·ma (ăs'trō-sī-tō'mə) *n., pl.* **-mas** or **-ma·ta** (-mə-tə). A malignant tumor of astrocytes.
as·tro·dome (ăs'trə-dōm') *n.* A transparent dome on the top of an aircraft, through which celestial observations are made for navigation.
as·tro·dy·nam·ics (ăs'trō-dī-năm'ĭks) *n. (used with a sing. verb).* The dynamics of celestial bodies.
as·tro·gate (ăs'trə-gāt') *intr.v.* **-gat·ed, -gat·ing, -gates.** To navigate a spacecraft. [ASTRO- + (NAVI)GATE.] **—as'tro·ga'tion** *n.* **—as'tro·ga'tor** *n.*
as·tro·ge·ol·o·gy (ăs'trō-jē-ŏl'ə-jē) *n.* The geology of celestial bodies.
as·tro·labe (ăs'trə-lāb') *n.* A medieval instrument used to determine the altitude of the sun or other celestial bodies. [ME *astrelabie* < OFr. *astrelabe* < Med. Lat. *astrolabium* < Gk. *astrolabon,* planisphere : *astron,* star + *lambanein,* to take.]
as·trol·o·gy (ə-strŏl'ə-jē) *n.* The study of the positions and aspects of heavenly bodies in the belief that they have an influence on the course of human affairs. [ME *astrologie* < OFr. < Lat. *astrologia,* astronomy < Gk. < *astrologos,* astronomer : *astron,* star + *logos,* speech.] **—as·trol'o·ger** *n.* **—as'tro·log'ic** (ăs'trə-lŏj'ĭk), **as'tro·log'i·cal** *adj.* **—as'tro·log'i·cal·ly** *adv.*
as·trom·e·try (ə-strŏm'ĭ-trē) *n.* The scientific measurement of the positions and motions of celestial bodies. **—as'tro·met'ric** (ăs'trō-mĕt'rĭk), **as'tro·met'ri·cal** *adj.*
as·tro·naut (ăs'trə-nôt') *n.* A person trained to pilot, navigate, or otherwise participate in the flight of a spacecraft. [ASTRO- + Gk. *nautēs,* sailor < *naus,* ship.]
as·tro·nau·tics (ăs'trə-nô'tĭks) *n. (used with a sing. verb).* The science and technology of space flight. [ASTRO- + Lat. *nautica,* neuter pl. of *nauticus,* nautical. —see NAUTICAL.] **—as'tro·nau'tic, as'tro·nau'ti·cal** *adj.* **—as'tro·nau'ti·cal·ly** *adv.*
as·tro·nav·i·ga·tion (ăs'trō-năv'ĭ-gā'shən) *n.* **1.** Navigation of spacecraft. **2.** Celestial navigation. **—as'tro·nav'i·ga'tor** *n.*
as·tron·o·mer (ə-strŏn'ə-mər) *n.* A scientist specializing in astronomy.
as·tro·nom·i·cal (ăs'trə-nŏm'ĭ-kəl) also **as·tro·nom·ic** (-nŏm'ĭk) *adj.* **1.** Of or pertaining to astronomy. **2.** Inconceivably large; immense. **—as'tro·nom'i·cal·ly** *adv.*
astronomical unit *n.* A unit of length used in measuring astronomical distances, equal to the mean distance of the earth from the sun, approximately 93 million miles.
as·tron·o·my (ə-strŏn'ə-mē) *n.* The scientific study of the universe beyond the earth, esp. the observation, calculation, and theoretical interpretation of the positions, dimensions, distribution, motion, composition, and evolution of celestial bodies and phenomena. [ME *astronomie* < OFr. < Lat. *astronomia* < Gk. : *astron,* star + *-nomia,* -nomy.]
as·tro·pho·tog·ra·phy (ăs'trō-fə-tŏg'rə-fē) *n.* Astronomical photography. **—as'tro·pho'to·graph'ic** (-fō'tə-grăf'ĭk) *adj.*
as·tro·phys·ics (ăs'trō-fĭz'ĭks) *n. (used with a sing. verb).* The physics of stellar phenomena. **—as'tro·phys'i·cal** *adj.* **—as'tro·phys'i·cist** (-fĭz'ĭ-sĭst) *n.*
as·tro·sphere (ăs'trō-sfîr') *n.* **1.** The central portion of a cell aster; the centrosphere. **2.** The entire cell aster with the exception of the centrosome.
As·tro·turf (ăs'trō-tûrf'). A trademark for an artificial grasslike ground covering.
as·tute (ə-sto͞ot', ə-styo͞ot') *adj.* Keen in judgment: shrewd; crafty. [Lat. *astutus* < *astus,* craft.] **—as·tute'ly** *adv.* **—as·tute'ness** *n.*
As·ty·a·nax (ə-stī'ə-năks') *n. Gk. Myth.* The young son of Hector and Andromache, killed by the conquering Greeks. [Gk. *Astuanax.*]
a·sty·lar (ā-stī'lər) *adj.* Not having columns or pilasters. [A-[1] + Gk. *stulos,* pillar + -AR.]
a·sun·der (ə-sŭn'dər) *adv.* **1.** Into separate parts or pieces. **2.** Apart from each other either in position or direction. [ME *asonder* < OE *onsundran* : *on,* on + *sundran,* separately < *sunder,* apart.] **—a·sun'der** *adj.*
a·swarm (ə-swôrm') *adj.* Filled to overflowing; teeming: *The playground was aswarm with children.*
a·swirl (ə-swûrl') *adj.* Moving with a swirling or whirling motion.
a·syl·lab·ic (ā'sĭ-lăb'ĭk) *adj.* Not syllabic.
a·sy·lum (ə-sī'ləm) *n.* **1.** An institution for the care of the mentally ill or aged. **2.** A place offering protection or safety; refuge. **3.** A temple or church affording sanctuary for criminals or debtors. **4.** Protection and immunity from extradition granted by a government to a political refugee from another country. [ME *asilum* < Lat. *asylum* < Gk. *asulon,* sanctuary < *asulos,* inviolable : *a-,* without + *sulē,* right of seizure.]
a·sym·met·ric (ā'sĭ-mĕt'rĭk) also **a·sym·met·ri·cal** (-rĭ-kəl) *adj.* Not symmetrical. **—a'sym·met'ri·cal·ly** *adv.*
a·sym·me·try (ā-sĭm'ĭ-trē) *n.* Lack of symmetry or balance.
a·symp·to·mat·ic (ā'sĭmp-tə-măt'ĭk) *adj.* Neither causing nor exhibiting symptoms. **—a'symp·to·mat'i·cal·ly** *adv.*
as·ymp·tote (ăs'ĭm-tōt', -ĭmp-) *n. Math.* A line considered a limit to a curve in the sense that the perpendicular distance from a moving point on the curve to the line approaches zero as the point moves an infinite distance from the origin. [NLat. *asymptota* < Gk. *asumptōtos,* not touching : *a-,* not + *sun-,* together + *ptōtos,* likely to fall.] **—as'ymp·tot'ic** (-tŏt'ĭk), **as'ymp·tot'i·cal** *adj.* **—as'ymp·tot'i·cal·ly** *adv.*
a·syn·chro·nism (ā-sĭng'krə-nĭz'əm) *n.* Lack of synchronism. **—a·syn'chro·nous** (-nəs) *adj.* **—a·syn'chro·nous·ly** *adv.*
a·syn·de·ton (ə-sĭn'dĭ-tŏn') *n.* The omission of conjunctions from constructions in which they would normally be used. [LLat. < Gk. *asundeton* < *asundetos,* without conjunctions : *a-,* not + *sundetos,* bound together < *sundein,* to bind together (*sun-,* together + *dein,* to bind).] **—as'yn·det'ic** (ăs'ĭn-dĕt'ĭk) *adj.* **—as'yn·det'i·cal·ly** *adv.*
a·syn·tac·tic (ā'sĭn-tăk'tĭk) *adj.* Not syntactic.
at[1] (ăt; ət *when unstressed*) *prep.* **1. a.** In the location of: *at the market.* **b.** In the position of: *at the center of the page.* **2.** To or toward the direction of: *Look at him.* **3.** Present; attending: *at the dance.* **4.** In the duration of; during: *at night.* **5.** In the state or condition of: *at peace with one's conscience.* **6.** In the manner of: *at a run.* **7.** To the extent or amount of: *at thirty cents a pound.* **8.** On or near the time or age of: *at three o'clock.* **9.** Because of: *rejoice at a victory.* **10.** Through; by way of. **11.** According to: *at one's discretion.* **12.** Dependent upon: *at the mercy of the court.* **13.** Occupied with: *at work.* [ME < OE *æt.*]
at[2] (ät) *n., pl.* **at.** See table at **currency.** [Thai.]
At The symbol for the element astatine.
at– *pref.* Variant of **ad-.** Used before *t.*
At·a·brine (ăt'ə-brĭn, -brēn'). A trademark for an antimalarial preparation, quinacrine hydrochloride.
at·a·ghan (ăt'ə-găn, -gən) *n.* Variant of **yataghan.**
At·a·lan·ta (ăt'ə-lăn'tə) *n. Gk. Myth.* A maiden who agreed to marry any man who could outrun her and was defeated by Hippomenes when he dropped three golden apples that she paused to pick up. [Lat. < Gk. *Atalantē.*]
at all *adv.* In any way whatsoever: *no good at all.*
at·a·man (ăt'ə-măn') *n., pl.* **-mans.** A Cossack chief. [R., prob. < Pol. *hetman,* captain.]
at·a·mas·co lily (ăt'ə-măs'kō) *n.* A plant, *Zephyranthes atamasco,* of eastern North America, having funnel-shaped white or pinkish flowers. [Algonquian (Virginia) *Attamusco.*]
at·a·rac·tic (ăt'ə-răk'tĭk) also **at·a·rax·ic** (-răk'sĭk) *adj.* Pertaining to or conducive of calmness and peace of mind. *—n.* A drug that reduces nervous tension; tranquilizer. [Gk. *ataraktos,* undisturbed : *a-,* not + *taraktos,* disturbed < *tarassein,* to disturb.]
at·a·rax·i·a (ăt'ə-răk'sē-ə) *n.* Peace of mind; emotional tranquillity. [Gk. < *ataraktos,* undisturbed. —see ATARACTIC.]
at·a·vism (ăt'ə-vĭz'əm) *n.* **1.** The reappearance of a characteristic in an organism after several generations of absence, caused by a recessive gene or complementary genes. **2.** An individual or part displaying atavism. [Fr. *atavisme* < Lat. *atavus,* ancestor : *atta,* father + *avus,* grandfather.] **—at'a·vist** *n.* **—at'a·vis'tic** *adj.* **—at'a·vis'ti·cal·ly** *adv.*
a·tax·i·a (ə-tăk'sē-ə) also **a·tax·y** (ə-tăk'sē) *n.* Loss or lack of muscular coordination. [Gk., disorder < *ataktos,* disorderly : *a-,* not + *taktos,* ordered < *tassein,* to arrange.]
a·tax·ic (ə-tăk'sĭk) *adj.* Of or pertaining to ataxia. *—n.* An individual exhibiting symptoms of ataxia.
ate (āt) *v.* Past tense of **eat.**
–ate[1] *suff.* **1. a.** Having: *nervate.* **b.** Characterized by: *Latinate.* **c.** Resembling: *lyrate.* **2. a.** One that is characterized by: *laminate.* **b.** Rank; office: *rabbinate.* **3.** To act upon in a specified manner: *acidulate.* [ME *-at* < OFr. < Lat. *-atus,* p.part. suffix of verbs in *-are.*]
–ate[2] *suff.* **1.** A derivative of a specified chemical compound or element: *aluminate.* **2.** A salt or ester of a specified acid: *acetate.* [NLat. *-atum* < Lat., neuter of *-atus,* p.part. suffix.]
at ease *n.* A position of silent rest with the right foot stationary, assumed by soldiers in ranks.
at·el·ier (ăt'l-yā') *n.* A workshop or studio, esp. an artist's studio. [Fr. < OFr. *astelier,* carpenter's shop < *astele,* splinter < LLat. *astella,* alteration of Lat. *astula,* dim. of *assis,* board.]
a tem·po (ä tĕm'pō) *adv. & adj. Mus.* In normal time; resuming the original tempo. [Ital., in time.]
a·tem·po·ral (ā-tĕm'pər-əl) *adj.* Independent of time; timeless.
Ath·a·na·sian (ăth'ə-nā'zhən) *adj.* Of or pertaining to Athanasius. *—n.* A follower of Athanasius and his doctrine of opposition to Arianism.
Ath·a·pas·can (ăth'ə-păs'kən) also **Ath·a·bas·can** (-băs'kən) *n.* **1.** A group of related North American Indian languages including Navaho and Apache and languages of Alaska, northwestern Canada, and coastal Oregon and California. **2.** A member of an Athapascan-speaking tribe. [Af-

astrolabe
13th-century Spanish

astronaut

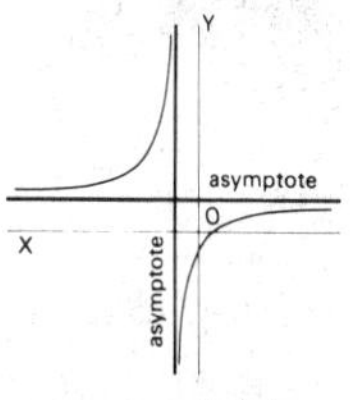

asymptote
Asymptotes of a hyperbola

Atalanta
Drawing illustrating Atalanta's race

ter Lake *Athabaska* in Canada < Cree *athapaskaaw,* there is scattered grass.] —**Ath'a·pas'can** *adj.*

a·the·ism (ā'thē-ĭz'əm) *n.* **1.** Disbelief in or denial of the existence of God. **2.** Godlessness. [OFr. *atheisme* < *athee,* atheist < Gk. *atheos,* godless : *a-,* without + *theos,* god.]

a·the·ist (ā'thē-ĭst) *n.* One who denies the existence of God.

a·the·is·tic (ā'thē-ĭs'tĭk) or **a·the·is·ti·cal** (-tĭ-kəl) *adj.* **1.** Pertaining to or characteristic of atheism or of atheists. **2.** Inclined to atheism. —**a'the·is'ti·cal·ly** *adv.* —**a'the·is'tic·ness** *n.*

ath·e·ling (ăth'ə-lĭng, ăth'-) *n.* An Anglo-Saxon nobleman or prince. [ME < OE *ætheling,* prince.]

A·the·na (ə-thē'nə) also **A·the·ne** (-nē) *n. Gk. Myth.* The goddess of wisdom and the arts. [Lat. < Gk. *Athenē.*]

ath·e·nae·um also **ath·e·ne·um** (ăth'ə-nē'əm) *n.* **1.** An institution, such as a literary club or scientific academy, for the promotion of learning. **2.** A library, reading room, or similar place. [LLat. *Athenaeum,* a Roman school, after Gk. *Athenaion,* the temple of Athena.]

Athena
1st-century A.D. Greek sculpture

ath·er·o·gen·e·sis (ăth'ər-ō-jĕn'ĭ-sĭs) *n.* The production of atheroma. [ATHERO(MA) + -GENESIS.] —**ath'er·o·gen'ic** *adj.*

ath·er·o·ma (ăth'ə-rō'mə) *n., pl.* **-mas** or **-ma·ta** (-mə-tə). **1.** A deposit or degenerative accumulation of pulpy, acellular, lipid-containing materials, esp. in arterial walls. **2.** A form of arteriosclerosis induced and characterized by such deposits. [Lat. < Gk. *athērōma,* tumor full of gruel like pus < *athēra,* gruel.] —**ath'er·o·ma·to'sis** (-tō'sĭs) *n.* —**ath'er·om'a·tous** (-rŏm'ə-təs, -rō'mə-) *adj.*

ath·er·o·scle·ro·sis (ăth'ə-rō-sklə-rō'sĭs) *n.* Atheromatous arteriosclerosis; atheroma. [ATHERO(MA) + SCLEROSIS.] —**ath'er·o·scle·rot'ic** (-rŏt'ĭk) *adj.*

a·thirst (ə-thûrst') *adj.* **1.** Strongly desirous; eager: *athirst for freedom.* **2.** *Archaic.* Thirsty.

ath·lete (ăth'lēt') *n.* **1.** One who takes part in competitive sports. **2.** A person possessing the natural aptitudes for physical exercises and sports, as strength, agility, and endurance. [ME < Lat. *athleta* < Gk. *athlētēs,* contestant < *athlein,* to contend < *athlon,* prize.]

athlete's foot *n.* A contagious skin infection caused by parasitic fungi usually affecting the feet and sometimes the hands and causing itching, blisters, cracking, and scaling.

ath·let·ic (ăth-lĕt'ĭk) *adj.* **1.** Of, pertaining to, or befitting athletics or athletes. **2.** Physically strong; muscular. —**ath·let'i·cal·ly** *adv.* —**ath·let'i·cism** (-lĕt'ĭ-sĭz'əm) *n.*

ath·let·ics (ăth-lĕt'ĭks) *n.* **1.** *(used with a pl. verb).* Athletic activities, as competitive sports. **2.** *(used with a sing. verb).* The principles or system of athletic exercises and training.

athletic supporter *n.* An elastic support for the male genitals, sometimes employing a rigid metallic cup, worn esp. in athletic or other strenuous activity.

ath·o·dyd (ăth'ə-dĭd') *n.* A simple, essentially tubular jet engine, as a ramjet. [A(ERO)- + TH(ERM)ODY(NAMIC) + D(UCT).]

at-home (ət-hōm') *n.* An informal reception at one's home.

a·thwart (ə-thwôrt') *adv.* **1.** From side to side; crosswise; transversely. **2.** So as to thwart or obstruct; perversely. —*prep.* **1.** From one side to the other of; across. **2.** Contrary to; against. **3.** *Naut.* Across the course, line, or length of. [ME : *a-,* on + *thwart,* across. —see THWART.]

Atlas

a·tilt (ə-tĭlt') *adj.* **1.** In a tilted position; inclined upward. **2.** Tilting with or as with a lance. —**a·tilt'** *adv.*

-ation *suff.* **1. a.** Action or process: *strangulation.* **b.** The result of an action or process: *acculturation.* **2.** State, condition, or quality of: *eburnation.* [ME *-acioun* < OFr. *-ation* < Lat. *-atio,* n. suffix < *-atus,* -ate.]

-ative *suff.* Of, relating to, or associated with: *talkative.* [ME < OFr. *-atif* < Lat. *-ativus* < *-atus,* -ate.]

At·ka mackerel (ăt'kə, ät'-) *n.* A food fish, *Pleurogrammus monopterygius,* of northern Pacific waters. [After *Atka* Island, Alaska.]

At·lan·te·an (ăt'lăn-tē'ən, ăt-lăn'tē-) *adj.* **1.** Of, pertaining to, or like Atlas. **2.** Of or pertaining to Atlantis. [< Gk. *Atlas, Atlant-,* Atlas.]

at·lan·tes (ăt-lăn'tēz') *n. Archit.* Plural of **atlas** (sense 6).

At·lan·tic (ăt-lăn'tĭk) *adj.* **1.** Of, in, near, upon, or pertaining to the Atlantic Ocean. **2.** Of or pertaining to Atlas or to the Atlas Mountains. [Lat. *(mare) Atlanticum,* Atlantic (sea) < Gk. *(pelagos) Atlantikos* < *Atlas,* Atlas.]

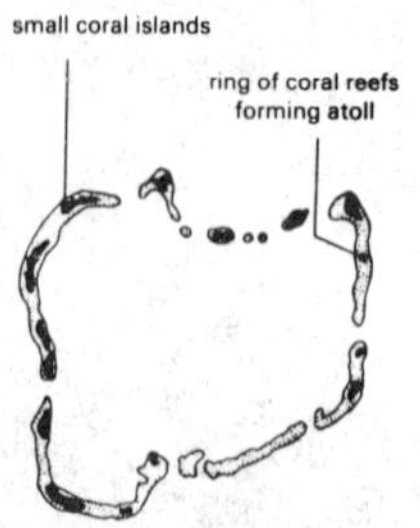

atoll

Atlantic salmon *n.* A food fish, *Salmo salar,* of northern Atlantic waters.

Atlantic Standard Time *n.* Standard time as reckoned in the region between the meridians at 52.5° and 67.5° west of Greenwich, England. The eastern edge of Canada is in this region.

At·lan·tis (ăt-lăn'tĭs) *n.* A legendary island in the Atlantic west of Gibraltar, said by Plato to have sunk beneath the sea during an earthquake. [Gk. < *Atlas,* Atlas.]

atomic bomb

At·las (ăt'ləs) *n.* **1.** *Gk. Myth.* A Titan condemned to support the heavens upon his shoulders. **2.** Any person supporting a great burden. **3. atlas.** A book or bound collection of maps. **4. atlas.** Any volume of tables, charts, or plates that systematically illustrates a particular subject: *an anatomical atlas.* **5. atlas.** A large size of drawing paper, measuring 26 by 33 or 34 inches. **6. atlas,** *pl.* **at·lan·tes** (ăt-lăn'tēz'). *Archit.* A figure of a man used as a masonry column on a building. **7. atlas.** *Anat.* The top or first cervical vertebra of the neck, which supports the head. **8.** A kind of intercontinental ballistic missile developed by the U.S. Air Force. [Gk. *Atlas.*]

at·man (ät'mən) *n. Hinduism.* **1.** The individual soul; the principle of life. **2. Atman.** The supreme and universal soul, from which all individual souls arise. [Skt. *ātman,* breath, spirit.]

at·mom·e·ter (ăt-mŏm'ĭ-tər) *n.* An instrument that measures the rate of water evaporation. —**at'mo·met'ric** (-mō-mĕt'rĭk) *adj.* —**at·mom'e·try** *n.*

at·mos·phere (ăt'mə-sfîr') *n.* **1.** The gaseous mass or envelope surrounding a celestial body, esp. that surrounding the earth, and retained by the body's gravitational field. **2.** The atmosphere or climate in a specific place. **3.** *Physics.* A unit of pressure equal to 1.01325 × 10^5 newtons per square meter. **4.** Environment or surroundings regarded as having a psychological, physical, or other influence: *the quiet atmosphere of a hospital; an atmosphere of austerity.* **5.** The predominant tone or mood of a work of art. **6.** *Informal.* A quality or effect considered to be exotic or romantic. [NLat. *atmosphaera* : Gk. *atmos,* vapor + Lat. *sphaera,* sphere.]

at·mos·pher·ic (ăt'mə-sfĕr'ĭk, -sfîr'ăk) also **at·mos·pher·i·cal** (-ĭ-kəl) *adj.* **1.** Of, pertaining to, or existing in the atmosphere. **2.** Produced by, dependent on, or coming from the atmosphere. —**at'mos·pher'i·cal·ly** *adv.*

atmospheric pressure *n.* An exerted pressure of 1 atmosphere.

at·mos·pher·ics (ăt'mə-sfĕr'ĭks, -sfîr'-) *n. (used with a sing. verb).* **1.** Electromagnetic radiation produced by natural phenomena such as lightning. **2.** Radio interference produced by electromagnetic radiation.

at·mo·spher·i·um (ăt'mə-sfîr'ē-əm) *n.* **1.** An optical device designed to project atmospheric phenomena, such as clouds, on the inside of a dome. **2.** A room containing an atmospherium. [ATMOSPHER(E) + (PLANETAR)IUM.]

a·toll (ăt'ôl', -ŏl', ā'tôl', ā'tŏl') *n.* A ringlike coral island and reef that nearly or entirely encloses a lagoon. [Malayalam *atoḷu,* reef.]

at·om (ăt'əm) *n.* **1.** Anything considered an irreducible constituent of a specified system. **2.** The irreducible, indestructible material unit of ancient atomism. **3.** *Physics & Chem.* **a.** A unit of matter, the smallest unit of an element, consisting of a dense, central, positively charged nucleus surrounded by a system of electrons, equal in number to the number of nuclear protons, the entire structure having an approximate diameter of 10^{-8} centimeter and characteristically remaining undivided in chemical reactions except for limited removal, transfer, or exchange of certain electrons. **b.** This unit regarded as a source of nuclear energy. [ME *attome* < Lat. *atomus* < Gk. *atomos,* indivisible : *a-,* not + *temnein,* to cut.]

atom bomb *n.* An atomic bomb.

a·tom·ic (ə-tŏm'ĭk) *adj.* **1.** Of or relating to an atom or atoms. **2.** Of or employing atomic energy: *an atomic submarine.* **3.** Very small; infinitesimal. —**a·tom'i·cal·ly** *adv.*

atomic age also **Atomic Age** *n.* The current era as characterized by the discovery, technological applications, and sociopolitical consequences of atomic energy.

atomic bomb *n.* **1.** An explosive weapon of great destructive power derived from the rapid release of energy in the fission of heavy atomic nuclei, as of uranium 235. **2.** Any bomb deriving its destructive power from the release of nuclear energy.

atomic clock *n.* An extremely precise timekeeping device regulated in correspondence with a characteristic invariant frequency of an atomic or molecular system.

atomic energy *n.* **1.** The energy released from an atomic nucleus in fission or fusion. **2.** Atomic energy regarded as a source of practical power.

at·o·mic·i·ty (ăt'ə-mĭs'ĭ-tē) *n.* **1.** The state of being composed of atoms. **2.** *Chem.* **a.** The number of atoms in a molecule. **b.** Valence.

atomic mass *n.* The mass of an atomic system or constituent, usually expressed in atomic mass units.

atomic mass unit *n.* A unit of mass equal to $^1/_{12}$ the mass of the carbon isotope with mass number 12, approximately 1.6604 × 10^{-24} gram.

atomic number *n.* The number of protons in an atomic nucleus.

atomic pile *n.* A nuclear reactor.

atomic theory *n.* **1.** The physical theory of the structure, properties, and behavior of the atom. **2.** Atomism.

atomic weight *n.* The average weight of an atom of an element, usually expressed relative to one atom of the carbon isotope taken to have a standard weight of 12.

at·om·ism (ăt'ə-mĭz'əm) *n.* **1.** The ancient theory of Democritus, Epicurus, and Lucretius, according to which simple, indivisible, and indestructible atoms are the basic components of the entire universe. **2.** A theory according to which social institutions and processes arise solely from the acts of individual people. **3. a.** The division or tendency to divide into subclasses, groups, or units of a given society. **b.** The foregoing tendency accompanied by or arising from a strong subjective individualism. —**at'om·ist** *n.* —**at'om·is'tic** (-ĭs'tĭk), **at'om·is'ti·cal** *adj.* —**at'om·is'ti·cal·ly** *adv.*

at·om·ize (ăt'ə-mīz') *tr.v.* **-ized, -iz·ing, -iz·es. 1.** To reduce or separate into atoms. **2. a.** To reduce (a liquid) to a spray.

b. To spray (a liquid) in this form. **3.** To subject to bombardment with atomic weapons. **—at'om·i·za'tion** *n.*
at·om·iz·er (ăt'ə-mī'zər) *n.* A device for producing a fine spray, esp. one of perfume or medicine.
atom smasher *n.* An atomic particle accelerator.
at·o·my[1] (ăt'ə-mē) *n., pl.* **-mies.** *Archaic.* **1.** A tiny particle. **2.** A tiny being. [< Lat. *atomi,* pl. of *atomus,* atom.]
at·o·my[2] (ăt'ə-mē) *n., pl.* **-mies.** *Archaic.* A skeleton or a gaunt person. [< *an atomy,* respelling of ANATOMY.]
a·to·nal (ā-tō'nəl) *adj. Mus.* Lacking a tonal center. **—a·to'nal·ly** *adv.*
a·to·nal·ism (ā-tō'nə-lĭz'əm) *n. Mus.* **1.** The lack of a tonal center or key as a principle of musical composition. **2.** The theory of atonal composition.
a·to·nal·i·ty (ā'tō-năl'ĭ-tē) *n.* A style of musical composition in which tonal center or key is disregarded.
at once *adv.* **1.** At one time; simultaneously: *everything happening at once.* **2.** Immediately; instantly: *Leave the room at once.*
a·tone (ə-tōn') *v.* **a·toned, a·ton·ing, a·tones.** *—intr.* **1.** To make amends, as for a sin or fault. **2.** *Archaic.* To agree. *—tr. Archaic.* **1.** To expiate. **2.** To reconcile or harmonize. **3.** To conciliate; appease. [ME *atonen,* to be reconciled < *at one,* in agreement : *at,* at + *one,* one.] **—a·ton'a·ble, a·tone'a·ble** *adj.* **—a·ton'er** *n.*
a·tone·ment (ə-tōn'mənt) *n.* **1.** Amends or reparation made for an injury or wrong; expiation. **2.** In the Hebrew Scriptures, man's reconciliation with God after having transgressed the covenant. **3. Atonement.** *Theol.* **a.** The redemptive life and death of Christ. **b.** The reconciliation of God and man thus brought about by Christ. **4.** In Christian Science, the radical obedience and purification, exemplified in the life of Jesus, by which humanity finds oneness with God. **5.** *Archaic.* Reconciliation; concord.
a·ton·ic (ā-tŏn'ĭk) *adj.* **1.** Not accented: *atonic words and syllables.* **2.** *Pathol.* Pertaining to, caused by, or characterized by atony. *—n.* A word, syllable, or sound that is unaccented. [Fr. *atonique* < Gk. *atonos.* —see ATONY.] **—at'o·nic'i·ty** (ăt'ə-nĭs'ĭ-tē) *n.*
at·o·ny (ăt'ə-nē) *n.* **1.** Insufficient muscular tone. **2.** In phonetics, lack of accent or stress. [LLat. *atonia* < Gk. < *atonos,* slack : *a-,* without + *tonos,* stretching, tone.]
a·top (ə-tŏp') *adv.* On or at the top. *—prep.* On top of. **—a·top'** *adj.*
-ator *suff.* One that acts in a specified manner: *radiator.* [ME *-atour* < OFr. < Lat. *-ator* : *-atus,* -ate + *-or,* -or.]
-atory *suff.* **1. a.** Of or relating to: *perspiratory.* **b.** Tending to: *amendatory.* **2.** One that is connected with: *reformatory.* [ME < Lat. *-atorius* : *-atus,* -ate + *-orius,* -ory.]
ATP (ā'tē'pē') *n.* An adenosine-derived nucleotide, $C_{10}H_{16}N_5O_{13}P_3$, that supplies energy to cells through its conversion to ADP. [A(DENOSINE) T(RI)PYHOSPHATE).]
ATP·ase (ā'tē-pē'ās) *n.* An enzyme that hydrolyzes ATP.
at·ra·bil·ious (ăt'rə-bĭl'yəs) also **at·ra·bil·i·ar** (-bĭl'ē-ər) *adj.* **1.** Inclined to melancholy. **2.** Having a peevish disposition; surly. [< Lat. *atra bilis,* black bile, transl. of Gk. *melankholia.* —see MELANCHOLY.] **—at'ra·bil'ious·ness** *n.*
A·treus (ā'trōōs', ā'trē-əs) *n. Gk. Myth.* A king of Mycenae, father of Agamemnon and Menelaus. [Gk.]
a·tri·a (ā'trē-ə) *n.* A plural of **atrium.**
a·tri·o·ven·tric·u·lar (ā'trē-ō-vĕn-trĭk'yə-lər) *adj.* Pertaining to the atria and the ventricles of the heart.
a·trip (ə-trĭp') *adj.* Just clear of the bottom, as an anchor. **—a·trip'** *adv.*
a·tri·um (ā'trē-əm) *n., pl.* **a·tri·a** (ā'trē-ə) or **-ums. 1.** An open central court, esp. in ancient Roman houses. **2.** A bodily cavity or chamber, as in the heart. [Lat. *atrium.*] **—a'tri·al** *adj.*
a·tro·cious (ə-trō'shəs) *adj.* **1.** Extremely evil or cruel; monstrous: *an atrocious crime.* **2.** Exceptionally bad; abominable: *atrocious decor; atrocious behavior.* [< Lat. *atrox, atroc-,* cruel.] **—a·tro'cious·ly** *adv.* **—a·tro'cious·ness** *n.*
a·troc·i·ty (ə-trŏs'ĭ-tē) *n., pl.* **-ties. 1.** Atrocious condition, quality, or behavior; monstrousness. **2.** An atrocious action, situation, or object.
at·ro·phy (ăt'rə-fē) *n., pl.* **-phies. 1.** *Pathol.* The emaciation or wasting of tissues, organs, or the entire body. **2.** Any wasting away or diminution: *intellectual atrophy.* *—v.* **-phied, -phy·ing, -phies.** *—tr.* To cause to wither; affect with atrophy. *—intr.* To waste away; wither. [LLat. *atrophia* < Gk. < *atrophos,* ill-nourished : *a-,* without + *trophē,* food.] **—a·troph'ic** (ā-trŏf'ĭk), **at'ro·phous** *adj.*
at·ro·pine (ăt'rə-pēn', -pĭn) also **at·ro·pin** (-pĭn) *n.* An extremely poisonous, bitter, crystalline alkaloid, $C_{17}H_{23}NO_3$, obtained from belladonna and related plants. It is used to dilate the pupil of the eye and as an anesthetic and antispasmodic. [G. *Atropin* < NLat. *Atropa,* genus name of belladonna < Gk. *atropos,* unchangeable.]
At·ro·pos (ăt'rə-pŏs', -pəs) *n. Gk. Myth.* One of the three Fates. [Gk. < *atropos,* inexorable.]
at·tach (ə-tăch') *v.* **-tached, -tach·ing, -tach·es.** *—tr.* **1.** To fasten on or affix to; connect or join. **2.** To connect as an adjunct or associated part. **3.** To affix or append; add, as a signature. **4.** To ascribe or assign: *attached no significance to the threat.* **5.** To bind by personal ties, as of affection or loyalty: *He's very attached to his family.* **6.** To appoint officially. **7.** To assign (personnel) to a military unit on a temporary basis. **8.** *Law.* To seize (persons or property) by legal writ. *—intr.* To adhere. [ME *attachen* < OFr. *attachier,* of Germanic orig.] **—at·tach'a·ble** *adj.* **—at·tach'er** *n.*
at·ta·ché (ăt'ə-shā', ă-tă'shā') *n.* A person officially assigned to the staff of a diplomatic mission to serve in some particular capacity: *a cultural attaché.* [Fr. < p.part. of *attacher,* to attach.]
attaché case *n.* A briefcase resembling a small suitcase, with hinges and flat sides.
at·tach·ment (ə-tăch'mənt) *n.* **1.** The act of attaching or the condition of being attached. **2.** Something that attaches one thing to another, as a tie, band, or fastening. **3.** A bond of affection or loyalty; fond regard. **4.** A supplementary part; accessory: *a food processor with attachments.* **5.** *Law.* **a.** The legal seizure of a person or property. **b.** The writ ordering such a seizure.
at·tack (ə-tăk') *v.* **-tacked, -tack·ing, -tacks.** *—tr.* **1.** To set upon with violent force; begin hostilities against or conflict with. **2.** To bombard with hostile criticism. **3.** To start work on with purpose and vigor: *attack a problem.* **4.** To begin to affect harmfully. *—intr.* To make an attack; launch an assault. *—n.* **1.** The act of attacking; assault. **2.** The occurrence or onset of a disease. **3.** The initial movement in a task or undertaking: *an attack on the work piled high on the desk.* **4.** *Mus.* The manner in which a passage or phrase is begun. [Fr. *attaquer* < OFr. < OItal. *attaccare,* of Germanic orig.] **—at·tack'er** *n.*

Synonyms: *attack, bombard, assail, storm, assault, beset.* These verbs mean to set upon physically or, in some cases, figuratively. *Attack* applies to any offensive action, physical or verbal, and especially to the beginning of planned aggression. *Bombard* suggests showering with bombs or shells or, figuratively, with words: *bombarded with questions. Assail,* literally and figuratively, implies repeated and violent attacks. *Storm* refers to a sudden, sweeping attempt for quick, total victory. *Assault* almost always implies physical contact and sudden, intense violence. *Beset* suggests encirclement by an enemy force or by adversity and attack from all sides.

at·tain (ə-tān') *v.* **-tained, -tain·ing, -tains.** *—tr.* **1.** To gain, reach, or accomplish by mental or physical effort. **2.** To arrive at, as in time. *—intr.* To succeed in gaining or reaching: *He attained to the highest office in the land.* [ME *atteignen* < OFr. *ataindre,* to reach to < Lat. *attingere* : *ad-,* to + *tangere,* to touch.] **—at·tain'a·ble** *adj.* **—at·tain'a·bil'i·ty, at·tain'a·ble·ness** *n.*
at·tain·der (ə-tān'dər) *n.* **1.** The loss of all civil rights legally consequent to a death sentence or to outlawry, esp. for treason. **2.** *Archaic.* Dishonor. [ME *attendre,* conviction < OFr. *ataindre,* to convict, affect. —see ATTAIN.]
at·tain·ment (ə-tān'mənt) *n.* **1.** The act of attaining or the condition of being attained. **2.** Something that is attained; accomplishment.
at·taint (ə-tānt') *tr.v.* **-taint·ed, -taint·ing, -taints. 1.** *Law.* To condemn by a sentence of attainder. **2.** *Archaic.* To impart stigma to; disgrace. **3.** *Obs.* To accuse. *—n.* **1.** Attainder. **2.** *Archaic.* A disgrace; stigma. [ME *attaynten* < OFr. *ataint,* p.part. of *ataindre,* to affect. —see ATTAIN.]
at·tar (ăt'ər) *n.* A fragrant essential oil or perfume obtained from the petals of flowers, such as roses. [Pers. *'aṭir,* perfumed < Ar. *'uṭūr,* pl. of *'iṭr,* perfume.]
at·tempt (ə-tĕmpt') *tr.v.* **-tempt·ed, -tempt·ing, -tempts. 1.** To try to do, make, or achieve. **2.** *Archaic.* To tempt. **3.** *Archaic.* To attack with the intention of subduing. *—n.* **1.** An effort or try. **2.** An attack; assault: *an attempt on one's life.* [ME *attempten* < OFr. *attempter* < Lat. *attemptare* : *ad-,* to + *temptare,* to test.] **—at·tempt'a·ble** *adj.* **—at·tempt'er** *n.*
at·tend (ə-tĕnd') *v.* **-tend·ed, -tend·ing, -tends.** *—tr.* **1.** To be present at. **2.** To accompany as a circumstance or follow as a result: *The speech was attended by wild applause.* **3. a.** To accompany or wait upon as an attendant or servant. **b.** To take care of (a sick person, for example). **4.** To take charge of. **5.** To listen to; heed. **6.** *Archaic.* To wait for; expect. *—intr.* **1.** To be present. **2.** To apply or direct oneself: *attended to the problem.* **3.** To pay attention; heed. **4.** To remain ready to serve; wait. **5.** *Obs.* To delay or wait. [ME *attenden* < OFr. *atendre* < Lat. *attendere,* to heed : *ad-,* to + *tendere,* to stretch.] **—at·tend'er** *n.*
at·ten·dance (ə-tĕn'dəns) *n.* **1.** The act of attending. **2.** The persons or number of persons that attend a function.
at·ten·dant (ə-tĕn'dənt) *n.* **1.** One who attends or waits on another. **2.** One who is present. **3.** An accompanying thing or circumstance; concomitant. *—adj.* Accompanying or following as a result: *attendant circumstances.* **—at·tend'ant·ly** *adv.*
at·ten·tion (ə-tĕn'shən) *n.* **1.** Concentration of the mental powers upon an object; a close or careful observing or listening. **2.** The ability or power to concentrate mentally. **3.** Observant consideration; notice: *Your suggestion has come to our attention.* **4.** Consideration or courtesy: *attention to others' feelings.* **5. attentions.** Acts of courtesy, consideration, or gallantry, esp. by a suitor. **6.** A military posture, with the body erect, eyes to the front, arms at the sides, and heels together. Used as a command. [ME *attencioun* < Lat.

atomizer

atrium

attentio < *attendere,* to heed. —see ATTEND.] **—at·ten'tion·al** *adj.*

attention key *n. Computer Sci.* A function key on terminals that interrupts program execution by the central processing unit.

at·ten·tive (ə-tĕn'tĭv) *adj.* **1.** Paying attention; observant. **2.** Mindful of the well-being of others; considerate. **—at·ten'tive·ly** *adv.* **—at·ten'tive·ness** *n.*

at·ten·u·ate (ə-tĕn'yo͞o-āt') *v.* **-at·ed, -at·ing, -ates.** *—tr.* **1.** To make slender, fine, or small. **2.** To reduce in force, value, or amount; weaken. **3.** To lessen the density of; rarefy. **4.** *Biol.* To make less virulent. *—intr.* To become thin, weak, or fine. *—adj.* (ə-tĕn'yo͞o-ĭt). **1.** Reduced or weakened, as in strength or value. **2.** *Bot.* Gradually tapering to a slender point. [Lat. *attenuare,* to make thin : *ad-,* to + *tenuis,* thin.] **—at·ten'u·a·ble** (-ə-bəl) *adj.* **—at·ten'u·a'tion** *n.*

at·ten·u·a·tor (ə-tĕn'yo͞o-ā'tər) *n.* A device that reduces the amplitude of an electrical signal with little or no distortion.

at·test (ə-tĕst') *v.* **-test·ed, -test·ing, -tests.** *—tr.* **1.** To affirm to be correct, true, or genuine. **2. a.** To certify by signature or oath. **b.** To certify in an official capacity. **3.** To supply or be evidence of: *a splendid tomb that attested his power.* **4.** To constitute documentary proof of. **5.** To put under oath. *—intr.* To bear witness; give testimony: *attested to his good faith.* *—n. Archaic.* Attestation. [Fr. *attester* < OFr. < Lat. *attestari* : *ad-,* to + *testis,* witness.] **—at·test'ant** *n.* **—at'tes·ta'tion** (ăt'ĕs-tā'shən, ăt'ə-stā'-) *n.* **—at·test'er, at·tes'tor** *n.*

at·tic (ăt'ĭk) *n.* **1.** A story or room directly below the roof of a house. **2.** *Archit.* A low wall or story above the cornice of a classical façade. [< *Attic story,* a decorative structure over an order in a classical style.]

At·tic (ăt'ĭk) *adj.* **1.** Of, pertaining to, or characteristic of ancient Attica, Athens, or the Athenians. **2.** Characterized by purity and simplicity. *—n.* The ancient Greek dialect used in Attica that became the literary language of ancient Greece.

At·ti·cism (ăt'ĭ-sĭz'əm) *n.* **1.** A characteristic feature of the Attic Greek language. **2.** An expression characterized by conciseness and elegance.

at·tire (ə-tīr') *tr.v.* **-tired, -tir·ing, -tires.** To dress or clothe, esp. in elaborate or splendid garments. *—n.* **1.** Clothing; array. **2.** In heraldry, the antlers of a deer. [ME *attiren* < OFr. *atirier,* to put in order : *a-,* to (< Lat. *ad-*) + *tire,* rank.]

at·ti·tude (ăt'ĭ-to͞od', -tyo͞od') *n.* **1.** A position of the body or manner of carrying oneself: *stood in a graceful attitude.* **2.** A state of mind or feeling with regard to some matter; disposition: *an attitude of open hostility.* **3.** The orientation of an aircraft's axes relative to some reference line or plane, such as the horizon. **4.** *Aerospace.* The orientation of a spacecraft relative to its direction of motion. **5.** A position in which a ballet dancer stands on one leg with the other bent backward at the knee. [Fr. < Ital. *attitudine,* disposition < LLat. *aptitudo,* faculty < Lat. *aptus,* fit < *apere,* to fasten.] **—at'ti·tu'di·nal** (ăt'ə-to͞od'n-əl, -tyo͞od'n-əl) *adj.*

at·ti·tu·di·nize (ăt'ĭ-to͞od'n-īz', -tyo͞od'n-īz') *intr.v.* **-nized, -niz·ing, -niz·es.** To assume an affected attitude; posture. [Ital. *attitudine,* attitude, posture + -IZE.]

atto– *pref.* One quintillionth (10^{-18}): *attotesla.* [< Dan. or Norw. *atten,* eighteen < ON *attjan.*]

at·torn (ə-tûrn') *intr.v.* **-torned, -torn·ing, -torns.** *Law.* To acknowledge a new owner as one's landlord. [ME *attournen* < OFr. *atorner,* to assign to : *a-,* to (< Lat. *ad-*) + *torner,* to turn. —see TURN.] **—at·torn'ment** *n.*

at·tor·ney (ə-tûr'nē) *n., pl.* **-neys.** A person legally appointed to act for another, esp. an attorney at law. **—idiom. by attorney.** By proxy. [ME *attourney* < OFr. *atorne,* p.part. of *atorner,* to attorne.] **—at·tor'ney·ship'** *n.*

attorney at law *n.* One who is qualified to represent clients in a court of law and to advise them on legal matters; a lawyer.

attorney general *n., pl.* **attorneys general.** The chief law officer and legal counsel of the government of a state or nation.

at·to·tes·la (ăt'ō-tĕs'lə) *n.* One-quintillionth (10^{-18}) of a tesla.

at·tract (ə-trăkt') *v.* **-tract·ed, -tract·ing, -tracts.** *—tr.* **1.** To cause to draw near or adhere. **2.** To draw or direct to oneself by some quality or action: *Sugar attracts insects.* **3.** To evoke by arousing interest or admiration; allure. *—intr.* To possess or use the power of attraction. [ME *attracten* < Lat. *attrahere* : *ad-,* to + *trahere,* to draw.] **—at·tract'a·ble** *adj.* **—at·trac'tor, at·tract'er** *n.*

at·trac·tion (ə-trăk'shən) *n.* **1.** The act or capability of attracting. **2.** The quality of attracting; charm. **3. a.** A feature or characteristic that attracts. **b.** Something, such as a public spectacle or entertainment, that is intended to attract.

at·trac·tive (ə-trăk'tĭv) *adj.* **1.** Having the power to attract. **2.** Pleasing to the eye or mind; charming. **—at·trac'tive·ly** *adv.* **—at·trac'tive·ness** *n.*

at·trib·ute (ə-trĭb'yo͞ot) *tr.v.* **-ut·ed, -ut·ing, -utes.** **1.** To assign to a particular cause or source; ascribe. **2.** To consider or indicate as a creator or possessor: *attributed the painting to Titian.* *—n.* (ăt'rə-byo͞ot'). **1.** A quality or characteristic of a person or thing. **2.** An object associated with and serving to identify a character, personage, or office: *Lightning bolts were the attributes of Zeus.* **3.** *Gram.* A word, esp. an adjective, used to ascribe a quality. [Lat. *attribuere, attribut-* : *ad-,* to + *tribuere,* to allot < *tribus,* tribe.] **—at·trib'ut·a·ble** *adj.* **—at·trib'ut·er, at·trib'u·tor** *n.*

Synonyms: *attribute, ascribe, impute, credit, assign, refer.* These verbs mean to declare as belonging to an owner, time, class, or other source. *Attribute* and *ascribe,* often interchangeable, have the widest application: *a saying attributed* (or *ascribed*) *to Jefferson; a distrust of big business attributed* (or *ascribed*) *to his father's failure in Wall Street.* *Impute* is often used in laying guilt or fault to another: *a prejudice imputed to rural courts of law.* *Credit* usually applies to an accomplishment or virtue: *an invention credited to Franklin; frugality credited to a childhood spent in poverty.* *Assign* and *refer* are often used to classify or categorize according to character or chronology: *experiments now assigned* (or *referred*) *to fakery; works assigned* (or *referred*) *to the Romantic era.*

at·tri·bu·tion (ăt'rə-byo͞o'shən) *n.* **1.** The act of attributing. **2.** Something that is ascribed.

at·trib·u·tive (ə-trĭb'yə-tĭv) *n. Gram.* A word or word group, such as an adjective, that is placed adjacent to the noun it modifies without a linking verb, as *pale* in *the pale girl.* *—adj.* **1.** *Gram.* Of or functioning as an attributive, as an adjective. **2.** Of or having the nature of an attribution or attribute. **—at·trib'u·tive·ly** *adv.* **—at·trib'u·tive·ness** *n.*

at·trit·ed (ə-trī'tĭd) *adj.* Worn down by attrition.

at·tri·tion (ə-trĭsh'ən) *n.* **1.** A rubbing away or wearing down by friction. **2.** A gradual diminution in number or strength due to constant stress. **3.** A gradual, natural reduction in membership or personnel, as through retirement, resignation, or death. **4.** *Theol.* Repentance for sin motivated by fear of punishment rather than by love of God. [ME *attricioun* < Lat. *attritio,* act of rubbing against < *atterere,* to rub against : *ad-,* to + *terere,* to rub.]

at·tune (ə-to͞on', ə-tyo͞on') *tr.v.* **-tuned, -tun·ing, -tunes.** **1.** To tune. **2.** To bring into harmony.

a·twit·ter (ə-twĭt'ər) *adj.* In a state of nervous excitement.

a·typ·i·cal (ā-tĭp'ĭ-kəl) also **a·typ·ic** (-ĭk) *adj.* Not conforming to type; unusual. **—a·typ'i·cal·ly** *adv.*

Au The symbol for the element gold [Lat. *aurum,* gold.]

au·bade (ō-bäd') *n.* A musical composition, such as a love song, to be played or sung at dawn or early in the morning. [Fr. < OFr. < OSp. *albada* < *alba,* dawn.]

au·ber·gine (ō'bĕr-zhēn', ō'bər-jĭn) *n.* The eggplant (sense 1.b.). [Fr. < Catalan *albergínia* < Ar. *albādinjān* < Pers. *bādin-gān.*]

au·burn (ô'bərn) *n.* A moderate reddish brown to brown. [ME < OFr. *auborne* < Lat. *alburnus,* whitish < *albus,* white.]

au cou·rant (ō' ko͞o-räN') *adj.* Informed on current affairs; up-to-date. [Fr.]

auc·tion (ôk'shən) *n.* **1.** A public sale in which property or items of merchandise are sold to the highest bidder. **2.** The bidding in the game of bridge. **3.** Auction bridge. *—tr.v.* **-tioned, -tion·ing, -tions.** To sell at or by an auction: *auctioned off the furniture.* [Lat. *auctio* < *augēre,* to increase.]

auction bridge *n.* A variety of the game of bridge in which tricks made in excess of the contract are scored toward game.

auc·tion·eer (ôk'shə-nîr') *n.* A person who conducts an auction. *—tr.v.* **-eered, -eer·ing, -eers.** To auction.

auctioneering device *n. Computer Sci.* A device designed to automatically select either the highest or the lowest input signal from among two or more signals.

auc·to·ri·al (ôk-tôr'ē-əl, -tōr'-) *adj.* Of or pertaining to an author. [< Lat. *auctor,* author.]

au·da·cious (ô-dā'shəs) *adj.* **1.** Fearlessly daring; bold. **2.** Unrestrained by convention or propriety; insolent. [Lat. *audax, audaci-* < *audēre,* to dare.] **—au·da'cious·ly** *adv.* **—au·da'cious·ness** *n.*

au·dac·i·ty (ô-dăs'ĭ-tē) *n., pl.* **-ties.** **1.** Boldness; daring. **2.** Unrestrained impudence; brashness. **3.** An act or instance of audacity.

au·di·ble (ô'də-bəl) *adj.* Capable of being heard. *—n. Football.* A new or substitute offensive play called by the quarterback or defensive formation called by a linebacker at the line of scrimmage as an adjustment to the opposing side's formation. [Med. Lat. *audibilis* < Lat. *audire,* to hear.] **—au'di·bil'i·ty** *n.* **—au'di·ble·ness** *n.* **—au'di·bly** *adv.*

au·di·ence (ô'dē-əns) *n.* **1.** A group of spectators, listeners, or readers of a work or performance. **2.** A formal hearing, as with a king or pope. **3.** An opportunity to be heard or to express one's views. **4.** The act of hearing or attending. [ME < OFr. < Lat. *audientia* < *audiens,* pr.part. of *audire,* to hear.]

au·di·ent (ô'dē-ənt) *adj.* Hearing; listening. [Lat. *audiens, audient-,* pr.part. of *audire,* to hear.] **—au'di·ent** *n.*

au·dile (ô'dīl') *adj.* Capable of learning chiefly from auditory, rather than tactile or visual, stimuli. *—n.* An audile person. [< Lat. *audire,* to hear.]

aud·ing (ô'dĭng) *n.* The process of hearing, acknowledging, and understanding a spoken language. [Lat. *audire,* to hear + -ING[2].]

au·di·o (ô'dē-ō') *adj.* **1.** Of or pertaining to audible sound. **2. a.** Of or pertaining to the broadcasting of sound. **b.** Of or pertaining to the high-fidelity reproduction of sound. *—n.* **1.** The part of television or motion picture equipment that

has to do with sound. **2.** Audio broadcasting or reception. **3.** Audible sound. [< AUDIO-.]
audio– *pref.* **1.** Hearing: *audio-lingual.* **2.** Sound: *audiophile.* [< Lat. *audire,* to hear.]
audio frequency *n.* A range of frequencies, usually from 15 hertz to 20,000 hertz, characteristic of signals audible to the normal human ear.
au·di·o-lin·gual (ô′dē-ō-lĭng′gwəl) *adj.* Relating to or involving listening and speaking in learning a language.
au·di·ol·o·gy (ô′dē-ŏl′ə-jē) *n., pl.* **-gies.** The science of hearing defects and their treatment. **—au′di·o·log′i·cal** (-ə-lŏj′ĭ-kəl) *adj.* **—au′di·ol′o·gist** *n.*
au·di·om·e·ter (ô′dē-ŏm′ĭ-tər) *n.* An instrument for measuring hearing thresholds for pure tones of normally audible frequencies. **—au′di·o·met′ric** (-ō-mĕt′rĭk) *adj.* **—au′di·om′e·try** *n.*
au·di·o·phile (ô′dē-ə-fīl′) *n.* One with an ardent interest in high-fidelity sound reproduction.
au·di·o·typ·ing (ô′dē-ō-tī′pĭng) *n.* Typing done directly from a tape recording. **—au′di·o·typ′ist** *n.*
au·di·o-vis·u·al (ô′dē-ō-vĭzh′o͞o-əl) *adj.* **1.** Both audible and visible. **2.** Of or pertaining to educational materials, such as sound filmstrips, that present information in audible and visible form.
au·di·o·vis·u·als (ô′dē-ō-vĭzh′o͞o-əlz) *pl.n.* Educational materials that use both sight and sound to present information.
au·dit (ô′dĭt) *n.* **1.** An examination of records or accounts to check their accuracy. **2.** An adjustment or correction of accounts. **3.** An examined and verified account. *—v.* **-dit·ed, -dit·ing, -dits.** *—tr.* **1.** To examine, verify, or correct (accounts, for example). **2.** To attend (a course) without receiving academic credit. *—intr.* To examine accounts. [ME < Lat. *auditus,* a hearing < p.part. of *audire,* to hear.]
au·di·tion (ô-dĭsh′ən) *n.* **1.** The sense or power of hearing. **2.** An act of hearing. **3.** A performance, as by an actor or musician, to demonstrate ability or skill. *—tr. & intr.v.* **-tioned, -tion·ing, -tions.** To evaluate or present an audition. [Lat. *auditio* < *audire,* to hear.]
au·di·tive (ô′dĭ-tĭv) *adj.* Auditory.
au·di·tor (ô′dĭ-tər) *n.* **1.** One who hears; listener. **2.** One who audits accounts. **3.** One who audits a course. [ME < AN *auditour* < Lat. *auditor* < *audire,* to hear.]
au·di·to·ri·um (ô′də-tôr′ē-əm, -tōr′-) *n., pl.* **-ri·ums** or **-ri·a** (-tôr′ē-ə, -tōr′-). **1.** A room to accommodate an audience in a building such as a school or theater. **2.** A large building for public meetings or artistic performances. [Lat. < *audire,* to hear.]
au·di·to·ry (ô′dĭ-tôr′ē, -tōr′ē) *adj.* Of or pertaining to the sense, the organs, or the experience of hearing. [Lat. *auditorius* < *audire,* to hear.]
auditory nerve *n. Anat.* The acoustic nerve.
au fait (ō fĕ′) *adj.* Skilled or knowledgeable; expert. [Fr., to the point.]
Auf·klä·rung (ouf′klā′ro͝ong) *n.* The Enlightenment. [G.]
auf Wie·der·seh·en (ouf vē′dər-zā′ən) *interj.* Used to express a farewell. [G.]
Au·ge·an (ô-jē′ən) *adj.* Exceedingly filthy from long neglect. [After *Augeas,* legendary Greek king who did not clean his stable for thirty years.]
au·gend (ô′jĕnd′) *n.* A quantity to which the addend is added. [LLat. *augendum* < *augendus,* gerund. of *augēre,* to increase.]
au·ger (ô′gər) *n.* **1.** A tool for boring holes in wood. **2.** A large tool for boring into the earth. [ME < *an auger,* alteration of *a nauger* < OE *nafogār,* auger.]
aught[1] (ôt) *pron. Archaic.* Anything whatever; any least part. *—adv. Archaic.* At all; in any respect. [ME < OE *āuht.*]
aught[2] (ôt) *n.* **1.** A cipher; zero. **2.** *Archaic.* Nothing. [Alteration of A NAUGHT.]
au·gite (ô′jīt′) *n.* A dark-green to black pyroxene mineral that contains large amounts of aluminum, iron, and magnesium. [Lat. *augites,* a precious stone < Gk. *augitēs* < *augē,* brightness.]
aug·ment (ôg-mĕnt′) *v.* **-ment·ed, -ment·ing, -ments.** *—tr.* **1.** To make greater, as in size, extent, or quantity; increase. **2.** To add an augment to. *—intr.* To become greater; enlarge. *—n.* (ôg′mĕnt′). **1.** An enlargement or increase. **2.** The prefixation of a vowel or the lengthening of an initial vowel to indicate the past tense, esp. of Greek and Sanskrit verbs. [ME *augmentem* < OFr. *augmenter* < LLat. *augmentare,* to increase < *augmentum,* an increase < *augēre,* to increase.] **—aug·ment′a·ble** *adj.* **—aug·ment′er** *n.*
aug·men·ta·tion (ôg′mĕn-tā′shən) *n.* **1.** The act or process of augmenting. **2.** The condition of being augmented. **3.** Something that augments. **4.** *Mus.* The repetition of a theme in notes of usually double time value.
aug·men·ta·tive (ôg-mĕn′tə-tĭv) *adj.* **1.** Having the tendency or ability to augment. **2.** *Gram.* Of, relating to, or designating esp. a word element that indicates an increase, as in size, force, or intensity, in the meaning of the original word. **—aug·men′ta·tive** *n.*
aug·men·ted (ôg-mĕn′tĭd) *adj. Mus.* Larger by a semitone than the corresponding major or perfect interval.
au gra·tin (ō grät′n, grăt′n) *adj.* Covered with bread crumbs or bread crumbs, butter, and sometimes grated cheese, and browned in an oven. [Fr.]
au·gur (ô′gər) *n.* **1.** One of a group of religious officials of ancient Rome who foretold events by observing and interpreting signs and omens. **2.** A seer or prophet; soothsayer. *—v.* **-gured, -gur·ing, -gurs.** *—tr.* **1.** To predict or prognosticate, as from signs or omens. **2.** To serve as an omen of; betoken. *—intr.* **1.** To conjecture or foretell from signs or omens. **2.** To be a sign or omen: *"traits that augured well for success"* (Philip Horton). [Lat.] **—au′gu·ral** (ô′gyə-rəl) *adj.*
au·gu·ry (ô′gyə-rē) *n., pl.* **-ries.** **1.** The art, ability, or practice of auguring; divination. **2.** A sign or omen; indication. [ME *augurie* < OFr. < Lat. *augurium* < *augur,* augur.]
au·gust (ô-gŭst′) *adj.* **1.** Inspiring awe or admiration; majestic. **2.** Venerable for reasons of age or high rank. [Lat. *augustus,* venerable.] **—au·gust′ly** *adv.* **—au·gust′ness** *n.*
Au·gust (ô′gəst) *n.* The eighth month of the year according to the Gregorian calendar. See table at **calendar.** [ME < OE < Lat. *(mensis) Augustus,* (month) of Augustus, after *Augustus* Caesar.]
Au·gus·tan (ô-gŭs′tən) *adj.* **1.** Pertaining to or characteristic of Augustus Caesar or his reign or times. **2.** Pertaining to or characteristic of English literature during the reign of Queen Anne. **—Au·gus′tan** *n.*
Au·gus·tin·i·an (ô′gə-stĭn′ē-ən) *adj.* **1.** Pertaining to Saint Augustine or his doctrines. **2.** Designating or belonging to any of several orders following or influenced by the rule of Saint Augustine. *—n.* **1.** A follower of the principles and doctrines of Saint Augustine. **2.** A monk or friar belonging to any of the Augustinian orders. **—Au′gus·tin′i·an·ism, Au·gus′tin·ism** *n.*
au jus (ō zhü′) *adj.* Served with the natural juices or gravy: *roast beef au jus.* [Fr.]
auk (ôk) *n.* Any of several sea birds of the family Alcidae, of northern regions, having a chunky body and short wings, such as the razor-billed auk. [Norw. *alk* < ON *alka.*]
auk·let (ôk′lĭt) *n.* Any of various small auks of the genus *Aethia* and related genera, of northern Pacific coasts and waters.
au lait (ō lĕ′) *adj.* With milk. [Fr.]
auld (ôld) *adj. Scot.* Old.
auld lang syne (ôld′ lăng zīn′, sīn′) *n.* The good old days long past. [Sc., old long since.]
au·lic (ô′lĭk) *adj.* Pertaining to a royal court; courtly. [Fr. *aulique,* Lat. *aulicus* < Gk. *aulikos* < *aulē,* court.]
au na·tu·rel (ō′ nä-tü-rĕl′) *adj.* **1. a.** In a natural state. **b.** Nude. **2.** Cooked simply. [Fr.]
aunt (ănt, änt) *n.* **1.** The sister of one's father or mother. **2.** The wife of one's uncle. [ME *aunte* < AN < OFr. *ante* < Lat. *amita,* paternal aunt.]
aunt·ie also **aunt·y** (ăn′tē, än′-) *n. Informal.* Aunt.
au pair also **au pair girl** (ō′ pâr′) *n.* A foreign girl or woman who works for a family in exchange for room and board and a chance to learn the family's language. [Fr.]
au·ra (ôr′ə) *n., pl.* **au·ras** or **au·rae** (ôr′ē). **1.** An invisible breath or emanation. **2.** A distinctive air or quality that characterizes a person or thing: *an aura of nobility.* **3.** *Pathol.* A sensation, as of a cold breeze, preceding the onset of certain nervous disorders. [ME, gentle breeze < Lat. < Gk.]
au·ral[1] (ôr′əl) *adj.* Of, pertaining to, or perceived by the ear. [< Lat. *auris,* ear.]
au·ral[2] (ôr′əl) *adj.* Characterized by or pertaining to an aura.
au·rar (œ′rär′) *n.* Plural of **eyrir.**
au·re·ate (ôr′ē-ĭt) *adj.* **1.** Of a golden color; gilded. **2.** Characterized by an inflated and pompous style. [ME *aureat* < Lat. *aureatus* < *aureus,* golden < *aurum,* gold.] **—au′re·ate·ly** *adv.* **—au′re·ate·ness** *n.*
au·re·ole (ôr′ē-ōl′) also **au·re·o·la** (ô-rē′ə-lə) *n.* **1.** A circle of light or radiance surrounding the head or body of a representation of a deity or holy person; halo. **2.** A bright band or region around a celestial body, such as the sun or moon, esp. when observed through a haze or fog. [ME < Med. Lat. *aureola (corona),* golden (crown) < Lat. *aureolus,* golden < *aurum,* gold.]
Au·re·o·my·cin (ôr′ē-ō-mī′sĭn). A trademark for chlortetracycline.
au re·voir (ō′ rə-vwär′) *interj.* Good-by. [Fr.]
au·ric (ôr′ĭk) *adj.* Of, pertaining to, derived from, or containing gold, esp. with valence 3. [< Lat. *aurum,* gold.]
au·ri·cle (ôr′ĭ-kəl) also **au·ric·u·la** (-lə) *n.* **1. a.** *Anat.* The external part of the ear; pinna. **b.** An atrium of the heart. **2.** *Biol.* An earlike part, process, or appendage, esp. at the base of an organ. [Lat. *auricula,* dim. of *auris,* ear.] **—au′ri·cled** (-kəld) *adj.*
au·ric·u·la (ô-rĭk′yə-lə) *n., pl.* **-las** or **-lae** (-lē′). **1.** A species of primrose, *Primula auricula,* native to the Alps, having clusters of variously colored flowers. **2.** Variant of **auricle.** [NLat. < Lat., auricle.]
au·ric·u·lar (ô-rĭk′yə-lər) *adj.* **1.** Of or pertaining to the sense or organs of hearing. **2.** Perceived by or spoken into the ear: *an auricular confession.* **3.** Having the shape of an ear. **4.** Of or pertaining to an auricle of the heart. *—n.* **auriculars.** The feathers covering the opening of a bird's ear. [Med. Lat. *auricularis* < *auricula,* auricle.] **—au·ric′u·lar·ly** *adv.*
au·ric·u·late (ô-rĭk′yə-lĭt, -lāt′) also **au·ric·u·lat·ed** (-lāt′ĭd)

auger
Auger bit

auk
Razor-billed auk

adj. Having ears or earlike parts or extensions. [< Lat. *auricula,* auricle.] **—au·ric'u·late·ly** *adv.*

au·rif·er·ous (ô-rĭf'ər-əs) *adj.* Containing gold; gold-bearing. [Lat. *aurifer* : *aurum,* gold + *ferre,* to carry.]

au·ri·form (ôr'ə-fôrm') *adj.* Ear-shaped. [Lat. *auris,* ear + -FORM.]

Au·ri·ga (ô-rī'gə) *n.* A constellation in the Northern Hemisphere near Lynx and Perseus. [Lat. *auriga,* charioteer.]

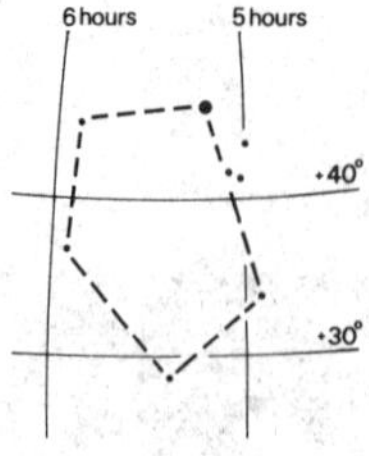

Auriga

Au·rig·na·cian (ôr'ĭg-nā'shən, ôr'ēn-yā'-) *adj. Archaeol.* Of or relating to the Old World Upper Paleolithic culture between Mousterian and Solutrean, associated with Cro-Magnon man, and characterized by artifacts such as figures of stone and bone, graphic art work, and the use of dress and adornment. [After *Aurignac,* a commune in France.]

au·rochs (ou'rŏks', ôr'ŏks') *n.* **1.** The urus. **2.** The wisent. [G.]

au·ro·ra (ô-rôr'ə, ô-rōr'ə, ə-) *n.* **1. Aurora.** *Rom. Myth.* The goddess of the dawn. **2.** The dawn. **3. a.** Aurora borealis. **b.** Aurora australis. [Lat.] **—au·ro'ral, au·ro're·an** (-ē-ən) *adj.* **—au·ro'ral·ly** *adv.*

aurora aus·tra·lis (ô-strā'lĭs) *n.* A luminous phenomenon of the southern regions that corresponds to the aurora borealis of the northern regions. [NLat., southern dawn.]

aurora bo·re·al·is (bôr'ē-ăl'ĭs, bōr'-) *n.* Luminous bands or streamers of light that are sometimes visible in the night skies of the northern regions and are thought to be caused by the ejection of charged particles into the magnetic field of the earth. [NLat., northern dawn.]

au·rous (ôr'əs) *adj.* Of or pertaining to gold, esp. with valence 1. [Lat. *aurum,* gold + -OUS.]

aus·cul·tate (ô'skəl-tāt') *tr.v.* **-tat·ed, -tat·ing, -tates.** *Med.* To examine by auscultation. [Back-formation < AUSCULTATION.] **—aus'cul·ta'tive** *adj.* **—aus·cul'ta·to'ry** (ô-skŭl'tə-tôr'ē, -tōr'ē) *adj.*

aus·cul·ta·tion (ô'skəl-tā'shən) *n.* **1.** The act of listening. **2.** *Med.* Diagnostic monitoring of the sounds made by internal organs or an internal bodily part. [Lat. *auscultatio* < *auscultare,* to listen to.]

aus·form (ôs'fôrm') *tr.v.* **-formed, -form·ing, -forms.** To subject a metal, esp. steel, to deformation, quenching, and tempering to improve its wear properties. [AUS(TENITIC) + (DE)FORM.]

aus·land·er (ou'slĕn'dər, -slăn'-) *n.* A foreigner. [G. *Ausländer* : *aus,* out + *Land,* land.]

aus·pex (ô'spĕks') *n., pl.* **aus·pi·ces** (ô'spĭ-sēz'). An augur of ancient Rome, esp. one who interpreted omens taken from the actions of birds. [Lat. —see AUSPICE.]

aus·pi·cate (ô'spĭ-kāt') *tr.v.* **-cat·ed, -cat·ing, -cates.** To begin or inaugurate with a ceremony designed to bring good luck. [Lat. *auspicari, aspicat-* < *auspex,* bird augur. —see AUSPICE.]

aus·pice (ô'spĭs) *n., pl.* **aus·pi·ces** (ô'spĭ-səz, -sēz'). **1. auspices.** Protection or support; patronage. **2.** A portent, omen, or augury, esp. when observed in the actions of birds. **3.** Observation of and divination from the actions of birds. [Lat. *auspicium,* bird divination < *auspex,* bird augur : *avis,* bird + *-spex,* watcher < *specere,* to look.]

aus·pi·cious (ô-spĭsh'əs) *adj.* **1.** Attended by favorable circumstances; propitious. **2.** Marked by success; prosperous. **—aus·pi'cious·ly** *adv.* **—aus·pi'cious·ness** *n.*

Aus·sie (ô'sē) *n. Informal.* A native or inhabitant of Australia. [AUS(TRALIAN) + -IE.] **—Aus'sie** *adj.*

aus·ten·ite (ôs'tən-īt') *n.* A nonmagnetic solid solution of ferric carbide or carbon in iron, used in making corrosive-resistant steel. [Fr., after Sir William Roberts-*Austen* (1843–1902).] **—aus'ten·it'ic** (-ĭt'ĭk) *adj.*

Aus·ter (ôs'tər) *n.* The personification of the south wind. [Lat.]

aus·tere (ô-stîr') *adj.* **1. a.** Severe or stern in disposition or appearance. **b.** Somber; grave. **2.** Strict or severe in discipline; ascetic. **3.** Without adornment or ornamentation; bare. [ME < OFr. < Lat. *austerus* < Gk. *austeros,* harsh.] **—aus·tere'ly** *adv.* **—aus·tere'ness** *n.*

aus·ter·i·ty (ô-stĕr'ə-tē) *n., pl.* **-ties. 1.** The quality of being austere. **2.** Severe and rigid economy: *wartime austerity.* **3.** An austere habit or practice.

aus·tral (ôs'trəl) *adj.* Of, pertaining to, or coming from the south. [< ME *auster,* south wind < Lat.]

Aus·tra·lian (ô-strāl'yən) *n.* **1.** A native or inhabitant of the Commonwealth of Australia. **2.** An aborigine of Australia. **3.** Any of the languages of the Australian aborigines. *—adj.* **1.** Of or pertaining to Australia or its inhabitants and their languages or cultures. **2.** *Ecol.* Of or designating the zoogeographic region that includes Australia and the islands adjacent to it, including New Guinea.

Australian ballot *n.* A printed ballot that bears the names of all candidates and the texts of propositions and is distributed to the voter at the polls and marked in secret.

Australian crawl *n.* A swimming stroke that is a variation of the crawl and executed with an flutter kick to each stroke.

Australian terrier *n.* A small dog of a breed developed in Australia, having a coarse blackish coat with tan markings.

Aus·tra·loid (ôs'trə-loid') *adj.* Of or relating to an ethnic group including the Australian aborigines. [AUSTRAL(IAN) + -OID.] **—Aus'tra·loid** *n.*

aus·tra·lo·pith·e·cine (ô-strā'lō-pĭth'ĭ-sīn') *n.* Any of several extinct manlike primates of the genera *Australopithecus* and *Paranthropus* or *Zinjanthropus,* known chiefly from Pleistocene fossil remains found in southern and eastern Africa. *—adj.* Of, pertaining to, or characteristic of the australopithecines. [< NLat. *Australopithecus* : Lat. *australis,* southern + *pithecus,* ape < Gk. *pithēkos.*] **—aus·tra'lo·pith'e·cine** *adj.*

Austro–[1] *pref.* Southern: *Austro-Asiatic.* [< Lat. *auster,* south.]

Austro–[2] *pref.* Austria; Austrian: *Austro-Hungarian.*

Aus·tro-A·si·at·ic (ôs'trō-ā'zhē-ăt'ĭk) *n.* A family of languages of southeastern Asia once dominant in northeastern India and Indochina. **—Aus'tro-A'si·at'ic** *adj.*

Aus·tro·ne·sian (ôs'trō-nē'zhən, -shən) *adj.* Of or pertaining to Austronesia, its peoples, or their languages. *—n.* A family of languages spoken in Austronesia, that includes the Indonesian, Melanesian, Micronesian, and Polynesian subfamilies.

aut– *pref.* Variant of **auto-.**

au·ta·coid also **au·to·coid** (ô'tə-koid') *n.* An organic substance, such as a hormone, formed in an organ and secreted into the blood, lymph, or sap, from which it acts on other parts of the organism. [AUT(O)- + Gk. *akos,* cure + -OID.] **—au'to·coid'al** (-koid'l) *adj.*

au·tar·chy (ô'tär'kē) *n., pl.* **-chies. 1. a.** Absolute rule or power; autocracy. **b.** A country under such rule. **2.** Variant of **autarky.** [Gk. *autarkhia* < *autarkhos,* self-governing : *autos,* self + *arkhos,* ruler.] **—au·tar'chic, au·tar'chi·cal** *adj.*

au·tar·ky (ô'tär'kē) *n., pl.* **-kies. 1.** A policy of national self-sufficiency and nonreliance on imports or economic aid. **2.** A self-sufficient region or country. [Gk. *autarkeia,* self-sufficiency < *autarkēs,* self-sufficient : *autos,* self + *arkein,* to suffice.] **—au·tar'kic, au·tar'ki·cal** *adj.*

au·te·col·o·gy (ô'tĭ-kŏl'ə-jē) *n.* The ecology of a species or of individual organisms in relation to the environment. **—au'te·co·log'i·cal** *adj.*

au·then·tic (ô-thĕn'tĭk) *adj.* **1. a.** Conforming to fact and therefore worthy of trust, reliance, or belief. **b.** Having an undisputed origin; genuine. **2.** *Law.* Executed with due process of law: *an authentic deed.* **3.** *Mus.* **a.** Designating a medieval mode having a range from its final tone to the octave above it. **b.** Designating a cadence with the dominant chord immediately preceding the tonic chord. **4.** *Obs.* Authoritative. [ME *autentik* < OFr. *autentique* < LLat. *authenticus* < Gk. *authentikos* < *authentēs,* author.] **—au·then'ti·cal·ly** *adj.*

au·then·ti·cate (ô-thĕn'tĭ-kāt') *tr.v.* **-cat·ed, -cat·ing, -cates.** To establish or prove as authentic. **—au·then'ti·ca'tion** *n.* **—au·then'ti·ca'tor** *n.*

au·then·tic·i·ty (ô'thĕn-tĭs'ə-tē) *n.* The condition or quality of being authentic, trustworthy, or genuine.

au·thor (ô'thər) *n.* **1. a.** The original writer of a literary work. **b.** One who practices writing as a profession. **2. a.** An originator or creator. **b. Author.** God. *—tr.v.* **-thored, -thor·ing, -thors. 1.** To be the author of; write. **2.** To originate; create. [ME *authour* < OFr. *autor* < Lat. *auctor,* creator < *augēre,* to create.]

au·thor·i·tar·i·an (ə-thôr'ĭ-târ'ē-ən, ə-thŏr'-, ô-) *adj.* Characterized by or favoring absolute obedience to authority, as against individual freedom. **—au·thor'i·tar'i·an** *n.* **—au·thor'i·tar'i·an·ism** *n.*

au·thor·i·ta·tive (ə-thôr'ĭ-tā'tĭv, ə-thŏr'-, ô-) *adj.* **1.** Having or arising from proper authority; official: *authoritative sources.* **2.** Wielding authority; commanding. **—au·thor'i·ta'tive·ly** *adv.* **—au·thor'i·ta'tive·ness** *n.*

au·thor·i·ty (ə-thôr'ĭ-tē, ə-thŏr'-, ô-) *n., pl.* **-ties. 1. a.** The power to command, enforce laws, exact obedience, determine, or judge. **b.** A person or group invested with this power. **c.** The officials of a political unit holding such power; government. **2.** Freedom or right granted to another; authorization. **3.** A public agency or corporation with administrative powers in a specified field: *the Port Authority.* **4. a.** An accepted source of expert information or advice. **b.** A quotation or citation from such a source. **5.** An expert in a given field: *an authority on plants.* **6.** Power to influence or persuade resulting from knowledge or experience: *write with authority.* **7.** Grounds for a particular course of action. **8.** An authoritative statement or decision that may be taken as a precedent. [ME *autority* < OFr. *autorite* < Lat. *auctoritas* < *auctor,* creator.]

au·thor·i·za·tion (ô'thər-ĭ-zā'shən) *n.* **1.** The act of authorizing. **2.** Something that authorizes; sanction.

au·thor·ize (ô'thə-rīz') *tr.v.* **-ized, -iz·ing, -iz·es. 1.** To grant authority or power to. **2.** To approve or give permission for; sanction: *authorize a highway project.* **3.** To be sufficient grounds for; justify. [ME *autorisen* < OFr. *autoriser* < Med. Lat. *auctorizare* < Lat. *auctor,* author.] **—au'thor·iz'er** *n.*

Authorized Version *n.* The King James Bible.

au·thor·ship (ô'thər-shĭp') *n.* **1.** The profession or occupation of writing. **2.** A source or origin, as of a book or idea.

au·tism (ô'tĭz'əm) *n.* **1.** Abnormal subjectivity; acceptance of fantasy rather than reality. **2.** A form of childhood schizophrenia characterized by acting out and withdrawal. **—au·tis'tic** (-tĭk) *adj. & n.*

au·to (ô'tō) *n., pl.* **-tos.** *Informal.* An automobile. *—intr.v.*

ă pat / ā pay / âr care / ä father / b bib / ch church / d deed / ĕ pet / ē be / f fife / g gag / h hat / hw which / ĭ pit / ī pie / îr pier / j judge / k kick / l lid, needle / m mum / n no, sudden / ng thing / ŏ pot / ō toe / ô paw, for / oi noise / ou out / ŏŏ took / ōō boot /

-toed, -to·ing, -tos. *Informal.* To go by or ride in an automobile. [Short for AUTOMOBILE.]
auto– *pref.* **1.** Self; same: *autogamy.* **2.** Automatic: *autopilot.* [Gk. < *autos,* self.]
au·to·an·ti·bod·y (ô′tō-ăn′tĭ-bŏd′ē) *n.* An antibody thought to act against cells of the organism in which it is formed.
au·to·bahn (ou′tō-bän′) *n.* A superhighway in Germany. [G. : *auto,* automobile + *Bahn,* road.]
au·to·bi·og·ra·phy (ô′tō-bī-ŏg′rə-fē, -bē-ŏg′rə-fē) *n., pl.* **-phies.** The biography of a person written by himself. **—au′to·bi·og′ra·pher** *n.* **—au′to·bi′o·graph′ic** (-bī′ə-grăf′ĭk), **au′to·bi′o·graph′i·cal** *adj.* **—au′to·bi′o·graph′i·cal·ly** *adv.*
au·to·bus (ô′tō-bŭs′) *n., pl.* **-bus·es** or **-bus·ses.** A bus.
au·to·ca·tal·y·sis (ô′tō-kə-tăl′ĭ-sĭs) *n., pl.* **-ses** (-sēz′). Catalysis of a chemical reaction by one of the products of the reaction. **—au′to·cat′a·lyt′ic** *adj.*
au·toch·thon (ô-tŏk′thən) *n., pl.* **-thons** or **-tho·nes** (-thə-nēz′). **1.** The earliest known or aboriginal inhabitant of a particular place. **2.** *Ecol.* An indigenous plant or animal. [Gk. *autokhthōn* : *autos,* self + *khthōn,* earth.]
au·toch·tho·nous (ô-tŏk′thə-nəs) also **au·toch·tho·nal** (-thə-nəl) or **au·toch·thon·ic** (-thŏn′ĭk) *adj.* Native to a particular place; indigenous. **—au·toch′thon·ism, au·toch′tho·ny** *n.* **—au·toch′tho·nous·ly** *adv.*
au·to·clave (ô′tō-klāv′) *n.* A strong, pressurized, steam-heated vessel, as for sterilization and for cooking. [Fr. : *auto-,* auto- + Lat. *clavis,* key.]
au·to·coid (ô′tə-koid′) *n.* Variant of **autacoid.**
au·toc·ra·cy (ô-tŏk′rə-sē) *n., pl.* **-cies. 1.** Government by a single person having unlimited power; despotism. **2.** A country or state that is governed by autocracy.
au·to·crat (ô′tə-krăt′) *n.* **1.** A ruler having absolute or unrestricted power; despot. **2.** A person with unlimited power or authority. [Fr. *autocrate* < Gk. *autokratēs,* ruling by oneself : *auto-,* self + *kratos,* authority.] **—au′to·crat′ic, au′to·crat′i·cal** *adj.* **—au′to·crat′i·cal·ly** *adv.*
au·to·cross (ô′tō-krôs′, -krŏs′) *n.* A competition for automobiles that tests driving skill and speed.
au·to-da-fé (ou′tō-də-fā′, ô′tō-) *n., pl.* **au·tos-da-fé** (ou′tōz-, ô′tōz-). **1.** The public announcement of the sentences imposed on persons tried by the Inquisition and the public execution of these sentences by the secular authorities. **2.** The burning of heretics at the stake. [Port. *auto da fé,* act of the faith.]
au·to·di·dact (ô′tō-dī′dăkt′) *n.* A person who is self-taught. [< Gk. *autodidaktos,* self-taught : *autos,* self + *didaktos,* taught. —see DIDACTIC.] **—au′to·di·dac′tic** *adj.*
au·to·dyne (ô′tə-dīn′) *n.* A heterodyne in which one tube serves simultaneously as oscillator and detector. **—au′to·dyne′** *adj.*
au·toe·cious (ô-tē′shəs) *adj. Biol.* Having all stages of a life cycle occur on the same host. [AUTO- + Gk. *oikos,* house.] **—au·toe′cism′** *n.*
au·to·er·o·tism (ô′tō-ĕr′ə-tĭz′əm) also **au·to·e·rot·i·cism** (-ĭ-rŏt′ĭ-sĭz′əm) *n.* **1.** Self-satisfaction of sexual desire, as by masturbation. **2.** The arousal of sexual feeling without external stimulation. **—au′to·e·rot′ic** (-ĭ-rŏt′ĭk) *adj.*
au·tog·a·my (ô-tŏg′ə-mē) *n.* **1.** *Bot.* Fertilization of a flower by its own pollen; self-fertilization. **2.** *Biol.* The union of nuclei within and arising from a single cell, as in certain protozoans.
au·to·gen·e·sis (ô′tō-jĕn′ĭ-sĭs) *n.* Abiogenesis. **—au′to·ge·ne′tic** (-jə-nĕt′ĭk) *adj.* **—au′to·ge·net′i·cal·ly** *adv.*
au·tog·e·nous (ô-tŏj′ə-nəs) also **au·to·gen·ic** (ô′tə-jĕn′ĭk) *adj.* Self-generated; self-produced. **—au·tog′e·nous·ly** *adv.*
au·to·gi·ro also **au·to·gy·ro** (ô′tō-jī′rō) *n., pl.* **-ros.** An aircraft powered by a conventional propeller and supported in flight by a freewheeling, horizontal rotor that provides lift. [AUTO- + Gk. *guros,* circle.]
au·to·graph (ô′tə-grăf′) *n.* **1.** A person's own signature or handwriting. **2.** A manuscript in the author's handwriting. —*tr.v.* **-graphed, -graph·ing, -graphs. 1.** To write one's name or signature on or in; sign. **2.** To write in one's own handwriting. [Lat. *autographus,* written with one's own hand < Gk. *autographos* : *autos,* self + *graphein,* to write.] **—au′to·graph′ic, au′to·graph′i·cal** *adj.* **—au′to·graph′i·cal·ly** *adv.*
au·tog·ra·phy (ô-tŏg′rə-fē) *n.* **1.** The writing of something in one's own handwriting. **2.** Autographs collectively.
Au·to·harp (ô′tō-härp′). A trademark for a musical instrument similar to a zither, on which a desired chord can be selected by depressing a particular damper.
au·to·hyp·no·sis (ô′tō-hĭp-nō′sĭs) *n.* **1.** The act or process of hypnotizing oneself. **2.** A self-induced hypnotic state. **—au′to·hyp·not′ic** (-nŏt′ĭk) *adj.*
au·to·im·mune (ô′tō-ĭ-myo͞on′) *adj.* Related to or caused by autoantibodies. **—au′to·im·mun′i·ty** *n.* **—au′to·im·mun·i·za′tion** (-ĭm′yə-nə-zā′shən) *n.* **—au′to·im′mun·ize′** *v.* **(-ized, -iz·ing, i·zes).**
au·to·in·dex (ô′tō-ĭn′dĕks′) *n.* **1.** The procedure for preparation of an index to a body of material by means of a computer program. **2.** An index prepared by autoindex.
au·to·in·fec·tion (ô′tō-ĭn-fĕk′shən) *n.* Infection, as with recurrent boils, caused by germs or viruses persisting on or in the body.
au·to·in·oc·u·la·tion (ô′tō-ĭn-ŏk′yə-lā′shən) *n.* **1.** Inoculation with a vaccine made from substances in the recipient's own body. **2.** A secondary infection caused by a disease already in the body.
au·to·in·tox·i·ca·tion (ô′tō-ĭn-tŏk′sĭ-kā′shən) *n.* Self-poisoning caused by endogenous microorganisms, metabolic wastes, or other toxins in the body.
au·to·load·ing (ô′tō-lō′dĭng) *adj.* Semiautomatic.
au·tol·y·sate (ô-tŏl′ĭ-sāt′, -zāt′) *n. Biochem.* An end product of autolysis.
au·tol·y·sin (ô-tŏl′ĭ-sĭn, ô′tə-lī′sĭn) *n.* A substance that causes autolysis.
au·tol·y·sis (ô-tŏl′ĭ-sĭs) *n.* The destruction of tissues or cells of an organism by autogenous substances, such as enzymes. **—au′to·lyt′ic** (ô′tə-lĭt′ĭk) *adj.*
au·to·mak·er (ô′tō-mā′kər) *n.* An automobile manufacturer.
Au·to·mat (ô′tə-măt′). A trademark for a restaurant in which the customers obtain food from closed compartments by depositing coins in the appropriate slots.
au·tom·a·ta (ô-tŏm′ə-tə) *n.* A plural of **automaton.**
au·to·mate (ô′tə-māt′) *v.* **-mat·ed, -mat·ing, -mates.** —*tr.* **1.** To convert to automation. **2.** To control or operate by automation. —*intr.* To convert to or make use of automation. [Back-formation from AUTOMATIC.]
automated teller *n.* An unattended data system and related equipment activated by a bank customer to obtain banking services.
au·to·mat·ic (ô′tə-măt′ĭk) *adj.* **1. a.** Acting or operating in a manner essentially independent of external influence or control; self-moving. **b.** Self-regulating. **2. a.** Without volition or conscious control. **b.** Acting or performing in a mechanical fashion. **3.** Capable of firing continuously until ammunition is exhausted. —*n.* **1.** An automatic firearm, esp. an automatic pistol. **2.** An automatic machine or device. **3.** *Football.* An audible. [Gk. *automatos,* self-acting.] **—au′to·mat′i·cal·ly** *adv.* **—au′to·ma·tic′i·ty** (-mə-tĭs′ĭ-tē) *n.*
automatic pilot *n.* A mechanism, as on an aircraft, that automatically maintains a preset course.
au·to·ma·tion (ô′tə-mā′shən) *n.* **1.** The automatic operation or control of a process, equipment, or a system. **2.** The techniques and equipment used to achieve automatic operation or control. **3.** The condition of being automatically controlled or operated. **—au′to·ma′tive** *adj.*
au·tom·a·tism (ô-tŏm′ə-tĭz′əm) *n.* **1. a.** The state or quality of being automatic. **b.** Automatic mechanical action. **2.** *Philos.* The theory that the body is a machine whose functions are accompanied but not controlled by consciousness. **3.** *Physiol.* **a.** The automatic operation of organs and cells, such as the beating of the heart. **b.** Performance of an act without conscious control, as in the operation of the reflexes. **4.** The suspension of consciousness in order to express subconscious ideas and feelings. **—au·tom′a·tist** *n.*
au·tom·a·ti·za·tion (ô-tŏm′ə-tĭ-zā′shən) *n.* Automation.
au·tom·a·tize (ô-tŏm′ə-tīz′) *tr.v.* **-tized, -tiz·ing, -tiz·es.** To make automatic.
au·tom·a·ton (ô-tŏm′ə-tən, -tŏn′) *n., pl.* **-tons** or **-ta** (-tə). **1.** A robot. **2.** One that behaves in an automatic or mechanical fashion. [Lat., self-operating machine < Gk. *automatos,* self-acting.] **—au·tom′a·tous** *adj.*
au·to·mo·bile (ô′tə-mō-bēl′, -mō′bēl′) *n.* A self-propelled passenger vehicle that usually has four wheels and an internal-combustion engine, used for land transport. —*adj.* Automotive. [Fr. : Gk. *autos,* self + *mobile,* mobile < OFr. —see MOBILE.] **—au′to·mo·bil′ist** *n.*
au·to·mo·tive (ô′tə-mō′tĭv) *adj.* **1.** Self-moving; self-propelling. **2.** Of or pertaining to self-propelled vehicles.
au·to·net·ics (ô′tō-nĕt′ĭks) *n. (used with a sing. verb).* The study of automatic guidance and control systems. [AUTO- + (CYBER)NETICS.]
au·to·nom·ic (ô′tə-nŏm′ĭk) *adj.* **1.** Independent; autonomous. **2.** *Physiol.* Of or pertaining to the autonomic nervous system. **3.** Resulting from internal causes; spontaneous. **—au′to·nom′i·cal·ly** *adv.*
autonomic nervous system *n.* The division of the vertebrate nervous system that regulates involuntary action, as of the intestines, heart, and glands, and comprises the sympathetic nervous system and the parasympathetic nervous system.
au·ton·o·mous (ô-tŏn′ə-məs) *adj.* **1. a.** Independent. **b.** Self-contained. **2. a.** Independent of the laws of another state or government; self-governing. **b.** Of or pertaining to an autonomy. **3.** Autonomic. [Gk. *autonomos,* self-ruling : *autos,* self + *nomos,* law.] **—au·ton′o·mous·ly** *adv.*
au·ton·o·my (ô-tŏn′ə-mē) *n., pl.* **-mies. 1.** The condition or quality of being self-governing. **2.** Self-government or the right of self-government; self-determination; independence. **3.** A self-governing state, community, or group. [Gk. *autonomia* < *autonomos,* autonomous.] **—au·ton′o·mist** *n.*
au·to·phyte (ô′tə-fīt′) *n.* An autotrophic plant. **—au′to·phyt′ic** (-fĭt′ĭk) *adj.*
au·to·pil·er (ô′tō-pī′lər) *n. Computer Sci.* A specific automatic compiler. [AUTO- + (COM)PILER.]
au·to·pi·lot (ô′tō-pī′lət) *n.* An automatic pilot.
au·to·plas·ty (ô′tō-plăs′tē) *n.* Surgical repair or replacement with tissue taken from the same body as that on which the surgery is performed. **—au′to·plas′tic** *adj.* **—au′to·plas′ti·cal·ly** *adv.*
au·top·sy (ô′tŏp′sē, ô′təp-) *n., pl.* **-sies.** The examination of a

Daniel Boone

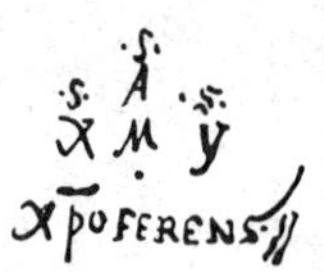
Christopher Columbus

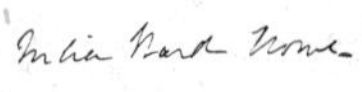
Julia Ward Howe

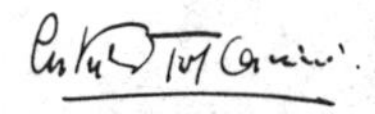
Arturo Toscanini

Thomas Hood

Emily Dickinson

Gertrude Stein

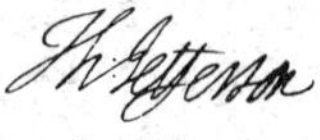
Thomas Jefferson

Napoleon

autograph

Autoharp

dead body to determine the cause of death. [Gk. *autopsia,* a seeing for oneself : *auto-,* self + *opsis,* sight.] —**au·top′sic, au·top′si·cal** *adj.* —**au·top′sist** *n.*

au·to·route (ô′tō-ro͞ot′) *n.* An expressway in France and French-speaking countries. [Fr. : *auto,* automobile + *route,* road.]

au·to·some (ô′tə-sōm′) *n.* A chromosome that is not a sex chromosome. —**au′to·so′mal** (-sō′məl) *adj.*

au·to·stra·da (ou′tō-strä′də, ô′tō-) *n.* An expressway in Italy. [Ital. : *auto,* automobile + *strada,* street < LLat. *strata,* paved road.]

au·to·sug·ges·tion (ô′tō-səg-jĕs′chən) *n. Psychol.* The process by which a person induces self-acceptance of an opinion, belief, or plan of action. —**au′to·sug·gest′i·bil′i·ty** *n.* —**au′to·sug·gest′i·ble** *adj.* —**au′to·sug·ges′tive** *adj.*

au·tot·o·mize (ô-tŏt′ə-mīz′) *tr. & intr.v.* **-mized, -miz·ing, -miz·es.** To cause the autotomy of or to undergo autotomy.

au·tot·o·my (ô-tŏt′ə-mē) *n. Zool.* The spontaneous casting off of a body part, as the tail of certain lizards, for self-protection. —**au′to·tom′ic** (ô′tə-tŏm′ĭk) *adj.*

au·to·tox·e·mi·a also **au·to·tox·ae·mi·a** (ô′tō-tŏk-sē′mē-ə) *n. Pathol.* Autointoxication.

au·to·tox·in (ô′tō-tŏk′sĭn) *n.* A poison that acts on the organism in which it is generated. —**au′to·tox′ic** *adj.*

au·to·trans·form·er (ô′tō-trăns-fôr′mər) *n.* An electrical transformer in which the primary and secondary coils have some or all windings in common.

au·to·troph (ô′tə-trŏf′) *n.* An autotrophic organism, such as a green plant. [Back-formation < AUTOTROPHIC.]

au·to·troph·ic (ô′tə-trŏf′ĭk, -trō′fĭk) *adj.* Designating or characterizing plants or plantlike organisms capable of manufacturing their own food by synthesis of inorganic materials, as in photosynthesis. —**au′to·troph′i·cal·ly** *adv.* —**au·tot′ro·phy** (ô-tŏt′rə-fē) *n.*

au·to·work·er (ô′tō-wûr′kər) *n.* A worker in the automobile industry.

au·tumn (ô′təm) *n.* **1.** The season of the year between summer and winter, lasting from the autumnal equinox to the winter solstice and from September to December in the Northern Hemisphere; fall. **2.** A period of maturity verging on decline. [ME *autumpne* < OFr. < Lat. *autumnus.*] —**au·tum′nal** (-tŭm′nəl) *adj.* —**au·tum′nal·ly** *adv.*

autumn crocus *n.* A plant, *Colchicum autumnale,* native to Europe and northern Africa, having pink or purplish flowers that bloom in the fall.

au·tun·ite (ō-tŭn′īt′, ô′tə-nīt′) *n.* A yellowish, fluorescent minor ore of uranium with composition $Ca(UO_2)_2(PO_4)_2 \cdot 10H_2O$. [After *Autun,* France.]

aux·e·sis (ôg-zē′sĭs, ôk-sē′-) *n.* An increase in the size of a cell without cell division. [Gk. *auxēsis,* growth < *auxanein,* to grow.] —**aux·et′ic** (-zĕt′ĭk) *adj.* —**aux·et′i·cal·ly** *adv.*

aux·il·ia·ry (ôg-zĭl′yə-rē, -zĭl′ə-rē) *adj.* **1.** Giving assistance or support; helping. **2.** Acting as a subsidiary; supplementary. **3.** Held in or used as a reserve: *auxiliary troops.* **4.** *Naut.* Equipped with a motor as well as sails. —*n., pl.* **-ries. 1.** An individual or group that assists or functions in an auxiliary capacity. **2.** A member of a foreign body of troops serving a country in war. **3.** An auxiliary verb. **4.** *Naut.* A sailing vessel equipped with a motor. **5.** A vessel designed for and used in other than combat services, such as a tug or a supply ship. [Lat. *auxiliarius* < *auxilium,* help.]

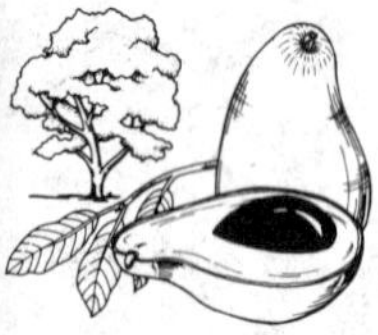

avocado

auxiliary verb *n. Gram.* A verb, such as *have, can,* or *will,* that accompanies particular forms of another verb of a clause to form a phrasal unit expressing person, number, tense, mood, voice, or aspect.

aux·in (ôk′sĭn) *n.* Any of several plant hormones, or similar substances produced synthetically, that affect growth by causing larger, elongated cells to develop. [< Gk. *auxein,* to grow.] —**aux·in′ic** *adj.* —**aux·in′i·cal·ly** *adv.*

Av (ôv, äb) also **Ab** (äb, äv, ôv) *n.* The 11th month of the year on the Hebrew calendar. See table at **calendar.** [Heb. *ābh* < Akkadian *abu.*]

a·vail (ə-vāl′) *v.* **a·vailed, a·vail·ing, a·vails.** —*tr.* To be of use or advantage to; help: *Nothing can avail him now.* —*intr.* To be of use, value, or advantage; serve. —*n.* Use, benefit, or advantage: *labored to no avail.* —**idiom. avail (oneself) of.** To make use of. [ME *availen* : *a-* (intensive) + OFr. *valoir, vail-,* to be worth < Lat. *valēre.*] —**a·vail′ing·ly** *adv.*

a·vail·a·ble (ə-vā′lə-bəl) *adj.* **1.** Accessible for use; at hand. **2.** Having the qualities and the willingness to take on a responsibility: *a list of available candidates.* **3.** *Archaic.* **a.** Capable of bringing about a desired end. **b.** Beneficial. —**a·vail′a·bil′i·ty, a·vail′a·ble·ness** *n.* —**a·vail′a·bly** *adv.*

av·a·lanche (ăv′ə-lănch′) *n.* **1.** A fall or slide of a large mass of snow, rock, or other material down a mountainside. **2.** Something resembling an avalanche: *received an avalanche of mail.* —*v.* **-lanched, -lanch·ing, -lanch·es.** —*intr.* To fall, as an avalanche. —*tr.* To overwhelm. [Fr. < dial. Fr. *avalantse.*]

avalanche lily *n.* A plant, *Erythronium montanum,* of western North America, having nodding white flowers. [So called because it grows near the snow line and blooms when the snow begins to melt.]

Av·a·lon (ăv′ə-lŏn′) *n.* A legendary island paradise in the western seas to which King Arthur went at his death.

a·vant-garde (ä′vänt-gärd′) *n.* A group active in the invention and application of new techniques in a given field, esp. in the arts. [Fr., vanguard.] —**a′vant-garde′** *adj.*

av·a·rice (ăv′ə-rĭs) *n.* An extreme desire for wealth; cupidity. [ME < OFr. < Lat. *avaritia* < *avarus,* greedy < *avēre,* to desire.]

av·a·ri·cious (ăv′ə-rĭsh′əs) *adj.* Immoderately greedy for wealth. —**av′a·ri′cious·ly** *adv.* —**av′a·ri′cious·ness** *n.*

a·vast (ə-văst′) *interj. Naut.* Used as a command to stop or desist.

av·a·tar (ăv′ə-tär′) *n.* **1. a.** An incarnation or embodiment, as of a quality or concept. **b.** A varying manifestation or aspect of a particular entity. **2.** The incarnation of esp. a Hindu deity in human form. [Skt. *avatāraḥ* : *ava,* down + *tarati,* he crosses.]

a·vaunt (ə-vônt′, ə-vänt′) *interj. Archaic.* A command to be gone. [ME < OFr. *avant.* —see VANGUARD.]

a·ve (ä′vā) *n.* **1.** An expression of greeting or farewell. **2. Ave.** The Ave Maria. [Lat., hail!]

A·ve Ma·ri·a (ä′vā mə-rē′ə) *n.* Hail Mary. [ME < Med. Lat., hail, Mary.]

a·venge (ə-vĕnj′) *v.* **a·venged, a·veng·ing, a·veng·es.** —*tr.* **1.** To take revenge or exact satisfaction for: *avenge a murder.* **2.** To take vengeance on behalf of: *avenge one's father.* [ME *avengen* < OFr. *avengier* : *a-,* to (< Lat. *ad-*) + *vengier,* to vindicate < Lat. *vindicare.*] —**a·veng′er** *n.* —**a·veng′ing·ly** *adv.*

av·ens (ăv′ənz) *n., pl.* **avens. 1.** Any of various plants of the genus *Geum,* having irregularly shaped leaves, white, yellow, or reddish flowers, and plumed seed clusters. **2.** Any of several plants of the genus *Dryas,* of mountainous and arctic regions, related to the avens. [ME *avence* < OFr.]

a·ven·tu·rine (ə-vĕn′chə-rēn′, -rĭn) also **a·ven·tu·rin** (-rĭn) *n.* **1.** An opaque or semitranslucent brown glass flecked with small metallic particles, often of copper or chromic oxide. **2.** Any of several varieties of quartz or feldspar flecked with particles of mica, hematite, or other materials. [Fr. < *aventure,* accident (so called because of its accidental discovery). —see ADVENTURE.] —**a·ven′tu·rine′** *adj.*

av·e·nue (ăv′ə-no͞o′, -nyo͞o′) *n.* **1.** A wide street or thoroughfare. **2. a.** A broad roadway lined with trees. **b.** *Chiefly Brit.* The drive leading from the main road up to a country house. **3.** A means of access or approach: *new avenues of trade.* [Fr. < OFr., p.part. of *avenir,* to approach < Lat. *advenire,* to come to. —see ADVENT.]

a·ver (ə-vûr′) *tr.v.* **a·verred, a·ver·ring, a·vers. 1.** To declare in a positive manner; affirm. **2.** *Law.* **a.** To assert formally as a fact. **b.** To justify or prove. [ME *averren* < OFr. *averer* < VLat. **adverare* : Lat. *ad-,* to + Lat. *verus,* true.] —**a·ver′ment** *n.* —**a·ver′ra·ble** *adj.*

av·er·age (ăv′ər-ĭj, ăv′rĭj) *n.* **1.** *Math.* **a.** A number that typifies a set of numbers of which it is a function. **b.** The arithmetic mean. **2.** A typical or usual level, degree, or kind. **3.** *Law.* **a.** The incurrence of and loss due to damage at sea to a ship or cargo. **b.** The equitable distribution of such a loss among concerned parties. **c.** Charges incurred through such a loss. **4.** Small expenses or charges that are usually paid by the master of a ship. —*adj.* **1.** Of, pertaining to, or constituting a mathematical average. **2.** Typical; usual. **3.** Assessed in compliance with the laws of average. —*v.* **-aged, -ag·ing, -ag·es.** —*tr.* **1.** To calculate the average of. **2.** To accomplish or obtain an average of: *average three hours work a day.* **3.** To distribute proportionately. —*intr.* **1.** To be or amount to an average. **2.** To buy or sell more goods or shares to obtain more than an average price. [Obs. *averie,* shipping charges < OFr. *avarie,* damage to shipping < OItal. *avaria* < Ar. *'awārīyah,* damaged goods < *'awar,* blemish.]

Synonyms: *average, medium, mediocre, fair, middling, indifferent, run-of-the-mill, so-so, tolerable.* These adjectives indicate rank or position on a scale of evaluation. *Average* and *medium* apply to what is midway between extremes on such a scale; usually they imply both sufficiency and lack of distinction. *Mediocre* stresses the undistinguished aspect of what is average. *Fair* suggests rank above the average but substantially below the highest. *Middling* refers to middle position, less favorably than *average* but less unfavorably than *mediocre. Indifferent* is close to *mediocre,* and suggests inadequacy. *Run-of-the-mill* suggests uniform mediocrity. *So-so* suggests what is just passable. *Tolerable* suggests more favorably what is acceptable.

a·verse (ə-vûrs′) *adj.* **1.** Having a feeling of great distaste or aversion: *was averse to sharing a table with them.* **2.** *Bot.* Turned away from the central stem or axis. [Lat. *aversus,* backward, p.part. of *avertere,* to avert.] —**a·verse′ly** *adv.* —**a·verse′ness** *n.*

Usage: *Averse* and *adverse* are often confused. *Averse* indicates opposition or strong disinclination on the subject's part: *He was averse to joining the party. Adverse* is used of something that opposes or hinders progress: *an adverse wind; adverse circumstances.*

a·ver·sion (ə-vûr′zhən, -shən) *n.* **1.** Intense dislike. **2.** A feeling of extreme repugnance. **3.** *Archaic.* One that is an object of aversion. **4.** *Obs.* The act of averting or turning away.

aversion therapy *n.* A therapy designed to modify antisocial habits or addictions by creating a strong association with a disagreeable stimulus.

a·ver·sive (ə-vûr′sĭv, -zĭv) *adj.* Causing avoidance of an unpleasant or punishing stimulus, as in techniques of behavior modification. **—a·ver′sive·ly** *adv.*

a·vert (ə-vûrt′) *tr.v.* **a·vert·ed, a·vert·ing, a·verts. 1.** To turn away: *avert one's eyes.* **2.** To ward off or prevent: *avert disaster.* [ME *averten* < OFr. *āvertir* < Lat. *avertere* : *ab-*, away from + *vertere,* to turn.] **—a·vert′i·ble, a·vert′a·ble** *adj.*

A·ves·ta (ə-vĕs′tə) *n.* The sacred writings of the ancient Persians. [Pers. *apastāk,* text.]

A·ves·tan (ə-vĕs′tən) *n.* The eastern dialect of Old Iranian and the language of the Avesta. *—adj.* Of or pertaining to the Avesta or Avestan.

a·vi·an (ā′vē-ən) *adj.* Of, pertaining to, or characteristic of birds. [< Lat. *avis,* bird.]

a·vi·ar·y (ā′vē-ĕr′ē) *n., pl.* **-ies.** A large enclosure for holding birds in confinement. [Lat. *aviarium* < *avis,* bird.] **—a′vi·a·rist** (-ə-rĭst, -ĕr′ĭst) *n.*

a·vi·a·tion (ā′vē-ā′shən, ăv′ē-) *n.* **1.** The operation of aircraft. **2.** The production of aircraft. **3.** Military aircraft. [Fr. < Lat. *avis,* bird.]

aviation medicine *n.* The branch of medicine comprising aeromedicine and space medicine.

a·vi·a·tor (ā′vē-ā′tər, ăv′ē-) *n.* A man who operates an aircraft; pilot. [Fr. *aviateur* < *aviation,* aviation.]

aviator glasses *pl.n.* Tinted eyeglasses with a lightweight metal frame.

a·vi·a·trix (ā′vē-ā′trĭks, ăv′ē-) *n.* A woman who operates an aircraft; pilot.

a·vi·cul·ture (ā′vĭ-kŭl′chər, ăv′ĭ-) *n.* The raising or keeping of birds. [Lat. *avis,* bird + -CULTURE.] **—a′vi·cul′tur·ist** *n.*

av·id (ăv′ĭd) *adj.* **1.** Ardently eager or greedy: *avid for adventure.* **2.** Marked by great enthusiasm: *an avid sportsman.* [Fr. *avide* < Lat. *avidus* < *avēre,* to desire.] **—av′id·ly** *adv.*

av·i·din (ăv′ĭ-dĭn) *n.* A protein in egg albumin, capable of inactivating biotin and consequently inhibiting the growth of certain bacteria. [AVID + -IN (from its affinity for biotin).]

a·vid·i·ty (ə-vĭd′ĭ-tē) *n.* **1. a.** Eagerness. **b.** Greed. **2.** *Chem.* **a.** The dissociation-dependent strength of an acid or base. **b.** Degree of affinity.

a·vi·fau·na (ā′və-fô′nə, ăv′ə-) *n.* All the birds of a specific region or time division. [Lat. *avis,* bird + FAUNA.] **—a′vi·fau′nal** *adj.*

av·i·ga·tion (ăv′ĭ-gā′shən) *n.* Navigation of aircraft. [AVI(ATION) + (NAVI)GATION.] **—av′i·ga′tor** *n.*

a·vi·on·ics (ā′vē-ŏn′ĭks, ăv′ē-) *n. (used with a sing. verb).* The science and technology of electronics applied to aeronautics and astronautics. [AVI(ATION) + (ELECTR)ONICS.] **—a′vi·on′ic** *adj.*

a·vir·u·lent (ā-vĭr′yə-lənt, ā-vĭr′ə-) *adj.* Not infective or virulent.

a·vi·ta·min·o·sis (ā-vī′tə-mĭ-nō′sĭs) *n.* A disease caused by deficiency of vitamins. **—a·vi′ta·min·ot′ic** (-nŏt′ĭk) *adj.*

a·vo (ä′vōō) *n., pl.* **a·vos.** See table at **currency.** [Port.]

av·o·ca·do (ăv′ə-kä′dō, ä′və-) *n., pl.* **-dos. 1.** A tropical American tree, *Persea americana,* cultivated for its edible fruit. **2.** The oval or pear-shaped fruit of the avocado, having leathery green or blackish skin, a large seed, and bland, greenish-yellow pulp. [Mex. Sp. *aguacate* < Nahuatl *ahuactl.*]

av·o·ca·tion (ăv′ō-kā′shən) *n.* **1.** An activity taken up in addition to one's regular work or profession, usually for enjoyment; hobby. **2.** *Archaic.* One's regular work or profession. [Lat. *avocatio,* diversion < *avocare,* to call away : *ab-*, away + *vocare,* to call.]

av·o·cet (ăv′ə-sĕt′) *n.* Any of several long-legged shore birds of the genus *Recurvirostra,* having a long, slender, upturned beak. [Fr. *avocette* < Ital. *avocetta.*]

A·vo·ga·dro number (ä′və-gä′drō, ăv′ə-) *n.* The number of molecules in a mole of a substance, approximately 6.0225×10^{23}. [After Amadeo *Avogadro* (1776–1856).]

A·vo·ga·dro's law (ä′və-gä′drōz, ăv′ə-) *n.* The principle that equal volumes of different gases under identical conditions of pressure and temperature contain the same number of molecules.

a·void (ə-void′) *tr.v.* **a·void·ed, a·void·ing, a·voids. 1.** To keep away from; shun. **2.** To keep from happening. **3.** *Law.* To annul or make void; invalidate. **4.** *Obs.* To void. [ME *avoiden* < AN *avoider,* to empty out < OFr. *esvuidier* : *es-*, out (< Lat. *ex-*) + *vuidier,* to empty < *voide,* empty. —see VOID.] **—a·void′a·ble** *adj.* **—a·void′a·bly** *adv.* **—a·void′er** *n.*

a·void·ance (ə-void′ns) *n.* **1.** The act of avoiding or shunning. **2.** *Law.* An annulment.

av·oir·du·pois (ăv′ər-də-poiz′) *n.* **1.** Avoirdupois weight. **2.** *Informal.* Weight or heaviness, esp. of a person. [ME *avoir de pois,* commodities sold by weight, alteration of OFr. *aveir de peis,* goods of weight.]

avoirdupois weight *n.* A system of weights and measures based on a pound containing 16 ounces or 7,000 grains and equal to 453.59 grams.

a·vouch (ə-vouch′) *tr.v.* **a·vouched, a·vouch·ing, a·vouch·es. 1.** To take responsibility for; guarantee. **2. a.** To assert positively; affirm. **b.** To establish; prove. **3. a.** To acknowledge one's responsibility for. **b.** To confess; avow. [ME *avouchen,* to cite as a warrant < OFr. *avochier* < Lat. *advocare,* to summon : *ad-*, to + *vocare,* to call.]

a·vow (ə-vou′) *tr.v.* **a·vowed, a·vow·ing, a·vows. 1.** To acknowledge openly; confess: *avow guilt.* **2.** To declare oneself to be. [ME *avowen* < OFr. *avouer* < Lat. *advocare,* to call upon. —see AVOUCH.] **—a·vow′a·ble** *adj.* **—a·vow′a·bly** *adv.* **—a·vow′ed·ly** (-ĭd-lē) *adv.* **—a·vow′er** *n.*

a·vow·al (ə-vou′əl) *n.* An admission or acknowledgment.

a·vulse (ə-vŭls′) *tr.v.* **a·vulsed, a·vuls·ing, a·vuls·es.** To tear off forcibly; rip away. [Lat. *avellere, avuls-*, to tear off : *ab-*, away + *vellere,* to pull.]

a·vul·sion (ə-vŭl′shən) *n.* **1. a.** A forcible separation. **b.** A part removed in this way. **2.** *Law.* The removal of a piece of land from one property onto another as a result of a shift in the course of a boundary stream.

a·vun·cu·lar (ə-vŭng′kyə-lər) *adj.* **1.** Of or pertaining to an uncle. **2.** Similar to an uncle, esp. in benevolence. [< Lat. *avunculus,* maternal uncle.]

aw (ô) *interj.* Used to express sympathy, disgust, or disbelief.

a·wait (ə-wāt′) *v.* **a·wait·ed, a·wait·ing, a·waits.** *—tr.* **1.** To wait for. **2.** To be in store for. **3.** *Obs.* To lie in ambush for. *—intr.* To wait. [ME *awaiten* < ONFr. *awaitier* : *a-*, to (< Lat. *ad-*) + *waitier,* to watch, of Germanic orig.]

a·wake (ə-wāk′) *v.* **a·woke** (ə-wōk′), **a·waked, a·wak·ing, a·wakes.** *—tr.* **1.** To rouse from sleep; waken. **2.** To stir the interest of; excite. **3.** To stir up (memories or fears, for example). *—intr.* **1.** To wake up. **2.** To become alert. **3.** To become aware or cognizant: *awoke to reality.* *—adj.* **1.** Not asleep. **2.** Alert; vigilant; watchful. [ME *awaken* < OE *āwacian.*]

a·wak·en (ə-wā′kən) *v.* **-ened, -en·ing, -ens.** *—tr.* To cause to wake up. *—intr.* To wake up. [ME *awakenen* < OE *āwæcnian* : *ā-*, on + *wæcnian,* to waken.] **—a·wak′en·er** *n.*

a·ward (ə-wôrd′) *tr.v.* **a·ward·ed, a·ward·ing, a·wards. 1.** To grant as merited or due. **2.** To declare as legally due: *awarded damages to the plaintiff.* *—n.* **1.** A decision, such as one made by a judge or arbitrator. **2.** Something awarded or granted, as for merit. [ME *awarden* < AN *awarder,* to decide (a legal question), of Germanic orig.] **—a·ward′a·ble** *adj.* **—a·ward′er** *n.*

a·ward·ee (ə-wôr-dē′) *n.* One that receives an award.

a·ware (ə-wâr′) *adj.* **1.** Having knowledge or cognizance: *aware of their limitations.* **2.** *Obs.* Vigilant; watchful. [ME < OE *gewær.*] **—a·ware′ness** *n.*

Synonyms: *aware, cognizant, conscious, sensible, alive, awake, alert, watchful, vigilant.* These adjectives mean to be mindful or heedful of something. *Aware* implies knowing something either by perception or by means of information. *Cognizant* is a rather formal equivalent of *aware* stressing sure knowledge and the recognition of it. *Conscious* emphasizes recognition of something sensed or felt. *Sensible* implies knowledge gained by sensing or perceiving, and suggests appreciation of it. *Alive* stresses keenness of perception, and *awake* suggests being aroused to the presence of something. *Alert* stresses both knowledge and capability of swift, apt response. *Watchful* and *vigilant* imply acute perception of what is dangerous or potentially so.

a·wash (ə-wŏsh′, ə-wôsh′) *adj.* **1.** Level with or washed by waves. **2.** Flooded. **3.** Floating on waves. **—a·wash′** *adv.*

a·way (ə-wā′) *adv.* **1.** From a particular place: *run away from home.* **2.** At a distance. **3.** In a different direction; aside: *He glanced away.* **4.** Out of existence: *The music faded away.* **5.** From one's possession: *gave the tickets away.* **6.** Continuously: *He worked away at his job.* **7.** Immediately: *Fire away!* *—adj.* **1.** Absent: *He is away from home.* **2.** At a distance: *He is miles away.* **3.** Played on an opponent's field or grounds: *an away game.* **4.** *Baseball.* Out: *bases loaded, two away.* **—*idioms.* away with. 1.** Take away. **2.** Go away. Often used imperatively: *Away with you!* **do (or make) away with. 1.** To get rid of. **2.** To murder. [ME < OE *aweg.*]

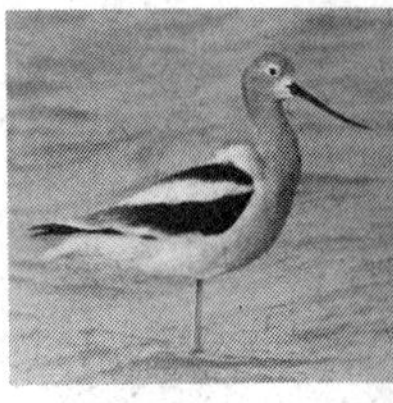

avocet

awe (ô) *n.* **1. a.** An emotion of mingled reverence, dread, and wonder. **b.** Fearful veneration or respect. **2.** *Archaic.* The power to inspire reverence or fear. **3.** *Obs.* Dread. *—tr.v.* **awed, aw·ing, awes.** To inspire with awe. [ME < ON *agi.*]

a·wea·ry (ə-wîr′ē) *adj.* Tired; weary.

a·weath·er (ə-wĕth′ər) *adv. Naut.* To windward.

a·weigh (ə-wā′) *adj. Naut.* Hanging just clear of the bottom. Used of an anchor.

awe·some (ô′səm) *adj.* **1.** Inspiring awe. **2.** Expressing or marked by awe. **—awe′some·ly** *adv.* **—awe′some·ness** *n.*

awe·struck (ô′strŭk′) or **awe·struck·en** (-strŭk′ən) also **awe·strick·en** (-strĭk′ən) *adj.* Full of awe.

aw·ful (ô′fəl) *adj.* **1.** Extremely bad or unpleasant; terrible. **2.** Commanding awe. **3.** Filled with awe. **4.** Great: *an awful burden.* *—adv. Informal.* Extremely; very: *was awful sick.* [ME *aweful,* awe-inspiring < OE *egefull.*] **—aw′ful·ly** *adv.* **—aw′ful·ness** *n.*

a·while (ə-hwīl′) *adv.* For a short time.

Usage: *Awhile,* an adverb, is never preceded by a preposition such as *for,* but the two-word form *a while* may be preceded by a preposition. In writing, each of the following is acceptable: *stay awhile; stay for a while; stay a while* (but not *stay for awhile*).

awk·ward (ôk′wərd) *adj.* **1.** Marked by a lack of dexterity and grace, esp. in physical movement. **2. a.** Clumsily lacking in the ability to do or perform; unskillful. **b.** Clumsily or unskillfully performed. **3.** Difficult to handle or manage: *an* *awkward bundle to carry.* **4. a.** Causing embarrassment and distress: *an awkward remark.* **b.** Marked by embarrassment or discomfort: *an awkward silence.* **5.** Needing tact and discretion: *an awkward situation.* [ME *awkeward,* in the wrong way < *awke,* wrong < ON *öfugr,* backward.] **—awk'ward·ly** *adv.* **—awk'ward·ness** *n.*

Synonyms: *awkward, clumsy, maladroit, inept, gauche, bungling, ungainly, unwieldy.* These adjectives refer to lack of grace or skill in movement, manner, or performance. *Awkward* and *clumsy,* the least specific, are often interchangeable. *Clumsy* emphasizes lack of dexterity in physical movement. *Awkward* applies both to physical movement and to embarrassing conditions and situations. *Maladroit* implies lack of tact or skill in relationships with other persons. *Inept* applies to inappropriate actions and speech. *Gauche* (French for "left") usually suggests boorishness. *Bungling* implies gross incompetence in performance. *Ungainly* suggests a visible lack of grace in form or movement. *Unwieldy* describes objects whose size or shape make them difficult to handle.

awl

awl (ôl) *n.* A pointed tool for making holes, as in wood or leather. [ME *aul* < OE *æl.*]

awl·wort (ôl'wûrt', -wôrt') *n.* A small aquatic plant, *Subularia aquatica,* of the Northern Hemisphere, having a tuft of narrow, pointed leaves and minute white flowers. [From its awl-shaped leaves.]

awning

awn (ôn) *n.* A slender, bristlelike terminal process such as those found at the tips of the spikelets in many grasses. [ME *awne* < ON *ōgn.*] **—awned** *adj.* **—awn'less** *adj.*

awn·ing (ô'nĭng) *n.* A rooflike structure, as over a window or door, that serves as a shelter. [Orig. unknown.]

a·woke (ə-wōk') *v.* Past tense of **awake.**

a·wok·en (ə-wō'kən) *v.* *Chiefly Brit.* Past participle of **awake.**

AWOL or **awol** (ā'wôl') *adj.* Absent without leave, esp. from military service. *—n.* One that is AWOL.

a·wry (ə-rī') *adv.* **1.** Turned or twisted toward one side; askew. **2.** Away from the correct course; amiss. **—a·wry'** *adj.*

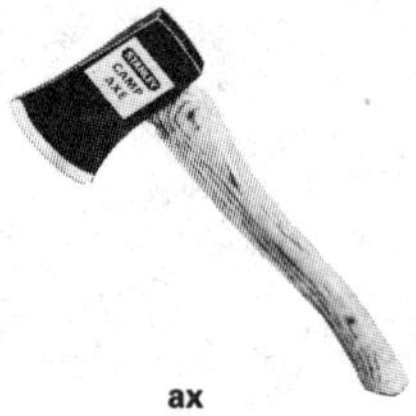

ax

ax or **axe** (ăks) *n., pl.* **ax·es** (ăk'sĭz). **1.** A tool with a bladed head mounted on a handle, used for felling or splitting lumber. **2.** A tool or weapon, such as a battle-ax, similar to an ax. **3.** *Informal.* **a.** A sudden termination of employment: *got the ax yesterday.* **b.** An abrupt or ruthless removal. *—tr.v.* **axed, ax·ing, ax·es. 1.** To use an ax. **2.** To remove ruthlessly or suddenly. ***—idiom.*** **have an ax to grind.** To pursue a selfish or subjective aim. [ME < OE *æxa.*]

ax·el (ăk'səl) *n.* A jump in figure skating with 1½ turns in the air. [After *Axel* Paulsen, 19th-cent. Norwegian figure skater.]

a·xen·ic (ā-zĕn'ĭk, ā-zē'nĭk) *adj.* Free of symbionts or parasites; uncontaminated. **—a·xen'i·cal·ly** *adv.*

ax·es *n.* **1.** (ăk'sēz'). Plural of **axis. 2.** (ăk'sĭz). Plural of **ax.**

ax·i·al (ăk'sē-əl) *adj.* **1.** Pertaining to or forming an axis. **2.** Located on, around, or in the direction of an axis. **—ax'i·al'i·ty** (-ăl'ĭ-tē) *n.* **—ax'i·al·ly** *adv.*

ax·il (ăk'sĭl) *n.* The angle between the upper surface of a leafstalk, flower stalk, branch, or similar part, and the stem or axis from which it arises. [Lat. *axilla,* armpit.]

ax·il·la (ăk-sĭl'ə) *n., pl.* **-il·lae** (-sĭl'ē). The armpit or an analogous part. [Lat.]

ax·il·lar (ăk-sĭl'ər, ăk'sə-lər) *adj.* Axillary. *—n.* One of the feathers in the axilla of a bird's wing.

ax·il·lar·y (ăk'sə-lĕr'ē) *adj.* **1.** *Anat.* Of, relating to, or near the axilla. **2.** *Bot.* Of, pertaining to, or located in an axil: *axillary buds.* *—n., pl.* **-ies.** An axillar.

azalea
Mountain azalea

ax·i·ol·o·gy (ăk'sē-ŏl'ə-jē) *n.* *Philos.* The study of the nature of values and value judgments. [Gk. *axios,* worth + -LOGY.] **—ax'i·o·log'i·cal** (-ə-lŏj'ĭ-kəl) *adj.* **—ax'i·o·log'i·cal·ly** *adv.* **—ax'i·ol'o·gist** *n.*

ax·i·om (ăk'sē-əm) *n.* **1.** A self-evident or universally recognized truth; maxim. **2.** An established rule, principle, or law. **3.** *Math. & Logic.* **a.** An undemonstrated proposition concerning an undefined set of elements, properties, functions, and relationships; postulate. **b.** A self-evident or accepted principle. [Lat. *axioma* < Gk. *axiōma* < *axios,* worthy.]

ax·i·o·mat·ic (ăk'sē-ə-măt'ĭk) also **ax·i·o·mat·i·cal** (-ĭ-kəl) *adj.* Of, pertaining to, or resembling an axiom; self-evident. **—ax'i·o·mat'i·cal·ly** *adv.*

ax·is (ăk'sĭs) *n., pl.* **ax·es** (ăk'sēz'). **1.** A straight line about which a body or geometrical object rotates or may be conceived to rotate. **2.** *Math.* **a.** An unlimited line, half-line, or line segment serving to orient a space or a geometrical object, esp. a line about which the object is symmetrical. **b.** A reference line from which distances or angles are measured in a coordinate system. **3.** A center line to which parts of a structure or body may be referred. **4.** An imaginary line to which elements of a work of art, as a picture, are referred for measurement or symmetry. **5.** *Anat.* **a.** The second cervical vertebra on which the head turns. **b.** Any of various central structures, as the spinal column, or standard abstract lines used as a positional referent. **6.** *Bot.* The main stem or central part about which organs or plant parts such as branches are arranged. **7. Axis.** The alliance of Germany and Italy (1936), later including Japan and other nations, that opposed the Allies in World War II. [ME < Lat.]

axis deer *n.* A deer, *Axis axis,* of central Asia, having a brown coat with white spots. [Lat. *axis,* a kind of animal.]

ax·ite (ăk'sīt') *n.* *Anat.* One of the terminal fibers of an axon. [AX(ON) + -ITE.]

ax·le (ăk'səl) *n.* **1.** A supporting shaft or member upon which a wheel or wheels revolve. **2. a.** The spindle of an axletree. **b.** Either end of an axletree. [ME *axel* < OE *eaxl.*]

ax·le·tree (ăk'səl-trē') *n.* A crossbar or rod supporting a vehicle, as a cart, and having terminal spindles on which the wheels revolve.

ax·man (ăks'mən) *n.* A man who wields an ax, esp. a worker who fells trees or chops logs.

Ax·min·ster (ăks'mĭn'stər) *n.* A kind of carpet with stiff jute backing and long, soft cut-wool pile. [After *Axminster,* England.]

ax·o·lotl (ăk'sə-lŏt'l) *n.* Any of several western North American and Mexican salamanders of the genus *Ambystoma,* which, unlike most amphibians, often retain their external gills and become sexually mature without undergoing metamorphosis. [Nahuatl : *atl,* water + *xolotl,* servant.]

ax·on (ăk'sŏn') also **ax·one** (-sōn') *n.* The core of a nerve fiber that generally conducts impulses away from the nerve cell. [Gk. *axōn,* axis.]

ax·seed (ăks'sēd') *n.* The crown vetch. [From its ax-shaped pods.]

ay1 (ī) *interj.* *Archaic.* Used to express surprise or distress.

ay2 (ī) *n. & adv.* Variant of **aye1.**

ay3 (ā) *adv.* Variant of **aye2.**

a·yah (ä'yə, ā'ə, ī'ə) *n.* A native maid or nurse in India. [Hindi *āyā* < Port. *aia,* nursemaid < Lat. *avia,* grandmother.]

a·ya·tol·lah (ī'ə-tō'lə, -tŏl'ə) *n.* An Islamic religious leader of the Shiite sect. [Pers. : Ar. *ayat,* sign + *allāh,* God.]

aye1 also **ay** (ī) *n.* An affirmative vote or voter. *—adv.* Yes; yea. [Prob. alteration of I.]

aye2 also **ay** (ā) *adv.* Always; ever. [ME *ai* < ON *ei.*]

aye-aye (ī'ī') *n.* A lemur, *Daubentonia madagascariensis,* of Madagascar, having large ears, a long, bushy tail, and rodentlike teeth. [Fr. < Malagasay *aiay,* prob. imit. of its cry.]

a·yin (ī'ĭn) *n.* The 16th letter of the Hebrew alphabet. See table at **alphabet.** [Heb. *'ayin.*]

Ay·ma·ra (ī'mä-rä') *n., pl.* **Aymara** or **-ras. 1. a.** An Indian people inhabiting Bolivia and Peru. **b.** A member of the Aymara. **2. a.** The language of the Aymara. **b.** A language family consisting of Aymara. **—Ay'ma·ran'** *adj. & n.*

Ayr·shire (âr'shĭr, -shər) *n.* One of a breed of brown and white dairy cattle originating in Ayr, Scotland.

az– *pref.* Variant of **azo-.**

a·zal·ea (ə-zăl'yə) *n.* Any of a group of deciduous or evergreen shrubs, part of the genus *Rhododendron,* of the North Temperate Zone, many of which are cultivated for their showy, variously colored flowers. [NLat. < Gk. *azaleos,* dry (so called because it grows in dry soil).]

a·zan (ä-zän') *n.* The Moslem summons to prayer, called by the muezzin from a minaret of a mosque five times a day. [Ar. *adhān* < *adhina,* to proclaim.]

A·za·zel (ə-zā'zəl, ăz'ə-zĕl') *n.* In ancient Hebrew tradition, the rebel leader of the angels who seduced mankind. [Heb. *'azāzēl.*]

A·zer·bai·ja·ni (ä'zər-bī-jä'nē, ăz'ər-) *n., pl.* **Azerbaijani** or **-nis. 1.** A native or inhabitant of Azerbaijan. **2.** The Turkic language of Azerbaijan.

A·zil·ian (ə-zĭl'yən) *adj.* *Archaeol.* Of or denoting a western European culture following the Magdalenian era and preceding the Neolithic. [After le Mas d'*Azil,* a village in France.]

az·i·muth (ăz'ə-məth) *n.* **1.** The horizontal angular distance from a fixed reference direction to a position, object, or object referent, as to a great circle intersecting a celestial body, usually measured clockwise in degrees along the horizon from a point due south. **2.** The lateral deviation of a projectile or bomb. [ME *azimut* < OFr. < Ar. *as-sumūt* : *as,* the + *sumūt,* pl. of *samt,* compass bearing.] **—az'i·muth'al** (-mŭth'əl) *adj.* **—az'i·muth'al·ly** *adv.*

azimuthal equidistant projection *n.* A map projection of the earth designed so that a straight line from a given point on the map to any other point gives the shortest distance between the two points.

az·ine (ăz'ēn', ā'zēn') *n.* A six-membered heterocyclic compound containing one or more atoms of nitrogen, such as pyridine.

azine dye *n.* Any of various dyes derived from phenazine.

az·o (ăz'ō, ā'zō) *adj.* Containing a nitrogen group. [< AZO-.]

azo– or **az–** *pref.* Containing a nitrogen group, esp. one attached at both ends in a covalent bond to other groups: *azole.* [< Fr. *azote,* nitrogen : Gk. *a-,* not + Gk. *zoē,* life.]

azo dye *n.* Any of various red, brown, or yellow acidic or basic dyes derived from azobenzene.

a·zo·ic (ā-zō'ĭk) *adj.* Of or pertaining to geological periods that precede the appearance of life.

az·ole (ăz'ōl', ā'zōl') *n.* An organic compound having a five-membered heterocyclic ring with two double bonds.

a·zon·ic (ā-zŏn'ĭk, ā-zō'nĭk) *adj.* Not restricted to a particular zone or region; not local.

az·o·te·mi·a (ăz'ə-tē'mē-ə, ā'zə-) *n.* Uremia. [Fr. *azote,* nitrogen + -EMIA.] **—az'o·te'mic** (-mĭk) *adj.*

az·oth (ăz′ŏth′, -ôth′) *n.* Mercury considered in alchemy to be the primary source of all metals. [Ar. *az-zā'ūq.*]
a·zo·to·bac·ter (ā-zō′tə-băk′tər) *n.* Any of various nitrogen-fixing bacteria of the family Azotobacteraceae. [Fr. *azote,* nitrogen + BACTER(IA).]
az·o·tu·ri·a (ăz′ə-to͝or′ē-ə, -tyo͝or′-) *n.* Increase of nitrogenous substances in the urine. [Fr. *azote,* nitrogen + -URIA.]
Az·ra·el (ăz′rā-ĕl′) *n.* The angel who separates the soul from the body at death in Moslem and Jewish legend. [Ar. *Azrā'īl* < Heb. *'Āzar'ēl,* God has helped.]
Az·tec (ăz′tĕk′) *n.* **1.** A member of an Indian people of Central Mexico noted for their advanced civilization before Cortés invaded Mexico in 1519. **2.** Nahuatl. —*adj.* Also **Az·tec·an** (-tĕk′ən). Of the Aztecs, their language, culture, or empire. [Sp. *Azteca* < Nahuatl *Aztecatl.*]
az·ure (ăzh′ər) *n.* **1.** A light purplish blue. **2.** An azure pigment. **3.** The blue sky. [ME < OFr. *azur* < Med. Lat. *azura* < Ar. *al-lāzaward* < Pers. *lājwārd,* lapis lazuli.]
az·ur·ite (ăzh′ə-rīt′) *n.* An azure-blue vitreous mineral of basic copper carbonate, $2CuCO_3 \cdot Cu(OH)_2$, used as a copper ore and as a gemstone.
a·zy·gous (ā-zī′gəs) *adj.* Occurring singly; unpaired.

B

Around 1000 B.C. the Phoenicians and other Semitic peoples began to use graphic signs to represent individual speech sounds instead of syllables or words. They used a symbol in the forms (1,2,3) to represent the sound of the consonant "b" and called it *bēth,* their word for "house." The Greeks, adapting the Phoenician alphabet, kept the phonetic value of *bēth* but varied its shape and orientation (4,5,6) and changed its name to *beta.* The Romans borrowed the alphabet from the Greeks via the Etruscans and adapted it for monumental inscriptions. Monumental script (8) is the prototype of modern capital letters (11,12). Medieval scribes adapted the Roman capitals to being quickly written on paper, parchment, and vellum. These uncial and cursive minuscules (9,10), in which the upper loop is reduced or omitted, are the prototypes of modern lower-case letters, both written and printed (14,13).

b

b or **B** (bē) *n., pl.* **b's** or **B's. 1.** The second letter of the modern English alphabet. **2.** Any of the speech sounds represented by the letter *b.* **3. B.** A human blood type of the ABO group. **4.** The second in a series. **5.** The second-best or second-highest in quality or rank: *grade B meat; a mark of B on an English theme.* **6.** *Mus.* **a.** The seventh tone in the scale of C major or the second tone in the relative minor scale. **b.** The key or a scale in which B is the tonic. **c.** A written or printed note representing this tone. **d.** A string, key, or pipe tuned to the pitch of this tone.

B The symbol for the element boron.

Ba The symbol for the element barium.

baa (bă, bä) *intr.v.* **baaed, baa·ing, baas.** To make a bleating sound, as a sheep does. *—n.* The bleat of a sheep. [Imit.]

Ba·al (bā'əl) *n., pl.* **-als** or **-al·im** (-ə-lĭm). **1.** Any of various local fertility and nature gods of the ancient Semitic peoples considered to be false idols by the Hebrews. **2.** Often **baal.** A false god or idol. [Heb. *bá'al,* lord.]

ba·ba (bä'bə) *n.* A leavened rum cake. [Fr. < Pol.]

ba·bas·su (bä'bə-so͞o') *n.* A Brazilian palm tree, *Orbignya martiana* (or *O. speciosa*), bearing hard nuts that yield an oil similar to coconut oil. [Port. *babaçú.*]

Bab·bitt[1] (băb'ĭt) *n.* A member of the American middle class whose attachment to its business and social ideals is such as to make him a model of narrow-mindedness and self-satisfaction. [After George F. *Babbitt,* the main character in the novel *Babbitt* by Sinclair Lewis.] **—Bab'bitt·ry** *n.*

Bab·bitt[2] (băb'ĭt). A trademark for a soft, silvery antifriction alloy composed of tin with small amounts of copper and antimony.

bab·ble (băb'əl) *v.* **-bled, -bling, -bles.** *—intr.* **1.** To utter a meaningless confusion of words or sounds. **2.** To talk foolishly or idly; chatter. **3.** To make a continuous low, murmuring sound, as flowing water. *—tr.* **1.** To utter rapidly and indistinctly. **2.** To blurt out impulsively; disclose without careful consideration. *—n.* **1.** Inarticulate or meaningless talk or sounds. **2.** Foolish or idle talk; prattle. **3.** A continuous low, murmuring sound. [ME *babelen.*] **—bab'bler** *n.*

babe (bāb) *n.* **1.** A baby; infant. **2.** An innocent or naive person. **3.** *Slang.* **a.** A young woman. **b.** A person. [ME.]

Ba·bel (bā'bəl, băb'əl) *n.* **1.** In the Old Testament, the site of a tower reaching to heaven whose construction was interrupted by the confusion of tongues. **2. babel. a.** A confusion of sounds or voices. **b.** A scene of noise and confusion. [Heb. *Bābhél* < Akkadian *Bāb-ilu,* gate of God.]

ba·be·sia (bə-bē'zhə) *n.* Any of the family Babesiidae of parasitic sporozoans that affect the blood of vertebrates, such as dogs and sheep. [NLat. *Babesia,* genus name, after Victor *Babes* (1854–1926).]

bab·e·si·a·sis (băb'ĭ-zī'ə-sĭs) also **ba·be·si·o·sis** (bə-bē'-ē-ō'sĭs) *n.* A disease or infection caused by babesia.

ba·bies'-breath (bā'bēz-brĕth') *n.* Variant of **baby's-breath.**

bab·i·ru·sa also **bab·i·rus·sa** or **bab·i·rous·sa** (băb'ə-ro͞o'-sə, bä'bə-) *n.* A wild pig, *Babyrousa babyrussa,* of the East Indies, having long, upward-curving tusks in the male. [Malay *bābīrūsa* : *bābī,* hog + *rūsa,* deer.]

bab·ka (bäb'kə) *n.* A coffee cake flavored with orange rind, rum, almonds, and raisins. [Pol.]

ba·boon (bă-bo͞on') *n.* **1.** Any of several chiefly African monkeys of the genus *Papio* (or *Chaeropithecus*) and related genera, having an elongated, doglike muzzle. **2.** *Slang.* A brutish person; boor. [ME *babewyne* < OFr. *babuin.*] **—ba·boon'ish** *adj.*

ba·boon·er·y (bă-bo͞o'nə-rē) *n.* Behavior characteristic of boors.

ba·bu (bä'bo͞o) *n.* **1.** A form of address in Hindi equivalent to *Mr.* **2. a.** A Hindu clerk who is literate in English. **b.** A native of India who has acquired some superficial education in English. [Hindi *bābū,* father.]

ba·bul (bə-bo͞ol') *n.* A tree, *Acacia arabica,* of northern Africa and India, that is a source of gum arabic, of a hardwood, and of tannin. [Pers. *babūl.*]

ba·bush·ka (bə-bo͝osh'kə) *n.* A woman's head scarf, folded triangularly and worn tied under the chin. [R., grandmother, dim. of *baba,* old woman.]

ba·by (bā'bē) *n., pl.* **-bies. 1. a.** A very young child; infant. **b.** The youngest member of a family or group. **c.** A very young animal. **2.** An adult or young person who behaves in an infantile way. **3.** *Slang.* A girl or young woman. **4.** *Slang.* An object of personal concern or interest. **—*modifier:*** *a baby girl; his baby sister.* *—tr.v.* **-bied, -by·ing, -bies.** To treat oversolicitously; coddle. [ME *babi.*] **—ba'by·hood'** *n.* **—ba'by·ish** *adj.*

baby blue *n.* A very light to very pale greenish or purplish blue.

ba·by-blue-eyes (bā'bē-blo͞o'īz') *n. (used with a sing. or pl. verb).* A low-growing plant, *Nemophila menziesii,* of California, having bell-shaped blue flowers.

baby bond *n.* A bond issued in an amount less than one thousand dollars.

baby grand *n.* A small grand piano approximately five feet long.

Bab·y·lon (băb'ə-lən, -lŏn') *n.* A city or place of great luxury and often corruption. [After *Babylon,* an ancient city of Babylonia, noted for its luxury.]

Bab·y·lo·ni·an (băb'ə-lō'nē-ən) *adj.* **1.** Of or pertaining to ancient Babylonia or Babylon or their people, culture, or language. **2.** Characterized by a luxurious, pleasure-seeking, and often immoral way of life. *—n.* **1.** A native or inhabitant of ancient Babylon or Babylonia. **2.** The form of Akkadian used in ancient Babylonia.

ba·by's-breath or **ba·bies'-breath** (bā'bēz-brĕth') *n.* **1.** A plant of the genus *Gypsophila,* esp. *G. paniculatum,* having numerous small white flowers in branching clusters. **2.** Any of several plants similar to the baby's breath, with small pleasantly scented flowers.

ba·by-sit (bā'bē-sĭt') *v.* **-sat** (-săt'), **-sit·ting, -sits.** *—intr.* To act as a baby sitter. *—tr.* To take care of: *babysit the children.*

baby sitter *n.* Someone engaged to care for one or more children when the parents are not at home.

ba·by-tears (bā'bē-tîrz') also **ba·by's-tears** (-bēz-) *n. (used with a sing. or pl. verb).* A creeping plant, *Helxine soleirolii,* native to Corsica, having numerous very small leaves and minute green flowers.

bac·ca·lau·re·ate (băk'ə-lôr'ē-ĭt) *n.* **1.** The degree of bachelor, conferred upon graduates of most U.S. colleges and universities. **2.** A farewell address in the form of a sermon delivered to a graduating class. [Med. Lat. *baccalaureatus* < *baccalarius,* bachelor.]

bac·ca·rat (bä'kə-rä', băk'ə-) *n.* A card game in which the winner is the player who holds two or three cards totaling closest to nine. [Fr. *baccara.*]

bac·cate (băk'āt') *adj.* **1.** Bearing berries. **2.** Resembling a berry in texture or form. [< Lat. *bacca,* berry.]

Bac·chae (băk'ē) *pl.n.* The priestesses and female followers of Bacchus. [Lat. < Gk. *bakkhai.*]

bac·cha·nal (băk'ə-năl', -näl', băk'ə-nəl) *n.* **1.** A participant in the Bacchanalia. **2.** Often **bacchanals.** The Bacchanalia. **3.** A drunken or riotous celebration. **4.** A reveler. *—adj.* Of, pertaining to, or typical of the worship of Bacchus. [Lat. *bacchanalis,* of Bacchus < *Bacchus,* Bacchus < Gk. *Bakkhos.*]

bac·cha·na·lia (băk'ə-nāl'yə, -nā'lē-ə) *n., pl.* **bacchanalia. 1. Bacchanalia.** The ancient Roman festival in honor of Bacchus. **2.** A riotous or drunken festivity; orgy. [Lat. < *bacchanalis,* of Bacchus < *Bacchus,* Bacchus < Gk. *Bakkhos.*] **—bac'cha·na'lian** (-nāl'yən, -nā'lē-ən) *adj. & n.*

bac·chant (bə-kănt', -känt', băk'ənt) *n., pl.* **bac·chants** or **bac·chan·tes** (bə-kăn'tēz, -kän'-, -kănts', -känts'). **1.** A priest or votary of Bacchus. **2.** A boisterous reveler. [Lat. *bacchans, bacchant-,* pr.part. of *bacchari,* to celebrate the festival of Bacchus < *Bacchus, Bakkhos,* Bacchus Gk.] **—bac·chan·tic** (-kăn'tĭk) *adj.*

bac·chan·te (bə-kăn'tē, -kän'-, -kănt', -känt') *n.* A priestess or female votary of Bacchus. [Fr. < Lat. *bacchans,* bacchant.]

bac·chan·tes (bə-kăn'tēz, -kän'-, kănts', -känts') *n.* A plural of **bacchant.**

Bac·chic (băk'ĭk) *adj.* **1.** Of or pertaining to Bacchus. **2. bacchic.** Drunken and carousing; bacchanalian.

Bac·chus (băk'əs) *n. Gk. Myth.* The god of grape-growing and of wine. [Lat. < Gk. *Bakkhos.*]

bac·cif·er·ous (băk-sĭf'ər-əs) *adj.* Bearing berries. [Lat. *baccifer* : *bacca,* berry + *ferre,* to carry.]

bac·ci·form (băk'sə-fôrm') *adj.* Having the shape of a berry. [Lat. *bacca,* berry + -FORM.]

bach also **batch** (băch) *intr.v.* **bached, bach·ing, bach·es** also **batched, batch·ing, batch·es.** *Slang.* To live alone and keep house as a bachelor. [Short for BACHELOR.] **—bach** *n.*

bach·e·lor (băch'ə-lər, băch'lər) *n.* **1.** An unmarried man. **2.** In feudal times, a young knight in the service of another knight. **3. a.** A college or university degree signifying completion of the undergraduate curriculum and graduation. **b.** A person holding such a degree. **4.** A young male fur seal who is kept from the breeding territory by older males. [ME *bacheler* < OFr., squire < Med. Lat. *baccalarius.*] **—bach'e·lor·dom, bach'e·lor·hood', bach'e·lor·ship'** *n.*

bach·e·lor's-but·ton (băch'ə-lərz-bŭt'n, băch'lərz-) *n.* **1.** The cornflower. **2.** The daisy (sense 2). **3.** Any of several plants similar to the bachelor's-button, having buttonlike flowers or flower heads.

bac·il·lar·y (băs'ə-lĕr'ē, bə-sĭl'ə-rē) also **ba·cil·lar** (bə-sĭl'ər, băs'ə-lər) *adj.* **1.** Rod-shaped. **2.** Of, pertaining to, or caused by bacilli. [< BACILLUS.]

ba·cil·li (bə-sĭl'ī') *n.* Plural of **bacillus.**

ba·cil·lo·pho·bi·a (bə-sĭl'ə-fō'bē-ə) *n.* A psychologically aberrant fear of bacilli. [BACILL(US) + -PHOBIA.]

bac·il·lu·ri·a (băs'ə-lo͝or'ē-ə) *n.* The presence of bacilli in the urine. [BACILL(US) + -URIA.]

ba·cil·lus (bə-sĭl'əs) *n., pl.* **-cil·li** (-sĭl'ī'). **1.** Any of various rod-shaped, aerobic bacteria of the genus *Bacillus,* often occurring in chainlike formations. **2.** Any of various bacteria, esp. a rod-shaped bacterium. [NLat. *Bacillus,* genus name < LLat., little rod, dim. of *baculum,* rod.]

bac·i·tra·cin (băs'ĭ-trā'sĭn) *n.* An antibiotic obtained from the bacterium *Bacillus subtilis* and used externally as a salve. [BACI(LLUS) + Margaret *Trac(y),* an American child in whose blood it was first isolated + -IN.]

back[1] (băk) *n.* **1. a.** The region of the vertebrate body located nearest the spine, in man consisting of the rear area from the neck to the pelvis. **b.** The analogous dorsal region

baboon

Bacchus

bachelor's-button

in other animals. **2.** The backbone or spine. **3.** The part or area farthest from the front. **4.** The part opposite the front. **5.** The reverse side, as of a coin. **6.** A part that supports or strengthens from the rear. **7. a.** The part of a book where the pages are stitched or glued together into the binding. **b.** The binding itself. **8.** *Sports.* **a.** In certain games, such as football, a player taking a position behind the front line of players. **b.** This position. —*v.* **backed, back·ing, backs.** —*tr.* **1.** To cause to move backward or in a reverse direction. **2.** To furnish or strengthen with a back or backing. **3.** To provide support, assistance, or encouragement for (a contending force). **4.** To adduce evidence in support of; substantiate: *backing up an argument with facts.* **5.** To bet on. **6.** To form the back or background of. **7.** To endorse by signing on the back of. —*intr.* **1.** To move backward. **2.** To shift to a counterclockwise direction. Used of the wind. —***phrasal verbs.*** **back down.** To withdraw from a position, opinion, or commitment. **back off.** To retreat or draw away. **back out. 1.** To withdraw from (an enterprise or plan) before completion. **2.** To fail to keep a commitment or promise. **back up.** To accumulate in a clogged state: *Traffic was backed up for blocks.* —*adj.* **1.** Located or placed in the rear. **2.** Distant from a center of activity; remote. **3.** Of a past date; not current. **4.** Owing or due from an earlier time; in arrears. **5.** In a backward direction. **6.** Articulated with the tongue positioned toward the rear of the mouth. —*adv.* **1.** At, to, or toward the rear or back; backward. **2.** In, to, or toward a former location. **3.** In, to, or toward a former condition. **4.** In, to, or toward a past time. **5.** In reserve or concealment. **6.** In check or under restraint. **7.** In reply or return. —***idioms.*** **back and fill. 1.** To maneuver a vessel in a narrow channel by adjusting the sails so as to let the wind in and out of them in alteration. **2.** To vacillate in one's actions or decisions. **go back on. 1.** To fail to keep (a promise or commitment). **2.** To betray or desert (a person). **turn (one's) back on. 1.** To reject, as in anger. **2.** To forsake. [ME *bak* < OE *bæc.*] —**backed** *adj.* —**back'less** *adj.*

Usage: The expression *back of* is an informal variant of *in back of* and is best avoided in writing: *There was a small stable in back of* (not simply *back of*) *the house.*

back[2] (băk) *n.* A shallow vat or tub used chiefly by brewers. [Du. *bak* < Fr. *bac,* ferry boat < OFr.]

back·ache (băk'āk') *n.* A pain or discomfort in the region of the spine or back.

back·bench·er (băk'bĕn'chər) *n. Chiefly Brit.* A junior member of Parliament who sits in the rear benches in the House of Commons behind government officeholders and their counterparts in the opposition party.

backgammon
Wood engraving by Erhard Ratdolt of Augsburg

back·bite (băk'bīt') *v.* **-bit** (-bĭt'), **-bit·ten** (-bĭt'n), **-bit·ing, -bites.** —*tr.* To speak spitefully or slanderously about (a person). —*intr.* To speak spitefully or slanderously about a person. —**back'bit'er** *n.*

back·board (băk'bôrd', -bōrd') *n.* **1.** A board placed under or behind something to provide firmness or support. **2.** *Basketball.* The elevated vertical board from which the basket projects.

back·bone (băk'bōn') *n.* **1.** The vertebrate spine or spinal column. **2.** Something, such as the keel of a ship, that resembles a backbone in appearance or position. **3.** A main support or major sustaining factor. **4.** Strength of character; determination. —**back'boned'** *adj.*

back·break·ing (băk'brā'kĭng) *adj.* Demanding great exertion, esp. physical exertion; arduous. —**back'break'er** *n.*

back·coun·try (băk'kŭn'trē) *n.* A sparsely inhabited rural region.

backhand

back·court (băk'kôrt', -kōrt') *n.* **1.** In tennis and other net games, the part of a court between the service line and the base line. **2.** In certain court games, such as handball, the part of the playing area farthest from the goal or target wall. **3.** *Basketball.* **a.** The half of the court that a team defends. **b.** The part of a team that comprises the two guard positions. **c.** The players in these positions.

back·cross (băk'krôs', -krŏs') *tr.v.* **-crossed, -cross·ing, -cross·es.** To mate (a first-generation hybrid) with a parent or member of the parental stock. —**back'cross'** *n.*

back·door (băk'dôr', -dōr') *adj.* Secret or surreptitious; clandestine.

back·drop (băk'drŏp') *n.* **1.** A painted curtain hung at the back of a stage set. **2.** The setting, as of a historical event; background.

back·er (băk'ər) *n.* One who supports or gives aid.

back·field (băk'fēld') *n. Football.* **1. a.** The players stationed behind the line of scrimmage. **b.** The positions filled by these players. **2.** The area in which the backfield lines up.

back·fire (băk'fīr') *n.* **1.** A fire started to extinguish an oncoming fire, as on a prairie, by clearing an area in its path. **2.** An explosion of prematurely ignited fuel or of unburned exhaust gases in an internal-combustion engine. —*intr.v.* **-fired, -fir·ing, -fires. 1.** To explode in or make the sound of a backfire. **2.** To produce an unexpected and undesired result.

backpack

back·for·ma·tion (băk'fôr-mā'shən) *n. Ling.* **1.** A new word created by removing from an existing word what is mistakenly thought to be an affix, as *laze* from *lazy* or *edit* from *editor.* **2.** The process of forming words by back-formation.

back·gam·mon (băk'găm'ən) *n.* A board game for two persons, played with pieces whose moves are determined by throws of dice. [BACK + GAMMON[1].]

back·ground (băk'ground') *n.* **1.** The ground located behind something. **2.** The part of a pictorial representation that appears as if in the distance and provides relief for objects in the foreground. **3.** A position of relative inconspicuousness or unimportance. **4.** The circumstances and events surrounding or leading up to something. **5.** A person's total experience, education, and knowledge. **6.** Subdued music played esp. as an accompaniment to dialogue in a dramatic performance. **7.** Sound or radiation present at a relatively constant low level at a specific location.

back·ground·er (băk'groun'dər) *n. Slang.* An informal meeting at which an official provides background information, as to news reporters, about a governmental issue.

back·hand (băk'hănd') *n.* **1.** *Sports.* A stroke or motion, as of a racket, made with the back of the hand facing outward and the arm moving forward. **2.** Handwriting characterized by letters that slant to the left. —*adv.* With a backhanded stroke or motion. —*tr.v.* **-hand·ed, -hand·ing, -hands.** To perform, catch, or hit backhand.

back·hand·ed (băk'hăn'dĭd) *adj.* **1.** Made with or using a backhand. **2.** Oblique or roundabout: *a backhanded compliment.* —**back'hand'ed·ly** *adv.* —**back'hand'ed·ness** *n.*

back·ing (băk'ĭng) *n.* **1.** Something forming a back. **2. a.** Support or aid. **b.** Approval or endorsement.

back·lash (băk'lăsh') *n.* **1.** A sudden or violent backward whipping motion. **2.** An antagonistic reaction to a prior action. **3.** A snarl in the part of a fishing line wound around the reel. **4.** The play resulting from loose connections between gears or other mechanical elements.

back·log (băk'lŏg', -lôg') *n.* **1.** A large log at the back of a fire in a fireplace. **2.** A reserve supply or source. **3.** An accumulation, esp. of unfinished work or unfilled orders. —*tr. & intr.v.* **-logged, -log·ging, -logs.** To acquire as or become a backlog.

back matter *n.* Material, such as an index or appendix, that follows the main body of a book.

back mutation *n.* A reversal process whereby a gene that has undergone mutation returns to its previous state. —**back'-mu'tate'** (băk'myo͞o'tāt', -myo͞o-tāt') *v.* **(-tat·ed, -tat·ing, -tates).**

back·pack (băk'păk') *n.* **1.** A knapsack, often mounted on a lightweight frame, that is worn on the back to carry camping supplies. **2.** A piece of equipment made for use while being carried on the back. —*v.* **-packed, -pack·ing, -packs.** —*intr.* To hike while carrying a backpack. —*tr.* To carry in a backpack. —**back'pack'er** *n.* —**back'pack'ing** *n.*

back·ped·al (băk'pĕd'l) *intr.v.* **-aled, -al·ing, -als** or **-alled, -al·ling, -als.** To move backward or withdraw: *He later backpedaled on the issue.*

back·rest (băk'rĕst') *n.* A rest for the back.

back·rush (băk'rŭsh') *n.* The seaward return of water after the landward motion of a wave.

back·saw (băk'sô') *n.* A saw that is reinforced by a metal band along its back edge.

back·scat·ter (băk'skăt'ər) *n.* The deflection of waves or particles through angles greater than 90 degrees by electromagnetic or nuclear forces. —**back'scat'ter** *v.* **(-tered, -ter·ing, -ters).**

back seat *n.* **1.** A seat in the back, esp. of a vehicle. **2.** *Informal.* A subordinate position.

back-seat driver (băk'sēt') *n. Informal.* **1.** An automobile passenger who constantly advises, corrects, or nags the driver. **2.** A person who persists in giving unsolicited advice.

back·set (băk'sĕt') *n.* A setback; reversal.

back·side (băk'sīd') *n. Informal.* The buttocks; rump.

back·slap (băk'slăp') *v.* **-slapped, -slap·ping, -slaps.** —*tr.* To demonstrate effusive good will for. —*intr.* To demonstrate effusive good will. —**back'slap'per** *n.*

back·slide (băk'slīd') *intr.v.* **-slid** (-slĭd'), **-slid** or **-slid·den** (-slĭd'n), **-slid·ing, -slides.** To revert to sin or wrongdoing, esp. in religious practice. —**back'slid'er** *n.*

back·spin (băk'spĭn') *n.* A spin that tends to retard, arrest, or reverse the linear motion of an object, esp. of a ball.

back·stage (băk'stāj') *adv.* **1.** In or toward the area, esp. the dressing rooms, behind the performing area in a theater. **2.** Secretly; privately. —*adj.* (băk'stāj'). **1.** Of, pertaining to, occurring in, or situated behind the performing area of a theater. **2.** Not open or known to the public; private or concealed.

back·stairs (băk'stârz') also **back·stair** (-stâr') *adj.* Furtively carried on; clandestine: *backstairs gossip.*

back·stay (băk'stā') *n.* **1.** *Naut.* A rope or shroud extending from the top of a mast aft to the ship's side or stern to help support the mast. **2.** A supporting device at or for the back of something.

back·stitch (băk'stĭch') *n.* A stitch made by inserting the needle at the midpoint of a preceding stitch so that the stitches overlap by half lengths. —*tr. & intr.v.* **-stitched, -stitch·ing, -stitch·es.** To sew with backstitches.

back·stop (băk'stŏp') *n.* **1.** A screen or fence used to prevent a ball from being thrown or hit far out of a playing area, as in baseball. **2.** *Baseball.* A catcher. —*tr.v.* **-stopped, -stop·ping, -stops. 1.** To serve as a backstop for. **2. a.** To support. **b.** To substitute for (another) in an emergency.

back-street (băk′strēt′) *adj.* Clandestine: *a back-street love affair.*
back•stretch (băk′strĕch′) *n.* The part of an oval racecourse farthest from the spectators and opposite the homestretch.
back•stroke (băk′strōk′) *n.* **1.** A backhanded stroke. **2.** A swimming stroke executed with the swimmer on his back.
back•swept (băk′swĕpt′) *adj.* Swept or angled backward.
back•swim•mer (băk′swĭm′ər) *n.* Any of various insects of the family Notonectidae that swim or float on their backs.
back•sword (băk′sôrd′, -sōrd′) *n.* **1.** A sword with only one cutting edge. **2.** A singlestick (sense 1).
back talk *n.* An insolent or impudent retort.
back•track (băk′trăk′) *intr.v.* **-tracked, -track•ing, -tracks. 1.** To go back over the course by which one has come. **2.** To reverse one's position or policy.
back-up (băk′ŭp′) *n.* **1.** A reserve or substitute. **2. a.** Support or backing. **b.** A background accompaniment, as for a musical performer. *—adj.* Extra; standby: *a back-up pilot.*
back•ward (băk′wərd) *adv.* **1.** To or toward the back. **2.** With the back leading. **3.** In a reverse manner or order. **4.** To, toward, or into the past. **5.** Toward a worse condition. *—adj.* **1.** Directed or facing toward the back. **2.** Done or arranged in a reverse manner or order. **3.** Behind others in progress or development. **—back′ward•ly** *adv.* **—back′ward•ness** *n.* **—back′wards** *adv.*
Usage: The adverb may be spelled *backward* or *backwards,* and the forms are interchangeable: *stepped backward; a mirror facing backwards.* Only *backward* is an adjective: *a backward view.*
back•wash (băk′wŏsh′, -wôsh′) *n.* **1.** A backward flow of water, as from the action of oars. **2.** A backward flow of air, as from the propeller of an airplane. **3.** A result of an event; aftermath.
back•wa•ter (băk′wô′tər, -wŏt′ər) *n.* **1. a.** Water held or pushed back by or as if by a dam or current. **b.** A body of water thus formed. **2.** A place or situation regarded as stagnant or backward: *a cultural backwater.*
back•woods (băk′wo͝odz′, -wo͝odz′) *pl.n.* Heavily wooded, uncultivated, thinly settled areas. **—back′woods′man** *n.*
back yard also **back•yard** (băk′yärd′) *n.* A yard at the rear of a house.
ba•con (bā′kən) *n.* The salted and smoked meat from the back and sides of a pig. [ME < OFr., of Germanic orig.]
Ba•co•ni•an (bā-kō′nē-ən) *adj.* **1.** Of, pertaining to, or characteristic of the works or thought of Francis Bacon. **2.** Of or designating the theory that Francis Bacon was the author of the plays attributed to Shakespeare.
bacter– *pref.* Variant of **bacterio-.**
bac•te•re•mi•a (băk′tə-rē′mē-ə) *n.* The presence of viable bacteria in the blood. **—bac′te•re′mic** (-mĭk) *adj.* **—bac′te•re′mi•cal•ly** *adv.*
bacteri– *pref.* Variant of **bacterio-.**
bac•te•ri•a (băk-tîr′ē-ə) *n.* Plural of **bacterium.**
bacterial capsule. A dense mucous protective layer that envelops some bacteria.
bac•te•ri•cide (băk-tîr′ĭ-sīd′) *n.* A substance that destroys bacteria. **—bac•te′ri•cid′al** (-sīd′l) *adj.*
bac•ter•in (băk′tə-rĭn) *n.* A vaccine prepared from dead bacteria.
bacterio– or **bacteri–** or **bacter–** *pref.* Bacteria; bacterial: *bacterioscopy.* [NLat. *bacterium,* bacterium.]
bac•te•ri•o•cin (băk-tîr′ē-ə-sĭn′) *n.* A bacterially produced anti-bacterial agent. [BACTERIO- + (COLI)CIN.]
bac•te•ri•o•gen•ic (băk-tîr′ē-ə-jĕn′ĭk) *adj.* Having bacteria as a cause.
bac•te•ri•ol•o•gy (băk-tîr′ē-ŏl′ə-jē) *n.* The study of bacteria, esp. in relation to medicine and agriculture. **—bac•te′ri•o•log′ic** (-ə-lŏj′ĭk), **bac•te′ri•o•log′i•cal** *adj.* **—bac•te′ri•o•log′i•cal•ly** *adv.* **—bac•te′ri•ol′o•gist** *n.*
bac•te•ri•ol•y•sis (băk-tîr′ē-ŏl′ĭ-sĭs) *n., pl.* **-ses** (-sēz′). The dissolution of bacteria. **—bac•te′ri•o•lyt′ic** (-ə-lĭt′ĭk) *adj.*
bac•te•ri•o•phage (băk-tîr′ē-ə-fāj′) *n.* A submicroscopic, usually viral organism that destroys bacteria. **—bac•te′ri•o•phag′ic** (-făj′ĭk), **bac•te′ri•oph′a•gous** (-ŏf′ə-gəs) *adj.* **—bac•te′ri•o•phag′i•cal•ly** *adv.*
bac•te•ri•os•co•py (băk-tîr′ē-ŏs′kə-pē) *n.* The study of bacteria with microscopes. **—bac•te′ri•o•scop′ic** (-ə-skŏp′ĭk), **bac•te′ri•o•scop′i•cal** *adj.* **—bac•te′ri•o•scop′i•cal•ly** *adv.* **—bac•te′ri•os′co•pist** *n.*
bac•te•ri•o•sta•sis (băk-tîr′ē-ō-stā′sĭs) *n., pl.* **-ses** (-sēz′). The arrestment or inhibition of bacterial growth without killing the bacteria. **—bac•te′ri•o•stat′ic** (-stăt′ĭk) *adj.* **—bac•te′ri•o•stat′i•cal•ly** *adv.*
bac•te•ri•o•stat (băk-tîr′ē-ə-stăt′) *n.* An agent that produces bacteriostasis.
bac•te•ri•um (băk-tîr′ē-əm) *n., pl.* **-ri•a** (ē-ə). Any of numerous unicellular microorganisms of the class Schizomycetes, occurring in a wide variety of forms, existing either as free-living organisms or as parasites, and having a wide range of biochemical, often pathogenic properties. [NLat. < Gk. *baktērion,* little rod, dim. of *baktron,* rod.] **—bac•te′ri•al** *adj.* **—bac•te′ri•al•ly** *adv.*
bac•te•ri•u•ri•a (băk-tîr′ē-yo͞or′ē-ə) *n.* The presence of bacteria in the urine.
bac•te•rize (băk′tə-rīz′) *tr.v.* **-rized, -riz•ing, -riz•es.** To change or cause a change in by means of bacteria. **—bac′te•ri•za′tion** *n.*
bac•te•roid (băk′tə-roid′) *adj.* Resembling bacteria in appearance or action. *—n.* Any of various structurally modified bacteria, such as those occurring on the roots of leguminous plants.
Bac•tri•an camel (băk′trē-ən) *n.* A two-humped camel, *Camelus bactrianus,* native to central and southwestern Asia.
bac•u•li•form (băk′yə-lə-fôrm′, bə-kyo͞o′lə-) *adj.* Rod-shaped. [Lat. *baculum,* stick + -FORM.]
bad[1] (băd) *adj.* **worse** (wûrs), **worst** (wûrst). **1.** Not achieving an adequate standard; poor. **2.** Evil or wicked. **3.** Disobedient or naughty. **4.** Disagreeable, unpleasant, or disturbing: *bad news.* **5.** Unfavorable: *bad reviews.* **6.** Not fresh; rotten or spoiled. **7.** Injurious in effect; detrimental: *bad habits.* **8.** Not working properly; defective: *a bad telephone connection.* **9.** Faulty or improper: *bad grammar.* **10.** Not valid or genuine: *a bad check.* **11.** Severe; intense: *a bad cold.* **12. a.** In poor health or in pain. **b.** In poor condition; diseased. **13.** Sorry; regretful. **14.** Comparative **bad•der,** superlative **bad•dest.** *Slang.* Very good; great. *—n.* **1.** Something that is bad: *weighing the good against the bad.* **2.** An unhappy or wicked state. *—adv. Informal.* Badly. [ME *badde,* prob. < OE *bæddel,* an effeminate person.] **—bad′ness** *n.*
Synonyms: *bad, evil, wicked.* These terms are compared as they pertain to departure from moral or ethical standards. *Bad* is most inclusive and generally weakest, although it can be applied with great stress. *Evil* emphasizes inherent capacity for harm or corruptive influence, and thereby more directly implies moral transgression. *Wicked* pertains not only to potential for wrong but to premeditated practice of it.
Usage: The adverb *badly* is often used idiomatically as an adjective in sentences like *I felt badly about the whole affair,* where grammar would seem to require *bad.* This usage is parallel to the use of the adverb *well* in sentences like *you're looking well,* however, and is accepted by a majority of the Usage Panel. The use of *bad* and *good* as adverbs, while common in informal speech, should be avoided in writing. Formal usage requires: *My tooth hurts badly* (not *bad*). *He drives well* (not *good*).
bad[2] (băd) *v. Archaic.* A past tense of **bid.**
bad blood *n.* Bitterness between persons.
bad•der•locks (băd′ər-lŏks′) *n. (used with a sing. or pl. verb).* An edible seaweed, *Alaria esculenta,* having long, yellowish-green fronds. [Orig. unknown.]
bade (băd, bād) *v.* A past tense of **bid.**
badge (băj) *n.* **1. a.** A device or emblem worn as an insignia of rank, office, or membership in an organization. **b.** An emblem given as an award or honor. **2.** A characteristic mark or sign. [ME *bagge.*] **—badge** *v.* **(badged, badg•ing, badg•es).**
badg•er (băj′ər) *n.* **1. a.** Any of several carnivorous, burrowing animals of the family Mustelidae, such as *Meles meles,* of Eurasia, or *Taxidea taxus,* of North America, having short legs, long claws on the front feet, and a heavy, grizzled coat. **b.** The fur or hair of a badger. **c.** Any of several mammals related to or resembling the badger, such as the honey badger. **2. Badger.** *Slang.* A native or inhabitant of Wisconsin. *—tr.v.* **-ered, -er•ing, -ers.** To harry persistently; pester. [Orig. unknown.]
bad•i•nage (băd′n-äzh′) *n.* Light, playful banter. [Fr. < *badin,* joker < Prov. *badar,* to gape < LLat. *badare.*]
bad•lands (băd′lăndz′) *pl.n.* An area of barren land characterized by roughly eroded ridges, peaks, and mesas.
bad•ly (băd′lē) *adv.* **1.** In a bad manner. **2.** Very much; greatly. —See Usage note at **bad**[1].
bad•min•ton (băd′mĭn′tən) *n.* A game played by volleying a shuttlecock back and forth over a high, narrow net by means of a light, long-handled racket. [After *Badminton,* the Duke of Beaufort's country seat in Gloucestershire, England.]
bad•mouth also **bad-mouth** (băd′mouth′, -mou*th*′) *tr.v.* **-mouthed, -mouth•ing, -mouths.** *Slang.* To criticize or disparage, often spitefully or unfairly; run down.
Bae•de•ker (bā′dĭ-kər) *n.* A guidebook. [After Karl *Baedeker* (1801–1859), publisher of guidebooks to Europe.]
baf•fle (băf′əl) *tr.v.* **-fled, -fling, -fles. 1.** To frustrate or check (a person) as by confusing or perplexing; stymie. **2.** To impede the force or movement of. *—n.* **1.** A usually static device that regulates the flow of a fluid or light. **2.** A partition that prevents interference between sound waves in a loudspeaker. [Perh. < Fr. *bafouer,* to ridicule.] **—baf′fle•ment** *n.* **—baf′fler** *n.*
bag (băg) *n.* **1. a.** A container in the form of a sack or pouch usually made from a flexible material such as paper or leather. **b.** A handbag; purse. **c.** A suitcase, satchel, or other piece of hand luggage. **d.** An organic sac or pouch, such as the udder of a cow. **2.** Something resembling a bag or pouch. **3.** *Naut.* The bulging part of a sail. **4.** The amount held in a bag; bagful. **5.** An amount of game taken or legally permitted to be taken. **6.** *Baseball.* A base. **7.** *Slang.* An area of interest or skill: *Cooking is not my bag.* *—v.* **bagged, bag•ging, bags.** *—tr.* **1.** To put into a bag. **2.** To cause to bulge like a bag. **3.** To capture or kill as game.

4. *Informal.* To gain possession of; capture. —*intr.* **1.** To hang loosely. **2.** To swell out; bulge. —***idioms.*** **bag and baggage.** **1.** With all one's belongings. **2.** Entirely; completely. **in the bag.** *Slang.* Assured of a successful outcome; virtually accomplished or won. [ME *bagge* < ON *baggi.*]

ba·gasse (bə-găs′) *n.* The dry pulp remaining from sugar cane after the juice has been extracted. [Fr. < Sp. *bagazo,* dregs < Lat. *baca,* berry.]

bag·a·telle (băg′ə-tĕl′) *n.* **1.** An unimportant or insignificant thing; trifle. **2.** A game played on an oblong table with a cue and balls. [Fr. < Ital., *bagatella,* poss. < Lat. *baca,* berry.]

ba·gel (bā′gəl) *n.* A glazed ring-shaped roll with a chewy texture. [Yiddish *beygel* < MHG *bouc,* ring < OHG *boug.*]

bag·gage (băg′ĭj) *n.* **1.** The trunks, bags, parcels, and suitcases in which one carries one's belongings while traveling; luggage. **2.** The movable equipment and supplies of an army. **3.** Superfluous or burdensome practices, regulations, or ideas. **4. a.** A wanton or immoral woman. **b.** An impudent girl or woman. [ME *bagage* < OFr. *bague,* bundle.]

bagpipe

bag·ging (băg′ĭng) *n.* Material used for making bags.

bag·gy (băg′ē) *adj.* **-gi·er, -gi·est.** Bulging or hanging loosely. —**bag′gi·ly** *adv.* —**bag′gi·ness** *n.*

bag lady *n.* A homeless woman esp. one in a big city, who carries all her possessions in a shopping bag.

bag·man (băg′mən) *n.* **1.** *Slang.* A person who collects money for racketeers. **2.** *Chiefly Brit.* A traveling salesman.

ba·gnio (băn′yō) *n., pl.* **-gnios.** **1.** A brothel. **2.** *Obs.* A prison for slaves in the Orient. [Ital. *bagno,* bath < Lat. *balneum* < Gk. *balaneion.*]

bag·pipe (băg′pīp′) *n.* Often **bagpipes.** A musical instrument having a flexible bag inflated either by a tube with valves or by bellows, a double-reed melody pipe, and from one to four drone pipes. —**bag′pip′er** *n.*

ba·guette (bă-gĕt′) *n.* **1. a.** A gem cut in the form of a narrow rectangle. **b.** The form of such a gem. **2.** *Archit.* A narrow, convex molding. [Fr., rod < Ital. *bacchetta,* dim. of *bacchio,* rod < Lat. *baculum,* stick.]

bag·wig (băg′wĭg′) *n.* A wig with the back hair encased in a small silk sack, worn in the 18th century.

bagworm

bag·worm (băg′wûrm′) *n.* The larva of any of several moths of the family Psychidae that encloses itself in a characteristic fibrous case and feeds upon and destroys tree foliage.

bah (bä, bă) *interj.* Used to express impatient rejection or contempt.

Ba·ha·i (bä-hä′ē, -hī′) *adj.* Of, pertaining to, or designating a religion founded in 1863 in Iran and emphasizing the spiritual unity of all mankind. —*n.* A teacher of or believer in the Bahai faith. [Pers. *bahā′ī,* of glory < *bahā-,* glory.] —**Ba·ha′ism** (bə-hä′ĭz′əm, -hī′-) *n.* —**Ba·ha′ist** *n.*

Ba·ha·sa Indonesia (bä-hä′sə) *n.* A dialect of Malay that is the official language of the Republic of Indonesia. [Indonesian, Indonesian language.]

baht (bät) *n., pl.* **bahts** or **baht.** See table at **currency.** [Thai, *bāt.*]

bail[1] (bāl) *n.* **1.** Security, usually a sum of money, exchanged for the release of an arrested person as a guarantee of his appearance for trial. **2.** Release from imprisonment provided by the payment of bail. **3.** A person who provides bail. —*tr.v.* **bailed, bail·ing, bails.** **1.** To secure the release of by providing bail. **2.** To release (a person) for whom bail has been paid. **3.** *Informal.* To extricate from a difficult situation: *always bailing her out of trouble.* **4.** To transfer (property) to another for a special purpose but without permanent transference of ownership. [ME *baile,* custody < OFr. *bail* < *baillier,* to take charge of < Lat. *bajulare,* to carry a load < *bajulus,* carrier of a burden.] —**bail′er** *n.*

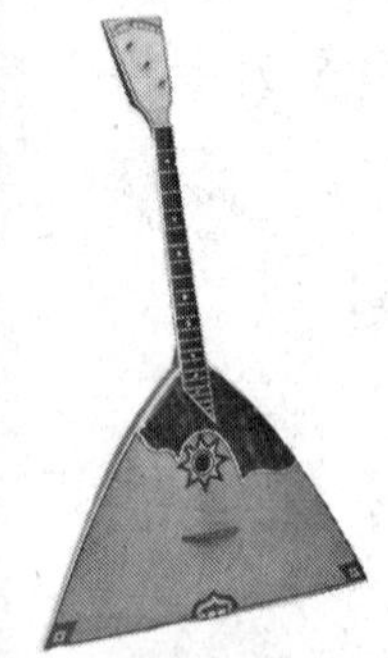

balalaika
20th-century Russian

bail[2] (bāl) *v.* **bailed, bail·ing, bails.** —*tr.* **1.** To remove (water) from a boat by repeatedly filling a container and emptying it over the side. **2.** To empty (a boat) of water by bailing. —*intr.* To empty a boat of water by bailing. —***phrasal verb.*** **bail out.** **1.** To parachute from an aircraft. **2.** *Slang.* To abandon a project or enterprise. —*n.* A container used for bailing. [< ME *baille,* bucket < OFr., poss. < Lat. *bajulus,* porter.] —**bail′er** *n.*

bail[3] (bāl) *n.* **1.** The arched, hooplike handle of a container, as a pail. **2.** An arch or hoop, such as those used to support the top of a covered wagon. **3.** A hinged bar on a typewriter that holds the paper against the platen. [ME *baill* prob. < ON *beygla.*]

bail[4] (bāl) *n.* **1.** *Chiefly Brit.* A pole or bar used to confine or separate animals. **2.** In cricket, one of the two crossbars that form the top of a wicket. [ME, bailey.]

bail·a·ble (bā′lə-bəl) *adj.* **1.** Eligible for bail. **2.** Allowing or admitting of bail: *a bailable offense.*

balance

bail·ee (bā-lē′) *n.* A person to whom property is bailed.

bai·ley (bā′lē) *n., pl.* **-leys.** **1.** The outer wall of a castle. **2.** The space enclosed by a bailey. [ME *baille* < OFr.]

Bai·ley bridge (bā′lē) *n.* A steel bridge designed to be shipped in parts and assembled rapidly. [After Sir Donald *Bailey* (b. 1901).]

bail·ie (bā′lē) *n.* **1.** A Scottish municipal officer corresponding to an English alderman. **2.** *Obs.* A bailiff. [ME *baillie* < OFr. *baillif,* bailiff.]

bail·iff (bā′lĭf) *n.* **1.** A court attendant entrusted with such duties as the maintenance of order in a courtroom during a trial. **2.** An official who assists a British sheriff and who has the power to execute writs, processes, and arrests. **3.** *Chiefly Brit.* An overseer of an estate; steward. [ME *baillif* < OFr. < Med. Lat. *bajulivus* < Lat. *bajulus,* carrier.]

bail·i·wick (bā′lə-wĭk′) *n.* **1.** The office or district of a bailiff. **2.** A person's specific area of interest, skill, or authority. [ME *bailliwik* : *baillif,* bailiff + *wik,* town < OE *wīc* < Lat. *vicus.*]

bail·ment (bāl′mənt) *n. Law.* **1.** The process of providing bail for an accused person. **2.** The act of delivering goods or personal property to another in trust.

bail·or (bā′lər, bā-lôr′) *n. Law.* A person who bails property to another.

bail·out (bāl′out′) *n.* A rescue from financial difficulties.

bails·man (bālz′mən) *n. Law.* One who provides bail or security for another.

bain-ma·rie (băn′mə-rē′) *n., pl.* **bains-ma·rie** (băn′mə-rē′). A device consisting of a large pan containing hot water in which smaller pans may be set to cook slowly or keep warm. [Fr. < Med. Lat. *balneum Mariae,* bath of Mary.]

bairn (bârn) *n. Scot.* A child. [ME *barn* < OE *bearn.*]

bait[1] (bāt) *n.* **1. a.** Food or other lure placed on a hook or in a trap and used in the taking of fish, birds, or other animals. **b.** Something, as a worm, used for this purpose. **2.** An enticement; temptation. **3.** *Archaic.* A stop for food or rest during a trip. —*v.* **bait·ed, bait·ing, baits.** —*tr.* **1.** To place bait in (a trap) or on (a fishing hook). **2.** To lure or entice, esp. by trickery or strategy. **3.** To set dogs upon (a chained animal, for example) for sport. **4.** To attack or torment, esp. with persistent insult, criticism, or ridicule. **5.** To tease. **6.** To feed (an animal) esp. on a journey. —*intr. Archaic.* To stop for food or rest during a trip. [ME, partly < ON *beita,* to hunt with dogs, and partly < ON *beita,* food.] —**bait′er** *n.*

Usage: The word *bait* is sometimes used improperly for *bate* in the phrase *bated breath.*

bait[2] (bāt) *v.* Variant of **bate[2].**

bait and switch *n.* A sales tactic in which a bargain-priced item is used to attract customers who are then encouraged to purchase a more expensive similar item.

bai·za (bī′zä) *n.* See table at **currency.** [Ar. < Hindi *paisā.*]

baize (bāz) *n.* A cotton or woolen material napped to imitate felt. [Fr. *baies* < *bai,* bay-colored < Lat. *badius.*]

bake (bāk) *v.* **baked, bak·ing, bakes.** —*tr.* **1.** To cook (food) with dry heat, esp. in an oven. **2.** To harden or dry by subjecting to heat in or as if in an oven. —*intr.* **1.** To cook food by baking. **2.** To become baked. —*n.* **1. a.** The act or process of baking. **b.** An amount baked. **2.** A social gathering at which food is baked and served. [ME *baken* < OE *bacan.*]

Ba·ke·lite (bā′kə-līt′). A trademark for any of a group of thermosetting plastics having high chemical and electrical resistance and used in a variety of manufactured articles.

bak·er (bā′kər) *n.* **1.** One who bakes. **2.** A portable oven.

baker's dozen *n.* A group of 13. [From the former custom of bakers to add an extra roll as a safeguard against the possibility of 12 weighing light.]

bak·er·y (bā′kə-rē) *n., pl.* **-ies.** A place where products such as bread, cake, and pastries are baked or sold.

bake·shop (bāk′shŏp′) *n.* A bakery.

baking powder *n.* Any of various mixtures of baking soda, starch, and at least one slightly acidic compound such as cream of tartar, used as a leavening agent in baking.

baking soda *n.* Sodium bicarbonate.

ba·kla·va (bä′klə-vä′) *n.* A dessert made of paper-thin layers of pastry, chopped nuts, and honey. [Turk.]

bak·sheesh (băk′shēsh′, băk-shēsh′) *n., pl.* **baksheesh.** In some Near Eastern countries, a gratuity; tip. [Pers. *bakhshīsh* < *bakhshīdan,* to give.]

BAL[1] (băl) *n.* A colorless, oily, viscous liquid, $C_3H_5(SH)_2(OH)$, used as an antidote for poisoning caused by lewisite, organic arsenic compounds, or heavy metals. [B(RITISH) + A(NTI-) + L(EWISITE).]

BAL[2] (bē′ā-ĕl′) *n. Computer Sci.* A low-level assembly language. [B(ASIC) A(SSEMBLY) L(ANGUAGE).]

Ba·laam (bā′ləm) *n.* An Old Testament prophet who was commanded to curse the Israelites but blessed them instead after being rebuked by the ass he rode. [Gk. < Heb. *Bil′ām.*]

bal·a·cla·va (băl′ə-klä′və) *n.* Sometimes **Balaclava.** **1.** A woolen hood almost completely covering the head and neck. **2.** A similar hood often covering the shoulders also, worn by soldiers and sailors, and originally used by soldiers in the Crimean War. Also called "balaclava helmet." [After *Balaklava,* U.S.S.R.]

bal·a·lai·ka (băl′ə-lī′kə) *n.* A Russian musical instrument with a triangular body and three strings. [R.]

bal·ance (băl′əns) *n.* **1.** A weighing device consisting of a rigid beam horizontally suspended by a low-friction support at its center, with identical weighing pans hung at either end, one of which holds an unknown weight while the effective weight in the other is increased by known amounts until the beam is level and motionless. **2.** A state of equilibrium or parity characterized by cancellation of all forces by equal opposing forces. **3.** The power or means to decide. **4.** A state of bodily equilibrium. **5.** A stable mental or psychological state; emotional stability. **6.** A harmonious or satisfying arrangement or proportion of parts or elements, as in a design. **7.** An influence or force tending to produce equilibrium; counterpoise. **8.** The difference in magnitude between opposing forces or influences. **9.** *Accounting.* **a.** Equality of totals in the debit and credit sides of an account. **b.** The difference between such totals, either on the credit or the debit side. **10.** Something that is left over; remainder. **11.** *Chem.* Equality of the number, kinds, and net electric charge of reacting species on each side of a chemical equation. **12.** *Math.* Equality with respect to the net number of reduced symbolic quantities on each side of an equation. **13.** A balance wheel. **14. Balance.** Libra. —*v.* **-anced, -anc·ing, -anc·es.** —*tr.* **1.** To weigh in or as if in a balance. **2.** To compare by or as if by weighing in the mind. **3.** To bring into or maintain in a state of equilibrium. **4.** To act as an equalizing weight or force to; counterbalance. **5.** *Accounting.* **a.** To compute the difference between the debits and credits of (an account). **b.** To reconcile or equalize the sums of the debits and credits of (an account). **c.** To settle by paying what is owed. **6.** To bring into or keep in equal or satisfying proportion or harmony. **7.** *Math.* To bring (an equation) into mathematical balance. **8.** *Chem.* To bring (a chemical equation) into chemical balance. **9.** To move toward and then away from (a dance partner). —*intr.* **1.** To be in or come into equilibrium. **2.** To be equal or equivalent. **3.** To sway or waver as if losing or regaining equilibrium. **4.** To move toward and then away from a dance partner. ***—idiom.* in the balance.** In an undetermined and often critical position. [ME *balaunce* < OFr. < VLat. **bilancia,* having two scale pans < Lat. *bilanx* : *bi-,* two + *lanx,* scale.]

balance beam *n.* **1.** A narrow horizontal wooden beam raised about four feet above the floor that is used in gymnastic competition for balancing exercises. **2.** A competitive gymnastics event in which various balancing feats are performed on the balance beam.

balance of payments *n.* A systematic record of a nation's total payments to foreign countries, including the price of imports, the outflow of capital and gold, and the total receipts from abroad, including the price of exports and the inflow of capital and gold.

balance of power *n.* A distribution of power whereby no one nation is able to dominate or interfere with others.

balance of trade *n.* The difference in value between the total exports and total imports of a nation.

bal·anc·er (băl′ən-sər) *n.* **1.** One that balances. **2.** A halter.

balance sheet *n.* A statement of the assets and liabilities of a business or individual at a specified date.

balance wheel *n.* A wheel that regulates rate of movement in machine parts, as in a watch.

bal·as (băl′əs) *n.* A rose-red to orange spinel. [ME < OF *balais* < Med. Lat. *balascus* < Ar. *bálakhsh* < Pers. *Badhakhshān,* a region in Afghanistan.]

ba·la·ta (bə-lä′tə) *n.* **1.** A tropical American tree, *Manilkara bidentata* (or *Mimusops balata*), that yields a latexlike sap. **2.** A tough, nonelastic, rubberlike gum obtained from the sap of the balata and used for golf-ball covers, industrial belting, and gaskets. [Am. Sp. (West Indies), of Cariban orig.]

bal·bo·a (băl-bō′ə) *n.* See table at **currency.** [After Vasco Núñez de *Balboa* (1475–1519).]

bal·brig·gan (băl-brĭg′ən) *n.* A knitted unbleached-cotton underwear fabric. [After *Balbriggan,* Ireland.]

bal·co·ny (băl′kə-nē) *n., pl.* **-nies. 1.** A platform that projects from the wall of a building and is surrounded by a railing, balustrade, or parapet. **2.** A gallery that projects over the main floor in a theater or auditorium. [Ital. *balcone* < OItal., scaffold, of Germanic orig.]

bald (bôld) *adj.* **-er, -est. 1.** Lacking hair on the top of the head. **2.** Lacking a natural or usual covering: *a bald spot on the lawn.* **3.** Having white feathers or markings on the head. **4.** Lacking ornament; unadorned. **5.** Undisguised; blunt: *a bald statement.* [ME *balled.*] **—bald′ly** *adv.* **—bald′ness** *n.*

bal·da·chin (bôl′də-kĭn, băl′-) also **bal·da·chi·no** (băl′-də-kē′nō) *n., pl.* **-chins** also **-chi·nos. 1.** A rich fabric of silk and gold brocade. **2.** A canopy of fabric carried in church processions or placed over an altar, throne, or dais. **3.** *Archit.* A stone or marble structure built in the form of a canopy, esp. over the altar of a church. [Ital. *baldacchino* < OItal. < *Baldacco,* Baghdad.]

bald cypress *n.* A cone-bearing but deciduous tree, *Taxodium distichum,* of the southeastern United States, growing in swamps and damp ground.

bald eagle *n.* A North American eagle, *Haliaeetus leucocephalus,* having a dark body and a white head and tail.

bal·der·dash (bôl′dər-dăsh′) *n.* Nonsense. [Orig. unknown.]

bald-faced (bôld′fāst′) *adj.* Brash; barefaced.

bald·head (bôld′hĕd′) *n.* **1.** A person whose head is bald. **2.** Any of several birds having white markings on the head.

bald·ing (bôl′dĭng) *adj. Informal.* Becoming bald.

bald·pate (bôld′pāt′) *n.* **1.** A baldheaded person. **2.** The widgeon.

bal·dric (bôl′drĭk) *n.* A belt, usually of ornamented leather, worn across the chest to support a sword or bugle. [ME *baudrik,* prob. < OFr. *baudre.*]

Bald·win (bôl′dwĭn) *n.* A red-skinned American variety of apple. [After Loammi *Baldwin* (1740–1807).]

bale[1] (bāl) *n.* A large bound and often wrapped package of raw or finished material. —*tr.v.* **baled, bal·ing, bales.** To wrap in bales. [ME, perh. < OFr., of Germanic orig.] **—bal′er** *n.*

bale[2] (bāl) *n.* **1.** Evil. **2.** Mental suffering; anguish. [ME < OE *balu.*]

ba·leen (bə-lēn′) *n.* Whalebone (sense 1). [ME *balene* < OFr. *baleine* < Lat. *ba-laena,* whale < Gk. *phalaina.*]

bale·ful (bāl′fəl) *adj.* **1.** Harmful or malignant in intent or effect. **2.** Portending evil; ominous. **—bale′ful·ly** *adv.* **—bale′ful·ness** *n.*

Usage: *Baleful* and *baneful* overlap in meaning, but *baleful* usually applies to that which menaces or foreshadows evil: *a baleful look. Baneful* is said most often of that which is actually harmful or destructive: *baneful effects of his foreign policy.*

Ba·li·nese (bä′lə-nēz′, -nēs′) *n.* **1.** A native or inhabitant of Bali. **2.** The Indonesian language of Bali. **—Ba′li·nese′** *adj.*

balk also **baulk** (bôk) —*v.* **balked, balk·ing, balks** also **baulked, baulk·ing, baulks.** —*intr.* **1.** To stop short and refuse to go on. **2.** To refuse obstinately or abruptly: *balked at the very idea of compromise.* **3. a.** To make an illegal motion before pitching a baseball. **b.** In other sports, to make an incomplete or misleading motion. —*tr.* **1.** To put obstacles in the way of; check or thwart. **2.** *Archaic.* To let go by; miss. **3.** To move one or more baseball runners ahead one base by balking. —*n.* **1.** A hindrance, check, or defeat. **2.** *Sports.* An incomplete or misleading motion, esp. an illegal move made by a baseball pitcher. **3. a.** An unplowed strip of land. **b.** A ridge between furrows. **4.** A wooden beam or rafter. **5.** One of the spaces between the cushion and the balk line on a billiard table. [ME *balken,* to plow up in ridges < *balk,* ridge < OE *balc.*] **—balk′er** *n.*

Bal·kan (bôl′kən) *adj.* **1.** Of or pertaining to the Balkan Peninsula or the Balkan Mountains. **2.** Of or pertaining to the Balkan States or their inhabitants.

Bal·kan·ize also **bal·kan·ize** (bôl′kə-nīz′) *tr.v.* **-ized, -iz·ing, -iz·es.** To divide (a region or territory) into small, often hostile units. [From the political division of the Balkans in the early 20th cent.] **—Bal′kan·i·za′tion** *n.*

balk line also **balk·line** (bôk′līn′) *n.* A line parallel to one end of a billiard table from behind which opening shots with the cue ball are made.

balk·y (bô′kē) *adj.* **-i·er, -i·est.** Tending to balk; obstinate: *a balky horse.* **—balk′i·ness** *n.*

ball[1] (bôl) *n.* **1. a.** A spherical or almost spherical body. **b.** A spherical entity: *a ball of flame.* **2. a.** Any of various rounded movable objects used in sports and games. **b.** A game, esp. baseball, played with such an object. **c.** A ball moving, thrown, hit, or kicked in a particular manner: *a low ball; a fair ball.* **d.** A pitched baseball not swung at by the batter that does not pass through the strike zone. **3. a.** A solid projectile of spherical or pointed shape, as that shot from a cannon. **b.** Projectiles of this kind collectively. **4.** A rounded part or protuberance, esp. of the body: *the ball of the foot.* **5. balls. a.** *Vulgar Slang.* The testicles. **b.** *Slang.* Courage, esp. of a reckless or presumptuous nature. —*v.* **balled, ball·ing, balls.** —*tr.* **1.** To form into a ball. **2.** *Vulgar Slang.* To have sexual intercourse with. —*intr.* **1.** To become formed into a ball. **2.** *Vulgar Slang.* To have sexual intercourse. ***—phrasal verb.* ball up.** *Slang.* To confuse or bungle. ***—idiom.* on the ball.** *Slang.* **1.** Alert, competent, or efficient. **2.** Having qualities, as competence, that might assure success: *had a lot on the ball; had nothing on the ball.* [ME *bal* < ON *böllr.*]

ball[2] (bôl) *n.* **1.** A formal gathering for social dancing. **2.** *Slang.* A very enjoyable time or experience. [Fr. *bal* < OFr. < *baller,* to dance < LLat. *ballare* < Gk. *ballizein.*]

bal·lad (băl′əd) *n.* **1.** A narrative poem, often of folk origin and intended to be sung, consisting of simple stanzas and usually having a recurrent refrain. **2.** The music for a ballad. **3.** A popular song esp. of a romantic or sentimental nature. [ME < OFr. *ballade* < OProv. *balada,* song sung while dancing < *balar,* to dance < LLat. *ballare,* to dance. —see BALL[2].] **—bal·lad′ic** (bə-lăd′ĭk, bă-) *adj.*

bal·lade (bə-läd′, bă-) *n.* **1.** A verse form usually consisting of three stanzas of eight or ten lines each, with the same concluding line in each stanza and an envoy, or brief final stanza, ending with the same last line as that of the preceding stanzas. **2.** A musical composition, usually for the piano, having the romantic or dramatic quality of a ballad. [ME < OFr., ballad.]

bal·lad·eer (băl′ə-dîr′) *n.* A ballad singer.

bal·lad·ist (băl′ə-dĭst′) *n.* A singer or writer of ballads.

bal·lad·ry (băl′ə-drē) *n.* Ballads collectively.

ballad stanza *n.* A four-line stanza often used in ballads, rhyming in the second and fourth lines and having four metrical feet in the first and third lines and three in the second and fourth.

ball-and-sock·et joint (bôl′ən-sŏk′ĭt) *n.* A joint consisting of a spherical knob or knoblike part fitted into a socket so that some degree of motion is possible in nearly any direction.

bal·last (băl′əst) *n.* **1.** Heavy material that is placed in the hold of a ship or the gondola of a balloon to enhance stability. **2.** Coarse gravel or crushed rock laid to form a bed for

balance beam

bald cypress

bale[1]

roads or railroads. **3.** Something that gives stability, esp. in character. —*tr.v.* **-last·ed, -last·ing, -lasts. 1.** To stabilize or provide with ballast. **2.** To fill (a railroad bed) with or as if with ballast. [Perh. < OSwed. or ODan. *barlast* : *bar,* bare + *last,* load.]

ball bearing *n.* **1.** A friction-reducing bearing consisting essentially of a ring-shaped track containing freely revolving hard metal balls against which a rotating shaft or other part turns. **2.** A hard ball used in a ball bearing.

ball carrier *n. Football.* The player carrying the ball on an offensive play.

ball cock *n.* A self-regulating device controlling the supply of water in a tank, cistern, or toilet by means of a float connected to a valve that opens or closes with a change in water level.

ball control *n. Sports.* An offensive strategy, esp. in football and basketball, in which a team attempts to keep possession of the ball for long periods of time or deliberately slows the pace of the game.

bal·le·ri·na (băl′ə-rē′nə) *n.* A female ballet dancer. [Ital. < *ballare,* to dance < LLat. < Gk. *ballizein.*]

bal·let (bă-lā′, băl′ā′) *n.* **1.** An artistic dance form characterized by grace and precision of movement and an elaborate formal technique. **2.** A theatrical presentation of group or solo dancing to a musical accompaniment, usually using costume and scenic effects and conveying a story, theme, or atmosphere. **3.** A musical composition written or used for ballet. **4.** A company or group that performs ballet. [Fr. < Ital. *balletto,* dim. of *ballo,* dance < *ballare,* to dance. —see BALLERINA.] —**bal·let′ic** (bă-lĕt′ĭk) *adj.*

bal·let·o·mane (bă-lĕt′ə-măn′) *n.* An ardent admirer of the ballet. [Back-formation < BALLETOMANIA.] —**bal·let′o·ma′ni·a** (-ə-mā′nē-ə, -mān′yə) *n.*

ball·flow·er (bôl′flou′ər) *n. Archit.* An ornament in the form of a ball cupped in the petals of a circular flower.

ball game *n.* **1.** A game, esp. baseball, that is played with a ball. **2.** *Informal.* **a.** A competition, such as a political race. **b.** A particular condition or situation.

bal·lis·ta (bə-lĭs′tə) *n., pl.* **-tae** (-tē′). A military engine used in ancient and medieval warfare to hurl heavy projectiles. [Lat. < Gk. *ballein,* to throw.]

bal·lis·tic (bə-lĭs′tĭk) *adj.* **1.** Of or pertaining to ballistics. **2.** Of or pertaining to projectiles, their motion, or their effects. [< BALLISTA.] —**bal·lis′ti·cal·ly** *adv.*

ballistic missile *n.* A projectile that assumes a free-falling trajectory after an internally guided, self-powered ascent.

bal·lis·tics (bə-lĭs′tĭks) *n. (used with a sing. verb).* **1. a.** The study of the dynamics of projectiles. **b.** The study of the flight characteristics of projectiles. **2. a.** The study of the functioning of firearms. **b.** The study of the firing, flight, and effect of ammunition. —**bal′lis·ti′cian** (băl′ĭ-stĭsh′ən) *n.*

bal·lis·to·car·di·o·gram (bə-lĭs′tō-kär′dē-ə-grăm′) *n.* A recording made by a ballistocardiograph. [BALLIST(IC) + CARDIOGRAM.]

bal·lis·to·car·di·o·graph (bə-lĭs′tō-kär′dē-ə-grăf′) *n.* A device used to measure the volume of blood passing through the heart in a specific period of time by measuring the body's recoil against the ejection movements of the heart's ventricular muscles. [BALLIST(IC) + CARDIOGRAPH.]

bal·lis·to·pho·bi·a (bə-lĭs′tə-fō′bē-ə) *n.* A psychologically aberrant fear of projectiles. [BALLIST(IC) + -PHOBIA.]

ball lightning *n.* A phenomenon associated with thunderstorms that is usually thought to consist of a moving luminous sphere of ionized gas.

ball of fire *n.* A highly energetic or dynamic person.

ball of wax *n. Informal.* An unspecified set of items or circumstances: *went shopping, had dinner, saw a play—the whole ball of wax.*

bal·lo·net (băl′ə-nā′) *n.* One of several small auxiliary gasbags placed inside a balloon or a nonrigid airship that can be inflated or deflated during flight to control and maintain shape and buoyancy. [Fr. *ballonnet,* dim. *ballon,* balloon.]

balloon
Hot-air balloons

bal·loon (bə-lo͞on′) *n.* **1 a.** A spherical, flexible, nonporous bag inflated with a gas lighter than air, such as helium, that causes it to rise and float in the atmosphere. **b.** Such a bag with sufficient capacity to lift a suspended gondola. **2.** Any of variously shaped, brightly colored inflatable rubber bags used as toys. **3.** A rounded or irregularly shaped outline containing the words a character in a cartoon is represented as saying. —*v.* **-looned, -loon·ing, -loons.** —*intr.* **1.** To ascend or ride in a balloon. **2.** To expand or swell out like a balloon. **3.** To increase or rise quickly. —*tr.* To cause to expand by or as if by inflating. —*adj.* Having periodic payments that are insufficient to pay back a note, thereby requiring a large final payment: *a balloon mortgage.* [Fr. *ballon* < Ital. *pallone,* aug. of *palla,* ball, of Germanic orig.] —**bal·loon′ist** *n.*

Baltimore oriole

balloon sail *n.* A comparatively large foresail used when going before the wind to supplement or replace a jib.

balloon tire *n.* A pneumatic tire with a wide tread, inflated to low pressure.

bal·lot (băl′ət) *n.* **1.** A sheet of paper used to cast or register a vote, esp. a secret vote. **2.** The act, process, or method of voting, esp. by the use of secret ballots. **3.** A list of candidates running for office; ticket. **4.** The total of all votes cast in an election. **5.** The right to vote; franchise. **6.** A small ball used to register a vote. —*intr.v.* **-lot·ed, -lot·ing, -lots. 1.** To cast a ballot; vote. **2.** To draw lots. [Ital. *ballotta,* dim. of *balla,* ball, of Germanic orig.] —**bal′lot·er** *n.*

bal·lotte·ment (bə-lŏt′mənt) *n.* A technique for detecting or examining a floating object in the body, as: **a.** The use of a finger to push sharply against the uterus and detect the presence or position of a fetus by its return impact. **b.** A test for a floating kidney in which the kidney is moved by alternating external digital pressures. [Fr. < *ballotter,* to toss < *ballotte,* dim. of *balle,* ball, of Germanic orig.]

ball·park also **ball park** (bôl′pärk′) *n.* A park or stadium in which ball games are played. —*idiom.* **in the ballpark.** *Informal.* Within the proper range; approximately right.

ball-point pen (bôl′point′) *n.* A pen having as its writing point a small ball bearing that transfers ink stored in a cartridge onto a writing surface.

ball·room (bôl′ro͞om′, -ro͝om′) *n.* A large room for dancing.

balls·y (bôl′zē) *adj.* **-i·er, -i·est.** *Slang.* Tough; gutsy.

ball valve *n.* A valve regulated by the position of a free-floating ball that moves in response to fluid or mechanical pressure.

bal·ly·hoo (băl′ē-ho͞o′) *Informal.* —*n., pl.* **-hoos. 1.** Sensational or clamorous advertising. **2.** Noisy shouting or uproar. —*tr.v.* **-hooed, -hoo·ing, -hoos.** To advertise by sensational methods. [Orig. unknown.]

bal·ly·rag (băl′ē-răg′) *v.* Variant of **bullyrag.**

balm (bäm) *n.* **1.** An aromatic, oily resin exuded by various chiefly tropical trees and shrubs and used in medicine. **2.** An aromatic ointment, oil, or unguent. **3. a.** An aromatic herb, *Melissa officinalis,* native to Eurasia, having clusters of small, fragrant white flowers. **b.** Any of several similar aromatic plants. **4.** A pleasing aromatic fragrance. **5.** Something that soothes, heals, or comforts. [ME *baume* < OFr. *basme* < Lat. *balsamum,* balsam.]

bal·ma·caan (băl′mə-kăn′, -kän′) *n.* A loose, full overcoat with raglan sleeves, originally made of rough woolen cloth. [After *Balmacaan,* an estate near Inverness, Scotland.]

balm of Gil·e·ad (gĭl′ē-əd, -ăd′) *n.* **1.** An aromatic evergreen tree of the genus *Commiphora,* esp. *C. opobalsamum,* of Africa and Asia Minor. **2.** A fragrant resin obtained from the balm of Gilead. **3.** A North American deciduous tree, *Populus candicans,* having broad, heart-shaped leaves. **4.** A fragrant resin obtained from the balsam fir. [After *Gilead,* region of ancient Palestine known for its balm.]

Bal·mor·al (băl-môr′əl, -mŏr′-) *n.* **1.** A brimless Scottish cap with a flat, round top. **2.** Often **balmoral.** A heavy, laced walking shoe. [After *Balmoral* Castle, Scotland.]

balm·y (bä′mē) *adj.* **-i·er, -i·est. 1.** Having the quality or fragrance of balm. **2.** Mild and pleasant: *a balmy breeze.* **3.** *Slang.* Eccentric in behavior. —**balm′i·ly** *adv.* —**balm′i·ness** *n.*

bal·ne·ol·o·gy (băl′nē-ŏl′ə-jē) *n.* Medical therapy with mineral baths. [Lat. *balneum,* bath + -LOGY.]

ba·lo·ney also **bo·lo·ney** (bə-lō′nē) *n., pl.* **-neys. 1.** *Informal.* Variant of **bologna. 2.** *Slang.* Nonsense.

bal·sa (bôl′sə) *n.* **1.** A tree, *Ochroma lagopus,* of tropical America, having wood that is unusually light in weight. **2.** The wood of the balsa tree. **3.** A raft consisting of a frame fastened to buoyant cylinders of wood or metal. [Sp.]

bal·sam (bôl′səm) *n.* **1. a.** An oily or gummy oleoresin, usually containing benzoic or cinnamic acids, obtained from the exudations of any of various trees and shrubs and used as a base for cough syrups, other medications, and perfumes. **b.** A similar substance, esp. a fragrant ointment used as medication. **2.** Any of various trees yielding an aromatic, resinous substance, esp. the balsam fir. **3.** Any of several plants of the genus *Impatiens,* esp. *I. balsamina,* cultivated for its double flowers of various colors. [Lat. *balsamum* < Gk. *balsamon.*] —**bal·sam′ic** (-săm′ĭk) *adj.*

balsam fir *n.* An evergreen tree, *Abies balsamea,* of northeastern North America, having small needles and cones about 2½ inches long.

balsam of Pe·ru (pə-ro͞o′) *n.* The aromatic resin of a tropical American tree, *Myroxylon pereirae,* used in the manufacture of perfumes and other products.

balsam of To·lu (tə-lo͞o′) *n.* The aromatic resin of a tropical American tree, *Myroxylon toluiferum,* used in cough remedies and in the manufacture of perfumes.

balsam pear *n.* A tropical vine, *Momordica charantia,* native to the Old World, having yellow-orange fruit.

balsam poplar *n.* A North American tree, *Populis balsamifera,* having large buds coated with a gummy, fragrant resin.

Balt (bôlt) *n.* A member of the Baltic-speaking people inhabiting the southeastern shores of the Baltic Sea and formerly occupying a wide area bounded by Danzig (Gdańsk), Riga, Moscow, and Kiev.

Bal·tic (bôl′tĭk) *adj.* **1.** Of or pertaining to the Baltic Sea or to the Baltic States and their inhabitants or cultures. **2.** Of or relating to the branch of the Indo-European language family that contains Latvian, Lithuanian, and Old Prussian. —*n.* The Baltic language branch.

Bal·ti·more oriole (bôl′tə-môr′, -mōr′) *n.* An American songbird, *Icterus galbula,* of which the male has bright orange, black, and white plumage. [After George Calvert (1580?–1632), 1st Lord *Baltimore.*]

Bal·to-Sla·vic (bôl′tō-slä′vĭk, -slăv′ĭk) *n.* A subfamily of the

Indo-European language family that consists of the Baltic and Slavic branches. **—Bal'to-Sla'vic** *adj.*

Ba·lu·chi (bə-lo͞o'chē) *n., pl.* **Baluchi** or **-chis. 1.** A native or inhabitant of Baluchistan. **2.** The Iranian language of the Baluchi.

bal·us·ter (băl'ə-stər) *n.* One of the posts or supports of a handrail. [Fr. *balustre* < Ital. *balaustro* < *balaustra,* pomegranate flower (from a resemblance to the post) < Lat. *balaustium* < Gk. *balaustion.*]

bal·us·trade (băl'ə-strād') *n.* A rail and the row of posts that support it, as along the edge of a staircase. [Fr. < Ital. *balustrade* < *balaustro,* baluster.]

Bam·ba·ra (bäm-bä'rä) *n., pl.* **Bambara** or **-ras. 1.** A Negroid people of the upper Niger River valley. **2.** A member of the Bambara. **3.** The Mande language of the Bambara.

bam·bi·no (băm-bē'nō, bäm-) *n., pl.* **-nos** or **-ni** (-nē). **1.** A child; baby. **2.** A representation of the infant Jesus. [Ital., dim. of *bambo,* child.]

bam·boo (băm-bo͞o') *n., pl.* **-boos. 1.** Any of various mostly tropical grasses of the genus *Bambusa,* having hard-walled stems with ringed joints. **2.** The hollow woody stems of the bamboo, used in a variety of constructions, crafts, and manufactures. **3.** Any of various tall, bamboolike grasses of the genera *Arundinaria, Phyllostachys,* and *Dendrocalamus.* [Orig. unknown.]

Bamboo Curtain *n.* A political and esp. an ideological barrier in Asia, esp. China.

bam·boo·zle (băm-bo͞o'zəl) *tr.v.* **-zled, -zling, -zles.** *Informal.* To trick or deceive by elaborate misinformation; hoodwink. [Orig. unknown.] **—bam·boo'zle·ment** *n.*

ban[1] (băn) *tr.v.* **banned, ban·ning, bans. 1.** To prohibit, esp. by official decree. **2.** *Archaic.* To curse; execrate. *—n.* **1.** In feudal times, a summons to arms. **2.** An excommunication or condemnation by church officials. **3.** A prohibition imposed by law or official decree. **4.** Censure, esp. through public opinion. **5.** A curse; imprecation. [ME *bannen,* to summon, banish, curse, partly < OE *bannan,* to summon, and partly < ON *banna,* to prohibit, curse.]

ban[2] (bän) *n., pl.* **ba·ni** (bä'nē). See table at **currency.** [Rum. < Serbo-Croatian *bān,* warlord.]

ba·nal (bə-näl', -năl', bā'nəl) *adj.* Lacking freshness or originality; hackneyed. [Fr. < OFr., shared by tenants in a feudal jurisdiction < *ban,* summons to military service, of Germanic orig.] **—ba·nal'i·ty** (bə-năl'ĭ-tē, bā-) *n.* **—ba·nal'ly** *adv.*

ba·nan·a (bə-năn'ə) *n.* **1.** Any of several treelike tropical or subtropical plants of the genus *Musa,* esp. *M. sapientum,* a widely cultivated species having long, broad leaves and hanging clusters of edible fruit. **2.** The crescent-shaped fruit of a banana plant, having white, pulpy flesh and thick, easily removed yellow or reddish skin. [Port. and Sp., of African orig.]

banana oil *n.* **1.** A liquid mixture of nitrocellulose and amyl acetate, or a similar solvent, having a bananalike odor. **2.** Amyl acetate.

ba·nan·as (bə-năn'əz) *adj. Slang.* Crazy.

banana seat *n.* An elongated bicycle seat that usually curves upward in the back. [From its shape.]

banana split *n.* Several scoops of ice cream and usually flavored syrups or sauces, nuts, fruit, and whipped cream served on a banana split lengthwise.

band[1] (bănd) *n.* **1.** A thin strip of flexible material used to encircle and bind one object or to hold a number of objects together. **2.** A strip or stripe that contrasts with something else, as in color. **3. a. bands.** *Archaic.* A physical restraint; fetter. **b.** Something that constrains or binds morally or legally. **4.** A simple ungrooved ring, esp. a wedding ring. **5.** A narrow strip of fabric used to trim, finish, or reinforce articles of clothing. **6.** A neckband or collar. **7.** *Biol.* A chromatically or functionally differentiated strip or stripe in or on an organism. **8.** *Physics.* **a.** A range of some physical variable, as of radiation wavelength or frequency. **b.** A range of very closely spaced electron energy levels in solids, the distribution and nature of which determine the electrical properties of a material. **9.** Any of the distinct grooves on a long-playing phonograph record that contains an individual selection or separate section of a whole. **10.** The cords across the back of a book to which the quires or sheets are attached. *—tr.v.* **band·ed, band·ing, bands. 1.** To tie, bind, or encircle with or as if with a band. **2.** To mark or identify with or as if with a band. [ME, partly < ON *band,* and partly < OFr. *bande,* both of Germanic orig.]

band[2] (bănd) *n.* **1. a.** A group of people. **b.** A group of animals. **2.** A group of musicians who play as an ensemble. *—v.* **band·ed, band·ing, bands.** *—tr.* To assemble or unite in a group. *—intr.* To form a group; unite: *banded together for protection.* [OFr., prob. of Germanic orig.]

band·age (băn'dĭj) *n.* A strip of fabric or other material used as a protective covering for a wound or other injury. *—tr.v.* **-aged, -ag·ing, -ag·es.** To apply a bandage to. [Fr. < *bande,* band, strip.] **—band'ag·er** *n.*

Band-Aid (bănd'ād'). A trademark for an adhesive bandage with a gauze pad in the center, used for protecting minor wounds.

ban·dan·na or **ban·dan·a** (băn-dăn'ə) *n.* A large handkerchief usually figured and brightly colored. [Prob. < Port. < Hindi *bāndhnū,* a dyeing process in which cloth is knotted < *bāndhnā,* to tie < Skt. *badhnāti,* he ties.]

band·box (bănd'bŏks') *n.* A lightweight cylindrical box used to hold small articles of apparel.

ban·deau (băn-dō') *n., pl.* **-deaux** (-dōz') or **-deaus. 1.** A narrow band for the hair. **2.** A brassiere. [Fr. < OFr. *bandel,* dim. of *bande,* band, strip.]

ban·de·ri·lla (băn'də-rē'ə, -rēl'yə) *n.* A decorated barbed dart that is thrust into the bull's neck or shoulder muscles by a banderillero in a bullfight. [Sp., dim. of *bandera,* banner.]

ban·de·ri·lle·ro (băn'də-rē-âr'ō, -rēl-yâr'ō) *n., pl.* **-ros.** One who implants the banderillas in a bullfight. [Sp. < *banderilla,* banderilla.]

ban·de·role or **ban·de·rol** (băn'də-rōl') also **ban·ne·rol** (băn'ə-rōl') *n.* **1.** A narrow forked flag or streamer. **2.** A long ribbon or scroll bearing an inscription. [Fr. < Ital. *banderoula,* dim. of *bandiera,* banner.]

ban·di·coot (băn'dĭ-ko͞ot') *n.* **1.** Any of several ratlike marsupials of the family Peramelidae, of Australia and adjacent islands, having a long tapering snout and long hind legs. **2.** Any of several large rats of the genera *Bandicota* and *Nesokia,* of southeastern Asia. [Telegu *pandi-kokku* : *pandi,* pig + *kokku,* rat.]

ban·dit (băn'dĭt) *n., pl.* **-dits** or **ban·dit·ti** (băn-dĭt'ē). **1.** A robber, esp. a highwayman. **2.** An outlaw; gangster. **3.** One who cheats or exploits others. [Ital. *bandito* < *bandire,* to band together, prob. of Germanic orig.] **—ban'dit·ry** *n.*

band·mas·ter (bănd'măs'tər) *n.* One who conducts a musical band.

ban·dog (băn'dôg', -dŏg') *n.* A dog kept chained as a watchdog or because of its ferocious nature. [ME *band-dogge.*]

ban·do·leer or **ban·do·lier** (băn'də-lîr') *n.* A belt fitted with small pockets or loops for carrying cartridges and worn across the chest by soldiers. [Fr. *bandoulière* < Sp. *bandolera,* dim. of *banda,* band, prob. of Germanic orig.]

ban·dore (băn'dôr', -dōr') also **ban·do·ra** (băn-dôr'ə, -dōr'ə) *n.* An ancient musical instrument resembling a guitar. [Port. *bandurra* < LLat. *pandura* < Gk. *pandoura.*]

band-pass filter (bănd'păs') *n.* An electric filter that blocks all signals but those within a selected frequency range.

band saw *n.* A power saw consisting essentially of a toothed metal band coupled to and continuously driven around the circumferences of two wheels.

band shell *n.* A bandstand with a concave, almost hemispheric wall at the rear that serves as a sounding board.

bands·man (băndz'mən) *n.* A musician in a band.

band·stand (bănd'stănd') *n.* A platform or stand, often roofed, for a band or orchestra.

band·wag·on (bănd'wăg'ən) *n.* **1.** An elaborately decorated wagon used to transport musicians in a parade. **2.** A cause or party that attracts increasing numbers of adherents.

band·width (bănd'wĭdth', -wĭth') *n.* The range of consecutive frequencies comprising a band.

ban·dy (băn'dē) *tr.v.* **-died, -dy·ing, -dies. 1. a.** To toss or throw back and forth. **b.** To hit (a ball, for example) back and forth. **2. a.** To give and take (words); exchange. **b.** To discuss in a casual or frivolous manner. **3.** To use lightly or indiscriminately. *—adj.* Bowed or bent in an outward curve: *bandy legs.* *—n., pl.* **-dies. 1.** A game similar to modern field hockey. **2.** A stick, bent at one end, used in playing bandy. [Orig. unknown.]

ban·dy-leg·ged (băn'dē-lĕg'ĭd) *adj.* Having legs that bend outward; bowlegged.

bane (bān) *n.* **1.** *Archaic.* Fatal injury or ruin. **2.** A cause of death, destruction, or ruin. **3.** A deadly poison. [ME, destroyer < OE *bana.*]

bane·ber·ry (bān'bĕr'ē) *n.* **1.** A plant of the genus *Actaea,* having clusters of white flowers and red or white poisonous berries. **2.** The berry of a baneberry plant.

bane·ful (bān'fəl) *adj.* Causing death, destruction, or ruin; harmful. —See Usage note at **baleful. —bane'ful·ly** *adv.*

bang[1] (băng) *n.* **1.** A sudden loud noise, as of an explosion. **2.** A sudden loud blow or bump. **3.** *Informal.* A sudden burst of action. **4.** *Slang.* A sense of excitement; thrill. *—v.* **banged, bang·ing, bangs.** *—tr.* **1.** To strike heavily and often repeatedly; bump. **2.** To close suddenly and loudly; slam. **3.** To handle noisily or violently. **4.** *Vulgar Slang.* To have sexual intercourse with. *—intr.* **1.** To make a sudden loud, explosive noise. **2.** To crash noisily against or into something. ***—phrasal verbs.*** **bang away. 1.** To assail insistently, esp. with questions. **2.** To work diligently and often at length. **bang up.** To damage extensively: *banged up the car.* *—adv.* Exactly; precisely: *The arrow hit bang on the target.* [Prob. of Scand. orig.]

bang[2] (băng) *n.* Often **bangs.** A fringe of hair cut short and straight across the forehead. *—tr.v.* **banged, bang·ing, bangs.** To cut in a bang. [Perh. short for BANGTAIL.]

bang[3] (băng) *n.* Variant of **bhang.**

ban·ga·lore torpedo (băng'gə-lôr') *n.* A piece of metal pipe filled with an explosive, used primarily to clear a path through barbed wire or to detonate land mines. [After *Bangalore,* India.]

bang·er (băng'ər) *n. Chiefly Brit.* **1.** A sausage. **2.** A noisy old car.

banana

bandoleer

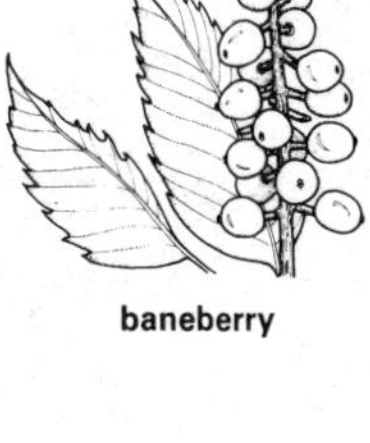

baneberry

bang·kok (băng′kŏk′, băng-kŏk′) *n.* A hat made of a fine straw. [After *Bangkok,* Thailand.]
ban·gle (băng′gəl) *n.* **1.** A rigid bracelet or anklet, esp. one with no clasp. **2.** An ornament that hangs from a bracelet or necklace. [Hindi *baṅgrī,* glass bracelet.]
Bang's disease (băngz) *n.* Brucellosis. [After Bernhard L. F. *Bang* (1848–1932).]
bang·tail (băng′tāl′) *n. Slang.* A racehorse. [BANG- + TAIL.]
bang-up (băng′ŭp′) *adj. Slang.* Very good; excellent: *a bang-up job.*
ba·ni (bä′nē) *n.* Plural of **ban[2]**.
ban·ian (băn′yən) *n.* **1.** A Hindu merchant or trader belonging to a caste whose members eat no meat. **2.** Variant of **banyan.** [Port. < Gujarati, *vāṇiyo* < Skt. *vāṇija,* a merchant.]
ban·ish (băn′ĭsh) *tr.v.* **-ished, -ish·ing, -ish·es. 1.** To force to leave a country or place by official decree; exile. **2.** To drive away; expel: *banish all doubts and fears.* [ME *banishen* < OFr. *banir, baniss-,* of Germanic orig.] **—ban′ish·er** *n.* **—ban′ish·ment** *n.*

Synonyms: *banish, exile, expatriate, deport, transport, extradite.* These verbs mean to send away from a place of residence. *Banish* applies broadly to forced departure from a country by official decree. *Exile* specifies departure from one's country, either through compulsion or voluntary action. *Expatriate* pertains to departure from one's native country, forced or voluntary, and usually implies formal change of citizenship. *Deport* denotes the act of sending an alien abroad by governmental order. *Transport* pertains to the sending abroad (usually to a penal colony) of one convicted of a crime. *Extradite* applies to the delivery of an accused or convicted person to the state or country having jurisdiction over him.

banjo

ban·is·ter also **ban·nis·ter** (băn′ĭ-stər) *n.* **1.** A baluster. **2.** The handrail or balustrade of a staircase. [Var. of BALUSTER.]
ban·jo (băn′jō) *n., pl.* **-jos** or **-joes.** A fretted stringed instrument having a narrow neck and a hollow circular body with a stretched diaphragm of vellum upon which the bridge rests. [Prob. of African orig.] **—ban′jo·ist** *n.*
bank[1] (băngk) *n.* **1.** A piled-up mass, as of snow or clouds. **2.** A steep natural incline. **3.** An artificial embankment. **4.** The slope of land adjoining a body of water. **5.** A large elevated area of a sea floor. **6.** The cushion of a billiard or pool table. **7.** The lateral tilting of an aircraft executed in a turn. *—v.* **banked, bank·ing, banks.** *—tr.* **1.** To border or protect with a ridge or embankment. **2.** To pile up; amass: *bank earth along a wall.* **3.** To cover (a fire), as with ashes or fresh fuel, to ensure continued low burning. **4.** To construct with a slope rising to the outside edge. **5.** To tilt (an aircraft) laterally in flight. **6.** In billiards, to strike (a ball) so that it rebounds from the table's cushion. *—intr.* **1.** To rise in or take the form of a bank. **2.** To tilt an aircraft laterally when turning. [ME, of Scand. orig.]
bank[2] (băngk) *n.* **1. a.** A business establishment in which money is kept for saving or commercial purposes or is invested, supplied for loans, or exchanged. **b.** The offices or building in which such an establishment is located. **2. a.** The funds of a gambling establishment. **b.** The funds held by a dealer or banker in some gambling games. **c.** The reserve pieces, cards, chips, or play money in some games, as poker, from which the players may draw. **3.** A supply or stock for use in emergencies: *a blood bank.* **4.** A place of safekeeping or storage: *a computer's memory bank.* **5.** *Obs.* A moneychanger's table or place of business. *—v.* **banked, bank·ing, banks.** *—tr.* To deposit in a bank. *—intr.* **1.** To transact business with a bank or maintain a bank account. **2.** To operate a bank. **—*phrasal verb.* bank on.** *Informal.* To have confidence in; rely on. [Fr. *banque* < Ital. *banca,* moneychanger's table, of Germanic orig.]
bank[3] (băngk) *n.* **1.** A set of similar or matched things arranged in a row, esp.: **a.** A set of elevators. **b.** A row of keys on a typewriter. **2.** A bench for rowers in a galley. **3.** The lines of type under a headline. *—tr.v.* **banked, bank·ing, banks.** To arrange or set up in a row: *streets banked with trees.* [ME, bench < OFr. *banc,* of Germanic orig.]
bank·a·ble (băng′kə-bəl) *adj.* **1.** Acceptable to or at a bank. **2.** Guaranteed to bring profit: *a bankable movie star.*
bank acceptance *n.* A draft or bill of exchange drawn upon and accepted by a bank.
bank account *n.* Funds deposited in a bank that are credited to and subject to withdrawal by the depositor.
bank annuities *pl.n. Chiefly Brit.* Consols.
bank·book (băngk′bo͝ok′) *n.* A book held by a depositor in which his deposits and withdrawals are recorded by the bank.
bank·card (băngk′kärd′) *n.* A credit card issued by a bank.
bank discount *n.* The interest on a loan computed in advance and deducted at the time the loan is made.
bank·er[1] (băng′kər) *n.* **1.** A person who owns or serves as an officer of a bank. **2.** The player in charge of the bank in some gambling games.
bank·er[2] (băng′kər) *n.* A person or boat engaged in cod fishing on the Newfoundland banks.
bank·er[3] (băng′kər) *n.* A workbench used by masons and sculptors. [< BANK[3], bench (obs.).]

banyan

banker's acceptance *n.* A bank acceptance.
bank holiday *n.* **1.** A day on which banks are legally closed. **2.** *Chiefly Brit.* A legal holiday when banks are ordered to remain closed.
bank·ing (băng′kĭng) *n.* **1.** The business of a bank. **2.** The occupation of a banker.
bank note *n.* A note issued by a bank representing its promise to pay a specific sum to the bearer on demand and acceptable as money.
bank paper *n.* **1.** Bank notes. **2.** Securities, drafts, bills of exchange, and other commercial paper acceptable by a bank.
bank rate *n.* The rate of discount established by a country's central bank.
bank·roll (băngk′rōl′) *n.* **1.** A roll of paper money. **2.** *Informal.* A person's ready cash. *—tr.v.* **-rolled, -roll·ing, -rolls.** To underwrite the expense of (a business venture, for example). **—bank′roll′er** *n.*
bank·rupt (băngk′rŭpt′, -rəpt) *n.* **1.** *Law.* A debtor who, upon voluntary petition or one invoked by his creditors, is judged legally insolvent and whose remaining property is administered for his creditors or distributed among them. **2.** A person who is devoid of a specific resource or quality: *an intellectual bankrupt.* *—adj.* **1.** Legally declared a bankrupt; insolvent. **2.** Financially ruined; impoverished. **3.** Depleted or destitute: *bankrupt of compassion.* *—tr.v.* **-rupt·ed, -rupt·ing, -rupts.** To cause to become bankrupt. [Fr. *banqueroute* < Ital. *bancarotta* : *banca,* moneychanger's table + *rotta,* p.part. of *rompere,* to break < Lat. *rumpere.*]
bank·rupt·cy (băngk′rŭpt′sē, -rəp-sē) *n.* **1.** The condition of being legally bankrupt. **2.** Impoverishment; destitution.
ban·ner (băn′ər) *n.* **1. a.** A piece of cloth attached to a staff and used as a standard by a monarch, knight, or military commander. **b.** The flag of a nation, state, army, or sovereign. **2.** A piece of cloth bearing a motto or legend, as of a club. **3.** A headline spanning the width of a newspaper page. **4.** A standard (sense 8.a.). *—adj.* Unusually good; outstanding: *a banner year for the company.* [ME *banere* < OFr. *baniere* < VLat. *bandaria < LLat. *bandum,* of Germanic orig.]
ban·ner·et[1] (băn′ər-ĭt, -ə-rĕt′) also **ban·ner·ette** (băn′ə-rĕt′) *n.* A small banner. [ME *baneret* < OFr. *banerete,* dim. of *baniere,* banner.]
ban·ner·et[2] (băn′ər-ĭt, -ə-rĕt′) *n.* A feudal knight entitled to lead men into battle under his own standard and ranking between knight bachelor and baron. [ME *baneret* < OFr. < *baniere,* banner.]
ban·ner·ette (băn′ə-rĕt′) *n.* Variant of **banneret[1]**.
ban·ner·ol (băn′ə-rōl′) *n.* Variant of **banderole.**
ban·nis·ter (băn′ĭ-stər) *n.* Variant of **banister.**
ban·nock (băn′ək) *n. Chiefly Brit. Regional.* A griddlecake, usually unleavened, made of oatmeal, barley, or wheat flour. [ME *bannok* < OE *bannuc* < Gael. *bannach.*]
banns (bănz) *pl.n.* An announcement, esp. in a church, of an intended marriage. [ME *banes,* pl. of *ban,* proclamation, partly < OE *gebann,* and partly < OFr. *ban,* of Germanic orig.]
ban·quet (băng′kwĭt) *n.* **1.** An elaborate and sumptuous repast. **2.** A ceremonial dinner honoring a particular guest or occasion. *—tr. & intr.v.* **-quet·ed, -quet·ing, -quets.** To entertain at or partake of a banquet. [OFr., dim. of *banc,* bench, of Germanic orig.] **—ban′quet·er** *n.*
banquet room *n.* A large room, as in a restaurant, suitable for banquets.
ban·quette (băng-kĕt′) *n.* **1.** A platform lining a trench or parapet wall on which soldiers may stand when firing. **2.** *Southern U.S.* A sidewalk. **3.** A long upholstered bench that is placed against or built into a wall. **4.** A ledge or shelf, as on a buffet. [Fr. < Prov. *banqueta,* dim. of *banca,* bench, of Germanic orig.]
ban·shee (băn′shē) *n.* A female spirit in Gaelic folklore believed to presage a death in the family by wailing. [Ir. Gael. *bean sidhe,* woman of the fairies.]
ban·tam (băn′təm) *n.* **1.** Any of various breeds of diminutive domestic fowl. **2.** A small but aggressive person. *—adj.* **1.** Diminutive; miniature. **2.** Spirited or aggressive. [After *Bantam,* Indonesia.]
ban·tam·weight (băn′təm-wāt′) *n.* A boxer in the weight class of 112 to 118 pounds.
ban·ter (băn′tər) *n.* Good-humored, playful conversation. *—v.* **-tered, -ter·ing, -ters.** *—tr.* To speak to in a playful or teasing way. *—intr.* To exchange mildly teasing remarks. [Orig. unknown.] **—ban′ter·er** *n.* **—ban′ter·ing·ly** *adv.*
bant·ling (bănt′lĭng) *n.* A young child. [Prob. alteration of G. *Bänkling,* bastard < *Bank,* bench < OHG.]
Ban·tu (băn′to͞o) *n., pl.* **Bantu** or **-tus. 1.** A member of any of several Negro tribes of central and southern Africa. **2.** A group of Niger-Congo languages spoken in central and southern Africa. **—Ban′tu** *adj.*
ban·yan also **ban·ian** (băn′yən) *n.* A tree, *Ficus benghalensis,* of tropical India and the East Indies, having large, oval leaves, reddish fruit, and many aerial roots that develop into additional trunks. [Var. of BANIAN.]
ban·zai (bän-zī′) *n.* A Japanese battle cry or patriotic cheer. [J., (may you live) ten thousand years < Chin. (Mandarin) *wan[4] sui[4]* : *wan[4],* ten thousand + *sui[4],* year.]

ban·zai attack *n.* A desperate attack by Japanese troops in World War II.
ba·o·bab (bā'ō-băb', bä'-) *n.* A tree, *Adansonia digitata,* of tropical Africa, having a trunk up to 30 feet in diameter, large, pendulous white flowers, and hard-shelled, fleshy fruit. [Prob. a native word in central Africa.]
bap·tism (băp'tĭz'əm) *n.* **1.** A Christian sacrament marked by the symbolic use of water to cleanse the recipient of original sin and resulting in admission into Christianity. **2.** A ceremony, trial, or experience by which one is initiated, purified, or given a name. **3.** In Christian Science, a submergence in Spirit or purification by Spirit. [ME *bapteme* < OFr. < LLat. *baptisma* < Gk. *baptismos* < *baptizein,* to baptize.] **—bap·tis'mal** (băp-tĭz'-məl) *adj.* **—bap·tis'mal·ly** *adv.*
baptism of fire *n.* **1.** A soldier's first experience of actual combat conditions. **2.** A severe ordeal experienced for the first time.
Bap·tist (băp'tĭst) *n.* **1.** A member of a Protestant denomination believing that the sacrament of baptism should be given only to adult members upon a profession of faith and usually by immersion. **2. baptist.** One who baptizes. **—Bap'tist** *adj.*
bap·tis·ter·y also **bap·tis·try** (băp'tĭ-strē) *n., pl.* **-ies** also **-tries. 1.** A part of a church or a separate building used for baptizing. **2.** A font used for baptism.
bap·tize (băp-tīz', băp'tīz') *v.* **-tized, -tiz·ing, -tiz·es.** *—tr.* **1.** To admit into Christianity by means of baptism. **2. a.** To cleanse or purify. **b.** To initiate. **3.** To give a first or Christian name to. *—intr.* To administer baptism. [ME *baptizen* < OFr. *baptiser* < LLat. *baptizare* < Gk. *baptizein* < *baptein,* to dip.] **—bap·tiz'er** *n.*
bar[1] (bär) *n.* **1.** A relatively long, straight, rigid piece of solid material used as a fastener, support, barrier, or structural or mechanical member. **2. a.** A solid oblong block of a substance, such as soap. **b.** A rectangular block of a precious metal. **3.** Something that impedes or prevents; obstacle. **4.** A ridge, as of sand or gravel, on a shore or stream bed that is formed by the action of tides or currents. **5.** A narrow marking, as a stripe or band. **6.** A pair of horizontal parallel lines across a heraldic shield. **7.** *Law.* **a.** The nullification, defeat, or prevention of a claim or action. **b.** The process by which this is accomplished. **8.** The railing in a courtroom enclosing the part of the room where the judges and lawyers sit, witnesses are heard, and prisoners are tried. **9.** A particular system of law courts. **10.** A tribunal or place of judgment. **11. a.** Lawyers collectively. **b.** The profession of law. **12.** *Mus.* **a.** A vertical line dividing a staff into equal measures. **b.** A measure. **13. a.** A counter at which drinks, esp. alcoholic drinks, and sometimes food are served. **b.** An establishment or room having such a counter. *—tr.v.* **barred, bar·ring, bars. 1.** To fasten securely with a bar. **2.** To shut in or out with or as if with bars. **3.** To obstruct or impede; block. **4.** To keep out; exclude. **5.** To mark with bars or stripes. **6.** *Law.* To stop (a claim or action) by legal objection. *—prep.* Excluding; except for: *his best performance, bar none.* [ME *barre* < OFr.]
bar[2] (bär) *n.* A unit of pressure equal to 10^5 newtons per square meter or 0.98697 standard atmosphere. [G. < Gk. *baros,* weight.]
bar– *pref.* Variant of **baro-.**
bar·a·the·a (băr'ə-thē'ə) *n.* A soft fabric of silk and cotton or silk and wool. [Orig. unknown.]
barb[1] (bärb) *n.* **1.** A sharp point projecting in reverse direction to the main point of a weapon or tool, as on an arrow. **2.** A cutting or biting remark. **3.** *Bot.* A hooked bristle or hairlike projection. **4.** One of the parallel filaments projecting from the main shaft of a feather. **5.** Any of various Old World freshwater fishes of the genus *Barbus* (or *Puntius*) and related genera. **6.** A linen covering for a woman's head, throat, and chin worn in medieval times. *—tr.v.* **barbed, barb·ing, barbs.** To provide or furnish with a barb. [ME *barbe* < OFr., beard < Lat. *barba.*]
barb[2] (bärb) *n.* **1.** A horse of a breed introduced into Spain from northern Africa by the Moors. **2.** One of a breed of domestic pigeons having dark plumage. [Fr. *barbe* < *Barbarie,* Barbary States.]
Bar·ba·dos cherry (bär-bā'dōs, -dəs) *n.* A tropical and semitropical American shrub, *Malpighia glabra,* bearing edible, acid red fruit.
bar·bar·i·an (bär-bâr'ē-ən) *n.* **1.** A member of a people considered by those of another nation or group to have a primitive civilization. **2.** A fierce, brutal, or cruel person. **3.** An insensitive, uncultured person; boor. [Fr. *barbarien* < Lat. *barbaria,* foreign country < *barbarus,* barbarous.] **—bar·bar'i·an·ism** *n.* **—bar·bar'i·cal·ly** *adv.*
bar·bar·ic (bär-băr'ĭk) *adj.* **1.** Of, pertaining to, or characteristic of barbarians. **2.** Marked by crudeness or lack of restraint in taste, style, or manner.
bar·ba·rism (bär'bə-rĭz'əm) *n.* **1.** An instance, act, trait, or custom characterized by brutality or coarseness. **2. a.** The use of words or forms considered incorrect or nonstandard in a language. **b.** A specific word or form so used. [OFr. *barbarisme* < Lat. *barbarismus* < Gk. *barbarismos,* foreign speech < *barbaros,* foreign.]
bar·bar·i·ty (bär-băr'ĭ-tē) *n., pl.* **-ties. 1.** Harsh or cruel conduct. **2.** An inhuman, brutal act. **3.** Crudity; coarseness.
bar·ba·rize (bär'bə-rīz') *tr. & intr.v.* **-rized, -riz·ing, -riz·es.** To make or become crude, savage, or barbarous. **—bar'ba·ri·za'tion** *n.*
bar·ba·rous (bär'bər-əs) *adj.* **1.** Primitive in culture and customs; uncivilized. **2.** Characterized by savagery; brutal. **3.** Lacking refinement or culture; coarse. **4.** Marked by the use or occurrence of barbarisms in language. [Lat. *barbarus* < Gk. *barbaros.*] **—bar'ba·rous·ly** *adv.* **—bar'ba·rous·ness** *n.*
Bar·ba·ry ape (bär'bə-rē) *n.* A tailless monkey, *Macaca sylvana,* of Gibraltar and northern Africa.
bar·bas·co (bär-băs'kō) *n., pl.* **-cos.** Any of several tropical American trees of the genus *Lonchocarpus,* used locally as the source of a poison for killing fish. [Am. Sp.]
bar·bate (bär'bāt') *adj.* Having a beard or tufted hairs resembling a beard. [Lat. *barbatus* < *barba,* beard.]
bar·be·cue (bär'bĭ-kyōō') *n.* **1.** A grill, pit, or outdoor fireplace for roasting meat. **2. a.** A whole animal carcass or section thereof roasted or broiled over an open fire or on a spit. **b.** A social gathering, usually held outdoors, at which food is prepared in this way. *—tr.v.* **-cued, -cu·ing, -cues.** To roast, broil, or grill (meat) over live coals or an open fire, often basting it with a seasoned sauce. [Am. Sp. *barbacoa* < Haitian, framework of sticks < Taino.]
barbed (bärbd) *adj.* **1.** Having barbs. **2.** Cutting; stinging: *barbed criticism.* **—barb'ed·ness** (bär'bĭd-nĭs) *n.*
barbed wire *n.* Twisted strands of fence wire with barbs at regular intervals.
bar·bel (bär'bəl) *n.* **1.** One of the slender, whiskerlike sensory organs on the head of certain fishes, such as catfish. **2.** Any of several Old World freshwater fish of the genus *Barbus.* [Obs. Fr. < OFr., dim. of *barbe,* beard < Lat. *barba.*]
bar·bell (bär'bĕl') *n.* A bar with adjustable weights at each end, lifted for sport or exercise.
bar·bel·late (bär'bə-lāt', bär-bĕl'ĭt, -āt') *adj.* Having minute, hooked bristles or hairs. [< NLat. *barbella,* dim. of Lat. *barbula,* little beard < *barba,* beard.]
bar·ber (bär'bər) *n.* One whose business is to cut hair and to shave or trim beards. *—v.* **-bered, -ber·ing, -bers.** *—tr.* **1.** To cut the hair of. **2.** To shave or trim the beard of. *—intr.* To work as a barber. [ME *barbour* < OFr. < Med. Lat. *barbator* < *barba,* beard < Lat.]
bar·ber·ry (bär'bĕr'ē) *n.* Any of various shrubs of the genus *Berberis,* having small leaves, clusters of yellow flowers, and small orange or red berries. [ME *berberie* < OFr. *berberis* < Ar. *barbārīs.*]
bar·ber·shop (bär'bər-shŏp') *n.* The place of business of a barber. *—adj.* Of, consisting of, or relating to the performance of sentimental songs in four-part harmony: *a barbershop quartet.*
barber's itch *n.* Any of various skin eruptions on the neck, esp. ringworm.
bar·bet (bär'bĭt) *n.* Any of various tropical birds of the family Capitonidae, having a broad bill bristled at the base and brightly colored plumage and related to the toucans. [Fr. *barbu* < Lat. *barbatus,* barbate < *barba,* beard.]
bar·bette (bär-bĕt') *n.* **1.** A platform or mound within a fort from which guns are fired over the parapet. **2.** An armored protective cylinder around a revolving turret on a warship. [Fr., dim. of *barbe,* beard < Lat. *barba.*]
bar·bi·can (bär'bĭ-kən) *n.* A tower or other fortification on the approach to a castle or town, esp. one at a gate or drawbridge. [ME < OFr. *barbacane* < Med. Lat. *barbacana,* perh. of Ar. or Pers. orig.]
bar·bi·cel (bär'bĭ-sĕl') *n.* One of many minute projections that fringe the edges of the barbules of feathers and interlock with those on adjacent barbules. [NLat. *barbicella,* dim. of Lat. *barba,* beard.]
bar·bi·tal (bär'bĭ-tôl') *n.* A white crystalline compound, $C_8H_{12}N_2O_3$, used as a sedative. [BARBIT(URIC ACID) + *-al* (as in *Veronal*).]
bar·bi·tu·rate (bär-bĭch'ər-ĭt, -ə-rāt', bär'bĭ-tŏŏr'ĭt, -āt', -tyŏŏr'-) *n.* **1.** A salt or ester of barbituric acid. **2.** Any of a group of barbituric acid derivatives used as sedatives or hypnotics. [BARBITUR(IC ACID) + -ATE.]
bar·bi·tu·ric acid (bär'bĭ-tŏŏr'ĭk, -tyŏŏr'-) *n.* An organic acid, $C_4H_4N_2O_3$, used in the manufacture of barbiturates and some plastics. [Partial transl. of G. *Barbitursäure.*]
bar·bule (bär'byōōl) *n.* A small barb or pointed projection, esp. one of the small projections fringing the edges of the barbs of feathers. [Lat. *barbula,* dim. of *barba,* beard.]
barb·wire (bärb'wīr') *n.* Barbed wire.
bar·ca·role also **bar·ca·rolle** (băr'kə-rōl) *n.* **1.** A Venetian gondolier's song with a rhythm suggestive of rowing. **2.** A musical composition imitating a barcarole. [Fr. < Ital. *barcaruola* < *barcaruolo,* gondolier < *barca,* boat < LLat.]
bar chart *n.* A bar graph.
bard[1] (bärd) *n.* **1.** One of an ancient Celtic order of singing poets who composed and recited verses on the legends and history of their tribes. **2.** A poet, esp. an exalted national poet. [ME < Ir. Gael. *bàrd* and Welsh *bardd.*] **—bard'ic** (bär'dĭk) *adj.*
bard[2] also **barde** (bärd) *n.* A piece of armor used to protect or ornament a horse. *—tr.v.* **bard·ed, bard·ing, bards.** To equip with bards. [ME *barde* < OFr., prob. < OItal. *barda* < Ar. *barda'ah,* stuffed packsaddle.]
bare[1] (bâr) *adj.* **bar·er, bar·est. 1.** Without the usual or ap-

baobab

Barbary ape

p pop / r roar / s sauce / sh ship, dish / t tight / th thin, path / *th* this, bathe / ŭ cut / ûr urge / v valve / w with / y yes / z zebra, size / zh vision / ə about, item, edible, gallop, circus / œ *Fr.* feu, *Ger.* schön / ü *Fr.* tu, *Ger.* über / KH *Ger.* ich, *Scot.* loch / N *Fr.* bon.

propriate covering or clothing; naked: *a bare head.* **2.** Exposed to view; undisguised: *laid bare the secret agreement.* **3.** Lacking the usual furnishings, equipment, or decoration: *walls bare of pictures.* **4.** Without addition, adornment, or qualification; plain: *the bare facts.* **5.** Just sufficient; mere: *the bare necessities of life.* **6.** *Obs.* Bareheaded. —*tr.v.* **bared, bar·ing, bares.** To make bare; strip of covering. [ME *bar* < OE *bær.*] **—bare'ness** *n.*

bare[2] (bâr) *v. Archaic.* Past tense of **bear.**

bare·back (bâr'băk') also **bare·backed** (-băkt') *adj. & adv.* On a horse, pony, or other animal with no saddle: *a bareback rider; rode bareback.*

bare bones *pl.n.* The barest elements or essentials: *outlined the bare bones of the plot.* **—bare'-bones'** (bâr'bōnz') *adj.*

bare·faced (bâr'fāst') *adj.* **1. a.** Having no covering over the face. **b.** Having no beard. **2.** Unconcealed; without disguise. **3.** Presumptuous and shameless: *a barefaced lie.* **—bare'fac'ed·ly** (-fā'sĭd-lē, -fāst'lē) *adv.* **—bare'fac'ed·ness** *n.*

bare·foot (bâr'fo͝ot') also **bare·foot·ed** (-fo͝ot'ĭd) *adj. & adv.* Wearing nothing on the feet: *a barefoot boy; walking barefoot in the grass.*

ba·rege also **ba·rège** (bə-rĕzh') *n.* A sheer fabric woven of silk or cotton and wool, used for women's apparel. [Fr. *barège* < *Barèges,* a town in France.]

bare·hand·ed (bâr'hăn'dĭd) *adj. & adv.* **1.** Having no covering on the hands. **2.** Unaided by tools or weapons: *fighting barehanded.* **—bare'hand'ed·ness** *n.*

bare·head·ed (bâr'hĕd'ĭd) *adj. & adv.* Having no covering on the head: *walking bareheaded in the rain.* **—bare'head'ed·ness** *n.*

bare·leg·ged (bâr'lĕg'ĭd, -lĕgd') *adj. & adv.* Having the legs uncovered. **—bare'leg'ged·ness** *n.*

bare·ly (bâr'lē) *adv.* **1.** By a very little; almost not; hardly: *could barely see the road in the fog.* **2.** In a scanty manner; sparsely: *a barely furnished room.*

barf (bärf) *intr.v.* **barfed, barf·ing, barfs.** *Slang.* To vomit. [Orig. unknown.]

bar·fly (bär'flī') *n. Slang.* One who frequents bars.

bar·gain (bär'gĭn) *n.* **1. a.** An agreement or contract, esp. one involving the purchase and sale of goods or services. **b.** The terms or conditions of such an agreement. **c.** The property acquired or services rendered as a result of such an agreement. **2.** Something offered or acquired at a price advantageous to the buyer. —*v.* **-gained, -gain·ing, -gains.** —*intr.* **1.** To negotiate the terms of a sale, exchange, or other agreement. **2.** To arrive at an agreement. —*tr.* To exchange; trade: *bargained his watch for a meal.* **—*phrasal verb.* bargain for.** To expect; count on. **—*idiom.* into** (or **in**) **the bargain.** Over and above what is expected; in addition. [ME *bargaine* < OFr., of Germanic orig.] **—bar'gain·er** *n.*

barge (bärj) *n.* **1.** A long, large, usually flat-bottomed boat that is unpowered and towed by other craft, used for transporting freight. **2.** A large pleasure boat. **3.** A powerboat reserved for the use of a flag officer. —*v.* **barged, barg·ing, barg·es.** —*tr.* To carry by barge. —*intr.* **1.** To move about clumsily. **2.** To enter rudely and abruptly; intrude: *barged into the meeting.* [ME, boat < OFr., poss. < Lat. *barca.*]

barge·board (bärj'bôrd', -bōrd') *n. Archit.* A board, often ornately carved, attached along the projecting edge of a gable roof. [Orig. unknown.]

barg·ee (bär-jē') *n. Chiefly Brit.* A bargeman.

bar·gel·lo (bär-zhĕl'ō) *n., pl.* **-los.** A needlepoint stitch that produces zigzag lines. [After the *Bargello,* a museum in Florence, Italy, which contains chairs upholstered in fabric worked in this stitch.]

barge·man (bärj'mən) *n.* The master or a crew member of a barge.

bar graph *n.* A graph consisting of parallel, usually vertical, bars or rectangles with lengths proportional to specified quantities in a set of data.

bar·hop (bär'hŏp') *intr.v.* **-hopped, -hop·ping, -hops.** To patronize a series of bars during an evening.

bar·i·at·rics (băr'ē-ăt'rĭks) *n.* (*used with a sing. verb*). A branch of medicine dealing with the treatment of obesity. **—bar'i·at'ric** *adj.* **—bar'i·a·tri'cian** (-ə-trĭsh'ən) *n.*

ba·ril·la (bə-rēl'yə, -rē'yə) *n.* **1.** Either of two Old World plants, *Salsola kali* or *S. soda,* or a similar plant, *Halogeton soda,* burned to obtain a form of sodium carbonate. **2.** The sodium carbonate obtained from a barilla. [Sp. *barrilla.*]

bar·ite (bâr'īt', băr'-) *n.* A colorless crystalline mineral of barium sulfate that is the chief source of barium chemicals. [Gk. *barus,* heavy + -ITE.]

bar·i·tone also **bar·y·tone** (băr'ĭ-tōn') *n.* **1. a.** A male singer or voice with a range higher than a bass and lower than a tenor. **b.** A part written for a voice with such a range. **2.** A brass wind instrument with a range similar to that of a baritone. [Ital. *baritono* < Gk. *barutonos,* deep sounding : *barus,* heavy + *tonus,* tone.]

bar·i·um (bâr'ē-əm, băr'-) *n. Symbol* **Ba** A soft, silvery-white alkaline-earth metal, used to deoxidize copper, in various alloys, and in rat poison. Atomic number 56; atomic weight 137.34; melting point 725°C; boiling point 1,140°C; specific gravity 3.50; valence 2. [BAR(YTA) + -IUM.] **—bar'ic** (-ĭk) *adj.*

barium sulfate *n.* A fine white powder, $BaSO_4$, used as a pigment, as a filler for textiles, rubbers, and plastics, and as an indicator in x-ray photography of the digestive tract.

barium yellow *n.* A pigment made of barium chromate, $BaCrO_4$.

bark[1] (bärk) *n.* **1.** The harsh, abrupt sound uttered by a dog. **2.** A sound, such as a cough, that is similar to a bark. —*v.* **barked, bark·ing, barks.** —*intr.* **1.** To utter a bark. **2.** To make a sound similar to a bark. **3.** To speak sharply; snap: *barked at his assistant.* **4.** *Informal.* To work as a barker. —*tr.* To utter in a loud, harsh voice. [< ME *berken,* to bark < OE *beorcan.*]

bark[2] (bärk) *n.* **1.** The outer covering of the woody stems, branches, roots, and main trunks of trees and other woody plants as distinguished from the cambium and inner wood. **2.** A specific kind of bark used for a special purpose, as in tanning or medicine. —*tr.v.* **barked, bark·ing, barks. 1.** To remove bark from (a tree or log). **2.** To rub off the skin of; abrade. **3.** To treat medically, tan, or dye using bark. [ME < ON *börkr.*]

bark[3] also **barque** (bärk) *n.* **1.** A sailing ship with from three to five masts, all of them square-rigged except the after mast, which is fore-and-aft rigged. **2.** A small sailing vessel. [ME *barke,* boat < OFr. *barque* < OItal. *barca* < LLat.]

bark beetle *n.* Any of various small insects of the family Scolytidae that damage trees by boring along the surface of the wood.

bar·keep·er (bär'kē'pər) also **bar·keep** (-kēp') *n.* **1.** A person who owns or runs a bar for the sale of alcoholic beverages. **2.** A bartender.

bar·ken·tine also **bar·quen·tine** (bär'kən-tēn') *n.* A sailing ship with from three to five masts of which only the foremast is square-rigged, the others being fore-and-aft rigged. [Prob. a blend of BARK[3] and BRIGANTINE.]

bark·er[1] (bär'kər) *n.* **1.** One that barks. **2.** *Informal.* An employee who stands before the entrance to a show and solicits customers with loud, colorful sales talk.

bark·er[2] (bär'kər) *n.* One that removes bark from trees or logs or prepares it for tanning.

bark·y (bär'kē) *adj.* **-i·er, -i·est.** Covered with, containing, or resembling bark.

bar-le-duc also **Bar-le-Duc** (bär'lĭ-do͞ok') *n.* A savory preserve made of white currants or gooseberries. [After *Bar-le-Duc,* France.]

bar·ley (bär'lē) *n.* **1.** A cereal grass, *Hordeum vulgare,* bearing bearded flower spikes with edible seeds. **2.** The grain of barley, used as food and in making beer, ale, and whiskey. [ME *barli* < OE *bærlic.*]

bar·ley·corn (bär'lē-kôrn') *n.* **1.** The seed or grain of barley. **2.** A unit of measure equal to the width of a grain of barley, or approximately $^1/_3$ inch.

barley sugar *n.* A clear, hard candy made by boiling down sugar.

barm (bärm) *n.* The yeasty foam that rises to the surface of fermenting malt liquors. [ME *berme* < OE *beorma.*]

bar·maid (bär'mād') *n.* A woman who serves drinks in a bar.

bar·man (bär'mən) *n.* A bartender.

Bar·me·cid·al (bär'mĭ-sīd'l) also **Bar·me·cide** (bär'mĭ-sīd') *adj.* Plentiful or abundant but only apparently: *a Barmecidal feast.* [After *Barmecide,* a nobleman in *The Arabian Nights,* who served a beggar an imaginary feast.]

bar mitz·vah (bär mĭts'və) *n.* **1.** A thirteen-year-old Jewish male, considered an adult and responsible for his moral and religious duties. **2.** The ceremony that initiates and recognizes a boy as a bar mitzvah. —*tr.v.* **-vahed, -vah·ing, -vahs.** To confirm in the ceremony of bar mitzvah. [Heb. *bar mitzvāh* : *bar,* son + *mitzvah,* commandment.]

barm·y (bär'mē) *adj.* **-i·er, -i·est. 1.** Full of barm; foamy. **2.** *Chiefly Brit. Slang.* Out of one's mind; crazy.

barn (bärn) *n.* **1.** A large farm building used for storing farm products and sheltering livestock. **2.** A large shed for the housing of vehicles, such as railroad cars. **3.** *Physics.* A unit of area equal to 10^{-24} square centimeter, used to express nuclear cross sections. [ME *bern* < OE *berern* : *bere,* barley + *ern,* house.]

bar·na·cle (bär'nə-kəl) *n.* **1.** Any of various marine crustaceans of the order Cirripedia that in the adult stage form a hard shell and remain attached to a submerged surface. **2.** The barnacle goose. [ME *bernak,* a kind of goose (from the belief that the geese were produced from the shellfish) < Med. Lat. *bernaca.*] **—bar'na·cled** *adj.*

barnacle goose *n.* A waterfowl, *Branta leucopsis,* of northern Europe and Greenland, having black, white, and gray plumage.

barn dance *n.* A social gathering, often held in a barn, with music and square dancing.

barn owl *n.* A predatory nocturnal bird, *Tyto alba,* having light-brown and white plumage and often frequenting barns and other buildings.

barn·storm (bärn'stôrm') *intr.v.* **-stormed, -storm·ing, -storms. 1.** To travel around the countryside presenting plays, lecturing, or making political speeches. **2.** To appear at county fairs and carnivals in exhibitions of stunt flying and parachute jumping. **—barn'storm'er** *n.*

barn swallow *n.* A widely distributed bird, *Hirundo rustica,* having a deeply forked tail, a dark-blue back, and tan underparts.

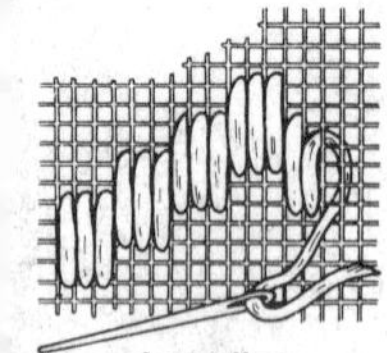

bargello

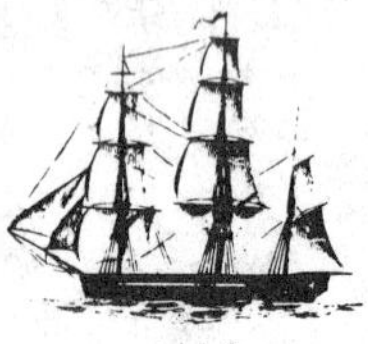

bark[3]

barkentine

barn

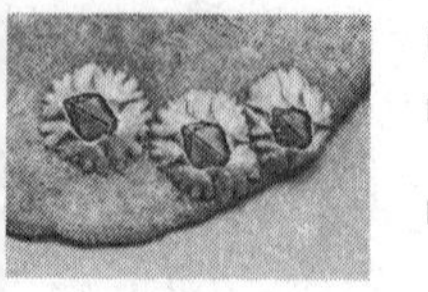

barnacle

George Miksch Sutton

barn owl

barn·yard (bärn′yärd′) *n.* The area surrounding a barn, often enclosed by a fence. *—adj.* Smutty; earthy: *barnyard humor.*
baro– or **bar–** *pref.* Weight; pressure: *barometer.* [< Gk. *baros,* weight.]
bar·o·gram (băr′ə-grăm′) *n.* A graphic record produced by a barograph.
bar·o·graph (băr′ə-grăf′) *n.* A recording barometer. **—bar′o·graph′ic** *adj.*
ba·rom·e·ter (bə-rŏm′ĭ-tər) *n.* **1.** An instrument for measuring atmospheric pressure, used in weather forecasting and in determining elevation. **2.** Something that gives notice of fluctuations; indicator: *Interest rates are an economic barometer.* **—bar′o·met′ric** (băr′ə-mĕt′rĭk), **bar′o·met′ri·cal** *adj.* **—bar′o·met′ri·cal·ly** *adv.* **—ba·rom′e·try** *n.*
bar·on (băr′ən) *n.* **1. a.** A feudal tenant holding his rights and title directly from the king or another feudal superior. **b.** A lord or nobleman; peer. **2. a.** A member of the lowest rank of nobility in Great Britain, certain European countries, and Japan. **b.** The rank or title of such a nobleman. **3.** A man with great wealth, power, and influence in a specified sphere of activity: *an oil baron.* [ME < OFr., prob. of Germanic orig.]
bar·on·age (băr′ə-nĭj) *n.* **1.** The rank, title, or dignity of a baron. **2.** All of the peers of a kingdom.
bar·on·ess (băr′ə-nĭs) *n.* **1.** The wife or widow of a baron. **2.** A woman holding a barony in her own right.
bar·on·et (băr′ə-nĭt, băr′ə-nĕt′) *n.* **1.** A British hereditary title of honor, ranking next below a baron, held by commoners. **2.** The bearer of a baronet. [ME, dim. of *baron,* baron.]
bar·on·et·age (băr′ə-nĭ-tĭj, -nĕt′ĭj) *n.* **1.** The rank or dignity of a baronet; baronetcy. **2.** Baronets collectively.
bar·on·et·cy (băr′ə-nĭt-sē, -nĕt′sē) *n.* The rank or dignity of a baronet.
ba·rong (bə-rông′, -rŏng′) *n.* A large, broad-bladed knife used by the Moros of the Philippines. [Native word in the Philippines.]
ba·ro·ni·al (bə-rō′nē-əl) *adj.* **1.** Of or pertaining to a baron or barony. **2.** Suited for or befitting a baron; stately: *a baronial mansion.*
bar·o·ny (băr′ə-nē) *n., pl.* **-nies. 1.** The domain of a baron. **2.** The rank or dignity of a baron.
ba·roque (bə-rōk′) *adj.* **1.** Of, pertaining to, or characteristic of a style in art and architecture developed in Europe from about 1550 to 1700 and typified by elaborate and ornate scrolls, curves, and other symmetrical ornamentation. **2.** Of, pertaining to, or characteristic of a style of musical composition that flourished in Europe from about 1600 to 1750, marked by chromaticism, strict forms, and elaborate ornamentation. **3.** Ornate or flamboyant in style; richly ornamented: *"his addiction to a baroque luxuriance of language"* (Orville Prescott). **4.** Irregular in shape: *baroque pearls.* *—n.* The baroque style or period in art, architecture, or music. [Fr. < Ital. *barocco.*] **—ba·roque′ly** *adv.*
bar·o·re·cep·tor (băr′ə-rĭ-sĕp′tər) *n.* A sensory nerve ending, as in the carotid sinus, that is sensitive to pressure change.
ba·rouche (bə-ro͞osh′) *n.* A four-wheeled carriage with a collapsible top, two double seats inside opposite each other, and a box seat outside in front for the driver. [G. *Barutsche* < Ital. *biroccio* < LLat. *birotus,* two-wheeled : *bi-,* two + *rota,* wheel.]
barque (bärk) *n.* Variant of **bark[3]**.
bar·quen·tine (bär′kən-tēn′) *n.* Variant of **barkentine.**
bar·rack[1] (băr′ək) *tr.v.* **-racked, -rack·ing, -racks.** To house in barracks.
bar·rack[2] (băr′ək) *tr.v.* **-racked, -rack·ing, -racks.** *Chiefly Brit.* To shout or jeer at. [Orig. unknown.] **—bar′rack·er** *n.*
bar·racks (băr′əks) *pl.n. (used with a sing. or pl. verb).* **1.** A building or group of buildings used to house soldiers. **2.** A large unadorned building, used for temporary occupancy. [Fr. *baraques* < Sp. *barraca,* soldier's tent < Catalan.]
barracks bag *n.* A soldier's cloth bag, usually with a drawstring, for the storage of clothing or laundry.
bar·ra·coon (băr′ə-ko͞on′) *n.* A barracks in which slaves or convicts were temporarily confined. [Sp. *barracón,* aug. of *barraca,* hut.]
bar·ra·cu·da (băr′ə-ko͞o′də) *n., pl.* **barracuda** or **-das.** Any of various voracious, mostly tropical marine fishes of the genus *Sphyraena,* having a long, narrow body and projecting jaws with fanglike teeth. [Mex. Sp.]
bar·rage[1] (bär′ĭj) *n.* An artificial obstruction in a watercourse, esp. one built to promote irrigation; dam. [Fr. < *barrer,* to bar < *barre,* bar < OFr.]
bar·rage[2] (bə-räzh′) *n.* **1.** A heavy curtain of artillery fire directed in front of friendly troops to screen and protect them. **2.** A rapid, concentrated discharge of missiles, as from small arms. **3.** An overwhelming, concentrated outpouring, as of words or blows: *a barrage of questions.* *—tr.v.* **-raged, -rag·ing, -rag·es.** To direct a barrage at. [Fr. *(tir de) barrage,* barrier (fire).]
barrage balloon *n.* A balloon anchored singly or in a series over a military objective to hinder the passage of enemy aircraft.
bar·ra·mun·da (băr′ə-mŭn′də) also **bar·ra·mun·di** (-dē) *n., pl.* **barramunda** or **-das** also **barramundi** or **-dis.** Any of several Australian food fishes, such as the river fish *Scleropages leichhardtdii* or the lungfish *Neoceratodus forsteri.* [Native word in Australia.]
bar·ran·ca (bə-răng′kə) *n. Southwestern U.S.* A deep ravine or gorge. [Sp., prob. < Iberian.]
bar·ra·tor also **bar·ra·ter** (băr′ə-tər) *n. Law.* A person who commits barratry. [ME *baratour* < OFr. *barateor,* swindler < *barater,* to cheat.]
bar·ra·try (băr′ə-trē) *n., pl.* **-tries. 1.** *Law.* The offense of inciting or stirring up quarrels or groundless lawsuits. **2.** An unlawful breach of duty on the part of a ship's master or crew resulting in injury to the ship's owner. **3.** The sale or purchase of positions in the church or state. [ME *barratrie,* the sale of church offices < OFr. *baraterie,* deception < *barater,* to cheat.] **—bar′ra·trous** (-trəs) *adj.* **—bar′ra·trous·ly** *adv.*
barred owl *n.* A North American owl, *Strix varia,* having barred, brownish plumage, a streaked belly, and a strident, hooting cry.
bar·rel (băr′əl) *n.* **1.** A large, cylindrical container, usually made of wooden staves bound together with hoops, with a flat top and bottom of equal diameter. **2.** The quantity that a barrel with a given or standard capacity will hold. **3.** Any of various units of volume or capacity. In the U.S. Customary System it varies, as a liquid measure, from 31 to 42 gallons as established by law or usage. **4.** The cylindrical part or hollow shaft of any of various mechanisms, as: **a.** The metal, cylindrical part of a firearm through which the bullet travels. **b.** A cylinder that contains a movable piston. **c.** The drum of a capstan. **d.** The cylinder within the mechanism of a timepiece that contains the mainspring. **5.** *Informal.* A large quantity: *a barrel of fun.* *—v.* **-reled, -rel·ing, -rels** or **-relled, -rel·ling, -rels.** *—tr.* To put or pack in a barrel. *—intr. Slang.* To move at a high speed. [ME *barel* < OFr. *baril.*]
barrel chair *n.* A large, upholstered chair having a high, rounded back resembling a half barrel.
bar·rel·house (băr′əl-hous′) *n.* **1.** A disreputable saloon or bawdyhouse. **2.** An early style of jazz characterized by free group improvisation and an accented two-beat rhythm.
barrel organ *n.* A portable musical instrument operated by the action of a revolving barrel with pegs or pins that open air valves leading from a bellows to a series of pipes.
barrel roll *n.* A flight maneuver in which an aircraft makes a complete rotation on its longitudinal axis while approximately maintaining its original direction.
bar·ren (băr′ən) *adj.* **1. a.** Not producing offspring; childless. **b.** Incapable of producing offspring; sterile. **2.** Lacking vegetation, esp. useful vegetation; fruitless. **3.** Unproductive of results or gains; unprofitable: *barren efforts.* **4.** Devoid of something specified; lacking: *writing barren of insight.* **5.** Lacking in liveliness or interest; dull. *—n.* Often **barrens.** A tract of unproductive land, often with a scrubby growth of trees. [ME *barreine* < OFr. *baraigne.*] **—bar′ren·ly** *adv.* **—bar′ren·ness** *n.*
barren strawberry *n.* A low-growing plant, *Waldsteinia fragarioides,* of eastern North America, having yellow flowers and small, dry, inedible fruit.
bar·rette (bə-rĕt′, bä-) *n.* A small clasp used by women for holding the hair in place. [Fr. < dim. of *barre,* bar < OFr.]
bar·ri·cade (băr′ĭ-kād′, băr′ĭ-kād′) *n.* **1.** A structure set up across a route of access for defense or the obstruction of passage. **2.** Something acting to obstruct passage; barrier. *—tr.v.* **-cad·ed, -cad·ing, -cades. 1.** To close off or block with a barricade. **2.** To keep in or out by means of a barricade. [Fr. < OFr. *barrique,* barrel < Sp. *barrica.*] **—bar′ri·cad′er** *n.*
bar·ri·er (băr′ē-ər) *n.* **1.** A fence, wall, or other structure built to bar passage. **2.** Something that acts to hinder or restrict: *spoke different languages, a real barrier to understanding.* **3.** A boundary or limit: *the sound barrier.* **4.** Something that separates or holds apart. **5.** A movable gate that keeps racehorses in line before the start of a race. **6. barriers.** The palisades or fences enclosing the lists of a medieval tournament. **7.** *Geol.* A section of the Antarctic ice shelf that extends beyond the coastline, resting partly on the ocean floor. [ME *barrer* < OFr. *barriere* < LLat. *barraria* < *barra,* bar.]
barrier reef *n.* A long, narrow ridge of coral or rock parallel to and relatively near a coastline, separated from the coastline by a lagoon too deep for coral growth.
bar·ring (bär′ĭng) *prep.* Apart from the occurrence of; excepting: *Barring strong headwinds, the plane will arrive on schedule.*
bar·ri·o (bä′rē-ō′, băr′-) *n., pl.* **-os. 1.** An enclave, ward, or district in a Spanish-speaking country. **2.** A chiefly Spanish-speaking community or neighborhood in a U.S. city. [Sp. < Ar. *barrī,* of an open area < *barr,* open area.]
bar·ris·ter (băr′ĭ-stər) *n. Chiefly Brit.* A lawyer admitted to plead at the bar in the superior courts. [Prob. < BAR[1] (railing).]
bar·room (bär′ro͞om′, -ro͝om′) *n.* A room or building in which alcoholic beverages are sold at a counter or bar.
bar·row[1] (băr′ō) *n.* **1.** A flat, rectangular tray or cart with handles at each end. **2.** A wheelbarrow. [ME *barowe* < OE *bearwe.*]
bar·row[2] (băr′ō) *n. Archaeol.* A large mound of earth or

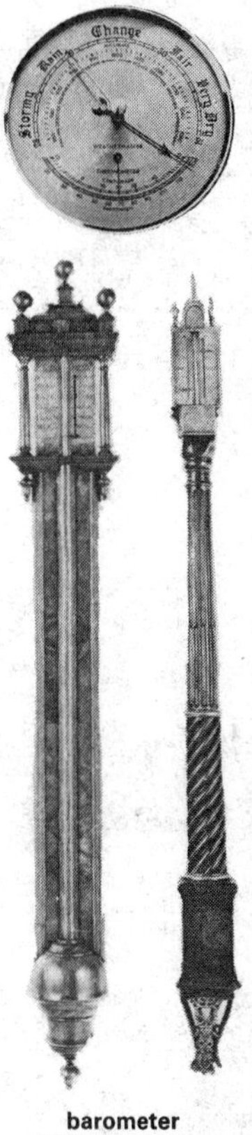

barometer
Above: 20th-century American
Below: 18th-century English (*left*), and 17th-century English (*right*)

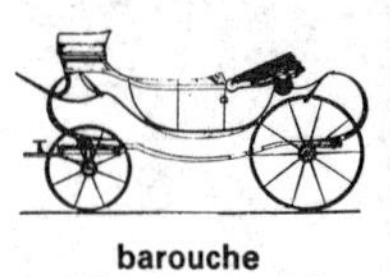

barouche
19th-century model

stones placed over a burial site. [ME *borewe* < OE *beorg.*]
bar·row[3] (băr′ō) *n.* A pig that has been castrated before reaching sexual maturity. [ME *barow* < OE *bearg.*]
bar sinister *n.* **1.** A heraldic bend or baton sinister held to signify bastardy. **2.** A hint or proof of illegitimate birth.
bar·tend·er (bär′tĕn′dər) *n.* One who mixes and serves alcoholic drinks at a bar.
bar·ter (bär′tər) *v.* **-tered, -ter·ing, -ters.** —*intr.* To trade goods or services without the exchange of money. —*tr.* To trade (goods or services) without the exchange of money: *bartered his watch for food.* —*n.* **1.** The act or practice of bartering. **2.** Something that is bartered. [ME *barteren,* prob. < OFr. *berator.*] —**bar′ter·er** *n.*
Bar·tho·lin's gland (bär′tl-ĭnz, -thə-lĭnz) *n.* Either of two small compound racemose glands located on either side of the lower vagina that secrete mucus during coitus. [After Kaspar *Bartholin* (1655–1738).]
bar·ti·zan also **bar·ti·san** (bär′tĭ-zən, bär′tĭ-zăn′) *n.* A small, overhanging turret on a wall or tower. [Alteration of *bratticing,* timberwork < BRATTICE.] —**bar′ti·zaned** *adj.*

bartizan

Bart·lett (bärt′lĭt) *n.* A widely grown variety of pear with large, juicy yellow fruit. [After Enoch *Bartlett* (1779–1860).]
bar·y·cen·ter (băr′ĭ-sĕn′tər) *n. Physics.* Center of mass. [Gk. *barus,* heavy + CENTER.]
bar·y·on (băr′ē-ŏn′) *n.* Any of a family of subatomic particles, including the nucleon and hyperon multiplets, that participate in strong interactions, have half-integral spins, and are generally more massive than mesons. [Gk. *barus,* heavy + -ON.] —**bar′y·on′ic** *adj.*
baryon number *n.* A quantum number equal to the difference between the number of baryons and the number of antibaryons in a system of subatomic particles.
bar·y·sphere (băr′ə-sfîr′) *n.* The centrosphere (sense 2).
ba·ry·ta (bə-rī′tə) *n.* Any of several barium compounds, such as barium sulfate. [NLat. < Gk. *barutēs,* weight < *barus,* heavy.]
ba·ry·tes (bə-rī′tēz′) *n.* Barite. [Gk. *barutēs,* weight < *barus,* heavy.]
bar·y·tone (băr′ĭ-tōn′) *n.* Variant of **baritone.**
bas·al (bā′səl, -zəl) *adj.* **1.** Of, pertaining to, located at, or forming a base. **2.** Of primary importance; basic. —**bas′al·ly** *adv.*
basal metabolic rate *n.* The rate at which energy is used by an organism at complete rest, measured in humans by the heat given off per unit time.
basal metabolism *n.* The least amount of energy required to maintain vital functions in an organism at complete rest.
ba·salt (bə-sôlt′, bā′sôlt′) *n.* A hard, dense, dark volcanic rock composed chiefly of plagioclase, augite, and magnetite and often having a glassy appearance. [Lat. *basaltes,* alteration of *basanites (lapis),* touchstone < Gk. *basanitēs* < *basanos,* of Egypt. orig.] —**ba·sal′tic** (-sôl′tĭk) *adj.*

bascule
Tower Bridge, London, England

bas·cule (băs′kyo͞ol) *n.* A device, such as a drawbridge, counterbalanced so that when one end is lowered the other is raised. [Fr., seesaw : *bas,* low + *cul,* bottom.]
base[1] (bās) *n.* **1.** The lowest or bottom part: *the base of a cliff.* **2.** A supporting part or layer; foundation: *built on a base of solid rock.* **3.** The fundamental principle or underlying concept of a system or theory; basis. **4.** A fundamental ingredient; chief constituent: *a paint with an oil base.* **5.** The fact, observation, or premise from which a reasoning process is begun. **6.** *Baseball.* Any one of the four corners of an infield, marked by a bag or plate, that must be touched by a runner before he can score a run. **7.** A center of organization, supply, or activity; headquarters. **8. a.** A fortified center of operations. **b.** A supply center for a large force. **9.** *Archit.* The lowest part of a structure, as a wall, considered as a separate architectural unit: *the base of a column.* **10.** In heraldry, the lower part of a shield. **11.** *Ling.* A morpheme or morphemes regarded as a form to which affixes or other bases may be added. **12.** *Math.* **a.** The side or face of a geometric figure to which an altitude is or is thought to be drawn. **b.** The number that is raised to various powers to generate the principal counting units of a number system. **c.** The number raised to the logarithm of a designated number in order to produce that designated number. **13.** A line used as a reference for measurement or computations. **14.** *Chem.* **a.** Any of a large class of compounds, including the hydroxides and oxides of metals, having a bitter taste, a slippery solution, the ability to turn litmus blue, and the ability to react with acids to form salts. **b.** A molecular or ionic substance capable of combining with a proton to form a new substance. **c.** A substance that provides a pair of electrons for a covalent bond with an acid. —*adj.* **1.** Forming or serving as a base. **2.** Situated at or near the base or bottom. —*tr.v.* **based, bas·ing, bas·es. 1.** To form or make a base for. **2.** To find a basis for; establish. —***idiom.* off base. 1.** Badly mistaken. **2.** In a state of unpreparedness. [ME < OFr. < Lat. *basis* < Gk.]

basenji

Synonyms: *base, basis, foundation, ground, groundwork.* These nouns all pertain to what underlies and supports. *Base* is applied chiefly to material things: *the base of a fountain.* *Basis* is used in a nonphysical sense: *the basis of a rumor.* *Foundation* applies physically and figuratively, and more comprehensively than either of the foregoing. It stresses firmness of support for something of relative magnitude: *a philosophy with a foundation in truth.* *Ground* may denote an actual working surface in arts and crafts; more often, in the plural, it is used figuratively in the sense of a justifiable reason: *grounds for complaint.* *Groundwork* is most often applied figuratively, with the sense of foundation or a neccessary preliminary.
base[2] (bās) *adj.* **bas·er, bas·est. 1.** Having or proceeding from low moral standards; mean or contemptible: *base instincts; a base act.* **2.** Inferior in quality or value. **3.** Containing inferior substances: *a base metal.* **4.** Valueless or greatly depreciated in value; debased. **5.** *Archaic.* Of low birth, rank, or position. **6.** *Obs.* Short in stature. —*n. Obs.* Bass[2]. [ME *bas* < OFr., low < Med. Lat. *bassus.*] —**base′ly** *adv.* —**base′ness** *n.*
base·ball (bās′bôl′) *n.* **1.** A game played with a bat and ball by two opposing teams of nine players, each team playing alternately in the field and at bat, the players at bat having to run a course of four bases laid out in a diamond pattern in order to score. **2.** The ball used in baseball.
base·board (bās′bôrd′, -bōrd′) *n.* A molding that conceals the joint between an interior wall and a floor.
base·born (bās′bôrn′) *adj.* **1.** Of humble birth. **2.** Born of unwed parents; illegitimate. **3.** Ignoble; contemptible.
base·burn·er (bās′bûr′nər) *n.* A stove or furnace that automatically replenishes consumed coal or other fuel from above.
Base Exchange. A trademark for a Post Exchange on a naval or air force base.
base hit *n. Baseball.* A hit by which the batter reaches base safely without an error or force play being made.
base·less (bās′lĭs) *adj.* Having no basis or foundation in fact; unfounded.
base level *n.* The lowest level to which a land surface can be reduced by the action of running water.
base line *n.* **1.** A line serving as a base, as for measurement. **2.** *Baseball.* An area within which a base runner must stay when running between successive bases. **3.** A line bounding each back end of a tennis court.
base·man (bās′mən) *n. Baseball.* A player assigned to first, second, or third base.
base·ment (bās′mənt) *n.* **1.** The substructure or foundation of a building. **2.** The lowest habitable story of a building, usually below ground level.
basement membrane also **basement lamina** *n.* A thin, primarily collagenous, delicate layer of connective tissue underlying the epithelium.
ba·sen·ji (bə-sĕn′jē) *n.* A dog of a breed originally from Africa, having a short, smooth coat, and characterized by the absence of a bark. [Bantu.]
base pair *n.* One of the pairs of compounds, as adenine and thymine, that along with a hydrogen bond form the connections between the complementary strands of DNA.
base runner *n. Baseball.* A member of the team at bat who has safely reached or is trying to reach a base.
ba·ses (bā′sēz′) *n.* Plural of **basis.**
bash (băsh) *tr.v.* **bashed, bash·ing, bash·es.** *Informal.* To strike with a heavy, crushing blow. —*n.* **1.** *Informal.* A heavy, crushing blow. **2.** *Slang.* A celebration; party. [Orig. unknown.]
ba·shaw (bə-shô′) *n. Obs.* A pasha.
bash·ful (băsh′fəl) *adj.* **1.** Timid with other people; shy. **2.** Characterized by, showing, or resulting from social shyness or self-consciousness. [(A)BASH + -FUL.] —**bash′ful·ly** *adv.* —**bash′ful·ness** *n.*
basi– or **baso–** *pref.* **1.** Base; lower part: *basipetal.* **2.** Chemical base; chemically basic: *basophil.* [< Lat. *basis,* base < Gk.]
ba·sic (bā′sĭk) *adj.* **1.** Of, pertaining to, or forming a base; fundamental. **2.** Of, being, or serving as a starting point or basis. **3.** *Chem.* **a.** Producing, resulting from, or pertaining to a base. **b.** Containing a base, esp. in excess of acid. **4.** *Geol.* Containing little silica, as igneous rocks. —*n.* Something that is basic; fundamental. —**ba′si·cal·ly** *adv.* —**ba·sic′i·ty** (-sĭs′ĭ-tē) *n.*
BA·SIC (bā′sĭk) *n. Computer Sci.* A common programming language often used with remote or time-sharing computer centers. [B(EGINNER'S) + A(LL-PURPOSE) + S(YMBOLIC) + I(NSTRUCTION) + C(ODE).]
ba·si·chro·mat·ic (bā′sĭ-krō-măt′ĭk) *adj.* Easily stained with basic dye.
basic oxide *n.* A metallic oxide that is a base or that forms a hydroxide if combined with water.
basic process *n.* A method of steel production that uses a furnace lined with a basic refractory material.
basic training *n.* The initial period of training of a recruit in the armed forces.
ba·sid·i·a (bə-sĭd′ē-ə) *n.* Plural of **basidium.**
ba·sid·i·o·my·cete (bə-sĭd′ē-ō-mī′sēt′, -mī-sēt′) *n.* A fungus of the class Basidiomycetes, which includes the mushrooms, puffballs, and other fungi that bear spores on a basidium. [NLat. *Basidiomycetes,* class name : BASIDIUM + Gk. *mukēs,* fungus.] —**ba·sid′i·o·my·ce′tous** (-mī-sē′təs) *adj.*
ba·sid·i·o·spore (bə-sĭd′ē-ə-spôr′, -spōr′) *n.* A spore formed on a basidium. —**ba·sid′i·o·spo′rous** *adj.*
ba·sid·i·um (bə-sĭd′ē-əm) *n., pl.* **-i·a** (-ē-ə). A club-shaped cell characteristic of basidiomycetous fungi on which sexual

spores, usually four, are borne at the tip. [NLat. < Lat. *basis,* base < Gk.] —**ba·sid'i·al** *adj.*
ba·si·fy (bā'sə-fī') *tr.v.* **-fied, -fy·ing, -fies.** *Chem.* To make basic. —**ba'si·fi·ca'tion** *n.* —**ba'si·fi'er** *n.*
bas·il (băz'əl, bā'zəl) *n.* **1.** An herb, *Ocimum basilicum,* native to the Old World, having spikes of small white flowers and aromatic leaves used as seasoning. **2.** A plant related to basil, *Satureja vulgaris,* native to Europe and widely naturalized in North America, having dense clusters of small pink or purplish flowers. [ME *basile* < OFr. < Med. Lat. *basilico* < Gk. *basilikon,* royal.]
bas·i·lar (băs'ə-lər) also **bas·i·lar·y** (-lĕr'ē) *adj.* Of, pertaining to, or located at or near the base, esp. the base of the skull. [NLat. *basilaris* < Lat. *basis,* base < Gk.]
ba·sil·i·ca (bə-sĭl'ĭ-kə) *n.* **1. a.** An oblong building of ancient Rome with a semicircular apse at one end, used as a court or place of assembly. **b.** A building of this design used as a Christian church. **2.** *Rom. Cath. Ch.* A church or cathedral accorded certain ceremonial rights by the pope. [Lat. < Gk. *basilikē (stoa),* royal (portico) < *basileus,* king.] —**ba·sil'i·can** (-kən) *adj.*
bas·i·lisk (băs'ə-lĭsk', băz'-) *n.* **1.** A legendary serpent or dragon with lethal breath and glance. **2.** Any of various tropical American lizards of the genus *Basiliscus,* having an erectile crest at the back of the head. [ME < Lat. *basiliscus* < Gk. *basiliskos,* dim. of *basileus,* king.]
ba·sin (bā'sĭn) *n.* **1. a.** A round, open, shallow container used esp. for holding liquids. **b.** The amount contained in a basin. **2.** A washbowl; sink. **3. a.** An artificially enclosed area of a river or harbor designed so that the water level remains unaffected by tidal changes. **b.** A small enclosed or partly enclosed body of water. **4.** A region drained by a single river system. **5.** *Geol.* **a.** A tract of land in which the rock strata are tilted toward a common center. **b.** A bowl-shaped depression in the surface of the land or ocean floor. [ME *bacin* < OFr.] —**ba'sin·al** *adj.*
bas·i·net (băs'ə-nĕt', băs'ə-nĭt) *n.* A light medieval helmet, often with a visor. [ME *bacinet* < OFr., dim. of *bacin,* basin.]
ba·sip·e·tal (bā-sĭp'ĭ-tl, -zĭp'-) *adj. Bot.* Developing or growing from the top toward the base, as certain forms of inflorescence. —**ba·sip'e·tal·ly** *adv.*
ba·sis (bā'sĭs) *n., pl.* **-ses** (-sēz'). **1.** A supporting element; foundation. **2.** The chief component of something. **3.** The essential principle. [Lat. < Gk.]
bask (băsk) *intr.v.* **basked, bask·ing, basks. 1.** To expose oneself to pleasant warmth. **2.** To thrive in the presence of a pleasant or advantageous influence or atmosphere. [ME *basken.*]
bas·ket (băs'kĭt) *n.* **1. a.** A container made of interwoven material, such as rushes or twigs. **b.** The amount a basket will hold. **2.** Something resembling a basket in shape or function. **3.** *Basketball.* **a.** Either of the two goals, each consisting of a metal hoop from which an open-bottomed circular net is suspended. **b.** The score, normally worth two points, made by throwing the ball through the basket. [ME.] —**bas'ket·ful'** (-fo͝ol') *n.*
bas·ket·ball (băs'kĭt-bôl') *n.* **1.** A game played between two teams of five players each, the object being to throw the ball through an elevated basket on the opponent's side of the rectangular court. **2.** The ball used in basketball.
basket case *n. Informal.* One that is in a completely hopeless or useless condition: *"Psychological basket cases desperately in search of love and identity"* (Village Voice).
basket fern *n.* **1.** An American tropical sword fern, *Nephrolepis pectinata.* **2.** A male fern.
basket hilt *n.* A sword hilt with a basket-shaped guard serving to cover and protect the hand.
bas·ket·ry (băs'kĭ-trē) *n.* **1.** The craft or process of making baskets. **2.** Baskets collectively.
basket star *n.* Any of various marine organisms of the class Ophiuroidea, related to the starfishes and having slender, many-branched arms.
basket weave *n.* A textile weave consisting of double threads interlaced to produce a checkered pattern similar to that of a woven basket.
basking shark *n.* A very large shark, *Cetorhinus maximus,* that feeds on plankton and often floats near the surface of water.
bas mitz·vah or **bas miz·vah** (bäs mĭts'və) *n.* Variants of **bat mitzvah.**
baso– *pref.* Variant of **basi-.**
ba·so·phil (bā'sə-fĭl, -zə-) *n.* A cell, esp. a white blood cell, having granules that exhibit an affinity for basic dyes. —**ba'so·phil'ic, ba·soph'i·lous** (bə-sŏf'ə-ləs) *adj.*
ba·so·pho·bi·a (bā'sə-fō'bē-ə, -zə-) *n.* An abnormal fear of standing erect or walking.
basque (băsk) *n.* A close-fitting bodice. [Fr. < Prov. *basta,* perh. of Germanic orig.]
Basque (băsk) *n.* **1.** One of a people of unknown origin inhabiting the western Pyrenees in France and Spain. **2.** The language of the Basques, of no known linguistic affiliation. [Fr. < Lat. *Vasco.*] —**Basque** *adj.*
bas-re·lief (bä'rĭ-lēf') *n.* Low relief. [Fr. < Ital. *bassorilievo* : *basso,* low (< Med. Lat. *bassus*) + *rilievo,* relief < *rilievare,* to raise < Lat. *relevare.* —see RELIEF.]
bass[1] (băs) *n., pl.* **bass** or **bass·es. 1.** Any of several North American freshwater fishes of the family Centrarchidae, related to but larger than the sunfishes. **2.** Any of various marine fishes of the family Serranidae, as the sea bass and the striped bass. [ME *bace,* var. of dial. *barse* < OE *bærs.*]
bass[2] (bās) *n.* **1.** A low-pitched sound or tone. **2.** The tones in the lowest register of a musical instrument. **3.** The lowest part in vocal or instrumental part music. **4. a.** A male singing voice of the lowest range. **b.** A man who has such a singing voice. **5.** A musical instrument, esp. a double bass that produces tones in a low register. —*adj.* **1.** Having a deep tone. **2.** Low in pitch. [ME *bas.*]
bass[3] (băs) *n.* Bast. [Var. of BAST.]
bass clef (bās) *n.* A musical clef that designates F below middle C as being on the fourth line above the bottom of the staff.
bass drum (bās) *n.* A large drum having a cylindrical body and two heads and producing a low, resonant sound.
bas·set (băs'ĭt) *n.* The basset hound. [Fr. < OFr., dim of *basse,* fem. adj. of *bas,* low.]
basset horn *n.* A tenor clarinet in F, having a range of 3½ octaves pitched between the range of an alto clarinet and that of a bass clarinet.
basset hound *n.* A short-haired dog of a breed originating in France and having a long body, short legs, and long, drooping ears.
bass horn (bās) *n.* A tuba.
bas·si·net (băs'ə-nĕt', băs'ə-nĕt') *n.* An oblong basketlike bed for an infant. [Fr., small basin.]
bass·ist (bā'sĭst) *n.* A double bass player.
bas·so (băs'ō, bä'sō) *n., pl.* **bas·sos** or **bas·si** (bä'sē). A bass singer, esp. an operatic bass. [Ital. < Med. Lat. *bassus,* low.]
bas·soon (bə-so͞on', bă-) *n.* A low-pitched woodwind instrument with a double reed, having a long wooden body attached to a lateral tube that leads to the mouthpiece. [Fr. *basson* < Ital. *bassone,* augmentative of *basso,* basso.] —**bas·soon'ist** *n.*
bas·so pro·fun·do (băs'ō prə-fŭn'dō, bä'sō prə-fo͞on'dō) *n., pl.* **basso pro·fun·dos** or **bas·si pro·fun·di** (bä'sē prə-fo͞on'dē). **1.** A bass voice of the lowest range. **2.** A singer having a basso profundo. [Ital.]
bas·so-re·lie·vo (băs'ō-rĭ-lē'vō) *n., pl.* **-vos.** Low relief. [Ital. *bassorilievo.* —see BAS-RELIEF.]
bass viol (bās) *n. Mus.* **1.** A double bass. **2.** A viola da gamba.
bass·wood (băs'wo͝od') *n.* **1.** Any of several linden trees of eastern North America, esp. *Tilia americana,* having clusters of fragrant yellowish flowers. **2.** The soft, light-colored wood of a basswood.
bast (băst) *n.* **1.** The fibrous or somewhat woody outer layer of the stems of such plants as flax, hemp, and ramie. **2.** Fibrous material obtained primarily from plants or from certain trees and used to make cordage and textiles. [ME, inner bark of the linden tree < OE *bæst.*]
bas·tard (băs'tərd) *n.* **1.** An illegitimate child. **2.** Something of irregular, inferior, or dubious origin. **3.** *Slang.* A mean or disagreeable person. —*adj.* **1.** Born of unwed parents; illegitimate. **2.** Not genuine; spurious. **3.** Of inferior breed or kind. **4.** Resembling a known kind or species but not truly such: *bastard toadflax.* [ME < OFr., perh. < *(fils de) bast,* (child of) a pack saddle.] —**bas'tard·ly** *adj.*
bas·tard·ize (băs'tər-dīz') *tr.v.* **-ized, -iz·ing, -iz·es.** To debase; corrupt. —**bas'tard·i·za'tion** *n.*
bastard toadflax *n.* A plant of the genus *Comandra,* esp. *C. umbellata,* of eastern North America, having rounded clusters of small greenish flowers.
bastard wing *n.* An alula.
bas·tard·y (băs'tər-dē) *n.* **1.** The condition of being of illegitimate birth; illegitimacy. **2.** The begetting of a bastard.
baste[1] (bāst) *tr.v.* **bast·ed, bast·ing, bastes.** To sew loosely with large running stitches so as to hold together temporarily. [ME *basten* < OFr. *bastir.*] —**bast'er** *n.*
baste[2] (bāst) *tr.v.* **bast·ed, bast·ing, bastes.** To moisten (meat, for example) periodically with a liquid, as butter or sauce, esp. while cooking. [Orig. unknown.] —**bast'er** *n.*
baste[3] (bāst) *tr.v.* **bast·ed, bast·ing, bastes. 1.** To beat vigorously; thrash. **2.** To berate. [Orig. unknown.]
bas·tille also **bas·tile** (bă-stēl') *n.* **1.** A prison; jail. **2. Bastille.** A fortress in Paris used as a prison until its capture at the outset of the French Revolution. [ME *bastel* < OFr. *bastille* < Med. Lat. *bastile* < *bastire,* to build.]
Bastille Day *n.* July 14 observed in France in commemoration of the destruction of the Bastille in 1789.
bas·ti·na·do (băs'tə-nā'dō, -nä'-) also **bas·ti·nade** (-nād', -näd') —*n., pl.* **-does** also **-nades. 1.** A beating with a stick or cudgel, esp. on the soles of the feet. **2.** A stick or cudgel. —*tr.v.* **-doed, -do·ing, -does** also **-nad·ed, -nad·ing, -nades.** To subject to a beating; thrash. [Sp. *bastonada* < *baston,* stick < LLat. *bastum.*]
bast·ing (bā'stĭng) *n.* **1.** The act of sewing together loosely. **2.** The thread used to baste. **3.** The loose stitches used to baste.
bas·tion (băs'chən, -tē-ən) *n.* **1.** A projecting part of a rampart or other fortification. **2.** A well-fortified position or area. **3.** Something regarded as a defensive stronghold. [Fr. < Ital. *bastione* < *bastire,* to build.] —**bas'tioned** *adj.*
bast·naes·ite (băst'nĭ-sīt') *n.* A yellowish to reddish-brown

basilisk

basket

bass[1]
Largemouth bass

basset hound

bassoon

mineral fluorocarbonate, used as a rare-earth ore. [Swed. *bastnäsit,* after *Bastnäs,* a region of Sweden.]

bat[1] (băt) *n.* **1.** A stout wooden stick or club; cudgel. **2.** A blow, as with a stick. **3. a.** A rounded, usually wooden club, wider and heavier at the hitting end and tapering at the handle, used to strike a baseball. **b.** A wooden club of similar function in cricket, having a broad, flat-surfaced hitting end and a distinct, narrow handle. **c.** The racket used in various other games, such as squash. **4.** *Slang.* A binge; spree. —*v.* **bat·ted, bat·ting, bats.** —*tr.* **1.** To hit with or as if with a club or bat. **2.** *Baseball.* To have (a certain percentage) as a batting average. **3.** *Informal.* To produce in a hurried manner: *bat out a speech.* **4.** *Informal.* To discuss or consider at length: *bat an idea around.* —*intr.* **1.** *Baseball.* **a.** To use a bat. **b.** To have a turn at bat. **2.** *Slang.* To go from place to place aimlessly; wander. —***idioms.*** **at bat.** Taking one's turn to bat, as in baseball. **go to bat for.** *Informal.* To give assistance to; support or defend. **right off the bat.** *Informal.* Without hesitation; immediately. [ME < OE *batt.*]

bat[2]

bat[2] (băt) *n.* Any of various nocturnal flying mammals of the order Chiroptera, having membranous wings that extend from the forelimbs to the hind limbs or tail. [Alteration of ME *bakke,* of Scand. orig.]

bat[3] (băt) *tr.v.* **bat·ted, bat·ting, bats.** To wink or flutter: *bat one's eyelashes.* [Prob. a var. of BATE[2].]

batch[1] (băch) *n.* **1.** An amount produced at one baking: *a batch of cookies.* **2.** The quantity produced as the result of one operation: *a batch of cement.* **3.** The quantity of material needed for one operation: *a batch of dough.* **4.** A group of persons or things: *a batch of tourists.* **5.** *Computer Sci.* A set of data or jobs to be processed in a single program run. [ME *bacche* < OE **bæcce* < *bacan,* to bake.]

bathyscaph

batch[2] (băch) *v.* Variant of **bach.**

bate[1] (bāt) *tr.v.* **bat·ed, bat·ing, bates. 1.** To lessen the force of; moderate. **2.** To take away; subtract. —See Usage note at **bait.** [ME *baten,* short for *abaten.* —see ABATE.]

bate[2] (bāt) *intr.v.* **bat·ed, bat·ing, bates.** To flap the wings wildly in impatience. Used of a falcon. [ME *baten* < OFr. *batre,* to beat.]

ba·teau (bă-tō′) *n., pl.* **-teaux** (-tōz′). A light, flat-bottomed boat, used esp. in Louisiana and Canada. [Fr., boat < OFr. *batel,* prob. < OE *bāt.*]

bateau bridge *n.* A pontoon bridge.

Bates·i·an mimicry (bāt′sē-ən) *n.* The resemblance of a harmless species to a species whose defense against predation is based on repellent traits. [After Henry W. *Bates* (1825–1892).]

bat·fish (băt′fĭsh′) *n., pl.* **batfish** or **-fish·es.** Any of various marine anglerfishes of the family Ogcocephalidae, having a retractable appendage above the mouth.

bat·fowl (băt′foul′) *intr.v.* **-fowled, -fowl·ing, -fowls.** To catch roosting birds at night by blinding them with a light.

bath[1] (băth, bäth) *n., pl.* **baths** (bă*th*z, bä*th*z, băths, bäths). **1.** The act of washing or soaking the body, as in water or steam. **2.** The water used for a bath. **3. a.** A bathtub. **b.** A bathroom. **4. a.** A building equipped for bathing. **b.** Often **baths.** A spa. **5.** A liquid or a liquid and its container in which something is dipped or soaked in order to process it in some way: *a bath of dye.* [ME < OE *bæð.*]

batter[2]

bath[2] (băth) *n.* An ancient Hebrew unit of liquid measure, equal to approximately ten U.S. gallons. [Heb.]

Bath chair (băth, bäth) *n.* A hooded wheelchair used esp. for invalids, as at a spa. [After *Bath,* England.]

bathe (bā*th*) *v.* **bathed, bath·ing, bathes.** —*intr.* **1.** To take a bath. **2.** To go into the water for swimming or recreation. **3.** To become immersed in or as if in liquid. —*tr.* **1.** To immerse in liquid; wet. **2.** To wash in a liquid. **3.** To apply a liquid to for soothing or healing purposes. **4.** To seem to wash or pour over; suffuse. [ME *bathen* < OE *baðian.*] —**bath′er** *n.*

ba·thet·ic (bə-thĕt′ĭk) *adj.* Characterized by bathos. [Prob. a blend of BATHOS and PATHETIC.]

bath·house (băth′hous′, bäth′-) *n.* **1.** A building equipped with facilities for bathing. **2.** A building with dressing rooms for swimmers.

bathing suit *n.* A swimsuit.

batho– *pref.* Variant of **bathy-.**

bath·o·lith (băth′ə-lĭth′) *n.* Igneous rock that has melted and intruded surrounding strata at great depths. —**bath′o·lith′ic** *adj.*

ba·thom·e·ter (bə-thŏm′ĭ-tər) *n.* An instrument used to measure the depth of water.

bath·o·pho·bi·a (băth′ə-fō′bē-ə) *n.* An abnormal fear of depths.

ba·thos (bā′thŏs′) *n.* **1. a.** A ludicrously abrupt transition from an elevated to a commonplace style. **b.** An anticlimax. **2. a.** Insincere or grossly sentimental pathos. **b.** Triteness or dullness. [Gk., depth.]

bath·robe (băth′rōb′, bäth′-) *n.* A loose-fitting robe worn before and after bathing and for lounging.

bath·room (băth′ro͞om′, -ro͝om′, bäth′-) *n.* A room equipped with facilities for taking a bath or shower and usually also containing a sink and toilet.

bath salts *pl.n.* A perfumed crystalline substance for softening bathwater.

bath·tub (băth′tŭb′, bäth′-) *n.* A tub for bathing, esp. one permanently installed in a bathroom.

bathy– or **batho–** *pref.* **1.** Deep; depth: *batholith.* **2.** Deep-sea: *bathysphere.* [< Gk. *bathus,* deep.]

ba·thym·e·try (bə-thĭm′ĭ-trē) *n.* The measurement of the depth of large bodies of water. —**bath′y·met′ric** (băth′-ə-mĕt′rĭk), **bath′y·met′ri·cal** *adj.* —**bath′y·met′ri·cal·ly** *adv.*

bath·y·pe·lag·ic (băth′ə-pə-lăj′ĭk) *adj.* Of, relating to, or living in the depths of the ocean, esp. below 2,000 feet.

bath·y·scaph (băth′ĭ-skăf′) also **bath·y·scaphe** (-skăf′, -skāf′) *n.* A free-diving, self-contained deep-sea research vessel consisting essentially of a large flotation hull with a manned observation capsule fixed to its underside. [Fr. *bathyscaphe* : Gk. *bathus,* deep + Gk. *scaphē,* boat.]

bath·y·sphere (băth′ĭ-sfîr′) *n.* A reinforced spherical deep-diving chamber.

ba·tik (bə-tēk′, băt′ĭk) *n.* **1. a.** A method of dyeing print into a fabric in which parts of the cloth not intended to be dyed are covered with removable wax. **b.** A design that is dyed into cloth by this method. **2.** A cloth dyed by batik. [Malay < Javanese, painted.]

ba·tiste (bə-tēst′, bă-) *n.* A fine, plain-woven fabric made from various fibers and used esp. for clothing. [Fr. < OFr.]

bat·man (băt′mən) *n.* An orderly of a British army officer. [Obs. *bat,* packsaddle < ME *batt* < OFr. *bat.*]

bat mitz·vah or **bat miz·vah** (băt mĭts′və) also **bas mitz·vah** or **bas miz·vah** (bäs) *n.* **1.** A Jewish girl of 12 to 14 years of age who assumes her Jewish duties and responsibilities. **2.** The ceremony that initiates and recognizes a girl as a bat mitzvah. [Heb. *baṭ mitzvāh* : *baṭ,* daughter + *mitzvāh,* commandment.]

ba·ton (bə-tŏn′, bă-, băt′n) *n.* **1.** A short staff carried by some public officials as a symbol of office. **2.** A slender wooden stick or rod used by a conductor to direct an orchestra or band. **3.** A hollow metal rod with heavy rubber tips twirled by a drum major or majorette. [Fr. *bâton* < OFr. *baston.*]

bat·o·pho·bi·a (băt′ə-fō′bē-ə) *n.* An abnormal fear of being near an object of great height, such as a skyscraper or mountain. [Gk. *batos,* passable + -PHOBIA.]

ba·tra·chi·an (bə-trā′kē-ən) *adj.* Of or pertaining to frogs and toads. —*n.* A frog or toad. [< NLat. *Batrachia,* former order name < Gk. *batrakhos,* frog.]

bats (băts) *adj. Slang.* Crazy; insane.

bats·man (băts′mən) *n.* A batter in baseball and cricket.

batt (băt) *n.* A mass of cotton fibers; batting.

bat·tal·ion (bə-tăl′yən) *n.* **1.** A tactical military unit typically consisting of a headquarters company and four infantry companies or a headquarters battery and four artillery batteries. **2.** A large body of military troops. **3.** A great number. [OFr. *battaillon* < OItal. *battaglione* < *battaglia,* a body of troops < VLat. **battalia.* —see BATTLE.]

bat·ten[1] (băt′n) *intr.v.* **-tened, -ten·ing, -tens. 1.** To become fat. **2.** To thrive and prosper, esp. at another's expense. [Ult. < ON *batna,* to improve.]

bat·ten[2] (băt′n) *n.* **1.** A narrow strip of wood used esp. for flooring. **2.** One of several flexible strips of wood placed in pockets at the outer edge of a sail to keep it flat. —*tr.v.* **-tened, -ten·ing, -tens. 1.** To furnish with battens. **2.** To fasten or make secure with battens: *batten down the hatches.* [Alteration of BATON.]

bat·ter[1] (băt′ər) *v.* **-tered, -ter·ing, -ters.** —*tr.* **1.** To beat heavily and repeatedly so as to hurt, bruise, or destroy. **2.** To damage, as by heavy wear. —*intr.* To hit heavily and repeatedly. —*n. Printing.* A damaged area on the face of type or on a plate. [ME *bateren* < OFr. *battre* < Lat. *battuere.*]

bat·ter[2] (băt′ər) *n.* The player at bat in baseball and cricket.

bat·ter[3] (băt′ər) *n.* A thick, beaten liquid mixture, as of flour, milk, and eggs, used in cooking. [ME *bater,* prob. < *bateren,* to batter, beat.]

bat·ter[4] (băt′ər) *n.* A slope, as of the outer side of a wall, that recedes from bottom to top. —*tr.v.* **-tered, -ter·ing, -ters.** To construct in a batter. [Orig. unknown.]

battered child syndrome *n.* A combination of serious physical injuries, such as bruises, scratches, hematomas, burns, or malnutrition, inflicted on a child through gross abuse usually by parents or guardians.

bat·ter·ing-ram also **battering ram** (băt′ər-ĭng-răm′) *n.* **1.** A heavy beam used in ancient warfare to batter down walls and gates. **2.** A device resembling a battering-ram or used for similar purposes.

bat·ter·y (băt′ə-rē) *n., pl.* **-ies. 1. a.** The act of beating or pounding. **b.** *Law.* The unlawful beating of another person. **2. a.** An emplacement for one or more pieces of artillery. **b.** A set of guns or other heavy artillery, as on a warship. **c.** The basic tactical artillery unit, corresponding to the company in the infantry. **3.** An array or grouping of like things to be used together. **4.** The pitcher and catcher on a baseball team. **5.** The percussion section of an orchestra. **6.** A device for generating an electric current by chemical reaction. [Fr. *batterie* < *battre,* to batter < OFr.]

bat·ting (băt′ĭng) *n.* **1.** The action of one who bats. **2.** Cotton or wool fiber wadded into rolls or sheets; and used for stuffing furniture and mattresses and lining quilts.

bat·tle (băt′l) *n.* **1. a.** A large-scale combat between two armed forces. **b.** Armed fighting; combat: *wounded in battle.* **2.** An intense competition, esp. between two persons; struggle. —*v.* **-tled, -tling, -tles.** —*intr.* To engage in or as if in battle. —*tr.* To fight against. [ME *bataille* < OFr. < VLat. **battalia* < LLat. *battualia,* fighting and fencing exercises < Lat. *battuere,* to batter.] —**bat'tler** *n.*

bat·tle-ax or **bat·tle-axe** (băt'l-ăks') *n.* **1.** A broad-headed ax formerly used as a weapon. **2.** *Informal.* A quarrelsome, overbearing woman.

battle cruiser *n.* A warship with less heavy armor than a battleship and with the speed of a cruiser.

battle cry *n.* **1.** A shout uttered by troops in battle. **2.** A slogan used by the proponents of a cause.

bat·tle·dore (băt'l-dôr', -dōr') *n.* **1.** An early form of badminton played with a flat wooden paddle and a shuttlecock. **2.** The paddle used in battledore. [ME *batildore,* perh. < OProv. *batedor.*]

battle fatigue *n.* Combat fatigue.

bat·tle·field (băt'l-fēld') *n.* **1.** A field or area where a battle is fought. **2.** A sphere of contention.

bat·tle·front (băt'l-frŭnt') *n.* The area where opponents meet or clash in battle: *a contest fought on political and military battlefronts.*

bat·tle·ground (băt'l-ground') *n.* A battlefield.

bat·tle·ment (băt'l-mənt) *n.* A parapet built on top of a wall, with indentations for defense or decoration. [ME *batelment* < OFr. *battillement.*] —**bat'tle·ment'ed** (-mĕn'tĭd) *adj.*

battle royal *n., pl.* **battles royal. 1.** A battle or confused fight in which numerous combatants participate. **2.** A fight to the finish. **3.** An intense altercation.

bat·tle·ship (băt'l-shĭp') *n.* Any of a class of modern warships of the largest size, carrying the greatest number of guns and batteries and clad with the heaviest armor.

battleship gray *n.* A medium gray. —**bat'tle·ship-gray'** *adj.*

bat·tle·wag·on (băt'l-wăg'ən) *n. Slang.* A battleship.

bat·ty (băt'ē) *adj.* **-ti·er, -ti·est.** *Slang.* Crazy; insane. —**bat'ti·ness** *n.*

bau·bee (bô-bē', bô'bē) *n.* Variant of **bawbee.**

bau·ble (bô'bəl) *n.* **1.** A small, showy ornament of little value; trinket. **2.** *Archaic.* A baton carried by a court jester as a mock scepter of his office. [ME *babel* < OFr., plaything.]

baud (bôd) *n. Computer Sci.* A unit of speed in data transmission, as one bit per second for binary signals. [After J.M.E. *Baudot* (d. 1903).]

Bau·haus (bou'hous') *adj.* Of, pertaining to, or characteristic of a 20th-century school of design whose aesthetic was influenced by and derived from techniques and materials employed esp. in industrial fabrication and manufacture. [G., an architecture school founded by Walter Gropius (1883–1969).]

baulk (bôk) *v. & n.* Variant of **balk.**

Bau·mé scale (bō-mā') *n.* A hydrometer scale that separately covers liquids with specific gravities greater and less than 1. [After Antoine *Baumé* (1728–1804).]

baux·ite (bôk'sīt') *n.* The principal ore of aluminum, 30 to 75 per cent $Al_2O_3{\cdot}nH_2O$, with ferric oxide and silica as impurities. [Fr., after Les Baux, France.]

Ba·var·i·an (bə-vâr'ē-ən) *n.* **1.** A native or inhabitant of Bavaria. **2.** The High German dialect of Bavaria and Austria. —**Ba·var'i·an** *adj.*

baw·bee also **bau·bee** (bô-bē', bô'bē) *n. Scot.* A halfpenny. [After Alexander Orrok, Laird of *Sillbawby,* 16th-cent. Scottish master of the mint.]

bawd (bôd) *n.* **1.** A woman who keeps a brothel; madam. **2.** A prostitute. [ME *bawde,* prob. < OFr. *baude,* bold < OHG *bald.*]

bawd·ry (bô'drē) *n.* Obscene, risqué, or coarse language. [ME *bawdery* < *bawde,* bawd.]

bawd·y (bô'dē) *adj.* **-i·er, -i·est. 1.** Humorously coarse; risqué. **2.** Vulgar; lewd. —**bawd'i·ly** *adv.* —**bawd'i·ness** *n.*

bawd·y·house (bô'dē-hous') *n.* A house of prostitution.

bawl (bôl) *v.* **bawled, bawl·ing, bawls.** —*intr.* **1.** To cry or sob loudly; wail. **2.** To cry out loudly and vehemently; shout. —*tr.* To utter in a loud, vehement voice. —***phrasal verb.*** **bawl out.** *Informal.* To reprimand or scold loudly or harshly. —*n.* A loud, bellowing cry; wail. [ME *baulen,* to bark, of Scand. orig.] —**bawl'er** *n.*

bay[1] (bā) *n.* **1.** A body of water partly enclosed by land but with a wide outlet to the sea. **2. a.** A broad stretch of low land between hills. **b.** An arm of prairie partly enclosed by woodland. [ME *baye* < OFr. *baie* < LLat. *baia,* perh. < Iberian.]

bay[2] (bā) *n.* **1.** *Archit.* A part of a building or other structure marked off by vertical elements. **2. a.** A bay window. **b.** An opening or recess in a wall. **3.** An extension of a building; wing. **4.** A compartment in a barn used for storing hay or grain. **5.** A ship's sickbay. **6.** A bomb bay in an aircraft. [ME < OFr. *baee,* an opening < *baer,* to gape.]

bay[3] (bā) *adj.* Reddish-brown: *a bay colt.* —*n.* **1.** A reddish brown. **2.** A reddish-brown animal, esp. a horse. [ME < OFr. *bai* < Lat. *badius.*]

bay[4] (bā) *n.* **1.** A deep, prolonged bark, as of hounds. **2.** The position of one cornered by pursuers and forced to turn and fight at close quarters. **3.** The position of one checked or kept at a safe distance. —*v.* **bayed, bay·ing, bays.** —*intr.* To utter a bay. —*tr.* **1.** To pursue with barking. **2.** To express by barking. **3.** To bring to bay. [ME < *baien,* to bark < OFr. *baiier.*]

bay[5] (bā) *n.* **1.** The laurel (sense 1). **2.** A crown or wreath made esp. of the leaves and branches of the bay and given as a sign of honor. **3.** Often **bays.** Renown; honor. [ME *bai,* laurel berry < OFr. *baie* < Lat. *baca,* berry.]

ba·ya·dere (bī'ə-dîr', -dâr') *n.* A fabric with contrasting horizontal stripes. [Fr. *bayadère* < Port. *bailadeira,* dancer < *bailar,* to dance < LLat. *ballare* < Gk. *ballizein.*]

bay·ber·ry (bā'bĕr'ē) *n.* **1.** Any of several aromatic shrubs or small trees of the genus *Myrica,* esp. *M. pensylvanica,* of eastern North America, bearing gray, waxy berries. **2.** A tropical American tree, *Pimenta acris,* yielding an oil used in making bay rum. **3.** The fruit of a bayberry.

bay leaf *n.* The dried aromatic leaf of the bay, *Laurus nobilis,* or of the bayberry, *Pimenta acris,* used as seasoning in cooking.

bay lynx *n.* The bobcat.

bay·o·net (bā'ə-nĭt, -nĕt', bā'ə-nĕt') *n.* A knife adapted to fit the muzzle end of a rifle and used in close combat. —*tr.v.* **-net·ed, -net·ing, -nets** or **-net·ted, -net·ting, -nets.** To stab or prod with a bayonet. [Fr. *baionnette* < *Bayonne,* a city in France.]

bay·ou (bī'ōō, bī'ō) *n.* A marshy, sluggish body of water tributary to a lake or river. [Louisiana Fr. < Choctaw *bayuk.*]

bay rum *n.* An aromatic liquid obtained by distilling the leaves of the bayberry tree, *Pimenta acris,* with rum or synthesized from alcohol, water, and various oils.

bay rum tree *n.* The bayberry.

bay window *n.* **1.** A large window or series of windows projecting from the outer wall of a building and forming a recess within. **2.** *Slang.* A protruding belly; paunch.

ba·zaar also **ba·zar** (bə-zär') *n.* **1.** An Oriental market consisting of a street lined with shops and stalls. **2.** A shop or part of a store for the sale of miscellaneous articles. **3.** A fair or sale at which miscellaneous articles are sold, often for charitable purposes. [Prob. < Ital. *bazarro* < Pers. *bāzār.*]

ba·zoo·ka (bə-zōō'kə) *n.* A portable military weapon consisting of a long metal smoothbore tube for firing small, armor-piercing rockets at short range. [After the *bazooka,* a crude wind instrument made of pipes, invented and named by Bob Burns (1896–1956).]

BB (bē'bē) *n.* A standard size of lead shot that measures about .46 cm., or 0.18 in., in diameter. [Perh. from the letter *b.*]

BB gun *n.* A small air rifle for firing BB shot.

B cell *n.* A lymphocyte derived from bone marrow that takes part in the immune responses. [BONE-MARROW-DERIVED + CELL.]

bdel·li·um (dĕl'ē-əm) *n.* An aromatic gum resin similar to myrrh, produced by various trees of the genus *Commiphora,* of western Asia and Africa. [Lat. < Gk. *bdellion,* of Semitic orig.]

be (bē) *intr.v.*

	1st person	2nd person	3rd person
Present Tense			
singular	**am** (ăm)	**are** (är)†	**is** (ĭz)
plural	**are**	**are**	**are**

†*Archaic 2nd person singular* **art** (ärt)

Past Tense			
singular	**was** (wŭz, wŏz)	**were** (wûr)‡	**was**
plural	**were**	**were**	**were**

‡*Archaic 2nd person singular* **wast** (wŏst) *or* **wert** (wûrt)

Present Participle: **being** (bē'ĭng) Present Subjunctive: **be**
Past Participle: **been** (bĭn) Past Subjunctive: **were**

1. To exist in actuality; have reality or life: *I think, therefore I am.* **2.** To occupy a specified position: *The food is on the table.* **3.** To take place; occur. **4.** To go. Used chiefly in the past and perfect tenses: *Have you ever been to Italy?* **5.** *Archaic.* To belong; befall. **6.** Used as a copula linking a subject and a predicate nominative, adjective, or pronoun, in such senses as: **a.** To equal in meaning or identity: *"To be a Christian was to be a Roman"* (James Bryce). **b.** To signify; symbolize: *A is excellent, C is passing.* **c.** To belong to a specified class or group: *Man is a primate.* **d.** To have or show a specified quality or characteristic: *She is lovely. All men are mortal.* —*aux.* **1.** Used with the past participle of a transitive verb to form the passive voice: *The mayoral election is held annually.* **2.** Used with the present participle of a verb to express a continuing action: *We are working to improve housing conditions.* **3.** Used with the infinitive of a verb to express intention, obligation, or future action: *She was to call before she left. He is to make the necessary changes.* **4.** *Archaic.* Used with the past participle of certain intransitive verbs of motion to form the perfect tense: *"Where be those roses gone which sweetened so our eyes?"* (Philip Sidney). [ME *been* < OE *bēon.*]

Usage: When pronouns follow a form of the verb *to be,* the nominative is traditionally required, on the grounds that the pronoun denotes the same entity as the subject. Thus, the rules require *it is I, that must be she,* and so forth. The rules create problems, however, when the pronoun after *to*

battlement
Caernarvon Castle, Wales

bayonet
Union soldiers at Appomatox Court House in April 1865

bay window

be denotes an entity that is also understood to be the object of some other verb or preposition. Shall we say *it is I she loves* or *it is me she loves?* There is no strict rule, but given the natural tendency to use objective forms like *me* rather than nominatives like *I* in undecidable cases, the use of *me* is entirely defensible here. It should also be noted that the use of the nominative following *to be* sounds stilted when the verb has been contracted. Nevertheless, a purist would say *it's I* rather than *it's me,* or *that's they* rather than *that's them.*

Be The symbol for the element beryllium.

be– *pref.* **1.** Completely; thoroughly; excessively. Used as an intensive: *bemoan.* **2.** On; around; over: *besmear.* **3.** Used to form transitive verbs from nouns, adjectives, and intransitive verbs, as: **a.** Make; cause to become: *besot.* **b.** Affect or provide with: *bespangle.* [ME < OE *bī-.*]

beach (bēch) *n.* **1.** The shore of a body of water, esp. when sandy or pebbly. **2.** The sand or pebbles on a shore. —*tr.v.* **beached, beach·ing, beach·es.** To haul or drive ashore. [Orig. unknown.]

beach buggy *n.* A dune buggy.

beach·comb·er (bēch'kō'mər) *n.* **1.** One who lives on what can be found on beaches or in wharf areas. **2.** A long wave rolling in toward a beach.

beach flea *n.* Any of various small, jumping crustaceans of the family Orchestiidae, living on sandy beaches at or near the tide line.

beach grass *n.* Any grass of the genus *Ammophila,* growing mostly on sandy shores and dunes and having spikelets in long, crowded clusters.

beach·head (bēch'hĕd') *n.* **1.** A position on an enemy shoreline captured by troops in advance of an invading force. **2.** A position that opens the way for further development; foothold.

beach pea *n.* Either of two similar North American plants, *Lathyrus maritimus,* of the Atlantic coast, or *L. littoralis,* of the Pacific coast, having purplish flowers and sprawling stems.

beach plum *n.* A seacoast shrub, *Prunus maritima,* of northeastern North America, having white flowers and edible, plumlike fruit.

beach wormwood *n.* A seacoast plant, *Artemisia stelleriana,* native to Asia, covered with dense white down and having small yellow flowers.

bea·con (bē'kən) *n.* **1.** A signal fire, esp. one used to warn of an enemy's approach. **2.** A lighthouse or other signaling or guiding device on a coast. **3.** A radio transmitter that emits a characteristic signal as a warning or guide. **4.** Something that warns or guides. —*tr. & intr.v.* **-coned, -con·ing, -cons.** To provide with or serve as a beacon. [ME *beken* < OE *bēacen.*]

bead (bēd) *n.* **1. a.** A small, ball-shaped piece of material pierced for stringing or threading. **b. beads.** A necklace made of such pieces. **c. beads.** A rosary. **2.** A small, round object, esp.: **a.** A small drop of moisture. **b.** A bubble of gas in a liquid. **c.** A small knob of metal on the muzzle of a rifle or gun, used for sighting. **3.** A strip of material, usually wood, with one molded edge placed flush against the inner part of a door or window frame. —*tr. & intr.v.* **bead·ed, bead·ing, beads.** To furnish with or collect into beads. [ME *bede,* rosary bead < OE *gebed,* prayer.]

beagle

bead·ing (bē'dĭng) *n.* **1.** Beads or material used for beads. **2.** Ornamentation with beads. **3.** A narrow, half-rounded molding. **4.** A narrow piece of openwork lace through which ribbon may be run.

bea·dle (bēd'l) *n.* A minor parish official in an English church whose duties include keeping order and ushering during services. [ME *bedele,* herald < OE *bydel.*]

bead·work (bēd'wûrk') *n.* **1.** Decorative work in beads. **2.** *Archit.* Beaded molding.

bead·y (bē'dē) *adj.* **-i·er, -i·est. 1.** Small, round, and shiny: *beady eyes.* **2.** Decorated or covered with beads.

bea·gle (bē'gəl) *n.* One of a breed of small hounds having short legs, drooping ears, and a smooth coat with white, black, and tan markings. [ME *begle.*]

beaker

beak (bēk) *n.* **1. a.** The horny, projecting structure forming the mandibles of a bird; bill. **b.** A part or organ resembling this, as in some turtles, insects, or fish. **2.** A hard, cone-shaped, or pointed structure or part. **3.** *Informal.* A person's nose. [ME *bek* < OFr. *bec* < Lat. *beccus,* of Celt. orig.] **—beaked** (bēkt) *adj.*

beak·er (bē'kər) *n.* **1.** A large drinking cup with a wide mouth. **2.** An open glass cylinder with a pouring lip, used as a laboratory container. [ME *biker* < ON *bikarr,* prob. < Med. Lat. *bicarius* < Gk. *bikos,* jug.]

bear[2]

beam (bēm) *n.* **1.** A squared-off log or large, oblong piece of timber, metal, or stone used esp. in construction. **2.** The breadth of a ship at the widest point. **3.** *Informal.* The width across a person's hips. **4.** A steel tube or wooden roller on which the warp is wound in a loom. **5.** An oscillating lever connected to an engine piston rod and used to transmit power to the crankshaft. **6.** The bar of a balance from which weighing pans are suspended. **7.** One of the main stems of a deer's antlers. **8.** The main horizontal bar on a plow to which the share, colter, and handles are attached. **9. a.** A ray of light. **b.** A group of particles traveling together in close parallel trajectories. **10.** A radio beam. —*v.* **beamed, beam·ing, beams.** —*intr.* **1.** To radiate light; shine. **2.** To smile expansively. —*tr.* To emit or transmit. **—idiom. on the beam. 1.** Following a radio beam, as an aircraft. **2.** *Informal.* On the right track; operating correctly. [ME < OE *bēam.*]

beam-ends (bēm'ĕndz') *pl.n.* The ends of a ship's beams.

beam·ish (bē'mĭsh) *adj.* Beaming; smiling. **—beam'ish·ly** *adv.*

beam·y (bē'mē) *adj.* **-i·er, -i·est. 1.** Broad in the beam. **2.** Emitting beams, as of light; radiant.

bean (bēn) *n.* **1. a.** Any of several plants of the genus *Phaseolus,* having compound leaves, white or yellow flowers, and seed-bearing pods. **b.** The edible seed or pod of any of these plants. **c.** Any of several related plants bearing similar pods and seeds. **d.** Any of various other seeds or pods resembling beans, as the coffee bean. **2.** *Slang.* The head. **3. beans.** *Slang.* A small amount: *don't know beans about the market.* **4.** *Chiefly Brit. Slang.* A fellow; chap. —*tr.v.* **beaned, bean·ing, beans.** *Slang.* To hit on the head with a thrown object, esp. a pitched baseball. **—idioms. full of beans.** Energetic. **spill the beans.** To disclose something that was not meant to be disclosed. [ME *bene* < OE *bēan.*]

bean·bag (bēn'băg') *n.* A small bag filled with dried beans and used for throwing in games.

bean ball *n.* A baseball pitch aimed at the batter's head.

bean blight *n.* A disease of the bean caused by the bacterium *Xanthomonas phaseoli,* which results in yellow-brown blotches on all parts of the plant.

bean caper *n.* A plant of the genus *Zygophyllum,* esp. *Z. fabago,* a shrub of the Middle East, bearing edible buds used as capers.

bean curd *n.* A soft, cheeselike food made from puréed soy beans. [Transl. of Chin. (Mandarin) *dou[4] fu[3]* : *dou[4],* bean + *fu[3],* curdled.]

bean·ie (bē'nē) *n.* A small brimless cap.

bean·o (bē'nō) *n., pl.* **-os.** A form of bingo, esp. one using beans as markers.

bean·pole (bēn'pōl') *n.* **1.** A thin pole used to support bean vines. **2.** *Slang.* A very tall, thin person.

bean sprout *n.* A young, tender shoot of certain beans, such as the soybean, used in cooking.

bean·stalk (bēn'stôk') *n.* The stem of a bean plant.

bean tree *n.* Any of various trees, such as the catalpa, that bear beanlike fruit.

bear[1] (bâr) *v.* **bore** (bôr, bōr), **borne** or **born** (bôrn, bōrn), **bear·ing, bears.** —*tr.* **1.** To hold up; support. **2.** To move while supporting; carry. **3.** To carry in the mind; harbor: *bore grudges.* **4.** To transmit; relate: *bearing glad tidings.* **5.** To have as a visible characteristic: *bore a scar on his arm.* **6.** To have as a quality; exhibit. **7.** To carry (oneself) in a specified way; conduct: *bore herself with grace.* **8.** To be accountable for; assume: *bearing heavy responsibilities.* **9.** To have a tolerance for; endure: *couldn't bear his lying.* **10.** To be susceptible to; admit of: *The case will bear investigation.* **11.** To give birth to. **12.** To produce; yield: *plants bearing flowers.* **13.** To offer; render: *bearing witness.* **14.** To move by steady pressure; push: *boats borne by the tides.* —*intr.* **1.** To yield a product; produce. **2.** To have relevance; apply: *how the relativity theory bears on the history of science.* **3.** To exert pressure. **4.** To exert oneself determinedly; forge. **5.** To proceed or extend in a specified direction: *bore right at the corner.* **—phrasal verbs. bear down. 1.** To overwhelm; vanquish: *bore down all opposition.* **2.** To apply maximum effort and concentration: *really bore down and finished the task.* **bear down on.** To affect in a harmful or adverse way: *Financial pressures are bearing down on him.* **bear out.** To prove right or justified; confirm: *results that bear out his claims.* **bear up.** To withstand stress, difficulty, or attrition: *bore up well during the long illness.* **bear with.** To be patient or tolerant with: *Please bear with me while I explain.* **—idiom. bear in mind.** To remember. [ME *beren* < OE *beran.*]

Synonyms: *bear, endure, stand, suffer, abide, tolerate.* These verbs are compared in the sense of withstanding, sustaining, or putting up with. *Bear* pertains broadly to capacity for such an act. *Endure* specifies a continuing capacity to face pain or harship. The remaining terms are more descriptive of the manner of withstanding or accepting. *Stand* implies resoluteness of spirit. *Suffer* and the less emphatic *abide* suggest resignation and forebearance. *Tolerate,* in its principal application (to something other than pain), connotes reluctant acceptance despite mental reservations.

Usage: In its literal sense the past participle *born* is used only of mammals and only in construction with *to be: The baby was born.* (It may also be used figuratively: *A star is born.) Borne,* said of the act of birth, refers only to the mother's role, but it can be used actively or passively: *She has borne three children. Three children were borne by her* (but *born to her*). In all other senses of *bear* the past participle is *borne: The soil has borne abundant crops. Such a burden cannot be borne by anyone.*

bear[2] (bâr) *n.* **1. a.** Any of various usually omnivorous mammals of the family Ursidae, having a shaggy coat and a short tail and walking with the entire lower surface of the foot touching the ground. **b.** Any of various animals, such as the koala, resembling a bear. **2.** A person who is awkward, clumsy, or ill-mannered. **3.** An investor or concern that sells securities or commodities in the expectation that prices will fall. [ME *bere* < OE *bera.*]

bear·a·ble (bâr′ə-bəl) *adj.* Capable of being borne; endurable. **—bear′a·bil′i·ty** *n.* **—bear′a·bly** *adv.*

bear·bait·ing (bâr′bā′tĭng) *n.* The former sport of setting dogs to attack or torment a chained bear.

bear·ber·ry (bâr′bĕr′ē) *n.* A trailing shrub, *Arctostaphylos uva-ursi,* of northern regions, having small evergreen leaves, white or pink flowers, and red berries.

beard (bîrd) *n.* **1.** The hair on the chin, cheeks, and throat of a man. **2.** A hairy or hairlike growth such as that on or near the face of certain mammals. **3.** A tuft or group of bristles on certain plants; awn. **4.** The part of a piece of type between the face and the shoulder; neck. *—tr.v.* **beard·ed, beard·ing, beards. 1.** To furnish with a beard. **2.** To grasp by the beard. **3.** To confront boldly. [ME *berd* < OE *beard.*] **—beard′ed** *adj.* **—beard′ed·ness** *n.* **—beard′less** *adj.* **—beard′less·ness** *n.*

bearded iris *n.* Any of many varieties of iris having beardlike growths at the bases of the three lower, recurved petals.

bearded vulture *n.* The lammergeier.

beard-tongue (bîrd′tŭng′) *n.* Any of various plants of the genus *Penstemon,* mostly of North America, having variously colored, tubular, two-lipped flowers.

bear·er (bâr′ər) *n.* **1.** One that carries or supports. **2.** A porter. **3.** A person who presents a check or other redeemable note for payment. **4.** A fruit-bearing plant.

bearer bond *n.* A bond payable to the holder.

bear grass *n.* **1.** A tall plant, *Xerophyllum tenax,* of northwestern North America, having narrow, grasslike leaves and white flowers in a large terminal cluster. **2.** Any of several plants similar or related to the bear grass, esp. any of several species of yucca.

bear hug *n.* A rough hug.

bear·ing (bâr′ĭng) *n.* **1.** The manner in which a person carries or conducts himself: *the poise and bearing of a champion.* **2. a.** A part that supports another machine part or structure. **b.** A device that supports, guides, and reduces the friction of motion between fixed and moving machine parts. **3.** Something that bears weight or acts as a support. **4.** The part of an arch or beam that rests on a support. **5. a.** The act, power, or period of producing fruit or offspring. **b.** The quantity produced; yield. **6.** Direction, esp. angular direction measured from one position to another using geographical or celestial reference lines. **7.** Often **bearings.** The awareness of one's position or situation relative to one's surroundings. **8.** Relevancy, relationship, or connection between persons, objects, or concepts: *facts with no bearing on our situation.* **9.** A charge or device on a heraldic field.

Synonyms: *bearing, carriage, manner, demeanor, air, mien, presence.* These nouns pertain to distinctive personal qualities. *Bearing,* the most inclusive, applies to both physical posture and conduct in general. *Carriage* denotes physical bearing. *Manner* denotes one's characteristic way of acting; the plural *manners* applies especially to the social proprieties. *Demeanor* is behavior considered as a mirror of personality. *Air* pertains broadly to distinctive appearance, and *mien* to bearing in general and to facial expression in particular. *Presence* denotes the quality of commanding respectful attention.

bearing rein *n.* A rein for a horse; checkrein.

bear·ish (bâr′ĭsh) *adj.* **1.** Like a bear in clumsiness, boorishness, or surliness. **2. a.** Causing, expecting, or characterized by falling stock-market prices. **b.** Pessimistic, negative, or skeptical. **—bear′ish·ly** *adv.* **—bear′ish·ness** *n.*

bé·ar·naise sauce (bā′är-nāz′, -ər-) *n.* A sauce similar to hollandaise but flavored with tarragon, shallots, and chervil.

bear·skin (bâr′skĭn′) *n.* **1.** Something, as a rug, made from the skin of a bear. **2.** A tall military headdress made of black fur.

beast (bēst) *n.* **1. a.** An animal as distinguished from man. **b.** A large, four-footed animal. **2.** The qualities of an animal; animal nature. **3.** A brutal or vile person. [ME *beste* < OFr. < Lat. *bestia.*]

beast epic *n.* A long verse narrative in which the characters are animals with human feelings and motives.

beast·ings (bē′stĭngz) *n.* Variant of **beestings.**

beast·ly (bēst′lē) *adj.* **-li·er, -li·est. 1.** Of or like a beast; bestial. **2.** Disagreeable; nasty: *beastly behavior. —adv. Chiefly Brit. Informal.* Used as an intensive: *a beastly hot month.* **—beast′li·ness** *n.*

beast of burden *n.* An animal, such as a donkey, used for transporting loads.

beat (bēt) *v.* **beat, beat·en** (bēt′n) or **beat, beat·ing, beats.** *—tr.* **1.** To strike or hit repeatedly. **2.** To punish by hitting or whipping; flog. **3.** To pound or strike against repeatedly: *waves beating the shore.* **4.** To shape or break by repeated blows; forge: *beat the glowing metal into a dagger.* **5.** To make flat by pounding or trampling. **6.** To mix rapidly with an instrument: *beat two eggs in a bowl.* **7.** To flap, as wings. **8.** To strike so as to produce a signal or music: *beat the drum.* **9.** To mark or count (time or rhythm) with the hands or with a baton. **10.** To defeat or subdue, as in a contest. **11.** *Informal.* To be superior; surpass: *Riding beats walking.* **12.** *Slang.* To perplex or baffle. **13.** *Informal.* To avoid or counter the effects of; circumvent: *beat the traffic. —intr.* **1.** To inflict repeated blows. **2.** To throb or pulsate rhythmically. **3.** *Physics.* To cause beating by superposing waves of different frequencies. **4.** To emit sound when struck: *The gong beat thunderously.* **5.** To sound a signal, as on a drum. **6.** To flap repeatedly. **7.** To hunt through woods or underbrush in search of game. **8.** *Naut.* To progress against the wind by tacking. ***—phrasal verbs.*** **beat back.** To force to retreat or withdraw. **beat down.** To force or persuade (a seller) to accept a lower price. **beat off.** To drive away. **beat out.** *Baseball.* To make a hit on a ground ball by fast running to first base. *—n.* **1.** A stroke or blow, esp. one that produces a sound or acts as a signal. **2.** A periodic pulsation or throb. **3.** *Physics.* An amplitude pulse produced by beating. **4.** *Mus.* **a.** A regular and rhythmical unit of time. **b.** The gesture used by a conductor to indicate this unit of time. **c.** The symbol representing this unit of time. **5.** The measured and rhythmical sound of verse; meter. **6.** The area regularly covered by a policeman, sentry, or newspaper reporter. **7.** *Slang.* The reporting of a news item obtained ahead of one's competitors. **8.** A beatnik *—adj.* **1.** *Informal.* Worn-out; fatigued. **2.** Of, pertaining to, or being a beatnik: *the beat generation.* ***—idioms.*** **beat around** (or **about**) **the bush.** To approach a subject in a roundabout manner. **beat it.** *Slang.* To get going; leave hurriedly. [ME *beten* < OE *bēaten.*]

beat·en (bēt′n) *adj.* **1.** Made thin or formed by hammering: *beaten gold.* **2.** Worn by continuous use; familiar and much traveled: *a beaten path.* **3.** Tired and worn-out. ***—idiom.*** **off the beaten path** (or **track**). Not well-known; unusual.

beat·er (bē′tər) *n.* **1.** One that beats, esp. an instrument for beating: *a carpet beater.* **2.** A person who drives wild game from under cover for a hunter.

be·a·tif·ic (bē′ə-tĭf′ĭk) *adj.* Showing or producing exalted joy or blessedness: *a beatific smile.* [LLat. *beatificus* : Lat. *beatus,* p.part. of *beare,* to bless + *facere,* to make.] **—be′a·tif′i·cal·ly** *adv.*

be·at·i·fy (bē-ăt′ə-fī′) *tr.v.* **-fied, -fy·ing, -fies. 1.** To make blessedly happy. **2.** *Rom. Cath. Ch.* To proclaim (a deceased person) to be one of the blessed and thus worthy of public religious honor. **3.** To exalt above all others. [Fr. *beatifier* < LLat. *beatificare* : Lat. *beatus,* p.part. of *beare,* to bless + Lat. *facere,* to make.] **—be·at′i·fi·ca′tion** *n.*

beat·ing (bē′tĭng) *n.* **1.** Punishment by whipping, flogging, or thrashing. **2.** A defeat. **3.** A throbbing or pulsation, as of the heart. **4.** *Physics.* The periodic alternation of amplitude maxima and minima produced by interference between two waves of different frequency.

be·at·i·tude (bē-ăt′ĭ-to͞od′, -tyo͞od′) *n.* **1.** Supreme blessedness or happiness. **2. Beatitude.** Any of nine declarations of blessedness made by Jesus in the Sermon on the Mount. [Fr. *béatitude* < Lat. *beatitudo* < *beare,* to bless.]

beat·nik (bēt′nĭk) *n.* A person who acts and dresses with pointed, often exaggerated disregard for what is thought proper and who is given to radical and extravagant social criticism or self-expression. [< *beat generation,* a group of unconventional young people of the 1950's + -NIK.]

beau (bō) *n., pl.* **beaus** or **beaux** (bōz). **1.** The sweetheart of a woman or girl. **2.** A man who is excessively interested in fine clothes and social etiquette; dandy. [Fr., handsome < Lat. *bellus.*]

Beau Brum·mell (bō brŭm′əl) *n.* A dandy; fop. [After George Bryan *("Beau") Brummell* (1778–1840).]

Beau·fort scale (bō′fərt) *n.* A scale on which successive ranges of wind velocities are assigned code numbers from 0 to 12 or from 0 to 17, corresponding to names from *calm* to *hurricane.* [After Sir Francis *Beaufort* (1774–1857).]

beau geste (bō zhĕst′) *n., pl.* **beaux gestes** (bō zhĕst′) or **beau gestes** (bō zhĕst′). **1.** A gracious gesture. **2.** A gesture noble in form but meaningless in substance. [Fr.]

beau i·de·al (bō′ ī-dē′əl) *n., pl.* **beau i·de·als. 1.** The concept of perfect beauty. **2.** An idealized type or model. [Fr. *beau idéal,* ideal beauty.]

Beau·jo·lais (bō′zhō-lā′) *n.* A red table wine of French origin. [After *Beaujolais,* a region of central France.]

beau monde (bō mŏnd′, mô**N**d′) *n., pl.* **beaux mondes** (bō mô**N**d′) or **beau mondes** (bō mŏndz′). The world of fashionable society. [Fr., fine world.]

beaut (byo͞ot) *n. Slang.* Something outstanding of its kind: *"When I make a mistake, it's a beaut"* (Fiorello H. La Guardia). [Short for BEAUTY.]

beau·te·ous (byo͞o′tē-əs) *adj.* Beautiful, esp. to the sight. **—beau′te·ous·ly** *adv.* **—beau′te·ous·ness** *n.*

beau·ti·cian (byo͞o-tĭsh′ən) *n.* One skilled in cosmetic treatments, as in a beauty parlor.

beau·ti·ful (byo͞o′tə-fəl) *adj.* Having beauty in any of its forms; pleasing to the senses or the mind. **—beau′ti·ful·ly** *adv.* **—beau′ti·ful·ness** *n.*

Synonyms: *beautiful, lovely, pretty, handsome, comely, fair.* All these adjectives apply to that which appeals to the senses or mind. *Beautiful,* the most comprehensive, applies to what stirs a heightened response of the senses and of the mind on its highest level. *Lovely* pertains to that which inspires ardent emotion rather than intellectual appreciation. *Pretty* suggests only sensory appeal of a limited and superfi-

bearskin
Sentry of the
Coldstream Guards

cial nature. *Handsome* stresses visual appeal by reason of conformity to ideals of form and proportion. *Comely* is usually restricted to wholesome physical attractiveness. *Fair,* in this context, emphasizes visual appeal deriving from freshness and purity.

beautiful people also **Beautiful People** *pl.n.* People who are prominent, esp. in international society.

beau·ti·fy (byo͞o′tə-fī′) *tr. & intr.v.* **-fied, -fy·ing, -fies.** To make or become beautiful. **—beau′ti·fi·ca′tion** *n.* **—beau′ti·fi′er** *n.*

beau·ty (byo͞o′tē) *n., pl.* **-ties. 1.** A pleasing quality associated with harmony of form or color, excellence of craftsmanship, truthfulness, originality, or another, often unspecifiable property. **2.** A person or thing that is beautiful, esp. a beautiful woman. **3.** A quality or feature that is most effective, gratifying, or telling: *The beauty of the venture is that we stand to lose nothing.* **4.** *Informal.* An outstanding or conspicuous example: *a beauty of a faux pas.* [ME *beaute* < OFr. *bealte* < *VLat.* **bellitas* < Lat. *bellus,* beautiful.]

beau·ty·bush (byo͞o′tē-bo͝osh′) *n.* A shrub, *Kolkwitzia amabilis,* native to China, widely cultivated for its profusely blooming pink flowers.

beauty parlor *n.* An establishment providing women with services that include hair treatment, manicures, and facials.

beauty salon *n.* A beauty parlor.

beauty shop *n.* A beauty parlor.

beauty spot *n.* **1.** A small black mark penciled or glued on a woman's face or shoulders to accentuate the fairness of her skin or conceal an imperfection. **2.** A mole or freckle.

beaux (bōz) *n.* A plural of **beau.**

beaux-arts (bō-zär′) *pl.n.* The fine arts. [Fr.]

beaux es·prits (bō′zĕ-sprē′) *n.* Plural of **bel esprit.**

beaux gestes (bō zhĕst′) *n.* A plural of **beau geste.**

beaux mondes (bō môNd′) *n.* A plural of **beau monde.**

beaver[1]

bea·ver[1] (bē′vər) *n.* **1. a.** A large aquatic rodent of the genus *Castor,* having thick brown fur, webbed hind feet, a paddlelike, hairless tail, and chisellike front teeth adapted for gnawing bark and felling trees used to build dams. **b.** The fur of a beaver. **2.** A top hat originally made of the beaver's underfur. **3.** A napped wool fabric, similar to felt, used for outer garments. [ME *bever* < OE *beofor.*]

bea·ver[2] (bē′vər) *n.* **1.** A piece of armor attached to a helmet or breastplate to protect the mouth and chin. **2.** The visor on a helmet. [ME *baviere* < OFr., child's bib < *bave,* saliva.]

bea·ver·board (bē′vər-bôrd′, -bōrd′) *n.* A light, semirigid building material of compressed wood pulp, used for walls and partitions. [Orig. a trademark.]

be·bop (bē′bŏp′) *n.* Bop[2]. [Imit. of a two-beat phrase in this music.]

be·calm (bĭ-käm′) *tr.v.* **-calmed, -calm·ing, -calms. 1.** To render motionless for lack of wind. **2.** To make calm or still; soothe.

be·came (bĭ-kām′) *v.* Past tense of **become.**

be·cause (bĭ-kôz′, -kŭz′) *conj.* For the reason that; since. [ME.]

Usage: *Because* is the most direct of the conjunctions used to express cause or reason. It is used to state an immediate and explicit cause: *He stayed behind because he was ill. Since, as,* and *for* are all less direct than *because;* they often express the speaker's or writer's view of the causal relation between circumstances or events. The clause introduced by *since* most frequently comes first in the sentence: *Since he stayed behind, he must have been ill* (his staying behind leads the speaker to conclude that he must have been ill). *As,* like *since,* often indicates that what follows is the speaker's basis for coming to a certain conclusion: *As I am ill, I would prefer to stay behind. For* is a coordinating conjunction, linking two independent statements. It expresses the speaker's reason for having said or concluded the previous statement: *The man definitely stole the book, for I was watching and I saw him do it. As* and *for* are now used primarily in formal levels of style. • *Because* is sometimes used in informal speech to mean "just because," as in *Because there's snow on the roof doesn't mean the fire is out in the basement.* This use of *because* should be avoided in writing. Traditional grammar holds that the expression *the reason is because* is redundant and so should be avoided at all levels. This usage is well established, however, and has perfectly acceptable equivalents in expressions like *the time was when.* • When *because* follows a negative verb or verb phrase, it should be preceded by a comma when the *because* clause gives the subject's reason for *not* doing something. *He didn't leave, because he was hungry* means roughly "He stayed in order to eat." When no comma is used, the *because* clause is understood as part of what is being negated. *He didn't leave because he was hungry* means "His reason for staying was not hunger, but something else." The conjunctions *since, as,* and *for,* when used to express a causal relation, must be preceded by commas: *He left, since he was hungry. I must go, as I have a great deal to do. There were no boats on the lake, for a strong wind had come up.*

because of *prep.* By reason of; on account of.

bec·ca·fi·co (bĕk′ə-fē′kō) *n., pl.* **-cos.** A small songbird or warbler of various genera, eaten as a delicacy in Italy. [Ital. : *beccare,* to peck (< *becco,* beak < Lat. *beccus*) + *fico,* fig (< Lat. *ficus*).]

bé·cha·mel sauce (bā′shə-mĕl′) *n.* A white sauce of butter, flour, and milk or cream. [Fr. *sauce béchamelle,* after Louis de *Béchamel* (d. 1703), its inventor.]

be·chance (bĭ-chăns′) *intr. & tr.v.* **-chanced, -chanc·ing, -chanc·es.** *Archaic.* To happen or happen to.

bêche-de-mer (bĕsh′də-mâr′) *n., pl.* **bêches-de-mer** (bĕsh′də-mâr′). **1.** The trepang. **2.** A lingua franca that combines Malay and English, spoken in the southwest Pacific. [Fr. : *bêche,* grub + *de,* of + *mer,* sea.]

Bech·u·a·na (bĕch′o͞o-ä′nə) *n., pl.* **Bechuana** or **-nas. 1.** A member of a Bantu people inhabiting Botswana in south-central Africa. **2.** The Bantu language of the Bechuana.

beck[1] (bĕk) *n.* A gesture of beckoning or summons. ***—idiom.*** **at (someone's) beck and call.** Ready to comply with any wish or command. [ME *bek,* an order < *bekken,* to beckon.]

beck[2] (bĕk) *n.* *Chiefly Brit.* A small brook. [ME < ON *bekkr.*]

beck·et (bĕk′ĭt) *n.* *Naut.* A device, such as a looped rope, hook and eye, strap, or grommet, for holding or fastening loose ropes, spars, or oars in position. [Orig. unknown.]

beck·on (bĕk′ən) *v.* **-oned, -on·ing, -ons.** *—tr.* **1.** To signal or summon, as by nodding or waving. **2.** To attract as if with gestures: *"a lovely, sunny country that seemed to beckon them on to the Emerald City"* (L. Frank Baum). *—intr.* **1.** To make a signaling or summoning gesture. **2.** To have a strong attraction; be enticing. *—n.* A gesture or motion of summons. [ME *beknen* < OE *bēcnan.*] **—beck′on·er** *n.* **—beck′on·ing·ly** *adv.*

be·cloud (bĭ-kloud′) *tr.v.* **-cloud·ed, -cloud·ing, -clouds.** To darken with or as if with clouds; obscure: *a development that beclouds the real issues.*

be·come (bĭ-kŭm′) *v.* **-came** (-kām′), **-come, -com·ing, -comes.** *—intr.* To grow or come to be: *"All women become like their mothers"* (Oscar Wilde). *—tr.* **1.** To be appropriate or suitable to: *"it would not become me . . . to interfere with parties"* (Jonathan Swift). **2.** To show to advantage; look good with: *a new dress that becomes you.* ***—phrasal verb.*** **become of.** To be the fate or subsequent condition of. [ME *becomen* < OE *becuman.*]

be·com·ing (bĭ-kŭm′ĭng) *adj.* **1.** Appropriate or suitable. **2.** Pleasing or attractive to the eye. **—be·com′ing·ly** *adv.* **—be·com′ing·ness** *n.*

Bec·que·rel ray (bĕ-krĕl′, bĕk′ə-rĕl′) *n.* *Obs.* Radiation associated with radioactivity. [After Antoine Henri *Becquerel* (1852–1908).]

be·crip·ple (bĭ-krĭp′əl) *tr.v.* **-pled, -pling, -ples.** To cause to become crippled.

bed (bĕd) *n.* **1. a.** A piece of furniture for reclining and sleeping, typically consisting of a flat, rectangular frame and a mattress resting on springs. **b.** A bedstead. **c.** A mattress. **2.** A place where one may sleep; lodging. **3.** A time at which one goes to sleep: *drank cocoa before bed.* **4.** A place for lovemaking. **5.** A marital relationship with its rights and intimacies. **6.** A small plot of cultivated or planted land: *a flower bed.* **7.** The bottom of a watercourse or other body of water. **8.** A supporting, underlying, or securing part, esp.: **a.** A layer of food surmounted by another kind of food. **b.** A foundation of crushed rock or a similar substance for a road or railroad; roadbed. **c.** A layer of mortar upon which stones or bricks are laid. **9.** *Geol.* **a.** A rock mass of large horizontal extent bounded, esp. above, by physically different material. **b.** A deposit, as of ore, parallel to the local stratification. *—v.* **bed·ded, bed·ding, beds.** *—tr.* **1.** To furnish with a bed or sleeping quarters: *bedded the guests down in the study.* **2.** To put to bed. **3.** To plant in a prepared bed of soil. **4.** To lay flat or arrange in layers. **5.** To embed. *—intr.* **1.** To go to bed. **2.** To form layers or strata. ***—idiom.*** **go to bed with.** To have sexual intercourse with. [ME < OE.]

be·daub (bĭ-dôb′) *tr.v.* **-daubed, -daub·ing, -daubs. 1.** To smear; soil. **2.** To ornament in a vulgar and showy fashion.

be·daz·zle (bĭ-dăz′əl) *tr.v.* **-zled, -zling, -zles.** To dazzle so completely as to confuse or blind. **—be·daz′zle·ment** *n.*

bed·bug also **bed bug** (bĕd′bŭg′) *n.* A wingless, bloodsucking insect, *Cimex lectularius,* that has a flat, reddish body and a disagreeable odor and that often infests human dwellings.

bed·cham·ber (bĕd′chām′bər) *n.* A bedroom.

bed·clothes (bĕd′klōz′, -klō*thz*′) *pl.n.* Coverings, such as sheets and blankets, ordinarily used on a bed.

bed·ding (bĕd′ĭng) *n.* **1.** Bedclothes. **2.** Straw or similar material for animals to sleep on. **3.** Something that forms a foundation or bottom layer. **4.** *Geol.* Stratification of rocks into beds.

be·deck (bĭ-dĕk′) *tr.v.* **-decked, -deck·ing, -decks.** To deck out or adorn in a showy fashion; cover with decorations.

bedes·man (bēdz′mən) *n.* An almsman. [ME *bedeman* : *bede,* prayer (< OE *gebed*) + *man,* man (< OE mann).]

be·dev·il (bĭ-dĕv′əl) *tr.v.* **-iled, -il·ing, -ils** or **-illed, -il·ling, -ils. 1.** To torment devilishly; plague. **2.** To worry, annoy, or frustrate. **3.** To possess with or as if with a devil; bewitch. **4.** To spoil; ruin. **—be·dev′il·ment** *n.*

be·dew (bĭ-do͞o′, -dyo͞o′) *tr.v.* **-dewed, -dew·ing, -dews.** To wet with or as if with dew.

bed·fast (bĕd′făst′) *adj.* Confined to bed; bedridden.

bed·fel·low (bĕd′fĕl′ō) *n.* **1.** A person with whom one shares a bed; bedmate. **2.** An associate, collaborator, or ally.
Bed·ford cord (bĕd′fərd) *n.* A heavy cotton or woolen fabric in a ribbed weave with wide or narrow raised cords much like corduroy. [After *Bedford,* England.]
be·dight (bĭ-dīt′) *tr.v.* **-dight** or **-dight·ed, -dight·ing, -dights.** *Archaic.* To dress or adorn. [ME *bidighten.*]
be·dim (bĭ-dĭm′) *tr.v.* **-dimmed, -dim·ming, -dims.** To make dim.
be·di·zen (bĭ-dī′zən, -dĭz′ən) *tr.v.* **-zened, -zen·ing, -zens.** To dress or ornament in a vulgar or tasteless manner. **—be·di′zen·ment** *n.*
bed·lam (bĕd′ləm) *n.* **1.** A place or situation of noisy uproar and confusion. **2.** *Archaic.* A lunatic asylum; madhouse. [ME *Bedlem,* Hospital of St. Mary of *Bethlehem,* London, an insane asylum.]
bed·lam·ite (bĕd′lə-mīt′) *n.* A madman; lunatic.
Bed·ling·ton terrier (bĕd′lĭng-tən) *n.* A dog of a breed developed in England, having a woolly grayish or brownish coat. [After *Bedlington,* England.]
bed·mate (bĕd′māt′) *n.* One with whom a bed is shared.
bed molding *n.* **1.** The molding between the corona and frieze of an entablature. **2.** A molding below a projecting part.
bed of roses *n.* A state of idyllic comfort or luxury.
Bed·ou·in also **Bed·u·in** (bĕd′o͞o-ĭn, bĕd′wĭn) *n.* An Arab of any of the nomadic tribes of the deserts of North Africa, Arabia, and Syria. [ME *Bedoin* < OFr. *beduin* < Ar. *badāwīn,* pl. of *badāwī* < *badw,* desert.]
bed·pan (bĕd′păn′) *n.* **1.** A metal, glass, or plastic receptacle for the excreta of bedridden persons. **2.** A warming pan.
bed·plate (bĕd′plāt′) *n.* A plate, frame, or platform serving as a base or support for a machine.
bed·post (bĕd′pōst′) *n.* A vertical post at the corner of a bed.
be·drag·gle (bĭ-drăg′əl) *tr.v.* **-gled, -gling, -gles.** To make wet and limp.
be·drag·gled (bĭ-drăg′əld) *adj.* **1. a.** Wet; limp. **b.** Soiled by or as if by dragging in the mud. **2.** In a condition of deterioration; dilapidated.
bed·rid·den (bĕd′rĭd′n) also **bed·rid** (-rĭd′) *adj.* Confined to bed because of illness or infirmity. [ME *bedreden* < OE *bedrida,* bedridden person : *bed,* bed + *rīda,* rider (< *rīdan,* to ride).]
bed·rock (bĕd′rŏk′) *n.* **1.** The solid rock that underlies all soil, sand, clay, gravel, and loose material on the earth's surface. **2.** The lowest or bottom level. **3.** Fundamental principles.
bed·roll (bĕd′rōl′) *n.* A portable roll of bedding used esp. by campers and others who sleep outdoors.
bed·room (bĕd′ro͞om′, -ro͝om′) *n.* A room for sleeping. *—adj.* **1.** Dealing with or suggestive of sexual relations: *a bedroom comedy; bedroom eyes.* **2.** Relating to or inhabited by commuters: *bedroom suburbs.*
bed·side (bĕd′sīd′) *n.* The space alongside a bed. *—adj.* Near a bed: *a bedside table.*
bedside manner *n.* The attitude and conduct of a doctor in the presence of a patient.
bed-sit (bĕd′sĭt′) *n. Chiefly Brit.* A bed-sitting-room.
bed-sit·ting-room (bĕd-sĭt′ĭng-ro͞om′, -ro͝om′) *n. Chiefly Brit.* A one-room apartment that serves as a bedroom and a sitting room.
bed·so·ni·a (bĕd-sō′nē-ə) *n.* Any of a group of intracellular parasites, as of the genus *Chlamydia,* including the causative agents of trachoma and psittacosis. [NLat., after Sir Samuel P. *Bedson* (d. 1969).]
bed·sore (bĕd′sôr′, -sōr′) *n.* A pressure-induced ulceration of the skin occurring during long confinement to bed.
bed·spread (bĕd′sprĕd′) *n.* A usually decorative bed covering.
bed·spring (bĕd′sprĭng′) *n.* The springs supporting the mattress of a bed.
bed·stead (bĕd′stĕd′) *n.* The frame supporting a bed.
bed·straw (bĕd′strô′) *n.* Any of various plants of the genus *Galium,* having whorled leaves, small white or yellow flowers, and prickly burrs.
bed·time (bĕd′tīm′) *n.* The time when one goes to bed.
bed-wet·ting (bĕd′wĕt′ĭng) *n.* Enuresis, esp. when occurring in bed at night. **—bed wetter** *n.*
bee¹ (bē) *n.* **1.** Any of various winged, hairy-bodied, usually stinging insects of the order Hymenoptera, including many solitary species as well as the social members of the family Apidae, characterized by specialized structures for sucking nectar and gathering pollen from flowers. **2.** A social gathering where people combine work, competition, and amusement: *a quilting bee.* [ME < OE *bēo.*]
bee² (bē) *n.* A bee block. [ME *bei,* a metal ring < OE *bēag.*]
bee³ (bē) *n.* The letter *b.*
bee balm *n.* Oswego tea.
bee block *n. Naut.* A piece of hardwood on either side of a bowsprit through which forestays are reeved.
bee·bread (bē′brĕd′) *n.* A brownish substance consisting of a mixture of pollen and nectar, fed by bees to their larvae.
beech (bēch) *n.* **1.** A tree of the genus *Fagus,* characterized by smooth, light-colored bark and edible nuts partly enclosed in a prickly husk, esp. *F. grandifolia,* of eastern North America, and *F. sylvatica,* of Europe. **2.** The wood of a beech. [ME *beche* < OE *bēce.*]
beech·drops (bēch′drŏps′) *n., pl.* **beechdrops.** A leafless plant, *Epifagus virginiana,* of eastern North America, that has brownish or purplish flowers and is parasitic on the roots of the beech tree.
beech·nut (bēch′nŭt′) *n.* The small, edible nut of the beech tree.
bee-eat·er (bē′ē′tər) *n.* Any of various chiefly tropical Old World birds of the family Meropidae, having brightly colored plumage and feeding chiefly on bees.
beef (bēf) *n., pl.* **beeves** (bēvz). **1. a.** A full-grown steer, bull, ox, or cow, esp. one intended for use as meat. **b.** The flesh of a slaughtered full-grown steer, bull, ox, or cow. **2.** *Informal.* Human muscle; brawn. **3.** *pl.* **beefs.** *Slang.* A complaint. *—intr.v.* **beefed, beef·ing, beefs.** *Slang.* To complain. ***—phrasal verb.* beef up.** *Slang.* To reinforce; build up. [ME < OFr. *boef* < Lat. *bos.*]
beef·a·lo (bē′fə-lō′) *n.* A hybrid resulting from a cross between the American buffalo and domestic cattle. [BEEF + (BUFF)ALO.]
beef bour·gui·gnon (bo͝or′gēn-yôn′) *n.* Braised beef cubes simmered in a seasoned red-wine sauce with mushrooms, carrots, and onions. [Fr. *boeuf bourguignon* < *Bourgogne,* Burgundy, a region of France.]
beef·burg·er (bēf′bûr′gər) *n.* A hamburger.
beef·cake (bēf′kāk′) *n. Informal.* Photographs of minimally attired men with muscular physiques. [BEEF + (CHEESE)CAKE.]
beef·eat·er (bēf′ē′tər) *n.* **1.** A yeoman of the royal guard in England. **2.** A warder of the Tower of London.
bee fly *n.* Any of various flies of the family Bombyliidae, resembling bees and having larvae that are parasitic on the young of bees, wasps, and other insects.
beef·steak (bēf′stāk′) *n.* A slice of beef, as from the loin or the hindquarters, suitable for broiling or frying.
beefsteak fungus *n.* An edible fungus, *Fistularia hepatica,* growing on decaying wood and having a large, irregularly shaped reddish cap.
beef stro·ga·noff (strō′gə-nôf′, -nŏf′) *n.* Thinly sliced beef fillet sautéed and served with mushrooms and sour cream. [After Count Paul *Stroganoff* (1744?–1817).]
beef·wood (bēf′wo͝od′) *n.* Any of various trees of the genus *Casuarina,* mostly native to Australia, having small, scalelike leaves and flowers. [Perh. from its reddish color.]
beef·y (bē′fē) *adj.* **-i·er, -i·est. 1.** Resembling beef. **2.** Muscular in build; brawny: *a beefy wrestler.* **—beef′i·ness** *n.*
bee gum *n.* **1.** A hollow gum tree in which bees hive. **2.** A beehive, esp. one in a hollow gum tree.
bee·hive (bē′hīv′) *n.* **1.** A hive, either natural or manmade, for bees. **2.** A place teeming with activity.
bee·keep·er (bē′kē′pər) *n.* One who keeps bees; apiarist.
bee·line (bē′līn′) *n.* A direct, straight course. [From the belief that a pollen-laden bee flies straight to its hive.]
Be·el·ze·bub (bē-ĕl′zə-bŭb′) *n.* The Devil. [LLat. *Beëlzebub* < Gk. *Beelzeboub* < Heb. *bá'al zbūb,* lord of the flies.]
bee moth *n.* Either of two moths, *Galleria mellonella* or *Achroia grisella,* that lay their eggs in beehives, where the larvae feed on the honeycombs and the young bees.
been (bĭn) *v.* Past participle of **be.**
beep (bēp) *n.* A signaling or warning sound, as from a horn or an electronic device. *—intr. & tr.v.* **beeped, beep·ing, beeps.** To make or cause to make a beep. [Imit.]
beep·er (bē′pər) *n.* **1.** One that beeps. **2.** A small portable electronic device that emits a beeping signal when the person carrying it is being paged.
bee plant *n.* Any of various fragrant, nectar-bearing plants that attract bees.
beer (bîr) *n.* **1.** A fermented alcoholic beverage brewed from malt and flavored with hops. **2.** Any of various drinks made from extracts of roots and plants: *birch beer.* [ME *bere* < OE *bēor.*]
beer·y (bîr′ē) *adj.* **-i·er, -i·est. 1.** Smelling or tasting of beer. **2.** Affected or produced by beer: *beery humor.*
beest·ings also **beast·ings** (bē′stĭngz) *n. (used with a sing. or pl. verb).* The first milk given by a cow or other mammal after parturition; colostrum. [ME *besting* < OE *bēost,* beestings.]
bees·wax (bēz′wăks′) *n.* **1.** The yellowish to dark-brown wax secreted by the honeybee for making honeycombs. **2.** Commercial wax obtained by processing and purifying the crude wax of the honeybee and used in making candles, crayons, and polishes.
beet (bēt) *n.* **1.** Any of several widely cultivated plants of the genus *Beta,* esp. *B. vulgaris,* having leaves sometimes eaten as greens and a thickened, fleshy root. **2.** The bulbous root of the beet, characteristically dark red in color, eaten as a vegetable. [ME *bete* < OE *bēte* < Lat. *beta.*]
beet armyworm *n.* An armyworm, *Spodoptera exigua,* feeding primarily on the foliage of alfalfa, beets, and other vegetables.
bee·tle¹ (bēt′l) *n.* **1.** Any of numerous insects of the order Coleoptera, having biting mouth parts and front wings modified to form horny wing covers that overlie the membranous rear wings when at rest. **2.** An insect resembling a beetle. [ME *bityl* < OE *bitela* < *bītan,* to bite.]

Bedlington terrier

George Miksch Sutton
bee-eater

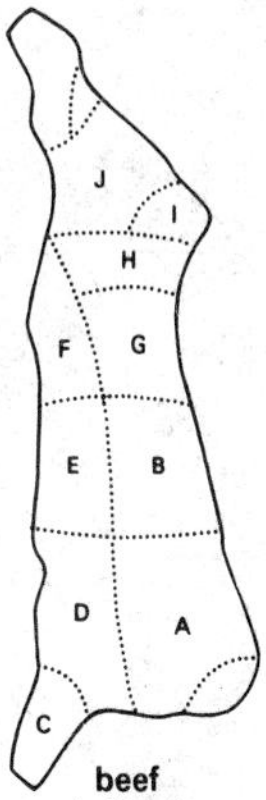

beef
A. Chuck
B. Ribs
C. Shank
D. Brisket
E. Plate
F. Flank
G. Loin (tenderloin and porterhouse)
H. Sirloin
I. Rump
J. Round

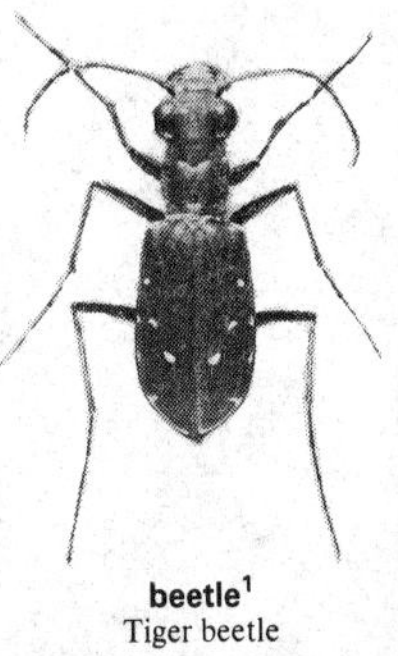

beetle¹
Tiger beetle

bee·tle² (bēt′l) *adj.* Jutting; overhanging: *beetle brows.* —*intr.v.* **-tled -tling, -tles.** To overhang. [ME *bitel-(brouwed),* having shaggy or protruding (eyebrows).]

bee·tle³ (bēt′l) *n.* **1.** A heavy mallet with a large wooden head. **2.** A small wooden household mallet. **3.** A heavy wooden club used in stamping and finishing handmade linen. **4.** A cloth-finishing machine that stamps cloth with revolving wooden hammers. [ME *betel* < OE *bīetel.*]

bee·tle·bung (bēt′l-bŭng′) *n.* The sour gum.

bee·tle·weed (bēt′l-wēd′) *n.* The galax.

bee tree *n.* **1.** A hollow tree in which bees live. **2.** A tree, such as the basswood, having flowers rich in nectar.

beet·root (bēt′ro͞ot′, -ro͝ot′) *n. Chiefly Brit.* The root of the beet.

beetroot purple *n.* A deep to very deep purplish red.

beeves (bēvz) *n.* A plural of **beef.**

be·fall (bĭ-fôl′) *v.* **-fell** (-fĕl′), **-fall·en** (-fô′lən), **-fall·ing, -falls.** —*intr.* To come to pass, esp. by chance; happen. —*tr.* To happen to. [ME *befallen* < OE *befeallen,* to fall.]

begonia

be·fit (bĭ-fĭt′) *tr.v.* **-fit·ted, -fit·ting, -fits.** To be suitable to or appropriate for.

be·fit·ting (bĭ-fĭt′ĭng) *adj.* **1.** Appropriate; suitable. **2.** Proper. —**be·fit′ting·ly** *adv.*

be·fog (bĭ-fôg′, -fŏg′) *tr.v.* **-fogged, -fog·ging, -fogs. 1.** To cover or obscure with or as if with fog. **2.** To cause confusion in; muddle.

be·fool (bĭ-fo͞ol′) *tr.v.* **-fooled, -fool·ing, -fools. 1.** To make a fool of. **2.** To hoodwink; deceive.

be·fore (bĭ-fôr′, -fōr′) *adv.* **1.** In the past; earlier. **2.** In front; ahead. —*prep.* **1.** Previous to in time; earlier than. **2.** In front of. **3.** In prospect for; awaiting: *Your happiness lies before you.* **4.** In the presence of: *She ordered the man to be brought before her.* **5.** Under the consideration or jurisdiction of: *the case before the court.* **6.** Superior to or in advance of, as in rank, condition, or development: *The prince is before his brother in the line of succession.* —*conj.* **1.** In advance of the time when: *before he went.* **2.** Rather than; sooner than: *He would die before he would betray his country.* [ME < OE *beforan.*]

be·fore·hand (bĭ-fôr′hănd′, -fōr′-) *adv. & adj.* **1.** In anticipation. **2.** In advance; early.

be·fore·time (bĭ-fôr′tīm′, -fōr′-) *adv. Archaic.* Formerly.

be·foul (bĭ-foul′) *tr.v.* **-fouled, -foul·ing, -fouls. 1.** To make dirty; soil. **2.** To speak badly of; cast aspersions upon.

be·friend (bĭ-frĕnd′) *tr.v.* **-friend·ed, -friend·ing, -friends.** To act as a friend to.

be·fud·dle (bĭ-fŭd′l) *tr.v.* **-dled, -dling, -dles. 1.** To confuse; perplex. **2.** To stupefy with or as if with alcoholic drink.

beg (bĕg) *v.* **begged, beg·ging, begs.** —*tr.* **1.** To ask for as charity. **2.** To ask earnestly for or of; entreat. —*intr.* **1.** To solicit alms. **2.** To make a humble or urgent plea. —***phrasal verb.* beg off.** To ask to be released from something, as an obligation. —***idiom.* beg the question. 1.** To assume the conclusion to one's argument to be true. **2.** To equivocate or dodge an issue. [ME *beggen,* prob. < OFr. *begart,* beggar, ult. < MDu. *beggaert.*]

Synonyms: *beg, crave, beseech, implore, entreat, importune. Beg* and *crave* apply to the act of asking for something one cannot claim as a right, in a way that is earnest, humble, and designed to stir pity. *Beseech* emphasizes earnestness and implies great anxiety. *Implore* intensifies the senses of earnestness, humility, and anxiety. *Entreat* pertains to persuasive pleading calculated to overcome opposition. *Importune* adds the sense of persistent and sometimes harassing pleading.

be·gan (bĭ-găn′) *v.* Past tense of **begin.**

be·gat (bĭ-găt′) *v. Archaic.* Past tense of **beget.**

be·get (bĭ-gĕt′) *tr.v.* **-got** (-gŏt′), **-got·ten** (-gŏt′n) or **-got, -get·ting, -gets. 1.** To father; sire. **2.** To cause to exist; produce. [ME *begete* < OE *begietan,* to obtain.] —**be·get′ter** *n.*

beg·gar (bĕg′ər) *n.* **1.** One who begs, esp. one who begs alms for a living. **2.** An impoverished person; pauper. **3.** A rascal; rogue. —*tr.v.* **-gared, -gar·ing, -gars. 1.** To make a beggar of; impoverish. **2.** To exhaust the resources of: *beauty that beggars all description.* [ME < OFr. *begart,* ult. < MDu. *beggaert.*]

beg·gar·ly (bĕg′ər-lē) *adj.* **1.** Of or pertaining to a beggar; very poor. **2.** Mean; contemptible. —**beg′gar·li·ness** *n.*

beg·gar's-lice (bĕg′ərz-līs′) *n.* **1.** *(used with a sing. or pl. verb).* Any of several plants, such as the stickseed, bearing small, prickly fruit that cling readily to clothing or the fur of animals. **2.** One of the seeds of a beggar's-lice.

beg·gar-ticks (bĕg′ər-tĭks′) *n.* **1.** *(used with a sing. or pl. verb).* Any of several plants having seeds that cling to clothing, often by means of barbed bristles, esp. the bur marigold and the tick trefoil. **2.** The seeds of a beggar-ticks.

beg·gar·weed (bĕg′ər-wēd′) *n.* A West Indian plant, *Desmodium purpureum,* grown as forage in the southern United States.

beg·gar·y (bĕg′ə-rē) *n.* **1.** Extreme poverty; penury. **2.** The state or condition of being a beggar. **3.** Beggars collectively.

be·gin (bĭ-gĭn′) *v.* **-gan** (-găn′), **-gun** (-gŭn′), **-gin·ning, -gins.** —*intr.* **1.** To start to do something; commence. **2.** To come into being: *when life began.* **3.** To do or be in the least degree: *That doesn't even begin to address the problem.* —*tr.* **1.** To start to do; commence. **2.** To cause to come into being; originate. [ME *beginnen* < OE *biginnan.*]

Synonyms: *begin, commence, start, initiate, inaugurate. Begin* and *commence* are equivalent in meaning, though *commence* is sometimes felt to be stronger in suggesting initiative. *Start* is often interchangeable with *begin* and *commence* but can specify a setting out from a specific point, following inaction, or (transitively) a setting in motion. *Initiate* applies to the act of taking the first steps in a process, without reference to what follows. *Inaugurate* pertains to a formal beginning.

be·gin·ner (bĭ-gĭn′ər) *n.* **1.** One who begins something. **2.** One who is just starting to learn or do something; novice.

be·gin·ning (bĭ-gĭn′ĭng) *n.* **1.** The act or process of bringing or being brought into being; start. **2.** The time when something begins or is begun. **3.** The place where something begins or is begun. **4.** A source; origin. **5.** The first part. **6.** Often **beginnings.** An early or rudimentary phase.

beginning rhyme *n.* **1.** Rhyme at the beginning of consecutive lines of verse. **2.** Alliteration.

be·gird (bĭ-gûrd′) *tr.v.* **-girt** (-gûrt′) or **-gird·ed, -girt, -gird·ing, -girds.** To gird or encircle; surround.

be·gone (bĭ-gôn′, -gŏn′) *interj.* Used as an order of dismissal. [ME *begone* : *be,* imper. of *been,* to be + *gone,* gone.]

be·go·nia (bĭ-gōn′yə) *n.* Any of various plants of the genus *Begonia,* mostly native to the tropics but widely cultivated, having leaves that are often brightly colored or veined and irregular, waxy flowers of various colors. [NLat. *Begonia,* genus name, after Michel *Bégon* (1638–1710).]

be·gor·ra (bĭ-gôr′ə, -gŏr′ə) *interj. Ir.* Used as a mild swearword. [Alteration of *by God.*]

be·got (bĭ-gŏt′) *v.* Past tense and a past participle of **beget.**

be·got·ten (bĭ-gŏt′n) *v.* A past participle of **beget.**

be·grime (bĭ-grīm′) *tr.v.* **-grimed, -grim·ing, -grimes.** To smear or soil with or as if with dirt or grime.

be·grudge (bĭ-grŭj′) *tr.v.* **-grudged, -grudg·ing, -grudg·es. 1. a.** To envy the possession or enjoyment of. **b.** To envy for a possession. **2.** To give with reluctance. —**be·grudg′er** *n.* —**be·grudg′ing·ly** *adv.*

be·guile (bĭ-gīl′) *tr.v.* **-guiled, -guil·ing, -guiles. 1.** To deceive by guile; delude. **2.** To take away from by guile; cheat. **3.** To distract the attention of; divert. **4.** To pass (time) pleasantly. **5.** To amuse or charm; delight. —**be·guile′ment** *n.* —**be·guil′er** *n.*

be·guine (bĭ-gēn′) *n.* **1.** A ballroom dance based on a native dance of Martinique and St. Lucia. **2.** The music for the beguine. [Fr. (West Indies) *béguine* < Fr. *béguin,* flirtation.]

Beg·uine (bā′gēn′, bā-gēn′) *n.* A member of any of several Roman Catholic lay sisterhoods existing in the Netherlands since the 12th century. [OFr.]

be·gum (bā′gəm, bē′-) *n.* A Moslem lady of rank. [Urdu < Turk. *begim,* possessive of *beg,* bey.]

be·gun (bĭ-gŭn′) *v.* Past participle of **begin.**

be·half (bĭ-hăf′, -häf′) *n.* Interest, support, or benefit. —***idioms.* in behalf of.** In the interest of; for the benefit of. **on behalf of.** On the part of; speaking for. [ME *bihalve* : *bi,* by + *half,* side. —see HALF.]

Usage: *In behalf of* and *on behalf of* have distinct senses and, according to a majority of the Usage Panel, should not be used interchangeably. *In behalf of* means "in the interest of" or "for the benefit of": *We raised money in behalf of the orphans. We acted in their behalf. On behalf of* means "as the agent of" or "on the part of": *The guardian sued on behalf of the minor child. On whose behalf did he act?*

be·have (bĭ-hāv′) *v.* **-haved, -hav·ing, -haves.** —*intr.* **1.** To act, react, function, or perform in a particular way. **2. a.** To conduct oneself in a specified way. **b.** To conduct oneself in a proper way. —*tr.* **1.** To conduct (oneself) properly. **2.** To conduct (oneself) in a specified way. [ME *behaven.*]

be·hav·ior (bĭ-hāv′yər) *n.* **1.** The manner in which one behaves. **2.** The actions or reactions of persons or things under specified circumstances. —**be·hav′ior·al** *adj.* —**be·hav′ior·al·ly** *adv.*

Synonyms: *behavior, conduct, deportment.* These all pertain to one's actions considered as a means of evaluation by others. *Behavior* applies to actions on specific occasions involving essentially external and sometimes superficial relationships. *Conduct* applies to actions in more significant relationships, considered from the standpoint of morals and ethics. *Deportment* more narrowly pertains to actions measured by a prevailing social code of behavior.

behavioral psychophysics *n.* A branch of psychology dealing primarily with the measurement of sensory capacities in nonaberrant animal specimens.

behavioral science *n.* A science, such as sociology or anthropology, that seeks to discover general truths about human social behavior. —**behavioral scientist** *n.*

be·hav·ior·ism (bĭ-hāv′yə-rĭz′əm) *n.* The psychological school holding that objectively observable organismic behavior constitutes the essential or exclusive scientific basis of psychological data and investigation and stressing the role of environment as a determinant of human and animal behavior. —**be·hav′ior·ist** *n.* —**be·hav′ior·is′tic** *adj.*

behavior modification *n.* The modification of behavioral traits through psychological means, as reinforcement and aversion therapy. —**behavior modifier** *n.*

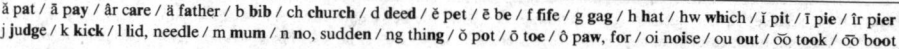

be·hav·iour (bĭ-hāv′yər) *n. Chiefly Brit.* Variant of **behavior.**
be·head (bĭ-hĕd′) *tr.v.* **-head·ed, -head·ing, -heads.** To separate the head from; decapitate. [ME *biheveden* < OE *beheāfdian* : *be-*, away from + *hēafod,* head.]
be·held (bĭ-hĕld′) *v.* Past tense and past participle of **behold.**
be·he·moth (bĭ-hē′məth, bē′ə-məth) *n.* **1.** A huge animal, possibly the hippopotamus, described in the Old Testament. **2.** Something enormous in size. [Heb. *bəhēmōth,* pl. of *bəhēmāh,* beast.]
be·hest (bĭ-hĕst′) *n.* **1.** An order or authoritative command. **2.** An urgent request. [ME *bihest,* promise < OE *behæs.*]
be·hind (bĭ-hīnd′) *adv.* **1.** In, to, or toward the rear: *He walked behind.* **2.** In a place or condition that has been passed or left: *He left his gloves behind.* **3.** In arrears; late: *behind in her payments.* **4.** Below the standard level; in or into an inferior position: *fall behind in class.* **5.** Slow: *His watch is running behind.* **6.** *Archaic.* In reserve; yet to come. —*prep.* **1.** At the back of or in the rear of: *She sat behind him.* **2.** On the farther side or other side of; beyond: *behind the door.* **3.** In a place or time that has been passed or left by: *Their worries are behind them.* **4.** Later than: *The plane was behind schedule.* **5.** Less advanced than: *behind us in technology.* **6. a.** Hidden or concealed by: *behind the scenes.* **b.** In the background of; underlying: *Behind his every action was greed.* **7.** Serving to support: *He had the army behind him.* **8.** In pursuit of: *the posse hard behind him.* —*n. Informal.* The buttocks. [ME *bihinde* < OE *behindan.*]
be·hind·hand (bĭ-hīnd′hănd′) *adv. & adj.* **1.** In arrears. **2.** Behind time; slow. **3.** In a backward state.
be·hind-the-scenes (bĭ-hīnd′thə-sēnz′) *adj.* Done, maintained, or held in secret.
be·hold (bĭ-hōld′) *tr.v.* **-held** (-hĕld′), **-hold·ing, -holds.** To gaze at; look upon. Often used as an interjection with exclamatory force. [ME *biholden* < OE *behealdan.*] **—be·hold′er** *n.*
be·hold·en (bĭ-hōl′dən) *adj.* Obliged, as for a favor; indebted. [ME *biholden.*]
be·hoof (bĭ-ho͞of′) *n.* Benefit; advantage. [ME *bihove* < OE *behōfe.*]
be·hoove (bĭ-ho͞ov′) *v.* **-hooved, -hoov·ing, -hooves.** —*tr.* To be necessary or proper for: *It behooved him to try.* —*intr.* To be necessary or proper. [ME *behoven* < OE *behōfian.*]
beige (bāzh) *n.* **1.** A soft fabric of undyed and unbleached wool. **2.** A light grayish brown or yellowish brown to grayish yellow. —*adj.* Light grayish brown or yellowish brown to grayish yellow. [Fr.]
be·ing (bē′ĭng) *n.* **1.** The state or quality of having existence. **2. a.** An object, idea, or symbol that exists, is thought to exist, or is represented as existing. **b.** A person: *"The artist after all is a solitary being"* (Virginia Woolf). **3.** One's basic or essential nature. **4.** *Philos.* **a.** That which can be conceived as existing. **b.** Absolute existence in its perfect and unqualified state; the essence of existence.
Be·ja (bā′jə) *n., pl.* **Beja. 1.** A pastoral tribe of people living as nomads in the area between the Nile River and the Red Sea. **2.** One of the Beja. **3.** The Cushitic language of the Beja.
bel (bĕl) *n.* The logarithm to the base 10 of the ratio of two levels of power, used to measure voltage or sound intensity and equal to 10 decibels. [After Alexander Graham *Bell* (1847–1922).]
be·la·bor (bĭ-lā′bər) *tr.v.* **-bored, -bor·ing, -bors. 1.** To attack with blows. **2.** To thrash or assail verbally. **3.** To go over repeatedly or for a long time; harp on: *belabor a point.*
be·la·bour (bĭ-lā′bər) *v. Chiefly Brit.* Variant of **belabor.**
be·lat·ed (bĭ-lā′tĭd) *adj.* Too late; tardy: *a belated birthday card.* **—be·lat′ed·ly** *adv.* **—be·lat′ed·ness** *n.*
be·lay (bĭ-lā′) *v.* **-layed, -lay·ing, -lays.** —*tr.* **1.** *Naut.* To secure or make fast (a rope, for example) by winding on a cleat or pin. **2.** To secure (a mountain climber) at the end of a length of rope. **3.** To cause to stop. —*intr.* **1.** To be made secure. **2.** To stop: *Belay there!* —*n.* In mountain climbing, the securing of a rope on a rock or other projection. [ME *beleggen,* to surround < OE *belecgan.*]
belaying pin *n.* A short, removable wooden or metal pin fitted in a hole in the rail of a boat and used for securing running gear.
bel can·to (bĕl kän′tō) *n.* A style of operatic singing characterized by rich tonal lyricism and brilliant display of vocal technique. [Ital., beautiful singing.]
belch (bĕlch) *v.* **belched, belch·ing, belch·es.** —*intr.* **1.** To expel gas noisily from the stomach through the mouth. **2.** To erupt or explode violently. **3.** To gush forth. —*tr.* **1.** To expel (gas) noisily from the stomach through the mouth; eruct. **2.** To eject violently. —*n.* An act or instance of belching, esp. an eructation. [ME *belchen* < OE *bealcan.*]
bel·dam also **bel·dame** (bĕl′dəm) *n.* An old woman, esp. one who is loathsome or ugly. [ME, grandmother : OFr. *bel,* beautiful (< Lat. *bellus*) + OFr. *dame,* woman. —see DAME.]
be·lea·guer (bĭ-lē′gər) *tr.v.* **-guered, -guer·ing, -guers. 1.** To besiege by surrounding with troops. **2.** To harass; beset: *beleaguered by problems.* [Du. *belegeren*: *be-*, around + *leger,* camp.]
bel·em·nite (bĕl′əm-nīt′) *n.* A cigar-shaped fossilized internal shell of any of various extinct cephalopods related to the cuttlefish. [NLat. *belemnites* < Gk. *belemnon,* dart.]
bel es·prit (bĕl′ĕ-sprē′) *n., pl.* **beaux es·prits** (bō′zĕ-sprē′). A cultivated person with a fine intellect. [Fr., fine mind.]
bel·fry (bĕl′frē) *n., pl.* **-fries. 1.** A bell tower, esp. one attached to a building. **2.** The part of a tower or steeple in which bells are hung. [ME *berfrei* < OFr., portable siege tower, of Germanic orig.] **—bel′fried** *adj.*
Bel·gae (bĕl′gī′, -jē′) *pl.n.* An ancient Gallic people who formerly inhabited what is now Belgium and northern France. [Lat.]
Bel·gian (bĕl′jən) *n.* A native or inhabitant of Belgium. **—Bel′gian** *adj.*
Belgian hare *n.* A large, reddish-brown rabbit of a domestic breed developed in England from Belgian stock.
Bel·gic (bĕl′jĭk) *adj.* **1.** Of or pertaining to Belgium or the Belgians. **2.** Of or pertaining to the Netherlands. **3.** Of or pertaining to the Belgae.
Be·li·al (bē′lē-əl, bēl′yəl) *n.* **1.** A satanic personification of wickedness and ungodliness alluded to in the New Testament. **2.** In Milton's *Paradise Lost,* one of the fallen angels who rebelled against God. [Heb. *blīyya′al,* uselessness: *blī,* without + *ya′al,* use.]
be·lie (bĭ-lī′) *tr.v.* **-lied, -ly·ing, -lies. 1.** To picture falsely; misrepresent. **2.** To show to be false. **3.** To disappoint or leave unfulfilled. **4.** *Archaic.* To tell lies about; defame. [ME *belīen* < OE *belēogan.*] **—be·li′er** *n.*
be·lief (bĭ-lēf′) *n.* **1.** The mental act, condition, or habit of placing trust or confidence in a person or thing. **2.** Mental acceptance of or conviction in the truth or actuality of something. **3.** Something believed or accepted as true, esp. a particular tenet or a body of tenets accepted by a group of persons. [ME *bileve,* alteration of OE *gelēafa.*]
be·lieve (bĭ-lēv′) *v.* **-lieved, -liev·ing, -lieves.** —*tr.* **1.** To accept as true or real. **2.** To credit with veracity. **3.** To expect or suppose; think: *I believe he will come shortly.* —*intr.* **1.** To have faith, esp. religious faith. **2.** To have faith or confidence; trust: *I believe in her ability.* **3.** To have confidence in the truth, value, or existence of something: *believed in free will.* **4.** To think or judge. [ME *bileven* < OE *belēfan.*] **—be·liev′a·ble** *adj.* **—be·liev′er** *n.*
be·like (bĭ-līk′) *adv. Archaic.* Perhaps; probably.
be·lit·tle (bĭ-lĭt′l) *tr.v.* **-tled, -tling, -tles. 1.** To represent or speak of as small or unimportant; disparage. **2.** To cause to seem less or little. **—be·lit′tle·ment** *n.* **—be·lit′tler** *n.*
bell[1] (bĕl) *n.* **1.** A hollow metal instrument, usually cup-shaped with a flared opening, that emits a metallic tone when struck. **2.** Something shaped like a bell, as: **a.** The round, flared mouth of some musical wind instruments. **b.** The corolla of a flower. **c.** A hollow, usually inverted vessel, such as a diving bell. **3.** *Naut.* **a.** A stroke on a bell to mark the hour. **b.** The time indicated by the striking of a bell, divided into half hours. **4. bells.** Bell-bottoms. —*v.* **belled, bell·ing, bells.** —*tr.* **1.** To put a bell on. **2.** To shape or cause to flare like a bell. —*intr.* To assume the form of a bell. —***idiom.*** **bell the cat.** To perform a daring action. [ME *belle* < OE.]
bell[2] (bĕl) *n.* The bellowing or baying cry of certain animals, such as a deer in rut or a beagle on the hunt. —*intr.v.* **belled, bell·ing, bells.** To bellow; bay. [< ME *bellen,* to bellow < OE *bellan.*]
bel·la·don·na (bĕl′ə-dŏn′ə) *n.* **1.** A poisonous Eurasian plant, *Atropa belladonna,* having purplish-red, bell-shaped flowers and small black poisonous berries. **2.** An atropine powder or tincture derived from the leaves and roots of the belladonna and used to treat asthma, colic, and hyperacidity. [Ital. : *bella,* beautiful + *donna,* lady.]
belladonna lily *n.* The amaryllis (sense 1).
bell·bird (bĕl′bûrd′) *n.* Any of various tropical American birds of the family Cotingidae, having a characteristic bell-like call.
bell-bot·tom (bĕl′bŏt′əm) *adj.* Having legs that flare out at the bottom: *bell-bottom trousers.*
bell-bot·toms (bĕl′bŏt′əmz) *pl.n.* Bell-bottom trousers.
bell·boy (bĕl′boi′) *n.* A boy or man employed by a hotel to assist guests, as by carrying luggage and running errands.
bell buoy *n.* A buoy fitted with a warning bell that is activated by the movement of the waves.
belle (bĕl) *n.* An attractive and much-admired girl or woman, esp. the most attractive at a given place: *the belle of the ball.* [Fr., beautiful < OFr. *bel* < Lat. *bella,* fem. of *bellus.*]
belle é·poque (ā-pŭk′) *n.* An era of artistic and cultural refinement in a society, esp. in France at the turn of the century. [Fr., beautiful age.]
Bel·ler·o·phon *n.* (bə-lĕr′ə-fən, -fŏn′) *n. Gk. Myth.* The Corinthian hero who, with the aid of the winged horse Pegasus, slew the Chimera. [Lat. < Gk. *Bellerophōn.*]
belles-let·tres (bĕl-lĕt′rə) *n. (used with a sing. verb).* Literature regarded for its aesthetic value rather than for its didactic or informative content. [Fr. : *belles,* fine + *lettres,* letters.]
bel·let·rist (bĕl-lĕt′rĭst) *n.* A writer of belles-lettres. **—bel·let′rism** *n.* **—bel′le·tris′tic** (bĕl′ĭ-trĭs′tĭk) *adj.*
bell·flow·er (bĕl′flou′ər) *n.* Any of various plants of the genus *Campanula,* characteristically having blue, bell-shaped flowers.
bell·hop (bel′hŏp′) *n.* A bellboy.

belfry

bell[1]
The Liberty Bell

belladonna

bel·li·cose (bĕl'ĭ-kōs') *adj.* Warlike in manner or temperament; pugnacious. [ME < Lat. *bellicosus* < *bellicus,* of war < *bellum,* war.] **—bel'li·cose'ly** *adv.* **—bel'li·cos'i·ty** (-kŏs'ĭ-tē), **bel'li·cose'ness** *n.*

bel·lig·er·ence (bə-lĭj'ər-əns) *n.* A warlike or hostile attitude, nature, or inclination.

bel·lig·er·en·cy (bə-lĭj'ər-ən-sē) *n.* **1.** The state of being at war or engaged in a warlike conflict. **2.** Belligerence.

bel·lig·er·ent (bə-lĭj'ər-ənt) *adj.* **1.** Inclined or eager to fight; hostile or aggressive. **2.** Of, pertaining to, or engaged in warfare. *—n.* **1.** One that is belligerent. **2.** One that is engaged in war. [Lat. *belligerans, belligerant-,* pr.part. of *belligerare,* to wage war : *bellum,* war + *gerere,* to make.] **—bel·lig'er·ent·ly** *adv.*

Synonyms: *belligerent, bellicose, pugnacious, contentious, quarrelsome. Belligerent* may specify actual combat, or conduct or temper conducive to hostilities. In the latter sense it is closely related to *bellicose* and *pugnacious,* although *pugnacious* more often applies to a natural inclination to aggressiveness than to a specific instance of hostility. *Contentious,* which implies chronic argumentativeness, and *quarrelsome,* which suggests perversity and bad temper, are weaker terms.

bell jar *n.* A cylindrical glass vessel with a rounded top and an open base used to protect and display fragile objects or to establish a controlled atmosphere or environment in scientific experiments.

bell·man (bĕl'mən) *n.* A town crier.

bell metal *n.* An alloy of tin and copper used to make bells.

Bel·lo·na (bə-lō'nə) *n.* The Roman goddess of war. [Lat. < *bellum,* war.]

bel·low (bĕl'ō) *v.* **-lowed, -low·ing, -lows.** *—intr.* **1.** To roar, as a bull. **2.** To shout in a deep voice. *—tr.* To utter in a loud and powerful voice. *—n.* **1.** The roar of a large animal, as a bull. **2.** A very loud utterance. [ME *belwen* < OE *belgan,* to be enraged.] **—bel'low·er** *n.*

bel·lows (bĕl'ōz, -əz) *n. (used with a sing. or pl. verb).* **1.** An apparatus for producing a strong current of air, as for sounding a pipe organ or increasing the draft to a fire, consisting of a flexible, valved air chamber that is contracted and expanded by pumping to force the air through a nozzle. **2.** Something resembling a bellows, as the pleated windbag of an accordion. **3.** The lungs. [ME *belows,* pl. of *below,* a bellows < OE *belg,* bag, belly.]

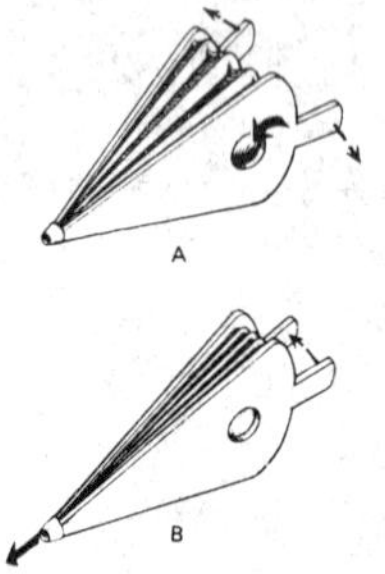

bellows
A. Air is admitted through open valve (*large arrow*) as bellows is expanded
B. Valve closes and air is expelled through nozzle (*large arrow*) as bellows is compressed

bell pepper *n.* **1.** A pepper plant, *Capsicum frutescens grossum,* cultivated for its edible fruit. **2.** The mild-flavored, bell-shaped fruit of the bell pepper, usually red when ripe but often eaten when green.

Bell's Law *n. Anat.* **1.** The law that in the spinal cord the dorsal roots are of sensory function and the ventral roots are of major function. **2.** The neurologic law that in any reflex arc nerve impulses are conducted in only one direction. [After Sir Charles *Bell* (1774–1842).]

Bell's palsy *n.* A suddenly occurring unilateral facial paralysis of unknown etiology, presumed to be caused by virally induced swelling of the seventh (facial) nerve. [After Sir Charles *Bell* (1774–1842).]

bell·weth·er (bĕl'wĕ*th*'ər) *n.* **1.** A male sheep, usually castrated, that wears a bell hung from its neck and is followed by a flock of sheep. **2.** Someone or something that leads or initiates.

bell·wort (bĕl'wûrt', -wôrt') *n.* A plant of the genus *Uvularia,* of eastern North America, having yellow, bell-shaped flowers.

bel·ly (bĕl'ē) *n., pl.* **-lies. 1.** The part of the body of mammals between the rib cage and the pelvis that contains the intestines; abdomen. **2.** The underside of the body of certain vertebrates, such as snakes and fish. **3. a.** The stomach. **b.** The appetite for food. **4.** A part that bulges or protrudes: *the belly of a sail.* **5.** The womb; uterus. **6.** The deep, hollow interior of something: *a ship's belly.* **7.** The bulging part of a muscle. **8.** The front part of the body of a stringed musical instrument; table. *—intr. & tr.v.* **-lied, -ly·ing, -lies.** To bulge or cause to bulge. [ME *beli* < OE *belg.*]

bel·ly·ache (bĕl'ē-āk') *n.* **1.** An ache or pain in the stomach or abdomen. **2.** *Slang.* A complaint. *—intr.v.* **-ached, -ach·ing, -aches.** *Slang.* To grumble or complain, esp. in a whining manner. **—bel'ly·ach'er** *n.*

bel·ly·band (bĕl'ē-bănd') *n.* **1.** A band passed around the belly of an animal to secure something, as a saddle. **2.** An encircling cloth band for holding in the protruding navel of a baby.

bel·ly·but·ton (bĕl'ē-bŭt'n) *n. Informal.* The navel.

belly dance *n.* A dance in which the performer makes sinuous movements of the belly. **—bel'ly-dance'** *v.* **(-danced, -danc·ing, -danc·es). —belly dancer** *n.*

belly flop *n.* A dive in which the front of the body hits flat against the surface of the water. **—bel'ly-flop'** *v.* **(-flopped, -flop·ping, -flops).**

bel·ly·ful (bĕl'ē-fo͝ol') *n. Informal.* An amount that exceeds what one desires or can endure.

bel·ly-land (bĕl'ē-lănd') *intr.v.* **-land·ed, -land·ing, -lands.** To land an airplane on its underside without the aid of landing gear. **—belly landing** *n.*

belly laugh *n.* A deep, jovial laugh.

bel·o·ne·pho·bi·a (bĕl'ə-nə-fō'bē-ə) *n.* An abnormal fear of sharply pointed objects. [Gk. *belonē,* needle + -PHOBIA.]

be·long (bĭ-lông', -lŏng') *intr.v.* **-longed, -long·ing, -longs. 1.** To have a proper, appropriate, or suitable place. **2. a.** To be naturally associated with something. **b.** To fit into a group naturally: *No matter what she did, she just didn't belong.* ***—phrasal verb.*** **belong to. 1.** To be the property or concern of: *"the earth belongs to the living"* (Jefferson). **2.** To be a member of (an organization): *belonged to a fraternity.* [ME *belongen.*]

be·long·ing (bĭ-lông'ĭng, -lŏng'-) *n.* **1. belongings.** Personal possessions; effects. **2.** Close and secure relationship: *a sense of belonging.*

be·lov·ed (bĭ-lŭv'ĭd, -lŭvd') *adj.* Dearly loved. *—n.* One that is beloved. [ME, p.part. of *beloven,* to love.]

be·low (bĭ-lō') *adv.* **1.** In or to a lower place; beneath. **2. a.** On or to a lower floor; downstairs. **b.** *Naut.* On or to a lower deck. **3.** Following or lower down on a page. **4.** Farther down, as along a slope or valley. **5.** In or to hell or Hades. **6.** On earth. **7.** In a lower rank or class. *—prep.* **1.** Underneath; beneath. **2.** Lower than, as on a graduated scale. **3.** Unworthy of or unsuitable to the rank or dignity of. [ME *biloogh*e : *bi,* by + *loogh,* low.]

Synonyms: *below, under, beneath, underneath. Below,* in its principal physical sense, denotes only position lower than a given point of reference. *Under* specifies position directly below, lower than the point of reference and in approximately vertical line with it. *Below* is also used to indicate direction and distance in a horizontal plane: *a town on the Hudson below Albany. Beneath* may have the basic sense of *below* or, more often, of *under. Underneath* combines the basic sense of *under* with that of at least partial concealment. Figuratively, *below* indicates deficiency or lesser status in a general way: *below normal; below one's rank. Under* indicates specific deficiency or explicitly subordinate relationship: *under legal age; serve under a captain. Beneath* applies to deficiency in moral or social senses: *beneath ordinary decency; beneath one's level.*

Bel·shaz·zar (bĕl-shăz'ər) *n.* In the Old Testament, the son of Nebuchadnezzar II and the last king of Babylon, who was warned of his downfall and death by the handwriting on the wall. [Heb. *Bēlshassar.*]

belt (bĕlt) *n.* **1.** A band, as of leather or cloth, worn around the waist to support clothing, secure tools or weapons, or serve as decoration. **2.** Something that resembles a belt: *a belt of outbuildings.* **3. a.** An encircling route or highway. **b.** A belt line. **4.** A strap that holds a person securely in a seat; seat belt. **5.** A continuous band or chain for transferring motion or power or conveying materials from one wheel or shaft to another. **6.** A band of tough reinforcing material beneath the tread of a tire. **7.** A geographic region that is distinctive in some specific way. **8.** *Slang.* A powerful blow; punch. **9.** *Slang.* A strong emotional reaction. **10.** *Slang.* A drink of hard liquor. *—tr.v.* **belt·ed, belt·ing, belts. 1.** To encircle; gird. **2.** To attach with or as if with a belt. **3.** To mark with or as if with a belt. **4.** To strike with a belt. **5.** *Slang.* To strike forcefully; punch. **6.** *Slang.* To sing in a loud and forceful manner: *belt out a song.* ***—idioms.*** **below the belt.** Not according to rule; unfairly. **tighten (one's) belt.** To become thrifty and frugal. **under (one's) belt.** Having become part of one's knowledge or experience. [ME < OE < Lat. *balteus.*]

Bel·tane (bĕl'tən) *n.* **1.** May Day in the old Scottish calendar. **2.** The ancient Celtic May Day celebration. [ME < Sc. Gael. *bealltainn.*]

belt highway *n.* A highway that skirts an urban area.

belt·ing (bĕl'tĭng) *n.* **1.** Belts collectively. **2.** The material used to make belts.

belt line *n.* A transportation line, as of trains, that makes a complete circuit of an urban area.

Belts·ville Small White (bĕlts'vĭl') *n.* A small white domestic turkey developed by the U.S. Department of Agriculture. [After *Beltsville,* Maryland.]

belt tightening *n.* A decrease in spending.

be·lu·ga (bə-lo͞o'gə) *n.* **1.** The white whale. **2.** A sturgeon, *Huso huso,* of the Black and Caspian seas, whose roe is used for caviar. [R. *byelukha* < *byelii,* white.]

bel·ve·dere (bĕl'vĭ-dîr') *n.* A structure, such as an open, roofed gallery, situated so as to command a view. [Ital. : *bel,* beautiful (< Lat. *bellus*) + *vedere,* view (< Lat. *vidēre,* to see).]

be·ma (bē'mə) *n., pl.* **-ma·ta** (-mə-tə). **1.** *Judaism.* The platform from which services are conducted in a synagogue. **2.** The enclosed area about the altar of an Eastern Orthodox church. [LLat. < Gk. *bēma,* platform.]

be·mire (bĭ-mīr') *tr.v.* **-mired, -mir·ing, -mires. 1.** To soil with mud. **2.** To cause to bog down in mud.

be·moan (bĭ-mōn') *v.* **-moaned, -moan·ing, -moans.** *—tr.* **1.** To mourn over; lament. **2.** To express pity or grief for. *—intr.* To mourn; lament.

be·muse (bĭ-myo͞oz') *tr.v.* **-mused, -mus·ing, -mus·es. 1.** To cause to be bewildered; confuse. **2.** To cause to be engrossed in thought. **—be·mus'ed·ly** (-myo͞o'zĭd-lē) *adv.*

ben[1] (bĕn) *Scot. —n.* The inner room or parlor of a house. *—adv.* Inside; within. *—prep.* Within. [ME *binne,* within < OE *binnan.*]

ben[2] (bĕn) *n.* Any of several Asiatic trees of the genus *Mo-*

ringa, bearing winged seeds that yield an oil used in perfumes and cosmetics. [Dial. Ar. *bēn* < Ar. *bān.*]

Bence-Jones protein (bĕns'jōnz') *n.* An abnormal globulin group that can appear in serum and in urine in association with multiple myeloma. [After Henry *Bence-Jones* (1814–1873).]

bench (bĕnch) *n.* **1.** A long seat, often without a back, for two or more persons. **2.** A thwart in a boat. **3. a.** The seat for judges in a courtroom. **b.** The office or position of a judge. **c.** The judge or judges composing a court. **4. a.** A seat occupied by a person in an official capacity. **b.** The office of such a person. **5.** A strong worktable, as one used in carpentry. **6.** A platform on which animals, esp. dogs, are exhibited. **7.** *Sports.* **a.** The place where the players on a team sit while they are not participating in a game. **b.** The reserve players on a team. **8. a.** A level, narrow stretch of land interrupting a declivity. **b.** A level elevation of land along a shore or coast, esp. one marking a former shoreline. —*tr.v.* **benched, bench·ing, bench·es. 1.** To furnish with benches. **2.** To seat on a bench. **3.** To show (dogs) in a bench show. **4.** *Sports.* To keep out of or remove from a game. [ME < OE *benc.*]

bench·er (bĕn'chər) *n.* **1.** One who sits on a bench. **2.** *Chiefly Brit.* A member of the inner or higher bar who acts as a governor of one of the Inns of Court. **3.** One who occupies an official bench, as a magistrate.

bench mark also **bench·mark** (bĕnch'märk') *n.* **1.** A surveyor's mark made on a stationary object of previously determined position and elevation and used as a reference point in tidal observations and surveys. **2. benchmark.** A standard by which something can be measured or judged.

bench show *n.* An indoor exhibition of small animals, esp. a competitive dog show.

bench warrant *n.* A warrant issued by a judge or court ordering the apprehension of an offender.

bend[1] (bĕnd) *v.* **bent** (bĕnt), **bend·ing, bends.** —*tr.* **1.** To bring into tension: *bend a bow.* **2. a.** To cause to assume a curved or angular shape. **b.** To force to assume a different shape or direction. **3.** To cause to swerve from a straight line; deflect. **4.** To turn or direct (one's attention, for example). **5.** To influence coercively; subdue. **6.** To apply (the mind) closely; concentrate. **7.** *Naut.* To fasten: *bend a mainsail onto the boom.* —*intr.* **1. a.** To turn or be altered from straightness or from an initial shape or position: *Wire bends easily.* **b.** To assume a curved, crooked, or angular form or direction: *The saplings bent in the wind.* **2.** To take a new direction; swerve. **3.** To incline the body; stoop. **4.** To bow in submission; yield. **5.** To apply oneself closely; concentrate: *She bent to her task.* —*n.* **1.** The act or fact of bending. **2.** The state of being bent. **3.** Something that is bent. **4.** *Naut.* **a. bends.** The thick planks in a ship's side; wales. **b.** A knot that joins a rope to a rope or another object. **5. bends** *(used with a sing. or pl. verb).* Caisson disease. —*idiom.* **bend over backward.** To make an effort greater than is required. [ME *benden* < OE *bendan.*]

bend[2] (bĕnd) *n. Heraldry.* A band passing from the upper dexter corner of an escutcheon to the lower sinister corner. [ME, prob. < OFr. *bende,* band.]

Ben Da·vis (bĕn dā'vĭs) *n.* A variety of large red winter apple grown in western North America and used for cooking.

Ben Day also **ben·day** or **Ben·day** (bĕn-dā') *n.* A method of adding a tone to a printed image by imposing a transparent sheet of dots or other patterns on the image at some stage of a photographic reproduction process. [After *Benjamin Day* (1838–1916), its inventor.]

bend·ed (bĕn'dĭd) *v. Archaic.* Past tense and past participle of **bend[1]**.

bend·er (bĕn'dər) *n.* **1.** One that bends. **2.** *Slang.* A drinking spree.

bend sinister *n. Heraldry.* A band passing from the upper sinister corner of an escutcheon to the lower dexter corner.

be·neath (bĭ-nēth') *adv.* **1.** In a lower place; below. **2.** Underneath. —*prep.* **1.** Lower than; below. **2.** Covered or concealed by: *The earth lay beneath a blanket of snow.* **3.** Under the force, control, or influence of. **4. a.** Lower than, as in rank or station. **b.** Unworthy of; unbefitting: *was beneath him to beg.* [ME *binethe* < OE *bineoðan.*]

ben·e·dict (bĕn'ĭ-dĭkt') *n.* A newly married man who has previously been considered a confirmed bachelor. [After *Benedick,* a character in *Much Ado About Nothing* by Shakespeare.]

Ben·e·dic·tine (bĕn'ĭ-dĭk'tĭn, -tēn') *adj.* Of or pertaining to Saint Benedict of Nursia or the order he founded. —*n.* A monk or nun belonging to the order founded by Saint Benedict.

ben·e·dic·tion (bĕn'ĭ-dĭk'shən) *n.* **1.** A blessing. **2.** An invocation of divine blessing, usually at the end of a church service. **3.** Often **Benediction.** *Rom. Cath. Ch.* A short service consisting of prayers, the singing of a Eucharistic hymn, and the blessing of the congregation with the host. **4.** The state of blessedness. [ME *benediccioun* < OFr. *benediction* < Lat. *benedictio* < *benedicere,* to bless : *bene,* well + *dicere,* to say.] —**ben'e·dic'tive, ben'e·dic'to·ry** (-dĭk'tə-rē) *adj.*

Ben·e·dic·tus (bĕn'ĭ-dĭk'təs) *n.* **1.** A canticle that begins *Benedictus qui venit in nomine Domini* ("Blessed is he that cometh in the name of the Lord"). **2.** A canticle that begins *Benedictus Dominus Deus Israel* ("Blessed be the Lord God of Israel"). [Lat., blessed.]

ben·e·fac·tion (bĕn'ə-făk'shən, bĕn'ə-făk'-) *n.* **1.** The act of conferring a benefit. **2.** A charitable gift or deed. [LLat. *benefactio* < Lat. *bene facere,* to do well.]

ben·e·fac·tor (bĕn'ə-făk'tər) *n.* One who gives financial or other aid. —**ben'e·fac'tress** *n.*

be·nef·ic (bə-nĕf'ĭk) *adj.* Beneficent. [Lat. *beneficus* < *bene facere,* to do well.]

ben·e·fice (bĕn'ə-fĭs) *n.* **1.** *Eccles.* **a.** A church office endowed with fixed capital assets that provide a living. **b.** The revenue from such assets. **2.** A landed estate granted in feudal tenure. —*tr.v.* **-ficed, -fic·ing, -fic·es.** To endow or provide with a benefice. [ME < OFr. < Med. Lat. *beneficium* < Lat., benefit < *beneficus,* benefic.]

be·nef·i·cence (bə-nĕf'ĭ-səns) *n.* **1.** The state or quality of being beneficent. **2.** A charitable act or gift. [OFr. < Lat. *beneficentia* < *beneficus,* benefic.]

be·nef·i·cent (bə-nĕf'ĭ-sənt) *adj.* **1.** Characterized by or performing acts of kindness or charity. **2.** Producing benefit; beneficial. —**be·nef'i·cent·ly** *adv.*

ben·e·fi·cial (bĕn'ə-fĭsh'əl) *adj.* **1.** Promoting a favorable result; enhancing well-being; advantageous. **2.** *Law.* Receiving or having the right to receive proceeds or other advantages. [Fr. *bénéficial* < LLat. *beneficialis* < Lat. *beneficium,* benefit < *beneficus,* benefic.] —**ben'e·fi'cial·ly** *adv.* —**ben'e·fi'cial·ness** *n.*

Synonyms: *beneficial, profitable, advantageous.* These adjectives apply to that which promotes gain. *Beneficial* is said of whatever enhances well-being; *profitable,* of what yields usually material gain; and *advantageous,* of that which affords improvement in relative position or in chances of success.

ben·e·fi·ci·ar·y (bĕn'ə-fĭsh'ē-ĕr'ē, -fĭsh'ə-rē) *n., pl.* **-ies. 1.** One that receives a benefit. **2.** *Law.* The recipient of funds, property, or other benefits, as from an insurance policy or will. **3.** *Eccles.* The holder of a benefice. —*adj.* Pertaining to or holding a feudal benefice.

ben·e·fit (bĕn'ə-fĭt) *n.* **1.** Something that promotes or enhances well-being; advantage. **2.** *Archaic.* A kindly deed. **3.** Payments made or entitlements available in accordance with a wage agreement, insurance contract, or public assistance program. **4.** A public entertainment, performance, or social event held to raise funds for a person or cause. —*v.* **-fit·ed, -fit·ing, -fits** also **-fit·ted, -fit·ting, -fits.** —*tr.* To be helpful or useful to. —*intr.* To gain advantage; profit: *benefit from her example.* [ME < OFr. *bienfait* < Lat. *benefactum,* good deed < *bene facere,* to do well.]

benefit of clergy *n.* **1.** Exemption from trial or punishment in a civil court given to the clergy in the Middle Ages. **2.** The authorized sanction of a religious rite: *cohabiting without benefit of clergy.*

benefit of the doubt *n.* A favorable judgment granted in the absence of full evidence.

be·nev·o·lence (bə-nĕv'ə-ləns) *n.* **1.** An inclination or tendency to do kind or charitable acts. **2.** A kindly act. **3.** A compulsory tax or payment exacted by some English sovereigns without the consent of Parliament.

be·nev·o·lent (bə-nĕv'ə-lənt) *adj.* **1.** Characterized by or suggestive of benevolence; kindly. **2.** Of, concerned with, or organized for the benefit of charity: *a benevolent fund.* [ME < Lat. *benevolens,* well-wishing : *bene,* well + *volens,* pr.part. of *velle,* to wish.] —**be·nev'o·lent·ly** *adv.*

Ben·ga·li (bĕn-gô'lē, bĕng-) *n.* **1.** An inhabitant of Bengal. **2.** An inhabitant of Bangladesh. **3.** The modern Indic language of West Bengal and Bangladesh. —*adj.* Of or characteristic of Bengal, its inhabitants, or its language.

ben·ga·line (bĕng'gə-lēn') *n.* A fabric having a crosswise ribbed effect made of silk, wool, or synthetic fibers. [Fr. < *Bengal,* Bengal.]

Ben·gal light (bĕn-gôl', bĕng-) *n.* A type of firework that burns with a brilliant, sustained blue light, formerly used for signaling.

be·night·ed (bĭ-nī'tĭd) *adj.* **1.** Overtaken by darkness or night. **2.** In moral or intellectual darkness; unenlightened. —**be·night'ed·ly** *adv.* —**be·night'ed·ness** *n.*

be·nign (bĭ-nīn') *adj.* **1.** Of a kind disposition. **2.** Manifesting gentleness and mildness. **3.** Tending to promote well-being; beneficial: *the benign influence of pure air.* **4.** *Pathol.* Not malignant: *a benign tumor.* [ME *benigne* < OFr. < Lat. *benignus* : *bene,* well + *genus,* born.] —**be·nign'ly** *adv.*

be·nig·nan·cy (bĭ-nĭg'nən-sē) *n., pl.* **-cies.** Benignity.

be·nig·nant (bĭ-nĭg'nənt) *adj.* **1.** Favorable; beneficial. **2.** Kind and gracious. —**be·nig'nant·ly** *adv.*

be·nig·ni·ty (bĭ-nĭg'nĭ-tē) *n., pl.* **-ties. 1.** The quality or condition of being benign. **2.** A kindly or gracious act.

ben·i·son (bĕn'ĭ-zən, -sən) *n.* A blessing; benediction. [ME *benisoun* < OFr. *beneisson* < Lat. *benedictio.* —see BENEDICTION.]

ben·ja·min (bĕn'jə-mĭn) *n.* Benzoin. [Var. of *benjoin,* benzoin.]

Ben·ja·min (bĕn'jə-mĭn) *n.* **1.** In the Old Testament, the youngest son of Jacob and Rachel, favorite son of Jacob.

bench mark

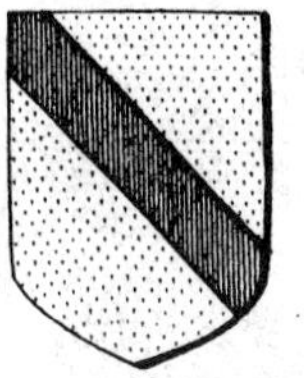
bend[2]

bend sinister

2. The tribe of Israel descended from Benjamin. [Heb. : *ben,* son + *yāmīn,* right hand.] —**Ben'ja·mite'** (-mīt') *n.*
benjamin bush *n.* The spicebush.
ben·ne or **ben·ni** (bĕn'ē) *n.* **1.** The sesame plant. **2.** The seeds or oil of the sesame plant. [Of African orig.]
ben·net (bĕn'ĭt) *n.* Herb bennet.
ben·ni (bĕn'ē) *n.* Variant of **benne.**
Ben·ning·ton or **Ben·ning·ton ware** (bĕn'ĭng-tən) *n.* Ceramic ware, as earthenware with a brown mottled glaze, made in Bennington, Vermont.
ben·ny (bĕn'ē) *n., pl.* **-nies.** *Slang.* An amphetamine tablet taken as a stimulant. [< BENZEDRINE.]
bent¹ (bĕnt) *v.* Past tense and past participle of **bend¹.** —*adj.* **1.** Not straight; crooked. **2.** On a fixed course of action; determined: *was bent on going to the theater.* —*n.* **1.** An individual tendency, disposition, or inclination: *"The natural bent of my mind was to science"* (Thomas Paine). **2.** The limit of endurance. **3.** A structural member or framework used for strengthening a bridge or trestle transversely.
bent² (bĕnt) *n.* **1.** Any of several grasses of the genus *Agrostis,* some species of which are used in lawn mixtures and for hay. **2.** The stiff stalk of various grasses. **3.** A moor; heath. [ME, grassy plain < OE *beonet.*]
Ben·tham·ism (bĕn'thə-mĭz'əm) *n.* The utilitarian philosophy of Jeremy Bentham, holding that pleasure is the chief end of life and that the greatest happiness for the greatest number should be the ultimate goal of man. —**Ben'tham·ite'** (-mīt') *n.*
ben·thos (bĕn'thŏs') *n.* **1.** The bottom of a sea or a lake. **2.** The organisms living on sea or lake bottoms. [Gk.] —**ben'thic** (bĕn'thĭk), **ben·thon'ic** (bĕn-thŏn'ĭk) *adj.*
ben·ton·ite (bĕn'tə-nīt') *n.* Either of two principally aluminum silicate clays, containing some magnesium and iron, distinguished by sodium or calcium content with corresponding high or low swelling capacity, and used in various adhesives, cements, and ceramic fillers. [After Fort *Benton,* Montana.] —**ben'ton·it'ic** (-nĭt'ĭk) *adj.*
bent·wood (bĕnt'wo͝od') *n.* Wood that has been steamed until pliable and then bent and shaped. —**modifier:** *a bentwood chair.*
be·numb (bĭ-nŭm') *tr.v.* **-numbed, -numb·ing, -numbs. 1.** To make numb, esp. by cold. **2.** To make inactive; dull: *"the anesthetic afternoon benumbs, sickens our senses"* (Karl Shapiro). [< ME *binomen,* p.part. of *benimen,* to take away < OE *beniman.*] —**be·numb'ment** *n.*
benz- *pref.* Variant of **benzo-.**
benz·al·de·hyde (bĕn-zăl'də-hīd') *n.* A colorless or yellowish, strongly reactive volatile oil, C_6H_5CHO, used as a solvent and flavoring and in perfumery.
Ben·ze·drine (bĕn'zĭ-drēn'). A trademark for a brand of amphetamine.
ben·zene (bĕn'zēn', bĕn-zēn') *n.* A clear, colorless, highly refractive flammable liquid, C_6H_6, derived from petroleum and used in or to manufacture a wide variety of chemical products including DDT, detergents, insecticides, and motor fuels.
benzene ring *n.* The hexagonal ring structure in the benzene molecule and its substitutional derivatives, each vertex of which is occupied and distinguished by a carbon atom.

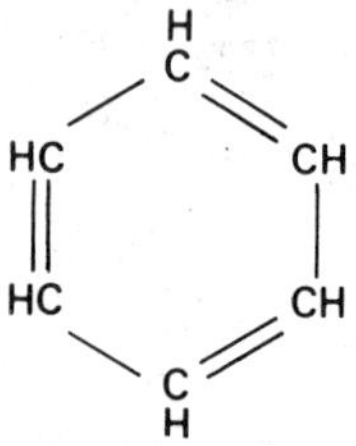

benzene ring
Each C represents a carbon atom, each H a hydrogen atom, and the straight lines are chemical bonds

beret

benzene series *n.* A series of chemically related aromatic hydrocarbons containing the benzene ring, the simplest member of which is benzene.
ben·zi·dine (bĕn'zĭ-dēn') *n.* A yellowish, white, or reddish-gray crystalline powder, $C_{12}H_{12}N_2$, used in dyes and to detect blood stains. [Prob. BENZ(ENE) + -ID(E) + -INE.]
ben·zine (bĕn'zēn', bĕn-zēn') also **ben·zin** (bĕn'zĭn) *n.* **1.** Ligroin. **2.** Benzene.
benzo- or **benz-** *pref.* Benzene; benzoic acid: *benzophenone.* [< BENZOIN.]
ben·zo·ate (bĕn'zō-āt') *n.* A salt or ester of benzoic acid.
benzoate of soda *n.* Sodium benzoate.
ben·zo·caine (bĕn'zə-kān') *n.* A white, odorless, tasteless crystalline ester, $C_9H_{11}NO_2$, used as a local anesthetic.
ben·zo·di·az·e·pine (bĕn'zō-dī-ăz'ə-pēn', -pĭn) *n.* Any of several chemical compounds used as sedatives and muscle relaxants. [BENZO- + DIAZEP(AM) + -INE.]
ben·zo·ic acid (bĕn-zō'ĭk) *n.* A white crystalline acid, C_6H_5COOH, used to season tobacco and in perfumes, dentifrices, and germicides.
ben·zo·in (bĕn'zō-ĭn, -zoin') *n.* **1.** Any of several resins containing benzoic acid, obtained as a gum from various trees of the genus *Styrax* and used in ointments, perfumes, and medicine. **2.** Any of various aromatic shrubs and trees of the genus *Lindera,* which includes the spicebush. **3.** A white or yellowish crystalline compound, $C_{14}H_{12}O_2$, derived from benzaldehyde and used as an antiseptic. [Fr. *benjoin* < Ital. *benzoino* < Ar. *lubān jāwī,* frankincense of Java.]
ben·zol (bĕn'zôl', -zōl') *n.* Benzene.
ben·zo·phe·none (bĕn'zō-fĭ-nōn', -fē'nōn') *n.* A white crystalline compound, $(C_6H_5)_2CO$, used in perfumery and in medicine.
ben·zo·py·rine (bĕn'zō-pī'rēn', -pī-rēn') *n.* A yellow, crystalline, aromatic hydrocarbon, $C_{20}H_{12}$, that is a carcinogen found in coal tar and cigarette smoke.
ben·zo·yl (bĕn'zō-ĭl') *n.* The univalent radical C_6H_5CO, derived from benzoic acid.
benzoyl peroxide *n.* A flammable white granular solid, $(C_6H_5CO)_2O_2$, used as a bleaching agent for flour, fats, waxes, and oils, as a polymerization catalyst, and in pharmaceuticals.
ben·zyl (bĕn'zĭl, -zēl') *n.* The univalent radical $C_6H_5CH_2$, derived from toluene.
Be·o·wulf (bā'ə-wo͝olf') *n.* The legendary hero of an anonymous Old English epic poem. [OE *Bēowulf.*]
be·queath (bĭ-kwēth', -kwēth') *tr.v.* **-queathed, -queath·ing, -queaths. 1.** *Law.* To leave or give by will. **2.** To pass on; hand down. [ME *bequethen* < OE *becweðan.*] —**be·queath'al** (-kwē'thəl, -thəl) *n.* —**be·queath'er** *n.* —**be·queath'ment** *n.*
be·quest (bĭ-kwĕst') *n.* **1.** The act of bequeathing. **2.** Something that is bequeathed; legacy. [ME *biqueste* < *bequethen,* to bequeath.]
be·rate (bĭ-rāt') *tr.v.* **-rat·ed, -rat·ing, -rates.** To rebuke or scold harshly.
Ber·ber (bûr'bər) *n.* **1.** A member of one of several Moslem tribes of North Africa. **2.** Any of the Afro-Asiatic languages of the Berbers. [Ar. *Barbar.*] —**Ber'ber** *adj.*
ber·ber·ine (bûr'bə-rēn') *n.* A bitter-tasting yellow alkaloid, $C_{20}H_{19}NO_5$, obtained from the root of a North American plant, *Hydrastis canadensis,* from the barberry, and from other plants, and used in medicine. [NLat. *Berberis,* barberry genus < OFr. *berberis,* barberry + -INE.]
ber·ceuse (bĕr-sœz') *n., pl.* **-ceuses** (-sœz'). **1.** A lullaby. **2.** A musical composition of a soothing nature. [Fr. < *bercer,* to rock.]
be·reave (bĭ-rēv') *tr.v.* **-reaved** or **-reft** (-rĕft'), **-reav·ing, -reaves.** *Archaic.* **1.** To deprive of (something valued). **2.** To deprive of (a loved one) by death. [ME *bireven* < OE *berēafian.*] —**be·reave'ment** *n.* —**be·reav'er** *n.*
be·reft (bĭ-rĕft') *adj.* **1. a.** Deprived of something: *bereft of his dignity.* **b.** Lacking something needed or expected: *a dictionary bereft of pictures.* **2.** Suffering the death of a loved one; bereaved. [< p.part. of BEREAVE.]
Ber·e·ni·ce's Hair (bĕr'ə-nī'sēz) *n.* Coma Berenices.
be·ret (bə-rā', bĕr'ā') *n.* A round, visorless cloth cap. [Fr. *béret* < OProv. *birret.* —see BIRETTA.]
berg (bûrg) *n.* An iceberg.
ber·ga·mot (bûr'gə-mŏt') *n.* **1. a.** A small, spiny tree, *Citrus aurantium bergamia,* bearing sour, pear-shaped fruit whose rind yields an aromatic oil. **b.** The oil of the bergamot, used in perfumery. **2.** Any of several plants of the genus *Monarda,* esp. the wild bergamot. [Fr. *bergamote* < Ital. *bergamotta,* prob. < Turk. *beg-armûdī,* prince's pear.]
Berg·mann's rule (bûrg'mənz) *n.* An axiom stating that in any warm-blooded animal species that is polytypic and wide-ranging, the body size of each geographic group varies with the average environmental temperature. [After Karl Georg L.C. *Bergmann* (1814–1865).]
Berg·son·ism (bĕrg'sə-nĭz'əm) *n.* The philosophy of Henri Bergson, which contends that all living forms arise from a persisting natural force, the élan vital. —**Berg·so'ni·an** (-sō'nē-ən) *n.*
ber·i·ber·i (bĕr'ē-bĕr'ē) *n.* A thiamine deficiency disease of the peripheral nervous system, endemic in eastern and southern Asia and characterized by partial paralysis of the extremities, emaciation, and anemia. [Singhalese, redup. of *beri,* weakness.]
Be·ring time (bîr'ĭng, bâr'-) *n.* The time in western Alaska and the Aleutian Islands, which lie in the 11th time zone west of Greenwich, England. [After the *Bering* Sea.]
Berke·le·ian·ism (bär'klē-ə-nĭz'əm, bûr'-) *n.* The philosophy of George Berkeley, which holds that material objects have no independent being but exist only as concepts of a human or divine mind. —**Berke'le·ian** *n.*
ber·ke·li·um (bər-kē'lē-əm, bûrk'lē-əm) *n. Symbol* **Bk** A synthetic transuranic element having 9 isotopes with mass numbers from 243 to 250 and half-lives from 3 hours to 1,380 years. Atomic number 97; valences 3, 4. [After *Berkeley,* California.]
Berk·shire (bûrk'shîr', -shər) *n.* One of a domestic breed of black swine with white feet and faces. [After *Berkshire,* a county in England.]
ber·lin (bər-lĭn') *n.* **1.** A light wool used in making clothing, esp. gloves. **2.** A four-wheeled covered carriage. **3.** Variant of **berline.** [After *Berlin,* Germany.]
ber·line also **ber·lin** (bər-lĭn') *n.* A limousine with a glass window between the front and rear seats. [Fr. < *Berlin,* Berlin, Germany.]
berm also **berme** (bûrm) *n.* **1. a.** A narrow ledge or shelf, as along a slope. **b.** A shoulder of a road. **2.** A ledge between the parapet and the moat in a fortification. [Fr. *berme* < MDu.]
Ber·mu·da grass (bər-myo͞o'də) *n.* A grass, *Cynodon dactylon,* that has wiry, creeping rootstocks and is used for lawns and pasturage in warm regions.
Bermuda lily *n.* A lily, *Lilium longiflorum,* cultivated extensively in Bermuda, having large, white, trumpet-shaped flowers.
Bermuda mulberry *n.* A species of beautyberry.
Bermuda onion *n.* A large, mild-flavored, yellow-skinned variety of onion.
Bermuda rig *n.* A fore-and-aft rig distinguished by a tall

triangular mainsail and widely used on cruising and racing vessels.

Ber·mu·das (bər-myōō′dəz) *pl.n.* Bermuda shorts.

Bermuda shorts *pl.n.* Shorts that end slightly above the knees.

Ber·noul·li distribution (bər-nōō′lē) *n. Statistics.* The binomial distribution. [After Jakob *Bernoulli* (1654–1705).]

Bernoulli effect *n.* The phenomenon of internal pressure reduction with increased stream velocity in a fluid. [After Daniel *Bernoulli* (1700–1782).]

Bernoulli's law *n.* **1.** *Statistics.* The probability theorem stating that for a very large number of independent repeated Bernoulli trials the observed relative frequency of successes will approximate the probability of success on each trial. **2.** *Physics.* The relationship between internal fluid pressure and fluid velocity, essentially a statement of the conservation of energy, that has as a consequence the Bernoulli effect. [Statistics law after Jakob *Bernoulli;* physics law after Daniel *Bernoulli.*]

Bernoulli trial *n. Statistics.* An experiment having just two possible results, usually denoted *success* and *failure,* with the property that the occurrence of one excludes the occurrence of the other in any given trial. [After Jakob *Bernoulli* (1654–1705).]

ber·ry (bĕr′ē) *n., pl.* **-ries. 1.** Any of various usually fleshy, edible fruits, such as the strawberry, blackberry, or raspberry. **2.** *Bot.* A fleshy fruit, such as the grape, blueberry, or tomato, developed from a single ovary and having few or many seeds but not a single stone. **3.** Any of various seeds or dried kernels, such as that of the coffee plant. **4.** The small, dark egg of certain crustaceans or fishes. *—intr.v.* **-ried, -ry·ing, -ries. 1.** To hunt for or gather berries. **2.** To produce or bear berries. [ME *berye* < OE *berie.*]

ber·seem (bər-sēm′) *n.* A clover, *Trifolium alexandrinum,* native to northern Africa and southwestern Asia, grown for soil improvement in dry regions of southwestern North America. [Ar. *birsīm* < Coptic *bersīm.*]

ber·serk (bər-sûrk′, -zûrk′) *adj.* **1.** Destructively or frenetically violent. **2.** Deranged. *—n.* A berserker. **—ber·serk′** *adv.*

ber·serk·er (bər-sûr′kər, -zûr′-) *n.* An ancient Scandinavian warrior who fought in battle with frenzied violence and fury. [ON *berserkr* : *björn,* bear + *serkr,* shirt.]

berth (bûrth) *n.* **1.** A built-in bed or bunk on a ship or train. **2.** A space at a wharf for a ship to dock or anchor. **3.** Sufficient space for a ship to maneuver. **4.** A position of employment, esp. on a ship. **5.** A place to sleep. **6.** A space where a vehicle can be parked. *—v.* **berthed, berth·ing, berths.** *—tr.* **1.** To bring (a ship) to a berth. **2.** To provide with a berth. *—intr.* To come to a berth; dock. **—idiom. give a wide berth to.** To stay at a substantial distance from; avoid. [Prob. < BEAR[1].]

ber·tha (bûr′thə) *n.* A wide, deep collar, often of lace, that covers the shoulders. [Fr. *berthe* < *Berthe,* the name Bertha.]

Ber·til·lon system (bûr′tl-ŏn′, bĕr′tē-yôN′) *n.* A system formerly used for identifying persons by means of a record of various body measurements, coloring, and markings. [After Alphonse *Bertillon* (1853–1914).]

ber·yl (bĕr′əl) *n.* A mineral, essentially aluminum beryllium silicate, $Be_3Al_2Si_6O_{18}$, occurring in hexagonal prisms and constituting the chief source of beryllium. [ME < OFr. < Lat. *beryllus* < Gk. *bērullos.*] **—ber′yl·line** (-ə-līn, -līn′) *adj.*

be·ryl·li·um (bə-rĭl′ē-əm) *n. Symbol* **Be** A high-melting, lightweight, corrosion-resistant, rigid, steel-gray metallic element used as an aerospace structural material, as a moderator and reflector in nuclear reactors, and in a copper alloy used for springs, electrical contacts, and nonsparking tools. Atomic number 4; atomic weight 9.0122; melting point 1,278°C; boiling point 2,970°C; specific gravity 1.848; valence 2. [< BERYL.]

be·seech (bĭ-sēch′) *tr.v.* **-sought** (-sôt′) or **-seeched, -seech·ing, -seech·es. 1.** To address an earnest or urgent request to; implore. **2.** To request earnestly; beg for. [ME *besechen* < OE *besēcan.*] **—be·seech′er** *n.*

be·seem (bĭ-sēm′) *tr.v.* **-seemed, -seem·ing, -seems.** *Archaic.* To be appropriate for; befit. [ME *besemen.*]

be·set (bĭ-sĕt′) *tr.v.* **-set, -set·ting, -sets. 1.** To attack from all sides; assail. **2.** To trouble persistently; harass: ". . . *beset by a ghostly band of doubts*" (Sherwood Anderson). **3.** To hem in; surround. **4.** To stud, as with jewels. [ME *besetten* < OE *besettan.*] **—be·set′ment** *n.*

be·set·ting (bĭ-sĕt′ĭng) *adj.* Constantly troubling or attacking.

be·shrew (bĭ-shrōō′) *tr.v.* **-shrewed, -shrew·ing, -shrews.** *Archaic.* To invoke evil upon; curse. [ME *beshrewen.*]

be·side (bĭ-sīd′) *prep.* **1.** At the side of; next to. **2.** In comparison with. **3.** Except for. **4.** Apart from; wide of: *a remark that was beside the point.* *—adv. Archaic.* **1.** In addition. **2.** Nearby. **—idiom. beside (oneself).** In a state of extreme agitation. [ME *biside* < OE *be sīdan* : *be,* by + *sīde,* side.]

be·sides (bĭ-sīdz′) *adv.* **1.** In addition; also. **2.** Moreover; furthermore. **3.** Otherwise; else. *—prep.* **1.** In addition to. **2.** Other than; except. [ME *bisides,* genitive of *biside,* beside.]

Usage: In modern usage the senses "in addition to" and "except for" are conveyed more often by *besides* than *beside.* Thus: *He had few friends besides us.*

be·siege (bĭ-sēj′) *tr.v.* **-sieged, -sieg·ing, -sieg·es. 1.** To surround with troops; lay siege to. **2.** To crowd around; hem in. **3.** To harass or importune, as with requests. **4.** To cause to feel distressed or worried: *was besieged by problems.* [ME *besegen.*] **—be·siege′ment** *n.* **—be·sieg′er** *n.*

be·smear (bĭ-smîr′) *tr.v.* **-smeared, -smear·ing, -smears.** To smear.

be·smirch (bĭ-smûrch′) *tr.v.* **-smirched, -smirch·ing, -smirch·es.** To soil; sully. **—be·smirch′er** *n.* **—be·smirch′ment** *n.*

be·som (bē′zəm) *n.* **1.** A bundle of twigs attached to a handle and used as a broom. **2.** A broom. **3.** The broom plant. [ME *besum* < OE *besema.*]

be·sot (bĭ-sŏt′) *tr.v.* **-sot·ted, -sot·ting, -sots.** To muddle or stupefy, esp. with liquor.

be·sought (bĭ-sôt′) *v.* A past tense and past participle of **beseech.**

be·spake (bĭ-spāk′) *v. Archaic.* Past tense of **bespeak.**

be·spat·ter (bĭ-spăt′ər) *tr.v.* **-tered, -ter·ing, -ters.** To spatter, as with mud.

be·speak (bĭ-spēk′) *tr.v.* **-spoke** (-spōk′), **-spo·ken** (-spō′kən) or **-spoke, -speak·ing. 1.** To be or give a sign of; indicate; signify. **2.** *Archaic.* To speak to; address. **3.** To engage or claim in advance; reserve. **4.** To foretell; portend. [ME *bespeken,* to speak out < OE *besprecan.*]

be·spec·ta·cled (bĭ-spĕk′tə-kəld) *adj.* Wearing eyeglasses.

be·spoke (bĭ-spōk′) *v.* The past tense and a past participle of **bespeak.** *—adj. Chiefly Brit.* **1.** Made-to-order. **2.** Dealing in custom-made articles.

be·spo·ken (bĭ-spō′kən) *v.* A past participle of **bespeak.** *—adj. Chiefly Brit.* Bespoke.

be·sprent (bĭ-sprĕnt′) *adj. Archaic.* Sprinkled over. [ME *bespreynt,* p.part. of *besprengen,* to besprinkle < OE *besprengan.*]

be·sprin·kle (bĭ-sprĭng′kəl) *tr.v.* **-kled, -kling, -kles.** To sprinkle.

Bes·se·mer converter (bĕs′ə-mər) *n.* A large pear-shaped container in which molten iron is converted to steel by the Bessemer process.

Bessemer process *n.* A method for making steel by blasting compressed air through molten iron, burning out excess carbon and other impurities. [After Henry *Bessemer* (1813–1898), its inventor.]

best (bĕst) *adj.* Superlative of **good. 1.** Surpassing all others in excellence, achievement, or quality; most excellent: *the best actor.* **2.** Most satisfactory, suitable, or useful; most desirable: *the best solution.* **3.** Greatest; largest: *the best part of a journey.* *—adv.* Superlative of **well. 1.** In the best way; most creditably or advantageously. **2.** To the greatest degree or extent; most. *—n.* **1.** Something that is best. **2.** The best condition or quality: *look your best.* **3.** One's best clothing. **4.** The best effort one can make: *doing his best.* **5.** One's warmest wishes or regards: *Give them my best.* *—tr.v.* **best·ed, best·ing, bests.** To get the better of; surpass. **—idiom. at best.** Under the most favorable conditions. [ME < OE *betst.*]

be·stead (bĭ-stĕd′) *Archaic.* *—tr.v.* **-stead·ed** or **-stead, -stead·ing, -steads. 1.** To be of service to; aid. **2.** To be of use to; avail. *—adj.* Placed; located.

bes·tial (bĕs′chəl, bĕst′yəl) *adj.* **1.** Of, pertaining to, or resembling an animal. **2.** Having the qualities or manners of a brute; savage. **3.** Lacking in intelligence. [ME < OFr. < LLat. *bestialis* < Lat. *bestia,* beast.] **—bes′tial·ly** *adv.*

bes·ti·al·i·ty (bĕs′chē-ăl′ĭ-tē, bēs′-) *n., pl.* **-ties. 1.** The quality of being bestial; animal nature. **2.** Conduct or an action marked by carnality or brutality. **3.** Sexual relations between a human being and an animal.

bes·tial·ize (bĕs′chə-līz′, bēs′-) *tr.v.* **-ized, -iz·ing, -iz·es.** To make bestial; brutalize.

bes·ti·ar·y (bĕs′chē-ĕr′ē, bēs′-) *n., pl.* **-ies.** A medieval collection of allegorical fables about the habits and traits of animals, each fable followed by an interpretation of its moral significance. [Med. Lat. *bestiarium* < Lat. *bestia,* beast.]

be·stir (bĭ-stûr′) *tr.v.* **-stirred, -stir·ring, -stirs.** To cause to become active; rouse. [ME *bestiren* < OE *bestyrian,* to pile up.]

best man *n.* The bridegroom's chief attendant at a wedding.

be·stow (bĭ-stō′) *tr.v.* **-stowed, -stow·ing, -stows. 1.** To present as a gift or honor; confer. **2.** To apply; use. **3.** *Archaic.* To store or house. [ME *bestowen.*] **—be·stow′a·ble** *adj.* **—be·stow′al, be·stow′ment** *n.*

be·strew (bĭ-strōō′) *tr.v.* **-strewed, -strewed** or **-strewn** (-strōōn′), **-strew·ing, -strews. 1.** To strew (a surface) with things so as to cover it. **2.** To lie scattered over or about.

be·stride (bĭ-strīd′) *tr.v* **-strode** (-strōd′), **-strid·den** (-strĭd′n), **-strid·ing, -strides. 1.** To sit or stand on with the legs astride; straddle. **2.** To step over. **3.** To stand high above; tower over. [ME *bestriden* < OE *bestrīdan.*]

best seller *n.* A book or other product that is among those sold in the largest numbers. **—best′-sell′ing** *adj.*

bet (bĕt) *n.* **1.** An agreement usually between two parties that the one who has made an incorrect prediction about an uncertain outcome will forfeit something stipulated to the other; wager. **2.** A fact, event, or outcome on which a wager

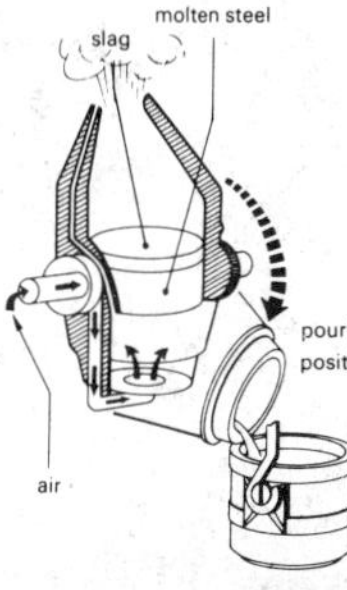

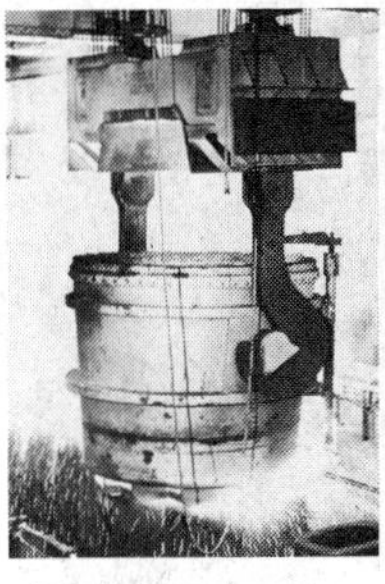

Bessemer converter
Above: Diagram
Below: Pouring molten iron

is made. **3.** An amount or object risked in a wager; stake. **4.** A person or thing on which a stake is placed. —*v.* **bet** or **bet·ted, bet·ting, bets.** —*tr.* **1.** To stake (an amount, for example) in a bet. **2.** To make a bet with. **3.** To make a bet on (a contestant or an outcome). **4.** To maintain confidently, as if making a bet. —*intr.* To make or place a bet. —***idiom.*** **you bet.** *Informal.* Of course; surely. [Orig. unknown.]

be·ta (bā'tə, bē'-) *n.* **1.** The 2nd letter of the Greek alphabet. See table at **alphabet. 2.** The second item in a series or system of classification. **3.** *Physics.* **a.** A beta particle. **b.** A beta ray. [Gk. *bēta,* of Phoenician orig.; akin to Heb. *bēth.*]

be·ta-ad·re·ner·gic (bā'tə-ăd'rə-nûr'jĭk, bē'-) *adj.* Of, pertaining to, or being a beta-receptor.

be·ta-block·er (bā'tə-blŏk'ər, bē'-) *n.* A drug that inhibits the absorption of adrenalin by interfering with beta-receptor action.

beta cell *n.* **1.** Any of the cells in the islands of Langerhans that produce insulin. **2.** Any of the basophilic chemophiles located in the anterior lobe of the adenohypophysis.

be·ta-en·dor·phin (bā'tə-ĕn-dôr'fĭn, bē'-) *n.* An endorphin that is a potent pain suppressant produced by the pituitary gland.

beta globulin *n.* Any of several globulins intermediate in their particulate motility response to electrophoresis as compared to alpha and gamma globulins.

be·ta·ine (bē'tə-ēn') *n.* A sweet crystalline alkaloid, $C_5H_{11}NO_2$, occurring in sugar beets and other plants and used in the treatment of muscular degeneration. [Lat. *beta,* beet + -INE.]

be·take (bĭ-tāk') *tr.v.* **-took** (-to͝ok'), **-tak·en, -tak·ing, -takes. 1.** To cause (oneself) to go or move. **2.** *Archaic.* To commit; apply.

be·ta-ox·i·da·tion (bā'tə-ŏk'sĭ-dā'shən, bē'-) *n.* The process of fatty-acid catabolism, in which two-carbon fragments are removed in succession from the carboxyl end of the chain.

beta particle *n.* A high-speed electron or positron, esp. one emitted in radioactive decay.

beta ray *n.* A stream of beta particles, esp. of electrons.

be·ta-re·cep·tor (bā'tə-rĭ-sĕp'tər, bē'-) *n.* A site in the autonomic nervous system that is activated by or strongly responds to adrenergic agents, such as epinephrine, by producing inhibitory action.

beta rhythm also **beta wave** *n.* The second most common waveform occurring in electroencephalograms of the adult brain, characteristically having a frequency from 18 to 30 cycles per second and associated with an alert waking state.

be·ta·tron (bā'tə-trŏn', bē'-) *n.* A fixed-radius magnetic induction electron accelerator capable of accelerating electrons to energies of a few million to a few hundred million electron volts.

be·tel (bĕt'l) *n.* A climbing Asiatic plant, *Piper betle,* whose leaves are chewed with the betel nut by people of southeastern Asia to induce both stimulating and narcotic effects. [Port. < Malayalam *veṭṭila.*]

Be·tel·geuse (bĕt'l-jo͞oz', bĕt'l-jœz') *n.* A bright-red intrinsic variable star, 527 light years from Earth, in the constellation Orion. [Fr. *Bételgeuse,* prob. < Ar. *bīt aljauzā.*]

betel palm

betel nut also **be·tel·nut** (bĕt'l-nŭt') *n.* The seed of the fruit of the betel palm, chewed, together with betel leaves and lime, by many people of southeastern Asia.

betel palm *n.* A palm tree, *Areca catechu,* of tropical Asia, having featherlike leaves and orange or scarlet fruit.

bête noire (bĕt nwär') *n.* Someone or something that one particularly dislikes or avoids. [Fr. : *bête,* beast + *noire,* black.]

beth (bĕt) *n.* The 2nd letter of the Hebrew alphabet. See table at **alphabet.** [Heb. *bēth.*]

beth·el (bĕth'əl) *n.* **1.** A hallowed or holy place. **2.** A chapel for seamen. [Heb. *bēth 'Ēl,* house of God.]

be·think (bĭ-thĭngk') *v.* **-thought** (-thôt'), **-think·ing, -thinks.** —*tr.* **1.** *Archaic.* To reflect on; think about. **2.** To remind (oneself); remember. —*intr. Archaic.* To meditate; ponder. [ME *bethinken* < OE *beðencan.*]

be·tide (bĭ-tīd') *v.* **-tid·ed, -tid·ing, -tides.** —*tr.* To happen to. —*intr.* To take place; befall. [ME *betiden* : *be-,* thoroughly + *tiden,* to happen < OE *tīdan.*]

be·times (bĭ-tīmz') *adv.* **1.** In good time; early. **2.** *Archaic.* Quickly; soon. [ME.]

bê·tise (bā-tēz') *n., pl.* **bê·tises** (-tēz'). **1.** Stupidity; foolishness. **2.** A stupid or foolish act. [Fr. < *bête,* foolish < *bête,* beast < OFr. *beste* < Lat. *bestia.*]

be·to·ken (bĭ-tō'kən) *tr.v.* **-kened, -ken·ing, -kens.** To be or give a sign or portent of. [ME *betokenen* : *be-,* thoroughly + *toknen,* to signify < OE *tacnian.*] —**be·to'ken·er** *n.*

bet·o·ny (bĕt'n-ē) *n., pl.* **-nies. 1.** Any of several plants of the genus *Stachys,* esp. *S. officinalis,* native to Eurasia, having a spike of reddish-purple flowers. **2.** The lousewort. [ME *betone* < OFr. *betoine* < Lat. *betonica,* prob. < *Vettones,* an ancient Iberian tribe.]

be·took (bĭ-to͝ok') *v.* Past tense of **betake.**

be·tray (bĭ-trā') *tr.v.* **-trayed, -tray·ing, -trays. 1.** To commit treason against or be a traitor to. **2.** To divulge in a breach of confidence. **3.** To make known unintentionally: *trembling hands betraying anxiety.* **4.** To reveal; indicate. **5.** To lead astray; deceive. [ME *betrayen* : *be-* thoroughly + *trayen,* to betray < OFr. *trair* < Lat. *tradee.* —see TRADITION.] —**be·tray'al** *n.* —**be·tray'er** *n.*

be·troth (bĭ-trōth', -trôth') *tr.v.* **-trothed, -troth·ing, -troths. 1.** To promise to give in marriage. **2.** To promise to marry. [ME *betrouthen* : *be-,* in relation to + *trouthe,* troth.]

be·troth·al (bĭ-trō'thəl, -trô'thəl) *n.* **1. a.** The act of betrothing. **b.** The fact of being betrothed. **2.** A mutual promise to marry; engagement.

be·trothed (bĭ-trōthd', -trôtht') *n.* A person to whom one is engaged to be married.

bet·ta (bĕt'ə) *n.* Any of a genus, *Betta,* of small, long-finned freshwater fishes of striking coloration, found in southeastern Asia. [NLat. *Betta,* genus name.]

bet·ter[1] (bĕt'ər) *adj.* Comparative of **good. 1.** Greater in excellence or higher in quality. **2.** More useful, suitable, or desirable. **3.** Larger; greater: *the better part of a summer.* **4.** Healthier than before. —*adv.* Comparative of **well. 1.** In a more excellent way. **2. a.** To a greater extent or degree. **b.** To greater use or advantage. **3.** More: *better than a year.* —*n.* **1.** Something that is better. **2.** A superior, as in rank or intelligence. —*v.* **-tered, -ter·ing, -ters.** —*tr.* **1.** To improve: *bettered his position.* **2.** To surpass or exceed. —*intr.* To become better. —***idioms.*** **better off.** In a better or wealthier condition. **for the better.** So as to improve. [ME < OE *betera.*]

Usage: *Better* is normally used in a comparison of two: *Which house of Congress has the better record?* However, *best* is used idiomatically with reference to two in certain locutions: *Put your best foot forward. May the best man win!* The phrase *had better* is accepted, so long as the *had* or its contraction is preserved: *You had better do it* or *you'd better do it,* but not *you better do it.* The use of *better* for *more,* as in *the distance is better than a mile,* is considered unacceptable in writing by a majority of the Usage Panel.

bet·ter[2] (bĕt'ər) *n.* Variant of **bettor.**

bet·ter·ment (bĕt'ər-mənt) *n.* **1.** An improvement. **2.** An improvement that is not merely a repair but that also adds to the value of real property.

bet·ter-off (bĕt'ər-ôf', -ŏf') *adj.* Being in a better or more prosperous condition.

bet·tor also **bet·ter** (bĕt'ər) *n.* One who bets.

be·tween (bĭ-twēn') *prep.* **1. a.** In the position or interval separating: *between the trees; between 11 o'clock and 12 o'clock.* **b.** Intermediate to, as in quantity, amount, or degree: *costs between fifteen and twenty dollars.* **2.** Connecting spatially: *a road between the house and the village.* **3. a.** By the combined effort or effect of: *Between them they succeeded.* **b.** In the combined ownership of: *They had three dollars between them.* **4.** As measured against. Used often to express a reciprocal relationship: *choose between riding and walking.* —*adv.* In an intermediate space, position, or time; in the interim. —***idioms.*** **between you and me.** In strictest confidence. **in between.** In an intermediate situation. [ME *betwene* < OE *betwēonum.*]

Usage: *Between* and *among* are often confused. *Between* is the only possible choice when only two entities are involved: *between* (never *among*) *good and evil; the rivalry between* (never *among*) *England and France.* When more than two entities are involved, the choice of *between* or *among* depends on the intended meaning. *Among* is used to indicate that an entity has been chosen from the members of a group: *the first among* (not *between*) *equals; Among* (not *between*) *the four chairs, I like the red one best. Among* is also used to indicate a relation of inclusion in a group: *He is among the best painters of our time; He took his place among the students waiting outside the door. Between,* on the other hand, is used to indicate the area bounded by several points: *We have narrowed the search to the area between* (not *among*) *Philadelphia, New York, and Scranton.* In other cases, either *between* or *among* may be used; one may speak of *an agreement between* or *among several merchants,* and one may say either that *the boy was lost among the trees* ("in the area of the trees") or *between the trees* (in which case we infer that the trees hid the boy from sight.)

be·tween·times (bĭ-twēn'tīmz') *adv.* At or during pauses.

be·twixt (bĭ-twĭkst') *adv. & prep. Archaic.* Between. —***idiom.*** **betwixt and between.** In an intermediate position; neither wholly one thing nor another. [ME < OE *betwyx.*]

Beu·lah (byo͞o'lə) *n.* **1.** In the Old Testament, the land of Israel. **2.** The land of peace described in Bunyan's *Pilgrim's Progress.*

bev·a·tron (bĕv'ə-trŏn') *n. Physics.* A proton synchrotron. [B(ILLION) + E(LECTRON) + V(OLTS) + -TRON.]

bev·el (bĕv'əl) *n.* **1.** The angle or inclination of a line or surface that meets another at any angle but 90 degrees. **2.** A rule with an adjustable arm used to measure or draw angles or to fix a surface at an angle. —*v.* **-eled, -el·ing, -els** or **-elled, -el·ling, -els.** —*tr.* To cut at an inclination that forms an angle other than a right angle. —*intr.* To be inclined; slope. [OFr. **bevel* < *baif,* open-mouthed < *bayer,* to gape.]

bevel gear *n.* Either of a pair of gears with teeth surfaces cut so that the gear shafts are not parallel.

bev·er·age (bĕv'ər-ĭj, bĕv'rĭj) *n.* Any of various liquids for drinking, usually excluding water. [ME *beverege* < OFr. *bevrage* < *beivre,* to drink < Lat. *biber.*]

bev·y (bĕv′ē) *n., pl.* **-ies. 1.** A group of animals or birds, esp. larks or quail; flock. **2.** A group or assemblage. [ME.]

be·wail (bĭ-wāl′) *tr.v.* **-wailed, -wail·ing, -wails. 1.** To express sorrow or regret over. **2.** To cry about. **—be·wail′er** *n.* **—be·wail′ment** *n.*

be·ware (bĭ-wâr′) *v.* **-wared, -war·ing, -wares.** *—tr.* To be cautious of. *—intr.* To be cautious: *Beware of the dog.* [ME *be ware* : *be,* imper. of *been,* to be + *ware,* on one's guard (< OE *wær*).]

be·whis·kered (bĭ-hwĭs′kərd, -wĭs′-) *adj.* Having whiskers.

be·wil·der (bĭ-wĭl′dər) *tr.v.* **-dered, -der·ing, -ders. 1.** To confuse or befuddle, esp. with numerous conflicting situations, objects, or statements. **2.** To cause to lose one's sense of where one is. **—be·wil′dered·ly** *adv.* **—be·wil′dered·ness** *n.* **—be·wil′der·ing·ly** *adv.*

be·wil·der·ment (bĭ-wĭl′dər-mənt) *n.* **1.** The condition of being bewildered. **2.** A situation of perplexity or confusion; tangle.

be·witch (bĭ-wĭch′) *tr.v.* **-witched, -witch·ing, -witch·es. 1.** To place under one's power by or as if by magic; cast a spell over. **2.** To captivate completely; fascinate. [ME *bewicchen* : *be-,* thoroughly + *wicchen,* to enchant < OE *wiccian* < *wicce,* witch and *wicca,* wizard.] **—be·witch′er** *n.* **—be·witch′er·y** *n.* **—be·witch′ing** *adj.*

be·witch·ment (bĭ-wĭch′mənt) *n.* **1. a.** The act of bewitching. **b.** The state of being bewitched. **2.** A spell that bewitches.

be·wray (bĭ-rā′) *tr.v.* **-wrayed, -wray·ing, -wrays.** *Archaic.* To disclose, esp. inadvertently; betray. [ME *bewreien* : *be-,* thoroughly + *wreien,* to accuse < OE *wregan.*]

bey (bā) *n.* **1.** A provincial governor in the Ottoman Empire. **2.** A native ruler of the former kingdom of Tunis. **3.** A Turkish title of honor and respect. [Turk.]

be·yond (bē-ŏnd′, bĭ-yŏnd′) *prep.* **1.** On the far side of; past. **2.** Later than. **3.** Past the understanding, reach, or scope of: *an evil beyond remedy.* **4.** To a degree or amount greater than: *rich beyond his wildest dreams.* **5.** In addition to: *asked for nothing beyond peace and quiet.* *—adv.* Farther along. [ME < OE *begeondan.*]

bez·ant (bĕz′ənt, bə-zănt′) **1.** A gold coin issued in Byzantium; solidus. **2.** *Archit.* A flat disk used as an ornament. [ME *besant* < OFr. < Lat. *Byzantius,* of Byzantium.]

bez·el (bĕz′əl) *n.* **1.** A slanting surface or bevel on the edge of a cutting tool. **2.** The upper, faceted portion of a cut gem, above the girdle. **3.** A groove or flange designed to hold a beveled edge, as of a watch crystal or a gem. [Orig. unknown.]

be·zique (bə-zēk′) *n.* A card game similar to pinochle that is played with a deck of 64 cards. [Fr. *bésique.*]

be·zoar (bē′zôr′, -zōr′) *n.* A hard gastric or intestinal mass found chiefly in ruminants and once considered an antidote to poison. [ME *bezear* < OFr. *bezar* < Ar. *bāzahr* < Pers. *pād-zahr* : *pād,* protecting against + *zahr,* poison.]

B-girl (bē′gûrl′) *n.* A woman who encourages customers in a bar to spend money freely. [B(AR) + GIRL.]

Bha·ga·vad-Gi·ta (bä′gə-väd-gē′tə) *n.* A sacred Hindu text in the form of a philosophical dialogue that is incorporated into the *Mahabharata,* an ancient Sanskrit epic. [Skt. *bhagavad-gītā,* song of the blessed one (Krishna).]

bhang also **bang** (băng) *n.* **1.** The hemp plant. **2.** Any of several narcotics made from the dried leaves and flowers of hemp. [Hindi *bhāng* < Skt. *bhaṅgā.*]

Bhu·tan·ese (bo͞o′tə-nēz′, -nēs′) *n., pl.* **Bhutanese. 1.** A native or inhabitant of Bhutan. **2.** The Sino-Tibetan language of Bhutan. *—adj.* Of or characteristic of Bhutan, its people, or their language and culture.

bi-[1] or **bin-** *pref.* **1. a.** Two: *biform.* **b.** Both: *binaural.* **c.** Both sides, parts, or directions: *biconcave.* **2. a.** Occurring at intervals of two: *bicentennial.* **b.** Occurring twice during: *biweekly.* **3. a.** Containing twice the proportion of a specified chemical element or group necessary for stability: *bicarbonate.* **b.** Containing two chemical atoms, radicals, or groups: *biphenyl.* [Lat. < *bis,* twice.]

Usage: *Bimonthly* and *biweekly* mean "once every two months" and "once every two weeks." For "twice a month" and "twice a week," the words *semimonthly* and *semiweekly* should be used. But there is a great deal of confusion over the distinction, and a writer is well advised to substitute expressions like "every two months" or "twice a month" where possible. However, used as nouns to denote "a publication that appears every two months," the words with *bi-* are unavoidable.

bi-[2] *pref.* Variant of **bio-**.

Bi The symbol for the element bismuth.

bi·a·ly (bē-ä′lē) *n., pl.* **-lys.** A flat, round baked roll topped with onion flakes. [After *Bialystok,* Poland.]

bi·an·nu·al (bī-ăn′yo͞o-əl) *adj.* Happening twice each year; semiannual. **—bi·an′nu·al·ly** *adv.*

bi·as (bī′əs) *n.* **1.** A line cutting diagonally across the grain of fabric. **2. a.** A preference or inclination, esp. one that inhibits impartial judgment; prejudice. **b.** A specified instance of this. **3. a.** A weight or irregularity in a ball that causes it to swerve, as in lawn bowling. **b.** The tendency of such a ball to swerve. **4.** The fixed voltage applied to an electrode. ***—modifier:*** *a bias fold.* *—tr.v.* **-ased, -as·ing, -as·es** or **-assed, -as·sing, -as·ses. 1.** To cause to have a prejudiced view. **2.** To apply a small voltage to (a grid). [OFr. *biais,* oblique.]

Usage: *Bias* has generally been defined as "uninformed or unintentional inclination"; as such it may operate either for or against someone or something. Recently *bias* has been used in the sense of "adverse action or discrimination": *Congress included a provision in the Civil Rights Act of 1964 banning racial bias in employment.* Less than half the members of the Usage Panel accept this meaning.

bi·ath·lon (bī-ăth′lən, -lŏn′) *n.* An athletic competition that combines events in cross-country skiing and rifle shooting. [BI- + Gk. *athlon,* contest.]

bi·ax·i·al (bī-ăk′sē-əl) *adj.* Having two axes. **—bi·ax′i·al′i·ty** (-ăl′ĭ-tē) *n.* **—bi·ax′i·al·ly** *adv.*

bib (bĭb) *n.* **1.** A kind of napkin tied under the chin and worn, esp. by small children, to protect the clothing during meals. **2.** The part of an apron or pair of overalls worn over the chest. *—v.* **bibbed, bib·bing, bibs.** *—tr.* To drink; imbibe. *—intr.* To indulge in drinking; tipple. [Prob. < ME *bibben,* to drink, perh. < Lat. *bibere.*]

bib and tucker *n. Informal.* Clothing; outfit: *put on her best bib and tucker.*

bibb (bĭb) *n.* **1.** A bracket on the mast of a ship to support the trestletrees. **2.** A bibcock. [Alteration of BIB.]

bib·ber (bĭb′ər) *n.* A tippler; drinker. [< BIB.]

Bibb lettuce (bĭb) *n.* A kind of lettuce forming a small head and having tender, dark-green leaves. [After Jack *Bibb,* 19th-cent. American vegetable grower.]

bib·cock (bĭb′kŏk′) *n.* A faucet with a nozzle that is bent downward.

bi·be·lot (bē′bə-lō′, bē-blō′) *n.* A small decorative object or trinket. [Fr. < OFr. *beubelet,* from a redup. of *bel,* beautiful < Lat. *bellus,* handsome.]

Bi·ble (bī′bəl) *n.* **1. a.** The sacred book of Christianity, a collection of ancient writings including the books of both the Old Testament and the New Testament. **b.** The Old Testament, the sacred book of Judaism. **c.** A particular copy of a Bible: *the old family Bible.* **d.** A book or collection of writings constituting the sacred text of a religion. **2. bible.** A book considered authoritative in its field: *the bible of French cooking.* [ME < OFr. < Med. Lat. *biblia* < Gk., pl. of *biblion,* book < *biblos,* papyrus < *Bublos,* a Phoenician port.]

Bible Belt *n.* Those sections of the United States, esp. in the South and Middle West, where Protestant fundamentalism prevails.

Bib·li·cal also **bib·li·cal** (bĭb′lĭ-kəl) *adj.* **1.** Of, pertaining to, or contained in the Bible. **2.** In keeping with the nature of the Bible, esp.: **a.** Suggestive of the personages or times depicted in the Bible. **b.** Suggestive of the prose or narrative style of the King James Bible. [Med. Lat. *biblicus* < *biblia,* Bible.] **—Bib′li·cal·ly** *adv.*

Bib·li·cist (bĭb′lĭ-sĭst) *n.* **1.** An expert on the Bible. **2.** A person who interprets the Bible literally. **—Bib′li·cism** *n.*

biblio– *pref.* Book: *bibliophile.* [< Gk. *biblion,* book. —see BIBLE.]

bib·li·o·film (bĭb′lē-ō-fĭlm′) *n.* A type of microfilm used esp. to photograph the pages of books.

bib·li·og·ra·pher (bĭb′lē-ŏg′rə-fər) *n.* **1.** An expert in the description and cataloguing of printed matter. **2.** One who compiles a bibliography.

bib·li·og·ra·phy (bĭb′lē-ŏg′rə-fē) *n., pl.* **-phies. 1. a.** A list of the works of a specific author or publisher. **b.** A list of writings relating to a single subject. **2. a.** The description and identification of the editions, dates of issue, authorship, and typography of books or other written material. **b.** A compilation of such information. **—bib′li·o·graph′i·cal** (-ə-grăf′ĭ-kəl), **bib′li·o·graph′ic** (-ĭk) *adj.* **—bib′li·o·graph′i·cal·ly** *adv.*

bib·li·ol·a·try (bĭb′lē-ŏl′ə-trē) *n.* **1.** Excessive adherence to a literal interpretation of the Bible. **2.** Extreme devotion to or concern with books. **—bib′li·ol′a·ter** *n.* **—bib′li·ol′a·trous** *adj.*

bib·li·o·man·cy (bĭb′lē-ə-măn′sē) *n., pl.* **-cies.** Divination by interpretation of a passage chosen at random from a book, esp. the Bible.

bib·li·o·ma·ni·a (bĭb′lē-ə-mā′nē-ə, -mān′yə) *n.* An exaggerated liking for acquiring and owning books. **—bib′li·o·ma′ni·ac′** (-ăk′) *n.* **—bib′li·o·ma·ni′a·cal** (-mə-nī′ə-kəl) *adj.*

bib·li·o·phile (bĭb′lē-ə-fīl′) also **bib·li·o·phil** (-fĭl′) or **bib·li·oph·i·list** (bĭb′lē-ŏf′ə-lĭst) *n.* **1.** One who loves books. **2.** A book collector. **—bib′li·oph′i·lism** *n.* **—bib′li·oph′i·lis′tic** *adj.*

bib·li·o·pho·bi·a (bĭb′lē-ə-fō′bē-ə) *n.* An abnormal fear of books. **—bib′li·o·phobe′** *n.* **—bib′li·o·pho′bic** *adj.*

bib·li·o·pole (bĭb′lē-ə-pōl′) also **bib·li·op·o·list** (bĭb′lē-ŏp′ə-lĭst) *n.* A person who deals in rare books. [Lat. *bibliopola* < Gk. *bibliopōlēs* : *biblion,* book + *pōlein,* to sell.] **—bib′li·o·pol′ic** (-pŏl′ĭk), **bib′li·o·pol′i·cal** *adj.*

bib·li·o·the·ca (bĭb′lē-ə-thē′kə) *n.* **1.** A book collection; library. **2.** A catalogue of books. [Lat. < Gk. *bibliothēkē* : *biblion,* book + *thēkē,* case.] **—bib′li·o·the′cal** *adj.*

bib·li·ot·ics (bĭb′lē-ŏt′ĭks) *n. (used with a sing. verb).* The examination of written documents to determine authorship or authenticity.

bib·u·lous (bĭb′yə-ləs) *adj.* **1.** Given to or marked by drinking. **2.** Very absorbent. [Lat. *bibulus* < *bibere,* to drink.] **—bib′u·lous·ly** *adv.* **—bib′u·lous·ness** *n.*

bevel gear
Spiral bevel gears

BOOKS OF THE BIBLE

Bible translation is one of the world's oldest scholarly activities; the tradition runs back to the 3rd century B.C. As of the present date, at least some books of the Bible have been translated into more than 1,400 languages. Since there are more than 3,000 languages in the world, it is reasonable to assume that the field will continue to expand. English has an uncommonly rich heritage in this respect; since the metrical paraphrases and Gospels of Anglo-Saxon times, the entire book has been translated again and again. The Jewish Publication Society *Holy Scriptures According to the Masoretic Text,* issued in 1916 by a committee of Jewish scholars, is accepted as standard in American Judaism, and its contents are listed here. For Roman Catholics the Douay Version (1582–1610) has for many centuries been the text officially approved for teaching and Church use. To serve two pressing needs facing the Church in the second half of the twentieth century—the need to keep abreast of the times and the need to deepen theological thought—changes have had to be made. The original texts were re-examined and re-evaluated with the assistance of the pioneer work of the School of Biblical Studies in Jerusalem; the result was the publication in France of *La Bible de Jerusalem* in the early 1960's. The English text of the *Jerusalem Bible,* published in 1966, owes a large debt to the work of the many scholars who collaborated to produce *La Bible de Jerusalem.* The *Jerusalem Bible* has gained wide acceptance in the light of the most recent research in the fields of history, archaeology, and literary criticism. Protestants may use either the King James Bible (or Authorized Version, as it is often called, especially in Great Britain), which appeared in 1611 under the patronage of James I; or they may use the Revised Standard Version (1946–52). The following table presents the contents as listed in the Jerusalem Bible and King James versions because they have the sanction of general acceptance.

HEBREW SCRIPTURES

Genesis	II Samuel	Joel	Haggai	Lamentations
Exodus	I Kings	Amos	Zechariah	Ecclesiastes
Leviticus	II Kings	Obadiah	Malachi	Esther
Numbers	Isaiah	Jonah	Psalms	Daniel
Deuteronomy	Jeremiah	Micah	Proverbs	Ezra
Joshua	Ezekiel	Nahum	Job	Nehemiah
Judges	THE TWELVE	Habakkuk	Song of Songs	I Chronicles
I Samuel	Hosea	Zephaniah	Ruth	II Chronicles

OLD TESTAMENT

Jerusalem Version	King James Version	Jerusalem Version	King James Version
Genesis	Genesis	Song of Solomon	Song of Solomon
Exodus	Exodus	Wisdom	
Leviticus	Leviticus	Ecclesiasticus	
Numbers	Numbers	Isaiah	Isaiah
Deuteronomy	Deuteronomy	Jeremiah	Jeremiah
Joshua	Joshua	Lamentations	Lamentations
Judges	Judges	Baruch	
Ruth	Ruth	Ezekiel	Ezekiel
I Samuel	I Samuel	Daniel	Daniel
II Samuel	II Samuel	Hosea	Hosea
I Kings	I Kings	Joel	Joel
II Kings	II Kings	Amos	Amos
I Chronicles	I Chronicles	Obadiah	Obadiah
II Chronicles	II Chronicles	Jonah	Jonah
Ezra	Ezra	Micah	Micah
Nehemiah	Nehemiah	Nahum	Nahum
Tobit		Habakkuk	Habakkuk
Judith		Zephaniah	Zephaniah
Esther	Esther	Haggai	Haggai
Job	Job	Zechariah	Zechariah
Psalms	Psalms	Malachi	Malachi
Proverbs	Proverbs	I Maccabees	
Ecclesiastes	Ecclesiastes	II Maccabees	

NEW TESTAMENT

Matthew	I Corinthians	II Thessalonians	I Peter
Mark	II Corinthians	I Timothy	II Peter
Luke	Galatians	II Timothy	I John
John	Ephesians	Titus	II John
Acts	Philippians	Philemon	III John
	Colossians	Hebrews	Jude
Romans	I Thessalonians	James	Revelation

bi·cam·er·al (bī-kăm′ər-əl) *adj.* Composed of two legislative chambers or branches: *a bicameral legislature.*

bi·cap·su·lar (bī-kăp′sə-lər) *adj. Bot.* **1.** Having two capsules. **2.** Having a capsule with two cells.

bi·car·bon·ate (bī-kär′bə-nāt′, -nĭt) *n.* The radical group HCO_3 or a compound, such as sodium bicarbonate, containing it.

bicarbonate of soda *n.* Sodium bicarbonate.

bi·cau·dal (bī-kôd′l) *adj.* Having two tails.

bi·cel·lu·lar (bī-sĕl′yə-lər) *adj.* Having two cells.

bi·cen·ten·a·ry (bī′sĕn-tĕn′ə-rē, bī-sĕn′tə-nĕr′ē) *n., pl.* **-ries.** A bicentennial. **—bi′cen·ten′a·ry** *adj.*

bi·cen·ten·ni·al (bī′sĕn-tĕn′ē-əl) *adj.* **1.** Happening once every 200 years. **2.** Lasting for 200 years. **3.** Pertaining to a 200th anniversary. *—n.* A 200th anniversary or its celebration.

bi·cen·tric (bī-sĕn′trĭk) *adj.* Having two centers. **—bi′cen·tric′i·ty** (-trĭs′ĭ-tē) *n.*

bi·ceph·a·lous (bī-sĕf′ə-ləs) *adj.* Having two heads.

bi·ceps (bī′sĕps′) *n., pl.* **biceps** or **-ceps·es** (-sĕp′sĭz). A muscle with two heads or points of origin, esp.: **a.** The large muscle at the front of the upper arm that flexes the elbow joint. **b.** The large muscle at the back of the thigh that flexes the knee joint. [NLat. < Lat., two-headed : *bi-,* two + *caput,* head.]

bi·chlo·ride (bī-klôr′īd′, -klōr′-) *n.* Dichloride.

bi·chro·mate (bī-krō′māt′, -mĭt) *n.* Dichromate.

bi·cil·i·ate (bī-sĭl′ē-ĭt, -āt′) *adj.* Having two cilia.

bi·cip·i·tal (bī-sĭp′ĭ-tl) *adj.* Of or pertaining to the biceps. [< NLat. *biceps, bicipit-,* biceps.]

bick·er (bĭk′ər) *intr.v.* **-ered, -er·ing, -ers. 1.** To engage in a petty quarrel; squabble. **2.** To flicker; quiver. *—n.* A petty quarrel; squabble. [ME *bikeren,* to attack.] **—bick′er·er** *n.*

bi·col·or (bī′kŭl′ər) also **bi·col·ored** (-ərd) *adj.* Having two colors.

bi·con·cave (bī′kŏn-kāv′, bī-kŏn′kāv′) *adj.* Concave on both sides or surfaces. **—bi′con·cav′i·ty** (-kăv′ĭ-tē) *n.*

bi·con·vex (bī′kŏn-vĕks′, bī-kŏn′vĕks′) *adj.* Convex on both sides or surfaces. **—bi′con·vex′i·ty** (-vĕk′sĭ-tē) *n.*

bi·corn (bī′kôrn′) also **bi·cor·nu·ate** (bī-kôr′nyo͞o-ĭt, -āt′) *adj.* **1.** Having two horns or horn-shaped parts. **2.** Shaped like a crescent. [Lat. *bicornis* : *bi-,* two + *cornu,* horn.]

bi·cor·po·ral (bī-kôr′pər-əl) also **bi·cor·po·re·al** (bī′kôr-pôr′ē-əl, -pōr′-) *adj.* Having two distinct bodies or main parts.

bi·cos·tate (bī-kŏs′tāt′) *adj. Bot.* Having two principal longitudinal ribs: *a bicostate leaf.* [BI- + COST(A) + -ATE.]

bi·cul·tur·al (bī-kŭl′chər-əl) *adj.* Of or relating to two discrete cultures in one nation or geographic region. **—bi·cul′tur·al·ism** *n.*

bi·cus·pid (bī-kŭs′pĭd) also **bi·cus·pi·date** (-pĭ-dāt′) *adj.* Having two points or cusps, as the crescent moon. *—n.* **bicuspid.** A bicuspid tooth, esp. a premolar. [NLat. *bicuspis, bicuspid-* : *bi-* two + *cuspis,* cusp.]

bicuspid valve *n.* The cardiac valve, composed of two triangular flaps, that is situated in the orifice connecting the left auricle and ventricle.

bi·cy·cle (bī′sĭk′əl, -sĭ′kəl) *n.* A vehicle consisting of a metal frame mounted on two wire-spoked wheels one behind the other and having a seat, handlebars for steering, and two pedals or a small motor by which it is driven. *—intr.v.* **-cled, -cling, -cles.** To ride or travel on a bicycle. [Fr. : *bi-,* two + Gk. *kuklos,* wheel.] **—bi′cy·clist** *n.*

bi·cy·clic (bī-sī′klĭk, -sĭk′lĭk) also **bi·cy·cli·cal** (-sī′klĭ-kəl, -sĭk′lĭ-) *adj.* **1.** Consisting of or having two cycles. **2.** *Bot.* Composed of or arranged in two distinct whorls, as the petals of a flower. **3.** *Chem.* Containing molecules consisting of two fused rings.

bid (bĭd) *v.* **bade** (băd, bād) or **bid, bid·den** (bĭd′n) or **bid, bid·ding, bids.** *—tr.* **1.** To order; command. **2.** To utter (a greeting or salutation). **3.** To invite to attend; summon. **4.** *Past tense and past participle* **bid.** To state one's intention to take (tricks of a certain number or suit in cards): *bid four hearts.* **5.** *Past tense and past participle* **bid.** To offer or propose (an amount) as a price. *—intr.* **1.** *Past tense and past participle* **bid.** To make an offer to pay or accept a specified price. **2.** *Past tense and past participle* **bid.** To seek to win or attain something; strive. *—n.* **1. a.** An offer or proposal of a price. **b.** The amount offered or proposed. **2.** An invitation, esp. one offering membership in a group or club. **3. a.** The act of bidding in card games. **b.** The number of tricks or points declared. **c.** The trump or no-trump declared. **d.** The turn of a player to bid. **4.** An earnest effort to win or attain something. **—*idiom.* bid fair.** To appear likely. [Partly < ME *bidden,* to ask, command (< OE *biddan*), and partly < ME *beden,* to offer (< OE *bēodan*).] **—bid′der** *n.*

bi·dar·ka (bī-där′kə) *n.* A hide-covered canoe used by Eskimos of Alaska. [R. *baidarka.*]

bid·da·ble (bĭd′ə-bəl) *adj.* **1.** Capable of being bid. **2.** Docile; tractable.

bid·den (bĭd′n) *v.* A past participle of **bid.**

bid·ding (bĭd′ĭng) *n.* **1.** A demand that something be done; command. **2.** A request to appear; summons. **3.** Bids collectively, as at an auction.

bid·dy[1] (bĭd′ē) *n., pl.* **-dies.** A hen; fowl. [Orig. unknown.]

bid·dy[2] (bĭd′ē) *n., pl.* **-dies.** *Slang.* A woman, esp. a garrulous old one. [Nickname for *Bridget.*]

Biddy Basketball *n.* Basketball for youngsters in which the baskets are at a height of 8½ feet. [Alteration of dial. *bitty,* small (BIT + -Y) + BASKETBALL.]

bide (bīd) *v.* **bid·ed** or **bode** (bōd), **bid·ed, bid·ing, bides.** *—intr.* **1.** To remain in a condition or state. **2. a.** To wait; tarry. **b.** To stay. **c.** To be left; remain. *—tr.* To await: *bide one's time.* [ME *biden* < OE *bīdan.*]

bi·den·tate (bī-dĕn′tāt′) *adj.* Having two teeth or toothlike processes.

bi·det (bē-dā′) *n.* A basinlike fixture designed to be straddled for bathing the genitals and the posterior parts. [Fr.]

bi·di·a·lec·tal (bī′dī-ə-lĕk′təl) *adj.* Using two dialects of the same language. **—bi′di·a·lec′tal·ism** *n.* **—bi′di·a·lec′tal·ist** *n.*

bi·don·ville (bē′dôN-vēl′) *n.* A shantytown on the outskirts of a city, as in France. [Fr. : *bidon,* tin can (< OFr., canteen, prob. of Scand. orig.) + *ville,* town. —see VILLAGE.]

Bie·der·mei·er (bē′dər-mī′ər) *adj.* Of or pertaining to a type of furniture developed in Germany during the first half of the 19th century and modeled after French Empire styles. [After Gottlieb *Biedermeier,* the imaginary author of poems written by Ludwig Eichroth (1827–1892).]

bi·en·ni·a (bī-ĕn′ē-ə) *n.* A plural of **biennium.**

bi·en·ni·al (bī-ĕn′ē-əl) *adj.* **1.** Lasting or living for two years. **2.** Happening every second year. **3.** Having a normal life cycle of two years. *—n.* **1.** An event that occurs once every two years. **2.** A plant that normally requires two years to reach maturity, producing leaves in the first year, blooming and producing fruit in the second year, and then dying. **—bi·en′ni·al·ly** *adv.*

bi·en·ni·um (bī-ĕn′ē-əm) *n., pl.* **-ni·ums** or **-ni·a** (-ē-ə). A two-year period. [Lat : *bi-,* two + *annus,* year.]

bier (bîr) *n.* A stand on which a corpse or a coffin containing a corpse is placed prior to burial. [ME *bere* < OE *bēr.*]

bi·fa·cial (bī-fā′shəl) *adj.* **1.** Having two faces, fronts, or facades. **2.** *Bot.* Having upper and lower surfaces that are distinct and dissimilar. **3.** Having two opposing surfaces that are alike.

biff (bĭf) *Slang.* *—tr.v.* **biffed, biff·ing, biffs.** To strike or punch. *—n.* A blow or punch. [Imit.]

bi·fid (bī′fĭd) *adj.* Divided into two equal parts or lobes by a median cleft. **—bi·fid′i·ty** (-fĭd′ĭ-tē) *n.* **—bi′fid·ly** *adv.*

bi·fi·lar (bī-fī′lər) *adj.* Fitted with or involving the use of two threads or wires. **—bi·fi′lar·ly** *adv.*

bi·flag·el·late (bī-flăj′ə-lĭt, -lāt′) *adj.* Having two flagella: *a biflagellate protozoan.*

bi·fo·cal (bī-fō′kəl) *adj.* **1.** Having two different focal lengths. **2.** Having one section that corrects for distant vision and another that corrects for near vision.

bi·fo·cals (bī-fō′kəlz) *pl.n.* Eyeglasses with bifocal lenses.

bi·fo·li·ate (bī-fō′lē-ĭt, -āt′) *adj.* Having two leaves.

bi·fo·li·o·late (bī-fō′lē-ə-lāt′, -lĭt) *adj.* Having two leaflets.

bi·fo·rate (bī-fôr′āt′, -fōr′-, bī′fə-rāt′) *adj. Biol.* Having two openings. [BI- + Lat. *forare, forat-,* to pierce.]

bi·form (bī′fôrm′) *adj.* Having a combination of features or qualities of two distinct forms.

bi·fur·cate (bī′fər-kāt′, bī-fûr′-) *v.* **-cat·ed, -cat·ing, -cates.** *—tr.* To divide into two parts or branches. *—intr.* To separate into two parts or branches; fork. *—adj.* (-kāt′, -kĭt). Forked or divided into two parts or branches. [Med. Lat. *bifurcare, bifurcat-,* to divide < Lat. *bifurcus,* two-pronged : *bi-,* two + *furcus,* fork.] **—bi′fur·cate′ly** *adv.* **—bi′fur·ca′tion** *n.*

big (bĭg) *adj.* **big·ger, big·gest. 1.** Of considerable size, number, quantity, magnitude, or extent; large. **2. a.** *Obs.* Of great force or violence. **b.** Of great intensity; strong. **3.** Grown-up; adult. **4.** Pregnant: *big with child.* **5.** Filled up; brimming over. **6.** Having or exercising considerable authority, control, or influence. **7.** Conspicuous in position, wealth, or importance; prominent. **8.** Of great significance; momentous. **9.** Loud and firm; resounding. **10.** Bountiful; generous. **11.** *Informal.* Self-important; boastful. *—adv.* **1.** In a pretentious or boastful way: *talked big about the job.* **2.** With considerable success. **—*idioms.* big on.** Enthusiastic about; partial to: *big on meat and potatoes.* **make it big.** To become very successful. [ME, prob. of Scand. orig.] **—big′gish** *adj.* **—big′ly** *adv.* **—big′ness** *n.*

bicycle

big·a·mous (bĭg′ə-məs) *adj.* **1.** Involving bigamy. **2.** Guilty of bigamy. **—big′a·mous·ly** *adv.*

big·a·my (bĭg′ə-mē) *n., pl.* **-mies.** *Law.* The criminal offense of marrying one person while still legally married to another. [ME *bigamie* < OFr. < *bigame,* bigamous < LLat. *bigamus* : Lat. *bi-,* two + Gk. *gamos,* marriage.] **—big′a·mist** *n.*

big·ar·reau (bĭg′ə-rō′) *n.* Any of several varieties of sweet cherry with firm, often light-colored flesh. [Fr. < *bigarrer,* to variegate.]

big bang *n.* The cosmic explosion that marked the origin of the universe according to the big bang theory.

big bang theory *n.* A cosmological theory holding that the universe originated billions of years ago from the violent eruption of a point source.

Big Bertha *n.* A large cannon used by Germany in World War I. [After *Bertha* Krupp von Bohlen und Halbach (1886–1957).]

big brother *n.* **1.** An older brother. **2.** A man who befriends a disadvantaged boy. **3. Big Brother.** A vague, threatening figure representing the all-seeing, omnipresent power of an authoritarian government. [After *Big Brother,* a character in the novel *Nineteen Eighty-Four* by George Orwell (1903–1950).]
Big Broth·er·ism (brŭth′ə-rĭz′əm) *n.* Authoritarian efforts at total control, as of an individual or a nation.
Big Dipper *n.* A cluster of seven stars in the constellation Ursa Major, four forming the bowl and three the handle of a dipper-shaped configuration.

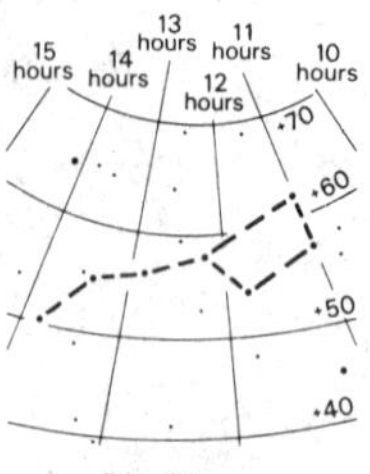

Big Dipper
In the constellation Ursa Major

bi·gem·i·nal (bī-jĕm′ə-nəl) *adj.* Occurring in pairs; twinned. [LLat. *bigeminus,* doubled : Lat. *bi-,* two + Lat. *geminus,* paired.]
bi·gem·i·ny (bī-jĕm′ə-nē) *n.* A cardiovascular condition wherein the pulse occurs in groups of two rapid beats with a pause following each pair of beats. [LLat. *bigeminus,* doubled + -Y.]
big·eye (bĭg′ī′) *n.* Any of several marine fishes of the family Priacanthidae, having large eyes and reddish scales.
Big·foot (bĭg′fo͝ot′) *n.* The sasquatch. [From the size of the footprints believed to belong to it.]
big game *n.* **1.** Large animals or fish hunted or caught for sport. **2.** *Slang.* An important objective. **—big′-game′** *adj.*
big·ge·ty (bĭg′ĭ-tē) *adj.* Variant of **biggity.**
big·gie (bĭg′ē) *n. Informal.* **1.** A bigwig; big wheel. **2.** Something, as a corporation, that is considered big or important.
big·gi·ty also **big·ge·ty** (bĭg′ĭ-tē) *adj. Informal.* Self-important; conceited. [< BIG.]
big·head (bĭg′hĕd′) *n.* **1.** *Informal.* Conceit; egotism. **2.** Any of various diseases of animals characterized by swelling of the head. **—big′head′ed** *adj.* **—big′head′ed·ness** *n.*
big-heart·ed (bĭg′här′tĭd) *adj.* Generous; kind. **—big′-heart′ed·ly** *adv.* **—big′-heart′ed·ness** *n.*
big·horn (bĭg′hôrn′) *n.* A wild sheep, *Ovis canadensis,* of the mountains of western North America, the male of which has massive, curved horns.

bighorn

big house *n. Slang.* A penitentiary.
bight (bīt) *n.* **1. a.** A loop in a rope. **b.** The middle or slack part of an extended rope. **2. a.** A bend or curve, esp. in a shoreline. **b.** A wide bay formed by such a bend or curve. —*tr.v.* **bight·ed, bight·ing, bights.** To tie in or secure with a bight. [ME, bend < OE *byht.*]
big league *n.* **1.** A major league. **2.** Big time. **—big leaguer** *n.*
big-league (bĭg′lēg′) *adj.* **1.** Major-league. **2.** Outstanding in one's field.
big·mouth (bĭg′mouth′) *n.* **1.** Any of various fishes having unusually large mouths. **2.** *Slang.* A loud-mouthed or gossipy person.
big·mouthed (bĭg′mou*th*d′, -moutht′) *adj.* **1.** Having a large mouth. **2.** Speaking loudly or indiscreetly; loud-mouthed.
big-name (bĭg′nām′) *adj.* **1.** Of superior status in popular acknowledgment. **2.** Of or involving one that is big-name.
big·no·ni·a (bĭg-nō′nē-ə) *n.* A plant of the genus *Bignonia,* esp. *B. capreolata,* a woody vine. [NLat. *Bignonia,* genus name, after Jean-Paul *Bignon* (1662–1743).]
big·ot (bĭg′ət) *n.* A person who is rigidly devoted to his own group, religion, race, or politics and is intolerant of those who differ. [Fr. < OFr.]
big·ot·ed (bĭg′ə-tĭd) *adj.* Being or characteristic of a bigot. **—big′ot·ed·ly** *adv.* **—big′ot·ed·ness** *n.*
big·ot·ry (bĭg′ə-trē) *n.* The attitude, state of mind, or behavior characteristic of a bigot; intolerance.
big shot *n. Slang.* An important or influential person.
big-tick·et (bĭg′tĭk′ĭt) *adj. Informal.* Having a high price.
big time *n. Slang.* The most prestigious level of attainment in a competitive field. **—big′-time′** *adj.* **—big′-tim′er** *n.*
big toe *n.* The largest and innermost toe of the human foot.
big top *n. Informal.* **1.** The main tent of a circus. **2.** The circus.
big tree *n.* The giant sequoia.
big wheel *n. Slang.* A person of importance or authority.
big·wig (bĭg′wĭg′) *n. Informal.* An important person; dignitary.
Bi·ha·ri (bĭ-hä′rē) *n., pl.* **-ris. 1.** A native or inhabitant of Bihar. **2.** The Indic language of the Biharis.
bi·jou (bē′zho͞o′) *n., pl.* **-joux** (-zho͞o′, -zho͞oz′). A small, exquisitely wrought trinket. [Fr. < Breton *bizou,* ring with a stone < *biz,* finger.]
bi·jou·te·rie (bē-zho͞o′tə-rē) *n.* A collection of jewelry or trinkets. [Fr.]
bike (bīk) *n.* **1.** A bicycle. **2.** A motorcycle. **3.** A motorbike. —*intr.v.* **biked, bik·ing, bikes.** To ride a bike. [Short for BICYCLE.]
bik·er (bī′kər) *n.* A motorcyclist, esp. one who belongs to a motorcycle gang.
bike·way (bīk′wā′) *n.* A roadway for bicycles.
bi·ki·ni (bĭ-kē′nē) *n.* **1.** A very brief two-piece bathing suit worn by women. **2.** Brief underpants that reach to the hips rather than to the waist. [Fr. < *Bikini,* an atoll in the Marshall Islands.]
bi·la·bi·al (bī-lā′bē-əl) *adj.* **1.** Pronounced or articulated with both lips, as the consonants *b, p, m,* and *w.* **2.** Pertaining to both lips. —*n.* A bilabial sound or consonant. **—bi·la′bi·al·ly** *adv.*
bi·la·bi·ate (bī-lā′bē-ĭt, -āt′) *adj. Bot.* Having two lips, as a flower or corolla.
bil·an·der (bĭl′ən-dər, bī′lən-) *n.* A small two-masted sailing vessel, used esp. on canals in the Low Countries. [Du. *bijlander*: *bij,* by (< MDu. *bie*) + *land,* land (< MDu.).]
bi·lat·er·al (bī-lăt′ər-əl) *adj.* **1.** Of, pertaining to, or having two sides; two-sided. **2.** Having two symmetrical sides. **3.** Affecting or undertaken by two sides equally; binding on both parties. **—bi·lat′er·al·ism** *n.* **—bi·lat′er·al·ly** *adv.* **—bi·lat′er·al·ness** *n.*
bil·ber·ry (bĭl′bĕr′ē) *n.* **1.** Any of several shrubby or woody plants of the genus *Vaccinium,* having edible blue or blackish berries. **2.** The fruit of a bilberry plant. [Prob. of Scand. orig.]
bil·bo (bĭl′bō) *n., pl.* **-boes.** An iron bar with sliding fetters formerly used to shackle the feet of prisoners. [Poss. after *Bilbao,* Spain.]
bile (bīl) *n.* **1.** A bitter, alkaline, brownish-yellow or greenish-yellow liquid that is secreted by the liver, stored in the gallbladder, and discharged into the duodenum and that aids in digestion, chiefly by saponifying fats. **2.** Ill temper; irascibility. [Fr. < Lat. *bilis.*]
bile acid *n.* Any of the liver-generated steroid acids that appear in the bile as sodium salts.
bile duct *n.* Any of the passages in the liver that convey bile from the liver to the hepatic duct, joining with the cystic duct to form the common bile duct.
bile salt *n.* **1.** Any of the sodium salts found in bile. **2.** A mixture of ox-gall salts used medicinally as a hepatic stimulant or laxative.
bilge (bĭlj) *n.* **1.** The lowest inner part of a ship's hull. **2.** Bilge water. **3.** The bulging part of a barrel or cask. **4.** *Slang.* Stupid talk; nonsense. —*v.* **bilged, bilg·ing, bilg·es.** —*intr.* **1.** To spring a leak in the bilge. **2.** To bulge or swell. —*tr.* To break open the bilge of. [Prob. alteration of BULGE.] **—bilg′y** *adj.*
bilge keel *n.* Either of two beams or fins fastened lengthwise along the outside of a ship's bilge to inhibit heavy rolling.
bilge water *n.* Water that collects in the bilge of a ship.
bil·har·zi·a·sis (bĭl′här-zī′ə-sĭs) *n.* Schistosomiasis. [< NLat. *Bilharzia,* genus name, after Theodor *Bilharz* (1825–1862).]
bil·i·ar·y (bĭl′ē-ĕr′ē) *adj.* Of or pertaining to bile.
biliary cirrhosis *n.* Progressive inflammatory disease of the liver caused by bile-duct obstruction.
bi·lin·e·ar (bī-lĭn′ē-ər) *adj. Math.* Linear with respect to each of two variables or positions.
bi·lin·gual (bī-lĭng′gwəl) *adj.* **1.** Able to speak two languages with equal skill. **2.** Of, pertaining to, or expressed in two languages. —*n.* A bilingual person. **—bi·lin′gual·ly** *adv.*
bi·lin·gual·ism (bī-lĭng′gwə-lĭz′əm) *n.* Habitual use of two languages, esp. in speaking.
bil·ious (bĭl′yəs) *adj.* **1.** Of, pertaining to, or containing bile; biliary. **2.** Pertaining to, characterized by, or experiencing gastric distress caused by sluggishness of the liver or gallbladder. **3.** Reminiscent of bile, esp. in color: *a bilious green.* **4.** Of a peevish disposition; irascible. **—bil′ious·ly** *adv.* **—bil′ious·ness** *n.*
bil·i·ru·bin (bĭl′ĭ-ro͞o′bĭn, bĭl′ĭ-ro͞o′-) *n.* A reddish-yellow organic compound, $C_{33}H_{36}O_6N_4$, derived from hemoglobin during normal and pathological destruction of erythrocytes. [Lat. *bilis,* bile + *ruber,* red + -IN.]
bil·i·ver·din (bĭl′ĭ-vûr′dĭn, bĭl′ĭ-vûr′-) *n.* A green compound, $C_{33}H_{34}O_6N_4$, occurring in bile, sometimes formed by oxidation of bilirubin. [Swed.: Lat. *bilis* + OFr. *verd,* green. —see VERDANT.]
bilk (bĭlk) *tr.v.* **bilked, bilk·ing, bilks. 1.** To defraud, cheat, or swindle. **2.** To evade payment of. **3.** To thwart or frustrate. **4.** To elude. —*n.* **1.** One who cheats. **2.** A hoax or swindle. [Perh. an alteration of BALK.] **—bilk′er** *n.*
bill[1] (bĭl) *n.* **1.** An itemized list or statement of fees or charges. **2.** A statement or list of particulars, such as a playbill or menu. **3.** The entertainment offered by a theater. **4.** An advertising poster or similar public notice. **5.** A piece of legal paper money. **6.** A bill of exchange or a similar commercial note. **7.** A draft of a proposed law presented for approval to a legislative body. **8.** *Law.* A document presented to a court and containing a formal statement of a case, complaint, or petition. —*tr.v.* **billed, bill·ing, bills. 1.** To present a statement of costs or charges to. **2.** To enter on a statement of costs or on a particularized list. **3.** To advertise, announce, or schedule by public notice or as part of a program. ***—idioms.*** **fill the bill.** *Informal.* To meet all necessary requirements. **foot the bill.** *Informal.* To pay the complete cost of. [ME *bille* < Norman Fr. < Med. Lat. *billa,* alteration of *bulla,* seal on a document < Lat., bubble.]
bill[2] (bĭl) *n.* **1.** The beak of a bird. **2.** A beaklike mouth part, as of a turtle. **3.** The visor of a cap. **4.** The tip of the fluke of an anchor. —*intr.v.* **billed, bill·ing, bills.** To touch beaks together. ***—idiom.*** **bill and coo.** To kiss and murmur amorously. [ME < OE *bile.*]
bill[3] (bĭl) *n.* **1.** A billhook. **2.** A halberd or similar weapon with a hooked blade and a long handle. [ME *bil* < OE.]
bil·la·bong (bĭl′ə-bông′, -bŏng′) *n. Austral.* **1.** A dead-end channel extending from the main stream of a river. **2.** A streambed filled with water only in the rainy season. **3.** A stagnant pool or backwater. [Native word in Australia.]

bill·board (bĭl′bôrd′, -bōrd′) *n.* A structure for the display of advertisements in public places or alongside highways.
bill·er (bĭl′ər) *n.* **1.** A clerk who makes out bills. **2.** A machine for making out bills.
bil·let[1] (bĭl′ĭt) *n.* **1. a.** Board and lodging for troops, esp. in a nonmilitary building. **b.** A written order directing that a billet be provided. **2.** *Informal.* A position of employment; job. **3.** *Archaic.* A short letter; note. —*v.* **-let·ed, -let·ing, -lets.** —*tr.* **1. a.** To quarter (soldiers), esp. in nonmilitary buildings. **b.** To serve (a person) with a written order to provide a billet. **2.** To assign lodging to. —*intr.* To be quartered; lodge. [ME, official register < OFr. *billette,* dim. of *bulle,* document < Med. Lat. *bulla,* document, seal < Lat., bubble.]
bil·let[2] (bĭl′ĭt) *n.* **1.** A short, thick piece of wood, as firewood. **2.** One of a series of square or log-shaped decorations forming part of a molding. **3. a.** A bar of iron or steel in an intermediate stage of manufacture. **b.** A small ingot of nonferrous metal. **4. a.** The part of a harness strap that passes through a buckle. **b.** A loop or pocket for securing the tongue of a harness strap. [ME < OFr. *billette,* dim. of *bille,* log < Med. Lat. *billus,* poss. of Celt. orig.]
bil·let-doux (bĭl′ā-do͞o′) *n., pl.* **bil·lets-doux** (-do͞oz′). A love letter. [Fr.: *billet,* short note + *doux,* sweet.]
bill·fish (bĭl′fĭsh′) *n., pl.* **billfish** or **-fish·es. 1.** Any of various fishes of the family Istiophoridae, such as a marlin or sailfish, having an elongated, swordlike or spearlike snout and upper jaw. **2.** Any of various other fishes having long, pointed jaws.
bill·fold (bĭl′fōld′) *n.* A folding pocket-sized case for carrying money and personal documents.
bill·head (bĭl′hĕd′) *n.* A sheet of paper with a business name and address printed at the top, used for billing costs or charges.
bill·hook (bĭl′ho͝ok′) *n.* An implement with a curved blade attached to a handle, used esp. for clearing brush and for rough pruning.
bil·liard (bĭl′yərd) *n.* A shot in billiards; carom. —*adj.* Of, pertaining to, or used in billiards.
bil·liards (bĭl′yərdz) *n.* *(used with a sing. verb).* **1.** A game played on a rectangular, cloth-covered table with raised, cushioned edges, in which a long, tapering cue is used to hit three small, hard balls against one another or the side cushions of the table. **2.** Any of several similar games, such as one played on a table with pockets. [Fr. *billard.*]
bill·ing (bĭl′ĭng) *n.* **1.** The relative importance of performers as indicated by the position and type size in which their names are listed on programs, theater marquees, or advertisements. **2. a.** Advertising. **b.** Often **billings.** The total amount of business done in a specific period, as by a company.
bil·lings·gate (bĭl′ĭngz-gāt′, -gĭt) *n.* Foul-mouthed, abusive language. [After *Billingsgate,* a fish market in London, England.]
bil·lion (bĭl′yən) *n.* **1.** The cardinal number equal to 10^9. **2.** *Chiefly Brit.* The cardinal number equal to 10^{12}. **3.** An indefinitely large number. [Fr., a million million : *bi-,* second power + *million,* million.] **—bil′lion** *adj. & pron.*
bil·lion·aire (bĭl′yə-nâr′) *n.* A person whose wealth amounts to at least a billion dollars, pounds, or other monetary units. [BILLION + (MILLION)AIRE.]
bil·lionth (bĭl′yənth) *n.* **1.** The ordinal number that matches the number one billion in a series. **2.** One of a billion equal parts. **—bil′lionth** *adj. & adv.*
bill of attainder *n.* A former legislative act pronouncing a person guilty of a crime, usually treason, without trial and subjecting him to capital punishment and attainder.
bill of exchange *n.* A written order directing that a specified sum of money be paid to a specified person.
bill of fare *n.* A menu.
bill of goods *n.* A consignment of goods.
bill of health *n.* A certificate stating whether or not there is infectious disease aboard a ship or in a port of departure, given to the ship's master. ***—idiom.*** **clean bill of health.** *Informal.* A satisfactory attestation as to condition.
bill of lading *n.* A document listing and acknowledging receipt of goods for shipment.
bill of rights *n.* **1.** A formal summary of those rights and liberties considered essential to a people or group of people: *a consumer bill of rights.* **2. Bill of Rights.** The first ten amendments to the Constitution of the United States. **3. Bill of Rights.** A declaration of rights restricting the power of the crown, enacted by the English Parliament in 1689.
bill of sale *n.* A document that attests a transfer of the ownership of personal property.
bil·lon (bĭl′ən) *n.* **1.** An alloy of gold or silver with a greater proportion of another metal, such as copper, used in making coins. **2.** An alloy of silver with a high percentage of copper, used in making medals and tokens. [Fr. < OFr., ingot, log. —see BILLET.]
bil·low (bĭl′ō) *n.* **1.** A large wave or ocean swell. **2.** A great swell or surge, as of smoke. —*v.* **-lowed, -low·ing, -lows.** —*intr.* **1.** To surge or roll in billows. **2.** To swell out or bulge. —*tr.* To cause to billow. [Prob. < ON *bylgja.*] **—bil′low·i·ness** *n.* **—bil′low·y** *adj.*
bill·post·er (bĭl′pō′stər) *n.* One who posts notices, posters, or advertisements. **—bill′post′ing** *n.*
bil·ly[1] (bĭl′ē) *n., pl.* **-lies.** A billy club. [Prob. < *Billy,* nickname for William.]
bil·ly[2] (bĭl′ē) *n., pl.* **-lies.** *Austral.* A metal pot or kettle used in camp cooking. [Prob. short for *billycan* : *billa,* water (native word in Australia) + CAN[2].]
billy club *n.* A short wooden club, esp. a policeman's club.
bil·ly·cock (bĭl′ē-kŏk′) *n.* *Chiefly Brit.* A man's felt hat with a low crown, similar to a derby. [Orig. unknown.]
billy goat *n.* *Informal.* A male goat.
bi·lo·bate (bī-lō′bāt′) also **bi·lo·bat·ed** (-bā′tĭd) or **bi·lobed** (bī′lōbd′) *adj.* Divided into or having two lobes.
bi·lob·u·lar (bī-lŏb′yə-lər, -lō′byə-) *adj.* Bilobate.
bi·loc·u·lar (bī-lŏk′yə-lər) also **bi·loc·u·late** (-lĭt, -lāt′) *adj.* Divided into or containing two chambers, cavities, or cells.
Bi·lox·i (bə-lŭk′sē, -lŏk′-) *n., pl.* **Biloxi** or **-is.** One of a tribe of North American Indians originally inhabiting the area of the lower Mississippi River.
bil·sted (bĭl′stĕd′) *n.* The sweet gum (sense 1). [Orig. unknown.]
bil·tong (bĭl′tŏng′, -tông′) *n.* *So. Afr.* Narrow strips of meat dried in the sun. [Afr. : *bil,* buttock (< MDu. *bille*) + *tong,* tongue (< MDu. *tonghe*).]
bi·man·u·al (bī-măn′yo͞o-əl) *adj.* Using or requiring the use of both hands. **—bi·man′u·al·ly** *adv.*
bi·max·il·lar·y (bī-măk′sə-lĕr′ē) *adj.* Pertaining to the two halves of the maxilla.
bi·mes·tri·al (bī-mĕs′trē-əl) *adj.* Bimonthly. [Lat. *bimestris* : *bi-,* two + *mensis,* month.]
bi·me·tal·lic (bī′mə-tăl′ĭk) *adj.* **1.** Consisting of two metals. **2.** Of, based on, or using the principles of bimetallism.
bi·met·al·lism (bī-mĕt′l-ĭz′əm) *n.* **1.** The use of gold and silver as the monetary standard of currency and value. **2.** The doctrine advocating bimetallism. **—bi·met′al·list** *n.* **—bi·met′al·lis′tic** *adj.*
bi·mod·al (bī-mōd′l) *adj.* Having two distinct statistical modes. **—bi′mo·dal′i·ty** (bī′mō-dăl′ĭ-tē) *n.*
bi·mo·lec·u·lar (bī′mə-lĕk′yə-lər) *adj.* Pertaining to, consisting of, or affecting two molecules. **—bi′mo·lec′u·lar·ly** *adv.*
bi·month·ly (bī-mŭnth′lē) *adj.* **1.** Happening every two months. **2.** Happening twice a month; semimonthly. —*adv.* **1.** Once every two months. **2.** Twice a month; semimonthly. —*n., pl.* **-lies.** A bimonthly publication.
bi·mor·phe·mic (bī′môr-fē′mĭk) *adj.* Consisting of two morphemes.
bin (bĭn) *n.* A container or enclosed space for storage. —*tr.v.* **binned, bin·ning, bins.** To place or store in a bin. [ME *binne* < OE.]
bin– *pref.* Variant of **bi-**[1].
bi·nal (bī′nəl) *adj.* Twofold; double. [NLat. *binalis,* twin < Lat. *bini,* two by two.]
bi·na·ry (bī′nə-rē) *adj.* **1.** Characterized by or composed of two different parts or components; twofold. **2.** Of or based on the number 2 or the binary numeration system: *a binary digit.* **3.** *Chem.* Consisting of or containing only molecules consisting of two kinds of atoms. **4.** Having two music sections or subjects. —*n., pl.* **-ries.** Something that is binary, esp. a binary star. [LLat. *binarius* < Lat. *bini,* two by two.]
binary digit *n.* Either of the digits 0 or 1, used in representing numbers in the binary numeration system.
binary fission *n.* Fission, esp. of a cell or of an atomic nucleus, that results in two approximately equal products.
binary numeration system *n.* A system of numeration, based on 2, in which the numerals are represented as sums of powers of 2 and in which all numerals can be written using the symbols 0 and 1.
binary operation *n.* An operation, such as addition, that is applied to two elements of a set to produce a single element of the set.
binary star *n.* A stellar system consisting of two stars orbiting about a common center of mass and often appearing as a single visual or telescopic object.
bi·nate (bī′nāt′) *adj.* Consisting of two parts or divisions; growing in pairs: *a binate leaf.* **—bi′nate′ly** *adv.*
bi·na·tion·al (bī-năsh′ə-nəl, -năsh′nəl) *adj.* Of, relating to, or involving two nations.
bin·au·ral (bī-nôr′əl, bĭn-ôr′-) *adj.* **1. a.** Having or related to two ears. **b.** Hearing with both ears. **2.** Of or pertaining to sound transmission from two sources, which may vary acoustically, as in tone or pitch, relative to a listener. **—bin·au′ral·ly** *adv.*
bind (bīnd) *v.* **bound** (bound), **bind·ing, binds.** —*tr.* **1.** To tie or secure, as with a rope or cord. **2.** To fasten or wrap by encircling, as with a belt. **3.** To bandage. **4.** To hold or restrain with or as if with bonds. **5.** To compel, obligate, or unite, as with a sense of moral duty. **6.** *Law.* To place under legal obligation by contract or oath. **7.** To make certain or irrevocable: *bind a bargain.* **8.** To hold or employ as an apprentice; indenture. **9.** To cause to cohere or stick together in a mass. **10.** To enclose and fasten (a book) between covers. **11.** To furnish with an edge or border for reinforcement or ornamentation. **12.** To constipate. —*intr.* **1.** To tie up or fasten something. **2.** To be tight and uncomfortable. **3.** To become compact or solid; cohere. **4.** To be obligatory or compulsory. ***—phrasal verbs.*** **bind off.** To cast off in knitting. **bind over.** *Law.* To hold on bail or place under bond. —*n.* **1. a.** Something that binds. **b.** The act of binding.

billiards

billy goat

c. The state of being bound. **2.** *Informal.* A difficult situation or dilemma. [ME *binden* < OE *bindan.*]
bind·er (bīn′dər) *n.* **1.** One who binds books; bookbinder. **2.** Something, such as a cord, used to bind. **3.** A notebook cover with rings or clamps for holding sheets of paper. **4.** Something that causes uniform consistency, solidification, or cohesion, as the eggs in batter. **5. a.** An attachment on a reaping machine that ties grain in bundles. **b.** A machine that reaps and ties grain. **6.** *Law.* A payment or written statement making an agreement legally binding until the completion of a formal contract, esp. an insurance contract.
bind·er·y (bīn′də-rē) *n., pl.* **-ies.** A place where books are bound.
bind·ing (bīn′dĭng) *n.* **1.** The action of one that binds. **2.** Something that binds or is used as a binder. **3.** The cover that holds together the pages of a book. **4.** A strip sewn or attached over or along the edge of something for protection, reinforcement, or ornamentation. —*adj.* **1.** Serving to bind. **2.** Uncomfortably tight and confining. **3.** Having the power to impose an agreement or commitment; obligatory. **—bind′ing·ly** *adv.* **—bind′ing·ness** *n.*
binding energy *n.* **1.** The energy released in binding a group of particles into a single system, esp. a group of nucleons into an atomic nucleus. **2.** The work required to remove an atomic electron to an infinitely remote position from its orbit.
binding force *n.* A strong interaction.
bin·dle·stiff (bĭn′dl-stĭf′) *Slang.* A migrant worker or hobo who carries his own bedroll. [E. *bindle,* alteration of BUNDLE + STIFF.]
bind·weed (bīnd′wēd′) *n.* **1.** Any of several trailing or twining plants of the genus *Convolvulus,* having pink or white trumpet-shaped flowers. **2.** Any of various trailing or twining plants similar to a bindweed.
bine (bīn) *n.* **1.** The flexible stem of any of various climbing and twining plants, such as the hop, woodbine, or bindweed. **2.** A plant whose stem is a bine. [Dial. of *bind.*]
Bi·net age (bĭ-nā′) *n.* A person's mental age as determined by the Binet-Simon scale.
Bi·net-Si·mon scale (bĭ-nā′sē-mōɴ′, -sī′mən) *n.* Any of a series of early psychological tests of childhood intelligence. [After Alfred *Binet* (1857–1911) and Théodore *Simon* (1873–1961).]
binge (bĭnj) *Slang.* —*n.* **1.** A drunken spree or revel. **2.** A period of uncontrolled self-indulgence: *an eating binge.* —*intr.v.* **binged, bing·ing, bing·es.** To be uncontrolled and self-indulgent: *binging on chocolate.* [Dial. *binge,* to soak.]
bin·go (bĭng′gō) *n., pl.* **-gos.** A game of chance in which players place markers on a pattern of numbered squares according to numbers drawn and announced by a caller. [Orig. unknown.]

binnacle

bin·na·cle (bĭn′ə-kəl) *n.* The nonmagnetic stand on which a ship's compass case is supported. [Alteration of ME *bitakil* < OSp. *bitácula* or OPort. *bitácola* < Lat. *habitaculum,* habitation < *habitare,* to inhabit.]
bin·oc·u·lar (bə-nŏk′yə-lər, bī-) *adj.* **1.** Pertaining to, used by, or involving both eyes at the same time. **2.** Having two eyes arranged to produce stereoscopic vision. —*n.* Often **binoculars.** An optical device, esp. a pair of field glasses, designed for use by both eyes at once. **—bin·oc′u·lar′i·ty** (-lăr′ĭ-tē) *n.* **—bin·oc′u·lar·ly** *adv.*

binocular

bi·no·mi·al (bī-nō′mē-əl) *adj.* Consisting of or pertaining to two names or terms. —*n.* **1.** *Math.* An expression consisting of two terms connected by a plus or minus sign. **2.** *Biol.* A taxonomic name in binomial nomenclature. [< NLat. *binomius*: BI- + Gk. *nomos,* part.] **—bi·no′mi·al·ly** *adv.*
binomial distribution *n.* The frequency distribution of the probability of a specified number of successes in an arbitrary number of repeated independent Bernoulli trials.
binomial nomenclature *n.* A system of classifying plants and animals by a double name, the first of which is the name of the genus and the second that of the species within the genus.
binomial theorem *n.* A mathematical theorem that specifies the expansion of a binomial to any power without requiring the explicit multiplication of the binomial terms.
bi·nu·cle·ate (bī-no͞o′klē-ĭt, -āt′, -nyo͞o′-) also **bi·nu·cle·at·ed** (-ā′tĭd) *adj.* Having two nuclei.
bio– or **bi–** *pref.* **1. a.** Life: *biolysis.* **b.** Living organism: *biome.* **2.** Biology; biological: *biophysics.* [Gk. < *bios,* life.]
bi·o·ac·tiv·i·ty (bī′ō-ăk-tĭv′ĭ-tē) *n.* The effect of a given agent, such as a vaccine, upon a living organism.
bi·o·as·say (bī′ō-ăs′ā′, -ă-sā′) *n.* Evaluation of a drug by comparison of its effect with that of a standard on a test organism.
bi·o·as·tro·nau·tics (bī′ō-ăs′trə-nô′tĭks) *n.* *(used with a sing. verb).* The study of the biological and medical effects of space flight.
bi·o·a·vail·a·bil·i·ty (bī′ō-ə-vā′lə-bĭl′ĭ-tē) *n.* The degree to which an agent, as a drug or nutrient, becomes available at the physiological site of activity.
bi·o·cat·a·lyst (bī′ō-kăt′l-ĭst) *n.* A substance that initiates or modifies the rate of a biological process. **—bi′o·cat′a·lyt′ic** (-ĭt′ĭk) *adj.*
bi·o·ce·nol·o·gy (bī′ō-sə-nŏl′ə-jē) *n.* *Ecol.* The study of communities and member interactions in nature.
biochemical oxygen demand *n.* The amount of dissolved oxygen required to meet the metabolic needs of microorganisms in a water environment rich in organic matter, such as sewage.
bi·o·chem·is·try (bī′ō-kĕm′ĭ-strē) *n.* The chemistry of biological substances and processes. **—bi′o·chem′i·cal** (-ĭ-kəl), **bi′o·chem′ic** *adj.* **—bi′o·chem′i·cal·ly** *adv.* **—bi′o·chem′ist** *n.*
bi·o·cide (bī′ə-sīd′) *n.* A substance, such as a pesticide or an antibiotic, that is capable of destroying living organisms. **—bi′o·cid′al** (-sīd′l) *adj.*
bi·o·cli·ma·tol·o·gy (bī′ō-klī′mə-tŏl′ə-jē) *n.* The study of the effects of climatic conditions on organic life. **—bi′o·cli·mat′ic** (-klī-măt′ĭk) *adj.*
bi·o·de·grad·a·ble (bī′ō-dĭ-grā′də-bəl) *adj.* Capable of being decomposed by natural biological processes: *a biodegradable detergent.*
bi·o·eth·ics (bī′ō-ĕth′ĭks) *n.* *(used with a sing. or pl. verb).* The study of the ethical and moral questions involved in the application of new biological and medical findings, as in the fields of genetic engineering, neurobiology, and drug research. **—bi′o·eth′ic** *adj.* **—bi′o·eth′i·cist** (-ĭ-sĭst) *n.*
bi·o·feed·back (bī′ō-fēd′băk′) *n.* A technique in which an attempt is made to consciously regulate a bodily function thought to be involuntary, as heartbeat or blood pressure, by using an instrument to monitor the function and to signal changes in it.
bi·o·fla·vo·noid (bī′ō-flā′və-noid′) *n.* Any of a group of biologically active substances found widely in plants and functioning in the maintenance of the walls of small blood vessels.
bi·o·gas (bī′ō-găs′) *n.* A mixture of methane and carbon dioxide produced through bacterial action.
bi·o·gen·e·sis (bī′ō-jĕn′ĭ-sĭs) also **bi·og·e·ny** (bī-ŏj′ə-nē) *n.* **1.** The doctrine that living organisms develop only from other living organisms and not from nonliving matter. **2.** The generation of living organisms from other living organisms. **—bi′o·ge·net′ic** (-jə-nĕt′ĭk), **bi′o·ge·net′i·cal, bi·og′e·nous** (bī-ŏj′ə-nəs) *adj.* **—bi′o·ge·net′i·cal·ly** *adv.*
bi·o·ge·og·ra·phy (bī′ō-jē-ŏg′rə-fē) *n.* The biological study of the geographic distribution of plants and animals. **—bi′o·ge′o·graph′ic** (-jē′ə-grăf′ĭk), **bi′o·ge′o·graph′i·cal** *adj.*
bi·og·ra·pher (bī-ŏg′rə-fər, bē-) *n.* One who writes a biography.
bi·o·graph·i·cal (bī′ə-grăf′ĭ-kəl) also **bi·o·graph·ic** (-grăf′ĭk) *adj.* **1.** Containing, consisting of, or pertaining to the facts or events in a person's life. **2.** Of or pertaining to biography as a literary form. **—bi′o·graph′i·cal·ly** *adv.*
bi·og·ra·phy (bī-ŏg′rə-fē, bē-) *n., pl.* **-phies. 1.** A written account of a person's life; life history. **2.** Biographies collectively, esp. when considered as a literary form. [Med. Gk. *biographia* : *bios,* life + *graphia,* -graphy.]
bi·o·haz·ard (bī′ō-hăz′ərd) *n.* A material of biological composition, esp. if infective in nature, that constitutes a threat to man or his environment.
bi·o·in·stru·men·ta·tion (bī′ō-ĭn′strə-mĕn-tā′shən) *n.* **1.** The use of instruments for the recording or transmission of physiological information. **2.** The instruments used in bioinstrumentation.
bi·o·log·i·cal (bī′ə-lŏj′ĭ-kəl) also **bi·o·log·ic** (-lŏj′ĭk) *adj.* **1.** Of or pertaining to biology. **2.** Of, pertaining to, caused by, or affecting life or living organisms. —*n.* **biologic.** A drug derived from a biological source. **—bi′o·log′i·cal·ly** *adv.*
biological clock *n.* An intrinsic biological mechanism responsible for the periodicity or other time-dependent aspects of certain classes of behavior in living organisms.
biological half-life *n.* Half-life (sense 2.a.).
biological warfare *n.* Warfare in which disease-producing microorganisms or organic biocides are used to destroy livestock, crops, or human life.
bi·ol·o·gy (bī-ŏl′ə-jē) *n.* **1.** The science of living organisms and life processes, including the study of structure, functioning, growth, origin, evolution, and distribution of living organisms. **2.** The life processes or characteristic phenomena of a group or category of living organisms. **3.** The plant and animal life of a specific region or place. [G. *Biologie* : Gk. *bios,* life + Gk. *logos,* reckoning.] **—bi·ol′o·gist** *n.*
bi·o·lu·mi·nes·cence (bī′ō-lo͞o′mə-nĕs′əns) *n.* The emission of visible light by living organisms such as the firefly and various fish, fungi, and bacteria. **—bi′o·lu′mi·nes′cent** *adj.*
bi·ol·y·sis (bī-ŏl′ĭ-sĭs) *n.* Death caused or accompanied by lysis. **—bi′o·lyt′ic** (bī′ə-lĭt′ĭk) *adj.*
bi·o·mass (bī′ō-măs′) *n.* The total mass of living matter within a given volume of environment.
bi·ome (bī′ōm′) *n.* A community of living organisms of a single major ecological region.
bi·o·med·i·cine (bī′ō-mĕd′ĭ-sĭn) *n.* **1.** The branch of medical science dealing with the ability of humans to survive in and functionally cope with abnormally stressful environments and with the medical concerns of protectively modifying those environments. **2.** The study of medicine as it relates to all biological systems. **—bi′o·med′i·cal** *adj.*
bi·o·met·rics (bī′ō-mĕt′rĭks) *n.* *(used with a sing. verb).* The statistical study of biological data. **—bi′o·met′ric, bi′o·met′ri·cal** *adj.* **—bi′o·met′ri·cal·ly** *adv.*
bi·om·e·try (bī-ŏm′ĭ-trē) *n.* Biometrics.
bi·on·ic (bī-ŏn′ĭk) *adj.* **1.** Consisting of or enhanced by or as

if by electronic or mechanical devices or components. **2.** Of or relating to biomics. [BIO- + (ELECTR)ONIC.]
bi·on·ics (bī-ŏn'ĭks) *n.* *(used with a sing. verb).* The application of biological principles to the study and design of engineering systems, esp. electronic systems. [BI(O)- + (ELECTR)ONICS.]
bi·o·nom·ics (bī'ə-nŏm'ĭks) *n.* *(used with a sing. verb).* Ecology. [< Fr. *bionomique,* pertaining to ecology < *bionomie,* ecology : Gk. *bios,* life + Gk. *nomos,* law.] **—bi'o·nom'ic, bi'o·nom'i·cal** *adj.* **—bi'o·nom'i·cal·ly** *adv.*
bi·ont (bī'ŏnt') *n.* A living organism. **—bi·on'tic** (bī-ŏn'tĭk) *adj.*
bi·o·phys·ics (bī'ō-fĭz'ĭks) *n.* *(used with a sing. verb).* The physics of biological processes. **—bi'o·phys'i·cal** *adj.* **—bi'o·phys'i·cal·ly** *adv.* **—bi'o·phys'i·cist** *n.*
bi·o·plasm (bī'ō-plăz'əm) *n.* Living protoplasm, esp. as distinguished from its nonliving content.
bi·op·sy (bī'ŏp'sē) *n., pl.* **-sies.** The study of tissue taken from a living person or organism, esp. in examination for the presence of disease. **—bi·op'sic** (bī-ŏp'sĭk) *adj.*
bi·o·rhythm (bī'ō-rĭth'əm) *n.* **1.** An intrinsically patterned cyclical biological process or function. **2.** The determining factor in a biorhythm.
bi·o·sci·ence (bī'ō-sī'əns) *n.* Life science.
bi·o·scope (bī'ə-skōp') *n.* An early motion-picture projector.
bi·os·co·py (bī-ŏs'kə-pē) *n., pl.* **-pies.** Medical examination of a body to determine whether it is dead.
-biosis *suff.* A way of living: *parabiosis.* [NLat. < Gk. *biōsis,* way of life < *bioun,* to live < *bios,* life.]
bi·o·sphere (bī'ə-sfîr') *n.* The part of the earth and its atmosphere in which living things exist.
bi·o·syn·the·sis (bī'ō-sĭn'thĭ-sĭs) *n.* The production of complex substances from simple ones by or with living organisms. **—bi'o·syn·thet'ic** (-thĕt'ĭk) *adj.* **—bi'o·syn·thet'i·cal·ly** *adv.*
bi·o·ta (bī-ō'tə) *n.* The animal and plant life of a particular region considered as a total ecological entity. [NLat. < Gk. *biotē,* way of life.]
bi·o·tech·nol·o·gy (bī'ō-tĕk-nŏl'ə-jē) *n.* The engineering and biological study of relationships between man and machines. **—bi'o·tech'no·log'i·cal** (-nə-lŏj'ĭ-kəl) *adj.*
bi·ot·ic (bī-ŏt'ĭk) *adj.* Pertaining to life or specific life conditions. [Gk. *biōtikos* < *bios,* life.]
biotic potential *n.* **1.** The likelihood of survival of a specific organism in a specific environment, esp. in an unfavorable environment. **2.** The growth rate of a population that maintains a stable age distribution.
bi·o·tin (bī'ə-tĭn) *n.* A colorless crystalline vitamin, $C_{10}H_{16}N_2O_3S$, often considered in the vitamin B complex and found in large quantities in liver, egg yolk, milk, and yeast. [Gk. *biotos,* life + -IN.]
bi·o·tite (bī'ə-tīt') *n.* A dark-brown to black mica, $K(Mg, Fe)_3AlSi_3O_{10}(OH)_2$, found in igneous and metamorphic rocks. [G. *Biotit,* after Jean Baptiste *Biot* (1774–1862).] **—bi'o·tit'ic** (-tĭt'ĭk) *adj.*
bi·o·tope (bī'ə-tōp') *n.* A limited ecological region or niche in which the environment is suitable for certain forms of life. [BIO- + Gk. *topos,* place.]
bi·o·trans·for·ma·tion (bī'ō-trăns'fər-mā'shən) *n.* A chemical transformation within a living system.
bi·o·tron (bī'ə-trŏn') *n.* A climate-control chamber used for studying a living organism's response to specific environmental conditions.
bi·o·type (bī'ə-tīp') *n.* A group of organisms having identical genetic but varying physical characteristics. **—bi'o·typ'ic** (-tĭp'ĭk) *adj.*
bi·o·vu·lar (bī-ō'vyə-lər, -ŏv'yə-) *adj.* Derived from two ova, as fraternal twins.
bip·a·rous (bĭp'ər-əs) *adj.* **1.** *Biol.* Producing two offspring in a single birth. **2.** *Bot.* Having two axes or branches, as certain flower clusters.
bi·par·ti·san (bī-pär'tĭ-zən, -sən) *adj.* Consisting of or supported by members of two parties, esp. two major political parties. **—bi·par'ti·san·ism** *n.* **—bi·par'ti·san·ship'** *n.*
bi·par·tite (bī-pär'tīt') *adj.* **1.** Having or consisting of two parts. **2.** Having two corresponding parts, one for each party: *a bipartite treaty.* **3.** *Bot.* Divided into two, almost to the base, as certain leaves. [< Lat. *bipartire, bipartit-,* to divide into two parts : *bi-,* two + *partire,* to part < *pars,* share.] **—bi·par'tite'ly** *adv.* **—bi'par·ti'tion** (-tĭsh'ən) *n.*
bi·ped (bī'pĕd') *n.* An animal with two feet. *—adj.* Having two feet; two-footed. [Lat. *bipes, biped-,* two-footed : *bi-,* two + *pes,* foot.] **—bi·ped'al** (bī-pĕd'l) *adj.*
bi·pet·al·ous (bī-pĕt'l-əs) *adj.* Having two petals; dipetalous.
bi·phen·yl (bī-fĕn'əl, -fē'nəl) *n.* A colorless crystalline compound, $C_{12}H_{10}$, used as a heat-transfer agent, in fungicides, and in organic synthesis.
bi·pin·nate (bī-pĭn'āt') *adj.* Having opposite leaflets that are subdivided into opposite leaflets, as compound leaves. **—bi·pin'nate'ly** *adv.*
bi·plane (bī'plān') *n.* An early aircraft with single or paired wings fixed at two different levels, esp. one above and one below the fuselage.
bi·pod (bī'pŏd') *n.* A supporting stand with two legs.
bi·po·lar (bī-pō'lər) *adj.* **1.** Pertaining to or having two poles. **2.** Relating to or involving both of the earth's poles. **3.** Having or expressing two opposite or contradictory ideas or qualities. **—bi'po·lar'i·ty** (-lăr'ĭ-tē) *n.*
bi·po·ten·ti·al·i·ty (bī'pə-tĕn'shē-ăl'ĭ-tē) *n.* The capacity to perform both the male and the female sexual functions.
bi·pro·pel·lant (bī'prə-pĕl'ənt) *n.* A two-component rocket propellant, such as liquid hydrogen and liquid oxygen, combined as fuel and oxidizer.
bi·quad·rat·ic (bī'kwŏ-drăt'ĭk) *Math.* *—adj.* Of or pertaining to the fourth degree. *—n.* An algebraic equation of the fourth degree.
bi·quar·ter·ly (bī-kwôr'tər-lē) *adj.* Happening or appearing two times during each three-month period of the year. **—bi·quar'ter·ly** *adv.*
bi·ra·cial (bī-rā'shəl) *adj.* Of, for, or consisting of members of two races. **—bi·ra'cial·ism** *n.*
bi·ra·di·al (bī-rā'dē-əl) *adj.* Both bilaterally and radially symmetrical.
bi·ra·mous (bī-rā'məs) *adj.* Having two branches, as in an arthropod appendage.
birch (bûrch) *n.* **1.** Any of several deciduous trees of the genus *Betula,* common in the Northern Hemisphere and having white, yellowish, or gray bark that can be separated from the wood in sheets. **2.** The hard, close-grained wood of a birch tree. **3.** A rod from a birch tree, used to administer a whipping. *—tr.v.* **birched, birch·ing, birch·es.** To whip with or as if with a birch rod. [ME < OE *birc.*]
Birch·er (bûr'chər) also **Birch·ite** (-chīt') or **Birch·ist** (-chĭst) *n.* A member or supporter of the John Birch Society. **—Birch'ism** *n.*
bird (bûrd) *n.* **1.** A member of the class Aves, which includes warm-blooded, egg-laying feathered vertebrates with forelimbs modified to form wings. **2.** A bird hunted as game. **3.** *Slang.* A rocket or guided missile. **4.** A clay pigeon. **5.** A shuttlecock. **6.** *Slang.* One who is odd or remarkable. **7.** *Chiefly Brit. Slang.* A young woman. **8.** *Slang.* A raspberry (sense 4). *—intr.v.* **bird·ed, bird·ing, birds. 1.** To observe and identify birds in their natural surroundings. **2.** To trap, shoot, or catch birds. **—*idiom.* for the birds.** Objectionable or worthless. [ME < OE, young bird.] **—bird'er** *n.*
bird·bath (bûrd'băth', -bäth') *n.* A basin filled with water for birds to bathe in.
bird·brain (bûrd'brān') *n.* *Slang.* A silly, light-minded person.
bird·cage (bûrd'kāj') *n.* A cage for birds.
bird·call (bûrd'kôl') *n.* **1.** The song of a bird. **2. a.** An imitation of the song of a bird. **b.** A small device for producing this.
bird cherry *n.* A cherry tree, *Prunus padus,* native to Eurasia, having clusters of white flowers and small black fruit.
bird colonel *n.* *Slang.* A full colonel. [From the eagle of the insignia.]
bird dog *n.* **1.** A dog used to hunt game birds; gun dog. **2.** *Slang.* One who seeks out something for another.
bird-dog (bûrd'dôg', -dŏg') *v.* **-dogged, -dog·ging, -dogs.** *—intr.* To watch closely. *—tr.* To seek out; follow.
bird·farm (bûrd'färm') *n.* *Slang.* An aircraft carrier.
bird·house (bûrd'hous') *n.* **1.** An aviary. **2.** A box made as a nesting place for birds.
bird·ie (bûr'dē) *n.* **1.** *Informal.* A small bird. **2.** One stroke under par for a hole in golf. **3.** A shuttlecock. *—tr.v.* **-ied, -ie·ing, -ies.** To shoot (a hole in golf) in one stroke under par.
bird·lime (bûrd'līm') *n.* **1.** A sticky substance smeared on branches or twigs to capture small birds. **2.** Something that captures and ensnares. *—tr.v.* **-limed, -lim·ing, -limes. 1.** To smear with birdlime. **2.** To catch with birdlime.
bird·man (bûrd'mən) *n.* **1.** (*also* -măn'). One who works with birds, as a fowler or ornithologist. **2.** *Slang.* An aviator.
bird of paradise *n.* Any of various birds of the family Paradisaeidae, native to New Guinea and adjacent areas, usually having brilliant plumage and long tail feathers in the male.
bird-of-par·a·dise flower (bûrd'əv-pâr'ə-dīs', -dīz') *n.* A perennial plant, *Strelitzia reginae,* having purple bracts and large orange or yellow flowers with blue tongues.
bird of passage *n.* **1.** A migratory bird. **2.** A person who moves from place to place frequently.
bird of prey *n.* Any of various predatory carnivorous birds such as the eagle or hawk.
bird pepper *n.* **1.** A plant, *Capsicum frutescens,* that is the probable ancestor of the mild peppers and many of the pungent peppers. **2.** The narrow, extremely pungent fruit of the bird pepper.
bird·seed (bûrd'sēd') *n.* A mixture of various kinds of seeds used for feeding birds, esp. caged birds.
bird's-eye (bûrdz'ī') *n.* **1.** Any of various plants having small, brightly colored flowers. **2. a.** A fabric woven with a pattern of small diamonds, each having a dot in the center. **b.** The pattern of such a fabric. *—adj.* **1.** Dappled or patterned with spots thought to resemble birds' eyes: *bird's-eye maple.* **2.** Seen from high above or from a distance: *a bird's-eye view.*
bird's-foot (bûrdz'fo͝ot') *n., pl.* **bird's-foots.** Any of various plants, such as the bird's-foot trefoil, that have flowers, leaves, or pods resembling a bird's foot or claw.

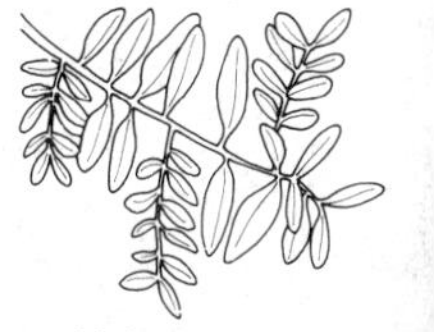
bipinnate
Honey locust leaf

biplane
Wilbur Wright in Kitty Hawk, North Carolina, 1903

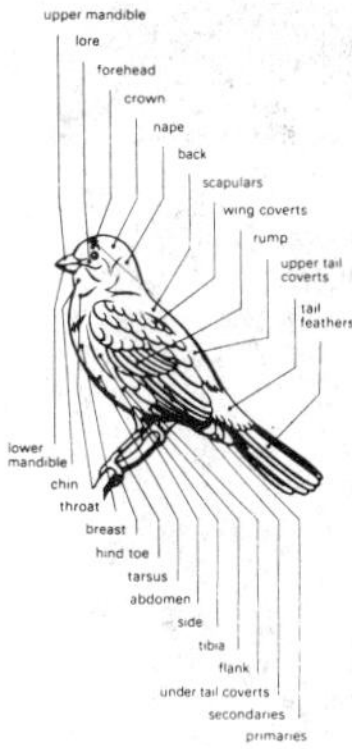

bird

George Miksch Sutton
bird of paradise

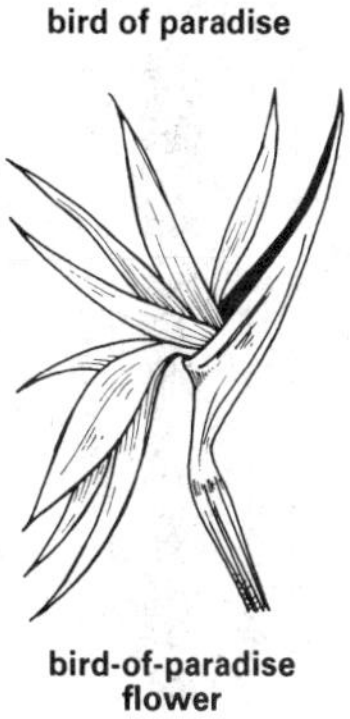
bird-of-paradise flower

bird's-foot fern *n.* A fern, *Pellaea mucronata,* native to California, having fronds with wiry leaves grouped to resemble a bird's foot.
bird's-foot trefoil *n.* A sprawling plant, *Lotus corniculatus,* having yellow flowers and clusters of seed pods resembling the claws of a bird.
bird's-nest fungus (bûrdz'nĕst') *n.* Any of various fungi of the family Nidulariaceae, having a cuplike fruiting body containing several round, egglike structures that enclose the spores.
bird watcher *n.* A person who observes and identifies birds in their natural surroundings. **—bird watching** *n.*
bird·y·back (bûr'dē-băk') *n.* The transporting of loaded truck trailers by airplane. [BIRD + -Y + (PIGGY)BACK.]
bi·re·frin·gence (bī'rĭ-frĭn'jəns) *n.* The resolution or splitting of a light wave into two waves with mutually perpendicular vibration directions by an optically anisotropic medium such as calcite or quartz. **—bi're·frin'gent** *adj.*
bi·reme (bī'rēm') *n.* An ancient galley equipped with two tiers of oars on each side. [Lat. *biremis* : *bi-,* two + *remus,* oar.]
bi·ret·ta (bə-rĕt'ə) *n.* A stiff square cap that is worn esp. by Roman Catholic clergy and is black for a priest, purple for a bishop, and red for a cardinal. [Ital. *berretta* < OProv. *birret,* cap < LLat. *birrus,* hooded cloak.]
birl (bûrl) *v.* **birled, birl·ing, birls.** *—tr.* To cause (a floating log) to spin rapidly by rotating with the feet. *—intr.* **1.** To participate in birling. **2.** To whirr or hum. *—n.* A whirring noise; hum. [Blend of BIRR and WHIRL.] **—birl'er** *n.*
birl·ing (bûr'lĭng) *n.* A game of skill, esp. among lumberjacks, in which two competitors try to balance on a floating log while spinning it with their feet.

bison

birr[1] (bûr) *n.* A whirring sound. [ME *bir,* strong wind < ON *byrr,* favorable wind.]
birr[2] (bîr) *n., pl.* **birr** or **birrs.** See table at **currency.** [Native word in Ethiopia.]
birth (bûrth) *n.* **1.** The beginning of existence; fact of being born. **2.** A beginning or origin. **3. a.** The act of bearing young; parturition. **b.** The passage of a child from the uterus. **4.** Ancestry; parentage: *a woman of noble birth.* **5.** Origin; lineage: *a Southerner by birth.* *—tr.v.* **birthed, birth·ing, births.** *Chiefly Regional.* **1.** To deliver (a baby). **2.** To bear (a child). **—*idiom.* give birth to.** To bring into being. [ME, of ON orig.]
birth canal *n.* The cavity of the uterus and the vagina traversed by the fetus in parturition.
birth certificate *n.* An official record of a person's parentage and the date, place, and time of birth.
birth control *n.* Voluntary limitation or control of the number of children conceived, esp. by planned use of contraceptive techniques.
birth·day (bûrth'dā') *n.* **1.** The day of one's birth. **2.** The anniversary of one's birth.
birthday suit *n.* The state of being naked.
birth·mark (bûrth'märk') *n.* A mole or blemish present on the body from birth; nevus.
birth pang *n.* **1.** Often **birth pangs.** One of the repetitive pains occurring in childbirth. **2. birth pangs.** Turmoil or tumult associated esp. with a major social change.
birth·place (bûrth'plās') *n.* The place where someone is born or where something originates.
birth·rate (bûrth'rāt') *n.* The number of births in a specified population per unit time, esp. per year.
birth·right (bûrth'rīt') *n.* **1.** A privilege granted a person by virtue of his birth. **2.** A special privilege accorded a firstborn.
birth·root (bûrth'ro͞ot', -ro͝ot') *n.* Any of several North American plants of the genus *Trillium,* esp. *T. erectum,* having purplish flowers with an unpleasant odor and tuberlike roots, formerly used as an aid in childbirth.
birth·stone (bûrth'stōn') *n.* A jewel associated with the specific month of a person's birth.
birth trauma *n.* **1.** An injury sustained by an infant during birth. **2.** An emotional shock sustained by an infant during birth.
birth·wort (bûrth'wûrt', -wôrt') *n.* Any of several tropical woody vines of the genus *Aristolochia,* having reddish or brownish, usually unpleasantly scented flowers.
bis (bĭs) *adv.* Again; encore. Used esp. as a direction in music. [Fr. < Lat., twice.]
bis·cuit (bĭs'kĭt) *n., pl.* **-cuits** or **biscuit. 1.** A small cake of shortened bread leavened with baking powder or soda. **2.** *Chiefly Brit.* A thin, crisp cracker. **3.** A pale brown; beige. **4.** Clay that has been fired once but not glazed. [ME *biscute* < OFr. *biscuit* < Med. Lat. *biscoctus* : Lat. *bis,* twice + Lat. *coquere,* to cook.]
bise (bēz) *n.* A cold north wind of the Swiss Alps, France, and Italy. [ME < OFr., of Germanic orig.]
bi·sect (bī'sĕkt', bī-sĕkt') *v.* **-sect·ed, -sect·ing, -sects.** *—tr.* To cut or divide into two equal parts. *—intr.* To split; fork. **—bi·sec'tion** *n.* **—bi·sec'tion·al** *adj.* **—bi·sec'tion·al·ly** *adv.*
bi·sec·tor (bī'sĕk'tər, bī-sĕk'-) *n.* Something that bisects, esp. a straight line that bisects an angle.

bit[2]

bi·ser·rate (bī-sĕr'āt') *adj. Biol.* **1.** Having serrations that are themselves serrated; doubly serrate. **2.** Serrated on both sides: *biserrate antennae.*
bi·sex·u·al (bī-sĕk'sho͞o-əl) *adj.* **1.** Of or pertaining to both sexes. **2.** Having both male and female organs; hermaphroditic. **3.** Sexually attracted to members of both sexes. *—n.* **1.** A bisexual organism; hermaphrodite. **2.** A person who is sexually attracted to members of both sexes. **—bi'sex·u·al'i·ty** (-ăl'ĭ-tē) *n.* **—bi·sex'u·al·ly** *adv.*
bish·op (bĭsh'əp) *n.* **1.** A high-ranking Christian clergyman, in modern churches usually in charge of a diocese and in some churches regarded as having received the highest ordination in unbroken succession from the apostles. **2.** A miter-shaped chessman that can move diagonally across any number of unoccupied spaces of the same color. **3.** Mulled port spiced with oranges, sugar, and cloves. [ME < OE *bisceop* < LLat. *episcopus* < LGk. *episkopos* < Gk., overseer : *epi,* over + *skopos,* watcher.]
bish·op·ric (bĭsh'ə-prĭk) *n.* **1.** The office or rank of a bishop. **2.** The diocese of a bishop. [ME *bishop-rik* < OE *bisceop-rīce.* the diocese of a bishop : *bisceop,* bishop + *rīce,* dominion.]
bish·op's-cap (bĭsh'əps-kăp') *n.* The miterwort.
bis·muth (bĭz'məth) *n. Symbol* **Bi** A white, crystalline, brittle, highly diamagnetic metallic element used in alloys to form sharp castings for objects sensitive to high temperatures and in various low-melting alloys for fire-safety devices. Atomic number 83; atomic weight 208.980; melting point 271.3°C; boiling point 1,560°C; specific gravity 9.747; valences 3, 5. [Obs. G. *Bismut,* alteration of *Wismut* : *Wise,* meadow + *Mut,* claim to a mine.] **—bis'muth·al** *adj.*
bis·na·ga (bĭs-nä'gə) *n.* Any of several spiny, globe-shaped or barrel-shaped cacti of the southwestern United States and Mexico. [Sp. *biznaga,* alteration of *vitznauac* (< Nahuatl *huitznahuac* : *huitztli,* spine + *nahuac,* around.]
bi·son (bī'sən, -zən) *n.* **1.** A hoofed mammal, *Bison bison,* of western North America, having a dark-brown coat, a shaggy mane, and short, curved horns; buffalo. **2.** An animal, *B. bonasus,* of Europe, that is similar to but somewhat smaller than the bison; wisent. [Fr. < Lat., of Germanic orig.]
bisque[1] (bĭsk) *n.* **1. a.** A thick, rich soup made from meat, fish, or shellfish. **b.** A thick cream soup made of vegetables that have been puréed. **2.** Ice cream mixed with crushed macaroons or nuts. [Fr.]
bisque[2] (bĭsk) *n.* **1.** Biscuit (sense 4). **2. a.** A pale orange yellow to yellowish gray. **b.** A color ranging in various industries from moderate yellowish pink to grayish yellow. [< BISCUIT.]
bisque[3] (bĭsk) *n.* An advantage allowed an inferior player in certain games, esp. a free point taken when desired in a tennis set. [Fr.]
bis·sex·tile (bī-sĕk'stĭl, -stīl', bĭ-) *adj.* **1.** Of or pertaining to a leap year. **2.** Of or pertaining to the extra day falling in a leap year. *—n.* A leap year. [LLat. *bissextilis* < Lat. *bissextus,* an intercalary day : *bi-,* twice + *sextus,* sixth.]
bi·state (bī'stāt') *adj.* Of, relating to, or involving two states.
bis·ter also **bis·tre** (bĭs'tər) *n.* **1.** A water-soluble, yellowish-brown pigment made from soot obtained from beech or other wood. **2.** A grayish to yellowish brown. [Fr. *bistre.*] **—bis'tered** *adj.*
bis·tort (bĭs'tôrt') *n.* Any of several plants of the genus *Polygonum,* esp.: **a.** A Eurasian plant, *P. bistorta,* having pointed clusters of small, pinkish flowers. **b.** A similar plant, *P. bistortoides,* of the mountains of western North America, having oval clusters of pink or white flowers. [OFr. *bistorte* < Med. Lat. *bistorta* : Lat. *bis,* twice + Lat. *torquēre,* to twist.]
bis·tou·ry (bĭs'tə-rē) *n., pl.* **-ries.** A surgical knife for minor incisions. [Fr. *bistouri* < OFr. *bistorie,* dagger.]
bis·tre (bĭs'tər) *n.* Variant of **bister.**
bis·tro (bē'strō, bĭs'trō) *n., pl.* **-tros.** A small bar, tavern, or nightclub. [Fr.]
bi·sul·cate (bī-sŭl'kāt') *adj.* Cleft or cloven, as a hoof.
bi·sul·fate (bī-sŭl'fāt') *n.* The inorganic acid group HSO_4 or a compound containing it.
bi·sul·fide (bī-sŭl'fīd') *n.* A disulfide.
bi·sul·fite (bī-sŭl'fīt') *n.* The inorganic acid group HSO_3 or a compound containing it.
bit[1] (bĭt) *n.* **1.** A small piece, portion, or amount. **2.** A brief amount of time; moment. **3. a.** An entertainment routine given regularly by a performer; act. **b.** A short scene or episode in a theatrical performance. **4.** A small and insignificant role, as in a play or movie, usually containing a few spoken lines. **5.** *Informal.* **a.** A particular kind of action, situation, or behavior: *She did the whole bit.* **b.** A matter being considered: *What's this bit about inflation?* **6.** *Informal.* An amount equal to 1/8 of a dollar: *two bits.* **7.** *Chiefly Brit.* A small coin: *a threepenny bit.* **—*idiom.* bit by bit.** Little by little; gradually. [ME *bite,* morsel < OE *bita.*]
bit[2] (bĭt) *n.* **1.** The sharp part of a tool, as the blade of a knife. **2.** A pointed and threaded tool for drilling and boring that is secured in a brace, bitstock, or drill press. **3.** The part of a key that enters the lock and engages the bolt or tumblers. **4.** The metal mouthpiece of a bridle, serving to control, curb, and direct an animal. **5.** Something that controls, guides, or curbs. *—tr.v.* **bit·ted, bit·ting, bits. 1.** To place a bit in the mouth of (a horse). **2.** To check or control as if with a bit. **3.** To make or grind a bit on (a key). [ME *bite* < OE, cut.]

bit[3] (bĭt) *n. Computer Sci.* **1.** A single character of a language having just two characters, as either of the binary digits 0 or 1. **2.** A unit of information equivalent to the choice of either of two equally likely alternatives. **3.** A unit of information storage capacity, as of a computer memory. [B(INARY) (DIG)IT.]
bit[4] (bĭt) *v.* The past tense and a past participle of **bite.**
bi·tar·trate (bī-tär′trāt′) *n.* The tartrate of an acid.
bitch (bĭch) *n.* **1.** A female dog or other canine animal. **2.** *Slang.* **a.** A spiteful woman. **b.** A lewd woman. **3.** *Slang.* A complaint. **4.** *Slang.* Something very unpleasant or difficult. —*v.* **bitched, bitch·ing, bitch·es.** *Slang.* —*intr.* To complain; grumble. —*tr.* To botch; bungle. [ME *bicche* < OE *bicce.*]
bitch·er·y (bĭch′ə-rē) *n.* Malevolent or tyrannical behavior.
bitch goddess *n.* Material success.
bitch·y (bĭch′ē) *adj.* **-i·er, -i·est.** *Slang.* Malicious, spiteful, or ill-tempered. **—bitch′i·ly** *adv.* **—bitch′i·ness** *n.*
bite (bīt) *v.* **bit** (bĭt), **bit·ten** (bĭt′n) or **bit, bit·ing, bites.** —*tr.* **1.** To cut, grip, or tear with or as if with the teeth. **2.** To pierce the skin of esp. with the teeth or fangs. **3.** To cut into with a sharp instrument. **4.** To grip, grab, or seize. **5.** To eat into; corrode. **6.** To cause to sting or smart. —*intr.* **1.** To cut, grip, or tear something with or as if with the teeth. **2.** To have a stinging effect. **3.** To have a sharp taste. **4.** To take or swallow bait. **5.** To be taken in by a ploy or deception. —*n.* **1.** The act of biting. **2.** A wound or injury resulting from biting. **3. a.** A stinging or smarting sensation. **b.** An incisive, penetrating quality. **4.** An amount of food taken into the mouth at one time; mouthful. **5.** *Informal.* A light meal or snack. **6.** A secure grip or hold applied by a tool or machine upon a working surface. **7.** The angle at which the upper and lower teeth meet. **8.** The corrosive action of acid upon an etcher's metal plate. **—*idioms.* bite the bullet.** To face a painful situation bravely and stoically. **bite the dust. 1.** To fall dead, esp. in combat. **2.** To be badly defeated. **3.** To become useless. **put the bite on.** *Slang.* To borrow money from. [ME *biten* < OE *bītan.*] **—bit′a·ble, bite′a·ble** *adj.* **—bit′er** *n.*
bite·wing (bīt′wĭng′) *n.* A dental x-ray plate that has a central flap for the patient to bite, holding the plate in position.
bit·ing (bī′tĭng) *adj.* **1.** Causing a stinging sensation. **2.** Incisive; penetrating. **—bit′ing·ly** *adv.*
bit·stock (bĭt′stŏk′) *n.* A brace or handle in which a drilling or boring bit is secured.
bitt (bĭt) *n.* A vertical post set on the deck of a ship and used to secure cables. —*tr.v.* **bitt·ed, bitt·ing, bitts.** To wind (a cable) around a bitt. [Orig. unknown.]
bit·ten (bĭt′n) *v.* A past participle of **bite.**
bit·ter (bĭt′ər) *adj.* **-er, -est. 1.** Having or being a taste that is sharp, acrid, and unpleasant. **2.** Causing sharp pain to the body or discomfort to the mind; harsh: *a bitter wind; bitter memories.* **3.** Difficult or distasteful to accept, admit, or bear: *the bitter truth.* **4.** Exhibiting or proceeding from strong animosity: *bitter foes.* **5.** Resulting from or expressive of severe grief, anguish, or disappointment: *cried bitter tears.* **6.** Marked by anguished resentfulness or rancor: *"He was already a bitter elderly man with a gray face"* (John Dos Passos). —*tr. & intr.v.* **-tered, -ter·ing, -ters.** To make or become bitter. —*n.* **bitters.** A bitter, usually alcoholic liquid made with herbs or roots and used in cocktails or as a tonic. [ME < OE.] **—bit′ter·ly** *adv.* **—bit′ter·ness** *n.*
bitter almond *n.* A variety of the common almond, *Prunus amygdalus amara,* having bitter kernels that yield a very poisonous oil.
bitter apple *n.* **1.** The colocynth. **2.** The fruit of the colocynth.
bitter end *n.* **1.** *Naut.* The end of a rope or cable that is wound around a bitt. **2.** A final, painful, or disastrous extremity.
bit·tern[1] (bĭt′ərn) *n.* Any of several wading birds of the genera *Botaurus* and *Ixobrychus,* having mottled, brownish plumage and a deep, resonant cry. [ME *biture* < OFr. *butor.*]
bit·tern[2] (bĭt′ərn) *n.* The solution of bromides, magnesium, and calcium salts remaining after sodium chloride is crystallized out of sea water. [< BITTER.]
bit·ter·nut (bĭt′ər-nŭt′) *n.* A hickory tree, *Carya cordiformis,* of eastern North America, having nuts with bitter kernels.
bitter principle *n.* Any of a large number of bitter substances, frequently of vegetable origin.
bit·ter·root (bĭt′ər-ro͞ot′, -ro͝ot′) *n.* A plant, *Lewisia rediviva,* of western North America, having showy pink or white flowers and a starchy, edible root.
bitter rot *n.* A fungal disease of fruit caused by *Glomerella cingulata.*
bit·ter·sweet (bĭt′ər-swēt′) *n.* **1.** A North American woody vine, *Celastrus scandens,* having orange or yellowish fruits that split open to expose seeds enclosed in fleshy scarlet arils. **2.** A sprawling vine, *Solanum dulcamara,* native to Eurasia, having purple flowers and poisonous scarlet berries. **3.** A dark to deep reddish orange color. —*adj.* **1.** Bitter and sweet at the same time. **2.** Producing a mixture of pain and pleasure. **3.** Dark to deep reddish orange.
bit·ter·weed (bĭt′ər-wēd′) *n.* Any of various plants that yield or contain a bitter principle, as the ragweed or plants of the genus *Picris.*
bi·tu·men (bĭ-to͞o′mən, -tyo͞o′-, bī-) *n.* Any of various mixtures of hydrocarbons and other substances, occurring naturally or obtained by distillation from coal or petroleum, found in asphalt and tar, and used for surfacing roads and for waterproofing. [ME *bithumen,* a mineral pitch from the Near East < Lat. *bitumen.*] **—bi·tu′mi·noid′** (-mə-noid′) *adj.*
bi·tu·mi·nize (bĭ-to͞o′mə-nīz′, -tyo͞o′-, bī-) *tr.v.* **-nized, -niz·ing, -niz·es.** To treat with bitumen. **—bi·tu′mi·ni·za′tion** *n.*
bi·tu·mi·nous (bĭ-to͞o′mə-nəs, -tyo͞o′-, bī-) *adj.* **1.** Like or containing bitumen. **2.** Of or pertaining to bituminous coal.
bituminous coal *n.* A mineral coal that burns with a smoky, yellow flame, yielding volatile bituminous constituents.
bi·va·lent (bī-vā′lənt) *adj.* **1.** *Chem.* Having valence 2. **2.** Composed of two homologous chromosomes or two sets of such chromosomes. **—bi·va′lence, bi·va′len·cy** *n.*
bi·valve (bī′vălv′) *n.* A mollusk, such as an oyster or clam, that has a shell consisting of two hinged parts. —*adj.* **1.** Having a shell consisting of two hinged parts. **2.** Consisting of two similar separable parts. **—bi′valved′** *adj.*
bi·var·i·ate (bī-vâr′ē-ĭt, -āt′) *adj.* Having two variables.
biv·ou·ac (bĭv′o͞o-ăk′, bĭv′wăk′) *n.* A temporary encampment often in the open air. —*intr.v.* **-acked, -ack·ing, -acks** or **-acs.** To camp in a bivouac. [Fr., prob. < dial. G. *beiwacht,* supplementary night watch.]
bi·week·ly (bī-wēk′lē) *adj.* **1.** Happening every two weeks. **2.** Happening twice a week; semiweekly. —*n., pl.* **-lies.** A publication issued every two weeks. —*adv.* **1.** Every two weeks. **2.** Twice a week; semiweekly.
bi·year·ly (bī-yîr′lē) *adj.* **1.** Happening every two years. **2.** Happening twice a year; semiyearly. —*adv.* **1.** Every two years. **2.** Twice a year; semiyearly.
bi·zarre (bĭ-zär′) *adj.* Strikingly unconventional or far-fetched, as in style or appearance; odd. [Fr. < Sp. *bizarro,* brave, prob. < Basque *bizar,* beard.] **—bi·zarre′ly** *adv.* **—bi·zarre′ness** *n.*
bi·zon·al (bī-zō′nəl) *adj.* Of or relating to the affairs of a zone under the joint administration of two powers.
Bk The symbol for the element berkelium.
blab (blăb) *v.* **blabbed, blab·bing, blabs.** —*tr.* To reveal (secret matters) esp. through indiscreet or unreserved talk. —*intr.* **1.** To reveal secret matters. **2.** To chatter indiscreetly. —*n.* **1.** A person who blabs. **2.** Lengthy chatter. [ME *blabben,* to talk foolishly.] **—blab′by** *adj.*
blab·ber (blăb′ər) *intr.v.* **-bered, -ber·ing, -bers.** To chatter. —*n.* **1.** Idle chatter. **2.** One who blabs. [ME *blaberen.*]
blab·ber·mouth (blăb′ər-mouth′) *n. Slang.* One who chatters indiscreetly and at length.
black (blăk) *adj.* **-er, -est. 1.** Being of the darkest achromatic visual value; producing or reflecting comparatively little light and having no predominant hue. **2.** Having little or no light: *a black, moonless night.* **3.** Often **Black.** Belonging to an ethnic group having dark skin, esp. Negroid. **4.** Dark in color: *a face black with anger.* **5.** Soiled, as from soot; dirty. **6.** Evil; wicked: *black deeds.* **7.** Cheerless and depressing; gloomy: *black thoughts.* **8.** Marked by anger or sullenness: *gave him a black look.* **9.** Often **Black.** Attended with disaster; calamitous: *the stock-market crash on Black Friday.* **10.** Deserving of, indicating, or incurring censure or dishonor: *"man . . . has written one of his blackest records as a destroyer on the oceanic islands"* (Rachel Carson). **11.** Wearing black clothing: *the black knight.* **12.** Served without milk or cream: *black coffee.* —*n.* **1.** An achromatic color value of minimum lightness or maximum darkness; one extreme of the neutral gray series, the opposite being white. Although strictly a response to zero stimulation of the retina, the perception of black appears to depend on contrast with surrounding color stimuli. **2.** Complete or almost complete absence of light; darkness. **3.** Black clothing, esp. such clothing worn for mourning. **4.** Often **Black.** A member of a Negroid people; Negro. **5.** A black-colored chess or checker piece. —*tr. & intr.v.* **blacked, black·ing, blacks.** To make or become black. **—*phrasal verb.* black out. 1.** To extinguish or conceal all lights that might help enemy aircraft find a target during an air raid. **2.** To lose consciousness or memory temporarily. **3.** To prohibit the dissemination of, esp. by censorship: *blacked out the news issuing from the rebel provinces.* **—*idiom.* in the black.** On the credit side of a ledger; prosperous. [ME *blak* < OE *blæc.*] **—black′ish** *adj.* **—black′ly** *adv.* **—black′ness** *n.*
Usage: The preferred term for a person today is *black* rather than *Negro.* Another acceptable term is *Afro-American.* The noun and the adjective *black* are usually but not invariably lower-cased: *"Together, blacks and whites can move our country beyond racism"* (Whitney Young, Jr.).
black alder *n.* **1.** A deciduous holly, *Ilex verticillata,* of eastern North America, bearing bright-scarlet berries. **2.** A tree, *Alnus glutinosa,* native to Eurasia, having dark bark.
black·a·moor (blăk′ə-mo͝or′) *n.* A dark-skinned person, esp. an African Negro. [BLACK + MOOR.]
black-and-blue (blăk′ən-blo͞o′) *adj.* Discolored from coagulation of blood below the surface of the skin.
Black and Tan *n.* A member of the Royal Irish Constabulary, a force of British soldiers sent to Ireland to suppress the Sinn Fein rebellion of 1919–21. [From the color of their uniform.]

bittern[1]

bittersweet

black-and-tan terrier (blăk'ən-tăn') *n.* A Manchester terrier.
black and white *n.* **1.** Writing or print. **2.** A picture or photograph in tones of black and white.
black-and-white (blăk'ənd-hwīt', -wīt') *adj.* **1.** Being in writing or print. **2.** Partially black and partially white: *a black-and-white cow.* **3.** Drawn or painted in dark pigment on a light background or vice versa. **4.** Reproducing visual images in tones of gray rather than in color: *black-and-white film.* **5.** Evaluating things as either totally good or totally bad: *black-and-white moralists.*
black art *n.* Black magic.
black·ball (blăk'bôl') *n.* **1.** A small black ball used as a negative ballot. **2.** A negative vote that blocks the admission of an applicant to an organization. —*tr.v.* **-balled, -ball·ing, -balls. 1.** To vote against, esp. to veto the admission of. **2.** To exclude from a social group. **—black'ball'er** *n.*
black bass *n.* Any of several North American freshwater game fishes of the genus *Micropterus.*
black bear *n.* Either of two black or dark-brown bears, *Euarctos* (or *Ursus*) *americanus,* of North America, or *Selenarctos thibetanus,* of Asia.
black belt *n.* **1. a.** The rank of expert in a system of self-defense such as judo or karate. **b.** The black-colored sash that symbolizes the black belt. **c.** A person who holds a black belt. **2.** A region of rich, black soil. **3.** A part of a state or city having a predominantly black population.

blackberry

black·ber·ry (blăk'bĕr'ē) *n.* **1.** Any of several woody plants of the genus *Rubus,* having canelike, usually thorny stems and black, glossy, edible berries. **2.** The fruit of a blackberry.
black bile *n.* One of the four humors of medieval physiology, supposed to cause melancholia.
black·bird (blăk'bûrd') *n.* **1.** Any of various New World birds of the family Icteridae, as the grackle or redwing, of which the male has black or predominantly black plumage. **2.** An Old World songbird, *Turdus merula,* of which the male is black with a yellow bill.
black·board (blăk'bôrd', -bōrd') *n.* A smooth, hard, often dark-colored panel for writing on with chalk.
black·bod·y (blăk'bŏd'ē) *n.* A theoretically perfect absorber of all incident radiation.
blackbody radiation *n.* The characteristic thermal radiation emitted by a blackbody at a specific temperature.
black book *n.* A record of people to blacklist or punish.
black box *n.* A device or theoretical construct, esp. an electric circuit, with known or specified performance characteristics but unknown or unspecified constituents and means of operation.
black bryony *n.* A climbing European plant, *Tamus communis,* having small, greenish flowers and poisonous red berries.

George Miksch Sutton
blackcap

black·buck (blăk'bŭk') *n.* An antelope, *Antilope cervicapra,* of India, of which the male has a dark back and spiral horns.
black·cap (blăk'kăp') *n.* **1.** The black raspberry. **2. a.** A small European bird, *Sylvia atricapilla,* of which the male is gray with a black crown. **b.** Any of various other black-crowned birds.
black·cock (blăk'kŏk') *n.* The male of the black grouse.
black cohosh *n.* A tall plant, *Cimicifuga racemosa,* of eastern North America, having long clusters of small, whitish flowers.
black comedy *n.* Comedy that uses black humor.
black crappie *n.* An edible North American fish, *Pomoxis nigromaculatus,* having dark, mottled coloring.
black·damp (blăk'dămp') *n.* A gas composed of a mixture of carbon dioxide and nitrogen, found in mines after fires and explosions of combustible gases.
Black Death *n.* A form of plague, caused by the bacillus *Yersina pestis,* that was pandemic throughout Europe and much of Asia for several years following 1353. [From the dark splotches it causes on its victims.]
black diamond *n.* **1.** Carbonado[2]. **2. black diamonds.** Coal.
black·en (blăk'ən) *v.* **-ened, -en·ing, -ens.** —*tr.* **1.** To make black. **2.** To sully or defame. —*intr.* To become black or dark. **—black'en·er** *n.*
Black English *n.* A distinctive nonstandard dialect of English spoken by many American blacks.

black-eyed Susan

black eye *n.* **1.** A bruised discoloration of the flesh surrounding the eye. **2.** A bad name; dishonored reputation.
black-eyed pea (blăk'īd') *n.* The cowpea (sense 2).
black-eyed Susan *n.* **1.** Any of several North American plants of the genus *Rudbeckia,* esp. *R. hirta,* having hairy stems and leaves and flowers with orange-yellow rays and dark-brown centers. **2.** A vine, *Thunbergia alata,* native to tropical Africa, having white or orange-yellow flowers with purple throats.
black·face (blăk'fās') *n.* **1.** Make-up for a conventionalized comic travesty of blacks, as in a minstrel show. **2.** An actor in a minstrel show. **3.** *Printing.* Boldface type.

Black
black letter

black·fish (blăk'fĭsh') *n., pl.* **blackfish** or **-fish·es. 1.** Any of various dark-colored fishes, such as: **a.** A freshwater fish, *Dallia pectoralis,* of far northern regions. **b.** The tautog. **2.** The pilot whale.
black flag *n.* A Jolly Roger.
black fly *n.* Any of various small, dark-colored biting flies of the family Simuliidae.
Black·foot (blăk'fo͝ot') *n., pl.* **Blackfoot** or **-feet** (-fēt'). **1.** Any of three tribes of Indians formerly inhabiting the regions of Montana, Alberta, and Saskatchewan. **2.** A member of one of the Blackfoot tribes. **3.** The Algonquian language of the Blackfoot. **—Black'foot'** *adj.*
black gold *n.* Petroleum.
black grouse *n.* A Eurasian game bird, *Lyrurus tetrix,* of which the male is black with white markings.
black·guard (blăg'ərd, -ärd') *n.* **1.** An unprincipled person; scoundrel. **2.** A foul-mouthed person. —*tr.v.* **-guard·ed, -guard·ing, -guards.** To abuse verbally; revile. **—black'-guard·ism** *n.* **—black'guard·ly** *adj. & adv.*
black gum *n.* The sour gum.
Black Hand *n.* A secret society organized for acts of terrorism and blackmail that was active in the United States in the early 20th century.
black haw *n.* A shrub, *Viburnum prunifolium,* with white flower clusters and purple-black fruit.
black·head (blăk'hĕd') *n.* **1.** A plug of dried fatty matter capped with blackened dust and epithelial debris that clogs a pore of the skin. **2.** An infectious, often fatal liver and intestinal disease of turkeys and some wildfowl. **3.** Any of various birds with dark head markings.
black·heart (blăk'härt') *n.* A disease of plants in which the inner tissues darken.
black-heart·ed (blăk'här'tĭd) *adj.* Evil by nature; wicked.
black hole *n.* A small celestial body with an intense gravitational field that is believed to be a collapsed star.
black horehound *n.* A strong-smelling plant, *Ballota nigra,* native to Europe, having clusters of purple flowers.
black humor *n.* Humor of the morbid and the absurd, esp. in its development as a literary genre. **—black humorist** *n.*
black·ing (blăk'ĭng) *n.* **1.** Lampblack. **2.** A black paste or liquid used as shoe polish.
black·jack[1] (blăk'jăk') *n.* **1.** A leather-covered bludgeon with a short flexible shaft or strap, used as a hand weapon. **2.** An oak tree, *Quercus marilandica,* of the southeastern United States, having blackish bark. **3.** A card game in which the object is to accumulate cards with a total count nearer to 21 than that of the dealer. **4.** Sphalerite. —*tr.v.* **-jacked, -jack·ing, -jacks. 1.** To hit with a blackjack. **2.** To coerce by threats.
black·jack[2] (blăk'jăk') *n.* A tankard made of tarred or waxed leather. [BLACK + ME *jakke,* leather container < OFr. *jacque.*]
black knot *n.* A disease of plum and cherry trees caused by a fungus, *Dibotryon morbosa,* and resulting in black, knotlike swellings on the branches.
black lead (lĕd) *n.* Graphite.
black·leg (blăk'lĕg') *n.* **1.** An infectious, usually fatal gas gangrene affecting the heavily muscled upper parts of the legs of sheep and cattle. **2.** A bacterial or fungous plant disease that causes the stems of plants to turn black. **3.** One who cheats at cards, esp. a professional gambler; cardsharp. **4.** *Chiefly Brit.* A strikebreaker; scab.
black letter *n.* A heavy typeface with very broad counters and thick, ornamental serifs.
black light *n.* Invisible ultraviolet or infrared radiation.
black·list (blăk'lĭst') *n.* A list of persons or organizations that are disapproved, boycotted, or suspected of disloyalty. —*tr.v.* **-list·ed, -list·ing, -lists.** To place (a name) on a blacklist. **—black'list'er** *n.*
black lung *n.* Pneumoconiosis caused by the long-term inhalation of coal dust.
black magic *n.* Magic in league with the Devil; witchcraft.
black·mail (blăk'māl') *n.* **1. a.** The extortion of money or something of value from a person by the threat of exposure of something criminal or discreditable. **b.** Something of value extorted in this manner. **2.** Tribute formerly paid to freebooters along the Scottish border for protection from pillage. [BLACK + MAIL[3].] **—black'mail'** *v.* **(-mailed, -mail·ing, -mails). —black'mail'er** *n.*
Black Ma·ri·a (mə-rī'ə) *n.* A patrol wagon. [BLACK + the name *Maria.*]
black market *n.* **1.** The illegal business of buying or selling goods in violation of restrictions such as price controls or rationing. **2.** A place where black market operations are carried on.
black-mar·ket (blăk'mär'kĭt) *tr.v.* **-ket·ed, -ket·ing, -kets.** To trade in the black market. **—black marketer, black marketeer** *n.*
black mass *n.* A travesty of the Roman Catholic Mass as part of the reputed observances of Satanism.
black measles *n.* A severe form of measles, characterized by a dark rash.
black medic or **black medick** *n.* A cloverlike plant, *Medicago lupulina,* native to Europe, having compound leaves, small yellow flower heads, and black pods.
black money *n.* Income, as from illegal activities, not reported to the government for tax purposes.
Black Muslim *n.* A member of a black religious group, the Nation of Islam, that advocates segregation of blacks and whites and the establishment of a black nation.
black mustard *n.* A plant, *Brassica nigra,* native to Eurasia,

having clusters of yellow flowers and pungent seeds that are a source of the condiment mustard.

Black Nationalist *n.* A member of a group of militant blacks who urge separatism from whites and the establishment of self-governing black communities. **—Black Nationalism** *n.*

black nightshade *n.* The belladonna (sense 1).

black oak *n.* A deciduous tree, *Quercus velutina,* of eastern North America, having hard, durable wood.

black·out (blăk′out′) *n.* **1.** The extinguishing or concealing of lights that might be visible to enemy aircraft during an air raid. **2.** Lack of illumination caused by an electrical power failure. **3. a.** The sudden extinguishing of all stage lights in a theater to indicate the passage of time or mark the end of an act or a scene. **b.** A short, comic vaudeville skit that ends with lights off. **4.** A temporary loss of memory or consciousness. **5.** A suppression or stoppage, as of news.

Black Panther *n.* A member of an organization of militant black Americans.

black pepper *n.* Pepper (sense 1.b.).

Black Plague *n.* Black Death.

black·poll (blăk′pōl′) *n.* A North American warbler, *Dendroica striata,* of which the male has a black cap.

black poplar *n.* A shade tree, *Populus nigra,* native to Eurasia, having spreading branches and pointed, triangular leaves.

Black Power *n.* A movement among black Americans emphasizing racial pride and social equality through the creation of black political and cultural institutions.

black raspberry *n.* **1.** A prickly shrub, *Rubus occidentalis,* of eastern North America, bearing black fruit. **2.** The fruit of the black raspberry.

Black Rod *n.* The chief usher of various British institutions, including the House of Lords.

black rot *n.* Any of various plant diseases caused by fungi or bacteria and resulting in darkening of the leaves and decay.

black sheep *n.* A person considered undesirable or disgraceful by a respectable group.

Black Shirt *n.* A member of a fascist party organization having a black shirt as part of its uniform.

black·smith (blăk′smĭth′) *n.* **1.** One who forges and shapes iron with an anvil and hammer. **2.** One who makes, repairs, and fits horseshoes. [From the color of iron.] **—black′smith′ing** *n.*

black·snake (blăk′snāk′) *n.* **1.** Any of various dark-colored, chiefly nonvenomous snakes, such as the black racer, *Coluber constrictor,* or the black rat snake, *Elaphe obsoleta,* of North America. **2.** A long, tapering braided rawhide or leather whip with a snapper on the end.

black spot *n.* Any of various plant diseases caused by fungi or bacteria and resulting in small black spots on the leaves.

black spruce *n.* An evergreen tree, *Picea mariana,* of northern North America, growing mostly in bogs.

black·strap (blăk′străp′) *n.* A dark, very thick molasses used in the manufacture of industrial alcohol and as an ingredient in cattle feed.

black studies *pl.n.* Studies that deal with Afro-American culture.

black-tailed deer (blăk′tāld′) also **black-tail deer** (-tāl′) *n.* The mule deer.

black tea *n.* A dark tea, the leaf of which is fully fermented or oxidized before drying.

black·thorn (blăk′thôrn′) *n.* A thorny Eurasian shrub, *Prunus spinosa,* having clusters of white flowers and bluish-black, plumlike fruit.

black thorn *n.* The pear haw.

black tie *n.* **1.** A black bow tie worn with a dinner jacket. **2.** Semiformal evening wear for men, typically requiring a dinner jacket. **—black′-tie′** *adj.*

black tip *n.* Any of several plant diseases characterized by the development of dark necrotic areas at the tip of the fruit or seed.

black·top (blăk′tŏp′) *n.* A bituminous material, such as asphalt, used to pave roads. *—tr.v.* **-topped, -top·ping, -tops.** To pave with blacktop.

black vomit *n.* **1.** Vomit consisting of bloody matter. **2.** Severe yellow fever with symptomatic regurgitation of black vomit.

black vulture *n.* A carrion-eating bird, *Coragyps atratus,* of central North America and South America, having black plumage and a bald, black head.

black walnut *n.* **1.** A deciduous tree, *Juglans nigra,* of eastern North America, having dark, hard wood and edible nuts. **2.** The wood of the black walnut. **3.** The nut of the black walnut.

black·wash (blăk′wŏsh′, -wôsh′) *tr.v.* **-washed, -wash·ing, -wash·es.** To bring from concealment; disclose. [BLACK + (WHITE)WASH.]

black·wa·ter fever *n.* (blăk′wô′tər, -wŏt′ər). A severe, frequently fatal malaria with symptomatic excretion of blood in the urine.

black widow *n.* A New World spider, *Latrodectus mactans,* of which the extremely venomous female is black with red markings. [From the fact that the female eats its mate.]

blad·der (blăd′ər) *n.* **1.** *Anat.* Any of various distensible membranous sacs found in most animals, esp. the urinary bladder. **2.** Something resembling a bladder: *the bladder of a football.* **3.** *Bot.* An inflated, hollow structure, such as the air sac in certain seaweeds. **4.** *Pathol.* A blister, pustule, or cyst filled with fluid or air. [ME *bladdre* < OE *blǣdre.*]

blad·der·nose (blăd′ər-nōz′) *n.* The hooded seal.

blad·der·nut (blăd′ər-nŭt′) *n.* Any of several shrubs or small trees of the genus *Staphylea,* of the North Temperate Zone, having small, whitish flowers and inflated seed pods.

bladder worm *n.* The bladderlike, encysted larva of the tapeworm.

blad·der·wort (blăd′ər-wûrt′, -wôrt′) *n.* Any of various aquatic plants of the genus *Utricularia,* having violet or yellow flowers and in most species small bladders that trap minute aquatic animals.

bladder wrack *n.* A rockweed, *Fucus vesiculosus,* having forked, brownish-green fronds with air-filled bladders.

blade (blād) *n.* **1.** The flat-edged cutting part of a sharpened tool or weapon. **2. a.** A sword. **b.** A swordsman. **3.** A dashing young man. **4.** A flat, thin part or section: *the blade of an oar.* **5.** The metal part of an ice skate. **6.** *Anat.* The scapula. **7.** *Bot.* **a.** The leaf of a grass or similar plant. **b.** The expanded, usually green part of a leaf as distinguished from the leafstalk. **8.** The upper surface of the tongue just behind the tip. [ME < OE *blæd.*] **—blad′ed** *adj.*

blade-ap·ple (blād′ăp′əl) *n.* A spiny, vinelike, tropical American cactus, *Pereskia aculeata,* having true leaves, white flowers, and pulpy yellow fruit.

blah (blä) *Slang.* *—n.* **1.** Worthless nonsense; drivel. **2. blahs.** A general feeling of physical or psychological discomfort or dissatisfaction. *—adj.* Dull and uninteresting. [Imit. of meaningless talk.]

blain (blān) *n.* A skin swelling or sore. [ME < OE *blegen.*]

blam·a·ble also **blame·a·ble** (blā′mə-bəl) *adj.* Deserving of blame; culpable. **—blam′a·ble·ness** *n.* **—blam′a·bly** *adv.*

blame (blām) *tr.v.* **blamed, blam·ing, blames. 1.** To hold (someone or something) at fault; think of as responsible or guilty. **2.** To find fault with; censure. **3.** To place responsibility for (something) on a person. *—n.* **1.** The responsibility or guilt for a fault or error. **2.** Censure; condemnation. **—*idiom.* to blame.** Deserving of censure; at fault. [ME *blamen* < OFr. *blasmer* < alteration of LLat. *blasphemare,* to reproach. —see BLASPHEME.] **—blam′er** *n.*

Synonyms: *blame, fault, guilt.* These nouns are compared in the sense of responsibility for an offense. *Blame* stresses censure arising from something for which one is held liable. *Fault* usually applies to a cause of failure ascribed specifically to a person or persons. *Guilt* applies to serious, willful breaches of a standard of conduct and stresses the moral culpability, rather than practical shortcoming, of the offender.

blame·a·ble (blā′mə-bəl) *adj.* Variant of **blamable.**

blamed (blāmd) *adj & adv.* Damned.

blame·ful (blām′fəl) *adj.* Deserving of blame; blameworthy. **—blame′ful·ly** *adv.* **—blame′ful·ness** *n.*

blame·less (blām′lĭs) *adj.* Free from blame or guilt; innocent. **—blame′less·ly** *adv.* **—blame′less·ness** *n.*

blame·wor·thy (blām′wûr′*th*ē) *adj.* **-thi·er, -thi·est.** Deserving of blame; reprehensible. **—blame′wor′thi·ness** *n.*

blanc fixe (blängk′ fēks′) *n.* Powdered barium sulfate used as a base for water-color pigments. [Fr. : *blanc,* white + *fixe,* fixed.]

blanch (blănch) also **blench** (blĕnch) *v.* **blanched, blanch·ing, blanch·es** also **blenched, blench·ing, blench·es.** *—tr.* **1.** To take the color from; bleach. **2.** To whiten (a growing food plant, such as celery) by covering to cut off direct light. **3.** To whiten (a metal) by soaking in acid or by coating with tin. **4. a.** To scald in order to loosen the skin of (almonds, for example). **b.** To scald (food) briefly, as before freezing. **5.** To cause to turn white or become pale. *—intr.v.* To turn white or become pale. [ME *blaunchen,* to make white < OFr. *blanchir* < *blanche,* fem. of *blanc,* white.] **—blanch′er** *n.*

blanc·mange (blə-mänj′, -mäNzh′) *n.* A flavored and sweetened milk pudding thickened with cornstarch. [ME *blankmanger,* white meat with rice < OFr. *blanc manger,* white food.]

bland (blănd) *adj.* **-er, -est. 1.** Characterized by a moderate, undisturbing, or tranquil quality, esp.: **a.** Pleasant in manner; ingratiating. **b.** Not irritating or stimulating; soothing: *a bland diet.* **c.** Mild; balmy. **2.** Lacking distinctive character; dull. [Lat. *blandus,* caressing.] **—bland′ly** *adv.* **—bland′ness** *n.*

blan·dish (blăn′dĭsh) *tr.v.* **-dished, -dish·ing, -dish·es.** To coax by flattery or wheedling; cajole. [ME *blandishen* < OFr. *blandir* < Lat. *blandiri* < *blandus,* flattering.] **—blan′dish·er** *n.* **—blan′dish·ment** *n.*

blank (blăngk) *adj.* **-er, -est. 1.** Bearing no writing, print, or marking of any kind. **2.** Not completed or filled in: *a blank questionnaire.* **3.** Without grooves or cuts: *a blank key.* **4.** Expressing nothing; vacant: *"Although his gestures were elaborate, his face was blank"* (Nathanael West). **5.** Appearing confused or dazed; bewildered. **6.** Devoid of activity or character; empty. **7.** Barren; fruitless: *blank efforts.* **8.** Absolute; complete: *a blank refusal.* *—n.* **1.** An empty space or place; void. **2. a.** An empty space to be filled in on a document. **b.** A document with one or more such spaces. **3.** An

black widow
With egg sac

unfinished material, part, or article, such as a key form, that is prepared and stored for eventual finishing. **4.** A gun cartridge with a charge of powder but no bullet. **5.** A lottery ticket that wins no prize. **6.** A mark, usually a dash (—), indicating the omission of a word or letter. **7.** The center white circle of a target; bull's eye. *—tr.v.* **blanked, blank·ing, blanks. 1.** To remove, as from view; obliterate: *"at times the strong glare of the sun blanked it from sight"* (Richard Wright). **2.** To delete; invalidate. **3.** *Sports.* To prevent (an opponent) from scoring. **4.** To punch or stamp from flat stock, esp. with a die. ***—idiom.* draw a blank.** To fail, esp. to fail to come up with an idea, answer or solution. [ME < OFr. *blanc,* white.] **—blank'ly** *adv.* **—blank'ness** *n.*

blank cartridge *n.* A blank (sense 4).

blank check *n.* **1.** A signed check with no amount filled in. **2.** Total freedom of action; carte blanche.

blank endorsement *n.* An endorsement on a check or negotiable note that names no payee, making it payable to the bearer.

blast furnace

blan·ket (blăng'kĭt) *n.* **1.** A large piece of woven material used as a covering for warmth, esp. on a bed. **2.** A thick layer that covers or encloses: *a blanket of snow.* *—adj.* Applying to or covering all conditions or requirements: *a blanket insurance policy.* *—tr.v.* **-ket·ed, -ket·ing, -kets. 1.** To cover with or as if with a blanket. **2.** To cover so as to inhibit or suppress. **3.** To apply to generally and uniformly without exception. [ME < OFr. < *blanc,* white.]

blan·ket·flow·er (blăng'kĭt-flou'ər) *n.* The gaillardia.

blanket stitch *n.* The buttonhole stitch as used for edging around a blanket or other heavy material.

blan·ket-stitch (blăng'kĭt-stĭch') *tr.v.* **-stitched, -stitch·ing, -stitch·es.** To sew with a blanket stitch.

blank verse *n.* Verse consisting of unrhymed lines, usually of iambic pentameter.

blare (blâr) *v.* **blared, blar·ing, blares.** *—intr.* To sound loudly and stridently. *—tr.* **1.** To cause to blare. **2.** To utter or exclaim loudly. *—n.* **1.** A loud, strident noise. **2.** Flamboyance. [ME *bleren.*]

blar·ney (blär'nē) *n.* **1.** Smooth, flattering talk. **2.** Nonsensical or deceptive talk. [After the *Blarney* Stone, in Blarney Castle, Blarney, Ireland, said to give skill in flattery to those who kiss it.] **—blar'ney** *v.* **(-neyed, -ney·ing, -neys).**

bla·sé (blä-zā') *adj.* **1.** Uninterested or unexcited because of frequent exposure or indulgence. **2.** Very sophisticated. [Fr., p.part. of *blaser,* to cloy.]

blas·pheme (blăs-fēm') *v.* **-phemed, -phem·ing, -phemes.** *—tr.* **1.** To speak of (God or something sacred) in an irreverent or impious manner. **2.** To revile; execrate. *—intr.* To speak blasphemy. [ME *blasfemen* < OFr. *blasfemer* < LLat. *blasphemare* < Gk. *blasphēmien* < *blasphēmos,* blasphemous.] **—blas·phem'er** *n.*

blastoff

blas·phe·mous (blăs'fə-məs) *adj.* Impiously irreverent. [LLat. *blasphemus* < Gk. *blasphēmos.*] **—blas'phe·mous·ly** *adv.* **—blas'phe·mous·ness** *n.*

blas·phe·my (blăs'fə-mē) *n., pl.* **-mies. 1. a.** A contemptuous or profane act, utterance, or writing concerning God. **b.** The act of claiming for oneself the attributes and rights of God. **2.** An irreverent or impious act, attitude, or utterance in regard to something considered inviolable or sacrosanct.

blast (blăst) *n.* **1. a.** A strong gust of wind. **b.** The effect of such a gust. **2.** A forcible stream of air, gas, or steam from an opening, esp. one in a blast furnace to aid combustion. **3. a.** The act of blowing a whistle or wind instrument. **b.** The sound or noise produced by this. **4. a.** An explosion, as of dynamite. **b.** The effect of such an explosion. **c.** The charge of dynamite or other explosive used. **5.** A disease of plants that results in failure of flowers to open or of fruit or seeds to mature. **6.** A destructive or damaging influence. **7.** A violent verbal assault or outburst. **8.** *Slang.* A satisfyingly exciting experience or event, as a big party. *—v.* **blast·ed, blast·ing, blasts.** *—tr.* **1.** To fragment by or as if by explosion; smash. **2.** To ruin; frustrate: *"Our hopes were all blasted at one blow"* (Frederick Douglass). **3.** To cause to shrivel, wither, or mature imperfectly by or as if by blast or blight. **4.** To make or open by or as if by explosion: *blast a channel through the reefs.* **5.** *Informal.* To attack or criticize vigorously. *—intr.* **1.** To detonate explosives. **2.** To emit a loud, strident noise. **3.** To wither, shrivel, or mature imperfectly. **4.** *Informal.* To attack or criticize with vigor. **5.** *Slang.* To shoot. **6.** *Electronics.* To distort sound recording or transmission by overloading a microphone or loudspeaker. ***—phrasal verb.* blast off.** To take off, as a rocket or space vehicle. ***—idiom.* (at) full blast.** At full speed, volume, or capacity. [ME < OE *blǣst.*] **—blast'er** *n.*

blast– *pref.* Variant of **blasto-.**

-blast *suff.* Bud; germ; cell; cell layer: *endoblast.* [< Gk. *blastos,* bud.]

blast·ed (blăs'tĭd) *adj.* **1.** Blighted; withered; shriveled. **2.** *Informal.* Extremely annoying; obnoxious: *these blasted flies.*

blas·te·ma (blă-stē'mə) *n., pl.* **-mas** or **-ma·ta** (-mə-tə). A segregated region of embryonic cells from which a specific organ develops. [Gk. *blastēma,* offspring < *blastos,* bud.] **—blas·te'mal** (blă-stē'məl), **blas'te·mat'ic** (blăs'tə-măt'ĭk), **blas·te'mic** (blă-stē'mĭk) *adj.*

blast furnace *n.* A furnace in which combustion is intensified by a blast of air.

-blastic *suff.* Having a specified number or kind of buds, germs, cells, or cell layers: *meroblastic.* [< -BLAST.]

blasting gelatin *n.* A dynamite containing nitrocellulose in addition to nitroglycerin.

blasto– or **blast–** *pref.* Bud; germ: *blastocyst.* [< Gk. *blastos,* bud.]

blas·to·coel or **blas·to·coele** (blăs'tə-sēl') *n.* The cavity of a blastula. [BLASTO- + -COEL.] **—blas'to·coe'lic** *adj.*

blas·to·cyst (blăs'tə-sĭst') *n.* The germinal vesicle. **—blas'to·cys'tic** *adj.*

blas·to·derm (blăs'tə-dûrm') *n.* The layer of cells surrounding the blastocoel and giving rise to the germinal disc from which the embryo develops in most placental vertebrates. **—blas'to·der·mat'ic** (-dər-măt'ĭk), **blas'to·der'mic** (-dûr'mĭk) *adj.*

blas·to·disc (blăs'tə-dĭsk') *n.* The germinal disc.

blast·off also **blast-off** (blăst'ôf') *n.* The launching of a rocket or space vehicle.

blas·to·gen·e·sis (blăs'tə-jĕn'ĭ-sĭs) *n.* **1.** The theory that inherited characteristics are transmitted from parent to offspring by germ plasm. **2.** Reproduction by budding. **—blas'to·ge·net'ic** (-jə-nĕt'ĭk), **blas'to·gen'ic** (-jĕn'ĭk) *adj.*

blas·to·ma (blă-stō'mə) *n., pl.* **-mas** or **-ma·ta** (-mə-tə). A neoplasm composed of immature and undifferentiated cells.

blas·to·mere (blăs'tə-mîr') *n.* A cell formed during the cleavage of a fertilized ovum. **—blas'to·mer'ic** (-mîr'ĭk, -mĕr'-) *adj.*

blas·to·pore (blăs'tə-pôr', -pōr') *n.* The mouthlike opening into the primitive intestinal cavity of the gastrula. [BLASTO- + PORE².] **—blas'to·por'al** (-pôr'əl, -pōr'-) *adj.*

blas·tu·la (blăs'chə-lə) *n., pl.* **-las** or **-lae** (-lē'). An early embryonic form consisting essentially of a hollow cellular sphere. [NLat. < Gk. *blastos,* bud.] **—blas'tu·lar** (-lər) *adj.* **—blas'tu·la'tion** (-lā'shən) *n.*

blat (blăt) *v.* **blat·ted, blat·ting, blats.** *—tr.* To utter without thinking; blurt. *—intr.* **1.** To cry, esp. as a sheep; bleat. **2.** To make a harsh or raucous noise. [Imit.] **—blat** *n.*

bla·tant (blāt'nt) *adj.* **1.** Unpleasantly and often vulgarly loud and noisy. **2.** Completely and often offensively conspicuous; obvious: *a blatant lie.* [Prob. < Lat. *blatire,* to blab.] **—bla'tan·cy** *n.* **—bla'tant·ly** *adv.*

Usage: *Blatant* and *flagrant* are often confused. In the sense that causes the confusion, *blatant* has the meaning of "outrageous" or "egregious." *Flagrant* emphasizes wrong or evil that is glaring or notorious. Therefore, one who blunders may be guilty of a *blatant* (but not a *flagrant*) error; one who intentionally and ostentatiously violates a pledge commits a *flagrant* act.

blath·er (blăth'ər) also **bleth·er** (blĕth'-) *—intr.v.* **-ered, -er·ing, -ers.** To talk nonsensically. *—n.* Absurd or foolish talk; nonsense. [ME < ON *blaðra* < *blaðr,* nonsense.] **—blath'er·er** *n.*

blath·er·skite (blăth'ər-skīt') *n.* **1.** A babbling, foolish person. **2.** Blather. [BLATHER + Sc. dial. *skate,* a contemptuous person.]

blaze¹ (blāz) *n.* **1.** A brilliant burst of fire; flame. **2.** A bright or steady light or glare: *the blaze of day.* **3.** A destructive fire. **4.** A brilliant or striking display: *flowers that were a blaze of color.* **5.** A sudden outburst, as of emotion: *a blaze of anger.* **6. blazes.** *Slang.* Hell. *—v.* **blazed, blaz·ing, blaz·es.** *—intr.* **1.** To burn with a bright flame. **2.** To shine brightly. **3.** To be resplendent: *a garden blazing with flowers.* **4.** To flare up suddenly: *His temper blazed.* **5.** To shoot rapidly and continuously: *entered the hideout with guns blazing.* *—tr.* **1.** To cause to blaze; burn. **2.** To shine or be resplendent with: *eyes that blazed fire.* [ME *blase* < OE *blæse.*] **—blaz'ing·ly** *adv.*

Synonyms: *blaze, flame, flare, flash, glare, incandescence, glow.* These nouns relate to the visible signs of combustion, especially to a brightly burning light. *Blaze* primarily stresses intensity and magnitude of combustion and especially implies vivid illumination. *Flame* more narrowly pertains to a jet or tongue of fire. *Flare* applies to a sudden, brief, intensely brilliant but unsteady burst of light, and *flash* to an even shorter burst. *Glare* emphasizes continuing intensity of blinding light. *Incandescence* suggests the intense brilliance of something white-hot. *Glow* primarily stresses light, often in the absence of visible flame; it particularly suggests steadiness of radiation and absence of intense brilliance.

blaze² (blāz) *n.* **1.** A white or light-colored spot on the face of a horse or other animal. **2.** A mark cut or painted on a tree to indicate a trail *—tr.v.* **blazed, blaz·ing, blaz·es. 1.** To mark (a tree) with or as if with blazes. **2.** To indicate (a trail) by marking trees with blazes. [Of Germanic orig.]

blaze³ (blāz) *tr.v.* **blazed, blaz·ing, blaz·es.** To make known publicly; proclaim: *blazed the news.* [ME *blasen* < MDu. *blāsen,* to blow.]

blaz·er (blā'zər) *n.* **1.** One that blazes. **2.** A lightweight, informal sports jacket, often striped or brightly colored.

blazing star *n.* **1.** A North American plant, *Chamaelirium luteum,* having a long cluster of small white flowers. **2.** Any of various North American plants of the genus *Liatris,* having clusters of tuftlike purple or pinkish flowers. **3.** A plant,

Mentzelia laevicaulis, of western North America, having large, pale-yellow flowers.,

bla·zon (blā′zən) *tr.v.* **-zoned, -zon·ing, -zons. 1.** To describe (a coat of arms) in proper heraldic terms. **2.** To paint or depict (a coat of arms) with accurate heraldic detail. **3.** To adorn or embellish with or as if with blazons: *"the stars and moons and suns blazoned on that sacred wall"* (G.K. Chesterton). **4.** To announce; proclaim. *—n.* **1.** A coat of arms. **2.** The heraldic description or representation of a coat of arms. **3.** An ostentatious or showy display. [ME *blasoun,* shield < OFr. *blason.*] **—bla′zon·er** *n.* **—bla′zon·ment** *n.*

bla·zon·ry (blā′zən-rē) *n., pl.* **-ries. 1.** The art of properly and accurately describing or representing armorial bearings. **2.** A coat of arms. **3.** A showy or brilliant display.

bleach (blēch) *v.* **bleached, bleach·ing, bleach·es.** *—tr.* **1.** To remove the color from, as by means of chemical agents. **2.** To make white or colorless. *—intr.* To become white or colorless. *—n.* **1.** A chemical agent used for bleaching. **2. a.** The act of bleaching. **b.** The degree of bleaching obtained. [ME *blechen* < OE *blǣcan.*]

bleach·er (blē′chər) *n.* **1.** One that bleaches. **2.** Often **bleachers.** An often unroofed outdoor grandstand for seating spectators.

bleaching powder *n.* A powder, such as chlorinated lime or calcium hypochlorite, used in solution as a bleach.

bleak[1] (blēk) *adj.* **-er, -est. 1.** Exposed to the elements; unsheltered and barren. **2.** Cold and cutting; raw. **3. a.** Gloomy and somber; dreary: *"Life in the Aran Islands has always been bleak and difficult"* (John M. Synge). **b.** Not encouraging; depressing: *a bleak prospect.* [ME *bleik* < ON *bleikr.*] **—bleak′ly** *adv.* **—bleak′ness** *n.*

bleak[2] (blēk) *n.* A European freshwater fish of the genus *Alburnus,* having silvery scales used in the manufacture of artificial pearls. [ME *bleke* < OE *blǣc,* bright.]

blear (blîr) *tr.v.* **bleared, blear·ing, blears. 1.** To blur (the eyes) with or as if with tears. **2.** To blur; dim. *—adj.* Bleary. [ME *bleren.*]

blear-eyed (blîr′īd′) *adj.* Variant of **bleary-eyed.**

blear·y (blîr′ē) *adj.* **-i·er, -i·est. 1.** Blurred or dimmed by or as if by tears: *bleary eyes.* **2.** Vaguely outlined; indistinct. **3.** Exhausted; worn-out. **—blear′i·ly** *adv.* **—blear′i·ness** *n.*

blear·y-eyed (blîr′ē-īd′) also **blear-eyed** (blîr′īd′) *adj.* **1.** With eyes blurred by or as if by tears. **2.** Dull of mind or perception.

bleat (blēt) *n.* **1.** The characteristic cry of a goat or sheep. **2.** A sound similar to a bleat, as a whining cry. *—v.* **bleat·ed, bleat·ing, bleats.** *—intr.* **1.** To utter a bleat. **2.** To utter a sound similar to a bleat, esp. a whine. *—tr.* To utter in a whining voice. [ME *blet* < *bleten,* to bleat < OE *blǣtan.*] **—bleat′er** *n.*

bleb (blĕb) *n.* **1.** A small blister or pustule. **2.** An air bubble. [Prob. var. of BLOB.] **—bleb′by** *adj.*

bleed (blēd) *v.* **bled** (blĕd), **bleed·ing, bleeds.** *—intr.* **1.** To lose or emit blood. **2.** To be wounded, esp. in battle. **3.** To feel sympathetic grief or anguish: *My heart bleeds for you.* **4.** To exude sap or a similar fluid, as a bruised plant does. **5.** *Slang.* To pay out money, esp. an exorbitant amount. **6.** To become mixed or run, as dyes in wet cloth. **7.** To show through a layer of paint, as a stain or resin in wood. **8.** To be printed so as to go off the edge or edges of a page after trimming. *—tr.* **1. a.** To take or remove blood from. **b.** To extract sap or juice from. **2. a.** To draw liquid or gaseous contents from; drain. **b.** To draw off (liquid or gaseous matter) from a container. **3.** *Slang.* To obtain money from, esp. by improper means. **4. a.** To cause (an illustration, for example) to bleed. **b.** To trim (a page, for example) so closely as to mutilate the printed or illustrative matter. *—n.* **1.** Illustrative matter that bleeds. **2. a.** A page trimmed so as to bleed. **b.** The part of the page that is trimmed off. [ME *bleden* < OE *blēdan.*]

bleed·er (blē′dər) *n.* **1.** A hemophiliac. **2.** A bloodletter. **3.** *Slang.* A blood vessel severed by trauma or surgery that requires attention for the arrest of blood flow.

bleed·ing-heart (blē′dĭng-härt′) *n.* **1.** Any of several plants of the genus *Dicentra,* having nodding pink flowers, esp. the widely cultivated species *D. spectabilis,* native to Japan. **2.** A person who is considered excessively sympathetic toward those who claim to be underprivileged or exploited.

bleep (blēp) *n.* A brief high-pitched sound, as from an electronic device. *—tr.v.* **bleeped, bleep·ing, bleeps.** To blip. [Imit.]

blem·ish (blĕm′ĭsh) *tr.v.* **-ished, -ish·ing, -ish·es.** To impair or spoil by a flaw; mar. *—n.* A flaw or defect, esp. one that adversely affects appearance. [ME *blemisshen* < OFr. *blemir,* to make pale, of Germanic orig.] **—blem′ish·er** *n.*

Synonyms: *blemish, imperfection, fault, defect, flaw.* All of these denote loss or absence of perfection. *Blemish* applies to some manifest characteristic that is held to mar the appearance of character of a thing, whereas *imperfection* and *fault* apply more comprehensively to any deficiency or shortcoming in make-up. *Defect* denotes serious functional or structural shortcoming; *flaw* refers to a small but fundamental weakness or dislocation, such as a fissure in a gem.

blench[1] (blĕnch) *intr.v.* **blenched, blench·ing, blench·es.** To draw back or shy away out of fear; quail. [ME *blenchen* < OE *blencan,* to deceive.] **—blench′er** *n.*

blench[2] (blĕnch) *v.* Variant of **blanch.**

blend (blĕnd) *v.* **blend·ed** or **blent** (blĕnt), **blend·ing, blends.** *—tr.* **1.** To combine or mix so as to render the constituent parts indistinguishable. **2.** To mix (different varieties or grades) thoroughly so as to obtain a new mixture of a particular quality or consistency: *blend whiskeys.* *—intr.* **1.** To form a uniform mixture; intermingle: *"The smoke blended easily into the odor of the other fumes"* (Norman Mailer). **2.** To become merged into one; unite. **3.** To go well together; harmonize: *picked a tie that blended with his jacket.* *—n.* **1.** Something that is blended; mixture. **2.** The act of blending. **3.** *Ling.* A word produced by combining parts of other words, as *smog* from *smoke* and *fog.* [ME *blenden* < OE *blandan.*]

blende (blĕnd) *n.* **1.** Any of various shiny minerals composed chiefly of metallic sulfides. **2.** Sphalerite. [G. < *blenden,* to deceive < OHG *blenten,* to blind.]

blended whiskey *n.* Whiskey that is either a blend of two or more straight whiskeys or a blend of whiskey and neutral spirits.

blend·er (blĕn′dər) *n.* **1.** One that blends. **2.** An electrical appliance with whirling blades for chopping, mixing, or liquefying foods.

blending inheritance *n.* Inheritance of characters intermediate between those of parents widely divergent in those characters.

blen·ny (blĕn′ē) *n., pl.* **-nies.** Any of numerous small, elongated marine fishes, chiefly of the families Blenniidae and Clinidae. [Lat. *blennius,* a kind of sea fish < Gk. *blennos.*]

blent (blĕnt) *v.* A past tense and past participle of **blend.**

bleph·a·ri·tis (blĕf′ə-rī′tĭs) *n.* Inflammation of the eyelid. [Gk. *blepharon,* eyelid + -ITIS.]

bleph·a·ro·spasm (blĕf′ə-rō-spăz′əm) *n.* Uncontrollable winking caused by the involuntary contraction of an eyelid muscle. [NLat. *blepharospasmus* : Gk. *blepharon,* eyelid + Gk. *spasmos,* cramp.]

bles·bok (blĕs′bŏk′) *n., pl.* **blesbok** or **-boks.** An African antelope, *Damaliscus albifrons,* having curved horns and a face marked with white. [Afr. : *bles,* white mark on an animal's face (< MDu.) + *bok,* buck (< MDu. *boc*).]

bless (blĕs) *tr.v.* **blessed** or **blest** (blĕst), **bless·ing, bless·es. 1.** To make holy by religious rite; sanctify. **2.** To make the sign of the cross over so as to sanctify. **3.** To invoke divine favor upon. **4.** To honor as holy; glorify: *Bless the Lord.* **5.** To confer well-being or prosperity upon. **6.** To endow, as with talent. [ME *blessen* < OE *blētsian.*] **—bless′er** *n.*

bless·ed (blĕs′ĭd) also **blest** (blĕst) *adj.* **1. a.** Worthy of worship; holy. **b.** Held in veneration; revered. **2.** *Rom. Cath. Ch.* Enjoying the eternal happiness of heaven. Used as a title for those who have been beatified. **3.** Enjoying happiness; fortunate. **4.** Bringing happiness; pleasurable. **5.** *Slang.* Used as an intensive: *not a blessed dime.* **—bless′ed·ly** *adv.* **—bless′ed·ness** *n.*

Blessed Sacrament *n. Rom. Cath. Ch.* The consecrated Host.

Blessed Virgin *n.* The Virgin Mary.

bless·ing (blĕs′ĭng) *n.* **1.** The act of one who blesses. **2.** Something promoting or contributing to happiness, well-being, or prosperity; boon. **3.** Approbation; approval: *This plan has my blessing.* **4.** A short prayer before or after a meal.

blest (blĕst) *v.* A past tense and past participle of **bless.** *—adj.* Variant of **blessed.**

bleth·er (blĕth′ər) *v. & n.* Variant of **blather.**

bleu cheese *n.* Blue cheese.

blew (blo͞o) *v.* Past tense of **blow[1].**

blight (blīt) *n.* **1.** Any of several plant diseases that result in the death of leaves, growing tips, or an entire plant. **2.** An adverse environmental condition, as air pollution. **3.** One that withers hopes or ambitions, impairs growth, or halts prosperity. **4.** The state or result of being blighted. *—v.* **blight·ed, blight·ing, blights.** *—tr.* **1.** To cause (a plant, for example) to be affected with blight. **2.** To cause to decline or decay. **3.** To ruin; destroy. *—intr.* To suffer blight. [Orig. unknown.]

blight·er (blī′tər) *n.* **1.** One that blights. **2.** *Chiefly Brit.* A fellow, esp. one considered of little worth.

blimp[1] (blĭmp) *n.* A nonrigid, buoyant aircraft. [Orig. unknown.]

blimp[2] (blĭmp) *n. Chiefly Brit.* One whose views exhibit a blend of ultraconservative jingoism and misinformation. [After Colonel *Blimp,* a cartoon character invented by David Low (1891–1963).]

blind (blīnd) *adj.* **-er, -est. 1.** Being without sight; sightless. **2.** Of, pertaining to, or for sightless persons. **3.** Performed by instruments and without the use of sight: *blind navigation.* **4.** Performed without preparation, forethought, or knowledge: *a blind attempt.* **5.** Unable or unwilling to perceive or understand: *blind to his faults.* **6.** Not based on reason or evidence: *blind faith.* **7.** *Slang.* Drunk. **8.** Independent of human control: *blind fate.* **9. a.** Difficult to comprehend or see; illegible: *blind writings.* **b.** Illegibly or incompletely addressed: *blind mail.* **10. a.** Hidden from sight: *a blind seam.* **b.** Screened from the view of an oncoming driver: *a blind intersection.* **11.** Closed at one end: *a blind socket.* **12.** Having no opening: *a blind wall.* **13.** *Bot.*

bleeding-heart

blesbok

blimp[1]

Failing to flower. *—n.* **1.** Something that hinders vision or shuts out light, as a window shade or Venetian blind. **2.** A shelter for concealing hunters, esp. duck hunters. **3.** Something intended to conceal the true nature, esp. of an activity; subterfuge. *—adv.* **1.** Without seeing; blindly: *fly blind.* **2.** *Informal.* Into a stupor: *drank themselves blind.* *—tr.v.* **blind·ed, blind·ing, blinds. 1.** To deprive of sight. **2.** To dazzle. **3.** To deprive of perception or judgment. **4.** To deprive of light. [ME < OE.] **—blind'ing·ly** *adv.* **—blind'ly** *adv.* **—blind'ness** *n.*

blind alley *n. Informal.* An undertaking that is mistaken or fails to produce results.

blind date *n. Informal.* **1.** A social engagement between a man and a woman who have not previously met. **2.** Either of the persons taking part in a blind date.

blind·er (blīn'dər) *n.* **1.** One that blinds. **2. blinders.** A pair of leather flaps attached to a horse's bridle to curtail side vision.

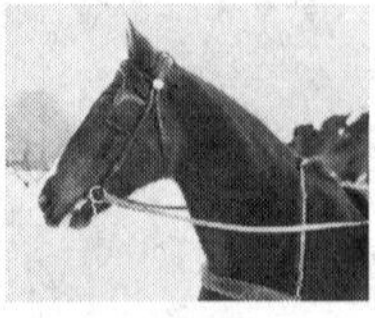

blinder
Blinders on a horse

blind·fish (blīnd'fĭsh') *n., pl.* **blindfish** or **-fish·es.** Any of various fishes having rudimentary, nonfunctioning eyes, esp. the cavefish.

blind·fold (blīnd'fōld') *tr.v.* **-fold·ed, -fold·ing, -folds. 1.** To cover the eyes of with or as if with a bandage. **2.** To prevent from seeing and esp. from comprehending. *—n.* A bandage to cover the eyes. *—adj.* **1.** With eyes covered. **2.** Reckless. [ME *blindfellen,* OE *geblindfellian,* to strike blind.]

blind gut *n.* **1.** A digestive cavity having only one opening. **2.** The cecum of the large intestine.

blind hinge *n.* A hinge constructed to allow the hinged piece to swing shut by its own weight unless held open.

blind·man's buff (blīnd'mănz') *n.* A game in which a blindfolded player tries to catch and identify one of the other players. [*Buff,* short for *buffet,* a blow.]

blind pig *n. Slang.* A speakeasy.

blind side *n.* The side away from which one is directing one's attention.

blind spot *n.* **1.** *Anat.* The small, optically insensitive region where the optic nerve enters the retina of the eye. **2.** A part of an area that cannot be directly observed. **3.** An area where radio reception is weak. **4.** A subject about which one is markedly ignorant or prejudiced.

blind staggers *n. (used with a sing. verb).* Staggers (sense 3.b.).

blind tiger *n. Slang.* A speakeasy.

blind·worm (blīnd'wûrm') *n.* The slowworm. [From its small eyes.]

bli·ni (blē'nē) *pl.n.* Small buckwheat pancakes served with caviar or sour cream. [R., pl. of *blin,* pancake.]

blink (blĭngk) *v.* **blinked, blink·ing, blinks.** *—intr.* **1.** To close and open the eyes rapidly. **2.** To look through half-closed eyes, as in a bright glare; squint. **3.** To shine with intermittent gleams; flash on and off. **4.** To be startled or dismayed. *—tr.* **1.** To close and open (the eyes) rapidly. **2.** To refuse to recognize or face; ignore or overlook: *blink ugly facts.* **3.** To signal (a message) with a flashing light. ***—phrasal verb.*** **blink at.** To look with pretended ignorance; pretend not to see: *blink at dishonest practices.* *—n.* **1.** The act or an instance of closing and opening the eyes rapidly. **2.** A quick look or glimpse; glance. **3.** The time it takes to blink. **4.** A flash of light; twinkle. **5.** An iceblink (sense 1). ***—idiom.*** **on the blink.** *Slang.* Not in proper working condition; out of order. [ME *blinken.*]

blister beetle

blink·er (blĭng'kər) *n.* **1.** A light that blinks in order to convey a message or warning. **2.** *Slang.* An eye. **3. blinkers.** Goggles. **4. blinkers.** Blinders (sense 2).

blintz (blĭnts) also **blin·tze** (blĭn'tsə) *n.* A thin, rolled pancake usually filled with cottage cheese and often served with sour cream. [Yiddish *blintse* < R. *blinyets,* dim. of *blin,* pancake.]

blip (blĭp) *tr.v.* **blipped, blip·ping, blips.** To interrupt recorded sounds, as on a videotape: *blipped the expletive from the TV show.* *—n.* **1.** A spot of light on a radar screen. **2.** A brief interruption of the sound received in a television program as a result of blipping. [Alteration of BLEEP.]

bliss (blĭs) *n.* **1.** Extreme happiness; joy. **2.** The ecstasy of salvation; spiritual joy. [ME *blisse* < OE *bliss.*] **—bliss'ful** *adj.* **—bliss'ful·ly** *adv.* **—bliss'ful·ness** *n.*

blis·ter (blĭs'tər) *n.* **1.** A thin, rounded swelling of the skin, containing watery matter, caused by burning or irritation. **2.** A swelling similar to a blister on a plant. **3.** An air bubble resembling a blister, as on a painted surface. **4.** A rounded, often transparent protuberance, as one used for observation on certain aircraft. *—v.* **-tered, -ter·ing, -ters.** *—tr.* **1.** To cause a blister to form on. **2.** To reprove harshly. *—intr.* To break out in blisters. [ME < OFr. *blestre,* boil, of Germanic orig.] **—blis'ter·y** *adj.*

block

blister beetle *n.* Any of various beetles of the family Meloidae that secrete a substance capable of blistering the skin.

blister copper *n.* An almost pure copper produced in an intermediate stage of copper refining. [From its blistered appearance.]

blis·ter·ing (blĭs'tər-ĭng) *adj.* **1.** Intensely hot: *a blistering sun.* **2.** Harsh; severe: *blistering criticism.* **3.** Very rapid: *a blistering pace.*

blister rust *n.* Any of several diseases of pine trees, caused by various fungi of the genus *Cronartium* and resulting in cankers and blisters on the bark.

blite (blīt) *n.* Strawberry blite. [ME, an herb < Lat. *blitum,* spinach < Gk. *bliton.*]

blithe (blīth, blīth) *adj.* **blith·er, blith·est. 1.** Filled with gaiety; cheerful. **2.** Casual; carefree: *blithe optimism.* [ME < OE *blīðe*] **—blithe'ly** *adv.* **—blithe'ness** *n.*

blith·er (blĭth'ər) *intr.v.* **-ered, -er·ing, -ers.** To blather. [Alteration of BLATHER.]

blithe·some (blīth'səm, blīth'-) *adj.* Cheerful; merry. **—blithe'some·ly** *adv.* **—blith'some·ness** *n.*

blitz (blĭts) *n.* **1.** A blitzkrieg. **2.** An intensive air raid or series of air raids. **3.** An intense campaign. *—tr.v.* **blitzed, blitz·ing, blitz·es.** To subject to a blitz. [Short for BLITZKRIEG.]

blitz·krieg (blĭts'krēg') *n.* **1.** A swift, sudden military offensive, usually by combined air and land forces. **2.** A swift, concerted effort. [G. : *Blitz,* lightning + *Krieg,* war.]

bliz·zard (blĭz'ərd) *n.* **1.** A violent windstorm accompanied by intense cold and driving snow. **2.** A very heavy snowstorm with high winds. **3.** A torrent or superabundance: *a blizzard of phone calls.* [Orig. unknown.]

bloat (blōt) *v.* **bloat·ed, bloat·ing, bloats.** *—tr.* **1.** To cause to swell up or inflate, as with liquid or gas. **2.** To puff up, as with vanity. **3.** To cure (fish) by soaking in brine and half-drying in smoke. *—intr.* To become swollen or inflated. *—n.* A swelling of the rumen or intestinal tract of a domestic animal, caused by the gases of fermentation of green forage. [< ME *blout,* soft, puffed < ON *blautr.*]

bloat·er (blō'tər) *n.* A mackerel or herring lightly smoked and salted.

blob (blŏb) *n.* **1.** A soft, amorphous mass. **2.** A shapeless splotch or daub, esp. of color. *—tr.v.* **blobbed, blob·bing, blobs.** To splash or mark with blobs; splotch. [ME *blober,* bubble.]

bloc (blŏk) *n.* **1.** A group of persons, parties, or nations united for common action. **2.** A coalition, often bipartisan, of U.S. legislators acting together for a common purpose or interest: *the farm bloc.* [Fr. < OFr., block.]

block (blŏk) *n.* **1. a.** A solid piece of wood or other hard substance having one or more flat sides. **b.** Such a piece used as a construction member or as a supporting or strengthening piece. **c.** Such a piece upon which chopping or cutting is done: *a butcher's block.* **d.** Such a piece upon which persons are beheaded. **2.** A stand from which articles are sold at an auction. **3.** A mold or form on which something is shaped or displayed: *a hat block.* **4.** A piece of wood, stone, or other substance prepared for engraving. **5. a.** A pulley or a system of pulleys set in a casing. **b.** An engine block. **6.** A group acting or regarded as a unit; bloc. **7.** A set of like items sold or handled as a unit, as shares of stock. **8.** A group of four or more unseparated postage stamps forming a rectangle. **9.** A group of townships in an unsurveyed area in Canada. **10. a.** A rectangular section of a city or town bounded on each side by consecutive streets. **b.** A segment of a street bounded by successive cross streets and including its buildings and inhabitants. **11.** A large building divided into separate units, such as apartments. **12.** A length of railroad track controlled by signals. **13.** An act of obstructing or hindering. **14.** An obstacle or hindrance. **15.** *Sports.* An act of bodily obstruction, esp. in football, legal interference with an opposing player to clear the path of the ballcarrier. **16.** *Med.* Interruption, esp. obstruction, of a neural, digestive, or other physiological process. **17.** *Psychol.* Sudden cessation of a thought process without an immediate observable cause, sometimes considered a consequence of repression. **18.** *Slang.* A person's head: *threatened to knock his block off.* **19.** A blockhead. *—v.* **blocked, block·ing, blocks.** *—tr.* **1.** To shape into a block. **2.** To support, strengthen, or retain in place by means of a block. **3.** To shape, mold, or form with or on a block: *block a hat.* **4.** To stop or impede the passage of or movement through; hinder or obstruct: *block traffic; block out the sun's rays.* **5.** To indicate broadly without great detail; sketch. **6.** *Sports.* To impede the movement of (an opponent or the ball) by physical interference. **7.** *Med.* To interrupt the proper functioning of (a physiological process). **8.** *Psychol.* To fail to remember. **9.** To run (trains) on the block system. *—intr. Sports.* To obstruct the movement of an opponent. ***—idiom.*** **on the block.** Up for sale, esp. at an auction. [ME *blok* < OFr. < MDu., of Germanic orig.] **—block'er** *n.*

block·ade (blŏ-kād') *n.* **1.** The closing off of an area, as a city or harbor, by hostile ships or forces in order to prevent the entrance and exit of traffic and communication. **2.** The forces used in a blockade. *—tr.v.* **-ad·ed, -ad·ing, -ades.** To set up a blockade against. **—block·ad'er** *n.*

block·ade-run·ner (blŏ-kād'rŭn'ər) *n.* A ship or person that goes through or past a blockade. **—block·ade'-run'ning** *n.*

block·age (blŏk'ĭj) *n.* **1.** The act of obstructing. **2.** An obstruction.

block and tackle *n.* An apparatus of pulley blocks and ropes or cables used for hauling and hoisting heavy objects.

block·bust·er (blŏk'bŭs'tər) *n. Informal.* **1.** A bomb capable of destroying a city block. **2.** Something of devastating effect. **3.** One that engages in blockbusting.

ă pat / ā pay / âr care / ä father / b bib / ch church / d deed / ĕ pet / ē be / f fife / g gag / h hat / hw which / ĭ pit / ī pie / îr pier / j judge / k kick / l lid, needle / m mum / n no, sudden / ng thing / ŏ pot / ō toe / ô paw, for / oi noise / ou out / ŏŏ took / ōō boot /

block·bust·ing (blŏk′bŭs′tĭng) *n. Informal.* The practice of persuading white homeowners to sell quickly and usually at a loss by appealing to the fear that minority groups and esp. blacks will move into the neighborhood, with a resulting decline in property values.
block·head (blŏk′hĕd′) *n.* A stupid person; dolt.
block·house (blŏk′hous′) *n.* **1.** A military fortification constructed of concrete or other sturdy material, with loopholes for defensive firing or for observation. **2.** A heavily reinforced building used for launch operations of missiles and space launch vehicles. **3.** A fort made of squared timbers with a projecting upper story.
block·ish (blŏk′ĭsh) *adj.* **1.** Like or resembling a block. **2.** Dull; stupid. **—block′ish·ly** *adv.* **—block′ish·ness** *n.*
block letter *n.* **1.** A letter printed or written sans serif. **2.** *Printing.* A sans-serif style of type.
block plane *n.* A small plane used by carpenters for cutting across the grain of wood.
block printing *n.* Printing from engraved or carved wooden or linoleum blocks.
block signal *n.* A fixed signal at the entrance to a railroad block, indicating whether or not trains may enter.
block system *n.* A system for controlling and safeguarding the flow of railway trains in which track is divided into blocks, each controlled by automatic signals.
block·y (blŏk′ē) *adj.* **-i·er, -i·est.** Resembling a block; stocky.
bloke (blōk) *n. Chiefly Brit. Slang.* A fellow; man. [Orig. unknown.]
blond (blŏnd) *adj.* **-er, -est. 1.** Having fair hair and skin and usually light eyes: *blond Scandinavians.* **2.** Of a flaxen or golden color or of any light shade of auburn or pale yellowish brown: *blond hair.* **3.** Light-colored: *blond furniture.* —*n.* **1.** A blond person. **2.** A light yellowish brown to dark grayish yellow. [OFr.] **—blond′ish** *adj.* **—blond′ness** *n.*

Usage: *Blond* as an adjective may be used of both sexes. *Blonde* and *brunette* as nouns are used only of females.

blonde (blŏnd) *adj.* **blond·er, blond·est.** Blond. —*n.* A blonde woman or girl. [OFr., fem. of *blond.*]
blood (blŭd) *n.* **1. a.** The fluid circulated by the heart through the vertebrate vascular system, carrying oxygen and nutrients throughout the body and waste materials to excretory channels. **b.** A functionally similar fluid in an invertebrate. **c.** A fluid resembling blood, such as the juice of certain plants. **2.** Life; lifeblood. **3.** Bloodshed; murder. **4.** Temperament or disposition. **5. a.** Descent from a common ancestor; parental lineage. **b.** Family relationship; kinship. **c.** Descent from noble or royal lineage: *a princess of the blood.* **d.** Recorded descent from purebred stock. **e.** Racial or national ancestry. **6.** Personnel: *new blood in the organization.* **7.** A dashing young man; dandy. ***—modifier:*** *a blood transfusion.* —*tr.v.* **blood·ed, blood·ing, bloods. 1. a.** To give (a hunting dog) its first taste of blood. **b.** To initiate (a novice hunter) by marking his face with the blood of the prey. **2.** To subject (recruits) to the baptism of fire. —*adj.* Purebred: *a blood mare.* ***—idiom.*** **in cold blood.** Dispassionately; deliberately and coldly. [ME *blod* < OE *blōd,* of Germanic orig.]
blood agar *n.* A culture medium containing whole blood for cultivation of bacteria.
blood bank *n.* **1.** A place where whole blood or plasma is typed, processed, and stored for future use in transfusion. **2.** Blood or plasma stored in a blood bank.
blood bath *n.* A savage and indiscriminate killing; massacre.
blood-brain barrier (blŭd′brān′) *n.* **1.** A physiologic differentiation phenomenon that deaccelerates the penetration of certain substances into the brain while allowing more rapid perfusion into other tissues. **2.** A membrane separating brain tissues from circulating blood.
blood brother *n.* **1.** A brother by birth. **2.** One of two individuals vowed to mutual fidelity and trust by a ceremony involving the mingling of each other's blood. **—blood brotherhood** *n.*
blood clot *n.* A solidified mass of blood caused by polymerization of fibrin molecules and trapped cells.
blood count *n.* **1.** The number of red and white corpuscles in a specific volume of blood. **2.** The determination of a blood count.
blood·cur·dling (blŭd′kûrd′lĭng) *adj.* Causing great horror; terrifying. **—blood′cur′dling·ly** *adv.*
blood·ed (blŭd′ĭd) *adj.* **1.** Having blood or a temperament of a specified kind: *a cold-blooded reptile; a hot-blooded person.* **2.** Thoroughbred.
blood fluke *n.* A schistosome.
blood group *n.* Any of several immunologically distinct, genetically determined classes of human blood, clinically identified by characteristic agglutination reactions.
blood·guilt (blŭd′gĭlt′) *n.* Guilt caused by murder or bloodshed.
blood heat *n.* The usual temperature (98.6°F) of human blood.
blood·hound (blŭd′hound′) *n.* **1.** One of a breed of hounds with a smooth coat, drooping ears, sagging jowls, and a keen sense of smell. **2.** *Informal.* A relentless pursuer.
blood·less (blŭd′lĭs) *adj.* **1.** Lacking or deficient in blood. **2.** Pale and anemic in color. **3.** Achieved without bloodshed. **4.** Lacking in vivacity or spirit. **—blood′less·ly** *adv.* **—blood′less·ness** *n.*
blood·let·ting (blŭd′lĕt′ĭng) *n.* **1.** The bleeding of a vein as a therapeutic measure. **2.** A draining away, as of lifeblood. **3.** Bloodshed. **—blood′let′ter** *n.*
blood·line (blŭd′līn′) *n.* **1.** Direct line of descent. **2.** Pedigree.
blood·mo·bile (blŭd′mə-bēl) *n.* A motor vehicle equipped for collecting blood from donors. [BLOOD + (AUTO)MOBILE.]
blood money *n.* **1.** Money paid as compensation to the next of kin of a murder victim. **2.** Money gained at the cost of another's life or livelihood.
blood plasma *n.* The pale-yellow or gray-yellow, protein-containing fluid portion of the blood in which the corpuscles are normally suspended.
blood platelet *n.* A platelet.
blood poisoning *n.* **1.** Toxemia. **2.** Septicemia.
blood pressure *n.* The pressure of the blood within the arteries, primarily maintained by contraction of the left ventricle.
blood pudding *n.* A sausage prepared from cooked swine's blood and suet.
blood red *n.* A moderate to vivid red. **—blood′-red′** (blŭd′-rĕd′) *adj.*
blood relation *n.* A person who is related by birth rather than by marriage. **—blood relationship** *n.*
blood·root (blŭd′ro͞ot′, -ro͝ot′) *n.* A woodland plant, *Sanguinaria canadensis,* of eastern North America, having a fleshy rootstock, red juice, and a single pale flower.
blood sausage *n.* Blood pudding.
blood serum *n.* Blood plasma with the fibrin removed.
blood·shed (blŭd′shĕd′) *n.* The shedding of blood, esp. the injury or killing of human beings.
blood·shot (blŭd′shŏt′) *adj.* Red and irritated: *bloodshot eyes.*
blood·stain (blŭd′stān′) *n.* A stain caused by blood. —*tr.v.* **-stained, -stain·ing, -stains.** To stain with blood.
blood·stone (blŭd′stōn′) *n.* A variety of deep-green chalcedony flecked with red jasper.
blood stream also **blood·stream** (blŭd′strēm′) *n.* The stream of blood flowing through the circulatory system of a living body.
blood·suck·er (blŭd′sŭk′ər) *n.* **1.** An animal, as a leech, that sucks blood. **2.** One who clings to or preys upon another; parasite. **—blood′suck′ing** *adj.*
blood test *n.* A usually diagnostic examination of a blood sample, esp. to detect syphilis.
blood·thirst·y (blŭd′thûr′stē) *adj.* Thirsting for or characterized by bloodshed; murderous. **—blood′thirst′i·ly** *adv.* **—blood′thirst′i·ness** *n.*
blood type *n.* Blood group.
blood vessel *n.* An elastic, tubular canal, such as an artery, vein, or capillary, through which blood circulates.
blood·worm (blŭd′wûrm′) *n.* Any of various segmented worms of the genera *Polycirrus* and *Enoplobranchus,* having bright-red bodies and often used for bait.
blood·wort (blŭd′wûrt′, -wôrt′) *n.* Any of various chiefly South American plants of the family Haemodoraceae, having roots that contain a red juice.
blood·y (blŭd′ē) *adj.* **-i·er, -i·est. 1.** Stained with blood. **2.** Of, characteristic of, or containing blood. **3.** Accompanied by or giving rise to bloodshed: *a bloody fight.* **4.** Bloodthirsty; cruel. **5.** Suggesting the color of blood; blood-red. **6.** Used as an intensive: *a bloody fool.* —*adv.* Used as an intensive: *bloody well right.* —*tr.v.* **-ied, -y·ing, -ies.** To stain, spot, or color with or as if with blood. **—blood′i·ly** *adv.* **—blood′i·ness** *n.*
bloody mary also **Bloody Mary** *n.* A cocktail usually made of vodka, tomato juice, and seasonings.
bloom¹ (blo͞om) *n.* **1.** The flower or blossoms of a plant. **2. a.** The condition or a time of being in flower: *a rose in bloom.* **b.** A condition or time of vigor, freshness, and beauty; prime: *"the radiant bloom of Greek genius"* (Edith Hamilton). **3.** A fresh, rosy complexion: *"She was short, plump, and fair, with a fine bloom"* (Jane Austen). **4. a.** *Bot.* A delicate, powdery coating, such as that on some fruits, as the plum, or on some leaves and stems. **b.** A similar coating, as on newly minted coins. **5.** An excessive planktonic growth in a body of water. —*v.* **bloomed, bloom·ing, blooms.** —*intr.* **1.** To bear flowers. **2.** To shine with health and vigor; glow. **3.** To grow or flourish. —*tr.* **1.** *Obs.* To cause to flower. **2.** To cause to flourish. [ME *blom* < ON *blōm.*] **—bloom′y** *adj.*
bloom² (blo͞om) *n.* **1.** A bar of steel, usually over 36 square inches in cross section, prepared for rolling. **2.** A mass of wrought iron ready for further working. [ME *blome,* lump of metal < OE *blōma.*]
bloom·er¹ (blo͞o′mər) *n.* **1. a.** A plant that blooms. **b.** One who attains full development of his abilities: *a late bloomer.* **2.** *Slang.* A blunder.
bloo·mer² (blo͞o′mər) *n.* **1.** A costume formerly worn by women and girls that was composed of loose trousers gathered about the ankles and worn under a short skirt. **2. bloomers. a.** Wide, loose trousers gathered at the knee and formerly worn by women and girls as an athletic cos-

blockhouse
Blockhouse at the site of the Battle of Saratoga, showing slits for rifles and openings for downward fire

bloodhound

bloodroot

bloomer²

tume. **b.** Women's underpants of similar design. [After Amelia *Bloomer* (1818–1894).]

bloom·ing (blo͞o′mĭng) *adj. Chiefly Brit. Slang.* Used as an intensive: *a blooming idiot.* [Prob. a euphemism for BLOODY.]

bloop·er (blo͞o′pər) *n.* **1.** *Baseball.* A short, weakly hit fly ball that carries just beyond the infield. **2.** *Informal.* A clumsy mistake, esp. one made in public; faux pas. [< *bloop,* imit. of the sound of such a hit.]

blos·som (blŏs′əm) *n.* **1.** A flower or mass of flowers, esp. of a plant that yields edible fruit. **2.** The condition or time of flowering: *peach trees in blossom.* —*intr.v.* **-somed, -som·ing, -soms. 1.** To come into flower; bloom. **2.** To develop; flourish: *She blossomed into a beauty.* [ME < OE *blōstm.*] **—blos′som·y** *adj.*

blot[1] (blŏt) *n.* **1.** A spot; stain. **2.** A moral stigma; disgrace: *"Let not the name of George the Third be a blot on the page of history"* (Jefferson). —*v.* **blot·ted, blot·ting, blots.** —*tr.* **1.** To spot or stain. **2.** *Obs.* To bring moral disgrace to. **3.** To obliterate; cancel. **4.** To make obscure; darken: *clouds blotting out the moon.* **5.** To dry or soak up with absorbent material. —*intr.* **1.** To spill or spread in a blot. **2.** To become blotted. —***phrasal verb.* blot out.** To destroy utterly; annihilate. [ME.]

blot[2] (blŏt) *n.* **1.** An exposed piece in backgammon. **2.** *Archaic.* A weak point. [Orig. unknown.]

blotch (blŏch) *n.* **1.** A spot or blot; splotch. **2.** A discoloration on the skin; blemish. **3.** Any of various plant diseases caused by fungi and resulting in brown or black dead areas on leaves or fruit. —*tr. & intr.v.* **blotched, blotch·ing, blotch·es.** To mark or become marked with blotches. [Prob. a blend of BLOT and BOTCH.] **—blotch′i·ness** *n.* **—blotch′y** *adj.*

blowtorch

blot·ter (blŏt′ər) *n.* **1.** A piece or pad of blotting paper. **2.** A book containing daily records of occurrences or transactions: *a police blotter.*

blotting paper *n.* Absorbent paper used to blot a surface by soaking up excess ink.

blouse (blous, blouz) *n.* **1.** A woman's or child's loosely fitting shirt extending to the waist or slightly below. **2.** A loosely fitting garment resembling a long shirt, worn esp. by European workmen. **3.** The service coat or tunic worn by members of the U.S. Army. —*intr. & tr.v.* **bloused, blous·ing, blous·es.** To hang or cause to hang loose and full. [Fr.]

blou·son (blou′sŏn′, blo͞o′zŏn′) *n.* A woman's garment, as a dress or blouse, with a fitted waistband over which material blouses. [Fr., dim. of *blouse,* blouse.]

blow[1] (blō) *v.* **blew** (blo͞o), **blown** (blōn), **blow·ing, blows.** —*intr.* **1.** To be in motion, as air. **2.** To move along or be carried by or as if by the wind. **3.** To expel a current of air, as from the mouth or from a bellows. **4.** To produce a sound by expelling a current of air, as in sounding a musical wind instrument. **5.** To breathe hard; pant. **6.** To burn out or melt, as a fuse. **7.** To burst suddenly, as a tire. **8.** To spout water and air, as a whale. **9.** *Slang.* To boast. **10.** *Slang.* To go away; depart. —*tr.* **1.** To cause to move by means of a current of air. **2.** To expel (air) from the mouth. **3.** To cause air to be expelled from. **4.** To drive a current of air on, in, or through. **5.** To clear out or make free of obstruction by forcing air through. **6.** To shape or form (glass, for example) by forcing air or gas through at the end of a pipe. **7. a.** To cause (a wind instrument) to sound. **b.** To sound: *a bugle blowing taps.* **8.** To cause (a horse) to be out of breath. **9.** To cause to explode: *An artillery shell blew apart our headquarters.* **10.** To lay or deposit eggs in. Used of a fly. **11.** To melt or disable (a fuse). **12.** *Slang.* To spend (money) freely. **13.** *Vulgar Slang.* To perform fellatio upon. **14.** *Slang.* To handle ineptly. **15.** *Slang.* To depart in a great hurry: *blew the city.* —***phrasal verbs.* blow away** *Slang.* **1.** To kill by shooting. **2.** To affect intensely; overwhelm. **blow in.** *Slang.* To arrive. **blow off. 1.** To release; let off: *a boiler blowing off steam.* **2.** *Slang.* To relieve through speech or action; give vent to. **blow out. 1.** To extinguish or be extinguished by blowing: *blow out a candle.* **2.** To fail, as an electrical apparatus. **blow over. 1.** To subside: *The storm blew over quickly.* **2.** To be forgotten: *The scandal will soon blow over.* **blow up. 1.** To come into being: *A storm blew up.* **2.** To fill with air; inflate. **3.** To enlarge (a photographic image or print). **4.** *Slang.* To lose one's temper. —*n.* **1. a.** A blast of air or wind. **b.** A storm. **2.** The act or an instance of blowing. **3.** *Slang.* An act of bragging. —***idioms.* blow hot and cold.** To change one's opinion often on a given matter; vacillate. **blow off steam.** To give vent to one's anger or other pent-up emotion. **blow (one's) mind.** To affect with intense emotion, as amazement, excitement, or shock. [ME *blowen* < OE *blāwan.*]

blow[2] (blō) *n.* **1.** A sudden hard stroke or hit, as with the fist or an instrument. **2.** A sudden unexpected shock or calamity. **3.** A sudden unexpected attack. —***idiom.* come to blows.** To begin to fight. [ME *blaw.*]

blow[3] (blō) *n.* A mass of blossoms: *peach blow.* —*intr. & tr.v.* **blew** (blo͞o), **blown** (blōn), **blow·ing, blows.** To bloom or cause to bloom. [ME *blowen* < OE *blōwan.*]

blow·ball (blō′bôl′) *n.* A fluffy seed ball, such as that of a dandelion.

blow-by-blow (blō′-bī-blō′) *adj.* Marked by close attention to details: *a blow-by-blow description.*

blow-dry (blō′drī′) *tr.v.* **-dried, -dry·ing, -dries.** To dry and often style with a hand-held hair dryer: *blow-dry damp hair.*

blow·er (blō′ər) *n.* **1.** One that blows, esp. a mechanical device such as a fan. **2.** *Slang.* A braggart. **3.** *Chiefly Brit. Slang.* A telephone.

blow·fish (blō′fĭsh′) *n., pl.* **blowfish** or **-fish·es.** The puffer (sense 2).

blow·fly (blō′flī′) *n.* Any of several flies of the family Calliphoridae that deposit their eggs in carcasses or carrion or in open sores and wounds.

blow·gun (blō′gŭn′) *n.* A long narrow pipe through which darts or pellets may be blown.

blow·hard (blō′härd′) *n. Slang.* A boaster; braggart.

blow·hole (blō′hōl′) *n.* **1.** A nostril at the highest point on the head of whales and other cetaceans. **2.** A hole in ice to which aquatic mammals, as dolphins, come to breathe. **3.** A vent to permit the escape of air or other gas.

blow·job (blō′jŏb′) *n. Vulgar Slang.* An act or instance of fellatio.

blown[1] (blōn) *v.* Past participle of **blow**[1]. —*adj.* **1.** Swollen or inflated; distended. **2.** Out-of-breath; panting. **3.** Flyblown. **4.** Formed by blowing: *blown glass.*

blown[2] (blōn) *v.* Past participle of **blow**[3]. —*adj.* Completely expanded or opened: *a full-blown flower.*

blow·out (blō′out′) *n.* **1. a.** A sudden rupture or bursting, as of an automobile tire. **b.** The hole made by such a rupture. **2.** A sudden escape of a confined gas. **3.** *Slang.* A large party or social affair.

blow·pipe (blō′pīp′) *n.* **1.** A metal tube in which a flow of gas is mixed with a controlled flow of air to concentrate the heat of a flame. **2.** A blowgun. **3.** A long, narrow iron pipe used to gather, work, and blow molten glass.

blow·sy (blou′zē) *adj.* Variant of **blowzy.**

blow·torch (blō′tôrch′) *n.* A usually portable gas burner that produces a flame typically hot enough to melt soft metals.

blow·up (blō′ŭp′) *n.* **1.** An explosion. **2.** A violent outburst of temper. **3.** A photographic enlargement.

blow·y (blō′ē) *adj.* **-i·er, -i·est.** Windy; breezy.

blow·zy also **blow·sy** (blou′zē) *adj.* **-zi·er, -zi·est** also **-si·er, -si·est. 1.** Having a coarsely ruddy and bloated appearance. **2.** Disheveled and frowzy; unkempt. [< Obs. *blowze,* beggar wench.]

BLT (bē′ĕl-tē′) *n.* A bacon, lettuce, and tomato sandwich.

blub·ber[1] (blŭb′ər) *v.* **-bered, -ber·ing, -bers.** —*intr.* To weep and sob noisily. —*tr.* **1.** To utter while crying and sobbing. **2.** To make wet and swollen by weeping. —*n.* A loud weeping and sobbing. [ME *bluberen,* to bubble < *bluber,* foam.] **—blub′ber·er** *n.* **—blub′ber·ing·ly** *adv.*

blub·ber[2] (blŭb′ər) *n.* **1.** The thick layer of fat between the skin and the muscle layers of whales and other marine mammals. **2.** Excessive body fat. **3.** A large invertebrate sea nettle or medusa. —*adj.* Swollen and protruding. [ME *bluber,* foam.] **—blub′ber·y** *adj.*

blu·cher (blo͞o′chər, -kər) *n.* **1.** A high shoe or half boot. **2.** A shoe having the vamp and tongue made of one piece and the top lapping over the vamp. [After Gebhard L. von *Blücher* (1742–1819).]

bludg·eon (blŭj′ən) *n.* A short, heavy club, usually of wood, that has one end loaded or thicker than the other. —*tr.v.* **-eoned, -eon·ing, -eons. 1.** To hit with or as if with a club or bludgeon. **2.** To threaten or bully. [Orig. unknown.] **—bludg′eon·er, bludg′eon·eer′** (-ə-nîr′) *n.*

blue (blo͞o) *n.* **1.** Any of a group of colors that may vary in lightness and saturation, whose hue is that of a clear sky; the hue of that portion of the spectrum lying between green and violet; one of the additive or light primaries; one of the psychological primary hues, evoked in the normal observer by radiant energy of wavelength approximately 475 nanometers. **2. a.** A pigment or dye imparting the color blue. **b.** Bluing. **3. a.** An object of the color blue. **b.** Blue dress or clothing: *the girls in blue.* **4.** A person who wears a blue uniform. **5.** Often **Blue. a.** A member of the Union Army in the Civil War. **b.** The Union Army. **6. blues.** The blue uniform of the U.S. Navy. **7.** A small blue butterfly of the family Lycaenidae. **8. a.** The sky. **b.** The sea. —*adj.* **blu·er, blu·est. 1.** Of the color blue. **2.** Bluish or having parts that are blue or bluish: *a blue spruce; the blue whale.* **3.** Having a gray or purplish color, as from cold or contusion. **4.** Wearing blue. **5. a.** Gloomy; depressed. **b.** Dismal; dreary: *a blue day.* **6.** Puritanical; strict. **7.** Aristocratic; patrician. **8.** Indecent; risqué: *a blue joke.* —*tr. & intr.v.* **blued, blu·ing, blues.** To make or become blue. —***idioms.* once in a blue moon.** Very seldom; rarely. **out of the blue. 1.** From an unexpected or unforeseen source. **2.** At a completely unexpected time. [ME < OFr. *bleu,* of Germanic orig.] **—blue′ly** *adv.* **—blue′ness** *n.*

blue baby *n.* An infant born with bluish skin caused by inadequate oxygenation of the blood, a symptom of a congenital cardiac or pulmonary defect.

blue·beard (blo͞o′bîrd′) *n.* A man who first marries and then murders one wife after another. [< *Bluebeard,* a character in a folk tale.]

blue·bell (blo͞o′bĕl′) *n.* Any of various plants having blue, bell-shaped flowers, esp.: **a.** A European plant, *Scilla non-*

scripta, having grasslike leaves and a one-sided cluster of fragrant, blue-violet flowers. **b.** The harebell. **c.** Any of various plants of the genus *Mertensia.*
blue·ber·ry (blo͞o'bĕr'ē) *n.* **1.** Any of several North American shrubs of the genus *Vaccinium,* having small, urn-shaped flowers and edible berries. **2.** The juicy blue, purplish, or blackish berry of a blueberry shrub.
blue·bill (blo͞o'bĭl') *n.* The scaup.
blue·bird (blo͞o'bûrd') *n.* Any of several North American birds of the genus *Sialia,* having blue plumage and in the male of most species a rust-colored breast.
blue-black (blo͞o'blăk') *adj.* Being very dark blue in color.
blue blood *n.* **1.** Noble or aristocratic descent. **2.** A member of the aristocracy or other high social group. [Transl. of Sp. *sangre azul;* prob. from the visible veins of fair-complexioned aristocrats.] **—blue'-blood'ed** *adj.*
blue·blos·som (blo͞o'blŏs'əm) *n.* A shrub, *Ceanothus thyrsiflorus,* of the west coast of the United States, having profuse clusters of small blue flowers.
blue·bon·net (blo͞o'bŏn'ĭt) *n.* **1. a.** A plant, *Lupinus subcarnosus,* of Texas and adjacent regions, having compound leaves and clusters of blue flowers. **b.** Any of several other plants similar to the bluebonnet and having blue flowers. **2. a.** A broad, blue woolen cap worn in Scotland. **b.** A person wearing such a cap.
blue book also **blue·book** (blo͞o'bo͝ok') *n.* **1.** An official list of persons in the employ of the U.S. government. **2.** *Informal.* A book listing the names of socially prominent people. **3.** A blank notebook with blue covers in which to write college examinations.
blue·bot·tle (blo͞o'bŏt'l) *n.* **1.** Any of several flies of the genus *Calliphora,* having a bright metallic-blue body and breeding in decaying organic matter. **2.** The cornflower.
blue cheese *n.* A semisoft cheese made of cow's milk, having a greenish-blue mold and flavor similar to Roquefort cheese.
blue chip *n.* **1.** A stock that sells at a high price because of public confidence in its long record of steady earnings. **2.** An extremely valuable asset or property.
blue·coat (blo͞o'kōt') *n.* A person who wears a blue uniform, esp. a policeman.
blue cohosh *n.* A plant, *Caulophyllum thalictroides,* of eastern North America, having compound leaves and a cluster of greenish or purplish flowers.
blue-col·lar (blo͞o'kŏl'ər) *adj.* Of or pertaining to wage earners, esp. as a class, whose jobs are performed in work clothes and often involve manual labor.
blue·curls also **blue curls** (blo͞o'kûrlz') *n. (used with a sing. or pl. verb).* Any of several North American plants of the genus *Trichostema,* having blue, two-lipped flowers with long, curved stamens.
blue devils *pl.n. Informal.* A feeling of depression or despondency.
blue-eyed grass (blo͞o'īd') *n.* Any of various plants of the genus *Sisyrinchium,* mostly of North America, having grass-like leaves and small, starlike blue flowers.
blue-eyed Mary *n.* A plant, *Collinsia verna,* of eastern North America, having two-lipped blue and white flowers.
blue·fish (blo͞o'fĭsh') *n., pl.* **bluefish** or **-fish·es. 1.** A voracious food and game fish, *Pomatomus saltatrix,* of temperate and tropical waters of the Atlantic and Indian oceans. **2.** Any of various fishes that are predominantly blue in color.
blue flag *n.* Any of several wild irises having blue flowers, esp. *Iris versicolor,* of eastern North America.
blue fox *n.* **1.** The arctic fox during its summer color phase, when its pelt is bluish gray. **2.** The fur of a blue fox.
blue·gill (blo͞o'gĭl') *n.* A common, edible sunfish, *Lepomis macrochirus,* of North American lakes and streams.
blue·grass (blo͞o'grăs') *n.* **1.** Any of several grasses of the genus *Poa,* esp. *P. pratensis,* native to Eurasia but naturalized throughout North America. **2.** A type of folk music that originated in the southern United States, typically played on banjos and guitars and characterized by rapid tempos and jazzlike improvisation.
blue-green alga (blo͞o'grēn') *n.* An alga of the division Cyanophyta (or Myxophyceae), considered to be among the simplest forms of plants.
blue grouse *n.* A wildfowl, *Dendragapus obscurus,* of western North America, having predominantly gray plumage.
blue gum *n.* A tall timber tree, *Eucalyptus globulus,* native to Australia, having aromatic leaves and outer bark that peels off in shreds.
blue·head (blo͞o'hĕd') *n.* A marine fish, *Thalassoma bifasciatum,* of tropical Atlantic waters, of which the male has a blue head and a green body.
blue·hearts (blo͞o'härts') *n. (used with a sing. or pl. verb).* A hairy plant, *Buchnera americana,* of central North America, having a spike of deep-purple flowers.
blue heron *n.* Any of several varieties of heron with blue or blue-gray plumage.
blue·ing (blo͞o'ĭng) *n.* Variant of **bluing.**
blue·ish (blo͞o'ĭsh) *adj.* Variant of **bluish.**
blue·jack (blo͞o'jăk') *n.* An oak tree, *Quercus cinerea,* of the southern United States, having narrow, unlobed leaves. [BLUE + (BLACK)JACK[1]]
blue·jack·et (blo͞o'jăk'ĭt) *n.* An enlisted man in the U.S. or British Navy; sailor.
blue jay *n.* A North American bird, *Cyanocitta cristata,* having a crested head and predominantly blue plumage.
blue jeans *pl.n.* Jeans (sense 2).
blue law *n.* **1.** One of a body of laws in colonial New England designed to enforce certain moral standards. **2.** A law designed to regulate Sunday activities.
blue mold *n.* Any of several fungi of the genus *Penicillium,* forming a bluish growth on food and other surfaces.
blue·nose (blo͞o'nōz') *n.* A puritanical person.
blue note *n. Mus.* A flatted note, esp. the third or seventh note of a chord, in place of an expected major interval. [From its use in blues music.]
blue-pen·cil (blo͞o'pĕn'səl) *tr.v.* **-ciled, -cil·ing, -cils** also **-cilled, -cil·ling, -cils.** To edit, revise, or correct with or as if with a blue pencil.
blue pe·ter (pē'tər) *n.* A blue flag with a white square in the center, flown to signal that a ship is ready to sail.
blue-plate (blo͞o'plāt') *adj.* Being a main course of a restaurant meal usually offered at a special price: *a blue-plate luncheon.*
blue point *n.* A type of edible oyster found chiefly off Blue Point, Great South Bay, Long Island, New York.
blue·print (blo͞o'prĭnt') *n.* **1.** A photographic reproduction, as of architectural plans or technical drawings, rendered as white lines on a blue background. **2.** A carefully designed plan. *—tr.v.* **-print·ed, -print·ing, -prints. 1.** To make a blueprint of. **2.** To lay a plan for.
blue ribbon *n.* **1.** A blue ribbon awarded as the first prize in a competition. **2.** An award or honor given for excellence. **—blue'-rib'bon** *adj.*
blue-rib·bon jury (blo͞o'rĭb'ən) *n.* A jury whose members have been selected as possessing special qualifications, as intelligence, that enable them to deal with complex legal issues.
blues (blo͞oz) *pl.n. (used with a sing. or pl. verb).* **1.** A state of depression or melancholy. **2.** A style of jazz evolved from southern American Negro secular songs and usually distinguished by slow tempo and flatted thirds and sevenths. [Short for BLUE DEVILS.]
blue shift *n.* An apparent decrease in the wavelength of radiation emitted by an approaching celestial body as a consequence of the Doppler effect.
blue-sky law (blo͞o'skī') *n.* A law designed to protect the public from buying fraudulent securities.
blue spruce *n.* An evergreen tree, *Picea pungens,* of the Rocky Mountain region, having bluish-green needles.
blues-rock (blo͞oz'rŏk') *n.* A style of music that combines the blues and rock 'n' roll.
blue·stock·ing (blo͞o'stŏk'ĭng) *n.* A pedantic or scholarly woman. [After the *Blue Stocking* Society, a nickname for a predominantly female literary club of 18th-cent. London.] **—blue'stock'ing** *adj.*
blue·stone (blo͞o'stōn') *n.* **1.** A bluish-gray sandstone used for paving and building. **2.** A stone similar to the bluestone.
blue streak *n. Informal.* **1.** Something moving very fast. **2.** A rapid and seemingly interminable stream of words.
blu·ets (blo͞o'ĭts) *n. (used with a sing. or pl. verb).* A slender, low-growing plant, *Houstonia caerulea,* of eastern North America, having small, light-blue flowers with yellow centers. [< Fr. *bluet,* cornflower.]
blue vitriol *n.* Copper sulfate.
blue·weed (blo͞o'wēd') *n.* Viper's bugloss.
blue whale *n.* A very large whale, *Sibbaldus musculus,* having a bluish-gray back and longitudinal grooves along the throat and belly.
bluff[1] (blŭf) *v.* **bluffed, bluff·ing, bluffs.** *—tr.* **1.** To mislead, deceive, or hoodwink. **2.** To impress, deter, or intimidate by a display of confidence greater than the facts support. **3.** To try to mislead (opponents) in poker by heavy betting on a poor hand or by little or no betting on a good one. *—intr.* To engage in a false display of strength or confidence. *—n.* **1.** The act or practice of bluffing. **2.** One who bluffs. **—*idiom.* call (someone's) bluff.** To challenge or expose a false display of strength or confidence. [Perh. < Du. *bluffen,* to boast.] **—bluff'a·ble** *adj.* **—bluff'er** *n.*
bluff[2] (blŭf) *n.* A steep headland, promontory, river bank, or cliff. *—adj.* **-er, -est. 1.** Having a broad, steep front. **2.** Having a rough and blunt but not unkind manner. [Orig. unknown.] **—bluff'ly** *adv.* **—bluff'ness** *n.*
blu·ing also **blue·ing** (blo͞o'ĭng) *n.* **1.** Any of various coloring agents used to counteract the yellowing of laundered fabrics. **2.** A rinsing agent used to give a silver tint to graying hair.
blu·ish also **blue·ish** (blo͞o'ĭsh) *adj.* Somewhat or slightly blue. **—blu'ish·ness** *n.*
blun·der (blŭn'dər) *n.* A stupid and serious mistake usually caused by ignorance, stupidity, or confusion. *—v.* **-dered, -der·ing, -ders.** *—intr.* **1.** To move awkwardly or clumsily. **2.** To make a blunder. *—tr.* **1.** To botch or bungle. **2.** To say stupidly or thoughtlessly. [ME *blunderen,* to go blindly, prob. < ON *blunda,* to doze.] **—blun'der·er** *n.* **—blun'der·ing·ly** *adv.*
blun·der·buss (blŭn'dər-bŭs') *n.* **1.** A short musket of wide bore and flaring muzzle, formerly used to scatter shot at

blueberry

blue jay

close range. **2.** A stupid, clumsy person. [Alteration of Du. *donderbus* : *donder,* thunder (< MDu. *doner*) + *bus,* gun (< MDu. *busse,* tube < Lat. *buxis,* box).]

blunt (blŭnt) *adj.* **-er, -est. 1.** Having a dull edge or end; not sharp. **2.** Abrupt and frank in manner; brusque. **3.** Slow to understand or perceive; dull. **4.** Lacking in feeling; insensitive. —*v.* **blunt·ed, blunt·ing, blunts.** —*tr.* **1.** To dull the edge of. **2.** To make less effective; weaken: *"Division of purpose blunted our offensive spirit"* (T.E. Lawrence). —*intr.* To become blunt. [ME.] **—blunt'ly** *adv.* **—blunt'ness** *n.*

blur (blûr) *v.* **blurred, blur·ring, blurs.** —*tr.* **1.** To make indistinct and hazy in outline or appearance; obscure. **2.** To smear or stain; smudge. **3.** To lessen the perception of; dim. —*intr.* **1.** To become indistinct. **2.** To make blurs. —*n.* **1.** A smear or blot; smudge. **2.** Something that is hazy and indistinct. [Orig. unknown.] **—blur'ri·ness** *n.* **—blur'ry** *adj.*

blurb (blûrb) *n.* A brief publicity notice, as on a book jacket. [Coined by Gelett Burgess (1866–1951).]

blurt (blûrt) *tr.v.* **blurt·ed, blurt·ing, blurts.** To utter suddenly and impulsively: *blurt out a confession.* [Prob. imit.]

blush (blŭsh) *intr.v.* **blushed, blush·ing, blush·es. 1.** To become red in the face esp. from modesty, embarrassment, or shame; flush. **2.** To become red or rosy. **3.** To feel embarrassed or ashamed: *blushed at his own audacity.* —*n.* **1.** A reddening of the face esp. from modesty, embarrassment, or shame. **2.** A red or rosy color. ***—idiom.*** **at (or on) first blush.** At first sight or glance. [ME *blushen* < OE *blyscan.*] **—blush'ful** *adj.* **—blush'ing·ly** *adv.*

blush·er (blŭsh'ər) *n.* **1.** One that blushes. **2.** Make-up used on the face and esp. on the cheekbones to give a usually rosy tint.

blus·ter (blŭs'tər) *v.* **-tered, -ter·ing, -ters.** —*intr.* **1.** To blow in loud, violent gusts, as wind in a storm. **2.** To speak or act with noisy boasts or threats. —*tr.* To force or bully with swaggering threats. —*n.* **1.** A violent, gusty wind. **2.** Turbulence or noisy confusion. **3.** Noisily boastful or threatening talk. [ME *blusteren* < MLG *blüsteren.*] **—blus'ter·er** *n.* **—blus'ter·y, blus'ter·ous** *adj.*

boa constrictor

bo (bō) *n., pl.* **bos.** *Slang.* A fellow; pal. [Prob. short for BOY.]

bo·a (bō'ə) *n.* **1.** Any of various large, nonvenomous, chiefly tropical snakes of the family Boidae, which includes the pythons, anaconda, boa constrictor, and other snakes that coil around and suffocate their prey. **2.** A long, fluffy scarf made of soft material such as feathers. [NLat. *Boa,* genus name < Lat. *boa,* a large water snake.]

boa constrictor *n.* A large, nonvenomous snake, *Constrictor constrictor,* of tropical America, having brown markings.

boar
Wild Russian boars

boar (bôr, bōr) *n.* **1.** An uncastrated male pig. **2.** A wild pig, *Sus scrofa,* of Eurasia and northern Africa, that has dense, dark bristles and is the ancestor of the domestic hog. [ME *bor* < OE *bār.*] **—boar'ish** *adj.* **—boar'ish·ness** *n.*

board (bôrd, bōrd) *n.* **1.** A long, flat slab of sawed lumber; plank. **2.** A flat piece of wood or similarly rigid material adapted for a special use. **3.** A flat surface on which a game is played. **4.** The hard pasteboard cover of a book. **5. boards.** A theater stage. **6. a.** A table, esp. one set for serving food. **b.** Food or meals collectively: *board and lodging.* **7.** A table at which official meetings are held; council table. **8.** An organized body of administrators or investigators: *a board of trustees.* **9.** An electrical-equipment panel. **10.** *Obs.* A border or edge. **11. boards.** The wooden structure enclosing an ice-hockey rink. **12.** *Naut.* **a.** The side of a ship. **b.** A leeboard. **c.** A centerboard. —*v.* **board·ed, board·ing, boards.** —*tr.* **1.** To cover or close with boards: *board up a door.* **2. a.** To furnish with meals in return for pay. **b.** To house where board is furnished. **3.** To enter or go aboard (a vehicle or ship). **4.** To come alongside (a ship). **5.** *Obs.* To approach. —*intr.* To receive meals in return for pay. ***—idioms.*** **across the board. 1.** Designating a bet that a horse or dog will win, place, or show. **2.** Affecting all members, divisions, or categories equally. **go by the board. 1.** To be swept overboard. **2.** To be ruined, unnoticed, or ignored. **on board.** Aboard. [ME *bord* < OE.]

boatbill

board·er (bôr'dər, bōr'-) *n.* One who boards, esp. one who pays a stipulated sum in return for regular meals or meals and lodging.

board foot *n., pl.* **board feet.** A unit of lumber measurement equal to one foot square by one inch thick.

board game *n.* A game of strategy, as chess or backgammon, played by moving pieces on a board.

boarding house also **board·ing·house** (bôr'dĭng-hous', bōr'-) *n.* A house that provides meals and lodging.

boarding school *n.* A school where pupils are provided with meals and lodging.

board measure *n.* Measurement in board feet.

board of education *n.* A school board.

board of trade *n.* **1.** An association of bankers and businessmen to promote common commercial interests. **2. Board of Trade.** A British governmental committee dealing with problems of trade and commerce.

board rule *n.* A measuring stick for determining board feet.

board·walk (bôrd'wôk', bōrd'-) *n.* **1.** A walk made of wooden planks. **2.** A promenade, esp. of planks, along a beach or waterfront.

bobcat

boast[1] (bōst) *v.* **boast·ed, boast·ing, boasts.** —*intr.* To speak with excessive pride about one's own accomplishments, talents, or possessions; brag. —*tr.* **1.** To speak about with excessive pride. **2.** To take pride in or be enhanced by the possession of: *The college boasts a fine new auditorium.* **3.** To possess; have. —*n.* **1.** The act or an instance of bragging. **2.** A source of pride. [ME *bosten* < *bost,* brag.] **—boast'er** *n.* **—boast'ful** *adj.* **—boast'ful·ly** *adv.* **—boast'ful·ness** *n.*

Synonyms: *boast, brag, crow, vaunt. Boast* is the most general of the verbs for the expression of vanity, primarily by vocal means. *Brag,* used in more informal contexts, implies exaggerated claims, blatancy, and often an air of insolence. *Crow,* also informal in tone, stresses exultation and noisy rejoicing over a victory or achievement. *Vaunt* is distinctive in emphasizing ostentatious display as strongly as vocal extravagance; it is appropriate to formal usage and often appears as the participle *vaunted,* used as an attributive adjective.

boast[2] (bōst) *tr.v.* **boast·ed, boast·ing, boasts.** To shape or form (stone) roughly with a broad chisel. [Orig. unknown.]

boat (bōt) *n.* **1.** A relatively small, usually open craft. **2.** A ship. **3.** A dish shaped like a boat: *a gravy boat.* —*v.* **boat·ed, boat·ing, boats.** —*intr.* To travel by boat. —*tr.* **1.** To transport by boat. **2.** To place in a boat. **3.** To ride a boat for pleasure. ***—idiom.*** **in the same boat.** In the same situation. [ME *boot* < OE *bāt.*]

boat·bill (bōt'bĭl') *n.* A tropical American wading bird, *Cochlearius cochlearius,* having a large bill shaped like an inverted boat.

boat·er (bō'tər) *n.* **1.** One who boats. **2.** A stiff straw hat with a flat crown.

boat hook *n.* A pole with a metal point and hook at one end used esp. to maneuver logs, rafts, and boats.

boat·house (bōt'hous') *n.* A house in which boats are kept.

boat·load (bōt'lōd') *n.* The number of passengers or quantity of cargo that a boat can safely carry.

boat·man (bōt'mən) *n.* One who works on, deals with, or operates boats. **—boat'man·ship'** *n.*

boat·swain also **bo's'n** or **bos'n** or **bo·sun** (bō'sən) *n.* A warrant officer or petty officer in charge of a ship's deck crew, rigging, anchors, and cables. [ME *botswein* < OE *bātswān.*]

boat-tailed grackle (bōt'tāld') *n.* A bird, *Cassidix mexicanus,* of the southern United States and Mexico, that has a long tail and the male of which has glossy black plumage.

boat train *n.* A train that regularly carries passengers between a city and a port.

bob[1] (bŏb) *v.* **bobbed, bob·bing, bobs.** —*tr.* **1.** To hit lightly and quickly; tap. **2.** To cause to move up and down: *bobbed his head.* —*intr.* **1.** To move up and down: *a cork bobbing on the water.* **2.** To grab at floating or hanging objects with the teeth: *bobbed for apples.* **3.** To curtsy or bow. ***—phrasal verb.*** **bob up.** To appear or arise unexpectedly or suddenly. —*n.* **1.** A tap or light blow. **2.** A quick, jerky movement of the head or body. [ME *bobben.*]

bob[2] (bŏb) *n.* **1.** A small knoblike pendent object, as a plumb bob. **2.** A fishing float or cork. **3.** A small lock or curl of hair. **4.** A short haircut on a woman or child. **5.** The docked tail of a horse. **6. a.** A bobsled. **b.** A bob skate. —*v.* **bobbed, bob·bing, bobs.** —*intr.* **1.** To fish with a bob. —*tr.* **2.** To cut short: *bobbed her hair.* [ME *bobbe.*] **—bob'ber** *n.*

bob[3] (bŏb) *n., pl.* **bob.** *Chiefly Brit. Slang.* A shilling. [Orig. unknown.]

bob·bin (bŏb'ĭn) *n.* **1.** A spool or reel that holds thread or yarn for spinning, weaving, knitting, sewing, or making lace. **2.** Narrow braid used as trimming. [Fr. *bobine.*]

bob·bi·net (bŏb'ə-nĕt') *n.* A machine-woven net fabric with hexagonal meshes. [BOBBI(N) + NET.]

bobbin lace *n.* An intricate handmade lace made by interlacing thread around small notched pins or bobbins stuck into a pillow.

bob·ble (bŏb'əl) *v.* **-bled, -bling, -bles.** —*intr.* To bob up and down. —*tr.* To fumble (a ball, for example). —*n.* A mistake; blunder. [Freq. of BOB[1].]

bob·by (bŏb'ē) *n., pl.* **-bies.** *Chiefly Brit. Slang.* A policeman. [After Sir *Robert* Peel (1788–1850).]

bobby pin *n.* A small metal hair clip with the ends pressed tightly together. [< BOB[2].]

bobby socks also **bobby sox** *pl.n. Informal.* Ankle socks worn by girls or women.

bob·by·sox·er also **bobby sox·er** (bŏb'ē-sŏk'sər) *n. Informal.* A teen-age girl of the 1940's who followed current fads.

bob·cat (bŏb'kăt') *n.* A wild cat, *Lynx rufus,* of North America, having spotted reddish-brown fur, tufted ears, and a short tail. [From its short tail.]

bob·o·link (bŏb'ə-lĭngk') *n.* An American migratory songbird, *Dolichonyx oryzivorus,* of which the male has black, white, and yellowish plumage. [Imit. of its cry.]

bob skate *n.* A skate with two parallel bearing edges.

bob·sled (bŏb'slĕd') *n.* **1.** A long racing sled with a steering mechanism controlling the front runners. **2. a.** A long sled made of two shorter sleds joined in tandem. **b.** Either of these two smaller sleds. —*intr.v.* **-sled·ded, -sled·ding, -sleds.** To ride or race in a bobsled.

bob·stay (bŏb'stā') *n.* A rope or chain used to steady the bowsprit of a ship. [Prob. < BOB[1].]

bob·tail (bŏb'tāl') *n.* **1.** A short or shortened tail. **2.** A horse or other animal having a bobtail. **3.** Something that has been cut short or abbreviated. **—bob'tailed'** *adj.*

bob·white (bŏb-hwīt', -wīt') *n.* A small North American quail, *Colinus virginianus,* having brown plumage with white markings. [Imit. of its cry.]

bo·cac·cio (bə-kä'chō, -chē-ō') *n., pl.* **-cios.** A rockfish, *Sebastodes paucispinis,* of American Pacific waters. [Mex. Sp., prob. < Sp. *bocachón,* big mouth, aug. of *boca,* mouth.]

boc·cie or **boc·ci** or **boc·ce** (bŏch'ē) *n.* A game of Italian origin similar to bowling that is played with wooden balls on a long narrow dirt or clay court. [Ital. *bocce,* pl. of *boccia,* ball.]

bock (bŏk) *n.* Bock beer.

bock beer *n.* A strong dark beer, the first that is drawn from the vats in springtime. [G. *Bockbier,* alteration of *Einbecker Bier,* after *Einbeck,* West Germany.]

bod (bŏd) *n. Slang.* Body.

bode[1] (bōd) *tr.v.* **bod·ed, bod·ing, bodes. 1.** To be an omen of: *a heavy sea that boded trouble for the small ship.* **2.** *Archaic.* To predict; foretell. [ME *boden* < OE *bodian,* to announce < *boda,* messenger.]

bode[2] (bōd) *v.* A past tense of **bide.**

bo·de·ga (bō-dā'gə) *n.* **1.** A small grocery store, sometimes combined with a wineshop. **2.** A warehouse for wine storage. [Sp. < Lat. *apotheca,* storehouse. —see APOTHECARY.]

bo·dhi·satt·va (bō'dĭ-sŭt'və) *n. Buddhism.* One who, out of compassion, forgoes nirvana in order to save others. [Skt. : *bodhih,* perfect knowledge + *sattvam,* reality.]

bod·ice (bŏd'ĭs) *n.* **1.** The fitted part of a dress that extends from the waist to the shoulder. **2.** A woman's laced outer garment, worn like a vest over a blouse. **3.** *Obs.* A corset. [Var. of *bodies,* pl. of BODY.]

bod·ied (bŏd'ēd) *adj.* Having a body, esp. of a specified kind: *strong-bodied.*

bod·i·less (bŏd'ē-lĭs) *adj.* Having no body, form, or substance; incorporeal.

bod·i·ly (bŏd'l-ē) *adj.* **1.** Of, pertaining to, within, or exhibited by the body: *bodily organs.* **2.** Physical as opposed to mental or spiritual: *bodily welfare.* —*adv.* **1.** In the flesh; in person: *bodily but not mentally present.* **2.** As a complete physical entity: *carried her bodily from the room.*

bod·ing (bō'dĭng) *n.* An omen or foreboding, esp. of evil.

bod·kin (bŏd'kĭn) *n.* **1.** A small, sharply pointed instrument for making holes in fabric or leather. **2.** A blunt needle for pulling tape or ribbon through a series of loops or a hem. **3.** A long hairpin, usually with an ornamental head. **4.** *Printing.* An awl or pick for extracting letters from set type. **5.** *Archaic.* A dagger or stiletto. [ME *boidekyn.*]

bod·y (bŏd'ē) *n., pl.* **-ies. 1. a.** The entire material structure and substance of an organism, esp. of a human being or an animal. **b.** The soma or physical part of man as distinguished from the mind or spirit. **c.** A corpse or carcass. **2. a.** The trunk or torso of a human being or animal. **b.** The part of a garment covering the torso. **3.** *Law.* **a.** A person. **b.** A group of individuals regarded as an entity; corporation. **4.** A number of persons, concepts, or things regarded collectively; group: *We walked out in a body.* **5.** The main or central part of something, as: **a.** The nave of a church. **b.** The content of a book or document exclusive of prefatory matter, codicils, indexes, or appendices. **c.** The passenger- and cargo-carrying part of an aircraft, ship, or vehicle. **d.** The sound box of a musical instrument. **6.** A bounded aggregate of matter: *a body of water.* **7.** Consistency of substance, as in paint, textiles, or wine: *a sauce with body.* **8.** *Printing.* The part of a block of type underlying the impression surface. —*tr.v.* **-ied, -y·ing, -ies. 1.** To furnish with a body. **2.** To give shape to. [ME < OE *bodig.*]

Synonyms: *body, corpse, remains, carcass, cadaver. Body* denotes the physical organism of a person or animal, alive or dead. *Corpse* and *remains* apply to the body of a dead person. *Carcass* primarily denotes the body of a dead animal; it is applied to a person, alive or dead, only derogatorily or humorously. *Cadaver* is a corpse used for dissection and study. *Remains* is considered genteel by some; others find its literal connotations clinical and rather grisly.

body bag *n.* A zippered usually rubber bag for transporting a human corpse.

body building *n.* The practice of developing the body through physical exercise and diet, esp. for competitive exhibition. **—body builder** *n.*

body cavity *n.* The coelom.

body corporate *n. Law.* A corporation (sense 1.a.).

body count *n.* A count of individual bodies, as those killed by enemy soldiers.

body English *n.* **1.** The natural or instinctive tendency of a person to try to influence the movement of a propelled object, such as a ball, by twisting his body toward the desired goal. **2.** The usually irregular movement or spin of a propelled object as if it were influenced by body English.

bod·y·guard (bŏd'ē-gärd') *n.* A person or group of persons, usually armed, responsible for the physical safety of one or more specific persons.

body language *n.* The bodily gestures, postures, and facial expressions by which an individual communicates nonverbally with others.

body louse *n.* A parasitic louse, *Pediculus humanus,* afflicting humans.

body politic *n.* The people collectively of a politically organized nation or state.

body shirt *n.* **1.** A woman's top that is made with a sewn-in or snapped crotch. **2.** A tight-fitting shirt or blouse.

body shop *n.* A shop or garage where the bodies of automotive vehicles are repaired.

body snatcher *n.* A person who steals corpses from graves.

body stocking *n.* A tight-fitting usually one-piece garment that covers the torso and sometimes has sleeves and legs.

body suit *n.* A tight-fitting one-piece garment for the torso.

bod·y·surf (bŏd'ē-sûrf') *intr.v.* **-surfed, -surf·ing, -surfs.** To ride on a wave without a surfboard. **—bod'y·surf'er** *n.*

body wall *n.* The external animal body surface made up of ectoderm and mesoderm, which encloses the body cavity.

body work *n.* The act or process of repairing the bodies of automotive vehicles.

boehm·ite (bā'mīt', bō'-) *n.* A white to dark reddish brown orthorhombic mineral, ALO(OH), present in bauxite. [G. *Böhmit,* after J. *Böhm,* 20th-cent. German scientist.]

Boer (bōr, bôr, bo͝or) *n.* A Dutch colonist or descendant of a Dutch colonist in South Africa. [Du., farmer < MDu. *gheboer.*]

bof·fo (bŏf'ō) *adj.* Extremely successful, excellent; great. [Short for slang *boffola,* hit, success.]

Bo·fors gun (bō'fôrz', bo͞o'-) *n.* A double-barreled, automatic antiaircraft gun. [After *Bofors,* Sweden.]

bog (bôg, bŏg) *n.* Soft, waterlogged ground; marsh. —*v.* **bogged, bog·ging, bogs.** —*tr.* To cause to sink in or as if in a bog: *were bogged down in a mass of detail.* —*intr.* To be hindered and slowed. [Ir. Gael. *bogach* < *bog,* soft.] **—bog'gy** *adj.*

bog asphodel *n.* Either of two related bog plants, *Narthecium americanum,* of the southeastern United States, or *N. ossifragum,* of Europe, having a cluster of yellow flowers.

bo·gey (bō'gē) *n., pl.* **-geys. 1.** Variant of **bogy[1]. 2. a.** An estimated standard golf score. **b.** One golf stroke over par on a hole. **3.** *Slang.* An unidentified flying aircraft.

bog·ey·man (bo͝og'ē-măn', bō'gē-, bo͞o'gē-) *n.* Variant of **boogieman.**

bog·gle (bŏg'əl) *v.* **-gled, -gling, -gles.** —*intr.* **1.** To hesitate or evade as if in fear or doubt. **2.** To shy away with fright or astonishment; be overcome. **3.** To botch; bungle. —*tr.* To cause to be overcome, as with fright or astonishment. [Prob. < *boggle,* dial. var. of BOGLE.] **—bog'gler** *n.*

bo·gie[1] also **bo·gy** (bō'gē) *n., pl.* **-gies. 1.** A railroad car or locomotive undercarriage with two, four, or six wheels that swivels so that curves can be negotiated. **2.** One of several wheels or supporting and aligning rollers inside the tread of a tractor or tank. [Orig. unknown.]

bo·gie[2] (bō'gē, bo͝og'ē, bo͞o'gē) *n.* Variant of **bogy[1].**

bo·gle (bō'gəl) *n.* A hobgoblin; bogy. [Sc. *bogill.*]

bog rosemary *n.* A low-growing evergreen shrub, *Andromeda glaucophylla,* of northern regions, growing in wet ground, and having small pink flowers.

bog·trot·ter (bôg'trŏt'ər, bŏg'-) *n.* **1.** A person who lives in or frequents bogs. **2.** *Offensive.* An Irishman.

bo·gus (bō'gəs) *adj.* Counterfeit; fake. [< E. *bogus,* a device for making counterfeit money.]

bog·wood (bôg'wo͝od', bŏg'-) *n.* Wood that has been preserved in a peat bog.

bo·gy[1] also **bo·gey** or **bo·gie** (bō'gē, bo͝og'ē, bo͞o'gē) *n., pl.* **-gies** also **-geys** or **-gies. 1.** An evil or mischievous spirit; hobgoblin. **2.** Something that causes annoyance or harassment. [Orig. unknown.]

bo·gy[2] (bō'gē) *n.* Variant of **bogie[1].**

bo·hea (bō-hē') *n.* A black Chinese tea. [Chin. (Fujian) *bu-i,* after *Wu-i Shan,* a range of hills on the border of Jiangxi and Fujan Provinces.]

bo·he·mi·a also **Bo·he·mi·a** (bō-hē'mē-ə) *n.* **1.** A community of persons with artistic or literary tastes who adopt manners and mores conspicuously different from those expected or approved of by the majority of society. **2.** The district in which bohemians live. [Back-formation < BOHEMIAN.]

Bo·he·mi·an (bō-hē'mē-ən) *n.* **1.** A native or inhabitant of Bohemia. **2.** A Gypsy. **3.** The Czech dialects of Bohemia. **4. bohemian.** A person with artistic or literary interests who disregards conventional standards of behavior. **—Bo·he'mi·an** *adj.*

Bohr theory (bôr, bōr) *n.* A model of atomic structure in which electrons travel around the nucleus in orbits determined by quantum conditions. [After Niels *Bohr* (1885–1962).]

boil[1] (boil) *v.* **boiled, boil·ing, boils.** —*intr.* **1. a.** To vaporize a liquid by the application of heat. **b.** To reach the boiling point. **c.** To undergo the action of boiling, esp. in being cooked. **2.** To be agitated like boiling water; churn: *water boiling through the rapids.* **3.** To be stirred up or greatly excited: *The mere idea made him boil.* —*tr.* **1.** To heat to the boiling point. **2.** To cook or clean by boiling. **3.** To separate by evaporation by boiling: *boil the maple sap.* **—*phrasal verbs.* boil away.** To evaporate by boiling. **boil down. 1.** To reduce in bulk or size by boiling. **2.** To condense or be condensed; reduce. **boil over. 1.** To overflow while boiling.

bobolink

bobwhite

bog
Cranberry bog

2. To explode in rage; lose one's temper. —*n.* The condition or act of boiling. [ME *boillen* < OFr. *boilir* < Lat. *bullire.*]

Synonyms: *boil, simmer, seethe, stew.* All of these verbs have physical senses and related figurative ones. *Boil* refers to heating up to the vaporizing (boiling) point, with consequent bubbling up of gases; figuratively, it pertains to the act of being stirred by intense emotion, especially anger. *Simmer* refers to the less agitated state of heating to or near the boiling point, and figuratively to being stirred by pent-up anger. *Seethe,* a strong term, emphasizes in both senses the turbulence of steady boiling at high temperature. *Stew* refers to slow, gentle boiling and to emotional upset that is persistent but not violent in expression.

boil² (boil) *n.* A painful, localized pus-filled swelling of the skin and subcutaneous tissue caused by bacterial infection. [ME *bile* < OE *bȳl.*]

boil·er (boi'lər) *n.* **1.** An enclosed vessel in which water is heated and circulated, either as hot water or as steam, for heating or power. **2.** A container, such as a kettle, for boiling liquids. **3.** A storage tank for hot water.

boil·er·mak·er (boi'lər-mā'kər) *n.* **1.** One who makes or repairs boilers. **2.** *Slang.* A drink of whiskey with beer as a chaser.

boil·er·plate (boi'lər-plāt') *n.* **1.** A steel plate used in making the shells of steam boilers. **2.** Journalistic material, such as syndicated features, available in plate or mat form.

boil·er-room (boi'lər-ro͞om', -ro͝om') *adj. Informal.* Of, relating to, or involving usually illegal, high-pressure telephone sales tactics, as used in selling stock, commodities, or land.

boiling point *n.* **1.** The temperature at which a liquid boils, esp. under standard atmospheric conditions. **2.** *Informal.* The point at which a person loses his temper.

boil-off (boil'ôf', -ŏf') *n.* The vaporization of liquid, such as a rocket fuel.

bois de rose (bwä' də rōz') *n.* A grayish red. [Fr. : *bois,* wood + *de,* of + *rose,* rose.]

bois·ter·ous (boi'stər-əs, -strəs) *adj.* **1.** Rough and stormy; violent. **2.** Loud, noisy, and lacking in restraint or discipline. [ME *boistres,* var. of *boistous,* rude.] **—bois'ter·ous·ly** *adv.* **—bois'ter·ous·ness** *n.*

bok choy (bŏk choi') *n.* Variant of **pak choi.**

Bok·mål (bo͝ok'môl', bŏk'-) *n.* Riksmål. [Norw. : *bok,* book + *mål,* language.]

bola
Argentine gaucho preparing to release bola

bo·la (bō'lə) also **bo·las** (-ləs) *n.* A rope with weights attached used esp. in South America to catch cattle or game by entangling the legs. [Sp. (South America) *bolas,* pl. of Sp. *bola,* ball.]

bola tie *n.* Variant of **bolo tie.**

bold (bōld) *adj.* **-er, -est. 1.** Fearless and daring; courageous. **2.** Requiring or exhibiting courage and bravery. **3.** Unduly forward and brazen in manner. **4.** Clear and distinct to the eye; conspicuous: *a bold handwriting.* **5.** Abrupt; steep, as a cliff. **6.** Designating boldface type. [ME < OE *bald.*] **—bold'ly** *adv.* **—bold'ness** *n.*

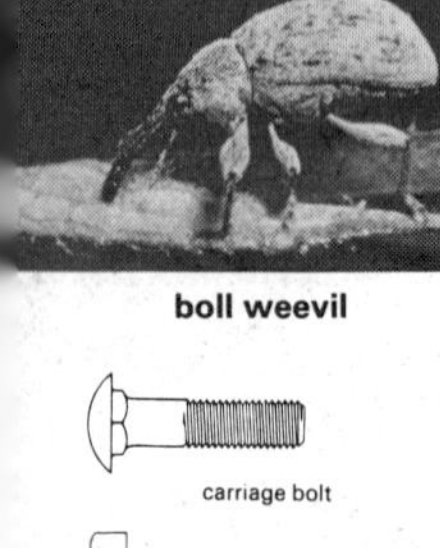

boll weevil

bold·face (bōld'fās') *n.* Type with thick, heavy lines. —*tr.v.* **-faced, -fac·ing, -fac·es. 1.** To mark (copy) for printing in boldface. **2.** To print or set in boldface.

bold-faced (bōld'fāst') *adj.* **1.** Impudent; brazen. **2. a.** Printed or set in boldface. **b.** Marked for printing in boldface.

bole (bōl) *n.* The trunk of a tree. [ME < ON *bolr.*]

bo·le·ro (bō-lâr'ō, bə-) *n., pl.* **-ros. 1.** A very short jacket worn open in the front. **2. a.** A Spanish dance in triple meter. **b.** The music for a bolero. [Sp.]

bo·le·tus (bō-lē'təs) *n., pl.* **-tus·es** or **-ti** (-tī'). A fungus of the genus *Boletus,* with an umbrella-shaped cap with spore-bearing tubules on the underside, of which some species are poisonous and others edible. [NLat. *Boletus,* genus name < Lat. *boletus,* mushroom.]

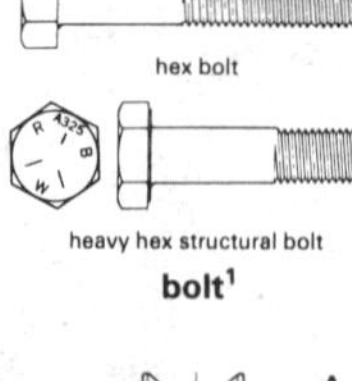

bolt¹

bo·li·var (bō-lē'vär', bŏl'ə-vər) *n., pl.* **bo·li·vars** or **bo·li·var·es** (bŏ'lē-vä'räs'). See table at **currency.** [After Simón *Bolívar* (1783–1830).]

boll (bōl) *n.* The rounded seed pod or capsule of certain plants, such as flax or cotton. [ME.]

bol·lard (bŏl'ərd) *n.* A thick post on a ship or wharf, used for securing ropes and hawsers. [ME, prob. < *bole,* tree trunk < ON *bolr.*]

bol·lix (bŏl'ĭks) *tr.v.* **-lixed, -lix·ing, -lix·es.** *Slang.* To throw into confusion; botch or bungle: *managed to bollix up the whole affair.* [Alteration of *ballocks,* testicles < ME *balloks* < OE *beallucas.*]

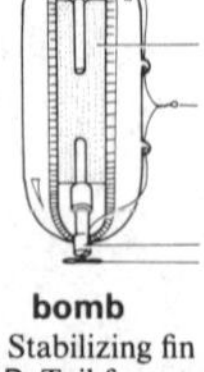

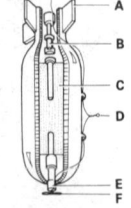

bomb
A. Stabilizing fin
B. Tail fuse
C. Explosive charge
D. Arming wire assembly
E. Explosive charge
F. Arming vane

boll weevil *n.* A small, grayish, long-snouted beetle, *Anthonomus grandis,* of Mexico and the southern United States, having destructive larvae that hatch in and damage cotton bolls.

boll·worm (bōl'wûrm') *n.* **1.** The larva of a moth, *Pectinophora gossypiella,* that is very destructive to growing cotton. **2.** The corn earworm.

bo·lo (bō'lō) *n., pl.* **-los.** A long, heavy, single-edged machete used in the Philippines. [Sp.]

bo·lo·gna (bə lō'nē, nə, nyə) also **ba·lo·ney** or **bo·lo·ney** (-nē) *n.* A seasoned smoked sausage made of mixed meats. [After *Bologna,* Italy.]

bo·lom·e·ter (bō-lŏm'ĭ-tər) *n.* An instrument that measures radiant heat by correlating the radiation-induced change in electrical resistance of a blackened metal foil with the amount of radiation absorbed. [Gk. *bolē,* ray + -METER.] **—bo'lo·met'ric** (bō'lə-mĕt'rĭk) *adj.*

bo·lo·ney (bə-lō'nē) *n.* Variant of **bologna.**

bolo tie also **bola tie** *n.* A necktie consisting of a piece of cord fastened with an ornamental bar or clasp. [Alteration of BOLA + TIE.]

Bol·she·vik (bōl'shə-vĭk', bŏl'-) *n., pl.* **-viks** or **-vi·ki** (-vē'kē). **1. a.** A participant in the Russian Revolution belonging to the Communist Party of the Soviet Union. **b.** A member of the left-wing majority group of the Russian Social Democratic Party adopting Lenin's theses on party organization (1903). **2.** Often **bolshevik.** An extreme radical. [R. *Bol'shevik* < *bol'shii,* comp. of *bol'shoi,* large.]

Bol·she·vism also **bol·she·vism** (bōl'shə-vĭz'əm, bŏl'-) *n.* **1.** The strategy developed by the Bolsheviks between 1903 and 1917 with a view to seizing state power and establishing the dictatorship of the proletariat. **2.** Soviet Communism.

Bol·she·vist also **bol·she·vist** (bōl'shə-vĭst, bŏl'-) *n.* A Bolshevik.

bol·ster (bōl'stər) *n.* A long, narrow pillow or cushion. —*tr.v.* **-stered, -ster·ing, -sters. 1.** To support or prop up with or as if with a bolster. **2.** To buoy up: *visitors that bolstered his morale.* [ME < OE.] **—bol'ster·er** *n.*

bolt¹ (bōlt) *n.* **1.** A bar made of wood or metal that slides into a socket and is used to fasten doors and gates. **2.** A metal bar or rod in the mechanism of a lock that is thrown or withdrawn by turning the key. **3.** A fastener consisting of a threaded pin or rod with a head at one end, designed to be inserted through holes in assembled parts and secured by a mated nut that is tightened by application of torque. **4. a.** A sliding metal bar that positions the cartridge in breech-loading rifles, closes the breech, and ejects the spent cartridge. **b.** A similar device in any breech mechanism. **5.** A short, heavy arrow with a thick head, used esp. with a crossbow. **6.** A flash of lightning; thunderbolt. **7.** A sudden or unexpected event. **8.** A sudden movement toward or away from something. **9.** A large roll of cloth of a definite length, esp. as it comes from the loom. —*v.* **bolt·ed, bolt·ing, bolts.** —*tr.* **1.** To secure or lock with or as if with a bolt. **2.** *Archaic.* To shoot or discharge (an arrow or other missile). **3.** To arrange or roll (lengths of cloth, for example) on a bolt. **4.** To eat hurriedly and with little chewing; gulp. **5.** To desert or withdraw support from (a political party). **6.** To utter impulsively; blurt out. —*intr.* **1.** To move or spring suddenly. **2.** To break from a rider's control and run away, as a horse. **3.** To make off suddenly; run away: *bolted from the room.* **4.** To break away from a political party or its policies. **5.** To flower or produce seeds prematurely. —***idiom.*** **bolt from the blue.** A sudden, often shocking surprise. [ME < OE, heavy arrow.]

bolt² (bōlt) *tr.v.* **bolt·ed, bolt·ing, bolts.** To pass through a sieve; sift. [ME *bulten* < OFr. *buleter,* of Germanic orig.]

bolt·er¹ (bōl'tər) *n.* **1.** A horse given to bolting. **2.** One who gives up membership in or withdraws support from a political party.

bolt·er² (bōl'tər) *n.* **1.** A machine used for sifting, esp. for sifting flour. **2.** One who operates a bolter.

bol·to·ni·a (bōl-tō'nē-ə) *n.* Any of several North American plants of the genus *Boltonia,* having daisylike flowers with white, violet, or pinkish rays. [NLat., genus name after James *Bolton* (d. 1799).]

bolt·rope (bōlt'rōp') *n.* A rope sewn into the outer edge of a sail to prevent the sail from tearing.

bo·lus (bō'ləs) *n., pl.* **-lus·es. 1.** A small round mass. **2.** *Pharm.* A large pill or tablet. **3.** A soft mass of chewed food in the mouth. [Med. Lat. *bolus* < Gk. *bōlos,* lump of earth.]

bomb (bŏm) *n.* **1. a.** An explosive weapon detonated by impact, proximity to an object, a timing mechanism, or other predetermined means. **b.** An atomic bomb. **2.** Any of various weapons detonated to release destructive material such as smoke or gas. **3.** *Football.* A very long forward pass designed to achieve great yardage in a single play. **4. a.** A container capable of withstanding high internal pressure. **b.** A vessel for storing compressed gas. **c.** A portable, manually operated container that ejects a spray, foam, or gas under pressure. **5.** *Slang.* A dismal failure or complete fiasco. **6.** *Chiefly Brit. Slang.* A large amount of money. **7.** *Chiefly Brit.* An old car. —*v.* **bombed, bomb·ing, bombs.** —*tr.* To attack, damage, or destroy with or as if with bombs. —*intr.* **1.** To drop bombs. **2.** *Slang.* To fail miserably: *The play bombed.* [Fr. *bombe* < Ital. *bomba,* prob. < Lat. *bombus,* a booming sound < Gk. *bombos.*]

bom·bard (bŏm'bärd') *n.* An early form of cannon that fired stone balls. —*tr.v.* (bŏm-bärd') **-bard·ed, -bard·ing, -bards. 1.** To attack with bombs, shells, or missiles. **2.** To attack persistently, as with questions. **3.** To irradiate (an atom). **4.** To attack with a bombard. [ME < OFr. *bombarde* < Med. Lat. *bombarda* prob. < Lat. *bombus,* a booming sound < Gk. *bombos.*] **—bom·bard'er** *n.* **—bom·bard'ment** *n.*

bom·bar·dier (bŏm'bər-dîr') *n.* **1.** The member of an aircraft crew who operates the bombing equipment. **2.** A noncommissioned British artillery officer. **3.** A soldier who operated a bombard. [Fr. < OFr. *bombarde,* bombard.]

bombardier beetle *n.* Any of various beetles of the genus

Brachinus and related genera that expel an acrid secretion from the posterior end of the abdomen.

bom·bar·don (bŏm′bər-dŏn′, bŏm-bär′dn) *n.* **1.** A brass musical instrument resembling a tuba but with a lower pitch; a bass or contrabass tuba. **2.** A 16-foot reed stop on the organ. [Fr. < Ital. *bombardone,* aug. of *bombardo,* alteration of *bombarda,* bombard < Med. Lat.]

bom·bast (bŏm′băst′) *n.* Grandiloquent and pompous speech or writing. [OFr. *bombace,* cotton padding < LLat. *bombax,* cotton < Lat. *bombyx,* silk < Gk. *bombux,* silkworm.] **—bom′bast′er** *n.* **—bom·bas′tic** (-băs′tĭk) *adj.* **—bom·bas′ti·cal·ly** *adv.*

Synonyms: *bombast, declamation, rant, fustian, claptrap, rodomontade.* All these terms designate speech or writing that emphasizes extravagance of style or delivery, usually at the expense of content. *Bombast,* applicable to speech and writing, stresses inflation of style without ruling out the possibility of substantial content. *Declamation* applies principally to formal oratory and the speaking of verse drama but may imply clamorous, empty display. *Rant,* said chiefly of speech, emphasizes turgidity and style of writing or speech and absurd or commonplace content. *Claptrap* is insincere, worthless speech or writing, calculated to win applause. *Rodomontade* is boastful speech and bluster.

Bom·bay duck (bŏm-bā′) *n.* **1.** A food fish, *Harpodon nehereus,* of India. **2.** The dried flesh of the Bombay duck or a dish prepared from it.

bom·ba·zine (bŏm′bə-zēn′) *n.* A fine twilled fabric of silk and worsted or cotton, often dyed black and used for mourning clothes. [Fr. *bombasin* < LLat. *bombacinum,* silken texture < Lat. *bombycinum* < *bombyx,* silk < Gk. *bombux,* silkworm.]

bomb bay *n.* The compartment in the fuselage of a military aircraft from which bombs are dropped.

bombe (bŏm, bôɴb) *n.* A dessert consisting of two or more layers of ice cream of different flavors frozen in a round or melon-shaped mold. [Fr.]

bombed (bŏmd) *adj. Slang.* Drunk.

bomb·er (bŏm′ər) *n.* **1.** A military aircraft designed to carry and drop bombs. **2.** One that bombs.

bomb·proof (bŏm′pro͞of′) *adj.* Designed and constructed to resist destruction by bombs.

bomb·shell (bŏm′shĕl′) *n.* **1.** A bomb. **2.** A shocking surprise.

bomb·sight (bŏm′sīt′) *n.* A device in aircraft for aiming bombs.

bom·by·cid (bŏm′bĭ-sĭd) *n.* A moth of the family Bombycidate, which includes the silkworms. [< NLat. *Bombycidae,* family name < Lat. *bombyx,* silkworm < Gk. *bombux.*]

bo·na fide (bō′nə fīd′, fī′dē, bŏn′ə) *adj.* **1.** Done or made in good faith; sincere: *a bona fide offer.* **2.** Authentic; genuine: *a bona fide Rembrandt.* [Lat., in good faith.]

bo·nan·za (bə-năn′zə) *n.* **1.** A rich mine, vein, or pocket of ore. **2.** A source of great wealth or prosperity. [Sp., exaggerated good, aug. of *bueno,* good < Lat. *bonus.*]

Bo·na·part·ist (bō′nə-pär′tĭst) *n.* A follower or supporter of Napoleon Bonaparte and his policies and dynastic claims or of the Bonaparte family. **—Bo′na·part′ism** *n.*

bon·bon (bŏn′bŏn′) *n.* A candy that often has a center of fondant, fruit, or nuts and is coated with chocolate or fondant. [Fr., redup. of *bon,* good < Lat. *bonus.*]

bon·bon·nière (bŏn′bŏn-yâr′) *n.* **1.** A small ornate box or dish for candy. **2.** A confectioner's store. [Fr. < *bonbon,* bonbon.]

bond (bŏnd) *n.* **1.** Something that binds, ties, or fastens together, as a fetter, cord, or band. **2.** Often **bonds.** *Archaic.* Captivity; confinement. **3.** A uniting force or tie; link: *bonds of friendship.* **4.** A binding agreement; covenant. **5.** A duty, promise, or obligation by which one is bound. **6. a.** A substance or an agent that causes two or more objects or parts to cohere. **b.** The union or cohesion brought about by such a substance or agent. **7.** A chemical bond. **8.** *Law.* **a.** A written and sealed obligation, esp. one requiring payment of a stipulated amount of money on or before a given day. **b.** A sum of money paid as bail or surety. **c.** One who acts as bail; bondsman. **9.** A certificate of debt issued by a government or corporation guaranteeing payment of the original investment plus interest by a specified future date. **10.** The condition of storing taxable goods in a warehouse until the taxes or duties due on them are paid. **11.** An insurance contract in which an agency guarantees payment to an employer in the event of unforeseen financial loss through the actions of an employee. **12.** An overlapping arrangement of bricks or other masonry components in a wall. **13.** Bond paper. *—v.* **bond·ed, bond·ing, bonds.** *—tr.* **1.** To mortgage or place a guaranteed bond on. **2.** To furnish bond or surety for. **3.** To place (an employee, for example) under bond or guarantee. **4.** To join securely, as with glue or cement. **5.** To lay (bricks, for example) in an overlapping pattern for solidity. *—intr.* To secure or hold together with or as if with a bond. [ME < ON *band.*] **—bond′a·ble** *adj.* **—bond′er** *n.*

bond·age (bŏn′dĭj) *n.* **1.** The condition of a slave or serf; servitude. **2.** A state of subjection to a force, power, or influence. **3.** Villeinage. [ME < AN < ME *bonde,* serf < OE *bōnda,* husbandman < ON *bondi.*]

bond·hold·er (bŏnd′hōl′dər) *n.* The owner of a bond or bonds.

bond·ing (bŏn′dĭng) *n. Anthropol.* The formation of close, specialized human relationships, such as those that link parent and child.

bond·maid (bŏnd′mād′) *n.* A female bondservant.

bond·man (bŏnd′mən) *n.* A male bondservant.

bond paper *n.* A superior grade of strong white paper made wholly or in part from rag pulp.

bond·ser·vant (bŏnd′sûr′vənt) *n.* **1.** A person obligated to service without wages. **2.** A slave or serf.

bonds·man (bŏndz′mən) *n.* **1.** A male bondservant. **2.** A person who provides bond or surety for another.

bond·wom·an (bŏnd′wo͝om′ən) *n.* A female bondservant.

bone (bōn) *n.* **1. a.** The dense, semirigid, porous, calcified connective tissue of the skeleton of most vertebrates. **b.** Any of numerous anatomically distinct skeletal structures made of bone. **c.** A piece of bone. **2. bones. a.** The skeleton. **b.** The body. **c.** Mortal remains. **3.** An animal structure or material, such as ivory, resembling bone. **4.** Something made of bone or of material resembling bone, esp.: **a.** A piece of whalebone or similar material used as a corset stay. **b. bones.** *Informal.* Dice. **5. bones.** The fundamental plan or design, as of the plot of a book. **6. a. bones.** Flat clappers made of bone or wood used by the end man in a minstrel show. **b. Bones** *(used with a sing. verb).* The end man in a minstrel show. *—v.* **boned, bon·ing, bones.** *—tr.* **1.** To remove the bones from. **2.** To stiffen (a piece of clothing) with stays, as of whalebone. *—intr. Slang.* To study intensely, usually at the last minute. **—idioms. bone of contention.** The subject of a dispute. **feel in (one's) bones.** To have an intuition of. **have a bone to pick.** To have grounds for a complaint or dispute. **make no bones about.** To be frank and candid about. [ME *bon* < OE *bān.*]

bomber
U.S. B-52 bomber plane

bone ash *n.* The white, powdery calcium phosphate ash of burned bones, used as a fertilizer, in making ceramics, and in cleaning and polishing compounds.

bone·black also **bone black** (bōn′blăk′) *n.* A black pigment containing about 10 per cent charcoal, made by roasting bones in an airtight container and used in polishes, as a filtering medium, and in decolorizing sugar.

bone charcoal *n.* Boneblack.

bone china *n.* Porcelain made of clay mixed with bone ash.

bone conduction *n.* The transmission of sound by bone, esp. to the inner ear by the bones of the skull.

bone-dry (bōn′drī′) *adj.* Without a trace of moisture; very dry.

bone·fish (bōn′fĭsh′) *n., pl.* **bonefish** or **-fish·es.** A marine game fish, *Albula vulpes,* of warm waters, having silvery scales.

bone·head (bōn′hĕd′) *n. Slang.* A stupid person; dunce. **—bone′head′ed** *adj.* **—bone′head′ed·ness** *n.*

bone meal *n.* Bones crushed and ground to a coarse powder and used as plant fertilizer and animal feed.

bon·er (bō′nər) *n. Slang.* A blunder.

bone·set (bōn′sĕt′) *n.* Any of various plants of the genus *Eupatorium,* esp. *E. perfoliatum,* of eastern North America, having broad clusters of small white flowers. [From its use as a folk medicine.]

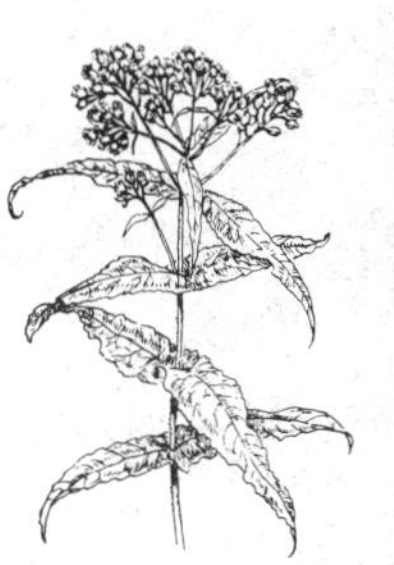

boneset

bon·fire (bŏn′fīr′) *n.* A large outdoor fire. [ME *bonfir* : *bon,* bone + *fir,* fire.]

bong (bŏng, bông) *n.* A deep ringing sound, as of a bell. *—tr. & intr.v.* **bonged, bong·ing, bongs.** To sound with a bong; ring. [Imit.]

bon·go¹ (bŏng′gō, bông′-) *n., pl.* **-gos.** An antelope, *Boocercus eurycerus,* of central Africa, having a reddish-brown coat with white stripes and spirally twisted horns. [Of Bantu orig.]

bon·go² (bŏng′gō, bông′-) *n., pl.* **-gos** also **-goes.** One of a pair of connected tuned drums that are played by beating with the hands. [Am. Sp. (West Indies) *bongó.*]

bongo²
Bongo drums

bon·ho·mie (bŏn′ə-mē′) *n.* A pleasant and affable disposition; geniality. [Fr. < *bonhomme,* good-natured man : *bon,* good (< Lat. *bonus*) + *homme,* man < Lat. *homo.*]

bon·i·face (bŏn′ə-fəs, -fās′) *n.* An innkeeper. [After *Boniface,* an innkeeper in *The Beaux' Strategem* by George Farquhar (1678–1707).]

boning knife *n.* A knife with a narrow blade and a sharp point for boning poultry, meat, and fish.

bo·ni·to (bə-nē′tō) *n., pl.* **bonito** or **-tos. 1.** Any of several marine food and game fishes of the genus *Sarda,* related to and resembling the tuna. **2.** Any of several fishes similar to the bonito. [Sp. < *bonito,* pretty < Lat. *bonus,* good.]

bon·kers (bŏng′kərz) *adj. Slang.* Crazy. [Orig. unknown.]

bon mot (bôɴ mō′) *n., pl.* **bons mots** (bôɴ mō′, mōz′). A clever saying; witticism. [Fr. : *bon,* good + *mot,* word.]

bonne (bôn) *n.* A French female servant or maid. [Fr., fem. of *bon,* good < Lat. *bonus.*]

bon·net (bŏn′ĭt) *n.* **1. a.** A hat that is held in place by ribbons tied under the chin, worn by women and girls. **b.** *Scot.* A brimless cap worn by men. **c.** A feather headdress worn by some American Indians. **2.** A removable metal plate over a valve or other machinery part. **3.** *Chiefly Brit.* The hood of an automobile. **4.** A wind screen for a chimney. **5.** A strip of canvas laced to a fore-and-aft sail to increase sail area.

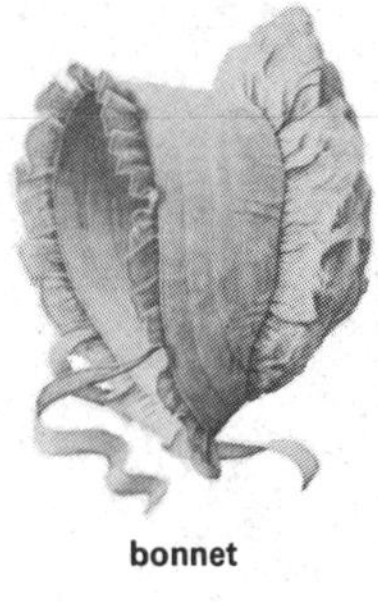

bonnet

—*tr.v.* **-net·ed, -net·ing, -nets.** To put a bonnet on. [ME *bonet,* cap < OFr.]

bon·ny also **bon·nie** (bŏn′ē) *adj.* **-ni·er, -ni·est.** *Chiefly Scot.* **1.** Pleasing or attractive to the eye; pretty. **2.** Vigorous; spirited. [Orig. unknown.] —**bon′ni·ly** *adv.* —**bon′ni·ness** *n.*

bon·ny·clab·ber (bŏn′ē-klăb′ər) *n. Chiefly Brit. Regional.* Sour clotted milk. [Ir. Gael. *bainne,* milk + *claba,* thick.]

bon·sai (bŏn-sī′) *n., pl.* **bonsai. 1.** The art of growing dwarfed, ornamentally shaped trees or shrubs in small, shallow pots. **2.** A tree or shrub grown by the methods of bonsai. [J., potted plant : *bon,* basin (< Chin. *pen*[2]) + *sai,* to plant (< Chin. *zai*[1]).]

bonsai

bon·spiel (bŏn′spēl′) *n. Scot.* A curling tournament or match. [Prob. of Du. orig.]

bon·te·bok (bŏn′tə-bŏk′) *n.* A nearly extinct South African antelope, *Damaliscus pygargus,* having a reddish coat, a white rump, and a white mark on the face. [Afr. : *bont,* spotted (< MDu.) + *bok,* buck < MDu. *boc*).]

bon ton (bŏn tŏn′) *n.* **1.** A sophisticated manner or style. **2.** Stylish or fashionable society. [Fr. : *bon,* good + *ton,* tone.]

bo·nus (bō′nəs) *n., pl.* **-nus·es. 1.** Something given or paid in addition to what is usual or expected. **2.** Money paid to a state by a company in return for a corporate charter. **3.** A grant from a government to veterans of the armed forces. **4.** An extra dividend paid to stockholders of a company from profits. **5.** A premium paid for a loan. [< Lat., good.]

Synonyms: *bonus, bounty, subsidy, dividend, premium, prize, reward, gratuity.* Each of these nouns designates some form of extra payment. *Bonus* usually applies to money in excess of what is normally received or strictly due, given in consideration of superior achievement or as a share in profits. *Bounty* generally pertains to a grant from a government, designed to encourage a specific desirable activity, such as the destruction of vermin. *Subsidy* refers to a large grant, usually by a government, in support of an enterprise regarded as in the public interest but not self-sustaining. *Dividend* usually refers to distribution of profits to shareholders or policyholders. *Premium* is generally something given as an incentive to business or commercial activity, as a discount or special wage rate. *Prize,* in this context, usually implies competitive achievement. *Reward* refers broadly to payment for a specific effort and emphasizes the merit of the accomplishment (or, less often, its evil). *Gratuity* pertains to voluntary payment in appreciation of services rendered, such as a tip, and emphasizes generosity.

bon vi·vant (bôN′ vē-väN′) *n., pl.* **bons vi·vants** (bôN′ vē-väN′). A person who has refined tastes and esp. one who enjoys good food and drink. [Fr. : *bon,* good + *vivant,* pr.part. of *vivre,* to live.]

bon voy·age (bôN′ vwä-yäzh′) *interj.* Used to wish a departing traveler a pleasant journey. [Fr. : *bon,* good + *voyage,* journey.]

bon·y (bō′nē) *adj.* **-i·er, -i·est. 1.** Of, pertaining to, resembling, or consisting of bone. **2.** Having an internal skeleton of bones. **3.** Full of bones: *a bony fish filet.* **4.** Having protruding or prominent bones; lean; gaunt. —**bon′i·ness** *n.*

bonze (bŏnz) *n.* A Mahayana Buddhist monk, esp. of China, Japan, and adjacent countries. [Fr. < Port. *bonzo* < J. *bonsō,* of Chin. orig.]

bon·zer (bŏn′zər) *adj. Austral. Slang.* Excellent; very good. [Poss. alteration of BONANZA.]

boo[1] (bōō) *n., pl.* **boos.** A vocal sound uttered to show contempt, scorn, or disapproval. —*interj.* Used to frighten or surprise or to express contempt, scorn, or disapproval. —*v.* **booed, boo·ing, boos.** —*intr.* To utter a boo. —*tr.* To express contempt, scorn, or disapproval of by booing. [Imit.]

boo[2] (bōō) *n. Slang.* Marijuana. [Orig. unknown.]

boob[1] (bōōb) *n. Slang.* A stupid or foolish person; dolt. [Short for BOOBY.]

boob[2] (bōōb) *n. Slang.* A woman's breast.

boob·oi·sie (bōōb′wä-zē′) *n.* A class of people composed of the stupid and gullible. [BOOB[1] + (BOURGE)OISIE.]

boo-boo (bōō′bōō) *n., pl.* **-boos.** *Slang.* **1.** A stupid or thoughtless mistake; blunder. **2.** A slight physical injury. [Perh. alteration of *boohoo,* to weep noisily.]

boob tube *n. Slang.* Television.

boo·by[1] (bōō′bē) *n., pl.* **-bies. 1.** A stupid person; dunce. **2.** Any of several tropical sea birds of the genus *Sula,* resembling and related to the gannets. [Prob. Sp. *bobo* < Lat. *balbus,* stammering.]

boo·by[2] (bōō′bē) *n., pl.* **-bies.** *Slang.* A woman's breast. [Orig. unknown.]

booby hatch *n.* **1.** *Naut.* A raised covering over a small hatchway. **2.** *Slang.* An asylum or hospital for the insane.

booby prize *n.* An insignificant or comical award given to the person who receives the lowest score in a game or contest.

booby trap *n.* **1.** A concealed or camouflaged device designed to be triggered by an unsuspecting action of the intended victim. **2.** A device or situation that catches a person off guard; trap.

boo·dle (bōōd′l) *Slang.* —*n.* **1. a.** Money, esp. counterfeit money. **b.** Money accepted as a bribe. **2.** Stolen goods; swag. **3.** A crowd of people; caboodle. —*tr. & intr.v.* **-dled, -dling, -dles.** To bribe or accept a bribe. [Du. *boedel,* estate < MDu. *bōdel.*] —**boo′dler** *n.*

boog·ie·man also **boog·y·man** or **bog·ey·man** (bŏŏg′ē-măn′, bō′gē-, bōō′gē-) *n.* A terrifying specter; hobgoblin. [Var. of BOGY + MAN.]

boog·ie-woog·ie (bŏŏg′ē-wŏŏg′ē, bōō′gē-wōō′gē) *n.* A style of jazz piano characterized by a repeated rhythmic and melodic pattern in the bass. [Orig. unknown.]

book (bŏŏk) *n.* **1.** A set of written or printed pages fastened along one side and encased between protective covers. **2.** A written or printed literary work. **3.** A bound volume of blank or ruled pages. **4. a.** A volume in which financial transactions are recorded. **b. books.** Such records collectively. **5.** A main division of a larger written or printed work: *a book of the Old Testament.* **6.** A libretto (sense 2). **7.** The script of a play. **8. Book.** The Bible. **9.** A set of rigid, prescribed rules: *runs the company by the book.* **10.** Something regarded as a source of knowledge. **11.** A small packet of similar items bound together: *a book of matches.* **12.** A record of bets placed on a race. **13.** *Games.* The number of card tricks needed before any tricks can have scoring value, as the first six tricks taken by the declaring side in bridge. **14.** A bundle of tobacco leaves sliced lengthwise. —***modifier:*** *a book report.* —*tr.v.* **booked, book·ing, books. 1.** To list or register in or as if in a book. **2.** To record charges against (a person) on a police blotter. **3.** To arrange for (tickets, for example) in advance; reserve. **4.** To hire (entertainers, for example). —***idioms.*** **bring to book.** To compel to explain or account for. **in (one's) book.** In one's opinion. **like a book.** Thoroughly; completely: *knows him like a book.* **one for the books.** *Informal.* Something noteworthy. **on the books.** Recorded or registered. **throw the book at.** *Slang.* **1.** To make all possible charges against (a lawbreaker, for example). **2.** To reprimand or punish severely. [ME *bok* < OE *bōc.*] —**book′er** *n.*

book·bind·er·y (bŏŏk′bīn′də-rē) *n., pl.* **-ies.** A business establishment where bookbinding is carried on.

book·bind·ing (bŏŏk′bīn′dĭng) *n.* The art, trade, or profession of binding books. —**book′bind′er** *n.*

book·case (bŏŏk′kās′) *n.* A piece of furniture with shelves for holding books.

book·end also **book end** (bŏŏk′ĕnd′) *n.* A prop placed at the end of a row of books to keep them upright.

book·ie (bŏŏk′ē) *n. Slang.* A bookmaker.

book·ing (bŏŏk′ĭng) *n.* **1.** An engagement, as for a performance by an entertainer. **2.** A reservation, as for accommodations at a hotel.

book·ish (bŏŏk′ĭsh) *adj.* **1.** Of, relating to, or resembling a book. **2.** Fond of books; studious. **3.** Relying on book learning. **4.** Pedantic; dull. —**book′ish·ly** *adv.* —**book′ish·ness** *n.*

book jacket *n.* A dust jacket.

book·keep·ing (bŏŏk′kē′pĭng) *n.* The art or practice of recording the accounts and transactions of a business. —**book′keep′er** *n.*

book learning *n.* Knowledge gained from books rather than from practical experience.

book·let (bŏŏk′lĭt) *n.* A small bound book or pamphlet, usually with paper covers.

book·lore (bŏŏk′lôr′, -lōr′) *n.* Book learning. [ME *boklore* < OE *bōklār* : *bōk,* book + *lār,* learning.]

book·louse (bŏŏk′lous′) *n.* Any of various small, often wingless insects of the order Psocoptera (or Corrodentia), some species of which damage books.

book lung *n.* A saccular respiratory organ found in some arachnids, consisting of a group of membranous folds resembling pages in a book.

book·mak·er (bŏŏk′mā′kər) *n.* **1.** One who edits, prints, publishes, or binds books. **2.** Someone who accepts and pays off bets, as on a horse race. —**book′mak′ing** *n.*

book·man (bŏŏk′mən) *n.* **1.** Someone who is fond of books and reading. **2.** Someone whose occupation is selling books.

book·mark (bŏŏk′märk′) *n.* A marker, such as a ribbon or a strip of leather, placed between the pages of a book.

book·mo·bile (bŏŏk′mō-bēl′) *n.* A small truck or trailer equipped to serve as a mobile lending library. [BOOK + (AUTO)MOBILE.]

Book of Common Prayer *n.* The book of services and prayers used in the Anglican church.

Book of Mormon *n.* The sacred text of the Mormon Church.

book·plate (bŏŏk′plāt′) *n.* A label usually pasted on the inside cover of a book that bears the owner's name or other identification.

book·rack (bŏŏk′răk′) *n.* **1.** A small rack or shelf for books. **2.** A frame or rack for supporting an open book.

book review *n.* A critical appraisal of a book.

book·sell·er (bŏŏk′sĕl′ər) *n.* A person who sells books.

book·shelf (bŏŏk′shĕlf′) *n.* A shelf or set of shelves for holding books.

book·shop (bŏŏk′shŏp′) *n.* A bookstore.

book·stall (bŏŏk′stôl′) *n.* A stall or stand where books are sold.

book·stand (bŏŏk′stănd′) *n.* **1.** A small counter where books are sold. **2.** A bookrack.

book·store (bŏŏk′stôr′, -stōr′) *n.* A store where books are sold.

book·worm (bo͝ok′wûrm′) *n.* **1.** The larva of any of various insects that infest books and feed on the paste in the bindings. **2.** One who spends much time reading or studying.
Bool·e·an (bo͞o′lē-ən) *adj.* Of or pertaining to an algebraic combinatorial system treating variables, such as propositions and computer logic elements, through the operators AND, OR, NOT, IF, THEN, and EXCEPT. [After George *Boole* (1815–1864).]
boom[1] (bo͞om) *v.* **boomed, boom·ing, booms.** —*intr.* **1.** To make a deep, resonant sound. **2.** To grow or develop rapidly; flourish: *Business is booming.* —*tr.* **1.** To give forth or utter with a deep, resonant sound. **2.** To cause to grow or flourish; boost. —*n.* **1.** A booming sound, as of an explosion. **2.** A time of prosperity. **3.** A sudden increase, as in wealth or popularity. [ME *bummen.*]
boom[2] (bo͞om) *n.* **1.** *Naut.* A long spar extending from a mast to hold or extend the foot of a sail. **2.** A long pole extending upward at an angle from the mast of a derrick to support or guide objects lifted or suspended. **3. a.** A barrier composed of a chain of floating logs enclosing other free-floating logs. **b.** The area enclosed by such a barrier. **4.** A floating barrier serving to obstruct navigation. **5.** A long, movable arm used to maneuver a microphone. [Du., pole < MDu.]
boo·mer·ang (bo͞o′mə-răng′) *n.* **1.** A flat, curved usually wooden missile that can be hurled so that it returns to the thrower. **2.** A statement or course of action that backfires against its originator. —*intr.v.* **-anged, -ang·ing, -angs.** To have the opposite effect from the one intended; backfire. [Native word in Australia.]
boom·let (bo͞om′lĭt) *n.* A small boom, as in business or politics.
boon[1] (bo͞on) *n.* **1.** Something beneficial that is bestowed; blessing. **2.** *Archaic.* A favor or request. [ME *bone* < ON *bōn,* prayer.]
boon[2] (bo͞on) *adj.* **1.** Jolly; convivial: *a boon companion.* **2.** *Archaic.* Kind; generous. [ME *bon,* good < OFr. < Lat. *bonus.*]
boon·docks (bo͞on′dŏks′) *pl.n. Slang.* **1.** Wild and dense brush; jungle. **2.** Rural country; backwoods. [Tagalog *bundok,* mountain.]
boon·dog·gle (bo͞on′dô′gəl, -dŏg′əl) *Informal.* —*n.* Pointless, unnecessary, and wasteful work. —*intr.v.* **-gled, -gling, -gles.** To waste time or money on pointless and unnecessary work. [< *boondoggle,* a plaited leather cord worn by Boy Scouts (coined by R.H. Link, 20th-cent. American scoutmaster).] **—boon′dog′gler** *n.*
boon·ies (bo͞o′nēz) *pl.n. Slang.* The boondocks (sense 2). [Shortening and alteration of BOONDOCKS.]
boor (bo͝or) *n.* **1.** A peasant. **2.** A crude person with rude or clumsy manners. [Du. *boer* < MDu. *gheboer.*]
boor·ish (bo͝or′ĭsh) *adj.* Resembling a boor; crude, rude, and offensive. **—boor′ish·ly** *adv.* **—boor′ish·ness** *n.*
boost (bo͞ost) *tr.v.* **boost·ed, boost·ing, boosts. 1.** To lift by or as if by pushing up from below. **2.** To increase; raise. **3.** To stir up enthusiasm for; promote vigorously. —*n.* **1.** A push upward or ahead. **2.** An increase: *a boost in salary.* [Orig. unknown.]
boost·er (bo͞o′stər) *n.* **1.** A device for increasing power or effectiveness. **2.** An enthusiastic promoter. **3.** *Electronics.* A radio-frequency amplifier. **4. a.** A rocket that assists the main propulsive system of an aircraft or spacecraft. **b.** A rocket used to launch a missile or space vehicle. **5.** A supplementary dose of a vaccine injected to maintain immunity.
booster cable *n.* An electric cable used to connect a discharged automobile battery to a power source for charging.
boot[1] (bo͞ot) *n.* **1.** A protective piece of footgear, usually leather, covering the foot and part or all of the leg. **2.** A protective sheath for a horse's leg. **3.** An instrument of torture used to crush the foot and leg. **4.** A protective covering or sheath, esp.: **a.** A protective flap for the driver of an open automobile or other vehicle. **b.** A patch for the inner casing of an automobile tire to protect a weak spot or break. **5.** *Chiefly Brit.* An automobile trunk. **6.** A scabbard on a saddle or vehicle to hold a gun. **7. a.** A kick. **b.** *Slang.* A swift, pleasurable feeling; thrill. **8.** A marine or navy recruit in basic training. **9.** *Slang.* A rude dismissal, as from work. **10. boots.** *Chiefly Brit.* A servant, esp. one in a hotel, who cleans and shines shoes. —*tr.v.* **boot·ed, boot·ing, boots. 1.** To put boots on. **2.** To kick. **3.** *Slang.* To discharge; dismiss. [ME *bote* < OFr.]
boot[2] (bo͞ot) *intr.v.* **boot·ed, boot·ing, boots.** *Archaic.* To be of help or advantage; avail. —*n.* **1.** *Regional.* Something given in addition. **2.** *Archaic.* Advantage; avail. **—*idiom.* to boot.** In addition; besides. [ME *boten* < OE *bōt,* help.]
boot·black (bo͞ot′blăk′) *n.* A person who cleans and polishes shoes for a living.
boot camp *n.* A training camp for marine or navy recruits.
boot·ed (bo͞o′tĭd) *adj.* Wearing boots.
boo·tee also **boo·tie** (bo͞o′tē) *n.* A soft, usually knitted shoe for a baby.
Bo·ö·tes (bō-ō′tēz) *n.* A constellation in the Northern Hemisphere near Virgo and Canes Venatici. [Lat. *Bootes* < Gk. *Boōtēs* < *boōtēs,* plowman < *boōtein,* to plow < *bous,* ox.]
booth (bo͞oth) *n., pl.* **booths** (bo͞o*th*z, bo͞oths). **1.** A small enclosed compartment, usually accommodating only one person and providing privacy: *a telephone booth.* **2.** A seating area in a restaurant that has a table and seats whose backs serve as partitions. **3.** A small stall or stand for the display and sale of goods. [ME *bothe,* prob. of Scand. orig.]
boo·tie (bo͞o′tē) *n.* Variant of **bootee.**
boot·jack (bo͞ot′jăk′) *n.* A forked device for holding a boot secure while the foot is being withdrawn.
boot·leg (bo͞ot′lĕg′) *v.* **-legged, -leg·ging, -legs.** —*tr.* To make, sell, or transport (alcoholic liquor, for example) for sale illegally. —*intr.* **1.** To engage in bootlegging. **2.** *Football.* To fake a handoff, conceal the ball on the hip, and roll out in order to pass or esp. to rush around the end. Used of a quarterback. —*n.* **1.** Goods smuggled or illicitly produced or sold. **2.** The part of a boot above the instep. **3.** *Football.* A bootleg play. —*adj.* Produced, sold, or transported illegally: *bootleg gin.* [From a smuggler's practice of carrying liquor in the legs of boots.] **—boot′leg′ger** *n.*
boot·less (bo͞ot′lĭs) *adj.* Without advantage or benefit; useless. **—boot′less·ly** *adv.* **—boot′less·ness** *n.*
boot·lick (bo͞ot′lĭk′) *v.* **-licked, -lick·ing, -licks.** —*tr.* To behave toward in a servile or obsequious manner. —*intr.* To behave in a servile or obsequious manner; fawn. **—boot′lick′er** *n.*
boot·strap (bo͞ot′străp′) *n.* **1.** A leather or cloth loop sewn at the side or the top rear of a boot to help in pulling the boot on. **2.** *Computer Sci.* A subroutine used to establish the full routine or another routine. —*tr.v.* **strapped, strap·ping, straps.** To establish (a program) with a bootstrap. —*adj.* **1.** Undertaken or accomplished with minimal resources or help. **2.** Being or relating to a process that is self-initiating or self-sustaining, as in a computer. **—*idiom.* by one's (own) bootstraps.** By one's own efforts.
boot tree *n.* A shoetree.
boo·ty (bo͞o′tē) *n., pl.* **-ties. 1.** Plunder taken from an enemy in time of war. **2.** Goods that have been stolen or seized. **3.** A valuable prize, award, or gain. [ME *bottyne* < OFr. *butin* < MLG *būte,* exchange.]
booze (bo͞oz) *Slang.* —*n.* **1.** Alcoholic beverages, esp. hard liquor. **2.** A drinking spree. —*intr.v.* **boozed, booz·ing, booz·es.** To drink alcoholic beverages excessively or chronically. [ME *bous* < MDu. *būse,* drinking vessel.] **—booz′er** *n.* **—booz′y** *adj.*
bop[1] (bŏp) *Informal.* —*tr.v.* **bopped, bop·ping, bops.** To hit or strike. —*n.* A blow; punch. [Imit.]
bop[2] (bŏp) *n.* A style of jazz characterized by rhythmic and harmonic complexity and a brilliant style of execution. [Short for BEBOP.]
bo·ra (bôr′ə, bōr′ə) *n.* A violent cold wind from the northeast blowing on the Dalmatian coast of Yugoslavia in winter. [Dial. Ital. < Lat. *Boreas,* Boreas.]
bo·rac·ic (bə-răs′ĭk) *adj.* Variant of **boric.** [< Med. Lat. *borax, borac-,* borax.]
bor·age (bôr′ĭj, bŏr′-) *n.* A plant, *Borago officinalis,* native to southern Europe and northern Africa, having hairy leaves sometimes used as seasoning and star-shaped blue flowers. [ME < OFr. *bourage* < Med. Lat. *borago,* perh. < Ar. *abū 'āraq,* father of sweat (from its use as a sudorific).]
bo·rane (bôr′ān′, bōr′-) *n.* Any of a series of boron-hydrogen compounds. [BOR(ON) + -ANE.]
bo·rate (bôr′āt′, bōr′-) *n.* A salt of boric acid.
bo·rax (bôr′ăks′, -əks, bōr′-) *n.* **1.** A hydrated sodium borate. **2.** An anhydrous sodium borate used in the manufacture of glass and various ceramics. [ME *boras* < OFr. *boreis* < Med. Lat. *borax* < Ar. *būraq* < Pers. *būrah.*]
Bo·ra·zon (bôr′ə-zŏn′, bōr′-). A trademark for an extremely hard boron nitride formed at very high pressures and temperatures.
Bor·deaux (bôr-dō′) *n., pl.* **Bordeaux** (bôr-dōz′). A red or white wine produced in the region around Bordeaux.
Bordeaux mixture *n.* A mixture of copper sulfate, lime, and water used as a fungicide. [Transl. of Fr. *bouillie bordelaise.*]
bor·del·lo (bôr-dĕl′ō) *n., pl.* **-los.** A house of prostitution. [Ital. < OFr. *bordel* < *borde,* wooden hut.]
bor·der (bôr′dər) *n.* **1.** A margin, rim, or edge. **2.** A design or a decorative strip around the edge or rim of something, as a fabric. **3.** A strip of ground in which ornamental plants or shrubbery is planted. **4.** The line or frontier area separating political divisions or geographic regions; boundary. —*tr.v.* **-dered, -der·ing, -ders. 1.** To put a border on. **2.** To lie along or adjacent to the border of. **—*phrasal verb.* border on (or upon). 1.** To adjoin. **2.** To be almost like; approach in character: *an act that borders on heroism.* [ME *bordure* < OFr. *bordëure* < *border,* to border < *bort,* border, of Germanic orig.] **—bor′der·er** *n.*

Synonyms: *border, margin, edge, verge, brink, brow, rim, brim.* All these words refer to the line or narrow area that marks the outmost bound of a surface. *Border* refers either to the boundary (limiting line) of a surface or, more often, to the area that immediately adjoins the boundary. *Margin* is an area, adjacent to the boundary, that is more or less precisely definable as to width and often distinguishable in other respects from the rest of the surface. *Edge* may refer specifically to the precise bounding line formed by the continuous convergence of two surfaces of a solid. *Verge* is an extreme terminating line or edge; figuratively it indicates

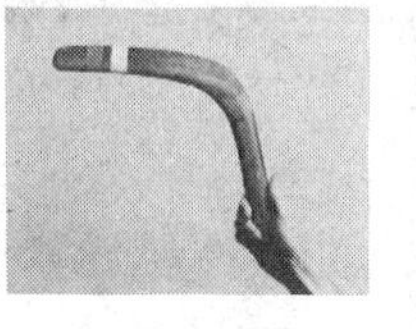

boomerang

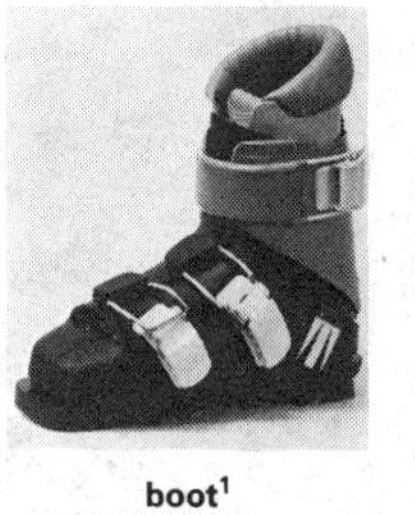

boot[1]
Ski boot

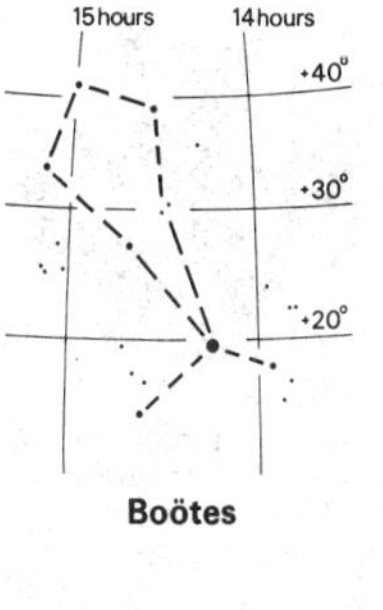

Boötes

extreme closeness to, or the imminence of, a thing or condition. *Brink* denotes the edge of a steep incline or slope; figuratively it indicates the imminence of an extreme condition, such as disaster or war. *Brow* is the upper edge of a steep incline. *Rim* denotes the edge of a surface that is circular or curved, such as a wheel or cymbal. *Brim* applies to the upper edge or inner side of the rim of a vessel or container, such as a cup.

bor·der·land (bôr′dər-lănd′) *n.* **1.** Land located on or near a border or frontier. **2.** An uncertain or indeterminate area, situation, or condition.

bor·der·line also **border line** (bôr′dər-līn′) *n.* **1.** A line that establishes or marks a border. **2.** An indefinite area between two qualities or conditions. *—adj.* Verging on a given quality or condition; dubious: *a borderline case of paranoia.*

bor·de·tel·la per·tus·sis (bôr′də-tĕl′ə pər-tŭs′ĭs) *n.* The coccobacillus that causes whooping cough. [NLat. : *Bordetella,* genus name (after Jules *Bordet,* 1870–1961) + *pertussis,* whooping cough.]

bor·dure (bôr′jər) *n.* A border around a heraldic shield. [ME. —see BORDER.]

bore[1] (bôr, bōr) *v.* **bored, bor·ing, bores.** *—tr.* **1.** To make a hole in or through, as with a drill. **2.** To form (a tunnel, for example) by drilling, digging, or burrowing. *—intr.* **1.** To make a hole in or through something by or as if by boring. **2.** To proceed or advance steadily or laboriously. *—n.* **1.** A hole or passage made by or as if by boring. **2.** The interior diameter of a hole, tube, or cylinder. **3.** The caliber of a firearm. **4.** A drilling tool. [ME *boren* < OE *borian.*]

bore[2] (bôr, bōr) *tr.v.* **bored, bor·ing, bores.** To make weary with dullness, repetition, or tediousness. *—n.* One that arouses boredom. [Orig. unknown.]

bore[3] (bôr, bōr) *n.* A high and often dangerous wave caused by the surge of a flood tide upstream in a narrowing estuary or by colliding tidal currents. [ME *bare,* wave < ON *bāra.*]

bore[4] (bôr, bōr) *v.* Past tense of **bear**[1].

bo·re·al (bôr′ē-əl, bōr′-) *adj.* **1.** Of or pertaining to the north; northern. **2.** Of or concerning the north wind. **3. Boreal.** Of or pertaining to the forest areas and tundras of the North Temperate Zone and Arctic region. [ME < LLat. *Boreālis* < Lat. *Boreas,* Boreas.]

borzoi

Bo·re·as (bôr′ē-əs, bōr′-) *n.* **1.** The north wind. **2.** *Gk. Myth.* The god personifying the north wind. [ME < Lat. *Boreas* < Gk.]

bore·cole (bôr′kōl′, bōr′-) *n.* Kale. [Du. *boerenkool* : *boer,* peasant + *kool,* cabbage.]

bore·dom (bôr′dəm, bōr′-) *n.* The condition of being bored; ennui.

bor·er (bôr′ər, bōr′-) *n.* **1. a.** A tool used for boring or drilling. **b.** One who works with such a tool. **2.** An insect or insect larva, such as the corn borer, that bores into plants. **3.** Any of various mollusks that bore into soft rock or wood.

bo·ric (bôr′ĭk, bōr′-) also **bo·rac·ic** (bə-răs′ĭk) *adj.* Of, pertaining to, derived from, or containing boron.

boric acid *n.* A white or colorless crystalline compound, H_3BO_3, used as an antiseptic and preservative and in fireproofing compounds, cosmetics, cements, and enamels.

bo·ride (bôr′īd′, bōr′-) *n.* A binary compound of boron with a more electropositive element or radical. [BOR(ON) + -IDE.]

bor·ing (bôr′ĭng, bōr′-) *adj.* Uninteresting and tiresome; dull. **—bor′ing·ly** *adv.*

Synonyms: *boring, monotonous, tedious, irksome, tiresome, humdrum, dismal, dreary.* These adjectives all mean to be burdensome in the sense of inducing discontent and mental weariness. *Boring* implies dullness that causes listlessness and lack of interest. *Monotonous* stresses unchanging lack of variety. *Tedious* suggests slowness, longwindedness, and dullness. *Irksome* describes what is demanding of time and effort and yet is dull, distasteful, or otherwise unrewarding. *Tiresome* intensifies the sense of *irksome,* and *humdrum* refers to what is commonplace, trivial, or characterized by unexciting routine. In this comparison *dismal* and *dreary* apply to what is depressingly dull.

born (bôrn) *v.* A past participle of **bear**[1]. *—adj.* **1.** Brought into life or being. **2.** Having from birth a particular quality or talent: *a born artist.* **3.** Resulting or arising: *wisdom born of experience.* —See Usage note at **bear**[1].

born-a·gain (bôrn′ə-gĕn′) *adj.* **1. a.** Of, relating to, or being an individual who has made a conversion or renewed a commitment to Jesus Christ as personal savior: *a born-again Christian.* **b.** Of or relating to evangelical Christianity: *a born-again religious experience.* **2.** Characterized by renewal, resurgence, or return: *born-again enthusiasm.*

borne (bôrn) *v.* A past participle of **bear**[1]. —See Usage note at **bear**[1].

boss[2]
13th-century French architectural boss

born·ite (bôr′nīt′) *n.* A brownish-bronze copper ore with composition Cu_5FeS_4. [After Ignaz von *Born* (1742–1791).]

bo·ron (bôr′ŏn′, bōr′-) *n. Symbol* **B** A soft, brown, amorphous or crystalline nonmetallic element, extracted chiefly from kernite and borax, and used in flares, propellant mixtures, nuclear reactor control elements, abrasives, and hard metallic alloys. Atomic number 5; atomic weight 10.811; melting point 2,300°C; sublimation 2,550°C; specific gravity (crystal) 2.34; valence 3. [BOR(AX) + (CARB)ON.]

boron carbide *n.* An extremely hard, black crystalline compound or solid solution, B_4C, used as an abrasive, in control rods for nuclear reactors, and as a reinforcing filament in composite structural materials.

bo·ro·sil·i·cate glass (bôr′ō-sĭl′ĭ-kĭt, bōr′-, -kāt′) *n.* A strong heat-resistant glass that contains a minimum of five per cent boric oxide.

bor·ough (bûr′ō, bŭr′-ō) *n.* **1.** A self-governing incorporated town in certain U.S. states. **2.** One of the five administrative units of New York City. **3.** *Chiefly Brit.* **a.** A town having a municipal corporation and certain rights, such as self-government. **b.** A town that sends one or more representatives to Parliament. [ME *burgh,* city < OE *burg.*]

bor·ough-Eng·lish (bûr′ō-ĭng′glĭsh, bŭr′-) *n.* A former custom in certain boroughs of England whereby the right to inherit an estate went to the youngest son or, in default of issue, to the youngest brother.

Bor·rel·i·a (bə-rĕl′ē-ə, -rē′lē-ə) *n.* A genus of locomotive helical bacteria of the family Spirochaetaceae, some of which cause relapsing fever in humans. [NLat., after Amédée *Borrel* (1867–1936).]

bor·row (bŏr′ō, bôr′ō) *v.* **-rowed, -row·ing, -rows.** *—tr.* **1.** To obtain or receive (something) on loan with the promise or understanding of returning it or its equivalent. **2.** To adopt or use as one's own: *borrowed his ideas.* **3.** In subtraction, to take (a unit of ten) from the next larger denomination in the minuend so as to make a number larger than the number to be subtracted. *—intr.* To obtain or receive something. [ME *borwen* < OE *borgian.*] **—bor′row·er** *n.*

Usage: In many dialects of American English, the expression *borrow off* is used in place of *borrow from.* This usage is not sufficiently well established to be used in writing, however; one writes *Ken borrowed twenty dollars from* (not *off*) *his brother.*

bor·row·ing (bŏr′ō-ĭng, bôr′-) *n.* Something that is borrowed, esp. a word borrowed from one language for use in another.

borscht also **borsht** (bôrsht) or **borsch** (bôrsh) *n.* A beet soup served hot or cold, often with sour cream. [R. *borshch.*]

borscht circuit *n. Slang.* The predominantly Jewish resort hotels of the Catskill Mountains that employ entertainers. [From the popularity of BORSCHT in their cuisine.]

bort (bôrt) *n.* **1.** Poorly crystallized diamonds used for industrial cutting and abrasion. **2.** A carbonado. [Prob. < Du. *boort.*] **—bort′y** *adj.*

bor·zoi (bôr′zoi′) *n.* A rather large, slenderly built dog of a breed originating in Russia, having a narrow, pointed head and a silky, predominantly white coat. [R. *borzaya.*]

bos·cage also **bos·kage** (bŏs′kĭj) *n.* A mass of trees or shrubs; thicket. [ME *boskage* < OFr. *boscage* < *bosc,* forest, of Germanic orig.]

bosh (bŏsh) *n. Informal.* Meaningless talk or opinions; nonsense. [Turk. *boş,* useless.]

bosk (bŏsk) *n.* A small wooded area or thicket. [Back-formation < *bosky.*]

bos·kage (bŏs′kĭj) *n.* Variant of **boscage.**

Bos·kop man (bŏs′kŏp′) *n.* A Stone Age man of southern Africa held to be ancestral to the Bushmen and Hottentots. [After *Boskop,* a region in the Transvaal where the remains were first found.]

bosk·y (bŏs′kē) *adj.* **-i·er, -i·est. 1.** Covered with bushes, shrubs, or trees; wooded. **2.** Shaded by trees or bushes. [< ME *bosk,* bush < Med. Lat. *bosca,* of Germanic orig.] **—bosk′i·ness** *n.*

bo's'n or **bos'n** (bō′sən) *n.* Variants of **boatswain.**

Bos·ni·an (bŏz′nē-ən) also **Bos·ni·ac** (-nē-ăk′) *—adj.* Of or pertaining to Bosnia. *—n.* **1.** A native of Bosnia. **2.** The Serbo-Croatian language of the Bosnians.

bos·om (bo͝oz′əm, bo͞o′zəm) *n.* **1.** The chest of a human being, esp. the female breasts. **2.** The part of a garment covering the chest. **3.** The center; heart: *in the bosom of the family.* **4.** The chest considered as the source of emotion. **—modifier:** *bosom friends.* [ME < OE *bōsm.*]

bo·son (bō′sŏn) *n.* A particle, such as a photon, pion, or alpha particle, having zero or integral spin and obeying statistical rules that permit any number of identical particles to occupy the same quantum state. [After Jagadis Chandra *Bose* (1858–1937).]

boss[1] (bôs, bŏs) *n.* **1. a.** An employer or supervisor of workers. **b.** Someone who makes decisions or exercises authority. **2.** A professional politician who controls a party or political machine. *—v.* **bossed, boss·ing, boss·es.** *—tr.* **1.** To supervise or control. **2.** To give orders to, esp. in an arrogant or domineering manner: *bossing us around.* *—intr.* To be or act as a boss. *—adj. Slang.* First-rate; topnotch. [Du. *baas,* master.]

boss[2] (bôs, bŏs) *n.* **1.** A circular protuberance or knoblike swelling. **2.** A raised area used as ornamentation. **3.** *Archit.* A raised ornament, as at the intersection of the ribs in vaulted roofs. **4. a.** An enlarged part of a shaft to which another shaft is coupled or to which a wheel or gear is keyed. **b.** A hub, esp. of a propeller. **5.** A metal ornament used for protecting the corners or centers of books. *—tr.v.* **bossed, boss·ing, boss·es. 1.** To decorate with bosses. **2.** To emboss. [ME *boce* < OFr.]

boss[3] (bôs, bŏs) *n.* A cow or calf. [Orig. unknown.]

bos·sa no·va (bŏs′ə nō′və) *n.* **1.** A lively Brazilian dance that is similar to the samba. **2.** Music that is a blend of jazz and samba. [Port. : *bossa,* trend + *nova,* new.]

boss·ism (bô′sĭz′əm, bŏs′ĭz′-) *n.* The domination of a political organization by a political boss.

boss·y[1] (bô′sē, bŏs′ē) *adj.* **-i·er, -i·est.** Given to ordering others around; domineering. **—boss′i·ly** *adv.* **—boss′i·ness** *n.*

boss·y[2] (bô′sē, bŏs′ē) *adj.* Decorated with studs or similar raised ornaments.

boss·y[3] (bô′sē, bŏs′ē) *n., pl.* **-ies.** *Informal.* A cow or calf.

Bos·ton bag (bô′stən) *n.* A handbag or satchel with handles on both sides of the top opening.

Boston bull *n.* A Boston terrier.

Boston cream pie *n.* A cake with a custard filling.

Boston fern *n.* A fern, *Nephrolepis exaltata bostoniensis,* having arching or drooping fronds with opposite leaflets.

Boston ivy *n.* A widely cultivated climbing woody vine, *Parthenocissus tricuspidata,* native to Asia, that has three-lobed leaves and that frequently covers the outer walls of buildings.

Boston lettuce *n.* A type of cultivated lettuce forming a rounded head and having soft-textured, yellow-green leaves.

Boston terrier *n.* A small dog of a breed that originated in New England as a cross between a bull terrier and a bulldog.

bo·sun (bō′sən) *n.* Variant of **boatswain.**

Bos·well (bŏz′wĕl′, -wəl) *n.* An assiduous and devoted admirer, student, and recorder of another's words and deeds. [After James *Boswell* (1740–1795).]

bot also **bott** (bŏt) *n.* The parasitic larva of a botfly. [ME.]

bo·tan·i·cal (bə-tăn′ĭ-kəl) also **bo·tan·ic** (-tăn′ĭk) *adj.* **1.** Of or pertaining to plants or plant life. **2.** Of or pertaining to the science of botany. *—n.* A drug, medicinal preparation, or similar substance obtained from a plant or plants. [Fr. *botanique* < LLat. *botanicus* < Gk. *botanikos* < *botanē,* plant.] **—bo·tan′i·cal·ly** *adv.*

bot·a·nist (bŏt′n-ĭst) *n.* One who specializes in the study of plants.

bot·a·nize (bŏt′n-īz′) *v.* **-nized, -niz·ing, -niz·es.** *—intr.* **1.** To secure plants for botanical study. **2.** To examine plants scientifically. *—tr.* To investigate (an area) for botanical study. **—bot′a·niz′er** *n.*

bot·a·ny (bŏt′n-ē) *n., pl.* **-nies. 1.** The biological science of plants. **2.** The plant life of a particular area or district. **3.** The characteristics and phenomena of a plant group or category. **4. a.** A book or scholarly work on botany. **b.** A particular system of botany.

botch (bŏch) *tr.v.* **botched, botch·ing, botch·es. 1.** To ruin through carelessness or clumsiness. **2.** To make or perform clumsily; bungle. **3.** To repair or mend clumsily. *—n.* **1.** A ruined or defective piece of work. **2.** A badly repaired part or flaw. [ME *bocchen,* to mend.] **—botch′er** *n.* **—botch′y** *adj.*

bot·fly also **bot fly** (bŏt′flī′) *n.* Any of various winged insects, chiefly of the genera *Gasterophilus* and *Oestrus,* having larvae that are parasitic on man and various animals.

both (bōth) *adj.* One and the other; relating to or being two in conjunction: *Both men arrived. —pron.* The one and the other: *Both of those men are patriots. —conj.* Used with *and* to indicate that each of two things in a coordinated phrase or clause is included: *both men and women.* [ME *bothe* < ON *bāðir.*]

Usage: *Both* is used to underscore that the activity or state denoted by a verb applies equally to two entities, where it might have been expected that it would apply only to one. *Both the cooks have exasperated me,* for example, emphasizes that neither cook escapes my impatience. As such, *both* is improperly used with a verb that can apply only to two or more entities. It is illogical to say *they are both alike,* since neither could be "alike" if the other were not. Similarly, *both* is unnecessary in a sentence like *they both appeared together,* since neither one can "appear together" by himself. And we cannot say *both of them accused each other,* since neither one of them can "accuse each other" by himself. • The expression *the both,* as in *he gave it to the both of them,* is best avoided in formal writing and speech. • In possessive constructions, *of both* is usually preferred: *the mothers of both* (rather than *both their mothers*); *the fault of both* (rather than *both their fault* or *both's fault*). • When *both* is used with *and* to link parallel elements in a sentence, the words or phrases that follow them should correspond grammatically: *in both India and China* or *both in India and in China* (not *both in India and China*).

both·er (bŏth′ər) *v.* **-ered, -er·ing, -ers.** *—tr.* **1.** To irritate, esp. by small annoyances. **2. a.** To make agitated or nervous; fluster. **b.** To make confused or perplexed; puzzle. **3.** To intrude without invitation or warrant; disturb. **4.** To give trouble to: *a back condition that bothers him constantly. —intr.* **1.** To take the trouble; concern oneself. **2.** To cause trouble. *—n.* A cause or state of disturbance. *—interj. Chiefly Brit.* Used to express annoyance or mild irritation. [Orig. unknown.]

both·er·a·tion (bŏth′ə-rā′shən) *n.* Something that bothers; vexation.

both·er·some (bŏth′ər-səm) *adj.* Causing bother; troublesome.

both·ri·um (bŏth′rē-əm) *n.* A suction groove on the scolex of the pseudophyllidean tapeworm. [NLat. < Gk. *bothrion,* dim. of *bothros,* pit.]

bo tree (bō) *n.* The peepul. [Singhalese *bo* < Pali *bodi(taru),* (tree of) wisdom < Skt. *bodhi,* enlightenment < *bodhati,* he awakes.]

bot·ry·oid·al (bŏt′rē-oid′l) also **bot·ry·oid** (bŏt′rē-oid′) *adj.* Shaped like a bunch of grapes. [Gk. *botruoeidēs* < *botrus,* bunch of grapes.] **—bot′ry·oid′al·ly** *adv.*

bots (bŏts) *n.* *(used with a sing. or pl. verb).* An ailment in mammals, as cattle and horses, caused by alimentary infestations of parasitic botfly larvae. [Perh. < Sc. Gael. *boiteag,* maggot.]

bott (bŏt) *n.* Variant of **bot.**

bot·tle (bŏt′l) *n.* **1.** A receptacle, usually glass, having a narrow neck and a mouth that can be plugged, corked, or capped. **2.** The quantity a bottle contains. **3.** A bottle filled with milk or formula and fed, as to babies, in place of mothers' milk. *—tr.v.* **-tled, -tling, -tles.** To place in a bottle. ***—phrasal verb.*** **bottle up. 1.** To hold in; restrain: *bottled up her emotions.* **2.** To seal up; block. ***—idiom.*** **hit the bottle.** *Slang.* To drink alcoholic liquor to excess. [ME *botel* < OFr. *botele* < Med. Lat. *buticula,* dim. of LLat. *butis,* cask.] **—bot′tler** *n.*

Boston terrier

bot·tle·brush (bŏt′l-brŭsh′) *n.* Any of various shrubs or trees of the genera *Callistemon* and *Melaleuca,* native to Australia, that have dense spikes of flowers with protruding stamens that suggest a brush used to clean bottles.

bottle club *n.* A private establishment where patrons may purchase bottles of liquor and keep them for consumption after legal closing hours.

bottled gas *n.* Gas, such as butane or propane, stored under pressure in portable tanks.

bot·tle-feed (bŏt′l-fēd′) *tr.v.* **-fed** (-fĕd′), **-feed·ing, -feeds.** To feed, as a baby, with a bottle.

bottle gentian *n.* A plant, *Gentiana andrewsii,* of eastern and central North America, having deep-blue flowers that remain closed.

bottle gourd *n.* **1.** The calabash vine. **2.** The fruit of the calabash vine.

bottle green *n.* A dark to moderate or grayish green. **—bot′tle-green′** *adj.*

bot·tle·neck (bŏt′l-nĕk′) *n.* **1.** The narrow part of a bottle near the top. **2.** A narrow or obstructed section of a highway or pipeline. **3.** A hindrance to production or progress. **4.** *Mus.* A style of guitar playing in which an object, as a piece of glass or metal, is pressed against the strings to achieve a gliding effect. *—tr.v.* **-necked, -neck·ing, -necks.** To impede or slow down by creating a bottleneck.

bottle-nosed dolphin

bot·tle·nose (bŏt′l-nōz′) *n.* A bottle-nosed dolphin.

bot·tle-nosed dolphin (bŏt′l-nōzd′) *n.* Any of several marine mammals of the genus *Tursiops,* having a short, protruding beak.

bottle tree *n.* Any of several trees of the genus *Stercula* (or *Brachychiton*), native to Australia, characterized by a bottle-like swelling of the trunk.

bot·tom (bŏt′əm) *n.* **1.** The lowest or deepest part of something. **2.** The underside. **3.** The supporting part of something; foundation. **4.** The basic quality underlying something; essence. **5.** The solid surface under a body of water. **6.** Often **bottoms.** Low-lying alluvial land adjacent to a river; bottomland. **7.** The part of a ship's hull below the water line. **8.** A ship. **9.** Often **bottoms.** The trousers of pajamas. **10.** *Informal.* The buttocks. **11.** The seat of a chair. **12.** Staying power, as of a horse; stamina. ***—modifier:*** *the bottom drawer. —v.* **-tomed, -tom·ing, -toms.** *—tr.* **1.** To provide with an underside or foundation. **2.** To establish; found. **3.** To grasp the meaning of; fathom. *—intr.* **1.** To be or become based or grounded. **2.** To rest on or touch the bottom. ***—phrasal verb.*** **bottom out.** To descend, as securities, to the lowest point possible, after which only a rise may occur. ***—idiom.*** **at bottom.** Basically. [ME *botme* < OE *botm.*] **—bot′tom·er** *n.*

bottom break *n.* A branch arising from the stem base of a plant.

bottom fauna *n.* Marine vegetation growing in the benthic region of the ocean depths.

bot·tom·land (bŏt′əm-lănd′) *n.* Low-lying land along a river.

bot·tom·less (bŏt′əm-lĭs) *adj.* **1.** Having no bottom. **2.** Too deep to be measured. **3.** Difficult or impossible to understand; unfathomable. **4.** Limitless. **—bot′tom·less·ly** *adv.*

bottom line *n.* **1.** The lowest line in a financial statement, showing net income or loss. **2.** The final result or statement; upshot. **3.** The main or essential point.

bot·tom-line (bŏt′əm-līn′) *adj.* Concerned exclusively with costs and profits.

bottom round *n.* A cut of meat, as a steak or roast, taken from the outer section of a round of beef.

bot·tom·ry (bŏt′əm-rē) *n.* A contract by which a shipowner borrows money to finance a voyage, pledging the ship as security. [Alteration of Du. *bodemerij* < *bodem,* ship.]

bot·u·lin (bŏch′ə-lĭn) *n.* Any of several nerve toxins produced by botulinum and found in improperly canned or improperly smoked foods. [Lat. *botulus,* sausage + -IN.]

bot·u·li·num (bŏch′ə-lī′nəm) *n.* A bacterium, *Clostridium botulinum,* that secretes botulin. [NLat. < Lat. *botulus,* sausage.]

bot·u·lism (bŏch′ə-lĭz′əm) *n.* An extremely virulent, dangerous food poisoning caused by botulin and characterized by vomiting, abdominal pain, coughing, muscular weakness, and visual disturbance. [G. *Botulismus* < Lat. *botulus,* sausage.]

bou·clé or **bou·cle** (bo͞o-klā′) *n.* **1.** A type of yarn, usually three-ply and having one thread looser than the others, that produces a rough-textured cloth. **2.** Fabric woven or knitted from bouclé. [Fr., p.part. of *boucler,* to curl < OFr. *boucle,* curl of hair.]

bou·doir (bo͞o′dwär′, -dwôr′) *n.* A woman's private sitting room, dressing room, or bedroom. [Fr. < OFr. *bouder,* to sulk.]

bouf·fant (bo͞o-fänt′) *adj.* Puffed-out; full: *a bouffant hair style.* [Fr., pr.part. of *bouffer,* to puff up < OFr.]

bouffe (bo͞of) *n.* Comic opera.

bou·gain·vil·le·a also **bou·gain·vil·lae·a** (bo͞o′gən-vĭl′ē-ə, -vĭl′yə) *n.* Any of several woody tropical American vines of the genus *Bougainvillea,* having inconspicuous flowers surrounded by showy red, purple, or orange bracts. [NLat. *Bougainvillea,* genus name after Louis Antoine de *Bougainville* (1729–1811).]

bough (bou) *n.* A large branch of a tree. [ME < OE *bōh.*]

bought (bôt) *v.* Past tense and past participle of **buy.**

bought·en (bôt′n) *v. Regional.* A past participle of **buy.**

bou·gie (bo͞o′zhē, -jē) *n.* **1.** A wax candle. **2.** *Med.* **a.** A slender, pliable implement inserted into a bodily canal, as the urethra or rectum. **b.** A suppository. [Fr. < OFr., a fine wax < *Bougie,* Bejaïa, Algeria.]

bouil·la·baisse (bo͞o′yə-bās′) *n.* A highly seasoned fish stew made of several kinds of fish and shellfish. [Fr. < Prov. *bouiabaisso* : *boui,* imper. of *bouie,* to boil (< Lat. *bullire*) + *abaisso,* imper. of *abeissa,* to lower.]

bouil·lon (bo͞o′yŏn′, bo͝ol′-, -yən) *n.* A clear, thin broth made typically by simmering beef or chicken in water with seasonings. [Fr. < OFr. < *boulir,* to boil < Lat. *bullire.*]

bouillon cube *n.* A small cube of evaporated seasoned meat, poultry, or vegetable stock.

boul·der also **bowl·der** (bōl′dər) *n.* A large rounded mass of rock lying on the surface of the ground or imbedded in the soil. [ME *bulder,* prob. of Scand. orig.]

bou·le¹ (bo͞o′lē, bo͞o-lā′) *n.* **1. a.** The senate of 400 founded in ancient Athens by Solon. **b.** A legislative assembly in any of the states of ancient Greece. **2.** The lower house of the modern Greek legislature. [Gk. *boulē.*]

boule² (bo͞ol) *n.* A pear-shaped synthetic sapphire, ruby, or other alumina-based gem, produced by fusing and tinting alumina. [Fr., ball < Lat. *bulla.*]

boule³ (bo͞ol) *n.* Variant of **buhl.**

boul·e·vard (bo͝ol′ə-värd′, bo͞o′lə-) *n.* A broad city street, often tree-lined and landscaped. [Fr. < OFr. *boloart,* rampart converted to a promenade < MDu. *bolwerc,* bulwark < MHG.]

bou·le·vard·ier (bo͞o′lə-vär-dyā′, bo͝ol′ə-, -dîr′) *n.* A man about town. [Obs. Fr. < *boulevard,* boulevard.]

bou·le·ver·se·ment (bo͞o′lə-vĕr′sə-mäɴ′) *n.* **1.** A reversal. **2.** A violent uproar; tumult. [Fr. < OFr. *bouleverser,* to overturn : *boule,* ball + *verser,* to overturn < Lat. *versare,* to turn.]

boulle (bo͞ol) *n.* Variant of **buhl.**

bounce (bouns) *v.* **bounced, bounc·ing, bounc·es.** *—intr.* **1. a.** To rebound elastically from a collision. **b.** To collide and rebound elastically several times in succession. **2.** To bound thumpingly: *a child bouncing into the room.* **3.** *Informal.* To be sent back by a bank as valueless: *a check that bounced.* *—tr.* **1.** To cause to collide and rebound. **2.** *Slang.* **a.** To expel by force. **b.** To dismiss from employment. **3.** To write on an overdrawn bank account: *bounce a check.* *—n.* **1.** A bound or rebound. **2.** A sudden spring or leap. **3.** Capacity to bounce; spring: *a ball with bounce.* **4.** Spirit; liveliness. **5.** *Slang.* Expulsion; dismissal. **6.** *Chiefly Brit.* Impudent bluster. [ME *bounsen,* to beat.]

bounc·er (boun′sər) *n.* **1.** One that bounces. **2.** *Slang.* A person employed to expel disorderly persons from a public place.

bounc·ing (boun′sĭng) *adj.* **1.** Vigorous; healthy: *a bouncing baby.* **2.** Spirited; lively. **—bounc′ing·ly** *adv.*

bouncing Bet (bĕt) *n.* A plant, *Saponaria officinalis,* native to the Old World, having rounded clusters of fragrant pink or white flowers. [< *Bet,* nickname for *Elizabeth.*]

bouncing Bet

bounc·y (boun′sē) *adj.* **-i·er, -i·est.** **1.** Tending to bounce. **2.** Springy; elastic. **3.** Lively; energetic: *bouncy tunes.* **—bounc′i·ly** *adv.*

bound¹ (bound) *intr.v.* **bound·ed, bound·ing, bounds. 1.** To leap forward or upward; spring. **2.** To progress by bounds. *—n.* **1.** A leap; jump. **2.** A bounce. [Fr. *bondir,* to bounce < OFr., to resound, perh. < Lat. *bombitare,* to hum < *bombus,* a humming sound < Gk. *bombos.*]

bound² (bound) *n.* **1.** Often **bounds.** A boundary; limit: *His joy knew no bounds.* **2. bounds.** The territory on, within, or near limiting lines: *the bounds of the kingdom.* *—v.* **bound·ed, bound·ing, bounds.** *—tr.* **1.** To provide a limit to. **2.** To constitute the boundary or limit of. **3.** To identify and set the boundaries of; demarcate. *—intr.* To border on another country, state, or place; adjoin. **—idiom. out of bounds.** Beyond boundaries or limits. [ME < OFr. *bunde* < Med. Lat. *bodina,* of Celtic orig.]

bound³ (bound) *v.* Past tense and past participle of **bind.** *—adj.* **1.** Confined by bonds; tied: *bound and gagged.* **2.** Under legal or moral obligation; under contract: *bound by his promise.* **3.** Indentured: *a bound apprentice.* **4.** Equipped with a cover or binding: *bound volumes.* **5.** Predetermined; certain: *bound to be late.* **6.** Determined; resolved: *He's bound to be mayor.* **7.** Constipated.

bound⁴ (bound) *adj.* Headed; on the way: *bound for home.* [ME *boun,* ready < ON *būinn,* p.part. of *būa,* to get ready.]

bound·a·ry (boun′də-rē, -drē) *n., pl.* **-ries. 1.** Something that indicates a border or limit. **2.** The border or limit indicated by a boundary.

Synonyms: *boundary, border, frontier, limit, bound, end, confine. Boundary* is usually applied geographically to a precisely defined terminating line of a country, city, or the like. *Border* may be used in this exact sense or more broadly to denote the territory immediately adjoining a boundary. *Frontier* denotes either the part of a country that faces toward or fronts an adjoining country or (within a country) the remote, imprecisely defined area that marks the farthest settlement. Figuratively the term applies to any newly explored branch of knowledge. *Limit* (often in the plural) is interchangeable with *boundary* in a physical sense; figuratively it indicates an extent beyond which an activity or function cannot or should not take place. *Bound* (usually plural) is interchangeable with *boundary,* physically: *The ball went out of bounds;* figuratively it has the sense of limit: *the bounds of good taste. End* (often plural) in this comparison emphasizes remoteness or extreme limit in all senses: *the ends of the earth; the end of his rope. Confine* (usually plural) is used physically and figuratively to denote enclosure or limitation.

boundary layer *n.* The nearly motionless fluid layer found immediately adjacent to a boundary, such as the surface of a solid, past which the fluid flows.

bound·en (boun′dən) *adj.* **1.** *Archaic.* Under obligation; obliged. **2.** Obligatory: *his bounden duty.* [ME, p.part. of *binden,* to bind < OE bindan.]

bound·er (boun′dər) *n.* **1.** One that bounds. **2.** *Chiefly Brit.* A vulgar, cocksure fellow.

bound form *n.* A linguistic element that always occurs as part of another word, as *-ly* in *lovely.*

bound·less (bound′lĭs) *adj.* Without limit; infinite. **—bound′less·ly** *adv.* **—bound′less·ness** *n.*

boun·te·ous (boun′tē-əs) *adj.* **1.** Giving generously and kindly. **2.** Copious; plentiful. [ME *bountevous* < OFr. *bontive,* benevolent < *bonte,* bounty.] **—boun′te·ous·ly** *adv.* **—boun′te·ous·ness** *n.*

boun·ti·ful (boun′tə-fəl) *adj.* **1.** Generous. **2.** Abundant; plentiful. **—boun′ti·ful·ly** *adv.* **—boun′ti·ful·ness** *n.*

boun·ty (boun′tē) *n., pl.* **-ties. 1.** Liberality in giving. **2.** Something that is given liberally. **3.** A reward, inducement, or payment, esp. one given by a government for acts beneficial to the state, such as killing predatory animals or enlisting for military service. [ME *bounte* < OFr. *bonte* < Lat. *bonitas,* goodness < *bonus,* good.]

bounty hunter *n.* One who hunts predatory animals or criminals and outlaws for a bounty.

bou·quet (bō-kā′, bo͞o-) *n.* **1.** A cluster of flowers; nosegay. **2.** The fragrance typical of a wine or a liqueur. [Fr. < OFr. *bosquet,* thicket, dim. of *bosc,* forest, of Germanic orig.]

bou·quet gar·ni (bō-kā′ gär-nē′, bo͞o-) *n., pl.* **bou·quets gar·nis** (bō-kāz′ gär-nē′, bo͞o-). A bunch of herbs tied together or wrapped in cheesecloth and immersed in a soup or stew as seasoning. [Fr. : *bouquet,* bunch + *garni,* p.part. of *garnir,* to garnish.]

bour·bon (bûr′bən) *n.* A whiskey distilled from a fermented mash containing not less than 51 per cent corn. [After *Bourbon* County, Kentucky.]

bour·don (bo͝or′dn) *n.* **1.** The monotonic drone bass of a bagpipe. **2.** An organ stop, commonly of the 16-foot pipes. [ME *burdoun* < OFr. *bourdon.*]

bourg (bo͝org) *n.* **1.** A medieval village, esp. one situated near a castle. **2.** A French market town. [ME < OFr. < Lat. *burgus,* fortress, of Germanic orig.]

bour·geois (bo͝or-zhwä′, bo͝or′zhwä′) *n., pl.* **bourgeois. 1.** A person belonging to the bourgeoisie. **2.** A person whose attitudes and behavior are marked by conformity to the standards and conventions of the middle class. **3.** In Marxist theory, a member of the property-owning class; a capitalist as opposed to a member of the proletariat. *—adj.* **1.** Of or typical of the middle class. **2.** Characterized by a preoccupation with respectability and material values. [Fr. < OFr. *burgeis* < *bourg,* bourg.]

bour·geoise (bo͝or-zhwäz′, bo͝or′zhwäz′) *n., pl.* **-geois·es** (-zhwä′zĭz). A woman belonging to the bourgeoisie. [Fr., fem. of *bourgeois,* bourgeois.] **—bour·geoise′** *adj.*

bour·geoi·sie (bo͝or′zhwä-zē′) *n.* **1.** The middle class. **2.** In Marxist theory, the social group opposed to the proletariat in the class struggle; the capitalist class. [Fr. < *bourgeois,* bourgeois.]

bour·geon (bûr′jən) *v.* Variant of **burgeon.**

bourn¹ also **bourne** (bôrn, bōrn, bo͝orn) *n.* A stream or small brook. [ME < OE *burna.*]

bourn² also **bourne** (bôrn, bōrn, bo͝orn) *n. Archaic.* **1.** The terminal point of a trip or course of action; goal. **2.** A boundary, as between properties. [Fr. *bourne* < OFr. *bodne, limit* < *Med. Lat. bodina,* of Celtic orig.]
bour·rée (bo͞o-rā′, bo͞o-) *n.* **1.** An old French dance resembling the gavotte, usually in quick duple time beginning with an upbeat. **2.** The music for a bourrée. [Fr.]
bourse (bo͝ors) *n.* The stock exchange of a city of continental Europe, esp. Paris. [Fr. < LLat. *bursa,* bag. —see PURSE.]
bouse also **bowse** (bouz) *v.* **boused, bous·ing, bous·es** also **bowsed, bows·ing, bows·es.** *Naut. —tr.* To hoist or pull up with a tackle. *—intr.* To hoist. [Orig. unknown.]
bou·stro·phe·don (bo͞o′strə-fēd′n, -fē′dŏn′) *n.* An ancient method of writing in which the lines are inscribed alternately from right to left and from left to right. [< Gk. *boustrophēdon,* turning like an ox while plowing: *bous,* ox + *strephein,* to turn.] **—bou·stroph′e·don′ic** (-strŏf′ĭ-dŏn′ĭk) *adj.*
bout (bout) *n.* **1.** A contest between antagonists; match: *a wrestling bout.* **2.** A period of time spent in a particular way; spell: *"His tremendous bouts of drinking had wrecked his health"* (Thomas Wolfe). [ME, bend.]
bou·tique (bo͞o-tēk′) *n.* A small retail shop that specializes in gifts, fashionable clothes, and accessories. [Fr. < OProv. *botica* < Lat. *apotheca,* storehouse. —see APOTHECARY.]
bou·ton (bo͞o-tôn′) *n.* A club-shaped enlargement at the end of a nerve fiber. [Fr., button.]
bou·ton·niere also **bou·ton·nière** (bo͞o′tə-nîr′, -tən-yâr′) *n.* A flower or small bunch of flowers worn in a buttonhole. [Fr. *boutonnière,* buttonhole < OFr. < *bouton,* button.]
bou·var·di·a (bo͞o-vär′dē-ə) *n.* Any of several tropical American shrubs of the genus *Bouvardia,* having clusters of white or red, often fragrant flowers. [NLat. *Bouvardia,* genus name, after Charles *Bouvard* (1572–1658).]
Bou·vier des Flan·dres (bo͞o-vyā′ də flăn′dərz, flän′drə) *n.* A rough-coated dog of a breed originally used in Belgium for herding and guarding cattle. [Fr. : *bouvier,* cowherd + *des,* of + *Flandres,* Flanders.]
bou·zou·ki (bo͞o-zo͞o′kē, bə-) *n. Mus.* A Greek stringed instrument resembling a mandolin. [Modern Gk. *mpouzouki.*]
bo·vid (bō′vĭd) *adj.* Of or belonging to the family Bovidae, which includes hoofed, hollow-horned ruminants such as cattle, sheep, goats, and buffaloes. *—n.* A member of the Bovidae. [< NLat. *Bovidae,* family name < Lat. *bōs,* cow.]
bo·vine (bō′vīn′, -vēn′) *adj.* **1.** Of, pertaining to, or resembling an ox, cow, or other animal of the genus *Bos.* **2.** Sluggish; dull; stolid. *—n.* A bovine animal. [LLat. *bovinus* < Lat. *bos,* cow.]
bow¹ (bou) *n.* **1.** The front section of a ship or boat. **2.** The oar or oarsman closest to the bow of a boat. [ME *boue,* of Germanic orig.]
bow² (bou) *v.* **bowed, bow·ing, bows.** *—intr.* **1.** To bend or curve downward; stoop. **2.** To incline the body or head or bend the knee in greeting, consent, courtesy, acknowledgment, submission, or veneration. **3.** To yield or comply; submit. *—tr.* **1.** To bend (the head, knee, or body) in order to express greeting, consent, courtesy, submission, or veneration. **2.** To convey (greeting, for example) by bowing. **3.** To escort deferentially and with bows: *bowed us into the restaurant.* **4.** To cause to acquiesce; submit. **5.** To cause to bend downward; overburden: *Grief bowed him down.* ***—phrasal verb.*** **bow out.** To remove oneself; withdraw or resign. *—n.* An inclination of the head or body, as in greeting, consent, courtesy, acknowledgment, submission, or veneration. [ME *bowen* < OE *būgan.*]
bow³ (bō) *n.* **1.** Something that is bent, curved, or arched. **2.** A weapon consisting of a curved, flexible strip of material, esp. wood, strung taut from end to end and used to launch arrows. **3. a.** An archer. **b.** Archers collectively. **4.** A rod having horsehair drawn tightly between its two raised ends, used in playing instruments of the violin and viol families. **5.** A knot usually having two loops and two ends; bowknot. **6. a.** A frame for the lenses of a pair of eyeglasses. **b.** The part of such a frame passing over the ear. **7.** A rainbow. **8.** An oxbow. *—v.* **bowed, bow·ing, bows.** *—tr.* **1.** To bend (something) into the shape of a bow. **2.** To play (a stringed instrument) with a bow. *—intr.* **1.** To bend into a curve or bow. **2.** To play a stringed instrument with a bow. [ME *bowe* < OE *boga.*]
bow compass (bō) *n.* A drawing compass with legs that are connected by an adjustable metal spring band.
bowd·ler·ize (bōd′lə-rīz′, boud′-) *tr.v.* **-ized, -iz·ing, -iz·es.** To expurgate (a book, for example) prudishly. [After Thomas *Bowdler* (1754–1825).] **—bowd′ler·ism** *n.* **—bowd′ler·i·za′tion** *n.* **—bowd′ler·iz′er** *n.*
bow·el (bou′əl, boul) *n.* **1. a.** An intestine, esp. of a human being. **b.** Often **bowels.** The part of the digestive tract below the stomach. **2. bowels.** The interior of something: *in the bowels of the ship.* **3. bowels.** *Archaic.* The seat of pity or the gentler emotions. *—tr.v.* **-eled, -el·ing, -els** or **-elled, -el·ling, -els.** To remove the bowels or entrails from; disembowel. [ME < OFr. *bouele* < LLat. *botellus,* small intestine, dim. of *botulus,* sausage.]
bow·er¹ (bou′ər) *n.* **1.** A shaded, leafy recess; arbor. **2.** A woman's private chamber in a medieval castle; boudoir. **3.** A rustic cottage; country retreat. *—tr.v.* **-ered, -er·ing, -ers.** To enclose in or as if in a bower; embower. [ME *bour,* a dwelling < OE *būr.*] **—bow′er·y** (-ə-rē) *adj.*
bow·er² (bou′ər) *n.* The heaviest of a ship's anchors, carried at the bow.
bow·er·bird (bou′ər-bûrd′) *n.* Any of various birds of the family Ptilonorhynchidae, of Australia and New Guinea, of which the males of many species build bowers of grasses, twigs, and colored materials to attract females.
bow·er·y (bou′ə-rē, bou′rē) *n., pl.* **-ies.** A farm or plantation owned by one of the early Dutch settlers of New York. [Du. *bouwerij* < *bouwen,* to cultivate < MDu.]
bow·fin (bō′fĭn′) *n.* A freshwater fish, *Amia calva,* of central and eastern North America, that is the only known living species of the family Amidae.
bow·front (bō′frŭnt′) *adj.* Having an outward-curving front: *a bowfront bureau.*
bow·head (bō′hĕd′) *n.* A whale, *Balaena mysticetus,* of Arctic seas, having a large head.
bow·ie knife (bō′ē, bo͞o′ē) *n.* A single-edged steel hunting knife, about 15 inches in length, having a hilt and a crosspiece. [After James *Bowie* (1790?–1836).]
bow·knot (bō′nŏt′) *n.* A knot with large, decorative loops.
bowl¹ (bōl) *n.* **1. a.** A hemispherical vessel, wider than it is deep, for food or fluids. **b.** The contents of such a vessel. **2.** A drinking goblet. **3.** A bowl-shaped part, as of a spoon. **4. a.** A bowl-shaped stadium or outdoor theater. **b.** Any of various football games played between specially selected teams after the regular season. **5.** A bowl-shaped topographic depression. [ME *bowle* < OE *bolla.*]
bowl² (bōl) *n.* **1.** A large, wooden ball weighted or slightly flattened so as to roll with a bias. **2.** A roll or throw of the ball, as in bowling. **3.** A revolving cylinder or drum in a machine. **4. bowls** *(used with a sing. verb).* The game of lawn bowling. *—v.* **bowled, bowl·ing, bowls.** *—intr.* **1.** To participate in a game of bowling. **2.** To throw or roll a ball in bowling. **3.** To move smoothly and rapidly: *a bus that was bowling along.* **4.** To hurl a cricket ball from one end of the pitch toward the batsman at the other in a manner distinguished from throwing. *—tr.* **1.** To throw or roll (a ball) in bowling. **2.** To make or achieve by bowling. ***—phrasal verbs.*** **bowl out.** To retire (a batsman in cricket) with a bowled ball that knocks the bails off the wicket. **bowl over.** To take by surprise; astound. [ME *boule* < OFr. < Lat. *bulla,* bubble.]
bowl·der (bōl′dər) *n.* Variant of **boulder.**
bow·leg (bō′lĕg′) *n.* A leg having an outward curvature in the region of the knee.
bow·leg·ged (bō′lĕg′ĭd, -lĕgd′) *adj.* Having bowlegs.
bowl·er¹ (bō′lər) *n.* One that bowls.
bowl·er² (bō′lər) *n. Chiefly Brit.* A derby hat. [After John *Bowler,* a 19th-cent. London hatmaker.]
bow·line (bō′lĭn, -līn′) *n.* **1.** A rope leading forward from the leech of a square sail to hold the leech forward when sailing close-hauled. **2.** A knot forming a loop that does not slip. [ME *bouline,* of Germanic orig.]
bowl·ing (bō′lĭng) *n.* **1.** A game played by rolling a ball down a wooden alley in order to knock down a triangular group of ten pins. **2.** Any of various games similar to bowling, such as skittles or ninepins.
bowling alley *n.* **1.** A smooth, level wooden alley used in bowling. **2.** A building or room containing bowling alleys.
bow·man¹ (bō′mən) *n.* An archer.
bow·man² (bou′mən) *n.* An oarsman stationed at the bow of a boat.
Bow·man's capsule (bo′mənz) *n.* The renal or malpighian corpuscle, which acts as a filter in urine formation in the kidney. [After Sir William *Bowman* (1816–1892).]
Bowman's glands *n.* The olfactory glands, which keep the olfactory surface moist. [After Sir William *Bowman* (1816–1892).]
bow·man's root (bō′mənz) *n.* A plant, *Gillenia trifoliata,* of eastern North America, having compound leaves and small white or pinkish flowers.
bow pen (bō) *n.* A bow compass with a pen at the end of one leg.
bowse (bouz) *v.* Variant of **bouse.**
bow·shot (bō′shŏt′) *n.* The distance an arrow can be shot.
bow·sprit (bou′sprĭt′, bō′-) *n.* A spar extending forward from the stem of a ship. [ME *bouspret.*]
bow·string (bō′strĭng′) *n.* The string of a bow.
bowstring hemp *n.* **1.** Any of various plants of the genus *Sansevieria,* having thick, erect leaves. **2.** The fiber from the leaves of bowstring hemp, used for cordage and in packing.
bow tie (bō) *n.* A man's small necktie tied in the shape of a bow.
bow window (bō) *n.* A bay window built in a curve.
bow-wow (bou′wou′) *n.* The bark of a dog. [Imit.]
bow·yer (bō′yər) *n.* **1.** An archer. **2.** One who makes bows.
box¹ (bŏks) *n.* **1. a.** A rectangular container typically having a lid or cover. **b.** The amount or quantity such a container can hold. **2.** A separated compartment in a public place, as a theater, for the accommodation of a small group. **3.** A small structure serving as a shelter: *a sentry box.* **4.** *Chiefly Brit.* A small country house in hunting country: *a shooting box.* **5.** A box stall. **6.** The raised seat for the driver of a coach or carriage. **7.** *Baseball.* **a.** An area on a diamond

bow³

George Miksch Sutton
bowerbird

bowie knife

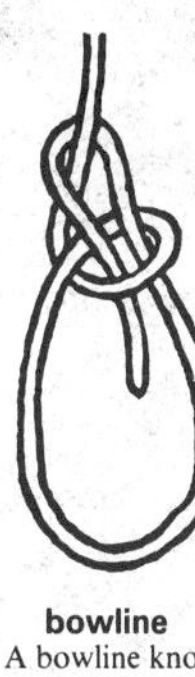

bowline
A bowline knot

marked by lines where the batter stands. **b.** Any of various designated areas for other team members, such as the pitcher, catcher, and coaches. **8.** Featured printed matter enclosed by hairlines, a border, or white space and placed within or between text columns. **9.** A cut in the side of a tree through which sap is collected. **10.** An insulating, enclosing, or protective casing or part in a machine. **11.** An awkward or perplexing situation; predicament. *—tr.v.* **boxed, box·ing, box·es. 1.** To pack in a box. **2.** To confine in or as if in a box. **3.** *Naut.* To boxhaul. ***—idiom.*** **box the compass. 1.** To name the points of the compass in proper order. **2.** To make a complete revolution or reversal. [ME < OE < LLat. *buxis* < Gk. *puxis* < *puxos,* box tree.]

box[2] (bŏks) *n.* A blow or slap with the hand. *—v.* **boxed, box·ing, box·es.** *—tr.* **1.** To hit with the hand or fist. **2.** To take part in a boxing match with. *—intr.* To fight with the fists; spar. [ME.]

box[3] (bŏks) *n., pl.* **box** or **box·es. 1. a.** An evergreen tree or shrub of the genus *Buxus,* esp. *B. sempervirens,* used for hedges, borders, and garden mazes. **b.** The wood of this tree. **2.** Any of several trees whose timber or foliage resembles that of box. [ME < OE < Lat. *buxus* < Gk. *puxos.*]

box calf *n.* Calfskin treated with chromium salts and having square markings on the grain. [After Joseph *Box,* a 19th-cent. London bootmaker.]

box·car (bŏks'kär') *n.* An enclosed and covered railway car for the transportation of freight.

box coat *n.* **1.** A heavy overcoat formerly worn by coachmen. **2.** A coat designed to hang loose from the shoulders. [BOX[1] + COAT.]

box·el·der (bŏks'ĕl'dər) *n.* A maple tree, *Acer negundo,* of North America, having compound leaves with lobed leaflets.

boxer[2]

box·er[1] (bŏk'sər) *n.* One that engages in fighting with the fists.

box·er[2] (bŏk'sər) *n.* A short-haired dog of a breed developed in Germany, having a brownish coat and a short, square-jawed muzzle. [G. < BOXER[1].]

Box·er (bŏk'sər) *n.* A member of a secret society in China that attempted in 1900 to drive foreigners from the country by violence and to force Chinese Christians to renounce their religion. [Approximate transl. of Chin. (Mandarin) *yi[4] he[2] quan[2],* righteous harmonious fists, alteration of *yi[4] he[2] tuan[2],* righteous harmonious society.]

boxer shorts *pl.n.* Men's full-cut undershorts.

box·fish (bŏks'fĭsh') *n., pl.* **boxfish** or **-fish·es.** The trunkfish.

box·haul (bŏks'hôl') *tr.v.* **-hauled, -haul·ing, -hauls.** To turn (a square-rigged ship) about on the heel by bracing the sails aback.

box·ing[1] (bŏk'sĭng) *n.* Material used for boxes.

box·ing[2] (bŏk'sĭng) *n.* The sport of fighting with the fists.

Boxing Day *n.* The first weekday after Christmas, observed in parts of the British Commonwealth as a holiday, when Christmas gifts or boxes are traditionally given to service workers.

boxing glove *n.* A heavily padded leather glove worn in boxing.

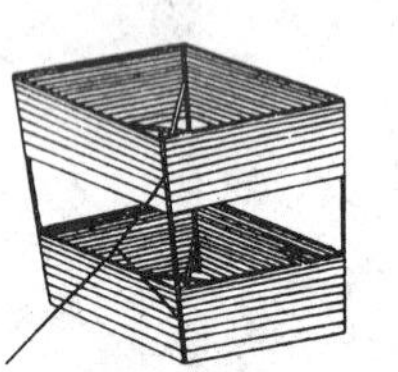
box kite

box kite *n.* A tailless kite consisting of a rectangular, box-shaped frame encircled with cloth or paper bands.

box lunch *n.* A lunch packed in a container, as a box, esp. for traveling.

box office *n.* **1.** A ticket office, as of a theater or stadium. **2.** The drawing power of a theatrical entertainment or of a performer; popular appeal.

box pleat *n.* A double pleat formed by two facing folds.

box score *n.* A printed summary, as of a baseball game, in the form of a table listing each player and the statistics for his performance.

box seat *n.* A seat in a box at a theater, concert hall, or stadium.

box set *n.* A stage set with a ceiling and three walls.

box spring *n.* A bedspring consisting of a frame enclosed with cloth and containing rows of coil springs.

box stall *n.* An enclosed stall for a single animal.

box·thorn (bŏks'thôrn') *n.* The matrimony vine.

box turtle *n.* Any of several North American turtles of the genus *Terrapene,* having a high-domed shell.

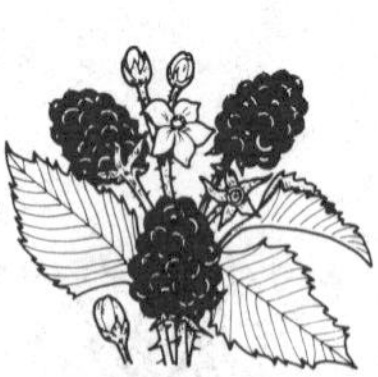
boysenberry

box·wood (bŏks'wo͝od') *n.* **1.** A box shrub or tree. **2.** The hard, light-yellow wood of the boxwood, used to make musical instruments, rulers, inlays, and engraving blocks.

box·y (bŏk'sē) *adj.* **-i·er, -i·est.** Like a box. **—box'i·ness** *n.*

boy (boi) *n.* **1.** A male child or youth. **2.** *Informal.* A grown man; fellow: *a night out with the boys.* **3.** A manservant. *—interj.* Used to express mild astonishment, elation, or disgust: *Oh boy, some car!* [ME *boi,* poss. < OFr. *embuié,* p.part. of *embuier,* to fetter.] **—boy'hood'** *n.*

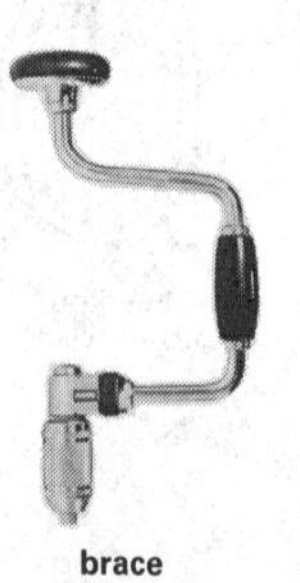
brace
Bit brace

bo·yar also **bo·yard** (bō-yär') *n.* A member of a former Russian aristocratic order abolished by Peter I. [R. *boyarin* < Old R., of Turkish orig.]

boy·cott (boi'kŏt') *tr.v.* **-cott·ed, -cott·ing, -cotts.** To abstain from using, buying, or dealing with to express protest or to coerce. *—n.* The act or an instance of boycotting. [After Charles C. *Boycott* (1832–1897).] **—boy'cott'er** *n.*

boy·friend also **boy friend** (boi'frĕnd') *n.* **1.** A male friend. **2.** *Informal.* A favored male companion or sweetheart.

boy·ish (boi'ĭsh) *adj.* Characteristic of or befitting a boy: *a boyish prank.* **—boy'ish·ly** *adv.* **—boy'ish·ness** *n.*

Boyle's law (boilz) *n.* The principle that at a fixed temperature the pressure of a confined ideal gas varies inversely with its volume. [After Robert *Boyle* (1627–1691), its formulator.]

Boy Scout *n.* A member of a worldwide organization of young men and boys, founded in England in 1908, for character development and citizenship training.

boy·sen·ber·ry (boi'zən-bĕr'ē) *n.* **1.** A prickly bramble hybridized from the loganberry and various blackberries and raspberries. **2.** The large, wine-red, edible berry of the boysenberry. [After Rudolph *Boysen* (d. 1950).]

bo·zo (bō'zō) *n., pl.* **-zos.** *Slang.* **1.** A fellow; guy. **2.** A dunce; fool. [Orig. unknown.]

Br The symbol for the element bromine.

bra (brä) *n.* A brassiere.

brab·ble (brăb'əl) *intr.v.* **-bled, -bling, -bles.** To quarrel noisily; wrangle. *—n.* A petty dispute; squabble. [Poss. < M. Du. *brabbelen,* to jabber.] **—brab'bler** *n.*

brace (brās) *n.* **1.** A device that holds or fastens two or more parts together or in place; clamp. **2.** A device that steadies or holds something erect, as a supporting beam in a building. **3. braces.** *Chiefly Brit.* A pair of suspenders. **4.** An appliance used to support a bodily part. **5.** Often **braces.** An arrangement of bands and wires fixed to the teeth to correct irregular alignment. **6.** A rope by which a yard is swung and secured on a square-rigged ship. **7.** A protective pad strapped to the bow arm of an archer. **8.** A leather loop that slides to change the tension on the cords of a drum. **9.** A set of connected musical staves. **10.** A cranklike handle with an adjustable aperture at one end for securing and turning a bit. **11.** One of two symbols, { }, used to connect written or printed lines. **12.** *Math.* Either of a pair of symbols, { }, used to indicate aggregation or to clarify the grouping of quantities when parentheses and square brackets have already been used. **13.** *pl.* **brace.** A pair of like things: *a brace of partridges.* **14.** An extremely stiff and erect position or bearing. *—v.* **braced, brac·ing, brac·es.** *—tr.* **1.** To furnish with a brace. **2.** To support or hold steady with or as if with a brace. **3.** To prepare or position so as to be ready for an impact or danger. **4.** To invigorate; stimulate: *cold, clear air that braced the skiers.* **5.** To turn (the yards of a ship) by the braces. *—intr.* To get ready; make preparations. ***—phrasal verb.*** **brace up.** To summon one's strength or endurance. [ME < OFr., two arms < Lat. *bracchia,* pl. of *bracchium,* arm < Gk. *brakhiōn.*]

brace·let (brās'lĭt) *n.* **1.** An ornamental band or chain encircling the wrist. **2.** Something, such as handcuffs, that resembles a bracelet. [ME < OFr., dim. of *bracel,* armlet < Lat. *bracchiale* < *bracchium,* arm < Gk. *brakhiōn.*]

brac·er[1] (brā'sər) *n.* **1.** One that braces. **2.** *Informal.* A stimulating drink; tonic.

bra·cer[2] (brā'sər) *n.* An arm or wrist guard worn by archers and fencers. [ME < OFr. *braceüre* < *bras,* arm < Lat. *bracchium* < Gk. *brakhiōn.*]

bra·ce·ro (brə-sâr'ō) *n., pl.* **-ros.** A Mexican laborer permitted to enter the United States and work for a limited period of time. [Sp., laborer < *brazo,* arm < Lat. *bracchium* < Gk. *brakhiōn.*]

brach (brăch) *n. Obs.* A bitch hound. [ME *brache,* back-formation < OFr. *brachez,* pl. of *brachet,* hunting dog < OHG *bracco.*]

bra·chi·a (brā'kē-ə, brăk'ē-ə) *n.* Plural of **brachium.**

bra·chi·al (brā'kē-əl, brăk'ē-) *adj.* Of, pertaining to, or resembling the arm or a similar or homologous part. [Lat. *bracchialis* < *bracchium,* arm < Gk. *brakhiōn.*]

bra·chi·ate (brā'kē-ĭt, -āt', brăk'ē-) *adj.* Having widely spreading branches arranged in pairs. *—intr.v.* (āt') **-at·ed, -at·ing, -ates.** To swing by the arms from branch to branch, as certain apes do. [Lat. *bracchiatus* < *bracchium,* arm < Gk. *brakhiōn.*] **—bra'chi·a'tion** *n.*

brach·i·o·pod (brăk'ē-ə-pŏd', brā'kē-) *n.* Any of various marine invertebrates of the phylum Brachiopoda, having bivalve dorsal and ventral shells and a pair of tentacled, armlike structures on either side of the mouth. [BRACHI(UM) + -POD.] **—brach'i·o·pod'** *adj.*

bra·chi·um (brā'kē-əm, brăk'ē-) *n., pl.* **bra·chi·a** (brā'kē-ə, brăk'ē-ə). An arm or a homologous anatomical structure, such as a flipper or wing. [Lat. *bracchium,* arm < Gk. *brakhiōn.*]

brachy– *pref.* Short: *brachydactylic.* [< Gk. *brakhus,* short.]

brach·y·ce·phal·ic (brăk'ĭ-sə-făl'ĭk) also **brach·y·ceph·a·lous** (-sĕf'ə-ləs) *adj.* Having a short, almost round head, the width of which is at least 80 per cent as great as the length. **—brach'y·ceph'a·ly** (-sĕf'ə-lē), **brach'y·ceph'a·lism** (-sĕf'ə-lĭz'əm) *n.*

brach·y·dac·tyl·ic (brăk'ĭ-dăk-tĭl'ĭk) also **brach·y·dac·ty·lous** (-dăk'tə-ləs) *adj.* Having abnormally short fingers or toes. **—brach'y·dac'ty·ly** (-dăk'tə-lē) *n.*

bra·chyl·o·gy (brə-kĭl'ə-jē) *n., pl.* **-gies. 1.** Brief, concise speech. **2.** A shortened or condensed phrase or expression. [Med. Lat. *brachylogia* < Gk. *brakhulogia* : *brakhus,* short + *logos,* speech.]

bra·chyp·ter·ous (brə-kĭp'tər-əs) *adj.* Having short wings,

ă pat / ā pay / âr care / ä father / b bib / ch church / d deed / ĕ pet / ē be / f fife / g gag / h hat / hw which / ĭ pit / ī pie / îr pier / j judge / k kick / l lid, needle / m mum / n no, sudden / ng thing / ŏ pot / ō toe / ô paw, for / oi noise / ou out / o͝o took / o͞o boot /

as certain insects. [Gk. *brakhupteros* : *brakhus,* short + *pteron,* wing.] **—bra·chyp'ter·ism** (-tə-rĭz'əm) *n.*

brach·y·u·ran (brăk'ē-yo͝or'ən) also **brach·y·u·ral** (-əl) or **brach·y·u·rous** (-əs) *adj.* Of or belonging to the Brachyura, a group of crustaceans characterized by a short abdomen concealed under the cephalothorax and including the true crabs. *—n.* A member of the Brachyura. [< NLat. *Brachyura,* name suborder : Gk. *brakhus,* short + Gk. *oura,* tail.]

brac·ing (brā'sĭng) *adj.* Invigorating. **—brac'ing·ly** *adv.*

brack·en (brăk'ən) *n.* **1.** A fern, *Pteridium aquilinum,* having tough stems and branching, finely divided fronds. **2.** An area overgrown with bracken. **3.** A large, coarse fern. [ME *braken,* prob. of Scand. orig.]

brack·et (brăk'ĭt) *n.* **1.** A simple rigid structure in the shape of an L, one arm of which is fixed to a vertical surface, the other projecting horizontally to support a shelf or other weight. **2.** A wall-anchored fixture adapted to support a load. **3.** A small shelf or shelves supported by brackets. **4. a.** Either of a pair of symbols, [ ], used to enclose written or printed material or to indicate a mathematical expression considered in some sense a single quantity. **b.** Either of a pair of symbols, < >, similarly used and in mathematics used esp. together to indicate the average of a contained quantity. **c.** *Math.* A brace (sense 12). **5.** A classification or grouping, esp. of taxpayers according to income. **6.** The space between two rounds of artillery, the first aimed beyond a target and the second aimed short of it, used to determine range. *—tr.v.* **-et·ed, -et·ing, -ets. 1.** To support with a bracket or brackets. **2.** To place within or as if within brackets. **3.** To classify or group together. **4.** To fire beyond and short of (a target) in order to determine range. [OFr. *braguette,* codpiece, dim. of *brague,* breeches < OProv. *braga* < Lat. *bracae.*]

bracket fungus *n.* Any of various fungi that form shelflike growths on tree trunks and wood structures.

brack·ish (brăk'ĭsh) *adj.* **1.** Containing some salt; briny: *brackish water.* **2.** Distasteful; unpalatable. [Du. *brak.*] **—brack'ish·ness** *n.*

bract (brăkt) *n.* A leaflike plant part, usually small but sometimes showy and sometimes brightly colored, located either below a flower or on the stalk of a flower cluster. [NLat. *bractea* < Lat. gold leaf.] **—brac'te·al** (brăk'tē-əl) *adj.*

brac·te·ate (brăk'tē-ĭt, -āt') *adj.* Bearing bracts. [NLat. *bracteatus* < *bractea,* gold leaf.]

brac·te·o·late (brăk'tē-ə-lĭt, -lāt') *adj.* Bearing bracteoles.

brac·te·ole (brăk'tē-ōl') *n.* A small or secondary bract. [NLat. *bracteola* < Lat., dim. of *bractea,* gold leaf.]

brad (brăd) *n.* A tapered nail with a small head or a slight side projection instead of a head. [ME < ON *broddr,* spike.]

brad·awl (brăd'ôl') *n.* A small awl with a chisel edge, used to make holes in wood for brads or screws.

brady– *pref.* Slow: *bradycardia.* [NLat. < Gk. *bradus,* slow.]

brad·y·car·di·a (brăd'ĭ-kär'dē-ə) *n.* Abnormally slow heartbeat, as less than 60 beats per minute. [BRADY- + Gk. *kardia,* heart.] **—brad'y·car'dic** (-dĭk) *adj.*

brad·y·lex·i·a (brăd'ĭ-lĕk'sē-ə) *n.* A slowness of reading not attributable to lack of intelligence. [BRADY- + Gk. *lexis,* speech < *legein,* to speak.]

brad·y·lo·gia (brăd'ə-lō'jə, -jē-ə) *n.* Abnormally slow speech. [NLat. : BRADY- + Gk. *-logia,* -logy.]

brae (brā) *n. Scot.* A hillside; slope. [ME *bra* < ON *brā,* eyelid.]

brag (brăg) *v.* **bragged, brag·ging, brags.** *—intr.* To talk boastfully. *—tr.* To assert boastfully. *—n.* **1.** Arrogant or boastful speech or manner. **2.** Something boasted of. **3.** A braggart; boaster. **4.** A card game similar to poker. *—adj.* **brag·ger, brag·gest.** Exceptionally fine. [ME *braggen* < *brag,* ostentatious.] **—brag'ger** *n.*

brag·ga·do·ci·o (brăg'ə-dō'sē-ō', -shē-ō', -shō) *n., pl.* **-os. 1.** A braggart. **2. a.** Empty or pretentious bragging. **b.** Swaggering manner; cockiness. [Alteration of *Braggadocchio,* the personification of vainglory in *The Fairie Queene* by Sir Edmund Spenser (1552–1599).]

Bragg angle (brăg) *n.* The angle between an incident x-ray beam and a set of crystal planes for which the secondary radiation displays maximum intensity as a result of constructive interference. [After William Henry *Bragg* (1862–1942) and William Lawrence *Bragg* (1890–1971).]

brag·gart (brăg'ərt) *n.* One given to loud, empty boasting; bragger. *—adj.* Boastful. [Fr. *bragard* < *braguer,* to brag, perh. < ME *braggen.*]

Bragg's law (brăgz) *n.* The fundamental law of x-ray crystallography, $n\lambda = 2d\sin\Theta$, where n is an integer, λ is the wavelength of a beam of x rays incident on a crystal with lattice planes separated by distance d, and Θ is the Bragg angle. [After William Henry *Bragg* (1862–1942) and William Lawrence *Bragg* (1890–1971).]

Brah·ma[1] (brä'mə) *n. Hinduism.* **1.** The personification of divine reality in its creative aspect as a member of the Hindu triad. **2.** Variant of **Brahman** (senses 1, 3). [Skt. *brahman.*]

Brah·ma[2] also **brah·ma** (brä'mə, brā'-) *n.* A large domestic fowl of a breed originating in Asia and having feathered legs. [After the *Brahmaputra* River in southern Asia.]

Brah·man (brä'mən) *n.* **1.** Also **Brah·ma** (-mə). *Hinduism.* The essential divine reality of the universe; the eternal spirit from which all being originates and to which all returns. **2.** Also **Brah·min** (-mĭn). *Hinduism.* A member of the highest caste, originally composed of priests but now occupationally diversified. **3.** Also **Brah·ma** (-mə) or **Brah·min** (-mĭn). One of a breed of domestic cattle developed in the southern United States from stock originating in India and having a hump between the shoulders and a pendulous dewlap. [Skt.] **—Brah·man'ic** (-măn'ĭk), **Brah·man'i·cal** *adj.*

Brah·man·ism (brä'mə-nĭz'əm) also **Brah·min·ism** (brä'mĭ-) *n.* **1.** The religious practices and beliefs of ancient India as reflected in the Vedas, the earliest religious texts. **2.** The social caste system of the Brahmans of India. **—Brah'man·ist** *n.*

Brah·min (brä'mĭn) *n.* **1.** A highly cultured and socially exclusive person, esp. a member of one of the old New England families. **2.** Variant of **Brahman** (senses 2, 3). **—Brah·min'ic** (-mĭn'ĭk), **Brah·min'i·cal** *adj.*

Brah·min·ism (brä'mĭ-nĭz'əm) *n.* **1.** The attitude or conduct typical of a social or cultural elite. **2.** Variant of **Brahmanism.**

braid (brād) *tr.v.* **braid·ed, braid·ing, braids. 1.** To interweave three or more strands of; plait. **2.** To decorate or edge with an ornamental trim. **3.** To produce by interweaving: *braid a rug.* **4.** To fasten or decorate (hair) with a band or ribbon. *—n.* **1.** A narrow length of fabric, hair, or other material that has been braided or plaited. **2.** A thin, flat woven strip of cloth used for binding or decorating fabrics. **3.** A ribbon or band used to fasten the hair. [ME *braiden* < OE *bregdan,* to weave.] **—braid'er** *n.*

braid·ed (brā'dĭd) *adj.* Flowing in an interconnected network of channels: *a braided stream.*

braid·ing (brā'dĭng) *n.* Braided embroidery.

brail (brāl) *n.* A line used to furl loose-footed sails. *—tr.v.* **brailed, brail·ing, brails.** To gather in (a sail) with brails. [ME *brayle* < OFr. *brail,* belt < Med. Lat. *bracale* < Lat. *bracae,* breeches.]

Braille also **braille** (brāl) *n.* A system of writing and printing for the blind, in which varied arrangements of raised dots representing letters and numerals can be identified by touch. [After Louis *Braille* (1809–1852).]

brain (brān) *n.* **1. a.** The portion of the central nervous system in the vertebrate cranium that is responsible for the interpretation of sensory impulses, the coordination and control of bodily activities, and the exercise of emotion and thought. **b.** A functionally similar portion of the invertebrate nervous system. **2. brains.** Intellectual capacity. **3.** *Informal.* A highly intelligent person. **4.** Often **brains.** The supreme planner, as of a movement. **5.** An automatic device, as a computer, that is central to a computation or control process. *—tr.v.* **brained, brain·ing, brains. 1.** To smash in the skull of. **2.** *Slang.* To hit on the head. **—idioms. on the brain.** Obsessively in mind. **rack** (or **beat**) **(one's) brains.** To think as hard as one can. [ME < OE *brægen.*]

brain case *n.* The brainpan.

brain child *n. Informal.* An original idea or plan attributed to a specific person or group.

brain coral *n.* Any of several corals of the genus *Meandrina,* forming rounded colonies that resemble the human brain.

brain death *n.* Death as evidenced by absence of central-nervous-system activity. **—brain'-dead'** (brān'dĕd') *adj.*

brain drain *n.* The emigration of professionals, as scientists or scholars, to countries that offer higher-paid positions and better living conditions.

brain-drain (brān'drān') *v.* **-drained, -drain·ing, -drains.** *—intr.* To emigrate to another country usually for a more highly paid position or better living conditions. *—tr.* To persuade (a scientist, for example) to brain-drain.

brain fever *n.* Encephalitis.

brain·less (brān'lĭs) *adj.* Devoid of intelligence; stupid. **—brain'less·ly** *adv.* **—brain'less·ness** *n.*

brain·pan (brān'păn') *n.* The part of the skull that contains the brain; cranium.

brain-pick·ing (brān'pĭk'ing) *n.* The act of probing another's mind for information. **—brain-pick'er** *n.*

brain·pow·er (brān'pou'ər) *n.* **1.** Intellectual power or ability. **2.** People with well-developed mental ability.

brain scanner *n.* A CAT scanner used to x-ray the brain. **—brain scan** *n.*

brain·sick (brān'sĭk') *adj.* Of, pertaining to, or induced by insanity; mad. **—brain'sick'ly** *adv.* **—brain'sick'ness** *n.*

brain·stem (brān'stĕm') *n.* The part of the brain consisting of the medulla oblongata, pons, and mesencephalon and connecting the spinal cord to the forebrain and cerebrum.

brain·storm (brān'stôrm') *n.* **1.** A sudden and violent disturbance in the brain. **2. a.** A sudden clever idea. **b.** A foolish idea.

brain·storm·ing (brān'stôr'mĭng) *n.* A method of shared problem-solving in which all members of a group spontaneously contribute ideas. **—brain'storm'** *v.* **(-stormed, -storm·ing, -storms). —brain'storm'er** *n.*

brains trust *n. Chiefly Brit.* A brain trust.

brain trust *n.* A group of experts who serve as unofficial advisers and policy planners, esp. in a government. **—brain truster** *n.*

brain·wash (brān'wŏsh', -wôsh') *tr.v.* **-washed, -wash·ing,**

bracket fungus

Braille
Blind girl reading Braille

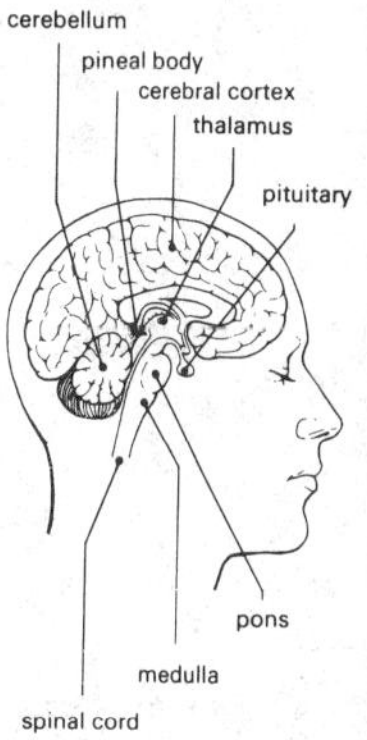

brain

-wash·es. To subject to brainwashing. [Back-formation < BRAINWASHING.]

brain·wash·ing (brān′wŏsh′ĭng, -wô′shĭng) *n.* Intensive indoctrination, usually political, aimed at changing a person's basic convictions and attitudes and replacing them with a fixed and unquestioned set of beliefs. [Transl. of Chin. (Mandarin) *xi*[3] *nao*[3] : *xi*[3], to wash + *nao*[3], brain.]

brain wave *n.* **1.** A rhythmic fluctuation of electric potential between parts of the brain. **2.** A sudden inspiration.

brain·y (brā′nē) *adj.* **-i·er, -i·est.** *Informal.* Intelligent; smart. **—brain′i·ly** *adv.* **—brain′i·ness** *n.*

braise (brāz) *tr.v.* **braised, brais·ing, brais·es.** To cook (meat or vegetables) by browning in fat, then simmering in a small quantity of liquid in a covered container. [Fr. *braiser* < *braise,* hot charcoal < OFr. *brese,* of Germanic orig.]

brake[1] (brāk) *n.* **1.** A device for separating the fibers of flax or hemp by crushing or beating. **2.** A heavy harrow for breaking clods of earth. **3.** A handle on a pump or other machine. **4.** A machine for bending and folding sheet metal. *—tr.v.* **braked, brak·ing, brakes. 1.** To crush (flax or hemp) in a brake. **2.** To break up (clods of earth) with a harrow. [ME.]

brake[2] (brāk) *n.* **1.** A device for slowing or stopping motion, as of a vehicle, esp. by contact friction. **2.** Something that slows or stops action. *—v.* **braked, brak·ing, brakes.** *—tr.* To reduce the speed of with or as if with a brake. *—intr.* To operate or apply a brake. [Perh. ME *breake,* bridle, curb.]

brake[3] (brāk) *n.* Any of several ferns, esp. bracken. [ME.]

brake[4] (brāk) *n.* An area overgrown with dense brushwood, briers, and undergrowth; thicket. [ME.]

brake[5] (brāk) *n.* Variant of **break** (sense 19).

brake[6] (brāk) *v. Archaic.* Past tense of **break.**

brake·age (brā′kĭj) *n.* The action or capacity of a brake.

brake band *n.* A flexible belt that is tightened around a brake drum to arrest the motion of a wheel or shaft.

brake drum *n.* A metal cylinder to which pressure is applied by a braking mechanism in order to arrest rotation of the wheel or shaft to which the cylinder is attached.

brake fluid *n.* The liquid used in a hydraulic brake cylinder.

brake horsepower *n.* The actual or useful horsepower of an engine, usually determined from the force exerted on a dynamometer connected to the drive shaft.

brand

brake·man (brāk′mən) *n.* A railroad employee who assists the conductor and checks on the operation of the train's brakes.

brake pad *n.* A flat block that presses against the disc of a disc brake.

brake shoe *n.* A curved metal block that presses against and arrests the rotation of a wheel or brake drum.

brakes·man (brāks′mən) *n. Chiefly Brit.* Variant of **brakeman.**

braking rocket *n.* A retrorocket.

bra·less (brä′lĭs) *adj. & adv.* Wearing no brassiere.

bram·ble (brăm′bəl) *n.* **1.** A prickly plant or shrub of the genus *Rubus,* esp. the blackberry or the raspberry. **2.** A prickly shrub or bush. [ME *brembel* < OE *bræmbel.*] **—bram′bly** *adj.*

bram·bling (brăm′blĭng) *n.* A finch, *Fringilla montifringilla,* of northern Eurasia, having black, white, and rust-brown plumage. [BRAMB(LE) + -LING[1].]

bran (brăn) *n.* **1.** The seed husk or outer coating of cereals such as wheat, rye, and oats, separated from the flour by sifting or bolting. **2.** Cereal by-products used as a food. [ME < OFr., of Celtic orig.]

branch (brănch) *n.* **1.** A secondary woody stem or limb growing from the trunk or main stem of a tree, bush, or shrub or from another secondary limb. **2.** A part resembling or structurally analogous to a branch. **3.** A limited part of a larger or more complex body, esp.: **a.** An academic or vocational field of specialization. **b.** A local unit of a business. **c.** A division of a family, tribe, or other group believed to stem from a common ancestor. **4.** *Ling.* A subdivision of a family of languages. **5. a.** A tributary of a river. **b.** A small stream, creek, or brook. **6.** *Math.* A part of a curve that is separated, as by discontinuities or extreme points. **7.** *Computer Sci.* **a.** A program instruction that causes a departure from the normal sequence of instructions. **b.** The instructions executed as the result of such a departure. *—v.* **branched, branch·ing, branch·es.** *—intr.* **1.** To put forth or spread out in branches. **2.** To separate into subdivisions; diverge. **3.** *Computer Sci.* To depart from a sequence of instructions as a result of a branch. *—tr.* **1.** To separate into or as if into branches. **2.** To embroider with a design of flowers or foliage. ***—phrasal verbs.*** **branch off.** To separate from the main part or course; diverge. **branch out.** To enlarge the scope of one's interests, business, or activities. [ME < OFr. *branche* < LLat. *branca,* paw.] **—branched** *adj.* **—branch′less** *adj.* **—branch′y** *adj.*

bran·chi·a (brăng′kē-ə) *n., pl.* **-chi·ae** (-kē-ē). A gill or similar breathing organ. [Lat. < Gk. *brankhia,* gills.] **—bran′chi·al** *adj.*

bran·chi·ate (brăng′kē-ĭt, -āt′) *adj.* Having branchiae or gills.

bran·chi·o·pod (brăng′kē-ə-pŏd′) *n.* Any of various crustaceans of the subclass Branchiopoda, characteristically having a segmented body and flattened, limblike appendages. [NLat. *Branchiopoda,* subclass name : Lat. *branchia,* gill + Gk. *pous,* foot.] **—bran′chi·o·pod′, bran′chi·op′o·dan** (-ŏp′ə-dən), **bran′chi·op′a·dous** (-ŏp′ə-dəs) *adj.*

branch water *n.* Plain water, esp. when mixed with liquor. [< *branch water,* water from a stream.]

brand (brănd) *n.* **1. a.** A trademark or distinctive name identifying a product or a manufacturer. **b.** The make of a product thus marked: *a popular brand of soap.* **2.** A mark indicating identity or ownership, burned on the hide of an animal with a hot iron. **3.** A mark formerly burned into the flesh of criminals. **4.** A mark of disgrace or notoriety; stigma. **5.** An iron that is heated and used for branding. **6.** A piece of burning or charred wood. **7.** *Archaic.* A sword. *—tr.v.* **brand·ed, brand·ing, brands. 1.** To mark with or as if with a brand. **2.** To mark with disgrace or infamy; stigmatize. [ME, torch < OE.] **—brand′er** *n.*

branding iron *n.* A metal rod heated and used for branding.

bran·dish (brăn′dĭsh) *tr.v.* **-dished, -dish·ing, -dish·es. 1.** To wave or flourish menacingly, as a weapon. **2.** To display ostentatiously. *—n.* A menacing or defiant wave or flourish. [ME *brandissen* < OFr. *brandir, bandiss-* < *brand,* sword, of Germanic orig.] **—bran′dish·er** *n.*

brand·ling (brănd′lĭng) *n.* A common reddish-brown earthworm, *Eisenia foetida,* often used as bait. [BRAND (from its markings) + -LING.]

brand name *n.* A trade name (sense 1).

brand-new (brănd′no͞o′, -nyo͞o′) *adj.* In fresh and unused condition; completely new.

bran·dy (brăn′dē) *n., pl.* **-dies.** An alcoholic liquor distilled from wine or fermented fruit juice. *—tr.v.* **-died, -dy·ing, -dies.** To mix, flavor, or preserve with brandy. [Short for *brandy-wine* < Du. *brandewijn* : *branden,* to distill + *wijn,* wine.]

branks (brăngks) *n. (used with a sing. or pl. verb).* A metal bridle with a bit to restrain the tongue, formerly used to punish scolds. [Orig. unknown.]

bran·ni·gan (brăn′ĭ-gən) *n. Slang.* **1.** A noisy or confused quarrel. **2.** A spree; binge. [Prob. from the name *Brannigan.*]

brant (brănt) also **brent** (brĕnt) *n., pl.* **brant** or **brants** also **brent** or **brents.** Any of several wild geese of the genus *Branta* that breed in arctic regions, esp. *B. bernicla,* having a black neck and head. [Orig. unknown.]

brash[1] (brăsh) *adj.* **-er, -est. 1.** Hasty and unthinking; rash. **2.** Impudent; saucy. **3.** Brittle: *brash timbers.* [Orig. unknown.] **—brash′ly** *adv.* **—brash′ness** *n.*

brash[2] (brăsh) *n.* A mass or pile of rubble or fragments, as of floating ice. [Perh. an alteration of Fr. *brèche,* breach.]

brass (brăs) *n.* **1.** An alloy of copper and zinc with other metals in varying lesser amounts. **2.** Ornaments, objects, or utensils made of brass. **3.** Often **brasses.** *Mus.* Wind instruments, such as the French horn and trombone, made of brass. **4.** A memorial plaque or tablet made of brass. **5.** A bushing sleeve or similar lining for a bearing, made from a copper alloy. **6.** *Informal.* Blatant self-assurance; effrontery. **7.** *Slang.* High-ranking military officers or other high officials. **8.** *Chiefly Brit. Slang.* Money. ***—modifier:*** *brass buttons; the brass players.* [ME *bras* < OE *bræs.*]

bras·sage (brăs′ĭj) *n.* A charge issued by a government to cover the cost of converting bullion to coins. [Fr., act of stirring, coining money, brassage < *brasser,* to brew, mix < OFr. *bracier* < Lat. *braces,* a kind of grain, of Celtic orig.]

bras·sard (brə-särd′, brăs′ärd′) *n.* **1.** A cloth badge worn around the upper arm. **2.** A piece of armor for the arm. [Fr. < Prov. *brassal* < *bras,* arm < Lat. *brācchium* < Gk. *brakhion.*]

brass·bound (brăs′bound′) *adj.* Firmly and inflexibly established; rigid: *a brassbound tradition.*

brass-col·lar (brăs′kŏl′ər) *adj.* Voting the straight party ticket with no variation.

bras·se·rie (brăs′ə-rē′, brăs-rē) *n.* A restaurant serving alcoholic beverages, esp. beer, as well as food. [Fr. < *brasser,* to brew. —see BRASSAGE.]

brass hat *n. Slang.* **1.** A high-ranking military officer. **2.** A high-ranking civilian official. [From the gold braid on his hat.]

brass·ie also **brass·y** (brăs′ē) *n., pl.* **-ies.** A wooden golf club with a brass-plated sole, used for long low shots.

bras·siere or **bras·sière** (brə-zîr′) *n.* A woman's undergarment worn to support and give contour to the breasts. [Fr. < OFr. *braciere,* armguard < *bras,* arm < Lat. *brācchium* < Gk. *brakhion.*]

brass knuckles *pl.n.* A weapon consisting of a metal strip or chain with holes or links into which the fingers fit.

brass tacks *pl.n. Informal.* Essential facts; basics: *getting down to brass tacks.*

brass·y[1] (brăs′ē) *adj.* **-i·er, -i·est. 1.** Of or decorated with brass. **2.** Resembling brass in color. **3.** Like or characterized by the sound of brass instruments. **4.** Cheap and showy; flashy. **5.** *Informal.* Brazen; insolent. **—brass′i·ly** *adv.* **—brass′i·ness** *n.*

brass·y[2] (brăs′ē) *n.* Variant of **brassie.**

brat (brăt) *n.* A child, esp. a nasty, spoiled, or ill-mannered one. [Poss. < *brat,* coarse garment < ME < OE *bratt,* of Celtic orig.] **—brat′ty** *adj.*

brat·tice (brăt′ĭs) *n.* A partition, esp. one erected in a mine for ventilation. *—tr.v.* **-ticed, -tic·ing, -tic·es.** To equip with a brattice. [ME *bretice,* defensive structure < OFr. *breteche* < Med. Lat. *brittisca.*]

brat·tle (brăt′l) *n.* A rattling or clattering sound. —*intr.v.* **-tled, -tling, -tles.** To make a brattle. [Imit.]

brat·wurst (brăt′wûrst′, -vŏŏrst′) *n.* A sausage made with finely chopped, seasoned fresh pork. [G. < OHG *brātwurst* : *brāto,* meat + *wurst,* sausage.]

Braun·schwei·ger (broun′shwī′gər) *n.* A smoked liver sausage. [G. < *Braunschweig,* Brunswick, West Germany.]

bra·va (brä′vä, brä-vä′) *interj.* Used to express approval in applauding a woman. —*n.* A shout or cry of "brava." [Ital., fem. of *bravo,* bravo.]

bra·va·do (brə-vä′dō) *n., pl.* **-does** or **-dos. 1.** Defiant or swaggering behavior. **2.** A pretense of courage; false bravery. [Sp. *bravada* < *bravo,* brave.]

brave (brāv) *adj.* **brav·er, brav·est. 1.** Possessing or displaying courage; valiant. **2.** Making a fine display; splendid. **3.** *Archaic.* Excellent. —*n.* **1.** A North American Indian warrior. **2.** A courageous person. **3.** *Obs.* A bully. **4.** *Obs.* A boast or challenge. —*v.* **braved, brav·ing, braves.** —*tr.* **1.** To undergo or face courageously. **2.** To defy; challenge: *"Together they would brave Satan and all his legions"* (Emily Brontë). **3.** *Obs.* To make splendid. —*intr. Obs.* To boast. [OFr. < OItal. *bravo.*] **—brave′ly** *adv.* **—brave′ness** *n.*

Synonyms: *brave, courageous, fearless, intrepid, bold, daring, audacious, gallant, valiant, valorous, doughty, game, gritty, mettlesome, plucky, dauntless, undaunted.* These adjectives all apply to admirable human action in difficult conditions. *Brave,* the least specific, is frequently associated with an innate quality, and *courageous* with the act of consciously rising to a specific test by drawing on a reserve of moral strength and righteousness. *Fearless* emphasizes, besides absence of fear, resolute self-possession; *intrepid* adds to this the sense of invulnerability to fear in any situation. *Bold* and *daring* stress not only readiness to meet danger but a desire to seize initiative; *audacious* intensifies those qualities, often to the point of recklessness. *Gallant* also implies indifference to danger, together with a noble display of courage, often in a losing cause. *Valiant,* said principally of persons, pertains to the bravery or courage of heroes, and *valorous* to their deeds. On a lower and perhaps more contemporary plane, *doughty* suggests formidableness (now usually humorously), and *game* and *gritty* imply dogged persistence and capacity for resisting pain. *Mettlesome* stresses spirit and love of challenge; *plucky* stresses spirit and heart in the face of unfavorable odds. *Dauntless* refers to courage that resists subjection or intimidation; *undaunted* more strongly suggests such courage that has been put to actual test.

brav·er·y (brā′və-rē, brāv′rē) *n., pl.* **-ies. 1.** The state or quality of being brave; courage. **2.** Splendor, as of attire; show.

bra·vis·si·mo (brä-vĭs′ə-mō′) *interj.* Used to express great approval. [Ital., superl. of *bravo,* fine.]

bra·vo[1] (brä′vō, brä-vō′) *interj.* Used to express approval. —*n., pl.* **-vos.** A shout or cry of "bravo." [Ital., fine.]

bra·vo[2] (brä′vō) *n., pl.* **-voes** or **-vos.** A hired assassin; killer. [Ital., brigand.]

bra·vu·ra (brə-vŏŏr′ə, -vyŏŏr′ə) *n.* **1.** *Mus.* Brilliant technique or style in performance. **2.** A showy manner or display. [Ital. < *bravo,* fine.] **—bra·vu′ra** *adj.*

braw (brô) *adj.* **-er, -est.** *Scot.* Fine or splendid. [Sc., alteration of BRAVE.]

brawl (brôl) *n.* **1.** A noisy quarrel or fight. **2.** *Slang.* A loud party. —*intr.v.* **brawled, brawl·ing, brawls. 1.** To quarrel noisily. **2.** To flow noisily, as water. [ME *brall* < *brallen,* to quarrel.] **—brawl′er** *n.* **—brawl′ing·ly** *adv.*

brawn (brôn) *n.* **1.** Solid and well-developed muscles. **2.** Muscular strength and power. **3.** *Chiefly Brit.* **a.** A pig. **b.** A pickled or preserved preparation made from meat of the head or feet of a pig. [ME, muscle < OFr. *bräon,* meat, of Germanic orig.]

brawn·y (brô′nē) *adj.* **-i·er, -i·est.** Strong and muscular. **—brawn′i·ly** *adv.* **—brawn′i·ness** *n.*

bray[1] (brā) *v.* **brayed, bray·ing, brays.** —*intr.* **1.** To utter the loud, harsh cry of a donkey. **2.** To sound loudly and harshly: *The foghorn brayed all night.* —*tr.* To utter loudly and harshly. —*n.* **1.** The loud, harsh cry of a donkey. **2.** A sound resembling a bray. [ME *brayen* < OFr. *braire,* prob. of Celtic orig.] **—bray′er** *n.*

bray[2] (brā) *tr.v.* **brayed, bray·ing, brays. 1.** To crush and pound in or as if in a mortar. **2.** To spread (ink) thinly over a surface. [ME *brayen* < OFr. *breier,* of Germanic orig.]

bray·er (brā′ər) *n. Printing.* A small hand roller used to spread ink thinly and evenly over type.

braze[1] (brāz) *tr.v.* **brazed, braz·ing, braz·es. 1.** To make of or decorate with brass. **2.** To make hard like brass. [ME *brasen* < OE *brasian* < *bræs,* brass.]

braze[2] (brāz) *tr.v.* **brazed, braz·ing, braz·es.** To solder (two pieces of metal) together using a hard solder with a high melting point. [Prob. < Fr. *braser* < OFr. < *brese,* hot coals.] **—braz′er** *n.*

bra·zen (brā′zən) *adj.* **1.** Made of brass. **2.** Resembling brass in color, quality, or hardness. **3.** Having a loud, resonant sound like that of a brass trumpet. **4.** Impudent; bold. —*tr.v.* **-zened, -zen·ing, -zens.** To face or undergo with bold self-assurance: *brazened out the crisis.* [ME *brasen* < OE *bræsen* < *bræs,* brass.] **—bra′zen·ly** *adv.* **—bra′zen·ness** *n.*

bra·zen-faced (brā′zən-fāst′) *adj.* Impudent and shameless.

bra·zier[1] (brā′zhər) *n.* One that works in brass. [ME *brasier* < *bras,* brass.]

bra·zier[2] (brā′zhər) *n.* A metal pan for holding burning coals or charcoal. [Fr. *brasier* < *braise,* hot coals.]

brazier[2]

braz·i·lin (brăz′ə-lĭn, brə-zĭl′ən) *n.* A crystalline compound, $C_{16}H_{14}O_5$, obtained from brazilwood and used as a dye. [Fr. *brésiline* < *brésil,* brazilwood < OFr. *bresil.*]

Bra·zil nut (brə-zĭl′) *n.* **1.** A tree, *Bertholletia excelsa,* of tropical South America, bearing hard, round, woody pods that contain about 20 to 30 nuts. **2.** The edible nut of the Brazil nut. [After *Brazil.*]

Brazil nut

bra·zil·wood (brə-zĭl′wŏŏd′) *n.* The red wood of any of several tropical trees of the genus *Caesalpinia,* used for cabinetwork and as the source of a red or purple dye. [Obs. *brazil,* brazilwood (< ME *brasil* < OFr. *bresil*) + WOOD.]

breach (brēch) *n.* **1.** A violation or infraction, as of a law, legal obligation, or promise. **2.** A gap or rift, esp. in a solid structure such as a dike or fortification. **3.** A breaking up or disruption of friendly relations; estrangement. **4.** A leap of a whale from the water. **5.** The breaking of waves or surf. **6.** *Obs.* A wound; injury. —*v.* **breached, breach·ing, breach·es.** —*tr.* To make a hole or gap in; break through. —*intr.* To leap from the water: *waiting for the whale to breach.* [ME *breche* < OE *brēc.*]

Synonyms: *breach, infraction, violation, transgression, trespass, encroachment, infringement.* These nouns apply to the act of one who commits a legal or moral offense. *Breach* and *infraction* are applied to any failure to keep the law or to fulfill one's duties, obligations, word, or the like, whether intentional or otherwise. *Violation* is broadly applicable to such an act committed willfully, and more strongly suggests injury. *Transgression* refers to violation, generally of divine or moral law, in which sense it denotes sin. *Trespass* refers either to violation of moral or statutory law; in the latter sense it denotes forceful violation of another's rights, possessions, or person. In all senses it implies willful intrusion. *Encroachment* is the act of gradual intrusion on another's rights, territory, or other possessions, generally by stealth. *Infringement* is used broadly in the sense of infraction or violation and specifically to denote encroachment on another's rights, such as the rights granted by a copyright.

breach of promise *n.* The failure to fulfill a promise, esp. a promise to marry.

bread (brĕd) *n.* **1.** A staple food made from flour or meal mixed with a liquid, usually combined with a leavening agent, and kneaded, shaped into loaves, and baked. **2.** Food in general, regarded as necessary for sustaining life. **3. a.** The necessities of life; livelihood: *earn one's bread.* **b.** Something that nourishes; sustenance. **c.** *Slang.* Money. —*tr.v.* **bread·ed, bread·ing, breads.** To coat with bread crumbs, as before cooking. [ME < OE *brēad.*]

bread and butter *n. Informal.* A means of support; livelihood.

bread-and-butter (brĕd′n-bŭt′ər) *adj.* **1.** Influenced by or undertaken out of necessity: *a bread-and-butter job.* **2.** Expressive of gratitude for hospitality: *a bread-and-butter note.*

bread·bas·ket (brĕd′băs′kĭt) *n.* **1.** A basket for serving bread. **2.** A geographic region serving as a principal source of grain supply. **3.** *Slang.* The stomach.

bread·board (brĕd′bôrd′, -bōrd′) *n.* **1.** A board on which bread is sliced. **2.** An experimental model, esp. of an electric circuit; prototype. —*tr.v.* **-board·ed, -board·ing, -boards.** To construct an experimental model of (an electric circuit, for example). **—bread′board′ing** *n.*

bread·fruit (brĕd′frōōt′) *n.* **1.** A tree, *Artocarpus communis* (or *A. incisa*), of Polynesia, having deeply lobed leaves and round, usually seedless fruit. **2.** The edible fruit of the breadfruit, having a texture like that of bread when baked or roasted.

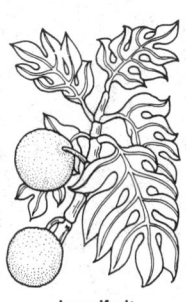

breadfruit

bread mold *n.* A fungus, *Rhizopus nigricans,* that forms a dense, cottony growth on bread and other foods.

bread·nut (brĕd′nŭt′) *n.* **1.** A tree, *Brosimum alicastrum,* of Central America and the West Indies, bearing round, nutlike fruit. **2.** The fruit of the breadnut, ground to produce a substitute for wheat flour.

bread·root (brĕd′rōōt′, -rŏŏt′) *n.* A plant, *Psoralea esculenta,* of the central North American plains, having an edible, starchy root.

bread·stuff (brĕd′stŭf′) *n.* **1.** Bread. **2.** Flour, meal, or grain used in the baking of bread.

breadth (brĕdth) *n.* **1.** The measure or dimension from side to side as distinguished from length or thickness; width. **2.** A piece of something usually produced in a standard width: *a breadth of canvas.* **3.** Wide extent or scope. **4.** Freedom from narrowness, as of views or interests. [ME *brede* < OE *brǣd.*]

breadth·wise (brĕdth′wīz′) also **breadth·ways** (-wāz′) *adv. & adj.* In the direction of the breadth.

bread·win·ner (brĕd′wĭn′ər) *n.* One who supports a family or household by his or her earnings.

break (brāk) *v.* **broke** (brōk), **bro·ken** (brō′kən), **break·ing, breaks.** —*tr.* **1.** To crack or split into two or more pieces with sudden or violent force; smash. **2.** To crack without actually separating into pieces. **3.** To render unusable or inoperative. **4.** To part or pierce the surface of: *break ground for a new hospital.* **5.** To cause to burst. **6.** To fracture a bone of. **7.** To force or make a way through; penetrate: *break the sound barrier.* **8.** To force one's way out of; escape from: *break jail.* **9.** To put an end to by force or strong opposition: *break a strike.* **10.** To fail to conform to; violate. **11.** To disrupt abruptly; interrupt: *A cry broke the silence.* **12.** To cause to give up a habit. **13.** To train to obey; tame. **14.** To disrupt or destroy the order or regularity of: *break ranks.* **15.** To destroy the completeness of: *break a set of books.* **16.** To lessen in force or effect: *break a fall.* **17.** To weaken or destroy, as in spirit or health: *"For a hero loves the world till it breaks him"* (Yeats). **18.** To overwhelm with grief or sorrow: *broke her heart.* **19.** To cause to be without money or go into bankruptcy. **20.** To reduce in rank; demote. **21.** To reduce to or exchange for smaller monetary units: *break a dollar.* **22.** To surpass or outdo: *break a record.* **23.** To make known, as news. **24.** To find the solution or key to. **25.** *Law.* To invalidate (a will) by judicial action. **26.** *Elect.* To open: *break a circuit.* —*intr.* **1.** To become separated into pieces or fragments; come apart. **2.** To become unusable or inoperative. **3.** To give way; collapse: *The dam broke.* **4.** To diminish or discontinue abruptly: *His fever broke.* **5.** To scatter or disperse. **6.** To move away or escape suddenly. **7.** To change direction suddenly. **8.** To come into being or notice, esp. suddenly. **9.** To emerge above the surface of water. **10.** To be overwhelmed with sorrow: *His heart broke when the last child died.* **11.** To begin abruptly to produce or utter something: *flowers breaking into bloom.* **12.** To come to an end; finish: *The game will break up in ten minutes.* **13.** To drop rapidly and considerably: *Stock prices broke at the news.* **14.** To collapse or crash into surf or spray, as waves. **15.** To change from one tone quality or musical register to another. **16.** To curve near or over a baseball plate: *The pitch broke sharply.* **17.** *Informal.* To occur in a particular way: *Things are breaking well for her.* —**phrasal verbs. break down.** **1.** To fail to function; cease to be useful or operable. **2.** To have a physical or mental collapse. **3.** To become or cause to become distressed or upset. **4.** To consider in parts; analyze. **5.** To decompose chemically. **6.** To undergo electrical breakdown. **break in. 1.** To train or adapt for some purpose. **2.** To loosen or soften with use: *break in new shoes.* **3.** To enter forcibly or suddenly. **4.** To interrupt. **break in on** (or **upon**). To interrupt or intrude on. **break into. 1.** To enter forcibly, suddenly, or illegally. **2.** To interrupt: *"No one would have dared to break into his abstraction"* (Alan Paton). **3.** To begin suddenly: *The horse broke into a wild gallop.* **break off. 1.** To stop suddenly, as in speaking. **2.** To discontinue (a relationship). **break out. 1.** To become affected with a skin eruption, as pimples. **2.** To develop suddenly and forcefully: *Fighting broke out in the prison cells.* **3. a.** To ready for action or use: *break out the rifles.* **b.** To produce for consumption: *break out the champagne.* **break up. 1.** To bring or come to an end: *break up a fight. The marriage broke up.* **2.** *Informal.* To burst or cause to burst into laughter. —*n.* **1.** The act of breaking; a separating into parts. **2.** The result of breaking; fracture or crack. **3.** A beginning or opening: *the break of day.* **4.** A dash, esp. to escape. **5.** An interruption or disruption of continuity or regularity. **6.** A pause or interval, as from work. **7.** A sudden or marked change. **8.** *Informal.* A chance occurrence, esp. an unexpected opportunity. **9.** A severing of ties. **10.** A sudden decline in prices. **11.** A caesura. **12.** *Printing.* **a.** The space between two paragraphs. **b.** A series of three dots (. . .) used to indicate an omission in a text. **13.** *Elect.* Interruption of a flow of current. **14.** *Mus.* **a.** The point at which a register or a tonal quality changes to another register or tonal quality. **b.** The change itself. **c.** A solo jazz cadenza played during the pause between the regular phrases or choruses of a melody. **15.** The swerving of a ball from a straight path of flight when thrown, as in baseball. **16.** The opening shot in billiards. **17.** A run or unbroken series of successful shots, as in billiards or croquet. **18.** Failure to score a strike or a spare in a given bowling frame. **19.** Also **brake.** A high, open horse-drawn carriage with four wheels. —**idiom. break camp.** To pack up equipment and leave a campsite. [ME *breken* < OE *brecan.*]

Synonyms: *break, crack, fracture, rupture, burst, split, splinter, shatter, shiver, smash, crush.* These verbs describe the effect of sudden application of force. *Break,* the least specific, usually involves separation of a rigid object into parts; sometimes, however, it is used in the sense of *crack,* which specifies adherence of parts. *Fracture* applies to breaking or cracking of a rigid body. *Rupture* refers to breaking apart or tearing of a soft or pliable substance; sometimes rupturing (as in the case of a blood vessel) results from internal force and thus has the basic sense of *burst. Split* refers to the breaking of a rigid substance lengthwise or in the direction of the grain. *Splinter* involves splitting into thin and sharp separate pieces. *Shatter* pertains to the breaking of a rigid object into many small, scattered pieces. *Shiver* indicates fragmentation by sudden force but especially suggests fine splinters. *Smash* stresses force of impact and complete change of form of a rigid body but is otherwise not specific. *Crush* refers to the effect of great external force, to change of form, or to reduction into fine particles.

breaker[1]

break·a·ble (brā'kə-bəl) *adj.* Capable of being broken. —*n.* Often **breakables.** Articles capable of being broken easily. —**break'a·ble·ness** *n.*

break·age (brā'kĭj) *n.* **1.** The act or process of breaking. **2.** A quantity broken. **3. a.** Loss or damage as a result of breaking. **b.** An allowance for such loss or damage.

break·a·way (brāk'ə-wā') *adj.* **1.** Designating a theatrical prop designed to fall apart easily. **2.** Capable of or favoring independent action: *a breakaway political group.* —*n.* **1.** One that breaks away. **2.** A breakaway object.

break·bone fever (brāk'bōn') *n.* Dengue.

break·down (brāk'doun') *n.* **1. a.** The act or process of breaking down and failing to function. **b.** The condition resulting from this. **2.** *Elect.* The failure of an insulator or insulating medium to prevent discharge or current flow. **3.** A collapse in physical or mental health. **4.** An analysis, outline, or summary consisting of itemized data or essentials. **5.** Disintegration or decomposition into parts or elements.

break·er[1] (brā'kər) *n.* **1.** One that breaks. **2.** A machine or plant for breaking up a substance, as rock. **3.** *Elect.* A circuit breaker. **4.** A wave that crests or breaks into foam, esp. against a shoreline.

brea·ker[2] (brā'kər) *n.* A small water cask for use on a ship's lifeboat. [Alteration of Sp. *barrica.*]

break·fast (brĕk'fəst) *n.* The first meal of the day. —**modifier;** *a breakfast tray.* —*intr.v.* **-fast·ed, -fast·ing, -fasts.** To eat breakfast. [ME *brekfast* : *breken,* to break + *faste,* a fast < ON *fasta.*] —**break'fast·er** *n.*

break·front (brāk'frŭnt') *n.* A high, wide cabinet or bookcase having a central section projecting beyond the end sections.

break-in (brāk'ĭn') *n.* **1.** Forcible entry, as into a dwelling, for an illegal purpose such as theft. **2.** A training or testing period intended to improve the performance of someone or something new.

break·ing (brā'kĭng) *n. Ling.* The change of a simple vowel to a diphthong, often caused by the influence of neighboring consonants. [Transl. of G. *Brechung.*]

breaking and entering *n. Law.* The gaining of an unauthorized access, as by forcing a lock, to another's premises for the purpose of committing a crime.

breaking point *n.* **1.** The point at which a person breaks down under stress. **2.** The point at which a condition or situation becomes critical.

break·neck (brāk'nĕk') *adj.* **1.** Dangerous: *breakneck speed.* **2.** Rapid.

break·out (brāk'out') *n.* A forceful break from a restrictive condition or situation.

break·through (brāk'thro͞o') *n.* **1.** An act of breaking through an obstacle or restriction. **2.** A military offensive that penetrates an enemy's lines of defense. **3.** A major achievement or success that permits further progress, as in technology.

break·up (brāk'ŭp') *n.* **1.** The act of breaking up; a separation or dispersal. **2.** *Informal.* A loss of control or composure.

break·wa·ter (brāk'wô'tər, -wŏt'ər) *n.* A barrier that protects a harbor or shore from the full impact of waves.

bream[1] (brēm) *n., pl.* **bream** or **breams. 1.** Any of several European freshwater fishes of the genus *Abramis,* having a flattened body and silvery scales. **2.** Any of several fishes similar or related to the bream. [ME *breme* < OFr., of Germanic orig.]

bream[2] (brēm) *tr.v.* **breamed, bream·ing, breams.** To clean (a wooden ship's hull) by applying heat to soften the pitch and then scraping. [Orig. unknown.]

breast (brĕst) *n.* **1. a.** The human mammary gland. **b.** A homologous organ in other mammals. **2.** The superior ventral surface of the body, extending from the neck to the abdomen. **3.** The seat of affection and emotion: *caused no pity in his breast.* **4.** Something likened to the breast: *the breast of a hill.* —*tr.v.* **breast·ed, breast·ing, breasts.** To encounter or advance against resolutely; confront boldly. [ME *brest* < OE *brēost.*]

breast-beat·ing (brĕst'bē'tĭng) *n.* A noisy demonstration, esp. of self-accusation.

breast·bone (brĕst'bōn') *n.* The sternum.

breast-feed (brĕst'fēd') *tr.v.* **-fed** (-fĕd'), **-feed·ing, -feeds.** To feed (a baby) mother's milk from the breast; suckle.

breast·plate (brĕst'plāt') *n.* **1.** A piece of armor plate that covers the breast. **2.** A square cloth set with 12 precious stones representing the 12 tribes of Israel, worn by a Jewish high priest. **3.** The plastron of a turtle's or tortoise's shell.

breast stroke *n.* A swimming stroke in which one lies face down in the water and extends the arms in front of the head, then sweeps them both back laterally under the surface of the water while performing a frog kick. —**breast'-strok'er** *n.*

breast·work (brĕst'wûrk') *n.* A temporary, quickly constructed fortification, usually breast-high.

breath (brĕth) *n.* **1.** The air inhaled and exhaled in respiration. **2.** The act or process of breathing; respiration. **3.** The capacity to breathe. **4.** A single respiration. **5.** Exhaled air, as evidenced by vapor, odor, or heat. **6.** A momentary pause or rest. **7. a.** A momentary stirring of air. **b.** A slight gust of fragrant air. **8.** A trace or suggestion. **9.** A soft-spoken sound; whisper. **10.** Exhalation of air without vibration of the vocal cords, as in the articulation of *p* and *s*. —***idioms.*** **hold (one's) breath.** To wait anxiously or excitedly. **in the same breath.** At or almost at the same time. **out of breath.** Breathless, as from exertion. **take (one's) breath away.** To leave one as if breathless from awe or surprise. **under (one's) breath.** In a whisper or muted voice. [ME *breth* < OE *brǣð*.]

breathe (brēth) *v.* **breathed, breath·ing, breathes.** —*intr.* **1.** To inhale and exhale air. **2.** To be alive; live. **3.** To move or blow gently, as air. **4.** To be exhaled or emanated, as a fragrance. **5.** To pause to rest or regain breath: *Give me a moment to breathe.* —*tr.* **1.** To inhale and exhale during respiration. **2.** To impart as if by breathing; instill: *breathe life into a portrait.* **3.** To exhale; emit. **4.** To utter, esp. quietly; whisper: *Don't breathe a word of this.* **5.** To make apparent; manifest. **6.** To allow (a person or animal) to rest or regain breath. —***idiom.*** **breathe (one's) last.** To die. [ME *brethen* < *breth,* breath.] —**breath'a·ble** *adj.*

breath·er (brē'thər) *n.* **1.** One that breathes, esp. in a specified manner. **2.** *Informal.* A short rest period.

breath·ing (brē'thĭng) *n.* **1.** The act or process of respiration. **2.** Either of two marks used in Greek to indicate aspiration of an initial sound (ʽ) or the absence of such aspiration (ʼ).

breathing space *n.* **1.** Sufficient space to permit ease of breathing or movement. **2.** An opportunity to rest or give thought to a situation.

breathing spell *n.* A breathing space (sense 2).

breath·less (brĕth'lĭs) *adj.* **1. a.** Without breath; not breathing. **b.** Dead. **2.** Having no air or breeze; still: *a breathless day.* **3.** Out-of-breath. **4.** Holding the breath from excitement or suspense: *a breathless audience.* **5.** Inspiring or marked by sudden excitement that takes the breath away: *a breathless flight.* —**breath'less·ly** *adv.* —**breath'less·ness** *n.*

breath·tak·ing (brĕth'tā'kĭng) *adj.* Inspiring awe; exciting. —**breath'tak'ing·ly** *adv.*

breath·y (brĕth'ē) *adj.* **-i·er, -i·est.** Marked by audible or noisy breathing: *a breathy voice.* —**breath'i·ly** *adv.* —**breath'i·ness** *n.*

brec·ci·a (brĕch'ē-ə, brĕch'ə) *n.* Rock composed of sharp-angled fragments cemented in a fine matrix. [Ital., of Germanic orig.]

brec·ci·ate (brĕch'ē-āt') *tr.v.* **-ci·at·ed, -ci·at·ing, -ci·ates.** To form (rock) into breccia. —**brec'ci·a'tion** *n.*

bred (brĕd) *v.* Past tense and past participle of **breed.**

brede (brēd) *n. Archaic.* An ornamental embroidered edging. [Alteration of BRAID.]

bred-in-the-bone (brĕd'ĭn-thə-bōn') *adj.* **1.** Deeply instilled: *bred-in-the-bone loyalty.* **2.** Firmly established; inveterate: *a bred-in-the-bone liberal.*

breech (brēch) *n.* **1.** The lower rear portion of the human trunk; buttocks. **2.** The lower part of a pulley. **3.** The part of a firearm to the rear of the bore. **3. breeches. a.** Trousers extending to or just below the knee. **b.** *Informal.* Trousers. —*tr.v.* **breeched, breech·ing, breech·es.** *Archaic & Regional.* To clothe with breeches. [ME *brech* < OE *brēc,* pl. of *brōc,* leg covering.]

breech·block (brēch'blŏk') *n.* The metal part that closes the breech end of the barrel of a breechloading gun and that is removed to insert a cartridge and replaced before firing.

breech·cloth (brēch'klôth', klŏth') also **breech·clout** (-klout') *n.* A cloth worn to cover the loins; loincloth.

breech delivery *n.* Delivery of a fetus with the buttocks or feet appearing first.

breeches buoy *n.* An apparatus used for rescues and transfers at sea, consisting of sturdy canvas breeches attached at the waist to a ring buoy that is suspended from a pulley running along a rope from ship to shore or from ship to ship.

breech·ing (brē'chĭng, brĭch'ĭng) *n.* **1.** The strap of a harness that passes behind a draft animal's haunches. **2.** The parts of a gun that make up the breech. **3.** A rope formerly used to secure the breech of a cannon to the side of a ship to control the recoil.

breech·load·er (brēch'lō'dər) *n.* A gun or firearm loaded at the breech. —**breech'load'ing** *adj.*

breech presentation *n.* The position of a fetus during labor in which the buttocks or feet appear first.

breed (brēd) *v.* **bred** (brĕd), **breed·ing, breeds.** —*tr.* **1.** To produce (offspring); give birth to or hatch. **2.** To bring about; engender. **3. a.** To cause to reproduce; raise. **b.** To develop new or improved strains in (animals or plants). **4.** To rear or train; bring up. —*intr.* **1.** To produce offspring. **2.** To originate and thrive: *Fads breed in empty heads and full purses.* —*n.* **1.** A genetic strain or type of organism, usually a domestic animal, having consistent and recognizable inherited characteristics, esp. such a strain developed and maintained by man. **2.** A kind; sort: *a new breed of politicians.* [ME *breden* < OE *brēdan.*]

breed·er (brē'dər) *n.* **1.** A person who breeds animals or plants. **2.** An animal kept to produce offspring. **3.** A cause or source. **4.** *Physics.* A breeder reactor.

breeder reactor *n.* A nuclear reactor that produces as well as consumes fissionable material, esp. one that produces more fissionable material than it consumes.

breed·ing (brē'dĭng) *n.* **1.** One's line of descent; ancestry: *a woman of noble breeding.* **2.** Training in the proper forms of social and personal conduct. **3.** The producing of offspring or young. **4.** The propagation of animals or plants.

breeding ground *n.* **1.** A place to which animals go to breed. **2.** A place or set of circumstances that encourages certain ideas or conditions.

breeks (brēks) *pl.n. Scot.* Breeches. [ME, var. of *breeches.*]

breeze[1] (brēz) *n.* **1.** A light air current; gentle wind. **2.** *Meteorol.* A wind of from 6.4 to 49.6 kilometers or 4 to 31 miles per hour. **3.** *Chiefly Brit. Informal.* A commotion or disturbance; argument. **4.** *Informal.* An easily accomplished task. —*intr.v.* **breezed, breez·ing, breez·es. 1.** To blow lightly. **2.** *Informal.* To progress swiftly and effortlessly: *breezed through the test.* [Perh. < OSp. *briza,* northeast wind.]

breeze[2] (brēz) *n.* The refuse left when coal, coke, or charcoal is burned, used in brickmaking and as a concrete filler. [Prob. < Fr. *braise,* hot coals < OFr. *brese.*]

breeze·way (brēz'wā') *n.* A roofed, open-sided passageway connecting two structures, such as a house and a garage.

breez·y (brē'zē) *adj.* **-i·er, -i·est. 1.** Exposed to breezes; windy. **2.** Fresh and animated; lively: *a breezy prose style.* —**breez'i·ly** *adv.* —**breez'i·ness** *n.*

breg·ma (brĕg'mə) *n., pl.* **-ma·ta** (-mə-tə). The junction of the sagittal and coronal sutures at the top of the skull. [NLat. < LLat., top of head < Gk.] —**breg·mat'ic** (-măt'ĭk) *adj.*

brems·strah·lung (brĕms'shträ'ləng) *n.* The electromagnetic radiation produced by an electrically charged subatomic particle, such as an electron, subjected to sudden deceleration in the electric field of an atomic nucleus. [G. : *Bremse,* brake + *Strahlung,* radiation < *Strahl,* ray.]

Bren gun (brĕn) *n.* A .303 caliber gas-operated, air-cooled submachine gun adopted by the British Army in World War II. [Blend of *Brno,* Czechoslovakia, and *Enfield,* England.]

brent (brĕnt) *n.* Variant of **brant.**

br'er (brûr, brĕr) *n. Southern U.S.* Brother.

breth·ren (brĕth'rən) *n. Archaic.* Plural of **brother.**

Bret·on (brĕt'n) *n.* **1.** A native or inhabitant of Brittany. **2.** The Celtic language of Brittany. [ME < OFr. < Lat. *Briton.*] —**Bret'on** *adj.*

breve (brĕv, brēv) *n.* **1.** A symbol placed over a vowel to show that it has a short sound, as the ă in *bat.* **2.** A symbol similar to a breve used to indicate that a syllable of verse is short or unstressed. **3.** *Mus.* A single note equivalent to two whole notes. [ME, short, var. of *bref* < OFr. < Lat. *brevis.*]

bre·vet (brə-vĕt', brĕv'ĭt) *n.* A commission, often granted as an honor, promoting a military officer in rank without an increase in pay or authority. —*tr.v.* **-vet·ted, -vet·ting, -vets** or **-vet·ed, -vet·ing, -vets.** To promote by brevet. [ME, official letter < AN, dim. of *bref,* letter < OFr. *brief* < Lat. *breve,* dispatch < *brevis,* short.] —**bre·vet'cy** (brə-vĕt'sē) *n.*

bre·vi·ar·y (brē'vē-ĕr'ē, brĕv'ē-) *n., pl.* **-ies.** *Eccles.* A book containing the hymns, offices, and prayers for the canonical hours. [ME *breviarie* < Med. Lat. *breviarium,* abridgment, ult. < Lat. *brevis,* short.]

brev·i·ty (brĕv'ĭ-tē) *n.* **1.** Briefness of duration. **2.** Concise expression; terseness. [Lat. *brevitas* < *brevis,* short.]

brew (bro͞o) *v.* **brewed, brew·ing, brews.** —*tr.* **1.** To make (ale or beer) from malt and hops by infusion, boiling, and fermentation. **2.** To make (a beverage) by boiling, steeping, or mixing various ingredients. **3.** To concoct; devise. —*intr.* **1.** To make ale or beer as an occupation. **2.** To be imminent; impend: *"In spite of storms brewing on every frontier"* (John Dos Passos). —*n.* **1.** A beverage made by brewing. **2.** The quantity of beverage brewed at one time. [ME *brewen* < OE *brēowan.*] —**brew'er** *n.*

brew·age (bro͞o'ĭj) *n.* **1.** Something prepared by brewing. **2.** The process of brewing.

brew·er's yeast (bro͞o'ərz) *n.* A yeast, *Saccharomyces cerevisiae,* used in brewing and as a source of B-complex vitamins.

brew·er·y (bro͞o'ə-rē, bro͞or'ē) *n., pl.* **-ies.** An establishment for the manufacture of malt liquors.

brew·house (bro͞o'hous') *n.* A brewery.

brew·is (bro͞o'ĭs, bro͞oz) *n. Regional.* **1.** A broth. **2.** Bread soaked in liquid, as broth or milk. [ME < OFr. *brouetz,* dim. of *brouet,* broth, of Germanic orig.]

bri·ar[1] also **bri·er** (brī'ər) *n.* **1.** A shrub or small tree, *Erica arborea,* of southern Europe, having a hard, woody root used to make tobacco pipes. **2.** A pipe made from briarroot or from a similar wood. [Fr. *bruyère,* heath.]

bri·ar[2] (brī'ər) *n.* Variant of **brier[1].**

bri·ard (brē-är', -ärd') *n.* A sturdily built, rough-coated dog of an ancient French breed. [Fr. < *Brie,* a region of France.]

Bri·ar·e·us (brī-âr'ē-əs) *n. Gk. Myth.* A giant who aided Zeus and the Olympians against the Titans. [Lat. < Gk. *Briareōs* < *briaros,* strong.]

bri·ar·root (brī'ər-ro͞ot', -ro͝ot') *n.* The hard, woody root of the briar.

bri·ar·wood (brī'ər-wo͝od') *n.* Wood from the root of the briar.

bribe (brīb) *n.* **1.** Something, such as money or a favor, offered or given to someone in a position of trust to induce

breastplate
16th-century steel breastplate

him to act dishonestly. **2.** Something offered or serving to influence or persuade. *—v.* **bribed, brib·ing, bribes.** *—tr.* **1.** To give, offer, or promise a bribe to. **2.** To gain influence over or corrupt by bribery. *—intr.* To give, offer, or promise bribes. [ME < OFr., alms.] **—brib'a·ble** *adj.* **—brib'er** *n.*

brib·er·y (brī'bə-rē) *n., pl.* **-ies.** The act or practice of giving, offering, or taking a bribe.

bric-a-brac (brĭk'ə-brăk') *n.* Small usually ornamental objects valued for their antiquity, rarity, or curiosity value. [Fr. *bric-à-brac.*]

brick (brĭk) *n.* **1.** A molded, rectangular block of clay baked by the sun or in a kiln until hard and used as a building and paving material. **2.** An object shaped like a brick: *a brick of cheese.* **3.** *Informal.* A splendid fellow. ***—modifier:*** *a brick wall.* *—tr.v.* **bricked, brick·ing, bricks. 1.** To construct, line, or pave with brick. **2.** To close or wall with brick: *bricked up the windows of the old house.* [ME *brike* < MDu. *bricke.*] **—brick'y** *adj.*

brick·bat (brĭk'băt') *n.* **1.** A piece of brick, esp. one used as a weapon or missile. **2.** An unfavorable remark or criticism.

brick·kiln (brĭk'kĭln', -kĭl') *n.* A kiln in which bricks are baked.

brick·lay·er (brĭk'lā'ər) *n.* A person skilled in building with bricks. **—brick'lay'ing** *n.*

brick red *n.* **1.** A moderate reddish brown. **2.** A moderate to strong brown. **—brick'-red'** *adj.*

brick·work (brĭk'wûrk') *n.* **1.** A structure made of bricks. **2.** Construction with bricks.

brick·yard (brĭk'yärd') *n.* A place where bricks are made.

bri·dal (brīd'l) *n.* A marriage ceremony; wedding. *—adj.* Of or pertaining to a bride or a marriage ceremony; nuptial. [ME *bridale,* wedding feast < OE *brȳdeala* : *brȳd,* bride + *ealu,* ale.]

bridal wreath *n.* Either of two related shrubs, *Spiraea prunifolia* or *S. vanhouttei,* cultivated for their profuse white flowers.

bridge
Covered bridge in Vermont

bride[1] (brīd) *n.* A woman who has recently been married or is about to be married. [ME < OE *brȳd.*]

bride[2] (brīd) *n.* A loop, bar, or tie connecting pattern segments in lacework or needlework. [Fr. < OFr., rein < MHG *brīdel* < OHG *brittil.*]

bride·groom (brīd'grōōm', -grŏŏm') *n.* A man who has recently been married or is about to be married. [Alteration of ME *bridegome* < OE *brȳdguma* : *brȳd,* bride + *guma,* man.]

brides·maid (brīdz'mād') *n.* A woman who attends the bride at a wedding.

bridge[1] (brĭj) *n.* **1.** A structure spanning and providing passage over a waterway, railroad, or other obstacle. **2.** Something resembling or analogous to a bridge in form or function. **3. a.** The upper bony ridge of the human nose. **b.** The part of a pair of eyeglasses that rests against this ridge. **4.** *Mus.* **a.** A thin, upright piece of wood in some stringed instruments that supports the strings above the soundboard. **b.** A transitional passage connecting two subjects or movements. **5.** A fixed or removable replacement for one or several but not all of the natural teeth, usually anchored at each end to a natural tooth. **6.** A crosswise platform above the main deck of a ship from which the ship is controlled. **7. a.** A piece of wood used to steady the cue in billiards. **b.** The hand used as a support to steady the cue in billiards. **8.** *Elect.* Any of various circuits containing a branch that connects two points of equal potential and consequently carries no current when the circuit is suitably adjusted. *—tr.v.* **bridged, bridg·ing, bridg·es. 1.** To build a bridge over. **2.** To cross by or as if by a bridge. [ME *brigge* < OE *brycge.*] **—bridge'a·ble** *adj.*

bridle

bridge[2] (brĭj) *n.* Any of several card games derived from whist and played with one deck of cards divided equally among four people. [Orig. unknown.]

bridge·board (brĭj'bôrd', -bōrd') *n.* A notched board at either side of a staircase that supports the treads and risers.

bridge·head (brĭj'hĕd') *n.* A military position established by advance troops on the enemy's side of a river or pass to afford protection for the main attacking force. [Transl. of Fr. *tête de pont.*]

bridge·work (brĭj'wûrk') *n.* **1.** A dental bridge. **2.** Dental prosthetics involving a bridge or bridges.

bridg·ing (brĭj'ĭng) *n.* Wooden braces between beams, as of a roof, that provide reinforcement and distribution of stress.

brig

bri·dle (brīd'l) *n.* **1.** The harness, consisting of a headstall, bit, and reins, fitted about a horse's head and used to restrain or guide the animal. **2.** A curb or check. **3.** *Naut.* A span of chain, wire, or rope that can be secured at both ends to an object and slung from its center point. *—v.* **-dled, -dling, -dles.** *—tr.* **1.** To put a bridle on. **2.** To control or restrain with or as if with a bridle: *Bridle your curiosity.* *—intr.* **1.** To lift the head and draw in the chin as an expression of scorn or resentment. **2.** To show anger or resentment; take offense: *bridled at the criticism.* [ME *bridel* < OE *brīdel.*] **—bri'dler** *n.*

bridle path *n.* A trail for saddle horses or pack horses.

bri·dle-wise (brīd'l-wīz') *adj.* Trained to respond to pressure of the rein on the neck rather than a pull on the bit, as a horse.

brigantine

bri·doon (brī-dōōn') *n.* A cavalry bit resembling a snaffle that can be reined independently of the curb bit. [Fr. *bridon* < *bride,* rein. —see BRIDE[2].]

Brie (brē) *n.* A mold-ripened, whole-milk cheese whose center is soft. [After *Brie,* a region of France.]

brief (brēf) *adj.* **-er, -est. 1.** Short in time or duration. **2.** Short in length or extent. **3.** Condensed in expression; succinct. **4.** Curt; abrupt. *—n.* **1.** A short or condensed statement. **2.** A condensation or abstract of a large document or series of documents. **3.** *Law.* **a.** An abstract of all of the documents affecting the title of real property. **b.** A document containing all facts and points of law pertinent to a specific case, filed by an attorney before arguing the case in court. **4.** *Rom. Cath. Ch.* A papal letter pertaining to matters of discipline. **5.** A briefing. **6. briefs.** Short, tight-fitting underpants. *—tr.v.* **briefed, brief·ing, briefs. 1.** To summarize. **2.** To give concise preparatory instructions or advice to. **3.** *Chiefly Brit.* To send a legal brief to. **4.** *Chiefly Brit.* To hire (an attorney) as counsel. ***—idiom.* in brief.** In short; in a few words. [ME *bref* < OFr. *bref* < Lat. *brevis,* short.] **—brief'ly** *adv.* **—brief'ness** *n.*

brief·case (brēf'kās') *n.* A portable rectangular case used for carrying books or papers. [< BRIEF (document).]

brief·ing (brē'fĭng) *n.* **1.** The act or procedure of giving or receiving concise preparatory instructions, information, or advice. **2.** The information conveyed during a briefing.

brief·less (brēf'lĭs) *adj.* Having no brief, thus no clients: *a briefless lawyer.*

bri·er[1] also **bri·ar** (brī'ər) *n.* Any of various thorny plants or bushes, esp. a prickly-stemmed rosebush. [ME *breir* < OE *brǣr.*] **—bri'er·y** *adj.*

bri·er[2] (brī'ər) *n.* Variant of **briar[1]**.

brig (brĭg) *n.* **1.** A two-masted sailing ship, square-rigged on both masts, carrying two or more headsails and a quadrilateral gaff sail or spanker aft of the mizzenmast. **2.** A ship's prison. **3.** A guardhouse. [Short for BRIGANTINE.]

bri·gade (brĭ-gād') *n.* **1. a.** A military unit consisting of a variable number of combat battalions. **b.** A former unit of the U.S. Army composed of two or more regiments commanded by a brigadier general. **2.** A group of persons organized for a specific purpose: *a fire brigade.* *—tr.v.* **-gad·ed, -gad·ing, -gades.** To form into a brigade. [Fr. < OFr., company < OItal. *brigata* < *brigare,* to fight < LLat. *briga,* strife.]

brig·a·dier (brĭg'ə-dîr') *n.* A brigadier general. [Fr. < *brigade,* brigade.]

brigadier general *n., pl.* **brigadier generals.** An officer ranking between a colonel and a major general in the U.S. Army, Air Force, and Marine Corps.

brig·and (brĭg'ənd) *n.* A robber or freebooter, esp. one of a band of bandits. [ME *brigaunt* < OFr., prob. < OItal. *brigante,* skirmisher < *brigare,* to fight. —see BRIGADE.] **—brig'and·age** (-ən-dĭj), **brig'and·ism** *n.*

brig·an·tine (brĭg'ən-tēn') *n.* A two-masted sailing ship, square-rigged on the foremast and having a fore-and-aft mainsail with square maintopsails. [Fr. *brigantin* < OFr. *brigandin* < OItal. *brigantino,* skirmishing ship < *brigante,* skirmisher. —see BRIGAND.]

bright (brīt) *adj.* **-er, -est. 1. a.** Emitting or reflecting light readily or in large amounts; shining. **b.** Comparatively high on the scale of brightness. **2.** Characterizing a dyestuff that produces a highly saturated color; brilliant in color; vivid. **3.** Glorious; splendid. **4.** Full of promise and hope; auspicious. **5.** Happy; cheerful. **6.** Smart; intelligent. *—n.* **1.** A thin, flat paintbrush used for highlighting. **2. brights.** High-beam headlights. *—adv.* In a bright manner. [ME < OE *beorht.*] **—bright'ly** *adv.*

Synonyms: *bright, brilliant, radiant, lustrous, lambent, luminous, incandescent, effulgent. Bright* can be applied to anything that emits or reflects light. The terms that follow are more specific. A *brilliant* object is intensely bright and striking by reason of the sparkle, glitter, or gleam that it emits or reflects; figuratively the term applies to outstanding personal qualities. A *radiant* object radiates light; figuratively the term applies to that which, like a smile, reveals inner light and warmth. A *lustrous* object originates no light but reflects an agreeable sheen. *Lambent* is said of that which, like a flame, casts soft, flickering light; figuratively it suggests a subtle playfulness, as of style or wit. Physically, *luminous* is broadly applicable to anything bright, but is said especially of that which shines in the dark or figuratively of that which is remarkably clear or enlightened. *Incandescent* stresses burning brilliance, as of something white-hot. *Effulgent,* physically and figuratively, means intensely radiant.

bright·en (brīt'n) *tr. & intr.v.* **-ened, -en·ing, -ens. 1.** To make or become bright or brighter. **2.** To make or become more cheerful. **—bright'en·er** *n.*

bright·ness (brīt'nĭs) *n.* **1.** The state or quality of being bright. **2.** The effect or sensation by means of which an observer is able to distinguish differences in luminance. **3.** The dimension of a color that represents its similarity to one of a series of achromatic colors ranging from very dim (dark) to very bright (dazzling).

Bright's disease (brīts) *n.* Chronic nephritis. [After Richard *Bright* (1789–1858).]

bright·work (brīt'wûrk') *n.* Metal parts or fixtures, esp. on a ship, made bright by polishing.

brill (brĭl) *n., pl.* **brill** or **brills.** An edible flatfish, *Scophthalmus rhombus,* of European waters. [Orig. unknown.]

bril·liance (brĭl'yəns) also **bril·lian·cy** (-yən-sē) *n.* **1.** Extreme brightness. **2.** Sharpness and clarity of musical tone. **3.** Splendor; magnificence. **4.** Exceptional clarity and agility of intellect or invention.

bril·liant (brĭl'yənt) *adj.* **1.** Full of light; shining. **2. a.** Brightly vivid in color. **b.** Designating a color that has a combination of high lightness and strong saturation. **3.** *Mus.* Sharp and clear in tone. **4.** Glorious; magnificent: *the brilliant court life of Versailles.* **5.** Superb; wonderful: *a brilliant performance.* **6.** Marked by extraordinary powers of intellect or invention. *—n.* A precious gem, esp. a diamond, finely cut in any of various forms with numerous facets. [Fr. *brillant,* pr.part. of *briller,* to shine < Ital. *brillare,* perh. < *brillo,* beryl < Lat. *beryllus.*] **—bril'liant·ly** *adv.* **—bril'liant·ness** *n.*

bril·lian·tine (brĭl'yən-tēn') *n.* **1.** An oily, perfumed hairdressing. **2.** A glossy fabric made from cotton and worsted or cotton and mohair. [Fr. *brillantine* < *brillant,* brilliant.]

Brill's disease (brĭlz) *n.* A form of epidemic typhus that is believed to be a recurrence of an earlier infection. [After Nathan E. *Brill* (1860–1925).]

brim (brĭm) *n.* **1.** The rim or uppermost edge of a cup or other vessel. **2.** A projecting rim or edge: *the brim of a hat.* **3.** A border or edge, esp. one surrounding a body of water. *—tr. & intr.v.* **brimmed, brim·ming, brims.** To fill or be full to the brim. ***—phrasal verb.* brim over.** To overflow. [ME *brimme,* of Germanic orig.]

brim·ful (brĭm'fo͝ol') *adj.* Full to the brim.

brim·stone (brĭm'stōn') *n. Obs.* Sulfur. [ME *brimston* < OE *brynstān.*]

brin (brĭn) *n.* One of the ribs of a fan. [Fr.]

brin·dle (brĭn'dl) *n.* **1.** A brindled color. **2.** A brindled animal. [Back-formation < BRINDLED.]

brin·dled (brĭn'dld) *adj.* Tawny or grayish with streaks or spots of a darker color. [Alteration of ME *brended,* perh. < *brende,* p.part. of *brennen,* to burn < ON *brenna.*]

brine (brīn) *n.* **1.** Water saturated with or containing large amounts of a salt, esp. of sodium chloride. **2. a.** The water of a sea or an ocean. **b.** A large body of salt water. **3.** Salt water used for preserving and pickling foods. *—tr.v.* **brined, brin·ing, brines.** To immerse, preserve, or pickle in brine. [ME < OE *brīne.*] **—brin'er** *n.*

Bri·nell hardness (brĭ-nĕl') *n.* The relative hardness of metals and alloys, determined by forcing a steel ball into a test piece under standard conditions and measuring the surface area of the resulting indentation. [After Johann A. *Brinell* (1849–1925).]

Brinell number *n.* The numerical value assigned to the Brinell hardness of metals and alloys.

brine shrimp *n.* Any of various small crustaceans of the genus *Artemia.*

bring (brĭng) *tr.v.* **brought** (brôt), **bring·ing, brings. 1.** To take with oneself to a place; convey or carry along: *brought enough money with him.* **2.** To carry as an attribute or contribution: *brought years of experience to his new post.* **3.** To lead or force into a specified state, situation, or location: *brought the water to a boil; was brought to grief.* **4.** To succeed in persuading; induce: *His confession brought others to confess.* **5.** To cause to occur as a consequence or concomitant: *Floods brought death to the valley.* **6.** To cause to become apparent to the mind; recall: *bring back memories.* **7.** *Law.* To advance or set forth (charges, for example) in a court. **8.** To sell for; fetch. ***—phrasal verbs.* bring about.** To cause to happen. **bring around (or round). 1.** To cause to adopt an opinion or course of action. **2.** To cause to recover consciousness. **bring down. 1.** To cause to fall or collapse. **2.** To kill. **bring forth. 1.** To give rise to; effect; produce. **2.** To bear (fruit or young). **bring forward. 1.** To present; produce: *bring forward proof.* **2.** *Accounting.* To carry (a sum) from one page or column to another. **bring in. 1.** To give or submit (a verdict). **2.** To produce or yield (profits or income). **bring off.** To accomplish successfully. **bring on. 1.** To result in; cause. **2.** To cause to appear: *bring on the dessert.* **bring out. 1.** To reveal or expose. **2.** To produce or publish. **bring over.** To win over. **bring to. 1.** To cause to recover consciousness. **2.** To cause (a ship) to turn into the wind and lose way. **bring up. 1.** To take care of and educate (a child); rear. **2.** To introduce into discussion; mention. **3.** To vomit or cough up. [ME *bringen* < OE *bringan.*] **—bring'er** *n.*

Usage: In most dialects of American English, *bring* is used to denote movement toward the place of speaking or the point from which the action is regarded: *Bring it to me now. He brought his children a present from his travels. Take* denotes movement away from such a place. Thus, one normally *takes* checks to the bank and *brings* home cash, though from the banker's point of view, one has *brought* him checks in order to *take* away cash.

bring·down (brĭng'doun') *n.* Something that disturbs or disappoints.

bring·ing-up (brĭng'ĭng-ŭp') *n.* The care, training, and education of a child; upbringing.

brink (brĭngk) *n.* **1. a.** The upper edge of a steep or vertical slope: *the brink of a cliff.* **b.** The margin of land bordering a body of water. **2.** The verge of something: *on the brink of discovery.* [ME, prob. of Scand. orig.]

brink·man·ship (brĭngk'mən-shĭp') *n.* The practice, esp. in international politics, of seeking advantage by creating the impression that one is willing and able to pass the brink of nuclear war rather than concede.

brin·y (brī'nē) *adj.* **-i·er, -i·est.** Of, pertaining to, or resembling brine; salty. *—n. Slang.* The sea. **—brin'i·ness** *n.*

bri·o (brē'ō) *n.* Vigor; vivacity. [Ital., of Celt. orig.]

bri·oche (brē-ôsh', -ŏsh') *n.* A soft, light-textured roll or bun made from eggs, butter, flour, and yeast. [Fr. < OFr. < dial. *brier,* var. of *broyer,* to knead, of Germanic orig.]

bri·o·lette (brē'ə-lĕt') *n.* A pear-shaped gem, esp. a diamond, cut with long triangular facets. [Fr.]

bri·quette also **bri·quet** (brĭ-kĕt') *n.* A block of compressed coal dust or charcoal, used for fuel and kindling. [Fr. *briquette,* dim. of *brique,* brick < MDu. *bricke.*]

bri·sance (brĭ-zäns', -zäNs') *n.* The shattering effect of a sudden release of energy, as in an explosion. [Fr. < *brisant,* pr.part. of *briser,* to break, of Celt. orig.] **—bri·sant'** (-zänt', -zäNt') *adj.*

brisk (brĭsk) *adj.* **-er, -est. 1.** Lively; energetic: *a brisk walk.* **2.** Keen or sharp in speech or manner: *a brisk greeting.* **3.** Stimulating and invigorating: *a brisk wind.* **4.** Pleasantly zestful: *a brisk tea.* [Orig. unknown.] **—brisk'ly** *adv.* **—brisk'ness** *n.*

bris·ket (brĭs'kĭt) *n.* **1.** The chest of an animal. **2.** The ribs and meat from the brisket. [ME *brusket,* poss. of Scand. orig.]

bris·ling (brĭz'lĭng, brĭs'-) *n.* The sprat (sense 1). [Norw. < LG *bretling* < *bret,* broad.]

bris·tle (brĭs'əl) *n.* A short, coarse, stiff hair or hairlike part. *—v.* **-tled, -tling, -tles.** *—intr.* **1.** To erect the bristles, as an angry, excited, or frightened animal: *The porcupine stood its ground and bristled.* **2.** To react with agitation to anger, excitement, or fear. **3.** To stand erectly on end like bristles. **4.** To be covered or thick with or as if with bristles: *The path bristled with thorns.* *—tr.* **1.** To cause to stand erect like bristles; stiffen. **2.** To furnish or supply with bristles. **3.** To ruffle; disturb. [ME *bristel.*] **—bris'tly** *adj.*

bris·tle·cone pine (brĭs'əl-kōn') *n.* A small pine, *Pinus aristata,* of the western United States, that is the longest-living conifer known.

bris·tle·tail (brĭs'əl-tāl') *n.* Any of various wingless insects of the order Thysanura, such as the silverfish, having bristlelike posterior appendages.

Bris·tol board (brĭs'təl) *n.* A smooth, heavy pasteboard of fine quality. [After *Bristol,* England.]

brit also **britt** (brĭt) *n.* **1.** The young of herring and similar fish. **2.** Minute marine organisms, such as crustaceans of the genus *Calanus,* that are a major source of food for many fish and whales. [Perh. < Cornish *brȳthel,* mackerel.]

Bri·tan·nia (brĭ-tăn'yə, -tăn'ē-ə) *n.* **1.** A poetic term for Great Britain. **2.** A female personification of Great Britain or the British Empire. **3.** Also **britannia.** Britannia metal. [Lat. < *Brittanni,* the Britons.]

britannia metal *n.* A white alloy of tin with copper, antimony, and sometimes bismuth and zinc. [After BRITANNIA.]

Bri·tan·nic (brĭ-tăn'ĭk) *adj.* British.

britch·es (brĭch'ĭz) *pl.n. Informal.* Breeches. ***—idiom.* too big for (one's) britches.** *Informal.* Overconfident; cocky. [Alteration of BREECHES.]

Brit·i·cism (brĭt'ĭ-sĭz'əm) also **Brit·ish·ism** (-shĭz'əm) *n.* A word, phrase, or idiom characteristic of or peculiar to English as it is spoken in Great Britain.

Brit·ish (brĭt'ĭsh) *adj.* **1.** Of, pertaining to, or characteristic of Great Britain, the United Kingdom, or the British Empire. **2.** Of, pertaining to, or characteristic of the ancient Britons. *—n.* **1.** *(used with a pl. verb).* The people of Great Britain. **2.** British English. **3.** The Celtic language of the ancient Britons. [ME *Brittish* < OE *Bryttisc,* pertaining to ancient Britons.]

British English *n.* The English language as used in England as distinguished from that used elsewhere.

Brit·ish·er (brĭt'ĭ-shər) *n. Informal.* A native or inhabitant of Great Britain.

Brit·ish·ism (brĭt'ĭ-shĭz'əm) *n.* Variant of **Briticism.**

British thermal unit *n.* The quantity of heat required to raise the temperature of one pound of water by one degree Fahrenheit.

Brit·on (brĭt'n) *n.* **1.** A native or inhabitant of Britain. **2.** One of a Celtic people who inhabited ancient Britain before the Roman invasion. [ME *Breton* < OFr. < Lat. *Britto,* Celt, of Celtic orig.]

britt (brĭt) *n.* Variant of **brit.**

Brit·ta·ny spaniel (brĭt'n-ē) *n.* A large spaniel of a breed originating in France. [After *Brittany,* a region of northwestern France.]

brit·tle (brĭt'l) *adj.* **-tler, -tlest. 1.** Likely to break; fragile: *brittle porcelain.* **2.** Difficult to deal with; snappish: *a brittle disposition.* *—n.* A confection of caramelized sugar to which nuts are added: *peanut brittle.* [ME *britel.*] **—brit'tle·ly** (brĭt'l-ē) *adv.* **—brit'tle·ness** *n.*

brittle star *n.* Any of various marine organisms of the class

Brittany spaniel

Ophiuroidea, related to and resembling the starfish but having long, slender, whiplike arms.

Brix scale (brĭks) *n.* A hydrometer scale for measuring the sugar content of a solution at a given temperature. [After Adolf F. *Brix* (d. 1870), its inventor.]

broach[1] (brōch) *n.* **1. a.** A tapered and serrated tool used to shape or enlarge a hole. **b.** The hole made by such a tool. **2.** A spit for roasting meat. **3.** A narrow mason's chisel. **4.** A gimlet for tapping or broaching casks. **5.** Variant of **brooch**. —*tr.v.* **broached, broach·ing, broach·es. 1. a.** To begin to talk about; bring up: *broach a subject.* **b.** To announce: *broached his plans for the next year.* **2.** To pierce in order to draw off liquid: *broach a keg of beer.* **3.** To draw off (a liquid) by piercing a hole in a cask or other container. **4.** To shape or enlarge (a hole) with a broach. [ME *broche* < OFr., spit.] —**broach'er** *n.*

broach[2] (brōch) *intr. & tr.v.* **broached, broach·ing, broach·es.** *Naut.* To veer or cause to veer broadside to the wind and waves: *tried to keep the boat from broaching to.* [Poss. < BROACH[1].]

broad (brôd) *adj.* **-er, -est. 1.** Wide from side to side: *broad hips.* **2.** Large in expanse; spacious: *a broad lawn.* **3.** Widely diffused; clear and bright: *broad daylight.* **4.** Covering a wide scope; general: *a broad rule.* **5.** Liberal or tolerant: *a broad point of view.* **6.** Main; essential: *the broad facts of the matter.* **7.** Plain and clear; obvious: *a broad hint.* **8.** Outspoken; unrestrained: *a broad hint.* **9.** Vulgar; ribald: *a broad joke.* **10.** Heavily regional: *a broad accent.* **11.** *Ling.* Indicating a vowel that is pronounced with the tongue placed low and flat and with the oral cavity wide open, esp. as when the *a* in *bath* is pronounced like the *a* in *bard.* —*n.* **1.** The broad part of something. **2.** *Slang.* A woman or girl. —*adv.* Fully; completely. [ME *brod* < OE *brād.*] —**broad'ly** *adv.* —**broad'ness** *n.*

broad arrow *n.* **1.** An arrow with a wide, barbed head. **2.** A wide arrowhead mark identifying British government property.

broad·ax also **broad·axe** (brôd'ăks') *n.* An ax with a wide, flat head and a short handle; battle-ax.

broad·band (brôd'bănd') *adj.* Of, having, or pertaining to a wide band of electromagnetic frequencies: *broadband communications.* —**broad'band'** *n.*

broad bean *n.* **1.** A plant, *Vicia faba,* native to the Old World, cultivated for its edible pods and seeds. **2.** The somewhat flattened seed of the broad bean.

broad·bill (brôd'bĭl') *n.* **1. a.** Any of various birds of the family Eurylaimidae, of Africa and tropical Asia, having a short, wide bill and brightly colored plumage. **b.** Any of several other broad-billed birds, as the shoveler. **2.** The swordfish.

George Miksch Sutton

broadbill

broad·brim (brôd'brĭm') *n.* **1.** A hat with a broad, flat brim, as those worn by Quakers. **2. Broadbrim.** *Informal.* A member of the Society of Friends; Quaker.

broad·cast (brôd'kăst') *v.* **-cast** or **-cast·ed, -cast·ing, -casts.** —*tr.* **1.** To transmit (a program) by radio or television. **2.** To make known over a wide area: *broadcast rumors.* **3.** To sow (seed) over a wide area, esp. by hand. —*intr.* **1.** To transmit a radio or television program. **2.** To participate in a radio or television program. —*n.* **1.** Transmission of a radio or television program or signal. **2. a.** A radio or television program. **b.** The duration of such a program. **3.** The act of scattering seed. —*adj.* Scattered over a wide area. —*adv.* In a scattered manner; far and wide. —**broad'cast'er** *n.*

Broad-Church (brôd'chûrch') *adj.* Of or pertaining to members of the Anglican Communion favoring liberalism of doctrine and ritual. —**Broad'Church'man** *n.*

broad·cloth (brôd'klôth', -klŏth') *n.* **1.** A densely textured woolen cloth with a plain or twill weave and a lustrous finish. **2.** A closely woven silk, cotton, or synthetic fabric with a narrow crosswise rib.

brocade
Fabric from an 18th-century Japanese kimono

broad·en (brôd'n) *tr. & intr.v.* **-ened, -en·ing, -ens.** To make or become broad or broader. —**broad'en·er** *n.*

broad gauge *n.* A railroad track with a width between the rails greater than the standard gauge of 56½ inches.

broad-gauge (brôd'gāj') *adj.* **1.** Having a broad gauge. **2.** *Informal.* Having a wide scope; liberal.

broad·head (brôd'hĕd') *n.* **1.** A flat steel arrowhead with two sharp edges. **2.** An arrow with a broadhead.

broad jump *n.* A long jump.

broad·leaf (brôd'lēf') *n.* Any of various tobacco plants having broad leaves. —*adj.* Broad-leaved.

broad-leaved (brôd'lēvd') also **broad-leafed** (-lēft') *adj.* Having relatively broad leaves, as evergreens such as the rhododendron and holly, rather than needles, as evergreens such as the pines and spruces.

broad·loom (brôd'lo͞om') *adj.* Designating carpet from 4½ to 18 feet in width that is woven on a wide loom. —*n.* A broadloom carpet.

broad-mind·ed (brôd'mīn'dĭd) *adj.* Having or characterized by liberal or tolerant views. —**broad'-mind'ed·ly** *adv.* —**broad'-mind'ed·ness** *n.*

broad seal *n.* The official public seal of a state or nation.

broad·sheet (brôd'shēt') *n.* A broadside (sense 4).

broad·side (brôd'sīd') *n.* **1.** The side of a ship above the water line. **2. a.** All the guns on one side of a warship. **b.** Their simultaneous discharge. **3.** An explosive verbal attack or denunciation. **4.** A large sheet of paper printed on one side. **5.** A broad, unbroken surface. —*adv.* With the side turned to a given object: *The wave caught them broadside and filled the canoe.*

broad-spec·trum (brôd'spĕk'trəm) *adj.* Widely applicable or effective: *a broad-spectrum drug.*

broad·sword (brôd'sôrd', -sōrd') *n.* A cutting sword with a wide blade.

broad·tail (brôd'tāl') *n.* **1.** The karakul. **2.** The black pelt of a prematurely born karakul sheep, having a flat surface with wavy markings.

Broad·way (brôd'wā') *n.* **1.** The principal theater district of New York City, located on or near Broadway, a thoroughfare extending the length of Manhattan Island. **2.** The American legitimate stage: *a career in motion pictures and on Broadway.* —**modifier:** *a Broadway musical.*

bro·cade (brō-kād') *n.* A heavy fabric interwoven with a rich, raised design. —*tr.v.* **-cad·ed, -cad·ing, -cades.** To weave brocade. [Sp. or Port. *brocado* < Ital. *brocato* < *brocco,* twisted thread < VLat. **brocca,* spike < Lat. *brocchus,* of Celt. orig.]

broc·a·tel also **broc·a·telle** (brŏk'ə-tĕl') *n.* A very heavy fabric resembling brocade but with a more highly raised design. [Fr. *brocatelle* < Ital. *broccatello,* dim. of *broccato,* brocade.]

broc·co·li also **broc·o·li** (brŏk'ə-lē) *n.* **1.** A plant, *Brassica oleracea italica,* closely related to the cabbage and cauliflower, having a branched, greenish flower head. **2.** The flower head of the broccoli, eaten as a vegetable before the green, tightly clustered buds have opened. [Ital., pl. of *broccolo,* cabbage top, dim. of *brocco,* shoot. —see BROCADE.]

bro·chette (brō-shĕt') *n.* A small spit or skewer upon which meat, fish, or vegetables are roasted or broiled. [Fr. < OFr., dim. of *broche,* spit.]

bro·chure (brō-sho͝or') *n.* A small pamphlet or booklet. [Fr. < *brocher,* to stitch < *broche,* knitting needle < OFr., spit.]

brock (brŏk) *n. Chiefly Brit.* A badger. [ME < OE *broc,* of Celt. orig.]

brock·et (brŏk'ĭt) *n.* **1.** A two-year-old stag with its first horns. **2.** Any of several small deer of the genus *Mazama,* of South America, having short, unbranched horns. [ME *broket* < OFr. *brocard* < *broque,* animal's horn, var. of *broche,* spit.]

broc·o·li (brŏk'ə-lē) *n.* Variant of **broccoli**.

bro·gan (brō'gən) *n.* A heavy, ankle-high work shoe. [Ir. Gael. *brōgan,* dim. of *brōg,* brogue.]

brogue (brōg) *n.* **1. a.** A heavy shoe of untanned leather, formerly worn in Scotland and Ireland. **b.** A strong oxford shoe, usually with ornamental perforations. **2.** A strong dialectal accent, esp. a strong Irish accent. [Ir.and Sc. Gael. *brōg,* OIr. *brōc,* shoe.]

broi·der (broi'dər) *tr.v.* **-dered, -der·ing, -ders.** *Obs.* To ornament with needlework; embroider. —**broi'der·y** (-də-rē) *n.*

broil[1] (broil) *v.* **broiled, broil·ing, broils.** —*tr.* **1.** To cook by direct radiant heat, as over a grill or under an electric coil. **2.** To expose to great heat. —*intr.* To be exposed to great heat. —*n.* **1.** The act or condition of broiling. **2.** Something broiled. [ME *broilen* < OFr. *bruler.*]

broil[2] (broil) *n.* A rowdy argument; brawl. —*intr.v.* **broiled, broil·ing, broils.** To engage in a broil. [< obs. *broil,* to brawl < ME *broilen* < OFr. *brouiller.*]

broil·er (broi'lər) *n.* **1.** One that broils. **2. a.** A small electric oven used for broiling. **b.** The part of a stove used for broiling. **3.** A tender young chicken suitable for broiling.

broke (brōk) *v.* Past tense and nonstandard past participle of **break**. —*adj. Informal.* **1.** Lacking funds. **2.** Bankrupt.

bro·ken (brō'kən) *v.* Past participle of **break**. —*adj.* **1.** Forcibly fractured into two or more pieces; shattered. **2.** Violated: *broken promises.* **3.** Fragmentary; incomplete: *a broken set of books.* **4.** Disorganized; routed: *broken troops.* **5.** Intermittently stopping and starting; discontinuous. **6.** Varying abruptly, as in pitch: *broken sobs.* **7.** Spoken with gaps and crude errors: *broken English.* **8.** Topographically rough; uneven. **9.** Subdued; humbled: *a broken spirit.* **10.** Tamed and trained: *a broken stallion.* **11.** Weakened; exhausted: *broken health.* **12.** Crushed by grief: *a broken heart.* **13.** Financially ruined; bankrupt. **14.** Not functioning. —**bro'ken·ly** *adv.* —**bro'ken·ness** *n.*

bro·ken-down (brō'kən-doun') *adj.* **1.** Out of working order. **2.** In poor condition, as from old age; infirm.

bro·ken·heart·ed (brō'kən-här'tĭd) *adj.* Grievously sad.

broken home *n.* A family in which the parents are separated or divorced.

broken wind *n.* Heaves (sense 5).

bro·ker (brō'kər) *n.* **1.** One who acts as an agent for others in negotiating contracts, purchases, or sales in return for a fee or commission. **2.** A stockbroker. —*tr.v.* **-kered, -ker·ing, -kers.** To arrange or manage as a broker. [ME < AN *brocour.*]

bro·ker·age (brō'kər-ĭj) *n.* **1.** The business of a broker. **2.** A fee or commission paid to a broker.

brom– *pref.* Variant of **bromo-**.

bro·mate (brō'māt') *n.* A salt of bromic acid. —*tr.v.* **-mat·ed, -mat·ing, -mates. 1.** To treat (a substance) chemically with a bromate. **2.** To combine (a substance) chemically with bromine.

brome (brōm) *n.* A grass of the genus *Bromus,* having spikelets in loose, often drooping clusters. [NLat. *Bromus,* genus name < Lat. *bromos,* oats < Gk.]

brome grass *n.* Brome.

bro·me·li·ad (brō-mē′lē-ăd′) *n.* Any of various mostly epiphytic plants of the family Bromeliaceae, which includes the pineapple, Spanish moss, and many species grown as house plants. [< NLat. *Bromelia,* type genus, after Olaf *Bromelius* (1639–1705).]

bro·mic acid (brō′mĭk) *n.* A corrosive, colorless liquid, $HBrO_3$, used in making dyes and pharmaceuticals.

bro·mide (brō′mīd′) *n.* **1.** A binary compound of bromine. **2.** Potassium bromide. **3. a.** A commonplace remark or notion; platitude. **b.** A tiresome person; bore. **4.** A photographic print on paper that has been treated with bromine and silver. **—bro·mid′ic** (-mĭd′ĭk) *adj.*

bro·mi·nate (brō′mə-nāt′) *tr.v.* **-nat·ed, -nat·ing, -nates.** To combine (a substance) with bromine or a bromine compound. **—bro′mi·na′tion** *n.*

bro·mine (brō′mēn′) *n. Symbol* **Br** A heavy, volatile, corrosive, reddish-brown, nonmetallic liquid element, having a highly irritating vapor. It is used in producing gasoline antiknock mixtures, fumigants, dyes, and photographic chemicals. Atomic weight 79.909; atomic number 35; melting point −7.2°C; boiling point 58.78°C; valences 1, 3, 5, 7. [Fr. *brome* < Gk. *brōmos,* stench + -INE.]

bro·mism (brō′mĭz′əm) also **bro·min·ism** (brō′mə-nĭz′əm) *n.* Poisoning from overuse of bromides.

bromo– or **brom–** *pref.* Bromine: *bromide.* [Prob. < Fr. *brome* < Gk. *brōmos,* stench.]

bronch– *pref.* Variant of **broncho-**.

bron·chi (brŏng′kī′) *n.* Plural of **bronchus.**

bron·chi·a (brŏng′kē-ə) *n.* Plural of **bronchium.**

bron·chi·al (brŏng′kē-əl) *adj.* Of or pertaining to the bronchi, the bronchia, or the bronchioles. **—bron′chi·al·ly** *adv.*

bronchial asthma *n.* A usually allergic asthma of the bronchi.

bronchial tube *n.* A bronchus or any of its branches.

bron·chi·ec·ta·sis (brŏng′kē-ĕk′tə-sĭs) *n.* Chronic dilation of the bronchial tubes, with cough and formation of mucopurulent matter. [Gk. *bronkhia,* bronchial tubes < *bronkhos,* windpipe + Gk. *ektasis,* extension (*ek-,* out + *teinein,* to stretch).]

bron·chi·ole (brŏng′kē-ōl′) *n.* Any of the fine, thin-walled, tubular extensions of a bronchus. **—bron′chi·o′lar** (-ō′lər) *adj.*

bron·chi·tis (brŏn-kī′tĭs, brŏng-) *n.* Chronic or acute inflammation of the mucous membrane of the bronchial tubes. **—bron·chit′ic** (-kĭt′ĭk) *adj.*

bron·chi·um (brŏng′kē-əm) *n., pl.* **-chi·a** (-kē-ə). A bronchial tube that is smaller than a bronchus and larger than a bronchiole. [NLat., sing. of LLat. *bronchia,* bronchial tubes < Gk. *bronkhia* < *bronkhos,* windpipe.]

broncho– or **bronch–** *pref.* Bronchus; bronchial: *bronchoscope.* [LLat. < Gk. *bronkho-* < *bronkhos,* windpipe.]

bron·cho·con·stric·tion (brŏng′kō-kən-strĭk′shən) *n.* Constriction of the bronchial tubes. **—bron′cho·con·stric′tor** *adj.*

bron·cho·pneu·mo·ni·a (brŏng′kō-nōō-mōn′yə, -nyōō-) *n.* Inflammation of the lungs spreading from and following infection of the bronchi.

bron·cho·scope (brŏng′kə-skōp′) *n.* A slender tubular instrument with a small light on the end for inspection of the interior of the bronchi. **—bron′cho·scop′ic** (-skŏp′ĭk) *adj.* **—bron′cho·scop′i·cal·ly** *adv.* **—bron·chos′co·pist** (brŏn-kŏs′kə-pĭst, brŏng-) *n.* **—bron·chos′co·py** (-kə-pē) *n.*

bron·chus (brŏng′kəs) *n., pl.* **-chi** (-kī′). Either of two main branches of the trachea, leading directly to the lungs. [NLat. < Gk. *bronkhos,* windpipe.]

bron·co (brŏng′kō) *n., pl.* **-cos.** A wild or semiwild horse or pony of western North America. [Mex. Sp. < Sp., wild.]

bron·co·bust·er (brŏng′kō-bŭs′tər) *n.* A cowboy who breaks wild horses to the saddle.

bron·to·saur (brŏn′tə-sôr′) also **bron·to·sau·rus** (brŏn′tə-sôr′əs) *n.* A very large, herbivorous dinosaur of the genus *Apatosaurus* (or *Brontosaurus*), of the Jurassic period. [NLat. *Brontosaurus,* genus name : Gk. *brontē,* thunder + Gk. *sauras,* lizard.]

Bronx cheer (brŏngks) *n. Slang.* A raspberry (sense 4). [After the *Bronx,* a borough of the City of New York.]

bronze (brŏnz) *n.* **1. a.** Any of various alloys of copper and tin, sometimes with traces of other metals. **b.** Any of various alloys of copper, with or without tin, and antimony, phosphorus, or other components. **2.** A work of art made of bronze. **3. a.** A moderate yellowish to olive brown. **b.** A pigment of this color. **—modifier:** *a bronze statue.* *—adj.* Of the color bronze. *—tr.v.* **bronzed, bronz·ing, bronz·es.** To give the appearance of bronze to. [Fr. < Ital. *bronzo.*] **—bronz′y** *adj.*

Bronze Age *n.* A period of human culture between the Stone Age and the Iron Age, characterized by weapons and implements made of bronze.

bronz·er (brŏn′zər) *n.* A cosmetic esp. for men that gives the skin a tanned appearance.

Bronze Star *n.* A U.S. Army decoration awarded for heroism or meritorious achievement in ground combat.

brooch also **broach** (brōch, brōōch) *n.* A large decorative pin or clasp. [ME *broche,* pointed tool. —see BROACH[1].]

brood (brōōd) *n.* **1.** The young of certain animals, esp. a group of young birds or fowl hatched at one time and cared for by the same mother. **2.** The children in one family. *—v.* **brood·ed, brood·ing, broods.** *—tr.* **1.** To sit on or hatch (eggs). **2.** To protect (young) by or as if by covering with the wings. *—intr.* **1.** To sit on or hatch eggs. **2.** To hover envelopingly. **3.** To think at length and unhappily; ponder. *—adj.* Kept for breeding: *a brood hen.* [ME < OE *brōd.*] **—brood′ing·ly** *adv.*

brood·er (brōō′dər) *n.* **1.** One that broods. **2.** A heated enclosure in which young chickens or other fowl are raised.

brood·mare (brōōd′mâr′) *n.* A mare kept for breeding.

brood·y (brōō′dē) *adj.* **-i·er, -i·est. 1.** Moody; meditative. **2.** Inclined to sit on eggs to hatch them: *a broody hen.* **—brood′i·ness** *n.*

brook[1] (brŏŏk) *n.* A small, natural freshwater stream. [ME < OE *brōc.*]

brook[2] (brŏŏk) *tr.v.* **brooked, brook·ing, brooks.** To put up with; tolerate: *will brook no delay.* [ME *brouken* < OE *brūcan,* to use, enjoy.]

brook·ite (brŏŏk′īt′) *n.* A red-brown to black titanium dioxide mineral with characteristic orthorhombic crystals. [After Henry J. *Brooke* (1771–1857).]

brook lamprey *n.* Any of several usually small lampreys that live mostly in brooks.

brook·let (brŏŏk′lĭt) *n.* A small brook.

brook·lime (brŏŏk′līm′) *n.* Either of two closely related trailing plants, *Veronica americana,* of North America, and *V. beccabunga,* native to Eurasia, growing in moist places and having small blue flowers. [ME *broke-lemok* : *broke,* brook + *lemok,* a kind of brooklime < OE *hleomoce.*]

brook trout *n.* A freshwater game fish, *Salvelinus fontinalis,* of eastern North America.

brook·weed (brŏŏk′wēd′) *n.* Either of two related plants, *Samolus valerandi,* of Europe, and *S. floribundus,* of North America, having small white flowers and growing in moist areas.

broom (brōōm, brŏŏm) *n.* **1.** A brush of twigs, straw, or bristles bound together, attached to a stick or handle, and used for sweeping. **2. a.** A shrub of the genus *Cytisus,* native to Eurasia, having compound leaves and yellow or white flowers. **b.** Any of several similar or related shrubs, esp. of the genus *Genista.* *—tr.v.* **broomed, broom·ing, brooms.** To sweep with or as if with a broom. [ME < OE *brōm.*] **—broom′y** *adj.*

broom·corn (brōōm′kôrn′, brŏŏm′-) *n.* A grass, *Sorghum vulgare technicum,* having flower clusters with stiff, branching stalks that are used to make brooms and brushes.

broom moss *n.* A moss of the genus *Dicranum,* esp. *D. scoparium,* having leaves turned to one side along the stem.

broom·rape (brōōm′rāp′, brŏŏm′-) *n.* Any of several leafless, parasitic plants of the genus *Orobanche,* having yellow, purple, or reddish-brown flowers and living on the roots of other plants. [Transl. of Lat. *rapum genistae,* broom tuber, from the resemblance of the parasitic growths to tubers on the roots of broom.]

broom·stick (brōōm′stĭk′, brŏŏm′-) *n.* The long handle of a broom.

broth (brôth, brŏth) *n., pl.* **broths** (brôths, brŏths, brôthz, brŏthz). **1.** The water in which meat, fish, or vegetables have been boiled; stock. **2.** A thin, clear soup based on stock, to which rice, barley, meat, or vegetables may be added. [ME < OE *broð.*]

broth·el (brŏth′əl, brô′thəl) *n.* A house of prostitution. [Short for *brothel-house* < ME *brothel,* prostitute < *brother,* p.part. of *brethen,* to go to ruin < OE *brēoðan,* to decay.]

broth·er (brŭth′ər) *n.* **1.** A male having the same parents as another or one parent in common with another. **2.** One who shares a common ancestry, allegiance, character, or purpose with another or others, esp.: **a.** A kinsman. **b.** A fellow man. **c.** A fellow member, as of a fraternity. **d.** A close male friend; comrade. **3.** *Eccles.* **a.** A member of a men's religious order who is not in holy orders but engages in the work of the order. **b.** A lay member of a religious order of men. [ME < OE *brōðor.*]

broth·er·hood (brŭth′ər-hŏŏd′) *n.* **1.** The state or relationship of being brothers. **2.** The quality of being brotherly; fellowship. **3.** An association of men united for common purposes, as a fraternity or union. **4.** All the members of a specific profession or trade.

broth·er-in-law (brŭth′ər-ĭn-lô′) *n., pl.* **broth·ers-in-law. 1.** The brother of one's husband or wife. **2.** The husband of one's sister. **3.** The husband of the sister of one's husband or wife.

broth·er·ly (brŭth′ər-lē) *adj.* Characteristic of or befitting brothers; fraternal. **—broth′er·li·ness** *n.* **—broth′er·ly** *adv.*

brougham (brōōm, brōō′əm, brōm, brō′əm) *n.* **1.** A closed four-wheeled carriage with an open driver's seat in front. **2.** An automobile with an open driver's seat. **3.** An electrically powered automobile resembling a coupé. [After Henry P. *Brougham* (1778–1868).]

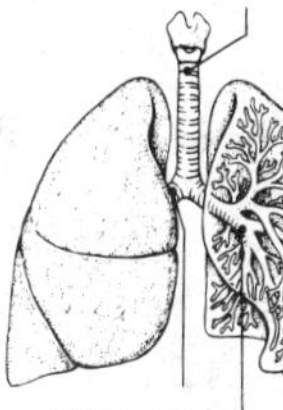

bronchus

brontosaur

brooch

brought (brôt) *v.* Past tense and past participle of **bring.**
brou·ha·ha (bro͞o'hä-hä') *n.* An uproar; hubbub. [Fr.]
brow (brou) *n.* **1. a.** The superciliary ridge over the eyes. **b.** The eyebrow. **c.** The forehead. **2.** A facial expression; countenance: *"Speak you this with a sad brow?"* (Shakespeare). **3.** The edge of a steep place. [ME < OE *brū.*]
brow·beat (brou'bēt') *tr.v.* **-beat, -beat·en** (-bēt'n), **-beat·ing, -beats.** To intimidate with an overbearing or imperative manner; domineer. **—brow'beat'er** *n.*
brown (broun) *n.* Any of a group of colors between red and yellow in hue that are medium to low in lightness and low to moderate in saturation. *—adj.* **-er, -est. 1.** Of the color brown. **2.** Deeply sun-tanned. *—tr. & intr.v.* **browned, brown·ing, browns.** To make or become brown. [ME < OE *brūn.*] **—brown'ish** *adj.* **—brown'ness** *n.*
brown alga *n.* A brownish, chiefly marine alga of the division Phaeophyta, which includes the rockweeds and the kelps.
brown bagging *n.* **1.** The practice of taking one's own liquor into a public establishment, as a restaurant, where setups are available. **2.** The practice of taking one's lunch to work, usually in a brown paper bag. **—brown bagger** *n.*
brown bear *n.* A very large bear, *Ursus arctos,* of Alaska and northern Eurasia, having brown to yellowish fur.
brown Bet·ty (bĕt'ē) *n.* A baked pudding of chopped or sliced apples, bread crumbs, raisins, sugar, butter, and spices. [*Betty,* nickname for *Elizabeth.*]
brown bread *n.* **1.** A bread made of a dark flour, such as graham or whole-wheat. **2.** A steamed bread usually made of cornmeal, flour, and molasses.
brown coal *n.* Lignite.
brown fat *n.* Adipose tissue whose oxidation is a major source of heat in mammals.
Brown·i·an motion (brou'nē-ən) *n.* The random motion of microscopic particles suspended in a liquid or gas, caused by collision with molecules of the surrounding medium. [After Robert *Brown* (1773–1858).]
Brownian movement *n.* Brownian motion.
brown·ie (brou'nē) *n.* **1.** A small sprite supposed to do helpful work at night. **2. Brownie.** A member of the Girl Scouts from 7 to 9 years of age. **3.** A square or bar of moist usually chocolate cake with nuts.
Brownie point *n.* Credit considered as earned, esp. by favorably impressing a superior. [From the practice of awarding points for achievement by Brownies in the Girl Scouts.]
Brown·ing automatic rifle (brou'nĭng) *n.* A .30 caliber air-cooled, automatic or semiautomatic, gas-operated, magazine-fed rifle used in World Wars I and II. [After John M. *Browning* (1855–1926).]
Browning machine gun *n.* A .30 or .50 caliber automatic belt-fed, water-cooled machine gun capable of firing ammunition at a rate of more than 500 rounds per minute. [After John M. *Browning* (1855-1926).]
brown lung disease *n.* Byssinosis.
brown·out (broun'out') *n.* A cutback or reduction in electric power, esp. as a result of a shortage. [BROWN + (BLACK)-OUT.]
brown patch *n.* A disease of grasses caused by a fungus, *Pellicularia filamentosa,* and resulting in circular dying areas.
brown rat *n.* The Norway rat.
brown rice *n.* Unpolished rice, retaining the germ and the yellowish outer layer containing the bran.
brown rot *n.* **1.** A disease of peaches and similar fruits, caused by fungi of the genus *Monolinia.* **2.** A disease of citrus trees, caused by fungi of the genus *Phytophthora.*
Brown Shirt *n.* A storm trooper. [Transl. of G. *Braunhemd.*]
brown·stone (broun'stōn') *n.* **1.** A brownish-red sandstone used as a building material. **2.** A house built or faced with brownstone. **3.** A grayish brown.
brown study *n.* A state of deep thought or reverie.
brown sugar *n.* Sugar whose crystals retain a thin coating of dark syrup.
Brown Swiss *n.* One of a hardy breed of dairy cattle that originated in Switzerland.
brown-tail moth (broun'tāl') *n.* A small white and brown moth, *Euproctis phaeorrhoea,* whose larvae damage shade-tree foliage and cause an irritating skin rash.
brown thrasher *n.* A North American bird, *Toxostoma rufum,* having a reddish-brown back and a dark-streaked breast.
brown trout *n.* A widely naturalized European freshwater fish, *Salmo trutta,* having yellow-brown sides with reddish spots.

Brussels sprout

browse (brouz) *v.* **browsed, brows·ing, brows·es.** *—intr.* **1. a.** To inspect in a leisurely and casual way. **b.** To read a book superficially by selecting passages at random. **2.** To feed on leaves, young shoots, and other vegetation. *—tr.* **1.** To look through or over casually. **2. a.** To nibble; crop. **b.** To graze on. *—n.* **1.** Young twigs, leaves, and tender shoots of plants or shrubs that are fit for animals to eat. **2.** An act of browsing. [Perh. < Fr. *broust,* young shoot < OFr. *brost,* of Germanic orig.] **—brows'er** *n.*
bru·cel·lo·sis (bro͞o'sə-lō'sĭs) *n.* **1.** Undulant fever. **2.** A disease of cattle caused by the bacillus *Brucella abortus* and resulting in abortions in newly infected animals. [NLat. *Brucella,* genus name (after Sir David *Bruce,* 1855–1931) + -OSIS.]
bru·cine (bro͞o'sēn', -sĭn) *n.* A poisonous white crystalline alkaloid, $C_{23}H_{26}O_4N_2 \cdot 2H_2O$, derived from nux vomica seeds. [After James *Bruce* (1730–1794).]
bru·in (bro͞o'ĭn) *n.* A bear. [Du., brown.]
bruise (bro͞oz) *v.* **bruised, bruis·ing, bruis·es.** *—tr.* **1.** To injure without breaking or rupturing. **2.** To dent or mar. **3.** To pound into fragments; crush. **4.** To hurt, esp. psychologically. *—intr.* To experience or undergo bruising. *—n.* **1.** An injury in which the skin is not broken; contusion. **2.** An injury, esp. to one's feelings. [ME *bruisen* < OE *brȳsan,* to crush, and OFr. *bruisier,* to crush.]
bruis·er (bro͞o'zər) *n. Slang.* A large, powerfully built man.
bruit (bro͞ot) *tr.v.* **bruit·ed, bruit·ing, bruits.** To spread news of; repeat. *—n.* **1.** *Archaic.* **a.** A rumor. **b.** A din; clamor. **2.** *Med.* An abnormal sound heard in auscultation. [< ME, noise < OFr., p.part. of *bruire,* to roar.]
bru·mal (bro͞o'məl) *adj.* Of, pertaining to, or characteristic of winter. [Lat. *brumalis* < *bruma,* winter.]
brume (bro͞om) *n.* Heavy fog or mist. [Fr., ult. < Lat. *bruma,* winter.] **—bru'mous** (bro͞o'məs) *adj.*
brum·ma·gem (brŭm'ə-jəm) *adj.* Cheap and showy; meretricious. *—n.* Something cheap and gaudy. [Alteration of *Birmingham,* England (from the counterfeit coins made there in the 17th century).]
brunch (brŭnch) *n.* A meal eaten as a combination of breakfast and lunch. [BR(EAKFAST) + (L)UNCH.]
bru·net (bro͞o-nĕt') *adj.* **1.** Of a dark complexion or coloring. **2.** Having dark brown or black hair or eyes. *—n.* A person with brown hair. [Fr. < OFr. < *brun,* brown, of Germanic orig.]
bru·nette (bro͞o-nĕt') *adj.* Having dark or brown hair. *—n.* A girl or woman with dark or brown hair.
Brun·hild (bro͞on'hĭlt') *n.* A queen of Iceland in Germanic legend who is won as a bride by Gunther. [G.]
Bruns·wick stew (brŭnz'wĭk) *n.* A stew that usually contains chicken and rabbit or squirrel meat cooked with vegetables. [After *Brunswick* County, Virginia.]
brunt (brŭnt) *n.* **1.** The main impact, force, or burden, as of a blow. **2.** *Obs.* A violent attack. [ME.]
brush[1] (brŭsh) *n.* **1.** Any of various devices consisting of bristles fastened into a handle, for such uses as scrubbing, polishing, or painting. **2.** The act of using a brush. **3.** A light touch in passing; graze. **4.** A brief contact or encounter. **5.** A bushy tail. **6.** A sliding connection completing a circuit between a fixed and a moving conductor. *—v.* **brushed, brush·ing, brush·es.** *—tr.* **1.** To use a brush on so as to clean, polish, or groom. **2.** To apply with or as if with motions of a brush. **3.** To remove with or as if with motions of a brush. **4.** To dismiss abruptly or curtly: *brushed the matter aside; brushed his friend off.* **5.** To touch lightly in passing; graze against. *—intr.* **1.** To use or apply a brush. **2.** To move past something so as to touch it lightly. ***—idiom.*** **brush up.** To refresh one's memory. [ME *brusshe* < OFr. *brosse,* perh. < *brosse,* brushwood.] **—brush'er** *n.* **—brush'y** *adj.*
brush[2] (brŭsh) *n.* **1. a.** A dense growth of bushes or shrubs. **b.** Land covered by such a growth. **2.** Cut or broken branches. [ME *brusshe* < OFr. *brosse,* brushwood.] **—brush'y** *adj.*
brush discharge *n.* A faintly visible, relatively slow crackling discharge of electricity without sparking.
brushed (brŭsht) *adj.* Of or designating fabrics that have a nap produced by brushing.
brush fire *n.* A fire in low-growing, scrubby trees and brush.
brush-off (brŭsh'ôf', -ŏf') *n. Slang.* An abrupt dismissal.
brush·wood (brŭsh'wo͝od') *n.* **1.** Cut or broken-off branches. **2. a.** Dense undergrowth. **b.** An area covered by such growth.
brush·work (brŭsh'wûrk') *n.* **1.** Work done with a brush. **2.** The manner in which an artist applies paint with his brush.
brusque also **brusk** (brŭsk) *adj.* Abrupt and curt in manner or speech, often to the point of rudeness; blunt. [Fr. < Ital. *brusco.*] **—brusque'ly** *adv.* **—brusque'ness** *n.*
brus·que·rie (brŭs'kə-rē') *n.* Brusqueness; curtness. [Fr. < *brusque,* brusque.]
Brus·sels carpet (brŭs'əlz) *n.* A machine-made carpet consisting of small, colored woolen loops that form a heavy, patterned pile. [After *Brussels,* Belgium.]
Brussels lace *n.* Net lace with an appliqué design, formerly made by hand but now usually made by machine.
Brussels sprout *n.* **1.** A variety of cabbage, *Brassica oleracea gemmifera,* having a stout stem studded with budlike heads. **2. Brussels sprouts.** The small edible heads of the Brussels sprout.
brut (bro͞ot) *adj.* Very dry, as a wine, esp. champagne. [Fr. < OFr., rough < Lat. *brutus,* heavy.]
bru·tal (bro͞ot'l) *adj.* **1.** Characteristic of or befitting a brute; cruel: *a brutal assault.* **2.** Disagreeably precise and trenchant: *told her the brutal facts.* **3.** Harsh; unrelenting: *a brutal winter.* **—bru'tal·ly** *adv.*
bru·tal·ism (bro͞ot'l-ĭz'əm) *n.* A style of architecture that achieves an effect of massiveness or power through the use of exaggeration. **—bru'tal·ist** *n.*

bru·tal·i·ty (bro͞o-tăl'ĭ-tē) *n., pl.* **-ties. 1.** The state or quality of being brutal. **2.** A brutal act.
bru·tal·ize (bro͞ot'l-īz') *tr.v.* **-ized, -iz·ing, -iz·es. 1.** To make brutal or unfeeling. **2.** To treat brutally. **—bru'tal·i·za'tion** *n.*
brute (bro͞ot) *n.* **1.** An animal other than man; beast. **2.** A brutal person. *—adj.* **1.** Of or relating to beasts; animal: *"None of the brute creation requires more than food and shelter"* (Thoreau). **2.** Characteristic of a brute, esp.: **a.** Entirely physical or instinctive: *brute force.* **b.** Lacking or showing a lack of reason or intelligence: *a brute impulse.* **c.** Savage; cruel: *brute coercion.* **3.** Gross; coarse. [< ME, nonhuman < OFr. *brut* < Lat. *brutus,* stupid.] **—brut'ism** *n.*
Synonyms: *brute, animal, brutish, brutal, beastly, bestial.* These adjectives apply to behavior characteristic of lower animals. *Brute,* the least derogatory, stresses the fundamental powers possessed by all creatures: *brute instinct. Animal* emphasizes physical nature distinguished from intellect or spirit: *animal vitality. Brutish,* said principally of manners, stresses marked lack of human refinement and sensibility. *Brutal,* said of physical acts, stresses unfeeling cruelty. *Beastly* is applied to what is considered beneath man and is often used as a counter word meaning merely very disagreeable. *Bestial* usually implies the vileness of moral degradation.
bru·ti·fy (bro͞o'tə-fī') *tr. & intr.v.* **-fied, -fy·ing, -fies.** To brutalize or become brutalized.
brut·ish (bro͞o'tĭsh) *adj.* **1.** Of or characteristic of a brute. **2.** Showing a lack of reason or intelligence. **3.** Crude in feeling or manner. **4.** Sensual; carnal. **—brut'ish·ly** *adv.* **—brut'ish·ness** *n.*
Bryn·hild (brĭn'hĭld') *n.* A Valkyrie who is revived from an enchanted sleep by Sigurd. [ON *Brynhildr.*]
bryo– *pref.* Moss: *bryology.* [NLat. < Gk. *bruon,* moss.]
bry·ol·o·gy (brī-ŏl'ə-jē) *n.* The botany of bryophytes. **—bry'o·log'i·cal** (-ə-lŏj'ĭ-kəl) *adj.*
bry·o·ny (brī'ə-nē) *n., pl.* **-nies. 1.** The black bryony. **2.** The white bryony. [Lat. *bryonia* < Gk. *bruōnia.*]
bry·o·phyte (brī'ə-fīt') *n.* A plant of the major botanical division Bryophyta, which includes the true mosses, peat mosses, and liverworts. **—bry'o·phyt'ic** (-fĭt'ĭk) *adj.*
bry·o·zo·an (brī'ə-zō'ən) *n.* Any of various small aquatic animals of the phylum Bryozoa that reproduce by budding and form mosslike or branching colonies. *—adj.* Of or belonging to the Bryozoa. [< NLat. *Bryozoa,* phylum name : Gk. *bruon,* moss + Gk. *zōa,* pl. of *zōon,* animal.]
Bryth·on (brĭth'ən, -ŏn') *n.* **1.** An ancient Celtic Briton of Cornwall, Wales, or Cumbria. **2.** One who speaks a Brythonic language. [Welsh.]
Bry·thon·ic (brĭ-thŏn'ĭk) *adj.* Of, pertaining to, or characteristic of the Brythons or their language. *—n.* The branch of the Celtic languages that includes Welsh, Breton, and Cornish.
bub·ble (bŭb'əl) *n.* **1.** A rounded, generally spherical, thin-walled, and typically hollow object, often occurring naturally in an otherwise homogeneous medium as a result of the local accumulation of gas: *a soap bubble.* **2.** A small globule of gas trapped in a liquid or solid, as in a carbonated beverage. **3.** A sound made by or as if by the forming and bursting of bubbles. **4.** Something insubstantial, groundless, or ephemeral, as a scheme that comes to nothing. **5.** A glass or plastic dome, usually transparent. *—v.* **-bled, -bling, -bles.** *—intr.* **1.** To form or give off bubbles. **2.** To move or flow with a gurgling sound: *a brook bubbling along its course.* **3.** To display irrepressible activity or emotion: *bubbling over with fun.* *—tr.* To cause to form bubbles. [< ME *bubelen,* to bubble.] **—bub'bly** *adj.*
bubble and squeak *n. Chiefly Brit.* Cabbage and potatoes fried together. [Imit. of the sounds made as it cooks.]
bubble chamber *n.* An apparatus for detecting the paths of charged particles or inferring the paths of electrically neutral particles by examination of trails of bubbles that form on ions produced in a superheated liquid.
bubble gum *n.* Chewing gum that can be blown into bubbles.
bubble memory *n.* A computer memory in which binary digits are represented by the presence or absence of magnetic bubbles.
bub·bler (bŭb'lər) *n.* A drinking fountain in which the water flows upward through a small nozzle.
bub·bly (bŭb'lē) *n., pl.* **-blies.** *Informal.* Champagne.
bub·by (bo͝ob'ē, bo͞ob'ē) *n., pl.* **-bies.** *Slang.* A breast of a woman. [Orig. unknown.]
bu·bo (bo͞o'bō, byo͞o'-) *n., pl.* **-boes.** An inflamed swelling of a lymphatic gland, esp. in the area of the armpit or groin. [ME < Med. Lat. < Gk. *boubōn.*] **—bu·bon'ic** (-bŏn'ĭk) *adj.*
bubonic plague *n.* A contagious, usually fatal epidemic disease caused by bacteria of the genus *Pasteurella,* transmitted by fleas from infected rats and characterized by chills, fever, vomiting, diarrhea, and buboes.
buc·cal (bŭk'əl) *adj.* Of or pertaining to the cheeks or mouth cavity. [< Lat. *bucca,* cheek.]
buc·ca·neer (bŭk'ə-nîr') *n.* A pirate, esp. one of the freebooters who preyed on Spanish shipping in the West Indies during the 17th century. [Fr. *boucanier* < *boucaner,* to cure meat < *boucan,* barbecue frame < Tupi *mocaen.*] **—buc'ca·neer'** *v.* **(-neered, -neer·ing, -neers).**
Bu·ceph·a·lus (byo͞o-sĕf'ə-ləs) *n.* The war horse of Alexander the Great. [Lat. *Bucephalus* < Gk. *Boukephalos* : *bous,* bull + *kephalē,* head.]
buck[1] (bŭk) *n.* **1.** The adult male of some animals, such as the deer or rabbit. **2.** *Informal.* **a.** A robust or high-spirited young man. **b.** A fop. *—v.* **bucked, buck·ing, bucks.** *—intr.* **1.** To leap forward and upward suddenly; rear up, as a horse. **2.** To move rapidly forward with the head lowered; butt. **3.** To move with sudden forward jerks; jolt. **4.** To resist stubbornly and obstinately; balk. **5.** *Informal.* To strive determinedly: *bucking for a promotion.* *—tr.* **1.** To throw (a rider or burden) by bucking. **2.** To butt against with the head. **3.** *Football.* To charge into (an opponent's line) carrying the ball. **4.** To oppose directly and stubbornly; turn against. ***—phrasal verb.*** **buck up.** *Informal.* To summon one's courage or spirits. *—adj.* Of the lowest rank in a specified military category: *a buck private.* [ME *bukke* < OE *buc.*] **—buck'er** *n.*
buck[2] (bŭk) *n.* **1.** A sawhorse. **2.** A leather-covered frame used for gymnastic vaulting. [Short for SAWBUCK.]
buck[3] (bŭk) *n. Slang.* A dollar. [Short for BUCKSKIN.]
buck[4] (bŭk) *n.* A counter or marker formerly placed before a poker player to mark him as the next dealer. ***—idiom.*** **pass the buck.** To shift responsibility or blame to someone else. [Short for *buckhorn knife.*]
buck and wing *n.* A fast solo tap dance with much springing of the legs and heel clicking.
buck·a·roo also **buck·er·oo** (bŭk'ə-ro͞o') *n., pl.* **-roos** also **-oos.** A cowboy. [Sp. *vaquero* < *vaca,* cow < Lat. *vacca.*]
buck·bean (bŭk'bēn') *n.* A marsh plant, *Menyanthes trifoliata,* having a creeping rootstock and white or reddish flowers. [Transl. of Flem. *bocks boonen.*]
buck·board (bŭk'bôrd', -bōrd') *n.* A four-wheeled open carriage with the seat attached to a flexible board extending from the front to the rear axle. [Obs. *buck,* body of a wagon (< ME *buke,* belly < OE *būc*) + BOARD.]
buck·er·oo (bŭk'ə-ro͞o') *n.* Variant of **buckaroo.**
buck·et (bŭk'ĭt) *n.* **1. a.** A cylindrical vessel used for holding or carrying liquids or solids; pail. **b.** The amount that a bucket will hold. **2.** Any of various machine compartments that receive and convey material, as the scoop of a steam shovel. *—v.* **-et·ed, -et·ing, -ets.** *—tr.* **1.** To hold, carry, or put in a bucket. **2.** To ride (a horse) long and hard. *—intr.* **1.** To move or proceed rapidly and jerkily: *bucketing over the unpaved lane.* **2.** To make haste; hustle. [ME < OFr. *buket.*]
bucket seat *n.* A seat with a rounded or molded back for one person, as in sports cars.
bucket shop *n.* A fraudulent brokerage operation that accepts orders to buy or sell securities or commodities but delays executing the orders on the gamble that prices will change adversely to the interests of the customer so that the broker can pocket what the customer thinks he has lost. [< *bucket shop,* a saloon selling small amounts of liquor in buckets, from its resemblance to the forerunner of such brokerage operations, which dealt in small units of stocks and commodities.]
buck·eye (bŭk'ī') *n.* **1.** Any of several North American trees of the genus *Aesculus,* having compound leaves and erect clusters of white or reddish flowers. **2.** The glossy brown nut of a buckeye. [From the seed's appearance.]
buck fever *n. Informal.* Nervous excitement felt by a novice hunter at the first sight of game.
buck·hound (bŭk'hound') *n.* A hound used for hunting deer.
buck·le[1] (bŭk'əl) *n.* **1.** A metal frame with one or more movable tongues used esp. for fastening two strap or belt ends. **2.** An ornament that resembles a buckle. *—tr. & intr.v.* **-led, -ling, -les.** To fasten or become fastened with a buckle. ***—phrasal verb.*** **buckle down.** To apply oneself with determination. [ME *bocle* < OFr. *boucle* < Lat. *buccula,* cheek strap of a helmet, dim. of *bucca,* cheek.]
buck·le[2] (bŭk'əl) *v.* **-led, -ling, -les.** *—intr.* **1.** To bend, warp, or crumple, as under pressure or heat. **2.** To give way; collapse: *struts buckling under the stress.* **3.** To surrender, as to another's authority; yield: *buckled from the excessive demands made on him.* *—tr.* To cause to bend, warp, or crumple. *—n.* A bend, bulge, or other distortion. [ME *boclen* < OFr. *boucler,* to fasten with a buckle < *boucle,* buckle.]
buck·ler (bŭk'lər) *n.* **1.** A small round shield either carried or worn on the arm. **2.** A means of protection; defense. *—tr.v.* **-lered, -ler·ing, -lers.** To shield with or as if with a buckler; protect. [ME *bokler* < OFr. *bocler* < *boucle,* boss on a shield < Lat. *buccula.*]
buck·o (bŭk'ō) *n., pl.* **-oes. 1.** A bully. **2.** *Chiefly Ir.* A young man; lad.
buck passer *n.* One who regularly tries to shift responsibility to another.
buck·ra (bŭk'rə) *n. Offensive Slang.* A white man. [Efik *mbakara,* white man.]
buck·ram (bŭk'rəm) *n.* **1.** A coarse cotton fabric heavily sized with glue, used for stiffening garments and in bookbinding. **2.** *Obs.* Stiffness; formality. *—adj.* Resembling buckram in stiffness. *—tr.v.* **-ramed, -ram·ing, -rams.** To stiffen with or as if with buckram. [ME *bokeram,* fine linen < OFr. *boquerant,* poss. after *Bukhara,* U.S.S.R.]

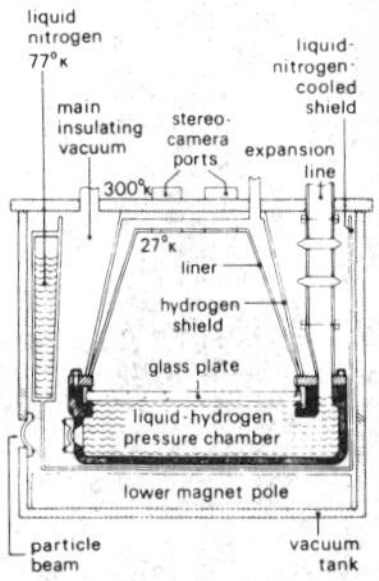

bubble chamber

buck[1]

buckboard

buck·saw (bŭk'sô') *n.* A wood-cutting saw, usually set in an H-shaped frame. [< BUCK[2].]
buck·shee (bŭk'shē) *n. Chiefly Brit. Slang.* **1.** A windfall or gratuity. **2.** An extra ration. [Var. of BAKSHEESH.]
buck·shot (bŭk'shŏt') *n.* A large lead shot for shotgun shells.
buck·skin (bŭk'skĭn') *n.* **1. a.** The skin of a male deer. **b.** A strong, grayish-yellow leather once made from deerskins but now usually made from sheepskins. **2. buckskins.** A pair of breeches or shoes made from buckskin. **3.** A person wearing clothes of buckskin, esp. an American soldier of the Revolutionary War. **4.** A horse of the grayish-yellow color of buckskin. **—*modifier:*** *buckskin shoes.*

Buddha
8th-century Korean sculpture

buck·thorn (bŭk'thôrn') *n.* A shrub or tree of the genus *Rhamnus,* esp. *R. cathartica,* native to Eurasia, having spine-tipped branches and small greenish flowers. [Transl. of NLat. *cervi spina.*]
buck·tooth (bŭk'to͞oth') *n.* A prominent, projecting front tooth. **—buck'toothed'** (-to͞otht') *adj.*
buck·wheat (bŭk'hwēt', -wēt') *n.* **1.** A plant of the genus *Fagopyrum,* esp. *F. esculentum,* native to Asia, having fragrant white flowers and small triangular seeds. **2.** The edible seeds of buckwheat, often ground into flour. [Partial transl. of MDu. *boecweite* : *boek,* beech + *weite,* wheat.]
bu·col·ic (byo͞o-kŏl'ĭk) *adj.* **1.** Of or characteristic of shepherds or flocks; pastoral. **2.** Of or characteristic of the countryside or its people; rustic. *—n.* A pastoral poem. [Lat. *bucolicus* < Gk. *boukolikos* < *boukolos,* cowherd < *bous,* cow.] **—bu·col'i·cal·ly** *adv.*
bud (bŭd) *n.* **1.** *Bot.* **a.** A small protuberance on a stem or branch, often enclosed in protective scales, containing an undeveloped shoot, leaves, or flowers. **b.** The stage or condition of having buds. **2.** *Biol.* **a.** An asexually produced protuberance, as on a polyp, that develops into a mature, complete organism. **b.** A small, rounded organic part resembling a plant bud. **3.** A person or thing that is not yet fully developed. *—v.* **bud·ded, bud·ding, buds.** *—intr.* **1.** To put forth or produce buds. **2.** To begin to develop or grow from or as if from a bud. **3.** To be in an undeveloped stage or condition. *—tr.* **1.** To cause to put forth buds. **2.** To graft a bud onto (a plant). **—*idioms.* in the bud.** In an incipient or undeveloped state. **nip in the bud.** To stop (something) in its initial stage. [ME *budde.*] **—bud'der** *n.*

budgerigar

Bud·dha (bo͞o'də, bo͝od'ə) *n.* **1.** A Buddhist sage who has achieved a state of perfect illumination in accordance with the teachings of Gautama Buddha. **2.** A representation of Gautama Buddha. [Skt., enlightened < *bodhati,* he awakes.]
Bud·dhism (bo͞o'dĭz'əm, bo͝od'ĭz'-) *n.* **1.** The doctrine, attributed to Gautama Buddha, that suffering is inseparable from existence but that inward extinction of the self and of the senses culminates in a state of illumination beyond both suffering and existence. **2.** The religion of eastern and central Asia represented by the many differing sects that profess Buddhism and venerate Gautama Buddha. **—Bud'dhist** *n.* **—Bud·dhis'tic** *adj.*
bud·dle (bŭd'l) *n.* An inclined trough in which ore is separated from waste by washing with running water. [Orig. unknown.]
bud·dle·ia (bŭd'lē-ə, bŭd-lē'ə) *n.* The butterfly bush. [After Adam *Buddle* (d. 1715).]
bud·dy (bŭd'ē) *n., pl.* **-dies.** *Informal.* **1.** A good friend; comrade. **2.** Brother; friend: *Watch it, buddy.* [Prob. alteration of BROTHER.]

buffalo

buddy system *n.* An informal arrangement in which persons are paired, as for mutual safety or assistance.
budge[1] (bŭj) *v.* **budged, budg·ing, budg·es.** *—intr.* **1.** To move or stir slightly: *was asleep and didn't budge.* **2.** To alter a position or attitude: *had made the decision and wouldn't budge.* *—tr.* **1.** To cause to move slightly. **2.** To cause to alter a position or attitude: *an adamant woman who couldn't be budged.* [OFr. *bouger* < VLat. **bullicare,* to bubble < Lat. *bullire,* to boil.]
budge[2] (bŭj) *n.* Fur, usually lambskin, formerly used to trim academic robes. *—adj. Archaic.* Extremely formal; solemn. [ME *buge.*]
budg·er·i·gar (bŭj'ə-rē-gär', bŭj'ə-rē'-) *n.* A parakeet, *Melopsittacus undulatus,* native to Australia, having green, yellow, or blue plumage. [Native word in Australia.]
budg·et (bŭj'ĭt) *n.* **1. a.** An itemized summary of probable expenditures and income for a given period. **b.** A systematic plan for meeting expenses in a given period. **c.** The total sum of money allocated for a particular purpose or time period. **2.** A stock or collection with definite limits. *—tr.v.* **-et·ed, -et·ing, -ets. 1.** To plan in advance the expenditure of (money, for example). **2.** To enter or plan for in a budget. [ME *bouget,* wallet < OFr. *bougette,* dim. of *bouge,* leather bag < Lat. *bulga,* of Celt. orig.] **—budg'et·ar'y** (bŭj'ĭ-tĕr'ē) *adj.* **—budg'et·er** *n.*
budg·ie (bŭj'ē) *n. Informal.* A budgerigar.
buff[1] (bŭf) *n.* **1. a.** A soft, thick, undyed leather made chiefly from the skins of buffalo, elk, or oxen. **b.** The color of buff; pale, light, or moderate yellowish pink to yellow, including moderate orange yellow to light yellowish brown. **c.** A military coat made of buff. **2.** *Informal.* The bare skin: *went swimming in the buff.* **3.** A polishing implement covered with a soft material, such as velvet. **—*modifier:*** *a buff jacket.* *—adj.* Of the color of buff. *—tr.v.* **buffed, buff·ing, buffs. 1.** To polish or shine with a buff. **2.** To make the color of buff. [OFr. *buffle,* buffalo.]
buff[2] (bŭf) *tr.v.* **buffed, buff·ing, buffs.** To deaden the shock of. [Prob. imit.]
buff[3] (bŭf) *n. Informal.* One who is enthusiastic and knowledgeable about a given subject: *a Civil War buff.* [From the buff-colored uniform worn by New York volunteer firemen at one time.]
buf·fa·lo (bŭf'ə-lō') *n., pl.* **-loes** or **-los** or **buffalo. 1. a.** Any of several oxlike Old World mammals of the family Bovidae, such as *Syncerus caffer,* of Africa, having massive, downward-curving horns. **b.** The bison. **2.** The buffalo fish. *—tr.v.* **-loed, -lo·ing, -loes.** *Slang.* **1.** To intimidate. **2.** To confuse; bewilder. [Ital. or Port. *bufalo* < VLat. **bufalus* < Lat. *bubalus* < Gk. *boubalos.*]
buffalo berry *n.* **1.** Either of two North American shrubs, *Shepherdia argentea* or *S. canadensis,* having small yellowish flowers and red or yellowish berries. **2.** The berry of a buffalo berry.
buffalo bug *n.* The carpet beetle.
buffalo fish *n.* Any of several North American freshwater fishes of the genus *Ictiobus,* having a humped back.
buffalo grass *n.* A short grass, *Buchloe dactyloides,* of the plains east of the Rocky Mountains.
buffalo robe *n.* The dressed skin of the North American bison, used as a lap robe, cape, or blanket.
buff·er[1] (bŭf'ər) *n.* An implement used to shine or polish, as a soft cloth.
buff·er[2] (bŭf'ər) *n.* **1.** Something that lessens or absorbs the shock of an impact. **2.** One that protects by intercepting or moderating adverse pressures or influences. **3.** Something that separates the entities, as an area between two rival powers that serves to lessen the danger of conflict. **4. a.** *Chem.* A substance capable of maintaining the relative concentrations of hydrogen and hydroxyl ions in a solution by neutralizing, within limits, added acids or bases. **b.** *Computer Sci.* A device or area used to store data temporarily and deliver at a rate different from that at which it was received. *—tr.v.* **-ered, -er·ing, -ers.** *Chem.* To treat (a solution) with a buffer. [Prob. < BUFF[2].]
buf·fet[1] (bə-fā', bo͞o-) *n.* **1.** A large sideboard with drawers and cupboards. **2. a.** A counter from which meals or refreshments are served. **b.** A restaurant having such a counter. **3.** A meal at which guests serve themselves from various dishes displayed on a table or sideboard. [Fr.]
buf·fet[2] (bŭf'ĭt) *n.* A blow or cuff with or as if with the hand. *—v.* **-fet·ed, -fet·ing, -fets.** *—tr.* **1.** To hit or club, esp. with the hand. **2.** To strike against forcefully; batter: *winds buffeting the tent.* **3.** To force (one's way) with or as if with crude blows. *—intr.* To force one's way, esp. with difficulty. [ME < OFr. *bufet,* dim. of *buffe,* blow.] **—buf'fet·er** *n.*
buf·fi (bo͞o'fē) *n.* A plural of **buffo.**
buffing wheel *n.* A wheel covered with a soft material, such as velvet or leather, for shining and polishing metal.
buf·fle·head (bŭf'əl-hĕd') *n.* A small North American duck, *Bucephala albeola,* having black and white plumage and a densely feathered, rounded head. [Obs. *buffle,* buffalo (< OFr. < VLat. **bufalus*) + HEAD.]
buf·fo (bo͞o'fō) *n., pl.* **-fi** (-fē) or **-fos.** A male singer of comic opera roles. [Ital. < *buffare,* to puff.]
buf·foon (bə-fo͞on') *n.* **1.** A clown; jester. **2.** A person given to making coarse jokes. [Fr. *bouffon* < OItal. *buffone* < *buffa,* jest < *buffare,* to puff.] **—buf·foon'er·y** (bə-fo͞o'nə-rē) *n.*
bug (bŭg) *n.* **1.** Any of various wingless or four-winged insects of the order Hemiptera, and esp. the suborder Heteroptera, having mouth parts adapted for piercing and sucking. **2.** An insect or similar organism. **3.** *Informal.* A disease-producing microorganism. **4.** A mechanical, electrical, or other systemic defect or difficulty. **5.** *Slang.* An enthusiast or devotee; buff: *a hi-fi bug.* **6.** A small hidden microphone or other device used for eavesdropping. *—v.* **bugged, bug·ging, bugs.** *—intr.* To protrude: *His eyes bugged when he saw the mess.* *—tr.* **1.** *Slang.* To annoy; pester. **2.** To equip (a telephone circuit, for example) with a concealed electronic listening device. [Orig. unknown.] **—bug'ger** *n.*
bug·a·boo (bŭg'ə-bo͞o') *n., pl.* **-boos. 1.** A bugbear. **2.** A steady source of concern. [Perh. of Celt. orig.]
bug·bane (bŭg'bān') *n.* Any of several plants of the genus *Cimicifuga,* esp. *C. americana,* of eastern North America, having clusters of small white flowers supposed to repel insects.
bug·bear (bŭg'bâr') *n.* **1.** An object of obsessive dread. **2.** *Archaic.* A hobgoblin or bogie. [Obs. *bug,* hobgoblin (< ME *bugge,* poss. < MWelsh *bwga,* ghost) + BEAR.]
bug-eyed (bŭg'īd') *adj. Slang.* Agog, as with amazement.
bug·ger (bŭg'ər, bo͝og'-) *n.* **1.** *Vulgar.* A sodomite. **2.** A contemptible or disreputable person. **3.** *Slang.* A fellow; chap. *—v.* **-gered, -ger·ing, -gers.** *Vulgar.* *—intr.* To practice buggery. *—tr.* To practice buggery with. [ME *bougre,* heretic < OFr. < Med. Lat. *Bulgarus,* Bulgarian.]
bug·ger·y (bŭg'ə-rē, bo͝og'-) *n. Vulgar.* Sodomy.
bug·gy[1] (bŭg'ē) *n., pl.* **-gies. 1.** A small, light, four-wheeled horse-drawn carriage. **2.** A baby carriage. [Orig. unknown.]
bug·gy[2] (bŭg'ē) *adj.* **-gi·er, -gi·est. 1.** Infested with bugs. **2.** *Slang.* Crazy. **—bug'gi·ness** *n.*

bug·house (bŭg′hous′) *Slang.* —*n.* An insane asylum. —*adj.* Mentally unsound; insane. [< BUGGY[2].]
bu·gle[1] (byōō′gəl) *n.* A brass wind instrument somewhat shorter than a trumpet and lacking keys or valves. —*intr.v.* **-gled, -gling, -gles. 1.** To play a bugle. **2.** To give forth a deep, prolonged sound similar to the bay of a hound. [ME < OFr. < Lat. *buculus,* steer, dim. of *bos,* ox.] **—bu′gler** *n.*
bu·gle[2] (byōō′gəl) *n.* A tubular glass or plastic bead used to trim clothing. [Orig. unknown.]
bu·gle[3] (byōō′gəl) *n.* Any of several plants of the genus *Ajuga,* native to Eurasia, having spikes or dense clusters of small blue or white flowers. [ME < OFr. < LLat. *bugula* < Lat. *bugillo.*]
bu·gle·weed (byōō′gəl-wēd′) *n.* **1.** A plant of the genus *Lycopus,* esp. *L. virginicus,* having small, whitish flowers and an aromatic odor. **2.** A bugle[3]. [Perh. from its tubular flowers.]
bu·gloss (byōō′glŏs′, -glôs′) *n.* Any of several plants of the genera *Lycopsis, Echium,* and *Anchusa,* having hairy stems and leaves and clusters of blue flowers. [ME *buglosse* < OFr. < Lat. *buglossa* < Gk. *bouglōssos* : *bous,* ox + *glōssa,* tongue.]
bug moss *n.* A moss of the genus *Buxbaumia,* characterized by a flattened, asymmetric capsule borne on a rough stalk.
bug·seed (bŭg′sēd′) *n.* Any of several low-growing plants of the genus *Corispermum,* having narrow leaves and flat seeds.
bug·sha (bōōg′shä′) *n.* See table at **currency.** [Ar.]
buhl also **boule** or **boulle** (bōōl) *n.* Inlaid furniture decoration of elaborate designs in tortoiseshell, ivory, and metals of various colors. [After André C. *Boule* (1642–1732).]
buhr·stone also **burr·stone** (bûr′stōn′) *n.* A tough limestone impregnated with silica, from which millstones were formerly made. [Var. of BURR[1] + STONE.]
build (bĭld) *v.* **built** (bĭlt), **build·ing, builds.** —*tr.* **1.** To form by combining materials or parts; construct. **2.** To give form to according to a definite plan or process; create. **3.** To establish and strengthen; create and add to: *build a savings account.* **4.** To establish a basis for; found or ground: *build an argument on fact.* —*intr.* **1.** To engage in construction. **2.** To be a builder. **3.** To develop in magnitude or extent: *The snow began to build and the wind to howl.* **4.** To progress toward a maximum, as of intensity: *suspense building from the opening scene to the climax.* **—*phrasal verbs.* build in.** To construct as an integral or permanent part of. **build up. 1.** To develop in stages or by degrees: *built up the business; building up the record collection.* **2.** To increase, as in value or reputation: *building up the product.* —*n.* The physical make-up of a person or thing: *an athletic build.* [ME *bilden* < OE **byldan* < *bold,* dwelling.]
build·er (bĭl′dər) *n.* **1.** One that builds, esp. a person who contracts for and supervises the construction of a building. **2.** An abrasive or filler used in a soap or detergent.
build·ing (bĭl′dĭng) *n.* **1.** Something that is built; structure. **2.** The act, process, art, or occupation of constructing.
Synonyms: *building, structure, edifice, pile.* All these nouns apply to something built. *Building* is the basic, broadly applicable term of this group. *Structure* usually implies considerable size and emphasizes physical make-up with respect to material and design. *Edifice* invariably implies something large or otherwise imposing; it may be applied figuratively to a receptacle of knowledge or ideals. *Pile* suggests the massiveness of stone and frequently indicates a cluster of buildings.
build-up also **build·up** (bĭld′ŭp′) *n.* **1.** The act or process of amassing or increasing. **2.** *Informal.* Widely favorable publicity, esp. by a systematic campaign.
built (bĭlt) *v.* Past tense and past participle of **build.**
built-in (bĭlt′ĭn′) *adj.* **1.** Constructed as part of a larger unit; not detachable: *a built-in cabinet.* **2.** Forming a permanent or essential element or quality: *a built-in escape clause.* **—built′-in′** *n.*
built-up (bĭlt′ŭp′) *adj.* **1.** Made by fastening several layers or sections one on top of the other: *a built-up roof.* **2.** Filled with buildings.
bulb (bŭlb) *n.* **1. a.** *Bot.* A modified underground stem, such as that of the onion or tulip, usually surrounded by scalelike modified leaves and containing stored food for the undeveloped shoots of the new plant enclosed within it. **b.** An underground stem or root resembling this, as a corm, rhizome, or tuber. **c.** A plant that grows from a bulb. **2.** A rounded projection or part: *the bulb of a syringe.* **3.** An incandescent lamp or its glass housing. **4.** *Anat.* Any of various rounded, enlarged, or bulb-shaped structures, esp. the medulla oblongata. [Lat. *bulbus* < Gk. *bolbos,* bulbous plant.]
bul·bar (bŭl′bər, -bär′) *adj.* Of, pertaining to, or characteristic of a bulb, esp. of the medulla oblongata: *bulbar poliomyelitis.*
bul·bil (bŭl′bəl, -bĭl′) *n.* A small bulblike part growing above ground on a flower stalk or in a leaf axil. [Fr. *bulbille,* dim. of *bulbe,* bulb < Lat. *bulbus.*]
bul·bous (bŭl′bəs) *adj.* **1.** Resembling a bulb in shape; rounded or swollen. **2.** *Bot.* Bearing bulbs or growing from a bulb. **—bul′bous·ly** *adv.*
bul·bul (bōōl′bōōl′) *n.* **1.** Any of various chiefly tropical Old World songbirds of the family Pycnonotidae, having grayish or brownish plumage. **2.** A songbird thought to be a nightingale, often mentioned in Persian poetry. [Pers. < Ar.]
Bul·gar (bŭl′gär′, bōōl′-) *n.* A Bulgarian (sense 1).
Bul·gar·i·an (bŭl-gâr′ē-ən, bōōl-) *adj.* Of, pertaining to, or characteristic of Bulgaria, its inhabitants, or their language. —*n.* **1.** A native or inhabitant of Bulgaria. **2.** The Slavic language of the Bulgarians.
bulge (bŭlj) *n.* **1.** A protruding part; outward curve or swelling. **2.** The rounded lower section of a ship's hull. **3.** *Slang.* An advantage. —*v.* **bulged, bulg·ing, bulg·es.** —*tr.* To cause to curve outward. —*intr.* To swell up; grow larger or rounder. [ME, pouch < OFr. *bouge* < Lat. *bulga,* bag, of Celt. orig.] **—bulg′i·ness** *n.* **—bulg′y** *adj.*
bul·gur (bōōl-gōōr′, bŭl′gər) *n.* Dried cracked wheat prepared for food. [Turk.]
bu·lim·i·a (byōō-lĭm′ē-ə) *n.* Insatiable appetite. [NLat. < Gk. *boulima* : *bous,* ox + *limos,* hunger.]
bulk[1] (bŭlk) *n.* **1.** Great size, mass, or volume. **2. a.** A distinct mass or portion of matter, esp. a large one. **b.** The body of a human being, esp. when large and corpulent. **3.** The major portion or greater part of something: *"the great bulk of necessary work can never be anything but painful"* (Bertrand Russell). **4.** Thickness of paper or cardboard in relation to weight. **5.** A ship's hold or the cargo stowed there. —*v.* **bulked, bulk·ing, bulks.** —*intr.* **1.** To be or appear to be massive in size, volume, importance, or consequence; loom: *Sightseeing bulks large in our vacation plans.* **2.** To grow or increase in size or importance. —*tr.* **1.** To cause to swell or expand. **2.** To cause to cohere or form a mass. **—*idiom.* in bulk. 1.** Unpackaged; loose. **2.** In large numbers, amounts, or volume. [ME < ON *bulki,* cargo.]
bulk[2] (bŭlk) *n.* A frame structure, such as a stall or booth, projecting from the front of a building. [Orig. unknown.]
bulk·age (bŭl′kĭj) *n.* A substance that stimulates peristalsis by increasing the bulk of material in the intestine.
bulk·head (bŭlk′hĕd′) *n.* **1.** One of the upright partitions dividing a ship into compartments and serving to prevent the spread of leakage or fire. **2.** A wall or embankment constructed in a mine or tunnel to protect against earth slides, fire, water, or gas. **3.** A horizontal or sloping structure providing access to a cellar stairway or to an elevator shaft. [BULK[2] + HEAD.]
bulk·y (bŭl′kē) *adj.* **-i·er, -i·est. 1.** Extremely large; massive. **2.** Clumsy; unwieldy. **—bulk′i·ly** *adv.* **—bulk′i·ness** *n.*
bull[1] (bōōl) *n.* **1. a.** An adult male bovine mammal. **b.** The uncastrated adult male of domestic cattle. **c.** The male of certain other mammals, such as the elephant and moose. **2.** An exceptionally large, strong, and aggressive man. **3.** A person who buys commodities or securities in anticipation of a rise in prices or who tries by speculative purchases to effect such a rise. **4. Bull.** Taurus. **5.** *Slang.* A policeman or detective. **6.** *Slang.* Empty, foolish talk; nonsense. —*v.* **bulled, bull·ing, bulls.** —*tr.* **1.** To engage in speculative buying so as to raise the price of (stocks) or prices in (a market). **2.** To push; force: *bulled his way through a crowded bus.* —*intr.* **1.** To rise in price. **2.** To push ahead or through forcefully. —*adj.* **1.** Male. **2.** Resembling a bull; large and strong. **3.** Characterized by rising prices: *a bull market.* [ME *bule* < OE **bulla* < ON *boli.*]
bull[2] (bōōl) *n.* **1.** An official document issued by the pope and sealed with a bulla. **2.** The bulla with which a bull is sealed. [ME *bulle* < OFr. < Med. Lat. *bulla.*]
bull[3] (bōōl) *n.* *Informal.* A blunder. [Orig. unknown.]
bul·la (bōōl′ə) *n., pl.* **bul·lae** (bōōl′ē). **1.** A round seal affixed to a papal bull. **2.** *Pathol.* A large blister or vesicle. [Med. Lat. < Lat., bubble, seal.]
bul·lace (bōōl′ĭs) *n.* The damson (sense 1.a.). [ME *bolas* < OFr. *buloce.*]
bul·lae (bōōl′ē) *n.* Plural of **bulla.**
bul·late (bōōl′āt′, bŭl′-) *adj.* Having a puckered or blistered appearance: *bullate leaves.* [< Lat. *bulla,* bubble.]
bull·bait·ing (bōōl′bā′tĭng) *n.* The formerly popular sport of baiting bulls with dogs.
bull·bat (bōōl′băt′) *n.* The nighthawk (sense 1). [From its roaring sound in flight.]
bull·dog (bōōl′dôg′, -dŏg′) *n.* **1.** A short-haired dog of a breed characterized by a large head, strong, square jaws with dewlaps, and a stocky body. **2.** A short-barreled revolver or pistol of a large caliber. **3.** A heat-resistant material used to line puddling furnaces. **4.** *Chiefly Brit.* A proctor's assistant at Oxford or Cambridge. —*adj.* Having the qualities of a bulldog; stubborn. —*tr.v.* **-dogged, -dog·ging, -dogs.** *Western U.S.* To throw (a steer) by seizing its horns and twisting its neck until the animal falls. **—bull′dog′ger** *n.*
bulldog edition *n.* The early morning edition of a daily newspaper.
bull·doze (bōōl′dōz′) *tr.v.* **-dozed, -doz·ing, -doz·es. 1.** *Slang.* To coerce by intimidation; bully. **2.** To clear, dig up, or move with a bulldozer. [Poss. < obs. *bulldose,* severe beating : BULL[1] + DOSE.]
bull·doz·er (bōōl′dō′zər) *n.* **1.** A tractor with a vertical metal scoop in front for moving earth and rocks, used esp. to clear or grade land. **2.** *Slang.* An overbearing person; bully.
bul·let (bōōl′ĭt) *n.* **1. a.** A spherical or pointed cylindrical metallic projectile that is fired from a pistol, rifle, or other

bugle[1]

George Miksch Sutton
bulbul

bulldog

bulldozer

relatively small firearm. **b.** Such a projectile in a metal casing; cartridge. **2.** An object resembling a bullet in shape, action, or effect. **3.** *Printing.* A heavy dot (•) used to call attention to a particular passage. [Fr. *boulette,* dim. of *boule,* ball < OFr. < Lat. *bulla.*]

bul·le·tin (bo͝ol′ĭ-tn, -tĭn) *n.* **1.** A printed or broadcast statement on a matter of public interest. **2.** A periodical, esp. one published by an organization or society. —*tr.v.* **-tined, -tin·ing, -tins.** To inform by bulletin. [Fr., prob. < OFr. *bullette* < *bulle,* bull. —see BULL[2].]

bulletin board *n.* A board on which notices are posted.

bul·let·proof (bo͝ol′ĭt-pro͞of′) *adj.* Impenetrable by bullets. —*tr.v.* **-proofed, -proof·ing, -proofs.** To make bulletproof.

bull fiddle *n.* A double bass.

bull·fight (bo͝ol′fīt′) *n.* A public spectacle, esp. in Spain and Mexico, in which a fighting bull is engaged in a series of traditional maneuvers culminating usually with the matador's ceremonial execution of the bull by sword. **—bull′fight′er** *n.* **—bull′fight′ing** *n.*

bull·finch (bo͝ol′fĭnch′) *n.* **1.** A European bird, *Pyrrhula pyrrhula,* having a short, thick bill and, in the male, a red breast. **2.** Any of several similar finches.

bullfrog

bull·frog (bo͝ol′frôg′, -frŏg′) *n.* Any of several large frogs, chiefly of the genus *Rana,* esp. *R. catesbeiana,* of North America, having a characteristic deep, resonant croak.

bull·head (bo͝ol′hĕd′) *n.* **1.** Any of several North American freshwater catfishes of the genus *Ictalurus.* **2.** Any of several fishes of the family Cottidae, such as the sculpin and the miller's thumb.

bull·head·ed (bo͝ol′hĕd′ĭd) *adj.* Very stubborn; obstinate. **—bull′head′ed·ly** *adv.* **—bull′head′ed·ness** *n.*

bull·horn (bo͝ol′hôrn′) *n.* An electric megaphone that amplifies the volume of a voice or other sounds.

bullmastiff

bul·lion (bo͝ol′yən) *n.* **1. a.** Gold or silver considered with respect to quantity rather than value. **b.** Gold or silver in the form of bars, ingots, or plates. **2.** A heavy lace trimming made of twisted gold or silver threads. [ME, an ingot of precious metal, partly < OFr. *billon* < *bille,* stick, bubble < *boilir,* to boil, and partly < OFr. *boillon,* molten metal.]

bull·ish (bo͝ol′ĭsh) *adj.* **1.** Like a bull; brawny or bullheaded. **2. a.** Causing, expecting, or characterized by rising stock-market prices. **b.** Optimistic or confident. **—bull′ish·ly** *adv.* **—bull′ish·ness** *n.*

bull·mas·tiff (bo͝ol′măs′tĭf) *n.* A heavy-set dog of a breed developed from the bulldog and the mastiff.

Bull Moose *n.* A member or supporter of the Bull Moose Party. [From the party's emblem.]

Bull Moose Party *n.* The Progressive Party (sense 1).

bull·necked (bo͝ol′nĕkt′) *adj.* Having a short, thick neck.

bull·nose (bo͝ol′nōz′) *n.* A contagious disease of swine caused by the bacillus *Actinomyces necrophorus* and characterized by an infection and swelling of the snout.

bul·lock (bo͝ol′ək) *n.* **1.** A castrated bull; steer. **2.** A young bull. [ME *bullok* < OE *bulluc.*]

bull·pen (bo͝ol′pĕn′) *n.* **1.** A pen for confining bulls. **2.** *Informal.* A place for the temporary detention of prisoners. **3.** *Baseball.* **a.** An area where relief pitchers warm up during a game. **b.** The relief pitchers of a team collectively.

bull·ring (bo͝ol′rĭng′) *n.* A circular arena for bullfights.

bullroarer
Hopi medicine man using a bullroarer in a ceremonial dance

bull·roar·er (bo͝ol′rôr′ər, -rōr′-) *n.* A small wooden slat, attached to a string, that makes a roaring noise when whirled.

bull session *n. Informal.* A random, informal group discussion.

bull's eye also **bull's-eye** (bo͝olz′ī′) *n.* **1. a.** The small central circle on a target. **b.** A shot that hits this circle. **2.** Something that precisely achieves a desired goal. **3.** A thick, circular piece of glass set, as in a roof, to admit light. **4.** A circular opening or window. **5. a.** A plano-convex lens used to concentrate light. **b.** A lantern or lamp having such a lens. **6.** A piece of round, hard candy.

bull snake *n.* Any of several nonvenomous North American snakes of the genus *Pituophis,* having yellow and brown or black markings.

bull terrier

bull terrier *n.* A dog of a breed developed by crossing a bulldog and a terrier, having a short, usually white coat.

bull thistle *n.* A coarse weed, *Cirsium vulgare,* native to Eurasia, having spiny stems and leaves and purple flowers. [From its large head.]

bull tongue *n.* A heavy plow with a single shovel, used chiefly in cotton fields.

bull·whip (bo͝ol′hwĭp′, -wĭp′) *n.* A long, plaited rawhide whip with a knotted end. —*tr.v.* **-whipped, -whip·ping, -whips.** To whip with a bullwhip.

bul·ly[1] (bo͝ol′ē) *n., pl.* **-lies. 1.** A person who is habitually cruel, esp. to smaller or weaker people. **2.** *Archaic.* A hired ruffian. **3.** *Obs.* A pimp. **4.** *Obs.* A fine fellow. **5.** *Obs.* A sweetheart. —*v.* **-lied, -ly·ing, -lies.** —*tr.* To intimidate with superior size or strength. —*intr.* To behave like a bully. —*adj. Informal.* Excellent; splendid. —*interj.* Used to express approval: *Bully for him!* [Poss. < MDu. *boele,* sweetheart.]

bul·ly[2] (bo͝ol′ē) *n.* Canned or pickled beef. [Perh. Fr. *bouilli,* boiled meat < *bouiller,* to boil.]

bul·ly·rag (bo͝ol′ē-răg′) also **bal·ly·rag** (băl′ē-) *tr.v.* **-ragged, -rag·ging, -rags.** To mistreat or intimidate by bullying.

bumblebee

bul·rush (bo͝ol′rŭsh′) *n.* **1.** Any of various grasslike sedges of the genus *Scirpus,* growing in wet places. **2.** Any of various marsh plants, such as the cattail. [ME *bulrish.*]

bul·wark (bo͝ol′wərk, bŭl′-, -wôrk′) *n.* **1.** A wall or similar structure raised as a defensive fortification; rampart. **2.** Something serving as a principal defense against attack or encroachment: "*We have seen the necessity of the Union, as our bulwark against foreign danger*" (James Madison). **3.** A breakwater. **4.** Often **bulwarks.** The part of a ship's side that is above the upper deck. —*tr.v.* **-warked, -wark·ing, -warks. 1.** To fortify with a bulwark. **2.** To provide defense or protection for. [ME *bulwerk* < MDu. *bolwerk* < MHG *bolwerc* : *bole,* plank + *werc,* work < OHG.]

Synonyms: *bulwark, barricade, breastwork, earthwork, rampart, bastion, parapet.* All of these nouns refer to structures used or regarded as a defense against attack. *Bulwark* applies to any wall-like fortification, and figuratively to anything relied upon heavily for protection. *Barricade* pertains broadly to any barrier but implies hasty construction to meet an imminent threat. *Breastwork* denotes a low defensive wall, especially a temporary one built in haste. *Earthwork* specifies a defensive embankment of earth, usually in the field. A *rampart,* the main defensive structure around a guarded place, is permanent, high, and broad. The projecting sections of a *rampart* are called *bastions,* from which defenders have a wide range of view and fire. Both terms are used figuratively, *bastion* implying great defensive strength. *Parapet* applies to any low fortification, typically a wall atop a *rampart.*

bum[1] (bŭm) *n.* **1.** A tramp; hobo. **2.** A person who avoids work and seeks to live off others. **3.** A person who performs poorly; incompetent: *called the pitcher a bum.* —*v.* **bummed, bum·ming, bums.** *Informal.* —*intr.* **1.** To live by begging or sponging, often while moving from place to place. **2.** To loaf. —*tr.* To acquire by begging or sponging. —*adj. Slang.* **1.** Invalid; worthless: *gave me bum information.* **2.** Disabled; malfunctioning: *a bum shoulder.* **—*idiom.* on the bum.** *Slang.* **1.** Living as a hobo or tramp. **2.** Out of order; broken. [Short for *bummer,* lazy person, prob. < G. *Bummler* < *bummeln,* to loaf.] **—bum′mer** *n.*

bum[2] (bŭm) *intr.v.* **bummed, bum·ming, bums.** *Chiefly Brit.* To make a humming sound; drone. [ME *bummen.*]

bum[3] (bŭm) *n. Chiefly Brit. Slang.* The buttocks. [ME *bom.*]

bum·ble[1] (bŭm′bəl) *v.* **-bled, -bling, -bles.** —*intr.* To speak or behave in a clumsy or faltering manner. —*tr.* To bungle; botch. [Prob. alteration of BUNGLE.]

bum·ble[2] (bŭm′bəl) *intr.v.* **-bled, -bling, -bles.** To make a humming or droning sound; buzz. —*n.* A humming or droning sound; buzz. [ME *bomblen.*]

bum·ble·bee (bŭm′bəl-bē′) *n.* Any of various large, hairy bees of the genus *Bombus.* [BUMBLE[2] + BEE.]

bum·boat (bŭm′bōt′) *n.* A small boat used to peddle provisions and small wares to ships anchored offshore. [Perh. BUM[3] + BOAT.]

bum·mer (bŭm′ər) *n. Slang.* **1. a.** A bad reaction to a hallucinogenic drug. **b.** A disagreeable person, event, or situation. **2.** A failure.

bump (bŭmp) *v.* **bumped, bump·ing, bumps.** —*tr.* **1.** To strike or collide with forcefully. **2.** To cause to knock against an obstacle. **3.** To knock to a new position; displace. **4.** *Informal.* To displace by right of seniority or authority. —*intr.* **1.** To hit or knock against something forcefully. **2.** To proceed with jerks and jolts. **—*phrasal verbs.* bump into.** To meet by chance. **bump off.** *Slang.* To murder. —*n.* **1.** A forceful blow, collision, or jolt. **2.** A slight swelling or lump. **3.** One of the natural protuberances on the human skull. **4.** A forward thrust of the pelvis as or as if in a burlesque striptease. [Imit.]

bump·er[1] (bŭm′pər) *n.* **1.** One that bumps. **2. a.** Either of two metal structures, typically horizontal bars, attached to the front and rear of an automobile to absorb the impact of a collision. **b.** A protective device used to absorb shocks.

bump·er[2] (bŭm′pər) *n.* **1.** A drinking vessel filled to the brim. **2.** Something unusually or extraordinarily large. —*adj.* Unusually full or abundant: *a bumper crop.* [Perh. < BUMP.]

bumper sticker *n.* A sticker bearing a printed message for display on a vehicle's bumper.

bump·kin (bŭmp′kĭn, bŭm′-) *n.* **1.** An awkward, unsophisticated rustic; yokel. **2.** A short spar projecting from the deck of a ship, used to extend a sail or secure a block or stay. [Orig. unknown.]

bump·tious (bŭmp′shəs) *adj.* Crudely forward and assertive in behavior; pushy. [Perh. a blend of BUMP and FRACTIOUS.] **—bump′tious·ly** *adv.* **—bump′tious·ness** *n.*

bump·y (bŭm′pē) *adj.* **-i·er, -i·est. 1.** Covered with or full of bumps or protuberances: *a bumpy head.* **2.** Marked by bumps and jolts: *a bumpy road.* **—bump′i·ly** *adv.* **—bump′i·ness** *n.*

bun[1] (bŭn) *n.* **1.** A small bread roll, often sweetened or spiced. **2.** A tight roll of hair worn at the back of a woman's head. [ME *bunne,* prob. < OFr. *bugne,* boil, of Celt. orig.]

bun[2] (bŭn) *n.* A drunken spree or revel. [Orig. unknown.]

Bu·na (bo͞o′nə, byo͞o′-). A trademark for synthetic rubber made by polymerization of butadiene and sodium.

bunch (bŭnch) *n.* **1.** A group of like items growing, fastened, or placed together; cluster. **2.** *Informal.* A group of people.

3. A lump or swelling. —*v.* **bunched, bunch·ing, bunch·es.** —*tr.* To gather or form into a bunch. —*intr.* **1.** To form a cluster or group. **2.** To swell; protrude. [ME *bunche,* prob. < OFr. *bonge,* bundle.] —**bunch'y** *adj.*

bunch·ber·ry (bŭnch'bĕr'ē) *n.* The dwarf cornel.

bunch·flow·er (bŭnch'flou'ər) *n.* A bog plant, *Melanthium virginicum,* of the eastern United States, having narrow leaves and a branching cluster of greenish flowers.

bun·co also **bun·ko** (bŭng'kō) *Informal.* —*n., pl.* **-cos** also **-kos.** A swindle in which an unsuspecting person is cheated; confidence game. —*tr.v.* **-coed, -co·ing, -cos** also **-koed, -ko·ing, -kos.** To swindle, as by a confidence game. [Sp. *banca,* card game < Ital. *banca,* bank.]

bun·combe (bŭng'kəm) *n.* Variant of **bunkum.**

bund[1] (bŭnd) *n.* **1.** An embankment or dike, esp. in India. **2.** A street running along a harbor or waterway, esp. in the Orient. [Hindi *band* < Pers.]

bund[2] (bo͝ond, bŭnd) *n.* **1.** An association, esp. a political association. **2.** Often **Bund.** A pro-Nazi German-American organization of the 1930's. [G. < MHG *bunt.*] —**bund'ist** *n.*

Bun·des·rat also **Bun·des·rath** (bo͝on'dəs-rät') *n.* **1.** The upper house of the federal legislature of West Germany. **2.** The federal council of certain countries, as of Switzerland and Austria. [G. : *Bundes,* genitive of *Bund,* confederation + *Rat,* council.]

Bun·des·tag (bo͝on'dəs-täg') *n.* The lower house of the federal legislature of West Germany. [G. : *Bund,* confederation + *-tag,* meeting < MHG *tagen,* to meet < *tag,* day < OHG *tac.*]

bun·dle (bŭn'dl) *n.* **1.** A group of objects tied, fastened, wrapped, or otherwise held together. **2.** Something wrapped or tied up for carrying; package. **3.** *Biol.* A cluster or strand of specialized cells. **4.** *Bot.* A vascular bundle. **5.** *Slang.* A large sum of money. —*v.* **-dled, -dling, -dles.** —*tr.* **1.** To tie, wrap, or fasten together. **2.** To dispatch quickly and with little fuss; hustle: *bundled her off to school.* **3.** To dress warmly: *bundled them up in winter clothes.* —*intr.* **1.** To leave hastily and unceremoniously. **2.** To sleep in the same bed while fully clothed, a custom practiced by engaged couples in early New England. [ME *bundel,* prob. < MDu. *bondel.*] —**bun'dler** *n.*

bung (bŭng) *n.* **1.** A stopper for the hole through which a cask, keg, or barrel is filled or emptied. **2.** A bunghole. —*tr.v.* **bunged, bung·ing, bungs.** To close with or as if with a cork or stopper. [ME *bunge* < MDu. *bonge,* perh. < LLat. *puncta,* hole < Lat. *pungere,* to prick.]

bun·ga·low (bŭng'gə-lō') *n.* A small cottage, usually of one story. [Hindi *baṅglā* < *Bengal,* a region in eastern India and Bangladesh.]

bung·hole (bŭng'hōl') *n.* The hole in a cask, keg, or barrel through which liquid is poured in or drained out.

bun·gle (bŭng'gəl) *v.* **-gled, -gling, -gles.** —*intr.* To work or act ineptly or inefficiently. —*tr.* To manage (a task) badly; mishandle. [Perh. of Scand. orig.] —**bun'gler** *n.* —**bun'gling·ly** *adv.*

bun·ion (bŭn'yən) *n.* A painful, inflamed swelling at the bursa of the big toe. [Poss. alteration of obs. *bunny,* swelling.]

bunk[1] (bŭngk) *n.* **1.** A narrow bed built like a shelf against a wall. **2.** A double-decker bed. **3.** *Informal.* A place for sleeping. —*v.* **bunked, bunk·ing, bunks.** —*intr.* **1.** To sleep in a bunk. **2.** To sleep, esp. in makeshift quarters. —*tr.* To provide with sleeping quarters. [Orig. unknown.]

bunk[2] (bŭngk) *n.* *Slang.* Empty talk; twaddle. [Short for BUNKUM.]

bunk bed *n.* A bunk[1] (sense 2).

bun·ker (bŭng'kər) *n.* **1.** A bin or tank for fuel storage, as on a ship. **2.** A sand trap serving as an obstacle on a golf course. **3.** A fortified earthwork, as for the protection of a gun emplacement. —*tr.v.* **-kered, -ker·ing, -kers.** To store or place in a bunker. [Sc. *bonker,* chest.]

bunk·house (bŭngk'hous') *n.* Sleeping quarters on a ranch or in a camp.

bunk·mate (bŭngk'māt') *n.* A person with whom one shares rough sleeping quarters.

bun·ko (bŭng'kō) *n.* Variant of **bunco.**

bun·kum also **bun·combe** (bŭng'kəm) *n.* Empty or meaningless talk; claptrap. [After *Buncombe* County, North Carolina.]

bun·ny (bŭn'ē) *n., pl.* **-nies.** *Informal.* A rabbit. [Dial. *bun,* rabbit.]

Bun·ra·ku (bo͝on-rä'ko͞o, bo͝on'rä'-) *n.* A traditional Japanese puppet theater featuring large wooden puppets. [J. : *bun,* literary composition + *raku,* easy.]

buns (bŭnz) *pl.n.* *Slang.* The buttocks. [< dial. *bun,* hind part of a rabbit or squirrel < Sc. Gael., stump, bottom.]

Bun·sen burner (bŭn'sən) *n.* A small laboratory burner consisting of a vertical metal tube connected to a gas source and producing a very hot flame from a mixture of gas and air let in through adjustable holes at the base. [After Robert W. *Bunsen* (1811–1899).]

bunt[1] (bŭnt) *v.* **bunt·ed, bunt·ing, bunts.** —*tr.* **1.** To push or strike with or as if with the horns or head; butt. **2.** *Baseball.* To bat (a pitched ball) with a half swing so that the ball rolls slowly in front of the infielders. —*intr. Baseball.* To bunt a pitch. —*n.* **1.** A butt with or as if with the horns or head. **2.** *Baseball.* **a.** The act of bunting. **b.** A bunted ball. [Orig. unknown.]

bunt[2] (bŭnt) *n.* **1.** The middle section of a square sail. **2.** The sagging middle part of a fishnet. [Orig. unknown.]

bunt[3] (bŭnt) *n.* A disease of wheat, rye, and other cereal grasses, caused by fungi of the genus *Tilletia* and resulting in sooty black spores in place of normal seeds. [Orig. unknown.]

bunt·ing[1] (bŭn'tĭng) *n.* **1.** A light cotton or woolen cloth used for making flags. **2.** Flags collectively. **3.** Long, colored strips of cloth used for festive decoration. [Orig. unknown.]

bunt·ing[2] (bŭn'tĭng) *n.* Any of various birds of the family Fringillidae, having short, cone-shaped bills. [ME.]

bunt·ing[3] (bŭn'tĭng) *n.* A snug-fitting, hooded sleeping bag for infants. [Orig. unknown.]

bunt·line (bŭnt'lĭn, -līn') *n.* A rope that keeps a square sail from bellying when it is being hauled up for furling.

bun·ya (bŭn'yə) also **bun·ya·bun·ya** (bŭn'yə-bŭn'yə) *n.* An evergreen tree, *Araucaria bidwilli,* native to Australia, having sharp-pointed, close-set leaves and large cones. [Native word in Australia.]

Bun·yan·esque (bŭn'yə-nĕsk') *adj.* **1.** Of, pertaining to, or suggestive of the allegorical writings of John Bunyan. **2. a.** Of, pertaining to, or suggestive of the stories about Paul Bunyan. **b.** Of astonishingly large size.

buoy (bo͞o'ē, boi) *n.* **1.** A float, often having a bell or light, moored in water as a warning of danger or as a marker for a channel. **2.** A device made of cork or other buoyant material for keeping a person afloat. —*tr.v.* **buoyed, buoy·ing, buoys.** **1.** To mark with or as if with a buoy. **2.** To keep afloat. **3.** To uplift the spirits of; hearten: *good news that buoyed her up.* [ME *boie* < OFr.]

buoy

buoy·ance (boi'əns, bo͞o'yəns) *n.* Buoyancy.

buoy·an·cy (boi'ən-sē, bo͞o'yən-) *n.* **1.** The tendency or capacity to remain afloat in a liquid or to rise in air or gas. **2.** The upward force that a fluid exerts on an object less dense than itself. **3.** The ability to recover quickly from setbacks. **4.** Lightness of spirit; cheerfulness.

buoy·ant (boi'ənt, bo͞o'yənt) *adj.* **1.** Capable of floating or keeping things afloat. **2.** Animated; sprightly. [Sp. *boyante,* pr.part. of *boyar,* to refloat a boat < *boya,* buoy < OFr. *boie.*] —**buoy'ant·ly** *adv.*

bu·pres·tid (byo͞o-prĕs'tĭd) *n.* Any of various often brightly colored beetles of the family Buprestidae, many of which are destructive wood borers as larvae. [NLat. *Buprestidae,* family name < *Buprestis,* type genus < Lat. *buprestis,* beetle harmful to cattle < Gk. *bouprestis* : *bous,* ox + *prēthein,* to swell up.]

bur[1] (bûr) *n.* **1. a.** The rough, prickly, or spiny fruit husk, seed pod, or flower of various plants, such as the chestnut or the burdock. **b.** A plant producing burs. **2.** A persistently clinging or nettlesome person or thing. **3.** A rough protuberance, esp. a burl on a tree. **4.** Variant of **burr**[1]. [ME *burre,* of Scand. orig.]

bur[2] (bûr) *n. & v.* Variant of **burr**[2].

bur[3] (bûr) *n.* Variant of **burr**[3].

bur·ble (bûr'bəl) *n.* **1.** A rushing or bubbling sound. **2.** A rapid, excited flow of speech. **3.** A separation in the boundary layer of air about a moving streamlined body, such as the wing of an airplane, causing a breakdown in the smooth airflow and resulting in turbulence. —*intr.v.* **-bled, -bling, -bles.** **1.** To bubble; gurgle. **2.** To speak quickly and excitedly. [ME *burblen,* to bubble.]

bur·bot (bûr'bət) *n., pl.* **burbot** or **-bots.** A freshwater fish, *Lota lota,* of the Northern Hemisphere, related to and resembling the cod. [ME < OFr. *borbote.*]

bur cucumber *n.* **1.** A climbing vine, *Sicyos angulatus,* of eastern North America, having lobed leaves, small greenish flowers, and bristly, egg-shaped fruit. **2.** The fruit of the bur cucumber.

bur·den[1] (bûr'dn) *n.* **1. a.** Something that is carried. **b.** Something that is difficult to bear physically or emotionally. **2.** A responsibility or duty. **3. a.** The amount of cargo that a vessel can carry. **b.** The weight of the cargo carried by a vessel at one time. **4.** The carrying of heavy loads. —*tr.v.* **-dened, -den·ing, -dens.** **1.** To load or overload. **2.** To weigh down; oppress. [ME < OE *byrðen.*]

bur·den[2] (bûr'dn) *n.* **1.** The bass accompaniment to a song. **2.** The chorus or refrain of a musical composition. **3.** The drone of a bagpipe. **4.** A recurring idea or theme. [Var. of BOURDON.]

burden of proof *n.* The responsibility of proving a disputed charge or allegation.

bur·den·some (bûr'dn-səm) *adj.* Being or imposing a burden. —**bur'den·some·ly** *adv.* —**bur'den·some·ness** *n.*

Synonyms: *burdensome, onerous, oppressive, harsh, arduous, demanding, rigorous, exacting.* These adjectives all apply to what taxes the body or mind. *Burdensome* is generally associated with actual hardship of body, and *onerous* with the figuratively heavy load imposed by something irksome, annoying, or otherwise unwelcome. *Oppressive* and *harsh* pertain to severe trial of body or spirit. The remaining adjectives imply active efforts to overcome hardship. *Arduous* emphasizes the expenditure of sustained, exhausting labor. *Demanding* and *rigorous* apply to that which imposes severe conditions, and *exacting* further intensifies the sense of un-

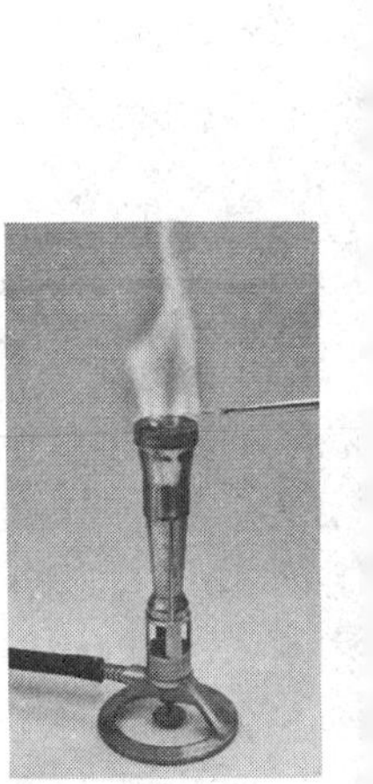

Bunsen burner

compromising demands, as for high standards of performance or for strict observance of rules.

bur·dock (bûr′dŏk′) *n.* Any of several coarse, weedy plants of the genus *Arctium,* native to Eurasia, having large, heart-shaped leaves and purplish flowers surrounded by hooked bristles. [BUR + DOCK⁴.]

bu·reau (byo͝or′ō) *n., pl.* **-reaus** or **-reaux** (-ōz). **1.** A chest of drawers, esp. one with a mirror. **2.** *Chiefly Brit.* A writing desk or writing table with drawers. **3. a.** A government department or subdivision of a department. **b.** An office, usually of a large organization, that performs a specific duty: *a news bureau.* **c.** A business that offers information of a specified kind: *a travel bureau.* [Fr., desk, cloth cover for desks < OFr. *burel,* woolen cloth, ult. < LLat. *burra,* shaggy garment.]

bu·reauc·ra·cy (byo͞o-rŏk′rə-sē) *n., pl.* **-cies. 1. a.** Administration of a government chiefly through bureaus staffed with nonelective officials. **b.** The departments and their officials as a group. **2.** Government marked by diffusion of authority among numerous offices and adherence to inflexible rules of operation. **3.** An administrative system in which the need to follow complex procedures impedes effective action. [Fr. *bureaucratie* : *bureau,* office (see BUREAU) + Gk. *-kratia,* rule < *kratos,* strength.]

bu·reau·crat (byo͝or′ə-krăt′) *n.* **1.** An official who insists on rigid adherence to rules, forms, and routines. **2.** An official of a bureaucracy. **—bu′reau·crat′ic** *adj.* **—bu′reau·crat′i·cal·ly** *adv.*

bu·reau·crat·ese (byo͝or′ə-kră-tēz′, -tēs′) *n.* A style of language used esp. by bureaucrats that is characterized by jargon and euphemism.

bu·reau·cra·tize (byo͞o-rŏk′rə-tīz′) *tr.v.* **-tized, -tiz·ing, -tiz·es.** To bring under bureaucratic influence or control.

bu·rette also **bu·ret** (byo͞o-rĕt′) *n.* A uniform-bore glass tube with fine gradations and a stopcock at the bottom, used esp. in laboratory procedures for accurate fluid dispensing and measurement. [Fr., dim. of *buire,* vase for liquors.]

burg (bûrg) *n.* **1.** A fortified or walled town. **2.** *Informal.* A city or town. [ME *burgh* < OE *burg.*]

bur·gage (bûr′gĭj) *n.* A tenure in England and Scotland under which property of the king or a lord in a town was held for a yearly rent. [ME < Med. Lat. *burgagium* < *burgus,* fortified town, of Germanic orig.]

bur·gee (bər-jē′, bûr′jē) *n.* A small distinguishing flag displayed by a yacht. [Perh. < dial. Fr. *bourgeais,* shipowner < OFr. *burgeis,* citizen < *bourg,* bourg.]

bur·geon also **bour·geon** (bûr′jən) *intr.v.* **-geoned, -geon·ing, -geons. 1. a.** To put forth new buds, leaves, or greenery; sprout. **b.** To begin to grow or blossom. **2.** To develop rapidly; flourish. [ME *burgeonen* < OFr. *borjoner.*]

Usage: The verb *burgeon* and its participle *burgeoning,* used as an adjective, are properly restricted to the actual or figurative sense of "to bud or sprout," or "to newly emerge": *the burgeoning talent of the young Mozart.* They are not mere substitutes for the more general *expand, grow,* or *thrive.* A slight majority of the Usage Panel rejects the following example: *the burgeoning population of Queens.*

burg·er (bûr′gər) *n. Informal.* **1.** A hamburger. **2.** A sandwich similar to a hamburger but with a nonbeef filling: *a crab burger.*

bur·gess (bûr′jĭs) *n.* **1.** A freeman or citizen of an English borough. **2.** Formerly, a member of the English Parliament representing a town, borough, or university. **3.** A member of the lower house of the legislature of colonial Virginia or Maryland. [ME *burgeis* < OFr. < LLat. *burgensis.*]

burgh (bûrg) *n.* A chartered town or borough in Scotland. [Sc., var. of BOROUGH.]

burgh·er (bûr′gər) *n.* **1.** A member of the mercantile class of a medieval city. **2.** A citizen of a town or borough. [Ult. < MHG *burgaere* < OHG *burgārī* < *burg,* city.]

bur·glar (bûr′glər) *n.* One who commits burglary. [AN *burgler* < Med. Lat. *burgulator,* var. of *burgator* < LLat. *burgus,* fortified town, of Germanic orig.]

bur·glar·i·ous (bər-glâr′ē-əs) *adj.* Of or pertaining to burglary.

bur·glar·ize (bûr′glə-rīz′) *tr.v.* **-ized, -iz·ing, -iz·es.** To break into, enter, and steal from.

bur·glar·proof (bûr′glər-pro͞of′) *adj.* Secure against burglary.

bur·gla·ry (bûr′glə-rē) *n., pl.* **-ries.** The crime of breaking into and entering a building with the intention of stealing.

bur·gle (bûr′gəl) *tr.v.* **-gled, -gling, -gles.** *Informal.* To burglarize. [Back-formation < BURGLAR.]

bur·go·mas·ter (bûr′gə-măs′tər) *n.* In the Netherlands, Flanders, Austria, and Germany, the principal magistrate of a city or town, comparable to a mayor. [Partial transl. of Du. *burgemeester* : *burg,* town (< MDu. *burch*) + *meester,* master.]

bur·go·net (bûr′gə-nĭt, bûr′gə-nĕt′) *n.* A 16th-century helmet. [OFr. *bourguignotte,* prob. < *Bourgogne,* Burgundy, a region of southeastern France.]

bur·goo (bûr′go͞o′, bər-go͞o′) *n., pl.* **-goos. 1.** Thick oatmeal gruel. **2. a.** A thick, spicy soup or stew of meat and vegetables. **b.** A picnic or gathering where burgoo is served. [Orig. unknown.]

Bur·gun·dy (bûr′gən-dē) *n., pl.* **-dies. 1. a.** Any of various red or white wines produced in Burgundy, France. **b.** Any of various similar wines produced elsewhere. **2. burgundy.** A dark grayish or blackish purple to dark purplish red or reddish brown.

bur·i·al (bĕr′ē-əl) *n.* The act or process of burying a dead body. ***—modifier:*** *burial rites.* [ME *buriel* < OE *byrgels.*]

bu·rin (byo͝or′ĭn, bûr′-) *n.* A pointed steel cutting tool used in engraving or in carving stone. [Fr.]

burke (bûrk) *tr.v.* **burked, burk·ing, burkes. 1.** To kill by suffocation or strangulation so as to leave the body intact and suitable for dissection. **2.** To suppress quietly. [After William *Burke* (1792–1829).]

burl (bûrl) *n.* **1.** A knot, lump, or slub in yarn or cloth. **2. a.** A large, rounded outgrowth on the trunk or branch of a tree. **b.** The strongly marked wood from such an outgrowth used as veneer. *—tr.v.* **burled, burl·ing, burls.** To dress or finish (cloth) by removing burls or loose threads. [ME *burle* < OFr. *bourle,* tuft of wool, dim. of *bourre,* coarse wool < LLat. *burra,* shaggy garment.] **—burl′er** *n.*

bur·lap (bûr′lăp′) *n.* A coarsely woven cloth made of fibers of jute, flax, or hemp and used to make bags, to reinforce linoleum, and in interior decoration. [Orig. unknown.]

bur·lesque (bər-lĕsk′) *n.* **1.** A literary or dramatic work that makes a subject appear ridiculous by treating it in an incongruous way, as by presenting a lofty subject with vulgarity or an inconsequential one with mock dignity. **2.** A ludicrous or mocking imitation; travesty. **3.** Vaudeville entertainment characterized by ribald comedy, dancing, and nudity. *—v.* **-lesqued, -lesqu·ing, -lesques.** *—tr.* To imitate mockingly or humorously: *"always bringing junk . . . home, as if he were burlesquing his role as provider"* (John Updike). *—intr.* To use the methods or techniques of burlesque. [< Fr., comical < Ital. *burlesco* < *burla,* joke < VLat. **burrula,* dim. of LLat. *burrae,* nonsense.] **—bur·lesque′ly** *adv.* **—bur·lesqu′er** *n.*

bur·ley (bûr′lē) *n., pl.* **-leys.** A light-colored tobacco grown chiefly in Kentucky. [Prob. < the name *Burley.*]

bur·ly (bûr′lē) *adj.* **-li·er, -li·est.** Heavy, strong, and muscular; husky. [ME *burlich.*] **—bur′li·ly** *adv.* **—bur′li·ness** *n.*

bur marigold *n.* Any of various plants of the genus *Bidens,* having yellow flowers and pointed seeds that cling to fur and clothing.

Bur·mese (bər-mēz′, -mēs′) *adj.* Of, pertaining to, or characteristic of Burma, its natives and inhabitants, their language, or their culture. *—n., pl.* **Burmese. 1.** A native or inhabitant of Burma. **2.** The Sino-Tibetan language of Burma.

burn¹ (bûrn) *v.* **burned** or **burnt** (bûrnt), **burn·ing, burns.** *—tr.* **1. a.** To cause to undergo combustion. **b.** To destroy with fire: *burned the rubbish.* **2.** *Physics.* To cause to undergo nuclear fission or fusion. **3.** To damage or injure by fire, heat, or a heat-producing agent: *burned his finger.* **4. a.** To kill with fire. **b.** *Slang.* To execute, esp. to electrocute. **5.** To produce by fire or heat: *burn a clearing in the brush.* **6.** To use as a fuel: *a furnace that burns coal.* **7.** To impart a sensation of intense heat to: *The chili burned his mouth.* **8.** To brand (an animal). **9.** To harden or impart a finish to by subjecting to intense heat; fire: *burn clay pots in a kiln.* **10.** To make angry: *remarks that burned me up.* **11.** *Slang.* **a.** To defeat in a contest, esp. by a narrow margin. **b.** To swindle or deceive; cheat. *—intr.* **1.** To undergo combustion. **2.** To be on fire; flame. **3.** To emit heat or light by or as if by fire: *the sun burning bright in the sky.* **4.** To be destroyed, injured, damaged, or changed by or as if by fire: *a house that burned to the ground.* **5.** To feel or look hot: *burning with fever.* **6.** To be consumed with strong emotion, esp.: **a.** To be or become angry: *always burns at every little remark.* **b.** To be very eager: *was burning to know what happened.* **7.** To be imprinted by or as if by burning: *criticism that burned in my mind.* **8.** *Slang.* To be electrocuted. **9.** To impart a sensation of heat. **10.** To become sunburned. ***—phrasal verb.*** **burn out. 1.** To stop burning from lack of fuel. **2.** To wear out or become inoperative as a result of heat or friction. **3.** To become exhausted, esp. as a result of long-term stress. *—n.* **1.** An injury produced by fire, heat, or a heat-producing agent. **2.** A burned place or area: *a cigarette burn in the tablecloth.* **3.** The process or result of burning, as in the manufacture of bricks. **4.** A stinging sensation: *the burn of alcohol on an open wound.* **5.** A sunburn. **6.** *Aerospace.* One firing of a rocket. **7.** *Slang.* A swindle. ***—idioms.*** **burn (one's) bridges (behind one).** To eliminate the possibility of retreat. **to burn.** In great amounts: *had money to burn.* [ME *burnen* < OE *beornan* and *bærnan.*]

Synonyms: *burn, scorch, singe, sear, char, parch.* These verbs mean to injure or alter by heat. *Burn* can apply to the effect of exposure to any source of heat. *Scorch* usually refers to contact with flame or heated metal, and involves superficial (surface) burning that discolors, damages texture, or makes brittle. *Singe* specifies superficial and momentary burning of edges through nearness to the heat source. *Sear* applies to surface burning of organic tissue, as by branding, cauterizing, or application of intense flame, as to meat. *Char* pertains to the reduction of a burning substance to carbon, or to any blackening or disintegration due to fire. *Parch* emphasizes surface drying and, often, fissuring by long exposure to flame or sun.

burn[2] (bûrn) *n. Chiefly Scot.* A small stream; brook. [ME < OE.]

burn·er (bûr′nər) *n.* **1.** One that burns. **2.** The part of a stove, furnace, or lamp that is lighted to produce a flame. **3.** A device, as a furnace, in which something is burned.

bur·net (bər-nĕt′, bûr′nĭt) *n.* Any of several plants of the genus *Sanguisorba,* having cucumber-flavored leaves and clusters of small white, brownish-red, or dark brown flowers. [ME < OFr. *burnette,* dark brown, dim. of *brun,* brown, of Germanic orig.]

burn·ing (bûr′nĭng) *adj.* **1.** Marked by intense heat: *a burning sun.* **2.** Characterized by intense emotion; passionate: *a burning desire for justice.* **3.** Of immediate import; urgent: *"the issues that seem so burning in Washington"* (John F. Kennedy). **—burn′ing·ly** *adv.*

burning bush *n.* **1.** Any of several plants or shrubs having foliage that turns bright red, as the wahoo and the summer cypress. **2.** The gas plant.

burning glass *n.* A convex lens used to focus the sun's rays and produce heat, esp. for ignition.

bur·nish (bûr′nĭsh) *tr.v.* **-nished, -nish·ing, -nish·es. 1.** To make smooth or glossy by or as if by rubbing; polish. **2.** To rub with a tool that serves esp. to smooth or polish. *—n.* A smooth, glossy finish or appearance; luster. [ME *burnishen* < OFr. *burnir, burniss-,* var. of *brunir* < *brun,* shining, of Germanic orig.] **—bur′nish·er** *n.*

bur·noose also **bur·nous** (bər-no͞os′) *n.* A hooded cloak worn esp. by Arabs. [Fr. *burnous* < Ar. *bournous* < Gk. *birros,* cloak < LLat. *birrus.*]

burn·out (bûrn′out′) *n.* **1.** A failure in a device attributable to burning, excessive heat, or friction. **2.** *Aerospace.* **a.** The termination of rocket or jet-engine operation because of fuel exhaustion or shutoff. **b.** The point at which this termination occurs. **3. a.** Physical or emotional exhaustion, esp. as a result of long-term stress. **b.** One who is burned out, as from long-term stress.

burn·sides (bûrn′sīdz′) *pl.n.* Heavy side whiskers and a moustache, worn with the chin clean-shaven. [After Ambrose E. *Burnside* (1824–1881).]

burnt (bûrnt) *v.* A past tense and past participle of **burn.**

burnt sienna *n.* **1.** A reddish-brown pigment prepared by calcining raw sienna. **2.** A dark reddish orange; sienna.

bur oak *n.* A timber tree, *Quercus macrocarpa,* of eastern North America, having acorns enclosed within a deep, fringed cup.

burp (bûrp) *n.* A belch. *—v.* **burped, burp·ing, burps.** *—intr.* To belch. *—tr.* To cause (a baby) to belch, esp. after feeding. [Imit.]

burp gun *n.* A portable, lightweight machine gun.

burr[1] (bûr) *n.* **1.** A rough edge or area remaining on metal or other material after it has been cast, cut, or drilled. **2.** A rotary cutting tool designed to be attached to a drill. **3.** Variant of **bur[1]**. *—tr.v.* **burred, burr·ing, burrs. 1.** To form a burr on. **2.** To remove burrs from. [ME *burre,* of Scand. orig.]

burr[2] also **bur** (bûr) *n.* **1.** A rough trilling of the letter *r,* as in Scottish pronunciation. **2.** A buzzing or whirring sound. *—v.* **burred, burr·ing, burrs** or **burs.** *—tr.* To pronounce with a burr. *—intr.* **1.** To speak with a burr. **2.** To make a buzzing or whirring sound. [Imit.]

burr[3] also **bur** (bûr) *n.* **1.** A washer that fits around the smaller end of a rivet. **2.** A blank punched from a sheet of metal. [Var. of obs. *burrow* < ME *burwhe.*]

bur reed *n.* Any of various marsh plants of the genus *Sparganium,* having narrow leaves and round, prickly fruit.

bur·ri·to (bo͞o-rē′tō, bə-) *n.* A flour tortilla wrapped around a filling, as beef, beans, or cheese. [Am. Sp. < Sp., little donkey, dim. of *burro,* burro.]

bur·ro (bûr′ō, bo͝or′ō, bŭr′ō) *n., pl.* **-ros.** A small donkey, esp. one used as a pack animal. [Sp. < *borrico,* donkey < LLat. *burricus,* small horse.]

bur·row (bûr′ō, bŭr′ō) *n.* A hole or tunnel dug in the ground by a small animal, such as a rabbit or a mole, for habitation or refuge. *—v.* **-rowed, -row·ing, -rows.** *—intr.* **1.** To dig a burrow. **2.** To live or hide in a burrow. **3.** To move or progress by or as if by digging or tunneling: *"Suddenly the train is burrowing through the pinewoods"* (William Styron). *—tr.* **1.** To make by or as if by tunneling. **2.** To dig a burrow in or through. **3.** *Archaic.* To hide in a burrow. [ME *borow.*] **—bur′row·er** *n.*

burr·stone (bûr′stōn′) *n.* Variant of **buhrstone.**

bur·ry (bûr′ē) *adj.* **-ri·er, -ri·est. 1.** Like a bur; prickly. **2.** Full of or covered with burs.

bur·sa (bûr′sə) *n., pl.* **-sae** (-sē) or **-sas.** A saclike bodily cavity, esp. one located between joints or at points of friction between moving structures. [NLat. < Med. Lat., purse < Gk.] **—bur′sal** (-səl) *adj.*

bur·sar (bûr′sər, -sär′) *n.* An official in charge of funds, as at a college or university; treasurer. [Med. Lat. *bursarius* < *bursa,* purse.]

bur·sa·ry (bûr′sə-rē) *n., pl.* **-ries. 1.** A treasury, esp. of a public institution or religious order. **2.** A scholarship granted to a student, esp. at a Scottish university. [Med. Lat. *bursaria* < *bursa,* purse.] **—bur·sar′i·al** (bər-sâr′ē-əl) *adj.*

burse (bûrs) *n.* **1.** A purse. **2.** *Eccles.* A flat cloth case for carrying the corporal that is used in celebrating the Eucharist. [Med. Lat. *bursa* < Gk., purse.]

bur·seed (bûr′sēd′) *n.* The stickseed.

bur·si·form (bûr′sə-fôrm′) *adj. Anat.* Shaped like a pouch or sac.

bur·si·tis (bər-sī′tĭs) *n.* Inflammation of a bursa, esp. in the shoulder, elbow, or knee joint.

burst (bûrst) *v.* **burst, burst·ing, bursts.** *—intr.* **1. a.** To come open or fly apart suddenly or violently, esp. from internal pressure. **b.** To explode. **2.** To be or seem to be full to the point of breaking open. **3.** To come forth, emerge, or arrive suddenly: *burst into the room.* **4.** To come apart from overwhelming emotion: *thought his heart would burst with happiness.* **5.** To give sudden utterance or expression: *burst out laughing; burst into tears.* *—tr.* **1.** To cause to burst. **2.** *Computer Sci.* To separate (a continuous roll of print-out) into individual sheets. *—n.* **1.** A sudden outbreak or outburst; explosion. **2.** The result of bursting. **3.** A sudden, vehement occurrence: *wind blowing in fitful bursts.* **4.** An abrupt, intense increase; rush: *a burst of speed.* **5.** The explosion of a projectile or bomb on impact or in the air. **6.** The number of bullets fired from an automatic weapon by one pull of the trigger. [ME *bursten* < OE *berstan.*]

burst·er (bûr′stər) *n. Computer Sci.* An offline device used to burst computer print-out.

bur·then (bûr′*th*ən) *n. Archaic.* Variant of **burden[1]**.

bur·ton (bûr′tn) *n. Naut.* A light tackle having double or single blocks, used to hoist or tighten rigging. [Orig. unknown.]

bur·weed (bûr′wēd′) *n.* Any of various plants, such as the burdock, that bear burs.

bur·y (bĕr′ē) *tr.v.* **-ied, -y·ing, -ies. 1.** To conceal by or as if by covering with earth: *bury a bone; buried the secret deep within himself.* **2.** To place (a dead body) in a grave, a tomb, or the sea; inter. **3.** To cover from view; hide: *buried her face in the pillow.* **4.** To occupy (oneself) with deep concentration; absorb: *buried himself in his studies.* **5.** To put an end to; abandon: *buried their quarrel and shook hands.* [ME *burien* < OE *byrgan,* to inter.] **—bur′i·er** *n.*

burying beetle *n.* Any of various black or black and orange beetles of the genus *Necrophorus* that bury dead mice and other small animals on which they feed and lay their eggs.

bus (bŭs) *n., pl.* **bus·es** or **bus·ses. 1.** A long motor vehicle for carrying passengers. **2.** *Informal.* A large or clumsy automobile. **3.** A four-wheeled cart for carrying dishes in a restaurant. **4.** *Elect.* A bus bar. *—v.* **bused, bus·ing, bus·es** or **bussed, bus·sing, bus·ses.** *—tr.* To transport in a bus. *—intr.* **1.** To travel in a bus. **2.** To work as a bus boy. [Short for OMNIBUS.]

Usage: *Bus* is now well established as a transitive verb. It has the general meaning of "to transport (passengers)" and the specialized meaning of "to transport (schoolchildren) to achieve racial integration."

bus bar *n. Elect.* A conducting bar that carries heavy currents to supply several electric circuits.

bus boy *n.* A restaurant employee who clears away dirty dishes and serves as a waiter's assistant.

bus·by (bŭz′bē) *n., pl.* **-bies.** A tall, full-dress fur hat worn in certain regiments of the British army. [Poss. < the name *Busby.*]

bush[1] (bo͝osh) *n.* **1.** A low, branching woody plant, usually smaller than a tree; shrub. **2.** A thick growth of shrubs; thicket. **3. a.** Land covered with a dense growth of shrubs. **b.** Land remote from settlement; backland. **4.** A shaggy mass, as of hair. **5.** A fox's tail. **6. a.** *Archaic.* A clump of ivy used as the sign of a tavern. **b.** *Obs.* A tavern. *—v.* **bushed, bush·ing, bushes.** *—intr.* **1.** To grow or branch out like a bush. **2.** To extend in a bushy growth. *—tr.* To decorate, protect, or support with bushes. [ME.]

bush[2] (bo͝osh) *tr.v.* **bushed, bush·ing, bush·es.** To furnish or line with a bushing. [< E. *bush,* bushing.]

bush baby *n.* The galago.

bush bean *n.* A shrubby plant, *Phaseolus vulgaris humilis,* a variety of the string bean.

bush·buck (bo͝osh′bŭk′) *n.* An African antelope, *Tragelaphus scriptus,* having white markings and twisted horns. [Transl. of Afr. *bosbok.*]

bush clover *n.* Any of various plants or shrubs of the genus *Lespedeza,* having compound leaves with three leaflets and clusters of purple or yellowish flowers.

bushed (bo͝osht) *adj. Informal.* Extremely tired; exhausted. [Orig. unknown.]

bush·el[1] (bo͝osh′əl) *n.* **1. a.** A unit of volume or capacity in the U.S. Customary System, used in dry measure and equal to 4 pecks, 35.24 liters, or 2,150.42 cubic inches. **b.** A unit of volume or capacity in the British Imperial System, used in dry and liquid measure and equal to 2,219.36 cubic inches. **2.** A container with the capacity of a bushel. **3.** *Informal.* A large amount; great deal. [ME < OFr. *boissel* < *boisse,* one sixth of a bushel, of Celt. orig.]

bush·el[2] (bo͝osh′əl) *tr.v.* **-eled, -el·ing, -els** or **-elled, -el·ling, -els.** To alter or mend (clothing). [Prob. < G. *bosseln,* to do odd jobs.] **—bush′el·man** (-mən) *n.*

bush honeysuckle *n.* Any of several North American shrubs of the genus *Diervilla,* having yellow flowers that turn reddish.

burnoose

p **pop** / r **roar** / s **sauce** / sh **ship, dish** / t **tight** / th **thin, path** / *th* **this, bathe** / ŭ **cut** / ûr **urge** / v **valve** / w **with** / y **yes** / z **zebra, size** / zh **vision** / ə **about, item, edible, gallop, circus** / œ *Fr.* **feu,** *Ger.* **schön** / ü *Fr.* **tu,** *Ger.* **über** / KH *Ger.* **ich,** *Scot.* **loch** / N *Fr.* **bon.**

Bu·shi·do also **bu·shi·do** (bo͝osh'ĭ-dō', bo͞o'shĭ-) *n.* The traditional code of the Japanese samurai, stressing self-discipline, bravery, and simple living. [J. *bushidō* : *bushi,* warrior (< Chin. *wu*^{3}*shi*^{4}) + *dō,* way (< Chin. *dao*^{4}).]
bush·ing (bo͝osh'ĭng) *n.* **1.** A fixed or removable metal lining used to constrain, guide, or reduce friction. **2.** An insulating lining for an aperture through which a conductor passes. **3.** An adapter threaded to permit joining of pipes with different diameters. [MDu. *busse.*]
bush jacket *n.* A long cotton shirtlike jacket usually with four flat pockets and a belt.
bush league *n. Slang.* A minor baseball league. **—bush leaguer** *n.*
bush-league (bo͝osh'lēg') *adj. Slang.* **1.** Of or belonging to a bush league. **2.** Mediocre; second-rate.
Bush·man (bo͝osh'mən) *n.* **1.** A member of a nomadic Negroid people of southwestern Africa, characteristically of short stature. **2.** Any of the Khoisan languages spoken by the Bushmen. **3. bushman.** *Austral.* A backwoodsman. [Transl. of Afr. *boschjeman.*]
bush·mas·ter (bo͝osh'măs'tər) *n.* A large, venomous snake, *Lachesis muta,* of tropical America, having brown and grayish markings.
bush pig *n.* A hog, *Potamochoerus porcus,* of southern Africa, having long tufts of hair on the face and ears. [Transl. of Afr. *bosvark.*]
bush pilot *n.* A pilot who flies a small airplane to and from areas inaccessible to larger aircraft or other means of transportation.
bush·rang·er (bo͝osh'rān'jər) *n.* **1.** A backwoodsman. **2.** *Austral.* An outlaw living in the bush.
bush·tit (bo͝osh'tĭt') *n.* Either of two small, long-tailed birds, *Psaltriparus minimus* or *P. melanotis,* of western North America, having predominantly gray plumage.
bush·whack (bo͝osh'hwăk', -wăk') *v.* **-whacked, -whack·ing, -whacks.** *—intr.* **1.** To make one's way through thick woods by cutting away bushes and branches. **2.** To travel through or live in the woods. **3.** To fight as a guerrilla in the bush. *—tr.* To attack suddenly from a place of concealment; ambush. **—bush'whack'er** *n.*
bush·y (bo͝osh'ē) *adj.* **-i·er, -i·est. 1.** Overgrown with bushes. **2.** Thick and shaggy. **—bush'i·ly** *adv.* **—bush'i·ness** *n.*
busi·ness (bĭz'nĭs) *n.* **1. a.** The occupation, work, or trade in which a person is engaged: *in the wholesale food business.* **b.** A specific occupation or pursuit: *really knew her business.* **2.** Commercial, industrial, or professional dealings: *new systems now being used in business.* **3.** A commercial enterprise or establishment: *bought his uncle's business.* **4.** Volume or amount of commercial trade: *Business had fallen off.* **5.** Commercial dealings; patronage: *kept his business by giving individual service.* **6.** One's rightful or proper concern or interest: *"The business of America is business"* (Calvin Coolidge). **7.** Serious work or endeavor: *got right down to business.* **8.** An affair or matter: *a peculiar business.* **9.** An incidental action performed by an actor on the stage to fill a pause between lines or to provide interesting detail. **10.** *Informal.* Verbal abuse; scolding: *got the business for being late.* **11.** *Obs.* The condition of being busy. ***—modifier:*** *a business suit.* [ME *businesse* < *bisi,* busy.]
Synonyms: *business, industry, commerce, trade, traffic.* These nouns apply to forms of activity that have the objective of supplying commodities. *Business* pertains broadly to all gainful activity, though it usually excludes the professions and farming. *Industry* is the production and manufacture of goods and commodities, especially on a large scale, and *commerce* and *trade,* the exchange and distribution of commodities. Often *commerce* is applied to exchange of commodities for money, as within a country, while *trade* refers to exchange of commodities for commodities, as between countries. *Traffic* may suggest illegal trade or commerce, as in narcotics.
business administration *n.* A college or university course of studies that offers instruction in general business principles and practices.
business card *n.* A small card that conveys information about a business or a business representative.
busi·ness·like (bĭz'nĭs-līk') *adj.* **1.** Showing or having characteristics advantageous to or of use in business; methodical and systematic. **2.** Purposeful; earnest.
busi·ness·man (bĭz'nĭs-măn') *n.* A man engaged in business.
busi·ness·wom·an (bĭz'nĭs-wo͝om'ən) *n.* A woman engaged in business.
bus·ing also **bus·sing** (bŭs'ĭng) *n.* The transportation of children by bus to schools outside their neighborhoods, esp. as a means of achieving racial integration.
busk[1] (bŭsk) *n.* **1.** A thin, flexible strip, as of whalebone, sewn into a woman's undergarment as stiffening. **2.** *Regional.* A corset. [Fr. *busc.*]
busk[2] (bŭsk) *intr.v.* **busked, busk·ing, busks.** *Chiefly Brit.* To entertain by singing and dancing, esp. in streets and public places. [Orig. unknown.] **—busk'er** *n.*
busk[3] (bŭsk) *tr.v.* **busked, busk·ing, busks.** *Chiefly Scot.* To make ready; prepare. [ME *busken* < ON *būask,* reflexive of *būa,* to prepare.]
bus·kin (bŭs'kĭn) *n.* **1.** A foot and leg covering reaching halfway to the knee, resembling a laced half boot. **2. a.** A thick-soled laced half boot worn by actors of Greek and Roman tragedies. **b.** Tragedy. [OFr. *bouzequin.*]
bus·man (bŭs'mən) *n.* One who runs a bus.
bus·man's holiday (bŭs'mənz) *n. Informal.* A vacation on which a person engages in activity that is similar to his usual work.
buss (bŭs) *tr. & intr.v.* **bussed, buss·ing, buss·es.** To kiss. *—n.* A kiss. [Prob. imit.]
bust[1] (bŭst) *n.* **1. a.** A woman's bosom. **b.** *Archaic.* The human chest. **2.** A piece of sculpture representing a person's head, shoulders, and upper chest. [Fr. *buste* < Ital. *busto,* poss. < Lat. *bustum,* sepulchral monument.]

bust[1]

bust[2] (bŭst) *v.* **bust·ed, bust·ing, busts.** *—tr.* **1.** To smash or break, esp. forcefully. **2.** To cause to come to an end; break up: *busted the steel trust; wasn't going to bust up their friendship.* **3.** To break or tame (a horse). **4.** To cause to become bankrupt or short of money. **5.** To reduce the rank of; demote. **6.** To hit or punch. **7. a.** To place under arrest. **b.** To make a raid on. *—intr.* **1.** To burst or break. **2.** To become bankrupt or short of money. *—n.* **1.** A failure; flop. **2.** A state of bankruptcy. **3.** A time or period of widespread financial depression. **4.** A punch or blow. **5.** A spree. **6. a.** An arrest. **b.** A raid. [Var. of BURST.]
bus·tard (bŭs'tərd) *n.* Any of various large Old World birds of the family Otididae, frequenting open, grassy regions. [ME < blend of OFr. *bistarde* and *oustarde,* both < Lat. *avis tarda.*]

George Miksch Sutton
bustard

bust·er (bŭs'tər) *n.* **1.** One who bursts or breaks up: *a crime buster.* **2.** One who breaks horses; broncobuster. **3. a.** Something very large or remarkable. **b.** A particularly large or robust child. **4.** A spree. **5.** Fellow. Used as a term of familiar address: *Say, buster, where are you going?*
bus·tle[1] (bŭs'əl) *intr. & tr.v.* **-tled, -tling, -tles.** To hurry or cause to hurry energetically and busily. *—n.* Excited and often noisy activity; stir. [Prob. var. of obs. *buskle,* freq. of BUSK[3].]
bus·tle[2] (bŭs'əl) *n.* **1.** A frame or pad to support and expand the fullness of the back of a woman's skirt. **2.** A bow, peplum, or gathering of material at the back of a skirt below the waist. [Orig. unknown.]
bust·y (bŭs'tē) *adj.* **-i·er, -i·est.** *Informal.* Full-bosomed. **—bust'i·ness** *n.*
bu·sul·fan (byo͞o-sŭl'fən) *n.* An antineoplastic drug, $C_6H_{14}O_6S_2$. [Blend of BUTANE and SULFONYL.]
bus·y (bĭz'ē) *adj.* **-i·er, -i·est. 1.** Actively engaged in some form of work; occupied. **2.** Crowded with activity: *a busy morning.* **3.** Meddlesome; prying. **4.** In use, as a telephone line. **5.** Cluttered with detail to the point of being distracting: *a busy design.* *—tr.v.* **-ied, -y·ing, -ies.** To make busy; occupy: *busied himself preparing his tax return.* [ME < OE *bisig.*] **—bus'i·ly** *adv.* **—bus'y·ness** *n.*
Synonyms: *busy, industrious, diligent, assiduous, sedulous.* All these words suggest active or sustained effort to accomplish something. *Busy* primarily applies to one engaged in present activity, without definite implication of kind, continuity, or duration of activity. *Industrious* implies continuing activity and a natural inclination to be so engaged. *Diligent* suggests intense activity in the accomplishment of a specific goal; often it implies keen interest in work of one's choosing. *Assiduous* emphasizes sustained devotion to work. *Sedulous* adds to assiduity the sense of earnest, persistent, painstaking labor.
bus·y·bod·y (bĭz'ē-bŏd'ē) *n.* A person who meddles or pries into the affairs of others.
busy signal *n.* A series of sharp buzzing tones heard over a telephone when the number dialed is in use.
bus·y·work (bĭz'ē-wûrk') *n.* Activity that takes up time but does not necessarily yield productive results.
but (bŭt; bət *when unstressed*) *conj.* **1.** On the contrary: *caused not prosperity but ruin.* **2.** Contrary to expectation; yet: *organized her work but accomplished very little.* **3.** Except; save: *No one but she saw the prowler.* **4.** With the exception that; except that. Used to introduce a dependent clause: *would have resisted but that they lacked courage.* **5.** Without the result that: *It never rains but it pours.* **6.** Other than: *I have no goal but to end war.* **7.** That. Often used after a negative: *no doubt but right will prevail.* **8.** That . . . not. Used after a negative or question: *There never is a tax law presented but someone will oppose it.* **9.** *Archaic.* Unless; if not: *"Beshrew me but I love her heartily"* (Shakespeare). **10. a.** Before; when. **b.** *Archaic & Nonstandard.* Than. *—prep.* **1.** With the exception of; barring. **2.** Other than: *the whole truth and nothing but the truth.* *—adv.* Merely; just: *hopes that lasted but a moment.* *—n.* An objection, restriction, or exception: *no ifs, ands, or buts.* ***—idiom.* but what.** *Informal.* That not: *don't know but what I'll go.* [ME < OE *būtan.*]
Synonyms: *but, however, still, yet, nevertheless.* Each of these words introduces a statement in opposition to what precedes it. *But,* which notes but does not stress the opposition, is the most widely applicable: *He was ill, but he kept the appointment.* In the same example, *however* would soften the contrast between the two elements. *Still, yet,* and *nevertheless,* in the same example, emphasize contrast.
Usage: *But* is used to mean "except" in sentences like

No one but John can read it. Some traditionalists have suggested that *but* is a conjunction in this use and so should be followed by nominative pronouns like *I* and *he* when the phrase in which it occurs is the subject of the sentence. But this use of *but* is perhaps better thought of as a preposition, since the verb always agrees with the subject preceding *but;* we say *no one but the boys has left,* (not *have left*), and traditionalists themselves do not say *everyone but I am leaving,* which is clearly ungrammatical. Accordingly, this use of *but* should properly be accompanied by pronouns in the objective case, like *me* and *him: Everyone but me has received an answer. But* is redundant when used in combination with *however,* as in *But the army, however, went on with its own plans* (eliminate either *but* or *however*). *But* is often used in informal speech together with a negative in sentences like *It won't take but an hour.* The construction should be avoided in formal style; write *It won't take an hour. But what* is informal in sentences like *I don't know but what we'll get there before the boys do.* In writing, substitute *whether* or *that* for *but. But* is also informal when used in place of *than* in sentences like *It no sooner started but it stopped* (in writing, use *than*). *But* is usually not followed by a comma. Write *Kim wanted to go, but we didn't want to,* not *Kim wanted to go, but, we didn't want to,* which is incorrect. *But* may be used to begin a sentence, even in formal style. But it should not be followed by a comma here, either. See also Usage notes at **doubt** and **than.**

but– *pref.* Containing a group of four carbon atoms: *butyl.* [< BUTYRIC.]

bu·ta·di·ene (byo͞o'tə-dī'ēn', -dī-ēn') *n.* A colorless, highly flammable hydrocarbon, C_4H_6, obtained from petroleum and used in the manufacture of synthetic rubber. [BUTA(NE) + DI- + -ENE.]

bu·tane (byo͞o'tān') *n.* Either of two isomers of a gaseous hydrocarbon, C_4H_{10}, produced synthetically from petroleum and used as a household fuel, refrigerant, and aerosol propellant, and in the manufacture of synthetic rubber.

bu·ta·no·ic acid (byo͞o'tə-nō'ĭk) *n.* Butyric acid.

bu·ta·nol (byo͞o'tə-nôl', -nōl') *n.* Either of two butyl alcohols derived from butane and used as solvents and in organic synthesis.

bu·ta·none (byo͞o'tə-nōn') *n.* A colorless, flammable ketone, C_4H_8O, used in lacquers, paint removers, cements and adhesives, celluloid, and cleaning fluids.

butch (bo͝och) *Slang.* —*n.* A female homosexual with mannish or aggressive traits. —*adj.* Very masculine in appearance or behavior. [Orig. unknown.]

butch·er (bo͝och'ər) *n.* **1. a.** One who slaughters and dresses animals for food or market. **b.** One who sells meats. **2.** One who takes a sadistic pleasure in killing. **3.** A vender, as of candy and magazines, on a train. **4.** One who bungles; botcher. —*tr.v.* **-ered, -er·ing, -ers. 1.** To slaughter or prepare (animals) for market. **2.** To kill cruelly or pointlessly. **3.** To spoil by botching; bungle. [ME *bucher* < OFr. *bouchier* < *boc,* he-goat.] **—butch'er·er** *n.*

butch·er·bird (bo͝och'ər-bûrd') *n.* Any of various birds, esp. the shrike, that impale their prey on thorns.

butcher knife *n.* A heavy-duty knife about 8 inches long with a broad blade.

butcher's broom *n.* A shrub, *Ruscus aculeatus,* native to Europe, having stiff, prickle-tipped, flattened stems resembling true leaves.

butch·er·y (bo͝och'ə-rē) *n., pl.* **-ies. 1.** The trade of a butcher. **2.** *Chiefly Brit.* A slaughterhouse. **3.** Wanton or cruel killing; carnage. **4.** Something that is botched; bungle.

bu·te·o (byo͞o'tē-ō') *n., pl.* **-os.** Any of various hawks of the genus *Buteo,* characterized by broad wings and broad, rounded tails. [NLat., genus name < Lat. *buteo,* a kind of hawk or falcon.]

but·ler (bŭt'lər) *n.* The head male servant in a household. [ME < OFr. *bouteillier,* bottle bearer < *bouteille, botele,* bottle.]

butler's pantry *n.* A serving and storage room between a kitchen and dining room.

butt¹ (bŭt) *v.* **butt·ed, butt·ing, butts.** —*tr.* To hit or push against with the head or horns; ram. —*intr.* **1.** To hit or push something with the head or horns. **2.** To project forward or out. **—*phrasal verb.* butt in.** *Informal.* To interfere or meddle in other people's affairs. —*n.* A push or blow with the head or horns. [ME *butten* < OFr. *bouter,* to strike, of Germanic orig.] **—butt'er** *n.*

butt² (bŭt) *tr. & intr.v.* **butt·ed, butt·ing, butts.** To join or be joined end to end; abut. —*n.* **1.** A butt joint. **2.** A butt hinge. [ME *butten* < OFr. *bouter,* to adjoin.]

butt³ (bŭt) *n.* **1.** One that serves as an object of ridicule or contempt: *was the butt of their jokes.* **2. a.** A target. **b. butts.** A target range. **c.** An obstacle behind a target for stopping the shot. **3.** *Obs.* A limit; goal. [ME *butte* < OFr.]

butt⁴ (bŭt) *n.* **1.** The larger or thicker end of something: *the butt of a rifle.* **2. a.** An unburned end, as of a cigarette. **b.** *Informal.* A cigarette. **3.** A short or broken remnant; stub. **4.** *Informal.* The buttocks; rear end. [ME *butte.*]

butt⁵ (bŭt) *n.* **1.** A large cask. **2.** A unit of volume equal to 126 U.S. gallons, or about 477 liters. [ME < OFr. *boute* < LLat. *buttis.*]

butte (byo͞ot) *n.* A hill that rises abruptly from the surrounding area and has sloping sides and a flat top. [Fr. < OFr. *butt,* mound behind targets.]

but·ter (bŭt'ər) *n.* **1.** A soft yellowish or whitish emulsion of butterfat, water, air, and sometimes salt, churned from milk or cream and processed for use as a food. **2.** Any of various substances similar to butter, esp.: **a.** A spread made from fruit, nuts, or other foods: *peanut butter.* **b.** A vegetable fat having a nearly solid consistency at ordinary temperatures: *cocoa butter.* **3.** *Informal.* Flattery. —*tr.v.* **-tered, -ter·ing, -ters.** To put butter on or in. **—*phrasal verb.* butter up.** To praise or flatter excessively: *always buttering up the boss.* [ME *butere* < OE < Lat. *butyrum* < Gk. *bouturon,* cow cheese : *bous,* cow + *turos,* cheese.]

but·ter-and-eggs (bŭt'ər-ən-ĕgz') *n. (used with a sing. or pl. verb).* A North American plant, *Linaria vulgaris,* having numerous narrow leaves and a spike of spurred pale-yellow and orange flowers.

but·ter·ball (bŭt'ər-bôl') *n.* **1.** A ball of butter. **2.** *Informal.* A fat or chubby person. **3.** The bufflehead.

butter bean *n.* **1.** The wax bean. **2.** *Regional.* The lima bean.

but·ter·bur (bŭt'ər-bûr') *n.* Any of several plants of the genus *Petasites,* having woolly leaves and stems and fragrant whitish or purple flowers.

but·ter·cup (bŭt'ər-kŭp') *n.* Any of various plants of the genus *Ranunculus,* characteristically having glossy yellow flowers.

but·ter·fat (bŭt'ər-făt') *n.* The oily content of milk from which butter is made, consisting largely of the glycerides of oleic, stearic, and palmitic acids.

but·ter·fin·gers (bŭt'ər-fĭng'gərz) *n. (used with a sing. verb).* A clumsy or awkward person who is apt to drop things. **—but'ter·fin'gered** *adj.*

but·ter·fish (bŭt'ər-fĭsh') *n., pl.* **butterfish** or **-fish·es. 1.** A marine food fish, *Poronotus triacanthus,* of the North American Atlantic coast, having a flattened body. **2.** Any of various fishes similar or related to the butterfish. [From its slippery mucous coating.]

but·ter·fly (bŭt'ər-flī') *n.* **1.** Any of various insects of the order Lepidoptera, characteristically having slender bodies, knobbed antennae, and four broad, usually colorful wings. **2.** A person interested principally in frivolous pleasure. **3.** The butterfly stroke. **4. butterflies.** A feeling of unease or mild nausea caused esp. by fearful anticipation. —*tr.v.* **-flied, -fly·ing, -flies.** To cut and spread open and flat, as shrimp. [ME *butterflye* < OE *butorflēoge.*]

butterfly bush *n.* Any of several shrubs of the genus *Buddleia,* cultivated for their clusters of purplish or white flowers.

butterfly fish *n.* Any of various tropical marine fishes of the family Chaetodontidae, most of which are brightly colored.

butterfly pea *n.* A twining vine, *Clitoria mariana,* of the eastern United States, having compound leaves and pale-blue flowers.

butterfly stroke *n.* A swimming stroke in which both arms are drawn upward out of the water and forward with a simultaneous up-and-down kick of the feet.

butterfly valve *n.* **1.** A disk turning on a diametrical axis inside a pipe, used as a throttle valve or damper. **2.** A valve composed of two semicircular plates hinged on a common spindle, used to permit flow in one direction only.

butterfly weed *n.* A North American plant, *Asclepias tuberosa,* having flat-topped clusters of bright-orange flowers.

but·ter·milk (bŭt'ər-mĭlk') *n.* **1.** The sour liquid that remains after the butterfat has been removed from whole milk or cream by churning. **2.** A cultured sour milk made by adding certain microorganisms to sweet milk.

but·ter·nut (bŭt'ər-nŭt') *n.* **1. a.** A tree, *Juglans cinerea,* of eastern North America, having compound leaves and egg-shaped nuts. **b.** The edible, oily nut of the butternut. **c.** The bark of the butternut. **d.** A brownish color or dye obtained from butternut bark. **e. butternuts.** Clothing dyed with butternut extract. **2.** *Informal.* A Confederate soldier or partisan in the Civil War. **3.** The souari nut. [From the nut's oiliness.]

but·ter·scotch (bŭt'ər-skŏch') *n.* A syrup, sauce, candy, or flavoring made by melting butter, brown sugar, and sometimes artificial flavorings.

but·ter·weed (bŭt'ər-wēd') *n.* **1.** A plant, *Senecio glabellus,* of the southern and central United States, having yellow flowers. **2.** The horseweed.

but·ter·wort (bŭt'ər-wûrt', -wôrt') *n.* A plant of the genus *Pinguicula,* esp. *P. vulgaris,* of wet places, having spurred violet-blue flowers and fleshy, greasy leaves. [From the leaves' oiliness.]

but·ter·y¹ (bŭt'ə-rē) *adj.* **1.** Resembling, containing, or spread with butter. **2.** *Informal.* Marked by effusive and insincere flattery. **—but'ter·i·ness** *n.*

but·ter·y² (bŭt'ə-rē, bŭt'rē) *n., pl.* **-ies.** *Chiefly Brit.* **1.** A pantry or wine cellar. **2.** A place in colleges and universities where students may buy provisions. [ME *buttrie* < OFr. *boterie* < LLat. *botaria* < *bota,* var. of *butta,* cask.]

butt hinge *n.* A hinge composed of two plates attached to abutting surfaces of a door and door jamb and joined by a pin. [< BUTT².]

butt·in·sky (bŭ-tĭn'skē) *n., pl.* **-skies.** *Slang.* One prone to

George Miksch Sutton
butcherbird

buttercup

butterfly
Monarch butterfly

butterfly fish

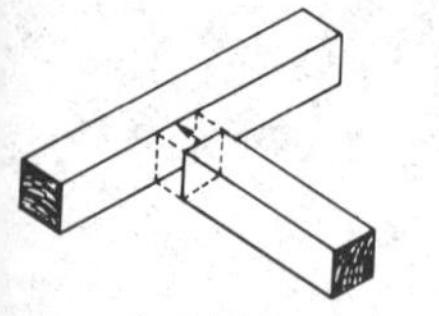

butt joint

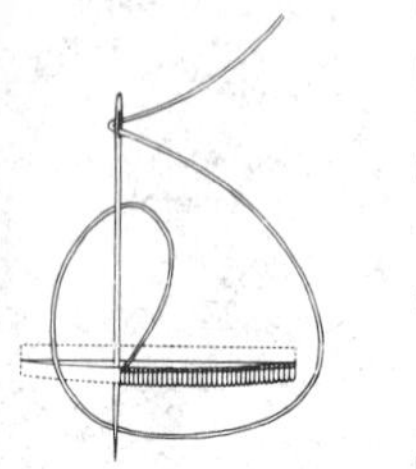

buttonhole stitch

George Miksch Sutton

buttonquail

butting in; meddler. [BUTT + IN + *-sky,* last syllable in many Slavic surnames.]

butt joint *n.* A joint formed by two abutting surfaces placed squarely together. [< BUTT².]

but·tock (bŭt′ək) *n.* **1.** Either of the two rounded, fleshy parts of the rump. **2. buttocks.** The rump. [ME < OE *buttuc,* end.]

but·ton (bŭt′n) *n.* **1. a.** A generally disk-shaped fastener used to join two parts of a garment by fitting through a buttonhole or loop. **b.** Such an object used for decoration. **2.** Any of various objects resembling a button, esp.: **a.** A push-button switch. **b.** The tip of a fencing foil. **c.** A fused metal or glass globule. **3.** Any of various knoblike organic structures, esp.: **a.** The head of a small mushroom. **b.** The tip of a rattlesnake's tail. **4.** A round flat badge bearing a design or printed information: *a campaign button.* **5.** *Slang.* The end of the chin. —*v.* **-toned, -ton·ing, -tons.** —*tr.* **1.** To fasten with buttons. **2.** To decorate or furnish with buttons. —*intr.* To admit of being fastened with buttons. ***—idiom.* on the button.** *Informal.* Exactly; precisely. [ME < OFr. *bouton* < *bouter,* to thrust, of Germanic orig.] **—but′ton·er** *n.* **—but′ton·y** *adj.*

but·ton·ball (bŭt′n-bôl′) *n.* The sycamore (sense 1). [From its button-shaped fruit.]

but·ton·bush (bŭt′n-bo͝osh′) *n.* A North American shrub, *Cephalanthus occidentalis,* having spherical clusters of small white flowers.

but·ton-down (bŭt′n-doun′) *adj.* **1.** Having the ends of the collar fastened down by buttons: *a button-down shirt.* **2.** Also **but·toned-down.** Conservative, conventional, or unimaginative: *buttoned-down diplomacy.*

but·ton·hole (bŭt′n-hōl′) *n.* **1.** A slit in a garment or piece of fabric for fastening a button. **2.** *Chiefly Brit.* A boutonniere. —*tr.v.* **-holed, -hol·ing, -holes. 1.** To make a buttonhole in. **2.** To sew with a buttonhole stitch. **3.** To accost and detain (a person) in conversation. **—but′ton·hol′er** *n.*

buttonhole stitch *n.* A loop stitch that forms a reinforced edge, as around a buttonhole.

but·ton·hook (bŭt′n-ho͝ok′) *n.* A small hook for buttoning shoes or gloves.

but·ton·mold (bŭt′n-mōld′) *n.* A piece of wood, plastic, or metal that is covered with fabric to form a button.

but·ton·quail (bŭt′n-kwāl′) *n.* Any of various small, quail-like Old World birds of the family Turnicidae.

button snakeroot *n.* **1.** The blazing star (sense 2). **2.** The rattlesnake master.

but·ton·wood (bŭt′n-wo͝od′) *n.* The sycamore (sense 1). [From its button-shaped fruit.]

but·tress (bŭt′rĭs) *n.* **1.** A structure, usually brick or stone, built against a wall for support or reinforcement. **2.** Something resembling a buttress. **3.** A horny growth on the heel of a horse's hoof. **4.** Something that serves to support, prop, or reinforce. —*tr.v.* **-tressed, -tress·ing, -tress·es. 1.** To support or reinforce with a buttress. **2.** To sustain, prop, or bolster: *buttress an argument with evidence.* [ME *buteras* < OFr. *bouteret* < *bouter,* to strike against, of Germanic orig.]

butt shaft *n.* A blunt, unbarbed arrow.

butt weld *n.* A welded butt joint.

butt-weld (bŭt′wĕld′) *tr.v.* **-weld·ed, -weld·ing, -welds.** To join by a butt weld.

bu·tut (bo͞o′to͞ot′) *n., pl.* **butut** or **-tuts.** See table at **currency.** [Native word in Gambia.]

bu·tyl (byo͞ot′l) *n.* A hydrocarbon radical, C_4H_9, with the structure of butane and valence 1.

butyl alcohol *n.* Any of four isomeric alcohols, C_4H_9OH, widely used as solvents and in organic synthesis.

bu·tyl·ate (byo͞ot′l-āt′) *tr.v.* **-at·ed, -at·ing, -ates.** To bring a butyl group into (a compound). **—bu′tyl·a′tion** *n.*

bu·tyl·ene (byo͞ot′l-ēn′) *n.* Any of three gaseous isomeric ethylene hydrocarbons, C_4H_8, used principally in making synthetic rubbers.

butyl rubber *n.* A synthetic rubber produced by copolymerization of a butylene with isoprene, outstanding in gaseous impermeability and used in tires, inner tubes, and insulation.

bu·ty·ra·ceous (byo͞o′tə-rā′shəs) *adj.* Resembling butter in appearance, consistency, or chemical properties. [Lat. *butyrum,* butter + -ACEOUS.]

bu·tyr·al·de·hyde (byo͞o′tə-răl′də-hīd′) *n.* A transparent, extremely flammable liquid, C_4H_8O, used in synthesizing resins. [BUTYR(IC) + ALDEHYDE.]

bu·ty·rate (byo͞o′tə-rāt′) *n.* A salt or ester of butyric acid. [BUTYR(IC) + -ATE.]

bu·tyr·ic (byo͞o-tîr′ĭk) *adj.* **1.** Of, pertaining to, containing, or derived from butter. **2.** Of, pertaining to, or derived from butyric acid. [< Lat. *butyrum,* butter.]

butyric acid *n.* Either of two colorless isomeric acids, C_3H_7COOH, occurring in animal milk fats and used in disinfectants, emulsifying agents, and pharmaceuticals.

bu·ty·rin (byo͞o′tər-ĭn) *n.* One of three isomeric glyceryl esters of butyric acid, naturally present in butter. [Fr. *butyrine* < Lat. *butyrum,* butter.]

bux·om (bŭk′səm) *adj.* **1.** Healthily plump and ample of figure: *a buxom woman.* **2.** *Archaic.* Lively; vivacious. **3.** *Obs.* Obedient; yielding. [ME, obedient < OE **būhsum* < *būgan,* to bow, submit.] **—bux′om·ly** *adv.* **—bux′om·ness** *n.*

buy (bī) *v.* **bought** (bôt), **buy·ing, buys.** —*tr.* **1.** To acquire in exchange for money or its equivalent; purchase. **2.** To be capable of purchasing: *money and what money buys.* **3.** To acquire by sacrifice, exchange, or trade: *tried to buy love with gifts.* **4.** To bribe. **5.** *Slang.* To accept the truth or feasibility of: *couldn't buy that story.* —*intr.* To purchase goods; act as a purchaser. ***—phrasal verbs.* buy in. 1.** To purchase stock or interest, as in a company. **2.** To purchase back for the original owner, as at an auction when the bidding is low. **buy off.** To bribe in order to proceed without interference or be exempted from an obligation or from prosecution. **buy out.** To purchase the controlling stock, business rights, or interests of. **buy up.** To purchase all that is available of. —*n.* **1.** Something bought or capable of being bought; purchase. **2.** *Informal.* Something that is underpriced; bargain. [ME < OE *bycgan.*] **—buy′a·ble** *adj.*

Usage: *Buy* as a noun denoting a purchase at a low price is appropriate chiefly to commercial usage. Its use in a more general context (as in *luxury gained at the expense of liberty is never a good buy*) is considered to be unacceptable in written usage to a majority of the Usage Panel.

buy·er (bī′ər) *n.* **1.** One that buys. **2.** A purchasing agent, esp. one who buys for a retail store.

buyers' market *n.* A market condition characterized by low prices occurring when a supply of commodities exceeds market demand.

buzz (bŭz) *v.* **buzzed, buzz·ing, buzz·es.** —*intr.* **1.** To make a low droning or vibrating sound like that of a bee. **2.** To talk, often excitedly, in low tones. **3.** To move quickly and busily; bustle. **4.** To make a signal with a buzzer. —*tr.* **1.** To cause to buzz. **2.** To utter in a rapid, low voice. **3.** *Informal.* To fly low over: *The plane buzzed the control tower.* **4.** To signal with a buzzer. **5.** *Informal.* To make a telephone call to. **6.** *Chiefly Brit. Regional.* To drink (a bottle or cup) to the last drop. ***—phrasal verb.* buzz off.** *Informal.* To leave quickly; go away: *told him in no uncertain terms to buzz off.* —*n.* **1.** A vibrating, humming, or droning sound. **2.** A low murmur: *a buzz of talk.* **3.** *Informal.* A telephone call. **4.** *Slang.* A pleasant intoxication, as from alcohol. [ME *bussen.*]

buz·zard (bŭz′ərd) *n.* **1.** Any of various North American vultures, such as the turkey buzzard. **2.** *Chiefly Brit.* A hawk of the genus *Buteo.* **3.** An avaricious or unpleasant person. [ME *busard* < OFr. < Lat. *buteo.*]

buzz bomb *n.* A robot bomb (sense 1).

buzz·er (bŭz′ər) *n.* Any of various electric signaling devices, such as a doorbell, that make a buzzing sound.

buzz saw *n.* A circular saw.

buzz session *n.* An informal group discussion, as in a workshop or classroom.

buzz word *n.* A usually important-sounding word or phrase connected with a specialized field that is used primarily to impress laymen.

bwa·na (bwä′nə) *n.* Sir; boss. Used chiefly in eastern Africa as a term of address. [Swahili < Ar. *abūna,* our father.]

BX (bē-ĕks′). Base Exchange.

by¹ (bī) *prep.* **1.** Next to; close to: *the window by the door.* **2.** With the help or use of; through: *He came by the back road.* **3.** Up to and beyond; past: *He drove by the house.* **4.** In the period of; during: *sleeping by day.* **5.** Not later than: *by 5:00 P.M.* **6. a.** In the amount of: *letters by the thousands.* **b.** To the extent of: *shorter by two inches.* **7. a.** According to. **b.** With respect to: *played by the rules.* **8.** In the name of: *swore by his honor as a gentleman.* **9.** Through the agency or action of: *killed by a bullet.* **10.** Used to indicate a succession of specified units of measure: *One by one they left. They were persuaded little by little.* **11. a.** Used in multiplication and division: *4 by 6.* **b.** Used with measurements: *a room 12 by 18 feet.* —*adv.* **1.** On hand; nearby: *stand by.* **2.** Aside; away: *He put it by for later.* **3.** Up to, alongside, and past: *The car raced by.* **4.** Into the past: *as years go by.* ***—idioms.* by and by.** A little later. **by and large.** On the whole; for the most part. [ME < OE *bi.*]

Synonyms: *by, through, with.* These prepositions indicate the agency or means by which something is accomplished. *By* usually introduces directly the agent (person) or agency (power): *named by him; struck by lightning. Through,* the least direct, is often followed by a person, in the sense of intermediary (*apply through a friend*), or by a word naming a condition as cause or means (*fail through indecision*). *With* is usually followed by an inanimate object denoting physical instrument (*fight with a sword*) or instrumentality (*soothe with kind words*).

by² (bī) *n.* Variant of **bye.**

by– or **bye–** *pref.* **1.** By: *bygone.* **2.** Secondary, incidental: *byway.*

by-and-by (bī′ən-bī′) *n.* **1.** Some future time or occasion. **2.** The hereafter.

by-bid·der (bī′bĭd′ər) *n.* A person who bids at an auction to raise prices for the owner.

by-blow (bī′blō′) *n.* **1.** An indirect or chance blow. **2.** An illegitimate child; bastard.

bye also **by** (bī) *n.* **1.** A secondary matter; side issue.

2. *Sports.* The position of one who draws no opponent for a round in a tournament and so advances to the next round. —*idiom.* **by the bye.** Incidentally; by the way. [< BY.]
bye– *pref.* Variant of **by-**.
bye-bye (bī'bī', bī-bī') *interj. Informal.* Used to express farewell. [Redup. of (GOOD-)BYE.]
by-e·lec·tion also **bye-e·lec·tion** (bī'ĭ-lĕk'shən) *n.* A special election, esp. in the United Kingdom, held between general elections to fill a vacancy in a legislature.
Byel·o·rus·sian (byĕl'ō-rŭsh'ən) also **Bel·o·rus·sian** (bĕl'-ō-) —*adj.* Of or pertaining to the Byelorussian S.S.R., its people, or their language. —*n.* **1.** A native or inhabitant of the Byelorussian S.S.R. **2.** The Slavic language of the Byelorussians.
by·gone (bī'gôn', -gŏn') *adj.* Gone by; past: *bygone days.* —*n.* A past occurrence. —*idiom.* **let bygones be bygones.** To let past differences be forgotten.
by-lane (bī'lān') *n.* A side road; byway.
by·law (bī'lô') *n.* **1.** A secondary law. **2.** A law or rule governing the internal affairs of an organization. [ME *bilawe,* local regulations, poss. of Scand. orig.]
by-line also **by·line** (bī'līn') —*n.* A line at the head of a newspaper or magazine article with the author's name. —*tr.v.* **-lined, -lin·ing, -lines.** To write (a newspaper or magazine article) under a by-line. —**by'-lin'er** *n.*
by-name (bī'nām') *n.* **1.** A surname. **2.** A nickname.
by-pass also **by·pass** (bī'păs') —*n.* **1.** A road or highway that passes around or to one side of an obstructed or congested area. **2.** A pipe or channel to conduct gas or liquid around another pipe or a fixture. **3.** A means of circumvention. **4.** *Elect.* A shunt (sense 3). **5.** *Med.* **a.** An alternative passage created surgically between two blood vessels, esp. to avoid an obstruction. **b.** An operation to create a by-pass. —*tr.v.* **-passed, -pass·ing, -pass·es. 1.** To avoid (an obstacle) by using a by-pass. **2.** To proceed heedless of; ignore: *by-passing office procedures.* **3.** To cause (piped liquid, for example) to follow a by-pass.
by·past (bī'păst') *adj.* Past; bygone.
by-path (bī'păth', -päth') *n.* An indirect or little-used path.
by-play (bī'plā') *n.* Secondary action or speech taking place while the main action proceeds, esp. on a theater stage.
by-prod·uct (bī'prŏd'əkt) *n.* **1.** Something produced in the making of something else. **2.** A secondary result; side effect.
byre (bīr) *n. Chiefly Brit.* A cowshed or barn. [ME < OE *bȳre.*]
by·road (bī'rōd') *n.* A side road; back road.
By·ron·ic (bī-rŏn'ĭk) *adj.* Of or characteristic of the poet Byron or his works. —**By·ron'i·cal·ly** *adv.*
bys·si·no·sis (bĭs'ĭ-nō'sĭs) *n.* Pneumoconiosis caused by the long-term inhalation of cotton dust and characterized by chronic bronchitis. [LLat. *byssinum,* linen garment (< Lat. *byssus,* a kind of cloth < Gk. *bussos,* flax, of Semitic orig.) + -OSIS.]
bys·sus (bĭs'əs) *n., pl.* **bys·sus·es** or **bys·si** (bĭs'ī'). **1.** *Zool.* A mass of filaments by means of which certain bivalve mollusks, such as mussels, attach themselves to fixed surfaces. **2.** A fine-textured linen of ancient times, used by the Egyptians as wrapping for mummies. [Lat., linen cloth < Gk. *bussos,* linen, of Semitic orig.]
by·stand·er (bī'stăn'dər) *n.* A person who is present at an event without participating in it.
by·street (bī'strēt') *n.* A side street or road.
byte (bīt) *n.* A sequence of adjacent binary digits operated on as a unit by a computer. [Alteration and blend of BIT[1] and BITE.]
by·way (bī'wā') *n.* **1.** A side road; byroad. **2.** A secondary or overlooked field of study.
by·word (bī'wûrd') *n.* **1.** A well-known saying; proverb. **2.** One that proverbially represents a type, class, or quality. **3.** An object of notoriety or note. **4.** A nickname or epithet. [ME *byworde* < OE *bīword* < transl. of Lat. *proverbium.*]
Byz·an·tine (bĭz'ən-tēn', -tīn', bĭ-zăn'tĭn) *adj.* **1.** Of, pertaining to, or characteristic of the ancient city of Byzantium, its inhabitants, or their culture. **2.** Of or designating the style of architecture developed from the 5th century A.D. in Byzantium, characterized by round arches, massive domes, intricate spires and minarets, and extensive use of mosaic. **3.** Of or designating the style of painting and design developed in Byzantium, characterized by formality of design, frontal, stylized presentation of figures, rich use of color, esp. gold, and generally religious subject matter. **4.** Of the Eastern Orthodox Church or the rites performed in it. **5. a.** Of, relating to, or characterized by intrigue; scheming or devious: *"A fine hand for Byzantine deals and cozy arrangements"* (New York). **b.** Highly complicated; intricate and involved: *"A financial empire of Byzantine complexity"* (Newsweek). —*n.* A native or inhabitant of Byzantium.

Byzantine
Byzantine-style architecture

C

Around 1000 B.C. the Phoenicians and other Semitic peoples began to use graphic signs to represent individual speech sounds instead of syllables or words. They used a symbol in the forms (1,2) to represent the sound of the consonant "g" and called it *gīmel,* their word for "camel." The Greeks, adapting the Phoenician alphabet, kept the phonetic value of *gīmel* but changed its shape and orientation (3,4,5,6,7) and altered its name to *gamma.* The Romans borrowed the alphabet from the Greeks via the Etruscans. Because the Etruscans did not distinguish between the sounds of the consonants "g" and "k," they used *gamma* to represent both. The Romans, who did distinguish the two sounds, used the letter C to represent only the sound of "k" and adapted its shape for monumental inscriptions. Their monumental script (10) is the prototype of modern capital letters (13,14). Medieval scribes adapted the Roman capitals to being quickly written on paper, parchment, and vellum. These uncial and cursive minuscules (11,12) are the prototypes of modern lower-case letters, both written and printed (16,15). Changes in pronunciation since ancient times have given the letter C several different phonetic values.

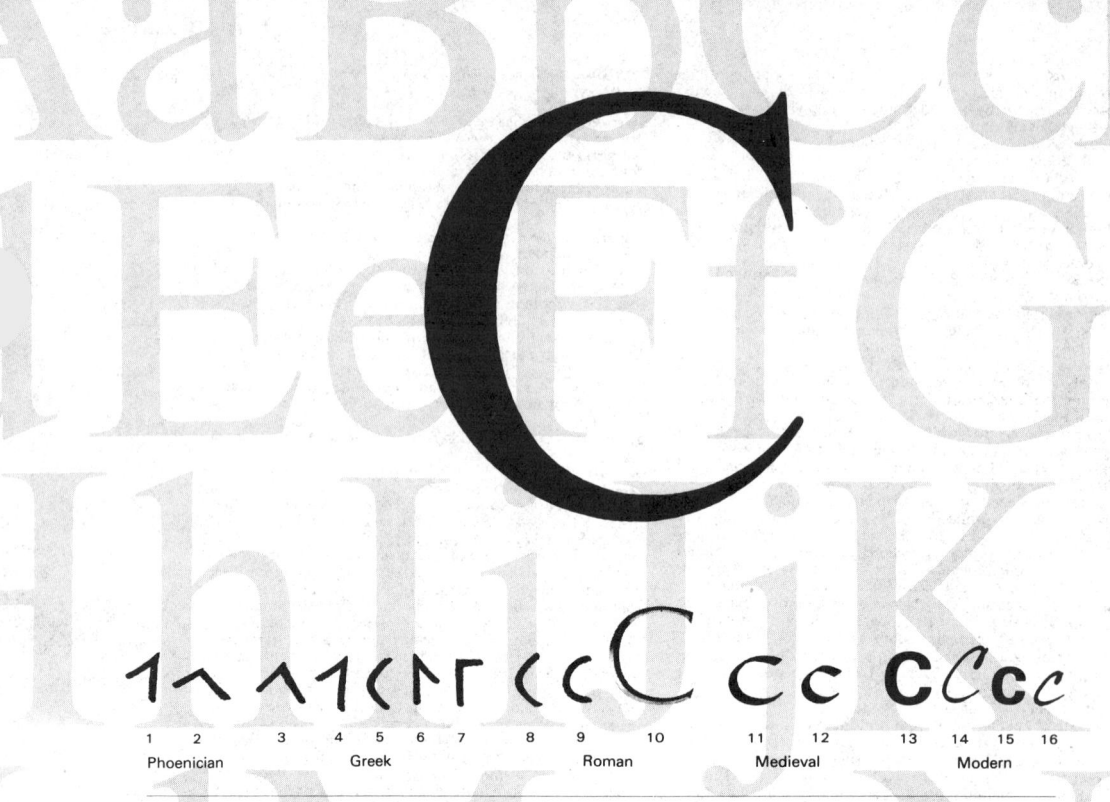

c

c or **C** (sē) *n., pl.* **c's** or **C's. 1.** The third letter of the modern English alphabet. **2.** Any of the speech sounds represented by the letter *c.* **3. C** The Roman numeral for 100 (Latin *centum*). **4.** The third in a series. **5. C** The third highest in quality or rank: *a mark of C on a term paper.* **6. C** *Mus.* **a.** The first tone in the scale of C major. **b.** The third tone in the relative minor scale. **c.** The key or a scale in which C is the tonic. **d.** A written or printed note representing this tone.

C The symbol for the element carbon.

Ca The symbol for the element calcium.

cab¹ (kăb) *n.* **1.** A taxicab. **2.** A one-horse vehicle for public hire. **3.** The covered compartment of a heavy vehicle or machine, such as a truck or locomotive, in which the operator or driver sits. [Short for TAXICAB.]

cab² (kăb) *n.* A Hebrew measure equal to about two quarts. [Heb. *qabh.*]

ca·bal (kə-băl′) *n.* **1.** A conspiratorial group of plotters or intriguers: *a cabal of political manipulators.* **2.** A secret scheme or plot. *—intr.v.* **-balled, -bal·ling, -bals.** To form a cabal. [Fr. *cabale* < Med. Lat. *cabala.* —see CABALA.]

cab·a·la or **cab·ba·la** (kăb′ə-lə, kə-bä′-) *n.* **1.** Often **Cabala.** An occult theosophy of rabbinical origin, widely transmitted in medieval Europe, based on an esoteric interpretation of the Hebrew Scriptures. **2.** A secret doctrine resembling the Cabala. [Med. Lat. < Heb. *qabbālāh,* received doctrine < *qābal,* he received.] **—cab′a·lism** *n.* **—cab′a·list** *n.*

cab·a·lis·tic (kăb′ə-lĭs′tĭk) *adj.* **1.** Of or relating to the Cabala. **2.** Having secret or hidden meaning; occult: *cabalistic symbols engraved in stone.* **—cab′a·lis′ti·cal·ly** *adv.*

cab·al·le·ro (kăb′ə-lâr′ō, -əl-yâr′ō) *n., pl.* **-ros. 1.** A Spanish gentleman; cavalier. **2.** *Southwestern U.S.* One who is skilled in riding and managing horses. [Sp. < LLat. *caballarius,* horse groom < Lat. *caballus,* horse.]

ca·ban·a also **ca·ba·ña** (kə-băn′ə, -băn′yə) *n.* A shelter on a beach or at a swimming pool used as a bathhouse. [Sp. *cabaña* < LLat. *capanna,* hut.]

cab·a·ret (kăb′ə-rā′) *n.* **1.** A restaurant or nightclub providing short programs of live entertainment. **2.** The floor show billed by a cabaret. [Fr. < ONFr., liquor store, perh. < LLat. *camera,* room. —see CHAMBER.]

cab·bage (kăb′ĭj) *n.* **1.** An edible plant, *Brassica oleracea capitata,* grown in temperate climates throughout the world and having a short, thick stalk and a large head formed by tightly overlapping green or reddish leaves. **2.** An edible leaf bud of the cabbage palm. **3.** *Slang.* Money, esp. in the form of bills. *—intr.v.* **-baged, -bag·ing, -bag·es.** To form or grow in a head, as cabbage does. [ME *caboche* < OFr. *caboce,* head.]

cabbage butterfly *n.* Any of several white butterflies of the genus *Pieris,* having larvae that feed on cabbage.

cabbage palm *n.* A tropical American palm tree, *Roystonea oleracea,* having leaf buds that are edible when young.

cabbage palmetto *n.* A palmetto.

cabbage rose *n.* A prickly shrub, *Rosa centifolia,* native to the Caucasus, having large, fragrant, many-petaled pink flowers.

cab·bage·worm (kăb′ĭj-wûrm′) *n.* Any of several caterpillars that feed on and are destructive to cabbage, esp. the bright-green larva of the cabbage butterfly.

cabbage yellow *n.* A disease of cabbage marked by the yellowing of leaves and caused by the fungus *Fusarium conglutinans.*

cab·ba·la (kăb′ə-lə, kə-bä′-) *n.* Variant of **cabala.**

cab·by (kăb′ē) *n., pl.* **-bies.** *Informal.* A cab driver.

ca·ber (kā′bər, kä′-) *n.* A heavy wooden pole heaved as a demonstration of strength in a Scottish sporting contest. [Sc. Gael. *cabar.*]

cab·er·net (kăb′ər-nā′) *n.* A dry red wine made from the grape variety *Cabernet sauvignon.* [Fr.]

cab·e·zon (kăb′ĭ-zŏn′) *n.* A large, edible fish, *Scorpaenichthys marmoratus,* of North American Pacific coastal waters. [Sp. *cabezón,* aug. of *cabeza,* head < VLat. **capitia* < Lat. *caput,* head.]

cab·in (kăb′ĭn) *n.* **1.** A small, roughly built house; cottage. **2. a.** A room in a ship used as living quarters by an officer or passenger. **b.** An enclosed compartment in a boat serving as a shelter or as living quarters. **c.** The enclosed space in an airplane for the crew, passengers, or cargo. *—tr. & intr.v.* **-ined, -in·ing, -ins.** To confine or live in a cabin or a small area. [ME *caban* < OFr. *cabane* < LLat. *capanna.*]

cabin boy *n.* A male servant aboard a ship.

cabin class *n.* A class of accommodations on some passenger ships, lower than first class and higher than tourist class.

cabin cruiser *n.* A powerboat with a cabin.

cab·i·net (kăb′ə-nĭt) *n.* **1.** An upright, cupboardlike repository with shelves, drawers, or compartments for the safekeeping or display of a collection of objects or materials. **2.** *Archaic.* A small or private room set aside for some specific activity. **3.** Often **Cabinet.** A body of persons appointed by a chief of state or a prime minister to head the executive departments of the government and to act as his official advisers. **—*modifier:*** *a cabinet minister; teak and other heavy cabinet woods.* [OFr., small room, dim. of ONFr. *cabine,* gambling house.]

cab·i·net·mak·er (kăb′ə-nĭt-mā′kər) *n.* A craftsman specializing in making fine articles of wooden furniture. **—cab′i·net·mak′ing** *n.*

cab·i·net·ry (kăb′ĭ-nĭ-trē) *n.* Cabinetwork: *finely detailed cabinetry.*

cab·i·net·work (kăb′ə-nĭt-wûrk′) *n.* Finished woodwork made by a cabinetmaker.

cabin fever *n.* Uneasiness or distress resulting from a lack of environmental stimulation, as when living in a remote, sparsely populated region or a small enclosed space.

ca·ble (kā′bəl) *n.* **1. a.** A strong, large-diameter heavy steel or fiber rope. **b.** Something that resembles a cable. **2.** *Elect.* A bound or sheathed group of mutually insulated conductors. **3. a.** *Naut.* A heavy rope or chain for mooring or anchoring a ship. **b.** A unit of nautical length equal to 720 feet in the United States and 608 feet in England. **4.** A cablegram. **5.** Cable television. *—v.* **-bled, -bling, -bles.** *—tr.* **1. a.** To send a cablegram to. **b.** To transmit (a message) by telegraph. **2.** To supply or fasten with a cable or cables. *—intr.* To send a cablegram. [ME < Norman Fr. < LLat. *capulum,* lasso < Lat. *capere,* to seize.]

cable car *n.* A car designed to operate on a cableway or cable railway.

ca·ble·cast (kā′bəl-kăst′) *n.* A telecast by cable television. **—ca′ble′cast′** *v.* **(-cast·ed, -cast·ing, -casts). —ca′ble·cast′er** *n.*

ca·ble·gram (kā′bəl-grăm′) *n.* A telegram sent by submarine cable.

ca·ble-laid (kā′bəl-lād′) *adj.* Made of three ropes of three strands each, twisted together counterclockwise.

cable railway *n.* A railroad on which the cars are moved by an endless cable driven by a stationary engine.

cable stitch *n.* A stitch in knitting that produces a twisted rope design.

ca·blet (kā′blĭt) *n.* A cable-laid rope with a circumference of less than ten inches.

cable television also **cable TV** *n.* A television distribution system in which station signals, picked up by elevated antennas, are delivered by cable to receivers of subscribers.

ca·ble·vi·sion (kā′bəl-vĭzh′ən) *n.* Cable television.

ca·ble·way (kā′bəl-wā′) *n.* A suspended cable used as a track for a cable car or similar vehicle.

cab·man (kăb′mən) *n.* The driver of a cab.

cab·o·chon (kăb′ə-shŏn′) *n.* **1.** A highly polished, convex-cut, unfaceted gem. **2.** The cabochon style of cutting. *—adv.* In the style of cabochon: *a sapphire cut cabochon.* [OFr., aug. of *caboche,* head.]

ca·boo·dle (kə-bōōd′l) *n.* *Informal.* The lot, group, or bunch: *donated the whole caboodle.* [Perh. alteration of *kit and boodle.*]

ca·boose (kə-bōōs′) *n.* **1.** The last car on a freight train, having kitchen and sleeping facilities for the train crew. **2.** *Obs.* **a.** A ship's galley. **b.** Any of various cast-iron cooking ranges used in such galleys during the early 19th century. **c.** An outdoor oven or fireplace. [Perh. < Du. *kabuis.*]

cab·o·tage (kăb′ə-täzh′) *n.* Trade or navigation in coastal waters. [Fr. < *caboter,* to coast.]

Cab·ot's ring (kăb′əts) *n.* Ringlike inclusions in the red blood cells sometimes found in cases of severe anemia. [After Richard C. *Cabot* (1868–1939).]

ca·bret·ta (kə-brĕt′ə) *n.* A soft, kidlike leather made from sheepskin having coarse, hairlike wool. [Sp. and Port. *cabra,* goat (< Lat. *capra,* she-goat) + Sp. *-etta,* -ette.]

ca·bril·la (kə-brē′yə, -brĭl′ə) *n.* Any of various sea basses, esp. *Epinephelus guttatus,* of tropical waters. [Sp., dim. of *cabra,* goat < Lat. *capra,* she-goat.]

cab·ri·ole (kăb′rē-ōl′) *n.* A form of furniture leg, characteristic of Queen Anne and Chippendale furniture, that curves outward and then narrows downward into an ornamental foot. [Fr., caper (from its resemblance to the foreleg of a capering animal). —see CABRIOLET.]

cab·ri·o·let (kăb′rē-ə-lā′) *n.* **1.** A two-wheeled, one-horse carriage with two seats and a folding top. **2.** An automobile with a folding top; a convertible coupe. [Fr., dim. of *cabriole,* caper < OFr. < OItal. *capriola* < *capriolo,* roebuck < Lat. *capreolus,* wild goat < *caper,* he-goat.]

cab·stand (kăb′stănd′) *n.* A place designated for taxicabs waiting for hire.

ca·ca·o (kə-kä′ō, -kā′ō) *n., pl.* **-os. 1.** An evergreen tropical American tree, *Theobroma cacao,* having yellowish flowers and reddish-brown seed pods. **2.** The seed of the cacao tree, used in making chocolate, cocoa, and cocoa butter. [Sp. < Nahuatl *cacahuatl,* cacao beans.]

cacao bean *n.* The seed of the cacao tree.

cacao butter *n.* Cocoa butter.

cach·a·lot (kăsh′ə-lŏt′, -ə-lō′) *n.* The sperm whale. [Fr.]

cache (kăsh) *n.* **1.** A hole or similar hiding place used for storing provisions and other necessities. **2.** A place for concealment and safekeeping, as of valuables. **3.** A store of goods hidden in a cache. **4.** *Computer Sci.* A fast storage buffer in the central processing unit of a computer. *—tr.v.* **cached, cach·ing, cach·es.** To store or hide in a cache. [Fr. < *cacher,* to hide < OFr. < VLat. **coactiare* < Lat. *coactare,* to constrain, freq. of *cogere,* to drive together. —see COGENT.]

ca·chec·tic (kə-kĕk′tĭk) *adj.* Pertaining to or characterized

cabin
Log cabin

cable car

cable stitch

cabriole
On a Chippendale lowboy

by cachexia. [Fr. *cachectique* < Lat. *cachecticus* < Gk. *kakhektikos* < *kakhexia,* bad condition of the body. —see CACHEXIA.]

cache·pot (kăsh′pŏt′, -pō′) *n.* An ornamental container for a flowerpot. [Fr. : *cacher,* to hide + *pot,* pot.]

ca·chet (kă-shā′) *n.* **1.** A seal on a letter or document. **2.** A mark or quality, as of distinction, individuality, or authenticity: *a profession with a cachet of glamour and prestige.* **3. a.** A commemorative design stamped on an envelope to mark some postal or philatelic event. **b.** A motto forming part of a postal cancellation. **4.** A kind of wafer capsule formerly used by pharmacists for presenting an unpleasant-tasting drug. [OFr. < *cacher,* to hide. —see CACHE.]

ca·chex·i·a (kə-kĕk′sē-ə) *n.* A general wasting of the body during a chronic disease. [LLat. < Gk. *kakhexia* : *kakos,* bad + *hexis,* condition < *ekhein,* to have.]

cach·in·nate (kăk′ə-nāt′) *intr.v.* **-nat·ed, -nat·ing, -nates.** To laugh loud, hard, or convulsively; guffaw. [Lat. *cachinnare, cachinnat-.*] **—cach′in·na′tion** *n.*

cacomistle
Bassariscus astutus

ca·chou (kă-shōō′, kăsh′ōō) *n.* **1.** Catechu. **2.** A pastille used to sweeten the breath. [Fr. < Port. *cachu* < Malayalam *kāccu.*]

ca·chu·cha (kə-chōō′chə) *n.* An Andalusian solo dance in 3/4 time. [Sp.]

ca·cique (kə-sēk′) *n.* **1.** An Indian chief, esp. in the Spanish West Indies and other parts of Latin America during colonial and postcolonial times. **2.** A local political boss in Spain or Latin America. **3.** Any of various tropical orioles. [Sp., of Arawakan orig.]

cack·le (kăk′əl) *v.* **-led, -ling, -les.** *—intr.* **1.** To make the shrill cry characteristic of a hen after laying an egg. **2.** To laugh or talk in a manner similar to a hen's cackle. *—tr.* To utter in cackles. *—n.* **1.** The act or sound of cackling. **2.** Shrill, brittle laughter. **3.** Foolish chatter. [ME *cakelen.*] **—cack′ler** *n.*

caco– *pref.* Bad: *cacography.* [Gk. *kako-* < *kakos,* bad.]

cac·o·dyl (kăk′ə-dĭl′) *n.* **1.** The arsenic group $As(CH_3)_2$. **2.** A poisonous oil, $As_2(CH_3)_4$, with an obnoxious garlicky odor. [Gk. *kakōdēs,* bad-smelling (*kakos,* bad + *ozein,* to smell) + -YL.] **—cac′o·dyl′ic** *adj.*

cac·o·ë·thes (kăk′ō-ē′thēz) *n.* A mania or irresistible compulsion; a pernicious habit. [Lat. *cacoethus* < Gk. *kakoēthes* : *kakos,* bad + *ēthos,* disposition.]

cac·o·gen·ics (kăk′ə-jĕn′ĭks) *n.* (*used with a sing. verb*). Dysgenics. **—cac′o·gen′ic** *adj.*

ca·cog·ra·phy (kə-kŏg′rə-fē) *n.* **1.** Bad handwriting as opposed to calligraphy. **2.** Bad spelling as opposed to orthography.

cac·o·mis·tle (kăk′ə-mĭs′əl) *n.* Either of two small, carnivorous mammals, *Bassariscus astutus* of the southwestern United States or *Jentinkia sumichrasti* of Central America, having grayish or brownish fur and a black-banded tail. [Mex. Sp. < Nahuatl *tlacomiztli* : *tlaco,* half + *miztli,* mountain lion.]

cactus

ca·coph·o·nous (kə-kŏf′ə-nəs) *adj.* Having a harsh, unpleasant sound; discordant. [Gk. *kakophōnos* : *kakos,* bad + *phōnē,* sound.] **—ca·coph′o·nous·ly** *adv.*

ca·coph·o·ny (kə-kŏf′ə-nē) *n., pl.* **-nies. 1.** Jarring, discordant sound; dissonance. **2.** Harsh or unharmonious use of language as opposed to euphony. [Fr. *cacophonie* < Gk. *kakophonia* < *kakophōnos,* cacophonous.]

cac·tus (kăk′təs) *n., pl.* **-ti** (-tī′) or **-tus·es.** Any of a large group of plants of the family Cactaceae, mostly native to arid regions of the New World and characterized by thick, fleshy, often prickly stems that function as leaves and in some species having showy flowers and edible fruit. [NLat. *Cactus,* type genus < Lat., cardoon < Gk. *kaktos.*]

caddis fly

ca·cu·mi·nal (kə-kyōō′mə-nəl) *adj.* Articulated with the tip of the tongue turned back and up toward the roof of the mouth; retroflex. [< Lat. *cacumen,* summit.]

cad (kăd) *n.* An ungentlemanly man. [Short for CADDIE.] **—cad′dish** *adj.* **—cad′dish·ly** *adv.* **—cad′dish·ness** *n.*

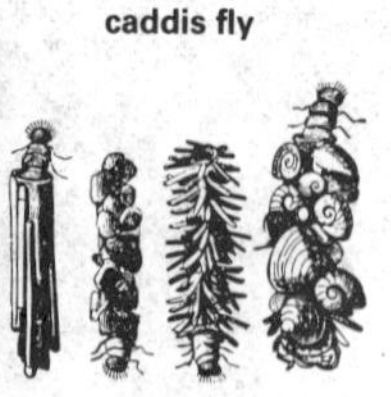

caddis worm
Larva cases of caddis worms

ca·das·ter also **ca·das·tre** (kə-dăs′tər) *n.* A public record, survey, or map of the value, extent, and ownership of land as a basis of taxation. [Fr. < Ital. *cadastro,* var. of OItal. *catastico* < LGk. *katastikhon,* register : *kata-,* by + *stikhos,* line.] **—ca·das′tral** *adj.*

ca·dav·er (kə-dăv′ər) *n.* A dead body, esp. one intended for dissection. [Lat. < *cadere,* to die.] **—ca·dav′er·ic** (-ə-rĭk) *adj.*

ca·dav·er·ine (kə-dăv′ə-rēn′) *n.* A syrupy, colorless fuming ptomaine, $NH_2(CH_2)_5NH_2$, formed by the carboxylation of lysine in decaying animal flesh.

ca·dav·er·ous (kə-dăv′ər-əs) *adj.* **1.** Suggestive of death; corpselike. **2. a.** Of corpselike pallor; pallid: *"I saw a cadaverous face appear at a small window"* (Dickens). **b.** Emaciated; gaunt: *a cadaverous dog picking through the trash.* **—ca·dav′er·ous·ly** *adv.* **—ca·dav′er·ous·ness** *n.*

caduceus

cad·dice (kăd′ĭs) *n.* Variant of **caddis.**

caddice fly *n.* Variant of **caddis fly.**

caddice worm *n.* Variant of **caddis worm.**

cad·die also **cad·dy** (kăd′ē) *—n., pl.* **-dies. 1.** One hired to serve as an attendant to a golfer, esp. by carrying his clubs. **2.** *Scot.* A boy who does odd jobs. *—intr.v.* **-died, -dy·ing, -dies.** To serve as a caddie. [French *cadet,* caddie, cadet.]

cad·dis also **cad·dice** (kăd′ĭs) *n.* A coarse woolen fabric, yarn, or ribbon binding. [ME *cadace* < AN *cadaz* < OProv. *cadarz.*]

caddis fly also **caddice fly** *n.* Any of various four-winged insects of the order Trichoptera, found near lakes and streams. [< obs. *cad,* var. of COD² (from the tube in which the larva lives).]

caddis worm also **caddice worm** *n.* The aquatic, wormlike larva of the caddis fly, enclosed in a cylindrical case covered with grains of sand, fragments of shell, and other debris.

Cad·do (kăd′ō) *n., pl.* **Caddo** or **-dos.** A member of a North American Indian confederacy of Caddoan linguistic stock, formerly living in Arkansas, Louisiana, and eastern Texas. [Prob. < Caddoan *Kädohädächo.*]

Cad·do·an (kăd′ō-ən) *n.* A family of North American Indian languages formerly spoken in the Dakotas, Nebraska, Kansas, Oklahoma, Arkansas, Texas, and Louisiana.

cad·dy¹ (kăd′ē) *n., pl.* **-dies.** A small box or other container, esp. one for holding tea. [Malay *kati,* catty.]

cad·dy² (kăd′ē) *n.* & *v.* Variant of **caddie.**

cade¹ (kād) *adj.* Left by its mother and reared by hand: *a cade calf.* [ME.]

cade² (kād) *n.* A shrub, *Juniperus oxycedrus,* of the Mediterranean region, whose wood yields an oily brown liquid used to treat skin ailments. [Fr. < OProv. < Med. Lat. *catanus.*]

–cade *suff.* Procession: *motorcade.* [< CAVALCADE.]

ca·delle (kə-dĕl′) *n.* A small blackish beetle, *Tenebroides mauritanicus,* both the larval and adult forms of which damage stored grain and packaged foods. [Fr. < Prov. *cadello* < Lat. *catella,* fem. of *catellus,* puppy < *catulus,* the young of animals.]

ca·dence (kād′ns) also **ca·den·cy** (kād′n-sē) *n., pl.* **-denc·es** also **-den·cies. 1.** Balanced, rhythmic flow, as of poetry or oratory. **2.** The measure or beat of movement, as in dancing or marching. **3. a.** A falling inflection of the voice, as at the end of a sentence. **b.** The general inflection or modulation of the voice. **4.** *Mus.* A progression of chords moving to a harmonic close or point of rest. [ME < OFr. < OItal. *cadenza* < *cadere,* to fall < Lat.] **—ca′denced** *adj.*

ca·dent (kād′nt) *adj.* **1.** Having cadence or rhythm. **2.** *Archaic.* Falling: *cadent tears.* [Lat. *cadens, cadent-,* pr. part. of *cadere,* to fall.]

ca·den·za (kə-dĕn′zə) *n.* **1.** An elaborate ornamental melodic flourish interpolated into an aria or other vocal piece. **2.** An extended virtuosic section for the soloist near the end of a movement of a concerto. [Ital. < OItal., cadence.]

ca·det (kə-dĕt′) *n.* **1.** A student at a military school. **2.** A younger son or brother. **3.** *Slang.* A pimp. [Fr. < dial *capdet,* captain < LLat. *capitellum,* dim. of Lat. *caput,* head.] **—ca·det′ship′** *n.*

cadge (kăj) *intr & tr.v.* **cadged, cadg·ing, cadg·es.** *Informal.* To beg or get by begging. [Perh. back-formation < obs. *cadger,* peddler < ME *cadgear.*] **—cadg′er** *n.*

cad·mi·um (kăd′mē-əm) *n.* *Symbol* **Cd** A soft, bluish-white metallic element, occurring primarily in zinc, copper, and lead ores. It is easily cut with a knife and is used in low-friction, fatigue-resistant alloys, solders, dental amalgams, nickel-cadmium storage batteries, and in rustproof electroplating. Atomic number 48; atomic weight 112.40; melting point 320.9°C; boiling point 765°C; specific gravity 8.65; valence 2. [NLat. < Lat. *cadmia,* calamine (from its being found with calamine in zinc ore).] **—cad′mic** (-mĭk) *adj.*

cadmium sulfate *n.* A compound, $CdSO_4$, that forms colorless crystals and is used as an antiseptic.

Cad·mus (kăd′məs) *n.* *Gk. Myth.* A Phoenician prince who killed a dragon and sowed its teeth, from which sprang up an army of men who fought one another until only five survived and with these five Cadmus founded the city of Thebes. [Lat. < Gk. *Kadmos.*]

cad·re (kăd′rē) *n.* **1.** A framework. **2.** A nucleus of trained personnel around which a larger organization can be built and trained: *a basic training cadre of sergeants and corporals.* [Fr. < Ital. *quadra* < Lat. *quadrum,* a square.]

ca·du·ce·us (kə-dōō′sē-əs, -shəs, -dyōō′-) *n., pl.* **-ce·i** (-sē-ī′). **1. a.** A herald's wand or staff, esp. in ancient times. **b.** *Myth.* A winged staff with two serpents twined around it, carried by Hermes. **2.** An insignia modeled on a caduceus and used as the symbol of the medical profession. [Lat. *caduceus,* alteration of Gk. *karukeion* < *karux,* herald.] **—ca·du′ce·an** (-sē-ən, -shən) *adj.*

ca·du·ci·corn (kə-dōō′sĭ-kôrn, -dyōō′-) *adj.* Having horns that are shed annually, as certain deer. [Lat. *caducus,* falling (< *cadere,* to fall) + *cornu,* horn.]

ca·du·ci·ty (kə-dōō′sĭ-tē, -dyōō′-) *n.* **1.** The frailty of old age; senility. **2.** The quality or state of being perishable; impermanence. [Fr. *caducité* < *caduc,* frail < Lat. *caducus.* —see CADUCOUS.]

ca·du·cous (kə-dōō′kəs, -dyōō′-) *adj.* *Biol.* Dropping off or shedding at an early stage of development, as the gills of amphibians or the leaves of certain plants. [Lat. *caducus,* falling < *cadere,* to fall.]

cae·cil·ian (sə-sĭl′yən, -sĭl′ē-ən, -sēl′-) *n.* Any of various legless, burrowing, wormlike amphibians of the order Gymnophiona, of tropical regions. [< Lat. *caecilia,* a kind of lizard < *caecus,* blind (from its small eyes).]

cae·cum (sē′kəm) *n.* Variant of **cecum.**

Cae·lum (sē′ləm) *n.* A constellation in the Southern Hemi-

sphere near Columba and Eridanus. [Lat. *caelum,* sculptor's chisel < *caedere,* to cut.]
caer·phil·ly (kär-fĭl'ē) *n.* A mild white cheese originating in Wales. [After *Caerphilly,* a district in Wales.]
Cae·sar (sē'zər) *n.* **1.** A surname of the early Roman emperors that after Hadrian became the title of the junior imperial colleague of the Augustus. **2.** Often **caesar.** A dictator or autocrat. [Lat., after Gaius Julius *Caesar* (100–44 B.C.).]
Cae·sar·e·an also **Cae·sar·i·an** or **Ce·sar·e·an** or **Ce·sar·i·an** (sĭ-zâr'ē-ən) *n.* A Caesarean section.
Caesarean section also **caesarean section** *n.* A surgical incision through the abdominal wall and uterus, performed to extract a fetus. [From the belief that Julius *Caesar* (100–44 B.C.) was delivered by this operation.]
Cae·sar·ism (sē'zə-rĭz'əm) *n.* Military or imperial dictatorship; political authoritarianism. **—Cae'sar·ist** *n.* **—Cae'sar·is'tic** *adj.*
caesar salad *n.* A tossed green salad of anchovies, croutons, and grated cheese with a dressing of olive oil, lemon juice, and a raw or coddled egg. [After *Caesar's,* a restaurant in Tijuana, Mexico.]
cae·si·um (sē'zē-əm) *n.* Variant of **cesium.**
caes·pi·tose (sĕs'pĭt-ōs') *adj.* Variant of **cespitose.**
caes·tus (sĕs'təs) *n.* Variant of **cestus²**.
cae·su·ra also **ce·su·ra** (sĭ-zhŏŏr'ə, -zŏŏr'ə) *n., pl.* **-su·ras** or **-su·rae** (-zhŏŏr'ē, -zŏŏr'ē). **1.** A pause in a line of verse dictated by sense or natural speech rhythm rather than by metrics. **2.** In Latin and Greek prosody, a break in a line caused by the ending of a word within a foot, esp. when this coincides with a sense division. **3.** *Mus.* A pause or breathing at a point of rhythmic division in a melody. [Lat. < *caedere,* to cut off.] **—cae·su'ral, cae·su'ric** *adj.*
ca·fé also **ca·fe** (kă-fā', kə-) *n.* A coffee house, restaurant, or bar. [Fr., café, coffee < Turk. *kahve.* —see COFFEE.]
ca·fé au lait (kă-fā' ō lā') *n.* **1.** Coffee served with hot milk. **2.** A light coffee color. [Fr., coffee with milk.]
café fil·tre (fĭl'trə) *n.* Coffee made by passing hot water through ground coffee and a filtering device underneath. [Fr., filter coffee.]
café noir (nwär') *n.* Coffee served without cream or milk. [Fr., black coffee.]
caf·e·te·ri·a (kăf'ĭ-tîr'ē-ə) *n.* A restaurant in which the customers are served at a counter and carry their meals on trays to tables. [Sp. *cafetería,* coffee shop < *café,* coffee < Turk. *kahve.* —see COFFEE.]
caf·feine also **caf·fein** (kă-fēn', kăf'ēn', kăf'ē-ĭn) *n.* A bitter white alkaloid, $C_8H_{10}N_4O_2 \cdot H_2O$, found in coffee, tea, and kola nuts and used as a stimulant and diuretic. [G. *Kaffein* < *Kaffee,* coffee < Fr. *café.* —see CAFÉ.]
caf·tan (kăf'tăn', kăf-tăn') *n.* A full-length tunic with long sleeves and a sash at the waist that is a characteristic garment of the Near East. [R. *kaftan* < Turk.]
cage (kāj) *n.* **1.** A structure for confining birds or animals, enclosed on at least one side by a grating of wires or bars in order to let in air and light. **2. a.** An enclosure that serves as a means of confining prisoners. **b.** Something resembling a cage in purpose or design. **3.** A framework having a cagelike appearance or construction. **4.** An elevator car. **5.** *Baseball.* **a.** A backstop used for batting practices. **b.** A catcher's mask. **6.** *Sports.* **a.** The basket in basketball. **b.** In hockey, the goal, made of a network frame. *—tr.v.* **caged, cag·ing, cag·es.** To put in a cage; lock up or confine. [ME < OFr. < Lat. *cavea* < *cavus,* hollow.]
cage·ling (kāj'lĭng) *n.* A bird kept in a cage as a pet.
cag·ey also **ca·gy** (kā'jē) *adj.* **-i·er, -i·est. 1.** Wary; careful. **2.** Crafty; shrewd. [Orig. unknown.] **—cag'i·ly** *adv.* **—cag'i·ness** *n.*
ca·hier (kä-yā') *n.* **1.** A number of pages gathered together, as in a loose-leaf binder; notebook. **2.** A report, as of the proceedings at a meeting. [Fr. < OFr. *caier* < Lat. *quaterni,* group of four < *quattuor,* four.]
ca·hoots (kə-hŏŏts') *pl.n. Informal.* Collaboration of a questionable nature: *in cahoots with a dishonest lawyer.* [Perh. < Fr. *cahute,* cabin < OFr.]
Ca·hui·lla (kə-wē'ə) *n., pl.* **Cahuilla** or **-llas.** A Shoshonean language of Southeastern California. [Sp., of Am. Indian orig.]
cai·man also **cay·man** (kā'mən, kā-măn', kī-) *n., pl.* **-mans.** Any of various tropical American crocodilians of the genus *Caiman* and related genera, resembling and closely related to the alligators. [Sp. *caimán* < Carib *acayuman.*]
Cain (kān) *n.* **1.** In the Old Testament, the eldest son of Adam and Eve, who killed his brother Abel out of jealousy. **2.** A murderer. **—*idiom.* raise Cain.** *Slang.* To create a great disturbance or uproar; make trouble. [Lat. < Gk. *Kain* < Heb. *Qayin.*]
-caine *suff.* A synthetic alkaloid anesthetic: *eucaine.* [< COCAINE.]
cai·no·to·pho·bi·a (kā-nō'tə-fō'bē-ə) *n.* An abnormal fear of newness. [Gk. *kainotēs,* newness + PHOBIA.]
ca·ïque (kä-ēk') *n.* **1.** A long, narrow rowboat used in the Middle East. **2.** A small sailing vessel used in the eastern Mediterranean. [Fr. < Ital. *caicco* < Turk. *kayiuk.*]
caird (kârd) *n. Scot.* An itinerant tinker or handyman. [Sc. Gael. *ceard,* craftsman < OIr. *cerd,* artist.]
cairn (kârn) *n.* A mound of stones erected as a landmark or memorial. [ME *carne* < Sc. Gael. *carn.*] **—cairned** (kârnd) *adj.*
cairn·gorm (kârn'gôrm') *n.* A smoky-brown or yellow variety of quartz, used as a semiprecious gem. [After the *Cairngorm* Mountains, Scotland.]
Cairn terrier *n.* A small dog of a breed developed in Scotland, having a broad head and a rough, shaggy coat. [So called because it hunts among cairns.]
cais·son (kā'sŏn', -sən) *n.* **1.** A watertight structure within which construction work is carried on under water. **2.** A camel (sense 2). **3.** A floating structure used to close off the entrance to a dock or canal lock. **4.** A large box open at the top and one side, designed to fit against the side of a ship and used to repair damaged hulls under water. **5. a.** A large box used to hold ammunition. **b.** A horse-drawn vehicle, usually two-wheeled, formerly used to carry ammunition. [Fr., aug. of *caisse,* box < OProv. *caisa* < Lat. *capsa* < *capere,* to hold.]
caisson disease *n.* A disorder, esp. in divers and caisson and tunnel workers, caused by the release of nitrogen bubbles in the tissues and blood upon too rapid a return from high pressure to atmospheric pressure, characterized by pains in the joints, cramps, paralysis, and eventual death unless treated by gradual decompression.
cai·tiff (kā'tĭf) *n.* A despicable coward; wretch. *—adj.* Despicable and cowardly. [ME *caitif* < Norman Fr. < Lat. *captivus,* prisoner. —see CAPTIVE.]
Ca·jan (kā'jən) *n.* Variant of **Cajun.**
ca·jole (kə-jōl') *tr.v.* **-joled, -jol·ing, -joles.** To coax gently and persistently; wheedle. [Fr. *cajoler.*] **—ca·jol'er** *n.* **—ca·jol'er·y** (-jō'lə-rē) *n.* **—ca·jol'ing·ly** *adv.*
Ca·jun also **Ca·jan** (kā'jən) *n.* A native of Louisiana believed to be descended from the French exiles from Acadia. [Alteration of ACADIAN.]
cake (kāk) *n.* **1.** A sweet baked mixture of flour, liquid, eggs, and other ingredients in loaf or rounded layer form. **2.** A flat, thin mass of dough or batter that is baked or fried, such as a pancake. **3.** A patty of fried food, such as a fishcake. **4.** A shaped or molded piece, as of soap or ice. *—tr. & intr.v.* **caked, cak·ing, cakes.** To form into a cake or compact mass. **—*idiom.* take the cake.** *Informal.* To win the prize; be outstanding. [ME < ON *kaka.*]
cake·walk (kāk'wôk') *n.* **1.** A promenade or walk, formerly executed as an entertainment by American blacks in which those performing the most complex and unusual steps won cakes as prizes. **2. a.** A strutting dance based on the cakewalk. **b.** The music for this dance. *—intr.v.* **-walked, -walk·ing, -walks.** To perform a cakewalk. **—cake'walk'er** *n.*
Cal·a·bar bean (kăl'ə-bär) *n.* The dark-brown, poisonous seed of a woody vine, *Physostigma venenosum,* of tropical Africa that is the source of the drug physostigmine [After *Calabar,* Nigeria.]
cal·a·bash (kăl'ə-băsh') *n.* **1.** A vine, *Lagenaria siceraria,* native to the Old World, bearing large, hard-shelled gourds. **2.** A tropical American tree, *Crescentia cujete,* bearing large, rounded fruit. **3.** The fruit of a calabash. **4.** A utensil, such as a dish or ladle, made from the fruit of a calabash. [Fr. *calabasse,* gourd < Sp. *calabaza.*]
cal·a·boose (kăl'ə-bōōs') *n. Regional.* A jail. [Louisiana Fr. *calabouse* < Sp. *calabozo,* dungeon.]
ca·la·di·um (kə-lā'dē-əm) *n.* Any of various tropical plants of the genus *Caladium,* widely cultivated as potted plants for their showy, variegated foliage. [NLat. *Caladium,* genus name < Malay *kĕladi,* an aroid.]
cal·a·man·co (kăl'ə-măng'kō) *n., pl.* **-coes.** A glossy woolen fabric with a checked pattern on one side. [Sp. *calamaco,* perh. < Lat. *calamancus,* felt cap.]
cal·a·man·der (kăl'ə-măn'dər) *n.* The hard, black-and-brown-striped wood of certain tropical Asiatic trees of the genus *Diospyros,* used for making furniture. [Prob. < Du. *kalamander.*]
cal·a·mi (kăl'ə-mī') *n.* Plural of **calamus.**
cal·a·mine (kăl'ə-mīn', -mĭn) *n.* **1.** A white or sometimes iron- or copper-stained mineral, essentially $Zn_4Si_2O_7(OH)_2 \cdot H_2O$. **2.** A pink, odorless, tasteless powder of zinc oxide with a small amount of ferric oxide, dissolved in mineral oils and used in skin lotions. [Fr. < Med. Lat. *calamina,* alteration of Lat. *cadmia* < Gk. *kadmeia* < *kadmeios,* Theban < *Kadmos,* Cadmus.]
cal·a·mint (kăl'ə-mĭnt') *n.* Any of several aromatic plants of the genus *Satureja,* esp. *S. calamintha,* native to Eurasia, having clusters of purplish or pink flowers. [ME *calaminte* < OFr. *calamente* < Med. Lat. *calamentum* < Lat. *calaminthe* < Gk. *kalaminthē.*]
cal·a·mite (kăl'ə-mīt') *n.* Any of various extinct treelike plants of the genus *Calamites,* resembling but much larger than the horsetails and known only as fossils. [NLat. *Calamites,* genus name < Lat. *calamus,* reed < Gk. *kalamos.*]
ca·lam·i·tous (kə-lăm'ĭ-təs) *adj.* Causing or involving calamity. **—ca·lam'i·tous·ly** *adv.* **—ca·lam'i·tous·ness** *n.*
ca·lam·i·ty (kə-lăm'ĭ-tē) *n., pl.* **-ties. 1.** An extraordinarily serious event marked by terrible loss, lasting distress, and affliction. **2.** A state of dire distress or misfortune. [ME *calamite* < OFr. < Lat. *calamitas.*]
cal·a·mon·din (kăl'ə-mŏn'dĭn) *n.* **1.** A citrus tree, *Citrus mitis,* of the Philippine Islands. **2.** The acid, globular fruit of

caïque

Cairn terrier

the calamondin, resembling a small orange. [Tagalog *kalamunding.*]

cal·a·mus (kăl'ə-məs) *n., pl.* **-mi** (-mī'). **1. a.** The sweet flag. **b.** The aromatic root of the sweet flag. **2.** Any of various tropical Asiatic palms of the genus *Calamus,* from some of which rattan is obtained. **3.** Quill (sense 1). [Lat., reed < Gk. *kalamos.*]

ca·lan·do (kə-län'dō) *Mus.* —*adj.* Gradually diminishing in tempo and volume. —*adv.* In a calando manner. [Ital. < *calare,* to let down < Lat. *chalare* < Gk. *khalan.*]

ca·lash (kə-lăsh') also **ca·lèche** (-lĕsh') *n.* **1. a.** A carriage with low wheels and a collapsible top. **b.** The top of such a carriage. **2.** A woman's folding bonnet of the late 18th century. [Fr. *calèche* < G. *Kalesche,* of Slavic orig.]

cal·a·thus (kăl'ə-thəs) *n., pl.* **-thi** (-thī'). A vase-shaped basket represented in Greek painting and sculpture. [Lat. < Gk. *kalathos.*]

calc– *pref.* Variant of **calci-**.

calash

cal·ca·ne·o·cu·boid ligament (kăl-kā'nē-ō-kyōō'boid') *n.* The ligament that connects the calcaneus and the cuboid bones.

cal·ca·ne·us (kăl-kā'nē-əs) also **cal·ca·ne·um** (-nē-əm) *n., pl.* **-ne·i** (-nē-ī') also **-ne·a** (-nē-ə). The quadrangular bone at the back of the tarsus. [LLat., heel < Lat. *calcaneum* < *calx.*] —**cal·ca'ne·al** *adj.*

cal·car¹ (kăl'kär') *n., pl.* **cal·car·i·a** (kăl-kâr'ē-ə). An anatomical spur or spurlike projection. [Lat., spur < *calx,* heel.]

cal·car² (kăl'kär') *n.* A furnace formerly used in glassmaking for preparing frit. [Ital. *calcara* < Lat. *calcaria* < *calx,* lime. —see CALX.]

cal·car·e·ous (kăl-kâr'ē-əs) *adj.* Composed of, containing, or characteristic of calcium carbonate, calcium, or limestone; chalky. [Lat. *calcarius* < *calx,* lime. —see CALX.]

cal·ca·rine fissure (kăl'kə-rīn') *n.* A calcarine sulcus.

cal·car·ine sul·cus (sŭl'kəs) *n.* A sulcus on the occipital lobe of the brain. [CALCAR¹ + -INE.]

cal·ce·i·form (kăl'sē-ə-fôrm') *adj. Bot.* Slipper-shaped; calceolate. [Lat. *calceus,* shoe + -FORM.]

cal·ce·o·lar·i·a (kăl'sē-ə-lâr'ē-ə) *n.* Any of various plants of the genus *Calceolaria,* native to tropical America and widely cultivated for their yellow, speckled, slipper-shaped flowers. [NLat. *Calceolaria,* genus name < Lat. *caleolus,* small shoe. —see CALCEOLATE.]

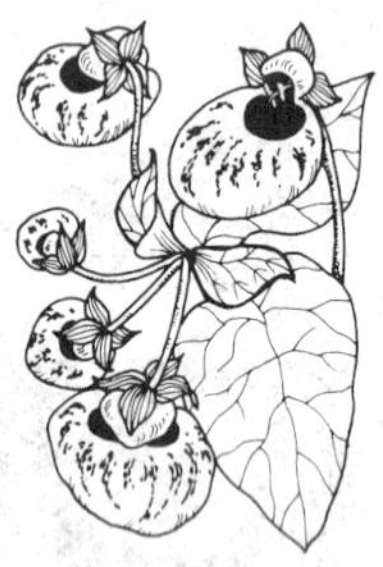
calceolaria

cal·ce·o·late (kăl'sē-ə-lāt') *adj.* Shaped like a slipper, as the blossoms of some orchids. [< Lat. *calceolus,* dim. of *calceus,* shoe.]

cal·ces (kăl'sēz) *n.* A plural of **calx**.

calci– or **calc–** *pref.* Calcium; calcium salt: *calciferous.* [< Lat. *calx, calc-,* lime < Gk. *khalix,* pebble.]

cal·cic (kăl'sĭk) *adj.* Composed of, containing, derived from, or pertaining to calcium or lime.

cal·ci·cole (kăl'sĭ-kōl') *n.* A plant that thrives in soil rich in lime. [CALCI- + Lat. *colere,* to inhabit.] —**cal·cic'o·lous** (-sĭk'ə-ləs) *adj.*

cal·ci·co·sis (kăl'sĭ-kō'sĭs) *n.* A pneumoconiosis resulting from the inhalation of calcium carbonate dust. [CALCI- + *-cosis* (as in *silicosis*).]

cal·cif·er·ol (kăl-sĭf'ə-rôl', -rōl') *n.* Vitamin D_2. [CALCIF(EROUS) + (ERGOST)EROL.]

cal·cif·er·ous (kăl-sĭf'ər-əs) *adj.* Of, forming, or containing calcium or calcium carbonate.

cal·cif·ic (kăl-sĭf'ĭk) *adj.* Producing salts of lime, as in the formation of eggshells in birds and reptiles.

cal·ci·fi·ca·tion (kăl'sə-fĭ-kā'shən) *n.* **1. a.** Impregnation with calcium or calcium salts, as with calcium carbonate. **b.** Hardening, as of tissue, by such impregnation. **2.** A calcified substance or part.

cal·ci·fuge (kăl'sə-fyōōj') *n.* A plant that does not thrive in lime-rich soil. —**cal·cif'u·gal** (-sĭf'yə-gəl), **cal·cif'u·gous** (-yə-gəs) *adj.*

cal·ci·fy (kăl'sə-fī') *tr. & intr.v.* **-fied, -fy·ing, -fies.** To make or become stony or chalky by deposition of calcium salts.

cal·ci·mine (kăl'sə-mīn') *n.* A white or tinted liquid containing zinc oxide, water, glue, and coloring matter, used as a wash for walls and ceilings. —*tr.v.* **-mined, -min·ing, -mines.** To cover or wash with calcimine. [Orig. unknown.]

cal·ci·na·tion (kăl'sə-nā'shən) *n.* **1.** The act or process of calcining. **2.** The state of being calcined.

cal·cine (kăl-sīn', kăl'sīn') *v.* **-cined, -cin·ing, -cines.** —*tr.* To heat (a substance) to a high temperature but below the melting or fusing point, causing loss of moisture, reduction, or oxidation. —*intr.* To undergo calcination. [ME *calcinen* < OFr. *calciner* < Med. Lat. *calcinare* < Lat. *calx,* lime. —see CALX.]

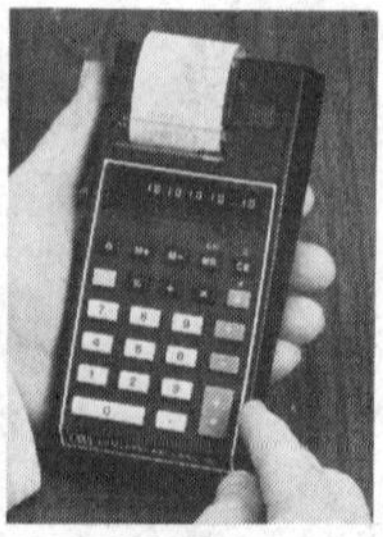
calculator

cal·ci·no·sis (kăl'sə-nō'sĭs) *n.* An abnormal condition in which calcium salts are deposited in a tissue of the body, as the skin. [CALCI- + -OSIS.]

cal·cite (kăl'sīt') *n.* A common crystalline form of natural calcium carbonate, the basic constituent of limestone, marble, and chalk. —**cal·cit'ic** (-sĭt'ĭk) *adj.*

cal·ci·to·nin (kăl'sĭ-tō'nĭn) *n.* A hormone that functions in calcium metabolism, produced by the thyroid gland. [CALCI- + TON(IC) + -IN.]

cal·ci·um (kăl'sē-əm) *n. Symbol* **Ca** A silvery, moderately hard metallic element, constituting approximately three per cent of the earth's crust, a basic component of bone, shells, and leaves. It occurs naturally in limestone, gypsum, and fluorite, and its compounds are used to make plaster, quicklime, Portland cement, and metallurgic and electronic materials. Atomic number 20; atomic weight 40.08; melting point 842 to 848°C; boiling point 1,487°C; specific gravity 1.55; valence 2. [NLat. < Lat. *calx,* lime. —see CALX.]

calcium carbide *n.* A grayish-black crystalline compound, CaC_2, obtained by heating pulverized limestone or quicklime with carbon and used to generate acetylene gas, as a dehydrating agent, and in the manufacture of graphite and hydrogen.

calcium carbonate *n.* A colorless or white crystalline compound, $CaCO_3$, occurring naturally as chalk, limestone, marble, and other forms and used in a wide variety of manufactured products including commercial chalk, medicines, and dentifrices.

calcium chloride *n.* A white deliquescent compound, $CaCl_2$, used chiefly as a drying agent, refrigerant, and preservative and for controlling dust and ice on roads.

calcium cyanamide *n.* A gray-black compound, $Ca(CN)_2$, used as a fertilizer and weed killer.

calcium fluoride *n.* A white powder, CaF_2, used in emery wheels, carbon electrodes, and cements.

calcium hydroxide *n.* A soft white powder, $Ca(OH)_2$, used in making mortar, cements, calcium salts, paints, hard rubber products, and petrochemicals.

calcium hypochlorite *n.* A white crystalline solid, $Ca(OCl)_2$, used as a bactericide, fungicide, and bleaching agent.

calcium light *n.* Limelight (sense 1.b.).

calcium oxide *n.* A white caustic lumpy powder, CaO, used as a refractory, as a flux, in manufacturing steel, glassmaking, waste treatment, insecticides, and as an industrial alkali.

calcium phosphate *n.* Any of several phosphate compounds, esp.: **a.** A white crystalline powder, $CaHPO_4$ or $CaHPO_4{\cdot}2H_2O$, used as a food, as a plastic stabilizer, and in glass. **b.** A colorless deliquescent powder, $CaH_4(PO_4)_2{\cdot}H_2O$, used in baking powders, as a plant food, plastic stabilizer, and in glass. **c.** A white amorphous powder, $Ca_3(PO_4)_2$, used in ceramics, rubber, fertilizers, plastic stabilizers, and as a food supplement.

calc·spar or **calc-spar** (kălk'spär') *n.* Calcite. [Partial transl. of Swed. *kalkspat* : *kalk,* lime < OSwed. < MLG < Lat. *calx,* lime. + *spat,* spar (mineral).]

calc-tu·fa (kălk'tōō'fə, -tyōō'fə) also **calc-tuff** (-tŭf') *n.* A porous or spongy deposit of calcium carbonate found in calcareous mineral springs. [CALC(AREOUS) + TUFA.]

cal·cu·la·ble (kăl'kyə-lə-bəl) *adj.* **1.** Capable of being calculated or estimated. **2.** Readily relied upon; dependable. —**cal'cu·la·bil'i·ty** *n.*

cal·cu·late (kăl'kyə-lāt') *v.* **-lat·ed, -lat·ing, -lates.** —*tr.* **1.** To ascertain by computation; reckon: *calculate the odds on winning.* **2.** To make an estimate of; evaluate. **3.** To fit for a purpose; make suitable for: *a car that is calculated to go 100 miles an hour.* **4.** *Regional.* **a.** To purpose; intend. **b.** To think; suppose. —*intr.* **1.** To execute a mathematical process. **2.** *Regional.* **a.** To suppose; guess. **b.** To count, depend, or rely on: *We're calculating on your help.* [Lat. *calculare, calculat-* < *calculus,* small stone used in reckoning, dim. of *calx,* small stone for gaming. —see CALX.]

Synonyms: *calculate, compute, reckon, estimate.* These verbs describe ways of getting more or less abstract results by mathematics. *Calculate,* the most comprehensive, can apply to all mathematical operations, simple or complex, but usually implies a relatively high level of abstraction or procedural complexity. *Compute* applies, in general, to essentially straightforward, though possibly lengthy, arithmetic operations. *Reckon* suggests simple arithmetic. *Estimate* implies rough approximation of a result without immediate need for exactness.

cal·cu·lat·ed (kăl'kyə-lā'tĭd) *adj.* **1.** Undertaken after careful estimation of the likely outcome: *a calculated risk.* **2.** Likely; apt: *a stratagem calculated to succeed.* **3.** Determined by mathematical calculation. —**cal'cu·lat'ed·ly** *adv.*

cal·cu·lat·ing (kăl'kyə-lā'tĭng) *adj.* **1.** Performing calculations: *a calculating machine.* **2. a.** Shrewd; crafty. **b.** Coldly scheming or conniving.

cal·cu·la·tion (kăl'kyə-lā'shən) *n.* **1.** The act, process, or result of calculating. **2.** An estimate based on probabilities. **3.** Deliberation; foresight. —**cal'cu·la'tive** *adj.*

cal·cu·la·tor (kăl'kyə-lā'tər) *n.* **1.** A person who performs calculations. **2.** A keyboard machine for the automatic performance of mathematical operations. **3.** A set of mathematical tables used to aid in calculating.

cal·cu·lous (kăl'kyə-ləs) *adj.* Pertaining to, caused by, or having a calculus or calculi.

cal·cu·lus (kăl'kyə-ləs) *n., pl.* **-li** (-lī') or **-lus·es.** **1.** *Pathol.* An abnormal concretion in the body, usually formed of mineral salts; a stone, as in the gall bladder, kidney, or urinary bladder. **2.** *Math.* **a.** A method of analysis or calculation using a special symbolic notation. **b.** The combined mathematics of differential and integral calculus. [Lat., small stone used in reckoning. —see CALCULATE.]

calculus of variations *n.* The mathematical analysis of the maxima and minima of definite integrals, the integrands of which are functions of independent variables, dependent variables, and the derivatives of one or more dependent variables.

cal·de·ra (kăl-dâr′ə, -dîr′ə, kôl-) *n.* A large crater formed by volcanic explosion or by collapse of a volcanic cone. [Sp., caldron < LLat. *caldaria.*]

cal·dron also **caul·dron** (kôl′drən) *n.* A large kettle or vat for boiling. [ME *caudroun* < Norman Fr. < LLat. *caldaria* < Lat. *caldarius,* suitable for warming < *calidus,* warm.]

ca·lèche (kə-lĕsh′) *n.* Variant of **calash.**

cal·en·dar (kăl′ən-dər) *n.* **1.** Any of various systems of reckoning time in which the beginning, length, and divisions of a year are arbitrarily defined or otherwise established. **2.** A table showing the months, weeks, and days in at least one specific year. **3.** A list or schedule, esp. one arranged in chronological order, as of cases on a court docket or bills to be considered by a legislature. **4.** *Obs.* A guide; example. —*tr.v.* **-dared, -dar·ing, -dars.** To enter on a calendar; schedule. [ME *calender* < OFr. *calendier* < Med. Lat. *calendra* < Lat., account book < *kalendae,* calends (from the fact that monthly interest was due on the calends).]

calendar month *n.* Month (sense 1).

calendar year *n.* Year (sense 1).

cal·en·der (kăl′ən-dər) *n.* A machine in which paper or cloth is made smooth and glossy by being pressed through rollers. —*tr.v.* **-dered, -der·ing, -ders.** To press in a calender. [Fr. *calendre* < Med. Lat. *calendra* < Lat. *cylindrus,* roller < Gk. *kulindros* < *kulindein,* to roll.] —**cal′en·der·er** *n.*

ca·len·dri·cal (kə-lĕn′drĭ-kəl) also **ca·len·dric** (-drĭk) *adj.* Of, pertaining to, or used in a calendar.

cal·ends (kăl′əndz) *n., pl.* **calends.** The day of the new moon and the first day of the month in the ancient Roman calendar. [ME *kalendes* < Lat. *kalendae.*] —**ca·len′dal** (kə-lĕn′dəl) *adj.*

ca·len·du·la (kə-lĕn′jə-lə) *n.* A plant of the genus *Calendula,* having orange-yellow flowers. [NLat. *Calendule,* genus name < Med. Lat., marigold < Lat. *kalendae,* calends.]

cal·en·ture (kăl′ən-cho͝or′) *n.* A mild tropical fever that is sometimes persistent. [Sp. *calentura* < *calentar,* to heat < Lat. *calens,* pr.part. of *calēre,* to be warm.]

calf[1] (kăf, käf) *n., pl.* **calves** (kăvz, kävz). **1. a.** A young cow or bull. **b.** The young of certain other mammals, such as the elephant or whale. **2.** Calfskin leather. **3.** A large, floating chunk of ice split from a glacier, iceberg, or floe. **4.** An awkward, callow youth. [ME < OE *cealf.*]

calf[2] (kăf, käf) *n., pl.* **calves** (kăvz, kävz). The fleshy, muscular back part of the human leg between the knee and ankle. [ME < ON *kalfi.*]

calf's-foot jelly also **calves'-foot jelly** (kăvz′fo͝ot′, kăfs′-, kävz′-, käfs′-) *n.* A gelatinous food made by boiling calves' feet.

calf·skin (kăf′skĭn′, käf′-) *n.* **1.** The hide of a calf. **2.** Fine leather made from the hide of a calf.

Cal·i·ban (kăl′ə-băn′) *n.* The grotesque, brutish slave in Shakespeare's *The Tempest.*

cal·i·ber (kăl′ə-bər) *n.* **1. a.** The diameter of the inside of a tube. **b.** The diameter of the bore of a gun. **c.** The diameter of a bullet or shell. **2.** Degree of worth or distinction: *a school of high caliber.* [OFr. *calibre* < OItal. *calibro* < Ar. *qālib,* mold.]

cal·i·brate (kăl′ə-brāt′) *tr.v.* **-brat·ed, -brat·ing, -brates. 1.** To check, adjust, or systematically standardize the graduations of a quantitative measuring instrument. **2.** To determine the caliber of (a tube). —**cal′i·bra′tion** *n.* —**cal′i·bra′tor** *n.*

cal·i·bre (kăl′ə-bər) *n. Chiefly Brit.* Variant of **caliber.**

ca·li·ces (kā′lĭ-sēz′, kăl′ĭ-) *n.* Plural of **calix.**

ca·li·che (kə-lē′chē) *n.* **1. a.** A crude sodium nitrate occurring naturally in Chile, Peru, and the southwestern United States, used as fertilizer. **b.** Sodium nitrate. **2.** A hard soil layer cemented by calcium carbonate and found in deserts and other arid or semiarid regions. [Sp., pebble in a brick < Lat. *calx,* pebble. —see CALX.]

cal·i·co (kăl′ĭ-kō′) *n., pl.* **-coes** or **-cos. 1.** A coarse cloth, usually printed with bright designs. **2.** *Chiefly Brit.* White cotton cloth. **3.** An animal with a mottled or blotched coat. [After *Calicut* (Kozhikode), India.]

calico bass *n.* The black crappie. [From the colored spots on its body.]

calico bush *n.* The mountain laurel.

ca·lif (kā′lĭf, kăl′ĭf) *n.* Variant of **caliph.**

Cal·i·for·nia laurel (kăl′ə-fôr′nyə) *n.* An aromatic evergreen tree, *Umbellularia californica,* of the North American Pacific Coast, having clusters of yellowish-green flowers and yellowish-green fleshy fruit.

California nutmeg *n.* An evergreen tree, *Torreya californica,* having spiny, pointed leaves and purple-streaked, greenish fruit.

California poppy *n.* A plant, *Eschscholtzia californica,* of the Pacific Coast of North America, having finely divided bluish-green leaves and orange-yellow flowers.

California quail *n.* A plump, chunky bird, *Lophortyx californicus,* of western North America, having gray and brown plumage and a curving black plume on the crown of the head.

cal·i·for·ni·um (kăl′ə-fôr′nē-əm) *n. Symbol* **Cf** A synthetic element produced in trace quantities by helium isotope bombardment of curium. All isotopes are radioactive, chiefly by emission of alpha particles. Atomic number 98; mass numbers 244 to 254; half-lives varying from 25 minutes to 800 years. [After *California.*]

MONTHS OF THREE PRINCIPAL CALENDARS

GREGORIAN		HEBREW (Months correspond approximately to those in parentheses)		MOSLEM (Beginning of year retrogresses through the solar year of the Gregorian calendar)	
name	**number of days**	**name**	**number of days**	**name**	**number of days**
January	31	Tishri (September–October)	30	Muharram	30
February in leap year	28 29	Heshvan in some years (October–November)	29 30	Safar	29
March	31	Kislev in some years (November–December)	29 30	Rabi I	30
April	30	Tevet (December–January)	29	Rabi II	29
May	31	Shevat (January–February)	30	Jumada I	30
June	30	Adar* in leap year (February–March)	29 30	Jumada II	29
July	31	Nisan (March–April)	30	Rajab	30
August	31	Iyar (April–May)	29	Sha'ban	29
September	30	Sivan (May–June)	30	Ramadan	30
October	31	Tammuz (June–July)	29	Shawwal	29
November	30	Av (July–August)	30	Dhu'l-Qa'dah	30
December	31	Elul (August–September)	29	Dhu'l-Hijja in leap year	29 30

*Adar is followed in leap year by the intercalary month Veadar, or Adar Sheni, having 29 days.

ca·lig·i·nous (kə-lĭj′ə-nəs) *adj. Archaic.* Dark; gloomy; shadowy. [< Lat. *caliginosus* < *caligo,* darkness.]

cal·i·pash (kăl′ə-păsh′, kăl′ə-păsh′) *n.* An edible, gelatinous, greenish substance lying beneath a turtle's upper shell. [Prob. alteration of Sp. *carapacho,* carapace.]

cal·i·pee (kăl′ə-pē′, kăl′ə-pē′) *n.* An edible, gelatinous, yellowish substance lying above a turtle's lower shell. [Prob. alteration of CALIPASH.]

cal·i·per also **cal·li·per** (kăl′ə-pər) *n.* **1.** Often **calipers.** An instrument consisting essentially of two curved hinged legs and used to measure internal and external dimensions. **2.** A large instrument having a fixed and a movable arm on a graduated stock, used for measuring the diameters of logs and similar objects. **3.** A vernier caliper. —*tr. & intr.v.* **-pered, -per·ing, -pers.** To measure or determine dimensions with calipers. [Alteration of CALIBER.]

ca·liph also **ca·lif** (kā′lĭf, kăl′ĭf) *n.* The secular and religious head of a Moslem state. [ME *calife* < OFr. < Ar. *khalīfa* < *khalafa,* he succeeded.]

ca·liph·ate (kā′lĭ-fāt′, kăl′ĭ-, -fĭt) *n.* The office, jurisdiction, or reign of a caliph.

cal·i·sa·ya (kăl′ĭ-sā′yə) *n.* The bark of a tree of the genus *Cinchona,* from which quinine is obtained, esp. *C. calisaya.* [Sp., prob. < *Calisaya,* an area of Bolivia where a species of quinine bark was first discovered.]

cal·is·then·ics (kăl′ĭs-thĕn′ĭks) *n.* **1.** *(used with a sing. or pl. verb).* Gymnastic exercises designed to develop muscular tone and promote physical well-being. **2.** *(used with a sing. verb).* The practice of calisthenics. [Gk. *kalli-* beautiful (< *kallos,* beauty) + *sthenos,* strength.] —**cal′is·then′ic** *adj.*

ca·lix (kā′lĭks, kăl′ĭks) *n., pl.* **ca·li·ces** (kā′lĭ-sēz′, kăl′ĭ-). *Eccles.* A chalice. [Lat. *calix, calic-,* cup.]

calk[1] (kôk) *n.* **1.** A pointed extension on the toe or heels of a horseshoe, designed to prevent slipping. **2.** A spiked plate fixed on the bottom of a shoe to prevent slipping and preserve the sole. —*tr.v.* **calked, calk·ing, calks. 1.** To supply with or fasten on calks. **2.** To cut or injure with a calk. [Short for obs. *calkin* < ME *kakun* < MDu. *kalkoen,* hoof < OFr. *calcain,* heel < Lat. *calcaneum* < *calx.*]

calk[2] (kôk) *v.* Variant of **caulk.**

call (kôl) *v.* **called, call·ing, calls.** —*tr.* **1.** To cry out in a loud tone; announce; proclaim: *called her name.* **2.** To summon: *call to dinner.* **3.** To convoke or convene (a meeting). **4.** To summon to a particular career or pursuit. **5.** To

caldron
15th-century woodcut of witches

California poppy

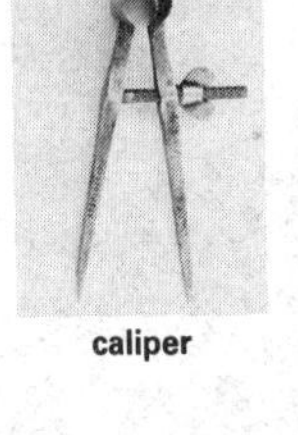

caliper

awaken. **6.** To telephone (someone). **7. a.** To make a characteristic cry, as a bird. **b.** To lure by imitating such a cry. **8.** To name: *What will you call the baby?* **9.** To estimate as being; consider: *I call that fair.* **10.** To designate; label: *Nobody calls me a liar.* **11.** To bring to action or under consideration: *call a case to court.* **12.** To demand payment of (a loan or bond issue). **13.** *Sports.* **a.** To stop or postpone (a game) because of bad weather, darkness, or other adverse conditions. **b.** To indicate a decision in regard to (a foul or play, for example). **c.** In baseball, to indicate a decision in regard to (a pitch). **d.** To choose or select (plays to be run): *cited the poor game called by the quarterback.* **14. a.** To predict (the outcome of a billiard shot) before playing. **b.** To ask (another player) to do so. **15.** To forecast or predict accurately: *He's called the game's outcome every time.* **16.** To demand to see the hand of (a poker opponent) by equaling his bet. **17.** To demand that a person make good a boast or support a statement with facts: *call a bluff.* **18.** To shout (directions) in rhythm for square dances. —*intr.* **1.** To telephone. **2.** To pay a short visit. **3.** To attract attention by shouting. —***phrasal verbs.*** **call back.** To telephone repeatedly or in return. **call down. 1.** To invoke, as from heaven. **2.** To find fault with or berate. **call for. 1.** To go and get or stop for. **2.** To be appropriate for; warrant: *This calls for a celebration.* **3.** To require; demand: *work that calls for patience.* **call forth.** To evoke. **call in. 1.** To take out of circulation: *calling in silver dollars.* **2.** To summon for assistance or consultation: *call in a specialist.* **call off. 1.** To cancel or postpone. **2.** To restrain or recall: *Call off your dogs.* **call on** (or **upon**). To request or order (someone) to do something. **call out.** To cause to assemble; summon: *call out the guard.* **call up. 1.** To summon into military service: *called up for active duty.* **2.** To remember or cause to remember: *calling up old times.* **3.** To bring forth for action or discussion. —*n.* **1.** A shout or loud cry. **2. a.** The characteristic cry of an animal, esp. a bird. **b.** An instrument or sound made to imitate such a cry, used as a lure: *a moose call.* **3.** Need or occasion: *There was no call for that remark.* **4.** Demand: *There isn't much call for buggy whips today.* **5.** A claim on a person's time or life: *the call of duty.* **6.** A short visit, esp. one made as a formality or for business or professional purposes. **7.** A summons or invitation. **8. a.** A signal, as made by a horn or bell. **b.** The sounding of a horn to encourage hounds during a hunt. **9.** A vocation, as to the ministry. **10.** A roll call. **11.** A notice of rehearsal times posted in a theater. **12.** *Sports.* The decision of an umpire or referee. **13.** An instruction in square dancing to begin a different step or set. **14.** A demand or request for payment of a debt, as by redeeming bonds. **15. a.** An agreement in which a trader may, for a fee, buy a certain quantity of a stock or commodity for a specified price within a limited period of time. **b.** A demand for payment due on stock bought on margin when the value has shrunk. —***idioms.*** **call into question.** To raise doubt about. **call to mind.** To remind of. **close call.** A narrow escape. **on call. 1.** Payable on demand. **2.** Available whenever summoned. **within call.** Close enough to come if summoned; accessible. [ME *callen* < ON *kalla.*]

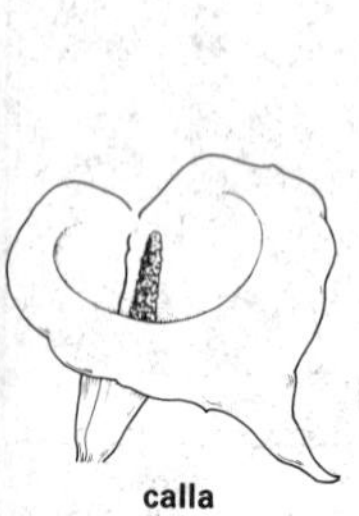

calla

cal·la (kăl'ə) *n.* **1.** Any of several tropical or semitropical plants of the genus *Zantedeschia,* esp. *Z. aethiopica,* widely cultivated for its large, showy white spathe that encloses a yellow spadix. **2.** A marsh plant, *Calla palustris,* of the North Temperate Zone, having small, densely clustered greenish flowers partly enclosed in a spreading white spathe. [NLat. *Calla,* genus name < Gk. *kallaia,* wattle of a cock.]

call·back (kôl'băk') *n.* A recall of a recently sold product by the manufacturer to correct a defect.

call·board (kôl'bôrd', -bōrd') *n.* A bulletin board backstage in a theater for posting instructions and notices.

call·boy (kôl'boi') *n.* **1.** One who tells actors when it is time for them to go on stage. **2.** A bellboy.

call·er[1] (kô'lər) *n.* One that calls.

cal·ler[2] (kăl'ər) *adj. Scot.* **1.** Fresh. Used of food, esp. fish. **2.** Cool and refreshing, as a breeze. [ME *calour.*]

call girl *n.* A female prostitute hired by telephone.

call house *n.* A house of prostitution.

cal·lig·ra·phy (kə-lĭg'rə-fē) *n.* **1.** The art of fine handwriting. **2.** Penmanship; handwriting. [Fr. *calligraphic* < Gk. *kalligraphia,* beautiful writing : *kalli-,* beautiful (< *kallos,* beauty) + *graphein,* to write.] —**cal·lig'ra·pher, cal·lig'ra·phist** *n.* —**cal'li·graph'ic** (kăl'ĭ-grăf'ĭk) *adj.*

call-in (kôl'ĭn') *adj.* Inviting listeners to make broadcasted telephone calls: *a call-in radio show.*

call·ing (kô'lĭng) *n.* **1.** An inner urge; a strong impulse. **2.** An occupation, profession, or career.

calling card *n.* A card bearing one's name and often one's address and telephone number, used for social or business purposes.

Cal·li·o·pe (kə-lī'ə-pē') *n.* **1.** *Gk. Myth.* The Muse of epic poetry. **2. calliope** (*also* kăl'ē-ōp'). A musical instrument fitted with steam whistles, played from a keyboard. [Lat. < Gk. *Kalliopē* : *kalli-,* beautiful (< *kallos,* beauty) + *ops,* voice.]

cal·li·op·sis (kăl'ē-ŏp'sĭs) *n.* The coreopsis.

cal·li·per (kăl'ə-pər) *n.* Variant of **caliper.**

cal·li·pyg·i·an (kăl'ə-pĭj'ē-ən) also **cal·li·py·gous** (-pī'gəs) *adj.* Having beautifully proportioned buttocks. [Gk. *kallipugos* : *kalli-,* beautiful (< *kallos,* beauty) + *pugē,* buttocks.]

Cal·lis·to (kə-lĭs'tō) *n.* **1.** *Gk. Myth.* A nymph, beloved of Zeus and hated by Hera. Hera changed her into a bear, and Zeus then placed her in the sky as the constellation Ursa Major. **2.** One of the moons of Jupiter, the largest known moon of any planet. [Lat. < Gk. *Kallistō* < *kallistos,* superl. of *kalos,* beautiful.]

call letters *pl.n.* The identifying code letters or numbers of a radio or television transmitting station.

call loan *n.* A loan repayable on demand at any time.

call market *n.* The market for call money.

call money *n.* Money lent by banks, usually to stockbrokers, subject to repayment on demand at any time.

call number *n.* A number used in libraries to classify a book and indicate its placement on the shelves.

cal·lose (kăl'ōs') *n.* A complex branched carbohydrate component of plant cell walls. [< Lat. *callosus,* callous.]

cal·los·i·ty (kə-lŏs'ĭ-tē) *n., pl.* **-ties. 1.** The condition of being calloused. **2.** Hardheartedness; insensitivity. **3.** A callus. [ME *callosite* < OFr. *callosité* < Lat. *callositas* < *callosus,* callous.]

cal·lous (kăl'əs) *adj.* **1.** Having calluses; toughened. **2.** Emotionally hardened; unfeeling. —*tr. & intr.v.* **-loused, -lous·ing, -lous·es.** To make or become callous. [ME < OFr. *calleuse* < Lat. *callosus* < *callum,* hard skin.] —**cal'lous·ly** *adv.* —**cal'lous·ness** *n.*

Usage: The noun form of this word is spelled *callus,* but the verb and adjective forms are spelled *callous.*

cal·low (kăl'ō) *adj.* **1.** Immature; inexperienced: *a callow youth.* **2.** Not yet having feathers; unfledged, as a bird. [ME *calwe,* bald < OE *calu.*] —**cal'low·ness** *n.*

call rate *n.* The rate of interest charged on call loans.

cal·lus (kăl'əs) *n., pl.* **-lus·es. 1. a.** A localized thickening and enlargement of the horny layer of the skin. **b.** The hard bony tissue that surrounds the ends of a fractured bone. **2.** *Bot.* Hardened tissue that develops over a wound or cut end of a woody stem. —*intr.v.* **-lused, -lus·ing, -lus·es.** To form or develop a callus. —See Usage note at **callous.** [Lat.]

calm (käm) *adj.* **-er, -est. 1.** Nearly or completely motionless; undisturbed: *the calm surface of the lake.* **2.** Not excited or agitated; composed: *remained calm throughout the trial.* —*n.* **1.** An absence or cessation of motion; stillness. **2.** Serenity; tranquillity; peace. **3.** A meteorological condition of little or no wind. —*tr. & intr.v.* **calmed, calm·ing, calms.** To make or become calm or quiet. [ME *calme* < OFr. < OItal. *calma* < LLat. *cauma,* heat of the day < Gk. *kauma* < *kaiein,* to burn.] —**calm'ly** *adv.* —**calm'ness** *n.*

Synonyms: *calm, tranquil, placid, serene, still, quiet, halcyon, peaceful.* These adjectives describe absence of movement, noise, or emotion. *Calm,* in both its physical and figurative senses, implies freedom from agitation. *Tranquil* adds to *calm* the idea of a more enduring state: *tranquil life.* A *placid* person is not easily shaken by emotion, and *placid* waters are unruffled. *Serene* suggests a lofty, even spiritual calm. *Still* and *quiet* are related in emphasizing absence of all noise. *Still* has the additional sense of absence of motion. *Halcyon* has the meaning of both *calm* and *tranquil* and suggests happiness: *halcyon days of youth. Peaceful* implies aversion to conflict.

calm·a·tive (kä'mə-tĭv, kăl'mə-) *adj.* Having relaxing or pacifying properties; sedative. —*n.* A sedative or tranquilizer.

cal·o·mel (kăl'ə-mĕl', -məl) *n.* A white, tasteless compound, Hg_2Cl_2, used as a purgative. [Fr. : Gk. *kalos,* beautiful + *melas,* black.]

cal·o·re·cep·tor (kăl'ə-rĭ-sĕp'tər) *n.* A sensory receptor that detects warmth. [Lat. *calor,* heat + RECEPTOR.]

ca·lor·ic (kə-lôr'ĭk, -lŏr'-) *adj.* Of or pertaining to heat or calories. —*n.* A hypothetically indestructible, uncreatable, highly elastic, self-repellent, all-pervading fluid formerly thought responsible for the production, possession, and transfer of heat. [Fr. *calorique* < Lat. *calor,* heat.] —**ca·lor'i·cal·ly** *adv.*

cal·o·rie (kăl'ə-rē) *n.* **1.** Any of several approximately equal units of heat, each measured as the quantity of heat required to raise the temperature of 1 gram of water by 1°C from a standard initial temperature, esp. from 3.98°C, 14.5°C, or 19.5°C, at 1 atmosphere pressure. **2.** The unit of heat equal to $^1/_{100}$ the quantity of heat required to raise the temperature of 1 gram of water from 0 to 100°C at 1 atmosphere pressure. **3.** The unit of heat equal to the amount of heat required to raise the temperature of 1 kilogram of water by 1°C at 1 atmosphere pressure. **4.** The unit of heat equal to 4.184 joules. [Fr. < Lat. *calor,* heat.]

cal·o·rif·ic (kăl'ə-rĭf'ĭk) *adj.* Pertaining to or generating heat or calories. [Fr. *calorifique* < Lat. *calorificus* : *calor,* heat + *facere,* to make.]

cal·o·rim·e·ter (kăl'ə-rĭm'ĭ-tər) *n.* **1.** An apparatus for measuring heat. **2.** The part of a calorimeter, usually a container for holding a sample, in which the heat measured causes a change of state. [Lat. *calor,* heat + -METER.] —**ca·lor'i·met'ric** (kə-lôr'ə-mĕt'rĭk, -lŏr'-) *adj.* —**ca·lor'i·met'ri·cal·ly** *adv.*

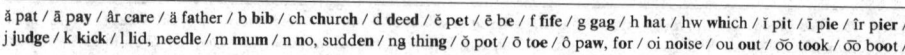

cal·o·rim·e·try (kăl'ə-rĭm'ĭ-trē) *n.* The measurement of the amount of heat evolved or absorbed in a chemical reaction, change of state, or formation of a solution. [Lat. *calor,* heat + -METRY.]

ca·lotte (kə-lŏt′) *n.* **1.** A skullcap, esp. one worn by Roman Catholic clergymen. **2.** *Biol.* A caplike structure. [Fr. dim. of OFr. *cale,* cap, of Germanic orig.]

ca·loy·er (kə-loi′ər, kăl′ə-yər) *n.* A monk of the Eastern Orthodox Church. [Fr. < obs. Ital. *caloiero* < LGk. *kalogēros,* venerable : Gk. *kalos,* beautiful + *gēros,* old age.]

cal·pac also **cal·pack** (kăl′păk′, kăl-păk′) *n.* A large black cap, usually of sheepskin or felt, worn in Turkey, Armenia, and other Near Eastern regions. [Turk. *kalpāk.*]

calque (kălk) *n. Ling.* **1.** A form of semantic borrowing in which a word is given a special extended meaning by analogy with that of a word having the same basic meaning in another language. **2.** A loan translation. —*tr.v.* **calqued, calqu·ing, calques.** To model (the meaning of a word) upon that of an analogous word in another language. [Fr. < *calquer,* to copy < Ital. *calcare,* to press < Lat., to tread on < *calx,* heel.]

cal·trop also **cal·trap** (kăl′trəp, kôl′-) *n.* **1.** An iron ball with four projecting spikes so arranged that when three of the spikes are on the ground, the fourth points upward, formerly used to delay the advance of mounted and unmounted troops. **2.** Any of several plants having spiny burs or bracts, such as members of the genera *Tribulus* and *Kallstroemia.* [ME *calketrappe,* partly < Norman Fr., and partly OE < *calcatrippe,* thistle, both < Med. Lat. *calcatrippa,* thistle.]

cal·u·met (kăl′yə-mĕt′, -mĭt, kăl′yə-mĕt′) *n.* A long-stemmed, ornamented pipe used by North American Indians for ceremonial purposes. [Canadian Fr. < dial. Fr., straw < LLat. *calamellus,* dim. of Lat. *calamus,* reed < Gk. *kalamos* straw.]

ca·lum·ni·ate (kə-lŭm′nē-āt′) *tr.v.* **-at·ed, -at·ing, -ates.** To make maliciously false statements about; slander. [Lat. *calumniari, calumniat-* < *calumnia,* calumny.] —**ca·lum′ni·a′tion** *n.* —**ca·lum′ni·a′tor** *n.*

ca·lum·ni·ous (kə-lŭm′nē-əs) *adj.* Containing or implying calumny; slanderous; defamatory. —**ca·lum′ni·ous·ly** *adv.*

cal·um·ny (kăl′əm-nē) *n., pl.* **-nies. 1.** A false statement maliciously made to injure someone. **2.** The utterance of calumny; slander. [ME *calumnie* < OFr. *calomnie* < Lat. *calumnia.* < *calvi,* to deceive.]

cal·va·dos (kăl′və-dōs′) *n.* A French brandy made from apples. [Fr., after *Calvados,* a department of France.]

cal·var·i·um (kăl-vâr′ē-əm) *n., pl.* **-i·ums** or **-i·a** (-ē-ə). The superior portion of the skull that lacks the lower jaw and facial parts. [NLat. < Lat. *calvaria,* skull < *calvus,* bald.]

cal·va·ry (kăl′və-rē) *n., pl.* **-ries. 1.** A sculptured depiction of the Crucifixion. **2.** An experience or ordeal marked by intense suffering or difficulty. [Fr. *calvaire* < *Calvaire,* Calvary, the hill outside Jerusalem where Jesus Christ was crucified.]

Calvary cross *n.* In heraldry, a Latin cross set on three steps.

calve (kăv, käv) *v.* **calved, calv·ing, calves.** —*intr.* **1.** To give birth to a calf. **2.** To break up and lose a portion of itself. Used of a glacier or an iceberg. —*tr.* **1.** To give birth to (a calf). **2.** To set loose (a mass of ice). [ME *calven* < OE *calfian.*]

calves (kăvz, kävz) *n.* Plural of **calf.**

calves′-foot jelly (kăvz′fo͝ot′, kăfs′-, kävz′-, käfs′-) *n.* Variant of **calf's-foot jelly.**

Cal·vin·ism (kăl′vĭ-nĭz′əm) *n.* The religious doctrines of John Calvin, emphasizing the omnipotence of God and the salvation of the elect by God's grace alone. —**Cal′vin·ist** *n.* —**Cal′vin·is′tic** *adj.* —**Cal′vin·is′ti·cal·ly** *adv.*

calx (kălks) *n., pl.* **calx·es** or **cal·ces** (kăl′sēz′). **1.** The crumbly residue left after a mineral or metal has been calcined or roasted. **2.** Lime; chalk. **3.** Calcium oxide. [Lat., lime < Gk. *khalix,* pebble.]

ca·ly·cine (kā′lĭ-sīn′, kăl′ĭ-) *adj.* Of, pertaining to, or resembling a calyx.

ca·ly·cle (kā′lĭ-kəl, kăl′ĭ-) *n. Bot.* An epicalyx. [Fr. *calicule* < Lat. *calyculus,* dim. of *calyx,* calyx.] —**ca·lyc′u·late′** (kə-lĭk′yə-lāt′, -lĭt) *adj.*

ca·lyc·u·lus (kə-lĭk′yə-ləs) *n., pl.* **-li** (-lī′). *Biol.* A small cup-shaped structure. [Lat. —see CALYCLE.] —**ca·lyc′u·lar** *adj.*

Ca·lyp·so (kə-lĭp′sō) *n.* **1.** *Gk. Myth.* A sea nymph who delayed Odysseus on her island, Ogygia, for seven years. **2.** An orchid, *Calypso bulbosa,* of the North Temperate Zone, having a pinkish flower with a slippershaped lip. **3.** A type of music that originated in the West Indies, notably in Trinidad, and is characterized by improvised lyrics on topical or broadly humorous subjects. [Lat. < Gk. *Kalupso* < *kaluptein,* to conceal.]

ca·lyp·tra (kə-lĭp′trə) *n.* **1.** The protective cap covering the spore case of a moss or related plant. **2.** A similar hoodlike or caplike structure. [Gk. *kaluptra,* vein < *kaluptein,* to cover.] —**ca·lyp′trate′** (-trāt′) *adj.*

ca·lyx (kā′lĭks, kăl′ĭks) *n., pl.* **ca·lyx·es** or **ca·ly·ces** (kā′lĭ-sēz′, kăl′ĭ-). **1.** The outer protective covering of a flower, consisting of a series of leaflike, usually green segments called sepals. **2.** A cuplike or funnel-shaped animal structure. **3.** A collecting structure in the kidney. [Lat. *calyx, calic-* < Gk. *kalux.*]

cam (kăm) *n.* An eccentric or multiply curved wheel mounted on a rotating shaft and used to produce variable or reciprocating motion in another engaged or contacted part. [Du. *cam,* comb, of Germanic orig.]

ca·ma·ra·der·ie (kä′mə-rä′də-rē, kăm′ə-răd′ə-) *n.* Good will and lighthearted rapport between or among friends; comradeship. [Fr. < *camarade,* comrade < OFr., roommate. —see COMRADE.]

cam·a·ril·la (kăm′ə-rĭl′ə, -rē′yə) *n.* **1.** Any of various secret and unofficial advisers to the Spanish kings. **2.** A group of confidential advisers; cabal. [Sp. < *cámara,* room < LLat. *camera* < Lat., arched roof < Gk. *kamara,* vault.]

cam·as also **cam·ass** (kăm′əs) *n.* **1.** Any of several North American plants of the genus *Camassia,* esp. *C. quamash,* of western North America, having a showy cluster of blue or white flowers and an edible bulb. **2.** The death camas. [Chinook Jargon *kamass.*]

cam·ber (kăm′bər) *n.* **1. a.** A slightly arched surface, as of a road, a ship's deck, or an airfoil. **b.** The condition of having an arched surface. **2.** A setting of automobile wheels closer together at the bottom than at the top. —*intr. & tr.v.* **-bered, -ber·ing, -bers.** To arch or cause to arch slightly. [ME *caumber,* curved < OFr. *cambre* < *cambrer,* to arch < *camerare,* to vault < *camera,* vault < Lat. —see CHAMBER.]

cam·bist (kăm′bĭst) *n.* **1.** A manual giving exchange rates of different currencies and equivalents of different weights and measures. **2.** A dealer in or expert on international exchange. [Fr. *cambiste,* exchange broker < Ital. *cambista* < *cambio,* exchange < LLat. *cambire,* to exchange.] —**cam′bism, cam′bis·try** *n.*

cam·bi·um (kăm′bē-əm) *n.* A layer of cells in the stems and roots of vascular plants that gives rise to phloem and xylem. [Med. Lat., change < LLat. *cambire,* to exchange.] —**cam′bi·al** *adj.*

Cam·bri·an (kăm′brē-ən) *adj.* **1.** Of or pertaining to Wales; Welsh. **2.** Of, belonging to, or designating the geologic time, system of rocks, and sedimentary deposits of the first period of the Paleozoic era, characterized by warm seas and desert land areas. —*n.* **1.** A Welshman. **2.** The Cambrian period. [< Med. Lat. *Cambria,* Wales < Welsh *Cymry.*]

cam·bric (kām′brĭk) *n.* A finely woven white linen or cotton fabric. [Obs. *cameryk* < obs. Flem. *kameryk* < *Kameryk,* Cambrai, a city in France.]

cambric tea *n.* A drink for children, made of hot water, milk, sugar, and usually a small amount of tea. [So called because it is thin and white like cambric.]

came[1] (kām) *n.* A slender, grooved lead bar used to hold together the panes in stained glass or latticework windows. [Orig. unknown.]

came[2] (kām) *v.* Past tense of **come.**

cam·el (kăm′əl) *n.* **1.** A humped, long-necked ruminant mammal of the genus *Camelus,* domesticated in Old World desert regions as a beast of burden and as a source of wool, milk, and meat. **2.** A device used to raise a sunken vessel. [ME < Lat. *camelus* < Gk. *kamēlos,* of Semitic orig.]

cam·el·back (kăm′əl-băk′) *adj.* Having a shape characterized by a hump or arching curve.

cam·el·eer (kăm′ə-lîr′) *n.* A person who drives or rides a camel.

ca·mel·lia (kə-mēl′yə) *n.* **1.** Any of several shrubs or trees of the genus *Camellia,* native to Asia, esp. *C. japonica,* having shiny evergreen leaves and showy, variously colored flowers. **2.** The flower of a camellia. [NLat. *Camellia,* genus name, after Georg Josef *Kamel* (1661–1706).]

ca·mel·o·pard (kə-mĕl′ə-pärd′) *n.* **1.** *Archaic.* A giraffe. **2.** In heraldry, a bearing resembling a giraffe but represented with long curved horns. [Med. Lat. *camelopardus* < Lat. *camelopardalis* < Gk. *kamēlopardalis* : *kamēlos,* camel + *pardalis,* var. of *pardos,* pard (so called because the giraffe has a head like a camel's and the spots of a leopard).]

Ca·mel·o·par·da·lis (kə-mĕl′ō-pär′dl-ĭs) *n.* A constellation in the Northern Hemisphere near Ursa Major and Cassiopeia. [Lat. *camelopardalis,* camelopard.]

Cam·e·lot (kăm′ə-lŏt′) *n.* **1.** The legendary town where King Arthur had his court. **2.** A place, time, or circumstance marked by idealized beauty, peacefulness, and enlightenment.

camel's hair *n.* **1.** The soft, fine hair of a camel or a substitute for it. **2.** A soft, heavy cloth, usually light tan, made chiefly of camel's hair.

Cam·em·bert (kăm′əm-bâr′) *n.* A creamy, mold-ripened cheese that softens on the inside as it matures. [Fr., after *Camembert,* France.]

cam·e·o (kăm′ē-ō′) *n., pl.* **-os. 1. a.** A technique of engraving in relief on a gem or other stone, esp. with layers of different hues, cut so the raised design is of one color and the background of another. **b.** A gem so cut. **c.** A medallion with a profile cut in raised relief. **2.** A brief but dramatic appearance of a prominent actor or actress in a single scene on a television show or in a motion picture. —*tr.v.* **-oed, -o·ing, -os. 1.** To make into or like cameo. **2.** To portray in sharp, delicate relief, as in a literary composition. [ME *cameu* < OFr. *camaieu* < OSp. *camafeo.*]

cam·er·a (kăm′ər-ə, kăm′rə) *n.* **1.** An apparatus for taking photographs, generally consisting of a lightproof enclosure having an aperture with a shuttered lens through which the

calumet
Crow Indian calumet

cam

camel

camellia

cameo

image of an object is focused and recorded on a photosensitive film or plate. **2.** The part of a television transmitting apparatus that receives the primary image on a light-sensitive cathode tube and transforms it into electrical impulses. **3.** A camera obscura. **4.** *pl.* **-er·ae** (-ə-rē). A judge's private chamber. [LLat., room. —see CHAMBER.]

cam·er·al (kăm'ər-əl) *adj.* **1.** Pertaining to a judge's chamber and to the judicial affairs that take place there. **2.** Pertaining to public finance and state business or to a council that manages such matters. [Med. Lat. *cameralis* < *camera,* office < LLat., room. —see CHAMBER.]

camera lu·ci·da (lo͞o'sĭ-də) *n.* An optical device that projects a virtual image of an object onto a plane surface, esp. for tracing. [NLat., light chamber.]

cam·er·a·man (kăm'ər-ə-măn', kăm'rə-) *n.* A person who operates a motion picture or television camera.

camera ob·scu·ra (əb-skyo͝or'ə) *n.* A darkened chamber in which the real image of an object is received through a small opening or lens and focused in natural color onto a facing surface. [NLat., dark chamber.]

cam·er·lin·go (kăm'ər-lĭng'gō) also **cam·er·len·go** (-lĕng'gō) *n., pl.* **-gos.** *Rom. Cath. Ch.* The cardinal who manages the pope's secular affairs. [Ital. *camarlingo.*]

cam·i·on (kăm'ē-ən, käm-yôɴ') *n.* **1.** A low, sturdy wagon. **2. a.** A truck. **b.** A bus. [Fr. < OFr. *chamion.*]

ca·mi·sa (kə-mē'sə) *n. Southwestern U.S.* A shirt or chemise. [Sp. < LLat. *camisia,* shirt.]

cam·i·sa·do (kăm'ĭ-sā'dō, -sä'-) *n., pl.* **-dos.** *Archaic.* A surprise attack by night. [Prob. < Sp. *encamisado,* shirted (so called because the attackers wore white shirts over their armor for identification) < *camisa,* shirt. —see CAMISA.]

ca·mise (kə-mēz', -mēs') *n.* A loose shirt, shift, or tunic. [Ar. *qamīs* < LLat. *camisia,* shirt.]

cam·i·sole (kăm'ĭ-sōl') *n.* **1.** A woman's sleeveless undergarment. **2.** A short negligee. [Fr. < OProv. *camisolla,* dim. of *camisa,* shirt < LLat. *camisia.*]

Cam·lan (kăm'lən) *n.* The legendary battlefield where King Arthur was mortally wounded.

cam·let (kăm'lĭt) *n.* **1.** A rich cloth of Oriental origin, supposed originally to have been made of camel's hair and silk and later made of goat's hair and silk or other combinations. **2.** A garment made from camlet. [ME *chamelet* < OFr. *chamelot* < Ar. *ḥamlat.*]

cam·o·mile (kăm'ə-mīl') *n.* Variant of **chamomile.**

Ca·mor·ra (kə-môr'ə, -mŏr'ə) *n.* **1.** A Neapolitan secret society organized about 1820, notorious for practicing violence and blackmail. **2.** An unscrupulous, clandestine group. [Ital., perh. < *camorra,* a kind of smock, said to have been worn by members of the society.]

cam·ou·flage (kăm'ə-fläzh', -fläj') *n.* **1.** The method or result of concealing personnel or materiel from an enemy by making them appear to be part of the natural surroundings. **2.** A means of concealment; dissimulation. —*tr. & intr.v.* **-flaged, -flag·ing, -flag·es.** To conceal by or use camouflage. [Fr. < *camoufler,* to disguise < Ital. *camuffare.*] —**cam'ou·flag'er** *n.*

camp¹ (kămp) *n.* **1. a.** A place where a group of people, such as soldiers, are temporarily lodged in tents, huts, or other makeshift shelters. **b.** The shelters in such a place. **c.** The persons using such shelters. **2.** A place consisting of more or less permanent cabins or other shelters, used for vacationing or other recreational purposes. **3.** Military service; army life: *recruits getting used to the routine in camp.* **4.** A group of persons, parties, or states favorable to a common cause, doctrine, or political system: *the socialist camp.* —*v.* **camped, camp·ing, camps.** —*tr.* To shelter or lodge in a camp; encamp. —*intr.* **1.** To make or set up a camp. **2.** To live in or as if in a camp; settle: *camped in the apartment until the furniture arrived.* [OFr. < Lat. *campus,* field.]

camp² (kămp) *n.* **1. a.** An affectation or appreciation of manners and tastes commonly thought to be outlandish, vulgar, or banal. **b.** Behavior exhibiting such affectation or appreciation. **2.** Banality or artificiality when appreciated for its humor. —*adj.* Having the qualities or style of camp. —*intr.v.* **camped, camp·ing, camps.** To act in an outlandish, vulgar, or banal manner. [Orig. unknown.] —**camp'y** *adj.*

cam·paign (kăm-pān') *n.* **1.** A series of military operations undertaken to achieve a specific objective within a given area. **2.** An operation undertaken, as by means of propaganda, to attain some political, social, or commercial goal. —*intr.v.* **-paigned, -paign·ing, -paigns.** To engage in a campaign. [Fr. *campagne* < OFr., battlefield < OItal. *campagna* < LLat. *campania,* open country < *campus,* field.] —**cam·paign'er** *n.*

cam·pa·ni·le (kăm'pə-nē'lē) *n., pl.* **-les** (-lēz) or **-li** (-lē). A bell tower, esp. one near but not attached to a church. [Ital. < *campana,* bell < LLat.]

cam·pa·nol·o·gy (kăm'pə-nŏl'ə-jē) *n.* The art or study of bell casting and ringing. [LLat. *campana,* bell + -LOGY.] —**cam'pa·nol'o·gist** *n.*

cam·pan·u·la (kăm-păn'yə-lə) *n.* Any of various plants of the genus *Campanula,* which includes the bellflowers. [NLat. *Campanula,* genus name, dim. of LLat. *campana,* bell.]

cam·pan·u·late (kăm-păn'yə-lĭt, -lāt') *adj. Bot.* Bell-shaped. [NLat. *campanula,* dim. of LLat. *campana,* bell + -ATE¹.]

camp·er (kăm'pər) *n.* **1.** One that camps. **2. a.** A compact, vanlike vehicle resembling an automobile-and-trailer combination, designed to serve as a dwelling and used for camping or on long motor trips. **b.** A portable shelter resembling the top part of a trailer, made to be mounted on a pickup truck to form such a vehicle.

cam·pes·tral (kăm-pĕs'trəl) *adj.* Of, pertaining to, or growing in uncultivated land or open fields. [Lat. *campester,* of a field < *campus,* field.]

cam·pes·tri·an (kăm-pĕs'trē-ən) *adj.* Pertaining to the northern Great Plains. [< Lat. *campestria,* a plain < *campus,* field.]

camp·fire (kămp'fīr') *n.* **1.** An outdoor fire in a camp, used for warmth or cooking. **2.** A meeting held around a campfire.

camp fire girl *n.* A member of the Camp Fire Girls, an organization for girls from 7 through 18 that strives to instill good values and character and develop practical skills.

camp follower *n.* **1.** A civilian who follows an army from place to place to sell goods or services. **2.** One who follows but does not belong to a main body or group.

camp·ground (kămp'ground') *n.* An area used for setting up a camp or holding a camp meeting.

cam·phene (kăm'fēn') *n.* A colorless crystalline compound, $C_{10}H_{16}$, used in the manufacture of synthetic camphor and insecticides. [CAMPH(OR) + -ENE.]

cam·phor (kăm'fər) *n.* A volatile crystalline compound, $C_{10}H_{16}O$, obtained from camphor tree wood or synthesized and used as an insect repellent, in the manufacture of film, plastics, lacquers, and explosives, and medicinally as a stimulant, expectorant, and diaphoretic. [ME *caumfre* < OFr. *camphre* < Med. Lat. *camphora* < Ar. *kāfūr.*] —**cam·phor'ic** (-fôr'ĭk, -fŏr'-) *adj.*

cam·phor·ate (kăm'fə-rāt') *tr.v.* **-at·ed, -at·ing, -ates.** To treat or impregnate with camphor.

camphor ice *n.* A skin ointment consisting of camphor, white wax, spermaceti, and castor oil.

camphor oil *n.* The oil obtained from the wood of the camphor tree.

camphor tree *n.* An evergreen tree, *Cinnamomum camphora,* native to eastern Asia, having aromatic wood that is a source of camphor.

cam·pi·on (kăm'pē-ən) *n.* Any of various plants of the genus *Lychnis* or related genera, having red, pink, or white flowers. [Orig. unknown.]

camp meeting *n.* An evangelistic gathering held in a tent or outdoors and often lasting a number of days.

cam·po (kăm'pō, käm'-) *n., pl.* **-pos.** A large, grassy plain in South America, with occasional bushes and small trees. [Am. Sp. < Sp., field < Lat. *campus.*]

camp·o·ree (kăm'pə-rē') *n.* An assembly or gathering of Boy Scouts on a local or district level. [CAMP + (JAMB)OREE.]

camp robber *n.* The Canada jay.

camp·site (kămp'sīt') *n.* An area suitable or used for camping.

camp·stool (kămp'sto͞ol') *n.* A light folding stool.

cam·pus (kăm'pəs) *n., pl.* **-pus·es.** **1.** The grounds of a school, college, or university. **2.** A field in ancient Rome used for various events, such as military exercises. [Lat., field.]

cam·py·lot·ro·pous (kăm'pə-lŏt'rə-pəs) *adj. Bot.* Having the ovule partially inverted and curved. [Gk. *kampulos,* curved + -TROPOUS.]

cam·shaft (kăm'shăft') *n.* An engine shaft fitted with a cam or cams.

can¹ (kăn; kən *when unstressed*) *aux.v.* Past tense **could** (ko͝od). **1.** Used to indicate: **a.** Physical or mental ability: *I can meet you today.* **b.** Possession of a specified power, right, or privilege: *The President can veto congressional bills.* **c.** Possession of a specified capacity or skill: *He can tune the harpsichord as well as play it.* **2.** Used to indicate possibility or probability: *I wonder if she can still be alive.* **3.** Used to request or grant permission: *Can I be excused? No, you cannot.* [ME < OE, first and third person pr. indicative of *cunnan,* to know how.]

Usage: Generations of grammarians and schoolteachers have insisted that *can* should be used only to express the capacity to do something, while *may* must be used to indicate permission. Technically, correct usage therefore requires: *The boss said that anyone who wants an extra day off may* (not *can*) *have one. May* (not *can*) *I have an extra blanket?* In speech, however, *can* is used to express permission by most speakers, and the "permission" use of *can* is even more frequent in British English. The negative contraction *can't* is frequently used in coaxing and wheedling questions like *Can't I have the car tonight?* Many members of the Usage Panel feel also that the alternative contraction *mayn't* is awkward and unnatural.

can² (kăn) *n.* **1.** A usually cylindrical metal container. **2. a.** An airtight container, usually made of tin-coated iron, in which foods or beverages are preserved. **b.** The contents of such a container. **3.** *Slang.* A jail or prison. **4.** *Slang.* A toilet or rest room. **5.** *Slang.* The buttocks. —*tr.v.* **canned, can·ning, cans.** **1.** To seal in a can or jar for future use;

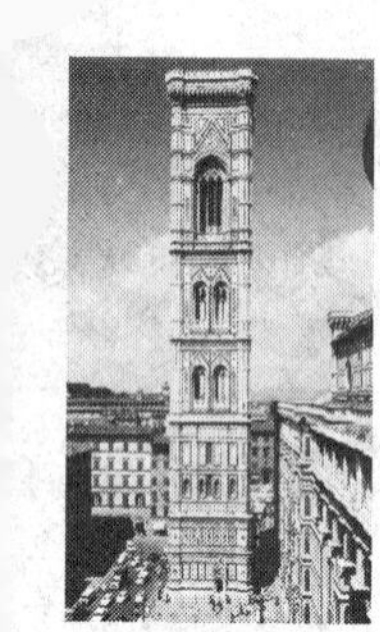

campanile
Campanile of Florence Cathedral designed by Giotto

camper

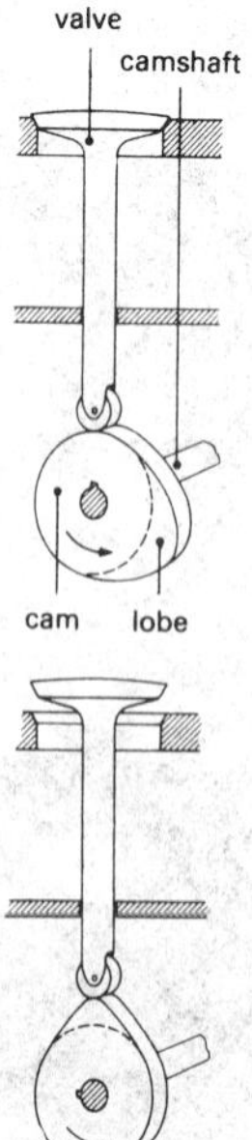

camshaft

preserve. **2.** *Slang.* To make a recording of: *can the audience's applause.* **3.** *Slang.* **a.** To dismiss from employment or school. **b.** To quit or dispense with: *can the chatter.* [ME *canne,* a water container < OE.] **—can'ner** *n.*
Can·a·da balsam (kăn'ə-də) *n.* **1.** The balsam fir. **2.** A viscous, yellowish, transparent resin obtained from the balsam fir and used as a mounting cement for microscopic specimens.
Canada goose *n.* A common wild goose, *Branta canadensis,* of North America, having grayish plumage, a black neck and head, and a white face patch.
Canada jay *n.* A bird, *Perisoreus canadensis,* of North American conifer forests, having gray plumage and a black-capped head.
Canada thistle *n.* A weedy plant, *Cirsium arvense,* native to Eurasia, having prickly leaves and clusters of purplish flowers.
Ca·na·di·an bacon (kə-nā'dē-ən) *n.* Cured rolled bacon from the loin of a pig.
Canadian French *n.* The language of the French-Canadians.
ca·naille (kə-nī', -nāl') *n.* The masses of common people; rabble; riffraff. [Fr. < Ital. *canaglia* < *cane,* dog < Lat. *canis.*]
ca·nal (kə-năl') *n.* **1.** A manmade waterway or artificially improved river used for irrigation, shipping, or travel. **2.** *Anat.* A tube or duct. **3.** *Astron.* One of the faint, hazy markings resembling straight lines on the surface of Mars. *—tr.v.* **-nalled, -nal·ling, -nals** or **-naled, -nal·ing, -nals. 1.** To dig an artificial waterway through. **2.** To provide with a canal or canals. [Partly < Fr., channel, and partly < ME, tube, both < Lat. *canalis,* tube, channel.]
can·a·lic·u·late (kăn'ə-lĭk'yə-lĭt, -lāt') *adj.* Having grooves or channels. [Lat. *canaliculatus* < *canaliculus,* dim. of *canalis,* channel.]
can·a·lic·u·lus (kăn'ə-lĭk'yə-ləs) *n., pl.* **-li** (-lī'). A small bodily channel, as a tear duct. [Lat., dim. of *canalis,* conduit.] **—can'a·lic'u·lar** (-lər) *adj.*
can·a·li·za·tion (kăn'ə-lĭ-zā'shən) *n.* **1.** The act or an instance of canalizing. **2.** A system of canals.
can·a·lize (kăn'ə-līz') *tr.v.* **-lized, -liz·ing, -liz·es. 1.** To furnish with, build, or convert into a canal or canals. **2.** To channel into a particular direction; provide an outlet for.
canal rays *pl.n.* Positively charged ions formed in a gas by electrical discharge and attracted to the cathode of the discharge tube. Not in current technical use. [Transl. of G. *Kanalstrahl* (from the fissures in the cathode, through which the ions pass).]
can·a·pé (kăn'ə-pā', -pē) *n.* A cracker or small, thin piece of bread or toast spread with cheese, meat, or relish and served as an appetizer. [Fr. < *canapé,* couch < Med. Lat. *canapeum,* mosquito net. —see CANOPY.]
ca·nard (kə-närd') *n.* An unfounded or false, deliberately misleading story. [Fr., prob. < the phrase *vendre un canard á moitié,* to half-sell a duck, to swindle.]
ca·nar·y (kə-nâr'ē) *n., pl.* **-ies. 1.** A songbird, *Serinus canaria,* native to the Canary Islands, that is greenish to yellow and has long been bred as a cage bird. **2.** *Slang.* An informer; stool pigeon. **3.** A sweet white wine, similar to Madeira, from the Canary Islands. **4.** A lively 16th-century court dance. **5.** A light to moderate or vivid yellow. [Fr. *canari* < OSp. *canario* < (*Islas*) *Canarias,* Canary (Islands) < LLat. *Canariae* (*Insulae*), (islands) of dogs < Lat. *canis,* dog.]
canary grass *n.* A grass, *Phalaris canariensis,* native to Europe, having straw-colored seeds used to feed birds.
ca·nas·ta (kə-năs'tə) *n.* A card game for two to six players, related to rummy and requiring two decks of cards. [Sp. < *canasto,* basket < Lat. *canistrum.* —see CANISTER.]
can·can (kăn'kăn') *n.* An exuberant dance, originating in France, performed by women and marked by high kicking. [Fr.]
can·cel (kăn'səl) *v.* **-celed, -cel·ing, -cels** also **-celled, -cel·ling, -cels.** *—tr.* **1.** To cross out with lines or other markings. **2.** To annul or invalidate: *cancel an invitation.* **3.** To mark or perforate (a postage stamp, for example) to indicate that it may not be used again. **4.** To equalize or make up for; offset. **5.** *Math.* **a.** To remove a common factor from the numerator and denominator of a fractional expression. **b.** To remove a common factor or term from both members of an equation or inequality. **6.** *Printing.* To omit or delete. *—intr.* To balance or neutralize one another: *two forces that canceled out.* *—n.* **1. a.** The omission or deletion of typed or printed matter. **b.** The matter omitted or deleted or its replacement. **2.** A part of a book used as a substitute for an original part of the book. [ME < Norman Fr. *canceler* < Lat. *cancellare,* to cross out < *cancelli,* lattice, dim. of *cancer,* lattice.] **—can'cel·a·ble** *adj.* **—can'cel·er** *n.*
can·cel·a·tion (kăn'sə-lā'shən) *n.* Variant of **cancellation.**
can·cel·late (kăn-sĕl'ĭt, kăn'sə-lāt') also **can·cel·lat·ed** (-lā'tĭd). *adj. Anat.* Cancellous. [Lat. *cancellatus,* p.part. of *cancellare,* to make like a lattice. —see CANCEL.]
can·cel·la·tion also **can·ce·la·tion** (kăn'sə-lā'shən) *n.* **1.** The act of canceling. **2.** Marks or perforations indicating canceling. **3.** Something that has been canceled.
can·cel·lous (kăn-sĕl'əs, kăn'sə-ləs) *adj. Anat.* Having a coarse netlike or spongy structure. Used of bone.
can·cer (kăn'sər) *n.* **1. a.** Any of various malignant neoplasms that manifest invasiveness and a tendency to metastasize to new sites. **b.** The pathological condition characterized by such growths. **2.** A pernicious, spreading evil: *A cancer of bigotry spread through the community.* **3. Cancer.** A constellation in the Northern Hemisphere near Leo and Gemini. **4. Cancer. a.** The fourth sign of the zodiac. **b.** One born under the astrological sign of Cancer. [Lat. *cancer, cancr-.*] **—can'cer·ous** (-sər-əs) *adj.*
can·croid (kăng'kroid') *adj.* **1.** Resembling a cancer. **2.** Similar to a crab. *—n.* A skin cancer.
can·del·a (kăn-dĕl'ə) *n.* A unit of luminous intensity equal to $^{1}/_{60}$ of the luminous intensity per square centimeter of a blackbody radiating at the temperature of solidification of platinum (2,046°K). [Lat. *candela,* candle.]
can·de·la·bra (kăn'dl-ä'brə, -ăb'rə, -ā'brə) *n.* A candelabrum.
can·de·la·brum (kăn'dl-ä'brəm, -ăb'rəm, -ā'brəm) *n., pl.* **-bra** (-brə) or **-brums.** A large decorative candlestick having several arms or branches. [Lat. < *candela,* candle.]
can·dent (kăn'dənt) *adj.* Having a white-hot glow; incandescent. [Lat. *candens, candent-,* pr.part. of *candēre,* to shine.]
can·des·cence (kăn-dĕs'əns) *n.* The state of being white hot; incandescence. [< Lat. *candescens,* pr.part. of *candescere,* inceptive of *candēre,* to shine.] **—can·des'cent** (-ənt) *adj.* **—can·des'cent·ly** *adv.*
can·did (kăn'dĭd) *adj.* **1.** Free from prejudice; impartial. **2.** Without pretense or reserve; straightforward: *candid opinions.* **3.** Not posed or rehearsed: *a candid picture.* *—n.* An unposed informal photograph. [Fr. *candide* < Lat. *candidus* < *candēre,* to shine.] **—can'did·ly** *adv.* **—can'did·ness** *n.*
can·di·da (kăn'dĭ-də) *n.* Any of the pathogenic yeastlike imperfect fungi of the genus *Candida.* [NLat. *Candida,* genus name < Lat., fem. of *candidus,* white.]
can·di·date (kăn'dĭ-dāt', -dĭt) *n.* **1.** A person who seeks or is nominated for an office, prize or honor. **2.** A person who seems likely to gain a certain position or come to a certain fate. [Lat. *candidatus,* clothed in white (from the white togas worn by Romans seeking office) < *candidus,* white. —see CANDID.] **—can'di·da·cy** (-də-sē), **can'di·da·ture'** (-də-cho͝or', -chər) *n.*
candid camera *n.* A small, easily operated camera with a fast lens for taking unposed or informal photographs.
can·di·di·a·sis (kăn'dĭ-dī'ə-sĭs) *n.* A fungous infection caused by a member of the genus *Candida.*
can·died (kăn'dēd) *adj.* Permeated, covered, encrusted, or cooked with sugar: *candied sweet potatoes.*
can·dle (kăn'dl) *n.* **1.** A solid, usually cylindrical mass of tallow, wax, or other fatty substance with an axially embedded wick that is burned to provide light. **2.** Something resembling a candle in shape or use. **3.** *Physics.* **a.** An obsolete unit of luminous intensity, originally defined in terms of a wax candle with standard composition and equal to 1.02 candelas. **b.** A candela. *—tr.v.* **-dled, -dling, -dles.** To examine (an egg) for freshness in front of a light. ***—idioms.*** **burn (one's) candle at both ends.** To expend too much of one's energy in too many directions. **not hold a candle to.** To be not nearly as good as. [ME *candel* < OE < Lat. *candela* < *candēre,* to shine.] **—can'dler** *n.*
can·dle·ber·ry (kăn'dl-bĕr'ē) *n.* The wax myrtle or its fruit.
can·dle·fish (kăn'dl-fĭsh') *n., pl.* **candlefish** or **-fish·es.** An oily, edible fish, *Thaleichthys pacificus,* of northern Pacific waters, formerly dried and used as a torch by Indians.
can·dle-foot (kăn'dl-fo͝ot') *n.* A foot-candle.
can·dle·hold·er (kăn'dl-hōl'dər) *n.* A candlestick.
can·dle·light (kăn'dl-līt') *n.* **1.** Illumination from a candle or candles. **2.** Dusk; twilight.
Can·dle·mas (kăn'dl-məs) *n.* A church festival celebrated on February 2 as the feast of the purification of the Virgin Mary and the presentation of the infant Christ in the temple. [ME *candelmasse* < OE *candelmæsse* : *candel,* candle + *mæsse,* mass (from the blessing of candles at the feast).]
can·dle·nut (kăn'dl-nŭt') *n.* **1.** A tree, *Aleurites moluccana,* of tropical Asia and Polynesia, bearing nuts that yield an oil used in paints and varnishes. **2.** The nut of the candlenut.
can·dle·pin (kăn'dl-pĭn') *n.* **1.** A slender bowling pin used in a variation of the game of tenpins. **2. candlepins** *(used with a sing. verb).* A bowling game using a ball smaller than that used in tenpins.
can·dle·pow·er (kăn'dl-pou'ər) *n.* Luminous intensity expressed in standard candles.
can·dle·stick (kăn'dl-stĭk') *n.* A holder, often ornamental, with cups or spikes for a candle or candles. [ME *candelstikke* < OE *candelsticca.*]
can·dle·wick (kăn'dl-wĭk') *n.* The wick of a candle.
can·dle·wick·ing (kăn'dl-wĭk'ĭng) *n.* **1.** Soft, heavy cotton thread similar to that used to make wicks for candles. **2.** Embroidery made of tufts of candlewicking.
can·dle·wood (kăn'dl-wo͝od') *n.* **1.** The ocotillo. **2.** The resinous wood of the ocotillo or similar plants.
can·dor (kăn'dər) *n.* **1.** Frankness of expression; straightforwardness. **2.** Freedom from prejudice; impartiality. [Lat. < *candēre,* to shine.]
can·dour (kăn'dər) *n. Chiefly Brit.* Variant of **candor.**

canal

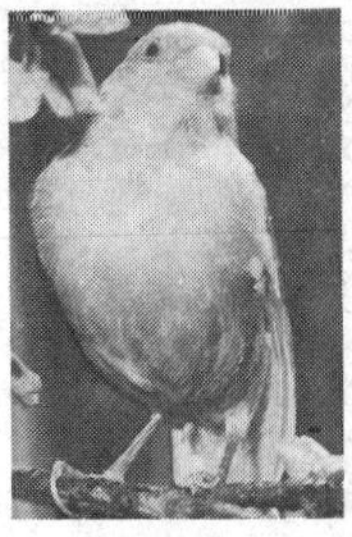
canary

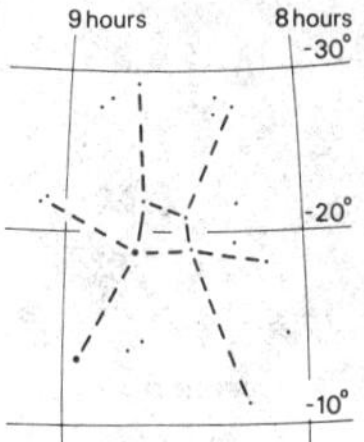

cancer
The constellation Cancer

candelabrum

candlestick
19th-century English candlesticks

can·dy (kăn′dē) *n., pl.* **-dies. 1.** Any of numerous kinds of rich, sweet confections made with sugar, corn syrup, or similar substances, often combined with chocolate, dairy products, fruits, or nuts. **2.** A single piece of such a confection. *—v.* **-died, -dy·ing, -dies.** *—tr.* **1.** To reduce to sugar crystals. **2.** To cook, preserve, saturate, or coat with sugar or syrup. **3.** To make pleasant or agreeable; sweeten. *—intr.* **1.** To crystallize, as sugar. **2.** To become coated with sugar or syrup. [Short for *sugar candy* < ME *sugre candie* < OFr. *sucre candi* < Ital. *zucchero candi* < Ar. *sukkar qandī* : *sukkar,* sugar + *qandī,* candied < *qand,* cane sugar, of Dravidian orig.]

candy striper *n.* A usually teen-age volunteer nurse's aid in a hospital. [From the resemblance of the volunteer's red and white striped uniform to a candy cane.]

can·dy·tuft (kăn′dē-tŭft′) *n.* Any of various plants of the genus *Iberis,* having clusters of white, red, or purplish flowers. [Obs. *Candy,* var. of *Candia,* Crete + TUFT.]

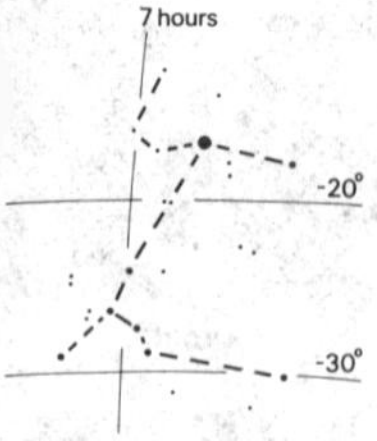

Canis Major

cane (kān) *n.* **1. a.** A slender, jointed stem, woody but usually flexible, as of bamboo, rattan, or certain palm trees. **b.** A plant having such a stem. **c.** Such stems or strips of such stems used for wickerwork. **2.** A grass, *Arundinaria gigantea,* of the southeastern United States, having long stiff stems and often forming canebrakes. **3.** The long, woody stem of a raspberry, blackberry, certain roses, or similar plants. **4.** Sugar cane. **5.** A stick used as an aid in walking. **6.** A rod used for flogging. *—tr.v.* **caned, can·ing, canes. 1.** To make, supply, or repair with cane. **2.** To hit or beat with a cane. [ME < Norman Fr. < Med. Lat. *canna* < Gk. *kanna,* reed.] **—can′er** *n.*

cane·brake (kān′brāk′) *n.* A dense thicket of cane.

ca·nes·cent (kə-nĕs′ənt) *adj.* **1.** *Biol.* Covered with whitish or grayish down; hoary. **2.** Turning white or grayish. [Lat. *canescens, canescent-,* p.part. of *canescere,* inchoative of *canēre,* to be white < *canus,* white.] **—ca·nes′cence** *n.*

cane sugar *n.* Sucrose.

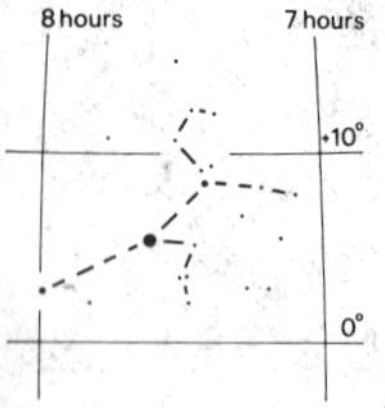

Canis Minor

Ca·nes Ve·nat·i·ci (kā′nēz vĭ-năt′ĭ-sī′) *n.* A constellation in the Northern Hemisphere near Ursa Major and Boötes, under the Big Dipper's handle. [Lat., hunting dogs.]

Ca·nic·u·la (kə-nĭk′yə-lə) *n.* Sirius. [Lat. < dim. of *canis,* dog.]

ca·nic·u·lar (kə-nĭk′yə-lər) *adj.* **1.** Of or pertaining to the Dog Star. **2.** Pertaining to the dog days of July and August.

ca·nine (kā′nīn′) *adj.* **1.** Of, pertaining to, or characteristic of a member of the family Canidae, which includes dogs, wolves, and foxes. **2.** Of or designating one of the conical teeth located between the incisors and the first bicuspids. *—n.* **1.** A canine animal. **2.** A canine tooth. [Lat. *caninus* < *canis,* dog.]

Ca·nis Ma·jor (kā′nĭs mā′jər, kăn′ĭs) *n.* A constellation in the Southern Hemisphere near Puppis and Lepus containing the star Sirius. [Lat., the larger dog.]

cannon

Canis Mi·nor (mī′nər) *n.* A constellation in the equatorial region of the Southern Hemisphere near Hydra and Monoceros containing the star Procyon. [Lat., the smaller dog.]

can·is·ter (kăn′ĭ-stər) *n.* **1.** A container, usually of thin metal, for holding dry foods. **2.** A metallic cylinder that when fired from a gun bursts and scatters the shot packed inside it. **3.** The part of a gas mask containing a filter for removing poison gas from the surrounding air. [Lat. *canistrum,* basket < Gk. *kanastron* < *kanna,* reed.]

can·ker (kăng′kər) *n.* **1.** An ulcerous sore of the mouth and lips. **2.** A necrotic area in a plant surrounded by healthy wood or bark. **3.** Any of several animal diseases characterized by chronic inflammatory processes. **4.** A source of spreading corruption or debilitation. *—v.* **-kered, -ker·ing, -kers.** *—tr.* **1.** To attack or infect with canker. **2.** To cause to decay or become corrupt. *—intr.* To become infected with or as if with canker. [ME < OE *cancer,* cancer and < OFr. *cancre,* cancer, both < Lat. *cancer.*]

can·ker·ous (kăng′kər-əs) *adj.* **1.** Of the nature of or infected with a canker; ulcerous. **2.** Causing canker; ulcerating.

canker sore *n.* A small, painful ulcer usually of the mouth.

can·ker·worm (kăng′kər-wûrm′) *n.* The larva of either of two moths, *Paleacrita vernata* or *Alsophila pometaria,* that are destructive to fruit and shade trees.

can·na (kăn′ə) *n.* Any of various tropical plants of the genus *Canna,* having broad leaves and showy red or yellow flowers. [NLat. *Canna,* genus name < Lat. *canna,* cane.]

can·na·bi·di·ol (kăn′ə-bĭ-dī′ôl′, -ōl′) *n.* A chemical constituent of cannabis, $C_{21}H_{28}(OH)_2$. [CANNABI(S) + DI-¹ + -OL.]

can·na·bin (kăn′ə-bĭn) *n.* A resinous material extracted from cannabis. [CANNAB(IS) + -IN.]

can·na·bis (kăn′ə-bĭs) *n.* **1.** The hemp plant. **2.** The dried flowering tops of the hemp plant. [Lat. < Gk. *kannabis.*] **—can′na·bic** (-bĭk) *adj.*

canned (kănd) *adj.* **1.** Preserved and sealed in a can or jar. **2.** *Informal.* Recorded or taped: *"So if television is to have canned laughter, how about canned tears?"* (Jack Paar).

canned heat *n.* Alcohol or paraffin fuel packed in small cans and used to heat food.

can·nel or **can·nel coal** (kăn′əl) *n.* A bituminous coal that burns brightly with much smoke. [Perh. short for *cannel coal,* var. of *candle coal* (from its bright flame).]

can·nel·lo·ni (kăn′ə-lō′nē) *n.* An Italian pasta dish of large-sized macaroni that is stuffed, baked, and served with tomato sauce or cream sauce. [Ital., pl. of *cannellone,* tubular soup noodle < *cannello,* small tube, dim. of *canna,* reed < Lat. < Gk. *kanna.*]

can·ner·y (kăn′ə-rē) *n., pl.* **-ies.** An establishment where meat, vegetables, or other foods are canned.

can·ni·bal (kăn′ə-bəl) *n.* **1.** A person who eats the flesh of human beings. **2.** An animal that feeds on others of is own kind. [< Sp. *Caníbalis,* name (as recorded by Christopher Columbus 1451–1506), of the man-eating Caribs of Cuba and Haiti, of Arawakan orig.] **—can′ni·bal·ism** *n.* **—can′ni·bal·is′tic** *adj.*

can·ni·bal·ize (kăn′ə-bə-līz′) *tr.v.* **-ized, -iz·ing, -iz·es. 1.** To remove serviceable parts from (damaged airplanes, tanks, or other machinery) for use in the repair of other equipment. **2.** To deprive (an organization) of personnel or equipment for use in another organization. **—can′ni·bal·i·za′tion** *n.*

can·ni·kin (kăn′ĭ-kĭn) *n.* **1.** A little can or cup. **2.** A wooden bucket. [Prob. < Du. *kanneken* < MDu. *canneken,* dim. of *canne,* can, of Germanic orig.]

can·ning (kăn′ĭng) *n.* The act, process, or business of preserving foods in airtight containers.

can·no·li (kə-nō′lē, kă-) *n.* A fried pastry roll with a usually sweet, creamy filling. [Ital., pl. of *cannolo,* tube, dim. of *canna* < Lat., reed. —see CANE.]

can·non (kăn′ən) *n., pl.* **cannon** or **-nons. 1.** A weapon for firing projectiles, consisting of a heavy metal tube mounted on a carriage. **2.** A heavy firearm larger than 0.60 caliber. **3.** The loop at the top of a bell by which the bell is suspended. **4.** A round bit for a horse. **5.** The section of leg containing the cannon bone. **6.** *Chiefly Brit.* A carom made in billiards. *—tr. & intr.v.* **-noned, -non·ing, -nons. 1.** To bombard with or fire cannon. **2.** *Chiefly Brit.* To carom or cause to carom, as in billiards. [ME *canon* < OFr. < OItal. *cannone* < *canna,* tube < Lat., reed. —see CANE.]

can·non·ade (kăn′ə-nād′) *tr. & intr.v.* **-ad·ed, -ad·ing, -ades.** To assault with or deliver heavy artillery fire. *—n.* An extended, usually heavy discharge of artillery. [Prob. < Fr. *canonade,* discharge of artillery < Ital. *cannonata* < *cannone,* cannon. < OItal.]

can·non·ball also **cannon ball** (kăn′ən-bôl′) *n.* **1.** A round projectile fired from a cannon. **2.** A jump into water made with the arms grasping the upraised knees. **3.** Something, such as a fast train, moving with great speed. *—intr.v.* **-balled, -ball·ing, -balls. 1.** To travel rapidly in the manner of a cannonball. **2.** To make a cannonball jump into water.

cannon bone *n.* A supporting bone of the leg in some hoofed mammals.

can·non·eer (kăn′ə-nîr′) *n.* A gunner or artilleryman. [OFr. *canonier* < *canon,* cannon.]

cannon fodder *n.* Soldiers considered as expendable materials of warfare. [Transl. of G. *Kanonenfutter.*]

can·non·ry (kăn′ən-rē) *n., pl.* **-ries. 1.** Artillery; cannons collectively. **2.** Artillery fire.

cannon shot *n.* **1.** Ammunition for a cannon. **2.** A shot or shots fired by cannon. **3.** The firing distance of a cannon.

can·not (kăn′ŏt, kə-nŏt′, kă-) *v.* The negative form of **can.**

Usage: In the phrase *cannot but,* which is sometimes criticized as a double negative, *but* is used in the sense of "except": *One cannot but admire his courage* (that is, "one cannot do otherwise than admire his courage".) Thus, the expression is not to be classed with the double negative that occurs when *but* in the sense of "only" is coupled with a negative. *Cannot but* is accepted in the preceding example by a majority of the Usage Panel. Alternative phrasings are: *can but admire, can only admire, cannot help admiring.* See also Usage notes at **help, seem.**

can·nu·la also **can·u·la** (kăn′yə-lə) *n., pl.* **-las** or **-lae** (-lē′). A tube inserted into a bodily cavity to drain fluid or insert medication. [Lat., dim. of *canna,* reed. —see CANE.]

can·nu·lar (kăn′yə-lər) *adj.* Cannulate.

can·nu·late also **can·u·late** (kăn′yə-lāt′) *—tr.v.* **-lat·ed, -lat·ing, -lates.** To insert a cannula in. *—adj.* Tubular; hollow. **—can′nu·la′tion** *n.*

can·ny (kăn′ē) *adj.* **-ni·er, -ni·est. 1.** Careful and shrewd, esp. where one's own interests are concerned. **2.** *Chiefly Scot.* **a.** Pleasant; attractive. **b.** Gentle; mild. [< CAN¹.] **—can′ni·ly** *adv.* **—can′ni·ness** *n.*

ca·noe (kə-no͞o′) *n.* A light, slender boat with pointed ends, propelled by paddles. *—v.* **-noed, -noe·ing, -noes.** *—tr.* To carry or send by canoe. *—intr.* **1.** To travel in a canoe. **2.** To propel a canoe. [Obs. *canoa* < Sp., of Cariban orig.] **—ca·noe′ist** *n.*

can of worms *n. Informal.* A complicated, often troublesome condition or situation.

can·on¹ (kăn′ən) *n.* **1.** An ecclesiastical law or code of laws established by a church council. **2.** A secular law, rule, or code of law. **3.** A basis for judgment; standard; criterion. **4.** The books of the Bible officially recognized as the Holy Scripture. **5.** The part of the Mass beginning after the Sanctus and ending just before the Lord's Prayer. **6.** The calendar of saints accepted by the Roman Catholic Church. **7.** An authoritative list, as of the works of an author. **8.** *Mus.* A composition or passage in which the same melody is repeated by one or more voices, overlapping in time in the same or a related key. [ME *canoun,* partly < OE, and partly < OFr. *canon,* both < Lat. *canon,* rule < Gk. *kanōn.*]

can·on[2] (kăn′ən) *n.* **1.** One of a chapter of priests serving in a cathedral or collegiate church. **2.** A member of a religious community living under common rules and bound by vows. [ME *canoun* < Norman Fr. *canun* < LLat. *canonicus* < *canon,* rule.]

ca·ñon (kăn′yən) *n.* Variant of **canyon.**

can·on·ess (kăn′ə-nĭs) *n.* A member of a religious community of women living under a common rule but not bound by vows.

ca·non·i·cal (kə-nŏn′ĭ-kəl) also **ca·non·ic** (-ĭk) *adj.* **1.** Pertaining to, required by, or abiding by canon law. **2.** Of or appearing in the Biblical canon. **3.** Officially approved; authoritative; orthodox. **—ca·non′i·cal·ly** *adv.* **—can′on·ic′i·ty** (kăn′ə-nĭs′ĭ-tē) *n.*

canonical hours *pl.n.* **1.** *Eccles.* **a.** A special form of prayer, prescribed by canon law, normally to be recited at specified times of the day, either in common or individually. They are matins (with lauds), prime, tierce, sext, nones, vespers, and complin. **b.** The times of day set aside for these prayers. **2.** *Chiefly Brit.* The hours between 8:00 A.M. and 3:00 P.M., during which marriages may legally take place in parish churches.

ca·non·i·cals (kə-nŏn′ĭ-kəlz) *pl.n.* The dress prescribed by canon for officiating clergy.

ca·non·i·cate (kə-nŏn′ĭ-kāt′, -kĭt) *n.* The office or dignity of a canon; canonry. [Med. Lat. *canonicatus* < LLat. *canonicus,* canon.]

can·on·ist (kăn′ə-nĭst) *n.* A person skilled in canon law. **—can′on·is′tic, can′on·is′ti·cal** *adj.*

can·on·ize (kăn′ə-nīz′) *tr.v.* **-ized, -iz·ing, -iz·es. 1.** To declare (a deceased person) to be a saint and entitled to be fully honored as such by the Roman Catholic Church. **2.** To include in the Biblical canon. **3.** To approve as being within canon law. **—can′on·i·za′tion** *n.* **—can′on·iz′er** *n.*

canon law *n.* The body of officially established rules governing the faith and practice of the members of a Christian church.

can·on·ry (kăn′ən-rē) *n., pl.* **-ries. 1.** The position or benefice of a canon. **2.** Canons collectively.

Ca·no·pic (kə-nō′pĭk, -nŏp′ĭk) *adj.* Designating an ancient Egyptian vase, urn, or jar used to hold the remains of the dead. [After *Canopus,* a city of ancient Egypt.]

Ca·no·pus (kə-nō′pəs) *n.* A star in the constellation Carina, 650 light-years from Earth, the second-brightest star in the sky. [Lat. < Gk. *kanōpos.*]

can·o·py (kăn′ə-pē) *n., pl.* **-pies. 1.** A cloth covering fastened or held horizontally above a person or an object for protection or ornamentation. **2.** *Archit.* An ornamental, rooflike structure. **3.** Any high, overarching covering: *"spreads out into a vast canopy of foliage"* (Thomas Huxley). **4. a.** The transparent, movable enclosure over an aircraft's cockpit. **b.** The hemispherical surface of a parachute. *—tr.v.* **-pied, -py·ing, -pies.** To cover with or as if with a canopy. [ME *canape* < Med. Lat. *canapeum,* mosquito net < Lat. *conopeum* < Gk. *kōnōpion* < *Kanōpos,* Canopus, a city of ancient Egypt.]

ca·no·rous (kə-nôr′əs, -nōr′-, kăn′ər-əs) *adj.* Agreeable to the ears; melodious. [Lat. *canorus* < *canor,* tune < *canere,* to sing.] **—ca·no′rous·ly** *adv.* **—ca·no′rous·ness** *n.*

canst (kănst) *v. Archaic.* Second person singular present tense of **can**[1].

cant[1] (kănt) *n.* **1.** Angular deviation from a vertical or horizontal plane or surface; inclination; slant; slope. **2. a.** A thrust or motion that tilts something. **b.** The tilt caused by such a thrust or motion. **3.** An outer corner, as of a building. **4.** A slanted edge or surface. *—v.* **cant·ed, cant·ing, cants.** *—tr.* **1.** To set at an oblique angle; cause to slant or tilt. **2.** To give a slanting edge to; bevel. **3.** To change the direction of suddenly. *—intr.* **1.** To tilt to one side; slant. **2.** To take an oblique direction or course; swing around, as a ship. [ME, side < Norman Fr.]

cant[2] (kănt) *n.* **1.** Whining, affected speech. **2.** Discourse recited monotonously or mechanically. **3.** Hypocritically pious language. **4.** The special vocabulary peculiar to the members of an underworld group; argot. **5.** The special terminology understood among the members of a profession, discipline, or class but obscure to the general population; jargon. *—intr.v.* **cant·ed, cant·ing, cants. 1.** To speak in a whining, pleading tone. **2.** To speak tediously or sententiously; moralize. **3.** To use special jargon or argot. [Prob. < Norman Fr., singing < *canter,* to sing < Lat. *cantare,* freq. of *canere,* to sing.] **—cant′ing·ly** *adv.* **—cant′ing·ness** *n.*

can't (kănt, känt). Cannot.

can·ta·bi·le (kän-tä′bə-lā′) *Mus. —adj.* Marked by a smooth, lyrical, flowing style. Used as a direction to the performer. *—n.* A cantabile passage or movement. [Ital. < LLat. *cantabilis,* worthy to be sung < Lat. *cantare,* freq. of *canere,* to sing.] **—can·ta′bi·le′** *adv.*

Can·ta·brig·i·an (kăn′tə-brĭj′ē-ən) *adj.* Of or pertaining to Cambridge University. *—n.* A student or graduate of Cambridge University. [< Med. Lat. *Cantabrigia,* Cambridge.]

can·ta·la (kăn-tä′lə) *n.* **1.** A century plant, *Agave cantula,* native to tropical America, cultivated for its coarse, tough fiber. **2.** The fiber of the cantala. [Orig. unknown.]

can·ta·loupe also **can·ta·loup** (kăn′tl-ōp′) *n.* **1.** A variety of melon, *Cucumis melo cantalupensis,* having fruit with a ribbed, rough rind and aromatic orange flesh. **2.** Any of several similar melons. **3.** The fruit of a cantaloupe. [Fr. *cantaloup* < Ital. *cantalupo* < *Cantalupo,* a former papal villa near Rome.]

can·tan·ker·ous (kăn-tăng′kər-əs) *adj.* Ill-tempered and quarrelsome; disagreeable. [Perh. ult. < ME *contek,* contentious.] **—can·tan′ker·ous·ly** *adv.* **—can·tan′ker·ous·ness** *n.*

can·ta·ta (kən-tä′tə) *n.* A vocal and instrumental composition comprising choruses, solos, and recitatives. [Ital. *(aria) cantata,* sung (aria) < *cantare,* to sing < Lat., freq. of *canere.*]

can·teen (kăn-tēn′) *n.* **1. a.** A store for on-base military personnel. **b.** *Chiefly Brit.* A club for soldiers. **2.** An institutional recreation hall or cafeteria. **3.** A temporary or mobile eating place, esp. one set up in an emergency. **4. a.** A mess kit. **b.** A box divided into compartments containing a set of cooking gear. **5.** A flask for drinking water of the kind carried by soldiers. [Fr. *cantine* < Ital. *cantina,* wine cellar < *canto,* corner.]

can·ter (kăn′tər) *n.* A gait slower than a gallop but faster than a trot. *—v.* **-tered, -ter·ing, -ters.** *—intr.* To move or ride at a canter. *—tr.* To cause (a horse) to go at a canter. [Short for *Canterbury gallop,* after *Canterbury,* England, toward which pilgrims rode at an easy pace.]

Can·ter·bur·y bells (kăn′tər-bĕr′ē) *n. (used with a sing. or pl. verb).* A plant, *Campanula medium,* native to Europe, widely cultivated for its showy, bell-shaped violet-blue flowers. [From the association of the flowers with the bells on the horses of Canterbury pilgrims.]

can·tha·ris (kăn′thər-ĭs) *n., pl.* **can·thar·i·des** (kăn-thăr′ĭ-dēz′). A toxic preparation of the crushed, dried bodies of the beetle *Lytta vesicatoria* (or *Cantharis vesicatoria*), formerly used as a counterirritant for skin blisters and as an aphrodisiac. [Lat., a kind of beetle < Gk. *kantharis.*]

cant hook *n.* A peavey. [< CANT[1].]

can·thi·tis (kăn-thī′tĭs) *n.* Inflammation of the canthus.

can·thus (kăn′thəs) *n., pl.* **-thi** (-thī′). The corner at either side of the eye, formed by the meeting of the upper and lower eyelids. [LLat. < Gk. *kanthos.*]

can·ti·cle (kăn′tĭ-kəl) *n.* A song or chant, esp. a nonmetrical hymn with words taken directly from a Biblical text. [ME < Lat. *canticulum,* dim. of *cantus,* song < *canere,* to sing.]

can·ti·le·ver (kăn′tl-ē′vər, -ĕv′ər) *n.* **1.** A projecting beam or other structure supported only at one end. **2.** A beam or other member projecting beyond a fulcrum and supported by a balancing member or a downward force behind the fulcrum. **3.** A bracket or block supporting a balcony or cornice. *—tr.v.* **-vered, -ver·ing, -vers.** To extend outward or build as a cantilever. [Perh. CANT[1] + LEVER.]

cantilever bridge *n.* A bridge formed by two projecting beams or trusses that are joined in the center by a connecting member and are supported on piers and anchored by counterbalancing members.

can·til·late (kăn′tl-āt′) *tr. & intr.v.* **-lat·ed, -lat·ing, -lates.** To chant or recite in a musical monotone, as in Jewish or other rituals. [Lat. *cantillare, cantillat-,* to hum < *cantare,* to sing, freq. of *canere.*] **—can′til·la′tion** *n.*

can·ti·na (kăn-tē′nə) *n. Southwestern U.S.* An establishment that serves liquor; a bar or saloon. [Sp., canteen < Ital., wine cellar < *canto,* corner.]

can·tle (kăn′tl) *n.* **1.** The rear part of a saddle. **2.** A corner or portion, esp. when cut off from something. [ME *cantel,* corner < Norman Fr., dim. of *cant,* corner.]

can·to (kăn′tō) *n., pl.* **-tos.** One of the principal divisions of a long poem. [Ital. < Lat. *cantus,* song. —see CANTICLE.]

can·ton (kăn′tən, -tŏn′) *n.* **1. a.** A small territorial division of a country, esp. one of the states of Switzerland. **b.** A subdivision of an arrondissement in France. **2.** A small, square division of a heraldic shield, usually in the upper right corner. **3.** A division of a flag, usually rectangular, occupying the upper corner next to the staff. *—tr.v.* **-toned, -ton·ing, -tons. 1.** To divide into parts, esp. into cantons or territorial districts. **2.** (kăn-tŏn′, -tōn′).To assign quarters to (troops); billet. [Fr. < OFr. < Ital. *cantone,* aug. of *canto,* corner.] **—can′ton·al** (kăn′tə-nəl, kăn-tŏn′əl) *adj.*

Can·ton crepe (kăn′tŏn′) *n.* A soft fabric of silk or similar material with a finely crinkled texture, similar to crêpe de Chine but heavier. [After *Canton* (Guangzhou), China.]

Can·ton·ese (kăn′tə-nēz′, -nēs′) *n.* The dialect of Chinese spoken in and around Guangzhou (formerly Canton), China. **—Can′ton·ese′** *adj.*

Canton flannel (kăn′tŏn′) *n.* Flannelette. [After *Canton* (Guangzhou), China.]

can·ton·ment (kăn-tōn′mənt, -tŏn′-) *n.* **1.** A group of more or less temporary buildings for housing troops. **2.** The assignment of troops to temporary quarters.

Canton ware *n.* Ceramic ware including blue-and-white enameled porcelain exported from China, esp. during the 18th and 19th centuries. [After *Canton* (Guangzhou), China.]

can·tor (kăn′tər) *n.* **1.** The official soloist or chief singer of the liturgy in a synagogue. **2.** The person who leads a church choir or congregation in singing. [Lat., singer < *canere,* to sing.]

can·trip (kăn′trĭp) *n. Scot.* **1.** A magic spell; a witch's trick. **2.** A mischievous trick; prank. [Orig. unknown.]

canopy
19th-century American canopy bed

cantaloupe

can·tus fir·mus (kăn′təs fîr′məs, fûr′-) *n.* A plainsong serving as the basis of a polyphonic composition by the addition of contrapuntal voices, as in 15th-century polyphony. [Med. Lat., fixed melody.]
Ca·nuck (kə-nŭk′) *n. Offensive Slang.* A Canadian, esp. a French Canadian. [Prob. alteration of Canadian.]
can·u·la (kăn′yə-lə) *n.* Variant of **cannula.**
can·u·late (kăn′yə-lāt′) *v. & adj.* Variant of **cannulate.**
can·vas (kăn′vəs) *n.* **1.** A heavy, coarse, closely woven fabric of cotton, hemp, or flax, used for making tents and sails. **2. a.** A piece of canvas on which a painting is made, esp. an oil painting. **b.** A painting of this kind. **3.** Sailcloth. **4.** A sail or sails collectively. **5. a.** A tent or tents collectively. **b.** A circus tent. **6.** A fabric of coarse open weave, used as a foundation for needlework. **7.** The floor of a ring in which boxing or wrestling takes place. [ME *canevas* < Norman Fr. *canevaz* < Lat. *cannabis,* hemp. —see CANNABIS.]
can·vas·back (kăn′vəs-băk′) *n.* A North American duck, *Aythya valisneria,* having a reddish-brown head and neck and a whitish back.

canvasback

canvas duck *n.* A fabric made of lightweight cotton or linen.
can·vass (kăn′vəs) *v.* **-vassed, -vass·ing, -vass·es.** —*tr.* **1.** To examine carefully or discuss thoroughly; scrutinize. **2. a.** To go through (a region) or go to (persons) to solicit votes, orders, or subscriptions. **b.** To conduct a survey of (public opinion) on a given subject; poll. —*intr.* **1.** To make a thorough examination or conduct a detailed discussion. **2.** To solicit political support, sales orders, or opinions. —*n.* **1.** An examination or discussion. **2. a.** A solicitation of votes, sales orders, or opinions. **b.** A survey of public opinion. [< obs. *canvass,* to toss in a canvas sheet as punishment < CANVAS.] **—can′vass·er** *n.*
can·yon also **ca·ñon** (kăn′yən) *n.* A narrow chasm with steep cliff walls, formed by running water; gorge. [Sp. *cañon,* aug. of *caña,* tube < Lat. *canna,* reed < Gk. *kanna.*]

canyon
The Grand Canyon, United States

can·zo·ne (kăn-zō′nē, känt-sō′nā) *n., pl.* **-nes** (-nēz, -nāz) or **-ni** (-nē). **1.** A lyric 13th-century Italian or Provençal poetic form. **2.** A polyphonic song form evolving from the canzone and resembling the madrigal in style. [Ital. < Lat. *cantio,* song < *canere,* to sing.]
can·zo·net (kăn′zə-nĕt′) *n.* A short, lighthearted song or air. [Ital. *canzonetta,* dim. of *canzone.* —see CANZONE.]
caou·tchouc (kou′cho͝ok′, -cho͞ok′) *n.* Rubber[1] (sense 1). [Fr. < obs. Sp. *cauchuc* < Quechua.]
cap (kăp) *n.* **1.** A usually soft and close-fitting head covering, either brimless or with a visor. **2. a.** A special head covering worn to indicate rank, occupation, or membership in a particular group: *a cardinal's cap.* **b.** A mortarboard (sense 2). **3. a.** An object similar to a cap in form, use, or position: *a bottle cap.* **b.** Something that limits or restrains: *a cap on government spending.* **4.** *Archit.* The capital of a column. **5.** The top part, or pileus, of a fungus such as a mushroom. **6. a.** A percussion cap. **b.** A small explosive charge enclosed in paper for use in a toy gun. **7.** Any of several sizes of writing paper, as foolscap. —*tr.v.* **capped, cap·ping, caps. 1.** To put a cap on. **2.** To lie over or on top of; cover: *Snow capped the hills.* **3.** To apply the finishing touch to; complete: *cap a meal with dessert.* **4.** To surpass; outdo. [ME *cappe* < OE *cæppe* < LLat. *cappa.*]

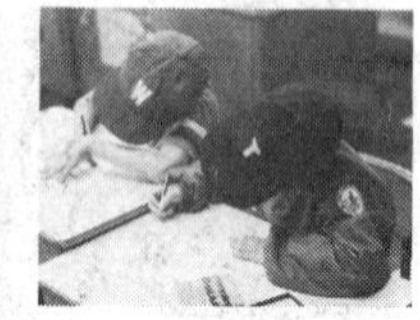
cap

ca·pa·bil·i·ty (kā′pə-bĭl′ĭ-tē) *n., pl.* **-ties. 1.** The quality or condition of being capable; ability. **2.** Potential ability: *lived up to her capabilities.* **3.** The capacity to be used, treated, or developed for a specific purpose.
ca·pa·ble (kā′pə-bəl) *adj.* **1.** Having capacity or ability; efficient; able. **2.** Having the mental or physical capacity for; qualified for. **3.** Open to; susceptible to: *an error capable of remedy.* [Fr. < OFr. < LLat. *capabilis,* spacious < *capere,* to take.] **—ca′pa·ble·ness** *n.* **—ca′pa·bly** *adv.*
ca·pa·cious (kə-pā′shəs) *adj.* Capable of containing a large quantity; spacious. [< Lat. *capax, capac-* < *capere,* to take.] **—ca·pa′cious·ly** *adv.* **—ca·pa′cious·ness** *n.*
ca·pac·i·tance (kə-păs′ĭ-təns) *n.* **1.** The ratio of charge to potential on an electrically charged, isolated conductor. **2.** The ratio of the electric charge transferred from one to the other of a pair of conductors to the resulting potential difference between them. **3. a.** The property of a circuit element that permits it to store charge. **b.** The part of the circuit exhibiting capacitance. [CAPACIT(Y) + -ANCE.] **—ca·pac′i·tive** (-tĭv) *adj.* **—ca·pac′i·tive·ly** *adv.*

caparison
16th-century German jousting armor

ca·pac·i·tate (kə-păs′ĭ-tāt′) *tr.v.* **-tat·ed, -tat·ing, -tates.** To render fit; make qualified; enable. [CAPACIT(Y) + -ATE[1].] **—ca·pac′i·ta′tion** *n.*
ca·pac·i·tor (kə-păs′ĭ-tər) *n.* An electric circuit element used to store charge temporarily, consisting in general of two metallic plates separated by a dielectric.
ca·pac·i·ty (kə-păs′ĭ-tē) *n., pl.* **-ties. 1. a.** The ability to receive, hold, or absorb. **b.** A measure of this ability; volume. **2.** The maximum amount that can be contained: *a trunk filled to capacity.* **3.** The maximum or optimum amount of production. **4.** The ability to learn or retain knowledge. **5.** The ability to do something; faculty: *a capacity for self-expression.* **6.** The quality of being suitable for or receptive to specified treatment: *the capacity of elastic to be stretched.* **7.** The position in which one functions; role: *his capacity as host.* **8.** Legal qualification or authority: *the capacity to make an arrest.* **9.** *Obs.* Capacitance. **—modifier:** *a capacity crowd.* [ME *capacite* < OFr. < Lat. *capacitas* < *capax,* spacious. —see CAPACIOUS.]
cap-a-pie or **cap-à-pie** (kăp′ə-pē′) *adv.* From head to foot. [OFr. *(de) cap a pie,* (from) head to foot < OProv. *(de) cap a pe.*]
ca·par·i·son (kə-păr′ĭ-sən) *n.* **1.** A usually ornamental covering for a horse's saddle or harness; trappings. **2.** Richly ornamented clothing; finery. —*tr.v.* **-soned, -son·ing, -sons.** To outfit with a caparison. [Obs. Fr. *caparasson* < Sp. *caparazón.*]
cape[1] (kāp) *n.* A sleeveless garment fastened at the throat and worn hanging over the shoulders. [Fr., partly < OProv. *cape,* and partly < Sp. *capa,* both < Med. Lat. *cappa,* cloak.]

cape[1]

cape[2] (kāp) *n.* A point or head of land projecting into a sea or other body of water; promontory. [ME *cap* < OFr. < OProv. < Lat. *caput,* head.]
Cape Cod cottage *n.* A compact one- or one-and-a-half-story house with a gabled roof and a central chimney. [After *Cape Cod,* Massachusetts.]
Cape cowslip *n.* Any of various bulbous South African plants of the genus *Lachenalia,* having clusters of drooping red or yellow flowers and widely cultivated as a potted plant. [After *Cape* of Good Hope, a province of the Republic of South Africa.]
Cape gooseberry *n.* A plant, *Physalis peruviana,* native to tropical America, having yellow flowers and edible yellow berries.
Cape jasmine *n.* The gardenia.
cap·e·lin (kăp′ə-lĭn, kăp′lĭn) also **cap·lin** (kăp′lĭn) *n.* A small, edible marine fish, *Mallotus villosus,* of northern Atlantic and Pacific waters, related to and resembling the smelts. [Canadian Fr. *capelan* < Fr., codfish < OProv.]
Ca·pel·la (kə-pĕl′ə) *n.* A double star in Auriga, the brightest star in the constellation, approximately 46 light-years from Earth. [Lat., dim. of *caper,* goat.]
ca·per[1] (kā′pər) *n.* **1.** A playful leap or hop. **2.** A wild escapade or prank. **3.** A criminal plot or enterprise. —*intr.v.* **-pered, -per·ing, -pers.** To leap or frisk about; frolic. [Alteration of CAPRIOLE.]
ca·per[2] (kā′pər) *n.* **1.** A spiny, trailing shrub, *Capparis spinosa,* of the Mediterranean region. **2. a.** A pickled flower bud of the caper, used as a condiment. **b.** A similar pickled bud or pod. [ME *caperis* < Lat. *capparis* < Gk. *kapparis.*]
cap·er·cail·lie (kăp′ər-kāl′yē, -kā′lē) also **cap·er·cail·zie** (-kāl′zē) *n.* A large grouse, *Tetrao urogallus,* of northern Europe, having dark plumage and a fanlike tail. [Sc. Gael. *capull coille* : *capull,* horse (prob. < Lat. *caballus*) + *coille,* forest.]
cape·skin (kāp′skĭn′) *n.* Soft leather made from sheepskin, used esp. for gloves. [After *Cape* of Good Hope, a province of the Republic of South Africa.]
Ca·pe·tian (kə-pē′shən) *adj.* Pertaining or belonging to the French dynasty (987–1328) founded by Hugh Capet. —*n.* A member of the Capetian dynasty.
cap·ful (kăp′fo͝ol′) *n., pl.* **fuls.** The amount a cap will hold.
cap gun *n.* A cap pistol.
ca·pi·as (kā′pē-əs) *n. Law.* A writ authorizing an officer to arrest the person specified therein. [ME < Med. Lat. < Lat., you may arrest (the first word of the writ) < *capere,* to seize.]
cap·il·lar·i·ty (kăp′ə-lăr′ĭ-tē) *n., pl.* **-ties.** The interaction between contacting surfaces of a liquid and a solid that distorts the liquid surface from a planar shape.
cap·il·lar·o·scope (kăp′ə-lăr′ə-skōp′) *n.* A microscope used in capillaroscopy. [CAPILLAR(Y) + -SCOPE.]
cap·il·la·ros·co·py (căp′ə-lə-rŏs′kə-pē) *n.* The diagnostic examination of the capillaries. [CAPILLAR(Y) + -SCOPY.]
cap·il·lar·y (kăp′ə-lĕr′ē) *adj.* **1.** Pertaining to or resembling a hair; fine and slender. **2.** Having a very small internal diameter, as a tube. **3.** *Anat.* In, of, or pertaining to the capillaries. **4.** *Physics.* Of or pertaining to capillarity. —*n., pl.* **-ies. 1.** *Anat.* One of the minute blood vessels that connect the arteries and veins. **2.** A tube with a small internal diameter. [Lat. *capillaris* < *capillus,* hair.]
capillary attraction *n.* The force that results from greater adhesion of a liquid to a solid surface than internal cohesion of the liquid itself and that causes the liquid to be raised against a vertical surface, as water is in a clean glass tube.
capillary bed *n.* The capillary network in a particular area or organ of the body.
cap·i·tal[1] (kăp′ĭ-tl) *n.* **1. a.** A town or city that is the official seat of government in a state, nation, or other political entity. **b.** A city or region that is the center of a specific activity. **2. a.** Wealth in the form of money or property, owned, used, or accumulated in business by an individual, partnership, or corporation. **b.** Any form of material wealth used or available for use in the production of more wealth. **3. a.** *Accounting.* The remaining assets of a business after all liabilities have been deducted; net worth. **b.** The funds contributed to a business by the owners or stockholders. **4.** Capitalists considered as a group or class. **5.** An asset or advantage. **6.** A capital letter. —*adj.* **1.** First and foremost; principal: *a decision of capital importance.* **2.** Of or pertaining to a political capital. **3.** First-rate; excellent: *a capital fellow.* **4.** Extremely serious: *a capital blunder.* **5.** Involving death or calling for the death penalty: *capital punishment; a*

capital offense. **6.** Of or pertaining to monetary capital. **7.** Designating an upper-case letter. [< ME, principal < OFr. < Lat. *capitalis* < *caput,* head.]

Usage: The term for a town or city that serves as a seat of government is spelled *capital.* The term for the building in which a legislative assembly meets is spelled *capitol.*

cap·i·tal[2] (kăp′ĭ-tl) *n.* The top part, or head, of a pillar or column. [ME < Norman Fr. < LLat. *capitellum,* dim. of *caput,* head.]

capital account *n.* **1.** An account stating the amount of funds and assets invested in a business by the owners or stockholders, including retained earnings; the owner's interest in the firm. **2.** *Accounting.* A statement of the net worth of a business enterprise at a given time.

capital assets *pl.n.* Long-term assets, as land or buildings.

capital expenditure *n.* Funds spent for additions or improvements to plant or equipment.

capital gain *n.* Profit from the sale of capital assets.

capital gains distribution *n.* A payment to shareholders realized from the sale of capital assets, as securities.

capital goods *pl.n.* Goods used in the production of commodities.

cap·i·tal-in·ten·sive (kăp′ĭ-tl-ĭn-tĕn′sĭv) *adj.* Requiring or having a large expenditure of capital in comparison to labor: *a capital-intensive industry.*

cap·i·tal·ism (kăp′ĭ-tl-ĭz′əm) *n.* **1.** An economic system, characterized by open competition in a free market, in which the means of production and distribution are privately or corporately owned and development is proportionate to increasing accumulation and reinvestment of profits. **2.** A political or social system regarded as being based on capitalism.

cap·i·tal·ist (kăp′ĭ-tl-ĭst) *n.* **1.** An investor of capital in business, esp. one having a major interest in an important enterprise. **2.** A person of great wealth. **3.** A person who supports capitalism.

cap·i·tal·is·tic (kăp′ĭ-tl-ĭs′tĭk) *adj.* Of or pertaining to capitalism or capitalists. **—cap′i·tal·is′ti·cal·ly** *adv.*

cap·i·tal·i·za·tion (kăp′ĭ-tl-ĭ-zā′shən) *n.* **1.** The act, practice, or result of capitalizing. **2. a.** The total value of owners' shares in a business firm. **b.** The authorized or outstanding stock or bonds in a corporation. **3.** The process of converting anticipated future income into present value. **4.** The use of upper-case letters in printing or writing.

cap·i·tal·ize (kăp′ĭ-tl-īz′) *v.* **-ized, -iz·ing, -iz·es.** *—tr.* **1.** To utilize as or convert into capital. **2.** To supply with capital or investment funds. **3.** To authorize a certain amount of capital stock of (a business). **4.** To convert (debt) into capital stock or shares. **5.** To estimate the present value of (an asset). **6.** *Accounting.* To include (expenditures) in business accounts as assets instead of expenses. **7. a.** To write or print in upper-case letters. **b.** To begin a word with an upper-case letter. *—intr.* To turn to advantage; profit by: *capitalize on an opponent's error.* **—cap′i·tal·iz′a·ble** *adj.*

capital letter *n.* A letter written or printed in a size larger than and often in a form differing from its corresponding lower-case letter; an upper-case letter.

capital levy *n.* A tax on capital assets or real property.

cap·i·tal·ly (kăp′ĭ-tl-ē) *adv.* In an excellent manner; admirably.

capital punishment *n.* The infliction of the death penalty for the commission of certain crimes.

capital ship *n.* A warship, such as a battleship, of the largest class.

capital stock *n.* **1.** The total amount of stock authorized for issue by a corporation. **2.** The total stated or par value of the permanently invested capital of a corporation.

cap·i·tate (kăp′ĭ-tāt′) *adj.* **1.** *Zool.* Enlarged or globular at an end, as some tentacles are. **2.** *Bot.* Forming a headlike mass or dense cluster, as the inflorescence of certain flowers. [Lat. *capitatus,* having a head < *caput,* head.]

cap·i·ta·tion (kăp′ĭ-tā′shən) *n.* A tax fixed at an equal sum per person; a per capita or poll tax. [Lat. *capitatio,* poll tax < *caput,* head.] **—cap′i·ta′tive** *adj.*

cap·i·tel·lum (kăp′ĭ-tĕl′əm) *n.* The rounded process of the humerus that articulates with the radius. [NLat. < LLat., dim. of Lat. *caput,* head.]

cap·i·tol (kăp′ĭ-tl) *n.* **1.** The building in which a state legislature assembles. **2. Capitol.** The building in Washington, D.C., occupied by the Congress of the United States. —See Usage note at **capital.** [ME *Capitol,* Jupiter's temple in Rome < Lat. *Capitolium.*]

Capitol Hill *n.* The U.S. Congress.

ca·pit·u·lar (kə-pĭch′ə-lər) *adj.* Of or pertaining to a chapter, esp. an ecclesiastical chapter. [Med. Lat. *capitularis* < *capitulum,* chapter. —see CHAPTER.] **—ca·pit′u·lar·ly** *adv.*

ca·pit·u·lar·y (kə-pĭch′ə-lĕr′ē) *n., pl.* **-ies. 1.** A member of an ecclesiastical chapter. **2. a.** An ecclesiastical or civil ordinance. **b.** A set of such ordinances, esp. those promulgated by Charlemagne and his successors.

ca·pit·u·late (kə-pĭch′ə-lāt′) *intr.v.* **-lat·ed, -lat·ing, -lates. 1.** To surrender under specified conditions; come to terms. **2.** To give up all resistance; acquiesce. [Med. Lat. *capitulare, capitulat-,* to draw up in chapters < *capitulum,* chapter. —see CHAPTER.] **—ca·pit′u·lant** *n.* **—ca·pit′u·la′tor** *n.*

ca·pit·u·la·tion (kə-pĭch′ə-lā′shən) *n.* **1.** The act of capitulating. **2.** A document or other instrument containing the terms of surrender. **3.** An enumeration of the main parts of a subject; summary. **—ca·pit′u·la·to′ry** (-lə-tôr′ē, -tōr′ē) *adj.*

ca·pit·u·lum (kə-pĭch′ə-ləm) *n., pl.* **-la** (-lə). **1.** *Bot.* A dense, headlike cluster of stalkless flowers. **2.** *Anat.* A small knob or head-shaped part, as the end of a bone or the knoblike tip of an insect's antenna. [NLat. < Lat., dim. of *caput,* head.]

cap·lin kăp′lĭn) *n.* Variant of **capelin.**

ca·po[1] (kā′pō) *n., pl.* **-pos.** A small movable bar placed across the fingerboard of a guitar or other similar instrument for altering the pitch of all the strings simultaneously. [Short for *capo tasto* < Ital. *capotasto* : *capo,* head + *tasto,* fret.]

ca·po[2] (kä′pō, kăp′ō) *n., pl.* **-pos.** The head of an organized crime syndicate or one of its branches. [Ital., head < Lat. *caput.*]

ca·pon (kā′pŏn′, -pən) *n.* A rooster castrated to improve the quality of its flesh for food. [ME *capoun,* partly < OE *capun,* and partly < OFr. *chapon,* both < Lat. *capo.*]

cap·o·ral (kăp′ər-əl, kăp′ə-răl′) *n.* A strong, dark tobacco. [Fr., short for *tabac de caporal,* corporal's tobacco.]

ca·pote (kə-pōt′) *n.* A long cloak or coat, usually hooded. [Fr., dim. of *cape,* cloak. —see CAPE[1].]

cap·per (kăp′ər) *n.* **1.** One that caps or makes caps. **2.** *Informal.* **a.** A climactic or unexpected point or resolution. **b.** A highlight. **3.** *Slang.* One who acts as a decoy, as in a confidence game; shill. **4.** A climax or ending.

cap pistol *n.* A toy pistol with a hammer action that detonates a mildly explosive cap.

cap·puc·ci·no (kăp′ə-chē′nō, kä′pə-) *n., pl.* **-nos.** Espresso coffee mixed or topped with steamed milk or cream. [Ital., Capuchin (from the resemblance of its color to the color of the monk's habit).]

cap·re·o·late (kăp′rē-ə-lāt′, kə-prē′-) *adj. Biol.* Having or like tendrils. [< Lat. *capreolus,* tendril, wild goat. —see CAPRIOLE.]

cap·ric acid (kăp′rĭk) *n.* A white crystalline compound, $CH_3(CH_2)_8COOH$, obtained by distilling coconut oil and used in the manufacture of perfumes and fruit flavors. [< Lat. *caper, capr-,* goat (from the acid's nasty smell).]

ca·pric·cio (kə-prē′chō, -chē-ō′) *n., pl.* **-cios. 1.** *Mus.* An instrumental work with an improvisatory style and a free form. **2.** A prank or caper. **3.** A fanciful whim. [Ital. —see CAPRICE.]

ca·pric·cio·so (kə-prē-chō′sō) *adj. Mus.* Lively and free. Used as a direction. [Ital. < *capriccio.* —see CAPRICE.]

ca·price (kə-prēs′) *n.* **1.** An impulsive change of mind. **2.** An inclination to change one's mind impulsively. **3.** *Mus.* A capriccio. [Fr. < Ital. *capriccio* : *capo,* head (< Lat. *caput*) + *riccio,* curly (< Lat. *ericius,* hedgehog).]

Synonyms: *caprice, whim, whimsy, vagary, freak.* These nouns denote an erratic or unexpected notion, act, or quality. *Caprice* strongly suggests lack of apparent motivation and can imply wanton or willful behavior. *Whim* and *whimsy* can both mean a quaint or fanciful idea, but *whim* reserves the suggestion of sudden inspiration, and *whimsy* more often refers to the literary quality or humor of being playful and fanciful. *Vagary* emphasizes the erratic and unpredictable, even irresponsible, nature of a notion or act. *Freak,* synonymous with *whim* and *vagary* in an old sense, now more commonly means a rare and highly improbable occurrence or a grotesque variation from a type.

ca·pri·cious (kə-prĭsh′əs, -prē′shəs) *adj.* Characterized by or subject to whim; impulsive and unpredictable; fickle. **—ca·pri′cious·ly** *adv.* **—ca·pri′cious·ness** *n.*

Cap·ri·corn (kăp′rĭ-kôrn′) *n.* **1.** A constellation in the equatorial region of the Southern Hemisphere, near Aquarius and Sagittarius. **2.** The tenth sign of the zodiac. [ME *Capricorne* < Lat. *Capricornus* : *Caper,* goat + *cornu,* horn.]

cap·ri·fi·ca·tion (kăp′rə-fĭ-kā′shən) *n.* A method of assuring pollination of the edible fig by having certain wasps carry pollen from the flowers of the caprifig to those of the edible variety. [Lat. *caprificatio* < *caprificare,* to ripen figs by caprification < *caprificus,* caprifig.]

cap·ri·fig (kăp′rə-fĭg′) *n.* A wild variety of fig, *Ficus carica sylvestris,* of the eastern Mediterranean region, used in the caprification of the edible fig. [ME < Lat. *caprificus* : *caper,* goat + *ficus,* fig.]

cap·ri·ole (kăp′rē-ōl′) *n.* **1.** An upward leap made by a trained horse without going forward and with all feet off the ground. **2.** A leap or jump. *—intr.v.* **-oled, -ol·ing, -oles.** To perform a capriole. [Fr. < Ital. *capriola,* somersault < *capriolo,* wild goat < Lat. *capreolus,* dim. of *caper,* goat.]

ca·pri pants (kä′prē, kə-prē′) also **ca·pris** (kä′prēz, kə-prēz′) *pl.n.* Tight-fitting nearly ankle-length pants with a slit on the outside of the leg bottoms. [After *Capri,* Italy.]

cap·ro·ic acid (kə-prō′ĭk, kă-) *n.* A liquid fatty acid, $C_6H_{12}O_2$, found in animal fats and oils and used in the manufacture of pharmaceuticals and flavors. [< Lat. *caper, capr-,* goat.]

ca·pryl·ic acid (kə-prĭl′ĭk, kă-) *n.* A liquid fatty acid, $C_8H_{16}O_2$, having a rancid taste and used in the manufacture of dyes and perfumes. [< E. *capryl,* a radical found in caprylic acid.]

cap·sa·i·cin (kăp-sā′ĭ-sĭn) *n.* Variant of **capsicin.**

capital[2]
12th-century French

capitol
The Capitol building in Washington, D.C.

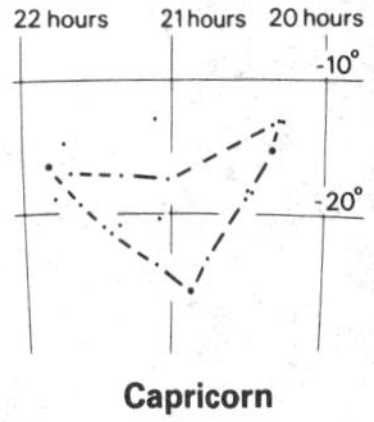

Capricorn

cap screw *n.* A long-threaded bolt, usually with a square head, used in fastening machine parts.
Cap·si·an (kăp'sē-ən) *adj.* Of or designating a Paleolithic culture of northern Africa and southern Europe. [Fr. *capsien* < Lat. *Capsa,* Gafsa, a town in Tunisia, near where remains of this culture were found.]
cap·si·cin (kăp'sĭ-sĭn) also **cap·sa·i·cin** (kăp-sā'ĭ-sĭn) *n.* A peppery, reddish-brown liquid, $C_{18}H_{27}O_3N$, obtained from plants of the genus *Capsicum* and used in flavoring vinegar and pickles and medicinally as an irritant. [CAPSIC(UM) + -IN.]
cap·si·cum (kăp'sĭ-kəm) *n.* **1.** Any of various tropical plants of the genus *Capsicum.* **2.** The dried fruit of pungent varieties of *C. frutescens,* used medicinally as a gastric stimulant and counterirritant. [NLat. *Capsicum,* genus name, perh. < Lat. *capsa,* box (from its podlike fruit).]
cap·sid (kăp'sĭd) *n.* The proteinaceous covering of a virus particle. [< Lat. *capsa,* box.]
cap·size (kăp'sīz', kăp-sīz') *intr. & tr.v.* **-sized, -siz·ing, -siz·es.** To overturn or cause to overturn. [Orig. unknown.]
cap·so·mere (kăp'sə-mîr') *n.* An individual subunit that comprises a capsid. [CAPS(ID) + -MERE.]
cap·stan (kăp'stən, stăn') *n.* **1.** *Naut.* An apparatus consisting of a vertical cylinder rotated manually or by motor, used for hoisting weights by winding in a cable. **2.** A small cylindrical pulley used to regulate the speed of magnetic tape in a tape recorder. [ME < Norman Fr. < OProv. *cabestan* < Lat. *capistrum,* halter < *capere,* to seize.]

capstan

cap·stone (kăp'stōn') also **cope·stone** (kōp'-) *n.* **1.** The top stone of a structure or wall. **2.** The crowning or final stroke; culmination; acme.
cap·su·lar (kăp'sə-lər) *adj.* Of, pertaining to, or resembling a capsule.
cap·su·late (kăp'sə-lāt', -lĭt) also **cap·su·lat·ed** (-lā'tĭd) *adj.* In or formed into a capsule. **—cap'su·la'tion** *n.*
cap·sule (kăp'səl, -so͞ol) *n.* **1.** A soluble container, usually of gelatin, enclosing a dose of an oral medicine. **2.** *Anat.* A fibrous, membranous, or fatty envelope that encloses an organ or part, such as the sac surrounding the kidney. **3.** *Microbiol.* A mucopolysaccharide layer enveloping certain bacteria. **4.** *Bot.* **a.** A fruit that contains two or more seeds and that dries and splits open. **b.** The spore case of a moss or other bryophyte. **5.** A pressurized modular compartment of an aircraft or spacecraft, esp. one designed to accommodate a crew or to be ejected if required. **6.** A brief summary or condensation. **—modifier:** *a capsule description.* —*tr.v.* **-suled, -sul·ing, -sules. 1.** To enclose in or furnish with a capsule. **2.** To condense or summarize: *capsuled the news.* [Fr.< Lat. *capsula,* dim. of *capsa,* box.]

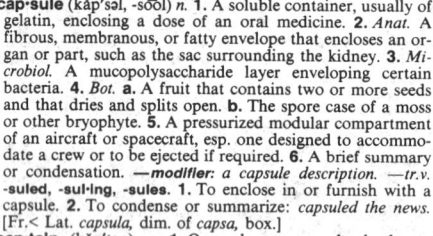

George Miksch Sutton
caracara

cap·tain (kăp'tən) *n.* **1.** One who commands, leads, or guides others, esp.: **a.** The officer in command of a ship. **b.** A precinct chief in a police or fire department. **c.** The designated leader of a team or crew in sports. **2. a.** A commissioned officer in the Army, Air Force, or Marine Corps who ranks below a major and above a first lieutenant. **b.** A commissioned officer in the Navy who ranks below a commodore or rear admiral and above a commander. **3.** A figure in the forefront; leader: *a captain of industry.* —*tr.v.* **-tained, -tain·ing, -tains.** To command or direct. [ME *capitain* < OFr. < LLat. *capitaneus* < Lat. *caput,* head.] **—cap'tain·cy** *n.* **—cap'tain·ship'** *n.*
cap·tan (kăp'tən, -tăn') *n.* An agricultural fungicide, $C_9H_8Cl_3NO_2S$. [Short for MERCAPTAN.]
cap·tion (kăp'shən) *n.* **1.** A title, short explanation, or description accompanying an illustration or photograph. **2.** A subtitle in a motion picture. **3.** A title or heading, as of a document. **4.** *Law.* The part of a legal document that states the time, place, and authority of its execution. —*tr.v.* **-tioned, -tion·ing, -tions.** To furnish a caption for. [CAPTION, an arrest (obs.) < Lat. *captio* < *capere,* to seize.]
cap·tious (kăp'shəs) *adj.* **1.** Inclined to find fault and make petty criticisms; carping. **2.** Intended to entrap or confuse; deceptive: *a captious question.* [ME *capcious* < Lat. *captiosus* < *captio,* sophism < *capere,* to take.] **—cap'tious·ly** *adv.* **—cap'tious·ness** *n.*
cap·ti·vate (kăp'tĭ-vāt') *tr.v.* **-vat·ed, -vat·ing, -vates. 1.** *Archaic.* To capture. **2.** To fascinate by special charm or beauty; enrapture. [LLat. *captivare, captivat-,* to capture < Lat. *captivus,* prisoner < *capere,* to seize.] **—cap'ti·va'tion** *n.* **—cap'ti·va'tor** *n.*
cap·tive (kăp'tĭv) *n.* **1.** One who is forcibly confined, restrained, or subjugated, as a prisoner. **2.** One who is enslaved by a strong emotion or passion. —*adj.* **1.** Held as prisoner. **2.** Under restraint or control. **3.** Captivated; enraptured. **4.** Obliged to be present: *a captive audience.* [ME *catif* < OFr. < Lat. *captivus* < *capere,* to seize.]
cap·tiv·i·ty (kăp-tĭv'ĭ-tē) *n., pl.* **-ties.** The state or a period of being captive.
cap·tor (kăp'tər, -tôr') *n.* One who takes or keeps a person or thing as a captive. [LLat., hunter < Lat. *capere,* to seize.]
cap·ture (kăp'chər) *tr.v.* **-tured, -tur·ing, -tures. 1.** To take captive; seize or catch by force or craft. **2.** To win possession or control of, as in a contest. **3.** To succeed in preserving in a permanent form: *capture a likeness in a painting.* —*n.* **1.** The act of capturing; seizure. **2.** One that is seized, caught, or won; a catch or prize. **3.** *Physics.* The phenomenon in which an atomic nucleus absorbs a subatomic particle, often with the subsequent emission of radiation. [Fr. < OFr. < Lat. *captura,* a catching of animals < *capere,* to seize.]
ca·puche (kə-po͞och', -po͞osh') *n.* A hood on a cloak, esp. the long, pointed cowl worn by a Capuchin monk. [Ital. *capuccio* < *cappa,* hood.]
cap·u·chin (kăp'yə-chĭn, kə-pyo͞o'-, -shĭn) *n.* **1. Capuchin.** A monk belonging to the Order of Friars Minor Capuchins, a branch that broke away from the Franciscans in 1525. **2.** A hooded cloak worn by women. **3.** Any of several long-tailed monkeys of the genus *Cebus,* of Central and South America, many of which have hoodlike tufts of hair on the head. [Fr. < Ital. *cappuccino* < *cappuccio,* hood. —see CAPUCHE.]
cap·y·ba·ra (kăp'ə-bä'rə, -băr'ə) *n.* A large, short-tailed semiaquatic rodent, *Hydrochoerus hydrochaeris,* of tropical South America, often attaining a length of four feet. [Port. *capibara* < Tupi.]
car (kär) *n.* **1.** An automobile. **2.** A conveyance, such as a streetcar, with wheels that runs along tracks. **3.** *Archaic.* A chariot. **4.** A boxlike enclosure for passengers on a conveyance, such as an elevator car. [ME *carre,* cart < Norman Fr., ult. < Lat. *carrus,* cart.]
car·a·bao (kăr'ə-bou', kä'rə-) *n., pl.* **-baos.** The water buffalo. [Sp. < Visayan *karabáw.*]
car·a·bid (kăr'ə-bĭd, kə-răb'ĭd) *n.* Any of various black carnivorous beetles of the family Carabidae. [NLat. *Carabidae,* family name < Gk. *karabos,* horned beetle.]
car·a·bi·neer or **car·a·bi·nier** (kăr'ə-bə-nîr') *n.* Variants of **carbineer.**
car·a·cal (kăr'ə-kăl') *n.* A wild cat, *Lynx caracal,* of Africa and southern Asia, having short, fawn-colored fur and long, tufted ears. [Fr. < Turk. *kara kūlāk* : *kara,* black + *kulak,* ear.]
car·a·car·a (kăr'ə-kăr'ə, -kə-rä') *n.* Any of several large, carrion-eating or predatory birds of the subfamily Caracarinae, of South and Central America and the southern United States, related to the hawks and falcons. [Sp., and Port. *caracará,* both < Tupi *caracara.*]
car·ack (kăr'ək) *n.* Variant of **carrack.**
car·a·cole (kăr'ə-kōl') also **car·a·col** (-kŏl) *n.* A half turn to either side performed by a horseman. —*intr.v.* **-coled, -col·ing, -coles.** To perform a caracole. [Fr. < Sp. *caracol,* snail.]
car·a·cul (kăr'ə-kəl) *n.* **1.** The loosely curled fur of a karakul lamb. **2.** Variant of **karakul.**
ca·rafe (kə-răf') *n.* A glass bottle, often with a flared lip, for serving water or wine. [Fr. < Ital. *caraffa* < Sp. *garaffa* < Ar. *gharrāf* < *gharafa,* he dipped.]
car·a·geen (kăr'ə-gēn') *n.* Variant of **carrageen.**
car·a·mel (kăr'ə-məl, -mĕl', kär'məl) *n.* **1.** A smooth, chewy candy made with sugar, butter, cream or milk, and flavoring. **2.** Burnt sugar, used for coloring and sweetening foods. [Fr. < Sp. *caramelo.*]
car·a·mel·ize (kăr'ə-mə-līz', kär'mə-līz') *tr. & intr.v.* **-ized, -iz·ing, -iz·es.** To convert into or change to caramel. **—car'a·mel·i·za'tion** *n.*
ca·ran·gid (kə-răn'jĭd, -răng'gĭd) *n.* Any of various fishes of the family Carangidae, which includes the jacks and pompanos. —*adj.* Of or belonging to the Carangidae. [NLat. *Carangidae,* family name < Fr. *carangue,* mackerel < Sp. *caranga.*]
car·a·pace (kăr'ə-pās') *n.* **1.** *Zool.* A hard bony or chitinous outer covering, such as the fused dorsal plates of a turtle or the portion of the exoskeleton covering the head and thorax of a crustacean. **2.** A protective covering similar to a carapace. [Fr. < Sp. *carapacho.*]
car·at (kăr'ət) *n.* **1.** A unit of weight for precious stones, equal to 200 milligrams. **2.** Variant of **karat.** [Fr. < OFr. < Med. Lat. *carratus* < Ar. *qīrāṭ,* weight of four grains < Gk. *keration,* a weight, dim. of *keras,* horn.]
car·a·van (kăr'ə-văn') *n.* **1.** A company of travelers journeying together, esp. across a desert. **2.** A single file of vehicles or pack animals. **3.** A large covered vehicle; van. **4.** *Chiefly Brit.* A trailer or home on wheels. [Fr. *caravane* < Pers. *kārwān.*]
car·a·van·sa·ry (kăr'ə-văn'sə-rē) also **car·a·van·se·rai** (-rī') *n., pl.* **-ries** also **-rais. 1.** In the Near or Far East, an inn built around a large court for accommodating caravans. **2.** A large inn or hostelry. [Pers. *kārwānsarāī* : *kārwān,* caravan + *sarāī,* palace.]
car·a·vel also **car·a·velle** (kăr'ə-vĕl') or **car·vel** (kär'vəl, -vĕl') *n.* A small, light sailing ship of the kind used by the Spanish and Portuguese in the 15th and 16th centuries. [OFr. *caravelle* < OPort. *caravela.*]
car·a·way (kăr'ə-wā') *n.* **1.** A plant, *Carum carvi,* native to Eurasia, having finely divided leaves and clusters of small, whitish flowers. **2.** The pungent, aromatic seeds of the caraway, used in baking and cooking. [ME *carewei,* prob. < Med. Lat. *carvi* < Ar. *karawyā* < Gk. *karon.*]
carb– *pref.* Variant of **carbo-.**
car·ba·mate (kär'bə-māt', kär-băm'āt') *n.* A salt or ester of carbamic acid, esp. one used as an insecticide. [CARBAM(IC ACID) + -ATE.]
car·bam·ic acid (kär-băm'ĭk) *n.* An acid, CH_3NO_2, used in the form of its derivatives and salts, such as urea. [CARB(O)- + AM(IDE) + -IC.]

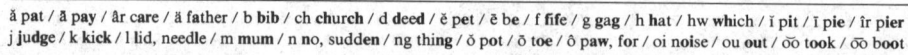

ă pat / ā pay / âr care / ä father / b bib / ch church / d deed / ĕ pet / ē be / f fife / g gag / h hat / hw which / ĭ pit / ī pie / îr pier / j judge / k kick / l lid, needle / m mum / n no, sudden / ng thing / ŏ pot / ō toe / ô paw, for / oi noise / ou out / o͝o took / o͞o boot /

car·ba·mide (kär′bə-mīd′, kär-băm′ĭd) *n.* Urea. [CARB(O)- + AMIDE.]

car·ban·i·on (kär-băn′ī′ən, -ī′ŏn′) *n.* A negatively charged ion located at a carbon position.

car·ba·ryl (kär′bə-rĭl′) *n.* A carbamate, $C_{11}H_{11}NO_2$, used as a general purpose insecticide. [CARB(AMATE) + AR(OMATIC) + -YL.]

car·ben·i·cil·lin (kär-bĕn′ĭ-sĭl′ĭn) *n.* A broad-spectrum antibiotic of the penicillin group. [CAR(BOXYL) + BEN(ZYL) + (PEN)ICILLIN.]

car·bide (kär′bīd′) *n.* A binary carbon compound, esp. calcium carbide, consisting of carbon and a more electropositive element.

car·bine (kär′bīn′, -bēn′) *n.* A light shoulder rifle with a short barrel, originally used by cavalry. [Fr. *carabine* < OFr. *carabin,* soldier armed with a musket.]

car·bi·neer (kär′bə-nîr′) also **car·a·bi·neer** or **car·a·bi·nier** (kär′ə-) *n.* A soldier armed with a carbine.

car·bi·nol (kär′bə-nôl′, -nōl′) *n.* **1.** Methanol. **2.** An alcohol derived from methanol.

carbo– or **carb–** *pref.* Carbon: *carbohydrate.* [Fr. < *carbone,* carbon.]

car·bo·cy·clic (kär′bō-sī′klĭk, -sĭk′lĭk) *adj. Chem.* Having a ring composed of carbon atoms, as benzene.

car·bo·hy·drase (kär′bō-hī′drās′, -drāz′) *n.* Any of various enzymes that catalyze the hydrolysis of a carbohydrate.

car·bo·hy·drate (kär′bō-hī′drāt′) *n.* Any of a group of chemical compounds, including sugars, starches, and cellulose, containing carbon, hydrogen, and oxygen only, with the ratio of hydrogen to oxygen atoms usually 2:1.

car·bo·lat·ed (kär′bə-lā′tĭd) *adj.* Containing or treated with carbolic acid.

car·bol·ic acid (kär-bŏl′ĭk) *n.* Phenol (sense 1). [CARB- + Lat. *oleum,* oil + -IC.]

car·bon (kär′bən) *n. Symbol* **C** **1.** A naturally abundant nonmetallic element that occurs in many inorganic and in all organic compounds, exists in amorphous, graphitic, and diamond allotropes, and is capable of chemical self-bonding to form an enormous number of chemically, biologically, and commercially important long-chain molecules. Atomic number 6; atomic weight 12.01115; sublimes above 3,500°C; boiling point 4,827°C; specific gravity of amorphous carbon 1.8 to 2.1, of diamond 3.15 to 3.53, of graphite 1.9 to 2.3; valences 2, 3, 4. **2. a.** A sheet of carbon paper. **b.** A copy made by using carbon paper. **3.** *Elect.* **a.** Either of two rods through which current flows to form an arc in lighting or in welding. **b.** A carbonaceous electrode in an electric cell. [Fr. *carbone* < Lat. *carbo,* charcoal.] **—car′bon·ous** (-bə-nəs) *adj.*

carbon 14 *n.* A naturally radioactive carbon isotope with atomic mass 14 and half-life 5,700 years, used in dating ancient carbon-containing objects.

car·bon-14 dating (kär′bən-fôr-tēn′, -fōr-) *n.* Carbon dating.

car·bo·na·ceous (kär′bə-nā′shəs) *adj.* Consisting of, containing, pertaining to, or yielding carbon.

car·bo·na·do[1] (kär′bə-nā′dō, -nä′-) *n., pl.* **-does** or **-dos.** A piece of scored and broiled fish, fowl, or meat. *—tr.v.* **-doed, -do·ing, -dos. 1.** To score and broil (fish, fowl, or meat). **2.** *Archaic.* To slice or cut. [Sp. *carbonada* < *carbón,* charcoal < Lat. *carbo.*]

car·bo·na·do[2] (kär′bə-nā′dō, -nä′-) *n., pl.* **-does.** A form of opaque or dark-colored diamond, chiefly Brazilian, used for drills. [Port. < *carbone,* carbon < Fr. —see CARBON.]

car·bon·ate (kär′bə-nāt′) *tr.v.* **-at·ed, -at·ing, -ates. 1.** To charge with carbon dioxide gas, as a beverage. **2.** To burn to carbon; carbonize. **3.** To change into a carbonate. *—n.* (-nāt′, -nĭt). A salt or ester of carbonic acid. **—car′bon·a′tion** *n.* **—car′bon·a′tor** *n.*

carbonated water *n.* Soda water (sense 1).

carbon bisulfide *n.* Carbon disulfide.

carbon black *n.* Any of various finely divided forms of carbon derived from the incomplete combustion of natural gas or petroleum oil and used principally in rubber and ink.

carbon copy *n.* **1.** A replica, as of a letter, made by using carbon paper. **2.** *Informal.* A close copy or reproduction; duplicate.

carbon cycle *n.* **1.** The carbon-nitrogen cycle. **2.** *Biol.* The cycle of natural processes in which atmospheric carbon in the form of carbon dioxide is converted to carbohydrates by photosynthesis, metabolized by animals, and ultimately returned to the atmosphere as a carbon dioxide waste or decomposition product.

carbon dating *n.* The determination of the approximate age of carbon-containing objects by use of the radiation rate of carbon 14.

carbon dioxide *n.* A colorless, odorless, incombustible gas, CO_2, formed during respiration, combustion, and organic decomposition and used in food refrigeration, carbonated beverages, inert atmospheres, fire extinguishers, and aerosols.

carbon disulfide *n.* A clear, flammable liquid, CS_2, used to manufacture viscose rayon and cellophane, as a solvent for fats, rubber, resins, waxes, and sulfur, and in matches, fumigants, and pesticides.

carbon fiber *n.* An extremely strong light fiber made by pyrolyzing synthetic fibers, as rayon, and used in high-strength composites.

car·bon·ic acid (kär-bŏn′ĭk) *n.* A weak, unstable acid, H_2CO_3, present in solutions of carbon dioxide in water.

carbonic acid gas *n.* Carbon dioxide.

car·bon·if·er·ous (kär′bə-nĭf′ər-əs) *adj.* **1.** Producing, containing, or pertaining to carbon or coal. **2. Carboniferous.** Of, belonging to, or designating a geologic division of the Paleozoic era following the Devonian and preceding the Permian, including the Mississippian and Pennsylvanian periods. It was characterized, esp. in the Pennsylvanian, by swamp formation and deposition of plant remains later hardened into coal. *—n.* **Carboniferous.** The Carboniferous period.

car·bo·ni·um (kär-bō′nē-əm) *n.* A positively charged organic ion, such as H_3C, having one less electron than a corresponding free radical and behaving chemically as if the positive charge were localized on the carbon atom.

car·bon·i·za·tion (kär′bə-nĭ-zā′shən) *n.* **1.** The process of carbonizing. **2.** The destructive distillation of bituminous coal to obtain coke and other fractions.

car·bon·ize (kär′bə-nīz′) *tr.v.* **-ized, -iz·ing, -iz·es. 1.** To reduce or convert to carbon, as by partial burning. **2.** To coat or combine with carbon. **—car′bon·iz′er** *n.*

carbon monoxide *n.* A colorless, odorless, highly poisonous gas, CO, formed by the incomplete combustion of carbon or a carbonaceous material, including gasoline.

car·bon-ni·tro·gen cycle (kär′bən-nī′trə-jən) *n.* A chain of thermonuclear reactions in which nitrogen isotopes are formed in intermediate stages and carbon acts essentially as a catalyst to convert four protons into one helium nucleus, the entire sequence thought to generate significant amounts of energy in certain classes of stars.

carbon paper *n.* A lightweight paper faced on one side with a dark waxy pigment that is transferred by the impact of typewriter keys or by writing pressure to a copying surface, as paper.

carbon process *n.* A photographic printing process using permanent pigments, such as carbon, contained in a sensitized tissue or film of gelatin.

carbon star *n.* Any of a class of carbon-rich stars with primarily low temperatures.

carbon tetrachloride *n.* A poisonous, nonflammable, colorless liquid, CCl_4, used in fire extinguishers and as a solvent.

car·bon·yl (kär′bə-nĭl′, -nēl′) *n.* **1.** The bivalent radical CO. **2.** A metal compound, such as $Ni(CO)_4$, containing the CO group. **—car′bon·yl′ic** (-nĭl′ĭk) *adj.*

carbonyl chloride *n.* Phosgene.

car·bo·rane (kär′bə-rān′) *n.* Any of a class of stable compounds containing carbon, hydrogen, and boron. [Blend of CARBON and BORANE.]

Car·bo·run·dum (kär′bə-rŭn′dəm). A trademark for a silicon carbide abrasive.

car·box·yl (kär-bŏk′səl) *n.* A univalent radical, COOH, characteristic of all organic acids. [CARB(O)- + OX(Y)- + -YL.] **—car′box·yl′ic** (-sĭl′ĭk) *adj.*

car·box·yl·ase (kär-bŏk′sə-lās′, -lāz′) *n.* A plant enzyme that produces acetaldehyde and carbon dioxide from pyruvic acid.

car·box·yl·a·tion (kär-bŏk′sə-lā′shən) *n.* The introduction of a carboxyl group into a compound or molecule.

car·box·yl·ic acid (kär′bŏk-sĭl′ĭk) *n.* An organic acid that contains one or more carboxyl groups.

car·boy (kär′boi′) *n.* A large glass or plastic bottle, usually encased in a protective basket or crate and often used to hold corrosive liquids. [Pers. *qarāba.*]

car·bun·cle (kär′bŭng′kəl) *n.* **1.** A painful, localized pus-producing infection of the skin and subcutaneous tissue. **2.** *Obs.* A deep-red garnet, unfaceted and convex. [ME < OFr. < Lat. *carbunculus,* dim. of *carbo,* coal.] **—car′bun′cled** *adj.* **—car·bun′cu·lar** (-kyə-lər) *adj.*

car·bu·ret (kär′bə-rāt′, -byə-, -rĕt′) *tr.v.* **-ret·ed, -ret·ing, -rets** or **-ret·ted, -ret·ting, -rets.** To combine or mix with carbon or hydrocarbons, so as to increase available fuel energy. [< obs. *carburet,* carbide < Fr. *carbure* < Lat. *carbo,* carbon.]

car·bu·re·tor (kär′bə-rā′tər, -byə-) *n.* A device used in gasoline engines to produce an efficient explosive vapor of fuel and air. [< CARBURET.]

car·bu·ret·tor (kär′bə-rĕt′ər, -byə-) *n. Chiefly Brit.* Variant of **carburetor.**

car·bu·rize (kär′bə-rīz′, -byə-) *tr.v.* **-rized, -riz·ing, -riz·es. 1.** To treat with carbon. **2.** To treat with hydrocarbons. [CARBUR(ET) + -IZE.] **—car′bu·ri·za′tion** *n.*

car·ca·jou (kär′kə-jo͞o′, -zho͞o′) *n.* The wolverine. [Canadian Fr. < Algonquian *karkajou.*]

car·ca·net (kär′kə-nĕt′, -nĭt) *n.* A jeweled necklace, collar, or headband. [OFr. *carcan,* collar.]

car·case (kär′kəs) *n. Archaic.* Variant of **carcass.**

car·cass (kär′kəs) *n.* **1.** The dead body of an animal, esp. one slaughtered for food. **2.** The living body of a human being. **3.** Something from which the substance or character is gone: *the carcass of a once-glorious empire.* **4.** A framework or basic structure, as of a ruined building. [Fr. *carcasse* < OFr. *carcois.*]

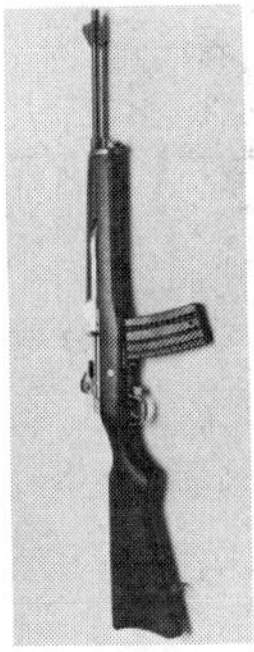

carbine

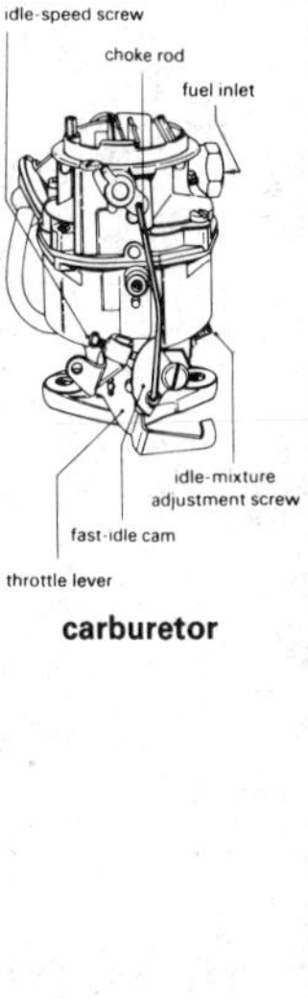

carburetor

carcino– *pref.* Cancer; cancerous: *carcinogen.* [Gk. *karkino-* < *karkinos,* crab, cancer.]

car·cin·o·gen (kär-sĭn′ə-jən, kär′sə-nə-jĕn′) *n.* A cancer-causing substance. **—car′ci·no·gen′e·sis** (kär′sə-nə-jĕn′ə-sĭs) *n.* **—car′cin·o·gen′ic** (kär′sə-nə-jĕn′ĭk) *adj.* **—car′ci·no·ge·nic′i·ty** (kär′sə-nə-jə-nĭs′ĭ-tē) *n.*

car·ci·no·ma (kär′sə-nō′mə) *n., pl.* **-mas** or **-ma·ta** (-mə-tə). A malignant tumor derived from epithelial tissue. [Lat., cancerous ulcer < Gk. *karkinōma* < *karkinos.*] **—car′ci·nom′a·tous** (-nŏm′ə-təs, -nō′mə-) *adj.* **—car′ci·no′ma·toid** (-nō′mə-toid′) *adj.*

car·ci·no·ma·to·sis (kär′sə-nō′mə-tō′sĭs) *n.* The existence of carcinomas at many bodily sites.

car coat *n.* A three-quarter-length coat.

card[1] (kärd) *n.* **1.** A small, flat, usually rectangular piece of stiff paper or thin pasteboard esp.: **a.** A playing card. **b.** A greeting card. **c.** A post card. **d.** One bearing a person's name and other information, used for purposes of identification or classification. **2. cards** *(used with a sing. or pl. verb).* **a.** A game played with cards. **b.** The playing of games with cards. **3.** A program, esp. for a sports event. **4.** A compass card. **5.** *Informal.* An amusing or eccentric person. *—tr.v.* **card·ed, card·ing, cards. 1.** To furnish with or attach to a card. **2.** To list on a card; catalogue. **3.** *Informal.* To check the identification of, esp. in order to verify legal age. ***—idioms.*** **have a card up (one's) sleeve.** To have a secret resource or plan held in reserve. **in the cards.** Likely or destined to occur. **put (or lay) (one's) cards on the table.** To make frank and clear revelation, as of one's motives. [ME *carde,* alteration < OFr. *carte* < Lat. *charta,* leaf of papyrus < Gk. *khartēs.*]

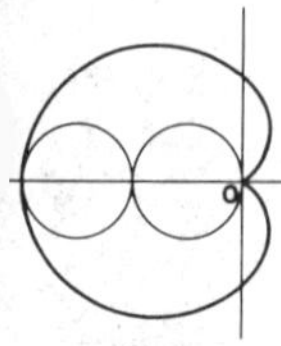

cardioid

card[2] (kärd) *n.* **1.** A wire-toothed brush or a machine fitted with rows of wire teeth used to disentangle fibers, as of wool, prior to spinning. **2.** A device used to raise the nap on a fabric. *—tr.v.* **card·ed, card·ing, cards.** To comb out or brush with a card. [ME *carde* < Med. Lat. *cardus* < Lat. *carduus,* thistle.] **—card′er** *n.*

car·da·mom or **car·da·mum** (kär′də-məm) also **car·da·mon** (-mən). *n.* **1.** A tropical Asiatic perennial plant, *Elettaria cardamomum,* having large, hairy leaves and capsular fruit whose seeds are used as a condiment and in medicine. **2.** An East Indian plant, *Amomum cardamomum,* whose seeds are used as an inferior substitute for true cardamom seed. [Lat. *cardamomum* < Gk. *kardamōmon* : *kardamon,* cress + *amōmon,* an Indian spice.]

card·board (kärd′bôrd′, -bōrd′) *n.* A thin, stiff pasteboard made of paper pulp, used for making cartons and signs.

card-car·ry·ing (kärd′kăr′ē-ĭng) *adj.* **1.** Being an enrolled member of a particular organization, esp. a member of the Communist party. **2.** Being strongly identified with or devoted to, as a particular cause or ideal: *a card-carrying liberal.* [From the assumption that such a person carries a membership card.]

card catalog *n.* An alphabetical listing, esp. of books in a library, made with a separate card for each item.

cardi– *pref.* Variant of **cardio-**.

car·di·a (kär′dē-ə) *n.* The opening of the esophagus into the stomach. [Gk. *kardia,* heart, cardiac orifice of the stomach.]

car·di·ac (kär′dē-ăk′) *adj.* **1.** Of, near, or pertaining to the heart. **2.** Of or pertaining to the cardia. *—n.* A person with a heart disorder. [Lat. *cardiacus* < Gk. *kardiakos* < *kardia,* heart.]

cardiac massage *n.* A resuscitative procedure marked by the rhythmic compression of the chest by an individual in an effort to restore proper circulation and respiration.

cardiac muscle *n.* The striated muscle of the heart.

car·di·al·gia (kär′dē-ăl′jə, -jē-ə) *n.* Heartburn. [Gk. *kardialgia* : *kardia,* heart + *algos,* pain.]

car·di·gan (kär′dĭ-gən) *n.* A sweater or knitted jacket opening down the front. [After the Seventh Earl of *Cardigan;* James Thomas Brudenell (1797–1868).]

car·di·nal (kär′dn-əl, kärd′nəl) *adj.* **1.** Of foremost importance; pivotal. **2.** Of a dark to deep or vivid red color. *—n.* **1.** *Rom. Cath. Ch.* A member of the Sacred College or College of Cardinals who is appointed by and ranks just below the pope. **2.** A dark to deep or vivid red. **3.** A North American bird, *Richmondena cardinalis,* having a crested head, a short, thick bill, and bright-red plumage in the male. **4.** A short, hooded cloak, originally of scarlet cloth, worn by women in the 18th century. **5.** A cardinal number. [ME < Lat. *cardinalis,* principal, pertaining to a hinge < *cardo,* hinge.] **—car′di·nal·ship′** *n.*

car·di·nal·ate (kär′dn-ə-lĭt, kärd′nə-, -lāt′) *n. Rom. Cath. Ch.* **1.** The College of Cardinals. **2.** The position, rank, dignity, or term of a cardinal.

cardinal flower *n.* A plant, *Lobelia cardinalis,* of eastern North America, having a terminal cluster of brilliant scarlet flowers.

cardinal number *n.* A number, such as 3 or 11 or 412, used to indicate quantity but not order.

cardinal point *n.* One of the four principal directions on a compass: north, south, east, or west.

cardinal virtues *pl.n.* The four qualities of justice, prudence, fortitude, and temperance.

cardio– or **cardi–** *pref.* Heart: *cardiovascular.* [Gk. *kardio-* < *kardia,* heart.]

car·di·o·ac·cel·er·a·tor (kär′dē-ō′ăk-sĕl′ə-rā′tər) *n.* An agent that increases the heart rate. **—car′di·o′ac·cel′er·a′tion** *n.*

car·di·o·gen·ic (kär′dē-ō-jĕn′ĭk, -jē′nĭk) *adj.* Having origin in a cardiac condition.

car·di·o·gram (kär′dē-ə-grăm′) *n.* The curve traced by a cardiograph, used in the diagnosis of heart defects.

car·di·o·graph (kär′dē-ə-grăf′) *n.* An instrument used to record the mechanical movements of the heart. **—car′di·og′ra·phy** (-ŏg′rə-fē) *n.*

car·di·oid (kär′dē-oid′) *n.* A heart-shaped plane curve, the locus of a fixed point on a circle that rolls on the circumference of another circle with the same radius.

car·di·ol·o·gy (kär′dē-ŏl′ə-jē) *n.* The medical study of the diseases and functioning of the heart. **—car′di·ol′o·gist** *n.*

car·di·o·meg·a·ly (kär′dē-ō-mĕg′ə-lē) *n.* Megalocardia.

car·di·o·pul·mo·nar·y (kär′dē-ō-po͝ol′mə-nĕr′ē) *adj.* Of or pertaining to the heart and the lungs.

cardiopulmonary resuscitation *n.* A procedure employed after cardiac arrest in which cardiac massage, drugs, and mouth-to-mouth resuscitation are used to restore breathing.

car·di·o·res·pi·ra·to·ry (kär′dē-ō-rĕs′pər-ə-tôr′ē, -rĭ-spīr′ə-tôr′ē, -tōr′ē) *adj.* Of or pertaining to the heart and the respiratory system.

car·di·o·vas·cu·lar (kär′dē-ō-văs′kyə-lər) *adj.* Of, pertaining to, or involving the heart and the blood vessels.

car·di·tis (kär-dī′tĭs) *n.* Inflammation of the heart.

car·doon (kär-do͞on′) *n.* A plant, *Cynara cardunculus,* of southern Europe, closely related to the artichoke and having spiny leaves, purple flowers, and an edible leafstalk. [Fr. *cardon* < Prov. < Lat. *carduus,* wild thistle.]

card·sharp (kärd′shärp′) also **card·sharp·er** (-shär′pər) *n.* A person expert in cheating at cards. **—card′sharp′ing** *n.*

care (kâr) *n.* **1.** Mental distress and uncertainty; worry. **2.** Mental suffering; grief. **3.** An object or source of worry, attention, or solicitude. **4.** Caution in avoiding harm or danger; heedfulness: *handling with care.* **5.** Protection; supervision; charge: *in the care of a nurse.* **6.** Attentiveness to detail; painstaking application. *—v.* **cared, car·ing, cares.** *—intr.* **1.** To be concerned or interested. **2.** To object or mind: *I won't care if you borrow my car.* **3.** To have a liking or attachment. *—tr.* **1.** To wish; be inclined: *We don't care to attend.* **2.** To be concerned to the degree of: *I don't care a bit what he thinks.* [ME < OE *cearu.*]

ca·reen (kə-rēn′) *v.* **-reened, -reen·ing, -reens.** *—intr.* **1.** To lurch or swerve while in motion. **2.** To lean to one side, as a ship sailing in the wind. **3.** *Naut.* To turn a ship on its side for cleaning, caulking, or repairing. *—tr. Naut.* **1.** To cause (a ship) to lean to one side; tilt. **2. a.** To lean (a ship) on one side for cleaning, caulking, or repairing. **b.** To clean, caulk, or repair (a ship in this position). *—n.* **1.** The act or process of careening a ship. **2.** The position of a careened ship. [< Fr. *(en) carene,* (on) the keel < OFr. *carene* < OItal. *carena* < Lat. *carina.*] **—ca·reen′er** *n.*

ca·reer (kə-rîr′) *n.* **1. a.** A chosen pursuit; a profession or occupation. **b.** The general course or progression of one's life, esp. in one's profession: *an officer with a distinguished career.* **2.** *Archaic.* **a.** A path or course. **b.** A rapid course or swift progression, as of the sun through the heavens. **3. a.** Speed: *"My hasting days fly on with full career"* (Milton). **b.** The moment of highest pitch or peak activity: *The Republic was now in the full career of its triumphs.* *—intr.v.* **-reered, -reer·ing, -reers.** To move or run at full speed; go headlong; rush: *"Thus the night fled away . . . and the careering on it"* (Hawthorne). [Fr. *carrière* < OFr., racecourse < OProv. *carriera,* street < Med. Lat. *(via) carraria,* (road) for carts < LLat. *carra,* cart. —see CAR.]

ca·reer·ism (kə-rîr′ĭz′əm) *n.* The practice of seeking one's professional advancement by all possible means. **—ca·reer′ist** *n.*

care·free (kâr′frē′) *adj.* Free of worries and responsibilities.

care·ful (kâr′fəl) *adj.* **1.** Cautious in thought, speech, or action; circumspect. **2.** Thorough and painstaking in execution; conscientious. **3.** Showing care; solicitous: *Be careful of her feelings.* **4.** *Archaic.* Full of cares or anxiety. **—care′ful·ly** *adv.* **—care′ful·ness** *n.*

care·less (kâr′lĭs) *adj.* **1.** Not taking sufficient care; negligent. **2.** Marked by or resulting from lack of forethought or thoroughness: *a careless mistake.* **3.** Showing a lack of consideration: *a careless remark.* **4.** Unconcerned or indifferent: *careless about her health.* **5.** Unstudied or effortless: *careless grandeur.* **6.** Free from cares; cheerful. **—care′less·ly** *adv.* **—care′less·ness** *n.*

Synonyms: *careless, heedless, thoughtless, inadvertent, indifferent.* These adjectives apply to actions or attitudes demonstrating little or no concern for what results. *Careless* pertains to lack of care or attentiveness and can imply negligence. *Heedless* implies inattentiveness to the point of recklessness. *Thoughtless* suggests action without consideration for others. *Inadvertent* applies only to actions that are unintentional. *Indifferent* emphasizes not caring one way or the other about consequences.

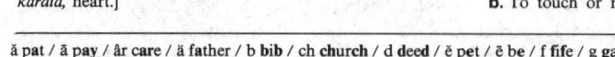

ca·ress (kə-rĕs′) *n.* A gentle touch or gesture of fondness, tenderness, or love. *—tr.v.* **-ressed, -ress·ing, -ress·es.** **1. a.** To touch or stroke in an affectionate or loving manner. **b.** To touch or move as if with a caress: *soft music that* *caressed her ears.* **2.** To treat fondly, kindly, or favorably. [Fr. *caresse* < Ital. *carezza* < *caro,* dear < Lat. *carus.*] **—ca·ress′er** *n.* **—ca·ress′ing·ly** *adv.* **—ca·res′sive** *adj.*

car·et (kăr′ĭt) *n.* A proofreading symbol used to indicate where something is to be inserted in a line of printed or written matter. [Lat., there is lacking < *carere,* to lack.]

care·tak·er (kâr′tā′kər) *n.* One that is employed to look after or take charge of goods, property, or a person; custodian.

care·worn (kâr′wôrn′, -wōrn′) *adj.* Showing the effects of care; weary from worry.

car·fare (kär′fâr′) *n.* Fare charged a passenger.

car·go (kär′gō) *n., pl.* **-goes** or **-gos.** The freight carried by a ship, airplane, or other vehicle. [Sp. < *cargar,* to load < LLat. *carricare* < Lat. *carrus,* cart, of Celtic orig.]

car·hop (kär′hŏp′) *n.* One who waits on customers at a drive-in restaurant.

Car·ib (kăr′ĭb) *n., pl.* **Carib** or **-ibs. 1.** Also **Car·i·ban** (kăr′ə-bən, kə-rē′bən). **a.** A group of peoples of American Indians of northern South America and the Lesser Antilles. **b.** A member of one of these peoples. **2.** Any of the languages of the Carib. [Sp. *Caribe,* of Cariban orig.] **—Car′ib** *adj.*

Car·i·ban (kăr′ə-bən, kə-rē′bən) *n., pl.* **Cariban** or **-bans. 1.** Variant of **Carib** (sense 1). **2.** A language family comprising the Carib languages. **—Car′i·ban** *adj.*

Car·ib·be·an (kăr′ə-bē′ən, kə-rĭb′ē-ən) *n.* A Carib Indian. *—adj.* **1.** Of or pertaining to the Caribbean Sea and its islands. **2.** Of or pertaining to the Carib or their language.

ca·ri·be (kə-rē′bē) *n.* The piranha. [Am. Sp. < Sp. *Caribe,* Carib.]

car·i·bou (kăr′ə-bo͞o′) *n., pl.* **caribou** or **-bous.** A deer, *Rangifer tarandus,* of arctic regions of the New World, having antlers in both sexes. [Canadian Fr., of Algonquian orig.]

car·i·ca·ture (kăr′ĭ-kə-cho͝or′) *n.* **1.** A representation, esp. pictorial, in which the subject's distinctive features or peculiarities are deliberately exaggerated or distorted to produce a comic or grotesque effect. **2.** The process or art of creating caricatures. **3.** An imitation so inferior as to be absurd. *—tr.v.* **-tured, -tur·ing, -tures.** To represent or imitate in or as if in a caricature. [Fr. < Ital. *caricatura* < *caricare,* to exaggerate, to load < Lat. *carrus,* cart, of Celtic orig.] **—car′i·ca·tur′ist** *n.*

Synonyms: *caricature, burlesque, parody, travesty, satire, lampoon, takeoff, spoof.* These nouns denote artistic forms in which a person or thing is imitated or otherwise depicted in an amusing and generally critical manner. A *caricature,* usually pictorial, grossly exaggerates a peculiar feature of a person, group, or thing with intent to ridicule. *Burlesque,* usually a stage work, suggests outlandish mimicry and broad comedy to provoke laughter. *Parody, travesty, satire,* and *lampoon* generally apply to written works or to their dramatizations. *Parody* implies ludicrous treatment of a generally trivial theme, employing the manner and style of a well-known composition or writer. A *travesty* keeps to the theme or subject of the original but treats it with a heavy hand and an ironic and absurd manner. *Satire* usually involves holding up to ridicule the follies and vices of a people or a time, and is often associated with social reform. *Lampoon* refers to an abusive attack in a broadly humorous vein. *Takeoff,* an informal term, suggests good-humored imitation in written or dramatic form. *Spoof* is often interchangeable with *parody* but stresses lightheartedness.

car·ies (kâr′ēz) *n., pl.* **caries.** Decay of a bone or tooth. [Lat.]

car·il·lon (kăr′ə-lŏn′, -lən) *n.* **1.** A stationary set of chromatically tuned bells in a tower, usually played from a keyboard. **2.** A composition written or arranged for the carillon. *—intr.v.* **-lonned, -lon·ning, -lons.** To play a carillon. [Fr., alteration of OFr. *quarregnon* < LLat. *quaternio,* set of four. —see QUATERNION.]

car·il·lon·neur (kăr′ə-lə-nûr′) *n.* A person who plays a carillon.

ca·ri·na (kə-rī′nə, -rē′-) *n., pl.* **-nae** (-nē′). A keel-shaped ridge, such as that on the breastbone of a bird or in the petals of certain flowers. [NLat. < Lat., keel.]

Ca·ri·na (kə-rī′nə) *n.* A constellation in the Southern Hemisphere near Volans and Vela and containing the star Canopus. [Lat. < *carina,* keel.]

car·i·nate (kăr′ə-nāt′, -nĭt) also **car·i·nat·ed** (-nā′tĭd) *adj. Biol.* Having or shaped like a keel; ridged.

Car·i·o·ca (kăr′ē-ō′kə) *n.* A native or resident of Rio de Janeiro, Brazil. [Port. < Tupi.] **—Car′i·o′can** *adj.*

car·i·ole (kăr′ē-ōl′) also **car·ri·ole** *n.* **1.** A small, open one-horse carriage with two wheels. **2.** A light, covered cart. [Fr. *carriole* < OProv. *carriola,* dim. of *carri,* chariot < Lat. *carrus,* cart, of Celtic orig.]

car·i·ous (kâr′ē-əs) *adj.* Having caries; decayed. **—car′i·os′i·ty** (-ŏs′ĭ-tē), **car′i·ous·ness** *n.*

carl or **carle** (kärl) *n.* **1.** *Archaic.* A peasant or farmer. **2.** *Obs.* A bondman; serf. **3.** *Regional.* A rude person; churl. [ME < ON *karl,* man.]

car·line or **car·lin** (kär′lĭn) *n. Scot.* A woman, esp. an old woman. [ME *kerling* < ON < *karl,* man.]

car·ling (kär′lĭng, -lĭn) *n.* One of the short timbers running fore and aft that connect the transverse beams supporting the deck of a ship. [Fr. *carlingue* < OFr. *calingue,* prob. < ON *kerling,* old woman < *karl,* man.]

Car·list (kär′lĭst) *n.* A supporter of Don Carlos, the pretender to the Spanish throne, or his heirs. **—Carl′ism** *n.*

car·load (kär′lōd′) *n.* **1.** The amount a car carries or is able to carry. **2.** The official minimum weight necessary to ship freight at the carload rate.

Car·lo·vin·gian (kär′lə-vĭn′jən, -jē-ən) *adj. & n.* Variant of **Carolingian.**

car·man (kär′mən) *n.* **1.** A motorman or conductor, as of a streetcar. **2.** A person who drives a car or cart.

Car·mel·ite (kär′mə-līt′) *n.* **1.** A monk or mendicant friar belonging to the order of Our Lady of Mount Carmel, founded in 1155. **2.** A member of a community of nuns of the Carmelite order, founded in 1452. **—Car′mel·ite′** *adj.*

car·min·a·tive (kär-mĭn′ə-tĭv, kär′mə-nā′-) *adj.* Inducing expulsion of gas from the stomach and intestines. *—n.* A carminative drug. [ME *carminatif* < Lat. *carminare,* to card wool < *carmen,* card for wool.]

car·mine (kär′mĭn, -mīn′) *n.* **1.** A strong to vivid red color. **2.** A crimson pigment derived from cochineal. *—adj.* Vivid-red or purplish-red. [Fr. *carmin* < Med. Lat. *carminium,* prob. a blend of Ar. *qirmiz,* kermes and Lat. *minium,* cinnabar.]

car·nage (kär′nĭj) *n.* **1.** Massive slaughter, as in war; massacre. **2.** *Obs.* Corpses, esp. of men killed in battle. [OFr. < OItal. *carnaggio* < LLat. *carnactium,* meat < Lat. *caro.*]

car·nal (kär′nəl) *adj.* **1.** Relating to the desires and appetites of the flesh or body; sensual. **2.** Worldly or earthly; temporal. [ME < Lat. *carnalis* < Lat. *caro,* flesh.] **—car·nal′i·ty** (kär-năl′ĭ-tē) *n.* **—car′nal·ly** *adv.*

carnal knowledge *n.* Sexual intercourse.

car·nall·ite (kär′nə-līt′) *n.* A white, brownish, or reddish mineral, $KCl \cdot MgCl_2 \cdot 6H_2O$, used to manufacture potash salts. [G. *Carnallit,* after Rudolf von *Carnall* (1804–1874).]

car·nas·si·al (kär-năs′ē-əl) *adj.* Adapted for tearing apart flesh. Used of teeth. *—n.* The last upper premolar and the first lower molar teeth in carnivorous mammals. [Fr. *carnassier,* carnivorous < Lat. *caro,* flesh.]

car·na·tion (kär-nā′shən) *n.* **1. a.** A plant, *Dianthus caryophyllus,* native to Eurasia, widely cultivated for its fragrant white, pink, or red flowers with fringed petals. **b.** The flower of this plant. **2.** A flesh-colored tint once used in painting. [Prob. < OFr., flesh-colored < OItal. *carnagione* < *carne,* flesh < Lat. *caro.*]

car·nau·ba (kär-nô′bə, -nou′-) *n.* **1.** A palm tree, *Copernica cerifera,* of tropical South America. **2.** Also **carnauba wax.** A hard wax obtained from the leaves of the carnauba, used as a polish and in candles. [Port., prob. of Tupi origin.]

car·nel·ian (kär-nēl′yən) also **cor·nel·ian** (kôr-) *n.* A pale to deep red or reddish-brown variety of clear chalcedony, used in jewelry. [ME *corneline* < OFr.]

car·net (kär-nā′) *n.* **1.** An official, esp. international, pass or permit. **2.** A book of postage stamps. [Fr., notebook < OFr. *quernet* < Lat. *quaterni,* group of four < *quattuor,* four.]

car·ney (kär′nē) *n.* Variant of **carny.**

car·ni·tine (kär′nĭ-tēn′) *n.* A betaine that commonly occurs in the liver and in skeletal muscle. [G. *Karnitin* < *Karnin,* a basic substance derived from meat.]

car·ni·val (kär′nə-vəl) *n.* **1.** The season just before Lent, marked by merrymaking and feasting. **2.** A time of revelry; festival. **3.** A traveling amusement show. [Ital. *carnevale* < OItal. *carnelevare,* Shrovetide : *carne,* meat (< Lat. *caro*) + *levare,* to remove < Lat.]

car·ni·vore (kär′nə-vôr′, -vōr′) *n.* **1.** An animal belonging to the order Carnivora, including predominantly flesh-eating mammals. **2.** A flesh-eating or predatory organism, such as a bird of prey or an insectivorous plant. [Fr. < Lat. *carnivorus,* carnivorous.]

car·niv·o·rous (kär-nĭv′ər-əs) *adj.* **1.** Belonging or pertaining to the order Carnivora. **2.** Flesh-eating or predatory. **3.** *Bot.* Capable of trapping and absorbing insects or other small organisms; insectivorous. Used of plants such as the pitcher plant and the Venus's-flytrap. [Lat. *carnivorus* : *caro,* flesh + *vorare,* to swallow up.] **—car·niv′o·rous·ly** *adv.* **—car·niv′o·rous·ness** *n.*

car·no·tite (kär′nə-tīt′) *n.* A yellow uranium ore with composition $K_2(UO_2)_2(VO_4)_2 \cdot 3H_2O$. [Fr., after M.A. *Carnot* (d. 1920), French inspector general of mines.]

car·ny also **car·ney** (kär′nē) *n., pl.* **-nies** also **-neys.** *Slang.* **1.** A carnival. **2.** A person who works with a carnival.

car·ob (kăr′əb) *n.* An evergreen tree, *Ceratonia siliqua,* of the Mediterranean region, having compound leaves and edible pods. [OFr. *carobe* < Med. Lat. *carrubium* < Ar. *kharrūbah.*]

ca·roche (kə-rōch′, -rōsh′) *n.* A stately carriage of the 16th and 17th centuries. [OFr. *carroche* < OItal. *carroccio,* aug. of *carro,* cart < Lat. *carrus,* of Celtic orig.]

car·ol (kăr′əl) *v.* **-oled, -ol·ing, -ols** also **-olled, -ol·ling, -ols.** *—tr.* **1.** To celebrate in song. **2.** To sing joyously. *—intr.* **1.** To sing in a joyous manner; warble. **2.** To go from house to house singing Christmas songs. *—n.* **1.** A song of praise or joy, esp. for Christmas. **2.** An old round dance often accompanied by singing. [ME *carolen* < OFr. *caroler* < *carole,* a carol < LLat. *choraula,* choral song < Lat. *choraules,* accompanist < Gk. *khoraulēs* : *khoros,* choral dance + *aulos,* reed instrument.] **—car′ol·er** *n.*

Car·o·le·an (kăr′ə-lē′ən) *adj.* Of or relating to Charles I or Charles II of England. [< Med. Lat. *Carolus,* Charles.]

Car·o·line (kăr′ə-līn′, -lĭn) *adj.* Relating to the life and times

caribou

caricature
Above: Theodore Roosevelt
Below: Roosevelt caricatured as a bull moose in a 1912 cartoon

carillon

carob
Above: Foliage and flowers
Below: Pod

p **pop** / r **roar** / s **sauce** / sh **ship, dish** / t **tight** / th **thin, path** / *th* **this, bathe** / ŭ **cut** / ûr **urge** / v **valve** / w **with** / y **yes** / z **zebra, size** / zh **vision** / ə **about, item, edible, gallop, circus** / œ *Fr.* **feu,** *Ger.* **schön** / ü *Fr.* **tu,** *Ger.* **über** / KH *Ger.* **ich,** *Scot.* **loch** / N *Fr.* **bon.**

of Charles I or Charles II of England. [NLat. *Carolinius* < Med. Lat. *Carolus,* Charles.]

Car·o·lin·gi·an (kăr'ə-lĭn'-jən, -jē-ən) also **Car·lo·vin·gi·an** (kär'lə-vĭn'jən, -jē-ən) *adj.* Related to or belonging to the Frankish dynasty that was founded by Pepin the Short in A.D. 751 and that lasted until A.D. 987 in France and A.D. 911 in Germany. *—n.* A member of the Carolingian dynasty. [Fr. *Carolingien,* alt. of *Carlovingian,* ult. < OHG *Karl,* Charles.]

Car·o·lin·i·an (kăr'ə-lĭn'ē-ən) *adj.* **1.** Caroline. **2.** Of or relating to Charlemagne and his times.

car·om (kăr'əm) *n.* **1. a.** A shot in billiards in which the cue ball successively strikes two other balls. **b.** A similar shot in related games, such as pool. **2.** A collision followed by a rebound. *—v.* **-omed, -om·ing, -oms.** *—intr.* **1.** To collide with and rebound: *The boat caromed off the dock.* **2.** To make a carom, as in billiards. *—tr.* To cause to carom. [Obs. *carambole* < Sp. *carambola* < Fr. *carambole.*]

car·o·te·nase (kăr'ə-tē-nās, -nāz) *n.* An enzyme that catalyzes the hydrolysis of a carotenoid.

car·o·tene (kăr'ə-tēn') also **car·o·tin** (-tĭn) *n.* An orange-yellow to red hydrocarbon, $C_{40}H_{56}$, existing in three isomeric forms, occurring in many plants as a pigment, and converted to vitamin A in the animal liver. [G. *Karotin* < Lat. *carota,* carrot.]

car·o·te·ne·mi·a (kăr'ə-tə-nē'mē-ə) *n.* A condition in which there is carotene in the blood, sometimes characterized by yellowing of the skin.

ca·rot·e·noid (kə-rŏt'n-oid') *n.* Any of a class of yellow- to deep-red pigments, such as the carotenes, occurring in many vegetable oils and some animal fats.

ca·rot·id (kə-rŏt'ĭd) *n.* Either of the two major arteries in the neck that carry blood to the head. *—adj.* Of or pertaining to either of the two carotids. [Fr. *carotide* < Gk. *karōtides* < *karoun,* to stupefy.]

carotid body *n.* A chemoreceptor located bilaterally in the bifurcations of the carotid arteries that contains cells that are responsive to changes in oxygen in the blood and help control respiratory activity.

carotid sinus *n.* An arterial enlargement located at the bifurcations of the carotid arteries that contains numerous baroreceptors that function in arterial pressure control.

car·o·tin (kăr'ə-tĭn) *n.* Variant of **carotene.**

ca·rous·al (kə-rou'zəl) *n.* A jovial, riotous drinking party; boisterous merrymaking; revelry.

ca·rouse (kə-rouz') *n.* Boisterous, drunken merrymaking; carousal. *—intr.v.* **-roused, -rous·ing, -rous·es. 1.** To drink excessively. **2.** To go on a drinking spree. [G. *garaus (trinken),* (to drink) all out.] **—ca·rous'er** *n.*

car·ou·sel or **car·rou·sel** (kăr'ə-sĕl', -zĕl') *n.* **1.** A merry-go-round. **2.** A tournament in which knights or horsemen engaged in various exercises and races. [Fr. *carrousel* < Ital. *carosello,* a kind of tournament.]

carp¹ (kärp) *intr.v.* **carped, carp·ing, carps.** To find fault and complain constantly. [ME *carpen* < ON *karpa,* to boast.] **—carp'er** *n.*

carp² (kärp) *n., pl.* **carp** or **carps. 1.** An edible freshwater fish, *Cyprinus carpio,* frequently bred in ponds and lakes. **2.** Any of various fishes of the family Cyprinidae. [ME *carpe,* partly < OFr. *carpe,* and partly < Med. Lat. *carpa,* both of Germanic orig.]

-carp *suff.* Fruit; fruitlike structure: *cystocarp.* [NLat. *-carpium* < Gk. *-karpion* < *karpos,* fruit.]

car·pal (kär'pəl) *adj.* Of, pertaining to, or near the carpus. *—n.* A bone of the carpus. [NLat. *carpalis* < Gk. *karpos,* wrist.]

car·pe di·em (kär'pĕ dē'ĕm', -əm, dī'-) *n.* The admonition to seize the pleasures of the moment without thought for the future. [Lat., seize the day.]

car·pel (kär'pəl) *n.* The central, ovule-bearing female organ of a flower, consisting of a modified leaf forming one or more sections of the pistil. [NLat. *carpellum* < Gk. *karpos,* fruit.] **—car'pel·lar'y** (-pə-lĕr'ē) *adj.*

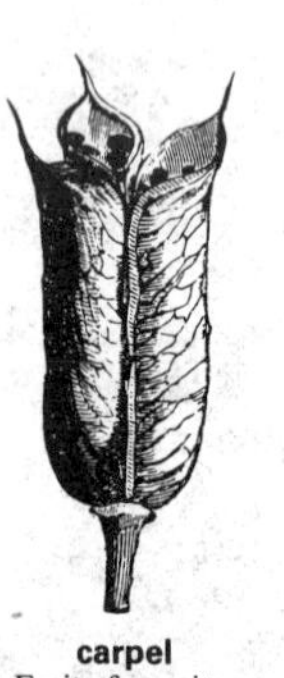

carpel
Fruit of aconite, composed of three carpels

car·pel·late (kär'pə-lāt', -lĭt) *adj. Bot.* Having carpels.

car·pen·ter (kär'pən-tər) *n.* One whose occupation is constructing, finishing, and repairing wooden objects and structures. *—v.* **-tered, -ter·ing, -ters.** *—tr.* To make, build, or repair (wooden structures). *—intr.* To work as a carpenter. [ME < Norman Fr. *carpentier* < LLat. *carpentarius (artifex),* (maker) of a carriage < *carpentum,* a two-wheeled carriage, of Celtic orig.] **—car'pen·try** (-trē) *n.*

carpenter ant *n.* Any of various ants of the genus *Camponotus* that nest in and are destructive to wood.

carpenter bee *n.* Any of various bees of the families Xylocopidae and Ceratinidae that do not live in colonies and that bore tunnels into wood to lay their eggs.

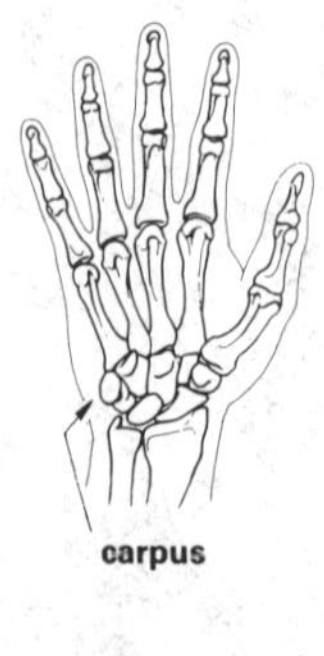

carpus

car·pet (kär'pĭt) *n.* **1. a.** A thick, heavy covering for a floor, usually made of wool or synthetic fibers; rug. **b.** The fabric used for this. **2.** A surface similar to a carpet in function or appearance: *a carpet of leaves and pine needles.* *—tr.v.* **-pet·ed, -pet·ing, -pets.** To cover with or as if with a carpet. **—*idiom.* on the carpet. 1.** Under discussion or consideration. **2.** In the position of being reprimanded by one in authority. [ME < OFr. *carpite* < OItal. *carpita* < *carpire,* to pluck < Lat. *carpere.*]

car·pet·bag (kär'pĭt-băg') *n.* An old-fashioned kind of traveling bag made of carpet fabric.

car·pet·bag·ger (kär'pĭt-băg'ər) *n.* **1.** A Northerner who went to the South after the Civil War for political or financial advantage. **2.** A nonresident politician who represents or seeks to represent a locality for political self-interest. [So called because they carried their belongings in a carpetbag.] **—car'pet·bag'ger·y** *n.*

carpet beetle *n.* Any of various small beetles of the genera *Anthrenus* and *Attagenus,* having larvae injurious to fabrics and furs.

car·pet·ing (kär'pĭ-tĭng) *n.* **1.** Material or fabric used for carpets. **2.** A carpet or carpets.

carpet knight *n.* A soldier, originally a knight, who has spent his life in ease away from battle.

car·pet·weed (kär'pĭt-wēd') *n.* A low-growing, weedy plant, *Mollugo verticillata,* forming dense mats and having whorled leaves and small, greenish-white flowers.

car·pi (kär'pī') *n.* Plural of **carpus.**

-carpic *suff.* -carpous. [Prob. < NLat. *-carpicus* < Gk. *karpos,* fruit.]

carp·ing (kär'pĭng) *adj.* Naggingly critical or complaining. **—carp'ing·ly** *adv.*

carpo- *pref.* Fruit: *carpophore.* [< Gk. *karpos,* fruit.]

car·po·go·ni·um (kär'pə-gō'nē-əm) *n., pl.* **-ni·a** (-nē-ə). *Bot.* The female structure producing sex cells in certain red algae. **—car'po·go'ni·al** (-əl) *adj.*

car·pol·o·gy (kär-pŏl'ə-jē) *n.* The area of botany concerned with fruit and seeds. **—car·pol'o·gist** *n.*

car·pool (kär'po͞ol') *n.* **1.** An arrangement whereby several commuters travel together in one car, sharing the costs and often taking turns providing the car used. **2.** A group, as of commuters, participating in a car-pool. *—intr.v.* **-pooled, -pool·ing, -pools.** To travel in a car-pool. *—tr.* To take turns driving, as in a car-pool: *car-pool the kids to school.* **—car'-pool'er** *n.*

car·poph·a·gous (kär-pŏf'ə-gəs) *adj.* Feeding on fruit; fruit-eating. [Gk. *karpophagos* : *karpos,* fruit + *phagein,* to eat.]

car·po·phore (kär'pə-fôr', -fōr') *n.* **1.** The elongated part of the axis of certain flowers to which the carpels are attached. **2.** A fruiting body or the stalk of a fruiting body in a fungus.

car·port (kär'pôrt', -pōrt') *n.* A roof projecting from the side of a building, used as a shelter for an automobile.

car·po·spo·ran·gi·um (kär'pə-spə-răn'jē-əm) *n., pl.* **-gi·a** (-jē-ə). A specialized sporangium in red algae in which carpospores are formed.

car·po·spore (kär'pə-spôr', -spōr') *n.* A nonmotile haploid or diploid spore formed within the carpogonium of red algae.

-carpous *suff.* A specified number or kind of fruit: *polycarpous.* [NLat. *-carpus* < Gk. *karpos,* fruit.]

car·pus (kär'pəs) *n., pl.* **-pi** (-pī'). **1. a.** The wrist. **b.** The bones of the wrist. **2.** A joint corresponding to the wrist in quadrupeds. [NLat. < Gk. *karpos,* wrist.]

car·rack also **car·ack** (kăr'ək) *n.* A large galleon used in the 14th, 15th, and 16th centuries. [ME *carik* < OFr. *caraque* < OSp. *carraca* < Ar. *qarāqīr,* pl. of *qurqūr,* merchant ship.]

car·ra·geen also **car·ra·gheen** or **car·a·geen** (kăr'ə-gēn') *n.* Irish moss. [After *Carragheen,* near Waterford, Ireland.]

car·ra·geen·in or **car·ra·geen·an** also **car·ra·gheen·in** (kăr'ə-gē'nən) *n.* A colloid derived from carrageen that is used as a clarifying and stabilizing agent in foods.

car·re·four (kăr'ə-fo͝or') *n.* **1.** A crossroads. **2.** A public square; plaza. [Fr. < OFr. *carrefor* < Lat. *quadrifurcus,* four forked : *quadri-,* four + *furca,* fork.]

car·rel also **car·rell** (kăr'əl) *n.* A nook near the stacks in a library, used for private study. [OFr. *carole* and Med. Lat. *carola.*]

car·riage (kăr'ĭj) *n.* **1.** A four-wheeled, usually horse-drawn passenger vehicle, often of an elegant design. **2.** *Chiefly Brit.* A railroad car for passengers. **3.** A perambulator; baby carriage. **4.** A wheeled support or frame for moving a heavy object, such as a cannon. **5.** A moving part of a machine for holding or shifting another part. **6. a.** The act or process of transporting or carrying. **b.** (kăr'ē-ĭj). The cost of or charge for transporting. **7.** The manner of holding and moving one's head and body; posture or bearing. **8.** *Archaic.* Management; administration. [ME *cariage* < Norman Fr. < *carier,* to carry. —see CARRY.]

carriage dog *n.* A Dalmatian (sense 1).

carriage trade *n.* Wealthy patrons, as of a restaurant.

car·rick bend (kăr'ĭk) *n. Naut.* A type of knot used to fasten two cables or hawsers together. [< Obs. *carrick,* carrack < ME *carik.*]

carrick bitt *n. Naut.* Either of the two posts that support the windlass on a ship's deck. [Prob. < obs. *carrick,* carrack. —see CARRICK BEND.]

car·ri·er (kăr'ē-ər) *n.* **1.** One that transports or conveys. **2.** A person, business or organization that deals in transporting passengers or goods. **3.** A mechanism or device by which something is conveyed or conducted. **4.** *Med.* A person or animal at least temporarily immune to a pathogen that it transmits directly or indirectly to others. **5.** *Electronics.* **a.** A carrier wave. **b.** A charge-carrying entity, esp. an electron or a hole in a semiconductor. **6.** An aircraft carrier.

carrier pigeon *n.* A homing pigeon, esp. one trained to carry messages.

carrier wave *n.* An electromagnetic wave that can be modulated in frequency, amplitude, phase, or otherwise to transmit speech, music, images, or other signals.

car·ri·ole (kăr′ē-ōl′) *n.* Variant of **cariole.**

car·ri·on (kăr′ē-ən) *n.* Dead and decaying flesh. [ME *careine* < AN < VLat. **caronia* < Lat. *caro,* flesh.]

carrion crow *n.* A European crow, *Corvus corone.*

carrion flower *n.* **1.** A climbing vine, *Smilax herbacea,* of eastern North America, having clusters of small, greenish flowers with an odor of decaying flesh. **2.** Any of several plants similar to the carrion flower having flowers with an unpleasant odor.

car·rot (kăr′ət) *n.* **1.** A widely cultivated plant, *Daucus carota sativa,* having finely divided leaves, flat clusters of small white flowers, and an edible, yellow-orange root. **2.** The long, tapering root of the carrot, eaten as a vegetable. **3.** Something held out as an attractive but often illusory inducement. [OFr. *carotte* < Lat. *carota* < Gk. *karōton.*]

car·rot-and-stick (kăr′ət-ən-stĭk′) *adj.* Combining a promised reward with a threat or punishment: *a carrot-and-stick approach to getting things done.*

car·rot·y (kăr′ə-tē) *adj.* **1.** Similar to a carrot in color. **2.** Having carrot-colored hair.

car·rou·sel (kăr′ə-sĕl′, -zĕl′) *n.* Variant of **carousel.**

car·ry (kăr′ē) *v.* **-ried, -ry·ing, -ries.** —*tr.* **1.** To bear or convey from one place to another; transport: *carry mail.* **2.** To make known, take, bring, or communicate (a message, for example). **3.** To serve as a means for the conveyance or transmission of; transmit. **4.** To hold or bear while moving: *carried the groceries.* **5.** To hold or be capable of holding. **6.** To support or sustain the responsibility of. **7.** To keep or have on one's person. **8.** To be pregnant with. **9. a.** To hold and move (the body or a part of it) in a particular way. **b.** To behave or conduct (oneself) in a specified manner. **10.** To extend or continue in a certain direction or to a given point or degree. **11.** To cause to move; drive; impel. **12.** To take or seize, esp. by force; capture. **13.** To gain victory, support, or acceptance for, esp. to secure the adoption of. **14.** To win most of the votes of: *Their candidate carried New England.* **15.** To be successful in; win. **16.** To win over; gain the interest of: *His enthusiasm carried the audience.* **17.** To support or corroborate (a claim, for example). **18. a.** To have as a customary or necessary attribute or accompaniment: *an appliance carrying a full-year guarantee.* **b.** To involve necessarily as a condition, consequence, or effect: *The crime carried a five-year sentence.* **19.** To transfer from one place, as a column, page, or book, to another. **20.** To keep in stock; offer for sale: *carry a line of dresses.* **21.** To keep in one's accounts as a debtor: *carried the customer while he was out of work.* **22.** To place before the public, as through a mass medium: *The press conference was carried by all networks.* **23.** To produce as a crop. **24.** To support or sustain (livestock). **25.** To sing (a melody, for example) on key: *carry a tune.* **26.** To cover (a distance) or advance beyond (a point or object) in one golf stroke. —*intr.* **1.** To act as a bearer: *teach a dog to fetch and carry.* **2. a.** To be transmitted or conveyed; cover a range: *a voice that carries well.* **b.** To have or exert propulsive force: *equipped with guns that carry well.* **3.** To admit of being transported in a certain manner: *Heavy loads do not carry easily.* **4.** To hold the neck and head in a certain way. Used of a horse. **5.** To be accepted or approved: *The proposal carried by a wide margin.* —**phrasal verbs. carry away.** To move or excite greatly: *carried away by desire.* **carry forward. 1.** To progress with: *carry forward the program.* **2.** *Accounting.* To transfer (an entry) to the next column, page, book or to another account. **carry off. 1.** To cause the death of: *carried off by a fever.* **2.** To seize and detain (a person) unlawfully. **3.** To handle (a situation, for example) successfully. **4.** To win, as a prize, award, or honor. **carry on. 1.** To conduct; administer. **2.** To engage in: *carry on a love affair.* **3.** To continue without halting: *carry on in the face of disaster.* **4.** To behave in an excited, improper, or silly manner; act hysterically or childishly. **carry out. 1.** To put into practice or effect. **2.** To follow or obey: *carry out instructions.* **3.** To bring to a conclusion; accomplish. **carry over. 1.** *Accounting.* To transfer (an entry) to another column, page, book, or account. **2.** To continue at another time; put off. **carry through. 1.** To accomplish; complete. **2.** To enable to endure; sustain. —*n., pl.* **-ries. 1.** The act or process of carrying. **2.** A portage, as between two navigable rivers or other bodies of water. **3. a.** The range of a gun or projectile. **b.** The distance traveled by a golf ball. **4.** *Football.* The act or an instance of rushing with the ball. [ME *carien* < Norman Fr. *carier* < *carre,* cart. —see CAR.]

car·ry·all (kăr′ē-ôl′) *n.* **1. a.** A covered one-horse carriage with two seats. **b.** A closed automobile with two lengthwise seats facing each other. **2.** A large bag, basket, or pocketbook.

carrying capacity *n.* The maximum number of individuals or inhabitants that an environment can support without detrimental effects.

carrying charge *n.* The interest charged on the balance owed when paying in installments.

car·ry·on (kăr′ē-ŏn′) *n.* An item, such as luggage, small or compact enough to be carried aboard an airplane by a passenger.

car·ry·out (kăr′ē-out′) *adj.* Take-out. —**car′ry·out′** *n.*

car·ry-o·ver (kăr′ē-ō′vər) *n.* **1.** A part or quantity, as of goods or commodities, left over or held for future use. **2.** *Accounting.* A sum transferred to a new column, page, book, or account.

car·sick (kär′sĭk′) *adj.* Nauseated by vehicular motion. —**car′sick′ness** *n.*

cart (kärt) *n.* **1.** A two-wheeled vehicle drawn by a horse or other animal and used for transporting goods. **2.** An open two-wheeled business or pleasure carriage. **3.** A small, light vehicle moved by hand, as a grocery cart. —*tr.v.* **cart·ed, cart·ing, carts. 1. a.** To convey in a cart. **b.** To convey laboriously, as in a cart; lug. **2.** To remove or transport (a person or thing) unceremoniously or forcibly: *carted him off to jail.* [ME, prob. < ON *kartr.*] —**cart′a·ble** *adj.* —**cart′er** *n.*

cart·age (kär′tĭj) *n.* **1.** The act or process of transporting by cart. **2.** The cost of transporting by cart.

carte blanche (kärt bläNsh′, blänch′) *n., pl.* **cartes blanches** (bläNsh′, bläN′shĭz, blänch′, blän′chĭz). Unrestricted power to act at one's own discretion; unconditional authority. [Fr. : *carte,* document + *blanche,* blank.]

car·tel (kär-tĕl′) *n.* **1.** A combination of independent business organizations formed to regulate production, pricing, and marketing of goods by the members. **2.** An official agreement between governments at war, esp. one concerning the exchange of prisoners. **3.** In some European countries, a political group united in a common cause; bloc. [G. *Kartell* < Fr. *cartel* < Ital. *cartello,* placard, dim. of *carta,* card < Lat. *charta,* leaf of papyrus. —see CARD.]

Car·te·sian (kär-tē′zhən) *adj.* Of or pertaining to the philosophy or methods of Descartes. [NLat. *Cartesianus* < *Cartesius,* René Descartes (1596–1650).] —**Car·te′sian·ism** *n.*

Cartesian coordinate *n.* A coordinate in a Cartesian coordinate system.

Cartesian coordinate system *n.* **1.** A two-dimensional coordinate system in which the coordinates of a point are its distances from two intersecting, often perpendicular straight lines, the distance from each being measured along a straight line parallel to the other. **2.** A three-dimensional coordinate system in which the coordinates of a point are its distances from each of three intersecting, often mutually perpendicular planes along lines parallel to the intersection of the other two.

Cartesian plane *n.* A plane having all points described by Cartesian coordinates.

Cartesian product *n.* A set of element pairs (x, y) constructed from given sets such that x belongs to X and y to Y.

Car·thu·sian (kär-thōō′zhən) *n. Rom. Cath. Ch.* A member of a contemplative order founded during the 11th century by St. Bruno. —*adj.* Of or pertaining to the Carthusian order. [Med. Lat. *Cartusiensis* < *Chartreuse,* the place in France where the order's first monastery was built.]

car·ti·lage (kär′tl-ĭj) *n.* A tough white fibrous connective tissue attached to the articular surfaces of bones, a major constituent of the fetal and young vertebrate skeleton that is largely converted to bone with maturation. [Lat. *cartilago.*]

cartilage bone *n.* A bone developed from cartilage.

car·ti·lag·i·nous (kär′tl-ăj′ə-nəs) *adj.* **1.** Of or pertaining to cartilage. **2.** Having a skeleton consisting mainly of cartilage.

cartilaginous fish *n.* A fish whose skeleton is composed mainly of cartilage.

cart·load (kärt′lōd′) *n.* The amount a cart carries or is able to carry.

car·to·gram (kär′tə-grăm′) *n.* A presentation of statistical data in geographical distribution on a map. [Fr. *cartogramme* : *carte,* map (< OFr., card) + *-gramme,* -gram.]

car·tog·ra·phy (kär-tŏg′rə-fē) *n.* The art or technique of making maps or charts. [Fr. *cartographie* : *carte,* map (< OFr., card) + *-graphie,* -graphy.] —**car·tog′ra·pher** *n.* —**car′to·graph′ic** (kär′tə-grăf′ĭk), **car′to·graph′i·cal** *adj.*

car·ton (kär′tn) *n.* **1. a.** A cardboard box. **b.** Any of various containers made from paper products: *a carton of milk.* **2.** The contents of a carton: *a carton of cigarettes.* —*tr.v.* **-toned, -ton·ing, -tons.** To place or pack in a carton. [Fr. < Ital. *cartone,* pasteboard, aug. of *carta,* card < Lat. *charta,* leaf of papyrus. —see CARD.]

car·toon (kär-tōōn′) *n.* **1.** A drawing depicting a humorous situation, often accompanied by a caption. **2.** A pictorial satire or comment on a subject of current public interest, usually accompanied by words; caricature. **3.** A preliminary sketch similar in size to the work, as a fresco, that is to be copied from it. **4.** An animated cartoon. **5.** A comic strip. —*v.* **-tooned, -toon·ing, -toons.** —*tr.* To sketch a humorous or satirical representation of; caricature. —*intr.* To draw satirical or humorous sketches. [Fr. *carton* < Ital. *cartone,* pasteboard. —see CARTON.] —**car·toon′ist** *n.*

car·touche or **car·touch** (kär-tōōsh′) *n.* **1.** *Archit.* A scroll-like tablet used either to provide space for an inscription or for ornamental purposes. **2.** In ancient Egyptian hieroglyphics, an oval or oblong figure that encloses characters

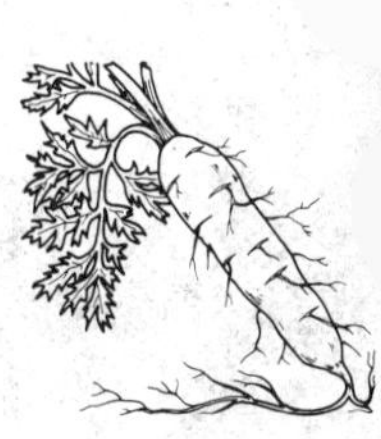

carrot

cart

cartwheel

casaba

cascade

casement

expressing the names or epithets of royal or divine personages. **3.** *Obs.* A heavy paper cartridge case. [Fr. < Ital. *cartoccio* < *carta,* card. —see CARTON.]

car·tridge (kär′trĭj) *n.* **1. a.** A tubular metal or cardboard and metal case containing the propellant powder and primer of small arms ammunition or shotgun shells. **b.** Such a case fitted with a projectile, such as a bullet. **2.** A small modular unit of equipment designed to be inserted into a larger piece of equipment. **3.** A removable case containing the stylus and electric conversion circuitry in a phonograph pickup. **4.** A case containing reeled magnetic tape, a pickup reel, and guide and feed mechanisms, used instead of separate reels in certain tape recorders and players. **5.** A case with photographic film that can be loaded directly into a camera. [Earlier *cartage,* var. of Fr. *cartouche.* —see CARTOUCHE.]

cartridge belt *n.* A belt with loops or pockets for carrying ammunition or other kinds of equipment.

cartridge clip *n.* A metal container or frame for holding cartridges to be loaded into an automatic rifle or pistol.

car·tu·lar·y also **char·tu·lar·y** (kär′chə-lĕr′ē) *n., pl.* **-ies.** A collection of deeds or charters, esp. a register of titles to all the property of an estate or monastery. [Med. Lat. *cartularium* < Lat. *cartula,* dim. of *carta,* leaf of papyrus. —see CARD.]

cart·wheel (kärt′hwēl′, -wēl′) *n.* **1.** A somersault or handspring in which the body turns over sideways with the arms and legs spread like the spokes of a wheel. **2.** *Slang.* A silver dollar or other large coin.

ca·run·cle (kə-rŭng′kəl, kăr′ŭng′-) *n.* **1.** A fleshy, naked outgrowth, such as a fowl's wattles. **2.** *Bot.* An excrescence on a seed at or near the hilum. [Obs. Fr. *caruncule* < Lat. *caruncula,* dim. of *caro,* flesh.] **—ca·run′cu·lar** (-lər) *adj.* **—ca·run′cu·late** (-lĭt, -lāt′), **ca·run′cu·lat′ed** (-lā′tĭd) *adj.*

car·va·crol (kär′və-krôl′, -krōl′) *n.* A liquid phenol, $C_{10}H_{14}O$, used in flavorings and fungicides. [NLat. *carvi,* specific epithet of *Carum carvi,* caraway + Lat. *acer, acr-,* sharp + -OL.]

carve (kärv) *v.* **carved, carv·ing, carves.** *—tr.* **1. a.** To divide into pieces by cutting; slice: *carve a turkey.* **b.** To divide by parceling out: *carve up an estate.* **2.** To cut into a desired shape; fashion by cutting: *carve the wood into a figure.* **3.** To make or form by or as if by cutting: *carve initials in the bark; carved out an empire.* **4.** To decorate by carving. *—intr.* **1.** To engrave or cut figures as a hobby or trade. **2.** To disjoint, slice, and serve meat or poultry. [ME *kerven* < OE *ceorfan.*] **—carv′er** *n.*

car·vel (kär′vəl, -vĕl′) *n.* Variant of **caravel.**

car·vel-built (kär′vəl-bĭlt′, -vĕl′-) *adj.* Built with the hull planks lying flush or edge to edge rather than overlapping: *a carvel-built ship.*

carv·en (kär′vən) *v. Archaic.* Past tense and past participle of **carve.**

carv·ing (kär′vĭng) *n.* **1.** The cutting of wood, stone, or other material to form a figure or design. **2.** The figure or design formed by carving.

car wash *n.* An area or a building equipped for washing cars.

car·y·at·id (kăr′ē-ăt′ĭd) *n., pl.* **-ids** or **-i·des** (-ĭ-dēz′). *Archit.* A supporting column sculptured in the form of a woman. [< Lat. *Caryatides,* caryatids, maidens of Caryae < Gk. *Karuatides* < *Karuai,* Caryae, a village in Greece.] **—car′y·at′i·dal** (-ĭ-dəl), **car′y·at′i·de′an** (-ĭ-dē′ən), **car′y·a·tid′ic** (-ə-tĭd′ĭk) *adj.*

caryo– *pref.* Variant of **karyo-.**

car·y·op·sis (kăr′ē-ŏp′sĭs) *n., pl.* **-op·ses** (-ŏp′sēz′) or **-op·si·des** (-ŏp′sĭ-dēz′). A one-celled, one-seeded dry fruit having its outer coat fused to its surface, as a grain of barley or wheat. [CARY(O)- + -OPSIS.]

ca·sa·ba also **cas·sa·ba** (kə-sä′bə) *n.* A variety of winter melon having a yellow rind and sweet, whitish flesh. [After *Kasaba,* former name for Turgutlu, Turkey.]

Cas·a·no·va (kăs′ə-nō′və, kăz′-) *n.* A promiscuous and unscrupulous man; libertine. [After G.J. *Casanova* de Seingalt (1725–1798).]

ca·sa·va (kə-sä′və) *n.* Variant of **cassava.**

Cas·bah (kăz′bä′, käz′-) *n.* **1.** In northern Africa, the citadel and palace of a sovereign. **2.** The native quarter in any of several cities in northern Africa. [Fr. < dial. Ar. *qaşbah* < Ar. *qasabah,* fortress.]

cas·cade (kă-skād′) *n.* **1.** A waterfall or a series of small waterfalls over steep rocks. **2.** Something resembling a cascade, esp. an arrangement or fall of material, as lace. **3.** A succession or series of processes, operations, or units. **4.** *Elect.* A series of components or networks the output of each of which serves as the input for the next. *—intr. & tr.v.* **-cad·ed, -cad·ing, -cades.** To fall or cause to fall from one level to another in a continuous series. [Fr. < Ital. *cascata* < *cascare,* to fall < VLat. **casicare* < Lat. *cadere.*]

cas·car·a (kă-skăr′ə) *n.* **1.** The cascara buckthorn. **2.** Cascara sagrada. [Sp. *cáscara,* bark < *cascar,* to break < VLat. **quassicare* < Lat. *quassare* < *quatere,* to shake.]

cascara buckthorn *n.* A shrub or tree, *Rhamnus purshiana,* of northwestern North America, whose bark is the source of cascara sagrada.

cascara sa·gra·da (sə-grä′də) *n.* The dried bark of the cascara buckthorn, used as a stimulant, cathartic, and laxative. [Am. Sp. *cáscara sagrada* : Sp. *cáscara,* bark + Sp. *sagrada,* sacred.]

cas·ca·ril·la (kăs′kə-rĭl′ə) *n.* **1.** A shrub, *Croton eluteria,* of the West Indies, having bitter, aromatic bark. **2.** Also **cascarilla bark.** The bark of the cascarilla, used as a tonic. [Sp., dim. of *cáscara,* bark. —see CASCARA.]

cascarilla oil *n.* An oil obtained from cascarilla bark that is used as a flavoring.

case¹ (kās) *n.* **1.** An instance or example of the existence or occurrence of something. **2. a.** An occurrence of disease or disorder. **b.** A client, as of a physician or attorney. **3.** A set of circumstances or state of affairs; situation. **4.** A set of reasons, arguments, or supporting facts offered in justification of a statement, action, situation, or thing. **5.** A question or problem; matter: *a case of honor.* **6.** A situation that requires investigation, esp. by a formal or official body. **7.** *Law.* **a.** An action or suit or just grounds for an action. **b.** The facts or evidence offered in support of a claim. **8.** *Informal.* A peculiar or eccentric person. **9.** *Ling.* **a.** The syntactic relationship of a noun, pronoun, or adjective to the other words of a sentence, indicated in inflected languages by the assumption of declensional endings and in noninflected languages by the position of the words within the sentence. **b.** The form or position of a word that indicates this relationship. **c.** Such forms, positions, or relationships collectively. **10. a.** *Ling.* A pattern of inflection of nouns, pronouns, and adjectives to express different syntactic functions in a sentence. **b.** The form of such an inflected word. *—tr.v.* **cased, cas·ing, cas·es.** *Slang.* To examine carefully, as in planning a crime: *case the bank before robbing it.* ***—idioms.*** **in any case.** Regardless of what occurred or will occur. **in case.** If it happens that; if. [ME *cas* < OFr. < Lat. *casus* < p.part. of *cadere,* to fall.]

case² (kās) *n.* **1.** A container or receptacle. **2.** A decorative or protective covering or cover. **3.** A box with its contents. **4.** A set or pair, as of pistols. **5.** The frame or framework of a window, door, or stairway. **6.** *Printing.* A shallow, compartmented tray for storing type or type matrices. *—tr.v.* **cased, cas·ing, cas·es.** To put into, cover, or protect with a case. [ME < Norman Fr. *casse* < Lat. *capsa.*]

ca·se·ate (kā′sē-āt′) *intr.v.* **-at·ed, -at·ing, -ates.** To undergo caseation. [< Lat. *caseus,* cheese.]

ca·se·a·tion (kā′sē-ā′shən) *n.* The necrotic degeneration of bodily tissue into a cheeselike substance. [< CASEATE.]

case·book (kās′bo͝ok′) *n.* A book containing source materials in a specific area, used as a reference and in teaching.

case·hard·en (kās′här′dn) *tr.v.* **-ened, -en·ing, -ens. 1.** To harden the surface of (iron or steel) by high-temperature shallow infusion of carbon followed by quenching. **2.** To make callous or insensitive.

case history *n.* An organized set of facts relevant to the development of an individual or group condition under study or treatment, esp. in sociology, psychiatry, or medicine.

ca·sein (kā′sēn′, kā′sē-ĭn) *n.* A white, tasteless, odorless milk and cheese protein, used to make plastics, adhesives, paints, and foods. [Ult. < Lat. *caseus,* cheese.]

case knife *n.* **1.** A knife kept in a sheath or case. **2.** A table knife.

case law *n.* Law based on judicial decision and precedent rather than statute.

case load *n.* The number of cases handled in a given period, as by a clinic or social services agency.

case·mate (kās′māt′) *n.* **1.** A fortified enclosure for artillery on a warship. **2.** An armored compartment for artillery on a rampart. [OFr. < OItal. *casamatta.*] **—case′mat′ed** *adj.*

case·ment (kās′mənt) *n.* **1. a.** A window sash that opens outward by means of hinges. **b.** A window with such sashes. **2.** A case or covering. [ME < Med. Lat. *casamentum* < *casa,* dwelling < Lat.] **—case′ment·ed** *adj.*

ca·se·ous (kā′sē-əs) *adj.* Resembling cheese. [< Lat. *caseus,* cheese.]

ca·sern also **ca·serne** (kə-zûrn′) *n.* A military barracks. [Fr. *caserne.*]

case shot *n.* **1. a.** A canister (sense 2). **b.** The shot in a canister. **2.** A shrapnel shell.

case study *n.* A detailed analysis of an individual or group, esp. as an exemplary model of medical, psychological, or social phenomena.

case system *n.* A method of teaching law that emphasizes the study of selected cases rather than the systematic study of legal textbooks.

case·work (kās′wûrk′) *n.* The part of a social worker's duties dealing with the problems of a particular case. **—case′work′er** *n.*

cash¹ (kăsh) *n.* **1.** Ready money; currency or coins. **2.** Payment for goods or services in money or by check. *—tr.v.* **cashed, cash·ing, cash·es.** To exchange for or convert into ready money: *cash a check.* ***—phrasal verb.*** **cash in. 1.** To withdraw from a venture by or as if by settling one's account. **2.** *Slang.* To die. ***—idiom.*** **cash in on.** To take advantage of. [OFr. *casse,* money box < Lat. *capsa,* case.]

cash² (kăsh) *n., pl.* **cash.** Any of various Oriental coins of small denomination, esp. a copper and lead coin with a

square hole in its center. [Port. *caixa* < Tamil *kācu,* a small coin < Skt. *karṣa,* a weight.]
cash·book (kăsh′bo͝ok′) *n.* A book in which a record of cash receipts and expenditures is kept.
cash crop *n.* A crop grown esp. for sale and usually providing an important source of income.
cash discount *n.* A reduction in the price of an item for sale allowed if payment is made within a stipulated period.
cash·ew (kăsh′o͞o, kə-sho͞o′) *n.* **1.** A tropical American evergreen tree, *Anacardium occidentale,* bearing kidney-shaped nuts that protrude from a fleshy receptacle. **2.** Also **cashew nut.** The nut of the cashew, edible only when roasted. [Port. *acajú* < Tupi.]
cash flow *n.* The cash receipts or net income after taxes and other disbursements from one or more assets for a given period, often used as a measure of corporate worth.
cash·ier[1] (kă-shîr′) *n.* **1.** The officer of a bank or business concern in charge of paying and receiving money. **2.** An employee who handles cash transactions for any of various business operations, such as a supermarket. [Du. *cassier* < Fr. *caissier* < *caisse,* money box < OFr. *casse.* —see CASH[1]]
ca·shier[2] (kă-shîr′) *tr.v.* **-shiered, -shier·ing, -shiers.** To dismiss from a position of command or responsibility, esp. for disciplinary reasons. [Du. *casseren* < OFr. *casser,* to dismiss. —see QUASH.]
cashier's check *n.* A check drawn by a bank on its own funds and signed by the bank's cashier.
cash·mere (kăzh′mîr′, kăsh′-) *n.* **1.** Fine, downy wool growing beneath the outer hair of the Cashmere goat. **2.** A soft fabric made of wool from the Cashmere goat or of similar fibers. [After *Kashmir,* a region in India.]
Cashmere goat *n.* A goat native to the Himalayan regions of India and Tibet, and prized for its wool.
cash register *n.* A machine that tabulates the amount of sales transactions, makes a permanent and cumulative record of them, and has a drawer in which cash may be kept.
cas·i·mere (kăz′ə-mîr′, kăs′-) *n.* Variant of **cassimere.**
cas·ing (kā′sĭng) *n.* **1.** The act of encasing. **2.** An outer cover. **3.** The cleaned intestines of cattle, sheep, or hogs, used to contain processed meat. **4.** The frame or framework for a window or door. **5.** A metal pipe or tube used as a lining for water, oil, or gas wells.
ca·si·no (kə-sē′nō) *n., pl.* **-nos. 1.** A summer or country house in Italy. **2.** A public room or house for entertainment, esp. for gambling. **3.** Also **cassino.** A card game for two to four players in which cards on the table are matched by cards in the hand. [Ital. < *casa,* house < Lat., hut.]
cask (kăsk) *n.* **1.** A barrel of any size. **2.** The quantity contained in a cask. [Sp. *casco,* helmet < *cascar,* to break. —see CASCARA.]
cas·ket (kăs′kĭt) *n.* **1.** A small case or chest, as for jewels or other valuables. **2.** A coffin. —*tr.v.* **-ket·ed, -ket·ing, -kets.** To enclose in a casket. [ME, poss. alteration of OFr. *cassette.* —see CASSETTE.]
casque (kăsk) *n.* **1.** A helmet or other armor for the head. **2.** *Zool.* A helmetlike structure or protuberance. [Fr. < Sp. *casco.* —see CASK.] **—casqued** (kăskt) *adj.*
cas·sa·ba (kə-sä′bə) *n.* Variant of **casaba.**
Cas·san·dra (kə-săn′drə) *n.* **1.** *Gk. Myth.* A daughter of Priam, King of Troy, endowed with the gift of prophecy but fated by Apollo never to be believed. **2.** A person who utters unheeded prophecies. [Lat. < Gk. *Kassandra.*]
cas·sa·tion (kă-sā′shən) *n.* Abrogation or annulment by a higher authority. [OFr. < *casser,* to annul. —see QUASH.]
cas·sa·va also **ca·sa·va** (kə-sä′və) *n.* **1.** Any of various tropical American plants of the genus *Manihot,* having a large, starchy root. **2.** A starch derived from the root of the cassava, used as an ingredient in tapioca and as a staple food in the tropics. [Sp. *cazabe,* cassava bread < Taino *caçábi.*]
cas·se·role (kăs′ə-rōl′) *n.* **1. a.** A dish, usually of earthenware, glass, or cast iron, in which food is both baked and served. **b.** Food prepared and served in such a dish. **2.** *Chem.* A small-handled, deep porcelain crucible used for heating and evaporating. [Fr., saucepan, dim. of OFr. *casse,* roasting pan < OHG *chezi.*]
cas·sette (kə-sĕt′, kă-) *n.* **1.** A light-proof camera cartridge for daylight loading of photographic film. **2.** *Electronics.* **a.** A small cartridge containing unlooped magnetic tape for use in certain recorders and players. **b.** A tape recorder or player designed to use cassettes. [Fr., small box < OFr., dim. of *casse,* case < Lat. *capsa.*]
cas·sia (kăsh′ə) *n.* **1.** Any of various chiefly tropical trees, shrubs, and plants of the genus *Cassia,* having compound leaves, usually yellow flowers, and long pods. **2. a.** A tree, *Cinnamomum cassia,* of tropical Asia, having bark similar to cinnamon but of inferior quality. **b.** The bark of this tree, used as a spice. [ME < Lat., a kind of plant < Gk., of Semitic orig.]
cassia oil *n.* An oil derived from the bark of the tree *Cinnamomum cassia.*
cas·si·mere also **cas·i·mere** (kăz′ə-mîr′, kăs′-) *n.* A plain or twilled woolen cloth for men's apparel. [Obs. *Cassimere,* var. of KASHMIR, a region in India.]
cas·si·no (kə-sē′nō) *n.* Variant of **casino** (sense 3).
Cas·si·o·pe·ia (kăs′ē-ə-pē′ə) *n.* A W-shaped constellation in the Northern Hemisphere near Camelopardalis and Cepheus. [Lat. < Gk. *Kassiopeia.*]
cas·sis (kə-sēs′) *n.* **1.** A European bush, *Ribes nigrum,* that bears black currants. **2.** A cordial made from the berries of the cassis. [Fr. < Lat. *cassia,* a kind of plant. —see CASSIA.]
cas·sit·er·ite (kə-sĭt′ə-rīt′) *n.* A light-yellow, red-brown, or black mineral, SnO_2, an important tin ore. [Fr. *casitérite* < Gk. *kasseritos,* tin.]
cas·sock (kăs′ək) *n.* A long garment reaching to the feet and worn by clergymen and others assisting in church services. [OFr. *casaque,* long coat, perh. < Pers. *kazagand,* padded jacket.]
cas·so·war·y (kăs′ə-wĕr′ē) *n., pl.* **-ies.** Any of several large, flightless birds of the genus *Casuarius,* of New Guinea and adjacent areas, having a large, bony projection on the top of the head and brightly colored wattles. [Malay *kĕsuari.*]
cast (kăst) *v.* **cast, cast·ing, casts.** —*tr.* **1.** To throw with violence or force; hurl; fling. **2.** To shed; molt. **3.** To throw forth; drop: *cast anchor.* **4.** To throw on the ground, as in wrestling. **5.** To deposit or give (a ballot). **6.** To turn or direct: *cast her eyes on the speaker.* **7.** To cause to fall upon or over something or in a certain direction, as if by throwing: *candles casting light; cast aspersions on her character.* **8.** *Archaic.* To bestow; confer: *"The government I cast upon my brother"* (Shakespeare). **9.** To throw (dice). **10.** To give birth to prematurely: *The cow cast a calf.* **11.** In hunting, to cause (hounds) to scatter and circle in search of a lost scent. **12. a.** To choose actors for (a play, for example). **b.** To assign a certain role to (an actor). **c.** To assign an actor to (a part). **13.** To form (liquid metal, for example) into a particular shape by pouring into a mold. **14.** To arrange in some system; formulate. **15.** To contrive; devise. **16.** To calculate or compute; add up (a column of figures). **17.** To calculate astrologically; forecast. **18.** To warp; twist. **19.** *Obs.* To consider; ponder. **20.** *Printing.* To stereotype or electroplate. **21.** *Naut.* To turn (a ship); change to the opposite tack. —*intr.* **1.** To throw, esp. to throw out a lure or bait at the end of a fishing line. **2. a.** To add a column of figures; make calculations. **b.** To conjecture or forecast. **3.** To receive form or shape in a mold. **4.** To search for a lost scent in hunting with hounds. **5.** *Naut.* **a.** To veer to leeward from a former course; fall off. **b.** To put about; tack. **6.** To choose the actors for a play, movie, or other theatrical presentation. **7.** *Obs.* To turn or revolve something in the mind; ponder; scheme. ***—phrasal verbs.*** **cast about. 1.** To search or look for. **2.** To devise means; contrive. **cast aside** (or **away**). **1.** To discard or reject as useless. **2.** To squander or waste. **cast off. 1.** To discard or reject. **2.** To let go; set loose. **3.** To make the last row of stitches in knitting. **4.** To estimate the space a manuscript will occupy when set into type. **cast on.** To make the first row of stitches in knitting. **cast out.** To drive out by force; expel. **cast up. 1.** To vomit. **2.** To add up; calculate. —*n.* **1. a.** The act of casting or throwing. **b.** The distance thrown. **2. a.** The throwing of a fishing line or net into the water. **b.** The line or net thrown. **c.** *Chiefly Brit.* The leader with flies or baited hooks attached. **3. a.** A throw of dice. **b.** The number thrown. **c.** A stroke of fortune or fate; lot. **4. a.** A turning of the eye in a certain direction. **b.** A slight squint. **5.** Something thrown off, out, or away, as the skin shed by an insect. **6. a.** The addition of a column of figures; calculation. **b.** A conjecture or forecast. **7. a.** The act of casting or founding. **b.** The amount of molten material poured into a mold at a single operation. **c.** Something formed by this means. **8.** An impression formed in a mold or matrix; a mold: *a cast of his face made in plaster.* **9.** The form in which something is made or constructed; arrangement; disposition. **10.** The actors in a theatrical presentation. **11.** A rigid dressing, usually made of gauze and plaster of Paris, as for a broken bone. **12.** A slight trace of color. **13.** Outward form or look; appearance. **14.** Sort or type: *fancies himself to be of a macho cast.* **15.** An inclination or tendency. **16.** A distortion of shape. **17.** The circling of hounds to pick up a scent in hunting. ***—idioms.*** **cast lots.** To draw lots in order to determine something by chance. **cast (one's) lot (in) with.** To join or side with for better or worse. [ME *casten* < ON *kasta.*]
cas·ta·nets (kăs′tə-nĕts′) *pl.n.* A rhythm instrument consisting of a pair of slightly concave shells of ivory or hardwood, held in the palm of the hand by a connecting cord over the thumb and clapped together with the fingers. [Sp. *castañeta* < *castaña,* chestnut < Lat. *castanea.* —see CHESTNUT.]
cast·a·way (kăst′ə-wā′) *adj.* **1.** Cast adrift or ashore; shipwrecked. **2.** Discarded; thrown away. —*n.* **1.** A shipwrecked person. **2.** A discarded or rejected person or thing.
caste (kăst) *n.* **1.** One of the four major hereditary classes into which Hindu society is divided, each caste distinctly separated from the others by restrictions placed upon occupation and marriage. **2. a.** A social class separated from others by distinctions of hereditary rank, profession, or wealth. **b.** A social system or the principle of grading society based on caste. **c.** The social position or status conferred by a system based on caste: *lose caste.* **3.** A specialized level in a colony of social insects, such as ants, in which its members, such as workers or soldiers, carry out a specific function. [Port. *casta,* race < *casto,* pure < Lat. *castus.*]
cas·tel·lan (kăs′tə-lən) *n.* The governor or keeper of a castle.

cashew

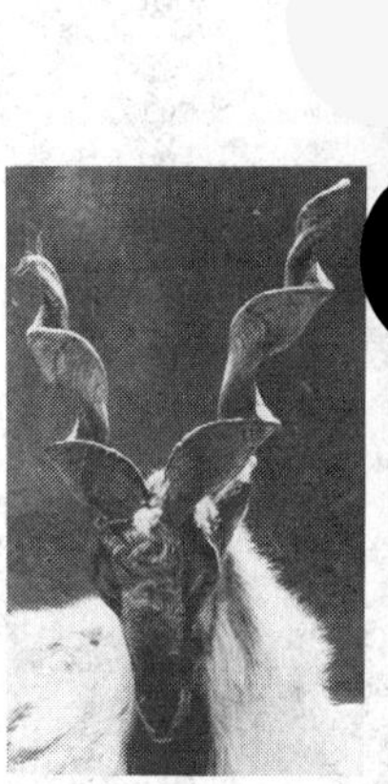
Cashmere goat

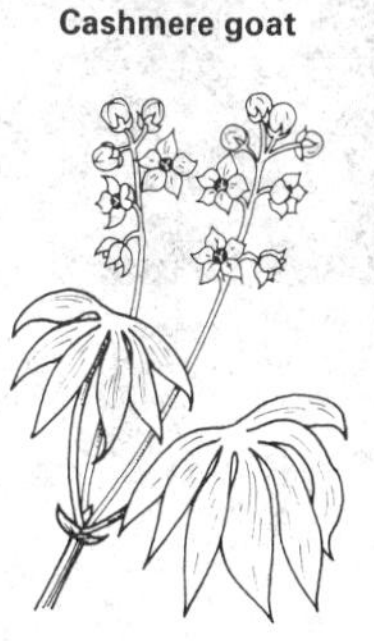
cassava

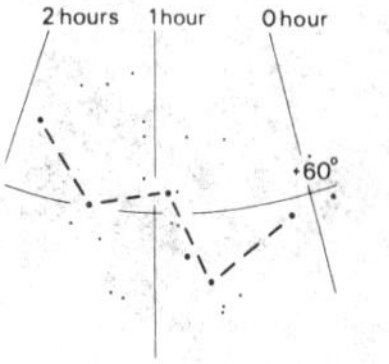

Cassiopeia

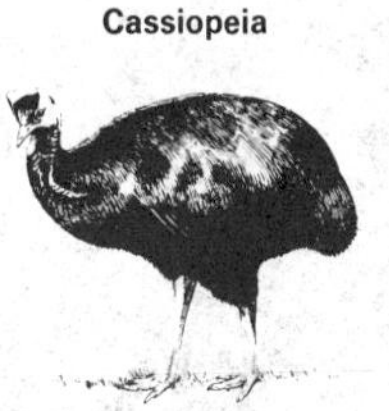
George Miksch Sutton
cassowary

castanets

[ME *castelain* < Norman Fr. < Lat. *castellanus,* of a castle < *castellum,* castle.]

cas·tel·la·ny (kăs′tə-lā′nē) *n., pl.* **-nies. 1.** The jurisdiction of a castellan. **2.** The lands appertaining to a castle.

cas·tel·lat·ed (kăs′tə-lā′tĭd) *adj.* **1.** Furnished with turrets and battlements in the style of a castle. **2.** Having a castle. [Med. Lat. *castellatus,* p.part of *castellare,* to fortify as a castle < Lat. *castellum,* castle.] **—cas′tel·la′tion** *n.*

cast·er (kăs′tər) *n.* **1.** One that casts. **2.** Also **cas·tor.** A small wheel on a swivel, attached under a piece of furniture or other heavy object to make it easier to move. **3.** Also **cas·tor. a.** A small bottle or cruet for condiments. **b.** A stand for holding a set of these bottles.

caster
18th-century American

cas·ti·gate (kăs′tĭ-gāt′) *tr.v.* **-gat·ed, -gat·ing, -gates. 1.** To punish or chastise. **2.** To criticize severely. [Lat. *castigare, castigat-* < *castus,* pure.] **—cas′ti·ga′tion** *n.* **—cas′ti·ga′tor** *n.*

Cas·tile soap also **cas·tile soap** (kă-stēl′) *n.* A fine, hard, white, odorless soap made with olive oil and sodium hydroxide. [After *Castile,* a province of Spain, where the soap was first made.]

Cas·til·ian (kă-stĭl′yən) *n.* **1. a.** The Spanish dialect of Castile. **b.** The standard literary and official form of Spanish, which is based on this dialect. **2.** A native or inhabitant of Castile. *—adj.* Of or pertaining to Castile, its people, or their language and culture.

cast·ing (kăs′tĭng) *n.* **1.** The act or process of making casts or molds. **2.** The throwing of a fishing line. **3.** The selection of actors or performers. **4.** Something that is cast in a mold. **5.** Something that is cast off or out.

casting vote *n.* The vote of a presiding officer in an assembly or council, given to break a tie.

cast iron *n.* A hard, brittle, nonmalleable iron-carbon alloy containing 2.0 to 4.5 per cent carbon, 0.5 to 3 per cent silicon, and lesser amounts of sulfur, manganese, and phosphorus.

cast-i·ron (kăst′ī′ərn) *adj.* **1.** Made of cast iron. **2.** Rigid or inflexible: *a cast-iron rule.*

castle
Neuschwanstein Castle built for King Ludwig II of Bavaria

cas·tle (kăs′əl) *n.* **1. a.** A fort or fortified group of buildings usually dominating the surrounding country and held by a vassal of a ruler in feudal societies. **b.** A fortified stronghold of this kind converted to residential use. **2.** A building similar to or resembling a castle. **3.** A place of privacy, security, or refuge. **4.** A rook in the game of chess. *—v.* **-tled, -tling, -tles.** *—tr.* **1.** To place in or as if in a castle. **2.** To move (the chess king) from his own square two squares to one side and then, in the same move, bring the rook from that side to the square immediately past the new position of the king. *—intr.* To move the chess king and rook by castling. [ME *castel,* partly < OE and partly < Norman Fr., both < Lat. *castellum,* dim. of *castrum,* fort.]

cas·tled (kăs′əld) *adj.* Castellated.

cast·off (kăst′ôf′, -ŏf′) *n.* **1.** One that has been discarded. **2.** *Printing.* A calculation of the amount of space a manuscript will occupy when set into type.

cast-off (kăst′ôf′, -ŏf′) *adj.* Discarded; rejected.

cas·tor¹ (kăs′tər) *n.* **1.** An oily, brown, odorous substance obtained from glands in the groin of the beaver and used as a perfume fixative. **2.** A beaver hat. **3.** A heavy wool fabric used esp. for overcoats. [ME, beaver < Lat. < Gk. *kastōr* < *Kastōr,* Castor.]

cas·tor² (kăs′tər) *n.* Variant of **caster** (senses 2 and 3).

catafalque

Cas·tor (kăs′tər) *n.* **1.** *Gk. Myth.* One of the Dioscuri. **2.** A double star in the constellation Gemini, the brightest star in the group, approximately 46 light-years from Earth. [Lat. < Gk. *Kastōr.*]

castor bean *n.* **1.** The castor-oil plant. **2.** The very poisonous seed of the castor bean. [CASTOR (OIL) + BEAN.]

castor oil *n.* A colorless or yellowish oil extracted from castor-oil plant seeds and used as a cathartic and a fine lubricant. [Poss. from a former use as a substitute for castor in medicine.]

cas·tor-oil plant (kăs′tər-oil′) *n.* A large plant, *Ricinus communis,* native to tropical Africa and Asia, grown for ornament and for the commercial extraction of castor oil from its poisonous seeds.

cas·trate (kăs′trāt′) *tr.v.* **-trat·ed, -trat·ing, -trates. 1.** To remove the testicles of; geld. **2.** To remove the ovaries of; spay. **3.** To remove the vitality or force of, esp. by expurgating. [Lat. *castrare, castrat-.*] **—cas·tra′tion** *n.*

Cas·tro·ism (kăs′trō-ĭz′əm) *n.* The governmental and socioeconomic principles and policies of the Cuban leader Fidel Castro. **—Cas′tro·ite′** (-īt′) *n.*

catalpa

ca·su·al (kăzh′o͞o-əl) *adj.* **1.** Occurring by chance; accidental. **2.** Occurring at irregular intervals; not planned; occasional. **3.** Showing little interest; nonchalant: *a casual manner.* **4. a.** Without ceremony or formality. **b.** Suited for everyday wear or use; informal. **5.** Not serious or thorough; superficial: *a casual inspection.* **6.** Not close or intimate: *a casual friendship.* *—n.* **1.** *Chiefly Brit.* A person who receives temporary welfare relief. **2.** A person who works at irregular intervals. **3.** A soldier temporarily attached to a unit while awaiting permanent assignment. [ME *casuel* < OFr. < LLat. *casualis* < Lat. *casus,* event. —see CASE¹.] **—ca′su·al·ly** *adv.* **—ca′su·al·ness** *n.*

ca·su·al·ty (kăzh′o͞o-əl-tē) *n., pl.* **-ties. 1.** An unfortunate accident, esp. one involving loss of life. **2.** One who is injured or killed in an accident. **3.** One injured, killed, captured, or missing in action against an enemy. [ME *casuelte* < OFr. < Lat. *casualis,* casual.]

ca·su·a·ri·na (kăzh′o͞o-ə-rī′nə) *n.* Any of various trees of the genus *Casuarina,* which includes the beefwoods. [NLat. *Casuarina,* genus name < Malay *kĕsuari,* cassowary (from the resemblance of its twigs to the drooping feathers of the cassowary).]

ca·su·ist (kăzh′o͞o-ĭst) *n.* A person who is expert in or given to casuistry. [Fr. *casuiste* < Sp. *casuista* < Lat. *casus,* case. —see CASE¹.]

ca·su·is·tic (kăzh′o͞o-ĭs′tĭk) also **ca·su·is·ti·cal** (-tĭ-kəl) *adj.* Of or pertaining to casuists or casuistry. **—ca′su·is′ti·cal·ly** *adv.*

ca·su·ist·ry (kăzh′o͞o-ĭ-strē) *n.* **1.** The determination of right and wrong in questions of conduct or conscience by the application of general principles of ethics. **2.** A subtle but misleading or false application of ethical principles. [< CASUIST.]

ca·sus bel·li (kā′səs bĕl′ī′, kä′səs bĕl′ē′) *n.* An act or event that justifies a declaration of war. [NLat., occasion of war.]

cat (kăt) *n.* **1. a.** A carnivorous mammal, *Felis catus* (or *F. domesticus*), domesticated since early times as a catcher of rats and mice and as a pet and existing in several distinctive breeds and varieties. **b.** Any of the other animals of the family Felidae, which includes the lion, tiger, leopard, and lynx. **c.** The fur of a domestic cat. **2.** A spiteful woman. **3.** A cat-o'-nine-tails. **4.** A catfish. **5.** *Naut.* **a.** A cathead. **b.** A device for raising an anchor to the cathead. **c.** A catboat. **6.** *Slang.* A man. *—tr.v.* **cat·ted, cat·ting, cats.** To hoist an anchor to the cathead. ***—idiom.*** **let the cat out of the bag.** To let a secret be known. [ME < OE *catt,* perh. < Lat. *cattus.*]

CAT (kăt) *n.* Computerized axial tomography.

cata– *pref.* **1.** Down: *catadromous.* **2.** Reverse; backwards; degenerative: *cataplasia.* [Gk. *kata-* < *kata,* down.]

ca·tab·o·lism (kə-tăb′ə-lĭz′əm) *n.* The metabolic change of complex into simple molecules. [< Gk. *katabolē,* a throwing down < *kataballein,* to throw down : *kata-,* down + *ballein,* to throw.] **—cat′a·bol′ic** (kăt′ə-bŏl′ĭk) *adj.* **—cat′a·bol′i·cal·ly** *adv.*

ca·tab·o·lite (kə-tăb′ə-līt′) *n.* A substance produced in the process of catabolism. [CATABOL(ISM) + -ITE.]

ca·tab·o·lize (kə-tăb′ə-līz′) *intr. & tr.v.* **-lized, -liz·ing, -liz·es.** To undergo or cause to undergo catabolism.

cat·a·chre·sis (kăt′ə-krē′sĭs) *n., pl.* **-ses** (-sēz′). **1. a.** Strained use of a word or phrase, as for rhetorical effect. **b.** A deliberately paradoxical figure of speech. **2.** The use of a wrong word in a context. [Lat. *catachresis* < Gk. *katakhrēsis,* excessive use < *katakhrēsthai,* to use up : *kata-,* completely + *khrēsthai,* to use.] **—cat′a·chres′tic** (-krĕs′tĭk) *adj.*

cat·a·clysm (kăt′ə-klĭz′əm) *n.* **1.** A violent and sudden change in the earth's crust. **2.** A violent upheaval or disaster. **3.** A devastating flood. [Fr. *cataclysme* < Lat. *cataclysmos,* deluge < Gk. *kataklusmos* < *katakluzein,* to inundate : *kata-,* down + *kluzein,* to wash.] **—cat′a·clys′mic** (-klĭz′mĭk), **cat′a·clys′mal** (-klĭz′məl) *adj.*

cat·a·comb (kăt′ə-kōm′) *n.* Often **catacombs.** An underground chamber or tunnel with recesses for graves. [OFr. *catacombe* < LLat. *catacumbae* (pl.).]

ca·tad·ro·mous (kə-tăd′rə-məs) *adj.* Migrating down river to breed in marine waters: *catadromous fish.*

cat·a·falque (kăt′ə-fălk′, -fôlk′) *n.* The raised structure upon which a coffin rests during a state funeral. [Fr. < Ital. *catafalco.*]

Cat·a·lan (kăt′l-ăn′, -ən) *adj.* Of or pertaining to Catalonia or its people, language, or culture. *—n.* **1.** A native or inhabitant of Catalonia. **2.** The Romance language of Catalonia.

cat·a·lase (kăt′l-ās′, -āz′) *n.* An enzyme in the blood and tissues that catalyzes the decomposition of hydrogen peroxide into water and oxygen. [CATAL(YSIS) + -ASE.]

cat·a·lec·tic (kăt′l-ĕk′tĭk) *adj.* Designating a verse that lacks part of the last foot. [LLat. *catalecticus* < Gk. *katalektikos,* incomplete < *katalēgein,* to leave off : *kata-,* off + *lēgein,* to stop.]

cat·a·lep·sy (kăt′l-ĕp′sē) *n., pl.* **-sies.** Muscular rigidity, lack of awareness of environment, and lack of response to external stimuli, often associated with epilepsy, schizophrenia, and hysteria. [ME *catalempsi* < Med. Lat. *catalempsia* < Gk. *katalēpsis* < *katalambanein,* to seize upon : *kata-,* (intensive) + *lambanein,* to seize.] **—cat′a·lep′tic** (-ĕp′tĭk) *adj.*

cat·a·logue also **cat·a·log** (kăt′l-ôg′, -ŏg′) *—n.* **1. a.** A systematized list, usually in alphabetical order, often with descriptions of the listed items. **b.** A publication, such as a book, containing such a list. **2.** A card catalog. *—tr. & intr.v.* **-logued, -logu·ing, -logues** also **-loged, -log·ing, -logs.** To list in or make a catalogue. [ME *cathaloge* < OFr. *catalogue* < LLat. *catalogus,* enumeration < Gk. *katalogos* < *katalegein,* to list : *kata-* (intensive) + *legein,* to count.] **—cat′a·logu′er, cat′a·log′er** *n.*

ca·tal·pa (kə-tăl′pə, -tôl′-) *n.* Any of several chiefly North American trees of the genus *Catalpa,* having large leaves, showy clusters of whitish flowers, and long, slender pods. [Creek *kutuhlpa.*]

ă pat / ā pay / âr care / ä father / b bib / ch church / d deed / ĕ pet / ē be / f fife / g gag / h hat / hw which / ĭ pit / ī pie / îr pier / j judge / k kick / l lid, needle / m mum / n no, sudden / ng thing / ŏ pot / ō toe / ô paw, for / oi noise / ou out / o͝o took / o͞o boot /

ca·tal·y·sis (kə-tăl′ĭ-sĭs) *n., pl.* **-ses** (-sēz′) The action of a catalyst, esp. modification of the rate of a chemical reaction by a catalyst. [Gk. *katalusis,* dissolution < *kataluein,* to dissolve : *kata-,* intensive + *luein,* to loosen.] **—cat′a·lyt′ic** (kăt′l-ĭt′ĭk) *adj.* **—cat′a·lyt′i·cal·ly** *adv.*

cat·a·lyst (kăt′l-ĭst) *n.* **1.** *Chem.* A substance, usually present in small amounts relative to the reactants, that modifies and esp. increases the rate of a chemical reaction without being consumed in the process. **2.** One that precipitates a process or event, esp. without being involved in or changed by the consequences. [< CATALYSIS.]

catalytic converter *n.* A reaction chamber typically containing a finely divided platinum-iridium catalyst into which exhaust gases from an automotive engine are passed together with excess air so that carbon monoxide and hydrocarbon pollutants are oxidized to carbon dioxide and water.

catalytic cracker *n.* An oil refinery unit in which the cracking of petroleum takes place in the presence of a catalyst.

cat·a·lyze (kăt′l-īz′) *tr.v.* **-lyzed, -lyz·ing, -lyz·es.** To modify the rate of (a chemical reaction) as a catalyst. [< CATALYSIS.] **—cat′a·lyz′er** *n.*

cat·a·ma·ran (kăt′ə-mə-răn′) *n.* **1.** A boat with two parallel hulls. **2.** A raft of logs or floats lashed together. [Tamil *kaṭṭumaram* : *kaṭṭu-,* to tie + *maram,* tree.]

cat·a·me·ni·a (kăt′ə-mē′nē-ə) *n. Physiol.* Menses. [Gk. *katamēnia* : *kata-,* according to + *mēn,* month.] **—cat′a·me′ni·al** (-nē-əl) *adj.*

cat·a·mite (kăt′ə-mīt′) *n.* A boy kept by a pederast. [Lat. *catamitus* < *Catamitus,* Ganymede < Etruscan *Catmite* < Gk. *Ganumēdēs.*]

cat·a·mount (kăt′ə-mount′) also **cat·a·moun·tain** (kăt′ə-moun′tən) *n.* Mountain lion. [Short for *catamountain,* var. of *cat of the mountain.*]

cat-and-mouse (kăt′n-mous′) *adj.* Of or using continual torment and teasing while probing the vulnerabilities of an opponent and waiting for an opportunity to attack.

cat·a·pho·re·sis (kăt′ə-fə-rē′sĭs) *n. Chem.* Electrophoresis. **—cat′a·pho·ret′ic** (-rĕt′ĭk) *adj.* **—cat′a·pho·ret′i·cal·ly** *adv.*

cat·a·phyll (kăt′ə-fĭl′) *n. Bot.* A modified or rudimentary leaf, such as a bud scale.

cat·a·pla·sia (kăt′ə-plā′zhə, -zhē-ə) *n.* Degenerative reversion of cells or tissue to a less differentiated form. **—cat′a·plas′tic** (-plăs′tĭk) *adj.*

cat·a·plasm (kăt′ə-plăz′əm) *n. Med.* A poultice. [OFr. *cataplasme* < LLat. *cataplasma* < Gk. *kataplasma* < *kataplassein,* to plaster over : *kata-* (intensive) + *plassein,* to mold.]

cat·a·plex·y *n.* A sudden state of immobility with loss of muscle tone usually caused by an extreme emotional stimulus. [Gk. *kataplēxis,* fixation (of the eyes in paralysis) < *kataplessein,* to amaze, terrify: *kata-,* down + *plessein,* to strike.]

cat·a·pult (kăt′ə-pŭlt′, po͝olt′) *n.* **1.** An ancient military machine for hurling large stones, arrows, or other missiles. **2.** A mechanism for launching aircraft without a runway, as from the deck of a ship. **3.** A slingshot. *—v.* **-pult·ed, -pult·ing, -pults.** *—tr.* To hurl or launch from or as if from a catapult. *—intr.* To become catapulted; spring up abruptly. [OFr. *catapulte* < Lat. *catapulta* < Gk. *katapaltēs* : *kata-,* down + *pallein,* to hurl.]

cat·a·ract (kăt′ə-răkt′) *n.* **1.** A very large waterfall. **2.** A great downpour. **3.** *Pathol.* Opacity of the lens or capsule of the eye, causing partial or total blindness. [Lat. *cataracta* < Gk. *kataraktēs* < *katarassein,* to dash down : *kata-,* down + *rassein,* to strike.]

ca·tarrh (kə-tär′) *n.* Inflammation of mucous membranes, esp. of the nose and throat. [OFr. *catarrhe* < LLat. *catarrhus* < Gk. *katarrous* < *katarrein,* to flow down : *kata-,* down + *rhein,* to flow.] **—ca·tarrh′al, ca·tarrh′ous** *adj.*

ca·tas·ta·sis (kə-tăs′tə-sĭs) *n., pl.* **-ses** (-sēz′). **1.** In classical tragedy, the intensified part of the action directly preceding the catastrophe. **2.** The climax of a play. [Gk. *katastasis,* settlement < *kathistanai,* to settle : *kata-,* down + *histanai,* to set.]

ca·tas·tro·phe (kə-tăs′trə-fē) *n.* **1.** A great and sudden calamity; disaster. **2.** A complete failure; fiasco **3.** A sudden violent change in the earth's surface; cataclysm. **4.** The dénouement of a play, esp. a classical tragedy. [Gk. *katastrophē,* an overturning < *katastrephein,* to overturn : *kata-,* down + *strephein,* to turn.] **—cat′a·stroph′ic** (kăt′ə-strŏf′ĭk) *adj.* **—cat′a·stroph′i·cal·ly** *adv.*

cat·a·to·ni·a (kăt′ə-tō′nē-ə) *n.* A schizophrenic disorder characterized by plastic immobility of the limbs, stupor, negativism, and mutism. [NLat. < G. *Katatonie* < Gk. *katatonos,* stretching down : *kata-,* down + *teinein,* to stretch.] **—cat′a·ton′ic** (-tŏn′ĭk) *adj. & n.*

Ca·taw·ba (kə-tô′bə) *n., pl.* **Catawba** or **-bas. 1. a.** A tribe of North American Indians formerly living along the Catawba River in the Carolinas. **b.** A member of this tribe. **c.** The Siouan language of the Catawba. **2. a.** *pl.* **-bas.** A light-red North American grape developed from the fox grape, *Vitis labrusca.* **b.** Wine made from these grapes.

cat·bird (kăt′bûrd′) *n.* A North American songbird, *Dumetella carolinensis,* having predominantly slate-gray plumage. [From the resemblance of one of its calls to the mewing of a cat.]

catbird seat *n.* A position of power or prominence.

cat·boat (kăt′bōt′) *n.* A broad-beamed sailboat carrying a single sail on a mast stepped well forward.

cat·bri·er (kăt′brī′ər) *n.* Any of several thorny vines of the genus *Smilax,* esp. *S. rotundifolia,* having heart-shaped leaves, small green flowers, and blackish berries.

cat·call (kăt′kôl′) *n.* A harsh or shrill call or whistle expressing disapproval or derision. **—cat′call′** *v.* **(-called, -call·ing, -calls).**

catch (kăch, kĕch) *v.* **caught** (kôt), **catch·ing, catch·es.** *—tr.* **1.** To capture or seize, esp. after a chase. **2.** To take by trapping or snaring. **3.** To discover or come upon suddenly, unexpectedly, or accidentally. **4. a.** To lay hold of forcibly or suddenly; grasp: *caught me by the arm.* **b.** To grab so as to stop the motion of: *catch a ball.* **5. a.** To overtake: *caught me on the straightaway.* **b.** To reach in time to board: *caught the bus.* **6. a.** To entangle; grip. **b.** To cause to become suddenly or accidentally hooked, entangled, or fastened. **7.** To hit; strike: *a punch that caught him in the stomach.* **8.** To check (oneself) during an action. **9.** To become subject to or contract, as by exposure or contagion: *catch a cold.* **10.** To become affected by or imbued with: *caught the joyous mood of the festival.* **11.** To take or get suddenly, momentarily, or quickly: *caught a glimpse of the queen.* **12.** To grasp mentally; apprehend. **13.** To apprehend and reproduce accurately by or as if by artistic means. **14.** To attract and fix; arrest: *couldn't catch her attention.* **15.** To charm or captivate. **16.** *Informal.* To see (a theatrical performance, for example). *—intr.* **1.** To become held, entangled, or fastened. **2.** To act or move so as to hold someone or something. **3.** To be communicable or infectious; spread. **4.** To take fire; kindle; burn. **5.** *Baseball.* To act as catcher. **—*phrasal verbs.*** **catch on.** *Informal.* **1.** To understand or perceive. **2.** To become popular. **catch up. 1.** To detect (someone) in a mistake. **2.** To come up from behind; overtake. **3.** To become involved with, often unwillingly: *caught up in the scandal.* **4.** To bring up to date: *catch up on my correspondence.* **5.** To absorb completely; engross: *caught up in his work.* *—n.* **1.** The act of catching; a taking and holding. **2.** Something that catches, esp. a device for fastening or for checking motion. **3.** Something that is caught. **4.** An amount that is caught. **5.** A choking or stoppage of the breath or voice. **6.** A stop or break in a mechanism. **7.** *Informal.* A person or thing worth catching. **8.** *Informal.* A tricky or unsuspected condition or drawback. **9.** A snatch or fragment. **10.** *Mus.* A canonical, often rhythmically intricate composition for three or more voices, popular esp. in the 17th and 18th centuries. **11.** *Sports.* **a.** The grabbing and holding of a thrown, kicked, or batted ball before it hits the ground. **b.** A game of throwing and catching a ball. **—*idioms.*** **catch it.** *Informal.* To receive some form of punishment or scolding. **catch (one's) breath.** To rest so as to be able to continue. [ME *cacchen* < AN *cachier,* to chase < Lat. *captare,* freq. of *capere,* to seize.]

catch·all (kăch′ôl′, kĕch′-) *n.* **1.** A receptacle for a variety of odds and ends. **2.** Something that covers a variety of situations.

catch-as-catch-can (kăch′əz-kăch-kăn′, kĕch′əz-kĕch-) *adj.* Seizing any opportunity or using any available means; not planned.

catch·er (kăch′ər, kĕch′-) *n.* **1.** One that catches. **2.** *Baseball.* The player whose position is behind home plate and who signals for and receives pitches.

catch·fly (kăch′flī′, kĕch′-) *n.* Any of several plants of the genus *Silene* and related genera, having white, pink, or red flowers with characteristically sticky stems and calyxes.

catch·ing (kăch′ĭng, kĕch′-) *adj.* **1.** Infectious. **2.** Attractive; alluring.

catch·ment (kăch′mənt, kĕch-) *n.* **1.** A catching or collecting of water. **2. a.** A structure, such as a basin, for collecting or draining water. **b.** The amount of water collected.

catch·pen·ny (kăch′pĕn′ē, kĕch-) *adj.* Designed and made to sell without concern for quality; cheap. *—n., pl.* **-nies.** A catchpenny item.

catch phrase *n.* An often repeated word or slogan.

catch·pole also **catch·poll** (kăch′pōl′, kĕch′-) *n.* A sheriff's officer, esp. one who arrests debtors. [ME *cacchepol* < Norman Fr. *cachepol,* prob. < OFr. *chacepol* : *chacier,* to hunt (< Lat. *captare,* freq. of *capere,* to seize.) + *poul,* rooster < Lat. *pullus,* chicken.]

Catch-22 (kăch′twĕn-tē-to͞o′, kĕch′-) *n.* A difficult situation or problem whose seemingly alternative solutions are logically invalid. [After *Catch-22,* a novel by Joseph Heller (b. 1923).]

catch·up (kăch′əp, kĕch′-) *n.* Variant of **ketchup.**

catch-up (kăch′ŭp′) *adj.* Designed or intended to catch up to a standard: *"catch-up increases in prices to restore profit margins"* (Newsweek).

catch·word (kăch′wûrd′, kĕch′-) *n.* **1.** A catch phrase. **2.** *Printing.* **a.** A word placed at the head of a column or page, as in a dictionary, to indicate the first or last entry on the page. **b.** The first word of a page printed at the bottom of the preceding page.

catch·y (kăch′ē, kĕch′ē) *adj.* **-i·er, -i·est. 1.** Attractive or alluring. **2.** Easily remembered. **3.** Tricky; deceptive. **4.** Fitful or spasmodic.

catamaran

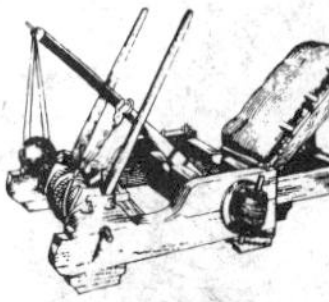
catapult
Roman catapult

catbird

catcher

cate (kāt) *n. Archaic.* A choice or dainty food; delicacy. [Short for *acate,* purchased food < ME < Norman Fr. *acat* < *acater,* to buy. —see CATER.]

cat·e·che·sis (kăt′ĭ-kē′sĭs) *n., pl.* **-ses** (-sēz′). Instruction of catechumens. [Gk. *katakhēsis* < *katekhein,* to teach by word of mouth. —see CATECHIZE.] **—cat′e·chet′i·cal** (-kĕt′ĭ-kəl) *adj.*

cat·e·chin (kăt′ĭ-kĭn′) *n.* A crystalline substance, $C_{15}H_{14}O_6$, derived from catechu and used in tanning and dyeing. [CATECH(U) + -IN.]

cat·e·chism (kăt′ĭ-kĭz′əm) *n.* **1.** A short book giving, in question-and-answer form, a brief summary of the basic principles of a religion. **2.** A book in question-and-answer form giving basic instruction in a subject. **3.** A question-and-answer examination, as of a political figure. [LLat. *catechismus* < LGk. *katēkhismos* < *katēkhizein,* to teach by word of mouth. —see CATECHIZE.]

cat·e·chist (kăt′ĭ-kĭst) *n.* A person who catechizes, esp. one who instructs catechumens in preparation for baptism. [LLat. *catechista* < LGk. *katēchistēs* < *katēkhizein,* to teach by word of mouth. —see CATECHIZE.] **—cat′e·chis′tic** (-kĭs′tĭk), **cat′e·chis′ti·cal** (-tĭ-kəl) *adj.*

catfish

cat·e·chize (kăt′ə-kīz′) *tr.v.* **-chized, -chiz·ing, -chiz·es. 1.** To teach esp. the principles of a religious creed by means of questions and answers. **2.** To question searchingly or persistently: *"Boswell was eternally catechizing him on all kinds of subjects"* (Macaulay). [ME *catecizen* < Med. Lat. *catechizare* < LGk. *katēkhizein* < Gk. *katēkhein,* to teach by word of mouth : *kata-,* according to + *ēkhein,* to sound < *ēkhē,* sound.] **—cat′e·chi·za′tion** *n.* **—cat′e·chiz′er** *n.*

cat·e·chol (kăt′ĭ-kôl′, -kōl′) *n.* **1.** Catechin. **2.** Pyrocatechol. [CATECH(U) + -OL.]

cat·e·cho·la·mine (kăt′ĭ-kō′lə-mēn′, -kô′-) *n.* Any of a group of amines, which include epinephrine, norepinephrine, and dopamine, that are derived from tyrosine and have a hormonal function.

cat·e·chu (kăt′ə-cho͞o′) *n.* Any of several water-soluble, resinous, astringent substances used in tanning and dyeing, as that obtained from a tree, *Acacia catechu,* of southern Asia, or from a woody vine, *Uncaria gambier,* of Malaya. [Prob. < Malay *kachu,* of Dravidian orig.]

cat·e·chu·men (kăt′ĭ-kyo͞o′mən) *n.* **1.** One who is being taught the principles of Christianity. **2.** One who is being instructed in any subject at an elementary level. [ME *cathecumine* < LLat. *catechumenus* < Gk. *katēkhoumenos,* pr. passive part. of *katēkhein,* to instruct. —see CATECHIZE.]

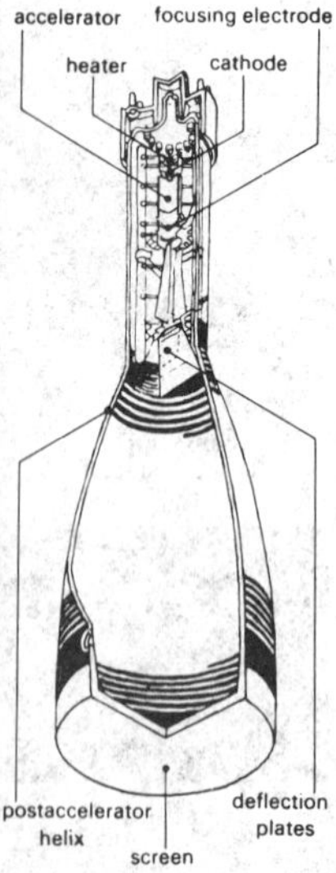

cathode-ray tube
Tube used in an oscilloscope

cat·e·gor·i·cal (kăt′ĭ-gôr′ĭ-kəl, -gŏr′-) or **cat·e·gor·ic** (-ĭk) *adj.* **1.** Without exception or qualification; absolute. **2.** Of, concerning, or included in a category. **—cat′e·gor′i·cal·ly** *adv.* **—cat′e·gor′i·cal·ness** *n.*

categorical imperative *n.* In Kant's ethical system, an absolute and universally binding moral law.

cat·e·go·rize (kăt′ĭ-gə-rīz′) *tr.v.* **-rized, -riz·ing, -riz·es.** To put into a category; classify. **—cat′e·go·ri·za′tion** *n.*

cat·e·go·ry (kăt′ĭ-gôr′ē, -gōr′ē) *n., pl.* **-ries. 1.** A specifically defined division in a system of classification; class. **2.** *Logic.* Any of the basic classifications into which all knowledge can be placed. [LLat. *categoria,* class of predicables < Gk. *katēgoria* < *katēgorein,* to predicate : *kata-,* against + *agora,* assembly.]

ca·te·na (kə-tē′nə) *n., pl.* **-nae** (-nē′) or **-nas.** A closely linked series. [Med. Lat., chain < Lat.]

cat·e·nar·y (kăt′n-ĕr′ē, kə-tē′nə-rē) *n., pl.* **-ies. 1.** The curve theoretically formed by a perfectly flexible, uniformly dense and thick, inextensible cable suspended from two points. **2.** Something having the shape of a catenary. *—adj.* Of or resembling a catenary. [< Lat. *catenarius,* of a chain < *catena,* chain.]

cat·e·nate (kăt′n-āt′) *tr.v.* **-nat·ed, -nat·ing, -nates.** To connect in a series of ties or links; form into a chain. [Lat. *catenare, catenat-* < *catena,* chain.] **—cat′e·na′tion** *n.*

ca·ten·u·late (kə-tĕn′yə-lĭt) *adj.* Consisting or formed of chainlike links. [< Lat. *catenula,* dim. of *catena,* chain.]

ca·ter (kā′tər) *v.* **-tered, -ter·ing, -ters.** *—intr.* **1.** To provide food or entertainment. **2.** To provide anything wished for or needed: *catered to his smallest desires. —tr.* To provide food service for: *catering a banquet.* [< obs. *cater,* a buyer of provisions < ME *catour,* short for *acatour* < Norman Fr. < *acater,* to buy < VLat.* *accaptare* : Lat. *ad-,* to + Lat. *captare,* to catch < *capere,* to take.] **—ca′ter·er** *n.*

cat·er·an (kăt′ər-ən) *n.* A former robber of the Scottish highlands. [ME *ketharan,* prob. < Sc. Gael. *ceathairneach.*]

cat·er·cor·nered (kăt′ər-kôr′nərd, kăt′ē-) also **cat·er·cor·ner** (-nər) or **cat·ty-cor·nered** (kăt′ē-kôr′nərd) *—adj.* Diagonal. *—adv.* Diagonally. [< obs. *cater,* four at dice < ME < OFr. *catre,* four < Lat. *quattuor.*]

cat·er·cous·in (kăt′ər-kŭz′ĭn) *n.* A very close friend. [Orig. unknown.]

cat·er·pil·lar (kăt′ər-pĭl′ər, kăt′ə-) *n.* **1.** The wormlike, often brightly colored, hairy, or spiny larva of a butterfly or moth. **2.** Any of various insect larvae similar to those of the caterpillar. [ME *catirpel,* prob. < OFr. *chatepelose* : *chate,* cat + *pelose,* hairy < Lat. *pilosus* < *pilus,* hair.]

cat·er·waul (kăt′ər-wôl′) *intr.v.* **-wauled, -waul·ing, -wauls. 1.** To cry or screech like a cat in heat. **2.** To make a discordant sound or shriek. **3.** To have a noisy argument. *—n.* A shrill, discordant cry. [ME *caterwawen.*]

cat·fish (kăt′fĭsh′) *n., pl.* **catfish** or **-fish·es.** Any of numerous scaleless, chiefly freshwater fishes of the order Siluriformes, characteristically having whiskerlike barbels extending from the upper jaw.

cat·gut (kăt′gŭt′) *n.* A tough, thin cord or thread made from the dried intestines of certain animals, used for stringing musical instruments and tennis rackets and for surgical ligatures.

ca·thar·sis (kə-thär′sĭs) *n., pl.* **-ses** (-sēz′). **1.** *Med.* Purgation, esp. for the digestive system. **2.** A purifying or figurative cleansing or release of the emotions or of tension, esp. through art. **3.** *Psychoanal.* **a.** A technique used to relieve tension and anxiety by bringing repressed material to consciousness. **b.** The result of this process; abreaction. [Gk. *katharsis* < *katharirein,* to purge < *katharos,* pure.]

ca·thar·tic (kə-thär′tĭk) *adj.* Inducing catharsis; purgative. *—n.* A cathartic agent, esp. a laxative. [LLat. *catharticus* < Gk. *kathartikos* < *kathairein,* to purge. —see CATHARSIS.]

cat·head (kăt′hĕd′) *n.* A beam projecting outward from the bow of a ship and used as a support to lift the anchor.

ca·the·dra (kə-thē′drə) *n., pl.* **-drae** (-drē). **1.** The official chair or throne of a bishop. **2.** The office or see of a bishop. **3.** The official chair of an office or position, as of a professor. [Lat., chair < Gk. *kathedra* : *kata-,* down + *hedra,* seat.]

ca·the·dral (kə-thē′drəl) *n.* **1.** The principal church of a bishop's see and one that contains his official throne. **2.** A large or important church. *—adj.* **1.** Of, pertaining to, or containing a bishop's official throne. **2.** Relating to or issuing from a chair of office or authority; authoritative. **3.** Of or pertaining to a cathedral. [Obs. *cathedral church* < ME *cathedral,* of a diocese < OFr. < Med.Lat. *cathedralis* < Lat. *cathedra,* chair. —see CATHEDRA.]

ca·thep·sin (kə-thĕp′sĭn) *n.* Any of various proteolytic enzymes that catalyze the hydrolysis of proteins into polypeptides. [G. *Kathepsin* < Gk. *kathepsein,* to digest : *kata-,* down + *hepsein,* to boil.]

cath·er·ine wheel (kăth′ər-ĭn, kăth′rĭn) *n.* Pinwheel (sense 2). [After St. *Catherine* of Alexandria (d. 307 A.D.).]

cath·e·ter (kăth′ĭ-tər) *n.* A slender, flexible tube inserted into a bodily channel, such as a vein, to distend or maintain an opening to an internal cavity. [LLat. < Gk. *kathetēr,* surgical instrument for emptying the bladder < *kathienai,* to drop : *kata-,* down + *hienai,* to send.]

cath·e·ter·ize (kăth′ĭ-tə-rīz′) *tr.v.* **-ized, -iz·ing, -iz·es.** To introduce a catheter into. **—cath′e·ter·i·za′tion** *n.*

ca·thex·is (kə-thĕk′sĭs) *n., pl.* **-thex·es** (-thĕk′sēz′). The concentration of emotional energy upon some object or idea. [Gk. *kathexis,* a holding < *katekhein,* to hold fast : *kata-,* down + *ekhein,* to hold.] **—ca·thec′tic** (-tĭk) *adj.*

cath·ode (kăth′ōd′) *n.* **1.** A negatively charged electrode, as of an electrolytic cell, storage battery, or electron tube. **2.** The positively charged terminal of a primary cell or of a storage battery that is supplying current. [Gk. *kathodos,* descent : *kata-,* down + *hodos,* way.] **—ca·thod′ic** (kă-thŏd′ĭk) *adj.* **—ca·thod′i·cal·ly** *adv.*

cathode ray *n.* **1.** A stream of electrons emitted by the cathode in electrical discharge tubes. **2.** One of the electrons that is emitted in a stream from a cathode-ray tube.

cath·ode-ray tube (kăth′ōd-rā′) *n.* A vacuum tube in which a hot cathode emits electrons that are accelerated as a beam through a relatively high voltage anode, further focused or deflected electrostatically or electromagnetically, and allowed to fall on a fluorescent screen.

cath·o·lic (kăth′ə-lĭk, kăth′lĭk) *adj.* **1.** Of broad or general scope; universal; all-inclusive **2.** Broad and comprehensive in interests, sympathies, or the like; liberal. **3. Catholic. a.** Of or pertaining to the universal Christian church. **b.** Of or pertaining to the ancient undivided Christian church. **c.** Of or designating those churches that have claimed to be representatives of the ancient undivided church. **d.** Of or concerning the Roman Catholic Church. *—n.* **Catholic.** A member of a Catholic church, esp. a Roman Catholic. [OFr. *catholique* < LLat. *catholicus* < Gk. *katholikos* < *katholou,* in general : *kata-,* according to + *holos,* whole.] **—ca·thol′i·cal·ly** (kə-thŏl′ĭ-kə-lē, -ĭk-lē) *adv.*

Catholic Church *n.* The Roman Catholic Church.

Ca·thol·i·cism (kə-thŏl′ĭ-sĭz′əm) *n.* The faith, doctrine, system, and practice of a Catholic church, esp. the Roman Catholic Church.

cath·o·lic·i·ty (kăth′ə-lĭs′ĭ-tē) *n.* **1.** The condition or quality of being catholic; broad-mindedness. **2.** General acceptance; universality. **3. Catholicity.** Roman Catholicism.

ca·thol·i·cize (kə-thŏl′ĭ-sīz′) *tr. & intr.v.* **-cized, -ciz·ing, -ciz·es. 1.** To make or become catholic. **2.** To convert or be converted to Catholicism.

ca·thol·i·con (kə-thŏl′ĭ-kŏn′) *n.* A universal remedy; panacea. [Fr. < Med. Lat. < Gk. *katholikon,* neuter of *katholikos,* universal. —see CATHOLIC.]

cat·house (kăt′hous′) *n. Slang.* A house of prostitution; brothel.

cat·i·on (kăt′ī′ən) *n.* An ion having a positive charge and, in electrolytes, characteristically moving toward a negative electrode. [Gk. *kation,* (a thing) going down : *kata-,* down + *ienai,* to go.] **—cat′i·on′ic** (kăt′ī-ŏn′ĭk) *adj.*

cation exchange *n.* A chemical process used in water softening in which cations of like charge are exchanged equally between a solid, as zeolite, and a solution, as water.

cat·kin (kăt'kĭn') *n. Bot.* A dense, often drooping flower cluster, such as that of a birch, consisting of small, scalelike flowers. [< obs. Du. *katteken,* dim. of *katte,* cat (from its resemblance to a cat's tail).]

cat·like (kăt'līk') *adj.* Like a cat; stealthy.

cat·nap (kăt'năp') *n.* A short nap; light sleep. **—cat'nap'** *v.* **(-napped, -nap·ping, -naps).**

cat·nip (kăt'nĭp') *n.* A hairy, aromatic plant, *Nepeta cataria,* native to Eurasia, to which cats are strongly attracted.

cat-o'-nine-tails (kăt'ə-nīn'tālz') *n.* A whip consisting of nine knotted cords fastened to a handle. [So called because it leaves marks like the scratches of a cat.]

ca·top·tric (kə-tŏp'trĭk) also **ca·top·tri·cal** (-trĭ-kəl) *adj.* Of or pertaining to mirrors and reflected images. [Gk. *katoptrikos* < *katoptron,* mirror.] **—ca·top'trics** *n.*

cat rig *n.* The rig of a catboat.

CAT scan *n.* A cross-sectional picture produced by a CAT scanner.

CAT scanner *n.* A device that produces cross-sectional x-rays of the body using computerized axial tomography. [C(OMPUTERIZED) A(XIAL) T(OMOGRAPHY).]

CAT scanning *n.* The act or process of using a CAT scanner.

cat's cradle *n.* A child's game in which an intricately looped string is transferred from the hands of one player to the next, resulting in a succession of different loop patterns.

cat scratch disease or **cat scratch fever** *n.* A disease in humans characterized by fever and lymphadenitis and thought to be transmitted by cats.

cat's-eye (kăts'ī') *n.* **1.** Any of various semiprecious gems displaying a band of reflected light that shifts position as the gem is turned. **2.** A colored reflector attached to the back of a vehicle to indicate its presence on the road at night. **3.** A marble marked with eyelike circles.

cat's-paw also **cats·paw** (kăts'pô') *n.* **1.** A person used by another as a dupe or tool. **2.** A light breeze that ruffles small areas of a water surface. **3.** *Naut.* A hitch in the bight of a rope, on which a tackle is hooked. [From a fable about a monkey that used a cat's paw to pull chestnuts out of a fire.]

cat·sup (kăt'səp, kăch'əp, kĕch'-) *n.* Variant of **ketchup.**

cat·tail (kăt'tāl') *n.* Any of several marsh plants of the genus *Typha,* esp. *T. latifolia,* having long, straplike leaves and a dense, cylindrical head of minute brown flowers.

cat·tle (kăt'l) *pl.n.* **1.** Various animals of the genus *Bos,* esp. those of the domesticated species *B. taurus,* raised in many breeds for meat and dairy products. **2.** Human beings, esp. when viewed as a mob. [ME *catel,* livestock, property < Norman Fr. < Med. Lat. *capitale,* property < Lat. *capitalis,* principal. —see CAPITAL.]

cat·tle·man (kăt'l-mən, -măn') *n.* A person who tends or raises cattle.

cattle prod *n.* An electrified prod designed for driving cattle.

cat·tle·ya (kăt'lē-ə) *n.* An orchid of the genus *Cattleya,* having showy rose-purple or white flowers. [NLat.*Cattleya,* genus name, after William *Cattley* (d. 1832).]

cat·ty[1] also **cat·tie** (kăt'ē) *n., pl.* **-ties.** An Asian unit of weight generally equivalent to 1 1/3 pounds avoirdupois. [Malay *kati.*]

cat·ty[2] (kăt'ē) *adj.* **-ti·er, -ti·est. 1.** Catlike; stealthy. **2.** Subtly cruel or malicious; spiteful: *a catty remark.* **—cat'ti·ly** *adv.* **—cat'ti·ness** *n.*

cat·ty-cor·nered (kăt'ē-kôr'nərd) *adj. & adv.* Variant of **cater-cornered.**

cat·walk (kăt'wôk') *n.* A narrow platform or pathway, as on the sides of a bridge.

Cau·ca·sian (kô-kā'zhən, -kăzh'ən) *n.* **1.** A native or inhabitant of the Caucasus. **2.** A member of the Caucasoid ethnic division. *—adj.* **1.** Of or pertaining to the Caucasus region, its people, or their culture. **2.** Caucasoid. [After the *Caucasus,* a mountain range in the Soviet Union.]

Cau·ca·soid (kô'kə-soid') *adj.* **1.** *Anthropol.* Of, pertaining to, or designating a major ethnic division of the human species having certain distinctive physical characteristics such as skin color varying from very light to brown and fine hair ranging from straight to wavy or curly. This division is considered to include groups of peoples indigenous to or inhabiting Europe, northern Africa, southwestern Asia, and the Indian subcontinent, and persons of this ancestry in other parts of the world. **2.** Of, pertaining to, or characteristic of Caucasoids. *—n.* A member of the Caucasoid ethnic division.

cau·cus (kô'kəs) *n., pl.* **-cus·es** or **-cus·ses. 1.** A closed meeting of the members of a political party to decide upon questions of policy and the selection of candidates for office. **2.** *Chiefly Brit.* A committee within a political party charged with determining policy. *—intr.v.* **-cused, -cus·ing, -cus·es** or **-cussed, -cus·sing, -cus·ses.** To assemble in or hold a caucus. [Poss. of Algonquian orig.]

cau·dad (kô'dăd') *adv. Anat.* Toward the tail or posterior part of the body. [Lat. *cauda,* tail + -AD.]

cau·dal (kôd'l) *adj.* **1.** *Anat.* Of, at, or near the tail or hind parts; posterior. **2.** *Zool.* Taillike. [NLat. *caudalis* < Lat. *cauda,* tail.] **—cau'dal·ly** *adv.*

caudal fin *n.* The tail fin of a fish.

cau·date (kô'dāt') also **cau·dat·ed** (-dā'tĭd) *adj.* Having a tail. [NLat. *caudatus* < Lat. *cauda,* tail.] **—cau·da'tion** *n.*

caudate nucleus *n.* A large ganglion in the lateral ventricle of the brain that functions in motor control.

cau·dex (kô'dĕks') *n., pl.* **-di·ces** (-dĭ-sēz') or **-dex·es. 1.** The thickened base of the stem of some perennial plants. **2.** A woody, trunklike stem, such as that of a tree fern. [Lat. *caudex, caudice,* tree trunk.]

cau·di·llo (kou-*th*ēl'yō, -*th*ē'yō) *n., pl.* **-llos.** In Spanish-speaking countries, a military leader who sets himself up as a dictator. [Sp., leader < LLat. *capitellum,* small head, dim. of Lat. *caput,* head.]

cau·dle (kôd'l) *n.* A warm beverage, consisting of wine or ale mixed with sugar, eggs, bread, and various spices, given to ailing persons. [ME *caudel* < Norman Fr. < *chaud,* warm < Lat. *calidus.*]

caught (kôt) *v.* Past tense and past participle of **catch.**

caul (kôl) *n.* **1.** A portion of the membrane that surrounds a fetus and that sometimes covers its head at birth. **2.** The large omentum covering the intestines. [ME *calle* < OE *cawl,* basket.]

caul·dron (kôl'drən) *n.* Variant of **caldron.**

cau·les·cent (kô-lĕs'ənt) *adj. Bot.* Having a stem showing above the ground. [Lat. *caulis,* stem + -ESCENT.]

cau·li·cle (kô'lĭ-kəl) *n. Bot.* A small stem. [Lat. *cauliculus,* dim. of *caulis,* stem.]

cau·li·flow·er (kô'lĭ-flou'ər, kŏl'ĭ-) *n.* **1.** A plant, *Brassica oleracea botrytis,* related to the cabbage and broccoli and having an enlarged, edible flower head. **2.** The compact, whitish flower head of the cauliflower. [Prob. < Ital. *cavolofiore : cavolo,* cabbage (< LLat. *caulus* < Lat. *caulis*) + *fiore,* flower < Lat. *flos.*]

cauliflower ear *n.* An ear deformed by repeated blows.

cau·line (kô'līn') *adj. Bot.* Of, having, or growing on a stem. [NLat. *caulinus* < Lat. *caulis,* stem.]

caulk also **calk** (kôk) *tr.v.* **caulked, caulk·ing, caulks** also **calked, calk·ing, calks. 1.** To make (a boat) watertight by packing seams with oakum or tar. **2.** To make (pipes, for example) watertight or airtight by filling in cracks. [OFr. *cauquer,* to press < Lat. *calcare,* to tread < *calx,* heel.] **—caulk'er** *n.*

caus·al (kô'zəl) *adj.* **1.** Pertaining to, involving, or constituting a cause: *the causal factor of the riot.* **2.** Indicating or expressing a cause. **3.** Originating from a cause. *—n.* A word or grammatical element expressing a cause or reason. **—caus'al·ly** *adv.*

cau·sal·i·ty (kô-zăl'ĭ-tē) *n., pl.* **-ties. 1.** The relationship between cause and effect. **2.** A causal agency, force, or quality.

cau·sa·tion (kô-zā'shən) *n.* **1.** The act or process of causing. **2.** A cause. **3.** Causality.

caus·a·tive (kô'zə-tĭv) *adj.* **1.** Functioning as an agent or cause. **2.** Designating a verb or verbal affix that expresses causation. **—caus'a·tive** *n.* **—caus'a·tive·ly** *adv.*

cause (kôz) *n.* **1. a.** Something that produces an effect, result, or consequence. **b.** The person, event, or condition responsible for an action or result. **2.** A basis for an action or decision; ground; reason. **3.** A goal or principle served with dedication and zeal. **4.** The interests of a person or group engaged in a struggle: *"The cause of America is in great measure the cause of all mankind"* (Thomas Paine). **5.** *Law.* **a.** A ground for legal action. **b.** A lawsuit. **6.** A subject under debate or discussion. *—tr.v.* **caused, caus·ing, caus·es.** To be the cause of; make happen; bring about; effect. [ME < OFr. < Lat. *causa,* reason.] **—caus'a·ble** *adj.* **—cause'less** *adj.* **—caus'er** *n.*

Synonyms: *cause, reason, occasion, antecedent.* These nouns denote things or prior conditions that bring about, or are associated with, certain effects. A *cause,* singly or as one of a series, must exist for an effect logically to occur; *Deficiency in vitamin C is the cause of scurvy. Reason* refers to what explains the occurrence or nature of an effect and suggests an effort of human thought: *There was no reason for the accident.* An *occasion* is the situation or time that permits existing causes to come in to play: *The occasion for the robbery was the absence of the regular night watchman. Antecedent* refers to that which has gone before. It implies a relationship, not necessarily causal, with the thing or effect in question.

cause cé·lè·bre (kōz' sā-lĕb'rə) *n., pl.* **causes cé·lè·bres** (kōz' sā-lĕb'rə). **1.** A celebrated legal case. **2.** An issue arousing heated public debate and partisanship. [Fr. : *cause,* case + *célèbre,* celebrated.]

cau·se·rie (kōz-rē') *n.* **1.** A chat. **2.** A short, conversational piece of writing. [Fr. < *causer,* to talk < Lat. *causari,* to discuss < *causa,* case.]

cause·way (kôz'wā') *n.* **1.** A raised roadway, as across water or marshland. **2.** A paved highway. [ME *caucewei* : *cauce,* raised road < Norman Fr. *caucie* < VLat. *calciata < Lat. *calx,* limestone. —see CALX.]

caus·tic (kô'stĭk) *adj.* **1.** Capable of burning, corroding, dissolving, or otherwise eating away by chemical action. **2.** Marked by sharp and bitter wit; cutting: *"Her new clothes were the subject of caustic comment"* (Willa Cather).

catwalk

cauliflower

C clef
Above: Soprano clef
Center: Alto clef
Below: Tenor clef

cedar
Genus *Juniperus*

3. Of or pertaining to light emitted from a point source and reflected or refracted from a curved surface. —*n.* A caustic material or substance. [Lat. *causticus* < Gk. *kaustikos* < *kaiein,* to burn.] —**caus'ti·cal·ly** *adv.* —**caus·tic'i·ty** (kô-stĭs'ĭ-tē) *n.*
caustic potash *n.* Potassium hydroxide.
caustic soda *n.* Sodium hydroxide.
cau·ter·ize (kô'tə-rīz') *tr.v.* **-ized, -iz·ing, -iz·es.** To burn or sear with a cautery. [OFr. *cauteriser* < LLat. *cauterizare,* to brand < Gk. *kautēriazein* < *kautērion,* branding iron. —see CAUTERY.] —**cau'ter·i·za'tion** *n.*
cau·ter·y (kô'tə-rē) *n., pl.* **-ies. 1.** A caustic agent or a very hot or very cold instrument used to destroy aberrant tissue. **2.** Cauterization. [Lat. *cauterium,* branding iron < Gk. *kautērion* < *kaiein,* to burn.]
cau·tion (kô'shən) *n.* **1.** Forethought to avoid danger or harm. **2.** A warning; admonishment. **3.** *Informal.* Someone or something that is striking or alarming. —*tr.v.* **-tioned, -tion·ing, -tions.** To warn against danger; put on guard. [ME *caucioun* < OFr. *caution* < Lat. *cautio* < *cavēre,* to take care.] —**cau'tion·ar'y** (-shə-nĕr'ē) *adj.*
cau·tious (kô'shəs) *adj.* Showing or practicing caution; careful. —**cau'tious·ly** *adv.* —**cau'tious·ness** *n.*
cav·al·cade (kăv'əl-kād', kăv'əl-kād') *n.* **1.** A ceremonial procession, esp. of horsemen or horse-drawn carriages. **2.** A colorful procession or display. [Fr. < OFr. < OItal. *cavalcata* < *cavalcare,* to ride on horseback < VLat. **caballicare* < Lat. *caballus,* horse.]
cav·a·lier (kăv'ə-lîr') *n.* **1.** An armed horseman; knight. **2.** A gallant or chivalrous gentleman. **3. Cavalier.** A supporter of Charles I of England in his struggles against Parliament; Royalist. —*adj.* **1.** Marked by or given to nonchalant disregard of what is important; disdainful; haughty. **2.** Carefree and gay; offhand. [OFr. < OItal. *cavaliere* < LLat. *caballarius,* horseman < Lat. *caballus,* horse.]
ca·val·la (kə-văl'ə) *n., pl.* **-las** or **cavalla. 1.** Any of various tropical marine food fishes of the family Carangidae. **2.** The king mackerel. [Sp. *caballa,* horse mackerel < LLat. *caballus,* horse.]
cav·al·ry (kăv'əl-rē) *n., pl.* **-ries.** Troops trained to fight on horseback or in armored vehicles. [OFr. *cavallerie* < OItal. *cavalleria* < *cavaliere,* cavalier.] —**cav'al·ry·man** *n.*
cave (kāv) *n.* A hollow beneath the earth's surface, often having an opening in the side of a hill or cliff. —*v.* **caved, cav·ing, caves.** —*tr.* To hollow out. —*intr. Informal.* **1.** To fall in; collapse, as from being undermined. **2.** To give up all opposition; yield: *caved in to our demands.* [ME < OFr. < Lat. *cava* < *cavus,* hollow.]
ca·ve·at (kā'vē-ăt', kăv'ē-, kä'vē-ät') *n.* **1.** *Law.* A formal notice filed by an interested party with a court or officer, requesting the postponement of a proceeding until he is heard. **2.** A warning or caution. —*v.* **-at·ed, -at·ing, -ats.** —*intr. Law.* To enter a caveat. —*tr. Slang.* To do or say (something) with an accompanying warning. [Lat., let him beware < *cavēre,* to beware.]
caveat emp·tor (ĕmp'tôr') *n.* The axiom that a person who buys something does so at his own peril. [Lat., let the buyer beware.]
cave·fish (kāv'fĭsh') *n., pl.* **cavefish** or **-fish·es.** Any of various freshwater fishes of the family Amblyopsidae, of subterranean waters, having rudimentary eyes.
cave-in (kāv'ĭn') *n.* **1.** An action of caving in. **2.** A place where the ground has caved in.
cave man *n.* **1.** A prehistoric man who lived in caves. **2.** *Informal.* One who is crude or brutal, esp. toward women. —**cave'-man'** *adj.*
cav·ern (kăv'ərn) *n.* A large cave. —*tr.v.* **-erned, -ern·ing, -erns. 1.** To enclose in or as if in a cavern. **2.** To hollow out. [ME *caverne* < OFr. < Lat. *caverna* < *cavus,* hollow.]
cav·er·nic·o·lous (kăv'ər-nĭk'ə-ləs) *adj.* Inhabiting caverns or caves.
cav·ern·ous (kăv'ər-nəs) *adj.* **1.** Filled with caverns. **2.** Like a cavern in depth or vastness. **3.** Filled with cavities; porous. —**cav'ern·ous·ly** *adv.*
ca·vet·to (kə-vĕt'ō) *n., pl.* **-vet·ti** (-vĕt'ē) or **-vet·tos.** A concave molding shaped like a circular quadrant. [Ital. < *cavo,* hollow < Lat. *cavus.*]
cav·i·ar also **cav·i·are** (kăv'ē-är', kä'vē-) *n.* The roe of a sturgeon or other large fish, salted, seasoned, and eaten as a relish or delicacy. [Prob. < OItal. *caviaro* < Turk. *havyār.*]
cav·il (kăv'əl) *v.* **-iled, -il·ing, -ils** also **-illed, -il·ling, -ils.** —*intr.* To find fault unnecessarily; raise trivial objections. —*tr.* To quibble about; detect petty flaws in. —*n.* A captious or trivial objection. [OFr. *caviller* < Lat. *cavillari,* to criticize < *cavilla,* a jeering.] —**cav'il·er** *n.*
cav·i·ta·tion (kăv'ĭ-tā'shən) *n.* **1.** The sudden formation and collapse of low-pressure bubbles in liquids by means of mechanical forces, as those resulting from rotation of a marine propeller. **2.** The formation of cavities in tissue or an organ, esp. as a result of disease. [< CAVITY.]
cav·i·ty (kăv'ĭ-tē) *n., pl.* **-ties. 1.** A hollow or hole. **2.** A hollow area within the body: *a sinus cavity.* **3.** A pitted area in a tooth caused by caries. [Fr. *cavité* < OFr. *cavete* < LLat. *cavitas* < Lat. *cavus,* hollow.]
ca·vort (kə-vôrt') *intr.v.* **-vort·ed, -vort·ing, -vorts. 1.** To bound or prance about in a sprightly manner; caper. **2.** To make merry; frolic. [Perh. var. of CURVET.]
ca·vy (kā'vē) *n., pl.* **-vies.** Any of various short-tailed or apparently tailless South American rodents of the family Caviidae, which includes the guinea pig and the capybara. [Prob. < Galibi *cabiai.*]
caw (kô) *n.* The hoarse, raucous sound characteristic of a crow or similar bird. —*intr.v.* **cawed, caw·ing, caws.** To utter a caw. [Imit.]
cay (kē, kā) *n.* A small, low islet composed largely of coral or sand. [Sp. *cayo,* prob. < OFr. *quai,* quay.]
cay·enne pepper (kī-ĕn', kā-) *n.* A condiment made from the very pungent fruit of a variety of the plant *Capsicum frutescens.* [Obs. *kian* < Tupi *kyinha.*]
cay·man (kā'mən, kā-măn', kī-măn') *n.* Variant of **caiman.**
Ca·yu·ga (kā-yōō'gə, kī-) *n., pl.* **Cayuga** or **-gas. 1.** A tribe of Indians formerly living around Cayuga and Seneca lakes in central New York. **2.** A member of the Cayuga. **3.** The Iroquoian language spoken by the Cayuga. —**Ca·yu'ga** *adj.*
Cay·use (kī-yōōs', kī'yōōs') *n., pl.* **Cayuse** or **-us·es. 1.** A tribe of Indians of Oregon. **2.** A member of the Cayuse. **3.** The Sahaptin language of the Cayuse. **4.** *Western U.S.* A horse, esp. an Indian pony. —**Cay·use'** *adj.*
Cb The symbol for the element columbium.
CB (sē-bē') *n., pl.* **CB's.** Citizens band.
CB·er (sē-bē'ər) *n.* One who uses a CB radio.
C clef *n.* A clef sign used to form any of three clefs, soprano, alto, or tenor, by locating the tone C (261.7 cycles per second) on, respectively, the lowest line of the staff, the middle line, or the fourth (next to the highest) line.
Cd The symbol for the element cadmium.
Ce The symbol for the element cerium.
cease (sēs) *v.* **ceased, ceas·ing, ceas·es.** —*tr.* To put an end to; discontinue: *The factory ceased production.* —*intr.* To come to an end; stop: *noise that at last ceased.* —*n.* Cessation: *experiencing pressure without cease.* [ME *cesen* < OFr. *cesser* < Lat. *cessare,* to stop, freq. of *cedere,* to yield.]
cease-fire (sēs'fīr') *n.* **1.** An order to cease firing. **2.** A suspension of active hostilities; truce.
cease·less (sēs'lĭs) *adj.* Without stop; endless. —**cease'less·ly** *adv.* —**cease'less·ness** *n.*
ce·cec·to·my (sē-sĕk'tə-mē) *n., pl.* **mies.** Surgical excision of the cecum. [CEC(UM) + -ECTOMY.]
ce·cro·pi·a moth (sĭ-krō'pē-ə) *n.* A large North American moth, *Hyalophora cecropia,* having wings with red, white, and black markings. [NLat. *cecropia,* specific name < Lat., fem of *Cecropius,* Athenian < Gk. *Kekropios* < *Kekrops,* Cecrops, a legendary Athenian king.]
ce·cum also **cae·cum** (sē'kəm) *n., pl.* **-ca** (-kə). **1.** A cavity with only one opening. **2.** *Anat.* The large blind pouch forming the beginning of the large intestine. [NLat. < Lat. (*intestinum*) *caecum,* blind (intestine) < *caecus,* blind.] —**ce'cal** (sē'kəl) *adj.*
ce·dar (sē'dər) *n.* **1. a.** Any of several coniferous evergreen trees of the genus *Cedrus,* native to the Old World, such as the cedar of Lebanon. **b.** Any of various similar evergreen trees, mostly of the genera *Thuja, Chamaecyparis,* and *Juniperus.* **2.** The durable, aromatic, often reddish wood of a cedar. [ME *cedre* < OFr. < Lat. *cedrus* < Gk. *kedros.*]
ce·dar·bird (sē'dər-bûrd') *n.* A cedar waxwing.
cedar of Lebanon *n.* A tall evergreen tree, *Cedrus libani,* of Asia Minor, having short dark needles and fragrant hard wood.
cedar waxwing *n.* A North American bird, *Bombycilla cedrorum,* having a crested head and predominantly brown plumage. [Prob. so called because it eats the berries of the red cedar.]
cede (sēd) *tr.v.* **ced·ed, ced·ing, cedes. 1.** To surrender possession of officially or formally. **2.** To yield; grant. [OFr. *ceder* < Lat. *cedere.*]
ce·di (sā'dē) *n., pl.* **cedi** or **-dis.** See table at **currency.**
ce·dil·la (sĭ-dĭl'ə) *n.* A mark (ç) placed beneath the letter *c,* as in the spelling of the French word *garçon,* to indicate that the letter is to be pronounced (s). [Obs. Sp., dim. of *ceda,* the letter *z* < LLat. *zeta,* zeta (so called because a small *z* was formerly used to make a hard *c* sibilant.]
cee (sē) *n.* The letter *c.*
cei·ba (sā'bə) *n.* Any of various large tropical trees of the genus *Ceiba,* which includes the silk-cotton tree, the source of the silky fiber kapok. [Sp., prob. < Arawakan.]
ceil (sēl) *tr.v.* **ceiled, ceil·ing, ceils. 1.** To make a ceiling for. **2.** To provide (a ship) with interior planking. [ME *celen* < OFr. *celer* < Lat. *caelare,* to carve < *caelum,* chisel. —see CAELUM.]
ceil·ing (sē'lĭng) *n.* **1. a.** The interior upper surface of a room. **b.** Material used to cover this surface. **2.** Something likened to a ceiling: *a ceiling of leaves over the arbor.* **3.** The planking applied to the interior framework of a ship. **4.** A maximum limit, esp. as prescribed by law: *wage and price ceilings.* **5.** Any of various vertical boundaries, esp. of atmospheric visibility, cloud cover altitude, or operable aircraft altitude. [ME *celing* < *celen,* to ceil.] —**ceil'inged** *adj.*
ceil·om·e·ter (sē-lŏm'ĭ-tər) *n.* A photoelectric instrument for ascertaining cloud heights. [CEIL(ING) + -METER.]
cel·a·don (sĕl'ə-dŏn') *n.* **1.** A pale to very pale green. **2.** A pale to very pale blue. [Fr., after *Céladon,* a character in

Astrée, a romance by Honoré d' d'Urfé (1568–1625).] **—cel′a·don′** *adj.*
cel·a·don·ite (sĕl′ə-dn-īt′) *n.* A soft mica having a green hue and a high iron content.
Ce·lae·no (sĭ-lē′nō) *n.* **1.** *Gk. Myth.* One of the Pleiades. **2.** One of the six stars in the Pleiades cluster visible to the naked eye. [Lat. < Gk. *Kelainō.*]
cel·an·dine (sĕl′ən-dīn′, -dēn′) *n.* **1.** A plant, *Chelidonium majus,* native to Eurasia, having deeply divided leaves, yellow flowers, and yellow-orange juice. **2.** The lesser celandine. [ME *celidoine* < OFr. < Med. Lat. *celidonia* < Lat. *chelidonia* < Gk. *khelidonion* < *khelidōn,* swallow (from the association by ancient writers of the plant with the habits of the swallow).]
-cele[1] *suff.* Tumor; hernia: *cystocele.*
-cele[2] *suff.* Variant of **-coel.**
cel·e·brant (sĕl′ə-brənt) *n.* **1.** The priest officiating at the celebration of the Eucharist. **2.** A participant in a celebration.
Usage: Strictly speaking, *celebrant* should be reserved for an official participant in a religious ceremony or rite: *celebrant of a mass.* In the general sense of "participant in a celebration" *(New Year's Eve celebrant)* it is acceptable to a bare majority of the Usage Panel. *Celebrator* is an undisputed alternative.
cel·e·brate (sĕl′ə-brāt′) *v.* **-brat·ed, -brat·ing, -brates.** *—tr.* **1.** To observe (a day or event) with ceremonies of respect, festivity, or rejoicing: *celebrated their anniversary.* **2.** To perform (a religious ceremony): *celebrate Mass.* **3.** To extol or praise publicly; honor: *a sonnet that celebrates love.* *—intr.* **1.** To observe an occasion with appropriate ceremony or festivity. **2.** To perform a religious ceremony. **3.** To engage in festivities: *went out and celebrated after the concert.* [Lat. *celebrare, celebrat-* < *celeber,* famous.] **—cel′e·bra′tion** *n.* **—cel′e·bra′tor** *n.*
cel·e·brat·ed (sĕl′ə-brā′tĭd) *adj.* Well and usually favorably known; famous.
ce·leb·ri·ty (sə-lĕb′rĭ-tē) *n., pl.* **-ties. 1.** A famous person. **2.** Renown; fame. [Lat. *celebritas,* fame < *celeber,* famous.]
ce·le·ri·ac (sə-lĭr′ē-ăk′, -lĕr′-) *n.* A variety of celery, *Apium graveolens rapaceum,* cultivated for its edible, turniplike root. [Alteration of CELERY.]
ce·ler·i·ty (sə-lĕr′ĭ-tē) *n.* Swiftness of action or motion; speed. [ME *celerite* < OFr. < Lat. *celeritas* < *celer,* swift.]
cel·er·y (sĕl′ə-rē) *n., pl.* **-ies.** A plant, *Apium graveolens dulce,* native to Eurasia and widely cultivated for its edible stalks. [Fr. *céleri* < dial. Ital. *seleri,* pl. of *selero,* alteration of Lat. *selinon,* parsley < Gk.]
celery cabbage *n.* Chinese cabbage.
ce·les·ta (sə-lĕs′tə) also **ce·leste** (sə-lĕst′) *n.* A musical instrument with a keyboard and metal plates struck by hammers that produce bell-like tones. [Fr. *célesta* < *céleste,* celestial < Lat. *caelestis.*]
ce·les·tial (sə-lĕs′chəl) *adj.* **1.** Of or pertaining to the sky or the heavens: *Planets are celestial bodies.* **2.** Of, from, or suggestive of heaven; spiritual; divine: *celestial beings.* **3.** Supreme in nature or kind; heavenly: *celestial happiness.* **4. Celestial.** Of or pertaining to the Chinese people or to the former Chinese Empire. *—n.* **1.** A heavenly being; a god or an angel. **2. Celestial.** A Chinese person. [ME < OFr. < Lat. *caelestis* < *caelum,* sky.] **—ce·les′tial·ly** *adv.*
celestial equator *n.* A great circle on the celestial sphere in the same plane as the earth's equator.
celestial globe *n.* A model of the celestial sphere showing the stars and other celestial bodies.
celestial horizon *n.* Horizon (sense 2.c.).
celestial mechanics *n. (used with a sing. verb).* The science of the motion of celestial bodies under the influence of gravitational forces.
celestial navigation *n.* Ship or aircraft navigation based on the positions of celestial bodies.
celestial pole *n.* Either of two diametrically opposite points at which the extensions of the earth's axis intersect the celestial sphere.
celestial sphere *n.* An imaginary sphere of infinite extent with the earth at its center on which the stars, planets, and other heavenly bodies appear to be located.
cel·es·tite (sĕl′ĭ-stīt′, sə-lĕs′-) *n.* An important white, red-brown, or light-blue strontium ore, essentially strontium sulfate, $SrSO_4$. [G. *Zölestin* < Lat. *caelestis,* celestial.]
ce·li·ac also **coe·li·ac** (sē′lē-ăk′) *adj.* Of or relating to the abdomen. *—n.* One who has celiac disease. [Lat. *coeliacus* < Gk. *koiliakos* < *koilia,* abdomen < *koilos,* hollow.]
celiac disease *n.* A chronic nutritional disturbance of infants and young children, caused by improper absorption of fats and resulting in malnutrition, distended abdomen, and diarrhea.
cel·i·ba·cy (sĕl′ə-bə-sē) *n.* **1.** The condition of being unmarried, esp. by reason of religious vows. **2.** Abstinence from sexual intercourse. [Lat. *caelibatus* < *caelebs,* unmarried.]
cel·i·bate (sĕl′ə-bĭt) *n.* **1.** One who remains unmarried, esp. by reason of religious vows. **2.** One who abstains from sexual intercourse. **—cel′i·bate** *adj.* [< Lat. *caelebs, caelib-,* unmarried.]
cell (sĕl) *n.* **1.** A narrow, confining room, as in a prison or convent. **2.** A small, one-room abode, such as a hut. **3.** A small religious house dependent on a larger one, as a priory within an abbey. **4.** The primary organizational unit of a movement, esp. of a political party of Leninist structure. **5.** *Biol.* The smallest structural unit of an organism that is capable of independent functioning, consisting of one or more nuclei, cytoplasm, various organelles, and inanimate matter, all surrounded by a semipermeable plasma membrane. **6.** *Biol.* A small, enclosed cavity or space, such as a compartment in a honeycomb or within a plant ovary or an area bordered by veins in an insect's wing. **7.** *Elect.* **a.** A single unit for electrolysis or for conversion of chemical into electric energy, usually consisting of a container with electrodes and an electrolyte. **b.** A single unit that converts radiant energy into electric energy: *a solar cell.* **8.** *Computer Sci.* A basic unit of storage in a computer memory that can hold one unit of information, as a character or word. *—v.* **celled, cell·ing, cells.** *—tr.* To store in a honeycomb. *—intr.* To live in a cell. [ME *celle,* partly < OE *cell,* and partly < OFr., both < Lat. *cella,* chamber.]
cel·la (sĕl′ə) *n., pl.* **cel·lae** (sĕl′ē′). The inner room of an ancient Greek or Roman temple. [Lat.]
cel·lar (sĕl′ər) *n.* **1.** A room used for storage, usually beneath the ground or under a building. **2. a.** A dark, cool room for storing wines. **b.** A stock of wines. **3.** *Informal.* The lowest level, esp. in the standing of an athletic team. *—tr.v.* **-lared, -lar·ing, -lars.** To store in a cellar. [ME *celer* < OFr. < LLat. *cellarium,* pantry < Lat. *cella,* storeroom.]
cel·lar·age (sĕl′ər-ĭj) *n.* **1.** A fee charged for storage in a cellar. **2.** A cellar or cellars collectively.
cel·lar·er (sĕl′ər-ər) *n.* A person, as in a monastic community, who is responsible for the maintenance of adequate supplies of food and drink. [ME *celerer* < OFr. < Lat. *cellarius,* steward < *cella,* storeroom.]
cel·lar·ette also **cel·lar·et** (sĕl′ə-rĕt′) *n.* A cabinet used for storing bottles of wine.
cell membrane *n.* Plasma membrane.
cel·lo (chĕl′ō) *n., pl.* **-los.** A four-stringed instrument of the violin family, pitched lower than the viola but higher than the double bass. [Short for VIOLONCELLO.] **—cel′list** (chĕl′ĭst) *n.*
cel·lo·bi·ose (sĕl′ə-bī′ōs′, -ōz′) *n.* A disaccharide that is produced from the partial hydrolysis of cellulose. [CELL(ULOSE) + BI- + -OSE.]
cel·loi·din (sə-loid′n) *n.* A pure pyroxylin in which specimen sections are embedded for microscopic examination. [CELL(ULOSE) + -OID + -IN.]
cel·lo·phane (sĕl′ə-fān′) *n.* A thin, flexible, transparent cellulose material made from wood pulp and used as a moistureproof wrapping. [Orig. a trademark.]
cel·lu·lar (sĕl′yə-lər) *adj.* **1.** Pertaining to or resembling a cell. **2.** Consisting of or containing a cell or cells. **—cel′lu·lar′i·ty** (-lăr′ĭ-tē) *n.* **—cel′lu·lar·ly** *adv.*
cel·lu·lase (sĕl′yə-lās′, -lāz′) *n.* Any of several enzymes, found in fungi, bacteria, and lower animals, that hydrolyze cellulose. [CELLUL(OSE) + -ASE.]
cel·lule (sĕl′yo͞ol) *n.* A small cell. [Fr. < Lat. *cellula,* dim. of *cella,* chamber.]
cel·lu·lite (sĕl′yə-līt′) *n.* A fatty deposit, as around the thighs and buttocks. [CELLUL(OSE) + -ITE.]
cel·lu·li·tis (sĕl′yə-lī′tĭs) *n.* Inflammation of subcutaneous tissue. [Lat. *cellula,* cell + -ITIS.]
cel·lu·loid (sĕl′yə-loid′) *n.* A colorless, flammable material made from nitrocellulose and camphor. [Orig. a trademark.]
cel·lu·lo·lyt·ic (sĕl′yə-lō-lĭt′ĭk) *adj.* Of, pertaining to, or causing the hydrolysis of cellulose. [CELLULO(SE) + -LYTIC.]
cel·lu·lose (sĕl′yə-lōs′, -lōz′) *n.* An amorphous carbohydrate polymer, $(C_6H_{10}O_5)_x$, the main constituent of all plant tissues and fibers, used in the manufacture of many fibrous products, including paper, textiles, and explosives. [Fr. < *cellule,* biological cell, cellule.] **—cel′lu·lo′sic** (-lō′sĭk, -zĭk) *adj.*
cellulose acetate *n.* A cellulose resin used in lacquers, photographic film, transparent sheeting, and cigarette filters.
cellulose nitrate *n.* Nitrocellulose.
cell wall *n.* The permeable, rigid outermost layer of a plant cell composed mainly of cellulose.
ce·lom (sē′ləm) *n.* Variant of **coelom.**
Cel·o·tex (sĕl′ə-tĕks′). A trademark for a building board made of compressed bagasse, used for insulation.
Cel·si·us (sĕl′sē-əs, -shəs) *adj.* Of or pertaining to a temperature scale that registers the freezing point of water as 0°C and the boiling point as 100°C under normal atmospheric pressure. [After Anders *Celsius* (1701-1744), its inventor.]
celt (sĕlt) *n.* A prehistoric axlike tool. [LLat. *celtis,* chisel.]
Celt (kĕlt, sĕlt) *n.* **1.** One of an ancient people of western and central Europe, including the Britons and the Gauls. **2.** A speaker or a descendant of a speaker of a Celtic language. [Fr. *Celte* < Lat. *Celta,* sing. of *Celtae.*]
Celt·ic (kĕl′tĭk, sĕl′-) *n.* A subfamily of the Indo-European language family comprising the Brythonic and the Goidelic branches. *—adj.* Of or pertaining to the Celtic people and languages.
Celtic cross *n.* An upright cross superimposed on a circle.
Celt·i·cism (kĕl′tĭ-sĭz′əm, sĕl′-) *n.* **1.** A Celtic custom. **2.** A fondness for Celtic customs. **3.** A Celtic idiom.

celery

cell

cello

Celtic cross

cenotaph

centaur
6th-century B.C. Greek vase

Centaurus

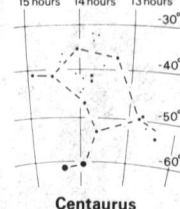

Celt·i·cist (kĕl′tĭ-sĭst, sĕl′-) *n.* A specialist in Celtic culture or Celtic languages.
cem·ba·lo (chĕm′bə-lō′) *n., pl.* **-los.** A harpsichord. [Ital., short for *clavicembalo* < Med. Lat. *clavicymbalum* : Lat. *clavis,* key + Lat. *cymbalum,* cymbal. —see CYMBAL.] **—cem′ba·list** *n.*
ce·ment (sĭ-mĕnt′) *n.* **1.** Any of various construction adhesives, consisting essentially of powdered, calcined rock and clay materials, that form a paste with water and can be molded or poured to set as a solid mass. **2.** A substance that hardens to act as an adhesive; glue. **3.** Something, such as a concern or feeling, that serves to unite: *Children were the cement that saved the marriage.* **4.** *Geol.* A chemically precipitated substance that binds particles of clastic rocks. **5.** Cementum. *—v.* **-ment·ed, -ment·ing, -ments.** *—tr.* **1.** To bind with or as if with cement. **2.** To cover or coat with cement. *—intr.* To become cemented. [ME *ciment* < OFr. < Lat. *caementum,* rough stone < *caedere,* to cut.] **—ce·ment′er** *n.*
ce·men·ta·tion (sē′mĕn-tā′shən) *n.* **1.** The act, process, or result of cementing. **2.** A metallurgical coating process in which iron or steel is immersed in a powder of another metal, such as zinc, chromium, or aluminum, and heated to a temperature below the melting point of either.
ce·ment·ite (sĭ-mĕn′tīt′) *n.* A hard, brittle iron carbide, Fe_3C, found in steel with more than 0.85 per cent carbon. [< CEMENT.]
ce·men·ti·tious (sē′mĕn-tĭsh′əs) *adj.* Of, relating to, or having the characteristics of cement.
cement mixer *n.* A concrete mixer.
ce·men·tum (sĭ-mĕn′təm) *n.* A bony substance covering the root of a tooth. [NLat. <Lat. *caementum,* rough stone < *caedere,* to cut.]
cem·e·ter·y (sĕm′ĭ-tĕr′ē) *n., pl.* **-ies.** A place for burying the dead; graveyard. [ME *cimiterie* < Med. Lat. *cimiterium* < LLat. *coemeterium* < Gk. *koimētērion* < *koiman,* to put to sleep.]
cen·a·cle (sĕn′ə-kəl) *n.* A small dining room, usually on an upper floor. [ME < OFr. < LLat. *cenaculum* < Lat. *cena,* dinner.]
-cene *suff.* Recent. Used in names of geological periods: *Oligocene.* [< Gk. *kainos,* new.]
ceno- *pref.* Variant of **coeno-**.
cen·o·bite also **coen·o·bite** (sĕn′ə-bīt′, sē′nə-) *n.* A member of a religious convent or community. [LLat. *coenobita* < *coenobium,* convent < Gk. *koinobion* < *koinobios,* living in community : *koinos,* common + *bios,* life.] **—cen′o·bit′ic** (-bĭt′ĭk), **cen′o·bit′i·cal** *adj.*
ce·no·gen·e·sis (sē′nō-jĕn′ĭ-sĭs, sĕn′ō-) also **coe·no·gen·e·sis** *n.* The environmentally determined development of characteristics or structures in an organism. [Gk. *kainos,* new + GENESIS.] **—ce′no·ge·net′ic** (-jə-nĕt′ĭk) *adj* **—ce′no·ge·net′i·cal·ly** *adv.*
ce·no·spe·cies (sē′nə-spē′shēz) *n.* A group of species capable of interbreeding.
cen·o·taph (sĕn′ə-tăf′) *n.* A monument erected in honor of a dead person whose remains lie elsewhere. [OFr. *cenotaphe* < Lat. *cenotaphium* < Gk. *kenotaphion* : *kenos,* empty + *taphos,* tomb.] **—cen′o·taph′ic** *adj.*
Ce·no·zo·ic (sē′nə-zō′ĭk, sĕn′ə-) *adj.* Of, belonging to, or designating the latest era of geologic time, which includes the Tertiary and Quaternary periods and is characterized by the evolution of mammals, birds, plants, modern continents, and glaciation. *—n.* The Cenozoic era. [Gk. *kainos,* new + -ZOIC.]
cense (sĕns) *tr.v.* **censed, cens·ing, cens·es. 1.** To perfume with incense. **2.** To offer incense to. [ME *censen,* short for *encensen* < *encens,* incense. —see INCENSE[2].]
cen·ser (sĕn′sər) *n.* An incense vessel. [ME, short for *encenser* < Norman Fr. *encensier* < *encens,* incense < OFr. —see INCENSE[2].]
cen·sor (sĕn′sər) *n.* **1.** A person authorized to examine literature, plays, or other material and who may remove or suppress what he considers morally or otherwise objectionable. **2.** An official, as in the military, who examines personal mail and official dispatches to remove information considered secret or improper. **3.** A person who condemns or censures. **4.** One of two officials in ancient Rome responsible for supervising the public census and public behavior and morals. **5.** *Psychoanal.* The agent responsible for censorship. *—tr.v.* **-sored, -sor·ing, -sors.** To examine and expurgate. [Lat., Roman censor < *censēre,* to assess.] **—cen·so′ri·al** (sĕn-sôr′ē-əl, -sōr′-) *adj.*
cen·so·ri·ous (sĕn-sôr′ē-əs, -sōr′-) *adj.* **1.** Tending to censure. **2.** Expressing censure. [Lat. *censorius,* of a censor < *censor,* Roman censor.] **—cen·so′ri·ous·ly** *adv.* **—cen·so′ri·ous·ness** *n.*
cen·sor·ship (sĕn′sər-shĭp′) *n.* **1.** The act, process, or policy of censoring. **2.** The office or authority of a Roman censor. **3.** *Psychoanal.* The inhibition by either ego or superego of conscious awareness of painful feelings or ideas.
cen·sur·a·ble (sĕn′shər-ə-bəl) *adj.* Deserving of or liable to censure. **—cen′sur·a·ble·ness, cen′sur·a·bil′i·ty** *n.* **—cen′sur·a·bly** *adv.*
cen·sure (sĕn′shər) *n.* **1.** An expression of blame or disapproval. **2.** An official rebuke. *—tr.v.* **-sured, -sur·ing, -sures.** To criticize severely; blame. [Lat. *censura,* severe judgment < *censor,* Roman censor.] **—cen′sur·er** *n.*
cen·sus (sĕn′səs) *n.* An official, usually periodic enumeration of population. [Lat., registration of citizens < *censēre,* to assess.]
cent (sĕnt) *n.* See table at **currency.** [OFr., hundred < Lat. *centum.*]
cen·tal (sĕn′təl) *n.* A hundredweight. [< Lat. *centum,* hundred.]
cen·taur (sĕn′tôr′) *n. Gk. Myth.* One of a race of monsters having the head, arms, and trunk of a man and the body and legs of a horse. [ME < Lat. *Centaurus* < Gk. *Kentauros.*]
Cen·tau·rus (sĕn-tôr′əs) *n.* A constellation in the Southern Hemisphere near Vela and Lupus. [Lat. *Centaurus,* centaur.]
cen·tau·ry (sĕn′tôr′ē) *n., pl.* **-ries. 1.** Any of several plants of the genus *Centaurium,* native to Eurasia, esp. *C. umbellatum,* having clusters of rose-purple flowers. **2.** A plant of the genus *Centaurea,* which includes the cornflower. [ME *centorie* < Lat. *centaureum* < Gk. *kentaureion* < *Kentauros,* centaur (from the legend that the plant's medicinal properties were discovered by a centaur).]
cen·ta·vo (sĕn-tä′vō) *n., pl.* **-vos.** See table at **currency.** [Sp. < Lat. *centum,* hundred.]
cen·te·nar·i·an (sĕn′tə-nâr′ē-ən) *n.* A person one hundred years old or older. [< Lat. *centenarius,* of a hundred. —see CENTENARY.] **—cen′te·nar′i·an** *adj.*
cen·ten·a·ry (sĕn-tĕn′ə-rē, sĕn′tə-nĕr′ē) *adj.* **1.** Of or pertaining to a 100-year period. **2.** Occurring once every 100 years. *—n., pl.* **-ries. 1.** A 100-year period. **2.** A centennial. [Lat. *centenarius,* of a hundred < *centum,* hundred.]
cen·ten·ni·al (sĕn-tĕn′ē-əl) *adj.* **1.** Of or pertaining to an age or period of 100 years. **2.** Occurring once every 100 years. **3.** Of or pertaining to a 100th anniversary. *—n.* A 100th anniversary or a celebration of this. [Lat. *centum,* hundred + (BI)ENNIAL.] **—cen·ten′ni·al·ly** *adv.*
cen·ter (sĕn′tər) *n.* **1.** A point equidistant or at the average distance from all points on the sides or outer boundaries of something; middle. **2. a.** A point equidistant from the vertexes of a regular polygon. **b.** A point equidistant from all points on the circumference of a circle or on the surface of a sphere. **3.** A point around which something revolves; axis. **4.** A part of an object that is surrounded by the rest; core. **5. a.** A place of concentrated activity or influence: *a financial center.* **b.** A place of dense population: *a metropolitan center.* **6.** A person or thing that is the chief object of attention, interest, activity, or emotion. **7.** A person, object, or group occupying a middle position. **8.** A political policy or group representing a compromise between the right and the left. **9.** In some team sports, a player who holds a middle position on the field, court, or forward line. *—v.* **-tered, -ter·ing, -ters.** *—tr.* **1.** To place in or on a center: *centered the vase on the table.* **2.** To concentrate at a center: *centering the discussion on the important issues.* **3.** *Football.* To pass (the ball) from the line to a back. *—intr.* **1.** To be concentrated; cluster. **2.** To have a central theme or concern; be focused. [ME *centre* < OFr. < Lat. *centrum* < Gk. *kentron.*]
Usage: *Center* as an intransitive verb may be used with *on, upon, in,* or *at.* Logically, it should not be used with *around,* since the word *center* refers to a point or focus. Thus: *The discussion centered on* (not *around*) *the meaning of the law* (a possible alternative, *revolved around*).
center bit *n.* A bit having a sharp center point, used in carpentry for boring holes.
cen·ter·board (sĕn′tər-bôrd′, -bōrd′) *n.* A flat board or metal plate that can be lowered through the bottom of a sailboat to prevent drifting and provide stability.
center field *n. Baseball.* **1.** The middle part of the outfield, behind second base. **2.** The position of center field. **—center fielder** *n.*
center of gravity *n.* The point in or near a body at which the gravitational potential energy of the body is equal to that of a single particle of the same mass located at that point and through which the resultant of the gravitational forces on the component particles of the body acts.
center of mass *n.* The point about which the sum of all the linear moments of mass of the particles in a body is zero.
cen·ter·piece (sĕn′tər-pēs′) *n.* A decorative object or arrangement placed at the center of a table.
center punch *n.* A tool with a sharp point used in metalworking to mark centers or center lines on pieces to be drilled.
cen·tes·i·mal (sĕn-tĕs′ə-məl) *adj.* **1.** Hundredth. **2.** Pertaining to or divided into hundredths. [< Lat. *centesimus* < *centum,* hundred.] **—cen·tes′i·mal·ly** *adv.*
cen·tes·i·mo[1] (sĕn-tĕs′ə-mō′) *n., pl.* **-mos** or **-mi** (-mē). See table at **currency.** [Ital. < Lat. *centesimus,* centesimal.]
cen·tes·i·mo[2] (sĕn-tĕs′ə-mō′) *n., pl.* **-mos.** See table at **currency.** [Sp. < Lat. *centesimus,* centesimal.]
cen·te·sis (sĕn-tē′sĭs), *pl.* **-ses** (-sēz′). The surgical puncture of a membrane or body cavity usually for diagnostic purposes. [Gk. *kentēsis,* act of pricking < *kentein,* to prick.]
centi- *pref.* One hundredth (10^{-2}): *centiliter.* [Fr. < Lat. *centum,* hundred.]
cen·ti·grade (sĕn′tĭ-grād′) *adj.* Celsius. [Fr. : Lat. *centum-,* hundred + Lat. *gradus,* degree.]

cen·ti·gram (sĕn′tĭ-grăm′) *n.* One hundredth (10^{-2}) of a gram.
cen·ti·li·ter (sĕn′tə-lē′tər) *n.* One hundredth (10^{-2}) of a liter.
cen·time (sän′tēm′, sĕn′) *n.* See table at **currency**. [Fr. < *cent,* hundred < Lat. *centum.*]
cen·ti·me·ter also **cen·ti·me·tre** (sĕn′tə-mē′tər, sän′-) *n.* A unit of length equal to 1/100 of a meter or 0.3937 inch.
cen·ti·me·ter-gram-sec·ond system (sĕn′tə-mē′tər-grăm′-sĕk′ənd) *n.* A coherent system of units for mechanics, electricity, and magnetism, in which the basic units of length, mass, and time are the centimeter, gram, and second.
cen·ti·mo (sĕn′tə-mō′) *n., pl.* **-mos.** See table at **currency**. [Sp. *céntimo* < Fr. *centime,* centime.
cen·ti·pede (sĕn′tə-pēd′) *n.* Any of various wormlike arthropods of the class Chilopoda, having numerous body segments, each with a pair of legs, the front pair modified into venomous biting organs. [Lat. *centipeda* : *centum,* hundred + *pes,* foot.]
cen·ti·poise (sĕn′tə-poiz′) *n.* One hundredth (10^{-2}) of a poise.
cent·ner (sĕnt′nər) *n.* **1.** A unit of weight corresponding to the hundredweight, equal to 110.23 pounds, used in several European countries. **2.** An assaying unit equal to one dram. [G. *Zentner* < Lat. *centenarius,* of a hundred. —see CENTENARY.]
cen·to (sĕn′tō) *n., pl.* **-tos.** A literary work pieced together from the works of several authors. [LLat. < Lat., patchwork.]
centr– *pref.* Variant of **centro-**.
cen·tral (sĕn′trəl) *adj.* **1.** At, in, near, or being the center. **2.** Having dominant or controlling power or influence: *the central office of the corporation.* **3.** Of great importance; essential: *the central theme of the novel.* **4.** Easily reached from various points: *a central location for the new store.* **5.** Of or constituting a single source controlling all components of a system: *central air conditioning.* **6.** *Anat. & Physiol.* **a.** Denoting that part of the nervous system constituted by the brain and spinal cord. **b.** Pertaining to a centrum. **7.** Pronounced with the tongue in a neutral position, as *e* in *mister.* —*n.* **1.** A telephone exchange. **2.** A telephone-exchange operator. [Lat. *centralis* < *centrum,* center.] —**cen′tral·ly** *adv.*
central angle *n.* An angle having radii as sides and the center of a circle as its vertex.
cen·tral·ism (sĕn′trə-lĭz′əm) *n.* The assignment of power and authority to a central leadership in an organization, as a political system. —**cen′tral·ist** *n.* —**cen′tral·is′tic** *adj.*
cen·tral·i·ty (sĕn-trăl′ĭ-tē) *n.* **1.** The state or quality of being central. **2.** The tendency to be or remain at the center.
cen·tral·ize (sĕn′trə-līz′) *v.* **-ized, -iz·ing, -iz·es.** —*tr.* **1.** To draw into or toward a center; consolidate. **2.** To bring under a single, central authority. —*intr.* To come together at a center; concentrate. —**cen′tral·i·za′tion** *n.* —**cen′tral·iz′er** *n.*
central nervous system *n.* The portion of the vertebrate nervous system consisting of the brain and spinal cord.
central processing unit *n.* The part of a computer that interprets and executes instructions.
Central Standard Time *n.* The local civil time of the 90th meridian west of Greenwich, England, six hours earlier than Greenwich time, observed in the central United States.
Central Time *n.* Central Standard Time.
cen·tre (sĕn′tər) *n. & v. Chiefly Brit.* Variant of **center**.
centri– *pref.* Variant of **centro-**.
cen·tric (sĕn′trĭk) also **cen·tri·cal** (-trĭ-kəl) *adj.* **1.** At, of, or having a center. **2.** *Physiol.* Of or originating at a nerve center. [Gk. *kentrikos* < *kentron,* center.] —**cen′tri·cal·ly** *adv.* —**cen·tric′i·ty** (sĕn-trĭs′ĭ-tē) *n.*
–centric *suff.* **1.** Having a specified kind or number of centers: *polycentric.* **2.** Having a specified object as the center: *geocentric.* [< Lat. *centrum,* center.]
cen·trif·u·gal (sĕn-trĭf′yə-gəl, -trĭf′ə-) *adj.* **1.** Moving or directed away from a center or axis. **2.** Operated by means of centrifugal force. **3.** *Physiol.* Pertaining to impulses transmitted away from a nerve center; efferent. **4.** *Bot.* Developing outward from a center or axis. **5.** Tending away from centralization: *centrifugal trends in urban society.* [< NLat. *centrifugus* : Lat. *centrum,* center + *fugere,* to flee.] —**cen·trif′u·gal·ly** *adv.*
centrifugal force *n.* The component of apparent force on a body in curvilinear motion, as observed from that body, that is directed away from the center of curvature or axis of rotation; the equilibrant of centripetal force.
cen·tri·fuge (sĕn′trə-fyo͞oj′) *n.* An apparatus consisting essentially of a compartment spun about a central axis to separate contained materials of different density or to simulate gravity with centrifugal force. —*tr.v.* **-fuged, -fug·ing, -fug·es.** To separate, dehydrate, or test by means of a centrifuge. [Fr. < NLat. *centrifugus,* centrifugal.] —**cen·trif′u·ga′tion** (sĕn-trĭf′yə-gā′shən, -trĭf′ə-) *n.*
cen·tri·ole (sĕn′trē-ōl′) *n.* A tiny cylindrical organelle, considered a pole of the mitotic figure and located at the center of a centrosome. [G. *Zentriol* < NLat. *centriolum,* dim. of Lat. *centrum,* center.]
cen·trip·e·tal (sĕn-trĭp′ĭ-tl) *adj.* **1.** Directed or moving toward a center or axis. **2.** Operated by centripetal force. **3.** *Physiol.* Pertaining to nerve impulses transmitted toward the central nervous system; afferent. **4.** *Bot.* Developing inward toward the center or axis, as some forms of inflorescence do. **5.** Tending to centralize: *the centripetal effects of a homogeneous population.* [Lat. *centrum,* center + -PETAL.] —**cen·trip′e·tal·ly** *adv.*
centripetal force *n.* The component of force acting on a body in curvilinear motion that is directed toward the center of curvature or axis of rotation.
cen·trism (sĕn′trĭz′əm) *n.* A political philosophy of avoiding extremes by taking a position in the center. —**cen′trist** *n.*
centro– or **centr–** or **centri–** *pref.* Center: *centroid.* [< Gk. *kentron,* center.]
cen·tro·bar·ic (sĕn′trə-băr′ĭk) *adj.* Of or relating to the center of gravity. [Gk. *kentrobarikē,* theory of the center of gravity : *kentron,* center + *baros,* weight.]
cen·troid (sĕn′troid′) *n.* **1.** The center of mass of an object having constant density. **2.** The point in a system of masses each of whose coordinates is a weighted mean of coordinates of the same dimension of points within the system, the weights being determined by the density function of the system.
cen·tro·lec·i·thal (sĕn′trə-lĕs′ə-thəl) *adj.* Having the yolk concentrated in the center of the egg cell. [CENTRO- + LECITH(IN) + -AL.]
cen·tro·mere (sĕn′trə-mîr′) *n.* The region of a chromosome to which the spindle fiber is attached during mitosis.
cen·tro·some (sĕn′trə-sōm′) *n.* A small mass of differentiated cytoplasm containing the centriole. —**cen′tro·so′mic** (-sō′mĭk) *adj.*
cen·tro·sphere (sĕn′trə-sfîr′) *n.* **1.** The mass of cytoplasm surrounding the centriole in a centrosome. **2.** The central core of the earth.
cen·trum (sĕn′trəm) *n., pl.* **-trums** or **-tra** (-trə). The major part of a vertebra, exclusive of the bases of the neural arch. [Lat., center.]
cen·tum (kĕn′təm) *adj.* Of, pertaining to, or comprising the group of Indo-European languages that retained the velar *k* and the labiovelar *kw* of primitive Indo-European. [Lat., hundred (a word whose initial sound illustrates the preservation of Indo-European velar *k.*]
cen·tu·ri·on (sĕn-to͝or′ē-ən, -tyo͝or′-) *n.* An officer commanding a century in the Roman army. [ME *centurioun* < OFr. *centurion* < Lat. *centurio* < *centuria,* century.] —**cen·tu′ri·al** *adj.*
cen·tu·ry (sĕn′chə-rē) *n., pl.* **-ries.** **1.** **a.** A period of 100 years. **b.** Each of the successive periods of 100 years before or since the advent of the Christian era. **2.** **a.** A unit of the Roman army originally consisting of 100 men. **b.** One of the 193 electoral divisions of the Roman people. **3.** A group of 100 things. [Lat. *centuria,* a group of a hundred < *centum,* hundred.]
century plant *n.* Any of several fleshy plants of the genus *Agave,* some species of which bloom only once in 10 to 20 years and then die, esp. *A. americana,* having large grayish leaves and greenish flowers.
ce·orl (chā′ôrl) *n.* A freeman of the lowest class in Anglo-Saxon England. [OE.]
cephal– *pref.* Variant of **cephalo-**.
ceph·a·lad (sĕf′ə-lăd′) *adv.* Toward the head or anterior section.
ceph·al·al·gia (sĕf′ə-lăl′jə, -jē-ə) *n.* Pain concentrated in the head region.
ce·phal·ic (sə-făl′ĭk) *adj.* **1.** Of or relating to the head or skull. **2.** Located on, in, or near the head. [OFr. *cephalique* < Lat. *cephalicus* < Gk. *kephalikos* < *kephalē,* head.] —**ce·phal′i·cal·ly** *adv.*
–cephalic *suff.* -cephalous. [-CEPHAL(OUS) + -IC.]
cephalic index *n.* The ratio of the maximum width of the head to its maximum length, multiplied by 100.
ceph·a·lin (sĕf′ə-lĭn) *n.* A phosphatide derived from the brain and spinal cord, usually of cattle, and used as a hemostatic agent.
ceph·a·li·za·tion (sĕf′ə-lĭ-zā′shən) *n.* The gradually increasing concentration of the brain and sensory organs in the head during animal evolution.
cephalo– or **cephal–** *pref.* Head: *cephalothorax.* [Lat. < Gk. *kephalo-* < *kephalē,* head.]
ceph·a·lo·chor·date (sĕf′ə-lə-kôr′dāt′) *adj.* Of or belonging to the subphylum Cephalochordata, which includes primitive forerunners of the vertebrates such as the lancelet. —*n.* A member of the Cephalochordata. [NLat. *Cephalochordata,* subphylum name : CEPHALO- + *Chordata,* chordate phylum name.]
ceph·a·lo·pod (sĕf′ə-lə-pŏd′) *n.* Any of various mollusks of the class Cephalopoda, such as an octopus or nautilus, having a beaked head, an internal shell in some species, and prehensile tentacles. —*adj.* Of, pertaining to, or belonging to the Cephalopoda. [NLat. *Cephalapoda,* class name : CEPHALO- + Gk. *pous,* foot.] —**ceph′a·lop′o·dan** (sĕf′ə-lŏp′ə-dən) *n. & adj.*
ceph·a·lo·spo·rin (sĕf-ə-lə-spôr′ĭn, -spōr′-) *n.* Any of various antibiotics produced by an imperfect fungus of the genus *Cephalosporium.* [< NLat. *Cephalosporium,* genus name : CEPHALO- + *spora,* spore.]
ceph·a·lo·tho·rax (sĕf′ə-lə-thôr′ăks′, -thōr′-) *n.* The anterior section of arachnids and many crustaceans, consisting of the fused head and thorax.

centipede

century plant

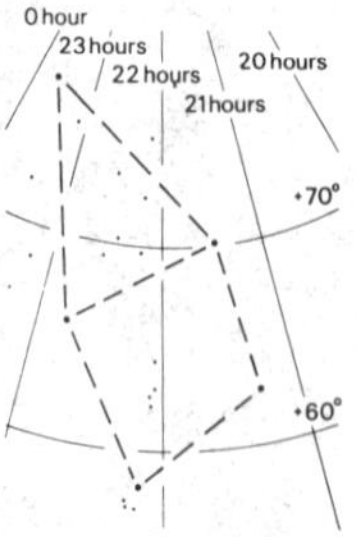

Cepheus

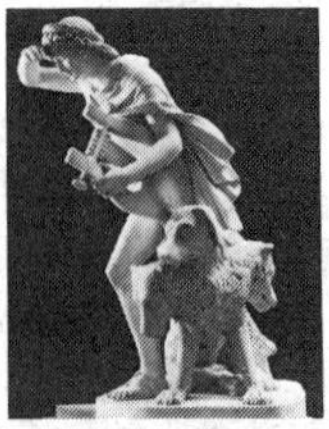
Cerberus
19th-century American sculpture of Orpheus and Cerberus

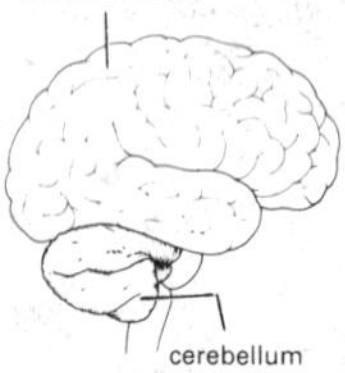

cerebellum

Ceres
16th-century woodcut

-cephalous *suff.* Having a specified kind of head or number of heads: *dicephalous.* [Gk. *-kephalos* < *kephalē,* head.]
-cephaly *suff.* A specified condition of the head: *microcephaly.* [< Gk. *kephalē,* head.]
Ce·phe·id (sē'fē-ĭd, sĕf'ē-) *n.* Any of a class of intrinsically variable stars with exceptionally regular periods of light pulsation. [< CEPHEUS.]
Ce·pheus (sē'fyo͞os', -fē-əs, sĕf'ē-) *n.* A constellation in the Northern Hemisphere near Cassiopeia and Draco. [Lat. *Cepheus* < Gk. *Kēpheus.*]
ce·ra·ceous (sə-rā'shəs) *adj.* Waxy or waxlike. [Lat. *cera,* wax + -ACEOUS.]
ce·ram·al (sə-răm'əl) *n.* Cermet. [CERAM(IC) + AL(LOY).]
ce·ram·ic (sə-răm'ĭk) *n.* **1.** Any of various hard, brittle, heat-resistant and corrosion-resistant materials made by shaping and then firing a nonmetallic mineral, such as clay, at a high temperature. **2. a.** An object made of ceramic. **b. ceramics** *(used with a sing. verb).* The art or technique of making objects of ceramic, esp. from fired clay or porcelain. [< Gk. *keramikos,* of pottery < *keramos,* potter's clay.] **—ce·ram'ic** *adj.* **—ce·ram'ist** *n.*
ce·ras·tes (sə-răs'tēz) *n., pl.* **cerastes.** Any of several venomous snakes of the genus *Cerastes,* such as the horned viper. [ME < Lat. < Gk. *kerastēs,* horned serpent < *keras,* horn.]
ce·rate (sîr'āt') *n.* A hard, unctuous, fat- or wax-based solid, sometimes medicated, formerly applied to the skin directly or on dressings. [Lat. *ceratum* < *cera,* wax.]
ce·rat·ed (sîr'ā'tĭd) *adj.* **1.** Coated with wax; waxed. **2.** Possessing a cere. [< Lat. *ceratus,* p. part. of *cerare,* to wax < *cera,* wax.]
cerato– or **cerat–** *pref.* Variants of **kerato-.**
ce·rat·o·dus (sə-răt'ə-dəs) *n., pl.* **-dus·es.** Any of various extinct lungfishes of the genus *Ceratodus,* of the Triassic and Cretaceous periods. [NLat. *Ceratodus,* genus name : Gk. *keras,* horn + Gk. *odous,* tooth.]
cer·a·toid (sĕr'ə-toid') *adj.* Hornlike.
Cer·ber·us (sûr'bər-əs) *n. Gk. & Rom. Myth.* A three-headed dog guarding the entrance of Hades. [Lat. < Gk. *Kerberos.*] **—Cer'ber·e'an** (sûr'bə-rē'ən) *adj.*
cer·car·i·a (sər-kâr'ē-ə) *n., pl.* **-i·ae** (-ē-ē') or **-i·as.** The parasitic larva of a trematode worm, having a tail that disappears in the adult stage. [NLat. < Gk. *kerkos,* tail.] **—cer·car'i·al** *adj.*
cer·co·pi·the·coid (sûr'kə-pĭ-thē'koid', -pĭth'ĭ-koid') *adj.* Of or belonging to the family Cercopithecidae, which includes monkeys such as the baboons, mandrills, macaques, and langurs. *—n.* A member of the Cercopithecidae. [< NLat. *Ceropithecidae,* family name < Lat. *cercopithecus,* long-tailed ape < Gk. *kerkopithēkos* : *kerkos,* tail + *pithēkos,* ape.]
cere¹ (sîr) *tr.v.* **cered, cer·ing, ceres.** To wrap in or as if in cerecloth. [ME *seren* < OFr. *cirer,* to cover with wax < Lat. *cerare* < *cera,* wax.]
cere² (sîr) *n.* A fleshy or waxlike swelling at the base of the upper part of the beak in certain birds, such as parrots. [ME *sere* < OFr. *cire* < Med. Lat. *cera* < Lat., wax.] **—cered** *adj.*
ce·re·al (sîr'ē-əl) *n.* **1.** An edible grain, such as wheat, oats, or corn. **2.** A grass producing grain. **3.** A food prepared from grain. *—adj.* Of or pertaining to cereals. [Lat. *cerealis,* of grain < *Ceres,* Ceres.]
cer·e·bel·lum (sĕr'ə-bĕl'əm) *n., pl.* **-bel·lums** or **-bel·la** (-bĕl'ə). The structure of the brain responsible for regulation and coordination of complex voluntary muscular movement, lying posterior to the pons and medulla oblongata and inferior to the occipital lobes of the cerebral hemispheres. [Med. Lat. < Lat., dim. of *cerebrum,* brain.] **—cer'e·bel'lar** (-bĕl'ər) *adj.*
cerebr– *pref.* Variant of **cerebro-.**
cer·e·bral (sə-rē'brəl, sĕr'ə-brəl) *adj.* **1.** Of or pertaining to the brain or cerebrum. **2.** Appealing to or marked by the workings of the intellect; intellectually refined. **—cer·e'bral·ly** *adv.*
cerebral cortex *n.* The extensive outer layer of gray tissue of the cerebral hemispheres, largely responsible for higher nervous functions.
cerebral hemisphere *n.* Either hemisphere of the cerebrum of the brain, divided by the longitudinal cerebral fissure.
cerebral palsy *n.* Impaired muscular power and coordination from brain damage usually occurring at or before birth. **—cer'e·bral-pal'sied** *adj.*
cer·e·brate (sĕr'ə-brāt') *intr.v.* **-brat·ed, -brat·ing, -brates.** To use the power of reason; think. [< Lat. *cerebrum,* brain.] **—cer'e·bra'tion** *n.*
cerebro– or **cerebr–** *pref.* Brain; cerebrum: *cerebroside.* [< CEREBRUM.]
cer·e·bro·side (sĕr'ə-brə-sīd', sə-rē'-) *n.* Any of various compounds found in the brain and other nerve tissue, yielding on decomposition a fatty acid, an unsaturated amino-alcohol, and a sugar. [CEREBR(O)- + -OS(E) + -IDE.]
cer·e·bro·spi·nal (sĕr'ə-brō-spī'nəl, sə-rē'brō-) *adj.* Of or pertaining to the brain and spinal cord.
cerebrospinal fluid *n.* The serumlike fluid that bathes the lateral ventricles of the brain and the cavity of the spinal cord.
cerebrospinal meningitis *n.* An acute infectious epidemic meningitis that is often fatal.
cer·e·bro·vas·cu·lar (sĕr'ə-brō-văs'kyə-lər, sə-rē'brō-) *adj.* Of or pertaining to the blood vessels supplying the brain.
cer·e·brum (sĕr'ə-brəm, sə-rē'brəm) *n., pl.* **-brums** or **-bra** (-brə). The large rounded structure of the brain occupying most of the cranial cavity, divided into two cerebral hemispheres by a deep median sagittal groove and joined at the bottom by the corpus callosum. [Lat., brain.]
cere·cloth (sîr'klôth', -klŏth') *n.* Cloth coated with wax, formerly used for wrapping the dead.
cere·ment (sĕr'ə-mənt, sîr'mənt) *n.* Cerecloth.
cer·e·mo·ni·al (sĕr'ə-mō'nē-əl) *adj.* Of, characterized by, or involved in ceremony. *—n.* **1.** A set of ceremonies prescribed for an occasion; rite. **2.** A ceremony. **—cer'e·mo'ni·al·ism** *n.* **—cer'e·mo'ni·al·ist** *n.* **—cer'e·mo'ni·al·ly** *adv.*
Usage: *Ceremonial* (adjective) is applicable chiefly to things; *ceremonious,* to persons and things. *Ceremonial* means simply "having to do with ceremony": *ceremonial occasions; ceremonial garb. Ceremonious,* when applied to a person, means "devoted to forms and ritual" or "standing on ceremony": *ceremonious courtiers.*
cer·e·mo·ni·ous (sĕr'ə-mō'nē-əs) *adj.* **1.** Of or pertaining to a ceremony. **2.** Fond of ceremony; elaborately polite. **3.** Characterized by ceremony; rigidly formal. —See Usage note at **ceremonial. —cer'e·mo'ni·ous·ly** *adv.* **—cer'e·mo'ni·ous·ness** *n.*
cer·e·mo·ny (sĕr'ə-mō'nē) *n., pl.* **-nies. 1.** A formal act or set of acts performed as prescribed by ritual, custom, or etiquette: *a wedding ceremony.* **2.** A conventional social gesture or act without intrinsic purpose: *ignored the ceremony of asking for comments.* **3.** Strict observance of formalities or etiquette: *was welcomed with ceremony.* [ME *cerimonie* < Lat. *caerimonia,* religious rite.]
Če·ren·kov effect (chə-rĕng'kôf) *n.* The emission of light by a particle passing through a transparent nonconducting solid at a speed greater than the speed of light in that solid. [After P. A. *Čerenkov* (1904–1958), its discoverer.]
Čerenkov radiation *n.* Light emitted in the Čerenkov effect.
Ce·res (sîr'ēz) *n.* **1.** *Rom. Myth.* The goddess of agriculture. **2.** The first asteroid to be discovered, having an orbit between Mars and Saturn. [Lat.]
ce·re·us (sîr'ē-əs) *n.* Any of several tall tropical American cacti esp. of the genus *Cereus,* such as the night-blooming cereus. [NLat. *Cereus,* genus name < Lat. *cereus,* taper (from the cacti's shape) < *cera,* wax.]
ce·ric (sîr'ĭk, sĕr'-) *adj.* Of, pertaining to, or containing cerium, esp. with valence 4. [CER(IUM) + -IC.]
ce·ric oxide (sîr'ĭk, sĕr'-) *n.* A pale yellow-white powder, CeO_2, used in ceramics, to polish glass, and to sensitize photosensitive glass.
cer·iph (sĕr'ĭf) *n. Chiefly Brit.* Variant of **serif.**
ce·rise (sə-rēs', -rēz') *n.* A deep to vivid purplish red. [Fr. < OFr., cherry. —see CHERRY.] **—ce·rise'** *adj.*
ce·ri·um (sîr'ē-əm) *n. Symbol* **Ce** A lustrous, iron-gray, malleable metallic rare-earth element that occurs chiefly in the minerals monazite and bastnaesite, exists in four allotropic states, is a constituent of lighter flint alloys, and is used in various metallurgical and nuclear applications. Atomic number 58; atomic weight 140.12; melting point 795°C; boiling point 3,468°C; specific gravity 6.67 to 8.23; valences 3, 4. [After CERES.]
cer·met (sûr'mĕt') *n.* A material consisting of processed ceramic particles bonded with metal and used in high-strength and high-temperature applications. [CER(AMIC) + MET(AL).]
cer·nu·ous (sûr'nyo͞o-əs) *adj. Bot.* Hanging downward; drooping. [Lat. *cernuus,* bowing forward.]
ce·ro (sîr'ō, sĕr'ō) *n., pl.* **-ros** or **cero. 1.** An edible fish, *Scomberomorus regalis,* of western Atlantic waters, having silvery sides and a dark-blue back. **2.** The king mackerel. [< Sp. *sierra,* sawfish. —see SIERRA.]
ce·ro·tic acid (sə-rō'tĭk, -rŏt'ĭk) *n.* An acid, $C_{25}H_{51}COOH$, occurring in waxes, such as beeswax. [< Lat. *ceratum,* cerate.]
ce·ro·type (sîr'ə-tīp', sĕr'ə-) *n.* The process of preparing a printing surface for electrotyping by first engraving on a wax-coated metal plate. [Gk. *kēros,* wax + -TYPE.]
ce·rous (sîr'əs) *adj.* Of, pertaining to, or containing cerium, esp. with valence 3. [CER(IUM) + -OUS.]
cer·tain (sûr'tn) *adj.* **1.** Definite; fixed: *set aside a certain sum each week.* **2.** Sure to come or happen; inevitable: *certain success.* **3.** Established beyond doubt or question; indisputable: *What is certain is that every effect must have a cause.* **4.** Unfailing; dependable: *a certain cure.* **5.** Confident; assured; positive. **6. a.** Not specified or identified but assumed to be known: *a certain woman.* **b.** Named but not familiar or well-known: *a certain Mr. Smith.* **7.** Appreciable but unspecified: *a certain degree; a certain charm.* *—pron.* An indefinite but limited number; some. **—idiom. for certain.** Surely; without doubt. [ME < OFr. < VLat. **certanus* < Lat. *certus,* p. part. of *cernere,* to determine.] **—cer'tain·ly** *adv.*
Usage: Although *certain* appears to be an absolute term, it is frequently qualified by adverbs, as in *fairly certain.* A great majority of the Usage Panel accepts this sentence: *Nothing is more certain than an extremist's hatred of compromise.*

cer·tain·ty (sûr′tn-tē) *n., pl.* **-ties. 1.** The fact, quality, or state of being certain. **2.** A clearly established fact.

Synonyms: *certainty, certitude, assurance, conviction.* These nouns mean freedom from any doubt. *Certainty,* the strongest, means a sure thing, belief in which is based on thorough examination of all evidence. *Certitude* implies a firm belief based more often on faith than on objective reasoning. *Assurance* relates closely to *certitude* and stresses as its foundation self-confidence, again resulting more from subjective experience than from objective examination. *Conviction* generally implies that a prior doubt existed and now has been removed because one has been convinced or assured of the truth.

cer·tes (sûr′tēz, sûrts) *adv. Archaic.* Certainly; truly. [ME < OFr. < *cert* < Lat. *certus,* certain.]

cer·tif·i·cate (sər-tĭf′ĭ-kĭt) *n.* **1.** A document testifying to the factuality or truth of something: *a birth certificate.* **2.** A document issued to a person completing a course of study not leading to a diploma. **3.** A document certifying that a person may officially practice in certain professions. **4.** A document certifying ownership. *—tr.v.* (-kāt′) **-cat·ed, -cat·ing, -cates.** To furnish with, testify to, or authorize by a certificate. [ME *certificat* < Med. Lat. *certificatum* < LLat. *certificare,* to certify.] **—cer·tif′i·ca·to′ry** (-kə-tôr′ē, -tōr′ē) *adj.*

certificate of deposit *n.* A certificate from a bank stating that the named person has a specified sum on deposit.

cer·ti·fi·ca·tion (sûr′tə-fĭ-kā′shən) *n.* **1.** The act of certifying. **2.** The state of being certified. **3.** A certified statement.

certified check *n.* A check guaranteed by a bank to be covered by sufficient funds on deposit.

certified mail *n.* Uninsured first-class mail whose delivery is recorded by having the addressee sign for it.

certified public accountant *n.* A public accountant who has received a certificate stating that he has met a state's legal requirements.

cer·ti·fy (sûr′tə-fī′) *v.* **-fied, -fy·ing, -fies.** *—tr.* **1. a.** To confirm formally as true, accurate, or genuine, esp. in writing. **b.** To guarantee as meeting a standard. **2.** To acknowledge in writing on the face of (a check) that the signature of the maker is genuine and that the depositor has sufficient funds on deposit for its payment. **3.** To declare legally insane. **4.** To assure or make certain; tell positively. **5.** To issue a license or certificate to. *—intr.* To testify: *certify to the facts.* [ME *certifien* < OFr. *certifier* < LLat. *certificare* : Lat. *certus,* certain + Lat. *facere,* to make.] **—cer′ti·fi′a·ble** *adj.* **—cer′ti·fi′a·bly** *adv.* **—cer′ti·fi′er** *n.*

cer·ti·o·rar·i (sûr′shē-ə-râr′ē, -rä′rē) *n. Law.* A writ from a higher court to a lower one requesting a transcript of the proceedings of a case for review. [ME < Lat., to be certified (from the word's occurrence in the writ) < *certiorare,* to certify < *certion,* comp. of *certus,* certain.]

cer·ti·tude (sûr′tĭ-to͞od′, -tyo͞od′) *n.* **1.** The condition of being certain; complete assurance. **2.** Inevitability. [ME < LLat. *certitudo* < Lat. *certus,* certain.]

ce·ru·le·an (sə-ro͞o′lē-ən) *adj.* Sky-blue; azure. [Lat. *caeruleus,* dark blue.]

ce·ru·lo·plas·min (sə-ro͞o′lō-plăz′mĭn) *n.* A blood glycoprotein that functions in the storage of copper. [CERUL(EAN) + PLASM(A) + -IN.]

ce·ru·men (sə-ro͞o′mən) *n.* A yellowish waxy secretion of the external ear; earwax. [NLat. < Lat. *cera,* wax.]

ce·ru·mi·nous gland (sə-ro͞o′mə-nəs) *n.* Any of the specialized sweat glands located in the external auditory canal that produce cerumen. [< NLat. *cerumen, cerumin-,* cerumen.]

ce·ruse (sə-ro͞os′, sĭr′o͞os′) *n.* White lead. [ME < OFr. < Lat. *cerussa.*]

ce·rus·site (sə-rŭs′īt′) *n.* Natural lead carbonate, $PbCO_3$, a lead ore. [G. *Zerussit* < Lat. *cerussa,* ceruse.]

cer·vi·cal (sûr′vĭ-kəl) *adj.* Of or pertaining to a neck or a cervix. [NLat. *cervicalis* < Lat. *cervix, cervic-,* neck.]

cer·vi·ci·tis (sûr′vĭ-sī′tĭs) *n.* Inflammation of the cervix of the uterus.

cer·vine (sûr′vīn′) *adj.* Pertaining to, resembling, or characteristic of a deer. [Lat. *cervinus* < *cervus,* deer.]

cer·vix (sûr′vĭks) *n., pl.* **cer·vix·es** or **cer·vi·ces** (sûr′vĭ-sēz′, sər-vī′sēz). **1.** The neck. **2.** A neck-shaped anatomical structure, such as the narrow outer end of the uterus. [Lat. *cervix, cervic-* neck.]

Ce·sar·e·an or **Ce·sar·i·an** (sĭ-zâr′ē-ən) *adj. & n.* Variants of **Caesarean.**

ce·si·um also **cae·si·um** (sē′zē-əm) *n. Symbol* **Cs** A soft, silvery-white ductile metal, liquid at room temperature, the most electropositive and alkaline of the elements, used in photoelectric cells and to catalyze hydrogenation of some organic compounds. Atomic number 55; atomic weight 132.905; melting point 28.5°C; boiling point 690°C; specific gravity 1.87; valence 1. [NLat. < Lat. *caesius,* bluish gray (from its blue spectral lines).]

ces·pi·tose also **caes·pi·tose** (sĕs′pĭ-tōs′) *adj.* Growing in dense tufts or turflike clumps; matted. [NLat. *caespitosus* < Lat. *caespes,* turf.] **—ces′pi·tose′ly** *adv.*

cess¹ (sĕs) *n.* A tax; levy. [Alteration of obs. *assess,* assessment < ASSESS.]

cess² (sĕs) *n. Ir.* Luck: *Bad cess to you!* [Poss. short for SUCCESS.]

ces·sa·tion (sĕ-sā′shən) *n.* The act or fact of ceasing; halt. [ME *cessacioun* < OFr. < Lat. *cessatio* < *cessare,* to stop. —see CEASE.]

ces·sion (sĕsh′ən) *n.* **1.** An act of ceding or surrendering, as of territory to another country by treaty. **2.** A ceded territory. [ME < OFr. < Lat. *cessio* < *cedere,* to yield.]

ces·sion·ar·y (sĕsh′ə-nĕr′ē) *n., pl.* **-ies.** One to whom a cession is made; assignee.

cess·pit (sĕs′pĭt′) *n.* A cesspool. [CESS(POOL) + PIT.]

cess·pool (sĕs′po͞ol′) *n.* A covered hole or pit for receiving waste or sewage. [Perh. alteration of obs. *cesperalle,* drainpipe < ME *suspiral* < OFr. *souspiral,* breathing hole < *souspirer,* to breathe < Lat. *suspirare,* to sigh. —see SUSPIRE.]

ces·tode (sĕs′tōd′) *n.* A flatworm of the class Cestoda, which includes the tapeworms. [NLat. *Cestoda,* class name < Lat. *cestus,* belt < Gk. *kestos.*]

ces·tus¹ (sĕs′təs) *n., pl.* **-ti** (-tī′). A belt or girdle. [Lat., belt < Gk. *kestos.*]

ces·tus² also **caes·tus** (sĕs′təs) *n., pl.* **-tus·es.** A covering for the hand, made of leather straps weighted with iron or lead, worn by ancient Roman boxers. [Lat. *caestus* < *caedere,* to strike.]

cestus²

ce·su·ra (sĭ-zho͝or′ə, -zo͝or′ə) *n.* Variant of **caesura.**

ce·ta·ce·an (sĭ-tā′shən) *adj.* Of or belonging to the order Cetacea, which includes fishlike aquatic mammals such as the whale and porpoise. *—n.* An aquatic mammal of the order Cetacea. [< NLat. *Cetacea,* order name < Lat. *cetus,* whale < Gk. *kētos.*]

ce·ta·ceous (sĭ-tā′shəs) *adj.* Cetacean. [Lat. *cetus,* whale (< Gk. *kētos*) + -ACEOUS.]

ce·tane (sē′tān′) *n.* A colorless liquid, $C_{16}H_{34}$, used as a solvent and in standardized hydrocarbons. [Lat. *cetus,* whale (so called because it is found in sperm whale oil) + -ANE.]

cetane number also **cetane rating** *n.* The performance rating of a diesel fuel, expressed as the percentage of cetane that must be mixed with liquid methylnaphthalene to produce the same ignition performance as the diesel fuel being rated.

ce·ter·is par·i·bus (kā′tər-ĭs păr′ə-bəs) *adv.* With all other factors or things being the same. [NLat, with other things equal.]

ce·tol·o·gy (sĭ-tŏl′ə-jē) *n.* The zoology of whales and related aquatic mammals. [Lat. *cetus,* whale (< Gk. *kētos*) + -LOGY.] **—ce′to·log′i·cal** (sēt′l-ŏj′ĭ-kəl) *adj.* **—ce·tol′o·gist** *n.*

Ce·tus (sē′təs) *n.* A constellation in the equatorial region of the Southern Hemisphere near Aquarius and Eridanus. [Lat. *cetus,* whale < Gk. *kētos.*]

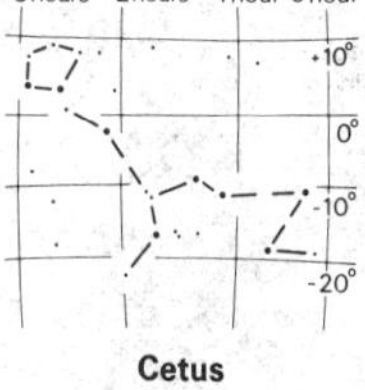

Cetus

ce·tyl alcohol (sēt′l) *n.* A waxy alcohol, $C_{15}H_{34}O$, used in cosmetics and pharmaceuticals. [Lat. *cetus,* whale + -YL.]

Cey·lon moss (sĭ-lŏn′) *n.* A red seaweed, *Gracilaria lichenoides,* of the East Indies, used for making agar. [After *Ceylon,* former name of Sri Lanka.]

Cf The symbol for the element californium.

Cha·blis (shă-blē′, shä-, shăb′lē) *n.* A very dry white Burgundy wine. [After *Chablis,* France.]

cha-cha (chä′chä) *n.* A rhythmic ballroom dance that originated in Latin America. *—intr.v.* **-chaed, -cha·ing, -chas.** To dance the cha-cha. [Sp. (Carribean) *chachachá.*]

chac·ma (chăk′mə) *n.* A grayish-black baboon, *Chaeropithecus ursinus* (or *Papio ursinus*), of southern and eastern Africa. [Hottentot.]

cha·conne (shä-kôn′, -kŏn′) *n.* **1.** A slow and stately dance of the 18th century. **2.** The music for the chaconne. **3.** A musical form consisting of variations based on a reiterated harmonic pattern. [Fr. < *chacona,* a kind of dance.]

chad (chăd) *n.* The small pieces of paper that result from the formation of holes in a punched tape or data card. [Orig. unknown.] **—chad′less** *adj.*

chae·ta (kē′tə) *n., pl.* **-tae** (-tē′). *Zool.* A bristle or seta of certain worms. [NLat. < Gk. *khaitē,* long hair.]

chae·tog·nath (kē′tŏg-năth′) *n.* Any of various marine worms of the phylum Chaetognatha, which includes the arrow worms. [NLat. *Chaetognatha,* phylum name : CHAETA + Gk. *gnathos,* jaw.]

chafe (chāf) *v.* **chafed, chaf·ing, chafes.** *—tr.* **1.** To wear away or irritate by rubbing. **2.** To annoy; vex. **3.** To heat or warm by rubbing. *—intr.* **1.** To cause friction; rub. **2.** To become worn or sore from rubbing. **3.** To be or become annoyed: *chafe at the delay.* *—n.* **1.** Warmth, wear, or soreness produced by friction. **2.** Annoyance; irritation; vexation. [ME *chafen* < OFr. *chaufer,* to warm < VLat. **calefare,* alteration of Lat. *calefacere* : *calēre,* to be warm + *facere,* to make.]

cha·fer (chā′fər) *n.* Any of various beetles of the family Scarabaeidae, such as a cockchafer. [ME, a kind of beetle < OE *ceafer.*]

chaff¹ (chăf) *n.* **1.** The husks of grain after separation from the seed. **2.** Finely cut straw or hay used as fodder. **3.** Trivial or worthless matter. **4.** Strips of metal foil released in the atmosphere to inhibit radar. [ME *chaf* < OE *ceaf.*]

chaff² (chăf) *tr.& intr.v.* **chaffed, chaff·ing, chaffs.** To subject to or engage in good-natured teasing. *—n.* Good-natured teasing; banter. [Perh. var. of CHAFE.] **—chaff′er** *n.*

chaf·fer (chăf′ər) *v.* **-fered, -fer·ing, -fers.** *—intr.* **1.** To bandy words. **2.** *Obs.* To bargain or haggle. *—tr.* **1.** To bargain or haggle for. **2.** *Obs.* To barter. *—n. Obs.* **1.** A bargaining or

chafing dish
18th-century American

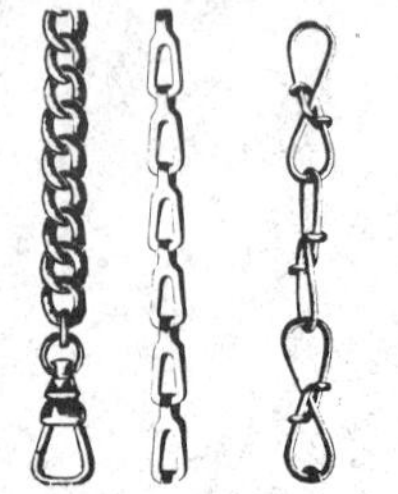
soldered link chain   brass chain   black japanned steel chain
chain

chalice
17th-century Spanish

haggling. **2.** A buying and selling; trade. [ME *chaffaren* < *chaffare,* bargaining : *chep,* trade (< OE *cēap*) + *fare,* business < OE *faru.*] **—chaf'fer·er** *n.*
chaf·finch (chăf'ĭnch) *n.* A small European songbird, *Fringilla coelebs,* having predominantly reddish-brown plumage. [ME *chaffinche* : *chaf,* chaff, husk + *finch,* finch.]
chafing dish *n.* A dish set above a heating device, used to cook or maintain the warmth of food at the table.
Cha·gas disease (shä'gəs) *n.* A South American form of trypanosomiasis caused by the protozoan *Trypanosoma cruzi.* [After Carlos *Chagas* (1879–1934).]
cha·grin (shə-grĭn') *n.* A feeling of embarrassment or humiliation caused by failure or disappointment. *—tr.v.* **-grined, -grin·ing, -grins.** To cause to feel chagrin; humiliate. [Fr. < *chagrin,* distressed.]
chain (chān) *n.* **1.** A connected, flexible series of links, usually of metal, used for binding, connecting, transmitting motion, or other purposes. **2.** Something that restrains or confines. **3. chains.** Bonds, fetters, or shackles. **4. chains.** Captivity or oppression; bondage. **5.** A series of connected or related things: *a chain of coincidences.* **6.** A number of establishments, such as stores or theaters, under common ownership or management. **7.** A mountain range. **8.** *Chem.* A group of atoms bonded in a spatial configuration resembling a chain. **9. a.** A measuring instrument for surveying, consisting of 100 linked pieces of iron or steel. **b.** A unit of length, equal to 100 links or 66 feet. **10. a.** A measuring instrument used in engineering. **b.** A unit of length, equal to 100 feet. *—tr.v.* **chained, chain·ing, chains. 1.** To bind or make fast with a chain or chains. **2.** To bind or fetter; confine. [ME *chaine* < OFr. < Lat. *catena.*]
Chain-A-Matic (chā'nə-măt'ĭk). A trademark for a balance with an adjustable calibrated chain suspended from the beam.
chain gang *n.* A group of convicts chained together.
chain letter *n.* A letter instructing the recipient to send out multiple copies so that its circulation increases in a geometrical progression as long as the instructions are followed.
chain mail *n.* Flexible armor of joined metal links or scales.
chain·man (chān'mən) *n.* Either of the two persons who hold a surveyor's measuring chain.
chain pump *n.* A pump that lifts water by means of containers, attached to an endless chain, that pass under water and up over a wheel.
chain-re·act (chān'rē-ăkt') *intr.v.* **-act·ed, -act·ing, -acts.** To undergo a chain reaction.
chain-reacting pile *n.* A nuclear reactor.
chain reaction *n.* **1.** A series of events each of which induces or influences its successor. **2.** *Physics.* A multistage nuclear reaction, esp. a self-sustaining series of fissions in which the average number of neutrons produced per unit of time exceeds the number absorbed or lost. **3.** *Chem.* A series of reactions in which one product of a reacting set is a reactant in the following set.
chain saw *n.* A power saw with teeth linked in an endless chain.
chain-smoke (chān'smōk') *v.* **-smoked, -smok·ing, -smokes.** *—intr.* To smoke cigarettes or cigars in continuing succession. *—tr.* To smoke (cigarettes or cigars) in continuing succession. **—chain smoker** *n.*
chain stitch *n.* A decorative stitch in which loops are connected like the links of a chain.
chain store *n.* One of a number of retail stores under the same ownership.
chair (châr) *n.* **1.** A piece of furniture consisting of a seat, legs, back, and often arms, designed to accommodate one person. **2.** A seat of office, authority, or dignity, as that of a bishop. **3. a.** The office or position of a person having authority. **b.** A person who holds such an office or position, esp. one who presides over a meeting. **4.** *Slang.* The electric chair. **5.** A seat carried about on poles; sedan chair. **6.** A metal block for supporting and holding railroad track in position. *—tr.v.* **chaired, chair·ing, chairs. 1.** To put or seat in a chair. **2.** To install in a position of authority, esp. as a presiding officer. **3.** To preside over (a meeting). **4.** *Chiefly Brit.* To carry (a person) aloft in triumph, usually in a chair. [ME *chaiere* < OFr. < Lat. *cathedra.* —see CATHEDRA.]
chair car *n.* A parlor car.
chair lift *n.* A cable-suspended, power-driven chair assembly used to transport people up or down mountains.
chair·man (châr'mən) *n.* **1.** One who presides over an assembly, meeting, committee, or board. **2.** One who carries or wheels others in a chair. *—tr.v.* **-manned, -man·ning, -mans.** To act as chairman of.
chair·man·ship (châr'mən-shĭp') *n.* The office or term of a chairman.
chair·per·son (châr'pûr'sən) *n.* A person who presides over an assembly, meeting, committee, or board.
chair·wom·an (châr'wo͝om'ən) *n.* A woman who presides over an assembly, meeting, committee, or board.
chaise (shāz) *n.* **1.** Any of various light, open carriages, often with a collapsible hood, esp. a two-wheeled carriage drawn by one horse. **2.** A post chaise. [Fr., chair, alteration of OFr. *chaiere.* —see CHAIR.]
chaise longue (shāz lông') *n., pl.* **chaise longues** or **chaises longues** (shāz lông'). A reclining chair with a seat long enough to support the outstretched legs of the sitter. [Fr. : *chaise,* chair + *longue,* long.]
chak·ra (chŭk'rə) *n.* One of the seven centers of spiritual energy in the human body according to yoga philosophy. [Skt. *cakram,* wheel.]
cha·lah (KHä'lə) *n.* Variant of **challah.**
cha·la·za (kə-lā'zə, -lăz'ə) *n., pl.* **-zae** (-zē') or **-zas. 1.** *Zool.* One of two spiral bands of tissue in an egg, connecting the yolk to the lining membrane. **2.** *Bot.* The part of an ovule that is opposite the micropyle and that serves as a point of attachment for the integuments and the nucellus. [Gk. *khalaza,* hailstone.]
cha·la·zi·on (kə-lā'zē-ən, -ŏn') *n.* A small hard tumor of the eyelid. [NLat. < Gk. *khalazion,* dim. of *khalaza,* hard lump.]
chal·ced·o·ny also **cal·ced·o·ny** (kăl-sĕd'n-ē) *n., pl.* **-nies.** A translucent to transparent milky or grayish quartz with distinctive microscopic crystals arranged in slender fibers in parallel bands. [ME *calcedoine* < LLat. *chalcedonius* < Gk. *khalkēdōn,* a mystical stone, perh. < *Khalkēdōn,* an ancient town in Asia Minor.] **—chal'ce·don'ic** (kăl'sĭ-dŏn'ĭk) *adj.*
chal·cid (kăl'sĭd) *n.* Any of various minute wasps of the superfamily Chalcidoidea, of which the larvae of many species are parasitic on the larval stages of other insects. [< NLat. *Chalcis,* genus name < Gk. *khalkos,* copper (from the wasp's metallic color).]
chal·co·cite (kăl'kə-sīt') *n.* An important copper ore, essentially CuS_2. [Alteration of obs. *chalcosine* < Gk. *khalkos,* copper.]
chal·co·py·rite (kăl'kə-pī'rīt') *n.* An important copper ore, essentially $CuFeS_2$. [Gk. *khalkos,* copper + PYRITES.]
chal·co·sis (kăl-kō'sĭs) *n.* Copper poisoning, sometimes with the formation of copper deposits in the tissues. [Gk. *khalkos,* copper + -OSIS.]
Chal·de·an also **Chal·dae·an** (kăl-dē'ən) or **Chal·dee** (kăl'dē') *n.* **1.** A member of an ancient Semitic people who ruled in Babylonia. **2.** The Semitic language of the Chaldeans. **3.** A person versed in occult learning. [< Lat. *Chaldaeus* < Gk. *Khaldaios* < *Khaldaia,* Chaldea, a region of ancient Babylonia.] **—Chal·da'ic** (-dā'ĭk) *n. & adj.* **—Chal·de'an** *adj.*
Chal·dee (kăl'dē') *n.* Variant of **Chaldean.**
chal·dron (chôl'drən) *n.* A unit of dry measure, as for coal, equal to 32 to 36 bushels, formerly used in England. [OFr. *chauderon* < *chaudiere,* kettle < LLat. *caldaria.* —see CALDRON.]
cha·let (shă-lā', shăl'ā) *n.* **1.** A dwelling with a gently sloping overhanging roof, common in Switzerland and other Alpine regions. **2.** The hut of a herdsman in the Alps. [Fr.]
chal·ice (chăl'ĭs) *n.* **1.** A cup or goblet. **2.** A cup for the consecrated wine of the Eucharist. **3.** A cup-shaped blossom. [ME < OFr. < Lat. *calix.*]
chal·i·co·sis (kăl'ĭ-kō'sĭs) *n.* Pneumoconiosis caused by the inhalation of stone dust. [Gk. *khalix, khalik-,* pebble + -OSIS.]
chal·i·co·there (kăl'ĭ-kə-thîr') *n.* Any of various extinct ungulate mammals of the Eocene to Pleistocene epochs, having distinctive three-clawed, three-toed feet. [NLat. *Chalicotherium,* genus name : Gk. *khalix,* stone + Gk. *thērion,* dim. of *thēr,* beast.]
chalk (chôk) *n.* **1.** A soft, compact calcium carbonate, $CaCO_3$, with varying amounts of silica, quartz, feldspar, or other mineral impurities, generally gray-white or yellow-white and derived chiefly from fossil seashells. **2.** A piece of chalk or chalklike substance, frequently colored, used for marking on a blackboard or other surface. **3.** A mark or picture made with chalk. **4.** A reckoning, as of credit given; tally. *—tr.v.* **chalked, chalk·ing chalks. 1.** To mark, draw, or write with chalk. **2.** To smear or cover with chalk. **3.** To make pale; whiten. **4.** To treat (soil, for example) with chalk. ***—phrasal verb.* chalk up. 1.** To earn or score: *chalk up points.* **2.** To credit: *Chalk that up to experience.* [ME < OE *cealk* < Lat. *calx,* lime. —see CALX.] **—chalk'i·ness** *n.* **—chalk'y** *adj.*
chalk·board (chôk'bôrd', -bōrd') *n.* A panel, usually green or black, for writing on with chalk; blackboard.
chalk·stone (chôk'stōn') *n. Pathol.* A tophus.
chalk talk *n.* A lecture, often informal, illustrated with diagrams chalked on a blackboard.
chal·lah also **cha·lah** (KHä'lə) *n.* A loaf of yeast-leavened, white egg bread, usually braided, traditionally eaten by Jews on the Sabbath, holidays, and ceremonial occasions. [Heb. *ḥallāh.*]
chal·lenge (chăl'ənj) *n.* **1.** A call to engage in a contest or fight. **2.** A demand for an explanation; a calling into question. **3.** A sentry's call for identification. **4.** The quality of requiring full use of one's abilities, energy, or resources: *a career that offers a challenge.* **5.** A claim that a vote is invalid or that a voter is unqualified. **6.** *Law.* A formal objection, esp. to the qualifications of a juror or jury. *—v.* **-lenged, -leng·ing, -leng·es.** *—tr.* **1.** To call to engage in a contest or fight. **2.** To take exception to; dispute: *challenged the statements.* **3.** To order to halt and be identified. **4.** *Law.* To take formal objection to (a juror, for example). **5.** To question the qualifications or validity of. **6.** To have due claim to; call for. **7.** To summon to action, effort, or use; stimulate: *a problem that challenges the imagination.* *—intr.* **1.** To make or give voice to a challenge. **2.** To begin barking

upon picking up the scent, as hunting dogs. [ME *chalenge* < OFr. < *chalanger,* to accuse < Lat. *calumniari,* to accuse falsely < *calumnia,* calumny < *calvi,* to deceive.] **—chal'lenge·a·ble** *adj.* **—chal'leng·er** *n.*

chal·lis (shăl'ē) *n.* A light clothing fabric made of wool, cotton, or rayon. [Poss. < the surname *Challis.*]

cha·lone (kā'lōn', kăl'ōn') *n.* A hormone that inhibits a metabolic process. [< Gk. *khalōn,* pr.part. of *khalan,* to slacken.]

cha·lyb·e·ate (kə-lĭb'ē-ĭt, -lē'bē-) *adj.* **1.** Impregnated with or containing salts of iron. **2.** Tasting like iron, as mineral-spring water. *—n.* Water or medicine containing iron in solution. [NLat. *chalybeatus* < Lat. *chalybs,* steel < Gk. *khalups* < *Khalups,* Chalybes, a people of Asia Minor famous for their steel.]

cham (kăm) *n. Archaic.* A Tatar or Mogul khan. [Fr. < Turk *khān.*]

Cha·mae·leon also **Cha·me·leon** (kə-mēl'yən, -mē'lē-ən) *n.* A constellation in the southern polar region near Apus and Mensa. [Lat. *chamaeleon,* chameleon.]

cham·ae·phyte (kăm'ə-fīt') *n.* A perennial plant that has its winter buds placed very close to the soil surface. [Gk. *khamai,* on the ground + -PHYTE.]

cham·ber (chām'bər) *n.* **1. a.** A room in a house, esp. a bedroom. **b. chambers.** *Chiefly Brit.* A suite of rooms; apartment. **2.** Often **chambers.** A judge's office. **3.** A room in a palace or official residence where an important personage receives visitors. **4.** A hall for the meeting of an assembly, esp. a legislative assembly. **5.** A legislative, judicial, or deliberative assembly. **6.** A board or council. **7.** A place where governmental funds are received and held; treasury. **8.** An enclosed space or compartment; cavity. **9. a.** An enclosed space at the bore of a gun that holds the charge. **b.** The part of a cylinder of a revolver that receives the cartridge. *—tr.v.* **-bered, -ber·ing, -bers. 1.** To put in or as if in a chamber; enclose; confine. **2.** To furnish with a chamber. [ME *chaumbre* < OFr. < LLat. *camera,* chamber < Lat., vault < Gk. *kamara.*]

chambered nautilus *n.* A cephalopod mollusk, *Nautilus pompilius,* of the Pacific and Indian oceans, having a coiled and partitioned shell lined with a pearly layer.

cham·ber·lain (chām'bər-lən) *n.* **1.** An official who manages the household of a sovereign or nobleman; chief steward. **2.** A high-ranking officer in various royal courts. **3.** An official who receives the rents and fees of a municipality; treasurer. **4.** *Rom. Cath. Ch.* An often honorary papal attendant. [ME *chaumberlein* < OFr. *chamberlene* < LLat. *camera,* chamber.]

cham·ber·maid (chām'bər-mād') *n.* A maid who cleans and cares for bedrooms, as in hotels.

chamber music *n.* Music appropriate for performance in a private room or small concert hall and composed for a group of instruments such as a trio or quartet.

chamber of commerce *n.* An association of businessmen and merchants for the promotion of business interests in the community.

chamber pot *n.* A portable vessel used as a toilet.

cham·bray (shăm'brā') *n.* A fine, lightweight type of gingham woven with white threads across a colored warp. [After *Cambrai,* France.]

cha·me·leon (kə-mēl'yən, -mē'lē-ən) *n.* **1.** Any of various tropical Old World lizards of the family Chamaeleonidae, characterized by their ability to change color. **2.** The anole. **3.** A changeable or inconstant person. **4. Chameleon.** Variant of **Chamaeleon.** [ME *camelioun* < Lat. *chamaeleon* < Gk. *khamaileōn* : *khamai,* on the ground + *leōn,* lion.] **—cha·me'le·on'ic** (-lē-ŏn'ĭk) *adj.*

cham·fer (chăm'fər) *tr.v.* **-fered, -fer·ing, -fers. 1.** To cut off the edge or corner of; bevel. **2.** To cut a groove in; flute. *—n.* **1.** A flat surface made by cutting off the edge or corner of something. **2.** A furrow or groove, as in a column. [Prob. ult. < OFr. *chanfreindre* : *chant,* edge + *fraindre,* to break < Lat. *frangere.*]

cham·fron (chăm'frən) *n.* Medieval armor for the front of a horse's head. [ME *shamfron* < OFr. *chanfrein.*]

cha·mi·so (chə-mē'sō) *n., pl.* **-sos.** A shrub, *Adenostoma fasciculatum,* of California, having clusters of small white flowers and forming dense thickets. [Sp. *chamiza,* wild brush < *chamizo,* dry brush gathered for firewood.]

cham·ois (shăm'ē) *n., pl.* **cham·ois** (shăm'ēz *also* shăm-wä') or **-mies. 1.** A hoofed mammal, *Rupricapra rupricapra,* of mountainous regions of Europe, having upright horns with backward-hooked tips. **2.** Also **cham·my,** *pl.* **-mies.** The soft leather made from the hide of the chamois or other animals such as deer or sheep. **3.** Moderate to grayish yellow. *—tr.v.* **-oised, -ois·ing, -ois·es. 1.** To dress or prepare like chamois. **2.** To polish or dry with chamois leather. [OFr.]

cham·o·mile or **cam·o·mile** (kăm'ə-mīl') *n.* **1.** Any of various plants of the genus *Anthemis,* esp. *A. nobilis,* an aromatic plant native to Eurasia, having finely dissected leaves and white flowers. **2.** Any of several similar plants of the genus *Matricaria,* esp. *M. chamomilla.* [ME *camomille* < LLat. *chamomilla* < Lat. *chamaemelon* < Gk. *khamaimēlon* : *khamai,* on the ground + *mēlon,* apple.]

champ[1] (chămp) also **chomp** (chŏmp) *v.* **champed, champ·ing, champs** also **chomped, chomp·ing, chomps.** *—tr.* **1.** To bite upon with restlessness or impatience. **2.** To chew upon noisily. **3.** *Scot.* To crush or trample. *—intr.* To work the jaws and teeth vigorously. *—n.* The act of chewing or biting vigorously. ***—idiom.*** **champ at the bit.** To be impatient. [Perh. imit.]

champ[2] (chămp) *n. Informal.* A champion.

cham·pagne (shăm-pān') *n.* **1. a.** A sparkling white wine produced in Champagne, a region of France. **b.** A similar wine made elsewhere. **2.** Pale orange yellow to grayish yellow or yellowish gray.

cham·paign (shăm-pān') *n.* Level and open country; a plain. *—adj.* Pertaining to or like champaign; level and open. [ME *champain* < OFr. *champaigne* < LLat. *campania,* open country. —see CAMPAIGN.]

cham·pak also **cham·pac** (chăm'păk', chŭm'pŭk) *n.* A tree, *Michelia champaca,* of India and the East Indies, that has yellow flowers and yields a camphorlike substance and an oil used in perfumes. [Hindi *campak* < Skt. *campakaḥ.*]

cham·per·ty (chăm'pər-tē) *n., pl.* **-ties.** *Law.* An illegal sharing in the proceeds of a lawsuit by an outside party who has promoted the litigation. [ME *champartie* < OFr. *champart,* the lord's share of the tenant's crop : *champ,* field (< Lat. *campus*) + *part,* share (< Lat. *pars*).] **—cham'per·tous** (-təs) *adj.*

cham·pi·gnon (shăm-pĭn'yən) *n.* An edible mushroom, esp. the common species *Agaricus campestris.* [Fr. < OFr. *champigneul,* prob. ult. < Lat. *campus,* field.]

cham·pi·on (chăm'pē-ən) *n.* **1.** One that holds first place or wins first prize in a contest, esp. in sports. **2.** One that defends, fights for, or supports a cause or another person. **3.** One who fights; warrior. *—tr.v.* **-oned, -on·ing, -ons. 1.** To fight as champion of; defend; support: *"championed the government and defended the system of taxation"* (Samuel Chew). **2.** *Obs.* To defy or challenge. *—adj.* Holding first place or prize; superior to all others. [ME *championn* < OFr. *champion* < Med. Lat. *campio.*]

cham·pi·on·ship (chăm'pē-ən-shĭp') *n.* **1.** The position or title of a champion. **2.** Defense or support; advocacy. **3.** A competition or series of competitions held to determine a winner.

chambered nautilus

chance (chăns) *n.* **1. a.** The abstract nature or quality shared by unexpected, random, or unpredictable events; contingency. **b.** This quality regarded as causing or deciding such events; luck. **2.** The likelihood of occurrence of an event; probability. **3. a.** An unexpected, random, or unpredicted event. **b.** A fortuitous event. **4. a.** An opportunity. **b.** A risk or hazard; gamble. **c.** A raffle or lottery ticket. **5.** *Baseball.* An opportunity to make a putout or an assist that counts as an error if unsuccessful. *—adj.* **1.** Happening unexpectedly: *a chance meeting with an old friend.* **2.** Determined or marked by whim or caprice; arbitrary. *—v.* **chanced, chanc·ing, chanc·es.** *—intr.* To happen by chance; occur by accident. *—tr.* To take the risk or hazard of. ***—phrasal verb.*** **chance on** (or **upon**). To find or meet accidentally; happen upon. [ME, unexpected event < OFr. < VLat. **cadentia* < Lat. *cadere,* to happen.]

Synonyms: *chance, random, casual, haphazard, desultory.* These adjectives apply to what lacks purposefulness or method. *Chance* implies total absence of design or predictability: *my chance meeting with a friend. Random* applies to things that happen to occur or be selected without the aid of a governing mind or design. *Casual* suggests lack of deliberation or formality; *haphazard,* a carelessness or a willful leaving to chance; and *desultory,* an absence of relation among things in a series.

chameleon

chance·ful (chăns'fəl) *adj.* **1.** Full of chance; eventful. **2.** *Archaic.* Dependent upon chance. **3.** *Obs.* Risky; dangerous.

chan·cel (chăns'fəl) *n.* The often enclosed space around the altar of a church for the clergy and choir. [ME *chauncel* < OFr. *chancel* < Lat. *cancelli,* lattice < *cancer.*]

chan·cel·ler·y (chăn'sə-lə-rē, -slə-rē, chän'-) *n., pl.* **-ies. 1.** The rank or position of a chancellor. **2. a.** The office or department of a chancellor. **b.** The building in which it is located. **3.** The official place of business of an embassy or consulate. [ME *chancelrie* < OFr. *chancelerie* < *chancelier,* chancellor.]

chan·cel·lor (chăn'sə-lər, -slər) *n.* **1.** Any of various officials of high rank, esp.: **a.** A secretary to a king or nobleman. **b.** *Chiefly Brit.* The chief secretary of an embassy. **c.** The chief minister of state in some European countries. **2. a.** *Chiefly Brit.* The honorary or titular head of a university. **b.** The president of certain American universities. **3.** The presiding judge of a court of chancery or equity in some states of the United States. [ME *chaunceler* < OFr. *chancelier* < LLat. *cancellarius,* doorkeeper < Lat. *cancelli,* lattice. —see CANCEL.] **—chan'cel·lor·ship'** *n.*

Chancellor of the Exchequer *n.* The highest minister of finance in the British government and a member of the cabinet.

chance-med·ley (chăns'mĕd'lē) *n.* **1.** *Law.* A sudden quarrel resulting in an unpremeditated homicide. **2.** A random or haphazard action. [ME *chaunce medley* < Norman Fr. *chance medlee,* mixed chance.]

chan·cer·y (chăn'sə-rē) *n., pl.* **-ies. 1. a.** A court with jurisdiction in equity as distinguished from one with jurisdiction in common law. **b.** The proceedings and practice of a court of chancery; equity. **2.** A court of public record; an office of archives. **3.** One of the five divisions of the High Court of Justice of Great Britain, presided over by the Lord High Chancellor. **4.** A chancellery. ***—idiom.* in chancery. 1.** *Law.* In litigation or pending in a court of chancery. **2.** With the head locked firmly in a wrestling opponent's arm and held against his chest. **3.** *Informal.* In an embarrassing or hopeless predicament. [ME *chauncerie* < OFr. *chancelerie,* chancellery < *chancelier,* chancellery.]

chan·cre (shăng′kər) *n.* **1.** A dull-red, hard, insensitive lesion that is the first manifestation of syphilis. **2.** An ulcer located at the initial point of entry of a pathogen. [Fr. < Lat. *cancer,* ulcer.]

chan·croid (shăng′kroid′) *n.* A soft, nonsyphilitic, usually venereal lesion of the genital region. [Fr. *chancroïde: chancre,* chancre + *-oïde,* -oid.] **—chan′crous** (-krəs) *adj.* **—chan′croid′al** (-kroid′l) *adj.*

chanc·y (chăn′sē, chän′-) *adj.* **-i·er, -i·est. 1.** Uncertain, as to outcome; risky; hazardous. **2.** *Scot.* Lucky; propitious.

chandelier

chan·de·lier (shăn′də-lîr′) *n.* A branched fixture that holds a number of light bulbs or candles and is usually suspended from a ceiling. [Fr. < OFr., prob < VLat. **candelarum* < Lat. *candelabrum,* candelabrum. —see CANDELABRUM.]

chan·delle (shăn-dĕl′) *n.* A sudden, steep climbing turn of an aircraft, executed to alter flight direction and gain altitude simultaneously. [Fr. < *chandelle,* candle < OFr. —see CHANDLER.]

chan·dler (chănd′lər) *n.* **1.** A person who makes or sells candles. **2.** A dealer in specified goods or equipment: *a ship chandler.* [ME *chaundeler* < OFr. *chandelier* < *chandelle,* candle < Lat. *candela.* —see CANDLE.]

Chan·dler Wobble (chănd′lər) or **Chan·dler's Wobble** (chănd′lərz) *n.* An oscillation in the rotational axis of the earth having a period of approximately 14 months. [After Seth C. *Chandler* (1846–1913).]

chan·dler·y (chănd′lə-rē) *n., pl.* **-ies. 1.** The stock or business of a chandler. **2.** A place where candles are stored.

change (chānj) *v.* **changed, chang·ing, chang·es.** *—tr.* **1. a.** To cause to be different; alter: *changed the spelling of a word.* **b.** To give a completely different form or appearance to; transform: *irrigation that changed the desert to fertile land.* **2.** To give and receive reciprocally; interchange: *Will you change places with me?* **3.** To exchange for or replace by another, usually of the same kind or category: *change one's name.* **4.** To lay aside, abandon, or leave for another; switch: *change methods; change planes.* **5.** To give or receive the equivalent of (money) in lower denominations or in foreign currency. **6.** To put fresh clothes or coverings on: *change a bed.* *—intr.* **1.** To become different or altered: *changed as he matured.* **2.** To go from one phase to another, as the moon. **3.** To make an exchange. **4.** To transfer from one vehicle to another: *changed in Chicago on his way to the coast.* **5.** To put on other clothing: *changed for dinner.* **6.** To become deeper in tone. Used of the voice. ***—phrasal verb.* change off. 1.** To alternate with another person in performing a task. **2.** To perform two tasks at once by alternating or a single task by alternate means. *—n.* **1. a.** The act, process or result of changing; alteration or modification: *a face that had undergone change with age.* **b.** The replacing of one thing for another; substitution: *went to Arizona for a change of atmosphere.* **2.** A transition from one state, condition, or phase to another: *the change of seasons.* **3.** Something different; variety: *ate early for a change.* **4.** A different or fresh set of clothing. **5.** Money of smaller denomination given or received in exchange for money of higher denomination. **b.** The balance of money returned when an amount given is more than what is due. **c.** Coins: *change jingling in his pocket.* **6.** *Mus.* A pattern or order in which bells are rung. **7.** A market or exchange where business is transacted. ***—idioms.* change hands.** To pass from one owner to another. **change (one's) mind.** To reverse an opinion or a decision. [ME *chaungen* < Norman Fr. *chaunger* < OFr. *changier* < LLat. *cambiare,* prob. of Celtic orig.] **—chang′er** *n.* **—change′less** *adj.*

Synonyms: *change, alter, vary, modify, transform, convert, transmute.* These verbs mean to make or become different. *Change* implies a fundamental difference or a substitution of one thing for another: *change his mind; change trains. Alter* usually means to make less of a difference or adjustment. *Vary* implies shifting circumstances or conditions that cause differences with some regularity. *Modify* can mean to restrict, limit, or qualify, and sometimes to make less extreme. *Transform* refers to complete change in outer form or appearance and often also in character and function. *Convert* can refer to moderate change designed to adapt something to new use or different conditions, to chemical change, to change in belief or doctrine, or to the exchange of something for equivalent value, either in the same form *(convert dollars into pounds)* or a different form *(convert real estate into cash). Transmute* suggests almost magical basic change that elevates something in value.

change·a·ble (chān′jə-bəl) *adj.* **1.** Liable to change; capricious: *changeable moods.* **2.** Capable of being altered: *changeable behavior.* **3.** Changing color or appearance when seen from different angles: *changeable taffeta.* **—change′a·bil′i·ty, change′a·ble·ness** *n.* **—change′a·bly** *adv.*

change·ful (chānj′fəl) *adj.* Having the tendency or ability to change; variable. **—change′ful·ly** *adv.* **—change′ful·ness** *n.*

change·ling (chānj′lĭng) *n.* **1.** A child secretly exchanged for another. **2.** *Archaic.* A changeable, fickle person. **3.** *Archaic.* A simple-minded person; idiot.

change of life *n.* The menopause.

change·o·ver (chānj′ō′vər) *n.* A conversion to a different purpose or from one system to another, esp. in equipment or production techniques.

change ringing *n.* The ringing of a set of chimes or bells with every possible unrepeated variation.

chan·nel[1] (chăn′əl) *n.* **1.** The bed of a stream or river. **2.** The deeper part of a river or harbor, esp. a deep navigable passage. **3.** A broad strait: *the English Channel.* **4.** A tubular passage for liquids. **5.** A course or passage through which something may be moved or directed: *a channel of thought.* **6. channels.** Official routes of communication. **7.** *Electronics.* A specified frequency band for the transmission and reception of electromagnetic signals, as for television signals. **8.** A trench, furrow, or groove. **9.** A rolled metal bar with a bracket-shaped section. *—tr.v.* **-neled, -nel·ing, -nels** also **-nelled, -nel·ling, -nels. 1.** To make or cut channels in. **2.** To form a channel or flute in. **3.** To direct or guide along some desired course: *channels her curiosity into research.* [ME *chanel* < OFr. < Lat. *canalis.*]

chan·nel[2] (chăn′əl) *n. Naut.* A wood or steel ledge projecting from a sailing ship's sides to spread the shrouds and keep them clear of the gunwales. [Alteration of obs. *chainwale* : CHAIN + WALE.]

channel bass *n.* The red drum.

channel black *n.* A finely divided carbon black, formed on iron plate by direct exposure to a natural gas flame and used in inks, paints, typewriter ribbons, crayons, and polishes. [< CHANNEL[1].]

chan·nel-lag deposit (chăn′əl-lăg′) *n.* The residue that is deposited in a channel as a stream runs its natural course.

chan·son (shäN-sôN′) *n., pl.* **-sons** (-sôN′, -sôNz′). A song, esp. a French cabaret song. [Fr. < OFr. < Lat. *cantio* < *cantare,* to sing. —see CHANTAGE.]

chan·son de geste (shäN-sôN′ də zhĕst′) *n., pl.* **chan·sons de geste** (-sôN′, -sôNz). A genre of Old French epic poem falling into cycles of poems celebrating the deeds of heroic or historical figures. [Fr.: *chanson,* song + *de,* of + *geste,* heroic exploit.]

chant (chănt) *n.* **1. a.** A short, simple melody in which a number of syllables or words are sung on the same note. **b.** A psalm or canticle sung in this manner. **2.** A song or melody. **3.** A monotonous rhythmic call or shout: *the chant of the crowd at the rally.* *—v.* **chant·ed, chant·ing, chants.** *—tr.* **1.** To sing or intone to a chant. **2.** To celebrate in song. **3.** To say in the manner of a chant. *—intr.* **1.** To sing, esp. in the manner of a chant. **2.** To speak monotonously. [Prob. < Fr., song < OFr. < Lat. *cantus* < *canere,* to sing.] **—chant′ing·ly** *adv.*

chant·age (shäN-täzh′) *n.* Blackmail. [Fr. < *chanter,* to sing < OFr. < Lat. *cantare,* freq. of *canere.*]

chant·er (chăn′tər) *n.* **1.** A person who chants, as a chorister. **2.** A priest who sings in a chantry. **3.** The pipe of a bagpipe on which the melody is played.

chan·te·relle (shăn′tə-rĕl′, shän′-) *n.* An edible yellow mushroom, *Cantharellus cibarius,* having a pleasant fruity odor. [Fr. < NLat. *cantharellus,* dim. of Lat. *cantharus,* cup (from the mushroom's shape) < Gk. *kantharos.*]

chan·teuse (shäN-tœz′) *n.* A woman singer, esp. a nightclub singer. [Fr., fem. of *chanteur,* singer < *chanter,* to sing. —see CHANTAGE.]

chan·tey also **chan·ty** (shăn′tē, chăn′-) *n., pl.* **-teys** also **-ties.** A song sung by sailors to the rhythm of their movements while working. [Prob. < Fr. *chantez,* imper. of *chanter,* to sing. —see CHANTAGE.]

chan·ti·cleer (chăn′tĭ-klîr′, shăn′-) *n.* A rooster. [ME *chauntecler* < OFr. *chantecler* : *chanter,* to sing + *cler,* clear < Lat. *clarus.*]

chan·try (chăn′trē) *n., pl.* **-tries.** *Eccles.* **1.** An endowment to cover expenses for the saying of masses and prayers, usually for the soul of the founder of the endowment. **2.** An altar or chapel endowed for the saying of masses and prayers. [ME *chaunterie* < OFr. < *chanter,* to sing. —see CHANTAGE.]

chan·ty (shăn′tē, chăn′-) *n.* Variant of **chantey.**

Cha·nu·kah (KHä′nə-kə, hä′-) *n.* An eight-day Jewish festival beginning on the 25th day of the month of Kislev and commemorating the victory of the Maccabees over the Syrians in 165 B.C. and the rededication of the Temple at Jerusalem. [Heb. *ḥanukkāh,* consecration.]

chao (dou) *n., pl.* **chao.** See table at **currency.**

cha·os (kā′ŏs′) *n.* **1.** A condition or place of total disorder or confusion: *emotions in complete chaos.* **2.** Often **Chaos.** The disordered state of unformed matter and infinite space supposed by some religious cosmological views to have existed prior to the ordered universe. **3.** *Obs.* A vast abyss or chasm. [Lat., formless matter < Gk. *khaos.*] **—cha·ot′ic** (-ŏt′ĭk) *adj.* **—cha·ot′i·cal·ly** *adv.*

chap[1] (chăp) *v.* **chapped, chap·ping, chaps.** *—tr.* To cause (the skin) to split or roughen, esp. as a result of cold or exposure: *The north wind chapped her lips.* *—intr.* To split or become rough and sore: *He has skin that chaps easily.* *—n.* A sore roughening or splitting of the skin, caused esp. by cold or exposure. [ME *chappen.*]

chap[2] (chăp) *n.* **1.** *Informal.* A man or boy; fellow. **2.** *Chiefly Brit. Regional.* A customer; purchaser. [Short for CHAPMAN.]

cha·pa·re·jos also **cha·pa·ra·jos** (shăp'ə-rā'ōs) *pl.n. Southwestern U.S.* Chaps. [Mex. Sp. *chaparreras,* chaps.]

chap·ar·ral (shăp'ə-răl') *n.* A dense thicket of shrubs and small trees, esp. in the southwestern United States and Mexico. [Sp. < *chaparro,* evergreen oak < Basque *txapar,* dim. of *saphar,* thicket.]

chaparral cock *n.* The roadrunner.

chaparral pea *n.* A thorny shrub, *Pickeringia montana,* of California, having showy reddish-purple flowers and forming dense thickets.

chap·book (chăp'bŏŏk') *n.* A small book or pamphlet containing poems, ballads, stories, or religious tracts. [CHAP(MAN) + BOOK, so called because it was originally sold by chapmen.]

chape (chāp, chăp) *n.* A metal tip or mounting on a scabbard or sheath. [ME < OFr., covering < LLat. *cappa.*]

cha·peau (shă-pō') *n., pl.* **-peaux** (-pōz') or **-peaus** (-pōz'). A hat. [Fr. < OFr. *chapel* < Med. Lat. *cappellus* < LLat. *cappa.*]

chap·el (chăp'əl) *n.* **1.** A place of worship that is smaller than and subordinate to a church. **2.** A place of worship in a college, hospital, or other institution. **3.** The services held at a chapel. **4.** A recess or room in a church set apart for special or small services. **5.** A place of worship for those not connected with or not members of an established church. **6.** A choir or orchestra connected with a chapel or royal court. **7. a.** An association of workers in a print shop. **b.** *Obs.* A printing house or print shop. [ME *chapele* < OFr. < Med. Lat. *capella,* chapel, cape (from a shrine containing the cape of St. Martin of Tours), dim. of *cappa,* cloak.]

chap·er·on also **chap·er·one** (shăp'ə-rōn') *n.* **1.** A person, esp. an older or married woman, who accompanies a young unmarried woman in public. **2.** An older person who attends and supervises a social gathering for young people. —*tr.v.* **-oned, -on·ing, -ons.** To act as chaperon to or for. [Fr. < *chaperon,* hood < OFr. < *chape,* covering. —see CHAPE.] **—chap'er·on'age** (-rō'nĭj) *n.*

chap·fall·en (chăp'fô'lən, chŏp'-) also **chop·fall·en** (chŏp'-) *adj.* In low spirits; dejected; disheartened. [< obs. *chaps,* alteration of CHOPS.]

chap·i·ter (chăp'ĭ-tər) *n. Archit.* The capital of a column. [ME *chapitre,* chapter, chapiter < OFr. < *chapitle* < Lat. *capitulum,* dim. of *caput,* head.]

chap·lain (chăp'lĭn) *n.* **1.** A clergyman attached to a chapel. **2.** A clergyman or layman who conducts religious services for a legislative assembly or other organization. **3.** A clergyman attached to a military unit. [ME *chapelein* < OFr. *chapelain* < Med. Lat. *cappellanus* < *capella,* chapel. —see CHAPEL.] **—chap'lain·cy, chap'lain·ship'** *n.*

chap·let (chăp'lĭt) *n.* **1.** A wreath or garland for the head. **2.** *Rom. Cath. Ch.* **a.** A string of prayer beads with one third the number of a rosary's beads. **b.** The prayers counted on such beads. **3.** A string of beads. **4.** *Archit.* A small molding carved so that it resembles a string of beads. [ME *chapelet* < OFr., dim. of *chapel,* hat. —see CHAPEAU.] **—chap'let·ed** *adj.*

chap·man (chăp'mən) *n.* **1.** *Chiefly Brit.* A peddler. **2.** *Archaic.* A dealer or merchant. [ME < OE *cēapman* : *cēap,* trade (ult. < Lat. *caupo,* tradesman) + *man* < OE *mann.*]

chaps (chăps, shăps) *pl.n.* Heavy leather trousers without a seat, worn over ordinary trousers by cowboys to protect their legs. [Short for Mex. Sp. *chaparreras.*]

chap·ter (chăp'tər) *n.* **1.** One of the main divisions of a book or other writing, usually numbered or titled. **2.** A period or sequence of events, as in history or a person's life, that marks a distinct change of pattern. **3.** A local branch of a club, fraternity, or other organization. **4.** *Eccles.* **a.** An assembly of the canons of a church. **b.** The canons collectively. **5.** *Eccles.* An assembly of the members or representatives of a religious house, community, or order. **6.** A meeting of society or order. **7.** A short Scriptural passage read after the psalms in certain church services. [ME *chapitre,* chapter, chapiter. —see CHAPITER.]

chapter house *n.* **1.** A building in which the chapter of a cathedral or monastery assembles. **2.** A house in which a chapter of a fraternity or sorority lives and holds its meetings.

char[1] (chär) *tr. & intr.v.* **charred, char·ring, chars. 1.** To scorch or become scorched. **2.** To reduce or become reduced to charcoal by incomplete combustion. —*n.* A substance that has been charred. [Back-formation < CHARCOAL.]

char[2] also **charr** (chär) *n., pl.* **char** or **chars** also **charr** or **charrs.** Any of several fishes of the genus *Salvelinus,* related to the trout, esp. the widely distributed species *S. alpinus.* [Orig. unknown.]

char[3] (chär) *n.* **1.** A chore or odd job, esp. a household task. **2.** A charwoman. —*intr.v.* **charred, char·ring, chars. 1.** To do small jobs, tasks, or chores. **2.** To work as a charwoman. [ME, a piece of work < OE *cierr,* a turning.]

char·a·banc (shăr'ə-băng') *n. Chiefly Brit.* A large bus, often used for sightseeing. [Fr. *char à bancs* : *char,* carriage + *à,* with + *bancs,* benches.]

char·a·cin (kăr'ə-sĭn) also **char·a·cid** (-sĭd) *n.* Any of numerous chiefly tropical freshwater fishes of the family Characidae, many of which are popular aquarium fishes. [NLat. *Characinidae,* former family name < Gk. *kharax,* a kind of fish.]

char·ac·ter (kăr'ək-tər) *n.* **1.** The combination of qualities or features that distinguishes one person, group, or thing from another. **2.** A distinguishing feature or attribute; characteristic. **3.** The combined moral or ethical structure of a person or group. **4.** Moral or ethical strength; integrity; fortitude. **5.** Public estimation of someone; reputation. **6.** Status, capacity, or role: *in his character as a father.* **7.** *Informal.* A person who is peculiar or eccentric. **8.** An important, influential person; personage. **9.** A person portrayed in a drama, novel, or other artistic piece. **10.** A description of a person's attributes, traits, or abilities. **11.** A formal written statement as to competency and dependability, given by an employer to a former employee; recommendation. **12.** A symbol or mark used in a writing system. **13.** *Computer Sci.* **a.** One of a set of symbols, as letters or numbers, arranged to express information. **b.** The multi-bit code representing such a character. **14.** A style of printing or writing. **15.** A symbol used in secret writing; a cipher or code. **16.** *Genetics.* A structure, function, or attribute determined by a gene or group of genes. —*adj.* **1.** Capable of acting in roles that emphasize traits markedly different from those of the performer himself: *a character actor.* **2.** Of or calling for the abilities of a character actor: *a character part.* —*tr.v.* **-tered, -ter·ing, -ters. 1.** To write, print, engrave, or inscribe. **2.** *Archaic.* To portray, describe, or represent. **—*idiom.* in** (or **out of**) **character.** Consistent (or not consistent) with someone's general character or behavior. [ME *carecter* < Lat. *character* < Gk. *kharaktēr* < *kharassein,* to inscribe.]

char·ac·ter·is·tic (kăr'ək-tə-rĭs'tĭk) *adj.* Pertaining to, indicating, or constituting a distinctive character, quality, or disposition; typical: *the characteristic quiet of the countryside.* —*n.* **1.** A distinguishing feature or attribute. **2.** *Math.* The integral part of a logarithm as distinguished from the mantissa: *6 is the characteristic of the logarithm 6.3214.* **—char'ac·ter·is'ti·cal·ly** *adv.*

char·ac·ter·i·za·tion (kăr'ək-tər-ĭ-zā'shən) *n.* **1.** The act of characterizing. **2.** A description or representation of a person's qualities or peculiarities. **3.** The creation or delineation of a character or characters on the stage or in writing, esp. by imitating or describing actions, gestures, or speeches.

char·ac·ter·ize (kăr'ək-tə-rīz') *tr.v.* **-ized, -iz·ing, -iz·es. 1.** To describe the qualities or peculiarities of: *characterized him as ruthless.* **2.** To be a distinguishing trait or mark of: *a novel characterized by its humor.* **—char'ac·ter·iz'er** *n.*

char·ac·ter·y (kăr'ək-tə-rē, kə-răk'-) *n., pl.* **-ies.** A system of characters or symbols used to express or convey thought and meaning.

cha·rade (shə-rād') *n.* **1. a. charades.** A game in which words or phrases are represented in pantomime, sometimes syllable by syllable, until they are guessed by the other players. **b.** An episode in this game or the word so represented. **2.** A pretense that is readily perceived; travesty. [Fr.]

char·broil (chär'broil') *tr.v.* **-broiled, -broil·ing, -broils.** To broil over charcoal: *charbroil a steak.* [CHAR[1] + BROIL.]

char·coal (chär'kōl') *n.* **1.** A black, porous carbonaceous material produced by the destructive distillation of wood and used as a fuel, filter, and absorbent. **2.** A drawing pencil or crayon made from charcoal. **3.** A drawing executed with a charcoal pencil or crayon. **4.** A dark grayish brown to black or dark purplish gray. —*tr.v.* **-coaled, -coal·ing, -coals.** To draw, write, or blacken with charcoal. [ME *charcol.*]

charcoal rot *n.* A disease of plants that is caused by a fungus, *Macrophomina phaseoli,* and results in black, decayed tissue.

Char·cot's disease (shär-kōz') *n.* Multiple sclerosis.

chard (chärd) *n.* A variety of beet, *Beta vulgaris cicla,* that has large, succulent leaves used as a vegetable. [Fr. *carde* < OProv. *cardon,* cardoon. —see CARDOON.]

charge (chärj) *v.* **charged, charg·ing, charg·es.** —*tr.* **1.** To entrust with a duty, responsibility, or obligation: *charged her with the task of supervising the beginners.* **2.** To instruct, command, or urge authoritatively: *charged him not to reveal the source of information.* **3.** To blame, accuse, or impute something to: *charged him with the crime.* **4.** To set or ask (a given amount) as a price: *charges ten dollars for a haircut.* **5.** To hold financially liable; demand payment from: *charged her for the balance due.* **6.** To postpone payment on (a service or purchase) by recording as a debt: *charging a new coat.* **7.** To attack violently. **8. a.** To direct or put (a weapon) into position for use. **b.** To load (a gun or other firearm). **9.** To instruct (a jury) about legal parts and the weight of evidence. Used of a judge. **10.** *Elect.* **a.** To cause formation of a net electric charge on or in (a conductor, for example). **b.** To energize (a storage battery). **11. a.** To furnish or fill to capacity: *an argument charged with emotion.* **b.** To cause to be saturated; impregnate: *The air was charged with perfume.* **12.** To place a heraldic bearing on. —*intr.* **1.** To rush forward in or as if in a violent attack.

chapman
16th-century German woodcut

chaps
Frederic Remington drawing of a cowboy wearing chaps

2. To demand or ask payment: *charged for the x-rays.* **3.** To make an entry to one's debit. **—phrasal verb. charge off.** To consider as a loss. *—n.* **1.** Care, custody, or supervision: *the scientist in charge of the experiment.* **2.** An obligation or responsibility. **3.** Someone or something entrusted to one's care or management. **4.** An order, command, or injunction. **5.** Instruction given by a judge to a jury about such matters as legal points and the weight of evidence. **6.** An accusation or indictment: *a charge of conspiracy to defraud.* **7. a.** Expense; cost. **b.** The price set or asked for something: *no charge for window-shopping.* **8.** A financial burden, as a tax or lien. **9.** A debt or an entry in an account recording a debt: *paying cash or is this a charge?* **10. a.** A rushing, forceful attack. **b.** The command to attack. **11.** *Informal.* A feeling of pleasant excitement; thrill: *got a real charge out of the movie.* **12.** The maximum quantity that an apparatus or container can hold at one time. **13.** A quantity of explosive to be set off at one time. **14. a.** The intrinsic property of matter responsible for all electric phenomena, in particular for the force of the electromagnetic interaction, occurring in two forms arbitrarily designated *negative* and *positive.* **b.** A measure of this property. **c.** By extension, the net measure of this property possessed by a body or contained in a bounded region of space. **15.** A heraldic bearing or figure. [ME < OFr. *chargier,* to load < LLat. *carricare* < Lat. *carrus,* cart, of Celtic orig.]

chariot
5th-century B.C. Greek vase

charge·a·ble (chär′jə-bəl) *adj.* **1.** Suitable to be charged, as to an account. **2.** Liable to be accused or indicted. **—charge′a·ble·ness** *n.*

charge account *n.* A business arrangement of credit in which the customer receives purchases or services prior to payment.

charge conjugation *n.* **1.** A mathematical operator that changes the sign of the charge and of the magnetic moment of every particle in the system to which it is applied. **2.** The theoretical conversion of matter to antimatter or of antimatter to matter.

charm
Above: From the New Hebrides
Below: 18th-century silver charm from New Hampshire

char·gé d'af·faires (shär-zhā′ də-fâr′) *n., pl.* **char·gés d'af·faires** (-zhā′, -zhāz′). **1.** A governmental official temporarily placed in charge of diplomatic affairs while the ambassador or minister is absent. **2.** A diplomatic representative of the lowest rank, accredited by his government to the minister of foreign affairs of another. [Fr. : *chargé,* charged + *d'affaires,* with affairs.]

charge density *n.* The electric charge per unit area or per unit volume of a body or of a region of space.

charg·er[1] (chär′jər) *n.* **1.** One that charges. **2.** A horse trained for battle; cavalry horse. **3.** An instrument that charges or replenishes storage batteries.

char·ger[2] (chär′jər) *n. Archaic.* A large, shallow dish; platter. [ME *chargeour* < OFr. < *chargier,* to load. —see CHARGE.]

char·i·ness (châr′ē-nĭs) *n.* **1.** The quality of being chary; carefulness; frugality. **2.** *Obs.* Strict integrity.

char·i·ot (chăr′ē-ət) *n.* **1.** An ancient horse-drawn two-wheeled vehicle used in war, races, and processions. **2.** A light four-wheeled carriage used for occasions of ceremony or for pleasure. *—tr. & intr.v.* **-ot·ed, -ot·ing, -ots.** To convey or ride in a chariot. [ME < OFr. *charriote* < *char,* cart < Lat. *carrus,* of Celtic orig.]

char·i·o·teer (chăr′ē-ə-tîr′) *n.* **1.** A person who drives a chariot. **2. Charioteer.** Auriga.

cha·ris·ma (kə-rĭz′mə) also **char·ism** (kăr′ĭz′əm) *n., pl.* **-ma·ta** (-mə-tə) also **-isms. 1. a.** A rare quality or power attributed to those persons who have demonstrated an exceptional ability for winning the devotion of large numbers of people. **b.** A special quality of personal magnetism or charm. **2.** *Theol.* A divinely inspired gift or power, such as the ability to perform miracles. [Gk. *kharisma,* divine gift < *kharizesthai,* to favor < *kharis,* favor.]

char·is·mat·ic (kăr′ĭz-măt′ĭk) *adj.* **1.** Of, relating to, or characterized by charisma. **2.** Of, relating to, or being a Christian religious movement that emphasizes divinely inspired powers or gifts, as of healing or prophecy. *—n.* A member of a charismatic group or movement.

char·i·ta·ble (chăr′ĭ-tə-bəl) *adj.* **1.** Generous in giving money or other help to the needy. **2.** Mild or tolerant in judging others; lenient. **3.** Of, for, or concerned with charity: *a charitable organization.* **—char′i·ta·ble·ness** *n.* **—char′i·ta·bly** *adv.*

char·i·ty (chăr′ĭ-tē) *n., pl.* **-ties. 1.** The provision of help or relief to the poor; almsgiving. **2.** Something that is given to help the needy; alms. **3.** An institution, organization, or fund established to help the needy. **4.** An act or feeling of benevolence, good will, or affection. **5.** Indulgence or forbearance in judging others; leniency. **6.** *Theol.* **a.** The benevolence of God toward man. **b.** The love of man for his fellow men; brotherly love. [ME *charite* < OFr., Christian love < Lat. *caritas,* affection < *carus,* dear.]

cha·ri·va·ri also **chiv·a·ree** (shĭv′ə-rē′, shĭv′ə-rē′) *n., pl.* **-ris** also **-rees.** A noisy mock serenade to newlyweds. [Fr. < LLat. *caribaria,* headache < Gk. *karēbaria* : *karē,* head + *barus,* heavy.]

char·kha also **char·ka** (chûr′kə, chär′-) *n.* In India, a spinning wheel, esp. one used for cotton. [Hindi *carkha.*]

char·la·tan (shär′lə-tən) *n.* A person who claims to possess knowledge or skill that he does not have; quack. [Fr. < Ital. *ciarlatano,* perh. < *ciarlare,* to prattle.] **—char′la·tan′ic** (-tăn′ĭk), **char′la·tan′i·cal** *adj.* **—char′la·tan·ism, char′la·tan·ry** *n.*

Charles's law (chärl′zĭz) *n.* The physical law that the volume of a fixed mass of gas held at a constant pressure varies directly with the absolute temperature. [After Jacques *Charles* (1746–1823), its formulator.]

Charles's Wain (wān) *n.* The Big Dipper. [After *Charlemagne* (742–814).]

Charles·ton (chärl′stən) *n.* A fast dance in 4/4 time, popular during the 1920's. [After *Charleston,* South Carolina.]

char·ley horse (chär′lē) *n. Informal.* A cramp or stiffness of various muscles in the body, esp. in the arm or leg, caused by injury or excessive exertion. [Orig. unknown.]

char·lock (chär′lək, -lŏk′) *n.* A weedy plant, *Brassica kaber,* native to Eurasia, having hairy stems, foliage, and yellow flowers. [ME *cherlok* < OE *cerlic.*]

char·lotte (shär′lət) *n.* A dessert consisting of a mold of sponge cake or bread with a filling, as of fruits, whipped cream, or custard. [Fr.< *Charlotte,* Charlotte.]

charlotte russe (ro͞os′) *n.* A cold dessert of Bavarian cream set in a mold lined with ladyfingers. [Fr. : *charlotte,* charlotte + *russe,* Russian.]

charm (chärm) *n.* **1.** The power or quality of pleasing, attracting, or fascinating. **2.** A particular quality or feature that fascinates or attracts: *"The charm of friendship is liberty"* (Gibbon). **3.** A trinket or small ornament worn on a bracelet or other jewelry. **4.** Something worn for its supposed magical effect, as in warding off evil; amulet. **5.** An action or formula thought to have magical power. **6.** The chanting of a magic word or verse; incantation. **7.** *Physics.* A quantum property of one of the quarks whose conservation explains the absence of certain strange-particle decay modes and that accounts for the longevity of the J particle. *—v.* **charmed, charm·ing, charms.** *—tr.* **1.** To attract or delight greatly or irresistibly; fascinate. **2.** To act upon with or as if with magic; bewitch. *—intr.* **1.** To be alluring or pleasing. **2.** To act as an amulet or charm. **3.** To employ spells. [ME *charme,* magic spell < OFr. < Lat. *carmen,* incantation.] **—charm′ing·ly** *adv.*

charm·er (chär′mər) *n.* **1.** A person, esp. an attractive woman, who charms or has the power to charm. **2.** A sorcerer.

char·mo·ni·um (chär-mō′nē-əm) *n.* Any of various elementary particles consisting of a charm quark and antiquark. [< CHARM.]

char·nel (chär′nəl) *n.* A charnel house. *—adj.* Resembling, suggesting, or suitable for receiving the dead. [ME < OFr. < LLat. *carnale* < Lat. *caro,* flesh.]

charnel house *n.* A building, room, or vault in which the bones or bodies of the dead are placed.

Char·on (kâr′ən) *n. Gk. Myth.* The ferryman who conveyed the dead to Hades over the river Styx. [Lat. < Gk. *Kharōn.*]

char·qui (chär′kē) *n.* Jerky[2]. [Sp. < Quechua *ch'arki.*]

charr (chär) *n.* Variant of **char**[2].

chart (chärt) *n.* **1.** A map showing coastlines, water depths, or other information of use to navigators. **2.** An outline map on which special information, as weather data, can be plotted. **3.** A sheet presenting information in the form of graphs or tables. **4.** A graph (sense 2). *—tr.v.* **chart·ed, chart·ing, charts. 1.** To make a chart of. **2.** To plan in detail. [< OFr. *charte* < Lat. *charta,* papyrus leaf. —see CARD[1].]

char·ta·ceous (kär-tā′shəs) *adj.* Resembling paper; papery. [LLat. *chartaceus* < Lat. *charta,* papyrus leaf. —see CARD[1].]

char·ter (chär′tər) *n.* **1.** A document issued by a sovereign, legislature, or other authority, creating a public or private corporation, as a city, college, or bank, and defining its privileges and purposes. **2.** A written grant from the sovereign power of a country conferring certain rights and privileges upon a person, a corporation, or the people. **3.** A document outlining the principles, functions, and organization of a corporate body; constitution. **4.** An authorization from a central organization to establish a local branch or chapter. **5.** A special privilege or immunity. **6.** A contract for the commercial leasing of a vessel or space on a vessel. **7.** The hiring or leasing of an aircraft, vessel, or other vehicle. **8.** A written instrument given as evidence of agreement, transfer, or contract; deed. *—tr.v.* **-tered, -ter·ing, -ters. 1.** To grant a charter to; establish by charter. **2.** To hire or lease by charter. **3.** To hire (a vehicle). [ME *chartre* < OFr. < Lat. *chartula,* dim. of *charta,* papyrus leaf. —see CARD[1].] **—char′ter·er** *n.*

chartered accountant *n. Chiefly Brit.* A member of one of the institutes of accountants granted a royal charter.

char·ter·house (chär′tər-hous′) *n.* A Carthusian monastery. [By folk ety. < OFr. *chartrouse.* —see CHARTREUSE.]

charter member *n.* An original member or founder of an organization.

Chart·ism (chär′tĭz′əm) *n.* The principles and practices of a party of social and political reformers, chiefly workingmen, active in England from 1838 to 1848.

chart·ist (chär′tĭst) *n.* **1.** A stock-market specialist who uses charts and graphic records to interpret market action, predict trends, or forecast price movements of individual stocks. **2. Chartist.** An advocate of Chartism.

char·treuse (shär-tro͞oz′, -tro͞os′, -trœz′) *n.* A strong to brilliant greenish yellow to moderate or strong yellow green. [< *Chartreuse*.] **—char·treuse′** *adj.*

Chartreuse. A trademark for a green or yellow liqueur.

char·treu·sin (shär-trōō′zĭn, -sĭn) *n.* An antibiotic, $C_{18}H_{18}O_{18}$, effective against some Gram-positive microorganisms and derived from a strain of *Streptomyces chartreusis.* [NLat. *chartreusis,* specific epithet of *Streptomyces chartreusis* + -IN.]

char·tu·lar·y (kär′chə-lĕr′ē) *n.* Variant of **cartulary**.

char·wom·an (chär′wōōm′ən) *n. Chiefly Brit.* A woman hired to do cleaning or similar work, usually in a large building.

char·y (châr′ē) *adj.* **-i·er, -i·est. 1.** Very cautious; wary: *chary of the risks involved.* **2.** Shy: *chary of meeting people.* **3.** Not giving or expending freely; sparing: *chary of compliments.* [ME *chari,* diligent < OE *cearig,* sorrowful.] **—char′i·ly** *adv.*

Cha·ryb·dis (kə-rĭb′dĭs) *n. Gk. Myth.* A whirlpool off the Sicilian coast, opposite the cave of Scylla. [Lat. < Gk. *Kharubdis.*]

chase[1] (chās) *v.* **chased, chas·ing, chas·es.** *—tr.* **1.** To pursue in order to catch or overtake. **2.** To follow (game) in order to capture or kill; hunt. **3.** To follow earnestly or regularly: *chasing one foolish scheme after another.* **4.** To put to flight; drive: *chased the dog away.* *—intr.* **1.** To go or follow in pursuit. **2.** *Informal.* To go hurriedly; rush: *chased all over looking for us.* *—n.* **1.** The act of chasing; pursuit. **2. a. the chase.** The sport of hunting. **b.** Something that is hunted or pursued; quarry. **3.** *Chiefly Brit.* **a.** A privately owned, unenclosed game preserve. **b.** The right to hunt or keep game on the land of others. [ME *chacen,* to hunt < OFr. *chacier* < Lat. *captare.* —see CATCH.]

chase[2] (chās) *n. Printing.* A rectangular steel or iron frame into which pages or columns of type are locked for printing or plate making. [Perh. < Fr. *chasse,* case < Lat. *capsa.*]

chase[3] (chās) *n.* **1. a.** A groove cut in an object; slot: *the chase for the quarrel on a crossbow.* **b.** A trench or channel for drainpipes or wiring. **c.** A longitudinal groove for a tenon or tongue. **2.** The part of a gun in front of the trunnions. *—tr.v.* **chased, chas·ing, chas·es. 1.** To decorate (metal) by engraving or embossing. **2. a.** To groove; indent. **b.** To cut (the thread of a screw). [Perh. < OFr. *chas,* enclosure < Lat. *capsa,* box.]

chas·er[1] (chā′sər) *n.* **1.** One that chases or pursues. **2.** *Informal.* A drink, as of beer, taken after hard liquor.

chas·er[2] (chā′sər) *n.* **1.** One who decorates metal by engraving or embossing. **2.** A steel tool for cutting or finishing screw threads.

chasm (kăz′əm) *n.* **1.** A deep cleft or crack in the earth's surface. **2.** A sudden interruption of continuity; gap. **3.** A pronounced difference of opinion, interests, or loyalty. [Lat. *chasma* < Gk. *khasma.*] **—chas′mal** (kăz′məl) *adj.*

chas·sé (shă-sā′) *n.* A dance movement consisting of one or more quick, gliding steps with the same foot always leading. *—intr.v.* **-séd, -sé·ing, -sés.** To make or perform a chassé. [Fr. < *chasser,* to chase < OFr. *chacier.* —see CHASE[1].]

chasse·pot (shăs′pō′) *n.* A type of breech-loading rifle introduced into the French army in 1866. [Fr., after Antoine *Chassepot* (1833–1905), its inventor.]

chas·seur (shă-sûr′) *n.* **1.** A soldier, esp. one of certain light cavalry or infantry troops trained for rapid maneuvers. **2.** A huntsman. **3.** A uniformed footman. [Fr. < OFr. *chaceor* < *chacier,* to pursue. —see CHASE[1].]

Chas·sid (KHă′sĭd) *n., pl.* **Chas·si·dim** (KHă-sē′dĭm). A member of a sect of Jewish mystics founded in Poland about 1750 in opposition to the formalistic Judaism of the period and to ritual laxity. [Heb. *hasīdh,* pious.] **—Chas·si′dic** *adj.* **—Chas′si′dism** *n.*

chas·sis (shăs′ē, chăs′ē) *n., pl.* **chas·sis** (-ēz). **1.** The rectangular steel frame, supported on springs and attached to the axles, that holds the body and motor of an automotive vehicle. **2.** The landing gear of an aircraft, including the wheels, floats, and other structures that support the aircraft on land or water. **3.** The frame on which a casement gun carriage moves forward and backward. **4.** The framework to which the functioning parts of a radio, television, phonograph, or other electronic equipment are attached. [Fr. *châssis* < OFr. < VLat. *capsicium* < Lat. *capsa,* box.]

chaste (chāst) *adj.* **chast·er, chast·est. 1.** Morally pure in thought and conduct; decent; modest. **2. a.** Not having experienced sexual intercourse; virginal. **b.** Abstaining from unlawful sexual intercourse. **c.** Abstaining from sexual intercourse; celibate. **3.** Pure or simple design or style; not ornate or extreme. [ME < OFr. < Lat. *castus.*] **—chaste′ly** *adv.* **—chaste′ness** *n.*

chas·ten (chā′sən) *tr.v.* **-tened, -ten·ing, -tens. 1.** To punish, either physically or morally; chastise. **2.** To restrain; moderate. **3.** To refine; purify: *chasten one's writing style.* [Alteration of obs. *chaste* < ME *chasten* < OFr. *chastiier, chastiss-* < Lat. *castigare* < *castus,* pure.] **—chas′ten·er** *n.*

chas·tise (chăs-tīz′) *tr.v.* **-tised, -tis·ing, -tis·es. 1.** To punish, usually by beating. **2.** To criticize severely. **3.** *Archaic.* To purify. [ME *chastisen* < OFr. *chastiier, chastiss-,* to chasten.] **—chas·tis′a·ble** *adj.* **—chas·tise′ment** (chăs-tīz′mənt, chăs′tĭz-mənt) *n.* **—chas·tis′er** *n.*

chas·ti·ty (chăs′tĭ-tē) *n.* **1.** The state or quality of being chaste or pure. **2. a.** Virginity. **b.** Virtuousness. **c.** Celibacy. [ME *chastite* < OFr. *chastete* < Lat. *castitas* < *castus,* pure.]

chastity belt *n.* A device worn by medieval women to prevent sexual intercourse.

chas·u·ble (chăz′ə-bəl, chăzh′ə-, chăs′ə-) *n.* A long, sleeveless vestment worn over the alb by a priest at Mass. [Fr. < OFr. < LLat. *casubla,* hooded garment.]

chat (chăt) *intr.v.* **chat·ted, chat·ting, chats.** To converse in an easy, informal, or familiar manner. *—n.* **1.** An informal or familiar conversation. **2.** Any of several birds known for their chattering call, as of the genera *Saxicola* or *Icteria.* [ME *chatten,* to jabber, short for *chateren.*]

cha·teau also **châ·teau** (shă-tō′) *n., pl.* **-teaux** (-tōz′). **1.** A French castle or manor house. **2.** A large country house. [Fr. *château* < OFr. *chastel* < Lat. *castellum,* castle. —see CASTLE.]

Châ·teau·bri·and also **châ·teau·bri·and** (shă-tō′-brē-äN′) *n.* **1.** A double-thick tender center cut of beef tenderloin. **2.** A cut of Châteaubriand in which a pocket is cut and filled with various seasonings before grilling. [After Vicomte de *Châteaubriand,* François René (1768–1848).]

chat·e·lain (shăt′l-ān′) *n.* The keeper of a castle; castellan. [ME *chatelein* < OFr. *chastelain* < Lat. *castellanus* < *castellum,* castle. —see CASTLE.]

chat·e·laine (shăt′l-ān′) *n.* **1. a.** The mistress of a castle or chateau. **b.** The mistress of a large, fashionable household. **2.** A clasp or chain worn at the waist for holding keys, a purse, or a watch. [Fr. *châtelaine,* fem. of *châtelain,* chatelain < OFr. *chastelain.*]

cha·toy·an·cy (shə-toi′ən-sē) *n.* The state or quality of being chatoyant.

cha·toy·ant (shə-toi′ənt) *adj.* Having a changeable luster. *—n.* A chatoyant stone or gemstone, such as the cat's-eye. [Fr., pr.part. of *chatoyer,* to shimmer < *chat,* cat.]

chat·tel (chăt′l) *n.* **1.** An article of personal, movable property. **2.** A slave. [ME *chatel,* property < OFr. < Med. Lat. *capitale.* —see CATTLE.]

chattel mortgage *n.* A mortgage on personal property as security for an obligation or debt.

chat·ter (chăt′ər) *v.* **-tered, -ter·ing, -ters.** *—intr.* **1.** To utter a rapid series of short, inarticulate, speechlike sounds: *birds chattering in the trees.* **2.** To talk rapidly, incessantly, and on a trivial subject; jabber. **3.** To click quickly and repeatedly: *teeth chattering from the cold; machine guns chattering in the distance.* **4.** To vibrate or rattle while in operation, as a power tool. *—tr.* To utter in a rapid and aimless way. *—n.* **1.** Idle or trivial talk. **2.** The sharp, rapid sounds made by some birds and animals. **3.** A series of quick rattling or clicking sounds. [ME *chateren.*] **—chat′ter·er** *n.*

chat·ter·box (chăt′ər-bŏks′) *n.* An extremely talkative person.

chatter mark also **chat·ter·mark** (chăt′ər-märk′) *n.* **1.** A riblike marking on wood or metal, caused by vibration of a cutting tool. **2.** *Geol.* One of a series of short scars on a glaciated rock surface.

chat·ty (chăt′ē) *adj.* **-ti·er, -ti·est. 1.** Given to informal conversation. **2.** Informal; familiar: *a chatty letter-writing style.* **—chat′ti·ly** *adv.* **—chat′ti·ness** *n.*

chaud·froid (shō-frwä′) *n.* **1.** A jellied white or brown sauce used as an aspic for cold meats or fish. **2.** Molded cold meat or fish dishes garnished with a chaudfroid sauce. [Fr. : *chaud,* hot + *froid,* cold.]

chauf·feur (shō′fər, shō-fûr′) *n.* One employed to drive a private automobile. *—v.* **-feured, -feur·ing, -feurs.** *—tr.* **1.** To serve as a driver for (someone). **2.** To convey as a chauffeur does: *chauffeured the guests around town.* *—intr.* To serve as a chauffeur. [Fr., stoker < *chauffer,* to heat < OFr. *chaufer.* —see CHAFE.]

chaul·moo·gra (chôl-mōō′grə) *n.* Any of several trees of tropical Asia, esp. *Taraktogenos kurzii* and those of the genus *Hydnocarpus,* having seeds that yield an oil used in treating leprosy. [Bengali *cāulmugrā* : *cāul,* rice + *mugrā,* hemp.]

chaunt (chônt, chänt) *n. & v. Archaic.* Variant of **chant**.

chausses (shōs) *pl.n.* Medieval armor of mail for the legs and feet. [ME *chauces* < OFr. < Lat. *calceus,* shoe.]

chau·vin·ism (shō′və-nĭz′əm) *n.* **1.** Militant devotion to and glorification of one's country; fanatical patriotism. **2.** Prejudiced belief in the superiority of one's own group: *male chauvinism.* [Fr. *chauvinisme,* after Nicholas *Chauvin,* a legendary French soldier.] **—chau′vin·ist** *n.* **—chau′vin·is′tic** (-nĭs′tĭk) *adj.* **—chau′vin·is′ti·cal·ly** *adv.*

chaw (chô) *Regional. —intr. & tr.v.* **chawed, chaw·ing, chaws.** To chew. *—n.* A chew. [Var. of CHEW.]

cha·yo·te (chä-yō′tā) *n.* **1.** A tropical American vine, *Sechium edule,* bearing edible squashlike fruit. **2.** The fruit of the chayote. [Sp. < Nahuatl *chayotli.*]

cha·zan or **chaz·zen** (KHä′zən) *n.* A cantor in a synagogue. [Heb. *hazzān.*]

cheap (chēp) *adj.* **-er, -est. 1.** Relatively low in cost; inexpensive or comparatively inexpensive. **2.** Charging low prices: *a cheap restaurant.* **3.** Requiring little effort: *a cheap victory.* **4.** Of or considered of small value: *Life was very cheap.* **5.** Of poor quality; inferior. **6.** Not worthy of respect; vulgar: *cheap jokes.* **7.** Stingy; miserly. **8.** *Econ.* **a.** Obtainable at a low rate of interest. **b.** Devalued, as in buying power: *cheap dollars.* *—adv.* Inexpensively. [< ME

chase[2]

chep, price, purchase < OE *cēap,* trade < Lat. *caupo,* tradesman.] **—cheap'ly** *adv.* **—cheap'ness** *n.*

cheap·en (chē'pən) *v.* **-ened, -en·ing, -ens.** *—tr.* **1.** To make cheap or cheaper. **2.** To deprecate, disparage, or belittle. *—intr.* To become cheap or cheaper. **—cheap'en·er** *n.*

cheap shot *n.* An unjust action or statement directed esp. at a vulnerable target, as a public figure.

cheap·skate also **cheap skate** (chēp'skāt') *n. Slang.* A stingy person; miser.

cheat (chēt) *v.* **cheat·ed, cheat·ing, cheats.** *—tr.* **1.** To deceive by trickery; swindle. **2.** To mislead; fool. **3.** To deprive by trickery; defraud: *cheated the Indians of their land.* **4.** To elude; escape: *cheat death.* *—intr.* **1.** To act dishonestly; practice fraud. **2.** *Informal.* To be sexually unfaithful: *cheating on his wife.* *—n.* **1.** A fraud or swindle. **2.** A swindler. **3.** *Law.* The fraudulent acquisition of another's property. **4.** A grass, *Bromus secalinus,* having rough blades and wheatlike ears. [ME *cheten,* to confiscate, short for *acheten,* var. of *escheten* < *eschete,* escheat. —see ESCHEAT.] **—cheat'er** *n.* **—cheat'ing·ly** *adv.*

check (chĕk) *n.* **1.** An abrupt halt or stop. **2.** A restraint or control: *kept a check on his impulses.* **3.** One that restrains or controls. **4.** Supervised control, as of accuracy or efficiency. **5.** A standard of comparison to verify accuracy; test. **6.** A mark to show verification or approval. **7.** A ticket or slip of identification: *a baggage check.* **8.** A bill at a restaurant or bar. **9.** A chip or counter used in gambling games. **10.** A written order to a bank to pay the amount specified from funds on deposit; draft. **11. a.** A pattern of small squares, as on a chessboard. **b.** One of the squares of such a pattern. **c.** A fabric patterned with such squares. **12.** A small crack or chink. **13. a.** A move in chess that directly attacks an opponent's king but does not constitute a checkmate. **b.** The position or tactical condition of a king so attacked. **14.** The act of impeding an opponent in control of the puck in ice hockey, either by blocking his progress with the body or by jabbing at the puck with the stick. *—interj.* **1.** Used to declare to a chess opponent that his king is in check. **2.** *Informal.* Used to express agreement or understanding. *—v.* **checked, check·ing, checks.** *—tr.* **1.** To arrest the motion of abruptly; halt. **2.** To hold in restraint; curb: *check an impulse.* **3.** To slow the growth of; retard. **4.** To rebuke; rebuff. **5.** To test or examine, as for accuracy or efficiency; verify; investigate. **6.** To put a check mark on or next to: *checked off each item on the list.* **7.** To deposit for temporary safekeeping: *check your hat.* **8.** To make cracks or chinks in. **9.** To move in chess so as to put (an opponent's king) under direct attack. **10.** To impede an opponent in control of the puck in ice hockey, either by using the body to block the opponent or by jabbing at the puck with the hockey stick. *—intr.* **1.** To come to an abrupt halt; stop. **2.** To have item-for-item correspondence; agree. **3.** To make an examination or investigation to determine accuracy or verification: *phoned to check on his departure time.* **4.** To write a check on a bank account. **5.** To undergo cracking in a pattern of checks, as paint. **6.** To pause to relocate a scent. Used of hunting dogs. **7.** To place a chess opponent's king in check. **8.** In falconry, to abandon the proper game and follow baser prey. ***—phrasal verbs.*** **check in.** To register, as at a hotel. **check out. 1.** To leave after going through a required procedure, as after paying a hotel bill. **2.** To take after a recording procedure: *check out books from the library.* ***—idiom.*** **in check.** Under restraint; in control. [ME *chek,* check in chess < OFr. *eschec* < Ar. *shāh* < Pers., king, king in chess.] **—check'a·ble** *adj.*

check·book (chĕk'bo͝ok') *n.* A book containing blank checks issued by a bank.

checked (chĕkt) *adj.* **1.** Having a pattern of checks or squares. **2.** Held in check; restrained. **3.** Situated in a stopped or closed syllable: *a checked vowel.*

check·er (chĕk'ər) *n.* **1. a. checkers** *(used with a sing. verb).* A game played on a checkerboard by two players, each using 12 pieces. **b.** One of the round, flat pieces used in this game. **2. a.** A pattern of checks or squares. **b.** One of the squares in such a pattern. **3.** One who checks, examines, or supervises. **4.** One who receives items for temporary storage or safekeeping: *a baggage checker.* **5.** A cashier. *—tr.v.* **-ered, -er·ing, -ers. 1.** To mark with a checked or squared pattern. **2.** To diversify in color, shading, or character; variegate. [ME *cheker,* chessboard < OFr. *eschequier* < *eschec,* check in chess. —see CHECK.]

checker

check·er·ber·ry (chĕk'ər-bĕr'ē) *n.* **1.** The wintergreen. **2.** The red, edible, spicy berry of the wintergreen. [CHECKER, the wild service tree (dial.) + BERRY.]

check·er·bloom (chĕk'ər-blo͞om') *n.* A plant, *Sidalcea malvaeflora,* of California, with long clusters of rose-pink flowers. [CHECKER, the wild service tree (dial.) + BLOOM.]

check·er·board (chĕk'ər-bôrd', -bōrd') *n.* A game board divided into 64 squares of two alternating colors on which chess and checkers are played.

check·ered (chĕk'ərd) *adj.* **1.** Divided into squares. **2.** Marked by light and dark patches; diversified in color. **3.** Marked by great changes or shifts in fortune: *a checkered career.*

checking account *n.* A bank account in which checks may be written against amounts on deposit.

check list *n.* A list in which items can be compared, scheduled, verified, or identified.

check·mate (chĕk'māt') *tr.v.* **-mat·ed, -mat·ing, -mates. 1.** To attack (a chess opponent's king) in such manner that no escape or defense is possible, thus ending the game. **2.** To defeat completely. *—n.* **1. a.** A move that constitutes an inescapable and indefensible attack on a chess opponent's king. **b.** The position or strategic condition of a king so attacked. **2.** Utter defeat. *—interj.* Used to declare the checkmate of an opponent's king in chess. [ME *chekmat* < OFr. *eschec mat* < Ar. *shāh māt,* the king is dead < Pers.]

check·off (chĕk'ôf', -ŏf') *n.* The collection of dues from members of a union by authorized deduction from their wages.

check·out (chĕk'out') *n.* **1.** The act, time, or place of checking out, as at a supermarket, library, or hotel. **2.** A test, as of a machine, for proper functioning. **3.** An investigation or inspection.

check·point (chĕk'point') *n.* A place where surface traffic is stopped for inspection.

check·rein (chĕk'rān') *n.* **1.** A short rein connected from a horse's bit to the saddle to keep a horse from lowering its head. **2.** A rein joining the bit of one of a span of horses to the driving rein of the other horse.

check·room (chĕk'ro͞om', -ro͝om') *n.* A place where hats, coats, packages, or other items can be stored temporarily.

check·row (chĕk'rō') *n.* A row, as of corn, in which the distance between plants is the same as the distance between adjacent rows to permit cross cultivation. *—tr.v.* **-rowed, -row·ing, -rows.** To plant in checkrows.

checks and balances *pl.n.* The system of maintaining a balance of power between various branches of a government.

check·up (chĕk'ŭp') *n.* **1.** A thorough examination, as for verification or accuracy. **2.** A physical examination.

Ched·dar also **ched·dar** (chĕd'ər) *n.* Any of several types of smooth, hard cheese varying in flavor from mild to extra sharp. [After *Cheddar,* England.]

cheek (chēk) *n.* **1.** The fleshy part of either side of the face below the eye and between the nose and ear. **2.** Something resembling the cheek in shape or position, as either of two sides of something. **3.** Either of the buttocks. **4.** Excessive, arrogant self-confidence. *—tr.v.* **cheeked, cheek·ing, cheeks.** *Informal.* To speak impudently to. ***—idiom.*** **cheek by jowl.** Side by side; in close contact. [ME *cheke* < OE *cēace.*]

cheek·bone (chēk'bōn') *n.* The zygomatic bone.

cheek pouch *n.* An enlargement in the cheeks of some rodents that functions as a means of carrying food.

cheek·y (chē'kē) *adj.* **-i·er, -i·est.** Saucy, impudent, or brazen. **—cheek'i·ly** *adv.* **—cheek'i·ness** *n.*

cheep (chēp) *n.* A faint, shrill sound like that of a young bird; chirp. *—tr. & intr.v.* **cheeped, cheep·ing, cheeps.** To chirp; peep. [Imit.] **—cheep'er** *n.*

cheer (chîr) *n.* **1.** Gaiety; animation; happiness. **2.** Something that gives joy or happiness; comfort. **3.** A shout of approval, encouragement, or congratulation. **4.** Food or drink; refreshment. *—interj.* **cheers.** Used as a toast. *—v.* **cheered, cheer·ing, cheers.** *—tr.* **1.** To make happier or more cheerful: *a warm fire that cheered us up.* **2.** To encourage with or as if with cheers; urge: *The fans cheered the runners on.* **3.** To salute or acclaim with cheers; applaud. *—intr.* **1.** To shout cheers; applaud. **2.** To become cheerful: *had lunch and soon cheered up.* [ME *chere,* mood < OFr. *chiere,* face < LLat. *cara* < Gk. *kara,* head.] **—cheer'er** *n.* **—cheer'ing·ly** *adv.*

cheer·ful (chîr'fəl) *adj.* **1.** Being in good spirits; happy. **2.** Producing a feeling of cheer; pleasant: *a cozy, cheerful room.* **3.** Willing; good-humored: *cheerful labor.* **—cheer'ful·ly** *adv.* **—cheer'ful·ness** *n.*

cheer·i·o (chîr'ē-ō') *interj. Chiefly Brit. Informal.* Used in greeting or parting. [< CHEER.]

cheer·lead·er (chîr'lē'dər) *n.* One who leads the cheering of spectators, as at a football game.

cheer·less (chîr'lĭs) *adj.* Lacking cheer; depressing. **—cheer'less·ly** *adv.* **—cheer'less·ness** *n.*

cheer·y (chîr'ē) *adj.* **-i·er, -i·est.** In good spirits; cheerful. **—cheer'i·ly** *adv.* **—cheer'i·ness** *n.*

cheese[1] (chēz) *n.* **1. a.** A solid food prepared from the pressed curd of milk, often seasoned and aged. **b.** A molded mass of this substance. **2.** Something like cheese in shape or consistency. **3. cheeses. a.** The common mallow, *Malva rotundifolia,* a creeping plant with pale-lavender or white flowers and flat, round, ridged fruits. **b.** The fruit of this plant. [ME *chese* < OE *cyse* < Lat. *caseus.*]

cheese[2] (chēz) *tr.v.* **cheesed, chees·ing, chees·es.** *Slang.* To stop. ***—idiom.*** **cheese it.** *Slang.* **1.** Look out. **2.** Get away fast; vamoose. [Orig. unknown.]

cheese[3] (chēz) *n. Slang.* An important person: *a big cheese.* [Perh. < Urdu *chīz,* thing < Pers.]

cheese·burg·er (chēz'bûr'gər) *n.* A hamburger topped with melted cheese.

cheese·cake (chēz'kāk') *n.* **1.** Also **cheese cake.** A cake made of sweetened cottage cheese or cream cheese, eggs, milk, sugar, and flavorings. **2.** *Slang.* **a.** A photograph of a

ă pat / ā pay / âr care / ä father / b bib / ch church / d deed / ĕ pet / ē be / f fife / g gag / h hat / hw which / ĭ pit / ī pie / îr pier / j judge / k kick / l lid, needle / m mum / n no, sudden / ng thing / ŏ pot / ō toe / ô paw, for / oi noise / ou out / o͝o took / o͞o boot /

pretty girl scantily clothed. **b.** Such photographs collectively.

cheese·cloth (chēz′klôth′, -klŏth′) *n.* A coarse, loosely woven cotton gauze, originally used for wrapping cheese.

cheese-par·ing (chēz′pâr′ĭng) *n.* **1.** Something of little or no value. **2.** Stinginess; parsimony. —*adj.* Miserly; stingy.

chees·y (chē′zē) *adj.* **-i·er, -i·est. 1. a.** Resembling cheese. **b.** Containing cheese. **2.** *Slang.* Of poor quality; shoddy. —**chees′i·ness** *n.*

chee·tah also **che·tah** (chē′tə) *n.* A long-legged, swift-running wild cat, *Acinonyx jubatus,* of Africa and southwestern Asia, that has black-spotted, tawny fur and nonretractile claws and is sometimes trained to pursue game. [Hindi *cītā* < Skt. *citrakāya,* tiger : *citra,* variegated + *kāyaḥ,* body.]

chef (shĕf) *n.* A cook, esp. the chief cook of a large kitchen staff. [Fr., short for *chef de cuisine,* head of the kitchen.]

chef-d'oeu·vre (shā-dœ′vrə, -dûrv′) *n., pl.* **chefs-d'oeuvre** (-dœ′vrə, -dûrv′, -dûrvz′). A masterpiece, esp. in literature or art. [Fr. : *chef,* head + *d'oeuvre,* of work.]

chef's salad *n.* A tossed green salad that usually includes raw vegetables, hard-boiled eggs, and julienne strips of cheese and meat.

chei·lo·sis (kī-lō′sĭs) *n.* Inflammation and fissuring of the lips with cracking at the angles of the mouth due to a deficiency of riboflavin. [Gk. *kheilos,* lip + -OSIS.]

cheiro– *pref.* Variant of **chiro-**.

chei·ro·plas·ty also **chi·ro·plas·ty** (kī′rō-plăs′tē) *n.* Plastic surgery of the hand. [CHIRO- + -PLASTY.]

che·la (kē′lə) *n., pl.* **-lae** (-lē). A pincerlike claw of a crustacean, as of a lobster or crab. [NLat. < Gk. *khēlē,* claw.]

che·late (kē′lāt′) *adj.* **1.** *Zool.* Having or characteristic of a chela. **2.** *Chem.* Of or pertaining to a heterocyclic ring containing a metal ion attached by coordinate bonds to at least two nonmetal ions in the same molecule. —*tr.v.* **-lat·ed, -lat·ing, -lates.** To form a ring compound by joining a chelating agent to a metal ion. —**che′late′** *n.* —**che·la′tion** *n.* —**che′la′tor** *n.*

che·lic·er·a (kĭ-lĭs′ər-ə) *n., pl.* **-er·ae** (-ə-rē′). Either of the first pair of appendages near the mouth of an arachnid, as a spider, often modified for grasping. [NLat. : CHELA + Gk. *keras,* horn.]

che·li·form (kē′lə-fôrm′) *adj.* Having the shape of a chela; pincerlike.

Chel·li·an or **Chel·le·an** (shĕl′ē-ən) *adj. Archaeol.* Abbevillian. [After *Chelles,* a commune in France.]

che·lo·ni·an (kĭ-lō′nē-ən) *adj. Zool.* Of or belonging to the order Chelonia, which includes the turtles and tortoises. —*n.* A member of the Chelonia. [< NLat. *Chelonia,* order name < Gk. *khelōnē,* tortoise.]

chem– or **chemi–** *pref.* Variants of **chemo-**.

chem·ic (kĕm′ĭk) *adj. Archaic.* **1.** Chemical. **2.** Alchemic. —*n. Obs.* An alchemist.

chem·i·cal (kĕm′ĭ-kəl) *adj.* **1.** Of or pertaining to chemistry. **2.** Of or pertaining to the properties or actions of chemicals. —*n.* A substance that is produced by or used in a chemical process. [Obs. *chimical* < *chimic,* alchemist < NLat. *chimicus* < Med. Lat. *alchimicus* < *alchymia,* alchemy. —see ALCHEMY.] —**chem′i·cal·ly** *adv.*

chemical bond *n.* Any of several forces or mechanisms, esp. the ionic bond, covalent bond, and metallic bond, by which atoms or ions are bound in a molecule or crystal.

chemical engineering *n.* The technology of large-scale chemical and chemical materials production. —**chemical engineer** *n.*

Chemical Mace. A trademark for a mixture of organic chemicals used in aerosol form as a weapon to disable with intense burning eye pain, blepharospasm, acute bronchitis, and respiratory irritation.

chemical warfare *n.* Warfare using as direct weapons chemicals other than explosives, esp. irritants, asphyxiants, contaminants, poisons, and incendiaries.

chem·i·lu·mi·nes·cence (kĕm′ə-lo͞o′mə-nĕs′əns) *n.* The emission of light as a result of a chemical reaction at environmental temperatures. —**chem′i·lu′mi·nes′cent** *adj.*

che·min de fer (shə-măN′ də fâr′) *n.* A gambling game that is a variation of baccarat. [Fr. : *chemin,* road + *de,* of + *fer,* iron.]

che·mise (shə-mēz′) *n.* **1.** A woman's loose, shirtlike undergarment. **2.** A shift (sense 7.a.). [ME < OFr., shirt < LLat. *camisia.*]

chem·i·sette (shĕm′ĭ-zĕt′) *n.* **1.** A short, sleeveless bodice, formerly worn by women. **2.** A blouse front formerly worn by women; a dickey. [Fr., dim. of *chemise,* shirt < OFr. —see CHEMISE.]

chem·i·sorb (kĕm′ĭ-sôrb′) also **chem·o·sorb** (-ə-sôrb′) *tr.v.* **-sorbed, -sorb·ing, -sorbs.** To take up and chemically bind (a substance) onto the surface of another substance. [CHEMI- + (AB)SORB.] —**chem′i·sorp′tion** (-sôrp′shən) *n.*

chem·ist (kĕm′ĭst) *n.* **1.** A scientist specializing in chemistry. **2.** *Chiefly Brit.* A pharmacist. **3.** *Obs.* An alchemist. [Obs. *chimist* < NLat. *chimista* < Med. Lat. *alchymista,* alchemist < *alchymia,* alchemy. —see ALCHEMY.]

chem·is·try (kĕm′ĭ-strē) *n., pl.* **-tries. 1.** The science of the composition, structure, properties, and reactions of matter, esp. of atomic and molecular systems. **2.** The composition, structure, properties, and reactions of a substance.

chemo– or **chemi–** or **chem–** *pref.* Chemicals; chemical: *chemotherapy.* [NLat. < LGk. *khēmeia,* alchemy. —see ALCHEMY.]

che·mo·au·to·troph (kē′mō-ô′tə-trŏf′, -trōf′, kĕm′ō-) *n.* An organism that obtains its nutritive substances through inorganic chemical oxidation as opposed to photosynthesis. —**che′mo·au′to·tro′phic** (-trō′fĭk) *adj.* —**che′mo·au′to·tro′phi·cal·ly** *adv.* —**che′mo·au·tot′ro·phy** (-ô-tŏt′rə-fē) *n.* [CHEMO- + AUTO- + Gk. *trophos,* feeder < *trephein,* to cause to grow.]

che·mo·pro·phy·lax·is (kē′mō-prō′fə-lăk′sĭs, kĕm′ō-) *n.* The use of chemicals to prevent infectious disease. —**che′mo·pro′phy·lac′tic** (-tĭk) *adj.*

che·mo·re·cep·tion (kē′mō-rĭ-sĕp′shən, kĕm′ō-) *n.* The reaction of a sense organ to a chemical stimulus. —**che′mo·re·cep′tive** *adj.* —**che′mo·re′cep·tiv′i·ty** (-rē′sĕp-tĭv′ĭ-tē) *n.*

che·mo·re·cep·tor (kē′mō-rĭ-sĕp′tər, kĕm′ō-) *n.* A nerve ending or sense organ, as of smell or taste, sensitive to chemical stimuli.

che·mo·sen·so·ry (kē′mō-sĕn′sə-rē, kĕm′ō-) *adj.* Of or pertaining to the sensory reception of a chemical stimulus.

chem·os·mo·sis (kĕm′ŏz-mō′sĭs, -ŏs-) *n.* The phenomenon of ionic or molecular transport across a membrane. —**chem′os·mot′ic** (-mŏt′ĭk) *adj.*

chem·o·sorb (kĕm′ə-sôrb′) *v.* Variant of **chemisorb.**

che·mo·sphere (kē′mə-sfîr′, kĕm′ə-) *n.* The region of the atmosphere between 20 and 120 miles altitude in which photochemical reactions initiated by solar radiation occur.

che·mo·sur·ger·y (kē′mō-sûr′jə-rē, kĕm′ō-) *n.* The selective destruction of tissue by use of chemicals.

che·mo·syn·the·sis (kē′mō-sĭn′thĭ-sĭs, kĕm′ō-) *n.* The synthesis of organic substances such as food nutrients, using the energy of chemical reactions. —**che′mo·syn·thet′ic** (-sĭn-thĕt′ĭk) *adj.* —**che′mo·syn·thet′i·cal·ly** *adv.*

che·mo·tax·is (kē′mō-tăk′sĭs, kĕm′ō-) *n.* Characteristic orientation or motion of a freely moving living organism relative to a chemical substance. —**che′mo·tac′tic** (-tăk′tĭk) *adj.* —**che′mo·tac′ti·cal·ly** *adv.*

che·mo·tax·on·o·my (kē′mō-tăk-sŏn′ə-mē, kĕm′ō-) *n.* The classification of organisms by use of biochemical criteria. —**che′mo·tax′o·nom′ic** (-tăk′sə-nŏm′ĭk) *adj.* —**chemo·tax′o·nom′i·cal·ly** *adv.* —**che′mo·tax·on′o·mist** *n.*

che·mo·ther·a·py (kē′mō-thĕr′ə-pē, kĕm′ō-) *n.* The treatment of disease with chemicals. —**che′mo·ther′a·peu′tic** (-pyo͞o′tĭk) *adj.*

che·mot·ro·pism (kĭ-mŏt′rə-pĭz′əm) *n.* Movement or growth of an organism, esp. a plant, in response to chemical stimuli. —**che′mo·trop′ic** (kē′mō-trŏp′ĭk, kĕm′ō-) *adj.*

chem·ur·gy (kĕm′ər-jē, kĭ-mûr′-) *n.* The development of new industrial chemical products from organic raw materials, esp. from those of agricultural origin. —**che·mur′gic** (kĭ-mûr′jĭk), **che·mur′gi·cal** *adj.*

che·nille (shə-nēl′) *n.* **1.** A soft, tufted cord of silk, cotton, or worsted used in embroidery or for fringing. **2.** Fabric made of chenille, commonly used for bedspreads or rugs. [Fr. *chenille,* caterpillar < Lat. *canicula,* dim. of *canis,* dog.]

che·no·pod (kē′nə-pŏd′, kĕn′ə-) *n.* A plant of the goosefoot family, Chenopodiaceae, which includes spinach and beets as well as many common weeds. [NLat. *Chenopodiaceae,* family name < *Chenopodium,* type genus : Gk. *khēn,* goose + Gk. *podion,* dim. of *pous,* foot.]

cheque (chĕk) *n. Chiefly Brit.* Variant of **check** (sense 10).

cheq·uer (chĕk′ər) *n. Chiefly Brit.* Variant of **checker.**

cher·i·moy·a (chĕr′ə-moi′ə) *n.* **1.** A tropical American tree, *Annona cherimola,* having yellow flowers and edible fruit with white, soft, aromatic pulp. **2.** The fruit of the cherimoya. [Am. Sp. *chirimoya* < Quechua *chirimuya.*]

cher·ish (chĕr′ĭsh) *tr.v.* **-ished, -ish·ing, -ish·es. 1.** To hold dear; treat with affection and tenderness. **2.** To keep fondly in mind; entertain: *cherish a memory.* [ME *cherishen* < OFr. *cherir, cheriss-* < *cher,* dear < Lat. *carus.*] —**cher′ish·er** *n.* —**cher′ish·ing·ly** *adv.*

cher·no·zem (chĕr′nə-zĕm′, chĕr′nə-zhôm′) *n.* A very black topsoil, rich in humus, typical of cool to temperate semiarid regions, such as the grasslands of European Russia. [R., short for *chërnaya zemlya,* black earth.]

Cher·o·kee (chĕr′ə-kē′, chĕr′ə-kē′) *n., pl.* **Cherokee** or **-kees. 1. a.** A tribe of North American Indians, formerly inhabiting North Carolina and northern Georgia and now settled in Oklahoma. **b.** A member of this tribe. **2.** The Iroquoian language of the Cherokee. [< Cherokee *tsalaki.*] —**Cher′o·kee′** *adj.*

Cherokee rose *n.* A climbing rose, *Rosa laevigata,* of Chinese origin, having large, white, fragrant flowers.

che·root (shə-ro͞ot′, chə-) *n.* A cigar with square-cut ends. [Tamil *śurruṭṭu* < *śuruḷ,* curl.]

cher·ry (chĕr′ē) *n., pl.* **-ries. 1. a.** Any of several trees of the genus *Prunus,* having small, fleshy, globe-shaped or heart-shaped fruit with a small, hard stone, esp. *P. avium,* the common sweet cherry, and *P. cerasus,* the sour cherry. **b.** The fruit or wood of any of these trees. **2.** A moderate or strong red to purplish red. **3.** *Vulgar Slang.* The hymen considered as a symbol of virginity. —*adj.* Of a moderate or strong red to purplish red. [ME *cheri* < Norman Fr. *cherise,*

cheetah

chef

cherry
Sour cherry

cherub

chess[1]
Illustration for a 15th-century treatise on playing chess

chestnut

chevron

var. of OFr. *cerise* < Med. Lat. *ceresia* < Lat. *cerasus* < Gk. *kerasos.*]

cherry birch *n.* Blackberry.

cherry laurel *n.* A frequently cultivated European shrub, *Prunus laurocerasus,* having evergreen foliage and white flowers.

cherry leaf spot *n.* A disease of the cherry caused by the fungus *Coccomyces hiemalis* that hinders the growth of the tree and causes spotting of the leaves.

cherry pepper *n.* The very pungent red, yellow, or purplish fruit of a tropical plant, *Capsicum frutescens cerasiforme.*

cherry picker *n.* Any of various large, usually mobile cranes with a long, maneuverable vertical boom often supporting a work platform.

cherry plum *n.* The myrobalan (sense 1).

cher·ry·stone (chĕr′ē-stōn′) *n.* The quahog clam when half-grown and of comparatively small size.

cherry tomato *n.* A variety of the common tomato, *Lycospermum esculentum cerasiforme,* having small red or yellow fruit.

cher·so·nese (kûr′sə-nēz′, -nēs′) *n.* A peninsula. [Lat. *chersonesus* < Gk. *khersonēsos* : *khersos,* dry land + *nēsos,* island.]

chert (chûrt) *n.* **1.** Any of various microscopically crystalline mineral varieties of silica. **2.** A siliceous rock of chalcedonic or opaline silica occurring in limestone. [Orig. unknown.]

cher·ub (chĕr′əb) *n., pl.* **cher·u·bim** (chĕr′ə-bĭm′, -yə-bĭm′). **1. a.** A winged celestial being. **b.** *Theol.* One of the second order of angels. **2.** A representation of an angelic cherub, portrayed as a winged child with a chubby, rosy face. **3.** A person, esp. a child, with an innocent or chubby face. [Heb. *kārūbh.*] **—che·ru′bic** (chə-ro͞o′bĭk) *adj.* **—che·ru′bi·cal·ly** *adv.*

cher·vil (chûr′vəl) *n.* **1.** An aromatic plant, *Anthriscus cerefolium,* native to Eurasia, having leaves used in soups and salads. **2.** Any of several related plants, esp. *Chaerophyllum bulbosum,* having an edible root. [ME *chervel* < OE *cerfille* < Lat. *chaerephylla* < Gk. *khairephullon.*]

Ches·a·peake Bay retriever (chĕs′ə-pēk′) *n.* A hunting dog of a breed developed in the United States, having a thick, short, brownish coat.

chesh·ire cheese (chĕsh′ər) *n.* A hard, yellow English cheese made from cow's milk. [After *Cheshire,* England.]

chess[1] (chĕs) *n.* A board game for two players, each possessing an initial force of a king, a queen, two bishops, two knights, two rooks, and eight pawns, all maneuvered following individual rules of movement with the objective of checkmating the opposing king. [ME *ches,* short for OFr. *esches,* pl. of *eschec,* check in chess. —see CHECK.]

chess[2] (chĕs) *n.* Any of several weedy grasses, esp. cheat. [Orig. unknown.]

chess[3] (chĕs) *n., pl.* **chess** or **chess·es.** One of the floor boards of a pontoon bridge. [ME *ches,* tier < OFr. *chasse,* frame < Lat. *capsa,* box.]

chess·board (chĕs′bôrd′, -bōrd′) *n.* A board used in playing chess, marked with 64 squares.

chess·man (chĕs′măn′, -mən) *n.* Any of the pieces used in playing the game of chess.

chest (chĕst) *n.* **1.** The part of the body between the neck and the abdomen, enclosed by the ribs and the breastbone. **2. a.** A sturdy box with a lid and often a lock, used esp. for storage. **b.** A small closet or cabinet with shelves for storing supplies. **3. a.** The treasury of a public institution. **b.** The funds kept there. **4. a.** A box for the shipping of certain goods, such as tea. **b.** The quantity packed in such a box. **5.** A sealed receptacle for liquid, gas, or steam. **6.** A bureau or dresser. [ME < OE *cest.*] **—chest′ed** (chĕs′tĭd) *adj.*

ches·ter·field (chĕs′tər-fēld′) *n.* **1.** A single-breasted or double-breasted overcoat, usually with concealed buttons and a velvet collar. **2.** A large, overstuffed sofa with upright armrests. [After a 19th-cent. Earl of *Chesterfield.*]

Ches·ter White (chĕs′tər) *n.* A white hog of a breed that originated in Chester County, Pennsylvania.

chest·nut (chĕs′nŭt′, -nət) *n.* **1. a.** Any of several trees of the genus *Castanea,* of the Northern Hemisphere, bearing nuts enclosed in a prickly bur. **b.** The nut of any of these trees, edible when cooked. **c.** The hard wood of these trees, used in furniture and as a building material. **2.** The horse chestnut. **3.** A grayish brown to moderate reddish brown. **4.** A reddish-brown horse. **5.** A small, hard callus on the inner surface of a horse's foreleg. **6. a.** An old and stale joke. **b.** Anything lacking freshness or originality, as a song or story. *—adj.* Of a grayish brown to moderate reddish brown. [ME *chesteine* < OFr. *chastaigne* < Lat. *castanea* < Gk. *kastenea.*]

chestnut blight *n.* A disease of the native American chestnut tree, caused by a fungus, *Endothia parasitica,* and resulting in cankers on the trunk and branches and eventual death.

chestnut oak *n.* A tree, *Quercus prinus,* of eastern and central North America, having leaves with wavy edges like those of the chestnut.

chest·y (chĕs′tē) *adj.* **-i·er, -i·est.** *Informal.* **1.** Having a large or well-developed chest. **2.** Arrogant; proud; conceited. **—chest′i·ness** *n.*

che·tah (chē′tə) *n.* Variant of **cheetah.**

chet·rum (chē′trəm, chĕt′rəm) *n.* See table at **currency.** [Native word in Bhutan.]

che·val-de-frise (shə-văl′də-frēz′) *n., pl.* **che·vaux-de-frise** (shə-vō′-). **1.** An obstacle composed of barbed wire or spikes attached to a wooden frame, used to block enemy advancement and, formerly, to hinder enemy cavalry. **2.** An obstacle in the form of jagged glass or spikes set in the masonry on the top of a wall. [Fr., Frisian horse, from its use by Frisians to compensate for a lack of cavalry.]

che·val·et (shə-văl′ā, shĕv′ə-lā′) *n.* The bridge of a stringed musical instrument. [Fr. < dim. of *cheval,* horse < Lat. *caballus.*]

che·val glass (shə-văl′) *n.* A long mirror mounted on swivels in a frame. [< Fr. *cheval,* support, horse. —see CHEVALET.]

chev·a·lier (shĕv′ə-lîr′) *n.* **1.** A member of certain orders of knighthood or merit, as the Legion of Honor in France. **2.** A French nobleman of the lowest rank. **3.** A knight. **4.** A chivalrous, gallant man. [ME *chevaler* < OFr. *chevalier* < LLat. *caballarius,* horseman < *caballus,* horse.]

che·ve·lure (shəv-lür′) *n.* A head of hair. [ME *cheveler* < OFr. *cheveleure* < Lat. *capillatura* < *capillus,* hair.]

Chev·i·ot (shĕv′ē-ət, chĕv′-) *n.* **1.** One of a breed of sheep with short, thick wool, originally raised in a range of hills along the border between England and Scotland. **2. cheviot.** A woolen fabric with a coarse twill weave, used chiefly for suits and overcoats and originally made from the wool of the Cheviot sheep. [After the *Cheviot* Hills, a range of hills between England and Scotland.]

chev·ron (shĕv′rən) *n.* **1.** A badge or insignia consisting of stripes meeting at an angle, worn on the sleeve of a military, naval, or police uniform to indicate rank, merit, or length of service. **2.** A heraldic device shaped like an inverted V. **3.** A V-shaped pattern, esp. a kind of fret used in architecture. [ME *cheveroun* < OFr., rafter (from the meeting of rafters at an angle) < Lat. *capra,* goat.]

chev·ro·tain (shĕv′rə-tān′) *n.* Any of several small, hornless ruminants of the genera *Hyemoschus* and *Tragulus* of central Africa and southeastern Asia. [Fr. *chevrotin* < OFr., dim. of *chevrot,* kid, dim. of *chevre,* goat < Lat. *capra,* she-goat.]

chew (cho͞o) *v.* **chewed, chew·ing, chews.** *—tr.* **1.** To bite and grind with the teeth; masticate. **2.** To meditate upon; ponder: *chew the problem over.* *—intr.* **1.** To make a crushing and grinding motion with the teeth. **2.** To cogitate; meditate. **3.** *Informal.* To use chewing tobacco. ***—phrasal verb.*** **chew out.** *Slang.* To scold or reprimand. *—n.* **1.** The act of chewing. **2.** Something held in the mouth and chewed: *a chew of tobacco.* ***—idiom.*** **chew the fat** (or **rag**). To talk casually or idly; chat. [ME *cheuen* < OE *cēowan.*] **—chew′er** *n.*

chewing gum *n.* A sweetened, flavored preparation for chewing, usually made of chicle.

che·wink (chĭ-wĭngk′) *n.* The towhee. [Imit. of its song.]

Chey·enne (shī-ăn′, -ĕn′) *n., pl.* **Cheyenne** or **-ennes. 1. a.** A tribe of North American Indians, formerly inhabiting central Minnesota and North and South Dakota, now settled in Montana and Oklahoma. **b.** A member of this tribe. **2.** The Algonquian language of the Cheyenne. [Canadian Fr. < Dakota *šahíyena.*] **—Chey·enne′** *adj.*

Cheyne-Stokes respiration (chān′stōks′, chā′nē-stōks′) *n.* An abnormal type of breathing characterized by slow rhythmic waxing and waning of respiratory depth. [After John *Cheyne* (1777–1836) and William *Stokes* (1804–1878).]

chi (kī) *n.* The 22nd letter of the Greek alphabet. See table at **alphabet.** [Gk. *khi.*]

Chi·an·ti (kē-än′tē, -ăn′-) *n.* A dry table wine, usually red. [After the *Chianti* Mountains, Italy.]

chiao (tyou) *n., pl.* **chiao.** See table at **currency.** [Chin. (Mandarin) *jiao*[3].]

chi·a·ro·scu·ro (kē-är′ə-sko͝or′ō, -skyo͝or′ō) *n., pl.* **-ros. 1.** The technique of using light and shade in pictorial representation. **2.** The arrangement of light and dark elements in a pictorial work of art. [Ital. : *chiaro,* light (< Lat. *clarus,* clear) + *oscuro,* dark < Lat. *obscurus.*] **—chi·a′ro·scu′rist** *n.*

chi·as·ma (kī-ăz′mə) also **chi·asm** (kī′ăz′əm) *n., pl.* **-ma·ta** (-mə-tə) or **-mas** also **-asms. 1.** *Anat.* A crossing or intersection of two tracts, as of nerves or ligaments. **2.** A point of contact between homologous chromosomes, considered the cytological manifestation of crossing over. [Gk. *khiasma, khiasmat-,* cross-piece < *khiazein,* to mark with an X < *khi,* chi, from the letter's shape.] **—chi·as′mal, chi·as′mic, chi′-as·mat′ic** (-măt′ĭk) *adj.*

chi·as·ma·ty·py (kī-ăz′mə-tī′pē) *n.* The meiotic twisting between pairs of homologous chromosomes that produces chiasmata. [CHIASMA + -TYP(E) + -Y[2].]

chi·as·mus (kī-ăz′məs) *n., pl.* **-mi** (-mī′). A rhetorical inversion of the second of two parallel structures, as *He went to the theater, but home went she.* [NLat. < Gk. *khiasmos* < *khiazein,* to mark with an X. —see CHIASMA.]

chi·as·to·lite (kī-ăs′tə-līt′) *n.* A mineral variety of andalusite with carbonaceous impurities regularly arranged along the longer axis of the crystal. [< Gk. *chiastos,* crossed, p.part. of *khiazein,* to mark with an X. —see CHIASMA.]

chiaus (chous, choush) *n.* An official Turkish messenger, emissary, or sergeant. [Turk. *çavuş* < *çav,* news.]

Chib·cha (chĭb′chə) *n., pl.* **Chibcha** or **-chas. 1. a.** An extinct tribe of Indians once inhabiting Colombia. **b.** A member of this tribe. **2.** The extinct language of the Chibcha.
Chib·chan (chĭb′chən) *n.* **1.** A South American or Central American Indian ethnic stock including the Chibcha. **2.** A language stock of Central and South America that includes Chibcha.
chi·bouk also **chi·bouque** (chĭ-bo͝ok′, shĭ-) *n.* A Turkish tobacco pipe with a long stem and a red clay bowl. [Fr. *chibouque* < Turk. *çibuk.*]
chic (shēk) *adj.* **-er, -est. 1.** Sophisticated; stylish. **2.** Dressed smartly and fashionably; modish. *—n.* **1.** Sophistication in dress and manner; elegance. **2.** Stylishness; fashionableness. [Fr.] **—chic′ly** *adv.* **—chic′ness** *n.*
chi·ca·lo·te (chē′kə-lō′tē) *n.* A prickly poppy, *Argemone platyceras,* of the southwestern United States and tropical America, having grayish foliage and large white flowers. [Sp. < Nahuatl *chicalotl.*]
Chi·ca·na (chĭ-kä′nə, shĭ-) *n.* A female Mexican-American. [Alteration of Sp. *Mejicana,* fem. of *Mejicano,* Mexican.] **—Chi·ca′na** *adj.*
chi·cane (shĭ-kān′, chĭ-) *v.* **-caned, -can·ing, -canes.** *—tr.* **1.** To trick; deceive. **2.** To quibble over; cavil. *—intr.* To use tricks or chicanery. *—n.* **1.** Chicanery. **2.** A bridge or whist hand without trumps. [Fr. *chicaner* < OFr., to quibble.] **—chi·can′er** *n.*
chi·can·er·y (shĭ-kā′nə-rē, chĭ-) *n., pl.* **-ies. 1.** Deception by trickery or sophistry. **2.** A trick; subterfuge.
Chi·ca·no (chĭ-kä′nō, shĭ-) *n. pl.* **-nos.** A Mexican-American. *—adj.* Of or pertaining to Chicanos. [Mex. Sp., var. of Sp. *Mejicano,* a Mexican < *Méjico,* Mexico.]
chi·chi (shē′shē) *adj.* Ostentatiously stylish; showy. [Fr.]
chick (chĭk) *n.* **1. a.** A young chicken. **b.** The young of any bird. **2.** A child. **3.** *Slang.* A girl or young woman. [ME *chike,* short for *chiken,* chicken < OE *cicen.*]
chick·a·dee (chĭk′ə-dē′) *n.* Any of several small, plump North American birds of the genus *Parus,* having predominantly gray plumage and a dark-crowned head. [Imit. of its song.]
chick·a·ree (chĭk′ə-rē′) *n.* A squirrel, *Tamiascurus douglasi,* of northwestern North America, resembling and closely related to the red squirrel. [Imit. of its song.]
Chick·a·saw (chĭk′ə-sô′) *n., pl.* **Chickasaw** or **-saws. 1. a.** A tribe of North American Indians, originally of Mississippi, later removed to Oklahoma. **b.** A member of this tribe. **2.** The Muskhogean language of the Chickasaw. **—Chick′a·saw′** *adj.*
chick·en (chĭk′ən) *n.* **1. a.** The common domestic fowl or its young. **b.** Any of various similar or related birds. **c.** The flesh of the common domestic fowl. **2.** *Slang.* A young woman. *—adj. Slang.* Afraid; timid. *—intr.v.* **-ened, -en·ing, -ens.** *Slang.* To act in a cowardly manner; lose one's nerve: *chickened out at the last moment.* [ME *chiken* < OE *cicen.*]
chicken breast *n.* A chest deformity marked by a projecting sternum, occurring as the result of rickets. **—chick′en-breast′ed** *adj.*
chicken feed *n. Slang.* A trifling amount of money.
chicken hawk *n.* Any of various hawks that prey on or have the reputation of preying on chickens.
chick·en-heart·ed (chĭk′ən-här′tĭd) *adj.* Lacking courage; cowardly; timid. **—chick′en·heart′ed·ness** *n.*
chick·en-liv·ered (chĭk′ən-lĭv′ərd) *adj.* Cowardly; timid.
chicken pox *n.* An acute contagious viral disease, usually of young children, characterized by skin eruption, slight fever, and mild constitutional symptoms.
chicken wire *n.* A light-gauge galvanized wire fencing, usually made with hexagonal mesh.
chick·pea (chĭk′pē′) *n.* **1.** A bushy plant, *Cicer arietenum,* grown in the Mediterranean region and central Asia and bearing edible seeds. **2.** One of the pealike seeds of the chickpea, widely used as food. [Obs. *chichpease* : ME *chiche,* chickpea (< OFr. < Lat. *cicer*) + *pease,* pea.]
chick·weed (chĭk′wēd′) *n.* Any of various plants of the genera *Cerastium* and *Stellaria,* esp. *S. media,* a weedy plant with white flowers. [So called because it is eaten by chickens.]
chic·le (chĭk′əl) *n.* The coagulated milky juice of the sapodilla, used as the principal ingredient of chewing gum. [Sp. < Nahuatl *chictli.*]
chi·co (chē′kō) *n., pl.* **-cos.** A species of greasewood, *Sarcobatus vermiculatus.* [Short for CHICALOTE.]
chic·o·ry (chĭk′ə-rē) *n., pl.* **-ries. 1.** A plant, *Cichorium intybus,* having usually blue flowers and leaves that are used in salads. **2.** The root of the chicory, dried, roasted, and ground for mixing with coffee or as a coffee substitute. [ME *cicoree* < OFr. < Lat. *cichorium* < Gk. *kikhora.*]
chide (chīd) *v.* **chid·ed** or **chid** (chĭd), **chid·ed** or **chid** or **chid·den** (chĭd′n), **chid·ing, chides.** *—tr.* **1.** To state one's disapproval to so as to correct or improve; scold; reprimand: *chided the boy for his sloppiness.* **2.** To goad; impel. *—intr.* To express disapproval. [ME *chiden* < OE *cīdan.*] **—chid′er** *n.* **—chid′ing·ly** *adv.*
chief (chēf) *n.* **1.** One who is highest in rank or authority; leader. **2.** Often **Chief.** *Naut.* A chief petty officer; the chief engineer of a ship. **3.** *Slang.* A boss. **4.** The upper section of a heraldic shield. **5.** The highest or most important part of something. *—adj.* **1.** Highest in rank, authority, or office. **2.** Principal; most important. *—adv. Archaic.* Chiefly. [ME *chef* < OFr. < Lat. *caput,* head.]

Synonyms: *chief, principal, main, leading, foremost, primary, prime.* These adjectives, often interchangeable, refer to being first, either in rank or in importance. *Chief* most commonly applies to a person who is highest in rank and authority: *chief magistrate.* Used figuratively, *chief* implies maximum importance: *the country's chief crop. Principal* usually stresses importance of persons or things rather than personal authority, but can be applied to persons in the sense of rank or standing. *Main* usually applies to things with reference to importance: *main building on a campus; main event of a boxing program. Leading,* applicable to persons and things, often suggests in the former a record of achievement, personal magnetism, or capacity for influencing others. *Foremost* is closely related to *leading,* but more strongly emphasizes first position and the sense of forging ahead of others in a given field. *Primary,* applicable to things, stresses first in the sense of origin, sequence, or development: *primary school.* It can also mean first in the sense of basic or fundamental. *Prime* emphasizes first in authority, power, or quality: *prime minister; prime ribs of beef.*

chief cell *n.* Any of the secretory cells of the gastric glands that produce pepsin.
chief justice also **Chief Justice** *n.* The presiding judge of a high court having several judges, esp. the U.S. Supreme Court.
chief·ly (chēf′lē) *adv.* **1.** Above all; especially. **2.** Mostly; mainly. *—adj.* Of or similar to a chief.
chief of staff *n.* **1.** Often **Chief of Staff.** The ranking officer of the U.S. Army, Navy, or Air Force, responsible to the secretary of his branch and to the President. **2.** The senior military staff officer at the division level or higher.
chief of state *n.* One who serves as the formal head of a nation.
chief·tain (chēf′tən) *n.* The leader or head of a group, esp. a clan or tribe. [ME *chevetain* < OFr. < LLat. *capitaneus* < Lat. *caput,* head.]
chiff·chaff (chĭf′chăf′) *n.* A small European warbler, *Phylloscopus collybita,* with yellowish plumage. [Imit. of its song.]
chif·fon (shĭ-fŏn′, shĭf′ŏn′) *n.* **1.** A fabric of sheer silk or rayon. **2.** Ribbons, laces, or other ornamental accessories for women's clothing. *—adj.* **1.** Of, relating to, or resembling chiffon. **2.** Having a light and fluffy consistency: *a lemon chiffon pie.* [Fr., chiffon, rag < *chiffe,* old rag.]
chif·fo·nier (shĭf′ə-nîr′) *n.* A narrow, high chest of drawers or bureau, often with a mirror attached. [Fr. < *chiffon,* rag. —see CHIFFON.]
chig·ger (chĭg′ər) *n.* **1.** Any of various small six-legged larvae of mites of the family Trombidiidae, causing intensely irritating itching when lodged on the skin. **2.** The chigoe (sense 1). [Var. of CHIGOE.]
chi·gnon (shēn-yŏn′, shēn′yŏn′) *n.* A roll or knot of hair worn at the back of the head or nape of the neck. [Fr. < OFr. *chaignon,* chain < Lat. *catena.*]
chig·oe (chĭg′ō, chē′gō) *n.* **1.** A small tropical flea, *Tunga penetrans,* of which the fertile female burrows under the skin, causing intense irritation and sores that may become severely infected. **2.** The chigger (sense 1). [Of Cariban orig.]
Chi·hua·hua (chĭ-wä′wä, -wə) *n.* A very small dog of a breed originating in Mexico, having pointed ears and a smooth coat. [After *Chihuahua,* Mexico.]
chil·blain (chĭl′blān′) *n.* An inflammation followed by itchy irritation on the hands, feet, or ears, resulting from exposure to moist cold. [CHIL(L) + BLAIN.] **—chil′blained′** *adj.*
child (chīld) *n., pl.* **chil·dren** (chĭl′drən). **1.** A person between birth and puberty. **2. a.** An unborn infant; fetus. **b.** An infant; baby. **3.** One who is childish or immature. **4.** A son or daughter; an offspring. **5.** Often **children.** Members of a tribe; descendants: *children of Abraham.* **6.** The figurative offspring of anything: *a child of nature.* **—idiom. with child.** Pregnant. [ME < OE *cild.*] **—child′less** *adj.* **—child′less·ness** *n.*
child·bear·ing (chīld′bâr′ĭng) *n.* The process of parturition.
child·bed (chīld′bĕd′) *n.* The state of a woman in childbirth.
childbed fever *n.* Puerperal fever.
child·birth (chīld′bûrth′) *n.* Parturition.
childe (chīld) *n. Archaic.* A child of noble birth. [ME *child,* child.]
child·hood (chīld′ho͝od′) *n.* The time or state of being a child.
child·ish (chīl′dĭsh) *adj.* **1.** Of, similar to, or suitable for a child: *a high, childish voice.* **2.** Marked by or indicating a lack of maturity; puerile: *childish remarks.* **—child′ish·ly** *adv.* **—child′ish·ness** *n.*
child labor *n.* The full-time employment of children under a minimum legal age.
child·like (chīld′līk′) *adj.* Like or befitting a child, as in innocence. **—child′like′ness** *n.*
child·proof (chīld′pro͞of′) *adj.* Designed to resist tampering by children: *a childproof aspirin bottle.*
chil·dren (chĭl′drən) *n.* Plural of **child.**

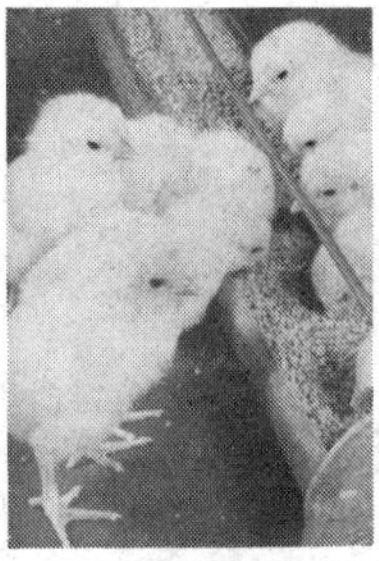
chick

chickpea

chicory

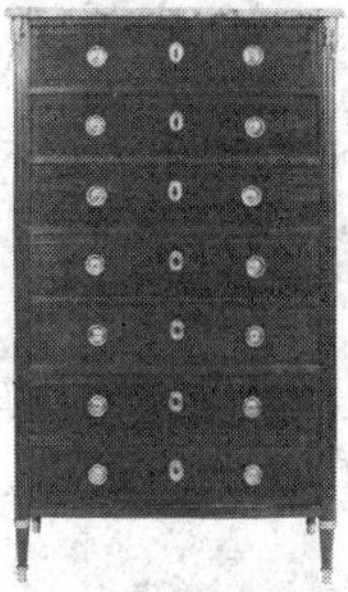
chiffonier
Louis XVI chiffonier

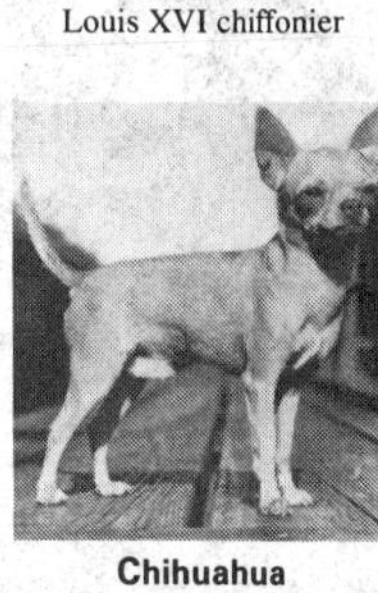
Chihuahua

chimera
5th-century B.C. bronze Chimera from Arezzo, Italy

chimney sweep

chimpanzee

chinchilla

child's play *n.* **1.** Something very easy to do. **2.** A trivial matter.

chil·e (chĭl'ē) *n.* Variant of **chili**.

chil·e con car·ne also **chil·i con car·ne** (chĭl'ē kŏn kär'nē) *n.* A highly spiced dish made of red peppers, meat, and sometimes beans. [Sp.: *chile,* chili + *con,* with + *carne,* meat.]

Chile saltpeter *n.* Sodium nitrate.

chil·i also **chil·e** or **chil·li** (chĭl'ē) *n., pl.* **-ies** also **-es** or **-lies. 1. a.** The very pungent fruit of several varieties of a woody plant, *Capsicum frutescens.* **b.** A condiment made from the dried fruits of the chili. **2.** Chile con carne. [Sp. *chile* < Nahuatl *chilli.*]

chil·i·ad (kĭl'ē-ăd', -əd) *n.* **1.** A group that contains one thousand elements. **2.** One thousand years. [LLat. *chilias, chiliad-* < Gk. *khilias* < *khilioi,* thousand.]

chil·i·asm (kĭl'ē-ăz'əm) *n. Theol.* The doctrine stating that Christ will reign on earth for 1,000 years. [NLat. *chiliasmus* < LLat. *chiliastes,* a chiliast < *chilias,* chiliad.] **—chil'i·ast'** (-ăst', -əst) *n.* **—chil'i·as'tic** *adj.*

chil·i·bur·ger (chĭl'ē-bûr'gər) *n.* A hamburger covered with chili.

chil·i·dog (chĭl'ē-dôg', -dŏg') *n.* A hot dog covered with chili.

chili sauce *n.* A spiced sauce made with chilies and tomatoes.

chill (chĭl) *n.* **1.** A moderate but penetrating coldness. **2.** A sensation of coldness, as with a fever. **3.** A checking or dampening of enthusiasm, spirit, or joy: *bad news that put a chill on the celebration.* **4.** A sudden numbing fear or dread. *—adj.* **1.** Chilly: *a chill wind.* **2.** Dispiriting; discouraging: *a chill response.* *—v.* **chilled, chill·ing, chills.** *—tr.* **1.** To affect with cold. **2.** To discourage; dispirit. **3.** To lower in temperature. **4.** *Metallurgy.* To harden (a metallic surface) by rapid cooling. *—intr.* **1.** To be seized with cold. **2.** To become cold: *jelly that chills quickly.* **3.** *Metallurgy.* To become hard by rapid cooling. [ME *chele* < OE *cēle.*] **—chill'ing·ly** *adv.* **—chill'ness** *n.*

chill·er (chĭl'ər) *n.* One that chills or frightens; a thriller.

chil·li (chĭl'ē) *n.* Variant of **chili**.

chill·y (chĭl'ē) *adj.* **-i·er, -i·est. 1.** Cool or cold enough to cause shivering. **2.** Seized with cold; shivering. **3.** Distant and cool; unfriendly. **—chill'i·ly** *adv.* **—chill'i·ness** *n.*

chi·lo·pod (kī'lə-pŏd') *n.* Any of various arthropods of the class Chilopoda, which includes the centipedes. [NLat. *Chilopoda,* class name : Gk. *kheilos,* lip + Gk. *pous,* foot (so called because the foremost pair of legs are jawlike appendages).]

chi·mae·ra (kī-mîr'ə, kĭ-) *n.* **1.** Any of the noncommercial fish of the family Chimaeridae. **2.** Variant of **chimera**. [NLat. *Chimaera,* type genus < Lat., *chimera.*]

chime[1] (chīm) *n.* **1.** An apparatus for striking a bell or bells to produce a musical sound. **2.** Often **chimes.** A set of bells tuned to the musical scale and used as an orchestral instrument. **3.** A single bell. **4.** The musical sound produced by a bell or bells. **5.** Agreement; accord. *—v.* **chimed, chim·ing, chimes.** *—intr.* **1.** To sound with a harmonious ring when struck. **2.** To make a musical sound by striking a chime. **3.** To agree; harmonize: *Their views chimed with ours.* *—tr.* **1.** To produce (music) by striking bells. **2.** To strike (a bell) to produce music. **3.** To make known (the hour) by ringing bells. **4.** To call, send, or welcome by ringing bells. ***—phrasal verb.* chime in. 1.** To break into, as a conversation; interrupt. **2.** To join in harmoniously. [ME *chimbe* < OFr., var. of *cimble,* cymbal < Lat. *cymbalum.* —see CYMBAL.] **—chim'er** *n.*

chime[2] (chīm) *n.* The rim of a cask. [ME *chimb.*]

chi·me·ra also **chi·mae·ra** (kī-mîr'ə, kĭ-) *n.* **1. Chimera.** *Gk. Myth.* A fire-breathing she-monster usually represented as a composite of a lion, a goat, and a serpent. **2.** A creation of the imagination; an impossible and foolish fancy. **3.** *Biol.* An organism, esp. a plant, containing tissues from at least two genetically distinct parents. [ME *chimere* < OFr. < Lat. *chimaera* < Gk. *khimaira.*]

chi·mer·i·cal (kī-mĕr'ĭ-kəl, -mîr'-, kĭ-) also **chi·mer·ic** (-mĕr'ĭk, -mîr'-) *adj.* **1.** Like a chimera; imaginary; unreal. **2.** Given to unrealistic fantasies; fanciful. **—chi·mer'i·cal·ly** *adv.*

chi·mer·ism (kī-mîr'ĭz'əm, kĭ-mə-rĭz'-) *n.* The condition of being a genetic chimera.

chim·ney (chĭm'nē) *n., pl.* **-neys. 1. a.** A passage through which smoke and gases escape from a fire or furnace; flue. **b.** The usually vertical structure containing a chimney. **c.** The part of such a structure that rises above a roof. **2.** *Chiefly Brit.* A smokestack, as of a ship or locomotive. **3.** A glass tube for enclosing the flame of a lamp. **4.** Something, as a narrow cleft in a cliff, resembling a chimney. [ME *chimene* < OFr. *cheminee* < LLat. *caminata,* fireplace < Lat. *caminus,* furnace < Gk. *kaminos.*]

chim·ney·piece (chĭm'nē-pēs') *n.* **1.** The mantel of a fireplace. **2.** A decoration over a fireplace.

chimney pot *n.* A pipe placed on the top of a chimney to improve the draft.

chimney sweep *n.* A worker employed to clean soot from chimneys.

chimney swift *n.* A small, dark, swallowlike New World bird, *Chaetura pelagica,* that frequently nests in chimneys.

chimp (chĭmp) *n. Informal.* A chimpanzee.

chim·pan·zee (chĭm'păn-zē', -pən-, chĭm-păn'zē) *n.* An anthropoid ape, *Pan troglodytes,* of tropical Africa, having gregarious, somewhat arboreal habits and a high degree of intelligence. [Of Bantu orig.]

chin (chĭn) *n.* The central forward portion of the lower jaw. *—v.* **chinned, chin·ning, chins.** *—tr.* **1.** To pull (oneself) up with the arms while grasping an overhead horizontal bar until one's chin is level with the bar. **2.** To place (a violin) under the chin. *—intr.* **1.** *Informal.* To chatter. **2.** To chin oneself. [ME < OE *cin.*]

chi·na (chī'nə) *n.* **1.** High-quality porcelain or ceramic ware, originally made in China. **2.** Any porcelain ware.

China aster *n.* A plant, *Callistephus chinensis,* native to China, widely cultivated for its showy, variously colored flowers.

chi·na·ber·ry (chī'nə-bĕr'ē) *n.* **1.** A spreading tree, *Melia azedarach,* native to Asia, widely grown for its white or purple flower clusters. **2.** A soapberry tree, *Sapindus marginatus* (or *S. saponaria*), of the West Indies, Mexico, and the southwestern United States. **3.** The fruit of a chinaberry.

Chi·na·man (chī'nə-mən) *n. Offensive.* A Chinese man.

China rose *n.* A shrub, *Rosa chinensis,* that has fragrant red or pink flowers and is the original ancestor of many cultivated hybrid roses.

Chi·na·town (chī'nə-toun') *n.* A neighborhood inhabited by Chinese people.

China tree *n.* The chinaberry (sense 1).

chi·na·ware (chī'nə-wâr') *n.* Tableware that is made of china.

chinch (chĭnch) *n. Regional.* A bedbug. [Sp. *chinche* < Lat. *cimex,* bug.]

chinch bug *n.* A small black-and-white insect, *Blissus leucopterus,* that is very destructive to grains and grasses.

chin·che·rin·chee (chĭn'chə-rĭn-chē', chĭng'kə-) *n.* A bulbous plant, *Ornithogalum thyrsoides,* of southern Africa, with long clusters or spikes of white or yellow flowers. [Orig. unknown.]

chin·chil·la (chĭn-chĭl'ə) *n.* **1. a.** A squirrellike rodent, *Chinchilla laniger,* native to the mountains of South America and widely raised in captivity for its soft pale-gray fur. **b.** The fur of this animal. **2.** A thick, twilled cloth of wool and cotton, used for overcoats. [Sp., prob. < Aymara.]

Chin·co·teague pony (shĭng'kə-tēg', chĭng'-) *n.* A type of small, inbred North American horse that runs wild on certain islands off the Virginia coast. [After *Chincoteague* Island, Virginia.]

chine (chīn) *n.* **1. a.** The backbone; spine. **b.** A cut of meat containing part of the backbone. **2.** A ridge or crest. **3.** The line of intersection between the side and bottom of a flat-bottom or V-bottom boat. [ME < OFr. *eschine,* of Germanic orig.]

Chi·nese (chī-nēz', -nēs') *adj.* Of or pertaining to China, its culture, people, or languages. *—n., pl.* **Chinese. 1. a.** A native or inhabitant of China. **b.** A person of Chinese ancestry. **2. a.** A branch of the Sino-Tibetan language family that consists of the various dialects spoken by the Chinese people. **b.** Any of the dialects spoken by the Chinese people.

Chinese anise *n.* Star anise (sense 2).

Chinese cabbage *n.* A Chinese plant, *Brassica pekinensis,* related to the common cabbage, having a cylindrical head of crisp, edible leaves.

Chinese calendar *n.* The lunar calendar of the Chinese people.

Chinese Chippendale *n.* Chippendale furniture characterized by certain Oriental influences.

Chinese date *n.* **1.** The jujube. **2.** The fruit of the jujube.

Chinese evergreen *n.* A plant, *Aglaonema simplex,* of tropical Asia, that has glossy, pointed green leaves and is widely grown as a house plant.

Chinese houses *n. (used with a sing. or pl. verb).* A plant, *Collinsia bicolor,* of California, having showy white and rose-purple flowers.

Chinese ink *n.* India ink.

Chinese lantern *n.* **1.** A decorative, collapsible lantern of thin, brightly colored paper. **2.** One of the papery, inflated seed cases of the winter cherry.

Chinese lantern plant *n.* The winter cherry.

Chinese puzzle *n.* **1.** A very intricate puzzle. **2.** Any very difficult problem.

Chinese red *n.* Vermilion.

Chinese restaurant syndrome *n* A complex of symptoms, including facial pressure, dizziness, perspiration, and headache, that may occur after ingesting food prepared with large amounts of monosodium glutamate.

Chinese sacred lily *n.* A variety of the polyanthus narcissus, *Narcissus tazetta orientalis,* that has fragrant yellow and white flowers and is frequently grown as a house plant.

Chinese white *n.* Zinc oxide.

Chinese wood oil *n.* Tung oil.

chink[1] (chĭngk) *n.* A crack or fissure; narrow opening. *—tr.v.* **chinked, chink·ing, chinks. 1.** To make chinks in. **2.** To fill chinks in. [Perh. alteration of obs. *chine* < ME, crack < OE *cine.*] **—chink'y** *adj.*

chink[2] (chĭngk) *n.* A short, metallic sound. *—intr. & tr.v.*

chinked, chink·ing, chinks. To make or cause to make a chink. [Imit.]
Chink (chĭngk) *n. Offensive Slang.* A Chinese. [Perh. alteration of CHINESE.]
chi·no (chē'nō, shē'-) *n., pl.* **-nos. 1.** A coarse, twilled cotton fabric used for uniforms and sports clothes. **2. chinos.** Boys' and men's trousers made of chino. [Am. Sp., toasted (from its original tan color).]
chi·noi·se·rie (shēn'wäz-rē') *n.* **1.** A style in art reflecting Chinese influence through use of elaborate decoration and intricate patterns. **2.** An object reflecting Chinese artistic influence. [Fr. < *chinois,* Chinese < *Chine,* China.]
Chi·nook (shĭ-no͝ok', chĭ-) *n., pl.* **Chinook** or **-nooks. 1. a.** A tribe of North American Indians formerly inhabiting the Columbia River basin in Oregon. **b.** A member of this tribe. **c.** The Chinookan language of the Chinook. **2. chinook.** A moist, warm wind blowing from the sea on the Oregon and Washington coasts. **3. chinook.** A warm, dry wind that descends from the eastern slopes of the Rocky Mountains, causing a rapid rise in temperature. [Salish *c'inuk.*]
Chi·nook·an (shĭ-no͝ok'ən, chĭ-) *n.* A North American Indian language family of Washington and Oregon. *—adj.* Of or pertaining to the Chinook Indians, their language, or their culture.
Chinook Jargon *n.* A pidgin language combining English, French, Chinook, and other Indian dialects that was formerly used by Indians and fur traders of the Pacific Northwest.
Chinook salmon *n.* A salmon, *Oncorhynchus tshawytscha,* of northern Pacific waters, valued as a food fish.
chin·qua·pin (chĭng'kə-pĭn') *n.* **1.** A small, shrubby tree, *Castanea pumila,* of the eastern United States. **2.** A large evergreen tree, *Castanopsis chrysophella,* of the Pacific Coast of North America. **3.** The nut of a chinquapin. [Of Algonquian orig.]
chintz (chĭnts) *n.* A printed and glazed cotton fabric, usually of bright colors. [Obs. *chints,* pl. of *chint,* calico cloth < Hindi *chīṇt* < Skt. *citra-,* variegated.]
chintz·y (chĭnt'sē) *adj.* **-i·er, -i·est. 1.** Of, relating to, or decorated with chintz. **2.** Gaudy; trashy; cheap.
chip[1] (chĭp) *n.* **1.** A small piece broken or cut off. **2.** A crack or other mark caused by chipping. **3. a.** A small disk or counter used in poker and other games to represent money. **b. chips.** *Slang.* Money. **4.** *Electronics.* A minute square of a thin semiconducting material, such as silicon or germanium, doped and otherwise processed to have specified electrical characteristics, esp. such a square before attachment of electrical leads and packaging as an electronic component or integrated circuit. **5.** A thin, brittle slice of a food: *a potato chip.* **6. chips.** *Chiefly Brit.* French-fried potatoes. **7.** Wood, palm leaves, straw, or similar material cut and dried for weaving. **8.** A fragment of dried animal dung, used as fuel. **9.** Something that is worthless. **10.** A chip shot in golf. *—v.* **chipped, chip·ping, chips.** *—tr.* **1.** To break a small piece from: *chip a tooth.* **2.** To chop or cut with an ax or other implement. **3.** To shape or carve by cutting or chopping: *chipped her name in the stone.* *—intr.* To become broken off. ***—phrasal verb.* chip in.** *Informal.* **1.** To contribute money or labor. **2.** To interject; interrupt. **3.** To put up chips or money as one's bet in poker and other games. ***—idioms.* chip off the old block.** A child who resembles either of his parents. **chip on (one's) shoulder.** A persistent feeling of resentment or bitterness. **in the chips.** *Slang.* Rich. [ME < OE *cyp,* beam.]
chip[2] (chĭp) *intr.v.* **chipped, chip·ping, chips.** To cheep, as a bird. [Imit.] **—chip** *n.*
chip[3] (chĭp) *n.* A trick method of throwing one's opponent in wrestling. [Orig. unknown.]
Chip·e·wy·an (chĭp'ə-wī'ən) *n., pl.* **Chipewyan** or **-ans. 1. a.** A tribe of North American Indians living in Canada in the area between Great Slave Lake and Lake Athabasca on the west and Hudson Bay on the east. **b.** A member of this tribe. **2.** The Athapascan language of the Chipewyan. [Cree *čīpwayān,* parka wearer : *cīpw-,* pointed + *-ayān,* skin.]
chip·munk (chĭp'mŭngk') *n.* A small rodent, *Tamias striatus,* of eastern North America, or any of several similar rodents of the genus *Eutamias,* of western North America and northern Asia, resembling a squirrel but smaller and having a striped back. [Alteration of obs. *chitmunk,* of Algonquian orig.]
chipped beef *n.* Dried beef smoked and sliced very thin.
Chip·pen·dale (chĭp'ən-dāl') *adj.* Of, pertaining to, or designating a type of furniture characterized by flowing lines and rococo ornamentation. [After Thomas *Chippendale* (1718–1779).]
chip·per[1] (chĭp'ər) *n.* One that chips or cuts.
chip·per[2] (chĭp'ər) *intr.v.* **-pered, -per·ing, -pers. 1.** To chirp or twitter, as a bird. **2.** To babble. [< CHIP[2].]
chip·per[3] (chĭp'ər) *adj. Informal.* Cheerful; pert. [Poss. alteration of Brit. dial. *kipper,* lively.]
Chip·pe·wa (chĭp'ə-wô', -wä', -wā', -wə) *n., pl.* **Chippewa** or **-was.** Ojibwa.
chipping sparrow *n.* A small North American sparrow, *Spizella passerina,* having a reddish-brown crown.
chip·py (chĭp'ē) *n., pl.* **-pies. 1.** The chipping sparrow. **2.** *Slang.* A prostitute. [< CHIP[2].]
chip shot *n.* A short, lofted golf stroke, used in approaching the green.
chi·ral (kī'rəl) *adj.* Of or pertaining to the handedness of an asymmetric molecule. **—chi·ral'i·ty** (kī-răl'ĭ-tē) *n.* [CHIRO- + -AL.]
chi-rho (kī'rō', kē'-) *n.* A monogram and symbol for Christ, consisting of the superimposed Greek letters chi (X) and rho (P), often embroidered on altar cloths and clerical vestments. [CHI + RHO, first two letters of Greek *Khristos,* Christ.]
chiro– or **cheiro–** *pref.* Hand: *chiropractic.* [Lat. < Gk. *kheir,* hand.]
chi·rog·ra·phy (kī-rŏg'rə-fē) *n.* Penmanship. **—chi·rog'ra·pher** *n.* **—chi'ro·graph'ic** (kī'rə-grăf'ĭk), **chi'ro·graph'i·cal** *adj.*
chi·ro·man·cy (kīr'ə-măn'sē) *n.* The art or practice of foretelling a person's future by studying the palm of his hand; palmistry. [ME *ciromancie* < Med. Lat. *chiromantia* < Gk. *kheiromantis,* palmist : *kheir,* hand + *mantis,* diviner.] **—chi'ro·man'cer** *n.*
Chi·ron (kī'rŏn') *n. Gk. Myth.* The wise centaur who tutored Achilles, Hercules, and Asclepius. [Lat. < Gk. *Kheirōn.*]
chi·ro·plas·ty (kī'ro-plăs'tē) *n.* Variant of **cheiroplasty.**
chi·rop·o·dy (kĭ-rŏp'ə-dē, shĭ-) *n.* Podiatry. [CHIR(O)- + -POD + -Y.] **—chi·rop'o·dist** *n.*
chi·ro·prac·tic (kīr'ə-prăk'tĭk) *n.* A system of therapy in which disease is considered the result of neural malfunction, and manipulation of the spinal column and other structures is the preferred method of treatment. [CHIRO- + Gk. *praktikos,* effective. —see PRACTICAL.] **—chi'ro·prac'tor** *n.*
chi·rop·ter·an (kī-rŏp'tər-ən) *n.* A flying mammal of the order Chiroptera, which includes the bats. [NLat. *Chiroptera,* order name : CHIRO- + -PTER.] **—chi·rop'ter·an** *adj.*
chirp (chûrp) *n.* A short, high-pitched sound like that made by a small bird. [Imit.] **—chirp** *v.* **(chirped, chirp·ing, chirps).**
chirr (chûr) *n.* A harsh, trilling sound, such as that made by crickets. [Imit.] **—chirr** *v.* **(chirred, chir·ring, chirs).**
chir·rup (chûr'əp, chĭr'-) *v.* **-ruped, -rup·ing, -rups.** *—intr.* **1.** To utter a series of chirps. **2.** To make clicking, clucking sounds with the lips, as in urging on a horse. *—tr.* **1.** To sound with chirps. **2.** To make clucking sounds to. *—n.* **1.** A series of chirps. **2.** A series of clucks or clicking sounds, such as those made to urge on a horse. [Var. of CHIRP.]
chi·rur·geon (kī-rûr'jən) *n. Archaic.* A surgeon. [ME *cirurgien* < OFr. *cirurgiien* < Lat. *chirurgia,* surgery. —see SURGERY.]
chis·el (chĭz'əl) *n.* A metal tool with a sharp, beveled edge, used to cut and shape stone, wood, or metal. *—v.* **-eled, -el·ing, -els** also **-elled, -el·ling, -els.** *—tr.* **1.** To shape or cut with a chisel. **2.** *Slang.* **a.** To cheat or swindle. **b.** To obtain by deception. *—intr.* **1.** To use a chisel. **2.** *Slang.* To use unethical methods; cheat. [ME < OFr., prob. ult. < Lat. *caedere,* to cut.] **—chis'el·er** *n.*
chi-square (kī'skwâr') *n.* A statistic used in testing a hypothesis concerning the difference between observed and expected results, that is calculated as the sum of the squares of observed values minus expected values divided by the expected values.
chit[1] (chĭt) *n.* **1.** A statement of an amount owed for food and drink; check. **2.** *Chiefly Brit.* A short letter; note. [Obs. *chitty* < Hindi *ciṭṭhi,* note, letter < Skt. **cista,* message.]
chit[2] (chĭt) *n.* A child, esp. a pert girl. [ME, young animal.]
chit·chat (chĭt'chăt') *n.* **1.** Casual conversation; small talk. **2.** Gossip. *—intr.v.* **-chat·ted, -chat·ting, -chats.** To indulge in chitchat. [Redup. of CHAT.]
chi·tin (kīt'n) *n.* A semitransparent horny substance, primarily a mucopolysaccharide, forming the principal component of crustacean shells, insect exoskeletons, and the cell walls of certain fungi. [Fr. *chitine* < NLat. *chiton,* mollusk < Gk. *khitōn,* chiton.] **—chi'tin·ous** *adj.*
chit·lins or **chit·lings** (chĭt'lĭnz) *n.* Variants of **chitterlings.**
chi·ton (kīt'n, kī'tŏn') *n.* **1.** A tunic worn by men and women in ancient Greece. **2.** Any of various marine mollusks of the class Amphineyra, living on rocks and having shells consisting of eight overlapping transverse plates. [Gk. *khitōn,* tunic, of Semitic orig.]
chit·tam·wood (chĭt'əm-wo͝od') *n.* Any of various North American trees, esp. a smoke tree. [Prob. of Muskhogean orig.]
chit·ter (chĭt'ər) *intr.v.* **-tered, -ter·ing, -ters.** To twitter or chatter, as a bird does. [ME *chiteren.*]
chit·ter·lings also **chit·lins** or **chit·lings** (chĭt'lĭnz) *pl.n.* The small intestines of pigs, cooked and eaten as food. [ME *chiterling.*]
chi·val·ric (shĭ-văl'rĭk, shĭv'əl-) *adj.* Chivalrous.
chiv·al·rous (shĭv'əl-rəs) *adj.* **1.** Having the qualities of gallantry and honor attributed to an ideal knight. **2.** Of or pertaining to chivalry. **3.** Characterized by consideration and courtesy, esp. toward women. **—chiv'al·rous·ly** *adv.* **—chiv'al·rous·ness** *n.*
chiv·al·ry (shĭv'əl-rē) *n., pl.* **-ries. 1. a.** The medieval institution of knighthood. **b.** The principles and customs of this institution. **2. a.** The qualities idealized by knighthood, such as bravery, courtesy, honor, and devotion to the weak. **b.** The manifestation of any of these qualities. **3.** A group of

chipmunk

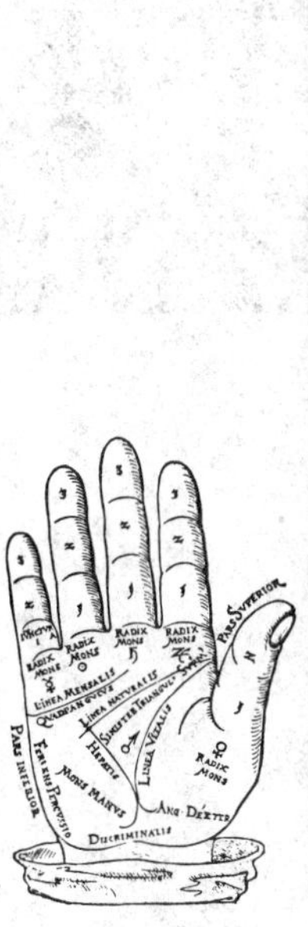

chiromancy
16th-century chart of the lines and mounts of the right hand

chisel
Cold chisel

knights or gallant gentlemen. [ME *chevalrie* < OFr. *chevalerie* < *chevalier,* knight. —see CHEVALIER.]
chiv·a·ree (shĭv′ə-rē′, shĭv′ə-rē′) *n.* Variant of **charivari.**
chive (chīv) *n.* **1.** A plant, *Allium schoenoprasum,* native to Eurasia, with purplish flowers and hollow, grasslike leaves. **2.** Often **chives.** The leaves of the chive, used as a seasoning. [ME *cive* < OFr. < Lat. *cepa,* onion.]
chiv·vy or **chiv·y** (chĭv′ē) *Chiefly Brit.* —*v.* **-vied, -vy·ing, -vies** also **-ied, -y·ing, -ies.** —*tr.* To chase or harass. —*intr.* To scurry. —*n., pl.* **-vies** or **-ies. 1.** A hunt or chase. **2.** A hunting cry. [< *chevy,* a hunting cry, prob. short for *chevy chase,* pursuit < *Chevy Chase,* title of a ballad about a border skirmish.]
chlam·y·date (klăm′ĭ-dāt′) *adj. Zool.* Having a mantle. Used of mollusks. [Lat. *chlamydatus,* cloaked < *chlamys,* cloak < Gk. *khlamus.*]
chla·myd·e·ous (klə-mĭd′ē-əs) *adj. Bot.* Having or pertaining to a floral envelope. [Lat. *chlamys, chlamyd-,* cloak + -EOUS.]
chla·myd·o·spore (klə-mĭd′ə-spôr′, -spōr′) *n.* A thick-walled fungus spore derived from a hyphal cell; resting spore. [Lat. *chlamys, chlamyd-,* cloak + SPORE.]
chlam·ys (klăm′ĭs, klā′mĭs) *n., pl.* **chlam·ys·es** or **chlam·y·des** (klăm′ĭ-dēz′). A short mantle fastened at the shoulder, worn by men in ancient Greece. [Lat. < Gk. *khlamus.*]
chlo·as·ma (klō-ăz′mə) *n., pl.* **-ma·ta** (-mə-tə). Skin discoloration of a patchy brown or black nature that usually occurs on the face. [NLat. < Gk. *khloasma,* greenness < *khloazein,* to be green < *khloos,* green color.]
chlor– *pref.* Variant of **chloro-.**
chlor·ac·ne (klôr-ăk′nē, klōr-) *n.* A skin condition resembling acne caused by the exposure to chlorinated hydrocarbons.
chlo·ral (klôr′əl, klōr′-) *n.* A colorless, mobile oily liquid, CCl_3CHO, a penetrating lung irritant, used to manufacture DDT and chloral hydrate.
chloral hydrate *n.* A colorless crystalline compound, $CCl_3CH(OH)_2$, used medicinally as a sedative and hypnotic.
chlo·ra·mine (klôr′ə-mēn′, klōr′-) *n.* Any of several compounds containing nitrogen and chlorine, esp. an unstable colorless liquid, NH_2Cl, used to make hydrazine.
chlo·ram·phen·i·col (klôr′ăm-fĕn′ĭ-kôl′, klōr′-, -kōl′) *n.* An antibiotic, $C_{11}H_{12}Cl_2N_2O_5$, derived from the soil bacterium *Streptomyces venezuelae* or synthesized. [CHLOR(O)- + AM(IDE) + PHE(NO)- + NI(TRO)- + (GLY)COL.]
chlo·rate (klôr′āt′, klōr′-) *n.* The inorganic group ClO_3 or a compound containing it.
chlor·dane (klôr′dān′, klōr′-) also **chlor·dan** (-dăn′) *n.* A colorless, odorless viscous liquid, $C_{10}H_6Cl_8$, used as an insecticide. [CHLOR(O)- + (IN)D(ENE) + -ANE.]
chlor·di·az·e·pox·ide (klôr′dī-ăz′ə-pŏk′sīd′, klōr′-) *n.* A compound, $C_{16}H_{14}ClN_3O$, whose hydrochloride is used as a tranquilizer. [CALOR(O)- + DI- + AZ(O) + EP(I)- + OXIDE.]
chlo·rel·la (klə-rĕl′ə) *n.* Any of various green algae of the genus *Chlorella,* widely used in studies of photosynthesis. [NLat. *Chlorella,* genus name < Gk. *khlōros,* green.]
chlo·ren·chy·ma (klə-rĕng′kə-mə) *n.* Plant tissue, esp. stem tissue, containing chlorophyll. [CHLOR(OPHYLL) + -ENCHYMA.]
chlo·ric (klôr′ĭk, klōr′-) *adj.* Of, pertaining to, or containing chlorine.
chloric acid *n.* A strongly oxidizing, unstable acid, $HClO_3 \cdot 7H_2O$.
chlo·ride (klôr′īd′, klōr′-) *n.* A binary compound of chlorine. **—chlo·rid′ic** (klə-rĭd′ĭk) *adj.*
chloride of lime *n.* Chlorinated lime.
chlo·ri·nate (klôr′ə-nāt′, klōr′-) *tr.v.* **-nat·ed, -nat·ing, -nates.** To treat or combine with chlorine or with a chlorine compound. **—chlo′ri·na′tion** *n.* **—chlo′ri·na′tor** *n.*
chlorinated lime *n.* A white powder of varying composition, as $CaCl(ClO) \cdot 4H_2O$, produced by chlorinating slaked lime and used as a bleach.
chlo·rine (klôr′ēn′, klōr′-, -ĭn) *n. Symbol* **Cl** A highly irritating, greenish-yellow gaseous halogen, capable of combining with nearly all other elements, produced principally by electrolysis of sodium chloride and used widely to purify water, as a disinfectant, a bleaching agent, and in the manufacture of many important compounds including chloroform and carbon tetrachloride. Atomic number 17; atomic weight 35.45; freezing point −100.98°C; boiling point −34.6°C; specific gravity 1.56 (−33.6°C); valences 1, 3, 5, 7.
chlo·rite¹ (klôr′īt′, klōr′-) *n.* A generally green or black secondary mineral, $(Mg, Fe, Al)_6(Si, Al)_4O_{10}(OH)_8$, often formed by metamorphic alteration of primary dark rock minerals. [Lat. *chloritis,* a green precious stone < Gk. *khlōritis* < *khlōros,* green.]
chlo·rite² (klôr′īt′, klōr′-) *n.* The inorganic group ClO_2 or a compound containing it.
chloro– or **chlor–** *pref.* **1.** Green: *chlorosis.* **2.** Chlorine: *chloroform.* [< Gk. *khlōros,* green.]
chlo·ro·ben·zene (klôr′ō-bĕn′zēn′, -bĕn-zēn′, klōr′-) *n.* A colorless, volatile flammable liquid, C_6H_5Cl, used to prepare phenol, DDT, and aniline, and used as a general solvent.
chlo·ro·car·bon (klôr′ō-kär′bən, klōr′-) *n.* A compound that consists of chlorine and carbon.
chlo·ro·fluor·o·car·bon (klôr′ō-flo͝or′ō-kär′bən, -flôr′-, -flōr′-, -flo͞o′ər-ō-, klōr′-) *n.* Any of various compounds consisting of carbon, hydrogen, chlorine, and fluorine, once used widely as aerosol propellants and refrigerants.
chlo·ro·form (klôr′ə-fôrm′, klōr′-) *n.* A clear, colorless, heavy liquid, $CHCl_3$, used in refrigerants, propellants, and resins, and as an anesthetic. —*tr.v.* **-formed, -form·ing, -forms. 1.** To anesthetize or kill with chloroform. **2.** To apply chloroform to. [CHLORO- + FORM(YL).]
chlo·ro·hy·drin (klôr′ō-hī′drĭn, klōr′-) *n.* An aliphatic organic chemical compound that is both an alkyl chloride and an alcohol, frequently containing a single chlorine atom and a single hydroxyl group on adjacent carbon atoms.
Chlo·ro·my·ce·tin (klôr′ō-mī-sēt′n, klōr′-). A trademark for chloramphenicol.
chlo·ro·phyll also **chlo·ro·phyl** (klôr′ə-fĭl, klōr′-) *n.* Any of a group of related green pigments found in photosynthetic organisms, esp.: **a.** *Chlorophyll a,* a waxy blue-black microcrystalline green-plant pigment, $C_{55}H_{72}MgN_4O_5$, with a characteristic blue-green alcohol solution. **b.** *Chlorophyll b,* a similar green-plant pigment, $C_{55}H_{70}MgN_4O_6$, having a brilliant green alcohol solution.
chlo·ro·pic·rin (klôr′ə-pĭk′rĭn, klōr′-) *n.* An oily colorless liquid, CCl_3NO_2, used to make poison gas and in dyestuffs, disinfectants, insecticides, and fumigants. [CHLORO- + PICR(O)- + -IN.]
chlo·ro·plast (klôr′ə-plăst′, klōr′-) also **chlo·ro·plas·tid** (klôr′ə-plăs′tĭd, klōr′-) *n. Bot.* A plastid containing chlorophyll in photosynthetic plants.
chlo·ro·prene (klôr′ə-prēn′, klōr′-) *n.* A colorless liquid, C_4H_5Cl, used as the monomer of neoprene rubber. [CHLORO- + (ISO)PRENE.]
chlo·ro·quine (klôr′ə-kwīn′, -kwēn′, klōr′-) *n.* A compound, $C_{18}H_{26}ClN_3$, used in the treatment of malaria and sometimes in the treatment of lupus erythematosus. [Blend of CHLORO- and QUINOLINE.]
chlo·ro·sis (klə-rō′sĭs) *n.* **1.** *Bot.* An abnormal condition of plants, characterized by absence of or deficiency in green pigment and caused by lack of light, mineral deficiency, or genetic disorders. **2.** *Pathol.* An iron-deficiency anemia chiefly affecting girls at puberty and characterized by greenish skin color. **—chlo·rot′ic** (-rŏt′ĭk) *adj.* **—chlo·rot′i·cal·ly** *adv.*
chlor·prom·a·zine (klôr-prŏm′ə-zēn′, -prō′mə-, klōr-) *n.* An oily liquid, $C_{17}H_{19}ClN_2S$, derived from phenothiazine and used as a sedative, tranquilizer, and antiemetic. [CHLOR(O)- + PRO(PYL) + METH(YL) + AZINE.]
chlor·tet·ra·cy·cline (klôr′tĕt-rə-sī′klēn′, klōr′-) *n.* An antibiotic, $C_{22}H_{23}ClN_2O_8$, obtained from the soil bacterium *Streptomyces aureofaciens.*
cho·a·na (kō′ə-nə) *n., pl.* **-nae** (-nē′). An opening with a funnel shape, esp. one of the internal nares. [Gk. *khoanē,* funnel < *khein,* to pour.]
cho·an·o·cyte (kō-ăn′ə-sīt′) *n. Biol.* One of the flagellated cells that line the body cavity of a sponge. [Gk. *khoanē,* funnel (< *khein,* to pour) + -CYTE.]
chock (chŏk) *n.* **1.** A block or wedge placed under something, such as a wheel, to keep it from moving. **2.** *Naut.* A heavy fitting of metal or wood with two jaws curving inward, through which a rope or cable may be run. —*tr.v.* **chocked, chock·ing, chocks. 1.** To fit with or secure by a chock. **2.** To place (a boat) on chocks. —*adv.* **1.** As completely as possible. **2.** As close as possible: *chock up against the railing.* [Orig. unknown.]
chock-a-block (chŏk′ə-blŏk′) *adj.* **1.** Drawn so close as to have the blocks touching. Used of a ship's hoisting tackle. **2.** Squeezed together; jammed: *The cheering fans were chock-a-block in the stands.* **—chock′a-block′** *adv.*
chock-full (chŏk′fo͝ol′, chŭk′-) *adj.* Completely filled; stuffed: *chock-full of candy.* [ME *chokkeful.*]
choc·o·late (chô′kə-lĭt, chôk′lĭt, chŏk′-) *n.* **1.** Husked, roasted, and ground cacao seeds, often combined with a sweetener or flavoring agent. **2.** A candy or beverage made from chocolate. **3.** A grayish to deep reddish brown to deep grayish brown. —*adj.* **1.** Flavored with chocolate. **2.** Of a grayish to deep reddish brown to deep grayish brown. [Sp. < Aztec *xocolatl* : *xococ,* bitter + *atl,* water.]
chocolate tree *n.* The cacao (sense 1).
Choc·taw (chŏk′tô) *n., pl.* **Choctaw** or **-taws. 1. a.** A tribe of Indians, formerly living in southern Mississippi and Alabama, now settled in Oklahoma. **b.** A member of this tribe. **2.** The Muskhogean language of the Choctaw. [Choctaw *Chahta.*]
choice (chois) *n.* **1.** The act of choosing; selection. **2.** The power, right, or liberty to choose; option. **3.** A person or thing that is chosen. **4.** A number or variety from which to choose: *a wide choice of styles and colors.* **5.** Something that is best or preferable above others; the best part. **6.** An alternative. —*adj.* **choic·er, choic·est. 1. a.** Of fine quality; select; excellent. **b.** Appealing to refined taste. **2.** Selected with care. **3.** Of the U.S. Government grade of meat higher than good and lower than prime. [ME *chois* < OFr. < *choisir,* to choose, of Gothic orig.] **—choice′ly** *adv.* **—choice′ness** *n.*

Synonyms: *choice, alternative, option, preference, selection, election.* Each of these terms involves the privilege of choosing. *Choice* implies broadly the freedom of choosing

choir

from a set of persons or things. *Alternative* emphasizes choice between only two possibilities or courses of action. *Option* stresses the power to choose and is widely used in the sense of granting exclusive rights to make a choice. *Preference* indicates choice based on one's values, bias, or predilections. *Selection* suggests a wide variety of things or persons to choose from. *Election* emphasizes use of judgment and wisdom in making a choice with an important end in view.

choir (kwīr) *n.* **1. a.** An organized company of singers, esp. one performing church music or singing in a church. **b.** The part of a church used by such singers. **2.** *Archit.* The part of a cruciform church between the nave and the main altar; chancel. **3. a.** A musical group or band. **b.** A section of a musical group or band. —*intr.v.* **choired, choir·ing, choirs.** To sing in chorus. [ME *quer* < OFr. *cuer* < Lat. *chorus.* —see CHORUS.]

choir·boy (kwīr'boi') *n.* A boy member of a choir.

choir loft *n.* A gallery for a church choir.

choir·mas·ter (kwīr'măs'tər) *n.* The director of a choir.

choke (chōk) *v.* **choked, chok·ing, chokes.** —*tr.* **1.** To interfere with or terminate the normal breathing of, esp. by constricting or breaking the windpipe or by polluting the air. **2.** To stop by or as if by strangling; suppress: *choke back tears; choked off debate.* **3.** To reduce the air intake of (a carburetor), thereby enriching the fuel mixture. **4.** To check or slow down the movement, growth, or action of. **5.** To block up or obstruct by filling or crowding; clog. **6.** To fill completely; jam. **7.** To grip (a bat, racket, or club) at a point nearer the hitting surface; shorten one's grip on. —*intr.* **1.** To become suffocated; have difficulty in breathing, swallowing, or speaking. **2.** To be blocked up or obstructed. ***—phrasal verb.* choke up.** *Informal.* **1.** To be unable to speak because of strong emotion. **2.** To fail to perform effectively because of nervous agitation or tension. —*n.* **1.** The act or sound of choking. **2. a.** Something that constricts or chokes. **b.** A narrow part, such as the chokebore of a gun. **3.** A device used in an internal-combustion engine to enrich the fuel mixture by reducing the flow of air to the carburetor. [ME *choken* < OE *āceōcian.*]

choke·ber·ry (chōk'bĕr'ē) *n.* **1.** Any of various North American shrubs of the genus *Aronia,* having bitter-tasting red, black, or purple fruit. **2.** The fruit of the chokeberry. [From its bitter fruit.]

choke·bore (chōk'bôr', -bōr') *n.* **1.** A shotgun bore that narrows toward the muzzle to prevent wide scattering of the shot. **2.** A gun with a chokebore.

choke·cher·ry (chōk'chĕr'ē) *n.* **1.** A North American shrub or tree, *Prunus virginiana,* with long clusters of white flowers and very astringent dark-red or blackish fruit. **2.** The fruit of the chokecherry. [From its bitter fruit.]

choke·damp (chōk'dămp') *n.* Blackdamp. [So called because it causes suffocation in mines.]

chok·er (chō'kər) *n.* **1.** One that chokes. **2. a.** A necklace that fits closely around the throat. **b.** A high, tight collar. **c.** A narrow fur neckpiece.

chol– *pref.* Variant of **chole-.**

cho·lan·gi·og·ra·phy (kō-lăn'jē-ŏg'rə-fē) *n.* Roentgenographic examination of the bile ducts. **—cho·lan'gi·o·graph'ic** (-ə-grăf'ĭk) *adj.* [CHOL(E)- + Gk. *angeion,* vessel + -GRAPHY.]

chole– or **chol–** *pref.* Bile: *cholesterol.* [< Gk. *kholē,* bile.]

cho·le·cyst (kō'lĭ-sĭst') *n.* The gallbladder.

cho·le·cys·tec·to·my (kō'lĭ-sĭ-stĕk'tə-me) *n., pl.* **-mies.** Surgical removal of the gallbladder.

cho·le·li·thi·a·sis (kō'lə-lĭ-thī'ə-sĭs) *n.* The presence of gallstones in the gallbladder.

chol·er (kŏl'ər, kō'lər) *n.* **1.** Anger; irritability. **2.** *Archaic.* **a.** One of the four humors of the body thought in the Middle Ages to cause anger and bad temper when present in excess; bile. **b.** Biliousness. [ME *colre* < OFr. < Lat. *cholera,* jaundice < Gk. *kholera.*]

chol·er·a (kŏl'ər-ə) *n.* An acute, often fatal, infectious epidemic disease caused by the microorganism *Vibrio comma,* that is characterized by watery diarrhea, vomiting, cramps, suppression of urine, and collapse. [Lat., jaundice. —see CHOLER.] **—chol'e·ra'ic** (-ə-rā'ĭk) *adj.* **—chol'e·roid'** (-ə-roid') *adj.*

cholera mor·bus (môr'bəs) *n.* Acute gastroenteritis occurring in summer and autumn and marked by severe cramps, diarrhea, and vomiting. [NLat. : Lat. *cholera,* jaundice + Lat. *morbus,* disease.]

cholera nos·tras (nŏs'trəs) *n.* Cholera morbus.

chol·er·ic (kŏl'ə-rĭk, kə-lĕr'ĭk) *adj.* **1.** Easily angered; bad-tempered **2.** Showing or expressing anger. **—chol'er·i·cal·ly, chol'er·ic·ly** *adv.*

cho·le·sta·sis (kō'lĭ-stā'sĭs) *n.* The suppression of bilary flow.

cho·les·ter·in (kə-lĕs'tər-ĭn) *n.* Cholesterol.

cho·les·ter·ol (kə-lĕs'tə-rōl', -rōl') *n.* A glistening white soapy crystalline substance, $C_{27}H_{45}OH$, the most common animal sterol, a precursor of a form of vitamin D and a universal tissue constituent, occurring notably in bile, gallstones, the brain, blood cells, plasma, egg yolk, and seeds. [Gk. *kholē,* bile + Gk. *stereos,* solid + -OL (so called because it was first found in gallstones).]

cho·lic acid (kō'lĭk) *n.* An abundant crystalline bile acid, $C_{24}H_{40}O_5$. [Gk. *kholikos,* bilious < *kholē,* bile.]

cho·line (kō'lēn') *n.* A natural amine, $C_5H_{15}NO_2$, often classed in the vitamin B complex and a precursor of acetylcholine.

cho·lin·er·gic (kō'lə-nûr'jĭk) *adj.* **1.** Activated by or capable of liberating the acetylcholine. **2.** Having physiological effects similar to acetylcholine. [(ACETYL)CHOLIN(E) + Gk. *ergon,* work.]

cho·lin·es·ter·ase (kō'lə-nĕs'tə-rās', -rāz') *n.* An enzyme that hydrolyzes acetylcholine to form acetic acid and choline. [CHOLIN(E) + ESTERASE.]

chol·la (choi'ə) *n.* Any of several very spiny cacti of the genus *Opuntia,* characterized by cylindrical rather than flattened stem segments. [Mex. Sp. < obs. Sp. *cholla,* upper part of the head, poss. < OFr. *cholle,* head, of Germanic orig.]

chomp (chŏmp) *v. & n.* Variant of **champ**[1].

chon (chŏn) *n., pl.* **chon.** See table at **currency.** [Korean.]

chondr– or **chondri–** *pref.* Variants of **chondro-.**

chon·dri·fy (kŏn'drə-fī') *tr. & intr.v.* **-fied, -fy·ing, -fies.** To change into cartilage. **—chon'dri·fi·ca'tion** *n.*

chon·dri·o·some (kŏn'drē-ə-sōm') *n.* A mitochondrion.

chon·drite (kŏn'drīt') *n.* A stone of meteoric origin characterized by chondrules. **—chon·drit'ic** (-drĭt'ĭk) *adj.*

chon·dri·tis (kŏn-drī'tĭs) *n.* Inflammation of cartilage.

chondro– or **chondri–** or **chondr–** *pref.* **1.** Cartilage: *chondrocranium.* **2.** Granule: *chondrite.* [< Gk. *khondros,* granule, cartilage.]

chon·dro·cra·ni·um (kŏn'drō-krā'nē-əm) *n., pl.* **-ni·ums** or **-ni·a** (-nē-ə). The embryonic cranium, esp. as distinguished from the osteocranium.

chon·dro·i·tin (kŏn-drō'ĭ-tĭn) *n.* A mucopolysaccharide that is found in cartilage in its sulfated form. [< *chondroitic acid,* an acid occurring in cartilage.]

chon·dro·ma (kŏn-drō'mə) *n., pl.* **-mas** or **-ma·ta** (-mə-tə). A cartilaginous growth.

chon·dro·ma·la·cia (kŏn'drō-mə-lā'shə) *n.* The abnormal softening of cartilage. [CHONDRO- + Gk. *malakia,* softness < *malakos,* soft.]

chon·drule (kŏn'drōōl) *n.* *Geol.* A small round granule of extraterrestrial origin found embedded in some meteorites.

choose (chōōz) *v.* **chose** (chōz), **chos·en** (chō'zən), **choos·ing, choos·es.** —*tr.* **1.** To select from a number of possible alternatives; decide upon and pick out. **2.** To prefer above others. **3.** To want; desire: *choose to go.* —*intr.* To make a choice; select: *did as he chose.* [ME *chesen* < OE *cēosan.*] **—choos'er** *n.*

Synonyms: *choose, select, elect, pick.* These verbs apply to making a choice. *Choose* implies the use of judgment in taking one of several persons, things, or courses. *Select* stresses care and comparison in choosing from a large variety. *Elect* strongly suggests deliberation in making a selection, usually between alternatives: *He elected to stay home. Pick,* like *select,* indicates some care in choosing but implies less deliberation than *elect.*

choos·y also **choos·ey** (chōō'zē) *adj.* **-i·er, -i·est.** Willing to settle for only the best; hard to please. **—choos'i·ness** *n.*

chop[1] (chŏp) *v.* **chopped, chop·ping, chops.** —*tr.* **1.** To cut by striking with a heavy, sharp tool, such as an axe: *chop wood.* **2.** To shape or form by chopping. **3.** To cut into bits; mince: *chop onions.* **4.** To cut short: *chopped off his sentence midway.* **5.** *Sports.* To hit or hit at with a short, swift downward stroke. —*intr.* **1.** To make heavy, cutting strokes. **2.** To move roughly or suddenly. —*n.* **1.** The act of chopping. **2.** A swift, short, cutting blow or stroke. **3.** A chopped-off piece, esp. a cut of meat, usually taken from the rib, shoulder, or loin and containing a bone. **4.** A short, irregular motion of waves. [ME *choppen.*]

chop[2] (chŏp) *intr.v.* **chopped, chop·ping, chops.** To change direction suddenly; swerve, as a ship in the wind. [*chop,* to exchange (obs.) < ME *choppen.*]

chop[3] (chŏp) *n.* **1.** An official stamp or permit in the Far East. **2.** Quality: *first chop.* [Hindi *chhāp,* seal.]

chop·fall·en (chŏp'fô'lən) *adj.* Variant of **chapfallen.**

chop·house (chŏp'hous') *n.* A restaurant that specializes in serving chops and steaks.

chop·per (chŏp'ər) *n.* **1.** One that chops. **2.** A device that interrupts an electric current or beam of radiation. **3.** *Slang.* A helicopter. **4. choppers.** *Slang.* Teeth, esp. a set of false teeth. **5.** A motorcycle, esp. one that is customized.

chopping block *n.* A wooden block on which food is prepared, as by chopping.

chop·py[1] (chŏp'ē) *adj.* **-pi·er, -pi·est.** **1.** Rough with many small waves: *choppy seas.* **2.** Marked by abrupt transitions; jerky: *choppy prose.* **—chop'pi·ness** *n.*

chop·py[2] (chŏp'ē) *adj.* **-pi·er, -pi·est.** Abruptly shifting; variable. Used of the wind.

chops (chŏps) *pl.n.* The jaws, cheeks, or jowls of animals or human beings. [Orig. unknown.]

chop·sticks (chŏp'stĭks') *pl.n.* A pair of slender sticks made of wood or ivory, used as eating utensils chiefly in Oriental countries. [Pidgin E. *chop,* fast (prob. < Cantonese *kap*) + STICKS.]

chop su·ey (chŏp sōō'ē) *n.* A Chinese-American dish consisting of small pieces of meat or chicken cooked with bean sprouts and other vegetables and served with rice. [Chin.

chokecherry

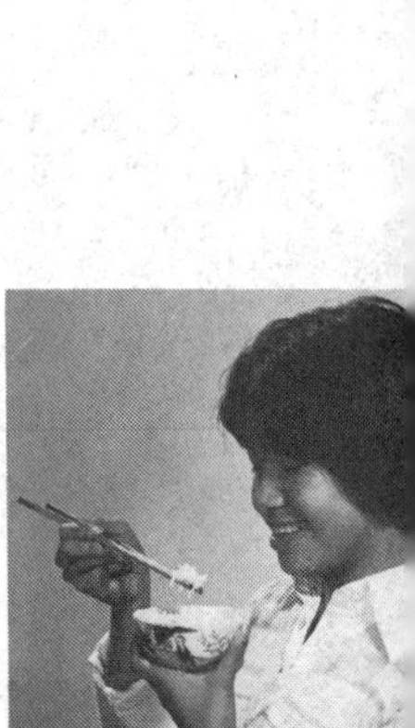

chopsticks

chorus
A chorus line from a Broadway musical

chow[1]

(Cantonese) *tsap[2] sui[4]*, mixed pieces : *tsap[2]*, mixed + *sui[4]*, to break up.]

cho·ra·gus (kə-rā′gəs) *n., pl.* **-gi** (-jī′). The leader of a chorus in Greek drama. [Lat. < Gk. *khoragos* : *khoros*, chorus + *agein*, to lead.] **—cho·rag′ic** (-răj′ĭk) *adj.*

cho·ral (kôr′əl, kōr′-) *adj.* **1.** Of or pertaining to a chorus or choir. **2.** Written for performance by a chorus. *—n.* Variant of **chorale.** [Med. Lat. *choralis* < *chorus*, choral dance < Lat. —see CHORUS.] **—cho′ral·ly** *adv.*

cho·rale also **cho·ral** (kə-răl′, -räl′) *n.* **1.** A Protestant hymn tune. **2.** A harmonized hymn, esp. one for organ. **3.** A chorus or choir. [G. *Choral(gesang)*, choral (song) < Med. Lat. *choralis*, choral.]

chorale prelude *n.* A musical composition for organ, chiefly in baroque style, characterized by an elaborate contrapuntal structure based on the melody of a hymn or chorale.

choral speaking *n.* The recitation of poetry or prose by a chorus.

chord[1] (kôrd, kōrd) *n.* **1.** A combination of three or more usually concordant tones sounded simultaneously. **2.** Harmony, as of color. **3.** An emotional feeling or response: *Her words struck a sympathetic chord.* *—tr. & intr.v.* **chord·ed, chord·ing, chords.** To furnish with or form a chord; harmonize. [ME *cord* < *accord*, agreement < OFr. *acorde* < *acorder*, to agree. —see ACCORD.]

chord[2] (kôrd, kōrd) *n.* **1.** A line segment that joins two points on a curve. **2.** A straight line connecting the leading and trailing edges of an airfoil. **3.** *Archaic.* The string of a musical instrument. **4.** Variant of **cord** (sense 5). [Alteration of CORD.]

chord·al (kôr′dl) *adj.* **1.** *Mus.* **a.** Of or pertaining to the strings of a musical instrument. **b.** Relating to or consisting of a harmonic chord. **c.** Giving prominence to harmonic rather than contrapuntal structure: *chordal music.* **2.** Of or pertaining to combinations of colors.

chor·date (kôr′dāt′, -dĭt) *n.* Any of numerous animals belonging to the phylum Chordata, which includes all vertebrates and certain marine animals, such as the lancelets, having a notochord. [NLat. *Chordata*, phylum name < Lat. *chorda*, cord. —see CORD.]

chord organ *n.* An electronic or reed organ equipped with buttons for producing chords.

chore (chôr, chōr) *n.* **1.** A routine or minor duty. **2. chores. a.** Daily or routine domestic tasks. **b.** The routine morning and evening tasks of a farmer, as the feeding of livestock. **3.** An unpleasant or burdensome task. *—intr.v.* **chored, chor·ing, chores.** To work at chores. [Var. of CHAR[3].]

-chore *suff.* A plant distributed by a specified agency: *zoochore.* [< Gk. *khōrein*, to move.]

cho·re·a (kô-rē′ə, kō-) *n.* A nervous disorder, esp. of children, marked by uncontrollable and irregular movements of the muscles of the arms, legs, and face. [Lat., dance < Gk. *khoreia*, choral dance < *khoros*.]

cho·re·o·graph (kôr′ē-ə-grăf′, kōr′-) *intr. & tr.v.* **-graphed, -graph·ing, -graphs.** To specialize in choreography or create the choreography of. **—cho′re·og′ra·pher** (kôr′ē-ŏg′rə-fər, kōr′-) *n.*

cho·re·og·ra·phy (kôr′ē-ŏg′rə-fē, kōr′-) *n.* **1.** The art of creating and arranging ballets or dances. **2.** The art and technique of dance notation. **3.** The art of dancing. [Fr. *chorégraphie* : Gk. *khoreia*, choral dance (< *khoros*) + *-graphie*, -graphy.] **—cho′re·o·graph′ic** (-ə-grăf′ĭk) *adj.* **—cho′re·o·graph′i·cal·ly** *adv.*

cho·ri·amb (kôr′ē-ămb′, -ăm′, kōr′-) *n.* **1.** A metrical foot consisting of a trochee followed by an iamb, much employed in Greek and Latin poetry. **2.** A foot of verse used in lyric poetry having two unstressed syllables flanked by the two rhythmic stresses marking the first and last syllables of the foot. [LLat. *choriambus* < Gk. *khoriambos* : *khoreios*, of a chorus (< *khoros*) + *iambos*, iamb.] **—cho′ri·am′bic** (-ăm′bĭk) *adj.*

cho·ric (kôr′ĭk, kōr′-, kŏr′-) *adj.* Of or pertaining to a chorus, esp. a Greek chorus. [Gk. *khorikos* < *khoros*, choral dance.]

cho·rine (kôr′ēn′, kōr′-) *n. Slang.* A chorus girl. [CHOR(US) + -INE[1].]

cho·ri·o·al·lan·to·is (kôr′ē-ō′ə-lăn′tō-ĭs, kōr′-) *n.* The highly vascular fetal membrane that consists of the fused chorion and allantois. [CHORIO(N) + ALLANTOIS.] **—cho′ri·o·al′lan·to′ic** (-ō-ăl′ən-tō′ĭk) *adj.*

cho·ri·oid (kôr′ē-oid′, kōr′-) *adj.* Choroid. [Gk. *khorioeidēs*, like an afterbirth : *khorion*, afterbirth + *-eidēs*, -oid.]

cho·ri·on (kôr′ē-ŏn′, kōr′-) *n.* The outer membrane enclosing the embryo in reptiles, birds, and mammals. [Gk. *khorion.*] **—cho′ri·on′ic** (-ŏn′ĭk) *adj.*

cho·ris·ter (kôr′ĭ-stər, kōr′-, kŏr′-) *n.* **1.** A choir singer, esp. a choirboy. **2.** A choir leader. [ME *queristre* < Norman Fr. **cueristre* < Med. Lat. *chorista* < *chorus*, chorus < Lat., choral dance. —see CHORUS.]

cho·ri·zo (chə-rē′zō, -sō) *n.* A spicy pork sausage. [Sp.]

cho·rog·ra·phy (kə-rŏg′rə-fē) *n.* **1.** The technique of mapping a region or district. **2.** *Archaic.* A description or map of a region. [Lat. *chorographia* < Gk. *khōrographia* : *khōros*, place + *-graphia*, writing < *graphein*, to write.] **—cho·rog′ra·pher** *n.* **—cho′ro·graph′ic** (kôr′ə-grăf′ĭk, kōr′-), **cho′ro·graph′i·cal** *adj.* **—cho′ro·graph′i·cal·ly** *adv.*

cho·roid (kôr′oid′, kōr′-) also **cho·roi·de·a** (kô-roi′dē-ə, kō-) *n.* The dark-brown vascular coat of the eye between the sclera and the retina. *—adj. Anat.* **1.** Resembling the chorion. **2.** Resembling the corium. **3.** Of or pertaining to the choroid. [< Gk. *khoroeidēs*, like an afterbirth, alteration of *khorioeidēs.* —see CHORIOID.]

chor·tle (chôr′tl) *n.* A snorting, joyful chuckle. *—intr. & tr.v.* **-tled, -tling, -tles.** To utter or express with a chortle. [Blend of CHUCKLE and SNORT.] **—chor′tler** *n.*

cho·rus (kôr′əs, kōr′-) *n., pl.* **-rus·es. 1.** *Mus.* **a.** A composition in four or more parts written for a large number of singers. **b.** A song refrain in which the audience joins the soloist. **c.** A repeat of the opening statement of a popular song played by the whole group. **d.** A solo section based on the main melody of a popular song and played by a member of the group. **e.** A body of singers who perform choral compositions. **f.** A body of vocalists and dancers who support the soloists and leading actors in operas, musical comedies, and revues. **2. a.** In drama or poetry recitation, a group of persons who speak or sing a given part or composition in unison. **b.** In Elizabethan drama, an actor who recites the prologue and epilogue to a play and sometimes comments on the action. **3.** In Greek poetry and drama: **a.** A ceremonial dance performed to the singing of odes. **b.** The portion of a drama consisting of choric dance and ode. **c.** The body of actors whose choric performance comments upon and accompanies the action of the play. **4. a.** A speech, song, or other utterance made in concert by many people. **b.** A simultaneous utterance by a number of individuals. *—tr. & intr.v.* **-rused, -rus·ing, -rus·es** or **-russed, -rus·sing, -rus·ses.** To sing or utter in chorus. **—*idiom.* in chorus.** With simultaneous utterance; all together. [Lat., choral dance < Gk. *khoros.*]

chorus girl *n.* A young woman who dances in a theatrical chorus.

chose[1] (chōz) *v.* Past tense of **choose.**

chose[2] (shōz) *n. Law.* An item of personal property; chattel. [Fr. < Lat. *causa*, thing.]

cho·sen (chō′zən) *v.* Past participle of **choose.** *—adj.* **1.** Selected from or preferred above others. **2.** *Theol.* Elect. *—n., pl.* **chosen. 1.** One of the elect. **2.** The elect collectively.

chott (shŏt) *n.* **1.** The depression surrounding a salt marsh, esp. in North Africa. **2.** The bed of a dried salt marsh. [Fr. < Ar. *shaṭṭ.*]

chough (chŭf) *n.* A crowlike Old World bird of the genus *Pyrrhocorax*, having black plumage and red legs. [ME.]

chow[1] (chou) also **chow chow** *n.* A heavy-set dog of a breed originating in China, having a long, dense, reddish-brown or black coat and a blackish tongue. [Pidgin E., prob. < Chin. (Mandarin) *kou[3]*, dog.]

chow[2] (chou) *Slang.* *—n.* Food; victuals. *—intr.v.* **chowed, chow·ing, chows.** To eat. [Pidgin E., prob < Chin. (Mandarin) *chao[3]*, to stir-fry.]

chow-chow (chou′chou′) *n.* A relish consisting of chopped vegetables pickled in mustard. [Pidgin E., prob. < Chin. (Mandarin) *chao[3]*, to stir-fry.]

chow chow *n.* Variant of **chow[1].**

chow·der (chou′dər) *n.* A thick soup or stew containing fish or shellfish, esp. clams, and vegetables, often in a milk base. [Fr. *chaudière*, stew pot < OFr. < LLat. *caldaria.* —see CALDRON.]

chow mein (chou′ mān′) *n.* A Chinese-American dish consisting of a combination of stewed vegetables and meat, served over fried noodles. [Chin. (Mandarin) *chao[3] mian[4]* : *chao[3]*, to stir-fry + *mian[4]*, noodles.]

chres·ard (krĕs′ərd) *n.* Water present in the soil and available for plant absorption. [Gk. *khrēsis*, use (< *khrēsthai*, to use) + Gk. *ardein*, to water.]

chres·tom·a·thy (krĕ-stŏm′ə-thē) *n., pl.* **-thies.** A selection of literary passages, used in studying literature or a language. [Gk. *khrēstomatheia* : *khrēstos*, useful (< *khrēsthai*, to use) + *-matheia*, learning < *manthanein*, to learn.] **—chres′to·math′ic** (krĕs′tə-măth′ĭk) *adj.*

chrism (krĭz′əm) *n. Eccles.* **1.** A mixture of oil and balsam consecrated by a bishop and used for anointing in various church sacraments, such as baptism. **2.** A sacramental anointing, esp. upon confirmation into the Eastern Orthodox Church. [ME *crisme*, chrism, chrisom < OE *crisma* < LLat. *chrisma* < Gk. *khrisma*, ointment < *khriein*, to anoint.] **—chris′mal** (krĭz′məl) *adj.*

chris·om (krĭz′əm) *n. Eccles.* **1.** A white cloth or robe worn by an infant at baptism. **2.** *Archaic.* An infant wearing a baptismal robe; baby. [ME *crisom*, var. of *crisme*, chrisom, chrism.]

Christ (krīst) *n.* **1.** The Anointed; the Messiah, as foretold by the prophets of the Old Testament. **2.** Jesus. **3.** *Christian Science.* "The divine manifestation of God, which comes to the flesh to destroy incarnate error." (Mary Baker Eddy). [ME *Crist* < OE *Crīst* < Lat. *Christus* < Gk. *Khristos* < *khristos*, anointed < *khriein*, to anoint.] **—Christ′li·ness** *n.* **—Christ′ly** *adj.*

chris·ten (krĭs′ən) *tr.v.* **-tened, -ten·ing, -tens. 1.** To baptize into a Christian church. **2.** To give a name to at baptism. **3.** To name and dedicate ceremonially: *christen a ship.* **4.** *Informal.* To use for the first time. [ME *cristnen* < OE *cristnian* < *Cristen*, Christian.]

Chris·ten·dom (krĭs′ən-dəm) *n.* **1.** Christians collectively. **2.** The Christian world. **3.** Christianity. [ME *Cristendom* < OE *Cristendōm* : *Cristen,* Christian + *-dom,* -dom.]

chris·ten·ing (krĭs′ə-nĭng) *n.* The Christian sacrament of baptism, including the bestowal of a name upon an infant.

Chris·tian (krĭs′chən) *adj.* **1.** Professing belief in Jesus as Christ or following the religion based on his teachings. **2.** Pertaining to or derived from Jesus or his teachings. **3.** Manifesting the qualities or spirit of Christ; Christlike. **4.** Pertaining to or characteristic of Christianity or its adherents. **5.** *Informal.* Neighborly; decent. —*n.* **1.** One who professes belief in Jesus as Christ or follows the religion based on his teachings. **2.** One who lives according to the teachings of Jesus. [ME *Cristen* < OE < Lat. *Christianus* < Gk. *Khristianos* < *Khristos,* Christ.] —**Chris′tian·ly** *adv.*

Christian era *n.* The period beginning with the birth of Jesus (conventionally in A.D. 1).

chris·ti·an·i·a (krĭs′tē-ăn′ē-ə, -ä′nē-ə, krĭs′chē-) *n.* A ski turn in which the body is swung from a crouching position to change direction or to make a stop. [Norw. < *Christiania,* the former name for Oslo, Norway.]

Chris·ti·an·i·ty (krĭs′chē-ăn′ĭ-tē, krĭs′tē-) *n., pl.* **-ties. 1.** The Christian religion, founded on the teachings of Jesus. **2.** Christians as a group; Christendom. **3.** The state or fact of being a Christian.

Chris·tian·ize (krĭs′chə-nīz′) *tr. & intr.v.* **-ized, -iz·ing, -iz·es.** To convert to or adopt Christianity. —**Chris′tian·i·za′tion** *n.* —**Chris′tian·iz′er** *n.*

Christian Science *n.* The church and the religious system founded by Mary Baker Eddy, emphasizing healing through spiritual means as an important element of Christianity and teaching pure divine goodness as underlying the scientific reality of existence. —**Christian Scientist** *n.*

Christ·like (krīst′līk′) *adj.* Having the spiritual qualities or attributes of Christ. —**Christ′like′ness** *n.*

Christ·mas (krĭs′məs) *n.* **1.** December 25, a holiday celebrated by Christians as the anniversary of the birth of Jesus. **2.** Christmastide. [ME *Cristemas* < OE *Crīstes mæsse* : *Crīst,* Christ + *mæsse,* mass. —see MASS.]

Christmas berry *n.* Toyon.

Christmas cactus *n.* A spineless, epiphytic cactus, *Zygocactus truncatus,* of South America, cultivated as a house plant for its showy red flowers.

Christmas disease *n.* A type of hemophilia that is caused by a deficiency of the plasma thromboplastin component. [After Stephen *Christmas,* the first patient in whom the disease was diagnosed and studied.]

Christmas Eve *n.* The evening before Christmas.

Christmas fern *n.* Dagger fern.

Christmas rose *n.* An evergreen plant, *Helleborus niger,* native to Europe, having a poisonous root and white or pinkish-green flowers that bloom in late fall or winter.

Christ·mas·tide (krĭs′məs-tīd′) *n.* The Christian church festival extending from December 24 through January 6.

Christmas tree *n.* An evergreen or artificial tree decorated with lights and ornaments during the Christmas season.

Chris·tol·o·gy (krĭ-stŏl′ə-jē) *n., pl.* **-gies. 1.** The study of Christ's person and qualities. **2.** A doctrine or theory based on Christ or his teachings. —**Chris′to·log′i·cal** (krĭs′-tə-lŏj′ĭ-kəl) *adj.*

Christ's-thorn (krīsts′thôrn′) *n.* Any of several plants of the Near East having spiny thorns and popularly believed to have been used for Christ's crown of thorns, as the jujube.

chris·ty (krĭs′tē) *n., pl.* **-ties.** A christiania.

chrom– *pref.* Variant of **chromo-**.

chro·ma (krō′mə) *n.* That aspect of color in the Munsell color system by which a sample appears to differ from a gray of the same lightness or brightness. Chroma corresponds to saturation of the perceived color. [Gk. *khrōma,* color.]

chro·maf·fin (krō′mə-fĭn) *adj.* Capable of being stained readily with chromium salts. [CHROMO- + Lat. *affinis,* related.]

chromat– *pref.* Variant of **chromato-**.

chro·mate (krō′māt′) *n.* A salt or ester of chromic acid.

chro·mat·ic (krō-măt′ĭk) *adj.* **1. a.** Pertaining to colors or color. **b.** Pertaining to color perceived to have a saturation greater than zero. **2.** *Mus.* **a.** Of, pertaining to, or based on the chromatic scale. **b.** Pertaining to chords or harmonies based on nonharmonic tones. [Gk. *khrōmatikos* < *khrōma,* color.] —**chro·mat′i·cal·ly** *adv.* —**chro·mat′i·cism** *n.*

chromatic aberration *n.* Color distortion in an image produced by a lens because of the dependence of lens refractivity on the wavelength of light and marked by a variation in the focusing of colors.

chro·ma·tic·i·ty (krō′mə-tĭs′ĭ-tē) *n.* The aspect of color that includes consideration of its dominant wavelength and purity.

chro·mat·ics (krō-măt′ĭks) *n.* *(used with a sing. verb).* The scientific study of color. —**chro′ma·tist** (-mə-tĭst) *n.*

chromatic scale *n. Mus.* A scale consisting of 12 semitones.

chro·ma·tid (krō′mə-tĭd) *n.* Either of two daughter strands of a duplicated chromosome while still joined by a single centromere.

chro·ma·tin (krō′mə-tĭn) *n.* A complex of nucleic acids and proteins characterized by intense staining with basic dyes. —**chro′ma·tin′ic** *adj.*

chromato– or **chromat–** *pref.* **1.** Color: *chromatophore.* **2.** Chromatin: *chromatolysis.* [< Gk. *khrōma, khrōmat-,* color.]

chro·mat·o·gram (krō-măt′ə-grăm′) *n.* The absorbent column or strip of material containing the stratographically differentiated constituents separated from a solution or mixture by chromatography.

chro·ma·tog·ra·phy (krō′mə-tŏg′rə-fē) *n.* Separation of complex mixtures by percolation through a selectively adsorbing medium, as through a column of magnesia, gelatin, or starch, yielding stratified, sometimes chromatically distinct constituent layers. —**chro·mat′o·graph′** *n.* —**chro′ma·tog′ra·pher** *n.* —**chro·mat′o·graph′ic** (krō-măt′ə-grăf′ĭk) *adj.* —**chro·mat′o·graph′i·cal·ly** *adv.*

chro·ma·tol·y·sis (krō′mə-tŏl′ĭ-sĭs) *n.* The solution and disintegration of stainable material, as of chromatin, within a cell. —**chro·mat′o·lyt′ic** (-măt′l-ĭt′ĭk) *adj.*

chro·mat·o·phore (krō-măt′ə-fôr′, -fōr′) *n. Biol.* A pigment-containing or pigment-producing cell, esp. a pigment-containing animal cell, as in certain lizards, that by expansion or contraction can change the overall color of the skin. —**chro·mat′o·phor′ic** (-fôr′ĭk, -fōr′-) *adj.*

chrome (krōm) *n.* **1. a.** Chromium. **b.** Something plated with a chromium alloy. **2.** A pigment containing chromium. —*tr.v.* **chromed, chrom·ing, chromes. 1.** To plate with chromium. **2.** To tan or dye with a chromium compound. [Fr. < Gk. *khrōma,* color (from the brilliant colors of chromium compounds).]

-chrome *suff.* **1.** Colored: *autochrome.* **2.** Color; pigment: *urochrome.* [< Gk. *khrōma,* color.]

chrome alum *n.* A violet-red crystalline compound, $CrK(SO_4)_2 \cdot 12H_2O$, used in tanning, as a mordant, and in photography.

chrome green *n.* **1.** Any of a class of green pigments consisting of chrome yellow and iron blue in various proportions. **2.** A very dark yellowish green to moderate or strong green.

chrome red *n.* A light orange to red pigment consisting of basic lead chromate with varying proportions of $PbCrO_4$ and PbO.

chrome yellow *n.* Lead chromate, $PbCrO_4$, a yellow pigment often combined with lead sulfate, $PbSO_4$, for lighter hues.

chro·mic (krō′mĭk) *adj.* Of, pertaining to, or containing chromium, esp. with valence 3.

chromic acid *n.* **1.** A corrosive, oxidizing acid, H_2CrO_4, known only in solution. **2.** The anhydride of chromic acid, CrO_3, a purplish crystalline material that reacts explosively with reducing agents and is used in chromium plating, as an oxidizing agent, and to color glass and rubber.

chromic oxide *n.* A bright-green crystalline powder, Cr_2O_3, used in metallurgy and as a paint pigment.

chro·mite (krō′mīt′) *n.* A widely distributed black to brownish-black chromium ore, $FeCr_2O_4$.

chro·mi·um (krō′mē-əm) *n. Symbol* **Cr** A lustrous, hard, steel-gray metallic element, resistant to tarnish and corrosion, and found primarily in chromite. It is used as a catalyst, to harden steel alloys, to produce stainless steels, in corrosion-resistant decorative platings, and as pigment in glass. Atomic number 24; atomic weight 51.996; melting point 1,890°C; boiling point 2,482°C; specific gravity 7.18; valences 2, 3, 6. [NLat. < Fr. *chrome.* —see CHROME.]

chromo– or **chrom–** *pref.* **1.** Color: *chromoplast.* **2.** Chromium: *chromous.* [< Gk. *khrōma,* color.]

chro·mo·dy·nam·ics (krō′mō-dī-năm′ĭks) *n. (used with a sing. verb).* The physics of the relationship between quarks and esp. the nature of the strong interaction, color, and the exchange of gluons.

chro·mo·gen (krō′mə-jən) *n.* **1.** *Chem.* A substance capable of chemical conversion into a pigment or dye. **2.** *Biol.* A strongly pigmented or pigment-generating organ or organelle. —**chro′mo·gen′ic** (-jĕn′ĭk) *adj.*

chro·mo·lith·o·graph (krō′mə-lĭth′ə-grăf′) *n.* A colored print produced by chromolithography.

chro·mo·li·thog·ra·phy (krō′mə-lĭ-thŏg′rə-fē) *n.* The art or process of printing color pictures from a series of stone or zinc plates by lithography. —**chro′mo·li·thog′ra·pher** *n.* —**chro′mo·lith′o·graph′ic** (-lĭth′ə-grăf′ĭk) *adj.*

chro·mo·mere (krō′mə-mîr′) *n.* One of the serially aligned chromatin granules forming a chromosome.

chro·mo·ne·ma (krō′mə-nē′mə) *n., pl.* **-ma·ta** (-mə-tə). The coiled filamentous core of a chromosome. [CHROMO- + Gk. *nēma,* thread.] —**chro′mo·ne′mal** (-nē′məl), **chro·mo′ne·mat′al** (-nē-măt′l), **chro′mo·ne·mat′ic** (-nə-măt′ĭk), **chro′mo·ne′mic** (-nē′mĭk) *adj.*

chro·mo·phil (krō′mə-fĭl′) *adj.* Capable of being stained readily with dyes.

chro·mo·phore (krō′mə-fôr′, -fōr′) *n.* A molecular group capable of selective light absorption resulting in coloration of aromatic compounds. —**chro′mo·phor′ic** (-fôr′ĭk, -fōr′-) *adj.*

chro·mo·plast (krō′mə-plăst′) *n.* A colored plastid containing a pigment other than or in addition to chlorophyll.

chro·mo·pro·tein (krō′mə-prō′tēn′, -tē-ĭn) *n.* A substance consisting of a protein and a chromophore or pigment.

Christmas cactus

Christmas rose

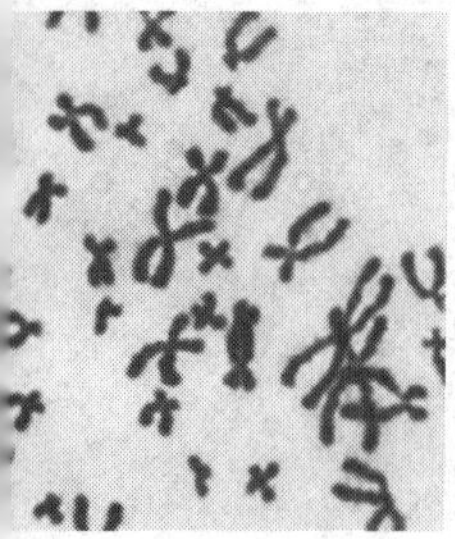

chromosome
Human female chromosomes

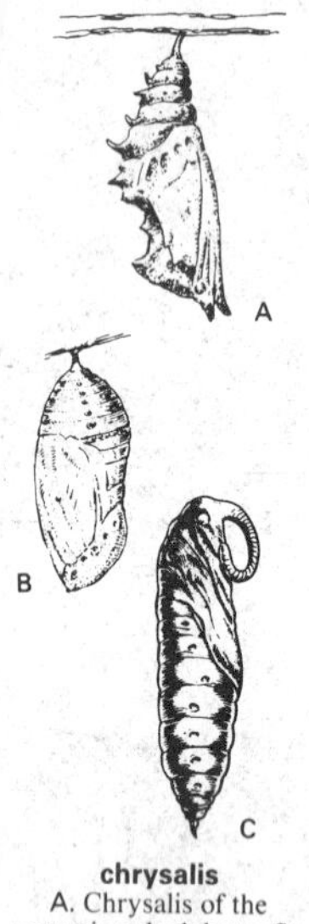

chrysalis
A. Chrysalis of the mourning cloak butterfly
B. Chrysalis of the monarch butterfly
C. Chrysalis of a hawk moth

chuck[2]

chukar

chro·mo·some (krō'mə-sōm') *n.* A DNA-containing linear body of the cell nuclei of plants and animals, responsible for the determination and transmission of hereditary characteristics. **—chro'mo·so'mal** (-sō'məl), **chro'mo·so'mic** (-sō'mĭk) *adj.* **—chro'mo·so'mal·ly** *adv.*

chro·mo·sphere (krō'mə-sfîr') *n.* **1.** An incandescent, transparent layer of gas, primarily hydrogen, several thousand miles in depth, that lies above and surrounds the photosphere of the sun but is distinctly separate from the corona. **2.** A gaseous layer similar to a chromosphere around a star. **—chro'mo·spher'ic** (-sfîr'ĭk, -sfĕr'-) *adj.*

chro·mous (krō'məs) *adj.* Of, pertaining to, or containing chromium, esp. with valence 2.

chron– *pref.* Variant of **chrono-**.

chro·nax·y also **chro·nax·ie** (krō'năk'sē, krŏn'ăk'-) *n., pl.* **-ies.** The time interval necessary to stimulate a muscle or nerve fiber electrically with twice the minimum current needed to elicit a threshold response. [Fr. *chronaxie* : Gk. *khronos,* time + Gk. *axia,* value < *axios,* worthy.]

chron·ic (krŏn'ĭk) *adj.* **1.** Of long duration; continuing; constant: *chronic money problems.* **2.** Prolonged; lingering, as certain diseases: *chronic colitis.* **3.** Subject to a disease or habit for a long time; inveterate: *a chronic liar.* [Fr. *chronique* < Lat. *chronicus* < Gk. < *khronos,* time.] **—chron'i·cal·ly** *adv.* **—chro·nic'i·ty** (krŏ-nĭs'ĭ-tē) *n.*

chron·i·cle (krŏn'ĭ-kəl) *n.* A chronological record of historical events. *—tr.v.* **-cled, -cling, -cles.** To record in or in the form of a chronicle. [ME *cronicle* < Norman Fr., var. of OFr. *cronique* < Lat. *chronica* < Gk. *khronika,* annals < *khronikos,* of time < *khronos,* time.] **—chron'i·cler** (-klər) *n.*

Chron·i·cles (krŏn'ĭ-kəlz) *pl.n.* See table at **Bible**.

chrono– or **chron–** *pref.* Time: *chronometer.* [< Gk. *khronos,* time.]

chron·o·bi·ol·o·gy (krŏn'ō-bī-ŏl'ə-jē) *n.* The study of biological rhythms.

chron·o·gram (krŏn'ə-grăm', krō'nə-) *n.* **1.** The record produced by a chronograph. **2.** An inscribed phrase in which certain letters can be read as Roman numerals indicating a specific date. **—chron'o·gram·mat'ic** (-grə-măt'ĭk) *adj.* **—chron'o·gram·mat'i·cal·ly** *adv.*

chron·o·graph (krŏn'ə-grăf', krō'nə-) *n.* An instrument that registers or graphically records time intervals such as the duration of an event. **—chron'o·graph'ic** *adj.* **—chron'o·graph'i·cal·ly** *adv.*

chron·o·log·i·cal (krŏn'ə-lŏj'ĭ-kəl, krō'nə-) also **chron·o·log·ic** (-lŏj'ĭk) *adj.* **1.** Arranged in order of time of occurrence. **2.** In accordance with or relating to chronology. **—chron'o·log'i·cal·ly** *adv.*

chronological age *n.* The number of years a person has lived, used in psychometrics as a comparison standard for various performance measures.

chro·nol·o·gy (krə-nŏl'ə-jē) *n., pl.* **-gies. 1.** The determination of dates and the sequence of events. **2.** The arrangement of events in time. **3.** A chronological list or table. **—chro·nol'o·gist** *n.*

chro·nom·e·ter (krə-nŏm'ĭ-tər) *n.* An exceptionally precise clock, watch, or other timepiece. **—chron'o·met'ric** (krŏn'ə-mĕt'rĭk, krō'nə-), **chron'o·met'ri·cal** *adj.* **—chron'o·met'ri·cal·ly** *adv.*

chro·nom·e·try (krə-nŏm'ĭ-trē) *n.* The scientific measurement of time.

chron·o·scope (krŏn'ə-skōp', krō'nə-) *n.* An optical instrument for measuring minute time intervals. **—chron'o·scop'ic** (-skŏp'ĭk) *adj.*

chrys– *pref.* Variant of **chryso-**.

chrys·a·lid (krĭs'ə-lĭd) *n.* A chrysalis. *—adj.* Pertaining to or resembling a chrysalis.

chrys·a·lis (krĭs'ə-lĭs) *n., pl.* **chrys·a·lis·es** or **chry·sal·i·des** (krĭ-săl'ĭ-dēz'). The third stage in the development of an insect, esp. a moth or butterfly, enclosed in a firm case or cocoon; pupa. [Lat. *chrysallis* < Gk. *khrusallis* < gold-colored pupa of a butterfly < *khrusos,* gold.]

chry·san·the·mum (krĭ-săn'thə-məm, -zăn'-) *n.* **1.** Any of several plants of the genus *Chrysanthemum,* the cultivated forms esp. having showy flowers of various colors and sizes. **2.** The flower of a chrysanthemum. [Lat. *chrysanthemum* < Gk. *khrusanthemon,* a kind of flower : *khrusos,* gold + *anthemon,* flower < *anthos.*]

chrys·a·ro·bin (krĭs'ə-rō'bĭn) *n.* A medicine obtained from a deposit found in the wood of the araroba tree and used to treat certain chronic skin conditions. [CHRYS(O)- (from its golden color) + (AR)AROB(A) + -IN.]

chrys·el·e·phan·tine (krĭ-sĕl'ə-făn'tēn', -tīn') *adj.* Made of gold and ivory. [Gk. *khruselephantinos* : *khrusos,* gold + *elephas,* ivory.]

chryso– or **chrys–** *pref.* Gold; golden: *chrysotherapy.* [< Gk. *khrusos,* gold.]

chrys·o·ber·yl (krĭs'ə-bĕr'əl) *n.* A green to yellow vitreous mineral, $BeAl_2O_4$, used as a gemstone. [Lat. *chrysoberyllus* < Gk. *khrusobērullos* : *khrusos,* gold + *bērullos,* beryl.]

chrys·o·lite (krĭs'ə-līt') *n.* Olivine (sense 1). [ME *crisolite* < OFr. < Lat. *chrysolithus* < Gk. *khrusolithos* : *khrusos,* gold + *lithos,* stone.]

chrys·o·prase (krĭs'ə-prāz') *n.* An apple-green chalcedony used as a gemstone. [ME *crisopase* < OFr. < Lat. *chrysoprasus* < Gk. *khrusoprasos* : *khrusos,* gold + *prason,* leek.]

chrys·o·ther·a·py (krĭs'ō-thĕr'ə-pē) *n.* The treatment of disease with gold compounds.

chrys·o·tile (krĭs'ə-tĭl') *n.* A fibrous mineral variety of serpentine forming part of commercial asbestos. [G. *Chrysotil* : Gk. *khrusos,* gold + Gk. *tilos,* something plucked < *tillein,* to pluck.]

chthon·ic (thŏn'ĭk) also **chtho·ni·an** (thō'nē-ən) *adj.* Pertaining to the gods and spirits of the underworld. [Gk. *khthonios,* under the earth < *khthōn,* earth.]

chub (chŭb) *n., pl.* **chub** or **chubs. 1.** Any of various freshwater fishes of the family Cyprinidae, related to the carps and minnows, esp. a Eurasian species, *Leuciscus cephalus.* **2.** Any of various fishes, such as a whitefish of the genus *Coregonus* or a marine fish of the genus *Kyphosus.* [ME *chubbe.*]

chub·by (chŭb'ē) *adj.* **-bi·er, -bi·est.** Rounded and plump. [Prob. < CHUB (from the plumpness of the fish).] **—chub'bi·ness** *n.*

chuck[1] (chŭk) *tr.v.* **chucked, chuck·ing, chucks. 1.** To pat or squeeze fondly or playfully, esp. under the chin. **2.** To throw; toss. **3.** *Informal.* To throw out; discard: *chucked her old sweater.* **4.** *Informal.* To force out; eject: *chucking out the troublemakers.* *—n.* **1.** An affectionate pat or squeeze under the chin. **2.** A throw, toss, or pitch. [Orig. unknown.]

chuck[2] (chŭk) *n.* **1.** A cut of beef extending from the neck to the ribs and including the shoulder blade. **2.** *Western U.S.* Food. **3.** A clamp that holds a tool or the material being worked in a machine such as a lathe. [Dial. *chuck,* lump.]

chuck[3] (chŭk) *intr.v.* **chucked, chuck·ing, chucks.** To make a clucking sound. *—n.* A clucking sound. [Imit.]

chuck-a-luck (chŭk'ə-lŭk') *n.* A gambling game in which players bet on the possible combinations of three thrown dice. [Prob. CHUCK[1] + LUCK.]

chuck·hole (chŭk'hōl') *n. Regional.* A rut or mudhole in a road. [Prob. < CHUCK[1].]

chuck·le (chŭk'əl) *intr.v.* **-led, -ling, -les. 1.** To laugh quietly or to oneself. **2.** To cluck or chuck, as a hen. *—n.* A quiet laugh of mild amusement or satisfaction. [Prob. freq. of CHUCK[3].] **—chuck'ler** *n.*

chuck·le·head (chŭk'əl-hĕd') *n. Informal.* A stupid and gauche person; blockhead. **—chuck'le·head'ed** *adj.*

chuck wagon *n.* A wagon equipped with food and cooking utensils, as in a lumber camp.

chuck·wal·la (chŭk'wŏl'ə) *n.* A lizard, *Sauromalus obesus,* of the southwestern United States and Mexico, related to the iguana. [Mex. Sp. *chacahuala* < Cahuilla *tcáxxwal.*]

chuck-will's-wid·ow (chŭk'wĭlz-wĭd'ō) *n.* A bird, *Caprimulgus carolinensis,* of the southern and central United States, related to and resembling the whippoorwill. [Imit. of its song.]

chu·fa (cho͞o'fə) *n.* A sedge, *Cyperus esculentus,* native to the Old World, having edible, nutlike tubers. [Sp. *chufar,* to make fun of < VLat. **sufilare,* var. of Lat. *sibilare,* to whistle at.]

chuff (chŭf) *n.* A rude, insensitive person. [ME *chuffe.*]

chug (chŭg) *n.* A dull explosive sound, usually short and repeated, made by or as if by a laboring engine. *—intr.v.* **chugged, chug·ging, chugs. 1.** To make chugs. **2.** To travel or move while making chugs. [Imit.]

chug·a·lug (chŭg'ə-lŭg') *v.* **-lugged, -lug·ging, -lugs.** *Slang.* *—tr.* To swallow the contents of (a container, as of beer) without pausing. *—intr.* To swallow liquid, as beer, without pausing. [Imit.]

chu·kar (chə-kär') *n.* An Old World partridge, *Alectoris graeca,* introduced into western North America. [Hindi *cakor* < Skt. *cakoraḥ.*]

Chuk·chi also **Chuk·chee** (cho͝ok'chē) *n., pl.* **Chukchi** or **-chis** also **Chukchee** or **-chees. 1.** A Mongoloid people of northeastern Siberia. **2.** A member of the Chukchi. **3.** The language of the Chukchi, noted for being pronounced differently by men and women.

chuk·ka (chŭk'ə) *n.* A short, ankle-length boot, usually made of suede, having two pairs of eyelets. [Alteration of CHUKKER (so called because polo players wear a similar boot).]

chuk·ker also **chuk·kar** (chŭk'ər) *n.* One of the periods of play, lasting 7½ minutes, in a polo match. [Hindi *cakkar,* circle < Skt. *cakram.*]

chum[1] (chŭm) *n.* An intimate friend or companion. *—intr.v.* **chummed, chum·ming, chums. 1.** To be an intimate friend. **2.** To share the same room. [Perh. short for *chamber fellow,* roommate.]

chum[2] (chŭm) *n.* Bait usually consisting of oily fish ground up and scattered on the water. *—intr.v.* **chummed, chum·ming, chums.** To fish with chum. [Orig. unknown.]

chum·my (chŭm'ē) *adj.* **-mi·er, -mi·est.** *Informal.* Intimate; friendly. **—chum'mi·ly** *adv.* **—chum'mi·ness** *n.*

chump[1] (chŭmp) *n.* A blockhead; dolt. [Perh. a blend of CHUNK and LUMP or STUMP.]

chump[2] (chŭmp) *tr. & intr.v.* **chumped, chump·ing, chumps.** To chew or make a chewing movement with the jaws. [Var. of CHAMP[1].]

chunk (chŭngk) *n.* **1.** A thick mass or piece: *a chunk of ice.* **2.** A substantial amount: *a chunk of money.* [Perh. var. of CHUCK[2].]

ă pat / ā pay / âr care / ä father / b **bib** / ch **church** / d **deed** / ĕ pet / ē be / f **fife** / g **gag** / h **hat** / hw **which** / ĭ pit / ī pie / îr pier / j **judge** / k **kick** / l lid, needle / m **mum** / n no, sudden / ng thing / ŏ pot / ō toe / ô paw, for / oi noise / ou **out** / o͝o **took** / o͞o **boot** /

chunk·y (chŭng′kē) *adj.* **-i·er, -i·est. 1.** Short and thick; stocky. **2.** In chunks. **—chunk′i·ness** *n.*

church (chûrch) *n.* **1.** Often **Church.** The company of all Christians regarded as a mystic spiritual body. **2.** A building for public, esp. Christian, worship. **3.** A congregation. **4.** Public divine worship in a church; a religious service. **5.** Often **Church.** A specified Christian denomination: *the Presbyterian Church.* **6.** Ecclesiastical power as distinguished from the secular: *the separation of church and state.* **7.** The clerical profession; clergy. **8.** *Christian Science.* "The structure of Truth and Love." (Mary Baker Eddy). *—tr.v.* **churched, church·ing, church·es.** To conduct a church service for, esp. to perform a religious service for (a woman after childbirth). *—adj.* Of or pertaining to the church; ecclesiastical. [ME *chirche* < OE *cirice* < LGk. *kuriakon* < Gk. *kuriakos,* of the lord < *kurios,* lord.]

church·go·er (chûrch′gō′ər) *n.* One who attends church regularly. **—church′go′ing** *adj. & n.*

church key *n. Informal.* A can or bottle opener with a triangular pointed head.

church·ly (chûrch′lē) *adj.* Of, pertaining to, or fit for a church. **—church′li·ness** *n.*

church·man (chûrch′mən) *n.* **1.** A clergyman; priest. **2.** A member of a church. **—church′man·ly** *adj.* **—church′man·ship′** *n.*

Church of Christ, Scientist *n.* The official name of the Christian Science Church.

Church of England *n.* The episcopal and liturgical national church of England, which withdrew its recognition of papal authority in the 16th century.

Church of Jesus Christ of Latter-day Saints *n.* The official name of the Mormon Church.

Church of Rome *n.* The Roman Catholic Church.

Church Slavonic *n.* The literary language of Slavic manuscripts written after the early 11th century and still used as a liturgical language by several churches of the Eastern Orthodoxy in Slavic countries.

church·war·den (chûrch′wôr′dn) *n.* **1.** A lay officer in the Anglican Church chosen annually by the vicar or the congregation to handle the secular and legal affairs of the parish. **2.** One of two elected chief lay officers of the vestry in the Episcopal Church.

church·wom·an (chûrch′wo͝om′ən) *n.* A woman who is a member of a church.

church·yard (chûrch′yärd′) *n.* A yard adjacent to a church, often used as a burial ground.

churl (chûrl) *n.* **1.** A rude, boorish person. **2.** A miser; niggard. **3. a.** A ceorl. **b.** A medieval English peasant. [ME < OE *ceorl,* peasant.]

churl·ish (chûr′lĭsh) *adj.* **1. a.** Of or like a churl; boorish. **b.** Befitting a churl; vulgar. **2.** Difficult to work with; intractable. **—churl′ish·ly** *adv.* **—churl′ish·ness** *n.*

churn (chûrn) *n.* A vessel or device in which cream or milk is agitated to separate the oily globules from the caseous and serous parts, used to make butter. *—v.* **churned, churn·ing, churns.** *—tr.* **1. a.** To stir or agitate (milk or cream) in a churn in order to make butter. **b.** To make by the agitation of milk or cream: *churn butter.* **2.** To shake or agitate vigorously: *Wind churned up the piles of leaves.* *—intr.* **1.** To make butter by operating a churn. **2.** To move with or produce great agitation: *waves churning in the storm.* **—phrasal verb. churn out.** To produce in an automatic manner and esp. abundantly: *churn out four novels a year.* [ME *chĭrne* < OE *cyrn.*] **—churn′er** *n.*

churr (chûr) *n.* The sharp, whirring or trilling sound made by some insects and birds. *—intr.v.* **churred, churr·ing, churrs.** To make a churr. [Imit.]

Chur·ri·gue·resque (cho͝or′ĭ-gə-rĕsk′) *adj.* Of or relating to a style of baroque architecture of Spain and its Latin-American colonies, characterized by elaborate and extravagant decoration. [Sp. *churrigueresco,* after José *Churriguera* (1650–1723).]

chute (sho͞ot) *n.* **1.** An inclined trough, passage, or channel through or down which things may pass. **2.** A waterfall or rapid. **3.** *Informal.* A parachute. [Fr., a fall < OFr. *cheoite,* p.part. of *cheoir,* to fall < Lat. *cadere.*]

chut·ney (chŭt′nē) *n.* A pungent relish made of fruits, spices, and herbs. [Hindi *caṭnī.*]

chutz·pah (KHo͝ot′spə) *n. Slang.* Brazenness; gall. [Yiddish.]

Chu·vash (cho͞o-väsh′) *n., pl.* **Chuvash** or **-vash·es. 1.** One of a Turkic-speaking Tartar people living chiefly in the Chuvash A.S.S.R. **2.** The Turkic language of the Chuvash. [R. < Chuvash *čăvaš.*]

chyle (kīl) *n.* A thick white or pale-yellow fluid, consisting of lymph and finely emulsified fat, that is taken up by the lacteals from the intestine in digestion. [Lat. *chylus* < Gk. *khulos,* juice < *khein,* to pour.] **—chy·la′ceous** (kī-lā′shəs), **chy′lous** (kī′ləs) *adj.*

chy·lo·mi·cron (kī′lō-mī′krŏn′) *n.* One of the microscopic fat particles found in the blood that are formed during the digestion of fat. [CHYL(E) + Gk. *mikron,* small thing < neuter of *mikros,* small.]

chyme (kīm) *n.* The thick semifluid mass of partly digested food that is passed from the stomach to the duodenum. [LLat. *chymus* < Gk. *khumos,* juice < *khein,* to pour.] **—chy′mous** (kī′məs) *adj.*

chy·mo·sin (kī′mə-sĭn) *n.* Rennin. [CHYM(E) + -OS(E) + -IN.]

chy·mo·tryp·sin (kī′mə-trĭp′sĭn) *n.* A pancreatic digestive enzyme. [CHYM(E) + TRYPSIN.]

ciao (chou) *interj.* Used to express greeting or farewell. [Ital. < dial. *schiavo,* (I am your) slave.]

ci·bo·ri·um (sĭ-bôr′ē-əm, -bōr′-) *n., pl.* **-bo·ri·a** (-bôr′ē-ə, -bōr′-). **1.** A vaulted canopy permanently placed over an altar. **2.** A covered receptacle for holding the consecrated wafers of the Eucharist. [Med. Lat. *ciborium* < Lat., a drinking cup < Gk. *kibōrion.*]

ci·ca·da (sĭ-kā′də, -kä′-) *n., pl.* **-das** or **-dae** (-dē′). Any of various insects of the family Cicadidae, having a broad head, membranous wings, and, in the male, a pair of resonating organs that produce a characteristic high-pitched, droning sound. [NLat. *Cicada,* type genus < Lat *cicada,* cicada.]

cicada killer *n.* A large wasp, *Sphecius speciosus,* that preys upon cicadas.

cic·a·trix (sĭk′ə-trĭks′, sĭ-kā′trĭks) *n., pl.* **cic·a·tri·ces** (sĭk′ə-trī′sēz, sĭ-kā′trĭ-sēz′). **1.** Recently formed connective tissue on a healing wound; scar tissue. **2.** *Bot.* A scar left where a leaf or a branch has been detached. [ME *cicatrice* < Lat. *cicatrix.*] **—cic′a·tri′cial** (sĭk′ə-trĭsh′əl), **ci·cat′ri·cose′** (sĭ-kăt′rĭ-kōs′) *adj.*

cic·e·ly (sĭs′ə-lē) *n., pl.* **-lies.** Sweet cicely. [ME *seseli* < Lat. *seselis* < Gk.]

cic·e·ro·ne (sĭs′ə-rō′nē, chē′chə-) *n., pl.* **-nes** or **-ni** (-nē). A guide who conducts sightseers. [Ital., after *Cicerone,* Marcus Tullius Cicero (106–43 B.C.).]

cich·lid (sĭk′lĭd) *n.* Any of various tropical freshwater fishes of the family Cichlidae, many of which are popular as aquarium fish. [NLat. *Cichlidae,* family name < Gk. *kikhlē,* a kind of fish.] **—cich′lid** *adj.*

-cide *suff.* **1.** Killer: *bactericide.* **2.** Act of killing: *ecocide.* [Fr., partly < Lat. *-cida,* killer, and partly < Lat. *-cidium,* killing, both < *caedere,* to kill.]

ci·der (sī′dər) *n.* The juice pressed from fruits, esp. apples, used to produce vinegar or as a beverage. [ME *sidre* < OFr. < LLat. *sicera,* intoxicating drink < Gk. *sikera* < Heb. *shēkār* < *shākar,* he drank deeply.]

ci·gar (sĭ-gär′) *n.* A small, compact roll of tobacco leaves prepared for smoking. [Sp. *cigarro,* poss. < Yucatec *sik,* to shred.]

cig·a·rette also **cig·a·ret** (sĭg′ə-rĕt′, sĭg′ə-rĕt′) *n.* A small roll of finely cut tobacco for smoking, enclosed in a wrapper of thin paper. [Fr., dim. of *cigare,* cigar < Sp. *cigarro.*]

cig·a·ril·lo (sĭg′ə-rĭl′ō) *n., pl.* **-los.** A small, narrow cigar. [Sp., dim. of *cigarro,* cigar.]

ci·gar-store Indian (sĭ-gär′stôr′, -stōr′) *n.* A wooden effigy of an American Indian brave holding a cluster of cigars and used formerly as the emblem of a tobacconist.

ci·lan·tro (sĭ-lăn′trō) *n.* The parsleylike leaves of fresh coriander used in cooking. [Sp., alteration of LLat. *coliandrum* < Lat. *coriandrum.* —see CORIANDER.]

cil·i·a (sĭl′ē-ə) *n.* Plural of **cilium.**

cil·i·ar·y (sĭl′ē-ĕr′ē) *adj.* **1.** Of, pertaining to, or resembling cilia. **2.** Of or pertaining to the ciliary body.

ciliary body *n.* The thickened part of the vascular tunic of the eye that connects the choroid with the iris.

ciliary movement *n.* A form of cellular motion characterized by rhythmic beating of cilia along the cell surface.

cil·i·ate (sĭl′ē-ĭt, -āt′) *adj.* Having cilia. *—n.* Any of various protozoans of the class Ciliata, having numerous cilia. **—cil′i·ate·ly** *adv.*

cil·i·a·ted (sĭl′ē-ā′tĭd) *adj.* Ciliate.

cil·ice (sĭl′ĭs) *n.* A coarse cloth; haircloth. [Fr. < Lat. *cilicium,* a covering made of Cilician goat's hair < *Cilicia,* a province in Asia Minor.]

cil·i·o·late (sĭl′ē-ə-lāt′) *adj.* Having minute cilia. [< NLat. *ciliolum,* dim. of *cilium,* cilium.]

cil·i·um (sĭl′ē-əm) *n., pl.* **-i·a** (-ē-ə). **1.** A microscopic hairlike process extending from a cell surface and often capable of rhythmical motion. **2.** An eyelash. [NLat. < Lat., eyelid.]

ci·met·i·dine (sĭ-mĕt′ĭ-dēn′, -dīn′) *n.* A drug that acts as a histamine receptor antagonist and that is used to treat gastrointestinal diseases, as peptic ulcers. [E. *ci-* (alteration of CYANO-) + MET(HYL) + -IDINE.]

ci·mex (sī′mĕks′) *n., pl.* **cim·i·ces** (sĭm′ĭ-sēz′). An insect of the genus *Cimex,* which includes the bedbugs. [NLat. *Cimex,* genus name < Lat. *cimex,* bug.]

cim·i·ces (sĭm′ĭ-sēz′) *n.* Plural of **cimex.**

Cim·me·ri·an (sĭ-mîr′ē-ən) *adj.* Very gloomy; dark. *—n.* One of a mythical people described by Homer as inhabiting a land of perpetual darkness. [< Lat. *Cimmerii,* the Cimmerians < Gk. *Kimmerioi.*]

cinch (sĭnch) *n.* **1.** A girth for a pack or saddle. **2.** *Informal.* A firm grip. **3.** *Slang.* **a.** Something easy to accomplish. **b.** A sure thing. *—v.* **cinched, cinch·ing, cinch·es.** *—tr.* **1.** To put a saddle girth on. **2.** *Informal.* To get a tight grip on. **3.** *Slang.* To make certain of: *cinch a victory.* *—intr.* To tighten a saddle girth. [Sp. *cincha* < Lat. *cingula* < *cingere,* to gird.]

cin·cho·na (sĭng-kō′nə, sĭn-chō′-) *n.* **1.** Any of various trees and shrubs of the genus *Cinchona,* native to South America, whose bark yields quinine and other medicinal alkaloids.

church

churn

ciborium
17th-century traveling ciborium

cicada

2. The dried bark of a cinchona tree. [NLat. *Cinchona,* genus name, after Francisca Henriquez de Ribera (1576–1639), Countess of *Chinchón.*] **—cin·chon'ic** (sĭng-kŏn'ĭk, sĭn-chŏn'-) *adj.*

cin·cho·nine (sĭng'kə-nēn', sĭn'chə-) *n.* An alkaloid, $C_{19}H_{22}N_2O$, derived from the bark of various cinchona trees and used as an antimalarial agent. [CINCHON(A) + -INE.]

cin·cho·nism (sĭng'kə-nĭz'əm, sĭn'chə-) *n.* A pathological condition resulting from an overdose of cinchona, marked by deafness, headache, giddiness, and dimming eyesight.

cinc·ture (sĭngk'chər) *n.* **1.** A belt; girdle. **2.** Something that encompasses or surrounds. *—tr.v.* **-tured, -tur·ing, -tures.** To gird or encompass. [Lat. *cinctura* < *cingere,* to gird.]

cin·der (sĭn'dər) *n.* **1.** A burned or partly burned substance, such as coal, that is not reduced to ashes but is incapable of further combustion. **2.** A partly charred substance that can burn further but without flame. **3. cinders.** Ashes. **4.** Scoria (sense 1). **5.** Slag (sense 1). *—tr.v.* **-dered, -der·ing, -ders.** To burn or reduce to cinders. [ME *sinder* < OE, dross.] **—cin'der·y** *adj.*

Cin·der·el·la (sĭn'də-rĕl'ə) *n.* **1.** The fairy-tale heroine who escapes from a life of drudgery through the intervention of a fairy godmother and marries a handsome prince. **2.** A person who achieves recognition or affluence after a period of obscurity and neglect. [< CINDER.]

cin·e·ast (sĭn'ē-ăst) also **cin·é·aste** (sĭn'ā-ăst') *n.* A motion-picture enthusiast. [Fr. *cinéaste* < *ciné,* cinema.]

cin·e·ma (sĭn'ə-mə) *n.* **1.** A motion picture. **2.** A motion-picture theater. **3. a.** Motion pictures collectively. **b.** The motion-picture industry. **4.** The art of making motion pictures. [Short for CINEMATOGRAPH.] **—cin'e·mat'ic** (sĭn'ə-măt'ĭk) *adj.* **—cin'e·mat'i·cal·ly** *adv.*

cin·e·mat·o·graph (sĭn'ə-măt'ə-grăf') *n. Chiefly Brit.* A motion-picture camera or projector. [Fr. *cinématographe* : Gk. *kinēma,* motion (< *kinein,* to move) + *-graphe,* -graph.] **—cin'e·mat'o·graph'ic** *adj.* **—cin'e·mat'o·graph'i·cal·ly** *adv.*

cin·e·ma·tog·ra·phy (sĭn'ə-mə-tŏg'rə-fē) *n.* The technique of making motion pictures. **—cin'e·ma·tog'ra·pher** *n.*

cin·e·mat·o·ra·di·og·ra·phy (sĭn'ə-măt'ə-rā'dē-ŏg'rə-fē) *n.* The radiography of a part or organ in motion. [Gk. *kinēma, kinēmat-,* movement (< *kinein,* to move) + RADIOGRAPHY.] **—cin'e·mat'o·ra'di·o·graph'ic** (-ə-grăf'ĭk) *adj.* **—cin'e·mat'o·ra'di·o·graph'i·cal·ly** *adv.*

ci·né·ma vé·ri·té (sē'nā-mä' vā'rē-tā') *n.* A type of film-making that stresses unbiased realism. [Fr. *cinéma-vérité* : *cinéma,* cinema + *vérité,* truth.]

cin·e·ol also **cin·e·ole** (sĭn'ē-ōl') *n.* Eucalyptol. [NLat. *cina,* wormseed + Lat. *oleum,* oil.]

Cin·er·am·a (sĭn'ə-răm'ə, -rä'mə). A trademark for a motion-picture process designed to produce a realistic effect.

cin·e·rar·i·a (sĭn'ə-râr'ē-ə) *n.* A plant, *Senecio cruentis,* native to the Canary Islands but widely cultivated as a house plant, having flat clusters of variously colored daisylike flowers. [NLat. *Cineraria,* genus name < Lat. *cinerarius,* of ashes (from the ash-colored down on its leaves) < *cinis,* ashes.]

cin·e·rar·i·um (sĭn'ə-râr'ē-əm) *n., pl.* **-i·a** (ē-ə). A place for keeping the ashes of a cremated body. [Lat. < *cinerarius,* of ashes < *cinis,* ashes.] **—cin'er·ar'y** (sĭn'ə-rĕr'ē) *adj.*

ci·ne·re·ous (sĭ-nîr'ē-əs) *adj.* **1.** Consisting of or like ashes. **2.** Of the color of ashes; gray tinged with black. [Lat. *cinereus* < *cinis,* ashes.]

cin·er·in (sĭn'ər-ĭn) *n.* Either of two compounds, $C_{20}H_{28}O_3$ or $C_{21}H_{28}O_5$, used in insecticides. [Lat. *cinis, ciner-,* ashes + -IN.]

cin·gu·lum (sĭng'gyə-ləm) *n., pl.* **-la** (-lə). *Biol.* A girdlelike structure, band, or marking. [NLat. < Lat., girdle < *cingere,* to gird.] **—cin'gu·late** (-lĭt), **cin'gu·la'ted** (-lā'tĭd) *adj.*

cin·na·bar (sĭn'ə-bär') *n.* **1.** A heavy reddish mercuric sulfide, HgS, that is the principal ore of mercury. **2.** Red mercuric sulfide used as a pigment. **3.** Vermilion (sense 2). [ME *cinabare* < Lat. *cinnabaris* < Gk. *kinnabari.*]

cin·na·mon (sĭn'ə-mən) *n.* **1.** Either of two trees, *Cinnamomum zeylanicum* or *C. lourerii,* of tropical Asia, having very aromatic bark. **2.** The yellowish-brown bark of a cinnamon tree, dried and often ground, used as a spice. **3.** Any of several trees yielding a spice similar to cinnamon. **4.** A light yellowish brown. *—adj.* Of a light yellowish brown. [ME *cinamome* < OFr. < Lat. *cinnamomum* < Gk. *kinnamōmon.*] **—cin·nam'ic** (sĭ-năm'ĭk) *adj.*

cinnamon bear *n.* The American black bear during the phase when its color is reddish-brown.

cinnamon stone *n.* Essonite.

cin·quain (sĭng'kān', săng'-) *n.* A five-line stanza. [Fr. : *cinq,* five (< Lat. *quinque*) + *quatrain,* quatrain.]

cinque (sĭngk, săngk) *n.* The number five in cards or dice. [ME *cink* < OFr. < Lat. *quinque,* five.]

cin·que·cen·to (chĭng'kwĭ-chĕn'tō) *n.* The 16th century, esp. in Italian art. [Ital., short for *millecinquecento,* one thousand five hundred.]

cinque·foil (sĭngk'foil', săngk'-) *n.* **1.** Any of various plants of the genus *Potentilla,* having compound leaves, often with five lobes. **2.** *Archit.* A design having five sides composed of converging arcs, usually used as a frame for glass or a panel. [ME *cinkfoil* < OFr. < Lat. *quinquefolium* : *quinque,* five + *folium,* leaf.]

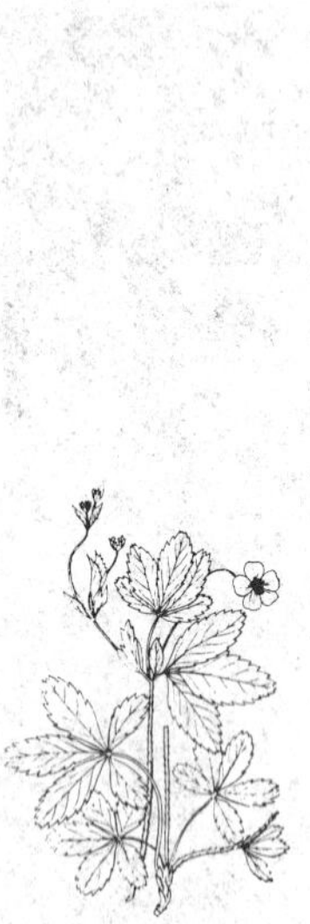

cinquefoil

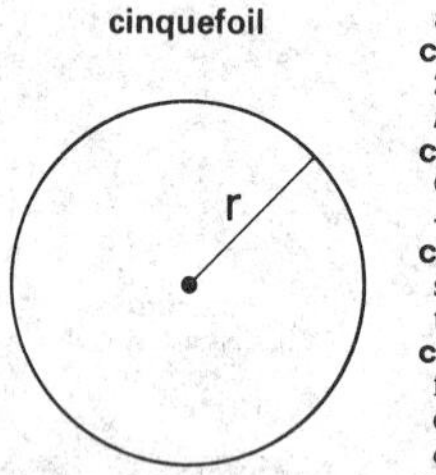

circle
Diameter = 2*r*
Area = πr^2 (π = 3.14)
Circumference = $2\pi r$

ci·on (sī'ən) *n.* Variant of **scion** (sense 2).

ci·pher also **cy·pher** (sī'fər) *—n.* **1.** The mathematical symbol (0) denoting absence of quantity; zero. **2.** An Arabic numeral or figure; number. **3.** The Arabic system of numerical notation. **4.** A person or thing without influence or value; nonentity. **5. a.** A cryptographic system in which units of plain text of regular length, usually letters, are arbitrarily transposed or substituted according to a predetermined key. **b.** The key to such a system. **c.** A message in cipher. **6.** A design combining or interweaving letters or initials; monogram. *—v.* **-phered, -pher·ing, -phers.** *—intr.* To solve problems in arithmetic; calculate. *—tr.* **1.** To put in secret writing; encipher. **2.** To solve by means of arithmetic. [ME *cifre* < OFr. < Med. Lat. *cifra* < Ar. *ṣifr.*]

cir·ca (sûr'kə) *prep.* In approximately: *born circa 1900.* [Lat. < *circum,* around < *circus,* circle.]

cir·ca·di·an (sər-kā'dē-ən, -kăd'ē-, sûr'kə-dī'ən, -dē'-) *adj. Biol.* Exhibiting approximately 24-hour periodicity. [Lat. *circa,* about + Lat. *dies,* day.]

circadian rhythm *n.* A daily rhythmic activity cycle, based on 24-hour intervals, that is exhibited by many organisms.

Cir·cas·sian (sər-kăsh'ən, -kăsh'ē-ən) *n.* **1.** An inhabitant of Circassia, esp. a member of a Caucasian people inhabiting Circassia. **2.** The non-Indo-European language of the Circassians. *—adj.* Of or pertaining to the people, language, or region of Circassia.

Circassian walnut *n.* The mottled or veined light-brown wood of the English walnut used esp. in decorative cabinetwork.

Cir·ce (sûr'sē) *n.* An enchantress described in the *Odyssey* who detained Odysseus for a year and turned his men into swine. [Lat. < Gk. *Kirkē.*] **—Cir'ce·an** (sûr'sē-ən, sər-sē'ən) *adj.*

cir·ci·nate (sûr'sə-nāt') *adj.* **1.** Ring-shaped. **2.** Rolled up from the tip, as a young fern frond. [Lat. *circinatus,* p.part. of *circinare,* to make circular < *circinus,* pair of compasses < *circus,* circle.] **—cir'ci·nate'ly** *adv.*

Cir·ci·nus (sûr'sə-nəs) *n.* A constellation in the Southern Hemisphere near Musca and Triangulum Australe. [Lat. *circinus,* pair of compasses < *circus,* circle.]

cir·cle (sûr'kəl) *n.* **1.** A plane curve everywhere equidistant from a given fixed point, the center. **2.** A planar region bounded by a circle. **3.** Something, such as a ring, shaped like a circle. **4.** A circular course, circuit, or orbit. **5.** A curved section or tier of seats in a theater. **6.** A series or process that finishes at its starting point or continuously repeats itself; cycle. **7.** A group of people sharing an interest, activity, or achievement: *a circle of friends; a sewing circle.* **8.** In some European countries, a territorial or administrative division, esp. of a province. **9.** A sphere of influence or interest; domain: *well-known in scientific circles.* **10.** *Logic.* A fallacy in reasoning in which the premise is used to prove the conclusion, and the conclusion used to prove the premise. *—v.* **-cled, -cling, -cles.** *—tr.* **1.** To make or form a circle around; enclose. **2.** To move in a circle around. *—intr.* To move in circles; revolve: *Crows circled overhead.* [ME *cercle* < OFr. < Lat. *circulus,* dim. of *circus,* circle.] **—cir'cler** (-klər) *n.*

Synonyms: *circle, coterie, set, clique, club, fraternity, society.* These nouns denote a group of associates. *Circle* can describe almost any group having common interests or activities on a scale large or small: *sewing circle; financial circles.* It can also designate the extent of personal relationships: *circle of friends. Coterie* applies to a small, intimate group of congenial persons. *Set* suggests a large, loosely bound group defined either by condition (*younger set*) or preoccupation with fashionable activity (*smart set; jet set*). *Clique* pertains to an exclusive group, usually social, with activities in which outsiders are denied participation. *Club* can imply exclusiveness but often means only a group devoted to a common interest best pursued in company: *Rotary Club; bridge club. Fraternity* most commonly denotes a Greek letter society of male students. It can also mean a professional group not actually organized: *medical fraternity. Society,* as compared here, is usually a rather large, formally organized group with common interests, often cultural.

cir·clet (sûr'klĭt) *n.* A small circle, esp. a circular ornament. [ME *cerclet* < OFr., dim. of *cercle,* circle.]

cir·cuit (sûr'kĭt) *n.* **1. a.** A closed, usually circular curve. **b.** The region enclosed by such a curve. **2. a.** A path or route the complete traversal of which without local change of direction requires returning to the starting point. **b.** The act of following such a path or route. **c.** A journey made on such a path or route. **3.** *Elect.* **a.** A closed path followed or capable of being followed by an electric current. **b.** A configuration of electrically or electromagnetically connected components or devices. **4. a.** A regular or accustomed course from place to place, as that of a salesman; round. **b.** The area or district thus covered, esp. a territory under the jurisdiction of a judge, in which he holds periodic court sessions. **5.** An association of theaters in which plays, acts, or films move from theater to theater for presentation. **6.** An association of teams, clubs, or arenas of competition. *—intr. & tr.v.* **-cuit·ed, -cuit·ing, -cuits.** To make a circuit or circuit of. [ME, circumference < OFr. < Lat. *circuitus,* a going around < *circumire,* to go around : *circum,* around + *ire,* to go.]

circuit breaker *n.* An automatic switch that stops the flow of electric current in a suddenly overloaded or otherwise abnormally stressed electric circuit.

circuit court *n.* In some states, the lowest court of record, in some instances holding sessions in different places.

cir·cu·i·tous (sər-kyo͞o′ĭ-təs) *adj.* Being or taking a roundabout, lengthy course. [Med. Lat. *circuitosus* < Lat. *circuitus,* a going round. —see CIRCUIT.] **—cir·cu′i·tous·ly** *adv.* **—cir·cu′i·ty, cir·cu′i·tous·ness** *n.*

circuit rider *n.* A clergyman who travels from church to church in a district, esp. a rural district.

cir·cuit·ry (sûr′kĭ-trē) *n.* **1.** The design of or detailed plan for an electric circuit. **2.** Electric circuits collectively.

cir·cu·lar (sûr′kyə-lər) *adj.* **1.** Of or pertaining to a circle. **2.** Shaped like or nearly like a circle; round. **3.** Moving in or forming a circle. **4.** Circuitous; indirect; roundabout. **5.** Marked by reasoning in a circle: *a circular theory.* **6.** Addressed or distributed to a large number of persons. *—n.* A printed advertisement, directive, or notice intended for mass distribution. **—cir′cu·lar′i·ty** (-lăr′ĭ-tē) *n.* **—cir′cu·lar·ly** *adv.*

circular file *n. Slang.* A wastebasket.

circular function *n.* Trigonometric function.

cir·cu·lar·ize (sûr′kyə-lə-rīz′) *tr.v.* **-ized, -iz·ing, -iz·es.** To publicize with circulars. **—cir′cu·lar·i·za′tion** *n.* **—cir′cu·lar·iz′er** *n.*

circular measure *n.* The measure of an angle in radians.

circular saw *n.* An electric saw consisting of a toothed disk rotated at high speed.

cir·cu·late (sûr′kyə-lāt′) *v.* **-lat·ed, -lat·ing, -lates.** *—intr.* **1.** To move in or flow through a circle or circuit: *blood circulating through the body.* **2.** To move around, as from person to person or place to place: *a guest circulating at a party.* **3.** To move about or flow freely; be diffused, as air. **4.** To spread widely among persons or places; disseminate: *Rumors tend to circulate quickly.* *—tr.* To cause to move about or be distributed. [Lat. *circulare, circulat-,* to make round < *circulus,* dim. of *circus,* circle.] **—cir′cu·la′tive** (-lā′tĭv) *adj.* **—cir′cu·la′tor** *n.* **—cir′cu·la·to′ry** (-lə-tôr′ē, -tōr′ē) *adj.*

circulating decimal *n.* A repeating decimal.

circulating library *n.* A lending library.

circulating medium *n.* Currency or coin that can be exchanged for goods without endorsement.

cir·cu·la·tion (sûr′kyə-lā′shən) *n.* **1.** Movement in a circle or circuit. **2.** The movement of blood through bodily vessels as a result of the heart's pumping action. **3.** Movement or passage through a system of vessels, as of water through pipes; flow. **4.** Free movement or passage. **5.** The passing of something, such as money or news, from place to place or from person to person. **6.** The condition of being passed about and widely known; distribution. **7. a.** The distribution of printed material, esp. copies of newspapers or magazines, among readers. **b.** The number of copies of a publication sold or distributed.

circulatory system *n.* The system of structures by which blood and lymph are circulated throughout the body.

circum– *pref.* Around; about: *circumlunar.* [Lat. < *circum,* around < *circus,* circle.]

cir·cum·am·bi·ent (sûr′kəm-ăm′bē-ənt) *adj.* Surrounding; enclosing. **—cir′cum·am′bi·ence, cir′cum·am′bi·en·cy** *n.* **—cir′cum·am′bi·ent′ly** *adv.*

cir·cum·cise (sûr′kəm-sīz′) *tr.v.* **-cised, -cis·ing, -cis·es.** To remove the prepuce of (a male) or clitoris of (a female). [ME *circumcisen* < Lat. *circumcidere,* to cut around : *circum-,* around (< *circus,* circle) + *caedere,* to cut.] **—cir′cum·cis′er** *n.*

cir·cum·ci·sion (sûr′kəm-sĭzh′ən) *n.* **1.** The act of circumcising. **2.** A religious ceremony in which someone is circumcised. **3. Circumcision.** A church festival celebrated on January 1 commemorating the circumcision of Jesus.

cir·cum·duc·tion (sûr′kəm-dŭk′shən) *n.* The movement of a limb such that the distal end of the limb delineates an arc. [Lat. *circumductio,* act of leading around < *circumducere,* to lead around: *circum-* around (< *circus,* circle) + *ducere,* to lead.]

cir·cum·fer·ence (sər-kŭm′fər-əns) *n.* **1.** The boundary line of a circle. **2. a.** The boundary line of a closed curvilinear figure; perimeter. **b.** The length of such a boundary. [ME < OFr. < Lat. *circumferentia* < *circumferre,* to carry around : *circum-,* around (< *circus,* circle) + *ferre,* to carry.] **—cir·cum′fer·en′tial** (-fə-rĕn′shəl) *adj.*

cir·cum·flex (sûr′kəm-flĕks′) *n.* A mark (ˆ) used over a vowel in certain languages or in phonetic keys to indicate quality of pronunciation. *—adj.* **1.** Marked with a circumflex. **2.** Curving around: *a circumflex blood vessel.* [Lat. *circumflexus,* a bending around < p.part. of *circumflectere,* to bend around : *circum-,* around (< *circus,* circle) + *flectere,* to bend.]

cir·cum·fuse (sûr′kəm-fyo͞oz′) *tr.v.* **-fused, -fus·ing, -fus·es.** **1.** To pour or diffuse around; spread. **2.** To surround, as with liquid; suffuse. [Lat. *circumfundere, circumfus-* : *circum-,* around (< *circus,* circle) + *fundere,* to pour.] **—cir′cum·fu′sion** *n.*

cir·cum·lo·cu·tion (sûr′kəm-lō-kyo͞o′shən) *n.* **1.** The use of prolix and indirect language. **2.** Evasion in speech or writing. **3.** A roundabout expression. [ME *circumlocucioun* < Lat. *circumlocutio* : *circum-* around (< *circus,* circle) + *loqui,* to speak.] **—cir′cum·loc′u·to′ri·ly** (-lŏk′yə-tôr′ə-lē, -tōr′-) *adv.* **—cir′cum·loc′u·to′ry** (-lŏk′yə-tôr′ē, -tōr′ē) *adj.*

cir·cum·lu·nar (sûr′kəm-lo͞o′nər) *adj.* Revolving about or surrounding the moon.

cir·cum·nav·i·gate (sûr′kəm-năv′ĭ-gāt′) *tr.v.* **-gat·ed, -gat·ing, -gates.** To sail completely around. **—cir′cum·nav′i·ga′tion** *n.* **—cir′cum·nav′i·ga′tor** *n.*

cir·cum·nu·tate (sûr′kəm-no͞o′tāt′, -nyo͞o′-) *intr.v.* **-tat·ed, -tat·ing, -tates.** *Bot.* To grow or move with an irregular elliptical or spiral motion. [CIRCUM- + Lat. *nutare, nutat-,* to sway.] **—cir′cum·nu·ta′tion** *n.*

cir·cum·po·lar (sûr′kəm-pō′lər) *adj.* **1.** Located or found in one of the polar regions. **2.** *Astron.* Designating a star that from a given observer's latitude does not go below the horizon.

cir·cum·ro·tate (sûr′kəm-rō′tāt′) *intr.v.* **-tat·ed, -tat·ing, -tates.** To turn like a wheel; revolve. **—cir′cum·ro·ta′tion** *n.* **—cir′cum·ro′ta·to′ry** (-tə-tôr′ē, -tōr′ē) *adj.*

cir·cum·scis·sile (sûr′kəm-sĭs′əl, -ĭl′) *adj. Bot.* Splitting or opening along a transverse circular line: *a circumscissile seed capsule.* [CIRCUM- + Lat. *scissilis,* able to be split < *scindere,* to split.]

cir·cum·scribe (sûr′kəm-skrīb′) *tr.v.* **-scribed, -scrib·ing, -scribes.** **1.** To draw a line around; encircle. **2.** To confine within bounds; restrict. **3.** To determine the limits of; define. **4. a.** To enclose (a polygon or polyhedron) within a configuration of lines, curves, or surfaces so that every vertex of the enclosed object is incident on the enclosing configuration. **b.** To be erected as such an enclosing configuration. [ME *circumscriben* < Lat. *circumscribere* : *circum-,* around (< *circus,* circle) + *scribere,* to write.] **—cir′cum·scrib′a·ble** *adj.* **—cir′cum·scrib′er** *n.*

cir·cum·scrip·tion (sûr′kəm-skrĭp′shən) *n.* **1. a.** The act of circumscribing. **b.** The state of being circumscribed. **2.** Something that circumscribes. **3.** A circumscribed space; a limited area. **4.** A circular inscription, as on a medallion. **—cir′cum·scrip′tive** *adj.* **—cir′cum·scrip′tive·ly** *adv.*

cir·cum·so·lar (sûr′kəm-sō′lər) *adj.* Revolving about or surrounding the sun.

cir·cum·spect (sûr′kəm-spĕkt′) *adj.* Heedful of circumstances or consequences; prudent. [ME < Lat. *circumspectus,* p.part. of *circumspicere,* to take heed : *circum-,* around (< *circus,* circle) + *specere,* to look.] **—cir′cum·spec′tion** *n.* **—cir′cum·spect′ly** *adv.*

cir·cum·stance (sûr′kəm-stăns′) *n.* **1.** A condition or fact attending an event and having some bearing upon it; a determining or modifying factor. **2.** A condition or fact that determines or must be considered in the determining of a course of action. **3.** The sum of determining factors beyond willful control: *a victim of circumstance.* **4.** Often **circumstances.** Financial status or means: *a man in comfortable circumstances.* **5.** Additional or accessory information; detail. **6.** Formal display; ceremony: *pomp and circumstance.* *—tr.v.* **-stanced, -stanc·ing, -stanc·es.** To place in particular circumstances or conditions; situate. ***—idioms.*** **under no circumstances.** In no case; never. **under (or in) the circumstances.** Given these conditions; such being the case. [ME < OFr. < Lat. *circumstantia* < *circumstare,* to stand around : *circum-,* around (< Lat. *circus,* circle) + *stare,* to stand.]

cir·cum·stan·tial (sûr′kəm-stăn′shəl) *adj.* **1.** Of, pertaining to, or dependent upon circumstances. **2.** Of no primary significance; incidental. **3.** Complete and particular; full of detail: *a circumstantial report about the debate.* **—cir′cum·stan′tial·ly** *adv.*

circumstantial evidence *n. Law.* Evidence not bearing directly on the fact in dispute but on various attendant circumstances from which the judge or jury might infer the occurrence of the fact in dispute.

cir·cum·stan·ti·al·i·ty (sûr′kəm-stăn′shē-ăl′ĭ-tē) *n., pl.* **-ties.** **1.** The quality of being fully or minutely detailed. **2.** A particular detail or circumstance.

cir·cum·stan·ti·ate (sûr′kəm-stăn′shē-āt′) *tr.v.* **-at·ed, -at·ing, -ates.** To set forth or verify with circumstances; give detailed proof or description of. [Lat. *circumstantia,* circumstance + -ATE[1].] **—cir′cum·stan′ti·a′tion** *n.*

cir·cum·ter·res·tri·al (sûr′kəm-tə-rĕs′trē-əl) *adj.* Revolving about or surrounding the earth.

cir·cum·val·late (sûr′kəm-văl′āt′) *tr.v.* **-lat·ed, -lat·ing, -lates.** To surround with or as if with a rampart or other defensive barrier. *—adj.* (-āt′, -ĭt). Surrounded with or as if with a rampart or other defensive barrier. [Lat. *circumvallare, circumvallat-* : *circum-,* around (< *circus,* circle) + *vallum,* rampart with palisades.] **—cir′cum·val·la′tion** *n.*

cir·cum·vent (sûr′kəm-vĕnt′) *tr.v.* **-vent·ed, -vent·ing, -vents.** **1.** To surround and entrap by craft. **2.** To overcome by artful maneuvering. **3.** To avoid by or as if by passing around. [Lat. *circumvenire, circumvent-* : *circum-,* around (< *circus,* circle) + *venire,* to come.] **—cir′cum·vent′er, cir′cum·ven′tor** *n.* **—cir′cum·ven′tion** *n.* **—cir′cum·ven′tive** *adj.*

cir·cum·vo·lu·tion (sər-kŭm′və-lo͞o′shən, sûr′kəm-vō-) *n.* **1.** An act of turning, coiling, or folding about a center, core, or axis. **2.** A single turn, coil, or fold; convolution. [ME

circus

cirrocumulus

cirrus

cithara
5th-century B.C. Greek vase showing Apollo holding a cithara

cittern

circumvolucioun < Med. Lat. *circumvolutio* < Lat. *circumvolvere,* to roll around. —see CIRCUMVOLVE.]

cir·cum·volve (sûr′kəm-vŏlv′) *intr. & tr.v.* **-volved, -volv·ing, -volves.** To revolve or cause to revolve. [Lat. *circumvolvere* : *circum-*, around (< *circus,* circle) + *volvere,* to roll.]

cir·cus (sûr′kəs) *n.* **1. a.** A public entertainment consisting typically of a variety of performances by acrobats, clowns, and trained animals. **b.** A traveling company that performs such entertainments. **c.** A circular arena, surrounded by tiers of seats and often covered by a tent, in which such shows are performed. **2.** A roofless, oval enclosure surrounded by tiers of seats and used in antiquity for public spectacles. **3.** *Chiefly Brit.* An open circular place where several streets intersect. **4.** *Informal.* A place or activity marked by rowdy or noisy disorder. [Lat., circle.]

cirque (sûrk) *n.* A steep hollow, often containing a small lake, occurring at the upper end of a mountain valley. [Fr. < Lat. *circus,* circle.]

cir·rate (sĭr′āt′) *adj. Biol.* Having or of the nature of a cirrus or cirri. [Lat. *cirratus,* curled < *cirrus,* curl.]

cir·rho·sis (sĭ-rō′sĭs) *n.* A chronic disease of the liver marked by progressive destruction and regeneration of liver cells and increased connective tissue formation that ultimately results in blockage of portal circulation, portal hypertension, liver failure, and death. [Gk. *kirros,* tawny (from the color of the diseased liver) + -OSIS.] —**cir·rhot′ic** (-rŏt′ĭk) *adj.*

cirri– *pref.* Variant of **cirro-**.

cir·ri·ped (sĭr′ə-pĕd′) also **cir·ri·pede** (-pēd′) *n.* Any of various crustaceans of the order Cirripedia, which includes the barnacles and similar organisms that attach themselves to objects or become parasitic in the adult stage. [NLat. *Cirripedia,* order name : CIRRUS + Lat. *pes,* foot.] —**cir′ri·ped′** *adj.*

cirro– or **cirri–** *pref.* Cirrus cloud: *cirrostratus.* [< CIRRUS.]

cir·ro·cu·mu·lus (sĭr′ō-kyo͞om′yə-ləs) *n.* A high-altitude cloud composed of a series of small, regularly arranged cloudlets in the form of ripples or grains.

cir·ro·stra·tus (sĭr′ō-strā′təs, -străt′əs) *n.* A high-altitude, thin hazy cloud, usually covering the sky and often producing a halo effect.

cir·rus (sĭr′əs) *n., pl.* **cir·ri** (sĭr′ī′). **1.** A high-altitude cloud composed of narrow bands or patches of thin, generally white, fleecy parts. **2.** *Bot.* A tendril or similar part. **3.** *Zool.* A slender, flexible appendage, such as a tentacle. [Lat., curl of hair.]

cis– *pref.* On this side: *cisatlantic.* [Lat. < *cis,* on this side of.]

cis·at·lan·tic (sĭs′ət-lăn′tĭk) *adj.* On this side of the Atlantic.

cis·co (sĭs′kō) *n., pl.* **-coes** or **-cos.** Any of several North American freshwater fishes of the genus *Coregonus* (or *Leucichthys*), related to and resembling the whitefish. [Canadian Fr. *ciscoette* < Ojibwa *pemitewiskawet,* oily-skinned fish.]

cis·lu·nar (sĭs-lo͞o′nər) *adj.* Between the earth and the moon.

cis·mon·tane (sĭs-mŏn′tān′) *adj.* On this side of the mountains. [Fr. *cismontain* < Lat. *cismontanus* : *cis-*, cis- + *montanus,* of the mountains < *mons,* mountain.]

cist[1] (sĭst) *n.* A wicker receptacle used in ancient Rome for carrying sacred utensils in procession. [Lat. *cista* < Gk. *kistē.*]

cist[2] (sĭst, kĭst) *n.* A Neolithic stone coffin. [Welsh, chest < Lat. *cista* < Gk. *kistē.*]

Cis·ter·cian (sĭ-stûr′shən) *n.* A member of a contemplative monastic order founded by reformist Benedictines in France in 1098. [Fr. *Cistertien* < Med. Lat. *Cistercium,* Cîteaux, France, site of an abbey.] —**Cis·ter′cian** *adj.*

cis·tern (sĭs′tərn) *n.* **1.** A receptacle for holding water or other liquid, esp. a tank for catching and storing rainwater. **2.** *Anat.* A cisterna. [ME *cisterne* < Lat. *cisterna* < *cista,* box < Gk. *kistē.*] —**cis·tern′al** (sĭ-stûr′nəl) *adj.*

cis·ter·na (sĭ-stûr′nə) *n., pl.* **-nae** (-nē′). **1.** A fluid-containing sac or space in the body of an organism. **2.** One of the saclike vesicles that comprise the endoplasmic reticulum. [NLat. < Lat., cistern.]

cis·tron (sĭs′trŏn′) *n.* A subunit of a gene that is complementary to another subunit on the same gene such that they form a single functional unit. —**cis·tron′ic** (sĭ-strŏn′ĭk) *adj.* [CIS- + TR(ANS)- + -ON[1].]

cit·a·del (sĭt′ə-dəl, -dĕl′) *n.* **1.** A fortress in a commanding position in or near a city. **2.** A stronghold or fortified place; bulwark. [OFr. *citadelle* < OItal. *citadella,* dim. of *cittade,* city < Lat. *civitas.*]

ci·ta·tion (sī-tā′shən) *n.* **1.** The act of citing. **2. a.** A quoting of an authoritative source for substantiation. **b.** A source so cited; quotation. **3.** *Law.* A reference to previous court decisions or authoritative writings. **4.** An official commendation for meritorious action, esp. in military service. **5.** Enumeration or mention, as of facts. **6.** An official summons, esp. one calling for appearance in court. —**ci·ta′tion·al** *adj.* —**ci′ta·to′ry** (sī′tə-tôr′ē, -tōr′ē) *adj.*

cite (sīt) *tr.v.* **cit·ed, cit·ing, cites. 1.** To quote as an authority or example. **2.** To mention or bring forward as support, illustration, or proof. **3.** To commend for meritorious action. **4.** To call to someone's attention; mention. **5.** To summon before a court of law. [ME *citen,* to summon < OFr. *citer* < Lat. *citare,* freq. of *ciēre,* to call.] —**cit′a·ble** *adj.*

cith·a·ra (sĭth′ər-ə, kĭth′-) *n.* An ancient musical instrument resembling the lyre. [Lat. < Gk. *kithara.*]

cith·er (sĭth′ər, sĭth′-) also **cith·ern** (-ərn) *n.* A cittern. [Fr. *cithare* < Lat. *cithara,* cithara < Gk. *kithara.*]

cit·ied (sĭt′ēd) *adj.* Having a city or cities.

cit·i·fied (sĭt′ĭ-fīd′) *adj.* Marked by or having customs, manners, fashions, or other characteristics attributed to city people.

cit·i·fy (sĭt′ĭ-fī′) *tr.v.* **-fied, -fy·ing, -fies. 1.** To cause to become urban. **2.** To impart the styles and manners of a city to. —**cit′i·fi·ca′tion** *n.*

cit·i·zen (sĭt′ĭ-zən) *n.* **1.** A person owing loyalty to and entitled by birth or naturalization to the protection of a given state. **2.** A resident of a city or town, esp. one entitled to vote and enjoy other privileges there. **3.** A civilian as distinguished from a person employed by a state. [ME *citisein* < AN *citesein,* prob. alteration of OFr. *citeain* < *cite,* city.] —**cit′i·zen·ly** *adj.*

cit·i·zen·ry (sĭt′ĭ-zən-rē) *n., pl.* **-ries.** Citizens collectively.

citizen's arrest *n.* An arrest made by a citizen who is authorized to do so by his status as a citizen.

citizens band *n.* A radio-frequency band allocated for private use.

cit·i·zen·ship (sĭt′ĭ-zən-shĭp′) *n.* The status of a citizen with its attendant duties, rights, and privileges.

cit·ral (sĭt′răl′) *n.* A mobile pale-yellow liquid, $C_{10}H_{16}O$, derived from lemon-grass oil and used in perfume and as a flavoring. [CITR(US) + -AL.]

cit·rate (sĭt′rāt′) *n.* A salt or ester of citric acid.

cit·ric (sĭt′rĭk) *adj.* Of or obtained from citrus fruits.

citric acid *n.* A colorless translucent crystalline acid, $C_6H_8O_7 \cdot H_2O$, principally derived by fermentation of carbohydrates or from lemon, lime, and pineapple juices and used to prepare citrates, in flavorings, and in metal polishes.

citric acid cycle *n.* Krebs cycle.

cit·ri·cul·ture (sĭt′rĭ-kŭl′chər) *n.* The cultivation of citrus fruits. [CITR(US) + CULTURE.] —**cit′ri·cul′tur·ist** *n.*

ci·trine (sĭ-trēn′, sĭt′rēn′) *n.* **1.** A pale-yellow variety of quartz resembling topaz. **2.** A light to moderate olive. [ME, yellow < OFr. *citrin* < Med. Lat. *citrinus* < Lat. *citrus,* citrus tree.] —**ci·trine′** *adj.*

cit·ron (sĭt′rən) *n.* **1. a.** A tree, *Citrus medica,* native to Asia, having lemonlike fruit with a thick, aromatic rind. **b.** The fruit of this tree. **2.** A variety of watermelon, *Citrullus vulgaris citroides,* having fruit generally considered inedible and a hard rind used as flavoring. **3.** The preserved or candied rind of the fruit of a citron, used esp. in baking. **4.** A grayish green yellow. [Fr. < OFr. < Lat. *citrus.*] —**cit′ron** *adj.*

cit·ro·nel·la (sĭt′rə-nĕl′ə) *n.* **1.** A tropical Eurasian grass, *Cymbopogon nardus,* having bluish-green, lemon-scented leaves. **2.** A light-yellow, aromatic oil obtained from citronella and used in insect repellents and perfumery. [NLat. < Fr. *citronnelle,* lemon oil, dim. of *citron,* citron.]

cit·ro·nel·lal (sĭt′rə-nĕl′ăl′) *n.* A colorless mixture of isomeric liquids, $C_9H_{17}CHO$, the chief constituent of citronella oil. [CITRONELL(A) + -AL.]

cit·rul·line (sĭt′rə-lēn′) *n.* An amino acid, $C_6H_{13}N_3O_3$, that is produced as an intermediate during urea formation in the liver. [NLat. *Citrullus,* plant genus + -INE.]

cit·rus (sĭt′rəs) *adj.* **1.** Of or pertaining to trees or shrubs of the genus *Citrus,* many of which bear edible fruit such as the orange, lemon, lime, and grapefruit. **2.** Of or characteristic of the fruits of citrus trees or shrubs. —*n., pl.* **-rus·es** or **citrus.** A citrus tree or shrub. [NLat., *Citrus,* genus name < Lat. *citrus,* citrus tree.]

cit·tern (sĭt′ərn) *n.* A 16th-century guitar with a pear-shaped body. [Ult. < Lat. *cithara,* cithara < Gk. *kithara.*]

cit·y (sĭt′ē) *n., pl.* **-ies. 1.** A center of population, commerce, and culture; a large and important town. **2. a.** In the United States, an incorporated municipality with definite boundaries and legal powers set forth in a charter granted by the state. **b.** In Canada, a municipality of high rank, usually determined by population but varying by province. **c.** In Great Britain, a large incorporated town, usually the seat of a bishop, with its title conferred by the Crown. **3.** The inhabitants of a city as a group. **4.** An ancient Greek city-state. [ME *cite* < OFr. < Lat. *civitas* < *civis,* citizen.]

city council *n.* The governing body of a city.

city desk *n.* The newspaper department handling local news.

city editor *n.* **1.** A newspaper editor responsible for handling local news and reporters' assignments. **2.** *Chiefly Brit.* The editor who handles commercial and financial news.

city father *n.* A municipal official, as a councilman.

city hall *n.* **1.** The building housing the administrative offices of a municipal government. **2.** The municipal government, esp. its officials considered as a group.

city manager *n.* An administrator appointed by a city council to manage the affairs of the municipality.

cit·y·scape (sĭt′ē-skāp′) *n.* **1.** An artistic representation, as a painting or photograph, of a city. **2.** A city regarded as a scene: *"the vast cityscape of lower Manhattan"* (The New Yorker).

city slicker *n. Informal.* A person exhibiting the smart and sophisticated style traditionally associated by rural people with the manners and mores of the city.

cit·y-state (sĭt'ē-stāt') *n.* A sovereign state consisting of an independent city and its surrounding territory.

civ·et (sĭv'ĭt) *n.* **1.** Any of various catlike mammals of the family Viverridae, of Africa and Asia, having anal scent glands that secrete a fluid with a musky odor. **2.** The fluid secreted by a civet, used in the manufacture of perfumes. **3.** The fur of a civet. [Fr. *civette* < OFr. < OItal. *zibetto* < Ar. *zabād.*]

civ·ic (sĭv'ĭk) *adj.* Of, pertaining to, or belonging to a city, a citizen, or citizenship; municipal or civil. [Lat. *civicus* < *civis,* citizen.]

civ·ics (sĭv'ĭks) *n. (used with a sing. verb).* The branch of political science that deals with civic affairs.

civ·ies (sĭv'ēz) *pl.n.* Variant of **civvies.**

civ·il (sĭv'əl) *adj.* **1.** Of, pertaining to, or befitting a citizen or citizens. **2.** Of or pertaining to citizens and their relations with the state. **3.** Of ordinary citizens or ordinary community life as distinguished from the military or the ecclesiastical: *civil authorities.* **4.** Of or in accordance with organized society; civilized. **5.** Observing or befitting accepted social usages; polite: *gave a civil reply.* **6.** Designating or according to legally recognized divisions of time: *a civil year.* **7.** *Law.* Pertaining to the rights of private individuals and to legal proceedings concerning these rights as distinguished from criminal, military, or international courts, proceedings, or rules. [ME < Lat. *civilis* < *civis,* citizen.] **—civ'il·ly** *adv.*

civil death *n. Law.* The total deprivation of civil rights resulting from conviction for treason or another serious offense.

civil defense *n.* The ensemble of emergency measures to be taken by an organized body of civilian volunteers for the protection of life and property in the case of a natural disaster or an attack or invasion by an enemy.

civil disobedience *n.* The refusal to obey civil laws regarded as unjust, usually by employing methods of passive resistance.

civil engineer *n.* An engineer trained in the design and construction of public works. **—civil engineering** *n.*

ci·vil·ian (sĭ-vĭl'yən) *n.* **1.** A person following the pursuits of civil life as distinguished from one serving in a police, fire-fighting, or military force. **2.** A student of or specialist in Roman or civil law. *—adj.* Of or pertaining to civilians or civil life; nonmilitary.

ci·vil·i·ty (sĭ-vĭl'ĭ-tē) *n., pl.* **-ties. 1.** Politeness; courtesy. **2.** A courteous act or utterance.

civ·i·li·za·tion (sĭv'ə-lĭ-zā'shən) *n.* **1.** An advanced stage of development in the arts and sciences accompanied by corresponding social, political, and cultural complexity. **2.** The type of culture and society developed by a particular nation or region or in a particular epoch: *the civilization of ancient Rome.* **3.** The act or process of civilizing or of reaching a civilized state. **4.** *Informal.* Modern society with its conveniences: *returned to civilization after camping.*

civ·i·lize (sĭv'ə-līz') *tr.v.* **-lized, -liz·ing, -liz·es. 1.** To bring out of a primitive or savage state. **2.** To educate or enlighten; refine. **—civ'i·liz'a·ble** *adj.* **—civ'i·liz'er** *n.*

civ·i·lized (sĭv'ə-līzd') *adj.* **1. a.** Having a highly developed society and culture. **b.** Of, pertaining to, or characteristic of a people or nation so developed. **2.** Polite or cultured; refined.

civil law *n.* **1.** The body of law dealing with the rights of private citizens in a particular state or nation as distinguished from criminal law, military law, or international law. **2.** The law of ancient Rome, esp. that which applied to private citizens. **3.** A system of law having its origin in Roman law as distinguished from common law or canon law.

civil liberty *n.* Liberty legally guaranteeing to the individual the rights of free speech, thought, and action, limited only insofar as their use does not interfere with the rights of others. **—civil libertarian** *n.*

civil marriage *n.* A marriage ceremony performed by a civil official.

civil rights *pl.n.* Rights belonging to a person by virtue of his status as a citizen or as a member of civil society. **—civil'-rights'** *adj.*

civil servant *n.* A person employed in the civil service.

civil service *n.* **1.** All branches of public service that are not legislative, judicial, military, or naval. **2.** Collectively, the persons employed by the civil branches of the government.

civil war *n.* A war between factions or regions of one country.

civ·vies also **civ·ies** (sĭv'ēz) *pl.n. Slang.* Civilian clothes as distinguished from military dress. [Shortening and alteration of CIVILIAN.]

Cl The symbol for the element chlorine.

clab·ber (klăb'ər) *n.* Sour, curdled milk. *—tr. & intr.v.* **-bered, -ber·ing, -bers.** To curdle. [Short for obs. *bonnyclabber* < Ir. Gael. *bainne clabair* : *bainne,* milk + *clabar,* thick sour milk.]

clack (klăk) *v.* **clacked, clack·ing, clacks.** *—intr.* **1.** To make an abrupt, dry sound, as of the collision of two hard surfaces. **2.** To chatter thoughtlessly or at length. **3.** To cackle or cluck, as a hen does. *—tr.* To cause to make an abrupt, dry sound. *—n.* **1.** A clacking sound: *the clack of a computer.* **2.** Something that makes a clacking sound. **3.** Thoughtless, prolonged talk; chatter. [ME *clakken* < ON *klaka.*] **—clack'er** *n.*

clack valve *n.* A hinged valve that permits fluids to flow in only one direction and clacks when the valve closes.

Clac·to·ni·an (klăk-tō'nē-ən) *adj. Archaeol.* Of or pertaining to a lower Paleolithic culture of northwestern Europe. [After *Clacton*-on-Sea, England.]

clad¹ (klăd) *tr.v.* **clad, clad·ding, clads.** To sheathe or cover (a metal) with a metal. [< CLAD².]

clad² (klăd) *v.* A past tense and past participle of **clothe.**

clad·ding (klăd'ĭng) *n.* A metal coating bonded onto another metal.

cla·doc·er·an (klə-dŏs'ər-ən) *n.* Any of various small aquatic crustaceans of the order Cladocera, which includes the water fleas. *—adj.* Of or belonging to the Cladocera. [NLat. *Cladocera,* order name : Gk. *klados,* branch + Gk. *keras,* horn.]

clad·ode (klăd'ōd') *n.* A cladophyll. [NLat. *cladodium* < Gk. *klados,* branch.] **—cla·do'di·al** (klə-dō'dē-əl) *adj.*

clad·o·gen·e·sis (klăd'ə-jĕn'ĭ-sĭs) *n.* A pattern of evolution in which the differentiation of two or more groups within a population give rise to additional taxa. [Gk. *klados,* branch + -GENESIS.] **—clad'o·ge·net'ic** (-jə-nĕt'ĭk) *adj.* **—clad'o·ge·net'i·cal·ly** *adv.*

clad·o·phyll (klăd'ə-fĭl') *n.* A branch or portion of a stem that resembles and functions as a leaf. [Gk. *klados,* twig + -PHYLL.]

clag (klăg) *tr. & intr.v.* **clagged, clag·ging, clags.** To clog. *—n.* A clog or clot. [Perh. < dial. *clag,* to cover with mud, of Scand. orig.]

claim (klām) *tr.v.* **claimed, claim·ing, claims. 1.** To demand or ask for as one's own or one's due; assert one's right to: *claim a reward.* **2.** To state to be true; assert or maintain: *claimed he could read while watching television.* **3.** To deserve or call for; require: *problems that claim her attention.* *—n.* **1.** A demand for something as one's rightful due: *filed a claim for losses.* **2.** A basis for demanding something; title or right. **3.** Something claimed, esp.: **a.** A tract of land staked out by a miner or homesteader. **b.** A sum of money demanded in accordance with an insurance policy or other formal arrangement. **4.** A statement of something as a fact; an assertion of truth: *advertising with false claims.* **—idiom. lay claim to.** To assert one's right to or ownership of. [ME *claimen* < OFr. *clamer* < Lat. *clamare,* to call.] **—claim'a·ble** *adj.* **—claim'er** *n.*

claim·ant (klā'mənt) *n.* A person making a claim.

claiming race *n.* A horse race in which each entry is available for purchase at a previously fixed price, the right to buy often being limited to those persons entering horses in that race.

clair de lune (klâr' də lo͞on') *n.* **1.** A pale, grayish-blue glaze applied to various kinds of Chinese porcelain. **2.** The color of clair de lune. [Fr. : *clair,* light + *de,* of + *lune,* moon.]

clair·voy·ance (klâr-voi'əns) *n.* **1.** The power to perceive things that are out of the natural range of human senses. **2.** Acute intuitive insight or perceptiveness. [Fr. : *clair,* clear (< Lat. *clarus*) + *voyant,* pr.part. of *voir,* to see < Lat. *vidēre.*] **—clair·voy'ant** *n.*

clam¹ (klăm) *n.* **1.** Any of various usually burrowing marine and freshwater bivalve mollusks of the class Pelecypoda, including members of the genera *Venus* and *Mya,* many of which are edible. **2.** *Informal.* An uncommunicative person. *—intr.v.* **clammed, clam·ming, clams.** To hunt for clams. **—phrasal verb. clam up.** To cease talking or remain silent. [Obs. *clam-shell,* clam < CLAM².]

clam² (klăm) *n.* A clamp or vise. [ME < OE, bond.]

cla·mant (klā'mənt, klăm'ənt) *adj.* **1.** Clamorous; loud. **2.** Urgent; compelling. [Lat. *clamans, clamant-,* pr.part. of *clamare,* to cry out.] **—cla'mant·ly** *adv.*

clam·bake (klăm'bāk') *n.* **1.** A seashore picnic where clams, fish, corn, and other foods are baked in layers on buried hot stones. **2.** *Informal.* A party, esp. a noisy and lively one.

clam·ber (klăm'bər, klăm'ər) *tr. & intr.v.* **-bered, -ber·ing, -bers.** To climb with difficulty, esp. on all fours. *—n.* The act of clambering. [ME *clambren.*] **—clam'ber·er** *n.*

clam chowder *n.* Any of various soups made of shucked clams, salt pork, potatoes, and onions.

clam·my (klăm'ē) *adj.* **-mi·er, -mi·est.** Disagreeably moist, sticky, and usually cold: *gave me a clammy handshake.* [ME *clammi,* sticky < *clam,* of MLG orig.] **—clam'mi·ly** *adv.* **—clam'mi·ness** *n.*

clam·or (klăm'ər) *n.* **1.** A loud outcry; hubbub. **2.** A vehement expression of discontent or protest; public outcry: *a clamor for pollution control.* **3.** A loud and sustained noise; din. *—v.* **-ored, -or·ing, -ors.** *—intr.* **1.** To make a clamor. **2.** To make insistent demands or complaints: *clamored for tax reforms.* *—tr.* **1.** To exclaim insistently and noisily. **2.** To drive or influence by clamor. [ME *clamour* < OFr. < Lat. *clamor,* shout < *clamare,* to cry out.] **—clam'or·er** *n.*

clam·or·ous (klăm'ər-əs) *adj.* Making, full of, or characterized by clamor. **—clam'or·ous·ly** *adv.* **—clam'or·ous·ness** *n.*

clam·our (klăm'ər) *n. & v. Chiefly Brit.* Variant of **clamor.**

clam·our·ous (klăm'ər-əs) *adj. Chiefly Brit.* Variant of **clamorous.**

clamp (klămp) *n.* A device used to join, grip, support, or

cityscape

civet

clam¹

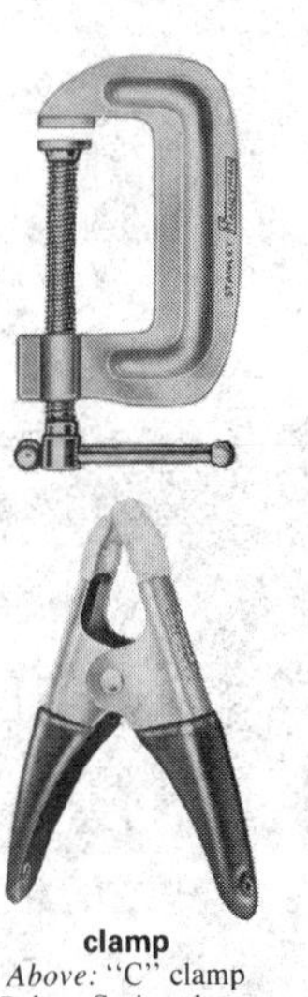

clamp
Above: "C" clamp
Below: Spring clamp

compress mechanical or structural parts. —*tr.v.* **clamped, clamp·ing, clamps.** To fasten, grip, or support with or as if with a clamp. —***phrasal verb.* clamp down.** *Informal.* To become more strict or repressive. [ME < MDu. *klampe.*]
clamp·er (klămʹpər) *n.* A spiked plate attached to the sole of a shoe to prevent slipping on ice.
clam·shell (klămʹshĕlʹ) *n.* **1.** The shell of a clam. **2.** A dredging bucket made of two hinged jaws.
clam·worm (klămʹwûrmʹ) *n.* Any of various segmented marine worms of the genus *Nereis.*
clan (klăn) *n.* **1.** A traditional social unit in the Scottish Highlands, consisting of a number of families claiming a common ancestor and following the same hereditary chieftain. **2.** A division of a tribe tracing descent from a common ancestor. **3.** A large group of relatives, friends, or associates. [Sc. Gael. *clann,* family < OIr. *cland,* offspring < Lat. *planta,* sprout.]
clan·des·tine (klăn-dĕsʹtĭn) *adj.* Concealed or kept secret, often for an illicit purpose. [Lat. *clandestinus* < *clam,* secretly.] —**clan·desʹtine·ly** *adv.* —**clan·desʹtine·ness** *n.*
clang (klăng) *intr. & tr.v.* **clanged, clang·ing, clangs.** To make or cause to make a loud, metallic, resonant sound. —*n.* **1.** A clanging sound. **2.** The strident call of a crane or goose. [Lat. *clangere.*]
clang·er (klăngʹər) *n. Chiefly Brit. Slang.* A blunder; faux pas: *drop a clanger.*
clan·gor (klăngʹər, klăngʹgər) *n.* A clang or repeated clanging; din. —*intr.v.* **-gored, -gor·ing, -gors.** To make a clangor. [Lat. < *clangere,* to clang.] —**clanʹgor·ous** *adj.* —**clanʹgor·ous·ly** *adv.*
clan·gour (klăngʹər, klăngʹgər) *n. & v. Chiefly Brit.* Variant of **clangor.**
clank (klăngk) *n.* A metallic sound, sharp and hard but not as resonant as a clang. —*intr.v.* **clanked, clank·ing, clanks.** To make a clanking sound. [Imit.]
clan·nish (klănʹĭsh) *adj.* **1.** Of, pertaining to, or characteristic of a clan. **2.** Inclined to cling together and to exclude outsiders. —**clanʹnish·ly** *adv.* —**clanʹnish·ness** *n.*
clans·man (klănzʹmən) *n.* A person belonging to a clan.
clap[1] (klăp) *v.* **clapped, clap·ping, claps.** —*intr.* **1.** To strike the palms of the hands together with a sudden explosive sound, as in applauding. **2.** To make a sudden sharp noise. —*tr.* **1. a.** To strike (the hands) together repeatedly with an abrupt, loud sound. **b.** To applaud in this manner. **2.** To tap with the open hand, as in greeting: *clapped him on the shoulder.* **3.** To put, move, or send promptly or suddenly: *clapped me in jail.* **4.** *Informal.* To put together hastily: *clap together a plan.* —*n.* **1. a.** The act or sound of clapping the hands. **b.** A loud, sharp, or explosive noise. **2.** A sharp blow with the open hand; slap. **3.** *Obs.* A sudden stroke, esp. of bad luck. [ME *clappen* < OE *clappan.*]
clap[2] (klăp) *n. Slang.* Gonorrhea. [Prob. < OFr. *clapoir,* bubo.]

clapboard

clap·board (klăbʹərd, klăpʹbôrdʹ, -bōrdʹ) *n.* A long, narrow board with one edge thicker than the other, overlapped to cover the outer walls of frame houses. —*tr.v.* **-board·ed, -board·ing, -boards.** To cover with clapboards. [Partial transl. of MDu. *clapholt* : *clappen,* to split + *holt,* board.]
clap·per (klăpʹər) *n.* **1.** One that claps, esp. the tongue of a bell. **2. clappers.** Two flat pieces of wood held between the fingers and struck together rhythmically. **3.** *Slang.* The tongue of a garrulous person.
clap·per·claw (klăpʹər-klôʹ) *tr.v.* **-clawed, -claw·ing, -claws.** *Archaic.* **1.** To claw or scratch. **2.** To berate or revile.
clapper rail *n.* A North American marsh bird, *Rallus longirostris,* having brownish plumage, a long bill, and a clattering cry.
clap·trap (klăpʹtrăpʹ) *n.* Pretentious, insincere, or empty language. [Obs. *claptrap,* a theatrical trick to win applause : CLAP[1] + TRAP[1].]
claque (klăk) *n.* **1.** A group of persons hired to applaud at a performance. **2.** A group of adulating or fawning admirers. [Fr. < *claquer,* to clap.]
clar·ence (klărʹəns) *n.* A four-wheeled closed carriage with seats for four passengers. [After the Duke of *Clarence* (1765–1837), later William IV of England.]
clar·et (klărʹĭt) *n.* **1. a.** The dry red table wine of Bordeaux, France. **b.** A similar wine made elsewhere. **2.** A dark or grayish purplish red to dark purplish pink. [Short for ME *claret win,* light-colored wine < OFr. *vin claret* : *vin,* wine (< Lat. *vinum*) + *claret,* light-colored < *clair,* clear < Lat. *clarus.*]
claret cup *n.* A chilled mixed drink of red wine variously combined with soda and fruit juices.
Cla·re·tian (klə-rēʹshən, klă-) *n.* A member of the Congregation of the Missionary Sons of the Immaculate Heart of Mary, founded in Spain in 1849. [After St. Anthony *Claret* (1807–1870).] —**Cla·reʹtian** *adj.*
clar·i·fy (klărʹə-fīʹ) *v.* **-fied, -fy·ing, -fies.** —*tr.* **1.** To make clear or easier to understand; elucidate. **2.** To make clear by removing impurities, often by heating gently: *clarify butter.* —*intr.* To become clear. [ME *clarifien* < OFr. *clarifier* < LLat. *clarificare* : Lat. *clarus,* clear + Lat. *facere,* to make.] —**clarʹi·fi·caʹtion** *n.* —**clarʹi·fiʹer** *n.*

clarinet

clar·i·net (klărʹə-nĕtʹ) also **clar·i·o·net** (klărʹē-ə-nĕtʹ) *n.* A woodwind instrument having a straight, cylindrical tube with a flaring bell and a single-reed mouthpiece, played by means of finger holes and keys. [Fr. *clarinette,* dim. of *clarine,* cattle bell < *clair,* clear < Lat. *clarus.*] —**clarʹi·netʹist, clarʹi·netʹtist** *n.*
clar·i·on (klărʹē-ən) *n.* **1.** A medieval trumpet with a shrill, clear tone. **2.** The sound made by the clarion or a sound resembling it. —*adj.* Shrill and clear. [ME *clarioun* < OFr. *clarion* < Med. Lat. *clario* < Lat. *clarus,* clear.]
clar·i·o·net (klărʹē-ə-nĕtʹ) *n.* Variant of **clarinet.**
clar·i·ty (klărʹĭ-tē) *n.* The state or quality of being clear; lucidity. [ME *clerte,* brightness < OFr. *clarte* < Lat. *claritas,* clearness < *clarus,* clear.]
clark·i·a (klärʹkē-ə) *n.* Any of several plants of the genus *Clarkia,* of western North America, having red, purple, or pink flowers. [NLat. *Clarkia,* genus name, after William *Clark* (1770–1838).]
clar·y (klârʹē) *n., pl.* **-ies.** Any of several European plants of the genus *Salvia,* esp. *S. sclarea,* an aromatic herb with bluish-white flowers. [ME *clare,* partly < Med. Lat. *sclarea,* and partly < OE *slaria.*]
clary sage *n.* The clary.
clash (klăsh) *v.* **clashed, clash·ing, clash·es.** —*intr.* **1.** To collide with a loud, harsh noise: *cymbals clashing.* **2.** To conflict; be in opposition: *political opponents who clashed on busing.* —*tr.* To strike together with a harsh, metallic noise. —*n.* **1.** A loud, resounding metallic noise, such as that made by two objects colliding. **2.** A state of disagreement or disharmony. **3.** An often heated discussion in which differences of opinion are expressed. [Imit.]
clas·mat·o·cyte (klăz-mătʹə-sītʹ) *n.* Histiocyte. [Gk. *klasma, klasmat-,* fragment (< *klan,* to break) + -CYTE.] —**clas·matʹo·cytʹic** *adj.*
clasp (klăsp) *n.* **1.** A fastening, such as a hook, used to hold two objects or parts together. **2. a.** An embrace; hug. **b.** A grip or grasp of the hand. **3.** A small metal bar attached to a military decoration indicating the action for which it was awarded. —*tr.v.* **clasped, clasp·ing, clasps.** **1.** To fasten with or as if with a clasp. **2.** To hold in a tight grasp; embrace. **3.** To grip firmly in or with the hand. [ME *claspe,* prob. of OE orig.] —**claspʹer** *n.*
clasp·er (klăsʹpər) *n.* A modified part of the pelvic fin of male elasmobranch fishes that aids in the transmission of sperm during copulation.
clasp knife *n.* A pocketknife with a folding blade.
class (klăs) *n.* **1. a.** A set, collection, group, or configuration containing members having or thought to have at least one attribute in common; kind; sort. **b.** *Statistics.* An interval in a frequency distribution. **2.** A division by quality, rank, or grade. **3. a.** A social stratum whose members share similar economic, political, and cultural characteristics: *the middle class.* **b.** Social rank or caste, esp. high rank. **4. a.** A group of students or alumni graduated in the same year. **b.** A group of students meeting to study the same subject. **c.** The period during which such a group meets. **5.** *Biol.* A taxonomic category ranking below a phylum and above an order. **6. a.** A grade of mail: *sent the letter by first class.* **b.** The quality of accommodation on a public vehicle: *travel third class.* **7.** *Slang.* Great style or quality: *a girl with class.* —*tr.v.* **classed, class·ing, class·es.** To arrange, group, or rate according to qualities or characteristics; classify. [Fr. *classe* < Lat. *classis,* class of citizens.]
class action *n.* A lawsuit in which the plaintiff or plaintiffs bring suit both on their own behalf and on behalf of many others who have the same claim against the defendant.
class-con·scious (klăsʹkŏnʹshəs) *adj.* Aware of belonging to a particular socioeconomic class. —**classʹconʹconʹscious·ness** *n.*
clas·sic (klăsʹĭk) *adj.* **1.** Of the highest rank or class. **2. a.** Serving as an outstanding representative of its kind; model. **b.** Well-known and typical: *the classic situation—boy meets girl.* **3.** Having lasting significance or recognized worth. **4.** Of or pertaining to ancient Greek or Roman literature or art; classical. **5.** Of or in accordance with established principles and methods in the arts and sciences. **6.** Of lasting historical or literary significance. —*n.* **1.** An artist, author, or work generally considered to be of the highest rank or excellence. **2.** A literary work of ancient Greece or Rome. **3.** Something considered to be typical or traditional.
clas·si·cal (klăsʹĭ-kəl) *adj.* **1. a.** Of or pertaining to the culture of ancient Greece and Rome, esp. the art, architecture, and literature. **b.** Pertaining to or versed in studies of antiquity. **2. a.** Pertaining to or designating the European music of the latter half of the 18th century. **b.** Designating music in the educated European tradition as distinguished from popular or folk music. **3.** Standard and authoritative rather than new or experimental: *classical methods of navigation.* **4.** Of or pertaining to nonrelativistic or nonquantum physics: *classical mechanics.* —**clasʹsi·calʹi·ty** (-kălʹĭ-tē), **clasʹsi·cal·ness** *n.* —**clasʹsi·cal·ly** *adv.*
clas·si·cism (klăsʹĭ-sĭzʹəm) *n.* **1.** Aesthetic attitudes and principles based on the culture, art, and literature of ancient Greece and Rome and characterized by emphasis on form, simplicity, proportion, and restrained emotion. **2.** Classical scholarship. **3.** A Greek or Latin expression or idiom.
clas·si·cist (klăsʹĭ-sĭst) *n.* A student of or specialist in the classics.

clas·si·fi·ca·tion (klăs′ə-fĭ-kā′shən) *n.* **1.** The act or result of classifying. **2.** *Biol.* The systematic grouping of organisms into categories based on shared characteristics or traits; taxonomy. **—clas′si·fi·ca·to′ry** (klăs′ə-fĭ-kə-tôr′ē, -tōr′ē, klə-sĭf′ĭ-, klăs′ə-fĭ-kā′tə-rē) *adj.*

classified advertisement *n.* An advertisement, usually brief and in small type, printed in a newspaper or magazine along with others of the same category.

clas·si·fy (klăs′ə-fī′) *tr.v.* **-fied, -fy·ing, -fies. 1.** To arrange or organize according to class or category. **2.** To designate (a document, for example) as secret and available only to authorized persons. **—clas′si·fi′a·ble** *adj.* **—clas′si·fi′er** *n.*

clas·sis (klăs′ĭs) *n., pl.* **-ses** (-ēz′). *Eccles.* **1.** A governing body of pastors and elders in certain Reformed churches having jurisdiction over local churches. **2.** The district or churches governed by a classis. [Lat., class of citizens.]

class mark *n. Statistics.* A mark[1] (sense 22).

class·mate (klăs′māt′) *n.* A member of the same academic class.

class·room (klăs′ro͞om′, -ro͝om′) *n.* A room in which classes are conducted in a school or college.

class·y (klăs′ē) *adj.* **-i·er, -i·est.** *Slang.* Stylish; elegant. **—class′i·ness** *n.*

clast (klăst) *n.* A rock fragment. [< Gk. *klastos,* broken < *klan,* to break.]

clas·tic (klăs′tĭk) *adj.* **1.** Separable into parts or having removable sections: *a clastic anatomical model.* **2.** *Geol.* Made up of fragments; fragmental. [< Gk. *klastos,* broken < *klan,* to break.] **—clas′tic** *n.*

clath·rate (klăth′rāt′) *adj.* **1.** *Biol.* Having a latticelike structure or appearance. **2.** *Chem.* Of or pertaining to inclusion complexes in which molecules of one substance are completely enclosed within the crystal structure of another. *—n.* A clathrate compound. [Lat. *clathratus,* p.part. of *clathrare,* to furnish with a lattice < Gk. *klēithron,* door bar < *kleiein,* to close.]

clat·ter (klăt′ər) *v.* **-tered, -ter·ing, -ters.** *—intr.* **1.** To make a rattling sound. **2.** To move with a rattling sound: *clattering along on roller skates.* **3.** To talk rapidly and noisily; chatter. *—tr.* To cause to make a rattling sound. *—n.* **1.** A rattling sound: *the clatter of dishes in the kitchen.* **2.** A loud disturbance; commotion. **3.** Noisy talk; chatter. [ME *clateren.*] **—clat′ter·er** *n.*

clau·di·ca·tion (klô′dĭ-kā′shən) *n.* A halt in a person's walk; limp. [ME *claudicacioun* < Lat. *claudicatio* < *claudicare,* to limp < *claudus,* lame.]

clause (klôz) *n.* **1.** A group of words containing a subject and a predicate and forming part of a compound or complex sentence. **2.** A distinct article, stipulation, or provision in a document. [ME < OFr. < Med. Lat. *clausa,* close of a rhetorical period < Lat. *claudere,* to close.] **—claus′al** (klô′zəl) *adj.*

claus·tral (klô′strəl) *adj.* Variant of **cloistral.**

claus·tro·pho·bi·a (klô′strə-fō′bē-ə) *n.* A pathological fear of confined spaces. [Lat. *claustrum,* enclosed place (< *claudere,* to close) + -PHOBIA.] **—claus′tro·pho′bic** (-fō′bĭk) *adj.*

cla·vate (klā′vāt′) *adj.* Having one end thickened; club-shaped; claviform. [NLat. *clavatus* < Lat. *clava,* club.] **—cla′vate′ly** *adv.*

clave[1] (klāv) *v. Archaic.* Past tense of **cleave**[1].

clave[2] (klāv) *v. Archaic.* Past tense of **cleave**[2].

cla·ver (klā′vər) *Scot. —intr.v.* **-vered, -ver·ing, -vers.** To gossip or talk idly. *—n.* Gossip; idle talk. [Perh. of Celt. orig.]

clav·i·chord (klăv′ĭ-kôrd′) *n.* An early musical keyboard instrument with a soft sound produced by tangents striking horizontal strings. [Med. Lat. *clavichordium* : Lat. *clavis,* key + Lat. *chorda,* string < Gk. *khordē.*]

clav·i·cle (klăv′ĭ-kəl) *n.* A bone that links the sternum and the scapula. [NLat. *clavicula* < Lat., dim. of *clavis,* key (from its shape).] **—cla·vic′u·lar** (klə-vĭk′yə-lər) *adj.* **—cla·vic′u·late′** (-lāt′) *adj.*

clav·i·corn (klăv′ĭ-kôrn′) *adj.* Belonging to or designating a group of beetles of the suborder Polyphaga, having club-shaped antennae. [NLat. *Clavicornia,* family name : Lat. *clava,* club + Lat. *cornu,* horn.]

cla·vier (klə-vîr′, klā′vē-ər, klăv′ē) *n.* **1.** A keyboard. **2.** A stringed keyboard instrument such as a harpsichord. [Fr. < OFr., key-bearer < Lat. *clavis,* key.]

clav·i·form (klăv′ə-fôrm′) *adj.* Club-shaped; clavate. [Lat. *clava,* club + -FORM.]

cla·vus (klā′vəs, klä′-) *n.* Corn[2]. [Lat., nail.]

claw (klô) *n.* **1.** A sharp, often curved nail on the toe of a mammal, reptile, or bird. **2. a.** A chela or similar pincerlike structure on the limb of a crustacean or other arthropod. **b.** A limb terminating in such a structure. **3.** Something resembling a claw, as the cleft end of a hammerhead. **4.** *Bot.* The narrowed basal part of certain petals or sepals. *—tr. & intr.v.* **clawed, claw·ing, claws.** To scratch or dig or make scratching or digging motions with or as if with claws. [ME *clave* < OE *clawu.*]

claw hammer *n.* **1.** A hammer having a head with one end forked for removing nails. **2.** A swallow-tailed coat.

claw hatchet *n.* A hatchet having one end of the head forked.

clay (klā) *n.* **1.** A fine-grained, firm natural material, plastic when wet, that consists primarily of hydrated silicates of aluminum and is widely used in making bricks, tiles, and pottery. **2.** An earth that forms a paste with water and hardens when heated, esp. one with grains smaller than 0.002 millimeters in diameter. **3.** Moist earth; mud. **4.** The human body as distinguished from the spirit. [ME *clei* < OE *clæg.*] **—clay′ey** (klā′ē), **clay′ish** (klā′ĭsh) *adj.*

clay mineral *n.* Any of various hydrous silicates that have a crystalline structure and are components of clay.

clay·more (klā′môr′, -mōr′) *n.* **1.** A large, double-edged broadsword formerly used by Scottish Highlanders. **2.** A claymore mine. [Gael. *claidheamh mōr* : *claidheamh,* sword + *mōr,* great.]

claymore mine *n.* A lens-shaped, ground-emplaced antipersonnel mine whose blast is focused only in the direction of the oncoming enemy.

clay pigeon *n.* A clay disk thrown as a flying target for skeet and trapshooting.

clay·to·ni·a (klā-tō′nē-ə) *n.* The spring beauty. [NLat. *Claytonia,* herb genus, after John *Clayton* (1693–1773).]

clean (klēn) *adj.* **-er, -est. 1.** Free from dirt, stain, or impurities; unsoiled. **2.** Free from foreign matter; unadulterated: *clean drinking water.* **3.** Producing little radioactive fallout or contamination: *a clean nuclear bomb.* **4.** Without imperfections or blemishes; regular: *a clean line.* **5.** Free from clumsiness; deft; adroit: *a clean throw.* **6.** Without restrictions or encumbrances. **7.** Entire; complete: *a clean escape.* **8.** Having few alterations or corrections; legible: *clean manuscript.* **9.** Blank: *a clean page.* **10.** Morally pure; sinless: *led a clean life.* **11.** Not ribald or obscene: *a clean joke.* **12.** Honest; fair, as in sports: *a clean fighter.* **13.** *Slang.* **a.** Not carrying concealed weapons. **b.** Free from narcotics addiction, use, or possession. **c.** Innocent of a suspected crime. *—adv.* **1. a.** So as to be clean: *wash dishes clean.* **b.** In a clean manner: *played the game clean.* **2.** *Informal.* Entirely; wholly: *clean forgot the appointment.* *—v.* **cleaned, clean·ing, cleans.** *—tr.* **1.** To rid of dirt or other impurities: *clean a room.* **2.** To remove (dirt or impurities) from: *clean a suit.* **3.** To prepare (fowl or other food) for cooking. **4.** To remove the contents from; empty: *cleaned his plate.* *—intr.* To undergo or perform the act of ridding of dirt and impurities. **—*phrasal verbs.* clean out. 1.** To drive or force out: *cleaned out subversives from the government.* **2.** To deprive completely, as of money; remove everything from: *The alimony payments had cleaned him out.* **clean up. 1.** To dispose of; settle: *cleaned up the unpaid bills.* **2.** *Informal.* To make a large profit, often in a short period of time. **—*idioms.* clean house.** To eliminate or discard what is undesirable: *The scandal forced the company to clean house.* **come clean.** *Slang.* To admit the truth; confess. [ME *clene* < OE *clǣne.*] **—clean′a·ble** *adj.* **—clean′ness** *n.*

clean-cut (klēn′kŭt′) *adj.* **1.** Clearly and sharply defined or outlined. **2.** Neat and trim in appearance; wholesome.

clean·er (klē′nər) *n.* **1.** One whose work or business is cleaning. **2.** A machine or substance used in cleaning.

clean-hand·ed (klēn′hăn′dĭd) *adj.* Innocent; guiltless.

clean-limbed (klēn′lĭmd′) *adj.* Having well-formed limbs.

clean·ly (klĕn′lē) *adj.* **-li·er, -li·est.** Habitually and carefully neat and clean. *—adv.* (klēn′lē). In a clean manner. **—clean′li·ness** (klĕn′lē-nĭs) *n.*

clean room *n.* A room that is kept contaminant-free, esp. for the handling of precision parts.

cleanse (klĕnz) *tr.v.* **cleansed, cleans·ing, cleans·es.** To free from dirt, defilement, or guilt; clean. [ME *clensen* < OE *clǣnsian.*]

cleans·er (klĕn′zər) *n.* **1.** One that cleans. **2.** A soap, detergent, or other preparation used for cleaning.

clean-shav·en (klēn′shā′vən) *adj.* **1.** Having the beard or hair shaved off. **2.** Having recently shaved.

clean·up (klēn′ŭp′) *n.* **1.** A thorough cleaning or ordering. **2.** *Informal.* A very large profit.

clear (klîr) *adj.* **-er, -est. 1.** Free from clouds, mist, or haze: *a clear day.* **2.** Free from anything that dims, obscures, or darkens; transparent: *clear water.* **3.** Free from flaw, blemish, or impurity: *a clear, perfect diamond.* **4.** Free from impediment, obstruction, or hindrance; open: *a clear view.* **5.** Plain or evident to the mind; unmistakable: *a clear case of cheating.* **6.** Easily perceptible to the eye or ear; distinct. **7.** Discerning or perceiving easily; keen: *a clear mind.* **8.** Free from doubt or confusion; certain. **9.** Free from qualification or limitation; absolute. **10.** Free from guilt; untroubled: *a clear conscience.* **11.** Freed from contact or connection; disengaged: *clear of danger.* **12.** Without charges or deductions; net: *earns a clear $15,000.* **13.** Containing nothing. *—adv.* **1.** Distinctly; clearly: *spoke loud and clear.* **2.** *Informal.* All the way; completely; entirely: *cried clear through the night.* *—v.* **cleared, clear·ing, clears.** *—tr.* **1.** To make clear, light, or bright. **2.** To rid of impurities, blemishes, muddiness, or foreign matter. **3.** To free from confusion, doubt, or ambiguity; make plain or intelligible: *cleared up the question of responsibility.* **4. a.** To rid of obstructions or entanglements: *clear the road of snow.* **b.** To remove or get rid of (obstructions or entanglements): *clear snow from the road.* **5.** To free from a legal charge or imputation of guilt; acquit: *was cleared of murder charges.* **6.** To pass by, under, or over without contact: *a runner clearing the hurdle.* **7.** To settle (a debt) by paying it. **8.** To gain (a

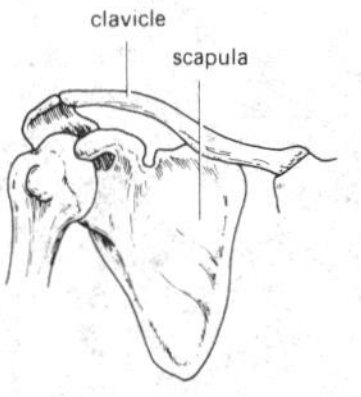

clavicle

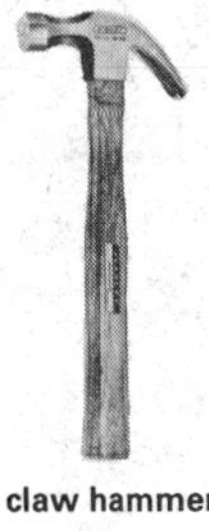

claw hammer

given amount) as net profit or earnings. **9.** To pass (a check or other bill of exchange) through a clearing-house. **10.** To free (a ship or cargo) from legal detention at a harbor by fulfilling customs and harbor requirements. **11.** To give (an aircraft) clearance or authorization: *cleared the plane for cruising at 30,000 feet.* **12.** To free (the throat) of phlegm by coughing. *—intr.* **1.** To become clear: *The sky cleared.* **2.** To pass through a clearing-house. **3.** To comply with customs and harbor requirements in discharging a cargo or in leaving or entering a port. ***—phrasal verb.*** **clear out.** *Informal.* To leave a place, often quickly. *—n.* **1.** A clear or open space. **2.** Clearance. ***—idioms.*** **clear the air.** To dispel emotional tensions or differences. **in the clear. 1.** Free from burdens or dangers. **2.** Not subject to suspicion or accusations of guilt: *The evidence showed him to be in the clear.* [ME *cler* < OFr. < Lat. *clarus.*] **—clear′a·ble** *adj.* **—clear′er** *n.* **—clear′ly** *adv.* **—clear′ness** *n.*

clear-air turbulence (klîr′âr′) *n.* A severe atmospheric turbulence that occurs under otherwise tranquil conditions and subjects aircraft to strong updrafts and downdrafts.

clear·ance (klîr′əns) *n.* **1.** The act or process of clearing. **2.** A space cleared; a clearing. **3.** The amount by which a moving object clears something. **4.** An intervening distance or space allowing free play, as between machine parts. **5.** Permission for a vehicle to proceed, as after an inspection of equipment or cargo. **6.** Official certification of blamelessness, trustworthiness, or suitability. **7.** A sale, generally at reduced prices, to dispose of old merchandise. **8.** The passage of checks and other bills of exchange through a clearing-house.

clear-cut (klîr′kŭt′) *adj.* **1. a.** Distinctly and sharply defined or outlined. **b.** Marked by or possessing keen intellect. **2.** Plain; evident: *a clear-cut victory.*

clear-eyed (klîr′īd′) *adj.* **1.** Having sharp, bright eyes; keen-sighted. **2.** Mentally acute or perceptive.

clear-head·ed (klîr′hĕd′ĭd) *adj.* Having a clear, orderly mind. **—clear′-head′ed·ly** *adv.* **—clear′-head′ed·ness** *n.*

clear·ing (klîr′ĭng) *n.* **1.** A tract of land from which the trees and other obstructions have been removed. **2. a.** The exchange among banks of checks, drafts, and notes and the settlement of differences arising from it. **b. clearings.** The total of claims presented daily at a clearing-house.

clear·ing-house also **clear·ing·house** (klîr′ĭng-hous′) *n.* An office where banks exchange checks and drafts and settle accounts.

clear-sight·ed (klîr′sī′tĭd) *adj.* **1.** Having sharp, clear vision. **2.** Perceptive; discerning. **—clear′-sight′ed·ly** *adv.* **—clear′-sight′ed·ness** *n.*

clear·sto·ry (klîr′stôr′ē, -stōr′ē) *n.* Variant of **clerestory.**

clear·weed (klîr′wēd′) *n.* A plant, *Pilea pumila,* of eastern North America, having small green flowers and translucent stems and leaves.

clear·wing (klîr′wĭng′) *n.* Any of various moths of the family Aegeriidae, having scaleless, transparent wings.

cleat (klēt) *n.* **1.** A strip of wood or iron used to strengthen or support the surface to which it is attached. **2.** A piece of iron, rubber, or leather attached to the underside of a shoe to preserve the sole or prevent slipping. **3.** A piece of metal or wood having projecting arms or ends on which a rope can be wound or secured. **4.** A wedge-shaped piece of wood or other material fastened onto something, such as a spar, to act as a support or to prevent slipping. **5.** A spurlike device used in gripping a tree or pole in climbing. *—tr.v.* **cleat·ed, cleat·ing, cleats.** To supply, support, secure, or strengthen with a cleat. [ME *clete,* of OE orig.]

cleav·age (klē′vĭj) *n.* **1.** The act of splitting or cleaving. **2.** The state of being split or cleft; a fissure or division. **3.** *Mineral.* The splitting or tendency to split of a crystallized substance along definite crystalline planes, yielding smooth surfaces. **4.** *Biol.* The process of or any of various stages in cell division that produce a blastula from a fertilized ovum. **5.** *Informal.* The separation between a woman's breasts.

cleave[1] (klēv) *v.* **cleft** (klĕft) or **cleaved** or **clove** (klōv), **cleft** or **cleaved** or **clo·ven** (klō′vən), **cleav·ing, cleaves.** *—tr.* **1.** To split or separate, as with an ax. **2.** To make or accomplish by or as if by cutting: *cleave a path through the forest.* **3.** To pierce or penetrate. *—intr.* **1.** To split or separate, esp. along a natural line of division. **2.** To make one's way; penetrate; pass. [ME *cleven* < OE *clēofan.*] **—cleav′a·ble** *adj.*

cleave[2] (klēv) *intr.v.* **cleaved** or **clove** (klōv), **cleaved, cleav·ing, cleaves. 1.** To adhere, cling, or stick fast. **2.** To be faithful. [ME *cleven* < OE *cleofian.*]

cleav·er (klē′vər) *n.* A heavy, axlike knife or hatchet used by butchers.

cleav·ers (klē′vərz) *n. (used with a sing. or pl. verb).* Any of several plants of the genus *Galium,* esp. *G. aparine,* having small white flowers and prickly stems and seeds. [ME *cliver* < OE *clīfe.*]

cleek (klēk) *n.* **1.** In golf, a number-one iron, having very little loft to the club face. **2.** *Scot.* A large hook. [ME *cleike,* large hook.]

clef (klĕf) *n.* A symbol on a musical staff indicating the pitch of the notes. [Fr. < Lat. *clavis,* key.]

cleft (klĕft) *v.* A past tense and past participle of **cleave[1]**. *—adj.* **1.** Divided; split. **2.** *Bot.* Having deeply divided lobes or divisions: *a cleft leaf.* *—n.* **1.** A crack, crevice, or split. **2.** A split or indentation between two parts, as of the chin.

cleaver

clematis

cleft palate *n.* A congenital fissure in the roof of the mouth.

cleis·tog·a·mous (klī-stŏg′ə-məs) also **cleis·to·gam·ic** (klī′stə-găm′ĭk) *adj. Bot.* Characterized by self-fertilization in an unopened, budlike state. [Gk. *kleistos,* closed (< *kleiein,* to close) + -GAMOUS.] **—cleis·tog′a·mous·ly** *adv.* **—cleis·tog′a·my** (-mē) *n.*

cleis·to·the·ci·um (klī′stə-thē′sē-əm) *n., pl.* **-ci·a** (-sē-ə). A closed, spherical ascocarp. [NLat. : Gk. *kleistos,* closed + Gk. *thēkion,* small case, dim. of *thēkē,* chest.]

clem·a·tis (klĕm′ə-tĭs) *n.* Any of various plants or vines of the genus *Clematis,* of eastern Asia and North America, having white or variously colored flowers and plumelike seeds. [NLat. *Clematis,* genus name < Lat. *clematis,* a creeping plant < Gk. *klēmatis* < *klēma,* twig.]

clem·en·cy (klĕm′ən-sē) *n., pl.* **-cies. 1.** Mercy, esp. toward an offender or enemy; leniency. **2.** A merciful, kind, or lenient act. **3.** Mildness, esp. of weather.

clem·ent (klĕm′ənt) *adj.* **1.** Inclined to be lenient or merciful. **2.** Mild: *clement weather.* [ME < Lat. *clemens.*] **—clem′ent·ly** *adv.*

clench (klĕnch) *tr.v.* **clenched, clench·ing, clench·es. 1.** To bring together (hands or teeth) tightly; close. **2.** To grasp or grip tightly. **3.** To clinch (a bolt, for example). **4.** *Naut.* To fasten with a clinch. *—n.* **1.** A tight grip or grasp. **2.** Something that clenches or holds fast, as a mechanical device. **3.** *Naut.* A clinch (sense 4). [ME *clenchen* < OE *(be)clencan.*]

cle·o·me (klē-ō′mē) *n.* Any of various mostly tropical plants of the genus *Cleome,* esp. *C. spinosa,* cultivated for its clusters of white or purplish flowers with long, conspicuous stamens. [NLat. *Cleome,* genus name.]

clepe (klēp) *tr.v.* **cleped** (klēpt, klĕpt), **cleped** or **clept** or **y·cleped** (ĭ-klēpt′, ī-klĕpt′) or **y·clept, clep·ing, clepes.** *Archaic.* To call by the name of; name. [ME *clepen* < OE *cleopian,* to cry out.]

clep·sy·dra (klĕp′sĭ-drə) *n., pl.* **-dras** or **-drae** (-drē′). An ancient device that measured time by marking the regulated flow of water through a small opening. [Lat. < Gk. *klepsudra* : *kleps-,* secretly (< *kleptein,* to steal) + *hudōr,* water.]

clere·sto·ry also **clear·sto·ry** (klîr′stôr′ē, -stōr′ē) *n., pl.* **-ries. 1.** The upper part of the nave, transepts, and choir of a church, containing windows. **2.** A windowed wall or construction similar to a clerestory, used for light and ventilation. [ME *clerestorie,* perh. : *cler,* giving light, clear + *storie,* tier. —see STORY.]

cler·gy (klûr′jē) *n., pl.* **-gies.** The body of people ordained for religious service. —See Usage note at **collective noun.** [ME *clergie* < OFr. < *clerc,* cleric. —see CLERK.]

cler·gy·man (klûr′jē-mən) *n.* A member of the clergy.

cler·ic (klĕr′ĭk) *n.* A clergyman. [LLat. *clericus.* —see CLERK.]

cler·i·cal (klĕr′ĭ-kəl) *adj.* **1.** Of or pertaining to clerks or office workers. **2.** Of, relating to, or characteristic of the clergy or a clergyman. *—n.* **1.** A clergyman. **2.** A person or party advocating clericalism. **—cler′i·cal·ly** *adv.*

cler·i·cal·ism (klĕr′ĭ-kə-lĭz′əm) *n.* A policy of supporting the power or influence of the clergy in political or secular matters. **—cler′i·cal·ist** *n.*

cler·i·hew (klĕr′ə-hyōō′) *n.* A humorous quatrain about a person who is generally named in the first line. [After Edmund *Clerihew* Bentley (1875–1956), its inventor.]

cler·i·sy (klĕr′ĭ-sē) *n.* Educated people as a class; the literati. [G. *klerisei,* clergy < Med. Lat. *clericia* < LLat. *clericus,* priest. —see CLERK.]

clerk (klûrk; *Brit.* klärk) *n.* **1.** A person who works in an office performing such tasks as keeping records, attending to correspondence, or filing. **2.** A person who keeps the records and performs the regular business of a court or legislative body. **3.** A salesperson in a store. **4.** *Archaic.* A clergyman. **5.** *Archaic.* **a.** A literate person. **b.** A scholar. *—intr.v.* **clerked, clerk·ing, clerks.** To work or serve as a clerk. [ME, clergyman, secretary < OE and OFr. *clerc,* clergyman, both < LLat. *clericus* < Gk. *klērikos,* belonging to the clergy < *klēros,* inheritance.] **—clerk′dom** *n.* **—clerk′ship′** *n.*

clerk·ly (klûrk′lē) *adj.* **-li·er, -li·est. 1.** Of or pertaining to a clerk or clerks. **2.** *Archaic.* Scholarly. **—clerk′li·ness** *n.*

clev·er (klĕv′ər) *adj.* **-er, -est. 1.** Mentally quick and original; bright. **2.** Nimble with the hands; dexterous. **3.** Showing quick-wittedness: *a clever story.* **4.** *Regional.* Handy; suitable. [Perh. < ME *cliver,* expert in seizing, perh. of ON orig.] **—clev′er·ly** *adv.* **—clev′er·ness** *n.*

Synonyms: *clever, cunning, ingenious, shrewd.* These adjectives describe quick-witted action or speech. *Clever,* the most comprehensive, stresses mental quickness or adeptness in handling a situation. *Cunning* adds to *clever* the idea of slyness or craftiness. *Ingenious* implies great originality and invention. *Shrewd* emphasizes mental cleverness and practical understanding.

clev·is (klĕv′ĭs) *n.* A U-shaped metal piece with holes in each end through which a pin or bolt is run, used for attaching a drawbar to a plow. [Obs. *clevi,* prob. of Scand. orig.]

clew[1] (klōō) *n.* **1.** A ball of yarn or thread. **2. clews.** The cords by which a hammock is suspended. **3. a.** One of the two lower corners of a square sail. **b.** The lower aft corner of a fore-and-aft sail. *—tr.v.* **clewed, clew·ing, clews. 1.** To roll

or coil into a ball. **2.** To raise the lower corners of (a square sail) by means of clew lines. [ME *cleve* < OE *clewe.*]
clew[2] (klo͞o) *n. & v.* Variant of **clue.**
clew line *n. Naut.* A rope used to raise the clew of a sail up to the yard or mast.
cli·ché (klē-shā′) *n.* **1.** A trite or overused expression or idea. **2.** *Printing.* A stereotype or electrotype plate. [Fr. < *clicher,* to stereotype.]
click (klĭk) *n.* **1.** A brief, sharp, nonresonant sound: *the click of a door latch.* **2.** A mechanical device, such as a detent, that snaps into position. **3.** An implosive speech sound, common in some African languages, produced by drawing air into the mouth and clicking the tongue. *—v.* **clicked, click·ing, clicks.** *—intr.* **1.** To produce a click or series of clicks. **2.** *Slang.* **a.** To become a success. **b.** To function well together. *—tr.* To cause to click. [Imit.] **—click′er** *n.*
click beetle *n.* A beetle of the family Elateridae, characterized by the ability to right itself from an overturned position by flipping into the air with a clicking sound.
cli·ent (klī′ənt) *n.* **1.** One for whom professional services are rendered, as by a lawyer. **2.** A customer or patron. **3.** One dependent on the patronage or protection of another: *Cuba—a client of the Soviet Union.* [ME < OFr. < Lat. *cliens.*] **—cli′ent·age** (-ən-tĭj) *n.* **—cli·en′tal** (klī-ĕn′tl, klī′ən-) *adj.*
cli·en·tele (klī′ən-tĕl′, klē′ən-, klē-äN-) *n.* **1.** The clients of a professional person taken collectively. **2.** A body of customers or patrons. [Fr. *clientèle* < Lat. *clientela,* clientship < *cliens,* client.]
cliff (klĭf) *n.* A high, steep, or overhanging face of rock. [ME *clif* < OE.] **—cliff′y** *adj.*
cliff dweller *n.* **1.** A member of certain prehistoric Indian tribes of the southwestern United States who lived in caves in the sides of cliffs. **2.** A person who lives in an apartment house, esp. in a city. **—cliff dwelling** *n.*
cliff·hang·er (klĭf′hăng′ər) *n.* **1.** A melodramatic serial in which each episode ends in suspense. **2.** A contest so closely matched that the outcome is uncertain until the end. **—cliff′hang′ing** *adj.*
cliff swallow *n.* A North American swallow, *Petrochelidon pyrrhonota,* that builds a bottle-shaped mud nest on the face of a cliff or bluff or under the eaves of a roof.
cli·mac·ter·ic (klī-măk′tər-ĭk, klī′măk-tĕr′ĭk) *n.* **1.** A period or year of life when physiological changes take place in the body. **2.** The menopause. **3.** A critical stage, period, or year. *—adj.* Pertaining to a critical stage, period, or year. [Lat. *climactericus,* of a dangerous period in life < Gk. *klimaktērikos* < *klimaktēr,* dangerous point, rung of a ladder < *klimax,* ladder.] **—cli′mac·ter′i·cal** (klī′măk-tĕr′ĭ-kəl) *adj.*
cli·mac·tic (klī-măk′tĭk) also **cli·mac·ti·cal** (-tĭ-kəl) *adj.* Pertaining to or constituting a climax. **—cli·mac′ti·cal·ly** *adv.*
cli·mate (klī′mĭt) *n.* **1.** The meteorological conditions, including temperature, precipitation, and wind, that characteristically prevail in a particular region. **2.** A region manifesting particular meteorological conditions. **3.** A prevailing condition or atmosphere: *a climate of hope.* [ME *climat* < OFr. < LLat. *clima* < Gk. *klima,* region of the earth.] **—cli·mat′ic** (-măt′ĭk), **cli·mat′i·cal** *adj.* **—cli·mat′i·cal·ly** *adv.*
cli·ma·tol·o·gy (klī′mə-tŏl′ə-jē) *n.* The meteorological study of climate. **—cli′ma·to·log′ic** (-tə-lŏj′ĭk) or **cli′ma·to·log′i·cal** *adj.* **—cli′ma·tol′o·gist** *n.*
cli·max (klī′măks′) *n.* **1.** The point of greatest intensity in a series or progression of events; culmination. **2.** Orgasm. **3. a.** A series of statements or ideas in an ascending order of rhetorical force or intensity. **b.** The final statement in such a series. **4.** The stage in ecological development or evolution in which a community of organisms becomes stable and begins to perpetuate itself. *—intr. & tr.v.* **-maxed, -max·ing, -max·es.** To reach or bring to a climax. [Lat., rhetorical climax < Gk. *klimax,* ladder.]
climb (klīm) *v.* **climbed, climb·ing, climbs.** *—tr.* To move up or mount, esp. by using the hands and feet; ascend: *climbed a mountain.* *—intr.* **1.** To rise or move up, esp. by using the hands and feet: *climbed up the ladder.* **2.** To reach a higher status, rank, or condition. **3.** To slant or slope upward: *a hill climbing steeply to the summit.* **4.** To grow in an upward direction, as some plants do, by twining around another object for support. ***—phrasal verb.* climb down.** To go down; descend, esp. by means of the hands and feet: *climbed down the tree.* *—n.* **1.** The act of climbing; ascent. **2.** A place to be climbed. [ME *climben* < OE *climban.*] **—climb′a·ble** (klī′mə-bəl) *adj.*
climb·er (clī′mər) *n.* **1.** One that climbs. **2.** A person who seeks to gain a higher social or professional position. **3.** A plant that grows upward by twining around another object. **4.** A climbing iron.
climbing fumitory *n.* A weak-stemmed climbing vine, *Adlumia fungosa,* of eastern North America, having spurred pinkish or white flowers.
climbing hempweed *n.* A twining vine, *Mikania scandens,* of eastern and central North America, having clusters of small white flowers.
climbing iron *n.* An iron bar with spikes or spurs attached, which can be strapped to a shoe or boot used in climbing.
climbing perch *n.* A freshwater fish, *Anabas testudineus,* of tropical Asia, capable of moving along the ground with the aid of its gill covers and pectoral fins.
clime (klīm) *n.* Climate. [ME, region of the earth < LLat. *clima* < Gk. *klima.*]
cli·mo·graph also **cli·ma·graph** (klī′mə-grăf′) *n.* A representation of climatic data in which one climatic factor, such as temperature, is plotted against another, such as moisture. [CLIM(ATE) + GRAPH.]
clin– *pref.* Variant of **clino-.**
-clinal *suff.* Sloping: *synclinal.* [< Gk. *klinein,* to lean.]
cli·nan·dri·um (klī-năn′drē-əm) *n., pl.* **-dri·a** (-drē-ə). *Bot.* A hollow containing the anther in the upper part of the column of an orchid. [NLat. : Gk. *klinē,* couch (< *klinein,* to recline) + NLat. *-andrium,* stamen < Gk. *anēr,* man.]
clinch (klĭnch) *v.* **clinched, clinch·ing, clinch·es.** *—tr.* **1. a.** To fix or secure (a nail, for example) by bending down or flattening the end that protrudes. **b.** To fasten together in this way. **2.** To settle definitely and conclusively; make final: *clinched the deal.* **3.** *Naut.* To fasten with a clinch. *—intr.* **1.** To be held together securely. **2.** To hold a boxing opponent's body with one or both arms to prevent or hinder his punches. **3.** *Slang.* To embrace. *—n.* **1.** Something, such as a clamp, that clinches. **2.** The clinched part of a nail, bolt, or rivet. **3.** The act or an instance of clinching in boxing. **4.** *Naut.* A knot in a rope made by a half hitch with the end of the rope fastened back by seizing. **5.** *Slang.* An amorous embrace. [Alteration of CLENCH.]
clinch·er (klĭn′chər) *n.* **1.** A person who clinches. **2.** A nail or bolt for clinching. **3.** A tool for clinching nails or bolts. **4.** *Informal.* A decisive point, fact, or remark, esp. one held in reserve.
cline (klīn) *n. Ecol.* A series of differing characteristics within members of a species or population, resulting from gradual changes or transitions in the environment. [< Gk. *klinein,* to lean.] **—clin′al** (klī′nəl) *adj.*
-cline *suff.* Slope: *anticline.* [< Gk. *klinein,* to lean.]
cling (klĭng) *intr.v.* **clung** (klŭng), **cling·ing, clings. 1.** To hold fast or adhere to something, as by grasping, sticking, or entwining. **2. a.** To stay near; remain close. **b.** To fit closely, as to the body: *fabrics that cling.* **c.** To resist separation. **3.** To hold on; remain attached: *cling to old-fashioned ideas.* *—n.* A clingstone. [ME *clingen* < *clingan.*] **—cling′er** *n.*
cling·fish (klĭng′fĭsh′) *n., pl.* **clingfish** or **-fish·es.** Any of various small marine fishes of the family Gobiesocidae, having an adhesive disk under the front part of the body by which it fastens itself to rocks and seaweed.
cling·stone (klĭng′stōn′) *n.* A fruit, esp. a peach, having pulp that adheres partially to the stone. **—cling′stone′** *adj.*
clin·ic (klĭn′ĭk) *n.* **1. a.** A training session for medical students in which they observe while patients are examined and treated. **b.** A class receiving such instruction. **2.** An institution associated with a hospital or medical school that deals chiefly with outpatients. **3.** A medical establishment run by several specialists working in cooperation. **4.** A center that offers counsel or instruction: *a vocational clinic; a tennis clinic.* [Fr. *clinique* < Lat. *clinicus,* physician < Gk. *klinikos* < *klinē,* bed < *klinein,* to recline.]
-clinic *suff.* **1.** Sloping: *isoclinic.* **2.** Having a specified number of oblique axial intersections: *triclinic.* [< Gk. *klinein,* to lean.]
clin·i·cal (klĭn′ĭ-kəl) *adj.* **1.** Of, pertaining to, or connected with a clinic. **2.** Of or pertaining to direct observation and treatment of patients. **3.** Very objective and devoid of emotion; analytical: *gave a clinical description of his financial predicament.* **—clin′i·cal·ly** *adv.*
clinical pathology *n.* The scientific study of the diagnosis and treatment of disease through laboratory analysis of clinical specimens, as tissue.
clinical thermometer *n.* A small self-registering glass thermometer used to measure body temperature.
cli·ni·cian (klĭ-nĭsh′ən) *n.* A physician, psychologist, or psychiatrist specializing in clinical studies or practice. [Fr. *clinicien* < *clinique,* clinic. —see CLINIC.]
clink[1] (klĭngk) *intr. & tr.v.* **clinked, clink·ing, clinks.** To make or cause to make a soft, sharp, ringing sound. *—n.* **1.** A clinking sound. **2.** *Chiefly Brit.* The shrill cry of some birds, such as the stonechat. [ME *clinken* < MDu.]
clink[2] (klĭngk) *n. Slang.* A prison; jail. [After *Clink,* a prison in London, England.]
clink·er (klĭng′kər) *n.* **1.** The incombustible residue, fused into an irregular lump, that remains after the combustion of coal. **2.** A partially vitrified brick or a mass of bricks fused together. **3.** An extremely hard burned brick. **4.** Vitrified matter expelled by a volcano. **5.** *Slang.* A mistake or fault, esp. in a musical performance. *—intr.v.* **-ered, -er·ing, -ers.** To create clinkers in burning, as coal does. [Obs. Du. *klinckaerd* < MDu. *klinken,* to clink.]
clink·er-built (klĭng′kər-bĭlt′) *adj.* Built with overlapping planks or boards, as a ship. [< obs. *clinker,* clinch-nail < ME *clinken,* prob. var. of *clenchen,* to clench < OE *(be)clencan.*]
clink·stone (klĭngk′stōn′) *n.* Phonolite.
clino– or **clin–** *pref.* Slope; slant: *clinometer.* [NLat. < Gk. *klinein,* to slope.]
cli·nom·e·ter (klī-nŏm′ĭ-tər) *n.* An instrument for measuring the angle of an incline, as of an embankment. **—cli′no·met′ric** (-nə-mĕt′rĭk), **cli′no·met′ri·cal** *adj.* **—cli·nom′e·try** *n.*

cliff
Dover, England

cliff dweller
An Indian cliff dwelling

climbing iron
A pair of climbing irons

climbing perch

clin·quant (klĭng′kənt, klăN-käN′) *adj.* Adorned with gold or silver; tinseled. —*n.* Imitation gold leaf; tinsel. [Fr., glistening, tinkling < obs. *clinquer,* to clink, perh. < MDu. *klinken.*]

clin·to·ni·a (klĭn-tō′nē-ə) *n.* A plant of the genus *Clintonia,* having broad leaves, white, greenish-yellow, or purplish flowers, and usually blue berries. [NLat. *Clintonia,* genus name, after DeWitt *Clinton* (1769–1828).]

Cli·o (klī′ō) *n.* **1.** *Gk. Myth.* The Muse of history. **2.** A statuette awarded annually for outstanding achievement in radio and television advertising. [Lat. < Gk. *Kleiō* < *kleiein,* to tell.]

cli·o·met·rics (klī′ə-mĕt′rĭks) *n.* *(used with a sing. verb).* The study of history using advanced mathematical methods of data processing and analysis. [CLIO + -METRICS.] —**cli′o·met′ric** *adj.* —**cli′o·me·tri′cian** (-mĭ-trĭsh′ən) *n.*

clip[1] (klĭp) *v.* **clipped, clip·ping, clips.** —*tr.* **1.** To cut, cut off, or cut out with shears or scissors. **2.** To make shorter by cutting; trim. **3.** To cut off the edge of: *clip a coin.* **4.** To cut short; curtail. **5.** To fail to pronounce or write fully: *clipped his words.* **6.** *Informal.* To hit with a sharp blow. **7.** *Slang.* To cheat or overcharge. —*intr.* **1.** To cut something. **2.** *Informal.* To move rapidly. —*n.* **1.** The act of clipping. **2.** Something clipped off, as a sequence from a movie film. **3. a.** The wool shorn at one shearing. **b.** A season's shearing. **4.** *Informal.* A quick, sharp blow. **5.** *Informal.* A brisk pace. **6. clips.** A pair of shears. [ME *clippen* < ON *klippa.*]

clip[2] (klĭp) *n.* **1.** A device for gripping; clasp; fastener. **2.** A piece of jewelry that fastens with a clasp or clip. **3.** A flange on the top of a horseshoe. **4.** A cartridge clip. —*tr.v.* **clipped, clip·ping, clips. 1.** To grip securely; fasten. **2.** To join (one thing) to another. **3.** *Football.* To block (an opponent who is not carrying the ball) illegally from the rear. [ME, hook < *clippen,* to embrace < OE *clyppan.*]

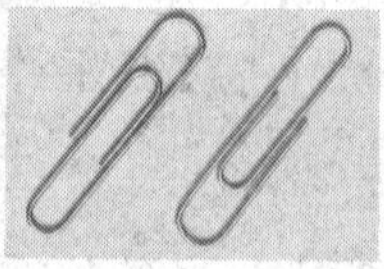

clip[2]
Paper clips

clip·board (klĭp′bôrd′, -bōrd′) *n.* A small writing board with a spring clip at the top for holding papers or a writing pad.

clip joint *n.* *Slang.* A restaurant or place of public entertainment where customers are overcharged or otherwise defrauded.

clip·per (klĭp′ər) *n.* **1.** One who cuts, shears, or clips. **2.** Often **clippers.** An instrument or tool for cutting, clipping, or shearing: *a barber's clippers.* **3.** A sharp-bowed sailing vessel of the mid-19th century, having tall masts and sharp lines and built for great speed. **4.** A fast-moving vehicle.

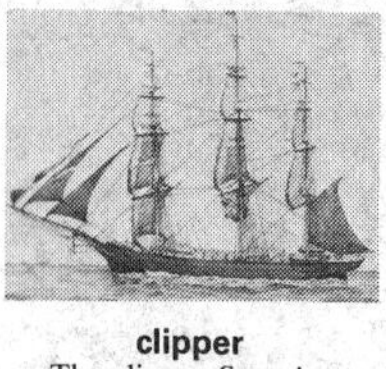

clipper
The clipper *Surprise*

clip·ping (klĭp′ĭng) *n.* Something, esp. an item from a newspaper, that is cut off or out.

clip·sheet (klĭp′shēt′) *n.* A sheet of paper containing news items and other newspaper material, usually printed on only one side for convenience in clipping and reprinting.

clique (klēk, klĭk) *n.* An exclusive group of friends or associates tending to remain aloof from others. —*intr.v.* **cliqued, cliqu·ing, cliques.** *Informal.* To form, associate in, or act as a clique. [Fr.] —**cliqu′ey, cliqu′y, cliqu′ish** *adj.* —**cliqu′ish·ly** *adv.* —**cliqu′ish·ness** *n.*

cli·tel·lum (klī-tĕl′əm) *n., pl.* **-tel·la** (-tĕl′ə). A swollen, glandular, saddlelike region in the epidermis of certain annelid worms, such as the earthworm. [NLat., alteration of Lat. *clitellae,* packsaddle.]

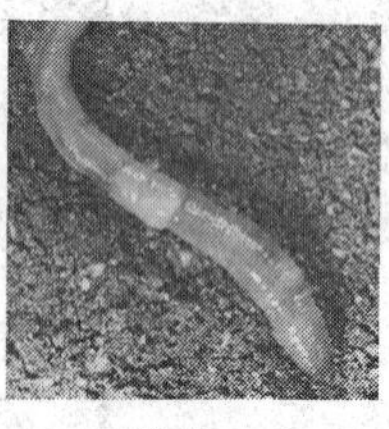

clitellum
Clitellum of an earthworm

clit·o·ris (klĭt′ər-ĭs, klī′tər-) *n.* A small, erectile organ at the upper end of the vulva, homologous with the penis. [Gk. *kleitoris,* poss. < *kleiein,* to shut.] —**clit′o·ral** (-əl) *adj.*

clo·a·ca (klō-ā′kə) *n., pl.* **-cae** (-sē′). **1.** A sewer. **2.** A latrine. **3.** *Zool.* **a.** The cavity into which the intestinal, genital, and urinary tracts open in vertebrates such as fish, reptiles, birds, and some primitive mammals. **b.** The posterior part of the intestinal tract in various invertebrates. [Lat.] —**clo·a′cal** (-kəl) *adj.*

cloak (klōk) *n.* **1.** A loose outer garment, usually sleeveless. **2.** Something that covers or conceals. —*tr.v.* **cloaked, cloak·ing, cloaks. 1.** To cover with or as if with a cloak. **2.** To hide; conceal. [ME *cloke* < OFr., var. of *cloche,* cloak, bell < Med. Lat. *clocca,* bell, from its shape.]

cloak-and-dagger (klōk′ən-dăg′ər) *adj.* Marked by melodramatic intrigue and often espionage.

cloak·room (klōk′rōōm′, -rŏŏm′) *n.* A room where coats and other articles may be left temporarily, as in a theater.

clob·ber (klŏb′ər) *tr.v.* **-bered, -ber·ing, -bers.** *Slang.* **1.** To strike violently and repeatedly; batter or maul. **2.** To defeat decisively. [Orig. unknown.]

cloche (klōsh) *n.* **1.** A bell-shaped glass vessel used to cover plants or food. **2.** A close-fitting woman's hat with a bell-like shape. [Fr., bell < OFr. < Med. Lat. *clocca.*]

clock[1] (klŏk) *n.* **1.** An instrument other than a watch for measuring or indicating time, esp. a mechanical device with a numbered dial and moving hands or pointers. **2.** A time clock. **3.** A metering device, as a speedometer or taxi meter. **4.** *Bot.* The downy flower head of a dandelion that has gone to seed. —*v.* **clocked, clock·ing, clocks.** —*tr.* To record the time or speed of, as with a stopwatch. —*intr.* To record working hours with a time clock: *clocks in at 8:00 A.M. and out at 4:00 P.M.* [ME *clokke* < OFr. *cloke,* var. of *cloche,* bell < Med. Lat. *clocca.*] —**clock′er** *n.*

clock[1]
18th-century English

clock[2] (klŏk) *n.* An embroidered or woven decoration on the side of a stocking or sock. [Perh. < CLOCK[1], bell (obs.), from an original bell-shaped appearance.]

clock radio *n.* A radio with a built-in clock that can be set to turn the radio on automatically.

clock·wise (klŏk′wīz′) *adv.* In the same direction as the rotating hands of a clock. —**clock′wise′** *adj.*

clock·work (klŏk′wûrk′) *n.* The mechanism of a clock or a similar mechanism. —*idiom.* **like clockwork.** With machinelike regularity and precision; perfectly.

clod (klŏd) *n.* **1.** A lump or chunk, esp. of earth or clay. **2.** Earth or soil. **3.** A dull, ignorant, or stupid person; dolt. [ME < OE.] —**clod′dish** *adj.* —**clod′dish·ly** *adv.* —**clod′dish·ness** *n.*

clod·hop·per (klŏd′hŏp′ər) *n.* **1.** A clumsy, coarse person; bumpkin. **2.** A big, heavy shoe.

clog (klŏg) *n.* **1.** An obstacle or hindrance. **2.** A weight, such as a block, that is attached to the leg of an animal to hinder movement. **3.** A heavy, usually wooden-soled shoe. —*v.* **clogged, clog·ging, clogs.** —*tr.* **1.** To block up; obstruct: *Heavy traffic clogged the highway.* **2. a.** To impede or encumber (an animal) with a clog. **b.** To impede or hamper. —*intr.* **1.** To become obstructed or choked up: *pipes clogging with rust.* **2.** To thicken or stick together so as to obstruct. **3.** To do a clog dance. [ME, block attached to an animal's leg.]

clog dance *n.* A dance performed while wearing clogs and characterized by heavy, stamping steps.

cloi·son·né (kloi′zə-nā′, klə-wä′zə-) *n.* **1.** A kind of enamelware in which the surface decoration is formed by different colors of enamel separated by thin strips of metal set on edge. **2.** The process or method of producing cloisonné. —*adj.* Of, denoting, or being cloisonné. [Fr., p.part. of *cloisonner,* to partition < *cloison,* partition < VLat. **clausio* < Lat. *claudere,* to close.]

clois·ter (kloi′stər) *n.* **1.** A covered walk with an open colonnade on one side, running along the inside walls of buildings that face a quadrangle. **2. a.** A place, esp. a monastery or convent, devoted to religious seclusion. **b.** Life in a monastery or convent. —*tr.v.* **-tered, -ter·ing, -ters. 1.** To confine in or as if in a cloister; seclude. **2.** To furnish (a building) with a cloister. [ME *cloistre* < OFr. < Lat. *claustrum,* enclosed place < *claudere,* to close.]

cloister

clois·tral (kloi′strəl) also **claus·tral** (klô′strəl) *adj.* **1.** Of, resembling, or suggesting a cloister; secluded. **2.** Living in a cloister.

clomb (klōm) *v.* *Archaic.* Past tense and past participle of **climb.**

clom·i·phene (klōm′ə-fēn, klō′mə-) *n.* A drug, $C_{26}H_{28}ClNO$, that is used in its citrate form to stimulate ovulation. [C(H)LO(RO)- + (A)MI(NE) + PHEN(YL).]

clomp (klŏmp) *intr.v.* **clomped, clomp·ing, clomps.** To walk heavily and noisily. [Imit.]

clone (klōn) *n.* **1.** A group of genetically identical cells descended from a single common ancestor. **2.** One or more organisms descended asexually from a single ancestor. **3.** One that is an exact replica of another. —*v.* **cloned, clon·ing, clones.** —*intr.* To create a genetic duplicate of an individual organism through asexual reproduction, as by stimulating a single cell. —*tr.* **1.** To duplicate (an organism) asexually by cloning. **2.** To create (a new organism) asexually by cloning. [Gk. *klōn,* twig.] —**clon′al** (klō′nəl) *adj.* —**clon′al·ly** *adv.* —**clon′er** *n.*

clo·nor·chi·a·sis (klō′nôr-kī′ə-sĭs) *n.* A parasitic infection of mammals usually caused by the ingestion of raw fish that is infected with the trematode *Opisthorchis sinensis.* [NLat. *Clonorchis,* former genus name + -IASIS.]

clo·nus (klō′nəs) *n., pl.* **-nus·es.** A convulsion characterized by rapidly alternating muscular contraction and relaxation. [< Gk. *klonos,* turmoil.] —**clo′nic** (klō′nĭk, klŏn′ĭk) *adj.* —**clo·nic′i·ty** (klō-nĭs′ĭ-tē, klŏ-), **clo′nism** (klō′nĭz′əm, klŏn′ĭz′əm) *n.*

clop (klŏp) *n.* The drumming sound of a horse's hoof striking pavement. —*intr.v.* **clopped, clop·ping, clops.** To make a clop. [Imit.]

close (klōs) *adj.* **clos·er, clos·est. 1.** Near in time or space. **2. a.** Near in relationship: *His closest living relative is a second cousin.* **b.** Bound by mutual interests, loyalties, or affections; intimate: *close friends.* **3.** With little or no space between elements or parts; tight; compact: *a close weave.* **4.** Near to the surface; short: *a close shot.* **5.** Almost even, as in tally or score: *a close election.* **6.** Very much like an original: *a close copy.* **7.** Rigorous; strict: *paid close attention.* **8.** Shut or shut in; not open. **9.** Enclosed or almost enclosed. **10.** Confining or narrow; crowded. **11.** Fitting tightly: *close garments.* **12.** Lacking fresh air; stuffy: *a close room.* **13.** Confined to specific persons or groups; restricted. **14.** Strictly confined or confining: *kept under close supervision.* **15.** Hidden from view; secluded. **16.** Taciturn in manner; reticent: *close about her personal life.* **17.** Averse to relinquishing possessions or money; stingy. **18.** Not easy to acquire; scarce: *close credit.* **19.** Uttered with the tongue near the palate. Used of vowels. **20.** Marked by more rather than less punctuation, esp. commas. —*v.* (klōz) **closed, clos·ing, clos·es.** —*tr.* **1.** To shut: *closed the door.* **2.** To fill or stop up: *closed the cracks with plaster.* **3.** To declare not open to the public: *The mayor closed the streets for snow removal.* **4.** To bring to an end: *close a letter.* **5.** To join or unite; bring into contact: *close a circuit.* **6.** To draw together: *It took eight stitches to close the wound.* **7.** To enclose on all sides; shut in. —*intr.* **1.** To become shut: *The door* *closed.* **2.** To come to an end: *a play that closed after four performances.* **3.** To discontinue operation: *The shop closes at six.* **4.** To engage in a one-on-one struggle; grapple: *The policeman closed with the thief.* **5.** To reach an agreement; come to terms. **6.** To come together: *His arms closed around her.* ***—phrasal verbs.*** **close in. 1.** To surround with an oppressive, isolating effect: *problems that closed in on her.* **2.** To surround and advance upon so as to eliminate the possibility of escape: *The enemy closed in on us.* **3.** To enshroud to such a degree that both entrance and exit are precluded: *an airport that was closed in by fog.* **close out.** To dispose of merchandise, usually at greatly reduced prices. *—n.* (klōz). **1.** The act of closing. **2.** A conclusion; finish: *The meeting came to a close.* **3.** An enclosed place, esp. land surrounding or beside a cathedral or other building. **4.** *Archaic.* A fight at close quarters. **5.** (klōs). *Scot. & Brit. Regional.* A narrow lane or alley. *—adv.* (klōs). In a close position; near: *stayed close together.* [ME *clos,* closed < OFr. < Lat. *clausus,* p.part. of *claudere,* to close.] **—close'ly** *adv.* **—close'ness** *n.* **—clos'er** *n.* **—clos'ing** *n.*

Usage: Strictly speaking, the expression *close proximity* says nothing that is not said by *proximity* itself.

close call (klōs) *n. Informal.* A narrow escape.

closed (klōzd) *adj.* **1.** Having boundaries; enclosed. **2.** Blocked or barred to passage or entry. **3.** Explicitly limited; restricted: *closed membership.* **4.** Self-contained. **5.** Carried on in secrecy without the presence of witnesses: *a closed session of the judiciary committee.* **6.** *Math.* **a.** Of or pertaining to a curve, such as a circle, having no end points. **b.** Of or pertaining to a surface having no boundary curves. **c.** Characterized by or possessing the property by which an operation acting on an element in a set produces an element within the set.

closed-cap·tioned (klōzd'kăp'shən d) *adj.* Being a telecast with captions that can be seen only on a specially equipped receiver: *a closed-captioned news program for the deaf.*

closed chain *n. Chem.* A ring (sense 14).

closed circuit *n.* **1.** A television transmission circuit with a limited number of reception stations and no broadcast facilities. **2.** An electric circuit providing an uninterrupted endless path for the flow of current.

closed corporation *n.* A corporation in which ownership of shares of stock is held by a relatively few persons and is rarely bought or sold on the open market.

closed-end investment company (klōzd'ĕnd') *n.* A company with fixed capitalization whose shares are bought and sold by investors and whose capital is invested in other companies.

closed gentian *n.* The bottle gentian.

closed interval *n.* An interval (sense 3.b.).

closed shop *n.* A union shop.

close-fist·ed (klōs'fĭs'tĭd) *adj.* Miserly; stingy.

close-grained (klōs'grānd') *adj.* Dense or compact in structure or texture: *close-grained wood.*

close-hauled (klōs'hôld') *adv. Naut.* With sails trimmed flat for sailing as close to the wind as possible. **—close'-hauled'** *adj.*

close-mind·ed (klōs'mīn'dĭd) *adj.* **1.** Intolerant of the beliefs and opinions of others. **2.** Very stubborn and unyielding.

close-mouthed (klōs'mou*th*d', -moutht') *adj.* Not disposed to talk; reticent.

close-or·der drill (klōs'ôr'dər) *n.* A military drill in marching, maneuvering, and formal handling of arms in which the participants perform at close intervals.

close-out (klōz'out') *n.* A sale in which all goods are disposed of, usually at greatly reduced prices.

close shave (klōs) *n. Informal.* A narrow escape.

clos·et (klŏz'ĭt, klô'zĭt) *n.* **1.** A small room, cabinet, or recess for storing linens, household supplies, or clothes. **2.** A small private chamber, as for studying. **3.** A water closet; toilet. *—tr.v.* **-et·ed, -et·ing, -ets.** To enclose or shut up in a private room, as for discussion: *closeted himself with an adviser.* *—adj.* **1. a.** Private; confidential. **b.** Secret; hidden: *a closet alcoholic.* **2.** Based upon theory and speculation rather than practice. [ME, private room < OFr., dim. of *clos,* enclosure < Lat. *clausum* < *clausus,* enclosed. —see CLOSE.]

closet drama *n.* A play to be read rather than performed.

closet queen *n. Slang.* A man who is latently or secretly homosexual.

close-up (klōs'ŭp') *n.* **1.** A picture, as a motion picture or television shot, taken at close range. **2.** A close or intimate look or view.

clos·trid·i·um (klŏ-strĭd'ē-əm) *n., pl.* **-i·a** (-ē-ə). Any of various rod-shaped, spore-forming, chiefly anaerobic bacteria of the genus *Clostridium,* such as the nitrogen-fixing bacteria found in soil and those causing botulism. [NLat. *Clostridium,* genus name < Gk. *klōstēr,* spindle < *klōthein,* to spin.] **—clos·trid'i·al** (-əl) *adj.*

clo·sure (klō'zhər) *n.* **1.** The act of closing or the condition of being closed. **2.** Something that closes or shuts. **3.** A finish; conclusion. **4.** Variant of **cloture. 5.** The property of being mathematically closed. *—v.* **-sured, -sur·ing, -sures.** To end by cloture. [ME < OFr. < Lat. *clausura* < *clausus,* enclosed. —see CLOSE.]

clot (klŏt) *n.* A thick, viscous, or coagulated mass or lump. *—v.* **clot·ted, clot·ting, clots.** *—intr.* To form into clots. *—tr.* **1.** To cause to clot. **2.** To fill or cover with clots. [ME < OE.]

cloth (klôth, klŏth) *n., pl.* **cloths** (klôths, klô*th*z, klŏths, klŏ*th*z). **1.** Fabric or material formed by weaving, knitting, pressing, or felting of natural or synthetic fibers. **2.** A piece of fabric or material used for a specific purpose, as a tablecloth. **3.** *Naut.* **a.** Canvas. **b.** A sail. **4.** Distinctive professional attire or mode of dress. **5. a.** The dress of the clergy. **b.** The clergy. [ME < OE *clāð.*]

cloth·bound (klôth'bound', klŏth'-) *adj.* Designating a book bound in thick paper boards covered with cloth.

clothe (klō*th*) *tr.v.* **clothed** or **clad** (klăd), **cloth·ing, clothes. 1.** To put clothes on; dress. **2.** To provide clothes for. **3.** To cover as if with clothes; invest. [ME *clothen* < OE *clāðian* < *clāð,* cloth.]

clothes (klōz, klō*th*z) *pl.n.* **1.** Articles of dress; wearing apparel; garments. **2.** Bedclothes. [ME < OE *clāðas* < *clāð,* cloth.]

clothes·horse (klōz'hôrs', klō*th*z'-) *n.* **1.** A frame on which clothes are hung to dry or air. **2.** A person considered excessively concerned with dress.

clothes·line (klōz'līn', klō*th*z'-) *n.* A cord, rope, or wire on which clothes are hung to dry or air.

clothes moth *n.* Any of various moths of the family Tineidae, whose larvae feed on wool, hair, fur, and feathers.

clothes·pin (klōz'pĭn', klō*th*z'-) *n.* A clip of wood or plastic for fastening clothes to a clothesline.

clothes·press (klōz'prĕs', klō*th*z'-) also **clothes press** *n.* A chest, closet, or wardrobe in which clothes are kept.

clothes tree *n.* An upright pole or stand with hooks or pegs on which to hang garments.

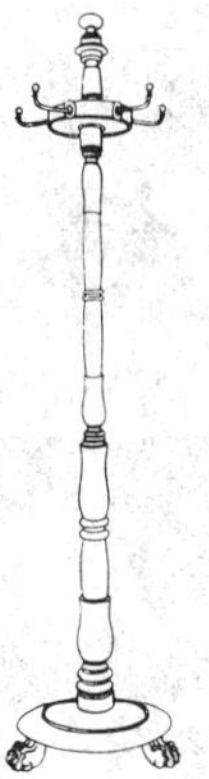

clothes tree

cloth·ier (klō*th*'yər, klō'*th*ē-ər) *n.* One who makes or sells clothing or cloth.

cloth·ing (klō'*th*ĭng) *n.* **1.** Clothes collectively; wearing apparel; attire. **2.** A covering.

Clo·tho (klō'thō) *n. Gk. Myth.* One of the three Fates, spinner of the thread of destiny. [Lat. < Gk. *Klōthō* < *klōthein,* to spin.]

cloth yard *n.* The standard unit of cloth measurement, equal to 36 inches, or 0.9144 meters.

clo·ture (klō'chər) also **clo·sure** (-zhər) *n.* A parliamentary procedure by which debate is ended and an immediate vote is taken on the matter under discussion. *—tr.v.* **-tured, -tur·ing, -tures.** To close (a parliamentary debate) by cloture. [Fr. *clôture,* alteration of OFr. *closure.* —see CLOSURE.]

cloud (kloud) *n.* **1. a.** A visible body of very fine droplets of water or particles of ice dispersed in the atmosphere above the earth's surface at various altitudes ranging up to several miles. **b.** A visible mass in the air, as of steam, smoke, or dust. **2.** A large moving body of things on the ground or in the air; swarm: *a cloud of locusts.* **3.** Something that darkens or fills with gloom. **4.** A dark region or blemish, as on a polished stone. **5.** Something that obscures. **6.** A charge or suspicion affecting a reputation. **7.** A collection of charged particles: *an electron cloud.* *—v.* **cloud·ed, cloud·ing, clouds.** *—tr.* **1.** To cover with or as if with clouds: *Mist clouded the hills.* **2.** To make gloomy or troubled. **3.** To cast aspersions on; sully: *Scandal clouded his reputation.* *—intr.* To become cloudy or overcast: *The sky clouded over.* ***—idiom.*** **in the clouds. 1.** Imaginary; unreal; fanciful. **2.** Impractical. [ME, hill, cloud < OE *clūd,* hill.] **—cloud'less** *adj.*

cloud·ber·ry (kloud'bĕr'ē) *n.* A creeping plant, *Rubus chamaemorus,* of northern regions, having white flowers and edible, reddish-orange fruit.

cloud·burst (kloud'bûrst') *n.* A sudden rainstorm.

cloud chamber *n.* A device in which the formation of chains of droplets on ions generated by the passage of charged subatomic particles through a supersaturated vapor is used to detect such particles, to infer the presence of neutral particles, and to study certain nuclear reactions.

cloud·land (kloud'lănd') *n.* A realm of imagination or fantasy.

cloud nine *n.* A state of elation or great happiness: *was on cloud nine after winning the marathon.*

cloud seeding *n.* A technique of stimulating rainfall, esp. by distributing quantities of dry ice crystals or silver iodide smoke through clouds; rainmaking.

cloud·y (klou'dē) *adj.* **-i·er, -i·est. 1.** Full of or covered with clouds; overcast. **2.** Of or like a cloud or clouds. **3.** Marked with indistinct masses or streaks: *cloudy marble.* **4.** Not transparent, as certain liquids. **5. a.** Liable to more than one interpretation. **b.** Not clearly perceived or perceptible. **6.** Troubled; gloomy. **—cloud'i·ly** *adv.* **—cloud'i·ness** *n.*

clout (klout) *n.* **1.** A blow, esp. with the fist. **2.** A long, powerful hit in baseball. **3.** *Informal.* **a.** Influence; pull: *political clout.* **b.** Power; muscle. **4.** An archery target. **5.** *Archaic & Regional.* A piece of cloth used for mending; patch. *—tr.v.* **clout·ed, clout·ing, clouts. 1.** To hit, esp. with the fist. **2.** *Archaic & Regional.* To patch or bandage. [ME, prob. < OE *clūt,* patch.]

clove[1] (klōv) *n.* **1.** An East Indian evergreen tree, *Eugenia aromatica,* whose aromatic unopened flower buds are used as a spice. **2.** Often **cloves.** A spice consisting of the dried flower buds of the clove, used whole or ground. [ME *clowes,*

clove[1]

clove spice < OFr. *clou (de girofle)*, nail (of the clove tree) < Lat. *clavus,* nail.]

clove[2] (klōv) *n.* One of the small sections of a separable bulb, such as that of garlic. [ME < OE *clufu.*]

clove[3] (klōv) *v.* A past tense and archaic past participle of **cleave[1]**.

clove[4] (klōv) *v. Archaic.* Past tense of **cleave[2]**.

clove hitch *n. Naut.* A knot used to secure a line to a spar, post, or other object, consisting of two turns with the second held under the first. [ME *clove,* split, p.part. of *cleven,* to split < OE *clēofan.*]

clo·ven (klō'vən) *v.* A past participle of **cleave[1]**. —*adj.* Split; divided.

cloven foot *n.* A cloven hoof. **—clo'ven-foot'ed** *adj.*

cloven hoof *n.* **1.** A divided or cleft hoof, as in deer or cattle. **2.** Evil, based on the usual depiction of Satan as a figure with cloven hoofs.

clo·ven-hoofed (klō'vən-ho͝oft', -ho͞oft', -ho͝ovd', -ho͞ovd') *adj.* **1.** Having cloven hoofs, as cattle do. **2.** Satanic; devilish.

clove oil *n.* An aromatic oil distilled from the dried flower buds of the clove tree, used in medicine as an antiseptic.

clove pink *n.* A variety of the carnation, *Dianthus caryophyllus,* having flowers with a spicy fragrance.

clo·ver (klō'vər) *n.* **1.** A plant of the genus *Trifolium,* having compound leaves with three leaflets and tight heads of small flowers. Many species provide valuable pasturage. **2.** Any of several plants related to the clover, such as the bush clover. —***idiom.* in clover.** Living a carefree life of ease, comfort, or prosperity. [ME < OE *clǣfre.*]

clo·ver·leaf (klō'vər-lēf') *n.* A highway interchange at which two highways crossing each other on different levels are provided with curving access and exit ramps enabling vehicles to go in any of four directions.

cloverleaf

clown (kloun) *n.* **1.** A buffoon or jester who entertains by jokes, antics, and tricks in a circus, play, or other presentation. **2.** A coarse, rude, vulgar person; boor. **3.** A rustic or peasant. —*intr.v.* **clowned, clown·ing, clowns. 1.** To behave like a clown or buffoon. **2.** To perform as a jester or clown. [Perh. of LG orig.] **—clown'ish** *adj.* **—clown'ish·ly** *adv.* **—clown'ish·ness** *n.*

clown

clox·a·cil·lin (klŏk'sə-sĭl'ĭn) *n.* A synthetic antibiotic of the penicillin group that is effective against staphylococci. [C(H)L(ORO)- + OX- + A(ZO) + (PENI)CILLIN.]

cloy (kloi) *v.* **cloyed, cloy·ing, cloys.** —*tr.* To supply with too much of something, esp. with something too rich or sweet; surfeit. —*intr.* To cause to feel surfeited. [Obs. *accloy* < ME *acloien.*] **—cloy'ing·ly** *adv.* **—cloy'ing·ness** *n.*

cloze (klōz) *n.* A test of reading comprehension in which the test taker is asked to supply words that have been systematically deleted from a text. [Alteration of CLOSURE.] **—cloze** *adj.*

club (klŭb) *n.* **1.** A stout, heavy stick, usually thicker at one end than at the other, suitable for use as a weapon; cudgel. **2.** A bat or stick used in certain games to drive a ball, esp. a stick with a curved head used in such games as golf and hockey. **3. a.** A black figure on a playing card, shaped like a trefoil or clover leaf. **b.** A card marked with such figures. **c. clubs.** The suit so marked. **4.** A group of people organized for a common purpose, esp. a group that meets regularly. **5.** The room, building, or other facilities used for the meetings of a club. —***modifier:*** *club regulations.* —*v.* **clubbed, club·bing, clubs.** —*tr.* **1.** To strike or beat with or as if with a club. **2.** To use (a rifle or similar firearm) as a club by holding the barrel and hitting with the butt end. **3.** *Archaic.* To gather or combine (hair, for example) into a clublike mass. **4.** To contribute for a joint or common purpose. —*intr.* **1.** *Archaic.* To form or gather into a mass. **2.** To join or combine for a common purpose; form a club. [ME < ON *klubba.*]

club

club·ba·ble also **club·a·ble** (klŭb'ə-bəl) *adj. Informal.* Suited to membership in a social club; sociable.

club·by (klŭb'ē) *adj.* **-bi·er, -bi·est. 1.** Typical of a club or club members. **2.** Friendly; sociable. **3.** Clannish; exclusive. **—club'bi·ness** *n.*

club car *n.* A railroad passenger car equipped with lounge chairs, tables, a buffet or bar, and other extra comforts.

club chair *n.* An upholstered easy chair with arms and a low back.

club·foot (klŭb'fo͝ot') *n.* **1.** Congenital deformity of the foot, marked by a misshapen appearance often resembling a club. **2.** A foot so deformed. **—club'foot'ed** *adj.*

club·house (klŭb'hous') *n.* **1.** A building occupied by a club. **2.** The locker room for a sports team.

Clumber spaniel

club·man (klŭb'mən, -măn') *n.* A man who is a member of a club or clubs, esp. one who is active in club life.

club moss *n.* Any of various evergreen, erect or creeping, mosslike plants of the genus *Lycopodium,* having tiny, scalelike, overlapping leaves and reproducing by spores. [From the club-shaped strobiles on some species of this plant.]

club root *n.* A disease of cabbage and related plants, caused by a fungus, *Plasmodiophora brassicae,* and resulting in large, distorted swellings on the roots.

club sandwich *n.* A sandwich, usually of three slices of bread, with a filling of various meats, tomato, lettuce, and dressing.

Clydesdale

club soda *n.* An effervescent, unflavored water used in various alcoholic and nonalcoholic drinks.

club steak *n.* Delmonico steak.

club·wom·an (klŭb'wo͝om'ən) *n.* A female member of a club or clubs, esp. one who is active in club life.

cluck (klŭk) *n.* **1. a.** The characteristic sound made by a hen when brooding or calling her chicks. **b.** A sound resembling a cluck. **2.** *Informal.* A stupid or foolish person. —*v.* **clucked, cluck·ing, clucks.** —*intr.* **1.** To utter a cluck. **2.** To make a sound similar to a cluck, as in coaxing a horse. —*tr.* **1.** To call by making a cluck. **2.** To express by clucking: *He clucked disapproval.* [Imit.]

clue also **clew** (klo͞o) —*n.* Something that guides or directs in the solution of a problem or mystery. —*tr.v.* **clued, clue·ing** or **clu·ing, clues** also **clewed, clew·ing, clews.** To give (someone) guiding information: *Clue me in on what's happening.* [Var. of CLEW (from Theseus' use of a thread as a guide through the Cretan labyrinth).]

Clum·ber spaniel also **clum·ber spaniel** (klŭm'bər) *n.* A dog of a breed developed in England, having short legs and a silky, predominantly white coat. [After *Clumber,* an estate in Nottinghamshire, England.]

clump (klŭmp) *n.* **1.** A clustered mass; lump. **2.** A thick grouping, as of trees or bushes. **3.** A heavy dull sound; thud. —*v.* **clumped, clump·ing, clumps.** —*intr.* **1.** To form clumps. **2.** To walk with a heavy dull sound. —*tr.* To gather into or form clumps of. [Prob. LG *klump* < MLG *klumpe.*] **—clump'y** *adj.*

clum·sy (klŭm'zē) *adj.* **-si·er, -si·est. 1.** Lacking physical coordination, skill, or grace; awkward. **2.** Awkwardly made; unwieldy: *clumsy wooden shoes.* **3.** Gauche; inept: *a clumsy excuse.* [< obs. *clumse,* to be numb with cold < ME *clomsen,* of ON orig.] **—clum'si·ly** *adv.* **—clum'si·ness** *n.*

clung (klŭng) *v.* Past tense and past participle of **cling.**

clunk (klŭngk) *n.* **1.** A dull sound; thump. **2.** A hefty blow. **3.** A stupid or dull person. —*v.* **clunked, clunk·ing, clunks.** —*intr.* **1.** To make or move with a clunk. **2.** To strike something with a clunk. —*tr.* To strike with a clunk. [Imit.]

clunk·er (klŭng'kər) *n.* **1.** A rattletrap, esp. an old car. **2.** A failure; flop.

clu·pe·id (klo͞o'pē-ĭd) *n.* Any of various oily, soft-finned fishes of the family Clupeidae, which includes the herrings and menhadens. —*adj.* Of or belonging to the Clupeidae. [NLat. *Clupeidae,* family name < Lat. *clupea,* a kind of small fish.]

clus·ter (klŭs'tər) *n.* **1.** A group of the same or similar elements gathered or occurring closely together; bunch. **2.** Two or more successive consonants in a word, as *cl* and *st* in the word *cluster.* —*v.* **-tered, -ter·ing, -ters.** —*intr.* To gather or grow into clusters. —*tr.* To cause to grow or form into clusters. [ME < OE *clyster.*]

cluster headache *n.* A severe headache similar to migraine that can occur several times daily for a period of weeks.

clutch[1] (klŭch) *v.* **clutched, clutch·ing, clutch·es.** —*tr.* **1.** To grasp and hold tightly. **2.** To seize or snatch. —*intr.* To attempt to grasp or seize: *clutch at the ring.* —*n.* **1.** A hand, claw, talon, or paw in the act of grasping. **2.** A tight grasp. **3.** Often **clutches.** Control or power: *the clutches of sin.* **4.** A device for gripping and holding. **5. a.** Any of various devices for engaging and disengaging two working parts of a shaft or of a shaft and a driving mechanism. **b.** The lever, pedal, or other apparatus that activates such a device. **6.** A tense or critical situation: *came through in the clutch.* [ME *clucchen,* var. of *clicchen* < OE *clyccan.*]

clutch[2] (klŭch) *n.* **1.** The number of eggs produced or incubated at one time. **2.** A brood of chickens. —*tr.v.* **clutched, clutch·ing, clutch·es.** To hatch (chicks). [Var. of dial. *cletch,* perh. < *cleck,* to hatch < ME *clekken* < ON *klekja.*]

clut·ter (klŭt'ər) *n.* **1.** A confused or disordered state or collection; jumble: *clutter in the attic.* **2.** A confused noise; clatter. —*v.* **-tered, -ter·ing, -ters.** —*tr.* To litter or pile in a disordered state: *cluttered up the garage with tools and boxes.* —*intr.* **1.** To run or move with bustle and confusion. **2.** To make a clatter. [Prob. < ME *cloteren,* to clot.]

Clydes·dale (klīdz'dāl') *n.* A large, powerful draft horse of a breed developed in the Clyde valley, Scotland.

clyp·e·ate (klĭp'ē-ĭt) also **clyp·e·at·ed** (-ā'tĭd) *adj.* **1.** Shaped like a round shield. **2.** Having a clypeus.

clyp·e·us (klĭp'ē-əs) *n., pl.* **-e·i** (-ē-ī'). *Biol.* A shieldlike structure, esp. a plate on the front of the head of an insect. [NLat. < Lat. *clipeus,* round shield.] **—clyp'e·al** *adj.*

clys·ter (klĭs'tər) *n. Med.* An enema. [ME *clister* < Lat. *clyster* < Gk. *klustēr,* clyster pipe < *kluzein,* to wash out.]

Cly·tem·nes·tra also **Cly·taem·nes·tra** (klī'təm-nĕs'trə) *n. Gk. Myth.* The wife of Agamemnon. [Lat. < Gk. *Klutaimnēstra.*]

Cm The symbol for the element curium.

cni·do·blast (nī'də-blăst') *n.* A modified interstitial cell in coelenterates that produces a nematocyst. [Gk. *knidē,* nettle + -BLAST.]

Co The symbol for the element cobalt.

co– *pref.* **1.** With, together, joint, jointly: *coeducation.* **2. a.** Partner or associate in an activity: *co-author.* **b.** Subordinate or assistant: *copilot.* **3.** To the same extent or degree: *coextend.* **4.** Complement of an angle: *cotangent.* [ME < Lat. < *com-,* com-.]

co·ac·er·vate (kō-ăs′ər-vāt′) *n. Chem.* A cluster of droplets separated out of a lyophilic colloid. [< Lat. *coacervatus,* p.part. of *coacervare,* to heap together : *co(m)-,* together + *acervare,* to heap < *acervus,* a heap.] **—co·ac′er·vate** *adj.* **—co·ac′er·va′tion** *n.*

coach (kōch) *n.* **1.** A large closed carriage with four wheels. **2.** A closed automobile, usually with two doors. **3.** A motorbus. **4.** A railroad passenger car. **5.** A low-priced class of passenger accommodations on a train or airplane. **6.** A person who trains athletes or athletic teams. **7.** A person who gives private instruction, as in singing or acting. **8.** A private tutor employed to prepare a student for an examination. *—tr. & intr.v.* **coached, coach·ing, coach·es. 1.** To train or act as a coach. **2.** To transport by or ride in a coach. [Fr. *coche,* ult. < Hung. *kocsi,* after *Kocs,* Hungary, where such carriages were first made.] **—coach′er** *n.*

coach dog *n.* Dalmatian (sense 1). [So called because it was trained to run behind a coach.]

coach·man (kōch′mən) *n.* **1.** A person who drives a coach. **2.** An artificial fishing fly having white wings, a multi-colored feather body with a brown hackle, and a gold tag.

co·ac·tion (kō-ăk′shən) *n.* **1.** An impelling or restraining force; compulsion. **2.** Joint action. [ME *coaccioun* < Lat. *coactio,* a collecting < *cogere,* to collect : *co(m)-,* together + *agere,* to drive.] **—co·ac′tive** *adj.* **—co·ac′tive·ly** *adv.*

co·ad·ju·tant (kō-ăj′ə-tənt) *n.* A helper; assistant.

co·ad·ju·tor (kō′ə-jo͞o′tər, kō-ăj′ə-tər) *n.* **1.** A coworker; assistant. **2.** The assistant to a bishop. [ME *coadjutour* < Lat. *coadjutor* : *co(m)-* (intensive) + *adjutor,* assistant < *adjutare,* to aid.]

co·ad·u·nate (kō-ăj′ə-nĭt, -nāt′) *adj.* Closely joined; united; grown together. [LLat. *coadunatus,* p.part. of *coadunare,* to combine : Lat. *co(m)-,* together + Lat. *adunare,* to unite (*ad-,* to + *unus,* one).] **—co·ad′u·na′tion** (-nā′shən) *n.* **—co·ad′u·na′tive** *adj.*

co·ag·u·lant (kō-ăg′yə-lənt) *n.* An agent that causes coagulation. **—co·ag′u·lant** *adj.*

co·ag·u·lase (kō-ăg′yə-lās′, -lāz′) *n.* An enzyme, as rennin or thrombin, that causes blood clotting. [COAGUL(ATE) + -ASE.]

co·ag·u·late (kō-ăg′yə-lāt′) *v.* **-lat·ed, -lat·ing, -lates.** *—tr.* To cause transformation of (a liquid or sol) into a soft, semisolid, or solid mass. *—intr.* To become coagulated. [ME *coagulaten* < Lat. *coagulare* < *coagulum,* coagulator. —see COAGULUM.] **—co·ag′u·la·bil′i·ty** *n.* **—co·ag′u·la·ble** *adj.* **—co·ag′u·la′tion** *n.* **—co·ag′u·la′tor** *n.*

co·ag·u·lum (kō-ăg′yə-ləm) *n., pl.* **-la** (-lə). A coagulated mass; clot; curd. [Lat., coagulator < *cogere,* to condense : *co(m)-,* together + *agere,* to drive.]

coal (kōl) *n.* **1. a.** A natural dark-brown to black solid used as a fuel, formed from fossilized plants and consisting of amorphous carbon with various organic and some inorganic compounds. **b.** A piece of this substance. **2.** A glowing or charred piece of coal, wood, or other solid fuel; ember. **3.** Charcoal. *—v.* **coaled, coal·ing, coals.** *—tr.* **1.** To burn (a combustible solid) to a charcoal residue. **2.** To provide with coal. *—intr.* To take on coal. [ME *col* < OE.]

coal·er (kō′lər) *n.* Something, as a ship or train, used for carrying or supplying coal.

co·a·lesce (kō′ə-lĕs′) *intr.v.* **-lesced, -lesc·ing, -lesc·es. 1.** To grow together; fuse. **2.** To come together so as to form one whole; unite: *The rebel units coalesced into one army to fight the invaders.* [Lat. *coalescere* : *co(m)-,* together + *alescere,* to grow, inceptive of *alere,* to nourish.] **—co′a·les′cence** *n.* **—co′a·les′cent** *adj.*

coal gas *n.* **1.** A gaseous mixture produced by the destructive distillation of bituminous coal and used as a commercial fuel. **2.** The gaseous mixture released by burning coal.

coal·i·fi·ca·tion (kō′lə-fĭ-kā′shən) *n.* The process by which coal is formed from plant materials. **—coal′i·fy** *v.* **(-fied, -fy·ing, -fies).**

co·a·li·tion (kō′ə-lĭsh′ən) *n.* **1.** An alliance, esp. a temporary one, of factions, parties, or nations. **2.** A combination into one body; union. [Med. Lat. *coalitio* < Lat. *coalescere,* to grow together. —see COALESCE.] **—co′a·li′tion·ist** *n.*

coal measures *pl.n. Geol.* **1. Coal Measures.** A stratigraphic unit equivalent to the Pennsylvanian or Upper Carboniferous periods. **2.** Strata of the Carboniferous period containing coal deposits.

coal oil *n.* Kerosene.

Coal·sack (kōl′săk′) *n.* **1.** A dark nebula near the Southern Cross, appearing as a hole in the Milky Way. **2.** A dark region of the sky, the Northern Coalsack, near the Northern Cross.

coal tar *n.* A viscous black liquid obtained by the destructive distillation of coal, used as a raw material for many dyes, drugs, and organic chemicals and for waterproofing, paints, roofing, and insulation materials.

coam·ing (kō′mĭng) *n.* A raised rim or curb around an opening, as in a ship's deck, designed to keep out water. [Orig. unknown.]

co-an·chor (kō-ăng′kər) *n.* Either of two news commentators who work as anchorpersons during a broadcast. **—co-anchor** *v.* **(-chored, -chor·ing, -chors).**

co·arc·tate (kō-ärk′tāt′) *adj.* **1.** Describing an insect pupa compressed in the larval shell. **2.** Having a constricted separation between the abdomen and thorax. [Lat. *coarctatus,* p.part. of *coarctare,* to compress : *co(m)-,* together + *artare,* to compress < *artus,* confined.] **—co′arc·ta′tion** *n.*

coarse (kôrs, kōrs) *adj.* **coars·er, coars·est. 1.** Of low, common, or inferior quality. **2.** Lacking in delicacy or refinement: *coarse language.* **3.** Consisting of large particles; not fine in texture: *coarse sand.* **4.** Rough; harsh: *a coarse tweed.* [ME *cors,* prob. < *course,* custom. —see COURSE.] **—coarse′ly** *adv.* **—coarse′ness** *n.*

Synonyms: *coarse, gross, crass, indelicate, vulgar, obscene, ribald.* These adjectives primarily describe offensive speech or writing and behavior. *Coarse* implies roughness and crudeness in manners, appearance, or expression. *Gross* implies excessive behavior approaching bestiality. *Crass* suggests stupidity combined with rudeness or other manifestation of lack of refinement: *crass ignorance. Indelicate* implies immodesty, tactless behavior, or lack of taste in expression: *an indelicate remark. Vulgar* emphasizes offensiveness to propriety and suggests boorishness and poor breeding. *Obscene* strongly stresses lewdness or indecency, particularly in reference to accepted standards of morality. *Ribald* implies vulgar, coarse, off-color language or behavior intended to provoke laughter.

coarse-grained (kôrs′grānd′, kōrs′-) *adj.* **1.** Having a rough or coarse texture. **2.** Not refined; indelicate; crude.

coars·en (kôr′sən, kōr′-) *intr. & tr.v.* **-ened, -en·ing, -ens.** To become or make coarse.

coast (kōst) *n.* **1.** The land next to the sea; seashore. **2.** *Obs.* The frontier or border of a country. **3.** A hill or other slope down which one may coast, as on a sled. **4.** The act of sliding or coasting; slide. **5. Coast.** The Pacific Coast of the United States. *—v.* **coast·ed, coast·ing, coasts.** *—intr.* **1. a.** To slide down an inclined slope, as on a sled. **b.** To move effortlessly and smoothly. **2.** To move without further acceleration. **3.** To sail near or along a coast. **4.** To act or move aimlessly or with little effort. *—tr.* To sail or move along the coast or border of. [ME *coste* < OFr. < Lat. *costa,* side.] **—coast′al** (kō′stəl) *adj.*

coast artillery *n.* Artillery for protecting coastal areas.

coast·er (kō′stər) *n.* **1.** One that coasts. **2.** A vessel engaged in coastal trade. **3.** A coasting sled or toboggan. **4.** A disk placed under a bottle, pitcher, or drinking glass to protect a table top or other surface beneath. **5.** A small tray, often on wheels, for passing something, as a wine decanter, around a table.

coaster brake *n.* A brake and clutch operating on the rear wheel and drive mechanism of a bicycle when pedaling is reversed.

coast guard also **Coast Guard** *n.* **1.** The military or naval coastal patrol of a nation, responsible for the protection of life and property at sea, coastal defense, and enforcement of customs, immigration, and navigation laws. **2.** A member of a coast guard; coastguardsman.

coast·guards·man (kōst′gärdz′mən) *n.* A member of a coast guard.

coast·line (kōst′līn′) *n.* The shape or boundary of a coast.

coast rhododendron *n.* An evergreen shrub, *Rhododendron californicum* (or *R. macrophyllum*), of the Pacific coast of North America, having rose-purple flowers.

coast·ward (kōst′wərd) *adv. & adj.* Toward or directed toward the coast. **—coast′wards** (-wərdz) *adv.*

coast·wise (kōst′wīz′) *adj. & adv.* Following, by way of, or along the coast. **—coast′ways′** (-wāz′) *adv.*

coat (kōt) *n.* **1. a.** An outer garment covering the body from the shoulders to the waist or below. **b.** A garment extending to just below the waist and usually forming the top part of a suit. **2.** A natural integument or outer covering, such as the fur of an animal. **3.** A layer of material covering something else; coating. *—tr.v.* **coat·ed, coat·ing, coats. 1.** To provide or cover with a coat. **2.** To cover with a layer, as of paint. [ME *cote* < OFr.] **—coat′ed** *adj.*

co·a·ti (kō-ä′tē) *n.* Any of several omnivorous mammals of the genus *Nasua,* of South and Central America and the southwestern United States, related to and resembling the raccoon but having a longer snout and tail. [Port. *coatí* < Tupi : *cua,* belt + *tim,* nose.]

co·a·ti·mun·di also **co·a·ti·mon·di** (kō-ä′tē-mŭn′dē) *n.* The coati. [Tupi.]

coat·ing (kō′tĭng) *n.* **1.** A layer of a substance spread over a surface for protection or decoration; a covering layer. **2.** Cloth for making coats.

coat of arms

coat of arms *n.* **1.** A tabard or surcoat blazoned with heraldic bearings. **2.** A representation of a coat of arms.

coat of mail *n., pl.* **coats of mail.** An armored coat made of chain mail, interlinked rings, or overlapping metal plates; hauberk.

coat·tail (kōt′tāl′) *n.* **1.** The loose back part of a coat below the waist. **2. coattails.** The skirts of a formal or dress coat. ***—idiom.*** **on (someone's) coattails.** As a result of the success of another.

co-au·thor (kō-ô′thər) *n.* A collaborating or joint author. *—tr.v.* **-thored, -thor·ing, -thors.** To be a co-author of.

coax (kōks) *v.* **coaxed, coax·ing, coax·es.** *—tr.* **1.** To persuade or try to persuade by pleading or flattery; cajole; wheedle. **2.** To obtain by persistent persuasion: *coaxed the secret out of him.* **3.** *Obs.* To caress or fondle. *—intr.* To use

p **p**op / r **r**oar / s **s**auce / sh **sh**ip, di**sh** / t **t**ight / th **th**in, pa**th** / *th* **th**is, ba**th**e / ŭ c**u**t / ûr **ur**ge / v **v**alve / w **w**ith / y **y**es / z **z**ebra, si**z**e / zh vi**s**ion / ə **a**bout, it**e**m, ed**i**ble, gall**o**p, circ**u**s / œ *Fr.* f**eu**, *Ger.* sch**ö**n / ü *Fr.* t**u**, *Ger.* **ü**ber / KH *Ger.* i**ch**, *Scot.* lo**ch** / N *Fr.* bo**n**.

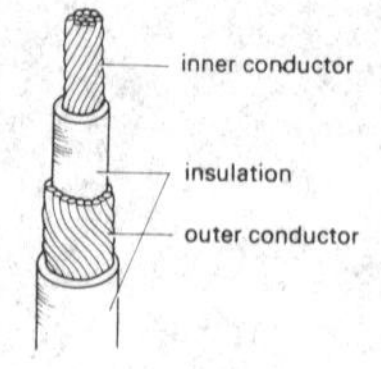

coaxial cable

persuasion or inducement. [Obs. *cokes,* to fool < *cokes,* fool.] —**coax'er** *n.* —**coax'ing·ly** *adv.*

co·ax·i·al (kō-ăk'sē-əl) *adj.* Having or mounted on a common axis.

coaxial cable *n.* A high-frequency telephone, telegraph, and television transmission cable consisting of a conducting outer metal tube enclosing and insulated from a central conducting core.

cob (kŏb) *n.* **1.** The central core of an ear of corn; corncob. **2.** A male swan. **3.** A thickset, stocky, short-legged horse. **4.** A small lump or mass, as of coal. [Prob. < obs. *cob,* round object.]

co·bal·a·min (kō-băl'ə-mĭn) also **co·bal·a·mine** (-mēn') *n.* Vitamin B_{12}. [COBAL(T) + (VIT)AMIN.]

co·balt (kō'bôlt') *n. Symbol* **Co** A hard, brittle metallic element, found associated with nickel, silver, lead, copper, and iron ores and resembling nickel and iron in appearance. It is used chiefly for magnetic alloys, high-temperature alloys, and in the form of its salts for blue glass and ceramic pigments. Atomic number 27; atomic weight 58.9332; melting point 1,495°C; boiling point 2,900°C; specific gravity 8.9; valences 2, 3. [G. *Kobalt* < MHG *Kobolt,* goblin (from the trouble it gave silver miners).]

cobra

cobalt 60 *n.* A radioactive isotope of cobalt with mass number 60 and exceptionally intense gamma-ray activity, used in radiotherapy, metallurgy, and materials testing.

cobalt blue *n.* **1.** A blue to green pigment consisting of a variable mixture of cobalt and aluminum oxides. **2.** A deep to vivid blue or strong greenish blue.

co·balt·ite (kō'bôl-tīt') also **co·balt·ine** (-tēn') *n.* A silver-white to gray mineral, CoAsS, that is an important cobalt ore and is used in ceramics.

cob·ber (kŏb'ər) *n. Austral.* A comrade; pal. [Orig. unknown.]

cob·ble[1] (kŏb'əl) *n.* **1.** A cobblestone. **2.** Cob coal (sense 2). —*tr.v.* **-bled, -bling, -bles.** To pave with cobblestones. [Back-formation < COBBLESTONE.]

cob·ble[2] (kŏb'əl) *tr.v.* **-bled, -bling, -bles. 1.** To make or mend (boots or shoes). **2.** To put together clumsily; bungle. [Prob. back-formation < COBBLER.]

cob·bler[1] (kŏb'lər) *n.* **1.** One who mends boots and shoes. **2.** *Archaic.* One who is clumsy at his work; bungler. [ME *cobeler.*]

Cochin China
A male Cochin China fowl

cob·bler[2] (kŏb'lər) *n.* **1.** A deep-dish fruit pie with a thick top crust. **2.** An iced drink made of wine or liqueur, sugar, and citrus fruit. [Orig. unknown.]

cob·ble·stone (kŏb'əl-stōn') *n.* A naturally rounded stone formerly used for paving streets and walls. [ME *cobelston.*]

cob coal *n.* **1.** Coal in rounded lumps of various sizes. **2.** A lump of coal about the size of a cobblestone.

co·bel·lig·er·ent (kō'bə-lĭj'ər-ənt) *n.* A nation associated with another or others in waging war.

co·bi·a (kō'bē-ə) *n.* A large game fish, *Rachycentron canadum,* of tropical and subtropical seas. [Orig. unknown.]

co·ble (kō'bəl) *n.* **1.** *Chiefly Brit.* A small, flat-bottomed fishing boat with a lugsail on a raking mast. **2.** *Scot.* A kind of flat-bottomed rowboat. [ME *cobel,* ult. < Lat. *caupulus,* a kind of small ship.]

cob·nut (kŏb'nŭt') *n.* **1.** A tree, *Corylus avellana grandis,* related to the hazel. **2.** The large, edible nut of the cobnut.

CO·BOL or **Co·bol** (kō'bôl') *n.* A language based on English words and phrases, used in programming digital computers for various business applications. [CO(MMON) B(USINESS) O(RIENTED) L(ANGUAGE).]

co·bra (kō'brə) *n.* **1.** Any of several venomous snakes of the genus *Naja* and related genera, of Asia and Africa, capable of expanding the skin of the neck to form a flattened hood. **2.** Leather made from the skin of a cobra. [Short for Port. *cobra (de capello),* snake (with a hood) < Lat. *colubra,* snake.]

cockade

cob·web (kŏb'wĕb') *n.* **1. a.** The web spun by a spider to catch its prey. **b.** A single thread of such a web. **2.** Something resembling a cobweb in gauziness or flimsiness. **3.** An intricate plot; snare: *caught in a cobweb of espionage and intrigue.* **4. cobwebs.** Confusion; disorder: *cobwebs in the brain.* —*tr.v.* **-webbed, -web·bing, -webs.** To cover with or as if with cobwebs. [ME *coppeweb* : *coppe,* spider (short for *attercoppe* < OE *āttercoppe* : *ātor,* poison + *copp,* head) + *web,* web < OE.] —**cob'web'by** *adj.*

co·ca (kō'kə) *n.* **1.** A South American tree, *Erythroxylon coca,* having leaves that contain cocaine and related alkaloids. **2.** The dried leaves of the coca or related plants, chewed by people of the Andes for their stimulating effect. [Sp. < Quechua *kúka.*]

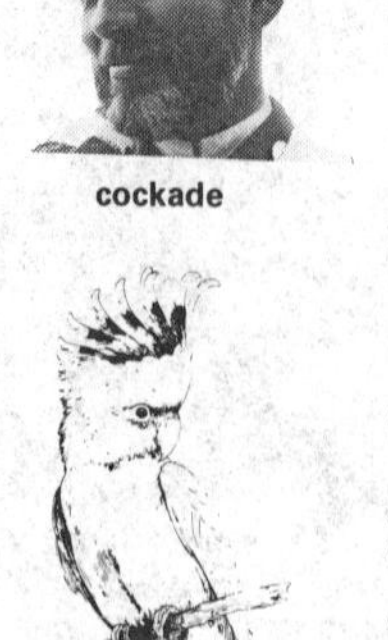

George Miksch Sutton

cockatoo

co·caine also **co·cain** (kō-kān', kō'kān') *n.* A colorless or white crystalline narcotic alkaloid, $C_{17}H_{21}NO_4$, extracted from coca leaves and used as a surface anesthetic.

co·cain·ism (kō-kā'nĭz'əm) *n.* The habitual use of cocaine.

co·cain·ize (kō-kā'nīz') *tr.v.* **-ized, -iz·ing, -iz·es.** To anesthetize (a body part) with cocaine. —**co·cain'i·za'tion** *n.*

co·car·box·y·lase (kō'kär-bŏk'sə-lās', -lāz') *n.* A coenzyme that functions in the catalysis of the decarboxylation of pyruvic acid in the Krebs cycle.

coc·ci (kŏk'sī, kŏk'ī') *n.* Plural of **coccus.**

coc·cid (kŏk'sĭd) *n.* An insect of the family Coccidae, including the scale insects and mealybugs. [NLat. *Coccidae,* family name < *Coccus,* genus name < Gk. *kokkos,* grain.]

coc·cid·i·oi·do·my·co·sis (kŏk-sĭd'ē-oi'dō-mī-kō'sĭs) *n.* A fungus disease of humans and other animals caused by the fungus *Coccidioides immitis* that usually affects the lungs. [NLat. *Coccidiodes,* genus name (< *Coccidia,* order name < COCCUS) + MYCOSIS.]

coc·cid·i·o·sis (kŏk-sĭd'ē-ō'sĭs) *n.* A disease of many animals, including cattle, swine, sheep, dogs, cats, and poultry, but rarely of man, resulting from an infection of the digestive tract by parasitic protozoa of the order Coccidia. [NLat. *Coccidia,* order name (< COCCUS) + -OSIS.]

coc·co·ba·cil·lus (kŏk'ō-bə-sĭl'əs) *n., pl.* **-cil·li** (-sĭl'ī'). A bacillus that is short and oval in shape. [COCC(US) + -O- + BACILLUS.]

coc·cus (kŏk'əs) *n., pl.* **coc·ci** (kŏk'sī', kŏk'ī'). **1.** A bacterium with a spherical or spheroidal shape. **2.** *Bot.* A division that contains a single seed and splits apart from a many-lobed fruit. [NLat. < Gk. *kokkos,* grain.] —**coc'coid'** (kŏk'oid'), **coc'cal** (kŏk'əl) *adj.*

-coccus *suff.* A microorganism of spherical or spheroidal shape: *streptococcus.* [NLat. < Gk. *kokkos,* berry.]

coc·cyg·e·al (kŏk-sĭj'ē-əl) *adj.* Of or pertaining to the coccyx. [< Gk. *kokkyx, kokkyg-,* coccyx.]

coc·cyx (kŏk'sĭks) *n., pl.* **coc·cy·ges** (kŏk-sī'jēz, kŏk'sĭ-jēz'). A small bone at the base of the spinal column, consisting of several fused rudimentary vertebrae. [Gk. *kokkux,* cuckoo, coccyx (from the resemblance of the bone to a cuckoo's beak).] —**coc·cyg'e·al** (kŏk-sĭj'ē-əl) *adj.*

Co·chin China (kō'chĭn, kŏch'ĭn) *n.* A large domestic fowl of a breed developed in Asia, having thickly feathered legs. [After *Cochin China,* a former name for a region of Vietnam.]

coch·i·neal (kŏch'ə-nēl', kŏch'ə-nēl', kō'chə-, kō'chə-) *n.* **1.** A brilliant red dye made by drying and pulverizing the bodies of the females of a tropical American scale insect, *Dactylopius coccus,* that feeds on certain species of cacti. **2.** A vivid red. [Fr. *cochenille* < Sp. *cochinilla,* prob. < Lat. *coccineus,* scarlet < Gk. < *kokkos,* kermes berry (from its use in making scarlet dye).] —**coch'i·neal'** *adj.*

cochineal insect *n.* A tropical American insect, *Dactylopius coccus,* that feeds on certain species of cacti.

coch·le·a (kŏk'lē-ə, kō'klē-ə) *n., pl.* **-le·ae** (-lē-ē'). A spiral tube of the inner ear resembling a snail shell and containing nerve endings essential for hearing. [NLat. < Lat., snail shell < Gk. *kokhlias,* snail < *kokhlos,* land snail.] —**coch'le·ar** *adj.*

cochlear nerve *n.* A division of the acoustic nerve.

coch·le·ate (kŏk'lē-ĭt, -āt', kō'klē-) also **coch·le·at·ed** (-ā'tĭd) *adj.* Shaped like a snail shell; spirally twisted. [Lat. *cochleatus* < *cochlea,* snail shell. —see COCHLEA.]

cock[1] (kŏk) *n.* **1. a.** The adult male of the domestic fowl; rooster. **b.** A male bird. **2.** A weather vane shaped like a rooster; weathercock. **3.** A leader or chief. **4.** A faucet or valve by which the flow of a liquid or gas can be regulated. **5. a.** The hammer in a firearm. **b.** Its position when ready for firing. **6.** A tilting or jaunty turn upward: *the cock of a hat.* **7.** *Slang.* The penis. —*v.* **cocked, cock·ing, cocks.** —*tr.* **1.** To set the hammer of (a firearm) in a position ready for firing. **2.** To tilt or turn up or to one side, usually in a jaunty or alert manner. **3.** To raise in preparation to throw or hit. —*intr.* **1.** To cock the hammer of a firearm. **2.** To turn or stick up. —***idiom.*** **cock of the walk.** An overbearing or domineering person. [ME *cok* < OE *coc.*]

cock[2] (kŏk) *n.* A cone-shaped pile of straw or hay. —*tr.v.* **cocked, cock·ing, cocks.** To arrange (straw or hay) in a cock. [ME *cok.*]

cock·ade (kŏ-kād') *n.* A rosette or knot of ribbon worn esp. on the hat as a badge. [Alteration of obs. *cockard* < Fr. *cocarde* < OFr. *coquarde,* vain < *coq,* cock.] —**cock·ad'ed** (kŏ-kā'dĭd) *adj.*

cock-a-hoop (kŏk'ə-ho͝op', -ho͞op') *adj.* **1.** In a state of elation or exultation. **2.** Boastful. **3.** Askew. [From the phrase *to set cock on hoop,* to drink festively.] —**cock'-a-hoop'** *adv.*

Cock·aigne (kŏ-kān') *n.* An imaginary land of easy and luxurious living. [ME *cokaigne* < OFr. < *(pais de) cokaigne,* land of plenty, prob. < MLG *kōkenje,* small cake, dim. of *kōke,* cake.]

cock-a-leek·ie also **cock·a·leek·ie** (kŏk'ə-lē'kē) *n.* A cream soup made with leeks and chicken. [Alteration of *cockie,* dim. of COCK[1] + *leekie,* dim. of LEEK.]

cock·a·lo·rum (kŏk'ə-lôr'əm, -lōr'-) *n.* **1.** A little man with an unduly high opinion of himself. **2.** Boastful talk; braggadocio. [Perh. alteration of obs. Flem. *kockeloeren,* to crow.]

cock·a·ma·mie also **cock·a·ma·my** (kŏk'ə-mā'mē) *adj. Slang.* **1.** Trifling; nearly valueless. **2.** Ludicrous; nonsensical: *gave me a cockamamie reason for not going.* [Prob. alteration of DECALCOMANIA.]

cock-and-bull story (kŏk'ən-bo͝ol') *n.* An absurd or highly improbable tale passed off as being true.

cock·a·tiel also **cock·a·teel** (kŏk'ə-tēl') *n.* A crested parrot, *Nymphicus hollandicus,* of Australia, having gray and yellow plumage. [Du. *kaketielje,* prob. ult. < Malay *kakatua,* cockatoo.]

cock·a·too (kŏk'ə-to͞o') *n., pl.* **-toos.** Any of various parrots of the genus *Kakatoe* and related genera, of Australia and adjacent areas, characterized by a long, erectile crest. [Du. *kaketoe,* < Malay *kakatua.*]

cock·a·trice (kŏk'ə-trĭs, -trīs') *n.* A mythical serpent that is hatched from a cock's egg and has the power of killing by its glance. [ME *cocatrice,* basilisk < OFr. *cocatris* < Med. Lat. *calcatrix* (< Lat. *calcare,* to track < *calx,* heel), transl. of Gk. *ikhneumōn,* tracker. —see ICHNEUMON.]
cock·boat (kŏk'bōt') *n.* A small rowboat, esp. one used as a tender, kept on a ship. [ME *cokbote* : *cok,* cockboat (< AN *coque*) + *bot,* boat < OE *bāt.*]
cock·chaf·er (kŏk'chā'fər) *n.* Any of various Old World beetles of the family Scarabaeidae, esp. *Melolontha melolontha,* a species destructive to plants.
Cock·croft-Wal·ton accelerator (kŏk'krôft-wôl'tən) *n.* *Physics.* A positive-ion accelerator, consisting essentially of several stages of a voltage-doubling circuit together with an ion source and a discharge tube, used in the first purely artificial disintegration of an atomic nucleus. [After Sir John Douglas *Cockcroft* (1897–1967) and Ernest Thomas Sinton *Walton* (b. 1903), its inventors.]
cock·crow (kŏk'krō') *n.* The time of day when the cock crows; dawn.
cocked hat *n.* A hat with the brim turned up in two or three places, esp. a three-cornered hat; tricorn.
cock·er[1] (kŏk'ər) *n.* **1.** A cocker spaniel. **2. a.** A person who keeps or trains gamecocks. **b.** A person who promotes or attends cockfights.
cock·er[2] (kŏk'ər) *tr.v.* **-ered, -er·ing, -ers.** To pamper, spoil, or coddle. [ME *cokeren.*]
cock·er·el (kŏk'ər-əl) *n.* A young rooster. [ME *cokerel,* dim. of *cok,* cock < OE *coc.*]
cocker spaniel *n.* A dog of a breed originally developed in England, having long, drooping ears and a variously colored silky coat. [From its original use in hunting woodcocks.]
cock·eye (kŏk'ī') *n.* A squinting eye.
cock·eyed (kŏk'īd') *adj.* **1.** Cross-eyed. **2.** *Slang.* **a.** Crooked; askew. **b.** Foolish; ridiculous; absurd: *a cockeyed idea.* **c.** Drunk.
cock·fight (kŏk'fīt') *n.* A fight between gamecocks that are often fitted with metal spurs. **—cock'fight'ing** *adj.* & *n.*
cock·horse (kŏk'hôrs') *n.* A rocking horse.
cock·le[1] (kŏk'əl) *n.* **1.** Any of various bivalve mollusks of the family Cardiidae, having rounded or heart-shaped shells with radiating ribs. **2.** The shell of a cockle; cockleshell. **3.** A wrinkle or pucker. **4.** A cockleshell (sense 2). *—intr.* & *tr.v.* **-led, -ling, -les.** To become or cause to become wrinkled or puckered. ***—idiom.* cockles of (one's) heart.** One's innermost feelings. [ME *cokel* < OFr. *coquille,* shell < VLat. **conchillia* < Lat. *conchyllium* < Gk. *konkhulion,* dim. of *konkhē,* mussel.]
cock·le[2] (kŏk'əl) *n.* Any of several plants often growing as weeds in grain fields. [ME *cokkel* < OE *coccel.*]
cock·le·boat (kŏk'əl-bōt') *n.* A cockboat.
cock·le·bur (kŏk'əl-bûr') *n.* **1.** Any of several coarse weeds of the genus *Xanthium,* bearing prickly burs. **2.** The bur of a cocklebur.
cock·le·shell (kŏk'əl-shĕl') *n.* **1. a.** The shell of a cockle. **b.** A shell similar to that of a cockle. **2.** A small, light boat.
cock·loft (kŏk'lôft', -lŏft') *n.* A small loft or garret. [Prob. from its use as a roosting place.]
cock·ney (kŏk'nē) *n., pl.* **-neys. 1.** Often **Cockney.** A native of the East End of London. **2.** The dialect or accent of cockneys. *—adj.* Of or like cockneys or their dialect. [ME *cokenei,* pampered child, prob. : *cok,* cock (< OE *coc*) + *ei,* egg < OE *ǣg.*]
cock-of-the-rock (kŏk'əv-*th*ə-rŏk') *n., pl.* **cocks-of-the-rock.** Either of two South American birds, *Rupicola rupicola* or *R. peruviana,* having a distinctive crest and bright-orange or reddish plumage in the male. [From its habit of nesting on rocks.]
cock·pit (kŏk'pĭt') *n.* **1.** A pit or enclosed space for cockfights. **2.** A place where many battles have been fought. **3. a.** An apartment in an old warship below the water line, used as quarters for junior officers and as a station for the wounded during a battle. **b.** In small decked vessels, an area toward the stern, lower than the rest of the deck, from which the vessel is steered. **4. a.** The space in the fuselage of a small airplane containing seats for the pilot, copilot, and sometimes passengers. **b.** The space set apart for the pilot and crew in a large airliner.
cock·roach (kŏk'rōch') *n.* Any of various oval, flat-bodied insects of the family Blattidae, several species of which are common household pests. [By folk ety. < Sp. *cucaracha.*]
cocks·comb (kŏks'kōm') *n.* **1.** The comb of a rooster. **2.** The cap of a jester, decorated to resemble the comb of a rooster. **3.** Any of several plants of the genus *Celosia,* esp. *C. argentea cristata,* having a showy crested or rolled flower cluster. **4.** Also **coxcomb.** A pretentious fop.
cock·shy (kŏk'shī') *n., pl.* **-shies.** *Chiefly Brit.* **1.** A mark aimed at in throwing contests. **2.** The throw in a throwing contest. [From an old game in which sticks were shied at a cock.]
cock·spur thorn (kŏk'spûr') *n.* A small, thorny North American tree, *Crataegus crus-galli,* having white flowers and small red fruit. [From the resemblance of its thorn to a cock's spur.]
cock·sure (kŏk'sho͝or') *adj.* **1.** Completely sure; certain. **2.** Too sure; overconfident. **—cock'sure'ly** *adv.* **—cock'sure'ness** *n.*
cock·tail (kŏk'tāl') *n.* **1.** Any of various mixed alcoholic drinks consisting usually of brandy, whiskey, or gin combined with fruit juices or other liquors and often served chilled. **2.** An appetizer, such as a juice or seafood served with a sharp sauce: *a clam cocktail.* *—adj.* **1.** Of or pertaining to cocktails. **2.** Suitable for wear on semiformal occasions: *a cocktail dress.*
cock·y (kŏk'ē) *adj.* **-i·er, -i·est.** *Informal.* Self-assertive or self-confident; conceited. **—cock'i·ly** *adv.* **—cock'i·ness** *n.*
co·co (kō'kō) *n., pl.* **-cos. 1.** The coconut palm. **2.** The coconut. *—adj.* Made of fibers from the coconut shell. [Sp. < Port., goblin, from the face suggested by holes on the inner coconut shell.]
co·coa (kō'kō) *n.* **1. a.** A powder made from cacao seeds after they have been roasted, ground, and freed of most of their fatty oil. **b.** A beverage made by combining this powder with water or milk and sugar. **2.** A moderate brown to reddish brown. [Var. of CACAO.] **—co'coa** *adj.*
cocoa butter *n.* A yellowish-white, waxy solid obtained from cacao seeds and used in the manufacture of pharmaceuticals, confections, and soap.
co·coa·nut (kō'kə-nŭt', -nət) *n.* Variant of **coconut.**
co·co·bo·lo (kō'kə-bō'lō) *n., pl.* **-los. 1.** A tropical American tree, *Dahlbergia retusa,* having hard, dark wood banded with light streaks. **2.** The wood of the cocobolo, used in cabinetwork. [Sp. < Arawakan *kakabali.*]
co·con·scious (kō'kŏn'shəs) *adj.* Being aware or conscious of the same things. *—n.* *Psychiat.* Mental processes outside the realm of conscious activity or awareness, as with schizophrenic individuals. **—co·con'scious·ness** *n.*
co·co·nut also **co·coa·nut** (kō'kə-nŭt', -nət) *n.* The fruit of the coconut palm, a large seed with a thick, hard shell that encloses edible white meat and has a milky fluid filling the hollow center.
coconut oil *n.* An oil extracted from coconuts that is used in foods and in the production of soaps.
coconut palm *n.* A tall palm tree, *Cocos nucifera,* native to the East Indies, bearing coconuts as fruit.
co·coon (kə-ko͞on') *n.* **1. a.** A covering of silk or similar fibrous material spun by the larvae of moths and other insects as protection for their pupal stage. **b.** A similar protective covering or structure, such as that of a spider or earthworm. **2.** A protective plastic coating placed over stored inactive military or naval equipment. [Fr. *cocon* < Prov. *coucoun,* dim. of *coco,* shell.]
co·cotte (kô-kôt') *n.* A prostitute. [Fr.]
Co·cy·tus (kō-sī'təs) *n.* *Gk. Myth.* One of the six rivers of Hades. [Lat. < Gk. *kōkutos* < *kōkutos,* lamentation < *kōkuein,* to wail.]
cod[1] (kŏd) *n., pl.* **cod** or **cods.** Any of various marine fishes of the family Gadidae, esp. *Gadus morhua* (or *G. callarias*), an important food fish of Northern Atlantic waters; codfish. [ME.]
cod[2] (kŏd) *n.* **1.** *Regional.* A husk or pod. **2.** *Obs.* A bag. **3.** *Archaic.* The scrotum. [ME < OE *codd.*]
co·da (kō'də) *n.* *Mus.* A passage at the end of a movement or composition that brings it to a formal close. [Ital. < Lat. *cauda,* tail.]
cod·dle (kŏd'l) *tr.v.* **-dled, -dling, -dles. 1.** To cook in water just below the boiling point. **2.** To treat indulgently; baby. [Poss. < CAUDLE.] **—cod'dler** *n.*
code (kōd) *n.* **1.** A systematically arranged and comprehensive collection of laws. **2.** A systematic collection of regulations and rules of procedure or conduct: *the military code.* **3. a.** A system of signals used to represent letters or numbers in transmitting messages. **b.** A system of symbols, letters, or words given certain arbitrary meanings, used for transmitting messages requiring secrecy or brevity. *—tr.v.* **cod·ed, cod·ing, codes. 1.** To systematize and arrange (laws and regulations) into a code. **2.** To convert (a message, for example) into code. [ME < OFr. < Lat. *codex.*]
co·deine (kō'dēn', -dē-ĭn) *n.* An alkaloid narcotic, $C_{18}H_{21}NO_3$, derived from opium or morphine, used for relieving coughing, as an analgesic, and as a hypnotic. [Fr. *codéine* : Gk. *kōdeia,* poppy head + *-ine,* -ine.]
Code Na·po·lé·on (kōd' nä-pō-lā-ôɴ') *n.* The code of French civil law, prepared under the direction of Napoleon Bonaparte between 1804 and 1807. [Fr.]
co·dex (kō'dĕks') *n., pl.* **co·di·ces** (kō'dĭ-sēz', kŏd'ĭ-). **1.** A manuscript volume, esp. of a classic work or of the Scriptures. **2.** *Obs.* A code of laws or statutes. [Lat.]
cod·fish (kŏd'fĭsh') *n., pl.* **codfish** or **-fish·es.** The cod[1].
codg·er (kŏj'ər) *n.* *Informal.* An old or somewhat eccentric man. [Perh. alteration of obs. *cadger,* peddler. —see CADGE.]
co·di·ces (kō'dĭ-sēz', kŏd'ĭ-) *n.* Plural of **codex.**
cod·i·cil (kŏd'ə-sĭl) *n.* **1.** *Law.* A supplement or appendix to a will. **2.** A supplement or appendix. [ME < Lat. *codicilis,* dim. of *codex,* codex.] **—cod'i·cil'la·ry** (kŏd'ə-sĭl'ə-rē) *adj.*
cod·i·fy (kŏd'ĭ-fī', kō'də-) *tr.v.* **-fied, -fy·ing, -fies. 1.** To reduce to a code: *codify laws.* **2.** To arrange or systematize. **—cod'i·fi·ca'tion** *n.* **—cod'i·fi'er** *n.*
cod·ling[1] (kŏd'lĭng) also **cod·lin** (-lĭn) *n.* *Chiefly Brit.* **1.** A long, tapering apple. **2.** An unripe apple. [ME *querdlyng.*]
cod·ling[2] (kŏd'lĭng) *n., pl.* **-lings** or **codling.** A young cod.

cocker spaniel

George Miksch Sutton
cock-of-the-rock

cockpit

cockroach

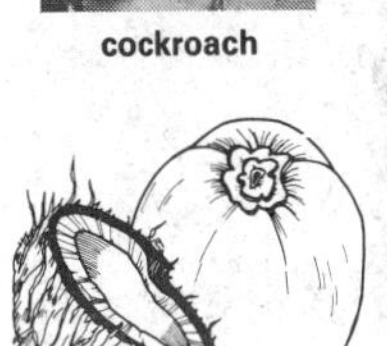
coconut

codpiece
Portrait of Charles V of Spain by Titian

coffee

codling moth also **codlin moth** *n.* A small, grayish moth, *Carpocapsa pomonella,* whose larvae are destructive to various fruits, esp. apples.

cod-liv·er oil (kŏd′lĭv′ər) *n.* An oil obtained from the liver of cod and containing a rich supply of vitamins A and D.

co·dom·i·nance (kō-dŏm′ə-nəns) *n.* The condition in which two different alleles in a gene pair appear together in a heterozygote. **—co·dom′i·nant** *adj.*

co·don (kō′dŏn′) *n.* A sequence of three adjacent nucleotides that specifies the insertion of an amino acid in a specific structural position during protein synthesis. [COD(E) + -ON[1].]

cod·piece (kŏd′pēs′) *n.* A pouch at the crotch of the tight-fitting breeches worn by men in the 15th and 16th centuries. [ME *codpece* : *cod,* scrotum (< OE *codd,* bag) + *pece,* piece. —see PIECE.]

cods·wal·lop (kŏdz′wŏl′əp) *n. Chiefly Brit. Slang.* Nonsense. [Orig. unknown.]

co·ed or **co-ed** (kō′ĕd′) *Informal.* —*n.* A woman student attending a coeducational college or university. —*adj.* Coeducational. [Short for *coeducational student.*]

co·ed·u·ca·tion also **co-ed·u·ca·tion** (kō-ĕj′ə-kā′shən) *n.* The system of education in which both men and women attend the same institution or classes. **—co·ed′u·ca′tion·al** *adj.* **—co·ed′u·ca′tion·al·ly** *adv.*

co·ef·fi·cient (kō′ə-fĭsh′ənt) *n.* **1.** *Math.* **a.** A numerical factor of an elementary algebraic term, as 4 in the term 4x. **b.** The product of all but one of the factors of an expression, the product being regarded as a distinct entity with respect to the excluded factor and to a designated operation. **2.** A numerical measure of a physical or chemical property that is constant for a system under specified conditions.

coefficient of correlation *n.* Correlation coefficient.

-coel or **-coele** or **-cele** *suff.* Chamber; cavity: *blastocoel.* [NLat. *-coela* < Gk. *koilos,* hollow.]

coe·la·canth (sē′lə-kănth′) *n.* Any of various fishes of the order Coelacanthiformes, known only in fossil form until a living species, *Latimeria chalumnae,* of African marine waters, was identified in 1938. [NLat. *Coelecanthus,* former genus name : Gk. *koilos,* hollow + Gk. *akantha,* spine.] **—coe′la·can′thine′** (-kăn′thīn′, -thĭn) *adj.* **—coe′la·can′thous** (-thəs) *adj.*

-coele *suff.* Variant of **-coel.**

coe·len·te·ra (sĭ-lĕn′tər-ə) *n.* Plural of **coelenteron.**

coe·len·ter·ate (sĭ-lĕn′tə-rāt′, -tər-ĭt) *n.* An invertebrate animal of the phylum Coelenterata, characterized by a radially symmetrical body with a saclike internal cavity, and including the jellyfishes, hydras, sea anemones, and corals. —*adj.* Of or belonging to the Coelenterata. [NLat. *Coelenterata,* phylum name : Gk. *koilos,* hollow + Gk. *enteron,* intestines.] **—coe·len·ter′ic** (sĭ-lĕn-tĕr′ĭk) *adj.*

coe·len·ter·on (sĭ-lĕn′tə-rŏn′, -tər-ən) *n., pl.* **-te·ra** (-tər-ə). The saclike body cavity of a coelenterate. [NLat. : Gk. *koilos,* hollow + Gk. *enteron,* intestine.]

coe·li·ac (sē′lē-ăk′) *adj.* Variant of **celiac.**

coe·lom also **ce·lom** or **coe·lome** (sē′ləm) *n.* The body cavity in all animals higher than the coelenterates and certain primitive worms, formed by the splitting of the mesoderm into two layers. [Gk. *koilōma,* cavity < *koilos,* hollow.]

coeno- or **ceno-** *pref.* Common: *coenocyte.* [NLat. < Gk. *koino-* < *koinos,* common.]

coen·o·bite (sĕn′ə-bīt′, sē′nə-) *n.* Variant of **cenobite.**

coe·no·cyte (sē′nə-sīt′) *n.* An organism consisting of a multinucleate protoplasmic mass resulting from nuclear division without the formation of a new cell wall or membrane, as in slime molds and certain fungi and algae. **—coe′no·cyt′ic** (-sĭt′ĭk) *adj.*

coe·no·gen·e·sis (sē′nō-jĕn′ĭ-sĭs, sĕn′ō-) *n.* Variant of **cenogenesis.**

coe·nu·rus (sĭ-nŏŏr′əs, -nyŏŏr′-) *n., pl.* **-nu·ri** (-nŏŏr′ī′, -nyŏŏr′ī′). The larval stage of a tapeworm, *Multiceps multiceps* (or *Taenia multiceps*), that attacks the central nervous system of ruminant animals. [COEN(O)- + -UR(O)US.]

co·en·zyme (kō-ĕn′zīm′) *n.* A heat-stable organic molecule that must be loosely associated with an enzyme for the enzyme to function. **—co·en·zy·mat·ic** (-zə-măt′ĭk) *adj.* **—co·en′zy·mat′i·cal·ly** *adv.*

coenzyme A *n.* A coenzyme present in all living cells that functions as an acetylating agent and is also necessary in fatty acid metabolism.

co·e·qual (kō-ē′kwəl) *adj.* Equal with one another, as in rank. —*n.* An equal. **—co′e·qual′i·ty** (-kwŏl′ĭ-tē) *n.* **—co·e′qual·ly** *adv.*

co·erce (kō-ûrs′) *tr.v.* **-erced, -erc·ing, -erc·es. 1.** To force to act or think in a given manner by pressure, threats, or intimidation; compel. **2.** To dominate, restrain, or control forcibly: *coerced the strikers into compliance.* **3.** To bring about by force: *efforts to coerce agreement.* [Lat. *coercēre,* to confine : *co(m)-,* together + *arcēre,* to restrain.] **—co·erc′er** *n.* **—co·erc′i·ble** *adj.*

co·er·cion (kō-ûr′zhən, -shən) *n.* **1.** The act or practice of coercing. **2.** The power to coerce. **—co·er′cion·ar′y** (-zhə-nĕr′ē, -shə-) *adj.*

co·er·cive (kō-ûr′sĭv) *adj.* Characterized by or inclined to coercion. **—co·er′cive·ly** *adv.* **—co·er′cive·ness** *n.*

co·es·sen·tial (kō′ĭ-sĕn′shəl) *adj.* Having the same nature or essence. **—co′es·sen′ti·al′i·ty** (-shē-ăl′ĭ-tē), **co′es·sen′tial·ness** *n.* **—co′es·sen′tial·ly** *adv.*

co·e·ta·ne·ous (kō′ĭ-tā′nē-əs) *adj.* Of equal age, duration, or period; coeval. [< LLat. *coaetaneus,* a contemporary : Lat. *co(m)-,* same + Lat. *aetas,* age.] **—co′e·ta′ne·ous·ly** *adv.* **—co′e·ta′ne·ous·ness** *n.*

co·e·ter·nal (kō′ĭ-tûr′nəl) *adj.* Equally eternal. **—co′e·ter′nal·ly** *adv.*

co·e·ter·ni·ty (kō′ĭ-tûr′nĭ-tē) *n.* Existence for eternity with another or others.

co·e·val (kō-ē′vəl) *adj.* Originating or existing during the same period of time; lasting through the same era. —*n.* One of the same era or period. [Lat. *coaevus* : *co(m)-,* same + *aevum,* age.] **—co·e′val·ly** *adv.*

co·ex·ist (kō′ĭg-zĭst′) *intr.v.* **-ist·ed, -ist·ing, -ists. 1.** To exist together, at the same time, or in the same place. **2.** To live in peace with another or others despite differences, esp. as a matter of policy. **—co′ex·is′tence** *n.* **—co′ex·is′tent** *adj.*

co·ex·tend (kō′ĭk-stĕnd′) *v.* **-tend·ed, -tend·ing, -tends.** —*tr.* To cause to extend through the same space or duration. —*intr.* To reach to or attain the same limit in space or time. **—co′ex·ten′sion** *n.*

co·ex·ten·sive (kō′ĭk-stĕn′sĭv) *adj.* Having the same limits, boundaries, or scope. **—co′ex·ten′sive·ly** *adv.*

co·fac·tor (kō′făk′tər) *n.* A substance, such as an inorganic ion, coenzyme, or vitamin, that activates an enzyme.

cof·fee (kô′fē, kŏf′ē) *n.* **1. a.** Any of several trees of the genus *Coffea,* native to eastern Asia and Africa, bearing berries containing beans used in the preparation of a beverage, esp. *C. arabica,* the chief commercial source of these beans. **b.** The seeds or beans of the coffee tree. **c.** An aromatic, mildly stimulating beverage prepared from coffee beans. **2.** A moderate brown to dark or dark grayish yellowish brown. **—*modifier:*** *a coffee cup.* [Turk. *kahve* < Ar. *qahwah.*]

coffee break *n.* A short break from work, as in midmorning, during which coffee or other refreshments may be consumed.

coffee cake *n.* A cake made of sweetened yeast dough, often containing nuts or raisins, and topped with powdered sugar or icing.

coffee house also **cof·fee·house** (kô′fē-hous′, kŏf′ē-) *n.* A restaurant where coffee and other refreshments are served and people often gather to socialize.

coffee klatch or **coffee klatsch** (klăch, kläch) *n.* A casual gathering for coffee and conversation. [Partial transl. of G. *Kaffeeklatsch* : *Kaffee,* coffee (< Ital. *caffè* < Turk. *kahve* < Ar. *qahwah*) + *Klatsch,* chat.]

coffee mill *n.* A device for grinding roasted coffee beans.

cof·fee·pot (kô′fē-pŏt′, kŏf′ē-) *n.* A pot for brewing or serving coffee.

coffee shop *n.* A small restaurant in which light meals are served.

coffee table *n.* A long, low table, often placed before a sofa.

cof·fee-ta·ble book (kô′fē-tā′bəl, kŏf′ē-) also **cof·fee-ta·bler** (-tā′blər) *n.* An oversize book of elaborate design that may be used for display, as on a coffee table.

coffee tree *n.* **1.** A tree of the genus *Coffea,* producing coffee beans. **2.** The Kentucky coffee tree.

cof·fer (kô′fər, kŏf′ər) *n.* **1.** A strongbox. **2.** Often **coffers.** Financial resources; funds; treasury. **3.** A decorative sunken panel in a soffit, ceiling, dome, or vault. **4.** A canal lock. **5.** A cofferdam. —*tr.v.* **-fered, -fer·ing, -fers. 1.** To put in a coffer. **2.** To supply with decorative sunken panels. [ME *cofre* < OFr. < Lat. *cophinus,* basket < Gk. *kophinos.*]

cof·fer·dam (kô′fər-dăm′, kŏf′ər-) *n.* **1.** A temporary watertight enclosure built in the water and pumped dry to expose the bottom so that construction, as of piers, may be undertaken. **2.** A watertight chamber attached to a ship's side to facilitate repairs below the water line.

cof·fin (kô′fĭn, kŏf′ĭn) *n.* **1.** An oblong box in which a corpse is buried. **2.** A horse's hoof. —*tr.v.* **-fined, -fin·ing, -fins.** To place in or as if in a coffin. [ME *cofin,* basket < OFr. < Lat. *cophinus* < Gk. *kophinos.*]

coffin bone *n.* The bone inside a horse's hoof.

coffin corner *n. Slang.* On a football field, any corner within 10 yards of the defending team's goal line. The ball may be deliberately punted out of bounds in this area, thus placing the receiving team very close to its goal line.

coffin nail *n. Slang.* A cigarette. [From the unhealthful effects of smoking cigarettes.]

cof·fle (kô′fəl, kŏf′əl) *n.* A file of animals, prisoners, or slaves, chained together in transit. —*tr.v.* **-fled, -fling, -fles.** To fasten together in a coffle. [Ar. *qāfilah,* caravan.]

cog[1] (kŏg) *n.* **1.** One of a series of teeth on the rim of a wheel that by engagement transmit motive force to a corresponding wheel. **2.** A cogwheel. **3.** A subordinate member of an organization who performs necessary but usually minor or routine functions. [ME *cogge.*] **—cogged** *adj.*

cog[2] (kŏg) *v.* **cogged, cog·ging, cogs.** —*tr.* To load or manipulate (dice) fraudulently. —*intr.* To cheat, esp. at dice. —*n.* An instance of cheating; swindle. [Orig. unknown.]

cog[3] (kŏg) *n.* A tenon projecting from a wooden beam and fitting into an opening in another beam to form a joint. —*tr.v.* **cogged, cog·ging, cogs.** To join with tenons. [Orig. unknown.]

co·gen·er·a·tion (kō-jĕn′ə-rā′shən) *n.* A process in which an industrial facility utilizes its waste energy to produce electricity.

co·gent (kō'jənt) *adj.* Making a strong appeal to the intellect or powers of reasoning; convincing: *a cogent argument.* [Lat. *cogens, cogent-,* pr.part. of *cogere,* to force : *co(m)-,* together + *agere,* to drive.] **—co'gen·cy** (-jən-sē) *n.* **—co'gent·ly** *adv.*

cog·i·tate (kŏj'ĭ-tāt') *intr. & tr.v.* **-tat·ed, -tat·ing, -tates.** To take careful thought or think carefully about; ponder. [Lat. *cogitare, cogitat-* : *co(m)-* (intensive) + *agitare,* to consider.] **—cog'i·ta·ble** (kŏj'ĭ-tə-bəl) *adj.* **—cog'i·ta'tor** *n.*

cog·i·ta·tion (kŏj'ĭ-tā'shən) *n.* **1.** The act of cogitating; thoughtful consideration. **2.** A serious thought.

cog·i·ta·tive (kŏj'ə-tā'tĭv) *adj.* **1.** Of or pertaining to cogitation. **2.** Inclined to or capable of cogitation. **—cog'i·ta'tive·ly** *adv.* **—cog'i·ta'tive·ness** *n.*

co·gnac (kōn'yăk', kŏn'-, kôn'-) *n.* **1.** A brandy produced in the vicinity of Cognac in western France. **2.** A fine brandy.

cog·nate (kŏg'nāt') *adj.* **1.** Related by blood; having a common ancestor. **2.** Related in origin, as certain words in different languages derived from the same root. **3.** Related or analogous in nature, character, or function. *—n.* A person or thing cognate with another, esp.: **a.** A person having a common ancestor with another. **b.** A word related to one in another language. [Lat. *cognatus* : *co(m),* together + *gnatus,* born, var. of *natus,* p.part. of *nasci,* to be born.] **—cog·na'tion** *n.*

cog·ni·tion (kŏg-nĭsh'ən) *n.* **1.** The mental process or faculty by which knowledge is acquired. **2.** Something that comes to be known, as through perception, reasoning, or intuition; knowledge. [ME *cognicioun* < Lat. *cognitio* < *cognoscere,* to learn : *co(m)-* (intensive) + *gnoscere,* to know.] **—cog·ni'tion·al, cog'ni·tive** (kŏg'nĭ-tĭv) *adj.*

cognitive dissonance *n. Psychol.* A condition of conflict resulting from inconsistency between one's beliefs and one's actions, as opposing the slaughter of animals and eating meat.

cog·ni·za·ble (kŏg'nĭ-zə-bəl, kŏg-nĭ'-) *adj.* **1.** Capable of being known or perceived. **2.** Capable of being tried before a particular court of law. **—cog'ni·za·bly** *adv.*

cog·ni·zance (kŏg'nĭ-zəns) *n.* **1.** Conscious knowledge or recognition; awareness. **2.** The range of what one can know or understand. **3.** Observance; notice: *took cognizance of his objections.* **4.** *Law.* **a.** The examination of a case by a court. **b.** The right or power of a court's jurisdiction. **c.** Admission of an action or fact; confession. **5.** A heraldic crest or badge worn to distinguish the bearer. [ME *conissaunce* < OFr. *conoissance* < *connoistre,* to know < Lat. *cognoscere,* to learn. —see COGNITION.]

cog·ni·zant (kŏg'nĭ-zənt) *adj.* Fully informed; aware: *cognizant of her rights.* [< COGNIZANCE.]

cog·no·men (kŏg-nō'mən) *n., pl.* **-mens** or **-nom·i·na** (-nŏm'ə-nə). **1.** A family name; surname. **2.** The third and usually last name of a citizen of ancient Rome, as *Caesar* in *Caius Julius Caesar.* **3.** A name, esp. a descriptive nickname acquired through usage. [Lat. : *co(m)-,* together + *gnomen, nomen,* name.] **—cog·nom'i·nal** (-nŏm'ə-nəl) *adj.*

co·gno·scen·te (kŏn'yə-shĕn'tē, kŏg'nə-) *n., pl.* **-ti** (-tē). A person of superior knowledge or taste; connoisseur. [Obs. Ital. < Lat. *cognoscens,* pr.part. of *cognoscere,* to know. —see COGNITION.]

cog·no·vit (kŏg-nō'vĭt) *n. Law.* A written admission by a defendant of his liability, made to avoid the expense of a trial. [Lat., he has acknowledged < *cognoscere,* to recognize. —see COGNITION.]

co·gon (kō-gōn') *n.* Any of various tall tropical grasses of the genus *Imperata,* esp. *I. cylindrica* or *I. exaltata,* of the Philippines and adjacent islands, used for thatching. [Sp. *cogón* < Tagalog *kugon.*]

cog railway *n.* A railway designed to operate on steep slopes, having locomotives with a center cogwheel that engages with a cogged center rail to provide traction.

Cogs·well chair (kŏgz'wĕl', -wəl) *n.* An upholstered easy chair, open under the armrests, with a sloping back and cabriole front legs. [Prob. < the name *Cogswell.*]

cog·wheel (kŏg'hwēl', -wēl') *n.* One of a set of cogged wheels within a given mechanism.

co·hab·it (kō-hăb'ĭt) *intr.v.* **-it·ed, -it·ing, -its. 1.** To live together as husband and wife. **2.** To live together in a sexual relationship when not legally married. [LLat. *cohabitare* : Lat. *co(m)-,* together + Lat. *habitare,* to dwell.] **—co·hab'i·tant** *n.* **—co·hab'i·ta'tion** *n.*

co·heir (kō-âr') *n.* A joint heir.

co·heir·ess (kō-âr'ĭs) *n.* A joint heiress.

co·here (kō-hîr') *v.* **-hered, -her·ing, -heres.** *—intr.* **1.** To stick or hold together in a mass. **2.** To be logically connected. *—tr.* To cause to form a united or orderly whole. [Lat. *cohaerēre* : *co(m)-,* together + *haerēre,* to cling.]

co·her·ence (kō-hîr'əns, -hĕr'-) also **co·her·en·cy** (-ən-sē) *n.* The quality or state of cohering, esp. logical or orderly relationship of parts.

co·her·ent (kō-hîr'ənt, -hĕr'-) *adj.* **1.** Sticking together; cohering. **2.** Marked by an orderly or logical relation of parts that affords comprehension or recognition: *coherent speech.* **3.** *Physics.* Of or pertaining to waves with a continuous relationship among phases. **4.** Of or pertaining to a system of units of measurement in which a small number of basic units are defined from which all others in the system are derived by multiplication or division only. **—co·her'ent·ly** *adv.*

co·he·sion (kō-hē'zhən) *n.* **1.** The act, process, or condition of cohering. **2.** *Physics.* The mutual attraction by which the elements of a body are held together. **3.** *Bot.* The congenital joining of two parts. [Fr. *cohésion,* ult. < Lat. *cohaerēre,* to cling together. —see COHERE.] **—co·he'sive** (-sĭv, -zĭv) *adj.* **—co·he'sive·ly** *adv.* **—co·he'sive·ness** *n.*

co·he·sion·less (kō-hē'zhən-lĭs) *adj.* Of or pertaining to a soil that is composed of particles that do not cohere.

co·hort (kō'hôrt') *n.* **1.** One of the ten divisions of a Roman legion, consisting of 300 to 600 men. **2.** A group or band united in a struggle. **3.** *Informal.* A companion or associate. [ME < Lat. *cohors.*]

Usage: Although *cohort* in the sense of "a companion or associate" occurs at all levels of usage, it still is not acceptable in formal writing to a majority of the Usage Panel.

co·ho salmon (kō'hō) *n.* A food and game fish, *Oncorhyncus kisutch,* originally of Pacific waters. [Orig. unknown.]

co·hosh (kō'hŏsh') *n.* The baneberry (sense 1). [Prob. of Algonquian orig.]

co·hune (kō-ho͞on') *n.* A tropical American palm tree, *Attalea cohune,* having long featherlike leaves and oily nuts. [Sp. (Central America) < Mosquito *ókhún.*]

cohune palm *n.* The cohune.

coif (koif) *n.* **1.** A tight-fitting cap worn under a veil, as by nuns. **2.** A white skullcap formerly worn by English lawyers. **3.** A heavy skullcap of steel or leather, formerly worn under a helmet or mail hood. **4.** (*also* kwäf). A coiffure. *—tr.v.* (koif) **coifed, coif·ing, coifs. 1.** To cover with or as if with a coif. **2.** (*also* kwäf). To arrange or dress (the hair). [ME < OFr. *coife* < LLat. *cofea,* helmet.]

coif·feur (kwä-fûr') *n.* A hairdresser. [Fr. < *coiffer,* to coif < OFr. *coife,* coif. —see COIF.]

coif·feuse (kwä-fûrz', -fyo͞oz') *n.* A female hairdresser. [Fr., fem. of *coiffeur,* coiffeur.]

coif·fure (kwä-fyo͝or') *n.* A way of arranging the hair; hair style. *—tr.v.* **-fured, -fur·ing, -fures.** To arrange or dress (the hair). [Fr. < *coiffer,* to coif. —see COIFFEUR.]

coil[1] (koil) *n.* **1. a.** A series of connected spirals or concentric rings formed by gathering or winding: *a coil of rope.* **b.** An individual spiral or ring within such a series. **2.** A spiral pipe or series of spiral pipes, as in a radiator. **3.** *Elect.* **a.** A wound spiral of two or more turns of insulated wire, used to introduce inductance into a circuit. **b.** Any device of which such a spiral is the major component. *—v.* **coiled, coil·ing, coils.** *—tr.* **1.** To wind in spirals or concentric rings. **2.** To wind into a shape resembling a coil. *—intr.* **1.** To form coils. **2.** To move in a spiral course. [Prob. < OFr. *coillir,* to gather < Lat. *colligere.* —see COLLECT.] **—coil'er** *n.*

coil[2] (koil) *n.* A disturbance; fuss. [Orig. unknown.]

coin (koin) *n.* **1.** A small piece of metal, usually flat and circular, authorized by a government for use as money. **2.** Metal money collectively. **3.** *Archit.* A corner or cornerstone. *—tr.v.* **coined, coin·ing, coins. 1.** To make (coins) from metal; mint; strike: *coin silver dollars.* **2.** To make coins from (metal): *coin gold.* **3.** To invent (a word or phrase). *—adj.* Requiring one or more coins for operation: *a coin washing machine.* [ME < OFr., die for stamping coins, wedge < Lat. *cuneus,* wedge.] **—coin'a·ble** *adj.* **—coin'er** *n.*

coin·age (koi'nĭj) *n.* **1.** The process or right of making coins. **2. a.** Metal currency. **b.** A system of metal currency. **3. a.** A coined word or phrase. **b.** The invention of new words.

co·in·cide (kō'ĭn-sīd') *intr.v.* **-cid·ed, -cid·ing, -cides. 1. a.** To occupy the same position simultaneously. **b.** To have identical dimensions. **2.** To happen at the same time or during the same period. **3.** To correspond exactly; be identical. [Med. Lat. *coincidere* : Lat. *co(m)-,* together + Lat. *incidere,* to occur. —see INCIDENT.]

co·in·ci·dence (kō-ĭn'sĭ-dəns, -dĕns') *n.* **1.** The state or fact of coinciding. **2.** A sequence of events that although accidental seems to have been planned or arranged.

coincidence gate *n.* Gate[1] (sense 7).

co·in·ci·dent (kō-ĭn'sĭ-dənt) *adj.* **1.** Occupying the same position. **2.** Happening at the same time. **3.** Matching point for point; coinciding: *coincident circles.*

co·in·ci·den·tal (kō-ĭn'sĭ-dĕn'təl) *adj.* Occurring as or resulting from coincidence. **—co·in'ci·den'tal·ly** *adv.*

co·in·sur·ance (kō'ĭn-sho͝or'əns) *n.* **1.** Insurance held jointly by two or more insurers. **2.** A form of insurance in which a person insures property for less than its full value and agrees to be responsible for the difference.

co·in·sure (kō'ĭn-sho͝or') *tr.v.* **-sured, -sur·ing, -sures. 1.** To insure jointly. **2.** To insure with coinsurance.

coir (koir) *n.* The fiber obtained from the husk of a coconut, used in making rope and matting. [Malayam *kāyar,* cord < *kāyaru,* to be twisted.]

co·i·tus (kō'ĭ-təs, kō-ē'-) also **co·i·tion** (kō-ĭsh'ən) *n.* The physical union of male and female sexual organs, leading to orgasm and ejaculation of semen. [Lat. < *coire,* to copulate : *co(m)-,* together + *ire,* to go.] **—co'i·tal** *adj.*

coitus in·ter·rup·tus (ĭn'tə-rŭp'təs) *n.* Sexual intercourse purposely interrupted by withdrawal of the male prior to

cogwheel

ejaculation. [Lat. : *coitus,* copulation + *interruptus,* interrupted.]
coke[1] (kōk) *n.* The solid carbonaceous residue obtained from bituminous coal after removal of volatile material by destructive distillation, used as fuel and in making steel. —*tr. & intr.v.* **coked, cok·ing, cokes.** To convert or change into coke. [Perh. < ME *colk,* core.]
coke[2] (kōk) *n. Slang.* Cocaine.
Coke (kōk). A trademark for a soft drink.
col (kŏl) *n.* A pass between two mountain peaks or a gap in a ridge. [Fr. < OFr., neck < Lat. *collum.*]
col–[1] *pref.* Variant of **com-**. Used before *l.*
col–[2] *pref.* Variant of **colo-**.
co·la[1] (kō′lə) *n.* A carbonated soft drink containing an extract prepared from kola nuts.
co·la[2] (kō′lə) *n.* A plural of **colon[1]** (sense 2).
co·la[3] (kō′lə) *n.* A plural of **colon[2]**.
co·la[4] (kō′lə) *n.* Variant of **kola.**
col·an·der (kŭl′ən-dər, kŏl′-) also **cul·len·der** (kŭl′ən-dər) *n.* A bowl-shaped kitchen utensil with perforations for draining off liquids and rinsing food. [ME *colyndore,* prob. alteration of OProv. *colador* < VLat. **colator* < Lat. *colare,* to strain < *colum,* sieve.]

colander

cola nut *n.* Variant of **kola nut.**
col·can·non (kŏl-kăn′ən) *n.* An Irish dish of mashed potatoes and cabbage. [Ir. Gael. *cal ceannan* : *cal,* cabbage (< OIr. < Lat. *caulis*) + *ceannan,* white-headed (*ceann,* head + *fionn,* white).]
col·chi·cine (kŏl′chĭ-sēn′, kŏl′kĭ-) *n.* A poisonous alkaloid, $C_{22}H_{25}NO_6$, used experimentally to induce chromosome doubling and medicinally to treat gout. [COLCHIC(UM) + -INE.]
col·chi·cum (kŏl′chĭ-kəm, kŏl′kĭ-) *n.* **1.** Any of various bulbous plants of the genus *Colchicum,* such as the autumn crocus. **2.** The dried seeds or corms of *C. autumnale,* a source of colchicine. [Lat., a plant with a poisonous root < Gk. *Kolkhikon,* meadow saffron, after *Kolkhos,* Colchis, a region east of the Black Sea.]
col·co·thar (kŏl′kə-thər, -thär′) *n.* A brownish-red iron oxide obtained as a residue after heating ferrous sulfate, used in glass polishing and as a pigment. [Sp. *colcotar* < Ar. *qolqoṭār.*]
cold (kōld) *adj.* **-er, -est. 1. a.** Having a low temperature. **b.** Having a temperature lower than normal body temperature. **c.** Feeling no warmth; uncomfortably chilled. **2. a.** Marked by a lack of heat: *a cold room.* **b.** At less than optimum warmth: *cold oatmeal.* **c.** Chilled by refrigeration or ice: *cold beer.* **3.** Not marked or affected by emotion; objective: *cold logic.* **4.** Without appeal to the senses or feelings; depressing: *a cold decor.* **5. a.** Not affectionate or friendly; aloof: *a cold person.* **b.** Not enthusiastic or interested: *a cold audience.* **c.** Without sexual desire; frigid. **6.** Designating a color or tone, such as pale gray, that suggests little warmth. **7. a.** *Informal.* Unconscious; insensible: *knocked cold.* **b.** Dead: *cold in his grave.* **8.** *Slang.* Not stolen or suspected of use in illegal activities: *a cold gun.* **9.** *Informal.* Marked by lack of advance preparation or introduction: *came in cold and got the job.* **10.** *Informal.* Marked by unqualified certainty: *had the cadenza cold.* **11.** So intense as to be almost uncontrollable: *cold fury.* —*adv. Informal.* **1.** Unqualifiedly; totally: *was cold sober.* **2.** Without advance preparation or introduction: *took the exam cold and passed.* —*n.* **1. a.** Relative lack of warmth. **b.** The sensation resulting from lack of warmth; chill. **2.** A viral infection characterized by inflammation of the mucous membranes of the respiratory passages and accompanying fever, chills, coughing, and sneezing. **3.** A condition of low air temperature; cold weather. —*idioms.* **in cold blood.** Without feeling, passion, or remorse. **(out) in the cold.** Lacking benefits given to others; neglected: *When others received raises, he was left in the cold.* [ME < OE *ceald.*] —**cold′ly** *adv.* —**cold′ness** *n.*

coleus

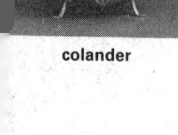

cold agglutinin *n.* An agglutinin found in human blood serum that induces agglutination only at low temperatures.
cold-blood·ed (kōld′blŭd′ĭd) *adj.* **1. a.** Lacking in feeling or emotion: *a cold-blooded killer.* **b.** Done without feeling or emotion: *a cold-blooded murder.* **2.** *Zool.* Having a body temperature that varies with the external environment; poikilothermous. —**cold′-blood′ed·ly** *adv.* —**cold′-blood′ed·ness** *n.*
cold chisel *n.* A chisel made of hardened, tempered steel and used for cutting cold metal.
cold cream *n.* An emulsion for cleansing and softening the skin.
cold cuts *pl.n.* Slices of assorted cold meats.
cold duck *n.* A beverage made of sparkling burgundy and champagne. [Transl. of G. *Kalte Ente,* a drink made from a mixture of wines.]
cold feet *n. Slang.* Fearfulness or timidity that prevents the completion of a course of action.
cold frame *n.* A structure consisting of a wooden frame and a glass top, used for protecting young plants from the cold.
cold front *n.* The leading portion of a cold atmospheric air mass moving against and eventually replacing a warm air mass.
cold-heart·ed (kōld′här′tĭd) *adj.* Lacking sympathy or feeling. —**cold′-heart′ed·ly** *adv.* —**cold′-heart′ed·ness** *n.*
cold light *n.* **1.** Light producing little or no heat. **2.** Light emitted by a process other than incandescence.
cold pack *n.* **1.** *Med.* A therapeutic pack consisting of a cold, damp sheet. **2.** A canning process in which uncooked food is packed in jars or cans, then sterilized by heat.
cold rubber *n.* A durable, strong synthetic rubber polymerized at low temperatures.
cold·shoul·der (kōld′shōl′dər) *tr.v.* **-dered, -der·ing, -ders.** *Informal.* To give (someone) the cold shoulder; slight; snub.
cold shoulder *n. Informal.* Deliberate coldness or disregard; snub.
cold sore *n.* A small sore on the lips that often accompanies a fever or cold; fever blister.
cold storage *n.* The protective storage, as of foods or furs, in a refrigerated place.
cold sweat *n.* Simultaneous perspiration and chill, usually induced by fear, pain, or shock.
cold turkey *n. Informal.* Immediate, complete withdrawal from something on which one has become dependent, as an addictive drug. —*idiom.* **talk cold turkey.** To speak frankly and bluntly.
cold type *n.* Typesetting, as photocomposition, done without the casting of metal.
cold war *n.* A state of political tension and military rivalry between nations that stops short of actual full-scale war. —**cold warrior** *n.*
cold-wa·ter (kōld′wô′tər, -wŏt′ər) *adj.* Lacking modern plumbing or heating facilities: *a cold-water flat.*
cold wave *n.* **1.** An abrupt onset of unusually cold weather. **2.** A form of permanent wave in which the hair is set by chemicals rather than heat.
cold welding *n.* The welding of two materials under high pressure or vacuum without the use of heat. —**cold′-weld′** *v.* **(-weld·ed, -weld·ing, -welds).**
cole (kōl) *n.* Any of various plants of the genus *Brassica,* as the cabbage or rape. [ME *col* < OE *cāl* < Lat. *caulis,* cabbage.]
co·lec·to·my (kə-lĕk′tə-mē) *n., pl.* **-mies.** Surgical removal of part or all of the colon.
cole·man·ite (kōl′mə-nīt′) *n.* A natural white or colorless hydrated calcium borate, $Ca_2B_6O_{11}\cdot5H_2O$, a principal source of borax. [After William T. *Coleman* (1824–1893).]
co·le·op·ter·a (kō′lē-ŏp′tər-ə) *n.* The beetles and weevils. [NLat. *Coleoptera,* order name < Gk. *koleopteros,* sheath-winged : *koleon,* sheath + *pteron,* wing.] —**co′le·op′ter·ist** *n.*
co·le·op·ter·an (kō′lē-ŏp′tər-ən, kŏl′ē-) also **co·le·op·ter·on** (-tə-rŏn′) *n.* An insect of the order Coleoptera, characterized by forewings modified to form tough protective covers for the hind wings, and including the beetles and weevils. —*adj.* Of or belonging to the Coleoptera. [NLat. *Coleoptera,* order name < Gk. *koleopteros,* sheath-winged : *koleon,* sheath + *pteron,* wing.] —**co′le·op′ter·ous** (-tər-əs) *adj.*
co·le·op·tile (kō′lē-ŏp′tĭl, kŏl′ē-) *n.* The first seedling leaf in grasses and similar monocotyledons, forming a protective sheath around the plumule. [NLat. *coleoptilum* : Gk. *koleon,* sheath + Gk. *ptilon,* plume.]
co·le·o·rhi·za (kō′lē-ə-rī′zə, kŏl′ē-) *n., pl.* **-zae** (-zē). A protective sheath around the embryonic root of grasses and similar monocotyledons. [Gk. *koleon,* sheath + Gk. *rhiza,* root.]
cole·slaw also **cole slaw** (kōl′slô′) *n.* A salad of finely shredded raw cabbage with a dressing. [Du. *koolsla* : *kool,* cabbage (< MDu. *cōle* < Lat. *caulis*) + *sla,* short for *salade,* salad < Fr. < OFr. —see SALAD.]
co·le·us (kō′lē-əs) *n.* Any of various plants of the genus *Coleus,* of Eurasia and Africa, cultivated for their showy leaves, which are often marked with red, yellow, or white. [NLat. *Coleus,* genus name < Gk. *koleos,* sheath (from the way its filaments are joined.]
cole·wort (kōl′wûrt′, -wôrt′) *n.* Cole.
coli– *pref.* Variant of **colo-**.
col·ic (kŏl′ĭk) *n.* **1.** Acute, paroxysmal pain in the abdomen, caused by spasm, obstruction, or distention of any of the hollow viscera. **2.** Severe abdominal pain in infants, usually resulting from accumulation of gas in the alimentary canal. [ME *colik,* suffering with colic < OFr. *colique* < Lat. *colicus* < Gk. *kōlikos* < *kōlon,* colon.] —**col′ick·y** (kŏl′ĭ-kē) *adj.*
col·i·cin (kŏl′ĭ-sĭn, kō′lĭ-) *n.* A protein produced by certain strains of the colon bacillus that is lethal to other strains of bacteria of the same species. [COL(ON) + -IC + -IN.]
col·i·ci·no·ge·nic·i·ty (kŏl′ĭ-sə-nə-jə-nĭs′ĭ-tē) *n.* The ability to produce colicin. —**col′i·ci·no·gen′ic** (-jĕn′ĭk) *adj.*
col·ic·root (kŏl′ĭk-rōōt′, -rŏŏt′) *n.* **1.** A plant, *Aletris farinosa,* of the eastern United States, having a cluster of tubular white flowers and a bitter root formerly used in medicine. **2.** Any of various other plants thought to cure or relieve colic.
col·ic·weed (kŏl′ĭk-wēd′) *n.* Any of several plants of the genera *Dicentra* or *Corydalis,* such as the squirrel corn.
co·li·form (kō′lə-fôrm′, kŏl′ə-) *adj.* Of, pertaining to, or resembling the colon bacillus. —**co′li·form′** *n.*
co·lin·e·ar (kō-lĭn′ē-ər) *adj. Genetics.* Containing elements

that correspond to one another and that are arranged in the same linear sequence. **—co·lin′e·ar′i·ty** (-ăr′ĭ-tē) *n.*
col·i·se·um also **col·os·se·um** (kŏl′ĭ-sē′əm) *n.* A large amphitheater for public entertainment or assemblies. [Med. Lat., an amphitheater in Rome, Italy < Lat. *colosseum,* neuter of *colosseus,* gigantic < *colossus,* huge statue < Gk. *kolossos.*]
co·lis·tin (kə-lĭs′tĭn, kō-) *n.* An antibiotic produced by the bacterium *Bacillus colistinus* that is effective against a wide range of Gram-positive microorganisms. [NLat. *Colistinus,* specific epithet of the bacterium that produces it.]
co·li·tis (kō-lī′tĭs) *n.* Inflammation of the mucous membrane of the colon.
coll– *pref.* Variant of **collo-**.
col·lab·o·rate (kə-lăb′ə-rāt′) *intr.v.* **-rat·ed, -rat·ing, -rates. 1.** To work together, esp. in a joint intellectual effort. **2.** To cooperate treasonably, as with an enemy occupying one's country. [LLat. *collaborare, collaborat-* : Lat. *com-,* together + Lat. *laborare,* to work < *labor,* work.] **—col·lab′o·ra′tion** *n.* **—col·lab′o·ra′tive** *adj.* **—col·lab′o·ra′tor** *n.*
col·lab·o·ra·tion·ist (kə-lăb′ə-rā′shə-nĭst) *n.* A person who collaborates with an enemy occupying his country. **—col·lab′o·ra′tion·ism** *n.*
col·lage (kō-läzh′, kə-) *n.* An artistic composition of materials and objects pasted over a surface, often with unifying lines and color. [Fr. < *coller,* to glue < *colle,* glue, ult. < Gk. *kolla.*]
col·la·gen (kŏl′ə-jən) *n.* The fibrous albuminoid constituent of bone, cartilage, and connective tissue. [Gk. *kolla,* glue + -GEN.] **—col′la·gen′ic** (kŏl′ə-jĕn′ĭk), **col·lag′e·nous** (kə-lăj′ə-nəs) *adj.*
col·lag·e·nase (kə-lăj′ə-nās′, -nāz′, kŏl′ə-jə-) *n.* Any of various enzymes that catalyze the breakdown of collagen and gelatin.
col·lap·sar (kə-lăp′sär′) *n.* A black hole. [COLLAPSE + *-ar,* as in *quasar.*]
col·lapse (kə-lăps′) *v.* **-lapsed, -laps·ing, -laps·es.** *—intr.* **1.** To fall down or inward suddenly; cave in. **2.** To cease to function; break down suddenly in strength or health: *a monarchy that collapsed.* **3.** To fold compactly: *chairs that collapse for storage.* *—tr.* To cause to collapse. *—n.* **1.** The act of falling down or inward, as from loss of supports. **2.** An abrupt failure of function, strength, or health; breakdown. [Lat. *collabi, collaps-,* to fall together : *com-,* together + *labi,* to fall.] **—col·laps′i·ble, col·laps′a·ble** *adj.* **—col·laps′i·bil′i·ty** *n.*
col·lar (kŏl′ər) *n.* **1.** The part of a garment that encircles the neck. **2.** A necklace. **3.** A restraining or identifying band of leather, metal, or plastic put around the neck of an animal. **4.** The cushioned part of a harness that presses against the shoulders of a draft animal. **5.** *Informal.* An arrest. **6.** *Biol.* An encircling structure or bandlike marking suggestive of a collar. **7.** Any of various ringlike devices used to limit, guide, or secure a machine part. *—tr.v.* **-lared, -lar·ing, -lars. 1.** To furnish with a collar. **2.** *Informal.* **a.** To seize or detain. **b.** To arrest. [ME *coler* < OFr. *colier* < Lat. *collare* < *collum,* neck.]
col·lar·bone (kŏl′ər-bōn′) *n. Anat.* The clavicle.
collar cell *n. Biol.* A choanocyte.
col·lard (kŏl′ərd) *n.* **1.** A variety of kale, *Brassica oleracea acephala,* having a crown of edible leaves. **2. collards.** The leaves of the collard used as a vegetable. [Var. of COLEWORT.]
col·late (kə-lāt′, kŏl′āt′, kō′lāt′) *tr.v.* **-lat·ed, -lat·ing, -lates. 1.** To examine and compare carefully in order to note points of disagreement. **2.** To assemble in proper numerical or logical sequence. **3.** To examine (gathered sheets) in order to arrange them in proper sequence before binding. **4.** To verify the order and completeness of (the pages of a volume). **5.** *Eccles.* To admit (a cleric) to a benefice. [Lat. *conferre, collat-,* to collect. —see CONFER.] **—col·la′tor** *n.*
col·lat·er·al (kə-lăt′ər-əl) *adj.* **1.** Situated or running side by side; parallel. **2.** Coinciding in tendency or effect; concomitant; accompanying. **3.** Serving to support or corroborate: *collateral evidence.* **4.** Of a secondary nature; subordinate. **5.** Of, designating, or guaranteed by a security pledged against the performance of an obligation: *a collateral loan.* **6.** Having an ancestor in common but descended from a different line. *—n.* **1.** Property acceptable as security for a loan or other obligation. **2.** A collateral relative. [ME < Med. Lat. *collateralis* : Lat. *co(m)-,* together + Lat. *latus,* side.] **—col·lat′er·al·ly** *adv.*
col·la·tion (kə-lā′shən, kŏ-, kō-) *n.* **1.** The act or process of collating. **2. a.** A light meal permitted on fast days. **b.** A light meal.
col·league (kŏl′ēg′) *n.* A fellow member of a profession, staff, or academic faculty; associate. [OFr. *collegue* < Lat. *collega* : *com-,* together + *legare,* to depute.] **—col′league·ship′** *n.*
col·lect[1] (kə-lĕkt′) *v.* **-lect·ed, -lect·ing, -lects.** *—tr.* **1.** To bring together in a group; gather; assemble. **2.** To accumulate as a hobby or for study: *collect stamps.* **3.** To call for and obtain payment of: *collect taxes.* **4.** To recover control of: *collect one's emotions.* *—intr.* **1.** To gather together; congregate; accumulate. **2.** To take in payments or donations: *collecting for charity.* *—adj.* With payment to be made by the receiver: *a collect phone call.* *—adv.* So that the receiver is charged: *send a telegram collect.* [ME *collecten* < Lat. *colligere* : *com-,* together + *legere,* to gather.] **—col·lect′i·ble, col·lect′a·ble** *adj.*
col·lect[2] (kŏl′ĭkt, -ĕkt′) *n. Eccles.* A brief formal prayer that is used in various Western liturgies before the epistle at Mass and varies with the day. [ME *collecte* < OFr. < Med. Lat. *collecta,* short for *oratio ad collectam,* prayer at the gathering.]
col·lec·ta·ne·a (kŏl′ĕk-tā′nē-ə) *pl.n.* A selection of passages from one or more authors; an anthology. [Lat. < *collectaneus,* gathered < *collectus,* p.part. of *colligere,* to gather. — see COLLECT[1].]
col·lect·ed (kə-lĕk′tĭd) *adj.* **1.** Self-possessed; composed: *calm, cool, and collected.* **2.** Brought or placed together from various sources: *the collected poems of W.H. Auden.* **—col·lect′ed·ly** *adv.* **—col·lect′ed·ness** *n.*
col·lec·tion (kə-lĕk′shən) *n.* **1.** The act or process of collecting. **2.** A group of objects or works to be seen, studied, or kept together. **3.** An accumulation; deposit. **4. a.** A collecting of money, as in church. **b.** The sum collected.
col·lec·tive (kə-lĕk′tĭv) *adj.* **1.** Formed by collecting; assembled or accumulated into a whole. **2.** Of, pertaining to, characteristic of, or made by a number of individuals taken or acting as a group: *a collective decision.* *—n.* **1.** A business or undertaking set up on the principle of ownership and control of the means of production and distribution by the worker involved, usually under the supervision of a government. **2.** *Gram.* A collective noun. **—col·lec′tive·ly** *adv.* **—col·lec′tive·ness** *n.*
collective bargaining *n.* Negotiation between the representatives of organized workers and their employer or employers to determine wages, hours, rules, and working conditions.
collective farm *n.* A farm or a group of farms organized as a unit and managed and worked cooperatively by a group of laborers under governmental supervision.
collective fruit *n. Bot.* A multiple fruit.
collective noun *n. Gram.* A noun that denotes a collection of persons or things regarded as a unit.

Usage: A collective noun takes a singular verb when it refers to the collection as a whole and a plural verb when it refers to the members of the collection as separate persons or things: *The orchestra was playing. The orchestra have all gone home.* (In British usage, however, collective nouns are most often construed as plural: *The government are committed to a policy.*) A collective noun should not be treated as both singular and plural in the same construction. Thus: *The family is determined to press its* (not *their*) *claim.* Among the most common collective nouns are *committee, company, clergy, enemy, group, family, flock, people, team.*

col·lec·tiv·ism (kə-lĕk′tə-vĭz′əm) *n.* The principle or system of ownership and control of the means of production and distribution by the people collectively. **—col·lec′tiv·ist** *n.* **—col·lec′tiv·is′tic** *adj.* **—col·lec′tiv·is′ti·cal·ly** *adv.*
col·lec·tiv·i·ty (kŏl′ĕk-tĭv′ĭ-tē, kə-lĕk′-) *n.* **1.** The condition or quality of being collective. **2.** The people as a whole.
col·lec·tiv·ize (kə-lĕk′tə-vīz′) *tr.v.* **-ized, -iz·ing, -iz·es.** To organize (an economy, industry, or enterprise) on the basis of collectivism. **—col·lec′tiv·i·za′tion** *n.*
col·lec·tor (kə-lĕk′tər) *n.* **1.** One that collects. **2.** A person employed to collect taxes, duties, or other payments. **3.** A person who makes a collection, as of stamps. **4. a.** *Elect.* A conducting contact between parts of an electric circuit in relative motion. **b.** *Electronics.* The output terminal of a three-terminal semiconducting device, esp. of a transistor. **—col·lec′tor·ship′** *n.*
col·leen (kŏ-lēn′, kŏl′ēn′) *n.* An Irish girl. [Ir. Gael. *cailīn,* dim. of *caile,* girl.]
col·lege (kŏl′ĭj) *n.* **1. a.** A school of higher learning that grants the bachelor's degree in liberal arts or science or both. **b.** Any of the undergraduate divisions or schools of a university offering courses and granting degrees in a particular field. **c.** A technical or professional school, often affiliated with a university, offering the bachelor's or master's degree: *a teachers' college.* **d.** The building or buildings occupied by any such school. **e.** *Chiefly Brit.* A self-governing society of scholars for study or instruction, incorporated within a university. **f.** In France, an institution for secondary education not supported by the state. **2.** A company or assemblage, esp. a body of persons having a common purpose or common duties: *a college of surgeons.* **3.** A body of clergymen living together on an endowment. [ME < OFr. < Lat. *collegium,* association < *collega,* colleague.]
College of Cardinals *n. Rom. Cath. Ch.* The body comprising all the cardinals that elects the pope, assists him in governing the church, and administers the Holy See when vacant.
col·le·gi·a (kə-lē′jē-ə, -lĕg′ē-ə) *n.* A plural of **collegium**.
col·le·gi·al (kə-lē′jē-əl, -jəl) *adj.* Variant of **collegiate**.
col·le·gi·al·i·ty (kə-lē′jē-ăl′ĭ-tē) *n.* **1.** Shared authority among colleagues. **2.** *Rom. Cath. Ch.* The doctrine that bishops collectively share collegiate authority. [< Lat. *collegiate,* of colleagues < *collegium,* association < *collega,* colleague.]
col·le·gian (kə-lē′jən, -jē-ən) *n.* A college student or recent college graduate.

coliseum
The Roman Colosseum

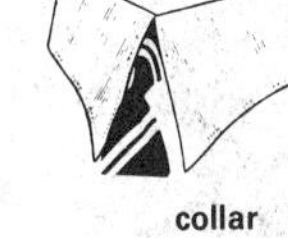
collar

college

col·le·giate (kə-lē′jĭt, -jē-ĭt) also **col·le·gi·al** (-jē-əl, -jəl) *adj.* **1.** Of, pertaining to, or resembling a college. **2.** Of, for, or typical of college students. **3.** Of or pertaining to a collegiate church. [Med. Lat. *collegiatus* < Lat. *collegium,* association. —see COLLEGE.]

collegiate church *n.* **1.** A Roman Catholic or Anglican church other than a cathedral, having a chapter of canons and presided over by a dean or provost. **2. a.** A church in the United States associated with others under a common body of pastors. **b.** An association of such churches. **3.** A church in Scotland served by two or more ministers at the same time.

col·le·gi·um (kə-lē′jē-əm, -lĕg′ē-) *n., pl.* **-le·gi·a** (-lē′jē-ə, -lĕg′ē-ə) or **-le·gi·ums.** An executive council or committee of equally empowered members, esp. one supervising an industry, commissariat, or other organization in the Soviet Union. [R. *kollegya* < Lat. *collegium,* association < *collega,* colleague.]

col·lem·bo·lan (kə-lĕm′bə-lən) *n.* The springtail. [COLL(O)- + Gk. *embolos,* peg.]

col·len·chy·ma (kə-lĕng′kə-mə) *n.* Supportive tissue of plants, consisting of elongated, approximately rectangular cells with cell walls thickened at the corners. [COLL(O)- + -ENCHYMA.] —**col′len·chym′a·tous** (kŏl′ən-kĭm′ə-təs) *adj.*

col·len·chyme (kŏl′ən-kīm′) *n.* A gelatinous mesenchyme that comprises a layer in the body wall of many coelenterates and ctenophores. [< COLLENCHYMA.]

col·let (kŏl′ĭt) *n.* **1.** A cone-shaped sleeve used in a lathe for holding circular or rodlike pieces. **2.** A metal collar used in watchmaking to join one end of a balance spring to the balance staff. **3.** A circular flange or rim, as in a ring, into which a gem is set. —*tr.v.* **-let·ed, -let·ing, -lets.** To set in or supply with a collet. [Fr., dim. of *col,* collar < Lat. *collum,* neck.]

collie

col·lide (kə-līd′) *intr.v.* **-lid·ed, -lid·ing, -lides. 1.** To come together with violent, direct impact. **2.** To meet in opposition; clash; conflict. [Lat. *collidere* : *com-,* together + *laedere,* to strike.]

col·lie (kŏl′ē) *n.* A large dog of a breed originating in Scotland as a sheep dog, having long hair and a long, narrow muzzle. [Sc.]

col·lier (kŏl′yər) *n. Chiefly Brit.* **1.** A coal miner. **2.** A coal ship. [ME *colier* < *col,* coal < OE.]

col·lier·y (kŏl′yə-rē) *n., pl.* **-ies.** *Chiefly Brit.* A coal mine.

col·li·gate (kŏl′ĭ-gāt′) *tr.v.* **-gat·ed, -gat·ing, -gates. 1.** To tie or group together. **2.** *Logic.* To bring (isolated observations) together by an explanation or hypothesis that applies to them all. [Lat. *colligare, colligat-* : *com-,* together + *ligare,* to tie.] —**col′li·ga′tion** *n.*

col·li·ga·tive (kŏl′ĭ-gā′tĭv) *adj.* Depending on the quantity of molecules but not on the chemical nature of them. [G. *kolligativ* < Lat. *colligatus,* p.part of *colligare,* to bind : *com-,* together + *ligare,* to tie.]

colophon
The colophon of Aldus Manutius

col·li·mate (kŏl′ə-māt′) *tr.v.* **-mat·ed, -mat·ing, -mates. 1.** To make parallel; line up. **2.** To adjust the line of sight of (an optical device). [NLat. *collimare, collimat-,* alteration of Lat. *collineare,* to aim : *com-* (intensive) + *lineare,* to make straight < *linea,* line.] —**col′li·ma′tion** *n.*

col·li·ma·tor (kŏl′ə-mā′tər) *n.* A device capable of collimating radiation, such as a long narrow tube in which strongly absorbing or reflecting walls permit only radiation traveling parallel to the tube axis to traverse the entire length.

col·lin·e·ar (kə-lĭn′ē-ər, kŏ-) *adj.* **1.** Lying on the same line. **2.** Containing a common line; coaxial. —**col·lin′e·ar′i·ty** (-ăr′ĭ-tē) *n.*

col·lins (kŏl′ənz) *n.* A tall iced drink made with liquor, as gin, and lemon or lime juice. [Prob. from the name *Collins.*]

col·lin·si·a (kə-lĭn′zē-ə) *n.* Any of various North American plants of the genus *Collinsia,* having blue-and-white or purplish flowers. [NLat. *Collinsia,* genus name, after Zaccheus *Collins* (1764–1831).]

col·li·sion (kə-lĭzh′ən) *n.* **1.** The act or process of colliding; crash. **2.** *Physics.* A dynamic event consisting of the interaction between two or more bodies, usually of very brief duration, resulting in a change of momentum of at least one participating body. [ME < Lat. *collisio* < *collidere,* to strike. —see COLLIDE.] — **col·li′sion·al** *adj.*

collision course *n.* A course, as of moving objects or opposing philosophies, that will end in conflict or collision if continued unchanged: *a meteor on a collision course with Earth.*

collo– or **coll–** *pref.* **1.** Glue: *collenchyma.* **2.** Colloid: *collotype.* [NLat. < Gk. *kolla,* glue.]

col·lo·cate (kŏl′ə-kāt′) *tr.v.* **-cat·ed, -cat·ing, -cates.** To place together or in proper order; arrange. [Lat. *collocare, collocat-* : *com-,* together + *locare,* to place < *locus,* place.]

col·lo·ca·tion (kŏl′ō-kā′shən) *n.* **1. a.** The act of collocating. **b.** The state of being collocated. **2.** An arrangement or juxtaposition, esp. of words. —**col′lo·ca′tion·al** *adj.*

col·lo·di·on (kə-lō′dē-ən) also **col·lo·di·um** (-əm) *n.* A highly flammable, colorless or yellowish syrupy solution of pyroxylin in ether and alcohol, used to hold surgical dressings, as a coating for certain skin diseases, and for making photographic plates. [NLat. *collodium* < Gk. *kollōdēs,* glutinous < *kolla,* glue.]

col·logue (kə-lōg′) *intr.v.* **-logued, -logu·ing, -logues.** *Chiefly Brit. Regional.* To confer secretly; conspire. [Orig. unknown.]

col·loid (kŏl′oid′) *n.* **1.** *Chem.* **a.** A suspension of finely divided particles in a continuous medium, esp. a gaseous, liquid, or solid substance, such as an atmospheric fog, a paint, or foam rubber, containing suspended particles that are approximately 5 to 5,000 angstroms in size, do not settle out of the substance rapidly, and are not readily filtered. **b.** The particulate matter so suspended. **2.** *Physiol.* A clear gelatinous secretion of the thyroid gland. **3.** *Pathol.* Gelatinous material resulting from colloid degeneration or colloid carcinoma. —*adj.* Of, relating to, or having the nature of a colloid. —**col·loid′al** (kə-loid′l, kŏ) *adj.* —**col·loid′al·ly** *adv.*

col·lop (kŏl′əp) *n.* **1.** A small portion or slice, esp. of meat. **2.** A roll of flesh on the body. [ME.]

col·lo·qui·al (kə-lō′kwē-əl) *adj.* **1.** Characteristic of or appropriate to the spoken language or to writing that seeks the effect of speech; informal. **2.** Relating to conversation; conversational. [< COLLOQUY.] —**col·lo′qui·al·ly** *adv.* —**col·lo′qui·al·ness** *n.*

col·lo·qui·al·ism (kə-lō′kwē-ə-lĭz′əm) *n.* **1.** Colloquial style or quality. **2.** A colloquial expression.

col·lo·qui·um (kə-lō′kwē-əm) *n., pl.* **-qui·ums** or **-qui·a** (-kwē-ə). **1.** An informal meeting for the exchange of views. **2.** An academic seminar on a broad field of study, usually led by a different lecturer at each meeting. [Lat., conversation < *colloqui,* to talk together : *com-,* together + *loqui,* to speak.]

col·lo·quy (kŏl′ə-kwē) *n., pl.* **-quies. 1.** A conversation, esp. a formal one. **2.** A written dialogue. [Lat. *colloquium,* conversation. —see COLLOQUIUM.]

col·lo·type (kŏl′ə-tīp′) *n.* **1.** A printing process utilizing a glass plate with a gelatin surface carrying the image to be reproduced. **2.** A print made by the collotype process.

col·lude (kə-lo͞od′) *intr.v.* **-lud·ed, -lud·ing, -ludes.** To be in collusion; act together secretly to achieve a deceitful or fraudulent purpose; connive. [Lat. *colludere* : *com-,* together + *ludere,* to play < *ludus,* play.] —**col·lud′er** *n.*

col·lu·sion (kə-lo͞o′zhən) *n.* A secret agreement between two or more persons for a deceitful or fraudulent purpose. [ME < Lat. *collusio* < *colludere,* to collude.]

col·lu·sive (kə-lo͞o′sĭv, -zĭv) *adj.* Given to, marked by, or acting in collusion. —**col·lu′sive·ly** *adv.* —**col·lu′sive·ness** *n.*

col·lu·vi·um (kə-lo͞o′vē-əm) *n., pl.* **-vi·a** (-vē-ə) or **-vi·ums.** A loose deposit of rock debris accumulated at the base of a cliff or slope. [Lat., collection of washings < *colluere,* to wash thoroughly : *com-* (intensive) + *lavere,* to wash.] —**col·lu′vi·al** *adj.*

col·lyr·i·um (kə-lîr′ē-əm) *n., pl.* **-i·ums** or **-i·a** (-ē-ə). A medicinal lotion applied to the eye; eyewash. [Lat. < Gk. *kollurion,* dim. of *kollura,* roll of bread.]

col·ly·wob·bles (kŏl′ē-wŏb′əlz) *pl.n. Informal.* A pain in the bowels or stomach; bellyache. [*Colly,* alteration of COLIC + WOBBLE.]

colo– or **coli–** or **col–** *pref.* Colon: *colostomy.* [NLat. < Lat. *colon* < Gk. *kolon,* large intestine.]

col·o·bo·ma (kŏl′ə-bō′mə) *n., pl.* **-ma·ta** (-mə-tə). A lesion or fissure of the eye or eyelid. [NLat. *coloboma, colobomat-* < Gk. *kolobos,* maimed, expressive suffixed variant of *kolos,* docked.]

col·o·cynth (kŏl′ə-sĭnth′) *n.* **1.** A vine, *Citrullus colocynthis,* of the Mediterranean region, bearing a small, bitter fruit. **2.** The fruit of the colocynth, used as a cathartic. [Lat. *colocynthis* < Gk. *kolokunthis.*]

co·logne (kə-lōn′) *n.* A scented liquid made of alcohol and various fragrant oils; eau de cologne. [Short for Fr. *eau de Cologne,* water of Cologne, after *Cologne,* Germany.]

co·lon¹ (kō′lən) *n., pl.* **-lons. 1. a.** A punctuation mark (:) used after a word introducing a quotation, explanation, example, or series and after the salutation of a business letter. **b.** The sign (:) used between numbers or groups of numbers in expressions of time (2:30 A.M.) and ratios (1:2). **2.** *pl.* **co·la** (-lə). A section of a rhythmical period in Greek and Latin verse, consisting of two to six feet and having one principal accent. [Lat., part of a verse < Gk. *kōlon,* metrical unit.]

co·lon² (kō′lən) *n., pl.* **-lons** or **-la** (-lə). The section of the large intestine extending from the cecum to the rectum. [ME < Lat. < Gk. *kolon.*] —**co·lon′ic** (kə-lŏn′ĭk) *adj.*

co·lon³ (kō-lōn′) *n., pl.* **-lons** or **-lo·nes** (-lō′nās′). See table at **currency.** [Sp. *colón* < *Christóbal Colón,* Christopher Columbus (1451–1506).]

colon bacillus *n.* A bacillus, *Escherichia coli,* found normally in all vertebrate intestinal tracts and occasionally virulent, causing pyelitis or infantile diarrhea.

colo·nel (kûr′nəl) *n.* **1. a.** An officer in the U.S. Army, Air Force, or Marine Corps ranking immediately above a lieutenant colonel and below a brigadier general. **b.** An officer of similar rank in other military or paramilitary organizations. **2.** An honorary title awarded by some states of the United States. [Alteration of obs. *coronel* < Fr. < OItal. *colonello,* dim. of *colonna,* column of soldiers < Lat. *columna,* pillar.] —**colo′nel·cy, colo′nel·ship′** *n.*

Colonel Blimp (blĭmp) *n.* An elderly, pompous, short-sighted reactionary, esp. an army officer or government official. [After *Colonel Blimp,* a cartoon character by David Low (1891–1963).]

co·lo·ni·al (kə-lō'nē-əl) *adj.* **1.** Of, pertaining to, possessing, or inhabiting a colony or colonies. **2.** Often **Colonial. a.** Of or relating to the 13 British colonies that became the original United States of America. **b.** Of or relating to the colonial period in the United States. **3.** Often **Colonial.** Designating an architectural style prevalent in the American colonies just before and during the Revolution. **4.** Living, forming, or consisting of a colony: *colonial organisms.* —*n.* An inhabitant of a colony. **—co·lo'ni·al·ly** *adv.*

co·lo·ni·al·ism (kə-lō'nē-ə-lĭz'əm) *n.* A policy by which a nation maintains or extends its control over foreign dependencies. **—co·lo'ni·al·ist** *n.*

col·o·nist (kŏl'ə-nĭst) *n.* **1.** An original settler or founder of a colony. **2.** An inhabitant of a colony.

co·lon·i·tis (kō'lə-nī'tĭs) *n.* Colitis.

col·o·ni·za·tion (kŏl'ə-nĭ-zā'shən) *n.* The act or process of establishing a colony or colonies.

col·o·nize (kŏl'ə-nīz') *tr.v.* **-nized, -niz·ing, -niz·es.** —*tr.* **1. a.** To establish a colony or colonies in. **b.** To migrate to and settle in; occupy as a colony. **2.** To establish in a new settlement; form a colony of. —*intr.* **1.** To set up or form a colony. **2.** To settle in a colony or colonies. **—col'o·niz'er** *n.*

col·on·nade (kŏl'ə-nād') *n. Archit.* A series of columns placed at regular intervals. [Fr. < Ital. *colonnato* < *colonna,* column < Lat. *columna.*] **—col'on·nad'ed** *adj.*

col·o·ny (kŏl'ə-nē) *n., pl.* **-nies. 1. a.** A group of emigrants or their descendants who settle in a distant land but remain subject to or intimately connected with the parent country. **b.** A territory thus settled. **2.** A region politically controlled by a distant country; dependency. **3. a.** A group of people with the same interests or ethnic origin concentrated in a particular area: *the American colony in Paris.* **b.** The area or place occupied by such a group. **4.** A group of the same kind of animals, plants, or one-celled organisms living or growing together. **5.** A visible growth of microorganisms in a nutrient medium. [ME *colonie* < Lat. *colonia* < *colonus,* settler < *colere,* to cultivate.]

col·o·phon (kŏl'ə-fŏn', -fən) *n.* **1.** An inscription placed usually at the end of a book, giving facts pertaining to its publication. **2.** A publisher's emblem or trademark placed usually on the title page of a book. [LLat. < Gk. *kolophōn,* finishing touch.]

col·or (kŭl'ər) *n.* **1.** That aspect of things that is caused by differing qualities of the light reflected or emitted by them. It may be defined in terms of the observer (sense a) or of the light (sense b): **a.** The appearance of objects or light sources described in terms of the individual's perception of them, involving hue, lightness, and saturation for objects and hue, brightness, and saturation for light sources. **b.** The characteristics of light by which the individual is made aware of objects or light sources through the receptors of the eye, described in terms of dominant wavelength, luminance, and purity. **2.** A dye, pigment, paint, or other substance that imparts color. **3. a.** The general appearance of the skin; complexion. **b.** A ruddy complexion. **c.** A reddening of the face; blush. **4.** The skin pigmentation of a person not classed as a Caucasian, esp. that of a Negro. **5. colors.** A flag or banner, as of a country or military unit. **6. colors.** A distinguishing symbol, badge, ribbon, or mark: *the colors of a college.* **7. colors.** One's opinion or position: *Stick to your colors.* **8.** Often **colors.** Character or nature: *revealed his true colors.* **9. a.** Outward, often deceptive appearance. **b.** Appearance of truth or authenticity; plausibility. **10.** Variety of effect or expression. **11.** Vivid and picturesque detail. **12.** Traits of personality or behavior that attract interest. **13.** The use or effect of color in painting as distinct from form. **14.** *Mus.* Tonal quality. **15.** *Law.* An apparent or prima-facie right, pretext, or ground. **16. colors.** The salute made during the ceremony of raising or lowering the flag. **17.** A particle or bit of gold found in auriferous gravel or sand. **18.** *Physics.* A quantum characteristic of quarks that determines their role in the strong interaction. **—*modifier:*** *color photography.* —*v.* **-ored, -or·ing, -ors.** —*tr.* **1.** To impart color to or change the color of. **2.** To give a distinctive character or quality to; modify or influence. **3.** To misrepresent, esp. by distortion or exaggeration. —*intr.* **1.** To take on color or become colored. **2.** To change color. **3.** To become red in the face; blush. [ME *colour* < OFr. < Lat. *color.*] **—col'or·er** *n.*

col·or·a·ble (kŭl'ər-ə-bəl) *adj.* **1.** Meant to deceive; specious. **2.** Seemingly true or genuine; plausible. **—col'or·a·bil'i·ty, col'or·a·ble·ness** *n.* **—col'or·a·bly** *adv.*

col·o·ra·do (kŏl'ə-rä'dō) *adj.* Of medium strength and color. Used of cigars. [Sp. reddish < *colorar, colorear,* to color < Lat. *colorare* < *color,* color.]

Col·o·ra·do potato beetle (kŏl'ə-rä'dō, -răd'ə) *n.* The potato beetle.

col·or·ant (kŭl'ər-ənt) *n.* Something, esp. a dye, pigment, ink, or paint that colors or modifies the color of something else.

col·or·a·tion (kŭl'ə-rā'shən) *n.* **1.** Arrangement of colors. **2.** The sum of the beliefs or principles of a person, group, or institution.

EXPLANATION OF THE COLOR DEFINITIONS

Definitions of color names used in this Dictionary follow the method recommended by the Inter-Society Color Council as it has been developed at the National Bureau of Standards (the ISCC-NBS system). The method is designed to provide a means of designating color sufficiently standardized to be acceptable and usable in science, sufficiently broad for art and industry, and sufficiently familiar to be understood, at least in a general way, by the public.

The method is simple in principle. The terms *light, medium,* and *dark* designate decreasing degrees of lightness, and the adverb *very* extends the lightness scale to *very light* and *very dark.* The adjectives *grayish, moderate, strong,* and *vivid* designate increasing degrees of saturation. These terms with the nouns *white, gray,* and *black,* and a series of hue names used both as nouns and in adjectival form, as shown in the table at the bottom of the column, combine to form names for describing color in terms of its three perceptual attributes: *hue, lightness,* and *saturation.* Certain adjectives cover combinations of lightness and saturation, as *brilliant* for *light* and *strong; pale* for *light* and *grayish;* and *deep* for *dark* and *strong.*

In the ISCC-NBS system the boundaries of each color name are fixed. These are defined in terms of the Munsell color notation, which specifies colors on numerical scales of *hue, value,* and *chroma,* which can be expressed as accurately as desired.

The Munsell system is represented by a collection of color chips, forming an atlas of charts that represent equal visual (not physical) intervals for a gray to white background, so that under set conditions the hue, value, and chroma of the chips correlate closely with the hue, lightness, and saturation of the perceived *color* (sense 1a).

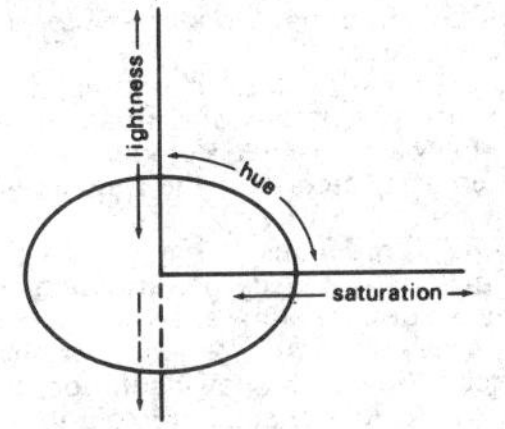

coordinates of color solid

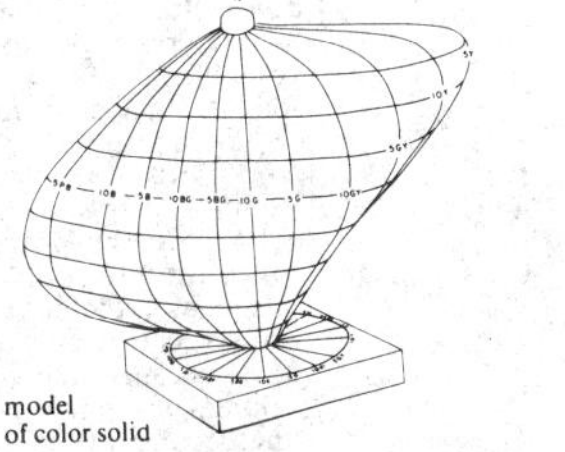

model of color solid

The relationship of these attributes can be explained by reference to what is known as a color solid, in which *hue* extends in a rotary direction clockwise about the neutral axis from red through the hues in spectrum order back to red; *lightness* extends in the vertical direction from black at the bottom through a series of grays to white at the top; and *saturation* extends in a radial direction horizontally from the central neutral axis, at which the saturation is zero, out to the strongest saturation, as far as it may extend from the central axis.

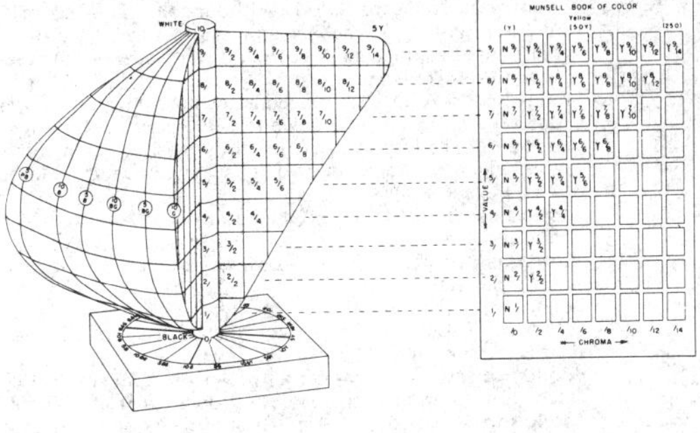

In the ISCC-NBS system the color solid is divided into 267 blocks, each of which defines a color name. These vary in size from the smaller and more tightly and irregularly packed blocks in the red, pink, orange, and brown regions to larger and more open blocks in the blue and purple regions. The method makes it possible to describe any color in a way that can be understood, and in a number of color names limited to 267, which cover about all the color differences that can be remembered.

If some of the color-name definitions in this Dictionary seem to cover a wider range than seems familiar, it is because different sources have based standards on different samples representing the same name. For further details on the method, especially with regard to colorimetry, consult National Bureau of Standards Special Publication 440, *Color: Universal Language and Dictionary of Names.*

Hue Names Used in ISCC-NBS System

red	purple
reddish orange	reddish purple
orange	purplish red
orange yellow	purplish pink
yellow	pink
greenish yellow	yellowish pink
yellow green	brownish pink
yellowish green	brownish orange
green	reddish brown
bluish green	brown
greenish blue	yellowish brown
blue	olive brown
purplish blue	olive
violet	olive green

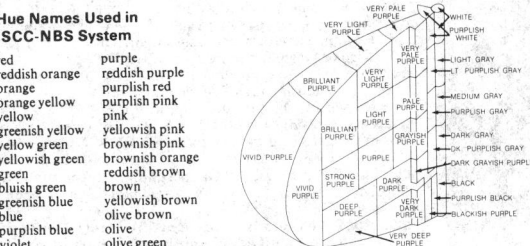

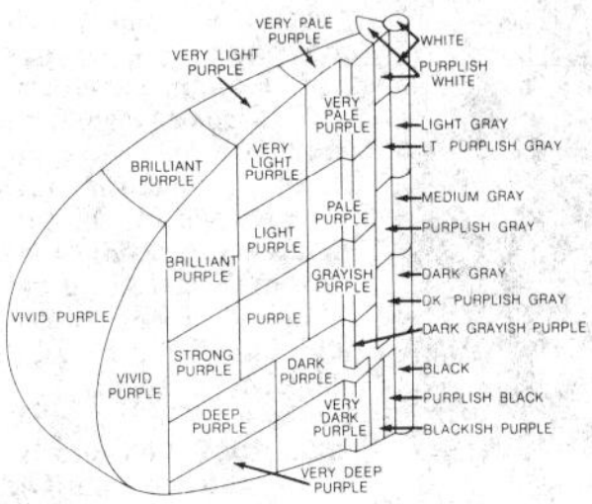

col·or·a·tu·ra (kŭl'ər-ə-to͝or'ə, -tyo͝or'ə) *n.* **1.** Florid ornamental trills and runs in vocal music. **2.** Music characterized by coloratura. **3.** A singer, esp. a soprano, specializing in coloratura. [Obs. Ital. < LLat., coloring < Lat. *colorare,* to color < *color,* color.]

color bar *n.* Color line.

col·or·blind (kŭl'ər-blīnd') *adj.* **1.** Partially or totally unable to distinguish certain colors. **2. a.** Not subject to racial prejudices. **b.** Not recognizing racial distinctions. **—col'or·blind'ness** *n.*

col·or·breed (kŭl'ər-brēd') *tr.v.* **-bred** (-brĕd'), **-breed·ing, -breeds.** To breed (plants or animals) selectively to produce new or desired colors.

col·or·cast (kŭl'ər-kăst') *v.* **-cast** or **-cast·ed, -cast·ing, -casts.** *—tr.* To broadcast (a television program) in color. *—intr.* To televise in color. *—n.* A television broadcast in color. [COLOR + (BROAD)CAST.]

col·or-code (kŭl'ər-kōd') *tr.v.* **-cod·ed, -cod·ing, -codes.** To color, as wires or papers, according to a code for easy identification.

col·ored (kŭl'ərd) *adj.* **1.** Having color. **2. a.** Of an ethnic group not regarded as Caucasian, esp. Negro. **b.** Of mixed racial strains. **3.** Distorted or biased, as by irrelevant or incorrect information. *—n.* A colored person or persons.

col·or·fast (kŭl'ər-făst') *adj.* Having color that will not run or fade with washing or wear: *a colorfast fabric.* **—col'or·fast'ness** *n.*

color filter *n.* A photographic filter used to increase contrast or take photographs through haze.

col·or·ful (kŭl'ər-fəl) *adj.* **1.** Full of color; abounding in colors. **2.** Characterized by rich variety; vivid; distinctive: *colorful language.* **—col'or·ful·ly** *adv.* **—col'or·ful·ness** *n.*

color guard *n.* The ceremonial escort for the flag, as of a country or organization.

col·or·if·ic (kŭl'ə-rĭf'ĭk) *adj.* Producing or imparting color.

col·or·im·e·ter (kŭl'ə-rĭm'ĭ-tər) *n.* **1.** Any of various instruments used to determine or specify colors, as by comparison with spectroscopic or visual standards. **2.** An instrument that measures the concentration of a known solution constituent by comparison with colors of standard solutions of that constituent. **—col'or·i·met'ric** (-ər-ə-mĕt'rĭk) *adj.* **—col'or·i·met'ri·cal·ly** *adv.* **—col'or·im'e·try** *n.*

col·or·ing (kŭl'ər-ĭng) *n.* **1.** The art, manner, or process of applying color. **2.** A substance used to color something. **3.** Appearance with regard to color. **4.** Characteristic aspect, tone, or style. **5.** False or misleading appearance.

col·or·ist (kŭl'ər-ĭst) *n.* **1.** A painter skilled in achieving special effects with color. **2.** A hairdresser who specializes in dyeing hair. **—col'or·is'tic** *adj.*

col·or·less (kŭl'ər-lĭs) *adj.* **1.** Without color. **2.** Weak or dull in color; pallid. **3.** Lacking animation, variety, or distinction; uninteresting; dull: *a colorless candidate.* **—col'or·less·ly** *adv.* **—col'or·less·ness** *n.*

color line *n.* A barrier, created by custom, law, or economic differences, separating nonwhite persons from whites.

co·los·sal (kə-lŏs'əl) *adj.* Enormous in size, extent, or degree; gigantic; tremendous. [Fr. < Lat. *colossus,* colossus.] **—co·los'sal·ly** *adv.*

col·os·se·um (kŏl'ə-sē'əm) *n.* Variant of **coliseum.**

co·los·si (kə-lŏs'ī') *n.* A plural of **colossus.**

Co·los·sians (kə-lŏsh'ənz, -lŏs'ē-ənz) *n. (used with a sing. verb).* See table at **Bible.**

co·los·sus (kə-lŏs'əs) *n., pl.* **-los·si** (-lŏs'ī') or **-los·sus·es. 1.** A huge statue. **2.** Something likened to a colossus, as in size or importance. [Lat. < Gk. *kolossos.*]

co·los·to·my (kə-lŏs'tə-mē) *n., pl.* **-mies.** The surgical construction of an artificial excretory opening from the colon.

co·los·trum (kə-lŏs'trəm) *n.* The first milk secreted by the mammary glands immediately after childbirth, lasting for a few days. [Lat.]

col·our (kŭl'ər) *n. & v. Chiefly Brit.* Variant of **color.**

–colous *suff.* Having a specified kind of habitat: *arenicolous.* [< Lat. *-cola,* inhabitant.]

col·pi·tis (kŏl-pī'tĭs) *n.* Inflammation of the vaginal mucous membrane. [Gk. *kolpos,* vagina + -ITIS.]

col·por·tage (kŏl'pôr'tĭj, -pōr'-) *n.* The work of a colporteur.

col·por·teur (kŏl'pôr'tər, -pōr'-) *n.* A peddler of devotional literature. [Fr., alteration of OFr. *comporteur* < *comporter,* to peddle, conduct. —see COMPORT.]

col·po·scope (kŏl'pə-skōp') *n.* A speculum that is used in the diagnostic examination of the vaginal and cervical tissues. [Gk. *kolpos,* vagina, womb + -SCOPE.]

col·pos·co·py (kŏl-pŏs'kə-pē) *n., pl.* **-pies.** The examination of the vaginal and cervical tissues by means of a colposcope. [Gk. *kolpos,* vagina, womb + -SCOPY.]

colt (kōlt) *n.* **1.** A young male horse. **2.** A youthful or inexperienced person; a novice or beginner. **3.** A rope whip formerly used for shipboard discipline. [ME < OE.]

col·ter also **coul·ter** (kōl'tər) *n.* A blade or wheel on a plow for making vertical cuts in the sod. [ME < OE *culter* ult. < Lat.]

colt·ish (kōl'tĭsh) *adj.* **1.** Of, pertaining to, or like a colt. **2.** Lively and playful; frisky. **—colt'ish·ly** *adv.* **—colt'ish·ness** *n.*

colts·foot (kōlts'fo͝ot') *n., pl.* **-foots.** A plant, *Tussilago farfara,* native to the Old World, having yellow flowers that appear before the heart-shaped leaves. [From the shape of its leaves.]

colt

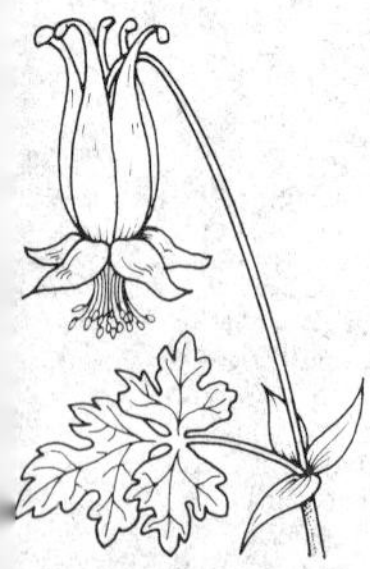

columbine

column

col·u·brid (kŏl'ə-brĭd, kŏl'yə-) *n.* Any of numerous chiefly nonvenomous snakes of the family Colubridae, which includes the king snakes and garter snakes. *—adj.* Of or belonging to the Colubridae. [NLat. *Colubridae,* family name, < Lat. *coluber,* snake.]

col·u·brine (kŏl'ə-brīn', kŏl'yə-) *adj.* Colubrid.

co·lu·go (kə-lo͞o'gō) *n., pl.* **-gos.** The flying lemur. [Malay.]

Co·lum·ba (kə-lŭm'bə) *n.* A constellation in the Southern Hemisphere near Caelum and Puppis. [NLat. < Lat. *columba,* dove.]

col·um·bar·i·um (kŏl'əm-bâr'ē-əm) also **col·um·bar·y** (kŏl'əm-bĕr'ē) *n., pl.* **-i·a** (-ē-ə) also **-ies. 1. a.** A vault with niches for urns containing ashes of the dead. **b.** One of the niches in such a vault. **2. a.** A dovecote. **b.** A pigeonhole in a dovecote. [Lat., sepulchre for urns, dovecote < *columba,* dove.]

Co·lum·bi·a (kə-lŭm'bē-ə) *n.* A feminine personification of the United States. [After Christopher COLUMBUS (1451–1506), its discoverer.]

Co·lum·bi·an (kə-lŭm'bē-ən) *adj.* **1.** Of or pertaining to the United States. **2.** Of or pertaining to Christopher Columbus.

col·um·bine (kŏl'əm-bīn') *n.* Any of several plants of the genus *Aquilegia,* having variously colored flowers with five conspicuously spurred petals. *—adj.* Dovelike. [ME < Med. Lat. *columbina* < Lat. *columbinus,* dovelike (from the resemblance of the inverted flower to a cluster of doves) < *columba,* dove.]

co·lum·bite (kə-lŭm'bīt') *n.* A black mineral, essentially $(Fe, Mn)(Nb, Ta)_2O_6$, used as a source of niobium and tantalum. [COLUMB(IUM) + -ITE.]

co·lum·bi·um (kə-lŭm'bē-əm) *n. Symbol* **Cb** Niobium. [< NLat. *Columbia,* the United States.]

Columbus Day *n.* October 12, a holiday celebrated officially on the second Monday in October in the United States in honor of Christopher Columbus.

col·u·mel·la (kŏl'yə-mĕl'ə, kŏl'ə-) *n., pl.* **-mel·lae** (-mĕl'ē). Any of several small, columnlike structures in various plants and animals. [Lat., dim. of *columna,* column.] **—col'u·mel'lar** (-mĕl'ər) *adj.* **—col'u·mel'late'** (-mĕl'āt') *adj.*

col·umn (kŏl'əm) *n.* **1.** A supporting pillar consisting of a base, a cylindrical shaft, and a capital. **2.** Something resembling a column in form or function: *a column of mercury in a thermometer.* **3. a.** One of two or more vertical sections of typed lines lying side by side on a page and separated by a rule or blank space. **b.** A feature article that appears regularly in a newspaper or other periodical. **4.** A formation, as of troops or vehicles, in which all elements follow one behind the other. **5.** *Bot.* An organ formed by the fusion of stamens or of stamens and pistils, as in the orchid. [ME *columne* < Lat. *columna.*] **—col'umned** (kŏl'əmd) *adj.*

co·lum·nar (kə-lŭm'nər) *adj* **1.** Having the shape of a column. **2.** Constructed with or having columns.

co·lum·ni·a·tion (kə-lŭm'nē-ā'shən) *n.* The use or arrangement of columns in a building.

col·um·nist (kŏl'əm-nĭst, -ə-mĭst) *n.* A writer of a newspaper or magazine column.

col·za (kŏl'zə, kōl'-) *n.* Rape². [Fr. < Du. *koolzaad* : *kool,* cabbage (< MDu. *cōle* < Lat. *caulis*) + *zaad,* seed < MDu. *saet.*]

com– or **col–** or **con–** *pref.* Together; with; joint; jointly: *commingle.* [ME < OFr. < Lat.]

co·ma¹ (kō'mə) *n., pl.* **-mas.** A deep, prolonged unconsciousness, usually the result of injury, disease, or poison. [Gk. *kōma, komat-,* deep sleep.]

co·ma² (kō'mə) *n., pl.* **-mae** (-mē). **1.** *Astron.* The nebulous luminescent cloud containing the nucleus and constituting the major portion of the head of a comet. **2.** *Bot.* A tuft of hairs, as on some seeds. **3.** *Optics.* A diffuse pear-shaped image of a point source. [Lat., hair < Gk. *komē.*] **—co'mal** *adj.*

Coma Ber·e·ni·ces (bĕr'ə-nī'sēz') *n.* A constellation in the northern sky near Boötes and Leo that contains the coma cluster of galaxies. [Lat., hair of Berenice.]

co·mae (kō'mē) *n.* Plural of **coma².**

Co·man·che (kə-măn'chē) *n., pl.* **Comanche** or **-ches. 1. a.** A tribe of North American Indians, formerly ranging over the western plains from Wyoming to Texas, now living in Oklahoma. **b.** A member of this tribe. **2.** The Uto-Aztecan language of the Comanche. [Sp. < Ute *kimanči.*] **—Co·man'che** *adj.*

Co·man·che·an (kə-măn'chē-ən) *adj.* Of, belonging to, or designating the geologic time, system of rocks, or sedimentary deposits of the Mesozoic era between the Jurassic and the Upper Cretaceous. *—n.* The Comanchean period. [After *Comanche,* a county in Texas.]

co·mate¹ (kō'māt') also **co·mose** (-mōs') *adj.* Having or resembling a tuft of hairs. [Lat. *comatus,* having long hair < *coma,* hair < Gk. *komē.*]

co·mate² (kō-māt', kō'māt') *n.* A mate; companion.

co·ma·tose (kō'mə-tōs', kŏm'ə-) *adj.* **1.** Of, pertaining to, or affected with coma; unconscious. **2.** Marked by lethargy; torpid. **—co'ma·tose'ly** *adv.*

co·mat·u·lid (kə-măch'ə-lĭd) also **co·mat·u·la** (-lə) *n., pl.*

-lids also **-lae** (-lē). Any of several marine invertebrates of the order Crinoidea that are attached to a surface by a stalk when young but are free-swimming as adults. [NLat. *Comatulidae,* former family name < LLat. *comatulus,* having neatly curled hair < Lat. *comatus,* having long hair. —see COMATE.]

comb (kōm) *n.* **1. a.** A thin, toothed strip, as of plastic or bone, used to smooth, arrange, or fasten the hair. **b.** Something resembling a comb in shape or use, as a card for dressing and cleansing wool or other fiber. **c.** A currycomb. **2. a.** The fleshy crest or ridge that grows on the crown of the head of domestic fowl and other birds and is most prominent in the male. **b.** Something suggesting a fowl's comb in appearance or position. **3.** A honeycomb. —*v.* **combed, comb·ing, combs.** —*tr.* **1.** To dress or arrange with or as if with a comb. **2.** To card (wool or other fiber). **3.** To search thoroughly; look through. —*intr.* To roll and break: *The waves combed thunderously.* [ME < OE.]

com·bat (kəm-băt′, kŏm′băt′) *v.* **-bat·ed, -bat·ing, -bats** also **-bat·ted, -bat·ting, -bats.** —*tr.* **1.** To fight against; oppose in battle. **2.** To oppose vigorously; resist: *drugs that combat infection.* —*intr.* To engage in fighting; contend; struggle. —*n.* (kŏm′băt′). Fighting, esp. armed battle; strife. [OFr. *combattre* < VLat. **combattere* : Lat. *com-,* with + Lat. *battuere,* to beat.]

com·bat·ant (kəm-băt′nt, kŏm′bə-tnt) *n.* One taking part in combat. —*adj.* Engaging in combat.

combat fatigue *n.* A nervous disorder, usually temporary but sometimes leading to a permanent neurosis, brought on by the exhaustion and stress of combat or similar situations and characterized by deep anxiety, depression, irritability, and other related symptoms.

com·bat·ive (kəm-băt′ĭv) *adj.* Eager or disposed to fight; belligerent. **—com·bat′ive·ly** *adv.* **—com·bat′ive·ness** *n.*

comb·er (kō′mər) *n.* **1.** One that combs. **2.** A long wave of the sea that has reached its peak or broken into foam; breaker.

com·bi·na·tion (kŏm′bə-nā′shən) *n.* **1. a.** The act of combining. **b.** The state of being combined. **2.** Something resulting from combining two or more things. **3.** An alliance or association of persons or parties for a common purpose; association. **4.** A sequence of numbers or letters used to open a combination lock. **5.** A one-piece undergarment consisting of an undershirt or chemise and underpants. **6.** *Math.* One or more elements selected from a set without regard to order of selection. **—com′bi·na′tion·al** *adj.*

combination lock *n.* A lock that will open only when its dial is turned through a predetermined sequence of positions identified on the dial face by numbers or letters.

com·bi·na·tive (kŏm′bə-nā′tĭv, kəm-bī′nə-tĭv) *adj.* **1.** Of, pertaining to, or resulting from combination. **2.** Tending, serving, or able to combine.

com·bi·na·to·ri·al (kŏm′bə-nə-tôr′ē-əl, -tōr′-, kəm-bī′nə-) *adj.* **1.** Relating to or involving combinations. **2.** Relating to the arrangement and manipulation of mathematical elements in sets.

com·bi·na·tor·ics (kŏm′bə-nə-tôr′ĭks, -tōr′-, kəm-bī′nə-) *n.* Combinatorial mathematics.

com·bine (kəm-bīn′) *v.* **-bined, -bin·ing, -bines.** —*tr.* **1.** To bring into a state of unity. **2.** To join (two or more substances) to make a single substance, as a chemical compound; mix. **3.** To possess or exhibit in combination. —*intr.* **1.** To become united; coalesce. **2.** To join forces for a common purpose. **3.** *Chem.* To form a chemical compound. —*n.* (kŏm′bīn′). **1.** A power-operated harvesting machine that cuts, threshes, and cleans grain. **2.** An association of persons or groups united for the furtherance of commercial or political interests. **3.** A combination. [ME *combinen* < OFr. *combiner* < LLat. *combinare* : Lat. *com-,* together + *bine,* two at a time.] **—com·bin′er** *n.*

comb·ings (kō′mĭngz) *pl.n.* Hairs, wool, or other material removed with a comb.

combining form *n. Gram.* A word element that combines with other word forms to create compounds, as *-logy* in *gynecology, macro-* in *macrochemistry,* or *Sino-* in *Sino-Soviet.*

combining weight *n.* Equivalent weight.

comb jelly *n.* A ctenophore.

com·bo (kŏm′bō) *n., pl.* **-bos. 1.** *Informal.* A small group of musicians. **2.** *Slang.* The result or product of combining; combination. [Short for COMBINATION.]

comb plate *n.* A locomotive apparatus in ctenophores that is comprised of a plate of fused cilia.

com·bus·ti·ble (kəm-bŭs′tə-bəl) *adj.* **1.** Capable of igniting and burning. **2.** Easily aroused or excited. —*n.* A combustible substance. **—com·bus′ti·bil′i·ty** *n.* **—com·bus′ti·bly** *adv.*

com·bus·tion (kəm-bŭs′chən) *n.* **1.** The process of burning. **2.** *Chem.* A chemical change, esp. oxidation, accompanied by the production of heat and light. **3.** Violent anger or agitation: *combustion slowly building up to the point of revolution.* [ME *combustion* < LLat. *combustio* < Lat. *comburere,* to burn up : *com-* (intensive) + *urere,* to burn.] **—com·bus′tive** (-tĭv) *adj.*

combustion chamber *n.* An enclosure in which combustion, esp. of a fuel or propellant, is initiated and controlled.

come (kŭm) *intr.v.* **came** (kām), **come, com·ing, comes. 1. a.** To advance toward the speaker or toward a specified place; approach: *Come to me.* **b.** To advance in a specified manner: *came reluctantly when I insisted.* **2.** To advance; make progress: *has come a very long way.* **3.** To reach a particular point in a series or as a result of orderly progression: *Dawn is coming.* **4.** To move into view; appear. **5.** To occur in time. **6. a.** To arrive at a particular result or end: *come to an understanding.* **b.** To arrive at or reach a particular state or condition: *came to her wits' end.* **c.** To move or be brought to a particular position: *came to an abrupt halt.* **7.** To extend; reach: *water that came to my waist.* **8. a.** To exist at a particular point or place: *The letter* T *comes before* U. **b.** To have priority; rank: *His work comes first.* **9. a.** To happen: *How did you come to know that?* **b.** To happen as a result: *This comes of your carelessness.* **10.** To fall to one: *No good can come of this.* **11.** To occur in the mind: *An idea came to him.* **12. a.** To issue from; descend: *comes from a good family.* **b.** To be derived; originate: *Oaks come from acorns.* **13.** To be a native or resident of: *comes from Chicago.* **14.** To add up; amount: *expenses came to more than income.* **15.** To become: *The knot came loose.* **16.** To be available or obtainable: *shoes that come in all sizes.* **17.** To prove or turn out to be: *a wish that may come true.* **18.** *Slang.* To experience orgasm. ***—phrasal verbs.* come about. 1.** To take place; happen. **2.** To turn around. **3.** *Naut.* To change tack. **come across. 1.** To meet or find by chance: *came across his old roommate today.* **2.** *Slang.* To do or give what is wanted. **3.** To give an impression: *came across as an aggressive businessman.* **come along.** To achieve success; advance. **come around** (or **round**). **1.** To recover; revive. **2.** To change one's opinion or position: *She came around after she heard the whole story.* **come at. 1.** To obtain; get. **2.** To attack; rush at. **come back. 1.** To return to past success after a period of misfortune. **2.** To retort; reply. **3.** To recur to the memory: *When he saw the picture, all his pain came back.* **come between.** To cause estrangement or separation. **come by. 1.** To acquire; get: *Mortgages are hard to come by.* **2.** To pay a visit. **come down. 1.** To lose wealth or position: *has really come down in the world.* **2.** To be descended or handed down: *a custom that comes down from colonial times.* **3.** To become sick: *came down with appendicitis.* **come forward.** To volunteer one's services. **come in. 1.** To arrive: *Fall clothes will be coming in soon.* **2.** To arrive among those who finish a contest or race: *came in fifth.* **come in for.** *Informal.* To be open to or the recipient of: *a performance that came in for adverse comment.* **come into.** To receive as an inheritance: *came into a small fortune.* **come off. 1.** To happen; occur: *The trip came off on schedule.* **2.** To acquit oneself: *is sure to come off badly if challenged to explain.* **3.** To turn out to be successful: *a party that came off.* **come on. 1.** To convey a particular personal image: *comes on as an old-fashioned reactionary.* **2.** To show sexual interest in someone. **come out. 1.** To become known: *The whole story came out at the trial.* **2.** To be issued or brought out: *His new book just came out.* **3.** To make a formal social debut. **4.** To result; end up: *Everything came out wrong.* **come out with. 1.** To disclose publicly; declare: *came out with the new tax program.* **2.** To put into words; say: *always comes out with the truth.* **come over. 1.** To happen to; seize: *Strange feelings came over me.* **2.** To change sides, as in a controversy. **3.** *Informal.* To pay a visit. **come through. 1.** *Informal.* To do what is required or anticipated: *I asked for his help, and he came through.* **2.** To become manifest: *His tenderness comes through in his facial expression.* **come to. 1.** To recover consciousness. **2.** *Naut.* **a.** To bring the bow into the wind. **b.** To anchor. **3.** To be a matter of: *When it comes to intelligence, she is outstanding.* **come up.** To manifest itself; arise: *The question never came up.* **come upon.** To discover or meet by accident. **come up to.** To be the equal of: *His work doesn't come up to yours.* **come up with.** *Informal.* To bring forth, esp. as a solution to a problem; produce; *Please try to come up with some new ideas.* —*interj.* Used to express anger, impatience, or remonstrance: *Come now, that's enough.* —*n. Slang.* Semen. ***—idioms.* come a cropper.** To fail utterly. **come alive.** To become responsive and animated. **come apart.** To disintegrate mentally or physically; go to pieces. **come clean.** To confess all. **come off it.** *Slang.* To stop acting or speaking foolishly or pretentiously. **come to grips with.** To wrestle with; face squarely: *came to grips with the problem.* [ME *comen* < OE *cuman.*]

combine

come·back (kŭm′băk′) *n.* **1.** A return to former prosperity or status. **2.** A return to popularity: *wide ties are making a comeback this year.* **3.** A reply, esp. a quick, witty one; retort. **4.** The act of making up a deficit, as in a contest or game.

co·me·di·an (kə-mē′dē-ən) *n.* **1.** A professional entertainer who tells jokes or performs various other comic acts. **2.** An actor in comedy. **3.** A comedy writer. **4.** A person who amuses or tries to be amusing; clown.

co·me·dic (kə-mē′dĭk) *adj.* Of or relating to comedy.

co·me·di·enne (kə-mē′dē-ĕn′) *n.* A female professional entertainer who tells jokes or performs various other comic acts. [Fr. *comédienne,* fem. of *comédien,* comedian < *comédie,* comedy < Lat. *comoedia.*]

com·e·do (kŏm′ĭ-dō′) *n., pl.* **-dos** or **-do·nes** (-dō′nēz). A blackhead. [Lat., glutton < *comedere,* to eat up : *com-* (intensive) + *edere,* to eat.]

come·down (kŭm′doun′) *n.* **1.** A decline or drop to a lower status or level. **2.** *Informal.* **a.** A feeling of disappointment or depression. **b.** Something that causes disappointment or depression.

com·e·dy (kŏm′ĭ-dē) *n., pl.* **-dies. 1. a.** A play, motion picture, or other work that is humorous in its treatment of theme and character and has a happy ending. **b.** The branch of drama made up of such plays. **2.** A literary composition with a theme appropriate to comedy or using the methods of comedy. **3.** The branch of literature dealing with comedies. **4.** The art or technique of composing comedy. **5.** A comic element of literature or life. **6.** A comic occurrence. [ME *comedie* < Lat. *comoedia* < Gk. *kōmōdia* < *kōmōidos,* comedian : *kōmos,* revel + *aoidos,* singer < *aeidein,* to sing.]

comedy of manners *n.* A comedy satirizing fashionable society.

come-hith·er (kŭm-hĭth′ər) *adj.* Seductive; alluring.

come·ly (kŭm′lē) *adj.* **-li·er, -li·est. 1.** Having a pleasing, attractive appearance. **2.** Suitable; proper; seemly: *comely behavior.* [ME *comli* < OE *cymlic,* lovely.] **—come′li·ness** *n.*

come-on (kŭm′ŏn′, -ôn′) *n.* **1.** Something offered to allure or attract; inducement. **2.** *Informal.* A sexual or romantic approach or proposal.

com·er (kŭm′ər) *n.* **1.** One that arrives or comes. **2.** *Informal.* One showing promise of attaining success.

co·mes·ti·ble (kə-mĕs′tə-bəl) *adj.* Fit to be eaten; edible. —*n.* Something that can be eaten as food. [OFr. < LLat. *comestibilis* < Lat. *comedere,* to eat up. —see COMEDO.]

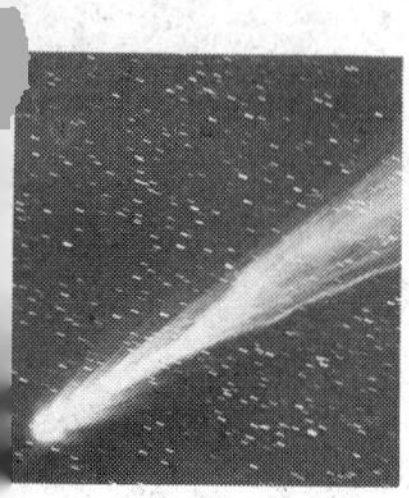

comet

com·et (kŏm′ĭt) *n. Astron.* A celestial body, observed only in that part of its orbit that is relatively close to the sun, having a head consisting of a solid nucleus surrounded by a nebulous coma up to 2.4 million kilometers or 1.5 million miles in diameter, an elongated curved vapor tail arising from the coma when sufficiently close to the sun, and thought to consist chiefly of ammonia, methane, carbon dioxide, and water. [ME *comete* < OE *comēta* < Lat. *cometa* < Gk. *komētēs* < *(astēr) komētēs,* long-haired (star) < *koman,* to grow hair long < *komē,* hair.] **—com′et·ar′y** (-ĭ-tĕr′ē), **co·met′ic** (kə-mĕt′ĭk) *adj.*

come·up·pance also **come·up·ance** (kŭm′ŭp′əns) *n. Informal.* A punishment or retribution that one deserves; one's just deserts.

com·fit (kŭm′fĭt, kŏm′-) *n.* A candy; confection. [ME *confit* < OFr. < Lat. *conficere,* to prepare : *com-* (intensive) + *facere,* to make.]

com·fort (kŭm′fərt) *tr.v.* **-fort·ed, -fort·ing, -forts. 1.** To soothe in time of grief or fear; console. **2.** To ease physically; relieve. —*n.* **1.** A condition of ease or well-being. **2.** Solace in time of grief or fear. **3.** Help; assistance: *gave comfort to the enemy.* **4.** One that brings comfort: *a child that was a comfort to his parents.* **5.** Capacity to give physical ease and well-being: *enjoying the comfort of his favorite chair.* [ME *comforten* < OFr. *conforter,* to strengthen < LLat. *confortare* : Lat. *com-* (intensive) + Lat. *fortis,* strong.] **—com′fort·ing·ly** *adv.*

com·fort·a·ble (kŭm′fər-tə-bəl, kŭmf′tə-bəl) *adj.* **1.** Providing or giving comfort: *a comfortable room.* **2.** Being in a state of comfort; at ease: *not comfortable in his presence.* **3.** *Informal.* Sufficient; adequate: *comfortable earnings.* **—com′fort·a·ble·ness** *n.* **—com′fort·a·bly** *adv.*

Synonyms: *comfortable, cozy, snug, restful.* These words mean affording pleasurable ease. *Comfortable* implies the deliberate removal of sources of pain or distress. *Cozy* evokes the image of a warm room in winter and suggests cheerful or reassuring closeness. *Snug* is even closer; the image is of a warm bed. *Restful* suggests a seclusion and quiet conducive to ease. Metaphorically, the terms may acquire ironic overtones. Thus, *comfortable* may suggest lethargy or complacency, and *cozy* a self-serving closeness of relationship.

com·fort·er (kŭm′fər-tər) *n.* **1.** One that comforts. **2. Comforter.** The Holy Spirit. **3.** A quilted bedcover. **4.** *Chiefly Brit.* A woolen neck scarf.

comfort station *n.* A public toilet or rest room.

com·frey (kŭm′frē) *n., pl.* **-freys.** Any of several usually hairy or bristly plants of the genus *Symphytum,* native to the Old World, having clusters of variously colored flowers. [ME *conferie* < OFr. *confirie* < Lat. *conferva.*]

com·fy (kŭm′fē) *adj.* **-fi·er, -fi·est.** *Informal.* Comfortable.

com·ic (kŏm′ĭk) *adj.* **1.** Of, characteristic of, or pertaining to comedy. **2.** Of or pertaining to comic strips. **3.** Amusing; humorous. —*n.* **1. a.** A comedian. **b.** A person who is comical. **2. a. comics.** Comic strips. **b.** A comic book. **3.** Something that provokes humor in art or life. [Lat. *comicus* < Gk. *kōmikos* < *kōmos,* revel.]

com·i·cal (kŏm′ĭ-kəl) *adj.* **1.** Provoking mirth or amusement; funny. **2.** Of or pertaining to comedy. **—com′i·cal′i·ty** (-kăl′ĭ-tē), **com′i·cal·ness** *n.* **—com′i·cal·ly** *adv.*

comic book *n.* A book of comic strips.

comic opera *n.* An opera or operetta with a humorous plot, spoken dialogue, and usually a happy ending.

com·ic-op·er·a (kŏm′ĭk-ŏp′rə, -ŏp′ər-ə) *adj.* That is not to be taken seriously: *comic-opera politics.*

comic strip *n.* A narrative series of cartoons.

com·ing (kŭm′ĭng) *adj.* **1.** Approaching; next: *the coming season.* **2.** *Informal.* Showing promise of fame or success. —*n.* Arrival; advent: *the coming of spring.*

com·ing-out (kŭm′ĭng-out′) *n. Informal.* A social debut.

Com·in·tern (kŏm′ĭn-tûrn′) *n.* The Third International (1919). [COM(MUNIST) INTERN(ATIONAL).]

co·mi·ti·a (kə-mĭsh′ē-ə, -mĭsh′ə) *n., pl.* **comitia.** A popular assembly in ancient Rome having legislative or electoral duties. [Lat. < pl. of *comitium,* assembly place : *com-,* together + *ire,* to go.] **—co·mi′tial** (-mĭsh′əl) *adj.*

com·i·ty (kŏm′ĭ-tē) *n., pl.* **-ties. 1.** An atmosphere of social harmony. **2.** Comity of nations. **3.** Courteous recognition accorded by the courts of one state or jurisdiction of the laws and judicial decisions of another. [Lat. *comitas* < *comis,* friendly.]

comity of nations *n.* **1.** Courteous recognition accorded by one nation to the laws and institutions of another. **2.** The nations observing international comity.

com·ix (kŏm′ĭks) *pl.n.* Comic books and comic strips, esp. of the underground press. [Alteration of COMICS.]

com·ma (kŏm′ə) *n.* **1.** A punctuation mark (,) used to indicate a separation of ideas or of elements within the structure of a sentence. **2.** A pause or separation; caesura. **3.** Any of several butterflies of the genus *Polygonia,* having wings with brownish coloring and irregularly notched edges. [LLat. < Gk. *komma,* short clause < *koptein,* to cut.]

comma bacillus *n.* A bacillus, *Vibrio comma,* that causes Asiatic cholera. [From its commalike shape.]

comma fault *n.* Improper use of a comma between independent clauses not joined by a conjunction.

com·mand (kə-mănd′) *v.* **-mand·ed, -mand·ing, -mands.** —*tr.* **1.** To direct with authority; give orders to. **2.** To have control or authority over; rule: *a general commanding an army.* **3.** To have at one's disposal: *commands seven languages.* **4.** To deserve and receive as due; exact: *His bravery commanded respect.* **5.** To dominate by position; overlook: *a mountain commanding the valley.* —*intr.* **1.** To give commands. **2.** To exercise authority as a commander; be in control. —*n.* **1.** The act of commanding. **2.** An order given with authority. **3.** A signal that actuates a device, as a computer. **4. a.** The authority to command: *an admiral in command.* **b.** The possession and exercise of the authority to command: *command of the seas.* **5.** Ability to control or use; mastery: *a command of four languages.* **6.** Dominance by location; extent of view. **7. a.** The jurisdiction of a commander. **b.** A military unit, post, district, or region under the control of one officer. **c.** A unit in the U.S. Air Force consisting of a specified number of wings, generally three or more, under the authority of an officer. **8.** *Chiefly Brit.* An invitation from a reigning monarch. ***—modifier:*** *command headquarters; a command performance.* [ME *commaunden* < OFr. *comander* < VLat. **commandare* : *com-* (intensive) + *mandare,* to entrust.]

Synonyms: *command, order, bid, enjoin, direct, instruct, charge.* These verbs, with varying degrees of authority, demand obedience on the part of the person or group addressed. *Command* and *order* are similar in emphasizing official authority of the person making the demand: *a general commands; a doctor orders. Bid* suggests an invitation to do something. In an earlier sense, *bid* has the force of *command: I bid you be seated. Enjoin, direct,* and *instruct* do not carry the full authority of *command* or *order. Enjoin* can apply both to demanding the execution of a given act and to demanding the prohibition of something: *Strikers were enjoined from picketing. Direct* implies ordering, but less strongly than *command. Instruct* suggests a mild order directing a person to do something in a specified way. *Charge* adds to *order* the imposition of a moral duty.

com·man·dant (kŏm′ən-dănt′, -dänt′) *n.* A commanding officer of a military organization.

com·man·deer (kŏm′ən-dîr′) *tr.v.* **-deered, -deer·ing, -deers. 1.** To force into military service. **2.** To seize for military use; confiscate. **3.** *Informal.* To take arbitrarily or by force. [Afr. *kommanderen* < Fr. *commander,* to command < OFr. *comander.* —see COMMAND.]

com·mand·er (kə-măn′dər) *n.* **1.** A person who commands; leader. **2. a.** An officer in the U.S. Navy who ranks next above a lieutenant commander and next below a captain. **b.** The chief commissioned officer of a military unit regardless of his rank. **3.** A chief or an officer in certain knightly or fraternal orders.

commander in chief *n.* **1.** Often **Commander in Chief.** The supreme commander of all the armed forces of a nation. **2.** The officer commanding a major armed force.

com·mand·er·y (kə-măn′də-rē) *n., pl.* **-ies. 1.** The district or office of a commander, esp. of an order of knights. **2.** A lodge or local branch of certain fraternal orders.

com·mand·ing (kə-măn′dĭng) *adj.* Dominating, as by magnitude or position: *took a commanding lead at the polls.* **—com·mand′ing·ly** *adv.*

commanding officer *n.* A U.S. Army officer in charge of a unit from company to regiment or of a post, camp, or station.

com·mand·ment (kə-mănd′mənt) *n.* **1.** A command; edict. **2.** One of the Ten Commandments.

command module *n.* The portion of a spacecraft in which the astronauts live and operate controls during a flight.
com·man·do (kə-măn′dō) *n., pl.* **-dos** or **-does. 1. a.** A small fighting force specially trained for making quick, destructive raids against enemy-held areas. **b.** A member of such a force. **2. a.** In South Africa, an organized force of Boer troops. **b.** A raid made by such a force. [Afr. *kommando* < Du. *commando,* unit of troops < Sp. *comando* < *comandar,* to command < VLat. **commandare.* —see COMMAND.]
command post *n.* The field headquarters used by the commander of a military unit.
comma splice *n.* A comma fault.
com·meas·ure (kə-mĕzh′ər) *tr.v.* **-ured, -ur·ing, -ures.** To coincide with; be coextensive with. **—com·meas′ur·a·ble** *adj.*
com·me·dia dell'ar·te (kə-mā′dē-ə dĕl-är′tē, -mĕd′ē-ə) *n.* A type of comedy developed in Italy in the 16th century and characterized by improvisation from a plot outline and the use of stock characters. [Ital., comedy of art.]
comme il faut (kŭm′ ēl fō′) *adj.* In accordance with conventions or accepted standards; proper. [Fr., as it should be.]
com·mem·o·rate (kə-mĕm′ə-rāt′) *tr.v.* **-rat·ed, -rat·ing, -rates. 1.** To honor the memory of with a ceremony. **2.** To serve as a memorial to. [Lat. *commemorare, commemorat-,* to remind : *com-* (intensive) + *memorare,* to remind < *memor,* mindful.] **—com·mem′o·ra′tor** *n.*
com·mem·o·ra·tion (kə-mĕm′ə-rā′shən) *n.* **1.** The act of commemorating. **2.** Something that commemorates.
com·mem·o·ra·tive (kə-mĕm′ər-ə-tĭv, -ə-rā′-) *adj.* Serving to commemorate. *—n.* Something that commemorates.
com·mem·o·ra·to·ry (kə-mĕm′ər-ə-tôr′ē, -tōr′ē) *adj.* Commemorative.
com·mence (kə-mĕns′) *v.* **-menced, -menc·ing, -menc·es.** *—tr.* To begin; start. *—intr.* To come into existence; have a beginning. [ME *commencen* < OFr. *comencier* < VLat. **cominitiare* : Lat. *com-* (intensive) + LLat. *initiare,* to begin < Lat. *initium,* beginning.] **—com·menc′er** *n.*
com·mence·ment (kə-mĕns′mənt) *n.* **1.** A beginning; start. **2. a.** A ceremony at which academic degrees or diplomas are conferred. **b.** The day on which such a ceremony takes place.
com·mend (kə-mĕnd′) *tr.v.* **-mend·ed, -mend·ing, -mends. 1.** To represent as worthy, qualified, or desirable; recommend. **2.** To express approval of; praise. **3.** To commit to the care of another; entrust. [ME *commenden* < Lat. *commendare* : *com-* (intensive) + *mandare,* to entrust.] **—com·mend′a·ble** *adj.* **—com·mend′a·ble·ness** *n.* **—com·mend′a·bly** *adv.*
com·men·da·tion (kŏm′ən-dā′shən) *n.* **1.** The act of commending. **2.** Something, esp. an official award or citation, that commends.
com·men·da·to·ry (kə-mĕn′də-tôr′ē, -tōr′ē) *adj.* Serving to commend or praise.
com·men·sal (kə-mĕn′səl) *adj.* **1.** Of or pertaining to those who customarily eat at the same table. **2.** *Biol.* Of, pertaining to, or characterized by commensalism. *—n.* **1.** A customary mealtime companion. **2.** *Biol.* An organism participating in a commensal relationship. [ME < Med. Lat. *commensalis* : Lat. *com-,* together + Lat. *mensa,* table.] **—com·men′sal·ly** *adv.*
com·men·sal·ism (kə-mĕn′sə-lĭz′əm) *n. Biol.* A relationship in which two or more organisms live in close association and in which one may derive some benefit but in which neither harms or is parasitic on the other.
com·men·su·ra·ble (kə-mĕn′sər-ə-bəl, -shər-) *adj.* **1.** Capable of being measured by a common standard. **2.** Properly proportioned; fitting. **3.** *Math.* Exactly divisible by the same unit an integral number of times. Used of two quantities. [LLat. *commensurabilis* : Lat. *com-,* together + *mensurabilis,* measurable < Lat. *mensura,* measure.] **—com·men′su·ra·bil′i·ty** *n.* **—com·men′su·ra·bly** *adv.*
com·men·su·rate (kə-mĕn′sər-ĭt, -shər-) *adj.* **1.** Of the same size, extent, or duration. **2.** Corresponding in size or degree; proportionate: *a salary commensurate with his performance.* **3.** Having a common measure or standard; commensurable. [LLat. *commensuratus* : Lat. *com-,* together + *mensuratus,* p.part. of *mensurare,* to measure < Lat. *mensura,* measure.] **—com·men′su·rate·ly** *adv.* **—com·men′su·ra′tion** *n.*
com·ment (kŏm′ĕnt′) *n.* **1.** A written note intended as an explanation, illustration, or criticism of a passage in a book or other writing; annotation. **2. a.** A brief statement of fact or opinion, esp. a remark that expresses a personal reaction or attitude: *made a comment on the governor's speech.* **b.** An implied conclusion or judgment: *a novel that is a comment on contemporary lawlessness.* **3.** Talk; gossip: *a divorce that caused much comment.* *—v.* **-ment·ed, -ment·ing, -ments.** *—intr.* To make a comment; remark. *—tr.* To make comments on; annotate. [ME < Lat. *commentum,* interpretation < neuter p.part. of *comminisci,* to devise.]
com·men·tar·y (kŏm′ən-tĕr′ē) *n., pl.* **-ies. 1.** A series of explanations or interpretations. **2.** Often **commentaries.** An expository treatise or series of annotations; exegesis. **3.** Something that explains or illustrates: *a scandal that is a sad commentary on city government.* **4.** Often **commentaries.** A personal narrative; memoir. **—com′men·tar′i·al** (-târ′ē-əl) *adj.*
com·men·tate (kŏm′ən-tāt′) *tr. & intr.v.* **-tat·ed, -tat·ing, -tates.** To make a commentary on or serve as commentator.
Usage: This verb has been in use for several hundred years in the sense of "to give a commentary." But in the sense "to provide a running commentary on," as in *she commentated the fashion show,* it is unacceptable to a large majority of the Usage Panel.
com·men·ta·tor (kŏm′ən-tā′tər) *n.* **1.** An author of commentaries. **2.** A writer or broadcaster who reports and analyzes events in the news. **3.** A member of the congregation who leads prayers and explains rituals during a service.
com·merce (kŏm′ərs) *n.* **1.** The buying and selling of goods, esp. on a large scale, as between nations. **2.** Intellectual exchange or social intercourse. **3.** Sexual intercourse. [OFr. < Lat. *commercium* : *com-,* together + *merx,* merchandise.]
com·mer·cial (kə-mûr′shəl) *adj.* **1. a.** Of or pertaining to commerce: *a commercial loan.* **b.** Engaged in commerce: *a commercial trucker.* **c.** Involved in work that is intended for the mass market: *a commercial artist.* **2.** Designating goods, often unrefined, produced and distributed in large quantities for use by industry. **3.** Having profit as a chief aim: *too scholarly to be a commercial book.* **4.** Sponsored by an advertiser or supported by advertising: *commercial television.* *—n.* An advertisement on radio or television. **—com·mer′cial·ly** *adv.*
commercial bank *n.* A bank whose principal functions are to receive demand deposits and to make short-term loans.
com·mer·cial·ism (kə-mûr′shə-lĭz′əm) *n.* **1.** The practices, methods, aims, and spirit of commerce or business. **2.** An attitude that emphasizes tangible profit or success. **—com·mer′cial·ist** *n.* **—com·mer′cial·is′tic** *adj.*
com·mer·cial·ize (kə-mûr′shə-līz′) *tr.v.* **-ized, -iz·ing, -iz·es. 1.** To apply methods of business to for profit. **2. a.** To exploit, do, or make mainly for financial gain. **b.** To sacrifice the quality of for profit. **—com·mer′cial·i·za′tion** *n.*
commercial paper *n.* Any of various short-term negotiable papers originating in business transactions.
commercial traveler *n.* A traveling sales representative.
com·mie also **Com·mie** (kŏm′ē) *n. Informal.* A Communist.
com·mi·na·tion (kŏm′ə-nā′shən) *n.* A formal denunciation. [ME *comminacioun* < Lat. *comminatio* < *comminari,* to threaten : *com-* (intensive) + *minari,* to threaten < *minae,* threats.] **—com·min′a·to′ry** (kə-mĭn′ə-tôr′ē, -tōr′ē, kŏm′ĭ-nə-) *adj.*
com·min·gle (kə-mĭng′gəl) *intr. & tr.v.* **-gled, -gling, -gles.** To blend or cause to blend together; mix.
com·mi·nute (kŏm′ə-no͞ot′, -nyo͞ot′) *tr.v.* **-nut·ed, -nut·ing, -nutes.** To reduce to powder; pulverize. [Lat. *comminuere, comminut-* : *com-* (intensive) + *minuere,* to lessen.] **—com′mi·nu′tion** *n.*
com·mis·er·ate (kə-mĭz′ə-rāt′) *v.* **-at·ed, -at·ing, -ates.** *—tr.* To feel or express sorrow or pity for; sympathize with. *—intr.* To feel or express sympathy: *commiserated over their failure.* [Lat. *commiserari, commiserat-* : *com-,* with + *miserari,* to pity < *miser,* wretched.] **—com·mis′er·a′tion** *n.* **—com·mis′er·a′tive** *adj.* **—com·mis′er·a′tive·ly** *adv.* **—com·mis′er·a′tor** *n.*
com·mis·sar (kŏm′ĭ-sär′) *n.* **1.** An official of the Communist Party in charge of political indoctrination and the enforcement of party loyalty. **2.** The head of a commissariat in the Soviet Union until 1946. [R. *komissar* < G. *Kommissar,* deputy < Med. Lat. *commissarius,* agent. —see COMMISSARY.]
com·mis·sar·i·at (kŏm′ĭ-sâr′ē-ĭt) *n.* **1.** A department of an army in charge of providing food and other supplies for the troops. **2.** A food supply. **3.** A major government department in the Soviet Union until 1946. [NLat. *commissariatus* < Med. Lat. *commissarius,* agent. —see COMMISSARY.]
com·mis·sar·y (kŏm′ĭ-sĕr′ē) *n., pl.* **-ies. 1. a.** A store where food and equipment are sold, as in a mining camp. **b.** A supermarket for the personnel of a military post. **2.** A lunchroom or cafeteria, esp. one in a motion-picture or television studio. **3.** A person to whom a special duty is given by a higher authority; deputy. [ME *commissarie* < Med. Lat. *commissarius,* agent < Lat. *committere,* to entrust. —see COMMIT.] **—com′mis·sar′y·ship′** *n.*
com·mis·sion (kə-mĭsh′ən) *n.* **1. a.** The act of granting certain powers or the authority to carry out a particular task or duty. **b.** The authority so granted. **c.** The matter or task so authorized: *Investigating fraud was their commission.* **d.** A document conferring such authorization. **2.** A group of people officially authorized to perform certain duties or functions: *The Federal Trade Commission investigates false advertising.* **3.** The act of committing or perpetrating: *the commission of a crime.* **4.** A fee or percentage allowed to a salesman or agent for his services. **5. a.** An official document issued by a government and conferring the rank of a commissioned officer in the armed forces. **b.** The rank and powers so conferred. *—tr.v.* **-sioned, -sion·ing, -sions. 1.** To grant a commission to: *was commissioned a captain.* **2.** To place an order for: *commissioned a new symphony for the festival.* **3.** To put (a ship) into active service. **—idioms. in commission. 1.** In active service, as a ship. **2.** In use or in usable condition. **out of commission. 1.** Not in active service. **2.** Not in use or in working condition. [ME *commissioun* < Lat. *commissio* < *committere,* to entrust. —see COMMIT.] **—com·mis′sion·al** *adj.*

com·mis·sion·aire (kə-mĭsh'ə-nâr') *n. Chiefly Brit.* A doorman. [Fr. < Med. Lat. *commissionarius* < Lat. *commissio,* commission.]

commissioned officer *n.* An officer who holds a commission and ranks as a second lieutenant or above in the U.S. Army, Air Force, or Marine Corps, or as an ensign or above in the U.S. Navy or Coast Guard.

com·mis·sion·er (kə-mĭsh'ə-nər) *n.* **1.** A person authorized by a commission to perform certain duties. **2.** A member of a commission. **3.** A governmental official in charge of a department: *a police commissioner.* **4.** An official selected by an athletic association or league to exercise judicial or regulatory powers: *a baseball commissioner.* **—com·mis'sion·er·ship'** *n.*

commission merchant *n.* A person who buys and sells goods for others on a commission basis.

commission plan *n.* A type of municipal government in which legislative and administrative functions and powers are vested in an elected commission rather than in a mayor and city council.

com·mis·sure (kŏm'ə-shŏŏr') *n.* **1.** A line or place at which two things are joined. **2.** *Anat.* **a.** A tract of nerve fibers passing from one side to the other of the spinal cord or brain. **b.** The angle or corner of such structures, such as the lips, eyelids, or cardiac valves. **3.** *Bot.* A surface by which adhering carpels are joined. [ME < Lat. *commissura* < *committere,* to join. —see COMMIT.] **—com'mis·su'ral** *adj.*

com·mis·sur·ot·o·my (kŏm'ə-shŏŏ-rŏt'ə-mē) *n., pl.* **-mies.** The surgical incision of a commissure of the brain, sometimes used in the treatment of certain psychiatric disorders. [COMMISSUR(E) + -TOMY.]

com·mit (kə-mĭt') *tr.v.* **-mit·ted, -mit·ting, -mits. 1.** To do, perform, or perpetrate: *commit a murder.* **2.** To place in trust or charge; entrust. **3.** To place officially in confinement or custody. **4.** To consign for future use or reference or for preservation: *commit to memory.* **5.** To put in a place to be disposed of or kept safe: *commit to the flames.* **6. a.** To pledge to a position on an issue: *never committed himself.* **b.** To bind or obligate, as by a pledge: *was committed to follow orders.* **7.** To refer (a legislative bill, for example) to a committee. [ME *committen* < Lat. *committere* : *com-,* together + *mittere,* to send.] **—com·mit'ta·ble** *adj.*

Synonyms: *commit, consign, entrust, confide, assign, relegate.* These verbs mean to place a person or thing in custody or safekeeping. *Commit* has the widest application and means to deliver a person or thing, physically or figuratively, into the charge of another. *Consign* states the formal act of transferring or delivering, especially goods or property. *Entrust* and *confide* both stress confidence in another. A child is entrusted to the care of a baby sitter; a secret is confided to a close friend. *Assign* refers to committing someone to a place, position, or task, or to transferring personal property or rights. *Relegate* refers to assigning a person or thing to a specific category or sphere and generally implies debasement or demotion.

com·mit·ment (kə-mĭt'mənt) *n.* **1.** The act of committing; a giving in charge or entrusting, esp.: **a.** The act of referring a legislative bill to committee. **b.** Official consignment, as to a prison or mental hospital. **c.** A court order authorizing consignment to a prison; mittimus. **2. a.** A pledge to do something. **b.** Something pledged, esp. an engagement by contract involving financial obligation. **3.** The state of being bound emotionally or intellectually to a course of action: *a deep commitment to liberal policies.*

com·mit·tal (kə-mĭt'l) *n.* **1.** The act of entrusting. **2.** The act of committing to confinement. **3.** The act of pledging oneself to a particular position.

com·mit·tee (kə-mĭt'ē) *n.* **1.** A group of people officially delegated to perform a function, as investigating, considering, reporting, or acting on a matter. **2.** *Law.* A person to whom the care of an estate or incompetent person is committed; trustee. —See Usage note at **collective noun.** [ME *committee,* trustee < AN *comité,* p.part. of *cometre,* to commit < L *committere.* —see COMMIT.]

com·mit·tee·man (kə-mĭt'ē-mən, -măn') *n.* **1.** A committee member. **2.** A ward or precinct party leader.

committee of the whole *n.* A committee consisting of all the members present of a legislative house.

com·mix (kə-mĭks', kŏ-) *intr. & tr.v.* **-mixed, -mix·ing, -mix·es.** To mix or cause to mix together; blend. [< ME *commixt,* mixed together < Lat. *commixtus,* p.part. of *commiscēre,* to mix together : *com-,* together + *miscēre,* to mix.]

commode
18th-century English

com·mix·ture (kə-mĭks'chər, kŏ-) *n.* **1.** The act or process of mixing. **2.** The result of mixing; mixture.

com·mode (kə-mōd') *n.* **1.** A low cabinet or chest of drawers, often elaborately decorated and usually on legs or short feet. **2. a.** A movable stand or cupboard containing a washbowl. **b.** A chair enclosing a chamber pot. **c.** A toilet. **3.** A woman's ornate headdress, fashionable around 1700. [Fr. < *commode,* convenient < Lat. *commodus.* —see COMMODIOUS.]

com·mo·di·ous (kə-mō'dē-əs) *adj.* **1.** Spacious; roomy. **2.** *Archaic.* Suitable; handy. [ME, convenient < Med. Lat. *commodiosus* < Lat. *commodus* : *com-,* with + *modus,* measure.] **—com·mo'di·ous·ly** *adv.* **—com·mo'di·ous·ness** *n.*

com·mod·i·ty (kə-mŏd'ĭ-tē) *n., pl.* **-ties. 1.** Something that is useful or can be turned to commercial or other advantage. **2.** An article of trade or commerce, esp. an agricultural or mining product, that can be transported. **3.** *Obs.* **a.** Convenience; expediency. **b.** A quantity of goods. [ME *commodite* < OFr., convenience < Lat. *commoditas* < *commodus,* convenient. —see COMMODIOUS.]

com·mo·dore (kŏm'ə-dôr', -dōr') *n.* **1.** An officer in the U.S. Navy ranking below rear admiral and above captain. This rank was abolished in 1899 but temporarily restored during World War II. **2.** An unofficial designation for a captain in the British Navy temporarily in command of a fleet division or squadron. **3. a.** The senior captain of a naval squadron or merchant fleet. **b.** The presiding officer of a yacht club. [Prob. < Du. *komandeur,* commander < Fr. *commandeur* < OFr. *commandeor* < *comander,* to command. —see COMMAND.]

com·mon (kŏm'ən) *adj.* **-er, -est. 1. a.** Belonging equally to or shared equally by two or more; joint: *common interests.* **b.** Of or pertaining to the community as a whole; public: *the common good.* **2.** Widespread; prevalent; general: *common knowledge.* **3. a.** Of frequent or habitual occurrence; usual: *a common phenomenon.* **b.** Most widely known or occurring most frequently; ordinary: *the common crow.* **4.** Without special designation, status, or rank: *a common sailor.* **5. a.** Not distinguished by superior or other characteristics; average: *the common spectator.* **b.** Of no special quality; standard: *common procedure.* **c.** Of mediocre or inferior quality; second-rate: *common cloth.* **6.** Unrefined or coarse in manner; vulgar: *behavior that branded him as common.* **7.** *Gram.* **a.** Either masculine or feminine in gender. **b.** Representing one or all the members of a class; not designating a unique entity. *—n.* **1. commons.** The common people; commonalty. **2. commons.** *(used with a sing. or pl. verb).* **a.** The political class comprising the commoners. **b.** The parliamentary representatives of this class. **c.** Often **Commons.** The House of Commons. **3.** A tract of land belonging to or used by a community as a whole. **4.** The legal right of a person to use the lands or waters of another, as for fishing. **5. commons.** *(used with a sing. verb).* A building or hall for dining. **6.** *Eccles.* A service used for a particular class of festivals. ***—idiom.* in common.** Equally with or by all. —See Usage note at **mutual.** [ME *commune* < OFr. < Lat. *communis.*] **—com'mon·ly** *adv.* **—com'mon·ness** *n.*

Synonyms: *common, ordinary, familiar, vulgar, prevalent.* These adjectives describe what is generally known or frequently seen, heard, or the like. *Common* implies that which is customary, takes place daily, is widely used, or is generally known. The term also suggests lack of distinction *(common man)* and can imply coarseness or crudeness. *Ordinary* implies plainness *(ordinary-looking)* or lack of distinctive quality *(ordinary ability).* In the latter sense it is sometimes derogatory. *Familiar* applies to what is well known or quickly recognized through frequent occurrence or regular association. *Vulgar* usually emphasizes the coarse sense of *common. Prevalent* describes a condition that is widespread.

com·mon·age (kŏm'ə-nĭj) *n.* **1.** The right to pasture animals on common land. **2.** The state of being held in common.

com·mon·al·ty (kŏm'ə-nəl-tē) also **com·mon·al·i·ty** (kŏm'ə-năl'ĭ-tē) *n., pl.* **-ties. 1.** The common people as opposed to the upper classes. **2.** A body corporate; corporation. **3.** An entire group; universal body. [ME *communalte* < OFr. *comunalte* < Med. Lat. *communalitas* < LLat. *communalis,* of the community. —see COMMUNAL.]

common bile duct *n.* The duct that carries bile from the liver to the duodenum.

common carrier *n.* A person or company in the business of transporting the public or goods for a fee.

common cold *n.* Coryza.

common denominator *n.* **1.** A quantity into which all the denominators of a set of fractions may be evenly divided. **2.** A commonly shared theme or trait.

common divisor *n.* A quantity that is a factor of two or more quantities.

com·mon·er (kŏm'ə-nər) *n.* **1.** One of the common people. **2.** A person without noble rank or title.

common fraction *n.* A fraction having an integer as a numerator and an integer as a denominator.

common gender *n.* Gender that may refer to either masculine or feminine categories, as *child* and *person.*

common law *n.* The system of laws originated and developed in England and based on court decisions, on the doctrines implicit in those decisions, and on customs and usages rather than on codified written laws.

common-law marriage (kŏm'ən-lô') *n.* A marriage existing by mutual agreement between a man and a woman without a civil or religious ceremony.

common logarithm *n.* A logarithm to the base 10, esp. as distinguished from a natural logarithm.

common measure *n.* **1.** *Mus.* Common time. **2.** A common divisor.

common multiple *n.* A quantity that is a multiple of each of two or more given quantities.

common noun *n. Gram.* A noun that can be preceded by the definite article and that represents one or all of the members of a class, as *book* and *man.*

com·mon·place (kŏm′ən-plās′) *adj.* Not remarkable; ordinary. —*n.* **1. a.** A trite or obvious remark; platitude. **b.** Something that is ordinary or common. **2.** *Archaic.* A passage marked for reference or entered in a commonplace book. [Transl. of Lat. *locus communis,* generally applicable theme, transl. of Gk. *koinos topos.*]
commonplace book *n.* A personal journal in which quotable passages, literary excerpts, and comments are written.
common pleas *n.* A court of common pleas (sense 1).
common salt *n.* **1.** Salt. **2.** Sodium chloride. **3.** Table salt (sense 1).
common school *n.* A public elementary school.
common sense *n.* Native good judgment. [Transl. of Lat. *sensus communis,* common feelings of humanity.]
common stock *n.* Ordinary capital shares of a corporation that have exclusive residual claim on the net assets and net income of the corporation after all prior claims have been paid.
common time *n. Mus.* A meter with four quarter notes to the measure.
com·mon·weal (kŏm′ən-wēl′) *n.* **1.** The public good or welfare. **2.** *Archaic.* A commonwealth.
com·mon·wealth (kŏm′ən-wĕlth′) *n.* **1.** The people of a nation or state; body politic. **2.** A nation or state governed by the people; republic. **3. Commonwealth. a.** The official title of some U.S. states, including Kentucky, Virginia, Massachusetts, and Pennsylvania. **b.** The official title of Puerto Rico, indicating its special status as a self-governing, autonomous political unit voluntarily associated with the United States. **4.** *Archaic.* Commonweal (sense 1). [ME *commune welthe* : *commune,* common + *welthe,* well-being. —see WEALTH.]
com·mo·tion (kə-mō′shən) *n.* **1.** A condition of turbulent motion. **2.** Civil disturbance or insurrection; disorder. **3.** An agitated disturbance; hubbub: *heard a commotion in the hall.* [ME *commocioun* < Lat. *commotio* < *commovēre,* to disturb : *com-* (intensive) + *movēre,* to move.] **—com·mo′tion·al** *adj.*
com·move (kə-mo͞ov′) *tr.v.* **-moved, -mov·ing, -moves.** To agitate; disturb. [ME *commeven* < OFr. *commovoir* < Lat. *commovere.* —see COMMOTION.]
com·mu·nal (kə-myo͞o′nəl, kŏm′yə-) *adj.* **1.** Of or pertaining to a commune. **2.** Of or pertaining to a community. **3. a.** Of or belonging to the people of a community; public. **b.** Marked by collective ownership and control of goods and property. [Fr. < LLat. *communalis* < Lat. *communis,* common.] **—com′mu·nal′i·ty** (kŏm′yə-năl′ĭ-tē) *n.* **—com·mu′nal·ly** *adv.*
com·mu·nal·ism (kə-myo͞o′nə-lĭz′əm, kŏm′yə-nə-) *n.* **1.** A theory or system of government in which virtually autonomous local communities are loosely bound in a federation. **2.** Belief in or practice of communal ownership, as of goods and property. **3.** Strong devotion to the interests of one's own ethnic group rather than those of society as a whole. **—com·mu′nal·ist** *n.* **—com·mu′nal·is′tic** *adj.*
com·mu·nal·ize (kə-myo͞o′nə-līz′, kŏm′yə-nə-) *tr.v.* **-ized, -iz·ing, -iz·es.** To convert into communal property.
Com·mu·nard (kŏm′yə-närd′) *n.* **1.** A member or advocate of the Commune of Paris of 1871. **2. communard.** One that lives in a commune. [Fr. < *commune,* division. —see COMMUNE².]
com·mune¹ (kə-myo͞on′) *intr.v.* **-muned, -mun·ing, -munes. 1. a.** To converse intimately; exchange thoughts and feelings. **b.** To be in accord: *communing with nature.* **2.** To receive the Eucharist. [ME *communen* < OFr. *communier* < *commune,* common.]
com·mune² (kŏm′yo͞on′, kə-myo͞on′) *n.* **1.** The smallest local political division of various European countries, governed by a mayor and municipal council. **2. a.** A local community organized with a government for promoting local interests. **b.** A municipal corporation in the Middle Ages. **3. a.** A small, often rural community whose members have common interests and in which property is shared or owned jointly. **b.** The people of a commune. [Fr. < Med. Lat. *communia,* community < Lat. *communis,* common.]
com·mu·ni·ca·ble (kə-myo͞o′nĭ-kə-bəl) *adj.* **1.** Capable of being communicated or transmitted: *communicable diseases.* **2.** Talkative. **—com·mu′ni·ca·bil′i·ty, com·mu′ni·ca·ble·ness** *n.* **—com·mu′ni·ca·bly** *adv.*
com·mu·ni·cant (kə-myo͞o′nĭ-kənt) *n.* **1.** A person who receives or is entitled to receive Communion. **2.** A person who communicates. —*adj.* Communicating.
com·mu·ni·cate (kə-myo͞o′nĭ-kāt′) *v.* **-cat·ed, -cat·ing, -cates.** —*tr.* **1. a.** To make known; impart: *communicate information.* **b.** To display; manifest. **2.** To spread to others; transmit (a disease, for example): *a carrier who communicated typhus.* —*intr.* **1.** To have an interchange, as of ideas. **2.** To express oneself in such a way that one is readily and clearly understood. **3.** To receive Communion. **4.** To be connected: *apartments that communicate.* [Lat. *communicare, communicat-* < *communis,* common.] **—com·mu′ni·ca′tor** *n.*
Usage: The newer intransitive sense denoting effective self-expression is now well established. Thus: *A fund of knowledge is secondary to a teacher's ability to communicate.* This example is acceptable to a majority of the Usage Panel.
com·mu·ni·ca·tion (kə-myo͞o′nĭ-kā′shən) *n.* **1.** The act of communicating; transmission. **2.** The exchange of thoughts, messages, or information, as by speech, signals, or writing. **3.** Something communicated; message. **4. communications.** A means of communicating, esp.: **a.** A system for sending and receiving messages, such as mail, telephone, or television. **b.** A network of routes for sending messages and transporting troops and supplies. **5. communications.** The art and technology of communicating. **—com·mu′ni·ca′tion·al** *adj.*
communications satellite *n.* An artificial satellite used to aid communications, as by reflecting or relaying a radio signal.
com·mu·ni·ca·tive (kə-myo͞o′nĭ-kā′tĭv, -kə-tĭv) *adj.* **1.** Inclined to communicate readily; talkative. **2.** Of or pertaining to communication. **—com·mu′ni·ca′tive·ly** *adv.* **—com·mu′ni·ca′tive·ness** *n.*
com·mun·ion (kə-myo͞on′yən) *n.* **1.** An act or instance of sharing, as of thoughts or feelings. **2.** A religious or spiritual fellowship. **3.** A body of Christians with a common religious faith who practice the same rites; denomination. **4. Communion. a.** The Christian sacrament in which consecrated bread and wine are partaken of in celebration of Christ's Last Supper. **b.** The consecrated elements of this sacrament. **c.** The part of the Mass or a liturgy in which this sacrament is received. [ME *communioun,* Christian fellowship, Eucharist < LLat. *communio,* Eucharist < Lat., mutual participation < *communis,* common.]
com·mu·ni·qué (kə-myo͞o′nĭ-kā′, -myo͞o′nĭ-kā′) *n.* An official announcement. [Fr. < *commiquer,* to announce < Lat. *communicare,* to communicate.]
com·mu·nism (kŏm′yə-nĭz′əm) *n.* **1.** A social system characterized by the common ownership of the means of production and subsistence and by the organization of labor for the common advantage of all members. **2. a.** A system of government in which the state controls the means of production and a single, often authoritarian party holds power with the intention of establishing a higher social order in which all goods are equally shared by the people. **b.** The Marxist-Leninist version of Communist doctrine that is the basis for the system of government in the Soviet Union. [Fr. *communisme* < *commun,* common < OFr. *commune.*]
Com·mu·nist (kŏm′yə-nĭst) *n.* **1. a.** A member of a Marxist-Leninist party. **b.** A supporter of such a party or movement. **2. communist.** A communalist. **3.** A Communard. **4.** Often **communist.** A radical viewed as a subversive or revolutionary. —*adj.* Also **communist.** Pertaining to, characteristic of, or resembling communism or Communists.
com·mu·nis·tic (kŏm′yə-nĭs′tĭk) *adj.* Of, characteristic of, or inclined to communism. **—com′mu·nis′ti·cal·ly** *adv.*
Communist Party *n.* A Marxist-Leninist party, usually one originally belonging to the Third International.
com·mu·ni·tar·i·an (kə-myo͞o′nĭ-târ′ē-ən) *n.* A member or supporter of a communistic community.
com·mu·ni·ty (kə-myo͞o′nĭ-tē) *n., pl.* **-ties. 1. a.** A group of people living in the same locality and under the same government. **b.** The district or locality in which such a group lives: *a small rural community.* **2.** A group or class having common interests: *the scientific community.* **3.** Similarity or identity: *a community of interests.* **4.** Society as a whole; the public. **5.** *Ecol.* **a.** A group of plants and animals living in a specific region under relatively similar conditions. **b.** The region in which they live. **6.** Common possession or participation. [ME *communite,* citizenry < OFr. *communite* < Lat. *communitas,* fellowship < *communis,* common.]
community antenna television *n.* Cable television.
community center *n.* A meeting place used by members of a community for social, cultural, or recreational purposes.
community chest *n.* A welfare fund financed by private contributions for aiding various charitable organizations.
community college *n.* A junior college without residential facilities that is often government-funded.
community property *n.* Property owned jointly by a husband and wife.
com·mu·nize (kŏm′yə-nīz′) *tr.v.* **-nized, -niz·ing, -niz·es. 1.** To subject to public ownership or control. **2.** To convert to Communist principles or control. [< Lat. *communis,* common.] **—com′mu·ni·za′tion** *n.*
com·mut·a·ble (kə-myo͞o′tə-bəl) *adj.* Capable of being commuted; interchangeable. **—com·mut′a·bil′i·ty** *n.*
com·mu·tate (kŏm′yə-tāt′) *tr.v.* **-tat·ed, -tat·ing, -tates.** To reverse the direction of (an alternating electric current) each half-cycle to produce a unidirectional current. [Back-formation < COMMUTATION.]
com·mu·ta·tion (kŏm′yə-tā′shən) *n.* **1.** A substitution, exchange, or interchange. **2. a.** The substitution of one kind of payment for another. **b.** The payment substituted. **3.** The travel of a commuter. **4.** *Elect.* **a.** The conversion of alternating to unidirectional current. **b.** The reversing of current direction. **5.** *Law.* A reduction of a penalty to a less severe one. [ME *commutacioun* < Lat. *commutatio* < *commutare,* to commute.]
commutation ticket *n.* A ticket issued at a reduced rate by a railroad, bus, or other transportation company for passage over a given route for a specified number of trips.
com·mu·ta·tive (kŏm′yə-tā′tĭv, kə-myo͞o′tə-tĭv) *adj.* **1.** Pertaining to, involving, or characterized by substitution, interchange, or exchange. **2.** Independent of order. Used of a

logical or mathematical operation that combines objects two at a time. **—com·mu'ta·tiv'i·ty** (kə-myōō'tə-tĭv'ĭ-tē) *n.*

commutative group *n.* A mathematical group in which the result of multiplying one member by another is independent of the order of multiplication.

com·mu·ta·tor (kŏm'yə-tā'tər) *n.* A cylindrical arrangement of insulated metal bars connected to the coils of an electric motor or generator to provide a unidirectional current from the generator or a reversal of current into the coils of the motor.

com·mute (kə-myōōt') *v.* **-mut·ed, -mut·ing, -mutes.** *—tr.* **1.** To substitute (one thing for another); exchange. **2.** To change (a penalty, debt, or payment) to a less severe one. *—intr.* **1. a.** To make substitution; exchange. **b.** To serve as a substitute. **2.** To pay in gross, usually at a reduced rate, rather than in individual payments. **3.** To travel as a commuter. **4.** *Math. & Logic.* To satisfy or engage in a commutative operation. *—n.* **1.** An act or instance of commuting. **2.** *Informal.* The trip made by a commuter: *a 22-mile commute.* [ME *commuten,* to change < Lat. *commutare* : *com-,* together + *mutare,* to change.]

com·mut·er (kə-myōō'tər) *n.* A person who travels regularly from one place to another, as from suburb to city and back.

co·mose (kō'mōs') *adj.* Variant of **comate¹**.

comp¹ (kŏmp) *intr.v.* **comped, comp·ing, comps.** *Mus.* To play a jazz accompaniment, as on a piano or guitar. [Short for ACCOMPANY.]

comp² (kŏmp) *n. Informal.* Something, as a theatre ticket, given free of charge. [Short for COMPLIMENTARY.]

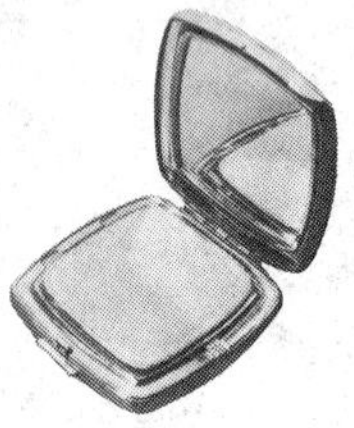

compact¹

com·pact¹ (kəm-păkt', kŏm-, kŏm'păkt') *adj.* **1.** Closely and firmly united or packed together; dense: *compact clusters of flowers.* **2.** Packed into or arranged within a relatively small space: *compact living quarters.* **3.** Briefly and to the point; concise: *a compact narration.* *—tr.v.* (kəm-păkt') **-pact·ed, -pact·ing, -pacts. 1.** To press or join firmly together; consolidate. **2.** To make by pressing or joining together; compose. *—n.* (kŏm'păkt'). **1.** A small case containing a mirror, face powder, a powder puff, and sometimes rouge. **2.** A relatively small automobile. [ME < Lat. *compactus,* p.part. of *compingere,* to put together : *com-,* together + *pangere,* to fasten.] **—com·pact'er** *n.* **—com·pact'ly** *adv.* **—com·pact'ness** *n.*

com·pact² (kŏm'păkt') *n.* An agreement or covenant. [Lat. *compactum* < *compactus,* p.part. of *compacisci,* to make an agreement : *com-,* together + *pacisci,* to agree.]

com·pac·tion (kəm-păk'shən) *n.* **1.** The process of compacting. **2.** The state of being compacted.

com·pac·tor (kəm-păk'tər, kŏm'păk'-) *n.* An apparatus that compresses refuse into relatively small packs for handy disposal.

com·pa·dre (kəm-pä'drā) *n. Southwestern U.S.* A friend or close companion. [Sp., godfather < Med. Lat. *compater* : Lat. *com-,* with + Lat. *pater,* father.]

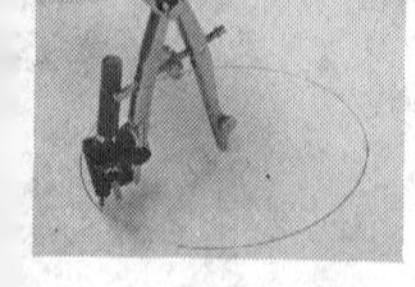

compass
Above: Directional device
Below: Drawing tool

com·pan·ion¹ (kəm-păn'yən) *n.* **1.** A person who accompanies or associates with another; comrade. **2.** A person employed to assist, live with, or travel with another. **3.** One of a pair or set of things; mate; match. *—tr.v.* **-ioned, -ion·ing, -ions.** To be a companion to; accompany. [ME *compaignoun* < OFr. *compaignon* < VLat. *companio : *com-,* together + *panis,* bread.]

com·pan·ion² (kəm-păn'yən) *n.* A companionway.

com·pan·ion·a·ble (kəm-păn'yə-nə-bəl) *adj.* **1.** Having the qualities of a good companion; friendly. **2.** Suggestive of companionship: *reading together in companionable silence.* **—com·pan'ion·a·ble·ness** *n.* **—com·pan'ion·a·bly** *adv.*

companion cell *n.* A specialized parenchyma cell, located in the phloem of angiosperms, that is closely associated in development and function with a cell that comprises the sieve tube.

com·pan·ion·ship (kəm-păn'yən-shĭp') *n.* The relationship of companions; fellowship.

com·pan·ion·way (kəm-păn'yən-wā') *n.* A staircase leading from a ship's deck to the cabins or area below. [Obs. Du. *kompanje,* poop deck.]

com·pa·ny (kŭm'pə-nē) *n., pl.* **-nies. 1.** A group; gathering: *the whole company of Nobel Prize winners.* **2. a.** One's companions or associates: *moving in fast company.* **b.** A guest or guests: *had company for the weekend.* **c.** Companionship; fellowship: *grateful for her company.* **3. a.** A business enterprise; firm. **b.** A partner or partners not specifically named in a firm's title: *John Rogers and Company.* **4.** A troupe of dramatic or musical performers: *a repertory company.* **5.** A subdivision of a regiment or battalion, the lowest administrative unit, usually under the command of a captain. **6.** A ship's crew and officers. *—tr.v.* **-nied, -ny·ing, -nies.** To accompany or associate with. *—Idioms.* **keep company.** To carry on courtship. **keep (someone) company.** To spend time with; associate with. **part company.** To end an association or friendship. —See Usage note at **collective noun.** [ME *compaignie* < OFr. < *compain,* companion < VLat. **companio.* —see COMPANION.]

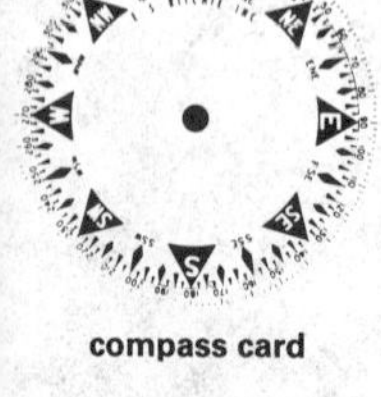

compass card

com·pa·ra·ble (kŏm'pər-ə-bəl) *adj.* **1.** Capable of being compared. **2.** Worthy of comparison. **3.** Similar or equivalent: *pianists of comparable ability.* *—pl.n.* **comparables.** Real properties that can be used to fix the value of a specific property by comparison. **—com'pa·ra·bil'i·ty, com'pa·ra·ble·ness** *n.* **—com'pa·ra·bly** *adv.*

com·par·a·tist (kəm-păr'ə-tĭst) *n.* A person who employs the comparative method, as in linguistics.

com·par·a·tive (kəm-păr'ə-tĭv) *adj.* **1.** Pertaining to, based on, or involving comparison. **2.** Estimated by comparison; relative: *a comparative newcomer.* **3.** *Gram.* Designating a degree of comparison of adjectives and adverbs higher than positive and lower than superlative. *—n. Gram.* **1.** The comparative degree. **2.** An adjective or adverb expressing the comparative degree. **—com·par'a·tive·ly** *adv.*

com·pa·ra·tor (kŏm'pə-rā'tər, kəm-păr'ə-) *n.* Any of various devices for comparing an aspect of an object, such as shape, color, or brightness, with a standard.

com·pare (kəm-pâr') *v.* **-pared, -par·ing, -pares.** *—tr.* **1.** To represent as similar, equal, or analogous; liken: *compared her eyes to sapphires.* **2.** To examine in order to note the similarities or differences of: *compared their writing styles.* **3.** *Gram.* To form the positive, comparative, or superlative degree of (an adjective or adverb). *—intr.* **1.** To be worthy of comparison; be considered as similar. **2.** To draw comparisons. *—n.* Comparison: *a musician beyond compare.* [ME *comparen* < Lat *comparare* < *compar,* equal : *com-,* together + *par,* equal.] **—com·par'er** *n.*

Usage: *Compare* usually takes *to* when it denotes the act of stating or representing that two things are similar: *He compared her to a summer's day. He compared the ships to tiny shells.* It usually takes *with* when it denotes the act of examining the ways in which two things are similar: *The paper compared the president's budget with the congressional version. The police compared the forged will with the original.* When *compared* means "worthy of comparison," *with* is used: *The reproduction can't be compared with the original.*

com·par·i·son (kəm-păr'ĭ-sən) *n.* **1. a.** The act of comparing or process of being compared. **b.** A statement or estimate of similarities and differences. **2.** The quality of being similar or equivalent; likeness: *no comparison between the two books.* **3.** *Gram.* The modification or inflection of an adjective or adverb to denote the positive, comparative, and superlative degrees. [ME *comparisoun* < OFr. *comparaison* < Lat. *comparatio* < *comparare,* to compare. —see COMPARE.]

comparison-shop (kəm-păr'ĭ-sən-shŏp') *intr.v.* **-shopped, -shop·ping, -shops.** To shop for bargains by comparing the prices of competing brands or stores.

com·part (kəm-pärt') *tr.v.* **-part·ed, -part·ing, -parts.** To divide into compartments or parts; partition. [Ult. < LLat. *compartiri,* to share : Lat. *com-,* with + Lat. *partiri,* to divide < *pars,* a part.]

com·part·ment (kəm-pärt'mənt) *n.* **1.** One of the parts or spaces into which an area is subdivided. **2.** A separate room, section, or chamber: *a storage compartment.* **—com'part·ment'al** (kŏm'pärt-mĕn'tl) *adj.*

com·part·men·tal·ize (kŏm'pärt-mĕn'tl-īz', kəm-pärt'-) *tr.v.* **-ized, -iz·ing, -iz·es.** To divide or partition into compartments or categories. **—com'part·men'tal·i·za'tion** *n.*

com·pass (kŭm'pəs, kŏm'-) *n.* **1. a.** A device used to determine geographical direction, usually consisting of a magnetic needle or needles horizontally mounted or suspended and free to pivot until aligned with the magnetic field of the earth. **b.** Any other device for determining geographical direction, as a radio compass or a gyrocompass. **c.** Often **compasses.** A V-shaped device for drawing circles or circular arcs, consisting of a pair of rigid, end-hinged, and continuously separable arms, one of which is equipped with a pen or pencil and the other with a sharp point providing a central anchor or pivot about which the drawing arm is turned. **2. a.** An enclosing line or boundary; circumference: *outside the compass of the fence.* **b.** A restricted space or area: *four huge crates within the compass of the elevator.* **c.** A range or scope; extent: *beyond the compass of your authority.* *—tr.v.* **-passed, -pass·ing, -pass·es. 1.** To make a circuit of; circle: *compassed the island.* **2.** To surround; encircle. **3.** To understand; comprehend. **4.** To achieve; obtain. **5.** To scheme; plot. *—adj.* Circular; round. [ME *compas,* compasses < OFr. < *compasser,* to measure < VLat **compassare* : Lat. *com-,* together + Lat. *passus,* step < *pandere,* to stretch.] **—com'pass·a·ble** *adj.*

compass card *n.* A freely pivoting circular disk carrying the magnetic needles of a compass and marked with the 32 points of the compass and the 360 degrees of the circle.

com·pas·sion (kəm-păsh'ən) *n.* The deep feeling of sharing the suffering of another, together with the inclination to give aid or support or to show mercy. [ME *compassioun* < LLat. *compassio* < *compati,* to sympathize : Lat. *com-,* with + Lat. *pati,* to suffer.]

com·pas·sion·ate (kəm-păsh'ə-nĭt) *adj.* Feeling or showing compassion; sympathetic. *—tr.v.* (-nāt') **-at·ed, -at·ing, -ates.** To have compassion for; pity. **—com·pas'sion·ate·ly** *adv.* **—com·pas'sion·ate·ness** *n.*

compass plant *n.* **1.** A tall plant, *Silphium laciniatum,* of central North America, having yellow flowers and lower leaves that tend to align in a north-south plane. **2.** Any of several plants similar to the compass plant.

com·pat·i·ble (kəm-păt'ə-bəl) *adj.* **1.** Capable of living or performing in harmonious, agreeable, or congenial combination with another or others. **2.** Capable of orderly, efficient integration and operation with other elements in a system. **3.** Capable of forming a chemically or biochemically stable system. **4.** Of or pertaining to a television system in which color broadcasts can be received in black and white by sets incapable of color reception. [ME < Med. Lat. *compatibilis* < LLat. *compati,* to sympathize. —see COMPASSION.] **—com·pat'i·bil'i·ty, com·pat'i·ble·ness** *n.* **—com·pat'i·bly** *adv.*

com·pa·tri·ot (kəm-pā'trē-ət, -ŏt') *n.* **1.** A fellow countryman. **2.** *Informal.* A colleague. [Fr. *compatriote* < LLat. *compatriota* : Lat. *com-,* with + *patriota,* countryman. —see PATRIOT.] **—com·pa'tri·ot'ic** (-ŏt'ĭk) *adj.*

com·peer (kŏm'pîr', kəm-pîr') *n.* **1.** A person of equal status or rank; peer or equal. **2.** A comrade, companion, or associate. [ME *comper* < OFr. < Lat. *compar,* equal. —see COMPARE.]

com·pel (kəm-pĕl') *tr.v.* **-pelled, -pel·ling, -pels. 1.** To force, drive, or constrain: *Duty compelled him to volunteer.* **2.** To necessitate or pressure by force; exact: *The energy crisis compels fuel conservation.* [ME *compellen* < Lat. *compellere* : *com-,* together + *pellere,* to drive.] **—com·pel'la·ble** *adj.* **—com·pel'la·bly** *adv.* **—com·pel'ler** *n.*

com·pel·la·tion (kŏm'pə-lā'shən, -pĕl-ā'-) *n.* **1.** An act of addressing or designating someone by name. **2.** A name; appellation. [Lat. *compellatio* < *compellare,* to address.]

com·pend (kŏm'pĕnd') *n.* A compendium.

com·pen·di·ous (kəm-pĕn'dē-əs) *adj.* Containing or stating briefly and concisely all the essentials; succinct. [ME < Med. Lat. *compendiosus* < Lat. *compedium,* a shortening. —see COMPENDIUM.] **—com·pen'di·ous·ly** *adv.* **—com·pen'di·ous·ness** *n.*

com·pen·di·um (kəm-pĕn'dē-əm) *n., pl.* **-di·ums** or **-di·a** (-dē-ə). A short, complete summary; abstract. [Lat., a shortening < *compendere,* to weigh together : *com-,* together + *pendere,* to weigh.]

com·pen·sa·ble (kəm-pĕn'sə-bəl) *adj.* **1.** Entitled to compensation. **2.** Capable of being compensated.

com·pen·sate (kŏm'pən-sāt') *v.* **-sat·ed, -sat·ing, -sates.** *—tr.* **1.** To make up for or offset; counterbalance. **2.** To make satisfactory payment or reparation to; recompense or reimburse: *compensated her for the time she worked.* **3.** To stabilize the purchasing power of (a monetary unit) by changing the gold content in order to counterbalance price variations. *—intr.* To provide with or serve as a substitute or counterbalance. [Lat. *compensare, compensat-* : *com-,* together + *pensare,* freq. of *pendere,* to weigh.] **—com'pen·sa'tive** (-sā'tĭv, kəm-pĕn'sə-tĭv) *adj.* **—com'pen·sa'tor** *n.* **—com·pen'sa·to'ry** (kəm-pĕn'sə-tôr'ē, -tōr'ē) *adj.*

com·pen·sa·tion (kŏm'pən-sā'shən) *n.* **1.** The act of compensating. **2.** Something given or received as payment or reparation, as for a service or loss. **3.** *Biol.* The counterbalancing of a functional defect by the supplementary development and activation of another organ or another part of the defective structure. **4.** *Psychol.* Behavior designed to compensate for real or imagined defects. **—com'pen·sa'tion·al** *adj.*

com·pete (kəm-pēt') *intr.v.* **-pet·ed, -pet·ing, -petes.** To strive or contend with another or others, as for profit or a prize; vie. [LLat. *competere,* to strive together : Lat. *com-,* together + Lat. *petere,* to strive.]

com·pe·tence (kŏm'pĭ-təns) *n.* **1.** The state or quality of being competent. **2.** Sufficient means for a comfortable existence. **3.** *Law.* The quality or condition of being legally qualified, eligible, or admissible. **4.** *Genetics.* The ability of bacteria to be genetically transformable.

com·pe·ten·cy (kŏm'pĭ-tən-se) *n., pl.* **-cies.** Competence.

com·pe·tent (kŏm'pĭ-tənt) *adj.* **1.** Properly or well qualified; capable: *a competent worker.* **2.** Adequate for the purpose; sufficient: *a competent performance.* **3.** *Law.* Legally qualified or fit; admissible. [ME, adequate < Lat. *competens,* pr.part. of *competere,* to be suitable : *com-,* together + *petere,* to seek.] **—com'pe·tent·ly** *adv.*

com·pe·ti·tion (kŏm'pĭ-tĭsh'ən) *n.* **1.** The act of competing, as for profit or a prize; rivalry. **2.** A contest or similar test of skill or ability: *a skating competition.* **3.** The rivalry between two or more businesses striving for the same customer or market. **4.** The one or ones against whom one competes: *The competition cornered the market.*

com·pet·i·tive (kəm-pĕt'ĭ-tĭv) *adj.* **1.** Of, involving, or determined by competition: *competitive games.* **2.** Liking or inclined to compete: *a highly competitive salesman.* **—com·pet'i·tive·ly** *adv.* **—com·pet'i·tive·ness** *n.*

com·pet·i·tor (kəm-pĕt'ĭ-tər) *n.* A person who competes, as in sports or business; rival.

com·pet·i·to·ry (kəm-pĕt'ĭ-tôr'ē, -tōr'ē) *adj.* Competitive.

com·pi·la·tion (kŏm'pə-lā'shən) *n.* **1.** The act of compiling. **2.** Something compiled, as a set of data, a report, or an anthology.

com·pile (kəm-pīl') *tr.v.* **-piled, -pil·ing, -piles. 1.** To gather into a single book. **2.** To put together or compose from materials gathered from several sources: *compile an encyclopedia.* **3.** To convert to machine language. [ME *compilen* < OFr. *compiler,* prob. < Lat. *compilare,* to plunder.]

com·pil·er (kəm-pī'lər) *n.* **1.** One that compiles. **2.** A computer program that converts a higher level language to machine language.

com·pla·cen·cy (kəm-plā'sən-sē) also **com·pla·cence** (-səns) *n.* **1.** A feeling of contentment or satisfaction; gratification. **2.** Self-satisfaction; smugness.

com·pla·cent (kəm-plā'sənt) *adj.* **1.** Contented to a fault; self-satisfied: *succeeded so often he had become complacent.* **2.** Complaisant. [Lat. *complacens, complacent-,* pr.part. of *complacēre,* to please : *com* (intensive) + *placere,* to please.] **—com·pla'cent·ly** *adv.*

com·plain (kəm-plān') *intr.v.* **-plained, -plain·ing, -plains. 1.** To express feelings of pain, dissatisfaction, or resentment. **2.** To make a formal accusation or bring a formal charge. [ME *compleinen* < OFr. *complaindre* < VLat. **complangere* : Lat. *com-* (intensive) + Lat. *plangere,* to lament.] **—com·plain'er** *n.*

com·plain·ant (kəm-plā'nənt) *n.* A person who makes a complaint or files a formal charge, as in a court of law; plaintiff.

com·plaint (kəm-plānt') *n.* **1.** An expression of pain, dissatisfaction, or resentment. **2.** A cause or reason for complaining; grievance. **3.** A cause of physical pain; malady; illness. **4.** *Law.* The presentation by the plaintiff in a civil action, setting forth the claim on which relief is sought. [ME *compleinte* < OFr. *complainte* < *complaindre,* to complain. —see COMPLAIN.]

com·plai·sance (kəm-plā'səns, -zəns) *n.* The inclination to comply willingly with the wishes of others; amiability.

com·plai·sant (kəm-plā'sənt, -zənt) *adj.* Showing a desire or willingness to please; cheerfully obliging. [Fr. < OFr., pr.part. of *complaire,* to please < Lat. *complacēre,* —see COMPLACENT.] **—com·plai'sant·ly** *adv.*

com·pleat (kəm-plēt') *adj.* Of or characterized by a highly developed or wide-ranging skill or proficiency: *She was the compleat tennis player, unparalleled in every facet of the game.* [Var. of COMPLETE.]

com·plect (kəm-plĕkt') *tr.v.* **-plect·ed, -plect·ing, -plects.** To join by weaving or twining together; interweave. [Lat. *complecti,* to entwine : *com-,* together + *plectere,* to plait.]

com·plect·ed (kəm-plĕk'tĭd) *adj. Regional.* Marked by or having a particular facial complexion: *light-complected.* [< COMPLEXION.]

com·ple·ment (kŏm'plə-mənt) *n.* **1. a.** Something that completes, makes up a whole, or brings to perfection. **b.** The quantity or number needed to make up a whole: *shelves with a full complement of books.* **c.** Either of two parts that complete the whole or mutually complete each other. **2.** An angle related to another so that the sum of their measures is 90 degrees. **3.** A word or words used after a verb to complete a predicate construction. **4.** An interval in music that completes an octave when added to a given interval. **5.** The full crew of officers and men required to man a ship. **6.** *Biochem.* The thermolabile substance found in normal blood serum that destroys pathogenic bacteria and materials. *—tr.v.* (-mĕnt') **-ment·ed, -ment·ing, -ments.** To add or serve as a complement to. [ME < Lat. *complementum* < *complere,* to fill out. —see COMPLETE.]

Usage: *Complement* and *compliment,* though quite distinct in meaning, are sometimes confused because of the context. *Complement* means "something that completes or brings to perfection": *The antique silver was a complement to the beautifully set table. Compliment* means "an expression of courtesy or praise": *He gave his hostess a compliment on her beautifully set table.*

com·ple·men·tal (kŏm'plə-mĕn'tl) *adj.* Complementary. **—com'ple·men'tal·ly** *adv.*

com·ple·men·ta·ry (kŏm'plə-mĕn'tə-rē, -trē) *adj.* **1.** Forming or serving as a complement; completing. **2.** Supplying mutual needs or lacks. **3.** Producing effects in concert different from those produced separately. Used of genes. **4.** Of or pertaining to the specific pairing of the purines and pyrimidines between the two strands of the DNA molecule. **—com'ple·men'ta·ri·ly** (-tə-rə-lē, -trə-lē, -mĕn-târ'ə-lē) *adv.* **—com'ple·men'ta·ri·ness** *n.* **—com'ple·men·tar'i·ty** (-tăr'ĭ-tē) *n.*

complementary angles *pl.n.* Two angles whose sum is 90 degrees.

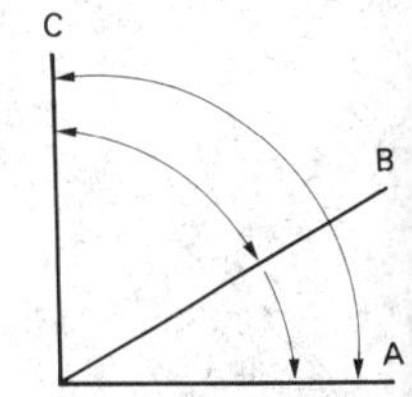

complementary angles
BOC (62°) and AOB (28°) are complementary

complementary color *n.* One of two colors that appears white or gray when ideally mixed in proper proportions, as the combination of blue-green with red.

complement fixation *n.* The joining of a complement to the antigen-antibody pair for which it is specific.

com·plete (kəm-plēt') *adj.* **-plet·er, -plet·est. 1.** Having all necessary or normal parts, components, or steps; entire; whole: *a complete meal.* **2.** *Bot.* Having all characteristic floral parts, including sepals, petals, stamens, and a pistil. **3.** Having come to an end; concluded. **4.** Thorough; consummate: *complete control.* **5.** Skilled; accomplished: *a complete musician.* *—tr.v.* **-plet·ed, -plet·ing, -pletes. 1.** To make whole or complete. **2.** To bring to an end; conclude. [ME < Lat. *completus,* p.part. of *complēre,* to fill out : *com-* (intensive) + *plēre,* to fill.] **—com·plete'ly** *adv.* **—com·plete'ness** *n.* **—com·ple'tive** *adj.*

Synonyms: *complete, close, end, finish, conclude, terminate.* These verbs mean to bring something to, or to arrive at, a stopping point or limit. *Complete* suggests the final stage in assembling parts into a whole: *complete a building,* or bringing a project to fruition: *complete a novel. Close* applies to stopping an action, either when it is completed: *The church service closes with a benediction,* or when it cannot be continued: *Lack of support caused the play to close. End* emphasizes finality: *end a career. Finish,* often interchangeable with *complete,* is especially applicable to what one has set oneself to do. *Conclude* adds to *complete* and *close* a sense of formality: *They concluded tariff negotiations. Terminate* more specifically suggests reaching an established limit in time or space.

Usage: *Complete* is sometimes held to be an absolute term like *perfect* or *chief,* which is not subject to comparison. It can be qualified by *more* or *less,* however, when its sense is "comprehensive, thorough," as in *A more complete failure than his could not be imagined.* A majority of the Usage Panel accepts the example *His book is the most complete treatment of the subject.*

complete blood count *n.* The determination of the quantity of each type of blood cell in circulation by extrapolation of the numbers found in a given blood sample.

com·ple·tion (kəm-plē′shən) *n.* **1.** The act of completing. **2.** The state of being completed.

com·plex (kəm-plĕks′, kŏm′plĕks′) *adj.* **1.** Consisting of interconnected or interwoven parts; composite. **2.** Involved or intricate, as in structure; complicated. **3.** *Gram.* **a.** Pertaining to or designating a word, such as *slowly,* consisting of at least one bound form. **b.** Pertaining to or designating a sentence consisting of an independent clause and one or more dependent clauses. —*n.* (kŏm′plĕks′). **1.** A whole composed of intricate or interconnected parts: *a complex of cities and suburbs.* **2.** *Psychiat.* A connected group of repressed ideas that compel characteristic or habitual patterns of thought, feeling, and action. **3.** *Informal.* An exaggerated or obsessive concern or fear. [Lat. *complexus,* p.part. of *complecti,* to entwine. —see COMPLECT.] **—com·plex′ly** *adv.* **—com·plex′ness** *n.*

Synonyms: *complex, complicated, intricate, involved, tangled, knotty.* These adjectives describe things having parts so interconnected as to make the whole difficult to understand. *Complex* and *complicated* are similar in indicating a challenge to the mind. *Complex,* however, often implies many varying parts; *complicated* stresses elaborate relationship of parts rather than number. *Intricate* refers to a pattern of intertwining parts that is difficult to follow. *Involved* stresses confusion arising from the commingling of parts and the consequent difficulty of separating them. *Tangled* strongly emphasizes the random twisting of many parts. *Knotty,* a less formal term applied to problems, stresses difficulty of solution.

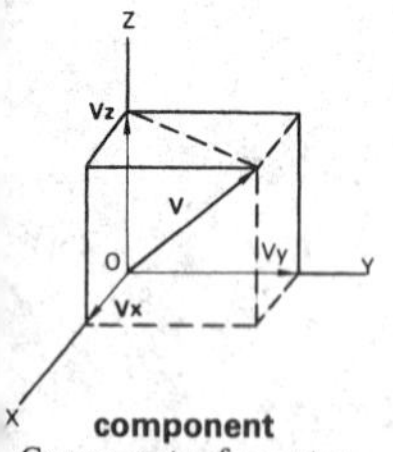

component
Components of a vector v along coordinate axes

complex conjugate *n.* **1.** A complex number that when multiplied by a given complex number yields a real number. **2.** A complex quantity that when multiplied by a given complex quantity yields a product free of imaginary terms.

complex fraction *n.* A fraction in which the numerator or denominator or both contain fractions.

com·plex·ion (kəm-plĕk′shən) *n.* **1.** The natural color, texture, and appearance of the skin, esp. of the face. **2.** General character, aspect, or appearance: *findings that will alter the complexion of the problem.* **3.** The combination of the four humors of cold, heat, moistness, and dryness in specific proportions thought in medieval physiology to control the temperament and the constitution of the body. [ME *complexioun,* physical constitution < LLat. *complexio* < Lat., combination < *complexus,* p.part. of *complecti,* to entwine. —see COMPLECT.] **—com·plex′ion·al** *adj.*

com·plex·ioned (kəm-plĕk′shənd) *adj.* Of or having a specified complexion: *fair-complexioned.*

com·plex·i·ty (kəm-plĕk′sĭ-tē) *n., pl.* **-ties. 1.** The quality or condition of being complex. **2.** Something complex: *the complexities of urban life.*

complex number *n.* A number of the form $a + bi$, where a and b are real numbers and $i^2 = -1$; a member of the set of ordered pairs (a,b) of real numbers in which a pair equals another pair if and only if corresponding members of the two pairs are identical and in which addition and multiplication are defined by $(a,b)+(c,d)=(a+c,\ b+d)$ and $(a,b)(c,d)=(ac-bd,\ ad+bc)$, respectively.

complex plane *n.* A plane that has complex numbers as its points.

complex variable *n.* An expression of the form $x+iy$, where x and y are real variables and $i^2=-1$.

com·pli·ance (kəm-plī′əns) also **com·pli·an·cy** (-ən-sē) *n.* **1.** An act of complying with a wish, request, or demand; acquiescence. **2.** A disposition or tendency to yield to others. **3. a.** The extension or displacement of a loaded structure per unit load. **b.** Flexibility.

com·pli·ant (kəm-plī′ənt) *adj.* Inclined or disposed to comply; acquiescent. **—com·pli′ant·ly** *adv.*

com·pli·ca·cy (kəm-plĭk′ə-sē) *n., pl.* **-cies. 1.** The state of being complicated. **2.** A complication.

com·pli·cate (kŏm′plĭ-kāt′) *tr. & intr.v.* **-cat·ed, -cat·ing, -cates. 1.** To make or become complex, intricate, or perplexing. **2.** To twist or become twisted together. —*adj.* (-kĭt). **1.** Complex; intricate; involved. **2.** *Biol.* Folded longitudinally one or several times, as certain leaves or the wings of some insects. [Lat. *complicare, complicat-,* to fold up : *com-,* together + *plicare,* to fold.]

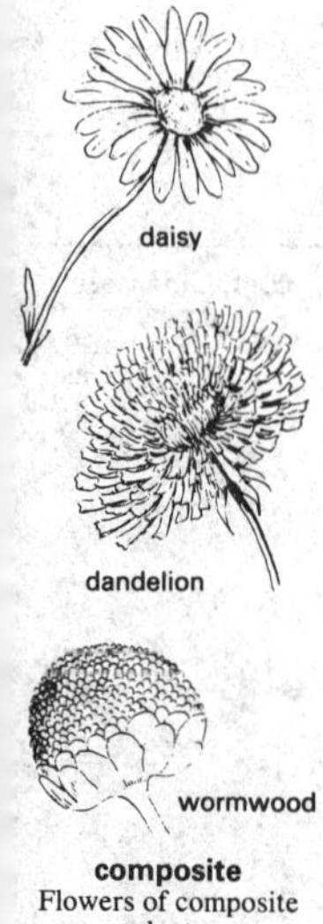

composite
Flowers of composite plants

com·pli·cat·ed (kŏm′plĭ-kā′tĭd) *adj.* **1.** Containing intricately combined or involved parts. **2.** Not easily understood or dealt with; perplexing. **—com′pli·cat′ed·ly** *adv.* **—com′pli·cat′ed·ness** *n.*

com·pli·ca·tion (kŏm′plĭ-kā′shən) *n.* **1.** The act of complicating. **2.** A confused or intricate relationship of parts. **3.** A factor, condition, or element that complicates. **4.** *Med.* A condition occurring during another disease and aggravating it.

com·plice (kŏm′plĭs) *n. Obs.* An associate or accomplice. [ME < OFr. < LLat. *complex,* closely connected : Lat. *com-,* together + Lat. *plicare,* to fold.]

com·plic·i·ty (kəm-plĭs′ĭ-tē) *n., pl.* **-ties.** Involvement as an accomplice in a crime or wrongdoing.

com·pli·er (kəm-plī′ər) *n.* One that complies.

com·pli·ment (kŏm′plə-mənt) *n.* **1.** An expression of praise, admiration, or congratulation. **2.** A formal act of civility, courtesy, or respect. **3. compliments.** Good wishes; regards: *Extend my compliments to your parents.* —*tr.v.* **-ment·ed, -ment·ing, -ments. 1.** To pay a compliment to. **2.** To show fondness, regard, or respect for by giving a gift or performing a favor. —See Usage note at **complement.** [Fr. < Sp. *cumplimento* < *cumplir,* to complete < Lat. *complēre,* to complete.]

com·pli·men·ta·ry (kŏm′plə-mĕn′tə-rē, -trē) *adj.* **1.** Expressing, using, or resembling a compliment: *a concert that received complimentary reviews.* **2.** Given free to repay a favor or as an act of courtesy: *complimentary copies of the new book.* **—com′pli·men′ta·ri·ly** *adv.*

com·plin (kŏm′plĭn) also **com·pline** (-plĭn, -plīn′) *n. Eccles.* The last of the seven canonical hours. [ME < OFr. *complie* < Med. Lat. (*hora*) *completa,* final hour < Lat. *completus,* p.part. of *complēre,* to complete.]

com·ply (kəm-plī′) *intr.v.* **-plied, -ply·ing, -plies. 1.** To act in accordance with another's command, request, rule, or wish. **2.** *Obs.* To be courteous or obedient. [Ital. *complire* < Sp. *cumplir,* to complete < Lat. *complēre.*]

com·po (kŏm′pō) *n., pl.* **-pos.** Any of various combined substances, such as mortar or plaster, formed by mixing ingredients. [Short for COMPOSITION.]

com·po·nent (kəm-pō′nənt) *n.* **1.** A constituent element, as of a system. **2.** A part of a mechanical or electrical complex. **3.** *Math.* One of a set of two or more vectors having a sum equal to a given vector. **4.** *Chem.* Any of the minimum number of substances required to specify completely the composition of all phases of a chemical system. —*adj.* Being or functioning as a component; constituent. [Lat. *componens, component-,* pr.part. of *componere,* to put together : *com-,* together + *ponere,* to put.] **—com′po·nen′tial** (kŏm′pə-nĕn′shəl) *adj.*

com·port (kəm-pôrt′, -pōrt′) *v.* **-port·ed, -port·ing, -ports.** —*tr.* To conduct or behave (oneself) in a particular manner: *comported herself with dignity.* —*intr.* To agree, correspond, or harmonize: *actions that comport with the principles of democracy.* [OFr. *comporter,* to conduct < Lat. *comportare,* to bring together : *com-,* together + *portare,* to carry.]

com·port·ment (kəm-pôrt′mənt, -pōrt′-) *n.* Bearing; deportment.

com·pose (kəm-pōz′) *v.* **-posed, -pos·ing, -pos·es.** —*tr.* **1.** To make up the constituent parts of; constitute or form: *an exhibit composed of French paintings.* **2.** To make or create by putting together parts or elements. **3.** To create or produce (a literary or musical piece). **4.** To make (one's mind or body) calm or tranquil; quiet: *compose yourself and deal with the problems.* **5.** To settle or adjust; reconcile: *composed their differences.* **6.** To arrange aesthetically or artistically. **7.** *Printing.* To arrange or set (type or matter to be printed). —*intr.* **1.** To create literary or musical pieces. **2.** *Printing.* To set type. [ME *composen* < OFr. *composer* < Lat. *componere.* —see COMPONENT.]

com·posed (kəm-pōzd′) *adj.* Not agitated; calm and self-possessed. **—com·pos′ed·ly** (-pō′zĭd-lē) *adv.* **—com·pos′ed·ness** *n.*

com·pos·er (kəm-pō′zər) *n.* A person who composes, esp. one who composes music.

composing room *n. Printing.* A room where typesetting is done.

composing stick *n. Printing.* A small shallow tray, usually metal and with an adjustable end, in which a compositor sets type by hand.

com·pos·ite (kəm-pŏz′ĭt) *adj.* **1.** Made up of distinct components; compound. **2.** *Math.* Having factors; factorable. **3.** *Bot.* Of, belonging to, or characteristic of the Compositae, a large plant family characterized by flower heads consisting of both ray flowers and disk flowers, as in the daisy, of disk flowers only, as in wormwood, or of ray flowers only, as in the dandelion. **4. Composite.** *Archit.* Pertaining to or designating the Composite order. —*n.* **1.** A composite structure or entity. **2.** A complex material, such as wood or fiber glass, in which two or more distinct, structurally complementary substances, esp. metals, ceramics, glasses, and polymers, combine to produce structural or functional properties not present in any individual component. **3.** A composite plant. [Lat. *compositus,* p.part. of *componere,* to put together. —see COMPONENT.] **—com·pos′ite·ly** *adv.* **—com·pos′ite·ness** *n.*

composite nerve *n.* A nerve that consists of both sensory and motor fibers.
composite number *n.* An integer exactly divisible by at least one number other than itself or 1.
Composite order *n. Archit.* A Roman capital formed by superimposing Ionic volutes on a Corinthian capital.
composite photograph *n.* A photograph made by combining two or more separate photographs.
com·po·si·tion (kŏm′pə-zĭsh′ən) *n.* **1. a.** A putting together of parts or elements to form a whole. **b.** The manner in which such parts are combined or related; constitution; make-up. **c.** The result or product of composing; mixture; compound. **2.** The arrangement of artistic parts so as to form a unified whole. **3. a.** The art or act of composing a literary or musical work. **b.** A work of art, literature, or music or its structure or organization. **4.** A short essay, esp. one written as a school exercise. **5.** *Law.* **a.** A settlement whereby the creditors of a debtor about to enter bankruptcy agree to accept partial payment in lieu of full payment for debts. **b.** The sum agreed upon. **6.** Settlement by mutual agreement or compromise. **7.** *Ling.* The formation of compounds from separate words. **8.** *Printing.* Typesetting. [ME *composicioun* < Lat. *compositio* < *componere,* to put together. —see COMPONENT.] **—com′po·si′tion·al** *adj.* **—com′po·si′tion·al·ly** *adv.*
composition of forces *n.* The finding or determination of a vector that is the resultant of a given set of forces.
com·pos·i·tive (kəm-pŏz′ĭ-tĭv) *adj.* Compounded; synthetic.
com·pos·i·tor (kəm-pŏz′ĭ-tər) *n. Printing.* A typesetter. **—com·pos′i·to′ri·al** (-tôr′ē-əl, -tōr′-) *adj.*
com·pos men·tis (kŏm′pəs mĕn′tĭs) *adj.* Of sound mind; sane. [Lat., having mastery of the mind.]
com·post (kŏm′pōst′) *n.* **1.** A mixture of decaying organic matter, such as leaves and manure, used as fertilizer. **2.** A composition; mixture. —*tr.v.* **-post·ed, -post·ing, -posts.** **1.** To fertilize with compost. **2.** To convert (vegetable matter) to compost. [ME, compote < OFr. —see COMPOTE.]
com·po·sure (kəm-pō′zhər) *n.* Tranquillity of mind; calmness and self-possession. [< COMPOSE.]
com·pote (kŏm′pōt) *n.* **1.** Fruit stewed or cooked in syrup. **2.** A long-stemmed dish used for holding fruit, nuts, or candy. [Fr. < OFr. *composte* < Lat. *compositus,* put together. —see COMPOSITE.]
com·pound[1] (kŏm-pound′, kəm-, kŏm′pound′) *v.* **-pound·ed, -pound·ing, -pounds.** —*tr.* **1.** To combine so as to form a whole; mix. **2.** To produce or create by combining two or more ingredients or parts: *pharmacists compounding prescriptions.* **3.** To settle (a debt, for example) by agreeing on an amount less than the claim; adjust. **4.** To compute (interest) on the principal and accrued interest. **5.** *Law.* To agree, for payment or other consideration, not to prosecute: *compound a felony.* **6.** To add to; increase: *High winds compounded the difficulties of the firefighters.* —*intr.* **1.** To combine in or form a compound. **2.** To come to terms; agree. —*adj.* (kŏm′pound′, kŏm-pound′, kəm-). Consisting of two or more substances, ingredients, elements, or parts. —*n.* (kŏm′pound′). **1.** A combination of two or more elements or parts. **2.** A word, as *loudspeaker* or *baby-sit,* containing two or more elements that have perceptible lexical meaning. **3.** *Chem.* A pure, macroscopically homogeneous substance consisting of atoms or ions of two or more different elements in definite proportions, and usually having properties unlike those of its constituent elements. [ME *compounen* < Lat. *componere.* —see COMPONENT.] **—com·pound′a·ble** *adj.* **—com·pound′er** *n.*
com·pound[2] (kŏm′pound′) *n.* **1.** A building or buildings, esp. a residence or group of residences, set off and enclosed by a barrier. **2.** A compound used for confining prisoners of war. [Malay *kampong,* village.]
com·pound-com·plex sentence (kŏm′pound-kŏm′plĕks′) *n.* A sentence consisting of at least two coordinate independent clauses and one or more dependent clauses.
compound eye *n.* The eye of most insects and some crustaceans, composed of many light-sensitive elements, each with its own refractive system and each forming a portion of an image.
compound flower *n.* A flower head of a composite plant, consisting of numerous small flowers appearing as a single bloom.
compound fraction *n.* A complex fraction.
compound fracture *n.* A fracture in which broken bone lacerates soft tissue.
compound interest *n.* Interest computed on the accumulated unpaid interest as well as on the original principal.
compound leaf *n.* A leaf consisting of two or more separate leaflets borne on a single leafstalk.
compound lens *n.* Lens (sense 1.b.).
compound microscope *n.* A microscope consisting of an objective and an eyepiece at opposite ends of an adjustable tube.
compound number *n.* A quantity, such as 10 pounds 5 ounces or 3 feet 4 inches, involving different units of measure.
compound sentence *n.* A sentence of two or more coordinate independent clauses, often joined by a conjunction or conjunctions, as *The problem was difficult, but I finally found the answer.*
com·pra·dor also **com·pra·dore** (kŏm′prə-dôr′) *n.* In China and certain other Asian countries, a native agent formerly employed by a foreign business to serve as an intermediary in commercial transactions. [Port. < LLat. *comparator,* buyer < Lat. *comparare,* to buy : *com-,* together + *parare,* to get.]
com·pre·hend (kŏm′prĭ-hĕnd′) *tr.v.* **-hend·ed, -hend·ing, -hends.** **1.** To grasp mentally; understand or know. **2.** To take in, include, or embrace; comprise: *Greater Boston comprehends the surrounding suburbs.* [ME *comprehenden* < Lat. *comprehendere : com-,* together + *prehendere,* to grasp.] **—com′pre·hend′i·ble** *adj.*
com·pre·hen·si·ble kŏm′prĭ-hĕn′sə-bəl) *adj.* Capable of being comprehended or understood; intelligible. [Lat. *comprehensibilis* < *comprehensus,* p.part. of *comprehendere,* to comprehend.] **—com′pre·hen′si·bil′i·ty, com′pre·hen′si·ble·ness** *n.* **—com·pre·hen′si·bly** *adv.*
com·pre·hen·sion (kŏm′prĭ-hĕn′shən) *n.* **1. a.** The act or fact of comprehending; understanding. **b.** Knowledge that is acquired through comprehending. **2.** The capacity to include; comprehensiveness. **3.** The attributes implied by a term in logic. [ME *comprehensioun* < Lat. *comprehensio* < *comprehensus,* p.part. of *comprehendere,* to comprehend.]
com·pre·hen·sive (kŏm′prĭ-hĕn′sĭv) *adj.* **1.** Including or comprehending much; large in scope or content: *a comprehensive history of the revolution.* **2.** Marked by or showing extensive understanding: *comprehensive knowledge.* —*n.* **1.** Often **comprehensives.** *Informal.* Examinations covering the entire field of major study, given in the final undergraduate or graduate year of college. **2.** An advertising layout showing all the elements planned for an advertisement but not ready for actual reproduction. [Lat. *comprehensivus* < *comprehensus,* p.part. of *comprehendere,* to comprehend.] **—com′pre·hen′sive·ly** *adv.* **—com′pre·hen′sive·ness** *n.*
com·press (kəm-prĕs′) *tr.v.* **-pressed, -press·ing, -press·es.** **1.** To press or squeeze together. **2.** To shorten or condense as if by pressing or squeezing. —*n.* (kŏm′prĕs′). **1.** *Med.* A soft pad of gauze or other material applied to a part of the body to control hemorrhage or, moistened with water or medication, to alleviate pain or reduce infection. **2.** A machine or establishment for baling cotton. [ME *compressen* < LLat. *compressare,* freq. of Lat. *comprimere : com-,* together + *premere,* to press.]

compote

com·pressed (kəm-prĕst′) *adj.* **1.** Pressed together or into less space; made compact. **2.** *Biol.* Flattened laterally or lengthwise, as certain seed pods or the bodies of many fish.
compressed air *n.* Air under greater than atmospheric pressure, esp. when used to power a mechanical device or provide a portable supply of oxygen.
com·press·i·ble (kəm-prĕs′ə-bəl) *adj.* Capable of being compressed. **—com·press′i·bil′i·ty, com·press′i·ble·ness** *n.*
com·pres·sion (kəm-prĕsh′ən) *n.* **1. a.** The act or process of compressing. **b.** The state of being compressed. **2. a.** The process by which the working substance in a heat engine, as the vapor mixture in the cylinder of an internal-combustion engine, is compressed. **b.** The engine cycle during which this process occurs. **—com·pres′sion·al** *adj.*
compression wave or **compressional wave** *n.* A wave, as of sound, propagated by means of the compression of an elastic medium.
com·pres·sive (kəm-prĕs′ĭv) *adj.* Compressing or capable of compressing. **—com·pres′sive·ly** *adv.*
com·pres·sor (kəm-prĕs′ər) *n.* One that compresses, esp. a machine used to compress gases.
com·prise (kəm-prīz′) *tr.v.* **-prised, -pris·ing, -pris·es.** **1.** To consist of; be composed of. **2.** To include; contain. [ME *comprisen* < *comprised,* included < OFr. *compris,* p.part. of *comprendre* < Lat. *comprehendere.* —see COMPREHEND.] **—com·pris′a·ble** *adj.*

Usage: The traditional rule states that the whole *comprises* the parts; the parts *compose* the whole. In strict usage: *The Union comprises fifty states. Fifty states compose* (or *constitute* or *make up*) *the Union.* While this distinction is still maintained by many writers, *comprise* is increasingly used, especially in the passive, in place of *compose: The Union is comprised of fifty states.* That use of *comprise* is considered unacceptable by a majority of the Usage Panel.

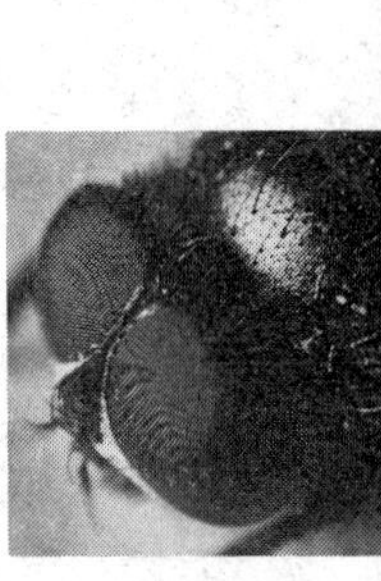

compound eye
Compound eyes of a fly

com·pro·mise (kŏm′prə-mīz′) *n.* **1. a.** A settlement of differences in which each side makes concessions. **b.** Something resulting from such a settlement. **2.** Something that combines certain qualities of different things. **3.** A concession to something that is detrimental or pejorative: *a compromise of morality.* —*v.* **-mised, -mis·ing, -mis·es.** —*tr.* **1.** To settle by concessions. **2.** To expose or make liable to danger, suspicion, or disrepute. **3.** *Obs.* To pledge mutually. —*intr.* To make a compromise. [ME *compromis* < OFr. < Lat. *compromissum,* mutual promise < *compromittere,* to promise mutually : *com-,* together + *promittere,* to promise. —see PROMISE.] **—com′pro·mis′er** *n.*
Compton effect (kŏmp′tən) *n.* The increase in wavelength of electromagnetic radiation, esp. of an x-ray or gamma-ray photon, scattered by an electron. [After A.H. *Compton* (1892–1962), its discoverer.]
comp·trol·ler (kən-trō′lər) *n.* Variant of **controller** (sense 2).

compound leaf
Of a cow vetch

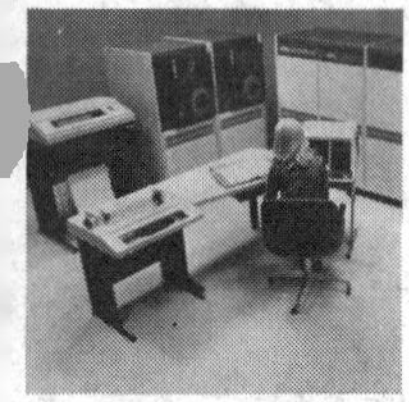

computer

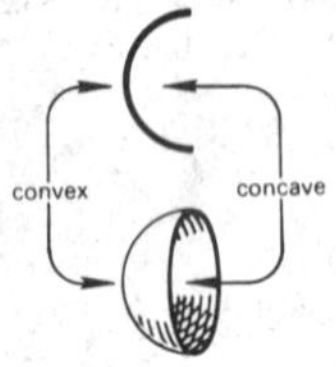

concave

com·pul·sion (kəm-pŭl′shən) *n.* **1. a.** The act of compelling. **b.** The state of being compelled. **2.** *Psychol.* **a.** An irresistible impulse to act, regardless of the rationality of the motivation. **b.** An act or acts performed in response to such an impulse. [ME < LLat. *compulsio* < Lat. *compellere,* to compel. —see COMPEL.]

com·pul·sive (kəm-pŭl′sĭv) *adj.* **1.** Having the capacity to compel. **2.** *Psychol.* Caused or conditioned by compulsion or obsession. **—com·pul′sive·ly** *adv.* **—com·pul′sive·ness** *n.*

com·pul·so·ry (kəm-pŭl′sə-rē) *adj.* **1.** Employing or exerting compulsion; coercive. **2.** Obligatory; required: *a compulsory examination.* **—com·pul′so·ri·ly** *adv.* **—com·pul′so·ri·ness** *n.*

com·punc·tion (kəm-pŭngk′shən) *n.* **1.** A strong uneasiness caused by a sense of guilt; remorse: *felt no compunctions about lying.* **2.** A feeling of uncertainty about the fitness or correctness of an action. [ME *compunccioun* < Med. Lat. *compunctio,* sting of conscience < Lat., puncture < *compungere,* to sting : *com-* (intensive) + *pungere,* to prick.] **—com·punc′tious** (-shəs) *adj.* **—com·punc′tious·ly** *adv.*

com·pur·ga·tion (kŏm′pər-gā′shən) *n. Law.* The practice of clearing an accused person of a charge by having a number of people swear to a belief in his innocence. [LLat. *compurgatio,* complete purification < Lat. *compurgare,* to purify completely : *com-* (intensive) + *purgare,* to purify.]

com·pu·ta·tion (kŏm′pyo͞o-tā′shən) *n.* **1. a.** The act or process of computing. **b.** A method of computing. **2.** The result of computing. **3.** The act of operating a computer. **—com′pu·ta′tion·al** *adj.* **—com′pu·ta′tion·al·ly** *adv.*

com·pute (kəm-pyo͞ot′) *v.* **-put·ed, -put·ing, -putes.** *—tr.* **1.** To determine by mathematics, esp. by numerical methods: *computed the tax due.* **2.** To determine by the use of a computer. *—intr.* **1.** To determine an amount or number. **2.** To use a computer. *—n.* Computation: *amounts beyond compute.* [Lat. *computare* : *com-,* together + *putare,* to reckon.] **—com·put′a·bil′i·ty** *n.* **—com·put′a·ble** *adj.*

com·put·er (kəm-pyo͞o′tər) *n.* **1.** A person who computes. **2.** A device that computes, esp. an electronic machine that performs high-speed mathematical or logical calculations or that assembles, stores, correlates, or otherwise processes and prints information derived from coded data in accordance with a predetermined program.

com·put·er·ese (kəm-pyo͞o′tə-rēz′,-rēs′) *n.* The technical language or jargon of the computer profession.

com·put·er·ize (kəm-pyo͞o′tə-rīz′) *tr.v.* **-ized, -iz·ing, -iz·es.** **1.** To process or store (information) with or in an electronic computer or system of computers. **2.** To furnish with a computer or computer system. **—com·put′er·iz′a·ble** *adj.* **—com·put′er·i·za′tion** *n.*

com·put·er·ized (kəm-pyo͞o′tə-rīzd′) *adj.* Of or pertaining to a computer or the use of a computer.

computerized axial tomography *n.* Tomography in which computer analysis of a series of cross-sectional scans made along a single axis of a structure is used to construct a three-dimensional image.

computer language *n.* A code used to provide data and instructions to computers.

com·rade (kŏm′răd′, -rəd) *n.* **1.** A person who shares one's interests or activities; friend; companion. **2.** Often **Comrade.** A fellow member of a group, esp. a fellow member of the Communist Party. [OFr. *camarade,* roommate < OSp. *camarada* < *camara,* room < LLat. *camera.* —see CHAMBER.] **—com′rade·ship′** *n.*

Com·sat (kŏm′săt′). A trademark for a communications satellite.

Com·stock·er·y (kŏm′stŏk′ə-rē, kŭm′-) *n.* Overzealous censorship of literature and the other arts because of alleged immorality. [After Anthony *Comstock* (1844–1915).]

Com·tism (kŏm′tĭz-əm) *n.* The philosophy of Auguste Comte; positivism. **—Com′tist** (kŏm′tĭst) *n.*

Co·mus (kō′məs) *n.* A classical deity of revelry. [Lat. < Gk. *Kōmos* < *kōmos,* revel.]

con[1] (kŏn) *adv.* In opposition to or disagreement with; against: *debate pro and con.* *—n.* **1.** An argument or opinion against something. **2.** A person or group holding an opposing opinion. [Short for CONTRA-.]

con[2] (kŏn) *tr.v.* **conned, con·ning, cons.** **1.** To study, peruse, or examine carefully. **2.** To learn or commit to memory. [ME *connen,* to know < OE *cunnan.*] **—con′ner** *n.*

con[3] also **conn** (kŏn) *Naut.* *—tr.v.* **conned, con·ning, cons** also **conns.** To direct the steering or course of (a vessel). *—n.* **1.** The station or post of the person who cons. **2.** The act or process of conning. [ME *conduen* < OFr. *conduire* < Lat. *conducere,* to lead together. —see CONDUCE.]

con[4] (kŏn) *Slang.* *—tr.v.* **conned, con·ning, cons.** To swindle or defraud (a victim) by first winning his confidence; dupe. *—n.* A swindle. [Short for CONFIDENCE.]

con[5] (kŏn) *n. Slang.* A convict.

con- *pref.* Variant of **com-.**

con a·mo·re (kŏn′ ə-môr′ē, -mōr′ē, kōn′ ä-mō′rā) *adv. Mus.* Lovingly; tenderly. Used as a direction. [Ital., with love.]

co·na·tion (kō-nā′shən) *n. Psychol.* The aspect of mental processes or behavior directed toward action or change and including impulse, desire, volition, and striving. [Lat. *conatio,* effort < *conatus,* p.part. of *conari,* to try.] **—co·na′tion·al** *adj.* **—co′na·tive** (kŏ′nə-tĭv, kōn′ə-) *adj.*

co·na·tus (kō-nā′təs) *n., pl.* **conatus.** A natural tendency, impulse, or directed effort. [Lat., effort < p.part. of *conari,* to try.]

con bri·o (kŏn brē′ō, kōn) *adv. Mus.* With spirit and vigor. Used as a direction. [Ital., with vigor.]

con·cat·e·nate (kŏn-kăt′n-āt′, kən-) *tr.v.* **-nat·ed, -nat·ing, -nates.** To connect or link in a series or chain. *—adj.* (-nĭt, -nāt′). Connected or linked in a series. [LLat. *concatenare, concatenat-* : *com-,* together + *catenare,* to bind < Lat. *catena,* chain.] **—con·cat′e·na′tion** *n.*

con·cave (kŏn-kāv′, kŏn′kāv′) *adj.* Curved like the inner surface of a sphere. *—n.* A concave surface, structure, or line. *—tr.v.* **-caved, -cav·ing, -caves.** To make concave. [ME < Lat. *concavus* : *com-* (intensive) + *cavus,* hollow.] **—con·cave′ly** *adv.* **—con·cave′ness** *n.*

con·cav·i·ty (kŏn-kăv′ĭ-tē) *n., pl.* **-ties.** **1.** The condition or state of being concave. **2.** A concave surface or structure.

con·ca·vo-con·cave (kŏn-kā′vō-kŏn-kāv′) *adj.* Concave on both surfaces, as certain lenses.

con·ca·vo-con·vex (kŏn-kā′vō-kŏn-vĕks′) *adj.* **1.** Concave on one side and convex on the other. **2.** Designating a lens with greater concave than convex curvature.

con·ceal (kən-sēl′) *tr.v.* **-cealed, -ceal·ing, -ceals.** To hide or keep from observation, discovery, or understanding; keep secret. [ME *concelen* < OFr. *conceler* < Lat. *concelare* : *com-* (intensive) + *celare,* to hide.] **—con·ceal′a·ble** *adj.* **—con·ceal′er** *n.* **—con·ceal′ment** *n.*

con·cede (kən-sēd′) *v.* **-ced·ed, -ced·ing, -cedes.** *—tr.* **1.** To acknowledge as true, just, or proper, often unwillingly; admit: *conceding defeat.* **2.** To yield or grant as a privilege or right. *—intr.* To make a concession: yield. [Fr. *concéder* < Lat. *concedere* : *com-* (intensive) + *cedere,* to yield.] **—con·ced′ed·ly** (-sē′dĭd-lē) *adv.* **—con·ced′er** *n.*

con·ceit (kən-sēt′) *n.* **1.** Too high an opinion of one's abilities, worth, or personality; vanity. **2.** An ingenious or witty thought or expression. **3. a.** An elaborate or exaggerated metaphor. **b.** The use of such metaphors. **4.** A fanciful thought or idea. **5.** A fancy article. *—tr.v.* **-ceit·ed, -ceit·ing, -ceits.** **1.** *Obs.* To understand; conceive. **2.** *Regional.* To imagine. **3.** *Chiefly Brit. Regional.* To take a fancy to; think well of. [ME *conceite,* mind < *conceiven,* to conceive.]

con·ceit·ed (kən-sē′tĭd) *adj.* **1.** Holding too high an opinion of oneself; vain. **2.** *Regional.* Inclined to be fanciful or whimsical. **—con·ceit′ed·ly** *adv.* **—con·ceit′ed·ness** *n.*

con·ceive (kən-sēv′) *v.* **-ceived, -ceiv·ing, -ceives.** *—tr.* **1.** To become pregnant with. **2.** To form or develop in the mind; devise: *conceive a plan to increase profits.* **3.** To apprehend mentally; understand: *can't conceive your meaning.* **4.** To think or believe; hold an opinion: *didn't conceive that such a tragedy could occur.* *—intr.* **1.** To form or hold an idea: *Ancient peoples conceived of the earth as flat.* **2.** To become pregnant. [ME *conceiven* < OFr. *concevoir* < Lat. *concipere* : *com-* (intensive) + *capere,* to take.] **—con·ceiv′a·bil′i·ty, con·ceiv′a·ble·ness** *n.* **—con·ceiv′a·ble** *adj.* **—con·ceiv′a·bly** *adv.* **—con·ceiv′er** *n.*

con·cel·e·brate (kən-sĕl′ə-brāt′) *intr.v.* **-brat·ed, -brat·ing, -brates.** To take part in a concelebration. **—con·cel′e·brant** (-brənt) *n.*

con·cel·e·bra·tion (kən-sĕl′ə-brā′shən) *n.* The celebration of the Eucharist by two or more clergymen.

con·cen·ter (kən-sĕn′tər, kŏn-) *tr. & intr.v.* **-tered, -ter·ing, -ters.** To direct toward or come together at a common center. [OFr. *concentrer,* to concentrate < VLat. **concentrare.* —see CONCENTRATE.]

con·cen·trate (kŏn′sən-trāt′) *v.* **-trat·ed, -trat·ing, -trates.** *—tr.* **1. a.** To direct or draw toward a common center; focus. **b.** To gather together in one main body or power: *Authority was concentrated in the president.* **2.** *Chem.* To increase the concentration of (a solution or mixture). *—intr.* **1.** To converge toward or meet in a common center. **2.** To direct one's thoughts or attention: *concentrating on the task before us.* *—n. Chem.* A product of concentration. *—adj.* Concentrated. [VLat. **concentrare, concentrat-* : Lat. *com-,* together + Lat. *centrum,* center. —see CENTER.] **—con′cen·tra′tive** *adj.* **—con′cen·tra′tive·ly** *adv.* **—con′cen·tra′tor** *n.*

con·cen·tra·tion (kŏn′sən-trā′shən) *n.* **1. a.** The act or process of concentrating, esp. close, undivided attention. **b.** The condition of being concentrated. **2.** Something that has been concentrated. **3.** *Chem.* The amount of a specified substance in a unit amount of another substance.

concentration camp *n.* A camp where prisoners of war, enemy aliens, and political prisoners are confined.

concentration gradient *n.* The difference in concentration of a solute per unit distance of a solution.

con·cen·tric (kən-sĕn′trĭk) also **con·cen·tri·cal** (-trĭ-kəl) *adj.* Having a common center. [ME *concentrik* < Med. Lat. *concentricus* : Lat. *com-,* same + *centrum,* center. —see CENTER.] **—con·cen′tri·cal·ly** *adv.* **—con′cen·tric′i·ty** (kŏn′-sĕn-trĭs′ĭ-tē) *n.*

con·cept (kŏn′sĕpt′) *n.* **1.** A general idea or understanding, esp. one derived from specific instances or occurrences. **2.** A thought or notion. [LLat. *conceptus* < p.part. of *concipere,* to conceive.]

Usage: *Concept* is frequently used as a synonym for *conception* or *idea.* Traditionally, *concept* is used for a general abstract idea: *The concept of democracy* (meaning "the general idea of a democratic state") *began with the Greeks. Conception* is used to refer to a particular mental picture or understanding of a concept: *Our conception of democracy* (meaning "our particular understanding of what democracy is") *is quite different from the Greeks.*

con·cep·ta·cle (kən-sĕp'tə-kəl) *n.* An external cavity containing reproductive structures in certain algae and fungi. [Fr. < Lat. *conceptaculum,* receptacle < *concipere,* to conceive.]

con·cep·tion (kən-sĕp'shən) *n.* **1. a.** The formation of a zygote capable of survival and maturation in normal conditions. **b.** The entity so formed; embryo; zygote. **2. a.** The ability to form or understand mental concepts. **b.** Something that is conceived in the mind; a concept, plan, design, idea, or thought. **3.** *Archaic.* A beginning; start. —See Usage note at **concept.** [ME *concepcioun* < Lat. *conceptio* < *concipere,* to conceive.] **—con·cep'tion·al** *adj.*

con·cep·tive (kən-sĕp'tĭv) *adj.* Capable of or pertaining to conceiving. **—con·cep'tive·ly** *adv.*

con·cep·tu·al (kən-sĕp'cho͞o-əl) *adj.* Of, consisting of, or pertaining to concepts or conception. **—con·cep'tu·al·ly** *adv.*

con·cep·tu·al·ism (kən-sĕp'cho͞o-ə-lĭz'əm) *n. Philos.* The doctrine, intermediate between nominalism and realism, that universals, or abstract concepts, exist only within the mind and have no external or substantial reality. **—con·cep'tu·al·ist** *n.* **—con·cep'tu·al·is'tic** *adj.* **—con·cep'tu·al·is'ti·cal·ly** *adv.*

con·cep·tu·al·ize (kən-sĕp'cho͞o-ə-līz') *v.* **-ized, -iz·ing, -iz·es.** *—tr.* To form a concept or concepts of. *—intr.* To form concepts. **—con·cep'tu·al·i·za'tion** *n.*

con·cern (kən-sûrn') *v.* **-cerned, -cern·ing, -cerns.** *—tr.* **1.** To pertain or relate to; be about: *an article concerning the energy crisis.* **2.** To have an effect on; be of interest or importance to: *a problem that concerns us all.* **3.** To engage the attention of; involve: *concerned herself with his health.* **4.** To cause anxiety or uneasiness in; trouble: *His unreliability concerns me.* *—intr. Obs.* To be of importance. *—n.* **1.** A matter that relates to or affects one. **2.** Regard for or interest in someone or something: *The doctor's concern sped her recovery.* **3.** Anxiety; worry: *filled with concern about his illness.* **4.** A business establishment or enterprise; company. **5.** *Informal.* A material article or contrivance. [ME *concernen* < Med. Lat. *concernere* < Lat., to mix : *com-,* together + *cernere,* to sift.]

con·cerned (kən-sûrnd') *adj.* **1.** Interested and involved: *concerned with foreign policy.* **2.** Anxious; troubled: *concerned about his future.*

con·cern·ing (kən-sûr'nĭng) *prep.* In reference to; regarding.

con·cern·ment (kən-sûrn'mənt) *n.* **1.** A matter that is of concern to one. **2.** Reference, relation, or importance. **3.** Anxiety; worry.

con·cert (kŏn'sûrt', -sərt) *n.* **1.** A musical performance given by one or more singers or instrumentalists or both. **2.** Agreement in purpose, feeling, or action. *—v.* (kən-sûrt') **-cert·ed, -cert·ing, -certs.** *—tr.* **1.** To plan or arrange by mutual agreement. **2.** To contrive or devise. *—intr.* To act together in harmony. **—idiom. in concert.** All together: *working in concert with colleagues.* [Fr. < Ital. *concerto* < OItal. *concertare,* to harmonize.]

con·cert·ed (kən-sûr'tĭd) *adj.* **1.** Planned or accomplished together; combined: *a concerted attempt to solve the problem.* **2.** *Mus.* Arranged in parts for voices or instruments. **—con·cert'ed·ly** *adv.*

concert grand *n.* The largest grand piano, being roughly nine feet in length.

con·cer·ti·na (kŏn'sər-tē'nə) *n.* A small, hexagonal accordion with bellows and with buttons for keys. [CONCERT + Ital. *-ina,* fem. dim. suffix.]

con·cer·ti·no (kŏn'chĕr-tē'nō) *n., pl.* **-nos.** *Mus.* **1.** A short concerto. **2.** The solo instrument group in a concerto grosso. [Ital., dim. of *concerto,* concert. —see CONCERT.]

con·cer·tize (kŏn'sər-tīz') *intr.v.* **-tized, -tiz·ing, -tiz·es.** To give or perform in concerts.

con·cert·mas·ter (kŏn'sərt-măs'tər) *n.* The first violinist and assistant conductor in a symphony orchestra.

con·cer·to (kən-chĕr'tō) *n., pl.* **-tos** or **-ti** (-tē). A composition for an orchestra and one or more solo instruments, typically in three movements. [Ital., concert.]

concerto gros·so (grō'sō) *n., pl.* **con·cer·ti gros·si** (kən-chĕr'tē grō'sē). A composition for a small group of solo instruments and a full orchestra. [Ital., great concerto.]

concert pitch *n.* **1.** A pitch to which orchestral instruments are tuned. **2.** The state of being ready and tensely alert.

con·ces·sion (kən-sĕsh'ən) *n.* **1.** The act of conceding. **2.** Something conceded. **3.** Something, such as a land tract or franchise, granted by a government or controlling authority to be used for a specific purpose. **4. a.** The privilege of maintaining a subsidiary business within certain premises. **b.** The space allotted for such a business. [ME < Lat. *concessio* < *concedere,* to concede. —see CONCEDE.] **—con·ces'sion·al** *adj.* **—con·ces'sion·ar'y** (-ə-nĕr'ē) *adj.*

con·ces·sion·aire (kən-sĕsh'ə-nâr') also **con·ces·sion·er** (-sĕsh'ə-nər) *n.* The operator of a concession. [Fr.]

con·ces·sive (kən-sĕs'ĭv) *adj.* **1.** Of the nature of or containing a concession. **2.** *Gram.* Expressing concession, as the conjunction *though.* [Lat. *concessivus* < *concessus,* p.part. of *concedere,* to concede. —see CONCEDE.] **—con·ces'sive·ly** *adv.*

conch (kŏngk, kŏnch) *n., pl.* **conchs** (kŏngks) or **conch·es** (kŏn'chĭz). **1.** Any of various tropical marine gastropod mollusks of the genus *Strombus* and other genera, having large, often brightly colored spiral shells and edible flesh. **2.** The shell of a conch, used for ornament, in making cameos, or as a horn. **3.** A concha. [ME *conche* < OFr. < Lat. *concha,* mussel < Gk. *konkhē.*]

conch– *pref.* Variant of **concho-.**

con·cha (kŏng'kə) *n., pl.* **-chae** (-kē'). **1.** *Anat.* A shell-like structure such as the external ear. **2.** *Archit.* The half dome over an apse. [Lat., mussel < Gk. *konkhē.*] **—con'chal** (-kəl) *adj.*

conchi- *pref.* Variant of **concho-.**

con·chif·er·ous (kŏng-kĭf'ər-əs) *adj.* Having or forming a shell.

con·chi·o·lin (kŏng-kī'ə-lĭn, kŏn-) *n.* A protein substance that is the organic basis of mollusk shells. [CONCH + -OL + -IN.]

concho– or **conchi–** or **conch–** *pref.* Shell: *conchology.* [Gk. *konkho-* < *konkhē,* shell.]

con·choi·dal (kŏng-koid'l) *adj.* Of or pertaining to rocks, such as flint or obsidian, having shell-like surfaces when fractured. [Gk. *konkhoeidēs,* mussellike : *konkhē,* mussel + *-eidēs,* -oid.] **—con·chol'dal·ly** *adv.*

con·chol·o·gy (kŏng-kŏl'ə-jē) *n.* The study of mollusks and shells. **—con'cho·log'i·cal** (-kə-lŏj'ĭ-kəl) *adj.* **—con·chol'o·gist** *n.*

con·cierge (kôɴ-syârzh') *n.* A person, esp. in France, who lives in a building, attends the entrance, and serves as a janitor. [Fr. < OFr. *cumcerges* < VLat. **conservius* < Lat. *conservus,* fellow slave : *com-* together + *servus,* slave.]

con·cil·i·ar (kən-sĭl'ē-ər) *adj.* Of or pertaining to a council. [< Lat. *concilium,* council.]

con·cil·i·ate (kən-sĭl'ē-āt') *tr.v.* **-at·ed, -at·ing, -ates. 1.** To overcome the distrust or animosity of; placate. **2.** To regain (friendship, for example) by pleasant behavior. **3.** To make consistent; reconcile. [Lat. *conciliare, conciliat-* < *concilium,* meeting.] **—con·cil'i·a·ble** (-ə-bəl) *adj.* **—con·cil'i·a'tion** *n.* **—con·cil'i·a'tor** *n.* **—con·cil'i·a·to'ry** (-ə-tôr'ē, -tōr'ē) *adj.*

con·cin·ni·ty (kən-sĭn'ĭ-tē) *n., pl.* **-ties. 1.** A skillful, harmonious arrangement of parts. **2.** Elegance of literary style. [< Lat. *concinnitas* < *concinnus,* deftly joined.]

con·cise (kən-sīs') *adj.* Expressing much in few words; clear and succinct. [Lat. *concisus,* p.part. of *concidere,* to cut up : *com-* (intensive) + *caedere,* to cut.] **—con·cise'ly** *adv.* **—con·cise'ness** *n.*

con·ci·sion (kən-sĭzh'ən) *n.* **1.** The state or quality of being concise. **2.** *Archaic.* A cutting apart or off.

con·clave (kŏn'klāv', kŏng'-) *n.* **1.** A confidential or secret meeting. **2. a.** The private rooms in which the cardinals of the Roman Catholic Church meet to elect a pope. **b.** The meeting held to elect a pope. [ME, private chamber < Lat. : *com-,* together + *clavis,* key.]

con·clude (kən-klo͞od') *v.* **-clud·ed, -clud·ing, -cludes.** *—tr.* **1.** To bring to an end; close: *concluded the rally with the national anthem.* **2.** To bring about an agreement or settlement; settle finally: *conclude a peace treaty.* **3.** To reach a decision or form an opinion about; infer or deduce: *The jury concluded that he was guilty.* **4.** To determine; decide; resolve: *concluded that he had to quit.* **5.** *Obs.* To confine or enclose. *—intr.* **1.** To come to an end; close. **2.** To form a final judgment; come to a decision or an agreement. [ME *concluden* < Lat. *concludere* : *com-* (intensive) + *claudere,* to close.] **—con·clud'er** *n.*

con·clu·sion (kən-klo͞o'zhən) *n.* **1.** The close or last part of something; end; finish. **2.** The outcome or result of an act or process. **3.** A judgment or decision reached after deliberation. **4.** A final arrangement or settlement, as of a treaty. **5.** *Law.* The close of a plea or deed. **6.** *Logic.* **a.** In a syllogism, the proposition that must follow from the major and minor premises. **b.** The proposition concluded from one or more premises; deduction. [ME *conclusioun* < Lat. *conclusio* < *concludere,* to end. —see CONCLUDE.]

con·clu·sive (kən-klo͞o'sĭv) *adj.* Serving to put an end to doubt, question, or uncertainty; decisive. **—con·clu'sive·ly** *adv.* **—con·clu'sive·ness** *n.*

con·coct (kən-kŏkt') *tr.v.* **-coct·ed, -coct·ing, -cocts. 1.** To prepare by mixing ingredients, as in cookery. **2.** To invent or devise; contrive: *concoct a mystery story.* [Lat. *concoquere, concoct-,* to boil together : *com-,* together + *coquere,* to cook.] **—con·coct'er, con·coc'tor** *n.* **—con·coc'tion** *n.* **—con·coc'tive** *adj.*

con·com·i·tance (kən-kŏm'ĭ-təns) *n.* **1.** Occurrence together or in connection with another; accompaniment. **2.** A concomitant.

con·com·i·tant (kən-kŏm'ĭ-tənt) *adj.* Existing or occurring concurrently; accompanying; attendant. *—n.* Something that exists or occurs concurrently with something else. [Lat. *concomitans, concomitant-,* pr.part. of *concomitari,* to accompany : *com-,* together + *comitari,* to accompany < *comes,* companion.] **—con·com'i·tant·ly** *adv.*

con·cord (kŏn'kôrd', kŏng'-) *n.* **1.** Harmony or agreement of interests or feelings; accord. **2.** A treaty establishing peaceful relations. **3.** *Gram.* Agreement between words in person,

concertina

conch

number, gender, and case. [ME *concorde* < OFr. < Lat. *concordia* < *concors,* agreeing : *com-,* same + *cors,* heart.]

con·cor·dance (kən-kôr′dns) *n.* **1.** A state of agreement; concord. **2.** An alphabetical index of all the words in a text or corpus of texts, showing every contextual occurrence of a word.

con·cor·dant (kən-kôr′dnt) *adj.* Harmonious; agreeing. [ME *concordaunt* < OFr. *concordant* < Lat. *concordans,* pr.part. of *concordare,* to agree < *concors,* agreeing. —see CONCORD.] **—con·cor′dant·ly** *adv.*

con·cor·dat (kən-kôr′dăt′) *n.* **1.** A formal agreement; compact. **2.** An agreement between the pope and a government for the regulation of church affairs. [Fr. < Med. Lat. *concordatum* < Lat. *concordare,* to agree. —see CONCORDANT.]

Con·cord grape (kŏng′kərd) *n.* A variety of grape having purple-black fruit with a bluish bloom, used for making jelly, juice, and wine. [After *Concord,* Massachusetts.]

con·course (kŏn′kôrs′, -kōrs′, kŏng′-) *n.* **1.** A great crowd; throng. **2.** An act of coming, moving, or flowing together. **3. a.** A large open space for the gathering or passage of crowds, as in a railroad station. **b.** A broad thoroughfare. [ME *concours* < OFr. < Lat. *concursus* < p.part. of *concurrere,* to assemble : *com-,* together + *currere,* to run.]

con·cres·cence (kən-krĕs′əns) *n.* The uniting, esp. the growing together, of related parts, as of physical particles or anatomical structures. [Lat. *concrescentia* < *concrescens,* pr.part. of *concrescere,* to grow together. —see CONCRETE.] **—con·cres′cent** *adj.*

concrete
Pouring concrete

con·crete (kŏn-krēt′, kŏn′krēt′) *adj.* **1.** Of or relating to an actual, specific thing or instance; particular: *concrete evidence.* **2.** Existing in reality or in real experience; perceptible by the senses; real: *concrete objects such as trees.* **3.** Designating a thing or group of things as opposed to an abstraction. **4.** Formed by the coalescence of separate particles or parts into one mass; solid. **5.** Made of concrete. *—n.* (kŏn′krēt′, kŏn-krēt′). **1.** A construction material consisting of conglomerate gravel, pebbles, broken stone, or slag in a mortar or cement matrix. **2.** A mass formed by the coalescence of particles. *—v.* (kŏn′krēt′, kŏn-krēt′) **-cret·ed, -cret·ing, -cretes.** *—tr.* **1.** To form into a mass by coalescence or cohesion of particles. **2.** To build, treat, or cover with concrete. *—intr.* To harden; solidify. [ME *concret* < Lat. *concretus,* p.part. of *concrescere,* to grow together, harden : *com-,* together + *crescere,* to grow.] **—con·crete′ly** *adv.* **—con·crete′ness** *n.*

concrete mixer *n.* A machine with a revolving drum in which cement, sand, gravel, and water are combined into concrete.

concrete music *n.* Musique concrète.

concrete poetry *n.* Poetry that visually conveys the poet's meaning through the graphic arrangement of letters, words, or symbols on the page.

condensation

con·cre·tion (kən-krē′shən) *n.* **1. a.** The act or process of concreting; coalescence. **b.** The state of being concreted. **2.** A solid or concrete mass. **3.** *Geol.* A rounded mass of mineral matter found in sedimentary rock. **4.** *Pathol.* **a.** A solid mass of inorganic material formed in a cavity or tissue of the body; calculus. **b.** An abnormal fusion of otherwise adjacent parts, as of toes. **—con·cre′tion·ar′y** (-shə-nĕr′ē) *adj.*

con·cret·ism (kŏn-krē′tĭz′əm) *n.* The theory or practice of concrete poetry. **—con·cret′ist** *n.*

con·cre·tize (kŏn′krĭ-tīz′) *tr.v.* **-tized, -tiz·ing, -tiz·es.** To make real or specific. **—con′cre·ti·za′tion** *n.*

con·cu·bi·nage (kŏn-kyōō′bə-nĭj, kən-) *n.* **1.** Cohabitation without legal marriage. **2.** The state of being a concubine.

con·cu·bine (kŏng′kyə-bīn′, kŏn′-) *n.* **1.** A woman who cohabits with a man without being married to him; mistress. **2.** In certain polygamous societies, a secondary wife, usually of inferior legal and social status. [ME < OFr. < Lat. *concubina* : *com-* with < *cubare,* to lie down.]

con·cu·pis·cence (kŏn-kyōō′pĭ-səns) *n.* A strong desire, esp. sexual desire; lust. [LLat. *concupiscentia* < Lat. *concupiscens,* pr.part. of *concupiscere,* inchoative of *concupere,* to desire strongly : *com-* (intensive) + *cupere,* to desire.] **—con·cu′pis·cent** *adj.*

con·cur (kən-kûr′) *intr.v.* **-curred, -cur·ring, -curs. 1.** To have or express the same opinion; agree. **2.** To act together; cooperate. **3.** To occur at the same time; coincide. **4.** *Obs.* To come together; converge. [ME *concurren* < Lat. *concurrere,* to meet : *com-,* together + *currere,* to run.]

con·cur·rence (kən-kûr′əns) *n.* **1.** Agreement in opinion; accordance. **2.** Cooperation, as of agents, circumstances, or events. **3.** Simultaneous occurrence; coincidence. **4.** *Law.* A power or claim jointly held.

con·cur·rent (kən-kûr′ənt) *adj.* **1.** Happening at the same time. **2.** Operating in conjunction. **3.** Meeting or tending to meet at the same point; convergent. **4.** In accordance; harmonious. [ME < Lat. *concurrens,* pr.part. of *concurrere,* to run together. —see CONCUR.] **—con·cur′rent** *n.* **—con·cur′rent·ly** *adv.*

concurrent resolution *n.* A resolution adopted by both houses of a bicameral legislature that does not have the force of law and does not require the signature of the chief executive.

con·cuss (kən-kŭs′) *tr.v.* **-cussed, -cuss·ing, -cuss·es.** To injure by concussion. [Lat. *concutere, concuss-,* to strike together : *com-,* together + *quatere,* to strike.]

con·cus·sion (kən-kŭsh′ən) *n.* **1.** A violent jarring; shock: *a concussion caused by the bomb's detonation.* **2.** An injury of a soft structure, esp. of the brain, resulting from a violent blow. **—con·cus′sive** (-kŭs′ĭv) *adj.* **—con·cus′sive·ly** *adv.*

con·demn (kən-dĕm′) *tr.v.* **-demned, -demn·ing, -demns. 1.** To express disapproval of; denounce. **2. a.** To judge to be guilty; convict. **b.** To pronounce judgment against; sentence. **3.** To judge or declare to be unfit for use or consumption, usually by official order: *condemn an old building.* **4.** *Law.* To declare appropriated for public use under the right of eminent domain. [ME *condemnen* < Lat. *condemnare* : *com-* (intensive) + *damnare,* to sentence < *damnum,* penalty.] **—con·dem′na·ble** (-dĕm′nə-bəl) *adj.* **—con·dem′na·to′ry** (-nə-tôr′ē, -tōr′ē) *adj.* **—con·demn′er** *n.*

con·dem·na·tion (kŏn′dĕm-nā′shən) *n.* **1. a.** The act of condemning. **b.** The state of being condemned. **2.** Severe reproof; strong censure. **3.** A reason or occasion for condemning.

con·den·sate (kŏn′dən-sāt′, -dĕn-, kən-dĕn′sāt′) *n.* A product of condensation. [Back-formation < CONDENSATION.]

con·den·sa·tion (kŏn′dĕn-sā′shən, -dən-) *n.* **1.** The act of condensing. **2.** The state of being condensed. **3.** A product of condensing. **4.** *Physics.* **a.** The physical process by which a liquid is removed from a vapor or vapor mixture. **b.** The liquid so removed; condensate. **5.** *Chem.* A chemical reaction in which water or another simple substance is released by the combination of two or more molecules. **6.** *Psychoanal.* The process by which a single idea or word is invested with the emotional content of a group of ideas. **—con′den·sa′tion·al** *adj.*

con·dense (kən-dĕns′) *v.* **-densed, -dens·ing, -dens·es.** *—tr.* **1.** To reduce the volume of; compress. **2.** To shorten or make more concise; abridge. **3. a.** To form a condensate from (a vapor, for example). **b.** To subject (a vapor, for example) to condensation. *—intr.* **1.** To become more compact. **2.** To undergo condensation. [ME *condensen* < OFr. *condenser* < Lat. *condensare* : *com-* (intensive) + *densare,* to thicken < *densus,* thick.] **—con·dens′a·bil′i·ty** *n.* **—con·dens′a·ble, con·dens′i·ble** *adj.*

condensed milk *n.* Cow's milk with sugar added, and reduced by evaporation to a thick consistency.

con·dens·er (kən-dĕn′sər) *n.* **1.** One that condenses. **2.** *Physics.* An apparatus used to condense vapor. **3.** A capacitor. **4.** A mirror, lens, or combination of lenses used to gather light and direct it upon an object or projection lens.

con·de·scend (kŏn′dĭ-sĕnd′) *intr.v.* **-scend·ed, -scend·ing, -scends. 1.** To agree to do something one regards as beneath one's rank or dignity; deign. **2.** To deal with people in a patronizing or superior manner. [ME *condescenden* < LLat. *condescendere* : Lat. *com-* (intensive) + *descendere,* to descend. —see DESCEND.] **—con′de·scend′er** *n.*

con·de·scen·dence (kŏn′dĭ-sĕn′dəns) *n.* Condescension.

con·de·scend·ing (kŏn′dĭ-sĕn′dĭng) *adj.* Marked by condescension; patronizing. **—con′de·scend′ing·ly** *adv.*

con·de·scen·sion (kŏn′dĭ-sĕn′shən) *n.* **1. a.** The act of condescending. **b.** An instance of condescending. **2.** Patronizing behavior or manner.

con·dign (kən-dīn′) *adj.* Deserved; adequate: *condign censure.* [ME *condigne* < Lat. *condignus* : *com-* (intensive) + *dignus,* worthy.] **—con·dign′ly** *adv.*

con·di·ment (kŏn′də-mənt) *n.* A seasoning for food, as mustard or various spices. [ME < Lat. *condimentum* < *condire,* to season < *condere,* to store.] **—con′di·men′tal** (-mĕn′tl) *adj.*

con·di·tion (kən-dĭsh′ən) *n.* **1.** The particular mode or state of being of a person or thing. **2. a.** A state of health. **b.** A state of readiness or physical fitness: *getting in condition for the tournament.* **3.** *Informal.* A disease or ailment: *a heart condition.* **4.** Rank or social position. **5.** Something indispensable to the appearance or occurrence of something else; prerequisite: *Compatibility is a condition of a successful marriage.* **6.** Something that restricts or modifies something else; qualification. **7.** Often **conditions.** The existing circumstances: *poor driving conditions.* **8.** *Gram.* The dependent clause of a conditional sentence. **9.** *Logic.* A proposition upon which another proposition depends; the antecedent of a conditional proposition. **10.** *Law.* **a.** A provision making the effect of a legal instrument contingent upon the occurrence of an uncertain future event. **b.** The event itself. **11.** An unsatisfactory grade given a student and serving notice that he can make up deficiencies by doing further work. **12.** *Obs.* Disposition of mind. *—tr.v.* **-tioned, -tion·ing, -tions. 1.** To make conditional. **2.** To render fit. **3.** To accustom (a person) to; adapt. **4.** To give the grade of condition to. **5.** *Psychol.* To cause to respond in a specific manner to a specific stimulus. [ME *condicioun* < OFr. *condicion* < Lat. *conditio,* stipulation, prob. < *condicere,* to agree : *com-,* together + *dicere,* to talk.]

Usage: *Condition* (noun) in the sense of "disease" or "ailment" (*a liver condition*) is not a scientific term and has been objected to as a euphemism.

con·di·tion·al (kən-dĭsh′ə-nəl) *adj.* **1.** Imposing, depending on, or containing a condition or conditions: *conditional approval.* **2.** *Gram.* Stating, containing, or implying a condition. **3.** *Psychol.* Brought about by conditioning. *—n. Gram.*

ă pat / ā pay / âr care / ä father / b bib / ch church / d deed / ĕ pet / ē be / f fife / g gag / h hat / hw which / ĭ pit / ī pie / îr pier / j judge / k kick / l lid, needle / m mum / n no, sudden / ng thing / ŏ pot / ō toe / ô paw, for / oi noise / ou out / ŏŏ took / ōō boot /

A mood, tense, clause, or word expressing a condition. **—con·di'tion·al'i·ty** (-dĭsh'ə-năl'ĭ-tē) *n.* **—con·di'tion·al·ly** *adv.*

conditional probability *n.* The probability that an event will take place, given that another event has occurred or will occur.

con·di·tioned (kən-dĭsh'ənd) *adj.* **1.** Subject to or dependent upon a condition or conditions. **2. a.** Physically fit; in good physical condition. **b.** Prepared for a specific action or process. **3.** *Psychol.* Exhibiting or trained to exhibit a conditioned response.

conditioned reflex *n.* A conditioned response.

conditioned response *n. Psychol.* A new or modified response elicited by a stimulus after conditioning.

conditioned stimulus *n. Psychol.* A stimulus rendered capable of eliciting a response like that of a specific unconditioned stimulus by conditioning.

con·di·tion·er (kən-dĭsh'ə-nər) *n.* **1.** One that conditions: *an air conditioner.* **2.** An additive or application that improves the quality or usability of a substance: *a soil conditioner; a hair conditioner.*

con·di·tion·ing (kən-dĭsh'ə-nĭng) *n. Psychol.* The process of or complex of organismic processes resulting from presenting an initially inadequate stimulus with an unconditioned stimulus until the former is capable of eliciting a response like that elicited by the latter.

con·do (kŏn'dō') *n. Informal.* A condominium (sense 2).

con·dole (kən-dōl') *intr.v.* **-doled, -dol·ing, -doles.** To express sympathy or sorrow: *I condoled with him in his loss.* [LLat. *condolēre,* to feel another's pain : Lat. *com-,* together + Lat. *dolēre,* to grieve.] **—con·do'la·to'ry** (-dō'lə-tôr'ē, -tōr'ē) *adj.* **—con·dol'er** *n.*

con·do·lence (kən-dō'ləns) *n.* **1.** Sympathy with a person who has experienced pain, grief, or misfortune. **2.** A formal declaration of condolence. **—con·do'lent** *adj.*

con·dom (kŏn'dəm, kŭn'-) *n.* A sheath, usually made of thin rubber, designed to cover the penis during sexual intercourse for antivenereal or contraceptive purposes. [Orig. unknown.]

con·do·min·i·um (kŏn'də-mĭn'ē-əm) *n.* **1. a.** Joint sovereignty, esp. joint rule of a territory by two or more states. **b.** A territory so governed. **2. a.** An apartment building in which the apartments are owned individually. **b.** An apartment in such a building. [COM- + Lat. *dominium,* property.]

con·do·na·tion (kŏn'də-nā'shən, -dō-) *n.* The act of condoning, esp. the implied forgiveness of an offense by ignoring it.

con·done (kən-dōn') *tr.v.* **-doned, -don·ing, -dones.** To forgive, overlook, or disregard (an offense) without protest or censure. [Lat. *condonare,* to pardon : *com-* (intensive) + *donare,* to give.] **—con·don'er** *n.*

con·dor (kŏn'dôr', -dər) *n.* **1.** Either of two very large New World vultures, *Vultur gryphus* of the Andes or *Gymnogyps californianus* of the mountains of California. **2.** A gold coin of some South American countries bearing the figure of a condor. [Sp. *cóndor* < Quechua *kúntur.*]

con·dot·tie·re (kŏn'də-tyâr'ē) *n., pl.* **-tie·ri** (-tyâr'ē). A leader of mercenary soldiers between the 14th and 16th centuries. [Ital. < *condotta,* troop of mercenaries < fem. p.part. of *condurre,* to conduct < Lat. *conducere,* to lead together. —see CONDUCE.]

con·duce (kən-do͞os', -dyo͞os') *intr.v.* **-duced, -duc·ing, -duces.** To contribute or lead to a specific result. [Lat. *conducere,* to lead together : *com-,* together + *ducere,* to lead.] **—con·duc'er** *n.* **—con·duc'ing·ly** *adv.*

con·du·cive (kən-do͞o'sĭv, -dyo͞o'-) *adj.* Tending to cause or bring about; contributive: *working conditions not conducive to productivity.* **—con·du'cive·ness** *n.*

con·duct (kən-dŭkt') *v.* **-duct·ed, -duct·ing, -ducts.** *—tr.* **1.** To direct the course of; control: *conduct a business; conduct a test.* **2.** To lead or guide: *conduct a tour.* **3.** To lead an orchestra or other musical group. **4.** To serve as a medium or channel for conveying; transmit: *Some metals conduct heat.* **5.** To behave or act: *conducted herself stoically in her grief.* *—intr.* **1.** To act as a conductor. **2.** To lead. *—n.* (kŏn'dŭkt'). **1.** The way a person acts; behavior. **2.** The act of directing or controlling; management. **3.** *Obs.* A guide or escort. [ME *conducten* < Lat. *conducere,* to lead together. —see CONDUCE.] **—con·duct'i·bil'i·ty** *n.* **—con·duct'i·ble** *adj.*

con·duc·tance (kən-dŭk'təns) *n.* A measure of a material's ability to conduct electric charge, the real part of the complex representation of admittance.

con·duc·tim·e·try (kŏn'dŭk-tĭm'ĭ-trē) *n.* The scientific measurement of solution conductance.

con·duc·tion (kən-dŭk'shən) *n.* The transmission or conveying of something through a medium or passage, esp. of electric charge or heat through a conducting medium without perceptible motion of the medium itself.

con·duc·tive (kən-dŭk'tĭv) *adj.* Exhibiting conductivity.

con·duc·tiv·i·ty (kŏn'dŭk-tĭv'ĭ-tē) *n.* **1.** The ability or power to conduct or transmit. **2.** A measure of the ability of a material to conduct an electric charge, the reciprocal of resistivity.

con·duc·to·met·ric titration (kən-dŭk'tə-mĕt'rĭk) *n.* Titration based on changes in the electrical conductance of a solution.

con·duc·tor (kən-dŭk'tər) *n.* **1.** A person who conducts, esp.: **a.** The person in charge of a railroad train, bus, or streetcar. **b.** The director of an orchestra or other musical ensemble. **2.** *Physics.* A substance or medium that conducts heat, light, sound, or esp. an electric charge. **3.** A lightning rod. **—con'duc·to'ri·al** (kŏn'dŭk-tôr'ē-əl, -tōr'-) *adj.* **—con·duc'tor·ship'** *n.*

con·duit (kŏn'dĭt, -do͞o-ĭt) *n.* **1.** A channel or pipe for conveying water or other fluids. **2.** A tube or duct for enclosing electric wires or cable. **3.** *Archaic.* A fountain. [ME < OFr., conveyance < Med. Lat. *conductus,* transportation < Lat., p.part. of *conducere,* to lead together. —see CONDUCT.]

con·du·pli·cate (kŏn-do͞o'plĭ-kĭt, -dyo͞o'-) *adj.* Folded in half lengthwise. Used of leaves and petals in the bud. [Lat. *conduplicatus,* p.part. of *conduplicare,* to double : *com-,* together + *duplicare,* to double < *duplex,* double.] **—con'du·pli·ca'tion** *n.*

con·dyle (kŏn'dīl', -dl) *n.* A rounded articulatory prominence at the end of a bone. [Lat. *condylus,* knuckle < Gk. *kondulos.*] **—con'dy·lar** (-də-lər) *adj.* **—con'dy·loid'** (-dl-oid') *adj.*

con·dy·lo·ma (kŏn'dl-ō'mə) *n., pl.* **-mas** or **-ma·ta** (-mə-tə). A wartlike growth near the anus or external genitalia. [Gk. *kondulōma* < *kondulos,* knuckle.] **—con'dy·lo'ma·tous** (-mə-təs) *adj.*

cone (kōn) *n.* **1. a.** A surface generated by a straight line, the generator, passing through a fixed point, the vertex, and moving along the intersection with a fixed curve, the directrix. **b.** The surface generated by such a generator passing through a vertex lying on the perpendicular axis of a circular directrix. **2. a.** The figure formed by a cone, bound or regarded as bound by its vertex and a plane section taken anywhere above or below the vertex. **b.** Something having the shape of this figure: *an ice-cream cone.* **3. a.** A conical, spheroidal, or cylindrical structure borne by certain trees, such as the pines, firs, and hemlocks, consisting of clusters of stiff, overlapping, woody scales, between which are the naked ovules. **b.** A similar fruit, such as that of the magnolia or hop. **4.** *Physiol.* A photoreceptor in the retina of the eye. **5.** Any of various gastropod mollusks of the family Conidae, of tropical seas, having a conical, often vividly marked shell. *—tr.v.* **coned, con·ing, cones.** To shape like a cone or cone segment. [Fr. *cône* < Lat. *conus* < Gk. *kōnos.*]

cone·flow·er (kōn'flou'ər) *n.* Any of various North American plants of the genera *Rudbeckia, Ratibida,* and *Echinacea,* having rayed flowers with a conelike center of tubular florets.

cone·nose (kōn'nōz') also **cone-nosed bug** (kōn'nōzd') *n.* Any of several assassin bugs, esp. *Triatoma sanguisuga,* of the southern and western United States and Mexico, having sucking mouth parts and capable of inflicting a painful, toxic bite.

Con·es·to·ga wagon (kŏn'ĭ-stō'gə) *n.* A heavy covered wagon with broad wheels, used by American pioneers for westward travel. [After *Conestoga,* Pennsylvania.]

co·ney (kō'nē, kŭn'ē) *n.* Variant of **cony.**

con·fab (kŏn'făb') *Informal. —n.* An informal talk; confabulation. *—intr.v.* (kən-făb', kŏn'făb') **-fabbed, -fab·bing, -fabs.** To engage in a confab.

con·fab·u·late (kən-făb'yə-lāt') *intr.v.* **-lat·ed, -lat·ing, -lates.** **1.** To talk informally; chat. **2.** *Psychiat.* To replace fact with fantasy in memory. [Lat. *confabulari, confabulat-* : *com-,* together + *fabulari,* to talk < *fabula,* conversation < *fari,* to speak.] **—con·fab'u·la'tion** *n.* **—con·fab'u·la'tor** *n.* **—con·fab'u·la·to'ry** (-lə-tôr'ē, -tōr'ē) *adj.*

con·fect (kən-fĕkt') *tr.v.* **-fect·ed, -fect·ing, -fects.** **1.** To put together by combining materials: *confected a movie scenario.* **2.** To make into a confection or preserve. *—n.* (kŏn'fĕkt'). A candy or other sweet confection. [ME *confecten* < Lat. *conficere,* to prepare : *com-* (intensive) + *facere,* to make.]

con·fec·tion (kən-fĕk'shən) *n.* **1.** The act or process of confecting. **2.** A sweet preparation, such as candy or preserves. **3.** A sweetened medicinal compound; an electuary. *—tr.v.* **-tioned, -tion·ing, -tions.** To make into a confection.

con·fec·tion·ar·y (kən-fĕk'shə-nĕr'ē) *adj.* Of, pertaining to, or resembling a confection. *—n., pl.* **-ies.** Variant of **confectionery** (sense 3).

con·fec·tion·er (kən-fĕk'shə-nər) *n.* One who makes or sells confections.

confectioners' sugar *n.* Finely pulverized sugar with some cornstarch added.

con·fec·tion·er·y (kən-fĕk'shə-nĕr'ē) *n., pl.* **-ies.** **1.** Candies and other confections collectively. **2.** The art or occupation of a confectioner. **3.** Also **con·fec·tion·ar·y.** A confectioner's shop.

con·fed·er·a·cy (kən-fĕd'ər-ə-sē) *n., pl.* **-cies.** **1. a.** A union of persons, parties, or states; league. **b.** The persons, parties, or states united in a league. **c. Confederacy.** The 11 Southern states that seceded from the United States (1860–61). **2.** A group of people who have united for unlawful practices; conspiracy. [ME *confederacie* < AN < LLat. *confoederatio,* agreement < *confoederare,* to unite. —see CONFEDERATE.]

con·fed·er·ate (kən-fĕd'ər-ĭt) *n.* **1.** A member of a confederacy; ally. **2.** One who assists in a plot; accomplice. **3. Confederate.** A supporter of the American Confederacy. *—adj.* **1.** United in a confederacy; allied. **2. Confederate.** Of or

condor
California condor

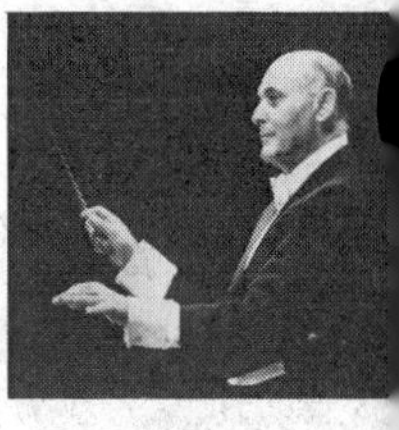

conductor
Georg Solti

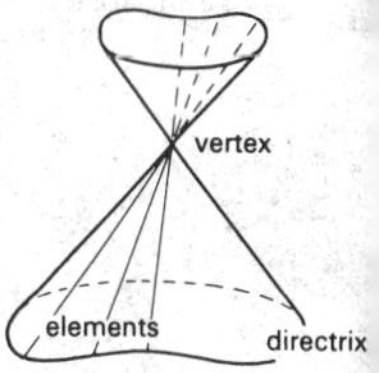

cone

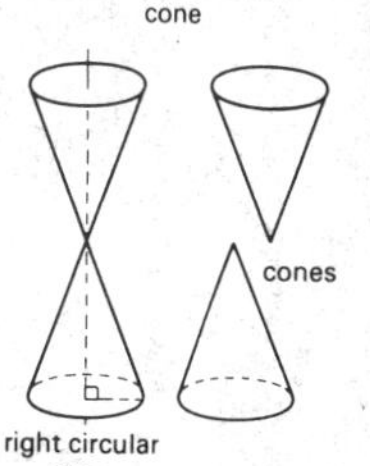

cone
Above: Geometric cones
Below: Ice-cream cones

Conestoga wagon

pertaining to the American Confederacy. —*tr. & intr.v.* (-ə-rāt′) **-at·ed, -at·ing, -ates.** To form into or become part of a confederacy. [< ME *confederat,* allied < LLat. *confoederatus,* p.part. of *confoederare,* to unite : Lat. *com-,* together + Lat. *foederare,* to unite < *foedus,* league.]

Confederate rose *n.* The cotton rose (sense 1).

con·fed·er·a·tion (kən-fĕd′ə-rā′shən) *n.* **1. a.** An act of confederating. **b.** A state of being confederated. **2.** A group of confederates, esp. of states or nations, united for a common purpose. **—con·fed′er·a′tion·ism** *n.* **—con·fed′er·a′tion·ist** *n.*

con·fer (kən-fûr′) *v.* **-ferred, -fer·ring, -fers.** —*tr.* **1.** To bestow (an honor, for example): *conferred a medal on the hero.* **2.** *Obs.* To compare. —*intr.* To hold a conference; consult together. [Lat. *conferre* : *com-,* together + *ferre,* to bring.] **—con·fer′ment** *n.* **—con·fer′ra·ble** *adj.* **—con·fer′ral** *n.* **—con·fer′rer** *n.*

con·fer·ee also **con·fer·ree** (kŏn′fə-rē′) *n.* **1.** A participant in a conference. **2.** One upon whom something is conferred.

con·fer·ence (kŏn′fər-əns, -frəns) *n.* **1. a.** A meeting for consultation or discussion. **b.** An exchange of views. **c.** A meeting of committees to settle differences between two legislative bodies. **2.** In various Protestant churches, an assembly of clerical or clerical and lay members from a particular district. **3.** An association of athletic teams. **4.** The act of conferring, as of a degree. [OFr. < Med. Lat. *conferentia* < Lat. *conferrens,* pr.part. of *conferre,* to bring together. —see CONFER.] **—con′fer·en′tial** (-fə-rĕn′shəl) *adj.*

conference call *n.* A conference by telephone in which several persons participate by a central switching unit.

con·fer·ree (kŏn′fə-rē′) *n.* Variant of **conferee.**

con·fer·va (kən-fûr′və) *n., pl.* **-vae** (-vē) or **-vas.** Any of various bright-green, threadlike freshwater algae. [Lat., comfrey.] **—con·fer′void′** (-void′) *n. & adj.*

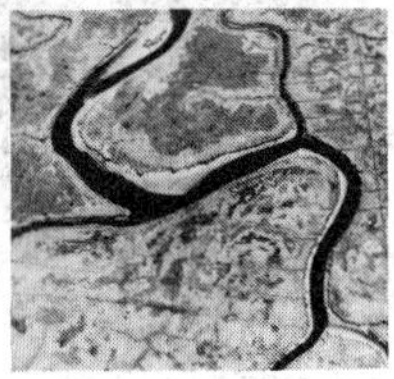

confluence

con·fess (kən-fĕs′) *v.* **-fessed, -fess·ing, -fess·es.** —*tr.* **1.** To disclose or acknowledge (something damaging or inconvenient to oneself); admit. **2.** To acknowledge belief or faith in. **3. a.** To make known (one's sins) to God or to a priest. **b.** To hear the confession of (a penitent). —*intr.* **1.** To admit or acknowledge: *The suspect confessed to the crime.* **2.** To tell one's sins to a priest. [ME *confessen* < OFr. *confesser* < VLat. **confessare* < Lat. *confiteri,* to acknowledge : *com-* (intensive) + *fateri,* to admit.] **—con·fess′a·ble** *adj.* **—con·fess′ed·ly** (-ĭd-lē) *adv.*

con·fess·er (kən-fĕs′ər) *n.* Variant of **confessor.**

con·fes·sion (kən-fĕsh′ən) *n.* **1.** An act of confessing. **2.** Something that is confessed. **3.** A formal declaration of guilt. **4.** The disclosure of sins to a priest for absolution. **5.** An avowal of belief in the doctrines of a particular faith; creed. **6.** A church or group of worshipers adhering to a particular creed.

con·fes·sion·al (kən-fĕsh′ə-nəl) *adj.* Of, pertaining to, or resembling confession. —*n.* A small enclosed stall in which a priest hears confessions.

con·fes·sor also **con·fess·er** (kən-fĕs′ər) *n.* **1.** A priest who hears confession and gives absolution. **2.** One who confesses. **3.** One who confesses faith in Christianity in the face of persecution but does not suffer martyrdom.

con·fet·ti (kən-fĕt′ē) *pl.n. (used with a sing. verb).* Small pieces or streamers of colored paper scattered around on festive occasions. [Ital., pl. of *confetto,* candy < Med. Lat. *confectum* < Lat. *confectus,* p.part. of *conficere,* to prepare. —see CONFECT.]

con·fi·dant (kŏn′fĭ-dănt′, -dänt′, kŏn′fĭ-dănt′, -dänt′) *n.* One to whom secrets or private matters are confided. [Fr. *confident* < Ital. *confidente* < Lat. *confidens,* p.part. of *confidere,* to rely on. —see CONFIDE.]

con·fi·dante (kŏn′fĭ-dănt′, -dänt′, kŏn′fĭ-dănt′, -dänt′) *n.* A woman to whom secrets or private matters are confided. [Fr. *confidente,* fem. of *confident,* confidant.]

con·fide (kən-fīd′) *v.* **-fid·ed, -fid·ing, -fides.** —*tr.* **1.** To tell (something) in confidence. **2.** To put into another's keeping; entrust. —*intr.* To tell private matters in confidence. [ME *confiden,* to rely on < OFr. *confider* < Lat. *confidere* : *com-* (intensive) + *fidere,* to trust.] **—con·fid′er** *n.*

con·fi·dence (kŏn′fĭ-dəns) *n.* **1.** Trust or reliance: *I am placing my confidence in you.* **2.** A trusting relationship: *took him into my confidence.* **3.** Something confided; secret. **4.** A feeling of assurance, esp. of self-assurance: *states his case with confidence.* **5.** The assurance that someone will keep a secret: *I am telling you this in strict confidence.*

Synonyms: *confidence, assurance, aplomb, self-confidence, self-possession, self-reliance.* These nouns imply trust and faith in oneself or in another. *Confidence* indicates a belief in a person or thing. *Assurance* implies a feeling of certainty and can suggest arrogance. *Aplomb* implies poise and self-assurance. *Self-confidence, self-possession,* and *self-reliance* all imply consciousness of one's own powers and abilities. *Self-confidence* stresses trust in one's own self-sufficiency. *Self-possession* implies control over one's own reactions and a tendency to be self-assured. *Self-reliance* stresses self-trust manifested in action and implies independence and self-sufficiency.

confidence game *n.* A swindle in which the victim is defrauded after his confidence has been won.

confidence interval *n.* A statistical range with a specified probability that a given parameter lies within the range.

confidence limit *n.* One of the two values that specify the range of a confidence interval.

confidence man *n.* One who swindles by using a confidence game.

con·fi·dent (kŏn′fĭ-dənt) *adj.* **1.** Marked by assurance, as of success. **2.** Marked by confidence in oneself; self-assured. **3.** Very bold; presumptuous. **4.** *Obs.* Confiding; trustful. [Lat. *confidens, confident-,* pr.part. of *confidere,* to rely on. —see CONFIDE.] **—con′fi·dent·ly** *adv.*

con·fi·den·tial (kŏn′fĭ-dĕn′shəl) *adj.* **1.** Done or communicated in confidence; secret. **2.** Entrusted with the confidence of another: *a confidential secretary.* **3.** Denoting confidence or intimacy: *a confidential tone of voice.* **—con′fi·den′ti·al′i·ty** (-shē-ăl′ĭ-tē), **con′fi·den′tial·ness** *n.* **—con′fi·den′tial·ly** *adv.*

confidential communication *n. Law.* A statement made to someone, such as one's doctor, lawyer, or spouse, who cannot be compelled to divulge the information in court.

con·fid·ing (kən-fī′dĭng) *adj.* Having a tendency to confide; trusting. **—con·fid′ing·ly** *adv.* **—con·fid′ing·ness** *n.*

con·fig·u·ra·tion (kən-fĭg′yə-rā′shən) *n.* **1. a.** The arrangement of the parts or elements of something. **b.** The form of a figure as determined by the arrangement of its parts; outline; contour. **2.** *Psychol.* A gestalt. **3.** *Chem.* The structural arrangement of atoms in a chemical compound or molecule. [LLat. *configuratio* < Lat. *configurare,* to form after : *com-,* with + *figurare,* to form < *figura,* shape.] **—con·fig′u·ra′tion·al·ly** *adv.* **—con·fig′u·ra′tive, con·fig′u·ra′tion·al** *adj.*

con·fig·ure (kən-fĭg′yər) *tr.v.* **-ured, -ur·ing, -ures.** To give configuration to; form; shape.

con·fig·ured (kən-fĭg′yərd) *adj.* Shaped, fashioned, or constructed.

con·fine (kən-fīn′) *v.* **-fined, -fin·ing, -fines.** —*tr.* **1.** To keep within bounds; restrict. **2.** To shut within an enclosure; imprison. **3.** To restrict in movement: *was confined to bed.* —*intr.* To border; abut. —*n.* (kŏn′fīn′). **1. confines.** The limits of a space or area; borders: *within the confines of one county.* **2.** *Obs.* A prison. [OFr. *confiner* < *confin,* boundary < Lat. *confine* < *confinis,* adjoining : *com-,* with + *finis,* border.] **—con·fin′a·ble, con·fine′a·ble** *adj.* **—con·fin′er** *n.*

con·fine·ment (kən-fīn′mənt) *n.* **1. a.** The act of confining. **b.** The state of being confined. **2.** Lying-in.

con·firm (kən-fûrm′) *tr.v.* **-firmed, -firm·ing, -firms.** **1.** To support or establish the certainty or validity of; verify. **2.** To make firmer; strengthen: *She confirmed his suspicions.* **3.** To make valid or binding by a formal or legal act; ratify. **4.** To administer the religious rite of confirmation to. [ME *confirmen* < OFr. *confermer* < Lat. *confirmare* : *com-* (intensive) + *firmare,* to strengthen < *firmus,* strong.] **—con·firm′a·bil′i·ty** *n.* **—con·firm′a·ble** *adj.* **—con·firm′a·to′ry** (-fûr′mə-tôr′ē, -tōr′ē) *adj.* **—con·firm′er** *n.*

Synonyms: *confirm, corroborate, substantiate, authenticate, validate, prove, establish, ratify, verify.* These verbs all mean to approve something, principally in the sense of attesting to its truth or vouching for its accuracy or genuineness. *Confirm* generally implies removal of all doubt about a matter heretofore considered uncertain or tentative. *Corroborate* refers to strengthening or supporting something, such as a statement or theory, by means of the evidence of another person or persons. *Substantiate* involves establishing something, such as a truth, claim, or position, by presenting substantial or tangible evidence. *Authenticate* implies doubt about the genuineness of something and the removal of such doubt by the act of an official or the testimony of an expert. *Validate* usually implies formal legal or official action (*validate a deed of sale*), but can refer to establishing any conclusion by detailed evidence or demonstration. *Prove* implies convincing evidence in the form of argument, reasoning, or demonstration. *Establish* adds to *prove* the securing of a position beyond all doubt. *Ratify* involves authoritative sanction, usually legal or official: *Treaties are ratified by the Senate. Verify* implies proving by comparison or by matching a contention against established fact: *verify a signature.*

con·fir·ma·tion (kŏn′fər-mā′shən) *n.* **1.** An act of confirming. **2.** Something that confirms; verification. **3. a.** A Christian rite admitting a baptized person to full membership in a church. **b.** A ceremony in Judaism that marks the completion of a young person's religious training.

con·firmed (kən-fûrmd′) *adj.* **1.** Ratified; verified. **2.** Firmly settled in habit; inveterate: *a confirmed bachelor.* **3.** Having received the rite of confirmation. **—con·firm′ed·ly** (-fûr′mĭd-lē) *adv.*

con·fis·ca·ble (kən-fĭs′kə-bəl) *adj.* Subject to confiscation.

con·fis·cate (kŏn′fĭ-skāt′) *tr.v.* **-cat·ed, -cat·ing, -cates.** **1.** To seize (private property) for the public treasury. **2.** To seize by or as if by authority. —*adj.* (kŏn′fĭ-skāt′, kən-fĭs′kət). **1.** Seized by a government; appropriated. **2.** Having lost property through confiscation. [Lat. *confiscare, confiscat-* : *com-,* together + *fiscus,* treasury.] **—con′fis·ca′tion** *n.* **—con′fis·ca′tor** *n.*

Con·fi·te·or (kən-fē′tē-ər, -ôr′) *n. Rom. Cath. Ch.* A prayer in which confession of sins is made. [Lat., I confess, the first word of the prayer.]

con·fi·ture (kŏn′fĭ-chŏŏr′) *n.* A confection, preserve, or sweetmeat. [Fr. < OFr. < *confit,* confection. —see COMFIT.]

con·fla·grant (kən-flā′grənt) *adj.* Burning intensely; blazing. [Lat. *conflagrans, conflagrant-,* pr.part. of *conflagrare,* to burn up : *com-* (intensive) + *flagrare,* to burn.]

con·fla·gra·tion (kŏn′flə-grā′shən) *n.* A large and destructive fire. [Lat. *conflagratio* < *conflagrare,* to burn up. —see CONFLAGRANT.]

con·flate (kən-flāt′) *tr.v.* **-flat·ed, -flat·ing, -flates.** To combine (two variant texts, for example) into one whole. [Lat. *conflare, conflat-,* to fuse : *com-,* together + *flare,* to blow.] **—con·fla′tion** *n.*

con·flict (kŏn′flĭkt′) *n.* **1.** A state of open fighting; warfare. **2.** A state of disagreement and disharmony; clash. **3.** *Psychol.* The opposition or simultaneous functioning of mutually exclusive impulses, desires, or tendencies. **4.** A collision. *—intr.v.* (kən-flĭkt′) **-flict·ed, -flict·ing, -flicts. 1.** To be in or come into opposition; differ. **2.** *Archaic.* To engage in warfare. [ME < Lat. *conflictus* < p.part. of *confligere,* to strike together : *com-,* together + *fligere,* to strike.] **—con·flic′tion** *n.* **—con·flic′tive** *adj.*

Synonyms: *conflict, contest, combat, fight, affray, melee, scuffle.* These nouns denote struggle between opposing forces. *Conflict* applies both to large-scale physical struggle between hostile forces and to a struggle within a person. *Contest* can mean either friendly competition or a struggle between hostile forces. In the latter case it is less forceful than *conflict. Combat* implies armed encounter between two persons or groups. *Fight* usually refers to a clash, physical or figurative, involving two persons or a small group, or to a struggle for a cause. *Affray, melee,* and *scuffle* all denote generally impromptu and disorderly physical clashes. *Affray* suggests street fighting and disturbing the peace. *Melee* implies confused, hand-to-hand fighting. *Scuffle* suggests hand-to-hand fighting on a small scale.

conflict of interest *n.* A conflict between the private interests and the public obligations of a person in an official position.

con·flu·ence (kŏn′flo͞o-əns) *n.* **1. a.** A flowing together of two or more streams. **b.** The point of juncture of such streams. **2.** A gathering or meeting together; crowd.

con·flu·ent (kŏn′flo͞o-ənt) *adj.* **1.** Flowing together; blended into one. **2.** *Pathol.* Merging together so as to form a mass, as sores in a rash. **3.** *Anat.* Coalesced, as two originally separate bones. *—n.* **1.** One of two or more confluent streams. **2.** A tributary. [ME < Lat. *confluens,* pr.part. of *confluere,* to flow together : *com-,* together + *fluere,* to flow.]

con·flux (kŏn′flŭks′) *n.* A confluence. [< Lat. *confluxus,* p.part. of *confluere,* to flow together. —see CONFLUENT.]

con·fo·cal (kŏn-fō′kəl) *adj.* Having the same focus or foci. **—con·fo′cal·ly** *adv.*

con·form (kən-fôrm′) *v.* **-formed, -form·ing, -forms.** *—intr.* **1.** To correspond in form or character; be similar. **2.** To act or be in compliance; comply. **3.** To act in accordance with current customs or modes. *—tr.* To bring into agreement or correspondence; make similar. [ME *conformen* < OFr. *conformer* < Lat. *conformare,* to shape after : *com-,* with + *formare,* to shape < *forma,* shape.] **—con·form′er** *n.* **—con·form′ist** *n.*

con·form·a·ble (kən-fôr′mə-bəl) *adj.* **1.** Corresponding; similar: *conformable to your wishes.* **2.** Quick to comply; submissive. **3.** *Geol.* Designating strata that are parallel to each other without interruption. **—con·form′a·bil′i·ty, con·form′a·ble·ness** *n.* **—con·form′a·bly** *adv.*

con·for·mal (kən-fôr′məl) *adj.* **1.** *Math.* Designating a depiction of a surface or region upon another surface so that all angles between intersecting curves remain unchanged. **2.** Of or pertaining to a map projection in which small areas are rendered with true shape. [LLat. *conformalis,* similar : Lat. *com-,* together + *forma,* shape.]

con·for·mance (kən-fôr′məns) *n.* Conformity.

con·for·ma·tion (kŏn′fər-mā′shən) *n.* **1.** The structure or outline of something as determined by the arrangement of its parts. **2.** A symmetrical arrangement of the parts of a thing. **3. a.** The act of conforming. **b.** The state of being conformed. **4.** One of the spatial arrangements of atoms in a molecule that can come about through free rotation of the atoms about a single chemical bond. **—con′for·ma′tion·al** *adj.* **—con′for·ma′tion·al·ly** *adv.*

con·form·i·ty (kən-fôr′mĭ-tē) *n., pl.* **-ties. 1.** Similarity in form or character; agreement: *acted in conformity with his principles.* **2.** Action or behavior in correspondence with current customs, rules, or styles: *conformity to university regulations.*

con·found (kən-found′, kŏn-) *tr.v.* **-found·ed, -found·ing, -founds. 1.** To cause (a person) to become confused; bewilder. **2.** To fail to distinguish; mix up: *confound fiction and fact.* **3.** To cause to be ashamed; abash: *an invention that confounded skeptics.* **4.** To damn. **5.** *Archaic.* To defeat; overthrow. [ME *confounden* < AN *confoundre* < Lat. *confundere,* to mix together : *com-,* together + *fundere,* to pour.] **—con·found′er** *n.*

con·found·ed (kən-foun′dĭd, kŏn-) *adj.* **1.** Confused; befuddled. **2.** Damned: *a confounded fool.* **—con·found′ed·ly** *adv.* **—con·found′ed·ness** *n.*

con·fra·ter·ni·ty (kŏn′frə-tûr′nĭ-tē) *n., pl.* **-ties.** An association of persons united in a common purpose or profession. [ME *confraternite* < OFr. < Med. Lat. *confraternitas* < *confrater,* colleague. —see CONFRERE.]

con·frere (kŏn′frâr′) *n.* A fellow member of a fraternity or profession; colleague. [ME < OFr. < Med. Lat. *confrater* : Lat. *com-,* together + Lat. *frater,* brother.]

con·front (kən-frŭnt′) *tr.v.* **-front·ed, -front·ing, -fronts. 1.** To come face to face with, esp. with defiance or hostility: *confronted his accuser.* **2.** To bring face to face: *Confronted with the evidence, he confessed.* **3.** To come up against; encounter: *confronted new difficulties daily.* [OFr. *confronter,* to adjoin < Med. Lat. *confrontare* : Lat. *com-,* together + Lat. *frons,* front.] **—con′fron·ta′tion** (kŏn′frŭn-ta′tion), **con·front′ment** *n.* **—con′fron·ta′tion·al** *adj.* **—con·front′er** *n.*

Con·fu·cian (kən-fyo͞o′shən) *adj.* Of, pertaining to, or characteristic of the Chinese philosopher Confucius, his teachings, or his followers. *—n.* One who adheres to the teachings of Confucius. **—Con·fu′cian·ism** *n.* **—Con·fu′cian·ist** *n.*

con·fuse (kən-fyo͞oz′) *tr.v.* **-fused, -fus·ing, -fus·es. 1.** To perplex or disconcert; throw off: *used camouflage to confuse the enemy.* **2. a.** To assemble without order or sense; jumble. **b.** To mistake (one thing for another): *confused effusiveness with affection.* **c.** To make unclear; blur: *statements that confuse the issue.* [ME *confusen* < *confus,* perplexed < Lat. *confusus,* p.part. of *confundere,* to mix together. —see CONFOUND.] **—con·fus′ed·ly** (-fyo͞o′zĭd-lē) *adv.* **—con·fus′ed·ness** *n.* **—con·fus′ing·ly** *adv.*

con·fu·sion (kən-fyo͞o′zhən) *n.* **1.** The act of confusing. **2.** The state of being confused. **3.** An early stage of psychosis involving mental and emotional disturbances. **—con·fu′sion·al** *adj.*

con·fu·ta·tion (kŏn′fyo͞o-tā′shən) *n.* **1.** The act of confuting. **2.** Something that confutes. **—con·fu′ta·tive** (kən-fyo͞o′tə-tĭv) *adj.*

con·fute (kən-fyo͞ot′) *tr.v.* **-fut·ed, -fut·ing, -futes. 1.** To prove to be wrong or in error; refute decisively. **2.** *Archaic.* To confound. [Lat. *confutare.*] **—con·fut′a·ble** *adj.* **—con·fut′er** *n.*

con·ga (kŏng′gə) *n.* **1.** A dance of Latin-American origin in which the dancers form a long, winding line. **2.** Music for the conga. *—intr.v.* **-gaed, -ga·ing, -gas.** To dance the conga. [Am. Sp. (Caribbean) *(danza) Conga,* Congo dance < Sp. *Congo,* of the Congo.]

con game *n. Slang.* A confidence game.

con·gé (kŏn′zhā′, -jā′, kôN-zhā′) also **con·gee** (kŏn′jē) *n.* **1.** Formal or authoritative permission to depart. **2.** An abrupt dismissal. **3. a.** *Archaic.* A formal bow. **b.** A leave-taking. **4.** *Archit.* A kind of concave molding. [Fr. < OFr. *congie* < Lat. *commeatus* < *commeare,* to come and go : *com-,* together + *meare,* to go.]

con·geal (kən-jēl′) *v.* **-gealed, -geal·ing, -geals.** *—intr.* **1.** To solidify, as by freezing. **2.** To coagulate; jell. *—tr.* To cause to solidify or coagulate. [ME *congelen* < Lat. *congelare* : *com-,* together + *gelare,* to freeze.] **—con·geal′a·ble** *adj.* **—con·geal′er** *n.* **—con·geal′ment** *n.*

con·gee (kŏn′jē) *intr.v.* **-geed, -gee·ing, -gees.** *Archaic.* **1.** To take ceremonious leave. **2.** To make a formal bow. *—n.* Variant of **congé.** [ME *congeien* < OFr. *congier* < *congie,* leave. —see CONGÉ.]

con·ge·la·tion (kŏn′jə-lā′shən) *n.* **1.** The process of congealing. **2.** The state of being congealed. **3.** A coagulation.

con·ge·ner (kŏn′jə-nər) *n.* **1.** A member of the same kind, class, or group. **2.** An organism belonging to the same genus as another or others. [Lat., of the same race : *com-,* same + *genus,* race.] **—con′ge·ner′ic** (-nĕr′ĭk), **con·gen′er·ous** (kən-jĕn′ər-əs, kŏn-) *adj.*

con·ge·net·ic (kŏn′jə-nĕt′ĭk) *adj.* Similar in origin.

con·gen·ial (kən-jēn′yəl) *adj.* **1.** Having the same tastes, habits, or temperament; sympathetic. **2.** Of a pleasant disposition; friendly and sociable: *a congenial host.* **3.** Suited to one's needs or nature; agreeable: *congenial surroundings.* **—con·ge′ni·al′i·ty** (-jē′nē-ăl′ĭ-tē), **con·gen′ial·ness** *n.* **—con·gen′ial·ly** *adv.*

con·gen·i·tal (kən-jĕn′ĭ-tl) *adj.* **1.** Existing at birth but not hereditary: *a congenital defect.* **2.** Being such as if by nature: *a congenital thief.* [< Lat. *congenitus* : *com-,* with + *genitus,* born, p.part. of *gignere,* to bear.] **—con·gen′i·tal·ly** *adv.*

congenital anomaly *n.* A physiological or structural abnormality that develops before birth.

con·ger or **con·ger eel** (kŏng′gər) *n.* Any of various large, scaleless marine eels of the family Congridae, esp. *Conger oceanicus,* of Atlantic waters. [ME *congre* < OFr. < Lat. *conger* < Gk. *gongros.*]

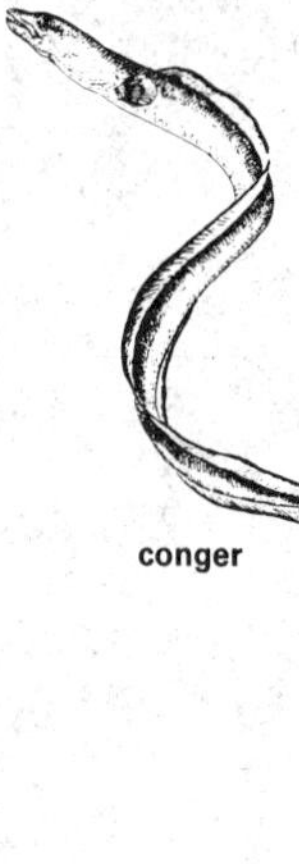

conger

con·ge·ries (kən-jîr′ēz′, kŏn′jə-rēz′) *n. (used with a sing. verb).* A collection; aggregation. [Lat. < *congerere,* to heap up. —see CONGEST.]

con·gest (kən-jĕst′) *v.* **-gest·ed, -gest·ing, -gests.** *—tr.* **1.** To overfill or overcrowd: *Trucks congested the tunnel.* **2.** *Pathol.* To cause excessive blood accumulation in (a vessel or organ). *—intr.* To become congested. [Lat. *congerere, congest-,* to heap up : *com-,* together + *gerere,* to carry.] **—con·ges′tion** *n.* **—con·ges′tive** *adj.*

con·gi·us (kŏn′jē-əs) *n., pl.* **-gi·i** (-jē-ī′). **1.** *Pharm.* A gallon. **2.** An ancient Roman measure for liquids, equal to about .84 of the U.S. gallon. [ME, a liquid measure < Lat.]

con·glo·bate (kŏn-glō′bāt′, kŏng′glō-) *tr.v.* **-bat·ed, -bat·ing, -bates.** To form into a globe or ball. *—adj.* Shaped like or formed into a ball. [Lat. *conglobare, conglobat-* : *com-*, together + *globus*, ball.] **—con'glo·ba'tion** *n.*

con·globe (kən-glōb') *tr.v.* **-globed, -glob·ing, -globes.** To conglobate.

con·glom·er·ate (kən-glŏm'ə-rāt') *intr. & tr.v.* **-at·ed, -at·ing, -ates.** To form or cause to form into an adhering or rounded mass. *—n.* (-ər-ĭt). **1.** A collected heterogeneous mass; cluster. **2.** *Geol.* A rock consisting of pebbles and gravel embedded in a loosely cementing material. **3.** A business corporation made up of a number of different companies that operate in widely diversified fields. *—adj.* (-ər-ĭt). **1.** Gathered into a mass; clustered. **2.** *Geol.* Made up of loosely cemented heterogeneous material. [Lat. *conglomerare, conglomerat-* : *com-*, together + *glomerare*, to wind into a ball < *glomus*, ball.] **—con·glom'er·at'ic** (-ə-răt'ĭk), **con·glom'er·it'ic** (-ə-rĭt'ĭk) *adj.*

con·glom·er·a·tion (kən-glŏm'ə-rā'shən) *n.* **1. a.** The process of conglomerating. **b.** The state of being conglomerated. **2.** A collection or accumulation of miscellaneous things.

con·glu·ti·nate (kən-glo͞ot'n-āt', kŏn-) *intr. & tr.v.* **-nat·ed, -nat·ing, -nates.** **1.** To become or cause to become stuck or glued together. **2.** *Med.* To become or cause to become reunited, as bones or tissues. [ME *conglutinaten* < Lat. *conglutinare*, to glue together : *com-*, together + *glutinare*, to glue < *gluten*, glue.] **—con·glu'ti·na'tion** *n.*

con·go dye (kŏng'gō) *n.* A nitrogen-containing dye that is usually derived from benzidine. [After *Congo*, a region of Africa.]

congo eel *n.* An eellike amphibian, *Amphiuma means*, of the southeastern United States, having two pairs of tiny, nonfunctioning legs.

Congo red *n.* A brownish-red powder, $C_{32}H_{22}N_6O_6S_2Na_2$, used in medicine and as a dye, indicator, and biological stain.

Congo snake *n.* Congo eel.

con·gou (kŏng'gō, -go͞o) *n.* A variety of black tea from China. [Chin. (Amoy) *kong hu (tē)*, elaborately prepared (tea).]

con·grat·u·late (kən-grăch'ə-lāt') *tr.v.* **-lat·ed, -lat·ing, -lates.** To express joy or acknowledgment for the achievement or good fortune of. [Lat. *congratulari, congratulat-* : *com-*, with + *gratulari*, to rejoice < *gratus*, pleasing.] **—con·grat'u·la'tor** *n.* **—con·grat'u·la·to'ry** (-lə-tôr'ē, -tōr'ē) *adj.*

con·grat·u·la·tion (kən-grăch'ə-lā'shən) *n.* **1.** The act of congratulating. **2.** Often **congratulations.** An expression of joy or acknowledgment for the achievement or good fortune of another.

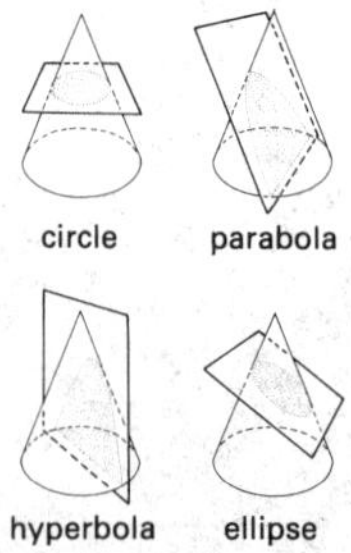

conic section

con·gre·gate (kŏng'grĭ-gāt') *tr. & intr.v.* **-gat·ed, -gat·ing, -gates.** To bring or come together in a crowd or assembly. *—adj.* (-gĭt). Gathered; assembled. [ME *congregaten* < Lat. *congregare* : *com-*, together + *gregare*, to assemble < *grex*, herd.] **—con'gre·ga'tive** *adj.* **—con'gre·ga'tive·ness** *n.* **—con'gre·ga'tor** *n.*

con·gre·ga·tion (kŏng'grĭ-gā'shən) *n.* **1.** An act of congregating. **2.** A body of assembled people or things; gathering. **3. a.** A group of people gathered for religious worship. **b.** The members of a specific religious group who regularly worship at a common church. **4.** *Rom. Cath. Ch.* **a.** A religious institute in which only simple vows, not solemn vows, are taken. **b.** A division of the Curia.

con·gre·ga·tion·al (kŏng'grĭ-gā'shə-nəl) *adj.* **1.** Of or pertaining to a congregation. **2. Congregational.** Of or pertaining to Congregationalism or Congregationalists.

con·gre·ga·tion·al·ism (kŏng'grĭ-gā'shə-nə-lĭz'əm) *n.* **1.** A type of church government in which each local congregation is self-governing. **2. Congregationalism.** The system of government and religious beliefs of a Protestant denomination in which each member church is self-governing. **—con'gre·ga'tion·al·ist** *n.*

con·gress (kŏng'grĭs) *n.* **1.** A formal assembly of representatives, as of various nations, to discuss problems. **2.** The national legislative bodies of certain nations, esp. of republics. **3. Congress. a.** The national legislative body of the United States, consisting of the Senate and the House of Representatives. **b.** The two-year session of this legislature between elections of the House of Representatives. **4.** The act of coming together; meeting. **5.** Sexual intercourse. [Lat. *congressus*, meeting < *congredi*, to meet : *com-*, together + *gradi*, to go.] **—con·gres'sion·al** (kən-grĕsh'ə-nəl) *adj.* **—con·gres'sion·al·ly** *adv.*

congress boot *n.* An ankle-high shoe with elastic material in the sides. [From its former popularity among members of the U.S. Congress.]

congress gaiter *n.* A congress boot.

Congressional Medal of Honor *n.* The Medal of Honor.

con·gress·man (kŏng'grĭs-mən) *n.* A member of the U.S. Congress, esp. of the House of Representatives.

con·gress·wom·an (kŏng'grĭs-wo͝om'ən) *n.* A female member of the U.S. Congress, esp. of the House of Representatives.

con·gru·ence (kŏng'gro͞o-əns, kən-gro͞o'-) also **con·gru·en·cy** (kŏng'gro͞o-ən-sē, kən-gro͞o'-) *n., pl.* **-enc·es** also **-en·cies. 1.** Agreement; conformity. **2.** *Math.* **a.** The state of being congruent. **b.** A mathematical statement that two quantities are congruent.

con·gru·ent (kŏng'gro͞o-ənt, kən-gro͞o'-) *adj.* **1.** Corresponding; congruous. **2.** *Math.* **a.** Coinciding exactly when superimposed: *congruent triangles.* **b.** Having a difference divisible by a modulus: *congruent numbers.* [ME < Lat. *congruens*, pr.part. of *congruere*, to agree.] **—con'gru·ent·ly** *adv.*

con·gru·i·ty (kən-gro͞o'ĭ-tē, kŏn-) *n., pl.* **-ties. 1.** The quality or fact of being congruous. **2.** The quality or fact of being congruent. **3.** A point of agreement.

con·gru·ous (kŏng'gro͞o-əs) *adj.* **1.** Corresponding in character or kind; appropriate; harmonious. **2.** *Math.* Congruent. [Lat. *congruus* < *congruere*, to agree.] **—con'gru·ous·ly** *adv.* **—con'gru·ous·ness** *n.*

con·ic (kŏn'ĭk) also **con·i·cal** (-ĭ-kəl) *adj.* **1.** Shaped like a cone. **2.** Of or pertaining to a cone. *—n. Math.* A conic section. [NLat. *conicus* < Gk. *konikos* < *konos*, cone.]

conic projection or **conical projection** *n.* A method of projecting pictures of parts of the earth's spherical surface on a surrounding cone, which is then flattened to a plane surface having concentric circles as parallels of latitude and radiating lines from the apex as meridians.

conic section *n.* One of a group of plane curves, including the circle, ellipse, hyperbola, and parabola, generated by: **a.** An intersection of a right circular cone and a plane. **b.** The plane locus of a point that moves so that the ratio of its distance to a fixed point to its distance from a fixed line is a positive constant. **c.** A graph of the general quadratic equation in two variables.

co·nid·i·o·phore (kə-nĭd'ē-ə-fôr', -fōr') *n.* A specialized hyphal filament in fungi, bearing conidia. [CONIDI(UM) + -PHORE.] **—co·nid'i·o·phor'ous** *adj.*

co·nid·i·um (kə-nĭd'ē-əm) *n., pl.* **-i·a** (-ē-ə). An asexual fungus spore, usually produced on a specialized sporophore. [NLat. < Gk. *konis*, dust.] **—co·nid'i·al** (-əl) *adj.*

con·i·fer (kŏn'ə-fər, kō'nə-) *n.* Any of various predominantly evergreen cone-bearing trees, such as a pine, spruce, hemlock, or fir. [< NLat. *Coniferae*, family name < Lat. *conifer*, cone-bearing : *conus*, cone (< Gk. *konos*) + *ferre*, to bear.] **—co·nif'er·ous** (kō-nĭf'ər-əs, kə-) *adj.*

co·ni·ine (kō'nē-ēn') also **co·nin** (kō'nĭn) or **co·nine** (-nēn') *n.* A poisonous, colorless liquid alkaloid, $C_8H_{17}N$, obtained from the poison hemlock and formerly used in the treatment of spasmodic disorders. [G. *Koniin* < LLat. *conium*, conium.]

co·ni·o·sis (kō'nē-ō'sĭs) *n.* A pathological condition caused by dust inhalation. [< Gk. *konia*, dust + -OSIS.]

co·ni·um (kō'nē-əm) *n.* Any of several poisonous plants of the genus *Conium*, including the poison hemlock. [LLat. *conium*, hemlock < Gk. *kōneion*.]

con·i·za·tion (kō'nĭ-zā'shən, kŏn'ĭ-) *n. Med.* The diagnostic excision of a cone of tissue.

con·jec·tur·al (kən-jĕk'chər-əl) *adj.* **1.** Based on or involving conjecture. **2.** Inclined to conjecture. **—con·jec'tur·al·ly** *adv.*

con·jec·ture (kən-jĕk'chər) *n.* **1.** Inference based on inconclusive or incomplete evidence. **2.** A statement, opinion, or conclusion based on inference. *—v.* **-tured, -tur·ing, -tures.** *—tr.* To infer from inconclusive evidence; guess. *—intr.* To make a conjecture. [ME < Lat. *conjectura* < *conicere*, to infer : *com-*, together + *jacere*, to throw.] **—con·jec'tur·a·ble** *adj.* **—con·jec'tur·a·bly** *adv.* **—con·jec'tur·er** *n.*

Synonyms: *conjecture, surmise, guess, speculate, presume, infer.* These verbs mean to reach a conclusion or judgment. *Conjecture* implies that a conclusion is based on incomplete evidence. *Surmise* suggests a conclusion reached by intuition or by interpretation of slender evidence. *Guess*, in formal usage, implies a haphazard attempt to answer or solve a problem and suggests substantial grounds for doubt. Informally the term implies a tentative conclusion reached in the absence of alternatives: *I guess I'll go to the movies. Speculate* implies an orderly process of reasoning based on inconclusive evidence, and is often interchangeable with *conjecture. Presume* and *infer* apply to conclusions about which less doubt is implied. *Presume* involves taking a conclusion for granted. In careful usage it is limited to what is considered worthy of trust; thus the term implies assumption based on experience or knowledge. *Infer* involves reaching a conclusion by reasoning from evidence about which no doubt is necessarily suggested.

con·join (kən-join') *tr. & intr.v.* **-joined, -join·ing, -joins.** To join or become joined together; unite. [ME *conjoinen* < OFr. *conjoindre* < Lat. *conjungere* : *com-*, together + *jungere*, to join.] **—con·join'er** *n.*

con·joint (kən-joint') *adj.* **1.** Joined together; united. **2.** Of, pertaining to, consisting of, or carried on by two or more joined or associated persons or things. [ME < OFr., p.part. of *conjoindre*, to conjoin.] **—con·joint'ly** *adv.*

con·ju·gal (kŏn'jə-gəl, kən-jo͞o'-) *adj.* Of or pertaining to marriage or the marital relationship. [Lat. *conjugalis* < *conjunx*, spouse < *conjungere*, to join in marriage. —see CONJOIN.] **—con'ju·gal'i·ty** (-găl'ĭ-tē) *n.* **—con'ju·gal·ly** *adv.*

con·ju·gant (kŏn'jə-gənt) *n.* Either of a pair of organisms, cells, or gametes undergoing conjugation. [< Lat. *conjugans, conjugant-*, pr.part. of *conjugare*, to unite. —see CONJUGATE.]

con·ju·gate (kŏn'jə-gāt') *v.* **-gat·ed, -gat·ing, -gates.** *—tr.* **1.** *Gram.* To give the various inflected forms of (a word, esp. a verb). **2.** To join together. *—intr.* **1.** *Biol.* To undergo conjugation. **2.** *Gram.* To give the various inflected forms of a word, esp. a verb. —*adj.* (-gĭt, -gāt′). **1.** Joined together, esp. in a pair or pairs; coupled. **2.** *Math. & Physics.* Inversely or oppositely related with respect to one of a group of otherwise identical properties, esp. designating either or both of a pair of complex numbers differing only in the sign of the imaginary term. **3.** *Gram.* Of or pertaining to words having the same derivation and usually a related meaning. —*n.* (-gĭt, -gāt′). **1.** *Gram.* One of two or more conjugate words. **2.** *Math. & Physics.* Either of a pair of conjugate quantities. [< ME *conjugat,* joined < Lat. *conjugatus,* p.part. of *conjugare,* to join together : *com-,* together + *jugare,* to join < *jugum,* yoke.] —**con′ju·gate′ly** *adv.* —**con′ju·ga′tive** *adj.* —**con′ju·ga′tor** *n.*

conjugated protein *n.* A compound of a protein with a nonprotein.

con·ju·ga·tion (kŏn′jə-gā′shən) *n.* **1. a.** The act of conjugating. **b.** The state of being conjugated. **2.** *Gram.* **a.** The inflection of a particular verb. **b.** A presentation of the complete set of inflected forms of a verb. **c.** A class of verbs having similar inflected forms. **3. a.** A process of sexual reproduction in which ciliate protozoans of the same species temporarily couple and exchange genetic material. **b.** Chromosome pairing in the first meiotic division. **c.** The fusion of gamete nuclei; karyogamy. **d.** The union of sex cells; syngamy. —**con′ju·ga′tion·al** *adj.* —**con′ju·ga′tion·al·ly** *adv.*

conjugation tube *n.* A slender protoplasmic tube in some algae through which gametes may move to sexually unite with other gametes.

con·junct (kən-jŭngkt′, kŏn′jŭngkt′) *adj.* **1.** Joined together; united. **2.** Designating adjacent successive tones of the musical scale. [ME < Lat. *conjunctus,* p.part. of *conjungere,* to join together. —see CONJOIN.] —**con·junct′ly** *adv.*

con·junc·tion (kən-jŭngk′shən) *n.* **1. a.** The act of joining. **b.** The state of being joined. **2.** A simultaneous occurrence in space or time; concurrence. **3.** *Gram.* In some languages, one of the parts of speech comprising words such as, in English, *and, but, because,* and *as,* that connect other words, phrases, clauses, or sentences. **4.** *Astron.* The position of two celestial bodies on the celestial sphere when they have the same celestial longitude. —**con·junc′tion·al** *adj.* —**con·junc′tion·al·ly** *adv.*

con·junc·ti·va (kŏn′jŭngk-tī′və) *n., pl.* **-vas** or **-vae** (-vē). The mucous membrane that lines the inner surface of the eyelid and the exposed surface of the eyeball. [ME < Med. Lat. *(membrana) conjunctiva,* connective (membrane) < LLat. *conjunctivus,* connective. —see CONJUNCTIVE.] —**con′junc·ti′val** (-vəl) *adj.*

con·junc·tive (kən-jŭngk′tĭv) *adj.* **1.** Joining; connective. **2.** Joined together; combined. **3.** *Gram.* **a.** Of or used as a conjunction. **b.** Serving to connect elements of meaning and construction in a sentence, as *and* and *moreover.* —*n. Gram.* A connective word, esp. a conjunction. [LLat. *conjunctivus* < Lat. *conjunctus,* p.part. of *conjungere,* to join together. —see CONJOIN.] —**con·junc′tive·ly** *adv.*

con·junc·ti·vi·tis (kən-jŭngk′tə-vī′tĭs) *n. Pathol.* Inflammation of the conjunctiva.

con·junc·ture (kən-jŭngk′chər) *n.* **1.** A combination of circumstances. **2.** A critical set of circumstances; crisis.

con·ju·ra·tion (kŏn′jə-rā′shən) *n.* **1. a.** The act of conjuring. **b.** A magic spell or incantation. **2.** Magic; legerdemain. **3.** A solemn appeal or invocation.

con·jure (kŏn′jər, kən-jŏŏr′) *v.* **-jured, -jur·ing, -jures.** —*tr.* **1.** To call upon or entreat solemnly, esp. by an oath. **2. a.** To summon (a devil or spirit) by oath, incantation, or magic spell. **b.** To cause or effect by or as if by magic. **c.** To call to mind; evoke: *a fragrance that conjures up images of the Old South.* —*intr.* **1.** To practice magic, esp. legerdemain. **2.** To summon a devil by oath, incantation, or magic spell. **3.** *Obs.* To conspire. [ME *conjuren* < OFr. *conjurer* < Lat. *conjurare,* to swear together : *com-,* together + *jurare,* to swear.]

con·jur·er also **con·jur·or** (kŏn′jər-ər, kŭn′-) *n.* One who practices magic or legerdemain.

conk[1] (kŏngk) *Slang. n.* **1.** The head. **2.** The nose. **3.** A blow, esp. on the head. —*v.* **conked, conk·ing, conks.** —*tr.* To hit, esp. on the head. —*intr.* **1.** To fail suddenly: *The engine conked out.* **2.** To fall asleep instantly: *conked out early.* **3.** To faint; pass out. [Orig. unknown.]

conk[2] (kŏngk) *n.* A hard, shelflike fruiting body of a fungus, esp. of the genera *Polyporus* and *Fomes,* found growing on tree trunks. [Perh. alteration of CONCH.]

conk[3] (kŏngk) *n.* A hair style in which the hair is straightened, usually by a chemical process. —*tr.v.* **conked, conk·ing, conks.** To straighten (kinky hair) usually by a chemical method. [Perh. alteration of *congolene,* a substance for straightening hair.]

con man *n. Slang.* A confidence man.

conn (kŏn) *v. & n.* Variant of **con**[3].

con·nate (kŏn′āt′, kŏ-nāt′) *adj.* **1.** Part of or existing in someone or something from birth; inborn; innate. **2.** Coexisting since or associated in birth or origin; cognate; related. **3.** *Biol.* Congenitally or firmly united, as like parts or organs. [LLat. *connatus,* p.part. of *connasci,* to be born with : Lat. *com-,* with + Lat. *nasci,* to be born.] —**con′nate′ly** *adv.* —**con′nate′ness** *n.*

con·nat·u·ral (kə-năch′ər-əl, kŏ-) *adj.* **1.** Innate; inborn. **2.** Related or similar in nature; cognate. [Med. Lat. *connaturalis* : Lat. *com-,* together + Lat. *naturalis,* by birth. —see NATURAL.] —**con·nat′u·ral′i·ty** (-ə-răl′ĭ-tē) *n.* —**con·nat′u·ral·ly** *adv.* —**con·nat′u·ral·ness** *n.*

con·nect (kə-nĕkt′) *v.* **-nect·ed, -nect·ing, -nects.** —*tr.* **1.** To join or fasten together; link; unite. **2.** To associate or consider as related: *no reason to connect the two events.* **3.** To join to a communications circuit. —*intr.* **1.** To become joined or united: *two streams connecting to form a river.* **2.** *Informal.* In sports such as baseball, to hit or make contact with the ball: *The batter connected for a home run.* [ME *connecten* < Lat. *conectere* : *com-,* together + *nectere,* to bind.] —**con·nect′ed·ly** (-nĕk′tĭd-lē) *adv.* —**con·nect′i·ble, con·nect′a·ble** *adj.* —**con·nec′tor, con·nect′er** *n.*

connecting rod *n.* A rod linking rotating parts of a machine in reciprocating motion connecting the crankshaft of an automobile to a piston.

con·nec·tion (kə-nĕk′shən) *n.* **1. a.** The act of connecting. **b.** The state of being connected. **2.** Something that connects; link: *a weak connection in the circuit.* **3.** An association or relationship: *no connection between the two crimes.* **4.** The logical ordering of words or ideas; coherence. **5.** The relation or association of a word or idea to the surrounding text; context: *In this connection let me say this.* **6.** A person with whom one is associated, as by kinship, interests in common, or marriage: *used his connections to land a job.* **7. a.** The meeting of various means of transportation for the transfer of passengers. **b.** A line of communication between two points in a telephone or similar wired system. **8.** *Slang.* **a.** A narcotics dealer. **b.** A narcotics purchase. —**con·nec′tion·al** *adj.*

con·nec·tive (kə-nĕk′tĭv) *adj.* Serving or tending to connect. —*n.* **1.** Something that connects. **2.** *Gram.* A word, such as a conjunction, that connects words, phrases, clauses, and sentences. **3.** *Bot.* The tissue of a stamen that forms the division between the two lobes of an anther. —**con·nec′tive·ly** *adv.* —**con′nec·tiv′i·ty** (kŏn′ĕk-tĭv′ĭ-tē) *n.*

connective tissue *n.* Tissue arising chiefly from the embryonic mesoderm, including mucous, fibrous, reticular, adipose, cartilage, and bone tissue, characterized by a highly vascular matrix structure and forming the supporting and connecting structures of the body.

connect time *n. Computer Sci.* The elapsed time during which a user of a remote terminal is connected with a time-sharing system.

con·nex·ion (kə-nĕk′shən) *n. Chiefly Brit.* Variant of **connection.**

conning tower *n.* **1.** The armored pilothouse of a warship. **2.** A raised, enclosed observation post in a submarine, often used as a means of entrance and exit. [< CON[3].]

conning tower

con·nip·tion (kə-nĭp′shən) *n. Informal.* A fit of anger or other violent emotion; tantrum. [Orig. unknown.]

con·niv·ance also **con·niv·ence** (kə-nī′vəns) *n.* **1.** The act of conniving. **2.** *Law.* Knowledge of and tacit consent to the commission of an illegal act by another.

con·nive (kə-nīv′) *intr.v.* **-nived, -niv·ing, -nives. 1.** To feign ignorance of or fail to take measures against a wrong, thus implying tacit encouragement or consent. **2.** To cooperate secretly. **3.** To conspire; plot. [Lat. *conivēre.*] —**con·niv′er** *n.* —**con·niv′er·y** *n.*

con·niv·ence (kə-nī′vəns) *n.* Variant of **connivance.**

con·ni·vent (kə-nī′vənt) *adj. Biol.* Converging and touching. Used esp. of stamens or an insect's wings. [Lat. *connivens, connivent-,* pr.part. of *conivere,* to close the eyes.]

con·nois·seur (kŏn′ə-sûr′) *n.* A person with informed and astute discrimination, esp. concerning the arts or matters of taste. [Obs. Fr. < OFr. *connoisseor* < *connoistre,* to know < Lat. *cognoscere,* to learn. —see COGNITION.] —**con′nois·seur′ship′** *n.*

con·no·ta·tion (kŏn′ə-tā′shən) *n.* **1.** The act or process of connoting. **2. a.** The configuration of suggestive or associative implications constituting the general sense of an abstract expression beyond its literal, explicit sense. **b.** A secondary meaning suggested by a word in addition to its literal meaning. **3.** *Logic.* The total of the attributes constituting the meaning of a term; intension. —**con′no·ta′tive** *adj.* —**con′no·ta′tive·ly** *adv.*

con·note (kə-nōt′) *tr.v.* **-not·ed, -not·ing, -notes. 1.** To suggest or imply in addition to literal meaning: *The word "Orient" often connotes mystery.* **2.** To involve as a condition or consequence: *Lying often connotes guilt.* —See Usage note at **denote.** [Med. Lat. *connotare,* to mark along with : Lat. *com-,* with + Lat. *notare,* to mark < *nota,* mark.]

con·nu·bi·al (kə-nōō′bē-əl, -nyōō′-) *adj.* Of marriage or the married state; conjugal. [Lat. *connubialis* < *connubium,* marriage : *com-,* together + *nubere,* to marry.] —**con·nu′bi·al·ism** *n.* —**con·nu′bi·al′i·ty** (-ăl′ĭ-tē) *n.* —**con·nu′bi·al·ly** *adv.*

co·noid (kō′noid′) also **co·noi·dal** (kō-noid′l) *adj.* Shaped like a cone. —**co′noid** *n.*

con·quer (kŏng′kər) *v.* **-quered, -quer·ing, -quers.** —*tr.* **1.** To defeat or subdue by force, esp. by force of arms. **2.** To gain control over by surmounting impediments: *scientists battling to conquer disease; a singer who conquered the operatic world.* **3.** To overcome or surmount by mental or moral force: *conquered his distaste.* —*intr.* To be victorious; win.

[ME *conqueren* < OFr. *conquerre* < VLat. **conquaerere* < Lat. *conquirere,* to procure : *com-* (intensive) + *quaerere,* to seek.] **—con'quer·a·ble** *adj.* **—con'quer·or** *n.*

con·quest (kŏn'kwĕst', kŏng'-) *n.* **1.** The act or process of conquering. **2.** Something, as territory, acquired by conquering. **3.** Someone whose love or favor has been captivated. [ME < OFr. < Lat. *conquisitus,* p.part. of *conquirere,* to procure. —see CONQUER.]

con·qui·an (kŏng'kē-ən) *n.* A card game for two players that resembles rummy. [Mex. Sp. *con quien* < Sp. *con quién,* with whom? : *con,* with (< Lat. *cum*) + *quien,* whom < Lat. *quem,* accusative of *quis,* who.]

con·quis·ta·dor (kŏn-kwĭs'tə-dôr', kŏng-kē'stə-) *n., pl.* **-dors** or **-dor·es** (-dôr'ās, -ēz). A conqueror, esp. one of the Spanish conquerors of Mexico and Peru in the 16th century. [Sp. < *conquistar,* to conquer < Med. Lat. *conquestare,* freq. of VLat. **conquaerere.* —see CONQUER.]

con·san·guine (kŏn-săng'gwĭn, kən-) *adj.* Consanguineous. [Lat. *consanguineus.* —see CONSANGUINEOUS.]

con·san·guin·e·ous (kŏn'săn-gwĭn'ē-əs, -săng-) *adj.* Of the same lineage or origin, esp. related by blood. [Lat. *consanguineus* : *com-,* together + *sanguis,* blood.] **—con'san·guin'e·ous·ly** *adv.*

con·san·guin·i·ty (kŏn'săn-gwĭn'ĭ-tē, -săng-) *n.* **1.** Blood relationship. **2.** A close connection or affinity.

con·science (kŏn'shəns) *n.* **1. a.** The faculty of recognizing the distinction between right and wrong in regard to one's conduct coupled with a sense that one should act accordingly. **b.** Conformity to one's own sense of right conduct. **2.** *Obs.* **a.** Consciousness. **b.** Inner thought. ***—idiom.*** **in (all) conscience.** In all truth or fairness. [ME < OFr. < Lat. *conscientia* < *consciens,* pr.part. of *conscire,* to know wrong : *com-* (intensive) + *scire,* to know.] **—con'science·less** *adj.*

conscience clause *n.* A clause in a law that relieves persons whose conscientious or religious scruples forbid compliance.

conscience money *n.* Money paid, often anonymously, to atone for a concealed dishonest act.

con·sci·en·tious (kŏn'shē-ĕn'shəs) *adj.* **1.** Governed by or accomplished according to conscience; scrupulous: *a conscientious governor.* **2.** Thorough and painstaking; careful: *a conscientious worker.* [Fr. *conscienteux* < Med. Lat. *conscientosus* < Lat. *conscientia,* conscience.] **—con'sci·en'tious·ly** *adv.* **—con'sci·en'tious·ness** *n.*

conscientious objector *n.* One who on the basis of religious and moral principles refuses to bear arms or participate in military service.

con·scio·na·ble (kŏn'shə-nə-bəl) *adj.* Conscientious. [Obs. *conscions,* var. of CONSCIENCE + -ABLE.]

con·scious (kŏn'shəs) *adj.* **1. a.** Having an awareness of one's own existence, sensations, and thoughts and of one's environment: *injured but conscious.* **b.** Capable of thought, will, or perception: *Man is a conscious being.* **2.** Subjectively known or felt: *conscious remorse.* **3.** Intentionally conceived or done; deliberate: *a conscious insult; made a conscious effort to speak clearly.* **4.** Having or showing self-consciousness; aware: *conscious of his shortcomings.* —*n. Psychoanal.* The component of waking awareness perceptible by an individual at any given instant; consciousness. [Lat. *conscius,* knowing with others : *com-,* together + *scire,* to know.] **—con'scious·ly** *adv.*

con·scious·ness (kŏn'shəs-nĭs) *n.* **1.** The state or condition of being conscious. **2.** The essence or totality of attitudes, opinions, and sensitivities held or thought to be held by an individual or group: *national consciousness.* **3.** *Psychoanal.* The conscious. **4. a.** A critical awareness of one's own identity and situation. **b.** Awareness; concern: *class consciousness.*

consciousness-raising *n.* **1.** A process of achieving greater awareness of one's needs in order to fulfill one's potential as an individual. **2.** A technique whereby one is made aware of discrimination against a particular class of people who have been oppressed. ***—modifier:*** *consciousness-raising groups.* **—con'scious·ness-rais'er** *n.*

con·script (kŏn'skrĭpt') *n.* One who is compulsorily enrolled for service; draftee. —*adj.* (kŏn'skrĭpt'). Enrolled compulsorily; drafted. —*tr.v.* (kən-skrĭpt') **-script·ed, -script·ing, -scripts.** To enroll compulsorily into service; draft. [Lat. *conscriptus,* p.part. of *conscribere,* to enroll : *com-,* together + *scribere,* to write.]

con·scrip·tion (kən-skrĭp'shən) *n.* **1.** Compulsory enrollment, esp. for the armed forces; draft. **2.** A monetary payment exacted by a government in wartime.

con·se·crate (kŏn'sĭ-krāt') *tr.v.* **-crat·ed, -crat·ing, -crates. 1.** To declare or set apart as sacred: *consecrate a church.* **2.** *Eccles.* **a.** To change (the elements of the Eucharist) into the body and blood of Christ. **b.** To initiate (a priest) into the order of bishops. **3.** To dedicate to a given goal or service: *consecrated his life to helping the poor.* **4.** To make venerable: *a tradition consecrated by time.* —*adj.* Consecrated to a sacred purpose; sanctified. [ME *consecraten* < Lat. *consecrare* : *com-* (intensive) + *sacrare,* to make sacred < *sacer,* sacred.] **—con'se·cra'tive** *adj.* **—con'se·cra'tor** *n.* **—con'se·cra·to'ry** (-krə-tôr'ē, -tōr'ē) *adj.*

con·se·cra·tion (kŏn'sĭ-krā'shən) *n.* **1.** The act, process, or ceremony of consecrating. **2.** The state of being consecrated.

con·se·cu·tion (kŏn'sĭ-kyo͞o'shən) *n.* **1.** A sequence or succession. **2.** *Logic.* The relation of consequent to antecedent; deduction; inference. [Lat. *consecutio* < *consequi,* to follow closely. —see CONSEQUENT.]

con·sec·u·tive (kən-sĕk'yə-tĭv) *adj.* **1.** Following successively without interruption. **2.** Marked by logical sequence. [Fr. *consecutif* < Med. Lat. *consecutivus* < Lat. *consequi,* to follow closely. —see CONSEQUENT.] **—con·sec'u·tive·ly** *adv.* **—con·sec'u·tive·ness** *n.*

con·sen·su·al (kən-sĕn'sho͞o-əl) *adj.* **1.** *Law.* Existing or brought about by consent, as a marriage. **2.** *Physiol.* Of or pertaining to an involuntary function or reflex that occurs on the opposite side of the body from the point of stimulation. [< CONSENSUS.] **—con·sen'su·al·ly** *adv.*

con·sen·sus (kən-sĕn'səs) *n.* **1.** Collective opinion: *the voters' consensus was that the tax bill was a good one.* **2.** General agreement or accord. [Lat. < *consentire,* to agree. —see CONSENT.]

Usage: The phrase *consensus of opinion* is held to be redundant because *consensus* by itself denotes a general opinion.

con·sent (kən-sĕnt') *intr.v.* **-sent·ed, -sent·ing, -sents. 1.** To give assent; agree. **2.** *Archaic.* To be of the same mind or opinion. —*n.* **1.** Voluntary allowance of what is planned or done by another; permission. **2.** Agreement and acceptance as to opinion or a course of action. [ME *consenten* < Lat. *consentire,* to agree : *com-,* together + *sentire,* to feel.] **—con·sent'er** *n.*

con·sen·ta·ne·ous (kŏn'sĕn-tā'nē-əs) *adj.* **1.** Manifesting agreement; accordant. **2.** Unanimous. [Lat. *consentaneus,* agreeing < *consentire,* to agree. —see CONSENT.] **—con·sen'ta·ne'i·ty** (kən-sĕn'tə-nē'ĭ-tē), **con'sen·ta'ne·ous·ness** *n.* **—con'sen·ta'ne·ous·ly** *adv.*

con·se·quence (kŏn'sĭ-kwĕns', -kwəns) *n.* **1.** Something that logically or naturally follows from an action or condition; effect. **2.** The relation of a result to its cause. **3.** A logical result or inference. **4.** Distinction or importance in rank: *a person of consequence.* **5.** Significance; importance: *an issue of consequence.*

con·se·quent (kŏn'sĭ-kwĕnt', -kwənt) *adj.* **1. a.** Following as a natural effect, result, or conclusion. **b.** Following as a logical conclusion. **2.** Logically correct or consistent. **3.** *Geol.* Having a position or direction relating to or resulting from the original slope of the earth's surface. —*n.* **1.** *Logic.* The conclusion, as of a syllogism. **2.** The second term of a ratio. [ME < Lat. *consequens,* pr.part. of *consequi,* to follow closely : *com-* (intensive) + *sequi,* to follow.]

con·se·quen·tial (kŏn'sĭ-kwĕn'shəl) *adj.* **1.** Following as an effect, result, or conclusion; consequent. **2.** Having consequence; important. **3.** Pompous; self-important. **—con'se·quen'ti·al'i·ty** (-shē-ăl'ĭ-tē), **con'se·quen'tial·ness** *n.* **—con'se·quen'tial·ly** *adv.*

con·se·quent·ly (kŏn'sĭ-kwĕnt'lē, -kwənt-lē) *adv.* As a result; therefore.

con·ser·van·cy (kən-sûr'vən-sē) *n., pl.* **-cies. 1.** Conservation, esp. of natural resources. **2.** *Chiefly Brit.* A commission supervising fisheries and navigation.

con·ser·va·tion (kŏn'sûr-vā'shən) *n.* **1.** The act or process of conserving. **2.** The controlled use and systematic protection of natural resources, such as forests and waterways. **—con'ser·va'tion·al** *adj.*

con·ser·va·tion·ist (kŏn'sûr-vā'shə-nĭst) *n.* One who practices or advocates conservation of natural resources.

conservation of charge *n.* An exact conservation law stating that the total electric charge of an isolated system remains constant regardless of changes within the system.

conservation of energy *n.* An exact conservation law stating that the total energy of an isolated system remains constant regardless of changes within the system.

conservation of mass *n.* The classical principle that the total mass of an isolated system is unchanged by interaction of its parts.

conservation of momentum *n.* An exact conservation law stating that the total linear momentum of an isolated system remains constant regardless of changes within the system.

con·ser·va·tism (kən-sûr'və-tĭz'əm) *n.* **1. a.** The disposition in politics to maintain the existing order and to resist or oppose change. **b.** The principles and practices of persons or groups so disposed. **2. Conservatism.** The principles and practices of the Conservative Party in the United Kingdom.

con·ser·va·tive (kən-sûr'və-tĭv) *adj.* **1. a.** Tending to oppose change; favoring traditional views and values. **b.** Traditional in style; not showy: *a conservative dark suit.* **2.** Moderate; cautious; restrained: *a conservative estimate.* **3. a.** Belonging to a conservative party or political group. **b. Conservative.** Adhering to or characteristic of the Conservative Party of the United Kingdom. **4. Conservative.** Of, pertaining to, or adhering to Conservative Judaism. **5.** Tending to conserve; preservative. —*n.* **1.** A person who favors traditional views and values. **2. a.** A person who supports political conservatism. **b. Conservative.** A member or supporter of the Conservative Party of the United Kingdom. **3.** A preservative. **—con·ser'va·tive·ly** *adv.* **—con·ser'va·tive·ness** *n.*

Conservative Judaism *n.* The branch of Judaism that holds a modified view of the sanctity of the Torah and is flexible in its submission to the authority of the rabbinical law, accepting some liturgical and ritual changes in the light of the needs of modern life.
Conservative Party *n.* A major political party of the United Kingdom.
con·ser·va·tor (kən-sûr′və-tər, kŏn′sər-vā′tər) *n.* **1.** One who conserves or preserves from injury, violation, or infraction; protector. **2.** *Law.* One who is responsible for the person and property of an incompetent. **—con·ser′va·to′ri·al** (-tôr′ē-əl, -tōr′-) *adj.*
con·ser·va·to·ry (kən-sûr′və-tôr′ē, -tōr′ē) *n., pl.* **-ries. 1.** A small glass-enclosed room or greenhouse in which plants are raised and displayed. **2.** A school of music or dramatic art.
con·serve (kən-sûrv′) *tr.v.* **-served, -serv·ing, -serves. 1. a.** To protect from loss or depletion: *conserved his supply of Cuban cigars.* **b.** To use carefully, avoiding waste: *tried to conserve fuel.* **2.** To preserve (fruits) with sugar. *—n.* (kŏn′sûrv′). A jam made of fruits stewed in sugar. [ME *conserven* < OFr. *conserver* < Lat. *conservare* : *com-* (intensive) + *servare,* to preserve.] **—con·serv′a·ble** *adj.* **—con·serv′er** *n.*
con·sid·er (kən-sĭd′ər) *v.* **-ered, -er·ing, -ers.** *—tr.* **1.** To think about carefully and seriously. **2.** To regard as; think or deem to be: *considered her a fool.* **3.** To believe after deliberation; judge: *considers waste criminal.* **4.** To take into account; bear in mind: *Consider the fact that he's a beginner.* **5.** To show consideration for: *considered others' feelings.* **6.** To esteem; regard. **7.** To look at thoughtfully. *—intr.* To think carefully; reflect: *Give me time to consider.* [ME *consideren* < Lat. *considerare.*] **—con·sid′er·er** *n.*

Synonyms: *consider, deem, regard, account, reckon.* These verbs refer to holding opinions or views that reflect evaluation of a person or thing. *Consider* suggests objective evaluation based on reflection and reasoning. *Deem* is more subjective through its emphasis on judgment distinguished from analytical thought. *Regard* may imply personal, subjective judgment or, especially in the passive, the sentiment of many. *Account* and *reckon* in this sense are rather literary in flavor and imply calculated judgment. Less formally, *reckon* is used in the related sense of suppose.

con·sid·er·a·ble (kən-sĭd′ər-ə-bəl) *adj.* **1.** Large in amount, extent, or degree: *a man of considerable influence.* **2.** Worthy of consideration; important; significant: *a considerable issue.* *—n. Informal.* A considerable amount, extent, or degree. **—con·sid′er·a·bly** *adv.*

Usage: *Considerable* is not properly used as an adverb: *She helped him considerable* (in correct usage, *considerably*). In some dialects of American English it is used as an intensive (*she acted considerable strange*), but this use is unacceptable in formal usage. Use of *considerable* as a noun is informal: *He did considerable for his sister's family.*

con·sid·er·ate (kən-sĭd′ər-ĭt) *adj.* **1.** Having regard for the needs or feelings of others; thoughtful. **2.** Characterized by careful thought; deliberate. [Lat. *consideratus,* p.part. of *considerare,* to consider.] **—con·sid′er·ate·ly** *adv.* **—con·sid′er·ate·ness** *n.*
con·sid·er·a·tion (kən-sĭd′ə-rā′shən) *n.* **1.** Careful thought; deliberation: *will give your proposal consideration.* **2.** A factor to be considered in forming a judgment or decision: *Health is the most important consideration.* **3.** Thoughtful concern for others; solicitude. **4.** A thought produced by considering; a thoughtful opinion. **5.** Payment given in exchange for a service rendered; recompense: *agreed to do it for a small consideration.* **6.** *Law.* Something promised, given, or done that has the effect of making an agreement a legally enforceable contract. **7.** High regard. **—idiom. in consideration of. 1.** In view of; on account of. **2.** In return for.
con·sid·ered (kən-sĭd′ərd) *adj.* **1.** Reached after deliberation or careful thought: *my considered opinion.* **2.** Regarded; esteemed.
con·sid·er·ing (kən-sĭd′ər-ĭng) *prep.* In view of; taking into consideration. *—adv. Informal.* All things considered.
con·sign (kən-sīn′) *v.* **-signed, -sign·ing, -signs.** *—tr.* **1.** To give over to the care of another; entrust. **2.** To turn over to another's charge or control; commit. **3.** To deliver (merchandise, for example) for custody or sale. *—intr. Obs.* To submit; consent. [OFr. *consigner* < Lat. *consignare,* to attest : *com-* (intensive) + *signare,* to mark < *signum,* mark.] **—con·sign′a·ble** *adj.* **—con′sig·na′tion** (kŏn′sĭ-nā′shən, -sĭg-) *n.* **—con·sig′nor, con·sign′er** *n.*
con·sign·ee (kŏn′sī-nē′, kən-sī′nē′) *n.* A person, such as an agent, to whom merchandise is consigned.
con·sign·ment (kən-sīn′mənt) *n.* **1.** The act of consigning. **2.** Something that is consigned. **—idiom. on consignment.** Sent to a retailer who is expected to pay following sale.
con·sist (kən-sĭst′) *intr.v.* **-sist·ed, -sist·ing, -sists. 1.** To be made up or composed: *New York City consists of five boroughs.* **2.** To have a basis; be inherent; lie: *The beauty of his style consists in its simplicity.* **3.** To be compatible; accord. [Lat. *consistere,* to stand still : *com-* (intensive) + *sistere,* to cause to stand.]
con·sis·tence (kən-sĭs′təns) *n.* Consistency.
con·sis·ten·cy (kən-sĭs′tən-sē) *n., pl.* **-cies. 1.** Agreement or logical coherence among things or parts. **2.** Compatibility or agreement among successive acts, ideas, or events. **3.** Degree or texture of density, firmness, or viscosity.
con·sis·tent (kən-sĭs′tənt) *adj.* **1.** In agreement; compatible. **2.** Conforming to the same principles or course of action; uniform. [Lat. *consistens, consistent-,* pr.part. of *consistere,* to stand still. —see CONSIST.] **—con·sis′tent·ly** *adv.*
con·sis·to·ry (kən-sĭs′tə-rē) *n., pl.* **-ries. 1. a.** *Rom. Cath. Ch.* A gathering presided over by the pope for the solemn promulgation of papal acts, as the canonization of a saint. **b.** In certain Reformed churches, a governing body of a local congregation. **c.** In Lutheran state churches, a court appointed to regulate ecclesiastical affairs. **d.** In the Anglican church, a diocesan court presided over by the bishop's chancellor or commissary. **2.** The meeting of a consistory. **3.** A council or tribunal. [ME *consistorie* < LLat. *consistorium,* assembly < Lat. *consistere,* to stand together. —see CONSIST.] **—con′sis·to′ri·al** (kŏn′sĭ-stôr′ē-əl, -stōr′ē-əl) *adj.*

conservatory

con·so·ci·ate (kən-sō′shē-āt′) *tr. & intr.v.* **-at·ed, -at·ing, -ates.** To bring or come into friendly association. *—adj.* (-ĭt). Associated; united. *—n.* (-ĭt). An associate; companion. [< ME *consociat,* associated < Lat. *consociatus,* p.part. of *consociare,* to associate : *com-,* together + *sociare,* to associate < *socius,* companion.] **—con·so′ci·a′tion** *n.*
con·so·la·tion (kŏn′sə-lā′shən) *n.* **1. a.** The act or an instance of consoling. **b.** The state of being consoled. **2.** Something that consoles; comfort.
con·sole¹ (kən-sōl′) *tr.v.* **-soled, -sol·ing, -soles.** To comfort in time of grief, defeat, or trouble; solace. [Fr. *consoler* < OFr. < Lat. *consolari* : *com-* (intensive) + *solari,* to comfort.] **—con·sol′a·ble** *adj.* **—con·so′la·to′ry** (-sō′lə-tôr′ē, -tōr′ē, -sŏl′ə-) *adj.* **—con·sol′er** *n.* **—con·sol′ing·ly** *adv.*
con·sole² (kŏn′sōl′) *n.* **1.** A decorative bracket for supporting a cornice, shelf, bust, or other object. **2.** A console table. **3.** The desklike part of an organ that contains the keyboard, stops, and pedals. **4.** A cabinet for a radio, television set, or phonograph, designed to stand on the floor. **5.** A panel housing the controls for electrical or mechanical equipment. **6.** The portion of a computer that houses the apparatus used to manually operate the machine and that provides a means of communication between the computer operator and the central processing unit. [Fr., perh. short for *consolider,* to strengthen < Lat. *consolidare.* —see CONSOLIDATE.]
con·sole table (kŏn′sōl′) *n.* **1.** A table supported by decorative consoles fixed to a wall. **2.** A small table, often with curved legs resembling consoles, designed to be set against a wall.

console table
Louis XVI console table

con·sol·i·date (kən-sŏl′ĭ-dāt′) *v.* **-dat·ed, -dat·ing, -dates.** *—tr.* **1.** To make firm or coherent; form into a compact mass. **2.** To make strong or stable; strengthen: *consolidated his political base.* **3.** To unite into one system or body; combine: *consolidated four small companies.* *—intr.* To become solidified or united. [Lat. *consolidare, consolidat-* : *com-* (intensive) + *solidare,* to make firm < *solidus,* firm.] **—con·sol′i·da′tor** *n.*
consolidated school *n.* A public school, usually rural, for pupils from several adjacent districts.
con·sol·i·da·tion (kən-sŏl′ĭ-dā′shən) *n.* **1. a.** The act or process of consolidating. **b.** The state of being consolidated. **2.** The merger of two or more commercial interests or corporations.
con·sols (kŏn′sŏlz′, kən-sŏlz′) *pl.n.* The perpetual governmental securities of Great Britain. [Short for *consolidated annuities.*]
con·so·lute (kŏn′sə-lo͞ot′) *adj.* Of or pertaining to liquid substances that are capable of being mixed in all proportions. [LLat. *consolutus,* dissolved together: Lat. *con-,* together + Lat. *solutus,* p.part. of *solvere,* to loosen, dissolve.]
con·som·mé (kŏn′sə-mā′, kŏn′sə-mā′) *n.* A clear soup made of meat or vegetable stock or both. [Fr. < *consommer,* to use up < Lat. *consummare,* to finish. —see CONSUMMATE.]
con·so·nance (kŏn′sə-nəns) *n.* **1.** Agreement; harmony; accord. **2. a.** Correspondence of sounds. **b.** A similarity or repetition of terminal consonants in two or more syllables, words, or lines, as in *rain* and *tone.* **3.** *Mus.* A simultaneous combination of sounds conventionally regarded as pleasing and final in effect.
con·so·nant (kŏn′sə-nənt) *adj.* **1.** In agreement or accord: *remarks consonant with his beliefs.* **2.** Corresponding in sound. **3.** Harmonious in sound. **4.** Consonantal. *—n.* **1.** A speech sound produced by a partial or complete obstruction of the air stream by any of various constrictions of the speech organs. **2.** A letter or character representing a consonant. [ME < Lat. *consonans,* pr.part. of *consonare,* to agree : *com-,* together + *sonare,* to sound.] **—con′so·nant·ly** *adv.*
con·so·nan·tal (kŏn′sə-năn′tl) *adj.* **1.** Of, relating to, or having the nature of a consonant. **2.** Containing a consonant or consonants. **—con′so·nan′tal·ly** *adv.*
con·sort (kŏn′sôrt′) *n.* **1.** A husband or wife, esp. the spouse of a monarch. **2.** A companion or partner. **3.** A ship accompanying another in travel. *—v.* (kən-sôrt′) **-sort·ed, -sort·ing, -sorts.** *—intr.* **1.** To keep company; associate: *consorts with gangsters.* **2.** To be in accord or agreement. *—tr.* **1.** To unite in company; associate. **2.** *Obs.* **a.** To escort; accompany. **b.** To espouse. [ME, colleague < OFr. < Lat. *consors,* partner : *com-,* together + *sors,* fate.]
con·sor·ti·um (kən-sôr′tē-əm, -shē-əm) *n., pl.* **-ti·a** (-tē-ə,

-shē-ə). **1.** An association of financial institutions or capitalists for effecting a venture requiring extensive financial resources, esp. in international finance. **2.** An association or partnership. **3.** *Law.* **a.** A husband's right to the company, help, and affection of his wife. **b.** A wife's right to the company, help, and affection of her husband. [Lat., fellowship < *consors,* partner. —see CONSORT.]

con·spe·cif·ic (kŏn'spĭ-sĭf'ĭk) *adj.* Of the same species.

con·spec·tus (kən-spĕk'təs) *n.* **1.** A general survey of a subject. **2.** A synopsis. [Lat., view < p.part. of *conspicere,* to observe. —see CONSPICUOUS.]

con·spic·u·ous (kən-spĭk'yo͞o-əs) *adj.* **1.** Easy to notice; obvious. **2.** Attracting attention by being unusual or remarkable. [Lat. *conspicuus* < *conspicere,* to observe : *com-* (intensive) + *specere,* to look.] **—con·spic'u·ous·ly** *adv.* **—con·spic'u·ous·ness** *n.*

con·spir·a·cy (kən-spîr'ə-sē) *n., pl.* **-cies. 1.** An agreement to perform together an illegal, treacherous, or evil act. **2.** A group of conspirators. **3.** A combining or acting together, as if by evil design: *a conspiracy of natural forces.* **4.** *Law.* An agreement between two or more persons to commit a crime or to accomplish a legal purpose through illegal action. [ME *conspiracie* < AN, prob. var. of OFr. *conspiraciou̇n* < Lat. *conspiratio* < *conspirare,* to conspire.]

Synonyms: *conspiracy, plot, machination, collusion, intrigue, cabal.* These nouns denote secret plans or schemes. *Conspiracy* refers to such a plan by a group intent usually on a bold purpose, such as overthrowing a government. *Plot* stresses sinister means and motives but may be small or large in number of participants and scope. *Machination,* usually in the plural, strongly implies crafty, underhand dealing by one or more persons, but is generally less forceful than the preceding terms. *Collusion* refers to secret agreement between persons, usually with intent to defraud others. *Intrigue* denotes a complex, clandestine scheme; usually it implies selfish, petty actions rather than criminal ends. *Cabal* refers to a conspiratorial group or to its actions, which usually are directed against a government or a political leader.

con·spir·a·tor (kən-spîr'ə-tər) *n.* A person engaged in a conspiracy; plotter.

con·spir·a·to·ri·al (kən-spîr'ə-tôr'ē-əl, -tōr'-) *adj.* Of, pertaining to, or characteristic of conspirators or a conspiracy. **—con·spir'a·to'ri·al·ly** *adv.*

con·spire (kən-spīr') *v.* **-spired, -spir·ing, -spires.** *—intr.* **1.** To plan together secretly to commit an illegal or evil act or to accomplish a legal purpose through illegal action. **2.** To work or act together; combine: *factors that conspired against his re-election.* *—tr.* To plan or plot secretly. [ME *conspiren,* < Lat. *conspirare* : *com-,* together + *spirare,* to breathe.] **—con·spir'er** *n.* **—con·spir'ing·ly** *adv.*

constable

con spi·ri·to (kŏn spîr'ĭ-tō', kōn) *adv. Mus.* With spirit and vigor. Used as a direction. [Ital.]

con·sta·ble (kŏn'stə-bəl, kŭn'-) *n.* **1.** A peace officer with less authority and smaller jurisdiction than a sheriff, empowered to serve writs and warrants and to make arrests. **2.** In medieval monarchies, an officer of high rank, usually serving as military commander in the ruler's absence. **3.** The governor of a royal castle. **4.** *Chiefly Brit.* A policeman. [ME < OFr. *conestable* < LLat. *comes stabuli* : Lat. *comes,* officer + Lat. *stabulum,* stable.] **—con'sta·ble·ship'** *n.*

con·stab·u·lar (kən-stăb'yə-lər) *adj.* Constabulary.

con·stab·u·lar·y (kən-stăb'yə-lĕr'ē) *n., pl.* **-ies. 1.** The body of constables of a district or city. **2.** The district under the jurisdiction of a constable. **3.** An armed police force organized like a military unit. *—adj.* Of or pertaining to constables or constabularies.

con·stan·cy (kŏn'stən-sē) *n.* **1.** Steadfastness, as in purpose; faithfulness. **2.** The quality of being constant; changelessness.

con·stant (kŏn'stənt) *adj.* **1.** Continually occurring or recurring; persistent. **2.** Unchanging in nature, value, or extent; invariable. **3.** Steadfast in purpose, loyalty, or affection; faithful. *—n.* **1.** Something that is unchanging or invariable. **2. a.** *Math.* A quantity taken to have a fixed value in a specified mathematical context. **b.** An experimental or theoretical condition, factor, or quantity that occurs, is held, or is regarded as invariant in specified circumstances. [ME < Lat. *constans,* pr.part. of *constare,* to stand firm : *com-* (intensive) + *stare,* to stand.] **—con'stant·ly** *adv.*

con·stan·tan (kŏn'stən-tăn') *n.* An alloy of equal parts of nickel and copper, used chiefly in electrical instruments because of its constant resistance. [< CONSTANT.]

constant dollars *pl.n.* A measure of the cost of goods or services with the effects of inflation removed.

con·stel·late (kŏn'stə-lāt') *intr. & tr.v.* **-lat·ed, -lat·ing, -lates.** To form or cause to form a group or cluster. [Back-formation < CONSTELLATION.]

con·stel·la·tion (kŏn'stə-lā'shən) *n.* **1.** *Astron.* **a.** Any of 88 stellar groups considered to resemble and named after various mythological characters, inanimate objects, and animals. **b.** An area of the celestial sphere occupied by such a group. **2.** *Astrol.* The position of the stars at the time of one's birth, regarded by astrologers as determining one's character or fate. **3.** A gathering or assemblage of similar or related persons or things. **4.** A set or configuration of objects, properties, or individuals, esp. a structurally or systematically related grouping. [ME *constellacioun* < OFr. *constellation* < LLat. *constellatio* : *com-,* together + *stella,* star.] **—con'stel·la'tion·al** *adj.* **—con·stel'la·to'ry** (-stĕl'ə-tôr'ē, -tōr'ē) *adj.*

con·ster·nate (kŏn'stər-nāt') *tr.v.* **-nat·ed, -nat·ing, -nates.** To cause consternation in. [Lat. *consternare, consternat-* : *com-* (intensive) + *sternere,* to throw down.]

con·ster·na·tion (kŏn'stər-nā'shən) *n.* Sudden confusion or amazement.

con·sti·pate (kŏn'stə-pāt') *tr.v.* **-pat·ed, -pat·ing, -pates.** To cause constipation in. [Lat. *constipare, constipat-,* to crowd together : *com-,* together + *stipare,* to cram.]

con·sti·pa·tion (kŏn'stə-pā'shən) *n.* Difficult, incomplete, or infrequent evacuation of the bowels.

con·stit·u·en·cy (kən-stĭch'o͞o-ən-sē) *n., pl.* **-cies. 1. a.** The body of voters represented by an elected legislator or executive. **b.** The district represented. **2.** A group of supporters.

con·stit·u·ent (kən-stĭch'o͞o-ənt) *adj.* **1.** Serving as part of a whole; component. **2.** Empowered to elect or designate. **3.** Authorized to make or amend a constitution. *—n.* **1.** Someone who authorizes another to represent him; client. **2.** A member of a group represented by an elected official. **3.** A constituent part; component. **4.** *Gram.* One of two or more elements into which a construction or compound may be divided by analysis, being either immediate, as *He/ works on the railroad,* or ultimate, as *He/ work/s/ on/ the/ rail/road.* [Lat. *constituens, constituent-,* pr.part. of *constituere,* to set up. —see CONSTITUTE.] **—con·stit'u·ent·ly** *adv.*

constituent structure *n.* An analysis, often in the form of a schematic representation, of the constituents of a grammatical construction, such as a sentence.

con·sti·tute (kŏn'stĭ-to͞ot', -tyo͞ot') *tr.v.* **-tut·ed, -tut·ing, -tutes. 1.** To be the elements or parts of; compose: *Ten members constitute a quorum.* **2.** To set up; enact (a law, for example). **3.** To establish formally; found (an institution, for example). **4.** To appoint to an office, dignity, function, or task; designate. [Lat. *constituere, constitut-,* to set up : *com-* (intensive) + *statuere,* to set up.] **—con'sti·tut'er, con'sti·tu'tor** *n.*

con·sti·tu·tion (kŏn'stĭ-to͞o'shən, -tyo͞o'-) *n.* **1.** The act or process of composing, setting up, or establishing. **2. a.** The composition or structure of something; make-up. **b.** The physical make-up of a person: *a man with a strong constitution.* **3. a.** The system of fundamental laws and principles that prescribes the nature, functions, and limits of a government or other institution. **b.** The document on which such a system is recorded.

con·sti·tu·tion·al (kŏn'stĭ-to͞o'shə-nəl, -tyo͞o'-) *adj.* **1.** Of or pertaining to a constitution: *a constitutional amendment.* **2.** Consistent with or permissible according to a constitution. **3.** Established by or operating under a constitution. **4.** Of or proceeding from the basic structure or nature of a person or thing; essential: *a constitutional inability to say "yes."* *—n.* A walk taken regularly for one's health. **—con'sti·tu'tion·al'i·ty** (-năl'ĭ-tē) *n.* **—con'sti·tu'tion·al·ly** *adv.*

con·sti·tu·tion·al·ism (kŏn'stĭ-to͞o'shə-nə-lĭz'əm, -tyo͞o'-) *n.* **1.** Government in which power is distributed and limited by a system of laws that must be obeyed by the rulers. **2.** Advocacy of constitutionalism. **—con'sti·tu'tion·al·ist** *n.*

constitutional monarchy *n.* A monarchy in which the powers of the ruler are restricted to those granted under the constitution and laws of the nation.

con·sti·tu·tive (kŏn'stĭ-to͞o'tĭv, -tyo͞o'-) *adj.* **1.** Making a thing what it is; essential. **2.** Having power to institute, establish, or enact. **—con'sti·tu'tive·ly** *adv.*

con·sti·tu·tive enzyme (kŏn'stĭ-to͞o'tĭv, -tyo͞o'-, kən-stĭch'ə-tĭv) *n.* An enzyme produced by a cell regardless of the presence of its substrate.

con·strain (kən-strān') *tr.v.* **-strained, -strain·ing, -strains. 1.** To compel by physical, moral, or circumstantial force; oblige: *felt constrained to object.* **2.** To keep within close bounds; confine. **3.** To check the freedom or mobility of; restrain. **4.** To compel or produce in a forced or artificial manner: *a constrained smile.* [ME *constreinen* < Lat. *constringere,* to restrain, compress : *com-,* together + *stringere,* to bind.] **—con·strain'a·ble** *adj.* **—con·strain'ed·ly** (-strā'nĭd-lē) *adv.* **—con·strain'er** *n.*

con·straint (kən-strānt') *n.* **1.** The threat or use of force to prevent, restrict, or dictate the action or thought of others. **2.** The state, quality, or sense of being restricted to a given course of action or inaction. **3.** Something that restricts, limits, or regulates. **4.** A lack of ease; embarrassed reserve or reticence: *"All constraint had vanished between the two, and they began to talk"* (Edith Wharton). [ME *constreinte* < OFr. *constraindre* < Lat. *constringere,* to restrain. —see CONSTRAIN.]

con·strict (kən-strĭkt') *v.* **-strict·ed, -strict·ing, -stricts.** *—tr.* **1.** To make smaller or narrower, as by shrinking or contracting. **2.** To squeeze or compress by or as if by narrowing or tightening. *—intr.* To become constricted. [Lat. *constringere, constrict-,* to compress. —see CONSTRAIN.] **—con·stric'tive** *adj.* **—con·stric'tive·ly** *adv.*

con·stric·tion (kən-strĭk'shən) *n.* **1. a.** The act or process of constricting. **b.** The condition of being constricted. **2.** Something that constricts.

con·stric·tor (kən-strĭk'tər) *n.* **1.** One that constricts. **2.** *Anat.* A muscle that contracts or compresses a part or organ of the body. **3.** Any of various snakes, such as a python or boa, that coil around and crush their prey.

con·stringe (kən-strĭnj') *tr.v.* **-stringed, -string·ing, -string·es.** To cause to contract; constrict. [Lat. *constringere,* to compress. —see CONSTRAIN.] **—con·strin'gen·cy** *n.* **—con·strin'gent** *adj.*

con·struct (kən-strŭkt') *tr.v.* **-struct·ed, -struct·ing, -structs.** **1.** To form by assembling parts; build. **2.** To create (a sentence, for example) by systematically arranging ideas or expressions. **3.** *Math.* To draw (a geometric figure) that meets specific requirements, usually with instruments limited to a straightedge and compass. *—n.* (kŏn'strŭkt'). Something, esp. a concept, that is synthesized or constructed from simple elements. [Lat. *construere, construct-* : *com-,* together + *struere,* to pile up.] **—con·struct'i·ble** *adj.* **—con·struc'tor, con·struct'er** *n.*

con·struc·tion (kən-strŭk'shən) *n.* **1. a.** The act or process of constructing. **b.** The condition of being constructed. **c.** The business or work of building. **2.** Something that is constructed; a structure or building. **3.** The way in which something is put together: *a shelter of simple construction.* **4.** The interpretation or explanation given an expression or statement. **5.** *Gram.* **a.** The arrangement of words to form a meaningful phrase, clause, or sentence. **b.** A group of words so arranged. **—con·struc'tion·al** *adj.* **—con·struc'tion·al·ly** *adv.*

con·struc·tion·ist (kən-strŭk'shə-nĭst) *n.* A person who construes a legal text or document in a specified way.

con·struc·tive (kən-strŭk'tĭv) *adj.* **1.** Serving to advance a good purpose; helpful. **2.** Of or pertaining to construction; structural. **3.** *Law.* Based on an interpretation; not directly expressed. **—con·struc'tive·ly** *adv.* **—con·struc'tive·ness** *n.*

con·struc·tiv·ism (kən-strŭk'tə-vĭz'əm) *n.* A movement in modern art in which glass, sheet metal, and other industrial materials are used to create nonrepresentational, often geometric objects. **—con·struc'tiv·ist** *n.*

con·strue (kən-strōō') *v.* **-strued, -stru·ing, -strues.** *—tr.* **1.** *Gram.* **a.** To analyze the structure of (a clause or sentence). **b.** To use syntactically: *The noun "fish" can be construed as singular or plural.* **2.** To place a certain meaning on; interpret. **3.** To translate, esp. aloud. *—intr.* To analyze grammatical structure. *—n.* (kŏn'strōō'). An interpretation or translation. [ME *construen* < LLat. *construere* < Lat., to build. —see CONSTRUCT.]

con·sub·stan·tial (kŏn'səb-stăn'shəl) *adj.* Having the same substance, nature, or essence. [ME *consubstancial* < LLat. *consubstantialis* : Lat. *com-,* same + LLat. *substantialis,* substantial < Lat. *substantia,* substance.]

con·sub·stan·ti·ate (kŏn'səb-stăn'shē-āt') *tr. & intr.v.* **-at·ed, -at·ing, -ates.** To unite or become united in one common substance, nature, or essence.

con·sub·stan·ti·a·tion (kŏn'səb-stăn'shē-ā'shən) *n.* *Theol.* The Lutheran doctrine that the body and blood of Christ coexist with the elements of bread and wine during the Eucharist.

con·sue·tude (kŏn'swĭ-tōōd', -tyōōd') *n.* Custom; usage. [ME < Lat. *consuetūdo.* —see CUSTOM.] **—con'sue·tu'di·nar'y** (-tōōd'n-ĕr'ē, -tyōōd'-) *adj.*

con·sul (kŏn'səl) *n.* **1.** Either of the two chief magistrates of the Roman Republic, elected for a term of one year. **2.** Any of the three chief magistrates of the French Republic from 1799 to 1804. **3.** An official appointed by a government to reside in a foreign city and represent his government's commercial interests and give assistance to its citizens there. —See Usage note at **council.** [ME *consulat* < Lat. *consulatus* < *consul,* consul.] **—con'su·lar** (-sə-lər) *adj.*

con·su·late (kŏn'sə-lĭt) *n.* **1. a.** Government by consuls. **b.** The office or term of office of a consul. **2.** The premises occupied by a consul. [ME *consulat* < Lat. *consulatus* < *consul,* consul.]

consul general *n., pl.* **consuls general.** A consular officer of the highest rank.

con·sult (kən-sŭlt') *v.* **-sult·ed, -sult·ing, -sults.** *—tr.* **1. a.** To seek advice or information of: *consult an attorney.* **b.** To refer to: *consult a directory.* **2.** To have an eye to; consider: *consult one's bankbook before making a major purchase.* *—intr.* **1.** To exchange views; confer. **2.** To give expert advice as a professional. *—n.* (kən-sŭlt', kŏn'sŭlt'). A consultation. [Lat. *consultare,* freq. of *consulere,* to take counsel.]

con·sult·ant (kən-sŭl'tənt) *n.* **1.** A person who gives expert or professional advice. **2.** A person who consults another.

con·sul·ta·tion (kŏn'səl-tā'shən) *n.* **1.** The act or procedure of consulting. **2.** A conference at which advice is given or views are exchanged.

con·sul·ta·tive (kən-sŭl'tə-tĭv) also **con·sul·ta·to·ry** (-tôr'ē, -tōr'ē) *adj.* Of or pertaining to consultation; advisory.

con·sume (kən-sōōm') *v.* **-sumed, -sum·ing, -sumes.** *—tr.* **1.** To eat or drink up; ingest. **2.** To expend (fuel, for example); use up. **3.** To waste; squander. **4.** To destroy totally, as by fire; level. **5.** To absorb; engross: *consumed with interest.* *—intr.* To be destroyed, expended, or wasted. [ME *consumen* < Lat. *consumere* : *com-* (intensive) + *sumere,* to take.] **—con·sum'a·ble** *adj. & n.*

con·sum·ed·ly (kən-sōō'mĭd-lē) *adv.* To an excessive degree.

con·sum·er (kən-sōō'mər) *n.* **1.** One that consumes. **2.** One who acquires goods or services; buyer. **3.** A heterotrophic organism in a food chain that ingests other organisms or organic matter. **—con·sum'er·ship'** *n.*

consumer credit *n.* Credit granted to a consumer, permitting him to own or use goods while he is making payments on them.

consumer goods *pl.n.* Goods, such as food and clothing, that satisfy human wants through their consumption or use.

con·sum·er·ism (kən-sōō'mə-rĭz'əm) *n.* **1.** The movement seeking to protect the rights of consumers by requiring such practices as honest packaging, labeling, and advertising, fair pricing, and improved safety standards. **2.** The theory that a progressively greater consumption of goods is economically beneficial. **—con·sum'er·ist** *n.*

consumer price index *n.* An index of prices used to measure the change in the cost of basic goods and services in comparison with a fixed base period.

con·sum·mate (kŏn'sə-māt') *tr.v.* **-mat·ed, -mat·ing, -mates.** **1.** To bring to completion, perfection, or fulfillment; conclude: *consummate a business transaction.* **2.** To fulfill (a marriage) with the first act of sexual intercourse after the ceremony. *—adj.* (kən-sŭm'ĭt). **1.** Complete or perfect in every respect: *consummate happiness.* **2.** Supremely accomplished or skilled: *a consummate artist.* **3.** Complete; utter: *a consummate bore.* [ME *consummaten* < Lat. *consummare* : *com-,* together + *summa,* sum.] **—con·sum'mate·ly** *adv.* **—con'sum·ma'tive** (kŏn'sə-mā'tĭv), **con·sum'ma·to'ry** (kən-sŭm'ə-tôr'ē, -tōr'ē) *adj.* **—con'sum·ma'tor** (kŏn'sə-mā'tər) *n.*

con·sum·ma·tion (kŏn'sə-mā'shən) *n.* **1.** The act of consummating; fulfillment. **2.** An ultimate end or goal.

con·sump·tion (kən-sŭmp'shən) *n.* **1. a.** The act or process of consuming. **b.** The state of being consumed. **c.** An amount consumed. **2.** *Econ.* The using up of consumer goods and services. **3.** *Pathol.* **a.** A wasting of tissue. **b.** Tuberculosis (sense 2). [Lat. *consumptio,* a consuming < *consumptus,* p.part. of *consumere,* to consume.]

con·sump·tive (kən-sŭmp'tĭv) *adj.* **1.** Tending to consume. **2.** Of, pertaining to, or afflicted with consumption. *—n.* A person afflicted with consumption. **—con·sump'tive·ly** *adv.*

con·tact (kŏn'tăkt') *n.* **1.** The coming together or touching of two objects or surfaces. **2.** The state of being in communication: *in contact with the right people.* **3.** A person who might be of use; connection. **4.** *Elect.* **a.** A connection between two conductors that permits a flow of current. **b.** A part or device that makes or breaks such a connection. **5.** *Med.* A person recently exposed to a contagious disease. **6.** *Informal.* A contact lens. *—v.* (kŏn'tăkt', kən-tăkt') **-tact·ed, -tact·ing, -tacts.** *—tr.* **1.** To bring or put in contact. **2.** *Informal.* To get in touch with; communicate with. *—intr.* To be in or come into contact. *—adj.* (kŏn'tăkt'). **1.** Of, sustaining, or making contact. **2.** Caused or transmitted by touching: *a contact skin rash.* [Lat. *contactus* < p.part. of *contingere,* to touch : *com-,* together + *tangere,* to touch.] **—con·tac'tu·al** (kən-tăk'chōō-əl) *adj.* **—con·tac'tu·al·ly** *adv.*

Usage: *Contact* (verb), meaning "to get in touch with," is widely used but is still considered inappropriate to formal use by a majority of the Usage Panel. *Contact* (noun), denoting "a person of possible usefulness," is better established and is acceptable to a majority of the Usage Panel.

contact dermatitis *n.* An acute skin inflammation caused by contact with an irritating substance, such as a chemical.

contact flight also **contact flying** *n.* Aircraft navigation by visual reference to the horizon or to landmarks.

contact inhibition *n.* The cessation of cellular growth and division due to contact with other cells.

contact lens *n.* A thin corrective lens fitted over the cornea of the eye.

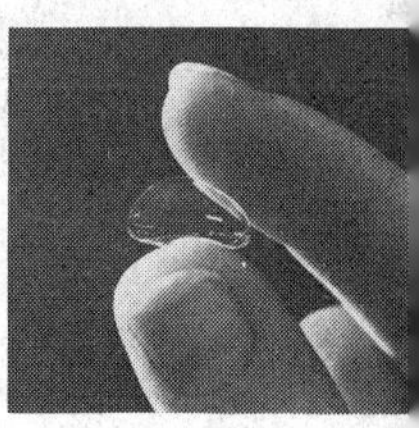
contact lens

contact print *n.* A print made by exposing a photosensitive surface in direct contact with a photographic negative.

con·ta·gion (kən-tā'jən) *n.* **1. a.** Disease transmission by direct or indirect contact. **b.** A disease that is or may be so transmitted. **c.** A contagium. **2.** A harmful or corrupting influence. **3.** The tendency to spread, as of an influence or emotional state. [ME *contagioun* < Lat. *contagio* < *contingere,* to touch. —see CONTACT.]

con·ta·gious (kən-tā'jəs) *adj.* **1.** Transmissible by direct or indirect contact. **2.** Carrying or capable of carrying disease. **3.** Spreading or tending to spread from one to another; catching. **—con·ta'gious·ly** *adv.* **—con·ta'gious·ness** *n.*

contagious abortion *n.* Brucellosis (sense 2).

con·ta·gium (kən-tā'jəm) *n., pl.* **-gia** (-jə). The direct cause, as a virus, of an infectious disease. [Lat., contagion < *contagio.*]

con·tain (kən-tān') *tr.v.* **-tained, -tain·ing, -tains.** **1.** To have within; enclose. **2.** To have as component parts; comprise; include. **3.** To be able to hold; have capacity for. **4.** *Math.* To be exactly divisible by. **5.** To hold or keep within certain limits; restrain: *contain one's emotions.* **6.** To restrict the strategic power of (a nation or bloc), as by encircling it with hostile alliances. [ME *conteinen* < OFr. *contenir* < Lat. *continēre* : *com-,* together + *tenēre,* to hold.] **—con·tain'a·ble** *adj.* **—con·tain'ment** *n.*

Synonyms: *contain, hold, accommodate.* These verbs mean to have within or to have capacity for. *Contain* refers

container
Railroad container cars

to what is actually within at a given time. *Hold* can be used in that sense, but primarily stresses capacity for enclosing a certain maximum. *Accommodate* can mean merely to contain but generally refers to capacity for holding comfortably: *The auditorium was built to accommodate 500.*

con·tain·er (kən-tā′nər) *n.* Something, as a box or barrel, in which material is held or carried; receptacle.

con·tain·er·ize (kən-tā′nə-rīz′) *tr.v.* **-ized, -iz·ing, -iz·es.** To package (cargo) in large, standardized containers to facilitate shipping and handling. **—con·tain′er·i·za′tion** *n.*

container ship *n.* A ship used for carrying containerized cargo.

con·tam·i·nant (kən-tăm′ə-nənt) *n.* Something that contaminates.

con·tam·i·nate (kən-tăm′ə-nāt′) *tr.v.* **-nat·ed, -nat·ing, -nates.** To make impure or corrupt by contact or mixture. *—adj.* (-nĭt). *Archaic.* Contaminated. [ME *contaminaten* < Lat. *contaminare.*] **—con·tam′i·na′tive** *adj.* **—con·tam′i·na′tor** *n.*

con·tam·i·na·tion (kən-tăm′ə-nā′shən) *n.* **1. a.** The act or process of contaminating. **b.** The state of being contaminated. **2.** One that contaminates.

conte (kôNT) *n., pl.* **contes** (kôNT). An adventure story. [Fr. < OFr. *conter,* to relate. —see COUNT[1].]

con·temn (kən-tĕm′) *tr.v.* **-temned, -temn·ing, -temns.** To view with contempt; despise. [ME *contempnen,* to slight < Lat. *contemnere* : *com-* (intensive) + *temnere,* to despise.] **—con·temn′er** (-tĕm′ər, -tĕm′nər) *n.*

con·tem·plate (kŏn′təm-plāt′) *v.* **-plat·ed, -plat·ing, -plates.** *—tr.* **1.** To look at pensively. **2.** To ponder or consider thoughtfully. **3.** To intend or anticipate: *contemplate marriage.* **4.** To regard as possible; take seriously. *—intr.* To ponder; meditate. [Lat. *contemplari, contemplat-* : *com-* (intensive) + *templum,* space for observing auguries.] **—con′tem·pla′tor** *n.*

con·tem·pla·tion (kŏn′təm-plā′shən) *n.* **1.** Thoughtful observation or meditation. **2.** Intention or expectation.

con·tem·pla·tive (kən-tĕm′plə-tĭv, kŏn′təm-plā′-) *adj.* Disposed to or characterized by contemplation. *—n.* **1.** A person given to contemplation. **2.** A member of a religious order dedicated to meditation. **—con·tem′pla·tive·ly** *adv.* **—con·tem′pla·tive·ness** *n.*

con·tem·po·ra·ne·ous (kən-tĕm′pə-rā′nē-əs) *adj.* Originating, existing, or happening during the same period of time: *the contemporaneous reigns of two kings.* [Lat. *contemporaneus* : *com-,* same + *tempus,* time.] **—con·tem′po·ra·ne′i·ty** (-rə-nē′ĭ-tē, -nā′-), **con·tem′po·ra′ne·ous·ness** *n.* **—con·tem′po·ra′ne·ous·ly** *adv.*

con·tem·po·rar·y (kən-tĕm′pə-rĕr′ē) *adj.* **1.** Belonging to the same period of time: *a fact documented by two contemporary sources.* **2.** Of about the same age. **3.** Current; modern: *contemporary trends in design.* *—n., pl.* **-ies. 1.** One of the same time or age. **2.** A person of the present age; a modern. [Med. Lat. *contemporarius* : Lat. *com-,* same + Lat. *tempus,* time.] **—con·tem′po·rar′i·ly** (-tĕm′pə-râr′ə-lē) *adv.*

Synonyms: *contemporary, contemporaneous, simultaneous, synchronous, concurrent, coincident, concomitant.* These adjectives mean existing or occurring at the same time. *Contemporary* and *contemporaneous* have this basic sense usually with reference to an age or period; *contemporary* applies especially to persons, and alone has the sense of modern or present-day. *Simultaneous* more narrowly specifies occurence of events at the same point in time. *Synchronous* generally refers to exact correspondence of events in time or rate of occurrence over a short period: *synchronous movements of dancers. Concurrent* usually refers to correspondence of events over a longer period; often it implies parallelism in character or length of the events involved: *concurrent prison terms. Coincident* applies to events occurring at the same time, without implying a relationship between them. *Concomitant* refers to coincidence in time of events so clearly related that one seems attendant on the other.

Usage: When *contemporary* is used in reference to something in the past, its meaning is not always clear. *Contemporary critics of Shakespeare* may mean critics in his time or critics in our time. When the context does not make the meaning clear, misunderstanding may be avoided by using such phrases as "critics in Shakespeare's time" or "modern critics."

con·tem·po·rize (kən-tĕm′pə-rīz′) *v.* **-rized, -riz·ing, -riz·es.** *—tr.* To relate in time; synchronize. *—intr.* To be contemporary. [< CONTEMPORARY.]

con·tempt (kən-tĕmpt′) *n.* **1.** Reproachful disdain, as for something vile or dishonorable; bitter scorn. **2.** The state of being despised or dishonored; disgrace. **3.** Open disrespect or willful disobedience of the authority of a court of law or a legislative body. [ME < Lat. *contemptus* < p.part. of *contemnere,* to despise. —see CONTEMN.]

con·tempt·i·ble (kən-tĕmp′tə-bəl) *adj.* **1.** Deserving of contempt; despicable. **2.** *Obs.* Contemptuous. **—con·tempt′i·bil′i·ty, con·tempt′i·ble·ness** *n.* **—con·tempt′i·bly** *adv.*

con·temp·tu·ous (kən-tĕmp′cho͞o-əs) *adj.* Manifesting or feeling contempt; scornful: *contemptuous of her opponents.* **—con·temp′tu·ous·ly** *adv.* **—con·temp′tu·ous·ness** *n.*

con·tend (kən-tĕnd′) *v.* **-tend·ed, -tend·ing, -tends.** *—intr.* **1.** To strive, as in battle; fight. **2.** To compete, as in a race; vie. **3.** To strive in controversy or debate; dispute. *—tr.* To maintain or assert. [ME *contenden* < Lat. *contendere* : *com-,* with + *tendere,* to strive.] **—con·tend′er** *n.*

con·tent[1] (kŏn′tĕnt′) *n.* **1.** Often **contents.** Something that is contained in a receptacle: *the contents of my desk drawer.* **2.** Often **contents.** Subject matter of a book or other written work. **3.** The meaning or significance of a literary or artistic work as distinguished from its form. **4.** The proportion of a specified substance: *Eggs have a high protein content.* [ME < Lat. *contentus,* p.part. of *continēre,* to contain.]

con·tent[2] (kən-tĕnt′) *adj.* **1.** Not desiring more than what one has; satisfied. **2.** Resigned to circumstances; assenting: *had to be content with a short answer.* *—tr.v.* **-tent·ed, -tent·ing, -tents.** To make content or satisfied: *contented himself with one piece of cake.* *—n.* Contentment; satisfaction. [ME < OFr. < Lat. *contentus* < p.part. of *continēre,* to restrain. —see CONTAIN.]

content analysis *n.* The systematic analysis of the content rather than the structure of a communication, esp. the determination for psychological study of the frequency of occurrence of thematic and symbolic elements, including ideas, feelings, assertions, and personal references, in responses to a test or in another communication.

con·tent·ed (kən-tĕn′tĭd) *adj.* Satisfied with things as they are; content: *a contented expression on her face.* **—con·tent′ed·ly** *adv.* **—con·tent′ed·ness** *n.*

con·ten·tion (kən-tĕn′shən) *n.* **1.** An act of contending. **2.** A striving to win in competition or rivalry. **3.** An assertion put forward in argument. [ME *contencioun* < OFr. *contention* < Lat. *contentio* < *contendere,* to contend.]

con·ten·tious (kən-tĕn′shəs) *adj.* **1.** Given to contention; quarrelsome. **2.** Involving contention. **—con·ten′tious·ly** *adv.* **—con·ten′tious·ness** *n.*

con·tent·ment (kən-tĕnt′mənt) *n.* The state of being contented; satisfaction.

con·ter·mi·nous (kən-tûr′mə-nəs) also **co·ter·mi·nous** (kō-) *adj.* **1.** Having a boundary in common; contiguous. **2.** Contained in the same boundaries; coextensive. [Lat. *conterminus* : *com-,* same + *terminus,* boundary.] **—con·ter′mi·nous·ly** *adv.* **—con·ter′mi·nous·ness** *n.*

con·test (kŏn′tĕst′) *n.* **1.** A struggle for superiority or victory between rivals. **2.** A competition, esp. one in which entrants perform separately and are rated by judges. *—v.* (kən-tĕst′, kŏn′tĕst′) **-test·ed, -test·ing, -tests.** *—tr.* **1.** To compete or strive for. **2.** To attempt to disprove or invalidate; challenge: *contest a will.* *—intr.* To struggle or compete; contend: *contested with other bidders for the antique.* [Prob. < OFr. *conteste* < *contester,* to call to witness < Lat. *contestari* : *com-* (intensive) + *testis,* witness.] **—con·test′a·ble** *adj.* **—con′tes·ta′tion** (kŏn′tĕ-stā′shən) *n.* **—con·test′er** *n.*

con·tes·tant (kən-tĕs′tənt, kŏn′tĕs′tənt) *n.* **1.** One who takes part in a contest; competitor. **2.** One who contests something, such as an election or a will.

con·text (kŏn′tĕkst′) *n.* **1.** The part of a written or spoken statement in which a word or passage at issue occurs and that often specifies its meaning. **2.** The circumstances in which a particular event occurs; situation. [ME, composition < Lat. *contextus* < p.part. of *contexere,* to join together : *com-,* together + *texere,* to plait.]

con·tex·tu·al (kən-tĕks′cho͞o-əl, kŏn-) *adj.* Of, pertaining to, or depending upon a context. **—con·tex′tu·al·ly** *adv.*

con·tex·ture (kən-tĕks′chər, kŏn′tĕks′-) *n.* **1.** The act of weaving or assembling parts into a whole. **2.** An arrangement of interconnected parts; structure. **—con·tex′tur·al** *adj.*

con·ti·gu·i·ty (kŏn′tĭ-gyo͞o′ĭ-tē) *n., pl.* **-ties. 1.** The state of being contiguous. **2.** A continuous mass or series.

con·tig·u·ous (kən-tĭg′yo͞o-əs) *adj.* **1.** Sharing an edge or boundary; touching. **2.** Nearby; neighboring; adjacent. **3.** Adjacent in time; immediately preceding or following. [Lat. *contiguus* < *contingere,* to touch. —see CONTACT.] **—con·tig′u·ous·ly** *adv.* **—con·tig′u·ous·ness** *n.*

con·ti·nence (kŏn′tə-nəns) *n.* **1.** Self-restraint; moderation. **2.** Partial or complete abstention from sexual activity. **3.** Voluntary control over bodily discharges.

con·ti·nent[1] (kŏn′tə-nənt) *n.* **1.** One of the principal land masses of the earth, usually regarded as including Africa, Antarctica, Asia, Australia, Europe, North America, and South America. **2. the Continent.** The mainland of Europe. [Lat. *(terra) continens,* continuous (land), pr.part. of *continēre,* to hold together. —see CONTAIN.]

con·ti·nent[2] (kŏn′tə-nənt) *adj.* Exercising continence. [ME < Lat. *continens,* pr.part. of *continēre,* to restrain. —see CONTAIN.] **—con′ti·nent·ly** *adv.*

con·ti·nen·tal (kŏn′tə-nĕn′tl) *adj.* **1.** Of, pertaining to, or like a continent. **2.** Often **Continental.** Of or relating to the mainland of Europe; European. **3. Continental.** Of or pertaining to the American colonies during and immediately after the Revolutionary War. *—n.* **1.** Often **Continental.** An inhabitant of the mainland of Europe; European. **2. Continental.** A soldier in the Continental Army during the Revolutionary War. **3.** A piece of paper money issued by the Continental Congress during the Revolutionary War. **—con′ti·nen′tal·ism** *n.* **—con′ti·nen′tal·ist** *n.* **—con′ti·nen·tal′i·ty** (-nĕn-tăl′ĭ-tē) *n.* **—con′ti·nen′tal·ly** *adv.*

continental code *n.* A form of Morse code having no spaces between the dot and dash signals, commonly used for telegraphic communication outside the United States and Canada.
continental divide *n.* An extensive stretch of high ground from each side of which the river systems of a continent flow in opposite directions.
continental drift *n.* The theoretical slow shifting of continents due to weakness in the suboceanic crust.
continental shelf *n.* A generally shallow, flat submerged portion of a continent, extending to a point of steep descent to the ocean floor.
continental slope *n.* The steep descent from the continental shelf to the ocean bottom.
con·tin·gence (kən-tĭn′jəns) *n.* **1.** A joining or touching. **2.** Contingency.
con·tin·gen·cy (kən-tĭn′jən-sē) *n., pl.* **-cies. 1. a.** An event that may occur but that is not likely or intended; possibility. **b.** A possibility that must be prepared against; future emergency. **2.** The condition of being dependent upon chance; uncertainty. **3.** Something incidental to something else. ***—modifier:*** *a contingency plan.*
contingency table *n.* A statistical table that shows the observed frequencies of a sample, with the rows indicating one variable and the columns another variable.
con·tin·gent (kən-tĭn′jənt) *adj.* **1.** Likely but not certain to occur; possible. **2.** Dependent upon conditions or events not yet established; conditional: *arms sales contingent on the approval of Congress.* **3.** Happening by chance or accident; fortuitous. **4.** *Logic.* Possessing a truth value derived from facts apart from the proposition itself; not necessarily true or false: *a contingent proposition.* —*n.* **1.** A contingent event or condition. **2.** A share or quota, as of troops, contributed to a general effort. **3.** A representative group forming part of an assemblage. [ME < Lat. *contingens,* pr.part. of *contingere,* to touch. —see CONTACT.] **—con·tin′gent·ly** *adv.*
con·tin·u·a (kən-tĭn′yo͞o-ə) *n.* A plural of **continuum.**
con·tin·u·al (kən-tĭn′yo͞o-əl) *adj.* **1.** Repeated regularly and frequently: *the continual banging of the shutters.* **2. a.** Not interrupted or broken; steady: *continual noise.* **b.** Continuous in time; incessant: *a continual diet of vegetables.* **—con·tin′u·al·ly** *adv.*
Synonyms: *continual, continuous, constant, ceaseless, incessant, perpetual, eternal, perennial, interminable.* These adjectives primarily mean occurring over and over during a long period of time or indefinitely. *Continual* can apply to uninterrupted action but is now chiefly restricted to what is intermittent or repeated at intervals: *the continual banging of the shutters. Continuous* implies either action without interruption in time or unbroken extent in space: *a continuous vigil; a continuous slope of terrain. Constant,* applied to action, stresses its steadiness or persistence and unvarying nature. *Ceaseless* and *incessant* pertain to uninterrupted action. *Perpetual* emphasizes both steadfastness and duration of action. *Eternal* refers to what is everlasting, especially to action seemingly without beginning or end in time. *Perennial* describes existence that goes on year after year, often with the suggestion of self-renewal. *Interminable* literally refers to what has no end, but more often is applied to a prolonged and wearisome action.
con·tin·u·ance (kən-tĭn′yo͞o-əns) *n.* **1.** The act or fact of continuing. **2.** The time during which something exists or lasts; duration. **3.** A continuation; sequel. **4.** *Law.* Postponement or adjournment to a future date.
Usage: *Continuance,* except in its legal sense, is sometimes interchangeable with *continuation. Continuance,* however, is used to refer to the duration of a state or condition, as in *his continuance in office. Continuation* applies especially to prolongation or resumption of action (*a continuation of the meeting*) or to physical extension (*the continuation of the street*). *Continuity* is used to refer to consistency over time; one speaks of the *continuity of foreign policy. The continuity of a story* is its internal coherence from one episode to the next; *the continuation of a story* is that part of the story that takes up after a break in its recitation.
con·tin·u·ant (kən-tĭn′yo͞o-ənt) *n.* A consonant, such as *s, z,* or *f,* that can be prolonged as long as the breath lasts without a change in quality.
con·tin·u·a·tion (kən-tĭn′yo͞o-ā′shən) *n.* **1. a.** The act or fact of continuing. **b.** The state of being continued. **2.** An extension by which something is carried to a further point. **3.** A recommencement after an interruption. —See Usage note at **continuance.**
con·tin·u·a·tive (kən-tĭn′yo͞o-ā′tĭv, -ə-tĭv) *adj.* Of, pertaining to, or serving to cause continuation. —*n.* Something that expresses or causes continuation. **—con·tin′u·a′tive·ly** *adv.*
con·tin·u·a·tor (kən-tĭn′yo͞o-ā′tər) *n.* One that continues, esp. a person who resumes the work of another.
con·tin·ue (kən-tĭn′yo͞o) *v.* **-ued, -u·ing, -ues.** —*intr.* **1.** To go on with a particular action or in a particular condition; persist. **2.** To exist over a prolonged period; last. **3.** To remain in the same state, capacity, or place: *She continued as representative for another term.* **4.** To go on after an interruption; resume. —*tr.* **1.** To carry forward; persist in: *The police will continue their investigation.* **2.** To carry further in time, space, or development; extend. **3.** To cause to remain or last; retain. **4.** To carry on after an interruption; resume. **5.** *Law.* To postpone or adjourn. [ME *continuen* < Lat. *continuare* < *continuus,* continuous < *continēre,* to hold together. —see CONTAIN.] **—con·tin′u·a·ble** *adj.* **—con·tin′u·er** *n.*
continued fraction *n.* A fraction whose denominator consists of an integer plus a fraction that likewise has a denominator consisting of an integer plus a fraction and so on.
continuing education *n.* **1.** An educational program that brings participants up to date in a particular area of knowledge or skills. **2.** Education courses designed esp. for part-time, adult students.
con·ti·nu·i·ty (kŏn′tə-no͞o′ĭ-tē, -nyo͞o′-) *n., pl.* **-ties. 1.** The state or quality of being continuous. **2.** An uninterrupted succession; unbroken course. **3. a.** A detailed shooting script consulted to avoid errors and discrepancies from shot to shot in a film. **b.** A script for all the spoken parts of a radio or television program. —See Usage note at **continuance.**
con·tin·u·o (kən-tĭn′yo͞o-ō′) *n., pl.* **-os.** A typically keyboard accompaniment for a solo instrument in which numerals indicate the successive chords, the actual notes played being left to the performer. [Ital. < Lat. *continuus,* continuous.]
con·tin·u·ous (kən-tĭn′yo͞o-əs) *adj.* **1.** Extending or prolonged without interruption or cessation; unceasing. **2.** *Math.* Designating a function of one or more variables in which the variation of its values can be made arbitrarily small in a sufficiently small neighborhood of every point in a given interval. [Lat. *continuus.* —see CONTINUE.] **—con·tin′u·ous·ly** *adv.* **—con·tin′u·ous·ness** *n.*
continuous creation theory *n.* Steady-state theory.
continuous spectrum *n.* A spectrum having no breaks, esp. a spectrum of radiation distributed over an uninterrupted range of wavelengths.
continuous wave *adj.* Emitting or capable of emitting continuously; not pulsed. Used esp. of lasers.
con·tin·u·um (kən-tĭn′yo͞o-əm) *n., pl.* **-tin·u·a** (-tĭn′yo͞o-ə) or **-tin·u·ums. 1.** A continuous extent, succession, or whole no part of which can be distinguished from neighboring parts except by arbitrary division. **2.** *Math.* A set having the same number of points as all the real numbers in an interval. [Lat., neuter of *continuus,* continuous.]
con·tort (kən-tôrt′) *v.* **-tort·ed, -tort·ing, -torts.** —*tr.* To twist or bend severely out of shape; wrench: *pain that contorted his face.* —*intr.* To become twisted into a strained shape or expression. [Lat. *contorquēre, contort-,* to twist : *com-* (intensive) + *torquēre,* to twist.] **—con·tor′tion** *n.* **—con·tor′tive** *adj.*
con·tort·ed (kən-tôr′tĭd) *adj.* **1.** Twisted or strained out of shape. **2.** *Bot.* Twisted or bent upon itself. **—con·tort′ed·ly** *adv.* **—con·tort′ed·ness** *n.*
con·tor·tion·ist (kən-tôr′shə-nĭst) *n.* An acrobat who can contort his body and limbs into extraordinary positions. **—con·tor′tion·is′tic** *adj.*

contortionist

con·tour (kŏn′to͝or′) *n.* **1. a.** The outline of a figure, body, or mass. **b.** A line that represents such an outline. **2.** Often **contours.** A surface, esp. of a curving form. **3.** A contour line. —*tr.v.* **-toured, -tour·ing, -tours. 1.** To make or shape the outline of; represent in contour. **2.** To build (a road, for example) to follow the contour of the land. —*adj.* **1.** Following the contour lines of uneven terrain to limit erosion of topsoil: *contour plowing.* **2.** Shaped to fit the outline or form of something: *a contour chair.* [Fr. < Ital. *contorno* < *contornare,* to draw in outline : Lat. *com-* (intensive) + Lat. *tornare,* to round off < *tornus,* lathe.]
contour feather *n.* Any of the outermost feathers of a bird, forming the visible body contour and plumage.
contour line *n.* An imaginary line, or its representation on a contour map, joining points of equal elevation.
contour map *n.* A map showing elevations and surface configuration by means of contour lines.

contour map
Map of a section of upper New York State

contra– *pref.* **1.** Against; opposite; contrasting: *contraposition.* **2.** Lower in pitch: *contrabassoon.* [ME < Lat. < *contra,* against.]
con·tra·band (kŏn′trə-bănd′) *n.* **1.** Goods prohibited by law or treaty from being imported or exported. **2. a.** Illegal traffic in contraband; smuggling. **b.** Smuggled goods. **3.** Goods that may be seized and confiscated by a belligerent if shipped to another belligerent by a neutral. **4.** During the Civil War, an escaped slave who fled to or was taken behind Union lines. —*adj.* Prohibited from being imported or exported. [Ital. *contrabbando* : *contra-,* against (< Lat.) + *bando,* proclamation < LLat. *bannus.*] **—con′tra·band′age** *n.* **—con′tra·band′ist** *n.*
con·tra·bass (kŏn′trə-bās′) *Mus.* —*n.* A double bass. —*adj.* Pitched an octave below the normal bass range. [Obs. Ital. *contrabasso* : *contra-,* below (< Lat., against) + *basso,* bass.] **—con′tra·bass′ist** *n.*
con·tra·bas·soon (kŏn′trə-bə-so͞on′, -bă-) *n.* The largest and lowest-pitched of the double-reed wind musical instruments, sounding an octave below the bassoon.
con·tra·cep·tion (kŏn′trə-sĕp′shən) *n.* Prevention of conception. [CONTRA- + (CON)CEPTION.]
con·tra·cep·tive (kŏn′trə-sĕp′tĭv) *adj.* Capable of preventing conception. —*n.* A contraceptive agent or device.
con·tract (kŏn′trăkt′) *n.* **1. a.** An agreement between two or more parties, esp. one that is written and enforceable by

law. **b.** The writing or document containing such an agreement. **2.** The branch of law dealing with contracts. **3.** Marriage as a formal agreement; betrothal. **4.** In the game of bridge: **a.** The last and highest bid of one hand. **b.** The number of tricks thus bid. **c.** Contract bridge. **5.** A paid assignment to murder someone: *put out a contract on the mobster's life.* —*v.* (kən-trăkt′, kŏn′trăkt′) **-tract·ed, -tract·ing, -tracts.** —*tr.* **1.** To enter into by contract; establish or settle by formal agreement: *contract a marriage.* **2.** To acquire or incur: *contract obligations.* **3.** To reduce in size by drawing together; shrink. **4.** To pull together; wrinkle. **5.** To shorten (a word or words) by omitting or combining some of the letters or sounds. —*intr.* **1.** To enter into or make a contract: *contract for garbage collection.* **2.** To become reduced in size by or as if by being drawn together: *The pupils of his eyes contracted.* [ME < Lat. *contractus* < p.part. of *contrahere,* to make a contract : *com-,* together + *trahere,* to draw.] —**con·tract′i·bil′i·ty, con·tract′i·ble·ness** *n.* —**con·tract′i·ble** *adj.*

Synonyms: *contract, condense, compress, constrict, shrink.* These verbs refer to decrease in size or content of a thing and sometimes to a resultant change in its form. *Contract* applies to internal drawing together that reduces the volume of a thing. *Condense* refers to an increase in compactness produced by the removal or reduction of parts or by a change in physical form of the thing involved, such as a change from gas to liquid or from liquid to solid. *Compress* applies to increased compactness brought about by external force; the term implies reduction of volume and change of form or shape. *Constrict* refers to decreasing the extent of a thing, usually by external pressure. *Shrink* refers to contraction that produces reduction in physical extent.

contract bridge *n.* A form of auction bridge in which tricks in excess of the contract may not count toward game bonuses.

con·trac·tile (kən-trăk′təl, -tīl′) *adj.* Capable of contracting or causing contraction. —**con′trac·til′i·ty** (kŏn′trăk-tĭl′ĭ-tē) *n.*

contractile vacuole *n.* A contracting vesicle in some protozoans that functions in fluid expulsion.

con·trac·tion (kən-trăk′shən) *n.* **1. a.** The act of contracting. **b.** The state of being contracted. **2.** *Gram.* **a.** A shortened word or words formed by omitting or combining some of the letters or sounds. **b.** The formation of such a word. **3.** *Physiol.* The shortening and often thickening of functioning muscle. **4.** A period of decreased business activity.

con·trac·tor (kŏn′trăk′tər, kən-trăk′-) *n.* **1.** One who agrees to furnish materials or perform services at a specified price, esp. for construction. **2.** Something that contracts, esp. a muscle.

con·trac·tu·al (kən-trăk′cho͞o-əl) *adj.* Of, pertaining to, or having the nature of a contract. —**con·trac′tu·al·ly** *adv.*

con·trac·ture (kən-trăk′chər) *n.* **1.** A drawing together, as of muscle or scar tissue, resulting in distortion or deformity. **2.** A deformity resulting from a contracture.

con·tra·cy·cli·cal (kŏn′trə-sī′klĭ-kəl, -sĭk′lĭ-) *adj.* Acting contrarily to an economic cycle.

con·tra·dance or **con·tra·danse** (kŏn′trə-dăns′) *n.* Variants of **contredanse.**

con·tra·dict (kŏn′trə-dĭkt′) *v.* **-dict·ed, -dict·ing, -dicts.** —*tr.* **1.** To assert or express the opposite of (a statement). **2.** To deny the statement of. **3.** To be contrary to; be inconsistent with. —*intr.* To utter a contradictory statement. [Lat. *contradicere, contradict-,* to speak against : *contra-,* against + *dicere,* to speak.] —**con′tra·dict′a·ble** *adj.* —**con′tra·dict′er, con′tra·dic′tor** *n.*

con·tra·dic·tion (kŏn′trə-dĭk′shən) *n.* **1. a.** The act of contradicting. **b.** The state of being contradicted. **2.** A denial. **3.** Inconsistency or discrepancy. **4.** Something that contains contradictory elements.

con·tra·dic·to·ry (kŏn′trə-dĭk′tə-rē) *adj.* **1.** Involving, having the nature of, or being a contradiction. **2.** Given to contradicting. —*n., pl.* **-ries.** *Logic.* Either of two propositions related in such a way that it is impossible for both to be true or both to be false. —**con′tra·dic′to·ri·ly** *adv.* —**con′tra·dic′to·ri·ness** *n.*

con·tra·dis·tinc·tion (kŏn′trə-dĭ-stĭngk′shən) *n.* Distinction by contrasting or opposing qualities. —**con′tra·dis·tinc′tive** *adj.* —**con′tra·dis·tinc′tive·ly** *adv.*

con·tra·dis·tin·guish (kŏn′trə-dĭ-stĭng′gwĭsh) *tr.v.* **-guished, -guish·ing, -guish·es.** To distinguish by contrasting qualities.

con·trail (kŏn′trāl′) *n.* A visible trail of water droplets or ice crystals sometimes forming in the wake of an aircraft. [CON(DENSATION) + TRAIL.]

con·tra·in·di·cate (kŏn′trə-ĭn′dĭ-kāt′) *tr.v.* **-cat·ed, -cat·ing, -cates.** To indicate the inadvisability of: *Allergic reactions contraindicated the use of penicillin.* —**con′tra·in′di·ca′tion** *n.* —**con′tra·in·dic′a·tive** (-ĭn-dĭk′ə-tĭv) *adj.*

con·tra·lat·er·al (kŏn′trə-lăt′ər-əl) *adj.* Taking place or originating in a corresponding part on an opposite side.

con·tral·to (kən-trăl′tō) *n., pl.* **-tos.** *Mus.* **1.** The lowest female voice or voice part, intermediate in range between soprano and tenor. **2.** A woman having a contralto voice. [Ital. : *contra-,* below (< Lat., against) + *alto,* alto.]

con·tra·po·si·tion (kŏn′trə-pə-zĭsh′ən) *n.* An opposite position; antithesis.

con·tra·pos·i·tive (kŏn′trə-pŏz′ĭ-tĭv) *n. Logic.* A proposition derived by negating and permuting the terms of another, equivalent proposition: "All not-Y is not-X" *is the contrapositive of* "All x is y."

con·trap·tion (kən-trăp′shən) *n.* A mechanical device; gadget. [Perh. blend of CONTRIVE and TRAP.]

con·tra·pun·tal (kŏn′trə-pŭn′tl) *adj. Mus.* Of, pertaining to, or incorporating counterpoint. [< Ital. *contrapunto,* counterpoint : *contra-,* against (< Lat.) + *punto,* point < Lat. *punctum* < *pungere,* to prick.] —**con′tra·pun′tal·ly** *adv.*

con·tra·pun·tist (kŏn′trə-pŭn′tĭst) *n.* A specialist in contrapuntal music.

con·tra·ri·e·ty (kŏn′trə-rī′ĭ-tē) *n., pl.* **-ties. 1.** The quality or condition of being contrary. **2.** Something that is contrary.

con·trar·i·ous (kən-trâr′ē-əs) *adj.* Perverse; inimical. —**con·trar′i·ous·ly** *adv.*

con·trar·i·wise (kŏn′trĕr′ē-wīz′, kən-trâr′-) *adv.* **1.** From a contrasting point of view. **2.** In the opposite way or reverse order. **3.** Perversely.

con·trar·y (kŏn′trĕr′ē) *adj.* **1.** Opposed, as in character or purpose; completely different. **2.** Opposite in direction or position: *playing scales in contrary motion.* **3.** Adverse; unfavorable: *a contrary wind.* **4.** (*also* kən-trâr′ē). Given to acting or speaking in opposition to others; perverse; willful. —*n., pl.* **-ies. 1.** Something that is contrary; opposite. **2.** Either of two contrary or opposing things. **3.** *Logic.* A proposition related to another in such a way that if the latter is true, the former must be false, but if the latter is false, the former is not necessarily true. —*adv.* In opposition; contrariwise. —***idioms.*** **by contraries.** In opposition to what is expected. **on the contrary.** In opposition to the previous statement; conversely. [ME *contrarie* < Lat. *contrarius* < *contra,* against.] —**con′trar·i·ly** *adv.* —**con′trar·i·ness** *n.*

Synonyms: *contrary, balky, stubborn, perverse, adverse, wayward, willful.* These adjectives refer to being in opposition to a prevailing order or to prescribed authority. *Contrary* applies especially to a person inherently self-willed and given to resisting authority. *Balky* describes the behavior of an animal that stops short and refuses to proceed, and is also applicable to related human behavior. *Stubborn* stresses inflexibility of mind or will and thus strongly implies resistance to authority. *Perverse* implies native disposition to depart from what is considered proper or morally right. *Adverse* is often applied to opposition, such as personal opinion or unfavorable circumstances, that is antagonistic to the progress or well-being of another person. *Wayward* suggests flouting of authority that leads to erratic, capricious, or morally reprehensible behavior. *Willful* implies headstrong self-determination and lack of susceptibility to either authority or reason.

con·trast (kən-trăst′) *v.* **-trast·ed, -trast·ing, -trasts.** —*tr.* To set in opposition in order to show or emphasize differences. —*intr.* To show differences when compared. —*n.* (kŏn′trăst′). **1. a.** The act of contrasting. **b.** The state of being contrasted. **2.** A striking dissimilarity between things compared. **3.** Something that shows a striking dissimilarity to something else. **4.** The use of opposing elements, such as colors, forms, or lines, in proximity to produce an intensified effect in a work of art. [Fr. *contrester* < Ital. *contrastare* < Med. Lat. : Lat. *contra-,* against + Lat. *stare,* to stand.] —**con·trast′a·ble** *adj.* —**con·trast′ing·ly** *adv.*

con·trast·y (kŏn′trăs′tē) *adj.* In photography, having or producing sharp contrasts between light and dark areas.

con·tra·vene (kŏn′trə-vēn′) *tr.v.* **-vened, -ven·ing, -venes. 1.** To act or be counter to; violate: *contravene a direct order.* **2.** To oppose in argument. [OFr. *contravenir* < LLat. *contravenire,* to oppose : Lat. *contra-,* against + Lat. *venire,* to come.] —**con′tra·ven′er** *n.*

con·tra·ven·tion (kŏn′trə-vĕn′shən) *n.* An act of contravening; violation.

con·tre·danse also **con·tre·dance** or **con·tra·dance** or **con·tra·danse** (kŏn′trə-dăns′) *n.* **1.** A dance performed in two lines with the partners facing each other. **2.** The music for a contredanse. [Fr. < COUNTRY-DANCE.]

con·tre·temps (kŏn′trə-täɴ′, kôɴ′trə-täɴ′) *n., pl.* **contre·temps** (-täɴz′, -täɴz′) An inopportune or embarrassing occurrence; mishap. [Fr. : *contre-,* against (< Lat. *contra-*) + *temps,* time < Lat. *tempus.*]

con·trib·ute (kən-trĭb′yo͞ot) *v.* **-ut·ed, -ut·ing, -utes.** —*tr.* **1.** To give or supply in common with others; give to a common fund or for a common purpose. **2.** To submit for publication. —*intr.* **1.** To make a contribution. **2.** To act as a determining factor; share responsibility: *Exercise contributes to better health.* **3.** To submit material for publication. [Lat. *contribuere, contribut-,* to bring together : *com-* together + *tribuere,* to grant. —see TRIBUTE.] —**con·trib′u·tive** *adj.* —**con·trib′u·tive·ly** *adv.* —**con·trib′u·tive·ness** *n.* —**con·trib′u·tor** *n.*

con·tri·bu·tion (kŏn′trĭ-byo͞o′shən) *n.* **1.** The act of contributing. **2.** Something contributed. **3.** An impost or levy for a special purpose.

con·trib·u·to·ry (kən-trĭb′yə-tôr′ē, -tōr′ē) *adj.* **1.** Of, pertaining to, or involving contribution. **2.** Contributing toward a result. **3.** Subject to an impost or levy. —*n., pl.* **-ries.** One that contributes.

con·trite (kən-trīt′, kŏn′trīt′) *adj.* **1.** Repentant for one's sins or inadequacies; penitent. **2.** Arising from contrition: *contrite words.* [ME *contrit* < Lat. *contritus,* p.part. of *conterere,* to crush : *com-* (intensive) + *terere,* to grind.] **—con·trite'ly** *adv.* **—con·trite'ness** *n.*

con·tri·tion (kən-trĭsh'ən) *n.* Sincere remorse for wrongdoing; repentance.

con·tri·vance (kən-trī'vəns) *n.* **1. a.** The act of contriving. **b.** The state of being contrived. **2.** Something contrived, as a mechanical device or a clever plan.

con·trive (kən-trīv') *v.* **-trived, -triv·ing, -trives.** *—tr.* **1.** To plan or devise with cleverness or ingenuity. **2.** To plot with evil intent; scheme. **3.** To invent or fabricate, esp. by improvisation. **4.** To manage, as by scheming. *—intr.* To plot or scheme: *contrive to gain admission.* [ME *contreven* < OFr. *controver* < Med. Lat. *contropare,* to compare : Lat. *com-,* with + Lat. *tropus,* trope < Gk. *tropos.*] **—con·triv'ed·ly** (-trī'vĭd-lē) *adv.* **—con·triv'er** *n.*

con·trol (kən-trōl') *tr.v.* **-trolled, -trol·ling, -trols. 1.** To exercise authority or dominating influence over; direct; regulate. **2.** To hold in restraint; check. **3. a.** To verify or regulate (a scientific experiment) by conducting a parallel experiment or by comparing with some other standard. **b.** To verify (an account, for example) by using a duplicate register for comparison. *—n.* **1.** Authority or ability to regulate, direct, or dominate. **2.** A restraining act or influence; curb: *price controls.* **3.** A standard of comparison for checking or verifying the results of an experiment. **4.** Often **controls.** An instrument or set of instruments used to operate, regulate, or guide a machine or vehicle. **5.** A spirit presumed to act through a spiritualist medium. [ME *countrollen* < AN < OFr. *contrarotulare* < Med. Lat. *contraretulare,* to check by duplicate register < *contrarotulus,* duplicate register : Lat. *contra,* against + Lat. *rotulus,* roll, dim. of *rota,* wheel.] **—con·trol'la·bil'i·ty** *n.* **—con·trol'la·ble** *adj.*

control chart *n.* A graph of a quantitative characteristic of a manufacturing process, usually determined from small, periodically repeated samples and evaluated with respect to control limits rendered as parallel horizontal lines above and below a line representing the expected or average value of the characteristic.

control experiment *n.* An experiment in which the variable factors are controlled so that the effects of changing one at a time can be observed.

controlled response *n.* A response to a military attack by limited military means in an effort to avoid nuclear war.

con·trol·ler (kən-trō'lər) *n.* **1.** One who controls. **2.** Also **comp·trol·ler.** An officer who audits accounts and supervises the financial affairs of a corporation or of a governmental body. **3.** A regulating mechanism, as in a vehicle or electric device. **—con·trol'ler·ship'** *n.*

control rocket *n.* A vernier rocket or similar missile used to change the attitude or trajectory of a rocket or spacecraft.

control stick *n.* A lever used in small aircraft to control the angle of the elevators and ailerons.

control surface *n.* A movable airfoil, esp. a rudder, aileron, or elevator, used to control or guide an aircraft, guided missile, or rocket.

control tower *n.* A usually glass-enclosed tower at an airport from which air traffic is controlled by radio.

con·tro·ver·sial (kŏn'trə-vûr'shəl, -sē-əl) *adj.* **1.** Of, subject to, or marked by controversy: *a controversial issue.* **2.** Fond of controversy; disputatious. **—con'tro·ver'sial·ist** *n.* **—con'tro·ver'sial·ly** *adv.*

con·tro·ver·sy (kŏn'trə-vûr'sē) *n., pl.* **-sies. 1.** A dispute, esp. a lengthy and public one, between sides holding opposing views. **2.** The act or practice of engaging in controversy. [ME *controversie* < Lat. *controversia* < *controversus,* disputed < *contro-,* against (var. of *contra-*) + *versus,* p.part. of *vertere,* to turn.]

con·tro·vert (kŏn'trə-vûrt', kŏn'trə-vûrt') *tr.v.* **-vert·ed, -vert·ing, -verts.** To raise arguments against; voice opposition to. [< CONTROVERSY.] **—con'tro·vert'i·ble** *adj.*

con·tu·ma·cious (kŏn'tə-mā'shəs, -tyə-) *adj.* Obstinately disobedient or rebellious; insubordinate. **—con'tu·ma'cious·ly** *adv.* **—con'tu·ma'cious·ness** *n.*

con·tu·ma·cy (kŏn'tōō-mə-sē, -tyōō-) *n., pl.* **-cies.** Obstinate or contemptuous resistance to authority; stubborn rebelliousness. [ME *contumacie* < Lat. *contumacia* < *contumax,* insolent.]

con·tu·me·ly (kŏn'tōō-mə-lē, -tyōō-, -təm-lē) *n., pl.* **-lies. 1.** Rudeness or contempt in behavior or speech; insolence. **2.** An insulting remark or act. [ME *contumelle* < Lat. *contumelia.*] **—con'tu·me'li·ous** (kŏn'tə-mē'lē-əs) *adj.* **—con'tu·me'li·ous·ly** *adv.*

con·tuse (kən-tōōz', -tyōōz') *tr.v.* **-tused, -tus·ing, -tus·es.** To injure without breaking the skin; bruise. [ME *contusen* < Lat. *contundere,* to beat : *com-* (intensive) + *tundere,* to beat.] **—con·tu'sion** *n.*

co·nun·drum (kə-nŭn'drəm) *n.* **1.** A riddle in which a fanciful question is answered by a pun. **2. a.** A problem admitting of no satisfactory solution. **b.** A difficult and complicated problem. [Orig. unknown.]

con·ur·ba·tion (kŏn'ər-bā'shən) *n.* A predominantly urban region including adjacent towns and suburbs; metropolitan area. [CON- + Lat. *urbs,* city + -ATION.]

co·nus ar·te·ri·o·sus (kō'nəs är-tîr'ē-ō'səs) *n.* **1.** A conical extension of the right ventricle in the heart of mammals from which the pulmonary arteries arise. **2.** An extension of the ventricle in the heart of amphibians and fish. [NLat., arterial cone.]

con·va·lesce (kŏn'və-lĕs') *intr.v.* **-lesced, -lesc·ing, -lesc·es.** To return to health after illness; recuperate. [Lat. *convalescere* : *com-* (intensive) + *valescere,* to grow strong < *valere,* to be strong.]

con·va·les·cence (kŏn'və-lĕs'əns) *n.* **1.** Gradual return to health after illness. **2.** The period needed for convalescence. **—con'va·les'cent** *adj.*

con·vec·tion (kən-vĕk'shən) *n.* **1.** The act or process of transmitting or conveying. **2.** *Physics.* **a.** Heat transfer by fluid motion between regions of unequal density that result from nonuniform heating. **b.** Fluid motion caused by an external force such as gravity. **3.** *Meteorol.* The transfer of heat or other atmospheric properties by massive motion within the atmosphere, esp. by such motion directed upward. [LLat. *convectio* < *convehere,* to carry together : Lat. *com-,* together + Lat. *vehere,* to carry.] **—con·vec'tion·al** *adj.* **—con·vec'tive** *adj.* **—con·vec'tive·ly** *adv.*

con·vec·tor (kən-vĕk'tər) *n.* A partly enclosed, directly heated surface from which warm air circulates by convection.

con·vene (kən-vēn') *v.* **-vened, -ven·ing, -venes.** *—intr.* To assemble, usually for an official or public purpose; meet formally. *—tr.* **1.** To cause to assemble; convoke. **2.** To summon to appear, as before a court of law. [ME *convenen* < Lat. *convenire* : *com-,* together + *venire,* to come.] **—con·ven'a·ble** *adj.* **—con·ven'er** *n.*

con·ven·ience (kən-vēn'yəns) *n.* **1.** The quality of being convenient; suitability or handiness. **2.** Personal comfort; material advantage. **3.** Something that increases comfort or makes work less difficult: *"If one's own car is a convenience, everybody else's is a nuisance"* (Joseph W. Krutch). **4.** *Chiefly Brit.* A lavatory.

convenience food *n.* A prepackaged food that can be prepared quickly and easily.

con·ven·ien·cy (kən-vēn'yən-sē) *n., pl.* **-cies.** *Archaic.* Convenience.

con·ven·ient (kən-vēn'yənt) *adj.* **1.** Suited or favorable to one's comfort, purpose, or needs. **2.** Easy to reach; accessible. **3.** *Obs.* Fitting and proper; appropriate. [ME < Lat. *conveniens,* pr.part. of *convenire,* to be suitable. —see CONVENE.] **—con·ven'ient·ly** *adv.*

con·vent (kŏn'vənt, -vĕnt') *n.* **1.** A community, esp. of nuns, bound by vows to a religious life under a superior. **2.** The building or buildings occupied by a convent, esp. a nunnery. [ME *covent* < OFr. < Med. Lat. *conventus* < Lat., assembly < *convenire,* to assemble. —see CONVENE.]

con·ven·ti·cle (kən-vĕn'tĭ-kəl) *n.* A religious meeting, esp. a secret or illegal one, such as those held by dissenters in England and Scotland in the 16th and 17th centuries. [ME < Lat. *conventiculum,* meeting, dim. of *conventus,* assembly. —see CONVENT.] **—con·ven'ti·cler** *n.*

con·ven·tion (kən-vĕn'shən) *n.* **1. a.** A formal assembly or meeting of members, representatives, or delegates of a group, such as a political party or fraternal society. **b.** The body of persons attending such an assembly. **2.** An agreement or compact, esp. an international agreement dealing with a specific subject: *the Geneva conventions on the treatment of war prisoners.* **3.** General agreement on or acceptance of certain practices or attitudes. **4.** A practice or procedure widely observed in a group, esp. to facilitate social intercourse; custom. **5.** A widely used and accepted device or technique, as in drama, literature, or painting: *the theatrical convention of the "aside."* [ME *convencioun* < Lat. *conventio,* meeting < *convenire,* to meet. —see CONVENE.]

con·ven·tion·al (kən-vĕn'shə-nəl) *adj.* **1.** Developed, established, or approved by general usage; customary. **2.** Conforming to established practice or accepted standards. **3.** Marked by or dependent upon conventions to the point of artificiality; stereotyped. **4.** Represented, as in a work of art, in simplified or abstract form. **5.** *Law.* Based upon consent or agreement; contractual. **6.** Of, pertaining to, or resembling an assembly. **7.** Using means other than nuclear weapons or energy. **—con·ven'tion·al·ism** *n.* **—con·ven'tion·al·ist** *n.* **—con·ven'tion·al·ly** *adv.*

con·ven·tion·al·i·ty (kən-vĕn'shə-năl'ĭ-tē) *n., pl.* **-ties. 1.** The state, quality, or character of being conventional. **2.** A conventional act, principle, or practice. **3. conventionalities.** The rules of conventional social behavior.

con·ven·tion·al·ize (kən-vĕn'shə-nə-līz') *tr.v.* **-ized, -iz·ing, -iz·es.** To make conventional. **—con·ven'tion·al·i·za'tion** *n.*

con·ven·tion·eer (kən-vĕn'shə-nîr') *n.* One who attends a convention.

con·ven·tu·al (kən-vĕn'chōō-əl) *adj.* Of or pertaining to a convent. *—n.* **1.** A member of a convent. **2. Conventual.** A member of a branch of the Franciscan order that permits the accumulation and possession of common property.

con·verge (kən-vûrj') *v.* **-verged, -verg·ing, -verg·es.** *—intr.* **1.** To approach the same point from different directions; tend toward a meeting or intersection. **2.** To tend or move toward union or toward a common conclusion or result. **3.** *Math.* To approach a limit. *—tr.* To cause to converge.

control tower

[LLat. *convergere,* to incline together : Lat. *com-,* together + Lat. *vergere,* to incline.]

con·ver·gence (kən-vûr′jəns) also **con·ver·gen·cy** (-jən-sē) *n., pl.* **-gen·ces** also **-gen·cies. 1.** The act, condition, quality, or fact of converging. **2.** *Math.* The property or manner of approaching a limit such as a point, line, surface, or value. **3.** The point or degree of converging. **4.** *Physiol.* The coordinated turning of the eyes inward to focus on a nearby point. **5.** *Biol.* The adaptive evolution of superficially similar structures, such as the wings of birds and insects, in unrelated species subjected to similar environments. **—con·ver′gent** *adj.*

convertible
1926 model

convergent evolution *n.* Convergence (sense 5).

con·ver·sance (kən-vûr′səns, kŏn′vər-) also **con·ver·san·cy** (kən-vûr′sən-sē) *n.* The state of being conversant; familiarity.

con·ver·sant (kən-vûr′sənt, kŏn′vər-) *adj.* Familiar, as by study or experience: *conversant with medieval history.* [ME *conversaunt,* associated with < OFr. *conversant,* pr.part. *converser,* to associate with < Lat. *conversari.*] **—con·ver′sant·ly** *adv.*

con·ver·sa·tion (kŏn′vər-sā′shən) *n.* **1.** A spoken exchange of thoughts, opinions, and feelings; talk. **2.** An informal discussion of a matter or an issue by representatives of governments, institutions, or organizations. **3.** A real-time interaction with a computer. **—con′ver·sa′tion·al** *adj.* **—con′ver·sa′tion·al·ly** *adv.*

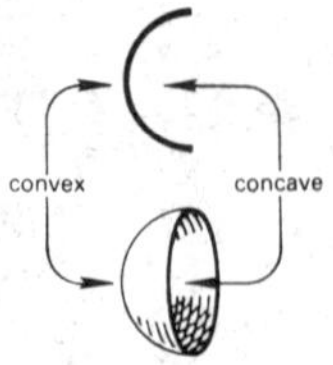

convex

con·ver·sa·tion·al·ist (kŏn′vər-sā′shə-nə-lĭst) also **con·ver·sa·tion·ist** (-shə-nĭst) *n.* One given to or skilled at conversation.

conversation piece *n.* **1.** A kind of genre painting, esp. popular in the 18th century, depicting a group of fashionable people. **2.** An unusual object that arouses comment or interest.

con·ver·sa·zi·o·ne (kŏn′vər-sät′sē-ō′nē, kōn′-) *n., pl.* **-nes** or **-ni** (-nē). A meeting for conversation or discussion, esp. of art. [Ital. < Lat. *conversatio,* dealings with persons < *conversari,* to associate with. —see CONVERSE[1].]

con·verse[1] (kən-vûrs′) *intr.v.* **-versed, -vers·ing, -vers·es. 1.** To engage in spoken exchange of thoughts and feelings; talk. **2.** To interact with a computer on-line. **3.** *Archaic.* To consort; associate. *—n.* (kŏn′vûrs′). **1.** Spoken interchange of thoughts and feelings; conversation. **2.** *Archaic.* Social intercourse. [ME *conversen,* to associate with < OFr. *converser* < Lat. *conversari* : *com-,* with + *versari,* to occupy oneself < *vertere,* to depend on.]

con·verse[2] (kən-vûrs′, kŏn′vûrs′) *adj.* Reversed, as in position, order, or action; contrary. *—n.* (kŏn′vûrs′). **1.** Something that has been reversed; opposite. **2.** *Logic.* A proposition obtained by conversion. [Lat. *conversus,* p.part. of *convertere,* to turn around. —see CONVERT.] **—con·verse′ly** *adv.*

con·ver·sion (kən-vûr′zhən, -shən) *n.* **1. a.** The act of converting. **b.** The state of being converted. **2.** A change in which one adopts a new religion. **3.** Something that is changed from one use, function, or purpose to another. **4.** *Law.* **a.** The unlawful appropriation of another's property. **b.** The changing of real property to personal property or vice versa. **5.** The exchange of one type of security or currency for another. **6.** *Logic.* The interchange of the subject and predicate of a proposition. **7.** *Football.* A score made on a try for a point or points after a touchdown. **8.** *Psychiat.* The symbolic manifestation of repressed ideas or impulses in motor or sensory abnormalities such as paralysis. [ME *conversioun,* religious conversion < OFr. *conversion* < Lat. *conversio,* a turning around < *convertere,* to turn around.] **—con·ver′sion·al, con·ver′sion·ar′y** (-zhə-nĕr′ē, -shə-) *adj.*

conveyer
Conveyer belt in a coffee factory

conversion factor *n.* A numerical factor used to multiply or divide a quantity expressed in one system of units in a conversion to another system.

conversion reaction *n.* A neurosis that is characterized by the presence of bodily symptoms that have no physical cause.

con·vert (kən-vûrt′) *v.* **-vert·ed, -vert·ing, -verts.** *—tr.* **1.** To change into another form, substance, state, or product; transform: *convert water into ice.* **2.** To persuade or induce to adopt a particular religion, faith, or belief. **3.** To change from one use, function, or purpose to another; adapt to a new or different purpose: *convert a forest into farmland.* **4.** To exchange for something of equal value. **5.** To exchange (a security, for example) by substituting an equivalent of another form. **6.** To express (a quantity) in alternative units. **7.** *Logic.* To transform (a proposition) by conversion. **8.** *Law.* **a.** To appropriate (another's property) without right to one's own use. **b.** To change (property) from real to personal or from joint to separate or vice versa. *—intr.* **1.** To be converted; undergo a change. **2.** *Football.* To make a conversion. *—n.* (kŏn′vûrt′). One who has been converted, esp. from one religion or belief to another. [ME *converten,* to convert to a religion < OFr. *convertir* < Lat. *convertere,* to turn around : *com-* (intensive) + *vertere,* to turn.]

con·vert·a·plane (kən-vûr′tə-plān′) *n.* Variant of **convertiplane.**

con·vert·er also **con·ver·tor** (kən-vûr′tər) *n.* **1.** One that converts. **2.** One that is employed in converting raw products into finished products. **3.** A furnace in which pig iron is converted into steel by the Bessemer process. **4. a.** A machine that changes electric current from one kind to another. **b.** An electronic device that changes the frequency of a radio signal. **c.** A device that transforms information from one code to another.

con·vert·i·ble (kən-vûr′tə-bəl) *adj.* **1.** Capable of being converted. **2.** Having a top that can be folded back or removed, as an automobile. **3.** Capable of being lawfully exchanged for gold or another currency: *dollars convertible into pounds.* *—n.* **1.** A convertible automobile. **2.** Something that can be converted. **—con·vert′i·bil′i·ty, con·vert′i·ble·ness** *n.* **—con·vert′i·bly** *adv.*

con·vert·i·plane also **con·vert·a·plane** (kən-vûr′tə-plān′) *n.* An airplane built to fly vertically as well as forward.

con·ver·tor (kən-vûr′tər) *n.* Variant of **converter.**

con·vex (kŏn′vĕks′, kən-vĕks′) *adj.* Having a surface or boundary that curves or bulges outward, as the exterior of a sphere. [Lat. *convexus* < *convehere,* to bring together.] **—con′vex′ly** *adv.*

con·vex·i·ty (kən-vĕk′sĭ-tē) *n., pl.* **-ties. 1.** The state of being convex. **2.** A convex surface, body, part, or line.

con·vex·o-con·cave (kən-vĕk′sō-kən-kāv′) *adj.* **1.** Having greater convex than concave curvature. Used of lenses. **2.** Concavo-convex (sense 1).

con·vex·o-con·vex (kən-vĕk′sō-kən-vĕks′) *adj.* Convex on both sides; doubly convex; biconvex.

con·vey (kən-vā′) *tr.v.* **-veyed, -vey·ing, -veys. 1.** To take or carry from one place to another; transport. **2.** To serve as a medium of transmission for; transmit. **3.** To communicate or make known; impart: *"a look intended to convey sympathetic comprehension"* (Saki). **4.** *Law.* To transfer ownership of or title to. **5.** *Obs.* To steal. [ME *conveien* < OFr. *conveier* < Med. Lat. *conviare,* to escort : Lat. *com-,* with + *via,* way.] **—con·vey′a·ble** *adj.*

Synonyms: *convey, carry, bear, transport, transmit, transfer.* These verbs refer to the movement of something from one place to another. When applied to physical objects, *convey* often implies continuous, regular movement or flow: *Pipelines convey water.* Figuratively *convey* means to serve as a medium for the movement or delivery of something, such as ideas or messages. *Carry* has broad application but is used principally with reference to movement of physical things. *Bear* has both physical and figurative use. Sometimes it suggests effort or burden; often it implies that the movement involves something important, such as valuable gifts or news. *Transport* is largely limited to movement of persons or material objects, often over a considerable distance. *Transmit* can refer to sending or dispatching material things, but more often applies to communicating (messages, news) or to serving as a medium for passage (of light, electricity, or sound). *Transfer* applies to movement of persons or things. It especially stresses change, as from one locality to another or from one means of travel to another.

con·vey·ance (kən-vā′əns) *n.* **1.** The act of conveying. **2.** A means of conveying, esp. a vehicle such as a car or bus. **3.** *Law.* **a.** The transfer of title to property from one person to another. **b.** The document by which this transfer is effected.

con·vey·anc·ing (kən-vā′ən-sĭng) *n.* The branch of legal practice dealing with the conveyance of property or real estate. **—con·vey′anc·er** *n.*

con·vey·er also **con·vey·or** (kən-vā′ər) *n.* **1.** One that conveys. **2.** A mechanical contrivance, such as a continuous moving belt, that transports bulk materials or packages from one place to another.

con·vict (kən-vĭkt′) *tr.v.* **-vict·ed, -vict·ing, -victs. 1.** To find or prove (someone) guilty of an offense or crime, esp. by the verdict of a court. **2.** To convince of wrongdoing or sinfulness. *—n.* (kŏn′vĭkt′). **1.** A person found or declared guilty of an offense or crime. **2.** A person serving a sentence of imprisonment. *—adj.* (kən-vĭkt′). *Archaic.* Found guilty; convicted. [ME *convicten* < Lat. *convincere.*]

con·vic·tion (kən-vĭk′shən) *n.* **1. a.** The act or process of finding or proving guilty. **b.** The state of being found or proved guilty. **2. a.** The act or process of convincing. **b.** The state of being convinced. **3.** A fixed or strong belief. **—con·vic′tion·al** *adj.*

con·vic·tive (kən-vĭk′tĭv) *adj.* Having power or serving to convince or convict. **—con·vic′tive·ly** *adv.*

con·vince (kən-vĭns′) *tr.v.* **-vinced, -vinc·ing, -vinc·es. 1.** To bring to belief by argument and evidence; cause to believe with certainty: *convinced of the need for action.* **2.** *Obs.* To convict. **3.** *Obs.* To conquer. [Lat. *convincere* : *com-,* (intensive) + *vincere,* to conquer.] **—con·vince′ment** *n.* **—con·vinc′er** *n.* **—con·vinc′i·ble** *adj.*

Usage: According to a traditional rule, one *persuades* someone to act but *convinces* someone of the truth of a statement or proposition: *By convincing me that no good could come of staying, he persuaded me to leave.* If the distinction is accepted, then *convince* should not be used with an infinitive: *He persuaded* (not *convinced*) *me to go.* This rule is supported by a majority of the Usage Panel, but the verbs are frequently used interchangeably at all levels.

con·vinc·ing (kən-vĭn′sĭng) *adj.* **1.** Serving to convince: *a* *convincing argument.* **2.** Believable; plausible: *a convincing story.* **—con·vinc'ing·ly** *adv.* **—con·vinc'ing·ness** *n.*

con·viv·i·al (kən-vĭv'ē-əl) *adj.* **1.** Fond of feasting, drinking, and good company; sociable. **2.** Relating to or of the nature of a feast; festive. [Lat. *convivialis* < Lat. *convivium,* banquet : *com-,* together + *vivere,* to live.] **—con·viv'i·al'i·ty** (-ăl'ĭ-tē) *n.* **—con·viv'i·al·ly** *adv.*

con·vo·ca·tion (kŏn'və-kā'shən) *n.* **1. a.** The act of convoking. **b.** A group of people convoked. **2.** A clerical assembly of the Anglican Church similar to a synod but assembling only when called. **3. a.** An assembly of the clergy and representative laity of a section of a diocese of the Episcopal Church. **b.** The district represented at such an assembly. **—con'vo·ca'tion·al** *adj.*

con·voke (kən-vōk') *tr.v.* **-voked, -vok·ing, -vokes.** To cause to assemble in a meeting; convene. [OFr. *convoquer* < Lat. *convocare* : *com-,* together + *vocare,* to call.] **—con·vok'er** *n.*

con·vo·lute (kŏn'və-lo͞ot') *adj.* Rolled or folded together with one part over another; coiled; twisted. *—tr. & intr.v.* **-lut·ed, -lut·ing, -lutes.** To coil; twist. [Lat. *convolutus,* p.part. of *convolvere,* to convolve.] **—con'vo·lute'ly** *adv.*

con·vo·lut·ed (kŏn'və-lo͞o'tĭd) *adj.* **1.** Exhibiting convolutions; coiled; twisted. **2.** Intricate; complicated.

con·vo·lu·tion (kŏn'və-lo͞o'shən) *n.* **1.** A convoluted formation or configuration. **2.** One of the convex folds of the surface of the brain. **—con'vo·lu'tion·al** *adj.*

con·volve (kən-vŏlv') *v.* **-volved, -volv·ing, -volves.** *—tr.* To roll together; coil up. *—intr.* To form convolutions. [Lat. *convolvere* : *com-,* together + *volvere,* to roll.]

con·vol·vu·lus (kən-vŏl'vyə-ləs) *n., pl.* **-lus·es** or **-li** (-lī'). Any of several trailing or twining plants of the genus *Convolvulus,* which includes the bindweeds. [NLat. *Convolvulus,* genus name < Lat. *covolvulus,* bindweed < *convolvere,* to intertwine. —see CONVOLVE.]

con·voy (kŏn'voi', kən-voi') *tr.v.* **-voyed, -voy·ing, -voys.** To accompany, esp. for protection; escort. *—n.* (kŏn'voi'). **1.** The act of convoying. **2.** An accompanying and protecting force, as of ships. **3.** Something, such as ships or troops, that is convoyed. **4.** A group, as of vehicles, traveling together for convenience. [ME *convoyen,* to escort < OFr. *convoier,* var. of *conveier.* —see CONVEY.]

con·vulse (kən-vŭls') *tr.v.* **-vulsed, -vuls·ing, -vuls·es. 1.** To shake or agitate violently: *"At that moment Darwin was convulsing society"* (Henry Adams). **2.** To affect with irregular and involuntary muscular contractions; throw into convulsions. [Lat. *convellere, convuls-,* to pull violently : *com-* (intensive) + *vellere,* to pull.]

con·vul·sion (kən-vŭl'shən) *n.* **1.** An intense paroxysmal involuntary muscular contraction. **2.** An uncontrolled fit, as of laughter; paroxysm. **3.** A violent turmoil.

con·vul·sion·ar·y (kən-vŭl'shə-nĕr'ē) *adj.* Of, pertaining to, affected with, or of the nature of convulsions. *—n., pl.* **-ies.** A person affected with convulsions, esp. as a result of religious fanaticism.

con·vul·sive (kən-vŭl'sĭv) *adj.* **1.** Marked by or of the nature of convulsions. **2.** Having or producing convulsions. **—con·vul'sive·ly** *adv.* **—con·vul'sive·ness** *n.*

co·ny also **co·ney** (kō'nē, kŭn'ē) *n., pl.* **-nies** also **-neys. 1.** A rabbit, esp. the Old World species *Oryctolagus cuniculus.* **2.** The fur of a rabbit. **3.** A pika. **4.** A hyrax. **5.** *Archaic.* A dupe. [ME < OFr. *conil* < Lat. *cuniculus.*]

coo (ko͞o) *v.* **cooed, coo·ing, coos.** *—intr.* **1.** To utter the characteristic murmuring sound of a dove or pigeon or a sound resembling this. **2.** To talk amorously or fondly in murmurs: *The lovers billed and cooed.* *—tr.* To express or utter gently or amorously, as with a murmuring sound. [Imit.] **—coo'er** *n.*

cook (ko͝ok) *v.* **cooked, cook·ing, cooks.** *—tr.* **1.** To prepare for eating by applying heat. **2.** To prepare or treat by heating. *—intr.* **1.** To prepare food for eating by applying heat. **2.** To undergo cooking. **3.** *Slang.* To happen, develop, or take place: *What's cooking in town?* **—phrasal verb. cook up.** *Informal.* To fabricate; concoct: *cook up an excuse.* *—n.* A person who prepares food for eating. [ME *coken* < *coke,* cook < OE *cōc* < LLat. *cocus* < Lat. *coquus* < *coquere,* to cook.]

cook·book (ko͝ok'bo͝ok') *n.* A book containing recipes and other information about the preparation of food.

cook·er (ko͝ok'ər) *n.* **1.** One that cooks, esp. a utensil or an appliance for cooking: *a pressure cooker.* **2.** A person employed to operate cooking apparatuses in the commercial preparation of food and drink.

cook·er·y (ko͝ok'ə-rē) *n., pl.* **-ies. 1.** The art or practice of preparing food. **2.** A place for cooking.

cook·out (ko͝ok'out') *n.* A meal cooked and served outdoors.

cook·y or **cook·ie** (ko͝ok'ē) *n., pl.* **-ies. 1.** A small, usually flat cake made from sweet dough. **2.** *Scot.* A bun. [Du. *koekje,* dim. of *koek,* cake < MDu. *koeke.*]

cool (ko͞ol) *adj.* **-er, -est. 1.** Moderately cold; neither warm nor very cold: *cool weather.* **2.** Affording or allowing relief from heat: *a cool breeze; a cool blouse.* **3.** Not excited; calm and controlled: *a cool head in a crisis.* **4.** Marked by indifference; unenthusiastic: *a cool greeting.* **5.** Marked by calm audacity; impudent: *gave him a cool look and walked away.* **6.** Designating or characteristic of colors, such as blue and green, that produce the impression of coolness. **7.** *Slang.* Excellent; first-rate. **8.** *Informal.* Entire; full: *He lost a cool million.* *—v.* **cooled, cool·ing, cools.** *—tr.* **1.** To make less warm. **2.** To make less ardent, intense, or zealous: *cooled his passion.* *—intr.* **1.** To become less warm: *took a dip to cool off.* **2.** To become calm. *—n.* **1.** Something that is cool or moderately cold: *the cool of early morning.* **2.** The state or quality of being cool. **3.** *Slang.* Composure: *recovered her cool.* **—idioms. cool it.** *Slang.* To calm down; relax. **cool (one's) heels.** *Slang.* To wait or be kept waiting. [ME *col* < OE *cōl.*] **—cool'ish** *adj.* **—cool'ly** *adv.* **—cool'ness** *n.*

Synonyms: *cool, composed, collected, unruffled, nonchalant, imperturbable, detached.* These adjectives apply to persons to indicate calmness, especially in time of stress. *Cool* has the widest application. Usually it implies merely a high degree of self-control, though it may also indicate aloofness. *Composed* and *collected* more strongly imply conscious display of self-discipline and absence of agitation. *Composed* also often suggests serenity or sedateness, and *collected,* mental concentration. *Unruffled* emphasizes calmness in the face of severe provocation that may have produced agitation in others present. *Nonchalant* describes a casual exterior manner that suggests, sometimes misleadingly, a lack of interest or concern. *Imperturbable* stresses unshakable calmness considered usually as an inherent trait rather than as a product of self-discipline. *Detached* implies aloofness and either lack of active concern or resistance to emotional involvement.

cool·ant (ko͞o'lənt) *n.* An agent that produces cooling, esp. a fluid that draws off heat by circulating through a machine or by bathing a mechanical part.

cool·er (ko͞o'lər) *n.* **1.** A device or container that cools or keeps cool. **2.** A cold drink. **3.** *Slang.* A jail or prison.

Coo·ley's anemia (ko͞o'lēz) *n.* An inherited form of anemia that results from a faulty synthesis of hemoglobin. [After Thomas B. *Cooley* (1871–1945).]

cool-head·ed (ko͞ol'hĕd'ĭd) *adj.* Not easily excited or flustered.

coo·lie also **coo·ly** (ko͞o'lē) *n., pl.* **-lies.** An unskilled Oriental laborer. [Hindi *kulī.*]

coon (ko͞on) *n.* **1.** *Informal.* A raccoon. **2.** *Offensive Slang.* A black person. [Short for RACCOON.]

coon·can (ko͞on'kăn') *n.* Conquian.

coon·hound (ko͞on'hound') *n.* A smooth-coated black and tan hound of a breed developed in the southeastern United States to hunt raccoons.

coon's age *n. Slang.* A long time.

coon·skin (ko͞on'skĭn') *n.* **1.** The pelt of a raccoon. **2.** An article, such as a hat, made of coonskin.

coon·tie (ko͞on'tē) *n.* An evergreen plant, *Zamia floridana,* of southern Florida, having underground stems that yield a starch resembling arrowroot. [Of Seminole orig.]

coop (ko͞op) *n.* **1.** An enclosure or cage, as for poultry or small animals. **2.** *Slang.* A place of confinement. *—tr.v.* **cooped, coop·ing, coops.** To confine in or as if in a coop: *hated being cooped up at home.* [ME *coupe.*]

co-op (kō'ŏp', kō-ŏp') *n.* A cooperative.

coo·per (ko͞o'pər) *n.* One who makes or repairs wooden tubs and casks. *—v.* **-pered, -per·ing, -pers.** *—tr.* To make or repair (wooden tubs and casks). *—intr.* To work as a cooper. [ME *couper* < MDu. *cūper* < *cūpe,* cask.]

coo·per·age (ko͞o'pər-ĭj) *n.* A cooper's work, shop, or products.

co·op·er·ate (kō-ŏp'ə-rāt') *intr.v.* **-at·ed, -at·ing, -ates. 1.** To work or act together toward a common end or purpose. **2.** To practice economic cooperation. [LLat. *cooperari, cooperat-* : *co(m)-,* together + *operari,* to work < *opus,* work.] **—co·op'er·a'tor** *n.*

co·op·er·a·tion (kō-ŏp'ə-rā'shən) *n.* **1.** An act of cooperating. **2.** An association of persons for mutual benefit. **—co·op'er·a'tion·ist** *n.*

co·op·er·a·tive (kō-ŏp'ər-ə-tĭv, -ŏp'rə-, -ə-rā'tĭv) *adj.* **1.** Done in cooperation with others: *a cooperative effort.* **2.** Marked by willingness to cooperate: *a cooperative patient.* **3.** Engaged in joint economic activity. *—n.* An enterprise that is owned jointly by those who use its facilities or services. **—co·op'er·a·tive·ly** *adv.* **—co·op'er·a·tive·ness** *n.*

co-opt (kō-ŏpt', kō'ŏpt') *tr.v.* **-opt·ed, -opt·ing, -opts. 1.** To elect as a fellow member of a group. **2.** To appoint summarily. **3.** To pre-empt; appropriate. **4.** To take or win over (an independent minority, for example) through assimilation into an established group or culture. [Lat. *cooptare* : *co(m)-,* together + *optare,* to choose.] **—co'op·ta'tion** (kō'ŏp-tā'shən) *n.* **—co-op'ta·tive** (-tə-tĭv) *adj.* **—co-op'tion** (-ŏp'shən) *n.* **—co-op'tive** *adj.*

co·or·di·nate (kō-ôr'dn-āt', -ĭt) *n.* **1.** One that is equal in importance, rank, or degree. **2.** *Math.* One of a set of numbers that determines the location of a point in a space of a given dimension. **3.** *Math.* Any of a set of two or more magnitudes used to determine the position of a point, line, curve, or plane. *—adj.* (-ĭt, -āt'). **1.** Of equal importance, rank, or degree. **2.** Of or involving coordination. **3.** Of or based on coordinates. *—v.* (-āt') **-nat·ed, -nat·ing, -nates.** *—tr.* **1.** To place in the same order, class, or rank. **2.** To harmonize in a common action or effort. *—intr.* To work together harmoniously. [Back-formation < COORDINATION.]

---

p **pop** / r **roar** / s **sauce** / sh **ship, dish** / t **tight** / th **thin, path** / *th* **this, bathe** / ŭ **cut** / ûr **urge** / v **valve** / w **with** / y **yes** / z **zebra, size** / zh **vision** / ə **about, item, edible, gallop, circus** / œ *Fr.* **feu,** *Ger.* **schön** / ü *Fr.* **tu,** *Ger.* **über** / KH *Ger.* **ich,** *Scot.* **loch** / N *Fr.* **bon.**

—**co·or′di·nate·ly** (-ĭt-lē) *adv.* —**co·or′di·nate·ness** (-ĭt-nĭs) *n.* —**co·or′di·na′tive** *adj.* —**co·or′di·na′tor** *n.*

coordinate bond *n.* A covalent chemical bond produced when an atom shares a pair of electrons with an atom lacking such a pair.

coordinate covalent bond *n.* Coordinate bond.

coordinating conjunction *n. Gram.* A conjunction that connects two identically constructed grammatical elements, such as *or* in *She doesn't know whether she's coming or going.*

co·or·di·na·tion (kō-ôr′dn-ā′shən) *n.* **1. a.** The act of coordinating. **b.** The state of being coordinate; harmonious adjustment or interaction. **2.** *Physiol.* The coordinated functioning of muscles or groups of muscles in the execution of a complex task. [Fr. or < LLat. *coordinatio* : *co(m)-*, same + *ordinatio,* arrangement < *ordinare,* to arrange in order < *ordo,* order.]

coordination complex *n.* Coordination compound.

coordination compound *n.* A chemical compound formed by joining independent molecules or ions to a central metallic atom.

coot (ko͞ot) *n.* **1.** Any of several dark-gray aquatic birds of the genus *Fulica,* esp. *F. americana,* of the New World, and *F. atra,* of the Old World. **2.** The scoter. **3.** *Informal.* A foolish old man. [ME *coote.*]

coot

coo·tie (ko͞o′tē) *n. Slang.* A body louse. [Perh. < Malay *kutu.*]

cop[1] (kŏp) *n.* **1.** A cone-shaped or cylindrical roll of yarn or thread wound on a spindle. **2.** *Archaic.* A summit or crest, as of a hill. [ME, summit < OE.]

cop[2] (kŏp) *n. Informal.* A policeman. —*tr.v.* **copped, cop·ping, cops.** *Slang.* **1.** To steal. **2.** To seize; catch. —***phrasal verb.*** **cop out.** *Slang.* **1.** To fail or refuse to commit oneself, esp. out of timidity. **2.** To back down, as on a promise; renege. —***idiom.*** **cop a plea.** *Informal.* To plead guilty to a lesser charge so as to avoid standing trial for a more serious charge. [Short for *copper,* prob. < *cop,* to catch.]

co·pa·cet·ic or **co·pa·set·ic** (kō′pə-sĕt′ĭk) *adj. Slang.* Excellent; first-rate. [Orig. unknown.]

co·pai·ba also **co·pai·ba balsam** (kō-pī′bə, -pā′-) *n.* A transparent, yellowish, viscous resin from South American trees of the genus *Copaifera,* used in varnishes and tracing papers and as an expectorant, diuretic, and stimulant. [Sp. < Port. *copaíba* < Tupi *copaiba.*]

co·pal (kō′pəl, -păl′) *n.* A brittle, aromatic, yellow to red resin of recent or fossil origin, obtained from various tropical trees and used in varnishes. [Sp. < Nahuatl *copalli,* resin.]

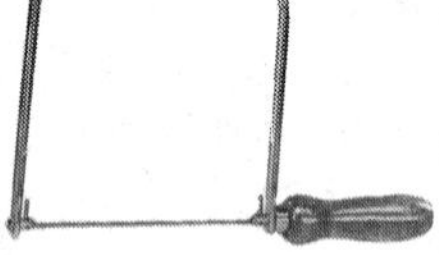

coping saw

co·par·ce·nar·y (kō-pär′sə-nĕr′ē) *n., pl.* **-ies. 1.** *Law.* Joint ownership of inherited property. **2.** Joint ownership. —*adj.* Of coparcenary or coparceners.

co·par·ce·ner (kō-pär′sə-nər) *n. Law.* One of two persons sharing an undivided inheritance.

co·part·ner (kō-pärt′nər) *n.* A partner, as in a business enterprise; associate. —**co·part′ner·ship′** *n.*

co·pa·set·ic (kō′pə-sĕt′ĭk) *adj.* Variant of **copacetic.**

cope[1] (kōp) *intr.v.* **coped, cop·ing, copes. 1.** To contend or strive, esp. on even terms or with success: *coping with child rearing and a full-time job.* **2.** *Informal.* To contend with difficulties and act to overcome them: *A successful social worker must be able to cope.* [ME *copen,* to strike < OFr. *couper* < *coup,* blow < LLat. *colpus* < Lat. *colaphus* < Gk. *kolaphos.*]

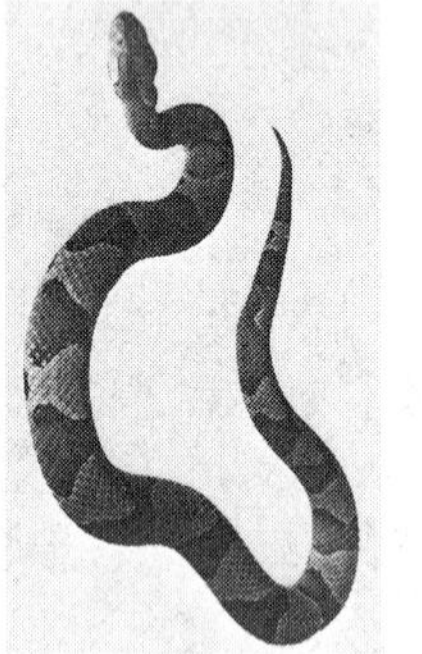

copperhead

cope[2] (kōp) *n.* **1.** A long ecclesiastical vestment worn over the alb or surplice. **2.** A covering resembling a cloak or mantle. **3.** A coping. —*tr.v.* **coped, cop·ing, copes. 1.** To cover or dress in a cope. **2.** To provide with coping: *cope a wall.* [ME *cope* < OE **cāp* < LLat. *capa,* cloak.]

co·peck (kō′pĕk′) *n.* Variant of **kopeck.**

co·pen·ha·gen (kō′pən-hā′gən, -hä′-) *n.* A grayish blue to purplish blue. [After *Copenhagen,* Denmark.] —**co′pen·ha′gen** *adj.*

co·pe·pod (kō′pə-pŏd′) *n.* Any of numerous small marine and freshwater crustaceans of the order *Copepoda.* [NLat. *Copepoda,* order name : Gk. *kōpē,* oar + Gk. *pous,* foot.]

Co·per·ni·can (kō-pûr′nĭ-kən) *adj.* Of or pertaining to the theory of Copernicus that the earth rotates on its axis and, with the other planets in the solar system, revolves around the sun.

cope·stone (kōp′stōn) *n.* Variant of **capstone.**

cop·i·er (kŏp′ē-ər) *n.* **1.** An office machine that makes copies. **2.** A copyist or transcriber.

co·pi·lot (kō′pī′lət) *n.* The second or relief pilot of an aircraft.

cop·ing (kō′pĭng) *n.* The top part of a wall or roof, usually with a slanting upper surface for drainage. [< COPE[2].]

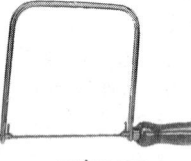

coping saw *n.* A narrow, short-bladed saw set in a recessed handle and used for cutting designs in wood. [Perh. < COPE[1], to strike (obs.).]

co·pi·ous (kō′pē-əs) *adj.* **1.** Yielding or containing plenty; affording ample supply: *a copious harvest.* **2.** Large in quantity; abundant: *copious rainfall.* **3.** Abounding in matter, thoughts, or words; wordy: *"I found our speech copious without order, and energetic without rules"* (Samuel Johnson). [ME < OFr. *copieux* < Lat. *copiosus* < *copia,* abundance.] —**co′pi·ous·ly** *adv.* —**co′pi·ous·ness** *n.*

co·pla·nar (kō-plā′nər) *adj.* Lying or occurring in the same plane. —**co′pla·nar′i·ty** (kō′plə-năr′ĭ-tē) *n.*

co·pol·y·mer (kō-pŏl′ə-mər) *n.* A polymer of two or more different monomers. —**co·pol′y·mer′ic** (-mĕr′ĭk) *adj.*

co·pol·y·mer·ize (kō-pŏl′ə-mə-rīz′, kō′pə-lĭm′ə-) *v.* **-ized, -iz·ing, -iz·es.** —*tr.* To polymerize (different monomers) together. —*intr.* To react to form a copolymer. —**co·pol′y·mer·i·za′tion** *n.*

cop·per[1] (kŏp′ər) *n.* **1.** *Symbol* **Cu** A ductile, malleable, reddish-brown metallic element that is an excellent conductor of heat and electricity and is widely used for electrical wiring, water piping, and corrosion-resistant parts either pure or in alloys such as brass and bronze. Atomic number 29; atomic weight 63.54; melting point 1,083°C; boiling point 2,595°C; specific gravity 8.96; valence 1, 2. **2.** A coin made of copper or a copper alloy. **3.** *Chiefly Brit.* A large boiler or pot made of copper or often of iron. **4.** Any of various small butterflies of the subfamily Lycaeninae, having predominantly copper-colored wings. —*tr.v.* **-pered, -per·ing, -pers. 1.** To coat or finish with a layer of copper. **2.** *Slang.* To bet against, as in faro. [ME *coper* < OE < LLat. *cuprum* < Lat. *Cyprium (aes),* Cyprian (metal).] —**cop′per·y** *adj.*

cop·per[2] (kŏp′ər) *n. Slang.* A policeman. [< COP[2].]

cop·per·as (kŏp′ər-əs) *n.* A greenish, crystalline, hydrated ferrous sulfate, $FeSO_4 \cdot 7H_2O$, used in the manufacture of fertilizers and inks and in water purification. [ME *coperose,* a metallic sulfate < OFr. < Med. Lat. *cuperosa,* prob. short for *aqua cuperosa,* copper water.]

cop·per·head (kŏp′ər-hĕd′) *n.* **1.** A venomous snake, *Agkistrodon contortrix* (or *Ancistron contortrix*), of the eastern United States, having reddish-brown markings. **2. Copperhead.** A Northerner who sympathized with the South during the Civil War.

cop·per·plate (kŏp′ər-plāt′) *n.* **1.** A copper printing plate engraved or etched to form a recessed pattern of the matter to be printed. **2.** A print or engraving made by using such a copperplate.

copper pyrites *n.* Chalcopyrite.

cop·per·smith (kŏp′ər-smĭth′) *n.* **1.** A worker or manufacturer of objects, esp. utensils, in copper. **2.** A brightly colored bird, *Megalaima haemacephala,* of southeastern Asia, having a ringing, metallic call.

copper sulfate *n.* A poisonous blue crystalline copper salt, $CuSO_4 \cdot 5H_2O$, used in agriculture, textile dyeing, leather treatment, electroplating, and the manufacture of germicides.

cop·per·ware (kŏp′ər-wâr′) *n.* Articles made of copper.

cop·pice (kŏp′ĭs) *n. Chiefly Brit.* A thicket; copse. [OFr. *copeiz* < *couper,* to cut, strike. —see COPE[1].]

co·pra (kō′prə, kŏp′rə) *n.* Dried coconut meat from which coconut oil is extracted. [Port. < Malayalam *koppara.*]

copro– *pref.* Excrement; dung: *coprolite.* [< Gk. *kopros,* dung.]

cop·ro·an·ti·bod·y (kŏp′rō-ăn′tē-bŏd′ē) *n.* An immunoglobulin that is present in the lumen of the intestine.

cop·ro·lite (kŏp′rə-līt′) *n.* Fossilized excrement. —**cop′ro·lit′ic** (-lĭt′ĭk) *adj.*

co·prol·o·gy (kō-prŏl′ə-jē) *n.* Pornography or scatology.

co·proph·a·gous (kō-prŏf′ə-gəs) *adj.* Feeding on excrement: *coprophagous insects.* —**co·proph′a·gy** (-ə-jē) *n.*

cop·ro·phil·i·a (kŏp′rə-fĭl′ē-ə) *n.* An abnormal attraction to fecal matter. —**cop′ro·phil′i·ac′** (-ē-ăk′) *n.*

co·proph·i·lous (kō-prŏf′ə-ləs) *adj.* Living in excrement.

copse (kŏps) *n.* A thicket of small trees or shrubs. [ME *copys* < OFr. *copeiz,* thicket for cutting < *couper,* to cut. —see COPE[1].]

Copt (kŏpt) *n.* **1.** A native of Egypt descended from ancient Egyptian stock. **2.** A member of the Coptic Church. [Ar. *Qubt,* Copts < Coptic *Gyptias* < Gk. *Aiguptios* < *Aiguptos,* Egypt.]

cop·ter (kŏp′tər) *n. Informal.* A helicopter.

Cop·tic (kŏp′tĭk) *n.* The Afro-Asiatic language of the Copts, which survives only as a liturgical language of the Coptic Church. —*adj.* Of or pertaining to the Copts or their language.

Coptic Church *n.* The Christian church of Egypt, adhering to the Monophysite doctrine.

cop·u·la (kŏp′yə-lə) *n.* **1.** A verb, as a form of *be* or *feel,* that identifies the predicate of a sentence with the subject. **2.** *Logic.* The word or set of words that serves as a link between the subject and predicate of a proposition. [Lat., link.] —**cop′u·lar** (-lər) *adj.*

cop·u·late (kŏp′yə-lāt′) *intr.v.* **-lat·ed, -lat·ing, -lates.** To engage in coitus. [Lat. *copulare, copulat-,* to join together < *copula,* link.] —**cop′u·la′tion** *n.* —**cop′u·la·to′ry** (-lə-tôr′ē, -tōr′ē) *adj.*

cop·u·la·tive (kŏp′yə-lā′tĭv, -lə-tĭv) *adj.* **1.** *Gram.* **a.** Serving to connect coordinate words or clauses: *a copulative conjunction.* **b.** Serving as a copula: *a copulative verb.* **2.** Of or pertaining to copulation. —*n. Gram.* A copulative word or group of words. —**cop′u·la′tive·ly** *adv.*

cop·y (kŏp′ē) *n., pl.* **-ies. 1.** An imitation or reproduction of something original; duplicate. **2.** One specimen or example of a printed text or picture: *an autographed copy of a novel.* **3.** A manuscript or other material to be set in type. **4.** Suit-

able source material, as for journalism: *Celebrities make good copy.* —*v.* **-ied, -y·ing, -ies.** —*tr.* **1.** To make a copy of. **2.** To follow as a model or pattern; imitate. —*intr.* **1.** To make a copy or reproduction. **2.** To admit of being copied. [ME < OFr. *copie* < Med. Lat. *copia* < Lat., abundance.]
cop·y·book (kŏp′ē-bo͝ok′) *n.* A book of models of penmanship for imitation. —*adj.* Unoriginal; trite: *a copybook phrase.*
copy boy *n.* An employee in a newspaper office who carries copy and runs errands.
cop·y·cat (kŏp′ē-kăt′) *n.* A mimic; imitator.
copy desk *n.* The desk in a newspaper office where copy is edited and prepared for typesetting.
cop·y-ed·it (kŏp′ē-ĕd′ĭt) *tr.v.* **-it·ed, -it·ing, -its.** To correct and prepare (a manuscript, for example) for typesetting and printing. **—copy editor** *n.*
cop·y·hold·er (kŏp′ē-hōl′dər) *n.* **1.** An assistant who reads manuscript aloud to a proofreader. **2.** A device that holds copy in place, esp. for a typesetter.
cop·y·ist (kŏp′ē-ĭst) *n.* One who makes written copies.
cop·y·read·er (kŏp′ē-rē′dər) *n.* One who edits and corrects newspaper copy for publication.
cop·y·right (kŏp′ē-rīt′) *n.* The legal right granted to an author, composer, playwright, publisher, or distributor, to exclusive publication, production, sale, or distribution of a literary, musical, dramatic, or artistic work. —*adj.* Protected by copyright. —*tr.v.* **-right·ed, -right·ing, -rights.** To secure a copyright for. **—cop′y·right′a·ble** *adj.* **—cop′y·right′er** *n.*
cop·y·writ·er (kŏp′ē-rī′tər) *n.* One who writes copy, esp. for advertising.
coq au vin (kōk′ ō văɴ′, kŏk′) *n.* A dish of chicken cooked in red wine. [Fr. : *coq,* cock + *au,* with + *vin,* wine.]
co·quet (kō-kĕt′) *intr.v.* **-quet·ted, -quet·ting, -quets. 1.** To engage in coquetry; flirt. **2.** To trifle; dally. [Fr. *coqueter* < *coquet,* flirtatious man, dim. of *coq,* cock < OFr. *coc* < LLat. *coccus* < Lat. *coco,* clucking.]
co·quet·ry (kō′kĭ-trē, kō-kĕt′rē) *n., pl.* **-ries.** Dalliance; flirtation. [Fr. *coquetterie* < *coquette,* coquette.]
co·quette (kō-kĕt′) *n.* A woman who flirts with men. [Fr., fem. of *coquet,* flirtatious man. —see COQUET.] **—co·quet′tish** *adj.* **—co·quet′tish·ly** *adv.* **—co·quet′tish·ness** *n.*
co·quil·la nut (kō-kēl′yə, -kē′yə) *n.* The nut of a South American palm tree, *Attalea funifera,* having a hard oval shell used for decorative carving or turning. [Port. *coquilho,* dim. of *côco,* coco.]
co·quille (kō-kēl′) *n.* A scallop-shaped dish or a scallop shell in which various seafood dishes are browned and served. [Fr. < Lat. *conchylia,* pl. of *conchylium,* shellfish < Gk. *konkhulion,* dim. of *konkhē.*]
co·qui·na (kō-kē′nə) *n.* **1.** Any of various small bivalve mollusks of warm marine waters, having variously colored, often striped or banded shells. **2.** A soft porous limestone, essentially of shell and coral fragments, used as a construction material. [Sp., cockle, dim. of *concha,* shell < Lat., mussel. —see CONCH.]
co·qui·to (kō-kē′tō) *n., pl.* **-tos.** A Chilean palm tree, *Jubaea spectabilis,* from whose sap a sweet edible syrup is obtained. [Sp., dim. of *coco,* coco palm < Port. *côco.*]
co·rac·i·i·form (kə-răs′ē-ə-fôrm′) *adj.* Of or pertaining to the order Coraciiformes that includes birds such as the kingfisher. [< NLat. *Coraciiformes,* order name : Gk. *korakias,* a kind of bird + Lat. *forma,* form.]
cor·a·cle (kôr′ə-kəl, kŏr′-) *n.* A small, rounded boat made of waterproof material stretched over a wicker or wooden frame. [Welsh *corwgl.*]
cor·a·coid (kôr′ə-koid′, kŏr′-) *n.* A bone or cartilage projecting from the scapula toward the sternum. [NLat. *coracoides* < Gk. *korakoeidēs,* like a raven : *korax,* raven + *-oeidēs,* -oid.] **—cor′a·coid′** *adj.*
cor·al (kôr′əl, kŏr′əl) *n.* **1. a.** Any of numerous chiefly colonial marine coelenterates of the class Anthozoa, characterized by calcareous skeletons massed in a wide variety of shapes and often forming reefs or islands. **b.** The often hard, rocklike structure formed by such organisms. **c.** The material forming such a structure, esp. the red-orange, pinkish, or white stony substance secreted by corals of the genus *Corallium,* used to make jewelry and ornaments. **2.** An object made of coral. **3.** A deep or strong pink to moderate red or reddish orange. **4.** The unfertilized eggs of a female lobster that turn a reddish color when cooked. —*adj.* Deep or strong pink to moderate red or reddish orange. [ME < OFr. < Lat. *corallium* < Gk. *korallion,* prob. of Semitic orig.]
cor·al-bells (kôr′əl-bĕlz′, kŏr′-) *n. (used with a sing. or pl. verb).* A plant, *Heuchera sanguinea,* of the western United States, often cultivated for its clusters of small, bell-shaped red flowers.
cor·al·ber·ry (kôr′əl-bĕr′ē, kŏr′-) *n.* **1.** A North American shrub, *Symphoricarpos orbiculatus,* having red or purplish fruit. **2.** The fruit of the coralberry.
cor·al·line (kôr′ə-lĭn, -līn′, kŏr′-) *adj.* **1.** Of, consisting of, or producing coral. **2.** Resembling coral, esp. in color. —*n.* **1.** A corallike animal, such as certain bryozoans or hydrozoans. **2.** Any of various red algae, esp. of the genus *Corallina,* covered with a calcareous substance and forming stony deposits. [Fr. *corallin* < Lat. *corallinus* < *corallium,* coral.]
cor·al·loid (kôr′ə-loid′, kŏr′-) *adj.* Resembling coral in appearance or form. [Lat. *corallium,* coral + -OID.] **—cor′al·loi′dal** (-loid′l) *adj.*
coral pink *n.* A moderate to deep yellowish pink.
coral reef *n.* An erosion-resistant marine ridge or mound consisting chiefly of compacted coral together with algal material and biochemically deposited magnesium and calcium carbonates.
cor·al·root (kôr′əl-ro͞ot′, -ro͝ot′, kŏr′-) *n.* Any of several orchids of the genus *Corallorhiza,* having small yellow-green or purplish flowers and branched roots that resemble coral.
coral snake *n.* Any of various venomous snakes of the genus *Micrurus,* of tropical America and the southern United States, characteristically having brilliant red, black, and yellow banded markings.
coral vine *n.* A climbing woody vine, *Antigonon leptopus,* native to Mexico and cultivated for its red or white flowers.
cor·ban (kôr′bən, -băn′) *n.* An offering to God among the ancient Hebrews. [ME < LLat. < Gk. *korban* < Heb. *qurbān.*]
cor·beil also **cor·beille** (kôr′bəl, kôr-bā′) *n.* A sculptured basket of flowers or fruits used as an architectural ornament. [Fr. *corbeille* < LLat. *corbicula,* little basket, dim. of *corbis,* basket.]
cor·bel (kôr′bəl, -bĕl′) *n.* A bracket of stone, wood, brick, or other building material, projecting from the face of a wall and generally used to support a cornice or an arch. —*tr.v.* **-beled, -bel·ing, -bels** also **-belled, -bel·ling, -bels.** To provide with or support by a corbel or corbels. [ME < OFr., dim. of *corp,* raven < Lat. *corvus.*]
cor·bel·ing (kôr′bəl-ĭng, -bĕl′) *n.* **1.** The building of a corbel. **2.** An overlapping arrangement of bricks or stones in which each course extends farther out from the vertical of the wall than the course below.
cor·bie gable (kôr′bē) *n.* A gable roof with corbie-steps.
cor·bie-step also **cor·bie·step** (kôr′bē-stĕp′) *n.* One of a series of steps or steplike projections on the top of a gable wall. [ME *corbie* < OFr. *corbin* < Lat. *corvinus,* ravenlike. —see CORBINA.]
cor·bi·na (kôr-bē′nə) also **cor·vi·na** (-vē′nə) *n.* **1.** A food and game fish, *Menticirrhus undulatus,* of North American Pacific coastal waters. **2.** Any of several marine fishes of the family Sciaenidae related to the corbina. [Mex. Sp. < Sp. *corvino,* ravenlike (from its color) < *corvus,* raven.]
cord (kôrd) *n.* **1.** A string or small rope of twisted strands or fibers. **2.** An insulated, flexible electric wire fitted with a plug or plugs. **3.** A hangman's rope. **4.** An influence, feeling, or force that binds or restrains. **5.** Also **chord.** *Anat.* A structure resembling a cord: *a spinal cord.* **6. a.** A raised rib on the surface of cloth. **b.** A fabric or cloth with such ribs. **7. cords.** Trousers made of corduroy. **8.** A unit of quantity for cut fuel wood, equal to 128 cubic feet in a stack measuring 4 by 4 by 8 feet. —*tr.v.* **cord·ed, cord·ing, cords. 1.** To fasten or bind with a cord. **2.** To furnish with a cord. **3.** To pile (wood) in cords. [ME < OFr. *corde* < Lat. *chorda* < Gk. *khordē.*] **—cord′er** *n.*
cord·age (kôr′dĭj) *n.* **1.** Ropes, esp. the ropes in the rigging of a ship. **2.** The amount of wood in an area as measured in cords.
cor·date (kôr′dāt′) *adj.* Having a heart-shaped outline: *a cordate leaf.* [NLat. *cordatus* < Lat. *cor,* heart.] **—cor′date′ly** *adv.*
cord·ed (kôr′dĭd) *adj.* **1.** Tied or bound with cords. **2.** Furnished with or made of cords. **3.** Ribbed or twilled, as corduroy. **4.** Stacked in cords, as firewood.
cor·dial (kôr′jəl) *adj.* **1.** Warm and sincere; hearty: *a cordial greeting.* **2.** Serving to invigorate; stimulating; reviving. —*n.* **1.** A stimulant. **2.** A liqueur. [ME < Med. Lat. *cordialis* < Lat. *cor,* heart.] **—cor·dial′i·ty** (-jăl′ĭ-tē, -jē-ăl′-, -dē-ăl′-), **cor′dial·ness** *n.* **—cor′dial·ly** *adv.*
cor·di·er·ite (kôr′dē-ə-rīt′) *n.* A dichroic violet-blue to gray mineral silicate of magnesium, aluminum, and sometimes iron. [Fr., after Pierre L.A. *Cordier* (1777–1861).]
cor·di·form (kôr′də-fôrm′) *adj.* Heart-shaped. [Lat. *cor, cord-,* heart + -FORM.]
cor·dil·le·ra (kôr′dl-yâr′ə, kôr-dĭl′ər-ə) *n.* A chain of mountains, esp. the principal mountain range or system of a large land mass. [Sp. < *cordilla,* dim. of *cuerda,* cord < Lat. *chorda.*] **—cor′dil·le′ran** (-yâr′ən) *adj.*
cord·ite (kôr′dīt′) *n.* A smokeless explosive powder consisting of nitrocellulose, nitroglycerin, and petrolatum dissolved in acetone, dried, and extruded in cords.
cord·less (kôrd′lĭs) *adj.* **1.** Having no cord. **2.** Using batteries as a source of power: *a cordless electric shaver.*
cord moss *n.* Any moss of the genus *Funaria,* esp. *F. hygrometrica,* usually growing in burned or waste places.
cor·do·ba (kôr′də-bə, -və) *n.* See table at **currency.** [After Francisco de *Córdoba* (1475–1526).]
cor·don (kôr′dn) *n.* **1.** A line of people, military posts, or ships stationed around an area to enclose or guard it. **2.** A cord or braid worn as a fastening or an ornament. **3.** A ribbon usually worn diagonally across the breast as a badge of honor or a decoration. **4.** *Archit.* A stringcourse. **5.** A fruit tree trained and pruned to grow along wires or other supports. —*tr.v.* **-doned, -don·ing, -dons.** To form a cordon around (an area) so as to prevent ingress or egress: *Troops*

coral

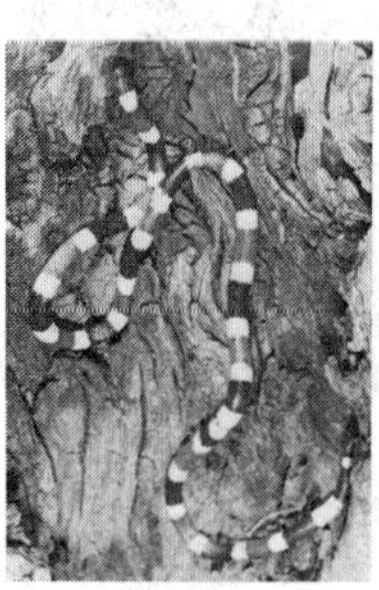
coral snake

corbie-step

cordate

cordoned off the riot zone. [Fr. < OFr., dim. of *corde,* cord.]
cor·don bleu (kôr'dôN blœ') *n., pl.* **cor·dons bleus** (kôr'dôN blœ'). A person highly distinguished in his field, esp. a master chef. [Fr. : *cordon,* ribbon + *bleu,* blue.]
cor·don sa·ni·taire (kôr-dôN' sä-nē-târ') *n., pl.* **cor·dons sa·ni·taires** (kôr-dôN' sä-nē-târ'). A chain of buffer states organized around a nation considered ideologically dangerous or potentially hostile. [Fr. : *cordon,* line + *sanitaire,* sanitary.]
cor·do·van (kôr'də-vən) *n.* A fine leather made originally at Córdoba, Spain, first of goatskin but now more frequently of split horsehide. *—**modifier:** cordovan shoes.* [Sp. *cordobán* < *Córdoba,* Córdoba, Spain.]
cor·du·roy (kôr'də-roi') *n.* **1.** A durable cut-pile fabric, usually made of cotton, with vertical ribs or wales. **2. corduroys.** Corduroy trousers. **3.** A road made of logs laid down crosswise. *—adj.* Made of logs laid down crosswise. *—tr.v.* **-royed, -roy·ing, -roys.** To build (a road) of logs laid down crosswise. [Prob. < CORD + obs. *duroy,* a coarse woolen fabric.]
cord·wood (kôrd'wŏŏd') *n.* **1.** Wood cut and piled in cords. **2.** Wood sold by the cord.
core (kôr, kōr) *n.* **1.** The hard or fibrous central part of certain fruits, such as the apple or pear, containing the seeds. **2.** The innermost or most important part of something; heart; center: *the core of the problem.* **3.** *Elect.* A soft iron rod in a coil or transformer that intensifies and provides a path for the magnetic field produced by the windings. **4.** Also **core memory.** A computer memory consisting of a series of doughnut-shaped masses of magnetic material. **5.** The central portion of the earth at a depth of approximately 2,900 kilometers or 1,800 miles. **6.** A mass of dry sand placed within a mold to provide openings or shape to a casting. **7.** The base, usually of soft or inferior wood, to which veneer woods are glued. *—tr.v.* **cored, cor·ing, cores.** To remove the core of: *core apples.* [ME.]
core city *n.* An inner city.
core dump *n.* A listing of the data stored in a computer core. **—core'-dump'** *v.* **(-dumped, -dump·ing, -dumps).**
co·re·lig·ion·ist (kō'rĭ-lĭj'ə-nĭst) *n.* One having the same religion as another.
cor·e·op·sis (kôr'ē-ŏp'sĭs, kōr-) *n.* Any of several plants of the genus *Coreopsis,* having daisylike yellow or variegated flowers. [NLat. *Coreopsis,* genus name : Gk. *koris,* bedbug + Gk. *opsis,* appearance.]
co·re·pres·sor (kō'rĭ-prĕs'ər) *n.* A substance that combines with a genetic repressor to activate it.
cor·er (kôr'ər, kōr'-) *n.* An implement for coring apples.
co·re·spon·dent (kō'rĭ-spŏn'dənt) *n. Law.* A person charged with having committed adultery with the defendant in a suit for divorce. **—co're·spon'den·cy** *n.*
corf (kôrf) *n., pl.* **corves** (kôrvz). *Chiefly Brit.* A truck, tub, or basket used in a mine. [ME, basket < MDu. *corf* or < MLG *korf,* both prob. < Lat. *corbis.*]
cor·gi (kôr'gē) *n.* A Welsh corgi. [Welsh : *cor,* dwarf + *ci,* dog.]
cor·i·a·ceous (kôr'ē-ā'shəs, kōr'-) *adj.* Of or like leather, esp. in texture; tough. [LLat. *coriaceus* < Lat. *corium,* leather.]
co·ri·an·der (kôr'ē-ăn'dər, kōr'-, kôr'ē-ăn'dər, kōr'-) *n.* **1.** An herb, *Coriandrum sativum,* widely cultivated for its aromatic seeds. **2.** The dried ripe seeds of the coriander, used as a condiment. [ME *coriandre* < OFr. < Lat. *coriandrum* < Gk. *koriandron.*]
Co·rin·thi·an (kə-rĭn'thē-ən) *adj.* **1.** Of or pertaining to ancient Corinth in Greece. **2.** Given to luxury; licentious; profligate. **3.** Elegantly or elaborately ornate. **4.** Pertaining to or designating the most ornate of the three classical orders of architecture, characterized by a slender fluted column having an ornate bell-shaped capital decorated with acanthus leaves. *—n.* **1.** A native or inhabitant of Corinth, Greece. **2.** A man about town. **3.** A wealthy amateur sportsman, esp. an amateur yachtsman. **4. Corinthians.** See table at **Bible.**
Co·ri·o·lis force (kôr'ē-ō'lĭs, kōr'-) *n.* A fictitious force used mathematically to describe motion, as of aircraft or cloud formations, relative to a noninertial, uniformly rotating frame of reference such as the earth. [After Gaspard G. de *Coriolis* (1792–1843).]
co·ri·um (kôr'ē-əm, kōr'-) *n., pl.* **-ri·a** (-ē-ə). The layer of the skin beneath the epithelium, containing nerve endings, sweat glands, and blood and lymph vessels. [Lat., skin.]
cork (kôrk) *n.* **1.** The light, porous, elastic outer bark of the cork oak used widely in industry and the arts. **2. a.** Something made of cork, esp. a bottle stopper. **b.** A bottle stopper made of other material, such as plastic. **3.** A small float used on a fishing line or net to buoy up the line or net or to indicate when a fish bites. **4.** *Bot.* A tissue of dead cells that forms on the outer side of the cambium in the stems of woody plants. *—tr.v.* **corked, cork·ing, corks. 1.** To stop or seal with or as if with a cork. **2.** To hold back; restrain or check. **3.** To blacken with burnt cork. [ME < Du. *kurk* or LG *korck,* both < Sp. *alcorque,* cork-soled shoe < dial. Ar. *al-qūrq* < Lat. *quercus,* oak.]
cork·age (kôr'kĭj) *n.* A charge exacted at a restaurant for every bottle of liquor served that was not bought on the premises.
cork·board (kôrk'bôrd', -bōrd') *n.* A construction and insulating sheet material made of compressed and baked granules of cork.
cork cambium *n. Bot.* Phellogen.
corked (kôrkt) *adj.* **1.** Sealed with a cork. **2.** Tainted in flavor by an unsound cork: *corked port.* **3.** Blackened by burnt cork.
cork·er (kôr'kər) *n.* **1.** One that corks. **2.** *Slang.* One that is remarkable or astounding.
cork·ing (kôr'kĭng) *adj. & adv. Slang.* Extremely splendid; fine. [< CORKER.]
cork oak *n.* An evergreen oak tree, *Quercus suber,* of the Mediterranean region, having porous outer bark that is the source of cork.
cork·screw (kôrk'skrōō') *n.* A device for drawing corks from bottles, consisting of a pointed metal spiral attached to a handle. *—adj.* Resembling a corkscrew in shape; spiral. *—intr. & tr.v.* **-screwed, -screw·ing, -screws.** To move or cause to move in a spiral or winding course.
cork·wood (kôrk'wŏŏd') *n.* **1. a.** A small tree or shrub, *Leitneria floridiana,* of the southeastern United States, having very light wood. **b.** Any of several other trees having light, porous wood. **2.** The wood of a corkwood.
cork·y (kôr'kē) *adj.* **-i·er, -i·est. 1.** Of or like cork. **2.** *Informal.* Lively; buoyant. **—cork'i·ness** *n.*
corm (kôrm) *n.* An underground stem, such as that of the gladiolus, similar to a bulb but without scales. [NLat. *cormus* < Gk. *kormos,* a trimmed tree trunk < *keirein,* to cut.]
cor·mel (kôr'məl, kôr-mĕl') *n.* A young corm that arises at the base of a fully developed corm.
cor·mo·rant (kôr'mər-ənt, -mə-rănt') *n.* **1.** Any of several widely distributed aquatic birds of the genus *Phalacrocorax,* having dark plumage, webbed feet, a hooked bill, and a distensible pouch. **2.** A greedy or rapacious person. *—adj.* Greedy; rapacious. [ME *cormoraunt* < OFr. *cormorant* : *corp,* raven (< Lat. *corvus*) + *marenc,* of the sea (< Lat. *marinus*).]
corn[1] (kôrn) *n.* **1. a.** Any of several varieties of a tall, widely cultivated cereal plant, *Zea mays,* bearing seeds or kernels on large ears. **b.** The seeds or kernels of this plant, used for food or fodder, and yielding an edible oil. **c.** The ears of the corn plant. **2.** *Chiefly Brit.* **a.** Any of several cereal plants producing edible seed, such as wheat, rye, oats, or barley. **b.** The seeds of such a plant or crop; grain. **3. a.** A single seed of a cereal plant; a grain. **b.** A seed or fruit of various other plants. **4.** *Informal.* Corn whiskey. **5.** *Slang.* Something considered trite, dated, melodramatic, or unduly sentimental. *—tr.v.* **corned, corn·ing, corns. 1.** To granulate or form into small grains. **2. a.** To preserve and season with granulated salt. **b.** To preserve in brine: *corned beef.* **3.** To feed (animals) with corn or grain. [ME, grain < OE.]
corn[2] (kôrn) *n.* A horny thickening of the skin, usually on or near a toe, resulting from pressure or friction. [ME *corne* < OFr., horn < Lat. *cornu.*]
corn·ball (kôrn'bôl') *Slang. —n.* One who behaves in a mawkish or unsophisticated manner. *—adj.* Mawkish or unsophisticated; corny. [< E. *corn ball,* a ball of popcorn and molasses.]
corn borer *n.* **1.** The larva of a moth, *Pyrausta nubilalis,* native to the Old World, that feeds on and destroys corn and other plants. **2.** Any of various insect larvae similar to the corn borer that infest corn.
corn bread also **corn·bread** (kôrn'brĕd') *n.* A kind of bread made from cornmeal.
corn·cake also **corn cake** (kôrn'kāk') *n.* A bread made with white cornmeal cooked either as small cakes on a griddle or oven-baked in a pan.
corn chip *n.* Often **corn chips.** A crisp piece of food made from cornmeal batter.
corn·cob (kôrn'kŏb') *n.* **1.** The woody core of an ear of corn, on which the kernels grow. **2.** A corncob pipe.
corncob pipe *n.* A pipe with a bowl made of a dried corncob.
corn cockle *n.* A plant, *Agrostemma githago,* native to Europe, having red flowers and growing in fields and by roadsides.
corn·crake (kôrn'krāk') *n.* A common Old World bird, *Crex crex,* having brownish plumage and frequenting grain fields and meadows.
corn·crib (kôrn'krĭb') *n.* A structure for storing and drying ears of corn.
corn·dodg·er (kôrn'dŏj'ər) *n.* A small, usually round corncake baked, fried, or broiled.
cor·ne·a (kôr'nē-ə) *n.* The transparent anterior portion of the outer fibrous tunic of the eye, a uniformly thick, nearly circular, convex structure covering the lens. [Med. Lat. *cornea (tela),* horny (tissue) < Lat. *corneus,* horny < *cornu,* horn.] **—cor'ne·al** (-əl) *adj.*
corn earworm *n.* The large, destructive larva of a moth, *Heliothis armigera,* that feeds on corn and many other plants.
cor·ne·i·tis (kôr'nē-ī'tĭs) *n.* Inflammation of the cornea.
cor·nel (kôr'nəl, -nĕl') *n.* Any of various shrubs, trees, or plants of the genus *Cornus,* which includes the dogwoods.

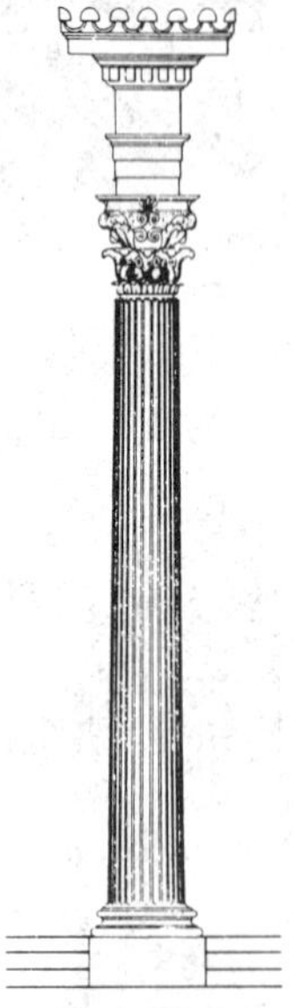

Corinthian
Above: Corinthian capital
Below: Corinthian column

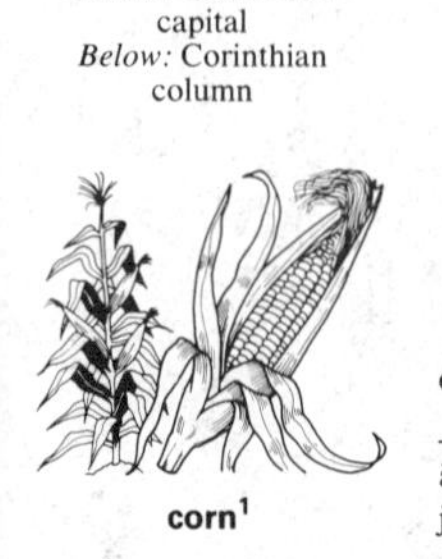

corn[1]

[G. *Kornel(baum)* : Lat. *cornus,* cornel tree + G. *Baum,* tree.]

cor·nel·ian (kôr-nēl′yən) *n.* Variant of **carnelian.**

cornelian cherry *n.* A shrub or small tree, *Cornus mas,* native to Eurasia, having very small yellow flowers and bright-red fruit. [< CORNEL.]

cor·ne·ous (kôr′nē-əs) *adj.* Made of horn or a hornlike substance; horny. [Lat. *corneus* < *cornu,* horn.]

cor·ner (kôr′nər) *n.* **1. a.** The position at which two lines or surfaces meet. **b.** The immediate interior or exterior region of the angle formed at this position, bounded by the two lines or surfaces. **2.** A vertex, esp. the interior region of a vertex, formed by the sides of roads or streets that join, meet, or intersect. **3.** A threatening or embarrassing position, esp. one from which escape is difficult or impossible: *got himself in a corner by boasting.* **4. a.** A part, quarter, or region: *the four corners of the earth.* **b.** A remote, secluded, or secret place: *a beautiful little corner of Paris.* **5.** A guard or decoration fitted on a corner, as of a bookbinding. **6.** A speculative monopoly of a stock or commodity created by purchasing all or most of the available supply in order to raise its price. ***—modifier:*** *a corner drugstore.* *—v.* **-nered, -ner·ing, -ners.** *—tr.* **1.** To furnish with corners. **2.** To place or drive into a corner: *cornered the thieves and captured them.* **3.** To form a corner in (a stock or commodity): *cornered the silver market.* *—intr.* **1.** To come together or be situated on or at a corner. **2.** To turn, as at a corner: *a truck that corners poorly.* ***—idiom.*** **cut corners.** *Informal.* **1.** To take the shortest route around obstacles, often dangerously or illegally. **2.** To reduce expenses; economize. [ME < OFr. < Lat. *cornu,* horn.]

cor·ner·back also **corner back** (kôr′nər-băk′) *n. Football.* Either of two defensive halfbacks stationed a short distance behind the linebackers and relatively near the sidelines.

cor·ner·stone also **corner stone** (kôr′nər-stōn′) *n.* **1. a.** A stone at the corner of a building uniting two intersecting walls; quoin. **b.** Such a stone ceremoniously laid, often hollowed to contain historical documents or objects and inscribed. **2.** The indispensable and fundamental basis of something: *the cornerstone of an argument.*

cor·ner·wise (kôr′nər-wīz′) also **cor·ner·ways** (-wāz′) *adv.* **1.** With a corner toward the front. **2.** So as to form a corner. **3.** From corner to corner; diagonally.

cor·net (kôr-nět′) *n.* **1.** A musical wind instrument of the trumpet class, having three valves operated by pistons. **2.** (kôr′nĭt). A piece of paper twisted into a cone and used to hold small wares such as candy or nuts. **3.** (kôr′nĭt). A headdress, often cone-shaped, worn by women in the 12th and 13th centuries. [ME < OFr., dim. of *corn,* horn < Lat. *cornu.*]

cor·net-à-pis·tons (kôr-nět′ə-pĭs′tənz) *n., pl.* **cor·nets-à-pis·tons** (kôr-něts′ə-pĭs′tənz). A cornet (sense 1). [Fr.]

cor·net·ist also **cor·net·tist** (kôr-nět′ĭst) *n.* One who plays a cornet.

corn-fed (kôrn′fěd′) *adj.* **1.** Fed on corn. **2.** *Slang.* Healthy and strong, but provincial and unsophisticated.

corn flakes *pl.n.* A crisp, flaky, commercially prepared cold cereal made from coarse cornmeal.

corn·flow·er (kôrn′flou′ər) *n.* A garden plant, *Centaurea cyanus,* native to Eurasia, having blue, purple, pink, or white flowers.

corn·husk (kôrn′hŭsk′) *n.* The leafy husk surrounding an ear of corn.

corn·husk·ing (kôrn′hŭs′kĭng) *n.* **1.** The husking of corn. **2.** A social gathering for husking corn. **—corn′husk′er** *n.*

cor·nice (kôr′nĭs) *n.* **1.** *Archit.* **a.** A horizontal molded projection that crowns or completes a building or wall. **b.** The uppermost part of an entablature. **2.** The molding at the top of the walls of a room, between the walls and ceiling. **3.** An ornamental horizontal molding or frame used to conceal rods, picture hooks, or other devices. *—tr.v.* **-niced, -nic·ing, -nic·es.** To supply, decorate, or finish with or as if with a cornice. [OFr. < OItal.]

cor·nic·u·late (kôr-nĭk′yə-lāt′, -lĭt) *adj.* Having horns or hornlike projections. [Lat. *corniculatus* < *corniculum,* little horn, dim. of *cornu,* horn.]

cor·ni·fi·ca·tion (kôr′nə-fĭ-kā′shən) *n.* The conversion of squamous epithelial cells into a horny material such as hair or nails. [Lat. *cornu,* horn + -FICATION.]

Cor·nish (kôr′nĭsh) *adj.* Of or pertaining to Cornwall in England, Cornishmen, or the Brythonic language of Cornwall, which has been extinct since the late 18th century. *—n.* The Cornish language.

Cornish hen *n.* A Rock Cornish hen.

Cor·nish·man (kôr′nĭsh-mən) *n.* A native or inhabitant of Cornwall, England.

Corn Law *n.* One of a series of British laws in force before 1846 regulating the grain trade and restricting imports of grain.

corn lily *n.* Any of several bulbous plants of the genus *Ixia,* native to southern Africa, having variously colored lilylike flowers.

corn marigold *n.* A Eurasian plant, *Chrysanthemum segetum,* cultivated for its yellow or white flowers.

corn·meal also **corn meal** (kôrn′mēl′) *n.* **1.** Meal made from corn. **2.** *Scot.* Oatmeal. ***—modifier:*** *cornmeal muffins.*

corn mint *n.* A widely distributed aromatic plant, *Mentha arvensis,* having small white or bluish flowers.

corn pone (pōn) *n. Southern U.S.* Corn bread made without milk or eggs.

corn poppy *n.* An Old World plant, *Papaver rhoeas,* having bright-red flowers, frequently a weed in cultivated fields.

corn rose *n. Chiefly Brit.* Any of several red-flowered plants growing in grain fields, as the corn poppy.

corn·row (kôrn′rō′) *tr.v.* To arrange or style (hair) by dividing into sections and braiding close to the scalp in rows. **—corn′row′** *n.*

corn salad *n.* Any of several plants of the genus *Valerianella,* esp. *V. locusta* (or *V. olitoria*), native to Europe, having leaves used in salad and small bluish flowers.

corn silk *n.* The styles and stigmas that appear as a silky tuft or tassel at the tip of an ear of corn.

corn snow *n.* Snow that has melted and refrozen into a rough, granular surface.

corn·stalk also **corn stalk** (kôrn′stôk′) *n.* A stalk or stem of corn, esp. maize.

corn·starch (kôrn′stärch′) *n.* **1.** Starch prepared from corn. **2.** A purified starchy flour used as a thickener in cooking.

corn sugar *n.* Dextrose.

corn syrup *n.* A syrup that is prepared from corn and contains glucose combined with dextrin and maltose.

cor·nu (kôr′no͞o, -nyo͞o) *n., pl.* **-nu·a** (-no͞o-ə, -nyo͞o-ə). A protuberance of bone resembling a horn. [Lat., horn.] **—cor′nu·al** (-əl) *adj.*

cor·nu·co·pi·a (kôr′nə-kō′pē-ə, -nyə-) *n.* **1.** A goat's horn overflowing with fruit, flowers, and corn, signifying prosperity; horn of plenty. **2.** A cone-shaped receptacle or ornament. **3.** An overflowing store; abundance. [LLat. : Lat. *cornu,* horn + Lat. *copia,* plenty.] **—cor′nu·co′pi·an** (-pē-ən) *adj.*

cor·nute (kôr-no͞ot′, -nyo͞ot′) also **cor·nut·ed** (-no͞o′tĭd, -nyo͞o′-) *adj.* **1.** Horn-shaped. **2.** Having horns or horn-shaped processes. [Lat. *cornutus* < *cornu,* horn.]

corn whiskey *n.* Whiskey distilled from corn.

corn·y (kôr′nē) *adj.* **-i·er, -i·est.** Trite, dated, melodramatic, or mawkishly sentimental. [< CORN[1].] **—corn′i·ly** *adv.* **—corn′i·ness** *n.*

co·rol·la (kə-rŏl′ə, -rō′lə) *n. Bot.* The inner envelope of a flower, consisting of fused or separate petals. [NLat. < Lat., small garland, dim. of *corona,* garland. —see CORONA.] **—co·rol′late′** (-rōl′āt′) *adj.*

cor·ol·lar·y (kôr′ə-lěr-ē, kŏr′-) *n., pl.* **-ies.** **1.** A proposition that follows with little or no proof required from one already proven. **2.** A deduction or inference. **3.** A natural consequence or effect; result. *—adj.* Consequent or resultant. [ME *corolarie* < Lat. *corollarium,* gratuity, money paid for a garland < *corolla,* small garland. —see COROLLA.]

co·ro·na (kə-rō′nə) *n., pl.* **-nas** or **-nae** (-nē). **1.** *Astron.* **a.** A faintly colored luminous ring around a celestial body visible through a haze or thin cloud, esp. such a ring around the moon or sun, caused by diffraction of light from suspended matter in the intervening medium. **b.** The luminous irregular envelope of highly ionized gas outside the chromosphere of the sun. **2.** *Archit.* The top projecting part of a cornice. **3.** A cigar with a long tapering body and blunt ends. **4.** *Anat.* A crownlike or upper part or structure, such as the top of the head. **5.** *Bot.* A crownlike part of a flower, usually between the petals and stamens but sometimes an appendage of the corolla, as in daffodils. **6.** *Elect.* A faint glow enveloping the high-field electrode in a corona discharge, often accompanied by streamers directed toward the low-field electrode. [Lat., crown < Gk. *korōnē.*]

Corona Aus·tra·lis (ô-strā′lĭs) *n.* A constellation in the Southern Hemisphere near Telescopium and Sagittarius. [Lat., southern crown.]

Corona Bo·re·al·is (bôr′ē-ăl′ĭs, -ā′lĭs, bōr′ē-) *n.* A constellation containing the Corona Borealis cluster of galaxies, in the Northern Hemisphere near Hercules and Boötes. [Lat., northern crown.]

corona discharge *n.* An electrical discharge characterized by a corona and occurring when one of two electrodes in a gas has a shape causing the electric field at its surface to be significantly greater than that between the electrodes.

co·ro·na·graph also **co·ro·no·graph** (kə-rō′nə-grăf′) *n.* A telescope used to examine the sun's corona.

cor·o·nal (kôr′ə-nəl, kŏr′-, kə-rō′nəl) *n.* **1.** A garland, wreath, or circlet. **2.** *Anat.* The coronal suture. *—adj.* **1.** Of or pertaining to a coronal. **2.** *Anat.* Of, designating, or having the direction of the coronal suture. [ME < Lat. *coronalis,* of a crown < *corona,* crown. —see CORONA.]

coronal suture *n.* The line of union of the two parietal bones with the frontal bone of the skull.

cor·o·nar·y (kôr′ə-něr′ē, kŏr′-) *adj.* **1.** Of, pertaining to, or designating either of two arteries that originate in the aorta and supply blood directly to the heart tissues. **2.** Of or pertaining to the heart. *—n., pl.* **-ies.** *Informal.* A coronary thrombosis. [Lat. *coronarius,* of a crown < *corona,* crown. —see CORONA.]

coronary artery *n.* One of the two arteries that supply blood to the heart.

coronary occlusion *n.* The complete obstruction of blood flow in a coronary artery.

cornflower

cornice

cornucopia

wild rose

wild potato-vine

corolla

coronation
Coronation of Elizabeth II of England, 1953

coronet

coronary thrombosis *n.* The occlusion of a coronary artery by a blood clot, often leading to destruction of heart muscle.

coronary vein *n.* Any of various blood vessels that drain the blood from the heart.

cor·o·na·tion (kôr′ə-nā′shən, kŏr′-) *n.* The act or ceremony of crowning a sovereign or his consort. [ME *coronacioun* < Med. Lat. *coronatio* < Lat. *coronare,* to crown < *corona,* crown. —see CORONA.]

cor·o·ner (kôr′ə-nər, kŏr′-) *n.* A public officer whose primary function is to investigate by inquest any death thought to be of other than natural causes. [ME, officer of the Crown < AN *corouner* < Lat. *corona,* crown. —see CORONA.] **—cor′o·ner·ship′** *n.*

cor·o·ner's jury (kôr′ə-nərz, kŏr-) *n.* A group of people summoned to attend a coroner's inquest and determine the cause of the death under investigation.

cor·o·net (kôr′ə-nĕt′, kŏr′-) *n.* **1.** A small crown worn by princes and princesses and by other nobles below the rank of sovereign. **2.** A chaplet or headband decorated with gold or jewels. **3.** The upper margin of a horse's hoof. [ME *coronette* < OFr., dim. of *corone,* crown < Lat. *corona.* —see CORONA.]

cor·o·noid (kôr′ə-noid′, kŏr′-) *adj.* Having a crownlike shape. [Lat. *corona,* wreath, crown (< Gk. *korōnē*) + -OID.]

co·ro·tate (kō-rō′tāt′) *intr.v.* **tat·ed, -tat·ing, -tates.** To rotate in conjunction with another body. **—co′ro·ta′tion** *n.* **—co′ro·ta′tion·al** *adj.*

cor·po·ra (kôr′pər-ə) *n.* Plural of **corpus.**

cor·po·ral[1] (kôr′pər-əl, kôr′prəl) *adj.* Of the body; bodily: *corporal punishment.* [ME < OFr. < Lat. *corporalis* < *corpus,* body.] **—cor′po·ral′i·ty** (-pə-răl′ĭ-tē) *n.* **—cor′po·ral·ly** *adv.*

cor·po·ral[2] (kôr′pər-əl, kôr′prəl) *n.* A noncommissioned officer ranking below sergeant and above private first class in the U.S. Army, Air Force, or Marine Corps. [OFr., lowest noncommissioned officer, var. of *caporal* < OItal. < *capo,* head < Lat. *caput.*]

cor·po·ral[3] (kôr′pər-əl, kôr′prəl) *n. Eccles.* A white linen cloth on which the consecrated elements are placed during the celebration of the Eucharist. [ME < OFr. and < Med. Lat. *corporale* < Lat. *corporalis,* of the body (from the Eucharistic bread being representative of Christ's body) < *corpus,* body.]

corporal's guard *n.* **1.** The squad commanded by a corporal. **2.** A small number of people.

cor·po·rate (kôr′pər-ĭt, kôr′prĭt) *adj.* **1.** Formed into a corporation; incorporated. **2.** Of or pertaining to a corporation: *corporate wealth.* **3.** United or combined into one body; collective: *corporate effort.* **4.** Variant of **corporative.** [Lat. *corporatus,* p.part. of *corporare,* to make into a body < *corpus,* body.] **—cor′po·rate·ly** *adv.*

cor·po·ra·tion (kôr′pə-rā′shən) *n.* **1. a.** A body of persons granted a charter legally recognizing them as a separate entity having its own rights, privileges, and liabilities distinct from those of its members. **b.** Such a body created for purposes of government. **2.** A group of people combined into or acting as one body.

cor·po·ra·tive (kôr′pər-ə-tĭv, -pə-rā′tĭv) also **cor·po·rate** (kôr′pər-ĭt, kôr′prĭt) *adj.* **1.** Of, pertaining to, or associated with a corporation. **2.** Of a government or political system in which the principal economic functions, such as banking, industry, labor, and government, are organized as corporate entities.

cor·po·ra·tor (kôr′pə-rā′tər) *n.* A member or stockholder of a corporation.

cor·po·re·al (kôr-pôr′ē-əl, -pōr′-) *adj.* **1.** Of, pertaining to, or characteristic of the body. **2.** Of a material nature; tangible. [< Lat. *corporeus* < *corpus,* body.] **—cor·po′re·al·ly** *adv.* **—cor·po′re·al·ness** *n.*

cor·po·re·i·ty (kôr′pə-rē′ĭ-tē, -rā′-) also **cor·po·re·al·i·ty** (kôr-pôr′ē-ăl′ĭ-tē, -pōr′-) *n.* The state of being material or corporeal; physical existence.

cor·po·sant (kôr′pə-zənt) *n.* St. Elmo's fire. [Port. and OSp. *corpo santo,* both < Lat. *corpus sanctum,* holy body.]

corps (kôr, kōr) *n., pl.* **corps** (kôrz, kōrz). **1. a.** A separate branch or department of the armed forces having a specialized function. **b.** A tactical unit of ground combat forces between a division and an army commanded by a lieutenant general and composed of two or more divisions and auxiliary service troops. **2.** A body of persons acting together or associated under common direction: *the press corps.* [Fr. < Lat. *corpus,* body.]

corps de bal·let (kôr′ də bă-lā′, kōr′) *n.* The dancers in a ballet troupe who perform as a group with no solo parts. [Fr.]

corpse (kôrps) *n.* A dead body, esp. the dead body of a human being. [ME *corps* < Lat. *corpus.*]

corps·man (kôr′mən, kōr′-, kôrz′mən, kōrz′-) *n.* An enlisted man in the U.S. Navy trained as a pharmacist or hospital assistant.

cor·pu·lence (kôr′pyə-ləns) *n.* The condition of being excessively fat; obesity. [ME, corporality < Lat. *corpulentia,* corpulence < *corpulentus,* corpulent < *corpus,* body.] **—cor′pu·lent** *adj.* **—cor′pu·lent·ly** *adv.*

cor pul·mo·na·le (kôr′ po͝ol′mə-nä′lē, -năl′ē, pŭl′-) *n.* A heart disease characterized by hypertrophy of the right ventricle that is caused by an obstruction in pulmonary circulation. [NLat., pulmonary heart.]

cor·pus (kôr′pəs) *n., pl.* **-po·ra** (-pər-ə). **1.** A human or animal body, esp. when dead. **2.** *Anat.* A structure constituting the main part of an organ. **3.** The principal or capital, as distinguished from the interest or income, as of a fund or estate. **4.** A large collection of writings of a specific kind or on a specific subject. [ME < Lat.]

corpus al·bi·cans (ăl′bĭ-kănz′) *n.* The white fibrous tissue in an ovary that results after the involution and regression of the corpus luteum. [NLat., white body.]

corpus cal·lo·sum (kə-lō′səm) *n., pl.* **corpora cal·lo·sa** (kə-lō′sə). *Anat.* A wide arched band of white matter connecting the cerebral hemispheres at the base of the longitudinal fissure. [NLat., callous body.]

Cor·pus Chris·ti (kôr′pəs krĭs′tē) *n. Rom. Cath. Ch.* A festival celebrated in honor of the Eucharist on the first Thursday after Trinity Sunday. [ME < Med. Lat. : Lat. *corpus,* body + Med. Lat. *Christus,* Christ.]

cor·pus·cle (kôr′pə-səl, -pŭs′əl) *n.* **1.** *Biol.* A cell, such as an erythrocyte or leukocyte, that is capable of free movement in a fluid or matrix, as distinguished from a cell fixed in tissue. **2.** A discrete particle such as a photon or electron. **3.** A minute globular particle. [Lat. *corpusculum,* little particle, dim. of *corpus,* body.] **—cor·pus′cu·lar** (kôr-pŭs′kyə-lər) *adj.*

corpus de·lic·ti (dĭ-lĭk′tī′) *n.* **1.** *Law.* **a.** The material substance upon which a crime has been committed. **b.** The material evidence, such as the discovered corpse of a murder victim, of the fact that a crime has been committed. **2.** The victim's corpse in a murder case. [NLat. : Lat. *corpus,* body + *delictum,* crime.]

corpus ju·ris (jo͝or′ĭs) *n.* The collective or comprehensive body of all the laws of a nation or state. [Lat., the body of law.]

Corpus Juris Ci·vil·is (sĭ-vĭl′ĭs) *n.* The body of civil or Roman law assembled and issued during Justinian's reign and forming the basis of most European law. [Lat., the body of civil law.]

corpus lu·te·um (lo͞o′tē-əm) *n., pl.* **corpora lu·te·a** (lo͞o′tē-ə). A yellow mass of endocrine cells in a ruptured mature Graafian follicle of the ovary, formed after the release of an ovum. [NLat., yellow body.]

corpus stri·a·tum (strī-ā′təm) *n., pl.* **corpora stri·a·ta** (strī-ā′tə). Either of two gray-and-white, striated ganglionic masses of the brain stem in the lower lateral wall of each cerebral hemisphere. [NLat., striated body.]

cor·rade (kə-rād′) *tr. & intr.v.* **-rad·ed, -rad·ing, -rades.** To erode or be eroded by abrasion. [Lat. *corradere,* to scrape together : *com-,* together + *radere,* to scrape.] **—cor·ra′sion** (-rā′zhən) *n.* **—cor·ra′sive** (-sĭv, -zĭv) *adj.*

cor·ral (kə-răl′) *n.* **1.** An enclosure for confining livestock. **2.** An enclosure formed by a circle of wagons for defense against attack during an encampment. *—tr.v.* **-ralled, -ral·ling, -rals. 1.** To drive into and hold in a corral. **2.** To arrange (wagons) in a corral. **3.** *Informal.* To take possession of; seize. [Sp. < Lat. *currus,* cart < *currere,* to run.]

cor·rect (kə-rĕkt′) *v.* **-rect·ed, -rect·ing, -rects.** *—tr.* **1. a.** To remove the errors or mistakes from. **b.** To indicate or mark the errors in. **2.** To admonish or punish for the purpose of improving. **3.** To remove, remedy, or counteract (a malfunction, for example). **4.** To adjust so as to meet a standard or other required condition: *correct the wheel alignment.* *—intr.* **1.** To make corrections. **2.** To make adjustments; compensate: *correcting for the effects of air resistance.* *—adj.* **1.** Free from error or fault; true or accurate. **2.** Conforming to standards; proper: *correct behavior.* [ME *correcten* < Lat. *corrigere,* to correct : *com-* (intensive) + *regere,* to rule.] **—cor·rect′a·ble, cor·rect′i·ble** *adj.* **—cor·rect′ly** *adv.* **—cor·rect′ness** *n.* **—cor·rec′tor** *n.*

Synonyms: *correct, rectify, remedy, redress, reform, revise, amend.* These verbs mean to make right or to improve. *Correct* can apply broadly to any such act but usually refers to eliminating error or defect. *Rectify* stresses the idea of bringing something into conformity with a standard of what is right. *Remedy* involves repairing or removing something considered a cause of harm or damage. *Redress* usually refers to setting right something considered morally or ethically wrong and involves making reparation to the wronged person. *Reform* implies broad change that improves character, as of a person or institution. *Revise* suggests change as a result of reconsideration of an earlier course. *Amend* adds to revision a more definite implication of improvement through alteration or addition.

cor·rec·tion (kə-rĕk′shən) *n.* **1.** The act or process of correcting. **2.** Something offered or substituted for a mistake or fault: *made corrections in the report.* **3.** Punishment intended to rehabilitate or improve. **4.** An amount or quantity that is added or subtracted to correct. **5.** A decline in stock-market prices or activity following a period of increases. **—cor·rec′tion·al** *adj.*

cor·rec·ti·tude (kə-rĕk′tĭ-to͞od′, -tyo͞od′) *n.* The state or quality of being correct, esp. in manners and behavior; propriety.

cor·rec·tive (kə-rĕk′tĭv) *adj.* Tending or intended to correct. *—n.* Something that corrects. **—cor·rec′tive·ly** *adv.*

cor·re·late (kôr′ə-lāt′, kŏr′-) *v.* **-lat·ed, -lat·ing, -lates.** *—tr.* **1.** To put or bring into causal, complementary, parallel, or reciprocal relation. **2.** To establish or demonstrate as having a correlation: *correlated drug abuse and crime. —intr.* To be related by a correlation. *—adj.* (-lĭt, -lāt′). Related by a correlation, esp. having corresponding characteristics. *—n.* (-lĭt, -lāt′). Either of two correlate entities; correlative. [Back-formation from CORRELATION.]

cor·re·la·tion (kôr′ə-lā′shən, kŏr′-) *n.* **1.** A causal, complementary, parallel, or reciprocal relationship, esp. a structural, functional, or qualitative correspondence between two comparable entities: *a correlation between recession and unemployment.* **2.** *Statistics.* **a.** The simultaneous increase or decrease in value of two numerically valued random variables: *the positive correlation between cigarette smoking and the incidence of lung cancer.* **b.** The simultaneous increase in the value of one and decrease in the value of the other of two numerically valued random variables: *the negative correlation between age and normal vision.* **3. a.** The act of correlating. **b.** The condition of being correlated. [Med. Lat. *correlatio* : Lat. *com-,* together + *relatio,* relation < *referre,* to carry back.] **—cor′re·la′tion·al** *adj.*

correlation coefficient *n.* A measure of the interdependence of two random variables that ranges in value from −1 to +1, indicating perfect negative correlation at −1, absence of correlation at 0, and perfect positive correlation at +1.

cor·rel·a·tive (kə-rĕl′ə-tĭv) *adj.* **1.** Related; corresponding. **2.** Indicating a reciprocal or complementary relationship: *a correlative conjunction. —n.* **1.** Either of two correlative entities; correlate. **2.** *Gram.* A correlative word or expression. **—cor·rel′a·tive·ly** *adv.*

cor·re·spond (kôr′ĭ-spŏnd′, kŏr′-) *intr.v.* **-spond·ed, -spond·ing, -sponds. 1.** To be in agreement, harmony, or conformity; be consistent or compatible: *Our goals corresponded.* **2.** To be similar, parallel, equivalent, or equal in character, quantity, origin, structure, or function: *English "navel" corresponds to Greek "omphalos."* **3.** To communicate by letter, usually over a period of time. [OFr. *correspondre* < Med. Lat. *correspondēre* : Lat. *com-,* together + *respondēre,* to respond.]

cor·re·spon·dence (kôr′ĭ-spŏn′dəns, kŏr′-) *n.* **1.** The act, fact, or state of agreeing or conforming. **2.** Similarity or analogy. **3. a.** Communication by the exchange of letters. **b.** The letters written or received.

correspondence principle *n.* The principle that predictions of quantum theory approach those of classical physics in the limit of large quantum numbers.

correspondence school *n.* A school that offers instruction by mail, sending lessons and examinations to a student.

cor·re·spon·den·cy (kôr′ĭ-spŏn′dən-sē, kŏr′-) *n.* Correspondence.

cor·re·spon·dent (kôr′ĭ-spŏn′dənt, kŏr′-) *n.* **1.** One who communicates by means of letters. **2.** Someone employed by a newspaper or magazine to supply news or articles: *a foreign correspondent.* **3.** A person or firm having regular business relations with another, esp. at a distance. **4.** Something that corresponds; correlative. *—adj.* Corresponding. **—cor′re·spon′dent·ly** *adv.*

correspondent banking *n.* A system of banking under which large banks perform various services for smaller banks in return for balances that the small banks keep with them.

cor·re·spond·ing (kôr′ĭ-spŏn′dĭng, kŏr′-) *adj.* **1.** Agreeing or conforming, as in degree or kind; consistent. **2.** Analogous or equivalent. **—cor′re·spond′ing·ly** *adv.*

cor·re·spon·sive (kôr′ĭ-spŏn′sĭv, kŏr′-) *adj.* Jointly responsive. **—cor′re·spon′sive·ly** *adv.*

cor·ri·da (kô-rē′də, *-thə*) *n.* A bullfight. [Sp. < *correr,* to run < Lat. *currere.*]

cor·ri·dor (kôr′ĭ-dər, -dôr′, kŏr′-) *n.* **1.** A narrow hallway, passageway, or gallery, often with rooms or apartments opening onto it. **2. a.** A tract of land forming a passageway, as one that allows an inland country access to the sea through another country. **b.** A lane for the passage of aircraft. [OFr. < OItal. *corridore* < *correre,* to run < Lat. *currere.*]

cor·rie (kôr′ē, kŏr′ē) *n. Scot.* A round hollow in a hillside; cirque. [Sc. Gael. *coire.*]

cor·ri·gen·dum (kôr′ə-jĕn′dəm, kŏr′-) *n., pl.* **-da** (-də). **1.** An error to be corrected, esp. a printer's error. **2. corrigenda.** A list of errors in a book with their corrections. [Lat., neuter gerund. of *corrigere,* to correct.]

cor·ri·gi·ble (kôr′ĭ-jə-bəl, kŏr′-) *adj.* Capable of being corrected, reformed, or improved. [ME < OFr. < Med. Lat. *corrigibilis* < Lat. *corrigere,* to correct.] **—cor′ri·gi·bil′i·ty** *n.* **—cor′ri·gi·bly** *adv.*

cor·ri·val (kə-rī′vəl, kō-) *n.* A rival or opponent. *—adj.* Rival or opposing. [OFr. or < Lat. *corrivalis* : *com-* (intensive) + *rivalis,* rival.] **—cor·ri′val·ry** (-rē) *n.*

cor·rob·o·rant (kə-rŏb′ər-ənt) *adj. Archaic.* Producing or stimulating physical vigor. Used of a medicine.

cor·rob·o·rate (kə-rŏb′ə-rāt′) *tr.v.* **-rat·ed, -rat·ing, -rates.** To support or confirm by new evidence; attest the truth or accuracy of. [Lat. *corroborare, corroborat-* : *com-* (intensive) + *roborare,* to strengthen < *robur,* strength.] **—cor·rob′o·ra′tion** *n.* **—cor·rob′o·ra′tive** (-ə-rā′tĭv, -ər′ə-tĭv) *adj.* **—cor·rob′o·ra′tor** *n.* **—cor·rob′o·ra·to′ry** (-ər-ə-tôr′ē, -tōr′ē) *adj.*

cor·rob·o·ree (kə-rŏb′ə-rē) *n. Austral.* **1.** An aboriginal dance festival held at night to celebrate tribal victories or other events. **2.** A large or noisy celebration. [< a native word in Australia.]

cor·rode (kə-rōd′) *v.* **-rod·ed, -rod·ing, -rodes.** *—tr.* **1.** To dissolve or wear away gradually, esp. by chemical action: *acid corroding metal.* **2.** To impair steadily; deteriorate. *—intr.* To be eaten or worn away; become corroded. [ME *corroden* < Lat. *corrodere,* to gnaw away : *com-* (intensive) + *rodere,* to gnaw.] **—cor·rod′i·ble** or **cor·ro′si·ble** (-rō′sə-bəl) *adj.*

cor·ro·sion (kə-rō′zhən) *n.* **1.** The act or process of corroding. **2.** A substance, such as rust, resulting from corrosion. **3.** The condition produced by corrosion. [ME *corosioun,* corrosion of tissue < OFr. *corrosion* < LLat. *corrosio,* the act of gnawing < Lat. *corrodere,* to gnaw away. —see CORRODE.]

cor·ro·sive (kə-rō′sĭv, -zĭv) *adj.* **1. a.** Capable of producing corrosion. **b.** Inclined to produce corrosion. **2.** Spiteful, malicious, or malevolent: *corrosive criticism. —n.* A corrosive substance. **—cor·ro′sive·ly** *adv.* **—cor·ro′sive·ness** *n.*

corrosive sublimate *n.* Mercuric chloride.

cor·ru·gate (kôr′ə-gāt′, kŏr′-) *v.* **-gat·ed, -gat·ing, -gates.** *—tr.* To shape into folds or parallel and alternating ridges and grooves. *—intr.* To become corrugated. [Lat. *corrugare, corrugat-,* to wrinkle up : *com-* (intensive) + *rugare,* to wrinkle < *ruga,* wrinkle.] **—cor′ru·gate′, cor′ru·gat′ed** (-gā′tĭd) *adj.*

corrugated iron *n.* A structural sheet iron, usually galvanized, shaped in parallel furrows and ridges for rigidity.

cor·ru·ga·tion (kôr′ə-gā′shən, kŏr′-) *n.* **1.** The act of corrugating. **2.** The state or process of being corrugated. **3.** A groove or ridge on a corrugated surface.

cor·rupt (kə-rŭpt′) *adj.* **1.** Marked by immorality and perversion; depraved. **2.** Marked by venality and dishonesty: *a corrupt mayor.* **3.** Decaying; putrid. **4.** Containing errors or alterations, as a text: *a corrupt translation. —v.* **-rupt·ed, -rupt·ing, -rupts.** *—tr.* **1.** To destroy or subvert the honesty or integrity of. **2.** To ruin morally; pervert. **3.** To taint; contaminate. **4.** To cause to become rotten; spoil. **5.** To change the original form of (a text, for example). *—intr.* To become corrupt. [ME < Lat. *corruptus,* p.part. of *corrumpere,* to destroy : *com-,* together + *rumpere,* to break.] **—cor·rupt′er, cor·rup′tor** *n.* **—cor·rup′tive** *adj.* **—cor·rupt′ly** *adv.* **—cor·rupt′ness** *n.*

cor·rupt·i·ble (kə-rŭp′tə-bəl) *adj.* Capable of being corrupted, as by bribery or depravity. **—cor·rupt′i·bil′i·ty, cor·rupt′i·ble·ness** *n.* **—cor·rupt′i·bly** *adv.*

cor·rup·tion (kə-rŭp′shən) *n.* **1.** The act or result of corrupting. **2.** The state of being corrupt. **3.** *Archaic.* Something that corrupts. **4.** Decay; rot.

cor·rup·tion·ist (kə-rŭp′shə-nĭst) *n.* One who defends or practices corruption.

cor·sage (kôr-säzh′, -säj′) *n.* **1.** A small bouquet of flowers worn by a woman at the shoulder or waist or on the wrist. **2.** The bodice or waist of a dress. [ME, torso < OFr. < *cors,* body < Lat. *corpus.*]

cor·sair (kôr′sâr′) *n.* **1.** A privateer, esp. along the Barbary Coast. **2.** A swift pirate ship, often operating with official sanction. **3.** A pirate. [OFr. *corsaire* < OProv. *corsari* < OItal. *corsaro* < Med. Lat. *cursarius* < *cursus,* plunder < Lat. *cursus,* course. —see COURSE.]

corse (kôrs) *n. Archaic.* A corpse. [ME *cors* < OFr. < Lat. *corpus.*]

corse·let (kôr′slĭt) *n.* **1.** Also **cors·let.** Body armor, esp. a breastplate. **2.** (kôr′sə-lĕt′). A light corset with few or no stays. [OFr. *corselet,* dim. of *corsel,* dim. of *cors,* body < Lat. *corpus.*]

cor·set (kôr′sĭt) *n.* **1.** A close-fitting undergarment, often reinforced by stays, worn to support and shape the waistline, hips, and breasts. **2.** A medieval outer garment, esp. a laced jacket or bodice. *—tr.v.* **-set·ed, -set·ing, -sets.** To enclose in or as if in a corset. [ME, bodice < OFr., dim. of *cors,* body < Lat. *corpus.*]

cor·se·tière (kôr′sĭ-tyâr′, -tîr′) *n.* A maker, fitter, or seller of corsets. [Fr. < *corset,* corset < OFr.]

cors·let (kôr′slĭt) *n.* Variant of **corselet** (sense 1).

cor·tege also **cor·tège** (kôr-tĕzh′) *n.* **1.** A train of attendants, as of a distinguished person; retinue. **2. a.** A ceremonial procession. **b.** A funeral procession. [Fr. *cortège* < OItal. *corteggio* < *corteggiare,* to pay honor < *corte,* court < Lat. *cohors,* throng.]

cortege
Funeral cortege

cor·tex (kôr′tĕks′) *n., pl.* **-ti·ces** (-tĭ-sēz′) or **-tex·es. 1.** *Anat.* **a.** The outer layer of an organ or part, as of the kidney, cerebrum, or cerebellum. **b.** The firm outer layer that comprises most of the adrenal gland. **2.** *Bot.* **a.** A layer of tissue in roots and stems lying between the epidermis and the vascular tissue. **b.** An external layer such as bark or rind. [Lat., bark.]

cortic- *pref.* Variant of **cortico-.**

cor·ti·cal (kôr′tĭ-kəl) *adj.* **1.** Of, pertaining to, or consisting of cortex. **2.** Of, pertaining to, associated with, or depending on the cerebral cortex. [NLat. *corticalis* < Lat. *cortex,* bark.] **—cor′ti·cal·ly** *adv.*

cor·ti·cate (kôr′tĭ-kĭt, -kāt′) also **cor·ti·cat·ed** (-kā′tĭd) *adj.*

Having a cortex or similar specialized outer layer. [Lat. *corticatus,* having bark < *cortex,* bark.]
cor·ti·ces (kôr′tĭ-sēz′) *n.* A plural of **cortex.**
cortico– or **cortic–** *pref.* Cortex: *corticotropin.* [< Lat. *cortex, cortic-,* bark, rind.]
cor·ti·coid (kôr′tĭ-koid′) *n.* Any of the steroids of the adrenal cortex.
cor·tic·o·lous (kôr-tĭk′ə-ləs) *adj. Biol.* Growing or living on tree bark: *corticolous mosses.*
cor·ti·co·spi·nal (kôr′tĭ-kō-spī′nəl) *adj.* Of or pertaining to the cerebral cortex and the spinal cord.
cor·ti·co·ste·roid (kôr′tĭ-kō-stîr′oid′) *n.* A corticoid.
cor·ti·cos·ter·one (kôr′tĭ-kŏs′tə-rōn′) *n.* A corticoid, $C_{21}H_{30}O_4$, that induces hyperglycemia and deposition of glycogen in the liver. [CORTICO- + STER(OL) + -ONE.]
cor·ti·co·tro·pin (kôr′tĭ-kō-trō′pən) also **cor·ti·co·tro·phin** (-trō′fĭn) *n.* ACTH. [CORTICO- + -TROP(IC) + -IN.]
cor·tin (kôr′tn) *n.* An adrenal cortex extract that contains several hormones and is used in medicine. [CORT(EX) + -IN.]
cor·ti·sol (kôr′tĭ-sôl′, -zôl′, -sōl′, -zōl′) *n.* A hormone of the adrenal cortex, hydrocortisone. [CORTIS(ONE) + -OL.]
cor·ti·sone (kôr′tĭ-sōn′, -zōn′) *n.* A corticoid, $C_{21}H_{28}O_5$, active in carbohydrate metabolism and used to treat rheumatoid arthritis, adrenal insufficiency, certain allergies, diseases of connective tissue, and gout. [Alteration of CORTICOSTERONE.]
co·run·dum (kə-rŭn′dəm) *n.* An extremely hard mineral, aluminum oxide, sometimes containing iron, magnesia, or silica, occurring in gem varieties such as ruby and sapphire and in a common gray, brown, or blue form used chiefly in abrasives. [Tamil *kuruntam,* prob. of Skt. orig.]
co·rus·cant (kə-rŭs′kənt) *adj.* Glittering. [Lat. *coruscans, coruscant-,* pr.part. of *coruscare,* to flash.]
cor·us·cate (kôr′ə-skāt′, kŏr′-) *intr.v.* **-cat·ed, -cat·ing, -cates.** To give forth flashes of light; sparkle; glitter. [Lat. *coruscare, coruscat-,* to flash.] **—cor′us·ca′tion** *n.*
cor·vée (kôr-vā′, kôr′vā′) *n.* **1.** A day of unpaid work required of a vassal by his feudal lord. **2.** Labor exacted by a local authority for little or no pay or instead of taxes and used esp. in the maintenance of roads. [ME *corve* < OFr. *corvée* < LLat. *(opera) corrogata,* work requested < Lat. *corrogare,* to bring together : *com-,* together + *rogare,* to ask.]
corves (kôrvz) *n.* Plural of **corf.**
cor·vette (kôr-vĕt′) *n.* **1.** A fast, lightly armed warship, smaller than a destroyer. **2.** An obsolete sailing warship, smaller than a frigate, usually armed with one tier of guns. [Fr., a kind of warship.]

corvette
Early 19th-century 20-gun corvette

cor·vi·na (kôr-vē′nə) *n.* Variant of **corbina.**
cor·vine (kôr′vīn′, -vĭn) *adj.* Of, resembling, or characteristic of crows, ravens, or related birds. [Lat. *corvinus* < *corvus,* raven.]
Cor·vus (kôr′vəs) *n.* A constellation in the Southern Hemisphere near Crater and Virgo. [NLat. < Lat. *corvus,* raven.]
co·ry (kō′rē, kŏr′ē) *n., pl.* **cory.** See table at **currency.**
Cor·y·bant (kôr′ə-bănt′, kŏr′-) *n., pl.* **Cor·y·bants** or **Cor·y·ban·tes** (kôr′ə-băn′tēz′, kŏr′-) *Gk. Myth.* A priest of the ancient Phrygian goddess Cybele whose rites were celebrated with music and ecstatic dances. [Lat. *Corybas, Corybant-* < Gk. *Korubas.*] **—Cor′y·ban′tic** (-băn′tĭk) *adj.*
co·ryd·a·lis (kə-rĭd′l-ĭs) *n.* Any of various plants of the genus *Corydalis,* having finely lobed leaves and spurred yellow or pinkish flowers. [NLat. *Corydalis,* genus name < Gk. *korudallis,* crested lark (from the shape of the flowers) < *korudos.*]
cor·ymb (kôr′ĭmb, -ĭm, kŏr′-) *n. Bot.* A flat-topped flower cluster in which the individual stalks grow upward from various points of the main stem to approximately the same height. [Fr. *corymbe* < Lat. *corymbus,* bunch of flowers < Gk. *korumbos.*] **—cor′ym·bose′** (-ĭm-bōs′), **co·rym′bous** (kə-rĭm′bəs) *adj.* **—cor′ym·bose′ly** *adv.*

corymb

co·ry·ne·bac·te·ri·um (kôr′ə-nē-băk-tîr′ē-əm, kə-rĭn′ə-) *n.* Any of the genus *Corynebacterium* of Gram-positive rod-shaped bacteria that include many animal and plant pathogens, including the causative agent of diphtheria in man. [NLat. *Corynebacterium,* genus name : Gk. *korynē,* club + *bacterium,* bacterium.]
co·ryn·e·form (kə-rĭn′ə-fôrm′) *adj.* Similar to a corynebacterium. [CORYNE(BACTERIUM) + -FORM.]
cor·y·phae·us (kôr′ə-fē′əs, kŏr′-) *n., pl.* **-phae·i** (-fē′ī′). **1.** The leader of the chorus in ancient Greek drama. **2.** A leader or spokesman. [Lat., leader < Gk. *koruphaios* < *koruphē,* head.]
cor·y·phée (kôr′ə-fā′) *n.* A ballet dancer ranking above the corps de ballet and below the soloists. [Fr. < Lat. *coryphaeus,* leader. —see CORYPHAEUS.]
co·ry·za (kə-rī′zə) *n.* An acute inflammation of the nasal mucous membrane marked by discharge of mucus, sneezing, and watering of the eyes. [Gk. *koruza,* catarrh.]
cos (kôs, kŏs) *n.* Romaine. [After *Cos,* the former name for Stanchio, an island in the Aegean.]
Co·sa Nos·tra (kō′sə nō′strə) *n.* A crime syndicate active throughout the United States, hierarchic in structure, comprising locally independent units known as families, and often believed to have an important relationship with the Sicilian Mafia. [Ital., our thing.]
co·se·cant (kō-sē′kănt′, -kənt) *n. Math.* The secant of the complement of a directed angle or arc.
co·seis·mal (kō-sīz′məl, -sīs′-) also **co·seis·mic** (-mĭk) *adj.* Pertaining to or designating a line connecting the points on a map that indicate the places simultaneously affected by an earthquake shock. *—n.* A coseismal line.
cosh (kŏsh) *Chiefly Brit. Slang. —n.* **1.** A blackjack. **2.** An attack with a blackjack. *—tr.v.* **coshed, cosh·ing, cosh·es.** To attack or hit with or as if with a cosh. [Prob. < Romany *kosh,* stick.]
cosh·er (kŏsh′ər) *tr.v.* **-ered, -er·ing, -ers.** To coddle; pamper. [Perh. < Ir. *cōisir,* feast.]
co·sign (kō-sīn′) *tr.v.* **-signed, -sign·ing, -signs. 1.** To sign (a document) jointly with another or others. **2.** To endorse (a signature), as for a loan. **—co·sign′er** *n.*
co·sig·na·to·ry (kō-sĭg′nə-tôr′ē, -tōr′ē) *adj.* Signed jointly with another or others. *—n., pl.* **-ries.** One who cosigns.
co·sine (kō′sīn′) *n.* **1.** The abscissa of the endpoint of an arc of a unit circle centered at the origin of a Cartesian coordinate system, the arc being of length *x* and measured counterclockwise from the point (1, 0) if *x* is positive or clockwise if *x* is negative. **2.** In a right triangle, the function of an acute angle that is the ratio of the adjacent side to the hypotenuse.
cos lettuce *n.* Romaine.
cosm– *pref.* Variant of **cosmo-.**
cos·met·ic (kŏz-mĕt′ĭk) *n.* A preparation, such as skin cream, designed to beautify the body by direct application. *—adj.* **1.** Serving to beautify the body. **2.** Serving to correct physical defects: *cosmetic surgery.* **3. a.** Decorative rather than functional: *cosmetic fenders on cars.* **b.** Lacking depth or significance; superficial: *made a few cosmetic changes when he took over the company.* [< Gk. *kosmētikos,* skilled in arranging < *kosmein,* to arrange < *kosmos,* order.] **—cos·met′i·cal·ly** *adv.*
cos·me·ti·cian (kŏz′mĭ-tĭsh′ən) *n.* A person whose occupation is manufacturing, selling, or applying cosmetics.
cos·met·i·cize (kŏz-mĕt′ĭ-sīz′) *tr.v.* **-cized, -ciz·ing, -ciz·es.** To make superficially attractive or acceptable.
cos·me·tol·o·gy (kŏz′mĭ-tŏl′ə-jē) *n.* The study or art of cosmetics and their use. [Fr. *cosmétologie* : *cosmétique,* cosmetic + *-logie,* -logy.] **—cos′me·tol′o·gist** *n.*
cos·mic (kŏz′mĭk) also **cos·mi·cal** (-mĭ-kəl) *adj.* **1.** Of or pertaining to the universe, esp. as distinct from the earth. **2.** Infinitely or inconceivably extended; vast: *an issue of cosmic dimensions.* [Gk. *kosmikos* < *kosmos,* universe.] **—cos′mi·cal·ly** *adv.*
cosmic dust *n.* Fine solid particles of matter in interstellar space.
cosmic noise *n.* Galactic noise.
cosmic ray *n.* A stream of ionizing radiation of extraterrestrial origin, chiefly of protons, alpha particles, and other atomic nuclei but including some high-energy electrons and photons, that enters the atmosphere and produces secondary radiation, principally pions, muons, electrons, and gamma rays.
cosmo– or **cosm–** *pref.* Universe; world: *cosmology.* [< Gk. *kosmos,* order, universe.]
cos·mo·chem·is·try (kŏz′mō-kĕm′ĭ-strē) *n.* The science of the chemical composition of the universe. **—cos′mo·chem′i·cal** (-ĭ-kəl) *adj.*
cos·mo·drome (kŏz′mə-drōm′) *n.* A Soviet spacecraft-launching center. [R. *kosmodrom: kosmo(naut)* + *-drome,* -drome.]
cos·mo·gen·ic (kŏz′mə-jĕn′ĭk) *adj.* Produced by cosmic rays. [COSM(IC RAY) + -GENIC.]
cos·mog·o·ny (kŏz-mŏg′ə-nē) *n., pl.* **-nies. 1.** The astrophysical study of the evolution of the universe. **2.** A specific theory or model of the evolution of the universe. [Gk. *kosmogonia,* creation of the world : *cosmos,* world + *gonos,* creation.] **—cos′mo·gon′ic** (-mə-gŏn′ĭk), **cos′mo·gon′i·cal** *adj.* **—cos′mo·gon′i·cal·ly** *adv.* **—cos·mog′o·nist** *n.*
cos·mog·ra·phy (kŏz-mŏg′rə-fē) *n., pl.* **-phies. 1.** The study of the constitution of nature. **2.** A description of the world or universe. [Gk. *kosmographia,* description of the world : *kosmos,* world + *-graphia,* -graphy.] **—cos·mog′ra·pher** *n.* **—cos′mo·graph′ic** (-mə-grăf′ĭk), **cos′mo·graph′i·cal** *adj.* **—cos′mo·graph′i·cal·ly** *adv.*
Cos·mo·line (kŏz′mə-lēn′). A trademark for petrolatum.
cos·mol·o·gy (kŏz-mŏl′ə-jē) *n., pl.* **-gies. 1.** A branch of philosophy dealing with the origin, processes, and structure of the universe. **2. a.** The astrophysical study of the structure and constituent dynamics of the universe. **b.** A specific theory or model of this structure and dynamics. **—cos′mo·log′ic** (-mə-lŏj′ĭk), **cos′mo·log′i·cal** *adj.* **—cos′mo·log′i·cal·ly** *adv.* **—cos·mol′o·gist** *n.*
cos·mo·naut (kŏz′mə-nôt′) *n.* An astronaut, esp. one from the Soviet Union. [R. *kosmonaut* : Gk. *kosmos,* universe + Gk. *nautēs,* sailor.]
cos·mo·pol·i·tan (kŏz′mə-pŏl′ĭ-tn) *adj.* **1.** Common to the whole world. **2.** Of the entire world or from many different parts of the world. **3.** At home in all parts of the world or in many spheres of interest. **4.** *Biol.* Growing or occurring in all or most parts of the world; widely distributed. *—n.* A cosmopolite. **—cos′mo·pol′i·tan·ism** *n.*
cos·mop·o·lite (kŏz-mŏp′ə-līt′) *n.* **1.** A cosmopolitan per-

son. **2.** *Biol.* A cosmopolitan organism. **3.** The painted lady. [Gk. *kosmopolitēs* : *kosmos,* world + *politēs,* citizen < *polis,* city.] **—cos·mop'o·lit'ism** (-lĭ'tĭz'əm, -lĭ-tĭz'-) *n.*

cos·mo·ra·ma (kŏz'mə-ră'mə, -răm'ə) *n.* An exhibition of scenes and pictures from all over the world. [Gk. *kosmos* + *horama,* spectacle.] **—cos'mo·ram'ic** (-răm'ĭk) *adj.*

cos·mos (kŏz'məs, -mŏs', -mōs') *n.* **1.** The universe regarded as an orderly, harmonious whole. **2.** An ordered, harmonious, and whole system. **3.** Harmony and order as distinct from chaos. **4.** Any of various tropical American plants of the genus *Cosmos,* having variously colored rayed flowers, esp. *C. bipinnatus,* widely cultivated as a garden plant. [Gk. *kosmos.*]

Cos·sack (kŏs'ăk') *n.* A member of a people of the southern Soviet Union in Europe and adjacent parts of Asia, noted as cavalrymen. *—adj.* Of or pertaining to the Cossacks. [R. *kazak* and Ukranian *kozak,* both < Turk. *kazak,* adventurer.]

cos·set (kŏs'ĭt) *tr.v.* **-set·ed, -set·ing, -sets.** To pamper; pet. *—n.* A pet, esp. a pet lamb. [Orig. unknown.]

cost (kôst) *n.* **1.** An amount paid or required in payment for a purchase; price. **2.** A loss, sacrifice, or penalty; detriment. **3. costs.** *Law.* The charges fixed for litigation, usually payable by the losing party. *—v.* **cost, cost·ing, costs.** *—intr.* To require a specified payment, expenditure, effort, or loss: *It costs more to live in the city.* *—tr.* **1.** To have as a price. **2.** To cause to lose, suffer, or sacrifice: *Participating in the strike cost him his job.* **3.** To estimate or determine the cost of. [ME < OFr. < *coster,* to cost < Lat. *constare.* —see CONSTANT.] **—cost'less** *adj.* **—cost'less·ness** *n.*

cos·ta (kŏs'tə) *n., pl.* **-tae** (-tē). *Biol.* A rib or a riblike part, such as the midrib of a leaf or a thickened anterior vein or margin of an insect's wing. [Lat.]

cost accountant *n.* An accountant who keeps records of the costs of production and distribution. **—cost accounting** *n.*

co·star also **co-star** (kō'stär') *—n.* A starring actor or actress given equal status with another or others in a play or motion picture. *—intr. & tr.v.* **-starred, -star·ring, -stars.** To act or present as a costar.

cos·tard (kŏs'tərd) *n.* **1.** An English variety of large apple. **2.** *Archaic Slang.* The head. [ME < AN, perh. < *coste,* rib (from its ribbed appearance) < Lat. *costa.*]

cost-ef·fec·tive (kôst'ĭ-fĕk'tĭv) *adj.* Economical in terms of the goods or services received for the money spent. **—cost'ef·fec'tive·ness** *n.*

cos·ter (kŏs'tər) *n. Chiefly Brit.* A costermonger.

cos·ter·mon·ger (kŏs'tər-mŭng'gər, -mŏng'-) *n. Chiefly Brit.* One who sells fruit, vegetables, fish, or other goods from a cart, barrow, or stand in the streets. [Obs. *costard-monger* : COSTARD + MONGER.]

cos·tive (kŏs'tĭv) *adj.* **1. a.** Suffering from constipation. **b.** Causing constipation. **2.** Slow; sluggish. **3.** Stingy. [ME *costif* < OFr. *costeve,* p.part. of *constever,* to constipate < Lat. *constipare.* —see CONSTIPATE.] **—cos'tive·ly** *adv.* **—cos'tive·ness** *n.*

cost·ly (kôst'lē) *adj.* **-li·er, -li·est.** **1.** Of high price or value; expensive: *costly jewelry.* **2.** Entailing loss or sacrifice: *a costly war.* **—cost'li·ness** *n.*

Synonyms: *costly, expensive, dear, valuable, precious, invaluable, priceless.* These adjectives apply to the measure of worth or value of things or, less often, of persons. *Costly, expensive,* and *dear* refer principally to the high price of things on sale. *Costly,* thus used, implies especially high quality or rarity of an object. *Valuable* stresses the quality and importance of the object without specifying the price. *Precious* implies uniqueness and irreplaceability. *Invaluable* and *priceless* describe worth beyond a person's power to estimate.

cost·mar·y (kôst'mâr'ē, kŏst'-) *n.* An herb, *Chrysanthemum balsamita,* native to Asia, having aromatic foliage sometimes used as seasoning. [ME *costmarie* : *cost,* costmary (< OE < Lat. *costum* < Gk. *kostos* < Skt. *kuṣṭhaḥ*) + *marie,* Mary, the mother of Jesus.]

cost of living *n.* **1.** The average cost of the basic necessities of life, such as food, shelter, and clothing. **2.** The cost of basic necessities as defined by an accepted standard.

cost-of-liv·ing adjustment (kôst'əv-lĭv'ĭng) *n.* An adjustment made in wages that corresponds with a change in the cost of living.

cost-of-living index *n.* The consumer price index.

cost-plus (kôst'plŭs', kŏst'-) *n.* The cost of production plus a fixed rate of profit. *—adj.* Paid or negotiated on the basis of cost-plus: *a cost-plus contract.*

cost-push (kôst'po͝osh', kŏst'-) *adj.* Designating a type of inflation in which increased production costs, as from higher wages, tend to drive prices up.

cos·trel (kŏs'trəl) *n.* A flat, pear-shaped drinking vessel with loops for attachment to the belt of the user. [ME < OFr. *costerel,* prob. < *costier,* at the side < *coste,* rib < Lat. *costa.*]

cos·tume (kŏs'to͞om', -tyo͞om') *n.* **1.** A prevalent fashion of dress, including garments, accessories, and hair style. **2.** A style of dress characteristic of a particular country, period, or people, often worn in a play or at a masquerade. **3.** A set of clothes appropriate for a particular occasion or season. ***—modifier:*** *a costume ball; a costume play.* *—tr.v.* (kŏ-sto͞om', -styo͞om', kŏs'to͞om', -tyo͞om') **-tumed, -tum·ing, -tumes.** **1.** To put a costume on; dress. **2.** To design or furnish costumes for. [Fr. < Ital. < Lat. *consuetudo,* custom. —see CUSTOM.]

cos·tum·er (kŏs'to͞o'mər, -tyo͞o'-, kŏ-sto͞o'mər, -styo͞o'-) also **cos·tum·i·er** (kŏ-sto͞om'yər, -styo͞om'-) *n.* A person who makes or supplies costumes, as for plays or masquerades.

co·sy (kō'zē) *adj. & n.* Variant of **cozy.**

cot[1] (kŏt) *n.* **1.** A narrow bed, esp. one made of canvas on a collapsible frame. **2.** *Chiefly Brit.* A crib. [Hindi *khāṭ,* couch < Skt. *khaṭvā,* of Dravidian orig.]

cot[2] (kŏt) *n.* **1. a.** A small house; cottage. **b.** A small shelter. **2.** A protective covering. [ME < OE.]

co·tan·gent (kō-tăn'jənt) *n. Math.* The tangent of the complement of a directed angle or arc. **—co'tan·gen'tial** (-jĕn'shəl) *adj.*

cot death *n. Chiefly Brit.* Sudden infant death syndrome.

cote[1] (kōt) *n.* **1.** A small shed or shelter for sheep or birds. **2.** *Regional.* A cottage; hut. [ME < OE.]

cote[2] (kōt) *tr.v.* **cot·ed, cot·ing, cotes.** *Archaic.* To go around by the side of; pass. [Orig. unknown.]

co·ten·ant (kō-tĕn'ənt) *n.* One of two or more tenants sharing common property. **—co·ten'an·cy** *n.*

co·ter·ie (kō'tə-rē, kō'tə-rē') *n.* A small group of persons who share interests and associate frequently. [Fr. < OFr., peasant association < *cotier,* cottager < Med. Lat. *cotarius* < ME *cot,* cot.]

co·ter·mi·nous (kō-tûr'mə-nəs) *adj.* Variant of **conterminous.**

co·thurn (kō'thûrn', kō-thûrn') *n.* A cothurnus (sense 1).

co·thur·nus (kō-thûr'nəs) *n., pl.* **-ni** (-nī'). **1.** A buskin worn by actors of classical tragedy. **2.** The ancient style of classic tragedy. [Lat. < Gk. *kothornos.*]

co·tid·al (kō-tīd'l) *adj.* **1.** Indicating coincidence of the tides. **2.** Denoting lines on a map that show where high or low tides occur simultaneously.

co·til·lion also **co·til·lon** (kō-tĭl'yən, kə-) *n.* **1. a.** A lively dance, originating in France in the 18th century, with varied, intricate patterns and steps. **b.** A quadrille. **c.** Music for these dances. **2.** A formal ball, esp. one at which girls are presented to society. [Fr. *cotillon* < OFr., petticoat, dim. of *cote,* coat.]

co·to·ne·as·ter (kə-tō'nē-ăs'tər) *n.* Any of various Old World shrubs of the genus *Cotoneaster,* having small white or pinkish flowers and frequently cultivated for ornament. [NLat. *Cotoneaster,* genus name < Lat. *cotoneum,* quince.]

cot·quean (kŏt'kwēn') *n. Archaic.* **1.** A vulgar woman; hussy. **2.** A man who does work regarded suitable only for women.

Cots·wold (kŏt'swōld') *n.* A sheep of a breed known for its long wool, originally developed in the Cotswold Hills of southwestern England.

cot·ta (kŏt'ə) *n., pl.* **cot·tae** (kŏt'ē) or **cot·tas.** A short ecclesiastical surplice. [Med. Lat., of Germanic orig.]

cot·tage (kŏt'ĭj) *n.* **1.** A small, single-storied house, esp. in the country. **2.** A small summer house used during vacations. [ME *cotage,* prob. < AN < ME *cot,* COT[2].]

cottage cheese *n.* A soft, white cheese made of strained and seasoned curds of skim milk.

cottage industry *n.* A usually small-scale industry carried on at home by family members using their own equipment.

cottage pudding *n.* Plain cake covered with a sweet sauce.

cot·tag·er (kŏt'ĭ-jər) *n.* A person who lives in a cottage.

cottage tulip *n.* A tall-stemmed garden tulip, usually having pointed petals.

cot·ter (kŏt'ər) *n.* **1.** A bolt, wedge, key, or pin inserted through a slot in order to hold parts together. **2.** A cotter pin. [Orig. unknown.]

cotter pin *n.* A split cotter inserted through holes in two or more pieces and bent at the ends to fasten.

cot·ti·er (kŏt'ē-ər) *n.* A peasant renting land directly from its owner, the rate having been fixed by public competition. [ME *cotier,* cottager < OFr. < ME *cot,* COT[2].]

cot·ton (kŏt'n) *n.* **1. a.** Any of various plants or shrubs of the genus *Gossypium,* cultivated in warm climates for the fiber surrounding their seeds. **b.** The soft, white, downy fiber attached to the seeds of the cotton plant, used in making textiles and other products. **c.** Cotton plants collectively. **d.** The crop of the cotton plants. **2.** Thread or cloth manufactured from cotton fiber. **3.** Any of various soft, downy substances found in other plants. ***—modifier:*** *a cotton fabric.* *—intr.v.* **-toned, -ton·ing, -tons.** *Informal.* To take a liking; become friendly: *doesn't cotton to strangers.* [ME *cotoun* < OFr. *coton* < dial. Ar. *qoṭon* < Ar. *quṭn.*]

cotton batting *n.* Batting.

cotton candy *n.* Spun sugar.

cotton flannel *n.* A soft, warm, napped fabric woven of cotton.

cotton gin *n.* A machine that separates the seeds, seed hulls, and other small objects from the fibers of cotton.

cotton grass *n.* Any of various grasslike bog plants of the genus *Eriophorum,* having densely tufted, cottony flower heads.

cotton leafworm *n.* The larva of a New World moth, *Alabama argillacea,* that feeds on and destroys cotton leaves.

cot·ton·mouth (kŏt'n-mouth') *n.* The water moccasin.

cotton rose *n.* **1.** A Chinese shrub, *Hibiscus mutabilis,* culti-

costume

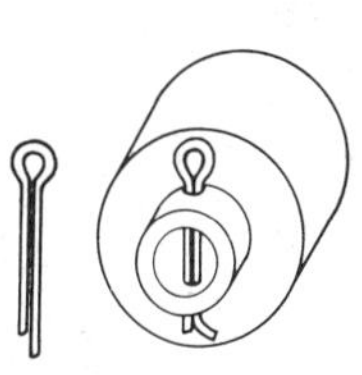

cotter pin
Left: Split cotter pin before use
Right: Cotter pin holding one shaft within another

vated in warm regions for its white or pink flowers that turn deep red. **2.** The cudweed (sense 2).
cotton rust *n.* A disease of the cotton plant caused by the fungus *Puccinia stakmanii* that produces yellowish discolorations on the leaves.
cot·ton·seed (kŏt'n-sēd') *n., pl.* **cottonseed** or **-seeds.** The seed of cotton, used as a source of oil and meal.
cottonseed meal *n.* Meal made from the residue of cottonseed after the oil has been removed and used as animal feed and fertilizer.
cottonseed oil *n.* A yellowish to dark-red oil obtained by crushing cottonseed, used in cooking, as salad oil, and in the manufacture of paints, soaps, and other products.
cotton stainer *n.* Any of various small, flat, red insects of the genus *Dysdercus* that pierce cotton bolls and stain the fibers.
cot·ton·tail (kŏt'n-tāl') *n.* Any of several New World rabbits of the genus *Sylvilagus,* having grayish or brownish fur and a tail with a white underside.
cotton tree *n.* A spiny tropical tree, *Bombax malabaricum,* having seeds surrounded by cottonlike fiber.
cot·ton·weed (kŏt'n-wēd') *n.* Any of various plants covered with cottony down or having cottonlike tufts.
cot·ton·wood (kŏt'n-wo͝od') *n.* Any of several softwood trees of the genus *Populus,* having seeds with cottonlike tufts, esp. *P. deltoides,* of eastern and central North America.
cotton wool *n.* **1.** Cotton in its natural or raw state. **2.** *Chiefly Brit.* Absorbent cotton.
cot·ton·y (kŏt'n-ē) *adj.* **1.** Of or resembling cotton; downy; fluffy. **2.** Covered with fibers resembling cotton; nappy.
cot·y·le·don (kŏt'l-ēd'n) *n.* **1.** *Bot.* A leaf of a plant embryo, being the first or one of the first to appear from a sprouting seed. **2.** *Anat.* A lobule of the placenta, esp. of ruminants. [Lat., navelwort < Gk. *kotulēdōn,* cup-shaped hollow < *kotulē,* anything hollow.] **—cot'y·le'don·al** (-ēd'n-əl), **cot'y·le'do·nous** (-ēd'n-əs) *adj.*

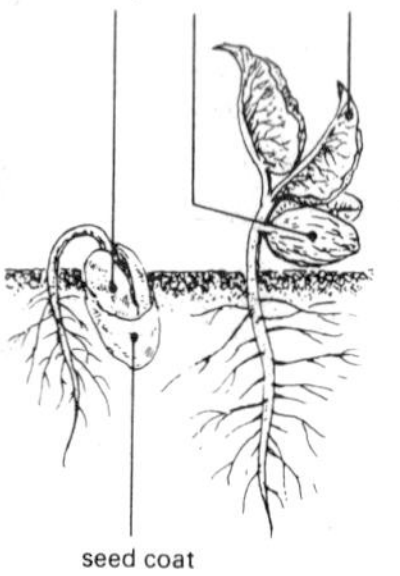

cotyledon
Dicotyledonous bean seedlings

cot·y·loid (kŏt'l-oid') also **cot·y·loid·al** (kŏt'l-oid'l) *adj.* Shaped like a cup. [Gk. *kotuloeidēs* : *kotulē,* anything hollow + *-oeidēs,* -oid.]
couch (kouch) *n.* **1.** An article of furniture, commonly upholstered and often having a back, on which one may sit or recline; sofa. **2. a.** The frame or floor on which grain, usually barley, is spread in malting. **b.** A layer of grain, usually barley, spread to germinate. *—v.* **couched, couch·ing, couch·es.** *—tr.* **1.** To cause (oneself) to lie down, as for rest. **2.** To lower (a spear or lance) to the position of attack. **3.** To embroider by laying thread flat on a surface and fastening it by stitches at regular intervals. **4.** To spread (grain) on a couch to germinate, as in malting. **5.** To word in a certain manner; phrase: *couched the complaint tactfully.* *—intr.* **1.** To lie down; recline, as for rest. **2.** To lie in ambush or concealment; lurk. **3.** To be in a heap or pile, as leaves for decomposition or fermentation. [ME *couche* < OFr. < *couchier,* to lay down < Lat. *collocare,* to lay. —see COLLOCATE.] **—couch'er** *n.*
couch·ant (kou'chənt) *adj. Heraldry.* Lying down with the head raised. [ME < OFr., pr.part. of *couchier,* to lay down. —see COUCH.]
couch grass *n.* A grass, *Agropyron repens,* having whitish-yellow rootstocks by means of which it multiplies rapidly, becoming a troublesome weed. [Alteration of QUITCH GRASS.]
couch·ing (kou'chĭng) *n.* A form of embroidery in which thread is sewn onto a material with stitches at regular intervals. [< ME *couchen,* to embroider < OFr. *couchier,* to lay down. —see COUCH.]
cou·gar (ko͞o'gər) *n.* The mountain lion. [Fr. *couguar,* ult. < Tupi *suasuarana.*]
cough (kôf, kŏf) *v.* **coughed, cough·ing, coughs.** *—intr.* **1.** To expel air from the lungs suddenly and noisily. **2.** To make a noise similar to that of coughing: *The motor coughed and died.* *—tr.* To expel by coughing: *coughed out phlegm.* ***—phrasal verb.*** **cough up.** *Slang.* To hand over (money or another possession), often reluctantly. *—n.* **1.** An act of coughing. **2.** An illness marked by frequent coughing. [ME *coughen.*]
cough drop *n.* A small, often medicated and sweetened lozenge taken to ease coughing or soothe a sore throat.
cough syrup *n.* A sweetened medicated liquid taken to ease coughing.
could (ko͝od) *v.* Past tense of **can[1].**
could·n't (ko͝od'nt). Could not.
cou·lee (ko͞o'lē) *n.* **1.** *Western U.S.* A deep gulch or ravine formed by rainstorms or melting snow, often dry in summer. **2. a.** A stream of molten lava. **b.** A sheet of solidified lava. [Canadian Fr. *coulée* < Fr., flow < *couler,* to flow < Lat. *colare,* to filter < *colum,* sieve.]
cou·lisse (ko͞o-lēs') *n.* **1.** A grooved timber in which something slides. **2. a.** One of the side scenes of the stage in a theater. **b.** The space between the side scenes. [Fr. < *coulis,* sliding < *couler,* to slide. —see COULEE.]
cou·loir (ko͞ol-wär') *n.* A deep mountainside gorge or gully, esp. in the Alps. [Fr. < *couler,* to flow. —see COULEE.]
cou·lomb[1] (ko͞o'lŏm', -lōm') *n.* A meter-kilogram-second unit of electrical charge equal to the quantity of charge transferred in one second by a steady current of one ampere. [After Charles A. de *Coulomb* (1736–1806).]
coulomb[2] or **cou·lom·bic** (ko͞o-lŏm'bĭk, -lōm'-) *adj.* Of or relating to the Coulomb force.
Coulomb field *n.* An electric field equivalent to that produced by a point charge so that the force at every point is described by Coulomb's law.
Coulomb force *n.* An attractive or repulsive electrostatic force described by Coulomb's law.
Coulomb potential *n.* The potential at any point in a Coulomb field.
Coulomb scattering *n.* The scattering of a charged particle from another charged particle, esp. from an atomic nucleus, principally or exclusively as a result of Coulomb forces.
Coulomb's law *n.* The fundamental law of electrostatics stating that the force between two charged particles is directly proportional to the product of their charges and inversely proportional to the square of the distance between them. [After Charles A. de *Coulomb,* its formulator.]
cou·lom·e·try (ko͞o-lŏm'ĭ-trē) *n.* An analytical method for determining the amount of a substance released during electrolysis in which the number of coulombs used is measured. [COULO(MB) + -METRY.] **—cou'lo·met'ric** (-lə-mĕt'rĭk) *adj.* **—cou'lo·met'ri·cal·ly** *adv.*
coul·ter (kōl'tər) *n.* Variant of **colter.**
cou·ma·rin (ko͞o'mər-ĭn) *n.* A fragrant organic compound, $C_9H_6O_2$, extracted from tonka beans or produced synthetically and used in perfumes, flavorings, and soaps. [Fr. *coumarine* < *coumarou,* tonka bean tree < Sp. *coumarú* < Tupi.] **—cou'ma·ric** (-mər-ĭk) *adj.*
coun·cil (koun'səl) *n.* **1.** An assembly of persons called together for consultation, deliberation, or discussion. **2.** A body of people elected or appointed to serve in an administrative, legislative, or advisory capacity. **3.** The discussion or deliberation that takes place in a council. **4.** An assembly of church officials and theologians convened for regulating matters of doctrine and discipline. ***—modifier:*** *a council chamber.* [ME *counceil* < OFr. *concile* < Lat. *concilium.*]
Usage: *Council, counsel,* and *consul* are never interchangeable as such, though their meanings are related. *Council* and *councilor* refer principally to a deliberative assembly (such as a city council or student council), its work and its membership. *Counsel* and *counselor* pertain chiefly to advice and guidance in general and to a person who provides it (such as a lawyer or camp counselor). *Consul* denotes an officer in the foreign service of a country.
coun·cil·lor (koun'sə-lər) *n.* Variant of **councilor.**
coun·cil·man (koun'səl-mən) *n.* A member of a council, esp. of the local governing body of a city or town. **—coun'cil·man'ic** (-măn'ĭk) *adj.*
coun·cil-man·ag·er plan (koun'səl-măn'ə-jər) *n.* A type of municipal government in which the chief executive official is a manager selected by the city council.
coun·cil·or also **coun·cil·lor** (koun'sə-lər) *n.* A member of a council. —See Usage note at **council.**
coun·cil·wom·an (koun'səl-wo͝om'ən) *n.* A female member of a council, esp. of the local governing body of a city or town.
coun·sel (koun'səl) *n.* **1.** An act of exchanging opinions and ideas; consultation. **2.** Advice or guidance, esp. as solicited from a knowledgeable person. **3.** A deliberate resolution; plan of action. **4.** A private purpose or opinion: *keep one's own counsel.* **5.** *pl.* **counsel.** A lawyer or group of lawyers, esp. an attorney engaged to conduct a case in court. *—v.* **-seled, -sel·ing, -sels** also **-selled, -sel·ling, -sels.** *—tr.* **1.** To give counsel to; advise. **2.** To urge the adoption of; recommend. *—intr.* To give or take counsel or advice. —See Usage note at **council.** [ME *counseil* < OFr. *conseil* < Lat. *consilium.*]
coun·sel·or also **coun·sel·lor** (koun'sə-lər) *n.* **1.** A person who gives counsel; adviser. **2.** An attorney, esp. a trial lawyer. **3.** A person supervising children at a summer camp. —See Usage note at **council.** **—coun'se·lor·ship'** *n.*
coun·sel·or-at-law (koun'sə-lər-ət-lô') *n., pl.* **coun·sel·ors-at-law.** A counselor (sense 2).
count[1] (kount) *v.* **count·ed, count·ing, counts.** *—tr.* **1. a.** To name or list (the units of a group or collection) one by one in order to determine a total; number. **b.** To recite numerals in ascending order up to and including: *count three before firing.* **c.** To include in a reckoning; take account of: *ten dogs, counting the puppies.* **2.** To believe or consider to be; deem: *counts himself lucky.* **3. a.** To include by or as if by counting: *count me in.* **b.** To exclude by or as if by counting: *counted him out.* *—intr.* **1.** To recite or list numbers in order or enumerate items by units or groups: *count by tens.* **2. a.** To have importance: *You really count with me.* **b.** To have a specified importance: *His opinions count for little.* **3.** *Mus.* To keep time by counting beats. ***—phrasal verb.*** **count on. 1.** To rely on; depend on: *You can count on my help.* **2.** To be confident of; anticipate: *counted on getting a raise.* *—n.* **1.** The act of counting or calculating. **2. a.** A number reached by counting. **b.** The totality of specific items in a particular sample: *a white cell count.* **3.** *Law.* Any of the separate and distinct charges in an indictment. **4.** The counting from one to ten seconds, during which time a boxer who has been knocked down must rise or be declared

the loser. **5.** The number of balls and strikes with which a baseball player is charged at one turn at bat. [ME *counten* < OFr. *conter* < Lat. *computare,* to compute : *com-,* together + *putare,* to think.]
count² (kount) *n.* In some European countries, a nobleman whose rank corresponds to that of an earl in England. [ME *counte* < OFr. *conte* < LLat. *comes,* occupant of any state office < Lat., companion.]
count·a·ble (koun′tə-bəl) *adj.* **1.** Capable of being counted. **2.** *Math.* Capable of being put in a one-to-one correspondence with the positive integers. **—count′a·bil′i·ty** *n.* **—count′a·bly** *adv.*
count·down (kount′doun′) *n.* **1.** The act or process of counting backward aloud from an arbitrary starting number to indicate the time remaining before an imminent deadline that will initiate an event or operation, as the launching of a missile or space vehicle. **2.** The checks and preparations carried out during a countdown.
coun·te·nance (koun′tə-nəns) *n.* **1.** Appearance, esp. the expression of the face. **2.** The face or facial features. **3. a.** A look or expression of apparent encouragement. **b.** Support or approval in general. **4.** Composure; bearing. *—tr.v.* **-nanced, -nanc·ing, -nanc·es.** To give or express approval to; condone: *wouldn't countenance cheating.* [ME *contenaunce* < OFr. < *contenir,* to behave. —see CONTAIN.] **—coun′te·nanc·er** *n.*
coun·ter¹ (koun′tər) *adj.* Contrary; opposing. *—n.* **1.** One that is counter; an opposite; contrary. **2.** A boxing blow given while receiving or parrying another. **3.** A fencing parry in which one foil follows the other in a circular fashion. **4.** A stiff piece of leather around the heel of a shoe. **5.** The portion of a ship's stern extending from the water line to the extreme outward swell. **6.** The depression between the raised lines of a typeface. *—v.* **-tered, -ter·ing, -ters.** *—tr.* **1.** To meet or return (a blow) by another blow. **2.** To move or act in opposition to; oppose. **3.** To offer in response: *countered that she was too pressed to be thorough.* *—intr.* To move, act, or respond so as to counter. *—adv.* **1.** In a contrary manner or direction. **2.** To or toward an opposite or dissimilar course or outcome: *a method running counter to traditional techniques.* [< COUNTER-.]
count·er² (koun′tər) *n.* **1.** A table or similar flat surface on which money is counted, business is transacted, or food is served. **2.** A piece, as of wood or ivory, used for keeping a count or a place in games. **3. a.** An imitation coin; token. **b.** A piece of money. [ME *countour* < AN < Med. Lat. *computatorium,* counting house < Lat. *computare,* to compute. —see COUNT.]
count·er³ (koun′tər) *n.* **1.** One that counts. **2.** An electronic or mechanical device that automatically counts occurrences or repetitions of phenomena or events.
counter- *pref.* **1.** Contrary; opposite; opposing: *counterclaim.* **2.** Corresponding; complementary: *counterfoil.* [ME *countre-* < OFr. *contre-* < *contre,* counter < Lat. *contra.*]
coun·ter·act (koun′tər-ăkt′) *tr.v.* **-act·ed, -act·ing, -acts.** To oppose and mitigate the effects of by contrary action; check. **—coun′ter·ac′tion** *n.* **—coun′ter·ac′tive** *adj.* **—coun′ter·ac′tive·ly** *adv.*
coun·ter·at·tack (koun′tər-ə-tăk′) *n.* A return attack. *—intr. & tr.v.* (koun′tər-ə-tăk′) **-tacked, -tack·ing, -tacks.** To deliver a counterattack or make a counterattack against.
coun·ter·bal·ance (koun′tər-băl′əns, koun′tər-băl′əns) *n.* **1.** A force or influence equally counteracting another. **2.** A weight that acts to balance another; counterpoise. *—tr.v.* (koun′tər-băl′əns, koun′tər-băl′əns) **-anced, -anc·ing, -anc·es. 1.** To act as a counterbalance to; counterpoise. **2.** To oppose with an equal force; offset.
coun·ter·change (koun′tər-chānj′) *tr.v.* **-changed, -chang·ing, -chang·es. 1.** To exchange; transpose. **2.** To make checkered; variegate.
coun·ter·charge (koun′tər-chärj′) *n.* A charge in opposition to another charge. *—tr. & intr.v.* (koun′tər-chärj′) **-charged, -charg·ing, -charg·es.** To bring a countercharge against or make a countercharge.
coun·ter·check (koun′tər-chĕk′) *n.* **1.** Something that serves to check something else. **2.** Something that confirms or denies the correctness of a previous check. *—tr.v.* (koun′ter-chĕk′) **-checked, -check·ing, -checks. 1.** To oppose or check by a counteraction. **2.** To check again in order to verify.
coun·ter·claim (koun′tər-klām′) *n.* A claim filed in opposition to another claim. *—intr. & tr.v.* (koun′tər-klām′) **-claimed, -claim·ing, -claims.** To plead a counterclaim or make a counterclaim against. **—coun′ter·claim′ant** (-klā′mənt) *n.*
coun·ter·clock·wise (koun′tər-klŏk′wīz′) *adv. & adj.* In a direction opposite to that of the movement of the hands of a clock.
coun·ter·con·di·tion·ing (koun′tər-kən-dĭsh′ən-ĭng) *n. Psychol.* Conditioning intended to replace a negative response to a stimulus with a positive response.
coun·ter·coup (koun′tər-ko͞o′) *n.* A coup to overthrow a government that gained power by a coup d'état.
coun·ter·cul·ture (koun′tər-kŭl′chər) *n.* A culture, esp. of young people, with values that run counter to those of the established culture. **—coun′ter·cul′tur·al** *adj.*
coun·ter·cur·rent (koun′tər-kûr′ənt, -kŭr′-) *n.* A current that flows in an opposite direction to the flow of another current. **—coun′ter·cur′rent** *adj.* **—coun′ter·cur′rent·ly** *adv.*
coun·ter·dem·on·stra·tion (koun′tər-dĕm′ən-strā′shən) *n.* A demonstration held in opposition to another demonstration. **—coun′ter·dem′on·stra′tor** *n.*
coun·ter·es·pi·o·nage (koun′tər-ĕs′pē-ə-näzh′, -nĭj) *n.* Espionage undertaken to detect and counteract enemy espionage.
coun·ter·ex·am·ple (koun′tər-ĭg-zăm′pəl) *n.* An example that refutes or disproves a hypothesis, proposition, or theorem.
coun·ter·feit (koun′tər-fĭt′) *v.* **-feit·ed, -feit·ing, -feits.** *—tr.* **1.** To make a copy of, usually with the intent to defraud; forge: *counterfeiting money.* **2.** To make a pretense of; feign: *counterfeited interest in the story.* *—intr.* **1.** To carry on a deception; dissemble. **2.** To make imitations. *—adj.* **1.** Made in imitation of what is genuine with the intent to defraud: *a counterfeit dollar bill.* **2.** Simulated; feigned: *a counterfeit illness.* *—n.* A fraudulent imitation or facsimile. [ME *countrefeten* < *countrefet,* made in imitation < OFr. *contrefait* < *contrefaire,* to counterfeit : *contre-,* counter- + *faire,* to make < Lat. *facere.*] **—coun′ter·feit′er** *n.*
coun·ter·foil (koun′tər-foil′) *n.* The part of a check or other commercial paper retained by the issuer as a record of a transaction.
coun·ter·glow (koun′tər-glō′) *n.* Gegenschein.
coun·ter·in·sur·gen·cy (koun′tər-ĭn-sûr′jən-sē) *n.* Political and military action undertaken to counter insurgency. **—coun′ter·in·sur′gent** *n.*
coun·ter·in·tel·li·gence (koun′tər-ĭn-tĕl′ə-jəns) *n.* The branch of an intelligence service charged with keeping valuable information from an enemy, preventing subversion and sabotage, and gathering political and military information.
coun·ter·ir·ri·tant (koun′tər-ĭr′ĭ-tənt) *n.* An agent that induces local irritation to counteract general or deep irritation.
coun·ter·man (koun′tər-măn′, -mən) *n.* One who tends a counter, as in a luncheonette.
coun·ter·mand (koun′tər-mănd′, koun′tər-mănd′) *tr.v.* **-mand·ed, -mand·ing, -mands. 1.** To cancel or reverse (a command or order). **2.** To recall by a contrary order. *—n.* (koun′tər-mănd′). An order or command reversing another. [ME *countremaunden* < OFr. *contremander* : *contr-,* counter- + *mander,* to command < Lat. *mandare.*]
coun·ter·march (koun′tər-märch′) *n.* **1.** A march back or in a reverse direction. **2.** A complete reversal of method or conduct. *—tr. & intr.v.* (koun′tər-märch′) **-marched, -march·ing, -march·es.** To conduct in or execute a countermarch.
coun·ter·mea·sure (koun′tər-mĕzh′ər) *n.* A measure taken to counter another measure.
coun·ter·mine (koun′tər-mīn′) *n.* **1. a.** A tunnel dug to intercept and destroy a tunnel dug by besiegers. **b.** A mine or charge of explosive placed so as to explode an enemy's mines. **2.** A plot to frustrate or defeat an attack. *—v.* (koun′tər-mīn′) **-mined, -min·ing, -mines.** *—tr.* **1.** To make or use a countermine against. **2.** To frustrate or defeat by secret and opposite measures. *—intr.* To make or lay down countermines.
coun·ter·move (koun′tər-mo͞ov′) *n.* A move countering another move. *—intr.v.* (koun′tər-mo͞ov′) **-moved, -mov·ing, -moves.** To make a countermove. **—coun′ter·move′ment** *n.*
coun·ter·of·fen·sive (koun′tər-ə-fĕn′sĭv) *n.* A large-scale attack by an army, designed to stop the offensive of an enemy force.
coun·ter·of·fer (koun′tər-ô′fər, -ŏf′ər) *n.* An offer made in return by one who rejects an unsatisfactory offer.
coun·ter·pane (koun′tər-pān′) *n.* A coverlet for a bed; bedspread. [Alteration of obs. *counterpoint* < ME *countrepoint.*]
coun·ter·part (koun′tər-pärt′) *n.* **1. a.** One that is markedly similar to another. **b.** One that has the same functions and characteristics as another; opposite number: *the Secretary of State and his counterpart, the Foreign Minister.* **2. a.** One of two parts that fit and complete each other. **b.** One that is a natural complement to another: *a fine wine that is a perfect counterpart to the dinner.*
coun·ter·plea (koun′tər-plē′) *n. Law.* A plaintiff's reply to a defendant's plea or counterclaim; answering plea.
coun·ter·plot (koun′tər-plŏt′) *n.* A plot intended to frustrate another plot. **—coun′ter·plot′** *v.* **(-plot·ted, -plot·ting, -plots).**
coun·ter·point (koun′tər-point′) *n.* **1.** *Mus.* **a.** Melodic material that is added above or below an existing melody. **b.** The technique of combining two or more melodic lines in such a way that they establish a harmonic relationship while retaining their linear individuality. **c.** Music incorporating or consisting of contrapuntal writing. **2.** A contrasting but parallel element, item, or theme.
coun·ter·poise (koun′tər-poiz′) *n.* **1.** A counterbalancing weight. **2.** A force or influence that balances or equally counteracts another. **3.** The state of being in equilibrium. *—tr.v.* **-poised, -pois·ing, -pois·es. 1.** To oppose with an equal weight; counterbalance. **2.** To act against with an equal force or power; offset.
coun·ter·pro·duc·tive (koun′tər-prə-dŭk′tĭv) *adj.* Tending to hinder rather than serve one's purpose; harmful, not helpful. **—coun′ter·pro·duc′tive·ly** *adv.*

coun·ter·pro·pos·al (koun'tər-prə-pō'zəl) *n.* A proposal offered to nullify or substitute for a previous one.
coun·ter·punch (koun'tər-pŭnch') *n.* A countering attack or blow, esp. a counter in boxing.
coun·ter·ref·or·ma·tion (koun'tər-rĕf'ər-mā'shən) *n.* A reformation in opposition to previous reformation.
Counter Reformation *n.* A reform movement within the Roman Catholic Church in response to the Protestant Reformation.
coun·ter·rev·o·lu·tion (koun'tər-rĕv'ə-lo͞o'shən) *n.* A movement arising in opposition to a revolution and aiming to restore the prerevolutionary state. **—coun'ter·rev'o·lu'tion·ar'y** (-shə-nĕr'ē) *adj. & n.* **—coun'ter·rev'o·lu'tion·ist** *n.*
coun·ter·shaft (koun'tər-shăft') *n.* An intermediate shaft between the powered and driven shafts in a belt drive.
coun·ter·sign (koun'tər-sīn') *tr.v.* **-signed, -sign·ing, -signs.** To sign (a previously signed document), as for authentication. *—n.* **1.** A second or confirming signature, as on a previously signed document. **2. a.** A secret sign or signal to be given to a sentry in order to obtain passage; password. **b.** A secret sign or signal given in answer to another. **—coun'ter·sig'na·ture** (-sĭg'nə-chər) *n.*
coun·ter·sink (koun'tər-sĭngk') *n.* **1.** A hole with the top part enlarged so that a screw or bolthead will lie flush with or below the surface. **2.** A tool for making a countersink. *—tr.v.* **-sunk** (-sŭngk'), **-sink·ing, -sinks. 1.** To make a countersink on or in. **2.** To drive a screw or bolt into (a countersink).
coun·ter·spy (koun'tər-spī') *n.* A spy working in opposition to enemy espionage.
coun·ter·stain (koun'tər-stān') *n.* A stain of a contrasting color used in addition to a principal stain that colors the components in a microscopic specimen that are not made visible by the principal stain.
coun·ter·sunk (koun'tər-sŭngk') *v.* Past tense and past participle of **countersink.**
coun·ter·ten·or (koun'tər-tĕn'ər) *n.* **1.** An adult male voice with a range above that of tenor. **2.** A singer with a countertenor voice.
coun·ter·vail (koun'tər-vāl', koun'tər-vāl') *v.* **-vailed, -vail·ing, -vails.** *—tr.* **1.** To act against with equal force; counteract. **2.** To compensate for; offset. *—intr.* To act against an often detrimental influence or power. [ME *countrevaillen* < OFr. *contrevaloir* : *contre,* counter- + *valoir,* to be worth < *valere,* to be strong.]

coupé

coun·ter·weigh (koun'tər-wā') *intr. & tr.v.* **-weighed, -weigh·ing, -weighs.** To counterbalance or cause to counterbalance.
coun·ter·weight (koun'tər-wāt') *n.* A weight used as a counterbalance. **—coun'ter·weight'ed** (-wā'tĭd) *adj.*
counter word *n.* A word, as *nice* or *awful,* commonly used without regard to its precise meaning.
count·ess (koun'tĭs) *n.* **1. a.** In various European countries, the wife or widow of a count. **b.** In Great Britain, the wife or widow of an earl. **2.** A woman holding the title of count or earl in her own right. [ME *countes* < OFr. *contesse,* fem. of *conte,* count. —see COUNT.]
counting house also **count·ing·house** (koun'tĭng-hous') *n.* An office in which a business firm carries on operations such as accounting and correspondence.
counting room *n.* A counting house.
count·less (kount'lĭs) *adj.* Too numerous to be counted; infinite; innumerable. **—count'less·ly** *adv.*
count noun *n.* A noun, such as *chair* or *pea,* that can form a plural and that can occur in a noun phrase construction with the indefinite article, with such terms as *many,* or with numerals.
count palatine *n.* A palatine[1] (sense 3).
coun·tri·fied also **coun·try·fied** (kŭn'trĭ-fīd') *adj.* **1.** Resembling or having the characteristics of country life; rural; rustic. **2.** Lacking in sophistication.
coun·try (kŭn'trē) *n., pl.* **-tries. 1.** A large tract of land distinguishable by features of topography, biology, or culture. **2.** A district outside of cities and towns; rural area. **3. a.** A nation or state. **b.** The territory of a nation or state; land. **c.** The people of a nation or state; populace. **4.** The land of a person's birth or citizenship. **5.** *Law.* A jury. *—modifier: country life.* [ME *countre* < OFr. *contree* < LLat. *contrata* < Lat. *contra,* opposite.]

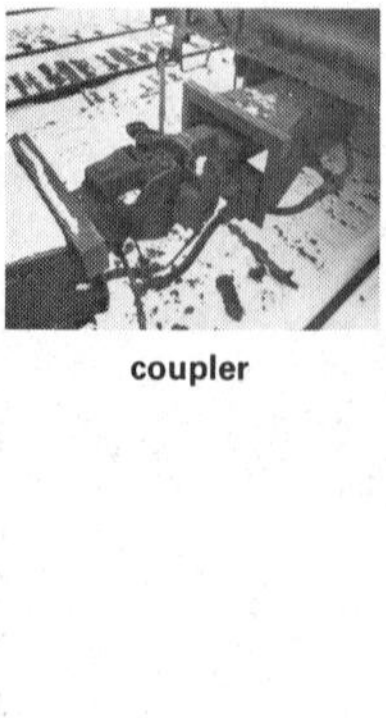
coupler

country and western *n.* Country music.
country club *n.* A suburban club with facilities for golf and other outdoor sports and social activities.
country cousin *n.* One whose ingenuousness or rustic ways may embarrass or amuse city dwellers.
coun·try-dance (kŭn'trē-dăns') *n.* A folk dance of English origin in which two lines of dancers face each other.
coun·try·fied (kŭn'trĭ-fīd') *adj.* Variant of **countrified.**
country gentleman *n.* **1.** The owner of a country estate. **2.** Often **Country Gentleman.** A variety of corn with small, sweet white kernels.
coun·try·man (kŭn'trē-mən) *n.* **1.** A person from one's own country; compatriot. **2.** A person from a particular country. **3.** One who lives in the country; rustic.
country music *n.* A style of popular music based on folk music of the rural United States, esp. of the southern or southwestern United States.
coun·try·seat (kŭn'trē-sēt') *n.* An estate or mansion in the country.
coun·try·side (kŭn'trē-sīd') *n.* **1.** A rural region. **2.** The inhabitants of a countryside.
coun·try·wom·an (kŭn'trē-wo͝om'ən) *n.* **1.** A woman from one's own country; compatriot. **2.** A woman from a particular country. **3.** A woman who lives in the country.
coun·ty (koun'tē) *n., pl.* **-ties. 1.** In the United States, an administrative subdivision of a state. **2.** In Great Britain and Ireland, a territorial division exercising administrative, judicial, and political functions. **3.** The people living in a county. **4.** The territory under the jurisdiction of a count or earl. [ME *counte,* territorial division < AN *counte* < OFr. *conte,* the territory of a count< Med. Lat. *comitatus* < LLat., an office of state < Lat., retinue < *comes,* companion.]
county palatine *n.* The domain of a count palatine.
county seat *n.* A town or city that is the center of government in its county.
county town *n. Chiefly Brit.* A county seat.
coup (ko͞o) *n., pl.* **coups** (ko͞oz). **1.** A brilliantly executed stratagem; masterstroke. **2.** A coup d'état. [Fr., stroke < OFr. < LLat. *colpus* < Lat. *colaphus* < Gk. *kolaphos.*]
coup de grâce (ko͞o' də gräs') *n.* **1.** A death blow or finishing stroke delivered to end the misery of someone who is mortally wounded. **2.** A finishing or decisive event or act. [Fr. : *coup,* stroke + *de,* of + *grace,* mercy.]
coup de main (ko͞o' də măN') *n.* A sudden action undertaken to surprise an enemy. [Fr. : *coup,* stroke + *de,* of + *main,* hand.]
coup d'é·tat (ko͞o' dā-tä') *n.* A sudden overthrow of a government by a group of persons in or previously in positions of authority in deliberate violation of constitutional forms. [Fr. : *coup,* stroke + *de,* of + *état,* state.]
coup de thé·â·tre (ko͞o' də tā-ä'trə) *n.* An unexpected and dramatic event, esp. one that overturns a given situation. [Fr. : *coup,* stroke + *de,* of + *théâtre,* theatre.]
coup d'oeil (ko͞o dœ'yə) *n.* A quick survey; glance. [Fr. : *coup,* stroke + *de,* of + *oeil,* eye.]
coupe[1] (ko͞op) *n.* **1. a.** A dessert of ice cream or fruit-flavored ice, variously garnished and served in a special dessert glass. **b.** The stemmed glass in which a coupe is served. **2.** A shallow, bowl-shaped dessert dish. [Fr., cup < LLat. *cuppa.*]
coupe[2] (ko͞op) *n.* Variant of **coupé** (sense 2).
cou·pé (ko͞o-pā') *n.* **1.** A closed four-wheel carriage with two seats inside and one outside. **2.** Also **coupe** (ko͞op). A closed two-door automobile. [Fr. < p.part. of *couper,* to cut < *coup,* blow. —see COUP.]
cou·ple (kŭp'əl) *n.* **1.** Two items of the same kind; pair. **2.** Something that joins or connects two things together; link. **3.** *(used with a sing. or pl.verb).* **a.** A man and woman united, as by marriage or betrothal. **b.** Two people together. **4.** A few; several: *a couple of days.* **5.** *Physics.* A pair of forces of equal magnitude acting in parallel but opposite directions, capable of causing rotation but not translation. *—v.* **-pled, -pling, -ples.** *—tr.* **1.** To link together; connect: *coupled her refusal with an explanation.* **2. a.** To join as man and wife; marry. **b.** To join in sexual union. **3.** *Elect.* To link (two circuits or currents) as by magnetic induction. *—intr.* **1.** To form pairs; join. **2.** To copulate. **3.** To join chemically. [ME < OFr. < Lat. *copula,* bond.]

Synonyms: *couple, pair, duo, brace, yoke.* These nouns denote two of something in association. *Couple* refers to two of the same kind or sort not necessarily closely associated, though often it does apply to close relationship. Less formally the term may mean "few." *Pair* stresses close association and often reciprocal dependence of things (as in the case of gloves or pajamas). Sometimes it denotes a single thing with interdependent parts (such as shears or spectacles). *Duo* refers to partners in a duet. *Brace* refers principally to certain game birds, and *yoke* to two joined draft animals.

Usage: *Couple,* when referring to a man and woman together, may be used with either a singular or a plural verb, but the plural is more common. Whatever the choice, usage should be consistent: *the couple are spending their honeymoon* (or *is spending its honeymoon*).

cou·pler (kŭp'lər) *n.* **1.** One that couples. **2.** A device for coupling two railroad cars. **3.** A device connecting two organ keyboards so that they may be played together.
cou·plet (kŭp'lĭt) *n.* **1.** A unit of verse consisting of two successive lines, usually rhyming and having the same meter. **2.** Two similar things; pair. [OFr., dim. of *couple,* couple.]
cou·pling (kŭp'lĭng) *n.* **1.** The act of forming couples. **2.** The act of copulating. **3.** Something that links or connects, as a railroad coupler. **4.** The part of the body connecting the hindquarters and forequarters of a four-footed animal.
cou·pon (ko͞o'pŏn', kyo͞o'-) *n.* **1.** A negotiable certificate attached to a bond that represents a sum of interest due. **2. a.** A detachable part, as of a ticket or advertisement, that entitles the bearer to certain benefits, such as a cash refund or a gift. **b.** A printed form, as in an advertisement, to be used as an order blank or for requesting information. **3.** A detachable slip calling for periodic payments, as for merchandise bought on an installment plan. [Fr. < OFr. *colpon,* piece cut off < *colper,* to cut < *coup,* blow. —see COUP.]

cour·age (kûr′ĭj, kŭr′-) *n.* The state or quality of mind or spirit that enables one to face danger with self-possession, confidence, and resolution; bravery. [ME *corage* < OFr. < *cuer,* heart < Lat. *cor.*]

cou·ra·geous (kə-rā′jəs) *adj.* Having or characterized by courage; valiant. **—cou·ra′geous·ly** *adv.* **—cou·ra′geous·ness** *n.*

cou·rante (ko͞o-ränt′) *n.* **1.** A French dance of the 17th century, characterized by running and gliding steps to an accompaniment in triple time. **2.** The second movement of the classical suite, typically following the allemande. [Fr. < fem. pr.part. of *courir,* to run < OFr. *courre* < Lat. *currere.*]

cour·gette (ko͝or-zhĕt′) *n. Chiefly Brit.* A zucchini. [Dial. Fr., dim. of *courge,* gourd < OFr. < Lat. *cucurbita.*]

cou·ri·er (ko͝or′ē-ər, kûr′-, kŭr′-) *n.* **1.** A messenger, esp. one on official diplomatic business. **2.** A personal attendant hired to make arrangements for a journey. [OFr. *courrier* < OItal. *corriere* < *correre,* to run < Lat. *currere.*]

cour·lan (ko͝or′lən) *n.* The limpkin. [Fr., alteration of *courliri* < Galibi *kurliri.*]

course (kôrs, kōrs) *n.* **1.** Onward movement in a particular direction; progress. **2.** The direction of continuing movement: *took a northern course.* **3.** The route or path taken by something, as a stream, that moves. **4.** A designated area of land or water on which a race is held or a sport played: *a golf course.* **5.** Movement in time; duration: *in the course of a year.* **6.** A mode of action or behavior: *followed the best course and waited.* **7.** A typical or natural manner of proceeding or developing: customary passage: *a fad that ran its course.* **8.** A systematic or orderly succession; sequence: *a course of medical treatments.* **9.** A continuous layer of building material, such as brick or tile, on a wall or roof of a building. **10. a.** A complete body of prescribed studies constituting a curriculum and leading toward an advanced degree. **b.** A unit of such a curriculum. **11.** A part of a meal served as a unit at one time. **12.** The lowest sail on a mast of a square-rigged ship. **13.** A point on the compass, esp. the one toward which a ship is sailing. *—v.* **coursed, cours·ing, cours·es.** *—tr.* **1.** To move swiftly through or over; traverse: *ships coursing the seas.* **2. a.** To hunt (game) with hounds. **b.** To set (hounds) to chase game. *—intr.* **1.** To proceed on a course; follow a direction. **2. a.** To move swiftly; race. **b.** To run; flow: *"Big tears now coursed down her face"* (Iris Murdoch). **3.** To hunt game with hounds. ***—idioms.*** **in due course.** At the proper or right time. **of course. 1.** In the natural order of things; naturally. **2.** Without any doubt; certainly. [ME *cours* < OFr. < Lat. *cursus* < *currere,* to run.]

cours·er[1] (kôr′sər, kōr′-) *n.* A dog trained for coursing.

cours·er[2] (kôr′sər, kōr′-) *n.* A swift horse; charger.

cours·ing (kôr′sĭng, kōr′-) *n.* The sport of hunting with dogs trained to chase game by sight instead of scent.

court (kôrt, kōrt) *n.* **1.** An extent of open ground partially or completely enclosed by walls or buildings; courtyard. **2.** A short street, esp. an alley walled by buildings on three sides. **3.** A large, open section of a building, often with a glass roof or skylight. **4.** A mansion or other large building standing in a courtyard. **5. a.** The place of residence of a sovereign or dignitary; a royal mansion or palace. **b.** The retinue of a sovereign, including the royal family and personal servants, advisers, and ministers. **c.** A sovereign's governing body, including the council of ministers and state advisers. **d.** A formal meeting or reception presided over by a sovereign. **6. a.** A person or body of persons whose task is to hear and submit a decision on cases at law. **b.** The building, hall, or room in which cases are heard and determined. **c.** The regular session of a judicial assembly. **d.** A similar authorized tribunal having military or ecclesiastical jurisdiction. **7.** An open, level area, marked with appropriate lines, upon which tennis, handball, basketball, or another game is played. **8.** The body of directors of a corporation, company, or other organization. **9.** A legislative assembly. ***—modifier:*** *a court jester; a court reporter.* *—v.* **court·ed, court·ing, courts.** *—tr.* **1.** To attempt to gain the favor of by flattery or attention. **2.** To attempt to gain the affections or love of; woo. **3.** To attempt to gain; seek. **4.** To behave, often unwittingly or foolishly, so as to invite or incur: *court disaster.* *—intr.* To woo. ***—idiom.*** **pay court to. 1.** To flatter with solicitous overtures in an attempt to obtain something or clear away antagonism. **2.** To woo. [ME < OFr. *cort* < Lat. *cohors.*]

cour·te·ous (kûr′tē-əs) *adj.* **1.** Characterized by graciousness and good manners. **2.** Characterized by consideration toward and respect for others. [ME *corteis* < OFr. < *cort,* court < Lat. *cohors.*] **—cour′te·ous·ly** *adv.* **—cour′te·ous·ness** *n.*

cour·te·san (kôr′tĭ-zən, kōr′-) *n.* A prostitute, esp. one associating with men of rank or wealth. [OFr. *courtisane* < OItal. *cortigiana,* female courtier, fem. of *cortigiano,* courtier < *corte,* court < Lat. *cohors.*]

cour·te·sy (kûr′tĭ-sē) *n., pl.* **-sies. 1. a.** Polite behavior; gracious manner or manners. **b.** A polite gesture or remark. **2.** Consent or agreement in spite of fact; indulgence: *was called "doctor" by courtesy.* [ME *courtesie* < OFr. < *corteis,* courteous.]

courtesy title *n. Chiefly Brit.* A title of nobility having no legal status. For example, the eldest son of the Duke of Bedford is called Marquis of Tavistock during his father's lifetime but is not a peer.

court·house (kôrt′hous′, kōrt′-) *n.* A building housing judicial courts.

courthouse

court·i·er (kôr′tē-ər, kōr′-, -tyər) *n.* **1.** An attendant at the court of a sovereign. **2.** One who seeks favor, esp. by flattery or obsequious behavior. [ME *courteour* < AN < OFr. *courteier,* to be at a royal court < *cort,* court < Lat. *cohors, cohort-,* courtyard.]

court·ly (kôrt′lē, kōrt′-) *adj.* **-li·er, -li·est. 1.** Suitable for a royal court; stately. **2.** Elegant in manners; refined. **3.** Flattering; obsequious. *—adv.* In a courtly manner; elegantly. **—court′li·ness** *n.*

courtly love *n.* A code of chivalrous devotion to a married lady that exerted an important influence in medieval and Renaissance literature.

court-mar·tial (kôrt′mär′shəl, kōrt′-) *n., pl.* **courts-mar·tial. 1.** A military or naval court of officers appointed by a commander to try persons for offenses under military law. **2.** A trial by court-martial. *—tr.v.* **-tialed, -tial·ing, -tials** also **-tialled, -tial·ling, -tials.** To try by court-martial.

court of appeals *n.* A court to which appeals are made on points of law resulting from the judgment of a lower court.

court of chancery *n.* A chancery (sense 1.a.).

court of claims *n.* A U.S. Federal court that determines claims of a specified sort by individuals against the United States.

court of common pleas *n.* **1.** In some states of the United States, a court having general jurisdiction. **2.** A court in Great Britain that formerly heard civil cases between commoners.

Court of Exchequer *n.* A court in Great Britain that formerly had jurisdiction in equity and common law, dealing originally with matters of revenue and later all kinds of cases, now merged in the Court of King's Bench.

court of law *n.* A court that hears and decides cases, proceeding in accordance with common law.

Court of St. James's (sānt -jāmz′, jām′zĭz) *n.* The British royal court.

court plaster *n.* An adhesive plaster used to cover cuts or scratches on the skin. [From its use by ladies at court to make beauty spots.]

court·room (kôrt′ro͞om′, kōrt′-, -ro͝om′) *n.* A room in which the proceedings of a court of law are carried on.

court·ship (kôrt′shĭp′, kōrt′-) *n.* The act or period of courting.

court tennis *n.* A form of tennis played in a large indoor court with a specially marked-out floor and high cement walls off which the ball may be played.

court·yard (kôrt′yärd′, kōrt′-) *n.* An open space surrounded by walls or buildings, adjoining or within a large building or castle.

courtyard

cous·cous (ko͞os′ko͞os′) *n.* A North African dish of crushed grain steamed and served with various meats and vegetables. [Fr. < Ar. *kouskous.*]

cous·in (kŭz′ĭn) *n.* **1.** A child of one's aunt or uncle. **2.** A relative descended from a common ancestor, such as a grandfather, by two or more steps in a diverging line. **3.** A relative by blood or marriage; kinsman or kinswoman. **4.** A member of a kindred group or country: *our Canadian cousins.* **5.** Used as a form of address by a sovereign to a nobleman. [ME *cosin,* a relative < OFr. < Lat. *consobrinus,* cousin : *com-,* together + *sobrinus,* cousin on the mother's side < *soror,* sister.] **—cous′in·ly** *adj.*

cous·in-ger·man (kŭz′ĭn-jûr′mən) *n., pl.* **cous·ins-ger·man.** A cousin (sense 1).

couth (ko͞oth) *adj.* Suave; knowledgeable. [Back-formation < UNCOUTH.]

cou·ture (ko͞o-to͝or′, -tür′) *n.* **1.** The business of a couturier. **2.** Dressmakers and fashion designers collectively. [Fr., sewing < OFr. *cousture* < VLat. **consutura* < Lat. *consuere,* to sew together : *com-,* together + *suere,* to sew.]

cou·tu·rier (ko͞o-to͝or′ē-ər, -ē-ā′) *n.* **1.** One who designs, makes, and sells fashionable, usually custom-made women's clothing. **2.** An establishment engaged in couture. [Fr. < OFr. *cousture,* sewing. —see COUTURE.]

cou·tu·rière (ko͞o-to͝or′ē-ər, -ē-âr′) *n.* A female couturier. [Fr. < OFr. *cousturiere,* fem. of *cousture,* sewing. —see COUTURE.]

cou·vade (ko͞o-väd′) *n.* A practice among certain primitive peoples in which the husband of a woman in labor takes to his bed as if he were bearing the child. [Fr. < OFr. < *couver,* to incubate < Lat. *cubare,* to lie down.]

co·va·lence (kō-vā′ləns) *n. Chem.* The number of electron pairs an atom can share with other atoms. **—co·va′len·cy** *n.* **—co·va′lent** *adj.* **—co·va′lent·ly** *adv.*

covalent bond *n.* A chemical bond formed by the sharing of one or more electrons, esp. pairs of electrons, between atoms.

co·var·i·ance (kō-vâr′ē-əns) *n.* **1.** *Physics.* The principle that the laws of physics have the same form regardless of the system of coordinates in which they are expressed. **2.** *Statistics.* The expected value of the product of the deviations of corresponding values of two variables from their respective means.

co·var·i·ant (kō-vâr′ē-ənt) *adj.* **1.** *Physics.* Expressing, exhib-

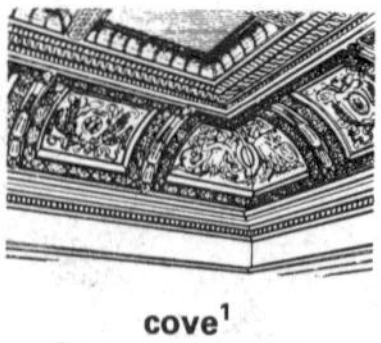

cove[1]
Coved ceiling of the Louvre in Paris, France

coveralls

covered bridge

covered wagon

cowbane

cowbird

cowboy
Drawing by Charles M. Russell

iting, or pertaining to covariance. **2.** *Math.* Varying with another variable quantity in a manner that leaves a specified relationship unchanged.

cove[1] (kōv) *n.* **1.** A small, sheltered bay in the shoreline of a sea, river, or lake. **2. a.** A recess or small valley in the side of a mountain. **b.** A cave or cavern. **3.** A narrow gap or pass between hills or woods. **4.** *Archit.* **a.** A concave molding. **b.** A curved surface forming a junction between a ceiling and a wall. —*tr.v.* **coved, cov·ing, coves.** To curve inward. [ME, chamber, cave < OE *cofa.*]

cove[2] (kōv) *n. Chiefly Brit.* A fellow. [Prob. < Romany *kova,* man.]

co·vel·lite (kō-vĕl′īt′, kō′və-līt′) *n.* An indigo-blue mineral, CuS, an important source of copper. [After Nicholas *Covelli* (1790–1829), its discoverer.]

cov·en (kŭv′ən, kō′vən) *n.* An assembly of 13 witches. [Perh. < ME *covent,* assembly < OFr. *convent* < Lat. *conventus.* —see CONVENT.]

cov·e·nant (kŭv′ə-nənt) *n.* **1.** A binding agreement made by two or more persons or parties; compact. **2.** *Law.* **a.** A formal sealed agreement or contract. **b.** A suit to recover damages for violation of such a contract. —*v.* **-nant·ed, -nant·ing, -nants.** —*tr.* To promise by a covenant. —*intr.* To enter into a covenant; contract. [ME < OFr. < pr.part. of *convenir,* to agree. —see CONVENE.] **—cov′e·nant′al** (-năn′tl) *adj.* **—cov′e·nant′al·ly** *adv.*

cov·e·nant·ee (kŭv′ə-năn-tē′, -nən-) *n.* The participant in a covenant to whom the promise is made.

cov·e·nant·er (kŭv′ə-năn′tər) *n.* **1.** One who makes a covenant. **2. Covenanter.** A Scottish Presbyterian who supported either of the agreements, National Covenant, 1638, or Solemn League and Covenant, 1643, intended to defend and extend Presbyterianism.

cov·e·nan·tor (kŭv′ə-năn′tər, -nən-, kŭv′ə-năn-tôr′) *n.* The party to a covenant by whom the obligation expressed in it is to be performed.

Cov·en·try (kŭv′ən-trē) *n.* A state of ostracism: *was sent to Coventry for talebearing.* [After *Coventry,* England, poss. from the sending of Royalist prisoners there during the English Civil War.]

cov·er (kŭv′ər) *v.* **-ered, -er·ing, -ers.** —*tr.* **1.** To place something upon or over, so as to protect or conceal. **2.** To overlay or spread with something. **3. a.** To put a covering on. **b.** To wrap up; clothe. **4.** To bring upon or invest (oneself): *covered himself with glory.* **5.** To serve as a covering for; occupy the surface of: *Dust covered the table.* **6.** To extend over: *a farm covering more than 100 acres.* **7.** To copulate with (a female). Used of animals, esp. horses. **8.** To sit on in order to hatch (eggs). **9.** To hide or screen from view or knowledge; conceal: *covered up his misdemeanors.* **10.** To protect or shield from harm, loss, or danger. **11.** To protect by insurance. **12.** To compensate or make up for. **13.** To be sufficient to defray, meet, or offset the cost or charge of: *cover a draft.* **14.** To make provision for; allow for: *Federal law does not cover all crimes.* **15.** To deal with; treat of. **16.** To travel or pass over; traverse. **17.** To have as one's territory or sphere of work. **18.** To hold within the range and aim of a weapon, such as a firearm. **19.** To protect, as from enemy attack, by occupying a strategic position. **20.** To be responsible for securing and reporting the details of (an event or situation): *cover a ball game.* **21.** *Sports.* **a.** To be responsible for guarding (an opponent). **b.** To be responsible for defending (a position): *cover left field.* **22.** To match (an opponent's stake) in a wager. **23.** To play a higher-ranking card than (the one previously played). **24.** *Obs.* To pardon or remit: *"Thou hast covered all their sins."* (Psalms 85:2). —*intr.* **1.** To spread over a surface to protect or conceal something. **2.** *Informal.* To act as a substitute or replacement during someone's absence. **3.** To hide something in order to save someone from censure or punishment: *cover up for a colleague.* **4.** *Games.* To play a higher card than the one previously played. —*n.* **1.** Something that covers or is laid, placed, or spread over or upon something else. **2. a.** A position offering shelter or protection from attack. **b.** Strategic protection given by armed units during military action: *a cover of mortar fire.* **3. a.** Vegetation covering an area, often serving to provide shade or prevent erosion. **b.** Underbrush or other vegetation serving as shelter for wild animals. **4.** Something that disguises or conceals. **5.** A table setting for one person. **6.** A cover charge. **7.** An envelope or wrapper for mail. **8.** Funds sufficient to meet an obligation or secure against loss. —***idioms.* break cover.** To come out of hiding. **cover (one's) tracks.** To conceal traces so as to elude pursuers. **cover (the) ground. 1.** To traverse a given distance with satisfying speed. **2.** To accomplish a task or assignment thoroughly and with efficiency. **take cover.** To seek concealment or protection, as from enemy fire. **under cover. 1.** Operating secretly or under a guise; covert. **2.** Hidden; protected. [ME *coveren* < OFr. *covrir* < Lat. *cooperire,* to cover completely : *co(m)-* (intensive) + *operire,* to cover.] **—cov′er·er** *n.*

cov·er·age (kŭv′ər-ĭj) *n.* **1.** The extent or degree to which something is observed, analyzed, and reported. **2.** The extent of protection afforded by an insurance policy. **3.** The amount of funds reserved to meet liabilities.

cov·er·alls (kŭv′ər-ôlz′) *pl.n.* A loose-fitting one-piece garment worn by workmen to protect their clothes.

cover charge *n.* A fixed amount added to the bill, at a nightclub, for entertainment or services.

cover crop *n.* A temporary crop, such as winter rye or clover, planted to protect the soil from erosion in winter and provide humus or nitrogen when plowed under in the spring.

covered bridge *n.* A bridge protected by a roof.

covered wagon *n.* A large wagon covered with an arched canvas top, used by American pioneers for prairie travel.

cover girl *n.* An attractive girl whose picture frequently appears on magazine covers.

cover glass *n.* A small thin piece of glass used to cover a specimen on a microscope slide.

cov·er·ing (kŭv′ər-ĭng) *n.* Something that covers, so as to protect or conceal.

cov·er·let (kŭv′ər-lĭt) also **cov·er·lid** (-lĭd) *n.* A bedspread.

co·ver·sine (kō-vûr′sīn′) *n.* Versed cosine.

cov·ert (kŭv′ərt, kō′vərt, kō-vûrt′) *adj.* **1.** Covered or covered over; sheltered. **2.** Concealed; hidden; secret. **3.** *Law.* Protected by a husband. —*n.* **1.** A covering or cover. **2.** A covered place or shelter; hiding place. **3.** Thick underbrush or woodland affording cover for game. **4.** Covert cloth. **5.** *Zool.* One of the feathers covering the bases of the longer main feathers of a bird's wings or tail. [ME < OFr. < *covrir,* to cover. —see COVER.] **—cov′ert·ly** *adv.* **—cov′ert·ness** *n.*

covert cloth *n.* A twilled cloth made of woolen or worsted yarn with cotton, silk, or rayon, used for garments.

cov·er·ture (kŭv′ər-chər, -chŏŏr′) *n.* **1. a.** A covering; shelter. **b.** Concealment; disguise. **2.** *Law.* The legal status of a married woman.

cov·er-up also **cov·er·up** (kŭv′ər-ŭp′) *n.* An effort or strategy designed to conceal something, such as a crime or scandal.

cov·et (kŭv′ĭt) *tr.v.* **-et·ed, -et·ing, -ets. 1.** To feel blameworthy desire for (that which is another's). **2.** To wish for excessively and longingly. [ME *coveiten* < OFr. *coveitier* < *covitie,* desire < Lat. *cupiditas* < *cupidus,* desirous < *cupere,* to desire.] **—cov′et·a·ble** *adj.* **—cov′et·er** *n.*

cov·et·ous (kŭv′ĭ-təs) *adj.* **1.** Excessively and culpably desirous of the possessions of another. **2.** Marked by extreme desire to acquire or possess: *covetous of learning.* **—cov′et·ous·ly** *adv.* **—cov′et·ous·ness** *n.*

cov·ey (kŭv′ē) *n., pl.* **-eys. 1.** A family of partridges. **2.** A small group, as of persons. [ME < OFr. *covee,* brood < *cover,* to incubate < *cubare,* to lie down.]

cov·ing (kō′vĭng) *n.* A cove (sense 4.b.).

cow[1] (kou) *n.* **1.** The mature female of cattle of the genus *Bos.* **2.** The mature female of other animals, such as whales, elephants, or moose. **3.** A domesticated bovine. **4.** *Slang.* A fat and slovenly woman. [ME *cou* < OE *cū.*]

cow[2] (kou) *tr.v.* **cowed, cow·ing, cows.** To frighten with threats or a show of force. [Prob. of Scand. orig.]

cow·ard (kou′ərd) *n.* One who shows ignoble fear in the face of danger or pain. [ME < OFr. *couard* < *coue,* tail < Lat. *cauda.*]

cow·ard·ice (kou′ər-dĭs) *n.* Lack of courage or resoluteness.

cow·ard·ly (kou′ərd-lē) *adj.* Like or befitting a coward. —*adv.* In the manner of a coward. **—cow′ard·li·ness** *n.*

cow·bane (kou′bān′) *n.* **1.** A plant, *Oxypolis rigidior,* of the southeastern and central United States, having poisonous roots and foliage, and clusters of small white flowers. **2.** Any of several plants related to the cowbane, as the water hemlock.

cow·bell (kou′bĕl′) *n.* A bell hung from a collar around a cow's neck to aid in locating her.

cow·ber·ry (kou′bĕr′ē) *n.* **1.** A creeping evergreen shrub, *Vaccinium vitis-idaea,* having pink or reddish flowers and edible, slightly acid red berries. **2.** A berry of the cowberry.

cow·bird (kou′bûrd′) *n.* Any of various blackbirds of the genus *Molothrus* and related genera that lay their eggs in the nests of other birds, esp. the common North American species *M. ater.* [From their habit of staying with cattle.]

cow·boy (kou′boi′) *n.* A hired man, esp. in the western United States, who tends cattle and performs many of his duties on horseback.

cowboy hat *n.* A ten-gallon hat.

cow·catch·er (kou′kăch′ər, -kĕch′-) *n.* The iron grille or frame that projects from the front of a locomotive or streetcar and serves to clear the track of obstructions.

cow college *n. Informal.* **1.** An agricultural college. **2.** A college or university considered to be provincial and unsophisticated.

cow·er (kou′ər) *intr.v.* **-ered, -er·ing, -ers.** To cringe or shrink away in fear. [ME *couren,* of Scand. orig.]

cow·fish (kou′fĭsh′) *n., pl.* **cowfish** or **-fish·es. 1.** Any of various small whales, porpoises, or similar aquatic mammals, esp. a whale of the genus *Mesopledon,* having a pointed snout. **2.** A fish, *Lactophrys quadricornis,* of warm Atlantic waters, having the body encased in a bony covering and hornlike spines over each eye.

cow·girl (kou′gûrl′) *n.* A hired woman, esp. in the western United States, who tends cattle and performs many of her duties on horseback.

cow·hand (kou′hănd′) *n.* A cowboy or cowgirl.

cow·herb (kou'ûrb', -hûrb') *n.* A plant, *Saponaria vaccaria,* native to Europe, having clusters of deep-pink flowers.
cow·herd (kou'hûrd') *n.* One who herds or tends cattle.
cow·hide (kou'hīd') *n.* **1. a.** The hide of a cow. **b.** The leather made from this hide. **2.** A strong, heavy, flexible whip, usually made of braided leather. *—tr.v.* **-hid·ed, -hid·ing, -hides.** To whip with a cowhide.
cowl (koul) *n.* **1. a.** The hood or the hooded robe worn esp. by a monk. **b.** A draped neckline on a woman's garment. **2.** A hood-shaped covering used to increase the draft of a chimney. **3.** The top portion of the front part of an automobile body, supporting the windshield and dashboard. **4.** An aircraft cowling. *—tr.v.* **cowled, cowl·ing, cowls.** To cover with or as if with a cowl. [ME *coule* < OE *cugele* < LLat. *cuculla* < Lat. *cucullus,* hood.]
cowled (kould) *adj.* **1.** Wearing or supplied with a cowl; hooded. **2.** Having the shape of a cowl.
cow·lick (kou'lĭk') *n.* A projecting tuft of hair on the head that grows in a different direction from the rest of the hair and will not lie flat. [From its appearance of having been licked by a cow.]
cowl·ing (kou'lĭng) *n.* A removable metal covering for an aircraft engine.
cow·man (kou'mən, -măn') *n.* **1.** An owner of cattle or a cattle ranch. **2. a.** A cowboy. **b.** *Chiefly Brit.* A cowherd.
co·work·er (kō'wûr'kər) *n.* A fellow worker.
cow parsnip *n.* Any of several tall, coarse plants of the genus *Heracleum,* such as *H. lanatum,* of North America.
cow·pea (kou'pē') *n.* **1.** A tropical vine, *Vigna sinensis,* bearing long, hanging pods and grown in the southern United States for soil improvement and as animal feed. **2.** The edible, pealike seed of the cowpea.
Cow·per's gland (kou'pərz, ko͞o'-) *n.* Either of a pair of small compound racemose glands lying alongside and discharging into the male urethra. [After William *Cowper* (1666–1709).]
cow pilot *n.* Pintano.
cow·poke (kou'pōk') *n. Informal.* A cowboy.
cow pony *n.* A small, agile horse used in roundups.
cow·pox (kou'pŏks') *n.* A contagious skin disease of cattle caused by a virus that is isolated and used to vaccinate humans against smallpox.
cow·punch·er (kou'pŭn'chər) *n. Informal.* A cowboy.
cow·ry also **cow·rie** (kou'rē) *n., pl.* **-ries.** Any of various tropical marine mollusks of the family Cypraeidae, having glossy, often brightly marked shells, some of which are used as money in the South Pacific and Africa. [Hindi *kauṛī* < Skt. *kapardaḥ,* shell, of Dravidian orig.]
cow shark *n.* Any of several sharks of the family Hexanchidae, of warm and temperate seas.
cow·shed (kou'shĕd') *n.* A shed for housing cows.
cow·slip (kou'slĭp') *n.* **1.** An Old World primrose, *Primula veris,* having fragrant yellow flowers. **2.** The marsh marigold. [ME *cowslyppe* < OE *cūslyppe* : *cū,* cow + *slyppe,* slime.]
cow town *n.* A small, unsophisticated town in a cattle-raising area.
cox (kŏks) *Informal.* *—n.* A coxswain. *—intr. & tr.v.* **coxed, cox·ing, cox·es.** To act as coxswain or serve as coxswain for.
cox·a (kŏk'sə) *n., pl.* **cox·ae** (kŏk'sē'). **1.** *Anat.* The hip or hip joint. **2.** *Zool.* The first segment of the leg of an insect or other arthropod, adjoining and attached to the body. [Lat.] **—cox'al** *adj.*
cox·al·gi·a (kŏk-săl'jē-ə, -jə) *n.* Pain in or disease of the hip. [COX(A) + -ALGIA.] **—cox·al'gic** (-jĭk) *adj.*
cox·comb (kŏks'kōm') *n.* **1.** A conceited dandy; fop. **2.** *Obs.* A cap resembling a cockscomb, worn by a professional jester. **3.** Variant of **cockscomb** (sense 4). [ME *cokkes comb,* cock's comb.]
cox·comb·ry (kŏk'skōm'rē, -skəm-) *n., pl.* **-ries.** Behavior characteristic of or appropriate to a coxcomb.
cox·i·tis (kŏk-sī'tĭs) *n.* Inflammation of the hip joint. [COX(A) + -ITIS.]
Cox·sack·ie virus (ko͝ok-sä'kē, -săk'ē) *n.* Any of a group of enteroviruses that produce a disease resembling poliomyelitis without paralysis. [After *Coxsackie,* New York.]
cox·swain (kŏk'sən, -swān') *n.* A person who steers a boat or racing shell or has charge of its crew. *—intr. & tr.v.* **-swained, -swain·ing, -swains.** To act as coxswain or serve as coxswain for. [ME *cokswaynne* : *cok,* cockboat + *swain,* servant.]
coy (koi) *adj.* **-er, -est. 1.** Shy and retiring. **2.** Artfully or affectedly demure. **3.** Annoyingly unwilling to make a commitment. [ME < OFr. *coi* < Lat. *quietus.*] **—coy'ly** *adv.* **—coy'ness** *n.*
coy·o·te (kī-ō'tē, kī'ōt') *n.* A wolflike carnivorous animal, *Canis latrans,* common in western North America and ranging eastward to Pennsylvania and New York. [Mex. Sp. < Nahuatl *cóyotl.*]
coy·o·til·lo (koi'ə-tĭl'ō, -tē'yō, kī'ə-) *n., pl.* **-los.** A poisonous shrub, *Karwinskia humboldtiana,* of the southwestern United States and Mexico. [Mex. Sp., dim. of *coyote,* coyote.]
coy·pu (koi'po͞o) *n., pl.* **-pus. 1.** A large, beaverlike South American rodent, *Myocaster coypu.* **2.** Nutria (sense 2). [Sp. (South America) *coipú* < Araucanian *kóypu.*]
coz (kŭz) *n. Informal.* Cousin.
coz·en (kŭz'ən) *v.* **-ened, -en·ing, -ens.** *—tr.* **1.** To deceive by means of a petty trick or fraud. **2.** To persuade or induce (someone) to do something by cajoling or wheedling. **3.** To obtain by cozening. *—intr.* To deceive. [Poss. < Ital. *cozzone,* horse-trader < Lat. *coctio,* trader.] **—coz'en·er** *n.*
coz·en·age (kŭz'ə-nĭj) *n.* **1.** The art or practice of cozening. **2.** An act or example of cozening.
co·zy also **co·sy** (kō'zē) *—adj.* **-zi·er, -zi·est** also **-si·er, -si·est. 1.** Snug and comfortable; warm. **2.** Marked by friendly intimacy. **3.** *Informal.* Marked by close association for devious purposes: *a cozy agreement.* *—intr.v.* **-zied, -zy·ing, -zies** also **-sied, -sy·ing, -sies.** *Informal.* To try to get on friendly or intimate terms; ingratiate oneself: *a candidate cozying up to business leaders.* *—n., pl.* **-zies** also **-sies.** A padded or knitted covering placed esp. over a teapot to keep the tea hot. [Prob. of Scand. orig.] **—co'zi·ly** *adv.* **—co'zi·ness** *n.*
CQ (sē'kyo͞o') *n.* Code letters used at the beginning of radio messages intended for all receivers. [C(ALL TO) Q(UARTERS).]
Cr The symbol for the element chromium.
crab¹ (krăb) *n.* **1. a.** Any of various predominantly marine crustaceans of the section Brachyura within the order Decapoda, characterized by a broad, flattened cephalothorax covered by a hard carapace and having the small abdomen concealed beneath it, and five pairs of legs, of which the anterior pair are large and pincerlike. **b.** Any of various similar related crustaceans, such as the hermit crab or the king crab. **2.** The horseshoe crab. **3. a.** The crab louse. **b. crabs.** Infestation by crab lice. **4. Crab.** Cancer (sense 4). **5.** The maneuvering of an aircraft partially into a crosswind in order to compensate for drift. **6.** Any of various machines for handling or hoisting heavy weights. *—v.* **crabbed, crab·bing, crabs.** *—intr.* **1.** To hunt or catch crabs. **2.** To move diagonally or sidewise. **3.** To direct an aircraft into a crosswind. *—tr.* **1.** To direct (an aircraft) partly into a crosswind to eliminate drift. **2.** To move or scurry sideways. ***—idiom.* catch a crab.** In rowing, to strike the water with an oar in recovering a stroke or to miss it in making one. [ME < OE *crabba.*] **—crab·ber** *n.*
crab² (krăb) *n.* **1.** The crab apple or its fruit. **2.** A quarrelsome, ill-tempered person. *—v.* **crabbed, crab·bing, crabs.** *—intr. Informal.* To criticize; find fault. *—tr.* **1.** *Informal.* To interfere with and ruin. **2.** *Informal.* To find fault with. **3.** To make ill-tempered. [ME.] **—crab'ber** *n.*
crab apple *n.* **1.** Any of several trees of the genus *Pyrus,* having white, pink, or red flowers. **2.** The small, tart, edible fruit of the crab apple, used for making jelly.
crab·bed (krăb'ĭd) *adj.* **1.** Irritable and perverse in disposition; ill-tempered. **2.** Difficult to understand. **3.** Difficult to read: *crabbed handwriting.* [ME.] **—crab'bed·ly** *adv.* **—crab'bed·ness** *n.*
crab·by (krăb'ē) *adj.* **-bi·er, -bi·est.** Grouchy; ill-tempered. **—crab'bi·ly** *adv.* **—crab'bi·ness** *n.*
crab cactus *n.* The Christmas cactus.
crab·grass (krăb'grăs') *n.* Any of various coarse grasses of the genus *Digitaria,* that tend to spread and displace other grasses in lawns.
crab louse *n.* A body louse, *Phthirus pubis,* that generally infests the pubic region and causes severe itching.
crab·stick (krăb'stĭk') *n.* **1.** A stick made of crab-apple wood. **2.** A crabby person.
crack (krăk) *v.* **cracked, crack·ing, cracks.** *—intr.* **1.** To break or snap apart. **2.** To make a sharp, snapping sound. **3.** To break without dividing into parts; split slightly. **4.** To change sharply in pitch or timbre, as from hoarseness or emotion. Used of the voice. **5.** To break down; fail; give out. **6.** To move or go rapidly: *was cracking along at 70 miles an hour.* **7.** *Informal.* To have a mental or physical breakdown: *cracked under the pressure.* **8.** *Chem.* To decompose into simpler compounds. *—tr.* **1.** To cause to make a sharp, snapping sound. **2.** To cause to break or split slightly or completely. **3.** To break with a sharp, snapping sound. **4.** To strike with a sudden, sharp sound. **5. a.** To break open or into: *crack a safe.* **b.** To open up for use or consumption. **6.** To discover the solution to, esp. after considerable effort: *crack a cipher.* **7.** To cause (the voice) to crack. **8.** *Informal.* To tell (a joke). **9.** *Informal.* To cause to have a mental or physical breakdown. **10.** To reduce (petroleum) to simpler compounds by cracking. ***—phrasal verbs.* crack down.** To act more forcefully to regulate or restrain: *cracked down on speeding.* **crack up. 1.** To praise highly: *He was simply not the genius he was cracked up to be.* **2.** To damage or wreck: *crack up a plane.* **3.** To have a mental or physical breakdown. **4.** To experience or cause to experience a great deal of amusement: *really cracked up when I heard that joke.* *—n.* **1.** A sharp, snapping sound, such as the report of a firearm. **2.** A partial split or break; fissure. **3.** A slight, narrow space: *The window was open a crack.* **4.** A sharp, resounding blow. **5.** A mental or physical impairment; defect. **6.** A cracking vocal tone or sound, as in hoarseness. **7.** An attempt; chance: *gave him a crack at the job.* **8.** A witty or sarcastic remark. **9.** A moment; instant: *at the crack of dawn.* *—adj.* Excelling in skill or achievement;

cowry

coxswain

coyote

crab¹

superior; first-rate: *a crack marksman.* [ME *craken* < OE *cracian.*]

crack·a·jack (krăk′ə-jăk′) *adj. & n. Slang.* Variant of **crackerjack.**

crack·brain (krăk′brān′) *n.* A foolish or insane person. —**crack′brained′** *adj.*

crack·down (krăk′doun′) *n.* An act or example of cracking down.

cracked stem *n.* A disease of the celery plant caused by a deficiency of boron and characterized by cracking of the stalks.

cradle
17th-century English

crack·er (krăk′ər) *n.* **1.** A thin, crisp wafer or biscuit, usually made of unsweetened dough. **2.** A firecracker. **3.** A small cardboard cylinder covered with decorative paper and containing candy or a favor and a weak explosive that makes a sharp popping noise when a paper strip is pulled at one or both ends and torn. **4.** *Offensive.* A poor white person of the rural esp. southeastern United States. **5.** One that cracks.

crack·er-bar·rel (krăk′ər-băr′əl) *adj.* Resembling or characteristic of the extended informal discussions carried on by persons assembled at a country store.

crack·er·jack (krăk′ər-jăk′) also **crack·a·jack** (krăk′ə-) *Slang.* —*adj.* Of excellent quality or ability; fine. —*n.* Someone or something of marked excellence. [< CRACK (first-rate) + JACK.]

Cracker Jack. A trademark for a candied popcorn confection.

crack·ers (krăk′ərz) *adj. Chiefly Brit. Slang.* Insane; mad.

crack·ing (krăk′ĭng) *n. Chem.* Thermal decomposition, sometimes with catalysis, of a complex substance, esp. such decomposition of petroleum to extract low-boiling fractions such as gasoline. —*adj.* Extremely good; great. —*adv.* Extremely; very.

crampon
Crampons on a hiking boot

crack·le (krăk′əl) *v.* **-led, -ling, -les.** —*intr.* **1.** To make a succession of slight sharp, snapping noises: *a small fire was crackling on the hearth.* **2.** To show liveliness or brilliance: *a book that crackles with humor.* **3.** To become covered with a network of cracks. —*tr.* **1.** To crush (paper, for example) with sharp, snapping sounds. **2.** To cause (china, for example) to become covered with a network of fine cracks. —*n.* **1.** The act or sound of crackling. **2. a.** A network of fine cracks on the surface of glazed pottery, china, or glassware. **b.** Ware bearing this network of cracks. [Freq. of CRACK.]

crack·le·ware (krăk′əl-wâr′) *n.* Ceramic ware made with a surface network of cracks.

crack·ling (krăk′lĭng) *n.* **1.** The production of a succession of slight sharp, snapping noises. **2. cracklings.** The crisp bits that remain after rendering fat from meat or after frying or roasting the skin, esp. of a pig or a goose.

crack·ly (krăk′lē) *adj.* Likely to crackle; crisp.

crack·nel (krăk′nəl) *n.* **1.** A hard, crisp biscuit. **2. cracknels.** Crisp bits of fried pork fat. [ME *craknel.*]

crack·pot (krăk′pŏt′) *n.* An eccentric person, esp. one with bizarre ideas.

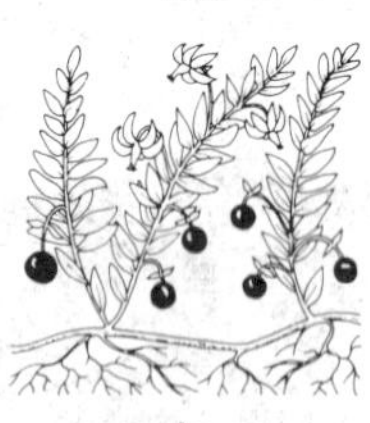

cranberry

crack·up (krăk′ŭp′) *n.* **1.** A collision, as of an airplane or automobile. **2.** A mental or physical breakdown.

-cracy *suff.* Government; rule: *meritocracy.* [OFr. *-cratie* < LLat. *-cratia* < Gk. *-kratia* < *kratos,* strength, power.]

cra·dle (krăd′l) *n.* **1.** A small, low bed for an infant, often furnished with rockers. **2. a.** The earliest period of one's life: *from the cradle to the grave.* **b.** A place of origin; birthplace. **3.** A framework of wood or metal used to support something, such as a ship undergoing construction or repair. **4.** A framework used to protect an injured limb. **5.** The part of a telephone that contains the connecting switch upon which the receiver and mouthpiece unit is supported. **6. a.** A frame projecting above a scythe, used to catch grain as it is cut so that it can be laid flat. **b.** A scythe equipped with such a frame. **7.** A low, flat framework that rolls on casters, used by a mechanic working beneath an automobile. **8.** A boxlike device furnished with rockers, used for washing gold-bearing dirt. —*v.* **-dled, -dling, -dles.** —*tr.* **1.** To place or hold in or as if in a cradle. **2.** To care for or nurture in infancy. **3.** To reap (grain) with a cradle. **4.** To place or support (a ship) in a cradle. **5.** To wash (gold-bearing dirt) in a cradle. —*intr. Obs.* To lie in or as if in a cradle. [ME *cradel* < OE.] —**cra′dler** *n.*

cradle cap *n.* A form of dermatitis that occurs in infants and is characterized by heavy yellow crusted lesions on the scalp.

cra·dle·song (krăd′l-sông′, -sŏng′) *n.* A lullaby.

craft (krăft) *n.* **1.** Skill or ability in something, esp. in handwork or the arts; expertness. **2.** Skill in evasion or deception; guile. **3. a.** An occupation or trade, esp. one requiring manual dexterity. **b.** The membership of such an occupation or trade; guild. **4.** *pl.* **craft.** A boat, ship, or aircraft. —*tr.v.* **craft·ed, craft·ing, crafts.** To make by or as if by hand. [ME < OE *cræft.*]

crane
Above: Stanley crane
Below: A transit crane

crafts·man (krăfts′mən) *n.* A skilled worker who practices a craft. —**crafts′man·ly** *adj.* —**crafts′man·ship′** *n.*

crafts·wom·an (krăfts′wo͝om′ən) *n.* A woman who is skilled in or practices a craft.

craft union *n.* A labor union limited in membership to workers engaged in the same craft.

craft·y (krăf′tē) *adj.* **-i·er, -i·est. 1.** Skillfully underhanded and deceptive; shrewd. **2.** *Archaic.* Skillful; ingenious; dexterous. —**craft′i·ly** *adv.* —**craft′i·ness** *n.*

crag (krăg) *n.* A steeply projecting mass of rock forming part of a rugged cliff or headland. [ME, of Celt. orig.] —**crag′ged** (krăg′ĭd) *adj.*

crag·gy (krăg′ē) *adj.* **-gi·er, -gi·est.** Having crags; steep and rugged. —**crag′gi·ly** *adv.* —**crag′gi·ness** *n.*

crake (krāk) *n.* Any of several birds of the family Rallidae, such as the corncrake or a marsh bird of the genus *Porzana.* [ME, crow, prob. < ON *krāka.*]

cram (krăm) *v.* **crammed, cram·ming, crams.** —*tr.* **1.** To force, press, or squeeze into an insufficient space; stuff. **2.** To fill too tightly. **3.** To gorge with food. **4.** *Informal.* To prepare hastily for an examination. —*intr.* **1.** To gorge oneself with food. **2.** *Informal.* To study hastily and concentratedly for an examination. —*n.* **1.** A group that has been crammed together; crush. **2.** *Informal.* Concentrated and usually hasty study for an examination. [ME *crammen* <OE *crammian.*] —**cram′mer** *n.*

cram·bo (krăm′bō) *n., pl.* **-bos. 1.** A word game in which a player or team must find and express a rhyme for a word or line presented by the opposing player or team. **2.** Doggerel. [Obs. *crambe,* cabbage < Lat. < Gk. *krambē.*]

cramp[1] (krămp) *n.* **1.** A sudden involuntary muscular contraction causing severe pain, often occurring in the leg or shoulder as the result of strain or chill. **2.** A temporary partial paralysis of habitually or excessively used muscles: *writer's cramp.* **3. cramps.** Sharp, persistent pains in the abdomen. —*tr.v.* **cramped, cramp·ing, cramps.** To affect with or as if with a cramp. [ME *crampe* < OFr., of Germanic orig.]

cramp[2] (krămp) *n.* **1.** A bar, usually of iron, with right-angle bends at both ends, used for permanently holding together stones, timber, and other materials used in building. **2.** A frame with an adjustable part to hold pieces together; clamp. **3.** Something that compresses or restrains. **4.** A confined position or part. —*tr.v.* **cramped, cramp·ing, cramps. 1.** To hold together with a cramp. **2.** To shut in so closely as to restrict the physical freedom of: *was cramped by the lack of space.* **3.** To restrict or prevent from free action or expression. **4. a.** To steer (the wheels of a vehicle) to make a turn. **b.** To jam (a wheel) by a short turn. —*adj.* **1.** Restricted; contracted; narrowed. **2.** Difficult to read or decipher, as some handwriting. —***idiom.*** **cramp one's style.** *Slang.* To interfere with or hamper one's usual confidence or skill. [MDu. crampe, hook.]

cramp·fish (krămp′fĭsh′) *n., pl.* **crampfish** or **-fish·es.** The electric ray. [< CRAMP[1], from its ability to give electric shocks.]

cram·pon (krăm′pŏn′, -pən) *n.* **1.** Often **crampons.** A hinged pair of curved iron bars for raising heavy objects, such as stones or timber. **2.** Often **crampons.** An iron spike attached to the shoe to prevent slipping when climbing or walking on ice. [OFr., of Germanic orig.]

cran·ber·ry (krăn′bĕr′ē) *n.* **1. a.** A slender, trailing North American shrub, *Vaccinium macrocarpon,* growing in damp ground and bearing tart red berries. **b.** The edible berry of this plant, often made into sauce or jelly. **2.** Any of various plants similar or related to the cranberry, esp. the European species *V. oxycoccous.* [Partial transl. of LG *kraanbere* : *kraan,* crane (< MLG *kran*) + *-bere,* berry.]

cranberry bush *n.* The high-bush cranberry.

cranberry tree *n.* The guelder rose.

crane (krān) *n.* **1.** Any of various large wading birds of the family Gruidae, having a long neck, long legs, and a long bill. **2.** A bird similar to a crane, such as a heron. **3.** A machine for hoisting and moving heavy objects by means of cables attached to a movable boom. **4.** Any of various devices with a swinging arm, as one in a fireplace for suspending a pot. —*v.* **craned, cran·ing, cranes.** —*tr.* **1.** To hoist or move with or as if with a crane. **2.** To strain and stretch (the neck). —*intr.* To stretch one's neck for a better view. [ME < OE *cran.*]

crane fly *n.* Any of numerous long-legged, slender-bodied flies of the family Tipulidae, having the general appearance of a large mosquito.

cranes·bill (krānz′bĭl′) *n.* A geranium (sense 1).

crani– *pref.* Variant of **cranio-.**

cra·ni·a (krā′nē-ə) *n.* A plural of **cranium.**

cra·ni·al (krā′nē-əl) *adj.* Of or pertaining to the skull. [< CRANIUM.] —**cra′ni·al·ly** *adv.*

cranial index *n.* The ratio of the maximum width to the maximum length of the cranium, multiplied by 100.

cranial nerve *n.* Any of several nerves that arise in pairs from the brainstem and reach the periphery through openings in the skull.

cra·ni·ate (krā′nē-ĭt, -āt′) *adj.* Having a skull. —*n.* An animal having a skull; vertebrate.

cra·ni·ec·to·my (krā′nē-ĕk′tə-mē) *n., pl.* **-mies.** The surgical removal of a portion of the cranium.

cranio– or **crani–** *pref.* Cranium: *craniometer.* [< CRANIUM.]

cra·ni·o·cer·e·bral (krā′nē-ō-sĕr′ə-brəl, -sə-rē′brəl) *adj.* Of or pertaining to the cranium and the brain.

cra·ni·ol·o·gy (krā′nē-ŏl′ə-jē) *n.* The scientific study of the characteristics of the skull, such as size and shape, esp. in

ă pat / ā pay / âr care / ä father / b **bib** / ch **church** / d **deed** / ĕ pet / ē be / f **fife** / g **gag** / h **hat** / hw **which** / ĭ pit / ī pie / îr pier / j **judge** / k **kick** / l lid, needle / m **mum** / n no, sudden / ng thing / ŏ pot / ō toe / ô paw, for / oi noise / ou out / o͝o took / o͞o boot /

humans. **—cra′ni·o·log′i·cal** (-ə-lŏj′ĭ-kəl) *adj.* **—cra′ni·o·log′i·cal·ly** *adv.* **—cra′ni·ol′o·gist** *n.*

cra·ni·om·e·ter (krā′nē-ŏm′ĭ-tər) *n.* An instrument or device for measuring skulls. **—cra′ni·o·met′ric** (-ə-mĕt′rĭk), **cra′ni·o·met′ri·cal** *adj.* **—cra′ni·om′e·try** *n.*

cra·ni·o·sac·ral system (krā′nē-ō-săk′rəl, -sā′krəl) *n.* The parasympathetic nervous system.

cra·ni·ot·o·my (krā′nē-ŏt′ə-mē) *n. pl.* **-mies. 1.** The surgical cutting or removal of part of the skull. **2.** The cutting or breaking of the fetal skull to reduce its size for removal when normal delivery is not possible.

cra·ni·um (krā′nē-əm) *n., pl.* **-ni·ums** or **-ni·a** (-nē-ə). **1.** The skull of a vertebrate. **2.** The portion of the skull enclosing the brain. [Med. Lat. < Gk. *kranion.*]

crank[1] (krăngk) *n.* **1.** A device for transmitting rotary motion, consisting of a handle or arm attached at right angles to a shaft. **2.** A turn of speech; verbal conceit. **3.** A peculiar or eccentric idea or action. **4.** *Informal.* **a.** A grouchy person. **b.** An eccentric. *—v.* **cranked, crank·ing, cranks.** *—tr.* **1.** To start or operate (an engine, for example) by turning a crank. **2.** To make into the shape of a crank; twist; bend. **3.** To provide with a crank. *—intr.* **1.** To turn a crank. **2.** To twist; wind. ***—phrasal verbs.* crank out.** To produce, esp. mechanically and rapidly: *cranks out memo after memo.* **crank up.** To cause to start or to get started as if by turning a crank: *cranking up a massive publicity campaign.* [ME < OE *cranc,* as in *crancstæf,* weaving implement.]

crank[2] (krăngk) *adj. Naut.* Liable to capsize; unstable. [Orig. unknown.]

crank[3] (krăngk) *adj.* **1.** Lively; cheerful; spirited. **2.** Overconfident. [ME *cranke.*]

crank·case (krăngk′kās′) *n.* The metal case enclosing the crankshaft and associated parts in a reciprocating engine.

crank·pin also **crank pin** (krăngk′pĭn′) *n.* A bar or cylinder in the arm of a crank to which a reciprocating member or connecting rod is attached.

crank·shaft (krăngk′shăft′) *n.* A shaft that turns or is turned by a crank.

crank·y[1] (krăng′kē) *adj.* **-i·er, -i·est. 1.** Ill-tempered; peevish. **2.** Odd; eccentric. **3.** Full of bends and turns; crooked. **—crank′i·ly** *adv.* **—crank′i·ness** *n.*

crank·y[2] (krăng′kē) *adj.* **-i·er, -i·est. 1.** *Naut.* Liable to capsize. **2.** Rickety; loose; shaky.

cran·ny (krăn′ē) *n., pl.* **-nies.** A small opening, as in a wall or rock face; crevice; fissure. [ME *crani* < OFr. *cran,* notch.] **—cran′nied** *adj.*

crap[1] (krăp) *Vulgar Slang. —n.* **1.** Excrement. **2.** An act of defecating. **3. a.** Worthless nonsense. **b.** Something useless; rubbish. *—intr.v.* **crapped, crap·ping, craps.** To defecate. [ME *crappe,* chaff < MDu., piece torn off < *crappen,* to break off.]

crap[2] (krăp) *n.* A losing throw in the game of craps. *—v.* **crapped, crap·ping, craps. —crap out.** To make a losing throw in the game of craps. [Back-formation < CRAPS.]

crape (krāp) *n.* **1.** Crepe (sense 1). **2.** A black band worn, as on the sleeve, as a sign of mourning. *—tr.v.* **craped, crap·ing, crapes.** To cover or drape with or as if with crape.

crape·hang·er (krāp′hăng′gər) *n.* A morose, gloomy, or pessimistic person.

crape jasmine *n.* A fragrant shrub, *Tabernaemontana coronaria,* of India, cultivated in warm regions for its white flowers. [From the crinkled lobes of the corolla.]

crape myrtle also **crepe myrtle** *n.* An Oriental shrub, *Lagerstroemia indica,* widely cultivated in warm climates for its showy pink, red, or white flowers.

crap·pie (krăp′ē) *n., pl.* **-pies.** Either of two edible North American freshwater fishes, *Pomoxis nigromaculatus,* the black crappie, or *P. annularis,* the white crappie, related to the sunfishes. [Canadian Fr. *crapet.*]

craps (krăps) *pl.n. (used with a sing. or pl. verb).* A gambling game played with two dice in which a first throw of 7 or 11 wins, a first throw of 2, 3, or 12 loses the bet, and a first throw of any other number (a point) must be repeated to win before a 7 is thrown, which loses both the bet and the dice. [Louisiana Fr. < Fr. *crabs* < E. *crabs,* the lowest throw at hazard.]

crap·shoot·er (krăp′shōō′tər) *n.* One who plays craps.

crap·u·lence (krăp′yə-ləns) *n.* **1.** Sickness caused by excessive eating or drinking. **2.** Excessive indulgence; intemperance. [< LLat. *crapulentus,* very drunk < Lat. *crapula,* intoxication < Gk. *kraipalē.*] **—crap′u·lent** *adj.* **—crap′u·lous** *adj.*

crash[1] (krăsh) *v.* **crashed, crash·ing, crash·es.** *—intr.* **1.** To fall or collide noisily; smash. **2.** To undergo sudden damage or destruction on impact. **3.** To make a sudden loud noise. **4.** To move noisily or so as to cause damage. **5.** To fail suddenly, as a business or an economy. **6.** *Slang.* To return to a normal mental state after an experience caused by the use esp. of a mind-altering drug. **7.** *Slang.* **a.** To find lodging or shelter. **b.** To go to sleep. *—tr.* **1.** To cause to crash. **2.** To dash to pieces; smash. **3.** *Informal.* To join or enter without invitation. *—n.* **1.** A sudden loud noise, as of something breaking. **2.** A wrecking; smashing; collision. **3.** A sudden business failure. *—adj. Informal.* Of or characterized by an intensive effort to produce or accomplish something: *a crash program.* [ME *crasschen.*] **—crash′er** *n.*

crash[2] (krăsh) *n.* **1.** A coarse, light, unevenly woven fabric of cotton or linen, used for towels and curtains. **2.** Starched reinforced fabric used to strengthen a book binding or the spine of a bound book. [R. *krashenina,* colored linen < *krashenie,* coloring < *krasit′,* to color < *krasa,* beauty.]

crash dive *n.* A rapid dive made by a submarine, esp. in an emergency.

crash helmet *n.* A padded helmet, as worn by motorcyclists and aviators, to protect the head in case of accident.

crash·ing (krăsh′ĭng) *adj.* Total; absolute: *a crashing bore.*

crash-land (krăsh′lănd′) *v.* **-land·ed, -land·ing, -lands.** *—tr.* To land (an aircraft) under emergency conditions, usually accompanied by damage to the aircraft. *—intr.* To crash-land an aircraft.

crash pad *n.* **1.** Padding inside automobiles, tanks, or other vehicles for protecting occupants in the event of an accident, sudden stop, or other quick movement. **2.** *Slang.* A place affording free and usually temporary lodging.

crash truck also **crash wagon** *n.* A truck specially designed and equipped to rescue victims of an airplane crash.

crash·wor·thy (krăsh′wûr′*th*ē) *adj.* Capable of withstanding the effects of a crash: *crashworthy cars.* **—crash′wor′thi·ness** *n.*

crass (krăs) *adj.* **-er, -est.** So crude and unrefined as to be lacking in discrimination and sensibility; coarse. [Lat. *crassus,* dense.] **—crass′i·tude′** (-ĭ-tōōd′, -tyōōd′), **crass′ness** *n.* **—crass′ly** *adv.*

-crat *suff.* A participant in or supporter of a specified form of government: *technocrat.* [Fr. *-crate* < Gk. *-kratēs* < *-kratia,* -cracy.]

crate (krāt) *n.* **1.** A container, such as a slatted wooden case, used for storing or shipping. **2.** *Slang.* An old, rickety vehicle, such as an automobile or aircraft. *—tr.v.* **crat·ed, crat·ing, crates.** To pack into a crate. [Lat. *cratis,* wickerwork.]

cra·ter (krā′tər) *n.* **1.** A bowl-shaped depression at the mouth of a volcano or geyser. **2.** A pit or hole in the ground created as by an explosion or the impact of a meteorite. [Lat. < Gk. *kratēr,* mixing vessel < *kerannunai,* to mix.]

Cra·ter (krā′tər) *n.* A constellation in the Southern Hemisphere near Hydra and Corvus.

cra·ter·let (krā′tər-lĭt) *n.* A small crater.

cra·vat (krə-văt′) *n.* A scarf or band of fabric worn as a necktie. [Fr. *cravate,* cravat, necktie worn by Croatian mercenaries in the service of France < *Cravate,* a Croatian < Serbo-Croatian *Hrvat.*]

crave (krāv) *v.* **craved, crav·ing, craves.** *—tr.* **1.** To have an intense desire for. **2.** To need urgently; require. **3.** To beg earnestly for; implore. *—intr.* To have an eager or intense desire. [ME *craven* < OE *crafian,* to beg.] **—crav′er** *n.* **—crav′ing·ly** *adv.*

cra·ven (krā′vən) *adj.* Characterized by abject fear; cowardly. *—n.* A coward. [ME *cravant.*] **—cra′ven·ly** *adv.* **—cra′ven·ness** *n.*

crav·ing (krā′vĭng) *n.* A consuming desire; yearning.

craw (krô) *n.* **1.** The crop of a bird. **2.** The stomach of an animal. [ME *crawe.*]

craw·fish (krô′fĭsh′) *intr.v.* **-fished, -fish·ing, -fish·es.** *Informal.* To withdraw from an undertaking. *—n.* Variant of **crayfish.**

crawl[1] (krôl) *intr.v.* **crawled, crawl·ing, crawls. 1.** To move slowly on the hands and knees or by dragging the body along the ground; creep. **2.** To advance slowly, feebly, or laboriously: *crawled along until we hit the open road.* **3.** To proceed or act servilely. **4.** To be or feel as if covered with crawling things: *flesh crawling in horror.* **5.** To swim the crawl. *—n.* **1.** The action of crawling. **2.** An extremely slow pace. **3.** A rapid swimming stroke consisting of alternating overarm strokes and a flutter kick. [ME *craulen* < ON *krafla.*] **—crawl′er** *n.* **—crawl′ing·ly** *adv.*

crawl[2] (krôl) *n.* A pen in shallow water, as for confining fish or turtles. [Afr. *kraal,* enclosure for animals. —see KRAAL.]

crawl·space (krôl′spās) *n.* A low or narrow space, as in the walls of a building, that gives workers access to plumbing or wiring equipment.

crawl·y (krô′lē) *adj.* **-i·er, -i·est.** *Informal.* **1.** Creepy. **2.** Feeling as if covered with crawling things.

cray·fish (krā′fĭsh′) also **craw·fish** (krô′-) *n., pl.* **crayfish** or **-fish·es** also **crawfish** or **-fish·es. 1.** Any of various freshwater crustaceans of the genera *Cambarus* and *Astacus,* resembling a lobster but considerably smaller. **2.** A spiny lobster. [By folk etymology < ME *crevis* < OFr. *crevise,* of Germanic orig.]

cray·on (krā′ŏn′, -ən) *n.* **1.** A stick of colored wax, charcoal, or chalk, used for drawing. **2.** A drawing made with crayons. *—tr.v.* **-oned, -on·ing, -ons.** To draw, color, or decorate with crayons. [Fr. < *craie,* chalk < Lat. *creta* < *Creta* (*terra*), Cretan (earth).] **—cray′on·ist** (-ə-nĭst) *n.*

craze (krāz) *v.* **crazed, craz·ing, craz·es.** *—tr.* **1.** To cause to become mentally deranged or obsessed; make insane. **2.** To produce a network of fine cracks in the surface or glaze of. *—intr.* **1.** To become mentally deranged or obsessed; go insane. **2.** To become covered with fine cracks. *—n.* **1.** A short-lived popular fashion; fad. **2.** A fine crack. [ME *crasen,* of Scand. orig.]

cra·zy (krā′zē) *adj.* **-zi·er, -zi·est. 1.** Affected with madness; insane. **2.** *Informal.* Departing from proportion or modera-

crater
Lunar craters

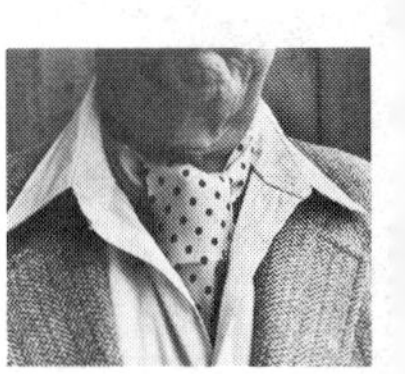

cravat

crazy quilt

tion, esp.: **a.** Possessed by enthusiasm or excitement. **b.** Immoderately fond; infatuated. **c.** Intensely involved or preoccupied. **d.** Not sensible; impractical. **3.** *Archaic.* Rickety or dilapidated. —*n.* One who is or appears crazy. —***idiom.*** **like crazy.** *Informal.* To an exceeding degree: *running around like crazy.* —**cra'zi·ly** *adv.* —**cra'zi·ness** *n.*

crazy bone *n. Informal.* The olecranon.

crazy quilt *n.* **1.** A patchwork quilt of pieces of cloth of various shapes, colors, and sizes, arranged in no definite pattern. **2.** A disorderly mixture; hodgepodge.

cra·zy·weed (krā'zē-wēd') *n.* Locoweed. [From its toxic effect on some animals.]

C-re·ac·tive protein (sē'rē-ăk'tĭv) *n.* A globulin that occurs in the blood in certain acute illnesses, such as rheumatic fever. [C(ARBOHYDRATE POLYSACCHARIDE) + REACTIVE.]

creak (krēk) *intr.v.* **creaked, creak·ing, creaks. 1.** To make a grating or squeaking sound. **2.** To move with a creaking sound. —*n.* A grating or squeaking sound. [ME *creken.*] —**creak'ing·ly** *adv.*

creak·y (krē'kē) *adj.* **-i·er, -i·est. 1.** Tending or liable to creak. **2.** Dilapidated; decrepit. —**creak'i·ly** *adv.* —**creak'i·ness** *n.*

cream (krēm) *n.* **1.** The yellowish fatty component of unhomogenized milk that tends to accumulate at the surface. **2.** A pale yellow to yellowish white. **3.** Any of various substances resembling or containing cream, as certain foods or cosmetics. **4.** The choicest part: *the cream of the crop.* —*v.* **creamed, cream·ing, creams.** —*intr.* **1.** To form cream. **2.** To form foam or froth at the top. —*tr.* **1.** To remove the cream from; skim. **2.** To select or remove the best part from. **3.** To beat into a creamy consistency. **4.** To prepare or cook in or with a cream sauce. **5.** To add cream to. **6.** *Slang.* To defeat overwhelmingly. [ME *creme* < OFr. *craime* < LLat. *cramum.*] —**cream** *adj.*

cream cheese *n.* A soft white cheese made of cream and milk.

cream-col·ored (krēm'kŭl'ərd) *adj.* Of the color of cream; yellowish white.

cream·cups (krēm'kŭps') *n. (used with a sing. or pl. verb).* A plant, *Platystemon californicus,* of the southwestern United States, having long-stalked cream-colored or light-yellow flowers.

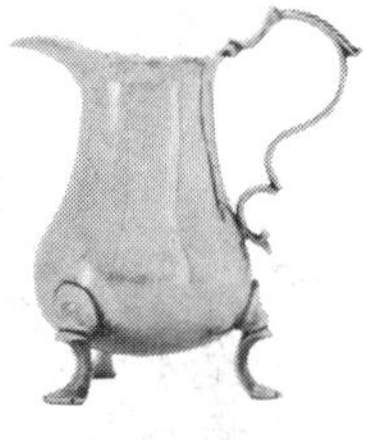

creamer
18th-century American

cream·er (krē'mər) *n.* **1.** A small jug or pitcher for cream. **2.** A machine or device for separating cream from milk. **3.** A refrigerator in which milk is placed to form cream.

cream·er·y (krē'mə-rē) *n., pl.* **-ies.** An establishment where dairy products are prepared or sold.

cream of tartar *n.* Potassium bitartrate.

cream puff *n.* **1.** A shell of light pastry filled with whipped cream, custard, or ice cream. **2.** *Slang.* A sissy.

cream sauce *n.* A white sauce made by cooking together a mixture of flour and butter with milk or cream.

cream·y (krē'mē) *adj.* **-i·er, -i·est.** Rich in or resembling cream. —**cream'i·ly** *adv.* —**cream'i·ness** *n.*

crease (krēs) *n.* **1.** A line made by pressing, folding, or wrinkling. **2.** In cricket, one of the lines marking off the positions of the bowler and batsman or the space between two of these lines. **3.** In hockey, a rectangular area marked off in front of the goal cage. —*v.* **creased, creas·ing, creas·es.** —*tr.* **1.** To make a crease in. **2.** To graze or wound superficially with a bullet. —*intr.* To become wrinkled. [Obs. *creast* < ME *crest,* ridge. —see CREST.] —**crease·less** *adj.* —**creas'er** *n.* —**creas'y** *adj.*

cre·ate (krē-āt') *tr.v.* **-at·ed, -at·ing, -ates. 1.** To cause to exist; bring into being. **2.** To give rise to; produce: *Her remark created a stir.* **3.** To invest with an office or title; appoint. **4.** To produce through artistic or imaginative effort: *create a poem; create a role.* —*adj. Archaic.* Created. [ME *createn* < Lat. *creare.*]

cre·a·tine (krē'ə-tēn', -tĭn) also **cre·a·tin** (-tĭn) *n.* A nitrogenous organic acid, $C_4H_9N_3O_2$, that is found in the muscle tissue of many vertebrates mainly in the form of phosphocreatine. [Gk. *kreas, kreat-,* flesh + -INE.]

creatine phosphate *n.* Phosphocreatine.

cre·at·i·nine (krē-ăt'n-ēn', -ĭn) *n.* The creatine anhydride $C_4H_7N_3O$, a normal metabolic waste. [CREATIN(E) + -INE.]

cre·a·tion (krē-ā'shən) *n.* **1. a.** The act of creating. **b.** The fact or process of being created. **2.** The act of investing with an office or title. **3. a.** The world and all things in it. **b.** All creatures or a class of creatures. **4.** An original product of human invention or artistic imagination. **5.** A new and usually specially designed garment. —**cre·a'tion·al** *adj.*

cre·a·tive (krē-ā'tĭv) *adj.* **1.** Having the ability or power to create. **2.** Creating; productive. **3.** Characterized by originality and expressiveness; imaginative. —**cre·a'tive·ly** *adv.* —**cre'a·tiv'i·ty** (-ĭ-tē), **cre·a'tive·ness** *n.*

cre·a·tor (krē-ā'tər) *n.* **1.** One that creates. **2. Creator.** God.

crea·ture (krē'chər) *n.* **1.** Something created. **2.** A living being, esp. an animal. **3.** A human being. **4.** One dependent upon or subservient to another; tool. —**crea'tur·al** *adj.* —**crea'ture·ly** *adj.*

creature comfort *n.* Something that contributes to physical comfort.

crèche

crèche (krĕsh) *n.* **1.** A representation of the Nativity scene. **2.** A foundling hospital. **3.** *Chiefly Brit.* A day nursery. [Fr. < OFr. crib, of Germanic orig.]

cre·dence (krēd'ns) *n.* **1.** Acceptance as true or valid; belief. **2.** Claim to acceptance; trustworthiness. **3.** Recommendation; credential: *a letter of credence.* **4.** A small table for holding the elements of the Eucharist. [ME < OFr. < Med. Lat. *credentia* < Lat. *credere,* to believe.]

cre·den·tial (krĭ-dĕn'shəl) *n.* **1.** That which entitles one to confidence, credit, or authority. **2. credentials.** Evidence or testimonials attesting one's right to credit, confidence, or authority. [< Med. Lat. *credentialis,* giving authority < *credentia,* trust < Lat. *credere,* to believe.]

cre·den·za (krĭ-dĕn'zə) *n.* A buffet or sideboard, esp. one without legs. [Ital. < Med. Lat. *credentia,* trust, from the practice of placing food and drink on a sideboard to be tasted by a servant before being served to ensure that they contained no poison.]

credibility gap *n.* **1.** Public skepticism about the truth esp. of official claims and pronouncements. **2.** Lack of trustworthiness. **3.** A discrepancy or disparity.

cred·i·ble (krĕd'ə-bəl) *adj.* **1.** Capable of being believed; plausible. **2.** Worthy of confidence; reliable. [ME < Lat. *credibilis* < *credere,* to believe.] —**cred'i·bil'i·ty** *n.* —**cred'i·ble·ness** *n.* —**cred'i·bly** *adv.*

cred·it (krĕd'ĭt) *n.* **1.** Belief or confidence in the truth of something; trust. **2.** A reputation for sound character or quality; standing. **3.** A source of honor or distinction: *He is a credit to his family.* **4.** Approval for an act, ability, or quality; praise. **5.** Influence based on the good opinion or confidence of others. **6.** Often **credits.** An acknowledgment of work done, as in the production of a motion picture or play. **7. a.** Official certification or recognition that a student has successfully completed a course of study. **b.** A unit of study so certified. **8.** Reputation for solvency and integrity entitling a person to be trusted in buying or borrowing. **9. a.** Confidence in a buyer's ability and intention to fulfill financial obligations. **b.** The time allowed for payment for something sold on trust. **10.** *Accounting.* **a.** The deduction of a payment made by a debtor from an amount due. **b.** The right-hand side of an account on which such amounts are entered. **c.** An entry or the sum of the entries on this side. **11.** The positive balance or amount remaining in a person's account. **12.** An amount placed by a bank at the disposal of a client. —*tr.v.* **-it·ed, -it·ing, -its. 1.** To believe in; trust: *"she refused steadfastly to credit the reports of his death"* (Agatha Christie). **2.** *Archaic.* To bring honor or distinction to. **3. a.** To give credit to for something: *credit him with the invention.* **b.** To ascribe to a person; attribute to: *credit the invention to him.* **4.** *Accounting.* **a.** To enter as a credit: *credited $500 to her account.* **b.** To make a credit entry in: *credit an account.* **5.** To give or award an educational credit to. [OFr. < OItal. *credito* < Lat. *creditum,* loan < *credere,* to entrust.]

cred·it·a·ble (krĕd'ĭ-tə-bəl) *adj.* **1.** Deserving of praise or commendation. **2.** Worthy of belief. **3.** Deserving of commercial credit. **4.** Capable of being assigned. —**cred'it·a·bil'i·ty, cred'it·a·ble·ness** *n.* —**cred'it·a·bly** *adv.*

credit bureau *n.* An organization to which business firms apply for credit information on prospective customers.

credit card *n.* A card authorizing the holder to buy goods or services on credit.

credit line *n.* **1.** A line of copy acknowledging the source or origin of a news dispatch, published article, motion picture, or other work. **2.** The maximum amount of credit to be extended to a customer.

cred·i·tor (krĕd'ĭ-tər) *n.* A person or firm to whom money or its equivalent is owed.

credit rating *n.* An estimate of the amount of credit that can be extended to a company or individual without undue risk.

credit union *n.* A cooperative organization that makes loans to its members at low interest rates.

cred·it·wor·thy (krĕd'ĭt-wûr'*th*ē) *adj.* Having an acceptable credit rating. —**cred'it·wor'thi·ness** *n.*

cre·do (krē'dō, krā'-) *n., pl.* **-dos.** Creed. [Lat., I believe (the first word of the Apostles' Creed) < *credere,* to believe.]

cre·du·li·ty (krĭ-dōō'lĭ-tē, -dyōō'-) *n.* A disposition to believe too readily; gullibility. [ME *credulite* < OFr. < Lat. *credulitas* < *credulus,* credulous.]

cred·u·lous (krĕj'ə-ləs) *adj.* **1.** Disposed to believe too readily; gullible. **2.** Arising from or characterized by credulity. [Lat. *credulus* < *credere,* to believe.] —**cred'u·lous·ly** *adv.* —**cred'u·lous·ness** *n.*

Cree (krē) *n., pl.* **Cree** or **Crees. 1. a.** A tribe of Indians formerly living in Ontario, Manitoba, and Saskatchewan. **b.** A member of this tribe. **2.** The Algonquian language of the Cree.

creed (krēd) *n.* **1.** A formal statement of religious belief; confession of faith. **2.** A system of belief, principles, or opinions. [ME *crede* < OE *creda* < Lat. *credo,* I believe. —see CREDO.] —**creed'al** (krēd'l) *adj.*

creek (krēk, krĭk) *n.* **1.** A small stream, often a shallow or intermittent tributary to a river. **2.** *Chiefly Brit.* A small inlet in a shoreline. —***idiom.*** **up the creek.** *Informal.* In a difficult or unfortunate position. [ME *creke,* prob. < ON *kriki,* bend.]

Creek (krēk) *n., pl.* **Creek** or **Creeks. 1. a.** A confederacy of several Indian tribes, formerly inhabiting parts of Georgia,

Alabama, and northern Florida. **b.** A member of any of these tribes. **2.** The Muskhogean language of the Creek.

creel (krēl) *n.* **1.** A wicker basket, esp. one used by anglers for carrying fish. **2.** A frame for holding bobbins or spools in a spinning machine. [ME *crelle.*]

creep (krēp) *intr.v.* **crept** (krĕpt), **creep·ing, creeps. 1.** To move with the body close to the ground, as a baby on hands and knees. **2. a.** To move stealthily or cautiously. **b.** To move or proceed very slowly. **3.** *Bot.* To grow along a surface, rooting at intervals or clinging by means of suckers or tendrils. **4.** To slip out of place; shift gradually. **5.** To have a tingling sensation: *made my flesh creep.* —*n.* **1.** The action of creeping; a creeping motion or progress. **2.** *Slang.* An obnoxious or insignificant person. **3.** A slow flow of metal when under high temperature or great pressure. **4.** *Geol.* The slow movement of rock debris and soil down a weathered slope. **5. creeps.** *Informal.* A sensation of fear or repugnance, as if things were crawling on one's skin. [ME *crepen* < OE *crēopan.*]

creep·er (krē'pər) *n.* **1.** One that creeps. **2.** *Bot.* A plant having stems that grow along a surface, either rooting at intervals or clinging for support. **3.** A grappling device for dragging lakes and similar bodies of water. **4. creepers.** A metal frame with spikes, attached to a shoe or boot to prevent slipping.

creep·ing (krē'pĭng) *adj.* Developing gradually over a period of time: *creeping insanity.*

creeping Char·lie (chär'lē) *n.* Moneywort.

creeping eruption *n.* A skin disease caused by larvae burrowing and creeping beneath the skin and characterized by eruptions in the form of reddish lines.

creeping Jen·nie also **creeping Jen·ny** (jĕn'ē) *n.* Moneywort.

creeping myrtle *n.* Periwinkle[2].

creep·y (krē'pē) *adj.* **-i·er, -i·est.** *Informal.* Inducing or having a sensation of repugnance or fear, as of things crawling on one's skin: *a creepy story.* **—creep'i·ness** *n.*

creese (krēs) *n.*. Variant of **kris.**

cre·mains (krĭ-mānz') *pl.n.* The ashes that remain after cremation of a corpse. [Blend of CREMATED and REMAINS.]

cre·mate (krē'māt', krĭ-māt') *tr.v.* **-mat·ed, -mat·ing, -mates.** To incinerate (a corpse). [Lat. *cremare, cremat-.*] **—cre·ma'tion** (krĭ-mā'shən) *n.* **—cre·ma'tor** *n.*

cre·ma·to·ri·um (krē'mə-tôr'ē-əm, -tōr'-) *n., pl.* **-to·ri·ums** or **-to·ri·a** (-tôr'ē-ə, -tōr'-). A crematory.

cre·ma·to·ry (krē'mə-tôr'ē, -tōr'ē, krĕm'ə-) *n., pl.* **-ries.** A furnace or establishment for the cremation of corpses. —*adj.* Of or pertaining to cremation. [NLat. *crematorium* < Lat. *cremare,* to cremate.]

crème de ca·cao (krĕm' də kə-kou', kə-kā'ō) *n.* A sweet liqueur with a chocolate flavor. [Fr. : *crème,* cream + *de,* of + *cacao,* cacao.]

crème de la crème (krĕm' də lä krĕm') *n.* **1.** Something that is superlative. **2.** People of the highest social level. [Fr. : *crème,* cream + *de,* of + *la,* the + *crème,* cream.]

crème de menthe (krĕm' də mäɴᴛ') *n.* A sweet green or white liqueur flavored with mint. [Fr. : *crème,* cream + *de,* of + *menthe,* mint.]

cre·nate (krē'nāt') also **cre·nat·ed** (-nā'tĭd) *adj. Biol.* Having a margin with rounded or scalloped projections: *a crenate leaf.* [NLat. *crenatus* < Med. Lat. *crena,* notch.] **—cre'nate'ly** *adv.*

cre·na·tion (krĭ-nā'shən) *n.* **1.** A rounded projection; crenature. **2.** The condition or fact of being crenate.

cren·a·ture (krĕn'ə-chər, krē'nə-) *n.* **1.** A crenation. **2.** A notch between crenations, as on a leaf.

cren·e·lat·ed also **cren·el·lat·ed** (krĕn'ə-lā'tĭd) *adj.* Having battlements. [< Fr. *crenel,* crenelation < OFr., poss. < Med. Lat. *crena,* notch.] **—cren'e·la'tion** *n.*

cren·u·late (krĕn'yə-lĭt, -lāt') also **cren·u·lat·ed** (-lā'tĭd) *adj.* Having minutely notched or scalloped projections. [NLat. *crenulatus* < *crenula,* dim. of Med. Lat. *crena,* notch.] **—cren'u·la'tion** *n.*

cre·o·dont (krē'ə-dŏnt') *n.* Any of various extinct carnivorous mammals of the suborder Creodonta, of the Paleocene to Pliocene epochs. [NLat. *Creodonta,* suborder name : Gk., *kreas,* flesh + Gk. *odous, odont,* tooth.]

Cre·ole (krē'ōl') *n.* **1.** A person of European descent born in the West Indies or Spanish America. **2. a.** A person descended from or culturally related to the original French settlers of the southern United States, esp. Louisiana. **b.** The French dialect spoken by these people. **3.** A person descended from or culturally related to the Spanish and Portuguese settlers of the Gulf States. **4.** A person of mixed European and Negro ancestry who speaks a Creole dialect. **5. creole.** A creolized language. **6.** Haitian Creole. —*adj.* **1.** Of, relating to, or characteristic of the Creoles. **2. creole.** Cooked with a spicy sauce containing tomatoes, onions, and peppers. [Fr. *créole* < Sp. *criollo* < Port. *crioulo,* prob. < *criar,* to bring up < Lat. *creare,* to beget.]

cre·o·lized language (krē'ə-līzd') *n.* A type of mixed language that develops when dominant and subordinate groups that speak different languages have prolonged contact, incorporating the basic vocabulary of the dominant language with the grammar and an admixture of words from the subordinate language and becoming the native tongue of the subordinate group.

Cre·on (krē'ŏn') *n. Gk. Myth.* King of Thebes, successor to Oedipus.

cre·o·sol (krē'ə-sôl', -sōl') *n.* A colorless to yellow aromatic liquid, $C_8H_{10}O_2$, that is a constituent of creosote and is obtained from beechwood tar. [CREOS(OTE) + -OL[1].]

cre·o·sote (krē'ə-sōt') *n.* **1.** A colorless to yellowish oily liquid obtained by the destructive distillation of wood tar, esp. from beechwood, and formerly used to treat tuberculosis and chronic bronchitis. **2.** A yellowish to greenish-brown oily liquid obtained from coal tar and used as a wood preservative and disinfectant. —*tr.v.* **-sot·ed, -sot·ing, -sotes.** To treat or paint with creosote. [G. *Kreosot* : Gk. *kreas,* flesh + Gk. *sōtēr, preserver* < *sōzein,* to save < *saos,* safe, from its antiseptic properties.]

creosote bush *n.* A resinous shrub, *Larrea tridentata,* of the western United States and Mexico, exuding an odor like that of creosote.

crepe also **crêpe** (krāp) *n.* **1.** A light, soft, thin fabric of silk, cotton, wool, or another fiber, with a crinkled surface. **2.** Crape (sense 2). **3.** Crepe paper. **4.** Crepe rubber. **5.** A very thin pancake. [Fr. *crêpe* < OFr. *crespe,* curly < Lat. *crispus.*]

crêpe de Chine (krāp' də shēn') *n.* A silk crepe used for women's dresses and blouses. [Fr. : *crêpe,* crepe + *de,* of + *Chine,* China.]

crepe myrtle *n.* Variant of **crape myrtle.**

crepe paper *n.* Crinkled tissue paper, resembling crepe, used for decorations.

crepe rubber *n.* Rubber with a crinkled texture, used esp. for shoe soles.

crêpe su·zette (krāp' so͞o-zĕt') *n., pl.* **crêpe su·zettes** or **crêpes su·zettes** (krāp' so͞o-zĕt'). A thin dessert pancake usually rolled with hot orange or tangerine sauce and often served with a flaming brandy or curaçao sauce. [Fr. : *crêpe,* pancake + *Suzette,* Suzy.]

crep·i·tate (krĕp'ĭ-tāt') *intr.v.* **-tat·ed, -tat·ing, -tates.** To make a creaking or rattling sound; crackle. [Lat. *crepitare, crepitat-,* to crackle, freq. of *crepare,* to creak.] **—crep'i·tant** (-tənt) *adj.* **—crep'i·ta'tion** *n.*

crept (krĕpt) *v.* Past tense and past participle of **creep.**

cre·pus·cu·lar (krĭ-pŭs'kyə-lər) *adj.* **1.** Of or like twilight; dim. **2.** *Zool.* Becoming active at twilight or before sunrise, as do certain insects and birds.

cre·pus·cule (krĭ-pŭs'kyo͞ol) also **cre·pus·cle** (-pŭs'əl) *n.* Twilight. [Lat. *crepusculum* < *creper,* dark.]

cres·cen·do (krə-shĕn'dō) *n., pl.* **-dos** or **-di** (-dē). **1.** A gradual increase, esp. in the volume or intensity of sound in a musical passage. **2.** A musical passage played in a crescendo. —*adj.* Gradually increasing in volume or intensity. —*adv.* With a crescendo. [Ital. < *crescere,* to increase < Lat.]

cres·cent (krĕs'ənt) *n.* **1.** The figure of the moon as it appears in its first quarter, with concave and convex edges terminating in points. **2.** Something shaped like a crescent. —*adj.* **1.** Crescent-shaped. **2.** Increasing; waxing, as the moon. [ME *cressant* < OFr. *creissant* < pr.part. of *creistre,* to grow < Lat. *crescere.*] **—cres·cen'tic** (krə-sĕn'tĭk) *adj.*

cre·sol (krē'sôl', -sōl') *n.* Any of three isomeric phenols, C_7H_8O, used in resins and as a disinfectant. [Alteration of CREOSOL.]

cress (krĕs) *n.* Any of various related plants, such as those of the genera *Cardamine* and *Arabis,* having pungent leaves often used in salads and as a garnish. [ME *cresse* < OE.]

cres·set (krĕs'ĭt) *n.* A metal cup, often suspended on a pole, containing burning oil or pitch and used as a torch. [ME < OFr. *craisset* < *craisse,* grease < VLat. *crassia* < Lat. *crassus,* fat, thick.]

Cres·si·da (krĕs'ĭ-də) *n.* In medieval romances, a Trojan woman who first returns the love of Troilus but later forsakes him for Diomedes.

crest (krĕst) *n.* **1.** A tuft, ridge, or similar projection on the head of a bird or other animal. **2. a.** A plume used as decoration on top of a helmet. **b.** A helmet. **3. a.** A heraldic device placed above the shield on a coat of arms. **b.** A representation of a heraldic crest. **4. a.** The top of something, as a mountain or wave; peak; summit. **b.** The highest point of a process or action: *the crest of his career.* **5.** The ridge on a roof. —*v.* **crest·ed, crest·ing, crests.** —*tr.* **1.** To decorate or furnish with a crest. **2.** To reach the crest of. —*intr.* To form into a crest, as a wave. [ME *creste* < OFr. < Lat. *crista.*]

crest·fall·en (krĕst'fô'lən) *adj.* Feeling dejected; dispirited; depressed. **—crest'fall'en·ly** *adv.* **—crest'fall'en·ness** *n.*

crest·ing (krĕs'tĭng) *n.* An ornamental ridge, as on top of a wall or roof.

cre·syl (krē'sĭl') *n.* Tolyl. [CRESO(L) + -YL.]

cre·syl·ic (krĭ-sĭl'ĭk) *adj. Chem.* Of or pertaining to creosote or cresol. [CRES(OL) + -YL + -IC.]

Cre·ta·ceous (krĭ-tā'shəs) *adj.* **1.** Of, belonging to, or designating the geologic time, system of rocks, and sedimentary deposits of the third and last period of the Mesozoic era, characterized by the development of flowering plants and the disappearance of dinosaurs. **2. cretaceous.** Of, containing, or resembling chalk. —*n. Geol.* The Cretaceous period.

creel

crenate
A crenate leaf

crescent

crest
On a bird

[Lat. *cretaceus* : *creta,* chalk < *Creta (terra),* Cretan (earth).] **—cre·ta'ceous·ly** *adv.*
Cret·an mullein (krēt'n) *n.* A plant, *Celsia cretica,* native to the Mediterranean region, having hairy foliage and yellow flowers splotched with purple.
cre·tin (krēt'n) *n.* **1.** One afflicted with cretinism. **2.** An idiot. [Fr. *crétin* < Swiss Fr. *crestin,* Christian, deformed idiot < *Christianus,* Christian. —see CHRISTIAN.] **—cre'tin·oid'** (-oid') *adj.* **—cre'tin·ous** (-əs) *adj.*
cre·tin·ism (krēt'n-ĭz'əm) *n.* Myxedema.
cre·tonne (krĭ-tŏn', krē'tŏn') *n.* A heavy unglazed cotton, linen, or rayon fabric, colorfully printed and used for draperies and slipcovers. [After *Creton,* France.]
Cre·ü·sa (krē-o͞o'zə). *n. Gk. Myth.* **1.** The bride of Jason, killed by Medea. **2.** The daughter of Priam and wife of Aeneas, lost in the flight from Troy. [Gk. *Kreousa.*]
cre·val·le (krĭ-văl'ē,) *n.* A food and game fish, *Caranx hippo,* of warm seas, having a laterally compressed silvery body. [Alteration of CAVALLA.]
crevalle jack *n.* The crevalle.
cre·vasse (krĭ-văs') *n.* **1.** A deep fissure, as in a glacier; chasm. **2.** A crack in a dike or levee. *—tr.v.* **-vassed, -vass·ing, -vass·es.** To make crevasses in; fissure. [Fr. < OFr. *crevace,* crevice.]
crev·ice (krĕv'ĭs) *n.* A narrow crack or opening; fissure; cleft. [ME < OFr. *crevace* < *crever,* to split < Lat. *crepare,* to crack.] **—crev'iced** *adj.*
crew[1] (kro͞o) *n.* **1. a.** A group of people working together; gang: *a crew of stage hands.* **b.** A group of people gathered together temporarily; crowd. **2. a.** All personnel manning a ship. **b.** All of a ship's personnel except the officers. **c.** All personnel manning an aircraft in flight. **d.** A team of oarsmen. *—intr.v* **crewed, crew·ing, crews.** To serve as a member of a crew. [ME *creue,* military reinforcement < OFr. *creue,* increase < *creistre,* to grow < Lat. *crescere.*]
crew[2] (kro͞o) *v.* A past tense of **crow[2]** (sense 1).
crew cut *n.* A close-cropped man's haircut. [So called because it was worn by oarsmen.]
crew·el (kro͞o'əl) *n.* Loosely twisted worsted yarn used for fancywork and embroidery. [ME *crule.*]

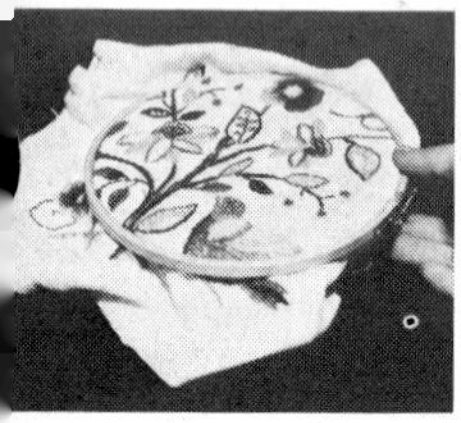

crewel
Crewel embroidery

crew neck *n.* A round close-fitting neckline, as on a sweater. [From the wearing of similarly-styled sweaters by oarsmen.]
crew sock *n.* A warm usually ribbed sock. [From its use by oarsmen.]
crib (krĭb) *n.* **1.** A child's bed with high sides. **2.** A small building, usually with slatted sides, for storing corn. **3.** A rack or trough for fodder; manger. **4.** A stall for cattle. **5.** A small, crude cottage or room. **6.** A framework to support or strengthen a mine or shaft. **7.** A wicker basket. **8.** *Informal.* **a.** A petty theft. **b.** Plagiarism. **c.** A pony (sense 4). **9.** A set of cards made up from discards by each player in cribbage, used by the dealer. *—v.* **cribbed, crib·bing, cribs.** *—tr.* **1.** To confine in or as if in a crib. **2.** To furnish with a crib. **3.** *Informal.* **a.** To plagiarize. **b.** To steal. *—intr. Informal.* To use a crib in examinations; cheat. [ME < OE *cribb,* manger.] **—crib'ber** *n.*
crib·bage (krĭb'ĭj) *n.* A card game for from two to four players in which the score is kept by inserting small pegs into holes arranged in rows on a small board. [< CRIB.]
crib·bing (krĭb'ĭng) *n.* A supporting framework, as of timber lining a shaft.
crib-bit·ing (krĭb'bī'tĭng) *n.* An injurious habit of horses of biting at the edge of a feed trough or other object and swallowing air at the same time.
crib death *n.* Sudden infant death syndrome.
crib·ri·form (krĭb'rə-fôrm') *adj.* Perforated like a sieve. [Lat. *cribrum,* sieve + -FORM.]
crib·work (krĭb'wûrk') *n.* A structural framework made of logs stacked one above the other, with the logs in each layer at right angles to those in the layer below.
cri·ce·tid (krĭ-sē'tĭd, -sĕt'ĭd) *n.* Any of various small rodents of the family Cricetidae, that includes muskrats and gerbils. [NLat. *Cricetidae,* family name < *Cricetus,* hamster genus, of Slav. orig.] **—cri·ce'tid** *adj.*

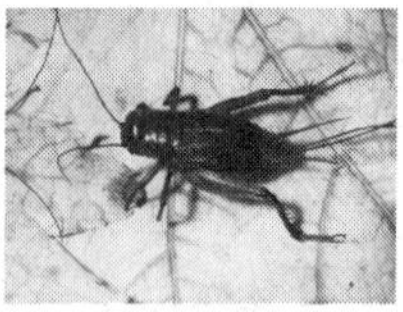

cricket[1]
Common field cricket

crick[1] (krĭk) *n.* A painful cramp or muscle spasm, as in the back or neck. *—tr.v.* **cricked, crick·ing, cricks.** To cause a crick in by turning or wrenching. [ME *crike.*]
crick[2] (krĭk) *n. Regional.* A creek.
crick·et[1] (krĭk'ĭt) *n.* Any of various insects of the family Gryllidae, having long antennae and legs adapted for leaping. The males of many species produce a shrill, chirping sound by rubbing the front wings together. [ME *criket* < OFr. *criquet* < *criquer,* to click.]
crick·et[2] (krĭk'ĭt) *n.* **1.** An outdoor game played with bats, a ball, and wickets by 2 teams of 11 players each. **2.** Good sportsmanship and fair conduct: *It's not cricket to cheat at cards.* *—intr.v.* **-et·ed, -et·ing, -ets.** To play cricket. [Poss. < OFr. *criquet,* target stick in a bowling game.] **—crick'et·er** *n.*
crick·et[3] (krĭk'ĭt) *n.* A small, low wooden footstool. [Orig. unknown.]
cri·coid (krī'koid') *n.* A ring-shaped cartilage of the lower larynx. [Gk. *krikoeidēs,* ring-shaped : *krikos,* ring + *-eidēs,* -oid.]
cried (krīd) *v.* Past tense and past participle of **cry.**
cri·er (krī'ər) *n.* **1.** A person who cries. **2.** A person who shouts out public announcements. **3.** A hawker.

cricket[2]

cries (krīz) *v.* Third person singular present tense of **cry.** *—n.* Plural of **cry.**
crime (krīm) *n.* **1.** An act committed or omitted in violation of a law forbidding or commanding it and for which punishment is imposed upon conviction. **2.** Unlawful activity: *Crime is on the rise.* **3.** A serious offense, esp. one in violation of morality. **4.** An unjust, senseless, or disgraceful act or condition. [ME < OFr. < Lat. *crimen.*]
crim·i·nal (krĭm'ə-nəl) *adj.* **1.** Of, involving, or having the nature of crime. **2.** Pertaining to the administration of penal law as distinguished from civil law. **3.** Guilty of crime. **4.** Shameful; disgraceful. *—n.* A person who has committed or been legally convicted of a crime. [ME < OFr. *criminel* < LLat. *criminalis* < Lat. *crimen,* accusation.] **—crim'i·nal·ly** *adv.*
criminal conversation *n. Law.* Adultery.
crim·i·nal·i·ty (krĭm'ə-năl'ĭ-tē) *n., pl.* **-ties. 1.** The state, quality, or fact of being criminal. **2.** A criminal action or practice.
crim·i·nal·ize (krĭm'ə-nə-līz') *tr.v.* **-ized, -iz·ing, -iz·es.** To impose a criminal penalty on or for; treat as criminal.
criminal law *n.* Law that deals with crime and its punishment.
crim·i·nate (krĭm'ə-nāt') *tr.v.* **-nat·ed, -nat·ing, -nates. 1.** To implicate in a crime; incriminate. **2.** To charge with a crime; accuse. **3.** To condemn as criminal; censure. [Lat. *criminari, criminat-,* to accuse < *crimen,* accusation.] **—crim'i·na'tion** *n.* **—crim'i·na'tive, crim'i·na·to'ry** (-nə-tôr'ē, -tōr'ē) *adj.* **—crim'i·na'tor** *n.*
crim·i·nol·o·gy (krĭm'ə-nŏl'ə-jē) *n.* The study of crime, criminals, and criminal behavior. [Ital. *criminologia* : Lat. *crimen,* accusation + *-logia,* -logy.] **—crim'i·no·log'i·cal** (-nə-lŏj'ĭ-kəl) *adj.* **—crim'i·no·log'i·cal·ly** *adv.* **—crim'i·nol'o·gist** *n.*
crimp[1] (krĭmp) *tr.v.* **crimped, crimp·ing, crimps. 1.** To press or pinch into small, regular folds or ridges. **2.** To bend or mold (leather) into shape. **3.** To cause (hair) to form tight curls or waves. **4.** To obstruct; hamper. *—n.* **1.** The act of crimping. **2.** Something that has been crimped, esp.: **a.** Hair that has been tightly curled or waved. **b.** A series of curls, as of wool fibers. **3.** Something that obstructs or hampers: *The blizzard put a crimp in surface traffic.* [ME *crimpen,* to wrinkle, prob. < LG *krimpen.*] **—crimp'er** *n.*
crimp[2] (krĭmp) *n.* A person who procures men to serve as sailors or soldiers by tricking or coercing them. *—tr.v.* **crimped, crimp·ing, crimps.** To procure (sailors or soldiers) by trickery or coercion. [Orig. unknown.]
crimp·y (krĭm'pē) *adj.* **-i·er, -i·est.** Full of crimps; wavy. **—crimp'i·ness** *n.*
crim·son (krĭm'zən) *n.* A deep to vivid purplish red to vivid red. *—tr. & intr.v.* **-soned, -son·ing, -sons.** To make or become crimson. [ME *cremesin* < OSp. < Ar. *qirmizī* < *quirmiz,* kermes insect.] **—crim'son** *adj.*
cringe (krĭnj) *intr.v.* **cringed, cring·ing, cring·es. 1.** To shrink back, as in fear; cower. **2.** To behave in a servile manner; fawn. *—n.* An act or instance of cringing. [ME *crengen,* prob. ult. < OE *cringan.*]
crin·gle (krĭng'gəl) *n.* A small ring or grommet of rope or metal fastened to the edge of a sail. [LG *kringel,* dim. of *kring,* ring < MLG.]
cri·nite (krī'nīt') *adj. Biol.* Hairy or having hairlike tufts. [Lat. *crinitus,* p.part. of *crinire,* to cover with hair < *crinis,* hair.]
crin·kle (krĭng'kəl) *v.* **-kled, -kling, -kles.** *—intr.* **1.** To form into wrinkles or ripples. **2.** To make a soft, crackling sound; rustle. *—tr.* To cause to crinkle. *—n.* A wrinkle or ripple; fold. [ME *crinkelen.*] **—crin'kly** *adj.*
crin·kle·root (krĭng'kəl-ro͞ot', -ro͝ot') *n.* A woodland plant, *Dentaria diphylla,* of eastern North America, having fleshy rootstocks and clusters of white or pinkish flowers.
cri·noid (krī'noid') *n.* Any of various marine invertebrates of the class Crinoidea, including the sea lilies and feather stars, characterized by feathery, radiating arms and a stalk by which they are attached to a surface. [NLat. *Crinoidea,* class name : Gk. *krinon,* lily + -OID.]
crin·o·line (krĭn'ə-lĭn) *n.* **1.** A coarse, stiff fabric of cotton or horsehair used esp. to line and stiffen garments. **2.** A petticoat made of crinoline. **3.** A hoop skirt. [Fr. < Ital. *crinolino* : *crino,* horsehair (< Lat. *crinis,* hair) + *lino,* flax (< Lat. *linum*).]
cri·num (krī'nəm) *n.* Any of several mostly tropical plants of the genus *Crinum,* having long, strap-shaped leaves and clusters of lilylike flowers. [NLat. *Crinum,* genus name < Gk. *krinon,* lily.]
crinum lily *n.* A crinum.
cri·o·sphinx (krī'ə-sfĭngks') *n.* A sphinx with the head of a ram. [Gk. *krios,* ram + SPHINX.]
crip·ple (krĭp'əl) *n.* **1.** One who is partly disabled or lame. **2.** Something that is damaged or defective. *—tr.v.* **-pled, -pling, -ples. 1.** To make into a cripple. **2.** To disable or damage. [ME *crepel* < OE *crypel.*] **—crip'pler** *n.*
cri·sis (krī'sĭs) *n., pl.* **-ses** (-sēz'). **1. a.** A crucial or decisive point or situation; turning point. **b.** An unstable condition in political, international, or economic affairs in which an abrupt or decisive change is impending. **2.** A sudden change in the course of an acute disease, either toward improve-

ment or deterioration. **3.** The point in a story or drama at which hostile forces are in the most tense state of opposition. [Lat. < Gk. < *krinein,* to separate.]

crisis center *n.* A center staffed esp. by volunteers who counsel individuals experiencing a personal crisis.

crisis management *n.* Special measures taken to solve problems caused by a crisis.

crisp (krĭsp) *adj.* **-er, -est. 1.** Firm but easily broken or crumbled; brittle. **2.** Firm and fresh: *crisp celery.* **3.** Brisk; invigorating: *crisp autumn air.* **4.** Animated; stimulating. **5.** Having small curls, waves, or ripples. *—tr. & intr.v.* **crisped, crisp·ing, crisps.** To make or become crisp. *—n. Chiefly Brit.* A potato chip. [ME, curly < OE < Lat. *crispus.*] **—crisp′ly** *adv.* **—crisp′ness** *n.*

cris·pate (krĭs′pāt′) also **cris·pat·ed** (-pā′tĭd) *adj.* Crimped, curled, or tightly waved. [Lat. *crispatus* < *crispare,* to curl < *crispus,* curly.]

cris·pa·tion (krĭs-pā′shən) *n.* **1. a.** The act of crisping or curling. **b.** The state of being crisped or curled. **2.** A slight involuntary contraction or constriction, as of the skin.

crisp·er (krĭs′pər) *n.* One that crisps, esp. a compartment in a refrigerator used for storing vegetables and keeping them fresh.

crisp·y (krĭs′pē) *adj.* **-i·er, -i·est.** Crisp. **—crisp′i·ness** *n.*

cris·sa (krĭs′ə) *n.* Plural of **crissum.**

criss·cross (krĭs′krôs′, -krŏs′) *v.* **-crossed, -cross·ing, -cross·es.** *—tr.* **1.** To mark with crossing lines. **2.** To move crosswise through or over. *—intr.* To move crosswise. *—n.* A mark or pattern made of crossing lines. *—adj.* Crossing one another or marked by crossings. *—adv.* In a crisscross manner or direction. [Alteration of obs. *christcross,* mark of a cross.]

cris·sum (krĭs′əm) *n., pl.* **cris·sa** (krĭs′ə). *Zool.* The feathers or area surrounding a bird's cloacal opening. [NLat. < Lat. *crissare,* to move the buttocks during intercourse.] **—cris′sal** (-əl) *adj.*

cris·ta (krĭs′tə) *n., pl.* **-tae** (-tē). *Biol.* **1.** A crest or ridge. **2.** One of the inward projections of the inner mitochondrial membrane. [NLat., crest.]

cris·tate (krĭs′tāt′) also **cris·tat·ed** (-tā′tĭd) *adj.* Having or forming a crest. [Lat. *cristatus* < *crista,* tuft.]

cri·te·ri·on (krī-tîr′ē-ən) *n., pl.* **-te·ri·a** (-tîr′ē-ə) or **-te·ri·ons.** A standard, rule, or test on which a judgment or decision can be based. [Gk. *kritērion* < *kritēs,* judge < *krinein,* to separate.] **—cri·te′ri·al** (-əl) *adj.*

Usage: *Criteria* is a plural form only. It should not be substituted for the singular *criterion.*

crit·ic (krĭt′ĭk) *n.* **1.** One who forms and expresses judgments of the merits, faults, value or truth of a matter. **2.** A specialist in the judgment of the worth of literary or artistic works, esp. one who does this as a profession. **3.** A person who finds fault; a severe judge. [Lat. *criticus* < Gk. *kritikos,* able to discern < *krinein,* to separate.]

crit·i·cal (krĭt′ĭ-kəl) *adj.* **1.** Inclined to judge severely and adversely. **2.** Characterized by careful and exact evaluation and judgment: *a critical reading.* **3.** Of, pertaining to, or characteristic of critics or criticism: *critical writings on Milton.* **4.** Forming or having the nature of a crisis; crucial: *a critical point in the campaign.* **5.** Designating materials and products essential to a condition or project but in short supply. **6.** *Med.* Of or pertaining to a crisis. **7.** *Math.* Of or pertaining to a point at which a curve has a maximum, minimum, or point of inflection. **8.** *Chem. & Physics.* Of or pertaining to a condition causing an abrupt change in a quality, property, or phenomenon. **9.** Of sufficient mass to sustain a nuclear chain reaction. **—crit′i·cal·ly** *adv.* **—crit′i·cal·ness** *n.*

critical angle *n.* **1.** The smallest angle of incidence at which a light ray passing from one medium to another less refractive medium can be totally reflected from the boundary between the two. **2.** The angle of attack of an airfoil at which airflow abruptly changes, causing changes in the lift and drag of an aircraft.

critical mass *n.* The smallest mass of a fissionable material that will sustain a nuclear chain reaction.

critical point *n.* **1.** *Physics.* The condition in which the liquid and vapor phases of a pure stable substance have the same density. **2.** *Math.* **a.** A maximum, minimum, or point of inflection. **b.** A point at which the derivative of a function is zero or infinite.

critical pressure *n.* The least applied pressure required at the critical temperature to liquefy a gas.

critical state *n.* Critical point (sense 1).

critical temperature *n.* The temperature above which a gas cannot be liquefied, regardless of the pressure applied.

crit·ic·as·ter (krĭt′ĭ-kăs′tər) *n.* A petty or inferior critic. [CRITIC + Lat. *-aster,* pejorative suffix.]

crit·i·cism (krĭt′ĭ-sĭz′əm) *n.* **1.** The act of criticizing, esp. adversely. **2.** A critical comment or judgment. **3. a.** The art, skill, or profession of making discriminating judgments and evaluations, esp. of literary or other artistic works. **b.** A review or other article expressing such judgment and evaluation. **4.** The detailed investigation of the origin and history of literary documents.

crit·i·cize (krĭt′ĭ-sīz′) *v.* **-cized, -ciz·ing, -ciz·es.** *—tr.* **1.** To judge the merits and faults of; analyze and evaluate. **2.** To judge with severity; find fault with. *—intr.* To act as a critic. **—crit′i·ciz′a·ble** *adj.* **—crit′i·ciz′er** *n.*

Synonyms: *criticize, blame, reprehend, censure, condemn, denounce.* These verbs are compared as they mean to express an unfavorable judgment. *Criticize,* the least specific, can mean merely to evaluate without necessarily finding fault, but usually it does imply detailed expression of disapproval. *Blame* emphasizes the finding of fault and the fixing of responsibility for it. *Reprehend* implies sharp disapproval, usually of the actions or attributes of a person. *Censure* refers to open and strong expression of disapproval; often it implies a reprimand, or formal criticism, of a person or persons by someone in authority. *Condemn* can refer broadly to any expression of severe disapproval or, more narrowly, to an official act of passing judgment, such as sentencing by a court. *Denounce* can apply to any strongly adverse judgment expressed openly and vehemently, or specifically to public proclamation of official criticism or repudiation.

cri·tique (krĭ-tēk′) *n.* **1.** A critical review or commentary, esp. one dealing with a literary or other artistic work. **2.** A critical discussion of a specified topic. **3.** The art of criticism. *—tr.v.* **-tiqued, -tiqu·ing, -tiques.** To criticize. [Fr. < Gk. *kritikē,* the art of criticism < *kritikos,* critical < *krinein,* to separate.]

Usage: *Critique* is widely used as a verb, but is still regarded by many as pretentious jargon. The use of phrases like *give a critique* or *offer a critique* will forestall objections.

crit·ter (krĭt′ər) *n. Regional.* **1.** A domestic animal, esp. a steer or horse. **2.** A living creature. [Alteration of CREATURE.]

croak (krōk) *n.* A low, hoarse sound, as that characteristic of frogs and crows. *—v.* **croaked, croak·ing, croaks.** *—tr.* **1.** To utter by croaking. **2.** *Slang.* To kill. *—intr.* **1.** To utter a croak. **2.** To speak with a low, hoarse voice. **3.** To mutter discontentedly; grumble. **4.** *Slang.* To die. [< ME *croken,* to croak.] **—croak′i·ly** *adv.* **—croak′y** *adj.*

croak·er (krō′kər) *n.* **1. a.** A croaking animal. **b.** A person who grumbles or habitually predicts evil. **2.** Any of various chiefly marine fishes of the family Sciaenidae that make croaking or grunting sounds.

Croat (krōt, krō′ăt′) *n.* **1.** A Slavic native or inhabitant of Croatia. **2.** Serbo-Croatian as used in Croatia, distinguished from Serbian primarily by its being written in the Latin alphabet. [NLat. *Croata* < Serbo-Croatian *Hrvat.*] **—Cro·a′tian** (krō-ā′shən) *n. & adj.*

cro·ce·in (krō′sē-ĭn) *n.* Any of various red or orange acid azo dyes. [Lat. *croceus,* saffron-colored (< *crocus,* saffron) + -IN.]

cro·chet (krō-shā′) *v.* **-cheted** (-shād′), **-chet·ing** (-shā′ĭng), **-chets** (-shāz′). *—intr.* To make a piece of needlework by looping thread with a hooked needle. *—tr.* To make by looping thread with a hooked needle. *—n.* Needlework made by crocheting. [< Fr., hook < OFr., dim. of *croc.*]

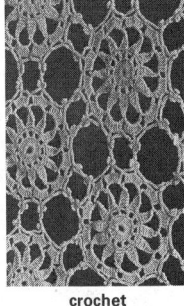

crochet

cro·cid·o·lite (krō-sĭd′l-īt′) *n.* A fibrous, lavender-blue or greenish mineral, a sodium iron silicate that is used as a commercial form of asbestos. [G. *Krokydolith* : Gk. *krokus,* nap of cloth + *-lith,* -lite.]

crock[1] (krŏk) *n.* **1.** An earthenware vessel. **2.** A broken piece of earthenware. [ME *crokke* < OE *crocc.*]

crock[2] (krŏk) *n. Chiefly Brit. Regional.* **1.** Soot. **2.** Coloring matter that rubs off from poorly dyed cloth. *—v.* **crocked, crock·ing, crocks.** *—tr.* To soil with or as if with crock. *—intr.* To give off soot or color. [Orig. unknown.]

crock[3] (krŏk) *n. Chiefly Brit.* One that is worn-out, decrepit, or impaired. *—intr.v.* **crocked, crock·ing, crocks.** *Chiefly Brit. Slang.* To become weak or disabled. [ME *crok,* prob. of Scand. orig.]

crocked (krŏkt) *adj. Slang.* Drunk. [Poss. < CROCK[3].]

crock·er·y (krŏk′ə-rē) *n.* Crocks collectively; earthenware.

crock·et (krŏk′ĭt) *n.* An ornamental device, usually in the form of a cusp or curling leaf, placed along outer angles of pinnacles and gables. [ME *croket* < ONFr. *croquet,* var. of OFr. *crochet,* hook. —see CROCHET.]

Crock·pot (krŏk′pŏt′). A trademark for an electric cooking pot.

croc·o·dile (krŏk′ə-dīl′) *n.* **1.** Any of various large aquatic reptiles of the genus *Crocodylus* and related genera, of tropical regions, having thick, armorlike skin and long, tapering jaws. **2.** A crocodilian reptile, such as an alligator, caiman, or gavial. **3.** Leather made from crocodile skin. [ME *cocodril* < OFr. < Med. Lat. *cocodrillus* < Lat. *crocodillus* < Gk. *krokodilos : krokē,* pebble + *drilos,* worm.]

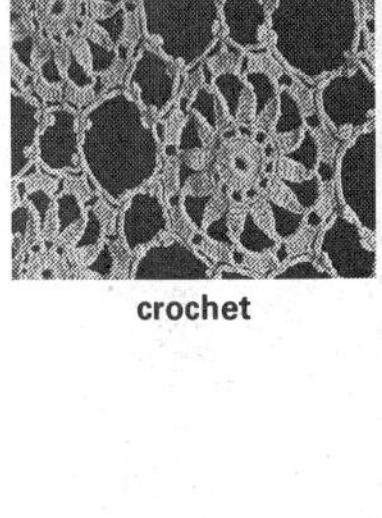

crocodile
Morlett's crocodile

crocodile bird *n.* A black and white African bird, *Pluvianus aegyptius,* that feeds on insects that infest crocodiles.

crocodile tears *pl.n.* False tears; an insincere display of grief. [From the belief that crocodiles weep after eating their victims.]

croc·o·dil·i·an (krŏk′ə-dĭl′ē-ən, -dĭl′yən) *n.* Any of various reptiles of the order Crocodylia, which includes the alligators, crocodiles, caimans, and gavials. *—adj.* **1.** Of or pertaining to a crocodile. **2.** Belonging to the order Crocodylia. [< NLat. *Crocodylia,* order name < Lat. *crocodilus,* crocodile.]

croc·oi·site (krŏk′wə-zīt′) *n.* Crocoite. [G. *Krokoisit* < Fr. *crocoise* < Gk. *krokoeis,* saffron-colored < *krokos,* saffron.]

crocus

croft

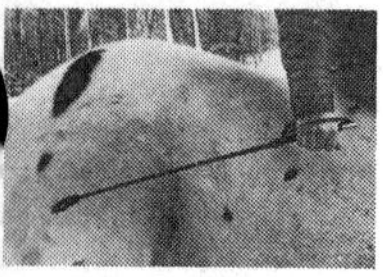
crop
A riding crop

crosier
12th-century Spanish crosier

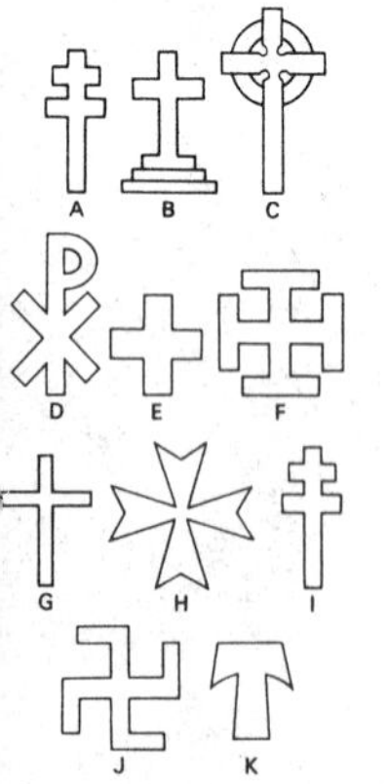

cross
A. Archiepiscopal cross
B. Calvary cross
C. Celtic cross
D. Chi-rho
E. Greek cross
F. Jerusalem cross
G. Latin cross
H. Maltese cross
I. Patriarchal cross
J. Swastika
K. Tau cross

croc·o·ite (krŏk′ō-īt′, krō′kō-) *n.* A rare orange to reddish mineral of lead chromate, $PbCrO_4$, found in oxidized lead deposits. [G. *Krokoit,* alteration of *Krokoisit,* crocoisite.]
cro·cus (krō′kəs) *n., pl.* **-cus·es** or **-ci** (-sī′). **1.** A plant of the genus *Crocus,* widely cultivated in gardens and having showy, variously colored flowers and grasslike leaves. **2.** A grayish to light reddish purple. **3.** A red variety of iron oxide, Fe_2O_3, used in the form of an abrasive powder for polishing. [Lat. < Gk. *krokos,* of Semitic orig.]
croft (krôft, krŏft) *n. Chiefly Brit. & Scot.* **1.** A small enclosed field or pasture near a house. **2.** A small farm, esp. a tenant farm. [ME < OE.]
croft·er (krôf′tər, krŏf′-) *n. Chiefly Brit. & Scot.* A person who rents and cultivates a croft; tenant farmer.
crois·sant (krwä-säN′) *n.* A rich, crescent-shaped roll of leavened dough or puff pastry. [Fr., crescent < OFr. *creissant.* —see CRESCENT.]
Croix de Guerre (krwä′ də gâr′) *n.* A French military decoration for bravery in battle. [Fr. : *croix,* cross + *de,* of + *guerre,* war.]
Cro-Mag·non (krō-măg′nən, -măn′yən) *n.* An early form of modern man, *Homo sapiens,* characterized by a rather robust physique and known from skeletal parts found in the Cro-Magnon cave in southern France. **—Cro-Mag′non** *adj.*
crom·lech (krŏm′lĕk′) *n.* **1.** A prehistoric monument consisting of monoliths encircling a mound. **2.** A dolmen. [Welsh : *crom,* fem. of *crwn,* arched + *llech,* stone.]
crone (krōn) *n.* A withered, witchlike old woman. [ME < ONFr. *carogne,* carrion < VLat. **caronia* < Lat. *caro,* flesh.]
Cro·nus (krō′nəs) *n. Gk. Myth.* A Titan who ruled the universe until dethroned by his son Zeus. [Gk. *Kronos.*]
cro·ny (krō′nē) *n., pl.* **-nies.** A close friend or companion. [Poss. < Gk. *khronios,* long lasting < *khronos,* time.]
cro·ny·ism (krō′nē-ĭz′əm) *n.* Favoritism shown to cronies without regard for their qualifications, as in political appointments to office.
crook (kro͝ok) *n.* **1.** Something bent or curved; hook or hooked part. **2.** An implement or tool, such as a bishop's crosier or a shepherd's staff, with a bent or curved part. **3.** A curve or bend; turn. **4.** *Informal.* A person who makes a living by dishonest methods; thief. *—tr. & intr.v.* **crooked, crook·ing, crooks.** To curve or become curved; bend. [ME *crok* < ON *krōkr,* hook.]
crook·back (kro͝ok′băk′) *n.* A hunchback. **—crook′backed′** *adj.*
crook·ed (kro͝ok′ĭd) *adj.* **1.** Having or marked by bends, curves, or angles. **2.** *Informal.* Dishonest or unscrupulous; fraudulent. **—crook′ed·ly** *adv.* **—crook′ed·ness** *n.*
Crookes tube (kro͝oks) *n.* A low-pressure discharge tube used to study the properties of cathode rays. [After Sir William *Crookes* (1832–1919).]
crook·neck (kro͝ok′nĕk′) *n.* A type of squash having a long, curved neck and yellow flesh.
croon (kro͞on) *v.* **crooned, croon·ing, croons.** *—intr.* **1.** To sing or hum softly. **2.** To sing popular songs in a soft, sentimental manner. **3.** *Chiefly Scot. & Brit. Regional.* To roar or bellow. *—tr.* To sing by crooning. *—n.* A soft singing or humming. [ME *croynen* < MDu. *kronen,* to lament.] **—croon′er** *n.*
crop (krŏp) *n.* **1. a.** Cultivated plants or agricultural produce, such as grain, vegetables, or fruit. **b.** The total yield of such produce in a particular season or place. **2.** A group, quantity, or supply appearing at one time: *a crop of new ideas.* **3.** A short haircut. **4.** An earmark on an animal. **5. a.** A short whip used in horseback riding, with a loop serving as a lash. **b.** The stock of a whip. **6.** *Zool.* **a.** A pouchlike enlargement of a bird's esophagus in which food is stored or partially digested. **b.** A similar organ in earthworms, insects, and other invertebrates. *—v.* **cropped, crop·ping, crops.** *—tr.* **1.** To cut off the stems or top of (a plant). **2.** To cut (hair, for example) very short. **3.** To clip (an animal's ears, for example). **4.** To reap; harvest. **5.** To cause to grow or yield a crop or crops. *—intr.* To plant, grow, or yield a crop or crops. ***—phrasal verb.* crop up.** To appear unexpectedly: *a name that cropped up early in the investigation.* [ME < OE *cropp,* ear of corn.]
crop-eared (krŏp′îrd′) *adj.* **1.** Having the ears cropped. **2.** Having the hair cut so short that the ears show.
crop·per[1] (krŏp′ər) *n.* **1.** One that crops. **2.** A person who works land in return for a share of the yield; sharecropper.
crop·per[2] (krŏp′ər) *n.* **1.** A heavy fall; tumble. **2.** A disastrous failure; fiasco. [Orig. unknown.]
crop rotation *n.* A method of maintaining and renewing the fertility of a soil by the successive planting of different crops on the same land.
cro·quet (krō-kā′) *n.* **1.** An outdoor game in which the players drive wooden balls through a series of wickets using long-handled mallets. **2.** The act of driving away an opponent's croquet ball by hitting one's own ball when the two are in contact. *—tr.v.* **-queted** (-kād′), **-quet·ing** (-kā′ĭng), **-quets** (-kāz′). To drive away (an opponent's ball) with a croquet. [Fr. < ONFr., hook. —see CROCKET.]
cro·quette (krō-kĕt′) *n.* A small cake of minced food, often coated with bread crumbs and fried in deep fat. [Fr. < *croquer,* to crunch.]
cro·qui·gnole (krō′kən-yōl′) *n.* A kind of permanent wave in which the hair is wound around metal rods. [Fr., a kind of biscuit < *croquer,* to crunch.]
cro·sier also **cro·zier** (krō′zhər) *n.* **1.** A staff with a crook or cross at the end, carried by or before an abbot, bishop, or archbishop as a symbol of office. **2.** *Bot.* A coiled tip of a plant stalk, as of a young fern frond. [ME *croser* < OFr. *crossier,* staff bearer < *crosse,* crosier, of Germanic orig.]
cross (krôs, krŏs) *n.* **1. a.** An upright post with a transverse piece near the top, upon which condemned persons were executed in ancient times. **b.** Often **Cross.** The cross upon which Jesus was crucified. **c.** A symbolic representation of the cross upon which Jesus was crucified. **d.** A crucifix. **2.** A sign made by tracing the outline of a cross with the right hand upon the forehead and chest as a devotional act. **3.** A trial or affliction: *Everyone has his own cross to bear.* **4.** A medal, emblem, or insignia in the form of a cross or modified cross. **5.** A mark or pattern formed by the intersection of two lines, esp. such a mark (X) used as a signature. **6.** A pipe fitting with four branches in the form of a cross, used as a junction for intersecting pipes. **7.** *Biol.* **a.** A plant or animal produced by crossbreeding; hybrid. **b.** The process of crossbreeding; hybridization. **8.** One that combines the qualities of two things: *a novel that is a cross between romance and satire.* **9.** *Slang.* A contest whose outcome has been dishonestly prearranged. *—v.* **crossed, cross·ing, cross·es.** *—tr.* **1.** To go or extend across; pass from one side of to the other: *crossed the room to greet him.* **2.** To carry or convey across. **3.** To extend or pass through or over; intersect. **4. a.** To delete or eliminate by or as if by drawing a line through: *crossing names off a list.* **b.** To make or put a line across: *Cross your t's.* **5.** To place crosswise: *crossed her legs.* **6.** To make the sign of the cross upon or over as a sign of devotion. **7.** To encounter in passing: *His path crossed mine.* **8.** *Informal.* To interfere with; thwart or obstruct: *Don't cross me.* **9.** *Biol.* To crossbreed or cross-fertilize (plants or animals). *—intr.* **1.** To lie or pass across; intersect. **2.** To move or extend from one side to another. **3.** To encounter in passing: *Our paths crossed.* **4.** *Biol.* To crossbreed or cross-fertilize. *—adj.* **1.** Lying or passing crosswise; intersecting: *a cross street.* **2.** Contrary or counter; opposing: *cross winds; cross purposes.* **3.** Showing ill humor; annoyed. **4.** Involving interchange; reciprocal. **5.** Crossbred; hybrid. *—adv.* Crosswise or across. ***—idiom.* cross swords.** To come to blows; fight. [ME *cros* < OE < ON *kross* < OIr. *cross* < Lat. *crux.*] **—cross′er** *n.* **—cross′ly** *adv.* **—cross′ness** *n.*
cross·bar (krôs′bär′, krŏs′-) *n.* A horizontal bar, line, or stripe.
cross·bill (krôs′bĭl′, krŏs′-) *n.* Any of several birds of the genus *Loxia,* having curved mandibles with narrow, crossed tips.
cross·bones (krôs′bōnz′, krŏs′-) *pl.n.* A representation of two bones placed crosswise, usually under a skull, symbolizing danger or death.
cross·bow (krôs′bō′, krŏs′-) *n.* A medieval weapon consisting of a bow fixed crosswise on a wooden stock, with grooves on the stock to direct the projectile. **—cross′bow′man** *n.*
cross·bred (krôs′brĕd′) *adj.* Produced by the mating of individuals of different breeds. **—cross′bred′** *n.*
cross·breed (krôs′brēd′, krŏs′-) *v.* **-bred** (-brĕd′), **-breed·ing, -breeds.** *—tr.* To produce (a hybrid) by the mating of individuals of different varieties or breeds; hybridize. *—intr.* To mate so as to produce a hybrid; interbreed. *—n.* A hybrid produced by crossbreeding.
cross·check (krôs′chĕk′, krŏs′-) *tr.v.* **-checked, -check·ing, -checks. 1.** To verify by comparing with parallel or supplementary data. **2.** To check illegally in ice hockey by thrusting with one's hockey stick at an opponent's arms or stick. *—n.* The act of crosschecking.
cross-coun·try (krôs′kŭn′trē, krŏs′-) *adj.* **1.** Moving or directed across open country rather than following tracks, roads, or runs: *a cross-country race.* **2.** From one side of a country to the opposite side: *a cross-country trip.* **—cross′-coun′try** *adv.*
cross-country skiing *n.* The sport of skiing over the countryside rather than on downhill runs.
cross-cul·tur·al (krôs′kŭl′chər-əl, krŏs′-) *adj.* Comparing or dealing with two or more different cultures: *a cross-cultural survey.*
cross·cur·rent (krôs′kûr′ənt, -kŭr′-, krŏs′-) *n.* **1.** A current flowing across another current. **2.** A conflicting movement, tendency, or inclination: *a crosscurrent of dissent.*
cross·cut (krôs′kŭt′, krŏs′-) *tr. & intr.v.* **-cut, -cut·ting, -cuts.** To cut or run across or crosswise. *—adj.* **1.** Used or constructed for cutting crosswise: *a crosscut saw.* **2.** Cut on the bias or across the grain. *—n.* **1.** A course or cut going crosswise. **2.** A path more direct than the main path; short cut. **3.** A level in a mine driven so that it intersects a vein of ore.
crosse (krôs, krŏs) *n.* A lacrosse stick. [Fr. < OFr. *crosse,* staff, of Germanic orig.]
cross-ex·am·ine (krôs′ĭg-zăm′ĭn, krŏs′-) *v.* **-ined, -in·ing, -ines.** *—tr.* **1.** To question closely, esp. in order to check the resulting answers against answers previously made. **2.** *Law.* To question (a witness already examined by the opposing

side). —*intr.* To question a person closely. —**cross′-ex·am′i·na′tion** *n.* —**cross′-ex·am′in·er** *n.*

cross-eye (krôs′ī′, krŏs′ī′) *n.* A form of strabismus in which one or both eyes deviate toward the nose. —**cross′-eyed′** *adj.*

cross-fer·til·i·za·tion (krôs′fûr′tl-ĭ-zā′shən, krŏs′-) *n.* **1.** *Biol.* Fertilization by the union of gametes from different individuals, often of different varieties or species. **2.** *Bot.* Fertilization of the ovule of one plant or flower by pollen nuclei from another. —**cross′-fer′tile** *adj.*

cross-fer·til·ize (krôs′fûr′tl-īz′, krŏs′-) *tr. & intr.v.* **-ized, -iz·ing, -iz·es.** To fertilize or be fertilized by means of cross-fertilization.

cross-file (krôs′fīl′, krŏs′-) *intr. & tr.v.* **-filed, -fil·ing, -files.** To register as a candidate in the primaries of more than one political party. —**cross′-fil′er** *n.*

cross·fire (krôs′fīr′, krŏs′-) *n.* **1.** Lines of fire from two or more positions crossing each other at a single point: *soldiers caught in crossfire.* **2.** A situation in which a number of things originating from different sources come together. **3.** A rapid, often agitated discussion.

cross-grained (krôs′grānd′, krŏs′-) *adj.* **1.** Having an irregular, transverse, or diagonal grain. **2.** Troublesome to deal with; contrary.

cross hair *n.* Either of two fine strands of wire crossed in the focus of the eyepiece of an optical instrument and used as a calibration or sighting reference.

cross·hatch (krôs′hăch′, krŏs′-) *tr.v.* **-hatched, -hatch·ing, -hatch·es.** To mark with two or more sets of intersecting parallel lines. —**cross′hatch′** *n.*

cross·head (krôs′hĕd′, krŏs′-) *n.* A beam that connects the piston rod to the connecting rod of a reciprocating engine.

cross-in·dex (krôs′ĭn′dĕks′, krŏs′-) *v.* **-dexed, -dex·ing, -dex·es.** —*tr.* To furnish (an index) with cross-references. —*intr.* To furnish cross-references. —**cross′-in′dex** *n.*

cross·ing (krô′sĭng, krŏs′ĭng) *n.* **1.** A place at which roads, lines, or tracks intersect; intersection. **2.** The place at which something, such as a river or highway, may be crossed. **3.** The intersection of the nave and transept in a cruciform church.

crossing over *n.* The exchange of genetic material between homologous chromosomes.

cross matching *n.* The process in which blood compatibilities are tested between a donor and a recipient before transfusion.

cross-mul·ti·ply (krôs′mŭl′tə-plī′, krŏs′-) *intr.v.* **-plied, -ply·ing, -plies.** To multiply the numerator of one of a pair of fractions by the denominator of the other. —**cross multiplication** *n.*

cross·o·ver (krôs′ō′vər, krŏs′-) *n.* **1.** A place at which or the means by which a crossing is made. **2.** A short connecting track by which a train can be transferred from one line to another. **3.** *Genetics.* **a.** A crossing over. **b.** A character resulting from crossing over. **4.** A registered member of one political party who votes in the primary of the other party. —**modifier:** *the crossover vote in California.*

cross·patch (krôs′păch′, krŏs′-) *n. Informal.* A peevish, irascible person. [CROSS + obs. *patch,* jester.]

cross·piece (krôs′pēs′, krŏs′-) *n.* A transverse piece, as of a structure.

cross-pol·li·nate (krôs′pŏl′ə-nāt′, krŏs′-) *tr.v.* **-nat·ed, -nat·ing, -nates.** *Bot.* To cross-fertilize (a plant or flower). —**cross′-pol′li·na′tion** *n.*

cross product *n.* Vector product.

cross-pur·pose (krôs′pûr′pəs, krŏs′-) *n.* A conflicting or contrary purpose. —**idiom. be at cross-purposes.** To have or act under a misunderstanding of each other's purposes.

cross-ques·tion (krôs′kwĕs′chən, krŏs′-) *tr.v.* **-tioned, -tion·ing, -tions.** To question closely; cross-examine. —*n.* A question asked in the process of cross-examination.

cross-re·ac·tion (krôs′rē-ăk′shən, krŏs′-) *n.* The reaction between an antigen and an antibody that was generated against a different antigen. —**cross′-re·act′** *v.* **(-act·ed, -act·ing, -acts).** —**cross′-re·ac′tive** *adj.* —**cross′-re·ac·tiv′i·ty** *n.*

cross-re·fer (krôs′rĭ-fûr′, krŏs′-) *v.* **-ferred, -fer·ring, -fers.** —*tr.* To refer from one part or passage to another. —*intr.* To make a cross-reference.

cross-ref·er·ence (krôs′rĕf′ər-əns, -rĕf′rəns, krŏs′-) *n.* A reference from one part of a book, index, catalogue, or file to another part containing related information.

cross·road (krôs′rōd′, krŏs′-) *n.* **1.** A road that intersects another road. **2. crossroads.** *(used with a sing. verb).* **a.** A place where two or more roads meet. **b.** A place where different cultures meet. **c.** A crucial point or place.

cross·ruff (krôs′rŭf′, -rŭf′, krŏs′-) *n.* A series of plays in games of the whist family where partnership hands alternately ruff suits led by the other partner. —*v.* **-ruffed, -ruff·ing, -ruffs.** —*intr.* To perform a crossruff or a series of crossruffs. —*tr.* To ruff (one's partner's lead or a lead from the dummy) in alternating plays.

cross section *n.* **1. a.** A section formed by a plane cutting through an object, usually at right angles to an axis. **b.** A piece so cut or a graphic representation of such a piece. **2.** *Physics.* A measure of the probability of occurrence of a particular atomic or nuclear reaction. **3.** A representative sample meant to be typical of the whole. —**cross′-sec′tion·al** *adj.*

cross-stitch (krôs′stĭch′, krŏs′-) *n.* **1.** In sewing and embroidery, a double stitch forming an X. **2.** Needlework made with cross-stitches. —*v.* **-stitched, -stitch·ing, -stitch·es.** —*tr.* To make or embroider with cross-stitches. —*intr.* To work in cross-stitch.

cross·talk (krôs′tôk′, krŏs′-) *n.* Noise or garbled sounds heard on a telephone or other electronic receiver, caused by interference from another channel.

cross·tie (krôs′tī′, krŏs′-) *n.* A transverse beam or rod serving as a support, esp. a beam that connects and supports the rails of a railroad.

cross-town (krôs′toun′, krŏs′-) *adj.* Running or extending across a city or town: *a cross-town bus.* —*adv.* Across a city or town.

cross·tree (krôs′trē′, krŏs′-) *n. Naut.* One of the two horizontal crosspieces at the upper ends of the lower masts in fore-and-aft-rigged vessels, serving to spread the shrouds.

cross vault *n.* A vaulting formed by the intersection of two or more simple vaults.

cross·walk (krôs′wôk′, krŏs′-) *n.* A path marked off for pedestrians crossing a street.

cross·way (krôs′wā′, krŏs′-) *n.* A crossroad.

cross·ways (krôs′wāz′, krŏs′-) *adv.* Variant of **crosswise.**

cross·wind (krôs′wĭnd′, krŏs′-) *n.* A wind blowing at right angles to a given direction, as to an aircraft's line of flight.

cross·wise (krôs′wīz′, krŏs′-) also **cross·ways** (-wāz′) *adv.* Across.

cross·word puzzle (krôs′wûrd′, krŏs′-) *n.* A puzzle in which an arrangement of numbered squares is to be filled with words running both across and down in answer to correspondingly numbered clues.

crotch (krŏch) *n.* **1.** The angle or region of the angle formed by the junction of two parts or members, such as two branches, limbs, or legs. **2.** The fork of a pole or other support. [Poss. alteration of CRUTCH.] —**crotched** (krŏcht) *adj.*

crotch·et (krŏch′ĭt) *n.* **1.** A small hook or hooklike structure. **2.** An odd, whimsical, or stubborn notion. **3.** *Mus.* A quarter note. [ME *crochet* < OFr. —see CROCHET.]

crotch·et·y (krŏch′ĭ-tē) *adj.* Capriciously stubborn or eccentric; perverse. —**crotch′et·i·ness** *n.*

cro·ton (krōt′n) *n.* **1.** Any of various chiefly tropical plants, shrubs, or trees of the genus *Croton.* **2.** Any of various tropical plants of the genus *Codiaeum,* esp. *C. variegatum pictum,* frequently grown as a house plant for its showy, varicolored foliage. [NLat. *Croton,* genus name < Gk. *kroton,* castor oil plant.]

Croton bug *n.* A small light-brown cockroach, *Blatella germanica,* that is a common household pest. [After the *Croton* River, New York.]

cro·ton·ic acid (krō-tŏn′ĭk) *n.* An organic acid, $C_4H_6O_2$, used in the preparation of pharmaceuticals and resins. [< NLat. *Croton,* plant genus. —see CROTON.]

croton oil *n.* A yellowish-brown, violently cathartic oil obtained from the seeds of a tree, *Croton tiglium,* of southeastern Asia.

crouch (krouch) *v.* **crouched, crouch·ing, crouch·es.** —*intr.* **1.** To stoop with the limbs pulled close to the body. **2.** To bend servilely or timidly; cringe. —*tr.* To cause to bend low, as in fear or humility. —*n.* The act or posture of crouching. [ME *crouchen* < OFr. *crochir,* to be bent < *croc,* hook.] —**crouch′ing·ly** *adv.*

croup[1] (kro͞op) *n.* A pathological condition affecting the larynx in children, characterized by respiratory difficulty and a harsh cough. [Orig. unknown.] —**croup′ous** (kro͞o′pəs), **croup′y** *adj.*

croup[2] also **croupe** (kro͞op) *n.* The rump of certain animals, esp. a horse. [ME *croupe* < OFr., of Germanic orig.]

crou·pi·er (kro͞o′pē-ər, -pē-ā′) *n.* An attendant at a gaming table who collects and pays bets. [Fr.< *croupe,* rump, croup < OFr.]

crou·ton (kro͞o′tŏn′, kro͞o-tŏn′) *n.* A small crisp piece of toasted or fried bread. [Fr. *croûton* < *croûte,* crust < OFr. *crouste* < Lat. *crusta.*]

crow[1] (krō) *n.* **1.** Any of several large, glossy, black birds of the genus *Corvus,* having a characteristic raucous call, esp. *C. brachyrhynchos,* of North America. **2.** A crowbar. —**idioms. as the crow flies.** In a straight line. **eat crow.** *Informal.* To be forced into a humiliating situation, as from having been in error. [ME *croue* < OE *crāwe.*]

crow[2] (krō) *intr.v.* **crowed, crow·ing, crows. 1.** *Past tense and past participle* **crowed** or **crew** (kro͞o). To utter the shrill cry characteristic of a cock or rooster. **2. a.** To exult blatantly, esp. over the misfortune of another. **b.** To brag or boast exultantly. **3.** To make a sound expressive of pleasure or well-being, characteristic of an infant. —*n.* **1.** The shrill cry of a cock. **2.** An inarticulate sound expressive of pleasure or delight. [ME *crouen* < OE *crāwan.*]

Crow (krō) *n., pl.* **Crow** or **Crows. 1. a.** A tribe of Indians, formerly inhabiting the region between the Platte and Yellowstone rivers and now settled in southeastern Montana. **b.** A member of this tribe. **2.** The Siouan language of the Crow.

crow·bar (krō′bär′) *n.* A straight bar of iron or steel, with the working end shaped like a forked chisel, used as a lever.

crosstree

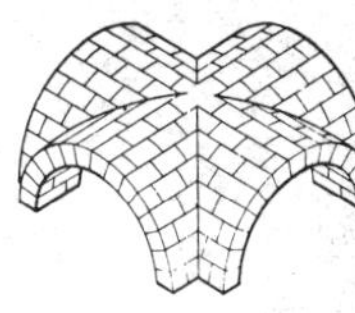
cross vault

crossword puzzle

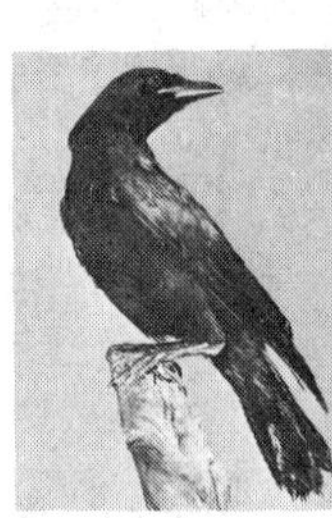
crow[1]

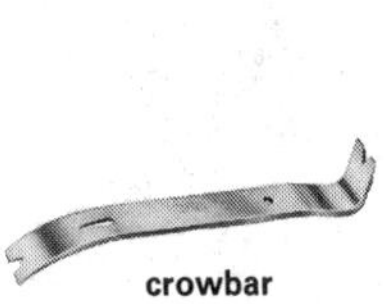
crowbar

[From the resemblance of its forked end to a crow's foot.]

crow·ber·ry (krō′bĕr′ē) *n.* **1. a.** A low-growing evergreen shrub, *Empetrum nigrum,* of cool regions of the Northern Hemisphere, having small, purplish flowers and black, berrylike fruit. **b.** Any of several similar or related plants, such as the bearberry. **2.** The fruit of a crowberry.

crow blackbird *n.* The grackle (sense 1).

crowd[1] (kroud) *n.* **1.** A large number of persons gathered together; throng. **2.** The common people; the populace. **3.** A particular social group; clique. **4.** A large number of things grouped or considered together. —*v.* **crowd·ed, crowd·ing, crowds.** —*intr.* **1.** To congregate in a close place; throng. **2.** To advance by shoving. —*tr.* **1.** To press or shove. **2.** To press, cram, or force tightly together. **3.** To fill or occupy to overflowing. **4.** *Informal.* To put pressure on. —***idiom.*** **crowd (on) sail.** *Naut.* To spread a large amount of sail to increase speed. [< ME *crowden,* to crowd < OE *crudan,* to hasten.] —**crowd′er** *n.*

crowd[2] (kroud, kro͞od) *n.* An ancient Celtic musical instrument, stringed and played with a bow. [ME *croud* < Welsh *crwth.*]

crow·foot (krō′fo͝ot′) *n.* **1.** *pl.* **-foots. a.** Any of various plants of the genus *Ranunculus,* which includes the buttercups and spearworts, esp. any of several similar plants, such as *R. abortivus* and *R. scleratus,* having small, inconspicuous yellow flowers. **b.** Any of various other plants having leaves or other parts resembling a bird's foot. **2.** *pl.* **-feet.** A caltrop. **3.** *pl.* **-feet.** *Naut.* **a.** A block used in supporting the middle section of an awning. **b.** A set of small lines passed through holes of a batten or fitting to help support the backbone of an awning.

crown (kroun) *n.* **1.** An ornamental circlet or head covering, often made of precious metal set with jewels, and worn as a symbol of sovereignty. **2.** Often **Crown. a.** The power, position, or empire of a monarch. **b.** The monarch as head of state. **3.** A distinction or reward for achievement, esp. a title signifying the championship in a sport. **4.** Anything resembling a crown in shape. **5.** A coin stamped with a crown or crowned head on the reverse side. **6. a.** A former British coin worth five shillings. **b.** Any of several coins with a name that means crown, such as the koruna, krona, and krone. **c.** See table at **currency. 7. a.** The top or highest part of the head. **b.** The head itself. **8.** The top or upper part of a hat. **9.** The highest point or summit. **10.** The highest or primary quality, attribute or state. **11. a.** The part of a tooth that is covered by enamel and projects beyond the gum line. **b.** An artificial substitute for the natural crown of a tooth. **12.** The lowest part of an anchor, where the arms are joined to it. **13. a.** The upper part of a tree, including the leaves and living branches. **b.** The part of a plant, usually at ground level, between the root and the stem. **c.** Corona (sense 5). **14.** The crest of an animal, esp. of a bird. **15.** The portion of a cut gem above the girdle. —*tr.v.* **crowned, crown·ing, crowns. 1.** To put a crown or garland upon the head of. **2.** To invest with regal power; enthrone. **3.** To confer honor, dignity, or reward upon. **4.** To surmount or be the highest part of. **5.** To form the crown, top, or chief ornament of. **6.** To bring to completion or successful conclusion; finish; consummate. **7.** To put a crown on (a tooth). **8.** In checkers, to make (a piece that has reached the last row) into a king by placing another piece upon it. **9.** *Informal.* To hit on the head. [ME *crowne* < OFr. *corone* < Lat. *corona,* wreath < Gk. *korōnē* < *korōnos,* curved.]

crown

crown canopy *n.* The canopy or cover formed by the upper branches of trees in a forest.

crown colony *n.* A British colony in which the sovereign has complete control of legislation, usually administered by an appointed governor.

crown cover *n.* Crown canopy.

crown glass *n.* **1.** A clear soda-lime-silica optical glass with low refraction. **2.** A form of window glass made by whirling a glass bubble to make a flat circular disk with a lump in the center formed by the craftsman's rod.

crown lens *n.* The crown-glass element in an achromatic lens.

crown-of-thorns (kroun′əv-thôrnz′) *n.* A spiny, vinelike desert plant, *Euphorbia splendens,* often grown as a potted plant for its scarlet flowers.

crown prince *n.* The heir apparent to a throne.

crown princess *n.* **1.** The wife of a crown prince. **2.** A female heir apparent to a throne.

crown rot *n.* A disease of plants that is characterized by the localized degeneration of the stem near ground level.

crown saw *n.* A cylindrical saw with teeth on the bottom edge of the cylinder.

crown vetch *n.* A sprawling plant, *Coronilla varia,* native to Europe, having compound leaves and clusters of pink flowers.

crow's-foot (krōz′fo͝ot′) *n., pl.* **-feet** (-fēt′). **1.** Often **crow's-feet.** Any of the wrinkles at the outer corner of the eye, common in many adults. **2.** A three-pointed embroidery stitch used as finishing, as at the end of a seam.

crow's-nest (krōz′nĕst′) *n.* **1.** *Naut.* A small lookout platform with a high protective railing and wind screen, located near the top of a ship's mast. **2.** A crow's-nest located ashore.

crow's-nest

croze (krōz) *n.* The groove at the ends of the staves of a barrel or cask into which the head is set. [Prob. < OFr. *crues,* groove.]

cro·zier (krō′zhər) *n.* Variant of **crosier.**

cru·ces (kro͞o′sēz′) *n.* A plural of **crux.**

cru·cial (kro͞o′shəl) *adj.* **1.** Of supreme importance; critical: *a crucial election.* **2.** Severe; difficult; trying. **3.** Having the form of a cross; cross-shaped. [OFr., cross-shaped < Lat. *crux,* cross.] —**cru′cial·ly** *adv.*

cru·ci·ate (kro͞o′shē-āt′) *adj.* **1.** Forming or arranged in a cross; cruciform. **2.** Overlapping or crossing, as the wings of some insects when at rest. [NLat. *cruciatus* < Lat. *crux,* cross.] —**cru′ci·ate′ly** *adv.*

cru·ci·ble (kro͞o′sə-bəl) *n.* **1.** A vessel made of a refractory substance such as graphite or porcelain, used for melting and calcining materials at high temperatures. **2.** The bottom of an ore furnace, in which the molten metal collects. **3.** A severe test or trial. [ME *crusible* < Med. Lat. *crucibulum,* crucible, night-light, poss. < Lat. *crux,* cross.]

crucible

crucible steel *n.* A high-grade steel made by fusing low-carbon steel with charcoal or cast iron in a graphite crucible and used in tools and dies.

cru·ci·fer (kro͞o′sə-fər) *n.* **1.** One who bears a cross in a religious procession. **2.** *Bot.* A plant of the family Cruciferae, such as a mustard or cress, having four-petaled flowers suggestive of a cross. [LLat. : Lat. *crux,* cross + Lat. *-fer,* -fer.] —**cru·cif′er·ous** (-sĭf′ər-əs) *adj.*

cru·ci·fix (kro͞o′sə-fĭks′) *n.* An image of Christ on the cross. [ME < LLat. *crucifixus* < p.part. of *crucifigere,* crucify.]

cru·ci·fix·ion (kro͞o′sə-fĭk′shən) *n.* **1.** The action of putting to death on a cross. **2.** A representation of Christ on the cross. **3. the Crucifixion.** The crucifying of Christ on Calvary.

cru·ci·form (kro͞o′sə-fôrm′) *adj.* Cross-shaped or marked with a cross; cruciate. [Lat. *crux, cruc-,* cross + -FORM.] —**cru′ci·form′** *n.* —**cru′ci·form′ly** *adv.*

cru·ci·fy (kro͞o′sə-fī′) *tr.v.* **-fied, -fy·ing, -fies. 1.** To put (a person) to death by nailing or binding to a cross. **2.** To mortify or subdue (the flesh). **3.** To treat cruelly; torment. [ME *crucifien* < OFr. *crucifier* < LLat. *crucifigere* : Lat. *crux,* cross + Lat. *figere,* to attach.] —**cru′ci·fi′er** *n.*

crud (krŭd) *n.* **1.** *Slang.* **a.** A coating or incrustation of filth or refuse. **b.** One that is contemptible or disgusting. **2.** A disease, imaginary or real, esp. one affecting the skin. **3.** *Regional.* A milk curd. [ME *crudde.*] —**crud′dy** *adj.*

crude (kro͞od) *adj.* **crud·er, crud·est. 1.** In an unrefined or natural state; raw: *crude oil.* **2.** *Archaic.* Unripe or immature. **3.** Lacking tact, refinement, or taste. **4.** Not carefully or completely made; rough. **5.** Displaying a lack of knowledge or skill. **6.** Undisguised or unadorned; blunt: *must face the crude truth.* —*n.* Petroleum in its unrefined state. [ME < Lat. *crudus.*] —**crude′ly** *adv.* —**cru′di·ty** (kro͞o′dĭ-tē), **crude′ness** *n.*

crude oil *n.* Petroleum.

cru·di·tés (kro͞o′dĭ-tā′) *pl.n.* Raw vegetables, as carrot sticks and pepper strips, served often with a dip as an appetizer. [Fr., pl. of *crudité,* indigestibility < Lat. *cruditas,* indigestion, undigested food < *crudus,* raw.]

cru·el (kro͞o′əl) *adj.* **-el·er, -el·est** or **-el·ler, -el·lest. 1.** Disposed to inflict pain or suffering. **2.** Causing suffering; painful. [ME < OFr. < Lat. *crudelis.*] —**cru′el·ly** *adv.*

Synonyms: *cruel, ferocious, barbarous, inhuman, sadistic, vicious, pitiless, ruthless.* These adjectives mean predisposed to inflict violence, pain, or hardship or to find satisfaction in the suffering of others. *Cruel* implies both disposition to harm and satisfaction in or indifference to suffering. *Ferocious* primarily stresses rough physical treatment and savagery, and *barbarous* adds the suggestion of behavior that befits only primitive or uncivilized men. *Inhuman* means markedly deficient in such qualities as tolerance and sympathy for one's fellow man. *Sadistic* implies the experiencing of satisfaction, especially sexual gratification, from cruelty inflicted on others. *Vicious* suggests native disposition to malicious and destructive behavior, and is sometimes associated with moral depravity. *Pitiless* refers specifically to absence of mercy. *Ruthless* also stresses lack of compassion and often implies relentless pursuit of personal ends regardless of hardship to others.

cru·el·ty (kro͞o′əl-tē) *n., pl.* **-ties. 1.** The quality or condition of being cruel. **2.** Something that causes pain or suffering, such as a cruel action or remark.

cru·et (kro͞o′ĭt) *n.* A small glass bottle for holding vinegar, oil, or other condiments at the table. [ME < AN, dim. of OFr. *crue,* flask, of Germanic orig.]

cruet

cruise (kro͞oz) *v.* **cruised, cruis·ing, cruis·es.** —*intr.* **1.** To sail or travel about, as for pleasure or reconnaissance. **2.** To travel at a speed providing maximum operating efficiency for a sustained period. **3. a.** To move leisurely about a place in search of something: *cabbies cruising for a fare.* **b.** *Informal.* To look for a sexual partner, as in a public place. **4.** To inspect a wooded area to determine its lumber yield. —*tr.* **1.** To cruise or journey over. **2.** To inspect in order to determine lumber yield. —*n.* A sea voyage for pleasure. [Du. *kruisen,* to cross < MDu. *crucen* < Lat. *crux,* cross.]

cruise missile *n.* A long-range, low-flying guided missile that can be launched from air, sea, or land.

cruis·er (kro͞o'zər) *n.* **1.** One of a class of fast warships of medium tonnage with a long cruising radius and less armor and firepower than a battleship. **2.** A large motorboat whose cabin is equipped with living facilities. **3.** A squad car.

cruis·ing (kro͞o'zĭng) *n.* The act or an instance of driving around a city or town in search of diversion or kicks.

cruising radius *n.* The longest distance a ship or aircraft can go and return at cruising speed without refueling.

crul·ler (krŭl'ər) *n.* A small cake of sweet dough fried in deep fat, usually ring-shaped or twisted. [Du. *krulle* < *krullen,* to curl < *krul,* curly < MDu. *crul.*]

crumb (krŭm) *n.* **1.** A small piece broken or fallen from cake, bread, or other baked goods. **2.** A small fragment or scrap. **3.** The soft inner portion of bread. **4.** *Slang.* A contemptible, untrustworthy, or loathsome person. —*tr.v.* **crumbed, crumb·ing, crumbs. 1.** To break into small pieces or crumbs; crumble. **2.** To cover or prepare with bread crumbs; bread. **3.** To brush (a table or cloth) clear of crumbs. —*intr.* To break apart in crumbs. [ME *crome* < OE *cruma.*]

crum·ble (krŭm'bəl) *v.* **-bled, -bling, -bles.** —*tr.* To break or cause to break into small parts or crumbs. —*intr.* To fall into tiny pieces; disintegrate. [ME *cremelen* < OE *(ge)crymian* < *cruma,* crumb.]

crum·bly (krŭm'blē) *adj.* **-bli·er, -bli·est.** Easily crumbled; friable. **—crum'bli·ness** *n.*

crumb·y (krŭm'ē) *adj.* Variant of **crummy.**

crum·mie (krŭm'ē) *n. Scot.* A cow with crooked horns. [< Sc. *crumb,* crooked < ME < OE.]

crum·my also **crumb·y** (krŭm'ē) *adj.* **-mi·er, -mi·est** also **-i·er, -i·est.** *Slang.* **1.** Miserable or wretched. **2.** Shabby or cheap. [< CRUMB.]

crump (krŭmp) *v.* **crumped, crump·ing, crumps.** —*tr.* **1.** To crush or crunch with the teeth. **2.** To strike heavily with a crunching sound. —*intr.* To make a crunching sound. —*n.* **1.** A crunching sound. **2.** A heavy blow. [Imit.]

crum·pet (krŭm'pĭt) *n. Chiefly Brit.* A light, soft bread similar to a muffin, baked on a griddle and often toasted. [Poss. < ME *crompid (cake),* curled (cake) < *crumpen,* to curl up < *crumb,* crooked < OE.]

crum·ple (krŭm'pəl) *v.* **-pled, -pling, -ples.** —*tr.* **1.** To crush together or press into wrinkles; rumple. **2.** To cause to fall apart. —*intr.* **1.** To become wrinkled; shrivel. **2.** To fall apart; collapse. —*n.* An irregular fold, crease, or wrinkle. [Prob. freq. of obs. *crump,* to curl up < ME *crumpen.* —see CRUMPET.]

crunch (krŭnch) *v.* **crunched, crunch·ing, crunch·es.** —*tr.* **1.** To chew with a noisy crackling sound. **2.** To crush, grind, or tread noisily. —*intr.* **1.** To chew noisily with a crackling sound. **2.** To move with a crushing sound. **3.** To produce or emit a crushing sound. —*n.* **1.** The act or sound of crunching. **2.** *Informal.* **a.** A decisive confrontation. **b.** A critical situation. [Imit.] **—crunch'y** *adj.*

crunch·er (crŭnch'ər) *n. Slang.* A finishing or decisive blow.

crup·per (krŭp'ər) *n.* **1.** A leather strap looped under a horse's tail and attached to a harness or saddle to keep it from slipping forward. **2.** The rump of a horse. [ME *crouper* < OFr. *cropiere* < *croup,* rump, of Germanic orig.]

cru·ra (kro͝or'ə) *n.* Plural of **crus.**

cru·ral (kro͝or'əl) *adj.* Of or pertaining to the leg, shank, or thigh. [Lat. *cruralis* < *crus,* leg.]

crus (kro͞os, krŭs) *n., pl.* **cru·ra** (kro͝or'ə). **1.** The section of the leg or hind limb between the knee and foot; shank. **2.** A leglike part. [NLat. *crus, crur-* < Lat., leg.]

cru·sade (kro͞o-sād') *n.* **1.** Often **Crusade.** Any of the military expeditions undertaken by European Christians in the 11th, 12th, and 13th centuries to recover the Holy Land from the Moslems. **2.** A holy war undertaken with papal sanction. **3.** A vigorous concerted movement for a cause or against an abuse. —*intr.v.* **-sad·ed, -sad·ing, -sades.** To engage in a crusade. [Partly < Fr. *croisade,* and partly < Sp. *cruzada,* both < Med. Lat. *cruciata* < Lat. *crux,* cross.] **—cru·sad'er** *n.*

cruse (kro͞oz, kro͞os) *n.* A small jar or pot for holding water, wine, or oil. [ME *crouse,* perh. < MDu. *cruyse,* pot.]

crush (krŭsh) *v.* **crushed, crush·ing, crush·es.** —*tr.* **1.** To press between opposing bodies so as to break or injure. **2.** To extract or obtain by pressing or squeezing: *crush juice from a grape.* **3.** To crumple or rumple. **4.** To hug forcibly. **5.** To break, pound, or grind (stone or ore, for example) into small fragments or powder. **6.** To press upon, shove, or crowd. **7.** To put down; subdue. **8.** To overwhelm or oppress severely: *Debt was crushing them.* —*intr.* **1.** To be or become crushed. **2.** To proceed or move by crowding or pressing. —*n.* **1.** The act of crushing; extreme pressure. **2.** The state of being crushed. **3.** A great crowd or throng. **4.** A substance prepared by or as if by crushing. **5.** *Informal.* **a.** An infatuation. **b.** The object of it. **6.** A decisive or critical moment or situation. [ME *crushen* < OFr. *croissir.*] **—crush'a·ble** *adj.* **—crush'er** *n.*

crust (krŭst) *n.* **1.** The hard outer portion or surface area of bread. **2.** A piece of bread consisting mostly of the hard outer portion. **3.** A pastry shell, as of a pie or tart. **4.** A hard, crisp covering or surface. **5.** A hard deposit produced by maturing wine on the interior of bottles. **6. a.** *Geol.* The exterior portion of the earth that lies above the Mohorovičić discontinuity. **b.** The outermost solid layer of a planet or moon. **7.** The hard outer covering or integument of certain plants and animals, such as lichens and crustaceans. **8.** *Pathol.* A coating or dry outer layer, as of pus or blood; scab. **9.** *Slang.* Insolence; audacity; gall. —*v.* **crust·ed, crust·ing, crusts.** —*tr.* **1.** To cover with a crust. **2.** To form (dough) into a crust. —*intr.* **1.** To become covered with a crust. **2.** To harden into a crust. [ME *cruste* < OFr. *crouste* < Lat. *crusta,* shell.]

crus·ta·cean (krŭ-stā'shən) *n.* Any of various predominantly aquatic arthropods of the class Crustacea, including lobsters, crabs, shrimps, and barnacles, characteristically having a segmented body, a chitinous exoskeleton, and paired, jointed limbs. —*adj.* Of or belonging to the Crustacea. [< NLat. *Crustacea,* class name < Lat. *crusta,* shell.]

crus·ta·ceous (krŭ-stā'shəs) *adj.* **1.** Having, resembling, or constituting a hard crust or shell. **2.** Crustacean. [Lat. *crusta,* shell + -ACEOUS.]

crust·al (krŭs'təl) *adj.* Of or pertaining to a crust, esp. that of the earth or the moon.

crus·tose (krŭs'tōs') *adj.* Pertaining to a lichen whose thallus is thin and crusty. [Lat. *crustosus,* crusted < *crusta,* crust.]

crust·y (krŭs'tē) *adj.* **-i·er, -i·est. 1.** Like or having a crust. **2.** Surly or brusk. **—crust'i·ly** *adv.* **—crust'i·ness** *n.*

crutch (krŭch) *n.* **1.** A staff or support used by the disabled as an aid in walking, usually designed to fit under the armpit and often used in pairs. **2.** A forked device similar to a crutch such as a forked leg rest on a sidesaddle. **3.** Anything depended upon for support. **4.** The human crotch. —*tr.v.* **crutched, crutch·ing, crutch·es.** To support on or as on crutches; to prop up. [ME *crucche* < OE *crycc.*]

crux (krŭks, kro͝oks) *n., pl.* **crux·es** or **cru·ces** (kro͞o'sēz'). **1.** A crucial or vital moment; critical point. **2.** The basic, essential, or central feature: *the crux of an argument.* **3.** A puzzling problem. **4. Crux.** A constellation in the Southern Hemisphere near Centaurus and Musca. [Lat., cross.]

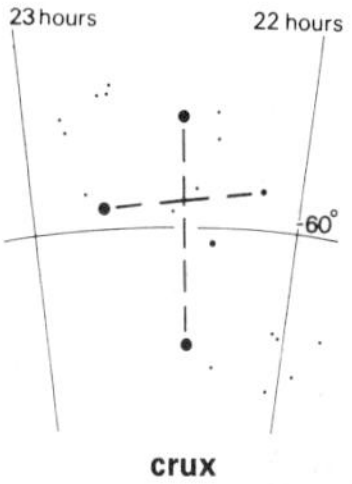

crux
The constellation Crux

cru·zei·ro (kro͞o-zâr'ō, -ro͞o) *n., pl.* **-ros.** See table at **currency.** [Port. < *cruz,* cross (from the figure on the coin) < Lat. *crux.*]

cry (krī) *v.* **cried, cry·ing, cries.** —*intr.* **1.** To make inarticulate sobbing sounds expressing grief, sorrow, or pain; weep. **2.** To call loudly; shout. **3.** To utter a characteristic sound or call. Used of an animal. **4.** To demand or require immediate action or remedy: *grievances crying out for redress.* —*tr.* **1.** To utter loudly. **2.** To proclaim or announce in public. **3.** To beg for; implore: *cry forgiveness.* **4.** To bring into a particular condition by weeping: *cry oneself to sleep.* ***—phrasal verbs.*** **cry down.** To belittle or disparage. **cry off.** To break or withdraw from a promise, agreement, or undertaking. **cry up.** To praise highly; extol. —*n., pl.* **cries. 1.** A loud utterance of some emotion, such as fear or anger. **2.** Any loud exclamation; a shout or call. **3.** A fit of weeping. **4.** An urgent entreaty or appeal. **5.** A public or general demand or complaint; clamor; outcry. **6.** An advertising of wares by calling out. **7.** A rallying call or signal. **8.** A political slogan. **9.** The characteristic call or utterance of an animal or bird. **10.** A pack of hounds. ***—idioms.*** **a far cry.** A long way. **cry havoc.** To sound an alarm. **cry over spilled milk.** To worry in vain about what cannot be undone or rectified. **in full cry.** In hot pursuit, as hounds hunting. [ME *crien* < OFr. *crier* < Lat. *quiritare,* to cry for help (from a citizen) < *Quirites,* Roman citizens.]

Synonyms: *cry, weep, wail, keen, moan, whimper, sob, blubber.* These verbs mean to express grief or pain by tears or voice or both. *Cry* and *weep* both involve tear-shedding; *cry* is the more common term and more strongly implies accompanying sound. *Wail* refers primarily to loud, sustained, inarticulate mournful sound. *Keen* suggests wailing associated with funeral dirges. *Moan* refers to sustained, low, inarticulate sound expressive of great suffering or grief. *Whimper* refers to broken or repressed cries in a low, whining voice. *Sob* describes weeping, or a mixture of broken speech and weeping, marked by convulsive breathing or gasping. *Blubber* refers to noisy shedding of tears accompanied by broken or inarticulate speech.

cry·baby (krī'bā'bē) *n.* A person who cries or complains frequently with little cause.

cry·ing (krī'ĭng) *adj.* Demanding or requiring immediate action or remedy: *a crying need.*

cry·mo·ther·a·py (krī'mō-thĕr'ə-pē) *n.* Variant of **cryotherapy.** [Fr. *crymothérapie* : *crymo-,* cryo- + *thérapie,* therapy.]

cryo– *pref.* Cold; freezing: *cryoscopy.* [< Gk. *kruos,* icy cold.]

cry·o·bi·ol·o·gy (krī'ō-bī-ŏl'ə-jē) *n.* The study of the effects of very low temperatures on living organisms. **—cry'o·bi'o·log'i·cal** (-bī'ə-lŏj'ĭ-kəl) *adj.* **—cry'o·bi'o·log'i·cal·ly** *adv.* **—cry'o·bi·ol'o·gist** *n.*

cry·o·gen (krī'ə-jən) *n.* A refrigerant used to obtain very low temperatures.

cry·o·gen·ic (krī'ə-jĕn'ĭk) *adj.* Of or pertaining to low temperatures. **—cry'o·gen'i·cal·ly** *adv.*

cry·o·gen·ics (krī'ō-jĕn'ĭks) *n. (used with a sing. verb).* The science of low-temperature phenomena.

cry·og·e·ny (krī-ŏj'ə-nē) *n.* Cryogenics.

cry·o·lite (krī'ə-līt') *n.* A white, vitreous natural fluoride of aluminum and sodium, Na_3AlF_6, used chiefly as an electrolyte in aluminum refining and in electrical insulation.

cry·om·e·ter (krī-ŏm'ĭ-tər) *n.* A thermometer capable of measuring very low temperatures.

cry·on·ics (krī-ŏn'ĭks) *n. (used with a sing. verb).* The process of freezing and storing a dead human body to prevent tissue decomposition so that at some time in the future the individual might be brought back to life when new medical cures have been developed. [CRY(O)- + *-onics,* as in *bionics.*] —**cry·on'ic** (-ĭk) *adj.*

cry·o·phil·ic (krī'ə-fĭl'ĭk) also **cry·oph·i·lous** (krī-ŏf'ə-ləs) *adj.* Having an affinity for or thriving at low temperatures.

cry·o·plank·ton (krī'ə-plangk'tən) *n.* Minute organisms living in snow, ice, or perpetually icy waters.

cry·o·probe (krī'ə-prōb') *n.* A surgical instrument used to apply extreme cold to tissues during cryosurgery.

cry·o·scope (krī'ə-skōp') *n.* An instrument used to measure the freezing point of a substance. [Back-formation < CRYOSCOPY.]

cry·os·co·py (krī-ŏs'kə-pē) *n.* The study of the freezing points of solutions. —**cry'o·scop'ic** (-ə-skŏp'ĭk) *adj.*

cry·o·stat (krī'ə-stăt') *n.* An apparatus used to maintain constant low temperature.

cry·o·sur·ger·y (krī'ō-sûr'jə-rē) *n.* The selective exposure of tissues to extreme cold to bring about cell destruction. —**cry'o·sur'geon** *n.* —**cry'o·sur'gi·cal** *adj.*

cry·o·ther·a·py (krī'ō-thĕr'ə-pē) also **cry·mo·ther·a·py** (krī'mō-) *n.* The use of low temperatures in medical therapy.

crypt (krĭpt) *n.* **1.** An underground vault or chamber, esp. one beneath a church that is used as a burial place. **2.** *Anat.* Any of various small pits, recesses, glandular cavities, or follicles in the body. [Lat. *crypta* < Gk. *kruptē* < *kruptos,* hidden < *kruptein,* to hide.]

crypt– *pref.* Variant of **crypto-.**

crypt·aes·the·sia (krĭp'təs-thē'zhə, -zhē-ə) *n.* Variant of **cryptesthesia.**

crypt·a·nal·y·sis (krĭp'tə-năl'ĭ-sĭs) *n.* The analysis and deciphering of cryptograms, ciphers, codes, or other secret writings. [CRYPT(OGRAM) + ANALYSIS.] —**crypt·an'a·lyst** (-tăn'ə-lĭst) *n.* —**crypt·an'a·lyt'ic** (-tăn'ə-lĭt'ĭk) *adj.*

crypt·es·the·sia or **crypt·aes·the·sia** (krĭp'təs-thē'zhə, -zhē-ə) *n. Psychol.* A term describing the various modes of paranormal perception, such as clairvoyance.

cryp·tic (krĭp'tĭk) also **cryp·ti·cal** (-tĭ-kəl) *adj.* **1.** Having an ambiguous or hidden meaning; enigmatic: *cryptic comments.* **2.** Of a secret or occult nature; mystifying. **3.** *Biol.* Tending to conceal or camouflage: *cryptic coloring.* [LLat. *crypticus* < Gk. *kruptikos* < *kruptos,* hidden < *kruptein,* to hide.] —**cryp'ti·cal·ly** *adv.*

crypto– or **crypt–** *pref.* Hidden; secret: *cryptoclastic.* [< Gk. *kruptos,* hidden < *kruptein,* to hide.]

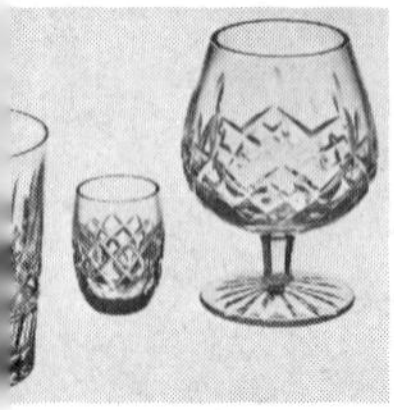

crystal
Crystal glassware

cryp·to·clas·tic (krĭp'tō-klăs'tĭk) *adj.* Composed of microscopic fragments. Used of rocks.

cryp·to·coc·co·sis (krĭp'tə-kŏ-kō'sĭs) *n.* A systemic infection caused by the fungus *Cryptococcus neoformans,* which can affect any organ of the body but most often occurs in the central nervous system. [NLat. *Cryptoccus,* fungus genus + -OSIS.]

cryp·to·crys·tal·line (krĭp'tō-krĭs'tə-lĭn) *adj.* Having a microscopic crystalline structure.

cryp·to·gam (krĭp'tə-găm') *n. Bot.* Any of the flowerless and seedless plants that reproduce by spores, such as fungi, algae, mosses, and ferns. [< NLat. *cryptogamia* : CRYPTO- + *-gamia,* -gamy.] —**cryp'to·gam'ic** or **cryp·tog'a·mous** (-tŏg'ə-məs) *adj.*

cryp·to·gen·ic (krĭp'tə-jĕn'ĭk) also **cryp·tog·e·nous** (krĭp-tŏj'ə-nəs) *adj.* Of obscure or unknown origin. Used of diseases.

crystal ball

cryp·to·gram (krĭp'tə-grăm') *n.* **1.** Something written in code or cipher. **2.** A figure having a secret or occult significance. —**cryp'to·gram'mic** *adj.*

cryp·to·graph (krĭp'tə-grăf') *n.* **1.** A cryptogram. **2.** A system of secret or cipher writing; cipher. **3. a.** A device for translating plain text into cipher. **b.** A device for deciphering codes and ciphers. [Back-formation < CRYPTOGRAPHY.]

cryp·tog·ra·phy (krĭp-tŏg'rə-fē) *n.* **1.** The art or process of writing in or deciphering secret code. **2.** A system of secret writing. —**cryp·tog'ra·pher, cryp·tog'ra·phist** *n.* —**cryp'to·graph'ic** (-tə-grăf'ĭk) *adj.* —**cryp'to·graph'i·cal·ly** *adv.*

cryp·to·me·ri·a (krĭp'tə-mîr'ē-ə) *n.* An evergreen tree, *Cryptomeria japonica,* native to Japan, having short, inward-curving needles and soft, durable, fragrant wood. [NLat. *Cryptomeria,* genus name : CRYPTO- + Gk. *meros,* part.]

crypt·or·chism (krĭp-tôr'kĭz'əm) also **crypt·or·chi·dism** (-kĭ-dĭz'əm) *n.* A condition marked by the failure of the testes to descend into the scrotum. [NLat. *cryptorchidismus* : CRYPT(O)- + *orchis,* testicle < Gk. *orkhis.*] —**crypt·or'chid** *n.*

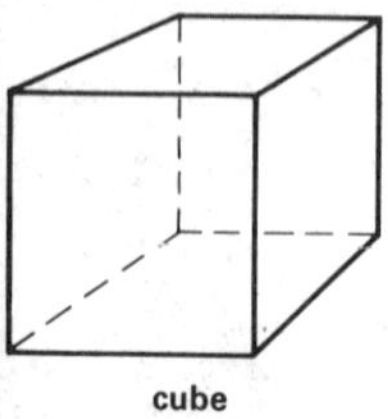

cube

cryp·to·zo·ite (krĭp'tə-zō'īt') *n.* A malaria parasite as it exists in bodily tissue prior to invasion of the red blood cells. [CRYPTO- + (SPORO)ZOITE.]

crys·tal (krĭs'təl) *n.* **1. a.** A three-dimensional atomic, ionic, or molecular structure consisting of periodically repeated, identically constituted, congruent unit cells. **b.** The unit cell of such a structure. **2.** A body, as a piece of quartz, having a crystalline structure, often characterized by external planar faces visible without magnification. **3.** An oscillator, detector, or other electronic device based on crystalline piezoelectricity, magnetism, semiconductivity, or other electric properties. **4. a.** A high-quality clear, colorless glass. **b.** An object, esp. a vessel or ornament, made of such glass. **c.** Such objects collectively. **5.** A clear glass or plastic protective cover for the face of a watch or clock. —*adj.* Clear or transparent: *a crystal lake; the crystal clarity of his reasoning.* [ME *cristal* < OFr. < Lat. *crystallum* < Gk. *krustallos.*]

crystal ball *n.* A glass globe used in crystal gazing.

crystal detector *n.* A rectifying detector used esp. in early radio receivers and consisting of a semiconducting crystal in point contact with a fine metal wire.

crystal gazing *n.* Divination by gazing into a crystal ball. —**crystal gazer** *n.*

crystall– *pref.* Variant of **crystallo-.**

crys·tal·lif·er·ous (krĭs'tə-lĭf'ər-əs) also **crys·tal·lig·er·ous** (-lĭj'-) *adj.* Producing or containing crystals.

crys·tal·line (krĭs'tə-lĭn, -līn') *adj.* **1.** Pertaining to or made of crystal. **2.** Resembling crystal; transparent. [ME *cristallin* < OFr. < Lat. *crystallinus* < Gk. *krustallinos* < *krustallos,* crystal.] —**crys'tal·lin'i·ty** (-lĭn'ĭ-tē) *n.*

crystalline lens *n.* Lens (sense 3).

crys·tal·lite (krĭs'tə-līt') *n.* Any of numerous minute rudimentary, crystalline bodies found in glassy igneous rocks. [G. *Kristallit* < Gk. *krustallos,* crystal.] —**crys'tal·lit'ic** (-lĭt'ĭk) *adj.*

crys·tal·lize also **crys·tal·ize** (krĭs'tə-līz') *v.* **-lized, -liz·ing, -liz·es** also **-ized, -iz·ing, -iz·es.** —*tr.* **1.** To cause to form crystals or to assume a crystalline structure. **2.** To give a definite and permanent form to: *paused to crystallize her ideas.* **3.** To coat with sugar. —*intr.* **1.** To assume a crystalline form. **2.** To take on a definite and permanent form. —**crys'tal·liz'a·ble** *adj.* —**crys'tal·li·za'tion** *n.* —**crys'tal·liz'er** *n.*

crystallo– or **crystall–** *pref.* Crystal: *crystallize.* [< Gk. *krustallos,* crystal.]

crys·tal·log·ra·phy (krĭs'tə-lŏg'rə-fē) *n.* The science of crystal structure and phenomena. —**crys'tal·lo·graph'ic** (-lə-grăf'ĭk), **crys'tal·lo·graph'i·cal** *adj.* —**crys'tal·lo·graph'i·cal·ly** *adv.* —**crys'tal·log'ra·pher** *n.*

crys·tal·loid (krĭs'tə-loid') *n.* **1.** *Chem.* A water-soluble crystalline substance capable of diffusion through a semipermeable membrane. **2.** *Bot.* Any of various minute crystallike particles consisting of protein, found in certain plant cells, esp. oily seeds. —*adj.* Resembling or having properties of a crystal or crystalloid. —**crys'tal·loi'dal** (-loid'l) *adj.*

crystal pickup *n.* A phonographic pickup that uses a piezoelectric crystal to convert stylus vibrations into electric impulses.

crystal set *n.* An early radio receiver using a crystal detector.

crystal violet *n.* A dye derived from rosaniline and used as a general biological stain.

Cs The symbol for the element cesium.

cte·nid·i·um (tĭ-nĭd'ē-əm) *n., pl.* **-i·a** (-ē-ə). *Zool.* A comblike structure, such as the respiratory apparatus of a mollusk or a row of spines in some insects. [NLat. < Gk. *kteis, kten-,* comb.]

cten·oid (tĕn'oid', tē'noid') *adj. Biol.* Having narrow segments or spines resembling the teeth of a comb; comblike: *fishes with ctenoid scales.* [Gk. *ktenoeidēs,* comblike : *kteis,* comb + *-eidēs,* -oid.]

cten·o·phore (tĕn'ə-fôr', -fōr') *n.* Any of various marine animals of the phylum Ctenophora, having transparent, gelatinous bodies bearing eight rows of comblike cilia used for locomotion. [NLat. *Ctenophora,* phylum name : Gk. *kteis,* comb + Gk. *pherein,* to bear.] —**cte·noph'o·ran** (tĭ-nŏf'ər-ən) *adj.*

Cu The symbol for the element copper. [Lat. *cuprum.* —see COPPER.]

cub (kŭb) *n.* **1.** The young of certain carnivorous animals, such as the bear, wolf, or lion. **2.** An inexperienced, awkward, or ill-mannered youth. **3.** A novice or learner, particularly in newspaper reporting. **4. Cub.** A Cub Scout. [Orig. unknown.]

cub·age (kyōō'bĭj) *n.* Cubic content or volume.

cu·ba·ture (kyōō'bə-chōōr', -chər) *n.* **1.** The determination of the cubic contents of a solid. **2.** Cubage. [CUB(E) + (QUADR)ATURE.]

cub·by (kŭb'ē) *n., pl.* **-bies.** A cubbyhole. [< obs. *cub,* stall, prob. of LG orig.]

cub·by·hole (kŭb'ē-hōl') *n.* **1.** A snug or cramped space or room. **2.** A small compartment. **3.** A small cupboard or closet.

cube (kyōōb) *n.* **1.** *Math.* A regular solid having six congruent square faces. **2.** Anything having the general shape of a cube. **3.** *Math.* The third power of a number or quantity. —*tr.v.* **cubed, cub·ing, cubes. 1.** To raise (a quantity or number) to the third power. **2.** To determine the cubic contents of. **3.** To form or cut into cubes; dice. **4.** To tenderize (meat) by breaking the fibers with superficial cuts in a pattern of squares. [OFr. < Lat. *cubus* < Gk. *kubos,* six-sided die.] —**cub'er** *n.*

cu·bé also **cu·be** (kyōō'bā', kyōō-bā') *n.* **1.** Any of various tropical American shrubs or plants, esp. of the genus *Lonchocarpus,* whose roots yield rotenone. **2.** An extract from the roots of the cubé plants, used as a fish poison and insecticide. [Am. Sp.]

cu·beb (kyo͞o′bĕb′) *n.* **1.** A treelike woody vine, *Piper cubeba,* of southeastern Asia, bearing brownish berries. **2.** The dried, unripe, spicy fruit of the cubeb, used as a stimulant and diuretic and sometimes smoked in cigarettes. [ME *cubibe* < OFr. *cubebe* < Med. Lat. *cubeba* < Ar. *kabābah.*]

cube root *n. Math.* A number whose cube is equal to a given number.

cube steak *n.* A thin slice of beef made tender by cubing.

cu·bic (kyo͞o′bĭk) *adj.* **1. a.** Having the shape of a cube. **b.** Having a shape approximating that of a cube. **2. a.** Having three dimensions. **b.** Having a volume equal to a cube whose edge is of a stated length: *a cubic foot.* **3.** *Math.* Of the third power, order, or degree. **4.** Isometric. *—n. Math.* A cubic expression, curve, or equation. **—cu′bic·ly** *adv.*

cu·bi·cal (kyo͞o′bĭ-kəl) *adj.* **1.** Cubic. **2.** Of or pertaining to volume. **—cu′bi·cal·ly** *adv.* **—cu′bi·cal·ness** *n.*

cu·bi·cle (kyo͞o′bĭ-kəl) *n.* **1.** A small sleeping compartment. **2.** A small compartment. [ME < Lat. *cubiculum,* bed chamber < *cubare,* to lie down.]

cubic measure *n.* A unit, as a cubic foot, or a system of units used to measure volume or capacity.

cu·bi·form (kyo͞o′bə-fôrm′) *adj.* Having the shape of a cube.

cub·ism (kyo͞o′bĭz′əm) *n.* A nonrepresentational school of painting and sculpture developed in Paris in the early 20th century, characterized by the reduction and fragmentation of natural forms into abstract and often geometric structures. [Fr. *cubisme* < *cube,* cube.] **—cub′ist** *n.* **—cu·bis′tic** *adj.* **—cu·bis′ti·cal·ly** *adv.*

cu·bit (kyo͞o′bĭt) *n.* An ancient unit of linear measure, originally equal to the length of the forearm from the tip of the middle finger to the elbow, or from 17 to 22 inches. [ME *cubite* < Lat. *cubitum,* elbow.]

cu·boid (kyo͞o′boid′) *adj.* **1.** Having the shape or approximate shape of a cube. **2.** *Anat.* Designating a bone on the side of the tarsus between the calcaneus and the fourth and fifth metatarsal bones of the foot. *—n. Anat.* **1.** The cuboid bone. **2.** *Math.* A rectangular parallelepiped. **—cu·boi′dal** (kyo͞o-boid′l) *adj.*

Cub Scout *n.* A member of the junior division of the Boy Scouts.

cu·chi·fri·to (ko͞o′chĭ-frē′tō) *n.* A small deep-fried cube of pork. [Am. Sp. : *cuchi,* pig (< Sp. *cochino*) + Sp. *frito,* p.part. of *freir,* to fry (< Lat. *frigere*).]

Cu·chul·ain (ko͞o′ho͝ol-ĭn) *n. Myth.* A tribal hero of Ulster who single-handedly defended it against the rest of Ireland. [OIr. *Cú Chulainn* : *Cú,* hound + *Culainn,* of Culann, a legendary Irish smith.]

cuck·ing stool (kŭk′ĭng) *n.* A former instrument of punishment, consisting of a chair in which the offender was tied and exposed to public derision or ducked in water. [ME *cukking stol* < *cukken,* to defecate, of Scand. orig.]

cuck·old (kŭk′əld, ko͝ok′-) *n.* A man whose wife has committed adultery. *—tr.v.* **-old·ed, -old·ing, -olds.** To make a cuckold of. [ME *cokewald* < OFr. **cucuald* < *cucu,* the cuckoo.] **—cuck′old·ry** (kŭk′əl-drē) *n.*

cuck·oo (ko͞o′ko͞o, ko͝ok′o͞o) *n., pl.* **-oos. 1. a.** An Old World bird, *Cuculus canorus,* having grayish plumage and a characteristic two-note call. **b.** Any of various related birds of the family Cuculidae, including several New World species. **2.** The call or cry of a cuckoo. **3.** A foolish person; simpleton. *—tr.v.* **-ooed, -oo·ing, -oos.** To repeat again and again. *—adj.* Crazy or foolish. [ME *cuccu.*]

cuckoo clock *n.* A wall clock having a mechanical cuckoo announcing intervals of time.

cuck·oo·flow·er (ko͞o′ko͞o-flou′ər, ko͝ok′o͞o-) *n.* **1.** A plant, *Cardamine pratensis,* of the North Temperate Zone, having white or rose-pink flowers. **2.** The ragged robin.

cuck·oo·pint (ko͞o′ko͞o-pĭnt′, ko͝ok′o͞o-) *n.* A European plant, *Arum maculatum,* having arrow-shaped leaves and a spadix enclosed in a purple-spotted spathe. [Obs. *cuckoopintle* < ME *cokkupyntel* : *cokku,* cuckoo + *pintle,* penis < OE *pintel.*]

cuckoo spit *n.* A frothy mass of liquid secreted on plant stems as a protective covering by nymphs of the spittlebug.

cu·cu·li·form (kyo͞o′kə-lə-fôrm′) *adj.* Of or belonging to the order Cuculiformes, which includes the cuckoos and related birds. [NLat. *Cuculiformes,* order name : Lat. *cuculus,* cuckoo + Lat. *forma,* shape.]

cu·cul·late (kyo͞o′kə-lāt′, kyo͞o-kŭl′āt′) also **cu·cul·lat·ed** (kyo͞o′kə-lā′tĭd) *adj.* Having the shape of a cowl or hood: *cucullate sepals.* [Med. Lat. *cucullatus* < Lat. *cucullus,* hood.] **—cu′cul·late′ly** *adv.*

cu·cum·ber (kyo͞o′kŭm′bər) *n.* **1.** A vine, *Cucumis sativus,* cultivated for its edible fruit. **2.** The usually cylindrical fruit of the cucumber vine, having a hard green rind and white succulent flesh. [ME *cucomer* < OFr. *coucombre* < Lat. *cucumis.*]

cucumber mosaic *n.* A viral disease of the cucumber plant that produces a variegated spotting of the leaves and fruits.

cucumber tree *n.* A tree, *Magnolia acuminata,* of eastern and central North America, having cup-shaped greenish-yellow flowers and brown or scarlet cucumber-shaped fruit.

cu·cur·bit (kyo͞o-kûr′bĭt) *n.* **1.** A gourd-shaped flask forming the body of an alembic, formerly used in distillation. **2.** Any of various vines of the family Cucurbitaceae, which includes the squash, pumpkin, and cucumber. [ME *cucurbite,* < OFr. < Lat. *cucurbita,* gourd.]

cud (kŭd) *n.* **1.** Food regurgitated from the first stomach to the mouth of a ruminant and chewed again. **2.** Something suitable to be held in the mouth and chewed, such as a quid of tobacco. ***—idiom.* chew the cud.** To ponder over; meditate. [ME < OE *cudu.*]

cud·bear (kŭd′bâr′) *n.* A purplish-red coloring substance derived from certain lichens. [After *Cuthbert* Gordon, 18th-cent. chemist.]

cud·dle (kŭd′l) *v.* **-dled, -dling, -dles.** *—tr.* To fondle in the arms; hug tenderly. *—intr.* To nestle; snuggle. *—n.* The act of cuddling; a hug or embrace. [Orig. unknown.] **—cud′dle·some** *adj.* **—cud′dly** *adj.*

cud·dy[1] (kŭd′ē) *n., pl.* **-dies. 1.** A small cabin or the cook's galley on a ship. **2.** A small room or cupboard. [Orig. unknown.]

cud·dy[2] (kŭd′ē) *n., pl.* **-dies.** *Scot.* **1.** A donkey. **2.** A fool; dolt. [Perh. < *Cuddy,* nickname for *Cuthbert.*]

cudg·el (kŭj′əl) *n.* A short, heavy club. *—tr.v.* **-eled, -el·ing, -els** also **-elled, -el·ling, -els.** To beat or strike with a cudgel. ***—idioms.* cudgel one's brains.** To think hard. **take up the cudgels (for).** To join in a dispute, esp. in defense of a participant. [ME *cuggel* < OE *cycgel.*] **—cudg′el·er** *n.*

cud·weed (kŭd′wēd′) *n.* **1.** Any of various woolly plants of the genus *Gnaphalium,* having clusters of whitish or yellow buttonlike flowers. **2.** An annual herb, *Filago germanica,* having capitate clusters of woolly heads.

cue[1] (kyo͞o) *n.* **1.** A long, tapered rod used to propel the ball in billiards and pool. **2.** A long stick with a concave attachment at one end for shoving disks in shuffleboard. **3.** A queue of hair. *—tr.v.* **cued, cu·ing, cues. 1.** To strike with a cue. **2.** To braid or twist (hair) into a cue. [Fr. *queue,* tail < OFr. *coue* < Lat. *cauda.*]

cue[2] (kyo͞o) *n.* **1.** A word or bit of stage business signaling the beginning of another action or speech. **2. a.** A reminder or a prompting as a signal to do something. **b.** A hint or suggestion. **3.** *Psychol.* A perceived signal for action, esp. one that produces an operant response. *—tr.v.* **cued, cu·ing, cues.** To give (a performer) a cue. ***—phrasal verb.* cue in.** To tell a latecomer what has happened up to now. [Orig. unknown.]

cue[3] (kyo͞o) *n.* The letter *q.*

cue ball *n.* The white ball that is propelled with the cue in billiards and pool.

cues·ta (kwĕs′tə) *n. Southwestern U.S.* A land elevation with a gentle slope on one side and a cliff on the other. [Sp., sloping side < Lat. *costa,* side.]

cuff[1] (kŭf) *n.* **1.** A fold or band used as trimming at the bottom of a sleeve. **2.** The turned-up fold at the bottom of a trouser leg. **3.** The part of a glove that extends over the wrist. **4.** A handcuff. ***—idioms.* off the cuff.** *Informal.* Extemporaneously. **on the cuff.** *Informal.* On credit. [ME *cuffe,* mitten.]

cuff[2] (kŭf) *tr.v.* **cuffed, cuff·ing, cuffs.** To strike with the open hand; slap. *—n.* A blow or slap with the open hand. [Orig. unknown.]

cuff links *n.* A pair of linked buttons or a similar device used to fasten the cuffs of a shirt.

Cu·fic (ko͞o′fĭk, kyo͞o′-) *adj.* Variant of **Kufic.**

cui·rass (kwĭ-răs′) *n.* **1. a.** A piece of armor for protecting the breast and back. **b.** The breastplate alone. **2.** *Zool.* A protective covering of bony plates or scales. *—tr.v.* **-rassed, -rass·ing, -rass·es.** To protect with a cuirass. [ME *curace* < OFr. *cuirasse* < Lat. *coriaceus,* of leather < *corium,* hide.]

cui·ras·sier (kwîr′ə-sîr′) *n.* A horse soldier in European armies whose equipment included the cuirass. [Fr. < *cuirasse,* cuirasse < OFr.]

Cui·se·naire (kwē′zə-nâr′). A trademark for a set of colored rods used to teach arithmetic.

cuish (kwĭsh) *n.* Variant of **cuisse.**

cui·sine (kwĭ-zēn′) *n.* **1.** A characteristic manner or style of preparing food. **2.** The food prepared. [Fr. < LLat. *coquina,* cookery, kitchen < *coquere,* to cook.]

cuisse (kwĭs) also **cuish** (kwĭsh) *n.* Plate armor worn to protect the thigh. [Back-formation < ME *cuisses* (pl.) < OFr. *cuisseaux,* pl. of *cuissel* < *cuisse,* thigh < Lat. *coxa,* hip.]

culch (kŭlch) *n.* **1.** A natural bed for oysters, consisting of gravel or crushed shells to which oyster spawn may adhere. **2.** The spawn of the oyster. **3.** Rubbish or refuse. [Perh. ult. < OFr. *culche,* couch.]

cul-de-sac (kŭl′dĭ-săk′, ko͝ol′-) *n., pl.* **cul-de-sacs. 1. a.** A dead-end street. **b.** An impasse. **2.** *Anat.* A saclike cavity or tube open only at one end. [Fr. : *cul,* bottom + *de,* of the + *sac,* sack.]

cu·let (kyo͞o′lĭt, kŭl′ĭt) *n.* **1.** The flat face of a gem cut as a brilliant. **2.** One of the plates of medieval armor covering the lower back. [Fr., dim. of *cul,* rump < Lat. *culus.*]

cu·lex (kyo͞o′lĕks′) *n., pl.* **-li·ces** (-lĭ-sēz′). Any of various mosquitoes of the genus *Culex,* which includes the common house mosquito, *C. pipiens.* [NLat. *Culex,* genus name < Lat. *culex,* gnat.]

cu·li·nar·y (kyo͞o′lə-nĕr′ē, kŭl′ə-) *adj.* Of or pertaining to a kitchen or to cookery. [Lat. *culinarius* < *culina,* kitchen, al-

cubeb

cubism
Detail from "Nature Morte" by Georges Braque

cuckoo
American yellow-billed cuckoo

cuckoo clock

cuckoopint

p **pop** / r **roar** / s **sauce** / sh **ship, dish** / t **tight** / th **thin, path** / *th* **this, bathe** / ŭ **cut** / ûr **urge** / v **valve** / w **with** / y **yes** / z **zebra, size** / zh **vision** / ə **about, item, edible, gallop, circus** / œ *Fr.* **feu,** *Ger.* **schön** / ü *Fr.* **tu,** *Ger.* **über** / KH *Ger.* **ich,** *Scot.* **loch** / N *Fr.* **bon.**

teration of *coquina.* —see CUISINE.] **—cu′li·nar′i·ly** (-nâr′ə-lē) *adv.*

cull (kŭl) *tr.v.* **culled, cull·ing, culls. 1.** To pick out from others; select. **2.** To gather; collect. *—n.* Something picked out from others, esp. something rejected because of inferior quality. [ME *cullen* < OFr. *cuillir* < Lat. *colligere.* —see COLLECT[1].] **—cull′er** *n.*

cul·len·der (kŭl′ən-dər) *n.*. Variant of **colander.**

cul·let (kŭl′ĭt) *n.* Scraps of broken or waste glass gathered for remelting. [Alteration of *collet,* neck of glass left on the blowing iron < Fr., collar, dim. of *col,* neck < OFr. < Lat. *collum.*]

cul·lis (kŭl′ĭs) *n.* A gutter or groove in a roof. [ME *colis* < OFr. *coleïs,* channel < *coler,* to pour < Lat. *colare,* to filter < *colum,* sieve.]

culm[1] (kŭlm) *n.* The jointed stem of a grass or sedge. [Lat. *culmus,* stalk.]

culm[2] (kŭlm) *n.* **1.** Waste from anthracite coal mines, consisting of fine coal, coal dust, and dirt. **2. a.** Carboniferous shale. **b.** Inferior anthracite coal. [ME *colme,* coal dust.]

cul·mi·nant (kŭl′mə-nənt) *adj.* **1.** Being at the highest altitude. **2.** Culminating; highest.

cul·mi·nate (kŭl′mə-nāt′) *intr.v.* **-nat·ed, -nat·ing, -nates. 1.** To reach the highest point or degree; climax. **2.** *Astron.* To reach the highest point above an observer's horizon. Used of stars and other celestial bodies. [LLat. *culminare, culminat-* < Lat. *culmen,* summit.] **—cul′mi·na′tion** *n.*

culottes

cu·lottes (ko͞o-lŏts′, kyo͞o-, ko͞o′lŏts′, kyo͞o′-) *pl.n.* A woman's full trousers cut to resemble a skirt. [Fr., breeches, dim. of *cul,* rump < Lat. *culus.*]

cul·pa (kŭl′pə, ko͝ol′-) *n. Law.* Fault; misconduct. [Lat.]

cul·pa·ble (kŭl′pə-bəl) *adj.* Responsible for wrong or error; blameworthy. [ME *coupable* < OFr. < Lat. *culpabilis* < *culpare,* to blame < *culpa,* fault.] **—cul′pa·bil′i·ty** *n.* **—cul′pa·bly** *adv.*

cul·prit (kŭl′prĭt) *n.* **1.** One charged with an offense or crime. **2.** One guilty of a fault or crime. [Prob. < AN *culpable,* culpable < Lat. *culpabilis.*]

cult (kŭlt) *n.* **1.** A system or community of religious worship and ritual. **2. a.** A religion or religious sect generally considered to be extremist or bogus. **b.** Followers of such a religion or sect. **3. a.** Obsessive devotion or veneration for a person, principle, or ideal, esp. when regarded as a fad. **b.** The object of such devotion. **4.** An exclusive group of persons sharing an esoteric interest. ***—modifier:*** *a cult figure.* [Fr. *culte* < Lat. *cultus,* worship < p.part. of *colere,* to cultivate.] **—cul′tic** (kŭl′tĭk) *adj.* **—cult′ish** *adj.* **—cult′ism** *n.* **—cult′ist** *n.*

cul·ti·gen (kŭl′tə-jən) *n.* An organism, esp. a cultivated plant, such as maize, of a kind not known to have a wild or uncultivated counterpart. [CULTI(VATED) + -GEN.]

cul·ti·va·ble (kŭl′tə-və-bəl) *adj.* Capable of being cultivated. **—cul′ti·va·bil′i·ty** *n.*

cultivator

cul·ti·var (kŭl′tə-vär′, -vâr′) *n.* A horticulturally or agriculturally derived variety of a plant, as distinguished from a natural variety. [CULTI(VATED) + VAR(IETY).]

cul·ti·vate (kŭl′tə-vāt′) *tr.v.* **-vat·ed, -vat·ing, -vates. 1. a.** To improve and prepare (land), as by plowing or fertilizing, for raising crops; till. **b.** To loosen or dig (soil) around growing plants. **2.** To grow or tend (a plant or crop). **3.** To promote the growth of (a biological culture, for example). **4.** To nurture; foster. **5.** To form and refine, as by education. **6.** To seek the acquaintance or good will of; make friends with. [Med. Lat. *cultivare, cultivat-* < *cultivus,* tilled < Lat. *cultus,* p.part. of *colere,* to till.] **—cul′ti·vat′a·ble** *adj.*

cul·ti·vat·ed (kŭl′tə-vā′tĭd) *adj.* Socially polished; cultured; refined.

cul·ti·va·tion (kŭl′tə-vā′shən) *n.* **1. a.** The act of cultivating. **b.** The state of being cultivated. **2.** Social polish; refinement.

cul·ti·va·tor (kŭl′tə-vā′tər) *n.* **1.** One that cultivates. **2.** An implement or machine for loosening the earth and destroying weeds around growing plants.

cumin

cul·trate (kŭl′trāt′) also **cul·trat·ed** (-trā′tĭd) *adj.* Sharp-edged and pointed; knifelike. [Lat. *cultratus* < *culter,* knife.]

cul·tur·al (kŭl′chər-əl) *adj.* **1.** Of or relating to culture. **2.** Obtained by specialized breeding, as certain plant varieties. **—cul′tur·al·ly** *adv.*

cultural anthropology *n.* The scientific study of human culture based on archaeological, ethnologic, ethnographic, linguistic, social, and psychological data and methods of analysis.

cul·ture (kŭl′chər) *n.* **1.** The totality of socially transmitted behavior patterns, arts, beliefs, institutions, and all other products of human work and thought characteristic of a community or population. **2.** A style of social and artistic expression peculiar to a society or class. **3.** Intellectual and artistic activity, and the works produced by it. **4.** The act of developing the social, moral, and intellectual faculties through education. **5.** A high degree of taste and refinement formed by aesthetic and intellectual training. **6.** The development of the body through special training: *physical culture.* **7.** The cultivation of the soil; tillage. **8.** The breeding of animals or growing of plants, esp. to produce improved stock. **9.** *Biol.* **a.** The growing of microorganisms in a nutrient medium. **b.** Such a growth or colony, as of bacteria. **c.** Medium (sense 6.b.). *—tr.v.* **-tured, -tur·ing, -tures. 1.** To cultivate; till. **2.** To develop (microorganisms or tissues, for example) in a culture medium. [ME, cultivation < OFr. < Lat. *cultura* < *cultus.* —see CULTIVATE.]

Synonyms: *culture, cultivation, breeding, refinement, gentility, taste.* These nouns are applied to personal achievement in the development of intellect, manners, and aesthetic appreciation. *Culture,* which overlaps the others, implies enlightenment attained through close association with and appreciation of the highest level of civilization. *Cultivation* usually refers to the self-improvement or self-development by which a person acquires culture. *Breeding* is the development of good character and behavior, and is especially revealed in manners, poise, and sensitivity to the feelings of others. *Refinement,* the highest product of breeding, stresses aversion to coarseness; sometimes it may imply a delicacy of feeling associated with fastidiousness. *Gentility* is sometimes still synonymous with refinement or good birth; in modern usage it may suggest extreme elegance in behavior or manners. *Taste* is the capacity for recognizing and appreciating what is aesthetically superior.

cul·tured (kŭl′chərd) *adj.* **1.** Cultivated. **2.** Produced under artificial and controlled conditions: *cultured pearls.*

culture shock *n.* A condition of confusion and anxiety that can affect an individual suddenly exposed to an alien culture or milieu.

cul·tus (kŭl′təs) *n., pl.* **-tus·es** or **-ti** (-tī′). A religious cult. [NLat. < Lat. —see CULT.]

cul·ver (kŭl′vər) *n.* A dove; pigeon. [ME < OE *culufre* < VLat. **columbra* < Lat. *columbula,* dim. of *columba,* dove.]

cul·ver·in (kŭl′vər-ĭn) *n.* **1.** An early, crudely made musket. **2.** A heavy cannon used in the 16th and 17th centuries. [ME < OFr. *coulevrine* < *couleuvre,* snake < Lat. *colubra,* fem. of *coluber.*]

Cul·ver's root (kŭl′vərz) *n.* **1.** A North American plant, *Veronicastrum virginicum,* having spikes of small white or purplish flowers. **2.** The root of the Culver's root, formerly used as a cathartic and emetic. [After Dr. *Culver,* 18th-cent. American physician.]

cul·vert (kŭl′vərt) *n.* A sewer or drain crossing under a road or embankment. [Orig. unknown.]

cum (ko͝om, kŭm) *prep.* Together with; plus: *her attic-cum-studio.* [Lat.]

cum·ber (kŭm′bər) *tr.v.* **-bered, -ber·ing, -bers. 1.** To weigh down; burden: *cumbered with many duties.* **2.** To hamper or hinder, as by being in the way: *cumbered with a long poncho.* **3.** To litter or pile in a disorderly state; clutter up: *The roofless temple walls still cumbered the new gardens.* *—n.* A hindrance; encumbrance. [ME *combren,* to annoy, short for *acombren,* perh. of OFr. orig.] **—cum′ber·er** *n.*

cum·ber·some (kŭm′bər-səm) *adj.* **1.** Difficult to handle or manage because of weight or bulk; unwieldy. **2.** Troublesome or onerous. **—cum′ber·some·ly** *adv.*

cum·brous (kŭm′brəs) *adj.* Cumbersome. [ME < *cumbren,* to annoy.]

cum gra·no sa·lis (ko͝om grä′nō sä′lĭs, kŭm grā′nō sā′lĭs) *adv.* With a grain of salt; with skepticism. [Lat.]

cum·in (kŭm′ĭn) *n.* **1.** An Old World plant, *Cuminum cyminum,* having finely divided leaves and small white or pinkish flowers. **2.** The aromatic seeds of the cumin, used as a condiment. [ME < OFr. < Lat. *cuminum* < Gk. *kuminon,* of Semitic orig.]

cum lau·de (ko͝om lou′də, lou′dē, kŭm lô′dē) *adv. & adj.* With honor. Used on diplomas as a mark of high standing. [NLat., with praise.]

cummerbund

cum·mer·bund (kŭm′ər-bŭnd′) *n.* A broad, pleated sash worn as an article of men's formal dress. [Hindi *kamarband* < Pers., waistband : *kamar,* loins + *band,* band.]

cum·quat (kŭm′kwŏt′) *n.* Variant of **kumquat.**

cum·shaw (kŭm′shô′) *n.* A tip; gratuity. [Pidgin E. < Chin. (Amoy) *kam sia,* an expression of thanks.]

cumul– *pref.* Variant of **cumulo-.**

cu·mu·late (kyo͞om′yə-lāt′) *v.* **-lat·ed, -lat·ing, -lates.** *—tr.* **1.** To gather in a heap; accumulate. **2.** To combine into one unit; merge. **3.** To expand by an increment in new material. *—intr.* To become massed. [Lat. *cumulare, cumulat-* < *cumulus,* heap.] **—cu′mu·la′tion** *n.*

cu·mu·la·tive (kyo͞om′yə-lā′tĭv, -yə-lə-tĭv) *adj.* **1.** Increasing or enlarging by successive addition. **2.** Acquired by or resulting from accumulation. **3.** Of or pertaining to interest or a dividend that is added to the next payment if not paid when due. **4.** *Law.* Designating additional or supporting evidence. **5.** *Statistics.* **a.** Of or pertaining to the sum of the frequencies of experimentally determined values of a random variable that are less than or equal to a specified value. **b.** Of or pertaining to experimental error that increases in magnitude with each successive measurement. **—cu′mu·la′tive·ly** *adv.* **—cu′mu·la′tive·ness** *n.*

cumulative voting *n.* A system of voting in proportional representation in which each voter is given as many votes as there are positions to be filled and allowed to cast those votes for one candidate or distributed in any way among the candidates.

cu·mu·li (kyo͞om′yə-lī′). Plural of **cumulus.**

cumuli– *pref.* Variant of **cumulo-.**

cu·mu·li·form (kyo͞om′yə-lə-fôrm′) *adj.* Having the shape of a cumulus.
cumulo– or **cumuli–** or **cumul–** *pref.* Cumulus: *cumulonimbus.* [< CUMULUS.]
cu·mu·lo·nim·bus (kyo͞om′yə-lō-nĭm′bəs) *n., pl.* **-bus·es** or **-bi** (-bī′). An extremely dense, vertically developed cumulus with a relatively hazy outline and a glaciated top, usually producing heavy rains, thunderstorms, or hailstorms.
cu·mu·lus (kyo͞om′yə-ləs) *n., pl.* **-li** (-lī′). **1.** A dense, white, fluffy, flat-based cloud with a multiple rounded top and a well-defined outline, usually formed by the ascent of thermally unstable air masses. **2.** A pile, mound, or heap. [NLat. < Lat., heap.] **—cu′mu·lous** *adj.*
cunc·ta·tion (kŭngk-tā′shən) *n.* A delay. [Lat. *cunctatio, cunctation-* < *cunctus,* p.part. of *cunctari,* to delay.] **—cunc′-ta′tive** (kŭngk′tā′tĭv, -tə-tĭv), **cunc′ta·to′ry** (-tə-tôr′ē, -tōr′ē) *adj.* **—cunc′ta′tor** *n.*
cu·ne·al (kyo͞o′nē-əl) *adj.* Wedge-shaped. [NLat. *cunealis* < Lat. *cuneus,* wedge.]
cu·ne·ate (kyo͞o′nē-ĭt, -āt′) also **cu·ne·at·ed** (-ā′tĭd) *adj.* Wedge-shaped. Used esp. of leaves that are narrow and triangular and taper toward the base. [Lat. *cuneatus* < *cuneus,* wedge.] **—cu′ne·ate′ly** *adv.*
cu·ne·i·form (kyo͞o′nē-ə-fôrm′, kyo͞o-nē′-) *adj.* **1.** Wedge-shaped. **2. a.** Designating the wedge-shaped characters used in ancient Sumerian, Akkadian, Assyrian, Babylonian, and Persian writing. **b.** Designating documents or inscriptions written in such characters. **3.** *Anat.* Denoting any of the three wedge-shaped bones in the tarsus of the foot. *—n.* **1.** Cuneiform writing. **2.** A cuneiform bone. [Fr. *cunéiforme* < Lat. *cuneus,* wedge.]
cun·ner (kŭn′ər) *n.* A marine fish, *Tautogolabrus adspersus,* of North American Atlantic waters. [Orig. unknown.]
cun·ni·lin·gus (kŭn′ə-lĭng′gəs) *n.* Oral stimulation of the clitoris or vulva. [NLat. < Lat., he who licks the vulva : *cunnus,* vulva + *lingere,* to lick.]
cun·ning (kŭn′ĭng) *adj.* **1.** Shrewd or crafty in manipulation or deception. **2.** Executed with or exhibiting ingenuity. **3.** *Regional.* Delicately pleasing; pretty; cute. *—n.* **1.** Skill in deception; guile. **2.** Skill or adeptness in performance; dexterity. [ME, pr.part. of *connen,* to know < OE *cunnan.*] **—cun′ning·ly** *adv.* **—cun′ning·ness** *n.*
cunt (kŭnt) *n. Obscene.* **1.** The female genital organs. **2.** A woman. [ME *cunte.*]
cup (kŭp) *n.* **1.** A small, open container, usually with a flat bottom and a handle, used for drinking. **2.** A cup and its contents. **3.** A measure of capacity equal to 1/2 pint, 8 ounces, or 16 tablespoons. **4.** The bowl of a drinking vessel. **5.** The chalice or the wine used in the celebration of the Eucharist. **6.** An ornamented cup-shaped vessel awarded as a prize or trophy. **7.** A golf hole or the metal container inside a hole. **8.** Either of the two parts of a brassiere that fit over the breasts. **9.** A rigid athletic supporter, usually made of plastic. **10.** Any of various beverages, usually combining wine, fruit, and spices. **11.** A dish served in a cup-shaped vessel: *fruit cup.* **12.** Anything resembling a cup. **13.** *Biol.* A cuplike structure or organ. **14.** A lot or portion to be suffered or enjoyed. *—tr.v.* **cupped, cup·ping, cups. 1.** To place in or as in a cup. **2.** To shape like a cup: *cup one's hand.* **—idioms. cup of tea.** Something that one enjoys or is expert in: *Opera is not my cup of tea.* **in one's cups.** Drunk. [ME *cuppe* < OE < LLat. *cuppa,* drinking vessel.]
cup·bear·er (kŭp′bâr′ər) *n.* One who serves wine, as in a royal household.
cup·board (kŭb′ərd) *n.* A closet or cabinet, usually with shelves for storing food, crockery, and other utensils.
cup·cake (kŭp′kāk′) *n.* A small cake baked in a cup-shaped container.
cu·pel (kyo͞o′pəl, kyo͞o-pĕl′) *n.* **1.** A small, shallow, porous vessel used in assaying to separate precious metals from less valuable elements such as lead. **2.** The bottom or receptacle in a silver-refining furnace. *—tr.v.* **-peled, -pel·ing, -pels** or **-pelled, -pel·ling, -pels.** To assay or separate from base metals in a cupel. [Fr. *coupelle,* dim. of *coupe,* cup < LLat. *cuppa,* drinking vessel.] **—cu′pel·er** *n.*
cu·pel·la·tion (kyo͞o′pə-lā′shən) *n.* A refining process for nonoxidizing metals, such as silver and gold, in which the components of a metallic mixture oxidized at high temperatures are separated by absorption into the walls of a cupel.
cup·ful (kŭp′fo͝ol′) *n., pl.* **-fuls. 1.** The amount a cup will hold. **2.** A measure of capacity equal to 1/2 pint, 8 ounces, or 16 tablespoons.
Cu·pid (kyo͞o′pĭd) *n. Rom. Myth.* The god of love. [Lat. *Cupido* < *cupido,* desire < *cupere,* to desire.]
cu·pid·i·ty (kyo͞o-pĭd′ĭ-tē) *n.* Excessive desire, esp. for wealth; avarice. [ME *cupidite* < OFr. < Lat. *cupiditas* < *cupidus,* desiring < *cupere,* to desire.]
cu·po·la (kyo͞o′pə-lə) *n.* **1. a.** A domed roof or ceiling. **b.** A small, usually domed structure surmounting a roof. **2.** A cylindrical shaft type of blast furnace used for remelting metals, usually iron, before casting. [Ital. < LLat. *cupula,* dim. of Lat. *cupa,* tub.]
cup·ping (kŭp′ĭng) *n.* A therapeutic process, rarely used in modern medicine, in which glass cups, partially evacuated by heating, are locally applied to the skin in order to draw blood toward or through the surface.
cup plant *n.* A coarse North American plant, *Silphium perfoliatum,* having yellow-rayed flowers. [From the cuplike configuration of its leaves.]
cupr– *pref.* Variant of **cupro-.**
cu·pre·ous (ko͞o′prē-əs, kyo͞o′-) *adj.* Of, concerning, resembling, or containing copper; coppery. [LLat. *cupreus* < *cuprum,* copper. —see COPPER[1].]
cupri– *pref.* Variant of **cupro-.**
cu·pric (ko͞o′prĭk, kyo͞o′-) *adj.* Of or containing divalent copper.
cu·prif·er·ous (ko͞o-prĭf′ər-əs, kyo͞o-) *adj.* Containing copper.
cu·prite (ko͞o′prīt′, kyo͞o′-) *n.* A natural red copper ore, essentially Cu_2O. [G. *Kuprit* < LLat. *cuprum,* copper. —see COPPER[1].]
cupro– or **cupri–** or **cupr–** *pref.* Copper: *cupriferous.* [LLat. *cuprum.* —see COPPER[1].]
cu·pro·nick·el (ko͞o′prō-nĭk′əl, kyo͞o′-) *n.* A copper-based alloy that contains 10 to 30 per cent nickel.
cu·prous (ko͞o′prəs, kyo͞o′-) *adj.* Of, pertaining to, or containing univalent copper.
cu·pu·late (kyo͞o′pyə-lāt′, -lĭt) also **cu·pu·lar** (-lər) *adj.* **1.** Resembling a small cup; cup-shaped. **2.** Having or bearing a cupule.
cu·pule (kyo͞o′pyo͞ol) *n. Biol.* A cup-shaped part, structure, or indentation, esp. the involucre of an acorn. [NLat. *cupula* < LLat., little cask, dim. of Lat. *cupa,* tub.]
cur (kûr) *n.* **1.** A dog considered to be inferior or undesirable; mongrel. **2.** A base or cowardly person. [ME *curre.*]
cur·a·ble (kyo͝or′ə-bəl) *adj.* Capable of being healed or cured. **—cur′a·bil′i·ty, cur′a·ble·ness** *n.* **—cur′a·bly** *adv.*
cu·ra·çao (kyo͝or′ə-sō′, -sou′, ko͝or′-) *n.* A liqueur flavored with the peel of the sour orange. [After *Curaçao,* an island in the Caribbean.]
cu·ra·cy (kyo͝or′ə-sē) *n., pl.* **-cies.** The office, duties, or term of office of a curate. [CURA(TE) + -CY.]
cu·ra·re or **cu·ra·ri** (ko͞o-rä′rē, kyo͞o-) *n.* **1.** Any of various resinous extracts of uncertain and variable chemical composition, obtained from several species of South American trees of the genera *Chondodendron* and *Strychnos,* used medicinally as a muscle relaxant and by some South American Indians as an arrow poison. **2.** Any of the trees from which curares are obtained. [Port. and Sp., both < Cariban *kurari.*]
cu·ra·rine (ko͞o-rä′rĭn, -rēn′, kyo͞o-) *n.* A poisonous alkaloid, $C_{19}H_{26}N_2O$, obtained from curare. [CURAR(E) + -INE[2].]
cu·ra·rize (ko͞o-rä′rīz′, kyo͞o-) *tr.v.* **-rized, -riz·ing, -riz·es. 1.** To poison with curare. **2.** To treat with curare so as to paralyze the motor nerves. **—cu·ra′ri·za′tion** *n.*
cu·ras·sow (ko͝or′ə-sō′, kyo͝or′-) *n.* Any of several long-tailed, crested tropical American birds of the family Cracidae, related to the pheasants and domestic fowl. [Alteration of *Curaçao,* an island in the Caribbean.]
cu·rate (kyo͝or′ĭt) *n.* **1.** A clergyman who has charge of a parish. **2.** A clergyman who assists a rector or vicar. [ME *curat* < Med. Lat. *curatus* < *cura,* spiritual charge < Lat., care.]
cu·ra·tive (kyo͝or′ə-tĭv) *adj.* **1.** Serving or tending to cure. **2.** Of or relating to the cure of disease. *—n.* Something that cures; remedy. **—cu′ra·tive·ly** *adv.* **—cu′ra·tive·ness** *n.*
cu·ra·tor (kyo͞o-rā′tər, kyo͝or′ə-tər) *n.* The administrative director of a museum, library, or other similar institution. [ME *curatour,* legal guardian < OFr. *curateur* < Lat. *curator,* overseer < *curare,* to take care of < *cura,* care.] **—cu′ra·to′ri·al** (kyo͝or′ə-tôr′ē-əl, -tōr′-) *adj.* **—cu·ra′tor·ship′** *n.*
curb (kûrb) *n.* **1.** Something that checks or restrains. **2.** A concrete border or row of joined stones forming part of a gutter along the edge of a street. **3.** An enclosing framework. **4.** A raised margin along an edge to confine or strengthen. **5.** A chain or strap serving in conjunction with the bit to restrain a horse. *—tr.v.* **curbed, curb·ing, curbs. 1.** To check, restrain, or control. **2.** To lead (a dog) off the sidewalk into the gutter so that it can excrete waste matter. **3.** To furnish with a curb. [OFr. *courbe,* horse bit < *courbe,* curved < Lat. *curvus.*] **—curb′er** *n.*
curb·ing (kûr′bĭng) *n.* **1.** The material used to construct a curb. **2.** A row of curbstones; curb.
curb roof *n.* A roof having two slopes on each side.
curb·stone (kûrb′stōn′) *n.* A stone or row of stones that constitutes a curb.
cur·cu·li·o (kər-kyo͞o′lē-ō′) *n., pl.* **-os.** Any of several weevils of the family Curculionidae, many of which are destructive to fruit, vegetables, and other plants. [Lat., a kind of weevil.]
cur·cu·ma (kûr′kyə-mə) *n.* Any of various Old World tropical plants of the genus *Curcuma,* having thick, aromatic rootstocks. *C. longa* is the source of turmeric. [NLat. *Curcuma,* genus name < Ar. *kurkum,* saffron.]
curd (kûrd) *n.* **1.** The coagulated part of milk, used to make cheese. **2.** A coagulation resembling curd. *—intr. & tr.v.* **curd·ed, curd·ing, curds.** To form or cause to form into curd; curdle; coagulate. [ME *crud.*] **—curd′y** *adj.*
curd cheese *n. Chiefly Brit.* Cottage cheese.
cur·dle (kûr′dl) *intr. & tr.v.* **-dled, -dling, -dles.** To change into or cause to change into curd. [Freq. of CURD.]
cure (kyo͝or) *n.* **1.** Restoration of health; recovery from disease. **2.** A method or course of medical treatment used to restore health. **3.** An agent, such as a drug, that restores

cumulonimbus

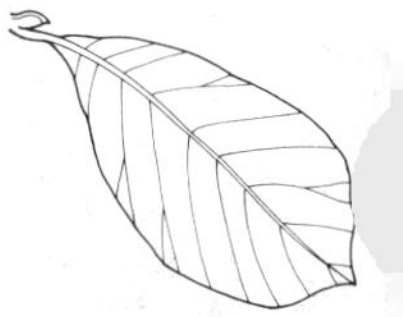
cuneate
Cuneate magnolia leaf

cuneiform

Cupid
Sculpture by Jean-Louis Lemoyne

cupola

George Miksch Sutton
curassow

p **pop** / r **roar** / s **sauce** / sh **ship, dish** / t **tight** / th **thin, path** / *th* **this, bathe** / ŭ **cut** / ûr **urge** / v **valve** / w **with** / y **yes** / z **zebra, size** / zh **vision** / ə **about,** item, edible, gallop, circus / œ *Fr.* **feu,** *Ger.* **schön** / ü *Fr.* **tu,** *Ger.* **über** / KH *Ger.* **ich,** *Scot.* **loch** / N *Fr.* **bon.**

health; remedy. **4.** Something that corrects or relieves a harmful or disturbing situation. **5.** *Eccles.* Spiritual charge or care of souls, as of a priest for his congregation. **6.** The office or duties of a curate. **7.** The act or process of preserving a product, such as fish, meat, and tobacco. —*v.* **cured, cur·ing, cures.** —*tr.* **1.** To restore to health. **2.** To get rid of; remedy: *cure an evil.* **3.** To preserve (meat, for example), as by salting, smoking, or aging. **4.** To prepare, preserve, or finish (a substance) by a chemical or physical process. **5.** To vulcanize (rubber). —*intr.* **1.** To effect a cure or recovery. **2.** To be prepared, preserved, or finished by a chemical or physical process. [ME, duty, care < OFr. < Lat. *cura.*] **—cure′less** *adj.* **—cur′er** *n.*

cu·ré (kyo͝o-rā′, kyo͝or′ā′) *n.* A parish priest. [Fr.]

cure-all (kyo͝or′ôl′) *n.* Something that cures all diseases or evils; panacea.

cu·ret (kyo͝o-rĕt′) *n.* Variant of **curette.**

cu·ret·tage (kyo͝or′ĭ-täzh′) *n.* Surgical scraping of a bodily cavity, as of the uterus, with a curette.

cu·rette also **cu·ret** (kyo͝o-rĕt′) *n.* A surgical instrument shaped like a scoop or spoon, used to remove dead tissue or growths from a bodily cavity. [Fr. < *curer,* to cure < OFr. < Lat. *curare,* to take care of < *cura,* care.]

cu·rette·ment (kyo͝o-rĕt′mənt) *n.* Curettage.

cur·few (kûr′fyo͞o) *n.* **1.** An order or regulation enjoining specified classes of the population to retire from the streets at a prescribed hour. **2. a.** The period during which a curfew regulation is in effect. **b.** The signal, as a bell, announcing it. [ME *curfeu* < OFr. *cuevrefeu,* cover the fire : *couvrir,* to cover + *feu,* fire < Lat. *focus,* hearth.]

cu·ri·a (ko͝or′ē-ə, kyo͝or′-) *n., pl.* **cu·ri·ae** (ko͝or′ē-ē′, kyo͝or′-). **1. a.** One of the ten primitive subdivisions of a tribe in early Rome, consisting of ten gentes. **b.** Its place of assembly. **2. a.** The Senate or any of the various buildings in which it met in republican Rome. **b.** The place of assembly of high councils in various Italian cities under Roman administration. **3.** The ensemble of central administrative and governmental services in imperial Rome. **4.** Often **Curia.** The central administration governing the Roman Catholic Church. **5. a.** A medieval assembly or council. **b.** A royal court of justice. [Lat., council.] **—cu′ri·al** *adj.*

cu·rie (kyo͝or′ē, kyo͝o-rē′) *n.* A unit of radioactivity, the amount of any nuclide that undergoes exactly 3.7×10^{10} radioactive disintegrations per second. [After Marie *Curie* (1867–1934).]

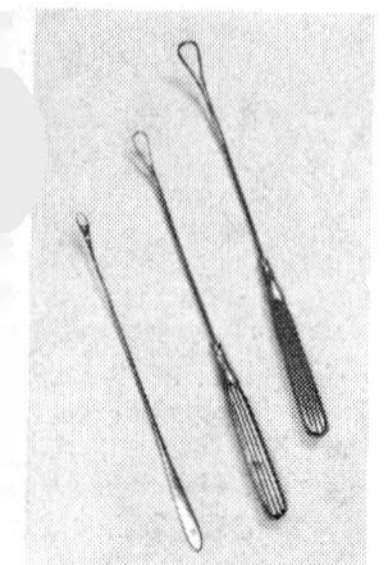

curette

Curie law *n.* The law that the magnetic susceptibility varies inversely with absolute temperature in a paramagnetic substance with negligible interactions among magnetic carriers. [After Pierre *Curie* (1859–1906).]

Curie point or **Curie temperature** *n.* A transition temperature marking a change in the magnetic properties of a substance, esp. the change from ferromagnetism to paramagnetism. [After Pierre *Curie.*]

Cu·rie-Weiss law (kyo͝or′ē-wīs′, -vīs′, kyo͝o-rē′-) *n.* The law that the magnetic susceptibility of a paramagnetic substance above the Curie point varies inversely with the excess of temperature above that point. [After Pierre *Curie* and Pierre-Ernest *Weiss* (1865–1940).]

cu·ri·o (kyo͝or′ē-ō′) *n., pl.* **-os.** A curious or unusual object of art or bric-a-brac. [Short for CURIOSITY.]

curlew

cu·ri·o·sa (kyo͝or′ē-ō′sə, -zə) *pl.n.* Books or other writings dealing with unusual, esp. pornographic, topics. [NLat., neut. pl. of Lat. *curiosus,* inquisitive. —see CURIOUS.]

cu·ri·os·i·ty (kyo͝or′ē-ŏs′ĭ-tē) *n., pl.* **-ties. 1.** A desire to know or learn. **2.** A desire to know about people or things that do not concern one; nosiness. **3.** Something that arouses interest, as by being novel or extraordinary. **4.** A strange or odd aspect. **5.** *Obs.* Fastidiousness.

cu·ri·ous (kyo͝or′ē-əs) *adj.* **1.** Eager to acquire information or knowledge. **2.** Unduly inquisitive; prying; nosy. **3.** Interesting because of novelty or rarity; singular; odd: *a curious fact.* **4.** *Obs.* **a.** Accomplished with skill or ingenuity. **b.** Extremely careful or scrupulous. [ME < OFr. *curios* < Lat. *curiosus,* careful, inquisitive < *cura,* care.] **—cu′ri·ous·ly** *adv.* **—cu′ri·ous·ness** *n.*

currant

Synonyms: *curious, inquisitive, snoopy, nosy, intrusive.* These adjectives apply to persons who show a marked desire for information or knowledge. *Curious* more often implies a legitimate desire to enlarge one's knowledge, but can suggest a less commendable urge to concern oneself in others' affairs. *Inquisitive* frequently suggests excessive curiosity and the asking of many questions. *Snoopy* implies an unworthy motive and underhandedness in implementing it. *Nosy* suggests excessive curiosity and impertinence in an adult; applied to a child, it may refer less unfavorably to habitual curiosity. *Intrusive* stresses unwarranted and unwelcome concern with another's affairs.

cu·ri·um (kyo͝or′ē-əm) *n. Symbol* **Cm** A silvery, metallic synthetic radioactive transuranic element having 13 isotopes with mass numbers from 238 to 250 and half-lives from 64 minutes to 16.4 million years. Atomic number 96. [After Marie *Curie* (1867–1934) and Pierre *Curie* (1859–1906).]

curl (kûrl) *v.* **curled, curl·ing, curls.** —*tr.* **1.** To twist (the hair, for example) into ringlets or coils. **2.** To form into the spiral shape of a ringlet or coil. **3.** To decorate with curls. —*intr.* **1.** To form ringlets or coils. **2.** To assume a spiral or curved shape. **3.** To move in a curve or spiral. **4.** To play the game of curling. ***—phrasal verb.*** **curl up. 1.** To assume a position with the legs drawn up. **2.** To make oneself comfortable. —*n.* **1.** Something with a spiral or coiled shape. **2.** A coil or ringlet of hair. **3. a.** The act of curling. **b.** The state of being curled. **4.** Any of various plant diseases in which the leaves roll up. **5.** *Math.* The vector product of the del operator and a vector function. [ME *curlen* < *crulle,* curly, perh. of MLG orig.]

curl·er (kûr′lər) *n.* **1.** One that curls. **2.** A device, such as a pin or roller, on which hair is wound for curling. **3.** A player of curling.

cur·lew (kûrl′yo͞o, kûr′lo͞o) *n.* Any of several brownish, long-legged shore birds of the genus *Numenius,* having long, slender, downward-curving bills. [ME *curleu* < OFr. *courlieu.*]

curl·i·cue also **curl·y·cue** (kûr′lĭ-kyo͞o′) *n.* A fancy twist or curl, such as a flourish made with a pen. [CURLY + CUE[1].]

curl·ing (kûr′lĭng) *n.* A Scottish game played on ice, in which two four-man teams slide heavy, oblate stones toward a fixed mark in the center of a circle at either end.

curling iron *n.* A rod-shaped metal implement used when heated to curl the hair.

curl paper *n.* A piece of soft paper on which a lock of hair is rolled up for curling.

curl·y (kûr′lē) *adj.* **-i·er, -i·est. 1.** Having curls. **2.** Having the tendency to curl. **3.** Having a wavy grain: *curly maple.* **—curl′i·ly** *adv.* **—curl′i·ness** *n.*

curl·y·cue (kûr′lĭ-kyo͞o′) *n.* Variant of **curlicue.**

curly top *n.* A disease of plants caused by a virus, *Ruga verrucosans,* and resulting in severe stunting of plants.

cur·mudg·eon (kər-mŭj′ən) *n.* A cantankerous person. [Orig. unknown.] **—cur·mudg′eon·ly** *adj.*

cur·rach also **cur·ragh** (kûr′əKH, kûr′ə) *n. Scot. & Ir.* A coracle. [ME *currok* < Ir. Gael. *curach.*]

cur·rant (kûr′ənt, kŭr′-) *n.* **1.** Any of various usually prickly shrubs of the genus *Ribes,* bearing clusters of red, black, or greenish fruit. **2.** The small, sour fruit of any of the currant plants, used chiefly for making jelly. **3.** A small, dried seedless grape of the Mediterranean region, used in cooking. [ME *(raysons of) coraunte,* (raisins of) Corinth.]

cur·ren·cy (kûr′ən-sē, kŭr′-) *n., pl.* **-cies. 1.** Any form of money in actual use as a medium of exchange. **2.** A passing from hand to hand, as a medium of exchange. **3.** General acceptance; prevalence. [Med. Lat. *currentia,* a flowing < Lat. *currens,* pr.part. of *currere,* to run.]

cur·rent (kûr′ənt, kŭr′-) *adj.* **1. a.** Belonging to the present time. **b.** Now in progress. **2.** Passing from one to another; circulating, as money. **3.** In general or widespread use; commonly accepted. **4.** Running; flowing. —*n.* **1.** A steady and smooth onward movement, as of water. **2.** The part of any body of liquid or gas that has a continuous onward movement: *a river current.* **3.** A general tendency, movement, or course. **4.** *Elect.* **a.** A flow of electric charge. **b.** The amount of electric charge flowing past a specified circuit point per unit time. [ME *curraunt* < OFr. *corant,* pr.part. of *courre,* to run < Lat. *currere.*] **—cur′rent·ly** *adv.* **—cur′rent·ness** *n.*

current assets *pl.n.* Cash or assets convertible into cash at short notice.

current density *n.* **1.** *Elect.* The ratio of the magnitude of current flowing in a conductor to the cross-sectional area perpendicular to the current flow. **2.** *Physics.* The number of subatomic particles per unit time crossing a unit area in a designated plane perpendicular to the direction of motion of the particles.

current ratio *n.* The arithmetic ratio of current assets to liabilities.

cur·ri·cle (kûr′ĭ-kəl) *n.* A light, open two-wheeled carriage, drawn by two horses abreast. [Lat. *curriculum,* racing chariot, course < *currere,* to run.]

cur·ric·u·lum (kə-rĭk′yə-ləm) *n., pl.* **-la** (-lə) or **-lums. 1.** All the courses of study offered by an educational institution. **2.** A particular course of study, often in a special field. [NLat. < Lat., course < *currere,* to run.] **—cur·ric′u·lar** (-lər) *adj.*

cur·ric·u·lum vi·tae (kə-rĭk′yə-ləm vī′tē, kə-rĭk′ə-ləm wē′tī′) *n.* A short résumé of one's career, as for an employer. [Lat., course of life.]

cur·rie (kûr′ē, kŭr′ē) *n.* Variant of **curry[2].**

cur·ri·er (kûr′ē-ər, kŭr′-) *n.* One who curries, esp. leather. [ME *curreiour* < OFr. < Lat. *coriarius,* a tanner < *corium,* leather.]

cur·ri·er·y (kûr′ē-ə-rē, kŭr′-) *n., pl.* **-ies.** The trade, work, or shop of a leather currier.

cur·rish (kûr′ĭsh) *adj.* Of or like a cur; snarling; bad-tempered. **—cur′rish·ly** *adv.*

cur·ry[1] (kûr′ē, kŭr′ē) *tr.v.* **-ried, -ry·ing, -ries. 1.** To groom (a horse) with a currycomb. **2.** To prepare (tanned hides) for use by soaking, coloring, or other processes. ***—idiom.*** **curry favor.** To seek or gain favor by fawning or flattery. [ME *curreien* < AN *curreier,* to arrange, curry.]

cur·ry[2] (kûr′ē, kŭr′ē) also **cur·rie** *n., pl.* **-ries. 1.** Curry powder. **2.** A heavily spiced sauce or relish made with curry powder and eaten with rice, meat, fish, or other food. **3.** A dish seasoned with curry powder. —*tr.v.* **-ried, -ry·ing, -ries.** To season with curry. [Tamil *kari,* relish.]

CURRENCY

Country, Basic Unit, or Subdivision	Country	Basic Unit	Subdivision
afghani	Afghanistan		100 puls
Afghanistan		afghani	100 puls
agora	Israel	shekel	100 agorot
Albania		lek	100 quintar
Algeria		dinar	100 centimes
Andorra		franc	100 centimes
		peseta	100 centimos
Angola		kwanza	100 lwei
Argentina		peso	100 centavos
at	Laos	kip	100 at
Australia		dollar	100 cents
Austria		schilling	100 groschen
avo	Macao	pataca	100 avos
Bahamas		dollar	100 cents
Bahrain		dinar	1000 fils
baht	Thailand		100 satang
baiza	Oman	riyal-omani	1000 baiza
balboa	Panama		100 centesimos
ban	Rumania	leu	100 bani
Bangladesh		taka	100 paisas
Barbados		dollar	100 cents
Belgium		franc	100 centimes
Belize		dollar	100 cents
Benin		franc	100 centimes
Bhutan		ngultrum	100 chetrums
birr	Ethiopia		100 cents
bolivar	Venezuela		100 centimos
Bolivia		peso	100 centavos
Brazil		cruzeiro	100 centavos
Brunei		dollar	100 cents
Bulgaria		lev	100 stotinki
Burma		kyat	100 pyas
Burundi		franc	100 centimes
butut	Gambia	dalasi	100 bututs
Cambodia		riel	100 sen
Cameroon		franc	100 centimes
Canada		dollar	100 cents
Cape Verde		escudo	100 centavos
Cayman Islands		dollar	100 cents
cedi	Ghana		100 pesewas
cent	Australia	dollar	100 cents
	Bahamas	dollar	100 cents
	Barbados	dollar	100 cents
	Belize	dollar	100 cents
	Brunei	dollar	100 cents
	Canada	dollar	100 cents
	Cayman Islands	dollar	100 cents
	China, Republic of (Taiwan)	yuan	100 cents
	Dominica	dollar	100 cents
	Ethiopia	birr	100 cents
	Fiji	dollar	100 cents
	Grenada	dollar	100 cents
	Guyana	dollar	100 cents
	Hong Kong	dollar	100 cents
	Kenya	shilling	100 cents
	Liberia	dollar	100 cents
	Malta	pound	100 cents
	Mauritius	rupee	100 cents
	Nauru	dollar	100 cents
	Netherlands	guilder	100 cents
	Netherlands Antilles	guilder	100 cents
	New Zealand	dollar	100 cents
	Saint Lucia	dollar	100 cents
	Saint Vincent	dollar	100 cents
	Seychelles	rupee	100 cents
	Sierra Leone	leone	100 cents
	Singapore	dollar	100 cents
	Solomon Islands	dollar	100 cents
	Somalia	schilling	100 cents
	South Africa	rand	100 cents
	Sri Lanka	rupee	100 cents
	Surinam	guilder	100 cents
	Swaziland	lilangeni	100 cents
		rand	100 cents
	Tanzania	shilling	100 cents
	Trinidad and Tobago	dollar	100 cents
	Uganda	shilling	100 cents
	United States	dollar	100 cents
	Western Samoa	tala	100 cents
	Zimbabwe	dollar	100 cents
centavo	Argentina	peso	100 centavos
	Bolivia	peso	100 centavos
	Brazil	cruzeiro	100 centavos
	Cape Verde	escudo	100 centavos
	Chile	peso	100 centavos
	Colombia	peso	100 centavos
	Cuba	peso	100 centavos

Country, Basic Unit, or Subdivision	Country	Basic Unit	Subdivision
	Dominican Republic	peso	100 centavos
	Ecuador	sucre	100 centavos
	El Salvador	colon	100 centavos
	Guatemala	quetzal	100 centavos
	Guinea-Bissau	peso	100 centavos
	Honduras	lempira	100 centavos
	Mexico	peso	100 centavos
	Nicaragua	cordoba	100 centavos
	Peru	sol	100 centavos
	Philippines	peso	100 centavos
	Portugal	escudo	100 centavos
centesimo	Italy	lira	100 centesimi
	Panama	balboa	100 centesimos
	San Marino	lira	100 centesimi
	Uruguay	peso	100 centesimos
	Vatican City	lira	100 centesimi
centime	Algeria	dinar	100 centimes
	Andorra	franc	100 centimes
	Belgium	franc	100 centimes
	Benin	franc	100 centimes
	Burundi	franc	100 centimes
	Cameroon	franc	100 centimes
	Central African Republic	franc	100 centimes
	Chad	franc	100 centimes
	Comoros	franc	100 centimes
	Congo	franc	100 centimes
	Djibouti	franc	100 centimes
	France	franc	100 centimes
	Gabon	franc	100 centimes
	Haiti	gourde	100 centimes
	Ivory Coast	franc	100 centimes
	Liechtenstein	franc	100 centimes
	Luxembourg	franc	100 centimes
	Madagascar	franc	100 centimes
	Mali	franc	100 centimes
	Monaco	franc	100 centimes
	Morocco	dirham	100 centimes
	Niger	franc	100 centimes
	Rwanda	franc	100 centimes
	Senegal	franc	100 centimes
	Switzerland	franc	100 centimes
	Togo	franc	100 centimes
	Upper Volta	franc	100 centimes
	Vanuatu	franc	100 centimes
centimo	Andorra	peseta	100 centimos
	Costa Rica	colon	100 centimos
	Equatorial Guinea	ekpwele	100 centimos
	Paraguay	guarani	100 centimos
	São Tomé and Principe	dobra	100 centimos
	Spain	peseta	100 centimos
	Venezuela	bolivar	100 centimos
Central African Republic		franc	100 centimes
Chad		franc	100 centimes
chao	Vietnam	dong	10 chao
chetrum	Bhutan	ngultrum	100 chetrums
chiao	People's Republic of China	renminbi	10 chiao
Chile		peso	100 centavos
China, People's Republic of		renminbi	10 chiao
China, Republic of (Taiwan)		yuan	100 cents
chon	South Korea	won	100 chon
colon	Costa Rica		100 centimos
	El Salvador		100 centavos
Colombia		peso	100 centavos
Comoros		franc	100 centimes
Congo		franc	100 centimes
cordoba	Nicaragua		100 centavos
cory	Guinea	syli	100 cory
Costa Rica		colon	100 centimos
crown	Czechoslovakia		100 halers
cruzeiro	Brazil		100 centavos
Cuba		peso	100 centavos
Cyprus		pound	1000 mils
Czechoslovakia		crown	100 halers
dalasi	Gambia		100 bututs
Denmark		kroner	100 öre
deutsche mark	West Germany		100 pfennigs
dinar	Algeria		100 centimes
	Bahrain		100 fils
	Iran	rial	100 dinars
	Iraq		1000 fils
	Jordan		1000 fils
	Kuwait		1000 fils
	Libya		1000 dirhams
	Southern Yemen		1000 fils
	Tunisia		1000 milliemes
	Yugoslavia		100 para
dirham	Morocco		100 centimes
	Qatar	riyal	100 dirhams
	United Arab Emirates		100 fils
Djibouti		franc	100 centimes
dobra	São Tomé and Principe		100 centimos
dollar	Australia		100 cents
	Bahamas		100 cents

Country, Basic Unit, or Subdivision	Country	Basic Unit	Subdivision
	Barbados		100 cents
	Brunei		100 cents
	Canada		100 cents
	Cayman Islands		100 cents
	Dominica		100 cents
	Fiji		100 cents
	Grenada		100 cents
	Guyana		100 cents
	Hong Kong		100 cents
	Jamaica		100 cents
	Liberia		100 cents
	Nauru		100 cents
	New Zealand		100 cents
	Saint Lucia		100 cents
	Saint Vincent		100 cents
	Singapore		100 cents
	Solomon Islands		100 cents
	Trinidad and Tobago		100 cents
	United States		100 cents
	Zimbabwe		100 cents
Dominica		dollar	100 cents
Dominican Republic		peso	100 centavos
dong	Vietnam		10 chao
drachma	Greece		100 lepta
East Germany		mark	100 pfennigs
Ecuador		sucre	100 centavos
Egypt		pound	100 piasters
ekpwele	Equatorial Guinea		100 cents
El Salvador		colon	100 centavos
Equatorial Guinea		ekpwele	100 cents
escudo	Cape Verde		100 centavos
	Portugal		100 centavos
Ethiopia		birr	100 cents
eyrir	Iceland	krona	100 aurar
Fiji		dollar	100 cents
fil	Bahrain	dinar	1000 fils
	Iraq	dinar	1000 fils
	Jordan	dinar	1000 fils
	Kuwait	dinar	1000 fils
	Southern Yemen	dinar	1000 fils
	United Arab Emirates	dinar	100 fils
	Yemen	riyal	100 fils
filler	Hungary	forint	100 fillér
Finland		markka	100 penni
forint	Hungary		100 fillér
franc	Andorra		100 centimes
	Belgium		100 centimes
	Benin		100 centimes
	Burundi		100 centimes
	Cameroon		100 centimes
	Central African Republic		100 centimes
	Chad		100 centimes
	Comoros		100 centimes
	Congo		100 centimes
	Djibouti		100 centimes
	France		100 centimes
	Gabon		100 centimes
	Ivory Coast		100 centimes
	Liechtenstein		100 centimes
	Luxembourg		100 centimes
	Madagascar		100 centimes
	Mali		100 centimes
	Monaco		100 centimes
	Niger		100 centimes
	Rwanda		100 centimes
	Senegal		100 centimes
	Switzerland		100 centimes
	Togo		100 centimes
	Upper Volta		100 centimes
	Vanuatu		100 centimes
France		franc	100 centimes
Gabon		franc	100 centimes
Gambia		dalasi	100 bututs
Ghana		cedi	100 pesewa
gourde	Haiti		100 centimes
Greece		drachma	100 lepta
Grenada		dollar	100 cents
groschen	Austria	schilling	100 groschen
grosz	Poland	zloty	100 groszy
guarani	Paraguay		100 centimos
Guatemala		quetzal	100 centavos
guilder	Netherlands		100 cents
	Netherlands Antilles		100 cents
	Surinam		100 cents
Guinea		syli	100 cory
Guinea-Bissau		peso	100 centavos
Guyana		dollar	100 cents
Haiti		gourde	100 centimes
haler	Czechoslovakia	crown	100 halers
Honduras		lempira	100 centavos
Hong Kong		dollar	100 cents
Hungary		forint	100 fillér
Iceland		krona	100 aurar

Country, Basic Unit, or Subdivision	Country	Basic Unit	Subdivision
India		rupee	100 paise
Indonesia		rupiah	100 sen
Iran		rial	100 dinars
Iraq		dinar	1000 fils
Ireland, Republic of		pound	100 pence
Israel		shekel	100 agorot
Italy		lira	100 centesimi
Ivory Coast		franc	100 centimes
Jamaica		dollar	100 cents
Japan		yen	100 sen
Jordan		dinar	1000 fils
jun	North Korea	won	100 jun
Kenya		shilling	100 cents
khoum	Mauritania	ouguiya	5 khoums
kina	Papua New Guinea		100 toea
kip	Laos		100 at
kobo	Nigeria	naira	100 kobo
kopeck	U.S.S.R.	rouble	100 kopecks
krona	Iceland		100 aurar
	Sweden		100 öre
krone	Norway		100 öre
kroner	Denmark		100 öre
kuru	Turkey	pound	100 kurus
Kuwait		dinar	1000 fils
kwacha	Malawi		100 tambala
	Zambia		100 ngwee
kwanza	Angola		100 lwei
kyat	Burma		100 pyas
Laos		kip	100 at
laree	Maldives	rupee	100 larees
Lebanon		pound	100 piasters
lek	Albania		100 quintar
lempira	Honduras		100 centavos
leone	Sierra Leone		100 cents
lepton	Greece	drachma	100 lepta
Lesotho		loti	100 lisente
leu	Rumania		100 bani
lev	Bulgaria		100 stotinki
Liberia		dollar	100 cents
Libya		dinar	1000 dirhams
Liechtenstein		franc	100 centimes
likuta	Zaire	zaire	100 makuta
lilangeni	Swaziland		100 cents
lira	Italy		100 centesimi
	San Marino		100 centesimi
	Vatican City		100 centesimi
lisente	Lesotho	loti	100 lisente
loti	Lesotho		100 lisente
Luxembourg		franc	100 centimes
lwei	Angola	kwanza	100 lwei
Macao		pataca	100 avos
Madagascar		franc	100 centimes
Malawi		kwacha	100 tambala
Malaysia		ringgit	100 sen
Maldives		rupee	100 larees
Mali		franc	100 centimes
Malta		pound	100 cents
mark	East Germany		100 pfennigs
markka	Finland		100 penni
Mauritania		ouguiya	5 khoums
Mauritius		rupee	100 cents
Mexico		peso	100 centavos
mil	Cyprus	pound	1000 mils
millieme	Tunisia	dinar	1000 milliemes
Monaco		franc	100 centimes
mongo	Mongolia	**tugrik**	100 mongo
Mongolia		**tugrik**	100 mongo
Morocco		dirham	100 centimes
naira	Nigeria		100 kobo
Nauru		dollar	100 cents
Nepal		rupee	100 paisas
Netherlands		guilder	100 cents
Netherlands Antilles		guilder	100 cents
New Zealand		dollar	100 cents
ngultrum	Bhutan		100 chetrums
ngwee	Zambia	kwacha	100 ngwee
Nicaragua		cordoba	100 centavos
Niger		franc	100 centimes
Nigeria		naira	100 kobos
North Korea		won	100 jun
Norway		krone	100 öre
Oman		riyal-omani	1000 baiza
öre	Denmark	kroner	100 öre
	Norway	krone	100 öre
	Sweden	krona	100 öre
ouguiya	Mauritania		5 khoums
pa'anga	Tonga		100 seniti
paisa	Bangladesh	taka	100 paisas
	India	rupee	100 paise
	Nepal	rupee	100 paisas
	Pakistan	rupee	100 paisas
Pakistan		rupee	100 paisas
Panama		balboa	100 centesimos
Papua New Guinea		kina	100 toea

Country, Basic Unit, or Subdivision	Country	Basic Unit	Subdivision
para	Yugoslavia	dinar	100 para
Paraguay		guarani	100 centimos
pataca	Macao		100 avos
penni	Finland	markka	100 penni
penny	Ireland, Republic of	pound	100 pence
	United Kingdom	pound	100 pence
Peru		sol	100 centavos
peseta	Andorra		100 centimos
	Spain		100 centimos
pesewa	Ghana	cedi	100 pesewas
peso	Argentina		100 centavos
	Bolivia		100 centavos
	Chile		100 centavos
	Colombia		100 centavos
	Cuba		100 centavos
	Dominican Republic		100 centavos
	Guinea-Bissau		100 centavos
	Mexico		100 centavos
	Philippines		100 centavos
	Uruguay		100 centesimos
pfennig	East Germany	mark	100 pfennigs
	West Germany	deutsche mark	100 pfennigs
Philippines		peso	100 centavos
piaster	Egypt	pound	100 piasters
	Lebanon	pound	100 piasters
	Sudan	pound	100 piasters
	Syria	pound	100 piasters
Poland		zloty	100 groszy
Portugal		escudo	100 centavos
pound	Cyprus		1000 mils
	Egypt		100 piasters
	Ireland, Republic of		100 pence
	Israel		100 agorot
	Lebanon		100 piasters
	Malta		100 cents
	Sudan		100 piasters
	Syria		100 piasters
	Turkey		100 kurus
	United Kingdom		100 pence
pul	Afghanistan	afghani	100 puls
pya	Burma	kyat	100 pyas
Qatar		riyal	100 dirhams
quetzal	Guatemala		100 centavos
quintar	Albania	lek	100 quintar
qurush	Saudi Arabia	riyal	20 qurush
rand	South Africa		100 cents
	Swaziland		100 cents
renminbi	China, People's Republic of		10 chiao
rial	Iran		100 dinars
riel	Cambodia		100 sen
riyal	Qatar		100 dirhams
	Saudi Arabia		20 qurush
	Yemen		100 fils
riyal-omani	Oman		1000 baiza
rouble	U.S.S.R.		100 kopecks
Rumania		leu	100 bani
rupee	India		100 paise
	Maldives		100 larees
	Mauritius		100 cents
	Nepal		100 paisas
	Pakistan		100 paisas
	Seychelles		100 cents
	Sri Lanka		100 cents
rupiah	Indonesia		100 sen
Rwanda		franc	100 centimes
Saint Lucia		dollar	100 cents
Saint Vincent		dollar	100 cents
San Marino		lira	100 centesimi
São Tomé and Principe		dobra	100 centimos
satang	Thailand	baht	100 satang
Saudi Arabia		riyal	20 qurush
schilling	Austria		100 groschen
	Somalia		100 cents
sen	Cambodia	riel	100 sen
	Indonesia	rupiah	100 sen
	Japan	yen	100 sen
	Malaysia	ringgit	100 sen
sene	Western Samoa	tala	100 sene
Senegal		franc	100 centimes
seniti	Tonga	pa'anga	100 seniti
Seychelles		rupee	100 cents
shekel	Israel		100 agorot
shilling	Kenya		100 cents
	Tanzania		100 cents
	Uganda		100 cents
Sierra Leone		leone	100 cents
Singapore		dollar	100 cents
sol	Peru		100 centavos
Solomon Islands		dollar	100 cents
Somalia		schilling	100 cents
South Africa		rand	100 cents
Southern Yemen		dinar	1000 fils
South Korea		won	100 chon
Spain		peseta	100 centimos

CURRENCY *(continued)*

Country, Basic Unit, or Subdivision	Country	Basic Unit	Subdivision
Sri Lanka		rupee	100 cents
stotinki	Bulgaria	lev	100 stotinki
sucre	Ecuador		100 centavos
Sudan		pound	100 piasters
Surinam		guilder	100 cents
Swaziland		lilangeni	100 cents
		rand	100 cents
Sweden		krona	100 öre
Switzerland		franc	100 centimes
syli	Guinea		100 cory
Syria		pound	100 piasters
taka	Bangladesh		100 paise
tala	Western Samoa		100 sene
tambala	Malawi	kwacha	100 tambala
Tanzania		shilling	100 cents
Thailand		baht	100 satang
toea	Papua New Guinea	kina	100 toea
Togo		franc	100 centimes
Tonga		pa'anga	100 seniti
Trinidad and Tobago		dollar	100 cents
tugrik	Mongolia		100 mongo
Tunisia		dinar	1000 milliemes
Turkey		pound	100 kurus
Uganda		shilling	100 cents
Union of Soviet Socialist Republics		rouble	100 kopecks
United Arab Emirates		dirham	100 fils
United Kingdom of Great Britain and Northern Ireland		pound	100 pence
United States of America		dollar	100 cents
Upper Volta		franc	100 centimes
Uruguay		peso	100 centesimos
Vanuatu (New Hebrides)		franc	100 centimes
Vatican City		lira	100 centesimi
Venezuela		bolivar	100 centimos
Vietnam		dong	100 chon
Western Samoa		tala	100 sene
West Germany		deutsche mark	100 pfennigs
won	North Korea		100 jun
	South Korea		100 chon
Yemen		riyal	100 fils
yen	Japan		100 sen
yuan	China, Republic of (Taiwan)		100 cents
Yugoslavia		dinar	100 para
zaire	Zaire		100 makuta
Zaire		zaire	100 makuta
Zambia		kwacha	100 ngwee
Zimbabwe		dollar	100 cents
zloty	Poland		100 groszy

cur·ry·comb (kûr′ē-kōm′, kŭr′-) *n.* A comb with metal teeth, used for grooming horses. —*tr.v.* **-combed, -comb·ing, -combs.** To groom with a currycomb.

curry powder *n.* A blended condiment prepared from cumin, coriander, turmeric, and other pungent spices.

curse (kûrs) *n.* **1.** An appeal or prayer for evil or injury to befall someone or something. **2.** The evil or injury that comes from or as if from an invocation. **3.** One that is accursed. **4.** Something that brings or causes evil; scourge. **5.** A profane oath or foul language; swear word. **6.** *Eccles.* A censure, ban, or anathema. **7. the curse.** *Slang.* Menstruation. —*v.* **cursed** or **curst** (kûrst), **curs·ing, curs·es.** —*tr.* **1.** To invoke evil, calamity, or injury upon; damn. **2.** To swear at. **3.** To bring evil upon; afflict. **4.** *Eccles.* To put under a ban or anathema; excommunicate. —*intr.* To utter curses; swear. [ME < OE *curs.*] —**curs′er** *n.*

curs·ed (kûr′sĭd, kûrst) also **curst** (kûrst) *adj.* Deserving to be cursed; wicked; detestable. —**curs′ed·ly** *adv.* —**curs′ed·ness** *n.*

cur·sive (kûr′sĭv) *adj.* Designating writing or printing in which the letters are joined together. —*n.* **1.** A cursive character or letter. **2.** A manuscript written in cursive characters. **3.** *Printing.* A type that imitates handwriting. [Med. Lat. *(scripta) cursiva,* flowing (script) < Lat. *cursus,* p.part. of *currere,* to run.] —**cur′sive·ly** *adv.* —**cur′sive·ness** *n.*

cur·sor (kûr′sər) *n.* A visual indicator on a video terminal showing the position of next entry. [Lat., runner < *cursus,* p.part. of *currere,* to run.]

cur·so·ri·al (kûr-sôr′ē-əl, -sōr′-) *adj.* Adapted to or specialized for running: *cursorial birds; cursorial legs.* [< LLat. *cursorius,* of running. —see CURSORY.]

cur·so·ry (kûr′sə-rē) *adj.* Hastily and superficially done; not thorough. [LLat. *cursorius,* of running < Lat. *cursor,* runner. —see CURSOR.] —**cur′so·ri·ly** *adv.* —**cur′so·ri·ness** *n.*

curst (kûrst) *adj.* Variant of **cursed.** —*v.* A past tense and past participle of **curse.**

curt (kûrt) *adj.* **-er, -est. 1.** Rudely brief or abrupt, as in speech or manner. **2.** Terse or concise. **3.** Shortened. [Lat. *curtus,* cut short.] —**curt′ly** *adv.* —**curt′ness** *n.*

cur·tail (kər-tāl′) *tr.v.* **-tailed, -tail·ing, -tails.** To cut short; abbreviate. [Obs. *curtal,* to dock a horse's tail < CURTAL.] —**cur·tail′er** *n.* —**cur·tail′ment** *n.*

curtail step *n.* The widened step or steps at the foot of a flight of stairs. [Orig. unknown.]

cur·tain (kûr′tn) *n.* **1.** A piece of cloth or similar material hanging in a window or other opening as a decoration, shade, or screen. **2.** Something that acts as a screen, cover, or barrier. **3. a.** The movable screen or drape that separates the stage from the auditorium in a theater or hall. **b.** The ascent or opening of a theater curtain at the beginning or its descent or closing at the end, as of a play or act. **c.** A line, speech, or situation in a play that occurs at the very end or just before the curtain closes. **d.** The time at which a theatrical performance begins or is scheduled to begin. **4.** The part of a rampart or parapet connecting two bastions or gates. **5.** *Archit.* An enclosing wall connecting two towers or similar structures. **6. curtains.** *Slang.* **a.** The end. **b.** Ruin. **c.** Death. —*tr.v.* **-tained, -tain·ing, -tains.** To provide or shut off with or as if with a curtain. [ME < OFr. *courtine* < LLat. *cortina.*]

curtain call *n.* The appearance of a performer or performers at the end of a performance in response to applause.

curtain lecture *n.* A private reprimand given to a husband by his wife. [So called because it was orig. given in a curtained bed.]

curtain raiser *n.* **1.** A short play presented before the principal dramatic production. **2.** A preliminary event.

curtain speech *n.* A talk given in front of the curtain at the conclusion of a theatrical performance.

cur·tal (kûr′tl) *Obs.* —*n.* **1.** An animal with a docked tail. **2.** Anything cut short or docked. —*adj.* **1.** Cut short or docked, as an animal's tail. **2.** Wearing a short frock. [OFr.

courtault, horse with a cropped tail < *court,* short < Lat. *curtus,* cut short.]

curtal ax *n. Archaic.* A cutlass. [By folk ety. < obs. *curtelace, coutelace,* cutlass < OFr. *coutelas.* —see CUTLASS.]

cur·tate (kûr′tāt′) *adj.* Shortened; abbreviated. [Lat. *curtatus,* p.part. of *curtare,* to shorten < *curtus,* cut short.]

cur·te·sy (kûr′tĭ-sē) *n., pl.* **-sies.** The life tenure which by common law is held by a man over the property of his deceased wife if children with rights of inheritance were born during the marriage. [ME *curtesie.* —see COURTESY.]

cur·ti·lage (kûr′tl-ĭj) *n. Law.* The enclosed land surrounding a house or dwelling. [ME < OFr. *courtillage* < *courtil,* dim. of *cort,* court. —see COURT.]

curt·sy (kûrt′sē) *n., pl.* **-sies.** A gesture of respect or reverence made by bending the knees with one foot forward and lowering the body. *—intr.v.* **-sied, -sy·ing, -sies.** To make a curtsy. [Var. of COURTESY.]

cu·rule (kyo͝or′o͞ol′) *adj.* Privileged to sit in a curule chair; of superior rank. [Lat. *curulis,* of a curule chair < *currus,* chariot < *currere,* to run.]

curule chair *n.* A seat with heavy, curved legs and no back, reserved for the use of the highest officials in ancient Rome.

cur·va·ceous (kûr-vā′shəs) *adj.* Having a full or voluptuous figure. **—cur·va′ceous·ly** *adv.* **—cur·va′ceous·ness** *n.*

cur·va·ture (kûr′və-cho͝or′, -chər) *n.* **1. a.** An act of curving. **b.** The state of being curved. **2.** *Math.* **a.** The ratio of the change in tangent inclination over a given arc to the length of the arc. **b.** The limit of this ratio as the length of the arc approaches zero. **3.** *Med.* A curving or bending, esp. an abnormal one: *curvature of the spine.* [Lat. *curvatura* < *curvatus,* p.part. of *curvare,* to bend < *curvus,* curved.]

curve (kûrv) *n.* **1. a.** A line that deviates from straightness in a smooth, continuous fashion. **b.** A surface that deviates from planarity in a smooth, continuous fashion. **2. a.** A rounded part, object, or region. **b.** A relatively smooth bend in a road or other course. **3. curves.** *Slang.* An appealing or well-proportioned female figure. **4. a.** A line representing data on a graph. **b.** A trend derived from or as if from such a graph. **5.** *Math.* **a.** The graph of a function on a coordinate plane. **b.** The intersection of two surfaces in three dimensions. **6.** A graphic representation showing the relative performance of individuals as measured against each other, used esp. as a method of grading students in which the range of grades is based on the proportion of students. **7.** A curve ball. *—v.* **curved, curv·ing, curves.** *—intr.* To move in or take the shape of a curve. *—tr.* **1.** To cause to curve. **2.** *Baseball.* To pitch a curve ball to. **3.** To grade on a curve. [ME, curved < Lat. *curvus.*] **—curv′ed·ly** (kûr′vĭd-lē) *adv.* **—curv′ed·ness** *n.*

curve ball *n.* **1.** *Baseball.* A pitched ball that veers or breaks to the left when thrown with the right hand and to the right when thrown with the left hand. **2.** *Slang.* A trick or deception.

cur·vet (kûr-vĕt′) *n.* A light leap by a horse, in which both hind legs leave the ground just before the forelegs are set down. *—v.* **-vet·ted, -vet·ting, -vets** or **-vet·ed, -vet·ing, -vets.** *—intr.* **1.** To leap in a curvet. **2.** To prance; frolic. *—tr.* To cause to leap in a curvet. [Ital. *corvetta* < OItal., dim. of *corva,* curve < Lat. *curvus,* curved.]

cur·vi·lin·e·ar (kûr′və-lĭn′ē-ər) also **cur·vi·lin·e·al** (-əl) *adj.* Formed, bounded, or characterized by curved lines. [Lat. *curvus,* curved + LINEAR.] **—cur′vi·lin′e·ar′i·ty** (-ē-ăr′ĭ-tē) *n.* **—cur′vi·lin′e·ar·ly** *adv.*

cus·cus (kŭs′kəs) *n.* Any of several marsupials of the genus *Phalanger,* of New Guinea and adjacent areas, having protruding eyes, a yellow nose, and a long, prehensile tail. [NLat., prob. < a native New Guinean word.]

cu·sec (kyo͞o′sĕk′) *n.* A unit of volumetric flow of liquids, equal to one cubic foot per second. [CU(BIC) + SEC(OND)[1].]

cu·shaw (kə-shô′, ko͞o′shô′) *n.* A squash, *Cucurbita moschata,* having variably shaped, often crook-necked fruit. [Of Algonquian orig.]

Cush·ing's disease also **Cushing's syndrome** (ko͝osh′ĭngz) *n.* A disease caused by an overgrowth of basophilic cells of the pituitary, characterized by obesity and muscular weakness. [After Harvey *Cushing* (1869–1939).]

cush·ion (ko͝osh′ən) *n.* **1.** A pad or pillow with a soft filling, used for resting or reclining. **2.** Something resilient used as a rest, support, or shock absorber. **3.** A padlike body part. **4.** The rim bordering a billiard table. **5.** A pillow used in lacemaking. **6.** Something that mitigates or relieves an adverse effect. *—tr.v.* **-ioned, -ion·ing, -ions. 1.** To provide with a cushion. **2.** To place or seat on a cushion. **3.** To cover or hide with or as if with a cushion. **4.** To protect against or absorb the shock of. [ME *cushin* < OFr. *cussin* < VLat. **coxinus* < Lat. *coxa,* hip.] **—cush′ion·y** *adj.*

Cush·it·ic (ko͝o-shĭt′ĭk) *n.* A group of Hamitic languages that includes Somali and other languages of Somalia and Ethiopia. **—Cush·it′ic** *adj.*

cush·y (ko͝osh′ē) *adj.* **-i·er, -i·est.** *Slang.* Making few demands; comfortable: *a cushy job.* [< Hindi *khush* < Pers. *khosh,* pleasant.] **—cush′i·ly** *adv.* **—cush′i·ness** *n.*

cusk (kŭsk) *n., pl.* **cusk** or **cusks.** A food fish, *Brosme brosme,* of North Atlantic coastal waters. [Prob. alteration of *tusk,* a kind of codfish.]

cusk eel *n.* Any of various eellike, chiefly marine fishes of the family Ophidiidae.

cusp (kŭsp) *n.* **1.** A point or pointed end. **2.** *Anat.* **a.** A prominence or projection on the chewing surface of a tooth. **b.** A fold or flap of a heart valve. **3.** *Math.* A point at which a curve crosses itself and at which the two tangents to the curve coincide. **4.** *Archit.* The pointed figure formed by two intersecting arcs or foils. **5.** *Astron.* Either point of a crescent moon. **6.** The transitional first or last part of an astrological house or sign. [Lat. *cuspis,* point.]

cus·pate (kŭs′pāt′) also **cus·pat·ed** (-pā′tĭd) *adj.* **1.** Having a cusp. **2.** Shaped like a cusp.

cus·pid (kŭs′pĭd) *n.* A tooth having one point; canine tooth. [Back-formation < BICUSPID.]

cus·pi·date (kŭs′pĭ-dāt′) also **cus·pi·dat·ed** (-dā′tĭd) *adj.* **1.** Having a cusp. **2.** *Biol.* Terminating in or tipped with a sharp point: *a cuspidate leaf.* [Lat. *cuspidatus,* p.part. of *cuspidare,* to make pointed < *cuspis,* point.]

cus·pi·da·tion (kŭs′pĭ-dā′shən) *n. Archit.* Decoration with cusps.

cus·pi·dor (kŭs′pĭ-dôr′, -dōr′) *n.* A spittoon. [Port. < *cuspir,* to spit < Lat. *conspuere,* to spit upon : *com-* (intensive) + *spuere,* to spit.]

cuss (kŭs) *Informal. —intr. & tr.v.* **cussed, cuss·ing, cuss·es.** To curse or cuss at. *—n.* **1.** A curse. **2.** An odd or perverse creature. [Var. of CURSE.]

cuss·ed (kŭs′ĭd) *adj. Informal.* **1.** Cursed. **2.** Perverse; vexatious. **—cuss′ed·ly** *adv.* **—cuss′ed·ness** *n.*

cus·tard (kŭs′tərd) *n.* A dessert of milk, sugar, eggs, and flavoring, boiled or baked until set. [ME *crustade,* a pie with a crust < AN < OProv. *croustado* < *crousta,* crust < Lat. *crusta.*]

custard apple *n.* **1.** A tropical American tree, *Annona reticulata,* bearing large, heart-shaped fruit. **2.** The fruit of the custard apple, having edible, fleshy pulp. **3.** The papaw (sense 2). [So called because its pulp resembles custard.]

cus·to·di·an (kŭ-stō′dē-ən) *n.* **1.** One who has charge of something; caretaker. **2.** A janitor. **—cus·to′di·an·ship′** *n.*

cus·to·dy (kŭs′tə-dē) *n., pl.* **-dies. 1.** The act or right of guarding, esp. such a right granted by a court. **2.** The state of being detained or held under guard, esp. by the police. [ME *custodie* < Lat. *custodia* < *custos,* guard.] **—cus·to′di·al** (-dē-əl) *adj.*

cus·tom (kŭs′təm) *n.* **1.** A practice followed as a matter of course among a people. **2.** A habitual practice of an individual. **3.** *Law.* A common tradition or usage so long established that it has the force or validity of law. **4.** Habitual patronage, as of a store. **5. customs.** *(used with a sing. verb).* **a.** A duty or tax imposed on imported and, less commonly, exported goods. **b.** The governmental agency authorized to collect these duties. **c.** The procedure for inspecting goods and baggage entering a country. **6.** Tribute, service, or rent paid by a feudal tenant to his lord. *—adj.* **1.** Made to order. **2.** Specializing in the making or selling of made-to-order goods. [ME *custume* < OFr. *costume* < Lat. *consuetudo* < *consuescere,* to accustom : *com-* (intensive) + *suescere,* to become accustomed.]

cus·tom·a·ble (kŭs′tə-mə-bəl) *adj.* Subject to tariffs.

cus·tom·ar·y (kŭs′tə-mĕr′ē) *adj.* **1.** Commonly practiced or used as a matter of course; usual. **2.** Based on custom or tradition rather than written law or contract. **—cus′tom·ar′i·ly** (-mâr′ə-lē) *adv.* **—cus′tom·ar′i·ness** *n.*

cus·tom-built (kŭs′təm-bĭlt′) *adj.* Built according to the specifications of the buyer.

cus·tom·er (kŭs′tə-mər) *n.* **1.** A person who buys goods or services, esp. on a regular basis. **2.** *Informal.* A person with whom one must deal: *a tough customer.*

cus·tom·house also **custom house** (kŭs′təm-hous′) *n.* A governmental building or office where customs are collected and ships are cleared for entering or leaving the country.

cus·tom·ize (kŭs′tə-mīz′) *tr.v.* **-ized, -iz·ing, -iz·es.** To alter to the tastes of the buyer: *customize a van.*

cus·tom-made (kŭs′təm-mād′) *adj.* Made according to the specifications of an individual purchaser. **—cus′tom-make′** *v.* **(-made, -mak·ing, -makes).**

customs union *n.* An international association organized to eliminate customs restrictions on goods exchanged between member nations and to establish a uniform tariff policy toward nonmember nations.

cut (kŭt) *v.* **cut, cut·ting, cuts.** *—tr.* **1.** To penetrate with a sharp edge; strike a narrow opening in. **2.** To separate into parts with or as if with a sharp-edged instrument; sever: *cut cloth with scissors.* **3.** To sever the edges or outer extensions of; shorten: *cut one's hair.* **4.** To reap; harvest: *cut grain.* **5.** To fell by sawing; hew. **6.** To have (a new tooth) grow through the gums. **7.** To form or shape by severing or incising: *a doll cut from paper.* **8.** To form by penetrating, probing, or digging. **9.** To separate or dissociate from a main body; detach: *cut a piece of meat.* **10.** To pass through or across; cross. **11.** To divide (a deck of cards) in two, as before dealing. **12.** To reduce or curtail the size, extent, or duration of: *cut a payroll.* **13.** To lessen the strength of; dilute: *cut whiskey.* **14.** To dissolve by breaking down the fat of: *Soap cuts grease.* **15.** To injure the feelings of; hurt keenly. **16.** *Informal.* To fail to attend purposely: *cut a class.* **17.** *Informal.* To cease; stop: *cut the noise; cut an engine.*

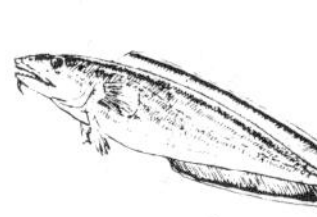

cusk

custard apple

customhouse
The customhouse in Charleston, South Carolina

cutlass

cutter
Pilot schooner *Bedouin*

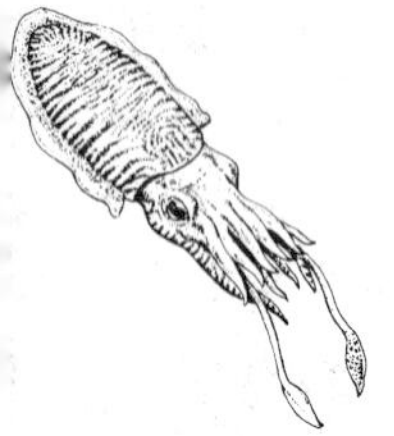

cuttlefish

18. *Sports.* To strike (the ball) so that it spins irregularly or is deflected. **19.** To perform: *cut a caper.* **20.** To terminate (a scene in a film). **21.** To record a performance on (a phonograph record). **22.** To edit (film or video tape). *—intr.* **1.** To make an incision or separation. **2.** To allow incision or severing: *Butter cuts easily.* **3.** To use a sharp-edged instrument. **4.** To grow through the gums. Used of teeth. **5.** To penetrate injuriously. **6.** To change direction abruptly: *cut to the left.* **7.** To go directly and often hastily: *cut across the field.* **8.** To divide a pack of cards into two parts. ***—phrasal verbs.*** **cut back. 1.** To shorten by cutting; prune. **2.** To reduce or decrease: *cut back production.* **cut down. 1.** To kill or strike down. **2.** To remove extra or additional fittings. **3.** To reduce or curtail. **cut in. 1.** To move into a line of people or things out of turn. **2.** To interrupt. **3.** To interrupt a dancing couple in order to dance with one of them. **4.** To connect or become connected into an electrical circuit. **5.** To mix into with or as if with cutting motions: *cut shortening into flour.* **6.** To include, esp. to give a share to. **cut off. 1.** To separate by or as if by cutting; sever. **2.** To stop suddenly; discontinue. **3.** To shut off; bar. **4.** To interrupt or break off. **5.** To disinherit. **cut out. 1.** To remove by cutting. **2.** To form or shape by or as if by cutting. **3.** To take the place of; supplant. **4.** To be suited: *I'm not cut out for this sort of work.* **5.** To be predetermined by necessity: *She's got her work cut out for her.* **6.** To deprive. **7.** To put an end to; desist. **8.** To stop; cease. **9.** *Informal.* To depart. **cut up.** *Informal.* **1.** To criticize severely. **2.** To clown or fool around. *—n.* **1.** The act of incising, severing, or separating. **2.** The result of cutting; an incision. **3.** A part that has been severed from a main body: *a cut of beef.* **4.** A passage resulting from excavating or probing. **5.** An elimination or excision of a part: *a cut in a speech.* **6.** A reduction: *a salary cut.* **7.** The style in which a garment is cut. **8.** *Informal.* A share of profits or earnings. **9.** *Informal.* A wounding remark; an insult. **10.** *Informal.* An unexcused absence, as from school or a class. **11.** *Printing.* **a.** An engraved block or plate. **b.** A print made from such a block. **12.** *Sports.* A stroke that causes a ball to spin irregularly or to deflect. **13.** The act of dividing a deck of cards into two parts, as before dealing. **14.** A sharp transition between shots or scenes in a film. **15.** One of the objects used in drawing lots. **16.** A single selection of music on a phonograph record. ***—idioms.*** **a cut above.** A little better than. **cut corners.** To do something in the easiest or most inexpensive way. **cut down to size.** To deflate the self-importance of. **cut loose.** To speak or act without restraint. **cut no ice.** To make no effect or impression. **cut (one's) losses.** To withdraw from a losing situation. **cut (one's) teeth on.** To learn or do as a beginner or at the start of one's career. **cut short.** To stop before the end; abbreviate. **cut the mustard.** To perform up to a required standard. [ME *cutten.*]

cut-and-dried (kŭt′ən-drīd′) *adj.* **1.** Prepared and arranged in advance; settled. **2. a.** Ordinary; routine. **b.** Lacking spontaneity.

cu·ta·ne·ous (kyo͞o-tā′nē-əs) *adj.* Of, pertaining to, or affecting the skin. [NLat. *cutaneus* < Lat. *cutis,* skin.] **—cu·ta′ne·ous·ly** *adv.*

cutaneous anaphylaxis *n.* Anaphylaxis characterized by a violent skin reaction upon contact with the sensitizing substance.

cut·a·way (kŭt′ə-wā′) *n.* A man's formal daytime coat, with front edges sloping diagonally from the waist and forming tails at the back.

cut·back (kŭt′băk′) *n.* **1.** A decrease; curtailment. **2.** A sharp reversal of direction, as of a ballcarrier in football.

cutch (kŭch) *n.* Catechu. [Malay *kachu,* of Dravidian orig.]

cute (kyo͞ot) *adj.* **cut·er, cut·est. 1.** Delightfully pretty or dainty. **2.** Obviously contrived to charm; precious. **3.** Shrewd; clever. [Short for ACUTE.] **—cute′ly** *adv.* **—cute′ness** *n.*

cut·ey (kyo͞o′tē) *n. Slang.* Variant of **cutie.**

cut glass *n.* Glassware shaped or decorated by cutting instruments or abrasive wheels.

cut·grass (kŭt′grăs′) *n.* Any of several swamp grasses of the genus *Leersia,* esp. *L. oryzoides,* having leaves with very rough margins.

cu·ti·cle (kyo͞o′tĭ-kəl) *n.* **1.** The epidermis. **2.** The strip of hardened skin at the base of a fingernail or toenail. **3.** *Zool.* The noncellular, often horny protective outer covering in many invertebrates. **4.** *Bot.* The layer of cutin covering the epidermis of plants. [Lat. *cuticula,* dim. of *cutis,* skin.] **—cu·tic′u·lar** (-tĭk′yə-lər) *adj.*

cut·ie also **cut·ey** (kyo͞o′tē) *n., pl.* **-ies** also **-eys.** *Slang.* A cute person.

cu·tin (kyo͞ot′n) *n. Bot.* A waxlike, water-repellent material present in the walls of some plant cells, and forming the cuticle which covers the epidermis. [Lat. *cutis,* skin + -IN.]

cut-in (kŭt′ĭn′) *n.* An inserted shot, often a still close-up, interrupting the continuity of the main action of a film.

cu·tin·ize (kyo͞ot′n-īz′) *tr. & intr.v.* **-ized, -iz·ing, -iz·es.** *Bot.* To coat or impregnate with cutin or become coated or impregnated with cutin. **—cu′tin·i·za′tion** *n.*

cu·tis (kyo͞o′tĭs) *n., pl.* **-tes** (-tēz) or **-tis·es.** *Anat.* The corium. [Lat., skin.]

cut·lass also **cut·las** (kŭt′ləs) *n.* A short, heavy sword with a curved single-edged blade, once used as a weapon by sailors. [OFr. *coutelas,* aug. of *coutel,* knife < Lat. *cultellus,* dim. of *culter,* knife.]

cutlass fish *n.* Any of several marine fishes of the genus *Trichiurus,* having a long, narrow body and a pointed tail.

cut·ler (kŭt′lər) *n.* A person who makes, repairs, or sells knives or other cutting instruments. [ME < OFr. *coutelier* < *coutel,* knife. —see CUTLASS.]

cut·ler·y (kŭt′lə-rē) *n.* **1.** Cutting instruments and tools. **2.** Implements used as tableware. **3.** The occupation of a cutler.

cut·let (kŭt′lĭt) *n.* **1.** A thin slice of meat, usually veal or lamb, cut from the leg or ribs of an animal. **2.** A flat croquette of chopped meat or fish. [Fr. *côtelette* < OFr. *costelette,* dim. of *coste,* rib < Lat. *costa.*]

cut·off (kŭt′ôf′, -ŏf′) *n.* **1.** A designated limit or point of termination. **2.** A short cut or by-pass. **3.** A new channel cut by a river across the neck of an oxbow. **4. a.** A checking or cutting off of a flow of steam, water, or other fluid. **b.** The device that cuts off. **5.** *Mus.* A conductor's signal indicating a stop or break in singing or playing.

cut-offs also **cut·offs** (kŭt′ôfs′, -ŏfs′) *pl.n.* Pants, as blue jeans, made into shorts by cutting off part of the legs.

cut·out (kŭt′out′) *n.* **1.** Something cut out or intended to be cut out. **2.** *Elect.* A device that interrupts, by-passes, or disconnects a circuit or circuit element.

cut·o·ver (kŭt′ō′vər) *adj.* Cleared of trees.

cut·purse (kŭt′pûrs′) *n. Archaic.* A pickpocket.

cut-rate (kŭt′rāt′) *adj.* Sold or on sale at a reduced price.

cut·ter (kŭt′ər) *n.* **1.** One that cuts, esp. in tailoring. **2.** A device or machine that cuts. **3.** *Naut.* **a.** A single-masted fore-and-aft-rigged sailing vessel with a running bowsprit, a mainsail, and two or more headsails which are usually set flying. **b.** A ship's boat, powered by a motor or oars, and used for transporting stores or passengers. **c.** A small, lightly armed motorboat used by the Coast Guard. **4.** A small sleigh, usually seating one person and drawn by a single horse.

cut·throat (kŭt′thrōt′) *n.* **1.** One who cuts throats; murderer. **2.** An unprincipled and ruthless person. *—adj.* **1.** Cruel; murderous. **2.** Relentless or merciless in competition. **3.** *Games & Sports.* Of or designating a form of a game in which each of three players acts and scores for himself.

cut time *n.* Alla breve.

cut·ting (kŭt′ĭng) *adj.* **1.** Capable of or designed for incising, shearing, or severing. **2.** Sharply penetrating; piercing and cold: *a cutting wind.* **3.** Bitterly sarcastic or insulting: *a cutting remark.* *—n.* **1.** A part cut off from a main body. **2.** An excavation made through high ground in the construction of a road, railway, or the like. **3.** *Chiefly Brit.* A clipping, as from a newspaper. **4.** The editing of film or audio tape. **5.** A twig or similar plant part removed to form roots and propagate a new plant.

cut·tle·bone (kŭt′l-bōn′) *n.* The calcareous internal shell of a cuttlefish, used as a dietary supplement for cage birds or ground into powder for use as a polishing agent.

cut·tle·fish (kŭt′l-fĭsh′) *n., pl.* **cuttlefish** or **-fish·es.** Any of various squidlike cephalopod marine mollusks of the genus *Sepia,* having ten arms, a calcareous internal shell, and secreting a dark, inky fluid. [ME *codel,* cuttlefish < OE *cudele* + FISH.]

cut·up (kŭt′ŭp′) *n. Informal.* A mischievous person; prankster.

cut·wa·ter (kŭt′wô′tər, -wŏt′ər) *n.* **1.** *Naut.* The forward part of a ship's prow. **2.** The wedge-shaped end of a bridge pier, designed to divide the current and break up ice floes.

cut·work (kŭt′wûrk′) *n.* Openwork embroidery in which the ground fabric is cut away from the design.

cut·worm (kŭt′wûrm′) *n.* The larva of any of various moths of the family Noctuidae, feeding on a wide variety of plants. [So called because many species eat through stems of plants.]

cu·vette (kyo͞o′vĕt) *n.* A small, often tubular laboratory vessel, often made of glass. [Fr., dim. of *cuve,* tub < Lat. *cupa.*]

cwm (ko͞om) *n. Welsh.* A cirque.

-cy *suff.* **1.** State; condition; quality: *bankruptcy.* **2.** Rank; office: *baronetcy.* **3.** Action; practice: *mendicancy.* [ME *-cie* < OFr. < Lat. *-cia, -tia* and Gk. *-kia, -tia.*]

cy·an (sī′ăn′, -ən) *n.* Greenish blue; one of the subtractive primary colors; a complement of red. [Gk. *kuanos,* blue.]

cyan– *pref.* Variant of **cyano-.**

cy·an·am·ide also **cy·an·am·id** (sī-ăn′ə-mĭd) *n.* **1.** An irritating caustic acidic crystalline compound, $NCNH_2$, prepared by treating calcium cyanamide with sulfuric acid. **2.** Calcium cyanamide. **3.** A salt or ester of cyanamide.

cy·a·nate (sī′ə-nāt′, -nət) *n.* A salt or ester of cyanic acid.

cy·an·ic (sī-ăn′ĭk) *adj.* **1.** Pertaining to or containing cyanogen. **2.** Blue or bluish.

cyanic acid *n.* A poisonous, unstable, highly volatile organic acid, HOCN, used to prepare certain cyanates.

cy·a·nide (sī′ə-nīd′) also **cy·a·nid** (-nĭd) *n.* Any of various salts or esters of hydrogen cyanide containing a CN group, esp. the extremely poisonous compounds potassium cyanide and sodium cyanide. *—tr.v.* **-nid·ed, -nid·ing, -nides. 1.** To treat (a metal surface) with cyanide to produce a hard surface. **2.** To treat (an ore) with cyanide to extract gold or silver.

cyanide process *n.* A process of extracting gold or silver from ores treated with a solution of sodium or calcium cyanide.

cy·a·nine (sī'ə-nēn', -nĭn) *n.* Any of various blue dyes, used to extend the range of color sensitivity of photographic emulsions.

cy·a·nite (sī'ə-nīt') *n.* Variant of **kyanite.**

cyano– or **cyan–** *pref.* **1.** Blue: *cyanotype.* **2. a.** Cyanogen: *cyanic.* **b.** Cyanide: *cyanogenesis.* [< Gk. *kuanos,* blue.]

cy·a·no·ac·ry·late (sī'ə-nō-ăk'rə-lāt', sī-ăn'ō-) *n.* An adhesive substance with an acrylate base that is used in industry and medicine.

cy·a·no·co·bal·a·min (sī'ə-nō'kō-băl'ə-mĭn) *n.* Vitamin B_{12}. [CYANO- + COBAL(T) + (VIT)AMIN.]

cy·an·o·gen (sī-ăn'ə-jən) *n.* **1.** A colorless, flammable, highly poisonous gas, C_2N_2, used as a rocket propellant, fumigant, military weapon, and in welding. **2.** The univalent radical CN found in simple and complex cyanide compounds. [Fr. *cyanogène* : *cyano-,* cyano- + *-gène,* -gen.]

cy·a·no·gen·e·sis (sī'ə-nō-jĕn'ĭ-sĭs, sī-ăn'ō-) *n.* The generation of cyanide. **—cy'a·no·ge·net'ic** (-jə-nĕt'ĭk), **cy'a·no·gen'ic** (-jĕn'ĭk) *adj.*

cy·a·no·hy·drin (sī'ə-nō-hī'drĭn, sī-ăn'ō-) *n.* Any of several compounds that contain both the CN and OH radicals. [CYANO- + HYDR(O)- + -IN.]

cy·a·nosed (sī'ə-nōzd') *adj.* Afflicted with cyanosis. [< CYANOSIS.]

cy·a·no·sis (sī'ə-nō'sĭs) *n.* A bluish discoloration of the skin, resulting from inadequate oxygenation of the blood. **—cy'a·not'ic** (-nŏt'ĭk) *adj.*

cy·an·o·type (sī-ăn'ə-tīp') *n.* A blueprint.

cy·a·nu·ric acid (sī'ə-nŏŏr'ĭk, -nyŏŏr'-) *n.* A white crystalline acid, $C_3N_3(OH)_3$, that decomposes with heating to form cyanic acid.

Cyb·e·le (sĭb'ə-lē) *n. Gk. Myth.* The goddess of nature of ancient Asia Minor. [Lat. < Gk. *Kubelē* < *kubelon,* mountain in Phrygia.]

cy·ber·nate (sī'bər-nāt') *v.* **-nat·ed, -nat·ing, -nates.** *—tr.* To control (an industrial process) automatically by computer. *—intr.* To become so controlled. [CYBERN(ETICS) + -ATE[1].] **—cy'ber·na'tion** *n.*

cy·ber·net·ics (sī'bər-nĕt'ĭks) *n. (used with a sing. verb).* The theoretical study of control processes in electronic, mechanical, and biological systems, esp. the mathematical analysis of the flow of information in such systems. [< Gk. *kubernētēs,* governor < *kubernan,* to govern.] **—cy'ber·net'ic** *adj.* **—cy'ber·net'i·cal·ly** *adv.* **—cy'ber·net'i·cist** *n.*

cy·borg (sī'bôrg') *n.* A human individual who has some of his vital bodily processes controlled by cybernetically operated devices. [CYB(ERNETIC) + ORG(ANISM).]

cy·cad (sī'kăd', -kəd) *n.* Any seed-bearing plant of the family Cycadaceae, resembling a palm tree but surmounted by fernlike leaves. [NLat. *Cycas,* genus name < Gk. *kukas,* alteration of *koïx,* a kind of palm tree.]

cycl– *pref.* Variant of **cyclo–.**

cy·cla·mate (sī'klə-māt', sĭk'lə-) *n.* A salt of cyclamic acid, esp. either of two very sweet crystalline compounds: **a.** Sodium cyclamate. **b.** Calcium cyclamate, $C_{12}H_{24}N_2O_6S_2Ca$.

cy·cla·men (sī'klə-mən, sĭk'lə-) *n.* Any of several plants of the genus *Cyclamen,* having showy white, pink, or red flowers with reflexed petals. [NLat. < Gk. *kuklaminos.*]

cyc·la·mic acid (sĭk'lə-mĭk', sī'klə-) *n.* A sour-sweet crystalline acid, $C_6H_{13}NO_3S$.

cy·clase (sī'klās', -klāz') *n.* An enzyme that acts as a catalyst in the cyclization of a compound.

cy·cle (sī'kəl) *n.* **1.** A time interval in which a characteristic, esp. a regularly repeated, event or sequence of events occurs. **2. a.** A single complete execution of a periodically repeated phenomenon. **b.** A periodically repeated sequence of events. **3.** The orbit of a celestial body. **4.** A long period of time; an age. **5. a.** The aggregate of traditional poems or stories organized around a central theme or hero: *the Arthurian cycle.* **b.** A series of poems or songs on the same theme: *Schubert's song cycles.* **6.** A bicycle or motorcycle. **7.** *Bot.* A circular arrangement of flower parts such as petals or sepals. *—v.* **-cled, -cling, -cles.** *—intr.* **1.** To occur in or pass through a cycle. **2.** To move in, or as if in, a circle. **3.** To ride a bicycle or motorcycle. *—tr.* To use or employ in a cycle: *cycle the most experienced workers.* [Fr. < LLat. *cyclus* < Gk. *kuklos,* circle.] **—cy'cler** *n.*

cy·cle·ry (sī'kəl-rē) *n.* A shop for the sale and service of bicycles.

cy·clic (sī'klĭk, sĭk'lĭk) also **cy·cli·cal** (sī'klĭ-kəl, sĭk'lĭ-kəl) *adj.* **1. a.** Of, relating to, or characterized by cycles. **b.** Recurring or moving in cycles. **2.** *Chem.* Of or pertaining to compounds having atoms arranged in a ring or closed-chain structure. **3.** *Bot.* **a.** Having parts arranged in a whorl. **b.** Forming a whorl. **—cy'cli·cal·ly** *adv.*

cyclic AMP *n.* A cyclic nucleotide that acts as a hormonal mediator on the cellular level in the control of various metabolic processes.

cyclic GMP *n.* A cyclic nucleotide of guanosine believed to act as an antagonist to cyclic AMP in cellular processes.

cy·clist (sī'klĭst) *n.* One who rides or races a bicycle, motorcycle, or similar vehicle.

cy·cli·za·tion (sī'klĭ-zā'shən, sĭk'lĭ-) *n.* The formation of rings in a hydrocarbon.

cyclo– or **cycl–** *pref.* **1.** Circle; cycle: *cyclorama.* **2.** A cyclic compound: *cyclohexane.* [< Gk. *kuklos,* circle.]

cy·clo·hex·ane (sī'klō-hĕk'sān') *n.* An extremely flammable, colorless, mobile liquid, C_6H_{12}, obtained from petroleum and benzene and used as a solvent, paint and varnish remover, and in the manufacture of nylon.

cy·clo·hex·i·mide (sī'klō-hĕk'sə-mīd', -mĭd) *n.* A compound, $C_{15}H_{23}NO_4$, that is used as an agricultural fungicide.

cy·cloid (sī'kloid') *adj.* **1.** Resembling a circle. **2.** *Zool.* Thin, rounded, and smooth-edged; disklike. Used of fish scales. **3.** *Psychiat.* Designating a person afflicted with cyclothymia. *—n. Math.* The curve traced by a point on the circumference of a circle that rolls on a straight line. [Fr. *cycloïde* < Gk. *kukloeidēs,* circular : *kuklos,* circle + *-eidēs,* -oid.] **—cy·cloi'dal** (-kloid'l) *adj.*

cy·clom·e·ter (sī-klŏm'ĭ-tər) *n.* **1.** An instrument that records the revolutions of a wheel in order to indicate distance traveled. **2.** An instrument that measures circular arcs. **—cy'clo·met'ric** (-klə-mĕt'rĭk) *adj.* **—cy·clom'e·try** *n.*

cy·clone (sī'klōn') *n.* **1.** *Meteorol.* A type of atmospheric disturbance characterized by masses of air rapidly circulating clockwise in the southern and counterclockwise in the northern hemisphere, about a low-pressure center, usually accompanied by stormy, often destructive, weather. **2.** A violent, rotating windstorm. **3.** Any of various devices using centrifugal force to separate materials. [Poss. < Gk. *kuklōma,* coil < *kuklos,* circle.] **—cy·clon'ic** (-klŏn'ĭk), **cy·clon'i·cal** *adj.*

cyclone cellar *n.* An underground shelter in or adjacent to a house, used for protection from cyclones or tornadoes.

cy·clo·pae·di·a (sī'klə-pē'dē-ə) *n.* Variant of **cyclopedia.**

cy·clo·par·af·fin (sī'klō-păr'ə-fĭn) *n.* Any of a class of hydrocarbons, including cyclopropane, cyclopentane, and cyclohexane, in which at least three carbon atoms per molecule are joined in a ring structure and each such carbon in the ring is bonded to two hydrogen atoms or alkyl groups.

cy·clo·pe·an (sī'klə-pē'ən, sī-klō'pē-) *adj.* **1.** Often **Cyclopean.** Pertaining to or suggestive of the Cyclopes. **2.** Pertaining to or designating a primitive style of masonry characterized by the use of massive stones of irregular shape and size.

cy·clo·pe·di·a also **cy·clo·pae·di·a** (sī'klə-pē'dē-ə) *n.* An encyclopedia. [Short for ENCYCLOPEDIA.] **—cy'clo·pe'dic** (-dĭk) *adj.* **—cy'clo·pe'dist** (-dĭst) *n.*

cy·clo·pen·tane (sī'klə-pĕn'tān', sĭk'lə-) *n.* A colorless flammable liquid, C_5H_{10}, derived from petroleum and used as a solvent and motor fuel.

Cy·clo·pes (sī-klō'pēz) *n.* Plural of **Cyclops.**

cy·clo·ple·gia (sī'klə-plē'jə) *n.* Loss of visual accommodation because of paralysis of the ciliary muscles of the eye.

cy·clo·pro·pane (sī'klə-prō'pān') *n.* A highly flammable, explosive, colorless gas, C_3H_6, used as an anesthetic.

Cy·clops (sī'klŏps') *n., pl.* **Cy·clo·pes** (sī-klō'pēz) *Gk. Myth.* **1.** Any of the three one-eyed Titans who forged thunderbolts for Zeus. **2.** Any of a race of one-eyed giants, reputedly descended from these Titans, inhabiting the island of Sicily. [Lat. < Gk. *kuklōps* : *kuklos,* circle + *ōps,* eye.]

cy·clo·ram·a (sī'klə-răm'ə, -rä'mə) *n.* **1.** A large composite picture placed on the interior walls of a cylindrical room so as to appear in natural perspective to a spectator standing in the center. **2.** A large curtain or wall, usually concave, placed or hung at the rear of a stage. [CYCL(O)- + (PAN)ORAMA.] **—cy'clo·ram'ic** *adj.*

cy·clo·ser·ine (sī'klō-sĕr'ēn') *n.* An antibiotic produced by a species of *Streptomyces* that is effective against many Gram-negative bacteria.

cy·clo·sis (sī-klō'sĭs) *n., pl.* **-ses** (-sēz). The streaming circulatory motion of protoplasm within certain cells and cell structures. [NLat. < Gk. *kuklōsis,* a surrounding < *kukloun,* to surround < *kuklos,* circle.]

cy·clo·stome (sī'klə-stōm') *n.* Any of various primitive eel-like vertebrates of the class Agnatha, such as a lamprey, lacking jaws and true teeth and having a circular, sucking mouth. [NLat. *Cyclostomi* and *Cyclostomata,* class names : CYCLO- + Gk. *stoma,* mouth.] **—cy·clos'to·mate'** (sī-klŏs'tə-māt'), **cy'clo·stom'a·tous** (sī'klə-stŏm'ə-təs, -stō'mə-) *adj.*

cy·clo·thyme (sī'klə-thīm') *n.* A person afflicted with cyclothymia.

cy·clo·thy·mi·a (sī'klə-thī'mē-ə) *n.* A form of manic-depressive psychosis characterized by alternating periods of activity and excitement with periods of inactivity and depression. **—cy'clo·thy'mic** (-mĭk) *adj. & n.*

cy·clo·tron (sī'klə-trŏn') *n.* A circular accelerator capable of generating particle energies between a few million and several tens of millions of electron volts, in which charged particles generated at a central source are accelerated spirally outward in a plane at right angles to a fixed magnetic field by an alternating electric field.

cy·der (sī'dər) *n. Chiefly Brit.* Variant of **cider.**

cy·e·sis (sī-ē'sĭs) *n., pl.* **-ses** (-sēz'). Pregnancy; gestation. [NLat. < Gk. *kuēsis* < *kuein,* to swell.]

cyclamen

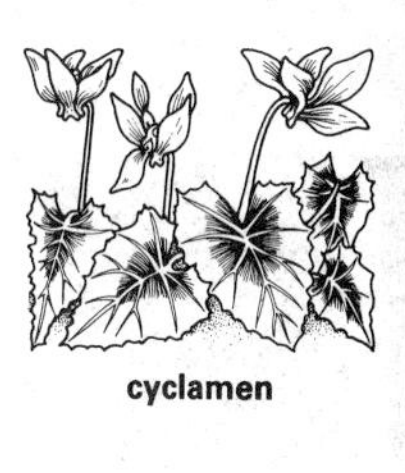

cycloid

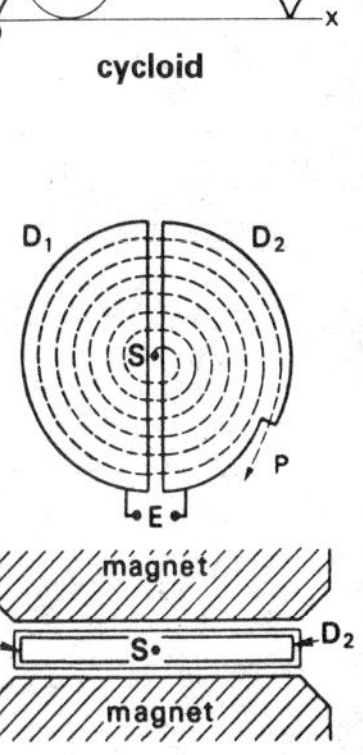

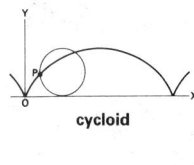

cyclotron
Above: Top view: D_1, D_2 form a hollow disk within which particles P from source S are accelerated outward by potential E
Below: Side view showing field magnets

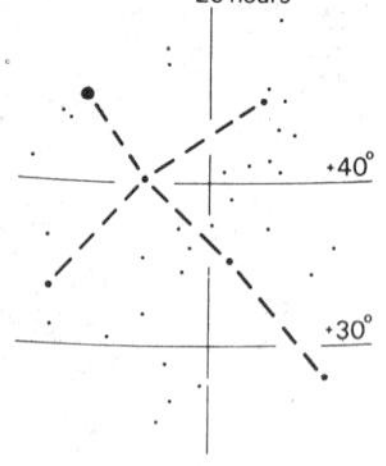

Cygnus

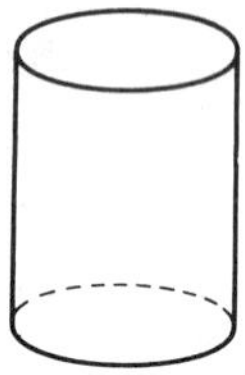
right circular cylinder

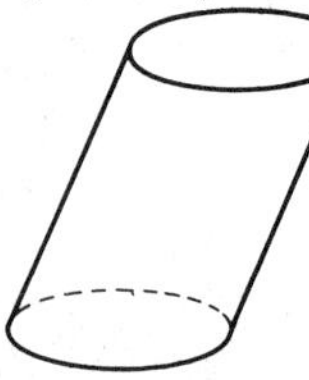
oblique circular cylinder
cylinder

cymbal
A pair of cymbals

cypress

cyg·net (sĭg′nĭt) *n.* A young swan. [ME *sygnett* < OFr. *cygne,* swan < Lat. *cygnus* < Gk. *kuknos.*]

Cyg·nus (sĭg′nəs) *n.* A constellation in the Northern Hemisphere near Lacerta and Lyra, containing the star Deneb. [Lat. *cygnus,* swan < Gk. *kuknos.*]

cyl·in·der (sĭl′ən-dər) *n.* **1.** *Math.* **a.** A surface generated by a straight line moving parallel to a fixed straight line and intersecting a plane curve. **b.** The portion of such a surface bounded by two parallel planes and the regions of the planes bounded by the surface. **c.** A solid bounded by two parallel planes and such a surface having a closed curve, esp. a circle, as a directrix. **2.** A cylindrical container or object. **3.** *Engineering.* **a.** The chamber in which a piston of a reciprocating engine moves. **b.** The chamber of a pump from which fluid is expelled by a piston. **4.** The rotating chamber of a revolver that holds the cartridges. **5.** Any of the rotating cylinders in a printing press that carry the paper or the curved printing plate or receive the ink or impression. **6.** *Archaeol.* A cylindrical stone or clay object with an engraved design or inscription. [OFr. *cylindre* < Lat. *cylindrus* < Gk. *kulindros* < *kulindein,* to roll.]

cylinder head *n.* The closed, often detachable, end of a cylinder or cylinders in an internal-combustion engine.

cy·lin·dri·cal (sə-lĭn′drĭ-kəl) also **cy·lin·dric** (-drĭk) *adj.* **1.** Having the shape of a cylinder, esp. of a circular cylinder. **2.** Of or pertaining to a cylinder. **3.** Of or pertaining to the coordinate system or to any of three coordinates in it, formed by two polar coordinates in a plane and a rectangular coordinate measured perpendicularly from the plane. **—cy·lin′dri·cal′i·ty** (-kăl′ĭ-tē) *n.* **—cy·lin′dri·cal·ly** *adv.*

cyl·in·droid (sĭl′ən-droid′) *n.* A cylindrical surface or solid all of whose sections perpendicular to the elements are elliptical. *—adj.* Resembling a cylinder.

cy·ma (sī′mə) *n.* A molding for a cornice, having a partly concave and partly convex curve in profile, used esp. in classical architecture. [Gk. *kuma* < *kuein,* to swell.]

cy·ma·tium (sĭ-mā′shəm, -shē-əm) *n., pl.* **-tia** (-shə, -shē-ə). **1.** A cyma. **2.** The topmost molding of a classical cornice. [Lat. < Gk. *kumation,* dim. of *kuma,* cyma.]

cym·bal (sĭm′bəl) *n.* **1.** One of a pair of concave brass plates that are struck together as percussion instruments. **2.** A single brass plate, sounded by hitting with a drumstick and often part of a set of drums. [ME < OFr. *cymbale* < Lat. *cymbalum* < Gk. *kumbalon* < *kumbē,* bowl.] **—cym′bal·eer′** (sĭm′bə-lîr′), **cym′bal·er, cym′bal·ist** *n.*

cym·bid·i·um (sĭm-bĭd′ē-əm) *n.* Any of various orchids of the genus *Cymbidium* having showy flowers that are often used for decoration. [NLat. *Cymbidium,* genus name < Lat. *cymba,* boat < Gk. *kumbē.*]

cyme (sīm) *n. Bot.* An often flat-topped flower cluster that blooms from the center toward the edges, and whose main axis is always terminated by a flower. [NLat. *cyma* < Lat., young cabbage sprout < Gk. *kuma,* cyma, sprout.] **—cy·mif′er·ous** (sī-mĭf′ər-əs) *adj.*

cy·mene (sī′mēn′) *n. Chem.* Any of three colorless isomeric liquid hydrocarbons, $C_{10}H_{14}$, obtained chiefly from the essential oils of various plants and used in the manufacture of synthetic resins. [Fr. *cymène* < Gk. *kuminon,* cumin, of Semitic orig.]

cym·ling (sĭm′lĭng) also **cym·lin** (-lĭn) *n.* A greenish-white, flat, round squash with a scalloped edge. [Alteration of SIMNEL.]

cy·mo·gene (sī′mə-jēn′) *n.* A flammable gaseous fraction of petroleum, chiefly butane. [CYM(ENE) + -GENE.]

cy·moid (sī′moid′) *adj.* Resembling a cyma or cyme.

cy·mo·phane (sī′mə-făn′) *n.* A variety of chrysoberyl having a shimmering luster. [Fr. : Gk. *kuma,* wave, cyma + Fr. *-phane,* -phane.]

cy·mose (sī′mōs′) also **cy·mous** (-məs) *adj.* **1.** Pertaining to or resembling a cyme. **2.** Bearing a cyme or cymes. [CYM(E) + -OSE[1].] **—cy′mose′ly** *adv.*

Cym·ric (kĭm′rĭk, sĭm′rĭk) *adj.* Of or pertaining to the Cymry. *—n.* **1.** Brythonic. **2.** Welsh (sense 2).

Cym·ry (kĭm′rē, sĭm′rē) *n.* The branch of the Celtic people to which the Welsh, the Cornish, and the Bretons belong. [Welsh.]

cyn·ic (sĭn′ĭk) *n.* **1. Cynic.** A member of a sect of ancient Greek philosophers who believed virtue to be the only good and self-control to be the only means of achieving virtue. **2.** A person who believes all people are motivated by selfishness. *—adj.* **1. Cynic.** Of or pertaining to the Cynics or their doctrines. **2.** Cynical. [Lat. *cynicus,* Cynic philosopher < Gk. *kunikos,* prob. ult. < *kuōn,* dog.]

cyn·i·cal (sĭn′ĭ-kəl) *adj.* **1.** Scornful of the motives or virtue of others. **2.** Bitterly mocking; sneering. **—cyn′i·cal·ly** *adv.* **—cyn′i·cal·ness** *n.*

cyn·i·cism (sĭn′ĭ-sĭz′əm) *n.* **1.** A cynical attitude or character. **2.** A cynical comment or act. **3. Cynicism.** The beliefs and doctrines of the Cynics.

cy·no·sure (sī′nə-shŏŏr′, sĭn′ə-) *n.* **1.** An object that serves as a focal point of attention and admiration. **2.** Something that serves to guide. [Fr., Ursa Minor (which contains the guiding star Polaris) < Lat. *cynosura* < Gk. *kunosoura,* dog's tail, Ursa Minor : *kuōn,* dog + *oura,* tail.] **—cy′no·sur′al** *adj.*

cy·pher (sī′fər) *n. & v.* Variant of **cipher.**

cy·press (sī′prəs) *n.* **1. a.** Any evergreen tree of the genus *Cupressus,* growing in warm climates, and having small, compressed needles. **b.** Any of several similar or related trees, as the bald cypress. **2.** The wood of any of the cypress trees. **3.** Cypress branches used as a symbol of mourning. [ME *cipres* < OFr. < LLat. *cypressus* < Gk. *kuparissos.*]

cypress spurge *n.* A plant, *Euphorbia cyparissias,* native to Eurasia, having densely crowded, narrow leaves and clusters of yellow-green flowers.

cypress vine *n.* A tropical American vine, *Quamoclit pennata,* having finely divided compound leaves and scarlet flowers.

Cyp·ri·an (sĭp′rē-ən) *adj.* **1.** Of or pertaining to Cyprus, its people, their customs, or their language. **2.** Characteristic of or resembling the ancient worship of Aphrodite on Cyprus; licentious; wanton. *—n.* **1.** A Cypriot. **2.** *Obs.* A wanton person, esp. a prostitute.

cyp·ri·nid (sĭp′rə-nĭd) *n.* Any of numerous often small freshwater fishes of the family Cyprinidae, which includes the minnows, carps, and shiners. *—adj.* Of, relating to, or belonging to the family Cyprinidae. [NLat. *Cyprinidae,* family name < *Cyprinus,* genus name < Lat. *cyprinus,* carp < Gk. *kuprinos.*]

cy·prin·o·dont (sĭ-prĭn′ə-dŏnt′, -prī′nə-) *n.* Any of various small, soft-finned fishes of the family Cyprinodontidae, which includes the killifishes, topminnows, and many species popular in home aquariums. [Lat. *cyprinus,* carp (< Gk. *kuprinos*) + -ODONT.]

cyp·ri·noid (sĭp′rə-noid′, sĭ-prī′-) *adj.* Of, pertaining to, or resembling a carp or related fish. *—n.* A cyprinoid fish. [NLat. *Cyprinoidea,* suborder name < *Cyprinus,* genus name. —see CYPRINID.]

Cyp·ri·ot (sĭp′rē-ət, -ŏt′) also **Cyp·ri·ote** (-ōt′, -ət) *—n.* **1.** A native or inhabitant of Cyprus. **2.** The ancient Greek dialect of Cyprus. *—adj.* **1.** Of or pertaining to Cyprus. **2.** Of or pertaining to the Cypriot language. [Fr. *cypriote* < *Cyprus,* Cyprus.]

cyp·ri·pe·di·um (sĭp′rĭ-pē′dē-əm) *n.* Any orchid of the genus *Cypripedium,* which includes the lady's-slippers. [NLat., *Cypripedium,* genus name : Gk. *Kupris,* Aphrodite (< *Kupros,* Cyprus, legendary birthplace of Venus) + Gk. *pedilon,* sandal.]

cy·prot·er·one (sĭ-prŏt′ə-rōn′) *n.* A hormone that inhibits the secretion of androgens. [Prob. Lat. *Cypris,* Venus (< Gk. *Kupris* < *Kupros,* Cyprus) + (TESTOS)TERONE.]

cyp·se·la (sĭp′sə-lə) *n., pl.* **-lae** (-lē′). An achene that does not separate from its calyx, characteristic of composite plants. [NLat. < Gk. *kupselē,* hollow vessel.]

Cyr·e·na·ic (sîr′ə-nā′ĭk, sīr′-) *adj.* **1.** Of or pertaining to Cyrenaica or Cyrene. **2.** Of or pertaining to a philosophy advocating pleasure as the only good in life. *—n.* **1.** A native or inhabitant of Cyrenaica or Cyrene. **2.** A disciple of the Cyrenaic school of philosophy.

Cy·ril·lic (sə-rĭl′ĭk) *adj.* Of or designating the old Slavic alphabet ascribed to Saint Cyril, presently used in modified form for Russian, Bulgarian, certain other Slavic languages, and other languages of the Soviet Union.

cyst (sĭst) *n.* **1.** *Pathol.* An abnormal membranous sac containing a gaseous, liquid, or semisolid substance. **2.** *Anat.* Any sac or vesicle in the body. **3.** *Biol.* A capsulelike membrane of certain organisms in a resting stage. **4.** *Bot.* Any of various cells of nonsexual origin in green algae, that germinate and produce new plants after a resting period. [NLat. *cystis* < Gk. *kustis,* bladder.]

cyst– *pref.* Variant of **cysto-.**

cys·tec·to·my (sĭ-stĕk′tə-mē) *n., pl.* **-mies. 1.** Surgical removal of a cyst. **2.** Surgical excision of the gall bladder or of a portion of the urinary bladder.

cys·te·ine (sĭs′tə-ēn′, -ĭn) *n.* An amino acid, $C_3H_7NO_2S$, found in most proteins, esp. in keratin. [CYST(INE) + -EIN.]

cys·tic (sĭs′tĭk) *adj.* **1.** Of, pertaining to, or like a cyst. **2.** Having or containing a cyst or cysts. **3.** Enclosed in a cyst. **4.** *Anat.* Pertaining to the gall bladder or urinary bladder.

cys·ti·cer·coid (sĭs′tĭ-sûr′koid) *n.* The larval stage of certain tapeworms, like a cysticercus but having the scolex completely filling the enclosing sac. [CYSTICERC(US) + -OID.]

cys·ti·cer·co·sis (sĭs′tĭ-sər-kō′sĭs) *n.* The condition of being infested with cysticerci. [CYSTICERC(US) + -OSIS.]

cys·ti·cer·cus (sĭs′tĭ-sûr′kəs) *n., pl.* **-ci** (-sī′). The larval stage of many tapeworms, consisting of a scolex enclosed in a fluid-filled sac. [NLat. : Gk. *kustis,* cyst + Gk. *kerkos,* tail.]

cystic fibrosis *n.* A congenital disease of mucous glands throughout the body, usually developing during childhood and causing pancreatic insufficiency and pulmonary disorders.

cys·tine (sĭs′tēn′) *n.* A white crystalline compound, $C_6H_{12}N_2O_4S_2$, the principal sulfur-containing amino acid of protein.

cys·ti·tis (sĭ-stī′tĭs) *n.* Inflammation of the urinary bladder.

cysto– or **cyst–** *pref.* Bladder; cyst; sac: *cystocele.* [< Gk. *kustis,* bladder.]

cys·to·carp (sĭs′tə-kärp′) *n.* A structure consisting of fertile filaments and carpospores, developed after fertilization of the carpogonium in red algae.

cys·to·cele (sĭs′tə-sēl′) *n.* Hernia of the bladder.
cys·toid (sĭs′toid′) *adj.* Formed like or resembling a cyst. —*n.* A cystoid structure.
cys·to·lith (sĭs′tə-lĭth′) *n.* **1.** *Bot.* A mineral concretion, usually calcium carbonate, formed in the cellulose wall of plant cells. **2.** *Pathol.* A urinary calculus.
cys·to·scope (sĭs′tə-skōp′) *n.* A tubular instrument fitted with a light and used to examine the urinary bladder and ureter. **—cys′to·scop′ic** (-skŏp′ĭk) *adj.* **—cys·tos′co·py** (sĭ-stŏs′kə-pē) *n.*
cys·tos·to·my (sĭ-stŏs′tə-mē) *n., pl.* **-mies.** The surgical formation of an opening into the bladder.
cyt– *pref.* Variant of **cyto-.**
-cyte *suff.* Cell: *leukocyte.* [NLat. *-cyta* < Gk. *kutos,* hollow vessel.]
Cyth·e·re·a (sĭth′ə-rē′ə) *n. Gk. Myth.* The goddess Aphrodite. [Lat. < Gk. *Kuthereia* < *Kuthēra,* one of the Ionian islands.]
cyto– or **cyt–** *pref.* Cell: *cytoplasm.* [< Gk. *kutos,* hollow vessel.]
cy·to·chem·is·try (sī′tō-kĕm′ĭ-strē) *n.* The chemistry of plant and animal cells. **—cy′to·chem′i·cal** (-kĕm′ĭ-kəl) *adj.*
cy·to·chrome (sī′tə-krōm′) *n.* Any of a class of iron-containing proteins important in cell metabolism.
cytochrome oxidase *n.* An oxidizing enzyme that functions in cell respiration by reacting with oxygen in the reduced state.
cy·to·gen·e·sis (sī′tō-jĕn′ĭ-sĭs) *n.* The formation and development of cells. **—cy′to·ge·net′ic** (sī′tō-jə-nĕt′ĭk) *adj.*
cy·to·ge·net·ics (sī′tō-jə-nĕt′ĭks) *n. (used with a sing. verb).* The study of heredity by cytological and genetic methods. **—cy′to·ge·net′i·cal** (-nĕt′ĭ-kəl) *adj.* **—cy′to·ge·net′i·cal·ly** *adv.* **—cy′to·ge·net′i·cist** (-nĕt′ĭ-sĭst) *n.*
cy·tog·e·ny (sī-tŏj′ə-nē) *n.* Cytogenesis.
cy·to·ki·ne·sis (sī′tō-kĭ-nē′sĭs, -kī-) *n.* The cleavage of cytoplasm during cell division. **—cy′to·ki·net′ic** (-nĕt′ĭk) *adj.*
cy·to·ki·nin (sī′tə-kī′nĭn) *n.* Any of various growth regulators that promote cell division in plants.
cy·tol·o·gy (sī-tŏl′ə-jē) *n.* The branch of biology dealing with the study of the formation, structure, and function of cells. **—cy′to·log′ic** (-tə-lŏj′ĭk), **cy′to·log′i·cal** *adj.* **—cy·tol′o·gist** *n.*
cy·tol·y·sin (sī-tŏl′ĭ-sĭn) *n.* An antibody capable of destroying an animal cell partially or completely. [CYTOLYS(IS) + -IN.]
cy·tol·y·sis (sī-tŏl′ĭ-sĭs) *n.* The dissolution of a cell. **—cy′to·lyt′ic** (sī′tə-lĭt′ĭk) *adj.*
cy·to·me·gal·ic (sī′tō-mĭ-găl′ĭk) *adj.* Pertaining to or characterized by greatly enlarged cells.
cy·to·meg·a·lo·vi·rus (sī′tə-mĕg′ə-lō-vī′rəs) *n.* Any of a group of viruses that cause cellular enlargement and also cause a disease of infants characterized by circulatory dysfunction and microcephaly.
cy·to·path·ic (sī′tə-păth′ĭk) *adj.* Of or pertaining to pathologic changes in cells.
cy·toph·a·gy (sī-tŏf′ə-jē) *n.* The devouring of other cells by the phagocytes. **—cy′to·phag′ic** (sī′tə-făj′ĭk), **cy·toph′a·gous** (-tŏf′ə-gəs) *adj.*
cy·to·pho·tom·e·try (sī′tə-fō-tŏm′ĭ-trē) *n.* The photometric study of a cell. **—cy′to·pho′to·met′ric** (-tə-mĕt′rĭk) *adj.*
cy·to·plasm (sī′tə-plăz′əm) *n.* The protoplasm outside a cell nucleus. **—cy′to·plas′mic** (-plăz′mĭk) *adj.* **—cy′to·plas′mi·cal·ly** *adv.*
cy·to·plast (sī′tə-plăst′) *n.* The cytoplasm within a single cell. **—cy′to·plas′tic** (-plăs′tĭk) *adj.*
cy·to·sine (sī′tə-sēn′) *n.* A pyrimidine base, $C_4H_5N_3O$, that is an essential constituent of both ribonucleic and deoxyribonucleic acids. [CYT(O)- + -OS(E)[2] + -INE[2].]
cy·to·tax·on·o·my (sī′tō-tăk-sŏn′ə-mē) *n.* The classification of organisms based on cellular structure, esp. on the comparative morphology of chromosomes. **—cy′to·tax′o·nom′ic** (-tăk′sə-nŏm′ĭk) *adj.* **—cy′to·tax·on′o·mist** *n.*
cy·to·tech·nol·o·gist (sī′tə-tĕk-nŏl′ə-jĭst) *n.* A technician who is trained in the medical examination and identification of cellular abnormalities.
czar (zär) *n.* **1.** A king or emperor, esp. one of the former emperors of Russia. **2.** A tyrant; autocrat. **3.** *Informal.* One in authority; leader: *a czar of finance.* [Pol. < R. *tsar′,* ult. < Lat. *Caesar,* emperor. —see CAESAR.] **—czar′dom** *n.*
czar·das (chär′dăsh′) *n.* **1.** An intricate Hungarian dance characterized by variations in tempo. **2.** Music for the czardas. [Hung. *csárdás.*]
czar·e·vitch (zär′ə-vĭch′) *n.* The eldest son of a czar. [Pol. < R. *tsarevich* : *tsar′,* czar + *-evich,* masc. patronymic suffix.]
cza·rev·na (zä-rĕv′nə) *n.* **1.** The daughter of a czar. **2.** The wife of a czarevitch. [Pol. < R. *tsarevna* : *tsar′,* czar + *-evna,* fem. patronymic suffix.]
cza·ri·na (zä-rē′nə) also **cza·rit·za** (-rĭt′sə, -rĕt′-) *n.* The wife of a czar. [Pol. < R. *tsarina* : *tsar′,* czar + *-ina,* fem. suffix.]
czar·ism (zär′ĭz′əm) *n.* The system of government in Russia under the czars; autocracy. **—czar′ist** *adj.*
cza·rit·za (zä-rĭt′sə, -rĕt′-) *n.* Variant of **czarina.**
Czech (chĕk) *n.* **1.** A native or inhabitant of Czechoslovakia, esp. a Bohemian, Moravian, or Slovak. **2.** The Slavic language of the Czechs. [Pol. < Czech *Čechy.*] **—Czech** *adj.*

cypress vine

D

1 2 3 4 5 6 7 8 9 10 11 12 13 14

Phoenician | Greek | Roman | Medieval | Modern

Around 1000 B.C. the Phoenicians and other Semitic peoples began to use graphic signs to represent individual speech sounds instead of syllables or words. They used a triangular symbol (1,2) to represent the sound of the consonant "d" and called it *dāleth,* their word for "door." The Greeks, adapting the Phoenician alphabet, kept the phonetic value of *dāleth* but altered its shape (3,4,5,6) and changed its name to *delta.* The Romans borrowed the alphabet from the Greeks via the Etruscans and adapted it for monumental inscriptions. Monumental script (8) is the prototype of modern capital letters (11,12). Medieval scribes adapted the Roman capitals to being quickly written on paper, parchment, and vellum. These uncial and cursive minuscules (9,10) are the prototypes of modern lower-case letters, both written and printed (14,13).

d

d or **D** (dē) *n., pl.* **d's** or **D's.** **1.** The fourth letter of the modern English alphabet. **2.** Any of the speech sounds represented by the letter *d.* **3.** Something shaped like the letter D. **4.** The fourth in a series. **5. D** The lowest passing grade given to a student in a school or college. **6. D** *Mus.* **a.** The second tone in the scale of C major or the fourth tone in the relative minor scale. **b.** The key or a scale in which D is the tonic. **c.** A written or printed note representing this tone. **d.** A string, key, or pipe tuned to the pitch of this tone. **7. D** The Roman numeral for 500.

-'d *suff.* **1.** Had: *He'd already left.* **2.** Would: *I'd rather walk than drive.* **3.** Did: *Who'd you ask?*

dab[1] (dăb) *v.* **dabbed, dab·bing, dabs.** *—tr.* **1.** To apply with short, poking strokes. **2.** To cover lightly with or as if with a moist substance. **3.** To strike or hit lightly. *—intr.* To tap gently; pat. *—n.* **1.** A small amount: *a dab of jelly.* **2.** A quick, light pat. [ME *dabben.*]

dab[2] (dăb) *n.* Any of various flatfishes, chiefly of the genera *Limanda* and *Hippoglossoides,* related to and resembling the flounders. [ME *dabbe.*]

dab[3] (dăb) *n. Chiefly Brit.* An expert. [Orig. unknown.]

dab·ber (dăb'ər) *n.* **1.** One that dabs. **2.** *Printing.* A cushioned pad used by printers and engravers to apply ink.

dab·ble (dăb'əl) *v.* **-bled, -bling, -bles.** *—tr.* To splash or spatter, as with a liquid. *—intr.* **1.** To splash liquid gently and playfully. **2.** To undertake something superficially or without serious intent. **3.** To bob forward and under in shoal water so as to feed off the bottom. [Perh. < Du. *dabbelen,* freq. of *dabben,* to strike, tap.] **—dab'bler** *n.*

dab·chick (dăb'chĭk') *n.* Any of various small grebes of the genus *Podiceps.*

da ca·po (dä kä'pō, də) *adv. Mus.* From the beginning. Used as a direction to repeat a passage. [Ital.]

dace (dās) *n., pl.* **dace** or **dac·es.** Any of various small freshwater fishes of the family Cyprinidae, related to and resembling the minnows. [ME *dars* < OFr.]

da·cha (dä'chə) *n.* A Russian country house. [R., gift, land.]

dachs·hund (däks'ho͝ont', däk'sənt) *n.* A small dog of a breed developed in Germany for hunting badgers, with a long body, a usually short-haired brown or black and brown coat, drooping ears, and very short legs. [G. : *Dachs,* badger + *Hund,* dog.]

Da·cron (dā'krŏn', dăk'rŏn'). A trademark for a synthetic polyester textile fiber.

dac·tyl (dăk'təl) *n.* **1.** A metrical foot consisting of one accented syllable followed by two unaccented or of one long syllable followed by two short. **2.** A finger, toe, or similar part or structure; digit. [ME *dactil* < Lat. *dactylus* < Gk. *daktulos,* finger, dactyl.] **—dac·tyl'ic** (-tĭl'ĭk) *adj. & n.* **—dac·tyl'i·cal·ly** *adv.*

dac·ty·li (dăk'tə-lī') *n.* Plural of **dactylus.**

dactylo- or **dactyl-** *pref.* Finger; toe; digit: *dactylogram.* [< Gk. *daktulos,* finger.]

dac·tyl·o·gram (dăk-tĭl'ə-grăm') *n.* A fingerprint.

dac·ty·log·ra·phy (dăk'tə-lŏg'rə-fē) *n.* The study of fingerprints as a method of identification. **—dac'ty·lo·graph'ic** (-lō-grăf'ĭk) *adj.*

dac·ty·lol·o·gy (dăk'tə-lŏl'ə-jē) *n.* The use of the fingers and hands to convey ideas, as in the manual alphabet used by deaf-mutes.

dac·ty·lus (dăk'tə-ləs) *n., pl.* **-li** (-lī'). **1.** A dactyl (sense 2). **2.** The tarsus of some insects following the first joint that usually consists of one or more joints. [NLat. < Gk. *daktulos,* finger.]

dad (dăd) *n. Informal.* Father. [Prob. of baby-talk orig.]

Da·da or **da·da** (dä'dä) also **Da·da·ism** (-ĭz'əm) *n.* A western European artistic and literary movement (1916–23) that sought the discovery of authentic reality through the abolition of traditional cultural and aesthetic forms by a technique of comic derision in which irrationality, chance, and intuition were the guiding principles. [Fr.] **—Da'da·ist** *n.* **—Da'da·is'tic** (dä'dä-ĭs'tĭk) *adj.*

dad·dy (dăd'ē) *n., pl.* **-dies.** *Informal.* Father.

daddy long·legs (lông'lĕgz', lŏng'-) *n., pl.* **daddy longlegs.** **1.** Any of various arachnids of the order Phalangida, with a small, rounded body and long, slender legs. **2.** The crane fly.

da·do (dā'dō) *n., pl.* **-does.** **1.** The section of a pedestal between the base and crown. **2.** The lower portion of the wall of a room, decorated differently from the upper section, as with panels. **3. a.** A rectangular groove cut into a board so that a like piece may be fitted into it. **b.** The groove so cut. *—tr.v.* **-doed, -do·ing, -does.** **1.** To furnish with a dado. **2. a.** To cut a dado in. **b.** To fit into a dado. [Ital. < Lat. *datum,* neuter p.part. of *dare,* to give.]

dae·dal (dēd'l) *adj.* **1.** Ingenious and complex in design or function; intricate. **2.** Finely or skillfully made or employed; artistic. [Lat. *daedalus* < Gk. *daidalos.*]

Dae·da·lus (dĕd'l-əs) *n. Gk. Myth.* A legendary artist and inventor, builder of the Labyrinth. [Lat. < Gk. *Daidalos* < *daidalos,* skillfully made.] **—Dae·da'li·an, Dae·da'le·an** (dĭ-dā'lē-ən, -dāl'yən) *adj.*

dae·mon (dē'mən) *n.* Variant of **demon** (senses 3, 4).

daf·fo·dil (dăf'ə-dĭl) *n.* **1. a.** A bulbous plant, *Narcissus pseudo-narcissus,* with showy, usually yellow flowers with a trumpet-shaped central crown. **b.** Its flower. **2.** A brilliant to vivid yellow. [Alteration of obs. *affodill* < ME *affodylle,* asphodel < Lat. *asphodilus.* —see ASPHODEL.]

daf·fy (dăf'ē) *adj.* **-fi·er, -fi·est.** *Informal.* **1.** Silly; foolish. **2.** Crazy. [< obs. *daff,* fool < ME *daffe.*]

daft (dăft) *adj.* **-er, -est.** **1.** Mad; crazy. **2.** Foolish; stupid. **3.** *Scot.* Frolicsome. [ME *dafte,* foolish < OE *gedæfte,* meek.] **—daft'ly** *adv.* **—daft'ness** *n.*

dag (dăg) *n.* **1.** A lock of matted or dung-coated wool. **2.** *Archaic.* A hanging end or shred. [ME *dagge,* shred.]

Da·gan (dä'gän') *n. Myth.* The Babylonian god of the earth. [Akkadian *Dagān.*]

dag·ger (dăg'ər) *n.* **1.** A short pointed weapon with sharp edges. **2.** Something that agonizes, torments, or wounds. **3.** *Printing.* **a.** An obelisk (sense 2). **b.** A double dagger. [ME *daggere.*]

da·go (dā'gō) *n., pl.* **-gos** or **-goes.** *Offensive Slang.* An Italian, Spaniard, or Portuguese. [Alteration of Sp. *Diego,* a given name < Lat. *Jacobus,* Jacob.]

Da·gon (dā'gŏn') *n. Myth.* The chief god of the ancient Philistines and later the Phoenicians, represented as half-man and half-fish. [ME < Lat. < Gk. *Dagōn* < Heb. *Dāgōn,* dim. of *dāg,* fish.]

da·guerre·o·type (də-gâr'ə-tīp') *n.* **1.** An early photographic process with the image made on a light-sensitive silver-coated metallic plate. **2.** A photograph made by daguerreotype. *—tr.v.* **-typed, -typ·ing, -types.** To make a daguerreotype of. [After Louis J. M. *Daguerre* (1787–1851), its inventor.] **—da·guerre'o·typ'er** *n.* **—da·guerre'o·typ'y** *n.*

dag·wood also **Dag·wood** (dăg'wo͝od') *n.* A multilayered sandwich with a variety of fillings. [After *Dagwood* Bumstead, a character who made such sandwiches in the comic strip *Blondie* by Murat B. Young (1901–1973).]

dah (dä) *n.* A dash in Morse code.

dahl·ia (dăl'yə, däl'-, dāl'-) *n.* **1.** Any of several plants of the genus *Dahlia,* native to Mexico and Central America, having tuberous roots and showy, variously colored flowers. **2.** The flower of a dahlia. [NLat. *Dahlia,* genus name, after Anders *Dahl* (d. 1789).]

da·hoon (də-ho͞on') *n.* An evergreen shrub or small tree, *Ilex cassine,* of the southeastern United States, having red fruit. [Orig. unknown.]

dai·ly (dā'lē) *adj.* **1.** Done, happening, or appearing every day or weekday: *a daily walk.* **2.** For each day: *a daily record.* **3.** Day-to-day; everyday: *for daily use.* *—adv.* **1.** Every day: *Exercise daily.* **2.** Once a day: *Wind the clock daily.* *—n., pl.* **-lies.** A newspaper published every day or every weekday. [ME *dayly* < OE *dæglic* < *dæg,* day.]

daily double *n.* A bet won by choosing both winners of two specified races on one day, as in horse racing.

dai·mi·o also **dai·my·o** (dī'mē-ō', dīm'yō') *n., pl.* **daimio** or **-mi·os** also **daimyo** or **-my·os.** A hereditary nobleman in feudal Japan. [J. *daimyo* : *dai,* great (< Chin. *da*[4]) + *myo,* name (< Chin. *ming*[2]).]

dai·mon (dī'mōn') *n.* Variant of **demon** (senses 3, 4).

dain·ty (dān'tē) *adj.* **-ti·er, -ti·est.** **1.** Delicately beautiful or charming; exquisite. **2.** Delicious or choice. **3.** Of refined taste; discriminating. **4.** Overly fastidious; squeamish. *—n., pl.* **-ties.** Something delicious; delicacy. [ME *deirte,* excellent < *deinte,* excellence, dignity < OFr. *deintie* < Lat. *dignitas* < *dignus,* worthy.] **—dain'ti·ly** *adv.* **—dain'ti·ness** *n.*

dai·qui·ri (dī'kə-rē, dăk'ə-) *n., pl.* **-ris.** An iced cocktail of rum, lime or lemon juice, and sugar. [After *Daiquirí,* Cuba.]

dair·y (dâr'ē) *n., pl.* **-ies.** **1.** A commercial establishment that processes or sells milk and milk products. **2.** A place where milk and cream are stored and processed. **3.** A dairy farm. **4.** The dairy business; dairying. [ME *daierie* < *daie,* dairymaid < OE *dæge.*]

dairy cattle *pl.n.* Cows bred and raised for milk rather than meat.

dairy farm *n.* A farm for producing milk and milk products.

dair·y·ing (dâr'ē-ĭng) *n.* The business of a dairy.

dair·y·maid (dâr'ē-mād') *n.* A female dairy worker.

dair·y·man (dâr'ē-mən) *n.* **1.** A dairy manager or owner. **2.** A male dairy worker.

da·is (dā'ĭs, dās) *n.* A raised platform, as in a lecture hall, for honored guests or speakers. [ME *deis* < OFr., platform < LLat. *discus,* table. —see DISK.]

dai·sy (dā'zē) *n., pl.* **-sies.** **1.** Any of several related plants having rayed flowers, esp. a widely naturalized Eurasian plant, *Chrysanthemum leucanthemum,* having flowers with a yellow center and white rays. **2.** A low-growing European plant, *Bellis perennis,* having flowers with pink or white rays. **3.** The flower of a daisy. **4.** *Slang.* Something excellent or notable. [ME *daisie* < OE *dægesēage* : *dæg,* day + *ēage,* eye.]

Da·kin's solution (dā'kĭnz) *n.* A dilute sodium hypochlorite solution used as a surgical disinfectant. [After Henry D. *Dakin* (1880–1952).]

Da·ko·ta (də-kō'tə) *n., pl.* **Dakota** or **-tas.** **1. a.** A large group of tribes of North American Plains Indians, commonly called Sioux, now living on reservations in North and South Dakota, Minnesota, and Montana. **b.** A member of any of the Dakota tribes. **2.** The Siouan language of the Dakota. **—Da·ko'tan** *adj. & n.*

Da·lai La·ma (dä'lī lä'mə) *n.* The traditional governmental ruler and highest priest of the Lamaist religion in Tibet and

dachshund

daffodil

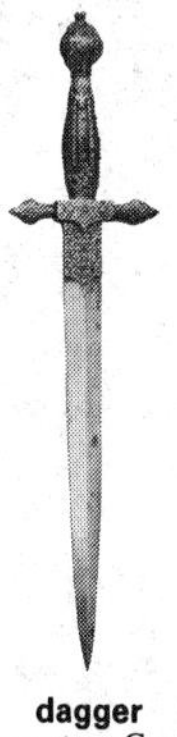
dagger
16th-century German

Dagon

daguerreotype

daisy
Oxeye daisy

Dalmatian

dam[1]
Dworshak Dam, Idaho

damascene
Damascene pendant

Mongolia. [Tibetan : Mongolian *dalai,* ocean + Tibetan *bla-ma,* monk.]
dal·a·pon (dăl'ə-pŏn') *n.* An organic acid used as a herbicide. [Blend of DI-, ALPHA, and PROPIONIC ACID.]
da·la·si (dä-lä'sē) *n., pl.* **dalasi.** See table at **currency.** [Native word in Gambia.]
dale (dāl) *n.* A valley. [ME < OE *dæl.*]
da·leth (dä'lĕth', -lĕt') *n.* The 4th letter of the Hebrew alphabet. See table at **alphabet.** [Heb. *dāleth* < *dālt,* door.]
dalles (dălz) *pl.n.* The steep precipices forming the sides of a gorge or narrow valley, usually having rapids at the bottom. [Fr., pl. of *dalle,* gutter < OFr. < ON *dæla.*]
dal·li·ance (dăl'ē-əns) *n.* **1.** Frivolous spending of time; dawdling. **2.** Amorous play; flirtation.
Dal·lis grass (dăl'ĭs) *n.* A South American grass, *Paspalum dilatatum,* grown for pasturage in the southern United States. [Prob. alteration of *Dallas,* Texas.]
dal·ly (dăl'ē) *v.* **-lied, -ly·ing, -lies.** —*intr.* **1.** To play amorously; flirt. **2.** To trifle; toy. **3.** To waste time; dawdle. —*tr.* To waste (time). [ME *dalien* < OFr. *dalier.*] **—dal'li·er** *n.* **—dal'ly·ing·ly** *adv.*
Dal·ma·tian (dăl-mā'shən) *n.* A dog of a breed believed to have originated in Dalmatia, having a short, smooth white coat covered with black or dark-brown spots.
dal·mat·ic (dăl-măt'ĭk) *n.* **1.** A wide-sleeved garment worn over the alb by a deacon, cardinal, bishop, or abbot at the celebration of Mass. **2.** A wide-sleeved garment worn by an English monarch at his coronation. [ME *dalmatik* < Med. Lat. *dalmatica* < Lat. *dalmaticus,* Dalmatian.]
dal se·gno (dăl sān'yō) *adv. Mus.* From a place marked by the sign § to a designated point. Used as a direction to repeat a passage. [Ital., from the sign.]
dal·ton (dôl'tən) *n.* A standard unit of mass equal to one-half the atomic mass of $^{12}_{6}C$ and used to express the masses of atoms, molecules, and nuclear particles. [After John *Dalton* (1766–1844).]
dal·ton·ism also **Dal·ton·ism** (dôl'tə-nĭz'əm) *n.* Red-green colorblindness. [After John *Dalton* (1766–1844).] **—dal·to'·ni·an** (dôl-tō'nē-ən), **dal·ton'ic** (-tŏn'ĭk) *adj.*
dam[1] (dăm) *n.* **1.** A barrier constructed across a waterway to control the flow or raise the level of water. **2.** A body of water controlled by a dam. **3.** An obstruction or hindrance. —*tr.v.* **dammed, dam·ming, dams. 1.** To construct a dam across; hold back by means of a dam. **2.** To obstruct or restrain; confine: *tried to dam up his grief.* [ME.]
dam[2] (dăm) *n.* **1.** A female parent. Used of a quadruped. **2.** *Archaic.* A mother. [ME *dam, dame.* —see DAME.]
dam·age (dăm'ĭj) *n.* **1.** Impairment of the usefulness or value of person or property; harm. **2. damages.** *Law.* Money ordered to be paid as compensation for injury or loss. **3.** *Informal.* Cost; price. —*v.* **-aged, -ag·ing, -ag·es.** —*tr.* To cause injury to; harm. —*intr.* To suffer or be susceptible to damage. [ME < OFr. < *dam,* loss < Lat. *damnum.*] **—dam'age·a·ble** *adj.* **—dam'ag·ing·ly** *adv.*
dam·ar (dăm'ər) *n.* Variant of **dammar.**
dam·as·cene (dăm'ə-sēn', dăm'ə-sēn') *tr.v.* **-cened, -cen·ing, -cenes.** To decorate (metal) with wavy patterns of inlay or etching. —*n.* Work decorated by damascening. —*adj.* Of or pertaining to damascening or damask. [OFr. *damasquiner* < *damasquin,* of Damascus.] **—dam'a·scen'er** *n.*
Da·mas·cus steel (də-măs'kəs) *n.* An early form of steel having wavy markings, developed in Near Eastern countries, esp. Persia, and used chiefly in sword blades.
dam·ask (dăm'əsk) *n.* **1.** A rich patterned fabric of cotton, linen, silk, or wool. **2.** A fine, twilled table linen. **3.** Damascus steel. **4.** The wavy pattern on Damascus steel. —*tr.v.* **-asked, -ask·ing, -asks. 1.** To damascene. **2.** To decorate or weave with rich patterns. **—*modifier:*** *a damask tablecloth.* [ME < Med. Lat. *(pannus de) damasco,* (cloth of) Damascus.]
damask rose *n.* A rose, *Rosa damascena,* native to Asia, having fragrant red or pink flowers used as a source of attar. [< obs. *Damask,* Damascan, Damascus.]
damask steel *n.* Damascus steel.
dame (dām) *n.* **1.** A title formerly given to a woman in authority or to the mistress of a household. **2.** A married woman; matron. **3.** *Slang.* A woman; female. **4.** *Brit.* **a.** *Archaic.* The legal title of the wife or widow of a knight or baronet. **b.** A title of a woman equivalent to that of a knight. [ME < OFr. < Lat. *domina,* fem. of *dominus,* lord, master.]
dame's rocket *n.* A plant, *Hesperis matronalis,* native to Europe, having clusters of fragrant purple or white flowers.
dame's violet *n.* Dame's rocket.
dam·mar or **dam·ar** also **dam·mer** (dăm'ər) *n.* Any of various hard resins obtained from Indo-Malayan trees of the genera *Shorea, Balanocarpus,* and *Hopea* and used in varnishes and lacquers. [Malay *damar,* resin.]
damn (dăm) *v.* **damned, damn·ing, damns.** —*tr.* **1.** To pronounce an adverse judgment upon. **2.** To bring about the failure of; ruin. **3.** To condemn as harmful, illegal, or immoral: *damn gambling and strong drink.* **4.** *Theol.* To condemn to everlasting punishment or a similar fate; doom. **5.** To swear at by using the word "damn." —*intr.* To swear; curse. —*interj.* Used to express anger, irritation, contempt, or disappointment. —*n.* **1.** The saying of "damn" as a curse. **2.** *Informal.* The least valuable bit; jot: *not worth a damn.* —*adj. & adv.* Damned. [ME *dampnen* < OFr. *dampner* < Lat. *damnare,* to condemn, inflict loss upon < *damnum,* loss.] **—damn'ing·ly** *adv.*
dam·na·ble (dăm'nə-bəl) *adj.* Deserving condemnation; odious. **—dam'na·ble·ness** *n.* **—dam'na·bly** *adv.*
dam·na·tion (dăm-nā'shən) *n.* **1.** The act of damning or the condition of being damned. **2.** *Theol.* **a.** Condemnation to everlasting punishment; doom. **b.** Everlasting punishment. **3.** Failure or ruination incurred by adverse criticism. —*interj.* Used to express anger or annoyance.
dam·na·to·ry (dăm'nə-tôr'ē, -tōr'ē) *adj.* Threatening with damnation; damning.
damned (dămd) *adj.* **-er, -est. 1.** Condemned, esp. to eternal punishment. **2.** *Informal.* Deserving condemnation; detestable: *this damned weather.* **3.** Used as an intensive: *a damned fool.* —*adv. Informal.* Very; extremely: *a damned poor excuse.* —*n. Theol.* Souls doomed to eternal punishment.
dam·ni·fy (dăm'nə-fī') *tr.v.* **-fied, -fy·ing, -fies.** *Law.* To cause loss or damage to. [OFr. *damnifier* < LLat. *damnificare* < Lat. *damnificus,* harmful : *damnum,* loss, harm + *facere,* to make.] **—dam'ni·fi·ca'tion** *n.*
dam·oi·selle (dăm'ə-zĕl') *n.* Variant of **damosel.**
Da·mon (dā'mən) *n. Rom. Myth.* A legendary figure who, out of devotion, pledged his life as a hostage for his condemned friend Pythias. [Lat. < Gk. *Damōn.*]
dam·o·sel also **dam·oi·selle** or **dam·o·zel** (dăm'ə-zĕl') *n. Archaic.* A damsel. [ME *damoysele* < OFr. *damoiselle,* damsel.]
damp (dămp) *adj.* **-er, -est. 1.** Slightly wet; moist. **2.** *Archaic.* Dejected. —*n.* **1.** Moisture in the air; humidity. **2.** Foul or poisonous gas that sometimes pollutes the air in mines. **3.** Lowness of spirits; depression. **4.** A restraint or check; discouragement. —*tr.v.* **damped, damp·ing, damps. 1.** To make damp or moist; moisten. **2.** To extinguish (a fire, for example) by cutting off air. **3.** To restrain or check; discourage. **4.** To provide (the strings of a keyboard instrument) with dampers as a means of reducing the dynamic level. **5.** *Physics.* To decrease the amplitude of (a wave). **—*phrasal verb.* damp off.** *Bot.* To be affected by damping off. [ME, poison gas, perh. < MLG, vapor.] **—damp'ish** *adj.* **—damp'·ly** *adv.* **—damp'ness** *n.*
damp·en (dăm'pən) *v.* **-ened, -en·ing, -ens.** —*tr.* **1.** To make damp. **2.** To deaden; depress: *dampen one's spirits.* —*intr.* To become damp. **—damp'en·er** *n.*
damp·er (dăm'pər) *n.* **1.** One that damps, restrains, or depresses. **2.** An adjustable plate, as in the flue of a furnace or stove, for controlling the draft. **3.** *Mus.* **a.** A device in various keyboard instruments for deadening the vibrations of the strings. **b.** A mute for various brass instruments. **4.** A device that eliminates or progressively diminishes oscillations.
damp·ing (dăm'pĭng) *n.* The capacity built into a mechanical or electrical device to prevent excessive correction and the resulting instability or oscillatory conditions.
damping off *n.* A disease of planted seeds or very young seedlings caused by fungi and resulting in death of the newly sprouted plants.
dam·sel (dăm'zəl) *n.* A young woman or girl; maiden. [ME *damisele* < OFr. *dameisele, damoiselle* < VLat. **dominicella,* dim. of Lat. *domina,* lady. —see DAME.]
dam·sel·fly (dăm'zəl-flī') *n.* Any of various slender-bodied, often brightly colored insects of the order Odonata, related to the dragonflies but differing in having wings that are folded together over the back when at rest.
dam·son (dăm'zən) *n.* **1.** A plum tree, *Prunus institia,* native to Eurasia, cultivated since ancient times for its edible fruit. **2.** The oval, bluish-black, juicy plum borne by the damson. [ME < Lat. *(prunum) Damascenum,* (plum) of Damascus.]
Dan[1] (dăn) *n.* **1.** In the Old Testament, the fifth son of Jacob. **2.** One of the 12 tribes of Israel, descended from Dan. [Heb. *Dān.*]
Dan[2] (dăn) *n. Obs.* A title of honor equivalent to *master* or *sir.* [ME < OFr. < Med. Lat. *Domnus* < Lat. *dominus,* master, lord.]
Dan·a·e also **Dan·a·ë** (dăn'ə-ē') *n. Gk. Myth.* The mother of Perseus by Zeus, who visited her in the form of a shower of gold during her imprisonment. [Lat. < Gk. *Danaē.*]
Dan·a·id also **Dan·a·ïd** (dăn'ə-ĭd) *n.* Any of the Danaides.
Da·na·i·des also **Da·na·ï·des** (də-nā'ĭ-dēz') *pl.n. Gk. Myth.* The daughters of Danaus, who at their father's command murdered their bridegrooms on their wedding night and were condemned in Hades to pour water eternally into a bottomless vessel. [Gk. < *Danaos,* Danaus.]
Dan·a·us also **Dan·a·üs** (dăn'ē-əs) *n. Gk. Myth.* A king of Argos, father of the Danaides. [Lat. < Gk. *Danaos.*]
dance (dăns) *v.* **danced, danc·ing, danc·es.** —*intr.* **1.** To move rhythmically to music, using prescribed or improvised steps and gestures. **2.** To leap or skip about excitedly; caper. **3.** To bob up and down. —*tr.* **1.** To engage in or perform (a dance). **2.** To cause to dance. **3.** To bring to a particular state or condition by dancing: *He danced her to exhaustion.* —*n.* **1.** A series of rhythmical motions and steps, usually to music. **2.** The art of dancing. **3.** A party or gathering of people for dancing; ball. **4.** One round or turn of dancing.

5. A musical or rhythmical accompaniment composed or played for dancing. **6.** An act or an instance of dancing. [ME *dauncen* < OFr. *danser.*] **—danc'er** *n.* **—danc'ing·ly** *adv.*

dance·a·ble (dăn'sə-bəl) *adj.* Suitable for dancing: *a danceable melody.*

dan·de·li·on (dăn'dl-ī'ən) *n.* **1.** A plant, *Taraxacum officinale,* native to Eurasia, widely naturalized as a weed in North America and having many-rayed yellow flowers and deeply notched basal leaves sometimes used in salads. **2.** Any of several plants similar or related to the dandelion. **3.** A brilliant to vivid yellow. [ME *dent-de-lion* < OFr., transl. of Med. Lat. *dens leonis,* lion's tooth (from its sharply indented leaves).]

dan·der[1] (dăn'dər) *n. Informal.* Temper or anger: *What got his dander up?* [Orig. unknown.]

dan·der[2] (dăn'dər) *n.* Scurf from the coat of various animals, such as dogs, cats, or horses, often of an allergenic nature. [Short for DANDRUFF.]

Dan·die Din·mont (dăn'dē dĭn'mŏnt') *n.* A small terrier of a breed developed in England, having a rough grayish or brownish coat and short legs. [After *Dandie Dinmont,* owner of two such dogs in *Guy Mannering,* a novel by Sir Walter Scott (1771–1832).]

dan·di·fy (dăn'də-fī') *tr.v.* **-fied, -fy·ing, -fies.** To dress as or cause to resemble a dandy. **—dan'di·fi·ca'tion** *n.*

dan·dle (dăn'dl) *tr.v.* **-dled, -dling, -dles. 1.** To move (a small child) up and down on the knees or in the arms. **2.** To pamper or pet. [Orig. unknown.] **—dan'dler** *n.*

dan·druff (dăn'drəf) *n.* A scaly scurf formed on and shed from the scalp, often caused by seborrhea. [Orig. unknown.] **—dan'druff·y** *adj.*

dan·dy (dăn'dē) *n., pl.* **-dies. 1.** A man who affects extreme elegance in clothes and manners; fop. **2.** *Informal.* Something very good or agreeable. **3.** A yawl (sense 1). *—adj.* **-di·er, -di·est. 1.** Like or dressed like a dandy; foppish. **2.** *Informal.* Fine; good. [Perh. short for *jack-a-dandy,* fop.] **—dan'dy·ish** *adj.*

dandy roll also **dandy roller** *n.* A cylinder of wire gauze pressed on moist pulp before it starts through the rollers and produces the watermarks in paper.

Dane (dān) *n.* **1.** A native or inhabitant of Denmark. **2.** A person of Danish ancestry. [ME *Dan* < ON *Danr.*]

Dane·geld (dān'gĕld') also **Dane·gelt** (-gĕlt') *n.* A tax levied in England from the 10th to the 12th century to finance protection against Danish invasion. [ME : *Dane,* Danes' + *geld,* tribute < OE *gield.*]

Dane·law also **Dane·lagh** (dān'lô') *n.* **1.** The body of law established by the Danish invaders and settlers in northeastern England in the ninth and tenth centuries. **2.** The sections of England under the jurisdiction of the Danelaw. [ME *Denelage* < OE *Dena lagu,* Danes' law.]

dan·ger (dān'jər) *n.* **1.** Exposure or vulnerability to harm or risk. **2.** A source or instance of risk or peril. **3.** *Obs.* Power, esp. power to harm. [ME *daunger,* power, dominion, peril < OFr. *dangier* < Lat. *dominium,* sovereignty < *dominus,* lord, master.]

Synonyms: *danger, peril, hazard, risk.* These nouns refer to exposure to harm or loss. *Danger,* the least specific, is applicable to any potentially harmful situation. *Peril* is much stronger through its suggestions of great potential for harm and of immediacy, or imminence, of the threat involved. *Hazard* less forcefully suggests the threat posed by chance or something largely beyond one's control. *Risk* also stresses chance or uncertainty, but often from the standpoint of one who weighs them against possible gain; the term therefore may imply voluntary exposure to harm or loss.

dan·ger·ous (dān'jər-əs) *adj.* **1.** Involving or fraught with danger; perilous. **2.** Able or apt to do harm. **—dan'ger·ous·ly** *adv.* **—dan'ger·ous·ness** *n.*

dan·gle (dăng'gəl) *v.* **-gled, -gling, -gles.** *—intr.* **1.** To hang loosely and swing or sway to and fro. **2.** To be a hanger-on. *—tr.* To cause to dangle. *—n.* **1.** The act of dangling. **2.** Something that is dangled. [Perh. of Scand. orig.] **—dan'gler** *n.*

dangling participle *n. Gram.* A participle usually in a subordinate clause that lacks a clear grammatical relation with the subject of its sentence, as *approaching* in the sentence *Approaching New York, the skyline came into view.*

Dan·iel (dăn'yəl) *n.* **1.** In the Old Testament, a Hebrew prophet during the Babylonian captivity. **2.** See table at **Bible.** [Heb. *Dānī'ēl,* God is my judge.]

da·ni·o (dā'nē-ō') *n., pl.* **-os.** Any of various small, often brightly colored freshwater fishes of the genera *Danio* and *Brachydanio,* native to Asia and popular as aquarium fish. [NLat. *Danio,* genus name.]

Dan·ish (dā'nĭsh) *adj.* Of or pertaining to Denmark, the Danes, their language, or their culture. *—n.* **1.** The North Germanic language of the Danes. **2.** *Informal.* Danish pastry. [ME < OE *Denisc* < *Dene,* the Danes.]

Danish pastry *n.* A sweet, buttery pastry made with raised dough.

Dan·ite (dăn'īt') *n.* In the Old Testament, a descendant of Dan. *—adj.* Of or pertaining to the Hebrew tribe descended from Dan.

dank (dăngk) *adj.* **-er, -est.** Uncomfortably damp; chilly and wet. [ME.] **—dank'ly** *adv.* **—dank'ness** *n.*

dan·seur (däN-sœr') *n., pl.* **-seurs** (-sœr'). A male ballet dancer. [Fr. < OFr. < *danser,* to dance.]

dan·seuse (däN-sœz') *n., pl.* **-seuses** (-sœz'). A female ballet dancer. [Fr., fem. of *danseur,* danseur.]

Dan·tesque (dăn-tĕsk') *adj.* Characterized by or having the exalted, visionary style of the Italian poet Dante.

Da·nu (thä'nōō) *n. Ir. Myth.* The goddess of death and mother of the gods. [Ir.]

dap (dăp) *intr.v.* **dapped, dap·ping, daps. 1.** To fish by letting a baited hook fall gently on the water. **2.** To dip lightly or quickly into water, as a bird does. **3.** To skip or bounce, esp. over the surface of water. [Prob. alteration of DAB[1].]

daph·ne (dăf'nē) *n.* Any of several shrubs of the genus *Daphne,* native to Eurasia, often cultivated for their glossy evergreen foliage and clusters of small, bell-shaped flowers. [NLat. *Daphne,* genus name < Lat., laurel < Gk. *daphnē.*]

Daph·ne (dăf'nē) *n. Gk. Myth.* A nymph who metamorphosed into a laurel tree as a means of escaping Apollo. [Lat. < Gk. *Daphnē,* Daphne, laurel.]

daph·ni·a (dăf'nē-ə) *n., pl.* **daphnia.** Any of various small freshwater crustaceans of the genus *Daphnia,* some species of which are commonly used as food for aquarium fish. [NLat. *Daphnia,* genus name.]

Daph·nis (daf'nĭs) *n. Gk. Myth.* A Sicilian shepherd and son of Hermes who was famed as a musician and reputed to be the inventor of pastoral poetry. [Lat. < Gk.]

dap·per (dăp'ər) *adj.* **1. a.** Neatly dressed; trim. **b.** Very stylish and current in dress. **2.** Small and active. [ME *dapyr,* elegant, prob. < MDu. *dapper,* quick, strong.] **—dap'per·ly** *adv.* **—dap'per·ness** *n.*

dap·ple (dăp'əl) *n.* **1. a.** Mottled or spotted marking, as on a horse's skin. **b.** An individual spot. **2.** An animal with a mottled or spotted skin or coat. *—tr.v.* **-pled, -pling, -ples.** To mark or mottle with spots. *—adj.* Also **dap·pled** (-əld). Spotted or mottled. [Back-formation < DAPPLE-GRAY.]

dap·ple-gray (dăp'əl-grā') *adj.* Gray with a mottled pattern of darker gray markings. *—n.* A dapple-gray horse. [ME *dappel-grai.*]

dap·sone (dăp'sōn', -zōn') *n.* An antimicrobial agent, $C_{12}H_{12}N_2OS$, used against leprosy. [Contraction of E. *diaminodiphenyl sulfone,* a drug used to treat leprosy.]

Dar·by and Joan (där'bē) *n.* An elderly married couple who live a placid, harmonious life together and are seldom seen apart. [Prob. after *Darby and Joan,* a couple in an 18th-cent. English ballad.]

Dard (därd) also **Dar·dic** (där'dĭk) *n.* A group of Indic languages spoken in the upper Indus River valley.

Dar·dan (där'dn) also **Dar·da·ni·an** (där-dā'nē-ən) *n.* A Trojan. [After *Dardanus,* the mythological founder of Troy.] **—Dar'dan** *adj.*

Dar·da·nus (där'dn-əs) *n. Gk. Myth.* The eponymous founder of Troy. [Lat. < Gk. *Dardanos.*]

Dar·dic (där'dĭk) *n.* Variant of **Dard.**

dare (dâr) *v.* **dared, dar·ing, dare** or **dares.** *—tr.* **1.** To have the courage required for. **2.** To challenge (someone) to do something requiring boldness. **3.** To confront or oppose boldly; defy. *—intr.* To be courageous or bold enough to do or try something. *—n.* An act of daring; challenge. ***—idiom.*** **dare say** also **dare·say** (dâr-sā'). To consider very likely or almost certain. [ME *daren* < OE *dear,* first and third person pr. indicative of *durran,* to venture, dare.] **—dar'er** *n.*

Usage: *Dare* has a set of irregular forms that coexist with its regular forms. The irregular *dare* differs from the regular *dare* in three ways: (1) It does not combine with any form of the verb *do: How dare you* (versus the regular *how do you dare)? They dare not* or *they daren't* (versus the regular *they don't dare).* (2) The third person singular lacks a final *s: Let him say that if he dare* (versus the regular *if he dares*). (3) It is followed by a verb without *to: If you dare say a word, I'll strike you down* (versus the regular *if you dare to say a word).* As the examples show, the irregular *dare* is used in questions, negations, and conditions. The regular and irregular forms are subtly different in meaning. *No one dares call her a liar* is a statement of fact and means roughly "Everybody is afraid to call her a liar." *No one dare call her a liar* is a warning and means roughly "No one had better call her a liar." In the sense of "challenge" only the regular form is used: *Anyone who dares* (not *dare*) *him to try* (not just *try*) *it will be sorry.* • The idiomatic form *dare say* (or *daresay*) is more common in British than in American English. It is never followed by *that: I daresay he'll be sorry he started up with her.* The expression is used only with *I* and only in the present tense; there is no equivalent *he dare say* or *I daresaid.*

dare·dev·il (dâr'dĕv'əl) *n.* One who is recklessly bold. *—adj.* Recklessly bold. **—dare'dev'il·ry, dare'dev'il·try** *n.*

dar·ing (dâr'ĭng) *adj.* Willing to take risks; bold. *—n.* Audacious bravery; boldness. **—dar'ing·ly** *adv.* **—dar'ing·ness** *n.*

Dar·jee·ling (där-jē'lĭng) *n.* A fine variety of black tea from Darjeeling, India.

dark (därk) *adj.* **-er, -est. 1.** With very little or no light. **2.** Reflecting only a small fraction of the incident light. **3.** Lacking light or brightness: *a dark day.* **4.** Of a shade tending toward black or brown in comparison with other

dandelion

Dandie Dinmont

Daphne
Apollo and Daphne

daredevil
A rope walker sits on the roof of a 1,350-foot building after walking along the rope from another building

shades: *dark meat.* **5.** Not fair in complexion; swarthy. **6.** Characterized by or producing gloom; dismal: *took a dark view of our chances for success.* **7.** Sullen or threatening: *a dark scowl.* **8.** Hard to understand; obscure. **9.** Concealed or secret; mysterious: *a dark scheme.* **10.** Without knowledge or enlightenment; uncivilized: *a dark era in history.* **11.** Evil or wicked; sinister: *a dark purpose.* **12.** Having richness or depth: *a dark, melancholy vocal tone.* **13.** Not giving performances; closed: *a dark theater.* —*n.* **1.** Absence of light. **2.** A place having little light. **3.** Night; nightfall. **4.** A dark hue or color. ***—idiom.* in the dark.** **1.** In secret: *things done in the dark.* **2.** In a state of ignorance; uninformed. [ME *derk* < OE *deorc.*] **—dark'ish** *adj.* **—dark'ly** *adv.* **—dark'ness** *n.*

Synonyms: *dark, dim, murky, dusky, obscure, opaque, shady, shadowy.* These adjectives indicate the absence of light or clarity. *Dark,* the most widely applicable, can refer to insufficiency of illumination for seeing, to deepness of shade of a color, as *dark brown,* or figuratively to absence of cheer or rectitude: *a dark day; a dark mood; dark comedy; dark deeds. Dim* suggests lack of clarity of outline of physical things or mental ones, such as memories or recollections, and can also apply to the source of light to indicate insufficiency. *Murky* usually implies darkness such as that produced by smoke or fog; less often it refers to extreme darkness or, figuratively, to unclear, sullen thoughts. *Dusky* applies principally to the dimness characteristic of twilight or to deepness of shade of a color. *Obscure* usually means unclear to the mind or senses but can refer to physical darkness. *Opaque* means incapable of being penetrated by light; figuratively it applies to what is incapable of perceiving reason and to what is unintelligible. *Shady* refers to what is sheltered from light, especially sunlight, or, figuratively, to what is covertly dishonest. *Shadowy* also implies obstructed light but suggests shifting illumination and indistinct vision.

dark adaptation *n.* The physical and chemical adjustments of the eye, including dilation of the pupil, that make vision possible in relative darkness. **—dark'-a·dapt'ed** (därk'ə-dăp'tĭd) *adj.*

Dark Ages *pl.n.* **1.** The early part of the Middle Ages. **2.** The entire period from the end of classical civilization to the revival of learning in the West.

dark·en (där'kən) *v.* **-ened, -en·ing, -ens.** —*tr.* **1.** To make dark or darker. **2.** To give a darker hue to. **3.** To fill with sadness; make gloomy. **4.** To render vague or uncertain; obscure. **5.** To tarnish or stain: *darken one's good name.* —*intr.* To become dark or darker. **—dark'en·er** *n.*

dark-field microscope (därk'fēld') *n.* An ultramicroscope.

dark horse *n.* **1.** A little-known entrant in a horse race or other contest. **2.** One who receives unexpected support as a candidate for the nomination in a political convention.

dark lantern *n.* A lantern whose light can be blocked by a panel or other device.

dar·kle (där'kəl) *intr.v.* **-kled, -kling, -kles.** **1.** To appear darkly or indistinctly. **2. a.** To grow dark. **b.** To become gloomy. [Back-formation < DARKLING.]

dark·ling (därk'lĭng) *adv.* In the dark. —*adj.* **1.** Being or happening in the dark or the night. **2.** Dim; obscure. [ME *derkeling* < *derk,* dark.]

darkling beetle *n.* A dark-colored, sluggish, nocturnal plant-eating beetle of the family Tenebrionidae.

dark·room (därk'ro͞om', -ro͝om') *n.* A room in which photographic materials are processed, either in complete darkness or with a safelight.

dark·some (därk'səm) *adj.* Dark; somber.

dark star *n.* A star that is normally obscured or too faint for direct visual observation, esp. the component of an eclipsing binary detectable by spectral analysis or in the eclipse of the bright component.

dar·ling (där'lĭng) *n.* **1.** A much-loved person. **2.** One that is greatly liked or preferred; favorite. —*adj.* **1.** Very dear; beloved. **2.** Regarded with special favor; favorite: "*Metaphysics and poetry . . . are my darling studies*" (Coleridge). **3.** *Informal.* Charming or amusing: *a darling hat.* [ME *dereling* < OE *dēorling* < *dēore,* dear.]

darn¹ (därn) *v.* **darned, darn·ing, darns.** —*tr.* To mend by weaving thread or yarn across a gap or hole. —*intr.* To mend or repair a hole or garment by darning. —*n.* **1.** A place repaired by darning. **2.** The act of darning. [Dial. Fr. *darner.*] **—darn'er** *n.*

darn² (därn) *interj.* Damn. —*adj. & adv.* Damn. —*tr. & intr.v.* **darned, darn·ing, darns.** To damn. [Alteration of DAMN.] **—darned** *adj & adv.*

dar·nel (där'nəl) *n.* Any of several grasses of the genus *Lolium,* native to the Old World, esp. *L. tementulum* or *L. perenne.* [ME.]

darning egg *n.* An egg-shaped object used to hold the shape of material being darned.

darning needle *n.* **1.** A long, large-eyed needle used in darning. **2.** *Informal.* A dragonfly.

dart (därt) *n.* **1.** A slender, pointed missile, often having tail fins, either thrown by the hand or shot from a blowgun or other device. **2.** Something like a dart in shape, use, or effect. **3.** An insect's stinger. **4. darts** *(used with a sing. verb).* A game in which darts are thrown at a target. **5.** A rapid, sudden movement. **6.** In sewing, a tapered tuck to adjust the fit of a garment. —*v.* **dart·ed, dart·ing, darts.** —*intr.* To move suddenly and swiftly. —*tr.* To throw or thrust suddenly or swiftly; shoot. [ME < OFr., of Germanic orig.]

dart

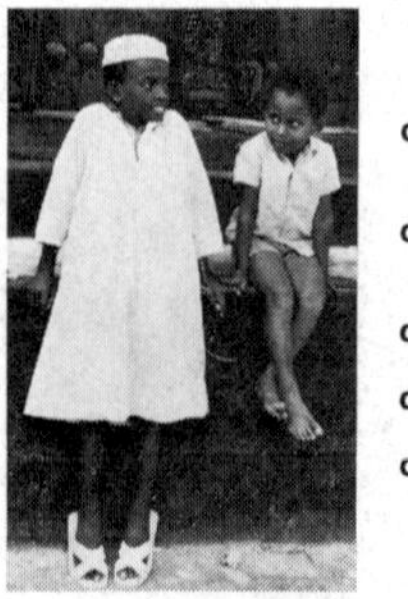

dashiki

dart·er (där'tər) *n.* **1.** One that moves suddenly and swiftly. **2.** Any of several long-necked, long-billed birds of the genus *Anhinga,* such as the water turkey. **3.** Any of various small, often brightly colored freshwater fishes of the family Percidae, of eastern North America.

dar·tle (där'tl) *tr.v.* **-tled, -tling, -tles.** To thrust or shoot out repeatedly. [Freq. of DART.]

Dar·win·ism (där'wĭ-nĭz'əm) *n.* A theory of biological evolution developed by Charles Darwin and others, stating that species of plants and animals develop through natural selection of variations that increase the organism's ability to survive and reproduce. **—Dar·win'i·an** (-wĭn'ē-ən) *adj.* **—Dar'win·ist** *n.* **—Dar'win·is'tic** *adj.*

dash¹ (dăsh) *v.* **dashed, dash·ing, dash·es.** —*tr.* **1.** To break or smash by striking violently. **2.** To hurl, knock, or thrust with sudden violence. **3.** To splash; bespatter. **4.** To perform or complete hastily: *dash off a letter.* **5.** To add an enlivening or altering element to; mix: "*Some truth there was, but dash'd and brew'd with lies*" (Dryden). **6.** To destroy; frustrate: *His dreams were dashed.* **7.** To confound; abash. —*intr.* **1.** To strike violently; smash. **2.** To move with haste; rush: *dashed through the crowd.* —*n.* **1.** A swift, violent blow or stroke. **2.** A splash. **3.** A small amount of an added ingredient: *a dash of salt.* **4.** A quick stroke, as with a pencil or brush. **5.** A sudden movement; rush. **6.** A foot race, usually less than a quarter-mile long, run at top speed from the outset. **7.** Spirited action or style; verve. **8.** A punctuation mark (—) used in writing and printing. **9.** In Morse and similar codes, the long sound or signal used in combination with the dot, a shorter sound, and silent intervals to represent letters or numbers. **10.** A dashboard. [ME *dashen,* prob. of Scand. orig.]

dash² (dăsh) *v., interj., adj., & adv.* Euphemism for **damn.**

dash·board (dăsh'bôrd', -bōrd') *n.* A panel under the windshield of a vehicle, containing indicator dials, compartments, and sometimes control instruments.

da·sheen (dă-shēn') *n.* The taro (sense 2). [Orig. unknown.]

dash·er (dăsh'ər) *n.* **1.** One that dashes. **2.** The plunger of a churn or ice-cream freezer. **3.** *Informal.* A spirited person.

da·shi·ki (də-shē'kē) *n., pl.* **-kis.** A loose, brightly colored African tunic, usually worn by men. [Yoruba *danshiki.*]

dash·ing (dăsh'ĭng) *adj.* **1.** Audacious and gallant; spirited. **2.** Marked by showy elegance; splendid: *a dashing coat.* **—dash'ing·ly** *adv.*

dash·pot (dăsh'pŏt') *n.* A piston-and-cylinder device used to damp motion.

das·sie (dăs'ē) *n.* The hyrax. [Afr., dim. of *das,* badger < MDu.]

das·tard (dăs'tərd) *n.* A base, sneaking coward. [ME, prob. < ON *dæstr,* p.part. of *dæsa,* to languish, decay.]

das·tard·ly (dăs'tərd-lē) *adj.* Cowardly and mean-spirited; base. **—das'tard·li·ness** *n.*

Usage: *Dastardly* is employed most precisely when it combines the meaning of "vicious" and "cowardly." It is loosely used to mean simply "base" or "reprehensible." Thus, a gunman who shoots his victim in the back is committing a *dastardly* act. The outlaw who faces the sheriff and beats him to the draw is better described as *wicked* or *vicious.*

das·y·ure (dăs'ē-yo͝or') *n.* Any of various marsupial mammals of the family Dasyuridae, of Australia and adjacent regions, ranging in size and appearance from that of a mouse to that of a dog. [NLat. *Dasyurus,* genus name : Gk. *dasus,* hairy + *oura,* tail.]

da·ta (dā'tə, dăt'ə, dä'tə) *pl.n. (used with a sing. or pl. verb).* **1.** Information, esp. information organized for analysis or used as the basis for a decision. **2.** Numerical information in a form suitable for processing by computer. **3.** Plural of **datum** (sense 1). [Lat., pl. of *datum.* —see DATUM.]

Usage: *Data* is the plural of the Latin word *datum* (something given) and traditionally takes a plural verb: *These data are inconclusive.* It is now widely used also with a singular verb: *This data is inconclusive.* The Usage Panel accepts the singular construction in casual speech but is evenly divided on its acceptability in writing.

data bank also **da·ta·bank** (dā'tə-băngk', dăt'ə-) *n.* **1.** A data base. **2.** An organization chiefly concerned with building, maintaining, and utilizing a data bank.

data base also **da·ta·base** (dā'tə-bās', dăt'ə-) *n.* A collection of data arranged for ease and speed of retrieval, as by a computer.

data carrier *n.* The medium, as magnetic tape, selected to transport or communicate data.

data processing *n.* **1.** The preparation of information for processing by computers. **2.** The storing or processing of raw data by a computer. **—data processor** *n.*

da·ta·ry (dā'tə-rē) *n., pl.* **-ries.** *Rom. Cath. Ch.* **1.** The duty, formerly an official office of the curia, of investigating the fitness of candidates for papal benefices. **2.** A cardinal assuming the duty of datary. [Med. Lat. *dataria* < *data,* date.]

data set *n.* **1.** An electronic device that provides an interface in the transmission of data to a remote station. **2.** A collection of related computer records. **3.** A modem.

date[1] (dāt) *n.* **1. a.** Time stated in terms of the day, month, and year. **b.** A statement of calendar time, as on a document. **2.** The day of the month. **3.** A particular point or period of time at which something happened or existed or is to happen. **4.** The time during which something lasts; duration. **5.** The time or historical period to which something belongs: *artifacts of a later date.* **6. a.** An appointment, esp. an engagement to go out socially with a member of the opposite sex. **b.** A person's companion on a date. **7.** An engagement for a performance: *have four singing dates this month.* —*v.* **dat·ed, dat·ing, dates.** —*tr.* **1.** To mark or supply with a date: *date a letter.* **2.** To determine the date of: *date a fossil.* **3.** To betray the age of. **4.** To go on a date with. —*intr.* **1.** To have origin in a particular time in the past: *This statue dates from 500* B.C. **2.** To become old-fashioned. **3.** To go on dates with a companion or as a couple. —***idiom.* to date.** Up to the present time. [ME < OFr. < Med. Lat. *data* < the phrase *data Romae,* issued at Rome (on a certain day) < Lat. *datus,* p.part. of *dare,* to give.] —**dat'a·ble, date'a·ble** *adj.* —**dat'er** *n.*

date[2] (dāt) *n.* **1.** The sweet, oblong, edible fruit of the date palm, containing a narrow, hard seed. **2.** The date palm. [ME < OFr. < OProv. *datil* < Lat. *dactylus* < Gk. *daktulos,* finger (from its shape).]

dat·ed (dā'tĭd) *adj.* **1.** Marked with or displaying a date. **2.** Old-fashioned; out-of-date. —**dat'ed·ly** *adv.* —**dat'ed·ness** *n.*

date·less (dāt'lĭs) *adj.* **1.** Having no date. **2.** Without limits; endless. **3.** Too old to be dated. **4.** Timeless or eternal.

date·line (dāt'līn') *n.* A phrase at the beginning of a newspaper or magazine article that gives the date and place of its origin.

date line *n.* An imaginary line through the Pacific Ocean roughly corresponding to 180 degrees longitude, to the east of which, by international agreement, the calendar date is one day earlier than to the west.

date palm *n.* A tree, *Phoenix dactylifera,* of tropical regions, having featherlike leaves and bearing clusters of dates as fruit.

dating bar *n.* A singles bar.

da·tive (dā'tĭv) also **da·ti·val** (dā-tī'vəl) *adj.* Designating or belonging to a grammatical case in Latin, Russian, and other inflected Indo-European languages that marks the indirect object of a verb and the object of any of certain verbs and prepositions. —*n.* **1.** The dative case. **2.** A word or form in the dative case. [ME *datif* < Lat. *(casus) dativus,* (case) of giving < *dare,* to give.] —**da'tive·ly** *adv.*

da·tum (dā'təm, dăt'əm, dä'təm) *n.* **1.** *pl.* **-ta** (-tə). An assumed, given, measured, or otherwise determined fact or proposition used to draw a conclusion or make a decision. **2.** *pl.* **-tums.** A point, line, or surface used as a reference, as in surveying, mapping, or geology. [Lat., something given < p.part. of *dare,* to give.]

da·tu·ra (də-to͝or'ə, -tyo͝or'ə) *n.* Any of several plants of the genus *Datura,* having large trumpet-shaped flowers. [NLat. *Datura,* genus name < Hindi *dhatūrā* < Skt. *dhattūraḥ.*]

daub (dôb) *v.* **daubed, daub·ing, daubs.** —*tr.* **1.** To cover or smear with an adhesive substance, such as plaster. **2.** To cover or smear with a dirty substance, such as mud or grease. **3.** To apply paint to with hasty or crude strokes. —*intr.* To apply paint or coloring with crude, unskillful strokes. —*n.* **1.** The act or a stroke of daubing. **2.** A soft adhesive coating material, such as plaster or mud. **3.** Something daubed on; smear. **4.** A crude or amateurishly inferior painting. [ME *dauben* < OFr. *dauber* < Lat. *dealbare,* to whitewash : *de-,* completely + *albus,* white.] —**daub'er** *n.* —**daub'er·y** (dô'bə-rē) *n.*

daugh·ter (dô'tər) *n.* **1.** One's female child. **2.** A female descendant. **3.** A woman considered as if in a relationship of child to parent: *a daughter of the nation.* **4.** Something personified or regarded as a female descendant: *"Culturally Japan is a daughter of Chinese civilization"* (Edwin Reischauer). **5.** The immediate product of the radioactive decay of an element. [ME *doughter* < OE *dohtor.*] —**daugh'ter·ly** *adj.*

daughter cell *n. Biol.* Either of two cells that form from the division of a cell.

daugh·ter-in-law (dô'tər-ĭn-lô') *n., pl.* **daugh·ters-in-law.** The wife of one's son.

daunt (dônt, dŏnt) *tr.v.* **daunt·ed, daunt·ing, daunts.** To drain the courage of and hence subdue; intimidate. [ME *daunten* < OFr. *danter* < Lat. *domitare,* freq. of *domare,* to tame.] —**daunt'er** *n.* —**daunt'ing·ly** *adv.*

daunt·less (dônt'lĭs, dŏnt'-) *adj.* Incapable of being intimidated or discouraged; bold. —**daunt'less·ly** *adv.* —**daunt'less·ness** *n.*

dau·phin (dô'fĭn) *n.* The eldest son of the king of France. Used as a title from 1349 to 1830. [Fr. < OFr. *dalphin,* title of the lords of Dauphiné.]

dau·phin·ess (dô'fĭ-nĭs) also **dau·phine** (dô-fēn') *n.* The wife of a dauphin.

dav·en·port (dăv'ən-pôrt', -pōrt') *n.* **1.** A large sofa, often convertible into a bed. **2.** *Chiefly Brit.* A small desk. [Orig. unknown.]

Da·vid (dā'vĭd) *n.* In the Old Testament, the second king of Judah and Israel (1010?–970? B.C.), successor to Saul, and father of King Solomon; reputed author of many of the Psalms. [Heb. *Dāwid.*] —**Da·vid'ic** (də-vĭd'ĭk, dā-) *adj.*

dav·it (dăv'ĭt, dā'vĭt) *n.* Any of various types of small cranes that project over the side of a ship and are used to hoist boats, anchors, and cargo. [ME *daviot* < OFr. *daviot,* dim. of *David,* David.]

Da·vy Jones (dā'vē jōnz') *n.* The spirit of the sea. [*Davy,* nickname for *David.*]

Davy Jones's locker *n.* The bottom of the sea, esp. as the grave of all who perish at sea.

Davy lamp *n.* An early safety oil lamp used by coal miners. [After Sir Humphrey *Davy* (1778–1829), its inventor.]

daw (dô) *n.* The jackdaw. [ME *dawe.*]

daw·dle (dôd'l) *v.* **-dled, -dling, -dles.** —*intr.* **1.** To take more time than necessary. **2.** To move aimlessly or lackadaisically: *dawdling on the way to work.* —*tr.* To waste (time) by idling: *dawdling away the hours.* [Perh. alteration of dial. *daddle,* to diddle.] —**daw'dler** *n.* —**daw'dling·ly** *adv.*

dawn (dôn) *n.* **1.** The time each morning when daylight first appears. **2.** A first appearance; beginning: *the dawn of history.* —*intr.v.* **dawned, dawn·ing, dawns. 1.** To begin to become light in the morning. **2.** To begin to appear or develop; emerge. **3.** To begin to be perceived or understood. [< ME *daunen,* to dawn, prob. back-formation < *dauning,* daybreak, alteration of *dauing* < OE *dagung* < *dagian,* to dawn.]

day (dā) *n.* **1.** The period of light between dawn and nightfall. **2. a.** The 24-hour period during which the earth completes one rotation on its axis. **b.** The period during which a celestial body makes a similar rotation. **3.** One of the numbered 24-hour periods into which a week, month, or year is divided. **4.** The portion of a day devoted to work: *an eight-hour day.* **5.** A day reserved for a certain activity: *a day of rest.* **6. a.** The period of activity or prominence in one's lifetime: *a writer who has had his day.* **b.** A period of opportunity: *Every dog has his day.* **7.** A period of time; era: *in Napoleon's day.* **8.** The contest or issue at hand: *carry the day.* —***idioms.* call it a day.** *Informal.* To stop one's work or activity for the day. **day after day.** For many days; continuously. **day in, day out.** Every day without fail; continuously. [ME < OE *dæg.*]

Day·ak (dī'ăk') *n.* Variant of **Dyak.**

day bed *n.* A couch or sofa convertible into a bed.

day·book (dā'bo͝ok') *n.* **1.** *Accounting.* A book in which daily transactions are recorded. **2.** A diary.

day·break (dā'brāk') *n.* Dawn (sense 1).

day care *n.* The providing of daytime supervision, training, and medical services for children of preschool age or for the elderly. —***modifier* (day-care)**: *a day-care center.*

day·dream (dā'drēm') *n.* A dreamlike musing or fantasy while awake, esp. of the fulfillment of wishes or hopes. —*intr.v.* **-dreamed** or **-dreamt** (-drĕmt'), **-dream·ing, -dreams.** To have daydreams. —**day'dream'er** *n.*

day·flow·er (dā'flou'ər) *n.* Any of various plants of the genus *Commelina,* having blue or purplish flowers that wilt quickly.

day·fly (dā'flī') *n.* The mayfly.

Day-Glo (dā'glō'). A trademark for fluorescent materials.

day labor *n.* Labor hired and paid by the day. —**day laborer** *n.*

day letter *n.* A telegram sent during the day, usually less expensive but slower than a regular telegram.

day·light (dā'līt') *n.* **1.** The light of day. **2. a.** Daybreak. **b.** Daytime. **3.** Exposure to public notice. **4.** Understanding or insight into what was formerly obscure. **5. daylights.** *Slang.* Mental stability; wits: *scare the daylights out of him.* —***idiom.* see daylight.** To approach the end of a difficult endeavor.

day·light-sav·ing time (dā'līt-sā'vĭng) *n.* Time during which clocks are set one hour or more ahead of standard time to provide more daylight at the end of the working day during late spring, summer, and early fall.

day lily *n.* **1.** Any of various plants of the genus *Hemerocallis,* native to Eurasia, having sword-shaped leaves and orange, yellow, or red funnel-shaped flowers. **2.** The plantain lily.

day·long (dā'lông', -lŏng') *adj.* Lasting the whole day. —*adv.* Through the whole day.

Day of Atonement *n.* Yom Kippur.

days (dāz) *adv.* Regularly or habitually in the daytime: *worked days.*

day sailer *n.* A small sailboat for day trips.

day school *n.* **1.** A private school for pupils living at home. **2.** A school that holds classes during the day.

day·side (dā'sīd') *n.* The side of a planet facing the sun.

days of grace *pl.n.* Extra days, usually three, allowed for payment of a note or bill after it has fallen due. [Transl. of Lat. *dies gratiae.*]

day·spring (dā'sprĭng') *n.* The early dawn; daybreak.

day·star (dā'stär') *n.* **1.** The morning star. **2.** The sun.

day·time (dā'tīm') *n.* The time between dawn and dark; day.

day-to-day (dā'tə-dā') *adj.* **1.** Occurring on a routine or daily basis: *day-to-day chores.* **2.** Characterized by subsistence a day at a time with little regard for the future: *lived a day-to-day existence.*

date line

date palm

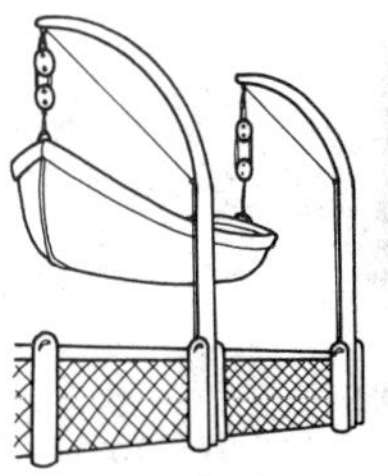
davit

dayflower

day lily

deadeye

day-trip·per (dā′trĭp′ər) *n.* One who takes a trip during the day without staying overnight.

daze (dāz) *tr.v.* **dazed, daz·ing, daz·es. 1.** To stun, as with a heavy blow or shock; stupefy. **2.** To dazzle, as with strong light. —*n.* A stunned or bewildered condition. [ME *dasen,* of Scand. orig.] **—daz′ed·ly** (dā′zĭd-lē) *adv.*

daz·zle (dăz′əl) *v.* **-zled, -zling, -zles.** —*tr.* **1.** To dim the vision of, esp. to blind with intense light. **2.** To bewilder, amaze, or overwhelm with spectacular display. —*intr.* **1.** To become blinded. **2.** To inspire admiration or wonder. —*n.* The act or quality of dazzling. [Freq. of DAZE.] **—daz′zler** *n.* **—daz′zling·ly** *adv.*

D-day (dē′dā′) *n.* The unnamed day on which a military offensive is to be launched, esp. June 6, 1944, the day on which the Allied forces invaded France during World War II. [D (abbr. of DAY) + DAY.]

DDT (dē′dē-tē′) *n.* A colorless contact insecticide, $(ClC_6H_4)_2CHCCl_3$, toxic to man and animals when swallowed or absorbed through the skin. [D(ICHLORO)D(IPHENYL)T(RICHLOROETHANE).]

de– *pref.* **1.** Reverse; do or make the opposite of: *decriminalize.* **2.** Remove or remove from: *delouse; dethrone.* **3.** Reduce; degrade: *declass.* **4.** Derived from: *deverbative.* [Lat. < *dē,* from.]

de-ac·ces·sion (dē′ăk-sĕsh′ən) *v.* **-sioned, -sion·ing, -sions.** —*tr.* To remove and sell (a work of art) from a museum's collection, esp. in order to purchase other works of art. —*intr.* To de-accession a work of art.

de·a·cid·i·fy (dē′ə-sĭd′ə-fī′) *tr.v.* **-fied, -fy·ing, -fies.** To remove the acid from or reduce the acid content of. **—de′a·cid′i·fi·ca′tion** *n.*

dea·con (dē′kən) *n.* **1.** In the Anglican, Eastern Orthodox, and Roman Catholic churches, a clergyman ranking just below a priest. **2.** In various other Christian churches, a layman who assists the minister in various functions. [ME *deken* < OE *dīacon* < LLat. *diaconus* < Gk. *diakonos,* attendant.]

dea·con·ess (dē′kə-nĭs) *n.* A woman appointed or elected to serve as an assistant in a church.

dea·con·ry (dē′kən-rē) *n., pl.* **-ries. 1.** The office or position of a deacon. **2.** Deacons collectively.

de·ac·ti·vate (dē-ăk′tə-vāt′) *tr.v.* **-vat·ed, -vat·ing, -vates. 1.** To render inactive or ineffective. **2.** To remove from active military status. **—de·ac′ti·va′tion** *n.*

dead (dĕd) *adj.* **-er, -est. 1.** No longer alive; having lost life. **2.** Marked for certain death; doomed. **3. a.** Having the physical appearance of death: *a dead pallor.* **b.** Lacking feeling or sensitivity; numb or unresponsive: *dead to her pleas for help.* **c.** Weary and worn-out; exhausted. **4. a.** Not having the capacity to live; inanimate: *as dead as a stone.* **b.** Not having the capacity to produce or sustain life; barren: *dead soil.* **5. a.** No longer in existence, use, or operation: *a dead language.* **b.** Not or no longer active; dormant: *a dead volcano.* **6. a.** Not productive; idle: *dead capital.* **b.** Not moving or circulating; stagnant: *dead water.* **7. a.** Without activity or traffic; quiet: *a dead town.* **b.** Without animation or activity; dull: *a dead party.* **c.** No longer having significance or relevance: *a dead issue.* **8.** Without resonance. Used of sounds. **9.** Extinguished: *a dead flame.* **10.** Lacking elasticity or bounce: *a dead ball.* **11.** Out of operation due to a fault or breakdown. **12. a.** Sudden; abrupt: *a dead stop.* **b.** Complete; utter: *dead silence.* **c.** Exact; unerring. **13.** *Sports.* Out of play. Used of a ball. **14. a.** Lacking connection to a source of electric current. **b.** Drained of electric charge, as a battery; discharged. —*n.* **1. a.** One who has died. **b.** Those who have died collectively. **2.** The period of greatest intensity, as of cold or darkness: *the dead of winter.* —*adv.* **1.** Absolutely; altogether. **2.** Directly; exactly: *dead ahead.* [ME *ded* < OE *dēad.*] **—dead′ness** *n.*

Synonyms: *dead, deceased, departed, extinct, lifeless, inanimate.* These adjectives all mean without life. *Dead,* which has the widest use, applies in general to whatever once had physical life, function, or usefulness but no longer does. *Deceased* refers only to nonliving human beings, as does *departed,* a euphemistic term. *Extinct* can refer to what has no living successors, such as an animal species, or to what is extinguished or inactive, such as a volcano. *Lifeless* applies to what no longer has physical life and to persons or things that lack animation or spirit. *Inanimate* is limited to what has never had physical life.

dead-air space (dĕd′âr′) *n.* An unventilated space.

dead·beat[1] (dĕd′bēt′) *adj.* Having an indicator that stops without oscillation.

dead·beat[2] (dĕd′bēt′) *n. Slang.* **1.** A person who does not pay his debts. **2.** A lazy person; loafer.

dead center *n.* Either of two points in the path of a moving crank and connecting rod at the ends of a stroke when the two lie in a straight line.

dead duck *n. Slang.* One that is doomed to failure.

dead·en (dĕd′n) *v.* **-ened, -en·ing, -ens.** —*tr.* **1.** To render less sensitive, intense, or vigorous. **2.** To make soundproof. **3.** To make less colorful. —*intr.* To become dead or as if dead. **—dead′en·er** *n.*

dead-end (dĕd′ĕnd′) *adj.* **1.** Not having an exit. **2.** Without opportunity for advancement: *a dead-end job.* **3.** *Informal.* Of or characteristic of the slums or life in the slums: *a dead-end gang.*

dead end *n.* **1.** An end of a passage, such as a street or pipe, that affords no outlet. **2.** A point beyond which no movement or progress can be made; impasse.

dead·en·ing (dĕd′n-ĭng) *n.* Material used for soundproofing.

dead·eye (dĕd′ī′) *n.* **1.** *Naut.* A flat hardwood disk with a grooved perimeter, pierced by three holes through which the lanyards are passed, used to fasten the shrouds. **2.** *Slang.* An expert marksman.

dead·fall (dĕd′fôl′) *n.* **1.** A trap for large animals in which a heavy weight is arranged to fall on and kill or disable the prey. **2.** A mass of fallen timber and tangled brush.

dead hand *n. Law.* Mortmain. [ME *dede hond,* transl. of OFr. *mortemain,* mortmain.]

dead·head (dĕd′hĕd′) *n. Informal.* **1.** A person who uses a free ticket for admittance, accommodation, or entertainment. **2.** A vehicle, such as a railroad car or an aircraft, carrying no passengers or freight. **3.** A dull-witted or sluggish person. —*tr.v.* **-head·ed, -head·ing, -heads. 1.** *Informal.* To drive or pilot (a vehicle) carrying no passengers or freight. **2.** To pull dead or dying blossoms off a flower. —*adv. Informal.* Without passengers or freight; empty.

dead heat *n.* A race in which two or more contestants finish at the same time; tie.

dead letter *n.* **1.** An unclaimed or undelivered letter that after a period of time is destroyed or returned to the sender by the post office. **2.** A law, directive, or factor still formally in effect but no longer valid or enforced.

dead·light (dĕd′līt′) *n.* **1.** *Naut.* **a.** A strong shutter or plate fastened over a ship's porthole or cabin window in stormy weather. **b.** A thick window set in a ship's side or deck. **2.** A skylight made so that it cannot be opened.

dead·line (dĕd′līn′) *n.* **1.** A time limit, as for payment of a debt or completion of an assignment. **2.** A boundary line in a prison that prisoners can cross only at the risk of being shot.

dead load *n.* The fixed weight of a structure or piece of equipment, such as a bridge on its supports.

dead·lock (dĕd′lŏk′) *n.* A stoppage or standstill resulting from the opposition of two unrelenting forces. —*tr. & intr.v.* **-locked, -lock·ing, -locks.** To bring or come to a deadlock.

dead·ly (dĕd′lē) *adj.* **-li·er, -li·est. 1.** Causing or tending to cause death; lethal: *deadly weapons.* **2.** Suggestive of death: *a deadly white.* **3.** Aiming or wanting to kill; implacable: *deadly enemies.* **4.** Destructive in effect: *gave the film a deadly review.* **5.** Absolute; utter: *deadly earnestness.* **6.** Extreme or terrible: *under deadly strain.* **7.** Extremely accurate; unerring: *a deadly shot.* **8.** *Informal.* Dull and boring. —*adv.* **1.** So as to suggest death. **2.** To an extreme: *deadly earnest.* **—dead′li·ness** *n.*

deadly nightshade *n.* The belladonna (sense 1).

dead march *n.* A slow, solemn march played for a funeral.

dead nettle *n.* Any of several weedy plants of the genus *Lamium,* native to the Old World, having clusters of small purplish, white, or yellow flowers.

dead·pan (dĕd′păn′) *n.* **1.** A blank, expressionless face. **2.** A person, esp. an actor, who has or assumes a deadpan. —*adj.* Characterized by a blank, expressionless face. —*adv. Slang.* With an emotionless face. —*v.* **-panned, -pan·ning, -pans.** —*tr.* To express in a deadpan. —*intr.* To express oneself in a deadpan manner.

dead point *n.* Dead center.

dead reckoning *n.* **1.** A method of estimating the position of an aircraft or ship without astronomical observations, as by applying to a previously determined position the course and distance traveled since. **2.** Calculation based on inference or guesswork.

dead spot *n.* A region where the reception of radio transmissions over a given frequency range is extremely weak.

dead weight *n.* **1.** The unrelieved weight of a heavy, motionless mass. **2.** An oppressive burden or difficulty affording no advantage whatever. **3.** A dead load.

dead·wood (dĕd′wo͝od′) *n.* **1.** Dead branches or wood on a tree. **2.** A burdensome or superfluous person or thing. **3.** *Naut.* The vertical planking between the keel of a vessel and the sternpost, serving merely as a reinforcement.

deaf (dĕf) *adj.* **-er, -est. 1.** Partially or completely incapable of hearing. **2.** Unwilling or refusing to listen; heedless. [ME < OE *dēaf.*] **—deaf′ly** *adv.* **—deaf′ness** *n.*

deaf·en (dĕf′ən) *v.* **-ened, -en·ing, -ens.** —*tr.* **1.** To make deaf, esp. momentarily by a loud noise. **2.** To make soundproof. —*intr.* To cause permanent or momentary deafness. **—deaf′en·ing·ly** *adv.*

deaf-mute also **deaf mute** (dĕf′myo͞ot′) *n.* A person who can neither speak nor hear. —*adj.* (dĕf-myo͞ot′). Unable to speak or hear.

deal[1] (dēl) *v.* **dealt** (dĕlt), **deal·ing, deals.** —*tr.* **1.** To give to someone as his share; apportion. **2.** To distribute or pass out among several people. **3.** To administer; deliver: *dealt a blow to the stomach.* **4. a.** To distribute (playing cards) among players. **b.** To give (a specific card) to a player while so distributing. —*intr.* **1.** To be occupied or concerned; treat: *a book dealing with the Middle Ages.* **2.** To behave in a specified way toward another or others; have transactions: *deal honestly with competitors.* **3.** To take action: *The com-*

mittee will deal with this complaint. **4.** To do business; trade: *dealing in diamonds.* **5.** To distribute playing cards. —*n.* **1.** The act or a round of apportioning or distributing. **2. a.** The distribution of playing cards. **b.** The cards distributed; hand. **c.** The right or turn of a player to distribute the cards. **d.** The playing of one hand. **3.** *Informal.* An indefinite quantity, extent, or degree: *a great deal of experience.* **4.** An agreement arranged secretly, as in business or politics. **5.** *Informal.* An agreement or business transaction. **6.** *Informal.* A bargain or favorable sale. **7.** *Informal.* Treatment received: *got a raw deal.* **8.** *Slang.* An important issue: *make a big deal out of nothing.* **9.** A program, such as a political platform, that offers some specified treatment for those participating: *Truman's Fair Deal.* [ME *delen* < OE *dǣlan,* to divide, share.]

deal^2 (dēl) *n.* **1. a.** A fir or pine board cut to standard dimensions. **b.** Such boards or planks collectively. **2.** Fir or pine wood. [ME *dele* < MLG *dele,* plank.]

de·a·late (dē-ā′lāt′) or **de·a·lat·ed** (-lā′tĭd) *adj.* Having lost the wings. Used of ants and other insects that shed their wings after a mating flight.

deal·er (dē′lər) *n.* **1.** One that is engaged in buying and selling: *a used-car dealer.* **2.** The person who distributes the cards in a card game.

deal·er·ship (dē′lər-shĭp′) *n.* A franchise to sell a particular item in a certain area.

deal·fish (dēl′fĭsh′) *n., pl.* **dealfish** or **-fish·es.** A marine fish, *Trachipterus arcticus,* of Atlantic waters, resembling the ribbonfishes. [< DEAL^2.]

deal·ing (dē′lĭng) *n.* **1. dealings.** Transactions or relations with others, usually in business. **2.** Method or manner of conduct in relation to others; treatment: *honest dealing.*

dealt (dĕlt) *v.* Past tense and past participle of **deal^1.**

de·am·i·nase (dē-ăm′ə-nās′, -nāz′) *n.* An enzyme that catalyzes the hydrolysis of amino compounds, as amino acids.

de·am·i·nate (dē-ăm′ə-nāt′) *tr.v.* **-nat·ed, -nat·ing, -nates.** To remove an amino group from (an organic compound). —**de·am′i·na′tion** *n.*

de·am·i·nize (dē-ăm′ə-nīz′) *tr.v.* **-nized, -niz·ing, -niz·es.** To deaminate. —**de·am′i·ni·za′tion** *n.*

dean (dēn) *n.* **1. a.** An administrative officer in charge of a college, faculty, or division in a university. **b.** An officer of a college or high school who counsels students and supervises the enforcement of rules. **2.** *Eccles.* The head of the chapter of canons governing a cathedral or collegiate church. **3.** *Chiefly Brit.* A priest appointed to oversee a group of parishes within a diocese. **4.** The senior member of a body: *the dean of the diplomatic corps.* [ME *deen* < OFr. *deien* < LLat. *decanus,* chief of ten < *decem,* ten.] —**dean′ship′** *n.*

dean·er·y (dē′nə-rē) *n., pl.* **-ies. 1.** The office, jurisdiction, or authority of a dean. **2.** A dean's official residence.

dean's list *n.* A list, issued periodically, of students in a college or university who have attained high academic rank.

dear^1 (dîr) *adj.* **-er, -est. 1. a.** Loved and cherished: *my dearest friend.* **b.** Greatly valued; precious: *lost everything dear to them.* **2.** Highly esteemed or regarded. Used in direct address, esp. in salutations: *Dear Sir.* **3. a.** High-priced; expensive. **b.** Charging high prices. **4.** Earnest; ardent: *"This good man was a dear lover and constant practiser of angling"* (Walton). **5.** *Obs.* Noble; worthy. —*n.* A greatly loved person. —*adv.* **1.** Fondly or affectionately. **2.** At a high cost. —*interj.* Used as a polite exclamation, chiefly of surprise or distress: *oh dear; dear me.* [ME *dere* < OE *dēore.*] —**dear′ly** *adv.* —**dear′ness** *n.*

dear^2 (dîr) *adj. Obs.* Severe; grievous. [ME *dere* < OE *dēor.*]

Dear John (jŏn) *n.* A letter, as to a soldier, in which a wife requests a divorce or a girlfriend terminates a friendship or engagement.

dearth (dûrth) *n.* **1.** Scarcity; lack. **2.** Shortage of food; famine. [ME < *dere,* dear.]

death (dĕth) *n.* **1.** The act of dying; termination of life. **2.** The state of being dead. **3.** Often **Death.** A personification of the destroyer of life, usually represented as a skeleton holding a scythe. **4.** Termination or extinction: *the death of imperialism.* **5.** The cause of dying. **6.** A manner of dying: *a hero's death.* **7. a.** Bloodshed or murder. **b.** Execution. **8.** Civil death. **9.** In Christian Science, the product of human belief of life in matter. —**idiom. to death.** To an intolerable degree: *worried to death.* [ME *deeth* < OE *dēað.*]

death·bed (dĕth′bĕd′) *n.* **1.** The bed on which a person dies. **2.** The last hours before death.

death·blow (dĕth′blō′) *n.* **1.** A blow or stroke that causes death. **2.** A fatal event or occurrence.

death camas also **death camass** *n.* Any of several plants of the genus *Zygadenus,* of western North America, having grasslike leaves and clusters of greenish-white flowers poisonous to livestock in the western U.S.

death cup *n.* A poisonous, usually white mushroom, *Amanita phalloides,* having a prominent bulbous base.

death duty *n. Chiefly Brit.* Inheritance tax.

death house *n.* A cell block or other part of a prison in which prisoners condemned to death await execution.

death·less (dĕth′lĭs) *adj.* Not subject to death; immortal. —**death′less·ly** *adv.* —**death′less·ness** *n.*

death·ly (dĕth′lē) *adj.* **1.** Of, resembling, or characteristic of death. **2.** Causing death; fatal. —*adv.* **1.** In the manner of death. **2.** Extremely; very.

death mask *n.* A cast of a person's face taken after death.

death point *n.* An environmental limit, as of temperature or radiation, beyond which a specified life form cannot survive.

death rate *n.* The ratio of total deaths to total population in a specified community.

death rattle *n.* A rare respiratory gurgling or rattling in the throat of a dying person, caused by loss of the cough reflex and passage of breath through accumulating mucus in the throat.

death's-head (dĕths′hĕd′) *n.* The human skull or a representation of it, symbolizing mortality or death.

deaths·man (dĕths′mən) *n. Archaic.* An executioner.

death tax *n.* Inheritance tax.

death·trap (dĕth′trăp′) *n.* **1.** An unsafe building or structure. **2.** A perilous circumstance or situation.

death warrant *n.* **1.** *Law.* An official order authorizing a person's execution. **2.** Something that destroys hope, joy, or expectation.

death·watch (dĕth′wŏch′) *n.* **1.** A vigil kept beside a dying or dead person. **2.** One who guards a condemned person before his execution. **3. a.** Any of several beetles of the family Anobiidae that strike their heads against the wood into which they burrow with a hollow, clicking sound. **b.** A booklouse that makes a similar sound.

death wish *n. Psychiat.* A conscious or unconscious desire for one's own death or the death of another.

de·ba·cle (dĭ-bä′kəl, -băk′əl) *n.* **1.** A sudden, disastrous collapse, downfall, or defeat; rout. **2.** A total, often ludicrous failure. **3.** The breaking up of ice in a river. **4.** A violent flood. [Fr. *débâcle* < *débâcler,* to unbar < OFr. *desbacler* : *des-,* away (< Lat. *de-*) + *bacler,* to bar < OProv. *baclar* < VLat. **bacclare* < Lat. *baculum,* rod.]

de·bar (dē-bär′) *tr.v.* **-barred, -bar·ring, -bars. 1.** To exclude or bar; shut out. **2.** To forbid, hinder, or prevent. [ME *debarren* < OFr. *desbarrer,* to unbar : *des-,* away (< Lat. *de-*) + *barrer,* to bar < *barre,* bar.] —**de·bar′ment** *n.*

de·bark (dĭ-bärk′) *v.* **-barked, -bark·ing, -barks.** —*tr.* To unload, as from a ship. —*intr.* To disembark. [Fr. *débarquer* < OFr. *debarquer* : *de-,* from (< Lat. *dē-*) + *barque,* ship. —see BARQUE.] —**de′bar·ka′tion** (dē′bär-kā′shən) *n.*

de·base (dĭ-bās′) *tr.v.* **-based, -bas·ing, -bas·es.** To lower in character, quality, or value. —**de·base′ment** *n.* —**de·bas′er** *n.*

de·bat·a·ble (dĭ-bā′tə-bəl) *adj.* **1.** Capable of being formally argued or discussed. **2.** Open to dispute; questionable. **3.** In dispute, as land. —**de·bat′a·bly** *adv.*

de·bate (dĭ-bāt′) *v.* **-bat·ed, -bat·ing, -bates.** —*intr.* **1.** To deliberate; consider. **2.** To engage in argument by discussing opposing points. **3.** To engage in a formal discussion or argument. **4.** *Obs.* To fight; quarrel. —*tr.* **1.** To deliberate upon; consider. **2.** To dispute or argue about. **3.** To discuss or argue (a question, for example) formally. **4.** *Obs.* To fight or argue for or over. —*n.* **1.** A discussion involving opposing points; argument. **2.** Deliberation; consideration. **3.** A formal contest of argumentation in which two opposing teams defend and attack a given proposition. **4.** *Obs.* Conflict; strife. [ME *debaten* < OFr. *debatre* : *de-,* apart (< Lat. *de-*) + *battre,* to fight < Lat. *battuere,* to batter.] —**de·bat′er** *n.*

de·bauch (dĭ-bôch′) *v.* **-bauched, -bauch·ing, -bauch·es.** —*tr.* **1. a.** To corrupt morally; seduce. **b.** To lead away from excellence or virtue. **2.** *Obs.* To cause to forsake allegiance. —*intr.* To indulge in dissipation. —*n.* **1.** An act or period of debauchery. **2.** An orgy. [Fr. *débaucher* < OFr. *desbaucher,* to lead astray, roughhew timber : *des-,* apart (< Lat. *de-*) + *bauch,* beam, of Germanic orig.] —**de·bauch′ed·ly** (-bô′chĭd-lē) *adv.* —**de·bauch′er** *n.*

de·bauch·ee (dĭ-bô′chē′, dĕb′ə-shē′, -shā′) *n.* A person who habitually indulges in dissipation or debauchery; libertine.

de·bauch·er·y (dĭ-bô′chə-rē) *n., pl.* **-ies. 1.** Extreme indulgence in sensual pleasures; dissipation. **2.** *Archaic.* Seduction from morality, allegiance, or duty.

de·ben·ture (dĭ-bĕn′chər) *n.* **1.** A certificate or voucher acknowledging a debt. **2.** An unsecured bond issued by a civil or governmental corporation or agency and backed only by the credit standing of the issuer. **3.** A customhouse certificate providing for the payment of a drawback. [ME *debentur* < Lat., they are due.]

de·bil·i·tate (dĭ-bĭl′ĭ-tāt′) *tr.v.* **-tat·ed, -tat·ing, -tates.** To make feeble; enervate. [Lat. *debilitare, debilitat-* < *debilis,* weak.] —**de·bil′i·ta′tion** *n.* —**de·bil′i·ta′tive** *adj.*

de·bil·i·ty (dĭ-bĭl′ĭ-tē) *n.* The state of abnormal bodily weakness; feebleness. [ME *debilite* < OFr. < Lat. *debilitas* < *debilis,* weak.]

deb·it (dĕb′ĭt) *n.* **1.** An item of debt as recorded in an account. **2. a.** An entry of a sum in the debit or left-hand side of an account. **b.** The sum of such entries. **3.** The left-hand side of an account or an accounting ledger where bookkeeping entries are made. **4.** A drawback or detriment. —*tr.v.* **-it·ed, -it·ing, -its. 1.** To enter (a sum) on the left-hand side of an account or accounting ledger. **2.** To charge with a debt. [ME *debite* < Lat. *debitum.* —see DEBT.]

deb·o·nair also **deb·o·naire** (dĕb′ə-nâr′) *adj.* **1.** Suave; ur-

death mask
Death mask of Napoleon

bane. **2.** Affable; genial. **3.** Carefree and gay; jaunty. [ME *debonaire,* gracious, kindly < OFr. < *de bonne aire,* of good disposition.] **—deb'o·nair'ly** *adv.* **—deb'o·nair'ness** *n.*

Deb·o·rah (dĕb'ər-ə) *n.* In the Old Testament, a prophetess and judge of Israel who helped the Israelites free themselves from the Canaanites. [Heb. *dĕvōrā,* bee.]

de·bouch (dĭ-bouch', -bo͞osh') *v.* **-bouched, -bouch·ing, -bouch·es.** *—intr.* **1.** To march from a narrow or confined area into the open. **2.** To emerge or issue. *—tr.* To cause to emerge or issue. [Fr. *déboucher* : *de-,* out of (< Lat. *de-*) + *bouche,* mouth < Lat. *bucca.*]

dé·bou·ché (dā'bo͞o-shā') *n.* **1.** An opening in military works for the passage of troops. **2.** An outlet, as for goods. [Fr. < *déboucher,* to debouch.]

de·bouch·ment (dĭ-bouch'mənt, -bo͞osh'-) *n.* **1.** The act or an instance of debouching. **2.** A debouchure.

de·bou·chure (dĭ-bo͞o'sho͝or') *n.* A mouth or opening, esp. of a river or channel.

dé·bride·ment (dā'brēd-mäɴ', dĭ-brēd'mənt) *n.* The surgical excision of dead and devitalized tissue and the removal of all foreign matter from a wound. [Fr. < *débrider* < OFr. *desbrider,* to unbridle : *des-,* away (< Lat. *de-*) + *bride,* bridle, of Germanic orig.]

de·brief (dē-brēf') *tr.v.* **-briefed, -brief·ing, -briefs. 1.** To question or interrogate to obtain knowledge or intelligence gathered esp. on a military mission. **2.** To instruct (a government agent or similar employee) not to reveal classified or secret information after his employment has ceased.

de·brief·ing (dē-brē'fĭng) *n.* **1.** The act or process of debriefing or being debriefed. **2.** The information conveyed during debriefing.

de·bris also **dé·bris** (də-brē', dā-, dā'brē') *n.* **1.** The scattered remains of something broken or destroyed; ruins. **2.** *Geol.* An accumulation of relatively large rock fragments. [Fr. *débris* < OFr. *desbrisier,* to break to pieces : *des-* (intensive < Lat. *dē-*) + *brisier,* to break.]

decanter

debt (dĕt) *n.* **1.** Something owed, such as money, goods, or services. **2. a.** An obligation or liability to pay or render something to someone else. **b.** The condition of having such an obligation: *always in debt.* **3.** *Theol.* An offense requiring forgiveness or reparation; trespass. [ME *dette* < OFr. < VLat. **debita,* fem. of Lat. *debitum,* debt < *debēre,* to owe.]

debt·or (dĕt'ər) *n.* **1.** One who owes something to another. **2.** One guilty of a trespass or sin; sinner. [ME *dettour* < OFr. *dettor* < Lat. *debitor* < *debēre,* to owe.]

de·bug (dē-bŭg') *tr.v.* **-bugged, -bug·ging, -bugs. 1.** To remove insects from. **2.** To remove a hidden electronic device, as a microphone, from: *debug a conference room.* **3.** To make (a hidden microphone, for example) ineffective. **4.** To search for and eliminate malfunctioning elements or error in: *debug a spacecraft before the launching date; debug a computer program.*

de·bunk (dē-bŭngk') *tr.v.* **-bunked, -bunk·ing, -bunks.** *Informal.* To expose or ridicule the falseness, sham, or exaggerated claims of. **—de·bunk'er** *n.*

de·but also **dé·but** (dā-byo͞o', dā'byo͞o') *n.* **1.** A first public appearance, as of an actor. **2.** The formal presentation of a girl to society. **3.** The beginning of a career or other course of action. *—tr. & intr.v.* **-buted** (-byo͞od'), **-but·ing** (-byo͞o'ĭng), **-buts** (-byo͞oz'). *Informal.* To present in or make a debut. [Fr. *début* < *débuter,* to lead off in a game, debut : *de-,* away (< Lat. *de-*) + *but,* target < OFr. *butte.*]

Usage: *Debut* is widely used as a verb, both intransitively in the sense "to make an appearance" (*the singer debuts here tonight*) and transitively in the sense "to present for the first time" (*the company will debut its new models at the auto show*). Both these uses are unacceptable to a large majority of the Usage Panel.

deb·u·tante also **dé·bu·tante** (dĕb'yo͞o-tänt', dā'byo͞o-) *n.* A young woman making a debut into society. [Fr. *débutante* < fem. pr.part. of *débuter,* to debut.]

deca– or **dec–** also **deka–** or **dek–** *pref.* Ten: *decane.* [Gk. *deka-* < *deka,* ten.]

dec·ade (dĕk'ād', dĕ-kād') *n.* **1.** A period of ten years. **2.** A group or series of ten. [ME, a group of ten < OFr. < LLat. *decas* < Gk. *dekas* < *deka,* ten.]

de·ca·dence (dĭ-kād'ns, dĕk'ə-dəns) *n.* A process, condition, or period of deterioration or decline, as in morals or art; decay. [OFr. < Med. Lat. *decadentia,* a falling : Lat. *de-,* down + *cadere,* to fall.]

de·ca·den·cy (dĭ-kād'n-sē, dĕk'ə-dən-) *n.* Decadence.

de·ca·dent (dĭ-kād'nt, dĕk'ə-dənt) *adj.* **1.** In a state or condition of decline or decay. **2.** Of or pertaining to the decadents. *—n.* **1.** A person in a condition or process of mental or moral decay. **2.** A member of a group of French and English writers of the 19th century who often sought inspiration in the morbid, neurotic, or macabre and tended toward overrefinement of style. **—de·ca'dent·ly** *adv.*

dec·a·gon (dĕk'ə-gŏn') *n.* A polygon with ten angles and ten sides. [NLat. *decagonum* < Gk. *dekagōnon* : *deka,* ten + *-gōnon,* -gon.] **—de·cag'o·nal** (dĭ-kăg'ə-nəl) *adj.* **—de·cag'o·nal·ly** *adv.*

dec·a·gram or **dek·a·gram** (dĕk'ə-grăm') *n.* Ten grams.

dec·a·he·dron (dĕk'ə-hē'drən) *n., pl.* **-drons** or **-dra** (-drə). A polyhedron with ten faces. **—dec'a·he'dral** *adj.*

de·cal (dē'kăl', dĭ-kăl') *n.* A picture or design transferred by the process of decalcomania.

de·cal·ci·fy (dē-kăl'sə-fī') *tr.v.* **-fied, -fy·ing, -fies.** To remove calcium or calcareous matter from (bones, for example). **—de·cal'ci·fi·ca'tion** *n.* **—de·cal'ci·fi'er** *n.*

de·cal·co·ma·ni·a (dē-kăl'kə-mā'nē-ə, -mān'yə) *n.* **1.** The process of transferring pictures or designs printed on specially prepared paper to glass, metal, or other material. **2.** A picture transferred by decalcomania; decal. [Fr. *décalcomanie* : *decalquer,* to transfer by tracing (*de-,* from + *calquer,* to trace < Ital. *calcare,* to trace, trample < Lat., to tread < *calx,* heel) + *manie,* madness < Lat. *mania* (from its popularity in the 19th cent.).]

de·ca·les·cence (dē'kə-lĕs'əns) *n.* In a metal being heated, a sudden slowing in the rate of temperature increase, as a result of endothermic structural changes. [DE- + Lat. *calescens,* pr.part. of *calescere,* to become warm < *calēre,* to be warm.] **—de'ca·les'cent** *adj.*

dec·a·li·ter or **dek·a·li·ter** (dĕk'ə-lē'tər) *n.* Ten liters.

Dec·a·logue or **Dec·a·log** (dĕk'ə-lôg', -lŏg') *n.* The Ten Commandments. [ME *decalog* < OFr. *decalogue* < LLat. *decalogus* < Gk. *dekalogos* : *deka,* ten + *logos,* speech, word.]

dec·a·me·ter or **dek·a·me·ter** (dĕk'ə-mē'tər) *n.* Ten meters.

dec·a·met·ric (dĕk'ə-mĕt'rĭk) *adj.* Of, relating to, or being a radio wave of wavelength between 1 and 10 decameters.

de·camp (dĭ-kămp') *intr.v.* **-camped, -camp·ing, -camps. 1.** To depart from a camping ground. **2.** To depart secretly or suddenly. [Fr. *décamper* < OFr. *descamper* : *des-,* away (< Lat. *dē-*) + *camper,* to camp < *camp,* camp < Lat. *campus.*] **—de·camp'ment** *n.*

dec·a·nal (dĕk'ə-nəl, dĭ-kā'nəl) *adj.* Of or pertaining to a dean or deanery. [< LLat. *decanus,* dean. —see DEAN.]

dec·ane (dĕk'ān') *n.* Any of various liquid isomers, $C_{10}H_{22}$, of the methane series.

dec·a·no·ic acid (dĕk'ə-nō'ĭk) *n.* Capric acid.

de·cant (dĭ-kănt') *tr.v.* **-cant·ed, -cant·ing, -cants. 1.** To pour off (wine, for example) without disturbing the sediment. **2.** To pour (a liquid) from one container into another. [Fr. *décanter* < Med. Lat. *decanthare* : Lat. *de-,* from + Lat. *canthus,* rim of a wheel, of Celtic orig.] **—de'can·ta'tion** (dē'kăn-tā'shən) *n.*

de·cant·er (dĭ-kăn'tər) *n.* **1.** A decorative bottle used for serving liquids, as wine. **2.** A vessel used for decanting.

de·cap·i·tate (dĭ-kăp'ĭ-tāt') *tr.v.* **-tat·ed, -tat·ing, -tates.** To cut off the head of; behead. [LLat. *decapitare, decapitat-* : Lat. *de-,* off + *caput,* head.] **—de·cap'i·ta'tion** *n.* **—de·cap'i·ta'tor** *n.*

dec·a·pod (dĕk'ə-pŏd') *n.* **1.** A crustacean of the order Decapoda, such as a crab, lobster, or shrimp, characteristically having five pairs of locomotor appendages, each joined to a segment of the thorax. **2.** A cephalopod mollusk, such as a squid or cuttlefish, having ten armlike tentacles. *—adj.* Of or pertaining to the Decapoda or a decapod. [< NLat. *Decapoda,* order name : DECA- + Gk. *pous,* foot.] **—de·cap'o·dal** (dĭ-kăp'ə-dəl), **de·cap'o·dan** (-dən), **de·cap'o·dous** (-dəs) *adj.*

de·car·bon·ate (dē-kär'bə-nāt') *tr.v.* **-at·ed, -at·ing, -ates.** To remove carbon dioxide or carbonic acid from. **—de·car'bon·a'tion** *n.*

de·car·bon·ize (dē-kär'bə-nīz') *tr.v.* **-ized, -iz·ing, -iz·es.** To remove carbon from; decarburize. **—de·car'bon·i·za'tion** *n.* **—de·car'bon·iz'er** *n.*

de·car·box·yl·ase (dē'kär-bŏk'sə-lās', -lāz') *n.* Any of various enzymes that hydrolize the carboxyl radical.

de·car·box·yl·a·tion (dē'kär-bŏk'sə-lā'shən) *n.* The removal of a carboxyl group from a chemical compound, with hydrogen usually replacing it.

de·car·bu·rize (dē-kär'bə-rīz', -byə-) *tr.v.* **-rized, -riz·ing, -riz·es.** To decarbonize. **—de·car'bu·ri·za'tion** *n.*

dec·are (dĕk'âr', -är') *n.* A metric unit of area measure equal to 10 ares, or 0.2471 acre.

dec·a·stere or **dek·a·stere** (dĕk'ə-stîr') *n.* Ten steres.

dec·a·syl·la·ble (dĕk'ə-sĭl'ə-bəl) *n.* A line of verse having ten syllables. **—dec'a·syl·lab'ic** (-sə-lăb'ĭk) *adj.*

de·cath·lon (dĭ-kăth'lən, -lŏn') *n.* An athletic contest in which each contestant participates in ten different track and field events. [Fr. *décathlon* : *déca-,* deca- + Gk. *athlon,* contest.]

de·cay (dĭ-kā') *v.* **-cayed, -cay·ing, -cays.** *—intr.* **1.** *Biol.* To decompose; rot. **2.** *Physics.* To disintegrate or diminish by radioactive decay. **3.** *Aerospace.* To decrease in orbit, as an artificial satellite. **4.** To fall into ruin. **5.** *Pathol.* To decline in health or vigor; waste away. **6.** To decline from a state of normality, excellence, or prosperity. *—tr.* To cause to decay. *—n.* **1.** The destruction or decomposition of organic matter as a result of bacterial or fungal action; rot. **2.** Radioactive decay. **3.** The decrease in orbital altitude of an artificial satellite due to conditions such as atmospheric drag. **4.** A gradual deterioration to an inferior state, as of health or mental capability. [ME *decayen* < AN *decair* < VLat. **decadere* : Lat. *de-,* down + Lat. *cadere,* to fall.]

Synonyms: *decay, rot, putrefy, spoil, crumble, molder, disintegrate, decompose.* These verbs all refer to gradual change marked by destruction or dissolution. *Decay,* which can apply to physical change or figuratively to breakdown of the mind, morals, or the like, usually implies a stage in deterioration short of destruction. *Rot* has both physical and figurative use, and *putrefy* largely physical; both stress later stages of deterioration marked in physical contexts by offensiveness to smell and sight. *Spoil* can refer to organic decay or figuratively (and transitively) to impairment of character of a person. *Crumble* and *molder* apply mostly to physical breakdown of a substance into small pieces or, in the case of *molder,* into dust. *Disintegrate,* which has physical and figurative use, refers to complete breakdown into component parts; it implies as well the destruction of usefulness or integrity. *Decompose* is largely restricted to the breakdown of substances into their chemical components.

de·cease (dĭ-sēs′) *intr.v.* **-ceased, -ceas·ing, -ceas·es.** To die. —*n.* Death. [ME *decesen* < *deces,* death < OFr. < Lat. *decessus* < p.part. of *decedere,* to depart : *de-,* away + *cedere,* to go.]

de·ceased (dĭ-sēst′) *adj.* No longer living; dead. —*n.* A dead person.

de·ce·dent (dĭ-sēd′nt) *n. Law.* The deceased. [Lat. *decedens, decedent-,* pr.part. of *decedere,* to die. —see DECEASE.]

de·ceit (dĭ-sēt′) *n.* **1.** The act or practice of deceiving; deception. **2.** A stratagem or trick. **3.** The quality of being deceitful; falseness. [ME < AN < Lat. *decepta,* fem. p.part. of *decipere,* to deceive.]

de·ceit·ful (dĭ-sēt′fəl) *adj.* **1.** Given to cheating or deceiving. **2.** Deliberately misleading; deceptive. **—de·ceit′ful·ly** *adv.* **—de·ceit′ful·ness** *n.*

de·ceive (dĭ-sēv′) *v.* **-ceived, -ceiv·ing, -ceives.** —*tr.* **1.** To cause (a person) to believe what is not true; mislead. **2.** *Archaic.* To catch by guile; ensnare. —*intr.* To practice deceit. [ME *deceiven* < AN *deceiver* < Lat. *decipere* : *de-* (pejorative) + *capere,* to seize.] **—de·ceiv′a·ble** *adj.* **—de·ceiv′er** *n.* **—de·ceiv′ing·ly** *adv.*

Synonyms: *deceive, betray, mislead, beguile, delude, dupe, hoodwink, bamboozle, outwit, double-cross.* These verbs mean to victimize persons, for the most part by underhand means. *Deceive* involves falsehood or the deliberate concealment or misrepresentation of truth with intent to lead another into error or to disadvantage. *Betray* implies faithlessness or treachery that brings another to grave disadvantage or into danger. *Mislead* means to lead into error and does not invariably imply intent to harm. *Beguile* suggests deceiving or misleading by means of allurement. *Delude* refers to deceiving or misleading to the point of rendering a person unable to detect falsehood or make sound judgment. *Dupe* means to delude by playing upon another's susceptibilities or naiveté. *Hoodwink* refers to deluding by trickery such as mental blinding or dazzling. *Bamboozle* less formally means to delude by trickery such as hoaxing, befuddling, or artful persuasion. *Outwit* means to frustrate another person by ingenuity and cunning and is less forceful in its suggestion of bad faith. *Double-cross,* a slang term, implies betrayal of a confidence or the willful breaking of a pledge.

de·cel·er·ate (dē-sĕl′ə-rāt′) *v.* **-at·ed, -at·ing, -ates.** —*tr.* To decrease the velocity of. —*intr.* To decrease in velocity. [DE- + (AC)CELERATE.] **—de·cel′er·a′tion** *n.* **—de·cel′er·a′tor** *n.*

De·cem·ber (dĭ-sĕm′bər) *n.* The 12th and last month of the year according to the Gregorian calendar. See table at **calendar.** [ME *decembre* < OFr. < Lat. *December,* the tenth month < *decem,* ten.]

De·cem·brist (dĭ-sem′brĭst) *n.* A participant in the unsuccessful conspiracy to overthrow Czar Nicholas I of Russia in December, 1825.

de·cem·vir (dĭ-sĕm′vər) *n., pl.* **-virs** or **-vi·ri** (-və-rī′). One of a body of ten Roman magistrates, esp. a member of one of two such bodies appointed in 451 and 450 B.C. to draw up a code of laws. [ME < Lat., back-formation < *decemviri,* commission of ten < *decem viri,* ten men.] **—de·cem′vi·ral** *adj.* **—de·cem′vi·rate** *n.*

de·cen·cy (dē′sən-sē) *n., pl.* **-cies. 1.** The state or quality of being decent; propriety. **2.** Conformity to prevailing standards of propriety or modesty. **3. decencies.** Social or moral proprieties.

de·cen·na·ry (dĭ-sĕn′ə-rē) *adj.* Of or pertaining to a ten-year period. —*n., pl.* **-ries.** A decennium; decade. [< Lat. *decennis,* of ten years. —see DECENNIUM.]

de·cen·ni·a (dĭ-sĕn′ē-ə) *n.* A plural of **decennium.**

de·cen·ni·al (dĭ-sĕn′ē-əl) *adj.* **1.** Pertaining to or lasting for ten years. **2.** Occurring every ten years. —*n.* A tenth anniversary. [< Lat. *decennium,* decennium.] **—de·cen′ni·al·ly** *adv.*

de·cen·ni·um (dĭ-sĕn′ē-əm) *n., pl.* **-cen·ni·ums** or **-cen·ni·a** (-sĕn′ē-ə). A period of ten years; decade. [Lat. < *decennis,* of ten years : *decem,* ten + *annus,* year.]

de·cent (dē′sənt) *adj.* **1.** Characterized by conformity to recognized standards of propriety or morality. **2.** Free from indelicacy; modest. **3.** Meeting accepted standards; adequate: *a decent salary.* **4.** Kind or obliging. **5.** *Informal.* Properly or modestly dressed. [Lat. *decens, decent-,* pr.part. of *decēre,* to be fitting.] **—de′cent·ly** *adv.* **—de′cent·ness** *n.*

de·cen·tral·ize (dē-sĕn′trə-līz′) *tr.v.* **-ized, -iz·ing, -iz·es. 1.** To distribute the administrative functions or powers of (a central authority) among several local authorities. **2.** To cause to withdraw from an area of concentration: *decentralize an industry.* **—de·cen′tral·i·za′tion** *n.*

de·cep·tion (dĭ-sĕp′shən) *n.* **1.** The use of deceit. **2.** The fact or state of being deceived. **3.** A ruse or trick. [ME *decepcioun* < OFr. *deception* < LLat. *deceptio* < Lat. *deceptus,* p.part. of *decipere,* to deceive.]

de·cep·tive (dĭ-sĕp′tĭv) *adj.* Intended or tending to deceive; misleading. **—de·cep′tive·ly** *adv.* **—de·cep′tive·ness** *n.*

deci- *pref.* One tenth (10^{-1}): *deciliter.* [Fr. *déci-* < Lat. *decimus,* tenth < *decem,* ten.]

dec·i·are (dĕs′ē-âr′, -är′) *n.* One-tenth (10^{-1}) of an are.

de·ci·bel (dĕs′ə-bəl, -bĕl′) *n.* A unit used to express relative difference in power, usually between acoustic or electric signals, equal to ten times the common logarithm of the ratio of the two levels.

de·cide (dĭ-sīd′) *v.* **-cid·ed, -cid·ing, -cides.** —*tr.* **1.** To conclude or settle. **2.** To influence or determine the conclusion of: *A few votes decided the election.* **3.** To cause to make or reach a decision. —*intr.* **1.** To pronounce a judgment; announce a verdict. **2.** To make up one's mind. [ME *deciden* < AN *decider* < Lat. *decidere* : *de-,* off + *caedere,* to cut.] **—de·cid′a·ble** *adj.* **—de·cid′er** *n.*

Synonyms: *decide, determine, settle, rule, conclude, resolve.* These verbs are compared in the sense of making decisions or judgments. *Decide,* the least specific, overlaps the other terms without conveying their more special meanings. *Determine* differs in that it often involves somewhat narrower issues and more detailed solutions. *Settle* stresses finality of decision, and *rule* implies that the decision is handed down by someone having recognized authority. *Conclude* suggests decision or judgment produced by careful consideration of all pertinent matters. *Resolve* implies formal deliberation and finality of decision or determination.

de·cid·ed (dĭ-sī′dĭd) *adj.* **1.** Without doubt or question; definite: *a decided success.* **2.** Free from hesitation or vacillation; resolute. **—de·cid′ed·ly** *adv.* **—de·cid′ed·ness** *n.*

de·cid·ing (dĭ-sī′dĭng) *adj.* **1.** Having the power or quality that decides: *Lack of money was the deciding factor.* **2.** Effecting a decision: *cast the deciding vote.*

de·cid·u·a (dĭ-sĭj′o͞o-ə) *n.* A mucous membrane of the uterus, modified during pregnancy and cast off during menstruation or at parturition. [NLat. *(membrana) decidua,* (membrane) that falls off < Lat. *deciduus,* deciduous.]

de·cid·u·ate (dĭ-sĭj′o͞o-ĭt) *adj.* **1.** Characterized by or having a decidua. **2.** Characterized by shedding.

de·cid·u·ous (dĭ-sĭj′o͞o-əs) *adj.* **1.** Falling off or shed at a specific season or stage of growth: *deciduous antlers; deciduous leaves.* **2.** Shedding or losing foliage at the end of the growing season: *deciduous trees.* **3.** Not lasting; temporary. [Lat. *deciduus* < *decidere,* to fall off : *de-,* off + *cadere,* to fall.] **—de·cid′u·ous·ly** *adv.* **—de·cid′u·ous·ness** *n.*

dec·i·gram (dĕs′ĭ-grăm′) *n.* One-tenth (10^{-1}) of a gram.

dec·ile (dĕs′īl′, -əl) *n. Statistics.* **1.** Any one of the numbers or values in a series dividing the distribution of the individuals in the series into ten groups of equal frequency. **2.** Any one of the ten groups. [< Lat. *decem,* ten.]

dec·i·li·ter (dĕs′ə-lē′tər) *n.* One-tenth (10^{-1}) of a liter.

de·cil·lion (dĭ-sĭl′yən) *n.* **1.** The cardinal number that is equal to 10^{33}. **2.** *Chiefly Brit.* The cardinal number that is equal to 10^{60}. [Lat. *decem,* ten + (M)ILLION.] **—de·cil′lionth** *adj & adv.*

dec·i·mal (dĕs′ə-məl) *n.* **1.** A linear array of integers that represents a fraction, every decimal place indicating a multiple of a positive or negative power of 10. For example, the decimal .1 = $^{1}/_{10}$, .12 = $^{12}/_{100}$, .003 = $^{3}/_{1000}$. **2.** A number written using base 10; a number containing a decimal point. —*adj.* **1.** Expressed or expressible as a decimal. **2. a.** Based on ten. **b.** Numbered or ordered by tens. [Med. Lat. *decimalis,* of tithes < Lat. *decimus,* tenth < *decem,* ten.] **—dec′i·mal·ly** *adv.*

decimal fraction *n.* A decimal (sense 1).

dec·i·mal·ize (dĕs′ə-mə-līz′) *tr.v.* **-ized, -iz·ing, -iz·es.** To change to a decimal system. **—dec′i·mal·i·za′tion** *n.*

decimal place *n.* The position of a digit to the right of a decimal point, usually identified by successive ascending ordinal numbers with the digit immediately to the right of the decimal point being first.

decimal point *n.* A period placed to the left of a decimal.

decimal system *n.* **1.** A number system using the base 10. **2.** A system of measurement in which all derived units are multiples of ten of fundamental units.

dec·i·mate (dĕs′ə-māt′) *tr.v.* **-mat·ed, -mat·ing, -mates. 1.** To destroy or kill a large part of. **2.** To select by lot and kill one in every ten of. [Lat. *decimare, decimat-* < *decimus,* tenth < *decem,* ten.] **—dec′i·ma′tion** *n.*

Usage: *Decimate* originally meant to kill every tenth person, a punishment sometimes inflicted by Roman commanders. The meaning has been extended to include the destruction of any large proportion of a group: *Famine decimated the population.* The Usage Panel accepts this extension but considers that *decimate* should not be used to describe the destruction of a single person, or an entire group, or any specified percentage other than one-tenth; avoid a sentence such as *The famine decimated 37 per cent of the population.*

dec·i·me·ter (dĕs′ə-mē′tər) *n.* One-tenth (10^{-1}) of a meter.

de·ci·pher (dĭ-sīʹfər) *tr.v.* **-phered, -pher·ing, -phers. 1.** To read or interpret (something ambiguous, obscure, or illegible). **2.** To convert from a code or cipher to plain text; decode. **—de·ciʹpher·a·ble** *adj.* **—de·ciʹpher·er** *n.* **—de·ciʹpher·ment** *n.*

de·ci·sion (dĭ-sĭzhʹən) *n.* **1.** The passing of judgment on an issue under consideration. **2.** The act of reaching a conclusion or making up one's mind. **3.** A conclusion or judgment reached or pronounced; verdict. **4.** Firmness of character or action; determination. **5.** In boxing, a victory won on points when no knockout has occurred. [ME *decisioun* < OFr. *decision* < Lat. *decisio* < *decidere,* to decide.]

de·ci·sive (dĭ-sīʹsĭv) *adj.* **1.** Having the power to decide; conclusive. **2.** Characterized by decision and firmness; resolute. **3.** Beyond doubt; unmistakable: *a decisive victory.* **—de·ciʹsive·ly** *adv.* **—de·ciʹsive·ness** *n.*

deck[1] (dĕk) *n.* **1.** *Naut.* A platform extending horizontally from one side of a ship to the other. **2.** A platform or surface similar to a ship's deck. **3. a.** A pack of playing cards. **b.** *Computer Sci.* A group of data processing cards. **4.** A tape deck. **5.** *Slang.* A packet of narcotics. *—tr.v.* **decked, deck·ing, decks. 1.** To furnish with a deck. **2.** To knock down: *decked him with one punch.* **—idioms. clear the deck.** To prepare for action. **hit the deck.** *Slang.* **1.** To get out of bed. **2.** To prepare for action. **3.** To fall or drop to a prone position. **on deck.** *Slang.* **1.** On hand; present. **2.** Waiting to take one's turn, esp. as a batter in baseball. [ME *dekke* < MDu. *dec,* covering.]

deck[2] (dĕk) *tr.v.* **decked, deck·ing, decks.** To clothe with finery; adorn: *decked out for a party.* [MDu. *dekken,* to cover.]

deck chair *n.* A folding chair that usually has arms and a leg rest.

deck hand *n.* A member of a ship's crew who works on deck.

deck·house (dĕkʹhousʹ) *n.* A superstructure on the upper deck of a ship.

deck·le (dĕkʹəl) *n.* **1.** A frame used in making paper by hand to form paper pulp into sheets of a desired size. **2.** A deckle edge. [G. *Deckel,* dim. of *Decke,* cover.]

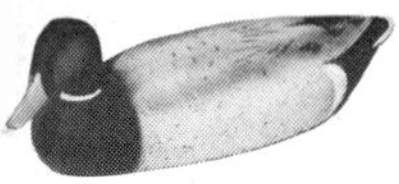

decoy

deckle edge *n.* The rough edge of handmade paper formed in a deckle. **—deckʹle-edgedʹ** *adj.*

deck tennis *n.* A game in which a small ring or quoit is tossed back and forth over a net.

de·claim (dĭ-klāmʹ) *v.* **-claimed, -claim·ing, -claims.** *—intr.* **1.** To deliver an elocutionary recitation. **2.** To speak loudly and vehemently; inveigh. *—tr.* To utter or recite with rhetorical effect. [ME *declamen* < Lat. *declamare* : *de-* (intensive) + *clamare,* to cry out.] **—de·claimʹer** *n.*

dec·la·ma·tion (dĕkʹlə-māʹshən) *n.* **1.** An elocutionary recitation. **2. a.** Vehement oratory. **b.** A harangue; tirade. [ME *declamacioun* < Lat. *declamatio* < *declamare,* to declaim.]

de·clam·a·to·ry (dĭ-klămʹə-tôrʹē, -tōrʹē) *adj.* **1.** Having the quality of a declamation. **2.** Pretentiously rhetorical; bombastic.

de·clar·ant (dĭ-klârʹənt) *n.* One who has signed a declaration of his intention to become a U.S. citizen.

dec·la·ra·tion (dĕkʹlə-rāʹshən) *n.* **1. a.** An explicit or formal statement or announcement. **b.** Such a statement in written form. **2.** The act or process of declaring. **3.** A statement of taxable goods or of properties subject to duty. **4.** *Law.* **a.** A formal statement by a plaintiff specifying the facts and circumstances constituting his cause of action. **b.** An unsworn statement of facts that is admissible as evidence. **5.** In certain card games, a bid, esp. the final bid of a hand.

de·clar·a·tive (dĭ-klârʹə-tĭv, -klărʹ-) also **de·clar·a·to·ry** (-tôrʹē, -tōrʹē) *adj.* Serving to declare or state. **—de·clarʹa·tive·ly** *adv.*

de·clare (dĭ-klârʹ) *v.* **-clared, -clar·ing, -clares.** *—tr.* **1.** To state officially or formally. **2.** To state with emphasis or authority; affirm. **3.** To reveal or manifest; prove. **4.** To make a full statement of (dutiable goods, for example). **5.** In bridge, to designate (a trump suit or no-trump) with the final bid of a hand. *—intr.* **1.** To make a declaration. **2.** To proclaim one's choice, opinion, or resolution: *declared against the bill's passage.* [ME *declaren* < OFr. *declarer* < Lat. *declarare* : *de-* (intensive) + *clarare,* to make clear < *clarus,* clear.] **—de·clarʹa·ble** *adj.* **—de·clarʹer** *n.*

de·class (dē-klăsʹ) *tr.v.* **-classed, -class·ing, -class·es.** To lower in class or status.

dé·clas·sé (dā′klă-sāʹ) *adj.* **1.** Lowered in rank or social position. **2.** Lacking high station or birth. [Fr., p.part. of *déclasser,* to lower in class : *de-,* down (< Lat. *dē-*) + *classe,* class < LLat. *classis.*]

de·clas·si·fy (dē-klăsʹə-fīʹ) *tr.v.* **-fied, -fy·ing, -fies.** To remove official security classification from (a document). **—de·clasʹsi·fiʹa·ble** *adj.* **—de·clasʹsi·fi·caʹtion** *n.*

de·clen·sion (dĭ-klĕnʹshən) *n.* **1.** *Ling.* **a.** In certain languages, the inflection of nouns, pronouns, and adjectives in categories such as case, number, and gender. **b.** A class of words of one language with the same or a similar system of inflections, as the first declension in Latin. **2.** A descending slope; descent. **3.** A decline or decrease; deterioration: *"States and empires have their periods of declension"* (Sterne). **4.** A deviation, as from a standard or practice. [ME *declenson* < OFr. *declinaison* < LLat. *declinatio,* grammatical declension < Lat., declination.] **—de·clenʹsion·al** *adj.*

dec·li·na·tion (dĕkʹlə-nāʹshən) *n.* **1.** A sloping or bending downward. **2.** A falling off, esp. from prosperity or vigor; decline. **3.** A deviation, as from a specific direction or standard. **4.** A refusal to accept. **5.** Magnetic declination. **6.** *Astron.* The angular distance to a point on the celestial sphere, measured north or south from the celestial equator along the hour circle to the point. [ME *declinacioun* < OFr. *declination* < Lat. *declinatio* < *declinare,* to turn aside. —see DECLINE.] **—decʹli·naʹtion·al** *adj.*

de·cline (dĭ-klīnʹ) *v.* **-clined, -clin·ing, -clines.** *—intr.* **1.** To refuse to do or accept something. **2. a.** To slope downward; descend. **b.** To bend downward; droop. **3.** To degrade or lower oneself; condescend. **4.** To deteriorate gradually; fail. **5. a.** To sink, as the setting sun. **b.** To draw to a gradual close; wane. *—tr.* **1.** To refuse (something). **2.** To cause to slope or bend downward. **3.** *Ling.* In certain languages, to give the inflected forms of (a noun, pronoun, or adjective). *—n.* **1.** The process or result of declining, esp. gradual deterioration. **2.** A downward movement. **3.** The period when something is tending toward an end. **4.** A downward slope; declivity. **5.** A disease, such as tuberculosis, that gradually weakens or wastes the body or a bodily part. [ME *declinen* < OFr. *decliner* < Lat. *declinare,* to turn aside : *de-,* away + *clinare,* to incline, bend.] **—de·clinʹa·ble** *adj.* **—de·clinʹer** *n.*

de·cliv·i·tous (dĭ-klĭvʹĭ-təs) *adj.* Rather steep.

de·cliv·i·ty (dĭ-klĭvʹĭ-tē) *n., pl.* **-ties.** A descending slope, as of a hill. [Lat. *declivitas* < *declivis,* sloping down : *de-,* down + *clivus,* slope.]

de·coct (dĭ-kŏktʹ) *tr.v.* **-coct·ed, -coct·ing, -cocts. 1.** To extract the flavor of by boiling. **2.** To concentrate; boil down. [ME *decocten,* to boil < *decoct,* boiled < Lat. *decoctus* < *decoquere,* to boil away : *de-* (intensive) + *coquere,* to cook.] **—de·cocʹtion** *n.*

de·code (dē-kōdʹ) *tr.v.* **-cod·ed, -cod·ing, -codes.** To convert from code into plain text. **—de·codʹer** *n.*

de·col·late[1] (dĭ-kŏlʹātʹ) *tr.v.* **-lat·ed, -lat·ing, -lates.** To behead. [Lat. *decollare, decollat-* : *de-,* off + *collum,* neck.] **—deʹcol·laʹtion** *n.*

de·col·late[2] (dĕkʹə-lātʹ, dē-kōʹlātʹ) *tr.v.* **-lat·ed, -lat·ing, -lates.** To separate the copies of. **—deʹcol·la·tor** *n.*

dé·colle·tage (dāʹkôl-täzhʹ) *n.* **1.** A low neckline on a garment. **2.** A décolleté garment. [Fr. < *décolleté,* décolleté.]

dé·colle·té (dāʹkôl-tāʹ) *adj.* **1.** Having a low neckline: *a décolleté dress.* **2.** Wearing a garment with a low neckline. [Fr., p.part. of *décolleter,* to cut a low neckline : *dé-,* off (< Lat. *de-*) + *collet,* collar, dim. of *col,* neck < OFr. < Lat. *collum.*]

de·col·o·nize (dē-kŏlʹə-nīzʹ) *tr.v.* **-nized, -niz·ing, -niz·es.** To free (a colony, for example) from dependent status. **—de·colʹo·ni·zaʹtion** *n.*

de·col·or·ant (dē-kŭlʹər-ənt) *n.* A bleaching agent.

de·col·or·ize (dē-kŭlʹə-rīzʹ) *tr.v.* **-ized, -iz·ing, -iz·es.** To remove the color from. **—de·colʹor·i·zaʹtion** *n.* **—de·colʹor·izʹer** *n.*

de·com·pose (dēʹkəm-pōzʹ) *v.* **-posed, -pos·ing, -pos·es.** *—tr.* **1.** To separate into component parts or basic elements. **2.** To cause to rot. *—intr.* **1.** To break down into component parts; disintegrate. **2.** To decay; putrefy. [Fr. *décomposer* : *dé-,* de- (< Lat.) + *composer,* to compose < OFr. —see COMPOSE.] **—deʹcom·posʹa·ble** *adj.* **—deʹcom·posʹer** *n.*

de·com·po·si·tion (dē-kŏmʹpə-zĭshʹən) *n.* **1.** The act or result of decomposing. **2. a.** *Chem.* Separation into constituents by chemical reaction. **b.** *Biol.* Organic decay. **—de·comʹpo·siʹtion·al** *adj.*

de·com·pound (dē-kŏmʹpoundʹ, dēʹkəm-poundʹ) *adj.* **1.** Compounded or consisting of things or parts that are already compound. **2.** Having or consisting of subdivided or compound leaflets: *a decompound leaf.*

de·com·press (dēʹkəm-prĕsʹ) *tr.v.* **-pressed, -press·ing, -press·es. 1.** To relieve of pressure. **2.** To bring (a person working in compressed air) back to normal air pressure.

de·com·pres·sion (dēʹkəm-prĕshʹən) *n.* **1.** The act or process of decompressing. **2.** A surgical procedure used to relieve pressure on an organ or part.

decompression sickness *n.* Caisson disease.

de·con·ges·tant (dēʹkən-jĕsʹtənt) *n.* A medication or treatment that breaks up congestion, as of the sinuses.

de·con·tam·i·nate (dēʹkən-tămʹə-nātʹ) *tr.v.* **-nat·ed, -nat·ing, -nates. 1.** To eliminate contamination in. **2.** To make safe by eliminating poisonous or otherwise harmful substances, such as noxious chemicals or radioactive material. **—deʹcon·tamʹi·nant** *n.* **—deʹcon·tamʹi·naʹtion** *n.*

de·con·trol (dēʹkən-trōlʹ) *tr.v.* **-trolled, -trol·ling, -trols.** To free from control, esp. from governmental control. **—deʹcon·trolʹ** *n.*

dé·cor also **de·cor** (dāʹkôrʹ, dā-kôrʹ) *n.* **1.** A decorative style or scheme, as of a room. **2.** A stage setting; scenery. [Fr. < *décorer,* to decorate < Lat. *decorare.*]

dec·o·rate (dĕkʹə-rātʹ) *tr.v.* **-rat·ed, -rat·ing, -rates. 1.** To furnish or adorn with fashionable or beautiful things. **2.** To confer a medal or other honor upon. [Lat. *decorare, decorat-* < *decus,* ornament.]

dec·o·ra·tion (dĕkʹə-rāʹshən) *n.* **1.** The act, process, technique, or art of decorating. **2.** An object or group of objects used to decorate. **3.** A medal, badge, or other emblem of honor.

Decoration Day *n.* Memorial Day.

dec•o•ra•tive (dĕk′ər-ə-tĭv, -ə-rā′-) *adj.* Serving to decorate; ornamental. **—dec′o•ra•tive•ly** *adv.* **—dec′o•ra•tive•ness** *n.*

dec•o•ra•tor (dĕk′ə-rā′tər) *n.* One that decorates, esp. an interior decorator.

dec•o•rous (dĕk′ər-əs, dĭ-kôr′əs, -kōr′-) *adj.* Characterized by or exhibiting decorum; proper. [Lat. *decorus* < *decor,* seemliness, beauty.] **—dec′o•rous•ly** *adv.* **—dec′o•rous•ness** *n.*

de•cor•ti•cate (dē-kôr′tĭ-kāt′) *tr.v.* **-cat•ed, -cat•ing, -cates. 1.** To remove the cortex from (an organ or structure), esp. as a surgical procedure. **2.** To remove the bark, husk, or outer layer from; peel. [Lat. *decorticare, decorticat-* : *de-,* off + *cortex,* bark, rind.] **—de•cor′ti•ca′tion** *n.* **—de•cor′ti•ca′tor** *n.*

de•co•rum (dĭ-kôr′əm, -kōr′-) *n.* **1.** Appropriateness of behavior or conduct; propriety. **2.** The conventions of polite behavior. **3.** In art and literature, something that is proper to the harmony, essence, or unity of a composition or to a subject, locale, time, or character being treated. [Lat. *decorum* < *decorus,* decorous.]

de•cou•page also **dé•cou•page** (dā′ko͞o-päzh′) *n.* **1.** The technique of decorating a surface with cutouts, as of paper. **2.** Something produced by decoupage. [Fr. < OFr. *decouper,* to cut out : *de-,* away (< Lat.) + *couper,* to cut < *coup,* stroke. —see COUP.]

de•cou•ple (dē-kŭp′əl) *tr.v.* **-pled, -pling, -ples. 1.** *Electronics.* To reduce or eliminate the coupling of circuits or mechanical parts. **2.** *Physics.* To decrease the seismic effect of (an explosion) by having it take place in an underground cavity. **—de•cou′pler** *n.*

de•coy (dē′koi′, dĭ-koi′) *n.* **1.** An enclosed place, such as a pond, into which wildfowl are lured for capture. **2.** A living or artificial bird or other animal used to entice game into a trap or within shooting range. **3.** A means used to mislead or lead into danger. *—tr.v.* (dĭ-koi′) **-coyed, -coy•ing, -coys.** To lure into danger or a trap by or as if by a decoy. [Poss. < Du. *de kooi,* the cage : *de,* the + *kooi,* cage < MDu. *cōie* < Lat. *cavea* < *cavus,* hollow.] **—de•coy′er** *n.*

de•crease (dĭ-krēs′) *intr. & tr.v.* **-creased, -creas•ing, -creas•es.** To grow or cause to grow gradually less or smaller, as in number, amount, or intensity. *—n.* (dē′krēs′). **1.** The act or process of decreasing. **2.** The amount by which something decreases. [ME *decresen* < OFr. *decreistre, decreiss-* < Lat. *decrescere* : *de-,* from, away + *crescere,* to grow.] **—de•creas′ing•ly** *adv.*

Synonyms: *decrease, reduce, lessen, dwindle, abate, diminish, shrink, subside.* These verbs mean to become smaller or less or to make something smaller. *Decrease* refers to gradual decline or making steadily smaller. *Reduce* emphasizes cutting down in size, time, cost, or rank. *Lessen* usually refers to decrease in number. *Dwindle* suggests decreasing bit by bit to a vanishing point. *Abate* stresses a decrease in quantity or strength and suggests there was originally too much. *Diminish* implies taking away or making or becoming perceptibly smaller by removal. *Shrink* applies specifically to reduction in original physical size. *Subside* implies decreasing to a more normal condition.

de•cree (dĭ-krē′) *n.* **1.** An authoritative order having the force of law. **2.** The judgment of a court of equity, admiralty, probate, or divorce. **3.** *Rom. Cath. Ch.* **a.** A doctrinal or disciplinary act of an ecumenical council. **b.** An administrative act applying or interpreting articles of canon law. *—v.* **-creed, -cree•ing, -crees.** *—tr.* To ordain, establish, or decide by decree. *—intr.* To issue a decree. [ME < OFr. *decret* < Lat. *decretum* < *decernere,* to decide : *de-,* away + *cernere,* to sift.] **—de•cree′a•ble** *adj.* **—de•cre′er** *n.*

de•cree-law (dĭ-krē′lô′) *n.* A decree having the force of a law enacted by a legislature but usually issued on the sole authority of an absolute ruler or the executive branch of a government.

dec•re•ment (dĕk′rə-mənt) *n.* **1.** The act or process of decreasing or becoming gradually less. **2.** The amount lost by gradual diminution or waste. **3.** *Math.* The amount by which a variable is decreased; negative increment. **4.** *Computer Sci.* A specific part of an instruction word. [Lat. *decrementum* < *decrescere,* to decrease.] **—dec′re•men′tal** (-mĕn′tl) *adj.*

de•crep•it (dĭ-krĕp′ĭt) *adj.* Weakened by old age, illness, or hard use; broken-down. [ME < OFr. < Lat. *decrepitus,* very old : *de-,* from, without + *crepitus,* p.part. of *crepare,* to rattle.] **—de•crep′it•ly** *adv.*

de•crep•i•tate (dĭ-krĕp′ĭ-tāt′) *v.* **-tat•ed, -tat•ing, -tates.** *—tr.* To roast or calcine (crystals or salts) until they emit a crackling sound or until crackling stops. *—intr.* To make a crackling sound when roasted. [Med. Lat. *decrepitare, decrepitat-* : Lat. *de-* (intensive) + *crepitare,* freq. of *crepare,* to crack.] **—de•crep′i•ta′tion** *n.*

de•crep•i•tude (dĭ-krĕp′ĭ-to͞od′, -tyo͞od′) *n.* The condition of being decrepit.

de•cre•scen•do (dā′krə-shĕn′dō, dē′-) *Mus.* *—n., pl.* **-dos. 1.** A gradual decrease in force or loudness. **2.** A passage marked or performed in a decrescendo. *—adj.* Gradually diminishing in force or loudness. *—adv.* With a decrescendo. [Ital., decreasing < Lat. *decrescendum,* gerund of *decrescere,* to decrease.]

de•cres•cent (dĭ-krĕs′ənt) *adj.* Becoming gradually less; waning. [Lat. *decrescens, decrescent-,* pr.part. of *decrescere,* to decrease.]

de•cre•tal (dĭ-krēt′l) *n.* *Rom. Cath. Ch.* **1.** A decree, esp. a papal letter giving a decision on a point or question of canon law. **2. Decretals.** The body of papal laws and decrees forming a part of canon law. [ME < OFr. < Med. Lat. (*epistola*) *decretalis,* (letter) of decree < Lat. *decretum,* decree.]

de•cre•tive (dĭ-krē′tĭv) *adj.* Having the force of a decree.

dec•re•to•ry (dĕk′rĭ-tôr′ē, -tōr′ē, dĭ-krē′tə-rē) *adj.* Of or resulting from a decree.

de•crim•i•nal•ize (dē-krĭm′ə-nə-līz′) *tr.v.* **-ized, -iz•ing, -iz•es.** To make no longer illegal or criminal. **—de•crim′i•nal•i•za′tion** *n.*

de•cry (dĭ-krī′) *tr.v.* **-cried, -cry•ing, -cries. 1.** To belittle or disparage openly. **2.** To depreciate (currency, for example) by official proclamation or by rumor. [Fr. *décrier* < OFr. *descrier* : *des-,* down (< Lat. *de-*) + *crier,* to cry. —see CRY.] **—de•cri′er** *n.*

Synonyms: *decry, disparage, belittle.* These verbs mean to express a low valuation of something or someone. *Decry* implies making public objection by condemnation. *Disparage* means to express slight regard for another's accomplishments, often by indirection. *Belittle* implies open depreciation.

de•cum•bent (dĭ-kŭm′bənt) *adj.* **1.** Lying down; reclining. **2.** *Bot.* Lying or growing along the ground but erect at or near the apex: *decumbent stems.* [Lat. *decumbens, decumbent-,* pr.part. of *decumbere,* to lie down.] **—de•cum′bence** (-bəns), **de•cum′ben•cy** (-bən-se) *n.*

dec•u•ple (dĕk′yə-pəl) *adj.* **1.** Ten times as great; tenfold. **2.** In groups of ten. [ME < OFr. < LLat. *decuplus* < Lat. *decem,* ten.]

de•cur•rent (dĭ-kûr′ənt, -kŭr′-) *adj.* Extending downward from the base along a stem: *decurrent leaves.* [Lat. *decurrens, decurrent-,* pr.part. of *decurrere,* to run down : *de-,* down + *currere,* to run.] **—de•cur′rent•ly** *adv.*

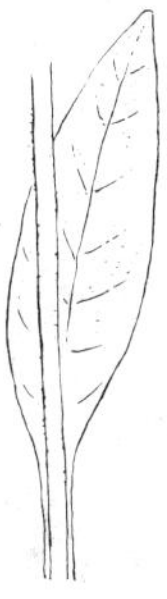

decurrent
Decurrent leaf

de•cus•sate (dĭ-kŭs′āt′, dĕk′ə-sāt′) *tr. & intr.v.* **-sat•ed, -sat•ing, -sates.** To cross so as to form an X; intersect. *—adj.* **1.** Intersected or crossed in the form of an X. **2.** *Bot.* Arranged on a stem in opposite pairs at right angles to those above or below. [Lat. *decussare, decussat-* < *decussis,* the number ten, intersection (from the Romans' use of X for the numeral 10) : *decem,* ten + *as,* unit.] **—de•cus′sate′ly** *adv.*

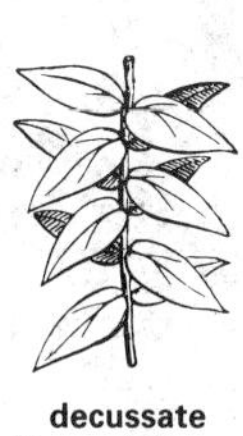

decussate
Decussate leaves

dec•us•sa•tion (dĕk′ə-sā′shən, dē′kə-) *n.* **1.** A crossing in the shape of an X. **2.** An X-shaped crossing of nerve fibers connecting dissimilar parts on the two sides of the spinal cord or brain.

de•dans (də-däN′) *n., pl.* **dedans** (-däN′, -däNz′). **1.** A screened gallery for spectators at the service end of a court-tennis court. **2.** The spectators at a court-tennis match. [Fr. < *dedans,* inside : *de,* from (< Lat.) + *dans,* within < LLat. *deintus* (*de,* from + *intus,* within).]

ded•i•cate (dĕd′ĭ-kāt′) *tr.v.* **-cat•ed, -cat•ing, -cates. 1.** To set apart for a deity or for religious purposes; consecrate. **2.** To set apart for a special use: *dedicated his money to scientific research.* **3.** To commit (oneself) to a particular course of thought or action: *dedicated herself to helping the poor.* **4.** To address or inscribe (a literary work, for example) to someone as a mark of respect or affection. **5. a.** To open (a building, for example) to public use. **b.** To unveil (a monument). [ME *dedicaten* < Lat. *dedicare* : *de-,* apart + *dicare,* to say.] **—ded′i•cat′ed•ly** (-kā′tĭd-lē) *adv.* **—ded′i•ca•tee′** (-kə-tē′) *n.* **—ded′i•ca′tive, ded′i•ca•to′ry** (-kə-tôr′ē, -tōr′ē) *adj.* **—ded′i•ca′tor** *n.*

ded•i•ca•tion (dĕd′ĭ-kā′shən) *n.* **1.** The act of dedicating or the state of being dedicated. **2.** A note prefixed to a literary, artistic, or musical composition dedicating it to someone in token of affection or esteem. **3.** A rite or ceremony of dedicating.

de•dif•fer•en•ti•a•tion (dē′dĭf-ə-rĕn′shē-ā′shən) *n.* *Biol.* The loss of specialized cellular form, esp. prior to redifferentiation.

de•duce (dĭ-do͞os′, -dyo͞os′) *tr.v.* **-duced, -duc•ing, -duc•es. 1.** To reach (a conclusion) by reasoning. **2.** To infer from a general principle; reason deductively. **3.** To trace the origin or derivation of. [ME *deducen* < Lat. *deducere,* to lead away : *de-,* away + *ducere,* to lead.] **—de•duc′i•ble** *adj.*

de•duct (dĭ-dŭkt′) *v.* **-duct•ed, -duct•ing, -ducts.** *—tr.* **1.** To take away (a quantity) from another; subtract. **2.** To derive by deduction; deduce. *—intr.* To detract; diminish: *Bad plumbing deducts from the value of his house.* [Lat. *deducere, deduct-,* to lead away. —see DEDUCE.]

de•duct•i•ble (dĭ-dŭk′tə-bəl) *adj.* **1.** Capable of being deducted. **2.** Allowable as a tax deduction. **—de•duct′i•bil′i•ty** *n.*

de•duc•tion (dĭ-dŭk′shən) *n.* **1.** The act of deducting; subtraction. **2.** An amount that is or may be deducted: *tax deductions.* **3. a.** The act of deducing; the drawing of a conclusion by reasoning. **b.** *Logic.* The process of reasoning in which a conclusion follows necessarily from the stated premises; inference by reasoning from the general to the specific. **c.** *Logic.* A conclusion reached by this process.

de·duc·tive (dĭ-dŭk′tĭv) *adj.* **1.** Of or based on deduction. **2.** Involving deduction in reasoning. **—de·duc′tive·ly** *adv.*
dee (dē) *n.* The letter *d.*
deed (dēd) *n.* **1.** An act. **2.** A feat; exploit. **3.** Action or performance in general, esp. as distinguished from words. **4.** *Law.* A document sealed as an instrument of bond, contract, or conveyance, esp. pertaining to property. *—tr.v.* **deed·ed, deed·ing, deeds.** To transfer by means of a deed. [ME *dede* < OE *dǣd.*]
deem (dēm) *v.* **deemed, deem·ing, deems.** *—tr.* To judge; consider: *We deem it advisable to wait.* *—intr.* To have an opinion; suppose. [ME *demen* < OE *dēman.*]
deep (dēp) *adj.* **-er, -est. 1. a.** Extending far downward below a surface: *a deep hole.* **b.** Extending far backward from front to rear: *a deep closet.* **c.** Extending far inward from an outer surface: *a deep cut.* **d.** Extending far from side to side from a center: *a deep yard surrounding the house.* **e.** Far distant down or in: *deep in the woods.* **f.** Coming from or penetrating to a depth: *a deep sigh.* **2.** Extending a specific distance in a given direction: *snow four feet deep.* **3.** Far distant in time or space: *deep in the future.* **4. a.** Difficult to penetrate or understand; recondite: *a deep theory.* **b.** Of a mysterious or obscure nature: *ancient and deep tribal rites.* **c.** Very learned or intellectual; wise: *a deep intellect.* **d.** Very cunning or crafty: *deep political machinations.* **5. a.** Of a grave or extreme nature: *deep trouble.* **b.** Very absorbed or involved: *deep in thought.* **c.** Showing strong feelings; profound: *a deep love.* **6.** Rich and vivid in shade: *a deep red.* **7.** Low in pitch; resonant: *a deep voice.* *—adv.* **1.** To a great depth; deeply: *dig deep; feelings that run deep.* **2.** Well on in time; late: *worked deep into the night.* *—n.* **1.** A deep place in land or in a body of water, esp. in the ocean. **2. a.** The extent of encompassing time or space. **b.** A vast, immeasurable extent; abyss. **3.** The most intense or extreme part: *the deep of night.* **4.** The ocean. **5.** A distance estimated in fathoms between successive marks on a sounding line. ***—idioms.*** **go off the deep end.** To act recklessly or hysterically. **in deep water.** In trouble. [ME *dep* < OE *dēop.*] **—deep′ly** *adv.* **—deep′ness** *n.*
deep·en (dē′pən) *tr. & intr.v.* **-ened, -en·ing, -ens.** To make or become deep or deeper.
Deep·freeze (dēp′frēz′). A trademark for a refrigerator designed to freeze food for long periods.
deep-fry (dēp′frī′) *tr.v.* **-fried, -fry·ing, -fries.** To fry by immersing in a deep pan of fat or oil.
deep-root·ed (dēp′ro͞o′tĭd, -ro͝ot′ĭd) *adj.* Firmly implanted.
deep-sea (dēp′sē′) *adj.* Pertaining to deep parts of the sea.
deep-seat·ed (dēp′sē′tĭd) *adj.* Deeply rooted; ingrained.
deep-six (dēp′sĭks′) *tr.v.* **-sixed, -six·ing, -six·es.** *Slang.* **1.** To toss overboard. **2.** To toss out; get rid of: *deep-sixed the incriminating papers.*
deep space *n.* The regions beyond the moon, encompassing interplanetary, interstellar, and intergalactic space.
deep structure *n. Ling.* An underlying structure that determines the semantic interpretation of a sentence.

deer

deer (dîr) *n., pl.* **deer. 1.** Any of various hoofed ruminant mammals of the family Cervidae, characteristically having deciduous antlers borne only by the males. **2.** Any of various smaller deerlike mammals, such as the mouse deer. [ME *der,* wild animal < OE *dēor.*]
deer fly *n.* Any of various blood-sucking flies of the genus *Chrysops,* having dark bars or spots on the wings.
deer grass *n.* Meadow beauty.

deerhound
Scottish deerhound

deer·hound (dîr′hound′) *n.* A dog of a breed developed in Scotland, resembling a greyhound but larger and having a wiry coat.
deer mouse *n.* Any of various New World mice of the genus *Peromyscus,* having large ears, white feet and underparts, and a long tail. [From its deerlike agility.]

deer mouse

deer·skin (dîr′skĭn′) *n.* **1.** Leather made from the hide of a deer. **2.** A garment made from deerskin.
deer·stalk·er (dîr-stô′kər) *n.* A tight-fitting hat with visors in the front and back, originally worn by hunters.
de-es·ca·late (dē-ĕs′kə-lāt′) *v.* **-lat·ed, -lat·ing, -lates.** *—tr.* To decrease the size, scope, or intensity of (a war, for example). *—intr.* To decrease or diminish in size, scope, or intensity: *The birth rate was de-escalating.* **—de-es′ca·la′tion** *n.* **—de-es′ca·la·tor′y** (-lə-tôr′ē, -tōr′ē) *adj.*
deet (dēt) *n.* A colorless, oily liquid, $C_{12}H_{17}NO$, that has a mild odor and is used as an insect repellent. [Pronunciation of *d.t.,* abbr. of DIETHYL TOLUAMIDE.]
de·face (dĭ-fās′) *tr.v.* **-faced, -fac·ing, -fac·es. 1.** To spoil or mar the surface or appearance of; disfigure. **2.** To impair the usefulness, value, or influence of. **3.** To efface or obliterate. [ME *defacen* < OFr. *desfacier* : *des-,* de- (< Lat *de-*) + *face,* face. —see FACE.] **—de·face′a·ble** *adj.* **—de·face′ment** *n.* **—de·fac′er** *n.*
de fac·to (dĭ făk′tō, dā) *adv.* In reality or fact; actually. *—adj.* **1.** Actual. **2.** Actually exercising power. [Lat., according to the fact.]
de·fal·cate (dĭ-făl′kāt′, -fôl′-, dĕf′əl-) *intr.v.* **-cat·ed, -cat·ing, -cates.** To misuse funds; embezzle. [Med. Lat. *defalcare, defalcat-* : Lat. *de-,* off + Lat. *falx,* sickle.] **—de′fal·ca′tion** (dē′făl-kā′shən, -fôl-, dĕf′əl-) *n.* **—de·fal′ca′tor** *n.*
def·a·ma·tion (dĕf′ə-mā′shən) *n.* Slander or libel; calumny. **—de·fam′a·to′ry** (dĭ-făm′ə-tôr′ē, -tōr′ē) *adj.*
de·fame (dĭ-fām′) *tr.v.* **-famed, -fam·ing, -fames. 1.** To attack the good name of by slander or libel. **2.** *Archaic.* To disgrace. [ME *defamen* < OFr. *defamer* < Lat. *diffamare* : *dis-,* apart + *fama,* reputation.] **—de·fam′er** *n.*
de·fault (dĭ-fôlt′) *n.* **1.** A failure to perform a task or fulfill an obligation, esp. failure to meet a financial obligation. **2.** Failure to make a required appearance in court. **3.** The failure of one or more competitors or teams to participate in a contest: *win by default.* *—v.* **-fault·ed, -fault·ing, -faults.** *—intr.* **1.** To fail to do what is required. **2.** To fail to pay money when it is due. **3.** *Law.* **a.** To fail to appear in court when summoned. **b.** To lose a case by not appearing. **4.** To fail to compete in or complete a scheduled contest. *—tr.* **1.** To fail to perform or pay. **2.** *Law.* To lose (a case) by failing to appear in court. **3.** To fail to take part in or complete (a contest, for example). ***—idiom.*** **in default of.** Through the failure, absence, or lack of. [ME *defaute* < OFr. < VLat. **defallita* : Lat. *de-* (intensive) + *fallere,* to fail.] **—de·fault′er** *n.*
de·fea·sance (dĭ-fē′zəns) *n.* **1.** An annulment or rendering void. **2.** The voiding of a contract or deed. **3.** A clause within a contract or deed providing for annulment. [ME *defesaunce* < AN < OFr. *defesance* < *defesant,* pr.part. of *desfaire,* to destroy. —see DEFEAT.]
de·fea·si·ble (dĭ-fē′zə-bəl) *adj.* Capable of being annulled or terminated. **—de·fea′si·bil′i·ty, de·fea′si·ble·ness** *n.*
de·feat (dĭ-fēt′) *tr.v.* **-feat·ed, -feat·ing, -feats. 1.** To win victory over; beat. **2.** To prevent the success of; thwart: *defeat one's purpose.* **3.** *Law.* To annul or make void. *—n.* **1.** The act of defeating or state of being defeated. **2.** Failure to win. **3.** A coming to naught; frustration. **4.** *Law.* The act of making null and void. [ME *defeten* < *defet,* disfigured < OFr. *desfait,* p.part. of *desfaire,* to destroy < Med. Lat. *disfacere* : Lat. *dis-,* asunder + *facere,* to do.] **—de·feat′er** *n.*

Synonyms: *defeat, conquer, vanquish, beat, rout, subdue, subjugate, overcome.* These verbs mean to get the better of an adversary. *Defeat,* the most general, does not necessarily imply finality of outcome. *Conquer* suggests decisive widescale victory. *Vanquish* emphasizes total and final mastery. *Beat,* less formal, is often the equivalent of *defeat,* though *beat* may convey greater emphasis. *Rout* implies not only complete victory but also putting an adversary to flight. *Subdue* suggests mastery and control by suppression or taming. *Subjugate* more strongly implies making an opponent subservient. *Overcome* stresses the importance of the conquest to the victor's well-being and often implies courage and perseverance.

de·feat·ism (dĭ-fē′tĭz′əm) *n.* Acceptance of or resignation to the prospect of defeat. **—de·feat′ist** *n.*
def·e·cate (dĕf′ĭ-kāt′) *v.* **-cat·ed, -cat·ing, -cates.** *—intr.* To void feces from the bowels. *—tr.* To clarify (a chemical solution). [Lat. *defaecare, defaecat-* : *de-,* away + *faex,* dregs.] **—def′e·ca′tion** *n.* **—def′e·ca′tor** *n.*
de·fect (dē′fĕkt′, dĭ-fĕkt′) *n.* **1.** The lack of something necessary or desirable for completion or perfection; deficiency. **2.** An imperfection; fault. *—intr.v.* (dĭ-fĕkt′) **-fect·ed, -fect·ing, -fects.** To leave, without consent or permission, an allegiance that one had espoused or acknowledged. [ME < Lat. *defectus* < p.part. of *deficere,* to depart, fail : *de-,* from + *facere,* to do.] **—de·fec′tion** *n.* **—de·fec′tor** *n.*
de·fec·tive (dĭ-fĕk′tĭv) *adj.* **1.** Having a defect; faulty. **2.** *Gram.* Lacking one or more of the inflected forms normal for a particular category of word, as the verb *may* in English. **3.** Of subnormal intelligence. *—n.* Someone physically or mentally incapacitated. **—de·fec′tive·ly** *adv.* **—de·fec′tive·ness** *n.*
de·fence (dĭ-fĕns′) *n. & v. Chiefly Brit.* Variant of **defense.**
de·fend (dĭ-fĕnd′) *v.* **-fend·ed, -fend·ing, -fends.** *—tr.* **1.** To protect from danger, attack, or harm; guard. **2.** To support or maintain, as by argument or action; justify. **3.** *Law.* **a.** To represent (the defendant) in a civil or criminal case. **b.** To contest (a legal action or claim). *—intr.* To make a defense. [ME *defenden* < OFr. *defendre* < Lat. *defendere,* to ward off.] **—de·fend′a·ble** *adj.* **—de·fend′er** *n.*

Synonyms: *defend, protect, guard, preserve, shield, safeguard.* These verbs mean to make safe from danger or attack. *Defend* implies use of countermeasures in repelling an actual attack. *Protect* suggests providing a cover to repel discomfort, injury, or attack. *Guard* suggests keeping watch over a person or thing. *Preserve* implies protective measures to maintain something as it is for an extended period. *Shield* suggests protection in the form of something or someone placed between the threat and the threatened. *Safeguard* stresses protection against potential or less imminent danger, often by preventive action.

de·fen·dant (dĭ-fĕn′dənt) *n. Law.* One against whom an action is brought.
de·fen·es·tra·tion (dē-fĕn′ĭ-strā′shən) *n.* An act of throwing something or someone out of a window. [DE- + Lat. *fenestra,* window.]
de·fense (dĭ-fĕns′) *n.* **1.** The act of defending against attack, danger, or injury; protection. **2.** Something that defends or protects. **3.** *Psychoanal.* A defense mechanism. **4.** An argument in support or justification of something. **5.** *Law.* **a.** The action of the defendant in opposition to complaints against him. **b.** The defendant and his legal counsel. **6.** The

science or art of defending oneself; self-defense. **7.** *Sports.* The team or those players on the team attempting to stop the opposition from scoring. —*tr.v.* **-fensed, -fens·ing, -fens·es.** *Sports.* To attempt to stop (the opposition) from scoring. [ME < OFr. < Lat. *defensa* < fem. p.part. of *defendere,* to ward off.] **—de·fense'less** *adj.* **—de·fense'less·ly** *adv.* **—de·fense'less·ness** *n.*

defense mechanism *n.* **1.** *Biol.* A reaction of an organism used in self-defense, as against germs. **2.** *Psychoanal.* A usually involuntary mental mechanism, such as repression or projection, that protects an individual from shame, anxiety, or loss of self-esteem.

de·fen·si·ble (dĭ-fĕn'sə-bəl) *adj.* Capable of being defended, protected, or justified. **—de·fen'si·bil'i·ty, de·fen'si·ble·ness** *n.* **—de·fen'si·bly** *adv.*

de·fen·sive (dĭ-fĕn'sĭv) *adj.* **1.** Intended or appropriate for defense. **2.** Done for defense. **3.** Of or pertaining to defense. —*n.* **1.** A means of defense. **2.** An attitude of defense. **—de·fen'sive·ly** *adv.* **—de·fen'sive·ness** *n.*

de·fer[1] (dĭ-fûr') *v.* **-ferred, -fer·ring, -fers.** —*tr.* **1.** To put off until a future time; postpone: *deferred writing until now.* **2.** To postpone the induction of (one eligible for the military draft). —*intr.* To procrastinate; delay. [ME *differren* < OFr. *diferer* < Lat. *differre.* —see DIFFER.] **—de·fer'ra·ble** *adj.* **—de·fer'rer** *n.*

de·fer[2] (dĭ-fûr') *intr.v.* **-ferred, -fer·ring, -fers.** To comply with or submit to the wishes, opinion, or decision of another: *deferred to his mother.* [ME *deferen* < OFr. *defere* < Lat. *deferre,* to carry away, bring to : *de-,* away + *ferre,* to carry.] **—de·fer'rer** *n.*

def·er·ence (dĕf'ər-əns, dĕf'rəns) *n.* **1.** Submission or courteous yielding to the opinion, wishes, or judgment of another. **2.** Courteous respect.

def·er·ent[1] (dĕf'ər-ənt, dĕf'rənt) *adj.* Showing deference; deferential.

def·er·ent[2] (dĕf'ər-ənt, dĕf'rənt) *adj.* **1.** Carrying down or away. **2.** Adapted to carry or transport. [Lat. *deferens, deferent-,* pr.part. of *deferre,* to carry away. —see DEFER[2].]

def·er·en·tial (dĕf'ə-rĕn'shəl) *adj.* Marked by deference: *a deferential attitude.* **—def'er·en'tial·ly** *adv.*

de·fer·ment (dĭ-fûr'mənt) also **de·fer·ral** (-fûr'əl) *n.* The act of delaying or putting off; postponement.

de·ferred (dĭ-fûrd') *adj.* **1.** Postponed or delayed. **2.** With benefits or payments withheld until a future date. **3.** Having had one's compulsory military service postponed.

de·fer·ves·cence (dē'fər-vĕs'əns) *n.* The abatement of a fever. [< Lat. *defervescens, defervescent-,* pr.part. of *defervescere,* to stop boiling : *de-,* off, away + *fervescere,* to begin to boil < *fervēre,* to boil.]

de·fi·ance (dĭ-fī'əns) *n.* **1.** Bold resistance to an opposing force or authority. **2.** Intentionally provocative behavior or attitude. [ME *defiaunce* < OFr. *desfiance* < *desfier,* to defy.]

de·fi·ant (dĭ-fī'ənt) *adj.* Marked by defiance. **—de·fi'ant·ly** *adv.*

de·fib·ril·late (dē-fĭb'rə-lāt') *tr.v.* **-lat·ed, -lat·ing, -lates.** To stop the fibrillating of (a heart). **—de·fib'ril·la'tion** *n.* **—de·fib'ril·la'tive** *adj.* **—de·fib'ril·la'tor** *n.* **—de·fib'ril·la·to'ry** (-lə-tôr'ē, -tōr'ē) *adj.*

de·fi·cien·cy (dĭ-fĭsh'ən-sē) *n., pl.* **-cies.** **1.** The quality or condition of being deficient. **2.** A lack or shortage; insufficiency.

deficiency disease *n.* A disease, as rickets or scurvy, caused by a dietary deficiency of specific vitamins and minerals.

de·fi·cient (dĭ-fĭsh'ənt) *adj.* **1.** Lacking an essential quality or element. **2.** Inadequate in amount or degree; insufficient. [Lat. *deficiens, deficient-,* pr.part. of *deficere,* to fail. —see DEFECT.] **—de·fi'cient·ly** *adv.*

def·i·cit (dĕf'ĭ-sĭt) *n.* The amount by which something, as a sum of money, falls short of the required or expected amount; shortage. [Fr. *déficit* < Lat. *deficit,* it is lacking.]

deficit spending *n.* The spending of public funds obtained by borrowing.

def·i·lade (dĕf'ə-lād', -läd') *tr.v.* **-lad·ed, -lad·ing, -lades.** To arrange (fortifications) so as to give protection from enfilading and other fire. —*n.* The act or procedure of defilading. [DE- + (EN)FILADE.]

de·file[1] (dĭ-fīl') *tr.v.* **-filed, -fil·ing, -files.** **1.** To make filthy or dirty; pollute. **2.** To render impure; corrupt. **3.** To profane or sully (a good name, for example). **4.** To make unclean or unfit for ceremonial use; desecrate. **5.** To violate the chastity of. [ME *defilen,* blend of *filen,* to defile (< OE *fȳlan*) and *defoulen,* to injure < OFr. *defouler* : *de-,* down (< Lat.) + *fouler,* to trample. —see FULL[2].] **—de·file'ment** *n.* **—de·fil'er** *n.* **—de·fil'ing·ly** *adv.*

de·file[2] (dĭ-fīl') *intr.v.* **-filed, -fil·ing, -files.** To march in single file or in files or columns. —*n.* **1.** A narrow gorge or pass that restricts lateral movement, as of troops. **2.** A march in a line or lines. [Fr. *défiler* : *dé-,* off (< Lat. *de-*) + *filer,* to march in files < OFr., to spin < LLat. *filare* < Lat. *filum,* thread.]

de·fine (dĭ-fīn') *v.* **-fined, -fin·ing, -fines.** —*tr.* **1.** To state the precise meaning of (a word or sense of a word, for example). **2.** To describe the nature or basic qualities of; explain: *define the properties of a new drug.* **3.** To delineate the outline or form of: *a shape defined by a line.* **4.** To specify distinctly: *define the weapons to be used in limited warfare.* **5.** To serve to distinguish; characterize. —*intr.* To make a definition. [ME *diffinen* < OFr. *definer* < Lat. *definire,* to limit : *de-,* off + *finis,* end.] **—de·fin'a·bil'i·ty** *n.* **—de·fin'a·ble** *adj.* **—de·fin'a·bly** *adv.* **—de·fine'ment** *n.* **—de·fin'er** *n.*

de·fin·i·en·dum (dĭ-fĭn'ē-ĕn'dəm) *n., pl.* **-da** (-də). A word or expression that is defined by a definiens. [Lat., neuter gerund. of *definire,* to define.]

de·fin·i·ens (dĭ-fĭn'ē-ĕnz') *n., pl.* **-fin·i·en·ti·a** (-fĭn'ē-ĕn'shē-ə, -shə). The word or words serving to define another word or expression, as in a dictionary entry. [Lat., pr.part. of *definire,* to define.]

def·i·nite (dĕf'ə-nĭt) *adj.* **1.** Having distinct limits: *definite restrictions on liquor sales.* **2.** Known positively; certain: *a definite victory.* **3.** Clearly defined; precise and explicit: *a definite statement of the terms of the will.* **4.** *Gram.* Limiting or particularizing. **5.** *Bot.* **a.** Of a specified number not exceeding 20, as certain floral organs, esp. stamens. **b.** Cymose; determinate. [ME *diffinite* < Lat. *definitus,* p.part. of *definire,* to define.] **—def'i·nite·ly** *adv.* **—def'i·nite·ness** *n.*

definite article *n. Gram.* The article *the,* which restricts or particularizes the noun or noun phrase following it.

definite integral *n.* The limit of sums with terms of the form $f(x_i)\Delta x_i$, where f is a function defined in the interval between two numbers a and b, Δx_i is the length of one of several intervals into which the interval from a to b is divided, x_i is a number in that interval, and the limit is taken as the lengths of the subintervals become smaller.

def·i·ni·tion (dĕf'ə-nĭsh'ən) *n.* **1.** The act of stating a precise meaning or significance. **2.** The statement of the meaning of a word, phrase, or term. **3.** The act of making clear and distinct: *a definition of one's intentions.* **4.** The state of being closely outlined or determined. **5.** A determination of outline, extent, or limits: *the definition of a nation's authority.* **6.** The degree of clarity with which a televised image is received or a radio receives a given station. **7.** The clarity of detail in an optically produced image, as a photograph, effected by a combination of resolution and contrast. [ME *diffinicioun* < OFr. *definition* < Lat. *definitio* < *definire,* to define.] **—def'i·ni'tion·al** *adj.*

de·fin·i·tive (dĭ-fĭn'ĭ-tĭv) *adj.* **1.** Precisely defining or outlining; explicit. **2.** Determining finally; decisive: *authority that has been influential but not definitive.* **3.** Authoritative and complete: *a definitive biography.* —*n. Gram.* A word that defines or limits, such as the definite article or a demonstrative pronoun. **—de·fin'i·tive·ly** *adv.* **—de·fin'i·tive·ness** *n.*

de·fin·i·tude (dĭ-fĭn'ĭ-to͞od', -tyo͞od') *n.* The quality of being definite or exact; precision.

def·la·grate (dĕf'lə-grāt') *intr. & tr.v.* **-grat·ed, -grat·ing, -grates.** To burn or cause to burn with great heat and intense light. [Lat. *deflagrare, deflagrat-* : *de-* (intensive) + *flagrare,* to burn.] **—def'la·gra'tion** *n.*

de·flate (dĭ-flāt') *v.* **-flat·ed, -flat·ing, -flates.** —*tr.* **1. a.** To release contained air or gas from. **b.** To collapse by releasing contained air or gas. **2.** To reduce or lessen the confidence, pride, self-esteem, or certainty of. **3.** *Econ.* To reduce the value or amount of (currency), effecting a decline in prices. —*intr.* To be or become deflated. [DE- + (IN)FLATE.] **—de·fla'tor** *n.*

de·fla·tion (dĭ-flā'shən) *n.* **1.** The act of deflating or the condition of being deflated. **2.** *Econ.* A reduction in available currency and credit that results in a decrease in the general price level. **—de·fla'tion·ar'y** (-shə-nĕr'ē) *adj.* **—de·fla'tion·ist** *n.*

de·flect (dĭ-flĕkt') *intr. & tr.v.* **-flect·ed, -flect·ing, -flects.** To turn aside or cause to turn aside; swerve. [Lat. *deflectere* : *de-,* away + *flectere,* to bend.] **—de·flect'a·ble** *adj.* **—de·flec'tive** *adj.* **—de·flec'tor** *n.*

de·flec·tion (dĭ-flĕk'shən) *n.* **1.** The act of deflecting or the condition of being deflected. **2.** Deviation or the amount of deviation. **3.** The deviation from zero shown by the indicator of a measuring instrument. **4.** The movement of a structure or structural part as a result of stress.

de·flexed (dĭ-flĕkst', dē'flĕkst') *adj. Bot.* Bent or turned downward at a sharp angle: *deflexed petals.* [< Lat. *deflexus,* p.part. of *deflectere,* to deflect.]

de·flex·ion (dĭ-flĕk'shən) *n. Chiefly Brit.* Variant of **deflection.**

def·lo·ra·tion (dĕf'lə-rā'shən) *n.* The act of deflowering. [ME *defloracioun* < LLat. *defloratio* < *deflorare,* to deflower.]

de·flow·er (dē-flou'ər) *tr.v.* **-ered, -er·ing, -ers.** **1.** To rupture the hymen of (a virgin) by sexual intercourse. **2.** To destroy the innocence of; violate. **3.** To spoil the appearance or nature of; mar. [ME *deflouren* < OFr. *deflorer* < LLat. *deflorare* : Lat. *de-,* away + Lat. *flos,* flower.] **—de·flow'er·er** *n.*

de·fo·cus (dē-fō'kəs) *tr.v.* **-cused, -cus·ing, -cus·es** also **-cussed, -cus·sing, -cus·ses.** To cause (a beam or a lens) to deviate from an accurate focus. —*n.* The result of defocusing.

de·fog (dē-fôg', -fŏg') *tr.v.* **-fogged, -fog·ging, -fogs.** To remove fog from. **—de·fog'ger** *n.*

de·fo·li·ant (dē-fō'lē-ənt) *n.* A chemical sprayed or dusted on plants to cause the leaves to fall off.

de·fo·li·ate (dē-fō'lē-āt') *v.* **-at·ed, -at·ing, -ates.** —*tr.* **1.** To deprive (a tree or other plant) of leaves. **2.** To cause the leaves of (a tree or other plant) to fall off, esp. by the use of a chemical spray or dust. —*intr.* To lose foliage. [LLat. *defoliare, defoliat-* : Lat. *de-*, off + Lat. *folium,* leaf.] —**de·fo'li·ate** (-ĭt) *adj.* —**de·fo'li·a'tion** *n.* —**de·fo'li·a'tor** *n.*

de·force (dē-fôrs', -fōrs') *tr.v.* **-forced, -forc·ing, -forc·es.** *Law.* To withhold (something) by force from the rightful owner. [ME *deforcen* < AN *deforcier* : *de-*, away (< Lat.) + *forcier,* to force < VLat. **fortiare* < Lat. *fortis,* strong.] —**de·force'ment** *n.*

de·for·ciant (dĭ-fôr'shənt, -fōr'-) *n. Law.* One who deforces a rightful owner.

de·for·est (dē-fôr'ĭst, -fŏr'-) *tr.v.* **-est·ed, -est·ing, -ests.** To clear away the trees or forests from. —**de·for'es·ta'tion** (-ĭ-stā'shən) *n.* —**de·for'est·er** *n.*

de·form (dĭ-fôrm') *v.* **-formed, -form·ing, -forms.** —*tr.* **1.** To spoil the natural form of; misshape. **2.** To deface; disfigure: *a body deformed by disease.* **3.** *Physics.* To alter the shape of by pressure or stress. —*intr.* To become deformed. [ME *deformen* < OFr. *deformer* < Lat. *deformare* : *de-*, off + *forma,* form.] —**de·form'a·bil'i·ty** *n.* —**de·form'a·ble** *adj.*

de·for·ma·tion (dē'fôr-mā'shən, dĕf'ər-) *n.* **1. a.** The act of deforming. **b.** The condition of being deformed. **2.** A change for the worse. **3.** *Physics.* **a.** An alteration of shape by pressure or stress. **b.** The altered shape that is the result of this.

de·formed (dĭ-fôrmd') *adj.* Misshapen or distorted in form.

de·for·mi·ty (dĭ-fôr'mĭ-tē) *n., pl.* **-ties. 1.** The state of being deformed. **2.** A bodily malformation. **3.** A deformed person or thing. **4.** Gross ugliness or distortion, esp. in art or morals.

de·fraud (dĭ-frôd') *tr.v.* **-fraud·ed, -fraud·ing, -frauds.** To take from or deprive of by fraud; swindle. [ME *defrauden* < OFr. *defrauder* < Lat. *defraudare* : *de-* (intensive) + *fraudare,* to cheat < *fraus,* fraud.] —**de'fraud·a'tion** (dē'frô-dā'shən) *n.* —**de·fraud'er** *n.*

de·fray (dĭ-frā') *tr.v.* **-frayed, -fray·ing, -frays.** To pay or provide for payment of (costs or expenses). [Fr. *défrayer* < OFr. *desfrayer* : *des-*, away (< Lat. *de-*) + **frai,* expense < Lat. *fractum,* neuter p.part. of *frangere,* to break.] —**de·fray'a·ble** *adj.* —**de·fray'al** *n.*

de·frock (dē-frŏk') *tr.v.* **-frocked, -frock·ing, -frocks.** To unfrock.

de·frost (dē-frôst', -frŏst') *v.* **-frost·ed, -frost·ing, -frosts.** —*tr.* **1.** To remove ice or frost from. **2.** To cause to thaw. —*intr.* To thaw out.

de·frost·er (dē-frô'stər, -frŏs'tər) *n.* A heating device designed to remove ice or frost or prevent its formation.

deft (dĕft) *adj.* **-er, -est.** Quick and skillful; adroit. [ME, gentle, humble, var. of *dafte,* foolish. —see DAFT.] —**deft'ly** *adv.* —**deft'ness** *n.*

de·funct (dĭ-fŭngkt') *adj.* Having ceased to live or exist. [Lat. *defunctus,* p.part. of *defungi,* to finish : *de-* (intensive) + *fungi,* to discharge.] —**de·func'tive** *adj.* —**de·funct'ness** *n.*

de·fuse (dē-fyo͞oz') *tr.v.* **-fused, -fus·ing, -fus·es. 1.** To remove the fuse from (an explosive device). **2.** To make less dangerous, tense, or hostile: *defuse an international crisis.*

de·fy (dĭ-fī') *tr.v.* **-fied, -fy·ing, -fies. 1.** To confront or stand up to; challenge. **2.** To resist successfully; withstand: *"so the plague defied all medicines"* (Defoe). **3.** To challenge or dare (someone) to perform something deemed impossible. [ME *defien* < OFr. *desfier* < VLat. **disfidare* : Lat. *dis-*, away + *fidere,* to trust.] —**de·fi'er** *n.*

dé·ga·gé (dā'gä-zhā') *adj.* Free and relaxed in manner; casual. [Fr., p.part. of *dégager,* to disengage < OFr. *desgagier* : *des-*, from (< Lat.) + *gage,* pledge, of Germanic orig.]

de·gas (dē-găs') *tr.v.* **-gassed, -gas·sing, -gas·ses** or **-gas·es.** To remove gas from.

de·gauss (dē-gous') *tr.v.* **-gaussed, -gauss·ing, -gauss·es.** To neutralize the magnetic field of (a ship, for example). —**de·gauss'er** *n.*

de·gen·er·a·cy (dĭ-jĕn'ər-ə-sē) *n., pl.* **-cies. 1.** The state of being degenerate. **2.** The process of degenerating. **3.** Degenerate behavior, esp. sexual perversion.

de·gen·er·ate (dĭ-jĕn'ər-ĭt) *adj.* **1.** Having declined, as in function or nature, from a former or original state. **2.** Having fallen or descended to a state below what is considered normal or desirable, esp. in mental or moral qualities. **3.** Marked by or exhibiting degeneracy. **4.** *Physics.* Taking on several discrete values or states. —*n.* **1.** A morally degraded person. **2. a.** A person lacking or having progressively lost normative biological or psychological characteristics. **b.** A person exhibiting antisocial, esp. sexually deviant, behavior. —*intr.v.* (-ə-rāt') **-at·ed, -at·ing, -ates. 1.** To decline from a former or original state; deteriorate: *old water pipes degenerating with age.* **2.** To fall below a normal or desirable state, esp. mentally or morally. **3.** To decline or go down in quality. **4.** *Physics.* To undergo degeneration. [Lat. *degenerare, degenerat-* : *de-*, from + *genus,* race.] —**de·gen'er·ate·ly** *adv.* —**de·gen'er·ate·ness** *n.* —**de·gen'er·a·tive** (-ə-tĭv) *adj.*

de·gen·er·a·tion (dĭ-jĕn'ə-rā'shən) *n.* **1.** The process of degenerating. **2.** The state of being degenerate. **3.** *Biol.* The usually irreversible deterioration of specific cells or organs with corresponding functional impairment, caused by injury or disease and often resulting in necrosis or death. **4.** *Electronics.* Negative feedback of output power to an input signal in an amplifying circuit.

de·glu·ti·nate (dĭ-glo͞ot'n-āt') *tr.v.* **-nat·ed, -nat·ing, -nates.** To extract the gluten from (wheat flour, for example). [Lat. *deglutinare, deglutinat-* : *de-*, away + *gluten,* glue.] —**de·glu'ti·na'tion** *n.*

de·glu·ti·tion (dē'glo͞o-tĭsh'ən) *n.* The process or act of swallowing. [Fr. < Lat. *deglutire,* to swallow down : *de-*, down + *glutire,* to gulp.] —**de·glu'ti·to'ry** (-tĭ-tôr'ē, -tōr'ē) *adj.*

de·grad·a·ble (dĭ-grā'də-bəl) *adj.* Capable of being chemically degraded.

deg·ra·da·tion (dĕg'rə-dā'shən) *n.* **1.** The act or process of degrading. **2.** A process of transition from a higher to a lower quality or level. **3.** The state of being degraded; degeneration. **4.** *Geol.* A general lowering of the earth's surface by erosion or transportation in running water. **5.** *Chem.* Decomposition of a compound by stages, exhibiting well-defined intermediate products.

de·grade (dĭ-grād') *tr.v.* **-grad·ed, -grad·ing, -grades. 1.** To reduce in grade, rank, or status, esp. to deprive of an office or dignity; demote. **2.** To lower in moral or intellectual character; debase. **3.** To reduce in worth or value. **4.** To expose to contempt, dishonor, or disgrace. **5.** *Geol.* To lower or wear by erosion. **6.** *Chem.* To decompose (a compound) by stages. [ME *degraden* < OFr. *degrader* < LLat. *degradare* : *de-*, down + *gradus,* step.] —**de·grad'er** *n.*

Synonyms: *degrade, abase, demean, humble, humiliate, discredit, mortify.* These verbs mean to cast down persons by reducing in dignity, respect, or rank. *Degrade* implies reduction to a state that incurs shame, disgrace, and contempt or to a state of actual corruption. *Abase* refers principally to loss of rank or prestige. *Demean* suggests placing a person in an inferior social position. *Humble* can refer to lowering in rank or estate or, more often, to driving out undue self-esteem. *Humiliate* involves subjecting one to shame, usually in public, and causing feelings of inferiority and loss of self-respect. *Discredit* refers to lowering of reputation or professional status. *Mortify* suggests causing extreme humiliation, chagrin, and embarrassment.

de·grad·ed (dĭ-grā'dĭd) *adj.* **1.** Reduced in rank, honor, or position. **2.** Reduced in quality or value. **3.** Having declined in moral qualities; depraved. **4.** Considered as below normal standards of civilization. —**de·grad'ed·ly** *adv.* —**de·grad'ed·ness** *n.*

de·grad·ing (dĭ-grā'dĭng) *adj.* Tending or intended to degrade; debasing. —**de·grad'ing·ly** *adv.*

de·gran·u·la·tion (dē-grăn'yə-lā'shən) *n.* The process of losing granules.

de·gree (dĭ-grē') *n.* **1.** One of a series of steps or stages in a process, course of action, progression, or retrogression. **2.** The relative distance, or a step, in a direct hereditary line of descent or ascent. **3.** Relative social or official rank, dignity, or position. **4.** Relative intensity or amount, as of a quality or attribute: *a high degree of accuracy.* **5.** The extent or measure of a state of being, action, or relation: *modernized their facilities to a large degree.* **6.** A unit division of a temperature scale. **7.** *Math.* A unit of angular measure equal in magnitude to the central angle subtended by $1/_{360}$ of the circumference of a circle. **8.** A unit of latitude or longitude, $1/_{360}$ of a great circle. **9. a.** The greatest sum of the exponents of the variables in a term of a polynomial or polynomial equation. **b.** The exponent of the derivative of highest order in a differential equation in standard form. **10. a.** An academic title given by a college or university to a student who has completed a course of study. **b.** A similar title conferred as an honorary distinction. **11.** *Law.* A division or classification of a specific crime according to its seriousness. **12.** *Gram.* One of the forms used in the comparison of adjectives and adverbs. **13.** *Mus.* **a.** One of the seven notes of a diatonic scale. **b.** A space or line of the staff. —***idioms.*** **by degrees.** Little by little; gradually. **to a degree. 1.** To a great extent. **2.** Somewhat. [ME *degre* < OFr. < VLat. **degradus* : Lat. *de-*, down + Lat. *gradus,* step.]

de·gree-day (dĭ-grē'dā') *n.* **1.** An indication of the extent of departure from a standard of mean daily temperature. **2.** A unit used in estimating quantities of fuel and power consumption, based on a daily ratio of consumption and the mean temperature below 65°F.

degree of freedom *n.* **1.** *Statistics.* Any of the unrestricted, independent random variables that constitute a statistic. **2.** *Physics.* **a.** Any of the minimum number of coordinates required to specify completely the motion of a mechanical system. **b.** Any of the independent thermodynamic variables, such as pressure, temperature, or composition, required to specify a system with a given number of phases and components.

de·gres·sion (dĭ-grĕsh'ən, dē-) *n.* A going down by steps; descent. [Med. Lat. *degressio,* descent < Lat. *degressus,* p.part. of *degredi,* to descend : *de-*, down + *gradi,* to step.] —**de·gres'sive** *adj.*

de·gust (dĭ-gŭst', dē-) *tr.v.* **-gust·ed, -gust·ing, -gusts.** To taste with relish; savor. [Lat. *degustare* : *de-* (intensive) + *gustare,* to taste < *gustus,* taste.] —**de'gus·ta'tion** (dē'gŭ-stā'shən) *n.*

de·hisce (dĭ-hĭs') *intr.v.* **-hisced, -hisc·ing, -hisc·es.** To burst or split open along a line or slit, as do the ripe capsules or pods of some plants. [Lat. *dehiscere* : *de-*, off + *hiscere,* to split, inchoative of *hiare,* to be open.]

de·his·cent (dĭ-hĭs′ənt) *adj.* Opening at pores or by splitting to release seeds within a fruit or pollen from an anther. **—de·his′cence** *n.*

de·horn (dē-hôrn′) *tr.v.* **-horned, -horn·ing, -horns. 1.** To remove the horns from. **2.** To prevent growth in the horns of, as by cauterization.

de·hu·man·ize (dē-hyo͞o′mə-nīz′) *tr.v.* **-ized, -iz·ing, -iz·es. 1.** To deprive of human qualities or attributes. **2.** To render mechanical and routine. **—de·hu′man·i·za′tion** *n.*

de·hu·mid·i·fy (dē′hyo͞o-mĭd′ə-fī′) *tr.v.* **-fied, -fy·ing, -fies.** To remove atmospheric moisture from. **—de′hu·mid′i·fi·ca′tion** *n.* **—de′hu·mid′i·fi′er** *n.*

de·hy·drase (dē-hī′drās′, -drāz′) *n. Biochem.* **1.** Dehydratase. **2.** Dehydrogenase.

de·hy·dra·tase (dē-hī′drə-tās′, -tāz′) *n. Biochem.* An enzyme that catalyzes the removal of oxygen and hydrogen from a metabolite in the ratio in which they occur in water.

de·hy·drate (dē-hī′drāt′) *v.* **-drat·ed, -drat·ing, -drates.** *—tr.* **1.** *Chem.* To eliminate water from or make anhydrous. **2.** To remove water from (vegetables, for example) for preservation. *—intr.* To lose water or moisture; become dry. **—de·hy′dra′tor** *n.*

de·hy·dra·tion (dē′hī-drā′shən) *n.* **1.** The process of removing water from a substance or compound. **2.** *Pathol.* Excessive loss of water from the body or from an organ or bodily part.

de·hy·dro·chlo·rin·ase (dē-hī′drə-klôr′ə-nās′, -nāz′, -klōr′-) *n. Biochem.* An enzyme that catalyzes the removal of hydrogen and chlorine from a chlorinated hydrocarbon.

de·hy·dro·chlo·rin·ate (dē-hī′drə-klôr′ə-nāt′, -klōr′-) *tr.v.* **-at·ed, -at·ing, -ates.** *Biochem.* To remove hydrogen and chlorine or hydrogen chloride from (a compound). **—de·hy′dro·chlo′ri·na′tion** *n.*

de·hy·dro·gen·ase (dē′hī-drŏj′ə-nās′, -nāz′, dē-hī′drə-jə-) *n.* An enzyme that removes hydrogen from metabolites.

de·hy·dro·ge·nate (dē′hī-drŏj′ə-nāt′, dē-hī′drə-jə-) *tr.v.* **-nat·ed, -nat·ing, -nates.** *Chem.* To remove hydrogen from; dehydrogenize. **—de·hy′dro·ge·na′tion** *n.*

de·hy·dro·ge·nize (dē′hī-drŏj′ə-nīz′, dē-hī′drə-jə-) *tr.v.* **-nized, -niz·ing, -niz·es.** To dehydrogenate. **—de·hy′dro·ge′ni·za′tion** *n.*

de·hyp·no·tize (dē-hĭp′nə-tīz′) *tr.v.* **-tized, -tiz·ing, -tiz·es.** To arouse from a hypnotic state.

de·ice (dē-īs′) *tr.v.* **-iced, -ic·ing, -ic·es.** To keep free of ice; melt ice from.

de·ic·er (dē-ī′sər) *n.* **1.** A device used on an aircraft in flight to keep certain surfaces free from ice or remove ice after it has formed. **2.** A compound used to prevent the formation of ice, as on windshields.

de·i·cide (dē′ĭ-sīd′) *n.* **1.** The killing of a god. **2.** One who kills a god. [Lat. *deus,* god + -CIDE.]

deic·tic (dīk′tĭk) *adj.* **1.** *Logic.* Directly proving by argument. **2.** *Ling.* Serving to point out or specify, as the demonstrative pronoun *this.* [Gk. *deiktikos* < *deiktos,* able to show directly < *deiknunai,* to show.] **—deic′ti·cal·ly** *adv.*

de·if·ic (dē-ĭf′ĭk) *adj.* **1.** Making or tending to make divine. **2.** Of or characterized by divine or godlike nature. [OFr. *deifique* < LLat. *deificus* : Lat. *deus,* god + *-ficus,* -fic.]

de·i·fi·ca·tion (dē′ə-fĭ-kā′shən) *n.* **1. a.** The act or process of deifying. **b.** The condition of having been deified. **2.** One who embodies the qualities of a god.

de·i·fy (dē′ə-fī′) *tr.v.* **-fied, -fy·ing, -fies. 1.** To raise to divine rank. **2.** To worship or revere as a god. **3.** To idealize; exalt. [ME *deifien* < OFr. *deifier* < LLat. *deificare* < *deificus,* deific.] **—de′i·fi′er** *n.*

deign (dān) *v.* **deigned, deign·ing, deigns.** *—intr.* To think it appropriate or suitable to one's dignity to do something: *wouldn't deign to answer the reporter's questions. —tr.* To condescend to give or grant. [ME *deinen* < OFr. *deignier,* to regard as worthy < Lat. *dignari* < *dignus,* worthy.]

deil (dēl) *n. Scot.* **1.** The devil. **2.** A mischievous person; imp. [Sc. < ME *dele,* alteration of *devel.* —see DEVIL.]

de·in·sti·tu·tion·al·ize (dē-ĭn′stĭ-to͞o′shə-nə-līz′, -tyo͞o′-) *tr.v.* **-ized, -iz·ing, -iz·es. 1.** To remove the status of an institution from. **2.** To enable (one who is developmentally disabled or mentally ill, for example) to live away from an institution. **—de·in′sti·tu′tion·al·i·za′tion** *n.*

Deir·dre (dîr′drə, -drē) *n. Ir. Myth.* A princess of Ulster who killed herself after her husband, Naoise, was murdered. [OIr. *Deidru.*]

de·ism (dē′ĭz′əm) *n.* The belief, based solely on reason, in the existence of God as the creator of the universe who after setting it in motion abandoned it, assumed no control over life, exerted no influence on natural phenomena, and gave no supernatural revelation. [Fr. *déisme* < Lat. *deus,* god.] **—de′ist** *n.* **—de·is′tic** *adj.* **—de·is′ti·cal·ly** *adv.*

de·i·ty (dē′ĭ-tē) *n., pl.* **-ties. 1.** A god or goddess. **2. a.** The essential nature or condition of being a god; divinity. **b. Deity.** God. [ME *deite* < OFr. < LLat. *deitas,* divine nature < Lat. *deus,* god.]

dé·jà vu (dā′zhä vü′) *n.* The illusion of having already experienced something actually being experienced for the first time. [Fr., already seen.]

de·ject (dĭ-jĕkt′) *tr.v.* **-ject·ed, -ject·ing, -jects.** To dishearten; dispirit. [ME *dejecten* < Lat. *dejectus,* p.part. of *deicere,* to cast down : *de-*, down + *jacere,* to throw.]

de·jec·ta (dĭ-jĕk′tə) *pl.n.* Excremental matter; feces. [NLat. < Lat. *dejectus,* p.part. of *deicere,* to cast down. —see DEJECT.]

de·ject·ed (dĭ-jĕk′tĭd) *adj.* In low spirits; depressed. **—de·ject′ed·ly** *adv.* **—de·ject′ed·ness** *n.*

de·jec·tion (dĭ-jĕk′shən) *n.* **1.** The state of being depressed; melancholy. **2.** *Med.* **a.** Evacuation of the bowels. **b.** Excrement.

de ju·re (dē jo͝or′ē, dā yo͝or′ā) *adv. & adj.* According to law; by right. [Lat.]

dek– or **deka–** *pref.* Variants of **deca-**.

dek·a·gram (dĕk′ə-grăm′) *n.* Variant of **decagram**.

dek·a·li·ter (dĕk′ə-lē′tər) *n.* Variant of **decaliter**.

dek·a·me·ter (dĕk′ə-mē′tər) *n.* Variant of **decameter**.

dek·a·stere (dĕk′ə-stîr′) *n.* Variant of **decastere**.

de·laine (də-lān′) *n.* A light dress fabric of wool or cotton and wool. [Short for Fr. *mousseline de laine,* muslin of wool.]

de·lam·i·nate (dē-lăm′ə-nāt′) *intr.v.* **-nat·ed, -nat·ing, -nates.** To split into thin layers.

de·lam·i·na·tion (dē-lăm′ə-nā′shən) *n.* **1.** The act of splitting or separating into layers. **2.** The splitting of the blastoderm into two layers of cells.

Del·a·ware[1] (dĕl′ə-wâr′) *n., pl.* **Delaware** or **-wares. 1. a.** A group of North American Indian tribes formerly inhabiting the Delaware River valley. **b.** A member of any of these tribes. **2.** The Algonquian language of the Delaware. **—Del′a·war′e·an** *adj.*

Del·a·ware[2] (dĕl′ə-wâr′) *n.* A variety of grape having sweet, light-red fruit. [After the state of *Delaware.*]

de·lay (dĭ-lā′) *v.* **-layed, -lay·ing, -lays.** *—tr.* **1.** To postpone until a later time; defer. **2.** To cause to be late or detained; hinder. *—intr.* To procrastinate or tarry; linger. *—n.* **1.** The act of delaying; postponement. **2.** The condition of being delayed; detainment. **3.** The period of time during which one is delayed. **4.** The time interval between two events. [ME *delaien* < OFr. *deslaier* : *des-*, off (< Lat. *de-*) + *laier,* alteration of *laissier,* to leave < Lat. *laxare,* to slacken < *laxus,* loose.] **—de·lay′er** *n.*

Synonyms: *delay, slow, retard, detain, check.* These verbs mean, transitively, to hold back and thus hinder or prevent action or progress. *Delay* applies either to putting behind schedule or to postponing or deferring action. *Slow* means to decrease in pace, often deliberately. *Retard* also stresses slackening of pace, intentional or otherwise; in the latter case it often refers to frustration of progress or development. *Detain* stresses holding at a particular point in time or place and thus preventing action. *Check* implies sudden impeding of action or progress in mid-course, usually by restraint.

de·le (dē′lē) *n.* A sign indicating that something is to be removed from typeset matter. *—tr.v.* **-led, -le·ing, -les. 1.** To take out or delete. **2.** To mark with a dele. [Lat., imper. of *delēre,* to delete.]

de·leave (dē-lēv′) *tr.v.* **-leaved, -leav·ing, -leaves.** To decollate.

de·lec·ta·ble (dĭ-lĕk′tə-bəl) *adj.* **1.** Greatly pleasing; delightful. **2.** Greatly pleasing to the taste; delicious. [ME < OFr. < Lat. *delectabilis* < *delectare,* to please. —see DELIGHT.] **—de·lec′ta·bil′i·ty, de·lec′ta·ble·ness** *n.* **—de·lec′ta·bly** *adv.*

de·lec·ta·tion (dē′lĕk-tā′shən) *n.* Pleasure; delight.

del·e·ga·cy (dĕl′ĭ-gə-sē) *n., pl.* **-cies. 1.** The authority, office, or position of a delegate. **2.** The act of delegating or state of being delegated. **3.** A body of delegates; delegation.

del·e·gate (dĕl′ĭ-gāt′, -gĭt) *n.* **1.** A person authorized to act as representative for another; deputy or agent. **2. a.** An elected or appointed representative of a U.S. territory in the House of Representatives who is entitled to speak but not vote. **b.** A member of the House of Delegates, the lower house of the Maryland, Virginia, and West Virginia legislatures. **c.** A representative to a conference or convention. *—tr.v.* (-gāt′) **-gat·ed, -gat·ing, -gates. 1.** To authorize and send (a person) as one's representative. **2.** To commit or entrust to another. **3.** *Law.* To appoint (one's debtor) as a debtor to one's creditor to replace oneself in satisfying a claim. [ME *delegat* < Med. Lat. *delegatus* < Lat., p.part. of *delegare,* to dispatch : *de-*, away + *legare,* to send < *lex,* law.]

del·e·ga·tion (dĕl′ĭ-gā′shən) *n.* **1. a.** The act of delegating. **b.** The condition of being delegated. **2.** A person or group of persons officially elected or appointed to represent another or others.

de·lete (dĭ-lēt′) *tr.v.* **-let·ed, -let·ing, -letes.** To strike out or cancel; omit. [Lat. *delēre, delet-*, to wipe out.]

del·e·te·ri·ous (dĕl′ĭ-tîr′ē-əs) *adj.* Having a harmful effect; injurious. [Med. Lat. < Gk. *dēlētērios* < *dēleisthai,* to harm.] **—del′e·te′ri·ous·ly** *adv.* **—del′e·te′ri·ous·ness** *n.*

de·le·tion (dĭ-lē′shən) *n.* **1.** An act of deleting; omission or erasure. **2.** A word, passage, or other matter that has been deleted from written or printed matter.

delft (dĕlft) *n.* **1. a.** A style of glazed earthenware, usually blue and white, originally made in Delft, Netherlands. **b.** A piece of pottery of this style. **2.** Pottery made in imitation of delft.

delft·ware (dĕlft′wâr′) *n.* Delft.

delft
Bristol delft plate

del·i (dĕl′ē) *n., pl.* **-is.** *Informal.* A delicatessen.
de·lib·er·ate (dĭ-lĭb′ər-ĭt) *adj.* **1. a.** Considered or planned in advance with a full awareness of everything involved; premeditated: *orchestrated a deliberate delay.* **b.** Done or said on purpose; intentional. **2.** Careful and thorough in deciding or determining: *a deliberate choice.* **3.** Leisurely or slow in motion or manner: *moved at a deliberate pace.* —*v.* (-ə-rāt′) **-at·ed, -at·ing, -ates.** —*intr.* **1.** To take careful thought; reflect. **2.** To consult with another or others as a process in reaching a decision. —*tr.* To consider (a matter) carefully, as by weighing alternatives. [Lat. *deliberatus,* resolved, p.part. of *deliberare,* to consider : *de-,* thoroughly + *librare,* to balance < *libra,* a balance, scales.] **—de·lib′er·ate·ly** *adv.* **—de·lib′er·ate·ness** *n.*
de·lib·er·a·tion (dĭ-lĭb′ə-rā′shən) *n.* **1.** The act or process of deliberating. **2.** Often **deliberations.** Formal discussion and debate of all sides of an issue. **3.** Thoughtfulness in decision or action.
de·lib·er·a·tive (dĭ-lĭb′ə-rā′tĭv, -ər-ə-tĭv) *adj.* **1.** Assembled or organized for deliberation or debate: *a deliberative legislature.* **2.** Characterized by or for use in deliberation or debate. **—de·lib′er·a′tive·ly** *adv.* **—de·lib′er·a′tive·ness** *n.*
del·i·ca·cy (dĕl′ĭ-kə-sē) *n., pl.* **-cies. 1.** The quality of being delicate. **2.** Something pleasing and appealing, esp. a choice food. **3.** Exquisite fineness or daintiness of appearance or structure. **4.** Frailty of bodily constitution or health. **5.** Sensitivity of perception, discrimination, or taste; refinement. **6. a.** Sensitivity to the feelings of others; tact. **b.** Sensitivity to what is proper; propriety. **c.** Undue sensitivity to or concern with what may be considered offensive or improper; squeamishness. **7.** The need for tact in treatment or handling: *a topic of some delicacy.* **8.** Fineness of touch: *the delicacy of an artist's brushstrokes.* **9.** Sensitivity or keenness of response or reaction: *the delicacy of a fine timepiece.* [ME *delicacie* < *delicat,* delicate.]
del·i·cate (dĕl′ĭ-kĭt) *adj.* **1.** Pleasing to the senses, esp. in a subtle way: *a delicate flavor; a delicate violin passage.* **2.** Exquisitely fine or dainty: *delicate china.* **3.** Frail in constitution or health. **4.** Easily broken or damaged. **5.** Marked by sensitivity of discrimination. **6. a.** Considerate of the feelings of others. **b.** Concerned with propriety. **c.** Squeamish or fastidious. **7.** Requiring tactful treatment. **8.** Fine or soft in touch or skill: *a surgeon's delicate touch.* **9.** Keenly accurate in response or reaction. **10.** Very subtle in difference or distinction. [ME *delicat* < Lat. *delicatus,* pleasing.] **—del′i·cate·ly** *adv.* **—del′i·cate·ness** *n.*
del·i·ca·tes·sen (dĕl′ĭ-kə-tĕs′ən) *n.* A shop that sells cooked or prepared foods ready for serving. [G. *Delikatessen,* pl. of *Delikatesse,* delicacy < Fr. *délicatesse* < Ital. *delicatezza* < *delicato,* delicate < Lat. *delicatus,* pleasing.]
de·li·cious[1] (dĭ-lĭsh′əs) *adj.* **1.** Highly pleasing or agreeable to the senses, esp. of taste or smell. **2.** Very pleasant; delightful. [ME < OFr. < LLat. *deliciosus,* pleasing < Lat. *delicia,* pleasure < *delicere,* to allure. —see DELIGHT.] **—de·li′cious·ly** *adv.* **—de·li′cious·ness** *n.*
de·li·cious[2] (dĭ-lĭsh′əs) *n.* Often **Delicious.** A variety of apple having sweet fruit often streaked with yellow and red.
de·lict (dĭ-lĭkt′) *n. Law.* A misdemeanor. [Lat. *delictum* < neuter p.part. of *delinquere,* to offend. —see DELINQUENT.]
de·light (dĭ-līt′) *n.* **1.** Great pleasure or gratification; joy. **2.** Something that gives great pleasure or enjoyment. —*v.* **-light·ed, -light·ing, -lights.** —*intr.* **1.** To take great pleasure or joy. **2.** To give great pleasure or joy. —*tr.* To please greatly. [ME *deliten* < OFr. *delitier* < Lat. *delectare,* freq. of *delicere,* to allure : *de-,* away + *lacere,* to entice.]
de·light·ed (dĭ-lī′tĭd) *adj.* **1.** Filled with delight. **2.** *Obs.* Delightful. **—de·light′ed·ly** *adv.* **—de·light′ed·ness** *n.*
de·light·ful (dĭ-līt′fəl) *adj.* Greatly pleasing. **—de·light′ful·ly** *adv.* **—de·light′ful·ness** *n.*
de·light·some (dĭ-līt′səm) *adj.* Delightful. **—de·light′some·ly** *adv.* **—de·light′some·ness** *n.*
De·li·lah (dĭ-lī′lə) *n.* In the Old Testament, a Philistine woman who betrayed Samson, her lover, to the Philistines by having his hair shorn as he slept, thus depriving him of his strength. [Heb. *Dĕlīlāh.*]
de·lim·it (dĭ-lĭm′ĭt) also **de·lim·i·tate** (-ĭ-tāt′) *tr.v.* **-it·ed, -it·ing, -its** also **-tat·ed, -tat·ing, -tates.** To establish the limit or boundaries of; demarcate. [Fr. *délimiter* < Lat. *delimitare* : *de-,* thoroughly + *limitare,* to limit < *limes,* limit.] **—de·lim′i·ta′tion** *n.* **—de·lim′i·ta′tive** *adj.*
de·lim·it·er (dĭ-lĭm′ĭ-tər) *n. Computer Sci.* A character marking the beginning or end of a unit of data.
de·lin·e·ate (dĭ-lĭn′ē-āt′) *tr.v.* **-at·ed, -at·ing, -ates. 1.** To draw or trace the outline of; sketch out. **2.** To represent pictorially; depict. **3.** To depict in words or gestures; portray. [Lat. *delineare, delineat-* : *de-,* thoroughly + *linea,* line < *linum,* flax.] **—de·lin′e·a′tion** *n.* **—de·lin′e·a′tor** *n.* **—de·lin′e·a′tive** *adj.*
de·lin·quen·cy (dĭ-lĭng′kwən-sē, -lĭn′-) *n., pl.* **-cies. 1.** Negligence or failure in doing what is required. **2.** An offense or misdemeanor; misdeed. **3.** Juvenile delinquency.
de·lin·quent (dĭ-lĭng′kwənt, -lĭn′-) *adj.* **1.** Failing to do what is required by law or obligation. **2.** Overdue in payment: *a delinquent account.* —*n.* **1.** A person who neglects or fails to do what law or obligation requires. **2.** A juvenile delinquent. [Lat. *delinquens, delinquent-,* pr.part. of *delinquere,* to offend : *de-* (intensive) + *linquere,* to leave, abandon.] **—de·lin′quent·ly** *adv.*
del·i·quesce (dĕl′ĭ-kwĕs′) *intr.v.* **-quesced, -quesc·ing, -quesc·es. 1.** To melt away or disappear as if by melting. **2.** *Chem.* To dissolve and become liquid by absorbing moisture from the air. **3.** *Bot.* **a.** To branch out into numerous subdivisions that lack a main axis. **b.** To become fluid or soft on maturing, as do certain fungi. [Lat. *deliquescere* : *de-,* thoroughly + *liquescere,* to melt, inchoative of *liquēre,* to be liquid.] **—del′i·ques′cence** *n.* **—del′i·ques′cent** *adj.*
de·lir·i·a (dĭ-lîr′ē-ə) *n.* A plural of **delirium.**
de·lir·i·ous (dĭ-lîr′ē-əs) *adj.* **1.** Suffering from delirium. **2.** Characteristic of or pertaining to delirium: *a delirious speech.* **—de·lir′i·ous·ly** *adv.* **—de·lir′i·ous·ness** *n.*
de·lir·i·um (dĭ-lîr′ē-əm) *n., pl.* **-i·ums** or **-i·a** (-ē-ə). **1.** A state of temporary mental confusion and clouded consciousness resulting from high fever, intoxication, or shock and characterized by anxiety, tremors, hallucinations, delusions, and incoherence. **2.** A state of uncontrolled excitement or emotion. [Lat. < *delirare,* to be deranged : *de-,* from + *lira,* furrow.] **—de·lir′i·ant** *adj.*
delirium tre·mens (trē′mənz) *n.* An acute delirium caused by alcohol poisoning. [NLat., trembling delirium.]
de·liv·er (dĭ-lĭv′ər) *v.* **-ered, -er·ing, -ers.** —*tr.* **1.** To release or rescue; set free: *deliver one from slavery.* **2. a.** To assist in giving birth: *The doctor delivered her of twins.* **b.** To assist or aid in the birth of: *The midwife delivered the twins.* **3.** To surrender to another; hand over: *delivered the criminal to the police.* **4.** To take to the intended recipient: *deliver groceries.* **5. a.** To send to an intended goal or target: *deliver a blow.* **b.** To throw or hurl: *The pitcher delivered the ball.* **6.** To give or utter (a lecture, for example). **7.** To secure (something promised or desired), as for a candidate or political party: *delivered the votes.* —*intr.* To do what is desired or expected; make good: *The senator delivered on his pledge.* —*idiom.* **deliver (oneself) of.** To pronounce; utter. [ME *deliveren* < OFr. *delivrer* < LLat. *deliberare* : Lat. *de-,* thoroughly + *liberare,* to free < *liber,* free.] **—de·liv′er·a·bil′i·ty** *n.* **—de·liv′er·a·ble** *adj.* **—de·liv′er·er** *n.*
de·liv·er·ance (dĭ-lĭv′ər-əns, -lĭv′rəns) *n.* **1. a.** The act of delivering. **b.** The condition of being delivered, esp. rescue from bondage or danger. **2.** A publicly expressed opinion or judgment, such as the verdict of a jury.
de·liv·er·y (dĭ-lĭv′ə-rē, -lĭv′rē) *n., pl.* **-ies. 1.** The act of delivering or conveying. **2.** Something that is delivered. **3.** The act of releasing or rescuing. **4.** The act of giving birth; parturition. **5.** The act of transferring to another. **6.** The act of giving up; surrender. **7. a.** Utterance. **b.** Manner of speaking or singing. **8.** The act or manner of throwing or discharging.
dell (dĕl) *n.* A small, secluded wooded valley. [ME *del* < OE *dell.*]
dells (dĕlz) *pl.n.* The rapids of a river. [By folk ety. < DALLES.]
Del·mon·i·co steak (dĕl-mŏn′ĭ-kō′) *n.* A small, often boned steak from the front section of the short loin of beef. [After the *Delmonico* Restaurant in New York City.]
de·lo·cal·ize (dē-lō′kə-līz′) *tr.v.* **-ized, -iz·ing, -iz·es. 1.** To remove (something) from its native or usual locality. **2.** To broaden the range or scope of. **—de·lo′cal·i·za′tion** *n.*
de·louse (dē-lous′) *tr.v.* **-loused, -lous·ing, -lous·es.** To rid of parasitic infestation by physical or chemical means.
Del·phic (dĕl′fĭk) also **Del·phi·an** (-fē-ən) *adj.* **1.** Of or pertaining to Delphi or to the oracle of Apollo at Delphi. **2.** Obscure in meaning; ambiguous.
del·phin·i·um (dĕl-fĭn′ē-əm) *n.* A plant of the genus *Delphinium,* esp. any of several tall cultivated varieties having spikes of showy, variously colored spurred flowers. [NLat. *Delphinium,* genus name < Gk. *delphinion,* larkspur, dim. of *delphis,* dolphin (from the shape of the nectary).]
Del·phi·nus (dĕl-fī′nəs) *n.* A constellation in the Northern Hemisphere near Pegasus and Aquila. [Lat. < *delphinus,* dolphin. —see DOLPHIN.]
del·ta (dĕl′tə) *n.* **1.** The 4th letter of the Greek alphabet. See table at **alphabet. 2. a.** A usually triangular alluvial deposit at the mouth of a river. **b.** A similar deposit at the mouth of a tidal inlet, caused by tidal currents. **3.** An object resembling a triangle in shape. **4.** *Math.* A finite increment in a variable. [Gk., of Phoenician orig.; akin to Heb. *dāleth,* daleth.] **—del·ta′ic** (-tā′ĭk), **del′tic** (-tĭk) *adj.*
delta ray *n.* An electron ejected from matter by ionizing radiation.
delta wave or **delta rhythm** *n.* A low-frequency brain wave that emanates from the forward portion of the brain during deep sleep in normal adults.
delta wing *n.* An aircraft with swept-back wings that give it the appearance of an isosceles triangle.
del·toid (dĕl′toid′) *n.* A thick, triangular muscle covering the shoulder joint, used to raise the arm from the side. —*adj.* **1.** Triangular. **2.** Pertaining to the deltoid. [NLat. *deltoides* < Gk. *deltoeidēs,* triangular : *delta,* delta + *-eides,* -oid.]
de·lude (dĭ-lōōd′) *tr.v.* **-lud·ed, -lud·ing, -ludes. 1.** To deceive the mind or judgment of. **2.** *Obs.* To elude or evade. **3.** *Obs.* To frustrate the hopes or plans of. [ME *deluden* < Lat. *deludere* : *de-* (pejorative) + *ludere,* to play < *ludus,* game.] **—de·lud′a·ble** *adj.* **—de·lud′er** *n.* **—de·lud′ing·ly** *adv.*

del·uge (dĕl′yo͞oj) *tr.v.* **-uged, -ug·ing, -ug·es. 1.** To overrun with water. **2.** To inundate in overwhelming numbers. —*n.* **1. a.** A great flood. **b.** A heavy downpour. **2.** Something that overwhelms as if by a great flood: *a deluge of fan mail.* **3. Deluge.** In the Old Testament, the great flood that occurred in the time of Noah. [< ME *deluge,* flood < OFr. < Lat. *diluvium* < *diluere,* to wash away : *dis-,* apart + *lavere,* to wash.]

de·lu·sion (dĭ-lo͞o′zhən) *n.* **1. a.** The act or process of deluding; deception. **b.** The state of being deluded. **2.** Something that is falsely disseminated or believed. **3.** A false belief held in spite of invalidating evidence, esp. as a condition of certain forms of mental illness. [ME *delusioun* < Lat. *delusio* < *deludere,* to delude.] **—de·lu′sion·al** *adj.*

de·lu·sive (dĭ-lo͞o′sĭv) also **de·lu·so·ry** (-lo͞o′sə-rē) *adj.* **1.** Tending to deceive or mislead; deceptive. **2.** Having the nature of a delusion; false. **—de·lu′sive·ly** *adv.* **—de·lu′sive·ness** *n.*

de luxe also **de·luxe** (dĭ-lo͝oks′, -lŭks′) —*adj.* Particularly elegant and luxurious; sumptuous: *a de luxe model.* —*adv.* In an elegant and luxurious manner; sumptuously. [Fr., of luxury.]

delve (dĕlv) *v.* **delved, delv·ing, delves.** —*intr.* **1.** To search carefully and laboriously. **2.** *Archaic.* To dig the ground, as with a spade. —*tr. Archaic.* To dig (ground) with a spade. [ME *delven,* to dig < OE *delfan.*] **—delv′er** *n.*

de·mag·net·ize (dē-măg′nĭ-tīz′) *tr.v.* **-ized, -iz·ing, -iz·es.** To remove magnetic properties from. **—de·mag′net·i·za′tion** *n.*

dem·a·gog (dĕm′ə-gôg′, -gŏg′) *n.* Variant of **demagogue.**

dem·a·gog·ic (dĕm′ə-gŏj′ĭk, -gŏg′-, -gō′jĭk) also **dem·a·gog·i·cal** (-gŏj′ĭ-kəl, -gŏg′-, -gō′jĭ-kəl) *adj.* Of, relating to, or characteristic of a demagogue. **—dem′a·gog′i·cal·ly** *adv.*

dem·a·gog·ism (dĕm′ə-gô′gĭz-əm, -gŏg′ĭz-) *n.* Demagoguery.

dem·a·gogue also **dem·a·gog** (dĕm′ə-gôg′, -gŏg′) *n.* **1.** A leader who obtains power by means of impassioned appeals to the emotions and prejudices of the populace. **2.** A leader of the common people in ancient times. [Gk. *dēmagōgos,* popular leader : *dēmos,* common people + *agōgos,* leading < *agein,* to lead.]

dem·a·gogu·er·y (dĕm′ə-gô′gə-rē, -gŏg′ə-) *n.* The practices or rhetoric of a demagogue.

dem·a·gog·y (dĕm′ə-gŏj′ē, -gô′jē, -gŏg′ē, -gō′jē) *n.* The quality or character of demagogues.

de·mand (dĭ-mănd′) *v.* **-mand·ed, -mand·ing, -mands.** —*tr.* **1.** To ask for urgently or firmly, leaving no chance for refusal or denial. **2.** To claim as just or due: *demand payment of the rent.* **3.** To ask to be informed of: *demand the cause of his action.* **4.** To need or require as useful, just, proper, or necessary. **5.** *Law.* **a.** To summon to court. **b.** To claim formally; lay legal claim to. —*intr.* To make a demand. —*n.* **1.** The act of demanding. **2.** Something that is demanded. **3. a.** The state of being sought after: *in great demand as a speaker.* **b.** An urgent requirement, need, or claim: *an increased demand for capital goods.* **4.** *Archaic.* An emphatic question or inquiry. **5.** *Law.* A formal claim. **6.** *Computer Sci.* A coding technique in which a read or write order is initiated as the need for a new block of data occurs. **7.** *Econ.* **a.** The desire to possess something combined with the ability to purchase it. **b.** The amount of a commodity that people are ready and able to buy at a given time for a given price. **—idiom. on demand.** On presentation. [ME *demanden* < OFr. *demander,* to charge with doing < Lat. *demandare,* to entrust : *de-* (intensive) + *mandare,* to entrust.] **—de·mand′a·ble** *adj.* **—de·mand′er** *n.*

de·mand·ant (dĭ-măn′dənt) *n.* A plaintiff.

demand deposit *n.* A bank deposit that can be withdrawn without advance notice.

de·mand·ing (dĭ-măn′dĭng) *adj.* **1.** Making rigorous demands. **2.** Requiring careful attention or constant effort. **—de·mand′ing·ly** *adv.*

demand loan *n.* A call loan.

demand note *n.* A bill or draft payable in lawful money on presentation or demand.

de·mand-pull (dĭ-mănd′po͝ol′) *adj.* Designating a type of inflation in which increased demand for a limited amount of goods and services tends to drive up prices.

de·man·toid (dĭ-măn′toid′) *n.* A transparent, green variety of garnet, used as a gem. [G. < obs. *Demant,* diamond < MHG *diemant* < OFr. *diamant.* —see DIAMOND.]

de·mar·cate (dĭ-mär′kāt′, dē′mär-kāt′) *tr.v.* **-cat·ed, -cat·ing, -cates. 1.** To set the boundaries of; delimit. **2.** To separate clearly as if by boundaries; discriminate. [Back-formation < DEMARCATION.] **—de·mar′ca′tor** *n.*

de·mar·ca·tion also **de·mar·ka·tion** (dē′mär-kā′shən) *n.* **1.** The setting or marking of boundaries or limits. **2.** A separation; distinction: *a line of demarcation.* [Sp. *demarcacion* < *demarcar,* to mark boundaries : *de-* (intensive < Lat.) + *marcar,* to mark < Ital. *marcare,* of Germanic orig.]

dé·marche (dā-mărsh′) *n.* **1.** A course of action; maneuver. **2.** A diplomatic representation or protest. **3.** A statement or protest addressed by citizens to public authorities. [Fr. < OFr. *demarche,* gait < *demarchier,* to march : *de-,* from (< Lat.) + *marchier,* to march, prob. of Germanic orig.]

de·mar·ka·tion (dē′mär-kā′shən) *n.* Variant of **demarcation.**

deme (dēm) *n.* **1.** One of the townships of ancient Attica. **2.** *Ecol.* A local, usually stable population of organisms of the same kind or species. [Gk. *dēmos.*]

de·mean[1] (dĭ-mēn′) *tr.v.* **-meaned, -mean·ing, -means.** To conduct or behave (oneself) in a particular manner. [ME *demeinen,* to govern < OFr. *demener* : *de-,* thoroughly (< Lat.) + *mener,* to conduct < Lat. *minare,* to drive < *minari,* to threaten < *minae,* threats.]

de·mean[2] (dĭ-mēn′) *tr.v.* **-meaned, -mean·ing, -means. 1.** To debase in dignity or stature. **2.** To humble (oneself).

de·mean·or (dĭ-mē′nər) *n.* The way in which a person behaves or conducts himself; deportment.

de·mean·our (dĭ-mē′nər) *n. Chiefly Brit.* Variant of **demeanor.**

de·ment (dĭ-mĕnt′) *tr.v.* **-ment·ed, -ment·ing, -ments.** To make insane. [LLat. *dementare* < Lat. *demens,* mad : *de-,* from + *mens,* mind.]

de·ment·ed (dĭ-mĕn′tĭd) *adj.* **1.** Insane. **2.** Afflicted with dementia. **—de·ment′ed·ly** *adv.* **—de·ment′ed·ness** *n.*

de·men·tia (dĭ-mĕn′shə) *n.* **1.** Irreversible deterioration of intellectual faculties with accompanying emotional disturbance resulting from organic brain disorder. **2.** Madness; insanity. [Lat., madness < *demens,* mad. —see DEMENT.] **—de·men′tial** *adj.*

dementia prae·cox (prē′kŏks′) *n.* Schizophrenia. [NLat., premature dementia.]

de·mer·it (dĭ-mĕr′ĭt) *n.* **1. a.** A quality or characteristic that deserves blame or censure; fault. **b.** Absence of merit. **2.** A mark made against one's record and usually involving some loss of privileges for bad conduct or failure. [ME *demerite,* offense < OFr. *desmerite* < Lat. *demeritum,* neuter p.part. of *demerēre,* to deserve : *de-* (intensive) + *merēre,* to earn.] **—de·mer′i·to′ri·ous** (-tôr′ē-əs, -tōr′-) *adj.* **—de·mer′i·to′ri·ous·ly** *adv.*

Dem·er·ol (dĕm′ə-rôl′, -rōl′). A trademark for a synthetic morphine.

de·mesne (dĭ-mān′, -mēn′) *n.* **1.** *Law.* Possession and use of one's own land. **2.** Lands retained by a feudal lord for his own use. **3.** The grounds belonging to a mansion or country house. **4.** An extensive piece of landed property; estate. **5.** A district; territory. **6.** A realm; domain. [ME *demeine* < OFr. *demaine.* —see DOMAIN.]

De·me·ter (dĭ-mē′tər) *n. Gk. Myth.* The goddess of agriculture, fertility, and marriage. [Gk. *Dēmētēr.*]

dem·e·ton (dĕm′ĭ-tŏn′) *n.* A pale-yellow, highly toxic organophosphorous liquid used as a systemic insecticide. [Blend of DIETHYL, MERCAPTAN, and THIONATE.]

demi– *pref.* **1.** Half: *demirelief.* **2.** Part; partly; to some degree: *demigod.* [Fr. < *demi,* half < Med. Lat. *dimedius* < Lat. *dimidius,* divided in half : *dis-,* apart + *medius,* half.]

dem·i·god (dĕm′ē-gŏd′) *n.* **1. a.** A mythological semidivine being, esp. the offspring of a god and a mortal. **b.** An inferior deity; minor god. **2.** A person with godlike attributes.

dem·i·god·dess (dĕm′ē-gŏd′ĭs) *n.* A woman regarded as a demigod.

dem·i·john (dĕm′ē-jŏn′) *n.* A large, narrow-necked bottle made of glass or earthenware, usually encased in wickerwork. [Prob. alteration of Fr. *dame-Jeanne,* lady Jane.]

demijohn

de·mil·i·ta·rize (dē-mĭl′ĭ-tə-rīz′) *tr.v.* **-rized, -riz·ing, -riz·es. 1.** To eliminate the military character of. **2.** To prohibit military forces or installations in. **3.** To replace military control of with civilian control. **—de·mil′i·ta·ri·za′tion** *n.*

dem·i·mon·daine (dĕm′ē-mŏn-dān′, -mŏn′dān′) *n.* A woman belonging to the demimonde. [Fr. < *demi-monde,* demimonde.]

dem·i·monde (dĕm′ē-mŏnd′) *n.* **1. a.** The social class of those who are kept by wealthy lovers or protectors. **b.** Prostitutes. **2.** A group that exists on the fringes of respectability: *the literary demimonde.* [Fr. : *demi-,* demi- + *monde,* world < Lat. *mundus.*]

dem·i·rep (dĕm′ē-rĕp′) *n.* A demimondaine. [DEMI- + REP(UTATION).]

de·mise (dĭ-mīz′) *n.* **1.** Death. **2.** The transfer of an estate by lease or will. **3.** The transfer of a ruler's authority by death or abdication. —*v.* **-mised, -mis·ing, -mis·es.** —*tr.* **1.** To transfer (an estate) by will or lease. **2.** To transfer (sovereignty) by abdication or will. —*intr.* **1.** To be transferred by will or descent. **2.** To die. [ME, transfer of property < OFr. *dimis,* p.part. of *demettre,* to release. —see DEMIT.] **—de·mis′a·ble** *adj.*

dem·i·sem·i·qua·ver (dĕm′ē-sĕm′ē-kwā′vər) *n. Chiefly Brit.* A thirty-second note.

de·mis·sion (dĭ-mĭsh′ən) *n.* The relinquishment of an office or function. [ME *dimissioun* < AN < Lat. *dimissio,* dismissal < *dimissus,* p.part. of *dimittere,* to release. —see DEMIT.]

de·mit (dĭ-mĭt′) *v.* **-mit·ted, -mit·ting, -mits.** —*tr.* **1.** To relinquish (an office or function). **2.** *Obs.* To dismiss. —*intr.* To resign. [ME *dimitten,* to release < OFr. *demettre* < Lat. *dimittere* : *dis-,* away + *mittere,* to send.]

dem·i·tasse (dĕm′ē-tăs′, -täs′) *n.* **1.** A small cup of strong black coffee. **2.** The cup used to serve demitasse. [Fr. : *demi-,* half + *tasse,* cup < OFr. < Ar. *tašt,* basin < Pers.]

dem·i·urge (dĕm′ē-ûrj′) *n.* **1. Demiurge.** The name used by Plato to designate the deity who fashions the material world. **2. Demiurge.** The Gnostic creator of the material world. **3.** A public magistrate in some ancient Greek states. [LLat. *demiurgus* < Gk. *dēmiourgos,* artisan : *dēmios,* public

(< *dēmos,* people) + *ergon,* work.] —**dem′i·ur′geous** (-ûr′-jəs), **dem′i·ur′gic** (-jĭk), **dem′i·ur′gi·cal** (-jĭ-kəl) *adj.* —**dem′i·ur′gi·cal·ly** *adv.*

dem·i·world (dĕm′ē-wûrld′) *n.* The demimonde.

dem·o (dĕm′ō) *n., pl.* **-os.** *Informal.* **1. a.** A demonstration, as of a product or service. **b.** A brief tape or recording used to illustrate the qualities of a performer, as a musician. **2.** A product, such as an automobile, used for demonstration and often sold later at a discount.

de·mob (dē-mŏb′) *Chiefly Brit. Informal.* —*tr.v.* **-mobbed, -mob·bing, -mobs.** To demobilize. —*n.* Demobilization.

de·mo·bil·ize (dē-mō′bə-līz′) *tr.v.* **-ized, -iz·ing, -iz·es. 1.** To dismiss from military service or use. **2.** To disband. —**de·mo′bil·i·za′tion** *n.*

de·moc·ra·cy (dĭ-mŏk′rə-sē) *n., pl.* **-cies. 1.** Government by the people, exercised either directly or through elected representatives. **2.** A political or social unit based upon democratic rule. **3.** The common people, esp. as the primary source of political power. **4.** Rule by the majority. **5.** The principles of social equality and respect for the individual within a community. **6. Democracy.** The ideology and policies of the Democratic Party in the United States. [OFr. *democratie* < LLat. *democratia* < Gk. *dēmokratia* : *dēmos,* people + *-kratia,* -cracy.]

dem·o·crat (dĕm′ə-krăt′) *n.* **1.** An advocate of democracy. **2. Democrat.** A member of the Democratic Party. [Fr. *démocrate,* back-formation < *democratie,* democracy < OFr.]

Usage: Republican politicians have long been in the habit of referring to the Democratic Party as the "Democrat Party," but this usage does not have wide acceptance off the campaign stump.

dem·o·crat·ic (dĕm′ə-krăt′ĭk) *adj.* **1.** Of, characterized by, or advocating democracy. **2. a.** Pertaining to, encompassing, or promoting the interests of the people. **b.** Carried on by the people in general. **3.** Believing in or practicing social equality: *"a proper democratic scorn for bloated dukes and lords"* (George Du Maurier). **4. Democratic.** Of, pertaining to, or characteristic of the Democratic Party. —**dem′o·crat′i·cal·ly** *adv.*

Democratic Party *n.* One of the two major political parties in the United States, owing its origin to a split in the Democratic-Republican Party under Andrew Jackson in 1828.

Dem·o·crat·ic-Re·pub·li·can Party (dĕm′ə-krăt′ĭk-rĭ-pŭb′lĭ-kən) *n.* A U.S. political party opposed to the Federalist Party, founded by Thomas Jefferson in 1792 and dissolved in 1828.

de·moc·ra·tize (dĭ-mŏk′rə-tīz′) *tr.v.* **-tized, -tiz·ing, -tiz·es.** To make democratic. —**de·moc′ra·ti·za′tion** *n.*

dé·mo·dé (dā′mō-dā′) *adj.* No longer in fashion; outmoded. [Fr.]

de·mod·u·late (dē-mŏj′ə-lāt′, -mŏd′yə-) *tr.v.* **-lat·ed, -lat·ing, -lates.** To extract (information) from a modulated carrier wave. —**de·mod′u·la′tion** *n.* —**de·mod′u·la′tor** *n.*

De·mo·gor·gon (dē′mə-gôr′gən, dĕ′mə-gôr′-) *n. Myth.* A terrifying deity or spirit, the very mention of whose name was thought to bring disaster or death. [LLat.]

dem·o·graph·ic (dĕm′ə-grăf′ĭk, dē′mə-) also **dem·o·graph·i·cal** (-ĭ-kəl) *adj.* Of or pertaining to demography. —**dem′o·graph′i·cal·ly** *adv.*

dem·o·graph·ics (dĕm′ə-grăf′ĭks, dē′mə-) *n. (used with a pl. verb).* Demographic data used esp. to identify consumer markets.

de·mog·ra·phy (dĭ-mŏg′rə-fē) *n.* The study of the characteristics of human populations, as size, growth, density, distribution, and vital statistics. [Fr. *démographie* : Gk. *dēmos,* people + Fr. *-graphie,* -graphy.] —**de·mog′ra·pher** *n.*

dem·oi·selle (dĕm′wə-zĕl′) *n.* **1.** A young lady. **2.** An Old World crane, *Anthropoides virgo,* having gray and black plumage and white plumes at the sides of the head. **3.** A damselfly. [Fr. < OFr. *dameisele.* —see DAMSEL.]

George Miksch Sutton

demoiselle

de·mol·ish (dĭ-mŏl′ĭsh) *tr.v.* **-ished, -ish·ing, -ish·es. 1.** To tear down completely; raze. **2.** To do away with completely; put an end to. **3.** To damage (someone's reputation, for example) severely. [OFr. *demolir, demoliss-* < Lat. *demoliri* : *de-,* apart + *moliri,* to build < *moles,* mass.]

dem·o·li·tion (dĕm′ə-lĭsh′ən, dē′mə-) *n.* **1.** The act or process of wrecking or destroying, esp. destruction by explosives. **2. demolitions.** Explosives, esp. when used or designed as weapons. [OFr. < Lat. *demolitio* < *demoliri,* to demolish.] —**dem′o·li′tion·ist** *n.*

demolition derby *n.* A sporting contest in which drivers crash old cars into each other until only one is left running.

de·mon (dē′mən) *n.* **1.** An evil being; devil. **2.** A persistently tormenting person, force, or passion. **3.** Also **dae·mon** or **dai·mon** (dī′mŏn′). *Gk. Myth.* An inferior divinity, such as a deified hero. **4.** Also **dae·mon** or **dai·mon** (dī′mŏn′). An attendant spirit; genius. **5.** One who is extremely zealous, skillful, or engrossed in a given activity. [ME < LLat. *daemon* < Lat., spirit < Gk. *daimōn,* divine power.]

de·mon·e·tize (dē-mŏn′ĭ-tīz′, -mŭn′-) *tr.v.* **-tized, -tiz·ing, -tiz·es. 1.** To divest (a coin, for example) of monetary value. **2.** To stop using (a metal) as a monetary standard. [Fr. *démonétiser* : *dé-,* de- + Lat. *moneta,* coin. —see MONEY.] —**de·mon′e·ti·za′tion** *n.*

de·mo·ni·ac (dĭ-mō′nē-ăk′) also **de·mo·ni·a·cal** (dē′mə-nī′ə-kəl) *adj.* **1.** Arising or seeming to arise from possession by a demon. **2.** Of, resembling, or suggestive of a devil; fiendish. —*n.* **demoniac.** One who is or seems to be possessed by a demon. [ME *demoniak* < LLat. *daemoniacus* < Gk. *daimoniakos* < *daimonios,* of a spirit < *daimōn,* divine power.] —**de′mo·ni′a·cal·ly** *adv.*

de·mon·ic (dĭ-mŏn′ĭk) *adj.* **1.** Befitting a demon; fiendish. **2.** Motivated by a spiritual force or genius; inspired. —**de·mon′i·cal·ly** *adv.*

de·mon·ize (dē′mə-nīz′) *tr.v.* **-ized, -iz·ing, -iz·es. 1.** To turn into or as if into a demon. **2.** To possess by a demon.

de·mon·ol·o·gy (dē′mə-nŏl′ə-jē) *n.* **1.** The study of demons. **2.** A treatise on demons or demon worship. **3.** Belief in demons. —**de′mon·ol′o·gist** *n.*

de·mon·stra·ble (dĭ-mŏn′strə-bəl) *adj.* **1.** Capable of being demonstrated. **2.** Obvious or apparent: *a shocking, demonstrable lie.* —**de·mon′stra·bil′i·ty, de·mon′stra·ble·ness** *n.* —**de·mon′stra·bly** *adv.*

dem·on·strate (dĕm′ən-strāt′) *v.* **-strat·ed, -strat·ing, -strates.** —*tr.* **1.** To prove or make evident by reasoning or adducing evidence. **2.** To describe or illustrate by experiment or practical application: *demonstrate the effect of a drug.* **3.** To show or reveal. **4.** To display, operate, and explain (a product). —*intr.* To present or participate in a demonstration. [Lat. *demonstrare, demonstrat-* : *de-,* completely + *monstrare,* to show < *monstrum,* divine portent < *monēre,* to warn.]

dem·on·stra·tion (dĕm′ən-strā′shən) *n.* **1.** The act of making evident or proving. **2.** Conclusive evidence; proof. **3.** An illustration or explanation, as of a theory or product, by exemplification or practical application. **4.** A manifestation, as of one's feelings. **5.** A public display of group opinion, as by a rally or march. **6.** A show of military strength.

de·mon·stra·tive (dĭ-mŏn′strə-tĭv) *adj.* **1.** Serving to manifest or prove. **2.** Involving or characterized by demonstration. **3.** Given to or marked by the open expression of emotion, esp. affection. **4.** *Gram.* Specifying or singling out the person or thing referred to. —*n. Gram.* A demonstrative pronoun or adjective. —**de·mon′stra·tive·ly** *adv.* —**de·mon′stra·tive·ness** *n.*

dem·on·stra·tor (dĕm′ən-strā′tər) *n.* **1.** One that demonstrates. **2.** A sample used in a demonstration.

dem·o·pho·bi·a (dĕm′ə-fō′bē-ə, dē′mə-) *n.* Abnormal fear of crowds. [Gk. *dēmos,* people + -PHOBIA.] —**dem′o·pho′bic** *adj.*

de·mor·al·ize (dĭ-môr′ə-līz′, -mŏr′-) *tr.v.* **-ized, -iz·ing, -iz·es. 1.** To debase the morals of; corrupt. **2.** To undermine the confidence or morale of; dishearten. **3.** To put into disorder; confuse. —**de·mor′al·i·za′tion** *n.* —**de·mor′al·iz′er** *n.*

de·mos (dē′mŏs′) *n.* **1.** The common people of an ancient Greek state. **2.** The common people; populace. [Gk. *dēmos,* district, people.]

de·mote (dĭ-mōt′) *tr.v.* **-mot·ed, -mot·ing, -motes.** To lower in rank or grade. [DE- + (PRO)MOTE.] —**de·mo′tion** *n.*

de·mot·ic (dĭ-mŏt′ĭk) *adj.* **1.** Of or pertaining to the common people; popular. **2.** Of, pertaining to, or written in the simplified form of ancient Egyptian hieratic writing. **3. Demotic.** Of or pertaining to a form of modern Greek based on colloquial use. —*n.* **Demotic.** Demotic Greek. [Gk. *dēmotikos* < *dēmotēs,* a commoner < *dēmos,* people.]

de·mount (dē-mount′) *tr.v.* **-mount·ed, -mount·ing, -mounts.** To remove (a motor, for example) from a position on a mounting or other support. —**de·mount′a·ble** *adj.*

de·mul·cent (dĭ-mŭl′sənt) *adj.* Soothing. —*n.* A soothing, usually mucilaginous or oily substance used esp. to relieve pain in inflamed or irritated mucous surfaces. [Lat. *demulcens, demulcent-,* pr.part. of *demulcēre,* to soften : *de-,* down + *mulcēre,* to stroke.]

de·mur (dĭ-mûr′) *intr.v.* **-murred, -mur·ring, -murs. 1.** To take exception; object. **2.** *Law.* To enter a demurrer. **3.** To delay. —*n.* **1.** The act of demurring. **2.** An objection. **3.** A delay. [ME *demuren,* to delay < OFr. *demorer* < Lat. *demorari* : *de-* (intensive) + *morari,* to delay < *mora,* delay.] —**de·mur′ra·ble** *adj.* —**de·mur′ral** (-mûr′əl, -mŭr′-) *n.*

de·mure (dĭ-myŏŏr′) *adj.* **-mur·er, -mur·est. 1.** Modest and reserved in manner or behavior. **2.** Feigning modesty or shyness; coy. [ME, prob. < AN.] —**de·mure′ly** *adv.* —**de·mure′ness** *n.*

de·mur·rage (dĭ-mûr′ĭj, -mŭr′-) *n.* **1.** The detention of a ship, freight car, or other cargo conveyance during loading or unloading beyond the scheduled time of departure. **2.** The compensation paid for demurrage.

de·mur·rer (dĭ-mûr′ər, -mŭr′-) *n.* **1.** A person who demurs; objector. **2.** *Law.* A plea to dismiss a lawsuit on the grounds that although the opposition's statements may be true, they are insufficient to sustain the claim. **3.** An objection.

de·my (dĭ-mī′) *n., pl.* **-mies.** Any of several standard sizes of paper, esp. paper measuring 16 by 21 inches. [Alteration of DEMI-.]

de·my·e·lin·ate (dē-mī′ə-lə-nāt′) *tr.v.* **-at·ed, -at·ing, -ates.** To destroy or remove the myelin from (a nerve fiber). —**de·my′e·lin·a′tion** *n.*

de·mys·ti·fy (dē-mĭs′tə-fī′) *tr.v.* **-fied, -fy·ing, -fies.** To make less difficult to understand. —**de·mys′ti·fi·ca′tion** *n.*

de·my·thol·o·gize (dē′mĭ-thŏl′ə-jīz′) *tr.v.* **-gized, -giz·ing, -giz·es. 1.** To rid of mythological elements in order to discover the underlying meaning: *demythologize biblical legends.* **2.** To remove mythical aspects from: *"providing an antiheroic age with heroes suitably demythologized, yet also grand"* (John Simon). **—de'my·thol'o·gi·za'tion** *n.* **—de'my·thol'o·giz'er** *n.*

den (dĕn) *n.* **1.** The shelter or retreat of a wild animal; lair. **2.** A cave used esp. as a refuge or hiding place. **3.** A residence or abode, esp. if hidden or squalid; haunt: *a den of thieves.* **4.** A small secluded room for study or relaxation. **5.** A unit of about eight to ten Cub Scouts. *—intr.v.* **denned, den·ning, dens.** To inhabit or hide in a den. [ME < OE *denn.*]

de·nar·i·us (dĭ-nâr'ē-əs) *n., pl.* **-i·i** (-ē-ī'). **1.** An ancient Roman silver coin. **2.** An ancient Roman gold coin valued at 25 silver denarii. [ME < Lat. —see DENARY.]

den·a·ry (dĕn'ə-rē) *adj.* **1.** Tenfold. **2.** Divided or counted by tens; decimal. [Lat. *denarius* < *deni,* by tens.]

de·na·tion·al·ize (dē-năsh'ə-nə-līz') *tr.v.* **-ized, -iz·ing, -iz·es. 1.** To deprive of national rights or characteristics. **2.** To return to private ownership. **—de·na'tion·al·i·za'tion** *n.*

de·nat·u·ral·ize (dē-năch'ər-ə-līz') *tr.v.* **-ized, -iz·ing, -iz·es. 1.** To make unnatural. **2.** To deprive of the rights of naturalization or citizenship. **—de·nat'u·ral·i·za'tion** *n.*

de·na·ture (dē-nā'chər) *tr.v.* **-tured, -tur·ing, -tures. 1.** To change the nature or natural qualities of. **2.** To render unfit to eat or drink without destroying usefulness in other applications, esp. to add methanol to ethyl alcohol. **3.** To alter the structure of (a protein), as with heat, alkali, or acid, so that some of the original properties are diminished or eliminated. **4.** To add nonfissionable matter to (fissionable material) to prevent use in an atomic weapon. **—de·na'tur·ant** *n.* **—de·na'tur·a'tion** *n.*

dendr– or **dendri–** *pref.* Variants of **dendro–.**

den·dri·form (dĕn'drə-fôrm') *adj.* Having the characteristic form or structure of a tree.

den·drite (dĕn'drīt') *n.* **1. a.** A mineral crystallizing in another mineral in the form of a branching or treelike mark. **b.** A rock or mineral bearing such a mark or marks. **2.** A branched part of a nerve cell that transmits impulses toward the cell body.

den·drit·ic (dĕn-drĭt'ĭk) also **den·drit·i·cal** (-ĭ-kəl) *adj.* **1.** Of, pertaining to, or resembling a dendrite. **2.** Treeshaped; dendriform. **—den·drit'i·cal·ly** *adv.*

dendro– or **dendri–** or **dendr–** *pref.* Tree; treelike: *dendrochronology.* [< Gk. *dendron,* tree.]

den·dro·chro·nol·o·gy (dĕn'drō-krə-nŏl'ə-jē) *n.* The study of the growth rings in trees to determine and date past events. **—den'dro·chron'o·log'i·cal** (-krŏn'ə-lŏj'ĭ-kəl) *adj.* **—den'dro·chron'o·log'i·cal·ly** *adv.*

den·droid (dĕn'droid') also **den·droid·al** (dĕn-droid'l) *adj.* Shaped like a tree.

den·drol·o·gy (dĕn-drŏl'ə-jē) *n.* The botanical study of trees. **—den'dro·log'ic** (-drə-lŏj'ĭk), **den'dro·log'i·cal** *adj.* **—den·drol'o·gist** *n.*

den·dron (dĕn'drŏn') *n.* A dendrite (sense 2). [Gk., tree.]

dene (dēn) *n. Chiefly Brit.* A sandy tract or dune by the seashore. [ME *den,* sandy seashore.]

De·neb (dĕn'ĕb') *n.* The brightest star in the constellation Cygnus, approximately 1,630 light years from Earth. [Ar. *dhanab,* tail.]

den·e·ga·tion (dĕn'ĭ-gā'shən) *n.* A denial. [Fr. < Lat. *denegatio* < *denegatus,* p.part. of *denegare,* to deny.]

den·gue (dĕng'gē, -gā') *n.* An infectious tropical disease transmitted by mosquitoes and characterized by fever, rash, and severe pains in the joints. [Sp., of African orig.]

de·ni·a·ble (dĭ-nī'ə-bəl) *adj.* Capable of being denied; questionable. **—de·ni'a·bly** *adv.*

de·ni·al (dĭ-nī'əl) *n.* **1.** A refusal to comply or satisfy a request. **2.** A refusal to grant the truth of a statement or allegation; contradiction. **3.** A rejection, as of a doctrine or belief. **4.** The act of disowning or disavowing; repudiation. **5.** *Law.* The opposing by a defendant of the allegation against him by the plaintiff. **6.** Abstinence; self-denial. [< DENY.]

de·ni·er¹ (dĭ-nī'ər) *n.* One who denies.

den·ier² (dən-yā') *n.* **1.** (*also* dĕn'yər). A unit of fineness for rayon, nylon, and silk yarns, based on a standard of 50 milligrams per 450 meters of yarn. **2.** (*also* də-nîr'). **a.** A small coin of varying composition and value current in France and western Europe from the eighth century until the French Revolution. **b.** *Archaic.* A small or trifling sum. [ME *denere,* a coin < OFr. *dener* < Lat. *denarius.* —see DENARIUS.]

den·i·grate (dĕn'ĭ-grāt') *tr.v.* **-grat·ed, -grat·ing, -grates. 1.** To deny the validity or importance of; belittle. **2.** To calumniate the character or reputation of; defame. [Lat. *denigrare, denigrat-,* to blacken, defame : *de-* (intensive) + *niger,* black.] **—den'i·gra'tion** *n.* **—den'i·gra'tor** *n.*

den·im (dĕn'ĭm) *n.* **1. a.** A coarse twilled cloth used for jeans, overalls, and work uniforms. **b. denims.** Garments made of coarse denim. **2.** A finer grade of denim material used in draperies and upholstery. [Fr. *(serge) de Nîmes,* (serge) of Nîmes, a city in southern France.]

de·ni·tri·fy (dē-nī'trə-fī') *tr.v.* **-fied, -fy·ing, -fies.** To remove nitrogen from (a material or chemical compound), as by bacterial action on soil. **—de·ni'tri·fi·ca'tion** *n.*

den·i·zen (dĕn'ĭ-zən) *n.* **1.** An inhabitant; resident. **2.** *Chiefly Brit.* A foreigner permitted certain rights and privileges of citizenship. **3.** One that frequents a particular place. **4.** *Ecol.* An animal or plant naturalized in a region to which it is not indigenous. *—tr.v.* **-zened, -zen·ing, -zens.** *Chiefly Brit.* To make a denizen of; naturalize. [ME *denisein* < AN *deinzein* < OFr. *deinz,* within < LLat. *deintus,* from within : Lat. *de-,* from + Lat. *intus,* within.] **—den'i·zen·a'tion** *n.*

den mother *n.* A woman who supervises a den of Cub Scouts.

de·nom·i·nate (dĭ-nŏm'ə-nāt') *tr.v.* **-nat·ed, -nat·ing, -nates.** To give a name to; designate. [Lat. *denominare, denominat-* : *de-* (intensive) + *nominare,* to name < *nomen,* name.] **—de·nom'i·na·ble** (-nə-bəl) *adj.*

de·nom·i·nate number (dĭ-nŏm'ə-nĭt) *n.* A number that designates a quantity as a multiple of a unit, as *12* in the expression *12 pounds.*

de·nom·i·na·tion (dĭ-nŏm'ə-nā'shən) *n.* **1.** The act of naming. **2.** A name; designation. **3.** The name of a class or group; classification. **4.** A class of units having specified values, as in a system of currency or weights. **5.** An organized group of religious congregations. **—de·nom'i·na'tion·al** *adj.* **—de·nom'i·na'tion·al·ly** *adv.*

de·nom·i·na·tion·al·ism (dĭ-nŏm'ə-nā'shə-nə-lĭz'əm) *n.* **1.** The tendency to separate into religious sects or denominations. **2.** Advocacy of the principles of denominationalism. **3.** Strict adherence to a denomination; sectarianism. **—de·nom'i·na'tion·al·ist** *n.*

de·nom·i·na·tive (dĭ-nŏm'ə-nā'tĭv, -nə-tĭv) *adj.* **1.** Giving or constituting a name; naming. **2.** *Gram.* Formed from a noun or adjective. *—n.* A word, esp. a verb, that is derived from a noun or adjective.

de·nom·i·na·tor (dĭ-nŏm'ə-nā'tər) *n.* **1.** *Math.* The quantity below the line indicating the number of units into which a whole is divided. **2.** A common trait or characteristic. **3.** An average level or standard: *The success of the film demonstrates the denominator of public taste.*

de·no·ta·tion (dē'nō-tā'shən) *n.* **1.** The act of denoting; indication. **2.** A sign, symbol, or reference that denotes; indicator. **3.** Something signified or referred to; a particular meaning of a symbol. **4.** The explicit meaning of a word as opposed to its connotation.

de·no·ta·tive (dĭ-nō'tə-tĭv, dē'nō-tā'-) *adj.* **1.** Able to denote; designative. **2.** Explicit. **—de·no'ta·tive·ly** *adv.*

de·note (dĭ-nōt') *tr.v.* **-not·ed, -not·ing, -notes. 1.** To reveal or indicate; mark. **2.** To serve as a symbol or name for; signify. **3.** To refer to specifically; mean explicitly. [OFr. *denoter* < Lat. *denotare* : *de-* (intensive) + *notare,* to mark < *nota,* mark.] **—de·not'a·ble** *adj.* **—de·no'tive** *adj.*

Usage: *Denote* means "to mark" or "to signify directly." *Connote* means "to suggest or convey to the mind what is not explicit." Thus: *Frost denotes the coming of winter. For us as children, winter connoted the beauty of frost on the window and the coming of Christmas.* In speaking of words, *denote* is used to indicate the thing a word names, and *connote* to indicate our associations with that thing: *The word* bachelor *denotes an unmarried man and connotes a life of parties and carefree amusements.*

dé·noue·ment also **de·noue·ment** (dā'nōō-mäN') *n.* **1.** The solution, clarification, or unraveling of the plot of a play or novel. **2.** The outcome or final solution of a sequence of events. [Fr. < OFr. *desnouement,* an untying < *desnouer,* to undo : *des-,* de- + *nouer,* to tie < Lat. *nodare* < *nodus,* knot.]

de·nounce (dĭ-nouns') *tr.v.* **-nounced, -nounc·ing, -nounc·es. 1.** To condemn openly, esp. as evil; censure. **2.** To accuse formally. **3.** To give formal announcement of the ending of (a treaty). [ME *denouncen,* to proclaim < OFr. *denoncier* < Lat. *denuntiare* : *de-* (intensive) + *nuntiare,* to announce < *nuntius,* messenger.] **—de·nounce'ment** *n.* **—de·nounc'er** *n.*

dense (dĕns) *adj.* **dens·er, dens·est. 1. a.** Having relatively high density. **b.** Crowded closely together; compact. **2.** Thick or impenetrable: *a dense fog.* **3.** Requiring effort to understand because of complexity in structure or content: *a dense novel.* **4.** Slow in understanding or perceiving; stupid. **5.** Opaque, with good contrast between light and dark areas. Used of a developed photographic negative. [Lat. *densus.*] **—dense'ly** *adv.* **—dense'ness** *n.*

den·sim·e·ter (dĕn-sĭm'ĭ-tər) *n.* An instrument used to determine density. [Lat. *densus,* dense + -METER.] **—den'si·met'ric** (-sə-mĕt'rĭk) *adj.*

den·si·tom·e·ter (dĕn'sĭ-tŏm'ĭ-tər) *n.* An apparatus for measuring the optical density of a material, such as a negative. [DENSIT(Y) + -METER.]

den·si·ty (dĕn'sĭ-tē) *n., pl.* **-ties. 1.** The quality or condition of being dense. **2.** *Physics.* **a.** The amount of something per unit measure, esp. per unit length, area, or volume. **b.** The mass per unit volume of a substance under specified or standard conditions of pressure and temperature. **3.** *Computer Sci.* The number of units of useful information contained within a linear dimension. **4.** The number of inhabitants per unit geographic region. **5.** The degree of optical opacity of a medium or material, as of a photographic negative. **6.** Thickness of consistency; impenetrability. **7.** Complexity of structure or content. **8.** Stupidity; dullness.

dentate
Dentate chestnut leaf

dent[1] (dĕnt) *n.* **1.** A depression in a surface made by pressure or a blow. **2.** A usually weakening effect or impression made by or as if by lessening. **3.** Meaningful progress; headway. *—v.* **dent·ed, dent·ing, dents.** *—tr.* To make a dent in. *—intr.* To become dented. [ME *dent,* alteration of *dint,* blow < OE *dynt.*]

dent[2] (dĕnt) *n.* A tooth (sense 3). [Fr. < Lat. *dens.*]

dent– *pref.* Variant of **denti-.**

den·tal (dĕn'tl) *adj.* **1.** Of, pertaining to, or for the teeth. **2.** Of, pertaining to, or intended for dentistry. **3.** Articulated with the tip of the tongue near or against the upper front teeth. Used of a speech sound. *—n.* A dental consonant. [NLat. *dentalis* < Lat. *dens,* tooth.]

dental floss *n.* A strong waxed or unwaxed thread used to clean areas between the teeth.

dental hygienist *n.* One who provides preventive dental services, as cleaning and taking x-rays, usually in conjunction with a dentist.

dental plate *n.* A denture.

dental technician *n.* One who makes dental appliances, as bridges or dentures.

den·tate (dĕn'tāt') *adj.* Edged with toothlike projections. [Lat. *dentatus* < *dens,* tooth.] **—den'tate'ly** *adv.*

den·ta·tion (dĕn-tā'shən) *n.* **1.** The condition of being dentate. **2.** A toothlike part or projection.

dent corn *n.* A tall-growing variety of corn, *Zea mays indentata,* having yellow or white kernels that are indented at the tip.

denti– or **dent–** *pref.* **1.** Tooth: *dentoid.* **2.** Dental: *dentilabial.* [< Lat. *dens, dent-,* tooth.]

den·ti·cle (dĕn'tĭ-kəl) *n.* A small tooth or toothlike projection. [ME < Lat. *denticulus,* dim. of *dens,* tooth.]

den·tic·u·late (dĕn-tĭk'yə-lĭt) also **den·tic·u·lat·ed** (-lā'tĭd) *adj.* **1.** Finely toothed; minutely dentate. **2.** *Archit.* Having dentils. [Lat. *denticulatus* < *denticulus,* denticle.] **—den·tic'u·late·ly** *adv.* **—den·tic'u·la'tion** *n.*

den·ti·form (dĕn'tə-fôrm') *adj.* Shaped like a tooth.

den·ti·frice (dĕn'tə-frĭs) *n.* A substance, such as a powder or paste, for cleaning the teeth. [OFr. < Lat. *dentifricium* : *dens,* tooth + *fricare,* to rub.]

den·tig·er·ous (dĕn-tĭj'ər-əs) *adj.* Bearing teeth. [DENTI- + Lat. *gerere,* to bear.]

den·til (dĕn'tĭl) *n. Archit.* One of a series of small rectangular blocks forming a molding or projecting beneath a cornice. [Obs. Fr. *dentille* < OFr., dim. of *dent,* tooth < Lat. *dens.*]

den·tine (dĕn'tēn') also **den·tin** (-tĭn) *n.* The calcareous part of a tooth, beneath the enamel, containing the pulp chamber and root canals. **—den·tin'al** (dĕn-tē'nəl, dĕn'tə-) *adj.*

den·tist (dĕn'tĭst) *n.* A person whose profession is dentistry. [Fr. *dentiste* < *dent,* tooth < Lat. *dens.*]

den·tist·ry (dĕn'tĭ-strē) *n.* The diagnosis, prevention, and treatment of diseases of the teeth and related structures.

den·ti·tion (dĕn-tĭsh'ən) *n.* **1.** *Biol.* The type, number, and arrangement of teeth, esp. in animals. **2.** The cutting of teeth; teething. [Lat. *dentitio* < *dentitus,* p.part. of *dentire,* to teethe < *dens,* tooth.]

den·toid (dĕn'toid') *adj.* Toothlike.

den·tu·lous (dĕn'chə-ləs) *adj.* Possessing teeth; toothed. [Back-formation < E. *edentulous,* toothless < Lat. *edentulus* : *ex-,* out + *dens,* tooth.]

den·ture (dĕn'chər) *n.* A set of artificial teeth. [Fr. < OFr. < *dent,* tooth < Lat. *dens.*]

de·nu·cle·ar·ize (dē-no͞o'klē-ə-rīz', -nyo͞o'-) *tr.v.* **-ized, -iz·ing, -iz·es.** To remove or ban nuclear arms from. **—de·nu'cle·ar·i·za'tion** *n.*

de·nu·date (dĭ-no͞o'dāt', -nyo͞o'-) *tr.v.* **-dat·ed, -dat·ing, -dates.** To denude. *—adj.* Bare; denuded. [Lat. *denudare, denudat-,* to denude.]

de·nude (dĭ-no͞od', -nyo͞od') *tr.v.* **-nud·ed, -nud·ing, -nudes.** **1.** To divest of covering. **2.** *Geol.* To expose (rock strata) by erosion. [Lat. *denudare* : *de-,* completely + *nudare,* to make bare < *nudus,* nude.] **—de'nu·da'tion** (dē'no͞o-dā'shən, -nyo͞o-, dĕn'yo͞o-) *n.*

de·nu·mer·a·ble (dĭ-no͞o'mər-ə-bəl, -nyo͞o'-) *adj.* Capable of being put into one-to-one correspondence with the positive integers; countable. **—de·nu'mer·a·bil'i·ty** *n.* **—de·nu'mer·a·bly** *adv.*

de·nun·ci·a·tion (dĭ-nŭn'sē-ā'shən, -shē-) *n.* **1.** The act of denouncing; open condemnation or censure. **2.** The act of accusing another of a crime before a public prosecutor. **—de·nun'ci·a'tive, de·nun'ci·a·to'ry** (-ə-tôr'ē, -tōr'ē) *adj.*

de·ny (dĭ-nī') *tr.v.* **-nied, -ny·ing, -nies.** **1.** To declare untrue; contradict. **2.** To refuse to believe; reject. **3.** To refuse to recognize or acknowledge; disavow. **4.** To refuse to grant; withhold. *—**idiom.*** **deny (oneself).** To abstain from indulging oneself in. [ME *denien* < OFr. *denier* < Lat. *denegare* : *de-* (intensive) + *negare,* to say no.]

de·o·dar (dē'ə-där') or **de·o·dar·a** (-där'ə) *n.* A tall cedar, *Cedrus deodara,* native to the Himalayas, having drooping branches and wood valued as timber. [Hindi *dē'odār* < Skt. *devadāru* : *deva-,* divine + *dāru,* wood.]

de·o·dor·ant (dē-ō'dər-ənt) *n.* **1.** A substance applied to counteract body odors. **2.** A chemical exposed to or sprayed into the air to counteract staleness. *—adj.* Capable of destroying or disguising odors.

de·o·dor·ize (dē-ō'də-rīz') *tr.v.* **-ized, -iz·ing, -iz·es.** To disguise or absorb the odor of. **—de·o'dor·i·za'tion** *n.* **—de·o'dor·iz'er** *n.*

de·on·tol·o·gy (dē'ŏn-tŏl'ə-jē) *n.* The theory or study of moral obligation or commitment; ethics. [Gk. *deon, deont-,* obligation, necessity < neuter p.part. of *dein,* to need, lack + -LOGY.] **—de·on'to·log'i·cal** (-tə-lŏj'ĭ-kəl) *adj.* **—de'on·tol'o·gist** *n.*

de·or·bit (dē-ôr'bĭt) *intr. & tr.v.* **-bit·ed, -bit·ing, -bits.** To go or cause to go out of orbit. *—n.* The process of deorbiting.

De·o vo·len·te (dē'ō və-lĕn'tē, dā'ō) *adv.* God willing. [Lat.]

de·ox·i·dize (dē-ŏk'sĭ-dīz') *tr.v.* **-dized, -diz·ing, -diz·es.** To remove oxygen, esp. chemically combined oxygen, from. **—de·ox'i·di·za'tion** *n.* **—de·ox'i·diz'er** *n.*

deoxy– *pref.* A molecule containing less oxygen than another to which it is closely related: *deoxycorticosterone.* [DE- + OXY-.]

de·ox·y·cor·ti·cos·ter·one (dē-ŏk'sē-kôr'tĭ-kŏs'tə-rōn') *n.* A steroid hormone, $C_{21}H_{30}O_3$, derived from the adrenal cortex and used to treat adrenal insufficiency.

de·ox·y·gen·ate (dē-ŏk'sə-jə-nāt') *tr.v.* **-at·ed, -at·ing, -ates.** To remove oxygen from. **—de·ox'y·gen·a'tion** *n.*

de·ox·y·ri·bo·nu·cle·ic acid (dē-ŏk'sē-rī'bō-no͞o-klē'ĭk, -nyo͞o-) *n.* DNA.

de·ox·y·ri·bo·nu·cle·o·tide (dē-ŏk'sē-rī'bō-no͞o'klē-ə-tīd', -nyo͞o'-) *n.* A nucleotide, containing deoxyribose, that is a constituent of DNA. [DEOXYRIBO(SE) + NUCLEOTIDE.]

de·ox·y·ri·bose (dē-ŏk'sē-rī'bōs') *n.* A sugar, $C_5H_{10}O_4$, that is a constituent of deoxyribonucleic acid.

de·part (dĭ-pärt') *v.* **-part·ed, -part·ing, -parts.** *—intr.* **1.** To go away; leave. **2.** To die. **3.** To vary, as from a regular course; deviate: *depart from custom.* *—tr.* To go away from; leave. [ME *departen* < OFr. *departir,* to divide : *de-,* away (< Lat.) + *partir,* to divide < Lat. *partire* < *pars,* part.]

de·part·ed (dĭ-pär'tĭd) *adj.* **1.** Bygone; past. **2.** Dead.

de·part·ment (dĭ-pärt'mənt) *n.* **1.** A distinct, usually specialized division of a large organization, such as a government or business. **2. Department.** One of the principal executive divisions of the federal government of the United States, headed by a cabinet officer. **3.** An administrative district in the government of France. **4.** A division of a school or college dealing with a particular field of knowledge: *the physics department.* **5.** *Informal.* An area of special knowledge or activity; sphere. [Fr. *département* < OFr., separation < *departir,* to divide. —see DEPART.] **—de'part·men'tal** (dē'pärt-mĕn'tl) *adj.* **—de'part·men'tal·ly** *adv.*

de·part·men·tal·ize (dē'pärt-mĕn'tl-īz') *tr.v.* **-ized, -iz·ing, -iz·es.** To organize into departments. **—de'part·men'tal·i·za'tion** *n.*

department store *n.* A large retail establishment offering a wide variety of merchandise and services and organized in separate departments.

de·par·ture (dĭ-pär'chər) *n.* **1.** The act of leaving. **2.** A starting out, as on a trip or a new course of action. **3.** A deviation or divergence, as from an established rule, plan, or procedure. **4.** The distance sailed due east or west by a ship on its course.

de·pend (dĭ-pĕnd') *intr.v.* **-pend·ed, -pend·ing, -pends.** **1.** To rely, as for support or aid: *depends on her scholarship.* **2.** To be assured; place trust: *You can depend on me.* **3.** To be determined, conditioned, or dependent. **4.** To hang down: *icicles depending from the tree branches.* **5.** *Informal.* To be pending or undecided. [ME *dependen,* to hang down < OFr. *dependre* < Lat. *dependēre* : *de-,* down + *pendēre,* to hang.]

Usage: *Depend,* indicating condition or contingency, is always followed by *on* or *upon,* as in *It depends on who is in charge.* Omission of the preposition is typical of casual speech.

de·pend·a·ble (dĭ-pĕn'də-bəl) *adj.* Capable of being depended upon; trustworthy. **—de·pend'a·bil'i·ty, de·pend'a·ble·ness** *n.* **—de·pend'a·bly** *adv.*

de·pend·ance (dĭ-pĕn'dəns) *n.* Variant of **dependence.**

de·pend·an·cy (dĭ-pĕn'dən-sē) *n.* Variant of **dependency.**

de·pend·ant (dĭ-pĕn'dənt) *adj. & n.* Variant of **dependent.**

de·pend·ence also **de·pend·ance** (dĭ-pĕn'dəns) *n.* **1.** The state of being dependent, as for support. **2.** Subordination to someone or something needed or greatly desired. **3.** The state of being determined, influenced, or controlled by something else. **4.** Trust; reliance.

de·pend·en·cy also **de·pend·an·cy** (dĭ-pĕn'dən-sē) *n., pl.* **-cies.** **1.** Dependence. **2.** Something dependent or subordinate. **3.** A territory or state under the jurisdiction of another country from which it is separated geographically.

de·pend·ent also **de·pend·ant** (dĭ-pĕn'dənt) *adj.* **1.** Contingent upon something or someone else. **2.** Subordinate. **3.** Relying on or requiring the aid of another for support: *dependent children.* **4.** Hanging down. *—n.* One who relies on another for support. **—de·pend'ent·ly** *adv.*

dependent clause *n. Gram.* A clause that cannot stand alone as a full sentence and that functions as a noun, adjective, or adverb within a sentence.

dependent variable *n.* A mathematical variable whose value is determined by the value assumed by an independent variable.

de·per·son·al·ize (dē-pûr'sə-nə-līz') *tr.v.* **-ized, -iz·ing, -iz·es.** **1.** To deprive of personal or individual character. **2.** To render impersonal. **—de·per'son·al·i·za'tion** *n.*

de·pict (dĭ-pĭkt′) *tr.v.* **-pict·ed, -pict·ing, -picts. 1.** To represent in a picture or sculpture. **2.** To represent in words; describe. [Lat. *depingere, depict-* : *de-*, completely + *pingere,* to picture.] **—de·pic′tion** *n.*

de·pig·men·ta·tion (dē-pĭg′mən-tā′shən, -mĕn-) *n.* Loss of normal pigmentation.

dep·i·late (dĕp′ə-lāt′) *tr.v.* **-lat·ed, -lat·ing, -lates.** To remove hair from (the body). [Lat. *depilare, depilat-* : *de-*, completely + *pilare,* to deprive of hair < *pilus,* hair.] **—dep′i·la′tion** *n.* **—dep′i·la′tor** *n.*

de·pil·a·to·ry (dĭ-pĭl′ə-tôr′ē, -tōr′ē) *adj.* Capable of removing hair. *—n., pl.* **-ries.** A liquid or cream used to remove unwanted hair from the body.

de·plane (dē-plān′) *intr.v.* **-planed, -plan·ing, -planes.** To disembark from an airplane.

de·plete (dĭ-plēt′) *tr.v.* **-plet·ed, -plet·ing, -pletes. 1.** To reduce or lessen in quantity, value, or effectiveness; exhaust. **2.** To empty. [Lat. *deplere, deplet-,* to empty : *de-* (reversal) + *plere,* to fill.] **—de·plet′a·ble** *adj.* **—de·ple′tion** *n.*

Synonyms: *deplete, drain, exhaust, impoverish, enervate.* These verbs all signify depletion of strength or resources to the point of functional impairment. *Deplete* refers to using up gradually and only hints at harmful consequences. *Drain* suggests reduction by gradually drawing off and is stronger in implying harm. *Exhaust* stresses reduction to a point of no further usefulness in a given activity. *Impoverish* refers to severe reduction of resources or qualities essential to adequate functioning. *Enervate* refers to weakening of vitality or moral strength.

de·plor·a·ble (dĭ-plôr′ə-bəl, -plōr′-) *adj.* **1.** Worthy of severe reproach. **2.** Lamentable; grievous. **3.** Wretched; bad. **—de·plor′a·ble·ness, de·plor′a·bil′i·ty** *n.* **—de·plor′a·bly** *adv.*

de·plore (dĭ-plôr′, -plōr′) *tr.v.* **-plored, -plor·ing, -plores. 1.** To feel or express sorrow over. **2.** To feel or express regret about. **3.** To feel or express strong disapproval of; censure. [OFr. *deplorer* < Lat. *deplorare* : *de-* (intensive) + *plorare,* to wail.]

de·ploy (dĭ-ploi′) *v.* **-ployed, -ploy·ing, -ploys.** *—tr.* **1.** To station (persons or forces) systematically over an area. **2.** To spread out (troops) to form an extended front. *—intr.* To be or become deployed. [Fr. *déployer* < OFr. *despleier* < Lat. *displicare,* to scatter : *dis-* (reversal) + *plicare,* to fold.] **—de·ploy′ment** *n.*

de·plume (dē-plo͞om′) *tr.v.* **-plumed, -plum·ing, -plumes. 1.** To pluck the feathers from. **2.** To deprive of honor or pride. [ME *deplumen* < OFr. *deplumer* < Med. Lat. *deplumare* : *de-*, off + *pluma,* feather.] **—de′plu·ma′tion** *n.*

de·po·lar·ize (dē-pō′lə-rīz′) *tr.v.* **-ized, -iz·ing, -iz·es.** To eliminate or counteract the polarization of. **—de·po′lar·i·za′tion** *n.*

de·po·lit·i·cize (dē′pə-lĭt′ĭ-sīz′) *tr.v.* **-cized, -ciz·ing, -ciz·es.** To remove the political aspect or status from; remove from the political sphere. **—de′po·lit′i·ci·za′tion** *n.*

de·pol·lute (dē′pə-lo͞ot′) *tr.v.* **-lut·ed, -lut·ing, -lutes.** To remove the pollution from: *depollute a river.*

de·pone (dĭ-pōn′) *v.* **-poned, -pon·ing, -pones.** *—tr.* To testify or declare under oath. *—intr.* To give testimony. [ME *deponen* < Med. Lat. *deponere* < Lat., to put down : *de-*, down + *ponere,* to put.]

de·po·nent (dĭ-pō′nənt) *adj. Gram.* Denoting a verb of active meaning but passive form, as certain Latin and Greek verbs. *—n.* **1.** *Gram.* A deponent verb. **2.** *Law.* A person who testifies under oath, esp. in writing. [LLat. *deponens, deponent-* < Lat., pr.part. of *deponere,* to put down. —see DEPONE.]

de·pop·u·late (dē-pŏp′yə-lāt′) *tr.v.* **-lat·ed, -lat·ing, -lates.** To reduce sharply the population of, as by disease, expulsion, or massacre. [Lat. *depopulari, depopulat-,* to lay waste : *de-* (intensive) + *populari,* to ravage < *populus,* people, throng.] **—de·pop′u·la′tion** *n.* **—de·pop′u·la′tor** *n.*

de·port (dĭ-pôrt′, -pōrt′) *tr.v.* **-port·ed, -port·ing, -ports. 1.** To expel from a country. **2.** To behave or conduct (oneself) in a given manner. [Partly < Fr. *déporter,* to banish, and partly < OFr. *deporter,* to behave, both < Lat. *deportare,* to carry away : *de-*, away + *portare,* to carry.]

de·port·a·ble (dĭ-pôr′tə-bəl, -pōr′-) *adj.* **1.** Subject to deportation. **2.** Punishable by deportation.

de·por·ta·tion (dē′pôr-tā′shən, -pōr-) *n.* **1.** The act or an instance of deporting. **2.** The expulsion from a country of an undesirable alien.

de·port·ee (dē′pôr-tē′, -pōr-) *n.* A deported person.

de·port·ment (dĭ-pôrt′mənt, -pōrt′-) *n.* Conduct; demeanor.

de·pos·al (dĭ-pō′zəl) *n.* The act of deposing from office.

de·pose (dĭ-pōz′) *v.* **-posed, -pos·ing, -pos·es.** *—tr.* **1.** To remove from office or a position of power. **2.** *Archaic.* To put or lay down; deposit. **3.** *Law.* To declare under oath, esp. in writing. *—intr. Law.* To testify, esp. in writing. [ME *deposen* < OFr. *deposer* : *de-*, away (< Lat.) + *poser,* to put. —see POSE[1].] **—de·pos′a·ble** *adj.*

de·pos·it (dĭ-pŏz′ĭt) *v.* **-it·ed, -it·ing, -its.** *—tr.* **1.** To lay or set down; place. **2.** To put down, esp. in a layer, by a natural process: *deposit sediment.* **3.** To give as partial payment or security. **4.** To entrust (money) to a bank. *—intr.* To become deposited; settle. *—n.* **1.** Something entrusted for safekeeping, as money in a bank. **2.** The condition of being deposited. **3.** A partial or initial payment of a cost or debt. **4.** A sum of money given as security for an item acquired for temporary use. **5.** A depository. **6.** Something deposited, particularly by a natural process, esp. mineral or sandy matter settled out of water or accumulated in a vein. [Lat. *deponere, deposit-* : *de-*, aside + *ponere,* to put.] **—de·pos′i·tor** *n.*

de·pos·i·tar·y (dĭ-pŏz′ĭ-tĕr′ē) *n., pl.* **-ies. 1.** A person entrusted with something. **2.** A repository; depository.

dep·o·si·tion (dĕp′ə-zĭsh′ən) *n.* **1.** The act of deposing, as from office. **2.** The act of depositing. **3.** Something deposited; deposit. **4.** *Law.* Testimony under oath, esp. a written statement by a witness for use in court in his absence. **—dep′o·si′tion·al** *adj.*

de·pos·i·to·ry (dĭ-pŏz′ĭ-tôr′ē, -tōr′ē) *n., pl.* **-ries. 1.** A place where something is deposited for safekeeping; repository. **2.** A trustee; depositary.

de·pot (dē′pō, dĕp′ō) *n.* **1.** A railroad or bus station. **2.** A warehouse or storehouse. **3. a.** A storage installation for military materials. **b.** A station for receiving, classifying, and assembling military personnel. [Fr. *dépôt* < OFr. *depost* < Lat. *depositum,* deposit < neuter p.part. of *deponere,* to deposit.]

depot
In Boise, Idaho

de·prave (dĭ-prāv′) *tr.v.* **-praved, -prav·ing, -praves.** To debase morally; corrupt. [ME *depraven,* to corrupt < OFr. *depraver* < Lat. *depravare* : *de-* (intensive) + *pravus,* crooked.] **—dep′ra·va′tion** (dĕp′rə-vā′shən) *n.* **—de·prav′er** *n.*

de·praved (dĭ-prāvd′) *adj.* Morally corrupt; perverted. **—de·prav′ed·ly** (-prā′vĭd-lē, -prāvd′lē) *adv.*

de·prav·i·ty (dĭ-prăv′ĭ-tē) *n., pl.* **-ties. 1.** Moral corruption. **2.** A wicked or perverse act.

dep·re·cate (dĕp′rĭ-kāt′) *tr.v.* **-cat·ed, -cat·ing, -cates. 1.** To express disapproval of. **2.** To depreciate; belittle. [Lat. *deprecari, deprecat-,* to ward off by prayer : *de-*, against + *precari,* to pray.] **—dep′re·ca′tion** *n.* **—dep′re·ca′tor** *n.*

Usage: The first and fully accepted meaning of *deprecate* is "to express disapproval of." But the word has steadily encroached upon the meaning of *depreciate.* It is now used, almost to the exclusion of *depreciate,* in the sense "to belittle or mildly disparage": *He deprecated his own contribution.* This newer sense is accepted by a majority of the Usage Panel.

dep·re·ca·to·ry (dĕp′rĭ-kə-tôr′ē, -tōr′ē) also **dep·re·ca·tive** (-kā′tĭv) *adj.* Expressing deprecation; disapproving. **—dep′re·ca·to′ri·ly** *adv.*

de·pre·cia·ble (dĭ-prē′shə-bəl) *adj.* Capable of being depreciated in value.

de·pre·ci·ate (dĭ-prē′shē-āt′) *v.* **-at·ed, -at·ing, -ates.** *—tr.* **1.** To lessen the price or value of. **2.** To make to seem less valuable or important; disparage. *—intr.* To diminish in value. [Med. Lat. *depreciare, depreciat-,* alteration of LLat. *depretiare* : Lat. *de-*, down + Lat. *pretium,* price.] **—de·pre′ci·a′tor** *n.*

de·pre·ci·a·tion (dĭ-prē′shē-ā′shən) *n.* **1.** A decrease or loss in value because of wear, age, or other cause. **2.** *Accounting.* An allowance made for a loss in value of property. **3.** A reduction in the purchasing value of money. **4.** An instance of disparaging.

de·pre·cia·to·ry (dĭ-prē′shə-tôr′ē, -tōr′ē) also **de·pre·cia·tive** (-shə-tĭv, -shē-ā′tĭv) *adj.* **1.** Diminishing in value. **2.** Disparaging.

dep·re·date (dĕp′rĭ-dāt′) *v.* **-dat·ed, -dat·ing, -dates.** *—tr.* To prey upon; plunder. *—intr.* To commit plunder. [LLat. *depraedari, depraedat-* : Lat. *de-* (intensive) + Lat. *praedari,* to plunder < *praeda,* booty.] **—dep′re·da′tion** *n.* **—dep′re·da′tor** *n.* **—de·pred′a·to′ry** (dĭ-prĕd′ə-tôr′ē, -tōr′ē, dĕp′rĭ-də-) *adj.*

de·press (dĭ-prĕs′) *tr.v.* **-pressed, -press·ing, -press·es. 1.** To lower in spirits; sadden. **2.** To press down; lower: *depress a brake pedal.* **3.** To lessen the activity or force of; weaken. **4.** To lower prices in (a stock market). [ME *depressen,* to push down < OFr. *depresser* < Lat. *depressus,* p.part. of *deprimere* : *de-*, down + *premere,* to press.] **—de·press′i·ble** *adj.*

de·pres·sant (dĭ-prĕs′ənt) *adj.* Serving to lower the rate of vital activities. *—n.* A depressant drug.

de·pressed (dĭ-prĕst′) *adj.* **1.** Low in spirits; dejected. **2.** *Bot.* Flattened downward, as if pressed from above. **3.** *Zool.* Flattened along the dorsal and ventral surfaces. **4.** Sunk below the surrounding region: *the depressed center of a crater.* **5.** Suffering from social and economic hardship.

de·press·ing (dĭ-prĕs′ĭng) *adj.* Dismal; gloomy. **—de·press′ing·ly** *adv.*

de·pres·sion (dĭ-prĕsh′ən) *n.* **1. a.** The act of depressing. **b.** The condition of being depressed. **2.** An area that is sunk below its surroundings; hollow. **3.** *Meteorol.* A region of low barometric pressure. **4.** The angular distance below the horizontal plane through the point of observation. **5.** *Astron.* The angular distance of a celestial body below the horizon. **6.** A reduction in activity or force. **7.** The condition of feeling sad or melancholy. **8.** *Psychiat.* A psychotic or neurotic condition characterized by an inability to concentrate, insomnia, and feelings of dejection and guilt. **9.** *Econ.* A period of drastic decline in the national economy, characterized by decreasing business activity, falling prices, and unemployment.

Depression glass *n.* Glassware of many colors and patterns produced in large quantities during the 1920's and

1930's. [After the Great *Depression,* a period of severe economic hardship during the 1930's.]

de·pres·sive (dĭ-prĕs′ĭv) *adj.* **1.** Causing depression. **2.** Of or pertaining to psychological depression. **—de·pres′sive·ly** *adv.* **—de·pres′sive·ness** *n.*

de·pres·sor (dĭ-prĕs′ər) *n.* **1.** Something that depresses or is used to depress. **2.** A depressor nerve. **3.** Any of several muscles that cause depression or contraction of a part. **4.** An instrument used to depress a part.

depressor nerve *n.* A nerve that lowers arterial blood pressure.

de·pres·sur·ize (dē-prĕsh′ə-rīz′) *tr.v.* **-ized, -iz·ing, -iz·es.** To release from pressure. **—de·pres′sur·i·za′tion** *n.*

de·priv·al (dĭ-prī′vəl) *n.* Deprivation.

dep·ri·va·tion (dĕp′rə-vā′shən) *n.* **1. a.** The act of depriving; loss. **b.** The condition of being deprived; privation. **2.** A removal of rank or office.

de·prive (dĭ-prīv′) *tr.v.* **-prived, -priv·ing, -prives. 1.** To take something away from; dispossess: *Redistricting deprived the state of two congressional seats.* **2.** To keep from possessing or enjoying; deny: *He was deprived of his just acclaim.* **3.** To remove from office. [ME *depriven* < OFr. *depriver* < Med. Lat. *deprivare* : Lat. *de-,* completely + Lat. *privare,* to rob < *privus,* without.] **—de·priv′a·ble** *adj.*

de·prived (dĭ-prīvd′) *adj.* Characterized by deprivation, esp. of economic or social necessities.

de·pro·gram (dē-prō′grăm′, -grəm) *tr.v.* **-grammed, -gram·ming, -grams** or **-gramed, -gram·ing, -grams.** To counteract or try to counteract the effect of an indoctrination, esp. a religious indoctrination. **—de·pro′gram′mer** *n.*

depth (dĕpth) *n.* **1.** The condition or quality of being deep. **2. a.** The extent, measurement, or dimension downward, backward, or inward. **b.** The linear measurement or sense of distance from an observation point, as perspective in painting. **3.** Often **depths.** A deep part of or place: *in the depths of the forest.* **4.** The most profound or intense part or stage: *the depth of despair.* **5.** The severest or worst part: *in the depth of winter.* **6.** A bad or deteriorated condition: *Production has fallen to incredible depths.* **7.** Intellectual complexity or penetration; profundity: *a novel of great depth.* **8.** The range of one's understanding or competence: *beyond one's depth.* **9.** The degree of richness or intensity: *depth of color.* **10.** Lowness in pitch. ***—idiom.* in depth.** With thoroughness: *a study in depth.* [ME *depthe* < *dep,* deep.]

depth charge *n.* A charge designed for explosion under water, used esp. against submarines.

depth perception *n.* Perception of spatial relationships, esp. of distances between objects, in three dimensions.

depth psychology *n.* **1.** Psychology of the unconscious, esp. as distinguished from the psychology of conscious behavior. **2.** Psychoanalysis.

dep·u·rate (dĕp′yə-rāt′) *tr. & intr.v.* **-rat·ed, -rat·ing, -rates.** To cleanse or purify or become cleansed or purified. [Med. Lat. *depurare, depurat-* : Lat. *de-,* away + *purus,* pure.] **—dep′u·ra′tion** *n.* **—dep′u·ra′tor** *n.*

dep·u·ta·tion (dĕp′yə-tā′shən) *n.* **1. a.** The act of deputing. **b.** The state of being deputed. **2.** A person or group appointed to represent another or others; delegation.

de·pute (dĭ-pyo͞ot′) *tr.v.* **-put·ed, -put·ing, -putes. 1.** To appoint or authorize as an agent or representative. **2.** To assign (authority or duties) to another; delegate. [ME *deputen* < OFr. *deputer* < LLat. *deputare,* to allot < Lat., to consider : *de-,* apart, away + *putare,* to trim, arrange.]

dep·u·tize (dĕp′yə-tīz′) *tr. & intr.v.* **-tized, -tiz·ing, -tiz·es.** To appoint as or serve as a deputy. **—dep′u·ti·za′tion** *n.*

dep·u·ty (dĕp′yə-tē) *n., pl.* **-ties. 1.** A person named or empowered to act for another. **2.** An assistant exercising full authority in the absence of his superior and equal authority in emergencies. **3.** A representative in a legislative body in certain countries. [ME *depute* < OFr. < p.part. of *deputer,* to depute.]

de·rac·i·nate (də-răs′ə-nāt′) *tr.v.* **-nat·ed, -nat·ing, -nates.** To pull out by or as if by the roots; uproot. [< Fr. *déraciner* < OFr. *desraciner* : *des-,* apart (< Lat. *dis-*) + *racine,* root < LLat. *radicina* < Lat. *radix.*] **—de·rac′i·na′tion** *n.*

de·rail (dē-rāl′) *intr. & tr.v.* **-railed, -rail·ing, -rails. 1.** To run or cause to run off the rails. **2.** To be thrown or throw off course. [Fr. *dérailler* : *dé-,* off (< Lat. *de-*) + *rail,* rail < E.] **—de·rail′ment** *n.*

de·rail·leur (dĭ-rā′lər) *n.* A gear mechanism on a bicycle that changes bicycle gear ratio by moving the chain from one sprocket to another. [Fr. *dérailler,* to become derailed : *dé-,* off (< Lat. *de-*) + *rail,* rail < E.]

de·range (dĭ-rānj′) *tr.v.* **-ranged, -rang·ing, -rang·es. 1.** To disturb the order or arrangement of. **2.** To disturb the normal condition or functioning of. **3.** To make insane. [Fr. *déranger* < OFr. *desrengier* : *des-,* apart (< Lat. *dis-*) + *reng,* line, of Germanic orig.] **—de·range′ment** *n.*

derby

der·by (dûr′bē; *Brit.* där′bē) *n., pl.* **-bies. 1.** Any of various annual horse races, esp. for three-year-olds. **2.** A formal race with a more or less open field of contestants: *a motorcycle derby.* **3.** A stiff felt hat with a round crown and a narrow, curved brim. [After Edward Smith Stanley (1752–1834), 12th Earl of *Derby,* founder of the English Derby.]

de·reg·u·late (dē-rĕg′yə-lāt′) *tr.v.* **-lat·ed, -lat·ing, -lates.** To decontrol. **—de·reg′u·la′tion** *n.*

der·e·lict (dĕr′ə-lĭkt′) *adj.* **1.** Neglectful of duty or obligation; remiss. **2.** Deserted by an owner or guardian; abandoned. *—n.* **1.** Abandoned property, esp. a ship abandoned at sea. **2.** A homeless or jobless person; vagrant. **3.** *Law.* Land left dry by a permanent recession of the water line. [Lat. *derelictus,* p.part. of *derelinquere,* to abandon : *de-,* completely + *relinquere,* to leave behind (*re-,* behind + *linquere,* to leave).]

der·e·lic·tion (dĕr′ə-lĭk′shən) *n.* **1.** Willful neglect, as of duty. **2.** Abandonment. **3.** *Law.* **a.** A gaining of land by the permanent recession of the water line. **b.** The land so gained.

de·ride (dĭ-rīd′) *tr.v.* **-rid·ed, -rid·ing, -rides.** To speak of or treat with contemptuous mirth. [Lat. *deridēre* : *de-* (pejorative) + *ridēre,* to laugh at.] **—de·rid′er** *n.* **—de·rid′ing·ly** *adv.*

de ri·gueur (də rē-gœr′) *adj.* Required by the current fashion or custom; socially obligatory. [Fr.]

de·ri·sion (dĭ-rĭzh′ən) *n.* **1. a.** An act of deriding; ridicule. **b.** A state of being derided. **2.** An object of ridicule; laughingstock. [ME *derisioun* < OFr. *derision* < LLat. *derisio* < Lat. *derisus,* p.part. of *deridēre,* to deride.]

de·ri·sive (dĭ-rī′sĭv, -zĭv, -rĭs′ĭv, -rĭz′-) *adj.* Mocking; scoffing. **—de·ri′sive·ly** *adv.* **—de·ri′sive·ness** *n.*

de·ri·so·ry (dĭ-rī′sə-rē, -zə-) *adj.* Derisive.

der·i·vate (dĕr′ə-vāt′) *adj.* Derivative.

der·i·va·tion (dĕr′ə-vā′shən) *n.* **1.** The act or process of deriving. **2.** The condition or fact of being derived. **3.** Something derived; derivative. **4.** The form or source from which something is derived; origin. **5.** The historical origin and development of a word; etymology. **6.** *Ling.* The process by which new words are formed from existing words, chiefly by the addition of affixes to roots, stems, or words. **7.** *Math.* A logical or mathematical process indicating through a sequence of statements that a result such as a theorem or a formula necessarily follows from the initial assumptions. **—der′i·va′tion·al** *adj.*

de·riv·a·tive (dĭ-rĭv′ə-tĭv) *adj.* **1.** Resulting from derivation. **2.** Copied or adapted from others: *a derivative prose style.* *—n.* **1.** Something derived. **2.** *Ling.* A word formed from another by derivation. **3.** *Math.* The limit, as the increment in the argument of a function approaches zero, of the ratio of the increment in its value to the corresponding increment in the argument; the instantaneous rate of change of a function with respect to a variable. **4.** *Chem.* A compound derived or obtained from known or hypothetical substances and containing essential elements of the parent substance. **—de·riv′a·tive·ly** *adv.* **—de·riv′a·tive·ness** *n.*

de·rive (dĭ-rīv′) *v.* **-rived, -riv·ing, -rives.** *—tr.* **1.** To obtain or receive from a source. **2.** To arrive at by reasoning; deduce or infer: *derive a conclusion from facts.* **3.** To trace the origin or development of (a word, for example). **4.** *Chem.* To produce or obtain (a compound) from another substance by chemical reaction. *—intr.* To issue from a source; originate. [ME *deriven,* to be derived from < OFr. *deriver* < Lat. *derivare,* to derive : *de-,* away + *rivus,* stream.] **—de·riv′a·ble** *adj.* **—de·riv′er** *n.*

derm (dûrm) *n.* Variant of **derma**[1].

derm– *pref.* Variant of **derma-.**

–derm *suff.* Skin; covering: *blastoderm.* [< Gk. *derma,* skin.]

der·ma[1] (dûr′mə) also **derm** (dûrm) or **der·mis** (dûr′mĭs) *n.* *Anat.* The corium. [NLat. < Gk., skin.]

der·ma[2] (dûr′mə) *n.* Beef casing stuffed with a seasoned mixture of matzo meal or flour, onion, and suet, prepared by boiling, then roasting. [Yiddish *derme,* pl. of *darm,* intestine < MHG < OHG.]

derma– or **derm–** or **dermo–** *pref.* Skin: *dermal.* [< Gk. *derma,* skin.]

–derma *suff.* Skin, skin disease: *scleroderma.* [NLat. < Gk. *derma,* skin.]

der·ma·bra·sion (dûr′mə-brā′zhən) *n.* A surgical procedure designed to remove skin imperfections, such as scars or wrinkles, through the abrasion of the frozen epidermis.

der·mal (dûr′məl) also **der·mic** (-mĭk) *adj.* Of or pertaining to the skin.

dermat– *pref.* Variant of **dermato-.**

der·ma·ti·tis (dûr′mə-tī′tĭs) *n.* Inflammation of the skin.

dermato– or **dermat–** *pref.* Skin: *dermatome.* [< Gk. *derma, dermat-,* skin.]

der·mat·o·gen (dûr-măt′ə-jən) *n.* *Bot.* The outer layer of meristem, from which the epidermis is formed.

der·ma·toid (dûr′mə-toid′) *n.* Resembling skin.

der·ma·tol·o·gy (dûr′mə-tŏl′ə-jē) *n.* The medical study of the physiology and pathology of the skin. **—der′ma·to·log′i·cal** (-tə-lŏj′ĭ-kəl) *adj.* **—der′ma·tol′o·gist** *n.*

der·ma·tome (dûr′mə-tōm′) *n.* The lateral wall of a somite, from which the corium is formed.

der·mat·o·phyte (dûr-măt′ə-fīt′, dûr′mə-tə-) *n.* Any of various fungi that cause skin disease. **—der·mat′o·phyt′ic** (-fĭt′ĭk) *adj.*

der·ma·to·phy·to·sis (dûr′mə-tō′fī-tō′sĭs) *n.* Athlete's foot.

der·ma·to·plas·ty (dûr′mə-tō-plăs′tē) *n.* The use of skin grafts in plastic surgery to correct defects or replace skin loss.

der·ma·to·sis (dûr′mə-tō′sĭs) *n., pl.* **-ses** (-sēz′). A skin disease.
–dermatous *suff.* Having a specified kind of skin: *sclerodermatous.* [< Gk. *derma, dermat-,* skin.]
der·mic (dûr′mĭk) *adj.* Variant of **dermal.**
der·mis (dûr′mĭs) *n.* Variant of **derma**¹.
dermo– *pref.* Variant of **derma-.**
der·nier cri (dĕr′nyā krē′) *n.* The latest thing; newest fashion. [Fr. : *dernier,* last + *cri,* cry.]
der·o·gate (dĕr′ə-gāt′) *v.* **-gat·ed, -gat·ing, -gates.** —*intr.* **1.** To take away; detract: *an error that will derogate from her reputation.* **2.** To deviate from a standard or expectation; go astray. —*tr.* To disparage; belittle. [Lat. *derogare, derogat-,* to take away : *de-,* away + *rogare,* to ask.] **—der′o·ga′tion** *n.* **—de·rog′a·tive** (dĭ-rŏg′ə-tĭv, dĕr′ə-gā′-) *adj.*
de·rog·a·to·ry (dĭ-rŏg′ə-tôr′ē, -tōr′ē) *adj.* Detracting or disparaging. **—de·rog′a·to′ri·ly** *adv.* **—de·rog′a·to′ri·ness** *n.*
der·rick (dĕr′ĭk) *n.* **1.** A large crane for hoisting and moving heavy objects, consisting of a movable boom equipped with cables and pulleys and connected to the base of an upright stationary beam. **2.** A tall framework over the opening of an oil well or other drilled hole, used to support boring equipment or to hoist and lower pipe lengths. [Obs. *derick,* gallows, hangman, after *Derick,* 16th-cent. English hangman.]
der·ri·ère also **der·ri·ere** (dĕr′ē-âr′) *n.* The buttocks; rear. [Fr. < *derrière,* behind < OFr. *deriere,* in back of < Lat. *de retro.*]
der·ring-do (dĕr′ĭng-do͞o′) *n.* Daring spirit and action; valor. [ME < *dorring don,* daring to do.]
der·rin·ger (dĕr′ĭn-jər) *n.* A short-barreled pistol with a large bore. [After Henry *Deringer,* 19th-cent. American gunsmith.]
der·ris (dĕr′ĭs) *n.* Any of various woody vines of the genus *Derris,* of tropical Asia, whose roots yield rotenone. [NLat. < Gk., covering.]
der·vish (dûr′vĭsh) *n.* A member of any of various Moslem orders of ascetics, some of which employ whirling dances and the chanting of religious formulas to produce a collective ecstasy. [Turk. *derviş,* mendicant < Pers. *därvīsh.*]
DES (dē′ē-ĕs′) *n.* Diethylstilbestrol.
de·sal·i·nate (dē-săl′ə-nāt′) *tr.v.* **-nat·ed, -nat·ing, -nates.** To desalinize. **—de·sal′i·na′tion** *n.* **—de·sal′i·na′tor** *n.*
de·sal·i·nize (dē-săl′ə-nīz′) *tr.v.* **-nized, -niz·ing, -niz·es.** To remove salts and other chemicals from sea water or saline water. **—de·sal′i·ni·za′tion** *n.*
de·salt (dē-sôlt′) *tr.v.* **-salt·ed, -salt·ing, -salts.** To desalinize.
des·cant (dĕs′kănt′) *n.* **1.** Also **dis·cant** (dĭs′-). *Mus.* **a.** An ornamental melody or counterpoint sung or played above a musical theme. **b.** The highest part sung in part music. **2.** A discussion or discourse on a theme. —*intr.v.* (dĕs′kănt′, dĕ-skănt′) **-cant·ed, -cant·ing, -cants. 1.** To comment at length; discourse: *"I have now descanted at some length on what I am going to talk about"* (William Dean Howells). **2.** Also **dis·cant** (dĭ-skănt′). *Mus.* **a.** To sing or play a descant. **b.** To sing melodiously. [ME < AN *descaunt* < Med. Lat. *discantus,* a refrain : Lat. *dis-,* apart + Lat. *cantus,* song < p.part. of *canere,* to sing.] **—des′cant′er** *n.*
de·scend (dĭ-sĕnd′) *v.* **-scend·ed, -scend·ing, -scends.** —*intr.* **1.** To move from a higher to a lower place. **2.** To slope, extend, or incline downward: *"A rough path descended like a steep stair into the plain"* (J.R.R. Tolkien). **3. a.** To come down from a source; derive: *descended from an old New England family.* **b.** To pass through inheritance: *The house has descended in the family.* **4.** To sink; stoop: *descended to lies and flattery.* **5.** To arrive or attack suddenly or overwhelmingly: *summer tourists descending on the seashore village.* —*tr.* To move from a higher to a lower part of; go down. [ME *descenden* < OFr. *descendre* < Lat. *descendere* : *de-,* down + *scandere,* to climb.] **—de·scend′i·ble, de·scend′a·ble** *adj.*
de·scen·dant (dĭ-sĕn′dənt) *n.* **1.** An individual descended from another. **2.** Something derived from a prototype or earlier form. —*adj.* Variant of **descendent.**
de·scen·dent also **de·scen·dant** (dĭ-sĕn′dənt) *adj.* **1.** Moving downward; descending. **2.** Proceeding by descent from an ancestor.
de·scend·er (dĭ-sĕn′dər) *n. Printing.* The part of certain letters, such as *g, p,* or *y,* that extends below the bottom of most lower-case letters.
de·scent (dĭ-sĕnt′) *n.* **1.** The act or an instance of descending. **2.** A way down. **3.** A downward incline or passage; slope. **4. a.** Hereditary derivation; lineage: *of native American descent.* **b.** The fact or process of coming down or being derived from a source: *can trace the descent of the novel from old picaresque tales.* **c.** Development in form or structure during transmission from an original source. **5.** One generation of a specific lineage. **6.** *Law.* Transference of property by inheritance. **7.** A lowering or decline, as in status or level. **8.** A sudden attack; onslaught. [ME < OFr. < *descendre,* to descend.]
de·scram·ble (dē-skrăm′bəl) *tr.v.* **-bled, -bling, -bles.** To decode.
de·scribe (dĭ-skrīb′) *tr.v.* **-scribed, -scrib·ing, -scribes. 1.** To give a verbal account of. **2. a.** To transmit a mental image or impression of with words. **b.** To present a lifelike image of. **3.** To trace or draw the figure of; outline: *describe a circle with a compass.* [Lat. *describere,* to delineate : *de-,* down + *scribere,* to write.] **—de·scrib′a·ble** *adj.* **—de·scrib′er** *n.*
de·scrip·tion (dĭ-skrĭp′shən) *n.* **1.** The act, process, or technique of describing. **2.** A statement or account describing something. **3.** The act of drawing or tracing a figure. **4.** A kind; sort: *costumes of every description.* [ME *descripcioun* < OFr. *description* < Lat. *descriptio* < *descriptus,* p.part. of *describere,* to delineate. —see DESCRIBE.]
de·scrip·tive (dĭ-skrĭp′tĭv) *adj.* **1.** Involving or characterized by description; serving to describe. **2.** Concerned with description or classification rather than explanation: *descriptive science.* **3.** *Gram.* Expressing an attribute of the modified noun, as *green* in *green grass.* Used of an adjective or adjectival clause. **—de·scrip′tive·ly** *adv.* **—de·scrip′tive·ness** *n.*
descriptive geometry *n.* The collection of mathematical techniques used to describe geometric relationships among three-dimensional structures on a plane surface.
descriptive linguistics *n.* The study of a language or languages at a specific stage of development, with emphasis on constructing a complete grammar rather than on historical development or comparison with other languages.
de·scrip·tor (dĭ-skrĭp′tər) *n. Computer Sci.* A word, phrase, or alphanumeric character used to identify an item in an information retrieval system. [LLat., describer < Lat. *descriptus,* p.part. of *describere,* to describe.]
de·scry (dĭ-skrī′) *tr.v.* **-scried, -scry·ing, -scries. 1.** To discern (something difficult to catch sight of): *"Through the mists they could descry the long arm of the mountains"* (J.R.R. Tolkien). **2.** To discover by careful observation or investigation. [ME *descrien,* to proclaim < OFr. *descrier.* —see DECRY.] **—de·scri′er** *n.*
des·e·crate (dĕs′ĭ-krāt′) *tr.v.* **-crat·ed, -crat·ing, -crates.** To abuse the sacredness of; profane. [DE- + (CON)SECRATE.] **—des′e·crat′er, des′e·cra′tor** *n.* **—des′e·cra′tion** *n.*
de·seg·re·gate (dē-sĕg′rĭ-gāt′) *v.* **-gat·ed, -gat·ing, -gates.** —*tr.* To abolish segregation, esp. racial segregation, in. —*intr.* To become desegregated. **—de·seg′re·ga′tion** *n.* **—de·seg′re·ga′tion·ist** *n.*
de·sen·si·tize (dē-sĕn′sĭ-tīz′) *tr.v.* **-tized, -tiz·ing, -tiz·es.** To render less sensitive or insensitive, as to light or pain. **—de·sen′si·ti·za′tion** *n.* **—de·sen′si·tiz′er** *n.*
des·ert¹ (dĕz′ərt) *n.* **1.** A dry, barren, often sandy region that because of environmental extremes can naturally support little or no vegetation. **2.** *Archaic.* A wild uncultivated and uninhabited region. **3.** A dismal or forbidding area: *a cultural desert.* **—*modifier:*** *desert heat; a desert island.* [ME < OFr. < LLat. *desertum* < p.part. of *deserere,* to desert.]
de·sert² (dĭ-zûrt′) *n.* **1.** Often **deserts.** Something that is deserved or merited, esp. a punishment: *He certainly received his just deserts.* **2.** The state or fact of deserving reward or punishment. [ME *deserte* < OFr. < fem. p.part. of *deservir,* to deserve.]
de·sert³ (dĭ-zûrt′) *v.* **-sert·ed, -sert·ing, -serts.** —*tr.* **1.** To forsake or leave, esp. when most needed; abandon. **2.** To abandon (a military post, for example) in violation of orders or oath. —*intr.* To forsake one's duty or post, esp. to be absent without leave from the armed forces with no intention of returning. [Fr. *déserter* < LLat. *desertare* < Lat. *desertus,* p.part. of *deserere,* to abandon : *de-,* apart + *serere,* to join.] **—de·sert′er** *n.*
de·ser·tion (dĭ-zûr′shən) *n.* **1. a.** The act of deserting. **b.** The state of being deserted. **2.** *Law.* Willful abandonment of one's spouse or children or both without their consent and with the intention of forsaking all legal obligation.
de·serve (dĭ-zûrv′) *v.* **-served, -serv·ing, -serves.** —*tr.* To be worthy of; merit. —*intr.* To be worthy. [ME *deserven* < OFr. *deservir* < Lat. *deservire,* to serve zealously : *de-* (intensive) + *servire,* to serve < *servus,* slave.]
de·served (dĭ-zûrvd′) *adj.* Merited or earned: *a deserved punishment.* **—de·serv′ed·ly** (-zûr′vĭd-lē) *adv.* **—de·serv′ed·ness** *n.*
de·serv·ing (dĭ-zûr′vĭng) *adj.* Worthy of reward, praise, or aid; meritorious. —*n.* Merit. **—de·serv′ing·ly** *adv.*
de·sex (dē-sĕks′) *tr.v.* **-sexed, -sex·ing, -sex·es.** To remove part or all of the reproductive organs of; spay or castrate.
de·sex·u·al·ize (dē-sĕk′sho͞o-ə-līz′) *tr.v.* **-ized, -iz·ing, -iz·es. 1.** To desex. **2.** To take away the sexual quality of. **—de·sex′u·al·i·za′tion** *n.*
des·ha·bille (dĕs′ə-bēl′, -bē′) *n.* Variant of **dishabille.**
des·ic·cant (dĕs′ĭ-kənt) *n.* A substance, such as calcium oxide, that has a high affinity for water and is used as a drying agent. [Lat. *desiccans, desiccant-,* pr.part. of *desiccare,* to desiccate.] **—des′ic·cant** *adj.*
des·ic·cate (dĕs′ĭ-kāt′) *v.* **-cat·ed, -cat·ing, -cates.** —*tr.* **1.** To dry out thoroughly. **2.** To preserve (foods) by removing the moisture. **3.** To divest of spirit, spontaneity, or animation. —*intr.* To become dry. —*adj.* Lacking spirit, spontaneity, or animation; arid: *"there was only the sun-bruised and desiccate feeling in his mind"* (J.R. Salamanca). [Lat. *desiccare, desiccat-* : *de-,* completely + *siccare,* to dry up < *siccus,* dry.] **—des′ic·ca′tion** *n.* **—des′ic·ca′tive** *adj.* **—des′ic·ca′tor** *n.*
de·sid·er·a·ta (dĭ-sĭd′ə-rā′tə, -rä′-) *n.* Plural of **desideratum.**
de·sid·er·ate (dĭ-sĭd′ə-rāt′) *tr.v.* **-at·ed, -at·ing, -ates.** To long

derrick

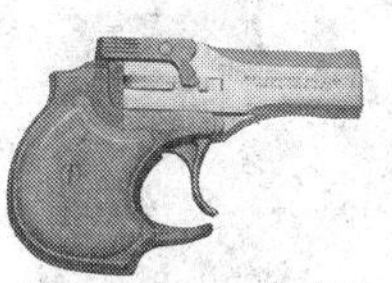
derringer

dervish

desert¹

for. [Lat. *desiderare, desiderat-,* to desire.] **—de·sid'er·a'tion** *n.* **—de·sid'er·a'tive** *adj.*

de·sid·er·a·tum (dĭ-sĭd'ə-rā'təm, -rä'-) *n., pl.* **-ta** (-tə). Something needed and desired: *"A journalist of spirit is a desideratum in a revolution"* (Hugh H. Brackenridge). [Lat., neuter p.part. of *desiderare,* to desire.]

de·sign (dĭ-zīn') *v.* **-signed, -sign·ing, -signs.** *—tr.* **1.** To conceive in the mind; invent: *designed his dream vacation.* **2.** To form a plan for: *designed a marketing strategy for the new product.* **3.** To have as a goal or purpose; intend. **4.** To plan by making a preliminary sketch, outline, or drawing. **5.** To create or execute in an artistic or highly skilled manner. *—intr.* **1.** To make or execute plans. **2.** To create designs. *—n.* **1.** A drawing or sketch. **2.** The invention and disposition of the forms, parts, or details of something according to a plan. **3.** A decorative or artistic work. **4.** A visual composition; pattern. **5.** The art of creating designs. **6.** A plan; project. **7.** A reasoned purpose; intention. **8.** Often **designs.** A sinister or hostile scheme: *He has designs on my job.* [OFr. *designer* < Lat. *designare,* to designate.] **—de·sign'a·ble** *adj.* **—de·sign'er** *n.*

des·ig·nate (dĕz'ĭg-nāt') *tr.v.* **-nat·ed, -nat·ing, -nates. 1.** To indicate or specify; point out. **2.** To give a name or title to; characterize. **3.** To select for a particular duty, office, or purpose; appoint. *—adj.* (-nĭt). Appointed but not yet installed in office. [Lat. *designare, designat-* : *de-,* out + *signare,* to mark < *signum,* sign.] **—des'ig·na'tive, des'ig·na·to'ry** (-nə-tôr'ē, -tōr'ē) *adj.* **—des'ig·na'tor** *n.*

designated hitter *n. Baseball.* A player designated at the start of a game to bat instead of the pitcher in the lineup.

des·ig·na·tion (dĕz'ĭg-nā'shən) *n.* **1.** The act of designating; a marking or pointing out. **2.** Nomination or appointment. **3.** A distinguishing name or mark; title.

de·sign·ed·ly (dĭ-zī'nĭd-lē) *adv.* On purpose; intentionally.

des·ig·nee (dĕz'ĭg-nē') *n.* A person who has been designated.

de·sign·ing (dĭ-zī'nĭng) *adj.* **1.** Conniving; crafty. **2.** Showing or exercising forethought. **—de·sign'ing·ly** *adv.*

de·sir·a·ble (dĭ-zīr'ə-bəl) *adj.* **1.** Of such quality as to be worth seeking; pleasing. **2.** Worth wanting or doing; advisable: *a desirable reform.* *—n.* A desirable person or thing. **—de·sir'a·bil'i·ty, de·sir'a·ble·ness** *n.* **—de·sir'a·bly** *adv.*

de·sire (dĭ-zīr') *tr.v.* **-sired, -sir·ing, -sires. 1.** To wish or long for; crave. **2.** To express a wish for; request. *—n.* **1.** A wish, longing, or craving. **2.** A request or petition. **3.** Something or someone longed for. **4.** Sexual appetite; passion. [ME *desiren* < OFr. *desirer* < Lat. *desiderare.*] **—de·sir'er** *n.*

desk
18th-century American Chippendale desk

de·sir·ous (dĭ-zīr'əs) *adj.* Having, expressing, or characterized by desire; desiring. **—de·sir'ous·ly** *adv.* **—de·sir'ous·ness** *n.*

de·sist (dĭ-zĭst', -sĭst') *intr.v.* **-sist·ed, -sist·ing, -sists.** To cease doing something; forbear. [OFr. *desister* < Lat. *desistere* : *de-,* from + *sistere,* to stop.]

desk (dĕsk) *n.* **1.** A piece of furniture usually with a flat top for writing and drawers or compartments. **2.** A table, counter, or booth at which specified, usually public services or functions are performed: *an information desk.* **3.** A lectern. **4.** A department of a large organization in charge of a specified operation: *a newspaper's city desk.* **5.** A music stand in an orchestra. [ME < Med. Lat. *desca* < OItal. *desco,* table < Lat. *discus,* quoit. —see DISK.]

desk·man (dĕsk'măn', -mən) *n.* A person who works at a desk, esp. a newspaper writer.

desman
Desmana moschata

des·man (dĕs'mən) *n., pl.* **-mans.** Either of two aquatic, insectivorous, molelike mammals, *Desmana moschata* of eastern Europe and western Asia or *Galemys pyrenaicus* of southwestern Europe, having dense, brownish fur, a long snout, and a flattened, scaly tail. [Short for Swedish *desmansråtta,* muskrat : *desman,* musk (< MLG *desem* < Med. Lat. *bisamum,* of Semitic orig.) + *råtta,* rat.]

des·mid (dĕs'mĭd) *n.* Any of various green, unicellular freshwater algae of the family Desmidiaceae, often forming chainlike colonies. [< NLat. *Desmidiaceae,* family name < *Desmidium,* genus name < Gk. *desmos,* bond < *dein,* to bind.]

des·o·late (dĕs'ə-lĭt, dĕz'-) *adj.* **1.** Devoid of inhabitants; deserted. **2.** Rendered unfit for habitation or use. **3.** Dreary; dismal. **4.** Without friends or hope; forlorn. *—tr.v.* (-lāt') **-lat·ed, -lat·ing, -lates. 1.** To rid or deprive of inhabitants. **2.** To lay waste; devastate. **3.** To forsake; abandon. **4.** To make lonely, forlorn, or wretched. [ME *desolat* < Lat. *desolatus,* p.part. of *desolare,* to abandon : *de-* (intensive) + *solus,* alone.] **—des'o·late·ly** *adv.* **—des'o·late·ness** *n.* **—des'o·lat'er, des'o·la'tor** *n.*

des·o·la·tion (dĕs'ə-lā'shən, dĕz'-) *n.* **1.** The act of rendering desolate. **2.** The state of being desolate; ruin. **3.** A wasteland. **4.** Loneliness or misery; wretchedness: *"an air of tranquil and unwitting desolation . . . as if she had never lived at all"* (Faulkner).

de·sorb (dē-sôrb', -zôrb') *tr.v.* **-sorbed, -sorb·ing, -sorbs.** To remove (an absorbed or adsorbed substance) from. **—de·sorp'tion** *n.*

de·spair (dĭ-spâr') *intr.v.* **-spaired, -spair·ing, -spairs.** To be overcome by a sense of futility or defeat. *—n.* **1.** Utter lack of hope. **2.** Something that destroys all hope. [ME *despeiren* < OFr. *desperer* < Lat. *desperare* : *de-* (reversal) + *sperare,* to hope.] **—de·spair'ing·ly** *adv.*

Synonyms: *despair, hopelessness, desperation, despondency, depression, discouragement, dejection.* These nouns denote emotional states marked by lowness of spirits or loss of hope. *Despair* and *hopelessness* stress the utter absence of hope and often imply a sense of powerlessness or resignation. *Desperation* implies absence of grounds for hope but adds the idea of fighting back, often blindly or recklessly. *Despondency* and *depression* emphasize lowness of spirits; *despondency* is usually stronger in suggesting cessation of hope, courage, or effort to recoup. *Discouragement* suggests loss of confidence or courage in the face of obstacles but is generally the weakest of these terms. *Dejection* is lowness of spirits, often of short duration and generally traceable to an external cause.

des·patch (dĭ-spăch') *v. & n.* Variant of **dispatch.**

des·per·a·do (dĕs'pə-rä'dō, -rā'-) *n., pl.* **-does** or **-dos.** A desperate, dangerous criminal. [Alteration of DESPERATE.]

des·per·ate (dĕs'pər-ĭt) *adj.* **1.** Reckless or violent because of despair: *a desperate criminal.* **2.** Undertaken as a last resort. **3.** Nearly hopeless; grave: *a desperate illness.* **4.** Marked by, arising from, or showing despair: *the desperate look of hunger.* **5.** Suffering unbearable need or anxiety: *desperate for recognition.* **6.** Extremely intense: *in desperate need.* [Lat. *desperatus,* p.part. of *desperare,* to despair.] **—des'per·ate·ly** *adv.* **—des'per·ate·ness** *n.*

des·per·a·tion (dĕs'pə-rā'shən) *n.* **1.** The condition of being desperate. **2.** Recklessness arising from despair.

des·pi·ca·ble (dĕs'pĭ-kə-bəl, dĭ-spĭk'ə-) *adj.* Deserving of contempt or scorn; vile. [LLat. *despicabilis* < Lat. *despicari,* to despise < *despicere.*] **—des'pi·ca·ble·ness** *n.* **—des'pi·ca·bly** *adv.*

de·spise (dĭ-spīz') *tr.v.* **-spised, -spis·ing, -spis·es. 1.** To look down on with contempt or scorn. **2.** To regard with extreme dislike and hostility. **3.** To regard as trivial or worthless. [ME *despisen* < OFr. *despire, despis-* < Lat. *despicere* : *de-,* down + *specere,* to look.] **—de·spis'er** *n.*

de·spite (dĭ-spīt') *prep.* In spite of; notwithstanding: *win despite overwhelming odds.* *—n.* **1.** Contemptuous defiance or disregard. **2.** Spite or malice. **3.** An act of contemptuous defiance; insult. **—*idiom.* in despite of.** In spite of. [ME *despit,* spite < OFr. < Lat. *despectus,* p.part. of *despicere,* to despise.]

de·spite·ful (dĭ-spīt'fəl) *adj.* Full of malice; spiteful. **—de·spite'ful·ly** *adv.* **—de·spite'ful·ness** *n.*

de·spit·e·ous (dĭ-spĭt'ē-əs) *adj. Obs.* Full of spite or malice; despiteful. **—de·spit'e·ous·ly** *adv.*

de·spoil (dĭ-spoil') *tr.v.* **-spoiled, -spoil·ing, -spoils.** To deprive of possessions or property by force; plunder. [ME *despoilen* < OFr. *despoiller* < Lat. *despoliare* : *de-,* away + *spoliare,* to plunder < *spolium,* booty.] **—de·spoil'er** *n.* **—de·spoil'ment** *n.*

de·spo·li·a·tion (dĭ-spō'lē-ā'shən) *n.* **1.** The act of despoiling. **2.** The condition of being despoiled. [LLat. *despoliatio* < Lat. *despoliatus,* p.part. of *despoliare,* to despoil.]

de·spond (dĭ-spŏnd') *intr.v.* **-spond·ed, -spond·ing, -sponds.** To become disheartened. [Lat. *despondere,* to give up : *de-,* away + *spondere,* to promise.] **—de·spond'ing·ly** *adv.*

de·spon·dence (dĭ-spŏn'dəns) *n.* Despondency.

de·spon·den·cy (dĭ-spŏn'dən-sē) *n.* Depression of spirits from loss of hope, confidence, or courage; dejection.

de·spon·dent (dĭ-spŏn'dənt) *adj.* Feeling or expressing despondency or dejection. **—de·spon'dent·ly** *adv.*

des·pot (dĕs'pət) *n.* **1. a.** A Byzantine emperor or prince. **b.** An Eastern Orthodox bishop or patriarch. **2.** A ruler with absolute power. **3.** A person who wields power oppressively or tyrannically. [OFr. < Gk. *despotēs.*] **—des·pot'ic** (dĭ-spŏt'ĭk) *adj.* **—des·pot'i·cal·ly** *adv.*

des·pot·ism (dĕs'pə-tĭz'əm) *n.* **1.** Rule by or as if by a despot; absolute power or authority. **2.** The actions of a despot; tyranny. **3. a.** A government or political system in which the ruler exercises absolute power. **b.** A state so ruled.

des·qua·mate (dĕs'kwə-māt') *intr.v.* **-mat·ed, -mat·ing, -mates.** To shed, peel, or scale off. Used of skin. [Lat. *desquamare, desquamat-* : *de-,* off + *squama,* scale.] **—des'qua·ma'tion** *n.*

des·sert (dĭ-zûrt') *n.* **1.** A portion of a sweet food, such as fruit, ice cream, or pastry, served as the last course of a lunch or dinner. **2.** *Chiefly Brit.* Fresh fruit, nuts, or sweetmeats served after the sweet course of a dinner. [OFr. < *desservir,* to clear the table : *des-,* away (< Lat. *de-*) + *servir,* to serve. —see SERVE.]

des·sert·spoon (dĭ-zûrt'spo͞on') *n.* A spoon intermediate in size between a tablespoon and a teaspoon, used for eating dessert. **—des·sert'spoon'ful** (-fo͝ol) *n.*

de·sta·bi·lize (dē-stā'bə-līz') *tr.v.* **-lized, -liz·ing, -liz·es.** To upset the stability or smooth functioning of. **—de·sta'bi·li·za'tion** *n.*

de·stain (dē-stān') *tr.v.* **-stained, -stain·ing, -stains.** To remove stain from (a specimen) to aid in microscopic study.

de·sta·lin·i·za·tion (dē-stä'lĭ-nĭ-zā'shən) *n.* The process of discrediting and eliminating the political policies, methods, and personal image of Stalin.

de·ster·i·lize (dē-stĕr′ə-līz′) *tr.v.* **-lized, -liz·ing, -liz·es.** To release (gold) from an inactive status and return it to use as a backing for credit and new currency.

de Stijl (də stīl′, stāl′) *n.* A school of art originated in the Netherlands in 1917 and characterized by the use of rectangular shapes and primary colors. [Du., the style.]

des·ti·na·tion (dĕs′tə-nā′shən) *n.* **1.** The place to which someone or something is going or directed. **2.** The purpose for which something is created or intended. **3.** *Archaic.* An act of appointing or setting aside for a specific purpose.

des·tine (dĕs′tĭn) *tr.v.* **-tined, -tin·ing, -tines. 1.** To determine beforehand; preordain: *a foolish scheme destined to fail.* **2.** To assign for a specific end, use, or purpose: *money destined to pay for her education.* **3.** To direct toward a given destination: *a flight destined for Tokyo.* [ME *destinen* < OFr. *destiner* < Lat. *destinare,* to determine.]

des·ti·ny (dĕs′tə-nē) *n., pl.* **-nies. 1.** The inevitable or necessary fate to which a particular person or thing is destined; lot. **2.** The predetermined or inevitable course of events considered as something beyond the power or control of man: *"Marriage and hanging go by destiny"* (Robert Burton). **3.** The power or agency thought to predetermine events; fate. [ME *destine* < OFr. *destinee* < fem. p.part. of *destiner,* to destine.]

des·ti·tute (dĕs′tĭ-to͞ot′, -tyo͞ot′) *adj.* **1.** Altogether lacking; devoid: *destitute of experience.* **2.** Utterly impoverished. [ME *destitut* < Lat. *destitutus,* p.part. of *destituere,* to abandon : *de-,* away + *statuere,* to place.] **—des′ti·tute′ness** *n.*

des·ti·tu·tion (dĕs′tĭ-to͞o′shən, -tyo͞o′-) *n.* **1.** Extreme want of resources or the means of subsistence; complete poverty. **2.** A deprivation or lack; deficiency.

des·tri·er (dĕs′trē-ər, dĭ-strîr′) *n. Archaic.* A war horse. [ME < OFr. < *destre,* right hand < Lat. *dexter,* right.]

de·stroy (dĭ-stroi′) *v.* **-stroyed, -stroy·ing, -stroys.** *—tr.* **1.** To ruin completely; spoil: *ancient manuscripts destroyed by fire.* **2.** To tear down or break up; demolish. **3.** To do away with; put an end to: *"In crowded populations, poverty destroys the possibility of cleanliness"* (G.B. Shaw). **4.** To kill: *destroy a rabid dog.* **5.** To render useless or ineffective: *destroyed the prosecution's chief witness.* **6.** To subdue or defeat completely; crush. *—intr.* To be destructive or harmful. [ME *destruyen* < OFr. *destruire* < VLat. **destrugere* < Lat. *destruere* : *de-,* away + *struere,* to pile up.]

de·stroy·er (dĭ-stroi′ər) *n.* **1.** One that destroys. **2.** A small, fast warship armed with guns, torpedos, and depth charges and noted for its high maneuverability.

destroyer escort *n.* A warship, usually smaller than a destroyer, used to convoy merchant vessels.

destroying angel *n.* Any of several poisonous mushrooms of the genus *Amanita.*

de·struct (dĭ-strŭkt′, dē′strŭkt′) *n.* The intentional destruction of a space vehicle, rocket, or missile after launching. [Back-formation < DESTRUCTION.]

de·struc·ti·ble (dĭ-strŭk′tə-bəl) *adj.* Subject to destruction; capable of being destroyed. **—de·struc′ti·bil′i·ty, de·struc′ti·ble·ness** *n.*

de·struc·tion (dĭ-strŭk′shən) *n.* **1.** The act of destroying. **2.** The condition or fact of being destroyed. **3.** The cause or means of destroying. [ME *destruccioun* < OFr. *destruction* < Lat. *destructio* < *destructus,* p.part. of *destruere,* to destroy.]

de·struc·tion·ist (dĭ-strŭk′shə-nĭst) *n.* A person who favors destruction, esp. of existing social institutions.

de·struc·tive (dĭ-strŭk′tĭv) *adj.* **1.** Causing or wreaking destruction; ruinous: *destructive to national safety.* **2.** Designed or tending to disprove or discredit: *destructive criticism.* **—de·struc′tive·ly** *adv.* **—de·struc′tive·ness, de′struc·tiv′i·ty** (dē′strŭk-tĭv′ĭ-tē) *n.*

destructive distillation *n.* The simultaneous decomposition by heat and distillation of substances such as wood, coal, and oil shale to produce useful by-products such as coke, charcoal, oils, and gases.

de·struc·tor (dĭ-strŭk′tər) *n.* **1.** An incinerator for refuse. **2.** An explosive device for effecting a destruct.

des·ue·tude (dĕs′wĭ-to͞od′, -tyo͞od′) *n.* The state or condition of disuse: *words fallen into desuetude.* [Fr. *désuétude* < Lat. *desuetudo* < *desuescere,* to put out of use : *de-* (reversal) + *suescere,* to become accustomed.]

de·sul·fur·ize (dē-sŭl′fə-rīz′) *tr.v.* **-ized, -iz·ing, -iz·es.** To eliminate sulfur from. **—de·sul′fur·i·za′tion** *n.*

des·ul·to·ry (dĕs′əl-tôr′ē, -tōr′ē, dĕz′-) *adj.* **1.** Moving or jumping from one thing to another; disconnected: *a desultory speech.* **2.** Occurring haphazardly; random. [Lat. *desultorius* < *desultor,* a leaper < *desultus,* p.part. of *desilire,* to leap down : *de-,* down + *salire,* to jump.] **—des′ul·to′ri·ly** *adv.* **—des′ul·to′ri·ness** *n.*

de·tach (dĭ-tăch′) *tr.v.* **-tached, -tach·ing, -tach·es. 1.** To separate; disconnect. **2.** To cut off from association with. **3.** To send (troops, for example) on a special mission. [Fr. *détacher* < OFr. *destachier* : *des-,* apart (< Lat. *de-*) + *attachier,* to attach, of Germanic orig.] **—de·tach′a·bil′i·ty** *n.* **—de·tach′a·ble** *adj.* **—de·tach′a·bly** *adv.*

de·tached (dĭ-tăcht′) *adj.* **1.** Standing apart from others; separate: *a detached house.* **2.** Free from emotional, intellectual, social, or other involvement; disinterested: *a detached opinion.* **—de·tach′ed·ly** (-tăch′ĭd-lē, -tăcht′lē) *adv.* **—de·tach′ed·ness** *n.*

de·tach·ment (dĭ-tăch′mənt) *n.* **1.** The act or process of disconnecting or detaching; separation. **2.** The state of being separate or apart. **3.** Indifference to worldly affairs or the concerns of others; aloofness. **4.** Absence of prejudice or bias; disinterest. **5. a.** The dispatch of military troops or ships selected from a larger unit for a special duty or mission. **b.** The unit of troops or ships so dispatched. **c.** A permanent unit, usually smaller than a platoon, organized for special duties.

de·tail (dĭ-tāl′, dē′tāl′) *n.* **1.** An individual part or item; particular. **2.** Particulars considered separately and in relation to a whole: *careful attention to detail.* **3.** The act of dealing with things item by item. **4.** A small or secondary part of a painting, statue, building, or other work of art, esp. when considered or represented in isolation. **5. a.** The selection of one or more troops for a particular duty, usually a fatigue duty. **b.** The personnel so selected. **c.** The duty assigned. *—tr.v.* (dĭ-tāl′) **-tailed, -tail·ing, -tails. 1.** To report or relate minutely or in particulars. **2.** To name or state explicitly. **3.** To select and dispatch for a particular duty. [Fr. *détail* < OFr. *detail,* a piece cut off < *detailler,* to cut up : *de-,* completely (< Lat. *de-*) + *tailler,* to cut. —see TAILOR.]

de·tailed (dĭ-tāld′, dē′tāld′) *adj.* Characterized by abundant use of detail or by thoroughness of treatment: *a detailed report on the state of the economy.*

detail man *n.* A representative of a manufacturer of drugs or medical supplies who calls on doctors, pharmacists, and other professional users to promote new drugs and supplies.

de·tain (dĭ-tān′) *tr.v.* **-tained, -tain·ing, -tains. 1.** To keep from proceeding; delay or retard. **2.** To keep in custody; confine. **3.** *Obs.* To retain or withhold. [ME *deteynen* < OFr. *detenir* < Lat. *detinēre* : *de-,* away + *tenēre,* to hold.] **—de·tain′ment** *n.*

de·tain·ee (dē′tā-nē′, dĭ-tā′-) *n.* A person held in custody: *a political detainee.*

de·tain·er (dĭ-tā′nər) *n. Law.* **1. a.** The unlawful withholding of the property of another. **b.** The detention of a person, esp. in custody. **2.** A writ authorizing the further detention of a person in custody pending action.

de·tect (dĭ-tĕkt′) *tr.v.* **-tect·ed, -tect·ing, -tects. 1.** To discover or discern the existence, presence, or fact of. **2.** To find out the true nature of. **3.** *Electronics.* To demodulate. [ME *detecten* < Lat. *detectus,* p.part. of *detegere,* to uncover : *de-,* off + *tegere,* to cover.] **—de·tect′a·ble, de·tect′i·ble** *adj.* **—de·tect′er** *n.*

de·tect·a·phone (dĭ-tĕk′tə-fōn′) *n.* A device used for secretly listening to another's telephone conversations.

de·tec·tion (dĭ-tĕk′shən) *n.* **1.** The act of finding out or the fact of being found out; discovery, as of something hidden or obscure. **2.** *Electronics.* Demodulation.

de·tec·tive (dĭ-tĕk′tĭv) *n.* A person, usually a policeman, whose work is investigating crimes, obtaining evidence, and performing similar duties. *—**modifier:** a detective novel; detective methods.*

de·tec·tor (dĭ-tĕk′tər) *n.* One that detects, esp. a mechanical, electrical, or chemical device that automatically identifies and records or registers a stimulus such as an environmental change in pressure or temperature, an electric signal, or radiation from a radioactive material.

de·tent (dĭ-tĕnt′) *n.* A pawl. [Fr. *détente,* a loosening < OFr. *destente* < *destendre,* to release : *des-,* apart (< Lat. *de-*) + *tendre,* to stretch < Lat. *tendere.*]

dé·tente (dā-tänt′, -tänt′) *n.* A relaxing or easing, as of tension between nations. [Fr. —see DETENT.]

de·ten·tion (dĭ-tĕn′shən) *n.* **1. a.** The act of detaining. **b.** The state of being detained, esp. a period of temporary custody while awaiting trial. **2.** A forced or punitive delay. [ME *detencioun,* act of withholding < OFr. *detention* < LLat. *detentio* < Lat. *detentus,* p.part. of *detinēre,* to detain.]

detention home *n.* A place where juvenile delinquents or offenders are held in custody, esp. for a temporary period while awaiting action by the court on their cases.

de·ter (dĭ-tûr′) *tr.v.* **-terred, -ter·ring, -ters.** To prevent or discourage from acting, as by means of fear or doubt. [Lat. *deterrēre* : *de-,* away + *terrēre,* to frighten.] **—de·ter′rer** *n.* **—de·ter′ment** *n.*

de·terge (dĭ-tûrj′) *tr.v.* **-terged, -terg·ing, -terg·es.** To wash or wipe off; cleanse. [Fr. *déterger* < Lat. *detergēre* : *de-,* off + *tergēre,* to wipe.]

de·ter·gen·cy (dĭ-tûr′jən-sē) also **de·ter·gence** (-jəns) *n.* Cleansing power or quality.

de·ter·gent (dĭ-tûr′jənt) *n.* A cleansing substance, esp. a synthetic one that acts as a wetting agent and emulsifier and is made from chemical compounds rather than from fats and lye. *—adj.* Having cleansing power.

de·te·ri·o·rate (dĭ-tîr′ē-ə-rāt′) *v.* **-rat·ed, -rat·ing, -rates.** *—tr.* To lower in quality, character, or value. *—intr.* To degenerate. [LLat. *deteriorare, deteriorat-* < Lat. *deterior,* worse.] **—de·te′ri·o·ra′tion** *n.* **—de·te′ri·o·ra′tive** *adj.*

de·ter·min·a·ble (dĭ-tûr′mə-nə-bəl) *adj.* **1.** Capable of being settled, fixed, or determined. **2.** *Law.* Liable to be terminated. **—de·ter′min·a·ble·ness** *n.* **—de·ter′min·a·bly** *adv.*

de·ter·mi·na·cy (dĭ-tûr′mə-nə-sē) *n.* **1.** The quality or condition of being determinate. **2.** The condition of being determined or characterized.

de·ter·mi·nant (dĭ-tûr′mə-nənt) *adj.* Determinative. *—n.*

1. An influencing or determining factor. **2.** *Math.* A square array of quantities or elements having a value determined by a rule of combination for the elements and used esp. in solving certain classes of simultaneous equations.

de·ter·mi·nate (dĭ-tûr′mə-nĭt) *adj.* **1.** Precisely limited or defined. **2.** Conclusively settled; final. **3.** Firm in purpose; resolute. **4.** *Bot.* **a.** Terminating in a flower and blooming in a sequence beginning with the uppermost or central flower: *a determinate inflorescence.* **b.** Not continuing indefinitely at the tip of an axis: *determinate growth.* [ME *determinat* < Lat. *determinatus,* p.part. of *determinare,* to determine.] **—de·ter′mi·nate·ly** *adv.* **—de·ter′mi·nate·ness** *n.*

de·ter·mi·nat·er (dĭ-tûr′mə-nā-tər) *n.* A determiner.

de·ter·mi·na·tion (dĭ-tûr′mə-nā′shən) *n.* **1. a.** The act of making or arriving at a decision. **b.** The decision arrived at. **2.** The quality of being resolute or firm in purpose; resoluteness. **3. a.** The act of settling a dispute, suit, or other question by an authoritative decision or pronouncement, esp. by a judicial body. **b.** The decision or pronouncement made. **4. a.** The ascertaining or establishing of the extent, quality, position, or character of something. **b.** The result of such ascertaining. **5.** A fixed movement or tendency toward an object or end. **6.** *Logic.* **a.** The rendering of a concept or proposition more definite by further qualification. **b.** The defining of a concept through its constituent elements.

de·ter·mi·na·tive (dĭ-tûr′mə-nā′tĭv, -nə-) *adj.* Tending, able, or serving to determine. *—n.* Something that determines. **—de·ter′mi·na′tive·ly** *adv.* **—de·ter′mi·na′tive·ness** *n.*

de·ter·mine (dĭ-tûr′mĭn) *v.* **-mined, -min·ing, -mines.** *—tr.* **1. a.** To decide or settle (a dispute, for example) conclusively and authoritatively. **b.** To end or decide by judicial or other final action. **2.** To establish or ascertain definitely, as after consideration, investigation, or calculation. **3.** To cause (someone) to come to a conclusion or resolution. **4.** To be the cause of; regulate: *Demand determines production.* **5.** To give direction to: *The board determines company policy.* **6.** To limit in scope or extent. **7.** *Math.* To fix or define the position, form, or configuration of. **8.** *Logic.* To explain or limit by adding differences. **9.** *Law.* To put an end to; terminate. *—intr.* **1.** To reach a decision; resolve. **2.** *Law.* To come to an end. [ME *determinen* < OFr. *determiner* < Lat. *determinare,* to limit : *de-,* off + *terminus,* boundary.]

de·ter·mined (dĭ-tûr′mĭnd) *adj.* **1.** Marked by or showing determination; resolute. **2.** Decided or resolved. **—de·ter′mined·ly** *adv.* **—de·ter′mined·ness** *n.*

de·ter·min·er (dĭ-tûr′mə-nər) *n.* **1.** One that determines. **2.** *Gram.* A word belonging to a group of noun modifiers generally considered to include articles, demonstratives, possessive adjectives, and a few other words such as *any, both, several,* and *whose* and that occupies the first position in a noun phrase or the second or third position after another determiner.

de·ter·min·ism (dĭ-tûr′mə-nĭz′əm) *n.* The philosophical doctrine that every event, act, and decision is the inevitable consequence of antecedents that are independent of the human will.

de·ter·rence (dĭ-tûr′əns, -tŭr′-) *n.* **1.** The act or a means of deterring. **2.** Measures taken by a state or an alliance of states to prevent hostile action by another state.

de·ter·rent (dĭ-tûr′ənt, -tŭr′-) *adj.* Tending to deter. *—n.* **1.** Something that deters: *a deterrent to theft.* **2.** A retaliatory means of discouraging enemy attack: *a nuclear deterrent.*

deuce[1]
Playing card

de·ter·sive (dĭ-tûr′sĭv, -zĭv) *adj.* Detergent. [OFr. *detersif* < Lat. *detersus,* p.part. of *detergēre,* to deterge.] **—de·ter′sive** *n.*

de·test (dĭ-tĕst′) *tr.v.* **-test·ed, -test·ing, -tests.** To dislike intensely; abhor. [Lat. *detestari,* to curse : *de-* (pejorative) + *testari,* to invoke < *testis,* witness.] **—de·test′er** *n.*

de·test·a·ble (dĭ-tĕs′tə-bəl) *adj.* Deserving abhorrence or execration; abominable. **—de·test′a·bil′i·ty, de·test′a·ble·ness** *n.* **—de·test′a·bly** *adv.*

de·tes·ta·tion (dē′tĕ-stā′shən) *n.* **1.** Strong dislike or hatred; abhorrence. **2.** Someone or something that is detested.

de·throne (dē-thrōn′) *tr.v.* **-throned, -thron·ing, -thrones.** **1.** To remove from the throne; depose. **2.** To remove from a prominent or powerful position. **—de·throne′ment** *n.*

det·i·nue (dĕt′n-ōō′, -yōō′) *n.* *Law.* **1. a.** An action to recover possession or the value of property wrongfully detained. **b.** The writ authorizing such action. **2.** *Obs.* The act of unlawfully detaining personal property. [ME *detenue* < OFr., detention < p.part. of *detenir,* to detain.]

det·o·na·ble (dĕt′n-ə-bəl) *adj.* Capable of being detonated.

det·o·nate (dĕt′n-āt′) *intr. & tr.v.* **-nat·ed, -nat·ing, -nates.** To explode or cause to explode suddenly and violently. [Lat. *detonare, detonat-,* to thunder down : *de-,* down + *tonare,* to thunder.] **—det′o·nat′a·ble** *adj.*

det·o·na·tion (dĕt′n-ā′shən) *n.* **1.** The act of detonating or exploding. **2.** An explosion.

det·o·na·tor (dĕt′n-ā′tər) *n.* **1.** A device, such as a fuse or percussion cap, used to set off explosives. **2.** An explosive.

de·tour (dē′tŏŏr′, dĭ-tŏŏr′) *n.* **1.** A roundabout way or course, esp. a road used temporarily instead of a main route. **2.** A deviation from a direct course of action. *—intr. & tr.v.* **-toured, -tour·ing, -tours.** To go or cause to go by a roundabout way. [Fr. *détour* < OFr. *destor* < *destorner,* to turn away : *des-,* away (< Lat. *de-*) + *tourner,* to turn. —see TURN.]

de·tox (dē-tŏks′) *Informal.* *—tr.v.* **-toxed, -tox·ing, -tox·es.** To subject to detoxification. *—n.* (dē′tŏks′). A section of a hospital or clinic in which patients are detoxified.

de·tox·i·fy (dē-tŏk′sə-fī′) also **de·tox·i·cate** (-sĭ-kāt′) *tr.v.* **-fied, -fy·ing, -fies** also **-cat·ed, -cat·ing, -cates.** **1.** To counteract or destroy the toxic properties of. **2.** To remove the effects of poison from. [DE- + TOXI(C) + -FY.] **—de·tox′i·fi·ca′tion** *n.*

de·tract (dĭ-trăkt′) *v.* **-tract·ed, -tract·ing, -tracts.** *—intr.* To take away a desirable part; diminish. *—tr.* **1.** To distract. **2.** *Archaic.* To speak ill of; belittle. [ME *detracten* < Lat. *detractus,* p.part. of *detrahere,* to remove : *de-,* away + *trahere,* to pull.] **—de·trac′tive** *adj.* **—de·trac′tor** *n.*

de·trac·tion (dĭ-trăk′shən) *n.* **1.** Disparagement. **2.** The act of detracting or taking away.

de·train (dē-trān′) *intr. & tr.v.* **-trained, -train·ing, -trains.** To leave or cause to leave a railroad train. **—de·train′ment** *n.*

de·trib·al·ize (dē-trī′bə-līz′) *tr.v.* **-ized, -iz·ing, -iz·es.** To cause to lose tribal customs. **—de·trib′al·i·za′tion** *n.*

det·ri·ment (dĕt′rə-mənt) *n.* **1.** Damage, harm, or loss: *pitched extra innings with no detriment to his effectiveness.* **2.** Something that causes damage, harm, or loss. [ME < OFr. < Lat. *detrimentum* < *deterere,* to lessen : *de-,* away + *terere,* to rub.]

det·ri·men·tal (dĕt′rə-mĕn′tl) *adj.* Causing damage or harm; injurious. **—det′ri·men′tal·ly** *adv.*

de·tri·tion (dĭ-trĭsh′ən) *n.* The act of wearing away by friction or rubbing. [Med. Lat. *detritio* < Lat. *detritus,* p.part. of *deterere,* to lessen. —see DETRIMENT.]

de·tri·tus (dĭ-trī′təs) *n., pl.* **detritus.** **1.** Loose fragments, particles, or grains that have been formed by the disintegration of rocks. **2.** Disintegrated matter; debris: *the detritus of past civilizations.* [Fr. *détritus* < Lat. *detritus,* p.part. of *deterere,* to lessen. —see DETRIMENT.]

de trop (də trō′) *adj.* Too much or too many; superfluous. [Fr.]

de·tu·mes·cence (dē′tōō-mĕs′əns, -tyōō-) *n.* Contraction following expansion, esp. restoration of a swollen organ or part to normal size. [< Lat. *detumescere,* to subside : *de-* (reversal) + *tumescere,* to swell up < *tumere,* to subside.] **—de′tu·mes′cent** *adj.*

Deu·ca·li·on (dōō-kā′lē-ən, dyōō-) *n.* *Gk. Myth.* A son of Prometheus who with his wife, Pyrrha, survived a deluge sent by Zeus and became the ancestor of the renewed human race. [Lat. < Gk. *Deukaliōn.*]

deuce[1] (dōōs, dyōōs) *n.* **1. a.** A playing card or side of a die bearing two spots. **b.** A cast of the dice totaling two. **2.** A tennis score in which each player or side has 40 points or 5 or more games each and either player or side must win 2 successive points or games to win the game or set. [OFr. *deus,* two < Lat. *duos,* accusative of *duo.*]

deuce[2] (dōōs, dyōōs) *n.* *Informal.* The devil. Used as a mild oath or exclamation of annoyance, impatience, or surprise. [Prob. < LG *duus,* a throw of two in dice games, bad luck, ult. < Lat. *duo,* two.]

deuc·ed (dōō′sĭd, dyōō′-) *adj.* *Informal.* Darned; confounded. [< DEUCE[2].] **—deuc′ed, deuc′ed·ly** *adv.*

de·us ex ma·chi·na (dā′əs ĕks mä′kə-nə, -nä′, măk′ə-nə) *n.* **1.** A deity in Greek and Roman drama who was brought in by stage machinery to intervene in a difficult situation. **2.** An unexpected, artificial, or improbable character, device, or event suddenly introduced to resolve a situation or untangle a plot. [NLat., god from a machine, transl. of Gk. *theos ek mēkhanēs.*]

deut– *pref.* Variant of **deuto-**.

deuter– *pref.* Variant of **deutero-**.

deu·ter·ag·o·nist (dōō′tə-răg′ə-nĭst) *n.* In classical Greek drama, the character second in importance to the protagonist. [Gk. *deuteragōnistēs* : *deuteros,* second + *agōnistēs,* actor. —see PROTAGONIST.]

deu·ter·a·no·pi·a (dōō′tər-ə-nō′pē-ə, dyōō′-) *n.* A form of colorblindness characterized by confusion of green, bluish red, and neutral. [DEUTER(O)- + AN- + -OPIA (so called from the blindness to green, which is considered the second of the primary colors).] **—deu′ter·a·nope′** (-nōp′) *n.* **—deu′ter·a·nop′ic** (-nŏp′ĭk, -nō′pĭk) *adj.*

deu·ter·ate (dōō′tə-rāt′, dyōō′-) *tr.v.* **-at·ed, -at·ing, -ates.** To introduce deuterium into. [DEUTER(IUM) + -ATE.] **—deu′te·ra′tion** *n.*

deu·te·ri·um (dōō-tîr′ē-əm, dyōō-) *n.* An isotope of hydrogen having an atomic weight of 2.0141.

deuterium oxide *n.* An isotopic form of water with composition D_2O, present in natural water as approximately 1 part in 6,500 and isolated for use as a moderator in certain nuclear reactors.

deutero– or **deuter–** *pref.* Second; secondary: *deuterocanonical.* [Gk. *deuteros,* second.]

deu·ter·o·ca·non·i·cal (dōō′tə-rō′kə-nŏn′ĭ-kəl, dyoo′-) *adj.* Of or pertaining to books or sections of books in the Old Testament considered canonical by the Eastern Orthodox and Roman Catholics and apocryphal by many Protestants.

deu·ter·og·a·my (dōō′tə-rŏg′ə-mē, dyōō′-) *n.* A second legal marriage, after the death or divorce of a first spouse.

deu·ter·on (do͞o′tə-rŏn′, dyo͞o′-) *n.* The nucleus of a deuterium atom, a composite of a proton and a neutron, regarded as a subatomic particle with unit positive charge. [DEUTER(IUM) + -ON.]

Deu·ter·on·o·my (do͞o′tə-rŏn′ə-mē, dyo͞o′-) *n.* See table at **Bible.** [LLat. *deuteronomium* < Gk. *deuteronomion* : *deuteros,* second + *nomos,* law.]

deuto– or **deut–** *pref.* Second; secondary: *deutoplasm.* [< DEUTERO-.]

deu·to·plasm (do͞o′tə-plăz′əm, dyo͞o′-) also **deu·ter·o·plasm** (-tə-rō-plăz′əm) *n.* Food substance or yolk in the cytoplasm of an ovum or other cell.

deut·sche mark also **deut·sche·mark** (doi′chə-märk′) *n.* See table at **currency.** [G., German mark.]

deut·zi·a (do͞ot′sē-ə, dyo͞ot′-) *n.* Any of various shrubs of the genus *Deutzia,* cultivated for their clusters of white or pinkish flowers. [NLat. *Deutzia,* genus name, after Jean *Deutz* (d. 1784?).]

de·val·u·ate (dē-văl′yo͞o-āt′) also **de·val·ue** (-văl′yo͞o) *tr.v.* **-at·ed, -at·ing, -ates** also **-ued, -u·ing, -ues. 1.** To lessen or annul the value of. **2.** To lower the exchange value of (currency) by lowering its gold equivalency. **—de·val′u·a′tion** *n.*

De·va·na·ga·ri (dā′və-nä′gə-rē) *n.* The alphabet in which Sanskrit and many modern Indian languages are written. [Skt. *devanāgarī* : *deva-,* divine + *nagaram,* city.]

dev·as·tate (dĕv′ə-stāt′) *tr.v.* **-tat·ed, -tat·ing, -tates. 1.** To lay waste. **2.** To overwhelm; confound: *a problem that devastated the family.* [Lat. *devastare, devastat-* : *de-* (intensive) + *vastare,* to lay waste < *vastus,* waste.] **—dev′as·tat′ing·ly** *adv.* **—dev′as·ta′tion** *n.* **—dev′as·ta′tor** *n.*

de·vel·op (dĭ-vĕl′əp) *v.* **-oped, -op·ing, -ops.** *—tr.* **1. a.** To realize the potentialities of: *developed her musical ability.* **b.** To aid in the growth of; strengthen: *develop muscles.* **2. a.** To cause to unfold gradually: *He slowly develops the novel's plot.* **b.** To cause to expand or grow gradually: *Centuries of erosion developed the ravine.* **3. a.** To bring into being; make active: *develop industry.* **b.** To make more available or effective: *develop natural resources.* **4. a.** To set forth or clarify by degrees: *develop a plan.* **b.** To elaborate or enlarge: *develop an idea.* **5.** *Mus.* To unfold (a theme) with rhythmic and harmonic variations. **6.** To convert (a tract of land) to a specific purpose, as by building extensively. **7.** To come to have gradually; acquire: *develop a taste for opera.* **8.** To become affected with; contract: *develop a disease.* **9.** To process (a photosensitive material), esp. with chemicals, in order to render a recorded image visible. *—intr.* **1.** To grow; expand. **2.** To come gradually into existence or activity. **3.** To be disclosed. **4.** *Biol.* **a.** To progress from earlier to later stages of individual maturation. **b.** To progress from earlier to later or from simpler to more complex stages of evolution. [Fr. *développer* < OFr. *desveloper* : *des-,* apart (< Lat. *dis-*) + *voloper,* to wrap.] **—de·vel′op·a·ble** *adj.*

de·vel·op·er (dĭ-vĕl′ə-pər) *n.* **1.** One that develops. **2.** A person who develops real estate. **3.** A chemical used to render visible the image recorded on a photosensitive surface.

de·vel·op·ing (dĭ-vĕl′ə-pĭng) *adj.* Underdeveloped: *developing nations.*

de·vel·op·ment (dĭ-vĕl′əp-mənt) *n.* **1.** The act of developing. **2.** The state of being developed. **3.** Something that has been developed, esp. a group of dwellings built by the same contractor. **4.** A significant event or occurrence. **—de·vel′op·men′tal** (-mĕn′tl) *adj.* **—de·vel′op·men′tal·ly** *adv.*

de·verb·a·tive (dē-vûr′bə-tĭv) *Gram. —adj.* **1.** Designating a word derived from a verb. For example, *worker* is a deverbative noun derived from the verb *work.* **2.** Designating an element used in derivation from a verb. For example, the suffix *-er* in *teacher* is deverbative. *—n.* A deverbative word or element.

de·vest (dĭ-vĕst′) *tr.v.* **-vest·ed, -vest·ing, -vests.** *Law.* To take (a right, for example) away. [OFr. *desvestir,* to undress < VLat. **disvestire* : Lat. *dis-,* apart + Lat. *vestis,* garment.]

De·vi (dā′vē) *n. Hinduism.* A general appellation for all feminine deities, used esp. for the wife of Shiva. [Skt. *devī,* fem. of *devaḥ,* god.]

de·vi·ant (dē′vē-ənt) *adj.* Differing from a norm or from the accepted standards of society. *—n.* A person whose behavior and attitudes differ from the norm or from accepted social and moral standards. [ME *deviaunt* < LLat. *devians,* pr.part. of *deviare,* to deviate.] **—de′vi·ance, de′vi·an·cy** *n.*

de·vi·ate (dē′vē-āt′) *v.* **-at·ed, -at·ing, -ates.** *—intr.* To turn or move increasingly away from a specified course or prescribed mode of behavior. *—tr.* To cause to turn aside or differ. *—n.* (-ĭt). A deviant. [LLat. *deviare, deviat-* : Lat. *de-,* away + Lat. *via,* road.] **—de′vi·a′tor** *n.*

de·vi·a·tion (dē′vē-ā′shən) *n.* **1.** The act of deviating or turning aside. **2.** An abnormality; departure: *"Vice was a deviation from our nature . . ."* (H. Fielding). **3.** Deviant behavior or attitudes. **4.** Divergence from an accepted political policy or party line. **5.** Deflection of a compass needle caused by a magnetic influence, as in a ship. **6.** *Statistics.* The difference, esp. the absolute difference, between one of a set of numbers and their mean. **—de′vi·a′tion·ism** *n.* **—de′vi·a′tion·ist** *n.*

de·vice (dĭ-vīs′) *n.* **1.** Something devised or constructed for a particular purpose, esp. a machine used to perform one or more relatively simple tasks. **2.** An artistic contrivance in a literary work used to achieve a particular effect. **3.** A plan or scheme, esp. a malign one. **4.** A decorative design, figure, or pattern, as one used in embroidery. **5.** A graphic symbol or motto, esp. in heraldry. **6.** *Archaic.* The act, state, or power of devising. ***—idiom.*** **leave to (one's) own devices.** To allow to do as one pleases. [ME < OFr. *devis,* division, and *devise,* design, both < *deviser,* to devise.]

dev·il (dĕv′əl) *n.* **1.** Often **Devil.** *Theol.* The major spirit of evil, ruler of Hell, and foe of God; Satan. **2.** A subordinate evil spirit; demon. **3.** A wicked or malevolent person. **4.** An unfortunate person; wretch: *poor devil.* **5.** A person who is energetic, mischievous, daring, or clever. **6.** A printer's devil. **7.** Any of various toothed machines, as for tearing up rags. **8.** *Informal.* Something difficult or hard to manage: *had the very devil of a time.* **9.** *Christian Science.* The opposite of Truth; error. *—v.* **-iled, -il·ing, -ils** or **-illed, -il·ling, -ils.** *—tr.* **1.** To season (food) heavily. **2.** To tear up (cloth or rags) in a toothed machine. **3.** To annoy, torment, or harass. *—intr.* To serve as a printer's devil. ***—idioms.*** **give the devil his due.** To acknowledge the ability or success of an evil or disliked person. **the devil.** *Informal.* An exclamation or expletive used to express surprise, anger, disgust, or vexation. **the devil to pay.** Trouble to be faced as a result of an action. [ME *devel* < OE *dēofol* < LLat. *diabolus* < LGk. *diabolos* < Gk., slanderer < *diaballein,* to slander : *dia-,* across + *ballein,* to throw.]

dev·il·fish (dĕv′əl-fĭsh′) *n., pl.* **devilfish** or **-fish·es. 1.** A manta (sense 2). **2.** An octopus (sense 1).

dev·il·ish (dĕv′ə-lĭsh) *adj.* **1.** Of, resembling, or characteristic of a devil; fiendish. **2.** *Informal.* Excessive; extreme: *devilish heat.* *—adv. Informal.* Extremely; very. **—dev′il·ish·ly** *adv.* **—dev′il·ish·ness** *n.*

dev·il·kin (dĕv′əl-kĭn) *n.* A little devil; imp.

dev·il-may-care (dĕv′əl-mā-kâr′) *adj.* **1.** Heedless of caution; reckless. **2.** Jovial and rakish in manner.

dev·il·ment (dĕv′əl-mənt) *n.* Devilish mischief.

dev·il·ry (dĕv′əl-rē) *n.* Variant of **deviltry.**

devil's advocate *n.* **1.** *Rom. Cath. Ch.* An official appointed to present arguments against a proposed canonization or beatification. **2.** A person who opposes an argument with which he does not necessarily disagree, as to determine its validity. **3.** An adverse critic, esp. of a good cause.

devil's bit *n.* The blazing star.

devil's club *n.* A spiny shrub, *Oplopanax horridus,* of western North America, having greenish-white flowers and scarlet fruit.

devil's darning needle *n.* **1.** A dragonfly. **2.** A damselfly.

dev·il's-food cake (dĕv′əlz-fo͝od′) *n.* A rich chocolate cake.

devil's paintbrush *n.* The orange hawkweed.

devil's walking stick *n.* The Hercules'-club.

dev·il·try (dĕv′əl-trē) also **dev·il·ry** (-əl-rē) *n., pl.* **-tries** also **-ries. 1.** Wanton or reckless mischief. **2.** Extreme cruelty; wickedness. **3.** Evil magic; witchcraft.

dev·il·wood (dĕv′əl-wo͝od′) *n.* A tree, *Osmanthus americanus,* of the southeastern United States, having fragrant greenish flowers and hard wood.

de·vi·ous (dē′vē-əs) *adj.* **1.** Deviating from the straight or direct course; roundabout. **2.** Departing from the correct or proper way; erring. **3.** Not straightforward; shifty: *a devious person.* [Lat. *devius,* out-of-the-way : *de-,* away from + *via,* road.] **—de′vi·ous·ly** *adv.* **—de′vi·ous·ness** *n.*

de·vi·sal (dĭ-vī′zəl) *n.* The act of devising.

de·vise (dĭ-vīz′) *tr.v.* **-vised, -vis·ing, -vis·es. 1.** To form or arrange in the mind; contrive. **2.** *Law.* To transmit or give (real property) by will. **3.** *Obs.* To suppose; imagine. *—n. Law.* **1.** The act of transmitting or giving real property by will. **2.** The property or lands transmitted by will. **3.** A will or clause in a will devising real property. [ME *devisen* < OFr. *deviser* < VLat. **divisare,* freq. of Lat. *dividere,* to divide.] **—de·vis′a·ble** *adj.* **—de·vis′er** *n.*

Devi

de·vi·see (dĭ-vī′zē′, dĕv′ī-zē′) *n. Law.* One to whom a devise is made.

de·vi·sor (dĭ-vī′zər, dĕv′ĭ-zôr′) *n. Law.* One who makes a devise.

de·vi·tal·ize (dē-vīt′l-īz′) *tr.v.* **-ized, -iz·ing, -iz·es.** To lower or destroy the vitality of. **—de·vit′al·i·za′tion** *n.*

de·vit·ri·fy (dē-vĭt′rə-fī′) *tr.v.* **-fied, -fy·ing, -fies. 1.** To remove or destroy the glassy quality of. **2.** To treat (material such as glass) so as to cause crystallization, brittleness, and loss of transparency. [Fr. *dévitrifier* : *dé-,* de- + *vitrifier,* to vitrify. —see VITRIFY.] **—de·vit′ri·fi′a·ble** *adj.* **—de·vit′ri·fi·ca′tion** *n.*

de·vo·cal·ize (dē-vō′kə-līz′) *tr.v.* **-ized, -iz·ing, -iz·es.** To devoice. **—de·vo′cal·i·za′tion** *n.*

de·voice (dē-vois′) *tr.v.* **-voiced, -voic·ing, -voic·es.** To unvoice (a speech sound).

de·void (dĭ-void′) *adj.* Completely lacking; destitute: *a novel devoid of wit and inventiveness.* [ME, p.part. of *devoiden,* to remove < OFr. *desvoidier* : *des-,* completely (< Lat. *de-*) + *voidier,* to empty < *voide,* empty. —see VOID.]

de·voir (dəv-wär′, dĕv′wär′) *n.* **1.** Often **devoirs.** An act or expression of respect or courtesy; civility. **2.** Duty or responsibility. [ME, duty < OFr. < *devoir,* to owe < Lat. *debēre.*]

de·vol·a·til·ize (dē-vŏl′ə-tl-īz′) *tr.v.* **-ized, -iz·ing, -iz·es.** To remove volatile material from. **—de·vol′a·til·i·za′tion** *n.*

dev·o·lu·tion (dĕv′ə-lo͞o′shən, dē′və-) *n.* **1.** A passing down through successive stages. **2.** The passing to a successor of something, such as properties, rights, and qualities. **3.** A delegating of authority or duties to a subordinate or substitute. **4.** A transfer of powers from a central government to local units. **5.** *Biol.* Degeneration as distinguished from evolution. [Med. Lat. *devolutio* < Lat. *devolutus,* p.part. of *devolvere,* to roll down. —see DEVOLVE.] **—dev′o·lu′tion·ar′y** (-shə-nĕr′ē) *adj.* **—dev′o·lu′tion·ist** *n.*

de·volve (dĭ-vŏlv′) *v.* **-volved, -volv·ing, -volves.** *—tr.* **1.** *Archaic.* To cause to roll onward or downward. **2.** To pass on or delegate to another. *—intr.* **1.** *Archaic.* To roll onward or downward. **2.** To be passed on or transferred to another. [ME *devolven,* to transfer < Lat. *devolvere,* to roll down : *de-,* down + *volvere,* to roll.] **—de·volve′ment** *n.*

Dev·on (dĕv′ən) *n.* Any of a breed of reddish cattle developed in Devonshire, England, and raised primarily for beef.

De·vo·ni·an (dĭ-vō′nē-ən) *adj.* Of, belonging to, or designating the geologic time, system of rocks, or sedimentary deposits of the fourth period of the Paleozoic era, preceded by the Silurian and followed by the Mississippian or Carboniferous period, and characterized by the appearance of forests and amphibians. *—n.* The Devonian period or system of deposits. [After *Devon,* a county in England.]

de·vote (dĭ-vōt′) *tr.v.* **-vot·ed, -vot·ing, -votes. 1.** To give or apply (one's time, attention, or self) entirely to a particular activity, pursuit, cause, or person. **2.** To set apart for a specific purpose or use: *land devoted to mining.* **3.** To set apart by or as if by a vow or solemn act; consecrate. [Lat. *devovēre, devot-,* to vow : *de-* (intensive) + *vovēre,* to vow.] **—de·vote′ment** *n.*

Synonyms: *devote, dedicate, consecrate, pledge.* These verbs are compared primarily in the sense of giving oneself or one's effort for a particular end. *Devote,* the most general, implies loyal and close attention to a cause, a job, another person, or the like. *Dedicate* adds the idea of a solemn and often formal commitment; in a related sense it means to set apart something, such as land or a structure, for special use. *Consecrate* stresses sacred commitment, as of a person to a cause or of a physical thing to religious use. *Pledge* refers to personal commitment backed by a solemn promise.

de·vot·ed (dĭ-vō′tĭd) *adj.* **1.** Feeling or displaying strong affection or attachment; ardent. **2.** Consecrated; dedicated. **—de·vot′ed·ly** *adv.* **—de·vot′ed·ness** *n.*

dev·o·tee (dĕv′ə-tē′, -tā′) *n.* **1.** A zealous follower or enthusiast: *a devotee of sports.* **2.** An ardent or fanatical adherent of a religion.

de·vo·tion (dĭ-vō′shən) *n.* **1.** Ardent attachment or affection. **2.** Religious ardor or zeal; piety. **3.** Often **devotions.** An act of religious observance or prayer, esp. when private. **4.** The act of devoting or the state of being devoted.

de·vo·tion·al (dĭ-vō′shə-nəl) *adj.* **1.** Of or pertaining to devotion. **2.** Used in worship. *—n.* A short service of worship. **—de·vo′tion·al·ly** *adv.*

de·vour (dĭ-vour′) *tr.v.* **-voured, -vour·ing, -vours. 1.** To eat up greedily. **2.** To destroy, consume, or waste: *Floods devoured the village.* **3.** To take in eagerly: *devour a novel.* **4.** To swallow up; engulf: *devoured by the crowd.* [ME *devouren* < OFr. *devourer* < Lat. *devorare* : *de-,* completely + *vorare,* to swallow.] **—de·vour′er** *n.* **—de·vour′ing·ly** *adv.*

de·vout (dĭ-vout′) *adj.* **-er, -est. 1.** Deeply religious; pious. **2.** Displaying reverence or piety. **3.** Sincere; earnest: *devout wishes for her success.* [ME < OFr. < LLat. *devotus* < Lat., p.part. of *devovere,* to vow. —see DEVOTE.] **—de·vout′ly** *adv.* **—de·vout′ness** *n.*

dew (do͞o, dyo͞o) *n.* **1.** Water droplets condensed from the air, usually at night, onto cool surfaces. **2.** Something moist, refreshing, or pure. **3.** Moisture appearing in small drops, as tears. *—tr.v.* **dewed, dew·ing, dews.** To wet with or as if with dew. [ME *deu* < OE *dēaw.*]

de·wan (dĭ-wän′) *n.* Any of certain governmental officials in India, esp. a prime minister. [Hindi *dīwān* < Pers. *divan,* account book.]

Dew·ar flask (do͞o′ər, dyo͞o′-) *n.* An insulated container used esp. to store liquefied gases, having a double wall with evacuated space between the walls and silvered surfaces. [After Sir James *Dewar* (1842–1923), its inventor.]

dew·ber·ry (do͞o′bĕr′ē, dyo͞o′-) *n.* **1.** Any of several trailing forms of the blackberry, such as *Rubus hispidus,* of North America, and *R. caesius,* of Europe. **2.** The fruit of a dewberry plant.

dew·claw (do͞o′klô′, dyo͞o′-) *n.* A vestigial digit, claw, or hoof on the foot of certain mammals.

dew·drop (do͞o′drŏp′, dyo͞o′-) *n.* A drop of dew.

Dew·ey decimal classification (do͞o′ē, dyo͞o′ē) *n.* A system used in libraries for the classification of books and other publications into ten major categories, each category being further subdivided by number. [After Melvil *Dewey* (1851–1931), its inventor.]

dew·fall (do͞o′fôl′, dyo͞o′-) *n.* **1.** The formation of dew. **2.** The time of evening when dew begins to form.

dew·lap (do͞o′lăp′, dyo͞o′-) *n.* **1.** A fold of loose skin hanging from the neck of certain animals. **2.** A pendulous part similar to a dewlap, such as the wattle of a bird. [ME *dewlappe.*]

dewlap
Brahman cow and calf

dhow

DEW line (do͞o, dyo͞o) *n.* A line of radar stations at about the 70th parallel across the North American continent, designed to give advance warning of approaching enemy aircraft and missiles. [*D(istant) E(arly) W(arning).*]

dew point *n.* The temperature at which air becomes saturated and produces dew.

dew-worm (do͞o′wûrm′, dyo͞o′-) *n.* An earthworm found on or near the surface of the ground and used as fishing bait.

dew·y (do͞o′ē, dyo͞o′ē) *adj.* **-i·er, -i·est. 1.** Moist with dew. **2.** Of or resembling dew. **3.** Suggestive of the freshness or purity of dew. **—dew′i·ly** *adv.* **—dew′i·ness** *n.*

dew·y-eyed (do͞o′ē-īd′, dyo͞o′-) *adj.* Innocent or naive.

dex (dĕks) *n.* Dextroamphetamine sulfate.

Dex·e·drine (dĕk′sĭ-drĭn, -drēn′). A trademark for a preparation of dextroamphetamine sulfate.

dex·ter (dĕk′stər) *adj.* **1.** Of or located on the right side. **2.** *Heraldry.* Located on the wearer's right and the observer's left. **3.** *Obs.* Auspicious; favorable. [Lat.]

dex·ter·i·ty (dĕk-stĕr′ĭ-tē) *n.* **1.** Skill in the use of the hands or body; adroitness. **2.** Mental skill or adroitness; cleverness. [OFr. *dexterite* < Lat. *dexteritas* < *dexter,* skillful, on the right side.]

dex·ter·ous (dĕk′stər-əs, -strəs) also **dex·trous** (-strəs) *adj.* **1.** Adroit or skillful in the use of the hands, body, or mind. **2.** Done with dexterity. [< Lat. *dexter,* skillful, on the right side.] **—dex′ter·ous·ly** *adv.* **—dex′ter·ous·ness** *n.*

Synonyms: *dexterous, deft, adroit, handy, nimble.* These adjectives refer to skill and ease in performance. *Dexterous* most often applies to manual ability. *Deft* suggests quickness, sureness, and lightness of touch in physical or mental activity. *Adroit* implies ease and natural skill, especially in meeting difficult situations. *Handy* implies a more modest aptitude, principally in manual work. *Nimble* stresses quickness and liveliness in physical or mental performance.

dextr– *pref.* Variant of **dextro-.**

dex·tral (dĕk′strəl) *adj.* **1.** Of, pertaining to, or located on the right side; right. **2.** Right-handed. **3.** *Zool.* Designating or pertaining to a gastropod shell that has its aperture to the right when facing the observer with the apex upward. **—dex·tral′i·ty** (-străl′ĭ-tē) *n.* **—dex′tral·ly** *adv.*

dex·tran (dĕk′străn′, -strən) *n.* Any of various heavy long-chain polymers of glucose that are used, depending on molecular weight, as a blood-plasma substitute and in confections, lacquers, and food additives.

dex·trin (dĕk′strĭn) also **dex·trine** (dĕk′strĭn, -strēn′) *n.* A white or yellow powder formed by the hydrolysis of starch, having colloidal properties, and used mainly as an adhesive and thickening agent.

dex·tro (dĕk′strō) *adj.* Dextrorotatory.

dextro– or **dextr–** *pref.* **1.** Right; on or to the right: *dextrorotation.* **2.** Dextrorotatory: *dextrose.* [Lat. < *dexter,* on the right side.]

dex·tro·am·phet·a·mine (dĕk′strō-ăm-fĕt′ə-mēn′, -mĭn) *n.* Amphetamine (sense 2).

dex·tro·glu·cose (dĕk′strə-glo͞o′kōs′, -kōz′) *n.* Dextrose.

dex·tro·ro·ta·ry (dĕk′strə-rō′tə-rē) *adj.* Variant of **dextrorotatory.**

dex·tro·ro·ta·tion (dĕk′strə-rō-tā′shən) *n.* A turning to the right. Used esp. of the plane of polarization of light.

dex·tro·ro·ta·to·ry (dĕk′strə-rō′tə-tôr′ē, -tōr′ē) also **dex·tro·ro·ta·ry** (-rō′tə-rē) *adj.* **1.** Turning or rotating the plane of polarization of light to the right or clockwise: *dextrorotatory crystals.* **2.** *Chem.* Of or pertaining to a solution that rotates the plane of polarized light to the right or clockwise.

dex·trorse (dĕk′strôrs′) *adj.* Growing upward in a spiral that turns from left to right: *a dextrorse vine.* [NLat. *dextrorsus* < Lat., turned toward the right : *dexter,* right + *versus,* p.part. of *vertere,* to turn.] **—dex′trorse′ly** *adv.*

dex·trose (dĕk′strōs′, -strōz′) *n.* A dextrorotatory sugar, $C_6H_{12}O_6 \cdot H_2O$, found in animal and plant tissue and derived synthetically from starch.

dex·trous (dĕk′strəs) *adj.* Variant of **dexterous.**

dey (dā) *n.* **1.** The title of the governor of Algiers before the French conquest in 1830. **2.** A title held by a ruler of the former states of Tunis or Tripoli. [Fr. < Turk. *dayi,* maternal uncle.]

dhar·ma (dûr′mə, där′-) *n.* *Hinduism & Buddhism.* **1.** The ultimate law of all things. **2.** Individual right conduct in conformity to dharma. [Skt. *darmaḥ,* law.]

Dhe·gi·ha (dā′jē-hä′) *n., pl.* **Dhegiha** or **-has. 1.** A Siouan language of the Osage, Omaha, and other neighboring tribes. **2. a.** The tribes speaking Dhegiha. **b.** A member of any of these tribes.

dhole (dōl) *n.* A doglike carnivorous mammal, *Cuon alpinus,* of Asia, having yellowish fur and often hunting in packs. [Perh. < Kanarese *tōla,* wolf.]

dho·ti (dō′tē) also **dhoo·ti** (do͞o′-) *n., pl.* **-tis. 1.** A loincloth worn by Hindu men in India. **2.** The cloth used in dhotis. [Hindi *dhōtī.*]

dhow (dou) *n.* A lateen-rigged Arabian vessel. [Ar. *dāw.*]

Dhul-Hij·ja (dül-hĭj′ä) *n.* The 12th month of the Moslem year. See table at **calendar.** [Ar. *dhū'l-ḥijja,* the one of the pilgrimage.]

Dhul-Qa·dah (dül-kä′dä) *n.* The 11th month of the Moslem year. See table at **calendar.** [Ar. *dhu'l-ga'dah,* the one of the sitting.]

Di The symbol for didymium.
di–¹ *pref.* **1.** Two; twice; double: *dichromatic.* **2.** Containing two atoms, radicals, or groups: *dichloride.* [Gk.]
di–² *pref.* Variant of **dia-.**
dia– or **di–** *pref.* **1.** Through: *diachronic.* **2.** Across: *diactinic.* [Gk. < *dia,* through.]
di·a·base (dī′ə-bās′) *n.* A dark-gray to black, fine-textured igneous rock composed mainly of feldspar and pyroxene and used for monuments and as crushed stone. [Fr. < Gk. *diabasis,* a crossing over < *diabainein,* to cross over : *dia-,* across + *bainein,* to go.]
di·a·be·tes (dī′ə-bē′tĭs, -tēz) *n.* Any of several metabolic disorders marked by excessive discharge of urine and persistent thirst. [ME *diabete* < Med. Lat. *diabetes* < Gk. *diabētēs,* a passing through < *diabainein,* to cross over. —see DIABASE.]
diabetes in·sip·i·dus (ĭn-sĭp′ĭ-dəs) *n.* A disease characterized by intense thirst and excessive urination, caused by a disorder of the pituitary gland. [NLat., insipid diabetes.]
diabetes mel·li·tus (mə-lī′təs, mĕl′ĭ-) *n.* A chronic disease of pancreatic origin, characterized by insulin deficiency, subsequent inability to utilize carbohydrates, excess sugar in the blood and urine, excessive thirst, hunger, and urination, weakness, emaciation, imperfect combustion of fats resulting in acidosis, and, without injection of insulin, eventual coma and death. [NLat., honey-sweet diabetes.]
di·a·bet·ic (dī′ə-bĕt′ĭk) *adj.* Of, relating to, or having diabetes. —*n.* One afflicted with diabetes mellitus.
di·a·ble·rie (dē-ä′blə-rē, -äb′lə-) *n.* **1.** Sorcery or witchcraft. **2.** The representation of devils or demons, as in paintings or fiction. **3.** Devilish conduct; deviltry. [Fr. < *diable,* devil < LLat. *diabolus.* —see DEVIL.]
di·a·bol·ic (dī′ə-bŏl′ĭk) also **di·a·bol·i·cal** (-ĭ-kəl) *adj.* **1.** Of, concerning, or characteristic of the devil; satanic. **2.** Appropriate to a devil; wicked or cruel. [ME *deabolik* < OFr. *diabolique* < LLat. *diabolicus* < *diabolus,* devil. —see DEVIL.] **—di′a·bol′i·cal·ly** *adv.* **—di′a·bol′i·cal·ness** *n.*
di·ab·o·lism (dī-ăb′ə-lĭz′əm) *n.* **1.** Dealings with or worship of the devil or demons; sorcery. **2.** Devilish conduct or character. **—di·ab′o·list** *n.*
di·ab·o·lize (dī-ăb′ə-līz′) *tr.v.* **-lized, -liz·ing, -liz·es. 1.** To cause to be diabolic or devilish. **2.** To represent as diabolic.
di·a·ce·tyl·mor·phine (dī′ə-sēt′l-môr′fēn′, dī-ăs′ĭ-tl-) *n.* Heroin.
di·a·chron·ic (dī′ə-krŏn′ĭk) *adj.* Of or concerned with phenomena, esp. of language, as they occur or change through time. [DIA- + Gk. *khronos,* time.] **—di′a·chron′i·cal·ly** *adv.*
di·ac·id (dī-ăs′ĭd) also **di·a·cid·ic** (dī′ə-sĭd′ĭk) *adj.* **1.** Capable of combining with two monoprotic acid molecules or one diprotic acid molecule to form a salt or ester. Used esp. of bases. **2.** Possessing two hydrogen atoms replaceable by metal atoms. Used of a salt. —*n.* **diacid.** An acid possessing two readily replaceable hydrogen atoms.
di·ac·o·nal (dī-ăk′ə-nəl) *adj.* Of or concerning a deacon or the diaconate. [LLat. *diaconalis* < *diaconus,* deacon.]
di·ac·o·nate (dī-ăk′ə-nĭt, -nāt′) *n.* **1.** The rank or office of a deacon. **2.** Deacons collectively. [LLat. *diaconatus* < *diaconus,* deacon.]
di·a·crit·ic (dī′ə-krĭt′ĭk) *adj.* **1.** Diacritical. **2.** *Med.* Diagnostic or distinctive. —*n.* A diacritical mark.
di·a·crit·i·cal (dī′ə-krĭt′ĭ-kəl) *adj.* Marking a distinction; distinguishing. [< Gk. *diakritikos,* distinguishing < *diakrinein,* to distinguish : *dia-,* apart + *krinein,* to separate.] **—di′a·crit′i·cal·ly** *adv.*
diacritical mark *n.* A mark, such as a circumflex, added to a letter to indicate a special phonetic value or to distinguish words that are otherwise graphically identical.
di·ac·tin·ic (dī′ăk-tĭn′ĭk) *adj.* Capable of transmitting chemically active or actinic radiation. **—di·ac′tin·ism** (-ăk′tə-nĭz′-əm) *n.*
di·a·del·phous (dī′ə-dĕl′fəs) *adj. Bot.* Having the filaments united so as to form two groups. Used of stamens.
di·a·dem (dī′ə-dĕm′, -dəm) *n.* **1.** A crown or headband worn as a sign of royalty. **2.** Royal power or dignity. —*tr.v.* **-demed, -dem·ing, -dems.** To adorn with or as if with a diadem. [ME *diademe* < OFr. < Lat. *diadema* < Gk. *diadēma* < *diadein,* to bind on either side : *dia-,* across + *dein,* to bind.]
di·aer·e·sis (dī-ĕr′ĭ-sĭs) *n.* Variant of **dieresis.**
di·a·gen·e·sis (dī′ə-jĕn′ĭ-sĭs) *n.* The process of chemical and physical change in deposited sediment during its conversion to rock. **—di′a·ge·net′ic** (-jə-nĕt′ĭk) *adj.*
di·a·ge·ot·ro·pism (dī′ə-jē-ŏt′rə-pĭz′əm) *n. Bot.* The tendency of growing parts, as roots, to become oriented at right angles to the direction of gravitational force. **—di′a·ge′o·trop′ic** (-ə-trŏp′ĭk, -trō′pĭk) *adj.*
di·ag·nose (dī′əg-nōs′, -nōz′) *v.* **-nosed, -nos·ing, -nos·es.** —*tr.* To distinguish or identify (a disease, for example) by diagnosis. —*intr.* To make a diagnosis. [Back-formation < DIAGNOSIS.]
di·ag·no·sis (dī′əg-nō′sĭs) *n., pl.* **-ses** (-sēz′). **1.** *Med.* **a.** The act or process of identifying or determining the nature of a disease through examination. **b.** The opinion derived from such an examination. **2. a.** A critical analysis of the nature of something. **b.** The conclusion reached by such analysis. **3.** *Biol.* A precise and detailed description of the characteristics of an organism for taxonomic classification. [NLat. < Gk. *diagnōsis,* discernment < *diagignoskein,* to distinguish : *dia-,* apart + *gignoskein,* to know.]
di·ag·nos·tic (dī′əg-nŏs′tĭk) *adj.* **1.** Of, pertaining to, or used in a diagnosis. **2.** Serving to identify a particular disease; characteristic. —*n.* **1.** Often **diagnostics.** The art or practice of medical diagnosis. **2.** A symptom serving as supporting evidence in a diagnosis. [Gk. *diagnostikos* < *diagnōstos,* to be distinguished < *diagignoskein,* to distinguish. —see DIAGNOSIS.] **—di′ag·nos′ti·cal·ly** *adv.*
di·ag·nos·ti·cian (dī′əg-nŏ-stĭsh′ən) *n.* A person who diagnoses, esp. a physician specializing in medical diagnostics.
di·ag·o·nal (dī-ăg′ə-nəl) *adj.* **1.** *Math.* **a.** Joining two nonadjacent vertices of a polygon. **b.** Joining two vertices of a polyhedron not in the same face. **2.** Having a slanted or oblique direction. **3.** Having oblique lines or markings. —*n.* **1.** *Math.* A diagonal line or plane. **2.** Something arranged obliquely, such as a row, course, or part. **3.** A fabric woven with diagonal lines. [Lat. *diagonalis* < Gk. *diagonios,* from angle to angle : *dia-,* across + *gonia,* angle.] **—di·ag′o·nal·ly** *adv.*
di·ag·o·nal·ize (dī-ăg′ə-nə-līz′) *tr.v.* **-ized, -iz·ing, -iz·es.** To order a matrix so that all the nonzero elements occur on the diagonal from upper left to lower right. **—di·ag′o·nal·iz′a·ble** *adj.* **—di·ag′o·nal·i·za′tion** *n.*
diagonal matrix *n.* A matrix that has been diagonalized.
di·a·gram (dī′ə-grăm′) *n.* **1.** A plan, sketch, drawing, or outline designed to demonstrate or explain how something works or to clarify the relationship between the parts of a whole. **2.** *Math.* A graphic representation of an algebraic or geometric relationship. **3.** A chart or graph. —*tr.v.* **-grammed, -gram·ming, -grams** or **-gramed, -gram·ing, -grams.** To indicate or represent by or as if by a diagram. [Lat. *diagramma* < Gk. < *diagraphein,* to mark out : *dia-,* apart + *graphein,* to write.] **—di′a·gram′ma·ble** *adj.* **—di′a·gram·mat′ic** (-grə-măt′ĭk), **di′a·gram·mat′i·cal** *adj.* **—di′a·gram·mat′i·cal·ly** *adv.*
di·a·ki·ne·sis (dī′ə-kə-nē′sĭs, -kī-) *n., pl.* **-ses** (-sēz′). *Genetics.* The final stage of the prophase in meiosis, characterized by the shortening, thickening, and dispersion of the chromosomes and the disappearance of the nucleolus. **—di′a·ki·net′ic** (-nĕt′ĭk) *adj.*
di·al (dī′əl) *n.* **1.** A graduated, usually circular face on which a measurement, such as speed, is indicated by a moving needle or pointer. **2. a.** The face of a clock. **b.** A sundial. **3. a.** The panel or face on a radio or television receiver on which the frequencies or channels are indicated. **b.** A movable control knob or other device on a radio or television receiver used to change the frequency. **4.** A rotatable disk on a telephone with numbers and letters, used to signal the number to which a call is made. —*v.* **-aled, -al·ing, -als** or **-alled, -al·ling, -als.** —*tr.* **1.** To measure with or as if with a dial. **2.** To point to, indicate, or register by means of a dial. **3.** To control or select by means of a dial. —*intr.* To use a dial, as on a telephone. [ME *diall* < Med. Lat. *diale* < *dialis,* daily < Lat. *dies,* day.] **—di′al·er** *n.*
di·a·lect (dī′ə-lĕkt′) *n.* **1. a.** A regional variety of a language distinguished by pronunciation, grammar, or vocabulary, esp. a variety of speech differing from the standard literary language or speech pattern of the culture in which it exists: *Cockney is a dialect of English.* **b.** A variety of language that with other varieties constitutes a single language of which no single variety is standard: *the dialects of Ancient Greek.* **2.** The language peculiar to an occupational group or a particular social class: *the dialect of science.* **3.** The manner or style of expressing oneself in language or the arts. **4.** A language considered as part of a larger family of languages or a linguistic branch: *Spanish and French are Romance dialects.* [OFr. *dialecte* < Lat. *dialectus* < Gk. *dialektos,* speech < *dialegesthai,* to discuss : *dia-,* between + *legesthai,* to speak < *legein,* to tell.] **—di′a·lec′tal** *adj.* **—di′a·lec′tal·ly** *adv.*

Synonyms: *dialect, vernacular, jargon, cant, argot, lingo, patois.* These nouns denote forms of language that vary from the accepted standard. *Dialect* applies to the words, usage, and pronunciation characteristic of specific localities. The *vernacular* is the colloquial language of a people. *Jargon* is the specialized language used in particular fields of activity and is often not understandable by persons outside those fields. *Cant* now usually refers to the specialized language of a group or trade and is often marked by stock phrases. *Cant* can also mean "insincere expression of piety." *Argot* is the language of the underworld or, by extension, that of any specific group. *Lingo* is applied humorously or contemptuously to language foreign to one or so specialized that it is difficult to understand. *Patois* refers to the dialect of a bilingual region and especially to a hybrid language used by the rustic or uneducated.

dialect atlas *n.* A linguistic atlas.
dialect geography *n.* Linguistic geography.
di·a·lec·tic (dī′ə-lĕk′tĭk) *n.* **1.** The art or practice of arriving at the truth by disclosing the contradictions in an opponent's argument and overcoming them. **2. a.** The Hegelian process of change whereby an ideational entity, a thesis, is transformed into its opposite, an antithesis, and preserved and fulfilled by it, the combination of the two being resolved in a higher form of truth, a synthesis. **b.** Hegel's criti-

cal method for the investigation of this process. **3. a.** Often **dialectics** *(used with a sing. verb).* The Marxian process of change through the conflict of opposing forces, whereby a given contradiction is characterized by a primary and a secondary aspect, the secondary succumbing to the primary, which is then transformed into an aspect of a new contradiction. **b.** The Marxian critique of this process. **4. dialectics** *(used with a sing. verb).* A method of argument or exposition that systematically weighs contradictory facts or ideas with a view to the resolution of their real or apparent contradictions. **5.** The contradiction between two conflicting forces viewed as the determining factor in their continuing interaction. [ME *dialetik* < OFr. *dialetique* < Lat. *dialectica* < Gk. *dialektikē (tekhnē),* (art of) debate < *dialektos,* speech. —see DIALECT.] **—di'a·lec'ti·cal, di'a·lec'tic** *adj.* **—di'a·lec'ti·cal·ly** *adv.*

dialectical materialism *n.* The Marxian interpretation of reality that views matter as the sole subject of change and all change as the product of a constant conflict between opposites arising from the internal contradictions inherent in all events, ideas, and movements.

di·a·lec·ti·cian (dī'ə-lĕk-tĭsh'ən) *n.* **1.** One who specializes in the study of dialects. **2.** One who practices or is skilled in dialectic.

di·a·lec·tol·o·gy (dī'ə-lĕk-tŏl'ə-jē) *n.* The study of dialects. **—di'a·lec'to·log'i·cal** (-tə-lŏj'ĭ-kəl) *adj.* **—di'a·lec'to·log'i·cal·ly** *adv.* **—di'a·lec·tol'o·gist** *n.*

di·a·log (dī'ə-lôg', -lŏg') *n. & v.* Variant of **dialogue.**

di·a·log·ic (dī'ə-lŏj'ĭk) also **di·a·log·i·cal** (-ĭ-kəl) *adj.* Of, pertaining to, or written in dialogue. **—di'a·log'i·cal·ly** *adv.*

di·al·o·gist (dī-ăl'ə-jĭst, dī'ə-lô'gĭst, -lŏg'ĭst) *n.* **1.** One who writes dialogue. **2.** One who speaks in a dialogue. **—di'a·lo·gis'tic** (dī'ə-lə-jĭs'tĭk), **di'a·lo·gis'ti·cal** *adj.*

di·a·logue also **di·a·log** (dī'ə-lôg', -lŏg') *—n.* **1.** A conversation between two or more people. **2.** A conversational passage in a play or narrative. **3.** A literary work written in the form of a conversation: *the dialogues of Plato.* **4.** A musical composition or passage for two or more parts that is suggestive of conversational interplay. **5.** An exchange of ideas or opinions. *—v.* **-logued, -logu·ing, -logues** also **-loged, -log·ing, -logs.** *—tr.* To express as or in a dialogue. *—intr.* To converse in a dialogue. [ME < OFr. < Lat. *dialogus* < Gk. *dialogos* < *dialegesthai,* to discuss. —see DIALECT.] **—di'a·log'uer** *n.*

dial tone *n.* A low, steady tone in a telephone receiver indicating that a number may be dialed.

di·al·y·sis (dī-ăl'ĭ-sĭs) *n., pl.* **-ses** (-sēz'). The separation of smaller molecules from larger molecules or of crystalloid particles from colloidal particles in a solution by selective diffusion through a semipermeable membrane. [NLat. < Gk. *dialusis,* separating < *dialuein,* to tear apart : *dia-,* apart + *luein,* to loosen.] **—di'a·lyt'ic** (-ə-lĭt'ĭk) *adj.* **—di'a·lyt'i·cal·ly** *adv.*

diamond
On a playing card

di·a·lyze (dī'ə-līz') *tr. & intr.v.* **-lyzed, -lyz·ing, -lyz·es.** To subject to or undergo dialysis. [Back-formation < DIALYSIS.] **—di'a·lyz'a·bil'i·ty** *n.* **—di'a·lyz'a·ble** *adj.* **—di'a·lyz'er** *n.*

di·a·mag·net (dī'ə-măg'nĭt) *n.* A diamagnetic substance. [< DIAMAGNETIC.]

di·a·mag·net·ic (dī'ə-măg-nĕt'ĭk) *adj.* Of or pertaining to a substance in which an induced magnetic field is in the opposite direction to and much weaker than the magnetizing field. **—di'a·mag'ne·tism** (-nĭ-tĭz'əm) *n.*

di·am·e·ter (dī-ăm'ĭ-tər) *n.* **1.** *Math.* **a.** A straight line segment passing through the center of a figure, esp. of a circle or sphere, and terminating at the periphery. **b.** The length of such a segment. **2.** The thickness or width of something. [ME *diametre* < OFr. < Lat. *diametros* < Gk. *diametros (grammē),* diagonal (line) : *dia-,* through + *metron,* measure.] **—di·am'e·tral** (-trəl) *adj.*

diamondback

di·a·met·ri·cal (dī'ə-mĕt'rĭ-kəl) also **di·a·met·ric** (-rĭk) *adj.* **1.** Of, pertaining to, or along a diameter. **2.** Exactly opposite; contrary. **—di'a·met'ri·cal·ly** *adv.*

di·am·ine (dī-ăm'ēn', -ĭn, dī'ə-mēn', -mĭn) *n.* Any of various chemical compounds containing two amino groups, esp. hydrazine.

di·a·mond (dī'ə-mənd, dī'mənd) *n.* **1.** An extremely hard, highly refractive colorless or white crystalline allotrope of carbon, used when pure as a gemstone and chiefly in abrasives otherwise. **2.** A figure with four equal sides forming two inner obtuse angles and two inner acute angles; rhombus or lozenge. **3. a.** A red, lozenge-shaped figure on certain playing cards. **b.** A playing card with this figure. **c. diamonds** *(used with a sing. or pl. verb).* The suit of cards represented by this figure. **4.** *Baseball.* **a.** An infield. **b.** The whole playing field. *—tr.v.* **-mond·ed, -mond·ing, -monds.** To adorn with or as if with diamonds. [ME *diamaunt* < OFr. *diamant* < LLat. *diamas* < Lat. *adamas* < Gk.]

di·a·mond·back (dī'ə-mənd-băk', dī'mənd-) *n.* **1.** Any of several large, venomous rattlesnakes of the genus *Crotalus,* of the southern and western United States and Mexico, having diamond-shaped markings. **2.** Any of several turtles of the genus *Malaclemys,* of the southern Atlantic and Gulf coasts of the United States, having edible flesh and a carapace with roughly diamond-shaped ridged or knobbed markings.

Diana

diamondback terrapin *n.* A diamondback (sense 2).

di·a·mond·if·er·ous (dī'ə-mən-dĭf'ər-əs, dī'mən-) *adj.* Bearing or yielding diamonds.

Di·an·a (dī-ăn'ə) *n. Rom. Myth.* **1.** The goddess of chastity, hunting, and the moon, identified with the Greek goddess Artemis. **2.** The moon. [ME < Lat.]

di·an·drous (dī-ăn'drəs) *adj. Bot.* Having two stamens.

di·an·thus (dī-ăn'thəs) *n.* A plant of the genus *Dianthus,* which includes carnations and pinks. [NLat. *Dianthus,* genus name : DI- + Gk. *anthos,* flower.]

di·a·pa·son (dī'ə-pā'zən, -sən) *n.* **1.** A full, rich outpouring of harmonious sound. **2. a.** The entire range of an instrument or voice. **b.** The entire range or scope of something. **3.** Either of the two principal stops on a pipe organ that form the tonal basis for the entire scale of the instrument. **4.** The musical interval and the consonance of an octave. **5.** A standard indication of musical pitch. **6.** A tuning fork. [ME *diapasoun* < Lat. *diapason* < Gk. *(hē) dia pasōn (khordōn sumphonia),* (concord) through all (the notes).]

di·a·pause (dī'ə-pôz') *n.* A period during which growth or development is suspended, as in certain insects. [Gk. *diapausis,* pause < *diapauein,* to pause : *dia-,* between + *pauein,* to stop.]

di·a·pe·de·sis (dī'ə-pĭ-dē'sĭs) *n., pl.* **-ses** (-sēz'). The passing of blood or any constituents, esp. erythrocytes, through intact blood-vessel walls. [NLat. < Gk. *diapēdēsis,* transudation < *diapēdan,* to ooze : *dia-,* through + *pēdan,* to leap.] **—di'a·pe·det'ic** (-dĕt'ĭk) *adj.*

di·a·per (dī'ə-pər, dī'pər) *n.* **1.** A folded piece of cloth or other absorbent material placed between a baby's legs and pinned at the waist. **2. a.** A white cotton or linen fabric patterned with small, duplicative diamond-shaped figures. **b.** A piece of such cloth. **c.** Such a pattern. *—tr.v.* **-pered, -per·ing, -pers. 1.** To put a diaper on (a baby). **2.** To weave or decorate in a diamond-shaped pattern. [ME, a patterned fabric < OFr. < Med. Lat. *diasprum* < Med. Gk. *diaspros,* pure white : *dia-,* thoroughly + *aspros,* white < Lat. *asper,* rough.]

di·aph·a·nous (dī-ăf'ə-nəs) *adj.* **1.** Of such fine texture as to be transparent or translucent. **2.** Characterized by delicacy of form. **3.** Vague or insubstantial: *diaphanous dreams of glory.* [Med. Lat. *diaphanus* Gk. *diaphanēs* < *diaphanein,* to be transparent : *dia-,* through + *phainein,* to show.] **—di'a·pha·ne'i·ty** (dī'ə-fə-nē'ĭ-tē), **di·aph'a·nous·ness** *n.* **—di·aph'a·nous·ly** *adv.*

di·a·pho·re·sis (dī'ə-fə-rē'sĭs, dī-ăf'ə-) *n.* Perspiration, esp. when copious and medically induced. [LLat. < Gk. *diaphorēsis* < *diaphorein,* to disperse : *dia-,* apart + *phorein,* to convey, freq. of *pherein,* to bear.]

di·a·pho·ret·ic (dī'ə-fə-rĕt'ĭk, dī-ăf'ə-) *adj.* Producing perspiration. *—n.* A diaphoretic medicine or agent.

di·a·phragm (dī'ə-frăm') *n.* **1.** *Anat.* A muscular membranous partition separating the abdominal and thoracic cavities and functioning in respiration. **2.** A membranous part that divides or separates. **3.** A thin disk, esp. in a microphone or telephone receiver, whose vibrations convert electric signals to sound waves or sound waves to electric signals. **4.** A contraceptive device consisting of a flexible disk that covers the uterine cervix. **5.** A disk having a fixed or variable opening used to restrict the amount of light traversing a lens or optical system. [ME *diafragma* < LLat. *diaphragma* < Gk. < *diaphrassein,* to barricade : *dia-,* completely + *phrassein,* to enclose.] **—di'a·phrag·mat'ic** (-frăg-măt'ĭk) *adj.* **—di'a·phrag·mat'i·cal·ly** *adv.*

di·aph·y·sis (dī-ăf'ĭ-sĭs) *n., pl.* **-ses** (-sēz'). The shaft of a long bone, esp. as distinguished from extremities and outgrowths. [NLat. < Gk. *diaphusis,* spinous process of the tibia < *diaphuesthai,* to grow between : *dia-,* between + *phuesthai,* to grow < *phuein,* to produce.] **—di'a·phys'i·al, di'a·phys'e·al** (dī'ə-fĭz'ē-əl) *adj.*

di·a·poph·y·sis (dī'ə-pŏf'ĭ-sĭs) *n., pl.* **-ses** (-sēz'). The superior or articular surface of a transverse vertebral process. **—di·ap'o·phys'i·al** (-ăp'ə-fĭz'ē-əl) *adj.*

di·ar·chy also **dy·ar·chy** (dī'är'kē) *n., pl.* **-chies.** Government by two joint rulers.

di·a·rist (dī'ə-rĭst) *n.* A person who keeps a diary.

di·ar·rhe·a also **di·ar·rhoe·a** (dī'ə-rē'ə) *n.* Pathologically excessive evacuation of watery feces. [ME *diaria* < Med. Lat. < LLat. *diarrhoea* < Gk. *diarrhoia* < *diarrhein,* to flow through : *dia-,* through + *rhein,* to flow.] **—di'ar·rhe'al** (-əl), **di'ar·rhe'ic** (-ĭk), **di'ar·rhet'ic** (-rĕt'ĭk) *adj.*

di·ar·thro·sis (dī'är-thrō'sĭs) *n., pl.* **-ses** (-sēz'). Any of several types of bone articulation permitting free motion in a joint. [NLat. < Gk. *diarthrōsis* < *diarthroun,* to articulate : *dia-,* between + *arthroun,* to fasten < *arthron,* joint.] **—di'ar·thro'di·al** (-dē-əl) *adj.*

di·a·ry (dī'ə-rē) *n., pl.* **-ries. 1.** A daily record, esp. a personal record of events, experiences, and observations; journal. **2.** A book for keeping a diary. [Lat. *diarium,* daily allowance, diary < *dies,* day.]

Di·as·po·ra (dī-ăs'pər-ə) *n.* **1.** Often **diaspora.** The body of Jews or Jewish communities outside of Palestine or modern Israel. **2.** The body of Jews living dispersed among the Gentiles after the Babylonian captivity. **3. diaspora.** A dispersion of an originally homogeneous people. [Gk., dispersion < *diaspeirein,* to disperse : *dia-,* apart + *speirein,* to scatter.]

di·a·spore (dī'ə-spôr', -spōr') *n.* A white to greenish, pearly hydrous aluminum oxide, $Al_2O_3 \cdot H_2O$, found in bauxite, corundum, and dolomite and used as a refractory and abrasive. [Gk. *diaspora,* dispersion. —see DIASPORA.]

di·a·stal·sis (dī′ə-stôl′sĭs, -stăl′-) *n., pl.* **-ses** (-sēz′). The peristaltic contraction of the small intestine in digestion. [DIA- + (PERI)STALSIS.] **—di′a·stal′tic** (-tĭk) *adj.*

di·a·stase (dī′ə-stās′, -stāz′) *n.* An amylase or a mixture of amylases that converts starch to maltose, found in certain germinating grains such as malt. [Fr. < Gk. *diastasis,* separation. —see DIASTASIS.] **—di′a·sta′sic** (-stā′sĭk, -zĭk) *adj.*

di·as·ta·sis (dī-ăs′tə-sĭs) *n., pl.* **-ses** (-sēz′). **1.** *Pathol.* Separation of normally adjacent, unjoined bones without fracture or of certain muscles during pregnancy. **2.** *Physiol.* The last stage of diastole in the heart, which occurs prior to contraction and during which little blood enters the filled ventricle. [NLat. < Gk., separation < *diistanai,* to separate : *dia-,* apart + *histanai,* to cause to stand.] **—di′a·stat′ic** (dī′ə-stăt′ĭk) *adj.*

di·a·ste·ma (dī′ə-stē′mə) *n., pl.* **-ma·ta** (-mə-tə). **1.** *Pathol.* A bodily fissure or cleft, esp. if congenital. **2.** An abnormally large space between teeth. [NLat. < LLat., interval < Gk. *diastēma* < *diistanai,* to separate. —see DIASTASIS.] **—di′a·ste·mat′ic** (-stə-măt′ĭk) *adj.*

di·as·to·le (dī-ăs′tə-lē) *n.* **1.** *Physiol.* The normal rhythmically occurring relaxation and dilatation of the heart cavities during which the cavities are filled with blood. **2.** The lengthening of a normally short syllable in Greek and Latin verse. [Gk. *diastolē,* dilation < *diastellein,* to expand : *dia-,* apart + *stellein,* to put.] **—di′a·stol′ic** (dī′ə-stŏl′ĭk) *adj.*

di·as·tro·phism (dī-ăs′trə-fĭz′əm) *n.* The process or series of processes by which the major features of the earth's crust, including continents, mountains, ocean beds, folds, and faults, are formed. [< Gk. *diastrophē,* distortion < *diastrephein,* to distort : *dia-,* apart + *strephein,* to twist.] **—di′a·stroph′ic** (dī′ə-strŏf′ĭk) *adj.*

di·a·tes·sa·ron (dī′ə-tĕs′ər-ən) *n.* The four Gospels combined into a single narrative. [Gk. *(evangelion) dia tessarōn,* (gospel) consisting of four parts.]

di·a·ther·my (dī′ə-thûr′mē) *n.* The therapeutic generation of local heat in body tissues by high-frequency electromagnetic waves. [DIA- + Gk. *thermē,* heat.] **—di′a·ther′mic** (-mĭk) *adj.*

di·ath·e·sis (dī-ăth′ĭ-sĭs) *n., pl.* **-ses** (-sēz′). A congenital, often hereditary predisposition of the body to a disease, group of diseases, or structural or metabolic abnormality. [NLat. < Gk., condition < *diatithenai,* to distribute : *dia-,* apart + *tithenai,* to put.] **—di′a·thet′ic** (dī′ə-thĕt′ĭk) *adj.*

di·a·tom (dī′ə-tŏm′) *n.* Any of various minute unicellular or colonial algae of the class Bacillariophyceae, having siliceous cell walls consisting of two overlapping symmetrical parts. [NLat. *diatoma* < Gk. *diatomos,* cut in half < *diatemnein,* to cut in half : *dia-,* through + *temnein,* to cut.]

di·a·to·ma·ceous (dī′ə-tə-mā′shəs, dī-ăt′ə-) *adj.* Consisting of diatoms or their siliceous skeletons.

diatomaceous earth *n.* A white or cream-colored siliceous earth composed of the shells of diatoms.

di·a·tom·ic (dī′ə-tŏm′ĭk) *adj.* **1.** Made up of two atoms: *a diatomic molecule.* **2.** Having two replaceable atoms or radicals.

di·at·o·mite (dī-ăt′ə-mīt′) *n.* A fine, powdered diatomaceous earth used in industry as a filler, filtering agent, absorbent, clarifier, and insulator.

di·a·ton·ic (dī′ə-tŏn′ĭk) *adj. Mus.* Of or using only the eight tones of a standard major or minor scale without chromatic deviations. [OFr. *diatonique* < LLat. *diatonicus* < Gk. *diatonikos* : *dia-,* through + *tonos,* tone.] **—di′a·ton′i·cal·ly** *adv.* **—di′a·ton′i·cism** (-ĭ-sĭz′əm) *n.*

di·a·tribe (dī′ə-trīb′) *n.* A bitter and abusive criticism or denunciation. [Lat. *diatriba,* learned discourse < Gk. *diatribē,* lecture, pastime < *diatribein,* to consume : *dia-,* completely + *tribein,* to rub.]

di·a·tron (dī′ə-trŏn′) *n.* A circuitry design that uses diodes.

di·at·ro·pism (dī-ăt′rə-pĭz′əm) *n.* The tendency of certain plants or their parts to arrange themselves at right angles to the line of force of a stimulus. **—di′a·trop′ic** (dī′ə-trŏp′ĭk, -trō′pĭk) *adj.*

di·az·e·pam (dī-ăz′ə-păm′) *n.* An antianxiety drug, $C_{16}H_{13}ClN_2O$. [DIAZ(O) + EP(OXIDE) + AM(MONIA).]

di·a·zine (dī′ə-zēn′, dī-ăz′ĭn) *n.* A compound containing a benzene ring in which two of the carbon atoms have been replaced by nitrogen atoms, esp. any of three compounds so structured and having the composition $C_4H_4N_2$. [DI- + AZ(O)- + -INE.]

di·az·o (dī-ăz′ō) *adj.* Of or relating to a pair of nitrogen atoms bonded together and to an organic compound.

di·a·zo·ni·um (dī′ə-zō′nē-əm) *n.* The univalent cation RN_2, where R is an aromatic hydrocarbon. [DIAZ(O) + (AMM)ONIUM.]

di·ba·sic (dī-bā′sĭk) *adj.* **1.** Containing two replaceable hydrogen atoms. **2.** Designating salts or acids forming salts with two atoms of a univalent metal.

dib·ber (dĭb′ər) *n.* A dibble. [Alteration of DIBBLE.]

dib·ble (dĭb′əl) *n.* A pointed gardening implement used to make holes in soil, esp. for planting bulbs or seedlings. —*tr.v.* **-bled, -bling, -bles. 1.** To make holes in (soil) with a dibble. **2.** To plant by means of a dibble. [ME *debylle.*] **—dib′bler** *n.*

di·bran·chi·ate (dī-brăng′kē-ĭt) *n.* Any of various cephalopod mollusks of the order Dibranchiata, which includes the octopuses, cuttlefish, and squids. —*adj.* Of or belonging to the Dibranchiata. [NLat. *Dibranchiata,* order name : DI- + Gk. *brankhia,* gills.]

di·bro·mide (dī-brō′mīd′, -mĭd) *n.* A binary chemical compound containing two bromine atoms per molecule.

dibs (dĭbz) *pl.n. Slang.* **1.** Money, esp. in small amounts. **2.** A claim; rights: *I have dibs on that last piece.* [Short for *dibstones,* counters used in a game, prob. < obs. *dib,* to tap.]

di·car·box·yl·ic (dī-kär′bŏk-sĭl′ĭk) *adj.* Containing two carboxyl groups per molecule.

di·cast (dī′kăst′, dĭk′ăst′) *n.* In ancient Athens, one of the 6,000 citizens chosen each year to sit in the law courts, with functions resembling those of a judge and juror. [Gk. *dikastēs,* judge < *dikazein,* to judge < *dikē,* right.] **—di·cas′tic** *adj.*

dice (dīs) *n., pl.* **dice. 1. a.** Plural of **die²** (senses 3, 4). **b.** A game of chance using dice. **2.** *pl.* also **dic·es.** A small cube, as of food. —*v.* **diced, dic·ing, dic·es.** —*intr.* To play or gamble with dice. —*tr.* **1.** To win or lose (money) by gambling with dice. **2.** To cut (food) into small cubes. **3.** To decorate with dicelike figures. **—*idiom.* no dice.** *Slang.* **1.** Of no use; futile. **2.** No. Used as a refusal to a request. [Pl. of DIE².]

di·cen·tra (dī-sĕn′trə) *n.* A plant of the genus *Dicentra,* which includes the bleeding-heart and Dutchman's-breeches. [NLat. *Dicentra,* genus name : DI- + Gk. *kentron,* center < *kentein,* to prick.]

di·ceph·a·lous (dī-sĕf′ə-ləs) *adj.* Having two heads, as a monster.

dic·er (dī′sər) *n.* **1.** A device used for dicing food. **2.** One who gambles with dice.

dic·ey (dī′sē) *adj.* **-i·er, -i·est.** Involving or fraught with danger or risk; chancy. [< DICE.]

dich– *pref.* Variant of **dicho-.**

di·cha·si·um (dī-kā′zē-əm, -zhē-əm, -zhəm) *n., pl.* **-si·a** (-zē-ə, -zhē-ə, -zhə). *Bot.* A cyme having two lateral stems branching from the main axis. [NLat. < Gk. *dikhasis,* division < *dikhazein,* to divide in two < *dikha,* in two.] **—di·cha′si·al** (-zē-əl, -zhē-əl, -zhəl) *adj.* **—di·cha′si·al·ly** *adv.*

di·chlo·ride (dī-klôr′īd′, -klōr′-) *n.* A binary chemical compound containing two chloride atoms per molecule.

di·chlo·ro·di·phen·yl·tri·chlo·ro·eth·ane (dī-klôr′ō-dī-fĕn′əl-trī-klôr′ō-ĕth′ān′, -klōr′-, -fē′nəl-, dī-klōr′-) *n.* DDT.

di·chlor·vos (dī-klôr′vŏs′, -vəs, -klōr′-) *n.* A nonpersistent organophosphorous pesticide, $C_4H_7Cl_2O_4P$, of low toxicity to humans. [DI- + CHLOR(O) + V(INYL) + (PH)OS(PHATE).]

dicho– or **dich–** *pref.* In two; into two parts: *dichogamous.* [LLat. < Gk. *dikho-* < *dikha,* in two.]

di·chog·a·mous (dī-kŏg′ə-məs) *adj. Bot.* Having pistils and stamens that mature at different times, thus ensuring cross-fertilization rather than self-pollination. **—di·chog′a·my** (-mē) *n.*

di·chot·o·mize (dī-kŏt′ə-mīz′) *v.* **-mized, -miz·ing, -miz·es.** —*tr.* To separate into two parts or classifications. —*intr.* To be or become divided into parts or branches; fork. **—di·chot′o·mist** *n.* **—di·chot′o·mi·za′tion** *n.*

di·chot·o·mous (dī-kŏt′ə-məs) *adj.* **1.** Divided or dividing into two parts or classifications. **2.** Characterized by dichotomy. **—di·chot′o·mous·ly** *adv.* **—di·chot′o·mous·ness** *n.*

di·chot·o·my (dī-kŏt′ə-mē) *n., pl.* **-mies. 1.** Division into two usually contradictory parts or opinions. **2.** *Astron.* The phase of the moon, Mercury, or Venus when half of the disk is illuminated. **3.** *Bot.* Branching characterized by successive forking into two approximately equal divisions. [Gk. *dikhotomia* < *dikhotomos,* divided : *dikha,* in two + *temnein,* to cut.]

di·chro·ic (dī-krō′ĭk) also **di·chro·it·ic** (dī′krō-ĭt′ĭk) *adj.* **1.** Manifesting dichroism. **2.** Dichromatic (sense 3). [< Gk. *dikhroos,* bicolored : *di-,* two + *khrōs,* color.]

di·chro·ism (dī′krō-ĭz′əm) *n. Chem.* **1.** The property of showing different colors depending on the thickness of the medium or the relative concentration of coloring matter in it. **2.** The property possessed by some crystals of exhibiting different colors, esp. two different colors, when viewed along different axes.

di·chro·ite (dī-krō′īt′) *n.* Cordierite. [DICHRO(IC) + -ITE.]

di·chro·it·ic (dī′drō-ĭt′ĭk) *adj.* Variant of **dichroic.** [DICHRO-I(SM) + -IT(E) + -IC.]

di·chro·mate (dī-krō′māt′, dī′krō-) *n.* A chemical compound with two chromium atoms per anion, usually having a characteristic orange-red color.

di·chro·mat·ic (dī′krō-măt′ĭk) *adj.* **1.** Possessing or exhibiting two colors. **2.** *Zool.* Having two distinct color phases in the adult, as do certain species of birds. **3.** *Pathol.* Capable of distinguishing only two colors.

di·chro·ma·tism (dī-krō′mə-tĭz′əm) also **di·chro·mism** (-mĭz′əm) *n.* The quality or condition of being dichromatic.

di·chro·mic (dī-krō′mĭk) *adj.* **1.** Dichromatic (sense 3). **2.** *Chem.* Containing two chromium atoms per molecule.

dichromic acid *n.* An acid, $H_2Cr_2O_7$, known only in solution.

di·chro·mism (dī-krō′mĭz′əm) *n.* Variant of **dichromatism.**

dick¹ (dĭk) *n. Slang.* A detective. [Shortening and alteration of DETECTIVE.]

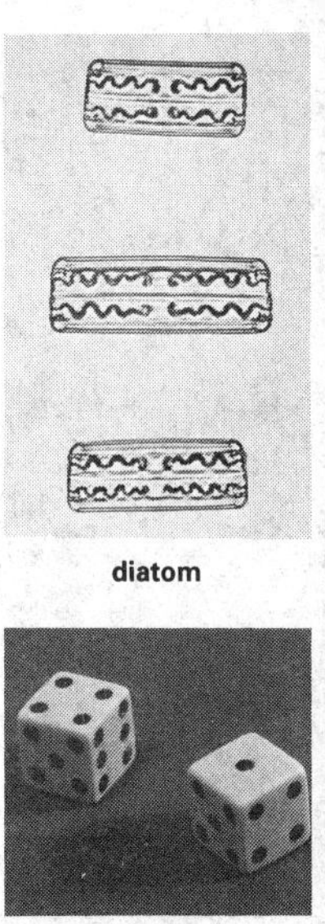

diatom

dice

dickcissel

dick^2 (dĭk) *n.* **1.** *Chiefly Brit. Slang.* A fellow; guy. **2.** *Vulgar Slang.* A penis. [< *Dick,* nickname for *Richard.*]

dick·cis·sel (dĭk-sĭs′əl, dĭk′sĭs′-) *n.* A sparrowlike bird, *Spiza americana,* of central North America, of which the male has a yellow breast marked with black. [Imit.]

dick·ens (dĭk′ənz) *n.* Deuce; devil. [Perh. alteration of OLD NICK.]

dick·er (dĭk′ər) *v.* **-ered, -er·ing, -ers.** —*intr.* To bargain; barter. —*tr.* To trade or exchange. —*n.* The act or process of dickering. [Perh. < *dicker,* a quantity of ten, ten hides < ME *diker,* ult. < Lat. *decuria,* set of ten < *decem,* ten.]

dick·ey also **dick·ie** or **dick·y** (dĭk′ē) *n., pl.* **-eys** also **-ies.** **1.** A woman's blouse front worn under a suit jacket or low-necked garment. **2.** A man's detachable shirt front. **3.** A collar for a shirt. **4.** A child's bib or pinafore. **5.** A donkey. **6.** A small bird. **7. a.** The forward outside driver's seat on a carriage. **b.** A rear seat for servants on a carriage. [< *Dick,* nickname for *Richard.*]

Dick test (dĭk) *n.* A test of susceptibility to scarlet fever. [After George *Dick* (1881–1967) and Gladys Henry *Dick* (1881–1963), its devisers.]

dick·y (dĭk′ē) *n.* Variant of **dickey.**

di·cli·nous (dī-klī′nəs) *adj. Bot.* **1.** Having stamens and pistils in separate flowers: *a diclinous plant.* **2.** Having pistils but not stamens or stamens but not pistils: *diclinous flowers.* [DI- + Gk. *klinē,* bed + -OUS.] —**di′cli′ny** (dī′klī′nē) *n.*

di·cot·y·le·don (dī′kŏt′l-ēd′n) also **di·cot** (dī′kŏt′) *n.* A plant of the subclass Dicotyledonae, one of the two major divisions of angiosperms, characterized by a pair of embryonic seed leaves that appear at germination. —**di′cot′y·le′don·ous** (-n-əs) *adj.*

di·cro·tism (dī′krə-tĭz′əm) *n.* A pathological doubling of the pulse with each beat of the heart. [< Gk. *dikrotos,* double-beating : *di-,* two + *krotein,* to strike.] —**di·crot′ic** (-krŏt′ĭk) *adj.*

dic·ta (dĭk′tə) *n.* A plural of **dictum.**

Dic·ta·belt (dĭk′tə-bĕlt′). A trademark for a plastic belt on which dictation is recorded in a dictating machine.

Dic·ta·phone (dĭk′tə-fōn′). A trademark for a phonographic apparatus that records and reproduces dictation for transcription.

dic·tate (dĭk′tāt′, dĭk-tāt′) *v.* **-tat·ed, -tat·ing, -tates.** —*tr.* **1.** To say or read aloud to be recorded or written by another. **2.** To prescribe with authority; impose: *dictate a command.* —*intr.* **1.** To say or read aloud material to be recorded or written by another. **2.** To issue orders or commands. —*n.* (dĭk′tāt′). **1.** A directive or command. **2.** A guiding principle: *followed the dictates of her conscience.* [Lat. *dictare, dictat-,* freq. of *dicere,* to say.]

dic·ta·tion (dĭk-tā′shən) *n.* **1. a.** The process of dictating material to another for transcription. **b.** The material dictated. **2.** An authoritative command or order.

dic·ta·tor (dĭk′tā′tər, dĭk-tā′-) *n.* **1. a.** A ruler having absolute authority and supreme jurisdiction over the government of a state. **b.** A tyrant. **2.** One who dictates. **3.** An ancient Roman magistrate appointed temporarily to deal with an immediate crisis or emergency.

dic·ta·to·ri·al (dĭk′tə-tôr′ē-əl, -tōr′-) *adj.* **1.** Tending to dictate; domineering. **2.** Of, pertaining to, or characteristic of a dictator or dictatorship; autocratic. —**dic′ta·to′ri·al·ly** *adv.* —**dic′ta·to′ri·al·ness** *n.*

Synonyms: *dictatorial, arbitrary, dogmatic, doctrinaire, imperious, authoritative, overbearing.* These adjectives mean tending to or disposed to assert authority or to impose one's will on other persons. *Dictatorial* stresses the idea of great power in the hands of one person, who usually exercises it in a highhanded, absolute manner. *Arbitrary* implies improper use of power by one motivated by selfishness, hasty judgment, or something other than sound reasoning. *Dogmatic* suggests the imposition of one's will or opinion as though these were beyond challenge. *Doctrinaire* implies belief in the theoretical rather than the practical; usually it also implies imposition of such theory or doctrine on others. *Imperious* suggests the manner of one accustomed to commanding. *Authoritative* can apply to exercise of official authority or authority based on acknowledged merit. Less often it implies unwarranted assumption of power. *Overbearing* implies a tendency to be domineering and arrogant.

dic·ta·tor·ship (dĭk-tā′tər-shĭp′, dĭk′tā′-) *n.* **1.** The office or tenure of office of a dictator. **2.** A state or government under dictatorial rule. **3.** Absolute or despotic control or power.

dic·tion (dĭk′shən) *n.* **1.** Choice and use of words in speech or writing. **2.** Degree of clarity and distinctness of pronunciation in speech or singing; enunciation. [Lat. *dictio* < *dictus,* p.part. of *dicere,* to say.] —**dic′tion·al** *adj.* —**dic′tion·al·ly** *adv.*

Synonyms: *diction, wording, vocabulary, articulation, enunciation.* These nouns refer to choice, arrangement, and expression of words. *Diction* refers to the selection and use of words in relation to effective written or oral expression. More narrowly it means quality of delivery of speech. *Wording* stresses style of expression with reference to choice and arrangement of words, especially in writing. *Vocabulary* is the aggregate of the words a person understands or uses. *Articulation* refers rather broadly to sound (clarity) and flow (coherence and organization) of speech, whereas *enunciation* refers to sound judged principally on the basis of distinctness of pronunciation.

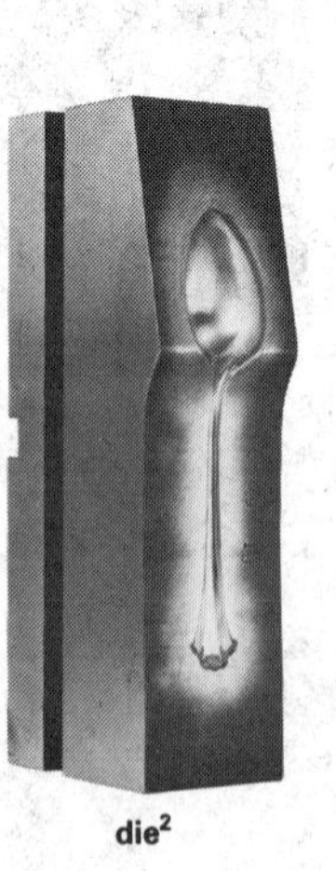

die^2

dic·tion·ar·y (dĭk′shə-nĕr′ē) *n., pl.* **-ies.** **1.** A reference book containing an explanatory alphabetical list of words, either comprehensive or limited to a particular category, with information given for each word, including meaning, pronunciation, etymology, and often usage guidance. **2.** A book listing the words of a language with translations into another language. **3.** A book listing words or other linguistic items, with specialized information about them: *a medical dictionary.* **4.** *Computer Sci.* A list stored in machine-readable form for reference by an automatic system. [Med. Lat. *dictionarium* < Lat. *dictio,* diction.]

Dic·to·graph (dĭk′tə-grăf′). A trademark for a telephonic instrument that reproduces or records sounds from a transmitter by means of a small, often concealed microphone.

dic·tum (dĭk′təm) *n., pl.* **-ta** (-tə) or **-tums.** **1.** A dogmatic and authoritative pronouncement. **2.** *Law.* An obiter dictum. **3.** A popular saying; maxim. [Lat. < neuter p.part. of *dicere,* to say.]

did (dĭd) *v.* Past tense of **do.**

di·dact (dī′dăkt′) *n.* A person who is didactic. [Back-formation < DIDACTIC.]

di·dac·tic (dī-dăk′tĭk) also **di·dac·ti·cal** (-tĭ-kəl) *adj.* **1.** Intended to instruct. **2.** Morally instructive. **3.** Inclined to teach or moralize excessively. [Gk. *didaktikos,* skillful in teaching < *didaktos,* taught < *didaskein,* to teach.] —**di·dac′ti·cal·ly** *adv.* —**di·dac′ti·cism** (-tĭ-sĭz′əm) *n.*

di·dac·tics (dī-dăk′tĭks) *n. (used with a sing. verb).* The art or science of teaching or instruction; pedagogy.

di·dap·per (dī′dăp′ər) *n.* A small grebe, such as the dabchick. [ME *didopper,* alteration of *divedap* < OE *dūfeedoppa* : *dūfan,* to dive + *-doppa,* a kind of bird.]

did·dle^1 (dĭd′l) *v.* **-dled, -dling, -dles.** —*tr.* To cheat; swindle. —*intr.* To waste time. [Orig. unknown.] —**did′dler** *n.*

did·dle^2 (dĭd′l) *v.* **-dled, -dling, -dles.** —*tr.* To jerk up and down or back and forth. —*intr.* To shake rapidly; jiggle. [Alteration of dial. *didder,* to quiver < ME *dideren.*]

did·n't (dĭd′nt). Did not.

di·do (dī′dō) *n., pl.* **-dos** or **-does.** *Informal.* A mischievous prank or antic; caper. [Orig. unknown.]

Di·do (dī′dō) *n. Rom. Myth.* A Tyrian princess, founder and queen of Carthage. [Lat. < Gk. *Didō.*]

didst (dĭdst) *v. Archaic.* Second person singular past tense of **do.**

di·dym·i·um (dī-dĭm′ē-əm) *n.* **1.** A metallic mixture, once considered an element, composed of neodymium and praseodymium. **2.** A mixture of rare-earth elements and oxides used chiefly in manufacturing and coloring various forms of glass. [NLat. < Gk. *didumos,* twin.]

did·y·mous (dĭd′ə-məs) *adj.* Arranged or occurring in pairs; twin. [Gk. *didumos,* twin.]

di·dyn·a·mous (dī-dĭn′ə-məs) *adj. Bot.* Having four stamens arranged in pairs that differ from one another, esp. in length. [< NLat. *Didynamia,* former class name : DI- + Gk. *dunamis,* power < *dunasthai,* to be able.]

die^1 (dī) *intr.v.* **died, dy·ing, dies.** **1.** To cease living; expire. **2.** To cease existing, esp. by degrees; fade: *The sunlight died in the west.* **3.** To lose vitality, activity, or force; subside: *The winds died down.* **4.** To cease existing completely: *tribal customs that died out centuries ago.* **5.** To experience an agony or suffering suggestive of that of death: *nearly died of embarrassment.* **6.** *Informal.* To desire greatly: *I am dying to go.* **7.** To cease operation; stop: *The motor suddenly died.* —***phrasal verbs.* die back.** To be affected by dieback. **die off.** To undergo a sudden, sharp decline in population: *rabbits dying off in that county.* [ME *deien* < ON *deyja.*]

die^2 (dī) *n., pl.* **dies.** **1.** A device used for cutting out, forming, or stamping material. **2. a.** An engraved metal piece used for impressing a design upon a softer metal, as in coining money. **b.** Any of several component pieces that are fitted into a diestock to cut threads on screws or bolts. **c.** A part on a machine that punches shaped holes in, cuts, or forms sheet metal, cardboard, or other stock. **d.** A metal block containing small conical holes through which plastic, metal, or other ductile stock is extruded or drawn. **3.** *pl.* **dice** (dīs). *Archit.* The dado of a pedestal, esp. when cube-shaped. **4.** *pl.* **dice.** A small cube marked on each side with from one to six dots, usually used in pairs in gambling and in various other games. —*tr.v.* **died, die·ing, dies.** To cut, form, or stamp with or as if with a die. [ME *de,* gaming dice < OFr. < Lat. *datum,* neuter p.part. of *dare,* to give.]

die·back (dī′băk′) *n.* The gradual dying of plant shoots, starting at the tips, as a result of various diseases or climatic conditions.

di·e·cious (dī-ē′shəs) *adj.* Variant of **dioecious.**

die-hard also **die·hard** (dī′härd′) *n.* One who stubbornly resists change or refuses to abandon a position. —**die′-hard′** *adj.* —**die′-hard′ism** *n.*

di·e·lec·tric (dī′ĭ-lĕk′trĭk) *n.* A nonconductor of electricity, esp. a substance with electrical conductivity less than a millionth (10^{-6}) of a mho. [DI(A)- + ELECTRIC.] —**di′e·lec′tric** *adj.* —**di′e·lec′tri·cal·ly** *adv.*

dielectric constant *n.* Permittivity.

dielectric heating *n.* The heating of electrically nonconducting materials by a rapidly varying electromagnetic field.

di·en·ceph·a·lon (dī'ĕn-sĕf'ə-lŏn', -lən) *n.* The posterior part of the forebrain that connects the midbrain with the cerebral hemispheres, encloses the third ventricle, and contains the pituitary gland. [DI(A)- + ENCEPHALON.]

di·er·e·sis also **di·aer·e·sis** (dī-ĕr'ĭ-sĭs) *n., pl.* **-ses** (-sēz'). **1.** A mark (¨) placed over the second of two adjacent vowels to indicate that two separate sounds are to be pronounced. **2.** A slight pause at the end of a line of verse that occurs when the end of a word and the end of a metric foot coincide. [LLat. *diaeresis* < Gk. *diairesis,* separation < *diairein,* to divide : *dia-,* apart + *hairein,* to take.]

die·sel (dē'zəl, -səl) *n.* **1.** A diesel engine. **2.** A vehicle powered by a diesel engine.

diesel engine *n.* An internal-combustion engine that uses the heat of highly compressed air to ignite a spray of fuel introduced after the start of the compression stroke. [After Rudolf *Diesel* (1858–1913), its inventor.]

die·sink·er (dī'sĭng'kər) *n.* One that makes stamping and shaping dies. **—die'sink'ing** *n.*

Di·es I·rae (dē'ās ĭr'ā') *n.* A medieval Latin hymn describing the Day of Judgment, used in some Masses for the dead. [Med. Lat., day of wrath, the first words of the hymn.]

di·e·sis (dī'ĭ-sĭs) *n., pl.* **-ses** (-sēz'). The double dagger. [ME, semitone (which was indicated by a double dagger) < Lat., quarter tone < Gk., a letting through < *diienai,* to send through : *dia-,* through + *hienai,* to send.]

die·stock (dī'stŏk') *n.* An apparatus for holding dies that cut threads on screws, bolts, pipes, or rods.

di·et[1] (dī'ĭt) *n.* **1.** The usual food and drink of a person or animal. **2.** A regulated selection of foods, esp. as prescribed for medical reasons. **3.** Something taken or provided regularly: *a diet of detective novels.* *—v.* **-et·ed, -et·ing, -ets.** *—tr.* To regulate or prescribe food and drink for. *—intr.* **1.** To eat and drink according to a prescribed regimen. **2.** To eat or feed. [ME *diete* < OFr. < Lat. *diaeta* < Gk. *diaita* < *diaitan,* to lead one's life.] **—di'et·er** *n.*

di·et[2] (dī'ĭt) *n.* **1.** A national or local legislative assembly in certain countries. **2.** A formal deliberative assembly of princes or other high personages. [ME *diete,* day's journey, day for meeting < Med. Lat. *dieta* < Lat. *dies,* day.]

di·e·tar·y (dī'ĭ-tĕr'ē) *adj.* Of or pertaining to diet. *—n., pl.* **-ies. 1.** A system or regimen of dieting. **2.** A regulated daily food allowance. **—di'e·tar'i·ly** (-târ'ə-lē) *adv.*

dietary law *n. Judaism.* One of the regulations prescribing the kinds and combinations of food that may be eaten.

di·e·tet·ic (dī'ĭ-tĕt'ĭk) *adj.* **1.** Of or pertaining to diet or its regulation. **2.** Specially prepared for restrictive diets. [LLat. *diaeteticus* < Gk. *diaitētikos* < *diaita,* diet.] **—di'e·tet'i·cal·ly** *adv.*

di·e·tet·ics (dī'ĭ-tĕt'ĭks) *n. (used with a sing. verb).* The study of diet and dieting as it relates to health and hygiene.

di·eth·yl ether (dī-ĕth'əl) *n.* Ether (sense 2).

di·eth·yl·stil·bes·trol (dī-ĕth'əl-stĭl-bĕs'trôl', -trōl') *n.* A synthetic estrogen, $C_{18}H_{20}O_2$, used as an estrogen substitute, esp. in the treatment of menstrual disorders.

diethyl tol·u·am·ide (tŏl'yōō-ăm'īd', -ĭd) *n.* Deet. [DIETHYL TOLU(ENE) + AMIDE.]

di·e·ti·tian also **di·e·ti·cian** (dī'ĭ-tĭsh'ən) *n.* A person specializing in dietetics.

dif·fer (dĭf'ər) *intr.v.* **-fered, -fer·ing, -fers. 1.** To be unlike or dissimilar in nature, quality, amount, or form: *Cricket differs from baseball in many respects.* **2.** To be of a different opinion; disagree: *differed with the author.* **3.** To quarrel; dispute. [ME *differen* < OFr. *differer* < Lat. *differre,* to differ, delay : *dis-,* apart + *ferre,* to carry.]

dif·fer·ence (dĭf'ər-əns, dĭf'rəns) *n.* **1.** The quality or condition of being different. **2. a.** An instance of disparity or unlikeness. **b.** A degree or amount of difference. **c.** A specific point or element that constitutes a difference. **d.** *Archaic.* A distinct mark or peculiarity. **3. a.** A disagreement or controversy. **b.** The cause of a disagreement or controversy. **4.** Discrimination in taste or choice; distinction. **5.** *Math.* **a.** The amount by which one quantity is greater or less than another. **b.** The amount that remains after one quantity is subtracted from another. *—tr.v.* **-enced, -enc·ing, -enc·es.** To distinguish or differentiate.

Synonyms: *difference, dissimilarity, unlikeness, divergence, variation, distinction, discrepancy.* These nouns refer to lack of correspondence, agreement, or equality, as revealed by comparison. *Difference,* the most general, applies to any such conditions. *Dissimilarity* points up difference between things otherwise alike or capable of close comparison. *Unlikeness* usually implies greater and more obvious difference. *Divergence* implies a gradually developing difference between things originally similar or alike. *Variation* is difference between things of the same class or species; often it refers to modification of something original, prescribed, or typical. *Distinction* usually means a slight difference in detail between like or related things, determined only by close inspection. The difference is also subjectively determined rather than palpable or factual. *Discrepancy* stresses the idea of difference, such as conflict or contradiction, that should not exist, as discrepancies in two accounts of an incident or between financial statements.

dif·fer·ent (dĭf'ər-ənt, dĭf'rənt) *adj.* **1.** Unlike in form, quality, amount, or nature; dissimilar: *took widely different approaches to the problem; a film quite different from her earlier work.* **2. a.** Distinct or separate: *That's a different issue altogether.* **b.** Various or assorted: *interviewed different members of the community.* **3.** Differing from all others; unusual: *a different kind of automobile.* [ME < OFr. < Lat. *differens,* pr.part. of *differe,* to differ.] **—dif'fer·ent·ly** *adv.* **—dif'fer·ent·ness** *n.*

dif·fer·en·ti·a (dĭf'ə-rĕn'shē-ə, -shə) *n., pl.* **-ti·ae** (-shē-ē'). An attribute that characterizes and distinguishes, esp. a characteristic that distinguishes a species from others of the same genus. [Lat., difference < *differens,* different.]

dif·fer·en·tia·ble (dĭf'ə-rĕn'shə-bəl, -shē-ə-) *adj.* **1.** Capable of being differentiated. **2.** *Math.* Possessing a derivative. **—dif'fer·en'tia·bil'i·ty** *n.*

dif·fer·en·ti·ae (dĭf'ə-rĕn'shē-ē') *n.* Plural of **differentia.**

dif·fer·en·tial (dĭf'ə-rĕn'shəl) *adj.* **1.** Of, pertaining to, or showing a difference. **2.** Constituting or making a difference; distinctive. **3.** Dependent on or making use of a difference or distinction. **4.** *Math.* Of or pertaining to differentiation. **5.** Involving differences in speed or direction of motion. *—n.* **1.** *Math.* **a.** An infinitesimal increment in a variable. **b.** The product of the derivative of a function of one variable multiplied by the independent variable increment. **2.** A differential gear. **3.** A differential rate **—dif'fer·en'tial·ly** *adv.*

differential analyzer *n.* A mechanical or electronic analog computer used to solve esp. complicated differential equations.

differential calculus *n.* The mathematics of the variation of a function with respect to changes in independent variables; the study of slopes of curves, accelerations, maxima, and minima by means of derivatives and differentials.

differential coefficient *n.* A derivative (sense 3).

differential equation *n.* An equation containing derivatives or differentials of an unknown function.

differential gear also **differential gearing** *n.* An arrangement of gears in an epicycle train permitting the rotation of two shafts at different speeds, used on the rear axle of automotive vehicles to allow different rates of wheel rotation on curves.

differential rate *n.* **1.** A difference in wage rate paid for the same work because of differing conditions. **2. a.** A difference in transportation rates to the same destination over different routes, to equalize traffic. **b.** A rate difference over the same route owing to differences in the commodities being shipped.

differential windlass *n.* A hoisting device that has two drums of different sizes on the same axis. A line wound on the larger and unwound from the smaller provides extra lifting power.

dif·fer·en·ti·ate (dĭf'ə-rĕn'shē-āt') *v.* **-at·ed, -at·ing, -ates.** *—tr.* **1.** To constitute the distinction between: *subspecies differentiated by the markings on their wings.* **2.** To perceive or show the difference in or between; discriminate. **3.** To develop differences in by alteration or modification. **4.** *Math.* To calculate the derivative or differential of. *—intr.* **1.** To become distinct or specialized. **2.** To make distinctions. **3.** To develop into specialized organs. Used esp. of embryonic cells or tissues. **—dif'fer·en'ti·a'tion** *n.*

dif·fi·cult (dĭf'ĭ-kŭlt', -kəlt) *adj.* **1. a.** Hard to do, achieve, or perform. **b.** Imposing a severe test of physical or spiritual strength; arduous. **c.** Causing difficulty or trouble. **2.** Hard to comprehend or solve. **3.** Hard to please, satisfy, or manage: *a difficult child.* **4.** Hard to persuade or convince. [ME, back-formation < *difficulte,* difficulty.] **—dif'fi·cult'ly** *adv.*

dif·fi·cul·ty (dĭf'ĭ-kŭl'tē, -kəl-) *n., pl.* **-ties. 1.** The condition or quality of being difficult. **2.** Something not easily done, accomplished, comprehended, or solved. **3.** Often **difficulties.** A troublesome or embarrassing state of affairs. **4.** A trouble; worry. **5.** A disagreement; dispute. **6.** An objection or reluctance; unwillingness. [ME *difficulte* < OFr. *dificulte* < Lat. *difficultas* < *difficilis,* difficult : *dis-,* not + *facilis,* easy.]

dif·fi·dence (dĭf'ĭ-dəns, -dĕns') *n.* The quality or state of being diffident.

dif·fi·dent (dĭf'ĭ-dənt, -dĕnt') *adj.* Hesitant to assert oneself from a lack of self-confidence; timid. [ME < Lat. *diffidens,* pr.part. of *diffidere,* to mistrust : *dis-,* not + *fidere,* to trust.] **—dif'fi·dent·ly** *adv.*

dif·fract (dĭ-frăkt') *intr. & tr.v.* **-fract·ed, -fract·ing, -fracts.** To undergo or cause to undergo diffraction. [Back-formation < DIFFRACTION.] **—dif·frac'tive** *adj.* **—dif·frac'tive·ly** *adv.* **—dif·frac'tive·ness** *n.*

dif·frac·tion (dĭ-frăk'shən) *n.* Modification of the behavior of light or of other waves resulting from limitation of their lateral extent, as by an obstacle or aperture. [NLat. *diffractio* < Lat. *diffractus,* p.part. of *diffringere,* to shatter : *dis-,* apart + *frangere,* to break.]

diffraction grating *n.* A usually glass or polished metal surface having a large number of very fine parallel grooves or slits cut in the surface and used to produce optical spectra by diffraction of transmitted or reflected light.

dif·fuse (dĭ-fyōōz') *v.* **-fused, -fus·ing, -fus·es.** *—tr.* **1.** To pour out and cause to spread freely. **2.** To spread about or scatter; disseminate. **3.** To make less brilliant; soften.

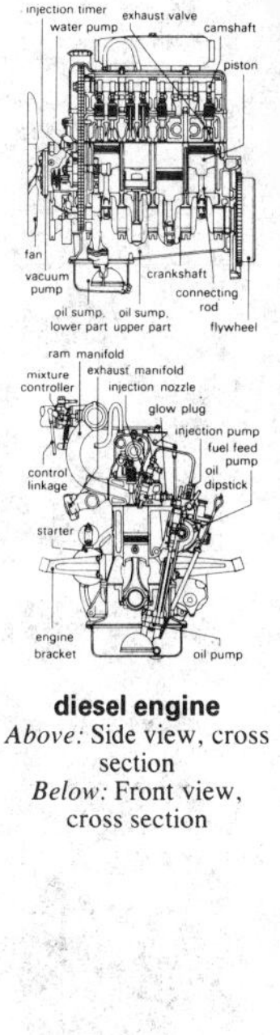

diesel engine
Above: Side view, cross section
Below: Front view, cross section

diffusion
Of blue ink through water

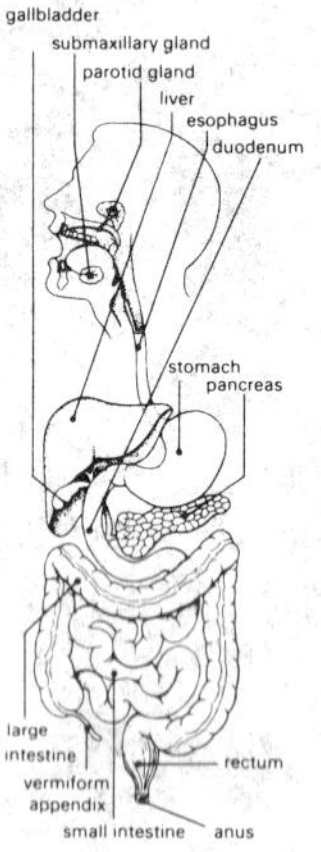

digestive system

digital
A digital watch

digitate
Digitate leaf

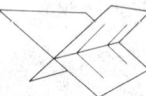

dihedral angle

—*intr.* **1.** To spread out or soften. **2.** *Physics.* To undergo diffusion. —*adj.* (dĭ-fyo͞os′). **1.** Widely spread or scattered; not concentrated. **2.** Characterized by verbosity; wordy. [ME, dispersed < OFr. *diffus* < Lat. *diffusus,* p.part. of *diffundere,* to spread : *dis-,* apart + *fundere,* to pour.] —**dif·fuse′ly** (-fyo͞os′lē) *adv.* —**dif·fuse′ness** (-fyo͞os′nĭs) *n.* —**dif·fus′i·ble** *adj.*

dif·fus·er (dĭ-fyo͞o′zər) *n.* **1.** One that diffuses. **2.** A lighting fixture, such as a frosted globe, that spreads light evenly. **3.** A flow passage in a wind tunnel that decelerates a stream of gas or liquid from a high to a low velocity.

dif·fu·sion (dĭ-fyo͞o′zhən) *n.* **1.** The process of diffusing or the condition of being diffused. **2.** *Physics.* The angular redistribution of radiation by a scattering, reflecting, or refracting system, ideally producing an isotropic distribution of intensity. **3.** *Physics.* The gradual mixing of the molecules of two or more substances, as a result of random thermal motion. **4.** Needless profusion of words; verbosity. —**dif·fu′sion·al** *adj.*

dif·fu·sive (dĭ-fyo͞o′sĭv, -zĭv) *adj.* Characterized by diffusion. —**dif·fu′sive·ly** *adv.* —**dif·fu′sive·ness** *n.*

dig (dĭg) *v.* **dug** (dŭg), **dig·ging, digs.** —*tr.* **1.** To break up, turn over, or remove (earth or sand, for example) with a tool or the hands. **2.** To make (an excavation) by or as if by digging. **3.** To obtain by digging: *dig coal.* **4.** To learn or discover by careful research or investigation. **5.** To force down and into, as for support: *The batter dug his foot in the ground and cocked the bat.* **6.** To force or prod against: *dug the gun into his back.* **7.** *Slang.* **a.** To comprehend and appreciate: *Can you dig what the man is saying?* **b.** To like or enjoy: *She digs horror films.* **c.** To notice, esp. in amusement or disbelief: *Did you dig that outfit?* —*intr.* **1.** To loosen or turn over the earth. **2.** To proceed along one's way by or as if by digging. **3.** *Informal.* To work hard and diligently. —***phrasal verb.*** **dig in. 1.** To dig holes or trenches. **2.** To entrench oneself. **3.** *Informal.* **a.** To begin to work intensively. **b.** To begin to eat. —*n.* **1.** A poke or punch. **2.** A sarcastic, taunting remark; gibe. **3.** An archaeological excavation. **4. digs.** *Chiefly Brit. Informal.* Lodgings; diggings. [ME *diggen.*]

di·ga·met·ic (dī′gə-mĕt′ĭk) *adj. Biol.* Having two types of gametes, one producing males and the other producing females.

di·gam·ma (dī-găm′ə) *n.* A letter occurring in certain early forms of Greek, transliterated in English as *w.* [Lat. < Gk. : *di-* two + *gamma,* gamma (from its shape).]

dig·a·my (dĭg′ə-mē) *n.* Remarriage after the death or divorce of one's first husband or wife. [LLat. *digamia* < Gk. : *di-,* two + *gamos,* marriage.] —**dig′a·mous** (-məs) *adj.*

di·gas·tric (dī-găs′trĭk) *adj.* Having two fleshy ends connected by a thinner tendinous portion. Used of certain muscles. —*n.* A lower jaw muscle that assists in lowering the jaw.

di·gen·e·sis (dī-jĕn′ĭ-sĭs) *n.* Metagenesis.

di·gest (dī-jĕst′, dĭ-) *v.* **-gest·ed, -gest·ing, -gests.** —*tr.* **1.** To transform (food) into an assimilable condition, as by chemical and muscular action in the alimentary canal. **2.** To absorb or assimilate mentally. **3.** To organize into a systematic arrangement, usually by summarizing or classifying. **4.** To endure or bear patiently. **5.** *Chem.* To soften or disintegrate by means of chemical action, heat, or moisture. —*intr.* **1.** To become assimilated into the body. **2.** To assimilate food substances. **3.** *Chem.* To undergo exposure to heat, liquids, or chemical agents. —*n.* (dī′jĕst′). **1.** A systematic arrangement of condensed data, esp. of literary or scientific material. **2.** *Law.* A systematic arrangement of statutes or court decisions. **3. Digest.** Pandect (sense 3). [ME *digesten* < Lat. *digestus,* p.part. of *digerere,* to separate, arrange : *dis-,* apart + *gerere,* to carry.]

di·gest·er (dī-jĕs′tər, dĭ-) *n.* **1.** One that organizes a digest. **2.** *Chem.* A vessel in which substances are softened or decomposed, usually for further processing.

di·gest·i·ble (dī-jĕs′tə-bəl, dĭ-) *adj.* Capable of being digested. —**di·gest′i·bil′i·ty, di·gest′i·ble·ness** *n.* —**di·gest′i·bly** *adv.*

di·ges·tion (dī-jĕs′chən, dĭ-) *n.* **1.** *Physiol.* **a.** The primarily enzymatic bodily process by which foodstuffs are decomposed into simple, assimilable substances. **b.** The ability to digest food. **c.** The result of this process. **2.** The process of decomposing organic matter in sewage by bacteria. **3.** The assimilation of ideas; understanding.

di·ges·tive (dī-jĕs′tĭv, dĭ-) *adj.* **1.** Pertaining to or aiding digestion. **2.** Functioning to digest food. —*n.* A digestive substance. —**di·ges′tive·ly** *adv.* —**di·ges′tive·ness** *n.*

digestive gland *n.* Any of various endocrine and exocrine glands that secrete enzymes necessary for digestion.

digestive system *n.* The alimentary canal together with accessory glands including the salivary glands, liver, and pancreas, regarded as an integrated system responsible for digestion.

dig·ger (dĭg′ər) *n.* **1.** One that digs, esp. a tool or machine for digging or excavating. **2.** *Informal.* A soldier from New Zealand or Australia.

digger wasp *n.* Any of various wasps of the family Sphecidae that burrow into the ground to build their nests.

dig·gings (dĭg′ĭngz) *pl.n.* **1.** An excavation site. **2.** Materials dug out. **3.** *Chiefly Brit. Informal.* Rooms; lodgings.

dight (dīt) *tr.v.* **dight** or **dight·ed, dight·ing, dights.** *Archaic.* To dress; adorn. [ME *dighten* < OE *dihtan,* to arrange < Lat. *dictare,* to dictate.]

dig·it (dĭj′ĭt) *n.* **1.** A finger or toe. **2.** The breadth of a finger, used as a unit of length, equal to about 3/4 inch. **3. a.** Any one of the ten Arabic number symbols, 0 through 9. **b.** Such a symbol used in a system of numeration. [ME < Lat. *digitus,* finger.]

dig·i·tal (dĭj′ĭ-tl) *adj.* **1.** Of, relating to, or resembling a digit, esp. a finger. **2.** Having digits. **3.** Expressed in digits, esp. for use by a computer. **4.** Using or giving a reading in digits. —*n.* A key played with the finger, as on a piano. —**dig′i·tal·ly** *adv.*

digital computer *n.* A computer that performs operations with quantities represented as digits, usually in the binary system.

dig·i·tal·in (dĭj′ĭ-tăl′ĭn) *n.* A poisonous white powder, $C_{36}H_{56}O_{14}$, used in the treatment of heart disease. [DIGITAL(IS) + -IN.]

dig·i·tal·is (dĭj′ĭ-tăl′ĭs) *n.* **1.** A plant of the genus *Digitalis,* which includes the foxgloves. **2.** A drug prepared from the seeds and dried leaves of digitalis, used as a cardiac stimulant. [NLat. *Digitalis,* genus name < Lat. *digitalis,* digital (from the finger-shaped corollas of foxglove) < *digitus,* finger.]

dig·i·tal·ize (dĭj′ĭ-tl-īz′) *tr.v.* **-ized, -iz·ing, -iz·es.** To treat with digitalis until the desired medical or physiological effect has been obtained. —**dig′i·tal·i·za′tion** *n.*

dig·i·tate (dĭj′ĭ-tāt′) also **dig·i·tat·ed** (-tā′tĭd) *adj.* **1.** Having digits or fingerlike parts. **2.** *Bot.* Having radiating fingerlike lobes or leaflets. —**dig′i·tate′ly** *adv.*

dig·i·ta·tion (dĭj′ĭ-tā′shən) *n.* **1.** Division into fingerlike parts; the condition of being digitate. **2.** A fingerlike part or process.

dig·i·ti·grade (dĭj′ĭ-tĭ-grād′) *adj.* Walking so that only the toes touch the ground, as do horses, cats, and dogs. —*n.* A digitigrade animal. [Fr. : Lat. *digitus,* digit + Lat. *gradus,* step.]

dig·it·ize (dĭj′ĭ-tīz′) *tr.v.* **-tized, -tiz·ing, -tiz·es.** To put (data, for example) into digital form. —**dig′i·ti·za′tion** *n.* —**dig′i·tiz′er** *n.*

dig·i·tox·in (dĭj′ĭ-tŏk′sĭn) *n.* A highly active glycoside, $C_{41}H_{64}O_{13}$, derived from digitalis. [DIGI(TALIS) + TOXIN.]

dig·ni·fied (dĭg′nə-fīd′) *adj.* Having or expressing dignity. —**dig′ni·fied′ly** (-fīd′lē, -fī′ĭd-lē) *adv.*

dig·ni·fy (dĭg′nə-fī′) *tr.v.* **-fied, -fy·ing, -fies. 1.** To give dignity or honor to. **2.** To add to the status or prestige of. [ME *dignifien* < OFr. *dignifier* < LLat. *dignificare* : Lat. *dignus,* worthy + Lat. *facere,* to do.]

dig·ni·tar·y (dĭg′nĭ-tĕr′ē) *n., pl.* **-ies.** A person of high rank.

dig·ni·ty (dĭg′nĭ-tē) *n., pl.* **-ties. 1. a.** The quality or condition of being esteemed or honored. **b.** Inherent nobility and worth: *the dignity of labor.* **2. a.** Poise and self-respect. **b.** Stateliness and reserve in deportment and appearance. **3.** The respect and honor associated with an important position. **4.** A high office or rank. **5. dignities.** The ceremonial symbols and observances attached to high office. [ME *dignite* < OFr. < Lat. *dignitas* < *dignus,* worthy.]

di·graph (dī′grăf′) *n.* **1.** A pair of letters that represents a single speech sound, such as the *ph* in *pheasant* or the *ea* in *beat.* **2.** Two letters run together to represent a special sound, such as Old English *æ.* —**di·graph′ic** (dī-grăf′ĭk) *adj.*

di·gress (dī-grĕs′, dĭ-) *intr.v.* **-gressed, -gress·ing, -gress·es.** To stray or turn aside from the main subject in writing or speaking. [Lat. *digredi, digress-* : *dis-,* apart + *gradi,* to go.]

di·gres·sion (dī-grĕsh′ən, dĭ-) *n.* **1.** The act of digressing. **2.** An instance of digressing in speech or writing. —**di·gres′sion·al** *adj.*

di·gres·sive (dī-grĕs′ĭv, dĭ-) *adj.* Characterized by digression. —**di·gres′sive·ly** *adv.* —**di·gres′sive·ness** *n.*

di·he·dral (dī-hē′drəl) *adj.* **1.** Formed by or having two plane faces; two-sided. **2.** Relating to, having, or forming a dihedral angle. —*n.* **1.** *Math.* A dihedral angle. **2.** The upward or downward inclination of an aircraft wing from true horizontal.

dihedral angle *n.* **1.** The angle formed by two intersecting planes. **2.** The dihedral of an aircraft wing.

di·hy·brid (dī-hī′brĭd) *n. Genetics.* An individual heterozygous for two pairs of genes.

di·hy·dric (dī-hī′drĭk) *adj.* Containing two hydroxyl radicals.

dik-dik (dĭk′dĭk′) *n.* Any of several very small African antelopes of the genus *Madoqua.* [Native word in East Africa.]

dike[1] also **dyke** (dīk) —*n.* **1.** An embankment of earth and rock built to prevent floods. **2.** *Chiefly Brit.* A low wall, often of sod, dividing or enclosing lands. **3.** A barrier blocking a passage, esp. for protection. **4.** A raised causeway. **5.** A ditch or channel. **6.** *Geol.* A long mass of igneous rock that cuts across the structure of adjacent rock. —*tr.v.* **diked, dik·ing, dikes** also **dyked, dyk·ing, dykes. 1.** To protect, enclose, or provide with a dike. **2.** To drain with dikes. [ME, partly < OE *dīc,* trench, and partly < ON *dīki,* ditch.] —**dik′er** *n.*

dike[2] also **dyke** (dīk) *n. Slang.* A lesbian. [Orig. unknown.]

dik·tat (dĭk-tät′) *n.* A unilaterally imposed settlement that deals harshly with a defeated party. [G. < Lat. *dictatum,* neuter p.part. of *dictare,* to dictate.]

Di·lan·tin (dī-lăn'tĭn). A trademark for diphenylhydantoin sodium, an anticonvulsant drug used to treat epilepsy.

di·lap·i·date (dĭ-lăp'ĭ-dāt') *tr. & intr.v.* **-dat·ed, -dat·ing, -dates.** To bring or fall into a state of ruin, decay, or disrepair. [Lat. *dilapidare, dilapidat-,* to throw away, destroy : *dis-,* apart + *lapidare,* to throw stones < *lapis,* stone.] **—di·lap'i·da'tion** *n.*

di·lap·i·dat·ed (dĭ-lăp'ĭ-dā'tĭd) *adj.* Fallen into a state of disrepair; broken-down.

di·la·tan·cy (dī-lāt'n-sē, dĭ-) *n.* **1.** The increase in volume of a fixed amount of certain materials, as of wet sand, subjected to a deformation that alters the interparticle distances of its constituents from their minimum-value configuration. **2.** Any of various phenomena, such as increase in viscosity or solidification, that result from dilatancy deformation.

di·la·tant (dī-lāt'nt, dĭ-) *adj.* **1.** Tending to dilate; dilating. **2.** Exhibiting dilatancy. *—n.* A dilator.

dil·a·ta·tion (dĭl'ə-tā'shən, dī'lə-) *n.* **1.** The act or process of dilating. **2.** The condition of being dilated or stretched. **3.** *Med.* The condition of being abnormally enlarged or dilated. **4.** Expatiation in writing or speech. **—dil'a·ta'tion·al** *adj.*

dil·a·ta·tor (dĭl'ə-tā'tər, dī'lə-) *n.* Variant of **dilator.**

di·late (dī-lāt', dī'lāt') *v.* **-lat·ed, -lat·ing, -lates.** *—tr.* To enlarge or expand; distend. *—intr.* **1.** To become wider or larger; expand. **2.** To speak or write at great length; expatiate. [ME *dilaten* < OFr. *dilater* < Lat. *dilatare,* to enlarge : *dis-,* apart + *latus,* wide.] **—di·lat'a·bil'i·ty** *n.* **—di·lat'a·ble** *adj.* **—di·lat'a·bly** *adv.* **—di·la'tion** *n.* **—di·la'tive** *adj.*

di·lat·ed (dī-lā'tĭd, dī'lā'-) *adj.* **1.** Widened; expanded. **2.** Distended. **—di·lat'ed·ly** *adv.* **—di·lat'ed·ness** *n.*

di·lat·er (dī-lā'tər, dī'lā'tər, dī-lā'tər) *n.* Variant of **dilator.**

dil·a·tom·e·ter (dĭl'ə-tŏm'ĭ-tər, dī'lə-) *n.* An instrument used to measure thermal expansion in solids, liquids, and gases. [DILATE + -METER.] **—dil'a·to·met'ric** (-tə-mĕt'rĭk) *adj.* **—dil'a·tom'e·try** *n.*

di·la·tor also **di·lat·er** (dī-lā'tər, dī'lā'tər, dī-lā'tər) or **dil·a·ta·tor** (dĭl'ə-tā'tər, dī'lə-) *n.* Something that dilates an object, organ, or part, esp. a drug, surgical instrument, or muscle that produces dilation.

dil·a·to·ry (dĭl'ə-tôr'ē, -tōr'ē) *adj.* **1.** Tending or intended to delay. **2.** Characterized by procrastination: *dilatory in his work habits.* **3.** Proceeding at a rate slower than desired. [ME *dilatorie* < Lat. *dilatorius* < *dilator,* delayer < *dilatus,* p.part. of *differre,* to delay. —see DIFFER.] **—dil'a·to'ri·ly** *adv.* **—dil'a·to'ri·ness** *n.*

dil·do also **dil·doe** (dĭl'dō) *n., pl.* **-dos** also **-does.** An object used as a substitute for an erect penis. [Orig. unknown.]

di·lem·ma (dĭ-lĕm'ə, dī-) *n.* **1. a.** A situation that requires one to choose between two equally balanced alternatives. **b.** A predicament that seemingly defies a satisfactory solution. **2.** *Logic.* An argument in which a choice of two or more alternatives, each being conclusive and fatal, is presented to an antagonist. [Lat. < Gk. *dilēmma,* ambiguous proposition : *di-,* two + *lēmma,* proposition.] **—dil'em·mat'ic** (dĭl'ə-măt'ĭk) *adj.*

Usage: *Dilemma* applies to a choice between evenly balanced alternatives, most often unattractive ones. It is not properly used as a synonym for *problem* or *predicament.* A sentence such as the following, therefore, is unacceptable to a large majority of the Usage Panel: *Juvenile delinquency represents the dilemma of our time.*

dil·et·tante (dĭl'ĭ-tänt', -tän'tē, -tănt', -tăn'tē, dĭl'ĭ-tänt') *n., pl.* **-tantes** or **-tan·ti** (-tän'tē, -tăn'-). **1.** A person with an amateurish or superficial interest in the arts or in a branch of knowledge. **2.** A lover of the fine arts; connoisseur. *—adj.* Superficial or amateurish. [Ital., lover of the arts, pr.part. of *dilettare,* to delight < Lat. *delectare.* —see DELIGHT.] **—dil'et·tan'tish** *adj.* **—dil'et·tan'tism** *n.*

dil·i·gence[1] (dĭl'ə-jəns) *n.* **1.** Persistent application to one's occupation or studies; assiduity. **2.** Attentive care; heedfulness. [ME < OFr. < Lat. *diligentia* < pr.part. of *diligere,* to esteem. —see DILIGENT.]

dil·i·gence[2] (dĭl'ə-jəns, dē'lē-zhäns') *n.* A large public stagecoach. [Fr. < *diligence,* speed < *diligent,* diligent.]

dil·i·gent (dĭl'ə-jənt) *adj.* Characterized by persevering, painstaking effort. [ME < OFr. < Lat. *diligens,* pr.part. of *diligere,* to esteem, love : *dis-,* apart + *legere,* to choose.] **—dil'i·gent·ly** *adv.*

dill (dĭl) *n.* **1.** An aromatic herb, *Anethum graveolens,* native to the Old World, having finely dissected leaves and small yellow flowers. **2.** The leaves or seeds of the dill plant, used as seasoning. [ME *dile* < OE.]

dill pickle *n.* A cucumber pickled and flavored with dill.

dil·ly (dĭl'ē) *n., pl.* **-lies.** *Slang.* One that is remarkable or startling: *what a dilly of a joke.* [Obs. *dilly,* delightful < DELIGHTFUL.]

dilly bag *n.* A bag or basket woven of rushes or bark, used in Australia. [< *dilli,* native word in Australia.]

dil·ly-dal·ly (dĭl'ē-dăl'ē) *intr.v.* **-lied, -ly·ing, -lies. 1.** To dawdle. **2.** To vacillate. [Redup. of DALLY.] **—dil'ly-dal'li·er** *n.*

dil·u·ent (dĭl'yo͞o-ənt) *adj.* Capable of diluting. *—n.* A substance used to dilute. [Lat. *diluens, diluent-,* pr.part. of *diluere,* to dilute.]

di·lute (dī-lo͞ot', dĭ-) *tr.v.* **-lut·ed, -lut·ing, -lutes. 1.** To thin or reduce the concentration of (a solution). **2.** To lessen the potency, strength, purity, or brilliance of by admixture. *—adj.* Weakened; diluted. [Lat. *diluere, dilut-* : *dis-,* apart + *lavere,* to wash.] **—di·lut'er** *n.*

di·lu·tion (dī-lo͞o'shən, dĭ-) *n.* **1. a.** The process of diluting. **b.** A dilute or weakened condition. **2.** A diluted substance.

di·lu·vi·al (dĭ-lo͞o'vē-əl) also **di·lu·vi·an** (-ən) *adj.* Of or produced by a flood. [LLat. *diluvialis* < Lat. *diluvium,* flood < *diluere,* to dilute.]

dim (dĭm) *adj.* **dim·mer, dim·mest. 1. a.** Deficient in brightness. **b.** Shedding a small amount of light; faint. **c.** Negative or unpromising: *took a dim view of our prospects.* **2.** Lacking brightness or luster; subdued; dull. **3.** Indistinct; obscure. **4.** Lacking sharpness or clarity of understanding or perception. **5.** Lacking keenness or vigor. *—v.* **dimmed, dim·ming, dims.** *—tr.* **1.** To make dim. **2.** To put on low beam: *dim the headlights of an automobile.* *—intr.* To become dim. *—pl.n.* **dims.** The parking lights on an automobile. [ME < OE *dimm.*] **—dim'ly** *adv.* **—dim'ness** *n.*

dime (dīm) *n.* A U.S. coin worth ten cents. [ME, tenth part < OFr. < Lat. *decima (pars),* tenth (part) < *decem,* ten.]

di·men·hy·dri·nate (dī'mĕn-hī'drə-nāt') *n.* An antihistamine, $C_{24}H_{28}ClN_5O_3$, used to treat motion sickness and allergic disorders. [DIME(THYL) + (AMI)N(E) + HYDR(O)- + -IN + -ATE.]

dime novel *n.* A cheap romance or adventure novel. **—dime novelist** *n.*

di·men·sion (dĭ-mĕn'shən, dī-) *n.* **1.** A measure of spatial extent, esp. width, height, or length. **2.** Often **dimensions.** Extent; magnitude; size; scope. **3.** *Math.* **a.** Any of the least number of independent coordinates required to specify a point in space uniquely. **b.** The range of any of these coordinates. **4.** *Physics.* A physical property, often mass, length, time, or a combination thereof, regarded as a fundamental measure or as one of a set of fundamental measures of a physical quantity: *Velocity has the dimensions of length divided by time.* *—tr.v.* **-sioned, -sion·ing, -sions.** To cut or shape to specified dimensions. [ME *dimensioun* < OFr. *dimension* < Lat. *dimensio,* extent < *dimensus,* p.part. of *dimetiri,* to measure : *dis-* (intensive) + *metiri,* to measure.] **—di·men'sion·al** *adj.* **—di·men'sion·al'i·ty** (-shə-năl'ĭ-tē) *n.* **—di·men'sion·al·ly** *adv.* **—di·men'sion·less** *adj.*

di·mer (dī'mər) *n.* **1.** A molecule consisting of two identical simpler molecules. **2.** A chemical compound consisting of dimers.

di·mer·ic (dī-mĕr'ĭk) *adj. Biol.* Composed of two parts or divisions.

dim·er·ous (dĭm'ər-əs) *adj.* **1.** Consisting of two parts or segments, as the tarsus in certain insects. **2.** *Bot.* Having flower parts, such as petals, sepals, and stamens, in sets of two. **—dim'er·ism** *n.*

dime store *n.* Five-and-ten.

dim·e·ter (dĭm'ĭ-tər) *n.* A verse consisting of two metrical feet or of two dipodies. [LLat. < Gk. *dimetros,* having two meters : *di-,* two + *metron,* meter.]

di·meth·yl (dī-mĕth'əl) *n.* Ethane.

di·meth·yl·sulf·ox·ide (dī-mĕth'əl-sŭl-fŏk'sīd') *n.* A colorless hygroscopic liquid, $(CH_3)_2SO$, obtained from lignin, used as a solvent and in medicine as a skin penetrant to convey medications into the tissues.

di·min·ish (dĭ-mĭn'ĭsh) *v.* **-ished, -ish·ing, -ish·es.** *—tr.* **1. a.** To make smaller or less or cause to appear smaller or less. **b.** To detract from the authority, rank, or prestige of. **2.** To cause to taper. **3.** *Mus.* To reduce (a perfect or minor interval) by a semitone. *—intr.* **1.** To become smaller or less. **2.** To taper. [ME *deminishen,* blend of *diminuen,* to lessen (< OFr. *diminuer* < Lat. *deminuere* : *de-,* from + *minuere,* to lessen) and *minishen,* to reduce (< OFr. *minuiser* < VLat. **minutiare* < Lat. *minutia,* smallness < *minutus,* small, p.part. of *minuere,* to lessen).] **—di·min'ish·a·ble** *adj.* **—di·min'ish·ment** *n.*

diminishing returns *pl.n.* The rate at which profits diminish in proportion to the amount of further investment after a certain point.

di·min·u·en·do (dĭ-mĭn'yo͞o-ĕn'dō) *n., adj., & adv. Mus.* Decrescendo. [Ital., diminishing < Lat. *deminuendum,* gerund of *deminuere,* to diminish.]

dim·i·nu·tion (dĭm'ə-no͞o'shən, -nyo͞o'-) *n.* **1. a.** The act or process of diminishing. **b.** The resulting reduction; decrease. **2.** *Mus.* The repetition of a theme in notes one-quarter or one-half the duration of the original. [ME *diminucioun* < OFr. *diminution* < Lat. *deminutio* < *deminuere,* to diminish.] **—dim'i·nu'tion·al** *adj.*

di·min·u·tive (dĭ-mĭn'yə-tĭv) *adj.* **1.** Of very small size; tiny. **2.** Designating certain suffixes that denote smallness, youth, familiarity, or affection, as *-let* in *booklet* or *-kin* in *lambkin.* *—n.* A diminutive suffix, word, or name. [ME *diminutif* < OFr. < Lat. *deminutivus* < *deminutus,* p.part. of *deminuere,* to diminish.] **—di·min'u·tive·ly** *adv.* **—di·min'u·tive·ness** *n.*

dim·i·ty (dĭm'ĭ-tē) *n., pl.* **-ties.** A sheer, crisp cotton fabric, usually corded or checked. [ME *demyt* < Med. Lat. *dimitum* < Med. Gk. *dimitos,* double-threaded : Gk. *di-,* two + *mitos,* thread.]

dilapidate
A dilapidated building

p **pop** / r **roar** / s **sauce** / sh **ship, dish** / t **tight** / th **thin, path** / *th* **this, bathe** / ŭ **cut** / ûr **urge** / v **valve** / w **with** / y **yes** / z **zebra, size** / zh **vision** / ə **about,** item, edible, gallop, circus / œ *Fr.* **feu,** *Ger.* **schön** / ü *Fr.* **tu,** *Ger.* **über** / KH *Ger.* **ich,** *Scot.* **loch** / N *Fr.* **bon.**

dim·mer (dĭm′ər) *n.* **1.** A device used to reduce the intensity of an electric light. **2. dimmers. a.** Parking lights on an automobile. **b.** Low-beam automobile headlights.
di·morph (dī′môrf′) *n.* Either of two dimorphic forms. [Back-formation < DIMORPHISM.]
di·mor·phic (dī-môr′fĭk) also **di·mor·phous** (-fəs) *adj.* Having two distinct forms.
di·mor·phism (dī-môr′fĭz′əm) *n.* **1.** *Bot.* The occurrence of two distinct forms of the same parts, such as leaves, flowers, or stamens, in a single plant or in plants of the same kind. **2.** *Chem. & Physics.* Dimorphic crystallization. **3.** *Zool.* The state of having two distinct forms in the same species when the sexes differ in secondary as well as primary sexual characteristics. [< Gk. *dimorphos,* having two forms : *di-,* two + *morphē,* shape.]
di·mor·phous (dī-môr′fəs) *adj.* Variant of **dimorphic.**
dim-out (dĭm′out′) *n.* **1.** The restricted use or exposure of lights at night, esp. to lessen the chance of air attack. **2.** The semidarkness resulting from a dim-out.
dim·ple (dĭm′pəl) *n.* **1.** A small natural indentation in the flesh on a part of the human body, esp. in a cheek. **2.** A slight depression in a surface: *the dimples of a mattress.* —*v.* **-pled, -pling, -ples.** —*tr.* To produce dimples in. —*intr.* To form dimples by smiling. [ME *dimpel.*] —**dim′ply** *adj.*
dim sum (dĭm′ sŏŏm′, sŭm′) *pl.n.* Light Chinese refreshments that include small steamed or fried dumplings and a variety of other delicacies. [Cantonese.]
dim·wit (dĭm′wĭt′) *n. Slang.* A stupid person. —**dim′wit′ted** *adj.* —**dim′wit′ted·ly** *adv.* —**dim′wit′ted·ness** *n.*
din (dĭn) *n.* A mixture of loud and discordant noises. —*v.* **dinned, din·ning, dins.** —*tr.* **1.** To stun with deafening noise. **2.** To impress by wearying repetition: *din an idea into one's head.* —*intr.* To make a din. [ME *dine* < OE *dyne.*]
di·nar (dĭ-när′, dē′när′) *n.* **1.** See table at **currency. 2.** Any of several units of gold and silver currency used in the Middle East from the 8th to the 19th century. [Ar. *dīnār* < LGk. *dēnarion* < Lat. *denarius,* denarius.]
dine (dīn) *v.* **dined, din·ing, dines.** —*intr.* To take dinner. —*tr.* To give dinner to. [ME *dinen* < OFr. *diner* < VLat. **disjejunare* : Lat. *dis-* (reversal) + Lat. *jejunus,* fast, hunger.]
din·er (dī′nər) *n.* **1.** One that dines. **2.** A railroad dining car. **3.** A restaurant with a long counter and booths, originally shaped like a railroad car.
di·nette (dī-nĕt′) *n.* **1.** A nook or alcove for informal meals. **2.** The table and chairs used in a dinette. [< DINE.]
ding (dĭng) *v.* **dinged, ding·ing, dings.** —*intr.* **1.** To ring; clang. **2.** To speak persistently and repetitiously. —*tr.* **1.** To cause to clang, as by striking. **2.** To hammer into or at with repetitious talk: *always dinging advice at me.* —*n.* A ringing sound. [Prob. imit.]
ding-a-ling (dĭng′ə-lĭng) *n. Informal.* A silly person; dingbat.
ding·bat (dĭng′băt′) *n.* **1.** A small object, such as a stick or stone, suitable for hurling at another object. **2.** *Printing.* A typographical ornament not further specified. **3.** *Informal.* A silly or foolish person. [Orig. unknown.]
ding-dong (dĭng′dông′, -dŏng′) *n.* The peal of a bell. —*intr.v.* **-donged, -dong·ing, -dongs.** To ring; jingle. —*adj.* Characterized by a hammering exchange, as of blows. [Imit.]
din·ghy (dĭng′ē) *n., pl.* **-ghies. 1.** A small boat powered by sails, oars, or a motor carried as a lifeboat or pleasure craft on a larger boat. **2.** A small rowboat. **3.** An inflatable rubber life raft. [Hindi *ḍiṅgī,* dim. of *ḍeṅgā,* long.]
din·gle (dĭng′gəl) *n.* A small, wooded valley; dell. [ME, dell, hollow.]
din·go (dĭng′gō) *n., pl.* **-goes.** A wild dog, *Canis dingo,* of Australia, having a yellowish-brown coat. [Native word in Australia.]
din·gus (dĭng′əs) *n. Slang.* A gadget or other article whose name is unknown or forgotten. [Du. *dinges,* prob. < G., genitive of *Ding,* thing.]
din·gy (dĭn′jē) *adj.* **-gi·er, -gi·est. 1.** Darkened with smoke and grime; dirty. **2.** Drab or squalid. **3.** Shabby or worn. [Orig. unknown.] —**din′gi·ly** *adv.* —**din′gi·ness** *n.*
dining car *n.* A railroad car in which meals are served.
dining room *n.* A room in which meals are served.
di·ni·tro·ben·zene (dī-nī′trō-bĕn′zēn′, -bĕn-zēn′) *n.* Any of three isomeric compounds, $C_6H_4(NO_2)_2$, made from a mixture of nitric acid, sulfuric acid, and heated benzene and used in celluloid manufacture, in dyes, and in organic syntheses.
dink (dĭngk) *n. Vulgar Slang.* The penis. [Perh. alteration of DICK.]
din·key also **din·ky** (dĭng′kē) *n., pl.* **-keys** also **-kies.** *Informal.* A small locomotive used in a railroad yard. [< DINKY.]
din·kum (dĭn′kəm) *Austral.* —*adj.* Genuine; real. —*adv.* Honestly; truly. [Orig. unknown.]
din·ky (dĭng′kē) *Informal.* —*adj.* **-ki·er, -ki·est.** Of small size or consequence; insignificant. —*n., pl.* **-kies.** A dinkey. [Prob. < Sc. *dink,* neat.]
din·ner (dĭn′ər) *n.* **1.** The chief meal of the day. **2.** A banquet or formal meal in honor of a person or commemorating an occasion. **3.** The food prepared for a dinner. **4.** A table d'hôte (sense 2). [ME *diner* < OFr. < *diner,* to dine.]

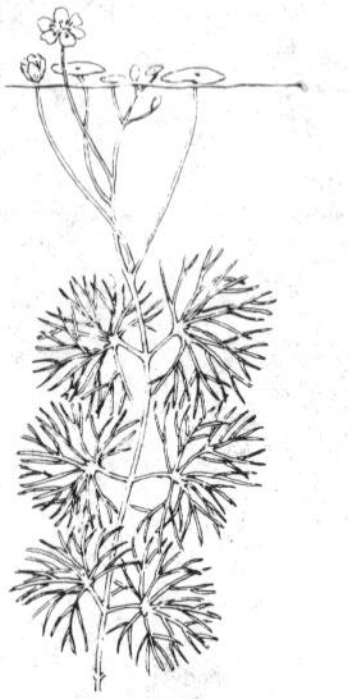

dimorphism
Exhibited in the distinction between the submerged and floating leaves of a plant

dinghy

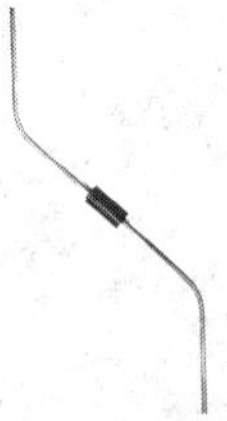

diode
Semiconductor

Dionysus

dinner jacket *n.* A tuxedo (sense 1).
dinner theater *n.* A restaurant that presents a play during or after dinner.
din·ner·ware (dĭn′ər-wâr′) *n.* **1.** The dishes, serving bowls, platters, and other tableware used in serving a meal. **2.** A set of dishes.
di·no·flag·el·late (dī′nō-flăj′ə-lĭt, -lāt′, -flə-jĕl′ĭt) *n.* Any of numerous minute, chiefly marine protozoans of the class Dinoflagellata, characteristically having two flagella and a cellulose outer envelope, and forming one of the chief constituents of plankton. [NLat. *Dinoflagellata,* class name : Gk. *dinos,* eddy (< *dinein,* to whirl) + NLat. *flagellum,* flagellum.]
di·no·saur (dī′nə-sôr′) *n.* Any of various extinct, often gigantic, reptiles of the orders Saurischia and Ornithischia, that existed during the Mesozoic era. [Gk. *deinos,* monstrous + Gk. *sauros,* lizard.] —**di′no·sau′ri·an** (-sôr′ē-ən) *adj. & n.* —**di′no·sau′ric** (-sôr′ĭk) *adj.*
di·no·there (dī′nə-thîr′) *n.* Any of various extinct elephantlike mammals of the genus *Dinotherium,* that existed during the Miocene, Pliocene, and Pleistocene epochs. [NLat. *Dinotherium,* genus name : Gk. *deinos,* monstrous + Gk *thērion,* dim. of *thēr,* beast.]
dint (dĭnt) *n.* **1.** Force or effort; exertion: *succeeded by dint of hard work.* **2.** A dent. —*tr.v.* **dint·ed, dint·ing, dints. 1.** To put a dent in. **2.** To impress or drive in forcibly. [ME < OE *dynt.*]
di·oc·e·san (dī-ŏs′ĭ-sən) *adj.* Of or pertaining to a diocese. —*n.* A bishop of a diocese.
di·o·cese (dī′ə-sĭs, -sēs′, -sēz′) *n.* The district or churches under the jurisdiction of a bishop; bishopric. [ME *diocise* < OFr. < LLat. *diocesis* < Lat. *dioecesis,* jurisdiction < Gk. *dioikēsis,* administration < *dioikein,* to keep house, administer : *dia-* (intensive) + *oikein,* to inhabit < *oikos,* house.]
di·ode (dī′ōd′) *n.* **1.** An electronic device that restricts current flow chiefly to one direction. **2.** A vacuum tube having two electrodes, a cathode, and an anode. **3.** A two-terminal semiconductor device used chiefly as a rectifier.
di·oe·cious also **di·e·cious** (dī-ē′shəs) *adj. Bot.* Having male and female flowers borne on separate plants. [DI- + Gk. *oikia,* a dwelling < *oikos,* house.] —**di·oe′cious·ly** *adv.*
di·oi·cous (dī-oi′kəs) *adj. Bot.* Having antheridia and archegonia on separate plants; unisexual. Used of mosses and related plants. [NLat. *dioecus* : DI- + Gk. *oikos,* house.]
Di·o·me·des (dī′ə-mē′dēz) *n. Gk. Myth.* A prince of Argos and one of the chief heroes at Troy. [Lat. < Gk. *Diomēdēs.*]
Di·o·ne (dī-ō′nē) *n. Gk. Myth.* The mother of Aphrodite by Zeus. [Lat. < Gk. *Diōnē.*]
Di·o·nys·i·a (dī′ə-nĭz′ē-ə, -nĭzh′ē-ə, -nĭs′ē-ə) *pl.n.* Any of various festivals of ancient Attica in honor of the god Dionysus, esp. the one held in the fall in which Greek tragedy is thought to have had its origin.
Di·o·nys·i·ac (dī′ə-nĭs′ē-ăk′) *adj.* **1.** Of or relating to Dionysus or the Dionysia. **2.** Often **dionysiac.** Ecstatic or wild; dionysian.
Di·o·nys·i·an (dī′ə-nĭsh′ən, -nĭzh′ən, -nĭs′ē-ən) *adj.* **1. a.** Of or relating to Dionysus or the Dionysia. **b.** Of or relating to any of several historical persons named Dionysus. **2. a.** Of or devoted to the worship of Dionysus **b.** Often **dionysian.** Of an ecstatic, orgiastic, or irrational nature; frenzied. **3.** Often **dionysian.** In the philosophy of Nietzsche, of or characteristic of creative-intuitive power as opposed to critical-rational power.
Di·o·ny·sus (dī′ə-nī′səs, nē′-) *n. Gk. Myth.* The god of wine and of an orgiastic religion celebrating the power and fertility of nature; identified with the Roman god Bacchus. [Lat. < Gk. *Dionusios.*]
di·o·phan·tine analysis (dī′ə-făn′tīn′, -tĭn) *n.* A method for determining integral solutions of certain algebraic equations. [After *Diophantus,* Greek mathematician of the 3rd cent. B.C.]
di·op·side (dī-ŏp′sīd′) *n.* A monoclinic pyroxene mineral, $CaMgSi_2O_6$, used as a gemstone and as a refractory. [Fr. : *di-,* two + Gk. *opsis,* appearance.]
di·op·ter (dī-ŏp′tər) *n.* A unit, equal to a reciprocal meter, of curvature and of the power of lenses, refracting surfaces, and other optical systems. [Obs. *diopter,* an instrument for measuring angles < Lat. *dioptra* < Gk. : *dia-,* through + *optos,* visible.] —**di·op′tral** (-trəl) *adj.*
di·op·tom·e·ter (dī′ŏp-tŏm′ĭ-tər) *n.* An instrument used for measuring ocular refraction. [DIOPT(ER) + -METER.] —**di′op·tom′e·try** *n.*
di·op·tric (dī-ŏp′trĭk) also **di·op·tri·cal** (-trĭ-kəl) *adj.* **1.** Of or relating to dioptrics. **2.** Pertaining to optical refraction; refractive.
di·op·trics (dī-ŏp′trĭks) *n. (used with a sing. verb).* The study of the refraction of light. [Gk. *dioptrikas* < *dioptra,* an instrument for measuring angles. —see DIOPTER.]
di·o·ram·a (dī′ə-răm′ə, -rä′mə) *n.* **1.** A three-dimensional miniature scene with painted modeled figures and background. **2.** A scene reproduced on cloth transparencies with various lights shining through the cloths to produce changes in effect, and viewed through a small aperture. [Fr. : *dia-,* dia- + *(pan)orama,* panorama < E.] —**di′o·ram′ic** (-răm′ĭk) *adj.*
di·o·rite (dī′ə-rīt′) *n.* Any of various granite-textured,

crystalline dark rocks rich in plagioclase and having little quartz. [Fr. < Gk. *diorizein,* to distinguish : *dia-,* apart + *horizein,* to divide < *horos,* boundary.] —**di'o·rit'ic** (-rĭt'ĭk) *adj.*

Di·os·cu·ri (dī-ŏs'kyə-rī', dī'ə-skyo͝or'ī') *pl.n. Gk. Myth.* Castor and Pollux, the twin sons of Leda and brothers of Helen and Clytemnestra, who were transformed by Zeus into the constellation Gemini. [Gk. *Dioskouroi* : *Dios,* genitive of *Zeus,* Zeus + *kouroi,* pl. of *kouros,* boy.]

di·ox·ane (dī-ŏk'sān') *n.* A flammable, potentially explosive, colorless liquid, $C_4H_8O_2$, used as a solvent for fats, greases, and resins and in various products including paints, lacquers, glues, cosmetics, and fumigants.

di·ox·ide (dī-ŏk'sīd') *n.* An oxide with two oxygen atoms per molecule.

di·ox·in (dī-ŏk'sĭn) *n.* Any of several carcinogenic or teratogenic heterocyclic hydrocarbons that occur as impurities in petroleum-derived herbicides. [DI- + OX(A)- + -IN.]

dip (dĭp) *v.* **dipped, dip·ping, dips.** —*tr.* **1.** To plunge briefly into a liquid, usually in order to wet, coat, or saturate. **2.** To color or dye by immersing: *dip Easter eggs.* **3.** To immerse (an animal) in a disinfectant solution. **4.** To make (a candle) by repeatedly immersing a wick in melted wax or tallow. **5.** To galvanize or plate (metal) by immersion. **6.** To scoop up by plunging the hand or a container into and out of a liquid; ladle. **7.** To lower and raise (a flag) in salute. **8.** To lower or drop suddenly: *dipped his head to avoid the branch.* —*intr.* **1.** To plunge into liquid and come out quickly. **2. a.** To plunge the hand or a container into a liquid, esp. to take something up or out. **b.** To make inroads for money: *dipped into her savings.* **3.** To drop or sink out of sight, esp. suddenly. **4.** To appear to sink. **5.** To drop suddenly before climbing. Used of an airplane. **6.** To slope downward; decline. **7.** To decline slightly and usually temporarily: *sales dipped after Christmas.* **8.** *Geol.* To lie at an angle to the horizontal plane, as a rock stratum or vein. **9. a.** To read here and there in a book or magazine; browse. **b.** To investigate a subject superficially; dabble. —*n.* **1.** A brief plunge or immersion. **2.** A liquid into which something is dipped. **3.** A smooth creamed preparation into which crackers or other foods may be dipped. **4.** An amount taken up by dipping. **5.** A container for dipping. **6.** A candle made by repeated dipping in tallow or wax. **7.** A downward slope. **8.** A downward course; drop: *a dip in prices.* **9.** *Geol.* The downward inclination of a rock stratum or vein in reference to the plane of the horizon. **10.** Magnetic dip. **11.** A hollow; depression. **12.** *Sports.* A gymnastic exercise on the parallel bars in which the body is lowered by bending the elbows until the chin reaches the level of the bars and then is raised by straightening the arms. **13.** *Slang.* A foolish or gullible person. [ME *dippen* < OE *dyppan.*]

di·pet·al·ous (dī-pĕt'l-əs) *adj.* Having two petals.

di·phase (dī'fāz') also **di·pha·sic** (dī-fā'zĭk) *adj.* Having two phases.

di·phen·yl (dī-fĕn'əl, -fē'nəl) *n.* Biphenyl.

di·phen·yl·a·mine (dī-fĕn'əl-ə-mēn', -ăm'ĭn, -fē'nəl-) *n.* A colorless crystalline compound, $(C_6H_5)_2NH$, used as a stabilizer for plastics and in the manufacture of dyes, explosives, pesticides, and pharmaceuticals.

di·phen·yl·a·mine·chlo·ro·ar·sine (dī-fĕn'əl-ə-mēn'klôr'ō-är-sēn', -är'sēn', -fē'nəl-, -klōr'-) *n.* Phenarsazine chloride.

di·phen·yl·hy·dan·to·in sodium (dī-fĕn'əl-hī-dăn'tō-ĭn, -fē'nəl-) *n.* A white powder, $C_{15}H_{11}N_2O_2Na$, used as an anticonvulsant.

di·phen·yl·ke·tone (dī-fĕn'əl-kē'tōn', -fē'nəl-) *n.* Benzophenone.

di·phos·gene (dī-fŏz'jēn') *n.* A colorless mobile liquid, $ClCOOCCl_3$, with a vapor used as a poison gas.

diph·the·ri·a (dĭf-thîr'ē-ə, dĭp-) *n.* An acute contagious disease caused by infection with the bacillus *Corynebacterium diphtheriae,* and characterized by the formation of false membranes in the throat and other air passages, causing difficulty in breathing, high fever, and weakness. [NLat. < Fr. *diphthérie* < Gk. *diphthera,* piece of leather.] —**diph'the·rit'ic** (-thə-rĭt'ĭk), **diph·ther'ic** (-thĕr'ĭk), **diph·the'ri·al** *adj.*

diph·thong (dĭf'thông', -thŏng', dĭp'-) *n.* **1.** A complex speech sound beginning with one vowel sound and moving to another vowel or semivowel position within the same syllable. For example, *oy* in the word *boy* is a diphthong. **2.** Either of the two ligatures *æ* or *œ,* originally pronounced as diphthongs in Classical Latin but now pronounced as single vowels. [ME *diptonge* < OFr. *diptongue* < LLat. *dipthongus* < Gk. *diphthongos* : *di-,* two + *phthongos,* sound.] —**diph·thon'gal** *adj.*

diph·thong·ize (dĭf'thông-īz', -thŏng-, dĭp'-) *v.* **-ized, -iz·ing, -iz·es.** —*tr.* To pronounce as a diphthong. —*intr.* To become a diphthong. —**diph'thong·i·za'tion** *n.*

diph·y·cer·cal (dĭf'ĭ-sûr'kəl) *adj.* Designating or having a tail fin in which the vertebral column extends to the tip, with symmetrical upper and lower parts. [< Gk. *diphuēs,* double (*di-,* two + *phuein,* to grow) + *kerkos,* tail.] —**diph'y·cer'cy** (-sûr'sē) *n.*

di·phy·let·ic (dī'fī-lĕt'ĭk) *adj.* Descended from two ancestral lines or individuals.

di·phyl·lous (dī-fĭl'əs) *adj.* Having two leaves.

di·phy·o·dont (dī-fī'ə-dŏnt') *adj.* Having two successive sets of teeth, as do most mammals. [Gk. *diphuēs,* double (*di-,* two + *phuein,* to grow) + -ODONT.]

dipl– *pref.* Variant of **diplo-.**

di·ple·gia (dī-plē'jə, -jē-ə) *n.* Paralysis of corresponding parts on both sides of the body.

di·plex (dī'plĕks') *adj.* Capable of simultaneous transmission or reception of two messages in the same radio channel. [DI- + (DU)PLEX.]

di·plex·er (dī'plĕk-sər) *n.* A coupling device that permits two radio transmitters to share the same antenna.

diplo– or **dipl–** *pref.* **1.** Double: *diploblastic.* **2.** Having double the basic number of chromosomes; diploid: *diplont.* [Gk. < *diploos,* double.]

dip·lo·blas·tic (dĭp'lō-blăs'tĭk) *adj.* Having two distinct cellular layers. Used of embryos and lower invertebrate animals such as sponges and coelenterates.

dip·lo·car·di·ac (dĭp'lō-kär'dē-ăk') *adj.* Having or characterizing a heart in which the two sides are distinctly separated, as in birds and mammals. [DIPLO- + Gk. *kardia,* heart.]

dip·lo·coc·cus (dĭp'lō-kŏk'əs) *n., pl.* **-coc·ci** (-kŏk'sī', -kŏk'ī'). Any of various paired spherical bacteria of the genus *Diplococcus,* some of which are pathogenic. [NLat. *Diplococcus,* genus name : DIPLO- + *coccus,* coccus.] —**dip'lo·coc'cal** (-kŏk'əl), **dip'lo·coc'cic** (-kŏk'sĭk, -kŏk'ĭk) *adj.*

di·plod·o·cus (dĭ-plŏd'ə-kəs, dī-) *n.* A very large, extinct, herbivorous dinosaur of the genus *Diplodocus,* that existed during the Jurassic period. [NLat. *Diplodocus,* genus name : DIPLO- + Gk. *dokos,* beam.]

dip·lo·e (dĭp'lō-ē') *n.* The spongy, bony tissue between the outer and inner bone layers of the cranium. [NLat. < Gk. *diploē* < *diploos,* double.] —**dip'lo·ic** (-lō-ĭk) *adj.*

dip·loid (dĭp'loid') *adj.* **1.** Double or twofold. **2.** *Genetics.* Having a homologous pair of chromosomes for each characteristic except sex, the total number of chromosomes being twice that of a gamete. —*n. Genetics.* **1.** A diploid cell. **2.** An individual characterized by a diploid chromosome number. —**dip'loid'ly** *adv.* —**dip'loi'dy** *n.*

di·plo·ma (dĭ-plō'mə) *n.* **1.** A document issued by a university or other school testifying that a student has earned a degree or completed a particular course of study. **2.** A certificate conferring a privilege or honor. **3.** An official document or charter. [Lat. < Gk. *diplōma,* document, folded paper < *diploos,* double.]

di·plo·ma·cy (dĭ-plō'mə-sē) *n., pl.* **-cies. 1.** The art or practice of conducting international relations, as in negotiating alliances, treaties, and agreements. **2.** Tact in dealing with people.

dip·lo·mat (dĭp'lə-măt') *n.* One skilled or working in diplomacy. [Fr. *diplomate,* back-formation < *diplomatique,* diplomatic.]

dip·lo·mate (dĭp'lə-māt') *n.* A physician certified as a specialist by a board of examiners.

dip·lo·mat·ic (dĭp'lə-măt'ĭk) *adj.* **1.** Of, pertaining to, or involving diplomacy. **2.** Characterized by tact and sensitivity in dealing with people. [Fr. *diplomatique* < NLat. *diplomaticus,* relating to documents < Lat. *diploma,* diploma.] —**dip'lo·mat'i·cal·ly** *adv.*

diplomatic corps *n.* The body of diplomatic personnel in residence at the capital of a nation.

diplomatic immunity *n.* Exemption from ordinary processes of law afforded to diplomatic personnel in a foreign country.

dip·lo·mat·ics (dĭp'lə-măt'ĭks) *n.* (*used with a sing. verb*). **1.** Diplomacy. **2.** The branch of paleography devoted to the study of ancient documents and the determination of their age and authenticity.

di·plo·ma·tist (dĭ-plō'mə-tĭst) *n.* A diplomat.

dip·lont (dĭp'lŏnt') *n.* An organism having somatic cells with diploid chromosomes. —**dip·lont'ic** (-lŏn'tik) *adj.*

dip·lo·pi·a (dĭ-plō'pē-ə) *n. Pathol.* A disorder of vision which causes objects to appear double. —**dip·lo'pic** (-plō'pĭk, -plŏp'ĭk) *adj.*

dip·lo·pod (dĭp'lə-pŏd') *n.* Any of various segmented, cylindrical arthropods of the class Diplopoda, which includes the millipedes. [NLat. *Diplopoda,* class name : DIPLO- + Gk. *pous,* foot.] —**di·plop'o·dous** (-lŏp'ə-dəs) *adj.*

dip·lo·sis (dĭ-plō'sĭs) *n.* The formation of the full number of chromosomes found in a somatic cell by the fusion of gamete nuclei containing haploid sets in fertilization. [NLat. < Gk. *diplōsis,* a doubling < *diploun,* to double < *diploos,* double.]

dip needle *n.* **1.** *Physics.* A magnetic needle vertically balanced and pivoted to rotate freely in order to indicate the local inclination of the earth's magnetic field. **2.** An inclinometer (sense 2).

dip·no·an (dĭp'nō-ən) *n.* Any of various fishes of the group Dipnoi, which includes the lungfishes, characterized by modified lungs that enable them to breathe atmospheric air. —*adj.* Of or belonging to the Dipnoi. [< NLat. *Dipnoi,* group name < Gk. *dipnoos,* having two apertures for breathing : *di-,* two + *pnoē,* breath < *pnein,* to breathe.]

dip·o·dy (dĭp'ə-dē) *n., pl.* **-dies.** A prosodic unit consisting of two feet. [LLat. *dipodia* < Gk. < *dipous,* two-footed : *di-,* two + *pous,* foot.]

di·po·lar (dī'pō'lər, dī-pō'-) *adj.* Of, pertaining to, or having a dipole.

diorama

di·pole (dī′pōl′) *n.* **1.** *Physics.* A pair of electric charges or magnetic poles, of equal magnitude but of opposite sign or polarity, separated by a small distance. **2.** *Electron.* An antenna, usually fed from the center, consisting of two equal rods extending outward in a straight line.

dipole moment *n.* **1.** The product of either charge in an electric dipole with the distance separating them. **2.** The product of the strength of either pole in a magnetic dipole with the distance separating them.

dipper

dip·per (dĭp′ər) *n.* **1.** One that dips. **2.** A container used for dipping, such as a long-handled cup for taking up water. **3. Dipper. a.** The Big Dipper in Ursa Major. **b.** The Little Dipper in Ursa Minor. **4.** The water ouzel.

dip·py (dĭp′ē) *adj.* **-pi·er, -pi·est.** *Slang.* Not sensible; foolish. [Orig. unknown.]

di·pro·pel·lant (dī′prə-pĕl′ənt) *n.* A bipropellant.

dip·so·ma·ni·a (dĭp′sə-mā′nē-ə, -mān′yə) *n.* An insatiable, often periodic craving for alcoholic liquors. [Gk. *dipsa,* thirst + -MANIA.] **—dip′so·ma′ni·ac** (-ăk′) *adj. & n.* **—dip′so·ma·ni′a·cal** (-mə-nī′ə-kəl) *adj.*

dip·stick (dĭp′stĭk′) *n.* A graduated rod for measuring the depth or amount of liquid in a container, as of oil in a crankcase.

dip·ter·an (dĭp′tər-ən) *n.* A dipterous insect. *—adj.* Of or belonging to the order Diptera; dipterous.

dip·ter·on (dĭp′tə-rŏn′) *n.* A dipteran. [Gk., neuter of *dipteros,* dipterous.]

dip·ter·ous (dĭp′tər-əs) *adj.* **1.** Of, pertaining to, or belonging to the Diptera, a large order of insects which includes the true flies and mosquitoes, characterized by a single pair of membranous wings and a pair of club-shaped balancing organs called halteres. **2.** Having two winglike parts: *the dipterous fruit of the maple.* [< NLat. *Diptera,* order name < Gk. *dipteros,* having two wings : *di-,* two + *pteron,* wing.]

diptych

dip·tych (dĭp′tĭk) *n.* **1.** An ancient writing tablet having two leaves hinged together. **2.** A pair of painted or carved panels hinged together. [LLat. *diptycha* < Gk. *diptukha* < *diptukhos,* folded double : *di-,* two + *ptukhē,* fold < *ptussein,* to fold.]

di·quat (dī′kwăt′) *n.* A strong, nonpersistent, yellow, crystalline herbicide, $C_{12}H_{12}Br_2N_2$, used to control water weeds. [DI- + QUAT(ERNARY).]

dire (dīr) *adj.* **dir·er, dir·est. 1.** Warning of or having dreadful or terrible consequences; calamitous: *a dire economic forecast; dire threats.* **2.** So extreme as to require quick remedial action or treatment: *in dire want; dire poverty.* [Lat. *dirus,* ill-omened.] **—dire′ly** *adv.* **—dire′ness** *n.*

di·rect (dĭ-rĕkt′, dī-) *v.* **-rect·ed, -rect·ing, -rects.** *—tr.* **1.** To conduct or regulate the affairs of; manage. **2.** To take charge of with authority; control. **3.** To order or command: *directed him to answer.* **4. a.** To move or guide (someone) toward a goal: *advice that helped direct the student's career choice.* **b.** To show or indicate the way to: *directed me to the airport.* **5.** To cause to move in or follow a direct or straight course: *direct your fire at the target.* **6.** To address (a communication, for example) to a destination. **7.** To address (remarks) to a person or audience. **8. a.** To give guidance and instruction to (actors or musicians) in the rehearsal and performance of a work. **b.** To supervise the performance of. *—intr.* **1.** To give commands or directions. **2.** To conduct a performance or rehearsal. *—adj.* **1.** Proceeding or lying in a straight course or line. **2.** Straightforward and candid in manner. **3.** Without intervening persons, conditions, or agencies; immediate: *direct sunlight; a direct answer.* **4.** By action of the voters, rather than through elected representatives or delegates. **5.** Of unbroken descent; lineal. **6.** Consisting of the exact words of the writer or speaker. **7.** Lacking compromising or mitigating elements; absolute: *direct opposites.* **8.** *Math.* Varying in the same manner as another quantity, esp. increasing if another quantity increases or decreasing if it decreases. **9.** *Astron.* Designating a west-to-east motion of a planet in the same direction as the sun's movement among the stars. *—adv.* In a direct manner; straight; directly. [ME *directen* < Lat. *directus,* p.part. of *dirigere,* to give direction to : *dis-,* apart + *regere,* to guide.]

dirndl

direct action *n.* The strategic use of immediately effective acts, such as strikes, demonstrations, or sabotage, to achieve a social or political end.

di·rect-ac·tion (dĭ-rĕkt′ăk′shən, dī-) *adj.* Operating without intermediate ingredients, components, stages, or processes.

direct current *n.* An electric current flowing in one direction.

directed angle *n.* An angle having an indicated positive sense.

directed distance *n.* A segment of a line having an indicated positive sense.

di·rec·tion (dĭ-rĕk′shən, dī-) *n.* **1.** The act or function of directing. **2.** Management, supervision, or guidance of an action or operation. **3.** The art or action of musical or theatrical directing. **4.** A word or phrase in a musical score indicating how a particular passage is to be played or sung. **5.** Often **directions.** An instruction or series of instructions for doing something. **6.** An order or command; authoritative indication. **7. a.** The distance-independent relationship between two points that specifies the angular position of either with respect to the other; the relationship by which the alignment or orientation of any position with respect to any other position is established. **b.** A position to which motion or another position is referred. **c.** A line leading to a place or point. **d.** The line or course along which a person or thing moves. **8.** The statement, in degrees, of the angle measured between due north and a given line or course on a compass. **9.** A course or area of development; tendency toward a particular end or goal: *charting a new direction for the company.* [ME, arrangement < OFr. < Lat. *directio* < *directus.* —see DIRECT.] **—di·rec′tion·less** *adj.*

di·rec·tion·al (dĭ-rĕk′shə-nəl, dī-) *adj.* **1.** Of or indicating direction: *an automobile's directional lights.* **2.** *Electronics.* Capable of receiving or sending signals in one direction only. **3.** Of or relating to guidance in effort or behavior: *directional training.* *—n.* A directional signal. **—di·rec′tion·al′i·ty** (-năl′ĭ-tē) *n.*

directional antenna *n.* An antenna adapted for receiving signals from or sending signals in a particular direction.

directional signal *n.* One of two flashing lights on an automotive vehicle that indicates the direction of a turn.

direction finder *n.* A device for determining the source of a transmitted signal, consisting mainly of a radio receiver and a coiled rotating antenna.

di·rec·tive (dĭ-rĕk′tĭv, dī-) *n.* An order or instruction, esp. one issued by a government or military unit. *—adj.* Serving to direct, indicate, or point out.

di·rect·ly (dĭ-rĕkt′lē, dī-) *adv.* **1.** In a direct line or manner; straight. **2.** Without anyone or anything intervening; immediately. **3.** Exactly or totally. **4. a.** At once; instantly. **b.** In a little while; shortly. *—conj. Chiefly Brit.* As soon as: *We'll go directly he's ready.*

direct object *n.* In English and some other languages, the word or words in a sentence designating the person or thing receiving the action of a transitive verb. For example, in *The boy broke the dish,* the direct object is *the dish.*

di·rec·tor (dĭ-rĕk′tər, dī-) *n.* **1.** One who supervises, controls, or manages. **2.** A member of a board of persons who control or govern the affairs of an institution or corporation. **3. a.** One whose profession is the supervision and instruction of the actors in a dramatic production. **b.** The conductor of an orchestra or chorus. **—di·rec′tor·ship′** *n.*

di·rec·tor·ate (dĭ-rĕk′tər-ĭt, dī-) *n.* **1.** The office or position of a director. **2.** A board of directors.

di·rec·to·ri·al (dĭ-rĕk′tôr′ē-əl, -tōr′, dī-) *adj.* **1.** Of or pertaining to a director or directorate. **2.** Serving to direct; directive. **—di·rec′to′ri·al·ly** *adv.*

director's chair *n.* A collapsible armchair having a back and seat usually made of canvas. [From its use by motion picture directors on the set.]

di·rec·to·ry (dĭ-rĕk′tə-rē, dī-) *n., pl.* **-ries. 1.** One that directs. **2.** A book listing names, addresses, and other data about a specific group of persons or organizations. **3.** A book of rules or directions. **4.** A group or body of directors. *—adj.* Serving to direct.

direct primary *n.* A preliminary election in which a party's candidates for public office are nominated by popular vote.

direct tax *n.* A tax, such as an income or property tax, levied directly on the taxpayer.

di·rec·trix (dĭ-rĕk′trĭks, dī-) *n., pl.* **di·rec·trix·es** or **di·rec·tri·ces** (dĭ′rĕk-trī′sēz). **1.** The fixed curve traversed by a generatrix in generating a conic or a cylinder. **2.** The median line in the trajectory of fire of an artillery piece.

dire·ful (dīr′fəl) *adj.* Dreadful or frightful. **—dire′ful·ly** *adv.* **—dire′ful·ness** *n.*

dirge (dûrj) *n.* **1.** A funeral hymn or lament. **2.** A slow, mournful musical composition or poem. [ME *dirige,* an antiphon in the Office for the Dead < Med. Lat. *dirige Domine Deus meus in conspectu tuo viam meam,* direct, O Lord my God, my way in your sight (the opening words of the antiphon).] **—dirge′ful** *adj.*

dir·ham (də-răm′) *n.* See table at **currency.** [Ar. < Gk. *drakhmē,* drachma.]

dir·i·gi·ble (dĭr′ə-jə-bəl, də-rĭj′ə-bəl) *n.* A steerable lighter-than-air craft; airship. *—adj.* Capable of being guided or steered. [< Lat. *dirigere,* to direct.] **—dir′i·gi·bil′i·ty** *n.*

dirk (dûrk) *n.* A dagger. *—tr.v.* **dirked, dirk·ing, dirks.** To stab with a dirk. [Sc. *durk.*]

dirn·dl (dûrn′dl) *n.* **1.** A full-skirted dress with a tight bodice, patterned after Tyrolean peasant wear. **2.** A full skirt similar to a dirndl. [G., short for *Dirndlkleid* : *Dirndl,* dim. of *Dirne,* girl + *Kleid,* dress.]

dirt (dûrt) *n.* **1.** Earth or soil. **2. a.** A filthy or soiling substance, such as mud or dust. **b.** Excrement. **3.** Something mean, contemptible, or vile. **4. a.** Obscene language. **b.** Malicious or scandalous gossip. **5.** A squalid or filthy condition. **6.** Unethical behavior or practice; corruption. **7.** Gravel, slag, or other material from which metal is extracted in mining. [ME *drit* < ON.]

dirt bike *n.* A lightweight motorbike designed for use on rough surfaces, as dirt roads or trails.

dirt-cheap (dûrt′chēp′) *adj. & adv.* Very cheap.

dirt farmer *n. Informal.* A farmer who does all his own work.

dirt·y (dûr′tē) *adj.* **-i·er, -i·est. 1. a.** Soiled, as with dirt; unclean. **b.** Causing to become soiled: *a dirty job.* **2. a.** Obscene or indecent. **b.** Malicious or scandalous: *a dirty lie.* **3.** Squalid or filthy; run-down. **4. a.** Unethical or corrupt;

sordid: *dirty politics.* **b.** Contrary to honor or rules; unsportsmanlike. **5. a.** Unavoidably offensive and distasteful: *laying off workers is the dirty part of this job.* **b.** Demanding, unpleasant, and thankless: *leaves the dirty work for me.* **c.** Unfortunate or regrettable: *a dirty shame.* **6.** Of a clouded or muddy appearance. **7.** Designating a nuclear weapon that produces an excessive amount of radioactive fallout. **8.** Stormy or rough. —*v.* **-ied, -y·ing, -ies.** —*tr.* **1.** To make dirty. **2.** To stain or tarnish with dishonor. —*intr.* To become dirty. —**dirt'i·ly** *adv.* —**dirt'i·ness** *n.*

Synonyms: *dirty, filthy, foul, nasty, squalid, soiled, grimy, slovenly, slatternly.* These adjectives apply to what is unclean, impure, or unkempt. *Dirty,* the most general, describes anything physically unclean or offensive to propriety by being off-color. *Filthy* intensifies these senses, as does *foul,* which suggests that which is revolting, particularly to the sense of smell or figuratively, to decency. *Nasty* can mean offensive to good taste, but often is applied to what is merely unpleasant. *Squalid* suggests, besides dirtiness, the neglect and untidiness characteristic of extreme poverty; figuratively it implies sordidness. *Soiled* suggests something stained or partly dirtied, and *grimy,* something whose surface is smudged with soot or other dirt. *Slovenly* and *slatternly* describe personal appearance. Both stress unkemptness and disorderliness, but *slatternly* is restricted to women.

dirty old man *n. Informal.* A lecherous man, esp. a middle-aged or older man.

dirty pool *n. Slang.* Unjust or dishonest conduct. [< POOL[2].]

dirty tricks *pl.n. Informal.* **1.** Covert intelligence operations. **2.** Unethical behavior, esp. in politics.

dirty word *n.* A word or expression that is inappropriate or offensive from a particular point of view.

dis- *pref.* **1.** Not: *dissimilar.* **2. a.** Absence of: *disinterest.* **b.** Opposite of: *disfavor.* **3.** Undo; do the opposite of: *disarrange.* **4. a.** Deprive of: *disfranchise.* **b.** Remove: *disbud.* **c.** Free from: *disintoxicate.* **5.** Used as an intensive: *disannul.* [Lat. < *dis,* apart, asunder.]

dis·a·bil·i·ty (dĭs'ə-bĭl'ĭ-tē) *n., pl.* **-ties. 1.** A disabled condition; incapacity. **2.** Something that disables; handicap. **3.** A legal incapacity or disqualification.

dis·a·ble (dĭs-ā'bəl) *tr.v.* **-bled, -bling, -bles. 1.** To weaken or destroy the normal physical or mental abilities of; incapacitate. **2.** To render legally disqualified. **3.** *Computer Sci.* To suppress an interrupt feature.

dis·a·buse (dĭs'ə-byo͞oz') *tr.v.* **-bused, -bus·ing, -bus·es.** To free from a falsehood or misconception. [Fr. *désabuser* : *dés-,* dis- + *abuser,* to delude < OFr., to abuse. —see ABUSE.]

di·sac·cha·ride (dī-săk'ə-rīd') *n.* Any of a class of carbohydrates, including lactose and sucrose, that yield two monosaccharides on hydrolysis.

dis·ac·cord (dĭs'ə-kôrd') *n.* Lack of harmony; disagreement. —*intr.v.* **-cord·ed, -cord·ing, -cords.** To disagree. [ME *disaccorden,* to disagree < OFr. *desacorder* : *des-,* not (Lat. *dis-*) + *acorder,* to agree. —see ACCORD.]

dis·ac·cus·tom (dĭs'ə-kŭs'təm) *tr.v.* **-tomed, -tom·ing, -toms.** To cause to become unaccustomed. [OFr. *desacostumer* : *dis-,* not (< Lat. *dis-*) + *acostumer,* to accustom. —see ACCUSTOM.]

dis·ad·van·tage (dĭs'əd-văn'tĭj) *n.* **1.** An unfavorable condition or circumstance; handicap. **2.** Damage or loss, esp. to reputation; detriment. —*tr.v.* **-taged, -tag·ing, -tag·es.** To put at a disadvantage; set back. [ME *disavauntage* < OFr. *desavantage* : *des-,* not (< Lat. *dis-*) + *avantage,* advantage.]

dis·ad·van·taged (dĭs'əd-văn'tĭjd) *adj.* Suffering under severe economic and social disadvantage. —*n.* A group that suffers under severe economic and social disadvantage.

dis·ad·van·ta·geous (dĭs-ăd'vən-tā'jəs, dĭs'ăd-vən-) *adj.* Detrimental; unfavorable; injurious. —**dis·ad'van·ta'geous·ly** *adv.* —**dis·ad'van·ta'geous·ness** *n.*

dis·af·fect (dĭs'ə-fĕkt') *tr.v.* **-fect·ed, -fect·ing, -fects.** To cause to lose affection or loyalty. —**dis'af·fec'tion** *n.*

dis·af·fect·ed (dĭs'ə-fĕk'tĭd) *adj.* No longer contented and loyal; resentful. —**dis'af·fect'ed·ly** *adv.*

dis·af·fil·i·ate (dĭs'ə-fĭl'ē-āt') *tr.v.* **-at·ed, -at·ing, -ates.** To disassociate from or sever an alliance or affiliation with. —**dis'af·fil'i·a'tion** *n.*

dis·af·firm (dĭs'ə-fûrm') *tr.v.* **-firmed, -firm·ing, -firms. 1.** To deny or contradict. **2.** *Law.* To repudiate. —**dis'af·fir'mance** (dĭs'ə-fûr'məns), **dis·af'fir·ma'tion** (dĭs-ăf'ər-mā'shən) *n.*

dis·ag·gre·gate (dĭs-ăg'rə-gĭt', -gāt') *intr.v.* **-gat·ed, -gat·ing, -gates.** To break up or break apart. —**dis·ag'gre·ga'tive** *adj.*

dis·a·gree (dĭs'ə-grē') *intr.v.* **-greed, -gree·ing, -grees. 1.** To fail to correspond: *our figures disagree.* **2. a.** To have a different opinion. **b.** To dispute; quarrel. **3.** To cause adverse effects: *fried foods disagree with me.* [ME *disagreen* < OFr. *desagreer* : *des-,* not (< Lat. *dis-*) + *agreer,* to agree. —see AGREE.]

dis·a·gree·a·ble (dĭs'ə-grē'ə-bəl) *adj.* **1.** Not to one's liking; unpleasant or offensive. **2.** Characterized by a quarrelsome manner; bad-tempered. —**dis'a·gree'a·ble·ness** *n.* —**dis'a·gree'a·bly** *adv.*

dis·a·gree·ment (dĭs'ə-grē'mənt) *n.* **1.** A failure or refusal to agree. **2.** A disparity or inconsistency. **3.** A conflict or difference of opinion.

dis·al·low (dĭs'ə-lou') *tr.v.* **-lowed, -low·ing, -lows. 1.** To refuse to allow. **2.** To reject as invalid, untrue, or improper. [ME *disallowen* < OFr. *desalouer,* to reprimand : *des-,* not (< Lat. *dis-*) + *alouer,* to approve. —see ALLOW.] —**dis'al·low'a·ble** *adj.* —**dis'al·low'ance** *n.*

dis·am·big·u·ate (dĭs'ăm-bĭg'yo͞o-at') *tr.v.* **-at·ed, -at·ing, -ates.** To establish a single grammatical or semantic interpretation for. —**dis'am·big'u·a'tion** *n.*

dis·an·nul (dĭs'ə-nŭl') *tr.v.* **-nulled, -null·ing, -nuls.** To annul; cancel. —**dis'an·nul'ment** *n.*

dis·ap·pear (dĭs'ə-pîr') *intr.v.* **-peared, -pear·ing, -pears. 1.** To pass out of sight; vanish. **2.** To cease to exist. —**dis'ap·pear'ance** *n.*

dis·ap·point (dĭs'ə-point') *tr.v.* **-point·ed, -point·ing, -points. 1.** To fail to satisfy the hope, desire, or expectation of. **2.** To frustrate or thwart. [ME *disappointen,* to remove from office < OFr. *desapointier* : *des-* (reversal < Lat. *dis-*) + *apointer,* to appoint.] —**dis'ap·point'ing·ly** *adv.*

dis·ap·point·ment (dĭs'ə-point'mənt) *n.* **1. a.** The act of disappointing. **b.** The condition or feeling of being disappointed. **2.** One that disappoints.

dis·ap·pro·ba·tion (dĭs-ăp'rə-bā'shən) *n.* Moral disapproval; condemnation.

dis·ap·prov·al (dĭs'ə-pro͞o'vəl) *n.* The act of disapproving; condemnation; censure.

dis·ap·prove (dĭs'ə-pro͞ov') *v.* **-proved, -prov·ing, -proves.** —*tr.* **1.** To have an unfavorable opinion of; condemn. **2.** To refuse to approve; reject. —*intr.* To have an unfavorable opinion: *disapproves of drinking.* —**dis'ap·prov'er** *n.* —**dis'ap·prov'ing·ly** *adv.*

dis·arm (dĭs-ärm') *v.* **-armed, -arm·ing, -arms.** —*tr.* **1.** To divest of weapons. **2.** To deprive of the means of attack or defense; render harmless. **3. a.** To overcome or allay the suspicion, hostility, or antagonism of. **b.** To win the confidence of. —*intr.* **1.** To lay down arms. **2.** To reduce or abolish armed forces. [ME *disarmen* < OFr. *desarmer* : *des-* (reversal < Lat. *dis-*) + *armer,* to arm < Lat. *armare* < *arma,* weapons.]

dis·ar·ma·ment (dĭs-är'mə-mənt) *n.* **1.** The act of laying down arms, esp. the reduction or abolition of a nation's military forces and armaments. **2.** The condition of being disarmed.

dis·arm·ing (dĭs-är'mĭng) *adj.* Tending to remove suspicion or hostility; endearing. —**dis·arm'ing·ly** *adv.*

dis·ar·range (dĭs'ə-rānj') *tr.v.* **-ranged, -rang·ing, -rang·es.** To upset the proper arrangement or order of. —**dis'ar·range'ment** *n.*

dis·ar·ray (dĭs'ə-rā') *n.* **1.** A state of disorder; confusion. **2.** Disorderly dress. —*tr.v.* **-rayed, -ray·ing, -rays.** To throw into confusion; upset. [ME *disaraien* < OFr. *desareer* : *des-* (reversal < Lat. *dis-*) + *areer,* to array.]

dis·ar·tic·u·late (dĭs'är-tĭk'yə-lāt') *v.* **-lat·ed, -lat·ing, -lates.** —*tr.* To separate at the joints; disjoint. —*intr.* To become disjointed. —**dis'ar·tic'u·la'tion** *n.* —**dis'ar·tic'u·la'tor** *n.*

dis·as·sem·ble (dĭs'ə-sĕm'bəl) *v.* **-bled, -bling, -bles.** —*tr.* To take apart. —*intr.* To come apart: *The unit disassembles easily.* —**dis'as·sem'bly** *n.*

dis·as·so·ci·ate (dĭs'ə-sō'shē-āt', -sē-) *tr.v.* **-at·ed, -at·ing, -ates.** To dissociate. —**dis'as·so'ci·a'tion** *n.*

dis·as·ter (dĭ-zăs'tər, -săs'-) *n.* **1. a.** An occurrence causing widespread destruction and distress. **b.** A grave misfortune. **2.** A total failure. **3.** *Obs.* An evil influence of a celestial body. [Fr. *désastre* < Ital. *disastro* : *dis-* (pejorative < Lat. *dis-*) + *astro,* star < Lat. *astrum* < Gk. *astron.*]

Synonyms: *disaster, calamity, catastrophe, cataclysm, debacle, holocaust.* These nouns refer to grave occurrences having destructive results. *Disaster* generally implies great destruction, hardship, or loss of life, while *calamity* emphasizes distress, grief, and the sense of loss more than widespread destruction. *Catastrophe* especially stresses the sense of tragic outcome with irreparable loss. *Cataclysm* refers to a sudden upheaval that brings an earthshaking change, physical, as an earthquake, or social, as a revolution. *Debacle* usually implies overwhelming defeat or sudden, chaotic collapse. *Holocaust* refers, in strict usage, to widespread destruction and loss of life caused especially by fire.

disaster area *n.* An area that officially qualifies for emergency governmental aid as a result of a disaster such as an earthquake or flood.

disaster dump *n. Computer Sci.* A printout that occurs as a result of a nonrecoverable program error.

dis·as·trous (dĭ-zăs'trəs, -săs'-) *adj.* Causing disaster; calamitous. —**dis·as'trous·ly** *adv.* —**dis·as'trous·ness** *n.*

dis·a·vow (dĭs'ə-vou') *tr.v.* **-vowed, -vow·ing, -vows.** To disclaim knowledge of, responsibility for, or association with. [ME *disavowen* < OFr. *desavouer* : *des-,* not (< Lat. *dis-*) + *avouer,* to avow.] —**dis'a·vow'al** *n.*

dis·band (dĭs-bănd') *v.* **-band·ed, -band·ing, -bands.** —*tr.* To break up; dissolve. —*intr.* To become disbanded; disperse. —**dis·band'ment** *n.*

dis·bar (dĭs-bär') *tr.v.* **-barred, -bar·ring, -bars.** To expel (a lawyer) from the legal profession by official action or procedure. —**dis·bar'ment** *n.*

dis·be·lief (dĭs'bĭ-lēf') *n.* Refusal or reluctance to believe.

dis·be·lieve (dĭs'bĭ-lēv') *v.* **-lieved, -liev·ing, -lieves.** —*tr.* To refuse to believe in; reject. —*intr.* To withhold belief. —**dis'be·liev'er** *n.* —**dis'be·liev'ing·ly** *adv.*

dis·bound (dĭs-bound') *adj.* Having a binding in poor condition or no longer having a binding: *a disbound library book.*

dis·branch (dĭs-brănch') *tr.v.* **-branched, -branch·ing, -branch·es. 1.** To cut or break a branch from (a tree). **2.** To remove (a limb or branch).

dis·bud (dĭs-bŭd') *tr.v.* **-bud·ded, -bud·ding, -buds. 1.** To remove buds from (a plant) to promote better blooms from remaining buds or to control the shape of the plant. **2.** To remove newly developing horns from (livestock).

dis·bur·den (dĭs-bûr'dn) *v.* **-dened, -den·ing, -dens.** —*tr.* **1.** To relieve of a burden. **2.** To unload or remove (a burden). —*intr.* To remove or unload a burden. —**dis·bur'den·ment** *n.*

dis·bur·sal (dĭs-bûr'səl) *n.* Disbursement.

dis·burse (dĭs-bûrs') *tr.v.* **-bursed, -burs·ing, -burs·es.** To pay out; expend, as from a fund. [OFr. *desbourser* : *des-* (reversal < Lat. *dis-*) + *bourse,* purse < Med. Lat. *bursa* < Gk.] —**dis·burs'a·ble** *adj.* —**dis·burs'er** *n.*

dis·burse·ment (dĭs-bûrs'mənt) *n.* **1.** The act of disbursing. **2.** Money paid out; expenditure.

disc (dĭsk) *n.* **1.** Also **disk.** A phonograph record. **2.** Variant of **disk.**

disc– *pref.* Variant of **disco-.**

dis·calced (dĭ-skălst') *adj.* Barefooted. Used of certain orders of monks. [< Lat. *discalceatus* : *dis-,* not + *calceatus,* shod < *calceus,* shoe < *calx,* heel.]

dis·cant (dĭs'kănt') *n.* & *v.* Variant of **descant.**

dis·card (dĭs-kärd') *v.* **-card·ed, -card·ing, -cards.** —*tr.* **1.** To throw away; reject. **2. a.** To throw out (a playing card) from one's hand. **b.** To play (a card other than a trump and different in suit from the card led). —*intr.* To discard a card. —*n.* (dĭs'kärd'). **1.** The act of discarding. **2.** A person or thing discarded, esp. a card in a card game. —**dis·card'er** *n.*

disc brake also **disk brake** *n.* A brake in which the retarding friction is generated between a set of stationary pads and a rotating disc.

dis·cern (dĭ-sûrn', -zûrn') *v.* **-cerned, -cern·ing, -cerns.** —*tr.* **1.** To perceive (something obscure or concealed); detect. **2.** To recognize or comprehend mentally. **3.** To perceive as separate and distinct; discriminate. —*intr.* To perceive differences. [ME *discernen* < OFr. *discerner* < Lat. *discernere* : *dis-,* apart + *cernere,* to perceive.] —**dis·cern'er** *n.* —**dis·cern'i·ble** *adj.* —**dis·cern'i·bly** *adv.*

dis·cern·ing (dĭ-sûr'nĭng, -zûr'-) *adj.* Showing insight and judgment; perceptive. —**dis·cern'ing·ly** *adv.*

dis·cern·ment (dĭ-sûrn'mənt, -zûrn'-) *n.* **1.** The act or process of discerning. **2.** Keenness of discrimination; perspicacity.

dis·charge (dĭs-chärj') *v.* **-charged, -charg·ing, -charg·es.** —*tr.* **1.** To relieve of a burden or of contents; unload. **2.** To unload or empty (contents). **3.** To release, as from confinement or duty. **4.** To dismiss from employment. **5.** To send or pour forth; emit. **6.** To shoot or fire (a projectile or weapon). **7.** To perform the obligations or demands of (an office, duty, or task). **8.** To comply with the terms of (a debt or promise, for example). **9.** *Law.* **a.** To release (a defendant, for example). **b.** To set aside; dismiss; annul: *discharge a court order.* **10.** To remove (color) from cloth, as by chemical bleaching. **11.** *Elect.* To cause electrical discharge in (a battery, for example). **12.** *Archit.* **a.** To apportion (weight) evenly, as over a door. **b.** To relieve (a part) of excess weight by distribution of pressure. —*intr.* **1.** To get rid of a burden, load, or weight. **2.** To go off; fire, as a gun. **3.** To pour forth contents. **4.** To become blurred; run. **5.** To undergo electrical discharge. —*n.* (dĭs'chärj', dĭs-chärj'). **1.** The act of removing a load or burden. **2.** The act of shooting or firing a projectile or weapon. **3. a.** An instance of pouring forth; emission: *a discharge of pus.* **b.** The amount or rate of emission or ejection. **4.** Something that is discharged, released, or emitted. **5.** An instance of relieving from or elimination of an obligation, burden, or responsibility. **6.** Fulfillment or performance. **7. a.** Dismissal or release from employment, service, or confinement. **b.** A document certifying such release, esp. from military service. **8.** *Law.* An annulment or acquittal; dismissal, as of a court order. **9.** *Elect.* **a.** The release of stored energy in a capacitor by the flow of electric current between its terminals. **b.** The conversion of chemical energy to electric energy in a storage battery. **c.** A flow of electricity in a dielectric, esp. in a rarefied gas. **d.** The elimination of net electric charge from a charged body. [ME *dischargen* < OFr. *deschargier* < VLat. **discarricare* : Lat. *dis-,* apart + LLat. *carricare,* to load < *carrus,* cart, of Celtic orig.] —**dis·charge'a·ble** *adj.* —**dis·charg'er** *n.*

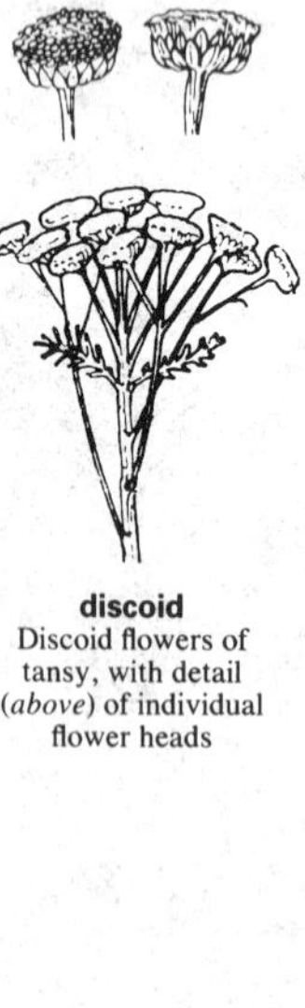

discoid
Discoid flowers of tansy, with detail (*above*) of individual flower heads

discharge lamp *n.* A lamp that generates light by means of an internal electrical discharge.

discharge tube *n.* A closed insulating vessel fitted with electrodes and containing a gas in which an electrical discharge is induced by high applied potentials.

dis·ci·ple (dĭ-sī'pəl) *n.* **1. a.** One who subscribes to the teachings of a master and assists in spreading them. **b.** An active adherent, as of a movement or philosophy. **2.** Often **Disciple.** One of the companions of Christ. **3. Disciple.** A member of the Disciples of Christ. [ME, partly < OE *discipul,* and partly < OFr. *desciple,* both < Lat. *discipulus,* pupil < *discere,* to learn.] —**dis·ci'ple·ship'** *n.*

Disciples of Christ *n.* A Christian denomination, founded in 1809, that accepts the Bible as the only rule of Christian faith and practice, rejects denominational creeds, and practices baptism by immersion.

dis·ci·plin·a·ble (dĭs'ə-plĭn'ə-bəl, dĭs'ə-plĭn'-) *adj.* **1.** Deserving of or subject to discipline. **2.** Responsive to training.

dis·ci·pli·nar·i·an (dĭs'ə-plə-nâr'ē-ən) *n.* A person who enforces or believes in strict discipline. —*adj.* Disciplinary.

dis·ci·pli·nar·y (dĭs'ə-plə-nĕr'ē) *adj.* **1.** Of, pertaining to, or used for discipline. **2.** Of or pertaining to a specific field of academic study. —**dis'ci·pli·nar'i·ly** (-nâr'ə-lē) *adv.*

dis·ci·pline (dĭs'ə-plĭn) *n.* **1.** Training that is expected to produce a specific character or pattern of behavior, esp. training that produces moral or mental improvement. **2.** Controlled behavior resulting from disciplinary training. **3.** A systematic method to obtain obedience: *a military discipline.* **4.** A state of order based upon submission to rules and authority. **5.** Punishment intended to correct or train. **6.** A set of rules or methods, as those regulating the practice of a church or monastic order. **7.** A branch of knowledge or of teaching. —*tr.v.* **-plined, -plin·ing, -plines. 1.** To train by instruction and control. **2.** To punish or penalize. **3.** To impose order upon: *needs to discipline her study habits.* [ME < OFr. *descepline* < Lat. *disciplina* < *discipulus,* pupil < *discere,* to learn.] —**dis'ci·pli·nal** (-plə-nəl) *adj.* —**dis'ci·plin'er** *n.*

disc jockey also **disk jockey** *n.* A radio announcer who presents and comments on popular phonograph records.

dis·claim (dĭs-klām') *v.* **-claimed, -claim·ing, -claims.** —*tr.* **1.** To deny or renounce any claim to or connection with; disown. **2.** To deny the validity of; repudiate. **3.** *Law.* To renounce one's right or claim to. —*intr. Law.* To renounce a right or claim. [ME *disclaimen* < AN *desclaimer* : *des-* (reversal < Lat. *dis-*) + *claimer,* to claim < OFr. *clamer.*]

dis·claim·er (dĭs-klā'mər) *n.* **1.** A repudiation or denial of responsibility or connection. **2.** *Law.* A renunciation of one's right or claim.

dis·cla·ma·tion (dĭs'klə-mā'shən) *n.* Disavowal or renunciation.

dis·cli·max (dĭs-klī'măks') *n.* An ecological community, normally stable under certain climatic conditions, that has been altered by man or other influences.

dis·close (dĭ-sklōz') *tr.v.* **-closed, -clos·ing, -clos·es. 1.** To expose to view, as by removing a cover; uncover. **2.** To make known; divulge. [ME *disclosen* < OFr. *desclore, desclos-* : *des-* (reversal < Lat. *dis-*) + *clore,* to close.] —**dis·clos'er** *n.*

dis·clo·sure (dĭ-sklō'zhər) *n.* **1.** The act or process of disclosing. **2.** Something disclosed; revelation.

dis·co (dĭs'kō') *n., pl.* **-cos. 1.** A nightclub that is usually characterized by showy decor and special lighting effects and that features recorded, electronically amplified music for dancing. **2. a.** Popular dance music characterized by strong repetitive bass rhythms. **b.** A style of dancing done esp. to disco music. —*intr.v.* **-coed, -co·ing, -cos.** To dance to disco music. [Short for DISCOTHEQUE.]

disco– or **disc–** *pref.* **1.** Disk: *discoid.* **2.** Phonograph record: *discophile.* [Lat. < Gk. *disko-* < *diskos,* disk.]

dis·cog·ra·phy (dĭ-skŏg'rə-fē) *n., pl.* **-phies. 1.** The study and cataloguing of phonograph records. **2.** A comprehensive list of the recordings made by a particular performer or of a particular composer's works. [Fr. *discographie* : *disco-,* disco- + *-graphie,* -graphy.] —**dis·cog'ra·pher** *n.*

dis·coid (dĭs'koid') also **dis·coi·dal** (dĭ-skoid'l) *adj.* **1.** Having the shape of a disk. **2.** *Bot.* Having disk flowers but no ray flowers. Used of a composite flower head. —**dis'coid'** *n.*

dis·col·or (dĭs-kŭl'ər) *v.* **-ored, -or·ing, -ors.** —*tr.* To alter or spoil the proper color of; stain. —*intr.* To become altered or spoiled in color. [ME *discolouren* < OFr. *discolerer* < LLat. *discolorare* : *dis-* (reversal) + *colorare,* to color < *color,* color.]

dis·col·or·a·tion (dĭs-kŭl'ə-rā'shən) *n.* **1. a.** The act of discoloring. **b.** The condition of being discolored. **2.** A stain.

dis·com·bob·u·late (dĭs'kəm-bŏb'yə-lāt') *tr.v.* **-lat·ed, -lat·ing, -lates.** *Slang.* To throw into a state of confusion. [Perh. alteration of DISCOMPOSE.] —**dis'com·bob'u·la'tion** *n.*

dis·com·fit (dĭs-kŭm'fĭt) *tr.v.* **-fit·ed, -fit·ing, -fits. 1.** To thwart the plans of; frustrate. **2.** To defeat in battle; vanquish. **3.** To make uneasy or perplexed; disconcert. —*n.* Discomfiture. [ME *discomfiten* < OFr. *disconfit,* p.part. of *desconfire,* to defeat < VLat. **disconficere* : Lat. *dis-* (reversal) + Lat. *conficere,* to prepare. —see COMFIT.]

Usage: *Discomfit* was once used strictly in the sense of "to defeat" or "to frustrate." Now, through confusion with the unrelated word *discomfort,* it has come to mean also "to disconcert, distress, or make uncomfortable." A large majority of the Usage Panel accepts this newer meaning.

dis·com·fi·ture (dĭs-kŭm'fĭ-chŏŏr', -chər) *n.* **1.** Frustration or disappointment. **2.** Defeat. **3.** Lack of ease; discomfort; embarrassment.

dis·com·fort (dĭs-kŭm'fərt) *n.* **1.** Mental or bodily distress. **2.** Something that disturbs one's comfort; annoyance. —*tr.v.* **-fort·ed, -fort·ing, -forts.** To make uncomfortable. —See Usage note at **discomfit.** [ME, distress < OFr. *desconfort*

< *desconforter,* to discourage : *des-* (reversal < Lat. *dis-*) + *conforter,* to strengthen. —see COMFORT.] **—dis·com'fort·a·ble** (-kŭm'fər-tə-bəl, -kŭmf'tə-bəl) *adj.*

dis·com·mend (dĭs'kə-mĕnd') *tr.v.* **-mend·ed, -mend·ing, -mends. 1.** To show or voice disapproval of. **2.** To cause to come into disfavor or ill regard. **—dis'com·mend'a·ble** *adj.*

dis·com·mode (dĭs'kə-mōd') *tr.v.* **-mod·ed, -mod·ing, -modes.** To put to inconvenience; trouble. [Fr. *discommoder* : Lat. *dis-* (reversal) + Fr. *commode,* convenient. —see COMMODE.]

dis·com·pose (dĭs'kəm-pōz') *tr.v.* **-posed, -pos·ing, -pos·es. 1.** To disturb the composure or calm of; perturb. **2.** To put into a state of disorder. **—dis'com·pos'ed·ly** (-pō'zĭd-lē) *adv.* **—dis'com·pos'ing·ly** *adv.*

dis·com·po·sure (dĭs'kəm-pō'zhər) *n.* Absence of composure.

dis·con·cert (dĭs'kən-sûrt') *tr.v.* **-cert·ed, -cert·ing, -certs. 1.** To upset the self-possession of; ruffle. **2.** To frustrate by throwing into disorder. [Obs. Fr. *disconcerter* < OFr. *desconcerter* : *des-* (reversal < Lat. *dis-*) + *concerter,* to bring into agreement < OItal. *concertare.*] **—dis'con·cert'ing·ly** *adv.*

dis·con·form·i·ty (dĭs'kən-fôr'mĭ-tē) *n., pl.* **-ties.** *Geol.* An interruption of sedimentation caused by erosion resulting in the formation of two parallel strata.

dis·con·nect (dĭs'kə-nĕkt') *tr.v.* **-nect·ed, -nect·ing, -nects. 1.** To sever or interrupt the connection of or between: *disconnected the hose.* **2.** *Elect.* To shut off the current in (an appliance) by removing its connection with the power source. **—dis'con·nec'tion** *n.*

dis·con·nect·ed (dĭs'kə-nĕk'tĭd) *adj.* Marked by unrelated parts; incoherent. **—dis'con·nect'ed·ly** *adv.* **—dis'con·nect'ed·ness** *n.*

dis·con·so·late (dĭs-kŏn'sə-lĭt) *adj.* **1.** Beyond consolation; hopelessly sad. **2.** Cheerless or gloomy: *a disconsolate landscape.* [ME < Med. Lat. *disconsolatus* : Lat. *dis-,* not + *consolatus,* p.part. of *consolari,* to console. —see CONSOLE.] **—dis·con'so·late·ly** *adv.* **—dis·con'so·late·ness, dis·con'so·la'tion** (-kŏn'sə-lā'shən) *n.*

dis·con·tent (dĭs'kən-tĕnt') *n.* **1.** Absence of contentment; dissatisfaction. **2.** A sense of resentment and grievance. —*adj.* Discontented. —*tr.v.* **-tent·ed, -tent·ing, -tents.** To make discontented. **—dis'con·tent'ment** *n.*

dis·con·tent·ed (dĭs'kən-tĕn'tĭd) *adj.* Not satisfied; restlessly unhappy. **—dis'con·tent'ed·ly** *adv.* **—dis'con·tent'ed·ness** *n.*

dis·con·tin·u·ance (dĭs'kən-tĭn'yo͞o-əns) *n.* **1.** The act of discontinuing or the condition of being discontinued; cessation. **2.** *Law.* The termination of an action by the plaintiff.

dis·con·tin·u·a·tion (dĭs'kən-tĭn'yo͞o-ā'shən) *n.* Discontinuance; cessation.

dis·con·tin·ue (dĭs'kən-tĭn'yo͞o) *v.* **-ued, -u·ing, -ues.** —*tr.* **1.** To put a stop to; terminate. **2.** To cease trying to accomplish or continue; abandon. **3.** *Law.* To terminate (an action) by discontinuance. —*intr.* To come to an end. [ME *discontinuen* < OFr. *descontinuer* < Med. Lat. *discontinuare* : Lat. *dis-* not + Lat. *continuare,* to continue. —see CONTINUE.]

dis·con·ti·nu·i·ty (dĭs-kŏn'tə-no͞o'ĭ-tē, -nyo͞o') *n., pl.* **-ties. 1.** A lack of continuity, logical sequence, or cohesion. **2.** A break or gap. **3.** *Math.* **a.** The property of being discontinuous. **b.** A point at which a function is defined but is not continuous. **c.** A point at which a function is undefined.

dis·con·tin·u·ous (dĭs'kən-tĭn'yo͞o-əs) *adj.* **1.** Marked by breaks or interruptions: *discontinuous applause.* **2.** *Math.* Possessing one or more discontinuities. **—dis'con·tin'u·ous·ly** *adv.* **—dis'con·tin'u·ous·ness** *n.*

dis·co·phile (dĭs'kə-fīl') *n.* A collector of or specialist in phonograph records.

dis·cord (dĭs'kôrd') *n.* **1. a.** Lack of agreement among persons, groups, or things. **b.** Tension and strife resulting from discord; dissension. **2.** A confused or harsh mingling of sounds. **3.** *Mus.* Inharmonious combination of simultaneously sounded tones; dissonance. —*intr.v.* (dĭ-skôrd', dĭs'kôrd') **-cord·ed, -cord·ing, -cords.** To fail to agree or harmonize; clash. [ME < OFr. *descorde* < Lat. *discordia,* strife < *discors,* disagreeing : *dis-,* apart + *cors,* heart.]

Synonyms: *discord, strife, contention, dissension, conflict, clash, dissonance, variance.* These nouns can all mean a condition marked by disagreement. *Discord* in general implies sharply opposing positions within a group, preventing united action. *Strife* usually implies outright fighting, often a destructive struggle between rivals or factions. *Contention* is largely limited to dispute in the form of heated debate or quarreling. *Dissension* implies rebellious unrest that disrupts unity within a group. *Conflict,* as compared here, suggests antagonism of ideas or interests that results in open hostility or divisiveness. *Clash* suggests sharp conflict involving ideas or interests that are irreconcilable. *Dissonance,* in this context, also stresses harsh disagreement between strongly opposed or incongruous positions. *Variance,* used chiefly in *at variance with,* usually suggests discrepancy or incompatibility between persons or things.

dis·cor·dant (dĭ-skôr'dnt) *adj.* **1.** Not in accord; conflicting. **2.** Disagreeable in sound; harsh or dissonant. **—dis·cor'dance, dis·cor'dan·cy** *n.* **—dis·cor'dant·ly** *adv.*

Dis·cor·di·a (dĭ-skôr'dē-ə) *n. Rom. Myth.* The goddess of strife. [Lat. < *discordia,* discord.]

dis·co·theque also **dis·co·thèque** (dĭs'kə-tĕk', dĭs'kə-tĕk') *n.* A disco. [Fr. : *disco-,* disco- + *(biblio)thèque,* library < Lat. *bibliotheca.* —see BIBLIOTHECA.]

dis·count (dĭs'kount', dĭs-kount') *v.* **-count·ed, -count·ing, -counts.** —*tr.* **1.** To deduct or subtract from a cost or price. **2. a.** To purchase or sell (a bill, note, or other commercial paper) after deducting the amount of interest that will accumulate before it matures. **b.** To loan money on (a commercial paper not immediately payable) after deducting the interest. **3.** To reduce in cost, quantity, or value. **4.** To leave out of account as being untrustworthy or exaggerated; disregard: *discount a rumor.* **5.** To underestimate the significance or effectiveness of. **6.** To anticipate and make allowance for. —*intr.* To lend money after deduction of interest. —*n.* (dĭs'kount'). **1.** A reduction from the full or standard amount of a price or debt. **2.** Discount rate. **3.** The act or an instance of discounting a bill of exchange, note, or other commercial paper. **—*modifier:*** *discount merchandise.* [OFr. *desconter* < Med. Lat. *discomputare* : Lat. *dis-* (reversal) + Lat. *computare,* to compute. —see COMPUTE.] **—dis'count'a·ble** *adj.* **—dis'count'er** *n.*

dis·coun·te·nance (dĭs-koun'tə-nəns) *tr.v.* **-nanced, -nanc·ing, -nanc·es. 1.** To view or treat with disfavor. **2.** To put out of countenance; abash; disconcert. —*n.* Disfavor or disapproval.

discount rate *n.* **1.** The interest deducted in advance in purchasing, selling, or lending a bill, note, or other commercial paper. **2.** The rate of interest deducted in a discount rate transaction.

discount store *n.* A store that sells merchandise, esp. consumer goods, at a discount from the manufacturer's suggested retail price.

dis·cour·age (dĭ-skûr'ĭj, -skŭr'-) *tr.v.* **-aged, -ag·ing, -ag·es. 1.** To deprive of confidence, hope, or spirit. **2.** To dissuade or deter: *wouldn't let past failures discourage him from trying again.* **3.** To hamper; hinder. **4.** To try to prevent by expressing disapproval or raising objections. [ME *discoragen* < OFr. *descoragier* : *des-* (reversal < Lat. *dis-*) + *corage,* courage. —see COURAGE.] **—dis·cour'ag·er** *n.* **—dis·cour'ag·ing·ly** *adv.*

dis·cour·age·ment (dĭ-skûr'ĭj-mənt, -skŭr'-) *n.* **1. a.** The act of discouraging. **b.** The condition of being discouraged. **2.** Something that discourages; deterrent.

dis·course (dĭs'kôrs', -kōrs') *n.* **1.** Verbal expression in speech or writing. **2.** Verbal exchange; conversation. **3.** A formal and lengthy discussion of a subject, either written or spoken. **4.** *Archaic.* The process or power of reasoning. —*v.* (dĭ-skôrs', -skōrs') **-coursed, -cours·ing, -cours·es.** —*intr.* **1.** To speak or write formally and at length. **2.** To engage in conversation or discussion; converse. —*tr. Archaic.* To narrate or discuss. [ME *discours* < LLat. *discursus,* discussion < p.part. of Lat. *discurrere,* to run about, to speak at length : *dis-,* apart + *currere,* to run.] **—dis·cours'er** *n.*

dis·cour·te·ous (dĭs-kûr'tē-əs) *adj.* Lacking courtesy; rude. **—dis·cour'te·ous·ly** *adv.* **—dis·cour'te·ous·ness** *n.*

dis·cour·te·sy (dĭs-kûr'tĭ-sē) *n., pl.* **-sies. 1.** Lack of courtesy; rudeness. **2.** A rude act or statement.

dis·cov·er (dĭ-skŭv'ər) *tr.v.* **-ered, -er·ing, -ers. 1.** To obtain knowledge of through observation, search, or study. **2.** To be the first to find, learn of, or observe. **3.** *Archaic.* To reveal; expose. [ME *discoveren,* to reveal < OFr. *descovrir* < LLat. *discooperire* : Lat. *dis-* (reversal) + *cooperire,* to cover. —see COVER.] **—dis·cov'er·a·ble** *adj.* **—dis·cov'er·er** *n.*

dis·cov·er·y (dĭ-skŭv'ə-rē) *n., pl.* **-ies. 1.** The act or an instance of discovering. **2.** Something that has been discovered. **3.** *Law.* Data or documents that a party to a legal action is compelled to disclose to another party either prior to or during a proceeding.

dis·cred·it (dĭs-krĕd'ĭt) *tr.v.* **-it·ed, -it·ing, -its. 1.** To damage in reputation; disgrace. **2.** To cause to be doubted or distrusted. **3.** To refuse to believe. —*n.* **1.** Loss of or damage to one's reputation. **2.** Lack or loss of trust or belief; doubt. **3.** Something damaging to one's reputation or stature.

dis·cred·it·a·ble (dĭs-krĕd'ĭ-tə-bəl) *adj.* Deserving of or resulting in discredit; blameworthy. **—dis·cred'it·a·bly** *adv.*

dis·creet (dĭ-skrēt') *adj.* **1.** Having or showing a judicious reserve in one's speech or behavior; prudent. **2.** Lacking ostentation or pretension; modest. [ME < OFr. *discret* < Med. Lat. *discretus* < Lat., p.part. of *discernere,* to discern, separate. —see DISCERN.] **—dis·creet'ly** *adv.* **—dis·creet'ness** *n.*

dis·crep·ance (dĭ-skrĕp'əns) *n.* Discrepancy.

dis·crep·an·cy (dĭ-skrĕp'ən-sē) *n., pl.* **-cies. 1.** Divergence or disagreement, as between facts or claims; inconsistency. **2.** An instance of discrepancy.

dis·crep·ant (dĭ-skrĕp'ənt) *adj.* Marked by discrepancy. [ME *discrepaunt* < Lat. *discrepans,* pr.part. of *discrepare,* to disagree : *dis-,* apart + *crepare,* to rattle.] **—dis·crep'ant·ly** *adv.*

dis·crete (dĭ-skrēt') *adj.* **1.** Constituting a separate thing; distinct. **2.** Consisting of unconnected distinct parts. [ME < Lat. *discretus.* —see DISCREET.] **—dis·crete'ly** *adv.* **—dis·crete'ness** *n.*

discrete variable *n.* A mathematical variable that assumes only whole number values.

dis·cre·tion (dĭ-skrĕsh′ən) *n.* **1.** The quality of being discreet; circumspection. **2.** Freedom to act or judge on one's own: *All the decisions were left to her discretion.* **—dis·cre′tion·al** *adj.* **—dis·cre′tion·al·ly** *adv.*

dis·cre·tion·ar·y (dĭ-skrĕsh′ə-nĕr′ē) *adj.* **1.** Left to or regulated by one's own discretion or judgment. **2.** Something that is to be used responsibly as needed: *a discretionary fund.* **—dis·cre′tion·ar′i·ly** (-nâr′ə-lē) *adv.*

discretionary account *n.* A stock or commodity account in which an agent is free to trade for the customer at his own discretion.

dis·cret·i·za·tion (dĭ-skrē′tə-zā′shən) *n.* The act of making mathematically discrete.

dis·crim·i·nate (dĭ-skrĭm′ə-nāt′) *v.* **-nat·ed, -nat·ing, -nates.** *—intr.* **1.** To make a clear distinction; distinguish; differentiate. **2.** To act on the basis of prejudice: *accused of discriminating against women.* *—tr.* **1.** To perceive the distinguishing features of. **2.** To serve to mark; differentiate. [Lat. *discriminare, discriminat-* < *discrimen,* distinction.] **—dis·crim′i·nate·ly** *adv.*

dis·crim·i·nat·ing (dĭ-skrĭm′ə-nā′tĭng) *adj.* **1.** Capable of recognizing or drawing fine distinctions; perceptive. **2.** Fastidiously selective. **3.** Serving to distinguish; distinctive. **4.** Discriminatory. **—dis·crim′i·nat′ing·ly** *adv.*

dis·crim·i·na·tion (dĭ-skrĭm′ə-nā′shən) *n.* **1.** The act of discriminating. **2.** The ability or power to see or make fine distinctions; discernment. **3.** An act based on prejudice.

dis·crim·i·na·tive (dĭ-skrĭm′ə-nā′tĭv, -nə-tĭv) *adj.* **1.** Drawing distinctions. **2.** Discriminatory. **—dis·crim′i·na′tive·ly** *adv.*

dis·crim·i·na·tor (dĭ-skrĭm′ə-nā′tər) *n.* **1.** One that discriminates. **2.** *Electronics.* A device that converts a property of a signal, such as frequency or phase, into an amplitude variation.

dis·crim·i·na·to·ry (dĭ-skrĭm′ə-nə-tôr′ē, -tōr′ē) *adj.* **1.** Marked by or showing prejudice; biased. **2.** Discriminating. **—dis·crim′i·na·to′ri·ly** *adv.*

dis·cur·sive (dĭ-skûr′sĭv) *adj.* **1.** Covering a wide field of subjects; rambling. **2.** Proceeding to a conclusion through reason rather than intuition. [Med. Lat. *discursivus* < Lat. *discursus,* discussion. —see DISCOURSE.] **—dis·cur′sive·ly** *adv.* **—dis·cur′sive·ness** *n.*

discus

dis·cus (dĭs′kəs) *n., pl.* **-cus·es. 1.** A disk, typically wooden with a metal rim and weighing 2 kilograms, about 4 1/2 pounds, thrown for distance in athletic competitions. **2.** A field event in which a discus is thrown. **3.** A small, brilliantly colored South American freshwater fish, *Symphysodon discus,* that has a disk-shaped body and is popular in home aquariums. [Lat. —see DISK.]

dis·cuss (dĭ-skŭs′) *tr.v.* **-cussed, -cuss·ing, -cuss·es. 1.** To speak together about; talk over. **2.** To examine (a subject) in speech or writing. [ME *discussen* < LLat. *discussus,* p.part. of *discutere,* to discuss < Lat., to break up : *dis-,* apart + *quatere,* to shake.] **—dis·cuss′er** *n.* **—dis·cuss′i·ble** *adj.*

Synonyms: *discuss, argue, debate, dispute, contend.* These verbs mean to speak with others in an effort to reach agreement, to ascertain truth, or to convince. *Discuss* involves close examination of a subject with interchange of opinions, and need not imply disagreement. *Argue* emphasizes the presentation of facts and reasons in support of a position opposed by others. *Debate* involves formal and often public argument. *Dispute* implies wide differences of opinion and sharp argument. *Contend* suggests a heated competition of arguments.

dis·cuss·ant (dĭ-skŭs′ənt) *n.* One who participates in a discussion.

dis·cus·sion (dĭ-skŭsh′ən) *n.* **1.** The consideration of a subject by a group; an earnest conversation. **2.** A formal discourse upon a topic; exposition.

dis·dain (dĭs-dān′) *tr.v.* **-dained, -dain·ing, -dains. 1.** To regard or treat with haughty contempt; despise. **2.** To consider or reject as unworthy of oneself. *—n.* A feeling, attitude, or show of contempt and aloofness; scorn. [ME *disdeinen* < OFr. *desdeignier* < Lat. *dedignari* : *de-,* not + *dignari,* to deem worthy < *dignus,* worthy.]

dis·dain·ful (dĭs-dān′fəl) *adj.* Feeling or showing disdain. **—dis·dain′ful·ly** *adv.* **—dis·dain′ful·ness** *n.*

dis·ease (dĭ-zēz′) *n.* **1.** An abnormal condition of an organism or part, esp. as a consequence of infection, inherent weakness, or environmental stress, that impairs normal physiological functioning. **2.** A condition or tendency, as of society, regarded as abnormal and harmful. **3.** *Obs.* Lack of ease. [ME *disese,* misery < OFr. : *des-,* not (< Lat. *dis-*) + *aise,* ease. —see EASE.]

dis·eased (dĭ-zēzd′) *adj.* **1.** Affected with disease. **2.** Unsound or disordered.

dis·em·bark (dĭs′ĕm-bärk′) *intr. & tr.v.* **-barked, -bark·ing, -barks.** To go ashore or cause to go ashore from a ship. **—dis·em′bar·ka′tion** *n.*

dis·em·bar·rass (dĭs′ĕm-băr′əs) *tr.v.* **-rassed, -rass·ing, -rass·es.** To free from something embarrassing, bothersome, or encumbering; relieve. **—dis′em·bar′rass·ment** *n.*

dis·em·bod·y (dĭs′ĕm-bŏd′ē) *tr.v.* **-ied, -y·ing, -ies.** To free (the soul or spirit) from the body. **—dis′em·bod′i·ment** *n.*

dis·em·bogue (dĭs′ĕm-bōg′) *v.* **-bogued, -bogu·ing, -bogues.** *—intr.* To empty its water at the mouth. Used of a river. *—tr.* To discharge (waters) at the mouth. Used of a river. [< Sp. *desembogue,* river mouth < *desembocar,* to flow out : des- (reversal < Lat. *dis-*) + *embocar,* to put into the mouth (*em-,* in + *boca,* mouth < Lat. *bucca,* cheek).] **—dis′em·bogue′ment** *n.*

dis·em·bow·el (dĭs′ĕm-bou′əl) *tr.v.* **-eled, -el·ing, -els** also **-elled, -el·ling, -els. 1.** To remove the entrails from. **2.** To deprive of meaning or substance by cutting or altering. **—dis′em·bow′el·ment** *n.*

dis·en·chant (dĭs′ĕn-chănt′) *tr.v.* **-chant·ed, -chant·ing, -chants.** To free from illusion or false belief; undeceive. **—dis′en·chant′er** *n.* **—dis′en·chant′ment** *n.*

dis·en·cum·ber (dĭs′ĕn-kŭm′bər) *tr.v.* **-bered, -ber·ing, -bers.** To relieve of burdens or hardships. **—dis′en·cum′ber·ment** *n.*

dis·en·fran·chise (dĭs′ĕn-frăn′chīz′) *tr.v.* **-chised, -chis·ing, -chis·es.** To disfranchise. **—dis′en·fran′chise′ment** (-chīz′mənt, -chĭz-) *n.*

dis·en·gage (dĭs′ĕn-gāj′) *v.* **-gaged, -gag·ing, -gag·es.** *—tr.* **1.** To release from something that holds fast, connects, or entangles. **2.** To release (oneself) from an engagement, pledge, or obligation. *—intr.* To free or detach oneself. **—dis′en·gage′ment** *n.*

dis·en·tail (dĭs′ĕn-tāl′) *tr.v.* **-tailed, -tail·ing, -tails.** *Law.* To release (an estate) from entail. **—dis′en·tail′ment** *n.*

dis·en·tan·gle (dĭs′ĕn-tăng′gəl) *v.* **-gled, -gling, -gles.** *—tr.* **1.** To extricate from entanglement or involvement; free. **2.** To clear up or resolve (a plot, for example); unravel. *—intr.* To become free of entanglement. **—dis′en·tan′gle·ment** *n.*

dis·en·tomb (dĭs′ĕn-to͞om′) *tr.v.* **-tombed, -tomb·ing, -tombs.** To remove from or as if from a tomb.

dis·en·twine (dĭs′ĕn-twīn′) *tr. & intr.v.* **-twined, -twin·ing, -twines.** To untwine or become untwined.

dis·e·qui·lib·ri·um (dĭs-ē′kwə-lĭb′rē-əm, -ĕk′wə-) *n.* Loss or lack of equilibrium or stability.

dis·es·tab·lish (dĭs′ĭ-stăb′lĭsh) *tr.v.* **-lished, -lish·ing, -lish·es. 1.** To alter the status of (something established by authority or general acceptance). **2.** To deprive (a church) of official governmental support. **—dis′es·tab′lish·ment** *n.*

dis·es·teem (dĭs′ĭ-stēm′) *tr.v.* **-teemed, -teem·ing, -teems.** To hold in disfavor. *—n.* Lack of esteem.

dis·fa·vor (dĭs-fā′vər) *n.* **1.** Unfavorable opinion or regard; disapproval. **2.** The condition of being regarded with disapproval. *—tr.v.* **-vored, -vor·ing, -vors.** To view or treat with dislike or disapproval.

dis·fea·ture (dĭs-fē′chər) *tr.v.* **-tured, -tur·ing, -tures.** To spoil the features of; disfigure. **—dis·fea′ture·ment** *n.*

dis·fig·ure (dĭs-fĭg′yər) *tr.v.* **-ured, -ur·ing, -ures.** To blemish or spoil the appearance or shape of; deform. [ME *disfiguren* < OFr. *desfigurer* < VLat. **disfigurare* : Lat. *dis-,* apart + Lat. *figura,* figure < *fingere,* to form.] **—dis·fig′u·ra′tion, dis·fig′ure·ment** *n.* **—dis·fig′ur·er** *n.*

dis·fran·chise (dĭs-frăn′chīz′) *tr.v.* **-chised, -chis·ing, -chis·es. 1.** To deprive (an individual) of a right of citizenship, esp. of the right to vote. **2.** To deprive (a corporation, for example) of a privilege or franchise. **—dis·fran′chise′ment** (-chīz′mənt, -chĭz-) *n.* **—dis·fran′chis′er** *n.*

dis·frock (dĭs-frŏk′) *tr.v.* **-frocked, -frock·ing, -frocks.** To unfrock.

dis·gorge (dĭs-gôrj′) *v.* **-gorged, -gorg·ing, -gorg·es.** *—tr.* **1.** To bring up and expel from the throat or stomach; vomit. **2.** To discharge violently; spew. *—intr.* To discharge or pour forth contents. **—dis·gorge′ment** *n.*

dis·grace (dĭs-grās′) *n.* **1.** Loss of honor, respect, or reputation; shame. **2.** The condition of being strongly and generally disapproved. **3.** Something that brings disfavor. *—tr.v.* **-graced, -grac·ing, -grac·es. 1.** To bring shame or dishonor upon: *disgraced the firm's reputation.* **2.** To put (someone) out of grace or favor. [Fr. *disgrâce* < Ital. *disgrazia* : *dis-,* not (< Lat. *dis-*) + *grazia,* favor < Lat. *gratia* < *gratus,* pleasing.] **—dis·grac′er** *n.*

Synonyms: *disgrace, dishonor, shame, infamy, ignominy, odium, scandal, obloquy, opprobrium, disrepute, discredit, degradation.* These nouns refer to the condition of being held in low regard. In current usage *disgrace* implies strong disfavor or ostracism. *Dishonor* implies loss of esteem or respect or loss of a good reputation. *Shame* suggests loss of status as a result of a moral offense. *Infamy* is public disgrace or notoriety. *Ignominy* often implies public contempt. *Odium* adds to disgrace the sense of being widely detested. *Scandal* in this comparison suggests open public disapproval in response to improper conduct. *Obloquy* implies being subjected to abuse and vilification. *Opprobrium* is the condition of being condemned with scorn. *Disrepute* involves lack of or loss of a good name but is weaker than dishonor in suggesting descent from previous high regard. *Discredit* implies doubt or distrust and applies to loss of professional status more often than to loss of esteem resulting from personal misconduct. *Degradation* involves reduction to a rank so low that it demoralizes or at least incurs extreme humiliation and contempt.

dis·grace·ful (dĭs-grās′fəl) *adj.* Bringing or warranting disgrace. **—dis·grace′ful·ly** *adv.* **—dis·grace′ful·ness** *n.*

dis·grun·tle (dĭs-grŭn′tl) *tr.v.* **-tled, -tling, -tles.** To make discontented or cross. [DIS- + dial. *gruntle,* to grumble < ME *grunilen,* freq. of *grunten,* to grunt.] **—dis·grun'tle·ment** *n.*

dis·guise (dĭs-gīz') *tr.v.* **-guised, -guis·ing, -guis·es. 1. a.** To modify the manner or appearance of in order to prevent recognition. **b.** To furnish with a disguise. **2.** To conceal or obscure by dissemblance or false show; misrepresent: *disguise one's true intentions.* —*n.* **1. a.** The act of disguising. **b.** The condition of being disguised. **2.** Clothes or accessories worn to conceal one's true identity. **3.** A pretense that conceals the truth. [ME *disguisen* < OFr. *disguiser* : *des-* (reversal < Lat. *dis-*) + *guise,* manner, of Germanic orig.] **—dis·guis'er** *n.*

dis·gust (dĭs-gŭst') *tr.v.* **-gust·ed, -gust·ing, -gusts. 1.** To excite nausea or loathing in; sicken. **2.** To offend the taste or moral sense of; repel. —*n.* Profound aversion or repugnance excited by something offensive. [OFr. *desgouster* : *des-,* not (< Lat. *dis-*) + *goust,* taste < Lat. *gustus.*]

dis·gust·ed (dĭs-gŭs'tĭd) *adj.* Filled with disgust or irritated impatience. **—dis·gust'ed·ly** *adv.*

dis·gust·ful (dĭs-gŭst'fəl) *adj.* **1.** Causing disgust; repugnant. **2.** Full of or marked by disgust. **—dis·gust'ful·ly** *adv.*

dis·gust·ing (dĭs-gŭs'tĭng) *adj.* Acutely repugnant; loathsome; repellent. **—dis·gust'ing·ly** *adv.*

dish (dĭsh) *n.* **1. a.** An open container, generally shallow and concave, for holding or serving food. **b.** The amount a dish holds. **2. a.** The food served or contained in a dish. **b.** A particular variety or preparation of food. **3. a.** A concavity or depression like that in a dish. **b.** The degree of such a concavity. **4.** A microwave transmitter or receiver consisting of a concave parabolic reflector. **5.** *Informal.* Something one particularly likes or excels in: *Golf is not my dish.* **6.** *Slang.* A good-looking person, esp. a woman. —*tr.v.* **dished, dish·ing, dish·es. 1.** To serve (food) in or as if in a dish. **2.** To hollow out; make concave: *dished out a depression in the sand.* **3.** *Chiefly Brit. Slang.* To foil; cheat; ruin. ***—phrasal verb.* dish out.** *Informal.* To give out; dispense: *dish out advice.* [ME < OE *disc,* plate < Lat. *discus,* quoit. —see DISK.]

dis·ha·bille (dĭs'ə-bēl', -bē') also **des·ha·bille** (dĕs'-) *n.* **1.** The state of being partially or very casually dressed; a state of undress. **2.** Casual or lounging attire. [Fr. *déshabillé* < p.part. of *déshabiller,* to undress : *des-* (reversal < Lat. *dis-*) + *habiller,* to clothe. —see HABILIMENT.]

dis·har·mo·ny (dĭs-här'mə-nē) *n.* Lack of harmony; discord. **—dis'har·mo'ni·ous** (-mō'nē-əs) *adj.*

dish·cloth (dĭsh'klôth', -klŏth') *n.* A cloth or rag used for washing dishes.

dishcloth gourd *n.* Loofa (sense 1).

dis·heart·en (dĭs-här'tn) *tr.v.* **-ened, -en·ing, -ens.** To shake or destroy the courage or resolution of; dispirit. **—dis·heart'en·ing·ly** *adv.* **—dis·heart'en·ment** *n.*

dished (dĭsht) *adj.* Slanting toward one another at the bottom. Used of a pair of wheels.

di·shev·el (dĭ-shĕv'əl) *tr.v.* **-eled, -el·ing, -els** also **-elled, -el·ling, -els. 1.** To loosen and let fall (hair or clothing) in disarray. **2.** To disarrange the hair or clothing of (a person). [Back-formation < DISHEVELED.] **—di·shev'el·ment** *n.*

di·shev·eled also **di·shev·elled** (dĭ-shĕv'əld) *adj.* **1.** Hanging in loose disarray; unkempt, as hair. **2.** Disordered or untidy. [ME *discheveled* < OFr. *deschevele,* p.part. of *descheveler,* to disarrange the hair : *des-,* apart (< Lat. *dis-*) + *chevel,* hair < Lat. *capillus.*]

dis·hon·est (dĭs-ŏn'ĭst) *adj.* **1.** Disposed to lie, cheat, defraud, or deceive. **2.** Arising from, gained by, or showing falseness or improbity. [ME *dishoneste* < OFr. *deshoneste* : *des-,* not (< Lat. *dis-*) + *honeste,* honest. —see HONEST.] **—dis·hon'est·ly** *adv.*

Synonyms: *dishonest, lying, untruthful, deceitful, mendacious, tricky, shady, underhand.* These adjectives mean lacking honesty or truthfulness. *Dishonest* is the least specific. *Lying,* applicable principally to persons, conveys a blunt accusation of untruth. *Untruthful* is a softer but closely related term applied to persons and even more to their statements. *Deceitful* implies misleading by falsehood or by concealment of truth. *Mendacious* suggests chronic inclination toward untruth. *Tricky* implies the use of cunning to fool a person. *Shady* suggests impropriety or illegality. *Underhand* is associated with unfairness and secrecy.

dis·hon·es·ty (dĭs-ŏn'ĭ-stē) *n., pl.* **-ties. 1.** Lack of integrity; improbity. **2.** A dishonest act or statement.

dis·hon·or (dĭs-ŏn'ər) *n.* **1.** Loss of honor, respect, or reputation. **2.** The condition of having lost honor, respect, or reputation. **3.** Something that causes loss of honor. **4.** Failure to pay a note, bill, or other commercial obligation. —*tr.v.* **-ored, -or·ing, -ors. 1.** To bring shame or disgrace upon. **2.** To treat in a disrespectful or demeaning manner. **3.** To fail to pay (a note, for example). [ME *dishonour* < OFr. *deshonor* < VLat. **dishonor* : Lat. *dis-,* not + Lat. *honor,* honor.] **—dis·hon'or·er** *n.*

dis·hon·or·a·ble (dĭs-ŏn'ər-ə-bəl) *adj.* **1.** Characterized by or causing dishonor or discredit. **2.** Lacking integrity; unprincipled. **—dis·hon'or·a·ble·ness** *n.* **—dis·hon'or·a·bly** *adv.*

dish·pan (dĭsh'păn') *n.* A basin or tub in which to wash dishes.

dish·rag (dĭsh'răg') *n.* A dishcloth.

dish·tow·el (dĭsh'tou'əl) *n.* A towel for drying dishes.

dish·ware (dĭsh'wâr') *n.* Dishes, as of china, used in serving food.

dish·wash·er (dĭsh'wŏsh'ər, -wô'shər) *n.* **1.** A person who washes dishes, esp. one hired to wash dishes in a restaurant. **2.** A machine that washes dishes.

dish·wa·ter (dĭsh'wô'tər, -wŏt'ər) *n.* Water in which dishes are or have been washed.

dish·y (dĭsh'ē) *adj.* **-i·er, -i·est.** *Chiefly Brit. Slang.* Good-looking; attractive.

dis·il·lu·sion (dĭs'ĭ-lo͞o'zhən) *tr.v.* **-sioned, -sion·ing, -sions.** To free or deprive of illusion. —*n.* **1.** The act of disenchanting. **2.** The condition or fact of being disenchanted. **—dis'il·lu'sion·ment** *n.* **—dis'il·lu'sive** (-sĭv, -zĭv) *adj.*

dis·in·cen·tive (dĭs'ĭn-sĕn'tĭv) *n.* A deterrent.

dis·in·cli·na·tion (dĭs-ĭn'klə-nā'shən) *n.* Lack of willingness or disposition; reluctance; aversion.

dis·in·cline (dĭs'ĭn-klīn') *v.* **-clined, -clin·ing, -clines.** —*tr.* To make reluctant or averse. —*intr.* To be reluctant or averse.

dis·in·clined (dĭs'ĭn-klīnd') *adj.* Unwilling or reluctant.

dis·in·fect (dĭs'ĭn-fĕkt') *tr.v.* **-fect·ed, -fect·ing, -fects.** To cleanse of harmful microorganisms. **—dis'in·fec'tion** *n.*

dis·in·fec·tant (dĭs'ĭn-fĕk'tənt) *n.* An agent that disinfects by destroying, neutralizing, or inhibiting the growth of harmful microorganisms. —*adj.* Serving to disinfect.

dis·in·fest (dĭs'ĭn-fĕst') *tr.v.* **-fest·ed, -fest·ing, -fests.** To rid of vermin. **—dis·in'fes·ta'tion** (-fĕ-stā'shən) *n.*

dis·in·fla·tion (dĭs'ĭn-flā'shən) *n.* The downward movement of inflated prices to a more normal level. **—dis'in·fla'tion·ar'y** (-shə-nĕr'ē) *adj.*

dis·in·for·ma·tion (dĭs-ĭn'fər-mā'shən) *n.* Incorrect and deliberately misleading information leaked esp. by an intelligence agency as a means of negating and discrediting authentic information that an enemy has obtained.

dis·in·gen·u·ous (dĭs'ĭn-jĕn'yo͞o-əs) *adj.* Not straightforward; crafty. **—dis'in·gen'u·ous·ly** *adv.* **—dis'in·gen'u·ous·ness** *n.*

dis·in·her·it (dĭs'ĭn-hĕr'ĭt) *tr.v.* **-it·ed, -it·ing, -its. 1.** To exclude from inheritance or the right to inherit. **2.** To deprive of a natural or established right or privilege. **—dis'in·her'i·tance** *n.*

dis·in·te·grate (dĭs-ĭn'tĭ-grāt') *v.* **-grat·ed, -grat·ing, -grates.** —*intr.* **1.** To separate into components; fragment. **2.** To decay or undergo a transformation, as an atomic nucleus. —*tr.* To cause (a body) to separate into components; destroy. **—dis·in'te·gra'tive** *adj.* **—dis·in'te·gra'tor** *n.*

dis·in·te·gra·tion (dĭs-ĭn'tĭ-grā'shən) *n.* **1.** The process of disintegrating or the state of being disintegrated. **2.** *Physics.* The natural or induced transformation of an atomic nucleus from a more massive to a less massive configuration by the emission of radiation, an electron, or a nuclear fragment.

dis·in·ter (dĭs'ĭn-tûr') *tr.v.* **-terred, -ter·ring, -ters. 1.** To dig up or remove from a grave or tomb; exhume. **2.** To remove from obscurity; expose. **—dis'in·ter'ment** *n.*

dis·in·ter·est (dĭs-ĭn'tər-ĭst, -ĭn'trĭst) *n.* **1.** Freedom from selfish bias or self-interest; impartiality. **2.** Lack of interest; indifference.

dis·in·ter·est·ed (dĭs-ĭn'trĭ-stĭd, -ĭn'tə-rĕs'tĭd) *adj.* **1.** Free of bias and self-interest; impartial: *disinterested criticism.* **2.** Uninterested; indifferent: "*supremely disinterested in all efforts to find a peaceful solution*" (C.L. Sulzberger). **—dis·in'ter·est·ed·ly** *adv.* **—dis·in'ter·est·ed·ness** *n.*

Usage: According to the traditional rule, a *disinterested* party is one who has no stake in a dispute and is therefore presumed to be impartial. One is *uninterested* in something, by contrast, when one is indifferent to it. A majority of the Usage Panel insists that *disinterested* should not be used for *uninterested,* despite an increasing tendency to use the two words interchangeably.

dis·in·ter·me·di·a·tion (dĭs-ĭn'tər-mē'dē-ā'shən) *n.* The process whereby savers by-pass banks and savings and loan associations and lend their money directly to borrowers, as the government or industry.

dis·in·tox·i·cate (dĭs'ĭn-tŏk'sĭ-kāt') *tr.v.* **-cat·ed, -cat·ing, -cates.** To free from the effects of intoxication or from dependence on intoxicating agents. **—dis'in·tox'i·ca'tion** *n.*

dis·in·vest·ment (dĭs'ĭn-vĕst'mənt) *n.* Diminution or consumption of capital investment.

dis·join (dĭs-join') *v.* **-joined, -join·ing, -joins.** —*tr.* To undo the joining of; separate. —*intr.* To become disconnected. [ME *disjoinen* < OFr. *desjoindre* < Lat. *disjungere* : *dis-* (reversal) + *jungere,* to join.]

dis·joint (dĭs-joint') *v.* **-joint·ed, -joint·ing, -joints.** —*tr.* **1.** To put out of joint; dislocate. **2.** To take apart at the joints. **3.** To destroy the coherence or connections of. **4.** To separate; disjoin. —*intr.* **1.** To come apart at the joints. **2.** To become dislocated. —*adj.* *Math.* Having no elements in common. [ME *disjointen,* to destroy < OFr. *desjoint,* p.part. of *desjoindre,* to disjoin.]

dis·joint·ed (dĭs-join'tĭd) *adj.* **1.** Separated at the joints. **2.** Out of joint; dislocated. **3.** Lacking order or coherence: *disjointed sentences.* **—dis·joint'ed·ly** *adv.* **—dis·joint'ed·ness** *n.*

dis·junct (dĭs-jŭngkt') *adj.* **1.** Characterized by separation. **2.** *Mus.* Pertaining to progression by intervals larger than major seconds. **3.** *Zool.* Having the head, thorax, and abdo-

dish
A 17th-century German marriage plate

men separated by deep constrictions. Used of insects. [ME *disjuncte* < Lat. *disjunctus,* p.part. of *disjungere,* to disjoin.]
dis·junc·tion (dĭs-jŭngk′shən) *n.* **1.** The act of disjoining or the condition of being disjointed. **2.** *Logic.* A proposition that presents two or more alternative terms, with the assertion that only one is true.
dis·junc·tive (dĭs-jŭngk′tĭv) *adj.* **1.** Serving to separate or divide. **2.** *Gram.* Serving to establish a relationship of contrast or opposition. The conjunction *but* in the phrase *poor but comfortable* is disjunctive. **3.** *Logic.* **a.** Of a proposition that presents two or more alternative terms. **b.** Of a syllogism that contains a disjunction as one premise. —*n. Gram.* A disjunctive conjunction. **—dis·junc′tively** *adv.*
dis·junc·ture (dĭs-jŭngk′chər) *n.* Disjunction.
disk also **disc** (dĭsk) *n.* **1.** A thin, flat, circular plate. **2.** Something resembling a disk, such as an astronomical body or an anatomical structure. **3.** *Bot.* The enlarged receptacle containing numerous tiny flowers in the flower head of many composite plants, such as the daisy and the coneflower. **4.** Variant of **disc** (sense 1). **5.** *Computer Sci.* A round flat plate coated with a magnetic substance on which data may be stored. **6.** A circular grid in a phototype setting machine. —*tr.v.* **disked, disk·ing, disks** also **disced, disc·ing, discs.** To work (soil) with a disk harrow. [Lat. *discus,* quoit < Gk. *diskos* < *dikein,* to throw.]
disk brake *n.* Variant of **disc brake.**
disk·ette (dĭ-skĕt′) *n.* A floppy disk.
disk flower *n.* Any of the tiny tubular flowers forming the center of the flower head of certain composite plants, such as the daisy.
disk harrow *n.* A harrow equipped with a series of disks set on edge or at an angle on one or more axles.
disk jockey *n.* Variant of **disc jockey.**
disk pack *n.* A computer storage device consisting of several magnetic disks that can be used and stored as a unit.
dis·like (dĭs-līk′) *tr.v.* **-liked, -lik·ing, -likes.** To regard with distaste or aversion. —*n.* An attitude or feeling of distaste or aversion; antipathy.
dis·lo·cate (dĭs′lō-kāt′, dĭs-lō′kāt′) *tr.v.* **-cat·ed, -cat·ing, -cates. 1.** To put out from the usual or proper relationship with contiguous parts. **2.** *Pathol.* To displace (a limb or organ) from the normal position, esp. to displace (a bone) from the socket or joint. **3.** To throw into confusion or disorder; disrupt. [ME *dislocare, dislocat-* : Lat. *dis-* (reversal) + Lat. *locare,* to place < *locus,* place.] **—dis′lo·ca′tion** *n.*
dis·lodge (dĭs-lŏj′) *v.* **-lodged, -lodg·ing, -lodg·es.** —*tr.* To remove or force out from a position or dwelling previously occupied. —*intr.* To move or go from a dwelling or former position. [ME *disloggen* < OFr. *deslogier* : *des-* (reversal < Lat. *dis-*) + *logier,* to lodge < *loge,* shed, of Germanic orig.] **—dis·lodge′ment, dis·lodg′ment** *n.*
dis·loy·al (dĭs-loi′əl) *adj.* Not true to duty or obligation. **—dis·loy′al·ly** *adv.*
dis·loy·al·ty (dĭs-loi′əl-tē) *n., pl.* **-ties. 1.** The quality of being disloyal; faithlessness. **2.** A disloyal act.
dis·mal (dĭz′məl) *adj.* **1.** Causing gloom or depression; dreary: *dismal weather.* **2.** Characterized by lack of hope. **3.** Causing dread or dismay; dire: *"We beheld the dismal spectacle, the whole city in dreadful flames"* (John Evelyn). **4.** Without substance or interest: *a dismal book.* [< ME, unlucky days < OFr. *dis mal* < Med. Lat. *dies mali* : Lat. *dies,* day + Lat. *malus,* evil.] **—dis′mal·ly** *adv.* **—dis′mal·ness** *n.*
dis·man·tle (dĭs-măn′tl) *tr.v.* **-tled, -tling, -tles. 1.** To strip of furnishings or equipment. **2. a.** To take apart; tear down. **b.** To put an end to in a gradual systematic way. **3.** To strip of clothing or covering. [OFr. *desmanteler* : *des-,* apart (< Lat. *dis-*) + *mantel,* cloak. —see MANTLE.] **—dis·man′tle·ment** *n.*
dis·mast (dĭs-măst′) *tr.v.* **-mast·ed, -mast·ing, -masts.** *Naut.* To remove or break off the mast of.
dis·may (dĭs-mā′) *tr.v.* **-mayed, -may·ing, -mays. 1.** To fill with dread or apprehension. **2.** To discourage or trouble greatly; dishearten. —*n.* A sudden or complete loss of courage or confidence in the face of trouble or danger. [ME *dismaien* : *dis-,* dis- + OFr. *esmaier,* to frighten, of Germanic orig.] **—dis·may′ing·ly** *adv.*

Synonyms: *dismay, appall, daunt, horrify, intimidate, cow.* These verbs mean to fill a person with fear. Usually they imply reducing him to inaction. *Dismay* can mean as little as to frighten or dishearten or as much as to overwhelm. *Appall* implies a sense of helplessness caused by an awareness of an enormity or a difficulty. *Daunt* suggests subduing by removing the courage necessary for action. *Horrify,* the strongest term, implies literally causing dread or revulsion; in a weaker sense it means to shock by some impropriety. *Intimidate* involves making a person fearful as a means of bringing about his submission or discouraging him from action. *Cow* stresses the breaking down of all resistance in another by a show of force.

dis·mem·ber (dĭs-mĕm′bər) *tr.v.* **-bered, -ber·ing, -bers. 1.** To cut, tear, or pull off the limbs of. **2.** To divide into pieces. [ME *dismembren* < OFr. *desmembrer* < VLat. **dismembrare* : Lat. *dis-,* apart + Lat. *membrum,* limb.] **—dis·mem′ber·ment** *n.*
dis·miss (dĭs-mĭs′) *tr.v.* **-missed, -miss·ing, -miss·es. 1.** To discharge, as from employment. **2.** To direct or allow to leave: *dismiss troops.* **3.** To rid one's mind of; dispel. **4.** To refuse to accept or recognize; repudiate: *"unanimous in dismissing the claim as highly improbable"* (Richard Aldington). **5.** To discontinue consideration of; drop. **6.** *Law.* To put (a claim or action) out of court without further hearing. [ME *dismissen* < Med. Lat. *dismissus,* p.part. of *dismittere,* alteration of Lat. *dimittere* : *dis-,* apart + *mittere,* to send.] **—dis·miss′i·ble** *adj.*
dis·miss·al (dĭs-mĭs′əl) *n.* **1. a.** The act of dismissing. **b.** The condition of being dismissed. **2.** An order or notice of discharge.
dis·mis·sion (dĭs-mĭsh′ən) *n.* Dismissal.
dis·mount (dĭs-mount′) *v.* **-mount·ed, -mount·ing, -mounts.** —*intr.* To get off or down, as from a horse or bicycle; alight. —*tr.* **1.** To remove from a support, setting, or mounting. **2.** To unseat, as from a horse. **3.** To take apart (a mechanism); disassemble. —*n.* (dĭs′mount′). The act or manner of dismounting esp. from a horse. **—dis·mount′a·ble** *adj.*
dis·o·be·di·ence (dĭs′ə-bē′dē-əns) *n.* Refusal or failure to obey. **—dis′o·be′di·ent** *adj.* **—dis′o·be′di·ent·ly** *adv.*
dis·o·bey (dĭs′ə-bā′) *v.* **-beyed, -bey·ing, -beys.** —*intr.* To refuse or fail to follow an order or rule. —*tr.* To refuse or fail to obey. [ME *disobeien* < OFr. *desobeir* < VLat. **disobedire* : Lat. *dis-,* not + Lat. *oboedire,* to obey. —see OBEY.] **—dis′o·bey′er** *n.*
dis·o·blige (dĭs′ə-blīj′) *tr.v.* **-bliged, -blig·ing, -blig·es. 1.** To refuse or neglect to act in accord with the wishes of. **2.** To slight; offend. **3.** To inconvenience. **—dis′o·blig′ing·ly** *adv.*
dis·or·der (dĭs-ôr′dər) *n.* **1.** A lack of order or regular arrangement; confusion. **2.** A breach of civic order or peace; public disturbance. **3.** An ailment that affects the function of mind or body. —*tr.v.* **-dered, -der·ing, -ders. 1.** To throw into disorder. **2.** To disturb the normal physical or mental health of; derange.
dis·or·dered (dĭs-ôr′dərd) *adj.* **1.** In a condition of disorder; disarranged. **2.** Physically or mentally ill; deranged. **—dis·or′dered·ly** *adv.* **—dis·or′dered·ness** *n.*
dis·or·der·ly (dĭs-ôr′dər-lē) *adj.* **1.** Lacking regular or logical order or arrangement. **2.** Undisciplined or unruly. **3.** *Law.* Disturbing the public peace or decorum. **—dis·or′der·li·ness** *n.*
disorderly conduct *n. Law.* A petty offense involving a disturbance of public peace and decorum.
dis·or·gan·ize (dĭs-ôr′gə-nīz′) *tr.v.* **-ized, -iz·ing, -iz·es.** To destroy the organization, systematic arrangement, or unity of. **—dis·or′gan·i·za′tion** *n.*
dis·o·ri·ent (dĭs-ôr′ē-ĕnt′, -ōr′-) *tr.v.* **-ent·ed, -ent·ing, -ents.** To cause to lose one's sense of direction, position, or relationship with one's surroundings. **—dis·o′ri·en·ta′tion** *n.*
dis·own (dĭs-ōn′) *tr.v.* **-owned, -own·ing, -owns.** To refuse to acknowledge or accept as one's own; repudiate.
dis·par·age (dĭ-spăr′ĭj) *tr.v.* **-aged, -ag·ing, -ag·es. 1.** To speak of as unimportant or small; belittle. **2.** To reduce in esteem or rank. [ME *disparagen,* to degrade < OFr. *desparager* : *des-,* apart (< Lat. *dis-*) + *parage,* rank < *per,* peer. —see PEER[2].] **—dis·par′age·ment** *n.* **—dis·par′ag·er** *n.* **—dis·par′ag·ing·ly** *adv.*
dis·pa·rate (dĭs′pər-ĭt, dĭ-spăr′ĭt) *adj.* Completely distinct or different in kind; entirely dissimilar. [Lat. *disparatus,* p.part. of *disparare,* to separate : *dis-,* apart + *parare,* to prepare.] **—dis′pa·rate·ly** *adv.* **—dis′pa·rate·ness** *n.*
dis·par·i·ty (dĭ-spăr′ĭ-tē) *n., pl.* **-ties. 1.** The condition or fact of being unequal in age, rank, or degree; difference. **2.** Unlikeness or incongruity. [OFr. *disparite* < LLat. *disparitas* : Lat. *dis-,* not + Lat. *paritas,* equality < *par,* equal.]
dis·pas·sion (dĭs-păsh′ən) *n.* Freedom from passion, bias, or emotion; objectivity.
dis·pas·sion·ate (dĭs-păsh′ə-nĭt) *adj.* Devoid of or unaffected by passion, emotion, or bias: *a dispassionate judgment.* **—dis·pas′sion·ate·ly** *adv.* **—dis·pas′sion·ate·ness** *n.*
dis·patch also **des·patch** (dĭ-spăch′) *tr.v.* **-patched, -patch·ing, -patch·es. 1.** To send off to a specific destination or on specific business. **2.** To complete or dispose of promptly. **3.** To put to death summarily. —*n.* **1.** The act of dispatching or sending off. **2.** The act of putting to death. **3.** Speed in performance or movement. **4.** A written message, particularly an official communication, sent with speed. **5.** A news item sent to a news organization, as by a correspondent. [Sp. *despachar* or Ital. *dispacciare,* both < OFr. *despeechier,* to set free : *des-,* apart (< Lat. *dis-*) + *(em)peechier,* to hinder < LLat. *impedicare,* to entangle (Lat. *in-,* in + Lat. *pedica,* shackle).]
dis·patch·er (dĭs-păch′ər) *n.* **1.** One that dispatches. **2.** A person who sends out trains, buses, trucks, or cars according to a schedule. **3.** *Computer Sci.* A routine that controls the order in which input and output devices obtain access to the processing system.
dis·pel (dĭ-spĕl′) *v.* **-pelled, -pel·ling, -pels.** —*tr.* **1.** To rid one's mind of: *managed to dispel her doubts.* **2.** To cause to separate and go in various directions; scatter. —*intr.* To disappear by or as if by rising; lift. [ME *dispellen* < Lat. *dispellere* : *dis-,* apart + *pellere,* to drive.]
dis·pen·sa·ble (dĭ-spĕn′sə-bəl) *adj.* Capable of being dispensed with. **—dis·pen′sa·bil′i·ty, dis·pen′sa·ble·ness** *n.*
dis·pen·sa·ry (dĭ-spĕn′sə-rē) *n., pl.* **-ries. 1.** An office in a hospital, school, or other institution from which medical

supplies and preparations are dispensed. **2.** A public institution that dispenses medicines or medical aid.

dis·pen·sa·tion (dĭs′pən-sā′shən, -pĕn-) *n.* **1.** The act of dispensing. **2.** Something that is dispensed or given out. **3.** A specific arrangement or system by which something is dispensed or administered. **4.** An exemption or release from an obligation or rule, granted by or as if by an authority. **5. a.** An exemption from a church law, a vow, or other similar obligation granted in a particular case by an ecclesiastical authority. **b.** The document containing this exemption. **6.** *Theol.* **a.** The divine ordering of worldly affairs. **b.** A religious system or code of commands considered to have been divinely revealed or appointed: *the Moslem dispensation.* **—dis′pen·sa′tion·al** *adj.*

dis·pen·sa·to·ry (dĭ-spĕn′sə-tôr′ē, -tōr′ē) *n., pl.* **-ries. 1.** A book in which the preparation, uses, and contents of medicines are described; pharmacopoeia. **2.** *Archaic.* A dispensary.

dis·pense (dĭ-spĕns′) *v.* **-pensed, -pens·ing, -pens·es.** *—tr.* **1.** To deal out or distribute in parts or portions. **2.** To prepare and give out (medicines). **3.** To administer (laws, for example). **4.** To exempt or release, as from a duty or religious obligation. *—intr.* To grant dispensation or exemption. ***—phrasal verb.* dispense with. 1.** To manage without; forgo. **2.** To dispose of. [ME *dispensen* < Med. Lat. *dispensare,* to exempt < Lat., to distribute, freq. of *dispendere,* to weigh out : *dis-,* apart + *pendere,* to weigh.]

dis·pens·er (dĭ-spĕn′sər) *n.* One that dispenses or gives out, esp. a machine or container that allows the contents to be taken out and used in convenient or prescribed amounts.

dis·peo·ple (dĭs-pē′pəl) *tr.v.* **-pled, -pling, -ples.** To depopulate.

dis·per·sal (dĭ-spûr′səl) *n.* The act or process of dispersing or the condition of being dispersed; distribution.

dis·perse (dĭ-spûrs′) *v.* **-persed, -pers·ing, -pers·es.** *—tr.* **1.** To break up and scatter in various directions: *police dispersed the crowd.* **2.** To cause to vanish or disappear; dispel. **3.** To disseminate (knowledge, for example). **4.** To separate (light) into spectral rays. *—intr.* **1.** To move or scatter in different directions. **2.** To vanish; dissipate: *The dark clouds dispersed by noon.* [ME *dispersen* < OFr. *disperser* < Lat. *dispersus,* p.part. of *dispergere,* to disperse : *dis-,* apart + *spargere,* to scatter.] **—dis·per′sant** *n.* **—dis·pers′ed·ly** (-spûr′sĭd-lē) *adv.* **—dis·pers′er** *n.* **—dis·pers′i·ble** *adj.*

disperse system *n.* A continuous medium containing dispersed entities of any size or state.

dis·per·sion (dĭ-spûr′zhən, -shən) *n.* **1. a.** The act or process of dispersing. **b.** The state of being dispersed. **2.** *Statistics.* The degree of scatter of data, usually about some mean or median value. **3.** *Physics.* **a.** The separation of a complex wave into component parts according to a given characteristic, such as frequency or wavelength. **b.** The separation of visible light into its color components by refraction or diffraction. **4.** *Chem.* A suspension, such as smog or homogenized milk, of solid, liquid, or gaseous particles, of colloidal size or larger, in a liquid, solid, or gaseous medium.

dis·per·sive (dĭ-spûr′sĭv, -zĭv) *adj.* **1.** Tending to become dispersed. **2.** Tending to produce dispersion. **—dis·per′sive·ly** *adv.* **—dis·per′sive·ness** *n.*

dis·pir·it (dĭ-spĭr′ĭt) *tr.v.* **-it·ed, -it·ing, -its.** To lower in or deprive of spirit; dishearten. [DI(S)- + SPIRIT.]

dis·pir·it·ed (dĭ-spĭr′ĭ-tĭd) *adj.* Characterized by low spirits; dejected. **—dis·pir′it·ed·ly** *adv.*

dis·place (dĭs-plās′) *tr.v.* **-placed, -plac·ing, -plac·es. 1.** To change the place or position of. **2.** To take the place of; supplant. **3.** To discharge from an office or position. **4.** To cause a displacement of (a body, for example). **—dis·place′a·ble** *adj.* **—dis·plac′er** *n.*

displaced person *n.* A person who has been driven from his homeland by war.

dis·place·ment (dĭs-plās′mənt) *n.* **1. a.** The act of displacing. **b.** The condition of being displaced. **2.** *Chem.* A reaction in which one kind of atom, molecule, or radical is removed from combination and replaced by another. **3.** *Physics.* **a.** The weight or volume of a fluid displaced by a floating body, used esp. as a measurement of the weight or bulk of ships. **b.** A vector or the magnitude of a vector from the initial position to a subsequent position assumed by a body. **4.** *Psychoanal.* The shifting of an emotional affect, as of anger, from an appropriate to an inappropriate object.

displacement ton *n. Naut.* A unit for measuring the displacement of a ship afloat, equivalent to one long ton or about one cubic meter of salt water.

dis·play (dĭ-splā′) *tr.v.* **-played, -play·ing, -plays. 1.** To hold up to view; exhibit: *display the latest fashions.* **2.** To make manifest or noticeable: *displayed his inexperience.* **3.** To exhibit ostentatiously; flaunt: *likes to display his wealth.* **4.** To be endowed with an identifiable form or character. **5.** To express, as by gestures or bodily posture. **6.** To spread out; unfurl. *—n.* **1.** The act of displaying, esp. a public exhibition. **2.** A demonstration or manifestation of something: *a display of temper.* **3.** Vulgar ostentation: *He made quite a display of himself.* **4.** An advertisement designed to catch the eye, as distinguished from a classified advertisement. **5.** *Computer Sci.* A device that gives information in a visual form, as on a cathode ray tube. [ME *displayen, displaien* < AN *despleier* < Med. Lat. *displicare* < Lat., to scatter : *dis-,* apart + *plicare,* to fold.]

dis·please (dĭs-plēz′) *v.* **-pleased, -pleas·ing, -pleas·es.** *—tr.* To cause annoyance or vexation to. *—intr.* To cause annoyance or displeasure. [ME *displesen* < OFr. *desplaisir* < VLat. ***displacare** : Lat. *dis-* (reversal) + Lat. *placare,* to calm.] **—dis·pleas′ing·ly** *adv.*

dis·pleas·ure (dĭs-plĕzh′ər) *n.* **1.** The condition or fact of being displeased or dissatisfied. **2.** *Archaic.* Discomfort; uneasiness. **3.** *Archaic.* An annoying or injurious offense. *—tr.v.* **-ured, -ur·ing, -ures.** *Archaic.* To displease.

dis·plode (dĭ-splōd′) *tr. & intr.v.* **-plod·ed, -plod·ing, -plodes.** *Archaic.* To explode. [Lat. *displodere,* to extend : *dis-,* apart + *plaudere,* to clap, beat.]

dis·port (dĭ-spôrt′, -spōrt′) *v.* **-port·ed, -port·ing, -ports.** *—intr.* To play; sport. *—tr.* To occupy (oneself) with diversion or amusement. *—n.* Diversion; sport. [ME *disporten* < OFr. *desporter,* to divert : *des,* apart (< Lat. *dis-*) + *porter,* to carry < Lat. *portare.*]

dis·pos·a·ble (dĭ-spō′zə-bəl) *adj.* **1.** Designed to be disposed of after use. **2.** Subject to use; available. *—n.* Something that can be disposed of after use, as a paper sheet or a hypodermic syringe. **—dis·pos′a·bil′i·ty** *n.*

dis·pos·al (dĭ-spō′zəl) *n.* **1.** A particular order, distribution, or placement: *a pleasing disposal of window trimming.* **2.** A particular method of attending to or settling matters. **3.** The transference of something by gift or sale. **4.** An act of throwing out or away. **5.** An apparatus or device for disposing of something, as garbage. **6.** The liberty or power to dispose of or use: *funds at our disposal.*

disposal
Cross section of an electric garbage disposal for a sink drain

dis·pose (dĭ-spōz′) *v.* **-posed, -pos·ing, -pos·es.** *—tr.* **1.** To place or set in a particular order; arrange. **2.** To put (business affairs, for example) into correct, definitive, or conclusive form. **3.** To make willing or receptive for; incline. *—intr.* To settle or decide a matter. ***—phrasal verb.* dispose of. 1.** To attend to; settle: *disposed of the problem quickly.* **2.** To transfer or part with, as by giving or selling. **3.** To get rid of. *—n. Obs.* **1.** Disposal. **2.** Disposition; demeanor. [ME *disposen* < OFr. *disposer* < Lat. *disponere,* to arrange : *dis-,* apart + *ponere,* to put.] **—dis·pos′er** *n.*

dis·po·si·tion (dĭs′pə-zĭsh′ən) *n.* **1.** One's usual mood; temperament: *a sweet disposition.* **2.** An habitual tendency or inclination: *a disposition to disagree.* **3.** Arrangement or distribution. **4.** A final settlement: *disposition of property.* **5.** An act of disposing of. **6.** The power or liberty to control, direct, or dispose.

Synonyms: *disposition, temperament, character, personality, nature.* These nouns refer to the sum of traits that identify a person. *Disposition* is approximately equivalent to habitual frame of mind. *Temperament* applies broadly to the sum of one's emotional characteristics. *Character* emphasizes moral and ethical qualities. *Personality* is the sum of distinctive traits or characteristics of a person that give him individuality, especially in his relationships with other persons. *Nature* suggests those inherent qualities that determine characteristic behavior or emotional response in people.

dis·pos·sess (dĭs′pə-zĕs′) *tr.v.* **-sessed, -sess·ing, -sess·es.** To deprive (another) of the possession or occupancy of something, such as real property. **—dis′pos·ses′sion** *n.* **—dis′pos·ses′sor** *n.* **—dis′pos·ses′so·ry** (-zĕs′ə-rē) *adj.*

dis·praise (dĭs-prāz′) *tr.v.* **-praised, -prais·ing, -prais·es.** To express disapproval of; censure. *—n.* Reproach; censure. [ME *dispreisen* < OFr. *despreiser* < Lat. *depretiare,* to depreciate. —see DEPRECIATE.] **—dis·prais′er** *n.* **—dis·prais′ing·ly** *adv.*

dis·prize (dĭs-prīz′) *tr.v.* **-prized, -priz·ing, -priz·es.** *Archaic.* To hold or regard in low esteem; disdain. [ME *dispreisen,* to dispraise.]

dis·proof (dĭs-pro͞of′) *n.* **1.** The act of disproving or refuting. **2.** Evidence that disproves or refutes.

dis·pro·por·tion (dĭs′prə-pôr′shən, -pōr-) *n.* **1.** The absence of due proportion; disparity. **2.** An instance of a disproportionate relation, as in size. *—tr.v.* **-tioned, -tion·ing, -tions.** To make disproportionate.

dis·pro·por·tion·al (dĭs′prə-pôr′shə-nəl, -pōr-) *adj.* Disproportionate. **—dis′pro·por′tion·al·ly** *adv.*

dis·pro·por·tion·ate (dĭs′prə-pôr′shə-nĭt, -pōr-) *adj.* Out of proportion, as in relative size, shape, or amount. **—dis′pro·por′tion·ate·ly** *adv.* **—dis′pro·por′tion·ate·ness** *n.*

dis·prove (dĭs-pro͞ov′) *tr.v.* **-proved, -prov·ing, -proves.** To prove to be false, invalid, or in error; refute. [ME *disproven* < OFr. *desprover* : *des-* (reversal < Lat. *dis-*) + *prover,* to prove. —see PROVE.] **—dis·prov′a·ble** *adj.* **—dis·prov′al** *n.*

dis·put·a·ble (dĭ-spyo͞o′tə-bəl, dĭs′pyə-) *adj.* Capable of being disputed; debatable. **—dis·put′a·bil′i·ty** *n.* **—dis·put′a·bly** *adv.*

dis·pu·tant (dĭ-spyo͞ot′nt, dĭs′pyə-tənt) *adj.* Engaged in argument or dispute. *—n.* A person who disputes; debater.

dis·pu·ta·tion (dĭs′pyə-tā′shən) *n.* **1.** The act of disputing; debate. **2.** An academic exercise consisting of a formal debate or an oral defense of a thesis.

dis·pu·ta·tious (dĭs′pyə-tā′shəs) *adj.* Inclined to dispute. **—dis′pu·ta′tious·ly** *adv.* **—dis′pu·ta′tious·ness** *n.*

dis·pute (dĭ-spyo͞ot′) *v.* **-put·ed, -put·ing, -putes.** *—tr.* **1.** To argue about; debate. **2.** To question the truth or validity of; doubt: *disputed his intentions.* **3.** To strive to win (a prize, for example); contest for: *disputed his position against all opponents.* **4.** To strive against; resist: *disputed the criticisms of his enemies.* —*intr.* **1.** To discuss; debate. **2.** To quarrel vehemently. —*n.* **1.** A verbal controversy; debate. **2.** A quarrel. [ME *disputen* < OFr. *desputer* < LLat. *disputare* < Lat., to examine : *dis-*, apart + *putare,* to reckon.] **—dis·put'er** *n.*

dis·qual·i·fi·ca·tion (dĭs-kwŏl'ə-fĭ-kā'shən) *n.* **1.** The act of disqualifying or the condition of being disqualified. **2.** Something that disqualifies.

dis·qual·i·fy (dĭs-kwŏl'ə-fī') *tr.v.* **-fied, -fy·ing, -fies. 1.** To render unfit or unqualified; disable. **2.** To declare ineligible or unqualified. **3.** To deprive of legal rights, powers, or privileges.

dis·qui·et (dĭs-kwī'ĭt) *tr.v.* **-et·ed, -et·ing, -ets.** To deprive of peace or rest; trouble. —*n.* The absence of mental peace or rest; restlessness; anxiety. —*adj.* Uneasy; restless. **—dis·qui'et·ing·ly** *adv.* **—dis·qui'et·ly** *adv.* **—dis·qui'et·ness** *n.*

dis·qui·e·tude (dĭs-kwī'ĭ-to͞od', -tyo͞od') *n.* A state of worry or uneasiness; anxiety.

dis·qui·si·tion (dĭs'kwĭ-zĭsh'ən) *n.* A formal discourse on a subject, often in writing. [Lat. *disquisitio,* investigation < *disquirere,* to investigate : *dis-* (intensive) + *quaerere,* to search for.]

dis·rate (dĭs-rāt') *tr.v.* **-rat·ed, -rat·ing, -rates.** To reduce in rating or rank; demote.

dis·re·gard (dĭs'rĭ-gärd') *tr.v.* **-gard·ed, -gard·ing, -gards. 1.** To pay no attention or heed to; ignore. **2.** To treat without proper respect or attentiveness. —*n.* Lack of thoughtful attention or due regard, esp. when willful. **—dis're·gard'er** *n.* **—dis're·gard'ful** *adj.*

dis·rel·ish (dĭs-rĕl'ĭsh) *tr.v.* **-ished, -ish·ing, -ish·es.** To have distaste for; dislike. —*n.* Distaste; aversion.

dis·re·mem·ber (dĭs'rĭ-mĕm'bər) *v.* **-bered, -ber·ing, -bers.** *Regional.* —*tr.* To fail to remember. —*intr.* To forget.

dis·re·pair (dĭs'rĭ-pâr') *n.* The condition of being in need of repairs: *a house in disrepair.*

dis·rep·u·ta·ble (dĭs-rĕp'yə-tə-bəl) *adj.* Not respectable in character, action, or appearance. **—dis·rep'u·ta·bil'i·ty, dis·rep'u·ta·ble·ness** *n.* **—dis·rep'u·ta·bly** *adv.*

dis·re·pute (dĭs'rĭ-pyo͞ot') *n.* The absence or loss of reputation; disgrace.

dis·re·spect (dĭs'rĭ-spĕkt') *n.* Lack of respect, esteem, or courteous regard. —*tr.v.* **-spect·ed, -spect·ing, -spects.** To show a lack of respect for.

dis·re·spect·a·ble (dĭs'rĭ-spĕk'tə-bəl) *adj.* Not worthy of respect. **—dis're·spect'a·bil'i·ty** *n.*

dis·re·spect·ful (dĭs'rĭ-spĕkt'fəl) *adj.* Having or demonstrating a lack of respect; rude; discourteous. **—dis're·spect'ful·ly** *adv.* **—dis're·spect'ful·ness** *n.*

dis·robe (dĭs-rōb') *v.* **-robed, -rob·ing, -robes.** —*tr.* To remove the clothing or covering from. —*intr.* To undress oneself. **—dis·robe'ment** *n.* **—dis·rob'er** *n.*

dis·rupt (dĭs-rŭpt') *tr.v.* **-rupt·ed, -rupt·ing, -rupts. 1.** To throw into confusion or disorder. **2.** To interrupt or impede the progress, movement, or procedure of. **3.** To break or burst; rupture. [Lat. *disrumpere, disrupt-,* to break apart : *dis-*, apart + *rumpere,* to break.] **—dis·rupt'er, dis·rup'tor** *n.* **—dis·rup'tion** *n.*

dis·rup·tive (dĭs-rŭp'tĭv) *adj.* Pertaining to, causing, or produced by disruption. **—dis·rup'tive·ly** *adv.*

dis·sat·is·fac·tion (dĭs-săt'ĭs-făk'shən) *n.* **1.** The condition or feeling of being displeased or not satisfied; discontent. **2.** Something that causes discontent.

dis·sat·is·fac·to·ry (dĭs-săt'ĭs-făk'tə-rē) *adj.* Unsatisfactory.

dis·sat·is·fied (dĭs-săt'ĭs-fīd') *adj.* Feeling or exhibiting a lack of contentment or satisfaction. **—dis·sat'is·fied'ly** *adv.*

dis·sat·is·fy (dĭs-săt'ĭs-fī') *tr.v.* **-fied, -fy·ing, -fies.** To fail to satisfy; disappoint.

dis·seat (dĭs-sēt') *tr.v.* **-seat·ed, -seat·ing, -seats.** *Archaic.* To unseat.

dis·sect (dĭ-sĕkt', dī-, dī'sĕkt') *tr.v.* **-sect·ed, -sect·ing, -sects. 1.** To cut apart or separate (tissue), esp. for anatomical study or in surgery. **2.** To examine, analyze, or criticize in minute detail: *dissected the plan afterward to learn why it had failed.* [Lat. *dissecare, dissect-,* to cut apart : *dis-*, apart + *secare,* to cut.] **—dis·sec'ti·ble** *adj.* **—dis·sec'tor** *n.*

dis·sect·ed (dĭ-sĕk'tĭd, dī-) *adj. Bot.* Divided into numerous narrow segments or lobes: *dissected leaves.*

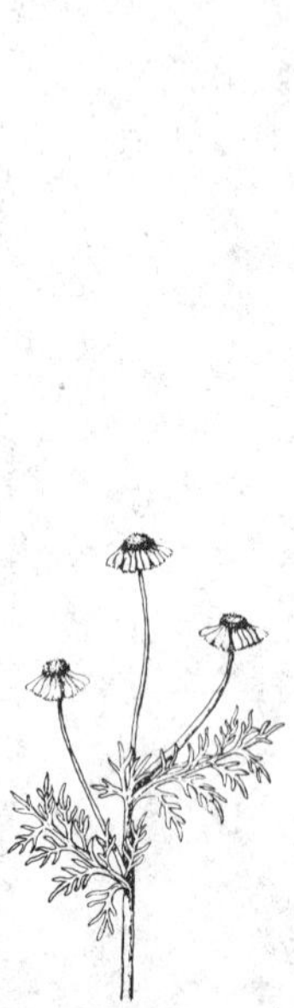

dissected
Dissected leaves of mayweed

dis·sec·tion (dĭ-sĕk'shən, dī-) *n.* **1.** The act of dissecting. **2.** Something that has been dissected, as tissue under study. **3.** A detailed examination or analysis.

dis·seise (dĭs-sēz') *v.* Variant of **disseize.**

dis·sei·sin (dĭs-sē'zĭn) *n.* Variant of **disseizin.**

dis·seize also **dis·seise** (dĭs-sēz') *tr.v.* **-seized, -seiz·ing, -seiz·es** also **-seised, -seis·ing, -seis·es.** *Law.* To dispossess unlawfully of real property. [ME *disseisen* < AN *disseisir* < OFr. *desseisir* : *des-* (reversal < Lat. *dis-*) + *seisir,* to seize, of Germanic orig.]

dis·sei·zin also **dis·sei·sin** (dĭs-sē'zĭn) *n. Law.* Wrongful usurpation of the powers and privileges of ownership. [ME *disseisine* < AN < OFr. *desseisine* : *des-* (reversal < Lat. *dis-*) + *seisine,* seisin. —see SEISIN.]

dis·sem·ble (dĭ-sĕm'bəl) *v.* **-bled, -bling, -bles.** —*tr.* **1.** To disguise or conceal behind a false appearance or semblance: *dissemble one's fears with laughter.* **2.** To make a false show of; feign. —*intr.* To conceal one's real motives, nature, or feelings under a pretense. [ME *dissemblen* < OFr. *dessembler,* to be different : *des-* (reversal < Lat. *dis-*) + *sembler,* to appear, seem. —see SEMBLABLE.] **—dis·sem'blance** *n.* **—dis·sem'bler** *n.* **—dis·sem'bling·ly** *adv.*

dis·sem·i·nate (dĭ-sĕm'ə-nāt') *v.* **-nat·ed, -nat·ing, -nates.** —*tr.* **1.** To scatter widely, as in sowing seed. **2.** To spread abroad; promulgate: *disseminate information.* —*intr.* To become diffused; spread. [Lat. *disseminare, disseminat-* : *dis-*, apart + *seminare,* to sow < *semen,* seed.] **—dis·sem'i·na'tion** *n.* **—dis·sem'i·na'tor** *n.*

dis·sem·i·nule (dĭ-sĕm'ə-nyo͞ol') *n.* A reproductive plant part, such as a seed, fruit, or spore, that is modified for dispersal. [DISSEMIN(ATE) + -ULE.]

dis·sen·sion (dĭ-sĕn'shən) *n.* A difference of opinion, esp. one that leads to contention or strife. [ME *dissencioun* < OFr. *dissension* < Lat. *dissensio* < *dissentire,* to dissent.]

dis·sent (dĭ-sĕnt') *intr.v.* **-sent·ed, -sent·ing, -sents. 1.** To differ in opinion or feeling; disagree. **2.** To withhold assent or approval. —*n.* **1.** Difference of opinion or feeling; disagreement. **2.** The refusal to conform to the authority or doctrine of an established church; nonconformity. [ME *dissenten* < Lat. *dissentire* : *dis-*, apart + *sentire,* to feel.] **—dis·sent'ing·ly** *adv.*

dis·sent·er (dĭ-sĕn'tər) *n.* **1.** One who dissents. **2.** Often **Dissenter.** One who refuses to accept the doctrines or usages of an established or national church, esp. a Protestant who dissents from the Church of England.

dis·sen·tient (dĭ-sĕn'shənt) *adj.* Dissenting, esp. from the sentiment or policies of a majority. —*n.* One who dissents. **—dis·sen'tience** *n.*

dis·sen·tious (dĭ-sĕn'shəs) *adj.* Given to dissension.

dis·sep·i·ment (dĭ-sĕp'ə-mənt) *n.* A membranous or calcareous partition between organs or parts; septum. [Lat. *dissaepimentum,* partition < *dissaepire,* to divide : *dis-*, apart + *saepire,* to enclose < *saepes,* fence.] **—dis·sep'i·men'tal** (-mĕn'tl) *adj.*

dis·ser·tate (dĭs'ər-tāt') also **dis·sert** (dĭ-sûrt') *intr.v.* **-tat·ed, -tat·ing, -tates** also **-sert·ed, -sert·ing, -serts.** To discourse formally. [Lat. *dissertare, dissertat-,* freq. of *disserere,* to discuss : *dis-*, apart + *serere,* to connect.] **—dis'ser·ta'tor** *n.*

dis·ser·ta·tion (dĭs'ər-tā'shən) *n.* A lengthy and formal treatise or discourse, esp. one written by a candidate for the doctoral degree at a university; thesis.

dis·serve (dĭs-sûrv') *tr.v.* **-served, -serv·ing, -serves.** To treat badly; harm.

dis·serv·ice (dĭs-sûr'vĭs) *n.* A harmful action; injury.

dis·sev·er (dĭ-sĕv'ər) *v.* **-ered, -er·ing, -ers.** —*tr.* **1.** To separate; sever. **2.** To divide into parts; break up. —*intr.* To become separated or disunited. [ME *disseveren* < OFr. *dessevrer* < LLat. *disseparare* : Lat. *dis-*, apart + Lat. *separare,* to separate. —see SEPARATE.] **—dis·sev'er·ance, dis·sev'er·ment** *n.*

dis·si·dence (dĭs'ĭ-dəns) *n.* Disagreement, as of opinion or belief; difference; dissent.

dis·si·dent (dĭs'ĭ-dənt) *adj.* Disagreeing, as in opinion or belief. —*n.* One who disagrees; dissenter. [Lat. *dissidens, dissident-,* pr.part. of *dissidēre,* to disagree : *dis-*, apart + *sedēre,* to sit.]

dis·sil·i·ent (dĭ-sĭl'ē-ənt) *adj.* Bursting apart, as some seed pods do when ripe. [Lat. *dissiliens, dissilient-,* pr.part. of *dissilire,* to burst apart : *dis-*, apart + *salire,* to leap.]

dis·sim·i·lar (dĭ-sĭm'ə-lər) *adj.* Unlike; different. **—dis·sim'i·lar·ly** *adv.*

dis·sim·i·lar·i·ty (dĭ-sĭm'ə-lăr'ĭ-tē) *n., pl.* **-ties. 1.** The quality of being distinct or unlike; difference. **2.** A point of distinction or difference.

dis·sim·i·late (dĭ-sĭm'ə-lāt') *v.* **-lat·ed, -lat·ing, -lates.** —*tr.* **1.** To make dissimilar or unlike. **2.** *Ling.* To cause to undergo dissimilation. —*intr.* **1.** To become dissimilar. **2.** *Ling.* To undergo dissimilation. [DIS- + (AS)SIMILATE.]

dis·sim·i·la·tion (dĭ-sĭm'ə-lā'shən) *n.* **1.** The act or process of making or becoming dissimilar. **2.** *Ling.* The process by which one of two similar phonemes is displaced or changed by the other; for example, the English form *marble* from French *marbre.*

dis·si·mil·i·tude (dĭs'ə-mĭl'ĭ-to͞od', -tyo͞od') *n.* Lack of resemblance; dissimilarity. [ME < Lat. *dissimilitudo* < *dissimilis,* different : *dis-*, not + *similis,* like.]

dis·sim·u·late (dĭ-sĭm'yə-lāt') *v.* **-lat·ed, -lat·ing, -lates.** —*tr.* To disguise (one's intentions, for example) under a feigned appearance. —*intr.* To conceal one's true feelings or intentions. [ME *dissimulaten* < Lat. *dissimulare* : *dis-* (reversal) + *simulare,* to simulate.] **—dis·sim'u·la'tion** *n.* **—dis·sim'u·la'tive** *adj.* **—dis·sim'u·la'tor** *n.*

dis·si·pate (dĭs'ə-pāt') *v.* **-pat·ed, -pat·ing, -pates.** —*tr.* **1.** To drive away or dispel by or as if by dispersing; scatter. **2.** To exhaust or expend intemperately; squander. **3.** To cause to lose (heat, for example) irreversibly. —*intr.* **1.** To vanish by dispersion. **2.** To disappear by or as if by rising. **3.** To indulge in intemperate pursuit of pleasure; carouse. [ME *dissipaten* < Lat. *dissipare,* to disperse : *dis-*, apart + *supare,* to throw.] **—dis'si·pat'er, dis'si·pa'tor** *n.* **—dis'si·pa'tive** *adj.*

dis·si·pat·ed (dĭs'ə-pā'tĭd) *adj.* **1.** Intemperate in the pursuit of pleasure; dissolute. **2.** Wasted or squandered. **—dis′si·pat′ed·ly** *adv.* **—dis′si·pat′ed·ness** *n.*

dis·si·pa·tion (dĭs′ə-pā′shən) *n.* **1. a.** The act of dissipating. **b.** The condition of being dissipated. **2.** Wasteful consumption or expenditure. **3.** Dissolute indulgence in pleasure; intemperance. **4.** An amusement; diversion.

dis·so·cia·ble (dĭ-sō′shə-bəl, -shē-ə-bəl) *adj.* Capable of being dissociated; separable. **—dis·so′cia·bil′i·ty, dis·so′cia·ble·ness** *n.* **—dis·so′cia·bly** *adv.*

dis·so·ci·ate (dĭ-sō′shē-āt′, -sē-) *v.* **-at·ed, -at·ing, -ates.** *—tr.* **1.** To remove from association; separate: *"Marx never dissociated man from his social environment"* (Sidney Hook). **2.** *Chem.* To cause to undergo dissociation. *—intr.* **1.** To cease associating; part. **2.** *Chem.* To undergo dissociation. [Lat. *dissociare, dissociat-* : *dis-* (reversal) + *sociare,* to unite < *socius,* companion.] **—dis·so′ci·a′tive** *adj.*

dis·so·ci·a·tion (dĭ-sō′sē-ā′shən, -shē-) *n.* **1. a.** The act of dissociating; removal. **b.** The condition of being dissociated; separation. **2.** *Chem.* **a.** The chemical process by means of which a change in physical condition, as in pressure or temperature, or the action of a solvent causes a molecule to split into simpler groups of atoms, single atoms, or ions. **b.** The separation of an electrolyte into ions of opposite sign. **3.** *Psychiat.* The separation of a group of related psychological activities into autonomously functioning units, as in the generation of multiple personalities.

dis·sol·u·ble (dĭ-sŏl′yə-bəl) *adj.* Capable of being dissolved. [Lat. *dissolubilis* < *dissolvere,* to dissolve.] **—dis·sol′u·bil′i·ty, dis·sol′u·ble·ness** *n.*

dis·so·lute (dĭs′ə-lo͞ot′) *adj.* Lacking in moral restraint. [ME < Lat. *dissolutus,* p.part. of *dissolvere,* to dissolve.] **—dis′so·lute′ly** *adv.* **—dis′so·lute′ness** *n.*

dis·so·lu·tion (dĭs′ə-lo͞o′shən) *n.* **1.** Decomposition into fragments or parts; disintegration. **2.** Excessive freedom and lack of restraint. **3.** Termination or extinction by deconcentration or dispersion. **4.** Extinction of life; death. **5.** Annulment or termination of a formal or legal bond, tie, or contract. **6.** Formal dismissal of an assembly or legislature. **7.** Reduction to a liquid form; liquefaction. **—dis′so·lu′tive** *adj.*

dis·solve (dĭ-zŏlv′) *v.* **-solved, -solv·ing, -solves.** *—tr.* **1.** To cause to pass into solution: *dissolve sugar in water.* **2.** To reduce to liquid form; melt. **3.** To cause to disappear or vanish; dispel. **4.** To break into component parts; disintegrate. **5.** To bring to an end by or as if by breaking up; terminate. **6.** To dismiss (a meeting or parliament, for example). **7.** To cause to give way emotionally or psychologically; upset. **8.** To cause to lose definition; blur; confuse: *"Morality has finally been dissolved in pity"* (Leslie Fiedler). **9.** *Law.* To render null; abrogate; annul. *—intr.* **1.** To pass into solution. **2.** To become liquid; melt. **3.** To break up or disperse. **4.** To become disintegrated; disappear. **5.** To collapse emotionally or psychologically. **6.** To lose clarity or definition; fade away. **7.** To shift scenes in a motion-picture film or videotape by having one scene fade out while the next appears behind it and grows clearer as the first dims. *—n.* A scene transition in a motion-picture film or videotape made by dissolving. [ME *dissolven* < Lat. *dissolvere* : *dis-,* apart + *solvere,* to release.] **—dis·solv′a·ble** *adj.* **—dis·solv′er** *n.*

dis·sol·vent (dĭ-zŏl′vənt) *adj.* Capable of dissolving. *—n.* A solvent.

dis·so·nance (dĭs′ə-nəns) also **dis·so·nan·cy** (-nən-sē) *n.* **1.** A harsh or disagreeable combination of sounds; discord. **2.** Lack of agreement, consistency, or harmony; conflict. **3.** *Mus.* A combination of tones conventionally considered to suggest unrelieved tension and to require resolution.

dis·so·nant (dĭs′ə-nənt) *adj.* **1.** Harsh or inharmonious in sound; discordant. **2.** Disagreeing or at variance. **3.** *Mus.* Constituting or producing a dissonance. [ME *dissonaunt* < OFr. *dissonant* < Lat. *dissonans,* pr.part. of *dissonare,* to be dissonant : *dis-,* apart + *sonare,* to sound.] **—dis′so·nant·ly** *adv.*

dis·suade (dĭ-swād′) *tr.v.* **-suad·ed, -suad·ing, -suades.** To deter (a person) from a purpose or course of action by persuasion or exhortation: *dissuaded him from his rash scheme.* [Lat. *dissuadēre* : *dis-* (reversal) + *suadēre,* to advise.] **—dis·suad′er** *n.*

dis·sua·sion (dĭ-swā′zhən) *n.* The act or an instance of dissuading. [Lat. *dissuasio* < *dissuadēre,* to dissuade.] **—dis·sua′sive** *adj.* **—dis·sua′sive·ly** *adv.* **—dis·sua′sive·ness** *n.*

dis·syl·la·ble (dĭ-sĭl′ə-bəl, dĭs′sĭl-, dī′sĭl′-) *n.* Variant of **disyllable.**

dis·sym·me·try (dĭs-sĭm′ĭ-trē) *n., pl.* **-tries.** Lack of symmetry. **—dis′sym·met′ric** (dĭ′sĭ-mĕt′rĭk), **dis′sym·met′ri·cal** *adj.* **—dis′sym·met′ri·cal·ly** *adv.*

dis·taff (dĭs′tăf′) *n.* **1.** A staff that holds on its cleft end the unspun flax, wool, or tow from which thread is drawn in spinning by hand. **2.** A woman's work and concerns. **3.** Women in general. [ME *distaf* < OE *distæf* : *dis-,* bunch of flax + *stæf,* staff.]

distaff side *n.* The female line or maternal branch of a family.

dis·tal (dĭs′təl) *adj.* Anatomically located far from the origin or line of attachment, as a bone. [DIST(ANT) + -AL.] **—dis′tal·ly** *adv.*

dis·tance (dĭs′təns) *n.* **1.** The fact or condition of being apart in space or time. **2. a.** A nonnegative number designating the magnitude of a path along a straight line or curve. **b.** The length of a line segment joining two points. **c.** The length of the perpendicular from a given point to a given line. **3.** The interval separating two specified instants in time. **4.** The extent of space between points on a linearly measured course. **5. a.** The degree of deviation or difference that separates two things in relationship. **b.** The degree of progress between two points in a trend or course. **6.** A stretch of linear space without designation of limit. **7.** A point removed in space or time. **8.** Chilliness of manner; aloofness. *—tr.v.* **-tanced, -tanc·ing, -tanc·es. 1.** To place or keep at a distance. **2.** To cause to appear at a distance. **3.** To leave far behind; outrun; outstrip.

dis·tant (dĭs′tənt) *adj.* **1.** Separate or apart in space or time. **2.** Far removed in space or time: *the distant past.* **3.** Located at, coming from, or going to a distance: *distant lands.* **4.** Far apart in relationship: *a distant cousin.* **5.** Far removed from the present situation: *distant thoughts.* **6.** Aloof or chilly in manner. [ME *distaunt* < OFr. < Lat. *distans,* pr.part. of *distare,* to be remote : *dis-,* apart + *stare,* to stand.] **—dis′tant·ly** *adv.*

Synonyms: *distant, far, far-off, faraway, remote, removed.* These adjectives mean to be widely apart in space or, less often, in time. *Distant* can be used (with a figure) to indicate a specific separation, or it can indicate an indefinite but sizable interval. *Far* implies a wide but indefinite interval, principally in space. *Far-off* and *faraway* imply a wider interval in either time or space. *Remote* not only means faraway but suggests isolation from the speaker's locality or point in time. *Removed* implies distinct separation in place, time, kind, or character with respect to the speaker.

dis·taste (dĭs-tāst′) *n.* Dislike or aversion. *—tr.v.* **-tast·ed, -tast·ing, -tastes.** *Archaic.* **1.** To feel repugnance for; dislike. **2.** To offend; displease.

dis·taste·ful (dĭs-tāst′fəl) *adj.* **1. a.** Unpleasant or disagreeable: *He finds cocktail parties distasteful.* **b.** Objectionable or offensive: *distasteful language.* **2.** Expressing aversion or dislike: *shot me a distasteful look.* **—dis·taste′ful·ly** *adv.* **—dis·taste′ful·ness** *n.*

dis·tem·per[1] (dĭs-tĕm′pər) *n.* **1. a.** An infectious virus disease occurring in certain mammals, esp. dogs, characterized by loss of appetite, a catarrhal discharge from the eyes and nose, and often partial paralysis and death. **b.** Any of various similar mammalian diseases. **2.** An illness or disease; ailment: *"He died . . . of a broken heart, a distemper which kills many more than is generally imagined"* (H. Fielding). **3.** Ill humor or testiness. **4.** Disorder or disturbance, esp. of a social or political nature. *—tr.v.* **-pered, -per·ing, -pers.** To upset or disturb. [ME *distemperen,* to upset the balance of the humors < OFr. *destemprer* < Med. Lat. *distemperare* : Lat. *dis-* (reversal) + Lat. *temperare,* to temper.]

dis·tem·per[2] (dĭs-tĕm′pər) *n.* **1. a.** A process of painting in which pigments are mixed with water and a glue-size or casein binder, used for flat wall decoration or for scenic and poster painting. **b.** The paint used in this process. **2.** A painting done in distemper. *—tr.v.* **-pered, -per·ing, -pers. 1.** To mix (powdered pigments or colors) with water and size. **2.** To paint in distemper. [ME *distemperen,* to dilute < Med. Lat. *distemperare.* —see DISTEMPER[1].]

dis·tend (dĭ-stĕnd′) *v.* **-tend·ed, -tend·ing, -tends.** *—intr.* To swell out or expand from or as if from internal pressure. *—tr.* **1.** To cause to expand by or as by internal pressure; dilate. **2.** To blow up, as in importance. **3.** To stretch out in all directions; extend. [ME *distenden* < Lat. *distendere* : *dis-,* apart + *tendere,* to stretch.]

dis·ten·si·ble (dĭ-stĕn′sə-bəl) *adj.* Capable of being distended. **—dis·ten′si·bil′i·ty** *n.*

dis·ten·tion also **dis·ten·sion** (dĭ-stĕn′shən) *n.* The act of distending or the condition of being distended. [ME *distensioun* < Lat. *distentio* < *distentus,* p.part. of *distendere,* to distend.]

dis·tich (dĭs′tĭk) *n., pl.* **-tichs.** A verse couplet, esp. one used in a Latin or Greek elegiac. [Lat. *distichon* < Gk. *distikhon* < *distikhos,* having two rows or verses : *di-,* two + *stikhos,* line of verse.]

dis·ti·chous (dĭs′tĭ-kəs) *adj.* Arranged in two vertical rows or ranks on opposite sides of an axis. Used of leaves. [LLat. *distichus,* having two rows < Gk. *distikhos.* —see DISTICH.] **—dis′ti·chous·ly** *adv.*

dis·til (dĭ-stĭl′) *v. Chiefly Brit.* Variant of **distill.**

dis·till (dĭ-stĭl′) *v.* **-tilled, -till·ing, -tills.** *—tr.* **1.** To subject (a substance) to distillation. **2.** To extract (a distillate) by distillation. **3.** To purify or refine by or as if by distillation. **4.** To separate or extract the core of: *distill the crucial points of the book.* **5.** To exude or give off in drops or small quantities. *—intr.* **1.** To undergo or be produced by distillation. **2.** To fall or exude in drops or small quantities. [ME *distillen* < OFr. *distiller* < Lat. *destillare,* to trickle : *de-,* down + *stillare,* to drip < *stilla,* drop.] **—dis·till′a·ble** *adj.*

dis·til·late (dĭs′tə-lāt′, -lĭt, dĭ-stĭl′ĭt) *n.* **1.** The liquid condensed from vapor in distillation. **2.** Something regarded as an essence or purified form.

dis·til·la·tion (dĭs′tə-lā′shən) *n.* **1.** Any of various heat-dependent processes used to purify or separate a fraction of

distaff

distichous
Distichous leaves of iris

p **pop** / r **roar** / s **sauce** / sh **ship, dish** / t **tight** / th **thin, path** / *th* **this, bathe** / ŭ **cut** / ûr **urge** / v **valve** / w **with** / y **yes** / z **zebra, size** / zh **vision** / ə **about, item, edible, gallop, circus** / œ *Fr.* **feu**, *Ger.* **schön** / ü *Fr.* **tu**, *Ger.* **über** / KH *Ger.* **ich**, *Scot.* **loch** / N *Fr.* **bon.**

a relatively complex substance, esp. the vaporization of a liquid mixture with subsequent collection of components by differential cooling to condensation. **2.** A distillate.

distillation column *n.* A tall cylindrical metal shell internally fitted with perforated horizontal plates used to promote separation of miscible liquids ascending in the shell as vapor.

dis·till·er (dĭ-stĭl′ər) *n.* **1.** One that distills, as a condenser. **2.** A maker of alcoholic liquors by the process of distillation.

dis·till·er·y (dĭ-stĭl′ə-rē) *n., pl.* **-ies.** An establishment or plant for distilling, esp. alcoholic liquors.

dis·tinct (dĭ-stĭngkt′) *adj.* **1.** Distinguishable from all others; separate; discrete: *on two distinct occasions.* **2.** Easily perceived by the senses or intellect; clear: *a distinct flavor; a distinct tragic element in the story.* **3.** Explicit or unquestionable: *a distinct disadvantage.* **4.** Very likely; probable: *a distinct possibility he won't come.* **5.** Distinguished or notable: *a distinct accomplishment.* [ME < OFr. < Lat. *distinctus,* p.part. of *distinguere,* to distinguish.] **—dis·tinct′ly** *adv.* **—dis·tinct′ness** *n.*

Usage: A thing is *distinct* if it is sharply distinguished from other things; a property or attribute is *distinctive* if it enables us to distinguish one thing from another. *The warbler has a distinctive song* means that the warbler's song enables us to distinguish the warbler from other birds. *The warbler is not a distinct species* means that the warbler is not a clearly defined type of bird.

dis·tinc·tion (dĭ-stĭngk′shən) *n.* **1.** The action of distinguishing; discrimination; differentiation. **2.** The condition or fact of being dissimilar or distinct; difference. **3.** A distinguishing factor, attribute, or characteristic. **4. a.** Excellence or eminence, as of performance, character, or reputation: *a man of distinction.* **b.** A special feature or quality conferring superiority. **5.** Recognition of achievement or superiority; honor: *graduate with distinction.*

dis·tinc·tive (dĭ-stĭngk′tĭv) *adj.* **1.** Serving to identify; distinguishing: *distinctive tribal tattoos.* **2.** Characteristic or typical: *distinctive habits.* **3.** *Ling.* Phonemically relevant. —See Usage note at **distinct. —dis·tinc′tive·ly** *adv.* **—dis·tinc′tive·ness** *n.*

dis·tin·gué (dēs′tăng-gā′, dĭs′-, dĭ-stăng′gā) *adj.* Distinguished in appearance, manner, or bearing. [Fr., p.part. of *distinguer,* to distinguish < OFr.]

dis·tin·guish (dĭ-stĭng′gwĭsh) *v.* **-guished, -guish·ing, -guish·es.** *—tr.* **1.** To recognize as being different or distinct. **2.** To perceive distinctly; make out. **3.** To detect or recognize; pick out. **4.** To make noticeable or different; set apart. **5.** To cause (oneself) to be eminent or recognized: *He distinguished himself as a statesman. —intr.* To perceive or indicate differences; discriminate: *distinguish between right and wrong.* [< ME *distinguen* < OFr. *distinguer* < Lat. *distinguere,* to separate.] **—dis·tin′guish·a·ble** *adj.* **—dis·tin′guish·a·bly** *adv.*

dis·tin·guished (dĭ-stĭng′gwĭsht) *adj.* **1.** Characterized by excellence or distinction; eminent; renowned. **2.** Dignified in conduct or appearance.

Distinguished Conduct Medal *n.* A British military decoration for distinguished conduct in the field.

Distinguished Flying Cross *n.* **1.** A U.S. military decoration awarded for heroism or extraordinary achievement in aerial combat. **2.** A British decoration awarded to officers of the Royal Air Force for extraordinary achievement.

Distinguished Service Cross *n.* **1.** A U.S. Army decoration awarded for exceptional heroism in combat. **2.** A British decoration awarded to officers of the Royal Navy for gallantry in action.

Distinguished Service Medal *n.* **1.** A U.S. military decoration awarded for distinguished performance in a duty of great responsibility. **2.** A British decoration awarded to noncommissioned officers and men in the Royal Navy and Royal Marines for distinguished conduct in war.

Distinguished Service Order *n.* A British military decoration for gallantry in action.

dis·tort (dĭ-stôrt′) *tr.v.* **-tort·ed, -tort·ing, -torts. 1.** To twist out of a proper or natural relation of parts; misshape; contort. **2.** To give a false or misleading account of; misrepresent. **3.** To cause to work in a twisted or disorderly manner; pervert. [Lat. *distorquēre, distort-* : *dis-,* apart + *torquēre,* to twist.] **—dis·tort′er** *n.*

Synonyms: *distort, twist, deform, contort, warp, gnarl.* These verbs mean to change the form or character of something, usually to its disadvantage. *Distort* applies to physical change in shape, as by bending, wrenching, or exaggerating certain features; to verbal or pictorial misrepresentation; and to alteration or perversion of meaning of something spoken or written. *Twist* has similar application but intensifies the idea of marked and deliberate change. *Deform* refers only to physical change that disfigures and usually deprives the object of attractiveness or capacity for normal functioning. *Contort* implies violent physical change that produces unnatural or grotesque effects. *Warp* can refer to physical turning or twisting out of shape or, figuratively, to turning something, such as the human mind or judgment, from a true course. *Gnarl* usually refers to making twisted or knotty in a physical sense.

distort
Distorted reflection of buildings in the mirrorlike windows of another building

dis·tor·tion (dĭ-stôr′shən) *n.* **1.** The act or an instance of distorting. **2.** The condition of being distorted. **3.** A statement that twists fact; misrepresentation. **4.** A distorted image resulting from imperfections in an optical system, such as a lens. **5.** *Electronics.* **a.** An undesired change in the waveform of a signal. **b.** A consequence of such a change, esp. diminished clarity in reception or reproduction. **6.** *Psychoanal.* The modification of unconscious impulses into forms acceptable by conscious or dreaming perception. **—dis·tor′tion·al** *adj.*

dis·tract (dĭ-străkt′) *tr.v.* **-tract·ed, -tract·ing, -tracts. 1.** To cause to turn away from the original focus of attention or interest; divert. **2.** To pull in conflicting emotional directions; unsettle. [ME *distracten* < Lat. *distractus,* p.part. of *distrahere,* to pull away : *dis-,* apart + *trahere,* to draw.] **—dis·trac′tive** *adj.* **—dis·tract′ing·ly** *adv.*

dis·tract·ed (dĭ-străk′tĭd) *adj.* **1.** Having the attention diverted. **2.** Suffering conflicting emotions; distraught. **—dis·tract′ed·ly** *adv.*

dis·tract·er also **dis·trac·tor** (dĭ-străk′tər) *n.* One of the incorrect answers presented as a choice in a multiple-choice test.

dis·trac·tion (dĭ-străk′shən) *n.* **1.** The act of distracting or the condition of being distracted. **2.** Something that distracts, esp. an amusement. **3.** Extreme mental or emotional disturbance; obsession: *loved her to distraction.*

dis·trac·tor (dĭ-străk′tər) *n.* Variant of **distracter.**

dis·train (dĭ-strān′) *v.* **-trained, -train·ing, -trains.** *Law. —tr.* **1.** To seize and hold (property) to compel payment or reparation, as of debts. **2.** To seize the property of (a person) in order to compel payment of debts; distress. *—intr.* To levy a distress. [ME *distreinen* < OFr. *destreindre,* to seize, compel < Med. Lat. *distringere* < Lat., to hinder : *dis-,* apart + *stringere,* to draw tight.] **—dis·train′a·ble** *adj.* **—dis·train′ment** *n.* **—dis·trai′nor, dis·train′er** *n.*

dis·train·ee (dĭs′trā-nē′) *n.* *Law.* One who has been distrained.

dis·traint (dĭ-strānt′) *n.* *Law.* The act or process of distraining; distress. [< DISTRAIN.]

dis·trait (dĭ-strā′) *adj.* Inattentive or absent-minded, esp. because of anxiety. [Fr. < Lat. *distractus.* —see DISTRACT.]

dis·traught (dĭ-strôt′) *adj.* **1.** Agitated with anxiety; worried. **2.** Crazed or mad. [ME alteration of *distract,* p.part. of *distracten,* to distract.]

dis·tress (dĭ-strĕs′) *tr.v.* **-tressed, -tress·ing, -tress·es. 1.** To cause strain, anxiety, or suffering to. **2.** *Archaic.* To constrain by harassment. **3.** *Law.* To hold the property of (a person) against the payment of debts; distrain. **4.** To mar or otherwise treat (furniture, for example) to give the appearance of an antique. *—n.* **1.** Anxiety or suffering. **2. a.** Severe strain resulting from exhaustion or an accident. **b.** Acute physical discomfort. **3.** The condition of being in need of immediate assistance: *a motorist in distress.* **4.** *Law.* **a.** The act of distraining or seizing to compel payment. **b.** The goods thus seized. ***—modifier:*** *distress merchandise; a distress sale.* [ME *distressen* < OFr. *destresser* < *destresse,* constraint < VLat. **districtia* < Lat. *districtus,* p.part. of *distringere,* to hinder. —see DISTRAIN.] **—dis·tress′ing·ly** *adv.*

dis·tress·ful (dĭ-strĕs′fəl) *adj.* **1.** Causing distress. **2.** Experiencing distress. **—dis·tress′ful·ly** *adv.* **—dis·tress′ful·ness** *n.*

dis·trib·u·tar·y (dĭ-strĭb′yə-tĕr′ē) *n., pl.* **-ies.** A branch of a river that flows away from the main stream and does not return to it.

dis·trib·ute (dĭ-strĭb′yo͞ot) *v.* **-ut·ed, -ut·ing, -utes.** *—tr.v.* **1.** To divide and dispense in portions. **2. a.** *Commerce.* To supply (goods) to retailers. **b.** To deliver or pass out: *distributing handbills on the street.* **3.** To spread or diffuse over an area. **4.** To separate into categories; classify. **5.** *Logic.* To use (a term) so as to include all individuals or entities of a given class. **6.** *Printing.* To separate (type) and replace in the proper boxes. *—intr.v.* To be mathematically distributive. [ME *distributen* < Lat. *distribuere* : *dis-,* apart + *tribuere,* to give. —see TRIBUTE.]

Synonyms: *distribute, divide, dispense, dole, deal, ration.* These verbs mean to give something as a portion or share. *Distribute* is the least specific. *Divide* implies giving out portions determined by plan and purpose, often equal parts or portions based on what is due or deserved. *Dispense* stresses even more the sense of careful determination of portions according to what is considered due or proper. *Dole* (usually followed by *out*) implies careful and scant measure of portions; often it applies to distribution of charity or something given reluctantly. *Deal* suggests orderly and equitable distribution, piece by piece. *Ration* refers to equitable division of scarce items, often necessities, by a system that limits individual portions.

dis·trib·ut·ed (dĭ-strĭb′yə-tĭd) *adj.* Characterized by a particular statistical distribution.

dis·tri·bu·tion (dĭs′trə-byo͞o′shən) *n.* **1.** The act of distributing or the condition of being distributed; apportionment. **2.** Something distributed; an allotment. **3.** The act of dispersing or the condition of being dispersed; diffusion. **4. a.** The geographic occurrence or range of an organism. **b.** The geographic occurrence or range of a custom, usage, or other feature. **5.** Division into categories; classification.

6. *Law.* The division of an estate or property among rightful heirs. 7. *Commerce.* The process of marketing and supplying goods, esp. to retailers. 8. A spatial or temporal array of objects or events: *the distribution of theaters on Broadway.* 9. *Statistics.* A set of numbers collected from a well-defined universe of possible measurements arising from a property or relationship under study. **—dis'tri·bu'tion·al** *adj.*

dis·trib·u·tive (dĭ-strĭb'yə-tĭv) *adj.* 1. Of or pertaining to distribution. 2. Serving to distribute. 3. Of or pertaining to the distributive property. 4. *Gram.* Referring to each individual or entity of a group separately rather than collectively; for example, *every* in the sentence *every employee attended the meeting.* —*n.* A distributive word or term. **—dis·trib'u·tive·ly** *adv.* **—dis·trib'u·tive·ness** *n.*

distributive education *n.* An educational program in which students receive both classroom instruction and on-the-job training.

dis·trib·u·tor (dĭ-strĭb'yə-tər) *n.* 1. One that distributes. 2. One that markets or sells merchandise, esp. a wholesaler. 3. A device that applies electric current in proper sequence to the spark plugs of an engine. 4. *Computer Sci.* The electronic circuitry that acts as an intermediate link between a computer's accumulator and drum storage.

dis·trict (dĭs'trĭkt) *n.* 1. A division of an area or geographic unit marked out by law for a particular purpose: *a school district; an electoral district.* 2. A distinctive area: *the lake district.* —*tr.v.* **-trict·ed, -trict·ing, -tricts.** To mark off or divide into districts. [Fr. < Med. Lat. *districtus,* jurisdiction < Lat., p.part. of *distringere,* to hinder. —see DISTRAIN.]

district attorney *n.* The prosecuting officer of a given judicial district.

district court *n.* 1. A U.S. Federal trial court serving a judicial district. 2. In some states, a state court of general jurisdiction.

dis·trust (dĭs-trŭst') *n.* Lack of trust; doubtfulness; suspicion. —*tr.v.* **-trust·ed, -trust·ing, -trusts.** To lack confidence in; doubt or suspect.

dis·trust·ful (dĭs-trŭst'fəl) *adj.* Feeling or showing doubt. **—dis·trust'ful·ly** *adv.* **—dis·trust'ful·ness** *n.*

dis·turb (dĭ-stûrb') *tr.v.* **-turbed, -turb·ing, -turbs.** 1. To break up or destroy the tranquillity or settled state of. 2. To trouble emotionally or mentally; upset. 3. a. To interfere with; interrupt: *disturb one's sleep.* b. To intrude upon; inconvenience: *constant calls disturbed her work.* 4. To put out of order; disarrange. [ME *destourben* < OFr. *destorber* < Lat. *disturbare* : *dis-* (intensive) + *turbare,* to agitate < *turba,* confusion < Gk. *turbē.*] **—dis·turb'er** *n.* **—dis·turb'ing·ly** *adv.*

dis·tur·bance (dĭ-stûr'bəns) *n.* 1. The act of disturbing or the condition of being disturbed. 2. Something that disturbs. 3. A commotion or scuffle, esp. a public tumult. 4. Unbalance or disorder, as of the mind. 5. A variation in a normal course or condition.

di·sul·fide (dī-sŭl'fīd') *n.* A chemical compound containing two sulfur atoms combined with other elements or radicals.

di·sul·fo·ton (dī-sŭl'fə-tŏn') *n.* A pale yellow, highly toxic, organophosphorous systemic insecticide, $C_8H_{19}O_2PS_3$. [DI(ETHYL) + SULFO- + T(HI)ON(ATE).]

dis·un·ion (dĭs-yo͞on'yən) *n.* 1. The state of being disunited; separation. 2. Lack of unity; discord.

dis·un·ion·ist (dĭs-yo͞on'yə-nĭst) *n.* One who advocates disunion, esp. a secessionist during the Civil War period.

dis·u·nite (dĭs'yo͞o-nīt') *v.* **-nit·ed, -nit·ing, -nites.** —*tr.* To disrupt the union of; separate. —*intr.* To become separate.

dis·u·ni·ty (dĭs-yo͞o'nĭ-tē) *n., pl.* **-ties.** Lack of unity; dissension.

dis·use (dĭs-yo͞os') *n.* The state of not being used or of being no longer in use; desuetude.

dis·u·til·i·ty (dĭs'yo͞o-tĭl'ĭ-tē) *n.* 1. Lack of utility; uselessness. 2. The quality of causing harm, inconvenience, or weariness.

dis·val·ue (dĭs-văl'yo͞o) *tr.v.* **-ued, -u·ing, -ues.** 1. To regard as of little or no value. 2. *Archaic.* To disparage. —*n.* Disesteem.

di·syl·la·ble (dī'sĭl'ə-bəl, dĭ-sĭl'-) also **dis·syl·la·ble** (dĭ-sĭl'-, dĭs'sĭl-, dī'sĭl'-) *n.* A word with two syllables. **—di'syl·lab'ic** (dī'sĭ-lăb'ĭk, dĭs'ĭ-) *adj.*

dit (dĭt) *n.* The oral representation of the dot in radio and telegraphic code. [Imit.]

ditch (dĭch) *n.* A long narrow trench or furrow dug in the ground, as for irrigation, drainage, or a boundary line. —*tr.v.* **ditched, ditch·ing, ditch·es.** 1. To dig or make a ditch in. 2. To surround with a ditch. 3. a. To drive (a vehicle) into a ditch. b. To derail (a train). 4. *Slang.* To throw aside; discard. 5. *Slang.* To escape from or avoid. 6. To bring (a land-based aircraft) down on water. [ME *dich* < OE *dīc.*]

dith·er (dĭth'ər) *n.* A state of agitation and indecision. —*intr.v.* **-ered, -er·ing, -ers.** To be nervously irresolute in acting or doing. [< ME *didderen,* to tremble.]

dith·y·ramb (dĭth'ĭ-răm', -rămb') *n.* 1. A frenzied and impassioned choric hymn and dance of ancient Greece in honor of Dionysus. 2. An irregular poetic expression suggestive of the ancient Greek dithyramb. [Lat. *dithyrambus* < Gk. *dithurambos.*] **—dith'y·ramb'ic** *adj.*

dit·ta·ny (dĭt'n-ē) *n., pl.* **-nies.** 1. An aromatic Old World plant, *Origanum dictamnus,* formerly believed to have magical powers. 2. The stone mint. 3. The gas plant. [ME *ditaine* < OFr. *ditain* < Med. Lat. *diptamnus* < Lat. *dictamnus* < Gk. *diktamnon.*]

dit·to (dĭt'ō) *n., pl.* **-tos.** 1. The same as stated above or before. Used to avoid repetition and indicated by a pair of small marks (") placed under the word that would otherwise be repeated. 2. A duplicate or copy. —*adv.* As before. —*tr.v.* **-toed, -to·ing, -tos.** To duplicate or repeat. —*interj.* Used to express sameness or agreement. [Dial. Ital. p.part. of Ital. *dire,* to say < Lat. *dicere.*]

dit·ty (dĭt'ē) *n., pl.* **-ties.** A simple song. [ME *dite,* a literary composition < OFr. *dite* < Lat. *dictatum,* p.part. of *dictare,* to dictate, freq. of *dicere,* to say.]

ditty bag *n.* A bag used by soldiers and sailors to carry small items such as sewing implements. [Orig. unknown.]

ditty box *n.* A box used like a ditty bag.

di·u·re·sis (dī'ə-rē'sĭs) *n.* Excessive discharge of urine. [NLat. < LLat. *diureticus,* diuretic.]

di·u·ret·ic (dī'ə-rĕt'ĭk) *adj.* Tending to increase the discharge of urine. —*n.* A diuretic drug. [ME *diuretik* < LLat. *diureticus* < Gk. *diouretikos* < *diourein,* to pass urine : *dia-,* through + *ourein,* to urinate < *ouron,* urine.] **—di'u·ret'ic·al·ly** *adv.*

di·ur·nal (dī-ûr'nəl) *adj.* 1. Pertaining to or occurring in a day or each day; daily. 2. Occurring or active during the daytime rather than at night. 3. *Bot.* Opening during daylight hours and closing at night. —*n. Archaic.* 1. A diary. 2. A daily newspaper. [ME < LLat. *diurnalis* < Lat. *diurnus* < *dies,* day.] **—di·ur'nal·ly** *adv.*

di·u·ron (dī'ə-rŏn') *n.* A persistent, white, crystalline solid, $C_9H_{10}Cl_2N_2O_3$, used as a pre-emergence herbicide. [DI- + UR(EA) + -ON.]

di·va (dē'və) *n., pl.* **-vas** or **-ve** (-vā). An operatic prima donna. [Ital. < Lat., goddess, fem. of *divus,* god.]

di·va·gate (dī'və-gāt', dĭv'ə-) *intr.v.* **-gat·ed, -gat·ing, -gates.** 1. To wander or drift about. 2. To ramble; digress. [LLat. *divagari, divagat-* : Lat. *dis-,* apart + Lat. *vagari,* to wander < *vagus,* wandering.] **—di'va·ga'tion** *n.*

di·va·lent (dī-vā'lənt) *adj.* Having a valence of 2; bivalent.

di·van (dĭ-văn') *n.* 1. (*also* dī'văn'). A long backless couch, esp. one against a wall with pillows. 2. a. (*also* dĭ-vän', dī-văn'). In Moslem countries, a counting room, tribunal, or public audience room. b. The seat used by an administrator when holding audience. c. A government bureau or council chamber. 3. (*also* dĭ-vän', dī-văn'). A coffee house or smoking lounge with divans. 4. (*also* dĭ-vän', dī-văn'). In the Middle East, a book of poems by one author. [Fr. < Turk. *dīvān* < Pers., register, office of accounts.]

di·var·i·cate (dī-văr'ĭ-kāt', dĭ-) *intr.v.* **-cat·ed, -cat·ing, -cates.** To diverge at a wide angle; spread apart. —*adj.* (dī-văr'ə-kĭt, -kāt', dĭ-). *Biol.* Branching or spreading widely from a point or axis; diverging. [Lat. *divaricare, divaricat-,* to be spread out : *dis-,* apart + *varicare,* to straddle < *varus,* bent.] **—di·var'i·cate'ly** *adv.*

di·var·i·ca·tion (dī-văr'ĭ-kā'shən, dĭ-) *n.* 1. The act of divaricating. 2. A divergence of opinion. 3. The point at which branching occurs.

dive[1] (dīv) *v.* **dived** or **dove** (dōv), **dived, div·ing, dives.** —*intr.* 1. a. To plunge headfirst into water, often as a sport. b. To go toward the bottom of a body of water; submerge. c. To submerge under power. Used of a submarine. d. To fall head down through the air. e. To descend nose down at an acceleration usually exceeding that of free fall. Used of an airplane. f. To engage in the sport of skydiving. g. To drop sharply and rapidly; plummet. 2. a. To rush headlong and vanish into: *dive into a crowd.* b. To plunge one's hand into. 3. To lunge: *dove for the loose ball.* 4. To plunge into an activity or enterprise with vigor and gusto. —*tr.* To cause (an aircraft or a submarine, for example) to dive. —*n.* 1. a. A headlong plunge into water, esp. one executed with athletic skill and form. b. A nearly vertical descent at an accelerated speed through water or space. c. A quick, pronounced drop. 2. *Slang.* A disreputable or run-down bar or nightclub. 3. *Slang.* A knockout feigned by prearrangement between prize fighters. [ME *diven* < OE *dȳfan,* to dip and *dūfan,* to sink.]

Usage: *Dove* as a past tense is actually a more recent form than the historically correct *dived. Dove* is widely used in speech and is acceptable in writing to about half of the Usage Panel.

diver

di·ve[2] (dē'vā) *n.* A plural of **diva.** [Ital.]

dive-bomb (dīv'bŏm') *tr.v.* **-bombed, -bomb·ing, -bombs.** To bomb from an airplane at the end of a steep dive toward the target. **—dive'-bomb'er** *n.*

div·er (dī'vər) *n.* 1. One that dives. 2. One who works under water, esp. one equipped with breathing apparatus and weighted clothing. 3. Any of several diving birds, esp. the loon.

di·verge (dĭ-vûrj', dī-) *v.* **-verged, -verg·ing, -verg·es.** —*intr.* 1. To go or extend in different directions from a common point; branch out. 2. To differ, as in opinion or manner. 3. To depart from a set course or norm; deviate. 4. *Math.* To fail to approach a limit. —*tr.* To cause to diverge; deflect. [LLat. *divergere,* to turn aside : Lat. *dis-,* apart + Lat. *vergere,* to bend.]

di·ver·gence (dĭ-vûr'jəns, dī-) also **di·ver·gen·cy** (-jən-sē) *n., pl.* **-genc·es** also **-gen·cies.** 1. a. The act of diverging.

b. The state of being divergent. **c.** The degree by which things diverge. **2.** Departure from a norm; deviation. **3.** Difference, as of opinion. **4.** *Math.* **a.** The property or manner of diverging; failure to approach a limit. **b.** The scalar product of the del operator and a vector function. **5.** A meteorological condition characterized by the uniform expansion in volume of a mass of air over a region, usually accompanied by fine dry weather.

di·ver·gent (dĭ-vûr′jənt, dī-) *adj.* **1. a.** Drawing apart from a common point; diverging. **b.** Causing divergence of radiation. **2.** Departing from convention; deviant. **3.** Differing from another: *a divergent opinion.* **4.** *Math.* Failing to approach a limit; not convergent. **—di·ver′gent·ly** *adv.*

di·vers (dī′vərz) *adj.* Various; several; sundry. [ME. —see DIVERSE.]

di·verse (dĭ-vûrs′, dī-, dī′vûrs′) *adj.* **1.** Distinct in kind; unlike. **2.** Having variety in form; diversified. [ME *divers, diverse* < OFr. *divers* < Lat. *diversus* < p.part. of *divertere,* to divert.] **—di·verse′ly** *adv.* **—di·verse′ness** *n.*

di·ver·si·form (dĭ-vûr′sə-fôrm′, dī-) *adj.* Having a variety of forms; variform.

di·ver·si·fy (dĭ-vûr′sə-fī′, dī-) *v.* **-fied, -fy·ing, -fies.** *—tr.* **1. a.** To give variety to; vary: *diversify a menu.* **b.** To extend (business activities) into disparate fields. **2.** To distribute (investments) among several companies in order to average the risk of loss. *—intr.* To spread out activities or investments, esp. in business. [ME *diversifien* < OFr. *diversifier* < Med. Lat. *diversificare* : Lat. *diversus,* diverse + Lat. *facere,* to make.] **—di·ver′si·fi·ca′tion** (-fĭ-kā′shən) *n.*

di·ver·sion (dĭ-vûr′zhən, -shən, dī-) *n.* **1.** An act or instance of diverting or turning aside; deviation. **2.** Something that distracts the mind and relaxes or entertains. **3.** A maneuver that draws the attention of an opponent away from the planned point of action, esp. as part of military strategy. **—di·ver′sion·ar′y** *adj.*

di·ver·sion·ist (dĭ-vûr′zhən-ĭst, -shən-, dī-) *n.* One engaged in diversionary, disruptive, or subversive activities.

di·ver·si·ty (dĭ-vûr′sĭ-tē, dī-) *n., pl.* **-ties. 1. a.** The fact or quality of being diverse; difference. **b.** A point or respect in which things differ. **2.** Variety or multiformity: *a healthy diversity in one's diet.*

di·vert (dĭ-vûrt′, dī-) *v.* **-vert·ed, -vert·ing, -verts.** *—tr.* **1.** To turn aside from a course or direction; deflect. **2.** To distract. **3.** To amuse; entertain. *—intr.* To turn aside. [ME *diverten* < OFr. *divertir* < Lat. *divertere* : *dis-,* aside + *vertere,* to turn.] **—di·vert′er** *n.* **—di·vert′ing·ly** *adv.*

di·ver·tic·u·la (dī′vûr-tĭk′yə-lə) *n.* Plural of **diverticulum.**

di·ver·tic·u·li·tis (dī′vûr-tĭk′yə-lī′tĭs) *n.* Inflammation of a diverticulum.

di·ver·tic·u·lo·sis (dī′vûr-tĭk′yə-lō′sĭs) *n.* A condition characterized by the presence of numerous diverticula in the colon. [DIVERTICUL(UM) + -OSIS.]

di·ver·tic·u·lum (dī′vûr-tĭk′yə-ləm) *n., pl.* **-la** (-lə). A pouch or sac branching out from a hollow organ or structure, such as the intestine. [NLat. < Lat. *deverticulum,* bypath < *devertere,* to turn aside : *de-,* away + *vertere,* to turn.] **—di′ver·tic′u·lar** *adj.*

di·ver·ti·men·to (dĭ-vĕr′tə-mĕn′tō) *n., pl.* **-tos** or **-ti** (-tē). *Mus.* A chiefly 18th-century form of instrumental chamber music having several short movements. [Ital., diversion < *divertire,* to divert < OFr. *divertir.*]

di·ver·tisse·ment (də-vûr′tĭs-mənt, dē-vĕr-tēs-mäN′) *n.* **1.** A short ballet or other performance given as an interlude in the opera or theater. **2.** *Mus.* A divertimento. **3.** A diversion; amusement. [Fr. < *divertir,* to divert < OFr.]

Di·ves (dī′vēz′) *n.* A man of wealth. [ME < Lat. < *dives,* rich.]

di·vest (dĭ-vĕst′, dī-) *tr.v.* **-vest·ed, -vest·ing, -vests. 1.** To strip, as of clothes. **2.** To deprive, as of rights or property; dispossess. **3.** *Law.* To devest. [Alteration of DEVEST.]

di·vide (dĭ-vīd′) *v.* **-vid·ed, -vid·ing, -vides.** *—tr.* **1. a.** To separate into parts, sections, groups, or branches. **b.** To sector into units of measurement; graduate. **c.** To separate and group according to kind; classify. **2. a.** To separate into opposing factions; disunite. **b.** *Chiefly Brit.* To cause (Parliamentary members) to vote by separating into groups, as pro and con. **3.** To separate from; cut off. **4.** To apportion among a number. **5.** *Math.* **a.** To subject to the process of division. **b.** To be an exact divisor of. *—intr.* **1. a.** To become separated into parts. **b.** To branch out, as a river. **c.** To form into factions; take sides. **d.** *Chiefly Brit.* To vote by dividing. **2.** To perform the mathematical operation of division. *—n.* **1.** A dividing point or line. **2.** A ridge of land; watershed. [ME *dividen* < Lat. *dividere.*] **—di·vid′a·ble** *adj.*

di·vid·ed (dĭ-vī′dĭd) *adj.* **1.** Separated into parts or pieces. **2.** In disagreement; disunited. **3.** Pulled by conflicting interests or activities. **4.** Separated by distance: *divided from her family and friends.* **5.** Having the lanes for opposing traffic separated. Used of a highway. **6.** *Bot.* Having indentations extending to the midrib or base and forming distinct divisions: *divided leaves.*

div·i·dend (dĭv′ĭ-dĕnd′) *n.* **1.** *Math.* A quantity to be divided. **2. a.** A share of profits received by a stockholder or by a policyholder in a mutual insurance society. **b.** A payment pro rata to a creditor of a person adjudged bankrupt. **3.** *Informal.* **a.** A share of a surplus; bonus. **b.** An unexpected gain, benefit, or advantage. [Lat. *dividendum,* neuter gerund. of *dividere,* to divide.]

di·vid·er (dĭ-vī′dər) *n.* **1.** One that divides, esp. a screen or other partition. **2. dividers.** A device resembling a compass, used for dividing lines and transferring measurements.

div·i-div·i (dĭv′ē-dĭv′ē) *n., pl.* **-is. 1.** A tropical American tree, *Caesalpina coriaria,* having compound leaves and long pods. **2.** The dried pods of the divi-divi, yielding an extract used in tanning leather. [Sp. *dividiví,* perh. of Cariban orig.]

div·i·na·tion (dĭv′ə-nā′shən) *n.* **1.** The art or act of foretelling future events or revealing occult knowledge by means of augury or alleged supernatural agency. **2.** An inspired guess or a presentiment. **3.** Something that has been divined. **—di·vin′a·to′ry** (dĭ-vĭn′ə-tôr′ē, -tōr′ē) *adj.*

di·vine[1] (dĭ-vīn′) *adj.* **-vin·er, -vin·est. 1. a.** Being or having the nature of a deity. **b.** Of, relating to, emanating from, or being the expression of a deity: *seek divine guidance through meditation.* **c.** In the service or worship of a deity or god; sacred; holy. **2.** Superhuman; godlike. **3.** Supremely good; magnificent. **4.** *Informal.* Heavenly; perfect. *—n.* **1.** A clergyman. **2.** A theologian. [ME < OFr. *devine* < Lat. *divinus* < *divus,* god.] **—di·vine′ly** *adv.* **—di·vine′ness** *n.*

di·vine[2] (dĭ-vīn′) *v.* **-vined, -vin·ing, -vines.** *—tr.* **1.** To foretell or reveal through the art of divination. **2. a.** To know by inspiration, intuition, or reflection. **b.** To guess. **3.** To locate (water) with a divining rod. *—intr.* **1.** To practice divination. **2.** To guess. [ME *divinen* < OFr. *deviner* < Lat. *divinare* < *divinus,* prophet < *divinus,* divine.] **—di·vin′er** *n.*

Divine Liturgy *n.* The Eastern Orthodox Eucharistic rite.

Divine Office *n. Rom. Cath. Ch.* The office of the breviary; the canonical hours.

divine right *n.* The doctrine that monarchs derive their right to rule directly from God and are accountable only to Him.

diving beetle *n.* Any of various predatory aquatic beetles of the family Dytiscidae.

diving bell *n.* A large vessel for underwater work, open on the bottom and supplied with air under pressure.

diving board *n.* A flexible board from which a dive may be executed, secured at one end and projecting over water at the other.

diving suit *n.* A heavy waterproof garment with a detachable air-fed helmet, used for underwater work.

divining rod *n.* A forked branch or stick that allegedly indicates subterranean water or minerals by bending downward when held over a source.

divining rod
16th-century woodcut

di·vin·i·ty (dĭ-vĭn′ĭ-tē) *n., pl.* **-ties. 1.** The state or quality of being divine. **2. a. the Divinity.** God; the godhead. **b.** A god or goddess; a deity. **3.** Godlike character. **4.** Theology. **5.** A soft, white candy, usually containing nuts.

di·vis·i·ble (dĭ-vĭz′ə-bəl) *adj.* Capable of being divided, esp. of being divided evenly with no remainder. **—di·vis′i·bil′i·ty, di·vis′i·ble·ness** *n.* **—di·vis′i·bly** *adv.*

di·vi·sion (dĭ-vĭzh′ən) *n.* **1. a.** The act or process of dividing. **b.** The state of being divided. **2.** The proportional distribution of a quantity or entity. **3.** Something that serves to divide or keep separate, as a boundary or partition. **4.** One of the parts, sections, or groups into which something is divided. **5. a.** An area of government or business activity organized as an administrative or functional unit. **b.** A territorial section marked off for political or governmental purposes. **6. a.** An administrative and tactical military unit that is smaller than a corps but is self-contained and equipped for prolonged combat activity. **b.** A group of several ships of similar type forming a tactical unit under a single command in the U.S. Navy. **c.** An air combat group of two or more combat wings and required service units in the U.S. Air Force. **7.** A major taxonomic category corresponding approximately to a phylum, used esp. in botany. **8.** A category created for purposes of competition, as in boxing. **9. a.** Variance of opinion; disagreement. **b.** A splitting into factions; disunion. **10.** *Chiefly Brit.* The physical separation and regrouping of members of Parliament according to their stand on an issue put to vote. **11.** *Math.* The operation of determining how many times one quantity is contained in another. **12.** A type of propagation characteristic of plants that spread by means of newly formed parts such as bulbs, suckers, or rhizomes. [ME *divisioun* < OFr. *division* < Lat. *divisio* < *divisus,* p.part. of *dividere,* to divide.] **—di·vi′sion·al** *adj.*

di·vi·sion·ism (də-vĭzh′ə-nĭz′əm) *n.* A branch of neo-impressionism in which colors are divided into their components and mechanically arranged so that the eye organizes the shape. **—di·vi′sion·ist** *n.*

division sign *n.* **1.** The symbol (÷) placed between two quantities to indicate the division of the first by the second. **2.** The symbol (/ or -) placed between two quantities to indicate a fraction.

di·vi·sive (dĭ-vī′sĭv) *adj.* Creating discord or dissension. **—di·vi′sive·ly** *adv.* **—di·vi′sive·ness** *n.*

di·vi·sor (dĭ-vī′zər) *n. Math.* The quantity by which another quantity, the dividend, is to be divided.

di·vorce (dĭ-vôrs′, -vōrs′) *n.* **1.** The legal dissolution of a marriage. **2.** A complete or radical separation of things closely connected. *—v.* **-vorced, -vorc·ing, -vorc·es.** *—tr.* **1.** To dissolve the marriage bond between. **2.** To shed (one's spouse) by legal divorce. **3.** To separate or remove; disunite.

—intr. To obtain a divorce. [ME < OFr. < Lat. *divortium,* separation < *divertere,* to divert.]

di·vor·cé (dĭ-vôr-sā′, -sē′, -vōr-, -vôr′sā′, -sē′, -vōr-) *n.* A divorced man. [Fr., masc. p.part. of *divorcer,* to divorce < OFr.]

di·vor·cée (dĭ-vôr-sā′, -sē′, -vōr-, -vôr′sā′, -sē′, -vōr′-) *n.* A divorced woman. [Fr., fem. p.part. of *divorcer,* to divorce < OFr.]

di·vorce·ment (dĭ-vôrs′mənt, -vōrs′-) *n.* A complete separation of things.

div·ot (dĭv′ət) *n.* **1.** A piece of turf torn up by a golf club in striking a ball. **2.** *Scot.* A thin square of turf or sod used for roofing. [Sc.]

di·vulge (dĭ-vŭlj′) *tr.v.* **-vulged, -vulg·ing, -vulg·es. 1.** To disclose (a secret); reveal. **2.** *Archaic.* To proclaim publicly. [ME *divulgen* < Lat. *divulgare,* to publish : *dis-,* among + *vulgus,* common people.] **—di·vul′gence** *n.* **—di·vulg′er** *n.*

di·vul·sion (dĭ-vŭl′shən) *n.* An act of tearing apart. [Lat. *divulsio* < *divulsus,* p.part. of *divellere,* to tear apart : *dis-,* apart + *vellere,* to pluck.] **—di·vul′sive** *adj.*

div·vy (dĭv′ē) *Slang. —tr.v.* **-vied, -vy·ing, -vies.** To divide: *divied up the loot. —n., pl.* **-vies.** A share or portion. [Shortening and alteration of DIVIDEND.]

Dix·ie (dĭk′sē) *n.* The Southern states, esp. those that joined the Confederacy during the Civil War. [After *Dixie,* a name for the Southern states in the song *Dixie* by Daniel D. Emmett (1815–1904).]

Dix·ie·crat (dĭk′sē-krăt′) *n.* A member of a dissenting group of Democrats in the South who formed the States' Rights Party in 1948. [DIXIE + (DEMO)CRAT.] **—Dix′ie·crat′ic** *adj.*

Dix·ie·land (dĭk′sē-lănd′) *n.* A style of instrumental jazz associated with New Orleans and characterized by a relatively fast two-beat rhythm and by group and solo improvisations.

di·zen (dī′zən, dĭz′ən) *tr.v.* **-zened, -zen·ing, -zens.** *Archaic.* To deck out in fine clothes or adornments; bedizen. [Obs. *disen,* to prepare a distaff with flax for spinning.] **—di′zen·ment** *n.*

di·zy·got·ic (dī′zī-gŏt′ĭk) *adj.* Derived from two separate and separately fertilized ova. Used esp. of fraternal twins. [DI- + ZYGOT(E) + -IC.]

diz·zy (dĭz′ē) *adj.* **-zi·er, -zi·est. 1.** Having a whirling sensation or feeling a tendency to fall. **2.** Bewildered or confused. **3. a.** Producing or tending to produce giddiness: *a dizzy height.* **b.** Caused by giddiness; reeling. **4.** Characterized by impulse and haste: *"The American language had begun its dizzy onward march before the Revolution"* (H.L. Mencken). **5.** *Informal.* Scatterbrained or silly. *—tr.v.* **-zied, -zy·ing, -zies. 1.** To make dizzy. **2.** To confuse or bewilder. [ME *dusie,* foolish < OE *dysig.*] **—diz′zi·ly** *adv.* **—diz′zi·ness** *n.*

djel·la·ba also **djel·la·bah** (jə-lä′bə) *n.* A long loose hooded garment with full sleeves, worn esp. in Moslem countries. [Ar. *jallabah.*]

djin·ni or **djin·ny** (jĭn′ē, jĭ-nē′) *n.* Variant of **jinni.**

D layer *n.* The lowest area of the ionosphere, existing only during the day as a layer in the D region.

DNA (dē′ĕn-ā′) *n.* A polymeric chromosomal constituent of living cell nuclei, consisting of two long chains of alternating phosphate and deoxyribose units twisted into a double helix and joined by hydrogen bonds between the complementary bases adenine and thymine or cytosine and guanine, each of which projects toward the axis of the helix from one of the strands where it is bonded in a sequence that determines individual hereditary characteristics; deoxyribonucleic acid. [D(EOXYRIBO)N(UCLEIC) A(CID).]

DNase (dē-ĕn′ās) also **DNAse** (dē′ĕn-ā′ās) *n.* An enzyme that hydrolyzes DNA to its component nucleotides. [DN(A) + -ASE.]

do[1] (do͞o) *v.* **did** (dĭd), **done** (dŭn), **do·ing, does** (dŭz). Present tense, first person, **do;** second person, **do;** third person singular, **does;** third person plural, **do.** *—tr.* **1.** To perform or execute. **2.** To carry out the requirements of. **3.** To produce, esp. by creative effort. **4.** To bring about; effect: *It won't do any good.* **5.** To bring or put forth; exert: *I'll do what I can.* **6.** To attend to so as to take care of or put in order: *do the bedrooms.* **7.** To deal with in order to prepare for use: *did the dishes.* **8.** To render or give: *do equal justice to the opposing sides.* **9.** To have as an occupation or profession. **10.** To work out by studying: *do a homework assignment.* **11.** To play the role of. **12.** To travel (a specified distance): *do a mile in four minutes.* **13.** To travel about in; tour: *do two cities in a week.* **14.** To meet the needs of sufficiently: *This room will do us very nicely.* **15. a.** To set or style (the hair). **b.** To apply cosmetics to: *did her face.* **16.** To decorate: *did the apartment in high tech.* **17.** *Informal.* To serve a prison term. **18.** *Slang.* To cheat or swindle: *do someone out of an inheritance. —intr.* **1.** To behave or conduct oneself; act. **2.** To act effectively or energetically; strive: *Do or die.* **3.** To get along; fare: *doing well at school.* **4.** To serve the purpose: *This coat will do for another season.* **5.** To be proper or fitting: *Such behavior won't do.* **6.** Used as a substitute for an antecedent verb: *worked as hard as everyone else did.* **7.** Used after a verb for emphasis: *Run quickly, do! —aux.* **1.** Used with a simple infinitive to indicate the tense in questions, negative statements, and inverted phrases: *Do you understand? I did not sleep well. Little did he suspect.* **2.** Used as a means of emphasis: *I do want to be sure. Do be still!* ***—phrasal verbs.*** **do away with. 1.** To make an end of; eliminate. **2.** To destroy; kill. **do by.** To behave with respect to; deal with. **do for. 1.** To care or provide for; take care of. **do in.** *Slang.* **1.** To tire completely; exhaust. **2.** To kill. **do up. 1.** To adorn or dress lavishly. **2.** To wrap and tie (a package). *—n., pl.* **do's** or **dos. 1.** *Regional.* Commotion; ado. **2.** *Chiefly Brit.* An entertainment; party. **3.** A statement of what should be done: *do's and don'ts.* **4.** *Chiefly Brit.* A swindle; cheat. **5.** *Archaic.* Duty. ***—idioms.*** **do a number on.** *Slang.* **1.** To confuse or defeat completely, esp. in an underhand manner. **2.** To make fun of. **do (oneself) proud.** To act or perform in a way that gives cause for pride. **do (one's) thing.** To do what one does best or finds most enjoyable. [ME *don* < OE *dōn.*]

do[2] (dō) *n. Mus.* The first tone of the diatonic scale in solfeggio. [Ital. —see GAMUT.]

do·a·ble (do͞o′ə-bəl) *adj.* Capable of being done.

do-all (do͞o′ôl′) *n.* A person employed to do all kinds of work; factotum.

dob·bin (dŏb′ĭn) *n.* A horse, esp. a workhorse. [< *Dobbin,* nickname for *Robert.*]

Do·bell's solution (dō′bĕlz′) *n.* An aqueous solution of sodium borate, sodium bicarbonate, glycerol, and phenol, used as an antiseptic and astringent for the mucous membranes, esp. of the nose and throat. [After Horace B. *Dobell* (1828–1917).]

Do·ber·man pin·scher (dō′bər-mən pĭn′shər) *n.* A fairly large dog of a breed originating in Germany, having a smooth, short, usually black coat. [G. *Dobermann* (after Ludwig *Dobermann,* 19th-cent. German dog breeder) + G. *Pinscher,* terrier.]

do·bra (dō′brə) *n.* See table at **currency.** [Port., ult. < Lat. *duplus,* double.]

dob·son (dŏb′sən) *n.* Hellgrammite. [Prob. < the name *Dobson.*]

dobson fly *n.* An insect, *Corydalus cornutus,* having four large, many-veined wings and long, pincerlike mandibles.

do·cent (dō′sənt, dō-sĕnt′) *n.* **1.** A teacher or lecturer at certain universities who is not a regular faculty member. **2.** A lecturer or tour guide in a museum. [Obs. G. < Lat. *Docens,* pr.part. of *docēre,* to teach.]

Do·ce·tism (dō-sē′tĭz′əm, dō′sə-tĭz′əm) *n.* The doctrine, espoused by a sect considered heretical in the early Christian Church, that Christ had no human body and only appeared to have died on the cross. [LLat. *Docetae,* espousers of Docetism < LGk. *Dokētai* < Gk. *dokein,* to seem.] **—Do·ce′tist** *n.*

doc·ile (dŏs′əl, -sīl′) *adj.* **1.** Easily taught; teachable. **2.** Submissive to training or management; tractable. [Lat. *docilis* < *docēre,* to teach.] **—doc′ile·ly** *adv.* **—do·cil′i·ty** (dŏ-sĭl′ə-tē, dō-) *n.*

dock[1] (dŏk) *n.* **1.** The area of water between two piers or alongside a pier that receives a ship for loading, unloading, or repairs. **2.** A pier or wharf. **3.** Often **docks.** A group of piers on a protected basin or other waterway serving as a general landing area for ships or boats. **4.** A platform at which trucks or trains load or unload cargo. *—v.* **docked, dock·ing, docks.** *—tr.* **1.** To maneuver (a vessel or other vehicle) into or next to a dock. **2.** *Aerospace.* To couple (two or more spacecraft, for example) in space. *—intr.* To move or come into a dock. [MDu. *docke,* prob. < Lat. *ductia,* act of leading < *ducere,* to lead.]

dock[2] (dŏk) *n.* **1.** The solid or fleshy part of an animal's tail. **2.** The tail of an animal after it has been bobbed or clipped. *—tr.v.* **docked, dock·ing, docks. 1.** To clip short or cut off (an animal's tail, for example). **2.** To withhold or deprive of a benefit or a part of the wages, esp. as a punishment. **3.** To deduct a part from (one's salary or wages). [ME *dok.*]

dock[3] (dŏk) *n.* An enclosed place where the defendant stands or sits in a criminal court. ***—idiom.*** **in the dock.** On trial or under intense scrutiny. [Flem. *docke,* cage.]

dock[4] (dŏk) *n.* Any of various weedy plants of the genus *Rumex,* having clusters of small greenish or reddish flowers. [ME < OE *docce.*]

dock·age (dŏk′ĭj) *n.* **1.** A charge for docking privileges. **2.** Facilities for docking vessels. **3.** The docking of ships.

dock·er[1] (dŏk′ər) *n.* One that docks something, as the tail of an animal.

dock·er[2] (dŏk′ər) *n.* A longshoreman.

dock·et (dŏk′ĭt) *n.* **1.** A summary or other brief statement of the contents of a document; abstract. **2.** *Law.* **a.** A brief entry of the proceedings in a court of justice. **b.** The book containing such entries. **c.** A calendar of the cases awaiting action in a court. **3.** A list of things to be done; agenda. **4.** A label on or ticket affixed to a package listing the contents or directions for assembling or operating. *—tr.v.* **-et·ed, -et·ing, -ets. 1.** To provide with a brief identifying statement. **2.** To enter in a docket. **3.** To label or ticket (a parcel). [ME *doggett.*]

dock·hand (dŏk′hănd′) *n.* A dock worker; longshoreman.

dock·mack·ie (dŏk′măk′ē) *n.* A shrub, *Viburnum acerifolium,* of eastern North America, having clusters of white flowers. [Prob. < Du. < Delaware *dogekumak.*]

dock·work·er (dŏk′wûr′kər) *n.* A longshoreman.

dock·yard (dŏk′yärd′) *n.* **1.** An area, often bordering a body

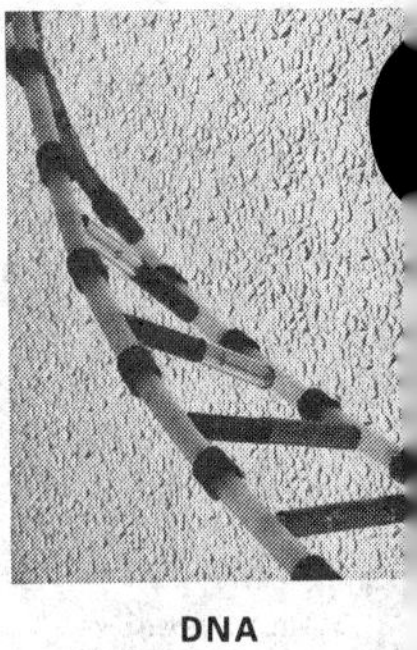

DNA
Model of DNA molecule showing the configuration and the four nucleotides that are building blocks of the DNA molecule

Doberman pinscher

p **pop** / r **roar** / s **sauce** / sh **ship, dish** / t **tight** / th **thin, path** / *th* **this, bathe** / ŭ **cut** / ûr **urge** / v **valve** / w **with** / y **yes** / z **zebra, size** / zh **vision** / ə **about, item, edible, gallop, circus** / œ *Fr.* **feu,** *Ger.* **schön** / ü *Fr.* **tu,** *Ger.* **über** / KH *Ger.* **ich,** *Scot.* **loch** / N *Fr.* **bon.**

of water, with facilities for building, repairing, or dry-docking ships. **2.** *Chiefly Brit.* A navy yard.

doc·tor (dŏk′tər) *n.* **1. a.** A person who has earned the highest academic degree awarded by a college or university in a specified discipline: *a Doctor of Music.* **b.** A person awarded an honorary degree by a college or university. **2.** A person trained in the healing arts and licensed to practice, esp. a physician, surgeon, dentist, or veterinarian. **3.** The title used in addressing a person who holds the degree of doctor. **4.** *Obs.* A learned person; teacher. **5.** A rig or device contrived for remedying an emergency situation or for doing a special task. **6.** Any of several brightly colored artificial flies used in fly fishing: *a silver doctor.* —*v.* **-tored, -tor·ing, -tors.** *Informal.* —*tr.* **1.** To give medical treatment to. **2.** To repair, esp. in a makeshift manner. **3.** To change or falsify so as to make favorable to oneself: *doctored the evidence.* **4.** To add ingredients to (food) in order to improve taste or appearance. **5.** To alter or modify for a specific end: *doctored his standard speech for the small-town audience.* —*intr.* **1.** To practice medicine. **2.** To receive medical treatment. [ME, an expert, authority < OFr. *docteur* < Lat. *doctor,* teacher < *docēre,* to teach.] **—doc′tor·al** *adj.*

doc·tor·ate (dŏk′tər-ĭt) *n.* The degree or status of a doctor as conferred by a university.

doc·tri·naire (dŏk′trə-nâr′) *n.* A person inflexibly attached to a practice or theory without regard to its practicality. —*adj.* Of, pertaining to, or characteristic of a doctrinaire; dogmatic. [Fr. < *doctrine,* doctrine < OFr.] **—doc′tri·nair′ism** *n.* **—doc′tri·nar′i·an** *n.*

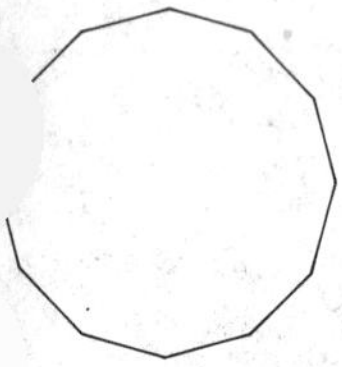

dodecagon

doc·tri·nal (dŏk′trə-nəl) *adj.* Belonging to, characterized by, or concerning doctrine. **—doc′tri·nal·ly** *adv.*

doc·trine (dŏk′trĭn) *n.* **1.** Something that is taught. **2.** A principle or body of principles presented for acceptance or belief, as by a religious, political, scientific, or philosophic group; dogma. **3.** A rule or principle of law, esp. when established by precedent. **4.** A statement of official government policy, esp. in foreign affairs. [ME < OFr. < Lat. *doctrina,* teaching, learning < *doctor,* teacher < *docēre,* to teach.]

doc·u·dra·ma (dŏk′yə-drä′mə, -drăm′ə) *n.* A television or motion-picture dramatization of events based on fact. [DOCU(MENTARY) + DRAMA.]

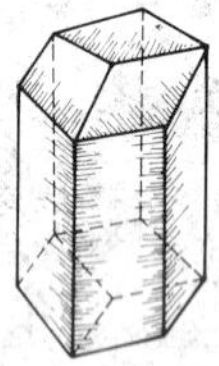

dodecahedron

doc·u·ment (dŏk′yə-mənt) *n.* **1.** A written or printed paper bearing the original, official, or legal form of something, and which can be used to furnish decisive evidence or information. **2.** Something serving as evidence or proof, esp. a material substance, as a coin, bearing a revealing symbol or mark. —*tr.v.* **-ment·ed, -ment·ing, -ments.** **1.** To furnish with a document. **2.** To support (an assertion or claim, for example) with evidence or decisive information. **3.** To support (statements in a book, for example) with written references or citations; annotate. [ME, precept < OFr. < Lat. *documentum,* lesson < *docēre,* to teach.] **—doc′u·ment′al** *adj.*

doc·u·ment·al·ist (dŏk′yə-mĕn′tl-ĭst′) *n.* One who specializes in documentation.

doc·u·men·ta·ry (dŏk′yə-mĕn′tə-rē) *adj.* **1.** Consisting of, concerning, or based upon documents. **2.** Presenting facts objectively without editorializing or inserting fictional matter, as in a book or film. —*n., pl.* **-ries.** A television or motion-picture presentation of factual, political, social, or historical events or circumstances, often consisting of actual news films accompanied by narration.

dodo

doc·u·men·ta·tion (dŏk′yə-mĕn-tā′shən) *n.* **1. a.** The act or an instance of the supplying of documents or supporting references or records. **b.** The documents or references supplied. **2.** The collation, synopsizing, and coding of printed material for future reference. **3.** *Computer Sci.* The orderly presentation, organization, and communication of recorded special knowledge to produce a historical record of changes in variables.

dod·der[1] (dŏd′ər) *intr.v.* **-dered, -der·ing, -ders.** **1.** To shake or tremble, as from old age; totter. **2.** To progress in a feeble, unsteady manner. [ME *daderen.*] **—dod′der·er** *n.*

dod·der[2] (dŏd′ər) *n.* Any of various parasitic vines of the genus *Cuscuta,* having slender, twining yellow or reddish stems with a few minute, scalelike leaves, and small whitish flowers. [ME *doder* < MLG, yolk of an egg.]

dod·dered (dŏd′ərd) *adj.* **1.** Lacking the top branches as a result of age or decay. **2.** Infirm or feeble. [Alteration of *dodded,* p.part.of dial. *dod,* to lop off < ME *dodden.*]

dod·der·ing (dŏd′ər-ĭng) *adj.* Feeble-minded from age; senile.

do·dec·a·gon (dō-dĕk′ə-gŏn′) *n.* A polygon with 12 sides. [Gk. *dōdekagōnon* : *dōdeka,* twelve (*duo,* two + *deka,* ten) + *-gōnon,* -gon.] **—do′de·cag′o·nal** (dō′dĕ-kăg′ə-nəl) *adj.*

do·dec·a·he·dron (dō′dĕk-ə-hē′drən) *n., pl.* **-drons** or **-dra** (-drə). A polyhedron with 12 faces. [Gk. *dōdekaedron* : *dōdeka,* twelve (*duo,* two + *deka,* ten) + *-edron,* -hedron.] **—do′dec·a·he′dral** *adj.*

do·dec·a·phon·ic (dō′dĕk-ə-fŏn′ĭk) *adj.* Pertaining to, composed in, or consisting of twelve-tone music. [Gk. *dōdeka,* twelve (*duo,* two + *deka,* ten) + PHONIC.] **—do·dec′a·phon·ist** (-fə-nĭst, dō′də-kăf′ə-) *n.* **—do·dec′a·phon′y** (-fō′nē, dō′də-kăf′ə-), **do·dec′a·phon·ism** *n.*

dodge (dŏj) *v.* **dodged, dodg·ing, dodg·es.** —*tr.* **1.** To avoid (a blow, for example) by moving or shifting quickly aside. **2.** To evade (an obligation, for example) by cunning, trickery, or deceit: *kept dodging the reporter's questions.* —*intr.* **1.** To move aside or in a given direction by shifting or twisting suddenly: *dodged through the throng.* **2.** To practice trickery or cunning; prevaricate. **3.** To blunt or reduce the intensity of (a section of a photograph) by shading during the printing process. —*n.* **1.** An act of dodging. **2.** A clever or evasive plan or device; stratagem. [Orig. unknown.]

dodg·er (dŏj′ər) *n.* **1.** A person who dodges or evades. **2.** A shifty or dishonest person; trickster. **3.** A small printed handbill. **4.** *Southern U.S.* A corndodger.

dodg·y (dŏj′ē) *adj.* **-i·er, -i·est.** *Chiefly Brit.* Evasive; shifty.

do·do (dō′dō) *n., pl.* **-does** or **-dos.** **1.** A large flightless bird, *Raphus cucullatus,* of the island of Mauritius in the Indian Ocean, that has been extinct since the late 17th century. **2.** *Informal.* One whose dress, lifestyle, and ideas are hopelessly passé. **3.** *Informal.* A stupid person; simpleton. [Port. *doudo* < *doudo,* stupid.]

doe (dō) *n., pl.* **doe** or **does.** **1.** The female of a deer or related animal. **2.** The female of various mammals, such as the hare or kangaroo. [ME *do* < OE *dā.*]

do·er (do͞o′ər) *n.* **1.** A person who does something, as an agent. **2.** A particularly active and energetic person.

does (dŭz) *v.* Third person singular present tense of **do**[1].

doe·skin (dō′skĭn′) *n.* **1. a.** The skin of a doe, deer, or goat. **b.** Leather made from this and used esp. for gloves. **2.** A fine, soft, smooth woolen fabric. **3.** A densely napped finish for certain woolen fabrics, such as flannel.

does·n't (dŭz′ənt). Does not.

do·est (do͞o′ĭst) *v. Archaic.* Second person singular present tense of **do**[1].

do·eth (do͞o′əth) *v. Archaic.* Third person singular present tense of do.

doff (dôf, dŏf) *tr.v.* **doffed, doff·ing, doffs.** **1.** To remove or take off: *doff one's clothes.* **2.** To tip or remove (one's hat) in salutation. **3.** To throw out or away; discard. [ME *doffen* < *don off,* to do off.]

dog (dôg, dŏg) *n.* **1.** A domesticated carnivorous mammal, *Canis familiaris,* raised in a wide variety of breeds and probably originally derived from several wild species. **2.** Any of various animals of the family Canidae, such as the dingo. **3.** A male canine animal, esp. of a domesticated breed or of the fox. **4.** Any of various mammals, such as the prairie dog. **5.** *Informal.* A fellow: *you lucky dog.* **6.** *Slang.* **a.** An uninteresting, unattractive, or unresponsive person. **b.** A hopelessly inferior product or creation: *That play was a real dog.* **c.** A contemptible wretched fellow. **7. dogs.** *Slang.* The feet. **8.** A firedog; andiron. **9.** *Slang.* A hot dog; wiener. **10.** Any of various hooked or U-shaped metallic devices used for gripping or holding heavy objects. **11.** *Astron.* Sun dog. —*adv.* Totally; completely: *dog-tired.* —*tr.v.* **dogged, dog·ging, dogs.** **1.** To track or trail persistently: *"A stranger then is still dogging us"* (Arthur Conan Doyle). **2.** To hold or fasten with a mechanical dog. ***—idioms.*** **go to the dogs.** *Informal.* To go to ruin; degenerate. **put on the dog.** *Informal.* To make an ostentatious display of elegance, wealth, or culture; feign refinement. [ME *dogge* < OE *docga.*]

dog·bane (dôg′bān′, dŏg′-) *n.* Any of several plants of the genus *Apocynum,* having milky juice and bell-shaped white or pink flowers.

dog·ber·ry (dôg′bĕr′ē, dŏg′-) *n.* **1.** A wild gooseberry, *Ribes cynosbati,* of eastern North America, bearing large, prickly berries. **2.** Any of several plants or shrubs bearing berrylike fruit. **3.** The fruit of any of the dogberries.

dog biscuit *n.* **1.** A hard cracker for dogs. **2.** *Slang.* A hard biscuit or cracker used as an army field ration.

dog·cart (dôg′kärt′, dŏg′-) *n.* **1.** A vehicle drawn by one horse and accommodating two persons seated back to back. **2.** A small cart pulled by dogs.

dog·catch·er (dôg′kăch′ər, dŏg′-) *n.* A dog officer.

dog collar *n.* **1.** A collar for a dog. **2.** *Slang.* A clerical collar. **3.** A choker (sense 2.a.).

dog days *pl.n.* **1.** The hot, sultry period between mid-July and September. **2.** A period of stagnation. [Transl. of LLat. *dies caniculares,* Dog Star days (so called because the Dog Star (Sirius) rises and sets with the sun during this time).]

doge (dōj) *n.* The elected chief magistrate of the former republics of Venice and Genoa. [Fr. < dial. Ital. < Lat. *dux,* leader < *ducere,* to lead.]

dog-ear (dôg′îr′, dŏg′-) *n.* A turned-down corner of the page of a book. —*tr.v.* **-eared, -ear·ing, -ears.** **1.** To turn down the corner of (a book page). **2.** To make worn or shabby from overuse. **—dog′-eared′** *adj.*

dog-eat-dog (dôg′ēt-dôg′, dŏg′ēt-dŏg′) *adj.* Ruthlessly competitive or acquisitive: *a dog-eat-dog society.*

dog·face (dôg′fās′, dŏg′-) *n. Slang.* An infantryman in the U.S. Army in World War II.

dog fennel *n.* **1.** Any of various strong-smelling plants of the genus *Anthemis,* such as the mayweed. **2.** A weedy plant, *Eupatorium capillifolium,* of the southeastern United States, having divided leaves and long clusters of greenish flowers.

dog·fight (dôg′fīt′, dŏg′-) *n.* **1.** A violent fight between or as if between dogs; brawl. **2.** An aerial battle between fighter planes.

dog·fish (dôg′fĭsh′, dŏg′-) *n., pl.* **dogfish** or **-fish·es.** **1.** Any of various small sharks, chiefly of the family Squalidae, of Atlantic and Pacific coastal waters. **2.** The bowfin.

dog·ged (dô'gĭd, dŏg'ĭd) *adj.* Not yielding readily; willful; stubborn. **—dog'ged·ly** *adv.* **—dog'ged·ness** *n.*

dog·ger·el (dô'gər-əl, dŏg'ər-) also **dog·grel** (dôg'rəl, dŏg'-) *—n.* Verse of a loose, irregular rhythm or of a trivial nature. *—adj.* Pertaining to or written in doggerel. [ME, poor, worthless < *dogge,* dog.]

dog·ger·y (dô'gə-rē, dŏg'ə-) *n., pl.* **-ies. 1.** Surly behavior; meanness. **2.** Rabble or riffraff. **3.** A cheap bar or saloon.

dog·gie (dô'gē, dŏg'ē) *n.* Variant of **doggy.**

doggie bag *n.* Variant of **doggy bag.**

dog·gish (dô'gĭsh, dŏg'ĭsh) *adj.* **1.** Pertaining to or suggestive of a dog. **2.** Surly or gruff. **3.** *Informal.* Showily stylish.

dog·gone (dôg'gôn', -gŏn', dŏg'-) *n.* Damn.

dog·grel (dôg'rəl, dŏg'-) *n. & adj.* Variant of **doggerel.**

dog·gy or **dog·gie** (dô'gē, dŏg'ē) *—n., pl.* **-gies.** A dog, esp. a small one. *—adj.* **-gi·er, -gi·est.** Of or like a dog.

doggy bag or **doggie bag** *n.* A bag for leftover food that a restaurant customer may take home. [From the assumption that such food would be given to the customer's dog.]

dog·house (dôg'hous', dŏg'-) *n.* A small house or shelter for a dog. *—idiom.* **in the doghouse.** *Slang.* In disfavor; in trouble.

do·gie also **do·gy** (dō'gē) *n., pl.* **-gies.** *Western U.S.* A motherless or stray calf. [Orig. unknown.]

dog in the manger *n.* One who prevents others from enjoying what he himself has no use for. [From a fable in which a dog prevented an ox from eating hay he did not want himself.]

dog·leg (dôg'lĕg', dŏg'-) *n.* **1.** Something that has a sharp bend, esp. a road that bends or curves abruptly. **2.** A golf hole in which the fairway is abruptly angled *—intr.v.* **-legged, -leg·ging, -legs.** To move along a dogleg course: *The fairway doglegs to the left.* **—dog'leg'ged** (-lĕg'ĭd, -lĕgd') *adj.*

dog·ma (dôg'mə, dŏg'-) *n., pl.* **-mas** or **-ma·ta** (-mə-tə). **1.** *Theol.* A system of doctrines proclaimed true by a religious sect: *Christian dogma.* **2.** A principle, belief, or statement of idea or opinion, esp. one authoritatively considered to be absolute truth. **3.** A system of principles or beliefs: *"The dogmas of the quiet past are inadequate to the stormy present"* (Abraham Lincoln). [Lat. < Gk., opinion, belief < *dokein,* to seem, think.]

dog·mat·ic (dôg-măt'ĭk, dŏg-) also **dog·mat·i·cal** (-ĭ-kəl). *adj.* **1.** Pertaining to or characteristic of dogma. **2.** Characterized by an authoritative, arrogant assertion of unproved or unprovable principles. [LLat. *dogmaticus* < Gk. *dogmatikos* < *dogma,* belief. —see DOGMA.] **—dog·mat'i·cal·ly** *adv.*

dog·mat·ics (dôg-măt'ĭks, dŏg-) *n. (used with a sing. verb).* The study of religious dogmas, esp. those of the Christian church.

dog·ma·tism (dôg'mə-tĭz'əm, dŏg'-) *n.* Dogmatic assertion of opinion or belief.

dog·ma·tist (dôg'mə-tĭst, dŏg'-) *n.* **1.** An arrogantly assertive person. **2.** One who expresses or sets forth dogma.

dog·ma·tize (dôg'mə-tīz', dŏg'-) *v.* **-tized, -tiz·ing, -tiz·es.** *—intr.* To express oneself dogmatically in writing or speech. *—tr.* To proclaim as dogma. **—dog'ma·ti·za'tion** *n.*

dog·nap (dôg'năp') *tr.v.* **-naped, -nap·ing, -naps** or **-napped, -nap·ping, -naps.** To steal (a dog), esp. for the purpose of selling it to a research laboratory. [DOG + KID(NAP).] **—dog'nap'per** *n.*

dog officer *n.* One appointed or elected to impound stray dogs.

do-good·er (do͞o'go͝od'ər) *n. Informal.* One who is naively idealistic in supporting philanthropic or humanitarian reforms. **—do'-good'ism** *n.*

dog paddle *n.* A prone swimming stroke in which the arms and legs remain submerged and each limb paddles in alternation.

dog rose *n.* A prickly wild rose, *Rosa canina,* native to Europe, having fragrant pink or white flowers.

dog's age *n. Informal.* A long time.

dogs·bod·y (dôgz'bŏd'ē, dŏgz'-) *n. Chiefly Brit. Slang.* One who does menial work; drudge. [Brit. slang, midshipman.]

dog's chance *n.* A very slim chance for one's success.

dog sled also **dog sledge** *n.* A sled pulled by one or more dogs.

dog's life *n. Informal.* An unhappy, slavish existence.

dog's mercury *n.* A creeping, ill-smelling Old World weed, *Mercurialis perennis,* having small greenish flowers.

Dog Star *n.* **1.** Sirius. **2.** Procyon.

dog tag *n.* **1.** A metal identification disk attached to a dog's collar. **2.** A military identification tag worn on a chain around the neck.

dog-tired (dôg'tīrd', dŏg'-) *adj.* Extremely tired; exhausted.

dog·tooth (dôg'to͞oth', dŏg'-) *n.* **1.** A canine tooth; eyetooth. **2.** *Archit.* A medieval architectural ornament consisting of four leaflike projections radiating from a raised center.

dogtooth violet *n.* Any of several plants of the genus *Erythronium,* esp. *E. americanum,* of North America, having leaves with reddish blotches and nodding, lilylike yellow flowers.

dog·trot (dôg'trŏt', dŏg'-) *n.* **1.** A steady trot like that of a dog. **2.** *Regional.* A roofed passage between two parts of a structure.

dog·watch (dôg'wŏch', dŏg'-) *n. Naut.* Either of two short periods of watch duty, from 4 to 6 P.M. or from 6 to 8 P.M.

dog·wood (dôg'wo͝od', dŏg'-) *n.* **1.** A tree, *Cornus florida,* of eastern North America, having small greenish flowers surrounded by showy white or pink bracts that resemble petals. **2.** Any of several trees or shrubs of the genus *Cornus.*

dogwood

do·gy (dō'gē) *n.* Variant of **dogie.**

doi·ly also **doy·ly** or **doy·ley** (doi'lē) *n., pl.* **-lies** also **-leys. 1.** A small ornamental mat, usually made of lace or linen. **2.** A small table napkin. [After *Doily* or *Doyly,* 18th-cent. London draper.]

do·ing (do͞o'ĭng) *n.* **1.** The act of performing something: *a job not worth the doing.* **2. doings.** Events or activities, esp. social activities.

doit (doit) *n.* **1.** A former Dutch coin worth about 1/4 cent. **2.** A small part of something; bit. [Du. *duit* < MDu.]

do-it-your·self (do͞o'ĭt-yər-sĕlf') *adj. Informal.* Of, relating to, or designed to be done by an amateur or as a hobby: *do-it-yourself home repairs; a do-it-yourself stereo kit.* **—do'-it-your·self'er** *n.*

do·jo (dō'jō) *n.* A school for training in Japanese arts of self-defense, such as judo and karate. [J. : *do,* art + *-jo,* ground.]

dol (dŏl) *n.* A unit used to measure pain, or by inference analgesia, based on application of heat to the skin. [< Lat. *dolor,* pain. —see DOLOR.]

do·lab·ri·form (dō-lăb'rə-fôrm') also **do·lab·rate** (-rāt') *adj. Biol.* Having the shape of the head of an ax. [Lat. *dolabra,* pickax < *dolare,* to hew + -FORM.]

Dol·by System (dōl'bē). A trademark for an electronic device that eliminates noise from recorded sound.

dol·ce (dōl'chā') *adv. Mus.* Gently and sweetly. Used as a direction. [Ital. < Lat. *dulcis,* sweet.] **—dol'ce** *adj.*

dolce vi·ta (vē'tä) *n.* A self-indulgent and sensual life. [Ital. : *dolce,* sweet + *vita,* life.]

doily

dol·drums (dōl'drəmz', dôl'-, dŏl'-) *n. (used with a sing. verb).* **1. a.** Ocean regions near the equator, characterized by calms or light winds. **b.** The calms characteristic of these areas. **2. a.** A period of inactivity or recession. **b.** A period or spell of listlessness or depression. [< Obs. *doldrum,* dullard < *dol,* var. of DULL.]

dole[1] (dōl) *n.* **1.** The distribution or dispensing of goods, esp. of money, food, or clothing as charity. **2.** A gift or share of money, food, or clothing distributed as charity. **3.** *Chiefly Brit.* The distribution by the government of relief payments to the unemployed. **4.** *Archaic.* One's fate. *—tr.v.* **doled, dol·ing, doles. 1.** To distribute or dispense as charity. **2.** To distribute in small portions. *—idiom.* **on the dole.** Receiving regular relief payments from or as if from the government. [ME *dol,* part, share < OE *dāl.*]

dole[2] (dōl) *n. Archaic.* Grief; sorrow; dolor. [ME *dol* < OFr. < LLat. *dolus* < Lat. *dolēre,* to feel pain, grieve.]

dole·ful (dōl'fəl) *adj.* **1.** Filled with or expressing grief; sad; melancholy: *a doleful song.* **2.** Causing grief: *a doleful loss.* **—dole'ful·ly** *adv.* **—dole'ful·ness** *n.*

dol·er·ite (dŏl'ə-rīt') *n.* **1.** *Chiefly Brit.* A coarse variety of basalt; diabase. **2.** A dark igneous rock with macroscopically indeterminate composition. [Fr. *dolérite* < Gk. *doleros,* deceitful < *dolos,* trick (from its easily being mistaken for diorite).] **—dol'er·it'ic** *adj.*

dol·i·cho·ce·phal·ic (dŏl'ĭ-kō-sə-făl'ĭk) also **dol·i·cho·ceph·a·lous** (-sĕf'ə-ləs) *adj.* Having a relatively long head; designating a skull that is longer than it is broad, with a cephalic index of 75.9 or less. [Gk. *dolikhas,* long + -CEPHALIC.] **—dol'i·cho·ceph'a·lism** (-sĕf'ə-lĭz'əm), **dol'i·cho·ceph'a·ly** (-sĕf'ə-lē) *n.*

dol·i·cho·cran·i·al (dŏl'ə-kō-krā'nē-əl) also **dol·i·cho·cran·ic** (-nĭk) *adj.* Having a relatively long head; designating a skull that is longer than it is broad, with a cranial index of 75.9 or less. [Gk. *dolikhos,* long + CRANIAL.] **—dol'i·cho·cran'y** *n.*

do-lit·tle (do͞o'lĭt'l) *n.* A lazy, self-indulgent person.

doll (dŏl) *n.* **1.** A child's toy representing a human being. **2.** A pretty child. **3.** *Slang.* **a.** An attractive person. **b.** A woman. **4. a.** A sweetheart or darling. **b.** A person regarded with fond familiarity: *My boss is a living doll.* *—v.* **dolled, doll·ing, dolls.** *Slang.* *—intr.* To dress up or adorn oneself smartly, as for a special occasion. *—tr.* To dress (oneself) up smartly, esp. for ostentation. [< *Doll,* nickname for *Dorothy.*]

dol·lar (dŏl'ər) *n.* **1.** See table at **currency. 2.** A coin or note worth one dollar. [LG *daler,* taler < G. *Taler,* short for *Joachimstaler,* after *Joachimstal,* a mining community in Bohemia where they were first minted.]

dol·lar-a-year (dŏl'ər-ə-yîr') *adj.* Designating U.S. Federal employees who receive token payment for patriotic service: *a dollar-a-year government consultant.*

dollar cost averaging *n.* The periodic investment of a fixed dollar amount in the stock market regardless of prevailing prices.

dollar diplomacy *n.* **1.** A policy aimed at furthering the interests of the United States abroad by encouraging the investment of U.S. capital in foreign countries. **2.** A policy designed to safeguard a nation's foreign investments.

dol·lar·fish (dŏl′ər-fĭsh′) *n., pl.* **dollarfish** or **-fish·es.** The moonfish (sense 1).

dollar sign *n.* The symbol ($) for a dollar when placed before a numeral.

dol·lop (dŏl′əp) *n.* **1.** A large lump or portion, as of ice cream. **2.** A small quantity or splash of liquid, as of whiskey. **3.** A small amount: *not a dollop of truth to the story.* [Orig. unknown.]

dolly

dol·ly (dŏl′ē) *n., pl.* **-lies. 1.** A doll (sense 1). **2. a.** A low mobile platform that rolls on casters, used for moving heavy loads. **b.** Such a platform as used by one working underneath an automobile or other vehicle. **3.** A wheeled apparatus used to move a motion-picture or television camera about a set. **4.** A small locomotive for use in a railroad yard, construction site, or similar area. **5.** A wooden implement for stirring clothes in a washtub. **6.** A tool used to hold one end of a rivet while the opposite end is being hammered to form a head. **7.** A small piece of wood or metal placed on the head of a pile to prevent damage while the pile is being driven. —*intr.v.* **-lied, -ly·ing, -lies.** To move the dolly on which a motion-picture or television camera is mounted toward or away from the scene of action.

Dol·ly Var·den (dŏl′ē vär′dn) *n.* **1.** A 19th-century ladies' costume consisting of a dress with a tight bodice and a flowered skirt draped over a brightly colored petticoat. **2.** A colorfully spotted trout, *Salvelinus malma,* of northwestern North America. [After *Dolly Varden,* a character in the novel *Barnaby Rudge* by Charles Dickens (1812–1870).]

dol·man (dŏl′mən) *n.* **1.** A long Turkish outer robe. **2.** A woman's cloak or coat with capelike arm pieces. **3.** A decorated jacket often worn like a cape as part of a hussar's uniform. [Fr. < G. < Turk. *dolaman,* robe < *dolamak,* to wind.]

dolman sleeve *n.* A full sleeve that is very wide at the armhole and narrow at the wrist.

dol·men (dŏl′mən) *n.* A prehistoric megalithic structure consisting of two or more upright stones with a capstone, typically forming a chamber. [Fr. : Breton *tol,* table (< Lat. *tabula*) + Breton *men,* stone.]

dol·o·mite (dŏl′ə-mīt′) *n.* **1.** A light-tinted, esp. gray, pink, or white mineral, essentially $CaMg(CO_3)_2$, used as a furnace refractory, a construction and ceramic material, and in fertilizer. **2.** A magnesia-rich sedimentary rock resembling limestone. [Fr., after Déodat de *Dolomieu* (1705–1801).] —**dol′o·mit′ic** (-mĭt′ĭk) *adj.* —**dol′o·mit′i·za′tion** (-mĭt′ĭ-zā′shən) *n.* —**dol′o·mit·ize′** (-mĭt-īz′) *v.* **(-ized, -iz·ing, -iz·es).**

do·lor (dō′lər) *n. Archaic.* Sorrow; grief. [ME *dolour* < OFr. < Lat. *dolor,* pain < *dolēre,* to feel pain.]

do·lo·ro·so (dō′lə-rō′sō) *Mus.* —*adj.* Mournful; plaintive. —*adv.* With a mournful or plaintive tempo or quality. Used as a direction to the performer. [Ital. < Lat. *dolorosus,* dolorous.]

do·lor·ous (dō′lə-rəs, dŏl′ə-) *adj.* Marked by or showing sorrow or pain. [ME < Lat. *dolorus* < *dolor,* dolor.] —**do′lor·ous·ly** *adv.* —**do′lor·ous·ness** *n.*

do·lour (dō′lər) *n. Chiefly Brit.* Variant of **dolor.**

dolphin

dol·phin (dŏl′fĭn, dôl′-) *n.* **1.** Any of various marine mammals, chiefly of the family Delphinidae, related to the whales but generally smaller and having a beaklike snout, esp. the common, widely distributed species *Delphinus delphis.* **2.** Either of two marine fishes, *Coryphaena hippurus* or *C. equisetis,* having iridescent coloring. [ME < OFr. *dalfin* < Med. Lat. *dalfinus* < Lat. *delphinus* < Gk. *delphis.*]

dolphin striker *n. Naut.* A small vertical spar under the bowsprit of a sailboat that extends and helps support the jib boom; martingale.

dolt (dōlt) *n.* A dullard; blockhead. [Perh. < ME *dol,* dull.] —**dolt′ish** *adj.* —**dolt′ish·ly** *adv.* —**dolt′ish·ness** *n.*

Dom (dŏm; *Portuguese* dōɴ) *n.* **1.** A title formerly bestowed in Portugal and Brazil. **2.** *Rom. Cath. Ch.* A title used before the names of monks of certain orders. [Port. < Lat. *dominus,* lord.]

-dom *suff.* **1.** State; condition: *stardom.* **2. a.** Domain; position; rank: *dukedom.* **b.** Those that collectively have a specified position, office, or character: *officialdom.* [ME < OE *-dōm.*]

do·main (dō-mān′) *n.* **1.** A territory over which rule or control is exercised. **2.** A sphere of activity, concern, or function; field: *the domain of history.* **3.** *Physics.* Any of numerous contiguous regions in a ferromagnetic material in which the direction of spontaneous magnetization is uniform and different from that in neighboring regions. **4.** *Law.* **a.** The ownership and right of disposal of property. **b.** The right of eminent domain. **5.** *Math.* **a.** The set of possible values of an independent variable of a function. **b.** An open connected set that contains at least one point. [Fr. *domaine* < OFr. *demaine* < Lat. *dominium,* property < *dominus,* lord.]

dome

dome (dōm) *n.* **1.** A hemispherical roof or vault. **2.** An object or structure resembling a dome. **3.** A large, stately building. **4.** *Slang.* The head (sense 1.a.). **5.** A form of crystal in which two similarly inclined faces intersect in a line parallel to the horizontal axis. —*v.* **domed, dom·ing, domes.** —*tr.* **1.** To cover with or as with a dome. **2.** To shape like a dome. —*intr.* To assume the shape of a dome by rising or swelling. [Fr. *dôme,* dome, cathedral < Ital. *duomo,* cathedral < Lat. *domus,* house.]

dome car *n.* A railroad passenger car with an elevated glassed-in section for scenic viewing.

Domes·day Book (do͞omz′dā′, dōmz′-) also **Dooms·day Book** (do͞omz′-) *n.* The written record of a census and survey of English landowners and their property made by order of William the Conqueror in 1085–86. [< ME *domesday,* doomsday.]

do·mes·tic (də-mĕs′tĭk) *adj.* **1.** Of or pertaining to the family or household: *domestic chores.* **2.** Fond of home life and household affairs. **3.** Tame or domesticated. Used of animals. **4.** Of or pertaining to a country's internal affairs. **5.** Produced in or indigenous to a particular country: *domestic oil.* —*n.* **1.** A household servant. **2.** Cotton cloth as distinguished from linen. **3.** A product of domestic origin. **4. domestics.** Household linens. [OFr. *domestique* < Lat. *domesticus* < *domus,* house.] —**do·mes′ti·cal·ly** *adv.*

do·mes·ti·cate (də-mĕs′tĭ-kāt′) *tr.v.* **-cat·ed, -cat·ing, -cates. 1.** To cause to feel comfortable at home; make domestic. **2.** To adopt for domestic use. **3. a.** To train or adapt (an animal or plant) to live in a human environment and be of use to man. **b.** To introduce and accustom (an animal or plant) into another region; naturalize. **4.** To bring down to the level of the common man. —**do·mes′ti·ca′tion** *n.*

do·mes·tic·i·ty (dō′mĕ-stĭs′ĭ-tē) *n., pl.* **-ties. 1.** The quality or condition of being domestic. **2.** Home life or devotion to it. **3. domesticities.** Household affairs.

do·mes·ti·cize (də-mĕs′tĭ-sīz′) *tr.v.* **-cized, -ciz·ing, -ciz·es.** To domesticate.

domestic prelate *n. Rom. Cath. Ch.* A priest who is an honorary member of the papal household.

domestic relations court *n.* In certain U.S. states, a court with jurisdiction over family disputes, esp. those involving the custody, support, and welfare of children.

do·mi·cal (dō′mĭ-kəl, dŏm′ĭ-) also **do·mic** (dō′mĭk, dŏm′ĭk) *adj.* Pertaining to, having, or shaped like a dome. —**do′mi·cal·ly** *adv.*

dom·i·cile (dŏm′ĭ-sīl′, -səl, dō′mĭ-) also **dom·i·cil** (-səl) *n.* **1.** A residence; home. **2.** One's legal residence. —*v.* **-ciled, -cil·ing, -ciles.** —*tr.* **1.** To establish (a person or oneself) in a residence. **2.** To provide with often temporary lodging. —*intr.* To reside or dwell. [OFr. < Lat. *domicilium* < *domus,* house.] —**dom′i·cil′i·ar′y** (dŏm′-ĭ-sĭl′ē-ĕr′ē, dō′mĭ-) *adj.*

dom·i·nance (dŏm′ə-nəns) also **dom·i·nan·cy** (-nən-sē) *n.* The condition or fact of being dominant.

dom·i·nant (dŏm′ə-nənt) *adj.* **1.** Exercising the most influence or control; governing. **2.** Most prominent in position or prevalence; ascendant. **3.** *Genetics.* Producing the same phenotypic effect whether paired with an identical or a dissimilar gene. **4.** *Ecol.* Designating or pertaining to the species that is most characteristic of a habitat and that may determine the presence and type of other species. **5.** *Mus.* Relating to or based upon the fifth tone of a diatonic scale. —*n.* **1.** *Genetics.* A dominant character. **2.** *Ecol.* A dominant species. **3.** *Mus.* The fifth tone of a diatonic scale. [OFr. < Lat. *dominans,* pr.part. of *dominare,* to dominate.] —**dom′i·nant·ly** *adv.*

Synonyms: *dominant, predominant, preponderant, paramount, pre-eminent.* These adjectives mean surpassing all others in power, influence, or the like. *Dominant* applies to what exercises principal control or is unmistakably outstanding. *Predominant* is often nearly identical with the preceding term but can mean uppermost at a particular time or for the time being. *Preponderant* implies superiority as the result of outweighing or outnumbering all others. *Paramount* means first in importance, rank, or regard. *Pre-eminent* especially suggests esteem and general recognition of supremacy in a given area.

dominant wavelength *n.* The wavelength of the light that when combined in specific proportions with an achromatic standard light matches a given color.

dom·i·nate (dŏm′ə-nāt′) *v.* **-nat·ed, -nat·ing, -nates.** —*tr.* **1.** To control, govern, or rule by superior authority or power. **2.** To occupy the pre-eminent position in or over: *ambition dominates her life.* **3.** To order or command arrogantly. **4.** To overlook from a height. —*intr.* To be dominant in position or authority. [Lat. *dominari,* to rule < *dominus,* lord.] —**dom′i·na′tive** *adj.* —**dom′i·na′tor** *n.*

dom·i·na·tion (dŏm′ə-nā′shən) *n.* **1.** The act of dominating or the condition of being dominated; rule; control. **2. dominations.** *Theol.* The fourth of the nine orders of angels.

dom·i·neer (dŏm′ə-nîr′) *v.* **-neered, -neer·ing, -neers.** —*tr.* To rule over arbitrarily or arrogantly; tyrannize. —*intr.* To govern tyrannically. [Du. *domineren* < Fr. *dominer* < Lat. *dominari,* to dominate.] —**dom′i·neer′ing·ly** *adv.*

dom·i·neer·ing (dŏm′ə-nîr′ĭng) *adj.* Tending to domineer; overbearing. —**dom′i·neer′ing·ly** *adv.*

do·min·i·cal (də-mĭn′ĭ-kəl) *adj.* **1.** Of or associated with the Christ as the Lord. **2.** Pertaining to Sunday as the Lord's day. [Med. Lat. *dominicalis* < Lat. *dominicus,* of a lord < *dominus,* lord.]

dominical letter *n.* One of the first seven letters of the alphabet applied to Sundays in the ecclesiastical calendar for a given year, the letter being the one that corresponds with the first Sunday in January when the first seven days of the month are lettered in order; for example, if the first Sunday is January 2, *B* will be the dominical letter for the year.

Do·min·i·can (də-mĭn'ĭ-kən) *adj.* Of or pertaining to the order of preaching friars established in 1215 by Saint Dominic. —*n.* A friar of the order of Saint Dominic.

dom·i·nie (dŏm'ə-nē', dō'mə-) *n.* **1.** A clergyman of the Dutch Reformed Church. **2.** *Informal.* A minister. **3.** *Scot.* A schoolmaster. [Obs. *domine,* clergyman < Lat., vocative of *dominus,* lord.]

do·min·ion (də-mĭn'yən) *n.* **1.** Control or the exercise of control; sovereignty: *"The devil . . . has their souls in his possession, and under his dominion"* (Jonathan Edwards). **2.** A territory or sphere of influence or control; realm. **3.** Often **Dominion.** One of the self-governing nations within the British Commonwealth. **4.** *Law.* Dominium. **5. dominions.** *Theol.* Dominations (sense 2). [ME *dominioun* < OFr. *dominion* < Med. Lat. *dominio* < Lat. *dominium,* property < *dominus,* lord.]

Dominion Day *n.* July 1, a legal holiday in Canada, the anniversary of the Dominion's formation in 1867.

Dom·i·nique (dŏm'ə-nēk', dŏm'ə-nĭk) also **Dom·i·nick** (dŏm'ə-nĭk) *n.* An American breed of domestic fowl having gray, barred plumage, yellow legs, and a rose-colored comb. [After *Dominica,* an island in the West Indies.]

do·min·i·um (də-mĭn'ē-əm) *n.* *Law.* Ownership of property, esp. of land, and the right to its disposition. [Lat., property < *dominus,* lord.]

dom·i·no[1] (dŏm'ə-nō') *n., pl.* **-noes** or **-nos. 1.** A hooded cape worn by clergymen. **2. a.** A hooded robe worn with an eye mask at a masquerade. **b.** The mask itself. **3.** One wearing a domino. [Fr. < Lat. *benedicamus domino,* let us bless the Lord.]

dom·i·no[2] (dŏm'ə-nō') *n., pl.* **-noes** or **-nos. 1.** A small, rectangular block whose face is divided into halves, each half being blank or marked by one to six dots. **2. dominoes** or **dominos** *(used with a sing. verb).* A game played with a set, generally 28, of dominoes. [Fr. < Lat.]

domino effect *n.* A cumulative effect produced when one event sets off a chain of similar events. [So-called from the fact that a row of dominoes stood on end will fall in succession if the first one is pushed.]

domino theory *n.* **1.** A theory that if one nation comes under Communist control, then neighboring nations will also come under Communist control. **2.** A theory that one event will set off a train of similar events.

don[1] (dŏn) *n.* **1. Don.** Sir. A title formerly affixed to the given name of a Spaniard of high rank, now used generally as a courtesy title. **2.** A Spanish gentleman. **3.** *Chiefly Brit.* A head, tutor, or fellow at a college of Oxford or Cambridge. [Sp. < Lat. *dominus,* lord.]

don[2] (dŏn) *tr.v.* **donned, don·ning, dons.** To put on (a piece of clothing). **2.** To assume or take on, as a role or posture. [Contraction of *do on.*]

do·ña (dō'nyä) *n.* **1. Doña.** Lady. A title of courtesy used with a woman's given name in Spanish-speaking countries. **2.** A Spanish gentlewoman. [Sp. < Lat. *domina,* fem. of *dominus,* lord.]

do·nate (dō'nāt', dō-nāt') *tr.v.* **-nat·ed, -nat·ing, -nates.** To present as a gift to a fund or cause; contribute. [Back-formation < DONATION.] **—do'na'tor** *n.*

do·na·tion (dō-nā'shən) *n.* **1.** The act of giving something to a fund or cause. **2.** A gift or grant; contribution. [ME, gift, benefice < OFr. < Lat. *donatio* < *donatus,* p.part. of *donare,* to give < *donum,* gift.]

Don·a·tist (dŏn'ə-tĭst, dō'nə-) *n.* A member of a schismatic Christian sect that arose in North Africa in the 4th century A.D. [Med. Lat. *Donatista,* after *Donatus,* 4th-cent. Bishop of Carthage.] **—Don'a·tism** *n.*

don·a·tive (dō'nə-tĭv, dŏn'ə-) *n.* **1.** A bounty or largess. **2.** A benefice. —*adj.* Constituting a benefice. [Lat. *donativum* < *donativus,* of a donation < *donatus,* p.part. of *donare,* to give < *donum,* gift.]

done (dŭn) *v.* Past participle of **do**[1]. —*adj.* **1.** Completely accomplished; finished. **2.** Cooked adequately. **3.** Socially acceptable: *not done in polite society.* —*interj.* Used to express concurrence. ***idiom.* done for. 1.** Doomed; dying. **2.** Physically or mentally exhausted. **—done'ness** *n.*

Usage: *Done,* in the sense of "completely accomplished" or "finished," is found most often, but not exclusively, in informal usage. It is acceptable in writing to a majority of the Usage Panel in the following example: *The entire project will not be done until next year.* In some contexts this use of *done* can be unclear, as in *The work will be done next week.* Alternatives, dependent on the meaning, would be: *The work will get done next week. The work will be done by next week.*

do·nee (dō-nē') *n.* A recipient of a gift. [DON(OR) + -EE.]

dong[1] (dŏng) *n.* See table at **currency.** [Vietnamese.]

dong[2] (dŏng) *n.* *Vulgar Slang.* The penis. [Orig. unknown.]

don·jon (dŏn'jən, dŭn'-) *n.* The fortified main tower of a castle; keep. [Variant of DUNGEON.]

Don Juan (dŏn wŏn', jo͞o'ən). **1.** A libertine; profligate. **2.** A man obsessed with seducing women. [After *Don Juan,* legendary Spanish nobleman and libertine.]

don·key (dŏng'kē, dŭng'-, dông'-) *n., pl.* **-keys. 1.** The domesticated ass, probably descended from the wild ass *Equus asinus.* **2.** *Informal.* An obstinate person. **3.** *Informal.* A stupid person. [Perh. DUN (dark) + *-key* as in *monkey.*]

donkey engine *n.* **1.** A small auxiliary steam engine used for hoisting or pumping, esp. aboard ship. **2.** A small locomotive.

don·na (dŏn'ə; *Italian* dôn'nä) *n.* **1. Donna.** Lady. A title of courtesy used with a woman's given name in Italian-speaking countries. **2.** An Italian gentlewoman. [Ital. < Lat. *domina,* fem. of *dominus,* lord.]

don·nish (dŏn'ĭsh) *adj.* Of, resembling, or characteristic of a university don; bookish; pedantic.

don·ny·brook (dŏn'ē-bro͝ok') *n.* A brawl or uproar; free-for-all. [After *Donnybrook* fair, held annually in Donnybrook, Ireland, and noted for its brawls.]

do·nor (dō'nər) *n.* **1.** One who contributes something, such as money, to a cause or fund. **2.** One from whom blood, tissue, or an organ is taken for use in a transfusion or transplant. **3.** *Electronics.* An element introduced into a semiconductor with a negative valence greater than that of the pure semiconductor. [AN *donour* < Lat. *donator* < *donare,* to give < *donum,* gift.]

do-no·thing (do͞o'nŭth'ĭng) *adj.* Offering no initiative for change, esp. in politics. —*n.* A person who is idle or lazy. **—do'-no'thing·ism** *n.*

Don Qui·xo·te (dŏn' kē-hō'tē, kwĭk'sət) *n.* An impractical idealist bent on righting incorrigible wrongs. [After *Don Quixote,* hero of a satirical chivalric romance by Miguel de Cervantes (1547–1616).]

don't (dōnt). Do not.

do·nut (dō'nŭt', -nət) *n.* Variant of **doughnut.**

doo·dad (do͞o'dăd') *n.* *Informal.* An unnamed or nameless gadget or trinket.

doo·dle (do͞od'l) *v.* **-dled, -dling, -dles.** *Informal.* —*intr.* **1.** To scribble aimlessly, esp. when preoccupied. **2.** To spend or kill time idly. —*tr.* To draw (figures) while preoccupied. —*n.* *Informal.* A figure, design, or scribble drawn or written absent-mindedly. [Dial. E., to fritter away time.]

doo·dle·bug (do͞od'l-bŭg') *n.* **1.** The larva of the ant lion. **2.** A divining rod. [Perh. dial. E. *doodle,* fool + BUG.]

doo·hick·ey (do͞o'hĭk'ē) *n., pl.* **-eys.** *Informal.* A doodad. [Perh. DOO(DAD) + HICKEY.]

doom (do͞om) *n.* **1.** A decision or judgment, esp. an official condemnation to a severe penalty. **2.** Fate or destiny, esp. a tragic or ruinous fate. **3.** Inevitable destruction or ruin; extinction. **4.** Judgment Day. **5.** *Archaic.* A statute or ordinance. **6.** *Informal.* A crucial judgment or reckoning, esp. a negative one. —*tr.v.* **doomed, doom·ing, dooms. 1.** To pronounce judgment against; condemn. **2.** To set the destiny of, esp. to destine to an unhappy end. [ME *dom* < OE *dōm.*]

domino[2]
Playing dominoes

doom·say·er (do͞om'sā'ər) *n.* One who is prone to predicting future calamity.

dooms·day (do͞omz'dā') *n.* **1.** The day of the Last Judgment. **2.** A dreaded day of judgment or reckoning. [ME *domesday* < OE *dōmes dæg* : *dōm,* judgment + *dæg,* day.]

Doomsday Book (do͞omz'dā') *n.* Variant of **Domesday Book.**

door (dôr, dōr) *n.* **1. a.** A movable structure used to close off an entrance, typically consisting of a panel that swings on hinges, slides, or rotates. **b.** A similar part on a piece of furniture or vehicle. **2.** The entranceway to a room, building, or passage. **3.** A means of approach or access: *looking for the door to success.* **4.** The room or building to which a door belongs: *three doors down the hall.* ***—idiom.* at one's door** (or **doorstep**). Within one's sphere of responsibility. [ME *dor* < OE *duru.*]

door·bell (dôr'bĕl', dōr'-) *n.* A buzzer or bell outside a door, used as a signal for admission.

door·jamb (dôr'jăm', dōr'-) *n.* Either of the two vertical pieces framing a doorway and supporting the lintel.

door·keep·er (dôr'kē'pər, dōr'-) *n.* A person employed to guard an entrance or gateway.

door·knob (dôr'nŏb', dōr'-) *n.* A knob-shaped handle for opening and closing a door.

door·man (dôr'măn', -mən, dōr'-) *n.* A person employed to attend the entrance of a hotel, apartment house, or building.

door·mat (dôr'măt', dōr'-) *n.* **1.** A mat placed before a doorway for wiping the shoes. **2.** *Slang.* A person who unprotestingly allows himself to be mistreated by others.

door·nail (dôr'nāl', dōr'-) *n.* A large-headed nail formerly used as a stud on doors. ***—idiom.* dead as a doornail.** Undoubtedly dead.

door·post (dôr'pōst', dōr'-) *n.* A doorjamb.

door prize *n.* A prize awarded by lottery to the holder of a ticket purchased at or before a function.

door·sill (dôr'sĭl', dōr'-) *n.* The threshold of a doorway.

door·step (dôr'stĕp', dōr'-) *n.* A step leading to a door.

door·stop (dôr'stŏp', dōr'-) *n.* **1.** A wedge inserted beneath a door to hold it open at a desired position. **2.** A weight or spring that prevents a door from slamming. **3.** A rubber-tipped projection attached to a wall to protect it from the impact of an opening door.

door·way (dôr'wā', dōr'-) *n.* The entranceway to a room or building.

door·yard (dôr'yärd', dōr'-) *n.* A yard in front of the door of a house.

do·pa (dō'pə) *n.* An amino acid, $C_9H_{11}NO_4$, that is converted to dopamine in the bloodstream and used to treat Parkinson's disease. [Contraction of E. *dihydroxyphenylalanine.*]

donkey

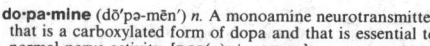

Doric
Columns in the style of the Doric order

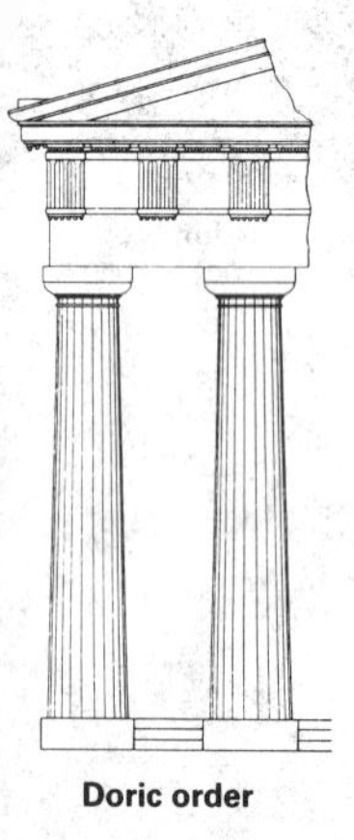
Doric order

dormer

dory[1]

dos-à-dos
19th-century double chair

do·pa·mine (dō′pə-mēn′) *n.* A monoamine neurotransmitter that is a carboxylated form of dopa and that is essential to normal nerve activity. [DOP(A) + AMINE.]
dop·ant (dō′pənt) *n.* A small quantity of a substance, such as phosphorus, added to another substance, such as a semiconductor, to alter the latter's properties. [DOP(E) + -ANT.]
dope (dōp) *n.* **1.** A viscid substance or liquid, esp. a lubricant, such as axle grease, or an absorbent material, such as the nitroglycerin used in manufacturing dynamite. **2.** Any of various preparations resembling varnish formerly used to protect, waterproof, and tauten the cloth surfaces of airplane wings. **3.** *Informal.* A narcotic, esp. an addictive. **4.** A narcotic preparation used to stimulate a race horse. **5.** *Slang.* A very stupid person. **6.** *Slang.* Factual information, esp. of a private nature. *—v.* **doped, dop·ing, dopes.** *—tr.* **1.** To add or apply dope to. **2.** *Informal.* To administer a narcotic to. **3.** *Informal.* To figure out (an outcome or puzzle). **4.** *Informal.* To make a rough plan of: *doped out his proposal.* *—intr. Informal.* To take drugs. [Du. *doop,* sauce < *doopen,* to dip.] **—dop′er** *n.*
dope sheet *n. Slang.* A publication giving information on the horses running in the day's races.
dope·ster (dōp′stər) *n.* One who analyzes and forecasts future events, as in sports or politics.
dop·ey also **dop·y** (dō′pē) *adj.* **dop·i·er, dop·i·est** *Slang.* **1.** Dazed or lethargic, as if drugged. **2.** Stupid or doltish. **3.** Silly or foolish.
dop·pel·gäng·er or **dop·pel·gang·er** (dŏp′əl-găng′ər, dôp′-əl-gĕng′ər) *n.* A ghostly double of a living person, esp. one that haunts its own fleshly counterpart. [G. : *doppel,* double + *gänger,* goer < *gehen,* to go.]
Dop·pler (dŏp′lər) *adj.* Of, relating to, or using the Doppler effect or Doppler radar.
Dop·pler effect (dŏp′lər) *n.* An apparent change in the frequency of waves, as of sound or light, occurring when the source and observer are in motion relative to one another, the frequency increasing when the source and observer approach one another and decreasing when they move apart. [After Christian *Doppler* (1803–1853).]
Doppler radar *n.* Radar that uses the Doppler effect to measure velocity.
Do·ra·do (də-rä′dō) *n.* A constellation of the Southern Hemisphere near Reticulum and Pictor, containing a great portion of the larger Magellanic Cloud.
dor·bee·tle (dôr′bēt′l) *n.* An Old World dung beetle, *Geotrupes stercorarius,* that flies with a droning sound. [Obs. *dor,* a buzzing bee or beetle (< ME *dorre* < OE *dora*) + BEETLE.]
Dor·cas society (dôr′kəs) *n.* A women's auxiliary group, often sponsored by a church, that provides clothes for the poor. [After *Dorcas,* a Christian woman of the 1st or 2nd cent. A.D.]
Do·ri·an (dôr′ē-ən, dōr′-) *n.* One of a Hellenic people that invaded Greece around 1100 B.C. and remained culturally and linguistically distinct within the Greek world, esp. in Sparta, Corinth, and Argos. **—Do′ri·an** *adj.*
Dor·ic (dôr′ĭk, dŏr′-) *n.* A dialect of ancient Greek spoken in the Peloponnesus, Crete, certain of the Aegean islands, Sicily, and in southern Italy. *—adj.* **1.** Of, pertaining to, characteristic of, or designating Doric. **2.** In the style of or designating the Doric order. [Lat. *Doricus* < Gk. *Dorikos* < *Doris,* a region of ancient Greece.]
Doric order *n.* The oldest and simplest of the three orders of classical Greek architecture, characterized by heavy, fluted columns having no base and plain, saucer-shaped capitals.
Dor·king (dôr′kĭng) *n.* A domestic fowl of a breed having a heavy body and raised chiefly for table use. [After *Dorking,* a town in England.]
dorm (dôrm) *n. Informal.* A dormitory.
dor·mant (dôr′mənt) *adj.* **1.** Asleep or lying as if asleep; inactive. **2.** Latent but capable of being activated: *"a harrowing experience which . . . lay dormant but still menacing"* (Charles Jackson). **3.** Temporarily quiescent: *a dormant volcano.* **4.** *Biol.* In a relatively inactive or resting condition in which some processes are slowed down or suspended. [ME *dormaunt* < OFr. *dormant* < pr.part. of *dormir,* to sleep < Lat. *dormire.*] **—dor′man·cy** *n.*
dor·mer (dôr′mər) *n.* **1.** A window set vertically in a small gable projecting from a sloping roof. **2.** The gable holding a dormer. [OFr. *dormeor,* bedroom < *dormir,* to sleep < Lat. *dormire.*]
dor·mie (dôr′mē) *adj.* Variant of **dormy.**
dor·min (dôr′mĭn) *n.* Abscisic acid. [DORM(ANCY) + -IN.]
dor·mi·to·ry (dôr′mĭ-tôr′ē, -tōr′ē) *n., pl.* **-ries. 1.** A room providing sleeping quarters for a number of persons. **2.** A building for housing a number of persons, as at a school or resort. **3.** A residential community whose inhabitants commute to a nearby metropolis for employment and recreation. [Lat. *dormitorium* < *dormitorius,* of sleep < *dormire,* to sleep.]
dor·mouse (dôr′mous′) *n.* Any of various small, squirrellike Old World rodents of the family Gliridae. [ME *dormowse.*]
dor·my also **dor·mie** (dôr′mē) *adj.* Ahead of an opponent by as many holes in a golf match as remain to be played. [Orig. unknown.]
dor·nick[1] (dôr′nĭk) *n.* A coarse damask cloth. [ME *dornick,* after *Doornik* (Tournai), Belgium.]
dor·nick[2] (dôr′nĭk) *n. Regional.* A small chunk of rock; stone. [Perh. of Celtic orig.]
do·ron·i·cum (də-rŏn′ĭ-kəm) *n.* A plant of the genus *Doronicum,* which includes the leopard's-bane. [NLat. < Ar. *dorūnaj.*]
dors– *pref.* Variant of **dorso–.**
dor·sad (dôr′săd′) *adv. Anat.* In the direction of the back.
dor·sal (dôr′səl) *adj.* **1.** *Anat.* Of, toward, on, in, or near the back. **2.** *Bot.* Of or on the outer surface, underside, or back of an organ. [LLat. *dorsalis* < Lat. *dorsualis* < *dorsum,* back.] **—dor′sal·ly** *adv.*
dorsal fin *n.* The main fin on the dorsal surface of fishes or certain marine mammals.
Dor·set Horn (dôr′sĭt) *n.* A domestic sheep of a breed having large horns and fine-textured wool. [After *Dorset,* a county in England.]
dorsi– *pref.* Variant of **dorso–.**
dor·si·ven·tral (dôr′sĭ-vĕn′trəl) *adj.* Having distinct upper and lower surfaces, as most leaves do.
dorso– or **dorsi–** or **dors–** *pref.* **1.** Back: *dorsad.* **2.** Dorsal: *dorsoventral.* [< Lat. *dorsum,* back.]
dor·so·ven·tral (dôr′sō-vĕn′trəl) *adj.* Extending from a dorsal to a ventral surface. [DORSO- + VENTRAL.]
dor·sum (dôr′səm) *n., pl.* **-sa** (-sə). *Anat.* **1.** The back. **2.** A part of an organ analogous to the back: *the dorsum of the foot.* [Lat., back.]
do·ry[1] (dôr′ē, dōr′ē) *n., pl.* **-ries.** A small, narrow, flat-bottomed fishing boat with high sides and a sharp prow. [Mosquito *dōri,* dugout.]
do·ry[2] (dôr′ē, dōr′ē) *n., pl.* **-ries. 1.** The John Dory. **2.** The walleye (sense 3). [ME *dorre* < OFr. *doree, gilded, fem. p.part. of dorer,* to gild < LLat. *deaurare* : Lat. *de-,* (intensive) + Lat. *aurum,* gold.]
dos-à-dos (dō′zä-dō′) *n., pl.* **dos-à-dos** (-dōz′, -dō′). **1.** A sofa or carriage that accommodates two people seated back to back. **2.** Also **do-si-do** (dō′sē-dō′) *pl.* **-dos. a.** A movement in square dancing in which two dancers approach each other and circle back to back, then return to their original positions. **b.** The call given for such a movement. [Fr. : *dos,* back + *à,* to + *dos,* back.]
dos·age (dō′sĭj) *n.* **1. a.** The administration of a therapeutic agent in prescribed amounts. **b.** The determination of the amount to be administered. **c.** The amount administered. **2.** The addition of an ingredient to a substance in a specific dose, esp. to wine.
dose (dōs) *n.* **1.** A specified quantity of a therapeutic agent prescribed to be taken at one time or at stated intervals. **2.** *Med.* The amount of radiation administered to a certain part. **3.** *Informal.* An amount, esp. of something unpleasant, to which one is subjected: *his dose of hard luck.* **4.** An ingredient added, esp. to wine, to impart flavor or strength. **5.** *Slang.* A venereal infection. *—tr.v.* **dosed, dos·ing, dos·es. 1.** To give (someone) a dose, as of medicine. **2.** To give or prescribe (medicine) in doses. [Fr. < LLat. *dosis* < Gk. < *didonai,* to give.] **—dos′er** *n.*
do·sim·e·ter (dō-sĭm′ĭ-tər) *n.* A device that measures and indicates the amount of x rays or radioactivity absorbed. [DOS(E) + -METER.]
do·sim·e·try (dō-sĭm′ĭ-trē) *n. Med.* The accurate measurement of doses. [DOS(E) + -METRY.] **—do·si·met′ric** *adj.*
doss (dŏs) *Chiefly Brit. Slang. —n.* **1.** A crude or makeshift bed. **2.** A cheap lodging house; flophouse. *—intr.v.* **dossed, doss·ing, doss·es.** To bed down; sleep. [Perh. alteration of *dorse,* back < Lat. *dorsum.*]
dos·sal also **dos·sel** (dŏs′əl) *n.* **1.** An ornamental hanging of rich fabric, as behind an altar. **2.** An ornamental covering for the back of a chair or throne. [Med. Lat. *dossale,* neuter of LLat. *dorsalis,* dorsal.]
dos·ser (dŏs′ər) *n.* **1.** A large pack basket. **2.** A dossal (sense 2). [ME *doser* < OFr. *dossier* < Med. Lat. *dorsarium* < Lat. *dorsum,* back.]
dos·si·er (dŏs′ē-ā′, dô′sē-ā′) *n.* A collection of papers giving detailed information about a particular person or subject. [Fr. < OFr., bundle of papers labeled on the back < *dos,* back < Lat. *dorsum.*]
dost (dŭst) *v. Archaic.* Second person singular present tense of **do**[1].
dot[1] (dŏt) *n.* **1. a.** A tiny round mark made by or as if by a pointed instrument; spot. **b.** Such a mark used in orthography, as above an *i.* **2.** A tiny amount. **3.** In Morse and similar codes, a short sound or signal used in combination with the dash and written as a dot to represent letters, numbers, or punctuation. **4.** *Math.* **a.** A decimal point. **b.** A symbol of multiplication. **5.** *Mus.* A mark after a note indicating an increase in time value by half. *—v.* **dot·ted, dot·ting, dots.** *—tr.* **1.** To mark with a dot. **2.** To form or make with dots. **3.** To cover with or as if with dots: *"Campfires, like red, peculiar blossoms, dotted the night"* (Stephen Crane). *—intr.* To make a dot. **—idiom. on (or at) the dot.** *Informal.* Absolutely punctual; on time. [ME **dot* < OE *dott,* head of a boil.] **—dot′ter** *n.*
dot[2] (dŏt, dō) *n.* A woman's marriage portion; dowry. [Fr. < Lat. *dos,* dowry.] **—do′tal** (dōt′l) *adj.*
dot·age (dō′tĭj) *n.* **1.** A feeble or foolish-minded condition

caused by mental deterioration; senility. **2.** Foolish or excessive fondness. [ME < *doten,* to dote.]

do·tard (dō'tərd) *n.* A senile person. [ME < *doten,* to dote.]

dote (dōt) *intr.v.* **dot·ed, dot·ing, dotes. 1.** To show excessive love or fondness: *dotes on his only child.* **2.** To be foolish or feeble-minded, esp. as a result of senility. [ME *doten.*] **—dot'er** *n.*

doth (dŭth) *v. Archaic.* Third person singular present tense of **do**[1].

dot product *n. Math.* Scalar product. [From the use of a dot to indicate the function, as in *x·y.*]

dot-se·quen·tial (dŏt'sĭ-kwĕn'shəl) *adj.* Pertaining to a color-television system in which the primary colors red, green, and blue are transmitted as dots in sequence and exhibited in the same sequence to produce a complete color image.

dotted swiss *n.* A crisp cotton fabric, embellished with woven, flocked, or embroidered dots.

dot·tle also **dot·tel** (dŏt'l) *n.* The plug of tobacco ash left in the bowl of a pipe after it has been smoked. [< DOT[1], lump (obs.).]

dot·ty (dŏt'ē) *adj.* **-ti·er, -ti·est. 1.** Having a feeble or unsteady gait; shaky. **2. a.** Mentally unbalanced; crazy: *gone absolutely dotty.* **b.** Eccentric or daft; *a dotty old lady.* **c.** Ridiculous or absurd: *a dotty scheme.* **3.** Obsessively infatuated. [Alteration of Sc. *dottle,* silly < ME *doten,* to dote.]

Dou·ay Bible (dōō-ā, dōō'ā) *n.* An English translation of the Latin Vulgate Bible by Roman Catholic scholars. [After *Douai,* France.]

Douay Version *n.* Douay Bible.

dou·ble (dŭb'əl) *adj.* **1.** Twice as much in size, strength, number, or amount: *a double dose.* **2.** Composed of two like parts: *double doors.* **3.** Composed of two unlike parts; dual: *a double meaning.* **4.** Accommodating or designed for two: *a double sleeping bag.* **5. a.** Acting two parts: *a double role.* **b.** Characterized by duplicity; deceitful: *speak with a double tongue.* **6.** *Bot.* Having many more than the usual number of petals, usually in a crowded or overlapping arrangement: *a double chrysanthemum.* *—n.* **1.** Something increased twofold. **2. a.** A duplicate of another; counterpart. **b.** An apparition; wraith. **3.** An actor's understudy. **4. a.** A sharp turn in running; reversal. **b.** An evasive reversal or shift in argument. **5. doubles.** A game, such as tennis or handball, having two players on each side. **6.** *Baseball.* A two-base hit. **7. a.** A bid in bridge indicating strength to one's partner; request for a bid. **b.** A bid doubling one's opponent's bid in bridge thus increasing the penalty for failure to fulfill the contract. **c.** A hand justifying such a bid. *—v.* **-bled, -bling, -bles.** *—tr.* **1.** To make twice as great. **2.** To be twice as much as. **3.** To fold in two. **4.** To duplicate; repeat. **5.** *Baseball.* **a.** To cause the scoring of (a run) by hitting a double. **b.** To advance or score (a runner) by hitting a double. **6.** *Baseball.* To put out (a runner) as the second part of a double play. **7.** To challenge (an opponent's bid) with a double in bridge. **8.** *Mus.* To duplicate (another part or voice) an octave higher or lower or in unison. **9.** *Naut.* To sail around: *double a cape.* *—intr.* **1.** To be increased twofold. **2.** To turn sharply backward; reverse: *double back on one's trail.* **3.** To serve in an additional capacity. **4.** To replace an actor in the execution of a given action or in the actor's absence. **5.** *Baseball.* To hit a double. **6.** To announce a double in bridge. ***—phrasal verb.*** **double up. 1.** To bend suddenly, as in pain or laughter. **2.** To share accommodations meant for one person. *—adv.* **1. a.** To twice the extent; doubly. **b.** To twice the amount: *double your money back.* **2.** Two together: *sleeping double.* **3.** In two: *bent double.* ***—idioms.*** **on** (or **at**) **the double.** *Informal.* **1.** In double time. **2.** Immediately. **see double.** To see two images of a single object, usually as a result of visual aberration. [ME < OFr. < Lat. *duplus.*] **—dou'ble·ness** *n.*

double agent *n.* A spy who infiltrates a government and pretends to work for it while actually working for another.

double bar *n. Mus.* A double vertical or heavy black line drawn through a staff to indicate the end of any of the main sections of a musical composition.

dou·ble-bar·reled (dŭb'əl-băr'əld) *adj.* **1.** Having two barrels mounted side by side: *a double-barreled shotgun.* **2.** Serving two purposes; twofold.

double bass *n.* The largest member of the violin family, shaped like a cello, played usually with a bow, and having a deep range of about three octaves.

double bassoon *n.* The contrabassoon.

double bed *n.* A bed accommodating two people.

dou·ble-blind (dŭb'əl-blīnd') *adj.* Of or designating an experimental testing procedure in which neither the researcher nor the subjects know who is receiving the substance or treatment being studied.

double boiler *n.* A cooking utensil consisting of two nested pans, designed to allow slow, even cooking or heating of food in the upper pan by the action of the water boiling in the lower.

dou·ble-breast·ed (dŭb'əl-brĕs'tĭd) *adj.* **1.** Fastened by lapping one half over the other, and usually having a double row of buttons with a single row of buttonholes. **2.** Having a double-breasted coat: *a double-breasted suit.*

double check *n.* A careful reinspection or re-examination to assure accuracy or efficiency; verification.

dou·ble-check (dŭb'əl-chĕk') *v.* **-checked, -check·ing, -checks.** *—tr.* To inspect or examine again; verify. *—intr.* To make a double check.

double chin *n.* A fold of fatty flesh beneath the chin.

dou·ble-cross (dŭb'əl-krôs', -krŏs') *Slang. —tr.v.* **-crossed, -cross·ing, -cross·es.** To betray by acting in contradiction to an agreed course of action. *—n.* An instance of betrayal. **—dou'ble-cross'er** *n.*

double dagger *n.* In writing and printing, a reference mark (‡).

double date *n.* A date in which two couples participate. **—dou'ble-date'** *v.* **(-dat·ed, -dat·ing, -dates).**

dou·ble-deal·ing (dŭb'əl-dē'lĭng) *adj.* Characterized by duplicity; deceitful; treacherous. *—n.* An act of treachery or duplicity. **—dou'ble-deal'er** *n.*

dou·ble-deck·er (dŭb'əl-dĕk'ər) *n.* **1.** A vehicle having two decks or tiers for passengers. **2.** Two beds, one built above the other. **3.** *Informal.* A sandwich having three slices of bread and two layers of filling.

double decomposition *n.* A chemical reaction between two compounds in which the first and second parts of one reactant are united, respectively, with the second and first parts of the other reactant.

dou·ble-dig·it (dŭb'əl-dĭj'ĭt) *adj.* Relating to percentage rates between 10 and 99 per cent: *double-digit inflation.*

double dipping *n.* The practice of drawing two incomes from the government, usually by holding a government job and receiving a pension. **—double dipper** *n.*

dou·ble-dome (dŭb'əl-dōm') *n. Slang.* An intellectual; egghead.

double dribble *n. Basketball.* An illegal dribble in which a player uses both hands simultaneously to dribble the ball or begins to dribble the ball a second time after having come to a complete stop.

double eagle *n.* A U.S. gold coin withdrawn from circulation in 1934 and having a face value of 20 dollars.

dou·ble-edged (dŭb'əl-ĕjd') *adj.* **1.** Having two cutting edges, as a sword or razor blade. **2.** Capable of being effective or interpreted in two ways: *double-edged praise.*

dou·ble-en·ten·dre (dŭb'əl-än-tän'drə, dōō-blän-tän'dr') *n.* **1.** A word or phrase having a double meaning, esp. when the second meaning is risqué. **2.** The use of double-entendres; ambiguity. [Fr.]

double entry *n.* A method of bookkeeping in which a transaction is entered both as a debit to one account and a credit to another account, so that the totals of debits and credits are equal.

dou·ble-faced (dŭb'əl-fāst') *adj.* **1.** Having two faces, aspects, or sides. **2.** Characterized by duplicity; hypocritical.

double feature *n.* A motion-picture program consisting of two full-length films.

dou·ble-head·er (dŭb'əl-hĕd'ər) *n.* **1.** Two games or events held in succession on the same program, esp. in baseball. **2.** A train pulled by two locomotives.

double indemnity *n.* A clause in an insurance policy that provides for payment of double the face value of the contract in case of accidental death.

double jeopardy *n. Law.* The act of putting a person through a second trial for an offense for which he has already been prosecuted.

dou·ble-joint·ed (dŭb'əl-join'tĭd) *adj.* Having unusually flexible joints permitting connected parts to be bent at unusual angles.

double knit *n.* A jerseylike fabric knitted on a machine equipped with two sets of needles so that a double thickness of fabric is produced in which the two sides of the fabric are interlocked.

double negative *n.* A syntactic construction that employs two negatives, esp. to express a single negation.

Usage: A double negative is properly used when it makes an affirmative statement: *He cannot just do nothing* (that is, "he must do something"). An affirmative meaning is also found when *not* is used before an adjective or adverb having a negative sense: *a not infrequent visitor; a not unwisely conceived plan.* In these expressions the double negative is used deliberately to convey a weaker affirmative sense than would the adjective *frequent* or the adverb *wisely.* • A double negative is generally considered unacceptable when it is intended to convey or reinforce a negative meaning, especially in a short sentence: *He didn't say nothing* (meaning "he said nothing"). *We aren't going neither* (meaning "we aren't going"). Formerly, such constructions were common in good writing as a form of intensified meaning; an example is Hamlet's advice to the players: *"Be not too tame neither, but let your discretion be your tutor."* • A double negative is still sometimes acceptable when it serves to reinforce a negative: *I will not surrender, not today, not tomorrow.* Less acceptable uses of the double negative are found in casual speech: *He's not coming, I don't think. Isn't he coming, don't you think?*

dou·ble-park (dŭb'əl-pärk') *v.* **-parked, -park·ing, -parks.** *—tr.* To park (a car or vehicle) alongside another vehicle already parked parallel to the curb. *—intr.* To double-park a vehicle.

double bass

double-decker
A double-decker bus in London, England

double play *n. Baseball.* A play in which two players are put out.
double pneumonia *n.* Pneumonia afflicting both lungs.
dou·ble-quick (dŭb′əl-kwĭk′) *adj.* Very quick; rapid. —*n.* Double time (sense 1). —*intr.v.* **-quicked, -quick·ing, -quicks.** To double-time.
dou·bler (dŭb′lər) *n.* A device that doubles the frequency of an input signal.
dou·ble-reed (dŭb′əl-rēd′) *n.* Any of a group of wind instruments that have a mouthpiece formed of two joined reeds that vibrate against each other.
double refraction *n.* Birefringence.
double salt *n. Chem.* A salt consisting or regarded as consisting of a molecular combination of two simple salts.
dou·ble-space (dŭb′əl-spās′) *v.* **-spaced, -spac·ing, -spac·es.** —*intr.* To type so that there is a full space between lines. —*tr.* To type (copy) so that there is a full space between lines.
dou·ble·speak (dŭb′əl-spēk′) *n.* Double talk (sense 2).
double standard *n.* A set of principles permitting greater opportunity or liberty to one than to another, esp. the granting of greater sexual freedom to men than to women.
double star *n.* A binary star.
dou·blet (dŭb′lĭt) *n.* **1.** A close-fitting jacket, with or without sleeves, worn by men between the 15th and 17th centuries. **2. a.** A pair of similar things. **b.** One of a pair. **c.** *Physics.* A multiplet with two members. **3.** *Ling.* One of two words derived from the same source by different routes of transmission. **4. doublets.** A throw of two dice in which the same number of dots appears on the upper face of each. [ME < OFr. < *double,* double.]
double take *n.* A delayed reaction to an unusual remark or circumstance, often used as a comic device.
double talk *n.* **1.** Meaningless speech that consists of nonsense syllables mixed with intelligible words; gibberish. **2.** Ambiguous or evasive language.
dou·ble-team (dŭb′əl-tēm′) *tr.v.* **-teamed, -team·ing, -teams.** *Sports.* To guard or cover an offensive player with two defensive players simultaneously
dou·ble·think (dŭb′əl-thĭngk′) *n.* The belief in two contradictory ideas or points of view at the same time.
double time *n.* **1.** A marching pace of 180 three-foot steps per minute. **2.** *Mus.* Duple time.
dou·ble-tongue (dŭb′əl-tŭng′) *intr.v.* **-tongued, -tongu·ing, -tongues.** *Mus.* To play a rapidly repeated series of notes on a wind instrument by placing the tongue alternately between the positions for *t* and *k.*
dou·ble·tree (dŭb′əl-trē′) *n.* A crossbar on a wagon or coach to which two whiffletrees are attached for harnessing two animals abreast.
dou·ble-u (dŭb′əl-yo͞o′) *n.* The letter *w.*
dou·ble·word (dŭb′əl-wûrd′) *n.* Two computer words considered as a single, 64-bit quantity.
dou·bloon (dŭ-blo͞on′) *n.* An obsolete Spanish gold coin. [Sp. *doblón,* aug. of *dobla,* Sp. coin < Lat. *dupla,* fem. of *duplus,* double.]
dou·blure (do͞o-blo͝or′) *n.* An ornamental lining, as of vellum or leather, on the inside face of a book cover. [Fr., lining < OFr. *doubler,* to double, line < Lat. *duplare,* to double < *duplus,* double.]
dou·bly (dŭb′lē) *adv.* **1.** To a double degree; twice. **2.** In a twofold manner.
doubt (dout) *v.* **doubt·ed, doubt·ing, doubts.** —*tr.* **1.** To be undecided or skeptical about. **2.** To tend to disbelieve; distrust: *doubts the promises of all politicians.* **3.** *Archaic.* To suspect; fear. —*intr.* To be undecided. —*n.* **1.** A lack of conviction or certainty. **2.** A lack of trust. **3.** A point about which one is uncertain or skeptical. **4.** An uncertain state of affairs: *an outcome still in doubt.* **—idioms. beyond** (or **without**) **doubt.** Without question; certainly; definitely. **no doubt. 1.** Certainly. **2.** Probably. [ME *douten* < OFr. *douter* < Lat. *dubitare,* to waver.] **—doubt′er** *n.*

Usage: *Doubt* and *doubtful* are often followed by clauses introduced by *that, whether,* or *if.* A choice among the three is guided by the intended meaning of the sentence, but considerable leeway exists. Generally, *that* is used when the intention is to express more or less complete rejection of a statement: *I doubt that he will even try* (meaning "I don't think he will even try"); or, in the negative, to express more or less complete acceptance: *I don't doubt that you are right.* On the other hand, when the intention is to express real uncertainty, the choice is usually *whether: We doubt whether they can succeed. It is doubtful whether he will come.* According to a majority of the Usage Panel, *whether* is the only acceptable choice in such examples; a minority would also accept *if* (which is more informal in tone) or *that.* In sum, *that* is especially appropriate to the denial of uncertainty or to implied disbelief but is sometimes used also when the intention is to express real uncertainty. *Doubt* is frequently used in informal speech, both as verb and as noun, together with *but: I don't doubt but* (or *but what*) *he will come. There is no doubt but it will be difficult.* These usages should be avoided in writing; substitute *that* or *whether* as the case requires.

doubt·ful (dout′fəl) *adj.* **1.** Subject to or tending to cause doubt; uncertain: *It's doubtful if we'll ever know what happened.* **2.** Experiencing doubt: *doubtful about his scheme.* **3.** Of uncertain outcome; undecided. **4.** Appearing in such a way as to raise questions about the honesty or value of; suspicious: *a man with a doubtful past.* —See Usage note at **doubt. —doubt′ful·ly** *adv.* **—doubt′ful·ness** *n.*

Synonyms: *doubtful, dubious, questionable.* These adjectives express a degree of uncertainty (as to the occurrence of something, for example) or they can imply reservations about persons or their attributes. *Doubtful* suggests pronounced uncertainty as to such an occurrence or as to the worth or fitness of a person. *Dubious* expresses uncertainty less directly and less forcefully; often it suggests hesitancy based on suspicion or mistrust rather than on something more tangible, such as fact or past performance. *Questionable* can mean uncertain in the sense of being open to doubt or debate, or it can imply, more strongly than the other terms, that the person or thing specified is not worthy of confidence or trust.

doubting Thom·as (tŏm′əs) *n.* One who is habitually doubtful. [After St. *Thomas,* an apostle who doubted Jesus' resurrection until he had proof of it.]
doubt·less (dout′lĭs) *adj.* Certain; assured. —*adv.* **1.** Certainly. **2.** Presumably; probably. **—doubt′less·ly** *adv.*

Usage: *Doubtless* and *no doubt* are relatively weak in expressing certainty (absence of doubt), since they can also indicate mere presumption or probability *(he will doubtless go)* or concession *(you are no doubt right in some details).* In contrast, *undoubtedly* and *without doubt* express a greater degree of certainty and conviction. *Indubitably* and *unquestionably* are even stronger.

dou·ceur (do͞o-sûr′) *n.* Money given as a tip, gratuity, or bribe. [Fr., < LLat. *dulcor,* sweetness < Lat. *dulcis,* sweet.]
douche (do͞osh) *n.* **1.** A stream of water or air applied to a body part or cavity for cleansing or medicinal purposes. **2.** The application of a douche. **3.** An instrument for applying a douche. —*tr. & intr.v.* **douched, douch·ing, douch·es.** To cleanse or treat or be cleansed or treated by a douche. [Fr., shower < Ital. *doccia,* conduit, douche < *doccione,* pipe < Lat. *ductio,* act of leading < *ductus,* p.part. of *ducere,* to lead.]
dough (dō) *n.* **1.** A soft, thick mixture of flour or meal, liquids, and various dry ingredients that is baked, esp. bread or pastry. **2.** A pasty mass similar to dough. **3.** *Slang.* Money. [ME *dogh* < OE *dāg.*]
dough·boy (dō′boi′) *n.* **1.** Bread dough that is rolled thin and cut into various shapes and then fried in deep fat. **2.** An infantryman in World War I.
dough·face (dō′fās) *n.* A Northerner who sided with the South in the Civil War, esp. a congressman who supported slavery.
dough·nut also **do·nut** (dō′nŭt′, -nət) *n.* A small, ring-shaped cake made of rich, light dough that is fried in deep fat.
dough·ty (dou′tē) *adj.* **-ti·er, -ti·est.** Characterized by courage; valiant. [ME < OE *dohtig.*] **—dough′ti·ly** *adv.* **—dough′ti·ness** *n.*
dough·y (dō′ē) *adj.* **-i·er, -i·est.** Having the consistency or appearance of dough.
Doug·las fir (dŭg′ləs) *n.* A tall evergreen timber tree, *Pseudotsuga taxifolia* (or *P. menziesii*), of northwestern North America, having short needles and egg-shaped cones. [After David *Douglas* (1798–1834).]

Douglas fir
Douglas fir cone

Dou·kho·bor (do͞o′kə-bôr′) *n.* Variant of **Dukhobor.**
dour (do͝or, dour) *adj.* **1.** Marked by intractable sternness or harshness; forbidding. **2.** Silently ill-humored; gloomy. **3.** Sternly obstinate; unyielding. [ME < Lat. *durus,* hard.]
dou·ra or **dou·rah** (do͝or′ə) *n.* Variants of **durra.**
dou·rine (do͞o-rēn′) *n.* A contagious venereal disease of horses, asses, and mules, caused by a microorganism. [Fr. < Ar. *darina,* to be dirty.]
douse[1] also **dowse** (dous) —*v.* **doused, dous·ing, dous·es** also **dowsed, dows·ing, dows·es.** —*tr.* **1.** To plunge into liquid; immerse. **2.** To wet thoroughly; drench. **3.** To put out (a light or fire); extinguish. —*intr.* To become thoroughly wet. —*n.* A thorough drenching. [Perh. < obs. *douse,* to strike.] **—dous′er** *n.*
douse[2] (douz) *v.* Variant of **dowse**[1].
dove[1] (dŭv) *n.* **1.** Any of various birds of the family Columbidae, which includes the pigeons. **2.** A gentle or innocent child or woman. **3.** In the Old Testament, a messenger of peace or deliverance from care. **4.** A person who advocates peace and conciliation in rigorous opposition to armed conflict. **5. Dove.** The constellation Columba. [ME *douve* < OE *dūfe.*] **—dov′ish** *adj.* **—dov′ish·ness** *n.*
dove[2] (dōv) *v.* A past tense of **dive**[1].
dove·cote (dŭv′kōt′, -kŏt′) also **dove·cot** (-kŏt′) *n.* A roost with compartments for domesticated pigeons.
dove·kie also **dove·key** (dŭv′kē) *n.* A small black-and-white sea bird, *Plautus alle,* of arctic and northern Atlantic regions. [Dim. of DOVE[1].]
Do·ver's powder (dō′vərz) *n.* A powdered drug, made essentially of ipecac and opium, formerly used to relieve pain and induce perspiration. [After Thomas *Dover* (1660–1742).]
dove·tail (dŭv′tāl′) *n.* **1.** A fan-shaped tenon that forms a tight interlocking joint when fitted into a corresponding mortise. **2.** A joint formed by interlocking dovetails and

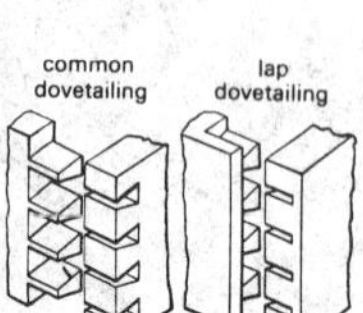

dovetail

mortises. —*v.* **-tailed, -tail·ing, -tails.** —*tr.* **1.** To cut into or join by means of dovetails. **2.** To connect or combine precisely or harmoniously. —*intr.* To combine or interlock into a unified whole.

dow·a·ger (dou'ə-jər) *n.* **1.** A widow who holds a title or property derived from her dead husband. **2.** An elderly woman of high social station. [OFr. *douagiere* < *douage,* dower < *douer,* to endow < Lat. *dotare* < *dos,* dowry.]

dow·dy (dou'dē) *adj.* **-di·er, -di·est.** **1.** Lacking in stylishness or neatness; shabby. **2.** Old-fashioned in appearance or manner. —*n., pl.* **-dies.** A dowdy woman; frump. [< ME *doude,* unattractive woman.] **—dow'di·ly** *adv.* **—dow'di·ness** *n.* **—dow'dy·ish** *adj.*

dow·el (dou'əl) *n.* **1.** A usually round pin that fits tightly into a corresponding hole to fasten or align two adjacent pieces. **2.** A piece of wood driven into a wall to act as an anchor for nails. —*tr.v.* **-eled, -el·ing, -els.** **1.** To fasten or align with dowels. **2.** To equip with dowels. [ME *doule,* part of a wheel.]

dow·er (dou'ər) *n.* **1.** The part or interest of a deceased man's real estate allotted by law to his widow for her lifetime. **2.** A dowry (sense 1). —*tr.v.* **-ered, -er·ing, -ers.** To assign a dower to; endow. [ME *douere* < OFr. *douaire* < Med. Lat. *dotarium* < Lat. *dos,* dowry.]

dow·itch·er (dou'ĭ-chər) *n.* Either of two shore birds, *Limnodromus griseus* or *L. scolopaeus,* of northern regions, having brownish plumage and a long, straight bill. [Of Iroquoian orig.]

Dow-Jones Averages (dou'jōnz'). A trademark used for an index of the relative price of selected industrial, transportation, and utility stocks based on a formula developed and periodically revised by Dow Jones & Company, Inc.

down[1] (doun) *adv.* **1. a.** From a higher to a lower place or position. **b.** Toward, to, or on the ground, floor, or bottom. **2. a.** Into a lower posture. **b.** In or into a prostrate position. **3.** Toward or in the south or in a southerly direction. **4. a.** Toward or in a center of activity: *going down to the office.* **b.** Away from the present place: *down on the farm.* **5.** To the source: *tracking a rumor down.* **6.** Toward or at a low or lower point on a scale. **7.** To or in a quiescent or subdued state. **8.** To or in a low status, as of subjection or disgrace. **9.** To an extreme degree. **10.** Seriously or vigorously: *get down to work.* **11.** From earlier times or people. **12.** To a reduced or concentrated form: *boiling down maple syrup.* **13.** In writing; on paper: *taking a statement down.* **14.** In partial payment at the time of purchase: *five dollars down.* —*adj.* **1. a.** Moving or directed downward: *a down elevator.* **b.** In a low position. **c.** At a reduced level. **2. a.** Sick: *He is down with a cold.* **b.** Low in spirit; depressed: *feel down.* **3. a.** In games, trailing an opponent by a specified number of points, goals, or strokes: *down two.* **b.** *Football.* Not in play. Used of the ball. **c.** *Baseball.* Having been put out. **4.** Being the first installment. —*prep.* **1.** In a descending direction along, upon, into, or through. **2.** Along the course of. **3.** Toward the mouth of a river. —*n.* **1.** A downward movement; descent. **2.** *Football.* Any of a series of four plays during which a team must advance at least ten yards to retain possession of the ball. —*v.* **downed, down·ing, downs.** —*tr.* **1.** To bring, put, strike, or throw down. **2.** To swallow hastily; gulp. **3.** *Football.* To put (the ball) out of play by touching it to the ground. —*intr.* To go or come down; descend. **—*idioms.* down and out.** Lacking friends or resources; destitute. **down in the mouth.** Discouraged; sad. **down on.** *Informal.* Hostile or negative toward; out of patience with. [ME *doun* < OE *dūne* < *adūne* : *a-,* from (< *of*) + *dūn,* hill.]

down[2] (doun) *n.* **1.** Fine, soft, fluffy feathers forming the first plumage of a young bird and underlying the contour feathers in adult birds. **2.** *Bot.* A covering of soft, short fibers, as on some leaves. **3.** A soft, silky, or feathery substance, such as the first growth of human beard. [ME *doun* < ON *dūnn.*]

down[3] (doun) *n.* **1.** Often **downs.** An expanse of rolling, grassy upland used for grazing. **2.** Often **Down.** Any of several breeds of sheep having short wool, developed in the downs of England. [ME *doune* < OE *dūn.*]

down-at-heel (doun'ət-hēl') or **down-at-the-heel** (-ət-thə-hēl') *adj.* Showing signs of wear and tear.

down·beat (doun'bēt') *n.* **1.** *Mus.* The downward stroke made by a conductor to indicate the first beat of a measure. **2.** *Informal.* A period of stagnation or inactivity. —*adj.* Cheerless or pessimistic.

down-bow (doun'bō') *n. Mus.* A stroke made by drawing a bow from handle to tip across the strings of a violin or other bowed instrument.

down·cast (doun'kăst') *adj.* **1.** Directed downward: *a downcast glance.* **2.** Low in spirits; depressed.

down·court (doun-kôrt', -kōrt') *adv. & adj. Sports.* To, into, or in the far end of the court, esp. in basketball.

Down East also **down East** *n.* New England, esp. Maine.

down·er (dou'nər) *n. Slang.* **1.** A depressant or sedative drug, as a barbiturate or tranquilizer. **2.** A depressing experience or predicament.

down·fall (doun'fôl') *n.* **1. a.** A sudden loss of wealth, rank, reputation, or happiness; ruin. **b.** Something causing this. **2.** A fall of rain or snow, esp. a heavy or unexpected one.

down·fall·en (doun'fô'lən) *adj.* Fallen, as from high estate; ruined.

down·field (doun-fēld) *adv. & adj. Sports.* To, into, or in the defensive team's end of the field.

down·grade (doun'grād') *n.* **1.** A descending slope, as in a road. **2.** A turn or trend downward. —*tr.v.* **-grad·ed, -grad·ing, -grades.** **1.** To lower the status and salary of. **2.** To lower or minimize the importance or reputation of. **—*idiom.* on the downgrade.** Declining, as in influence, reputation, or wealth.

down·haul (doun'hôl') *n.* A rope or set of ropes for hauling down or securing a sail or spar.

down·heart·ed (doun'här'tĭd) *adj.* Low in spirit; depressed. **—down'heart'ed·ly** *adv.* **—down'heart'ed·ness** *n.*

down·hill (doun'hĭl') *adv.* Down the slope of a hill. —*adj.* (doun'hĭl'). Sloping downward; descending. **—*idiom.* go downhill.** To decline, as in one's career or health.

down-home (doun'hōm') *adj.* Of, relating to, or characteristic of the rural southern U.S. or its people, as in simplicity, informality, or earthiness.

Down·ing Street (dou'nĭng) *n.* The British government. [From the location of the prime minister's residence at No. 10 Downing Street, London.]

down·play (doun'plā') *tr.v.* **-played, -play·ing, -plays.** To minimize or ignore the significance of.

down·pour (doun'pôr', -pōr') *n.* A heavy fall of rain.

down·range (doun'rānj') *adv.* In a direction away from the launch site and along the flight line of a missile test range. —*adj.* (doun'rānj'). Designating the area and airspace along the flight line of a missile test range.

down·right (doun'rīt') *adj.* **1.** Thoroughgoing or unequivocal: *a downright lie.* **2.** Forthright; candid. —*adv.* Thoroughly; absolutely.

down·size (doun'sīz') *tr.v.* **-sized, -siz·ing, -siz·es.** To make in a smaller size: *downsize automobiles.*

Down's syndrome (dounz) *n.* A congenital disorder characterized by moderate to severe mental retardation, a short flattened skull, and slanting eyes. [After John L. H. *Down* (1828–1896).]

down·stage (doun'stāj') *adv.* Toward or at the front part of a stage. —*adj.* (doun'stāj'). Relating to the front part of a stage. —*n.* (doun'stāj'). The front half of a stage.

down·stairs (doun'stârz') *adv.* **1.** Down the stairs. **2.** To or on a lower floor. —*adj.* (doun'stârz') also **down·stair** (-stâr'). Located on a lower or main floor. —*n.* (doun'stârz') *(used with a sing. verb).* The lower or main floor.

down·state (doun'stāt') *n.* The southerly section of a state in the U.S. —*adv. & adj.* To, from, or in the southerly section of a state. **—down'stat'er** *n.*

down·stream (doun'strēm') *adj.* In the direction of a stream's current. —*adv.* (doun'strēm'). Down a stream.

down·swing (doun'swĭng') *n.* **1.** A swing downward. **2.** A business decline.

down·tick (doun'tĭk') *n.* A transaction in a stock market security below the price of the previous transaction.

down·time (doun'tīm') *n.* The period of time when something, as a factory or its equipment, is inactive.

down-to-earth (doun'to͞o-ûrth', -tə-) *adj.* Realistic; sensible.

down·town (doun'toun') *n.* The lower part or the business center of a city or town. —*adv.* (doun'toun'). To, toward, or in the lower part or the business center of a city or town. —*adj.* (doun'toun'). Of, relating to, or located downtown.

down·trend (doun'trĕnd') *n.* A downturn.

down·trod·den (doun'trŏd'n) *adj.* Oppressed; tyrannized.

down·turn (doun'tûrn') *n.* A tendency downward, esp. in business or economic activity.

down under *n. Informal.* Australia or New Zealand.

down·ward (doun'wərd) *adv.* **1.** From a higher to a lower place, point, level, or condition. **2.** From an earlier to a more recent time. —*adj.* **1.** Descending from a higher to a lower place, point, level, character, or condition. **2.** Descending from a source or origin. **—down'wards, down'ward·ly** *adv.*

down·wind (doun'wĭnd') *adv.* In the direction in which the wind blows; leeward. **—down'wind'** *adj.*

down·y (dou'nē) *adj.* **-i·er, -i·est.** **1.** Made of or covered with down. **2. a.** Resembling down. **b.** Quietly soothing; soft.

downy mildew *n.* A disease of plants caused by fungi of the order Peronosporales and characterized by gray, velvety patches of spores on the lower surfaces of leaves.

dow·ry (dou'rē) *n., pl.* **-ries.** **1.** Money or property brought by a bride to her husband at marriage. **2.** *Archaic.* A dower (sense 1). **3.** A sum of money required of a postulant at a convent; dower. **4.** A natural endowment or gift; talent. [ME *douerie* < AN *dowarie,* ult. < Med. Lat. *dotarium,* dower.]

dowse[1] also **douse** (douz) *intr.v.* **dowsed, dows·ing, dows·es** also **doused, dous·ing, dous·es.** To use a divining rod to find underground water or minerals. [Orig. unknown.] **—dows'er** *n.*

dowse[2] (dous) *v. & n.* Variant of **douse**[1].

Dow theory (dou) *n.* A theory of stock market forecasting based on the activity of the market itself. [After Charles H. *Dow* (1851–1902).]

dox·ol·o·gy (dŏk-sŏl'ə-jē) *n., pl.* **-gies.** A liturgical formula of praise to God. [Med. Lat. *doxologia* < Gk., praise : *doxa,* glory, honor (< *dokein,* to seem) + *logos,* speech.] **—dox'o·log'i·cal** (-sə-lŏj'ĭ-kəl) *adj.* **—dox'o·log'i·cal·ly** *adv.*

dox·y (dŏk'sē) *n., pl.* **-ies.** *Slang.* **1.** A loose woman; prostitute. **2.** A paramour. [Perh. < obs. Du. *docke,* doll.]

dox·y·cy·cline (dŏk'sĭ-sī'klēn') *n.* A broad-spectrum antibiotic, $C_{22}H_{24}N_2O_8$, derived from tetracycline. [D(E)- + OX(Y)- + (TETRA)CYCLINE.]

dracaena

doy·en (doi-ĕn', doi'ən, dwä-yăN') *n.* The eldest or senior male member of a group. [Fr. < LLat. *decanus,* chief of ten. —see DEAN.]

doy·enne (doi-ĕn', dwä-yĕn') *n.* The eldest or senior female member of a group.

doy·ly or **doy·ley** (doi'lē) *n.* Variants of **doily.**

doze (dōz) *v.* **dozed, doz·ing, doz·es.** *—intr.* To sleep lightly and intermittently. *—tr.* To spend (time) dozing or as if dozing: *dozed the summer away.* **—phrasal verb. doze off.** To fall into a light sleep. *—n.* A short, light sleep. [Prob. of Scand. orig.] **—doz'er** *n.*

doz·en (dŭz'ən) *n.* **1.** *pl.* **dozen.** A set of 12. **2.** *pl.* **-ens.** An indefinite number: *dozens of errands to run.* *—adj.* Twelve. [ME *dozeine* < OFr. *dozaine* < *doze,* twelve < Lat. *duodecim* : *duo,* two + *decem,* ten.] **—doz'enth** *adj.*

do·zy (dō'zē) *adj.* **-zi·er, -zi·est.** Drowsy; half asleep. **—doz'i·ly** *adv.* **—do'zi·ness** *n.*

drab[1] (drăb) *adj.* **drab·ber, drab·best. 1. a.** Of a dull light brown. **b.** Of a light olive brown or khaki color. **2.** Faded and dull in appearance. **3.** Of a commonplace character; dreary. *—n.* **1.** Cloth of a light dull brown or grayish brown or unbleached natural color, esp. a heavy woolen or cotton fabric. **2.** A moderate to grayish or light grayish yellowish brown or light olive brown. [Obs. *drap,* cloth < OFr. —see DRAPE.] **—drab'ly** *adv.* **—drab'ness** *n.*

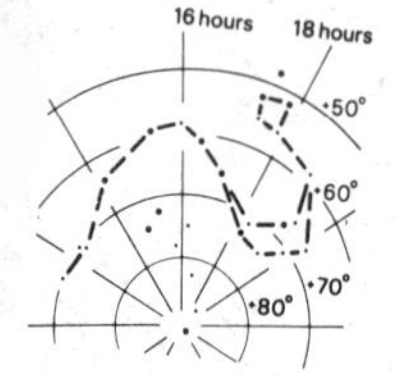

Draco

drab[2] (drăb) *n.* **1.** A slattern. **2.** A whore. *—intr.v.* **drabbed, drab·bing, drabs.** To consort with whores. [Of Celtic orig.]

drab·bet (drăb'ĭt) *n.* A coarse, unbleached linen. [< DRAB[1].]

drab·ble (drăb'əl) *v.* **-bled, -bling, -bles.** *—intr.* To draggle. *—tr.* To bedraggle. [ME *drabelen.*]

dra·cae·na (drə-sē'nə) *n.* Any of several tropical plants of the genera *Dracaena* and *Cordyline,* some species of which are cultivated as house plants for their decorative foliage. [NLat. *Dracaena,* genus name < LLat. *dracaena,* female dragon < Gk. *drakaina,* fem. of *drakōn,* serpent.]

drachm (drăm) *n. Chiefly Brit.* **1.** A dram. **2.** A drachma.

drach·ma (drăk'mə) *n., pl.* **-mas** or **-mae** (-mē). **1.** See table at **currency. 2.** A silver coin of ancient Greece. **3.** One of several modern units of weight, esp. the dram. [Lat. < Gk. *drakhmē.*]

Dra·co (drā'kō) *n.* A constellation in the polar region of the Northern Hemisphere near Cepheus and Ursa Major. [Lat. —see DRAGON.]

dra·co·ni·an (drā-kō'nē-ən, drə-) also **dra·con·ic** (-kŏn'ĭk) *adj.* **1.** Of or designating a law or code of extreme severity. **2.** Exceedingly harsh; rigorous: *a draconian penalty.* [After *Draco,* Athenian lawgiver of the 7th cent. B.C., whose laws were proverbially harsh.] **—dra·con'i·cal·ly** *adv.*

dra·con·ic[1] (drā-kŏn'ĭk) *adj.* Of or pertaining to a dragon. [< Lat. *draco, dracon-,* dragon < Gk. *drakōn,* serpent.]

dra·con·ic[2] (drā-kŏn'ĭk, drə-) *adj.* Variant of **draconian.**

dragon
Arthur Rackham cover design for Edgar Allan Poe's *Tales of Mystery and Imagination*

draft (drăft, dräft) *n.* **1. a.** A current of air in an enclosed area. **b.** A device in a flue controlling the circulation of air. **2. a.** A pull or traction of a load. **b.** Something that is pulled or drawn. **c.** A team of animals used to pull or draw a load. **3.** The depth of a vessel's keel below the water line, esp. when loaded. **4.** A heavy demand upon resources. **5.** A documentary instrument for transferring money. **6. a.** A gulp, swallow, or inhalation. **b.** The amount taken in by a single act of drinking or inhaling. **c.** A measured portion; dose. **7. a.** The drawing of a liquid, as from a cask or keg. **b.** The amount drawn. **8. a.** A selection of one or more individuals from a group for a particular purpose or duty: *the convention drafted a candidate.* **b.** Conscription for military service. **c.** The body of a people selected or conscripted. **d.** *Sports.* A system in which professional teams get the exclusive rights to new players. **9. a.** The act of drawing in a fishnet. **b.** The catch. **10. a.** A preliminary outline of a plan, document, or picture: *the first draft of a report.* **b.** A representation of something to be constructed. **11.** A narrow line chiseled on a stone to guide the stonecutter in leveling its surface. **12.** A slight taper given a die to facilitate the removal of a casting. **13.** *Commerce.* An allowance made for loss in weight of merchandise. *—v.* **draft·ed, draft·ing, drafts.** *—tr.* **1.** To select and draw from a group for some usually compulsory assignment, as military service. **2. a.** To draw up a preliminary version of or plan for. **b.** To compose: *draft a speech.* *—intr.* To drive close behind another vehicle to take advantage of the reduced air pressure in the wake of the leading vehicle. *—adj.* **1.** Suited for or used for drawing heavy loads. **2.** Drawn from a cask or tap. **—*idiom.* on draft.** Tapped from the keg; not bottled. [Me *draught,* act of drawing or pulling.]

dragonet

draft board *n.* A local board of civilians in charge of the selection of men for compulsory military service.

draft·ee (drăf-tē', dräf-) *n.* One drafted, esp. for military service.

dragonfly

draft·er (drăf'tər, dräf'-) *n.* A person who drafts, esp.: **a.** A person who draws plans or designs. **b.** A person who draws up documents.

draft·ing (drăf'tĭng, dräf'-) *n.* The systematic representation and dimensional specification of mechanical and architectural structures.

drafts·man (drăfts'mən, dräfts'-) *n.* **1.** A man who functions as a drafter. **2.** One who excels in drawing. **—drafts'man·ship'** *n.*

drafts·per·son (drăfts'pûr'sən, dräfts'-) *n.* A drafter.

drafts·wom·an (drăfts'wo͝om'ən, dräfts'-) *n.* A woman who functions as a drafter.

draft·y (drăf'tē, dräf'-) *adj.* **-i·er, -i·est.** Having or exposed to drafts of air. **—draft'i·ly** *adv.* **—draft'i·ness** *n.*

drag (drăg) *v.* **dragged, drag·ging, drags.** *—tr.* **1. a.** To pull or draw along the ground by force. **b.** To cause to trail along the ground. **2. a.** To search or sweep the bottom of (a body of water), as with a grappling hook or dragnet. **b.** To bring up or catch by such means. **3.** To bring forcibly to or into: *always have to drag him to the dentist.* **4.** To cause to move with great reluctance, weariness, or difficulty. **5.** To prolong tediously: *dragged the story out.* **6.** To introduce gratuitously into a discussion. **7.** *Baseball.* To hit (a bunt) down either foul line by pushing or pulling the ball with the bat while taking the first step to first base. *—intr.* **1.** To trail along the ground. **2.** To move slowly or with effort. **3.** To lag behind. **4.** To pass or proceed slowly, tediously, or laboriously. **5.** To search or dredge the bottom of a body of water. **6.** *Baseball.* To hit a drag bunt. **7.** To take part in or as if in a drag race. **8.** *Slang.* To draw on a cigarette, pipe, or cigar. *—n.* **1.** The act of dragging. **2.** Something that is dragged along the ground, as a harrow or an implement for spreading manure. **3.** A device for dragging under water, as a grappling hook. **4.** A heavy sledge or cart for conveying loads. **5.** A large four-horse coach with seats inside and on top. **6.** Something that retards motion, as a sea anchor or a brake on a fishing reel. **7.** One that prohibits or hinders progress; drawback; burden. **8.** The degree of resistance involved in dragging or hauling. **9.** The retarding force exerted on a moving body by a fluid medium in aviation. **10.** A slow, laborious motion or movement. **11. a.** The scent or trail of a fox or other animal. **b.** Something that provides an artificial scent. **12.** *Slang.* One that is obnoxiously tiresome; bore. **13.** *Slang.* A puff on a cigarette, pipe, or cigar. **14.** *Slang.* A street or road: *the main drag.* **15.** *Slang.* The clothing characteristic of one sex when worn by a member of the opposite sex: *in drag.* [ME *draggen* < ON *draga.*]

drag bunt *n. Baseball.* A bunt in which the batter tries to push or pull the ball down either foul line by hitting it with the bat trailing behind after he has already taken the first step toward first base, used esp. by left-handed batters.

dra·gée (drä-zhā') *n.* A small, often medicated candy. [Fr. < OFr. *dragie.* —see DREDGE[2].]

drag·ger (drăg'ər) *n.* **1.** One that drags. **2.** A fishing vessel that makes its catch in nets dragged along the bottom.

drag·gle (drăg'əl) *v.* **-gled, -gling, -gles.** *—tr.* To make wet and dirty by dragging in mud. *—intr.* **1.** To become muddy by being trailed. **2.** To follow slowly; straggle. [< DRAG.]

drag·gle·tail (drăg'əl-tāl') *n.* A bedraggled or slatternly woman.

drag·gy (drăg'ē) *adj.* **-gi·er, -gi·est. 1.** Dull and listless. **2.** *Slang.* Obnoxiously tiresome.

drag·line (drăg'līn') *n.* **1.** A line used for dragging. **2.** A kind of dredging machine.

drag link *n.* A link for transmitting rotary motion between cranks on two parallel but slightly offset shafts, as the rod connecting the lever of the steering gear to the steering arm in an automobile.

drag·net (drăg'nĕt') *n.* **1. a.** A net for trawling; trawl. **b.** A net for catching small game. **2.** A system of coordinated procedures used in apprehension, esp. of criminal suspects.

drag·o·man (drăg'ə-mən) *n., pl.* **-mans** or **-men.** An interpreter or guide in countries where Arabic, Turkish, or Persian is spoken. [ME *drugeman* < OFr. < Med. Lat. *dragumannus* < Gk. *dragoumanos* < Ar. *targumān* < Aram. *tūrgemānā* < Akkadian *targumānu,* interpreter < *ragāmu,* to call.]

drag·on (drăg'ən) *n.* **1.** A fabulous monster represented as a gigantic reptile having a lion's claws, the tail of a serpent, wings, and a scaly skin. **2.** *Archaic.* A large snake or serpent. **3.** A fiercely vigilant or intractable person. **4.** Any of various lizards, such as one of the genus *Draco.* **5. Dragon.** Draco. [ME < OFr. < Lat. *draco* < Gk. *drakōn,* serpent.]

drag·on·et (drăg'ə-nĭt) *n.* Any of various small, often brightly colored marine fishes of the family Callionymidae, having a slender body and a flattened head. [ME < *dragon,* dragon.]

drag·on·fly (drăg'ən-flī') *n., pl.* **-flies.** Any of various large insects of the order Odonata, having two pairs of narrow, net-veined wings and a long, slender body.

drag·on·head (drăg'ən-hĕd') *n.* Any of several plants of the genera *Dracocephalum* or *Physostegia,* having terminal spikes of rose-pink or purplish flowers.

drag·on·root (drăg'ən-ro͞ot', -ro͝ot') *n.* The green dragon.

dragon's blood (drăg'ənz) *n.* **1.** A red, resinous substance obtained from the fruit of a tree, *Daemonorops draco,* of

ă **pat** / ā **pay** / âr **care** / ä **father** / b **bib** / ch **church** / d **deed** / ĕ **pet** / ē **be** / f **fife** / g **gag** / h **hat** / hw **which** / ĭ **pit** / ī **pie** / îr **pier** / j **judge** / k **kick** / l **lid, needle** / m **mum** / n **no, sudden** / ng **thing** / ŏ **pot** / ō **toe** / ô **paw, for** / oi **noise** / ou **out** / o͝o **took** / o͞o **boot** /

tropical Asia, formerly used in the manufacture of varnishes and lacquers. **2.** Any of several resins similar to dragon's blood.

dragon tree *n.* A tree, *Dracaena draco,* of the Canary Islands, having a thick trunk, clusters of sword-shaped leaves, and orange fruit.

dra·goon (drə-go͞on', dră-) *n.* A heavily armed trooper in some European armies of the 17th and 18th centuries. —*tr.v.* **-gooned, -goon·ing, -goons. 1.** To persecute by the use of troops. **2.** To coerce by violent measures; harass. [Fr. *dragon,* dragoon, carbine < OFr., dragon. —see DRAGON.]

drag queen *n. Slang.* A male homosexual who dresses in women's clothing.

drag race *n.* A race between cars to determine which can accelerate faster from a standstill. **—drag racing** *n.*

drain (drān) *v.* **drained, drain·ing, drains.** —*tr.* **1.** To draw off (a liquid) by a gradual process: *drained water from the sink.* **2. a.** To cause liquid substance to go out from; empty: *drained the sink; drain the pond.* **b.** To draw off the surface water of. **3.** To drink all the contents of. **4. a.** To consume totally; exhaust: *expenses that drained our savings.* **b.** To fatigue or spend emotionally or physically. —*intr.* **1.** To flow off or go out of. **2.** To become empty or dry by the drawing off of liquid. **3.** To discharge surface waters through natural drainage channels in a given tract of land or region. —*n.* **1.** A pipe or channel by which liquid is drawn off. **2.** A device, such as a tube, inserted into the opening of a wound or cavity to facilitate discharge of fluid. **3.** The action or process of draining. **4.** A gradual outflow or loss; consumption or depletion: *a drain on the oil reserves.* **5.** Something that causes a depletion: *prolonged fighting caused a drain on the national treasury.* **—idiom. down the drain.** Used wastefully or proving fruitless. [ME *dreinen* < OE *drēahnian.*] **—drain'a·ble** *adj.* **—drain'er** *n.*

drain·age (drā'nĭj) *n.* **1.** The action or a given method of draining. **2.** A natural or artificial system of drains. **3.** Something that is drained off.

drainage basin *n.* The area drained by a river system.

drain·pipe (drān'pīp') *n.* A pipe for carrying off rainwater or sewage.

drake¹ (drāk) *n.* A male duck. [ME.]

drake² (drāk) *n.* A mayfly used as fishing bait. [ME, dragon < OE *draca* < Lat. *draco.* —see DRAGON.]

dram (drăm) *n.* **1. a.** A unit of weight in the U.S. Customary System, an avoirdupois unit equal to 1.771 grams or 0.0625 ounce. **b.** A unit of apothecary weight, equal to 3.889 grams or 0.125 ounce. **2. a.** A small draft: *a dram of cordial.* **b.** A bit: *not a dram of compassion.* [ME *dragme* < OFr. < Med. Lat. *dragma* < *Lat. drachma.* —see DRACHMA.]

dra·ma (drä'mə, drăm'ə) *n.* **1.** A prose or verse composition, esp. one telling a serious story, written for or as if for performance by actors; play. **2.** Dramatic art of a particular kind or period: *Elizabethan drama.* **3.** The art or practice of writing or producing plays. **4.** A situation or succession of events in real life having the dramatic progression or emotional content characteristic of a play. **5.** The quality or condition of being dramatic. [LLat. < Gk. < *dran,* to do.]

Dram·a·mine (drăm'ə-mēn'). A trademark for dimenhydrinate, a drug used to treat motion sickness.

dra·mat·ic (drə-măt'ĭk) *adj.* **1.** Of or pertaining to drama or the theater. **2.** Resembling a drama in emotional content or progression. **3.** Striking in appearance or forcefully effective. [LLat. *dramaticus* < Gk. *dramatikos* < *drama,* drama.] **—dra·mat'i·cal·ly** *adv.*

dramatic monologue *n.* A literary work, esp. in verse, in which a figure reveals his character in a monologue addressed directly to the reader or to another person.

dra·mat·ics (drə-măt'ĭks) *n.* *(used with a sing. or pl. verb).* **1.** The art and practice of acting and stage craft. **2.** Dramatic or histrionic behavior.

dram·a·tis per·so·nae (drăm'ə-tĭs pər-sō'nē, drä'mə-tĭs pər-sō'nī') *pl.n.* **1.** The characters in a play or story. **2.** A list of the characters in a play or story. [NLat., persons of the drama.]

dram·a·tist (drăm'ə-tĭst, drä'mə-) *n.* A playwright.

dram·a·ti·za·tion (drăm'ə-tĭ-zā'shən, drä'mə-) *n.* **1.** The act or art of transforming into a play or drama. **2.** A dramatic version of something.

dram·a·tize (drăm'ə-tīz', drä'mə-) *v.* **-tized, -tiz·ing, -tiz·es.** —*tr.* **1.** To adapt for presentation as a drama. **2.** To present or view in a dramatic or melodramatic way. —*intr.* **1.** To be adaptable to dramatic form. **2.** To indulge in self-dramatization.

dram·a·turge (drăm'ə-tûrj', drä'mə-) *n.* A playwright. [Fr. < Gk. *dramatourgos* : *drama,* drama + *ergon,* work.]

dram·a·tur·gy (drăm'ə-tûr'jē, drä'mə-) *n.* The art of the theater. **—dram'a·tur'gic, dram'a·tur'gi·cal** *adj.*

drank (drăngk) *v.* Past tense of **drink.**

drape (drāp) *v.* **draped, drap·ing, drapes.** —*tr.* **1.** To dress or hang with or as if with cloth in loose folds. **2.** To arrange or let fall in loose folds, as a garment. **3.** To hang or rest limply: *draped his legs over the chair.* —*intr.* To fall or hang in loose folds. —*n.* **1.** Often **drapes. a.** A drapery. **b.** A cloth arranged in a hospital operating room to keep the site of maximum sterility as small as possible. **2.** The way in which cloth falls or hangs. [ME *drapen,* to weave < OFr. < *drap,* cloth < LLat. *drappus,* of Celtic orig.]

drap·er (drā'pər) *n. Chiefly Brit.* A dealer in cloth or clothing and dry goods. [ME, weaver < OFr. *drapier* < *drap,* cloth. —see DRAPE.]

drap·er·y (drā'pə-rē) *n., pl.* **-ies. 1.** Cloth or clothing gracefully arranged in loose folds. **2.** Often **draperies.** Curtains, usually of heavy fabric, that hang straight in loose folds. **3.** Cloth; fabric. **4.** *Chiefly Brit.* The business of a draper.

dras·tic (drăs'tĭk) *adj.* **1.** Taking effect violently or rapidly. **2.** Quite severe or radical in nature; extreme: *took drastic steps.* [Gk. *drastikos,* active < *dran,* to do.] **—dras'ti·cal·ly** *adv.*

drat (drăt) *interj.* Used to express annoyance. [Short for *God rot.*]

draught (drăft) *n., v., & adj. Chiefly Brit.* Variant of **draft.**

draughts (drăfts, dräfts) *n. (used with a sing. verb). Chiefly Brit.* The game of checkers. [ME *draughtes,* pl. of *draught,* move at chess, act of pulling.]

Dra·vid·i·an (drə-vĭd'ē-ən) *n.* **1.** A large family of languages spoken esp. in southern India and northern Sri Lanka that includes Tamil, Telegu, Malayalam, and Kanarese. **2.** A member of any of the peoples that speak one of the Dravidian languages, esp. a member of the aboriginal population of southern India. [< Skt. *drāviḍah,* a Dravidian.] **—Dra·vid'i·an, Dra·vid·ic** (-vĭd'ĭk) *adj.*

draw (drô) *v.* **drew** (dro͞o), **drawn** (drôn), **draw·ing, draws.** —*tr.* **1. a.** To cause to move after or toward one by applying continuous force; pull; drag. **b.** To cause to move in a given direction or to a given position, as by leading: *She drew us into the room.* **c.** To move or pull so as to cover or uncover: *draw the drapes.* **2.** To cause to flow forth: *a pump drawing water.* **3.** To suck or take in (air); inhale. **4.** To displace (a specified depth of water) in floating: *a boat drawing 18 inches.* **5. a.** To take or pull out: *drew the gun from his belt.* **b.** To eviscerate; disembowel. **c.** To extract or take from for one's own use: *drew strength from her example.* **6. a.** To allure or attract: *afraid the casino will draw undesirable elements to the town.* **b.** To select or take in from a given group, type, or region: *draw clients from all levels of society.* **7. a.** To induce to act: *Frustration drew me into the squabble.* **b.** To bring on oneself as a result; provoke: *drew enemy fire.* **c.** To evoke as a response; elicit: *drew jeers and taunts from the audience.* **8. a.** To earn or bring in: *draw interest.* **b.** To withdraw (money). **c.** To use (a check, for example) when paying. **d.** To receive on a regular basis or at a specified time: *draw a salary.* **9.** To take or receive by chance: *draw lots.* **10. a.** To take (cards) from a dealer or central stack. **b.** To force (a card) to be played. **11.** To end or leave (a contest) tied or undecided. **12.** To hit or strike (a ball) so as to give it backspin. **13.** To pull back the string of (a bow). **14.** To distort the shape of. **15.** To stretch taut. **16. a.** To flatten, stretch, or mold (metal) by hammering or die stamping. **b.** To shape or elongate (a wire, for example) by drawing through dies. **17. a.** To describe (a line or figure) with a drafting implement. **b.** To draft or sketch (a picture). **18. a.** To portray by writing, speech, or imitative actions: *a poet who draws moving scenes of ghetto life.* **b.** To formulate or devise from evidence or data at hand: *draw a comparison.* **c.** To compose or write in a set form: *draw a contract.* —*intr.* **1. a.** To proceed or move steadily: *a ship drawing near the shore.* **b.** To wield an attracting force: *His new film is drawing poorly.* **2. a.** To pour forth liquid: *Her veins don't draw easily.* **b.** To take in a draft of air: *The flue isn't drawing.* **3. a.** To cause suppuration. **b.** To steep in the manner of tea. **4.** To pull out a weapon for use. **5.** To use or call upon part of a fund or supply: *drawing on an account; drew from the experience of his fellow workers.* **6.** To contract or tighten: *material that draws when it dries.* **7.** To tie in a contest. **8.** To describe forms and figures; sketch. ***—phrasal verbs.* draw away.** To move ahead of (as of a competitor). **draw back.** To pull back in order to avoid; retreat. **draw down.** To deplete by consuming or spending: *drew down our oil reserves.* **draw in.** To sketch roughly. **draw on.** To approach: *Dawn draws on.* **draw out. 1.** To cause to converse easily. **2.** To prolong; drag out. **draw up. 1.** To bring into order (as troops). **2.** To write in set or proper form. **3.** To bring or come to a halt. **4.** To bring (oneself) into an erect posture, often as a result of indignation. —*n.* **1.** An act of drawing. **2.** The result of drawing. **3.** Something drawn. **4.** The cards received as replacements in draw poker. **5.** Something that attracts interest or a crowd. **6.** The movable part of a drawbridge. **7.** A special advantage; edge: *have the draw on one's enemies.* **8.** A contest ending in a tie. **9.** A natural drainage basin; gully. ***—idioms.* draw a blank.** To fail to find or remember something. **draw and quarter. 1.** To execute (a prisoner) by tying each limb to a horse and driving the horses in different directions. **2.** To disembowel and dismember after hanging. **draw straws.** To decide by a lottery with straws of unequal lengths. **draw the line.** To set a limit, as of acceptable behavior. [ME *drawen* < OE *dragan.*]

draw·back (drô'băk') *n.* **1.** A disadvantage or inconvenience. **2.** A refund or remittance, such as a discount on duties or taxes for goods destined for favored uses.

drawbridge
In Chicago

draw·bar (drô′bär′) *n.* **1.** A bar across the rear of a tractor for hitching machinery. **2.** A railroad coupler.
draw·bridge (drô′brĭj′) *n.* A bridge that can be raised or drawn aside either to prevent access or to permit passage beneath it.
draw·down (drô′doun′) *n.* **1.** A lowering of the water level in a reservoir. **2.** The act, process, or result of depleting.
draw·ee (drô′ē′) *n.* A person on whom an order for the payment of money is drawn.
draw·er (drô′ər) *n.* **1.** One who draws, esp. a person who draws an order for the payment of money. **2.** (*also* drôr). A boxlike compartment in furniture that can be drawn on slides. **3. drawers** (drôrz). Underpants.
draw·ing (drô′ĭng) *n.* **1.** The act or an instance of drawing. **2.** The art of depicting forms or figures on a surface by lines. **3.** A portrayal in lines on a surface of a form or figure.
drawing account *n.* An account recording cash payments to a partner or employee to cover expenses or as advances on commissions.
drawing card *n.* An attraction drawing large audiences.
drawing pin *n. Chiefly Brit.* A thumbtack.
drawing room *n.* **1.** A formal reception room. **2.** A ceremonial reception. **3.** A private room on a railroad sleeping car. [Short for *withdrawing room.*]
draw·knife (drô′nīf′) *n.* A knife with a handle at each end of the blade, used with a drawing motion to shave a surface.
drawl (drôl) *v.* **drawled, drawl·ing, drawls.** —*intr.* To speak with lengthened or drawn-out vowels. —*tr.* To utter with a drawl. —*n.* The speech or manner of speaking of one who drawls. [Perh. < DRAW.] **—drawl′er** *n.*
drawn (drôn) *v.* Past participle of **draw.** —*adj.* Haggard, as from fatigue or ill health.
drawn butter *n.* Melted butter, often seasoned and used as a sauce.

drawknife

draw poker *n.* A kind of poker in which each player is dealt five cards face down and may then discard and get replacements for a specified number of cards after the first round of betting.
draw·shave (drô′shāv′) *n.* A drawknife.
draw·string (drô′strĭng′) *n.* A cord or ribbon run through a hem or casing and pulled to tighten or close an opening.
draw·tube (drô′to͞ob′, -tyo͞ob′) *n.* A tube that slides within another tube.
dray (drā) *n.* A low, heavy cart without sides, used for haulage. —*tr.v.* **drayed, dray·ing, drays.** To haul by dray. [ME *draye,* sled < OE *dræge,* dragnet.]
dray·age (drā′ĭj) *n.* **1.** Transport by dray. **2.** A charge for transport by dray.
dray·man (drā′mən) *n.* A driver of a dray.
dread (drĕd) *v.* **dread·ed, dread·ing, dreads.** —*tr.* **1.** To be in terror of. **2.** To hold in awe or reverence. **3.** To anticipate with alarm, anxiety, or reluctance. —*intr.* To be very afraid. —*n.* **1.** Profound fear; terror. **2.** Awe; reverence. **3.** Anxious or fearful anticipation. **4.** The object of fear, awe, or reverence. —*adj.* **1.** Causing terror or fear. **2.** Inspiring awe. [ME *dreden* < OE *drǣdan.*]
dread·ful (drĕd′fəl) *adj.* **1.** Inspiring dread; terrible. **2.** Extremely unpleasant; distasteful or shocking. **—dread′ful·ly** *adv.* **—dread′ful·ness** *n.*

dreadnought

dread·nought (drĕd′nôt′) *n.* A heavily armed battleship.
dream (drēm) *n.* **1.** A series of images, ideas, and emotions occurring in certain stages of sleep. **2.** A daydream; reverie. **3.** A state of abstraction; trance. **4.** A wild fancy or hope. **5.** An aspiration; ambition. **6.** One that is extremely beautiful, fine, or pleasant. —*v.* **dreamed** or **dreamt** (drĕmt), **dream·ing, dreams.** —*intr.* **1.** To experience a dream in sleep. **2.** To daydream. **3.** To have a deep aspiration: *dream of wealth and success.* —*tr.* **1.** To experience an image sequence of in sleep. **2.** To conceive of; imagine. **3.** To pass (time) idly or in reverie. ***—phrasal verbs.*** **dream of.** To consider something feasible or practical: *wouldn't dream of going.* **dream up.** To invent; concoct. [ME *drem* < OE *drēam,* joy and ON *draumr,* dream.]
dream·er (drē′mər) *n.* **1.** One who dreams. **2. a.** A visionary. **b.** An idealist. **3.** A habitually impractical person.
dream·land (drēm′lănd′) *n.* **1.** An ideal or imaginary land. **2.** A state of sleep.
dream·scape (drēm′skāp′) *n.* A dreamlike scene or picture having surreal qualities.
dreamt (drĕmt) *v.* A past tense and past participle of **dream.**
dream·y (drē′mē) *adj.* **-i·er, -i·est. 1.** Resembling a dream; vague. **2.** Given to daydreams or reverie. **3.** Soothing and serene. **4.** *Informal.* Inspiring delight; wonderful. **—dream′i·ly** *adv.* **—dream′i·ness** *n.*

dredge[1]

drear (drîr) *adj.* Dreary.
drea·ry (drîr′ē) *adj.* **-ri·er, -ri·est. 1.** Dismal or bleak. **2.** Boring or dull: *dreary tasks.* [ME *dreri* < OE *drēorig,* sad, bloody < *drēor,* gore.] **—drea′ri·ly** *adv.* **—drea′ri·ness** *n.*
dreck (drĕk) *n. Slang.* **1.** Excrement. **2.** Trash, esp. inferior merchandise. [Yiddish *drek* and G. *Dreck,* dung < MHG *drec.*] **—dreck′y** *adj.*
dredge[1] (drĕj) *n.* **1.** Any of various machines equipped with scooping or suction devices used in deepening harbors and waterways and in underwater mining. **2.** A boat or barge equipped with a dredge. **3.** An implement consisting of a net on a frame, used for gathering shellfish. —*v.* **dredged, dredg·ing, dredg·es.** —*tr.* **1.** To clean, deepen, or widen with a dredge. **2.** To bring up with a dredge. **3.** To come up with; unearth: *dredged up bitter memories.* —*intr.* To use a dredge. [Sc. *dreg.*] **—dredg′er** *n.*
dredge[2] (drĕj) *tr.v.* **dredged, dredg·ing, dredg·es.** To coat (food) by sprinkling with a powder, such as flour or powdered sugar. [< obs. *dredge,* a sweetmeat < ME *dragge* < OFr. *dragie* < Med. Lat. *dragia* < Lat. *tragemata,* confectionery < Gk. *tragēmata,* pl. of *tragēma,* sweetmeat < *trōgein,* to gnaw.] **—dredg′er** *n.*
D region *n.* The region of the ionosphere approximately 40 to 65 kilometers or 25 to 40 miles above the earth.
dregs (drĕgz) *pl.n.* **1.** The sediment of a liquid; lees. **2.** The basest or least desirable portion; trash. **3.** A small amount; residue. [ME *dregges* < ON *dregg.*]
drei·del also **drei·dl** (drād′l) *n.* **1.** A toy similar to a top with four sides marked with Hebrew letters. **2.** A game of chance played by children at Hanukah. [Yiddish *dreydl* < *dreyen,* to turn < MHG *drǣjen* < OHG *drāen.*]
drench (drĕnch) *tr.v.* **drenched, drench·ing, drench·es. 1.** To wet through and through; saturate. **2.** To administer a dose of liquid medicine to (an animal). **3.** To soak or fill completely as if by drenching. —*n.* **1.** An act of drenching. **2.** A large dose of liquid medicine. [ME *drenchen,* to drown < OE *drencan,* to cause to drink.] **—drench′er** *n.*
Dres·den china (drĕz′dən) *n.* Meissen. [After *Dresden,* a city in East Germany.]
dress (drĕs) *v.* **dressed, dress·ing, dress·es.** —*tr.* **1. a.** To put on (clothes). **b.** To furnish with clothing. **2.** To decorate or adorn. **3.** To arrange a display in: *dress a store window.* **4.** To arrange (troops) in ranks; align. **5.** To apply therapeutic materials to (a wound). **6.** To do up (the hair). **7.** To groom (an animal); curry. **8.** To cultivate (land or plants). **9.** To clean (fish or fowl) for cooking or sale. **10.** To put a finish on. —*intr.* **1.** To put on clothes. **2.** To wear clothes. **3.** To wear formal clothes. **4.** To get into proper alignment. **—phrasal verbs. dress down.** To scold; reprimand. **dress up. 1.** To wear formal or fancy clothes. **2.** To arrange in ranks. —*n.* **1.** Clothing; apparel. **2.** A one-piece outer garment for women. **3.** Outer covering or appearance. **4.** A style of clothing: *conservative in dress.* ***—modifier:*** *a dress coat.* **—idiom. dress ship.** To display the ensign, signal flags, and bunting on a ship. [ME *dressen,* to prepare < OFr. *dresser,* to arrange < VLat. **directiare* < Lat. *directus,* p.part. of *dirigere,* to direct.]
dres·sage (drə-säzh′, drĕ-) *n.* The guiding of a horse through a series of complex maneuvers by slight movements of the hands, legs, and weight. [Fr., preparation < *dresser,* to arrange < OFr. —see DRESS.]
dress circle *n.* A section of seats in a theater or opera house, usually the first tier above the orchestra.
dress code *n.* A set of rules, as in a school, indicating the approved manner of dress.
dress·er[1] (drĕs′ər) *n.* **1.** One that dresses. **2.** A wardrobe assistant, as for an actor; valet. **3.** One who dresses well or in a specified way.
dress·er[2] (drĕs′ər) *n.* **1.** A chest of drawers with a mirror. **2.** A cupboard or set of shelves for dishes or kitchen utensils. [ME *dressour,* table for preparing food < OFr. *dreceur* < *dresser,* to arrange. —see DRESS.]
dress·ing (drĕs′ĭng) *n.* **1.** The act of one that dresses. **2.** Therapeutic material applied to a wound. **3.** A sauce for certain dishes, such as salads. **4.** A stuffing, as for poultry or fish. **5.** Manure used to dress soil.
dressing gown *n.* A robe worn for lounging or before dressing.
dressing room *n.* A room in a theater or a home for changing costumes or clothes and applying make-up.
dressing table *n.* A low table with a mirror at which one sits while applying make-up.
dress·mak·er (drĕs′mā′kər) *n.* One who makes women's dresses. ***—modifier:*** *a dressmaker suit.* **—dress′mak′ing** *n.*
dress parade *n.* A military parade in dress uniform.
dress rehearsal *n.* A final, uninterrupted run-through, as of a play with costumes and stage properties.
dress suit *n.* A man's formal suit.
dress uniform *n.* A military uniform used for formal occasions.
dress·y (drĕs′ē) *adj.* **-i·er, -i·est. 1.** Showy or elegant in dress or appearance. **2.** Smart or stylish. **—dress′i·ness** *n.*
drew (dro͞o) *v.* Past tense of **draw.**
drib·ble (drĭb′əl) *v.* **-bled, -bling, -bles.** —*intr.* **1.** To flow or fall in drops or an unsteady stream; trickle. **2.** To let saliva drip from the mouth; drool. **3.** *Sports.* **a.** To dribble a ball. **b.** To advance by dribbling. —*tr.* **1.** To let flow or fall in drops or an unsteady stream. **2.** *Sports.* **a.** To move (a ball or puck) by repeated light bounces or kicks, as in basketball or soccer. **b.** To hit a ball so as to cause it to bounce slowly. —*n.* **1.** A trickle; drip. **2.** A small quantity; bit. **3.** *Sports.* The act of dribbling a ball. [Freq. of *drib,* var. of DRIP.] **—drib′bler** *n.*
drib·let (drĭb′lĭt) *n.* **1.** A tiny falling drop of liquid. **2.** A small amount or portion. [< obs. *drib,* drop < *drib,* var. of DRIP.]
dribs and drabs (drĭbz′n drăbz′) *pl.n.* Small and sporadic amounts. [Redup. of obs. *drib,* drop. —see DRIBLET.]

dribble

dri·er[1] also **dry·er** (drī′ər) *n.* **1.** One that dries. **2.** A substance added to paint, varnish, or ink to speed drying.
dri·er[2] (drī′ər) *adj.* A comparative of **dry**.
dri·est (drī′ĭst) *adj.* A superlative of **dry**.
drift (drĭft) *v.* **drift·ed, drift·ing, drifts.** —*intr.* **1.** To be carried along by or as by currents of air or water. **2.** To proceed or move unhurriedly and smoothly. **3.** To move leisurely or sporadically from place to place, esp. without regular employment and with no particular goal. **4. a.** To wander from a set course or point of attention; stray. **b.** To vary from or oscillate randomly about a fixed setting, position, or mode of operation. **5.** To be piled up in banks or heaps by the force of a current. —*tr.* **1.** To cause to drift. **2.** To cover with drifts. **3.** *Western U.S.* To drive (livestock) slowly or far afield, esp. for grazing. —*n.* **1.** The act or condition of drifting. **2.** Something moving along on a current of air or water. **3.** A bank or pile, as of sand or snow, heaped up by currents of air or water. **4.** *Geol.* Rock debris transported and deposited by or from ice, esp. by or from a glacier. **5. a.** A trend or general bearing; direction. **b.** General meaning or purport; tenor. **6. a.** A gradual change in position or opinion. **b.** A deviation from an original model, method, or intention. **7. a.** Lateral displacement or deviation of an object or vehicle from a planned course, esp. as a result of wind, ocean current, or other disturbance in the medium of travel. **b.** Variation or random oscillation about a fixed setting, position, or mode of behavior. **8.** A change in the output of a circuit or amplifier that takes place slowly. **9.** The rate of flow of a water current. **10. a.** A tool for ramming or driving something down. **b.** A tapered steel pin for enlarging and aligning holes. **11. a.** A horizontal or nearly horizontal passageway in a mine running through or parallel to a vein. **b.** A secondary mine passageway between two main shafts or tunnels. **12.** A drove or herd, esp. of swine. [< ME, drove, herd, act of driving.] **—drift′er** *n.* **—drift′y** *adj.*
drift·age (drĭf′tĭj) *n.* **1.** Deviation from a set course caused by drifting. **2.** Something that has been carried along or deposited by air or water currents.
drift·wood (drĭft′wo͝od′) *n.* **1.** Wood floating in or washed up by the water. **2.** A collection of worthless or trivial elements.
drill[1] (drĭl) *n.* **1. a.** An implement with cutting edges or a pointed end for boring holes in hard materials, usually by a rotating abrasion or by repeated blows. **b.** The hand-operated or hand-powered holder for this tool. **2.** Disciplined, repetitious exercise as a means of teaching and perfecting a skill or procedure, esp. as part of military training. **3.** Any of several marine gastropod mollusks, chiefly of the genus *Urosalpinx,* that drill holes into the shells of bivalve mollusks. —*v.* **drilled, drill·ing, drills.** —*tr.* **1.** To make a hole in (a hard material) with a drill. **2.** To strike or hit with a hard jabbing blow. **3. a.** To instruct thoroughly by repetition in a skill or procedure. **b.** To infuse knowledge of or skill in by repetitious instruction. —*intr.* **1.** To make a hole with a drill. **2.** To perform an exercise. [Du. *dril* < *drillen,* to drill.]
drill[2] (drĭl) *n.* **1.** A trench or furrow in which seeds are planted. **2.** A row of planted seeds. **3.** A machine or implement for planting seeds in holes or furrows. —*tr.v.* **drilled, drill·ing, drills. 1.** To sow (seeds) in rows. **2.** To plant (a field) in drills. [Perh. < DRILL[1], rill (obs.).]
drill[3] (drĭl) *n.* Durable cotton or linen twill of varying weights, generally used for work clothes. [Short for *drilling* < G. *Drillich* < OHG *drilīch* < Lat. *trilix,* triple-twilled : *tri-,* three + *licum,* thread.]
drill[4] (drĭl) *n.* A monkey, *Mandrillus leucophaeus,* of western Africa, related to and resembling the mandrill. [Native word in West Africa.]
drill instructor *n.* A noncommissioned officer who instructs recruits in military drill and discipline.
drill·mas·ter (drĭl′măs′tər) *n.* **1.** A drill instructor. **2.** An instructor given to severely rigorous training.
drill press *n.* A powered vertical drilling machine in which the drill is pressed to the work automatically or by a hand lever.
drill·ship (drĭl′shĭp′) *n.* A ship equipped for ocean floor drilling.
drill·stock (drĭl′stŏk′) *n.* The part of a drilling tool or machine that holds the shank of a drill or bit.
drink (drĭngk) *v.* **drank** (drăngk), **drunk, drink·ing, drinks.** —*tr.* **1.** To take into the mouth and swallow (a liquid). **2.** To soak up (liquid or moisture): *drank the fresh air.* **3.** To take in eagerly through the senses or intellect: *drank in her every word.* **4.** To swallow the liquid contents of (a vessel). **5. a.** To give or make (a toast). **b.** To toast (a person or occasion, for example). **6.** To bring to a specific state by drinking alcoholic liquors: *drank himself into a stupor.* —*intr.* **1.** To swallow liquid. **2.** To imbibe alcoholic liquors. **3.** To salute a person or occasion with a toast. —*n.* **1.** A liquid that is fit for drinking; beverage. **2.** An alcoholic beverage. **3.** An amount of liquid swallowed. **4.** Excessive or habitual indulgence in alcoholic liquor. **5.** *Slang.* A body of water; the sea: *slipped off the cliff and into the drink.* [ME *drinken* < OE *drincan.*]
drink·a·ble (drĭng′kə-bəl) *adj.* Suitable for drinking; potable. —*n.* A beverage.
drink·er (drĭng′kər) *n.* **1.** One who drinks. **2.** One who drinks alcoholic liquors excessively or habitually.
drip (drĭp) *v.* **dripped, drip·ping, drips.** —*intr.* **1.** To fall in drops. **2.** To shed drops. **3.** To ooze or be saturated with or as if with liquid: *a pompous fool dripping with hypocrisy.* —*tr.* To let fall in or as if in drops: *a dagger dripping blood.* —*n.* **1.** The process of forming and falling in drops. **2.** Liquid or moisture that falls in drops. **3.** The sound made by dripping liquid. **4.** A projection on a cornice or sill that protects the area below from rainwater. **5.** *Slang.* A tiresomely dull person. [ME *drippen* < OE *dryppan.*]
drip-dry (drĭp′drī′) *adj.* Made of a fabric that will not wrinkle when hung dripping wet for drying. —*intr.v.* **-dried, -dry·ing, -dries.** To dry with no wrinkles when hung dripping wet.
drip pan *n.* A pan for catching the drippings from roasting meat.
drip·ping (drĭp′ĭng) *n.* **1.** The act or sound of something that drips. **2.** Often **drippings.** The fat and juice exuded from roasting meat. —*adv.* Completely; thoroughly: *dripping wet.*
drip·py (drĭp′ē) *adj.* **-pi·er, -pi·est. 1.** Very wet; drizzly. **2.** *Slang.* Mawkishly sentimental. **—drip′pi·ness** *n.*
drip·stone (drĭp′stōn′) *n.* **1.** A drip made of stone, as on a cornice over a door or window. **2.** Calcium carbonate in the form of stalactites or stalagmites.
drive (drīv) *v.* **drove** (drōv), **driv·en** (drĭv′ən), **driv·ing, drives.** —*tr.* **1.** To push, propel, or press onward forcibly. **2.** To repulse by authority or force: *drove the attackers away.* **3.** To force to work, usually excessively. **4.** To force into or from a particular act or state: *She drives me crazy.* **5.** *Sports.* **a.** To throw, strike, or cast (a ball, for example) hard or rapidly. **b.** *Basketball.* To move with the ball directly through: *drove the lane.* **6.** *Baseball.* To cause (a baserunner or run) to be scored. **7.** To force to go through or penetrate. **8.** To create or produce by penetrating forcibly. **9.** To guide, control, or direct (a vehicle). **10.** To convey or transport in a vehicle. **11.** To supply the motive force to and cause to function: *Steam drives the engine.* **12.** To carry through vigorously to a conclusion: *drove home his point.* **13. a.** To chase (game) into the open or into traps or nets. **b.** To search (an area) for game in this manner. —*intr.* **1.** To move along or advance quickly as if pushed by an impelling force. **2.** To rush, dash, or advance violently against an obstruction: *The wind drove into my face.* **3.** To hit, throw, or impel a ball or other missile forcibly. **4.** *Basketball.* To move directly to the basket with the ball. **5.** To operate a car or other vehicle. **6.** To go or be transported in a car or other vehicle. **7.** To make an effort to reach or achieve a particular objective; aim. ***—phrasal verb.* drive at.** To mean to do or say. —*n.* **1.** The act of driving. **2.** A road for automobiles and other vehicles. **3.** A trip or journey in a vehicle. **4. a.** The means or apparatus for transmitting motion to a machine or machine part. **b.** The means by which automotive power is applied to a roadway: *four-wheel drive.* **c.** The means or apparatus for controlling and directing an automobile: *right-hand drive.* **5.** An organized effort to accomplish a purpose, such as raising money. **6.** Energy, push, or aggressiveness. **7.** *Psychoanal.* A strong motivating tendency or instinct, esp. of sexual or aggressive origin, that prompts activity toward a particular end. **8.** A massive and sustained military offensive. **9.** *Sports.* **a.** The act of hitting, knocking, or thrusting the ball very swiftly. **b.** The stroke or thrust by which the ball is driven. **c.** *Basketball.* The act of moving with the ball directly to the basket. **10. a.** A rounding-up and driving of cattle to new pastures or to market. **b.** A gathering and driving of logs down a river. **c.** The cattle or logs thus driven. [ME *driven* < OE *drīfan.*]
drive-in (drīv′ĭn′) *n.* A retail establishment designed to permit customers to remain in their automobiles while being accommodated. —*adj.* Designating or pertaining to a drive-in.
driv·el (drĭv′əl) *v.* **-eled, -el·ing, -els** or **-elled, -el·ling, -els.** —*intr.* **1.** To slobber; drool. **2.** To flow like spittle or saliva. **3.** To talk stupidly or childishly. —*tr.* **1.** To allow to flow from the mouth. **2.** To say (something) stupidly. —*n.* **1.** Saliva flowing from the mouth. **2.** Stupid or senseless talk. [ME *drivelen* < OE *dreflian.*] **—driv′el·er** *n.*
drive·line (drīv′līn′) *n.* The components of an automotive vehicle that connect the transmission with the driving axles and include the universal joint and drive shaft.
driv·en (drĭv′ən) *v.* Past participle of **drive.** —*adj.* **1.** Piled up or carried along by a current: *driven snow.* **2.** Having or motivated by a compulsive quality or need: *a driven man.*
driv·er (drī′vər) *n.* **1.** One that drives, esp. a chauffeur. **2.** A tool or device used for driving, as a hammer. **3.** A machine part that transmits motion or force to another part. **4.** A wooden-headed golf club with a long shaft, used for making long shots from the tee.
driver ant *n.* Any of various rapacious tropical Old World ants of the subfamily Dorylinae, that move in huge groups.
driver's seat *n.* A position of control or authority.
drive shaft *n.* A rotating shaft that transmits mechanical power to a point or region of application.
drive-up (drīv′ŭp′) *adj.* Enabling customers to remain in their automobiles while being served: *a drive-up window at the bank.*

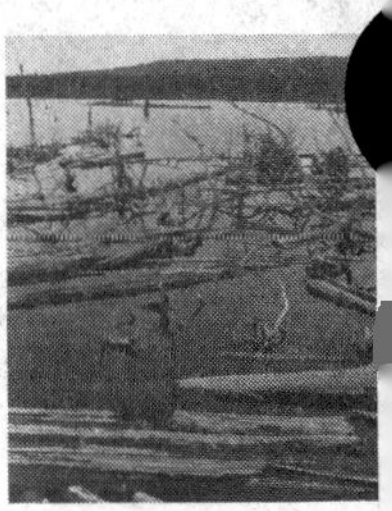
driftwood

drill[1]
Drilling for oil

drive·way (drīv′wā′) *n.* A private road connecting a house, garage, or other building with the street.
driv·ing (drī′vĭng) *adj.* **1.** Transmitting power or motion. **2.** Violent, intense, or forceful: *a driving rain.* **3.** Energetic or active: *a driving personality.*
driz·zle (drĭz′əl) *v.* **-zled, -zling, -zles.** —*intr.* To rain gently in fine, mistlike drops. —*tr.* **1.** To let fall in fine drops or particles. **2.** To moisten with fine drops. —*n.* A fine, gentle rain. [Perh. < ME *dresen,* to fall < OE *drēosan.*] **—driz′zly** *adj.*
drogue (drōg) *n.* **1.** A sea anchor. **2.** A drogue parachute. **3.** A funnel- or cone-shaped device towed behind an aircraft as a target. **4.** A funnel-shaped device at the end of the hose of a tanker aircraft, used as a stabilizer and receptacle for the probe of a receiving aircraft. [Perh. alteration of DRAG.]
drogue parachute *n.* **1.** A parachute used in decelerating a fast-moving object, esp. a small parachute used to slow down a re-entering spacecraft or satellite prior to deployment of the main parachute. **2.** A small parachute used to pull a main parachute from its storage pack.
droit (droit, drə-wä′) *n.* **1.** A legal right. **2.** Something to which one has legal right. [ME, a fee allowed by law < OFr., right < LLat. *directum* < Lat. *directus,* right, p.part. of *dirigere,* to direct.]
droll (drōl) *adj.* **-er, -est.** Amusingly odd or whimsically comical. —*n.* A buffoon. [Fr. *drôle* < *drôle,* buffoon < MDu. *drol,* little man.] **—droll′ness** *n.* **—drol′ly** *adv.*
droll·er·y (drō′lə-rē) *n., pl.* **-ies. 1.** A droll quality. **2.** A droll way of acting, talking, or behaving. **3. a.** The act of joking; clowning. **b.** Something droll, as a story.
-drome *suff.* **1. a.** Racecourse: *motordrome.* **b.** Field; arena: *airdrome.* **2.** Running: *acrodrome.* [Lat. *-dromos* < Gk. *dromos,* racecourse.]

drogue parachute
Apollo 16 landing in the Pacific Ocean in 1972

drom·e·dar·y (drŏm′ĭ-dĕr′ē, drŭm′-) *n., pl.* **-ies.** The one-humped domesticated camel, *Camelus dromedarius,* widely used as a beast of burden in northern Africa and western Asia. [ME *dromedarie* < OFr. *dromedaire* < LLat. *dromedarius* < Lat. *dromas* < Gk., running.]
drom·ond (drŏm′ənd, drŭm′-) *n.* A large medieval sailing galley. [ME < OFr. *dromont* < LLat. *dromo,* a kind of ship < LGk. *dromōn* < Gk. *dromos,* race.]
-dromous *suff.* Running; moving: *catadromous.* [NLat. *-dromus* < Gk. *-dromos* < *dromos,* act of running.]
drone¹ (drōn) *n.* **1.** A male bee, esp. a honeybee, characteristically stingless, performing no work, and producing no honey. **2.** An idle person who lives off others; loafer. **3.** A pilotless aircraft operated by remote control. [ME < OE *drān.*]
drone² (drōn) *v.* **droned, dron·ing, drones.** —*intr.* **1.** To make a continuous low dull humming sound. **2.** To speak in a monotonous tone. **3.** To pass or act in a monotonous way: *a lecture that droned on for hours.* —*tr.* To utter in a monotonous low tone. —*n.* **1.** A continuous low humming or buzzing sound. **2.** Any of the pipes of a bagpipe tuned to produce a single tone. **3.** *Mus.* A single sustained tone. [< DRONE¹ (from the bee's humming sound).]

dromedary

drool (dro͞ol) *v.* **drooled, drool·ing, drools.** —*intr.* **1.** To let saliva run from the mouth; drivel. **2.** *Informal.* To make an extravagant show of appreciation or desire. **3.** *Informal.* To talk nonsense. —*tr.* To let run from the mouth. —*n.* **1.** Saliva; drivel. **2.** *Informal.* Silly talk; nonsense. [Perh. alteration of DRIVEL.]
droop (dro͞op) *v.* **drooped, droop·ing, droops.** —*intr.* **1.** To bend or hang downward. **2.** To bend or sag gradually. **3.** To sag in dejection, exhaustion, or lifelessness. —*tr.* To let bend or hang down. —*n.* The act or condition of drooping. [ME *droupen* < ON *drūpa.*] **—droop′i·ly, droop′ing·ly** *adv.* **—droop′y** *adj.*
drop (drŏp) *n.* **1.** The smallest quantity of liquid heavy enough to fall in a spherical mass. **2.** A minute quantity of a substance. **3. drops.** Liquid medicine administered in drops. **4.** A trace or hint of something abstract: *not a drop of pity.* **5. a.** Something shaped or hanging like a drop. **b.** A small globular piece of hard candy. **6.** The act of falling; descent. **7.** A swift decline or decrease, as in quality, quantity, or intensity. **8. a.** The vertical distance from a higher to a lower level. **b.** The distance through which something falls or drops. **9.** A sheer incline, such as the face of a cliff. **10. a.** A descent by parachute. **b.** Personnel and equipment landed by means of parachute. **11.** Something arranged to fall or be lowered, as a trap door on a gallows. **12.** A drop curtain. **13.** A slot through which something is deposited in a receptacle. **14.** *Electronics.* A connection made available for a terminal unit on a transmission line. **15.** A central place or establishment where something, such as mail, is brought and subsequently distributed. —*v.* **dropped, drop·ping, drops.** —*intr.* **1.** To fall in drops. **2.** To fall from a higher to a lower place or position. **3.** To become less, as in number, intensity, or volume. **4.** To descend from one level to another. **5.** To fall or sink into a state of exhaustion or death. **6.** To pass or slip into a specified state or condition: *dropped into a doze.* **7.** *Sports.* To fall or roll into a basket or hole. Used of a ball. —*tr.* **1.** To let fall by releasing hold of. **2.** To let fall in drops. **3.** To cause to become less; reduce: *drop the rate of production.* **4.** To cause to fall, as by hitting or shooting. **5.** *Sports.* To hurl or strike (a ball) into a basket or hole. **6.** To give birth to. Used of animals. **7.** To say or offer casually: *drop a hint.* **8.** To write at one's leisure: *drop me a note.* **9.** To cease consideration or treatment of: *dropped the matter altogether.* **10.** To terminate an association or relationship. **11.** To leave unfinished: *drop everything and help her.* **12.** To leave out (a letter, for example) in speaking or writing. **13.** To leave or set down at a particular place; unload. **14.** To parachute. **15.** To lower the level of (the voice). **16.** To lose (a game or contest, for example). **17.** *Slang.* To take, as a drug, by mouth: *drop acid.* **—phrasal verbs. drop behind.** To fall behind. **drop by** (or **in**). To stop in for a short visit. **drop off. 1.** To fall asleep. **2.** To decrease. **drop out. 1.** To withdraw from participation, as in a game, club, or school. **2.** To withdraw from established society, esp. because of disillusion with conventional values. **—idiom. get** (or **have**) **the drop on.** To get (or have) a distinct advantage over. [ME < OE *dropa.*]
drop cloth *n.* A sheet, as of cloth or plastic, for protection against spills or dripping, used esp. by painters.
drop curtain *n.* **1.** An unframed curtain that forms part of the scenery on a stage. **2.** A theater curtain that can be lowered or raised.
drop-forge (drŏp′fôrj′, -fōrj′) *tr.v.* **-forged, -forg·ing, -forg·es.** To forge (a metal) between dies by the force of a drop hammer.
drop hammer *n.* A machine used to forge or stamp metal, consisting of an anvil or base aligned with a hammer that is forced down upon the molten metal.
drop-in (drŏp′ĭn′) *n.* **1.** One who casually drops in, as to visit. **2.** An informal social event.
drop kick *n. Football.* A kick made by dropping the ball to the ground and kicking it just as it starts to rebound.
drop-kick (drŏp′kĭk′) *intr. & tr.v.* **-kicked, -kick·ing, -kicks.** *Football.* To make or kick with a drop kick.
drop leaf *n.* A hinged wing on a table that can be folded down when not in use.
drop·let (drŏp′lĭt) *n.* A tiny drop.
drop letter *n.* A letter mailed and delivered from the same post office.
drop·light (drŏp′līt′) *n.* A hanging lamp that can be lowered and raised on its cord.
drop-off (drŏp′ôf′, -ŏf′) *n.* **1.** A very steep slope. **2.** A noticeable decrease: *a drop-off in attendance.*
drop·out (drŏp′out′) *n.* **1.** One who quits school. **2.** One who has withdrawn from a given social group, environment, or from established society. **3.** *Computer Sci.* A segment of magnetic tape on which expected information is absent.
drop·per (drŏp′ər) *n.* **1.** One that drops. **2.** A small tube with a suction bulb at one end for drawing in a liquid and releasing it in drops.
drop·ping (drŏp′ĭng) *n.* **1.** Something dropped. **2. drop·pings.** The dung of animals.
drop·shot (drŏp′shŏt′) *n. Sports.* A shot in various racquet games in which a ball or shuttlecock drops quickly after crossing the net or hitting the wall.
drop·sy (drŏp′sē) *n.* Pathological accumulation of diluted lymph in body tissues and cavities. [ME *dropesie,* short for *ydropesie* < OFr. < Lat. *hydropsis* < Gk. *hudrōpsis* < *hudrōps* < *hudōr,* water.] **—drop′si·cal** (-sĭ-kəl) *adj.* **—drop′si·cal·ly** *adv.*
drop·wort (drŏp′wôrt′, -wûrt′) *n.* A plant, *Filipendula hexapetala,* native to Eurasia, having finely divided leaflets and clusters of small white flowers.
dros·er·a (drŏs′ə-rə) *n.* Sundew. [NLat. < Gk., fem. of *droseros,* dewy < *drosos,* dew.]
drosh·ky (drŏsh′kē) also **dros·ky** (drŏs′kē) *n., pl.* **-kies.** An open, four-wheeled, horse-drawn carriage formerly common in Russia. [R. *drozhki,* dim. of *drogi,* wagon.]
dro·soph·i·la (drō-sŏf′ə-lə) *n.* A small fly of the genus *Drosophila,* esp. the fruit fly *D. melanogaster,* used extensively in genetic studies. [NLat. *Drosophila,* genus name : Gk. *drosos,* dew + NLat. *-philus,* -phile.]
dross (drŏs, drôs) *n.* **1.** Waste product or impurities formed on the surface of molten metal. **2.** Worthless, commonplace, or trivial matter. [ME *dros* < OE *drōs,* dregs.] **—dross′y** *adj.*
drought (drout) also **drouth** (drouth) *n.* **1.** A long period with no rain. **2.** A dearth or shortage of something. [ME < OE *drūgoð.*] **—drought′y** *adj.*
drove¹ (drōv) *v.* Past tense of **drive.**
drove² (drōv) *n.* **1.** A flock or herd being driven in a body. **2. a.** A large mass of people moving or acting as a body. **b.** A large body of like things. **3. a.** A stonemason's broad-edged chisel used for rough hewing. **b.** A stone surface dressed with a drove. [ME < OE *drāf* < *drīfan,* to drive.]
drov·er (drō′vər) *n.* A driver of cattle or sheep.
drown (droun) *v.* **drowned, drown·ing, drowns.** —*tr.* **1.** To kill by submerging and suffocating in water or another liquid. **2.** To drench thoroughly or cover with or as if with a liquid. **3.** To deaden one's awareness of, as by immersion: *drowned his troubles in drink.* **4.** To overwhelm and blur (a sound) by a louder sound: *screams that were drowned out by the passing train.* —*intr.* To die by suffocating in water or another liquid. [ME *drounen,* of Scand. orig.]
drowse (drouz) *v.* **drowsed, drows·ing, drows·es.** —*intr.* To be half-asleep. —*tr.* **1.** To make drowsy. **2.** To pass (time)

drum
Snare drum

by drowsing. —*n.* The condition of being sleepy. [Perh. ult. < OE *drusian,* to be sluggish.]
drows·y (drou'zē) *adj.* **-i·er, -i·est. 1.** Dull with sleepiness; sluggish. **2.** Produced or characterized by sleepiness. **3.** Inducing sleepiness; soporific. **—drows'i·ly** *adv.* **—drows'i·ness** *n.*
drub (drŭb) *v.* **drubbed, drub·bing, drubs.** —*tr.* **1.** To thrash with a stick. **2.** To instill or rout forcefully: *drubbed the lesson into her head; drubbed the idea right out of my mind.* **3. a.** To defeat emphatically. **b.** To berate harshly. **4.** To stamp (the feet). —*intr.* **1.** To beat the ground; stamp. **2.** To pound; throb. —*n.* A blow with a stick. [Ar. *ḍáraba,* to beat.] **—drub'ber** *n.*
drub·bing (drŭb'ĭng) *n.* **1.** A severe thrashing. **2.** A total defeat.
drudge (drŭj) *n.* A person who does tedious, menial, or unpleasant work. —*intr.v.* **drudged, drudg·ing, drudg·es.** To do the work of a drudge. [< ME *druggen,* to labor.] **—drudg'er** *n.* **—drudg'ing·ly** *adv.*
drudg·er·y (drŭj'ə-rē) *n., pl.* **-ies.** Tedious, menial, or unpleasant work.
drug (drŭg) *n.* **1.** A substance used as medicine in the treatment of disease. **2.** A narcotic, esp. one that is addictive. **3.** *Obs.* A chemical or dye. —*tr.v.* **drugged, drug·ging, drugs. 1.** To administer a drug to. **2.** To poison or mix (food or drink) with drugs. **3.** To stupefy or dull with or as if with a drug. [ME *drogge* < OFr. *drogue,* a chemical substance.]
drug·get (drŭg'ĭt) *n.* **1.** A heavy felted fabric of wool or wool and cotton, used for floor covering. **2.** A coarse rug of drugget, made in India. **3.** A fabric woven wholly or partly of wool, formerly used for clothing. [OFr. *droguet,* dim. of *drogue,* stuff.]
drug·gist (drŭg'ĭst) *n.* **1.** A pharmacist. **2.** One who sells drugs.
drug·store also **drug store** (drŭg'stôr', -stōr') *n.* A store where prescriptions are filled and drugs and other articles are sold.
dru·id also **Dru·id** (dro͞o'ĭd) *n.* A member of an order of priests in ancient Gaul and Britain who appear in Welsh and Irish legend as prophets and sorcerers. [Lat. *druides,* druids, prob. of Celtic orig.] **—dru·id'ic** (dro͞o-ĭd'ĭk), **dru·id'i·cal** *adj.* **—dru'id·ism** *n.*
drum (drŭm) *n.* **1.** A percussion instrument consisting of a hollow cylinder or hemisphere with a membrane stretched tightly over one or both ends, played by beating with the hands or sticks. **2.** A sound produced by a drum. **3.** Something resembling a drum in shape or structure, esp. a metal cylinder wound with cable, wire, or heavy rope, or a barrel-like metal container. **4.** Any of various marine and freshwater fishes of the family Sciaenidae, that make a drumming sound. **5.** The tympanic membrane. —*v.* **drummed, drum·ming, drums.** —*intr.* **1.** To play drums. **2.** To thump or tap rhythmically or continually. **3.** To produce a booming, reverberating sound by beating the wings, as certain birds do. —*tr.* **1.** To perform (a piece or tune) on or as if on a drum. **2.** To summon by or as if by beating a drum. **3.** To make known to or force upon (a person) by constant repetition: *drummed the answers into my head.* **4.** To expel or dismiss in disgrace: *drummed out of the army.* **—*phrasal verb.* drum up. 1.** To bring about by continuous, persistent effort: *drum up new business.* **2.** To devise; invent. [Prob. < Du. *trom.*]
drum·beat (drŭm'bēt') *n.* **1.** The sound produced by beating a drum. **2.** A cause supported ardently and esp. vehemently.
drum·beat·er (drŭm'bē'tər) *n.* One who supports a cause, esp. vehemently. **—drum'beat'ing** *n.*
drum·fire (drŭm'fīr') *n.* Heavy, continuous gunfire.
drum·head (drŭm'hĕd') *n.* **1.** The membrane stretched over the open end of a drum. **2.** *Naut.* The circular top part of a capstan, used to hold bars for turning.
drumhead court-martial *n.* A court-martial held for the summary trial of an offense committed during military operations. [So called because it was sometimes held around a drumhead.]
drum·lin (drŭm'lĭn) *n.* A streamlined hill or ridge of glacial drift. [Ir. Gael. *druim,* ridge < OIr. + -LIN(G)[1].]
drum major *n.* A man who leads a marching band or drum corps, often prancing before it and twirling a baton.
drum majorette *n.* A woman who leads a marching band or drum corps, often prancing before it and twirling a baton.
drum memory *n.* A computer memory device consisting of a magnetizable coating on the outer surface of a rotating cylinder.
drum·mer (drŭm'ər) *n.* **1.** One who plays a drum, as in a band. **2.** A traveling salesman.
drum printer *n.* A line printer in which a revolving drum acts as the printing element.
drum·stick (drŭm'stĭk') *n.* **1.** A stick for beating a drum. **2.** The lower part of the leg of a cooked fowl.
drunk (drŭngk) *v.* Past participle of **drink.** —*adj.* **1.** Intoxicated with alcoholic liquor to the point of impairment of physical and mental faculties. **2.** Caused or influenced by intoxication; drunken. **3.** Overcome by strong feeling or emotion: *drunk with power.* —*n.* **1.** A drunkard. **2.** A bout of drinking.

Usage: *Drunk* (adjective) is used predicatively: *He was drunk.* For attributive use before a noun, the choice is usually *drunken: a drunken guest.* The attributive use of *drunk,* as in *drunk driver,* is unacceptable to a great majority of the Usage Panel. But in its legal sense it is supported by usage and statute to the extent that the two expressions *drunk driver* (one who has exceeded the legal limit of alcohol consumption while driving) and *drunken driver* (one who is inebriated) are not synonymous.

drunk·ard (drŭng'kərd) *n.* One who is habitually drunk.
drunk·en (drŭng'kən) *adj.* **1.** Delirious with or as if with strong drink; intoxicated. **2.** Habitually drunk. **3.** Of, pertaining to, or occurring during intoxication: *drunken driving.* —See Usage note at **drunk. —drunk'en·ly** *adv.* **—drunk'en·ness** *n.*
drunk·o·me·ter (drŭng'kə-mē'tər, drŭng-kŏm'ĭ-tər) *n.* A device for determining the alcoholic content of the blood by analysis of the breath.
dru·pa·ceous (dro͞o-pā'shəs) *adj.* **1.** Pertaining to or consisting of a drupe: *drupaceous fruit.* **2.** Producing drupes: *a drupaceous tree.*
drupe (dro͞op) *n.* A fleshy fruit, such as the peach, plum, or cherry, usually having a single hard stone that encloses a seed. [NLat. *drupa* < Lat. *druppa,* overripe olive < Gk. < *drupepēs,* overripe : *drus,* tree + *peptein,* to cook, ripen.]
drupe·let (dro͞op'lĭt) *n.* A small drupe, such as one of the many subdivisions of the raspberry or the blackberry.
druse (dro͞oz) *n.* **1.** A crust of tiny crystals lining a rock cavity. **2.** A cavity lined by a druse. [G. < OHG *druos,* bump.]
Druse also **Druze** (dro͞oz) *n.* A member of a sect in Syria and Lebanon whose primarily Moslem religion contains some elements of Christianity. [Ar. *durūz,* pl. of *darazi,* a Druse, after Ismail al-*Darazi* (d. 1019).] **—Dru'si·an, Dru'se·an** *adj.*
druth·ers (drŭth'ərz) *pl.n. Informal.* A choice or preference: *if I had my druthers.* [Alteration of the phrase *I would rather.*]
Druze (dro͞oz) *n.* Variant of **Druse.**
dry (drī) *adj.* **dri·er, dri·est** also **dry·er, dry·est. 1.** Free from liquid or moisture. **2.** Having or characterized by little or no rain: *a dry climate.* **3.** Marked by the absence of natural or normal moisture: *a dry month.* **4.** Not under water: *dry land.* **5.** Having all the water or liquid drained away, evaporated, or exhausted: *a dry river.* **6.** No longer yielding liquid, esp. milk: *a dry cow.* **7.** Lacking a mucous or watery discharge: *a dry cough.* **8.** Not shedding tears: *dry sobs.* **9.** Needing or desiring drink; thirsty. **10.** No longer wet: *the paint is dry.* **11.** Of or pertaining to solid rather than liquid substances or commodities. **12.** Not sweet as a result of the decomposition of sugar during fermentation. Used of wines. **13.** Having a large proportion of strong liquor to other ingredients: *a dry martini.* **14.** Eaten without butter, gravy, or other garnish: *dry toast.* **15.** Without adornment or coloration; plain: *the dry facts.* **16.** Without bias or personal concern: *presented us with a dry critique.* **17.** Without tenderness, warmth, or involvement; severe: *a dry reading of the symphony.* **18.** Characterized by a matter-of-fact or indifferent manner: *rattled off the facts in a dry mechanical tone.* **19.** Wearisome and dull: *a dry lecture filled with trivial details.* **20.** Humorous or sarcastic in a shrewd, impersonal way: *dry wit.* **21.** *Informal.* Prohibiting or opposed to the sale or consumption of alcoholic beverages: *a dry town.* **22.** Not producing the expected results: *a mind dry of new ideas.* —*v.* **dried, dry·ing, dries.** —*tr.* **1.** To make dry. **2.** To preserve (meat or other foods, for example) by extracting the moisture. —*intr.* To become dry. **—*phrasal verbs.* dry out.** *Informal.* To undergo a cure for alcoholism. **dry up. 1.** To make or become unproductive, esp. to do so gradually. **2.** *Slang.* To stop talking. —*n., pl.* **drys.** *Informal.* A prohibitionist. [ME *drie* < OE *drȳge.*] **—dry'ly, dri'ly** *adv.* **—dry'ness** *n.*
dry·ad (drī'əd, -ăd') *n. Gk. Myth.* A nature divinity presiding over forests and trees; wood nymph. [Lat. *dryas, dryad-* < Gk. *druas* < *drus,* tree.] **—dry·ad'ic** *adj.*
dry·as·dust (drī'əz-dŭst') *n.* A dull, pedantic speaker or writer. [After Dr. Jonas *Dryasdust,* a fictitious character to whom Sir Walter Scott (1771–1832) dedicated some of his novels.]
dry battery *n.* An electric battery consisting of two or more dry cells.
dry cell *n.* A primary cell having an electrolyte in the form of moist paste. [So called because its contents are not spillable.]
dry-clean (drī'klēn') *tr.v.* **-cleaned, -clean·ing, -cleans.** To clean (clothing or fabrics) with chemical solvents having little or no water. **—dry cleaner** *n.* **—dry cleaning** *n.*
dry dock *n.* A large dock in the form of a basin from which the water can be emptied, used for building or repairing a ship below the water line.
dry-dock (drī'dŏk') *tr. & intr.v.* **-docked, -dock·ing, -docks.** To place in or go into a dry dock.
dry·er (drī'ər) *n.* **1.** An appliance that removes moisture by heating or another process: *a hair dryer.* **2.** Variant of **drier**[1].
dry farming *n.* A type of farming practiced in arid areas without irrigation by maintaining a fine surface tilth or

drum major

drum majorette

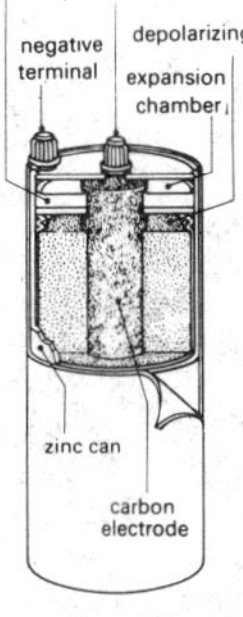

dry cell

dry dock

mulch that protects the natural moisture of the soil from evaporation. **—dry-farm** (drī′färm′) *v.* **(-farmed, -farm·ing, -farms).** **—dry farm** *n.* **—dry farmer** *n.*

dry fly *n.* An artificial fly used in fishing that floats on the water's surface when cast.

dry gangrene *n.* Gangrene that develops as a result of arterial obstruction and is characterized by mummification of the dead tissue and asepsis.

dry goods *pl.n.* Textiles, clothing, and related articles of trade.

dry ice *n.* Solid carbon dioxide that evaporates directly to gas at −78.5°C (−110°F) and is used primarily as a refrigerant. [Orig. a trademark.]

drying oil *n.* Any of various oily organic liquids, such as linseed oil, that forms a tough plastic layer when exposed to air in a thin film, used as a binder in paints and varnishes.

dry kiln *n.* A heated chamber in which cut lumber is dried and seasoned.

dry measure *n.* A system of units for measuring dry quantities such as grains, fruits, and vegetables.

dry nurse *n.* A nurse employed to care for an infant without breast-feeding it.

dry·o·pith·e·cine (drī′ō-pĭth′ĭ-sēn′) *n.* An extinct ape of the genus *Dryopithecus,* known from Old World fossil remains of the Miocene and Pliocene epochs, and believed to be an ancestor of the chimpanzees, gorillas, and man. *—adj.* Of or belonging to the genus *Dryopithecus.* [< NLat. *Dryopithecus,* genus name : Gk. *drus,* tree + Gk. *pithēkos,* ape.]

dry point *n.* **1.** A technique of intaglio engraving in which a hard steel needle is used to incise lines in the metal plate, with the burr at the side of the furrows retained. **2.** An engraving or print made with dry point.

dry rot *n.* **1.** A fungous disease of timber, causing it to become brittle and crumble into powder. **2.** A plant disease in which the plant tissue remains relatively dry while fungi invade and ultimately decay bulbs, fruit, or woody tissue.

duck[1]

dry run *n.* **1.** A test exercise in combat skills without the use of live ammunition. **2.** A trial exercise; rehearsal.

dry-salt·er (drī′sôlt′ər) *n. Chiefly Brit.* A dealer in chemical products and dyes. **—dry′salt′er·y** *n.*

dry socket *n.* A painful inflamed condition of a tooth socket after the tooth has been extracted.

dry wall *n.* A wall or section of a wall constructed of a prefabricated material, such as wallboard.

dry wash *n.* Laundry that has been washed and dried but not ironed.

D.T.'s (dē′tēz′) *pl.n.* Delirium tremens.

du·ad (do͞o′ăd′, dyo͞o′-) *n.* A unit of two objects; pair. [Gk. *duas, duad-,* two < *duo.*]

du·al (do͞o′əl, dyo͞o′-) *adj.* **1.** Composed of two parts; double; twofold. **2.** Having a double character, nature, or purpose. **3.** *Gram.* Designating or pertaining to a number category that indicates two persons or things, as in Greek, Sanskrit, and Old English. *—n. Gram.* **1.** The dual number. **2.** A word or expression in the dual number. [Lat. *dualis* < *duo,* two.] **—du′al·ly** *adv.*

ducking stool

du·al·ism (do͞o′ə-lĭz′əm, dyo͞o′-) *n.* **1.** The condition of being twofold; duality. **2.** *Philos.* The view that the world consists of or is explicable as two fundamental entities, such as mind and matter. **3.** *Psychol.* The view that there is a phenomenal distinction between mental and physical processes. **4.** *Theol.* **a.** The concept that the world is ruled by the antagonistic forces of good and evil. **b.** The concept that man has two basic natures, the physical and the spiritual. **—du′al·ist** *n.*

du·al·is·tic (do͞o′ə-lĭs′tĭk, dyo͞o′-) *adj.* **1.** Pertaining to or having the nature of dualism. **2.** Dual. **—du′al·is′ti·cal·ly** *adv.*

du·al·i·ty (do͞o-ăl′ĭ-tē, dyo͞o-) *n.* The quality or character of being twofold; dichotomy.

du·al-pur·pose (do͞o′əl-pûr′pəs, dyo͞o′-) *adj.* Designed for or serving two purposes.

dub[1] (dŭb) *tr.v.* **dubbed, dub·bing, dubs. 1.** To tap lightly on the shoulder by way of conferring knighthood. **2.** To honor with a new title or description. **3.** To name facetiously or playfully; nickname. **4.** To strike, cut, or rub (timber or leather, for example) so as to make even or smooth. **5.** To dress (a fowl). **6.** *Slang.* To execute (a golf stroke, for example) poorly. *—n. Slang.* An awkward person or player. [ME *dubben* < OE *dubbian.*]

dub[2] (dŭb) *v.* **dubbed, dub·bing, dubs.** *—tr.* **1.** To thrust at; poke. **2.** To beat (a drum). *—intr.* **1.** To make a thrust. **2.** To beat on a drum. *—n.* **1.** The act of dubbing. **2.** A drumbeat. [Perh. < LG *dubben,* to hit, strike.]

dub[3] (dŭb) *tr.v.* **dubbed, dub·bing, dubs. 1.** To make a new recording from the original of (a record or tape). **2.** To insert a new sound track, often a synchronized translation of the original dialogue, into (a film). **3.** To insert (sound) into a film or tape: *dub in strings behind the vocal. —n.* The new sounds added by dubbing. [Short for DOUBLE.] **—dub′ber** *n.*

dub[4] (dŭb) *n. Scot.* A puddle or small pool. [ME *dubbe.*]

dub·bin (dŭb′ĭn) also **dub·bing** (-ĭng) *n.* An application of tallow and oil for dressing leather. [< DUB[1].]

du·bi·e·ty (do͞o-bī′ĭ-tē, dyo͞o-) also **du·bi·os·i·ty** (do͞o′bē-ŏs′ĭ-tē, dyo͞o′-) **1.** The quality of being dubious. **2.** A matter of doubt. [LLat. *dubietas* < Lat. *dubius,* dubious.]

du·bi·ous (do͞o′bē-əs, dyo͞o′-) *adj.* **1.** Causing doubt or uncertainty; equivocal: *uneasy over his dubious response.* **2.** Reluctant to agree; skeptical: *dubious of the President's economic program.* **3. a.** Questionable as to quality or validity: *a person of dubious honesty.* **b.** Bordering on impropriety. **4.** Not yet determined; undecided: *still dubious as to what course to follow.* [Lat. *dubius.*] **—du′bi·ous·ly** *adv.* **—du′bi·ous·ness** *n.*

du·bi·ta·ble (do͞o′bĭ-tə-bəl, dyo͞o′-) *adj.* Subject to doubt or question; uncertain. [Lat. *dubitabilis* < *dubitare,* to doubt.] **—du′bi·ta·bly** *adv.*

du·bi·ta·tion (do͞o′bĭ-tā′shən, dyo͞o′-) *n. Archaic.* Doubt.

Du·bon·net (do͞o′bə-nā′, dyo͞o′-). A trademark for a fortified sweet wine that originated in France.

du·cal (do͞o′kəl, dyo͞o′-) *adj.* Of or pertaining to a duke or dukedom. [OFr. < LLat. *ducalis* < Lat. *dux,* leader. —see DUKE.] **—du′cal·ly** *adv.*

duc·at (dŭk′ət) *n.* **1.** Any of various gold coins formerly used in European countries. **2.** *Slang.* An admission ticket. [ME < OFr. < OItal. *ducato* < Med. Lat. *ducatus,* duchy (a word used on one of the early ducats).]

du·ce (do͞o′chā) *n.* A leader or commander; chief. [Ital. < Lat. *dux* < *ducere,* to lead.]

duch·ess (dŭch′ĭs) *n.* **1.** The wife or widow of a duke. **2.** A woman holding title to a duchy in her own right. [ME *duchesse* < OFr. < Med. Lat. *ducissa* < Lat. *dux,* leader. —see DUKE.]

duch·y (dŭch′ē) *n., pl.* **-ies.** The territory ruled by a duke or duchess; dukedom. [ME *duchie* < OFr. *duche* < Med. Lat. *ducatus* < Lat. *dux,* leader. —see DUKE.]

duck[1] (dŭk) *n.* **1.** Any of various wild or domesticated aquatic birds of the family Anatidae, characteristically having a broad, flat bill, short legs, and webbed feet. **2.** A female duck, as distinguished from a drake. **3.** The flesh of a duck used as food. **4.** *Slang.* A person, esp. a peculiar one. **5.** Often **ducks** *(used with a sing. verb). Chiefly Brit. Informal.* A dear. [ME *doke* < OE *duce.*]

duck[2] (dŭk) *v.* **ducked, duck·ing, ducks.** *—tr.* **1.** To lower quickly, esp. so as to avoid something. **2.** To evade; dodge: *duck responsibility.* **3.** To push suddenly under water. *—intr.* **1.** To lower the head or body. **2.** To move swiftly, esp. so as to escape being seen. **3.** To submerge the head or body briefly in water. *—n.* **1.** A quick lowering of the head or body. **2.** A plunge into water. [ME *douken.*] **—duck′er** *n.*

duck[3] (dŭk) *n.* **1.** A very durable, closely woven heavy cotton or linen fabric. **2. ducks.** Clothing made of duck, esp. white trousers. [Du. *doek,* cloth.]

duck[4] (dŭk) *n.* An amphibious military truck used during World War II. [< *DUKW,* its code designation.]

duck·bill (dŭk′bĭl′) *n.* The platypus.

duck blind *n.* A structure of wood or canvas, often camouflaged with reeds and grasses, behind which a duck hunter can hide and shelter himself from winds while awaiting a flight of ducks.

duck·board (dŭk′bôrd′, -bōrd′) *n.* A board or boardwalk laid across wet or muddy ground or flooring.

duck hawk *n.* The peregrine falcon.

ducking stool *n.* A punishment device formerly used in Europe and New England, consisting of a chair in which an offender was tied and ducked into water.

duck·ling (dŭk′lĭng) *n.* A young duck.

duck·pin (dŭk′pĭn′) *n.* **1.** A bowling pin, shorter and squatter than a tenpin. **2. duckpins** *(used with a sing. verb).* A bowling game played with duckpins and small balls. [From its squat appearance.]

ducks and drakes *n.* The game of skipping flat stones along the surface of water. ***—idiom.* make ducks and drakes of** or **play ducks and drakes with.** To squander; waste.

duck soup *n. Slang.* Something easy to accomplish.

duck·weed (dŭk′wēd′) *n.* Any of various small, free-floating, stemless aquatic plants of the genus *Lemna.*

duck·y (dŭk′ē) *adj.* **-i·er -i·est.** *Slang.* Excellent; fine.

duct (dŭkt) *n.* **1.** A tubular passage through which a substance, esp. a fluid, is conveyed. **2.** A bodily passage, esp. one for a secretion. **3.** *Elect.* A tube or pipe for carrying cables or wires. [Lat. *ductus,* act of leading < p.part. of *ducere,* to lead.]

duc·tile (dŭk′təl, -tĭl′) *adj.* **1.** Capable of being drawn into wire or hammered thin: *ductile metals.* **2.** Capable of being easily molded or shaped; plastic. **3.** Readily persuaded or influenced; tractable. [OFr. < Lat. *ductilis* < *ductus,* p.part. of *ducere,* to lead.] **—duc·til′i·ty** (-tĭl′ĭ-tē), **duc′ti·li·bil′i·ty** (-lə-bĭl′ĭ-tē) *n.*

duct·less gland (dŭkt′lĭs) *n.* An endocrine gland.

duct·ule (dŭk′to͞ol′) *n.* A small duct.

dud (dŭd) *n. Informal.* **1.** A bomb, shell, or explosive round that fails to detonate. **2.** One that is disappointingly ineffective or unsuccessful. **3. duds. a.** Clothing. **b.** Personal belongings. [ME *dudde,* an article of clothing.]

dude (do͞od, dyo͞od) *n.* **1.** *Informal.* An Easterner or city person who vacations on a Western ranch. **2.** *Informal.* A man who is very fancy or sharp in dress and demeanor. **3.** *Slang.* A fellow; chap. [Orig. unknown.]

du·deen (do͞o-dēn′) *n.* A short-stemmed clay pipe. [Ir. Gael. *dúidīn,* dim. of *dúd,* pipe.]

dude ranch *n.* A resort patterned after a Western ranch, featuring camping, horseback riding, and other outdoor activities.

dudg·eon[1] (dŭj′ən) *n.* A sullen, angry, or indignant humor: *"Slamming the door in Meg's face, Aunt March drove off in high dudgeon"* (Louisa May Alcott). [Orig. unknown.]

dudg·eon[2] (dŭj′ən) *n.* **1.** *Obs.* A kind of wood used in making knife handles. **2.** *Archaic.* **a.** A dagger with a hilt made of dudgeon. **b.** The hilt of a dagger. [ME *dogeon* < AN.]

due (do͞o, dyo͞o) *adj.* **1.** Payable immediately or on demand. **2.** Owed as a debt; owing: *the amount still due.* **3.** In accord with right, convention, or courtesy; appropriate: *due esteem.* **4.** Meeting special requirements; sufficient: *We have due cause to honor him.* **5.** Expected or scheduled, esp. appointed to arrive. **6.** Capable of being attributed. —*n.* **1.** Something that is owed or deserved: *finally received her due.* **2. dues.** A charge or fee for membership, as in a club or organization. —*adv.* **1.** Straight; directly: *due west.* **2.** *Archaic.* Duly. [ME < OFr. *deu* < VLat. **debutus* < Lat. *debitus,* p.part. of *debēre,* to owe.]

Usage: The phrase *due to* is always acceptable when *due* functions as a predicate adjective following a linking verb: *His hesitancy was due to fear.* But objection is often made when *due to* is used as a prepositional phrase: *He hesitated due to fear.* Such a construction is termed unacceptable in written usage by a large majority of the Usage Panel, though it is widely used. Generally accepted alternatives are *because of* or *on account of.*

due bill *n.* A written acknowledgment of indebtedness to a particular party, but not payable to his order or transferable by endorsement.

du·el (do͞o′əl, dyo͞o′-) *n.* **1.** A prearranged, formal combat between two persons, usually fought to settle a point of honor. **2.** A struggle for ascendancy between two contending persons, groups, or ideas. —*v.* **-eled, -el·ing, -els** or **-elled, -el·ling, -els.** —*tr.* **1.** To fight with in a duel. **2.** To oppose actively and forcefully. —*intr.* To fight a duel. [Med. Lat. *duellum* < Lat., war.] **—du′el·er, du′el·ist** *n.*

du·el·lo (do͞o-ĕl′ō, dyo͞o-) *n.* The art or rules of the duel. [Ital. < Lat. *duellum,* war.]

du·en·de (do͞o-ĕn′dā′) *n.* The ability to attract others through personal magnetism and charm. [Dial. Sp., charm < Sp., ghost.]

du·en·na (do͞o-ĕn′ə, dyo͞o-) *n.* **1.** An elderly woman retained by a Spanish or Portuguese family to act as governess and companion to the daughters. **2.** A chaperon. [Sp. *dueña* < Lat. *domina,* lady, fem. of *dominus,* lord.]

due process *n.* An established course for judicial proceedings or other governmental activities designed to safeguard the legal rights of the individual.

du·et (do͞o-ĕt′, dyo͞o-) *n.* **1.** A musical composition for two voices or instruments. **2.** The two performers of a duet. **3.** A pair. [Ital. *duetto,* dim. *duo* < Lat., two.]

due to *prep.* **1.** Attributable to; caused by. **2.** Because of. —See Usage note at **due.**

duff[1] (dŭf) *n.* A stiff flour pudding boiled in a cloth bag or steamed: *plum duff.* [Dial. var. of DOUGH.]

duff[2] (dŭf) *n.* **1.** Decaying leaves and branches covering a forest floor. **2.** Fine coal; slack. [Back-formation < DUFFER.]

duff[3] (dŭf) *n. Slang.* The buttocks. [Orig. unknown.]

duf·fel also **duf·fle** (dŭf′əl) *n.* **1.** A blanket fabric made of low-grade woolen cloth with a nap on both sides. **2.** Clothing and other personal gear carried by a camper. [Du., after *Duffel,* a town in Belgium.]

duffel bag *n.* A large cloth bag of canvas or duck for carrying personal belongings.

duf·fer (dŭf′ər) *n.* **1.** *Informal.* An incompetent or dull-witted person. **2.** *Slang.* A peddler of cheap merchandise. **3.** *Slang.* Something worthless or useless. [Orig. unknown.]

duf·fle (dŭf′əl) *n.* Variant of **duffel.**

dug[1] (dŭg) *n.* An udder, breast, or teat of a female animal. [Orig. unknown.]

dug[2] (dŭg) *v.* Past tense and past participle of **dig.**

du·gong (do͞o′gŏng′, -gông′) *n.* A herbivorous marine mammal, *Dugong dugon,* of tropical coastal waters of the Old World, having flipperlike forelimbs and a deeply notched tail fin. [NLat. *Dugong,* genus name < Malay *duyong.*]

dug·out (dŭg′out′) *n.* **1.** A boat or canoe made by hollowing out a log. **2.** A pit dug into the ground or on a hillside and used as a shelter. **3.** *Baseball.* Either of two usually sunken shelters at the side of a field where the players stay while not on the field.

dui·ker (dī′kər) *n.* Any of various small African antelopes, chiefly of the genus *Cephalopus,* having short, backward-pointing horns. [Afr. < Du. *duiken,* to dive.]

duke (do͞ok, dyo͞ok) *n.* **1.** A nobleman with the highest hereditary rank, esp. a man of the highest grade of the peerage in Great Britain. **2.** A prince who rules an independent duchy. **3.** A type of cherry intermediate between a sweet and a sour cherry. [ME < OFr. *duc* < Lat. *dux,* leader < *ducere,* to lead.]

duke·dom (do͞ok′dəm, dyo͞ok′-) *n.* **1.** A duchy. **2.** The office, rank, or title of a duke.

dukes (do͞oks, dyo͞oks) *pl.n. Slang.* The fists: *Put up your dukes!* [Short for *Duke of Yorks,* rhyming slang for *forks,* fingers.]

Du·kho·bor also **Dou·kho·bor** (do͞o′kə-bôr′) *n.* A member of an 18th-century Russian Christian sect, many of whom migrated to Canada in the 1890's to escape persecution. [R. *dukhoborets* : *dukh,* spirit + *borets,* wrestler < *borot',* to overcome.]

dul·cet (dŭl′sĭt) *adj.* **1. a.** Pleasing to the ear; melodious. **b.** Having a soothing and agreeable quality. **2.** *Archaic.* Sweet to the taste. [ME *doucet* < OFr. < *doux,* sweet < Lat. *dulcis.*]

dul·ci·fy (dŭl′sə-fī′) *tr.v.* **-fied, -fy·ing, -fies. 1.** To make agreeable or gentle; mollify. **2.** To sweeten. [LLat. *dulcificare,* to sweeten : Lat. *dulcis,* sweet + *facere,* to do.] **—dul′ci·fi·ca′tion** *n.*

dul·ci·mer (dŭl′sə-mər) *n.* A musical instrument with wire strings of graduated lengths stretched over a sound box, played with two padded hammers or by plucking. [ME *doucemer* < OFr. *doulcemer.*]

dull (dŭl) *adj.* **-er, -est. 1.** Lacking mental agility; stupid. **2.** Lacking responsiveness or alertness; insensitive. **3.** Dispirited; depressed. **4.** Not brisk or rapid; sluggish: *Business is dull.* **5.** Not having a sharp edge or point; blunt. **6.** Not intensely or keenly felt: *a dull ache.* **7.** Arousing no interest or curiosity; unexciting; boring. **8.** Not bright or vivid; dim: *a dull brown.* **9.** Cloudy or overcast: *a dull sky.* **10.** Not clear or resonant: *a dull thud.* —*v.* **dulled, dull·ing, dulls.** —*tr.* **1.** To make less sharp. **2.** To make less bright or distinct. **3.** To make (the senses, for example) less keen or receptive. —*intr.* To become dull. [ME *dul* < OE *dol.*] **—dull′ish** *adj.* **—dull′ness, dul′ness** *n.* **—dul′ly** *adv.*

dull·ard (dŭl′ərd) *n.* A mentally dull person; dolt.

du·ly (do͞o′lē, dyo͞o′-) *adv.* **1.** In a proper manner. **2.** At the expected time. [ME *duely* < *due,* due.]

Du·ma (do͞o′mə) *n.* A Russian national parliament, convened and dissolved four times between 1905 and 1917. [R., of Germanic orig.]

dumb (dŭm) *adj.* **-er, -est. 1.** Lacking the power of speech; mute. **2.** Temporarily speechless with shock or fear. **3.** Unwilling to speak. **4.** Not producing or accompanied by speech or sound. **5.** *Naut.* Not self-propelling. **6.** *Informal.* Stupid. [ME < OE.] **—dumb′ly** *adv.* **—dumb′ness** *n.*

dumb·bell (dŭm′bĕl′) *n.* **1.** A weight consisting of a short bar with a metal ball or disk at each end that is lifted for muscular development and exercise. **2.** *Slang.* A dull, stupid person; dolt.

dumb·found (dŭm′found′) *v.* Variant of **dumfound.**

dumb show *n.* **1.** A part of a dramatic performance unaccompanied by speech; pantomime. **2.** Communication by means of gestures.

dumb·struck (dŭm′strŭk′) *adj.* Shocked or astonished into speechlessness.

dumb·wait·er (dŭm′wā′tər) *n.* **1.** A small elevator used to convey food or other goods from one floor to another. **2.** A portable serving table.

dum–dum (dŭm′dŭm) *n. Slang.* A stupid person. [Redup. and alteration of DUMB.]

dum·dum bullet (dum′dum′) *n.* A small-arms bullet with a soft nose designed to expand upon contact, inflicting a gaping wound. [After *Dum-Dum,* town in India.]

dum·found or **dumb·found** (dŭm′found′) *tr.v.* **-found·ed, -found·ing, -founds.** To confound with astonishment or amazement. [DUM(B) + (CON)FOUND.]

dum·my (dŭm′ē) *n., pl.* **-mies. 1.** An imitation of a real or original object, intended to be used as a practical substitute. **2. a.** A mannequin used in displaying clothes. **b.** A stuffed or pasteboard figure used as a target. **c.** A figure of a person or an animal manipulated by a ventriloquist. **3.** A stupid person; dolt. **4.** A person or agency secretly in the service of another. **5.** *Printing.* **a.** A model of a work being published, indicating its general appearance and dimensions. **b.** A model page with text and illustrations pasted into place to direct the printer. **6. a.** In bridge, the partner who exposes his hand to be played by the declarer. **b.** The hand thus exposed. ***—modifier:*** *a dummy pocket; a dummy corporation.* —*tr.v.* **-mied, -my·ing, -mies.** *Printing.* To make a dummy of (a publication or page). [< DUMB.]

dummy variable *n.* A mathematical variable that can be replaced arbitrarily by another.

du·mor·ti·er·ite (do͞o-môr′tē-ə-rīt′, dyo͞o-) *n.* A greenish-blue aluminum borosilicate mineral, used in spark-plug porcelain and in special refractories. [Fr., after Eugène *Dumortier* (d.1876).]

dump (dŭmp) *v.* **dumped, dump·ing, dumps.** —*tr.* **1.** To release or throw down in a large mass. **2. a.** To empty (material) out of a container or vehicle. **b.** To empty out (a container or vehicle), as by overturning or tilting. **3. a.** To get rid of; jettison. **b.** To discard or reject unceremoniously. **4.** To place (goods) on the market, esp. in a foreign country, in large quantities and at a low price. **5.** *Computer Sci.* To reproduce (data stored internally in a computer) onto an external storage medium, as a printout. **6.** *Slang.* To knock down; beat. —*intr.* **1.** To fall or drop abruptly. **2.** To discharge cargo or contents; unload. —*n.* **1.** A place where refuse is dumped. **2.** A storage place for goods or supplies; depot. **3.** An unordered accumulation; pile. **4.** *Computer Sci.* An instance or the result of dumping data stored in a computer. **5.** *Slang.* A poorly maintained or disreputable place. [ME *dumpen,* of Scand. orig.] **—dump′er** *n.*

duel
19th-century illustration of the duel between Burr and Hamilton

dugong

dulcimer

dump·ling (dŭmp′lĭng) *n.* **1.** A small ball of dough cooked with stew or soup. **2.** Sweetened dough wrapped around an apple or other fruit, baked and served as a dessert. **3.** *Informal.* A short, chubby creature. [Orig. unknown.]
dumps (dŭmps) *pl.n.* A gloomy, melancholy state of mind; depression: *felt down in the dumps.* [< Du. *domp,* haze < MDu. *damp,* vapor.]
dump truck *n.* A heavy-duty truck having a bed that tilts backward to dump loose material.
dump·y[1] (dŭm′pē) *adj.* **-i·er, -i·est.** Short and stout; squat. [< dial. *dump,* lump.] **—dump′i·ly** *adv.* **—dump′i·ness** *n.*
dump·y[2] (dŭm′pē) *adj.* **-i·er, -i·est.** Depressed or discontented.
dumpy level *n.* A surveyor's instrument having a short telescope fixed rigidly to a horizontally rotating table.
dun[1] (dŭn) *tr.v.* **dunned, dun·ning, duns.** To importune (a debtor) persistently for payment. *—n.* **1.** One who duns. **2.** An importunate demand for payment. [Orig. unknown.]
dun[2] (dŭn) *n.* **1.** A color ranging from almost neutral brownish gray to dull grayish brown. **2.** A dun-colored fishing fly. **3.** A dun-colored horse. [ME < OE *dunn.*]
dunce (dŭns) *n.* A slow-witted or stupid person. [After John *Duns* Scotus (1265?–1308), whose writings and philosophy were ridiculed in the 16th cent.]
dunce cap also **dunce's cap** *n.* A cone-shaped paper cap, formerly placed upon the head of a slow or lazy pupil.
dun·der·head (dŭn′dər-hĕd′) *n.* A numbskull; dunce. [Perh. Du. *donder,* thunder + HEAD.]
dun·drear·ies (dŭn-drîr′ēz) *pl.n.* Long sideburns with a clean-shaven chin. [After Lord *Dundreary,* a character in the play *Our American Cousin* by Tom Taylor (1817–1880).]
dune (do͞on, dyo͞on) *n.* A hill or ridge of wind-blown sand. [Fr. < OFr. < MDu. *dūne.*]

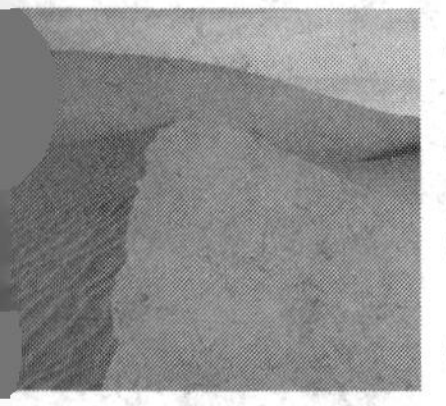
dune

dune buggy *n.* A small, light automobile, often without doors and roof, and usually equipped with a souped-up engine and oversize tires for driving on sand dunes.
dung (dŭng) *n.* **1.** The excrement of animals. **2.** Manure. **3.** Something foul or abhorrent. *—tr.v.* **dunged, dung·ing, dungs.** To fertilize with manure. [ME < OE.] **—dung′y** *adj.*
dun·ga·ree (dŭng′gə-rē′) *n.* **1.** A sturdy, usually blue denim fabric. **2. dungarees.** Overalls or trousers made of dungaree. [Hindi *dungri.*]
dung beetle *n.* Any of various beetles of the family Scarabaeidae, that form balls of dung on which they feed and in which they lay their eggs.
dun·geon (dŭn′jən) *n.* **1.** A dark, often underground chamber or cell used to confine prisoners. **2.** A donjon. [ME *donjon,* castle keep, dungeon < OFr., keep < Med. Lat. *dominio,* lordship < Lat. *dominus,* master.]
dung·hill (dŭng′hĭl′) *n.* **1.** A heap of animal excrement. **2.** A foul, degraded place or condition.
du·nite (do͞o′nīt′, dŭn′īt′) *n.* A dense igneous rock consisting mainly of olivine. [After Mt. *Dun* in New Zealand, where it is found.] **—du·nit·ic** (do͞o-nĭt′ĭk, də-) *adj.*
dunk (dŭngk) *v.* **dunked, dunk·ing, dunks.** *—tr.* **1.** To plunge into liquid; immerse. **2.** To dip (food) into a liquid before eating it. **3.** *Basketball.* To slam (a ball) through the basket from above. *—intr.* **1.** To submerge oneself briefly in water. **2.** *Basketball.* To dunk a basketball. *—n.* **1.** The act or an instance of dunking. **2.** *Basketball.* A shot made by jumping and slamming the ball down through the basket. [Pennsylvania Dutch *dunke* < MHG *dunken* < OHG *dunkōn.*] **—dunk′er** *n.*
Dun·ker (dŭng′kər) also **Dun·kard** (-kərd) *n.* A member of the German Baptist Brethren, a sect of German-American Baptists opposed to military service and the taking of legal oaths. [Pennsylvania Dutch < *dunke,* to dunk (from the practice of baptism by immersion).]
dunk shot *n. Basketball.* A dunk (sense 2).
dun·lin (dŭn′lĭn) *n.* A brown and white sandpiper, *Erolia* (or *Calidris*) *alpina,* of northern regions. [DUN[2] + -LIN(G)[1].]
dun·nage (dŭn′ĭj) *n.* **1.** Loose packing material protecting a ship's cargo from damage during transport. **2.** Personal belongings or baggage. [ME *dennage.*]
du·o (do͞o′ō, dyo͞o′ō) *n., pl.* **-os. 1.** *Mus.* **a.** A duet. **b.** Two performers singing or playing together. **2.** Two people in close association. [Ital. < Lat., two.]
duo– *pref.* Two: *duopsony.* [Lat. < *duo,* two.]
du·o·dec·i·mal (do͞o′ə-dĕs′ə-məl, dyo͞o′-) *adj.* **1.** Of, pertaining to, or based on the number 12: *the duodecimal system.* **2.** Of or pertaining to twelfths. *—n.* A twelfth. [< Lat. *duodecimus,* twelfth < *duodecim,* twelve : *duo,* two + *decem,* ten.]
du·o·dec·i·mo (do͞o′ə-dĕs′ə-mō′, dyo͞o′-) *n., pl.* **-mos. 1.** The page size (5 by 7 3/4 inches) of a book, formed by folding a single printer's sheet into 12 leaves. **2.** A book composed of duodecimos. [Lat., ablative of *duodecimus,* twelfth. —see DUODECIMAL.]
du·o·de·num (do͞o′ə-dē′nəm, dyo͞o′-, do͞o-ŏd′n-əm, dyo͞o-) *n., pl.* **du·od·e·na** (do͞o-ŏd′n-ə, dyo͞o-) or **du·o·de·nums.** The beginning portion of the small intestine, starting at the lower end of the stomach and extending to the jejunum. [ME < Med. Lat., short for *duodenum digitorum,* intestine of twelve fingers (in length) < Lat. *duodeni,* twelve each < *duodecim,* twelve. —see DUODECIMAL.] **—du′o·de′nal** (do͞o′ə-dē′nəl, dyo͞o′-, do͞o-ŏd′n-əl, dyo͞o-) *adj.*
du·op·so·ny (do͞o-ŏp′sə-nē, dyo͞o-) *n., pl.* **-nies.** A stock-market condition wherein two rival buyers exert a controlling influence on numerous sellers. [DUO- + Gk. *opsōnia,* purchasing of provisions : *opson,* food + *ōneisthai,* to buy.]
dupe (do͞op, dyo͞op) *n.* **1.** A person who is easily deceived. **2.** A person who is the tool of another person or a power. *—tr.v.* **duped, dup·ing, dupes.** To make a dupe of. [Fr. < OFr., prob. alteration of *huppe,* hoopoe.] **—dup′a·bil′i·ty** *n.* **—dup′a·ble** *adj.* **—dup′er** *n.*
dup·er·y (do͞o′pə-rē, dyo͞o′-) *n., pl.* **-ies. 1.** The action of duping. **2.** The state of being duped.
du·ple (do͞o′pəl, dyo͞o′-) *adj.* **1.** Consisting of two; double. **2.** *Mus.* Consisting of two or a multiple of two beats to the measure. [Lat. *duplus.*]
du·plex (do͞o′plĕks′, dyo͞o′-) *adj.* **1.** Twofold or double. **2.** Designating machinery that has two identical units that operate in a single frame, each capable of operating independently. **3.** *Electronics.* Able to transmit two messages simultaneously in the same or opposite directions over a single wire. *—n.* A duplex apartment or house. [Lat.] **—du·plex′i·ty** (do͞o-plĕk′sĭ-tē, dyo͞o-) *n.*
duplex apartment *n.* An apartment having rooms on two adjoining floors connected by an inner staircase.
duplex house *n.* A house divided into two living units.
du·pli·cate (do͞o′plĭ-kĭt, dyo͞o′-) *adj.* **1.** Identically copied from an original. **2.** Existing or growing in two corresponding parts; double. **3.** Designating a manner of play in certain card games in which all partnerships play the same hands and compare scores at the end. *—n.* **1.** An identical copy; facsimile. **2.** Something that corresponds exactly to something else, esp. an original. **3.** A duplicate card game. *—tr.v.* (-kāt′) **-cat·ed, -cat·ing, -cates. 1.** To make an identical copy of. **2.** To double; make twofold. **3.** To make or perform again; repeat: *a hard feat to duplicate.* *—intr.* To become duplicate. [ME < Lat. *duplicatus,* p.part. of *duplicare,* to double < *duplex,* twofold.] **—du′pli·cate·ly** *adv.* **—du′pli·ca′tive** *adj.*
du·pli·ca·tion (do͞o′plĭ-kā′shən, dyo͞o′-) *n.* **1. a.** The act or procedure of duplicating. **b.** The condition of being duplicated. **2.** A duplicate; replica.
du·pli·ca·tor (do͞o′plĭ-kā′tər, dyo͞o′-) *n.* A machine that reproduces printed or written material.
du·plic·i·tous (do͞o-plĭs′ĭ-təs, dyo͞o-) *adj.* Given to or marked by duplicity. **—du·plic′i·tous·ly** *adv.* **—du·plic′i·tous·ness** *n.*
du·plic·i·ty (do͞o-plĭs′ĭ-tē, dyo͞o-) *n., pl.* **-ties. 1.** Deliberate deceptiveness in behavior or speech; double-dealing. **2.** The quality or state of being twofold or double. [ME *duplicite* < OFr. < LLat. *duplicitas* < Lat. *duplex,* twofold.]
du·ra·ble (do͝or′ə-bəl, dyo͝or′-) *adj.* Capable of withstanding wear and tear or decay: *a durable fabric.* [ME < OFr. < Lat. *durabilis* < *durare,* to last.] **—du′ra·bil′i·ty, du′ra·ble·ness** *n.* **—du′ra·bly** *adv.*
durable goods *pl.n.* Manufactured products capable of long utility, as refrigerators and automobiles.
durable press *n.* **1.** A chemical process in which fabrics are permanently shaped and treated for wrinkle resistance. **2.** A fabric treated by durable press.
du·ral (do͝or′əl, dyo͝or′-) *adj.* Pertaining to the dura mater.
du·ral·u·min (do͞o-răl′yə-mĭn, dyo͞o-) *n.* An alloy of aluminum containing copper, manganese, magnesium, iron, and silicon that is resistant to corrosion by acids and sea water. [Orig. a trademark.]
du·ra ma·ter (do͝or′ə mā′tər, mä-, dyo͝or′ə) *n.* A tough fibrous membrane, lying over the arachnoid and the pia mater, that covers the brain and the spinal cord. [ME < Med. Lat. *dura mater* (*cerebri*), hard mother (of the brain).]
du·ra·men (do͞o-rā′mən, dyo͞o-) *n.* Heartwood. [NLat. < Lat., hardness < *durare,* to harden < *durus,* hard.]
du·rance (do͝or′əns, dyo͝or′-) *n.* Forced confinement; imprisonment. [ME *duraunce,* duration < OFr. *durance* < *durer,* to last < Lat. *durare.*]
du·ra·tion (do͞o-rā′shən, dyo͞o-) *n.* **1.** Continuance or persistence in time. **2.** The period of time during which something exists or persists: *sat quietly through the duration of the speech.* [Med. Lat. *duratio, duration-* < Lat. *durare,* to last.]
dur·bar (dûr′bär′) *n.* **1.** A state reception given formerly by an Indian prince or by a British governor in India. **2.** The court of an Indian prince. [Hindi *darbār* < Pers., court : *dar,* door + *bār,* admission, audience.]
du·ress (do͞o-rĕs′, dyo͞o-) *n.* **1.** Constraint by threat; coercion: *confessed under duress.* **2.** *Law.* **a.** Coercion illegally applied. **b.** Forcible confinement; durance. [ME *duresse,* harshness, compulsion < OFr. *durece,* hardness < Lat. *duritia* < *durus,* hard.]
Dur·ham (dûr′əm) *n.* A shorthorn. [After *Durham,* a county in England.]
du·ri·an (do͝or′ē-ən, dyo͝or′-, -än′) *n.* **1.** A tree, *Durio zibethinus,* of southeastern Asia, bearing edible fruit. **2.** The fruit of the durian, having a hard, prickly rind and soft pulp with an offensive odor but a pleasant taste. [Malay.]
dur·ing (do͝or′ĭng, dyo͝or′-) *prep.* **1.** Throughout the course or duration of: *suffered food shortages during the war.* **2.** At some time in: *born during a blizzard.* [ME < *duren,* to last < OFr. *durer* < Lat. *durare.*]
dur·mast (dûr′măst′) *n.* A European oak, *Quercus petraea,*

having tough, elastic wood. [Perh. alteration of *dun mast* : DUN[2] + MAST[2].]
durn (dûrn) *v. & interj.* Variant of **darn**[2]. **—durn, durned** *adj. & adv.*
du·roc also **Du·roc** (do͞o'rŏk', dyo͞o'-) *n.* A large red hog of a breed developed during the 19th century in the United States. [After *Duroc,* a horse owned by the developer of the breed.]
dur·ra (do͝or'ə) *n.* A cereal grain, *Sorghum vulgare durra,* of Asia and northern Africa, much cultivated in dry regions. [Ar. *dhurah.*]
durst (dûrst) *v. Archaic.* Past tense and past participle of **dare.**
du·rum (do͝or'əm, dyo͝or'-, dûr'-, dŭr'-) *n.* A hardy wheat, *Triticum aestivum durum,* used chiefly in making pasta. [NLat. < Lat., neuter of *durus,* hard.]
dusk (dŭsk) *n.* The darker stage of twilight, esp. in the evening. *—adj.* Tending to darkness; dusky. *—v.* **dusked, dusk·ing, dusks.** *—intr.* To become dark or dusky. *—tr.* To darken. [ME, dark < OE *dox.*]
dusk·y (dŭs'kē) *adj.* **-i·er, -i·est. 1.** Characterized by little or inadequate light; shadowy. **2.** Rather dark in color: *dusky skin.* **—dusk'i·ly** *adv.* **—dusk'i·ness** *n.*
dusky grouse *n.* The blue grouse.
dust (dŭst) *n.* **1.** Fine, dry particles of matter. **2.** A cloud of dust. **3.** Particles of matter regarded as the result of disintegration. **4. a.** Earth, esp. when regarded as the substance of the grave. **b.** The surface of the ground. **5.** A debased or despised condition. **6.** Something of no worth. **7.** *Chiefly Brit.* Household dirt or rubbish readied for disposal. **8.** Confusion or agitation resulting from a commotion: *won't go back in till the dust settles.* *—v.* **dust·ed, dust·ing, dusts.** *—tr.* **1.** To remove dust from by wiping, brushing, or beating. **2.** To sprinkle with a powdery substance. **3.** To strew like dust: *Freckles dusted her nose.* **4.** *Baseball.* To deliver a pitch so close to (the batter) as to make him back away. **5.** To restore to use: *dust off last year's winter coat.* **6.** *Archaic.* To cover with dust. *—intr.* **1.** To clean by removing dust. **2.** To cover itself with dust. Used of a bird. [ME < OE *dūst.*]
dust·bin (dŭst'bĭn') *n. Chiefly Brit.* A can for trash or garbage.
dust bowl *n.* A region reduced to aridity by drought and dust storms.
dust cover *n.* **1.** A removable or hinged plastic cover used to protect a turntable. **2.** A dust jacket (sense 1).
dust devil *n.* A small whirlwind that swirls dust, debris, and sand to great heights.
dust·er (dŭs'tər) *n.* **1.** One that dusts. **2.** A cloth or brush used to remove dust. **3.** A device for sifting or scattering a powdered substance. **4.** A smock worn to protect one's clothing from dust. **5.** A woman's loose dress-length housecoat.
dust jacket *n.* **1.** A removable paper cover used to protect the binding of a book. **2.** A cardboard sleeve in which a phonograph record is packaged.
dust·man (dŭst'mən) *n. Chiefly Brit.* A person employed to remove trash.
dust·pan (dŭst'păn') *n.* A short-handled pan into which dust is swept.
dust storm *n.* A severe windstorm that sweeps clouds of dust across an extensive area, esp. in an arid region.
dust·up (dŭst'ŭp') *n.* A row; argument.
dust·y (dŭs'tē) *adj.* **-i·er, -i·est. 1.** Covered or filled with dust. **2.** Consisting of or resembling dust; powdery. **3.** Tinged with gray. **—dust'i·ly** *adv.* **—dust'i·ness** *n.*
dusty miller *n.* Any of various plants having leaves and stems covered with dustlike down.
Dutch (dŭch) *adj.* **1.** Of or pertaining to the Netherlands, its inhabitants, or their language. **2.** *Archaic.* German. *—n.* **1. a.** The people of the Netherlands. **b.** *Archaic.* The Germans. **2. a.** The West Germanic language of the Netherlands. **b.** *Archaic.* German (sense 2). **c.** Pennsylvania Dutch. **3.** *Slang.* Anger or temper. ***—idioms.*** **go Dutch.** To go on an outing with each person paying his own way. **in Dutch.** *Informal.* In trouble or disfavor. [ME *Duch,* German, Dutch < MDu. *Duutsch.*]
Dutch cheese *n.* Cottage cheese.
Dutch clover *n.* The white clover.
Dutch courage *n. Informal.* Courage acquired from drinking liquor.
Dutch door *n.* A door divided in half horizontally so that either part can be left open or closed.
Dutch elm disease *n.* A disease of elm trees caused by a fungus, *Ceratocystis ulmi,* and resulting in brown streaks in the wood and eventual death of the tree.
Dutch·man (dŭch'mən) *n.* **1. a.** A native or inhabitant of the Netherlands. **b.** A person of Dutch descent. **2.** *Archaic.* A German. **3. dutchman.** Something used to conceal faulty construction.
Dutch·man's-breech·es (dŭch'mənz-brĭch'ĭz) *n.* A woodland plant, *Dicentra cucullaria,* of eastern North America, having finely divided leaves and yellowish-white flowers with two spurs.
Dutch·man's-pipe (dŭch'mənz-pīp') *n.* The pipe vine.
Dutch metal *n.* An alloy of copper and zinc used in thin sheets as a cheap imitation of gold leaf.
Dutch oven *n.* **1.** A large, heavy pot or kettle, usually of cast iron and with a tight lid, used for slow cooking. **2.** A metal utensil open on one side and equipped with shelves, placed before an open fire for baking or roasting food. **3.** A wall oven in which food is baked by means of preheated brick walls.
Dutch treat *n.* An outing, as for dinner or a movie, in which each person pays his own expenses.
Dutch uncle *n.* A stern and candid critic or adviser.
du·te·ous (do͞o'tē-əs, dyo͞o'-) *adj.* Obedient or dutiful. [< DUTY.] **—du'te·ous·ly** *adv.*
du·ti·a·ble (do͞o'tē-ə-bəl, dyo͞o'-) *adj.* Subject to import tax.
du·ti·ful (do͞o'tĭ-fəl, dyo͞o'-) *adj.* **1.** Careful to perform duties. **2.** Expressing or filled with a sense of duty. **—du'ti·ful·ly** *adv.* **—du'ti·ful·ness** *n.*
du·ty (do͞o'tē, dyo͞o'-) *n., pl.* **-ties. 1.** An act or a course of action that is required of one by position, social custom, law, or religion. **2. a.** Moral obligation. **b.** The compulsion felt to meet such obligation. **3.** A service, function, or task assigned to one, esp. in the armed forces. **4.** Function or work; service. **5.** A tax charged by a government, esp. on imports. **6. a.** The work capability of a machine under specified conditions. **b.** A measure of efficiency expressed as work per unit energy input. **7.** The amount of water required to irrigate a given area for the cultivation of some crop. [ME *duete* < AN < OFr. *deu,* due. —see DUE.]
du·ty-free (do͞o'tē-frē', dyo͞o'-) *adj.* Exempt from customs duties. **—du'ty-free'** *adv.*
du·um·vir (do͞o-ŭm'vər, dyo͞o-) *n.* A member of a duumvirate. [Lat., alteration of *duovir* : *duo,* two + *vir,* man.]
du·um·vi·rate (do͞o-ŭm'vər-ĭt, dyo͞o-) *n.* **1.** Any of various two-man executive boards in the Roman Republic. **2.** A regime or partnership of two persons.
du·ve·tyn also **du·ve·tyne** (do͞o'və-tēn', dyo͞o'-, do͞o'və-tēn', dyo͞o'-) *n.* A soft, short-napped fabric with a twill weave, made of wool, cotton, rayon, or silk. [Fr. *duvetine* < *duvet,* down < OFr. < *dum, dun* < ON *dūnn.*]
dwarf (dwôrf) *n., pl.* **dwarfs** or **dwarves** (dwôrvz). **1. a.** A very small person, esp. one afflicted with dwarfism. **b.** An atypically small animal or plant. **2.** A diminutive, often ugly, manlike creature of fairy tales and legend. **3.** A dwarf star. ***—modifier:*** *a dwarf tree.* *—v.* **dwarfed, dwarf·ing, dwarfs.** *—tr.* **1.** To check the natural growth or development of; stunt: *"The oaks were dwarfed from lack of moisture"* (John Steinbeck). **2.** To cause to appear small by comparison: *"Together these two big men dwarfed the tiny Broadway office"* (Saul Bellow). *—intr.* To become stunted or grow smaller. [ME *dwerf* < OE *dweorh.*] **—dwarf'ish** *adj.* **—dwarf'ish·ness** *n.*
dwarf cornel *n.* A woody plant, *Cornus canadensis,* of northern North America, having inconspicuous greenish flowers surrounded by white, petallike bracts, and scarlet fruit.
dwarf·ism (dwôr'fĭz'əm) *n.* A pathological condition of arrested growth having various causes.
dwarf star *n.* A star, such as the sun, having relatively low mass and average or below average luminosity.
dwarves (dwôrvz) *n.* A plural of **dwarf.**
dwell (dwĕl) *intr.v.* **dwelt** (dwĕlt) or **dwelled, dwell·ing, dwells. 1.** To live as a resident; reside. **2.** To exist in a given place or state. **3. a.** To fasten one's attention: *kept dwelling on what went wrong.* **b.** To treat at length; expatiate: *dwelt on the need to trim the budget.* *—n. Computer Sci.* A programmed time delay of variable duration. [ME *dwellen* < OE *dwellan,* to delay.] **—dwell'er** *n.*
dwell·ing (dwĕl'ĭng) *n.* A place to live in; abode.
dwelt (dwĕlt) *v.* A past tense and past participle of **dwell.**
dwin·dle (dwĭn'dl) *v.* **-dled, -dling, -dles.** *—intr.* To become gradually less until little remains; diminish. *—tr.* To make continuously smaller or less. [Freq. of obs. *dwine,* to diminish < ME *dwinen,* to shrink < OE *dwīnan.*]
Dy The symbol for the element dysprosium.
dy·ad (dī'ăd', -əd) *n.* **1.** Two units regarded as a pair. **2.** *Biol.* One pair of chromosomes separated from a tetrad in meiosis. **3.** *Chem.* A divalent atom or radical. **4.** A mathematical operator represented as a pair of vectors juxtaposed without multiplication. *—adj.* Made up of two units. [< Gk. *duas, duad-,* pair < *duo,* two.]
dy·ad·ic (dī-ăd'ĭk) *adj.* **1.** Twofold. **2.** Of or relating to a dyad. *—n. Math.* The direct product *(B·C) AD* of two dyads *AB* and *CD.*
Dy·ak also **Day·ak** (dī'ăk') *n.* **1.** A member of any of various Indonesian peoples of Borneo and the Sulu Sea islands. **2.** The language of the Dyaks. [Malay *Dayak* < *darat,* land.]
dy·ar·chy (dī'är'kē) *n.* Variant of **diarchy.**
dyb·buk (dĭb'ək) *n.* In Jewish folklore, the wandering soul of a deceased person that enters the body of a living person and controls his behavior. [Yiddish *dibek* < Heb. *dibbūq.*]
dye (dī) *n.* **1.** A substance used to color materials. **2.** A color imparted by dyeing. *—v.* **dyed, dye·ing, dyes.** *—tr.* To color (a material) with or as if with a dye, esp. by soaking in a coloring solution. *—intr.* To take on or impart color.

dust
Dust storm in Elkhart, Kansas, in 1937

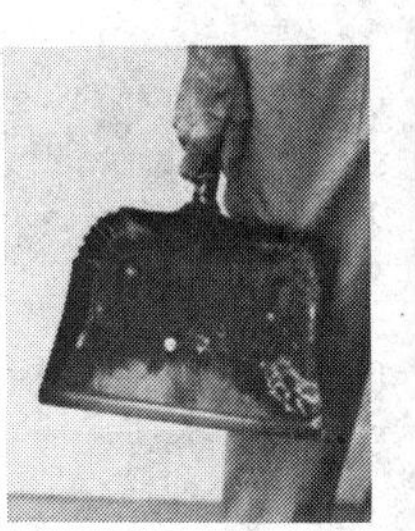

dustpan

Dutchman's-breeches

Dutch oven
Baking bread in a Dutch oven

—idiom. of the deepest dye. Of the most extreme sort. [ME *deie* < OE *dēah,* hue.] **—dy'er** *n.*
dyed-in-the-wool (dīd'ĭn-*thə*-wo͝ol') *adj.* **1.** Dyed before being woven into cloth. **2.** Thoroughgoing; out-and-out.
dy·er's broom (dī'ərz) *n.* The dyer's greenweed.
dyer's greenweed *n.* A small shrub, *Genista tinctoria,* native to Eurasia, having clusters of yellow flowers.
dyer's rocket *n.* A plant, *Reseda luteola,* native to Europe, having long spikes of small, yellowish-green flowers and yielding a yellow dye.
dy·er's-weed (dī'ərz-wēd') *n.* Any of various plants yielding coloring matter used as dye.
dye·stuff (dī'stŭf') *n.* A material used as or yielding a dye.
dye·wood (dī'wo͝od') *n.* A wood used as a dyestuff.
dy·ing (dī'ĭng) *adj.* **1.** About to die. **2.** Drawing to an end; declining. **3.** Done or uttered just before death.
dyke[1] (dīk) *n. & v.* Variant of **dike[1]**.
dyke[2] (dīk) *n.* Variant of **dike[2]**.
dy·nam·ic (dī-năm'ĭk) also **dy·nam·i·cal** (-ĭ-kəl) *adj.* **1. a.** Of or pertaining to energy, force, or motion in relation to force. **b.** Of or pertaining to dynamics. **2.** Characterized by continuous change, activity, or progress: *a dynamic market.* **3.** Characterized by vigor and energy; forceful: *a dynamic personality.* **4.** Of or pertaining to variation of intensity, as in musical sound. [Fr. *dynamique* < Gk. *dunamikos,* powerful < *dunamis,* power < *dunasthai,* to be able.] **—dy·nam'i·cal·ly** *adv.*
dy·nam·ics (dī-năm'ĭks) *n.* *(used with a sing. or pl. verb).* **1. a.** The study of the relationship between motion and the forces affecting motion. **b.** The combined study of kinetics and kinematics. **2.** The physical, intellectual, or moral forces that produce motion, activity, and change in a given sphere. **3.** Variation in force or intensity, esp. in musical sound. **4.** *Psychoanal.* **a.** The action of psychic forces or mechanisms. **b.** The psychological aspect or conduct of an interpersonal relationship.
dy·na·mism (dī'nə-mĭz'əm) *n.* **1.** Any of various theories or philosophical systems that explain the universe in terms of force or energy. **2.** A process or mechanism responsible for the development or motion of a system. **3.** The quality of being dynamic. [Fr. *dynamisme* < Gk. *dunamis,* power < *dunasthai,* to be able.] **—dy'na·mist** *n.* **—dy'na·mis'tic** *adj.*
dy·na·mite (dī'nə-mīt') *n.* **1.** A powerful explosive composed of nitroglycerin or ammonium nitrate dispersed in an absorbent medium with a combustible dope, such as wood pulp, and an antacid, such as calcium carbonate. **2.** *Slang.* Something that is exceptionally exciting or wonderful. **—modifier:** *a dynamite explosion; a dynamite dress.* —*tr.v.* **-mit·ed, -mit·ing, -mites. 1.** To blow up, shatter, or destroy with or as if with dynamite. **2.** To charge with dynamite. [Swed. *dynamit* < Gk. *dunamis,* power < *dunasthai,* to be able.] **—dy'na·mit'er** *n.*
dy·na·mo (dī'nə-mō') *n., pl.* **-mos. 1.** A generator, esp. one for producing direct current. **2.** An extremely energetic and forceful person. [Short for *dynamoelectric machine.*]
dy·na·mo·e·lec·tric (dī'nə-mō'ĭ-lĕk'trĭk) also **dy·na·mo·e·lec·tri·cal** (-trĭ-kəl) *adj.* Of or relating to the interconversion of mechanical energy and electrical energy. [Gk. *dunamis,* power + ELECTRIC.]
dy·na·mom·e·ter (dī'nə-mŏm'ĭ-tər) *n.* Any of several instruments used to measure force or power. [Fr. *dynamomètre* : Gk. *dunamis,* power + *-mètre,* meter.] **—dy'na·mo·met'ric** (-mō-mĕt'rĭk), **dy'na·mo·met'ri·cal** *adj.* **—dy'na·mom'e·try** *n.*
dy·na·mo·tor (dī'nə-mō'tər) *n.* A rotating electric machine with two armatures, used to convert alternating to direct current. [Gk. *dunamis,* power + MOTOR.]
dy·nast (dī'năst', -nəst) *n.* A ruler, esp. a hereditary ruler. [Lat. *dynastes* < Gk. *dunastēs,* lord < *dunasthai,* to be able.]
dy·nas·ty (dī'nə-stē) *n., pl.* **-ties. 1.** A succession of rulers from the same family or line. **2.** A family or group that maintains power for several generations. [Fr. *dynastie* < Gk. *dunasteia,* lordship < *dunastēs,* dynast.] **—dy·nas'tic** (dī-năs'tĭk) *adj.* **—dy·nas'ti·cal·ly** *adv.*
dy·na·tron (dī'nə-trŏn') *n.* *Electronics.* A tetrode with grid and plate potentials so arranged that plate current decreases when plate potential increases. [Gk. *dunamis,* power + -TRON.]
dyne (dīn) *n.* A centimeter-gram-second unit of force, equal to the force required to impart an acceleration of one centimeter per second per second to a mass of one gram. [Fr. < Gk. *dunamis,* power. —see DYNAMIC.]
Dy·nel (dī-nĕl'). A trademark for a copolymer of vinyl chloride and acrylonitrile, used to make fire-resistant, insect-resistant, and easily dyed textile fiber.
dy·node (dī'nōd') *n.* An electrode used in certain electron tubes to provide secondary emission. [Gk. *dunamis,* power + -ODE.]
dys– *pref.* **1.** Abnormal: *dysplasia.* **2. a.** Impaired: *dysgraphia.* **b.** Difficult: *dysphonia.* **3.** Bad: *dyslogistic.* [ME *dis-,* bad < OFr. < Lat. *dys-* < Gk. *dus-.*]
dys·cra·sia (dĭs-krā'zhə, -zhē-ə) *n.* An abnormal bodily condition caused by poisons in the blood. [NLat. < Med. Lat., disease < Gk. *duskrasia* : *dus-,* bad + *krasis,* mixing.]
dys·en·ter·y (dĭs'ən-tĕr'ē) *n.* An infection of the lower intestinal tract producing pain, fever, and severe diarrhea, often with the passage of blood and mucus. [ME *dissenterie* < Lat. *dysenteria* < Gk. *dusenteria* : *dus-,* bad + *enteron,* intestine.] **—dys'en·ter'ic** *adj.*
dys·func·tion (dĭs-fŭngk'shən) *n.* Disordered or impaired functioning of a bodily system or organ. **—dys·func'tion·al** *adj.*
dys·gen·ic (dĭs-jĕn'ĭk) *adj.* Pertaining to or causing the deterioration of hereditary qualities.
dys·gen·ics (dĭs-jĕn'ĭks) *n.* *(used with a sing. verb).* The biological study of the factors producing degeneration in offspring.
dys·graph·ia (dĭs-grăf'ē-ə) *n.* Impairment of the ability to write. [NLat. : DYS- + *-graphia,* -graphy.]
dys·lex·i·a (dĭs-lĕk'sē-ə) *n.* Impairment of the ability to read. [NLat. DYS- + Gk. *lexis,* speech < *legein,* to speak.] **—dys·lec'tic** (-lĕk'tĭk) *n.* **—dys·lex'ic** *adj.*
dys·lo·gis·tic (dĭs'lə-jĭs'tĭk) *adj.* Conveying censure; disapproving. [DYS- + (EU)LOGISTIC.] **—dys'lo·gis'ti·cal·ly** *adv.*
dys·men·or·rhe·a also **dys·men·or·rhoe·a** (dĭs-mĕn'ə-rē'ə) *n.* Difficult or painful menstruation. [DYS- + Gk. *mēn,* month + -RRHEA.] **—dys·men'or·rhe'al** (-rē'əl), **dys·men'or·rhe'ic** (-rē'ĭk) *adj.*
dys·pep·sia (dĭs-pĕp'shə, -sē-ə) *n.* Disturbed digestion; indigestion. [Lat. < Gk. *duspepsia* : *dus-,* bad + *pepsis,* digestion < *peptein,* to cook.]
dys·pep·tic (dĭs-pĕp'tĭk) *adj.* **1.** Pertaining to or having dyspepsia. **2.** Of or displaying a morose disposition. —*n.* One who suffers from dyspepsia. **—dys·pep'ti·cal·ly** *adv.*
dys·pha·gia (dĭs-fā'jə, -jē-ə) *n.* Difficulty in swallowing. **—dys·phag'ic** (-făj'ĭk) *adj.*
dys·pha·sia (dĭs-fā'zhə, -zhē-ə) *n.* Impairment of speech and verbal comprehension, esp. when associated with brain injury. **—dys·pha'sic** (-zĭk) *adj. & n.*
dys·pho·ni·a (dĭs-fō'nē-ə) *n.* Difficulty in speaking, usually evidenced by hoarseness. [NLat. DYS- + Gk. *phonē,* sound.] **—dys·phon'ic** (-fŏn'ĭk) *adj.*
dys·pho·ri·a (dĭs-fôr'ē-ə, -fōr'-) *n.* An emotional state characterized by anxiety, depression, and restlessness. [NLat. < Gk. *dusphoria,* distress < *dusphoros,* hard to bear : *dus-,* bad + *pherein,* to bear.] **—dys·phor'ic** (-fôr'ĭk, -fŏr'ĭk) *adj.*
dys·pla·sia (dĭs-plā'zhə, -zhē-ə) *n.* Abnormal development of tissues, organs, or cells. [NLat. DYS- + Gk. *plasis,* formation < *plassein,* to mold.] **—dys·plas'tic** (-plăs'tĭk) *adj.*
dysp·ne·a (dĭsp-nē'ə) *n.* A sense of difficulty in breathing, often associated with lung or heart disease. [NLat. < Gk. *duspnoia* < *duspnoos,* short of breath : *dus-,* bad + *pnoē,* breathing < *pnein,* to breathe.] **—dysp·ne'ic** (-nē'ĭk) *adj.*
dys·pro·si·um (dĭs-prō'zē-əm, -zhē-əm) *n.* *Symbol* **Dy** A soft, silvery rare-earth metal used in nuclear research. Atomic number 66; atomic weight 162.50; melting point 1,407°C; boiling point 2,600°C; specific gravity 8.536; valence 3. [NLat. < Gk. *dusprositos,* difficult to approach : *dus-,* bad + *prositos,* approachable < *prosienai,* to approach (*pros-,* toward + *ienai,* to go).]
dys·tel·e·ol·o·gy (dĭs-tĕl'ē-ŏl'ə-jē, -tē'lē-) *n.* **1.** The doctrine of purposelessness in nature. **2.** Purposelessness in natural structures, as manifested by the existence of vestigial or nonfunctional organs or parts. [G. *Dysteleologie* : *dys-,* dys- + *Teleologie,* teleology.] **—dys·tel'e·o·log'i·cal** (-ə-lŏj'ĭ-kəl) *adj.* **—dys·tel'e·ol'o·gist** *n.*
dys·to·pi·a (dĭs-tō'pē-ə) *n.* An imaginary place, as a country, of total misery and wretchedness. [DYS- + (U)TOPIA.] **—dys·to'pi·an** *adj.*
dys·tro·phy (dĭs'trə-fē) also **dys·tro·phi·a** (dĭ-strō'fē-ə) *n.* **1.** Defective nutrition. **2.** A disorder caused by defective nutrition. **—dys·troph'ic** (-trŏf'ĭk, -trō'fĭk) *adj.*
dys·u·ri·a (dĭs-yo͝or'ē-ə) *n.* Painful or difficult urination. **—dys·u'ric** (-yo͝or'ĭk) *adj.*

E

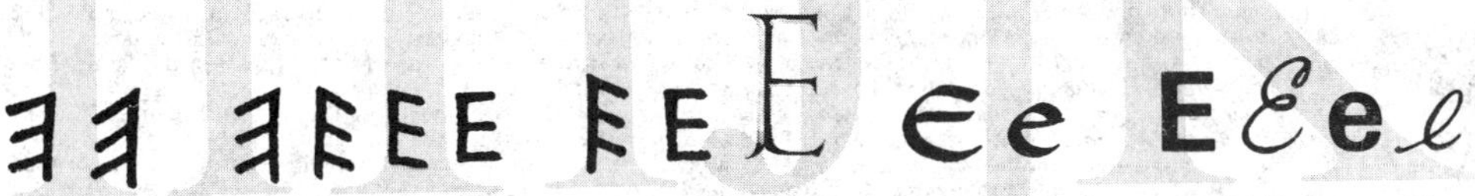

Around 1000 B.C. the Phoenicians and other Semitic peoples began to use graphic signs to represent individual speech sounds instead of syllables or words. They used a symbol in the forms (1,2) to represent the sound of the consonant "h" and called it *hē.* The Greeks, adapting the Phoenician alphabet, varied the orientation of *hē.* (3,4,5,6). They used it to represent the sound of the vowel "e" and called it *epsilon,* or "simple e," to distinguish it from long "e," which they called *ēta.* The Romans borrowed the alphabet from the Greeks via the Etruscans and adapted it for monumental inscriptions. Monumental script (9) is the prototype of modern capital letters (12,13). Medieval scribes adapted the Roman capitals to being quickly written on paper, parchment, and vellum. These uncial and cursive minuscules (10,11) are the prototypes of modern lower-case letters, both written and printed (15,14).

e

p **pop** / r **roar** / s **sauce** / sh **ship, dish** / t **tight** / th **thin, path** / *th* **this, bathe** / ŭ **cut** / ûr **urge** / v **valve** / w **with** / y **yes** / z **zebra, size** / zh **vision** / ə **about, item, edible, gallop, circus** / œ *Fr.* **feu,** *Ger.* **schön** / ü *Fr.* **tu,** *Ger.* **über** / KH *Ger.* **ich,** *Scot.* **loch** / N *Fr.* **bon.**

e or **E** (ē) *n., pl.* **e's** or **E's. 1.** The fifth letter of the modern English alphabet. **2.** Any of the speech sounds represented by the letter *e.* **3.** Something like an E in shape. **4. e** *Math.* The base of the natural system of logarithms, having a numerical value of approximately 2.718... . **5.** The fifth in a series. **6. E** *Mus.* The third tone in the scale of C major. **7.** A grade that indicates a student has failed to meet the standard for acceptable performance.

each (ēch) *adj.* Being one of two or more considered individually; every. *—pron.* Every one of a group considered individually; each one. *—adv.* For or to each one; apiece: *ten cents each.* [ME *ech* < OE *ælc.*]

Usage: When the subject of a sentence begins with *each,* it is traditionally held to be grammatically singular, and the verb and following pronouns must be singular as well: *Each of the pitchers has* (not *have*) *his* (not *their*) *good curve ball.* When *each* follows a plural subject, however, the verb and following pronouns generally remain in the plural: *The boys each have their jobs to do.* The expression *each and every* is likewise followed by a singular verb and singular pronouns in formal style: *Each and every driver knows what his or her job is supposed to be.* —See also Usage note at **everyone.**

each other *pron.* Each the other. Used to indicate a reciprocal relationship or action.

Usage: According to some traditional grammarians, *each other* is used of two, *one another* of more than two. This distinction has been ignored by many of the best writers, however, and a majority of the Usage Panel finds these examples acceptable: *The four partners regarded each other with suspicion. A husband and wife should confide in one another.* When speaking of an ordered series of events or stages, only *one another* can be used: *The Caesars exceeded one another* (not *each other*) *in cruelty* means that each Caesar was crueler than the last. • *Each other* cannot be used as the subject of a clause in formal writing. Instead of *we know what each other are thinking,* one should write *each of us knows what the other is thinking.* Instead of *the men know that each other are coming,* write *each of the men knows that the other is coming.* Instead of *we are all each other has,* write *each of us is all the other has.* • The possessive forms of *each other* and *one another* are written *each other's* and *one another's: The boys wore each other's* (not *each others'*) *coats. They had forgotten one another's* (not *one anothers'*) *names.*

ea·ger[1] (ē'gər) *adj.* **-er, -est. 1.** Intensely desirous of something; impatiently expectant: *an eager search for a familiar face in the crowd.* **2.** *Obs.* Tart; sharp; cutting. —See Usage note at **anxious.** [ME *eger* < OFr. *aigre,* sharp < Lat. *acer.*] **—ea'ger·ly** *adv.* **—ea'ger·ness** *n.*

Synonyms: *eager, avid, keen, anxious, earnest, fervid, zealous.* These adjectives describe a condition of mind marked by great interest, desire, or concern, or a manifestation of such a condition. *Eager* primarily suggests strong interest or desire. *Avid,* an intensification of *eager,* implies enthusiasm and unbounded craving. *Keen* suggests acuteness or intensity of interest or emotional drive. *Anxious* applies to interest or desire tinged by concern or fear. *Earnest* stresses seriousness of purpose and sincerity of motivation. *Fervid* emphasizes intensity of interest or desire, expressed in behavior that may be compulsive or overwrought. *Zealous* makes an even stronger implication of unbridled enthusiasm or concern, sometimes verging on fanaticism and unrestrained behavior.

ea·ger[2] (ē'gər, ā'-) *n.* Variant of **eagre.**

eager beaver *n. Informal.* An excessively industrious or zealous person.

eagle
Golden eagle

ea·gle (ē'gəl) *n.* **1.** Any of various large birds of prey of the family Accipitridae, including members of the genera *Aquila* and *Haliaeetus,* or characterized by a powerful hooked bill, long broad wings, and strong, soaring flight. **2.** A representation of an eagle used as an emblem or insignia. **3.** A former gold coin of the United States having a face value of ten dollars. **4.** A golf score of two below par on a hole. [ME *egle* < OFr. < Lat. *aquila.*]

ea·gle-eyed (ē'gəl-īd') *adj.* Having keen eyesight.

eagle owl *n.* A large Eurasian owl, *Bubo bubo,* having brownish plumage and prominent ear tufts.

Eagle Scout *n.* One who has achieved the highest rank in the Boy Scouts.

ea·glet (ē'glĭt) *n.* A young eagle.

ea·gre also **ea·ger** (ē'gər, ā'-) *n.* Bore[3]. [Orig. unknown.]

eal·dor·man (ôl'dər-mən) *n.* The chief magistrate of a district in Anglo-Saxon England. [OE. —see ALDERMAN.]

-ean *suff.* Variant of **-ian.**

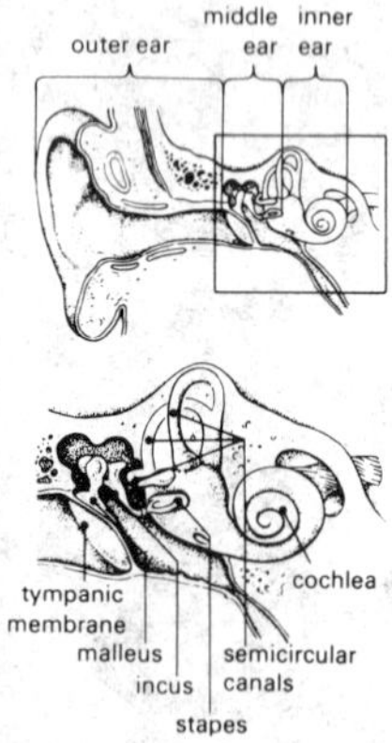

ear[1]
The human ear

ear[1] (îr) *n.* **1.** *Anat.* **a.** The vertebrate organ of hearing, responsible, in general, for maintaining equilibrium as well as sensing sound, and divided in man into the external ear, the middle ear, and the internal ear. **b.** The part of this organ that is externally visible. **2.** An organ analogous to the mammalian ear in invertebrates. **3.** The sense of hearing. **4.** Keenness of hearing. **5.** Sympathetic or favorable attention. **6.** Something resembling the external ear in position or shape, esp.: **a.** One of the tufts of feathers on the head of certain birds. **b.** A projecting handle, as on a vase or pitcher. **7.** A small box that appears in the upper corner of the page in a periodical, such as a newspaper and often contains an advertisement or weather information. **—*idioms.* all ears.** Acutely attentive: *If you want to tell your story, we're all ears.* **give** (or **lend**) **an ear.** To pay close attention to. **have** (or **keep**) **an ear to the ground.** To give attention to or watch for trends or coming events. **in one ear and out the other.** Heard but without influence or effect. **by ear.** Without reference to a score. **play it by ear.** To improvise. **up to one's** (or **the**) **ears.** Deeply involved: *up to one's ears in debt.* [ME *ere* < OE *ēare.*] **—ear'less** *adj.*

ear[2] (îr) *n.* The seed-bearing spike of a cereal plant, such as corn. *—intr.v.* **eared, ear·ing, ears.** To form or grow ears. [ME *ere* < OE *ær.*]

ear·ache (îr'āk') *n.* An ache in the ear.

ear·drop (îr'drŏp') *n.* An earring, esp. one with a pendent ornament.

ear·drum (îr'drŭm') *n. Anat.* The tympanic membrane.

eared (îrd) *adj.* **1.** Having ears or earlike projections. **2.** Having a specified kind or number of ears: *a lop-eared puppy.*

eared seal *n.* Any of various seals of the family Otariidae, which includes the sea lions and fur seals, characterized by external ears, oarlike front flippers, and hind flippers that can be turned forward for walking on land.

ear·flap (îr'flăp') *n.* A flap that is attached to a cap and may be turned down to cover the ears.

ear·ful (îr'fo͝ol') *n.* **1.** A flow of information or gossip. **2.** A scolding or reprimand.

ear·ing (îr'ĭng) *n.* A short line attaching an upper corner of a sail to the yard. [Perh. < EAR[1].]

earl (ûrl) *n.* A British peer next in rank above a viscount and below a marquis. [ME *erl,* nobleman of high rank < OE *eorl.*]

ear·lap (îr'lăp') *n.* An earflap.

earl·dom (ûrl'dəm) *n.* **1.** The rank or title of an earl. **2.** The territory of an earl. [ME *erldom* < OE *eorldōm.*]

earless seal *n.* Any of various seals of the family Phocidae, which includes the hair seals, characterized by the lack of external ears, short fore flippers, and reduced hind flippers specialized for swimming.

ear lobe *n.* The soft, fleshy tissue at the lowest portion of the external ear.

ear·ly (ûr'lē) *adj.* **-li·er, -li·est. 1.** Near the beginning of a given series, period of time, or course of events. **2.** Belonging to a distant or remote period of time; primitive. **3.** Occurring, developing, or appearing before the expected or usual time. **4.** Occurring in the near future. *—adv.* **1.** Near the beginning of a given series, period of time, or course of events. **2.** Far back in time. **3.** Before the expected or usual time. [ME *erli* < *ēr,* before, soon < OE *ær* and ON *ār.*] **—ear'li·ness** *n.*

early bird *n.* **1.** A person who arises early. **2.** One who arrives early or before others.

early on *adv.* At or during an early stage: *The new program developed problems early on.*

ear·mark (îr'märk') *n.* **1.** An identifying mark on the ear of a domestic animal. **2.** An identifying feature or characteristic. *—tr.v.* **-marked, -mark·ing, -marks. 1.** To mark the ear of (a domestic animal) for identification. **2.** To place an identifying or distinctive mark on. **3.** To reserve or set aside for a particular purpose: *We earmarked the merchandise for special customers.*

ear·muff (îr'mŭf') *n.* Either of a pair of ear coverings often attached to an adjustable headband and worn to protect esp. against the cold.

earn[1] (ûrn) *tr.v.* **earned, earn·ing, earns. 1.** To gain esp. for the performance of service, labor, or work. **2. a.** To acquire as a result of effort or action: *earned the disapproval of his peers.* **b.** To make worthy of. **3.** To produce as return or profit. [ME *ernen* < OE *earnian.*] **—earn'er** *n.*

earn[2] (ûrn) *intr.v.* **earned, earn·ing, earns.** *Obs.* To yearn. [Var. of YEARN.]

ear·nest[1] (ûr'nĭst) *adj.* **1.** Marked by or showing deep sincerity or seriousness: *an earnest gesture of good will.* **2.** Of an important or weighty nature; grave. **—*idiom.* in earnest.** With a purposeful or serious intent. [ME *ernest* < OE *eornoste.*] **—ear'nest·ly** *adv.* **—ear'nest·ness** *n.*

ear·nest[2] (ûr'nĭst) *n.* **1.** Money paid in advance as part payment to bind a contract or bargain. **2.** A token of something to come; promise or assurance. [ME *ernest* < OFr. *erres,* pl. of *erre,* pledge < Lat. *arra,* short for *arrabo* < Gk. *arrabōn* < Heb. *'ērābhōn* < *'ārabh,* he pledged.]

earn·ings (ûr'nĭngz) *pl.n.* Something earned, esp.: **a.** The salary or wages of a person. **b.** The profits of a business enterprise. **c.** Gains from investment.

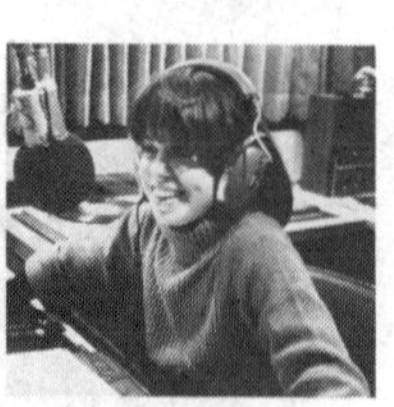

earphone

ear·phone (îr'fōn') *n.* A device that converts electric signals, as from a telephone or radio receiver, to audible sound and that fits over or in the ear.

ear·ring (îr'rĭng, îr'ĭng) *n.* An ornament worn on or pendent from the ear lobe.

ear rot *n.* Any of various fungus diseases of corn characterized by decay and molding of the ears.

ear shell *n.* The shell of the abalone.

ear·shot (îr'shŏt') *n.* The range within which sound can be heard; hearing distance.

ear·split·ting (îr'splĭt'ĭng) *adj.* Loud and shrill enough to hurt the ears.

earth (ûrth) *n.* **1. a.** The land surface of the world, as distin-

ă pat / ā pay / âr care / ä father / b bib / ch church / d deed / ĕ pet / ē be / f fife / g gag / h hat / hw which / ĭ pit / ī pie / îr pier / j judge / k kick / l lid, needle / m mum / n no, sudden / ng thing / ŏ pot / ō toe / ô paw, for / oi noise / ou out / o͝o took / o͞o boot /

guished from the oceans and air. **b.** The softer, friable part of land; soil, esp. productive soil. **2. Earth.** The third planet from the sun, having a sidereal period of revolution about the sun of 365.26 days at a mean distance of 92.96 million miles, an axial rotation period of 23 hours 56.07 minutes, an average radius of 3,959 miles, and a mass of 13.17 x 10^{24} pounds. **3.** The dwelling place of mortal men, as distinguished from heaven and hell; the temporal world. **4.** All of the human inhabitants of the world: *The earth received the news with joy.* **5.** Worldly affairs and pursuits, as distinguished from spiritual concerns. **6.** The material body of a human being. **7.** The lair of a burrowing animal. **8.** *Chiefly Brit.* The ground of an electrical circuit. **9.** *Chem.* Any of several metallic oxides, such as alumina or zirconia, that are difficult to reduce and were formerly regarded as elements. —*v.* **earthed, earth·ing, earths.** —*tr.* **1.** To cover or heap (plants) with soil for protection. **2.** To chase into an underground hiding place. —*intr.* To burrow or hide in the ground. Used of a hunted animal. —***idioms.* down to earth.** Sensible; realistic. **run to earth.** To hunt and run down. [ME *erthe* < OE *eorðe.*]

earth·born (ûrth′bôrn′) *adj.* **1. a.** Springing from or born on the earth. **b.** Human; mortal. **2.** Of, relating to, or connected with earthly life.

earth·bound also **earth-bound** (ûrth′bound′) *adj.* **1.** Fastened in or to the soil. **2. a.** Attached or confined to earthly interests. **b.** Unimaginative; ordinary. **3.** Headed for the earth: *an earthbound meteor.*

earth·en (ûr′thən, *-thən*) *adj.* **1.** Made of earth. **2.** Earthly; worldly.

earth·en·ware (ûr′thən-wâr′, *-thən-*) *n.* Ware, such as dishes or pots, made from a porous baked clay.

earth·light (ûrth′līt′) *n.* Earthshine.

earth·ling (ûrth′lĭng) *n.* **1.** One who inhabits the earth; human being. **2.** A person devoted to the world; worldling.

earth·ly (ûrth′lē) *adj.* **1.** Of or relating to this earth. **2. a.** Not heavenly or divine; secular. **b.** Terrestrial. **3.** Conceivable; possible: *no earthly meaning whatever.* **—earth′li·ness** *n.*

Synonyms: *earthly, terrestrial, worldly, mundane, earthy.* These adjectives all indicate relationship to the earth, but are not always interchangeable. *Earthly* is used principally in opposition or contrast to heavenly. *Terrestrial* is in opposition to celestial or specifies Earth distinguished from other planets or land distinguished from water. *Worldly,* in opposition to spiritual, describes the actions and concerns of people, especially as they pertain to this life (distinguished from afterlife); the term is associated with the pursuit of pleasure, wealth, or success. *Mundane* likewise refers to what is secular rather than spiritual or eternal and especially to the more ordinary, routine aspects of life on the earth. *Earthy,* in opposition to spiritual, suggests what is down to earth, especially the satisfaction of material wants and the more primitive human instincts.

earth·nut (ûrth′nŭt′) *n.* **1. a.** An Old World plant, *Conopodium denudatum,* having edible, nutlike tubers. **b.** The tuber of this plant. **2.** Any of various other plants, such as the peanut, similar to the earthnut.

earth·quake (ûrth′kwāk′) *n.* A series of elastic waves in the crust of the earth, caused by sudden relaxation of strains accumulated along geologic faults and by volcanic action, and resulting in movements in the earth's surface.

earth·rise (ûrth′rīz′) *n.* The rising of the earth from the horizon as seen from the moon.

earth satellite *n.* A satellite that orbits the earth.

earth science *n.* Any of several essentially geologic sciences concerned with the origin, structure, and physical phenomena of the earth.

earth·shak·ing (ûrth′shā′kĭng) *adj.* Of enormous or fundamental importance. **—earth′shak′ing·ly** *adv.*

earth·shine (ûrth′shīn′) *n.* The sunlight reflected from the earth's surface that illuminates part of the moon not directly lighted by the sun.

earth·star (ûrth′stär′) *n.* A fungus of the genus *Geastrum,* related to and resembling the puffballs and having an outer covering that splits open in a starlike form.

earth station *n.* An on-ground terminal linked to a spacecraft or satellite by an antenna and associated electronic equipment, for the purpose of transmitting or receiving messages, tracking, or control.

earth·ward (ûrth′wərd) *adj. & adv.* To or toward the earth. **—earth·wards** (-wərdz) *adv.*

earth·work (ûrth′wûrk′) *n.* **1.** An earthen embankment, esp. when used as a military fortification. **2.** *Engineering.* Excavation and embankment of earth.

earth·worm (ûrth′wûrm′) *n.* Any of various terrestrial annelid worms of the class Oligochaeta and esp. of the family Lumbricidae, that burrow into and help aerate and enrich soil.

earth·y (ûr′thē) *adj.* **-i·er, -i·est. 1.** Consisting of or resembling earth or soil. **2.** Pertaining to or characteristic of this world; worldly. **3.** Crude or coarse; unrefined. **—earth′i·ness** *n.*

ear trumpet *n.* A horn-shaped instrument formerly used to direct sound into the ear of a partially deaf person.

ear·wax (îr′wăks′) *n.* The waxlike secretion of certain glands lining the canal of the outer ear; cerumen.

ear·wig (îr′wĭg′) *n.* Any of various insects of the order Dermaptera, having pincerlike appendages protruding from the rear of the abdomen. —*tr.v.* **-wigged, -wig·ging, -wigs. 1.** To annoy by persistent and confidential solicitation. **2.** To attempt to influence by private or secret communications. [ME *erwig* < OE *ēarwicga* : *eare,* ear + *wicga,* insect.]

ear·worm (îr′wûrm′) *n.* The corn earworm.

ease (ēz) *n.* **1. a.** The condition of being without discomfort. **b.** Freedom from pain, worry, or agitation. **2.** Freedom from constraint or embarrassment; naturalness. **3. a.** Freedom from difficulty, hard work, or great effort. **b.** Readiness in performance; facility. **4.** Freedom from financial difficulty; affluence. —*v.* **eased, eas·ing, eas·es.** —*tr.* **1.** To free from pain, worry, or trouble. **2.** To lessen the discomfort or pain of; alleviate. **3.** To slacken the strain, pressure or tension of; loosen. **4.** To move into place slowly and carefully: *eased the car into a narrow space.* —*intr.* To lessen in discomfort, stress, pressure, or the like. [ME *ese* < OFr. *aise* < Lat. *adjacens,* pr.part. of *adjacēre,* to lie near. —see ADJACENT.]

ease·ful (ēz′fəl) *adj.* Affording or characterized by comfort and peace; restful. **—ease′ful·ly** *adv.* **—ease′ful·ness** *n.*

ea·sel (ē′zəl) *n.* An upright frame for displaying or supporting something, such as an artist's canvas. [Du. *ezel,* ass < MDu. *esel* < Lat. *asinus.*]

ease·ment (ēz′mənt) *n.* **1.** The act of easing or the condition of being eased. **2.** Something that affords ease or comfort. **3.** *Law.* A right, such as a right of way, afforded a person to make limited use of another's real property.

eas·i·ly (ē′zə-lē) *adv.* **1.** Without difficulty or stress. **2.** Without doubt or question; certainly: *easily the best play this season.*

east (ēst) *n.* **1. a.** The direction of the earth's axial rotation. **b.** The cardinal point on the mariner's compass 90 degrees clockwise from north and directly opposite west. **2.** Often **East.** The eastern part of a country or region, esp. the Orient. —*adj.* **1.** To, toward, of, facing, or in the east. **2.** Coming from or originating in the east. —*adv.* In, from, or toward the east. [ME < OE *ēast.*]

east·bound (ēst′bound′) *adj.* Going toward the east.

east by north *n.* The direction or point on the mariner's compass halfway between due east and east-northeast. It is 78 degrees 45 minutes east of due north. —*adv. & adj.* Toward or from east by north.

east by south *n.* The direction or point on the mariner's compass halfway between due east and east-southeast. It is 101 degrees 15 minutes east of due north. —*adv. & adj.* Toward or from east by south.

Eas·ter (ē′stər) *n.* **1.** A festival in the Christian Church commemorating the Resurrection of Christ, celebrated on the first Sunday following the full moon that occurs on or next after March 21. **2.** The Sunday on which the festival of Easter is held. [ME *ester* < OE *ēastre.*]

Easter egg *n.* A dyed or painted egg, traditionally associated with Easter.

Easter lily *n.* Any of various white-flowered lilies that bloom in the Easter season.

east·er·ly (ē′stər-lē) *adj.* **1.** Situated toward the east. **2.** From the east. —*n., pl.* **-lies.** A storm or wind from the east. **—east′er·ly** *adv.*

Easter Monday *n.* The Monday following Easter.

east·ern (ē′stərn) *adj.* **1.** Situated toward, in, or facing the east. **2.** Coming from the east. **3.** Growing in the east. **4.** Often **Eastern.** Of, pertaining to, or characteristic of eastern regions or the East. **5. Eastern.** Of, pertaining to, or characteristic of the Orient. **6. Eastern. a.** Of or pertaining to the Eastern Church. **b.** Of or relating to the Eastern Orthodox Church. [ME *estern* < OE *ēasterne.*]

Eastern Church *n.* **1.** The church of the Eastern Roman Empire, as distinguished from the Western Church, including the patriarchates of Constantinople, Antioch, Alexandria, and Jerusalem. **2.** The Eastern Orthodox Church. **3.** The Uniat Church.

east·ern·er also **East·ern·er** (ē′stər-nər) *n.* A native or inhabitant of the east, esp. of the eastern United States.

Eastern Hemisphere *n.* The part of the earth including the continents of Europe, Africa, Asia, and Australia.

east·ern·most (ē′stərn-mōst′) *adj.* Farthest east.

Eastern Orthodox Church *n.* The body of modern churches, including the Greek and Russian Orthodox, that is derived from the church of the Byzantine Empire and adheres to the Byzantine rite and primacy of the patriarch of Constantinople.

Eastern Standard Time *n.* The time in the zone that includes the eastern part of North America and is in the fifth time zone west of Greenwich, England.

Eas·ter·tide (ē′stər-tīd′) *n.* The Easter season, extending from Easter to Ascension Day, Whitsunday, or Trinity Sunday.

East Germanic *n.* The subdivision of the Germanic languages that includes Gothic.

east·ing (ē′stĭng) *n.* **1.** *Naut.* **a.** The distance sailed by a ship on an easterly course. **b.** The longitudinal distance from a given meridian on an easterly course. **2.** An easterly direction.

east-north·east (ēst′nôrth-ēst′) *n.* The direction or point on

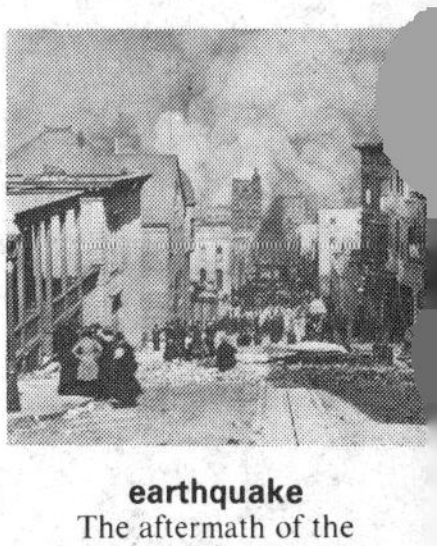

earthquake
The aftermath of the 1906 earthquake in San Francisco

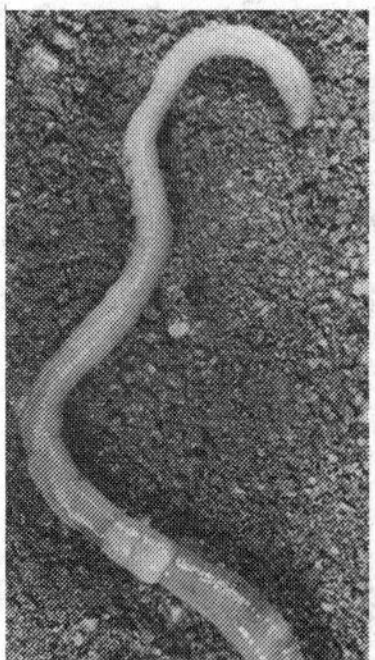

earthworm

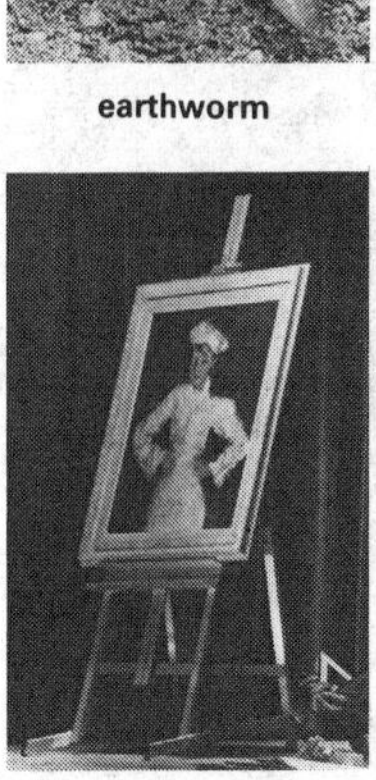

easel

the mariner's compass halfway between due east and northeast. It is 67 degrees 30 minutes east of due north. —*adj. & adv.* In, from, or toward east-northeast.
east-south·east (ēst′south′ēst′) *n.* The direction or point on the mariner's compass halfway between due east and southeast. It is 112 degrees 30 minutes east of due north. —*adj. & adv.* In, from, or toward east-southeast.
east·ward (ēst′wərd) *adj. & adv.* Toward, to, or in the east. —*n.* An eastward direction, point, or region. **—east′ward·ly** *adv.* **—east′wards** (-wərdz) *adv.*
eas·y (ē′zē) *adj.* **-i·er, -i·est. 1.** Capable of being accomplished or acquired with ease; posing no difficulty. **2.** Free from worry, anxiety, trouble, or pain. **3.** Conducive to rest or comfort. **4.** Socially at ease: *an easy, sociable manner.* **5. a.** Relaxed in attitude; easygoing. **b.** Not strict or severe; lenient: *an easy teacher.* **6.** Readily persuaded or influenced. **7.** Not hurried or forced; moderate. **8.** *Econ.* **a.** Less in demand and therefore readily obtainable: *Commodities are easier.* **b.** Plentiful and therefore at low interest rates: *easy money.* —*adv.* **1.** Without haste or agitation: *take it easy.* **2.** Easily: *success that came too easy.* [ME *esi* < OFr. *aaisie,* p.part. of *aaisier,* to put at ease : *a-,* to (< Lat. *ad-*) + < *aise* ease.] **—eas·i·ness** *n.*
Synonyms: *easy, simple, facile, effortless, smooth, light.* These adjectives mean not requiring much effort or not reflecting effort or difficulty in performance. *Easy* applies both to tasks that require little effort and to persons who are not demanding. *Simple* describes tasks that are not complex and hence not demanding intellectually. *Facile* and *effortless* apply to performance and stress readiness and fluency of execution. *Facile,* however, sometimes has unfavorable connotations, as of haste or lack of care in action, glibness or lack of sincerity in speech, or superficiality of thought. *Effortless* can imply actual lack of effort but often refers to performance in which application of great strength or skill makes the execution seem easy. *Smooth* describes performance whose progress is even and unimpeded. *Light* refers to tasks or impositions that involve no taxing burdens or responsibilities.
easy chair *n.* A large, comfortable, well-upholstered chair.
eas·y·go·ing also **eas·y-go·ing** (ē′zē-gō′ĭng) *adj.* **1. a.** Living without worry or concern; placid. **b.** Lazy and careless. **c.** Lax in moral attitude. **d.** Undemanding: *an easygoing life.* **2.** Having or moving at an unhurried, comfortable pace.
easy street *n. Slang.* A condition of financial security or independence.
eat (ēt) *v.* **ate** (āt; *Nonstandard.* ĕt), **eat·en** (ēt′n), **eat·ing, eats.** —*tr.* **1.** To take into the mouth, chew, and swallow as food. **2.** To consume, ravage, or destroy by or as if by eating. **3.** To erode or corrode. **4.** *Slang.* To bother or annoy: *What's eating him?* —*intr.* **1. a.** To consume food. **b.** To have or take a meal. **2.** To wear away or corrode by or as if by eating or gnawing. **—*idioms.* eat crow.** *Informal.* To be forced to accept a humiliating defeat. **eat one's heart out.** To feel bitter, hopeless anguish or longing. **eat one's words.** To retract something that one has said. [ME *eten* < OE *etan.*] **—eat′er** *n.*
eat·a·ble (ē′tə-bəl) *adj.* Fit to be eaten; edible. —*n.* **1.** Something fit to be eaten. **2. eatables.** Food.
eat·er·y (ē′tə-rē) *n., pl.* **-ies.** *Informal.* A restaurant.
eat·ing (ē′tĭng) *adj.* Suitable for eating raw: *eating apples.*
eats (ēts) *pl.n. Slang.* Food.
eau de co·logne (ō′ də kə-lōn′) *n., pl.* **eaux de cologne** (ō′, ōz′). Cologne. [Fr., water of Cologne < *Cologne,* Köln, West Germany.]
eau de vie (ō′ də vē′) *n., pl.* **eaux de vie** (ō′, ōz′). Brandy. [Fr. *eau-de-vie* : *eau,* water + *de,* of + *vie,* life.]
eaves (ēvz) *n. (used with a pl. verb).* The projecting overhang at the lower edge of a roof. [ME *eves* < OE *efes.*]

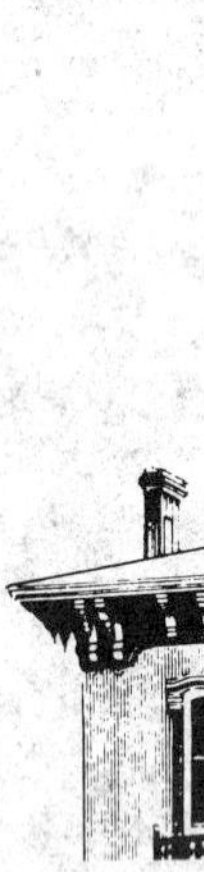
eaves

eaves·drop (ēvz′drŏp′) *intr.v.* **-dropped, -drop·ping, -drops.** To listen secretly to a private conversation of others. [Prob. back-formation < *eavesdropper,* one who eavesdrops < ME *evesdropper* < *evesdrop,* place where water falls from eaves < OE *yfæs drypæ.*] **—eaves′drop′per** *n.*
ebb (ĕb) *n.* **1.** Ebb tide. **2.** A period of decline, or diminution: *"insistence upon rules of conduct marks the ebb of religious fervor"* (A.N. Whitehead). —*intr.v.* **ebbed, ebb·ing, ebbs. 1.** To fall back from the flood. **2.** To fall away or decline. [ME *ebbe* < OE *ebba.*]
ebb tide *n.* The period of a tide between high water and a succeeding low water.
EBCDIC (ĕb′sə-dĭk) *n.* A code for representing alphanumeric information. [E(XTENDED) + B(INARY) + C(ODED) + D(ECIMAL) + I(NTERCHANGE) + C(ODE).]
Eb·lis (ĕb′lĭs) *n.* The principal evil spirit or devil of Islamic mythology. [Ar. *Iblīs* < LGk. *diabolos,* devil. —see DEVIL.]
eb·on (ĕb′ən) *adj.* **1.** Made of ebony. **2.** Black. —*n.* Ebony. [ME *eban,* ebony wood < Lat. *ebenus,* ebony tree < Gk. *ebenos,* of Egypt. orig.]
eb·on·ite (ĕb′ə-nīt′) *n.* A hard rubber.
eb·on·ize (ĕb′ə-nīz′) *tr.v.* **-ized, -iz·ing, -iz·es.** To stain black like ebony.
eb·on·y (ĕb′ə-nē) *n., pl.* **-ies. 1.** Any of several chiefly tropical trees of the genus *Diospyros,* esp. *D. ebenum,* of southern Asia, having hard, dark-colored heartwood. **2.** The wood of the ebony, used in cabinetwork and for piano keys. —*adj.* **1.** Made of or suggesting ebony. **2.** Black. [ME *hebenyf,* ebony wood < LLat. *ebeninus,* of ebony < Gk. *ebeninos* < *ebenos,* ebony tree, of Egypt. orig.]
e·brac·te·ate (ē-brăk′tē-āt′) *adj. Bot.* Without bracts. [NLat. *ebracteatus* : Lat. *ex-,* without + Lat. *bractea,* bract.]
e·bul·lience (ĭ-bo͝ol′-yəns, ĭ-bŭl′-) *n.* The quality of expressing feelings or ideas in an enthusiastic and lively manner. [< Lat. *ebulliens,* pr.part. of *ebullire,* to boil up : *ex-,* up + *bullire,* to boil.]
e·bul·lien·cy (ĭ-bo͝ol′yən-sē, ĭ-bŭl′-) *n.* Ebullience.
e·bul·lient (ĭ-bo͝ol′yənt, ĭ-bŭl′-) *adj.* **1.** Boiling; bubbling. **2.** Marked by ebullience. **—e·bul′lient·ly** *adv.*
eb·ul·li·tion (ĕb′ə-lĭsh′ən) *n.* **1.** The process or state of bubbling or boiling. **2.** A sudden, violent outpouring, as of emotion. [LLat. *ebullitio* < Lat. *ebullire,* to boil up. —see EBULLIENT.]
ec·ce ho·mo (ĕk′sē hō′mō, ĕk′ē) *n.* A picture depicting Christ wearing the crown of thorns. [LLat., behold the man.]
ec·cen·tric (ĭk-sĕn′trĭk) *adj.* **1. a.** Departing or deviating from the conventional or established norm. **b.** Departing from a direct or charted course; erratic. **2.** Deviating from a circular form or path. **3.** Not situated at or in the geometric center. **4.** Having the axis located elsewhere than at the geometric center. **5.** Not having the same center. —*n.* **1.** An eccentric person. **2.** A disk or wheel having its axis of revolution displaced from its center so that it is capable of imparting reciprocating motion. [ME *eccentrik,* planetary orbit of which the earth is not center < Med. Lat. *eccentricus* < *eccentricus,* not having the same center < Gk. *ekkentros* : *ek-,* out + *kentron,* center.] **—ec·cen′tri·cal·ly** *adv.*
ec·cen·tric·i·ty (ĕk′sĕn-trĭs′ĭ-tē) *n., pl.* **-ties. 1. a.** The quality of being eccentric. **b.** Deviation from the normal, expected, or established. **2.** An example or instance of eccentric behavior. **3.** The distance between the center of an eccentric and its axis. **4.** *Math.* The ratio of the distance of any point on a conic section from a focus to its distance from the corresponding directrix.
Synonyms: *eccentricity, idiosyncrasy, quirk.* These nouns refer to peculiarity of behavior. *Eccentricity* implies divergence from the usual or customary that, in extreme form, may suggest a disordered mind. *Idiosyncrasy* more often refers to such divergence viewed as peculiar to the temperament of a ruggedly individualistic person and serving as an identifying trait. *Quirk,* a milder term, suggests an odd trait or mannerism.
ec·chy·mo·sis (ĕk′ĭ-mō′sĭs) *n.* The passage of blood from ruptured blood vessels into subcutaneous tissue, marked by a purple discoloration of the skin. [NLat. < Gk. *ekkhumōsis* < *ekkhumousthai,* to extravasate blood : *ek-,* out + *khumos,* juice < *khein,* to pour.] **—ec′chy·mot′ic** (-mŏt′ĭk) *adj.*
ec·cle·si·a (ĭ-klē′zhē-ə, -zē-ə) *n., pl.* **-si·ae** (-zhē-ē′, -zē-ē′). **1.** The political assembly of citizens of an ancient Greek state. **2.** A church or congregation. [Lat. < Gk. *ekklēsia* < *ekkalein,* to summon : *ek-,* out + *kalein,* to call.]
Ec·cle·si·as·tes (ĭ-klē′zē-ăs′tēz′) *n.* See table at **Bible.** [LLat. < Gk. *Ekklēsiastēs,* preacher (transl. of Heb. *Qoholeth*) < *ekklēsiastēs,* a member of the ecclesia.]
ec·cle·si·as·tic (ĭ-klē′zē-ăs′tĭk) *adj.* Ecclesiastical. —*n.* A clergyman; priest.
ec·cle·si·as·ti·cal (ĭ-klē′zē-ăs′tĭ-kəl) *adj.* **1.** Of or pertaining to a church, esp. as an organized institution. **2.** Appropriate for use in a church. **—ec·cle′si·as′ti·cal·ly** *adv.*
ec·cle·si·as·ti·cism (ĭ-klē′zē-ăs′tə-sĭz′əm) *n.* **1.** Ecclesiastical principles, practices, and activities. **2.** Excessive adherence to ecclesiastical principles and forms.
Ec·cle·si·as·ti·cus (ĭ-klē′zē-ăs′tĭ-kəs) *n.* See table at **Bible.** [LLat. < *ecclesiasticus,* ecclesiastical < Gk. *ekklēsiastikos,* ecclesiastical, of an ecclesia.]
ec·cle·si·ol·o·gy (ĭ-klē′zē-ŏl′ə-jē) *n.* The study of ecclesiastical architecture and ornamentation. [ECCLESI(A) + -LOGY.] **—ec·cle′si·o·log′i·cal** (-ə-lŏj′ĭ-kəl) *adj.*
ec·crine (ĕk′rĭn, -rīn′, -rēn′) *adj.* **1.** Secreting externally, esp. pertaining to an eccrine gland or its secretion. **2.** Exocrine. [< Gk. *ekkrinein,* to secrete : *ek-,* out + *krinein,* to separate.]
eccrine gland *n.* Any of the small sweat glands distributed over the body's surface.
ec·crin·ol·o·gy (ĕk′rə-nŏl′ə-jē) *n.* The study of eccrine secretions and secretory organs.
ec·dys·i·ast (ĕk-dĭz′ē-ăst′, -əst) *n.* A stripteaser. [< ECDYSIS; coined by Henry L. Mencken (1880–1956).]
ec·dy·sis (ĕk′dĭ-sĭs) *n., pl.* **-ses** (-sēz′). The shedding of an outer integument or layer of skin, as in insects, crustaceans, and snakes. [NLat. < Gk. *ekdusis,* a stripping < *ekduein,* to take off : *ek-,* out + *duein,* to put on.]
ec·dy·sone (ĕk′də-sōn′) *n.* Any of various hormones of insects that control molting. [ECDYS(IS) + (HORM)ONE.]
e·ce·sis (ĭ-sē′sĭs) *n.* The successful establishment of an organism in a new environment. [Gk. *oikēsis,* inhabitation < *oikein,* to dwell < *oikos,* house.]
ec·hard (ĕk′härd′) *n. Ecol.* Soil water not available for absorption by plants. [Gk. *ekhein,* to hold back + *ardein,* to irrigate.]
ech·e·lon (ĕsh′ə-lŏn′) *n.* **1. a.** A formation of troops in which parallel units are arranged to the left or right of the

rear unit in a steplike fashion. **b.** A similar formation of groups, units, or individuals. **c.** A flight formation or arrangement of vessels in this manner. **2.** A level of command or authority, as in a military or naval force or in an organization. **3.** A diffraction grating consisting of parallel glass plates of successively varying sizes, used to examine extremely fine structures. —*tr. & intr.v.* **-loned, -lon·ing, -lons.** To arrange or take place in an echelon. [Fr. *échelon* < OFr. *eschelon,* rung of a ladder < *eschile,* ladder < Lat. *scala.*]

ech·e·ve·ri·a (ĕch′ə-və-rē′ə) *n.* Any of various tropical American plants of the genus *Echeveria,* having thick, succulent leaves often clustered in a rosette. [NLat. *Echeveria,* genus name, after *Echeveria,* a 19th-cent. Mexican botanical illustrator.]

e·chid·na (ĭ-kĭd′nə) *n.* Any of several burrowing, egg-laying mammals of the genera *Tachyglossus* and *Zaglossus,* of Australia, Tasmania, and New Guinea, having a spiny coat, slender snout, and a sticky tongue used for catching insects. [NLat. < Lat., viper < Gk. *ekhidna.*]

echin– *pref.* Variant of **echino-.**

ech·i·nate (ĕk′ə-nāt′) *adj.* Bearing or covered with spines; prickly.

echino– or **echin–** *pref.* **1.** Spiny; prickle: *echinate.* **2.** Echinoderm: *echinoid.* [NLat. < Lat. *echinus,* sea urchin < Gk. *ekhinos.*]

e·chi·no·coc·co·sis (ĭ-kī′nə-kə-kō′sĭs) *n., pl.* **-ses** (-sēz′). Infestation with echinococci. [ECHINOCOCC(US) + -OSIS.]

e·chi·no·coc·cus (ĭ-kī′nə-kŏk′əs) *n., pl.* **-coc·ci** (-kŏk′sī′). Any of several parasitic tapeworms of the genus *Echinococcus,* the larvae of which infect mammals and form large, spherical cysts, causing serious or fatal disease. [NLat. *Echinococcus,* genus name : ECHINO- + COCCUS.]

e·chi·no·derm (ĭ-kī′nə-dûrm′) *n.* Any of numerous radially symmetrical marine invertebrates of the phylum Echinodermata, which includes the starfishes, sea urchins, and sea cucumbers, having a body often covered with spines. —**e·chi′no·der′mal, e·chi′no·der′ma·tous** *adj.*

e·chi·noid (ĭ-kī′noid′) *n.* Any echinoderm of the class Echinoidea, which includes the sand dollars and sea urchins.

e·chi·nus (ĭ-kī′nəs) *n., pl.* **-ni** (-nī′). *Archit.* A curved molding just below the abacus of a Doric capital. [Lat. < Gk. *ekhinos,* echinus, sea urchin, hedgehog.]

ech·o (ĕk′ō) *n., pl.* **-oes. 1. a.** Repetition of a sound by reflection of sound waves from a surface. **b.** The sound produced in this manner. **2.** A repetition or imitation of something: *a fashion that is an echo of an earlier style.* **3.** One who imitates another, as in opinions, speech, or dress. **4.** A sympathetic response. **5.** The repetition of certain sounds or syllables in poetry. **6.** The soft repetition of a musical note or phrase. **7.** *Electronics.* A reflected wave received by a radio or radar. **8. Echo.** *Aerospace.* One of a series of U.S. passive satellites that are often visible at night. **9. Echo.** *Gk. Myth.* A nymph whose unrequited love for Narcissus caused her to pine away until nothing but her voice remained. —*v.* **-oed, -o·ing, -oes.** —*tr.* **1.** To repeat by or as by an echo. **2.** To repeat or imitate: *followers echoing the thoughts of the leader.* —*intr.* **1.** To produce an echo. **2.** To resound with an echo; reverberate. [ME < OFr. < Lat. < Gk. *ēkhō.*] —**ech′o·er** *n.*

ech·o·car·di·o·graph·y (ĕk′ō-kär′dē-ŏg′rə-fē) *n., pl.* **-phies.** *Med.* A diagnostic technique utilizing ultrasound to visualize the internal structure of the heart. —**ech′o·car′di·o·graph** (-kär′dē-ə-grăf′) *n.* —**ech′o·car·di·o·graph′ic** *adj.*

echo check *n.* An error control technique in which the receiving terminal or computer returns the original message to verify its correct reception.

e·cho·ic (ĭ-kō′ĭk) *adj.* **1.** Being like or resembling an echo. **2.** Imitative of sounds; onomatopoeic.

ech·o·la·li·a (ĕk′ō-lā′lē-ə) *n.* Involuntary repetition of words or phrases just spoken by others. [ECHO + Gk. *lalia,* talk < *lalos,* talkative.] —**ech′o·la′lic** (-lĭk) *adj.*

ech·o·lo·ca·tion (ĕk′ō-lō-kā′shən) *n.* **1.** The ability of an animal, such as a bat or dolphin, to orient itself by the reflection of the sound that it has produced. **2.** *Electronics.* Ranging by acoustical echo analysis. —**ech′o·lo·cate′** *v.* **(-cat·ed, -cat·ing, -cates).**

echo sounder *n.* A device for measuring sea depth by sending pressure waves down from the surface and recording the time until the echo returns from the sea floor.

é·clair (ā-klâr′, ā′klâr′) *n.* A tube-shaped cream puff that has a cream or custard filling and is usually iced with chocolate. [Fr. < OFr. *esclair,* lightning < *esclairier,* to flash < VLat. **exclariare* : Lat. *ex-,* completely + Lat. *clarus,* clear.]

é·clair·cisse·ment (ā-klâr-sēs-mäN′) *n.* A clarification; enlightenment. [Fr. < OFr. *ésclarcir,* to clarify < VLat. **exclaricire* : Lat. *ex-,* completely + Lat. *clarus,* clear.]

e·clamp·si·a (ĭ-klămp′sē-ə) *n.* Coma and convulsions arising from any of several conditions during or immediately after pregnancy. [NLat. < Gk. *eklampsis,* a shining forth < *eklampein,* to shine forth : *ek-,* out + *lampein,* to shine.] —**e·clamp′tic** (-tĭk) *adj.*

é·clat (ā-klä′, ā′klä′) *n.* **1.** Great brilliance, as of performance or achievement. **2.** Conspicuous success. **3.** Great acclamation or applause. **4.** *Archaic.* Notoriety; scandal. [Fr. < OFr. *esclat* < *esclater,* to burst, prob. of Germanic orig.]

e·clec·tic (ĭ-klĕk′tĭk) *adj.* **1.** Choosing what appears to be the best from diverse sources, systems, or styles. **2.** Consisting of components selected from diverse sources. —*n.* One that follows an eclectic method. [Gk. *eklektikos,* selective < *eklegein,* to select : *ek-,* out + *legein,* to choose.] —**e·clec′ti·cal·ly** *adv.*

e·clec·ti·cism (ĭ-klĕk′tə-sĭz′əm) *n.* An eclectic system or method.

e·clipse (ĭ-klĭps′) *n.* **1. a.** The partial or complete obscuring, relative to a designated observer, of one celestial body by another. **b.** The period of time during which an eclipse occurs. **2.** A temporary or permanent dimming or cutting off of light. **3. a.** A fall into obscurity; decline. **b.** A disgrace; downfall. —*tr.v.* **e·clipsed, e·clips·ing, e·clips·es. 1. a.** To cause an eclipse of. **b.** To obscure; darken. **2. a.** To obscure or diminish in importance, fame, or reputation. **b.** To surpass; outshine. [ME < OFr. < Lat. *eclipsis* < Gk. *ekleipsis* < *ekleipein,* to fail to appear : *ek-* out + *leipein,* to leave.]

eclipsing binary *n.* A binary star, the components of which pass in front of each other as viewed from the earth.

e·clip·tic (ĭ-klĭp′tĭk) *n.* **1.** The apparent path of the sun among the stars; the intersection plane of the earth's solar orbit with the celestial sphere. **2.** A great circle on a terrestrial globe inclined at an approximate angle of 23 degrees 27 minutes to the equator. [ME < LLat. *ecliptica* (*linea*), (line) of eclipses < Lat. *eclipticus,* of an eclipse < Gk. *ekleiptikos* < *ekleipein,* to fail to appear. —see ECLIPSE.]

ec·logue (ĕk′lôg′, -lŏg′) *n.* A poem usually in the form of a pastoral dialogue. [ME *eclog* < Lat. *ecloga* < Gk. *eklogē,* selection < *eklegein,* to select. —see ECLECTIC.]

e·clo·sion (ĭ-klō′zhən) *n.* The emergence of an adult insect from a pupal case or of an insect larva from an egg. [Fr. *éclosion* < *éclore,* to open < Lat. *excludere,* to shut out : *ex-,* out + *claudere,* to shut.]

eco– *pref.* Ecology; ecological: *ecosystem.* [< ECOLOGY.]

ec·o·cide (ĕk′ō-sīd′, ē′kō-) *n.* Deliberate destruction of the natural environment, as by pollutants.

ec·o·ge·o·graph·ic (ĕk′ō-jē′ə-grăf′ĭk) or **ec·o·ge·o·graph·i·cal** (-ĭ-kəl) *adj.* Of or relating to both the ecology and geography of the environment. —**ec′o·ge′o·graph′i·cal·ly** *adv.*

e·col·o·gy (ĭ-kŏl′ə-jē) *n.* **1.** The science of the relationships between organisms and their environments. **2.** The relationship between organisms and their environment. [G. *Ökologie* : Gk. *oikos,* house + G. *-logie,* -logy.] —**ec′o·log′i·cal** (ĕk′ə-lŏj′ĭ-kəl, ē′kə-), **ec′o·log′ic** (-ĭk) *adj.* —**ec′o·log′i·cal·ly** *adv.* —**e·col′o·gist** *n.*

e·con·o·met·rics (ĭ-kŏn′ə-mĕt′rĭks) *n.* (*used with a sing. verb*). The application of statistical techniques to economics in the study of problems, the analysis of data, and the development of theory. [ECONO(MICS) + -METR(Y) + -ICS.] —**e·con′o·met′ric** *adj.*

ec·o·nom·ic (ĕk′ə-nŏm′ĭk, ē′kə-) *adj.* **1.** Of or pertaining to the production, development, and management of material wealth, as of a country, household, or business enterprise. **2.** Of or pertaining to economics. **3.** Of or pertaining to matters of finance. **4.** Of or pertaining to the necessities of life; utilitarian.

ec·o·nom·i·cal (ĕk′ə-nŏm′ĭ-kəl, ē′kə-) *adj.* **1.** Not wasteful or extravagant; prudent and thrifty in management. **2.** Economic. —**ec′o·nom′i·cal·ly** *adv.*

economic rent *n.* Rent (sense 2.b.).

ec·o·nom·ics (ĕk′ə-nŏm′ĭks, ē′kə-) *n.* (*used with a sing. verb*). The science that deals with the production, distribution, and consumption of commodities.

e·con·o·mist (ĭ-kŏn′ə-mĭst) *n.* **1.** A specialist in economics. **2.** *Archaic.* One who is economical.

e·con·o·mize (ĭ-kŏn′ə-mīz′) *v.* **-mized, -miz·ing, -miz·es.** —*intr.* To be thrifty; practice economy. —*tr.* To use or manage with thrift. —**e·con′o·miz′er** *n.*

e·con·o·my (ĭ-kŏn′ə-mē) *n., pl.* **-mies. 1. a.** The careful or thrifty use or management of resources, such as income, materials, or labor. **b.** An example of this. **2.** The management of the resources of a country, community, or business. **3. a.** A system for the management and development of resources. **b.** The economic system of a country or area. **4.** The functional arrangement of elements within a structure or system: *the economy of an organism.* —***modifier:*** *economy cars.* [OFr. *economie,* management of household < Lat. *oeconomia* < Gk. *oikonomia* < *oikonomos,* household manager : *oikos,* house + *nemein,* to manage.]

ec·o·spe·cies (ĕk′ə-spē′shēz, -sēz, ē′kə-) *n.* A taxonomic species considered in terms of its ecological characteristics and usually including several ecotypes.

ec·o·sphere (ĕk′ō-sfîr′) *n.* The regions of the universe that are capable of supporting living organisms.

ec·o·sys·tem (ĕk′ə-sĭs′təm, ē′kə-) *n.* An ecological community together with its physical environment, considered as a unit.

ec·o·tone (ĕk′ə-tōn′, ē′kə-) *n.* An ecological community of mixed vegetation formed by the overlapping of adjoining communities. [ECO- + Gk. *tonos,* tension.]

ec·o·type (ĕk′ə-tīp′, ē′kə-) *n.* The smallest taxonomic subdivision of an ecospecies, consisting of subspecies or varieties adapted to a particular set of environmental conditions. —**ec′o·typ′ic** (-tĭp′ĭk) *adj.*

ec·ru (ĕk′rōō, ā′krōō) *n.* Grayish to pale yellow or light gray-

echidna

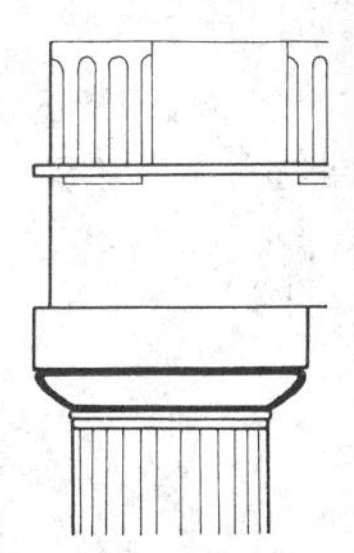

echinus
Echinus of a Doric column

echo
Narcissus and Echo

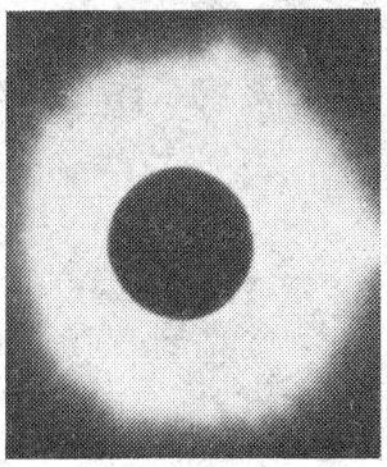

eclipse
Solar eclipse

edelweiss

edh

ish yellowish brown. [Fr. *écru* : *é-*, completely (< Lat. *ex-*) + *cru,* crude (< Lat. *crudus*).]

ec·sta·sy (ĕk'stə-sē) *n., pl.* **-sies. 1.** A state of intense joy or delight. **2.** A state of emotion so intense that one is carried beyond rational thought and self-control: *an ecstasy of anger.* **3.** The trance or rapture of mystic or prophetic exaltation. [ME *extasie* < OFr. < LLat. *extasis,* terror < Gk. *ekstasis* < *existanai,* to drive out of one's senses : *ek-,* out + *histanai,* to place.]

Synonyms: *ecstasy, rapture, transport, exaltation, euphoria, bliss.* These nouns all have reference to extremely strong emotion. The first four are now often used interchangeably in the approximate sense of joy. Even in general usage, however, *ecstasy* retains some of its original sense of a trancelike condition marked by loss of orientation toward rational experience and by concentration on a single emotion, and *rapture* that of attainment of an elevated state permitting superhuman sensory or emotional experience. *Transport* implies violence of feeling and sometimes of accompanying action. *Exaltation* and *euphoria* both involve a sense of extreme personal well-being, but *exaltation* is the stronger and more elevated term. *Bliss* is extreme happiness or joy, considered usually as a relatively tranquil state.

ec·stat·ic (ĕk-stăt'ĭk) *adj.* **1.** Of or relating to ecstasy. **2.** In a state of ecstasy; enraptured. **—ec·stat'i·cal·ly** *adv.*

ecto– *pref.* Outer; external: *ectoparasite.* [Gk. *ekto-* < *ektos,* outside < *ek,* out.]

ec·to·com·men·sal (ĕk'tə-kə-mĕn'səl) *n.* A commensal organism that lives on the outer body surface of another organism.

ec·to·derm (ĕk'tə-dûrm') *n.* The outermost of the three primary germ layers of an embryo, developing the epidermis, nervous tissue, and, in vertebrates, sense organs. **—ec'to·derm'al** (-dûr'məl), **ec'to·der'mic** (-mĭk) *adj.*

ec·tog·e·nous (ĕk-tŏj'ə-nəs) *adj.* Able to live and develop outside a host. Used of certain pathogenic microorganisms.

ec·to·mere (ĕk'tə-mîr') *n.* A blastomere that develops into ectoderm. **—ec'to·mer'ic** (-mîr'ĭk, -mĕr'-) *adj.*

ec·to·morph (ĕk'tə-môrf') *n.* An ectomorphic individual.

ec·to·mor·phic (ĕk'tə-môr'fĭk) *adj.* Lean and slightly muscular. [ECTO(DERM) + -MORPHIC.] **—ec'to·mor'phy** *n.*

–ectomy *suff.* Surgical removal: *adenectomy.* [NLat. *-ectomia* : Gk. *ek-,* out + NLat. *-tomia,* -tomy.]

ec·to·par·a·site (ĕk'tə-păr'ə-sīt') *n.* A parasite, such as a flea, that lives on the exterior of another organism. **—ec'to·par'a·sit'ic** (-sĭt'ĭk) *adj.*

ec·to·pi·a (ĕk-tō'pē-ə) *n.* Congenital positional abnormality of an organ or part. [NLat. < Gk. *ektopos,* away from a place : *ek-,* out + *topos,* place.] **—ec·top'ic** (-tŏp'ĭk) *adj.*

ectopic pregnancy *n.* Gestation outside the uterus, often in a Fallopian tube.

ec·to·plasm (ĕk'tə-plăz'əm) *n.* **1.** *Biol.* A portion of the continuous phase of cytoplasm distinguishable in some cells as a relatively rigidly gelled cortex limited on the outside by the cell membrane. **2.** The luminous substance that is believed to emanate from a spiritualistic medium.

ec·to·sarc (ĕk'tə-särk') *n.* The relatively clear outermost layer of protoplasm of certain protozoans, such as the amoeba. [ECTO- + Gk. *sarx,* flesh.]

ec·to·therm (ĕk'tə-thûrm') *n.* Poikilotherm. **—ec'to·therm'ic** *adj.*

ec·type (ĕk'tīp') *n.* A reproduction of an original; copy. [Gk. *ektupos,* worked in relief : *ek-,* out of + *tupos,* mold.] **—ec'ty·pal** (-tə-pəl) *adj.*

é·cu (ā-kyōō') *n., pl.* **é·cus** (ā-kyōō'). Any of various old French coins, esp. a silver five-franc piece. [Fr. < OFr. *escu* < Lat. *scutum,* shield (from the shield stamped on the coin).]

ec·u·men·i·cal (ĕk'yə-mĕn'ĭ-kəl) or **ec·u·men·ic** (-mĕn'ĭk) *adj.* **1.** Worldwide in range or applicability; universal. **2.** Of or pertaining to the worldwide Christian church, esp. in regard to unity. [LLat. *oecumenicus* < Gk. *oikoumenikos* < *oikoumenē,* the inhabited world < *oikein,* to inhabit < *oikos,* house.] **—ec'u·men'i·cal·ism** *n.* **—ec'u·men'i·cal·ly** *adv.*

ecumenical patriarch *n.* The patriarch of Constantinople who is the highest ecclesiastical official of the Eastern Orthodox Church.

ec·u·me·nism (ĕk'yə-mə-nĭz'əm, ĭ-kyōō'-) *n.* A movement seeking to achieve worldwide unity among religions through greater cooperation and improved understanding. **—ec'u·men'ist** *n.*

ec·ze·ma (ĕk'sə-mə, ĭg-zē'-) *n.* A noncontagious inflammation of the skin, marked mainly by redness, itching, and the outbreak of lesions that discharge serous matter and become encrusted and scaly. [NLat. < Gk. *ekzema* < *ekzein,* to break out : *ek-,* out + *zeein,* to boil.] **—ec·zem'a·tous** (ĕg-zĕm'ə-təs, -zē'mə-təs, ĭg-) *adj.*

–ed[1] *suff.* **1.** Used to form the past participle of regular verbs: *absorbed.* **2.** Having; characterized by; resembling: *blackhearted.* [ME *-ed* < OE *-ad, -ed, -od.*]

–ed[2] *suff.* Used to form the past tense of regular verbs: *inhabited.* [ME *-ede* < OE *-ade, -ede, -ode.*]

e·da·cious (ĭ-dā'shəs) *adj.* Characterized by voracity; devouring. [< Lat. *edax, edāc-* < *edere,* to eat.] **—e·dac'i·ty** (ĭ-dăs'ə-tē) *n.*

E·dam cheese (ē'dəm, ē'dăm') *n.* A mild, yellow Dutch cheese, pressed into balls and usually covered with red wax. [After *Edam,* Netherlands.]

e·daph·ic (ĭ-dăf'ĭk) *adj.* Of or pertaining to soil, esp. as it affects living organisms. [< Gk. *edaphos,* soil.]

Ed·da (ĕd'ə) *n.* **1.** A collection of Old Norse poems called the Elder or Poetic Edda, assembled in the early 13th century. **2.** A manual of Icelandic poetry, called the Younger or Prose Edda. [ON.] **—Ed'dic** *adj.*

ed·do (ĕd'ō) *n., pl.* **-does.** The taro. [Of African orig.]

ed·dy (ĕd'ē) *n., pl.* **-dies. 1.** A current, as of water or air, moving contrary to the direction of the main current, esp. in a circular motion. **2.** A current that runs contrary to the main current or tradition. *—v.* **-died, -dy·ing, -dies.** *—intr. & tr.v.* To move or cause to move against the main current, as in an eddy. [ME *ydy,* prob. < ON *iða.*]

e·del·weiss (ā'dəl-vīs', -wīs') *n.* A plant, *Leontopodium alpinum,* growing high in the Alps, and having leaves covered with whitish down and small flowers surrounded by conspicuous whitish bracts. [G. : *edel,* noble (< OHG *edili*) + *weiss,* white (< OHG *wīz*).]

e·de·ma (ĭ-dē'mə) *n., pl.* **-mas** or **-ma·ta** (-mə-tə). **1.** *Pathol.* An excessive accumulation of serous fluid in the tissues. **2.** *Bot.* Extended swellings in plant organs caused primarily by an excessive accumulation of water. [NLat. < Gk. *oidēma,* a swelling < *oidein,* to swell.] **—e·dem'a·tous** (-dĕm'ə-təs) *adj.*

E·den (ēd'n) *n.* **1.** In the Old Testament, the first home of Adam and Eve. **2.** A delightful place or dwelling; paradise. **3.** A state of bliss or ultimate happiness. [ME < LLat. < Gk. *Ēdēn* < Heb. *'Ēdhen* < *'ēdhen,* delight.]

e·den·tate (ē-dĕn'tāt') *adj.* **1.** *Biol.* Lacking teeth. **2.** Of or belonging to the order Edentata, which includes mammals, such as anteaters, armadillos, and sloths, having few or no teeth. *—n.* A member of the Edentata. [Lat. *edentatus,* p.part. of *edentare,* to knock out the teeth : *ex-,* out + *dens,* tooth.]

e·den·tu·lous (ē-dĕn'chə-ləs) *adj.* Having no teeth; toothless. [Lat. *edentulus* : *ex-,* without + *dens,* tooth.]

edge (ĕj) *n.* **1. a.** The usually thin, sharpened side of the blade of a cutting instrument. **b.** The degree of sharpness of a cutting blade. **2.** Keenness, as of desire or enjoyment; zest. **3.** A rim, brink, or crest, as of a cliff or ridge of hills. **4.** A dividing line or point of transition: *the edge of war.* **5.** The line of intersection of two surfaces of a solid: *the edge of a brick.* **6.** A margin of superiority; advantage: *a slight edge over the opposition.* *—v.* **edged, edg·ing, edg·es.** *—tr.* **1.** To give an edge to; sharpen. **2.** To put a border or edge on. **3.** To advance or push gradually. *—intr.* To move gradually or hesitantly: *She edged toward the door.* **—idiom. on edge.** Highly tense or nervous; irritable. [ME *egge* < OE *ecg.*] **—edge'less** *adj.*

edg·er (ĕj'ər) *n.* **1.** One that edges. **2.** A tool for trimming the edge of a lawn.

edge tool *n.* A tool, such as a chisel, with a cutting edge.

edge·wise (ĕj'wīz') also **edge·ways** (-wāz') *adv.* **1.** With the edge foremost. **2.** On, by, with, or toward the edge.

edg·ing (ĕj'ĭng) *n.* Something that forms or serves as an edge or border.

edg·y (ĕj'ē) *adj.* **-i·er, -i·est. 1.** On edge; tense; nervous. **2.** With a sharp edge. **3.** With excessively sharp definition, as in painting. **—edg'i·ness** *n.*

edh also **eth** (ĕth) *n.* **1.** A letter (ð)appearing in Old English, Old Saxon, Old Norse, and modern Icelandic to represent an interdental fricative. **2.** The symbol in the International Phonetic Alphabet representing the interdental voiced fricative, as in *the, with.* [Icel. *eð.*]

ed·i·ble (ĕd'ə-bəl) *adj.* Capable of being eaten; fit to eat. *—n.* Something fit to be eaten; food. [LLat. *edibilis* < Lat. *edere,* to eat.] **—ed'i·bil'i·ty, ed'i·ble·ness** *n.*

e·dict (ē'dĭkt') *n.* **1.** A decree or proclamation issued by an authority and having the force of law. **2.** A formal proclamation, command, or decree. [Lat. *edictum* < neuter p.part of *edicere,* to declare : *ex-,* out + *dicere,* to speak.]

ed·i·fi·ca·tion (ĕd'ə-fə-kā'shən) *n.* Intellectual, moral, or spiritual improvement; enlightenment.

ed·i·fice (ĕd'ə-fĭs) *n.* A building, esp. one of imposing appearance or size. [ME < OFr. < Lat. *aedificium* < *aedificare,* to build : *aedis,* a building + *facere,* to make.]

ed·i·fy (ĕd'ə-fī') *tr.v.* **-fied, -fy·ing, -fies.** To instruct or enlighten so as to encourage intellectual, moral, or spiritual improvement. [ME *edifien* < OFr. *edifier* < LLat. *aedificare* < *Lat.,* to build. —see EDIFICE.] **—ed'i·fi'er** *n.*

ed·it (ĕd'ĭt) *tr.v.* **-it·ed, -it·ing, -its. 1. a.** To prepare for publication or presentation, as by correcting or adapting. **b.** To prepare an edition of for publication: *edit a collection of short stories.* **2.** To supervise the publication of. **3.** To eliminate; delete: *edited the best scene out.* **4.** To put together the component parts of (a film, for example) by cutting, combining, and splicing. *—n.* An instance of editing. [Back-formation < EDITOR.]

e·di·tion (ĭ-dĭsh'ən) *n.* **1. a.** The entire number of copies of a publication printed from a single typesetting or other form of reproduction. **b.** A single copy from this group. **c.** A facsimile of an earlier publication having substantial changes or additions. **2. a.** Any of the various forms in which something, such as a publication, is issued or produced: *a vari-*

orum edition of Keats. **b.** One closely similar to an original; version: *The boy was a smaller edition of his father.* **3.** All the copies of a single press run of a newspaper: *the morning edition.* [OFr. < Lat. *editio,* publication < *edere,* to publish : *ex-,* out + *dare,* to give.]

ed·i·tor (ĕd′ĭ-tər) *n.* **1.** A person who edits, esp. as an occupation. **2.** One who writes editorials. **3.** A device for editing film, consisting basically of a splicer and viewer. **4.** *Computer Sci.* A routine that performs editing functions. [LLat., publisher < Lat. *edere,* to publish. —see EDITION.]

ed·i·to·ri·al (ĕd′ĭ-tôr′ē-əl, -tōr′-) *n.* **1.** An article in a publication expressing the opinion of its editors or publishers. **2.** A commentary on radio or television expressing the opinion of the station or network. —*adj.* **1.** Of, concerning, or relating to an editor. **2.** Of the nature of an editorial. **—ed′i·to′ri·al·ly** *adv.*

ed·i·to·ri·al·ize (ĕd′ĭ-tôr′ē-ə-līz′, -tōr′-) *intr.v.* **-ized, -iz·ing, -iz·es. 1.** To express an opinion in or as if in an editorial. **2.** To present an opinion in the guise of an objective report. **—ed′i·to′ri·al·i·za′tion** *n.* **—ed′i·to′ri·al·i′zer** *n.*

editor in chief *n., pl.* **editors in chief.** The editor having final responsibility for the operations and policies of a publication.

ed·i·tor·ship (ĕd′ĭ-tər-shĭp′) *n.* The position, functions, or guidance of an editor.

E·dom·ite (ē′də-mīt′) *n.* A member of a Semitic people inhabiting an area southeast of the Dead Sea in ancient times. [After *Edom,* a region of ancient Palestine.] **—E′dom·it′ish** *adj.*

EDTA (ē′dē-tē-ā′) *n.* A crystalline acid, $C_{10}H_{16}N_2O_8$, used as a chelating agent. [Abbr. of *ethylenediaminetetraacetic acid.*]

ed·u·ca·ble (ĕj′ə-kə-bəl) *adj.* Capable of being educated. [EDUC(ATE) + -ABLE.]

ed·u·cate (ĕj′ə-kāt′) *v.* **-cat·ed, -cat·ing, -cates.** —*tr.* **1.** To provide with knowledge or training, esp. through formal schooling; teach. **2.** To provide with training for some particular purpose: *educated him for the priesthood.* **3.** To provide with information; inform. **4.** To stimulate or develop the mental or moral growth of. —*intr.* To teach or instruct a person or group. [ME *educaten* < Lat. *educare.*]

ed·u·cat·ed (ĕj′ə-kā′tĭd) *adj.* **1.** Having an education, esp. one above the average. **2. a.** Showing evidence of schooling or instruction. **b.** Cultivated; cultured. **3.** Based on experience and some factual knowledge: *an educated guess.*

ed·u·ca·tion (ĕj′ə-kā′shən) *n.* **1. a.** The act or process of educating or being educated. **2.** The knowledge or skill obtained or developed by a learning process. **3.** The field of study that is concerned with teaching and learning pedagogy.

ed·u·ca·tion·al (ĕj′ə-kā′shən-əl) *adj.* **1.** Of or relating to education. **2.** Serving to educate; instructive: *an educational film.* **—ed′u·ca′tion·al·ly** *adv.*

educational television *n.* **1.** Public television. **2.** A video system that provides instructional material.

ed·u·ca·tive (ĕj′ə-kā′tĭv) *adj.* Educational.

ed·u·ca·tor (ĕj′ə-kā′tər) *n.* **1.** One trained in teaching; teacher. **2.** A specialist in the theory and practice of education.

e·duce (ĭ-do͞os′, ĭ-dyo͞os′) *tr.v.* **e·duced, e·duc·ing, e·duc·es. 1.** To draw or bring out; elicit. **2.** To assume or work out from given facts; deduce. [Lat. *educere* : *ex-,* out + *ducere,* to lead.] **—e·duc′i·ble** *adj.* **—e·duc′tion** (ĭ-dŭk′shən) *n.*

Ed·ward·i·an (ĕd-wôr′dē-ən, -wär′-) *adj.* Of, relating to, or characteristic of the reign of Edward VII of England, during whose reign the styles and views were opulent, elegant, ornate, and refined.

-ee[1] *suff.* **1. a.** One that receives or benefits from a specified action: *addressee.* **b.** One that possesses a specified thing: *mortgagee.* **2.** One that performs a specified action: *absentee.* [ME *-e* < OFr. < Lat. *-atus,* -ate.]

Usage: The suffix *-ee* has generally been used to indicate a person to whom something has been done or upon whom some right has been conferred: *appointee, grantee.* It has come to be used also with reference to a person in a specified condition (*absentee, refugee, amputee*) or even a person performing some action (*escapee, standee*). The Usage Panel accepts the use of *standee* and *escapee* in speech and is about evenly divided on their acceptability in writing. Less well established coinages, such as *returnee,* are best avoided.

-ee[2] *suff.* **1. a.** One resembling: *goatee.* **b.** A particular kind of: *bootee.* Used often as a diminutive. **2.** One connected with: *bargee.* [Alteration of -Y[1].]

eel (ēl) *n., pl.* **eel** or **eels. 1.** Any of various long, snakelike marine or freshwater fishes of the order Anguilliformes or Apodes, esp. *Anguilla rostrata,* of eastern North America, or *A. anguilla,* of Europe, characteristically migrating from fresh water to the Sargasso Sea to spawn. **2.** Any of several fishes similar or related to the eel. [ME *ele* < OE *ǣl.*]

eel·grass (ēl′grăs′) *n.* **1.** Any of several submerged aquatic plants of the genus *Zostera,* growing along the North Atlantic coast and having narrow, grasslike leaves. **2.** Any of several similar or related plants, such as tape grass.

eel·pout (ēl′pout′) *n., pl.* **eelpout** or **-pouts.** Any of various marine fishes of the family Zoarcidae, having an elongated body and a large head. [ME **elepout* < OE *ǣle-puta.*]

eel·worm (ēl′wûrm′) *n.* Any of various, often parasitic nematode worms, such as the vinegar eel.

e'en[1] (ēn) *n.* Evening.

e'en[2] (ēn) *adv.* Even.

-eer *suff.* One associated with, concerned with, or engaged in: *balladeer.* [OFr. *-ier* < Lat. *-arius,* -ary.]

e'er (âr) *adv.* Ever.

ee·rie or **ee·ry** (îr′ē) *adj.* **-ri·er, -ri·est. 1. a.** Inspiring fear or dread; weird. **b.** Supernatural in aspect or character; mysterious. **2.** *Scot.* Frightened or intimidated by superstition. [ME *eri,* fearful < OE *earg,* cowardly.] **—ee′ri·ness** *n.*

ef (ĕf) *n.* The letter *f.*

ef·face (ĭ-fās′) *tr.v.* **-faced, -fac·ing, -fac·es. 1.** To erase or make indistinct by or as if by rubbing; wipe out. **2.** To conduct (oneself) inconspicuously. [Fr. *effacer* < OFr. : Lat. *ex-,* out + Lat. *facies,* face.] **—ef·face′a·ble** *adj.* **—ef·face′ment** *n.* **—ef·fac′er** *n.*

ef·fect (ĭ-fĕkt′) *n.* **1.** Something brought about by a cause or agent; result. **2.** The way in which something acts upon or influences an object: *the effect of a drug on the nervous system.* **3.** The power or capacity to achieve the desired result; influence. **4.** The condition of being in full force or execution: *goes into effect tomorrow.* **5. a.** Something that produces a specific impression or supports a general design or intention: *sound effects.* **b.** A particular impression: *an effect of spaciousness.* **c.** The production of a particular impression: *She cries just for effect.* **6. a.** The basic meaning. **b.** Intention; purport. **7. effects.** Movable goods; property. —*tr.v.* **-fect·ed, -fect·ing, -fects. 1.** To produce as a result; bring into existence. **2.** To bring about. —*idioms.* **in effect. 1.** In fact; actually. **2.** In essence; virtually. **3.** In active force; in operation. **take effect.** To become operative. —See Usage note at **affect**[1]. [ME < OFr. < Lat. *effectus,* p.part. of *efficere,* to accomplish : *ex-,* out + *facere,* to make.] **—ef·fect′er** *n.* **—ef·fect′i·ble** *adj.*

Synonyms: *effect, consequence, result, outcome, upshot, sequel, consummation.* These nouns denote occurrences, situations, or conditions that are traceable to something antecedent. An *effect* is that which is produced by the action of an agent or cause and follows it in time, either immediately or shortly. A *consequence* also follows the action of an agent and is traceable to it, but the relationship between them is less sharply definable and less immediate than that between a cause and its effect. A *result* is an effect, or the last in a series of effects, that follows a cause and that is viewed as the end product of the operation of the cause. An *outcome* is a result that has clear definition; the term is even stronger than *result* in implying finality, and may suggest operation of a cause over a relatively long period. An *upshot* is a decisive result, often arrived at abruptly or in the nature of a climax. A *sequel* is a logical but relatively long-range consequence of an antecedent action. *Consummation* refers to the final, decisive stage of an action directed toward achievement of a specific end.

ef·fec·tive (ĭ-fĕk′tĭv) *adj.* **1.** Having an intended or expected effect. **2.** Producing or designed to produce the desired impression or response: *an effective speech.* **3.** Operative; in effect: *The law is effective immediately.* **4.** Existing in fact; actual: *a decline in the effective demand.* **5.** Prepared for use or action, esp. in warfare. —*n.* A soldier or a piece of military equipment that is ready for combat. **—ef·fec′tive·ly** *adv.* **—ef·fec′tive·ness, ef′fec·tiv′i·ty** *n.*

ef·fec·tor (ĭ-fĕk′tər) *n.* **1.** An organ at the end of a nerve that activates either gland secretion or muscular contraction. **2.** *Computer Sci.* A device used to produce a desired change in an object in response to input.

ef·fec·tu·al (ĭ-fĕk′cho͞o-əl) *adj.* Producing or sufficient to produce a desired effect; fully adequate. **—ef·fec′tu·al′i·ty, ef·fec′tu·al·ness** *n.* **—ef·fec′tu·al·ly** *adv.*

ef·fec·tu·ate (ĭ-fĕk′cho͞o-āt′) *tr.v.* **-at·ed, -at·ing, -ates.** To bring about; effect. [Med. Lat. *effectuare* < Lat. *efficere.* —see EFFECT.] **—ef·fec′tu·a′tion** *n.*

ef·fem·i·na·cy (ĭ-fĕm′ə-nə-sē) *n.* The quality or condition of being effeminate.

ef·fem·i·nate (ĭ-fĕm′ə-nĭt) *adj.* **1.** Having qualities or characteristics more often associated with women than men; unmanly. **2.** Characterized by weakness and excessive refinement. [ME *effeminat* < Lat. *effeminatus,* p.part. of *effeminare,* to make feminine : *ex,* from + *femina,* woman.] **—ef·fem′i·nate** *n.* **—ef·fem′i·nate·ly** *adv.* **—ef·fem′i·nate·ness** *n.*

ef·fen·di (ĭ-fĕn′dē) *n.* Sir. Used as a title of respect in Turkey. [Turk. *efendi* < Mod. Gk. *aphentēs,* master, alteration of Gk. *authentēs,* master.]

ef·fer·ent (ĕf′ər-ənt) *adj.* **1.** Directed away from a central organ or section. **2.** Carrying impulses from the central nervous system to an effector. [Fr. *efférent* < Lat. *efferens,* pr.part. of *efferre,* to carry off : *ex,* away + *ferre,* to carry.] **—ef′fer·ent** *n.* **—ef′fer·ent·ly** *adv.*

eel

ef·fer·vesce (ĕf′ər-vĕs′) *intr.v.* **-vesced, -vesc·ing, -vesc·es. 1.** To emit small bubbles as gas comes out of a liquid. **2.** To show high spirits or vivacity. [Lat. *effervescere* : *ex-* (intensive) + *fervescere,* to start boiling < *fervēre,* to boil.] **—ef′-**

fer·ves′cence, ef′fer·ves′cen·cy *n.* **—ef′fer·ves′cent** *adj.* **—ef′fer·ves′cent·ly** *adv.*

ef·fete (ĭ-fēt′) *adj.* **1.** No longer productive; infertile. **2.** Exhausted of vitality, force, or effectiveness; worn-out. **3.** Characterized by self-indulgence, weakness, or decadence. **4.** Overrefined; effeminate. [Lat. *effetus,* worn out by childbearing : *ex-,* out + *fetus,* childbearing.] **—ef·fete′ly** *adv.* **—ef·fete′ness** *n.*

ef·fi·ca·cious (ĕf′ĭ-kā′shəs) *adj.* Capable of producing a desired effect. [Lat. *efficax, efficac-* < *efficere,* to effect.] **—ef′fi·ca′cious·ly** *adv.* **—ef′fi·ca′cious·ness** *n.*

ef·fi·ca·cy (ĕf′ĭ-kə-sē) *n.* Power or capacity to produce a desired effect; effectiveness. [Lat. *efficacia* < *efficax,* efficacious.]

ef·fi·cien·cy (ĭ-fĭsh′ən-sē) *n., pl.* **-cies. 1. a.** The quality or property of being efficient. **b.** The degree to which this quality is exercised. **2. a.** The ratio of the effective or useful output to the total input in any system. **b.** The ratio of the energy delivered by a machine to the energy supplied for its operation. **3.** *Informal.* An efficiency apartment.

efficiency apartment *n.* A small, usually furnished apartment with a private bathroom and kitchenette.

efficiency expert *n.* An expert who analyzes esp. industrial operations in order to improve efficiency and productivity.

ef·fi·cient (ĭ-fĭsh′ənt) *adj.* **1.** Acting directly to produce an effect: *an efficient cause.* **2. a.** Acting or producing effectively with a minimum of waste, expense, or unnecessary effort. **b.** Exhibiting a high ratio of output to input. [ME < OFr. < Lat. *efficiens,* pr.part. of *efficere,* to effect.] **—ef·fi′cient·ly** *adv.*

egg[1]
Black skimmer eggs

egg-and-dart
Fragment of a frieze

ef·fi·gy (ĕf′ə-jē) *n., pl.* **-gies. 1.** A painted or sculptured representation, esp. of a person. **2.** A crude figure of a hated or despised person. ***—idiom.* hang** (or **burn**) **in effigy.** To hang or burn in public the effigy of a hated person. [ME *effigie* < Lat. *effigies* < *effingere,* to portray : *ex-,* from + *fingere,* to shape.]

ef·flo·resce (ĕf′lə-rĕs′) *intr.v.* **-resced, -resc·ing, -resc·es. 1.** To blossom; bloom. **2.** *Chem.* **a.** To become a powder by losing water of crystallization. **b.** To become covered with a powdery deposit. [Lat. *efflorescere* : *ex-,* out + *florescere,* inchoative of *florēre,* to blossom < *flos,* flower.]

ef·flo·res·cence (ĕf′lə-rĕs′əns) *n.* **1.** A state or time of flowering. **2. a.** A gradual process of unfolding or developing. **b.** The highest point; culmination. **3.** *Chem.* **a.** The process of efflorescing. **b.** The deposit that results from this process. **c.** A growth of salt crystals on a surface due to evaporation of salt-laden water. **—ef′flo·res′cent** *adj.*

ef·flu·ence (ĕf′lo͞o-əns) *n.* **1.** The act or an instance of flowing out. **2.** Something that flows out or forth; emanation.

ef·flu·ent (ĕf′lo͞o-ənt) *adj.* Flowing out or forth. *—n.* Something that flows out or forth, esp.: **a.** A stream flowing out of a lake or other body of water. **b.** An outflow or discharge of waste, as from a sewer. [ME < Lat. *effluens,* pr.part. of *effluere,* to flow out : *ex-,* out + *fluere,* to flow.]

ef·flu·vi·um (ĭ-flo͞o′vē-əm) *n., pl.* **-vi·a** (-vē-ə) or **-ums. 1.** A usually foul-smelling outflow or rising vapor. **2.** An invisible outflow of radiation or vapor; aura. [Lat. < *effluere,* to flow out. —see EFFLUENT.] **—ef·flu′vi·al** *adj.*

ef·flux (ĕf′lŭks′) *n.* **1.** An outward flow. **2.** Something that flows out or forth; effluence. **3.** An expiration; ending. [< Lat. *effluxus,* p.part. of *effluere,* to flow out. —see EFFLUENT.] **—ef·flux′ion** *n.*

ef·fort (ĕf′ərt) *n.* **1.** The use of physical or mental energy to do something; exertion. **2.** A difficult exertion of the strength or will: *It was an effort to get up.* **3.** A usually earnest attempt: *Make an effort to arrive promptly.* **4.** Something done or produced through exertion; achievement: *a play that was his finest effort.* **5.** *Physics.* Force applied against inertia. [OFr. < *efforcier,* to force < Med. Lat. *exfortiare* : Lat. *ex-,* out + Lat. *fortis,* strong.] **—ef′fort·ful** *adj.* **—ef′fort·ful·ly** *adv.*

Synonyms: *effort, exertion, endeavor, application, strain.* These nouns refer to the expenditure of physical or mental power as a means to an end. *Effort* can apply to any such act, great or small; where it is not qualified, the term usually implies a substantial expenditure of one's time, strength, or faculties. *Exertion* always implies great expenditure, usually of physical strength. *Endeavor* suggests earnest striving to achieve a serious goal. *Application* refers to devoting one's full attention to the mastery of something; it is closely associated with diligence, persistence, and hard work. *Strain* can denote excessive effort or exertion or a by-product of this, such as tension or muscular pain.

ef·fort·less (ĕf′ərt-lĭs) *adj.* Requiring or showing little or no effort. **—ef′fort·less·ly** *adv.* **—ef′fort·less·ness** *n.*

ef·front·er·y (ĭ-frŭn′tə-rē) *n., pl.* **-ies.** Impudent boldness; audacity. [Fr. *effronterie* < LLat. *effrons,* shameless : *ex-,* from + *frons,* forehead.]

ef·ful·gence (ĭ-fo͝ol′jəns, ĭ-fŭl′) *n.* A brilliant radiance.

ef·ful·gent (ĭ-fo͝ol′jənt, ĭ-fŭl′-) *adj.* Shining brilliantly; resplendent. [Lat. *effulgens, effulgent-,* pr.part. of *effulgere,* to shine out : *ex-,* out + *fulgēre,* to shine.]

ef·fuse (ĭ-fyo͞os′) *adj. Bot.* Spreading out loosely on a surface. *—v.* (ĭ-fyo͞oz′) **-fused, -fus·ing, -fus·es.** *—tr.v.* To pour or spread out; disseminate. *—intr.v.* **1.** To spread or flow out. **2.** To exude. [Lat. *effusus,* p.part. of *effundere,* to pour out : *ex-,* out + *fundere,* to pour.]

ef·fu·sion (ĭ-fyo͞o′zhən) *n.* **1. a.** The act or an instance of effusing. **b.** Something that is poured forth. **2.** An unrestrained outpouring of feeling, as in speech or writing. **3.** *Pathol.* **a.** The seeping of serous, purulent, or bloody fluid into a cavity. **b.** The effused fluid.

ef·fu·sive (ĭ-fyo͞o′sĭv) *adj.* Unrestrained or excessive in emotional expression; gushy. **—ef·fu′sive·ly** *adv.* **—ef·fu′sive·ness** *n.*

Ef·ik (ĕf′ĭk) *n.* **1.** One of a people of southern Nigeria. **2.** The Ibibio language of the Efik people. **—Ef′ik** *adj.*

eft (ĕft) *n.* A newt. [ME *evete* < OE *efeta.*]

eft·soons (ĕft-so͞onz′) *adv. Archaic.* **1.** Soon afterward; presently. **2.** Once again. [ME *eftsone* < OE *eftsōna* : *eft,* again + *sōna,* soon.]

e·gad (ĭ-găd′) *interj.* Used as a mild oath expressing surprise or enthusiasm. [Alteration of *ah God.*]

e·gal·i·tar·i·an (ĭ-găl′ĭ-târ′ē-ən) *n.* An adherent of the doctrine of equal political, economic, and legal rights for all human beings. [Fr. *égalitaire,* an egalitarian < *égalité,* equality < Lat. *aequalitas* < *aequalis,* equal.] **—e·gal′i·tar′i·an** *adj.* **—e·gal′i·tar′i·an·ism** *n.*

E·ge·ri·a (ĭ-jîr′ē-ə) *n.* A woman counselor or adviser. [After *Egeria,* an adviser to Numa Pompilius, legendary Roman king.]

e·gest (ē-jĕst′) *tr.v.* **e·gest·ed, e·gest·ing, e·gests.** To discharge or excrete from the body. [Lat. *egerere, egest-,* to carry out : *ex-,* out + *gerere,* to carry.] **—e·ges′tion** *n.* **—e·ges′tive** *adj.*

e·ges·ta (ē-jĕs′tə) *pl.n.* Egested matter, esp. excrement. [Lat. < *egerere,* to carry out. —see EGEST.]

egg[1] (ĕg) *n.* **1.** A female gamete; ovum. **2.** One of the female reproductive cells of various animals, consisting usually of an embryo surrounded by nutrient material with a protective covering. **3.** The oval, thin-shelled ovum of a bird, esp. of a domestic fowl, used as food. **4.** Something having the characteristically ovoid shape of a hen's egg. **5.** *Slang.* A fellow; person: *a good egg.* *—tr.v.* **egged, egg·ing, eggs. 1.** To cover with beaten egg, as in cooking. **2.** *Informal.* To throw eggs at. ***—idioms.* put** (or **have**) **all one's eggs in one basket.** To risk everything on a single venture. **with egg on one's face.** *Informal.* Embarrassed. [ME *egge,* bird's egg < ON *egg.*]

egg[2] (ĕg) *tr.v.* **egged, egg·ing, eggs. —egg on.** To encourage or incite to action. [ME *eggen* < ON *eggja.*]

egg-and-dart (ĕg′ən-därt′) *n.* A decorative molding consisting of a series of egg-shaped figures alternating with dart, anchor, or tongue-shaped figures.

egg·beat·er (ĕg′bē′tər) *n.* A kitchen utensil with rotating blades for beating, whipping, or mixing.

egg case *n.* A protective capsule in some animals that contains eggs.

egg·cup (ĕg′kŭp′) *n.* A cup for a usually soft-boiled egg.

eg·ger also **eg·gar** (ĕg′ər) *n.* Any of various moths of the family Lasiocampidae, whose larvae often construct tentlike webs.

egg·head (ĕg′hĕd′) *n. Slang.* An intellectual; highbrow: *an egghead who lives in an ivory tower.*

egg·nog (ĕg′nŏg′) *n.* A drink consisting of milk and beaten eggs, commonly mixed with rum, brandy, or wine. [EGG[1] + obs. *nog,* ale.]

egg·plant (ĕg′plănt′) *n.* **1. a.** A tropical Old World plant, *Solanum melongena,* cultivated for its edible fruit. **b.** The glossy, ovoid fruit of the eggplant. **2.** A blackish purple.

egg roll *n.* A cylindrical case made of an egg dough that has been filled with minced vegetables and sometimes with seafood or meat, and then fried.

eggs Ben·e·dict (bĕn′ĭ-dĭkt′) *n.* A dish consisting of poached eggs on slices of toast and ham, and covered with hollandaise sauce. [Prob. < the name *Benedict.*]

egg·shell (ĕg′shĕl′) *n.* **1.** The thin, brittle, exterior covering of a bird's egg. **2.** A pale yellow to yellowish white. **—egg′shell′** *adj.*

egg white *n.* The albumen of an egg.

e·gis (ē′jĭs) *n.* Variant of **aegis.**

eg·lan·tine (ĕg′lən-tīn′, -tēn′) *n.* The sweetbrier. [ME *eglentin* < OFr. *aiglent,* prob. ult. < Lat. *acus,* needle.]

e·go (ē′gō, ĕg′ō) *n.* **1.** The self, esp. as distinct from the world and other selves. **2.** *Psychoanal.* The personality component that is conscious, most immediately controls behavior, and is most in touch with external reality. **3. a.** Self-love; egotism. **b.** Self-confidence; self-esteem. [NLat. < Lat., I.]

e·go·cen·tric (ē′gō-sĕn′trĭk, ĕg′ō-) *adj.* **1.** Holding the view that the ego is the center, object, and norm of all experience. **2.** Self-centered; selfish. **3.** *Philos.* Viewed or perceived from one's own mind as a center. **—e′go·cen′tric** *n.* **—e′go·cen·tric′i·ty** (-trĭs′ĭ-tē) *n.*

ego ideal *n. Psychoanal.* The entirety of an individual's positive identifications with loving, reassuring parents or parental substitutes, regarded as a differentiated component of the mature ego.

e·go·ism (ē′gō-ĭz′əm, ĕg′ō-) *n.* **1. a.** The ethical doctrine that morality has its foundations in self-interest. **b.** The ethical belief that self-interest is the just and proper motive for all human conduct. **2.** Egotism.

e·go·ist (ē′gō-ĭst, ĕg′ō-) *n.* **1.** One devoted to his own interests and advancement. **2.** An adherent of egoism. **3.** An egotist. [Fr. *égoiste* < *égo*, ego < Lat. *ego*, I.] **—e′go·is′tic, e′go·is′ti·cal** *adj.* **—e′go·is′ti·cal·ly** *adv.*

e·go·ma·ni·a (ē′gō-mā′nē-ə, -măn′yə, ĕg′ō-) *n.* Obsessive preoccupation with the self. **—e′go·ma′ni·ac′** (-nē-ăk′) *n.* **—e′·go·ma·ni′a·cal** (-mə-nī′ə-kəl) *adj.* **—e′go·ma·ni′a·cal·ly** *adv.*

e·go·tism (ē′gə-tĭz′əm, ĕg′ə-) *n.* **1.** The tendency to speak or write of oneself excessively and boastfully. **2.** An inordinately large sense of self-importance; conceit. [EGO + *-tism*, as in *nepotism.*]

e·go·tist (ē′gə-tĭst, ĕg′ə-) *n.* **1.** A conceited, boastful person. **2.** A person who acts selfishly; egoist. **—e′go·tis′tic, e′go·tis′ti·cal** *adj.* **—e′go·tis′ti·cal·ly** *adv.*

ego trip *n. Slang.* Something that gratifies the ego.

e·go-trip (ē′gō-trĭp′, ĕg′ō-) *intr.v.* **-tripped, -trip·ping, -trips.** *Slang.* To act in an egotistic or self-seeking manner. **—e′-go-trip′per** *n.*

e·gre·gious (ĭ-grē′jəs, -jē-əs) *adj.* Outstandingly bad; flagrant. [Lat. *egregius*, distinguished : *ex-*, out from + *grex*, herd.] **—e·gre′gious·ly** *adv.* **—e·gre′gious·ness** *n.*

e·gress (ē′grĕs′) *n.* **1.** The act of going out; emergence. **2.** The right of going out. **3.** The path or opening by means of which one goes out; exit. **4.** *Astron.* The emergence of a celestial body from eclipse or occultation. [Lat. *egressus* < *egredi*, to go out : *ex-*, out + *gradi*, to go.]

e·gres·sion (ĭ-grĕsh′ən) *n.* Egress.

e·gret (ē′grĭt, ĕg′rĭt) *n.* Any of several usually white wading birds of the genera *Bubulcus, Casmerodius, Leucophoyx*, and related genera, characteristically having long, showy, drooping plumes during the breeding season. [ME < OFr. *aigrette* < Prov. *aigreta* < *aigron*, heron, of Germanic orig.]

E·gyp·tian (ĭ-jĭp′shən) *n.* **1.** A native or citizen of Egypt. **2.** The Afro-Asiatic language of the ancient Egyptians. **—E·gyp′tian** *adj.*

Egyptian clover *n.* Berseem.

Egyptian corn *n.* Durra.

Egyptian cotton *n.* A long-staple, fine cotton grown chiefly in northern Africa.

E·gyp·tol·o·gy (ē′jĭp-tŏl′ə-jē) *n.* The study of the culture and artifacts of the ancient Egyptian civilization. **—E′gyp·tol′o·gist** *n.*

eh (ā, ĕ) *interj.* **1.** Used interrogatively: *Eh? What was that?* **2.** Used in asking for confirmation: *He is a shrewd one, eh?*

ei·der (ī′dər) *n.* Any of several sea ducks of the genus *Somateria* and related genera, of northern regions, having soft, commercially valuable down and predominantly black and white plumage in the males. [Ult. < Icel. *æður* < ON *æðr.*]

ei·der·down also **eider down** (ī′dər-doun′) *n.* **1.** The down of the eider duck, used as stuffing for quilts and pillows. **2.** A quilt stuffed with eiderdown. **3.** A warm, napped fabric.

ei·det·ic (ī-dĕt′ĭk) *adj.* Of, relating to, or marked by extraordinarily detailed and vivid recall of visual images. [G. *eidetisch* < Gk. *eidētikos*, relating to images < *eidēsis*, knowledge < *eidos*, form.] **—ei·det′i·cal·ly** *adv.*

ei·do·lon (ī-dō′lən) *n., pl.* **-lons** or **-la** (-lə). **1.** A phantom; apparition. **2.** An image of an ideal. [Gk. *eidōlon* < *eidos*, form.]

eight (āt) *n.* **1.** The cardinal number that is next after the number 7 and equal to the sum of 7 + 1. **2.** The eighth in a set or sequence. **3.** Something having eight parts, units, or members, esp.: **a.** An eight-oared racing shell. **b.** An eight-cylinder engine or automobile. [ME *eighte* < OE *eahta* ; akin to G. *acht*, Lat. *octo*, Gk. *oktō*, Skt. *aṣṭā.*] **—eight** *adj. & pron.*

eight ball *n.* A black pool ball bearing the number eight that may place a player at a disadvantage. **—idiom. behind the eight ball.** *Slang.* In an unfavorable or uncomfortable position.

eight·een (ā-tēn′) *n.* The cardinal number that is next in order after the number 17 and equal to the sum of 17 + 1. [ME *eightetene* < OE *eahtatīene.*] **—eight·een′** *adj. & pron.*

eight·een·mo (ā-tēn′mō) *n., pl.* **-mos.** An octodecimo.

eight·eenth (ā-tēnth′) *n.* **1.** The ordinal number that matches the number 18 in a series. **2.** One of 18 equal parts. **—eight·eenth′** *adj. & adv.*

eighth (ātth, āth) *n.* **1.** The ordinal number that matches the number eight in a series. **2.** One of eight equal parts. [ME < OE < *eahta*, eight.] **—eighth** *adj. & adv.*

eighth note *n. Mus.* A note having one-eighth the time value of a whole note.

eight·i·eth (ā′tē-ĭth) *n.* **1.** The ordinal number that matches the number 80 in a series. **2.** One of 80 equal parts. **—eight′i·eth** *adj. & adv.*

eight·vo (āt′vō′) *n., pl.* **-vos.** An octavo. [EIGHT + (OCTA)VO.]

eight·y (ā′tē) *n.* The cardinal number equal to 8 x 10. [ME *eighti* < OE *hundeahtatig* : *hund*, hundred + *eahta*, eight + *-tig*, -ty.] **—eight′y** *adj. & pron.*

-ein *suff.* A chemical compound related to a specified compound with a similar name ending in *-in* : *phthalein.* [Alteration of -IN.]

ein·korn (īn′kôrn′) *n.* A one-seeded wheat, *Triticum monococcum*, grown in arid regions. [G. *Einkorn* : *ein*, one (< OHG) + *Korn*, grain (< OHG).]

ein·stein·i·um (īn-stī′nē-əm) *n. Symbol* **Es** A synthetic transuranic element first produced by neutron irradiation of uranium in a thermonuclear explosion. It has 12 known isotopes with half-lives ranging between 1.2 minutes and 270 days and mass numbers from 245 to 256. Atomic number 99. [After Albert *Einstein* (1879–1955).]

eis·tedd·fod (ā-stĕ*th*′vŏd, ĕs-tĕ*th*′-) *n.* An annual assembly of Welsh poets and musicians. [Welsh : *eistedd*, to sit (< *sedd*, seat) + *bod*, to be.]

ei·ther (ē′*th*ər, ī′*th*ər) *pron.* One or the other. *—conj.* Used before the first of two or more coordinates or clauses linked by *or: Either we go now, or remain here forever.* *—adj.* **1.** One or the other; any one of two: *Wear either coat.* **2.** One and the other; each: *rings on either hand.* *—adv.* Likewise; also. Used as an intensifier following negative statements: *If you don't order a dessert, I won't either.* [ME < OE *ǣgðer.*]

Usage: *Either* is normally used to mean "one of two," although it is sometimes used of three or more: *either corner of the triangle.* When referring to more than two, *any* or *any one* is preferred. • *Either* takes a singular verb: *Either plant grows in the shade.* Sometimes it is used informally with a plural verb, especially when followed by *of* and a plural: *I doubt whether either of them are available.* But such use is unacceptable in formal writing to a majority of the Usage Panel. • In *either . . . or* constructions, the two conjunctions should be followed by parallel elements. The following is held to be incorrect: *You may either have the ring or the bracelet* (properly, *you may have either the ring or the bracelet*). The following is also incorrect: *He can take either the examination offered to all applicants or ask for a personal interview* (properly, *he can either take . . .*). • When all the elements in an *either . . . or* construction are singular, the verb is singular: *Either Mary's father or Tom's mother is coming.* When one element is singular and the other plural, it is sometimes suggested that the verb should agree with whichever element is closest to it: *Either Kim or the boys are going* but *Either the boys or Kim is going.* Some traditionalists, however, insist that such constructions should be avoided entirely, and that substitutes must be found for them, such as *Either Kim is going, or the boys are.* There is no generally accepted rule in these cases. See also Usage notes at **everyone** and **neither.**

either-or (ē′*th*ər-ôr, ī′*th*ər-) *adj.* Marked by a choice between only two possibilities: *an either-or situation—fight or die.*

e·jac·u·late (ĭ-jăk′yə-lāt′) *v.* **-lat·ed, -lat·ing, -lates.** *—tr.* **1.** To eject or discharge abruptly, esp. to discharge (semen) in orgasm. **2.** To utter suddenly and passionately; exclaim. *—intr.v.* To eject semen. *—n.* (ĭ-jăk′yə-lĭt). Semen ejaculated in orgasm. [Lat. *ejaculari, ejaculat-* : *ex-*, out + *jaculari*, to throw < *jaculum*, dart.] **—e·jac′u·la′tor** *n.*

e·jac·u·la·tion (ĭ-jăk′yə-lā′shən) *n.* **1.** The act of ejaculating. **2.** An abrupt discharge of fluid, esp. of seminal fluid. **3. a.** A sudden, short utterance; exclamation. **b.** A brief, pious utterance or prayer.

e·jac·u·la·to·ry (ĭ-jăk′yə-lə-tôr′ē, -tōr′ē) *adj.* **1.** Of or pertaining to ejaculation. **2.** Pertaining to or constituting a sudden, brief utterance; exclamatory.

e·ject (ĭ-jĕkt′) *v.* **e·ject·ed, e·ject·ing, e·jects.** *—tr.* **1.** To throw out forcefully; expel. **2. a.** To compel to leave: *was ejected for creating a disturbance.* **b.** To evict. *—intr.* To make an emergency exit by ejection capsule or seat. [ME *ejecten* < Lat. *eicere* : *ex-*, out + *jacere*, to throw.]

Synonyms: *eject, expel, evict, dismiss, oust, throw out.* These verbs refer in various senses to removing things or persons. *Eject* applies principally to the hurling out of things or to the forcible physical removal of persons. *Expel* usually refers to permanent removal of a person from membership in a group; with reference to things, it is frequently interchangeable with *eject. Evict* generally refers to the dispossessing of persons, or putting them out of property by legal means. *Dismiss* refers to sending persons away as a matter of routine, as a teacher dismisses pupils, or to exercising the power to discharge subordinates from service or office. *Dismiss* also can refer to putting a person or thing out of one's mind or, in law, to refusing him or it further consideration. *Oust* is applied chiefly to the removal of persons from office by means lawful or otherwise. *Throw out* refers literally to the discarding of things; with reference to persons it is sometimes used as an informal substitute for any of the foregoing terms that imply forcible removal.

e·jec·ta (ĭ-jĕk′tə) *pl.n.* Ejected matter, as that from an erupting volcano. [NLat. < Lat. *ejectus*, p.part. of *eicere*, to throw out. —see EJECT.]

e·jec·tion (ĭ-jĕk′shən) *n.* **1.** The act of ejecting or the condition of being ejected. **2.** Ejected matter.

ejection seat *n.* A seat designed to eject clear of an aircraft and parachute to the ground in an emergency.

e·ject·ment (ĭ-jĕkt′mənt) *n.* **1.** The act of ejecting; dispossession. **2.** An action to regain possession of real estate held by another.

e·jec·tor (ĭ-jĕk′tər) *n.* **1.** One that ejects. **2.** A device in a gun that ejects the empty shell after each firing.

eke[1] (ēk) *tr.v.* **eked, ek·ing, ekes. 1.** To supplement with great effort; strain to fill out: *eked out his income by working*

egret

eider
American eider

at night. **2.** To earn with great effort or strain: *eke out a living.* **3.** To make (a supply) last by careful management. [ME *eken,* to increase < OE *ēcan.*]

eke[2] (ēk) *adv. Archaic.* Also. [ME < OE *ēc.*]

e·kis·tics (ĭ-kĭs′tĭks) *n. (used with a sing. verb).* The science of human settlements, including city or community planning and design. [< Gk. *oikistikos,* of settlements < *oikizein,* to settle < *oikos,* house.] **—e·kis′tic, e·kis′ti·cal** *adj.* **—ek′is·ti′cian** (ĕk′ĭ-stĭsh′ən) *n.*

ek·pwe·le (ĕk-pwē′lē) *n.* See table at **currency.**

el[1] also **ell** (ĕl) *n.* The letter *l.*

el[2] (ĕl) *n. Informal.* An elevated railway.

e·lab·o·rate (ĭ-lăb′ər-ĭt) *adj.* **1.** Planned or executed with painstaking attention to numerous parts or details. **2.** Characterized by intricacy and richness of detail. *—v.* (ĭ-lăb′ə-rāt′) **-rat·ed, -rat·ing, -rates.** *—tr.* **1.** To work out with care and detail; develop thoroughly. **2.** To produce by effort; create. *—intr.* **1.** To become elaborate. **2.** To express at greater length or in greater detail. [Lat. *elaborare, elaborat-* : *ex-,* out + *laborare,* to work < *labor,* work.] **—e·lab′o·rate·ly** *adv.* **—e·lab′o·rate·ness** *n.* **—e·lab′o·ra′tion** (ĭ-lăb′ə-rā′shən) *n.* **—e·lab′o·ra′tor** *n.*

Elaine (ĭ-lān′) *n.* One of two women in Arthurian legend who loved Lancelot: **a.** One who died of unrequited love for him. **b.** One who was the mother of Galahad by Lancelot.

é·lan (ā-läN′, ā-län′) *n.* **1.** Enthusiastic vigor and liveliness. **2.** Style; flair. [Fr. < OFr. *eslan,* rush < *eslancer,* to throw out : *es-,* out (< Lat. *ex-*) + *lancer,* to throw (< LLat. *lanceare,* to throw a lance < Lat. *lancea,* lance).]

e·land (ē′lənd) *n.* Either of two large African antelopes, *Taurotragus oryx* or *T. derbianus,* having a light-brown or grayish coat and spirally twisted horns. [Afr. < Du., elk < obs. G. *elen,* prob. < Lith. *élnis.*]

eland

élan vi·tal (vē-tăl′) *n.* The vital force hypothesized by Henri Bergson as a source of efficient causation and evolution in nature. [Fr.]

el·a·pid (ĕl′ə-pĭd) *n.* Any of various venomous snakes of the family Elapidae, which includes the cobras and coral snakes. [NLat. *Elapidae,* family name < Gk. *elaps,* fish, var. of *ellops.*]

e·lapse (ĭ-lăps′) *intr.v.* **e·lapsed, e·laps·ing, e·laps·es.** To pass; slip by: *Weeks elapsed before we could act.* *—n.* Lapse; passage. [Lat. *elabi, elaps-* : *ex-,* away + *labi,* to slip.]

elapsed time *n.* The measured duration of an event, esp. the actual time spent in transit, as in flight, by a moving body.

e·las·mo·branch (ĭ-lăz′mə-brăngk′) *n.* Any of numerous fishes of the subclass Elasmobranchii within the class Chondricthyes, characterized by a cartilaginous skeleton, and including the sharks, rays, and skates. [NLat. *Elasmobranchii,* subclass name : Gk. *elasmos,* metal plate (< *elaunein,* to beat) + Lat. *branchia,* gill < Gk., gills.] **—e·las′mo·branch′** *adj.*

elderberry

e·las·tic (ĭ-lăs′tĭk) *adj.* **1.** *Physics.* Returning or capable of returning to an initial form or state after deformation. **2.** Capable of adapting to change or a variety of circumstances; flexible: *an elastic schedule.* **3.** Quick to recover or revive: *an elastic spirit.* **4.** Springy; firm. *—n.* **1. a.** A flexible stretchable fabric made with interwoven strands of rubber or an imitative synthetic fiber. **b.** Something made of this fabric. **2.** A rubber band. [NLat. *elasticus* < Gk. *elastos,* impulsive < *elaunein,* to drive.] **—e·las′ti·cal·ly** *adv.*

elastic collision *n.* A collision of particles in which the total kinetic energy of translation is conserved.

e·las·tic·i·ty (ĭ-lă-stĭs′ĭ-tē, ē′lă-) *n.* **1.** The condition or property of being elastic; flexibility. **2.** *Physics.* **a.** The property of returning to an initial form or state following deformation. **b.** The degree to which this property is exhibited.

e·las·ti·ci·zer (ĭ-lăs′tə-sī′zər) *n.* An additive that increases the elasticity of a solid propellant to prevent cracking of the propellant grain in the combustion chamber.

e·las·tin (ĭ-lăs′tĭn) *n.* The albuminoid base of elastic tissue such as tendons, cartilage, and connective tissue. [ELAST(IC) + -IN.]

e·las·to·mer (ĭ-lăs′tə-mər) *n.* Any of various polymers having the elastic properties of natural rubber. [ELAST(IC) + -O- + -MER(E).] **—e·las′to·mer′ic** (-mĕr′ĭk) *adj.*

e·late (ĭ-lāt′) *tr.v.* **e·lat·ed, e·lat·ing, e·lates.** To excite pride or joy in. *—adj.* Elated; joyful. [Lat. *effere, elat-,* to carry out : *ex-,* out + *ferre,* to carry.] **—e·la′tion** *n.*

e·lat·ed (ĭ-lā′tĭd) *adj.* Exultant; joyful. **—e·lat′ed·ly** *adv.* **—e·lat′ed·ness** *n.*

el·a·ter (ĕl′ə-tər) *n.* **1.** An elaterid beetle. **2.** *Bot.* An elongated, often spirally thickened filament occurring among the spores of liverworts. [NLat. < Gk. *elatēr,* driver < *elaunein,* to drive.]

e·lat·er·id (ĭ-lăt′ər-ĭd) *n.* Any of numerous beetles of the family Elateridae, which includes the click beetles. [NLat. *Elateridae,* family name < Gk. *elatēr,* driver. —see ELATER.]

e·lat·er·ite (ĭ-lăt′ə-rīt′) *n.* A brown, elastic hydrocarbon resin. [G. *Elaterit* < Gk. *elatēr,* driver < *elaunein,* to drive.]

E layer *n.* A region, or any of various layers in the region, of the ionosphere, occurring between about 90 and 150 kilometers or 55 and 95 miles above the earth and influencing long-distance communications by strongly reflecting radio waves in the range from one to three megahertz.

Electra
4th-century B.C. Greek amphora

el·bow (ĕl′bō′) *n.* **1. a.** The joint or bend of the arm between the forearm and the upper arm. **b.** The bony outer projection of this joint. **2.** A joint, as of a bird or quadruped, corresponding to the human elbow. **3.** Something having a bend or angle similar to an elbow, esp.: **a.** A length of pipe with a sharp bend in it. **b.** A sharp bend in a river or a road. *—v.* **-bowed, -bow·ing, -bows.** *—tr.* **1. a.** To push or jostle with the elbow. **b.** To shove aside with the elbow. **2.** To make (one's way) by pushing, jostling, or shoving with one's elbow. *—intr.* To push, jostle, or shove one's way. ***—idiom.*** **at one's elbow.** Close at hand; nearby. [ME *elbowe* < OE *elnboga.*]

elbow grease *n. Informal.* Strenuous physical effort.

el·bow·room (ĕl′bō-ro͞om′, -ro͝om′) *n.* **1.** Room enough to move around or function in. **2.** Ample scope.

eld·er[1] (ĕl′dər) *adj.* A comparative of **old.** *—n.* **1.** An older person. **2.** An older, influential man of a family, tribe, or community. **3.** One of the governing officers of the church, often having pastoral or teaching functions. **4.** *Mormon Ch.* A member of the higher order of priesthood. [ME *eldre* < OE *eldra.*] **—el′der·ship′** *n.*

Usage: *Elder* and *eldest* apply only to persons, unlike *older* and *oldest,* which also apply to things. *Elder* and *eldest* are used principally with reference to seniority: *elder brother; elder statesman; John the Elder.* Unlike *older, elder* is also a noun: *the town elders; ought to listen to your elders.*

el·der[2] (ĕl′dər) *n.* Any of various shrubs or small trees of the genus *Sambucus,* having clusters of small white flowers and red or blackish berrylike fruit. [ME < OE *ellen.*]

el·der·ber·ry (ĕl′dər-bĕr′ē) *n.* **1.** The small, edible fruit of an elder, sometimes used to make wine or preserves. **2.** A shrub or tree that bears elderberries.

eld·er·ly (ĕl′dər-lē) *adj.* Approaching old age; rather old. **—el′der·li·ness** *n.*

elder statesman *n.* A prominent and experienced older person, esp. a statesman acting as an unofficial adviser.

eld·est (ĕl′dĭst) *adj.* Greatest in age or seniority. —See Usage note at **elder.** [ME < OE *eldesta.*]

El Do·ra·do (ĕ′l də-rä′dō) *n.* **1.** A legendary kingdom or city in Spanish America rich in precious metals and jewels, sought after by 16th-century explorers. **2.** A place of fabulous wealth or opportunity. [Sp., the gilded (land).]

el·dritch (ĕl′drĭch) *adj.* Strange or unearthly. [Of Sc. orig.]

El·e·at·ic (ĕl′ē-ăt′ĭk) *adj.* Of or characteristic of the school of philosophy founded by Xenophanes and Parmenides and holding the belief that immutable being is the only knowable reality and change is the subject of mere opinion. [Lat. *Eleaticus* < Gk. *Eleatikos* < *Elea,* Velia, an ancient town in south Italy.] **—El′e·a′tic** *n.* **—El′e·at′i·cism** *n.*

el·e·cam·pane (ĕl′ĭ-kăm-pān′) *n.* A tall, coarse plant, *Inula helenium,* native to Eurasia, having rayed yellow flowers. [ME *elecampana* < Med. Lat. *enula campana* : Lat. *inula,* elecampane (< Gk. *helenion*) + Lat. *campanea,* fem. of *campaneus,* of the field < *campus,* field.]

e·lect (ĭ-lĕkt′) *v.* **e·lect·ed, e·lect·ing, e·lects.** *—tr.* **1.** To select by vote for an office or for membership. **2.** To choose; pick out: *elect an art course.* **3.** To decide on: *elected to remain.* *—intr.* To make a choice or selection. *—adj.* **1.** Chosen deliberately; singled out. **2.** Elected but not yet installed: *the governor-elect.* **3.** Chosen for marriage: *the bride-elect.* **4.** *Theol.* Selected by the divine will for salvation. *—n.* **1.** One that is chosen or selected. **2.** *Theol.* One selected by the divine will for salvation. **3.** *(used with a pl. verb).* An exclusive group: *one of the elect who have power.* [ME *electen* < Lat. *eligere,* to select : *ex-,* out + *legere,* to choose.] **—e·lect′a·bil′i·ty** *n.* **—e·lect′a·ble** *adj.*

e·lec·tion (ĭ-lĕk′shən) *n.* **1. a.** The act or power of electing. **b.** The fact of being elected. **2.** The right or ability to make a choice. **3.** *Theol.* Predestined salvation, esp. as conceived by Calvinists.

Election Day *n.* A day set by law for the election of public officials.

e·lec·tion·eer (ĭ-lĕk′shə-nîr′) *intr.v.* **-eered, -eer·ing, -eers.** To work actively for a particular candidate or political party.

e·lec·tive (ĭ-lĕk′tĭv) *adj.* **1.** Of or pertaining to a selection by vote. **2.** Filled or obtained by election: *elective office.* **3.** Having the power or authority to elect; electoral. **4.** Permitting or involving a choice; optional: *elective surgery.* *—n.* An academic course or subject that is optional rather than obligatory. **—e·lec′tive·ly** *adv.* **—e·lec′tive·ness** *n.*

e·lec·tor (ĭ-lĕk′tər) *n.* **1.** A qualified voter in an election. **2.** A member of the Electoral College of the United States. **3.** One of the German princes in the Holy Roman Empire entitled to elect the emperor.

e·lec·tor·al (ĭ-lĕk′tər-əl) *adj.* **1.** Of, pertaining to, or composed of electors. **2.** Of or relating to election.

Electoral College *n.* A body of electors chosen to elect the President and Vice President of the United States.

e·lec·tor·ate (ĭ-lĕk′tər-ĭt) *n.* **1.** A body of qualified voters. **2.** The dignity or territory of an elector of the Holy Roman Empire.

electr- *pref.* Variant of **electro-.**

E·lec·tra (ĭ-lĕk′trə) *n. Gk. Myth.* A daughter of Clytemnestra and Agamemnon who assisted her brother Orestes in avenging the murder of Agamemnon by killing their mother and her lover. [Lat. < Gk. *Ēlektra.*]

Electra complex *n. Psychoanal.* Unconscious libidinal feeling on the part of a daughter, directed toward her father.
e·lec·tret (ĭ-lĕk′trĭt) *n.* A solid dielectric that exhibits persistent dielectric polarization. [ELECTR(ICITY) + (MAGN)ET.]
e·lec·tric (ĭ-lĕk′trĭk) or **e·lec·tri·cal** (-trĭ-kəl) *adj.* **1.** Of, pertaining to, or operated by electricity. **2. a.** Emotionally exciting; thrilling. **b.** Exceptionally tense; charged with emotion: *an atmosphere electric with suspicion.* —*n.* An electrically powered machine, esp. a vehicle. [NLat. *electricus* < Lat. *electrum,* amber < Gk. *ēlektron.*] —**e·lec′tri·cal·ly** *adv.*
electrical engineering *n.* The scientific technology of electricity, esp. the design and application of circuitry and equipment for power generation and distribution, machine control, and communications. —**electrical engineer** *n.*
electrical storm *n.* Thunderstorm.
electric chair *n.* **1.** A chair used to electrocute an individual sentenced to death by law. **2.** Execution by means of electrocution. **3.** The sentence of death by electrocution.
electric displacement *n.* The product of electric intensity and permittivity.
electric eel *n.* A long, eellike freshwater fish, *Electrophorus electricus,* of northern South America, having organs capable of producing a powerful electric discharge.
electric eye *n.* A photoelectric cell.
electric field *n.* A region of space characterized by the existence of a detectable electric intensity at every point.
electric flux *n.* The integral over a designated surface of the component of electric displacement normal to the surface.
electric flux density *n.* Electric displacement.
electric furnace *n.* An industrial or laboratory furnace heated by an electric arc, electric induction, or electric resistance.
electric guitar *n.* A guitar that transmits tones to an amplifier by means of an electronic pickup placed under the strings.
e·lec·tri·cian (ĭ-lĕk-trĭsh′ən, ē′lĕk-) *n.* A person whose occupation is the installation, maintenance, repair, or operation of electric equipment and circuitry.
electric intensity *n.* The ratio of the electrostatic force exerted on a body to the charge on the body.
e·lec·tric·i·ty (ĭ-lĕk-trĭs′ə-tē, ē′lĕk-) *n.* **1. a.** The class of physical phenomena arising from the existence and interactions of electric charge. **b.** The physical science of such phenomena. **2.** Electric current used or regarded as a source of power. **3.** Intense emotional excitement.
electric lamp *n.* A lamp that uses electricity to produce light.
electric light *n.* **1.** An electric lamp. **2.** Light produced electrically.
electric moment *n.* The dipole moment of an electric dipole.
electric motor *n.* A motor powered by electricity.
electric ray *n.* Any of various fishes of the family Torpedinidae, having a rounded body and a pair of organs capable of producing a fairly strong electric discharge.
e·lec·tri·fy (ĭ-lĕk′trə-fī′) *tr.v.* **-fied, -fy·ing, -fies. 1.** To produce electric charge on or in (a conductor). **2. a.** To wire or equip (a building, for example) for the use of electric power. **b.** To provide with electric power. **3.** To thrill, startle greatly, or shock. [ELECTRI(C) + -FY.] —**e·lec′tri·fi′a·ble** *adj.* —**e·lec′tri·fi·ca′tion** *n.* —**e·lec′tri·fi′er** *n.*
electro– or **electr–** *pref.* **1. a.** Electricity: *electromagnet.* **b.** Electric; electrically: *electrocute.* **2.** Electrolysis: *electrodeposit.* **3.** Electron: *electronegative.* [NLat. < Lat. *electrum,* amber < Gk. *ēlektron.*]
e·lec·tro·a·cous·tics (ĭ-lĕk′trō-ə-ko͞o′stĭks) *n.* (*used with a sing. verb*). The science of the interaction or interconversion of electric and acoustic phenomena. —**e·lec′tro·a·cous′tic** *adj.* —**e·lec′tro·a·cous′tic·al·ly** *adv.*
e·lec·tro·a·nal·y·sis (ĭ-lĕk′trō-ə-năl′ĭ-sĭs) *n., pl.* **-ses** (-sēz′). Chemical analysis using electrolytic techniques. —**e·lec′tro·an′a·lyt′ic** (-trō-ăn′ə-lĭt′ĭk), **e·lec′tro·an·a·lyt′i·cal** *adj.*
e·lec·tro·car·di·o·gram (ĭ-lĕk′trō-kär′dē-ə-grăm′) *n.* The curve traced by an electrocardiograph, used to diagnose heart disease.
e·lec·tro·car·di·o·graph (ĭ-lĕk′trō-kär′dē-ə-grăf′) *n.* An instrument used to record electric potentials associated with the electric currents that traverse the heart. —**e·lec′tro·car′di·o·graph′ic** (-grăf′ĭk) *adj.* —**e·lec′tro·car′di·o·graph′i·cal·ly** *adv.* —**e·lec′tro·car′di·og′ra·phy** (-kär′dē-ŏg′rə-fē) *n.*
e·lec·tro·chem·is·try (ĭ-lĕk′trō-kĕm′ĭs-trē) *n.* The science of the interaction or interconversion of electric and chemical phenomena. —**e·lec′tro·chem′i·cal** (-kĕm′ĭ-kəl) *adj.* —**e·lec′tro·chem′i·cal·ly** *adv.* —**e·lec′tro·chem′ist** *n.*
e·lec·tro·co·ag·u·la·tion (ĭ-lĕk′trō-kō-ăg′yə-lā′shən) *n. Med.* The use of a high frequency electric current to bring about the coagulation and destruction of tissue.
e·lec·tro·cute (ĭ-lĕk′trə-kyo͞ot′) *tr.v.* **-cut·ed, -cut·ing, -cutes. 1.** To kill with electricity. **2.** To execute (a condemned criminal) by means of electricity. [ELECTRO- + (EXE)CUTE.] —**e·lec′tro·cu′tion** (-kyo͞o′shən) *n.*
e·lec·trode (ĭ-lĕk′trōd′) *n.* **1.** A solid electric conductor through which an electric current enters or leaves a medium such as an electrolyte, a nonmetallic solid, a molten metal, a gas, or a vacuum. **2.** A collector or emitter of electric charge or electric-charge carriers, as in a semiconducting device.
e·lec·tro·de·pos·it (ĭ-lĕk′trō-dĭ-pŏz′ĭt) *tr.v.* **-it·ed, -it·ing, -its.** To deposit (a dissolved or suspended substance) on an electrode by electrolysis. —*n.* The substance deposited on an electrode by electrolysis. —**e·lec′tro·dep′o·si′tion** (-dĕp′ə-zĭsh′ən, -dē′pə-zĭsh′ən) *n.*
e·lec·tro·di·al·y·sis (ĭ-lĕk′trō-dī-ăl′ĭ-sĭs) *n., pl.* **-ses** (-sēz′). Dialysis at a rate speeded by the application of an electric potential across the dialysis membrane, used esp. to remove electrolytes from a colloidal suspension.
e·lec·tro·dy·nam·ics (ĭ-lĕk′trō-dī-năm′ĭks) *n.* (*used with a sing. verb*). The physics of the relationship between electric, magnetic, and mechanical phenomena. —**e·lec′tro·dy·nam′ic** *adj.*
e·lec·tro·dy·na·mom·e·ter (ĭ-lĕk′trō-dī′nə-mŏm′ə-tər) *n.* An instrument that uses the interaction of the magnetic fields of fixed and moving sets of coils to measure current, voltage, or power.
e·lec·tro·en·ceph·a·lo·gram (ĭ-lĕk′trō-ĕn-sĕf′ə-lə-grăm′) *n.* A graphic record of the electrical activity of the brain as recorded by the electroencephalograph.
e·lec·tro·en·ceph·a·lo·graph (ĭ-lĕk′trō-ĕn-sĕf′ə-lə-grăf′) *n.* An instrument that records the electrical activity of the brain. —**e·lec′tro·en·ceph′a·lo·graph′ic** *adj.* —**e·lec′tro·en·ceph′a·log′ra·phy** (-lŏg′rə-fē) *n.*
e·lec·tro·form (ĭ-lĕk′trə-fôrm′) *tr.v.* **-formed, -form·ing, -forms.** To produce or reproduce by electrodeposition in a mold.
e·lec·tro·gas·dy·nam·ics (ĭ-lĕk′trə-găs′dī-năm′ĭks) *n.* (*used with a sing. verb*). The generation of electrical energy based on the conversion of the kinetic energy contained in a high-pressure, ionized, moving combustion gas. —**e·lec′tro·gas′dy·nam′ic** *adj.*
e·lec·tro·graph (ĭ-lĕk′trə-grăf′) *n.* **1.** An electrically produced graph or tracing. **2.** Equipment used to produce electrographs in facsimile transmission.
e·lec·tro·hy·drau·lic (ĭ-lĕk′trō-hī-drô′lĭk) *adj.* Of, relating to, or involving a combination of electric and hydraulic mechanisms. —**e·lec′tro·hy·drau′lic·al·ly** *adv.*
e·lec·tro·kin·et·ics (ĭ-lĕk′trō-kĭ-nĕt′ĭks) *n.* (*used with a sing. verb*). The electrodynamics of heating effects and of current distribution in electric networks.
e·lec·trol·o·gist (ĭ-lĕk-trŏl′ə-jĭst, ē′lĕk-) *n.* One that removes esp. body hair by means of an electric current.
e·lec·tro·lu·mi·nes·cence (ĭ-lĕk′trō-lo͞o′mə-nĕs′əns) *n.* **1.** The direct conversion of electric energy to light by a solid phosphor subjected to an alternating electric field. **2.** The emission of light caused by electric discharge in a gas. —**e·lec′tro·lu′mi·nes′cent** *adj.*
e·lec·trol·y·sis (ĭ-lĕk-trŏl′ə-sĭs, ē′lĕk-) *n.* **1.** Chemical change, esp. decomposition, produced in an electrolyte by an electric current. **2.** Destruction of living tissue, as of hair roots, by an electric current.
e·lec·tro·lyte (ĭ-lĕk′trə-līt′) *n.* A substance that dissociates into ions in solution or when fused, thereby becoming electrically conducting.
e·lec·tro·lyt·ic (ĭ-lĕk′trə-lĭt′ĭk) *adj.* **1. a.** Of or pertaining to electrolysis. **b.** Produced by electrolysis. **2.** Of or pertaining to an electrolyte. —**e·lec′tro·lyt′i·cal·ly** *adv.*
electrolytic cell *n.* **1.** A cell containing an electrolyte through which an externally generated electric current is passed by a system of electrodes in order to produce an electrochemical reaction. **2.** A cell containing an electrolyte in which an electrochemical reaction produces an electromotive force.
e·lec·tro·lyze (ĭ-lĕk′trə-līz′) *tr.v.* **-lyzed, -lyz·ing, -lyz·es.** To decompose by electrolysis.
e·lec·tro·mag·net (ĭ-lĕk′trō-măg′nĭt) *n.* A magnet consisting essentially of a soft-iron core wound with a current-carrying coil of insulated wire, the current in which produces the magnetization of the core.
e·lec·tro·mag·net·ic (ĭ-lĕk′trō-măg-nĕt′ĭk) *adj.* Of or exhibiting electromagnetism. —**e·lec′tro·mag·net′i·cal·ly** *adv.*
electromagnetic field *n.* The field of force associated with electric charge in motion, having both electric and magnetic components and containing a definite amount of electromagnetic energy.
electromagnetic spectrum *n.* The entire range of radiation extending in frequency approximately from 10^{23} cycles per second to 0 cycles per second (or, in corresponding wavelengths, from 10^{-13} centimeter to infinity) and including, in order of decreasing frequency, cosmic-ray photons, gamma rays, x-rays, ultraviolet radiation, visible light, infrared radiation, microwaves, radio waves, heat, and electric currents.
electromagnetic unit *n.* Any of a system of units for electricity and magnetism based on a system of equations in which the permeability of free space is taken as unity and by means of which the abampere is defined as the fundamental unit of current.
electromagnetic wave *n.* A wave propagating as a periodic disturbance of the electromagnetic field and having a frequency in the electromagnetic spectrum.
e·lec·tro·mag·net·ism (ĭ-lĕk′trō-măg′nə-tĭz′əm) *n.* **1.** Magnetism arising from electric charge in motion. **2.** The physics of electricity and magnetism.
e·lec·tro·met·al·lur·gy (ĭ-lĕk′trō-mĕt′l-ûr′jē) *n.* The use of

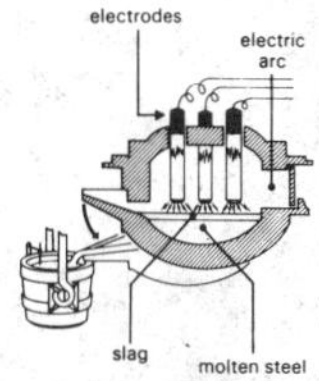

electric furnace

electric guitar

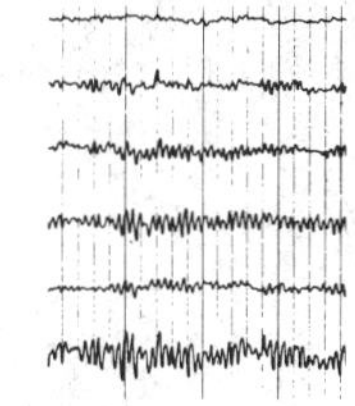
electroenceph-alogram

electromagnet

electricity to purify metals or to reduce metallic compounds to metals. —**e·lec'tro·met'al·lur'gi·cal** *adj.*

e·lec·trom·e·ter (ĭ-lĕk'trŏm'ĭ-tər, ē'lĕk-) *n.* An instrument for detecting or measuring potential differences, electric charge, or, indirectly, electric current by means of mechanical forces exerted between electrically charged bodies.

e·lec·tro·mo·tive (ĭ-lĕk'trō-mō'tĭv) *adj.* Of, pertaining to, or producing electric current.

electromotive force *n.* The energy per unit charge that is converted reversibly from chemical, mechanical, or other forms of energy into electrical energy in a conversion device such as a battery or dynamo.

e·lec·tro·my·o·gram (ē-lĕk'trō-mī'ō-grăm') *n.* A graphic recording of a muscle response as a result of electrical stimulation.

e·lec·tro·my·og·ra·phy (ĭ-lĕk'trō-mī-ŏg'rə-fē) *n.* The preparation and study of electromyograms. —**e·lec'tro·my'o·graph'ic** (-mī'ə-grăf'ĭk) *adj.* —**e·lec'tro·my'o·graph'ic·al·ly** *adv.*

e·lec·tron (ĭ-lĕk'trŏn') *n.* A subatomic particle in the lepton family having a rest mass of 9.1066 × 10^{-28} gram and a unit negative electric charge of approximately 1.602 × 10^{-19} coulomb.

e·lec·tro·neg·a·tive (ĭ-lĕk'trō-nĕg'ə-tĭv) *adj.* **1.** Having a negative electric charge. **2.** Tending to attract electrons to form a chemical bond.

electron gun *n.* An electron-emitting electrode and associated elements, esp. in a cathode-ray tube, that produce a beam of accelerated electrons.

e·lec·tron·ic (ĭ-lĕk-trŏn'ĭk, ē'lĕk-) *adj.* **1.** Of or pertaining to electrons. **2.** Of, pertaining to, based on, operated by, or otherwise involving the controlled conduction of electrons or other charge carriers, esp. in a vacuum, gas, or semiconducting material. **3.** Of or pertaining to electronics. —**e·lec'tron'i·cal·ly** *adv.*

electronic flash *n.* A strobe light.

electronic music *n.* Music produced by means of an electronic device, such as a tape recorder.

e·lec·tron·ics (ĭ-lĕk'trŏn'ĭks, ē'lĕk-) *n.* *(used with a sing. verb).* **1.** The science and technology of electronic phenomena. **2.** The commercial industry of electronic devices and systems.

electronic stylus *n.* A penlike input device that signals the computer by means of an electronic pulse and that is commonly used in conjunction with a cathode-ray tube.

electron lens *n.* Any of various devices that use an electric or a magnetic field to focus a beam of electrons.

electron micrograph *n.* A micrograph made by an electron microscope.

electron microscope *n.* Any of a class of microscopes that use electrons rather than visible light to produce magnified images, esp. of objects having dimensions smaller than the wavelengths of visible light, with linear magnification up to or exceeding a million (10^6).

electron multiplier *n.* A vacuum tube in which a single electron produces a large number of secondary electrons by collision with an anode, the process generally being repeated through a number of stages to achieve great amplification.

electron optics *n. (used with a sing. verb).* The science of the control of electron motion by electron lenses in systems or under conditions analogous to those involving or affecting visible light.

electron pair *n.* **1.** Two electrons functioning or regarded as functioning in concert, esp. two electrons shared by two atoms joined by a covalent chemical bond. **2.** The combination of an electron and a positron as produced by a high-energy photon.

electron tube *n.* A sealed enclosure, either highly evacuated or containing a controlled quantity of gas, in which electrons can be made sufficiently mobile to act as the principal carriers of current between at least one pair of electrodes, often under the control of one or more additional electrodes.

electron volt *n.* A unit of energy equal to the energy acquired by an electron falling through a potential difference of one volt, approximately 1.602 × 10^{-19} joule.

e·lec·tro·pho·rese (ĭ-lĕk'trō-fə-rēs') *tr.v.* **-resed, -res·ing, -res·es.** To subject to electrophoresis. [Back-formation < ELECTROPHORESIS.]

e·lec·tro·pho·re·sis (ĭ-lĕk'trō-fə-rē'sĭs) *n.* The motion of charged particles, esp. colloidal particles, through a relatively stationary liquid under the influence of an applied electric field provided, in general, by immersed electrodes.

e·lec·tro·pho·ret·o·gram (ĭ-lĕk'trō-fə-rē'tə-grăm') *n.* A record consisting of the separated components of a mixture produced by electrophoresis. [ELECTROPHORET(IC) + -GRAM.]

e·lec·troph·o·rus (ĭ-lĕk'trŏf'ər-əs, ē'lĕk-) *n., pl.* **-o·ri** (-ə-rī'). An apparatus for generating static electricity, consisting of a disk that is given a negative charge by friction and a metal plate that is charged by induction when in contact with the disk. [NLat. : ELECTRO- + Gk. *phoros,* bearer < *pherein,* to bear.]

e·lec·tro·plate (ĭ-lĕk'trə-plāt') *tr.v.* **-plat·ed, -plat·ing, -plates.** To coat or cover with a thin layer of metal by electrodeposition.

e·lec·tro·pos·i·tive (ĭ-lĕk'trō-pŏz'ĭ-tĭv) *adj.* **1.** Having a positive electric charge. **2.** Tending to release electrons to form a chemical bond.

e·lec·tro·scope (ĭ-lĕk'trə-skōp') *n.* An instrument used to detect the presence, sign, and in some configurations the magnitude of an electric charge by the mutual attraction or repulsion of metal foils or pith balls. —**e·lec'tro·scop'ic** (-skŏp'ĭk) *adj.*

e·lec·tro·shock (ĭ-lĕk'trō-shŏk') *n.* Shock therapy in which an electric current is passed through the brain.

e·lec·tro·stat·ic (ĭ-lĕk'trō-stăt'ĭk) *adj.* **1. a.** Of or pertaining to stationary electric charges. **b.** Produced or caused by such charges. **2.** Of or pertaining to electrostatics. —**e·lec'tro·stat'i·cal·ly** *adv.*

electrostatic generator *n.* Any of various devices, including the electrophorus, the Wimshurst machine, and esp. the Van de Graaff generator that generate high voltages by accumulating large quantities of electric charge.

electrostatic precipitation *n.* The removal of particles suspended in a gas by electrostatic charging and subsequent precipitation onto a collector in a strong electric field.

electrostatic printing *n.* A process for printing or copying in which electrostatic forces are used to form the image in powder or ink directly on the surface to be printed.

e·lec·tro·stat·ics (ĭ-lĕk'trō-stăt'ĭks) *n. (used with a sing. verb).* The physics of electrostatic phenomena.

electrostatic unit *n.* Any of a system of units for electricity and magnetism based on a system of equations in which the permittivity of empty space is defined as unity and by means of which a fundamental unit of charge is defined.

e·lec·tro·ther·a·peu·tics (ĭ-lĕk'trō-thĕr'ə-pyōō'tĭks) *n. (used with a sing. verb).* Electrotherapy.

e·lec·tro·ther·a·py (ĭ-lĕk'trō-thĕr'ə-pē) *n.* Medical therapy, such as diathermy, using electric currents.

e·lec·tro·ther·mal (ĭ-lĕk'trō-thûr'məl) *adj.* **1.** Of, pertaining to, or involving both electricity and heat. **2.** Of or pertaining to the production of heat by electricity. —**e·lec'tro·ther'mal·ly** *adv.*

e·lec·trot·o·nus (ĭ-lĕk'trŏt'ə-nəs, ē'lĕk-) *n.* The alteration in excitability and conductivity of a nerve caused by the passage of an electric current. —**e·lec'tro·ton'ic** (-trə-tŏn'ĭk) *adj.*

e·lec·tro·type (ĭ-lĕk'trə-tīp') *n.* **1.** A duplicate metal plate used in letterpress printing, made by electroplating a lead or plastic mold of the original plate. **2.** The process of making such a plate. —*tr.v.* **-typed, -typ·ing, -types.** To make an electrotype of. —**e·lec'tro·typ'er** *n.* —**e·lec'tro·typ'ic** (-trō-tĭp'ĭk) *adj.*

e·lec·tro·va·lence (ĭ-lĕk'trō-vā'ləns) also **e·lec·tro·va·len·cy** (-lən-sē) *n.* **1.** Valence characterized by the transfer of electrons from atoms of one element to atoms of another. **2.** The number of electric charges lost or gained by an atom in such a transfer. —**e·lec'tro·va'lent** *adj.*

electrovalent bond *n. Chem.* An ionic bond.

e·lec·trum (ĭ-lĕk'trəm) *n.* An alloy of silver and gold. [ME *electrum* < Lat., amber < Gk. *ēlektron.*]

e·lec·tu·ar·y (ĭ-lĕk'chōō-ĕr'ē) *n.* A drug mixed with sugar and water or honey into a pasty mass suitable for oral administration. [ME *electuarie* < LLat. *electuarium,* prob. alteration of Gk. *ekleikton* < *ekleikhein,* to lick up : *ek-,* out + *leikhein,* to lick.]

el·ee·mos·y·nar·y (ĕl'ə-mŏs'ə-nĕr'ē, ĕl'ē-ə-) *adj.* **1.** Of or pertaining to alms or the giving of alms. **2.** Dependent upon or supported by alms. **3.** Contributed as an act of charity; gratuitous. [Med. Lat. *eleemosynarius* < LLat. *eleemosyna,* alms. —see ALMS.]

el·e·gance (ĕl'ĭ-gəns) also **el·e·gan·cy** (-gən-sē) *n.* **1. a.** Refinement and grace in movement, appearance, or manners. **b.** Tasteful opulence in form, decoration, or presentation. **2 a.** Restraint and grace of style. **b.** Scientific exactness and precision. **3.** Something that is elegant.

el·e·gant (ĕl'ĭ-gənt) *adj.* **1.** Characterized by or exhibiting elegance. **2.** Excellent. [OFr. < Lat. *elegans.*] —**el'e·gant·ly** *adv.*

el·e·gi·ac (ĕl'ə-jī'ək, ĭ-lē'jē-ăk') *adj.* **1. a.** Pertaining to an elegy. **b.** Expressing sorrow; mournful. **2.** Of, pertaining to, or composed in couplets whose first line is a dactylic hexameter and second a pentameter. [LLat. *elegiacus* < Gk. *elegeiakos* < *elegeia,* elegy.] —**el'e·gi'ac** *n.* —**el'e·gi'a·cal** *adj.* —**el'e·gi'ac·al·ly** *adv.*

e·le·git (ĭ-lē'jĭt) *n. Law.* A writ of execution against a debtor by which the debtor's goods or property are delivered to the plaintiff until the debtor can settle the debt. [Lat. *elegit,* he has chosen, the first word of a phrase frequently used in the writ.]

el·e·gize (ĕl'ə-jīz') *v.* **-gized, -giz·ing, -giz·es.** —*intr.* To compose an elegy. —*tr.* To compose an elegy upon or for.

el·e·gy (ĕl'ə-jē) *n.* **1.** A poem composed in elegiac couplets. **2.** A poem or song composed esp. as a lament for one who is dead. **3.** A musical composition or poem that is melancholy or pensive in tone. [Fr. *élégie* < Lat. *elegia* < Gk. *elegeia* < *elegos,* mournful song.]

el·e·ment (ĕl'ə-mənt) *n.* **1.** A fundamental, essential, or irreducible constituent of a composite entity. **2. elements.** The

PERIODIC TABLE OF THE ELEMENTS

KEY

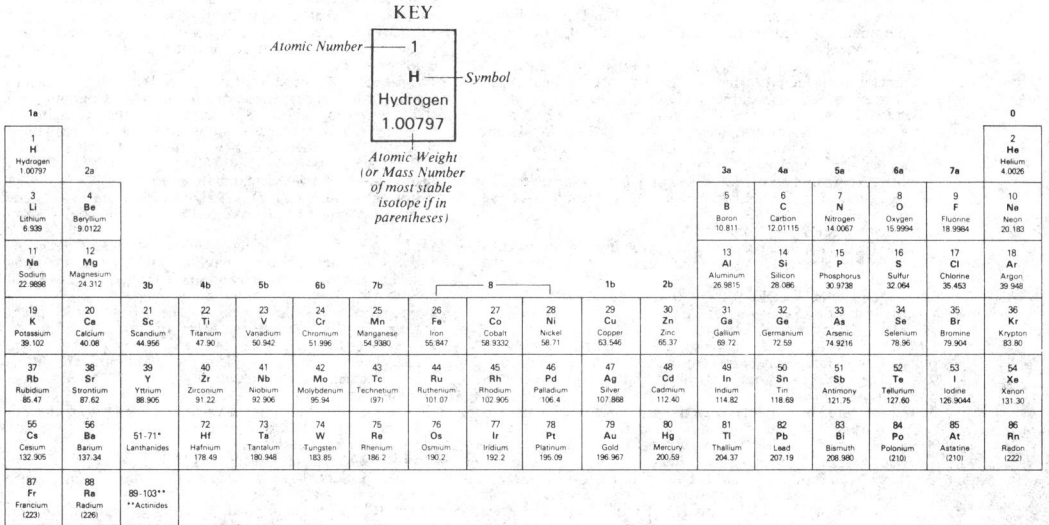

Atomic Number — 1
H — Symbol
Hydrogen
1.00797 — Atomic Weight (or Mass Number of most stable isotope if in parentheses)

1a	2a	3b	4b	5b	6b	7b	8	8	8	1b	2b	3a	4a	5a	6a	7a	0
1 **H** Hydrogen 1.00797																	2 **He** Helium 4.0026
3 **Li** Lithium 6.939	4 **Be** Beryllium 9.0122											5 **B** Boron 10.811	6 **C** Carbon 12.01115	7 **N** Nitrogen 14.0067	8 **O** Oxygen 15.9994	9 **F** Fluorine 18.9984	10 **Ne** Neon 20.183
11 **Na** Sodium 22.9898	12 **Mg** Magnesium 24.312											13 **Al** Aluminum 26.9815	14 **Si** Silicon 28.086	15 **P** Phosphorus 30.9738	16 **S** Sulfur 32.064	17 **Cl** Chlorine 35.453	18 **Ar** Argon 39.948
19 **K** Potassium 39.102	20 **Ca** Calcium 40.08	21 **Sc** Scandium 44.956	22 **Ti** Titanium 47.90	23 **V** Vanadium 50.942	24 **Cr** Chromium 51.996	25 **Mn** Manganese 54.9380	26 **Fe** Iron 55.847	27 **Co** Cobalt 58.9332	28 **Ni** Nickel 58.71	29 **Cu** Copper 63.546	30 **Zn** Zinc 65.37	31 **Ga** Gallium 69.72	32 **Ge** Germanium 72.59	33 **As** Arsenic 74.9216	34 **Se** Selenium 78.96	35 **Br** Bromine 79.904	36 **Kr** Krypton 83.80
37 **Rb** Rubidium 85.47	38 **Sr** Strontium 87.62	39 **Y** Yttrium 88.905	40 **Zr** Zirconium 91.22	41 **Nb** Niobium 92.906	42 **Mo** Molybdenum 95.94	43 **Tc** Technetium (97)	44 **Ru** Ruthenium 101.07	45 **Rh** Rhodium 102.905	46 **Pd** Palladium 106.4	47 **Ag** Silver 107.868	48 **Cd** Cadmium 112.40	49 **In** Indium 114.82	50 **Sn** Tin 118.69	51 **Sb** Antimony 121.75	52 **Te** Tellurium 127.60	53 **I** Iodine 126.9044	54 **Xe** Xenon 131.30
55 **Cs** Cesium 132.905	56 **Ba** Barium 137.34	51-71* Lanthanides	72 **Hf** Hafnium 178.49	73 **Ta** Tantalum 180.948	74 **W** Tungsten 183.85	75 **Re** Rhenium 186.2	76 **Os** Osmium 190.2	77 **Ir** Iridium 192.2	78 **Pt** Platinum 195.09	79 **Au** Gold 196.967	80 **Hg** Mercury 200.59	81 **Tl** Thallium 204.37	82 **Pb** Lead 207.19	83 **Bi** Bismuth 208.980	84 **Po** Polonium (210)	85 **At** Astatine (210)	86 **Rn** Radon (222)
87 **Fr** Francium (223)	88 **Ra** Radium (226)	89-103** **Actinides															

*Lanthanides	57 **La** Lanthanum 138.91	58 **Ce** Cerium 140.12	59 **Pr** Praseodymium 140.907	60 **Nd** Neodymium 144.24	61 **Pm** Promethium (145)	62 **Sm** Samarium 150.35	63 **Eu** Europium 151.96	64 **Gd** Gadolinium 157.25	65 **Tb** Terbium 158.924	66 **Dy** Dysprosium 162.50	67 **Ho** Holmium 164.930	68 **Er** Erbium 167.26	69 **Tm** Thulium 168.934	70 **Yb** Ytterbium 173.04	71 **Lu** Lutetium 174.97
**Actinides	89 **Ac** Actinium (227)	90 **Th** Thorium 232.038	91 **Pa** Protactinium (231)	92 **U** Uranium 238.03	93 **Np** Neptunium (237)	94 **Pu** Plutonium (244)	95 **Am** Americium (243)	96 **Cm** Curium (247)	97 **Bk** Berkelium (247)	98 **Cf** Californium (251)	99 **Es** Einsteinium (254)	100 **Fm** Fermium (257)	101 **Md** Mendelevium (256)	102 **No** Nobelium (254)	103 **Lw** Lawrencium (257)

basic assumptions or principles of a subject. **3.** *Math.* **a.** A member of a set. **b.** A point, line, or plane. **c.** A part of a geometric configuration, as an angle in a triangle. **d.** The generatrix of a geometric figure. **e.** Any of the terms in the rectangular array of terms that constitute a matrix or determinant. **4.** *Chem. & Physics.* A substance composed of atoms having an identical number of protons in each nucleus. **5.** One of four substances, earth, air, fire, or water, formerly regarded as a fundamental constituent of the universe. **6. elements.** The forces that constitute the weather, esp. severe or inclement weather. **7.** An environment naturally suited to or associated with an individual. **8. elements.** The bread and wine of the Eucharist. [ME < OFr. < Lat. *elementum.*]

el·e·men·tal (ĕl'ə-mĕn'tl) *adj.* **1.** Of, pertaining to, or being an element. **2. a.** Fundamental or essential; basic. **b.** Of or pertaining to the fundamentals; elementary. **c.** Belonging to inherently. **3.** Resembling a force of nature in power or effect. **—el'e·men'tal** *n.* **—el'e·men'tal·ly** *adv.*

el·e·men·ta·ry (ĕl'ə-mĕn'tə-rē, -trē) *adj.* **1.** Fundamental, essential, or irreducible. **2.** Of, involving, or introducing the fundamental or simplest aspects of a subject: *an elementary problem.* **3.** Of or relating to an elementary school: *the elementary grades.* **—el'e·men·ta'ri·ly** (-tĕr'ə-lē) *adv.* **—el'e·men'ta·ri·ness** *n.*

elementary particle *n.* A subatomic particle hypothesized or regarded as an irreducible constituent of matter.

elementary school *n.* **1.** The first six to eight years of a child's formal education. **2.** A school usually for the first six or eight grades.

el·e·mi (el'ə-mē) *n., pl.* **-mis.** Any of various oily resins derived from certain tropical trees, esp. *Canarium luzonicum,* of the Philippines, and used in making varnishes and inks. [Sp. *elemí* < Ar. *elemī,* var. of *allāmi,* the elemi.]

el·e·phant (ĕl'ə-fənt) *n.* Either of two very large herbivorous mammals, *Elephas maximus,* of south-central Asia, or *Loxodonta africana,* of Africa, having thick, almost hairless skin, a long, flexible, prehensile trunk, upper incisors forming long, curved tusks, and, in the African species, large, fan-shaped ears. [ME *elefaunt* < OFr. *olifant* < VLat. **olifantus* < Lat. *elephantus* < Gk. *elephas.*]

elephant folio *n.* A book or publication of the largest size, often approximately two feet in height.

el·e·phan·ti·a·sis (ĕl'ə-fən-tī'ə-sĭs) *n.* A chronic, often extreme enlargement and hardening of the cutaneous and subcutaneous tissue, esp. of the legs and the scrotum, resulting from lymphatic obstruction, and usually caused by a nematode worm, *Wuchereria bancrofti.* [Lat. < Gk.: *elephas,* elephant + *-iasis,* -iasis.]

el·e·phan·tine (ĕl'ə-făn'tēn, -tīn', ĕl'ə-fən-) *adj.* **1.** Of or pertaining to an elephant. **2 a.** Enormous in size or strength. **b.** Ponderous; heavy-footed.

elephant seal *n.* Either of two large seals, *Mirounga angustirostris* or *M. leonina,* of Pacific coastal waters of North and South America, having a trunklike proboscis.

El·eu·sin·i·an mysteries (ĕl'yo͞o-sĭn'ē-ən) *pl.n.* The ancient religious rites celebrated at Eleusis in honor of Demeter.

el·e·vate (ĕl'ə-vāt') *tr.v.* **-vat·ed, -vat·ing, -vates. 1.** To raise to a higher place or position; lift up. **2.** To increase the amplitude, intensity, or volume of. **3.** To promote to a higher rank. **4.** To raise to a higher moral, cultural, or intellectual level. **5.** To lift the spirits of; elate. [ME *elevaten* < Lat. *elevare* : *ex-,* up + *levare,* to raise.]

elephant
Asian elephant

el·e·vat·ed (ĕl'ə-vā'tĭd) *adj.* **1.** Raised above a given level. **2. a.** Morally or intellectually superior. **b.** Exalted; lofty: *elevated language.* **3.** Elated; high-spirited. *—n. Informal.* An elevated railway.

elevated railway *n.* A railway that operates on a raised structure in order to permit passage of vehicles or pedestrians beneath it.

el·e·va·tion (ĕl'ə-vā'shən) *n.* **1. a.** The act or an example of elevating. **b.** The condition of being elevated. **2.** An elevated place or position. **3.** The height to which something is elevated above a point of reference, such as the ground. **4.** Loftiness of thought or feeling. **5.** A scale drawing of the side, front, or rear of a given structure. **6.** Altitude. **7. a.** A leap, as by a dancer, in which the performer appears to be suspended. **b.** The ability of a performer to execute an elevation.

elevated railway

el·e·va·tor (ĕl'ə-vā'tər) *n.* **1. a.** A platform or enclosure raised and lowered in a vertical shaft to transport freight or people. **b.** The enclosure or platform with its operating equipment, motor, cables, and accessories. **2.** A mechanism, often with buckets or scoops attached to a conveyor, used for hoisting materials. **3.** A granary equipped with devices for hoisting and discharging grain. **4.** A movable control surface, usually attached to the horizontal stabilizer of an aircraft, and used to produce up or down motion.

e·lev·en (ĭ-lĕv'ən) *n.* **1.** The cardinal number that is next after 10 and equal to the sum of 10 + 1. **2.** Something, esp. a football team, with 11 members.[ME *elleven* < OE *endleofan.*] **—e·lev'en** *adj. & pron.*

e·lev·ens·es (ĭ-lĕv′ən-zəz) *pl.n. Chiefly Brit.* Tea or coffee, often accompanied by a snack, and taken at midmorning.
e·lev·enth (ĭ-lĕv′ənth) *n.* **1.** The ordinal number 11 in a series. **2.** One of 11 equal parts. **—e·lev′enth** *adj. & adv.*
eleventh hour *n.* The latest possible time.
el·e·von (ĕl′ə-vŏn′) *n.* An airplane control surface combining the functions of an elevator and an aileron. [ELEV(ATOR) + (AILER)ON.]
elf (ĕlf) *n., pl.* **elves** (ĕlvz). **1.** A small, often mischievous creature considered to have magical powers. **2.** A mischievous child. **3.** A dwarf. [ME < OE *ælf.*]
elf·in (ĕl′fĭn) *adj.* **1. a.** Of, pertaining to, or like an elf. **b.** Made, done, or produced by an elf. **2. a.** Small and sprightly; mischievous. **b.** Fairylike; magical. [Prob. < ME *elvene,* genitive pl. of *elf,* elf.]
elf·ish (ĕl′fĭsh) also **elv·ish** (ĕl′vĭsh) *adj.* **1.** Of or pertaining to elves. **2.** Prankish; mischievous. **—elf′ish·ly** *adv.* **—elf′ish·ness** *n.*
elf·lock (ĕlf′lŏk′) *n.* A tangled lock of hair.
el·hi (ĕl′hī′) *adj.* Of, pertaining to, involving, or designed for use in elementary school and high school. [EL(EMENTARY) + HI(GH SCHOOL).]
E·li (ē′lī) *n.* In the Old Testament, a judge of Israel who was the teacher of Samuel. [Heb. *'Ēlī*]
E·li·as (ĭ-lī′əs) *n.* Elijah. [Gk. < Heb. *Ēliyyāh.*]
e·lic·it (ĭ-lĭs′ĭt) *tr.v.* **-it·ed, -it·ing, -its. 1.** To bring out; evoke. **2.** To call forth (a reaction, for example). **3.** To educe. [Lat. *elicere, elicit-* : *ex-,* out + *lacere,* to entice.] **—e·lic′i·ta′tion** *n.* **—e·lic′i·tor** *n.*
e·lide (ĭ-līd′) *tr.v.* **e·lid·ed, e·lid·ing, e·lides. 1.** To omit or slur over (a syllable, for example) in pronunciation. **2. a.** To eliminate or leave out. **b.** To suppress. [Lat. *elidere,* to strike out : *ex-,* out + *laedere,* to strike.]
el·i·gi·ble (ĕl′ĭ-jə-bəl) *adj.* **1.** Qualified, as for an office or position. **2.** Desirable and worthy of choice, esp. for marriage. [ME < OFr. < VLat. **eligibilis* < Lat. *eligere,* to select. —see ELECT.] **—el′i·gi·bil′i·ty** *n.* **—el′i·gi·ble** *n.* **—el′i·gi·bly** *adv.*
E·li·jah (ĭ-lī′jə) *n.* A Hebrew prophet of the 9th century B.C. [Heb. *Ēliyyāh* : *Ēl,* Lord + *Yāh,* God.
e·lim·i·nate (ĭ-lĭm′ə-nāt′) *tr.v.* **-nat·ed, -nat·ing, -nates. 1.** To get rid of; remove: *eliminated luxuries from the budget.* **2. a.** To leave out or omit from consideration; reject. **b.** To remove from consideration by defeating, as in a contest. **3.** To remove by combining equations. **4.** *Physiol.* To excrete as waste. [Lat. *eliminare, eliminat-,* to banish : *ex-,* out + *limen,* threshold.] **—e·lim′i·na′tion** *n.* **—e·lim′i·na′tive, e·lim′i·na·to′ry** (-nə-tôr′ē, -tōr′ē) *adj.* **—e·lim′i·na′tor** *n.*
E·li·sha (ĭ-lī′shə) *n.* A Hebrew prophet of the 9th century B.C. [Heb. *Ĕlīshā* : *Ēl,* God + *yesha',* salvation.]
e·li·sion (ĭ-lĭzh′ən) *n.* **1.** The action of eliding. **2.** The omission of an unstressed vowel or syllable, as in scanning a verse. **3.** An omission. [Lat. *elisio, elision-* < *elidere,* to strike out. —see ELIDE.]
e·lite or **é·lite** (ĭ-lēt′, ā-lēt′) *n.* **1. a.** The best or most skilled members of a given social group. **b.** A small and privileged group. **2.** A size of type on a typewriter, equal to 12 characters per inch. [Fr. *élite* < OFr. *eslite* < fem. p.part. of *eslire,* to choose < Lat. *eligere.* —see ELECT.] **—e·lite′** *adj.*
e·lit·ism or **é·lit·ism** (ĭ-lē′tĭz′əm, ā-lē-) *n.* **1. a.** Belief in rule by an elite. **b.** Rule or domination by an elite. **2.** A sense of being part of an elite. **—e·lit′ist** *adj. & n.*
e·lix·ir (ĭ-lĭk′sər) *n.* **1.** A sweetened aromatic solution of alcohol and water, serving as a vehicle for medicine. **2.** A medicine believed to cure all ills. **3.** The philosophers' stone. **4.** The quintessence or underlying principle of something. [ME, a substance of transmutative properties < Med. Lat. < Ar. *al-iksīr* : *al,* the + *iksīr,* elixir, prob. < Gk. *xērion,* desiccative powder < *xēros,* dry.]
E·liz·a·be·than (ĭ-lĭz′ə-bē′thən, -bĕth′ən) *adj.* Of, pertaining to, or characteristic of the reign of Elizabeth I of England.
Elizabethan sonnet *n.* A Shakespearean sonnet.
elk (ĕlk) *n., pl.* **elks** or **elk. 1.** The wapiti. **2.** A large deer, *Alces alces,* of northern regions, having large, palmate antlers. **3.** A light, pliant leather of horsehide or calfskin, tanned and finished to resemble elk hide. [ME, prob. < OE *eolh.*]
elk·hound (ĕlk′hound′) *n.* A hunting dog of a breed developed in Scandinavia, having a grayish coat and a tail curled up over the back.
ell[1] (ĕl) *n.* A wing of a building at right angles to the main structure. [From its resemblance to the shape of the capital letter L.]
ell[2] (ĕl) *n.* An English linear measure equal to 114 centimeters or 45 inches. [ME < OE *eln,* the length from elbow to the middle finger's tip.]
ell[3] (ĕl) *n.* Variant of **el**[1].
el·lag·ic acid (ĭ-lăj′ĭk) *n.* A yellow crystalline compound, $C_{14}H_6O_8$, that is obtained from tannins. [Fr. *ellagique* < *ellag,* backward spelling of *galle,* plant gall < Lat. *galla.*]
el·lipse (ĭ-lĭps′) *n.* **1.** A plane curve, esp.: **a.** A conic section taken neither parallel to an element nor parallel to the axis of the intersected cone. **b.** The locus of points the sum of the distances of each of which from two fixed points is the same constant. **2.** Ellipsis. [Gk. *elleipsis,* ellipse, ellipsis.]
el·lip·sis (ĭ-lĭp′sĭs) *n., pl.* **-ses** (-sēz′). **1. a.** The omission of a word or phrase necessary for a complete syntactical construction but not necessary for understanding. **b.** An example of ellipsis. **2.** A mark or series of marks (. . . or ***, for example) used in writing or printing to indicate an omission, esp. of letters or words. [Lat. *ellipsis* < Gk. *elleipsis* < *elleipein,* to fall short : *en-,* in + *leipein,* to leave.]
el·lip·soid (ĭ-lĭp′soid′) *n.* A geometric surface whose plane sections are all either ellipses or circles. **—el·lip′soid′, el·lip·soid′al** (-soid′l) *adj.*
el·lip·tic (ĭ-lĭp′tĭk) or **el·lip·ti·cal** (-tĭ-kəl) *adj.* **1.** Of, pertaining to, or having the shape of an ellipse. **2.** Containing or characterized by ellipsis. **3. a.** Of or pertaining to economy of expression. **b.** Marked by an obscurity of style or expression. [Gk. *elleiptikos,* defective < *elleipein,* to fall short. —see ELLIPSIS.] **—el·lip′ti·cal·ly** *adv.*
elliptic geometry *n.* Riemannian geometry.
el·lip·tic·i·ty (ĭ-lĭp′-tĭs′ĭ-tē) *n.* **1.** Deviation from perfect circular or spherical form toward elliptic or ellipsoidal form. **2.** The degree of ellipticity.
elm (ĕlm) *n.* **1.** Any of various deciduous trees of the genus *Ulmus,* characteristically having arching or curving branches and widely planted as shade trees. **2.** The wood of an elm. [ME < OE.]
el·o·cu·tion (ĕl′ə-kyōō′shən) *n.* **1.** The art of public speaking, emphasizing gesture, vocal production, and delivery. **2.** A style or manner, esp. of public speaking. [ME *elocucion* < Lat. *elocutio, elocution-* < *eloqui,* to speak out : *ex-,* out + *loqui,* to speak.] **—el′o·cu′tion·ar′y** (-shə-nĕr′ē) *adj.* **—el′o·cu′tion·ist** *n.*
e·lo·de·a (ĭ-lō′dē-ə) *n.* Any of various small aquatic herbs of the genus *Elodea.* [NLat. *Elodea,* genus name < Gk. *helōdēs,* marshy < *helos,* marsh.]
E·lo·him (ĕ-lō′hĭm, ĕl′ō-hēm′) *n.* A Hebrew name for God in the Old Testament. [Heb. *'Elōhim,* pl. of *'Elōah,* God.] **—E·lo′hism** *n.*
e·loign (ĭ-loin′) *tr.v.* **e·loigned, e·loign·ing, e·loigns.** *Archaic.* **1.** To remove or carry away to a distance, esp. to conceal. **2.** To remove oneself; abscond. [ME *elongen* < OFr. *esloigner* < LLat. *elongare* : *ex-,* away + *longe,* distant < *longus,* long.]
e·lon·gate (ĭ-lông′gāt′, ĭ-lŏng′-) *tr. & intr.v.* **-gat·ed, -gat·ing, -gates.** To make or grow longer. *—adj.* **1.** Lengthened; extended. **2.** Slender. [LLat. *elongare, elongat-* : *ex-,* out + *longus,* long.]
e·lon·ga·tion (ĭ-lông′-gā′shən, ĭ-lŏng′-, ē′lông-, ē′lŏng-) *n.* **1.** The act of elongating or the condition of being elongated. **2.** Something that elongates; extension.
e·lope (ĭ-lōp′) *intr.v.* **e·loped, e·lop·ing, e·lopes. 1.** To run away with a lover, esp. with the intention of getting married. **2.** To run away; abscond. [AN *aloper,* to run away from one's husband with a lover.] **—e·lope′ment** *n.* **—e·lop′er** *n.*
el·o·quence (ĕl′ə-kwəns) *n.* **1.** Persuasive and fluent discourse. **2.** The ability or power to persuade with discourse.
el·o·quent (ĕl′ə-kwənt) *adj.* **1.** Persuasive, fluent, and graceful in discourse. **2.** Vividly or movingly expressive: *a look eloquent with compassion.* [ME < OFr. < Lat. *eloquens,* pr.part. of *eloqui,* to speak out. —see ELOCUTION.] **—el′o·quent·ly** *adv.* **—el′o·quent·ness** *n.*
else (ĕls) *adj.* **1.** Other; different: *somebody else.* **2.** Additional; more: *Would you like anything else? —adv.* **1.** In a different time, place, or manner; differently: *How else could it be done?* **2.** If not; otherwise: *Be careful, or else you will make a mistake.* [ME *elles* < OE.]

Usage: *Else* is often used redundantly in combination with prepositions such as *but, except,* and *besides: No one else but Sam saw the accident* (omit *else*). • When a pronoun is followed by *else,* the possessive form is generally written thus: *someone else's* (not *someone's else*). Both *who else's* and *whose else* are in use, but not *whose else's: Who else's book could it have been? Whose else could it have been?*

else·where (ĕls′hwâr′, -wâr′) *adv.* To or in a different or other place.
el·u·ant (ĕl′yōō-ənt) *n.* A substance used as a solvent in the process of elution. [< Lat. *eluere,* to wash out. —see ELUTE.]
e·lu·ci·date (ĭ-lōō′sĭ-dāt′) *v.* **-dat·ed, -dat·ing, -dates.** *—tr.* To make clear or plain; clarify. *—intr.* To give a clarification. [LLat. *elucidare, elucidat-,* : *ex-* (intensive) + *lucidus,* bright.] **—e·lu′ci·da′tion** *n.* **—e·lu′ci·da′tive** *adj.* **—e·lu′ci·da′tor** *n.*
e·lude (ĭ-lōōd′) *tr.v.* **e·lud·ed, e·lud·ing, e·ludes. 1.** To evade or escape from, as by daring or artifice: *elude capture.* **2.** To escape the understanding or grasp of: *a memory that eluded him.* [Lat. *eludere* : *ex-,* away + *ludere,* to play < *ludus,* play.]
E·lul (ĕ-lōōl′, ĕl′ōōl) *n.* The 12th month of the year of the Hebrew calendar. [Heb. *'Elul* < Akkadian *elūlu,* harvest time.]
e·lu·sive (ĭ-lōō′sĭv, -zĭv) *adj.* **1.** Tending to elude perception or comprehension: *an elusive theory.* **2.** Difficult to define or describe: *an elusive charm.* [< Lat. *eludere, elus-,* to elude.] **—e·lu′sive·ly** *adv.* **—e·lu′sive·ness** *n.*
e·lute (ĭ-lōōt) *tr.v.* **e·lut·ed, e·lut·ing, e·lutes.** To extract one material from another, usually by means of a solvent. [< Lat. *elutus,* p.part. of *eluere,* to wash out : *ex-,* out + *lavere,* to wash.] **—e·lu′tion** *n.*
e·lu·tri·ate (ĭ-lōō′trē-āt′) *tr.v.* **-at·ed, -at·ing, -ates.** To purify,

elk

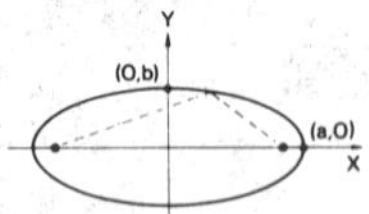

ellipse
The equation of the ellipse shown is

$$\frac{x^2}{a^2} + \frac{y^2}{b^2} = 1$$

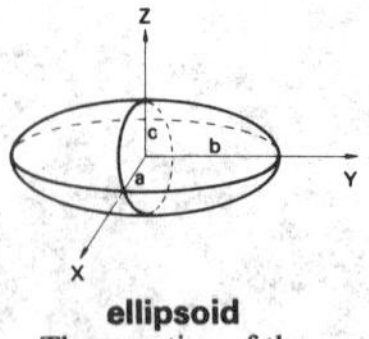

ellipsoid
The equation of the ellipsoid shown is

$$\frac{x^2}{a^2} + \frac{y^2}{b^2} + \frac{z^2}{c^2} = 1$$

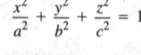

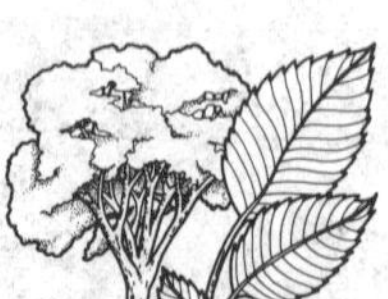
elm

separate, or remove by washing, decanting, and settling. [Lat. *elutriare, elutriat-* < *eluere,* to wash out. —see ELUVIUM.] **—e·lu′tri·a′tion** *n.*

e·lu·vi·a·tion (ĭ-lo͞o′vē-ā′shən) *n.* Internal movement of soil from place to place when rainfall exceeds evaporation. [ELUVI(UM) + -ATION.]

e·lu·vi·um (ĭ-lo͞o′vē-əm) *n.* Residual deposits of soil, dust, and rock particles produced by the action of the wind. [NLat. < Lat. *eluere,* to wash out : *ex-,* out + *lavere,* to wash.] **—e·lu′vi·al** *adj.*

el·ver (ĕl′vər) *n.* A young or immature eel. [Alteration of *eelfare,* the passage of young eels up a river.]

elves (ĕlvz) *n.* Plural of **elf.**

elv·ish (ĕl′vĭsh) *adj.* Variant of **elfish.**

E·ly·sian (ĭ-lĭzh′ən) *adj.* **1.** Pertaining to or suggestive of Elysium. **2.** Blissful; delightful.

Elysian Fields *pl.n.* Elysium.

E·ly·si·um (ĭ-lĭz′ē-əm, ĭ-lĭzh′-) *n.* **1.** *Gk. Myth.* The abode of the blessed after death. **2.** A place or condition of ideal happiness. [Lat. < Gk. *Ēlusion (pedion),* Elysian (fields).]

el·y·tron (ĕl′ə-trŏn′) *n., pl.* **-tra** (-trə). One of the leathery or chitinous forewings of a beetle or related insect, serving to encase the thin, membranous hind wings used in flight. [NLat. < Gk. *elutron,* sheath.] **—el′y·troid′** *adj.*

em (ĕm) *n.* **1.** The letter *m.* **2.** *Printing.* The square of the body size of any type, used as a unit of measure, esp. of a pica M.

′em (əm) *pron. Informal.* Them. [ME *hem* < OE *heom,* dative and accusative pl. of *hē,* he.]

em-[1] *pref.* Variant of **en-**[1]. Used before *b, m,* and *p.*

em-[2] *pref.* Variant of **en-**[2]. Used before *b, m,* and *p.*

e·ma·ci·ate (ĭ-mā′shē-āt′) *intr. & tr.v.* **-at·ed, -at·ing, -ates.** To become or make extremely thin, esp. as a result of starvation. [Lat. *emaciare, emaciat-* : *ex-* (intensive) + *maciare,* to make thin < *macer,* thin.] **—e·ma′ci·a′tion** *n.*

em·a·nate (ĕm′ə-nāt′) *intr. & tr.v.* **-nat·ed, -nat·ing, -nates.** To come or send forth, as from a source. [Lat. *emanare, emanat-,* flow out : *ex-,* out + *manare,* to flow.] **—em′a·na′tive** *adj.*

em·a·na·tion (ĕm′ə-nā′shən) *n.* **1.** An act or instance of emanating. **2. a.** Something that emanates or issues from a source; effluence. **b.** *Chem.* A gaseous product of radioactive disintegration.

e·man·ci·pate (ĭ-măn′sə-pāt′) *tr.v.* **-pat·ed, -pat·ing, -pates. 1.** To free from oppression, bondage, or restraint; liberate. **2.** *Law.* To release (a child) from the control of parents or guardian. [Lat. *emancipare, emancipat-* : *ex-,* out of, + *mancipium,* ownership < *manceps,* purchaser.] **—e·man′ci·pa′tive** *adj.* **—e·man′ci·pa′tor** *n.*

e·man·ci·pa·tion (ĭ-măn′sə-pā′shən) *n.* **1.** The act of emancipating. **2.** The condition of being emancipated.

Emancipation Proclamation *n.* A proclamation issued by President Abraham Lincoln, effective January 1, 1863, freeing all slaves in territory still at war with the Union.

e·mar·gi·nate (ĭ-mär′jə-nĭt, -nāt′) *adj.* With a notched tip, as a leaf. [Lat. *emarginare, emarginat-,* to take the edge away : *ex-,* away + *margo,* margin.] **—e·mar′gi·na′tion** (-nā′shən) *n.*

e·mas·cu·late (ĭ-măs′kyə-lāt′) *tr.v.* **-lat·ed, -lat·ing, -lates. 1.** To castrate. **2.** To deprive of strength or vigor; make weak. [Lat. *emasculare, emasculat-* : *ex-,* away + *masculus,* manly.] **—e·mas′cu·late′** (-lĭt, -lāt′) *adj.* **—e·mas′cu·la′tion** *n.* **—e·mas′cu·la′tive, e·mas′cu·la·to′ry** (-lə-tôr′ē, -tōr′ē) *adj.* **—e·mas′cu·la′tor** *n.*

em·balm (ĕm-bäm′) *tr.v.* **-balmed, -balm·ing, -balms. 1.** To prevent the decay of (a corpse) by treatment with preservatives. **2.** To preserve the memory of. **3.** To impart fragrance to. [ME *embaumen* < OFr. *embasmer* : *en-,* in (< Lat. *in-*) + *basme,* balm. —see BALM.] **—em·balm′er** *n.* **—em·balm′ment** *n.*

em·bank (ĕm-băngk′) *tr.v.* **-banked, -bank·ing, -banks.** To confine, support, or protect with an embankment.

em·bank·ment (ĕm-băngk′mənt) *n.* **1.** A mound of earth or stone built to hold back water or to support a roadway. **2.** The act of embanking.

em·bar·go (ĕm-bär′gō) *n., pl.* **-goes. 1.** A government order prohibiting the movement of merchant ships into or out of its ports. **2.** A suspension of trade, esp. in a particular commodity. **3.** A prohibition. *—tr.v.* **-goed, -go·ing, -goes.** To impose an embargo upon. [Sp. < *embargar,* to impede, of Lat. orig.]

em·bark (ĕm-bärk′) *v.* **-barked, -bark·ing, -barks.** *—tr.* **1.** To cause to board a vessel or aircraft. **2.** To enlist or invest in an enterprise. *—intr.* **1.** To go aboard a vessel, esp. at the start of a journey. **2.** To set out on a venture; commence. [OFr. *embarquer* < LLat. *imbarcare* : Lat. *in-,* in + *barca,* boat.] **—em′bar·ka′tion, em·bark′ment** *n.*

em·bar·rass (ĕm-băr′əs) *tr.v.* **-rassed, -rass·ing, -rass·es. 1.** To cause to feel self-conscious or ill at ease; disconcert. **2.** To involve in or hamper with financial difficulties. **3. a.** To beset with difficulties. **b.** To hinder; impede. **4.** To complicate. [Fr. *embarrasser,* to impede < Sp. *embarazar* < Ital. *imbarazzare,* of Lat. orig.] **—em·bar′rass·ing·ly** *adv.*

em·bar·rass·ment (ĕm-băr′əs-mənt) *n.* **1.** The state of being embarrassed. **2.** The act or an instance of embarrassing. **3.** Something that embarrasses. **4.** An overabundance: *an embarrassment of riches.*

em·bas·sage (ĕm′bə-sĭj) *n. Archaic.* Embassy. [ME *ambassage,* the function of a messenger, perh. < OFr. *ambassee,* vassal < Lat. *ambactia,* ult. of Celt. orig.]

em·bas·sy (ĕm′bə-sē) *n., pl.* **-sies. 1.** The position, function, or assignment of an ambassador. **2.** A mission to a foreign government headed by an ambassador. **3.** An ambassador and his staff. **4.** The official headquarters of an ambassador and his staff. [OFr. *ambassee.* —see EMBASSAGE.]

em·bat·tle (ĕm-băt′l) *tr.v.* **-tled, -tling, -tles. 1.** To prepare or array for battle. **2.** To prepare to struggle or resist. **3.** To furnish with battlements for defense. [ME *embatailen* < OFr. *embataillier* : *en-,* in < Lat. *in-,* + *batailler,* to battle < *bataille,* battle, battlement. —see BATTLE.]

em·bat·tle·ment (ĕm-băt′l-mənt, ĭm-) *n.* A battlement.

em·bay (ĕm-bā′) *tr.v.* **-bayed, -bay·ing, -bays. 1.** To put, shelter, or detain in a bay. **2.** To enclose in or as if in a bay.

em·bay·ment (ĕm-bā′mənt) *n.* **1.** A bay or baylike shape. **2.** The formation of a bay.

em·bed (ĕm-bĕd′) *v.* **-bed·ded, -bed·ding, -beds.** *—tr.* **1. a.** To fix firmly in a surrounding mass. **b.** To enclose in a matrix. **2.** To enclose snugly or firmly. **3.** To make an integral part of. *—intr.* To become embedded. **—em·bed′ment** *n.*

em·bel·lish (ĕm-bĕl′ĭsh) *tr.v.* **-lished, -lish·ing, -lish·es. 1.** To make beautiful, as by ornamentation; adorn. **2.** To add fanciful or ornamental details to: *embellish a story with anecdotes about famous people.* [ME *embelishen* < OFr. *embellir, embelliss-* : *en* (causative < Lat. *in-,* in) + *bel,* beautiful (< Lat. *bellus*).] **—em·bel′lish·er** *n.*

em·bel·lish·ment (ĕm-bĕl′ĭsh-mənt) *n.* **1.** An act of embellishing or the condition of being embellished. **2.** Something that embellishes. **3.** *Mus.* A note that embellishes a melody.

em·ber (ĕm′bər) *n.* **1.** A small piece of live coal or wood, as in a dying fire. **2. embers.** The smoldering coal or ash of a dying fire. [ME *embre* < OE *ǣmerge.*]

Ember day *n.* A day reserved for prayer and fasting by some Christian churches, observed on the Wednesday, Friday, and Saturday after the first Sunday of Lent, after Whitsunday, after September 14, and after December 13. [ME *Ymber Dayes* < OE *Ymbrendagas* : *ymbryne,* revolution of time (*ymbe,* around + *ryne,* running) + *dæg,* day.]

em·bez·zle (ĕm-bĕz′əl) *tr.v.* **-zled, -zling, -zles.** To take (money, for example) for one's own use in violation of a trust. [ME *embesilen* < AN *enbesiler* : OFr. *en-* (intensive) + OFr. *besillier,* to ravage.] **—em·bez′zle·ment** *n.* **—em·bez′zler** *n.*

em·bit·ter (ĕm-bĭt′ər) *tr.v.* **-tered, -ter·ing, -ters. 1.** To make bitter in flavor. **2.** To arouse bitter feelings in. **—em·bit′ter·ment** *n.*

em·blaze[1] (ĕm-blāz′) *tr.v.* **-blazed, -blaz·ing, -blaz·es. 1.** To set on fire. **2.** To cause to glow; light up.

em·blaze[2] (ĕm-blāz′) *tr.v.* **-blazed, -blaz·ing, -blaz·es.** *Archaic.* To emblazon.

em·bla·zon (ĕm-blā′zən) *tr.v.* **-zoned, -zon·ing, -zons. 1.** To ornament richly, esp. with heraldic devices. **2.** To make resplendent with brilliant colors. **3.** To make illustrious; celebrate. **—em·bla′zon·er** *n.* **—em·bla′zon·ment** *n.* **—em·bla·zon·ry** *n.*

em·blem (ĕm′bləm) *n.* **1.** An object or representation that functions as a symbol. **2.** A distinctive badge, design, or device. **3.** An allegorical picture usually inscribed with a verse or motto presenting a moral lesson. [ME, pictorial fable < Lat. *emblema,* raised ornament < Gk. *emblēma* < *emballein,* to insert : *en-,* in + *ballein,* to throw.]

em·blem·at·ic (ĕm′blə-măt′ĭk) or **em·blem·at·i·cal** (-ĭ-kəl) *adj.* Of, relating to, or serving as an emblem; symbolic. **—em′blem·at′i·cal·ly** *adv.*

em·blem·a·tize (ĕm-blĕm′ə-tīz′) also **em·blem·ize** (ĕm′blə-mīz′) *tr.v.* **-tized, -tiz·ing, -tiz·es** also **-ized, -iz·ing, -iz·es.** To represent with or as if with an emblem; symbolize.

em·ble·ments (ĕm′blə-mənts) *pl.n. Law.* The crops or products of the land legally belonging to a tenant. [ME *emblaiment* < OFr. *emblaement* < *emblaer,* to sow with grain < Med. Lat. *imbladare* : Lat. *in-,* in + *bladum,* grain.]

em·bod·i·ment (ĕm-bŏd′ē-mənt, ĭm-) *n.* **1.** The act of embodying or the condition of being embodied. **2.** One that embodies something: *considered him the embodiment of virtue.*

em·bod·y (ĕm-bŏd′ē) *tr.v.* **-bod·ied, -bod·y·ing, -bod·ies. 1.** To invest with or as if with bodily form. **2. a.** To represent in concrete form. **b.** To personify: *young men and women who embodied the ideals of a new era.* **3.** To make part of a system or whole.

em·bold·en (ĕm-bōl′dən) *tr.v.* **-ened, -en·ing, -ens.** To foster boldness in; encourage.

em·bo·lec·to·my (ĕm′bə-lĕk′tə-mē) *n., pl.* **-mies.** The removal of an embolus. [EMBOL(US) + -ECTOMY.]

em·bo·li (ĕm′bə-lī′) *n.* Plural of **embolus.**

em·bol·ic (ĕm-bŏl′ĭk) *adj.* Of or relating to an embolus or an embolism.

em·bo·lism (ĕm′bə-lĭz′əm) *n.* Obstruction or occlusion of a blood vessel by an embolus. [ME *embolisme,* insertion of one or more days in a calendar < LLat. *embolismus* < Gk.

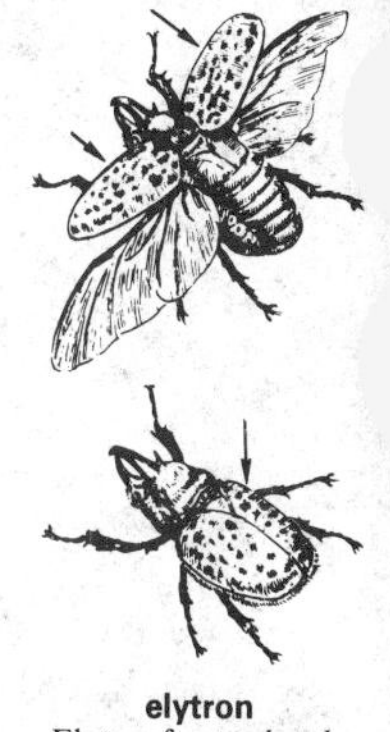

elytron
Elytra of a stag beetle
Above: Open
Below: Closed

emarginate
Emarginate leaf

embankment

embolismos < *emballein,* to insert. —see EMBLEM.] **—em′bo·lis′mic** *adj.*

em·bo·lus (ĕm′bə-ləs) *n., pl.* **-li** (-lī′). An air bubble, detached clot, mass of bacteria, or other foreign body that occludes a blood vessel. [NLat. < Lat., pump's piston < Gk. *embolos,* stopper < *emballein,* to insert. —see EMBLEM.]

em·bo·ly (ĕm′bə-lē) *n.* Development of a gastrula from a blastula by invagination. [Gk. *embolē,* insertion < *emballein,* to insert. —see EMBLEM.]

em·bon·point (äN′-bôN-pwăN′) *n.* Plumpness. [Fr. < OFr. < *en bon point,* in good condition.]

em·bos·om (ĕm-bo͝oz′əm, -bo͞o′zəm) *tr.v.* **-omed, -om·ing, -oms. 1.** *Archaic.* To clasp to or hold in the bosom. **2.** To envelop or enclose protectively; shelter.

em·boss (ĕm-bôs′, -bŏs′) *tr.v.* **-bossed, -boss·ing, -boss·es. 1.** To mold or carve in relief. **2.** To decorate with or as if with a raised design; raise the surface of in relief. **3.** To ornament lavishly. [ME *embosen* < OFr. *embocer* : *en-,* in (< Lat. *in-*) + *boce,* knob.] **—em·boss′er** *n.*

em·boss·ment (ĕm-bôs′mənt, -bŏs′-) *n.* The distance between the nondeformed part of a document surface and a specified point on a printed character in optical character recognition.

em·bou·chure (äm′bo͞o-sho͝or′) *n.* **1.** The mouth of a river. **2. a.** The mouthpiece of a wind instrument. **b.** The manner in which the lips and tongue are applied to such a mouthpiece. [Fr. < OFr. *emboucher,* to occlude : *en-,* in (< Lat. *in-*) + *bouche,* mouth < Lat. *bucca,* cheek.]

em·bowed (ĕm-bōd′) *adj.* **1.** Bent or curved like a bow. **2.** *Archit.* **a.** Arched. **b.** Protruding in an outward curve so as to form a recess.

em·bow·el (ĕm-bou′əl) *tr.v.* **-eled, -el·ing, -els** or **-elled, -el·ling, -els. 1.** To disembowel. **2.** *Obs.* To bury deeply.

em·bow·er (ĕm-bou′ər) *tr.v.* **-ered, -er·ing, -ers.** To enclose in or as if in a bower.

em·brace (ĕm-brās′) *v.* **-braced, -brac·ing, -brac·es.** —*tr.* **1.** To clasp or hold to one with the arms, usually as a display of affection. **2. a.** To encircle or surround. **b.** To twine around. **3.** To include, comprise, or contain; encompass. **4.** To take up willingly or eagerly: *embrace a cause.* **5.** To avail oneself of: *embrace an opportunity.* —*intr.* To join in an embrace. —*n.* **1.** An act of embracing; hug. **2.** An enclosure or encirclement. **3.** Eager acceptance. [ME *embracen* < OFr. *embracer* : *en-,* in (< Lat. *in-*) + *brace,* arms < Lat. *bracchium,* arm < Gk. *brakhiōn.*] **—em·brace′ment** *n.* **—em·brac′er** *n.*

em·brac·er (ĕm-brā′sər) *n. Law.* One guilty of attempting to influence a court illegally. [ME *embracer* < *embracen,* to influence a jury by illegal means. —see EMBRACE.]

em·brac·er·y (ĕm-brā′sə-rē) *n., pl.* **-ies.** An attempt to corrupt a jury, as with bribery. [ME *embracerie* < *embracen,* to influence a jury by illegal means, to embrace.]

em·branch·ment (ĕm-brănch′mənt) *n.* **1.** A branching out, as of a mountain range or river. **2.** A subdivision; ramification.

em·bran·gle (ĕm-brăng′gəl) *tr.v.* **-gled, -gling, -gles.** To entangle; embroil. [EN-[1] + dial. *brangle,* to wrangle.] **—em·bran′gle·ment** *n.*

em·bra·sure (ĕm-brā′zhər) *n.* **1.** *Archit.* An opening in a wall for a door or window. **2.** A flared opening for a gun in a wall or parapet. [Fr. < *embraser,* to widen an opening.]

em·bro·cate (ĕm′brə-kāt′) *tr.v.* **-cat·ed, -cat·ing, -cates.** To moisten and rub with a liniment or lotion. [Med. Lat. *embrocare, embrocat-* < LLat. *embrocha,* lotion < Gk. *embrokhē* < *embrekhein,* to foment : *en-,* in + *brekhein,* to wet.]

em·bro·ca·tion (ĕm′brə-kā′shən) *n.* A liniment.

em·broi·der (ĕm-broi′dər) *v.* **-dered, -der·ing, -ders.** —*tr.* **1.** To ornament with needlework. **2.** To create by means of needlework. **3.** To add embellishment to. —*intr.* **1.** To make embroidery. **2.** To supply embellishments. [ME *embrouderen* < OFr. *embroder* : *en-,* in (< Lat. *in-*) + *broder,* to embroider, of Germanic orig.] **—em·broi′der·er** *n.*

embroidery
17th-century Spanish

em·broi·der·y (ĕm-broi′də-rē) *n., pl.* **-ies. 1.** The art or act of embroidering. **2.** Ornamentation of fabric with needlework. **3.** A piece of embroidered fabric. **4.** Embellishment with fanciful details.

em·broil (ĕm-broil′) *tr.v.* **-broiled, -broil·ing, -broils. 1.** To involve in argument, contention, or hostile actions: *actions that embroiled their department with the administration.* **2.** To throw into confusion or disorder; entangle. [Fr. *embrouiller* : *en-,* in (< Lat. *in-*) + *brouiller,* to confuse, of Germanic orig.] **—em·broil′ment** *n.*

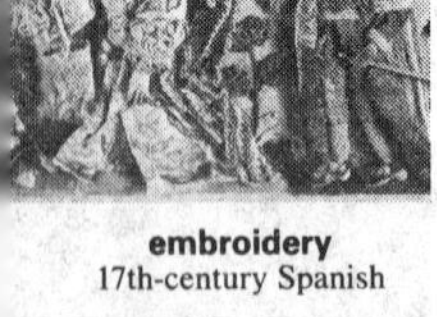

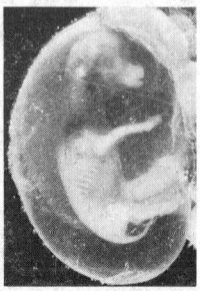

embryo
Cow embryo

em·brown (ĕm-broun′) *tr.v.* **-browned, -brown·ing, -browns. 1.** To make brown or dusky. **2.** To darken.

em·brue (ĕm-bro͞o′) *v.* Variant of **imbrue.**

em·bry·ec·to·my (ĕm′brē-ĕk′tə-mē) *n., pl.* **-mies.** The surgical removal of an extrauterine embryo.

em·bry·o (ĕm′brē-ō′) *n., pl.* **-os. 1.** *Biol.* **a.** An organism in its early stages of development, esp. before it has reached a distinctively recognizable form. **b.** Such an organism at any time before full development, birth, or hatching. **2. a.** The fertilized egg of a vertebrate animal. **b.** In humans, the prefetal product of conception up to the beginning of the third month of pregnancy. **3.** *Bot.* The minute, rudimentary plant contained within a seed or archegonium. **4.** A rudimentary or beginning stage. [Med. Lat. < Gk. *embruon* : *en-,* in + *bruein,* to grow.]

em·bry·o·gen·e·sis (ĕm′brē-ō-jĕn′ə-sĭs) also **em·bry·og·e·ny** (-ŏj′ə-nē) *n.* The development and growth of an embryo. **—em′bry·o·ge·net′ic** (-ō-jə-nĕt′ĭk) *adj.*

em·bry·ol·o·gy (ĕm′brē-ŏl′ə-jē) *n.* The science dealing with the formation, early growth, and development of living organisms. **—em′bry·o·log′ic** (-ə-lŏj′ĭk), **em′bry·o·log′i·cal** *adj.* **—em′bry·o·log′i·cal·ly** *adv.* **—em′bry·ol′o·gist** *n.*

em·bry·on·ic (ĕm′brē-ŏn′ĭk) also **em·bry·on·al** (ĕm′-brē-ə-nəl) *adj.* **1.** Of, pertaining to, or in the state of being an embryo. **2.** Rudimentary; incipient. **—em′bry·on′ic·al·ly** *adv.*

embryonic layer *n.* The germ layer.

em·bry·op·a·thy (ĕm′brē-ŏp′ə-thē) *n., pl.* **-thies.** Abnormal development of an embryo.

embryo sac *n.* A structure formed by the female gametophyte of a seed plant, in which the embryo develops.

em·cee (ĕm′sē′) *Informal.* —*n.* A master of ceremonies. —*v.* **-ceed, -cee·ing, -cees.** —*tr.* To serve as master of ceremonies of. —*intr.v.* To act as master of ceremonies. [Pronunciation of *M.C.,* abbr. of *master of ceremonies.*]

-eme *suff.* A distinctive unit of linguistic structure: *semanteme.* [Fr. *-ème* < *phonème,* phoneme.]

e·meer (ĭ-mîr′, ā-mîr′) *n.* Variant of **emir.**

e·mend (ĭ-mĕnd′) *tr.v.* **e·mend·ed, e·mend·ing, e·mends. 1.** To improve by critical editing. **2.** *Archaic.* To free from faults; correct. [ME *emenden* < Lat. *emendare* : *ex-,* away + *mendum,* fault.] **—e·mend′er** *n.*

e·men·date (ē′mĕn-dāt′, ĭ-mĕn′-) *tr.v.* **-dat·ed, -dat·ing, -dates.** To make textual corrections in. [Lat. *emendare, emendat-,* to emend.] **—e′men·da′tor** (-dā′tər) *n.* **—e·men′da·to′ry** (ĭ-mĕn′də-tôr′e, -tōr′ē) *adj.*

e·men·da·tion (ĭ-mĕn′dā′shən, ē′mĕn-) *n.* **1.** The act of emending. **2.** An alteration designed to improve.

em·er·ald (ĕm′ər-əld, ĕm′rəld) *n.* **1.** A brilliant, transparent green beryl used as a gemstone. **2.** A strong yellowish green. —*adj.* Of a strong yellowish-green color. [ME *emeraude* < OFr. < Lat. *smaragdus* < Gk. *smaragdos.*]

e·merge (ĭ-mûrj′) *intr.v.* **e·merged, e·merg·ing, e·merg·es. 1.** To rise up or come forth from or as if from immersion. **2.** To become evident or obvious. **3.** To issue, as from obscurity. **4.** To come into existence. [Lat. *emergere* : *ex-,* out + *mergere,* to immerse.]

e·mer·gence (ĭ-mûr′jəns) *n.* **1.** The act or process of emerging. **2.** *Bot.* A superficial outgrowth of plant tissue, as a thorn.

e·mer·gen·cy (ĭ-mûr′jən-sē) *n., pl.* **-cies.** An unexpected situation or sudden occurrence of a serious and urgent nature that demands immediate action.

emergency brake *n.* A separate brake system in a vehicle for use in case of failure of the regular brakes and commonly used as a parking brake.

emergency room *n.* The section of a hospital where emergency cases are treated.

e·mer·gent (ĭ-mûr′jənt) *adj.* **1.** Coming unexpectedly into existence. **2.** Demanding prompt action. **3.** Coming into being as a logical result. **4.** Newly created.

emergent evolution *n.* A theory holding that completely new types of organisms, modes of behavior, and consciousness appear at certain stages of the evolutionary process, usually as a result of an unpredictable rearrangement of the pre-existing elements.

e·mer·i·ta (ĭ-mĕr′ĭ-tə) *adj.* Emeritus. Used of a woman. [Lat., fem. of *emeritus.*] **—e·mer′i·ta** *n.*

e·mer·i·tus (ĭ-mĕr′ĭ-təs) *adj.* Retired but retaining an honorary title corresponding to that held immediately before retirement: *a professor emeritus.* —*n., pl.* **-ti** (-tī′). One who is emeritus. [Lat. *emeritus,* p.part. of *emereri,* to earn by service : *ex-* (intensive) + *mereri,* to earn.]

e·mersed (ĭ-mûrst′) *adj. Bot.* Rising above the surface of a fluid: *emersed aquatic plants.*

e·mer·sion (ĭ-mûr′zhən, -shən) *n.* The act of emerging; emergence. [< Lat. *emersus* < *emergere,* to emerge.]

em·er·y (ĕm′ə-rē, ĕm′rē) *n.* A fine-grained impure corundum used for grinding and polishing. [ME < OFr. *emeri* < LLat. *smericulum* < Gk. *smeris.*]

emery board *n.* A nail file consisting of a strip of cardboard coated with powdered emery.

emery cloth *n.* Cloth coated with powdered emery, used as a fine abrasive.

em·e·sis (ĕm′ĭ-sĭs) *n.* Vomiting. [NLat. < Gk. < *emein,* to vomit.]

e·met·ic (ĭ-mĕt′ĭk) *n.* An agent that causes vomiting. [Lat. *emetica* < Gk. *emetikos,* provoking vomiting < *emetos,* vomiting < *emein,* to vomit.] **—e·met′ic** *adj.* **—e·met′i·cal·ly** *adv.*

em·e·tine (ĕm′ĭ-tēn′) *n.* A bitter-tasting, crystalline alkaloid, $C_{29}H_{40}O_4N_2$, derived from ipecac root, and used as an emetic. [Fr. *émétine* : *émétique,* emetic + *-ine,* -ine.]

e·meu (ē′myo͞o) *n.* Variant of **emu.**

-emia *suff.* Blood: *leukemia.* [NLat. < Gk. *-aimia* < *haima,* blood.]

em·i·grant (ĕm′ĭ-grənt) *n.* One that emigrates. —*adj.* **1.** Emigrating. **2.** Of or pertaining to emigration or emigrants.

em·i·grate (ĕm′ĭ-grāt′) *intr.v.* **-grat·ed, -grat·ing, -grates.** To leave one country or region to settle in another. —See Usage note at **migrate.** [Lat. *emigrare, emigrat-* : *ex-,* away + *migrare,* to move.] **—em'i·gra'tion** (ĕm'ĭ-grā'shən) *n.*

é·mi·gré (ĕm'ĭ-grā') *n.* An emigrant, esp. one who has emigrated for political reasons. [Fr. < p.part. of *émigrer,* to emigrate < Lat. *emigrare.*]

em·i·nence (ĕm'ə-nəns) also **em·i·nen·cy** (-nən-sē) *n., pl.* **-cies. 1.** A position of great distinction or superiority. **2.** A rise of ground; hill. **3. a.** A person of high station or great achievements. **b. Eminence.** Used as a title of honor, esp. for a cardinal in the Roman Catholic Church.

em·i·nent (ĕm'ə-nənt) *adj.* **1.** Towering or standing out above others; prominent. **2.** Outstanding in performance, rank, or attainments; distinguished: *an eminent historian.* **3.** Possessing or displaying eminence; noteworthy. [ME < OFr. or < Lat. *eminens,* pr.part. of *eminēre,* to project.] **—em'i·nent·ly** *adv.*

eminent domain *n. Law.* The right of a government to appropriate private property for public use, usually with compensation to the owner.

e·mir or **e·meer** (ĭ-mîr', ā-mîr') *n.* A prince, chieftain, or governor, esp. in the Middle East. [Fr. *émir* < Sp. *emir* < Ar. *'amīr,* commander < *amara,* he commanded.]

e·mir·ate (ĭ-mîr'ĭt, -āt') *n.* **1.** The office of an emir. **2.** The nation or territory ruled by an emir.

em·is·sar·y (ĕm'ĭ-sĕr'ē) *n., pl.* **-ies.** An agent sent to represent or advance the interests of another. [Lat. *emissarius* < *emissus,* p.part of *emittere,* to send out. —see EMIT.]

e·mis·sion (ĭ-mĭsh'ən) *n.* **1.** An act or example of emitting. **2.** Something that is emitted. **3.** The substance discharged into the air, esp. by an internal combustion engine. [< Lat. *emittere, emiss-,* to send out. —see EMIT.]

emission nebula *n.* A nebula that absorbs ultraviolet radiation from stars and re-emits it as visible light.

emission spectrum *n.* The spectrum of bright lines, bands, or continuous radiation characteristic of and determined by a specific emitting substance subjected to a specific kind of excitation.

e·mis·sive (ĭ-mĭs'ĭv) *adj.* Having the power or tendency to send forth; emitting.

em·is·siv·i·ty (ĕm'ĭ-sĭv'ĭ-tē) *n.* The ratio of radiation intensity from a surface to the radiation intensity at the same wavelength from a blackbody at the same temperature.

e·mit (ĭ-mĭt') *tr.v.* **e·mit·ted, e·mit·ting, e·mits. 1.** To give or send out (radiation, for example). **2. a.** To utter; express. **b.** To give out as sound: *emitted a giggle.* **3.** To issue with authority, esp. to put into circulation (currency, for example). [Lat. *emittere,* to send out : *ex-,* out + *mittere,* to send.] **—e·mit'ter** *n.*

em·men·a·gogue (ĭ-mĕn'ĭ-gôg', -gŏg') *n.* A medicine that induces or hastens the menstrual flow. [Gk. *emmēna,* the menses (*en-,* in + *mēn,* month) + -AGOGUE.]

em·mer (ĕm'ər) *n.* A Eurasian wheat, *Triticum dicoccum,* cultivated as a cereal grain and as livestock feed. [G. < OHG *amaro.*]

em·met (ĕm'ĭt) *n. Archaic.* An ant. [ME *emete* < OE *ǣmete.*]

em·me·tro·pi·a (ĕm'ĭ-trō'pē-ə) *n.* The condition of the normal eye when parallel rays are focused exactly on the retina and vision is perfect. [Gk. *emmetros,* in measure (*en,* in + *metron,* measure) + -OPIA.] **—em'me·trop'ic** (-trŏp'ĭk) *adj.*

Em·my (ĕm'ē) *n., pl.* **-mys** or **-mies.** A statuette awarded annually by the Academy of Television Arts and Sciences for outstanding achievement in television. [Alteration of *Immy,* nickname for *image orthicon tube.*]

em·o·din (ĕm'ə-dĭn') *n.* An orange crystalline compound, $C_{15}H_{10}O_5$, obtained from plants and used as a laxative. [NLat. *emodi,* specific epithet of a species of rhubarb + -IN.]

e·mol·lient (ĭ-mŏl'yənt) *adj.* **1.** Softening and soothing, esp. to the skin. **2.** Making less harsh or abrasive; mollifying. *—n.* **1.** An agent that softens or soothes the skin. **2.** Something that assuages or mollifies. [Lat. *emolliens, emollient-,* pr.part. of *emollire,* to soften : *ex-* (intensive) + *mollire,* to soften < *mollis,* soft.]

e·mol·u·ment (ĭ-mŏl'yə-mənt) *n.* Compensation or payment from an office or employment. [ME < Lat. *emolumentum,* gain, perh. < *emoliri,* to bring about by effort.]

e·mote (ĭ-mōt') *intr.v.* **e·mot·ed, e·mot·ing, e·motes.** *Informal.* To express emotion in an excessive and theatrical manner. [Back-formation < EMOTION.]

e·mo·tion (ĭ-mō'shən) *n.* **1. a.** A complex and usually strong subjective response, as love or fear. **b.** Such a response involving physiological changes as a preparation for action. **2.** A state of agitation or disturbance: *controlled her emotions with effort.* **3.** The part of the consciousness that involves feeling or sensibility: *a choice determined by emotion rather than reason.* [Fr. *émotion* < OFr. *esmovoir,* to excite < VLat. **exmovēre* < Lat. *emovēre,* to move out : *ex-,* out + *movēre,* to move.]

e·mo·tion·al (ĭ-mō'shə-nəl) *adj.* **1.** Of or pertaining to emotion. **2.** Readily affected with or stirred by emotion. **3.** Capable of stirring the emotions: *an emotional appeal.* **4.** Marked by or exhibiting emotion; agitated. **—e·mo'tion·al'i·ty** (-năl'ĭ-tē) *n.* **—e·mo'tion·al·ly** *adv.*

e·mo·tion·al·ism (ĭ-mō'shə-nə-lĭz'əm) *n.* **1.** An inclination to rely on or place too much value on emotion. **2.** Undue display of emotion.

e·mo·tion·al·ist (ĭ-mō'shə-nə-lĭst) *n.* **1.** One whose conduct, thought, or rhetoric is governed by emotion rather than reason, often as a matter of policy. **2.** An excessively emotional person. **—e·mo'tion·al·is'tic** *adj.*

e·mo·tion·al·ize (ĭ-mō'shə-nə-līz') *tr.v.* **-ized, -iz·ing, -iz·es.** To impart an emotional character to.

e·mo·tion·less (ĭ-mō'shən-lĭs) *adj.* Devoid of apparent emotion. **—e·mo'tion·less·ness** *n.*

e·mo·tive (ĭ-mō'tĭv) *adj.* **1.** Of or pertaining to emotion. **2.** Expressing or exciting emotion. **—e·mo'tive·ly** *adv.* **—e·mo'tive·ness, e'mo·tiv'i·ty** *n.*

em·pale (ĕm-pāl') *v.* Variant of **impale.**

em·pan·el (ĕm-păn'əl) *v.* Variant of **impanel.**

em·pa·thet·ic (ĕm'pə-thĕt'ĭk) *adj.* Empathic. **—em'pa·thet'i·cal·ly** *adv.*

em·path·ic (ĕm-păth'ĭk) *adj.* Of, pertaining to, or characterized by empathy.

em·pa·thize (ĕm'pə-thīz') *intr.v.* **-thized, -thiz·ing, -thiz·es.** To feel or experience empathy.

em·pa·thy (ĕm'pə-thē) *n.* **1.** Identification with and understanding of another's situation, feelings, and motives. **2.** The attribution of one's own feelings to an object. [Transl. of G. *Einfühlung,* transl. of Gk. *empatheia,* passion.]

em·pen·nage (ĕm'pĭ-nĭj) *n.* The tail of an airplane. [Fr. < *empenner,* to feather an arrow : *en-,* in (< Lat. *in-*) + *penne,* feather < Lat. *penna.*]

em·per·or (ĕm'pər-ər) *n.* **1.** The male ruler of an empire. **2. a.** Any of several brightly colored butterflies of the family Nymphalidae, such as *Asterocampa clyton,* having orange-tawny wings with dark markings. **b.** Any of several moths of the family Saturniidae, esp. an Old World species, *Saturnia pavonia,* with distinctively patterned wings. [ME *emperour* < OFr. *empereor* < Lat. *imperator* < *imperare,* to command : *in-,* in + *parare,* to prepare.] **—em'per·or·ship'** *n.*

emperor butterfly *n.* Emperor (sense 2.a.).

emperor moth *n.* Emperor (sense 2.b.).

emperor penguin *n.* A large penguin, *Aptenodytes forsteri,* of Antarctic regions.

em·per·y (ĕm'pə-rē) *n., pl.* **-ies.** Absolute dominion or jurisdiction; sovereignty. [ME *emperie* < OFr. < Lat. *imperium.*]

em·pha·sis (ĕm'fə-sĭs) *n., pl.* **-ses** (-sēz'). **1.** Special weight or importance placed upon something: *an emphasis upon neatness.* **2.** Stress applied, as to a syllable or word. **3.** Force or intensity of expression. [Lat. < Gk. < *emphainein,* to indicate : *en-,* in + *phainein,* to show.]

em·pha·size (ĕm'fə-sīz') *tr.v.* **-sized, -siz·ing, -siz·es.** To give emphasis to; stress. [< EMPHASIS.]

em·phat·ic (ĕm-făt'ĭk) *adj.* **1.** Expressed or performed with emphasis. **2.** Forceful and definite in expression or action. **3.** Standing out in a striking and clearly defined way. [Med. Lat. *emphaticus* < Gk. *emphatikos* < *emphainein,* to indicate. —see EMPHASIS.] **—em·phat'i·cal·ly** *adv.*

em·phy·se·ma (ĕm'fĭ-sē'mə) *n.* **1.** A condition of the lungs marked by dilation of the air vesicles following atrophy of the septa, resulting in labored breathing and increased susceptibility to infection. **2.** A distention of connective tissues due to retention of air. [NLat. < Gk. *emphusēma,* inflation < *emphusan,* to blow in : *en-,* in + *phusan,* to blow.] **—em'phy·sem'a·tous** (-sĕm'ə-təs) *adj.*

em·pire (ĕm'pīr') *n.* **1. a.** A political unit, often comprising a number of territories or nations, ruled by a single supreme authority. **b.** The territory included in such a unit. **2.** An extensive enterprise under a unified authority: *a publishing empire.* [ME < OFr. < Lat. *imperium* < *imperare,* to command. —see EMPEROR.]

Em·pire (ŏm-pîr', ĕm'pīr') *adj.* Of, relating to, or characteristic of a neoclassic style, as in clothing or the decorative arts, prevalent in France during the first part of the 19th century. [After the 1st *Empire* of France (1804–1815).]

em·pir·ic (ĕm-pîr'ĭk) *n.* **1.** One who believes that practical experience is the sole source of knowledge. **2.** *Archaic.* A charlatan. [Lat. *empiricus* < Gk. *empeirikos* < *empeirikos,* experienced < *empeiros* : *en-,* in + *peiran,* to try.]

em·pir·i·cal (ĕm-pîr'ĭ-kəl) *adj.* **1. a.** Relying upon or derived from observation or experiment: *empirical methods.* **b.** Capable of proof or verification by means of observation or experiment. **2.** Relying solely on practical experience and without regard for system or theory. **—em·pir'i·cal·ly** *adv.*

empirical formula *n.* A type of chemical formula that indicates the ratio of the elements rather than the total number of atoms in a molecule.

em·pir·i·cism (ĕm-pîr'ĭ-sĭz'əm) *n.* **1.** The view that experience, esp. of the senses, is the only source of knowledge. **2. a.** The employment of empirical methods, as in science. **b.** An empirical conclusion. **3.** The practice of medicine that is based upon practical experience rather than scientific theory. **—em·pir'i·cist** *n.*

em·place (ĕm-plās') *tr.v.* **-placed, -plac·ing, -plac·es.** To put in place or position.

em·place·ment (ĕm-plās'mənt) *n.* **1.** A prepared position, such as a mounting or platform, for guns or other military equipment. **2.** The action of putting in a certain position; placement. **3.** Position; location. [Fr. < obs. *emplacer,* to place in position : *en-,* in (< Lat. *in-*) + OFr. *place,* open space. —see PLACE.]

George Miksch Sutton
emu

em·plane (ĕm-plān′) *v.* Variant of **enplane.**

em·ploy (ĕm-ploi′) *tr.v.* **-ployed, -ploy·ing, -ploys. 1.** To put to use or service. **2.** To devote or apply (time, for example) to some activity. **3. a.** To engage the services of; put to work. **b.** To provide with gainful work. *—n.* **1.** The state of being employed. **2.** *Archaic.* Occupation. [ME *emploien* < OFr. *emploier* < Lat. *implicare,* to involve : *in-,* in + *plicare,* to fold.] **—em·ploy′a·bil′i·ty** *n.* **—em·ploy′a·ble** *adj.* **—em·ploy′er** *n.*

em·ploy·ee also **em·ploy·e** or **em·ploy·é** (ĕm-ploi′ē, ĭm-, ĕm′ploi-ē′) *n.* A person who works for another in return for financial or other compensation.

em·ploy·ment (ĕm-ploi′mənt) *n.* **1. a.** The act of employing. **b.** The state of being employed. **2.** The work in which one is engaged; business. **3.** An activity to which one devotes time.

employment agency *n.* An agency that is in the business of finding jobs for people and of finding people to fill particular jobs.

em·poi·son (ĕm-poi′zən) *tr.v.* **-soned, -son·ing, -sons. 1.** To fill with venom; embitter. **2.** *Archaic.* To poison. [ME *empoisounen* < OFr. *empoisoner* : *en-,* in + *poison,* poison.]

em·po·ri·um (ĕm-pôr′ē-əm, -pōr′-) *n., pl.* **-ri·ums** or **-ri·a** (-ə, -ē-ə). **1.** A place that is an important trade center; marketplace. **2.** A large retail store carrying a wide variety of merchandise. [Lat. < Gk. *emporion* < *emporos,* merchant : *en-,* in + *poros,* journey.]

em·pow·er (ĕm-pou′ər) *tr.v.* **-ered, -er·ing, -ers.** To invest with legal power; authorize.

em·press (ĕm′prĭs) *n.* **1.** The female sovereign of an empire. **2.** The wife or widow of an emperor. [ME *emperesse* < OFr., fem. of *empereor,* emperor.]

em·presse·ment (äN′prĕs-mäN′) *n.* Effusive cordiality. [Fr. < *s'empresser,* to be eager.]

empress tree *n.* A tree, *Paulownia tomentosa,* native to China, having large, hairy leaves and lavender flowers.

em·prise also **em·prize** (ĕm-prīz′) *n.* **1.** An undertaking, esp. one of a chivalrous or adventurous nature. **2.** Chivalrous daring or prowess. [ME < OFr., fem. p.part. of *emprendre,* to undertake < VLat. **imprendere* : Lat. *in-,* in + Lat. *prendere,* to take.]

emp·ty (ĕmp′tē) *adj.* **-ti·er, -ti·est. 1. a.** Holding or containing nothing. **b.** Having no elements or members; null. **2.** Having no occupants or inhabitants; vacant: *an empty chair.* **3.** Lacking force or power: *an empty threat.* **4.** Lacking purpose or substance; meaningless: *an empty life.* **5.** Idle: *empty hours.* **6.** Vacuous; inane: *an empty mind.* **7.** Needing nourishment; hungry. **8.** Devoid; destitute: *empty of pity.* *—v.* **-tied, -ty·ing, -ties.** *—tr.* **1.** To remove the contents of; make empty. **2.** To transfer or pour off: *empty the ashes into a pail.* **3.** To unburden; relieve: *empty oneself of doubt.* *—intr.* **1.** To become empty. **2.** To discharge: *The river empties into a bay.* *—n., pl.* **-ties.** An empty container. [ME < OE *ǣmtig* < *ǣmetta,* leisure.] **—emp′ti·ly** *adv.* **—emp′ti·ness** *n.*

Synonyms: *empty, vacant, blank, void, vacuous, bare, barren.* These adjectives describe that which has nothing in it or on it and inferentially lacks what it could or should have. *Empty* applies physically and figuratively to what is without contents, content (substance), or occupants (persons): *an empty box; empty promises; an empty room. Vacant,* in physical usage, is largely limited to what is without an occupant or incumbent; in this sense, much more than *empty,* it suggests a condition of some duration. Figuratively *vacant* refers to absence of intellectual content, sometimes momentary: *a vacant stare; a vacant mind. Blank* stresses absence of something on a surface that would convey meaning or content: *a blank page; a blank expression. Void* appears principally in the expression *void of,* to indicate absence of the object specified, or in the legal sense of lacking force or validity. *Vacuous* means containing a vacuum, literally or, more often, figuratively in the sense of being silly or inane. *Bare* refers to lack of surface covering or detail or to the condition of being stripped of contents or furnishings. *Barren* stresses lack of productivity in both literal and figurative applications: *barren land; a barren scheme; barren ideas.*

emp·ty-hand·ed (ĕmp′tē-hăn′dĭd) *adj.* **1.** Bearing no gift, possessions, or impedimenta. **2.** Having received or gained nothing.

emp·ty-head·ed (ĕmp′tē-hĕd′ĭd) *adj.* Lacking sense or discretion; scatterbrained.

em·pur·ple (ĕm-pûr′pəl) *tr. & intr.v.* **-pled, -pling, -ples.** To make or become purple.

em·py·e·ma (ĕm′pī-ē′mə) *n., pl.* **-ma·ta** (-mə-tə). Pus in a body cavity, such as the pleural cavity or gall bladder. [Med. Lat. < Gk. *empuēma* < *empuein,* to suppurate.] **—em′py·e′mic** *adj.*

em·pyr·e·al (ĕm-pĭr′ē-əl, ĕm′pī-rē′əl, ĕm-pīr′ē-əl) *adj.* **1.** Empyrean. **2.** Of or pertaining to the sky; celestial. **3.** Elevated; sublime. [ME *imperyale* < Med. Lat. *empyreus* < Gk. *empurios,* fiery : *en-,* in + *pur,* fire.]

em·py·re·an (ĕm′pī-rē′ən, ĕm-pîr′ē-ən) *n.* **1. a.** The highest reaches of heaven, believed by the ancients to be a realm of pure fire or light. **b.** The abode of God and the angels; paradise. **2.** The sky. *—adj.* Of or pertaining to the empyrean of ancient belief. [< Med. Lat. *empyreum* < *empyreus,* empyreal.]

e·mu also **e·meu** (ē′myo͞o) *n.* A large, flightless Australian bird, *Dromiceius novaehollandiae,* related to and resembling the ostrich. [Port. *ema,* rhea.]

em·u·late (ĕm′yə-lāt′) *tr.v.* **-lat·ed, -lat·ing, -lates. 1.** To strive to equal or excel, esp. through imitation. **2.** To compete with or rival successfully. **3.** *Computer Sci.* To imitate one system with another so that both accept the same data, execute the same programs, and achieve the same results. *—adj. Obs.* Ambitious; emulous. [Lat. *aemulari, aemulat-* < *aemulus,* emulous.] **—em′u·la′tive** *adj.* **—em′u·la′tive·ly** *adv.* **—em′u·la′tor** *n.*

em·u·la·tion (ĕm′yə-lā′shən) *n.* **1.** Effort or ambition to equal or surpass another. **2.** Imitation of another. **3.** *Obs.* Jealous rivalry.

em·u·lous (ĕm′yə-ləs) *adj.* **1.** Eager or ambitious to equal or surpass another. **2.** Characterized or prompted by a spirit of rivalry. **3.** *Obs.* Covetous of power or honor; envious. [Lat. *aemulus.*] **—em′u·lous·ly** *adv.* **—em′u·lous·ness** *n.*

e·muls·i·ble (ĭ-mŭl′sə-bəl) *adj.* Capable of being emulsified.

e·mul·si·fy (ĭ-mŭl′sə-fī′) *tr.v.* **-fied, -fy·ing, -fies.** To make into an emulsion. [EMULSI(ON) + -FY.] **—e·mul′si·fi·ca′tion** *n.* **—e·mul′si·fi′er** *n.*

e·mul·sion (ĭ-mŭl′shən) *n.* **1.** *Chem.* A suspension of small globules of one liquid in a second liquid with which the first will not mix, such as milk fats in milk. **2.** A light-sensitive coating, usually of silver halide grains in a thin gelatin layer, on photographic film, paper, or glass. [NLat. < Lat. *emulgēre, emuls-,* to milk out : *ex,* out + *mulgēre,* to milk.] **—e·mul′sive** *adj.*

e·munc·to·ry (ĭ-mŭngk′tə-rē) *adj.* Serving to carry waste matter out of the body; excretory. *—n., pl.* **-ries.** An emunctory organ or passage. [ME *emunctorie* < Med. Lat. *emunctorius* < Lat. *emungere,* to blow the nose : *ex-* (intensive) + *mungere,* to blow the nose.]

en (ĕn) *n.* **1.** The letter *n.* **2.** *Printing.* A space equal to half the width of an em.

en–[1] or **em–** *pref.* **1. a.** To put into or onto: *encapsulate.* **b.** To go into or onto: *entrain.* **2.** To cover or provide with: *enrobe.* **3.** To cause to be: *endear.* **4.** Thoroughly. Used often as an intensive: *entangle.* [ME < OFr. < Lat. *in-,* in.]

en–[2] or **em–** *pref.* In; into; within: *enzootic.* [ME < Lat. < Gk.]

–en[1] *suff.* **1 a.** To cause to be: *cheapen.* **b.** To become: *redden.* **2. a.** To cause to have: *hearten.* **b.** To come to have: *lengthen.* [ME *-nen* < OE *-nian.*]

–en[2] *suff.* Made of; resembling: *earthen.* [ME < OE.]

en·a·ble (ĕn-ā′bəl) *tr.v.* **-bled, -bling, -bles. 1. a.** To supply with the means, knowledge, or opportunity to be or do something. **b.** To make feasible or possible. **2.** To give legal power, capacity, or sanction to.

en·act (ĕn-ăkt′) *tr.v.* **-act·ed, -act·ing, -acts. 1.** To make (a bill, for example) into law. **2.** To act out, as on a stage; represent. **—en·act′a·ble** *adj.* **—en·ac′tor** *n.*

en·act·ment (ĕn-ăkt′mənt) *n.* **1.** The act of enacting. **2.** The state of being enacted. **3.** Something, such as a law or statute, that has been enacted.

en·am·el (ĭ-năm′əl) *n.* **1.** A vitreous, usually opaque, protective or decorative coating baked on metal, glass, or ceramic ware. **2.** An object with an enameled surface, such as a piece of cloisonné. **3.** A paint that dries to a hard, glossy surface. **4.** A glossy, hard coating resembling enamel. **5.** *Anat.* The hard, calcareous substance covering the exposed portion of a tooth. *—tr.v.* **-eled, -el·ing, -els** or **-elled, -el·ling, -els. 1.** To coat, inlay, or decorate with enamel. **2.** To give a glossy or brilliant surface to. **3.** To adorn, as with bright colors. [< ME *enamelen,* to put on enamel < AN *enamailler* : *en-,* en- + *amail,* enamel < OFr. *esmail,* of Germanic orig.] **—en·am′el·er, en·am′el·ist** *n.*

en·am·el·ware (ĭ-năm′əl-wâr′) *n.* Ware coated with enamel.

en·a·mine (ĕn′ə-mēn′, ĭ-năm′ēn) *n.* An unsaturated amine that contains the double bond linkage C=C–N. [E. *en-,* chemically unsaturated + -AMINE.]

en·am·or (ĭ-năm′ər) *tr.v.* **-ored, -or·ing, -ors.** To inspire with love; captivate: *enamored of his surroundings.* [ME *enamouren* < OFr. *enamourer* : *en-,* in (< Lat. *in-*) + *amour,* love < Lat. *amor* < *amare,* to love.]

en·am·our (ĭ-năm′ər) *v. Chiefly Brit.* Variant of **enamor.**

en·an·ti·o·mer (ĭ-năn′tē-ə-mər) *n.* Enantiomorph. [Gk. *enantios,* opposite + -MER.] **—en·an′ti·o·mer′ic** (-mĕr′ĭk) *adj.*

en·an·ti·o·morph (ĕn-ăn′tē-ə-môrf′) *n.* Either of a pair of crystals that are similar in form but cannot be superimposed, one crystal being the mirror image of the other. [Gk. *enantios,* opposite + -MORPH.] **—en·an′ti·o·mor′phic, en·an′ti·o·mor′phous** *adj.* **—en·an′ti·o·morph′ism** *n.*

en·ar·thro·sis (ĕn′är-thrō′sĭs) *n., pl.* **-ses** (-sēz′). *Anat.* An articulation, such as the hip joint, wherein the rounded head of one bone fits into the rounded cavity of another bone, thus permitting movement in any direction. [NLat. < Gk. *enarthrōsis* < *enarthros,* jointed : *en-,* in + *arthron,* joint.]

e·nate (ĭ-nāt′, ē′nāt′) *adj.* **1.** Growing outward. **2.** Also **e·nat·ic** (ĭ-năt′ĭk). Related on the mother's side. *—n.* A relative on one's mother's side. [Lat. *enatus,* p.part. of *enasci,* to issue forth : *ex-,* out + *nasci,* to be born.]

en bro·chette (äɴ′ brô-shĕt′) *adv.* On a skewer. [Fr.]
en·cage (ĕn-kāj′) *tr.v.* **-caged, -cag·ing, -cag·es.** To confine in or as if in a cage.
en·camp (ĕn-kămp′) *v.* **-camped, -camp·ing, -camps.** —*intr.* To set up or live in a camp. —*tr.* To provide quarters for in a camp.
en·camp·ment (ĕn-kămp′mənt) *n.* **1. a.** The act of encamping. **b.** The state of being encamped. **2.** A camp or campsite.
en·cap·su·lant (ĕn-kăp′sə-lənt) *n.* A material used for encapsulating.
en·cap·su·late (ĕn-kăp′sə-lāt′) *v.* **-lat·ed, -lat·ing, -lates.** —*tr.* To encase in or as if in a capsule. —*intr.* To become encapsulated. **—en·cap′su·la′tion** *n.*
en·cap·su·lat·ed (ĕn-kăp′sə-lā′təd) *adj.* Enclosed by a protective coating or membrane, as in certain bacteria.
en·case (ĕn-kās′) *tr.v.* **-cased, -cas·ing, -cas·es.** To enclose in or as if in a case. **—en·case′ment** *n.*
en·caus·tic (ĕn-kô′stĭk) *adj.* A paint consisting of pigment mixed with beeswax and fixed with heat after its application. —*n.* **1.** The art of painting with encaustic. **2.** A painting produced with the use of encaustic. [Lat. *encausticus* < Gk. *enkaustikos* < *enkaiein,* to paint in encaustic : *en-,* in + *kaiein,* to burn.]
-ence *suff.* **1.** State or condition: *dependence.* **2.** Action: *emergence.* [ME < OFr. < Lat. *-entia* < *-ens,* -ent.]
en·ceinte[1] (ĕn-sānt′) *adj.* Being with child; pregnant. [Fr. < OFr. < VLat. **incienta* < Lat. *inciens.*]
en·ceinte[2] (ĕn-sānt′, äɴ-säɴt′) *n.* **1.** An encircling fortification around a fort, castle, or town. **2.** The structures or area protected by an encircling fortification. [Fr. < LLat. *incincta,* fem. p.part. of *incingere,* to surround closely : *in-,* in + *cingere,* to gird.]
encephal- *pref.* Variant of **encephalo-.**
en·ceph·a·la (ĕn-sĕf′ə-lə) *n.* Plural of **encephalon.**
en·ce·phal·ic (ĕn′sə-făl′ĭk) *adj.* **1.** Of or pertaining to the brain. **2.** Located within the cranial cavity.
en·ceph·a·li·tis (ĕn-sĕf′ə-lī′tĭs) *n.* Inflammation of the brain. **—en·ceph′a·lit′ic** (-lĭt′ĭk) *adj.*
encephalitis le·thar·gi·ca (lə-thär′jĭ-kə) *n.* A viral epidemic encephalitis often associated with influenza and marked by apathy, double vision, and extreme muscular weakness. [NLat., lethargic encephalitis.]
encephalo- or **encephal-** *pref.* Brain: *encephalitis.* [NLat. < Gk. *(muelos) enkephalos,* (marrow) in the head: *en-,* in + *kephalē,* head.]
en·ceph·a·lo·gram (ĕn-sĕf′ə-lō-grăm′) *n.* **1.** An x-ray picture of the brain taken by encephalography. **2.** An electroencephalogram.
en·ceph·a·log·ra·phy (ĕn-sĕf′ə-lŏg′rə-fē) *n., pl.* **-phies.** Roentgenography of the brain. **—en·ceph′a·lo·graph′** (-lō-grăf′) *n.* **—en·ceph′a·lo·graph′ic** *adj.* **—en·ceph′a·lo·graph′i·cal·ly** *adv.*
en·ceph·a·lo·ma (ĕn-sĕf′ə-lō′mə) *n., pl.* **-mas** or **-ma·ta** (-mə-tə). A tumor of the brain.
en·ceph·a·lo·my·e·li·tis (ĕn-sĕf′ə-lō-mī′ə-lī′tĭs) *n.* Any of several viral diseases causing inflammation of the brain and the spinal cord.
en·ceph·a·lon (ĕn-sĕf′ə-lŏn′) *n., pl.* **-la** (-lə). The brain of a vertebrate. [NLat. < Gk. *enkephalon,* neuter of *enkephalos,* in the head. —see ENCEPHALO-.] **—en·ceph′a·lous** *adj.*
en·ceph·a·lop·a·thy (ĕn-sĕf′ə-lŏp′ə-thē) *n., pl.* **-thies.** A disease of the brain. **—en·ceph′a·lo·path′ic** (-lə-păth′ĭk) *adj.*
en·chain (ĕn-chān′) *tr.v.* **-chained, -chain·ing, -chains.** To bind with or as if with chains. [ME *encheinen* < OFr. *enchäener* : *en-,* in (< Lat. *in-*) + *chäeine,* chain < Lat. *catena.*] **—en·chain′ment** *n.*
en·chant (ĕn-chănt′) *tr.v.* **-chant·ed, -chant·ing, -chants.** **1.** To cast under a spell; bewitch. **2.** To attract and delight completely; charm. [ME *enchanten* < OFr. *enchanter* < Lat. *incantare* : *in-* against + *cantare,* to sing.]
en·chant·er (ĕn-chăn′tər) *n.* **1.** One that enchants. **2.** A sorcerer or magician.
en·chant·ing (ĕn-chăn′tĭng) *adj.* Having the power to enchant. **—en·chant′ing·ly** *adv.*
en·chant·ment (ĕn-chănt′mənt) *n.* **1. a.** An act of enchanting. **b.** The state of being enchanted. **2.** Something that enchants.
en·chant·ress (ĕn-chăn′trĭs) *n.* **1. a.** A woman who practices magic. **b.** A sorceress. **2.** A woman of great charm or fascination.
en·chase (ĕn-chās′) *tr.v.* **-chased, -chas·ing, -chases.** **1.** To set (a gem, for example). **2.** To set with or as if with gems. **3.** To decorate or ornament by inlaying or engraving. [ME, to engrave < OFr. *enchasser,* to set gems : *en-,* in (< Lat. *in-*) + *chasse,* case < Lat. *capsa,* box.]
en·chi·la·da (ĕn′chə-lä′də) *n.* A tortilla rolled and stuffed usually with a mixture containing meat or cheese and served with a sauce spiced with chili. [Mex. Sp. : *en-,* in (< Lat. *in-*) + *chile,* chili pepper < Nahuatl *chilli.*]
en·chi·rid·i·on (ĕn′kī-rĭd′ē-ən) *n., pl.* **-i·ons** or **-i·a** (-ē-ə). A handbook; manual. [Gk. *enkheiridion* : *en-,* in + *kheir,* hand + *-idion,* dim. suffix.]
-enchyma *suff.* Cellular tissue: *chlorenchyma.* [< PARENCHYMA.]
en·ci·na (ĕn-sē′nə) *n.* An evergreen oak, *Quercus agrifolia,* of southwestern North America, often cultivated as a shade tree. [Sp., holm oak < LLat. *ilicina* < Lat. *ilex.*]
en·ci·pher (ĕn-sī′fər) *tr.v.* **-phered, -pher·ing, -phers.** To put into cipher. **—en·ci′pher·er** *n.* **—en·ci′pher·ment** *n.*
en·cir·cle (ĕn-sûr′kəl) *tr.v.* **-cled, -cling, -cles.** **1.** To form a circle around; surround. **2.** To move or go around completely; make a circuit of. **—en·cir′cle·ment** *n.*
en·clasp (ĕn-klăsp′) *tr.v.* **-clasped, -clasp·ing, -clasps.** To embrace.
en·clave (ĕn′klāv′, ŏn′-) *n.* **1.** A country or part of a country lying wholly within the boundaries of another. **2.** A distinctly bounded area enclosed within a larger unit. [Fr. < OFr. *enclaver,* to enclose < VLat. **inclavare* : Lat. *in-,* in + Lat. *clavis,* key.]
en·clit·ic (ĕn-klĭt′ĭk) *n. Ling.* A word or particle that has no independent accent and forms an accentual and sometimes also graphemic unit with the preceding word: In "*Give 'em the works,*" the particle *'em* is an enclitic. [LLat. *encliticus,* being an enclitic < Gk. *enklitikos* < *enklinein,* to lean on : *en-,* in + *klinein,* to lean.]
en·close (ĕn-klōz′) *tr.v.* **-closed, -clos·ing, -clos·es.** **1.** To surround on all sides; close in. **2. a.** To place within a container. **b.** To insert in the same envelope or package. **3.** To fence in or place an enclosure around so as to prevent common use. [ME *enclosen* < OFr. *enclos,* p.part. of *enclore* < Lat. *includere,* to include : *in-,* in + *claudere,* to close.]
en·clo·sure (ĕn-klō′zhər) *n.* **1.** The act of enclosing. **2.** The state of being enclosed. **3.** Something that is enclosed. **4.** Something that encloses.
en·code (ĕn-kōd′) *tr.v.* **-cod·ed, -cod·ing, -codes.** **1.** To put (a message) into code. **2.** *Computer Sci.* To convert a character into its equivalent combination of bits. **—en·cod′er** *n.*
en·co·mi·ast (ĕn-kō′mē-ăst′, -əst) *n.* A person who delivers or writes an encomium; eulogist. [Gk. *enkōmiastēs* < *enkōmiazein,* to praise < *enkōmion,* encomium.] **—en·co′mi·as′tic** (ĕn-kō′mē-ăs′tĭk), **en·co′mi·as′ti·cal** (-tĭ-kəl) *adj.*
en·co·mi·um (ĕn-kō′mē-əm) *n., pl.* **-mi·ums** or **-m·ia** (-mē-ə). **1.** Warm or glowing praise. **2.** A formal expression of praise; tribute. [Lat. *encomium* < Gk. *enkōmion (epos),* (speech) praising a victor < *enkōmios,* of the victory procession : *en-,* in + *kōmos,* celebration.]
en·com·pass (ĕn-kŭm′pəs) *tr.v.* **-passed, -pass·ing, -pass·es.** **1.** To form a circle or ring about; surround. **2.** To enclose; envelop. **3.** To comprise; include. **4.** To accomplish; achieve. **—en·com′pass·ment** *n.*
en·core (ŏn′kôr′, -kōr′) *n.* **1.** A demand by an audience for an additional performance. **2.** An additional performance in response to the demand of an audience. —*tr.v.* **-cored, -cor·ing, -cores.** To demand an encore of. —*interj.* Used to demand an additional performance. [Fr., again.]
en·coun·ter (ĕn-koun′tər) *n.* **1.** An unplanned or unexpected meeting. **2.** A usually brief meeting. **3. a.** A hostile confrontation. **b.** An often violent meeting; clash. —*v.* **-tered, -ter·ing, -ters.** —*tr.* **1.** To meet or come upon, esp. unexpectedly. **2.** To confront in battle or contention. **3.** To come up against; be faced with: *encounter numerous obstacles.* —*intr.* To meet, esp. unexpectedly. [ME *encountre* < OFr. < *encontrer,* to meet < LLat. *incontrare* : Lat. *in-,* in + Lat. *contra,* against.]
encounter group *n.* A typically unstructured therapy group in which individuals seek to increase their sensitivity and responsiveness, reveal their feelings, and relate to others openly and intimately, as by touching or verbalizing freely.
en·cour·age (ĕn-kûr′ĭj, -kŭr′) *tr.v.* **-aged, -ag·ing, -ag·es.** **1.** To inspire with hope, courage, or confidence; hearten. **2.** To give support to; foster. **3.** To stimulate. [ME *encouragen* < OFr. *encoragier* : *en-* (causative) < Lat. *in-,* in + *corage,* courage < Lat. *cor,* heart.] **—en·cour′ag·er** *n.*
en·cour·age·ment (ĕn-kûr′ĭj-mənt, -kŭr′-) *n.* **1.** The act of encouraging. **2.** The state of being encouraged. **3.** One that encourages.
en·cour·ag·ing (ĕn-kûr′ə-jĭng, -kŭr′-) *adj.* Giving courage, confidence, or hope. **—en·cour′ag·ing·ly** *adv.*
en·croach (ĕn-krōch′) *intr.v.* **-croached, -croach·ing, -croach·es.** **1.** To intrude gradually upon the possessions or rights of another: *encroach upon a neighbor's land.* **2.** To advance beyond proper or prescribed limits. [ME *encrochen,* to seize illegally < OFr. *encrochier,* to seize : *en-,* in (< Lat. *in-*) + *croc,* hook, of Scand. orig.] **—en·croach′er** *n.* **—en·croach′ment** *n.*
en·crust (ĕn-krŭst′) *tr.v.* **-crust·ed, -crust·ing, -crusts.** To cover or surmount with or as if with a crust: *a scepter encrusted with diamonds.* [Prob. < Fr. *incruster* < Lat. *incrustare* : *in-* upon + *crusta,* crust.] **—en′crust·a′tion** *n.*
en·cryp·tion (ĕn-krĭp′shən) *n.* A process for scrambling access codes to computer programs to prevent illicit entry into and control of the system. **—en·crypt** *v.* **(-crypt·ed, -crypt·ing, -crypts).**
en·cum·ber (ĕn-kŭm′bər) *tr.v.* **-bered, -ber·ing, -bers.** **1.** To weigh down unduly; burden. **2.** To hinder or impede the action or performance of. **3.** To burden, as with legal claims. [ME *encombren* < OFr. *encombrer,* to block up : *en-,* in (< Lat. *in-*) + *combre,* hindrance.]
en·cum·brance (ĕn-kŭm′brəns) *n.* **1.** One that encumbers; burden or impediment. **2.** *Law.* A lien or claim upon property.

en·cum·branc·er (ĕn-kŭm′brən-sər) *n. Law.* One that holds an encumbrance.
–ency *suff.* -ence. [Lat. *-entia.* —see -ENCE.]
en·cyc·li·cal (ĕn-sĭk′lĭ-kəl) *adj.* Intended for general or wide circulation. —*n. Rom. Cath. Ch.* A papal letter on a specific subject addressed to the bishops of the Church or to the hierarchy of a particular country. [LLat. *encyclicus,* circular < Gk. *enkuklios* : *en-,* in + *kuklos,* circle.]
en·cy·clo·pe·di·a or **en·cy·clo·pae·di·a** (ĕn-sī′klə-pē′dē-ə) *n.* A comprehensive reference work containing articles on a wide range of subjects or on numerous aspects of a particular field, usually arranged alphabetically. [Med. Lat. *encyclopaedia,* general education course < Gk. *enkuklopaideiā* < *enkuklios paideia,* general education.]
en·cy·clo·pe·dic or **en·cy·clo·pae·dic** (ĕn-sī′klə-pē′dĭk) *adj.* **1.** Of, pertaining to, or characteristic of an encyclopedia. **2.** Embracing many subjects; comprehensive: *encyclopedic knowledge.* **—en·cy′clo·pe′di·cal·ly** *adv.*
en·cy·clo·pe·dism or **en·cy·clo·pae·dism** (ĕn-sī′klə-pē′dĭz′əm) *n.* Encyclopedic learning.
en·cy·clo·pe·dist or **en·cy·clo·pae·dist** (ĕn-sī′klə-pē′dĭst) *n.* **1.** A person who writes for or compiles an encyclopedia. **2. Encyclopedist.** One of the writers of the French *Encyclopédie* (1751–72), including its editors, Diderot and d'Alembert.
en·cyst (ĕn-sĭst′) *v.* **-cyst·ed, -cyst·ing, -cysts.** —*tr.* To enclose in or as if in a cyst. —*intr.* To form or become enclosed in a cyst. **—en·cyst′ment, en′cys′ta′tion** *n.*

endive

end (ĕnd) *n.* **1.** Either extremity of something that has length. **2.** The outside or extreme edge or limit of something; boundary. **3.** The point in time at which an action, event, or phenomenon ceases or is completed; conclusion: *the end of a day.* **4.** A result; outcome. **5.** The termination of life or existence; death. **6.** An ultimate extent; limit: *the end of one's patience.* **7.** A goal toward which one strives. **8.** A remainder or remnant. **9. a.** A share of a responsibility or obligation: *your end of the bargain.* **b.** A particular area of responsibility: *in charge of the business end of the campaign.* **10.** *Football.* **a.** Either of the players in the outermost position at the line of scrimmage. **b.** The position played by such a player. —*v.* **end·ed, end·ing, ends.** —*tr.* **1.** To bring to an end; finish. **2.** To form the end or concluding part of. **3.** To destroy. —*intr.* **1.** To come to an end; cease. **2.** To die. **—idioms. go off the deep end.** *Informal.* To behave or proceed in an impulsive, reckless, or distraught manner. **make (both) ends meet.** To manage to live within one's means. **no end.** *Informal.* A great deal: *no end of stories to tell.* [ME *ende* < OE.]
end– *pref.* Variant of **endo-.**
en·da·moe·ba or **en·da·me·ba** (ĕn′də-mē′bə) *n.* Variants of **entamoeba.**
en·dan·ger (ĕn-dān′jər) *tr.v.* **-gered, -ger·ing, -gers.** To expose to danger or harm; imperil. **—en·dan′ger·ment** *n.*
en·dan·gered (ĕn-dān′jərd) *adj.* Faced with the danger of extinction: *an endangered species.*

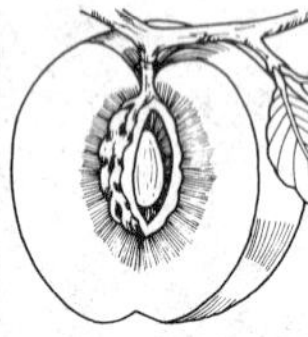
endocarp

end·ar·te·rec·to·my (ĕn′där-tə-rĕk′tə-mē) *n., pl.* **-mies.** The surgical excision of the inner lining of an artery that is clogged with atherosclerotic buildup. [NLat. *endarterium,* inner lining of an artery + -ECTOMY.]
end·ar·te·ri·tis (ĕn′där-tə-rī′tĭs) *n.* Inflammation of the inner lining of an artery. [NLat. *endarterium,* inner lining of an artery + -ITIS.]
end·brain (ĕnd′brān′) *n.* The telencephalon.
en·dear (ĕn-dîr′) *tr.v.* **-deared, -dear·ing, -dears.** **1.** To make beloved. **2.** *Obs.* To increase the cost or value of.
en·dear·ing (ĕn-dîr′ĭng) *adj.* Inspiring affection or warm sympathy. **—en·dear′ing·ly** *adv.*
en·dear·ment (ĕn-dîr′mənt) *n.* **1.** The act of endearing. **2.** An expression of affection, such as a caress.
en·deav·or (ĕn-dĕv′ər) *n.* A conscientious or concerted effort toward a given end; an earnest attempt. —*intr.v.* **-ored, -or·ing, -ors.** To make an earnest attempt: *endeavor to keep abreast of events.* [ME *endevour* < *endeveren,* to make an effort : *en-,* en- + *dever,* duty < OFr. *devoir,* duty. —see DEVOIR.] **—en·deav′or·er** *n.*
en·deav·our (ĕn-dĕv′ər) *n. & v. Chiefly Brit.* Variant of **endeavor.**
en·dem·ic (ĕn-dĕm′ĭk) *adj.* **1.** Prevalent in or peculiar to a particular locality or people. **2.** *Ecol.* Native or confined to a certain region. **3.** *Med.* Peculiar to a particular locality: *an endemic disease.* —*n. Ecol.* An endemic plant or animal. [Gk. *endēmos* : *en-,* in + *dēmos,* people.] **—en·dem′i·cal·ly** *adv.* **—en·dem′ism** *n.*
end·er·gon·ic (ĕn′dər-gŏn′ĭk) *adj.* Requiring energy. [END(O)- + Gk. *ergon,* work + -IC.]
en·der·mic (ĕn-dûr′mĭk) *adj.* Acting medicinally by absorption through the skin. **—en·der′mi·cal·ly** *adv.*
end·ing (ĕn′dĭng) *n.* **1.** A conclusion or termination. **2.** The concluding part; finale: *a happy ending.* **3.** The letter or letters added to a word base, esp. to make a derivative or inflectional form.
en·dive (ĕn′dīv′, ŏn′dēv′) *n.* **1.** A plant, *Cichorium endivia,* cultivated for its crown of crisp, succulent leaves, used in salads. **2.** A variety of the common chicory, *Cichorium intybus,* cultivated to produce a narrow, pointed cluster of whitish leaves used in salads. [ME < OFr. < Lat. *intibum.*]
end leaf *n.* An endpaper.
end·less (ĕnd′lĭs) *adj.* **1.** Being or seeming to be without an end; boundless. **2.** Incessant; interminable: *an endless conversation.* **3.** Formed with the ends joined; continuous: *endless acres of forest.* **—end′less·ly** *adv.* **—end′less·ness** *n.*
end·long (ĕnd′lông′, -lŏng′) *adv. Archaic.* Lengthwise.
end man *n.* **1.** The person at the end of a line or row. **2.** The man in a minstrel show who sits at one end of the company and engages in banter with the interlocutor.
end matter *n.* Back matter.
end·most (ĕnd′mōst′) *adj.* Being at or closest to the end; last.
endo– or **end–** *pref.* Inside; within : *endometrium.* [Gk. < *endon,* within.]
en·do·bi·ot·ic (ĕn′də-bī-ŏt′ĭk) *adj.* Living within the tissues of a host.
en·do·blast (ĕn′də-blăst′) also **en·to·blast** (ĕn′tə-) *n.* The inner layer of the blastoderm. **—en′do·blas′tic** *adj.*
en·do·car·di·tis (ĕn′dō-kär-dī′tĭs) *n.* Inflammation of the endocardium. [ENDOCARD(IUM) + -ITIS.] **—en′do·car·dit′ic** (-dĭt′ĭk) *adj.*
en·do·car·di·um (ĕn′dō-kär′dē-əm) *n., pl.* **-di·a** (-dē-ə). The thin, endothelial, serous membrane that lines the interior of the heart. [NLat. : ENDO- + Gk. *kardia,* heart.] **—en′do·car′di·al** *adj.*
en·do·carp (ĕn′də-kärp′) *n.* The often hard or leathery inner layer of the pericarp of many fruits. **—en′do·car′pal** *adj.*
en·do·cra·ni·um (ĕn′dō-krā′nē-əm) *n., pl.* **-ni·a** (-nē-ə). The dura mater.
en·do·crine (ĕn′də-krĭn, -krēn′, -krīn′) also **en·do·crin·ic** (-krĭn′ĭk) or **en·doc·ri·nous** (-dŏk′rə-nəs) *adj.* **1.** Secreting internally. **2.** Of or pertaining to any of the ductless or endocrine glands. —*n.* **1.** The internal secretion of a gland. **2.** An endocrine gland. [ENDO- + Gk. *krinein,* to separate.]
endocrine gland *n.* Any of the ductless glands, such as the thyroid or adrenal, the secretions of which pass directly into the bloodstream from the cells of the gland.
en·do·cri·nol·o·gy (ĕn′də-krə-nŏl′ə-jē) *n.* The physiology of the endocrine glands. **—en′do·cri′no·log′ic** (-krĭn′ə-lŏj′ĭk) *adj.* **—en′do·cri·nol′o·gist** *n.*
en·do·derm (ĕn′də-dûrm′) also **en·to·derm** (ĕn′tə-) *n.* The innermost of the three primary germ layers of an embryo, developing into the intestinal tract and associated structures. **—en′do·der′mal** *adj.*
en·do·der·mis (ĕn′də-dûr′mĭs) *n. Bot.* The innermost layer of the cortex in many plants. [NLat. : ENDO + Gk. *derma,* skin.]
en·do·don·tics (ĕn′dō-dŏn′tĭks) also **en·do·don·tia** (-shə, -shē-ə) *n. (used with a sing. verb).* The branch of dentistry dealing with diseases of the tooth pulp. **—en′do·don′tic** *adj.* **—en′do·don′tist** *n.*
en·do·en·zyme (ĕn′dō-ĕn′zīm′) *n.* An enzyme that acts inside the cell that produces it.
en·do·er·gic (ĕn′dō-ûr′jĭk) *adj.* Endothermic. [ENDO- + Gk. *ergon,* work + -IC.]
en·dog·a·my (ĕn-dŏg′ə-mē) *n.* **1.** Marriage within a particular group, caste, class, or tribe in accordance with set custom or law. **2.** *Bot.* Fertilization in which pollen is transferred to another flower of the same plant. **—en·dog′a·mous** *adj.*
en·dog·e·nous (ĕn-dŏj′ə-nəs) *adj.* **1.** Produced from within. **2.** *Biol.* Originating within an organ or part. **—en·dog′e·nous·ly** *adv.* **—en·dog′e·ny** *n.*
en·do·lymph (ĕn′də-lĭmf′) *n.* The fluid in the cochlear duct of the labyrinth of the ear. **—en′do·lym·phat′ic** *adj.*
en·do·me·tri·um (ĕn′dō-mē′trē-əm) *n., pl.* **-tri·a** (-trē-ə). The mucous membrane lining the uterus. **—en′do·me′tri·al** *adj.*
en·do·morph (ĕn′də-môrf′) *n.* **1.** A mineral found as an inclusion in another, such as rutile or tourmaline in quartz. **2.** *Physiol.* An endomorphic person.
en·do·mor·phic (ĕn′də-môr′fĭk) *adj.* **1. a.** Of or pertaining to an endomorph. **b.** Created through endomorphism. **2.** *Physiol.* Characterized by relative prominence of the abdomen and other soft body parts developed from the embryonic endodermal layer. **—en′do·mor′phy** *n.*
en·do·morph·ism (ĕn′də-môr′fĭz′əm) *n.* **1.** The metamorphism of igneous rock as it cools, resulting from contact with and the assimilation of the wall rock. **2.** *Math.* A homomorphism that maps a mathematical set into itself.
en·do·par·a·site (ĕn′dō-păr′ə-sīt′) *n.* An organism, such as a tapeworm, that lives parasitically within another organism.
en·do·phyte (ĕn′də-fīt′) *n.* A plant, such as certain fungi, growing within another plant. **—en′do·phyt′ic** (-dō-fĭt′ĭk) *adj.*
en·do·plasm (ĕn′də-plăz′əm) *n.* A low-viscosity portion of the continuous phase of cytoplasm distinguishable within some cells.
en·do·ra·di·o·sonde (ĕn′də-rā′dē-ō-sŏnd′) *n.* A microelectronic device that is introduced into the body by swallowing to record physiological data.
end organ *n.* The expanded functional termination of a sensory nerve or of a motor nerve in tissue.
en·dor·phin (ĕn-dôr′fĭn) *n.* Any of a group of hormones with pain-killing and tranquilizing ability that are secreted by the brain. [END(O)- + (M)ORPHIN(E).]
en·dorse (ĕn-dôrs′) *tr.v.* **-dorsed, -dors·ing, -dors·es.** **1.** To

write one's signature on the back of (a check, for example) as evidence of the legal transfer of its ownership, esp. in return for the cash or credit indicated on its face. **2.** To place (one's signature), as on a contract, to indicate approval of its contents or terms. **3.** To acknowledge (receipt of payment) by signing a bill, draft, or other instrument. **4.** To give approval of or support to; sanction. [ME *endosen* < AN *endosser* < Med. Lat. *indorsare* : Lat. *in-*, upon + Lat. *dorsum,* back.] **—en·dors'a·ble** *adj.* **—en·dors'er, en·dor'sor** *n.*

en·dor·see (ĕn'dôr-sē') *n.* One to whom ownership of a negotiable document is transferred by endorsement.

en·dorse·ment (ĕn-dôrs'mənt) *n.* **1.** An act of endorsing. **2.** Something that endorses or validates, as a signature or voucher. **3.** Approbation; sanction; support. **4.** An amendment to a contract, such as an insurance policy, permitting a change in the original terms.

endorsement in blank *n.* A blank endorsement.

en·do·scope (ĕn'də-skōp') *n.* An instrument for examining the interior of a bodily canal or hollow organ.

en·do·scop·ic (ĕn'də-skŏp'ĭk) *adj.* Pertaining to or performed by means of an endoscope. **—en'do·scop'ic·al·ly** *adv.*

en·do·skel·e·ton (ĕn'dō-skĕl'ĭ-tən) *n.* An internal supporting skeleton characteristic of vertebrates. **—en'do·skel'e·tal** *adj.*

en·dos·mo·sis (ĕn'dŏz-mō'sĭs, -dŏs-) *n.* Osmosis toward the interior of a cell or cavity. **—en'dos·mot'ic** (-mŏt'ĭk) *adj.*

en·do·some (ĕn'də-sōm') *n.* A discrete, cellular particle of chromatin situated near the center of a nucleus.

en·do·sperm (ĕn'də-spûrm') *n.* The nutritive tissue of a plant seed, surrounding and absorbed by the embryo.

en·do·spore (ĕn'də-spôr', -spōr') *n.* **1.** A small asexual spore, as that formed by some bacteria. **2.** The inner layer of the wall of a spore.

en·dos·te·um (ĕn-dŏs'tē-əm) *n., pl.* **-te·a** (-tē-ə). The membrane that lines the medullary cavity of a bone. [NLat. : END(O)- + Gk. *osteon,* bone.] **—en·dos'te·al** *adj.*

en·do·sul·fan (ĕn'də-sŭl'fən) *n.* A highly toxic crystalline insecticide, $C_9H_6Cl_6O_3S$, that is used in the control of crop insects and mites. [E. *endrin,* an insecticide + -SULF- + -AN.]

en·do·the·ci·um (ĕn'dō-thē'sē-əm, -shē-əm) *n., pl.* **-ci·a** (-sē-ə, -shē-ə). *Bot.* The inner tissue of an anther or a moss capsule. [NLat. : ENDO- + Gk. *thēkion,* dim. of *thēkē,* chest.]

en·do·the·li·o·ma (ĕn'dō-thē'lē-ō'mə) *n., pl.* **-ma·ta** (-mə-tə) or **-mas.** Any of various neoplasms derived from endothelial tissue. [ENDOTHELI(UM) + -OMA.]

en·do·the·li·um (ĕn'dō-thē'lē-əm) *n., pl.* **-li·a** (-lē-ə). A thin layer of flat cells that lines serous cavities, lymph vessels, and blood vessels. [NLat. : ENDO- + Gk. *thēlē,* nipple.] **—en'do·the'li·al, en'do·the'li·oid'** *adj.*

en·do·therm (ĕn'də-thûrm') *n.* Homoiotherm.

en·do·ther·mic (ĕn'dō-thûr'mĭk) also **en·do·ther·mal** (-məl) *adj.* Characterized by or causing the absorption of heat.

en·do·tox·in (ĕn'dō-tŏk'sən) *n.* A toxin produced within a microorganism and released upon destruction of the cell in which it is produced.

en·do·tra·che·al (ĕn'də-trā'kē-əl) *adj.* Within the trachea.

en·dow (ĕn-dou') *tr.v.* **-dowed, -dow·ing, -dows. 1.** To provide with property, income, or a source of income. **2.** To equip or supply with a talent or quality. **3.** *Obs.* To provide with a dower. [ME *endowen* < AN *endouer* : OFr. *en-* (intensive < Lat. *in-*) + *douer,* to provide with a dowry (< Lat. *dotare* < *dos,* dowry).]

en·dow·ment (ĕn-dou'mənt) *n.* **1.** An act of endowing. **2.** Funds or property donated to an institution, individual, or group as a source of income. **3.** A natural gift, ability, or quality.

end·pa·per also **end paper** (ĕnd'pā'pər) *n.* Either of two folded sheets of heavy paper having one half pasted to the inside front or back cover of a book and the other half pasted to the base of the first or last page to form a flyleaf.

end·plate (ĕnd'plāt') *n.* A motor nerve terminal that transmits nerve impulses to muscle.

end·point (ĕnd'point') *n.* **1.** Either of two points marking the end of a line segment. **2.** *Chem.* The point in a volumetric titration at which the amount of added reagent is chemically equivalent to the solution titrated.

end table *n.* A small table, usually placed at either end of a couch or beside a chair.

en·due (ĕn-do͞o', -dyo͞o') *tr.v.* **-dued, -du·ing, -dues. 1.** To provide with some quality or trait. **2.** To put on. [Partly < ME *enduen* < OFr. *enduire,* to lead in < Lat. *inducere* and partly < ME *induen,* to clothe (< Lat. *induere*).]

en·dur·a·ble (ĕn-do͝or'ə-bəl, -dyo͝or'-) *adj.* Capable of being endured; bearable. **—en·dur'a·bly** *adv.*

en·dur·ance (ĕn-do͝or'əns, -dyo͝or'-) *n.* **1.** The act, quality, or power of withstanding hardship or stress. **2.** The state or fact of persevering. **3.** Continuing existence; duration.

en·dure (ĕn-do͝or', -dyo͝or') *v.* **-dured, -dur·ing, -dures.** *—tr.* **1.** To carry on through, despite hardships; undergo: *endure an Arctic winter.* **2.** To bear with tolerance: *could not endure his whining.* *—intr.* **1.** To continue in existence; last: *buildings that endure for centuries.* **2.** To suffer patiently without yielding. [ME *enduren* < OFr. *endurer* < Lat. *indurare,* to make hard : *in-* (intensive) + *durare,* to harden < *durus,* hard.]

en·dur·ing (ĕn-do͝or'ĭng, -dyo͝or'-) *adj.* **1.** Lasting; durable. **2.** Chronic; unresolved: *an enduring problem.* **3.** Long-suffering. **—en·dur'ing·ly** *adv.* **—en·dur'ing·ness** *n.*

en·dur·o (ĕn-do͝or'ō, -dyo͝or'ō) *n., pl.* **-os.** A race, as of automobiles or runners, that tests endurance. [Shortening and alteration of ENDURANCE.]

end·wise (ĕnd'wīz') also **end·ways** (-wāz') *adv.* **1.** On end. **2.** With the end foremost. **3.** Lengthwise. **4.** End to end.

En·dym·i·on (ĕn-dĭm'ē-ən) *n. Gk. Myth.* A handsome young man who was loved by a moon goddess and whose youth was preserved by eternal sleep. [Lat. < Gk. *Endumiōn.*]

-ene *suff.* An unsaturated organic compound, esp. one containing a double bond: *acetylene.* [< Gk. *-ēnē,* fem. adj. suffix.]

en·e·ma (ĕn'ə-mə) *n., pl.* **en·e·mas** or **en·e·ma·ta** (ĕn'ə-mä'tə). **1.** The injection of liquid into the rectum through the anus for cleansing, as a laxative, or for other therapeutic purposes. **2.** The fluid injected as an enema. [LLat. < Gk. < *enienai,* to inject : *en-,* in + *hienai,* to send.]

en·e·my (ĕn'ə-mē) *n., pl.* **-mies. 1.** One that feels malice or hostility toward another; foe. **2. a.** A hostile power or force. **b.** A member or unit of such a force. **3.** Something destructive or injurious in its effects: *Fear is our chief enemy.* *—adj.* Of or pertaining to a hostile power or force. —See Usage note at **collective noun.** [ME *enemi* < OFr. < Lat. *inimicus* : *in-,* not + *amicus,* friend.]

en·er·co·log·i·cal (ĕn'ər-kə-lŏj'ĭ-kəl) *adj.* Of or pertaining to the achievement of a balance between energy use and ecological concerns. [ENER(GY) + (E)COLOGICAL.]

en·er·get·ic (ĕn'ər-jĕt'ĭk) *adj.* Possessing, exerting, or displaying energy; vigorous. [Gk. *energētikos* < *energein,* to be active < *energos,* active. —see ENERGY.] **—en'er·get'i·cal·ly** *adv.*

en·er·get·ics (ĕn'ər-jĕt'ĭks) *n. (used with a sing. verb).* The physics of energy and its transformations.

en·er·gid (ĕn'ər-jĭd') *n.* A unit consisting of a nucleus surrounded by cytoplasm, with or without a cell wall, that does not constitute a cell. [ENERG(Y) + -ID.]

en·er·gize (ĕn'ər-jīz') *v.* **-gized, -giz·ing, -giz·es.** *—tr.* To give energy to; charge. *—intr.* To release or put out energy. **—en'er·giz'er** *n.*

en·er·gy (ĕn'ər-jē) *n., pl.* **-gies. 1. a.** Vigor or power in action. **b.** Vitality and intensity of expression. **2.** The capacity for action or accomplishment: *lacked energy to finish the job.* **3.** *Physics.* The work that a physical system is capable of doing in changing from its actual state to a specified reference state, the total including, in general, contributions of potential energy, kinetic energy, and rest energy. **4.** Usable heat or electric power. [LLat. *energia* < Gk. *energeia* < *energos,* active : *en-,* at + *ergon,* work.]

energy density *n.* The energy per unit volume of a region of space.

energy level *n.* **1.** The energy characteristic of a stationary state of a quantum mechanical system. **2.** The stationary state of a quantum mechanical system.

en·er·vate (ĕn'ər-vāt') *tr.v.* **-vat·ed, -vat·ing, -vates.** To deprive of strength or vitality; weaken. *—adj.* (ĭ-nûr'vĭt). Deprived of strength; devitalized. [Lat. *enervare, enervat-* : *ex-,* out + *nervus,* sinew.] **—en'er·va'tion** *n.* **—en'er·va'tor** *n.*

en·face (ĕn-fās') *tr.v.* **-faced, -fac·ing, -fac·es.** To write on the face of (a check, for example). **—en·face'ment** *n.*

en·fant ter·ri·ble (äN-fäN' tĕ-rē'blə) *n., pl.* **en·fants ter·ri·bles** (äN-fäN' tĕ-rē'blə). One whose startlingly unconventional behavior and ideas are a source of embarrassment or dismay. [Fr. : *enfant,* child + *terrible,* terrible.]

en·fee·ble (ĕn-fē'bəl) *tr.v.* **-bled, -bling, -bles.** To make feeble; deprive of strength. [ME *enfeblen* < OFr. *enfeblir* : *en-* (causative < Lat. *in-,* in) + *feble,* feeble. —see FEEBLE.] **—en·fee'ble·ment** *n.* **—en·fee'bler** *n.*

en·feoff (ĕn-fĕf', -fēf') *tr.v.* **-feoffed, -feoff·ing, -feoffs. 1.** To invest with a feudal estate or fee. **2.** To surrender or give up. [ME *enfeffen* < OFr. *enfeffer* : *en-,* in (< Lat. *in-*) + *fief,* fee.] **—en·feoff'ment** *n.*

en·fet·ter (ĕn-fĕt'ər, ĭn-) *tr.v.* **-tered, -ter·ing, -ters.** To bind in fetters; enchain.

En·field rifle (ĕn'fēld') *n.* Any of several rifles of varying calibers used formerly by British and American troops, esp. the .30 or .303 bolt-action, breechloading model. [After *Enfield,* England.]

en·fi·lade (ĕn'fə-lād', -läd') *n.* The firing of a gun or guns so as to sweep the length of a target, such as a column of troops. *—tr.v.* **-lad·ed, -lad·ing, -lades.** To rake with gunfire in a lengthwise direction. [Fr. < *enfiler,* to rake with gunfire < OFr. to thread : *en-,* in (< Lat. *in-*) + *fil,* thread < Lat. *filum.*]

en·fleu·rage (ŏn'flə-räzh', -räj') *n.* A process in the making of perfume by which odorless fats or oils are exposed to the exhaled fragrance of fresh flowers. [Fr. < *enfleurer,* to saturate with the perfume of flowers : *en-* (< Lat. *in-*) + *fleur,* flower < OFr. *flour* < Lat. *flos.*]

en·flur·ane (ĕn-flo͝or'ān') *n.* A nonexplosive anesthetic, $C_3H_2ClF_5O$. [EN- + (TRI)FLU(O)R(OETH)ANE.]

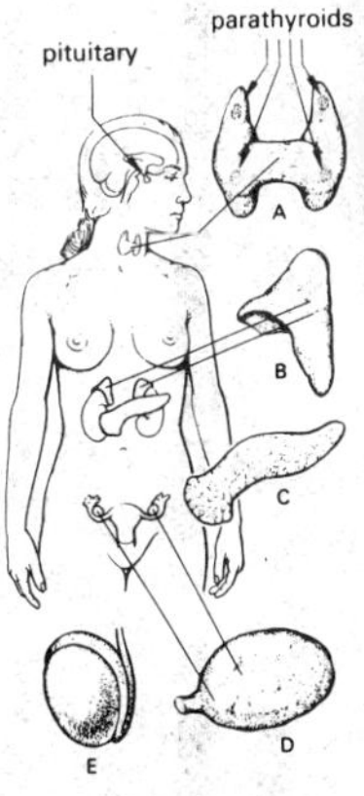

endocrine gland
A. Thyroid
B. Adrenal gland
C. Islands of Langerhans in pancreas
D. Ovary
E. Testis (in male)

en·fold (ĕn-fōld′) *tr.v.* **-fold·ed, -fold·ing, -folds. 1.** To cover with or as if with folds; envelop. **2.** To hold within limits; enclose. **3.** To embrace. **—en·fold′er** *n.*

en·force (ĕn-fôrs′, -fōrs′) *tr.v.* **-forced, -forc·ing, -forc·es. 1.** To compel observance of or obedience to: *enforce a regulation.* **2.** To compel. **3.** To give force to; reinforce. [ME *enforcen* < OFr. *enforcier,* to make strong < VLat. **infortiare* : *in-,* in + *fortis,* strong.] **—en·force′a·ble** *adj.* **—en·force′ment** *n.* **—en·forc′er** *n.*

en·fran·chise (ĕn-frăn′chīz′) *tr.v.* **-chised, -chis·ing, -chis·es. 1.** To bestow a franchise upon. **2.** To endow with the rights of citizenship, esp. the right to vote. **3.** To free, as from bondage. [ME *enfraunchisen* < OFr. *enfranchir, enfranchiss-* : *en-* (causative < Lat. *in-,* in) + *franc,* free. —see FRANK[1]]

en·gage (ĕn-gāj′) *v.* **-gaged, -gag·ing, -gag·es.** *—tr.* **1.** To obtain or contract for the services of; employ: *engage a carpenter.* **2.** To contract for the use of; reserve: *engage a room.* **3.** To obtain and hold the attention of; engross: *engaged her interest for months.* **4.** To require the use of; occupy: *Studying engages most of a student's time.* **5.** To pledge or promise, esp. to marry. **6.** To enter or bring into conflict with: *We have engaged the enemy.* **7.** To interlock or cause to interlock; mesh. **8.** To attract; win. **9.** To entangle; involve: *engage someone in idle chatter.* **10.** *Archaic.* To give or take as security. *—intr.* **1.** To involve oneself or become occupied; participate: *engage in conversation.* **2.** To assume an obligation; agree. **3.** To enter into conflict or battle. **4.** To become meshed or interlocked. [ME *engagen,* to pledge something as security for repayment of debt < OFr. *engager* : *en-,* in (< Lat. *in-*) + *gage,* pledge, of Germanic orig.] **—en·gag′er** *n.*

en·ga·gé (ăn′gä-zhā′) *adj.* Actively committed, as to a political cause. [Fr., p.part. of *engager,* to engage < OFr.]

en·gaged (ĕn-gājd′) *adj.* **1.** Employed, occupied, or busy. **2.** Committed to. **3.** Pledged to marry: *an engaged couple.* **4.** Involved in conflict or battle. **5.** Being in gear; meshed. **6.** Partly sunk, built into, or attached to another part, as columns on a wall.

en·gage·ment (ĕn-gāj′mənt) *n.* **1.** An act of engaging or the state of being engaged. **2.** Betrothal. **3.** One that engages. **4.** A promise or commitment to appear at a certain time; appointment. **5. a.** Employment, esp. for a specified time. **b.** The period of employment. **6.** A battle or encounter. **7.** The condition of being in gear.

en·gag·ing (ĕn-gā′jĭng) *adj.* Tending to attract; charming. **—en·gag′ing·ly** *adv.*

en garde (äɴ gärd′) *interj.* Used to warn a fencer to assume the first position preparatory to a match. [Fr. : *en,* on + *garde,* guard.]

en·gar·land (ĕn-gär′lənd) *tr.v.* **-land·ed -land·ing, -lands.** To encircle or deck with or as if with a garland.

en·gen·der (ĕn-jĕn′dər) *v.* **-dered, -der·ing, -ders.** *—tr.* **1.** To bring into existence; give rise to. **2.** To procreate; propagate. *—intr.* To come into existence. [ME *engendren* < OFr. *engendrer* < Lat. *ingenerare* : *in-,* in + *generare,* to produce < *genus,* birth.]

en·gine (ĕn′jĭn) *n.* **1. a.** A machine that converts energy into mechanical motion. **b.** A mechanical appliance, instrument, or tool: *engines of war.* **2.** A locomotive. **3.** *Archaic.* An agent, instrument, or means of accomplishment. [ME *engin* < OFr., skill < Lat. *ingenium.*]

engine block *n.* The cast metal block containing the cylinders of an internal-combustion engine.

en·gi·neer (ĕn′jə-nîr′) *n.* **1.** A person trained or professionally engaged in a branch of engineering. **2.** A person who skillfully or shrewdly manages an enterprise. **3.** A person who operates an engine. *—tr.v.* **-neered, -neer·ing, -neers. 1.** To plan, construct, and manage as an engineer. **2.** To plan, manage, and put through by skillful acts or contrivance; maneuver. [ME *enginer* < OFr. *engigneor* < Med. Lat. *ingeniator,* contriver < *ingeniare,* to contrive < *ingenium,* skill.]

en·gi·neer·ing (ĕn′jə-nîr′ĭng) *n.* **1.** The application of scientific and mathematical principles to practical ends such as the design, construction, and operation of efficient and economical structures, equipment, and systems. **2.** The profession of or the work performed by an engineer.

en·gine·ry (ĕn′jĭn-rē) *n.* **1.** Machines and tools; machinery. **2.** Engines or instruments of war.

en·gird (ĕn-gûrd′) *tr.v.* **-girt** (-gûrt′) or **-gird·ed, -gird·ing, -girds.** To encircle.

en·gir·dle (ĕn-gûr′dl) *tr.v.* **-dled, -dling, -dles.** To encircle or surround with or as if with a girdle.

en·gla·cial (ĕn-glā′shəl) *adj.* Located or occurring within a glacier.

Eng·lish (ĭng′glĭsh) *adj.* **1.** Of, pertaining to, derived from, or characteristic of England, its people, or its culture. *—n.* **1.** The people of England. **2. a.** The West Germanic language of England, the United States, and other countries that are or have been under English influence or control. **b.** The English language of a particular time, region, person, or group of persons: *American English.* **3.** A translation into or an equivalent in the English language. **4.** A course or individual class in the study of English literature, language, or composition. **5.** *Printing.* A size of type, 14-point. **6.** Often **english.** The spin given to a ball by striking it on one side or releasing it with a sharp twist. *—tr.v.* **-lished, -lish·ing, -lish·es. 1.** To translate into English. **2.** To adapt into English; Anglicize. [ME *Englisch* < OE *Englisc* < *Engle,* the Angles.]

English horn

English daisy *n.* The daisy (sense 2).

English finish *n.* A smooth, nonglossy finish for paper.

English horn *n.* A double-reed woodwind musical instrument similar to but larger than the oboe and pitched lower by a fifth.

Eng·lish·man (ĭng′glĭsh-mən) *n.* A man who is English by birth, descent, or naturalization.

English muffin *n.* A flat round of yeast dough that has been baked on a griddle and is usually split and toasted before eating.

English plantain *n.* Ribgrass.

English setter *n.* A dog of a breed developed in England, having a silky white coat usually with black or brownish markings.

English sheepdog *n.* The Old English sheepdog.

English sonnet *n.* A Shakespearean sonnet.

English sparrow *n.* The house sparrow.

English walnut *n.* **1.** A Eurasian tree, *Juglans regia,* cultivated in southern Europe and California. **2.** The large edible nut of the English walnut tree.

Eng·lish·wom·an (ĭng′glĭsh-wo͝om′ən) *n.* A woman who is English by birth, descent, or naturalization.

en·glut (ĕn-glŭt′) *tr.v.* **-glut·ted, -glut·ting, -gluts.** To gulp down; swallow greedily. [OFr. *englotir* < LLat. *inglutire* : Lat. *in-,* in + Lat. *gluttire,* to swallow.]

en·gorge (ĕn-gôrj′) *v.* **-gorged, -gorg·ing, -gorg·es.** *—tr.* **1.** To devour greedily. **2.** To gorge; glut. **3.** To fill to excess, as with blood or other fluid. *—intr.* To feed ravenously. [OFr. *engorgier* : *en-,* in (< Lat. *in-*) + *gorge,* throat < Lat. *gurges,* gulf.] **—en·gorge′ment** *n.*

en·graft (ĕn-grăft′) *tr.v.* **-graft·ed, -graft·ing, -grafts. 1.** To graft (a scion) onto or into another plant. **2.** To plant firmly; establish. **—en·graft′ment** *n.*

en·grailed (ĕn-grāl′d) *adj.* **1.** Indented along the edge with small curves. **2.** Having an edge or margin formed by a ring of dots. [ME *engrelen* < OFr. *engresler* : *en-,* in (< Lat. *in-*) + *gresle,* slender < Lat. *gracilis.*]

en·grain (ĕn-grān′) *tr.v.* **-grained, -grain·ing, -grains.** To ingrain. [ME *engreinen,* to dye red < OFr. *engrainer,* to dye < *en graine,* in cochineal dye.]

en·gram also **en·gramme** (ĕn′grăm′) *n.* A hypothetical alteration of living neural tissue, posited as an explanation for memory.

en·grave (ĕn-grāv′) *tr.v.* **-graved, -grav·ing, -graves. 1.** To carve, cut, or etch into a material. **2. a.** To carve, cut, or etch into a block or surface used for printing. **b.** To print from a block or plate made by such a process. **3.** To impress deeply. **—en·grav′er** *n.*

en·grav·ing (ĕn-grā′vĭng) *n.* **1.** The art or technique of one that engraves. **2.** An engraved surface for printing. **3.** A print made from an engraved plate or block.

en·gross (ĕn-grōs′) *tr.v.* **-grossed, -gross·ing, -gross·es. 1.** To occupy the complete attention of; absorb. **2.** To acquire most or all of a commodity; monopolize a market. **3. a.** To write or transcribe in a large, clear hand. **b.** To prepare the text of (an official document) by writing or printing. [Partly < ME *engrossen,* to collect in large quantity < OFr. *engrossier* < *en gros,* in large quantity, and partly < ME *engrossen,* to write in a large hand < AN *engrosser,* prob. < Med. Lat. *ingrossare : Lat. in-,* in + *grossa,* a copy in a large hand < Lat. *grossus,* thick.] **—en·gross′er** *n.*

en·gross·ing (ĕn-grō′sĭng) *adj.* Occupying one's complete attention; wholly absorbing. **—en·gross′ing·ly** *adv.*

en·gross·ment (ĕn-grōs′mənt) *n.* **1.** The act of engrossing. **2.** The state of being completely absorbed, occupied, or monopolized.

en·gulf (ĕn-gŭlf′) *tr.v.* **-gulfed, -gulf·ing, -gulfs. 1.** To surround and enclose completely. **2.** To swallow up or overwhelm by or as if by overflowing and enclosing. **—en·gulf′ment** *n.*

en·hance (ĕn-hăns′) *tr.v.* **-hanced, -hanc·ing, -hanc·es.** To increase or make greater, as in value, beauty, or reputation; augment. [ME *enhauncen* < AN *enhauncer* < OFr. *enhaucier* < VLat. **inaltiare* : Lat. *in-* (intensive) + *altus,* high.] **—en·hance′ment** *n.* **—en·hanc′er** *n.* **—en·hanc′ive** *adj.*

en·har·mon·ic (ĕn′här-mŏn′ĭk) *adj. Mus.* Of, relating to, or involving the use of two different written representations, such as C# to D♭, for the same tone. [Fr. *enharmonique* < OFr., of a scale employing quarter tones < Gk. *enarmonios* : *en-,* in + *harmonia,* harmony.] **—en′har·mon′i·cal·ly** *adv.*

e·nig·ma (ĭ-nĭg′mə) *n.* **1.** An obscure speech or writing. **2.** One that is puzzling, ambiguous, or inexplicable. [Lat. *aenigma* < Gk. *ainigma* < *ainissesthai,* to speak in riddles < *ainos,* fable.]

en·ig·mat·ic (ĕn′ĭg-măt′ĭk) or **en·ig·mat·i·cal** (-ĭ-kəl) *adj.* Of or resembling an enigma; puzzling. **—en′ig·mat′i·cal·ly** *adv.*

en·isle (ĕn-īl′) *tr.v.* **-isled, -isl·ing, -isles. 1.** To make into an island. **2.** To set apart from others; isolate.

en·jamb·ment or **en·jambe·ment** (ĕn-jăm′mənt, -jămb′mənt) *n.* The continuation of a sentence from one line or

ă pat / ā pay / âr care / ä father / b bib / ch church / d deed / ĕ pet / ē be / f fife / g gag / h hat / hw which / ĭ pit / ī pie / îr pier / j judge / k kick / l lid, needle / m mum / n no, sudden / ng thing / ŏ pot / ō toe / ô paw, for / oi noise / ou out / o͝o took / o͞o boot /

couplet of a poem to the next. [Fr. *enjambement* < OFr. *enjamber,* to straddle : *en-,* in (< Lat. *in-*) + *jambe,* leg < Lat. *gamba,* hoof, perh. < Gk. *kampē,* bend.]

en·join (ĕn-join′) *tr.v.* **-joined, -join·ing, -joins. 1.** To direct with authority and emphasis; command. **2.** To prohibit or forbid. [ME *enjoinen* < OFr. *enjoindre* < Lat. *injungere* : *in-,* in + *jungere,* to join.] **—en·join′er** *n.* **—en·join′ment** *n.*

en·joy (ĕn-joi′) *tr.v.* **-joyed, -joy·ing, -joys. 1.** To receive pleasure from; relish. **2.** To have the use or benefit of: *enjoys good health.* **3.** To make happy: *always enjoyed himself at their house.* [ME *enjoien* < OFr. *enjoir* : *en-,* in (< Lat. *in-*) + *joir,* to rejoice < Lat. *gaudere.*] **—en·joy′a·ble** *adj.* **—en·joy′a·bly** *adv.* **—en·joy′er** *n.*

en·joy·ment (ĕn-joi′mənt) *n.* **1.** The act or state of enjoying. **2.** The use or possession of something beneficial or pleasurable. **3.** Something that gives pleasure.

en·keph·a·lin (ĕn-kĕf′ə-lĭn′) *n.* One of two closely related proteins occurring in the brain and having opiate qualities. [Gk. *enkephalos,* in the head (*en-,* in + *kephalē,* head) + -IN.]

en·kin·dle (ĕn-kĭn′dl) *v.* **-dled, -dling, -dles.** *—tr.* **1.** To set afire; light. **2.** To incite; arouse. **3.** To make luminous and glowing. *—intr.* To catch fire. **—en·kin′dler** *n.*

en·lace (ĕn-lās′) *tr.v.* **-laced, -lac·ing, -lac·es. 1.** To wrap or wind about with or as if with a lace or laces; encircle. **2.** To interlace; entwine. **—en·lace′ment** *n.*

en·large (ĕn-lärj′) *v.* **-larged, -larg·ing, -larg·es.** *—tr.* **1.** To make larger; add to. **2.** To give greater scope to; expand. *—intr.* **1.** To become larger; grow. **2.** To speak or write at greater length or in greater detail: *enlarged upon his plan.* [ME *enlargen* < OFr. *enlargier* : *en-,* in (< Lat. *in-*) + *large,* large < Lat. *largus.*] **—en·larg′er** *n.*

en·large·ment (ĕn-lärj′mənt) *n.* **1.** An act of enlarging or the state of being enlarged. **2.** Something that enlarges. **3.** A photographic reproduction or copy larger than the original.

en·light·en (ĕn-līt′n) *tr.v.* **-ened, -en·ing, -ens. 1.** To furnish with spiritual understanding. **2.** To give information to; inform. **—en·light′en·er** *n.*

en·light·en·ment (ĕn-līt′n-mənt) *n.* **1.** An act or means of enlightening. **2.** The state of being enlightened. **3. Enlightenment.** A philosophical movement of the 18th century, concerned with the critical examination of previously accepted doctrines and institutions from the point of view of rationalism.

en·list (ĕn-lĭst′) *v.* **-list·ed, -list·ing, -lists.** *—tr.* **1.** To obtain or engage for service in the armed forces. **2.** To engage the support or cooperation of. *—intr.* **1.** To enter the armed forces voluntarily. **2.** To participate actively in some cause or enterprise. [EN- + LIST[1].] **—en·list′ment** *n.*

enlisted man *n.* A man or woman who has enlisted in the armed forces without an officer's commission or warrant.

en·liv·en (ĕn-lī′vən) *tr.v.* **-ened, -en·ing, -ens.** To make lively or spirited; animate. **—en·liv′en·er** *n.* **—en·liv′en·ment** *n.*

en masse (ŏn măs′) *adv.* In one group or body; all together. [Fr. : *en,* on + *masse,* crowd.]

en·mesh (ĕn-mĕsh′) *tr.v.* **-meshed, -mesh·ing, -mesh·es.** To entangle, involve, or catch in or as if in a mesh.

en·mi·ty (ĕn′mĭ-tē) *n., pl.* **-ties.** Deep-seated mutual hatred. [ME *enemite* < OFr. *enemitie* < VLat. **inimicitas* < Lat. *inimicus,* enemy. —see ENEMY.]

Synonyms: *enmity, hostility, antagonism, animosity, rancor, antipathy, animus.* These nouns refer to the feeling or expression of ill will. *Enmity* and *hostility* both denote the ill will of one person or group toward another or, more often, mutual bad feeling. *Hostility,* in addition, can refer to clear expression of this in the form of threats or violent acts. The remaining terms denote conditions of ill will likely to produce such acts. *Antagonism* makes the strongest implication of active opposition or combat or the imminence of it. *Animosity* and, to a greater degree, *rancor* suggest the harboring of hatred and resentment; such feelings typically trace to past differences that have produced grievances and the desire for revenge. *Antipathy* is deep-seated aversion or repugnance. *Animus* is ill will of a distinctively personal and sometimes irrational nature, based on one's prejudices or peculiarity of character or temperament.

en·ne·ad (ĕn′ē-ăd′) *n.* A group or set of nine. [Gk. *enneas, ennead-* < *ennea,* nine.]

en·no·ble (ĕn-nō′bəl) *tr.v.* **-bled, -bling, -bles. 1.** To make noble. **2.** To raise in rank to the nobility. [ME *ennoblen* < OFr. *ennoblir* : *en-,* in (< Lat. *in-*) + *noble,* noble < Lat. *nobilis.*] **—en·no′ble·ment** *n.* **—en·no′bler** *n.*

en·nui (ŏn-wē′, ŏn′wē) *n.* Listlessness and dissatisfaction; boredom. [Fr. < OFr. *enui* < Lat. *in odio,* odious : *in,* in + *odium,* hate.]

e·nol (ē′nôl′, ē′nōl′) *n.* An organic compound containing a hydroxyl group bonded to a carbon atom which in turn is doubly bonded to another carbon atom. [< -EN(E) + -OL.] **—e·nol′ic** (ē-nŏl′ĭk) *adj.*

e·no·lase (ē′nə-lās′) *n.* An enzyme present in muscle tissue that acts in carbohydrate metabolism.

e·nol·o·gy (ē-nŏl′ə-jē) *n.* Variant of **oenology.**

e·nor·mi·ty (ĭ-nôr′mĭ-tē) *n., pl.* **-ties. 1.** The quality of passing all moral bounds; excessive wickedness or outrageousness. **2.** A monstrous offense or evil; outrage.

e·nor·mous (ĭ-nôr′məs) *adj.* **1.** Very great in size, extent, number, or degree; immense. **2.** *Archaic.* Very wicked; heinous. [ME *enorme* < Lat. *enormis* : *ex-,* out of + *norma,* norm.] **—e·nor′mous·ly** *adv.* **—e·nor′mous·ness** *n.*

Synonyms: *enormous, immense, huge, gigantic, colossal, mammoth, tremendous, stupendous, gargantuan, vast.* These adjectives describe what is extraordinarily large or great in some respect. *Enormous* specifies a marked excess beyond the norm in size, amount, or degree. *Immense* literally means infinite and generally refers to size or extent that is beyond the usual means of measurement. *Huge* especially implies greatness of physical size or capacity. *Gigantic* implies abnormal deviation from the usual physical size or capacity of a given kind. *Colossal* suggests hugeness that creates awe or taxes belief. *Mammoth* is applied to anything on an extremely large or extravagant scale. *Tremendous,* in careful usage, refers to what inspires awe or fear; less strictly it describes greatness of quantity, extent, or degree. *Stupendous* implies size that astounds or defies description. *Gargantuan* stresses greatness of capacity, especially for food or pleasure. *Vast* often makes reference to greatness of extent or scope; less frequently it refers to quantity or amount.

e·nough (ĭ-nŭf′) *adj.* Sufficient to meet a need or satisfy a desire; adequate. *—pron.* An adequate quantity: *had enough of everything.* *—adv.* **1.** To a satisfactory amount or degree; sufficiently. **2.** Very; fully; quite: *We were glad enough to leave.* **3.** Tolerably; rather: *She sang well enough, but the show was a failure.* [ME *enogh* < OE *genōg*]

e·nounce (ĭ-nouns′) *tr.v.* **e·nounced, e·nounc·ing, e·nounc·es. 1.** To declare formally; state. **2.** To pronounce clearly; enunciate. [Fr. *énoncer* < Lat. *enuntiare,* to speak out : *ex-,* out + *nuntiare,* to declare.] **—e·nounce′ment** *n.*

e·now (ĭ-nou′) *adj. Archaic.* Enough. [ME *inow* < OE *genōg.*] **—e·now′** *adv.*

en pas·sant (äN′ pä-säN′) *adv.* In passing; by the way; incidentally. *—n.* The capture of a chess pawn after an initial move of two squares by an enemy pawn in a position to make a capture on the first of the two squares so crossed. [Fr.]

en·phy·tot·ic (ĕn′fī-tŏt′ĭk) *adj.* Designating or characterizing a plant disease that causes a relatively constant amount of damage each year. [EN- + -PHYT(E) + -OTIC.] **—en′phy·tot′ic** *n.*

en·plane (ĕn-plān′) also **em·plane** (ĕm-) *intr.v.* **-planed, -plan·ing, -planes.** To board an airplane.

en·quire (ĕn-kwīr′) *v.* Variant of **inquire.**

en·rage (ĕn-rāj′) *tr.v.* **-raged, -rag·ing, -rag·es.** To put in a rage; infuriate.

en·rapt (ĕn-răpt′) *adj.* **1.** Enraptured. **2.** Enthralled.

en·rap·ture (ĕn-răp′chər) *tr.v.* **-tured, -tur·ing, -tures.** To fill with rapture or delight. **—en·rap′ture·ment** *n.*

en·rich (ĕn-rĭch′) *tr.v.* **-riched, -rich·ing, -rich·es. 1.** To make rich or richer. **2.** To make fuller, more meaningful, or more rewarding: *studied in an enriched program at school.* **3.** To add fertilizer to. **4.** To add nutrients to. **5.** To add to the beauty or character of; adorn: *the carved moldings enriched the walls.* **6.** *Physics.* To increase the ratio of radioactive isotopes in. [ME *enrichen* < OFr. *enricher* : *en-* (causative < Lat. *in-,* in) + *riche,* rich, of Germanic orig.] **—en·rich′er** *n.*

engraving
Engraved face of an 18th-century tankard

en·rich·ment (ĕn-rĭch′mənt) *n.* **1. a.** The act of enriching. **b.** The state of being enriched. **2.** Something that enriches.

en·robe (ĕn-rōb′) *tr.v.* **-robed, -rob·ing, -robes.** To dress in or as if in a robe.

en·roll also **en·rol** (ĕn-rōl′) *v.* **-rolled, -roll·ing, -rolls** also **-rolled, -rol·ling, -rols.** *—tr.* **1.** To enter the name of in a register, record, or roll. **2.** To roll or wrap up. *—intr.* To place one's name on a roll or register. [ME *enrollen* < OFr. *enroller* : *en-,* in (< Lat. *in-*) + *rolle,* roll < Lat. *rotulus,* dim. of *rota,* wheel.] **—en·roll·ee′** *n.*

en·roll·ment or **en·rol·ment** (ĕn-rōl′mənt) *n.* **1. a.** The action of enrolling. **b.** The state or process of being enrolled. **2.** A record or entry. **3.** The number enrolled.

en·root (ĕn-ro͞ot′, -ro͝ot′) *tr.v.* **-root·ed, -root·ing, -roots.** To establish firmly by or as if by roots; implant.

en route (ŏn ro͞ot′, ĕn) *adv. & adj.* On or along the way. [Fr.]

en·sam·ple (ĕn-săm′pəl) *n. Archaic.* An example. [ME < OFr. *example.* —see EXAMPLE.]

en·san·guine (ĕn-săng′gwĭn) *tr.v.* **-guined, -guin·ing, -guines. 1.** To cover or stain with blood. **2.** To make crimson.

en·sconce (ĕn-skŏns′) *tr.v.* **-sconced, -sconc·ing, -sconc·es. 1.** To settle (oneself) securely or comfortably: *She ensconced herself in an armchair.* **2.** To place or conceal in a secure place.

en·sem·ble (ŏn-sŏm′bəl) *n.* A unit or group of complementary parts that contribute to a single effect, esp.: **a.** A coordinated outfit or costume. **b.** A group of supporting musicians, singers, dancers, or actors who perform together. **c.** Music for two or more vocalists or instrumentalists. **d.** The musicians who perform in a musical ensemble. [Fr. < LLat. *insimul,* at the same time : *in,* in + *simul,* at the same time.]

en·shrine (ĕn-shrīn′) *tr.v.* **-shrined, -shrin·ing, -shrines. 1.** To enclose in or as if in a shrine. **2.** To cherish as sacred. **—en·shrine′ment** *n.*

en·shroud (ĕn-shroud′) *tr.v.* **-shroud·ed, -shroud·ing, -shrouds.** To cover with or as if with a shroud.

ensiform
Ensiform iris leaves

en·si·form (ĕn′sə-fôrm′) *adj.* Sword-shaped, as the leaf of an iris. [Lat. *ensis,* sword + -FORM.]

en·sign (ĕn′sən) *n.* **1.** (*also* ĕn′sīn′). A national flag displayed on ships and aircraft, often with the special insignia of a branch or unit of the armed forces: *the naval ensign.* **2.** (*also* ĕn′sīn′). A standard or banner, as of a military unit. **3.** (*also* ĕn′sīn′). *Archaic.* A standard-bearer. **4.** A commissioned officer of the lowest rank in the U.S. Navy or Coast Guard. **5.** (*also* ĕn′sīn′). **a.** A badge; emblem. **b.** A sign; token. [ME *ensigne* < OFr. *enseigne* < Lat. *insignia,* insignia. —see INSIGNIA.]

en·si·lage (ĕn′sə-lĭj) *n.* **1.** The process of storing and fermenting green fodder in a silo. **2.** Fodder preserved in a silo; silage. —*tr.v.* **-laged, -lag·ing, -lag·es.** To ensile. [Fr. < *ensiler,* to ensile.]

en·sile (ĕn-sīl′) *tr.v.* **-siled, -sil·ing, -siles.** To store (fodder) in a silo for preservation. [Fr. *ensiler* < Sp. *ensilar* : *en-,* in (< Lat. *in-*) + *silo,* silo. —see SILO.]

en·slave (ĕn-slāv′) *tr.v.* **-slaved, -slav·ing, -slaves.** To make into or as if into a slave. **—en·slave′ment** *n.* **—en·slav′er** *n.*

en·snare (ĕn-snâr′) *tr.v.* **-snared, -snar·ing, -snares.** To take or catch in or as if in a snare. **—en·snare′ment** *n.* **—en·snar′er** *n.*

en·soul (ĕn-sōl′) *tr.v.* **-souled, -soul·ing, -souls. 1.** To endow with a soul. **2.** To unite with the soul.

en·sphere (ĕn-sfîr′) *tr.v.* **-sphered, -spher·ing, -spheres. 1.** To enclose in or as if in a sphere. **2.** To give spherical form to.

en·sta·tite (ĕn′stə-tīt′) *n.* A variety of orthorhombic pyroxene having a magnesium silicate base, mainly $Mg_2Si_2O_6$, usually found embedded in igneous rocks. [Gk. *enstatēs,* adversary + -ITE.]

ensign

en·sue (ĕn-so͞o′) *intr.v.* **-sued, -su·ing, -sues.** To follow as a consequence or result. [ME *ensuen* < OFr. *ensuir* < Lat. *insequi* to pursue : *in-,* in + *sequi,* to follow.]

en·sure (ĕn-sho͝or′) *tr.v.* **-sured, -sur·ing, -sures.** To make sure or certain; insure. —See Usage note at **assure.**

ent– *pref.* Variant of **ento-.**

-ent *suff.* **1. a.** Performing, promoting, or causing a specified action: *absorbent.* **b.** Being in a specified state or condition: *bivalent.* **2.** One that performs, promotes, or causes a specified action: *referent.* [ME < OFr. < Lat *-ens,* pr.part. suffix.]

en·tab·la·ture (ĕn-tăb′lə-cho͝or′) *n. Archit.* **1.** The upper section of a classical order, resting on the capital and including the architrave, frieze, and cornice. **2.** A raised, horizontal structure, esp. a support for machinery. [Obs. Fr. < Ital. *intavolatura* < *intavolare,* to put on a table : *in-,* in (< Lat.) + *tavola,* table < Lat. *tabula,* board.]

entablature

en·ta·ble·ment (ĕn-tā′bəl-mənt) *n.* A platform that supports a statue and is located above the base and the dado. [Fr. < OFr. : *en-,* in (< Lat. *in-*) + *table,* table (< Lat. *tabula,* board) + *-ment,* -ment.]

en·tail (ĕn-tāl′, ĭn-) *tr.v.* **-tailed, -tail·ing, -tails. 1.** To have, impose, or require as a necessary accompaniment or consequence: *a battle plan that entailed heavy casualties.* **2.** To limit the inheritance of (property) to a specified succession of heirs. —*n.* **1. a.** The act of entailing, esp. property. **b.** The state of being entailed. **2.** An entailed estate. **3.** A predetermined order of succession, as to an estate or to an office. **4.** Something transmitted as if by unalterable inheritance. [ME *entaillen,* to limit inheritance to specific heirs : *en-,* in (< Lat. *in-*) + *taille,* tail. —see TAIL2.] **—en·tail′ment** *n.*

en·ta·moe·ba or **en·ta·me·ba** (ĕn′tə-mē′bə) also **en·da·moe·ba** or **en·da·me·ba** (ĕn′də-) *n., pl.* **-bas** or **-bae** (-bē). Any of several parasitic amoebas of the genus *Entamoeba,* esp. *E. histolytica,* causing dysentery and ulceration of the colon and liver.

en·tan·gle (ĕn-tăng′gəl) *tr.v.* **-gled, -gling, -gles. 1.** To make tangled; snarl. **2.** To complicate; confuse. **3.** To involve in or as if in a tangle. **—en·tan′gle·ment** *n.* **—en·tan′gler** *n.*

en·tel·e·chy (ĕn-tĕl′ĭ-kē) *n., pl.* **-chies. 1.** In the philosophy of Aristotle, the condition of a thing whose essence is fully realized; actuality as distinguished from potentiality. **2.** In some philosophical systems, a vital force urging an organism toward self-fulfillment. [LLat. *entelechia* < Gk. *entelekheia* : *entelēs,* complete (*en-,* in + *telos,* perfection) + *ekhein,* to have.]

en·tente (ŏn-tŏnt′) *n.* **1.** An agreement between two or more governments or powers for cooperative action or policy. **2.** The parties to an entente. [Fr. < OFr. *entendre,* to understand. —see INTEND.]

en·ter (ĕn′tər) *v.* **-tered, -ter·ing, -ters.** —*tr.* **1.** To come or go into. **2.** To penetrate; pierce. **3.** To introduce; insert. **4.** To become an element in or a part of. **5.** To begin; embark upon. **6. a.** To obtain admission to. **b.** To gain admission for. **c.** To enroll. **7. a.** To register as an entry in an exhibition or competition: *enter dahlias in a flower show.* **b.** To become a participant in: *enter a debate.* **c.** To take part as a contestant in: *enter a primary.* **8.** To take up; make a beginning in: *enter the medical profession.* **9.** *Law.* **a.** To place formally upon the records: *enter a plea.* **b.** To go upon in order to take possession of (land). **10.** To report (a ship, for example) to customs. —*intr.* **1.** To come or go in. **2.** To gain entry. **3.** To become a member of a group. **4. a.** To participate: *enter into a discussion.* **b.** To be a component or part. **5.** To consider; investigate: *a report that entered into the effect of high interest rates upon the free market.* **6.** To become party to a contract. **7.** To set out; embark. **8.** To go upon in order to take legal possession of land. **9.** To begin to consider or deal with a subject. [ME *entren* < OFr. *entrer* < Lat. *intrare* < *intra,* within.]

enter– *pref.* Variant of **entero-.**

en·ter·al (ĕn′tər-əl) *adj.* Enteric. **—en′ter·al·ly** *adv.*

en·ter·ic (ĕn-tĕr′ĭk) *adj.* Of or within the intestine. [Gk. *enterikos* < *enteron,* intestine.]

enteric fever *n.* Typhoid fever.

en·ter·i·tis (ĕn′tə-rī′tĭs) *n.* Inflammation of the intestinal tract.

entero– or **enter–** *pref.* Intestine: *enteritis.* [NLat. < Gk. *enteron,* intestine.]

en·ter·o·bac·te·ri·um (ĕn′tə-rō-băk-tîr′ē-əm) *n., pl.* **-i·a** (-ē-ə). Any of various gram-negative rod-shaped bacteria of the family Enterobacteriaceae that includes some pathogens of plants and animals.

en·ter·o·bi·a·sis (ĕn′tə-rō-bī′ə-sĭs) *n.* Infestation of the intestine with pinworms *(Enterobius vermicularis).* [NLat. *Enterobius,* pinworm genus + -IASIS.]

en·ter·o·coc·cus (ĕn′tə-rō-kŏk′əs) *n., pl.* **-coc·ci** (-kŏk′sī′, -kŏk′ī′). A streptococcus that inhabits the intestine. **—en′ter·o·coc′cal** *adj.*

en·ter·o·gas·trone (ĕn′tə-rō-găs′trōn′) *n.* A hormone found in the upper intestinal mucosa that inhibits gastric motility and secretion. [ENTERO- + GASTR(O)- + (HORM)ONE.]

en·ter·o·ki·nase (ĕn′tə-rō-kī′nās′, -kĭn′ās′) *n.* An enzyme found in intestinal juice that converts trypsinogen to trypsin.

en·ter·on (ĕn′tə-rŏn′) *n.* The alimentary canal; intestine. [NLat. < Gk.]

en·ter·o·path·o·gen·ic (ĕn′tə-rō-păth′ə-jĕn′ĭk) *adj.* Capable of causing disease in the intestinal tract.

en·ter·op·a·thy (ĕn′tə-rŏp′ə-thē) *n.* A disease of the intestinal tract.

en·ter·os·to·my (ĕn′tə-rŏs′tə-mē) *n., pl.* **-mies.** Surgical formation of an opening into the intestine through the abdominal wall.

en·ter·ot·o·my (ĕn′tə-rŏt′ə-mē) *n., pl.* **-mies.** Surgical incision into the intestine.

en·ter·o·tox·in (ĕn′tə-rō-tŏk′sĭn) *n.* A toxin produced by bacteria that is specific for intestinal cells and causes the symptoms of food poisoning.

en·ter·prise (ĕn′tər-prīz′) *n.* **1.** An undertaking, esp. one of some scope, complication, and risk. **2.** A business organization. **3.** Industrious and systematic activity. **4.** Readiness to venture; initiative. [ME < OFr. *entreprise* < *entreprendre,* to undertake : *entre-,* between (< Lat. *inter-*) + *prendre,* to take < Lat. *prendere.*] **—en′ter·pris′er** *n.*

en·ter·pris·ing (ĕn′tər-prī′zĭng) *adj.* Showing imagination, initiative, and readiness to undertake or venture. **—en′ter·pris′ing·ly** *adv.*

en·ter·tain (ĕn′tər-tān′) *v.* **-tained, -tain·ing, -tains.** —*tr.* **1.** To hold the attention of; amuse. **2.** To extend hospitality toward: *entertain friends at dinner.* **3.** To consider; contemplate: *entertain an idea.* **4.** To hold in mind; harbor: *entertained few illusions.* **5.** *Archaic.* To continue with; maintain. —*intr.* **1.** To show hospitality to guests. **2.** To provide entertainment. [ME *entertinen,* to maintain < OFr. *entretenir* < VLat. **intertenēre* : Lat. *inter,* among + Lat. *tenēre,* to hold.] **—en′ter·tain′er** *n.*

en·ter·tain·ing (ĕn′tər-tā′nĭng) *adj.* Agreeably diverting; amusing. **—en′ter·tain′ing·ly** *adv.*

en·ter·tain·ment (ĕn′tər-tān′mənt) *n.* **1.** The act of entertaining. **2.** The art or field of entertaining. **3.** Something that entertains, esp. a performance or show. **4.** The pleasure afforded by being entertained; amusement. **5.** *Obs.* **a.** Maintenance; support. **b.** Employment.

en·thal·py (ĕn′thăl′pē, ĕn-thăl′-) *n., pl.* **-pies.** A thermodynamic function of a system, equivalent to the internal energy plus the product of the pressure and the volume. [< Gk. *enthalpein,* to heat in : *en-,* in + *thalpein,* to heat.]

en·thrall (ĕn-thrôl′) *tr.v.* **-thralled, -thrall·ing, -thralls. 1.** To hold spellbound; captivate. **2.** To enslave. [ME, to put in bondage : *en-,* en- + *thral,* slave. —see THRALL.] **—en·thrall′ment** *n.*

en·throne (ĕn-thrōn′) *tr.v.* **-throned, -thron·ing, -thrones. 1. a.** To seat on a throne. **b.** To invest with sovereign power or with the authority of high office. **2.** To raise to a lofty position; exalt. **—en·throne′ment** *n.*

en·thuse (ĕn-tho͞oz′) *v.* **-thused, -thus·ing, -thus·es.** *Informal.* —*tr.* To stimulate enthusiasm in. —*intr.* To show enthusiasm. [Back-formation from ENTHUSIASM.]

en·thu·si·asm (ĕn-tho͞o′zē-ăz′əm) *n.* **1. a.** Great or intense feeling for a subject or cause. **b.** Ardent eagerness; zeal. **2.** Something that inspires enthusiasm. **3.** *Archaic.* **a.** Excess of esp. religious feeling. **b.** Fanatical religious zeal. [LLat. *enthusiasmus* < Gk. *enthousiasmos* < *enthousiazein,* to be inspired by a god < *entheos,* possessed : *en-,* in + *theos,* god.]

en·thu·si·ast (ĕn-tho͞o′zē-ăst′) *n.* **1.** A person who is intensely involved or preoccupied with a particular subject: *a baseball enthusiast.* **2.** A zealot; fanatic. [Gk. *enthousiastēs* < *enthousiazein,* to be inspired. —see ENTHUSIASM.]

en·thu·si·as·tic (ĕn-tho͞o′zē-ăs′tĭk) *adj.* Having or demonstrating enthusiasm. **—en·thu′si·as′ti·cal·ly** *adv.*

en·thy·meme (ĕn′thə-mēm′) *n. Logic.* A syllogism with one of the premises implicit. [Lat. *enthymema* < Gk. *enthumēma,* a rhetorical argument < *enthumeisthai,* to consider : *en-,* in + *thumos,* mind.]

en·tice (ĕn-tīs′) *tr.v.* **-ticed, -tic·ing, -tic·es.** To attract by arousing hope or desire; lure. [ME *enticen* < OFr. *enticier,* to instigate < VLat. **intitiare* : Lat. *in-,* in + Lat. *titio,* firebrand.] **—en·tice′ment** *n.* **—en·tic′er** *n.* **—en·tic′ing·ly** *adv.*

en·tire (ĕn-tīr′) *adj.* **1.** Having no part excluded or left out; whole. **2.** Without reservation or limitation; complete: *gave us his entire attention.* **3.** All in one piece; intact. **4.** Of one piece; continuous. **5.** Not castrated. **6.** *Bot.* Not having an indented margin. *—n.* **1.** The whole of something; entirety. **2.** An uncastrated horse. [ME < OFr. *entir* < Lat. *integer* : *in-,* not + *tangere,* to touch.] **—en·tire′ness** *n.*

en·tire·ly (ĕn-tīr′lē) *adv.* **1.** Wholly; completely. **2.** Solely or exclusively: *He was entirely to blame.*

en·tire·ty (ĕn-tī′rə-tē) *n., pl.* **-ties. 1.** The state of being entire or complete. **2.** The entire amount or extent; total.

en·ti·tle (ĕn-tīt′l) *tr.v.* **-tled, -tling, -tles. 1.** To give a name or title to. **2.** To furnish with a right or claim to something. [ME *entitlen* < OFr. *entiteler* < Med. Lat. *intitulare.* : Lat. *in-,* in + Lat. *titulus,* title.] **—en·ti′tle·ment** *n.*

en·ti·ty (ĕn′tə-tē) *n., pl.* **-ties. 1.** The fact of existence; being. **2.** The existence of something considered apart from its properties. **3.** Something that exists as a particular and discrete unit: *Persons and corporations are equivalent entities under the law.* [Med. Lat. *entitas* < Lat. *ens,* pr.part. of *esse,* to be.]

ento– or **ent–** *pref.* Inside; within: *entozoan.* [NLat. < Gk. *entos,* within.]

en·to·blast (ĕn′tə-blăst′) *n.* Variant of **endoblast.**

en·to·derm (ĕn′tə-durm′) *n.* Variant of **endoderm.**

en·toil (ĕn-toil′) *tr.v.* **-toiled, -toil·ing, -toils.** *Archaic.* To ensnare; entrap. **—en·toil′ment** *n.*

en·tomb (ĕn-to͞om′) *tr.v.* **-tombed, -tomb·ing, -tombs. 1.** To place in or as if in a tomb or grave; bury. **2.** To serve as a tomb for. [OFr. *entoumber* : *en-,* in (< Lat. *in-*) + *tombe,* tomb. —see TOMB.] **—en·tomb′ment** *n.*

entomo– *pref.* Insect: *entomology.* [Fr. < Gk. *entomon,* insect : *en-,* in + *temnein,* to cut (from the insect's segmented body).]

en·to·mol·o·gy (ĕn′tə-mŏl′ə-jē) *n.* The scientific study of insects. **—en′to·mo·log′ic** (-mə-lŏj′ĭk), **en′to·mo·log′i·cal** *adj.* **—en′to·mo·log′i·cal·ly** *adv.* **—en′to·mol′o·gist** *n.*

en·to·moph·a·gous (ĕn′tə-mŏf′ə-gəs) *adj.* Feeding on insects; insectivorous.

en·to·moph·i·lous (ĕn′tə-mŏf′ə-ləs) *adj.* Pollinated by insects. **—en′to·moph′i·ly** *n.*

en·tou·rage (ŏn′to͞o-räzh′) *n.* **1.** A train of attendants or associates; retinue. **2.** One's environment or surroundings. [Fr. < *entourer,* to surround < OFr. *entour,* surroundings : *en-,* in + *tour,* circuit.]

en·to·zo·an (ĕn′tə-zō′ən) *n., pl.* **-zo·a** (-zō′ə). Any of various animals, such as tapeworms, that live within other animals, usually as parasites. **—en′to·zo′ic** *adj.*

en·tr'acte (ŏn′trăkt′, äN-trăkt′) *n.* **1.** The interval between two acts of a theatrical performance. **2.** An entertainment, such as a musical performance, provided between two acts of a play. [Fr. : OFr. *entre,* between + *acte,* act.]

en·trails (ĕn′trālz′, -trəlz) *pl.n.* The internal organs, esp. the intestines; viscera. [ME *entraille* < OFr. < Med. Lat. *intralia* < Lat. *inter,* within.]

en·train[1] (ĕn-trān′) *tr.v.* **-trained, -train·ing, -trains.** To pull or draw along after itself. [OFr. *entrainer* : *en-,* away (< Lat. *inde,* thence) + *trainer,* to drag < Lat. *trahere.*]

en·train[2] (ĕn-trān′) *tr. & intr.v.* **-trained, -train·ing, -trains.** To go aboard a train. **—en·train′ment** *n.*

en·trance[1] (ĕn′trəns) *n.* **1.** The act or an instance of entering. **2.** A means or opening that affords entry. **3.** Permission or power to enter; admission. **4.** The point, as in a musical score, at which a performer is to begin. **5.** The first entry of an actor into a scene. [ME *entraunce,* right to enter < OFr. < *entrer,* to enter. —see ENTER.]

en·trance[2] (ĕn-trăns′) *tr.v.* **-tranced, -tranc·ing, -tranc·es. 1.** To put into a trance. **2.** To fill with delight, wonder, or enchantment: *a child entranced by his own reflection.* **—en·trance′ment** *n.* **—en·tranc′ing·ly** *adv.*

en·trant (ĕn′trənt) *n.* One who enters, esp. one who enters a competition. [Fr. < pr.part. of *entrer,* to enter. —see ENTER.]

en·trap (ĕn-trăp′) *tr.v.* **-trapped, -trap·ping, -traps. 1.** To catch in or as if in a trap. **2.** To lure into danger or difficulty. [OFr. *entraper* : *en-,* in + *trappe,* trap.] **—en·trap′ment** *n.*

en·treat (ĕn-trēt′) *v.* **-treat·ed, -treat·ing, -treats.** *—tr.* **1.** To make an earnest request of. **2.** To ask for earnestly; petition for. **3.** *Archaic.* To treat. *—intr.* To make an earnest request or petition; plead. [ME *entreten* < OFr. *entraitier* : *en-,* in (< Lat. *in-*) + *traiter,* to treat < Lat. *trahere,* to drag.] **—en·treat′ing·ly** *adv.* **—en·treat′ment** *n.*

en·treat·y (ĕn-trē′tē) *n., pl.* **-ies.** An earnest request or petition; plea.

en·tre·chat (ŏn′trə-shä′) *n.* A leap in ballet during which the dancer crosses the feet a number of times, often beating them together. [Fr. < Ital. *(capriola) intrecciata,* intricate (caper) < *intrecciare,* to complicate : *in-,* in (< Lat.) + *treccia,* tress.]

en·trée or **en·tree** (ŏn′trā, ŏn-trā′) *n.* **1. a.** The act of entering. **b.** The power, permission, or liberty to enter; admittance. **2.** The main course of a meal. [Fr. < fem. p.part. of *entrer,* to enter < OFr. —see ENTER.]

en·tre·mets (ŏn′trə-mā′) *n., pl.* **-mets** (-māz′). A side dish served in addition to the principal course. [Fr. < OFr. *entremes* < Lat. *intermissus,* p.part. of *intermittere,* to intermit. —see INTERMIT.]

en·trench (ĕn-trĕnch′) *v.* **-trenched, -trench·ing, -trench·es.** *—tr.* **1.** To provide with a trench, esp. for the purpose of fortifying or defending. **2.** To fix firmly or securely: *arguments that only entrench him more firmly in error.* *—intr.* **1.** To dig a trench. **2.** To encroach, infringe, or trespass. **—en·trench′ment** *n.*

en·tre·pôt (ŏn′trə-pō′) *n.* **1.** A place where goods are stored or deposited and from which they are distributed. **2.** A trading or market center. [Fr. < *entreposer,* to store : *entre-,* among (< Lat. *inter-*) + *poser,* to place < OFr. —see POSE[1].]

en·tre·pre·neur (ŏn′trə-prə-nûr′) *n.* A person who organizes, operates, and assumes the risk for a business venture. [Fr. < OFr. < *entreprendre,* to undertake. —see ENTERPRISE.] **—en′tre·pre·neu′ri·al** *adj.*

en·tre·sol (ĕn′tər-sŏl′, ĕn′trə-) *n.* The floor just above the ground floor; mezzanine. [Fr. : *entre-,* between (< Lat. *inter-*) + *sol,* floor < Lat. *solum.*]

en·tro·py (ĕn′trə-pē) *n., pl.* **-pies. 1.** A measure of the capacity of a system to undergo spontaneous change, thermodynamically specified by the relationship $dS = dQ/T$, where dS is an infinitesimal change in the measure for a system absorbing an infinitesimal quantity of heat dQ at absolute temperature T. **2.** A measure of the disorder in a system specified in statistical mechanics by the relationship $S = k\ln P + c$, where S is the value of the measure for a system in a given state, P is the probability of occurrence of that state, and k is a fixed and c an arbitrary constant. [G. *Entropie* : Gk. *en-,* in + Gk. *tropē,* transformation.]

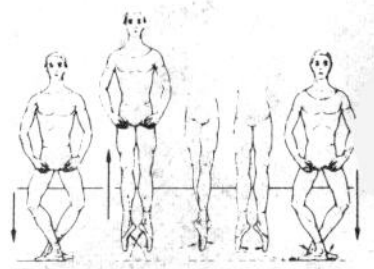

entrechat

en·trust (ĕn-trŭst′) *tr.v.* **-trust·ed, -trust·ing, -trusts. 1.** To give over (something) to another for care, protection, or performance: *entrusted the task to his aides.* **2.** To give as a trust to (someone): *entrusted his aides with the task.*

en·try (ĕn′trē) *n., pl.* **-tries. 1. a.** The act or an instance of entering. **b.** The privilege or right of entering. **2.** A means or place of entrance. **3. a.** The act of entering an item, as in a record. **b.** An item entered in this way. **4. a.** A word, term, or phrase entered in a dictionary. **b.** Such an item along with its related text. **5.** One entered in a competition. [ME < OFr. *entree,* fem. p.part. of *entrer,* to enter. —see ENTER.]

en·try·way (ĕn′trē-wā′) *n.* A passage or opening serving as an entrance.

en·twine (ĕn-twīn′) *v.* **-twined, -twin·ing, -twines.** *—tr.* To twine around or together. *—intr.* To twine or twist together.

entwine
Vine entwined around a downspout

en·twist (ĕn-twĭst′) *tr.v.* **-twist·ed, -twist·ing, -twists.** To twist together; entwine.

e·nu·cle·ate (ĭ-no͞o′klē-āt′, ĭ-nyo͞o′-) *tr.v.* **-at·ed, -at·ing, -ates. 1.** *Archaic.* To explain or elucidate. **2.** *Med.* To remove from an enveloping cover or sac. **3.** *Biol.* To remove the nucleus of. *—adj.* (-ĭt, -āt′). Lacking a nucleus. [Lat. *enucleare, enucleat-,* to take out the kernel : *ex-,* out + *nucleus,* kernel.] **—e·nu′cle·a′tion** *n.* **—e·nu′cle·a′tor** *n.*

e·nu·mer·a·ble (ĭ-no͞o′mər-ə-bəl, ĭ-nyo͞o′-) *adj.* Denumerable.

e·nu·mer·ate (ĭ-no͞o′mə-rāt′, ĭ-nyo͞o′-) *tr.v.* **-at·ed, -at·ing, -ates. 1.** To count off or name one by one; list. **2.** To determine the number of; count. [Lat. *enumerare, enumerat-,* to count out : *ex-,* out + *numerus,* number.] **—e·nu′mer·a′tion** *n.* **—e·nu′mer·a′tive** *adj.* **—e·nu′mer·a′tor** *n.*

e·nun·ci·ate (ĭ-nŭn′sē-āt′) *v.* **-at·ed, -at·ing, -ates.** *—tr.* **1.** To pronounce; articulate. **2.** To state or set forth precisely or systematically: *enunciate a doctrine.* **3.** To announce; proclaim. *—intr.* To make articulate sounds. [Lat. *enuntiare, enuntiat-* : *ex-,* out + *nuntiāre,* to announce < *nuntius,* messenger.] **—e·nun′ci·a·ble** (-ə-bəl) *adj.* **—e·nun′ci·a′tion** *n.* **—e·nun′ci·a′tive** (-sē-ā′tĭv, -sē-ə-tĭv) *adj.* **—e·nun′ci·a′tive·ly** *adv.* **—e·nun′ci·a′tor** *n.*

en·ure (ĭn-yo͝or′) *v.* Variant of **inure.**

en·u·re·sis (ĕn′yə-rē′sĭs) *n.* Involuntary urination. [NLat. < Gk. *enourein,* to urinate in : *en-,* in + *ourein,* to urinate < *ouron,* urine.] **—en′u·ret′ic** (-rĕt′ĭk) *adj.*

en·vel·op (ĕn-vĕl′əp) *tr.v.* **-oped, -op·ing, -ops. 1.** To enclose or encase completely with or as if with a covering. **2.** To attack (an enemy's flank). [ME *envolupen,* to be involved in < OFr. *envoloper* : *en-,* in (< Lat. *in-*) + *voloper,* to wrap up.] **—en·vel′op·er** *n.* **—en·vel′op·ment** *n.*

en·ve·lope (ĕn′və-lōp′, ŏn′-) *n.* **1.** Something that envelops; wrapping. **2.** A flat, folded paper container esp. for a letter. **3.** *Biol.* An enclosing covering, such as a membrane or shell. **4.** The bag containing the gas in a balloon. **5.** *Math.* A curve or surface that is tangent to all curves or surfaces of a family of curves or surfaces. [Fr. *enveloppe* < *envelopper,* to envelop < OFr. *envoloper.*]

en·ven·om (ĕn-vĕn′əm) *tr.v.* **-omed, -om·ing, -oms. 1.** To make poisonous or noxious. **2.** To embitter. [ME *envenimen* < OFr. *envenimer* : *en-,* in + *venim,* venom. —see VENOM.]

en·vi·a·ble (ĕn′vē-ə-bəl) *adj.* Extremely desirable: *"the envi-*

Eos

epaulet
Worn by Alexander I of Russia

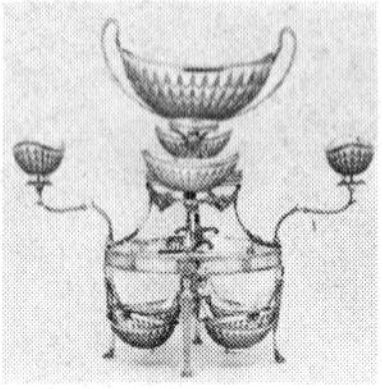

epergne
18th-century English

able English quality of being able to be mute without unrest" (Henry James). **—en'vi·a·bly** *adv.*

en·vi·ous (ĕn'vē-əs) *adj.* **1.** Feeling, expressing, or characterized by envy. **2.** *Obs.* Eager to emulate; emulous. **—en'vi·ous·ly** *adv.* **—en'vi·ous·ness** *n.*

en·vi·ron (ĕn-vī'rən) *tr.v.* To encircle; surround. [ME *environen* < OFr. *environner* < *environ,* round about : *en-,* in (< Lat. *in-*) + *viron,* circle < *virer,* to turn, poss. of Celt. orig.]

en·vi·ron·ment (ĕn-vī'rən-mənt) *n.* **1.** The circumstances or conditions that surround one; surroundings. **2.** The total of circumstances surrounding an organism or group of organisms, esp.: **a.** The combination of external or extrinsic physical conditions that affect and influence the growth and development of organisms. **b.** The complex of social and cultural conditions affecting the nature of an individual or community. **3.** An artistic or theatrical work that surrounds or involves the audience. **—en·vi'ron·men'tal** (-mĕn'tl) *adj.* **—en·vi'ron·men'tal·ly** *adv.*

en·vi·ron·men·tal·ism (ĕn-vī'rən-mĕn'tl-ĭz'əm) *n.* The theory that environment rather than heredity is the primary influence upon intellectual growth and cultural development.

en·vi·ron·men·tal·ist (ĕn-vī'rən-mĕn'tl-ĭst) *n.* **1.** A person who seeks to protect the natural environment. **2.** An adherent of environmentalism.

en·vi·rons (ĕn-vī'rənz) *pl.n.* **1.** A surrounding area, esp. of a city. **2.** Surroundings; environment. [Fr. < OFr. *environ,* about. —see ENVIRON.]

en·vis·age (ĕn-vĭz'ĭj) *tr.v.* **-aged, -ag·ing, -ag·es. 1.** To conceive an image or picture of, esp. as a future possibility. **2.** To consider or regard in a certain way. [Fr. *envisager* : OFr. *en-,* in (< Lat. *in-*) + *visage,* face. —see VISAGE.]

en·vi·sion (ĕn-vĭzh'ən) *tr.v.* **-sioned, -sion·ing, -sions.** To picture in the mind.

en·voi also **en·voy** (ĕn'voi', ŏn'-) *n.* The closing stanza of certain verse forms, such as the ballade, serving to dedicate the poem to a patron or to summarize the poem. [ME *envoie* < OFr. *envoier,* to send. —see ENVOY.]

en·voy¹ (ĕn'voi', ŏn'-) *n.* **1.** A messenger; agent. **2.** A representative of a government sent on a special diplomatic mission. **3.** A minister plenipotentiary assigned to a foreign embassy, ranking next below the ambassador. [Fr. *envoyé* < *envoyer,* to send < OFr. *envoier* < LLat. *inviare,* to put on the way : Lat. *in-,* on + Lat. *via,* way.]

en·voy² (ĕn'voi', ŏn'-) *n.* Variant of **envoi.**

en·vy (ĕn'vē) *n., pl.* **-vies. 1.** A feeling of discontent and resentment aroused by another's desirable possessions or qualities, accompanied by a strong desire to have them for oneself. **2.** One that is the object of envy: *the envy of all their friends.* **3.** *Obs.* Malevolence. *—tr.v.* **-vied, -vy·ing, -vies. 1.** To feel envy toward. **2.** To feel envy because of. [ME *envie* < OFr. < Lat. *invidia* < *invidus,* envious < *invidēre* to envy : *in-,* in + *vidēre,* to see.] **—en'vi·er** *n.* **—en'vy·ing·ly** *adv.*

Synonyms: *envy, begrudge, covet.* These verbs mean to resent another's good fortune or to desire to have what is his. *Envy* is wider in range than the others, since it combines both resentment and desire. *Begrudge* stresses resentment toward the possessor and unwillingness to acknowledge his right or claim. *Covet* stresses desire for another's possession, especially when the desire is a secret or shameful longing.

en·wind (ĕn-wīnd') *tr.v.* **-wound** (-wound'), **-wind·ing, -winds.** To wind around or about.

en·womb (ĕn-wo͞om') *tr.v.* **-wombed, -womb·ing, -wombs.** *Archaic.* To enclose in or as if in a womb.

en·wrap (ĕn-răp') *tr.v.* **-wrapped, -wrap·ping, -wraps. 1.** To wrap up; enclose. **2.** To envelop. **3.** To absorb completely; engross.

en·wreathe (ĕn-rē*th*') *tr.v.* **-wreathed, -wreath·ing, -wreathes.** To surround with or as if with a wreath.

en·zo·ot·ic (ĕn'zō-ŏt'ĭk) *adj.* Affecting or peculiar to animals of a specific area or limited district. Used of a disease. *—n.* An enzootic disease.

en·zyme (ĕn'zīm') *n.* Any of numerous proteins or conjugated proteins produced by living organisms and functioning as biochemical catalysts in living organisms. [G. *Enzym* < Med. Gk. *enzumos,* leavened : Gk. *en-,* in + *zumē,* leaven.] **—en'zy·mat'ic** (-zə-măt'ĭk) *adj.* **—en'zy·mat'i·cal·ly** *adv.*

en·zy·mol·o·gy (ĕn'zə-mŏl'ə-jē) *n.* The biochemistry of enzymes. **—en'zy·mol'o·gist** *n.*

eo- *pref.* Earliest; most primitive: *eohippus.* [Gk. *ēō-* < *ēōs,* dawn.]

E·o·cene (ē'ə-sēn') *adj.* Of, pertaining to, or designating the geologic time, rock series, sedimentary deposits, and fossils of the second oldest of the five major epochs of the Cenozoic era or Tertiary period, extending from the end of the Paleocene to the beginning of the Oligocene, and characterized by the rise of mammals. **—E'o·cene'** *n.*

e·o·hip·pus (ē'ō-hĭp'əs) *n.* An extinct, small, herbivorous mammal of the genus *Hyracotherium* (or *Eohippus*), of the Eocene epoch, having four-toed front feet and three-toed hind feet, and related ancestrally to the horse. [EO- + Gk. *hippos,* horse.]

e·o·li·an (ē-ō'lē-ən) *adj.* Pertaining to, caused by, or carried by the wind. [After AEOLUS.]

e·o·lith (ē'ə-lĭth') *n.* A crude stone artifact, such as a flint.

E·o·lith·ic (ē'ə-lĭth'ĭk) *adj.* Of or relating to the postulated earliest period of human culture preceding the Lower Paleolithic.

e·on (ē'ŏn', ē'ən) *n.* **1.** An indefinitely long period of time; age. **2.** *Geol.* The longest division of geologic time, containing two or more eras. [LLat. *aeon* < Gk. *aiōn.*] **—e·o'ni·an** (ē-ō'nē-ən) *adj.*

E·os (ē'ŏs') *n. Gk. Myth.* The goddess of the dawn. [Gk. *Ēōs* < *ēōs,* dawn.]

e·o·sin (ē'ə-sən) *n.* A red crystalline powder, $C_{20}H_8Br_4O_5$, used in textile dyeing, ink manufacturing, and in coloring gasoline. [Gk. *ēōs,* dawn + -IN.]

e·o·sin·o·phil (ē'ə-sĭn'ə-fĭl') also **e·o·sin·o·phile** (-fīl') *n.* **1.** *Physiol.* A type of leukocyte in vertebrate blood that accepts an eosin stain. **2.** *Biochem.* Any microorganism, cell, or histological element easily stained by eosin dye. **—e'o·sin'o·phil', e'o·sin'o·phil'ic, e'o·si·noph'i·lous** (ē'ō-sĭ-nŏf'ə-ləs) *adj.*

e·o·sin·o·phil·i·a (ē'ə-sĭn'ə-fĭl'ē-ə) *n.* An increase in the number of eosinophils in the blood.

-eous *suff.* Resembling; having the nature of: *gaseous.* [Lat. *-eus.*]

ep- *pref.* Variant of **epi-.**

e·pact (ē'păkt') *n.* The period of time necessary to bring the solar calendar into harmony with the lunar calendar. [OFr. *epacte* < Lat. *epacta* < Gk. *epaktai* < *epagein,* to intercalate : *epi-,* on + *agein,* to lead.]

ep·arch (ĕp'ärk') *n.* **1.** The chief administrator of an eparchy. **2.** A bishop or metropolitan of an Eastern Orthodox Church. [Gk. *eparkhos,* commander : *epi-,* over + *arkhein,* to rule.] **—e·par'chi·al** (ĭ-pär'kē-əl) *adj.*

ep·ar·chy (ĕp'är'kē) *n., pl.* **-chies. 1.** An administrative subdivision of Greece. **2.** A diocese of an Eastern Orthodox Church.

ep·au·let also **ep·au·lette** (ĕp'ə-lĕt', ĕp'ə-lĕt') *n.* A shoulder ornament, esp. a fringed strap formerly worn on a military uniform. [Fr. *épaulette,* dim. of *épaule,* shoulder < OFr. *espaule* < Med. Lat. *spatula.* —see ESPALIER]

e·pée also **e·pee** (ā-pā') *n.* **1.** A fencing sword with a bowl-shaped guard and a long, narrow, fluted blade that has no cutting edge and tapers to a blunted point. **2.** The sport or art of fencing with the épée. [Fr. < Lat. *spatha,* sword.] **—é·pée'ist** *n.*

ep·ei·rog·e·ny (ĕp'ī-rŏj'ə-nē) *n., pl.* **-nies.** The deformation of the crust of the earth by which continents and oceanic basins, or parts of these, are formed. [Gk. *ēpeiros,* continent + -GENY.] **—e·pei'ro·gen'ic** (ĭ-pī'rō-jĕn'ĭk) *adj.* **—e·pei'ro·gen'i·cal·ly** *adv.*

e·pen·the·sis (ĭ-pĕn'thə-sĭs) *n., pl.* **-ses** (-sēz'). The insertion of a sound or letter into a word. [LLat. < Gk. < *epentithenai,* to insert : *epi-,* in addition to + *en-,* in + *tithenai,* to place.] **—ep'en·thet'ic** (ĕp'ĭn-thĕt'ĭk) *adj.*

e·pergne (ĭ-pûrn', ā-pârn') *n.* A large table centerpiece consisting of a frame with extended arms or branches supporting holders, as for flowers, fruit, or sweetmeats. [Perh. alteration of Fr. *épargne,* saving < *épargner,* to save.]

ep·ex·e·ge·sis (ĕp-ĕk'sə-jē'sĭs) *n.* Additional explanation or explanatory material. [Gk. *epexēgēsis* < *epexēgeisthai,* to explain in detail : *epi-,* in addition to + *exēgeisthai,* to explain. —see EXEGESIS.] **—ep·ex'e·get'ic** (-jĕt'ĭk), **ep·ex'e·get'i·cal** *adj.* **—ep·ex'e·get'i·cal·ly** *adv.*

e·phah also **e·pha** (ē'fə) *n.* An ancient Hebrew unit of dry measure equal to slightly more than a bushel. [Heb. *'ēphāh,* prob. of Egypt. orig.]

e·phebe (ĕf'ēb', ĭ-fēb') *n.* In ancient Greece, a youth between 18 and 20 years of age. [Lat. *ephebus* < Gk. *ephēbos* : *epi-,* upon + *hēbē,* early manhood.] **—e·phe'bic** *adj.*

e·phe·bus (ĭ-fē'bəs) *n., pl.* **-bi** (-bī'). An ephebe. [Lat.]

e·phed·rine (ĭ-fĕd'rĭn, ĕf'ĭ-drēn') *n.* A white, odorless, crystalline alkaloid, $C_{10}H_{15}NO$, isolated from the mahuang shrub or made synthetically, used to treat allergies and asthma and as a vasoconstrictor. [< NLat. *Ephedra,* genus name < Lat. *ephedra,* horsetail < Gk. *ephedros,* sitting upon : *epi-,* upon + *hedra,* seat).]

e·phem·er·al (ĭ-fĕm'ər-əl) *adj.* **1.** Lasting for a brief time; short-lived; transitory. **2.** Living or lasting only one day. *—n.* An ephemeral thing or organism. [Gk. *ephēmeros* : *epi-,* on + *hēmera,* day.] **—e·phem'er·al'i·ty** *n.* **—e·phem'er·al·ly** *adv.*

e·phem·er·id (ĭ-fĕm'ər-ĭd) *n.* An insect of the order Ephemeroptera, which includes the mayflies. [NLat. *Ephemeridae,* former order name < Gk. *ephēmeron,* mayfly < *ephēmeros,* ephemeral.]

e·phem·er·is (ĭ-fĕm'ər-ĭs) *n., pl.* **eph·e·mer·i·des** (ĕf'ə-mĕr'ə-dēz'). A table giving the coordinates of a celestial body at a number of specific times during a given period. [LLat., diary < Gk. < *ephēmeros,* daily, ephemeral.]

ephemeris time *n.* A highly accurate astronomical system for the measurement of time based on the period of the earth's orbit, but in practice relying on lunar observations and an accurate lunar ephemeris to calculate corrections to be applied to clocks.

e·phem·er·on (ĭ-fĕm'ə-rŏn') *n., pl.* **-er·a** (-ər-ə) or **-er·ons. 1.** A short-lived thing or organism. **2.** *pl.* **ephemera.** Printed matter of passing interest, such as handbills or postcards. [Gk. *ephemēron*, mayfly. —see EPHEMERIS.]

E·phe·sians (ĭ-fē′zhənz) *pl.n.* *(used with a sing. verb).* See table at **Bible**.

eph·od (ĕf′ŏd′, ē′fŏd′) *n.* A vestment worn by ancient Hebrew priests. [ME < Med. Lat. < Heb. *ēphōdh*.]

eph·or (ĕf′ôr′, -ər) *n., pl.* **-ors** or **-o·ri** (-ə-rī′). One of a body of five elected magistrates exercising a supervisory power over the kings of Sparta. [Lat. *ephorus* < Gk. *ephoros* < *ephoran*, to oversee : *epi-*, over + *horan*, to see.]

epi– or **ep–** *pref.* **1. a.** On; upon: *epiphyte.* **b.** Over; above: *epicenter.* **c.** Around: *epicarp.* **d.** Near; close to: *epicalyx.* **e.** Besides: *epiphenomenon.* **f.** After: *epicrisis.* **2.** A chemical substance related to a specified chemical substance: *epicholesterol.* [Gk. < *epi*, upon.]

ep·i·blast (ĕp′ə-blăst′) *n.* Ectoderm. **—ep′i·blast′ic** *adj.*

e·pib·o·ly (ĭ-pĭb′ə-lē) *n.* Gastrulation by the differential growth of the cells of one embryonic part over and around another. [Gk. *epibolē*, addition < *epiballein*, to throw on : *epi-*, on + *ballein*, to throw.] **—ep′i·bol′ic** (ĕp′ə-bŏl′ĭk) *adj.*

ep·ic (ĕp′ĭk) *n.* **1.** An extended narrative poem in elevated or dignified language, celebrating the feats of a legendary or traditional hero. **2.** A literary or dramatic composition that resembles an epic. **3.** A series of events considered appropriate to an epic: *the epic of the Old West.* **—modifier:** *an epic poem.* [Lat. *epicus* < Gk. *epikos* < *epos*, song.]

ep·i·ca·lyx (ĕp′ĭ-kā′lĭks, -kăl′ĭks) *n., pl.* **-ca·lyx·es** or **-ca·ly·ces** (-kā′lĭ-sēz′, -kăl′ĭ-). A set of bracts close to and resembling a calyx.

ep·i·can·thic fold (ĕp′ĭ-kăn′thĭk) *n.* A fold of skin of the upper eyelid that tends to cover the inner corner of the eye.

ep·i·can·thus (ĕp′ĭ-kăn′thəs) *n., pl.* **-thi** (-thī, -thē). Epicanthic fold. [NLat. : EPI- + Gk. *kanthos*, corner of the eye.]

ep·i·car·di·um (ĕp′ĭ-kär′dē-əm) *n., pl.* **-di·a** (-dē-ə). The inner layer of the pericardium that is in actual contact with the heart. [NLat. : EPI- + Gk. *kardia*, heart.] **—ep′i·car′di·al** *adj.*

ep·i·carp (ĕp′ĭ-kärp′) *n.* Exocarp.

epic drama *n.* Modern narrative drama that encourages the audience to consider social problems analytically rather than emotionally.

ep·i·cene (ĕp′ə-sēn′) *adj.* **1. a.** Belonging to or having the characteristics of both the male and the female. **b.** Effeminate; womanish. **c.** Sexless; neuter. **2.** Having only one form of the noun for both the male and the female. [ME, having only one form of the noun for either gender < Lat. *epicoenus* < Gk. *epikoinos* : *epi-*, on + *koinos*, common.] **—ep′i·cene′** *n.* **—ep′i·cen′ism** *n.*

ep·i·cen·ter (ĕp′ĭ-sĕn′tər) *n.* **1.** The part of the earth's surface directly above the origin of an earthquake. **2.** A focal point. **—ep′i·cen′tral** *adj.*

ep·i·chlo·ro·hy·drin (ĕp′ĭ-klôr′ə-hī′drĭn, -klōr′-) *n.* A colorless liquid, C_3H_5OCl, used as a solvent in making resins.

ep·i·cot·yl (ĕp′ĭ-kŏt′l) *n.* The part of the stem of a seedling or embryonic plant that is above the cotyledons and below the first true leaves. [EPI- + COTYL(EDON).]

ep·i·crit·ic (ĕp′ĭ-krĭt′ĭk) *adj.* Pertaining to sensory nerve fibers that enable acute thermal and tactile sensitivity. [Gk. *epikritikos*, decisive < *epikritos*, decided on < *epikrinein*, to decide : *epi-*, over + *krinein*, to judge.]

epic theater *n.* Epic drama.

ep·i·cure (ĕp′ĭ-kyŏŏr′) *n.* **1.** A person with refined taste esp. in food and wine. **2.** *Archaic.* A person devoted to sensuous pleasure and luxurious living. —See Usage note at **gourmand**. [After *Epicurus*, (341–270 B.C.).]

ep·i·cu·re·an (ĕp′ĭ-kyŏŏ-rē′ən) *adj.* **1. Epicurean.** Of or relating to Epicurus or Epicureanism. **2.** Suited to the tastes of an epicure: *an epicurean repast.* —*n.* **1. Epicurean.** A follower of Epicurus. **2.** An epicure.

Ep·i·cu·re·an·ism (ĕp′ĭ-kyŏŏ-rē′ə-nĭz′əm) *n.* The philosophy advanced by Epicurus who sought freedom from pain and emotional disturbance, rejected a belief in the afterlife or the influence of gods on human affairs, and subscribed to the atomic theory of Democritus.

ep·i·cur·ism (ĕp′ĭ-kyŏŏ-rĭz′əm) *n.* The beliefs, tastes, or manner of living of an epicure.

ep·i·cu·ti·cle (ĕp′ĭ-kyŏŏ′tĭ-kəl) *n.* The outermost layer of cuticle of an insect exoskeleton, composed mostly of wax.

ep·i·cy·cle (ĕp′ĭ-sī′kəl) *n.* In Ptolemaic cosmology, a small circle, the center of which moves on the circumference of a larger circle at whose center is the earth, and the circumference of which describes the orbit of one of the planets around the earth. [ME *epicicle* < LLat. *epicyclus* < Gk. *epikuklos* : *epi-*, on + *kuklos*, circle.] **—ep′i·cy′clic** (-sī′klĭk, -sĭk′lĭk) *adj.*

epicyclic train *n.* A system of gears in which at least one wheel axis revolves about another.

ep·i·cy·cloid (ĕp′ĭ-sī′kloid′) *n.* The curve described by a point on the circumference of a circle as it rolls on the outside of the circumference of a fixed circle. **—ep′i·cy·cloid′al** (-kloid′l) *adj.*

ep·i·dem·ic (ĕp′ĭ-dĕm′ĭk) also **ep·i·dem·i·cal** (-ĭ-kəl) *adj.* **1.** Spreading rapidly and extensively by infection among many individuals in an area. **2.** Widely prevalent. —*n.* **epidemic. 1.** An outbreak of contagious disease that spreads rapidly. **2.** A rapid spread, growth, or development. [Fr. *épidémique* < *épidémie*, an epidemic < OFr. *espydymie* < LLat. *epidemia* < Gk. *epidēmia* < *epidēmos*, prevalent : *epi-*, on + *dēmos*, people.] **—ep′i·dem′i·cal·ly** *adv.*

ep·i·de·mi·ol·o·gy (ĕp′ĭ-dē′mē-ŏl′ə-jē, -dĕm′ē-) *n.* The study of epidemics and epidemic diseases. [LLat. *epidemia*, an epidemic + -LOGY.] **—ep′i·de′mi·o·log′ic** (-ə-lŏj′ĭk), **ep′i·de′mi·o·log′i·cal** (-ĭ-kəl) *adj.* **—ep′i·de′mi·ol′o·gist** *n.*

ep·i·der·mis (ĕp′ĭ-dûr′mĭs) *n.* **1. a.** *Anat.* The outer, protective, nonvascular layer of the skin. **b.** An integument or outer layer of various organisms. **2.** *Bot.* The outermost layer of cells or protective covering of a plant or plant part. [NLat. < Gk. : *epi-*, on + *derma*, skin.] **—ep′i·der′mal** (-məl) *adj.*

ep·i·der·moid (ĕp′ĭ-dûr′moid′) also **ep·i·der·moid·al** (-dər-moid′l) *adj.* Having the characteristics of or relating to the epidermis. [EPIDERM(IS) + -OID.]

ep·i·di·a·scope (ĕp′ĭ-dī′ə-skōp′) *n.* A machine for projecting the images of opaque objects or transparencies upon a screen.

ep·i·did·y·mis (ĕp′ĭ-dĭd′ə-mĭs) *n., pl.* **-mi·des** (-mĭ-dēz′). A long, narrow, flattened convoluted body that is part of the spermatic duct system, lying on the lateral edge of the posterior border of the testis. [Gk. : *epi-*, at + *didumos*, testicle.] **—ep′i·did′y·mal** *adj.*

ep·i·dote (ĕp′ĭ-dōt′) *n.* A natural, yellow, green, or black mineral consisting mainly of a silicate of calcium, aluminum, and iron, commonly found in metamorphic rock. [Fr. *épidote* < Gk. *epididonai*, to increase : *epi-*, upon + *didonai*, to give.] **—ep′i·dot′ic** (-dŏt′ĭk) *adj.*

ep·i·du·ral (ĕp′ĭ-dŏŏr′əl, -dyŏŏr′-) *adj.* Located upon or over the dura mater.

ep·i·gas·tri·um (ĕp′ĭ-găs′trē-əm) *n., pl.* **-tri·a** (-trē-ə). The upper middle region of the abdomen. [NLat. < Gk. *epigastrion* : *epi-*, above + *gastēr*, stomach.] **—ep′i·gas′tric** (-trĭk) *adj.*

ep·i·ge·al (ĕp′ə-jē′əl) also **ep·i·ge·an** (-ən) or **ep·i·ge·ous** (-əs) *adj.* **1.** *Biol.* Living or occurring on or near the surface of the ground. **2.** *Bot.* Designating or characterized by cotyledons that appear above the surface of the ground. [Gk. *epigaios*, on the earth : *epi-*, on + *gē*, earth.]

ep·i·gene (ĕp′ə-jēn′) *adj.* **1.** Formed, originating, or occurring on or just below the surface of the earth. **2.** Foreign to the material in which found. Used of a crystal. [Fr. *épigène* < Gk. *epigenēs*, arising after : *epi-*, upon + *genos*, birth.]

ep·i·gen·e·sis (ĕp′ə-jĕn′ĭ-sĭs) *n.* **1.** *Biol.* The theory that the individual is developed by structural elaboration of the unstructured egg rather than by a simple enlarging of a preformed entity. **2.** *Geol.* Change in the mineral characteristics of a rock due to outside influence. **—ep′i·ge·net′ic** (-jə-nĕt′ĭk) *adj.*

e·pig·e·nous (ĭ-pĭj′ə-nəs) *adj.* *Bot.* Developing or growing on an upper surface, as fungi on leaves.

ep·i·glot·tis (ĕp′ĭ-glŏt′ĭs) *n., pl.* **-glot·tis·es** or **-glot·ti·des** (-glŏt′ĭ-dēz′). An elastic cartilage located at the root of the tongue that folds over the glottis to prevent food from entering the windpipe during the act of swallowing. [Gk. *epiglōttis* : *epi-*, over + *glōttis*, glottis.] **—ep′i·glot′tal** (-glŏt′l), **ep′i·glot′tic** (-glŏt′ĭk) *adj.*

ep·i·gone (ĕp′ĭ-gōn′) *n.* A second-rate imitator or follower, esp. of an artist or philosopher. [< Gk. *Epigonoi*, sons of the seven heroes against Thebes < pl. of *epigonos*, born after : *epi-*, after + *gignesthai*, to be born.] **—ep′i·gon′ic** (-gŏn′ĭk) *adj.* **—e·pig′on·ism** (ĭ-pĭg′ə-nĭz′əm) *n.*

ep·i·gram (ĕp′ĭ-grăm′) *n.* **1.** A short poem expressing a single thought or observation with terseness and wit. **2.** A concise, clever, and often paradoxical statement. **3.** Epigrammatic discourse or expression. [OFr. *epigramme* < Lat. *epigramma* < Gk. < *epigraphein*, to write on : *epi-*, on + *graphein*, to write.]

ep·i·gram·mat·ic (ĕp′ĭ-grə-măt′ĭk) also **ep·i·gram·mat·i·cal** (-ĭ-kəl) *adj.* **1.** Of or having the nature of an epigram. **2.** Full of or given to the use of epigrams. **—ep′i·gram·mat′i·cal·ly** *adv.*

ep·i·gram·ma·tism (ĕp′ĭ-grăm′ə-tĭz′əm) *n.* Literary style marked by the use of epigrams. **—ep′i·gram′ma·tist** *n.*

ep·i·gram·ma·tize (ĕp′ĭ-grăm′ə-tīz′) *v.* **-tized, -tiz·ing, -tiz·es.** —*tr.* To express in an epigram. —*intr.* To create an epigram.

ep·i·graph (ĕp′ĭ-grăf′) *n.* **1.** An inscription, as on a statue or building. **2.** A motto or quotation, as at the beginning of a literary composition, setting forth a theme. [Gk. *epigraphē* < *epigraphein*, to write on. —see EPIGRAM.] **—ep′i·graph′ic, ep′i·graph′i·cal** *adj.* **—ep′i·graph′i·cal·ly** *adv.*

e·pig·ra·phy (ĭ-pĭg′rə-fē) *n.* **1.** Inscriptions collectively. **2. a.** The study of inscriptions. **b.** The decipherment esp. of ancient inscriptions. **—e·pig′ra·pher, e·pig′ra·phist** *n.*

e·pig·y·nous (ĭ-pĭj′ə-nəs) *adj.* Having or characterizing floral parts or organs attached to or near the summit of the ovary. **—e·pig′y·ny** (-nē) *n.*

ep·i·lep·sy (ĕp′ə-lĕp′sē) *n.* A disorder characterized by recurring attacks of motor, sensory, or psychic malfunction with or without unconsciousness or convulsive movements. [OFr. *epilepsie* < Lat. *epilepsia* < Gk. < *epilambanein*, to lay hold of : *epi-*, upon + *lambanein*, to take.]

ep·i·lep·tic (ĕp′ə-lĕp′tĭk) *adj.* **1.** Affected with epilepsy. **2.** Of, characteristic of, or associated with epilepsy. **—ep′i·lep′tic** *n.*

epicycloid
An epicycloid of three cusps;
$r = \frac{R}{3}$

ep·i·lep·toid (ĕp'ə-lĕp'toid') *adj.* Resembling epilepsy or any of its symptoms. [EPILEPT(IC) + -OID.]
ep·i·logue also **ep·i·log** (ĕp'ə-lôg', -lŏg') *n.* **1. a.** A short poem or speech spoken directly to the audience following the conclusion of a play. **b.** The performer or performers who speak this. **2.** A short addition or concluding section at the end of literary work, often dealing with the future of its characters. [ME *epiloge* < OFr. *epilogue* < Lat. *epilogus* < Gk. *epilogos* < *epilegein,* to say more : *epi-,* in addition to + *legein,* to say.]
ep·i·mor·pho·sis (ĕp'ə-môr'fə-sĭs) *n.* Regeneration of a part of an organ characterized by proliferation of new tissue.
ep·i·mys·i·um (ĕp'ə-mĭz'ē-əm, -mĭzh'ē-) *n., pl.* **-mys·i·a** (-mĭz'ē-ə, -mĭzh'ē-ə). The fibrous sheath enclosing a muscle. [NLat. : EPI- + Gk. *mus,* muscle.]
ep·i·nas·ty (ĕp'ə-năs'tē) *n., pl.* **-ties.** A downward bending of leaves or other plant parts, resulting from excessive growth of the upper side. **—ep'i·nas'tic** (-tĭk) *adj.*
ep·i·neph·rine also **ep·i·neph·rin** (ĕp'ə-nĕf'rĭn) *n.* **1.** An adrenal hormone that stimulates autonomic nerve action. **2.** A white to brownish crystalline compound, $C_9H_{13}NO_3$, isolated from the adrenal glands of certain mammals or synthesized, and used as a heart stimulant, vasoconstrictor, and in the treatment of asthma.
ep·i·neu·ri·um (ĕp'ə-nŏŏr'ē-əm, -nyŏŏr'-) *n., pl.* **-neu·ri·a** (-nŏŏr'ē-ə, -nyŏŏr'-). The connective tissue sheath of a nerve trunk, containing blood and lymph vessels. [NLat. : EPI- + Gk. *neuron,* nerve.] **—ep'i·neu'ri·al** (-ē-əl) *adj.*
ep·i·pe·lag·ic (ĕp'ə-pə-lăj'ĭk) *adj.* Of or pertaining to the part of the oceanic zone into which enough sunlight enters for photosynthesis to take place.
e·piph·a·ny (ĭ-pĭf'ə-nē) *n., pl.* **-nies. 1. Epiphany.** A Christian festival held on January 6 in celebration of the manifestation of the divine nature of Christ to the Gentiles as represented by the Magi. **2.** A revelatory manifestation of a divine being. **3. a.** A sudden manifestation of the essence or meaning of something. **b.** A comprehension or perception of reality by means of a sudden intuitive realization. [ME *epiphanie* < OFr. < LLat. *epiphania* < Gk. *epiphaneia,* appearance < *epiphainein,* to manifest : *epi-,* to + *phainein,* to show.]
ep·i·phe·nom·e·nal·ism (ĕp'ə-fĭ-nŏm'ə-nə-lĭz'əm) *n. Philos.* The doctrine that mental activities are simply epiphenomena of the neural processes of the brain.
ep·i·phe·nom·e·non (ĕp'ə-fĭ-nŏm'ə-nŏn') *n., pl.* **-na** (-nə). **1.** A secondary phenomenon that results from and accompanies another. **2.** *Pathol.* An additional condition in the course of a disease, not necessarily connected with the disease. **—ep'i·phe·nom'e·nal** (-nəl) *adj.* **—ep'i·phe·nom'e·nal·ly** *adv.*
e·piph·y·sis (ĭ-pĭf'ĭ-sĭs) *n., pl.* **-ses** (-sēz'). *Anat.* A part of a bone, often an end of a long bone, that initially develops separated from the main portion by cartilage. [Gk. *epiphusis* : *epi-,* upon + *phusis,* growth < *phuein,* to grow.] **—ep'i·phys'i·al** (ĕp'ə-fĭz'ē-əl), **ep'i·phys'e·al** *adj.*
ep·i·phyte (ĕp'ə-fīt') *n.* A plant, such as certain orchids or ferns, that grows on another plant upon which it depends for mechanical support but not for nutrients. **—ep'i·phyt'ic** (-fĭt'ĭk), **ep'i·phyt'i·cal** *adj.* **—ep'i·phyt'i·cal·ly** *adv.*
ep·i·phy·tot·ic (ĕp'ə-fī-tŏt'ĭk) *adj.* Of, pertaining to, or characterizing a sudden or abnormally destructive outbreak of a plant disease, usually over an extended geographic area. **—ep'i·phy·tot'ic** *n.*
e·pis·co·pa·cy (ĭ-pĭs'kə-pə-sē) *n., pl.* **-cies. 1.** An episcopate. **2.** A system of church government in which bishops are the chief ministers. [< EPISCOPATE.]
e·pis·co·pal (ĭ-pĭs'kə-pəl) *adj.* **1.** Of or pertaining to a bishop. **2.** Of, relating to, or involving church government by bishops. **3. Episcopal.** Designating or pertaining to the Protestant Episcopal Church. [ME < LLat. *episcopalis* < *episcopus,* bishop < Gk. *episkopos,* overseer : *epi-,* over + *skopos,* watcher.] **—e·pis'co·pal·ly** *adv.*
Episcopal Church *n.* The Protestant Episcopal Church.
E·pis·co·pa·lian (ĭ-pĭs'kə-pā'lē-ən, -pāl'yən) *adj.* **1.** Of, pertaining to, or belonging to the Protestant Episcopal Church. **2. episcopalian.** Of or advocating church government by bishops. **—E·pis'co·pa'lian** *n.*
e·pis·co·pate (ĭ-pĭs'kə-pĭt, -pāt') *n.* **1.** The position, term, or office of a bishop. **2.** The area of jurisdiction of a bishop; diocese. **3.** Bishops collectively. [LLat. *episcopatus* < *episcopus,* bishop. —see EPISCOPAL.]
ep·i·si·ot·o·my (ĭ-pē'zē-ŏt'ə-mē) *n., pl.* **-mies.** The surgical incision of the perineum during childbirth to facilitate delivery. [Gk. *epision,* pubic region + -TOMY.]
ep·i·sode (ĕp'ĭ-sōd') *n.* **1. a.** An incident that is part of a narrative but forms a separate unit within the whole. **b.** One of a series of related events in the course of a continuous account. **2.** A portion of a narrative that relates an event or series of connected events and forms a coherent story in itself; an incident: *an episode of a picaresque novel.* **3.** A separate part of a serialized work, such as a novel or play. **4.** A section of a classic Greek tragedy that occurs between two choric songs. **5.** *Mus.* A passage between statements of a main subject or theme, as in a rondo or fugue. [Gk. *epeisodion,* parenthetic story < *epeisodios,* coming in besides : *epi-,* in addition + *eisodios,* entering (*eis,* into + *hodos,* way).]
ep·i·sod·ic (ĕp'ĭ-sŏd'ĭk) also **ep·i·sod·i·cal** (-ĭ-kəl) *adj.* **1.** Pertaining to or resembling an episode. **2.** Composed of a series of episodes. **3.** Limited to the duration of an episode; temporary. **—ep'i·sod'i·cal·ly** *adv.*
ep·i·spas·tic (ĕp'ĭ-spăs'tĭk) *adj.* Causing blisters. *—n.* A blistering agent; vesicatory. [NLat. *epispasticus* < Gk. *epispastikos,* drawing toward oneself < *epispan,* to draw toward : *epi-,* toward + *span,* to draw.]
e·pis·ta·sis (ĭ-pĭs'tə-sĭs) *n., pl.* **-ses** (-sēz'). **1.** *Genetics.* A nonreciprocal interaction between nonalternative forms of gene in which one gene suppresses the expression of another affecting the same part of an organism. **2.** *Med.* Matter that rises to the surface of a body discharge. [Gk., stoppage < *ephistanai,* to stop : *epi-,* upon + *histanai,* to place.] **—ep'i·stat'ic** (ĕp'ĭ-stăt'ĭk) *adj.*
ep·i·stax·is (ĕp'ĭ-stăk'sĭs) *n.* Nosebleed. [Gk. < *epistazein,* to bleed from the nose : *epi-,* upon + *stazein,* to drip.]
ep·i·ste·mic (ĕp'ĭ-stē'mĭk) *adj.* Of, relating to, or involving knowledge or the act of knowing. [Gk. *epistēmikos,* of knowledge < *epistēmē,* knowledge. —see EPISTEMOLOGY.] **—ep'i·ste'mi·cal·ly** *adv.*
e·pis·te·mol·o·gy (ĭ-pĭs'tə-mŏl'ə-jē) *n., pl.* **-gies. 1.** The division of philosophy that investigates the nature and origin of knowledge. **2.** A theory of the nature of knowledge. [Gk. *epistēmē,* knowledge < *epistanai,* to understand (*epi-,* upon + *histanai,* to stand) + -LOGY.] **—e·pis'te·mo·log'i·cal** (-mə-lŏj'ĭ-kəl) *adj.* **—e·pis'te·mo·log'i·cal·ly** *adv.* **—e·pis'te·mol'o·gist** *n.*
e·pis·tle (ĭ-pĭs'əl) *n.* **1.** A letter, esp. a formal one. **2. Epistle. a.** One of the letters included as a book in the New Testament. **b.** An excerpt from one of these letters, read as part of a religious service. **3.** A literary composition in the form of a letter. [ME < OFr. < Lat. *epistola* < Gk. *epistolē* < *epistellein,* to send to : *epi-,* to + *stellein,* to send.]
e·pis·tler (ĭ-pĭs'lər) *n.* A writer of an epistle.
e·pis·to·lar·y (ĭ-pĭs'tə-lĕr'ē) *adj.* **1.** Of or associated with letters or letter writing. **2.** In the form of a letter. **3.** Carried on by or made up of letters: *an epistolary friendship.* [Lat. *epistolaris* < *epistola,* epistle.]
ep·i·style (ĕp'ĭ-stīl') *n. Archit.* An architrave (sense 1). [Lat. *epistylium* < Gk. *epistulion* : *epi-,* upon + *stulos,* pillar.]
ep·i·taph (ĕp'ĭ-tăf') *n.* **1.** An inscription on a tombstone in memory of the one buried there. **2.** A brief literary piece commemorating a dead person. [ME < OFr. *epitaphe* < Lat. *epitaphium* < Gk. *epitaphion* : *epi-,* upon + *taphos,* tomb.] **—ep'i·taph'ic** (-tăf'ĭk) *adj.*
e·pit·a·sis (ĭ-pĭt'ə-sĭs) *n., pl.* **-ses** (-sēz'). The middle part of a play that develops the action leading to the catastrophe. [Gk. < *epiteinein,* to intensify : *epi-,* upon + *teinein,* to stretch.]
ep·i·tha·la·mi·um (ĕp'ə-thə-lā'mē-əm) or **ep·i·tha·la·mi·on** (-ən) *n., pl.* **-mi·ums** or **-mi·a** (-mē-ə). A lyric ode in honor of a bride and bridegroom. [Lat. < Gk. *epithalamion* : *epi-,* upon + *thalamos,* bridal chamber.]
ep·i·the·li·oid (ĕp'ə-thē'lē-oid') *adj.* Resembling epithelium.
ep·i·the·li·o·ma (ĕp'ə-thē'lē-ō'mə) *n., pl.* **-ma·ta** (-mə-tə) or **-mas.** A carcinoma derived from the epithelium. **—ep'i·the'li·om'a·tous** (-ŏm'ə-təs) *adj.*
ep·i·the·li·um (ĕp'ə-thē'lē-əm) *n., pl.* **-li·ums** or **-li·a** (-lē-ə). Membranous tissue, usually in a single layer, composed of closely arranged cells separated by very little intercellular substance and forming the covering of most internal surfaces and organs and the outer surface of an animal body. [NLat. : EPI- + Gk. *thēlē,* nipple.] **—ep'i·the'li·al** (-əl) *adj.*
ep·i·thet (ĕp'ə-thĕt') *n.* **1. a.** A term used to characterize a person or thing. **b.** A term used as a descriptive substitute for the name or title of a person. **2.** An abusive or contemptuous word or phrase. [Lat. *epitheton* < Gk. < *epithetos,* added < *epitithenai,* to place upon : *epi-,* upon + *tithenai,* to place.] **—ep'i·thet'ic, ep'i·thet'i·cal** *adj.*
e·pit·o·me (ĭ-pĭt'ə-mē) *n.* **1.** A brief summary, as of a book or article; abstract. **2.** A representative or example of a class or type. [Lat. < Gk. *epitomē* < *epitemnein,* to cut short : *epi-,* upon + *temnein,* to cut.]
e·pit·o·mize (ĭ-pĭt'ə-mīz') *tr.v.* **-mized, -miz·ing, -miz·es. 1.** To make an epitome of; sum up. **2.** To be a typical example of.
ep·i·zo·ic (ĕp'ĭ-zō'ĭk) *adj.* Living or growing on the exterior of a living animal. **—ep'i·zo'ism** *n.* **—ep'i·zo'ite'** *n.*
ep·i·zo·ot·ic (ĕp'ĭ-zō-ŏt'ĭk) *adj.* **1.** Attacking a large number of animals simultaneously. Used of a disease. **2.** Prevalent among a group of animals. Used of a disease. *—n.* An epizootic disease. **—ep'i·zo·ot'i·cal·ly** *adv.*
ep·och (ĕp'ək, ē'pŏk') *n.* **1. a.** A particular period of history, esp. one considered remarkable or noteworthy. **b.** A notable event that marks the beginning of such a period. **2.** *Geol.* A unit of geologic time that is a division of a period. **3.** *Astron.* An instant in time that is arbitrarily selected as a point of reference. [LLat. *epocha,* a point in time < Gk. *epokhē* < *epekhein,* to stop : *epi-,* upon + *ekhein,* hold.]
ep·och·al (ĕp'ə-kəl, -ŏk'əl) *adj.* **1.** Of, pertaining to, or characteristic of an epoch. **2.** Highly significant or important; momentous.
ep·ode (ĕp'ōd') *n.* **1.** The strophe that follows the strophe and the apostrophe to complete the triad that forms the basic compositional unit of a lyric ode. **2.** A lyric poem

characterized by couplets formed by a long line followed by a shorter one. [Lat. *epodos,* a type of lyric poem < Gk. *epōidos* < *epōidos,* sung after < *epaidein,* to sing after : *epi-,* upon + *aidein,* to sing.]

ep·o·nym (ĕp′ə-nĭm′) *n.* A person whose name is or is thought to be the source of the name of something, such as a city, country, or era: *"Romulus" is the eponym of Rome.* [Gk. *epōnumos* < *epōnumos,* named after : *epi-,* to + *ōnuma,* name.] **—ep′o·nym′ic** *adj.*

e·pon·y·mous (ĭ-pŏn′ə-məs) *adj.* Of, relating to, or constituting an eponym.

e·pon·y·my (ĭ-pŏn′ə-mē) *n.* The derivation of a name of a city, country, era, institution, or other place or thing from that of a person.

ep·o·pee (ĕp′ə-pē′) *n.* **1.** Epic poetry, esp. as a literary genre. **2.** An epic poem. [Fr. *épopée* < Gk. *epopoiia* < *epopoios,* epic poet : *epos,* epic + *poiein,* to make.]

ep·os (ĕp′ŏs′) *n.* **1.** Unwritten epic poetry. **2.** An epic poem. [Lat. < Gk.]

ep·ox·y (ĕp′ŏk′sē, ĭ-pŏk′-) *n., pl.* **-ies.** Any of various usually thermosetting resins capable of forming tight cross-linked polymer structures characterized by toughness, strong adhesion, and high corrosion and chemical resistance, used esp. in surface coatings and adhesives. *—tr.v.* **-ied, -y·ing, -ies.** To fasten together with epoxy. [EP(I)- + OXY(GEN).]

ep·si·lon (ĕp′sə-lŏn′, -lən) *n.* The 5th letter in the Greek alphabet. See table at **alphabet.** [Gk. *e psilon,* simple e.]

Ep·som salts also **Ep·som salt** (ĕp′səm) *n.* Hydrated magnesium sulfate used as a cathartic. [After *Epsom,* England.]

eq·ua·ble (ĕk′wə-bəl, ē′kwə-) *adj.* **1. a.** Unvarying; steady. **b.** Free from extremes. **2.** Not easily disturbed; serene: *an equable temper.* [Lat. *aequabilis* < *aequare,* to make even < *aequus,* even.] **—eq′ua·bil′i·ty, eq′ua·ble·ness** *n.* **—eq′ua·bly** *adv.*

e·qual (ē′kwəl) *adj.* **1.** Having the same quantity, measure, or value as another. **2.** *Math.* Being the same or identical to in value. **3. a.** Having the same privileges, status, or rights: *equal before the law.* **b.** Being the same for all members of a group: *gave every player an equal chance to win.* **4. a.** Having the qualities, such as strength or ability, necessary for a task or situation. **b.** Adequate in extent, amount, or degree. **5.** *Archaic.* Impartial; just; equitable. **6.** *Archaic.* Tranquil; equable. **7.** *Archaic.* Flat, level, and smooth. *—n.* One that is equal to another. *—tr.v.* **e·qualed, e·qual·ing, e·quals** or **e·qualled, e·qual·ling, e·quals. 1.** To be equal to, esp. in value. **2.** To do, make, or produce something equal to: *equaled the world record in the mile run.* [Lat. *aequalis* < *aequus,* even.] **—e′qual·ly** *adv.*

e·qual·i·tar·i·an (ĭ-kwŏl′ĭ-târ′ē-ən) *adj.* Egalitarian. **—e·qual′i·tar′i·an·ism** *n.*

e·qual·i·ty (ĭ-kwŏl′ĭ-tē) *n., pl.* **-ties. 1.** The state or quality of being equal. **2.** A mathematical statement, usually an equation, that one thing equals another. [ME *equalite* < OFr. *equalite* < Lat. *aequalitas* < *aequalis,* equal.]

e·qual·ize (ē′kwə-līz′) *v.* **-ized, -iz·ing, -iz·es.** *—tr.* **1.** To make equal. **2.** To make uniform. *—intr.* To constitute or induce equality, equilibrium, or balance. **—e′qual·i·za′tion** (ē′-kwə-lĭ-zā′shən) *n.*

e·qual·iz·er (ē′kwə-lī′zər) *n.* **1.** One that equalizes. **2.** A device for equalizing pressure or strain. **3.** A tone control system designed to compensate for frequency distortion in audio systems. **4.** *Slang.* A weapon, esp. a revolver.

equal sign *n.* The symbol (=) used to indicate logical or mathematical equivalence.

equal temperament *n. Mus.* The modification of the intervals of just intonation in the tuning of instruments of fixed intonation to permit the modulation of harmony.

e·qua·nim·i·ty (ē′kwə-nĭm′ĭ-tē, ĕk′wə-) *n.* The quality of being calm and even-tempered; composure. [Lat. *aequanimitas* < *aequanimis,* calm : *aequus,* even + *animus,* mind.]

Synonyms: *equanimity, composure, sang-froid, serenity, nonchalance.* These nouns are closely related to calmness and self-control. *Equanimity* implies mental balance and evenness of temperament, usually as a characteristic state. *Composure* is calmness that suggests the exercise of self-control and maintenance of dignity. *Sang-froid* is coolness, especially in trying circumstances. *Serenity* is tranquillity of nature that suggests imperviousness to agitation or turmoil. *Nonchalance* is the absence not only of agitation but of close interest, customarily manifested by an indifferent or casual air or manner.

e·quate (ĭ-kwāt′) *v.* **e·quat·ed, e·quat·ing, e·quates.** *—tr.* **1.** To make equal or equivalent. **2.** To reduce to a standard or average; equalize. **3.** To consider, treat, or depict as equal or equivalent: *equates old age with wisdom.* *—intr.* To be or seem to be equal; correspond. [ME *equaten* < Lat. *aequare* < *aequus,* even.]

e·qua·tion (ĭ-kwā′zhən, -shən) *n.* **1.** The process or act of equating or of being equated. **2.** The state of being equal. **3.** *Math.* A linear array of mathematical symbols separated into left and right sides that are designated at least conditionally equal by an equal sign. **4.** *Chem.* A symbolic representation of a chemical reaction as a linear array of symbols for the reacting atomic and molecular species, separated into left and right sides by an equal sign, arrow, or opposing arrows. **5.** A complex of variable elements or factors: *personal equation.* **—e·qua′tion·al** *adj.* **—e·qua′tion·al·ly** *adv.*

e·qua·tor (ĭ-kwā′tər) *n.* **1. a.** The great circle circumscribing the earth's surface, the reckoning datum of latitudes and dividing boundary of Northern and Southern hemispheres, formed by the intersection of a plane passing through the earth's center perpendicular to its axis of rotation. **b.** A similar great circle drawn on the surface of a celestial body at right angles to the axis of rotation. **2.** *Astron.* The celestial equator. [ME < Med. Lat., equalizer < Lat. *aequare,* to equate.]

e·qua·to·ri·al (ē′kwə-tôr′ē-əl, -tōr′-, ĕk′wə-) *adj.* **1.** Of, relating to, or like the equator. **2.** Pertaining to conditions that exist at the earth's equator: *equatorial heat.* **3.** Having or constituting a support with two perpendicular axles, one of which is parallel to the earth's rotational axis. *—n. Astron.* An equatorial telescope. **—e′qua·to′ri·al·ly** *adv.*

equatorial current *n.* One of the surface currents drifting westward through the oceans at the equator.

eq·uer·ry (ĕk′wə-rē) *n., pl.* **-ries. 1.** An officer charged with supervision of the horses belonging to a royal or noble household. **2.** A personal attendant to the British royal household. [Fr. *écurie,* stable < OFr. *escurie* < *escuier,* squire. —see ESQUIRE.]

e·ques·tri·an (ĭ-kwĕs′trē-ən) *adj.* **1.** Of or pertaining to horsemanship or horseback riding. **2.** Depicted or represented on horseback: *the equestrian statue of General Grant.* **3.** Of, pertaining to, or composed of knights or horsemen. *—n.* One who rides a horse or performs on horseback. [< Lat. *equester* < *equus,* horse.]

e·ques·tri·enne (ĭ-kwĕs′trē-ĕn′) *n.* A woman who rides a horse or performs on horseback. [EQUESTRI(AN) + *-enne,* as in *comedienne.*]

equi- *pref.* Equal; equally: *equiangular.* [ME < Lat. *aequi-* < *aequus,* equal.]

e·qui·an·gu·lar (ē′kwē-ăng′gyə-lər, ĕk′wē-) *adj.* Having all angles equal.

e·qui·dis·tant (ē′kwē-dĭs′tənt, ĕk′wē-) *adj.* Equally distant. [OFr. < LLat. *aequidistans* : *aequus-,* equal + *distans,* distant.] **—e′qui·dis′tance** (-təns) *n.* **—e′qui·dis′tant·ly** *adv.*

e·qui·lat·er·al (ē′kwə-lăt′ər-əl, ĕk′wə-) *adj.* Having all sides or faces equal. *—n.* **1.** A side exactly equal to others. **2.** A geometric figure having equal sides. [LLat. *aequilateralis* : *aequus,* equal + *latus,* side.] **—e′qui·lat′er·al·ly** *adv.*

e·quil·i·brant (ĭ-kwĭl′ə-brənt) *n.* A force capable of balancing a system of forces to produce equilibrium.

e·quil·i·brate (ĭ-kwĭl′ə-brāt′) *v.* **-brat·ed, -brat·ing, -brates.** *—intr.* To be in or bring about equilibrium. *—tr.* To maintain in or bring into equilibrium. **—e·quil′i·bra′tion** *n.* [EQUILIBR(IUM) + -ATE[1].]

e·quil·i·bra·tor (ĭ-kwĭl′ə-brā′tər) *n.* A device that brings about and helps maintain equilibrium. **—e·quil′i·bra·to′ry** *adj.*

e·quil·i·brist (ĭ-kwĭl′ə-brĭst) *n.* A person who performs feats of balance, such as tightrope walking. [Fr. *équilibriste* < Lat. *aequilibrium,* equilibrium.] **—e·quil′i·bris′tic** *adj.*

e·qui·lib·ri·um (ē′kwə-lĭb′rē-əm, ĕk′wə-) *n.* **1.** A condition in which all acting influences are canceled by others, resulting in a stable, balanced, or unchanging system. **2.** *Physics.* The condition of a system in which the resultant of all acting forces is zero and the sum of all torques about any axis is zero. **3.** *Chem.* The state of a reaction in which its forward and reverse reactions occur at equal rates so that the concentration of the reactants does not change with time. **4.** Mental or emotional balance; poise. [Lat. *aequilibrium* : *aequus,* level + *libra,* balance.]

e·qui·mo·lar (ē′kwə-mō′lər) *adj. Chem.* Having an equal number of moles.

e·quine (ē′kwīn′, ĕk′wīn′) *adj.* **1.** Of, pertaining to, or characteristic of a horse. **2.** Of or belonging to the family Equidae, which includes the horses, asses, and zebras. [Lat. *equinus* < *equus,* horse.] **—e′quine′** *n.*

e·qui·noc·tial (ē′kwə-nŏk′shəl, ĕk′wə-) *adj.* **1.** Pertaining to an equinox. **2.** Relating to the celestial equator. **3.** *Bot.* Having or characterizing flowers that open and close at specific times. *—n.* **1.** A violent storm of wind and rain occurring, supposedly, at or near the time of the equinox. **2.** The celestial equator. [ME *equinoxial* < OFr. < Lat. *aequinoctialis* < *aequinoctium,* equinox.]

equinoctial circle *n.* The celestial equator.

e·qui·nox (ē′kwə-nŏks′, ĕk′wə-) *n.* **1.** Either of two points on the celestial sphere where the ecliptic intersects the celestial equator. **2.** Either of the two times during a year when the sun crosses the celestial equator and when the length of day and night are approximately equal: the vernal equinox and the autumnal equinox. [ME < OFr. *equinoxe* < Med. Lat. *aequinoxium* < Lat. *aequinoctium* : *aequus,* equal + *nox,* night.]

equinox

e·quip (ĭ-kwĭp′) *tr.v.* **e·quipped, e·quip·ping, e·quips. 1. a.** To supply with necessities such as tools or provisions. **b.** To furnish with the qualities necessary for performance: *an education that equipped him to handle such problems.* **2.** To dress up. [Fr. *équiper,* of Germanic orig.]

eq·ui·page (ĕk′wə-pĭj) *n.* **1.** Equipment or furnishings; outfit. **2. a.** A horse-drawn carriage. **b.** A carriage that is equipped with horses and attendants. **3.** *Archaic.* A retinue, as of a person of royalty or nobility. **4.** *Archaic.* A set of small household articles, such as a dinner or tea service. **5.** *Archaic.* A collection of small articles for personal use. [Fr. < *équiper,* to equip.]

e·quip·ment (ĭ-kwĭp′mənt) *n.* **1.** The act of equipping or the state of being equipped. **2.** Something with which a person, organization, or thing is equipped. **3.** The rolling stock esp. of a transportation system. **4.** The qualities or traits that make up the mental and emotional resources of an individual.

e·qui·poise (ē′kwə-poiz′, ĕk′wə-) *n.* **1.** Equality in distribution, as of weight, relationship, or emotional forces; equilibrium. **2.** A counterpoise; counterbalance.

e·qui·pol·lence (ē′kwə-pŏl′əns, ĕk′wə-) *n.* Equality, as in effectiveness or validity; equivalence.

e·qui·pol·lent (ē′kwə-pŏl′ənt, ĕk′wə-) *adj.* **1.** Equal in power, effectiveness, or significance. **2.** *Logic.* Validly derived from each other; deducible. **3.** Equivalent. —*n.* An equivalent. [ME < OFr. < Lat. *aequipollens* : *aequus,* even + *pollens,* pr.part. of *pollēre,* to be strong.] **—e′qui·pol′lent·ly** *adv.*

e·qui·pon·der·ance (ē′kwə-pŏn′dər-əns, ĕk′wə-) *n.* Equality of weight; equipoise. [Med. Lat. *aequiponderans,* pr.part. of *aequiponderare,* to equiponderate.] **—e′qui·pon′der·ant** *adj.*

e·qui·pon·der·ate (ē′kwə-pŏn′də-rāt′, ĕk′wə-) *tr.v.* **-at·ed, -at·ing, -ates. 1.** To counterbalance. **2.** To give equal balance or weight to. [Med. Lat. *aequiponderare, aequiponderat-* : Lat. *aequus,* equal + Lat. *ponderare,* to weigh.]

e·qui·po·ten·tial (ē′kwə-pə-tĕn′shəl, ĕk′wə-) *adj.* **1.** Having equal potential. **2.** *Physics.* Having the same potential at every point.

eq·ui·se·tum (ĕk′wə-sē′təm) *n.* Any of the flowerless, seedless plants of the genus *Equisetum,* which includes the horsetails. [NLat. *Equisetum,* genus name < Lat. *equisaetum,* horsetail : *equus,* horse + *saeta,* bristle.]

eq·ui·ta·ble (ĕk′wĭ-tə-bəl) *adj.* **1.** Exhibiting or characterized by equity; impartial or reasonable in judgment or treatment. **2.** *Law.* Possessing existence or validity in equity, as distinguished from statute and common law. [Fr. *équitable* < OFr. < *equite,* equity.] **—eq′ui·ta·ble·ness** *n.* **—eq′ui·ta·bly** *adv.*

eq·ui·tant (ĕk′wĭ-tənt) *adj.* Overlapping at the base to form a flat, fanlike arrangement, as the leaves of some irises. [Lat. *equitans, equitant-,* pr.part. of *equitare,* to ride < *eques,* rider < *equus,* horse.]

Erlenmeyer flask

eq·ui·ta·tion (ĕk′wĭ-tā′shən) *n.* The art and practice of riding a horse; horsemanship. [Lat. *equitatio* < *equitare,* to ride. —see EQUITANT.]

eq·ui·ty (ĕk′wĭ-tē) *n., pl.* **-ties. 1.** The state, ideal, or quality of being just, impartial, and fair. **2.** Something that is just, impartial, and fair. **3.** The residual value of a business or property beyond any mortgage thereon and liability therein. **4.** *Law.* **a.** Justice applied in circumstances not covered by law. **b.** A system of jurisprudence supplementing common law. **c.** An equitable right or claim. **5.** *Law.* Equity of redemption. [ME *equite* < OFr. < Lat. *aequitas* < *aequus,* even, fair.]

equity of redemption *n. Law.* The right of one who has mortgaged his property to redeem that property upon payment of the sum due within a reasonable amount of time after the due date.

equity stock *n.* Common stock.

e·quiv·a·lence (ĭ-kwĭv′ə-ləns) *n.* **1.** The state or condition of being equivalent; equality. **2.** *Math.* A reflexive, symmetric, and transitive relation between elements of a set that establishes any two elements in the set as equivalent or nonequivalent.

equivalence relationship *n.* Equivalence (sense 2).

e·quiv·a·len·cy (ĭ-kwĭv′ə-lən-sē) *n., pl.* **-cies.** Equivalence.

e·quiv·a·lent (ĭ-kwĭv′ə-lənt) *adj.* **1. a.** Equal, as in value, force, or meaning. **b.** Having similar or identical effects. **2.** To the extent or degree of; practically equal: *a wish that was equivalent to a command.* **3.** *Math.* **a.** Capable of being put into a one-to-one relationship. Used of two sets. **b.** Having virtually identical or corresponding parts. **4.** *Chem.* Having the same ability to combine. —*n.* **1.** Something that is equivalent. **2.** *Chem.* Equivalent weight. [ME < LLat. *aequivalens,* pr.part. of *aequivalēre,* to be equal in value : *aequi-,* equi- + *valēre,* to be strong.] **—e·quiv′a·lent·ly** *adv.*

equivalent weight *n.* The number of parts by weight of any element combining with or replacing the equivalent of half the atomic weight of oxygen or with one atomic weight of hydrogen.

e·quiv·o·cal (ĭ-kwĭv′ə-kəl) *adj.* **1.** Capable of two or more interpretations and often intended to mislead. **2.** Of uncertain significance. **3.** Of a doubtful or uncertain nature. [LLat. *aequivocus* : *aequus,* same + *vocare,* to call.] **—e·quiv′o·cal·ly** *adv.* **—e·quiv′o·cal·ness** *n.*

e·quiv·o·cate (ĭ-kwĭv′ə-kāt′) *intr.v.* **-cat·ed, -cat·ing, -cates. 1.** To use equivocal language intentionally. **2.** To avoid making an explicit statement. [ME *equivocaten* < Med. Lat. *aequivocare* < LLat. *aequivocus,* equivocal.] **—e·quiv′o·ca′tor** *n.*

e·quiv·o·ca·tion (ĭ-kwĭv′ə-kā′shən) *n.* **1.** The use of equivocal language. **2.** An equivocal statement or expression.

eq·ui·voque also **eq·ui·voke** (ĕk′wə-vōk′, ē′kwə-) *n.* **1.** An equivocal word, phrase, or expression. **2.** A pun. **3.** A double meaning. [LLat. *aequivocus,* equivocal.]

-er[1] *suff.* **1. a.** One that performs a specified action: *swimmer.* **b.** One that undergoes or is capable of undergoing a specified action: *broiler.* **c.** One that provides: *porker.* **d.** One that has: *ten-pounder.* **2. a.** One associated or involved with: *banker.* **b.** Native or resident of: *New Yorker.* **c.** One that is: *foreigner.* [ME < OE *-ere* < Lat. *-arius,* -ary.]

-er[2] *suff.* Used to form the comparative degree of adjectives and adverbs: *darker, faster.* [ME *-ere* < OE *-ra.*]

Er The symbol for the element erbium.

e·ra (îr′ə, ĕr′ə) *n.* **1.** A period of time as reckoned from a specific date serving as the basis of its chronological system. **2. a.** A period of time marked or characterized by particular circumstances, events, or personages: *the Colonial era of U.S. history.* **b.** A point in time that marks the beginning of such a period of time. **3.** *Geol.* The longest division of geologic time comprising one or more periods. [LLat. *aera* < Lat., counters, pl. of *aes,* money.]

e·rad·i·cate (ĭ-răd′ĭ-kāt′) *tr.v.* **-cat·ed, -cat·ing, -cates. 1.** To pull or tear up by or as if by the roots. **2.** To get rid of completely: *Their goal was to eradicate poverty.* [Lat. *eradicare, eradicat-* : *ex-,* out + *radix,* root.] **—e·rad′i·ca·ble** (-kə-bəl) *adj.* **—e·rad′i·ca′tion** *n.* **—e·rad′i·ca′tive** *adj.* **—e·rad′i·ca′tor** *n.*

e·rase (ĭ-rās′) *tr.v.* **e·rased, e·ras·ing, e·ras·es. 1. a.** To remove (something written, for example) by rubbing, wiping, or scraping. **b.** To remove recorded material from: *erase a tape.* **2.** To remove all traces of. **3.** To remove or destroy as if by wiping out. **4.** *Computer Sci.* To replace all the binary digits in a storage device by binary zeros. [Lat. *eradere, eras-* : *ex-,* out + *rādere,* to scratch.] **—e·ras′a·bil′i·ty** *n.* **—e·ras′a·ble** *adj.*

Synonyms: *erase, expunge, efface, delete, cancel, blot.* These verbs mean to remove or eliminate, especially what is written down or otherwise recorded. Though related, they are not always interchangeable. *Erase* refers to rubbing out, literally or figuratively. *Expunge* implies thoroughgoing removal that leaves no trace, as by wiping away something written down or by putting a thing out of mind or memory. *Efface* also can refer to removal of every trace, or it can mean to remove gradually and partially by making indistinct, as lettering on a tombstone is worn away. *Delete* is used principally in the sense of removing a passage from a manuscript. *Cancel* refers to invalidating, by drawing lines through something written or marking it in a way that indicates that its force or effect has been terminated. *Blot,* usually followed by *out,* refers literally to rendering illegible by covering over or smearing a written passage. In extended senses it means to remove by covering, as *Night blots out a view,* or by putting something out of mind. In every usage it implies complete removal.

e·ras·er (ĭ-rā′sər) *n.* Something, such as a piece of rubber or a pad of felt, used to erase.

e·ra·sure (ĭ-rā′shər) *n.* An act or example of erasing.

Er·a·to (ĕr′ə-tō′) *n. Gk. Myth.* The Muse of lyric poetry and mime. [Lat. < Gk. *Eratō* < *eratos,* loved < *eran,* to love.]

er·bi·um (ûr′bē-əm) *n. Symbol* **Er** A soft, malleable, silvery rare-earth element, used in metallurgy, nuclear research, and to color glass and porcelain. Atomic number 68; atomic weight 167.26; melting point 1,497°C; boiling point 2,900°C; specific gravity 9.051; valence 3. [After *Ytterby,* Sweden.]

ere (âr) *Archaic.* —*prep.* Previous to; before. —*conj.* **1.** Before. **2.** Sooner than; rather than. [ME *er* < OE *ǣr* and ON *ār.*]

Er·e·bus (ĕr′ə-bəs) *n. Gk. Myth.* The dark region of the underworld through which the dead must pass before they reach Hades. [Lat. < Gk. *Erebos.*]

e·rect (ĭ-rĕkt′) *adj.* **1. a.** Not lying down; upright. **b.** Vertical. **2.** Being in a stiff, rigid condition: *every hair erect.* **3.** *Archaic.* Wide-awake; alert. —*v.* **e·rect·ed, e·rect·ing, e·rects.** —*tr.* **1.** To construct by assembling: *erect a skyscraper.* **2.** To raise to an upright or rigid condition. **3.** To fix in an upright position. **4.** To set up; establish: *erect a dynasty.* **5.** *Math.* To construct (a perpendicular, for example) from or upon a given base. [ME < Lat. *erectus,* p.part. of *erigere,* to set up : *ex-* up from + *regere,* to guide.] **—e·rect′a·ble** *adj.* **—e·rect′ly** *adv.* **—e·rect′ness** *n.*

e·rec·tile (ĭ-rĕk′təl, -tīl′) *adj.* **1.** Capable of being erected. **2.** *Physiol.* Of or pertaining to vascular tissue that is capable of filling with blood and becoming rigid. **—e·rec·til′i·ty** (-tĭl′ĭ-tē) *n.*

e·rec·tion (ĭ-rĕk′shən) *n.* **1.** The act of erecting. **2.** Something erected; construction. **3.** *Physiol.* **a.** The condition of erectile tissue when filled with blood. **b.** An erect penis.

e·rec·tor also **e·rect·er** (ĭ-rĕk′tər) *n.* **1.** One that erects. **2.** *Anat.* A muscle that causes or maintains the erection of a body part.

E region *n.* The E layer.

ere·long (âr-lông′, -lŏng′) *adv. Archaic.* Before long; soon.

er·e·mite (âr′ə-mīt′) *n.* One who isolates himself from society esp. as a religious recluse. [ME < LLat. *eremita* < LGk. *erēmitēs* < *erēmia,* desert < *erēmos,* uninhabited.] **—er′e·mit′ic** (-mĭt′ĭk), **er′e·mit′i·cal** *adj.*

ă **pat** / ā **pay** / âr **care** / ä **father** / b **bib** / ch **church** / d **deed** / ĕ **pet** / ē **be** / f **fife** / g **gag** / h **hat** / hw **which** / ĭ **pit** / ī **pie** / îr **pier** / j **judge** / k **kick** / l **lid, needle** / m **mum** / n **no, sudden** / ng **thing** / ŏ **pot** / ō **toe** / ô **paw, for** / oi **noise** / ou **out** / o͝o **took** / o͞o **boot** /

er·e·mur·us (ĕr′ə-myo͝or′əs) *n.* Foxtail lily. [NLat. *Eremurus,* genus name : Gk. *erēmos,* solitary + Gk. *oura,* tail.]
ere·now (âr-nou′) *adv. Archaic.* Before now; heretofore.
e·rep·sin (ĭ-rĕp′sən) *n.* A mixture of peptidases in the small intestines that acts to produce amino acids. [Lat. *eripere,* to snatch away (*ex-,* away + *rapere,* to snatch) + (P)EPSIN.]
er·e·thism (ĕr′ə-thĭz′əm) *n.* Abnormal irritability and sensibility to stimulation in any part of the body. [Fr. *éréthisme* < Gk. *erethismos,* irritation < *erethizein,* to irritate.] **—er′e·this′mic** (-mĭk) *adj.*
ere·while (âr-hwīl′, -wīl′) also **ere·whiles** (-hwīlz′, -wīlz′) *adv. Archaic.* Some time ago; formerly.
erg (ûrg) *n.* A centimeter-gram-second unit of energy or work equal to the work done by a force of one dyne acting over a distance of one centimeter. [Gk. *ergon,* work.]
er·go (ûr′gō, âr′-) *conj.* Consequently; therefore. *—adv.* Consequently; hence. [Lat.]
er·go·cal·cif·er·ol (ûr′gō-kăl-sĭf′ə-rôl′, -rōl′) *n.* Vitamin D_2. [ERGO(T) + CALCIFEROL.]
er·go·graph (ûr′gə-grăf′) *n.* A device for determining the work capacity of a muscle or group of muscles by measuring the extent of movement. [Gk. *ergon,* work + -GRAPH.]
er·gom·e·ter (ûr-gŏm′ĭ-tər) *n.* An apparatus for measuring the amount of work done by a group of muscles under control conditions. [Gk. *ergon,* work + -METER.] **—er′go·met′ric** *adj.*
er·gos·ter·ol (ûr-gŏs′tə-rôl′, -rōl′) *n.* A crystalline sterol, $C_{28}H_{44}O$, synthesized by yeast from sugars or derived from ergot and converted under ultraviolet irradiation to vitamin D_2. [ERGO(T) + STEROL.]
er·got (ûr′gət, -gŏt′) *n.* **1.** Any of various fungi of the genus *Claviceps,* infecting various cereal plants and forming black sclerotia, or compact masses of branching filaments, that replace many of the seeds of the host plant. **2.** The disease caused by the ergot. **3.** The dried sclerotia of ergot, usually obtained from rye seed, and used as a source of several medicinally important alkaloids and as the basic source of lysergic acid. [Fr. < OFr. *argor,* cock's spur.]
er·got·a·mine (ûr-gŏt′ə-mēn′, -mĭn) *n.* A crystalline alkaloid, $C_{33}H_{35}N_5O_5$, derived from ergot, that induces vasoconstriction and is used in the treatment of migraine.
er·got·ism (ûr′gə-tĭz′əm) *n.* Poisoning by ergot-infected grain or grain products, characterized by lameness and necrosis of the extremities.
E·rie (îr′ē) *n., pl.* **Erie** or **E·ries. 1.** A tribe of North American Indians formerly inhabiting the region around Lake Erie. **2.** A member of the Erie tribe. **3.** The Iroquoian language of the Erie.
E·rin·y·es (ĭ-rĭn′ē-ēz′) *pl.n. Gk. Myth.* The Furies. [Lat. < Gk. *Erinues.*]
E·ris (îr′ĭs, ĕr′-) *n. Gk. Myth.* The goddess of discord. [Gk. < *eris,* strife.]
e·ris·tic (ĭ-rĭs′tĭk) also **e·ris·ti·cal** (-tĭ-kəl) *adj.* **1.** Of or relating to argument or controversy. **2.** Given to argument or polemics. *—n.* **1.** One given to or expert in argument or dispute. **2.** The art or practice of debate. [Gk. *eristikos* < *erizein,* to wrangle < *eris,* strife.]
Er·len·mey·er flask (ûr′lən-mī′ər, âr′-) *n.* A conical laboratory flask with a narrow neck and flat, broad bottom. [After Emil *Erlenmeyer* (1825–1909).]
er·mine (ûr′mĭn) *n.* **1.** A weasel, *Mustela erminea,* of northern regions, having brownish fur that turns white in winter. **2.** The valuable white fur of the ermine. [ME *ermin* < OFr., perh. of Germanic orig.]
erne also **ern** (ûrn) *n.* Any of several sea eagles, esp. *Haliaeetus albicella,* of the Old World. [ME *ern* < OE *earn.*]
e·rode (ĭ-rōd′) *v.* **e·rod·ed, e·rod·ing, e·rodes.** *—tr.* **1.** To wear (something) away by or as if by abrasion: *Waves erode the shore.* **2.** To eat into or corrode. **3.** To make or form by wearing away: *The river eroded a deep valley.* *—intr.* To become eroded or worn. [Lat. *erodere,* to gnaw off : *ex-,* off + *rodere,* to gnaw.]
e·rog·e·nous (ĭ-rŏj′ə-nəs) also **er·o·gen·ic** (ĕr′ə-jĕn′ĭk) *adj.* Responsive to sexual stimulation: *erogenous zones.* [Gk. *erōs,* sexual love + -GENOUS.]
Er·os (ĕr′ŏs′, îr′-) *n.* **1.** *Gk. Myth.* The god of love, son of Aphrodite. **2.** *Psychoanal.* The sum of all self-preservative, as contrasted with self-destructive, instincts. [Lat. Eros < Gk. *erōs,* sexual love.]
e·rose (ĭ-rōs′) *adj.* Irregularly notched, toothed, or indented. [Lat. *erosus,* p.part. of *erodere,* to gnaw off. —see ERODE.] **—e·rose′ly** *adv.*
e·ro·sion (ĭ-rō′zhən) *n.* **1.** The condition of being eroded or the process of eroding. **2.** Natural processes, including weathering, dissolution, abrasion, corrosion, and transportation, by which material is removed from the earth's surface. **—e·ro′sion·al** *adj.* **—e·ro′sion·al·ly** *adv.*
e·ro·sive (ĭ-rō′sĭv) *adj.* Causing erosion: *the erosive effect of the waves.* **—e·ro′sive·ness, e·ro′siv′i·ty** *n.*
e·rot·ic (ĭ-rŏt′ĭk) *adj.* **1.** Of or concerning sexual love and desire; amatory. **2.** Tending to arouse sexual desire. **3.** Dominated by sexual love or desire. [Gk. *erōtikos* < *erōs,* sexual love.] **—e·rot′ic** *n.* **—e·rot′i·cal·ly** *adv.*
e·rot·i·ca (ĭ-rŏt′ĭ-kə) *pl.n. (used with a sing. or pl. verb).* Literature or art intended to arouse sexual desire. [Gk. *erōtika,* neuter pl. of *erōtikos,* erotic.]
e·rot·i·cism (ĭ-rŏt′ĭ-sĭz′əm) also **er·o·tism** (ĕr′ə-tĭz′əm) *n.* **1.** An erotic quality or theme. **2.** Sexual excitement. **3.** Abnormally persistent sexual excitement. **—e·rot′i·cist** *n.*
e·ro·to·ma·ni·a (ĭ-rō′tə-mā′nē-ə, ĭ-rŏt′ə-) *n.* Excessive sexual desire. [Gk. *erōs, erōt-,* sexual love + -MANIA.]
err (ûr, ĕr) *intr.v.* **erred, er·ring, errs. 1.** To make an error or mistake. **2.** To violate accepted moral standards; sin. **3.** *Archaic.* To go astray. [ME *erren* < OFr. *errer* < Lat. *errare.*]
er·ran·cy (ĕr′ən-sē) *n., pl.* **-cies.** The state or an instance of erring.
er·rand (ĕr′ənd) *n.* **1. a.** A short trip taken to perform a specified task, usually for another. **b.** The purpose or object of such a trip: *His errand was to mail a letter.* **2.** *Archaic.* A mission. [ME *erand* < OE *ǣrend.*]
er·rant (ĕr′ənt) *adj.* **1.** Roving, esp. in search of adventure: *knights errant.* **2.** Straying from the proper course or standards. **3.** Wandering outside the established limits. [ME *erraunt* < AN, partly < OFr. *errer,* to travel (< VLat. **iterare* < LLat. *itinerare*), and partly < OFr. *errer,* to err (< Lat. *errare).*] **—er′rant** *n.* **—er′rant·ly** *adv.*
er·rant·ry (ĕr′ən-trē) *n.* The condition of traveling or roving about, esp. in search of adventure.
er·ra·ta (ĭ-rä′tə, ĭ-rā′-) *n.* Plural of **erratum.**
Usage: The plural *errata* is sometimes employed in the collective sense of a list of errors. Nevertheless, according to a large majority of the Usage Panel, *errata* always takes a plural verb: *The errata are* (not *is*) *noted in an appendix.*
er·rat·ic (ĭ-răt′ĭk) *adj.* **1.** Having no fixed or regular course; wandering. **2.** Lacking consistency, regularity, or uniformity. **3.** Deviating from the customary course in conduct or opinion; eccentric: *erratic behavior.* [ME *erratik* < OFr. *erratique* < Lat. *erraticus* < *errare,* to wander.] **—er·rat′i·cal·ly** *adv.*
er·ra·tum (ĭ-rä′təm, ĭ-rā′-) *n., pl.* **-ta** (-tə). An error in printing or writing, esp. such an error noted in a list of corrections and bound into a book. [Lat. < neuter p.part. of *errare,* to stray.]
er·rhine (ĕr′īn′) *adj.* Promoting nasal discharge. *—n.* An errhine medicine. [NLat. *errhinum,* an errhine medicine < Gk. *errhinon* : *en-,* in + *rhis,* nostril.]
er·ro·ne·ous (ĭ-rō′nē-əs) *adj.* Containing or derived from error; mistaken. [ME < Lat. *erroneus* < *errare,* to err.] **—er·ro′ne·ous·ly** *adv.* **—er·ro′ne·ous·ness** *n.*
er·ror (ĕr′ər) *n.* **1.** An act, assertion, or belief that unintentionally deviates from what is correct, right, or true. **2.** The condition of having incorrect or false knowledge. **3.** The act or an instance of deviation from an accepted code of behavior. **4.** A mistake. **5.** The difference between a computed or measured value and a correct value. **6.** *Baseball.* A defensive fielding or throwing misplay by a player when a play normally should have resulted in an out or prevented an advance by a base runner. [ME < OFr. < Lat. < *errare,* to err.]
Synonyms: *error, mistake, oversight.* These nouns refer to what is not in accordance with truth, accuracy, right, or propriety. In many examples *error* and *mistake* may be used interchangeably. *Error* is clearly preferable to indicate belief in untruth or departure from what is morally or ethically right or proper. *Mistake* often implies misunderstanding, misinterpretation, and resultant poor judgment, and is usually weaker than *error* in imputing blame or censure. *Oversight* refers to an omission or a faulty act that results from one's lack of attention.
er·satz (ĕr′zäts′, ĕr-zäts′) *adj.* Substitute; artificial. [< G. *Ersatz,* replacement < *ersetzen,* to replace < OHG *irsezzen.*] **—er′satz′** *n.*
Erse (ûrs) *n.* **1.** Irish Gaelic. **2.** Scottish Gaelic. *—adj.* Of or pertaining to the Scottish or Irish Celts or their language. [ME *Erisch,* Irish.]
erst (ûrst) *Archaic.* *—adv.* **1.** At first. **2.** Formerly. *—adj.* First. [ME *erest* < OE *ǣrest.*]
erst·while (ûrst′hwīl′, -wīl′) *adj.* Former. **—erst′while** *adv.*
er·u·bes·cence (ĕr′ə-bĕs′əns, ĕr′yə-) *n.* A blush. [< Lat. *erubescens,* pr.part. of *erubescere,* to blush : *ex-* (intensive) + *rubescere,* to redden < *rubere,* to be red.] **—er′u·bes′cent** *adj.*
e·ruct (ĭ-rŭkt′) *tr. & intr.v.* **e·ruct·ed, e·ruct·ing, e·ructs.** To belch. [Lat. *eructare* : *ex-,* out + *ructare,* to belch.]
e·ruc·ta·tion (ĭ-rŭk-tā′shən, ē′rŭk-) *n.* The act or an instance of belching. **—e·ruc′ta·tive** (ĭ-rŭk′tə-tĭv) *adj.*
er·u·dite (ĕr′yə-dīt′, ĕr′ə-) *adj.* Characterized by erudition; learned. [ME *erudit* < Lat. *eruditus,* p.part. of *erudire,* to instruct : *ex-,* out + *rudis,* rude.] **—er′u·dite′ly** *adv.* **—er′u·dite′ness** *n.*
er·u·di·tion (ĕr′yə-dĭsh′ən, ĕr′ə-) *n.* Deep and extensive learning.
e·rum·pent (ĭ-rŭm′pənt) *adj.* Bursting through or as if through a surface or covering. [Lat. *erumpens,* pr. part of *erumpere, erumpent-,* to burst. —see ERUPT.]
e·rupt (ĭ-rŭpt′) *v.* **e·rupt·ed, e·rupt·ing, e·rupts.** *—intr.* **1.** To emerge violently from limits or restraint; explode. **2.** To become violently active. **3.** To force out or release something, such as steam, with violence or suddenness. **4. a.** To pierce the gum in developing. Used of a tooth. **b.** To appear as a blemish on the skin. *—tr.* To force out violently. [Lat. *erumpere, erupt-* : *ex-,* out + *rumpere,* to break.] **—e·rup′tive** *adj.* **—e·rup′tive·ly** *adv.*
e·rup·tion (ĭ-rŭp′shən) *n.* **1.** An act, process, or instance of

ermine
Above: The animal
Below: An ermine robe

Eros
5th-century Greek statue

erosion
Above: Before replanting
Below: After replanting

erupting. **2.** A sudden, often violent outburst. **3.** A rash or blemish on the skin.

-ery *suff.* **1.** A place for: *bakery.* **2.** A collection or class: *finery.* **3.** A state or condition: *slavery.* **4.** Act; practice: *bribery.* **5.** Characteristics or qualities of: *snobbery.* [ME *-erie* < OFr. : *-er,* -ary (< Lat. *-arius*) + *-ie,* -ia (< Lat. *-ia*).]

e•ryn•go (ĭ-rĭng′gō) *n., pl.* **-goes. 1.** Any of several plants of the genus *Eryngium,* having spiny leaves and dense clusters of small bluish flowers. **2.** *Obs.* The candied root of *E. maritimum,* the sea holly, formerly considered an aphrodisiac. [NLat. *Eryngium,* genus name < Lat. *eryngion,* sea holly < Gk. *ērungion.*]

er•y•sip•e•las (ĕr′ĭ-sĭp′ə-ləs, ĭr′-) *n.* An acute disease of the skin and subcutaneous tissue caused by a streptococcus and marked by spreading inflammation. [ME *erisipila* < Lat. *erysipelas* < Gk. *erusipelas* : *erisi-,* red + *-pelas,* skin.] **—er′y•si•pel′a•tous** (-sĭ-pĕl′ə-təs) *adj.*

er•y•sip•e•loid (ĕr′ĭ-sĭp′ə-loid′, ĭr′ə-) *n.* An infectious disease of the hands characterized by red lesions and caused by the bacterium *Erysipelothrix rhusiopathiae,* found in infected meat or fish. [ERYSIPEL(AS) + -OID.]

er•y•the•ma (ĕr′ə-thē′mə) *n.* A redness of the skin, as caused by chemical poisoning or sunburn. [Gk. *eruthēma* < *eruthainein,* to be red < *eruthros,* red.] **—er′y•them′a•tous** (-thĕm′ə-təs, -thē′mə-təs), **er′y•the•mat′ic** (-thĭ-măt′ĭk), **er′y•the′mic** *adj.*

er•y•thor•bic acid (ĕr′ə-thôr′bĭk) *n.* An optical isomer of ascorbic acid used as an antioxidant. [ERYTH(RO)- + (ASC)ORBIC ACID.]

erythr– *pref.* Variant of **erythro-.**

er•y•thrism (ĕr′ə-thrĭz′əm) *n.* Unusual redness of pigmentation, as of hair or plumage. **—er′y•thris′mal** (ĕr′ə-thrĭz′məl) *adj.*

er•y•thrite (ĕr′ə-thrīt′) *n.* A reddish hydrated arsenate of cobalt found in veins bearing cobalt and arsenic and used in coloring glass.

erythro– or **erythr–** *pref.* **1.** Red: *erythrocyte.* **2.** Erythrocyte: *erythropoiesis.* [Gk. *eruthros,* red.]

e•ryth•ro•blast (ĭ-rĭth′rə-blăst′) *n.* Any of the nucleated cells in bone marrow that develop into erythrocytes. **—e•ryth′ro•blas′tic** *adj.*

e•ryth•ro•blas•to•sis (ĭ-rĭth′rō-blă-stō′sĭs) *n., pl.* **-ses** (-sēz′). The abnormal presence of erythroblasts in the blood.

erythroblastosis fe•tal•is (fə-tăl′əs) *n.* A hemolytic disease of the fetus and newborn usually caused by the production of antibodies from an Rh-negative mother against an Rh-positive fetus, characterized by anemia, jaundice, and the progressive destruction of circulating erythrocytes. [NLat., fetal erythroblastosis.]

e•ryth•ro•cyte (ĭ-rĭth′rə-sīt′) *n.* The yellowish, nonnucleated, disk-shaped blood cell that contains hemoglobin and is responsible for the color of blood. **—e•ryth′ro•cyt′ic** (-sĭt′ĭk) *adj.*

e•ryth•ro•cy•tom•e•ter (ĭ-rĭth′rə-sī-tŏm′ĭ-tər) *n.* A hemacytometer.

e•ryth•ro•my•cin (ĭ-rĭth′rə-mī′sĭn) *n.* An antibiotic agent from cultures of the bacterium *Streptomyces erythreus,* effective esp. against Gram-positive bacteria.

e•ryth•ro•poi•e•sis (ĭ-rĭth′rō-poi-ē′sĭs) *n.* The formation and production of erythrocytes. **—e•ryth′ro•poi•et′ic** (-ĕt′ĭk) *adj.*

e•ryth•ro•poi•e•tin (ĭ-rĭth′rō-poi-ē′tĭn) *n.* A hormone that regulates erythropoiesis. [ERYTHROPOIET(IC) + -IN.]

Es The symbol for the element einsteinium.

-es¹ *suff.* Variant of **-s¹.** Used after *s, z, ch, sh,* and postconsonantal *y.*

-es² *suff.* Variant of **-s².** Used after *s, z, ch, sh,* and postconsonantal *y.*

es•ca•drille (ĕs′kə-drĭl′, -drē′) *n.* A unit of a European air command, as in France during World War I. [Fr. < Sp. *escuadrilla,* dim. of *escuadrón,* squadron < *escuadrar,* to square, of Lat. orig.]

es•ca•lade (ĕs′kə-lăd′, -läd′) *n.* The act of scaling a fortified wall or rampart. *—tr.v.* **-lad•ed, -lad•ing, -lades.** To climb up and over (a wall or fortified place). [Fr. < Ital. *scalata* < *scalare,* to climb < *scala,* ladder < Lat. < *scalae,* steps.] **—es′ca•lad′er** *n.*

escalator

es•ca•late (ĕs′kə-lāt′) *v.* **-lat•ed, -lat•ing, -lates.** *—tr.* To increase, enlarge, or intensify. *—intr.* To increase in intensity or extent. [Back-formation < ESCALATOR.] **—es′ca•la′tion** *n.*

es•ca•la•tor (ĕs′kə-lā′tər) *n.* **1.** A moving stairway consisting of steps attached to a continuously circulating belt. **2.** An escalator clause. [Orig. a trademark.]

escalator clause *n.* A provision in a contract stipulating an increase or decrease, as in wages, benefits, or prices, under certain conditions, such as changes in the cost of living.

es•cal•lop (ĭ-skŏl′əp, ĭ-skăl′-) *n. & v.* Variant of **scallop.**

es•ca•pade (ĕs′kə-pād′) *n.* An adventurous action that usually violates conventional standards of behavior. [Fr. < OFr. < OSp. or OPort. *escapada* < *escapar,* to escape.]

es•cape (ĭ-skāp′) *v.* **-caped, -cap•ing, -capes.** *—intr.* **1.** To break loose from confinement; get free. **2.** To issue from confinement or an enclosure; leak or seep out. **3.** To avoid capture, danger, or harm. **4.** To grow beyond a cultivated area. *—tr.* **1.** To break loose from; get free of. **2.** To succeed in avoiding. **3.** To elude the memory or comprehension of: *Her name escapes me. The book's significance escaped him.* **4.** To issue involuntarily from: *A sigh escaped her lips.* *—n.* **1.** The act or an instance of escaping. **2.** A means of escaping. **3.** A means of obtaining temporary freedom from worry, care, or unpleasantness: *Television is his escape from worry.* **4.** A gradual effusion from an enclosure; leakage. **5.** A cultivated plant that has become established away from cultivation. [ME *escapen* < ONFr. *escaper* : Lat. *ex-,* out + Med. Lat. *cappa,* cloak.] **—es•cap′a•ble** *adj.* **—es•cap′er** *n.*

Synonyms: *escape, avoid, shun, eschew, evade, elude.* These verbs mean to get away from or keep away from persons or things. *Escape* can mean to get free from confinement by fleeing or to remain untouched or unaffected by something unwanted, such as death, punishment, or notice. The second sense does not invariably imply flight or even conscious effort to keep away. *Avoid,* in contrast, always involves such an effort to keep away from persons or things considered a source of danger or difficulty. *Shun* involves deliberately keeping clear of persons or things one dislikes. *Eschew* refers to staying clear of things because to do otherwise would be unwise or morally wrong. *Evade* applies both to getting clear of persons by adroit maneuvering and avoiding distasteful things by similar means. In the latter sense the term sometimes implies dishonesty or irresponsibility. To *elude* is to get away from artfully or by a small margin, or, metaphorically, to escape another's understanding by being perplexing.

es•cap•ee (ĭ-skā′pē′, ĕs′kā-) *n.* One that has escaped, esp. an escaped prisoner. —See Usage note at **-ee¹.**

es•cape•ment (ĭ-skāp′mənt) *n.* **1.** A mechanism consisting in general of an escape wheel and anchor, used esp. in timepieces to control the wheel movement and to provide periodic energy impulses to a pendulum or balance. **2.** A mechanism, as in a typewriter, that controls the lateral movement of the carriage. **3.** An escape. **4.** A means or way of escape.

escape velocity *n.* The minimum velocity that a body must attain to overcome the gravitational attraction of another body, such as the earth.

escape wheel *n.* The rotating notched wheel periodically engaged and disengaged by the anchor in an escapement.

es•cap•ism (ĭ-skā′pĭz′əm) *n.* **1.** The tendency to escape from unpleasant realities in fantasy or entertainment. **2.** Behavior characterized by escapism.

es•cap•ist (ĭ-skā′pĭst) *n.* One whose conduct or thought is characterized by escapism.

es•cap•ol•o•gy (ĕs′kā-pŏl′ə-jē) *n.* The art of escaping. **—es′cap•ol′o•gist** (-jĭst) *n.*

es•car•got (ĕs′kär-gō′) *n., pl.* **-gots** (-gō′). An edible snail, esp. when prepared for eating. [Fr. < OFr. < OProv. *escaragol.*]

es•ca•role (ĕs′kə-rōl′) *n.* A variety of *Cichorium endivia,* having leaves with irregular, frilled edges and often used in salads. [Fr. < OFr. *scariole* < LLat. *escariola* < Lat. *escarius,* of food < *esca,* food < *edere,* to eat.]

es•carp (ĭ-skärp′) *n.* **1.** A steep slope or cliff; escarpment. **2.** The inner wall of a ditch or trench dug around a fortification. *—tr.v.* **-carped, -carp•ing, -carps. 1.** To cause to form a steep slope. **2.** To furnish with an escarp or escarps. [Fr. *escarpe* < OFr. < OItal. *scarpa.*]

es•carp•ment (ĭ-skärp′mənt) *n.* **1.** A steep slope or long cliff resulting from erosion or faulting and separating two relatively level areas of differing elevations. **2.** A steep slope in front of a fortification.

-escence *suff.* The process or quality of emitting or reflecting light in a specified way: *fluorescence.* [OFr. < Lat. *-escentia* < *-escens,* -escent.]

-escent *suff.* **1.** Beginning to be; becoming: *juvenescent.* **2.** Resembling; characterized by: *opalescent.* [OFr. < Lat. *-escens, -escent-,* pr.part. suffix of inchoative verbs in *-escere.*]

esch•a•lot (ĕsh′ə-lŏt′) *n.* A shallot. [Obs. Fr. *eschallotte.* — see SHALLOT.]

es•char (ĕs′kär′) *n.* A dry scab or slough formed on the skin as a result of a burn or by the action of a corrosive or caustic substance. [ME *escare,* ult. < Lat. *eschara* < Gk. *eskhara.*]

es•cha•rot•ic (ĕs′kə-rŏt′ĭk) *adj.* Producing or capable of producing an eschar. *—n.* A caustic or corrosive substance or drug.

es•cha•tol•o•gy (ĕs′kə-tŏl′ə-jē) *n.* The branch of theology that is concerned with the ultimate or last things, such as death. [Gk. *eskhatos,* last + -LOGY.] **—es•chat′o•log′i•cal** (ĭ-skăt′l-ŏj′ĭ-kəl, ĕs′kə-tə-lŏj′-) *adj.* **—es•chat′o•log′i•cal•ly** *adv.* **—es′cha•tol′o•gist** *n.*

es•cheat (ĭs-chēt′) *n.* **1.** The reversion of land held under feudal tenure to the manor in the absence of legal heirs or claimants. **2.** The reversion of property to the state in the absence of legal heirs or claimants. **3.** Property that has reverted to the state when no legal heirs or claimants exist. *—intr. & tr.v.* **-cheat•ed, -cheat•ing, -cheats.** To revert or cause to revert by escheat. [ME *eschete* < OFr. < *escheoir,* to fall out < VLat. **excadere* : Lat. *ex-,* out + Lat. *cadere,* to fall.] **—es•cheat′a•ble** *adj.*

es•cheat•age (ĭs-chē′tĭj) *n.* The right of the state to acquire property by escheat.

es·chew (ĭs-cho͞o′) *tr.v.* **-chewed, -chew·ing, -chews.** To avoid; shun. [ME *eschewen* < OFr. *eschivir,* of Germanic orig.] **—es·chew′al** (-əl) *n.*

es·co·lar (ĕs′kə-lär′) *n., pl.* **escolar** or **-lars.** Any of several slender fishes of the family Gempylidae, esp. *Lepidocybium flavobrunneum,* of warm marine waters. [Sp., student (from the spectacle-like rings around its eyes) < LLat. *scholaris,* of a school. —see SCHOLAR.]

es·cort (ĕs′kôrt′) *n.* **1.** One or more persons accompanying another to guide, protect, or to pay honor. **2.** A man who is the companion of a woman, esp. on a social occasion. **3. a.** One or more vehicles accompanying another vehicle to guide, protect, or honor its passengers. **b.** A warship or plane or a group of warships or planes used to defend or protect other craft from enemy attack. **4.** The state of being accompanied by a person or protective guard. *—tr.v.* (ĭ-skôrt′, ĕ-skôrt′, ĕs′kôrt′) **-cort·ed, -cort·ing, -corts.** To accompany as an escort. [Fr. *escorte* < OFr. < OItal. *scorta* < *scorgere,* to conduct < VLat. **excorrigere* : Lat. *ex-,* out + Lat. *corrigere,* to set right.]

es·cri·toire (ĕs′krĭ-twär′) *n.* **1.** A writing table or desk. **2.** A desk with a top section for books. [Obs. Fr. < OFr. *escriptoire,* study < Med. Lat. *scriptorium* < Lat. *scribere,* to write.]

es·crow (ĕs′krō′, ĕ-skrō′) *n.* Money, property, a deed, or a bond put into the custody of a third party for delivery to a grantee only after the fulfillment of the conditions specified. [AN *escrowe* < OFr. *escroe,* scroll, of Germanic orig.]

es·cu·do (ĭ-sko͞o′dō) *n., pl.* **-dos.** See table at **currency.** [Port. and Sp., shield, escudo < Lat. *scutum,* shield.]

es·cu·lent (ĕs′kyə-lənt) *adj.* Suitable for eating; edible. [Lat. *esculentus* < *esca,* food < *edere,* to eat.] **—es′cu·lent** *n.*

es·cutch·eon (ĭ-skŭch′ən) *n.* **1.** A shield or shield-shaped emblem bearing a coat of arms. **2.** An ornamental or protective plate, as for a keyhole. **3.** The plate on the stern of a ship inscribed with the ship's name. [ME *escochon* < OFr. *escuchon* < VLat. **scutio* < Lat. *scutum,* shield.] **—es·cutch′eoned** *adj.*

Es·dras (ĕz′drəs) *n.* See table at **Bible.**

-ese *suff.* **1.** Of, relating to, characteristic of, or originating in a specified place: *Vietnamese.* **2.** Native or inhabitant of: *Taiwanese.* **3. a.** Language or dialect of: *Chinese.* **b.** Literary style or diction of: *journalese.* [OFr. *-eis* and Ital. *-ese* < Lat. *-ensis,* originating in.]

es·er·ine (ĕs′ə-rēn′) *n. Biochem.* Physostigmine. [Fr. *ésère,* Calabar bean (< Kongo *anzadi)* + -INE².]

es·ker (ĕs′kər) *n.* A long, narrow ridge of coarse gravel deposited by a stream flowing in an ice-walled valley or tunnel in a decaying glacial ice sheet. [Ir. Gael. *eiscir* < OIr. *escir.*]

Es·ki·mo (ĕs′kə-mō′) *n., pl.* **Eskimo** or **-mos. 1.** One of a people native to the Arctic coastal regions of North America and to parts of Greenland and northeastern Siberia. **2.** The language of the Eskimo people. [Dan. < Fr. *Esquimaux* (pl.), of Algonquian orig.] **—Es·ki·mo·an** (es′kə-mō′ən) *adj.*

Eskimo dog *n.* A large dog of a breed used in Arctic regions as a sled dog, having a thick coat and a plumed tail.

e·soph·a·gus (ĭ-sŏf′ə-gəs) *n., pl.* **-gi** (-jī′). A muscular, membranous tube for the passage of food from the pharynx to the stomach; gullet. [ME *ysophagus* < Gk. *oisophagos.*] **—e·soph′a·ge′al** (ĭ-sŏf′ə-jē′əl) *adj.*

es·o·ter·ic (ĕs′ə-tĕr′ĭk) *adj.* **1.** Intended for or understood by only a particular group: *an esoteric cult.* **2. a.** Known by a restricted number. **b.** Confined to a small group. **3.** Not publicly disclosed; confidential. [Gk. *esōterikos* < *esōterō,* comp. of *esō,* within.] **—es′o·ter′i·cal·ly** *adv.*

ESP (ē′ĕs-pē′) *n.* Extrasensory perception. [E(XTRA) S(ENSORY) P(ERCEPTION).]

es·pa·drille (ĕs′pə-drĭl′) *n.* A sandal having a rope sole and a canvas upper part. [Fr. < Prov. *espardilho,* dim. of *espart,* esparto < Lat. *spartum.*]

es·pal·ier (ĭ-spăl′yər, -yā′) *n.* **1.** A tree or shrub that is trained to grow in a flat plane against a wall, often in a symmetrical pattern. **2.** A trellis or other framework upon which an espalier is grown. *—tr.v.* **-iered, -ier·ing, -iers. 1.** To train on an espalier. **2.** To provide with an espalier. [Fr. < Ital. *spalliera,* stakes at shoulder's height < *spalla,* shoulder < Med. Lat. *spatula* < Lat., dim. of *spatho,* broad sword < Gk. *spathē,* broad blade.]

es·par·to (ĭ-spär′tō) *n., pl.* **-tos.** A tough, wiry grass, *Stipa tenacissima,* of northern Africa, yielding a fiber used in making paper and as cordage. [Sp. < Lat. *spartum* < Gk. *sparton,* rope.]

es·pe·cial (ĭ-spĕsh′əl) *adj.* **1.** Standing above or apart from others; exceptional. **2.** Pertaining to a particular person or thing; particular. —See Usage note at **special.** [ME < OFr. < Lat. *specialis* < *species,* species.] **—es·pe′cial·ly** *adv.*

es·per·ance (ĕs′pər-əns) *n. Obs.* Hope. [ME *esperaunce* < OFr. < Lat. *sperans,* pr. part. of *sperare,* to hope.]

Es·pe·ran·to (ĕs′pə-răn′tō, -rän′-) *n.* An artificial language with a vocabulary based on word roots common to many European languages and a regularized system of inflection. [After Dr. *Esperanto,* pseudonym of L.L. Zamenhof (1859–1917).]

es·pi·al (ĭ-spī′əl) *n.* **1.** The act of noticing or observing. **2.** The fact of being seen or noticed. [ME *espiaille* < OFr. < *espier,* to watch, of Germanic orig.]

es·pi·o·nage (ĕs′pē-ə-näzh′, -nĭj) *n.* The act or practice of spying or of using spies to obtain secret information, as about another government or a business competitor. [Fr. *espionnage* < OFr. < *espionner,* to spy < *espion,* spy < OItal. *spione,* of Germanic orig.]

es·pla·nade (ĕs′plə-näd′, -nād′) *n.* A flat, open stretch of pavement or grass, esp. one designed as a promenade along the shore. [Fr. < Ital. *spianala* < *spianare,* to level < Lat. *explanare* : *ex-,* out + *planus,* level.]

es·pous·al (ĭ-spou′zəl) *n.* **1. a.** A betrothal. **b.** A wedding ceremony. **2.** The adoption of an idea or cause; adoption.

es·pouse (ĭ-spouz′) *tr.v.* **-poused, -pous·ing, -pous·es. 1.** To take in marriage; marry. **2.** To give in marriage. **3.** To give one's loyalty or support to; adopt. [ME *espousen* < OFr. *espouser* < Lat. *sponsare* < *spondere,* to betroth.] **—es·pous′er** *n.*

es·pres·so (ĭ-sprĕs′ō) *n., pl.* **-sos.** A strong coffee brewed by forcing steam under pressure through darkly roasted, powdered coffee beans. [Ital., p.part. of *esprimere,* to press out < Lat. *exprimere* : *ex-,* out + *premere,* to press.]

es·prit (ĕ-sprē′) *n.* **1.** Spirit. **2.** Liveliness of mind and expression; wit. [Fr. < Lat. *spiritus,* spirit.]

es·prit de corps (ĕ-sprē′ də kôr′) *n.* A common spirit of comradeship, enthusiasm, and devotion to a cause among the members of a group. [Fr. : *esprit,* spirit + *de,* of + *corps,* body.]

es·py (ĭ-spī′) *tr.v.* **-pied, -py·ing, -pies.** To catch sight of; glimpse. [ME *espien* < OFr. *espier,* to watch, of Germanic orig.]

-esque *suff.* Resembling; in the manner of: *Lincolnesque.* [Fr. < Ital. *-esco,* of Germanic orig.]

Es·qui·mau (ĕs′kə-mō′) *n., pl.* **Esquimau** or **-maux** (-mōz′). Eskimo. **—Es′qui·mau′** *adj.*

es·quire (ĕs′kwīr′, ĭ-skwīr′) *n.* **1.** A candidate for knighthood in medieval times, serving a knight as attendant and shield-bearer. **2.** A member of the English gentry ranking below a knight. **3.** *Archaic.* An English country gentleman; squire. **4.** Used as a title of courtesy usually in its abbreviated form after a man's full name, esp. an attorney: *Martin Chuzzlewit, Esq.* [ME < OFr. *esquier* < LLat. *scutarius* < Lat. *scutum,* shield.]

Usage: The term *Esquire,* and its abbreviation *Esq.,* traditionally reserved for men, is now sometimes used in correspondence addressed to women, especially female attorneys: *Jane Roe, Esq.*

ess (ĕs) *n.* The letter *s.*

-ess *suff.* Female: *lioness.* [ME *-esse* < OFr. < LLat. *-issa* < Gk.]

es·say (ĕ-sā′, ĕs′ā′) *tr.v.* **-sayed, -say·ing, -says. 1.** To make an attempt at; try. **2.** To subject to a test. *—n.* (ĕs′ā′, ĕ-sā′). **1.** An attempt; endeavor. **2.** A testing or trial of the value or nature of a thing: *an essay of his capabilities.* **3.** (ĕs′ā′) **a.** A short literary composition on a single subject, usually presenting the personal view of the author. **b.** Something resembling this: *a photojournalistic essay.* [OFr. *essaier* < *essai, assai,* trial < LLat. *exagium,* a weighing : Lat. *ex-,* out + Lat. *agere,* to drive.] **—es·say′er** *n.*

es·say·ist (ĕs′ā′ĭst) *n.* A writer of essays.

es·sence (ĕs′əns) *n.* **1.** The intrinsic or indispensable properties that serve to characterize or identify something. **2.** The most important ingredient; crucial element. **3.** The inherent, unchanging nature of a thing or class of things, as distinguished from its existence. **4. a.** An extract that has the fundamental properties of a substance in concentrated form. **b.** Such an extract in a solution of alcohol. **c.** A perfume or scent. **5.** An existing thing, esp. a spiritual or incorporeal entity. [ME *essencia* < Lat. *essentia* < *esse,* to be.]

Es·sene (ĕs′ēn′, ĭ-sēn′) *n.* A member of an ascetic Jewish sect that existed in ancient Palestine from the 2nd century B.C. to the 3rd century A.D. **—Es·se′ni·an** (ĕ-sē′nē-ən), **Es·sen′ic** (ĕ-sĕn′ĭk) *adj.*

es·sen·tial (ĭ-sĕn′shəl) *adj.* **1.** Constituting or part of the nature of something; inherent. **2.** Basic or indispensable; necessary: *essential ingredients.* *—n.* **1.** Something that is fundamental. **2.** Something that is necessary or indispensable. **—es·sen′ti·al′i·ty** (-shē-ăl′ĭ-tē) **es·sen′tial·ness** *n.* **—es·sen′tial·ly** *adv.*

essential amino acid *n.* An amino acid that is required by the body for optimum growth and that must be supplied by dietary protein.

essential oil *n.* A volatile oil, usually having the characteristic odor or flavor of the plant from which it is obtained, used to make perfumes and flavorings.

es·so·nite (ĕs′ə-nīt′) *n.* A brown or yellowish-brown variety of garnet. [Fr. < Gk. *hēssōn,* inferior, from its being softer than true hyacinth.]

-est¹ *suff.* Used to form the superlative degree of adjectives and adverbs: *greatest, earliest.* [ME < OE *-est, -ast, -ost.*]

-est² *suff.* Used to form the archaic second person singular of English verbs: *comest.* [ME < OE *-est, -ast.*]

es·tab·lish (ĭ-stăb′lĭsh) *tr.v.* **-lished, -lish·ing, -lish·es. 1.** To make firm or secure. **2.** To settle in a secure position or condition: *established her in her own business.* **3.** To cause to be recognized and accepted: *a discovery that established his reputation.* **4.** To found. **5.** To make a state institution of (a church). **6.** To introduce and put (a law, for example) into

escritoire
Louis XVI escritoire

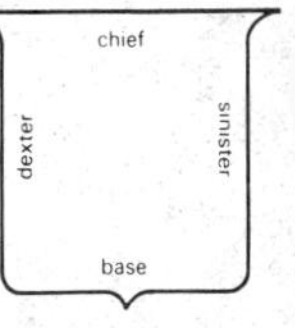

escutcheon
Above: Coat of arms
Below: On a boat

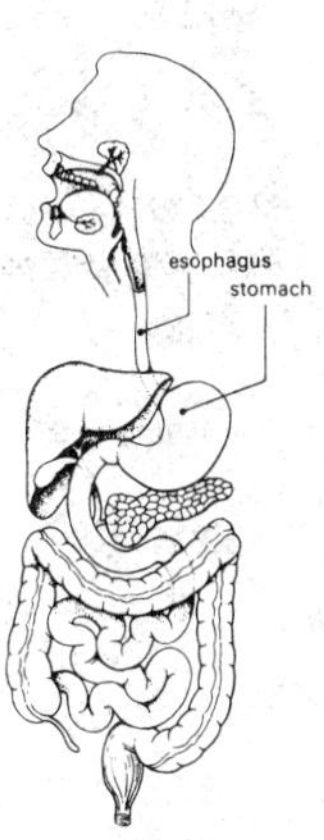

esophagus

esplanade

force. **7.** To prove the validity or truth of. [ME *establissen* < OFr. *establir, establiss-* < Lat. *stabilire* < *stabilis,* firm.] **—es·tab'lish·er** *n.*

established church *n.* A church that is officially recognized and given support as a national institution by a government.

es·tab·lish·ment (ĭ-stăb'lĭsh-mənt) *n.* **1.** The act of establishing. **2.** The condition or fact of being established. **3. a.** A business firm, club, institution, or residence, including its members or occupants. **b.** A place of business, including the possessions and employees. **c.** An organized group, such as a government, political party, or military force. **4.** An established church. **5.** Often **Establishment. a.** An exclusive group of powerful people who rule a government or society. **b.** A powerful group that controls a given field of activity: *the literary establishment.*

es·ta·mi·net (ĕ-stä'mē-nā') *n.* A small café. [Fr.]

es·tan·cia (ĕ-stän'syä) *n.* A large estate or cattle ranch in Spanish America. [Am. Sp. < Sp., enclosure < VLat. **stantia* < Lat. *stare,* to stand.]

es·tate (ĭ-stāt') *n.* **1.** A landed property, usually of considerable size. **2.** The whole of one's possessions, esp. all of the property and debts left by a dead person. **3.** *Law.* The nature and extent of an owner's rights with respect to his property. **4.** The situation of circumstances of one's life: *man's estate.* **5. a.** Social position or rank. **b.** *Obs.* High rank or status. **6.** *Archaic.* Display of wealth or power; pomp. **7.** A class, such as the nobility, commons, or clergy, formerly possessing distinct political rights. [ME *estat,* condition < OFr. < Lat. *status* < *stare,* to stand.]

Es·tates-Gen·er·al (ĭ-stāts'jĕn'ər-əl) *n.* The States-General. [Transl. of Fr. *états généraux.*]

es·teem (ĭ-stēm') *tr.v.* **-teemed, -teem·ing, -teems. 1.** To regard with respect; prize. **2.** To regard as; consider. *—n.* **1.** Favorable regard; respect: *He is held in high esteem.* **2.** *Archaic.* Judgment; opinion. [ME *estemen,* to appraise < OFr. *estimer* < Lat. *aestimare.*]

es·ter (ĕs'tər) *n.* Any of a class of organic compounds corresponding to the inorganic salts formed from an acid by the replacement of hydrogen by an alkyl radical. [G., prob. short for *Essigäther* : *Essig,* vinegar (< MHG *ezzich* < OHG *ezzīh* < Lat. *acetum)* + *Äther,* ether (< Lat. *aether*).]

es·ter·ase (ĕs'tə-rās') *n.* An enzyme that catalyzes the hydrolysis of an ester.

es·ter·i·fi·ca·tion (ĕ-stĕr'ə-fĭ-kā'shən) *n.* A reaction resulting in the formation of at least one ester product.

es·ter·i·fy (ĕ-stĕr'ə-fī') *intr. & tr.v.* **-fied, -fy·ing, -fies.** To change or cause to change to an ester.

Es·ther (ĕs'tər) *n.* **1.** A Jewish queen of Persia who saved her people from massacre. **2.** See table at **Bible.** [Heb. *Estēr* < Pers. *sitareh.*]

étagère
19th-century American

es·the·sia (ĕs-thē'zhə, -zhē-ə, ĭs-) *n.* The ability to receive sense impressions. [Back-formation from ANESTHESIA.]

es·the·si·om·e·ter (ĕs-thē'zē-ŏm'ə-tər) *n.* An instrument used to determine tactile discrimination. [ESTHESI(A) + -METER.]

es·thete (ĕs'thēt) *n.* Variant of **aesthete.**

es·thet·ic (ĕs-thĕt'ĭk) *adj.* Variant of **aesthetic.**

es·thet·ics (ĕs-thĕt'ĭks, ĭs-) *n.* Variant of **aesthetics.**

es·ti·ma·ble (ĕs'tə-mə-bəl) *adj.* **1.** Capable of being estimated. **2.** Deserving of esteem; admirable. **—es'ti·ma·ble·ness** *n.* **—es'ti·ma·bly** *adv.*

es·ti·mate (ĕs'tə-māt') *tr.v.* **-mat·ed, -mat·ing, -mates. 1.** To calculate approximately the extent or amount of. **2.** To form an opinion about; evaluate: *"While an author is yet living we estimate his powers by his worst performance"* (Samuel Johnson). *—n.* (ĕs'tə-mĭt). **1.** A tentative evaluation or rough calculation. **2. a.** A preliminary calculation of the cost of a project. **b.** The statement of such a calculation. **3.** A judgment based upon one's impressions; opinion. [Lat. *aestimare.*] **—es'ti·ma'tive** *adj.* **—es'ti·ma'tor** *n.*

Synonyms: *estimate, appraise, assess, assay, evaluate, rate.* These verbs mean to form a judgment of worth or significance. *Estimate* may imply judgment based on rather rough calculation. In general it lacks the definitiveness of the other terms, especially *appraise,* which stresses expert judgment. *Assess* implies authoritative judgment; it involves setting a monetary value on something as a basis for taxation. *Assay* likewise refers to careful examination, such as chemical analysis of ore to determine its content. In extended senses, *appraise, assess,* and *assay* can refer to any critical analysis or appraisal. *Evaluate* implies considered judgment in setting a value on a person or thing. *Rate* involves determining the rank of a person or thing when he or it is judged in relation to others of the same kind.

es·ti·ma·tion (ĕs'tə-mā'shən) *n.* **1.** The act or an instance of estimating. **2.** An opinion; judgment. **3.** Favorable regard; esteem.

es·ti·val (ĕs'tə-vəl) *adj.* Variant of **aestival.**

es·ti·vate (ĕs'tə-vāt') *v.* Variant of **aestivate.**

es·ti·va·tion (ĕs'tə-vā'shən) *n.* Variant of **aestivation.**

Es·to·ni·an (ĕ-stō'nē-ən) *n.* **1.** The Finno-Ugric language of Estonia. **2.** A native or inhabitant of Estonia. **—Es·to'ni·an** *adj.*

es·top (ĕ-stŏp') *tr.v.* **-topped, -top·ping, -tops. 1.** *Law.* To prohibit or impede by estoppel. **2.** *Archaic.* To stop up. [ME *estoppen* < AN *estopper,* perh. < STOP.] **—es·top'page** (ĕ-stŏp'ĭj) *n.*

es·top·pel (ĕ-stŏp'əl) *n. Law.* A bar against an allegation or denial that is contrary to one's previous allegation or denial of a fact. [Perh. < OFr. *estouppail,* stopper < *estouper,* to stop up, ult. < Lat. *stuppa,* tow < Gk. *stuppē.*]

es·tra·di·ol (ĕs'trə-dī'ôl', -ōl') *n.* An estrogenic hormone, $C_{18}H_{24}O_2$, found in the follicle cells of ovaries and isolated commercially from sow ovaries or the urine of pregnant mares, used in treating estrogen deficiency. [ESTR(US) + DI- + -OL.]

es·tral (ĕs'trəl) *adj.* Estrous.

estral cycle *n.* Estrous cycle.

es·trange (ĭ-strānj') *tr.v.* **-tranged, -trang·ing, -trang·es. 1.** To remove from an accustomed place or relation. **2.** To alienate the affections of; make hostile or unsympathetic. [OFr. *estranger* < Lat. *extraneare* < *extraneus,* strange.] **—es·trange'ment** *n.* **—es·trang'er** *n.*

Synonyms: *estrange, alienate, disaffect.* These verbs refer to the disrupting of love, friendship, loyalty, or a similar bond. *Estrange* and *alienate* are often used with reference to two persons, typically a husband and wife or partners or coworkers, whose harmonious relationship has been replaced by hostility or indifference. *Estrange* generally implies separation. *Alienate* sometimes refers to a break caused by a third person. Both terms also can apply to disruption of a bond that existed between one or more persons and a group or institution. *Disaffect* usually refers to the disruption of loyalty or allegiance within the membership of a group.

es·tray (ĭ-strā') *n.* **1.** *Archaic.* A stray. **2.** *Law.* A stray domestic animal. *—intr.v.* **-trayed, -tray·ing, -trays.** *Archaic.* To stray. [AFr. < *estraier,* to stray < OFr.]

es·tri·ol (ĕs'trī-ôl', -ōl', ĕ-strī'-) *n.* An estrogenic hormone, $C_{18}H_{24}O_3$, that is found in the ovaries of mammals, obtained commercially from the urine of pregnant animals and used in treating estrogen deficiency. [ES(TRUS) + TRI- + -OL2.]

es·tro·gen (ĕs'trə-jən) *n.* Any of several steroid hormones produced chiefly by the ovary and responsible for promoting estrus and the development and maintenance of female secondary sex characteristics. [ESTR(US) + -GEN.] **—es'tro·gen'ic** (-jĕn'ĭk) *adj.* **—es'tro·gen'i·cal·ly** *adv.*

es·trone (ĕs'trōn') *n.* An estrogenic hormone, $C_{18}H_{22}O_2$, found in the mammalian ovary, isolated commercially from the urine of pregnant females for use in treating estrogen deficiency. [ESTR(US) + -ONE.]

es·trous (ĕs'trəs) *adj.* **1.** Of or pertaining to estrus. **2.** Being in heat.

estrous cycle *n.* The series of chemical and physiological changes in female mammals from one period of estrus to the next.

es·trus (ĕs'trəs) *n.* A regularly recurrent period of ovulation and sexual excitement in female mammals other than humans. [NLat. < Lat. *oestrus,* frenzy < Gk. *oistros.*]

es·tu·a·rine (ĕs'cho͞o-ə-rīn', -rēn') *adj.* Of, pertaining to, or found in an estuary.

es·tu·ar·y (ĕs'cho͞o-ĕr'ē) *n., pl.* **-ies. 1.** The part of the wide lower course of a river where its current is met by the tides. **2.** An arm of the sea that extends inland to meet the mouth of a river. [Lat. *aestuarium* < *aestus,* tide.] **—es'tu·ar'i·al** (-âr'ē-əl) *adj.*

e·su·ri·ent (ĭ-so͝or'ē-ənt, ĭ-zo͝or'-) *adj.* Hungry; greedy. [Lat. *esuriens, esurient-,* pr.part. of *esurire,* desiderative of *edere,* to eat.] **—e·su'ri·ence** (-əns), **e·su'ri·en·cy** (-ən-sē) *n.* **—e·su'ri·ent·ly** *adv.*

-et *suff.* Small: *falconet.* [ME < OFr.]

e·ta (ā'tə, ē'tə) *n.* The 7th letter of the Greek alphabet. See table at **alphabet.** [Gk. *ēta,* of Phoenician orig.; akin to Heb. *ḥēth,* heth.]

é·ta·gère also **e·ta·gere** (ā'tä-zhâr') *n.* A piece of furniture with open shelves for ornaments; whatnot. [Fr. < OFr. *estagiere,* estage, floor. —see STAGE.]

eta particle *n.* An elementary particle that is neutral, spinless, and has a mass 1,074 times that of an electron.

et cet·er·a also **et·cet·er·a** (ĕt-sĕt'ər-ə, -sĕt'rə). And other unspecified things of the same class; and so forth. *—n.* **et·cet·er·a. 1.** A number of unspecified persons or things. **2. etceteras.** A miscellany of extras; additional odds and ends. [Lat., and the rest.]

Usage: The use of *et cetera* and its abbreviation *etc.* is principally appropriate to informal writing or to special areas such as technical reporting or business correspondence. It is not appropriate to formal writing in general.

etch (ĕch) *v.* **etched, etch·ing, etch·es.** *—tr.* **1. a.** To cut into the surface of (glass, for example) by the action of acid. **b.** To make or create by this method: *etch a design on glass.* **2.** To impress or imprint clearly. *—intr.* To practice etching. [Du. *etsen* < G. *ätzen* < MHG *etzen* < OHG *ezzen,* to be eaten.] **—etch'er** *n.*

etch·ing (ĕch'ĭng) *n.* **1.** The art of preparing etched plates, esp. metal plates, from which designs and pictures are printed. **2.** A design etched on a plate. **3.** An impression made from an etched plate.

e·ter·nal (ĭ-tûr'nəl) *adj.* **1.** Without beginning or end; existing outside of time: *God, the eternal Father.* **2.** Having a beginning but without interruption or end: *an eternal flame.*

3. Unaffected by time; timeless: *eternal truths.* **4.** Seemingly endless; interminable. **5.** Of or relating to spiritual communion with God, esp. after death: *eternal life.* —*n.* **1.** Something eternal. **2. the Eternal.** God. [ME < OFr. < LLat. *aeternalis* < Lat. *aeternus* < *aevum,* age.] **—e·ter'nal'i·ty** (ē' tər-năl'ĭ-tē), **e·ter'nal·ness** *n.* **—e·ter'nal·ly** *adv.*

e·ter·nal·ize (ĭ-tûr'nə-līz') *tr.v.* **-ized, -iz·ing, -iz·es.** To eternize.

e·terne (ĭ-tûrn') *adj. Archaic.* Eternal. [ME < OFr. < Lat. *aeternus* < *aevum,* age.]

e·ter·ni·ty (ĭ-tûr'nĭ-tē) *n., pl.* **-ties. 1.** The totality of time without beginning or end; infinite time. **2.** The state or quality of being eternal. **3. a.** The endless period of time following death. **b.** The afterlife; immortality. **4.** A seemingly endless or very long time. [ME *eternite* < OFr. *eternité* < Lat. *aeternitas* < *aeternus,* eternal.]

e·ter·nize (ĭ-tûr'nīz') *tr.v.* **-nized, -niz·ing, -niz·es. 1.** To make eternal. **2.** To make perpetually famous; immortalize. [OFr. *eterniser* < Med. Lat. *aeternizare* < *aeternus,* eternal < *aevum,* age.]

e·te·sian (ĭ-tē'zhən) *adj.* Recurring annually. Used of prevailing northerly summer winds of the Mediterranean. [Lat. *etesius* < Gk. *etēsios* < *etos,* year.] **—e·te'sian** *n.*

eth (ĕth) *n.* Variant of **edh.**

-eth¹ *suff.* Used to form the archaic third person present singular indicative of verbs: *leadeth.* [ME < OE -eð.]

-eth² *suff.* Variant of **-th².**

eth·a·cryn·ic acid (ĕth'ə-krĭn'ĭk) *n.* A compound, $C_{13}H_{12}Cl_2O_4$, used as a diuretic in the treatment of edema. [ETH(YL) + AC(ETIC) + (BUTY)RY(L) + (PHE)N(OL) + -IC.]

eth·ane (ĕth'ān') *n.* A colorless, odorless gas, C_2H_6, occurring as a constituent of natural gas and used as a fuel and refrigerant. [ETH(YL) + -ANE.]

eth·a·nol (ĕth'ə-nôl', -nōl') *n. Chem.* Alcohol (sense 1). [ETHAN(E) + -OL.]

eth·a·nol·a·mine (ĕth'ə-nŏl'ə-mēn', -nōl'-) *n.* A colorless liquid, C_2H_7NO, used as a solvent in dry cleaning and in paints.

eth·ene (ĕth'ēn') *n. Chem.* Ethylene. [ETH(YL) + -ENE.]

e·ther (ē'thər) *n.* **1.** Any of a class of organic compounds in which two hydrocarbon groups are linked by an oxygen atom. **2.** A volatile, highly flammable liquid, $C_4H_{10}O$, derived from the distillation of ethyl alcohol with sulfuric acid, and widely used in industry and as an anesthetic. **3.** The regions of space beyond the earth's atmosphere; the heavens. **4.** *Physics.* An all-pervading, infinitely elastic, massless medium formerly postulated as the medium of propagation of electromagnetic waves. [ME, upper air < Lat. *aethēr* < Gk. *aithēr.*] **—e·ther'ic** (ĭ-thĕr'ĭk, -thîr'-) *adj.*

e·the·re·al (ĭ-thîr'ē-əl) *adj.* **1.** Characterized by lightness and insubstantiality; intangible. **2.** Highly refined; delicate. **3. a.** Of the celestial spheres; heavenly. **b.** Unearthly; spiritual. **4.** *Chem.* Of or pertaining to ether. [Lat. *aetherius* < Gk. *aitherios* < *aithēr,* upper air.] **—e·the're·al'i·ty** (-ăl'ĭ-tē), **e·the're·al·ness** *n.* **—e·the're·al·ly** *adv.*

e·the·re·al·ize (ĭ-thîr'ē-ə-līz') *tr. & intr.v.* **-ized, -iz·ing, -iz·es.** To make or become ethereal. **—e·the're·al·i·za'tion** *n.*

e·ther·i·fy (ĭ-thĕr'ə-fī') *tr.v.* **-fied, -fy·ing, -fies.** To convert (an alcohol) into ether. **—e·ther'i·fi·ca'tion** *n.*

e·ther·ize (ē'thə-rīz') *tr.v.* **-ized, -iz·ing, -iz·es. 1.** To subject to the fumes of ether; anesthetize. **2.** *Chem.* To etherify. **—e'ther·i·za'tion** *n.* **—e'ther·iz'er** *n.*

eth·ic (ĕth'ĭk) *n.* **1.** A principle of right or good conduct. **2.** A system of moral principles or values. **3. ethics** *(used with a sing. verb).* The study of the general nature of morals and of the specific moral choices to be made by the individual in his relationship with others. **4. ethics.** The rules or standards governing the conduct of the members of a profession. [ME *ethik* < OFr. *ethique,* < LLat. *ethica* < Lat. *ethice* < Gk. *ēthikē* < *ēthikos,* ethical < *ēthos,* character.]

eth·i·cal (ĕth'ĭ-kəl) *adj.* **1.** Of, pertaining to, or dealing with ethics. **2.** In accordance with the accepted principles of right and wrong that govern the conduct of a profession. **3.** Designating a drug dispensed solely on the prescription of a physician. **—eth'i·cal·ly** *adv.* **—eth'i·cal·ness, eth'i·cal'i·ty** (-kăl'ĭ-tē) *n.*

eth·i·on (ĕth'ē-ŏn') *n.* A highly toxic, liquid, organophosphate pesticide, $C_9H_{22}O_4P_2S_4$. [Blend of ETHYL and THION-.]

E·thi·op (ē'thē-ŏp') also **E·thi·ope** (-ōp') *n. Archaic.* Ethiopian. [Lat. *Aethiops* < Gk. *Aithiops.*]

E·thi·o·pi·an (ē'thē-ō'pē-ən) *adj.* **1.** *Ecol.* Of or designating the zoogeographic region that includes Africa and most of Arabia. **2.** Of, relating to, or typical of Ethiopia or of the inhabitants of Ethiopia.

E·thi·op·ic (ē'thē-ŏp'ĭk, -ō'pĭk) *n.* The Afro-Asiatic language of ancient Ethiopia that is still used as a liturgical language in the Christian Church in Ethiopia. —*adj.* **1.** Of or pertaining to Ethiopic. **2.** Ethiopian.

eth·moid (ĕth'moid') also **eth·moid·al** (ĕth-moid'l) *adj.* Of or pertaining to a light spongy bone located between the orbits that forms part of the walls of the superior nasal cavity. —*n.* **ethmoid.** The ethmoid bone. [Fr. *ethmoide* < Gk. *ēthmoeidēs,* sievelike < *ēthmos,* strainer < *ēthein,* to strain.]

eth·narch (ĕth'närk') *n.* The ruler of a province or a people. [Gk. *ethnarkhēs* : *ethnos,* nation + *arkhos,* ruler.] **—eth'nar'chy** *n.*

eth·nic (ĕth'nĭk) also **eth·ni·cal** (-nĭ-kəl) *adj.* **1.** Of or pertaining to a religious, racial, national, or cultural group. **2.** Pertaining to a people not Christian or Jewish; heathen. —*n.* **ethnic.** *Informal.* A member of a particular ethnic group. [ME, heathen < LLat. *ethnicus* < Gk. *ethnikos* < *ethnos,* nation.] **—eth'ni·cal·ly** *adv.*

eth·nic·i·ty (ĕth-nĭs'ĭ-tē) *n.* The condition of belonging to a particular ethnic group.

ethno- *pref.* Race; people: *ethnology.* [Fr. < Gk. *ethnos,* people.]

eth·no·cen·trism (ĕth'nō-sĕn'trĭz'əm) *n.* **1.** Belief in the superiority of one's own ethnic group. **2.** Overriding concern with race. **—eth'no·cen'tric** (-trĭk) *adj.* **—eth'no·cen'tri·cal·ly** *adv.*

eth·nog·ra·phy (ĕth-nŏg'rə-fē) *n., pl.* **-phies. 1.** The descriptive anthropology of technologically primitive societies. **2.** Ethnology. **—eth·nog'ra·pher** *n.* **—eth'no·graph'ic** (ĕth'nə-grăf'ĭk), **eth'no·graph'i·cal** *adj.* **—eth'no·graph'i·cal·ly** *adv.*

eth·nol·o·gy (ĕth-nŏl'ə-jē) *n.* The anthropological study of socio-economic systems and cultural heritage in technologically primitive societies, esp. the study of cultural origins and factors influencing cultural growth and change. **—eth'no·log'ic** (ĕth'nə-lŏj'ĭk), **eth'no·log'i·cal** *adj.* **—eth'no·log'i·cal·ly** *adv.* **—eth·nol'o·gist** *n.*

eth·no·mu·si·col·o·gy (ĕth'nō-myōō'zĭ-kŏl'ə-jē) *n.* The study of music of different cultures. **—eth'no·mu'si·col'o·gist** (-jĭst) *n.*

e·thol·o·gy (ĭ-thŏl'ə-jē, ē-) *n.* The scientific study of animal behavior. [Lat. *ethologia,* art of depicting character < Gk. : *ēthos,* ethos + *-logia,* -logy.] **—eth'o·log'i·cal** (ĕth'ə-lŏj'ĭ-kəl) *adj.* **—e·thol'o·gist** *n.*

e·thos (ē'thŏs') *n.* The disposition, character, or fundamental values peculiar to a specific people, culture, or movement: *"The revolutionary ethos had become corrupted"* (Irving Howe). [Gk. *ēthos,* custom.]

eth·ox·yl (ĭ-thŏk'səl) also **eth·ox·y** (ĭ-thŏk'sē) *n.* The univalent radical C_2H_5O. [ETH(YL) + OX- + -YL.]

eth·yl (ĕth'əl) *n.* A univalent organic radical, C_2H_5. [ETHER + -YL.] **—eth·yl'ic** (ĕ-thĭl'ĭk) *adj.*

ethyl acetate *n.* A colorless, volatile, flammable liquid, $CH_3COOC_2H_5$, used in perfumes, flavorings, lacquers, pharmaceuticals, and rayon, and as a general solvent.

ethyl alcohol *n. Chem.* Alcohol (sense 1).

eth·yl·a·mine (ĕth'ə-lə-mēn') *n.* A colorless, volatile liquid, $C_2H_5NH_2$, used in petroleum refining, detergents, and organic synthesis.

eth·yl·ate (ĕth'ə-lāt') *tr.v.* **-at·ed, -at·ing, -ates.** *Chem.* To introduce the ethyl group into (a compound). **—eth'yl·a'tion** *n.*

ethyl chloride *n.* A chemical compound, C_2H_5Cl, a gas at ordinary temperatures and a colorless, volatile, flammable liquid when compressed, used as a solvent, refrigerant, and in the manufacture of tetraethyl lead.

eth·yl·ene (ĕth'ə-lēn') *n.* **1.** A colorless, flammable gas, C_2H_4, derived from natural gas and petroleum and used as a source of many organic compounds, in welding and cutting metals, to color citrus fruits, and as an anesthetic. **2.** The bivalent organic radical C_2H_4. **—eth'yl·e'nic** (-ə-lē'nĭk, -lĕn'ĭk) *adj.*

ethylene glycol *n.* A colorless, syrupy alcohol, $C_2H_6O_2$, used as an antifreeze in cooling and heating systems.

ethyl ether *n.* Ether (sense 2).

ethyl mercaptan *n.* Mercaptan.

-etic *suff.* Used to form adjectives usually from nouns ending in *-esis,* as *aphaeretic* from *aphaeresis.* [Lat. *-eticus* < Gk. *-etikos* < *-etos,* verbal ending.]

e·ti·o·late (ē'tē-ə-lāt') *v.* **-lat·ed, -lat·ing, -lates.** —*tr.* **1.** To cause (a plant) to develop without normal green coloring by preventing exposure to sunlight. **2.** To make weak by stunting the growth or development of. —*intr.* To become blanched or whitened, as when grown without sunlight. [Fr. *étioler* < Norman Fr. *étieuler,* to grow into haulm < *éteule,* stalk < OFr. *esteule* < Lat. *stipula.*] **—e'ti·o·la'tion** *n.*

e·ti·ol·o·gy (ē'tē-ŏl'ə-jē) *n., pl.* **-gies. 1.** The study of causes or origins. **2.** The branch of medicine that deals with the causes of disease. **3. a.** The assignment of a cause, origin, or reason for something. **b.** The cause of a disease or disorder as determined by medical diagnosis. [LLat. *aetiologia* < Gk. *aitiologia* : *aitia,* cause + *-logia,* -logy.] **—e'ti·o·log'ic** (-ə-lŏj'ĭk), **e'ti·o·log'i·cal** *adj.* **—e'ti·o·log'i·cal·ly** *adv.* **—e'ti·ol'o·gist** *n.*

et·i·quette (ĕt'ĭ-kĕt', -kĭt) *n.* The practices and forms prescribed by social convention or by authority. [Fr., etiquette, label < OFr. *estiquet,* label. —see TICKET.]

Synonyms: *etiquette, propriety, decorum, protocol.* These nouns refer to codes governing correct behavior. *Etiquette* consists of the prescribed forms of conduct in polite society, a code also denoted by the plural form *the proprieties.* The singular *propriety* and *decorum* are usually interchangeable with the foregoing terms, both implying in a more general way the standards to be observed by one who makes claim to good breeding. *Protocol* refers to etiquette as

Eton collar

it relates to affairs of state, especially to diplomatic exchange.

E·ton collar (ēt'n) *n.* A broad white collar worn over the lapels of a jacket. [After *Eton* College, England.]

Eton jacket *n.* A waist-length jacket that has wide lapels and is cut square at the hips. [After *Eton* College, England.]

E·tru·ri·an (ĭ-tro͝or'ē-ən) *n.* Etruscan.

E·trus·can (ĭ-trŭs'kən) *n.* **1.** A person who lived in ancient Etruria. **2.** The extinct language of the Etruscans, of unknown linguistic affiliation. **—E·trus'can** *adj.*

-ette *suff.* **1.** Small; diminutive: *dinette.* **2.** Female: *usherette.* [ME < OFr., fem. of *-et,* -et.]

e·tude (ā'to͞od', -tyo͞od') *n.* **1.** A piece of music for the development of a given point of technique. **2.** An artistic composition embodying some point of technique but performed because of its artistic merit. [Fr. *étude* < OFr. *estudie,* study.]

é·tui (ā-twē') *n., pl.* **é·tuis** (ā-twēz'). A small, usually ornamental case for holding small articles such as needles. [Fr. < OFr. *estui,* prison < *estuier,* to guard.]

et·y·mo·log·i·cal (ĕt'ə-mə-lŏj'ĭ-kəl) also **et·y·mo·log·ic** (-lŏj'ĭk) *adj.* Of or pertaining to etymology or based upon the principles of etymology. **—et'y·mo·log'i·cal·ly** *adv.*

et·y·mol·o·gist (ĕt'ə-mŏl'ə-jĭst) *n.* A specialist in etymology.

et·y·mol·o·gize (ĕt'ə-mŏl'ə-jīz') *v.* **-gized, -giz·ing, -giz·es.** *—tr.* To trace and state the etymology of. *—intr.* To give or suggest the etymology of a word.

et·y·mol·o·gy (ĕt'ə-mŏl'ə-jē) *n., pl.* **-gies. 1.** The origin and historical development of a linguistic form as shown by determining its basic elements, earliest known use, and changes in form and meaning, tracing its transmission from one language to another, and identifying its cognates in other languages. **2.** The branch of linguistics that deals with etymologies. [ME *ethimologie* < OFr. < Med. Lat. *ethimologia* < Lat. *etymologia* < Gk. *etumologia* : *etumon,* true sense of a word (< *etumos,* true) + *-logia,* -logy.]

et·y·mon (ĕt'ə-mŏn') *n., pl.* **-mons** or **-ma** (-mə). **1.** An earlier form of a word in the same language or in an ancestor language. **2.** A word or morpheme from which compounds and derivatives are formed. **3.** A foreign word from which a particular loan-word is derived. [Lat. < Gk. *etumon,* true sense of a word < *etumos,* true.]

eu- *pref.* **1.** Good; well; true: *euplastic.* **2.** A derivative of a specified substance: *eucaine.* [ME < Lat. < Gk. < *eus,* good.]

Eu The symbol for the element europium.

eu·caine (yo͞o'kān') *n.* A crystalline substance, $C_{15}H_{21}NO_2$, formerly used as a local anesthetic.

eu·ca·lyp·tol (yo͞o'kə-lĭp'tôl', -tōl') also **eu·ca·lyp·tole** (-tōl') *n.* A colorless oily liquid, $C_{10}H_{18}O$, derived from eucalyptus oil and used in pharmaceuticals, flavoring, and perfumery.

eu·ca·lyp·tus (yo͞o'kə-lĭp'təs) *n., pl.* **-tus·es** or **-ti** (-tī'). Any of numerous tall trees of the genus *Eucalyptus,* native to Australia, having aromatic leaves that yield an oil used medicinally and wood valued as timber. [NLat. *Eucalyptus,* genus name : Gk. *eu-,* well + Gk. *kaluptos,* covered < kaluptein, to cover.]

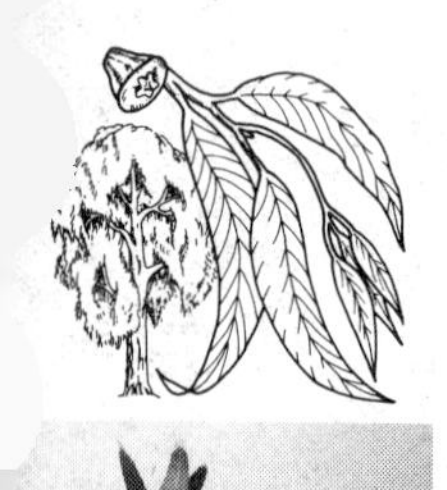

eucalyptus
Above: Tree, leaves, and berries
Below: Flowers and leaves

eu·car·y·ote also **eu·kar·y·ote** (yo͞o-kăr'ē-ōt', -ē-ət) *n.* An organism composed of one or more cells which contain well-defined nuclei. [EU- + Gk. *karyōtos,* having nuts < *karyon,* nut.] **—eu·car'y·ot'ic** (-ŏt'ĭk) *adj.*

Eu·cha·rist (yo͞o'kər-ĭst) *n.* **1.** Communion (sense 4.a.). **2.** *Christian Science.* Spiritual communion with God. [ME *eukarist* < OFr. *eucariste* < LLat. *eucharistia* < Gk. *eukharistia,* gratitude < *eukharistos,* grateful, thankful : *eu-,* well + *kharizesthai,* to show favor < *kharis,* grace.] **—Eu'cha·ris'tic, Eu'cha·ris'ti·cal** *adj.*

eu·chre (yo͞o'kər) *n.* **1.** A card game in which each player is dealt five cards and the player making the trump is required to take at least three tricks to win. **2.** The action of euchring an opponent. *—tr.v.* **-chred, -chring, -chres. 1.** To prevent (an opponent) from taking three tricks in euchre. **2.** *Informal.* To deceive by sly or underhand means; cheat: *euchred him out of his meager savings.* [Orig. unknown.]

eu·chro·ma·tin (yo͞o-krō'mə-tĭn') *n.* Chromatin that is genetically active. **—eu·chro·mat·ic** (yo͞o'krō-măt'ĭk) *adj.*

Eu·clid·e·an also **Eu·clid·i·an** (yo͞o-klĭd'ē-ən) *adj.* Of or pertaining to Euclid's geometric principles.

eu·de·mon also **eu·dae·mon** (yo͞o-dē'mən) *n.* A good or benevolent spirit.

eu·de·mon·ism also **eu·dae·mon·ism** (yo͞o-dē'mə-nĭz'əm) *n.* A system of ethics that evaluates the morality of actions in terms of their capacity to produce happiness. **—eu·de'mo·nist** *n.* **—eu·de'mon·is'tic, eu·de'mon·is'ti·cal** *adj.*

eu·gen·ic (yo͞o-jĕn'ĭk) *adj.* **1.** Of or relating to eugenics. **2.** Relating or adapted to the production of good offspring.

eu·gen·i·cist (yo͞o-jĕn'ĭ-sĭst) also **eu·gen·ist** (yo͞o'jə-nĭst) *n.* An advocate of or specialist in eugenics.

eu·gen·ics (yo͞o-jĕn'ĭks) *n. (used with a sing. verb).* The study of hereditary improvement by genetic control.

eu·ge·nol (yo͞o'jə-nôl', -nōl') *n.* A colorless aromatic oil, $C_{10}H_{12}O_2$, found in cloves and used in perfumes and germicides. [< NLat. *Eugenia,* genus of the clove plant, after *Eugene,* Prince of Savoy (1663–1736).]

eu·gle·na (yo͞o-glē'nə) *n.* Any of various minute unicellular freshwater organisms of the genus *Euglena,* characterized by the presence of chlorophyll, a reddish eyespot, and a single anterior flagellum. [NLat. : Gk. *eu-,* good + Gk. *glēnē,* eyeball.]

eu·glob·u·lin (yo͞o-glŏb'yə-lĭn) *n.* A globulin that is soluble in dilute salt solutions and insoluble in distilled water.

eu·he·mer·ism (yo͞o-hē'mə-rĭz'əm, -hĕm'ə-) *n.* A theory attributing the origin of the gods to the deification of historical heroes. [After *Euhemerus,* a Greek philosopher of the 4th cent. B.C.] **—eu·he'mer·ist** *n.* **—eu·he'mer·is'tic** *adj.* **—eu·he'mer·is'ti·cal·ly** *adv.*

eu·he·mer·ize (yo͞o-hē'mə-rīz', -hĕm'ə-) *tr.v.* **-ized, -iz·ing, -iz·es.** To explain or interpret euhemeristically.

eu·la·chon (yo͞o'lə-kŏn') *n., pl.* **eulachon** or **-chons.** The candlefish. [Chinook *vlâkân.*]

eu·lo·gize (yo͞o'lə-jīz') *tr.v.* **-gized, -giz·ing, -giz·es.** To write or deliver a eulogy for. **—eu'lo·gist** (-jĭst), **eu'lo·giz'er** *n.*

eu·lo·gy (yo͞o'lə-jē) *n., pl.* **-gies. 1.** A laudatory speech or written tribute. **2.** Great praise or commendation. [ME *euloge* < Med. Lat. *eulogium* < Gk. *eulogia,* praise : *eu-* well + *-logia,* discourse.] **—eu'lo·gis'tic** (-jĭs'tĭk) *adj.*

Eu·men·i·des (yo͞o-mĕn'ĭ-dēz') *pl.n. Gk. Myth.* The Furies. [Lat. < Gk. < *eumenēs,* kindly : *eu-,* good + *menos,* spirit.]

eu·nuch (yo͞o'nək) *n.* **1.** A castrated man employed as a harem attendant or functionary in certain Oriental courts. **2.** A man whose testes have not developed. [ME *eunuk* < Lat. *eunuchus* < Gk. *eunoukhos* : *eunē,* bed + *ekhein,* to keep.]

eu·on·y·mus (yo͞o-ŏn'ə-məs) *n.* Any of various trees, shrubs, or vines of the genus *Euonymus,* cultivated for their decorative foliage or fruits. [NLat. *Euonymus,* genus name < Lat. *euonymus* < Gk. *euōnumos,* of good name : *eu-,* good + *onoma,* name.]

eu·pat·rid (yo͞o-păt'rĭd, yo͞o'pə-trĭd) *n., pl.* **eu·pat·ri·dae** (yo͞o-păt'rĭ-dē') or **eu·pat·rids.** A member of the hereditary aristocracy of ancient Athens. [Gk. *eupatridēs* : *eu-,* good + *patēr,* father + *-idēs,* patronymic suffix.] **—eu·pat'rid** *adj.*

eu·pep·si·a (yo͞o-pĕp'sē-ə, -shə) *n.* Good digestion. [Gk. < *eupeptos,* eupeptic.]

eu·pep·tic (yo͞o-pĕp'tĭk) *adj.* **1.** Pertaining to or having good digestion. **2.** Conducive to digestion. [Gk. *eupeptos* : *eu-,* well + *peptein,* to digest.] **—eu·pep'ti·cal·ly** *adv.*

eu·phe·mism (yo͞o'fə-mĭz'əm) *n.* The act or an example of the substitution of an inoffensive term for one considered offensive: *"Euphemisms such as 'slumber room' . . . abound in the funeral business"* (Jessica Mitford). [Gk. *euphēmismos* < *euphēmos,* using auspicious words : *eu-,* good + *phēmē,* speech.] **—eu'phe·mist** *n.* **—eu'phe·mis'tic** (-mĭs'tĭk) *adj.* **—eu'phe·mis'ti·cal·ly** *adv.*

eu·phe·mize (yo͞o'fə-mīz') *v.* **-mized, -miz·ing, -miz·es.** *—tr.* To speak of or refer to by means of a euphemism. *—intr.* To speak with euphemisms. **—eu'phe·miz'er** *n.*

eu·phen·ics (yo͞o-fĕn'ĭks) *n. (used with a sing. verb).* The study of phenotypic improvement of humans after birth.

eu·phon·ic (yo͞o-fŏn'ĭk) *adj.* **1.** Pertaining or relating to euphony. **2.** Euphonious. **—eu·phon'i·cal·ly** *adv.*

eu·pho·ni·ous (yo͞o-fō'nē-əs) *adj.* Pleasing or agreeable to the ear. **—eu·pho'ni·ous·ly** *adv.*

eu·pho·ni·um (yo͞o-fō'nē-əm) *n.* A brass wind instrument, similar to the tuba, but having a somewhat higher pitch and a mellower sound. [< Gk. *euphōnos,* sweet-voiced. —see EUPHONY.]

eu·pho·nize (yo͞o'fə-nīz') *tr.v.* **-nized, -niz·ing, -niz·es.** To make euphonious.

eu·pho·ny (yo͞o'fə-nē) *n., pl.* **-nies.** Agreeable sound, esp. in the phonetic quality of words. [Fr. *euphonie* < LLat. *euphonia* < Gk. < *euphōnos,* sweet-voiced : *eu-,* good + *phōnē,* sound.]

eu·phor·bi·a (yo͞o-fôr'bē-ə) *n.* Any plant of the genus *Euphorbia,* which includes the spurges. [NLat. *Euphorbia,* genus name < Lat. *euphorbea,* after *Euphorbus,* Greek physician of the 1st cent. A.D.]

eu·pho·ri·a (yo͞o-fôr'ē-ə, -fōr'-) *n.* A feeling of great happiness or well-being. [NLat. < Gk. < *euphoros,* healthy : *eu-,* well + *pherein,* to bear.] **—eu·phor'ic** (-fôr'ĭk, -fōr'-) *adj.* **—eu·phor'i·cal·ly** *adv.*

eu·phot·ic (yo͞o-fŏt'ĭk) *adj.* Pertaining to, designating, or characterizing the uppermost layer of a body of water that receives sufficient light for photosynthesis and the growth of green plants.

Eu·phros·y·ne (yo͞o-frŏs'ə-nē) *Gk. Myth.* One of the Three Graces. [Lat. *Euphrosyne* < Gk. *Euphrosunē* < *euphrōn,* cheerful : *eu ,* good + *phrēn,* mind.]

eu·phu·ism (yo͞o'fyo͞o-ĭz'əm) *n.* **1.** An affectedly elegant literary style of the late 16th and early 17th centuries, characterized by elaborate alliteration, antitheses, and similes. **2.** Affected elegance of language. [After *Euphues,* a character in *Euphues: the Anatomy of Wit* and *Euphues and his England* by John Lyly (1554?–1606).] **—eu'phu·ist** *n.* **—eu'phu·is'tic, eu'phu·is'ti·cal** *adj.* **—eu'phu·is'ti·cal·ly** *adv.*

eu·plas·tic (yo͞o-plăs'tĭk) *adj.* Healing readily.

eu·ploid (yo͞o'ploid') *adj.* Having a chromosome complement that is an exact multiple of the haploid complement. **—eu'ploid** *n.* **—eu'ploi'dy** *n.*

eup·ne·a (yo͞op-nē'ə) *n.* Normal, unlabored breathing. [NLat. < Gk. *eupnoia* < *eupnoos,* breathing well : *eu-,* well + *pnein,* to breathe.] **—eup·ne'i·cal·ly** *adv.*

eu·re·ka (yo͞o-rē'kə) *interj.* Used to express triumph upon finding or discovering something. [Gk. *heurēka,* I have found (it), supposedly exclaimed by Archimedes upon discovering how to measure the volume of an irregular solid and thereby determine the purity of a gold object.]

eu·rhyth·mics (yo͞o-rĭ*th*′mĭks) *n.* Variant of **eurythmics**.

eu·rhyth·my (yo͞o-rĭ*th*′mē) *n.* Variant of **eurythmy**.

eu·ri·pus (yo͞o-rī′pəs) *n., pl.* **-pi** (-pī′). A sea channel characterized by turbulent and unpredictable currents in either direction. [Lat. < Gk. *euripos* : *eu-*, good + *ripē*, rush < *riptein*, to throw.]

Eu·ro·bond (yo͝or′ō-bŏnd′) *n.* A bond of a United States corporation issued in Europe. [EURO(PE) + BOND.]

eu·ro·cur·ren·cy (yo͝or′ō-kûr′ən-sē, -kŭr′-) *n., pl.* **-cies.** Currency used in the European money market. [EURO(PE) + CURRENCY.]

Eu·ro·dol·lar (yo͝or′ō-dŏl′ər) *n.* A United States dollar on deposit with a bank abroad, esp. in Europe. [EURO(PE) + DOLLAR.]

Eu·ro·pa (yo͞o-rō′pə) *n. Gk. Myth.* A Phoenician princess abducted to Crete by Zeus, who had assumed the form of a white bull. [Lat. < Gk. *Eurōpē*.]

Europa
Europa with Zeus as a bull

Eu·ro·pe·an (yo͝or′ə-pē′ən) *adj.* Of, pertaining to, or derived from Europe. **—Eu′ro·pe′an** *n.*

Eu·ro·pe·an·ize (yo͝or′ə-pē′ə-nīz′) *tr.v.* **-ized, -iz·ing, -iz·es.** To make European. **—Eu′ro·pe′an·i·za′tion** *n.*

European plan *n.* A hotel plan in which the rates include only the charges for a room and services and not for meals.

eu·ro·pi·um (yo͞o-rō′pē-əm) *n. Symbol* **Eu** A silvery-white, soft, rare-earth element occurring in monazite and bastnaesite and used as a laser dopant and to absorb neutrons in research. Atomic number 63; atomic weight 151.96; melting point 826°C; boiling point 1,439°C; specific gravity 5.259; valences 2, 3. [After *Europe*.]

Eu·rus (yo͝or′əs) *n. Gk. Myth.* The god of the east or southeast wind. [Lat. < Gk. *Euros*.]

eury– *pref.* Wide; broad: *eurythermal*. [NLat. < Gk. *eurus*, wide.]

eu·ry·bath·ic (yo͝or′ə-băth′ĭk) *adj.* Capable of dwelling at the bottom of a body of water in a wide range of depths.

Eu·ryd·i·ce (yo͞o-rĭd′ĭ-sē) *n. Gk. Myth.* The wife of Orpheus, whom he failed to rescue from Hades when he looked back at her and so violated the command of Pluto on their journey back to the upper world of the living. [Lat. < Gk. *Eurudikē* : *eurus*, wide + *dikē*, justice.]

eu·ry·ha·line (yo͝or′ə-hā′līn′, -hăl′-īn′) *adj.* Capable of tolerating a wide range of saltwater concentrations.

eu·ryp·ter·id (yo͞o-rĭp′tər-ĭd) *n.* Any of various large, extinct, segmented aquatic arthropods of the order Eurypterida, existing from the Ordovician to the Permian period. [NLat. *Eurypterida*, order name < *Eurypterus*, genus name : EURY- + Gk. *pteron*, wing.]

eu·ry·ther·mal (yo͝or′ə-thûr′məl) also **eu·ry·ther·mic** (-mĭk) or **eu·ry·ther·mous** (-məs) *adj.* Adaptable to a wide range of temperatures. Used of an organism. **—eu′ry·therm′** *n.*

eu·ryth·mics also **eu·rhyth·mics** (yo͞o-rĭth′mĭks) *n.* (*used with a sing. verb*). The choreographic art of interpreting musical composition by a rhythmical, free-style graceful movement of the body in response to the rhythm of the music. **—eu·ryth′mic** *adj.*

eu·ryth·my also **eu·rhyth·my** (yo͞o-rĭ*th*′mē) *n.* **1.** Harmony of proportion in architecture. **2.** A system of rhythmical body movements in harmony with the rhythm of the spoken word. [Lat. *eurythmia* < Gk. *euruthmia* < *euruthmos*, graceful : *eu-*, good + *ruthmos*, proportion.]

Eu·sta·chian tube (yo͞o-stā′shən, -shē-ən, -stā′kē-ən) *n.* A bony and cartilaginous tube through which the tympanic cavity communicates with the nasal part of the pharynx. [After Bartolommeo *Eustachio* (1524?–1574).]

eu·tec·tic (yo͞o-tĕk′tĭk) *adj.* **1.** Of, pertaining to, or formed at the lowest possible temperature of solidification for any mixture of specified constituents. Used esp. of alloys. **2.** Exhibiting the constitution or properties of a eutectic solid. *—n.* **1.** A eutectic mixture, solution, or alloy. **2.** The eutectic temperature. [< Gk. *eutēktos*, easily melted : *eu-*, well + *tēkein*, to melt.]

Eu·ter·pe (yo͞o-tûr′pē) *n. Gk. Myth.* The Muse of lyric poetry and music. [Gk. *Euterpē* : *eu-*, well + *terpein*, to please.]

eu·tha·na·sia (yo͞o′thə-nā′zhə, -zhē-ə) *n.* The action of killing an individual for reasons considered to be merciful. [Gk. : *eu-*, good + *thanatos*, death.]

eu·then·ics (yo͞o-thĕn′ĭks) *n.* (*used with a sing. verb*). The study of the improvement of human functioning and well-being by improvement of environment. [< Gk. *euthenein*, to flourish.]

eu·ther·i·an (yo͞o-thîr′ē-ən) *adj.* Of or pertaining to the Eutheria, a division of mammals to which all the placental mammals belong. [< NLat. *Eutheria*, a subdivision of the class Mammalia.]

eu·troph·ic (yo͞o-trŏf′ĭk, -trō′fĭk) *adj.* Designating a body of water in which the increase of mineral and organic nutrients has reduced the dissolved oxygen, producing an environment that favors plant over animal life. [Prob. < G. *Eutroph* < Gk. *eutrophos*, well-nourished < *eutrophein*, to thrive : *eu-*, well + *trephein*, to nourish.] **—eu·troph′i·ca′tion** *n.* **—eu′tro·phy** (yo͞o′trə-fē) *n.*

eux·e·nite (yo͞ok′sə-nīt′) *n.* A lustrous blackish-brown mineral consisting primarily of cerium, erbium, titanium, uranium, and yttrium. [G. *Euxenit* < Gk. *euxenos*, kind to strangers : *eu-*, good + *xenos*, stranger (so called because the mineral contains unusual elements).]

e·vac·u·ant (ĭ-văk′yo͞o-ənt) *adj.* Causing evacuation of an organ, esp. of the bowels. **—e·vac′u·ant** *n.*

e·vac·u·ate (ĭ-văk′yo͞o-āt′) *v.* **-at·ed, -at·ing, -ates.** *—tr.* **1. a.** To empty or remove the contents of. **b.** To create a vacuum in. **2.** To excrete or discharge (waste matter), esp. from the bowels. **3. a.** To relinquish military possession or occupation of (a town, for example). **b.** To withdraw or send away (troops or inhabitants) from a threatened area. **4.** To withdraw or depart from; vacate. *—intr.* **1.** To withdraw from or vacate a place or area, esp. a threatened area. **2.** To excrete waste matter from the body. [Lat. *evacuare*, *evacuat-*, to empty out : *ex-*, out + *vacuus*, empty < *vacare*, to be empty.] **—e·vac′u·a′tor** *n.*

e·vac·u·a·tion (ĭ-văk′yo͞o-ā′shən) *n.* **1.** The act of evacuating or the condition of being evacuated. **2.** *Physiol.* **a.** The excretion of waste materials from the excretory passages, esp. from the bowels. **b.** The material thus discharged.

e·vac·u·ee (ĭ-văk′yo͞o-ē′) *n.* A person evacuated from a dangerous area.

e·vade (ĭ-vād′) *v.* **e·vad·ed, e·vad·ing, e·vades.** *—tr.* **1.** To escape or avoid by cleverness or deceit. **2. a.** To avoid the fulfillment or performance of: *evaded his duty.* **b.** To fail to make payment of: *evade taxes.* **3.** To avoid giving a direct answer to. **4.** To baffle or elude: *The accident evades explanation.* *—intr.* To use cleverness or deceit in avoiding or escaping. [OFr. *evader* < Lat. *evadere* : *ex-*, out + *vadere*, to go.] **—e·vad′a·ble, e·vad′i·ble** *adj.* **—e·vad′er** *n.*

e·vag·i·nate (ĭ-văj′ə-nāt′) *v.* **-nat·ed, -nat·ing, -nates.** *—intr.* To turn inside out by eversion of an inner surface of a part or organ. *—tr.* To cause (a body part) to turn inside out; protrude by inversion. [Lat. *evaginare*, *evaginat-*, to unsheath : *ex-*, from + *vagina*, sheath.] **—e·vag′i·na′tion** *n.*

e·val·u·ate (ĭ-văl′yo͞o-āt′) *tr.v.* **-at·ed, -at·ing, -ates. 1.** To ascertain or fix the value or worth of. **2.** To examine and judge carefully. **3.** *Math.* To calculate or set down the numerical value of; express numerically. [Back-formation < E. *evaluation* < Fr. *évaluation* < OFr. *evaluation* < *evaluer*, to evaluate : *e-*, out (< Lat. *ex-*) + *value*, value. —see VALUE.] **—e·val′u·a′tion** *n.*

ev·a·nesce (ĕv′ə-nĕs′) *intr.v.* **-nesced, -nesc·ing, -nesc·es.** To dissipate or disappear like vapor. [Lat. *evanescere*, to vanish : *ex-* (intensive) + *vanescere*, to disappear < *vanus*, empty.] **—ev′a·nes′cence** *n.*

ev·a·nes·cent (ĕv′ə-nĕs′ənt) *adj.* Vanishing or likely to vanish; fleeting. **—ev′a·nes′cent·ly** *adv.*

e·van·gel (ĭ-văn′jəl) *n.* **1.** The Christian gospel. **2.** An evangelist. [ME *evangelie* < LLat. *evangelium* < Gk. *euangelion*, good news < *euangelos*, bringing good news : *eu-*, good + *angelos*, messenger.]

e·van·gel·i·cal (ē′văn-jĕl′ĭ-kəl, ĕv′ən-) also **e·van·gel·ic** (-jĕl′ĭk) *adj.* **1.** Of, pertaining to, or in accordance with the Christian gospel, esp. the four gospels of the New Testament. **2.** Protestant. **3.** Of, pertaining to, or being a Protestant group emphasizing the authority of the gospel and holding that salvation is from faith and grace rather than from good works and sacraments alone. **4. Evangelical.** Of or pertaining to the Evangelical Church in Germany. **5.** Pertaining or belonging to the Low Church party in the Church of England. *—n.* **Evangelical.** A member of an evangelical church or party. **—e·van·gel′i·cal·ly** *adv.*

e·van·gel·i·cal·ism (ē′văn-jĕl′ĭ-kə-lĭz′əm, ĕv′ən-) *n.* **1.** Evangelical beliefs or doctrines. **2.** Adherence to a church or party professing evangelical beliefs or doctrines.

e·van·gel·ism (ĭ-văn′jə-lĭz′əm) *n.* **1.** The zealous preaching and dissemination of the gospel, as through missionary work. **2.** Militant zeal for a cause.

e·van·gel·ist (ĭ-văn′jə-lĭst) *n.* **1.** Often **Evangelist.** Any of the authors of the four New Testament Gospels: Matthew, Mark, Luke, or John. **2.** One who practices evangelism, esp. a Protestant preacher or missionary. **—e·van′gel·is′tic** *adj.* **—e·van′gel·is′ti·cal·ly** *adv.*

e·van·gel·ize (ĭ-văn′jə-līz′) *v.* **-ized, -iz·ing, -iz·es.** *—tr.* **1.** To preach the gospel to. **2.** To convert to Christianity. *—intr.* To preach the gospel. **—e·van′gel·i·za′tion** *n.* **—e·van′gel·iz′er** *n.*

e·vap·o·ra·ble (ĭ-văp′ər-ə-bəl) *adj.* Capable of being evaporated. **—e·vap′o·ra·bil′i·ty** *n.*

e·vap·o·rate (ĭ-văp′ə-rāt′) *v.* **-rat·ed, -rat·ing, -rates.** *—tr.* **1. a.** To convert or change into a vapor. **b.** To draw off in the form of vapor. **2.** To draw moisture from, leaving only the dry solid portion. **3.** To deposit (a metal) on a substrate by vacuum sublimation. *—intr.* **1. a.** To change into vapor. **b.** To pass off in or as vapor. **2.** To produce vapor. **3.** To disappear; vanish: *His fears evaporated.* [ME *evaporaten* < Lat. *evaporare* : *ex-*, out + *vapor*, steam.] **—e·vap′o·ra′tion** *n.* **—e·vap′o·ra′tive** *adj.* **—e·vap′o·ra′tive·ly** *adv.* **—e·vap′o·ra·tiv′i·ty** (-rə-tĭv′ĭ-tē) *n.* **—e·vap′o·ra′tor** *n.*

evaporated milk *n.* Concentrated, unsweetened milk made by evaporating some of the water from whole milk.

e·vap·o·rite (ĭ-văp′ə-rīt′) *n.* A sedimentary deposit that results from the evaporation of sea water. [EVAPOR(ATION) + -ITE.] **—e·vap′o·rit′ic** (-rĭt′ĭk) *adj.*

e·va·sion (ĭ-vā′zhən) *n.* **1.** The act of evading. **2.** A means of

evading. [ME *evasioun* < OFr. *evasion* < LLat. *evasio* < Lat. *evadere,* to evade.]
e·va·sive (ĭ-vā′sĭv) *adj.* **1.** Characterized by or exhibiting evasion. **2.** Intentionally vague or ambiguous; equivocal: *an evasive statement.* **—e·va′sive·ly** *adv.* **—e·va′sive·ness** *n.*
eve (ēv) *n.* **1.** The evening or day preceding a special day, such as a holiday. **2.** The period immediately preceding a certain event: *the eve of war.* **3.** Evening. [ME, OE *ǣfen.*]
Eve (ēv) *n.* In the Old Testament, the first woman and wife of Adam. [ME < OE *Ēfe* < LLat. *Eva* < Heb. *Ḥawwah* < *ḥāwa,* he lived.]
e·vec·tion (ĭ-vĕk′shən) *n.* Solar perturbation of the lunar orbit. [Lat. *evectio,* a going up < *evehere,* to raise up : *ex-,* up from + *vehere,* to carry.] **—e·vec′tion·al** *adj.*
e·ven¹ (ē′vən) *adj.* **1. a.** Having a horizontal surface; flat: *an even floor.* **b.** Having no irregularities, roughness, or indentations; smooth. **2.** Having the same plane or line; level: *The picture is even with the window.* **3.** Having no variations or fluctuations; uniform: *an even tempo.* **4.** Of uniform thickness; uniformly distributed: *an even application of varnish.* **5.** Equally matched or balanced: *an even fight.* **6.** Equal or identical in degree, extent, or amount. **7.** Having equal probability: *an even chance of winning.* **8. a.** Having an equal score: *The teams are even.* **b.** Being equal for each opponent. Used of a score. **9.** Neither owing nor being owed; having nothing due: *Give him five dollars, and you will be even.* **10.** Having exacted full revenge. **11. a.** *Math.* Exactly divisible by 2. **b.** Characterized or indicated by a number exactly divisible by 2. **12. a.** Having an even number in a series. **b.** Having an even number of members. **13.** Having an exact amount, extent, or number: *an even pound.* *—adv.* **1.** To a higher degree or extent. Used as an intensive: *an even worse condition.* **2.** At the same time as; just: *Even as we watched, the building collapsed.* **3.** In spite of; notwithstanding: *Even with his head start, I soon overtook him.* **4.** Indeed; moreover. Used as an intensive: *unhappy, even weeping.* **5.** To a degree that extends to: *loyal even unto death.* **6.** *Nonstandard.* Smoothly; evenly. *—v.* **e·vened, e·ven·ing, e·vens.** *—tr.* To make even. *—intr.* To become even. **—*idioms.* break even.** *Informal.* To have neither losses nor gains. **get even.** To exact a full measure of revenge. [ME < OE *efen.*] **—e′ven·ly** *adv.* **—e′ven·ness** *n.*
e·ven² (ē′vən) *n. Archaic.* Evening. [ME < OE *ǣfen.*]
e·ven·fall (ē′vən-fôl′) *n.* The beginning of evening; twilight.
e·ven·hand·ed (ē′vən-hăn′dĭd) *adj.* Dealing equitably with all; impartial. **—e′ven·hand′ed·ly** *adv.* **—e′ven·hand′ed·ness** *n.*
eve·ning (ēv′nĭng) *n.* **1.** The period of decreasing daylight between afternoon and night. **2. a.** The period between sunset and bedtime. **b.** This period occupied in a given manner: *an evening at home.* **3.** A period or time of decline: *in the evening of his life.* *—adv.* **evenings.** Regularly or habitually in the evening. [ME < OE *ǣfnung* < *ǣfnian,* to become evening < *ǣfen,* evening.]
evening dress *n.* Clothing, esp. formal clothing, worn for evening social events.
evening gown *n.* A woman's formal dress, usually long, and worn esp. in the evening.
Evening Prayer *n.* A daily evening service in the Anglican Church.
evening primrose *n.* Any of various North American plants of the genus *Oenothera,* characteristically having four-petaled yellow flowers that open in the evening.
evening star *n.* A planet, esp. Venus or Mercury, that crosses the local meridian before midnight and is prominent in the west shortly after sunset.
evening stock *n.* A plant, *Mathiola bicornis,* native to Eurasia, having fragrant purple flowers that bloom at night.
e·ven·song (ē′vən-sông′, -sŏng′) *n.* **1.** A song sung in the evening. **2.** A vesper service. **3.** *Archaic.* Evening. **4.** Evening Prayer.
e·vent (ĭ-vĕnt′) *n.* **1. a.** Something that takes place; occurrence. **b.** A significant occurrence or happening. **2.** The actual outcome or final result. **3.** One of the items in a program of sports. **4.** *Physics.* A coincidence of two or more point objects at a particular position in space at a particular instant of time, regarded as the fundamental observational entity in relativity theory. **—*idioms.* at all events.** In any case. **in any event.** In any case. **in the event.** If it should happen; in case. [Lat. *eventus* < *evenire,* to happen : *ex-,* out + *venire,* to come.]
e·vent·ful (ĭ-vĕnt′fəl) *adj.* **1.** Full of events: *an eventful week.* **2.** Important; momentous: *an eventful decision.* **—e·vent′ful·ly** *adv.* **—e·vent′ful·ness** *n.*
e·ven·tide (ē′vən-tīd′) *n.* Evening. [ME < OE *ǣfentid* : *ǣfen,* evening + *tīd,* time.]
e·ven·tu·al (ĭ-vĕn′cho͞o-əl) *adj.* **1.** Occurring at an unspecified time in the future; ultimate: *his eventual failure.* **2.** Dependent on circumstance; contingent. [< EVENT.] **—e·ven′tu·al·ly** *adv.*
e·ven·tu·al·i·ty (ĭ-vĕn′cho͞o-ăl′ĭ-tē) *n., pl.* **-ties.** Something that may occur; possibility.
e·ven·tu·ate (ĭ-vĕn′cho͞o-āt′) *intr.v.* **-at·ed, -at·ing, -ates.** To result ultimately.
ev·er (ĕv′ər) *adv.* **1.** At all times; always: *was ever courteous.* **2.** At any time: *Have you ever seen a circus?* **3.** In any possible way or case; at all. Used for emphasis: *was ever so sorry.* **—*idioms.* ever and again** (or **anon**). Now and then; occasionally. **for ever and a day.** Always; forever. [ME < OE *ǣfre.*]
ev·er·glade (ĕv′ər-glād′) *n.* A tract of marshland, esp. of southern Florida, usually under water and covered in places with tall grass. [After the *Everglades,* Florida.]

everglade

ev·er·green (ĕv′ər-grēn′) *adj.* **1.** Having foliage that persists and remains green throughout the year. **2.** Remaining fresh. *—n.* **1.** An evergreen tree, shrub, or plant. **2. evergreens.** Twigs or branches of evergreen plants used as decorations.
ev·er·last·ing (ĕv′ər-lăs′tĭng) *adj.* **1.** Lasting forever; eternal. **2. a.** Continuing indefinitely or for a long period of time. **b.** Persisting too long; tedious: *his everlasting whining.* **3.** Retaining color and form for a long time when cut or dried, as certain plants. *—n.* **1. The Everlasting.** God. **2.** Eternal duration; eternity. **3.** Any of various plants, such as the strawflower or one of the genus *Anaphalis,* that retain form and color long after they are dry. **—ev′er·last′ing·ly** *adv.* **—ev′er·last′ing·ness** *n.*
ev·er·more (ĕv′ər-môr′, -mōr′) *adv.* **1.** *Archaic.* Forever. **2.** In a future time.
e·vert (ĭ-vûrt′) *tr.v.* **e·vert·ed, e·vert·ing, e·verts.** To turn inside out or outward. [Lat. *evertere,* to overturn : *ex-,* out + *vertere,* to turn.] **—e·ver′si·ble** (ĭ-vûr′sə-bəl) *adj.* **—e·ver′sion** (-zhən, -shən) *n.*
ev·er·y (ĕv′rē) *adj.* **1.** Constituting each and all members of a class without exception. **b.** Being each and all of a limited class or range. **2.** Being each of a specified succession of objects or intervals: *every third seat; every two hours.* **3.** The highest degree or expression of: *showed him every attention.* **—*idioms.* every bit.** *Informal.* In all ways; quite; equally: *He is every bit as mean as she is.* **every now and then** (or **again**). Occasionally. **every so often.** Occasionally. **every which way.** *Informal.* In complete disorder. —See Usage note at **everyone.** [ME < OE *ǣfre ǣlc* : *ǣfre,* ever + *ǣlc,* each.]
ev·er·y·bod·y (ĕv′rē-bŏd′ē, -bŭd′ē) *pron.* Every person; everyone. —See Usage note at **everyone.**
ev·er·y·day (ĕv′rē-dā′) *adj.* **1.** Suitable for ordinary days or routine occasions: *an everyday suit.* **2.** Commonplace; ordinary: *everyday worries.*
ev·er·y·one (ĕv′rē-wŭn′) *pron.* Every person; everybody.

Usage: There are a large number of words and expressions in English that are singular in form but felt to be plural in sense, so that speakers are uncertain as to whether to use a singular or plural pronoun in referring back to them. For example, strict grammarians have long insisted that it is correct to say *everyone took his coat,* not *their coat* or *their coats,* and that we must say *no one is happy when he is abandoned,* and not *when they are abandoned.* Yet speakers persist in using the plural pronouns, and the most thoughtful grammarians, like Fowler, have recognized that there is no entirely happy solution to the problem. • The constructions affected fall into three classes. First, there are words formed with the word elements *-one* and *-body,* such as *anyone, somebody, everyone, nobody,* together with the two-word form *no one.* Second, there are the words *either, each, none,* and *any,* either used alone, as in *each found his seat,* or together with a noun, as in *each of the boys has his notebook* and *none of the books has its cover intact.* Finally, there are the words *whoever, whatever,* and *whichever,* either used as indefinite pronouns, as in *whoever talks out of turn will have his name sent to the office,* or together with a noun, as in *whichever nation is attacked first will find itself at a disadvantage.* • The traditional rule is that only a singular pronoun can be used in referring back to these constructions, as in the preceding examples of correct usage. But the rule as stated creates grammatical complications. For one thing, a pronoun outside the sentence containing the element it refers to *cannot* be in the singular. Thus, it is simply not English to say: *Everybody left in a hurry. He took his coat with him.* Nor can one say: *No one could be seen. He must have been hiding behind a rock.* Constructions with *whoever* are exceptions. One says: *Whoever is elected will take office in January. I am sure he will do a good job.* Writers who do not want to risk a violation of the traditional rule will have to find other ways of expressing the meaning. One may rephrase so as to get the pronoun into the same sentence as its antecedent, saying, for example, *Everybody left carrying his raincoat with him.* One may also substitute other words, for example the plural *all,* as in *All the guests left. They took their coats with them.* • *Each* presents some special problems. When it precedes the noun, a following pronoun is correctly singular: *Each of the actors has learned his* (not *their*) *part.* When *each* follows the noun, however, the pronoun is generally plural: *The actors have each learned their parts* (not *his part*). It should also be noted that *none* has for centuries been used by the best writers as if it were a plural form, taking both plural verb and plural pronouns: *None of them have learned their parts* must be considered an entirely acceptable variant of *None of them has learned his part.* Only the mixture of singular verb and plural pronoun would be considered incorrect, as in *None of them has learned their parts.* • The traditional rule may also be politically offensive to many speakers. When referring back to a group consisting of both men and women, strict grammarians have insisted that the masculine singular *him* or *his* be used as a "neutral" form; one is thus required to say *Every one of the actors and actresses has learned his part.* Since the last century, however, feminists and their allies have objected to this presumption. The writer who finds the singular *he* and *his* distasteful in these cases has the choice of flying in the face of traditional grammar and using *they* and *their* or of using the somewhat clumsier variants *his and her* (or *her and his*); attempts to introduce new pronouns like *s/he* appear unlikely to win general acceptance. The entire matter is properly outside the scope of grammar. In the end, as Fowler put it, "everyone must decide for himself (or for himself and herself, or for themselves)."

eve·ry·place (ĕv′rē-plās′) *adv.* Everywhere.

Usage: *Everyplace* and *every place* used adverbially for *everywhere* are appropriate principally to informal writing or speech: *Everyplace* (or *every place*) *I go, I see her* (in formal writing, preferably *everywhere I go*). *Every place,* as a combination of adjective and noun, is, of course, standard English: *I searched in every place he suggested.*

eve·ry·thing (ĕv′rē-thĭng′) *pron.* **1.** All things or factors that exist or pertain to a given instance. **2.** The most important fact or consideration: *Her children meant everything to her.*

eve·ry·where (ĕv′rē-hwâr′, -wâr′) *adv.* In any or every place; in all places.

Usage: The only acceptable word is *everywhere* (not *everywheres*). The use of *that* with *everywhere* (*everywhere that I go*) is superfluous. See also Usage note at **everyplace.**

e·vict (ĭ-vĭkt′) *tr.v.* **e·vict·ed, e·vict·ing, e·victs. 1.** To expel or put out (a tenant) by legal process. **2.** To force out; eject. **3.** To recover (property, for example) by a superior claim or legal process. [ME *evicten* < Lat. *evincere* to vanquish : *ex-* (intensive) + *vincere,* to defeat.] **—e·vic′tion** *n.* **—e·vic′tor** *n.*

ev·i·dence (ĕv′ĭ-dəns) *n.* **1.** The data on which a judgment or conclusion may be based; something that furnishes proof: *fossilized evidence of climatic change.* **2.** Something that indicates: *His reaction was evidence of guilt.* **3.** *Law.* The documentary or verbal statements and the material objects admissible as testimony in a court of law. *—tr.v.* **-denced, -denc·ing, -denc·es. 1.** To indicate clearly; exemplify or prove. **2.** To support by testimony; attest. ***—idiom.* in evidence.** Present and plainly visible; conspicuous: *He was very much in evidence at the convention.* [ME < OFr. < LLat. *evidentia* < Lat. *evidens,* evident.]

ev·i·dent (ĕv′ĭ-dənt) *adj.* Easily seen or understood; obvious. [ME < OFr. < Lat. *evidens* : *ex-,* out + *videns,* pr.part. of *vidēre,* to see.]

ev·i·den·tial (ĕv′ĭ-dĕn′shəl) *adj.* Pertaining to, providing, or having the nature of evidence. **—ev′i·den′tial·ly** *adv.*

ev·i·den·tia·ry (ĕv′ĭ-dĕn′shə-rē, -shē-ĕr′ē) *adj.* Evidential.

ev·i·dent·ly (ĕv′ĭ-dənt-lē, ĕv′ĭ-dĕnt′lē) *adv.* **1.** Obviously; clearly. **2.** According to the evidence available: *She's evidently going to be late.*

e·vil (ē′vəl) *adj.* **1.** Morally bad or wrong; wicked. **2.** Causing ruin, injury, or pain; harmful. **3.** Characterized by or indicating future misfortune; ominous: *evil omens.* **4.** Purportedly bad or blameworthy; infamous: *an evil reputation.* **5.** Characterized by anger or spite; malicious: *an evil temper.* *—n.* **1.** Something that causes harm, misfortune, or destruction. **2.** Something morally bad or wrong; wickedness. **3.** An evil force or power. **4.** Something that is a cause or source of suffering, injury, or destruction: *the evils of war.* *—adv. Archaic.* In an evil manner. [ME < OE *yfel.*] **—e′vil·ly** *adv.* **—e′vil·ness** *n.*

e·vil·do·er (ē′vəl-do͞o′ər) *n.* A person who does evil. **—e′vil·do′ing** *n.*

evil eye *n.* **1.** A look or a stare believed to cause injury or misfortune to others. **2.** A person believed to have the power of the evil eye.

e·vil-mind·ed (ē′vəl-mīn′dĭd) *adj.* Having evil thoughts, opinions, or intentions. **—e′vil-mind′ed·ly** *adv.* **—e′vil-mind′ed·ness** *n.*

e·vince (ĭ-vĭns′) *tr.v.* **e·vinced, e·vinc·ing, e·vinc·es.** To show or demonstrate clearly or convincingly; manifest. [Lat. *evincere,* to prove. —see EVICT.] **—e·vinc′i·ble** *adj.*

e·vis·cer·ate (ĭ-vĭs′ə-rāt′) *v.* **-at·ed, -at·ing, -ates.** *—tr.* **1.** To remove the entrails of; disembowel. **2.** To take away a vital or essential part of. **3.** *Med.* **a.** To remove the contents of (an eyeball). **b.** To remove an organ, such as an eye, from (a patient). *—intr. Med.* To protrude through an incision after an operation. [Lat. *eviscerare, eviscerat-,* to disembowel : *ex-,* out + *viscera,* internal organs.] **—e·vis′cer·a′tion** *n.*

ev·i·ta·ble (ĕv′ĭ-tə-bəl) *adj.* Avoidable. [Lat. *evitabilis* < *evitare,* to shun : *ex-* (intensive) + *vitare,* to avoid.]

ev·o·ca·tion (ĕv′ə-kā′shən ē′və-) *n.* **1.** The act of evoking. **2.** Creation anew through the power of the memory or imagination. **—ev′o·ca′tor** *n.*

e·voc·a·tive (ĭ-vŏk′ə-tĭv) *adj.* Tending or having the power to evoke. **—e·voc′a·tive·ly** *adv.* **—e·voc′a·tive·ness** *n.*

e·voke (ĭ-vōk′) *tr.v.* **e·voked, e·vok·ing, e·vokes. 1.** To summon or call forth: *the sight evoked childhood memories.* **2. a.** To call to mind or memory. **b.** To create anew, esp. by means of the imagination. [Lat. *evocare* : *ex-,* out + *vocare,* to call.] **—ev·o·ca·ble** (ĕv′ə-kə-bəl, ĭ-vō′kə-) *adj.*

ev·o·lute (ĕv′ə-lo͞ot′, ē′və-) *n.* The locus of the centers of curvature of a given curve. [< Lat. *evolutus,* p.part. of *evolvere,* to unroll. —see EVOLVE.]

ev·o·lu·tion (ĕv′ə-lo͞o′shən, ē′və-) *n.* **1.** A gradual process in which something changes into a different and usually more complex or better form. **2.** *Biol.* **a.** The theory that groups of organisms, as species, may change with passage of time so that descendants differ morphologically and physiologically from their ancestors. **b.** The historical development of a related group of organisms. **3.** The gradual process of the development or growth of something, such as a social institution. **4.** A movement that is part of a set of ordered movements. **5.** *Math.* The extraction of a root of a quantity. [Lat. *evolutio* < *evolvere,* to unroll. —see EVOLVE.] **—ev′o·lu′tion·al, ev′o·lu′tion·ar′y** (-shə-nĕr′ē) *adj.* **—ev′o·lu′tion·ar′i·ly** *adv.* **—ev′o·lu′tion·ism** *n.* **—ev′o·lu′tion·ist** *n.*

e·volve (ĭ-vŏlv′) *v.* **e·volved, e·volv·ing, e·volves.** *—tr.* **1. a.** To develop or achieve gradually. **b.** To work out; devise. **2.** *Biol.* To develop by evolutionary processes from a primitive to a more highly organized form. **3.** To yield, give, or throw off. *—intr.v.* **1.** To experience evolutionary change. **2.** To undergo change or development. [Lat. *evolvere,* to unroll : *ex-* + *volvere,* to roll.] **—e·volv′a·ble** *adj.* **—e·volve′ment** *n.*

e·vul·sion (ĭ-vŭl′shən) *n.* A forcible extraction. [Lat. *evulsio* < *evellere,* to pull out : *ex-* + *vellere,* to pull.]

ev·zone (ev′zōn′) *n.* An infantryman of a special corps of the Greek army. [Mod. Gk. *euzōnos* < Gk., dressed for exercise : *eu-,* good + *zōnē,* girdle.]

ewe (yo͞o) *n.* A female sheep, esp. when full-grown. [ME < OE *ēowu.*]

E·we (ā′wā′, ā′vā′) *n.* **1. a.** A Negro people of Togo, Ghana, and parts of Dahomey. **b.** A member of the Ewe people. **2.** The Niger-Congo language of the Ewe people.

ewe-neck (yo͞o′nĕk′) *n.* A defect in a horse or dog in which the neck is thin and has a concave arch. **—ewe′-necked′** *adj.*

ew·er (yo͞o′ər) *n.* A large, wide-mouthed pitcher or jug. [ME *ever* < AN < OFr. *eviere* < VLat. **aquaria* < Lat. *aquarius,* relating to water < *aqua,* water.]

ewer
19th-century American

ex[1] (ĕks) *prep.* **1.** Out of; from. **2.** *Commerce.* Free of charge to the purchaser until removed from (a particular place or thing). [Lat.]

ex[2] (ĕks) *n.* The letter *x.*

ex[3] (ĕks) *n. Slang.* A former wife or husband.

ex- *pref.* **1.** Outside; out of; away from: *exodontia.* **2.** Not; without: *excaudate.* **3.** Former: *ex-president.* [ME < OFr. < Lat. *ex,* out of.]

ex·ac·er·bate (ĭg-zăs′ər-bāt′) *tr.v.* **-bat·ed, -bat·ing, -bates. 1.** To increase the severity of; aggravate: *exacerbate pain.* **2.** To embitter or irritate. [Lat. *exacerbare, exacerbat-* : *ex-* (intensive) + *acerbare,* to make harsh < *acerbus,* harsh.] **—ex·ac′er·ba′tion** *n.*

ex·act (ĭg-zăkt′) *adj.* **1.** Accurate and precise. **2.** Strictly and completely in accord with fact. **3.** Characterized by meticulous observation of or adherence to a standard. *—tr.v.* **-act·ed, -act·ing, -acts. 1.** To force the payment or yielding of; extort. **2.** To demand and obtain by or as if by force or authority. [Lat. *exactus,* p.part. of *exigere,* to demand : *ex-,* out + *agere,* to impel.] **—ex·act′a·ble** *adj.* **—ex·act′ness** *n.* **—ex·ac′tor, ex·act′er** *n.*

ex·act·a (ĭg-zăk′tə) *n.* A method of betting, as on a horse race, in which the bettor must correctly pick those finishing in the first and second places in precisely that sequence. [< Am. Sp. *quiniela exacta,* exact quiniela (a game of chance).]

ex·act·ing (ĭg-zăk′tĭng) *adj.* **1.** Making severe or rigorous demands: *an exacting instructor.* **2.** Requiring great care, effort, or attention: *an exacting task.* **—ex·act′ing·ly** *adv.* **—ex·act′ing·ness** *n.*

ex·ac·tion (ĭg-zăk′shən) *n.* **1. a.** The act of exacting. **b.** The act of demanding or requiring that which is not justly due; extortion. **2.** Something that is exacted.

ex·ac·ti·tude (ĭg-zăk′tĭ-to͞od, -tyo͞od′) *n.* The state or quality of being exact.

ex·act·ly (ĭg-zăkt′lē) *adv.* **1.** In an exact manner; accurately. **2.** In all respects; just: *Do exactly as you please.* **3.** As you say. Used to indicate agreement.

ex·ag·ger·ate (ĭg-zăj′ə-rāt′) *v.* **-at·ed, -at·ing, -ates.** *—tr.* **1.** To enlarge or increase to an abnormal degree. **2.** To make greater than is actually the case; overstate: *exaggerated his own importance.* *—intr.* To distort through overstatement. [Lat. *exaggerare* : *ex-* (intensive) + *aggerare,* to pile up < *agger,* pile.] **—ex·ag′ger·at′ed·ly** *adv.* **—ex·ag′ger·a′tion** *n.* **—ex·ag′ger·a′tive, ex·ag′ger·a·to′ry** (-ə-tôr′ē, -tōr′ē) *adj.* **—ex·ag′ger·a′tor** *n.*

ex·alt (ĭg-zôlt′) *tr.v.* **-alt·ed, -alt·ing, -alts. 1.** To raise in rank, character, or status; elevate. **2.** To glorify; praise; honor. **3.** To increase the effect or intensity of; heighten. **4.** *Obs.* To fill with an intensified feeling such as joy or pride; elate. [ME *exalten* < Lat. *exaltare* : *ex-,* up + *altus,* high.] **—ex·alt′er** *n.*

ex·al·ta·tion (ĕg′zôl-tā′shən) *n.* **1.** The act of exalting or the condition of being exalted. **2.** A feeling of intense, often excessive exhilaration and well-being; elation.

ex·alt·ed (ĭg-zôl′tĭd) *adj.* **1.** Elevated in rank, character, or status. **2.** Lofty; sublime; noble. **—ex·alt′ed·ly** *adv.* **—ex·alt′ed·ness** *n.*

ex·am (ĭg-zăm′) *n.* An examination; test.

ex·a·men (ĭg-zā'mən) *n.* Examination. [Lat. < *exigere,* to examine.]

ex·am·i·nant (ĭg-zăm'ə-nənt) *n.* **1.** One who examines. **2.** An examinee.

ex·am·i·na·tion (ĭg-zăm'ə-nā'shən) *n.* **1.** The act of examining or the state of being examined. **2.** An exercise testing knowledge or skill. **3.** Formal interrogation. **—ex·am'i·na'tion·al** *adj.*

ex·am·ine (ĭg-zăm'ĭn) *tr.v.* **-ined, -in·ing, -ines. 1. a.** To inspect in detail. **b.** To observe or analyze carefully. **2.** To test the state or condition of. **3.** To determine the qualifications, aptitude, or skills of by means of questions or exercises. **4.** To interrogate or question formally. [ME *examinen* < OFr. *examiner* < Lat. *examinare* < *examen,* a weighing < *exigere,* to weigh. —see EXACT.] **—ex·am'in·a·ble** *adj.* **—ex·am'in·er** *n.*

ex·am·in·ee (ĭg-zăm'ə-nē') *n.* One that is examined.

ex·am·ple (ĭg-zăm'pəl) *n.* **1.** One that is representative of a group as a whole. **2.** One that serves as a pattern of a specific kind: *a bad example.* **3.** A case or situation serving as a model or precedent for another that is the same or similar. **4. a.** A punishment given as a warning or deterrent. **b.** One that has been given such a punishment. **5.** A problem or exercise used to illustrate a principle or method. **—*idiom.* for example.** Serving as an illustration, a model, or an instance. [ME < OFr. *example, essample* < Lat. *exemplum* < *eximere,* to take out : *ex-,* out + *emere,* to take.]

Synonyms: *example, instance, case, illustration, sample, specimen.* Each of these nouns refers to what is representative of, or serves to explain, something larger. The first four are sometimes interchangeable. An *example* represents, usually typically and concretely, something of which it is a part, and thereby demonstrates the nature or operation of what it represents. An *instance* is an action, occurrence, event, or, less often, a person that is representative of a general subject and that is cited in some way bearing on the subject. A *case* is an action, occurrence, event, or condition that constitutes a specific instance: *a typical case of child neglect.* An *illustration* demonstrates or explains in detail all or part of a broad subject of which it is itself a part. *Sample* and *specimen* are often interchangeable. A *sample* is an actual part of something larger, presented as evidence of the quality of the whole. A *specimen* is either such a part of a whole or an individual and representative member of a group or class of persons or things.

ex·an·the·ma (ĕg'zăn-thē'mə) also **ex·an·them** (ĭg-zăn'thəm) *n., pl.* **-them·a·ta** (-thĕm'ə-tə) or **-the·mas** also **-thems. 1.** A skin eruption. **2.** A disease, such as measles or scarlet fever, accompanied by a skin eruption. [LLat. *exanthema* < Gk. *exanthēma* eruption < *exanthein,* to burst forth : *ex-,* out + *anthein,* to blossom < *anthos,* flower.] **—ex·an'the·mat'ic** (ĭg-zăn'-thə-măt'ĭk), **ex'an·them'a·tous** (ĕg'zăn-thĕm'ə-təs) *adj.*

ex·arch (ĕk'särk') *n.* **1.** The ruler of a province in the Byzantine Empire. **2.** A bishop in an Eastern Orthodox Church ranking immediately below a patriarch. [LLat. < Gk. *exarkhos* < *exarkhein,* to lead : *ex-,* out + *arkhein,* to rule.] **—ex·arch'al** *adj.* **—ex'ar'chate** (ĕk'sär'kāt), **ex'ar'chy** (ĕk'sär'kē) *n.*

ex·as·per·ate (ĭg-zăs'pə-rāt') *tr.v.* **-at·ed, -at·ing, -ates. 1.** To make very angry or irritated. **2.** To increase the gravity or intensity of. [Lat. *exasperare, exasperat-* : *ex-* (intensive) + *asperare,* to make rough < *asper,* rough.] **—ex·as'per·at'er** *n.* **—ex·as'per·at'ing·ly** *adv.*

ex·as·per·a·tion (ĭg-zăs'pə-rā'shən) *n.* **1.** An act or instance of exasperating. **2.** The state of being exasperated.

Ex·cal·i·bur (ĭk-skăl'ə-bər) *n.* The legendary sword belonging to King Arthur. [ME < OFr. *Escalibor* < Med. Lat. *Caliburnus* < Welsh *Caledvwlch.*]

ex ca·the·dra (ĕks' kə-thē'drə) *adj. & adv.* With the authority derived from one's office or position. [Lat. : *ex,* from + *cathedra,* chair. —see CATHEDRA.]

ex·cau·date (ĕk-skô'dāt') *adj.* Tailless; without a tail.

ex·ca·vate (ĕk'skə-vāt') *v.* **-vat·ed, -vat·ing, -vates.** *—tr.* **1.** To make a cavity or hole in; hollow out. **2.** To form by hollowing out. **3.** To remove by digging or scooping out. **4.** To expose or uncover by or as if by digging. *—intr.* To engage in digging, hollowing out, or removing. [Lat. *excavare, excavat-,* to hollow out : *ex-,* out + *cavare,* to hollow < *cavus,* hollow.]

excavation

ex·ca·va·tion (ĕk'skə-vā'shən) *n.* **1.** The act or process of excavating. **2.** A cavity formed by excavating.

ex·ca·va·tor (ĕk'skə-vā'tər) *n.* One that excavates, esp. a power shovel.

excavator

ex·ceed (ĭk-sēd') *tr.v.* **-ceed·ed, -ceed·ing, -ceeds. 1.** To be greater than; surpass. **2.** To go beyond the limits of. [ME *exceden* < Lat. *excedere* : *ex-,* out + *cedere,* to go.]

ex·ceed·ing (ĭk-sē'dĭng) *adj.* Extreme; extraordinary. *—adv. Archaic.* Exceedingly.

ex·ceed·ing·ly (ĭk-sē'dĭng-lē) *adv.* To an advanced or unusual degree; extremely.

ex·cel (ĭk-sĕl') *v.* **-celled, -cel·ling, -cels.** *—tr.* To be better than; surpass. *—intr.* To surpass or do better than others. [ME *excellen* < Lat. *excellere.*]

Synonyms: *excel, surpass, exceed, transcend, outdo, outstrip.* These verbs mean to go beyond a limit or standard, usually in the sense of being superior. *Excel* and *surpass* are generally applied to performance or achievement in things that reflect credit on a person. To *excel* is to be pre-eminent in a general sense or to be or perform at a level higher than that of another or others specified. To *surpass* another is to be superior in performance, quality, or degree. *Exceed* can also refer to superiority in quality, but more often applies to what is greater in sheer size or quantity: *He surpasses* (or *excels*) *me in knowledge, but my wealth exceeds his.* In a related sense *exceed* means to go beyond a proper limit: *exceed one's authority; exceed the speed limit. Transcend* usually refers to marked superiority in quality or degree; often it implies attainment of a level so high that comparison is hardly possible: *Great art transcends mere rules of composition. The national interest must transcend regional goals. Outdo* and *outstrip* refer to superiority in performance. *Outstrip,* the stronger, implies obvious superiority.

ex·cel·lence (ĕk'sə-ləns) *n.* **1.** The state, quality, or condition of excelling; superiority. **2.** Something in which a person or thing excels. **3. Excellence.** Excellency. [ME < OFr. < Lat. *excellentia* < *excellens,* excellent.]

Ex·cel·len·cy (ĕk'sə-lən-sē) *n., pl.* **-cies.** A title or form of address for certain high officials, such as ambassadors or bishops.

ex·cel·lent (ĕk'sə-lənt) *adj.* **1.** Of the highest or finest quality; exceptionally good of its kind. **2.** *Archaic.* Surpassing; superior. [ME < OFr. < Lat. *excellens,* pr.part. of *excellere,* to surpass.] **—ex'cel·lent·ly** *adv.*

ex·cel·si·or (ĭk-sĕl'sē-ər) *n.* Slender, curved wood shavings used esp. for packing. [Lat., comp. of *excelsis,* high < *excellere,* to rise.]

ex·cept (ĭk-sĕpt') *prep.* With the exclusion of; but: *everyone except me.* *—conj.* **1.** If it were not for the fact that; only: *He would buy the suit, except that it costs too much.* **2.** Otherwise than: *didn't open his mouth except to complain.* **3.** *Archaic.* Unless. *—v.* **-cept·ed, -cept·ing, -cepts.** *—tr.* To leave out; exclude. *—intr.* To object. —See Usage note at **than.** [ME < Lat. *excipere* : *ex-,* out + *capere,* to take.]

Usage: *Except* in the sense of "with the exclusion of" or "other than" is generally construed as a preposition, not a conjunction. A personal pronoun that follows *except* is therefore in the objective case: *No one except me knew it. Every member of the original cast was signed except her.* See also Usage note at **but.**

ex·cept·ing (ĭk-sĕp'tĭng) *prep.* Excluding; except. *—conj. Archaic.* Except; unless.

ex·cep·tion (ĭk-sĕp'shən) *n.* **1.** The act of excepting or state of being excepted. **2.** One that is excepted, esp. a case that does not conform to normal rules. **3.** An objection or criticism: *open to exception.* **4.** *Law.* A formal objection taken in the course of an action or proceeding. **—*idiom.* take exception. 1.** To object to; take issue with: *I take exception to your remarks.* **2.** *Archaic.* To take offense; resent.

ex·cep·tion·a·ble (ĭk-sĕp'shə-nə-bəl) *adj.* Open or liable to objection. **—ex·cep'tion·a·bil'ity** *n.* **—ex·cep'tion·a·bly** *adv.*

ex·cep·tion·al (ĭk-sĕp'shə-nəl) *adj.* **1.** Being an exception; uncommon. **2.** Being above average. **3. a.** Pertaining to or describing one whose ability deviates from the norm. **b.** Being below average. **—ex·cep'tion·al·ly** *adv.*

ex·cep·tive (ĭk-sĕp'tĭv) *adj.* **1.** Of, being, or containing an exception. **2.** *Archaic.* Captious; faultfinding.

ex·cerpt (ĕk'sûrpt') *n.* A passage or scene, as from a speech or book. *—tr.v.* (ĭk-sûrpt') **-cerpt·ed, -cerpt·ing, -cerpts.** To select or take out, as from a book, speech or play. [Lat. *excerptum* < *excerpere,* to pick out : *ex-,* out + *carpere,* to pluck.]

ex·cess (ĭk-sĕs', ĕk'sĕs') *n.* **1.** The state of exceeding what is normal or sufficient. **2.** An amount or quantity beyond what is normal or sufficient; superfluity. **3.** The amount or degree by which one quantity exceeds another; remainder. **4.** Intemperance; overindulgence. *—adj.* Being more than is usual, required, or permitted. *—tr.v.* **-cessed, -ces·sing, -ces·ses.** To eliminate the job or position of. **—*idioms.* in excess of.** Greater than; more than. **to excess.** To an extreme degree or extent; too much. [ME < OFr. < Lat. *excessus,* p.part. of *excedere,* to exceed.]

ex·ces·sive (ĭk-sĕs'ĭv) *adj.* Exceeding what is normal, proper, or reasonable. **—ex·ces'sive·ly** *adv.* **—ex·cess'ive·ness** *n.*

Synonyms: *excessive, exorbitant, extravagant, immoderate, inordinate, extreme, unreasonable.* These adjectives mean beyond a normal or proper limit. *Excessive,* which has the widest range, describes a quantity, amount, or degree that is beyond what is specified, required, reasonable, or just. *Exorbitant* usually refers to a quantity or amount that far exceeds what is customary, right, or just. *Extravagant* sometimes specifies excessive or unwise expenditure of money; in a more general sense it means beyond the bounds of truth, sound judgment, proper conduct, or the like: *extravagant claims. Immoderate* suggests what violates reason or good taste. *Inordinate* implies lack of balance and an overstepping of bounds imposed by authority or implied by good sense. *Extreme* implies great departure from a norm governing behavior, speech, or quality or degree in general. *Unreasonable* applies to what exceeds a limit set by custom, good judgment, fairness, or decent regard for others.

ex·change (ĭks-chānj') *v.* **-changed, -chang·ing, -chang·es.** —*tr.* **1.** To give or take in return for something else: *exchange ideas.* **2.** To give up for a substitute: *exchange a career in business for a government post.* **3.** To turn in for replacement by something more satisfactory: *exchange defective merchandise.* **4.** To provide or transfer in return for something of equal value; trade. —*intr.* **1.** To trade for something of equal value. **2.** To take part in a mutual trade, as of goods or services. —*n.* **1.** An act or instance of exchanging. **2.** One that is exchanged. **3.** A place where things are exchanged, esp. a center where securities and commodities are bought and sold: *a stock exchange.* **4.** A telephone exchange. **5. a.** A system of payments using instruments, such as negotiable drafts, instead of money. **b.** The fee or percentage charged for participating in such a system of payment. **6.** A bill of exchange. **7.** Rate of exchange. **8.** The amount of difference in the actual value of two or more currencies, or between values of the same currency at two or more places. [ME *eschaungen* < AN *eschaungier* < OFr. *eschangier* < VLat. **excambiare* : Lat. *ex-*, out + LLat. *cambiare,* to barter, prob. of Celtic orig.] **—ex·change'a·bil'i·ty** *n.* **—ex·change'a·ble** *adj.* **—ex·chang'er** *n.*

exchange force *n.* A force arising between two elementary particles as a result of the continuous interchange of space or spin coordinates.

exchange rate *n.* The rate of exchange.

ex·cheq·uer (ĕks'chĕk'ər, ĭks-chĕk'ər) *n.* **1. Exchequer.** The British governmental department charged with the collection and care of the national revenue. **2. Exchequer.** The Court of Exchequer. **3.** A treasury, as of a nation or an organization. **4.** Financial resources; funds. [ME *escheker* < OFr. *eschequier,* counting table, chessboard < *eschec,* check in chess. —see CHECK.]

ex·ci·mer (ĕk'sə-mər) *n.* A dimer existing in an energy level above the ground state. [EXC(ITED) + (D)IMER.]

ex·cip·i·ent (ĭk-sĭp'ē-ənt) *n.* An inert substance used as a diluent or vehicle for a drug. [Lat. *excipiens, excipient-,* pr.part. of *excipere,* to take out. —see EXCEPT.]

ex·cis·a·ble (ĭk-sī'zə-bəl) *adj.* Subject to an excise.

ex·cise¹ (ĕk'sīz') *n.* **1.** An internal tax levied on the production, sale, or consumption of certain commodities, such as tobacco or liquor, within a country. **2.** A tax often levied in the form of a licensing charge or a fee for certain privileges. —*tr.v.* **-cised, -cis·ing, -cis·es.** To levy an excise on. [Obs. Du. *excijs* < MDu., prob. < OFr. *acceis* < LLat. *accensare,* to tax : Lat. *ad-*, to + Lat. *census,* tax. —see CENSUS.]

ex·cise² (ĭk-sīz') *tr.v.* **-cised, -cis·ing, -cis·es.** To remove by or as if by cutting. [Lat. *excidere, excis-* : *ex-*, out + *caedere,* to cut.] **—ex·ci'sion** (-sĭzh'ən) *n.*

ex·cise·man (ĭk'sīz'mən, ĭk-sīz'-) *n. Chiefly Brit.* An officer who collects excise taxes or enforces excise laws.

ex·cit·a·ble (ĭk-sī'tə-bəl) *adj.* **1.** Capable of being easily excited. **2.** Capable of responding to stimuli. **—ex·cit'a·bil'i·ty, ex·cit'a·ble·ness** *n.* **—ex·cit'a·bly** *adv.*

ex·ci·tant (ĭk-sīt'nt) also **ex·ci·ta·tive** (-sī'tə-tĭv) or **ex·ci·ta·to·ry** (-sī'tə-tôr'ē, -tōr'ē) *adj.* Capable of exciting or stimulating. **—ex·ci'tant** *n.*

ex·ci·ta·tion (ĕk'sī-tā'shən) *n.* **1.** The act or process of exciting. **2.** Something that excites or stimulates. **3.** The state or condition of being excited.

ex·cite (ĭk-sīt') *tr.v.* **-cit·ed, -cit·ing, -cites. 1.** To stir to activity; put into motion. **2.** To elicit, as a reaction or emotion: *excited their curiosity.* **3.** To arouse strong feeling in; provoke: *She excited him to anger.* **4.** *Biol.* To produce increased activity in (an organism or part); stimulate. **5.** *Physics.* **a.** To increase the energy of. **b.** To raise (an atom, for example) to a higher energy level. [ME *exciten* < Lat. *excitare,* freq. of *exciēre* : *ex-*, out + *ciēre,* to call.]

ex·cit·ed (ĭk-sī'tĭd) *adj.* **1.** In a state of excitement; emotionally aroused; stirred. **2.** *Physics.* At an energy level higher than the ground state. **—ex·cit'ed·ly** *adv.*

ex·cite·ment (ĭk-sīt'mənt) *n.* **1. a.** The action or process of exciting. **b.** The state or condition of being excited; agitation. **2.** Something that excites.

ex·cit·er (ĭk-sī'tər) *n.* **1.** One that excites. **2.** *Elect.* **a.** An auxiliary generator used to provide field current for a larger generator or alternator. **b.** An oscillator for generating the carrier frequency of a transmitter.

ex·cit·ing (ĭk-sī'tĭng) *adj.* Creating or producing excitement. **—ex·cit'ing·ly** *adv.*

ex·ci·ton (ĕk'sĭ-tŏn', -sī-) *n.* An electrically neutral excited state of a crystal, often regarded as a bound state of an electron and a hole. [EXCIT(ATION) + -ON.]

ex·ci·ton·ics (ĕk'sə-tŏn'ĭks, -sī-) *n.* *(used with a sing. verb).* The study of excitons and their behavior in semiconductors and dielectrics.

ex·ci·tor (ĭk-sī'tər) *n.* A stimulant.

ex·claim (ĭk-sklām') *tr. & intr.v.* **-claimed, -claim·ing, -claims.** To cry out or utter suddenly or vehemently, as from surprise or emotion. [OFr. *exclamer* < Lat. *exclamare* : *ex-*, out + *clamare,* to call.] **—ex·claim'er** *n.*

ex·cla·ma·tion (ĕk'sklə-mā'shən) *n.* **1.** An abrupt, forceful utterance. **2.** An outcry, as of protest.

exclamation point *n.* A punctuation mark (!) used after an exclamation.

ex·clam·a·tory (ĭk-sklăm'ə-tôr'ē, -tōr'ē) *adj.* Constituting, containing, relating to, or using exclamation.

ex·clave (ĕk'sklāv') *n.* A portion of a country that is isolated from the main part and exists as an enclave in alien territory. [EX- + (EN)CLAVE.]

ex·clude (ĭk-sklōōd') *tr.v.* **-clud·ed, -clud·ing, -cludes. 1.** To keep or shut out; bar. **2.** To omit from consideration or notice; disregard. **3.** To put out; expel. [ME *excluden* < Lat. *excludere* : *ex-*, out + *claudere,* to shut.] **—ex·clud'a·bil'i·ty** *n.* **—ex·clud'a·ble, ex·clud'i·ble** *adj.* **—ex·clud'er** *n.*

ex·clu·sion (ĭk-sklōō'zhən) *n.* **1.** The act of excluding; rejection. **2.** The state of being excluded. [Lat. *exclusio* < *excludere,* to shut out. —see EXCLUDE.] **—ex·clu'sion·ar'y** (-zhə-nĕr'ē) *adj.*

ex·clu·sion·ist (ĭk-sklōō'zhə-nĭst) *n.* One who advocates excluding others from rights or privileges. **—ex·clu'sion·ism** *n.* **—ex·clu'sion·is'tic** *adj.*

exclusion principle *n.* The principle that no two particles of a given type, such as electrons, protons, or neutrons, can occupy a particular quantum state.

ex·clu·sive (ĭk-sklōō'sĭv) *adj.* **1.** Pertaining to or characterized by exclusion. **2.** Not divided or shared with others: *exclusive publishing rights.* **3.** Single or independent; sole. **4.** Complete; undivided. **5.** Excluding certain people, as from membership or participation. **6.** Catering to a wealthy clientele; expensive: *exclusive shops.* —*n.* **1.** A news item released to only one person or publication. **2.** An exclusive right or privilege, as to market a product. **—ex'clu·siv'i·ty** (ĕk'sklōō-sĭv'ĭ-tē) *n.* **—ex·clu'sive·ly** *adv.* **—ex·clu'sive·ness** *n.*

exclusive of *prep.* Not including or considering.

ex·cog·i·tate (ĭk-skŏj'ĭ-tāt') *tr.v.* **-tat·ed, -tat·ing, -tates.** To think out in great detail; devise. [Lat. *excogitare, excogitat-,* to find out by thinking : *ex-*, out + *cogitare,* to think. —see COGITATE.] **—ex·cog'i·ta'tion** *n.* **—ex·cog'i·ta'tive** *adj.*

ex·com·mu·ni·ca·ble (ĕks'kə-myōō'nĭ-kə-bəl) *adj.* Liable to, meriting, or punishable by excommunication.

ex·com·mu·ni·cate (ĕks'kə-myōō'nĭ-kāt') *tr.v.* **-cat·ed, -cat·ing, -cates. 1.** To deprive of the right of church membership by ecclesiastical authority. **2.** To exclude from membership or participation in a group. —*n.* (ĕks'kə-myōō'nĭ-kĭt). A person who has been excommunicated. —*adj.* (ĕks'kə-myōō'nĭ-kĭt, -kāt'). Excommunicated. [ME *excommunicaten* < LLat. *excommunicare* : Lat. *ex-*, out + Lat. *communis,* common.] **—ex·com·mu·ni·ca·tive** (ĭks'kə-myōō'nĭ-kā'tĭv, -kə-tĭv), **ex·com·mu'ni·ca·to'ry** (-kə-tôr'ē, -tōr'ē) *adj.* **—ex'com·mu'ni·ca'tor** *n.*

ex·com·mu·ni·ca·tion (ĕks'kə-myōō'nĭ-kā'shən) *n.* **1.** The act of excommunicating. **2.** The state of being excommunicated. **3.** A formal ecclesiastical censure that deprives a person of the right to belong to a church.

ex·co·ri·ate (ĭk-skôr'ē-āt', -skōr'-) *tr.v.* **-at·ed, -at·ing, -ates. 1.** To tear or wear off the skin of; abrade. **2.** To censure strongly; denounce. [ME *excoriaten* < Lat. *excoriare,* to strip of its skin : *ex-*, off + *corium,* skin.] **—ex·co'ri·a'tion** *n.*

ex·cre·ment (ĕk'skrə-mənt) *n.* Waste material expelled from the body after digestion, esp. fecal matter. [Lat. *excrementum* < *excernere,* to excrete.] **—ex'cre·ment'al** (ĕk'skrə-mĕn'tl) *adj.* **—ex'cre·men·ti'tious** (-mĕn-tĭsh'əs) *adj.*

ex·cres·cence (ĭk-skrĕs'əns) *n.* An abnormal outgrowth or enlargement. [ME < Lat. *excrescentia* < *excrescere,* to grow out : *ex-*, out + *crescere,* to grow.]

ex·cres·cen·cy (ĭk-skrĕs'ən-sē) *n., pl.* **-cies.** An excrescence.

ex·cres·cent (ĭk-skrĕs'ənt) *adj.* **1.** Growing out abnormally, excessively, or superfluously. **2.** *Ling.* Epenthetic. **—ex·cres'cent·ly** *adv.*

ex·cre·ta (ĭk-skrē'tə) *pl.n.* Waste matter, such as sweat, urine, or feces, excreted from the body. [Lat. < *excernere,* to discharge. —see EXCREMENT.] **—ex·cre'tal** *adj.*

ex·crete (ĭk-skrēt') *tr.v.* **-cret·ed, -cret·ing, -cretes.** To eliminate (waste matter) from the blood, tissues, or organs. [Lat. *excernere, excret-* : *ex-*, out + *cernere,* to separate.]

ex·cre·tion (ĭk-skrē'shən) *n.* **1.** The process or act of excreting undigested food residues or metabolic wastes. **2.** Matter excreted esp. as waste.

ex·cre·to·ry (ĕk'skrĭ-tôr'ē, -tōr'ē) *adj.* **1.** Of or pertaining to excretion. **2.** Having the function of excreting: *excretory organs.*

ex·cru·ci·ate (ĭk-skrōō'shē-āt') *tr.v.* **-at·ed, -at·ing, -ates. 1.** To inflict with severe pain; torture. **2.** To inflict great mental pain upon. [Lat. *excruciare* : *ex-* (intensive) + *cruciare,* to crucify < *crux,* cross.] **—ex·cru'ci·a'tion** *n.*

ex·cru·ci·at·ing (ĭk-skrōō'shē-ā'tĭng) *adj.* **1.** Intensely painful; agonizing. **2.** Marked by great intensity. **—ex·cru'ci·at'ing·ly** *adv.*

ex·cul·pate (ĕk'skəl-pāt', ĭk-skŭl'-) *tr.v.* **-pat·ed, -pat·ing, -pates.** To clear of guilt or blame. [Med. Lat. *exculpare* : Lat. *ex-*, away + *culpa,* guilt.] **—ex·cul'pa·ble** (ĭk-skŭl'pə-bəl) *adj.* **—ex'cul·pa'tion** *n.*

ex·cul·pa·to·ry (ĭk-skŭl'pə-tôr'ē, -tōr'ē) *adj.* Acting or tending to exculpate.

ex·cur·rent (ĭk-skûr'ənt, -skŭr'-) *adj.* **1. a.** Running or flowing in an outward direction. **b.** Marked by an outward flow of current. **2.** *Bot.* **a.** Having a single, undivided trunk with lateral branches, as many coniferous trees. **b.** Extending beyond the apex of a leaf, as a midrib or vein. [Lat. *excurrens, excurrent-*, pr.part. of *excurrere.* —see EXCURSION.]

ex·cur·sion (ĭk-skûr′zhən) *n.* **1.** A usually short journey made for pleasure; outing. **2. a.** A pleasure tour, esp. one of limited duration and at a special low fare. **b.** The party on such a tour. **3.** A diversion or deviation from the main topic; digression. **4. a.** A movement from a mean position or axis in an oscillating or alternating motion. **b.** The distance traversed in such a movement. [Lat. *excursio* < *excurrere,* to run out : *ex-*, out + *currere,* to run.]

ex·cur·sion·ist (ĭk-skûr′zhə-nĭst) *n.* A person who goes on an excursion.

ex·cur·sive (ĭk-skûr′sĭv) *adj.* Of, given to, characterized by, or having the nature of digression. **—ex·cur′sive·ly** *adv.* **—ex·cur′sive·ness** *n.*

ex·cur·sus (ĭk-skûr′səs) *n., pl.* **-sus·es. 1.** A lengthy, appended exposition of a topic or point. **2.** A digression. [Lat. < *excurrere,* to run out. —see EXCURSION.]

ex·cus·a·to·ry (ĭk-skyo͞o′zə-tôr′ē, -tōr′ē) *adj.* Tending or serving to excuse.

ex·cuse (ĭk-skyo͞oz′) *tr.v.* **-cused, -cus·ing, -cus·es. 1. a.** To apologize for. **b.** To seek to remove the blame from: *excused herself for her tardiness.* **2. a.** To grant pardon to; forgive: *excused him for his clumsiness.* **b.** To make allowance for; overlook. **3.** To serve as justification for: *Her brilliance does not excuse her rudeness.* **4.** To free, as from an obligation or duty; exempt. **5.** To give permission to leave; release. —*n.* (ĭk-skyo͞os′). **1.** An explanation offered to justify or elicit forgiveness. **2.** The reason or grounds for excusing. **3.** An act of excusing. **4.** A note explaining an absence. **5.** *Informal.* An inferior example: *He's a poor excuse for a poet.* [ME *excusen* < OFr. *excuser* < Lat. *excusare* : *ex-*, away from + *causa,* accusation.] **—ex·cus′a·ble** *adj.* **—ex·cus′a·ble·ness** *n.* **—ex·cus′a·bly** *adv.* **—ex·cus′er** *n.*

Usage: The expression *excuse away* has no meaning beyond that of *excuse* (unlike *explain away,* which has a different meaning from *explain*). *Excuse away* is unacceptable to a large majority of the Usage Panel: *His behavior cannot be excused* (not *excused away*).

ex·e·cra·ble (ĕk′sĭ-krə-bəl) *adj.* **1.** Deserving of execration. **2.** Extremely inferior; very bad: *an execrable meal.* [ME < Lat. *execrabilis* < *execrari,* to execrate.] **—ex′e·cra·ble·ness** *n.* **—ex′e·cra·bly** *adv.*

ex·e·crate (ĕk′sĭ-krāt′) *tr.v.* **-crat·ed, -crat·ing, -crates. 1.** To declare to be hateful or abhorrent; denounce. **2.** To feel loathing for; abhor. **3.** *Archaic.* To invoke a curse upon. [Lat. *execrari, execrat-* : *ex-*, away from + *sacrare,* to consecrate < *sacer,* sacred.] **—ex′e·cra′tive** *adj.* **—ex′e·cra′tor** *n.* **—ex′e·cra·to′ry** (-krə-tôr′ē, -tōr′ē) *adj.*

ex·e·cra·tion (ĕk′sĭ-krā′shən) *n.* **1.** The act of cursing. **2.** A curse. **3.** Something that is cursed or loathed.

ex·ec·u·tant (ĭg-zĕk′yə-tənt) *n.* One who performs or carries out, esp. a skilled performer.

ex·e·cute (ĕk′sĭ-kyo͞ot′) *tr.v.* **-cut·ed, -cut·ing, -cutes. 1.** To carry out; put into effect: *execute a law.* **2.** To perform. **3.** To create (a work of art, for example) in accordance with a prescribed design. **4.** To make valid, as by signing: *execute a deed.* **5.** To perform or carry out what is required by: *execute a will.* **6.** To put to death, esp. by carrying out a legal sentence. [ME *executen* < OFr. *executer* < Med. Lat. *executare* < Lat. *exequi* : *ex-*, out + *sequi,* to follow.] **—ex′e·cut′a·ble** *adj.* **—ex′e·cut′er** *n.*

ex·e·cu·tion (ĕk′sĭ-kyo͞o′shən) *n.* **1.** The act of executing. **2.** The state of being executed. **3.** The manner, style, or result of performance. **4.** The act or an instance of putting or being put to death as a legal penalty. **5.** *Law.* **a.** The carrying into effect of a court judgment. **b.** A writ empowering an officer to enforce a judgment. **6.** *Law.* The validation of a legal document by the performance of the necessary formalities. **7.** Effective, punitive, or destructive action.

ex·e·cu·tion·er (ĕk′sĭ-kyo͞o′shən-ər) *n.* **1.** One who executes. **2.** One who puts another to death.

execution time *n.* The time required for a computer to decode and perform an instruction.

ex·ec·u·tive (ĭg-zĕk′yə-tĭv) *n.* **1.** A person or group having administrative or managerial authority in an organization. **2.** The chief officer of a government, state, or political division. **3.** The branch of government charged with putting into effect a country's laws and the administering of its functions. **4.** *Computer Sci.* A set of coded instructions designed to process and control other coded instructions. —*adj.* **1.** Of, pertaining to, capable of, or suited for carrying out or executing. **2.** Of or pertaining to the branch of government charged with the execution and administration of the nation's laws. **3.** Of or pertaining to an executive.

executive agreement *n.* An agreement made between heads of state without senatorial ratification.

executive council *n.* **1.** A council that advises or assists a political executive. **2.** A council having the highest executive power or authority.

executive officer *n.* **1.** The officer second in command of a military unit smaller than a division. **2.** The officer second in command of a naval unit. **3.** A person holding executive power in an organization.

executive order *n.* A regulation (sense 3).

executive routine *n.* A set of coded instructions designed to utilize a computer to develop or control other routines.

executive secretary *n.* A secretary having administrative duties and responsibilities.

executive session *n.* A legislative session that is usually closed to the public.

ex·ec·u·tor (ĭg-zĕk′yo͞o-tər, ĕk′sĭ-kyo͞o′tər) *n.* **1.** A person who carries out or performs something. **2.** *Law.* A person who is appointed by a testator to execute his will. **—ex·ec′u·to′ri·al** (-tôr′ē-əl, -tōr′-) *adj.* **—ex·ec′u·tor·ship′** *n.*

ex·ec·u·to·ry (ĭg-zĕk′yə-tôr′ē) *adj.* **1.** Administrative. **2.** Operative; in effect. **3.** *Law.* Intended to go into effect or having the potential of becoming effective at some future time; contingent.

ex·ec·u·trix (ĭg-zĕk′yə-trĭks′) *n., pl.* **-trix·es** or **-tri·ces** (ĭg-zĕk′yə-trī′sēz′). *Law.* A woman who is appointed by a testator to execute his will.

ex·e·dra (ĕk′sĭ-drə, ĭk-sē′-) *n.* **1.** An often semicircular portico with seats that was used in ancient Greece and Rome as a place in which discussions were held. **2.** A usually curved outdoor bench with a high back. [Lat. < Gk. : *ex-*, out + *hedra,* seat.]

ex·e·ge·sis (ĕk′sə-jē′sĭs) *n., pl.* **-ses** (-sēz). Critical explanation or analysis, esp. of a text. [Gk. *exēgēsis* < *exēgeisthai,* to interpret : *ex-*, out + *hēgeisthai,* to lead.]

ex·e·gete (ĕk′sə-jēt′) also **ex·e·ge·tist** (ĕk′sə-jĕt′ĭst) *n.* A person skilled in exegesis. [Gk. *exēgētēs* < *exēgeisthai,* to interpret. —see EXEGESIS.]

ex·e·get·ic (ĕk′sə-jĕt′ĭk) also **ex·e·get·i·cal** (-ĭ-kəl) *adj.* Of or pertaining to exegesis; analytic. **—ex′e·get′i·cal·ly** *adv.*

ex·em·pla (ĭg-zĕm′plə) *n.* Plural of **exemplum.**

ex·em·plar (ĭg-zĕm′plär′, -plər) *n.* **1.** One that is worthy of imitation; model. **2.** One that is typical or representative; example. **3.** An ideal that serves as a pattern; archetype. **4.** A copy, as of a book. [ME < LLat. *exemplarium* < Lat. *exemplum,* example.]

ex·em·pla·ry (ĭg-zĕm′plə-rē) *adj.* **1.** Worthy of imitation; commendable: *exemplary behavior.* **2.** Serving as a model. **3.** Serving as an illustration; typical. **4.** Serving as a warning. **—ex′em·plar′i·ly** (ĕg′zəm-plâr′ə-lē) *adv.* **—ex·em′pla·ri·ness, ex′em·plar′i·ty** (ĕg′zəm-plăr′ĭ-tē) *n.*

ex·em·pli·fi·ca·tion (ĭg-zĕm′plə-fĭ-kā′shən) *n.* **1.** The act of exemplifying. **2.** One that exemplifies; example. **3.** *Law.* An official and certified copy of a document.

ex·em·pli·fy (ĭg-zĕm′plə-fī′) *tr.v.* **-fied, -fy·ing, -fies. 1. a.** To illustrate by example. **b.** To serve as an example of. **2.** *Law.* To make a certified copy of (a document.) [ME *exemplifien* < Med. Lat. *exemplificare* : Lat. *exemplum,* example + *facere,* to make.] **—ex·em′pli·fi′a·ble** *adj.* **—ex·em′pli·fi′er** *n.*

ex·em·pli gra·ti·a (ĭg-zĕm′plē′ grä′tē-ä′) *adv.* For example.

ex·em·plum (ĭg′zĕm′pləm) *n., pl.* **-pla** (-plə). **1.** An example. **2.** A short story used to make a point in an argument or to illustrate a moral truth. [Lat. —see EXAMPLE.]

ex·empt (ĭg-zĕmpt′) *tr.v.* **-empt·ed, -empt·ing, -empts. 1.** To free from an obligation or duty required of others. **2.** To isolate. —*adj.* **1.** Freed from an obligation or duty required of others; excused. **2.** *Obs.* Isolated; set apart. —*n.* One who is exempted from an obligation. [ME *exempten* < Lat. *eximere, exempt-*. —see EXAMPLE.] **—ex·empt′i·ble** *adj.*

ex·emp·tion (ĕg-zĕmp′shən) *n.* **1.** An act of exempting. **2.** The state of being exempt; immunity. **3. a.** Something that is exempted, esp. from taxable income. **b.** One that is so exempted or is a source of such an exemption.

ex·en·do·sperm·ous (ĕk-sĕn′də-spûr′məs) *adj. Bot.* Lacking an endosperm.

ex·en·ter·ate (ĭk-zĕn′tə-rāt′) *tr.v.* **-at·ed, -at·ing, -ates. 1.** To disembowel; eviscerate. **2.** *Med.* To remove the contents of (an organ). [Lat. *exenterare, exenterat-*, to disembowel : *ex,* from + Gk. *enteron,* intestines.] **—ex·en′ter·a′tion** *n.*

ex·er·cise (ĕk′sər-sīz′) *n.* **1.** An act of employing or putting into play; use. **2.** The discharge of a duty, function, or office. **3.** Activity that requires physical or mental exertion, esp. when performed to develop or maintain fitness. **4.** Something designed to increase one's skill or fitness through performance and practice: *a piano exercise.* **5. exercises.** A religious or secular ceremony that includes speeches, awards, and other traditional rites: *graduation exercises.* —*v.* **-cised, -cis·ing, -cis·es.** —*tr.* **1.** To put into play or operation; employ. **2.** To bring to bear; exert: *exercised the power of veto.* **3. a.** To subject to practice or exertion in order to train, strengthen, or develop: *exercise the memory.* **b.** To put through exercises: *exercise a platoon.* **4.** To carry out the functions of: *exercise the role of disciplinarian.* **5. a.** To absorb the attentions of, esp. by worry or anxiety. **b.** To arouse the anger of: *was exercised by their rudeness.* —*intr.* To take exercise. [ME < OFr. *exercice* < Lat. *exercitium* < *exercēre,* to exercise : *ex-*, out of + *arcēre,* to restrain.] **—ex′er·cis′a·ble** *adj.*

ex·er·cis·er (ĕk′sər-sī′zər) *n.* **1.** One that exercises. **2.** A device for exercising the body.

ex·er·ci·ta·tion (ĭg-zûr′sĭ-tā′shən) *n.* The action or an instance of exercising. [ME *exercitacioun* < Lat. *exercitatio* < *exercitare,* to exercise often, freq. of *exercēre,* to exercise.]

ex·er·gon·ic (ĕk′sər-gŏn′ĭk) *adj.* Releasing energy. [EX(O)- + Gk. *ergon,* work + -IC.]

ex·ergue (ĕk′sûrg′, ĕg′zûrg′) *n.* The space on the reverse of a coin or medal, usually below the central design and often giving the date and place of engraving. [Fr. < NLat. *exergum* : Gk. *ex-*, out of + Gk. *ergon,* work.]

ex·ert (ĭg-zûrt′) *tr.v.* **-ert·ed, -ert·ing, -erts. 1.** To put forth (strength, for example). **2.** To bring to bear; exercise: *exert influence.* **3.** To put (oneself) to a strenuous effort. **4.** To make use of; employ. [Lat. *exserere, exsert-,* to put forth : *ex-*, out + *serere,* to bring forth.]

ex·er·tion (ĭg-zûr′shən) *n.* An act or instance of exerting, esp. a strenuous effort.

ex·e·unt (ĕk′sē-ənt, -o͝ont′). Used as a stage direction to indicate that two or more actors leave the stage. [Lat., 3rd pers. pl. of *exire,* to go out : *ex-*, out + *ire,* to go.]

ex·fo·li·ate (ĕks-fō′lē-āt′) *v.* **-at·ed, -at·ing, -ates.** —*tr.* **1.** To remove (bark, for example) in flakes or scales; peel. **2.** To cast off in scales, flakes, or splinters. —*intr.* To come off or separate as scales, flakes, sheets, or layers. [Lat. *exfoliare, exfoliat-,* to strip of leaves : *ex-*, off + *folium,* leaf.] **—ex·fo′li·a′tion** *n.* **—ex·fo′li·a′tive** *adj.*

ex·ha·lant also **ex·ha·lent** (ĕks-hā′lənt, ĕk-sā′-) *adj.* Capable of or functioning in exhalation.

ex·ha·la·tion (ĕks′hə-lā′shən, ĕk′sə-) *n.* **1.** An act of exhaling. **2.** Something that is exhaled.

ex·hale (ĕks-hāl′, ĕk-sāl′) *v.* **-haled, -hal·ing, -hales.** —*intr.* **1. a.** To breathe out. **b.** To emit air or vapor. **2.** To be given off or emitted. —*tr.* **1.** To blow forth or breathe out. **2.** To give off; emit. **3.** To draw out or off; evaporate. [ME *exhalen* < Lat. *exhalare* : *ex-*, out + *halare,* to breathe.]

ex·haust (ĭg-zôst′) *v.* **-haust·ed, -haust·ing, -hausts.** —*tr.* **1.** To let out or draw off. **2.** To draw out the contents of; drain. **3.** To use up; consume: *exhaust one's money.* **4.** To wear out completely; tire. **5.** To drain of resources or properties; deplete: *cotton crops that exhausted the soil.* **6.** To deal with comprehensively: *exhaust a topic.* —*intr.* To escape or pass out, as steam. —*n.* **1. a.** The escape or release of vaporous waste material, as from an engine. **b.** The fumes or gases so released. **2.** A device or part, such as a pipe, through which waste material is emitted. **3.** An apparatus for drawing out noxious air or waste material by means of a partial vacuum. [Lat. *exhaurire, exhaust-* : *ex-*, out + *haurire,* to draw.] **—ex·haust′er** *n.* **—ex·haust′i·bil′i·ty** *n.* **—ex·haust′i·ble** *adj.*

ex·haus·tion (ĭg-zôs′chən) *n.* **1.** An act or instance of exhausting. **2.** The state of being exhausted.

ex·haus·tive (ĭg-zô′stĭv) *adj.* **1.** Tending to exhaust. **2.** Comprehensive; thorough: *an exhaustive survey.* **—ex·haus′tive·ly** *adv.* **—ex·haus′tive·ness** *n.* **—ex·haus·tiv′i·ty** *n.*

ex·haust·less (ĭg-zôst′lĭs) *adj.* Impossible to exhaust; inexhaustible. **—ex·haust′less·ly** *adv.* **—ex·haust′less·ness** *n.*

ex·hib·it (ĭg-zĭb′ĭt) *v.* **-it·ed, -it·ing, -its.** —*tr.* **1.** To show externally; display. **2. a.** To present for the public to view. **b.** To enter or show in an exhibition or contest. **3.** To give an instance or evidence of; demonstrate. **4.** *Law.* **a.** To submit (evidence or documents) in a court. **b.** To present or introduce officially. —*intr.* To put something on public display. —*n.* **1.** An act of exhibiting. **2.** Something that is exhibited. **3.** *Law.* Something, such as a document, formally introduced as evidence in court. [ME *exhibiten* < Lat. *exhibere* : *ex-*, out + *habēre,* to hold.] **—ex·hib′it·er, ex·hib′i·tor** *n.* **—ex·hib′i·to′ry** (-ĭ-tôr′ē, -tōr′ē) *adj.*

ex·hi·bi·tion (ĕk′sə-bĭsh′ən) *n.* **1.** An act of exhibiting. **2.** Something exhibited. **3.** A display for the public, as of art objects, industrial achievements, or agricultural products. **4.** *Chiefly Brit.* A grant given to scholars by a school or university.

ex·hi·bi·tion·er (ĕk′sə-bĭsh′ə-nər) *n. Chiefly Brit.* A student who receives an exhibition.

ex·hi·bi·tion·ism (ĕk′sə-bĭsh′ə-nĭz′əm) *n.* **1.** The act or practice of flaunting oneself in order to attract attention. **2.** *Psychol.* Compulsive exposure of the sexual organs in public. **—ex′hi·bi′tion·ist** *n.* **—ex′hi·bi′tion·is′tic** *adj.*

ex·hib·i·tive (ĭg-zĭb′ĭ-tĭv) *adj.* Tending to exhibit; serving as an exhibition: *behavior exhibitive of his lack of interest.* **—ex·hib′i·tive·ly** *adv.*

ex·hil·a·rant (ĭg-zĭl′ər-ənt) *adj.* Exhilarating.

ex·hil·a·rate (ĭg-zĭl′ə-rāt′) *tr.v.* **-rat·ed, -rat·ing, -rates. 1.** To make cheerful; elate. **2.** To invigorate; stimulate. [Lat. *exhilarare, exhilarat-* : *ex-* (intensive) + *hilarare,* to make cheerful < *hilaris,* cheerful < Gk. *hilaros.*] **—ex·hil′a·rat′ive** *adj.* **—ex·hil′a·ra′tor** *n.*

ex·hil·a·rat·ing (ĭg-zĭl′ə-rā′tĭng) *adj.* Causing exhilaration. **—ex·hil′a·rat′ing·ly** *adv.*

ex·hil·a·ra·tion (ĭg-zĭl′ə-rā′shən) *n.* **1.** The state of being exhilarated. **2.** The action of exhilarating.

ex·hort (ĭg-zôrt′) *v.* **-hort·ed, -hort·ing, -horts.** —*tr.v.* To urge or incite by strong argument, advice, or appeal. —*intr.* To make urgent appeal. [ME *exhorten* < Lat. *exhortari* : *ex-* (intensive) + *hortari,* to encourage.] **—ex·hort′er** *n.*

ex·hor·ta·tion (ĕg′zôr-tā′shən, ĕk′sôr-) *n.* **1.** An act of exhorting. **2.** The practice of exhorting. **3.** A speech or discourse that encourages or incites.

ex·hor·ta·tive (ĭg-zôr′tə-tĭv) also **ex·hor·ta·to·ry** (-tôr′ē, -tōr′ē) *adj.* **1.** Pertaining to exhortation. **2.** Serving to exhort; intended to incite or advise.

ex·hume (ĭg-zo͞om′, -zyo͞om′, ĭk-syo͞om′, ĕks-hyo͞om′) *tr.v.* **-humed, -hum·ing, -humes. 1.** To remove from a grave; disinter. **2.** To bring to light, esp. after a period of obscurity. [Fr. *exhumer* < Med. Lat. *exhumare* : Lat. *ex-*, out of + Lat. *humus,* ground.] **—ex′hu·ma′tion** (ĕg′zyo͞o-mā′shən) *n.* **—ex·hum′er** *n.*

ex·i·gence (ĕk′sə-jəns) *n.* Exigency.

ex·i·gen·cy (ĕk′sə-jən-sē, ĭg-zĭj′ən-) *n., pl.* **-cies. 1.** The state or quality of being exigent. **2.** A pressing or urgent situation. **3.** Often **exigencies.** Urgent requirements; pressing needs.

ex·i·gent (ĕk′sə-jənt) *adj.* **1.** Requiring immediate attention or remedy; urgent. **2.** Requiring or demanding a great deal. [Lat. *exigens,* pr.part. of *exigere,* to demand. —see EXACT.] **—ex′i·gent·ly** *adv.*

ex·i·gu·i·ty (ĕk′sĭ-gyo͞o′ĭ-tē) *n.* The quality or condition of being exiguous; scantiness.

ex·ig·u·ous (ĭg-zĭg′yo͞o-əs, ĭk-sĭg′-) *adj.* Extremely scanty; meager. [Lat. *exiguus,* measured < *exigere,* to weigh. —see EXACT.] **—ex·ig′u·ous·ly** *adv.* **—ex·ig′u·ous·ness** *n.*

ex·ile (ĕg′zīl′, ĕk′sīl′) *n.* **1. a.** Enforced removal from one's native country. **b.** Self-imposed absence from one's country. **2. a.** The state or circumstance of being in exile. **b.** The period of time in exile. **3. a.** One who has been sent into exile by an official decree. **b.** One who has voluntarily left his country. —*tr.v.* **-iled, -il·ing, -iles.** To send into exile; banish. [ME *exil* < OFr. < Lat. *exilium* < *exul,* exiled person.] **—ex·il′ic** (ĕg-zĭl′ĭk, ĭk-sĭl′-), **ex·il′ian** (-zĭl′yən, -zĭl′ē-ən, ĭk-sĭl′yən, -sĭl′ē-ən) *adj.*

ex·ine (ĕk′sēn′, -sīn′) *n. Bot.* The outer layer of the wall of a spore or pollen grain. [EX(O)- + Gk. *is, in-*, tendon.]

ex·ist (ĭg-zĭst′) *intr.v.* **-ist·ed, -ist·ing, -ists. 1.** To have being or actuality of a material or spiritual nature. **2. a.** To have life; live. **b.** To continue to be. **3.** To live at a level that is below an expected or desirable standard: *were so poor that they did not live but merely existed.* **4.** To be present under certain circumstances or in a specified place; occur. [Lat. *existere* : *ex-*, out + *sistere,* to stand.]

ex·is·tence (ĭg-zĭs′təns) *n.* **1.** The fact or state of existing; being. **2.** The fact or state of continued being; life. **3. a.** All that exists. **b.** A thing that exists; entity. **4.** A mode or manner of existing: *a meager existence.* **5.** Occurrence; specific presence: *the existence of life on other planets.*

ex·is·tent (ĭg-zĭs′tənt) *adj.* **1.** Having life or being; existing. **2.** Occurring or present at the moment; current. —*n.* One that exists.

ex·is·ten·tial (ĕg′zĭ-stĕn′shəl, ĕk′sĭ-) *adj.* **1.** Of, pertaining to, or dealing with existence. **2.** Based on experience; empirical. **3.** Pertaining to existentialism. **—ex′is·ten′tial·ly** *adv.*

ex·is·ten·tial·ism (ĕg′zĭ-stĕn′shə-lĭz′əm, ĕk′sĭ-) *n.* A philosophy that emphasizes the uniqueness and isolation of the individual experience in a hostile or indifferent universe, regards human existence as unexplainable, and stresses freedom of choice and responsibility for the consequences of one's acts. **—ex′is·ten′tial·ist** *n.*

ex·it[1] (ĕg′zĭt, ĕk′sĭt). Used as a stage direction for a specified actor to leave the stage. [Lat., 3rd. person sing. of *exire,* to go out : *ex-*, out + *ire,* to go.]

ex·it[2] (ĕg′zĭt, ĕk′sĭt) *n.* **1. a.** The act of going away or out. **b.** Death. **2.** A passage or way out. **3.** The departure of a performer from the stage. —*intr.v.* **-it·ed, -it·ing, -its.** To make one's exit. [Lat. *exire, exit-* : *ex-*, out + *ire,* to go.]

ex li·bris (ĕks lī′brĭs, lē′-) *n., pl.* **ex libris.** A bookplate. [Lat., from the books.]

ex ni·hi·lo (ĕks nē′ə-lō′, nī′-, nĭ′-) *adj. & adv.* Out of nothing. [Lat.]

exo– *pref.* Outside; external: *exoskeleton.* [Gk. *exō,* outside of < *ex,* out of.]

ex·o·bi·ol·o·gy (ĕk′sō-bī-ŏl′ə-jē) *n.* **1.** A branch of biology that deals with the search for and study of extraterrestrial living organisms. **2.** A branch of biology that deals with the effects of extraterrestrial space on living organisms. **—ex′o·bi′o·log′i·cal** (-ə-lŏj′ĭ-kəl) *adj.* **—ex′o·bi·ol′o·gist** *n.*

ex·o·carp (ĕk′sō-kärp′) *n. Bot.* The outermost layer of the pericarp of fruit.

ex·o·crine (ĕk′sə-krĭn, -krēn, -krīn′) *adj.* **1.** Having or secreting through a duct. Used of a gland. **2.** Of or pertaining to the secretion of a gland having a duct. [EXO- + Gk. *krinein,* to separate.]

ex·o·cy·clic (ĕk′sō-sī′klĭk, -sĭk′lĭk) *adj.* Occurring outside of a chemical ring structure.

ex·o·derm (ĕk′sō-dûrm′) *n.* The ectoderm.

ex·o·don·tia (ĕk′sə-dŏn′shə, -shē-ə) *n.* Dentistry involving the extraction of teeth. **—ex′o·don′tist** *n.*

ex·o·dus (ĕk′sə-dəs) *n.* **1.** A departure, usually of a large number of people. **2. Exodus.** The departure of the Israelites from Egypt. **3.** See table at **Bible.** [LLat. < Gk. *exodos* : *ex-*, out + *hodos,* way.]

ex·o·en·zyme (ĕk′sō-ĕn′zīm′) *n.* An enzyme, such as a digestive enzyme, that functions outside a cell.

ex·o·er·gic (ĕk′sō-ûr′jĭk) *adj.* Exothermic. [EXO- + Gk. *ergon,* work + -IC.]

ex of·fi·ci·o (ĕks′ ə-fĭsh′ē-ō′) *adj. & adv.* By virtue of office or position. [Lat.]

ex·og·a·my (ĕk-sŏg′ə-mē) *n.* **1.** The custom of marrying outside the tribe, family, clan, or other social unit. **2.** *Biol.* Reproduction by the fusion of gametes of different ancestries. **—ex'o·gam'ic** (ĕk'sə-găm'ĭk), **ex·og'a·mous** (ĕk-sŏg'ə-məs) *adj.*

ex·og·e·nous (ĕk-sŏj'ə-nəs) *adj.* **1.** *Biol.* Derived or developed from external causes. **2.** *Bot.* Characterized by the addition of layers of woody tissue. **3.** Having a cause external to the body. Used of diseases. [Fr. *exogène* : *exo-*, exo- + *gène*, born < Gk. *-genēs*.] **—ex·og'e·nous·ly** *adv.*

ex·on·er·ate (ĭg-zŏn'ə-rāt') *tr.v.* **-at·ed, -at·ing, -ates. 1.** To free from blame. **2.** To free from a responsibility, obligation, or task. [ME *exoneraten* < Lat. *exonerare, exonerat-*, to free from a burden : *ex-*, off + *onus*, burden.] **—ex·on'er·a'tion** *n.* **—ex·on'er·a·tive** *adj.*

ex·o·nu·cle·ase (ĕk'sō-nōō'klē-ās', -āz', -nyōō'-) *n.* Any of a group of enzymes that remove nucleotides sequentially from the end of a DNA chain.

ex·oph·thal·mic goiter (ĕk'səf-thăl'mĭc) *n.* A disease caused by the excessive production of thyroid hormone and characterized by an enlarged thyroid gland, protrusion of the eyeballs, tachycardia, and nervous excitability.

ex·oph·thal·mos also **ex·oph·thal·mus** (ĕk'səf-thăl'məs) *n.* Abnormal protrusion of the eyeball. [Gk., with prominent eyes : *ex-*, out + *ophthalmos*, eye.] **—ex'oph·thal'mic** *adj.*

ex·or·bi·tance (ĭg-zôr'bĭ-təns) *n.* **1.** Excessiveness, as of price, demand, or need; extravagance. **2.** An exorbitant act, esp. one that deviates from what is right or proper.

ex·or·bi·tant (ĭg-zôr'bĭ-tənt) *adj.* **1.** Exceeding the appropriate limits or bounds; immoderate. **2.** *Law.* Exceeding the established limits of right or propriety. [ME, aberrant < OFr. < Med. Lat. *exorbitans*, pr.part. *exorbitare*, to deviate : *ex*, out of + *orbita*, path < *orbis*, ring.] **—ex·or'bi·tant·ly** *adv.*

ex·or·cise (ĕk'sôr-sīz', -sər-) *tr.v.* **-cised, -cis·ing, -cis·es. 1.** To expel (an evil spirit) by or as if by incantation or adjuration. **2.** To free from evil spirits. [ME *exorcisen* < Med. Lat. *exorcizare* < Gk. *exorkizein* : *ex-*, out + *horkos*, oath.] **—ex'or·cis'er** *n.*

ex·or·cism (ĕk'sôr-sĭz'əm, -sər-) *n.* **1.** The act of exorcising. **2.** A formula used in exorcising. **—ex'or·cist** *n.*

ex·or·di·um (ĭg-zôr'dē-əm, ĭk-sôr'-) *n., pl.* **-di·ums** or **-di·a** (-dē-ə). A beginning or introductory part, esp. of a speech or treatise. [Lat. < *exordiri*, to begin : *ex-* (intensive) + *ordiri*, to begin.] **—ex·or'di·al** *adj.*

ex·o·skel·e·ton (ĕk'sō-skĕl'ĭ-tən) *n.* An external protective or supporting structure of many invertebrates, such as insects and crustaceans. **—ex'o·skel'e·tal** *adj.*

ex·os·mo·sis (ĕk'sŏz-mō'sĭs, -sŏs-) *n.* The flow of a fluid through a permeable membrane into a less dense fluid. [EX(O)- + OSMOSIS.] **—ex'os·mot'ic** (-mŏt'ĭk) *adj.*

ex·o·sphere (ĕk'sō-sfîr') *n.* The outermost portion of the atmosphere, estimated to begin 300 to 600 miles above the earth, characterized by the ability of constituent molecules with appropriate velocities to escape from the earth without colliding with other molecules. **—ex'o·spher'ic** *adj.*

ex·o·spore (ĕk'sō-spôr', -spōr') *n. Bot.* The outermost layer of a spore in some algae and fungi.

ex·o·spor·i·um (ĕk'sō-spôr'ē-əm, -spōr'-) *n., pl.* **-i·a** (ē-ə). *Bot.* Exine. [NLat. : EXO- + *spora*, spore.]

ex·os·to·sis (ĕk'sŏ-stō'sĭs) *n., pl.* **-ses** (-sēz'). A bony tumor on the surface of a bone. [Gk. *exostōsis* : *ex-*, out of + *osteon*, bone.]

ex·o·ter·ic (ĕk'sə-tĕr'ĭk) *adj.* **1.** Not confined to an inner circle of disciples or initiates. **2.** Comprehensible to or suited to the public; popular. **3.** Pertaining to the outside; external. [Lat. *exotericus*, external < Gk. *exōterikos* < *exōterō*, comp. of *exō*, outside < *ex*, out.] **—ex'o·ter'i·cal·ly** *adv.*

ex·o·ther·mic (ĕk'sō-thûr'mĭk) also **ex·o·ther·mal** (-məl) *adj.* Releasing, as opposed to absorbing, heat. **—ex'o·ther'mi·cal·ly** *adv.*

ex·ot·ic (ĭg-zŏt'ĭk) *adj.* **1.** From another part of the world; foreign. **2.** Having the charm of the unfamiliar; strikingly and intriguingly unusual or different. **3.** Of or relating to striptease. *—n.* **1.** One that is exotic. **2.** A striptease performer. [Lat. *exoticus* < Gk. *exōtikos* < *exō*, outside < *ex*, out.] **—ex·ot'i·cal·ly** *adv.* **—ex·ot'ic·ness** *n.*

ex·ot·i·cism (ĭg-zŏt'ĭ-sĭz'əm) *n.* The quality or condition of being exotic.

ex·o·tox·in (ĕk'sō-tŏk'sĭn) *n.* A toxin excreted by a microorganism into a surrounding medium and recoverable from a culture without destruction of the producing agent.

ex·pand (ĭk-spănd') *v.* **-pand·ed, -pand·ing, -pands.** *—tr.* **1.** To increase the size, volume, quantity, or scope of. **2.** To express at length or in detail; enlarge upon. **3.** *Math.* To write (a quantity) as a sum of terms, as a continued product, or as another extended form. *—intr.* **1.** To open up or out. **2.** To become greater in size, volume, or scope. **3.** To speak or write at length or in detail. **4.** To feel expansive. [ME *expanden*, to spread out < Lat. *expandere* : *ex-*, out + *pandere*, to spread.] **—ex·pand'a·ble** *adj.* **—ex·pand'er** *n.*

expanding universe theory *n.* **1.** The interpretation of the shifts of the lines in the spectra of galaxies as resulting from a Doppler effect, with the experimental results that all galaxies are retreating from each other at speeds proportional to the distance separating them and that the universe is expanding. **2.** The cosmological theory in which violent eruption from a point source leads to the formation of elementary particles, the subsequent formation of hydrogen and helium, and the dispersion of the galaxies that develop from this matter.

ex·pan·dor (ĭk-spăn'dər) *n.* A transducer designed for a given range of input voltages which produces a larger range of output voltages.

ex·panse (ĭk-spăns') *n.* **1.** A wide and open extent, as of land, sky, or water. **2. a.** Expansion. **b.** The distance or amount of expansion. [Lat. *expansum* < *expandere*, to spread out. —see EXPAND.]

ex·pan·si·ble (ĭk-spăn'sə-bəl) *adj.* Capable of expanding or of being expanded. **—ex·pan'si·bil'i·ty** *n.*

ex·pan·sile (ĭk-spăn'səl, -sīl') *adj.* Of, pertaining to, or capable of expansion.

ex·pan·sion (ĭk-spăn'shən) *n.* **1.** The act or process of expanding. **2.** The state of being expanded. **3. a.** An expanded part. **b.** A product of expanding. **4.** The extent or amount by which something has expanded. **5.** Increase in the dimensions of a body. **6.** *Math.* **a.** A quantity written in an extended form, as a sum of terms or as a continued product. **b.** The process of obtaining this form. **7.** An expanse.

ex·pan·sion·ar·y (ĭk-spăn'shə-nĕr'ē) *adj.* Tending toward expansion.

expansion bolt *n.* A bolt having an attachment that expands as the bolt is driven into a surface.

ex·pan·sion·ism (ĭk-spăn'shə-nĭz'əm) *n.* The practice or policy of esp. territorial or economic expansion by a nation. **—ex·pan'sion·ist** *n.*

ex·pan·sive (ĭk-spăn'sĭv) *adj.* **1.** Capable of expanding or tending to expand. **2.** Broad or comprehensive in extent. **3.** Disposed to be open and generous; outgoing. **4.** Marked by euphoria and delusions of grandeur. **5.** Grand in scale. **—ex·pan'sive·ly** *adv.* **—ex·pan'sive·ness** *n.* **—ex'pan·siv'i·ty** (ĕk'spăn-sĭv'ĭ-tē) *n.*

ex par·te (ĕks pär'tē) *adj.* & *adv.* **1.** *Law.* From or on one side only. **2.** One-sided; partisan.

ex·pa·ti·ate (ĭk-spā'shē-āt') *intr.v.* **-at·ed, -at·ing, -ates. 1.** To speak or write at length: *expatiated on the subject until everyone was bored.* **2.** *Archaic.* To wander freely. [Lat. *expatiari, expatiat-* : *ex-*, out + *spatiari*, to spread < *spatium*, space.] **—ex·pa'ti·a'tion** *n.*

ex·pa·tri·ate (ĕk-spā'trē-āt') *v.* **-at·ed, -at·ing, -ates.** *—tr.* **1.** To send into exile. **2.** To remove (oneself) from residence in one's native land. *—intr.* **1.** To give up residence in one's homeland. **2.** To renounce one's allegiance to one's homeland. *—n.* (-ĭt, -āt'). **1.** A person who has taken up residence in a foreign country. **2.** A person who has renounced his native land. *—adj.* Residing in a foreign country; expatriated. [Med. Lat. *expatriare, expatriat-* : Lat. *ex-*, out of + Lat. *patria*, native land < *pater*, father.] **—ex·pa'tri·a'tion** (ĕks-pā'trē-ā'shən) *n.*

ex·pect (ĭk-spĕkt') *tr.v.* **-pect·ed, -pect·ing, -pects. 1.** To look forward to the probable occurrence or appearance of. **2.** To consider likely or certain: *expect to see him soon.* **3.** To consider reasonable or due: *I expect an apology.* **4.** To consider obligatory; require. **5.** *Informal.* To presume; suppose. —See Usage note at **anticipate.** [Lat. *expectare* : *ex-*, out + *spectare*, look at, freq. of *specere*, to see.] **—ex·pect'a·ble** *adj.* **—ex·pect'a·bly** *adv.* **—ex·pect'ed·ly** *adv.* **—ex·pect'ed·ness** *n.*

Synonyms: *expect, anticipate, hope, await, foresee.* These verbs are related in various ways to the idea of looking ahead to something in the future. To *expect* is to look forward to the occurrence of something with little reservation as to its likelihood. To *anticipate* usually involves something more than expectation. In some contexts it refers to taking appropriate action in advance of something expected, so as to forestall or prevent its occurrence, or so as to meet an order or request: *anticipate trouble; anticipate one's wishes.* The term can also refer to looking forward to something and experiencing it beforehand: *anticipate pleasure.* To *hope* is to desire, usually with confidence in the likelihood of gaining what is desired. To *await*, in this comparison, is to look forward to without doubt as to occurrence. To *foresee* is to know of an occurrence in advance of its coming into existence, by means of insight, intuition, study, or inference.

ex·pec·tan·cy (ĭk-spĕk'tən-sē) *n., pl.* **-cies. 1.** The act or state of expecting; expectation. **2.** The state of being expected. **3. a.** Something expected. **b.** An expected amount calculated on the basis of statistical probability: *a life expectancy of 70 years.* **—ex·pec'tance** *n.*

ex·pec·tant (ĭk-spĕk'tənt) *adj.* **1.** Having or marked by expectation: *expectant of praise.* **2.** Expecting the birth of a child. **—ex·pec'tant** *n.* **—ex·pec'tant·ly** *adv.*

ex·pec·ta·tion (ĕk'spĕk-tā'shən) *n.* **1. a.** The act or state of expecting. **b.** Eager anticipation: *eyes shining with expectation.* **2.** The state of being expected. **3. a. expectations.** Prospects, esp. of inheritance. **b.** Something expected. **4.** The expected value of a random variable, esp. the mean. **5.** Expectancy (sense 3.b.).

ex·pec·ta·tive (ĭk-spĕk'tə-tĭv) *adj.* Of, relating to, or characterized by expectation.

ex·pect·ing (ĭk-spĕk'tĭng) *adj.* Pregnant.

ex·pec·to·rant (ĭk-spĕk'tər-ənt) *adj.* Promoting or facilitating secretion or expulsion from the mucous membrane of the air passages. *—n.* An expectorant medicine.

ex·pec·to·rate (ĭk-spĕk′tə-rāt′) *v.* **-rat·ed, -rat·ing, -rates.** —*tr.* **1.** To eject from the mouth; spit. **2.** To cough up and eject by spitting. —*intr.* **1.** To spit. **2.** To clear out the chest and lungs by coughing up and spitting out matter. [Lat. *expectorare, expectorat-,* to drive from the breast : *ex-,* out of + *pectus,* breast.] **—ex·pec′to·ra′tion** *n.*

ex·pe·di·ence (ĭk-spē′dē-əns) *n.* Expediency.

ex·pe·di·en·cy (ĭk-spē′dē-ən-sē) *n., pl.* **-cies. 1.** Appropriateness to the purpose at hand. **2.** Adherence to self-serving means. **3.** An expedient. **4.** *Obs.* Speed.

ex·pe·di·ent (ĭk-spē′dē-ənt) *adj.* **1.** Appropriate to a particular purpose. **2. a.** Serving to promote one's interest. **b.** Based on or marked by a concern for policy rather than principle. **3.** *Obs.* Speedy; expeditious. —*n.* **1.** Something that is a means to an end. **2.** A contrivance adopted to meet an urgent need. [ME < Lat. *expediens,* pr.part. of *expedire,* to make ready. —see EXPEDITE.] **—ex·pe′di·ent·ly** *adv.*

ex·pe·di·en·tial (ĭk-spē′dē-ĕn′shəl) *adj.* Of, pertaining to, or concerned with what is expedient. **—ex·pe′di·en′tial·ly** *adv.*

ex·pe·dite (ĕk′spĭ-dīt′) *tr.v.* **-dit·ed, -dit·ing, -dites. 1.** To speed up the progress of; facilitate. **2.** To perform quickly and efficiently. **3.** To issue officially; dispatch. [Lat. *expedire, expedit-,* to free from entanglement : *ex-,* out + *pes,* foot.] **—ex′pe·dit′er, ex′pe·di′tor** *n.*

ex·pe·di·tion (ĕk′spĭ-dĭsh′ən) *n.* **1. a.** A journey undertaken by an organized group of people with a definite objective. **b.** The group undertaking such a journey. **2.** Speed in performance; promptness. [ME *expedicioun,* military campaign < OFr. *expedition* < Lat. *expeditio* < *expedire,* to extricate. —see EXPEDITE.]

ex·pe·di·tion·ar·y (ĕk′spĭ-dĭsh′ə-nĕr′ē) *adj.* Relating to or constituting an esp. military expedition.

ex·pe·di·tious (ĕk′spə-dĭsh′əs) *adj.* Acting or done with speed and efficiency. **—ex′pe·di′tious·ly** *adv.* **—ex′pe·di′tious·ness** *n.*

ex·pel (ĭk-spĕl′) *tr.v.* **-pelled, -pel·ling, -pels. 1.** To force or drive out. **2.** To discharge from or as if from some receptacle: *expelled a huge sigh of relief.* **3.** To dismiss, as from a society. [ME *expellen* < Lat. *expellere* : *ex-,* out + *pellere,* to drive.] **—ex·pel′la·ble** *adj.* **—ex·pel′ler** *n.*

ex·pel·lant also **ex·pel·lent** (ĭk-spĕl′ənt) *adj.* Expelling or tending to expel. **—ex·pel′lant** *n.*

ex·pel·lee (ĕk′spĕl-lē′) *n.* One who is expelled.

ex·pend (ĭk-spĕnd′) *tr.v.* **-pend·ed, -pend·ing, -pends. 1.** To lay out; spend. **2.** To use up; consume. [ME *expenden* < Lat. *expendere* : *ex,* out + *pendere,* pay.]

ex·pend·a·ble (ĭk-spĕn′də-bəl) *adj.* **1.** Subject to use or consumption. **2.** Viewed as not worth keeping or maintaining. —*n.* Something that is expendable.

ex·pen·di·ture (ĭk-spĕn′də-chər) *n.* **1.** The act or process of expending; outlay. **2. a.** The amount expended. **b.** An expense.

ex·pense (ĭk-spĕns′) *n.* **1. a.** Something paid out to attain a goal or accomplish a purpose. **b.** Something given up for the sake of something else; sacrifice. **2. expenses. a.** Charges incurred by an employee in the performance of his work. **b.** *Informal.* Money allotted for payment of such charges. **3.** Something requiring the expenditure of money. **4.** *Archaic.* An act of expending; expenditure. —*tr.v.* **-pensed, -pens·ing, -pens·es. 1.** To charge with expenses. **2.** To write off as an expense. [ME < AN *expense* < Lat. *expensa* < fem. p.part. of Lat. *expendere,* to expend.]

expense account *n.* An account of expenses for repayment to an employee.

ex·pen·sive (ĭk-spĕn′sĭv) *adj.* Involving a large expenditure; costly. **—ex·pen′sive·ly** *adv.* **—ex·pen′sive·ness** *n.*

ex·pe·ri·ence (ĭk-spîr′ē-əns) *n.* **1.** The apprehension of an object, thought, or emotion through the senses or mind. **2. a.** Active participation in events or activities, leading to the accumulation of knowledge or skill. **b.** The knowledge or skill so derived. **3. a.** An event or series of events participated in or lived through. **b.** The totality of such events in the past of an individual or group. —*tr.v.* **-enced, -enc·ing, -enc·es.** To participate in personally; undergo: *experienced a feeling of loneliness.* [ME < OFr. or < Lat. *experientia* < *experiens,* pr.part. of *experiri,* to try.]

ex·pe·ri·enced (ĭk-spîr′ē-ənst) *adj.* **1.** Skilled as the result of observation, use, or practice. **2.** Knowledgeable or wise because of experience.

experience table *n.* A table compiled from life-insurance statistics to indicate life expectancy.

ex·pe·ri·en·tial (ĭk-spîr′ē-ĕn′shəl) *adj.* Pertaining to or derived from experience. **—ex·pe′ri·en′tial·ly** *adv.*

ex·per·i·ment (ĭk-spĕr′ə-mənt) *n.* **1.** A test made to demonstrate a known truth, to examine the validity of a hypothesis, or to determine the efficacy of something previously untried. **2.** The process of conducting a test. —*intr.v.* (-mĕnt′) **-ment·ed, -ment·ing, -ments.** To conduct an experiment. [ME < OFr. or < Lat. *experimentum* < *experiri,* to try.] **—ex·per′i·ment′er** *n.*

ex·per·i·men·tal (ĭk-spĕr′ə-mĕn′tl) *adj.* **1. a.** Pertaining to or based upon experiment. **b.** Given to experimenting. **2.** Of the nature of an experiment. **3.** Founded upon experience; empirical. **—ex·per′i·men′tal·ly** *adv.*

ex·per·i·men·tal·ism (ĭk-spĕr′ə-mĕn′tl-ĭz′əm) *n.* The use of empirical or experimental methods in determining the validity of an idea. **—ex·per′i·men′tal·ist** *n.*

ex·per·i·men·ta·tion (ĭk-spĕr′ə-mĕn-tā′shən) *n.* The act, process, or practice of experimenting.

experiment station *n.* An establishment in which scientific experiments are conducted in a specific field, such as agriculture, and practical uses are developed.

ex·pert (ĕk′spûrt′) *n.* **1.** A person with a high degree of skill in or knowledge of a certain subject. **2. a.** The highest grade that can be achieved in marksmanship. **b.** A person who has achieved this grade. —*adj.* (ĕk′spûrt, ĭk-spûrt′). Having or demonstrating great skill, dexterity, or knowledge as the result of experience or training. [ME < OFr., experienced < Lat. *expertus,* p.part. of *experiri,* to try.] **—ex′pert′ly** *adv.* **—ex′pert′ness** *n.*

ex·per·tise (ĕk′spûr-tēz′) *n.* **1.** Expert advice or opinion. **2.** Specialized knowledge or skill. [Fr. < OFr. < *expert,* experienced. —see EXPERT.]

ex·pi·a·ble (ĕk′spē-ə-bəl) *adj.* Capable of being expiated.

ex·pi·ate (ĕk′spē-āt′) *v.* **-at·ed, -at·ing, -ates.** —*tr.* To make atonement for. —*intr.* To make expiation. [Lat. *expiare, expiat-* : *ex-* (intensive) + *piare,* to atone < *pius,* devout.] **—ex′pi·a′tor** *n.*

ex·pi·a·tion (ĕk′spē-ā′shən) *n.* **1.** The act of expiating; atonement. **2.** The means of atonement. **—ex′pi·a·to′ry** (-ə-tôr′ē, -tōr′ē) *adj.*

ex·pi·ra·tion (ĕk′spə-rā′shən) *n.* **1.** The act of coming to a close; termination. **2.** The act of breathing out. **3.** *Obs.* Death.

ex·pi·ra·to·ry (ĭk-spī′rə-tôr′ē, -tōr′ē) *adj.* Of, pertaining to, or involving the expiration of air from the lungs.

ex·pire (ĭk-spīr′) *v.* **-pired, -pir·ing, -pires.** —*intr.* **1.** To come to an end; terminate: *His membership expired.* **2.** To breathe one's last breath; die. **3.** To exhale; breathe out. —*tr.* **1.** To breathe out. **2.** *Archaic.* To give off. [ME *expiren* < Lat. *exspirare* : *ex-,* out + *spirare,* to breathe.]

ex·pi·ry (ĭk-spīr′ē) *n., pl.* **-ries. 1.** An expiration, esp. of a contract or agreement. **2.** Death.

ex·plain (ĭk-splān′) *v.* **-plained, -plain·ing, -plains.** —*tr.* **1.** To make plain or comprehensible. **2.** To define; expound: *He explained his plan.* **3.** To offer reasons for or a cause of; justify: *explain an error.* —*intr.* To give an explanation. ***—phrasal verb.* explain away. 1.** To dismiss or get rid of by or as if by explaining. **2.** To minimize by explanation. [ME *explanen* < Lat. *explanare* : *ex-* (intensive) + *planus,* clear.] **—ex·plain′a·ble** *adj.*

Synonyms: *explain, elucidate, expound, explicate, interpret, construe.* These verbs mean to make the nature or meaning of something clear. *Explain* is most widely applicable, since it has the fewest special implications. *Elucidate* is used most appropriately in contexts that suggest an attempt to throw light in some way on a complex subject. *Expound* and *explicate* imply detailed and usually learned and lengthy exploration or analysis of such a subject. *Interpret* can refer to translation of a foreign tongue or, by extension, to translation of complexities into understandable terms. It often also implies the disclosure of underlying meaning by the application of special knowledge or insight. *Construe* involves putting a construction or interpretation on something: *a law construed strictly by the Supreme Court; construe silence as a sign of disapproval.*

ex·pla·na·tion (ĕk′splə-nā′shən) *n.* **1.** The act or process of explaining. **2.** Something that explains. **3.** A mutual clarification of misunderstandings; reconciliation.

ex·plan·a·tive (ĭk-splăn′ə-tĭv) *adj.* Explanatory. **—ex·plan′a·tive·ly** *adv.*

ex·plan·a·to·ry (ĭk-splăn′ə-tôr′ē, -tōr′ē) *adj.* Serving or intended to explain. **—ex·plan′a·to′ri·ly** *adv.*

ex·plant (ĕk-splănt′) *tr.v.* **-plant·ed, -plant·ing, -plants.** To take (living tissue) from the natural site of growth and place in a medium or culture. —*n.* Material explanted. **—ex′plan·ta′tion** *n.*

ex·ple·tive (ĕk′splĭ-tĭv) *adj.* Added or inserted in order to fill out something, such as a metrical line or sentence. —*n.* **1.** An exclamation or oath, esp. one that is profane or obscene. **2. a.** A word or phrase added to a sentence that does not contribute any meaning but is added only to fill out a sentence or metrical line. **b.** A word that stands in place of and anticipates a following word or phrase; in the sentence *"There are many books on the table,"* the word *"there"* functions as an expletive. [LLat. *expletivus* < Lat. *expletus* < *explēre,* to fill out : *ex-,* out + *plēre,* to fill.]

ex·ple·to·ry (ĕk′splĭ-tôr′ē) *adj.* Expletive.

ex·pli·ca·ble (ĕk′splĭ-kə-bəl) *adj.* Capable of being explained. **—ex′pli·ca·bly** *adv.*

ex·pli·cate (ĕks′plĭ-kāt′) *tr.v.* **-cat·ed, -cat·ing, -cates.** To make clear the meaning of; explain. [Lat. *explicare,* to unfold : *ex-,* out + *plicare,* to fold.] **—ex·pli·ca′tion** *n.* **—ex′pli·ca′tor** *n.*

ex·pli·ca·tion de texte (ĕk-splē-kä-syôɴ′ də tĕkst′) *n., pl.* **ex·pli·ca·tions de texte** (ĕk-splē-kä-syôɴ′ də tĕkst′). A method of literary criticism in which a detailed reading and analysis of a given text in each of its linguistic, compositional, and expressive parts and aspects is followed by a synthesizing exposition of these with relation to each other and to the

experiment

whole work. [Fr. : *explication,* explanation + *de,* of + *texte,* text.]

ex·pli·ca·tive (ĕk′splĭ-kā′tĭv) *adj.* Serving to explain; explanatory. —**ex′pli·ca·tive** *n.* —**ex′pli·ca·tive·ly** *adv.*

ex·plic·it (ĭk-splĭs′ĭt) *adj.* **1. a.** Expressed with clarity and precision. **b.** Clearly defined or formulated. **2.** Forthright and unreserved in expression: *was explicit in his criticism.* [Fr. *explicite* < Lat. *explicitus,* p.part. of *explicare,* to unfold. —see EXPLICATE.] —**ex·plic′it·ly** *adv.* —**ex·plic′it·ness** *n.*

Usage: *Explicit* and *express* both apply to something that is clearly stated rather than implied. *Explicit* applies more particularly to that which is carefully spelled out: *explicit instructions. Express* applies particularly to a clear expression of intention or will: *an express promise* or *an express prohibition.*

ex·plode (ĭk-splōd′) *v.* **-plod·ed, -plod·ing, -plodes.** —*intr.* **1.** To release mechanical, chemical, or nuclear energy in an explosion. **2.** To burst violently as a result of internal pressure. **3.** To burst forth or break out suddenly and often violently. **4.** To increase suddenly, sharply, and without control. —*tr.* **1.** To cause to explode or burst violently and noisily. **2.** To show to be false or unreliable: *explode a hypothesis.* **3.** *Obs.* To drive off the stage by the unrestrained expression of dissatisfaction. [Lat. *explodere,* to drive out by clapping : *ex-,* out + *plaudere,* to clap.] —**ex·plod′er** *n.*

exploded view *n.* An illustration or diagram of a construction that shows its parts separately but in positions that indicate their proper relationships to the whole.

ex·ploit (ĕk′sploit′, ĭk-sploit′) *n.* An act or deed, esp. a brilliant or heroic feat. —*tr.v.* (ĭk-sploit′, ĕk′sploit′) **-ploit·ed, -ploit·ing, -ploits. 1.** To employ to the greatest possible advantage. **2.** To make use of selfishly or unethically: *exploit peasant labor.* [ME < OFr. < Lat. *explicitum,* neuter p.part. of *explicare,* to explicate.] —**ex·ploit′a·ble** *adj.* —**ex·ploit′a·tive** *adj.* —**ex·ploit′er** *n.*

ex·ploi·ta·tion (ĕk′sploi-tā′shən) *n.* **1.** The act of exploiting. **2.** The utilization of another person for selfish purposes. **3.** An advertising or publicity program.

ex·plo·ra·tion (ĕk′splə-rā′shən) *n.* The act or an instance of exploring. —**ex·plor′a·to′ry** (ĭk-splôr′ə-tôr′ē, -splōr′ə-tōr′ē) *adj.*

ex·plore (ĭk-splôr′, -splōr′) *v.* **-plored, -plor·ing, -plores.** —*tr.* **1.** To investigate systematically; examine: *explore every possibility.* **2.** To search into or range over for the purpose of discovery. **3.** *Med.* To examine for diagnostic purposes. —*intr.* To make a careful examination or search. [Lat. *explorare.*]

ex·plor·er (ĭk-splôr′ər, -splōr′-) *n.* **1.** One who explores, esp. one who explores a geographic area. **2.** An implement or tool used for exploring; probe. **3. Explorer.** Any of a series of early U.S. satellites, two of which were instrumental in the discovery of the Van Allen belts.

ex·plo·sion (ĭk-splō′zhən) *n.* **1. a.** The act or an example of exploding. **b.** The loud, sharp sound made by this. **2.** A sudden and often vehement outburst, as of emotion. **3.** A sudden and great increase: *the cultural explosion.* **4.** Plosion. [Lat. *explosio* < *explodere,* to drive out by clapping. —see EXPLODE.]

ex·plo·sive (ĭk-splō′sĭv) *adj.* **1.** Pertaining to or of the nature of an explosion. **2.** Tending to explode. —*n.* **1.** A substance, esp. a prepared chemical, that explodes or causes explosion. **2.** A stop (sense 12). [< Lat. *explodere, explos-,* to drive out by clapping. —see EXPLODE.] —**ex·plo′sive·ly** *adv.* —**ex·plo′sive·ness** *n.*

ex·po·nent (ĭk-spō′nənt, ĕk′spō′nənt) *n.* **1.** One that expounds or interprets. **2.** One that speaks for, represents, or advocates. **3.** *Math.* A number or symbol, as 3 in $(x+y)^3$, placed to the right of and above another number, symbol, or expression, denoting the power to which the latter is to be raised. —*adj.* Expository; explanatory. [Lat. *exponens, exponent-,* pr.part. of *exponere,* to put forward : *ex-,* out + *ponere,* to put.]

ex·po·nen·tial (ĕk′spə-nĕn′shəl) *adj.* **1.** *Math.* **a.** Containing, involving, or expressed as an exponent. **b.** Expressed in terms of a designated power of *e,* the base of natural logarithms. **2.** Of or pertaining to an exponent. —**ex′po·nen′tial·ly** *adv.*

ex·po·nen·ti·a·tion (ĕk′spə-nĕn′shē-ā′shən) *n. Math.* The act of raising a quantity to a power.

ex·port (ĭk-spôrt′, -spōrt′, ĕk′spôrt′, -spōrt′) *v.* **-port·ed, -port·ing, -ports.** —*tr.* To send or carry (a commodity, for example) abroad, esp. for trade or sale. —*intr.* To send or carry abroad merchandise, esp. for sale or trade. —*n.* (ĕk′spôrt′, -spōrt′). **1.** The act of exporting. **2.** Something that is exported. [Lat. *exportare* : *ex-,* out + *portare,* to carry.] —**ex·port′a·bil′i·ty** *n.* —**ex·port′a·ble** *adj.* —**ex·port′er** *n.*

ex·por·ta·tion (ĕk′spôr-tā′shən, -spōr-) *n.* **1.** The act of exporting. **2.** Something that is exported.

ex·pose (ĭk-spōz′) *tr.v.* **-posed, -pos·ing, -pos·es. 1. a.** To take shelter or protection away from. **b.** To lay open, as to something undesirable or injurious. **2.** To subject (a photographic film, for example) to the action of light. **3.** To make visible: *Cleaning exposed the grain of the wood.* **4. a.** To make known (a crime, for example). **b.** To reveal the guilt or wrongdoing of: *expose a criminal.* **5.** To put out or abandon without food or shelter. [ME *exposen* < OFr. *exposer* < Lat. *exponere.* —see EXPOUND.] —**ex·pos′er** *n.*

ex·po·sé (ĕk′spō-zā′) *n.* **1.** An exposure or revelation of something discreditable. **2.** An exposition of facts. [Fr. < p.part. of *exposer,* to expose < OFr.]

ex·po·si·tion (ĕk′spə-zĭsh′ən) *n.* **1.** A setting forth of meaning or intent. **2.** A precise statement intended to give information about or an explanation of difficult material. **3. a.** *Mus.* The first part of a composition in sonata form that introduces the themes. **b.** The opening section of a fugue. **4.** The part of a play that introduces the theme and chief characters. **5.** The act or an example of exposing. **6.** A public exhibition or show, as of artistic or industrial developments. [ME *exposicioun* < OFr. *exposition* < Lat. *expositio* < *exponere,* to expound.] —**ex·pos′i·tive** (ĭk-spŏz′ĭ-tĭv), **ex·pos′i·to′ry** (-tôr′ē, -tōr′ē) *adj.* —**ex·pos′i·tor** *n.*

ex post fac·to (ĕks′ pōst făk′tō) *adj.* Formulated, enacted, or operating retroactively. Used esp. of a law. [Med. Lat. *ex postfacto,* from what is done afterward.]

ex·pos·tu·late (ĭk-spŏs′chə-lāt′) *intr.v.* **-lat·ed, -lat·ing, -lates.** To reason earnestly with someone in an effort to dissuade or correct; remonstrate. [Lat. *expostulare, expostulat-,* to demand strongly : *ex-* (intensive) + *postulare,* to demand.] —**ex·pos′tu·la′tion** *n.* —**ex·pos′tu·la′tor** *n.* —**ex·pos′tu·la·to′ry** (-lə-tôr′ē, -tōr′ē), **ex·pos′tu·la′tive** *adj.*

ex·po·sure (ĭk-spō′zhər) *n.* **1.** The act or an instance of exposing. **2.** The condition of being exposed, esp. to the forces of nature. **3.** A position in relation to climatic or weather conditions or points of the compass: *a southern exposure.* **4. a.** The act of exposing sensitized photographic film or plate. **b.** A film or plate so exposed. **c.** The amount of radiant energy needed to expose a photographic film. **5.** An act of abandoning without food or shelter.

exposure meter *n.* A photoelectric instrument that measures light intensity in a given area and, in photographic use, indicates the proper exposure for each of several shutter speeds.

ex·pound (ĭk-spound′) *v.* **-pound·ed, -pound·ing, -pounds.** —*tr.* **1.** To give a detailed statement of; set forth. **2.** To explain by presenting in detail. —*intr.* To make a detailed statement: *was expounding on his favorite topic.* [ME *expounden* < AN *espoundre* < Lat. *exponere* : *ex-,* out + *ponere,* to place.] —**ex·pound′er** *n.*

ex·press (ĭk-sprĕs′) *tr.v.* **-pressed, -press·ing, -press·es. 1.** To make known or set forth in words. **2.** To manifest or communicate, as by a gesture; show. **3. a.** To make known (one's opinion, for example): *expressed his objections forcefully.* **b.** To communicate (one's feelings, for example), esp. through artistic activity. **4.** To make a representation of; depict. **5.** To represent by a sign or symbol; symbolize. **6.** To squeeze or press out, as juice from a fruit. **7.** To send by special messenger or rapid transport. —*adj.* **1.** Definitely and explicitly stated: *his express wish.* **2.** Particular; specific: *an express purpose.* **3. a.** Sent out with or moving at high speed. **b.** Direct, rapid, and usually nonstop: *express mail delivery.* **c.** Of, relating to, or appropriate for rapid travel. —*adv.* By express delivery or transport. —*n.* **1. a.** A special messenger. **b.** A message delivered by special courier. **2. a.** A rapid, efficient system for the delivery of goods and mail. **b.** Goods and mail conveyed by such a system. **3.** A means of transport, such as a train, that travels rapidly and makes few or no stops before its destination. —See Usage note at **explicit.** [ME *expressen* < OFr. *expresser* < Med. Lat. *expressare* : Lat. *ex-,* out + Lat. *pressare,* to press, freq. of *premere,* to press.] —**ex·press′er** *n.* —**ex·press′i·ble** *adj.*

ex·press·age (ĭk-sprĕs′ĭj) *n.* **1.** The conveyance of goods by express. **2.** The amount charged for goods conveyed by express.

ex·pres·sion (ĭk-sprĕsh′ən) *n.* **1.** The act of expressing, conveying, or representing in words, art, music, or movement; manifestation. **2.** Something that expresses or communicates. **3.** *Math.* A designation of any symbolic mathematical form, such as an equation. **4.** The manner in which one expresses oneself, esp. in speaking, depicting, or performing. **5.** A particular word or phrase: *a slang expression.* **6.** The outward manifestation of a mood or disposition: *Her tears were an expression of her grief.* **7.** A facial aspect or look that conveys a special feeling: *an expression of scorn.* **8.** The act of pressing or squeezing out.

ex·pres·sion·ism (ĭk-sprĕsh′ə-nĭz′əm) *n.* A movement in the arts during the latter part of the 19th and early part of the 20th centuries that emphasized the subjective expression of the inner experiences of the artist. —**ex·pres′sion·ist** *n.* —**ex·pres′sion·is′tic** *adj.* —**ex·pres′sion·is′ti·cal·ly** *adv.*

ex·pres·sion·less (ĭk-sprĕsh′ən-lĭs) *adj.* Lacking expression.

ex·pres·sive (ĭk-sprĕs′ĭv) *adj.* **1.** Of, pertaining to, or characterized by expression. **2.** Serving to express or indicate: *actions expressive of frustration.* **3.** Full of expression; significant: *an expressive glance.* —**ex·pres′sive·ly** *adv.* —**ex·pres′sive·ness** *n.*

ex·pres·siv·i·ty (ĕk′sprĕs-ĭv′ĭ-tē) *n.* **1.** The quality of being expressive. **2.** *Genetics.* The degree to which a particular gene can affect the phenotype of an organism.

ex·press·ly (ĭk-sprĕs′lē) *adv.* **1.** In an express or definite manner; explicitly: *expressly ordered him to leave.* **2.** Especially; particularly: *designed expressly for left-handed craftsman.*

ex·press·man (ĭk-sprĕs′mən) *n.* A worker employed by an express agency.

express rifle *n.* A hunting rifle having low trajectory, high velocity, and a long pointblank range.

express train *n.* A train that travels at high speed and makes a minimum of stops.

ex·press·way (ĭk-sprĕs′wā′) *n.* A major divided highway designed for fast travel.

ex·pro·pri·ate (ĕk-sprō′prē-āt′) *tr.v.* **-at·ed, -at·ing, -ates. 1.** To deprive of possession. **2.** To transfer (another's property) to oneself. [Med. Lat. *expropriare, expropriat-* : Lat. *ex-*, away + Lat. *proprius,* one's own.] **—ex·pro′pri·a′tion** *n.* **—ex·pro′pri·a′tor** *n.* **—ex·pro′pri·a·to′ry** (-ə-tôr′ē, -tōr′ē) *adj.*

ex·pul·sion (ĭk-spŭl′shən) *n.* The act of expelling or the state of being expelled.

ex·punc·tion (ĭk-spŭngk′shən, -spŭng′shən) *n.* The act of expunging or the condition of being expunged; deletion. [< Lat. *expungere, expunct-,* to strike out. —see EXPUNGE.]

ex·punge (ĭk-spŭnj′) *tr.v.* **-punged, -pung·ing, -pung·es. 1.** To erase or strike out. **2.** To obliterate completely; annihilate. [Lat. *expungere,* to strike out : *ex-*, out + *pungere,* to prick.] **—ex·pung′er** *n.*

ex·pur·gate (ĕk′spər-gāt′) *tr.v.* **-gat·ed, -gat·ing, -gates.** To remove obscene, objectionable, or erroneous material from prior to publication. [Lat. *expurgare, expurgat-,* to purify : *ex-* (intensive) + *purgare,* to cleanse.] **—ex′pur·ga′tion** *n.* **—ex′pur·ga′tor** *n.*

ex·pur·ga·to·ry (ĭk-spûr′gə-tôr′ē, -tōr′ē) also **ex·pur·ga·to·ri·al** (-tôr′ē-əl, -tōr′ē-əl) *adj.* Of or pertaining to expurgation or an expurgator.

ex·qui·site (ĕk′skwĭ-zĭt, ĭk-skwĭz′ĭt) *adj.* **1.** Characterized by intricate and beautiful design or execution: *an exquisite chalice.* **2.** Of such beauty or delicacy as to arouse delight: *an exquisite sunset.* **3.** Acutely perceptive or discriminating: *an exquisite sense of color.* **4.** Intense; keen: *an exquisite pain.* **5.** *Obs.* Ingeniously devised or thought out. *—n.* One who is excessively fastidious in dress, manners, or taste. [ME *exquisit* < Lat. *exquisitus,* choice < *exquirere,* to search out : *ex-*, out + *quaerere,* to seek.] **—ex′qui·site·ly** *adv.* **—ex′qui·site·ness** *n.*

ex·san·gui·nate (ĕks-săng′gwə-nāt′) *tr.v.* **-nat·ed, -nat·ing, -nates.** To drain of blood. [< Lat. *exsanguinatus,* bloodless : *ex-*, without + *sanguis,* blood.] **—ex·san′gui·na′tion** *n.*

ex·san·guine (ĕks-săng′gwĭn) also **ex·san·gui·nous** (-gwĭ-nəs) *adj.* Lacking blood; anemic. [Lat. *exsanguis* : *ex-*, without + *sanguis,* blood.]

ex·scind (ĭk-sĭnd′) *tr.v.* **-scind·ed, -scind·ing, -scinds.** To excise or cut out. [Lat. *exscindere* : *ex-*, out + *scindere,* to cut.]

ex·sert (ĭk-sûrt′) *tr.v.* **-sert·ed, -sert·ing, -serts.** To thrust out or forth. *—adj.* Also **ex·sert·ed** (-sûr′tĭd). *Biol.* Thrust outward; protruding. [Lat. *exserere, exsert-.*] **—ex·ser′tion** *n.*

ex·sic·cate (ĕk′sĭ-kāt′) *intr. & tr.v.* **-cat·ed, -cat·ing, -cates.** To dry up or cause to dry up. [Lat. *exsiccare, exsiccat-,* to dry out : *ex-*, out + *siccare,* to dry < *siccus,* dry.] **—ex′sic·ca′tion** *n.* **—ex′sic·ca′tive** *adj.* **—ex′sic·ca′tor** *n.*

ex·stip·u·late (ĕks-stĭp′yə-lĭt) *adj. Bot.* Having no stipules.

ex·tant (ĕk′stənt, ĕk-stănt′) *adj.* **1. a.** Still in existence. **b.** Not destroyed, lost, or extinct: *extant manuscripts.* **2.** *Archaic.* Standing out; projecting. [Lat. *extans, extant-,* pr.part. of *extare,* to stand out : *ex-*, out + *stare,* to stand.]

ex·tem·po·ral (ĭk-stĕm′pər-əl) *adj. Archaic.* Extemporaneous.

ex·tem·po·ra·ne·ous (ĭk-stĕm′pə-rā′nē-əs) *adj.* **1.** Done with little or no preparation or practice; impromptu: *an extemporaneous recital.* **2.** Prepared in advance but delivered without notes or text: *an extemporaneous sermon.* **3.** Skilled at or given to unrehearsed speech or performance. **4.** Provided, made, or adapted as an expedient; makeshift. [LLat. *extemporaneus* < Lat. *ex tempore,* of the time.] **—ex·tem′po·ra′ne·ous·ly** *adv.* **—ex·tem′po·ra′ne·ous·ness** *n.*

Synonyms: *extemporaneous, impromptu, offhand, unrehearsed, unpremeditated.* These adjectives mean without formal preparation and sometimes without previous thought or study. They principally describe a form of expression or action. *Extemporaneous* is applied most often to public speaking without a written text. *Impromptu* even more strongly suggests lack of preparation, as in action or expression that comes on the spur of the moment to fill an unforeseen need. *Offhand* implies not only a spontaneous response but also an unceremonious or even casual manner of delivery. *Unrehearsed* describes performance without formal preparation, though it does not rule out forethought. *Unpremeditated* applies to action taken without prior thought or plan; often the term implies impulsiveness prompted by strong feeling.

ex·tem·po·rar·y (ĭk-stĕm′pə-rĕr′ē) *adj.* Extemporaneous. [< Lat. *ex tempore,* of the time.] **—ex·tem′po·rar′i·ly** (-râr′ə-lē) *adv.*

ex·tem·po·re (ĭk-stĕm′pə-rē) *adj.* Extemporaneous. *—adv.* Extemporaneously. [Lat. *ex tempore* : *ex,* of + *tempus,* time.]

ex·tem·po·rize (ĭk-stĕm′pə-rīz′) *v.* **-rized, -riz·ing, -riz·es.** *—tr.* To do or perform (something) extemporaneously. *—intr.* To perform or utter extemporaneously; improvise. **—ex·tem′po·ri·za′tion** *n.* **—ex·tem′po·riz′er** *n.*

ex·tend (ĭk-stĕnd′) *v.* **-tend·ed, -tend·ing, -tends.** *—tr.* **1.** To open or straighten out; unbend. **2.** To stretch or spread out to fullest length. **3. a.** To exert (oneself) vigorously or to full capacity. **b.** To cause to move at full gallop. **4. a.** To increase in quantity or bulk by adding a cheaper substance. **b.** To adulterate. **5. a.** To enlarge the area or scope of. **b.** To expand the influence of. **c.** To make more comprehensive or inclusive. **6. a.** To offer: *extend one's greetings.* **b.** To make available; provide. **7.** To prolong the time of repayment of. **8.** *Law.* **a.** *Chiefly Brit.* To appraise or assess; value. **b.** To seize or make a levy upon for the purpose of settling a debt. *—intr.* To be or become extended: *influence that extended to other continents.* [ME *extenden* < Lat. *extendere* : *ex-*, out + *tendere,* to stretch.] **—ex·tend′i·bil′i·ty** *n.* **—ex·tend′i·ble** *adj.*

ex·tend·ed (ĭk-stĕn′dĭd) *adj.* **1.** Stretched or pulled out. **2.** Continued for a long period of time; protracted. **3.** Enlarged or extensive in meaning, scope, or influence. **—ex·tend′ed·ly** *adv.*

extended family *n.* A family unit making up one household that consists of parents, children, and other close relatives, such as grandparents or aunts.

ex·tend·er (ĕk-stĕn′dər) *n.* A substance added to another substance to modify, dilute, or adulterate.

ex·ten·si·ble (ĭk-stĕn′sə-bəl) *adj.* Capable of being extended or protruded. [< Lat. *extendere, extens-,* to hold out. —see EXTEND.] **—ex·ten′si·bil′i·ty** *n.*

ex·ten·sile (ĭk-stĕn′sĭl) *adj.* Extensible.

ex·ten·sion (ĭk-stĕn′shən) *n.* **1. a.** The act of extending or the condition of being extended. **b.** Something that is extended. **2.** The amount, degree, or range to which something extends or can extend. **3. a.** The act of straightening or extending a limb. **b.** The position assumed by an extended limb. **4.** *Med.* The application of traction to a fractured or dislocated limb to restore the normal position. **5.** An addition to a main structure. **6.** An additional telephone connected to the main line. **7. a.** An allowance of extra time, esp. for the repayment of a debt. **b.** The period of this extra time. **8.** The property of an object by which it occupies space. **9.** *Logic.* The class of objects designated by a specific term or concept; denotation. **10.** *Math.* A set that includes a given and similar set as a subset. [ME *extensioun* < Lat. *extensio* < *extensus,* p.part. of *extendere,* to extend.] **—ex·ten′sion·al** *adj.*

ex·ten·si·ty (ĭk-stĕn′sĭ-tē) *n.* **1.** The quality of having extension or being extensive. **2.** The attribute of sensation that enables one to perceive space or size.

ex·ten·sive (ĭk-stĕn′sĭv) *adj.* **1.** Large in extent, range, or amount. **2.** Designating or pertaining to the cultivation of vast areas of land with a minimum of labor or expense. **3.** *Physics.* Having a value that is the sum of the values for subdivisions of a thermodynamic system. Used of volume, for example. **—ex·ten′sive·ly** *adv.* **—ex·ten′sive·ness** *n.*

ex·ten·som·e·ter (ĕk′stĕn-sŏm′ĭ-tər) *n.* An instrument used to measure minute deformations in a test specimen of a material. [EXTENS(ION) + -METER.]

ex·ten·sor (ĭk-stĕn′sər) *n.* A muscle that extends or stretches a limb. [NLat. < Lat. *extendere,* to stretch out. —see EXTEND.]

ex·tent (ĭk-stĕnt′) *n.* **1. a.** The range, magnitude, or distance over which a thing extends. **b.** The degree to which it extends. **2.** An extensive space or area: *an extent of desert.* **3.** *Archaic.* An assessment or valuation, as of land, esp. for taxation. **4.** *Law.* **a.** *Chiefly Brit.* A writ allowing a creditor to seize a debtor's property temporarily. **b.** *Chiefly Brit.* The seizure in execution of such a writ. **c.** A writ allowing a creditor to assume temporary ownership of a debtor's property. [ME *extente,* assessment < AN < Lat. *extenta,* fem. p.part. of *extendere,* to extend.]

ex·ten·u·ate (ĭk-stĕn′yo͞o-āt′) *tr.v.* **-at·ed, -at·ing, -ates. 1.** To lessen or attempt to lessen the magnitude or seriousness of by providing partial excuses. **2.** *Obs.* To belittle. **3.** To make thin or emaciated. **4.** To reduce the strength of. [Lat. *extenuare, extenuat-,* to diminish : *ex-*, out + *tenuare,* to make thin < *tenuis,* thin.] **—ex·ten′u·a′tive** *adj. & n.* **—ex·ten′u·a′tor** *n.* **—ex·ten′u·a·to′ry** (-ə-tôr′ē, -tōr′ē) *adj.*

ex·ten·u·a·tion (ĭk-stĕn′yo͞o-ā′shən) *n.* **1.** The act of extenuating or the condition of being extenuated; partial justification. **2.** Something that extenuates; a partial excuse.

ex·te·ri·or (ĭk-stîr′ē-ər) *adj.* **1.** Outer; external. **2.** Originating or acting from the outside. **3.** Suitable for use outside: *an exterior paint.* *—n.* **1.** A part or surface that is outside. **2.** An external or outward appearance: *a friendly exterior.* [Lat., comparative of *exterus,* outward.] **—ex·te′ri·or·ly** *adv.*

exterior angle *n.* **1.** The angle between any side of a polygon and an extended adjacent side. **2.** Any of the four angles that do not include a region of the space between two lines intersected by a transversal.

ex·te·ri·or·i·ty (ĭk-stîr′ē-ôr′ĭ-tē, -ŏr′-) *n.* Externality.

ex·te·ri·or·ize (ĭk-stîr′ē-ə-rīz′) *tr.v.* **-ized, -iz·ing, -iz·es.** To externalize.

ex·ter·mi·nate (ĭk-stûr′mə-nāt′) *tr.v.* **-nat·ed, -nat·ing, -nates.** To get rid of by destroying completely. [Lat. *exterminare, exterminat-,* to drive out : *ex-*, out of + *terminus,*

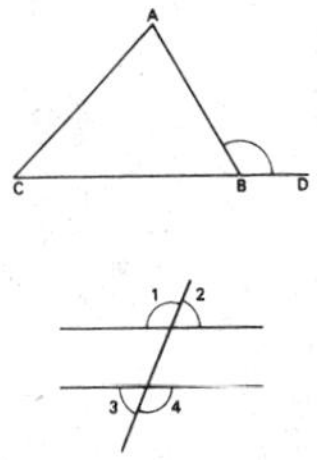

exterior angle
Above: Exterior angle of a triangle (angle ABD)
Below: Exterior angles of parallel lines (angles 1, 2, 3, and 4)

boundary.] **—ex·ter′mi·na′tion** *n.* **—ex·ter′mi·na′tive, ex·ter′mi·na·to′ry** (-nə-tôr′ē, -tōr′ē) *adj.*

ex·ter·mi·na·tor (ĭk-stûr′mə-nā′tər) *n.* One that exterminates, esp. one whose occupation is the extermination of vermin.

ex·tern or **ex·terne** (ĕk′stûrn′) *n.* A person associated with but not officially residing in an institution, esp. a nonresident doctor on a hospital staff. [OFr. *externe* < Lat. *externus,* external.]

ex·ter·nal (ĭk-stûr′nəl) *adj.* **1.** Pertaining to, existing on, or connected with the outside or an outer part; exterior. **2.** Suitable for application to the outside. **3.** Existing independently of the mind: *external objects.* **4.** Acting or coming from the outside: *external pressures.* **5.** Of or pertaining to outward appearance; superficial. **6.** Of or pertaining to foreign affairs or foreign countries. *—n.* **1.** An exterior part or surface. **2. externals. a.** External circumstances. **b.** Outward appearances. [ME < Lat. *externus,* outward.] **—ex·ter′nal·ly** *adv.*

ex·ter·nal-com·bus·tion engine (ĭk-stûr′nəl-kəm-bŭs′chən) *n.* An engine, such as a steam engine, in which the fuel is burned outside the engine cylinder.

external ear *n.* The portion of the ear including the auricle and the external acoustic meatus.

ex·ter·nal·ism (ĭk-stûr′nə-lĭz′əm) *n.* Excessive concern with externals. **—ex·ter′nal·ist** *n.*

ex·ter·nal·i·ty (ĕk′stər-năl′ĭ-tē) *n., pl.* **-ties. 1.** The condition or quality of being external or externalized. **2.** Something that is external.

ex·ter·nal·ize (ĭk-stûr′nə-līz′) *tr.v.* **-ized, -iz·ing, -iz·es. 1. a.** To make external. **b.** To manifest externally. **2.** To attribute to outside causes. **—ex·ter′nal·i·za′tion** *n.*

ex·ter·o·cep·tor (ĕk′stə-rō-sĕp′tər) *n.* A sense organ receiving and responding to external stimuli. [Lat. *exter,* outside + RECEPTOR.] **—ex′ter·o·cep′tive** *adj.*

ex·ter·ri·to·ri·al (ĕks′tĕr-ĭ-tôr′ē-əl, -tōr′) *adj.* Extraterritorial. **—ex′ter·ri·to′ri·al′i·ty** (-ăl′ĭ-tē) *n.* **—ex′ter·ri·to′ri·al·ly** *adv.*

ex·tinct (ĭk-stĭngkt′) *adj.* **1.** Extinguished or inactive: *an extinct volcano.* **2.** No longer existing or living. **3.** Lacking a claimant; void: *an extinct title.* **4.** No longer in use: *an extinct custom.* [ME < Lat. *extinguere,* to extinguish.]

ex·tinc·tion (ĭk-stĭngk′shən) *n.* **1.** The act of extinguishing or making extinct. **2.** The fact or condition of being extinguished or extinct.

ex·tinc·tive (ĭk-stĭngk′tĭv) *adj.* Tending to extinguish or make extinct.

ex·tin·guish (ĭk-stĭng′gwĭsh) *tr.v.* **-guished, -guish·ing, -guish·es. 1.** To put out (a fire, for example); quench. **2.** To put an end to; destroy. **3.** To obscure; eclipse. **4.** *Law.* **a.** To settle or discharge (a debt). **b.** To nullify. [Lat. *extinguere* : *ex-,* out + *stinguere,* to quench.] **—ex·tin′guish·a·ble** *adj.* **—ex·tin′guish·ment** *n.*

ex·tin·guish·er (ĭk-stĭng′gwĭ-shər) *n.* One that extinguishes, esp.: **a.** A small metal cone on a long handle, used for snuffing out candles. **b.** Any of various portable mechanical devices for spraying and extinguishing a fire with chemicals.

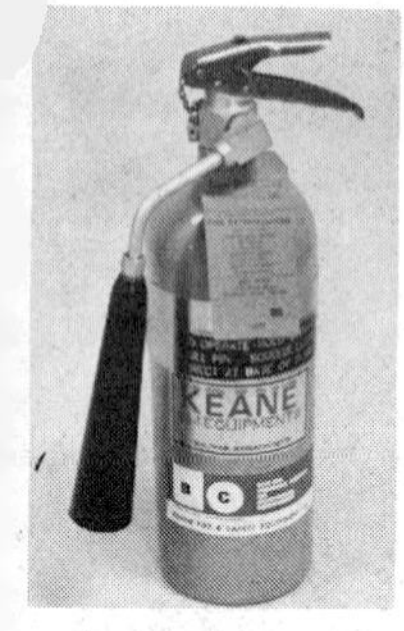

extinguisher
Fire extinguisher

ex·tir·pate (ĕk′stər-pāt′) *tr.v.* **-pat·ed, -pat·ing, -pates. 1.** To pull up by the roots. **2.** To destroy; exterminate. **3.** To remove by surgery. [Lat. *extirpare, extirpat-,* to root out : *ex-,* out + *stirps,* root.] **—ex′tir·pa′tion** *n.* **—ex′tir·pa′tive** *adj.* **—ex′tir·pa′tor** *n.*

ex·tol also **ex·toll** (ĭk-stōl′) *tr.v.* **-tolled, -tol·ling, -tols** also **-tolled, -toll·ing, -tolls.** To praise lavishly. [ME *extollen* < Lat. *extollere,* to lift up : *ex-,* up from + *tollere,* to lift.] **—ex·tol′ler** *n.* **—ex·tol′ment** *n.*

ex·tort (ĭk-stôrt′) *tr.v.* **-tort·ed, -tort·ing, -torts.** To obtain from another by coercion or intimidation. [Lat. *extorquēre, extort-,* to wrench out : *ex-,* out + *torquēre,* to twist.] **—ex·tort′er** *n.* **—ex·tor′tive** *adj.*

ex·tor·tion (ĭk-stôr′shən) *n.* **1.** The act or an instance of extorting. **2.** The illegal use of one's official position or powers to obtain property, funds, or patronage. **3.** An exorbitant or excessive charge. **4.** Something extorted. **—ex·tor′tion·ar′y** (-shə-nĕr′ē) *adj.* **—ex·tor′tion·ist, ex·tor′tion·er** *n.*

ex·tor·tion·ate (ĭk-stôr′shə-nĭt) *adj.* **1.** Characterized by extortion. **2.** Exorbitant. **—ex·tor′tion·ate·ly** *adv.*

ex·tra (ĕk′strə) *adj.* **1.** More or beyond what is usual, normal, expected, or necessary. **2.** Better than ordinary; superior: *extra fineness.* **3.** Liable to an additional charge. *—n.* **1.** Something more than what is usual or necessary. **2.** Something for which an additional charge is made, as an accessory on an automobile. **3.** A special edition of a newspaper. **4.** An additional or alternate worker. **5.** An actor hired to play a minor part, as in a crowd scene. **6.** Something of exceptional quality. *—adv.* Exceptionally; unusually: *extra dry.* [Prob. short for EXTRAORDINARY.]

extra– or **extro–** *pref.* Outside; beyond: *extraordinary.* [Lat. *extra,* outside < *exterus,* outward.]

ex·tra-base hit (ĕk′strə-bās′) *n. Baseball.* A double, triple, or home run.

ex·tra·cel·lu·lar (ĕk′strə-sĕl′yə-lər) *adj.* Located or occurring outside a cell. **—ex′tra·cel′lu·lar·ly** *adv.*

ex·tra·code (ĕk′strə-kōd′) *n. Computer Sci.* A sequence of machine code instructions used to simulate hardware functions.

ex·tra·cra·ni·al (ĕk′strə-krā′nē-əl) *adj.* Located or occurring outside the cranium.

ex·tract (ĭk-străkt′) *tr.v.* **-tract·ed, -tract·ing, -tracts. 1.** To draw or pull out forcibly. **2. a.** To obtain despite resistance: *extract a promise.* **b.** To draw forth by great effort. **3.** To obtain from a substance by chemical or mechanical action, as by pressure, distillation, or evaporation. **4.** To remove for separate consideration or publication; excerpt. **5.** *Math.* To determine or calculate (the root of a number). *—n.* (ĕk′străkt′). **1.** A passage from a literary work; excerpt. **2.** A concentrated preparation of the essential constituents of a food, flavoring, or other substance; concentrate: *maple extract.* [ME *extracten* < Lat. *extrahere,* to draw out : *ex-,* out + *trahere,* to draw.] **—ex·tract′a·ble, ex·tract′i·ble** *adj.* **—ex·tract′or** *n.*

ex·trac·tion (ĭk-străk′shən) *n.* **1.** The act of extracting or the condition of being extracted. **2.** Something obtained by extracting; extract. **3.** Origin; lineage: *of Asian extraction.*

ex·trac·tive (ĭk-străk′tĭv) *adj.* **1.** Used in or obtained by extraction. **2.** Capable of being extracted. *—n.* **1.** Something that may be extracted. **2.** The insoluble portion of an extract. **—ex·trac′tive·ly** *adv.*

ex·tra·cur·ric·u·lar (ĕk′strə-kə-rĭk′yə-lər) *adj.* **1.** Being outside the regular curriculum of a school or college. **2.** Outside the usual duties of a job or profession.

ex·tra·dit·a·ble (ĕk′strə-dī′tə-bəl) *adj.* **1.** Subject to extradition. **2.** Making liable to extradition: *an extraditable crime.*

ex·tra·dite (ĕk′strə-dīt′) *tr.v.* **-dit·ed, -dit·ing, -dites. 1.** To surrender to extradition. **2.** To obtain as a result of the extradition of. [Back-formation < EXTRADITION.]

ex·tra·di·tion (ĕk′strə-dĭsh′ən) *n.* The legal surrender of an alleged criminal to the jurisdiction of another state, country, or government for trial. [Fr. : Lat. *ex-,* out + *traditio,* surrender.]

ex·tra·dos (ĕk′strə-dŏs′, -dō′, -dŏs′) *n., pl.* **ex·tra·dos** (-dōz′) or **ex·tra·dos·es.** The upper or exterior curve of an arch. [Fr. : Lat. *extra,* outside + Fr. *dos,* back.]

ex·tra·ga·lac·tic (ĕk′strə-gə-lăk′tĭk) *adj.* Located or originating beyond the galaxy.

ex·tra·he·pat·ic (ĕk′strə-hĭ-păt′ĭk) *adj.* Located or occurring outside the liver.

ex·tra·ju·di·cial (ĕk′strə-jo͞o-dĭsh′əl) *adj.* **1.** Outside of the authority of a court. **2.** Outside of usual judicial proceedings. **—ex′tra·ju·di′cial·ly** *adv.*

ex·tra·le·gal (ĕk′strə-lē′gəl) *adj.* Not governed or permitted by law. **—ex′tra·le′gal·ly** *adv.*

ex·tra·mar·i·tal (ĕk′strə-măr′ĭ-tl) *adj.* Adulterous.

ex·tra·mun·dane (ĕk′strə-mŭn-dān′, -mŭn′dān′) *adj.* Occurring or existing outside of the physical world or universe.

ex·tra·mu·ral (ĕk′strə-myo͝or′əl) *adj.* Occurring or situated outside of the walls or boundaries, as of a community.

ex·tra·ne·ous (ĭk-strā′nē-əs) *adj.* **1.** Coming from the outside. **2.** Not essential or vital; accidental. **3.** Irrelevant. [Lat. *extraneus* < *extra,* outside.] **—ex·tra′ne·ous·ly** *adv.* **—ex·tra′ne·ous·ness** *n.*

ex·tra·nu·cle·ar (ĕk′strə-no͞o′klē-ər, -nyo͞o′-) *adj.* Located or occurring outside a nucleus.

ex·traor·di·nar·y (ĭk-strôr′dn-ĕr′ē, ĕk′strə-ôr′-) *adj.* **1.** Beyond what is ordinary or usual. **2.** Highly exceptional; remarkable. **3.** Used for a special service or occasion. **—ex·traor′di·nar′i·ly** (-âr′ə-lē) *adv.*

ex·trap·o·late (ĭk-străp′ə-lāt′) *v.* **-lat·ed, -lat·ing, -lates.** *—tr.* **1.** *Math.* To estimate (a value or values of a function) for values of the argument not used in the process of estimation; infer (a value or values) from known values. **2.** To infer or estimate by extending or projecting known information. *—intr.* To engage in the process of extrapolating. [EXTRA- + (INTER)POLATE.] **—ex·trap′o·la′tion** *n.* **—ex·trap′o·la′tive** *adj.* **—ex·trap′o·la·tor** *n.*

ex·tra·sen·so·ry (ĕk′strə-sĕn′sə-rē) *adj.* Outside the normal range or bounds of the senses.

ex·tra·sys·to·le (ĕk′strə-sĭs′tə-lē) *n. Med.* A premature contraction of the heart.

ex·tra·ter·res·tri·al (ĕk′strə-tə-rĕs′trē-əl) *adj.* Originating, located, or occurring outside the earth or its atmosphere.

ex·tra·ter·ri·to·ri·al (ĕk′strə-tĕr′ĭ-tôr′ē-əl, -tōr′-) *adj.* **1.** Located outside territorial boundaries. **2.** Of or pertaining to persons exempt from the legal jurisdiction of the country in which they reside. **—ex′tra·ter′ri·to′ri·al·ly** *adv.*

ex·tra·ter·ri·to·ri·al·i·ty (ĕk′strə-tĕr′ĭ-tôr′ē-ăl′ĭ-tē, -tōr′-) *n.* Exemption from local legal jurisdiction, such as is granted to foreign diplomats.

ex·tra·u·ter·ine (ĕk′strə-yo͞o′tər-ĭn, -tə-rīn′) *adj.* Located or occurring outside the uterus: *extrauterine pregnancy.*

ex·trav·a·gance (ĭk-străv′ə-gəns) *n.* **1.** The quality of being extravagant. **2.** An immoderate expense or display. **3.** Something extravagant.

ex·trav·a·gan·cy (ĭk-străv′ə-gən-sē) *n., pl.* **-cies.** Extravagance.

ex·trav·a·gant (ĭk-străv′ə-gənt) *adj.* **1.** Given to lavish or imprudent expenditure. **2.** Exceeding reasonable bounds; unrestrained: *extravagant demands.* **3.** Extremely abundant; profuse: *extravagant vegetation.* **4.** Unreasonably high; exorbitant. **5.** *Archaic.* Straying beyond limits or bounds; wandering. [ME *extravagaunt,* unusual < Med. Lat. *extravagans,* pr.part. of *extravagari,* to wander : Lat. *extra,* outside

+ Lat. *vagari,* to wander.] —**ex·trav'a·gant·ly** *adv.* —**ex·trav'a·gant·ness** *n.*

ex·trav·a·gan·za (ĭk-străv'ə-găn'zə) *n.* **1.** A light orchestral composition marked by freedom and diversity of form, often with burlesque elements. **2.** An elaborate, spectacular entertainment. [Ital. *estravaganza* < *estravagant,* extravagant < Med. Lat. *extravagans.*]

ex·trav·a·gate (ĭk-străv'ə-gāt') *intr.v.* **-gat·ed, -gat·ing, -gates. 1.** To wander or roam at will; stray. **2.** To exceed reasonable limits or bounds. [Med. Lat. *extravagari, extravagat-,* to wander. —see EXTRAVAGANT.]

ex·trav·a·sate (ĭk-străv'ə-sāt') *v.* **-sat·ed, -sat·ing, -sates.** —*tr.* **1.** *Pathol.* To force the flow of (blood or lymph) out into surrounding tissue. **2.** *Geol.* To cause (molten lava) to pour forth from a volcanic vent. —*intr.* **1.** *Pathol.* To exude into the surrounding tissues. **2.** *Geol.* To erupt.

ex·trav·a·sa·tion (ĭk-străv'ə-sā'shən) *n.* **1.** The act of extravasating or the condition of being extravasated. **2.** The matter extravasated.

ex·tra·vas·cu·lar (ĕk'strə-văs'kyə-lər) *adj.* **1.** Located or occurring outside a blood vessel or the vascular system. **2.** Lacking vessels; nonvascular.

ex·tra·ve·hic·u·lar activity (ĕk'strə-vē-hĭk'yə-lər) *n.* Activity or maneuvers performed by an astronaut outside a spacecraft in space.

ex·tra·ver·sion (ĕk'strə-vûr'zhən) *n.* Variant of **extroversion.**

ex·tra·vert (ĕk'strə-vûrt') *n.* Variant of **extrovert.**

ex·treme (ĭk-strēm') *adj.* **1.** Outermost or farthest; most remote in any direction: *the extreme edge of the field.* **2.** Final; last. **3.** Being in or attaining the greatest or highest degree; very intense: *extreme pleasure; extreme degradation.* **4.** Extending far beyond the norm: *an extreme conservative.* **5.** Of the greatest severity; drastic. —*n.* **1.** The greatest or utmost degree or point. **2.** Either of the two things situated at opposite ends of a range: *the extremes of boiling and freezing.* **3.** An extreme condition. **4.** A drastic or immoderate expedient: *resorted to extremes in the emergency.* **5.** *Math.* The first or last term of a ratio or series. **6.** *Logic.* The major or minor term of a syllogism. [ME < OFr. < Lat. *extremus.*] —**ex·treme'ly** *adv.* —**ex·treme'ness** *n.*

extremely high frequency *n.* A radio-frequency band with a range of 30,000 to 300,000 megahertz.

extreme unction *n. Rom. Cath. Ch.* The sacrament in which a priest anoints and prays for one in danger of death.

ex·trem·ist (ĭk-strē'mĭst) *n.* A person who advocates or resorts to extreme measures, esp. in politics. —**ex·trem'ism** *n.*

ex·trem·i·ty (ĭk-strĕm'ĭ-tē) *n., pl.* **-ties. 1.** The outermost or farthest point or portion. **2.** The greatest or utmost degree: *the extremity of despair.* **3.** Grave danger, necessity, or distress. **4.** A moment at which death or ruin is imminent. **5.** An extreme or severe measure. **6.** A bodily limb or appendage. **7.** A hand or a foot.

ex·tri·cate (ĕk'strĭ-kāt') *tr.v.* **-cat·ed, -cat·ing, -cates. 1.** To release from an entanglement or difficulty; disengage. **2.** *Archaic.* To distinguish from something related. [Lat. *extricare, extricat-* : *ex-,* out + *tricae,* hindrances, perplexities.] —**ex'tri·ca·ble** (-kə-bəl) *adj.* —**ex'tri·ca'tion** *n.*

ex·trin·sic (ĭk-strĭn'sĭk, -zĭk) *adj.* **1.** Not forming an essential part of a thing; extraneous. **2.** Not inherent; accessory. **3.** Originating from the outside; external. [LLat. *extrinsecus,* from outside.] —**ex·trin'si·cal·ly** *adv.*

Synonyms: *extrinsic, extraneous, foreign, alien.* These adjectives mean not inherently part of a thing or not compatible with it. What is *extrinsic* is either literally apart from the thing in question or derived from something external to it: *Sympathy is extrinsic to impartial judgment.* What is *extraneous* is not an integral part and is inessential or harmful: *extraneous matter in foodstuffs; an issue extraneous to the debate.* Something *foreign* is markedly different from the thing in question or out of place: *a technique foreign to classical ballet.* What is *alien* is generally irreconcilably different or adverse: *an economic theory alien to the spirit of capitalism.*

extrinsic factor *n.* Vitamin B_{12}.

extro– *pref.* Variant of **extra-.**

ex·trorse (ĕk'strôrs') *adj. Bot.* Facing outward; turned away from the axis. Used esp. of anthers. [LLat. *extrorsus,* turned outward : *extra,* outside + *versus,* p.part of *vertere,* to turn.]

ex·tro·ver·sion also **ex·tra·ver·sion** (ĕk'strə-vûr'zhən) *n.* **1.** Interest in one's environment or in others as opposed to or to the exclusion of oneself. **2.** A turning inside out, as of an organ or part. —**ex'tro·ver'sive** *adj.* —**ex'tro·ver'sive·ly** *adv.*

ex·tro·vert also **ex·tra·vert** (ĕk'strə-vûrt') *n.* An individual interested in others or in the environment as opposed to or to the exclusion of self. [EXTRO- + Lat. *vertere,* to turn.] —**ex'tro·vert'ed** *adj.*

ex·trude (ĭk-strōōd') *v.* **-trud·ed, -trud·ing, -trudes.** —*tr.* **1.** To push or thrust out. **2.** To shape by forcing through a die. —*intr.* To protrude or project. [Lat. *extrudere,* to thrust out : *ex-,* out + *trudere,* to thrust.]

ex·tru·sion (ĭk-strōō'zhən) *n.* **1.** The act or process of extruding. **2.** Something produced by extruding. [Med. Lat. *extrusio* < Lat. *extrudere,* to thrust out. —see EXTRUDE.]

ex·tru·sive (ĭk-strōō'sĭv, -zĭv) *adj.* **1.** Tending to extrude. **2.** *Geol.* Derived from magma. Used of rock.

ex·u·ber·ance (ĭg-zōō'bər-əns) *n.* **1.** The condition or quality of being exuberant. **2.** An exuberant act or expression.

ex·u·ber·ant (ĭg-zōō'bər-ənt) *adj.* **1.** Full of unrestrained enthusiasm or joy. **2.** Lavish; overflowing. **3.** Growing or producing abundantly; luxuriant. [ME, overabundant < Lat. *exuberans,* pr.part. of *exuberare,* to exuberate.] —**ex·u'ber·ant·ly** *adv.*

ex·u·ber·ate (ĭg-zōō'bə-rāt') *intr.v.* **-at·ed, -at·ing, -ates. 1.** To be exuberant. **2.** *Archaic.* To abound or overflow. [Lat. *exuberare* : *ex-* (intensive) + *uberare,* to be fruitful (< *uber,* fertile).]

Usage: In its newer sense of "to feel or experience exuberance," this word is unacceptable to a large majority of the Usage Panel.

ex·u·date (ĕks'yōō-dāt') *n.* An exuded substance. [Lat. *exudatum,* neuter p.part. of *exudare,* to exude.]

ex·u·da·tion (ĕks'yōō-dā'shən) *n.* **1.** The act or an instance of exuding. **2.** An exudate. —**ex'u·da'tive** *adj.*

ex·ude (ĭg-zōōd', ĭk-sōōd') *v.* **-ud·ed, -ud·ing, -udes.** —*intr.* To ooze forth. —*tr.* **1.** To discharge or emit gradually. **2.** To exhibit in abundance: *exude menace.* [Lat. *exudare* : *ex-,* out + *sudare,* to sweat.]

ex·ult (ĭg-zŭlt') *intr.v.* **-ult·ed, -ult·ing, -ults. 1.** To rejoice greatly; be jubilant or triumphant. **2.** *Obs.* To leap upward, esp. for joy. [Lat. *exultare,* freq. of *exsilire,* to spring out : *ex-,* out + *salire,* to leap.] —**ex·ul'tance, ex·ul'tan·cy** *n.* —**ex·ult'ing·ly** *adv.*

ex·ul·tant (ĭg-zŭl'tənt) *adj.* Marked by great joy or jubilation; triumphant. —**ex·ul'tant·ly** *adv.*

ex·ul·ta·tion (ĕk'səl-tā'shən, ĕg'zəl-) *n.* The act or condition of exulting.

ex·urb (ĕk'sûrb') *n.* A region lying beyond the suburbs of a city, inhabited principally by those who are well-to-do. [EX- + (SUB)URB).] —**ex·ur'ban** *adj.*

ex·ur·ban·ite (ĕk-sûr'bə-nīt, ĕg-zûr'-) *n.* A resident of an exurb.

ex·ur·bi·a (ĕk-sûr'bē-ə, ĕg-zûr'-) *n.* A typically exurban area.

ex·u·vi·ae (ĭg-zōō'vē-ē') *pl.n.* The cast skins or coverings of various animals, esp. the larvae and nymphs of insects. [Lat. < *exuere,* to take off.] —**ex·u'vi·al** (-vē-əl) *adj.*

ex·u·vi·ate (ĭg-zōō'vē-āt') *v.* **-at·ed, -at·ing, -ates.** —*tr.* To shed or cast off (a covering). —*intr.* To shed or cast off exuviae. [< EXUVIAE.] —**ex·u'vi·a'tion** *n.*

-ey *suff.* Variant of **-y**[1].

ey·as (ī'əs) *n.* A nestling hawk or falcon, esp. one to be trained for falconry. [Alteration of ME *a nias,* an eyas < OFr. *niais* < Lat. *nidus,* nest.]

eye (ī) *n.* **1.** An organ of vision or of light sensitivity. **2. a.** The vertebrate organ of vision; either of a pair of hollow structures located in fixed bony sockets of the skull, functioning together or independently, each having a lens capable of focusing incident light on an internal photosensitive retina. **b.** The external, visible portion of this organ together with its associated structures, such as the eyelids, eyelashes, and eyebrows. **c.** The pigmented iris of this organ. **3.** The faculty of seeing; vision. **4.** The ability to make intellectual or aesthetic judgments: *a good eye for fashion.* **5. a.** A look; gaze. **b.** A way of regarding something; point of view. **6.** Something suggestive of an eye in appearance, esp.: **a.** An opening in a needle. **b.** A circular marking on a peacock feather. **c.** A loop, as in a hook. **7.** *Bot.* **a.** A bud on a twig or tuber: *the eye of a potato.* **b.** The often differently colored center of the corolla of some flowers. **8.** *Meteorol.* The circular area of relative calm at the center of a cyclone. **9.** Something construed as a center or focal point. **10.** *Informal.* A detective. —*tr.v.* **eyed, eye·ing** or **ey·ing, eyes. 1.** To concentrate the eyes on. **2.** To watch closely. **3.** To supply with an eye. —***idioms.*** **an eye for an eye.** Punishment requiring that the offender suffer what he has caused another to suffer. **catch (someone's) eye.** *Informal.* To attract someone's attention. **eye to eye.** In agreement. **give (someone) the eye.** *Informal.* To look at with admiration or invitation. **in a pig's eye.** *Slang.* Never; under no condition. **my eye.** *Slang.* In no way; not at all. **with an eye to.** With a view to. [ME < OE *ēage.*]

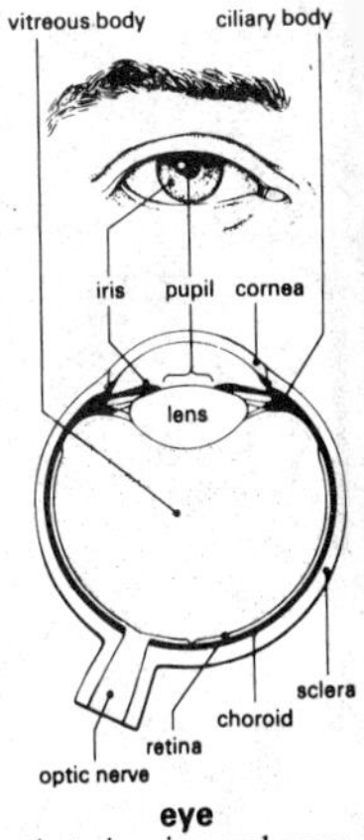

eye
Anterior view and cross section of the human eye

eye·ball (ī'bôl') *n.* **1.** The ball-shaped portion of the eye enclosed by the socket and eyelids. **2.** The eye itself. —*tr.v.* **-balled, -ball·ing, -balls.** *Informal.* To look over carefully; scrutinize.

eye·ball-to-eye·ball (ī'bôl'tə-ī'bôl') *adj. & adv. Informal.* Face to face.

eye bank *n.* A place at which corneas taken from human cadavers immediately after death are stored and preserved for subsequent transplantation to individuals with corneal defects.

eye bath *n.* Eyecup.

eye·bolt (ī'bōlt') *n.* A bolt having a looped head designed to receive a hook or rope.

eye·bright (ī'brīt') *n.* Any of several plants of the genus *Euphrasia,* esp. *E. officinalis,* native to the Old World, having small white and purplish flowers.

eye·brow (ī'brou') *n.* **1.** The bony ridge extending over the eye. **2.** The arch of short hairs covering this ridge.
eyebrow pencil *n.* A cosmetic pencil used for extending or darkening the eyebrows.
eye contact *n.* Direct visual contact with another's eyes.
eye·cup (ī'kŭp') *n.* A small cup with a rim contoured to fit the orbit of the eye, used for applying a liquid medicine or wash to the eye.
eyed (īd) *adj.* Having eyes of a specified number or kind: *blue-eyed.*
eye dialect *n.* The use of misspellings, such as *wimmin* for *women,* to represent dialectal or nonstandard speech.
eye·drop·per (ī'drŏp'ər) *n.* A dropper for administering liquid eye medicines.
eye·ful (ī'fo͝ol') *n.* **1.** A complete view. **2.** One that is pleasing to the sight, esp. a beautiful woman. **3.** Sufficient observation to reveal more than expected or enough to satisfy.
eye·glass (ī'glăs') *n.* **1. a. eyeglasses.** Glasses (sense 4.b.). **b.** A monocle. **2.** An eyepiece. **3.** An eyecup.
eye·hole (ī'hōl') *n.* **1.** The orbit of the eye. **2.** A peephole.
eye·hook (ī'ho͝ok') *n.* A hook attached to a ring at the end of a rope or chain.
eye·lash (ī'lăsh') *n.* **1.** One of a row of short hairs fringing the edge of the eyelid. **2.** A row of the hairs fringing the eyelid.

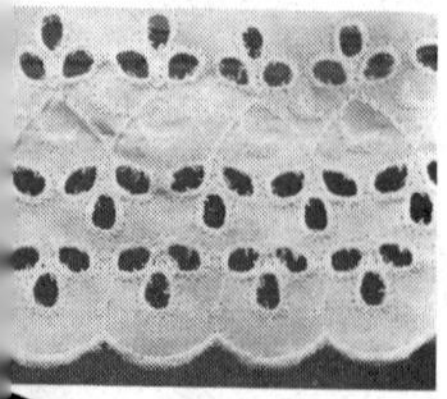

eyelet

eye·let (ī'lĭt) *n.* **1. a.** A small hole or perforation, usually rimmed with metal, cord, fabric, or leather, used for fastening with a cord or hook. **b.** A metal ring designed to reinforce such a hole; grommet. **2.** A small hole edged with embroidered stitches as part of a design. **3.** A peephole. **4.** A small eye. [ME *oilet* < OFr. *oillet,* dim. of *oil,* eye < Lat. *oculus.*]
eye·lid (ī'lĭd') *n.* Either of two folds of skin and muscle that can be closed over an eye.
eye·lin·er (ī'lī'nər) *n.* Make-up used to outline the eyes.
eye opener *n.* **1.** A startling or shocking revelation. **2.** A drink of liquor, taken to stimulate, esp. upon awakening.
eye·piece (ī'pēs') *n.* The lens or lens group closest to the eye in an optical instrument; ocular.
eye rhyme *n.* A false rhyme consisting of words, such as *lint* and *pint,* with similar spellings but different sounds.
eye shadow *n.* A cosmetic available in various colors or tints and applied esp. to the eyelids to enhance the eyes.
eye·shot (ī'shŏt') *n.* The range of vision; sight.
eye·sight (ī'sīt') *n.* **1.** The faculty of sight; vision. **2.** The range of vision; view.
eyes-on·ly (īz'ŏn'lē) *adj.* Of or relating to private or top-secret information: "*a secret eyes-only memo*" (Jeff Kamen).
eye·sore (ī'sôr', ī'sōr') *n.* Something that is offensive to the sight.
eye·spot (ī'spŏt') *n.* **1.** A light-sensitive, pigmented area in certain algae, protozoans, and other organisms. **2.** A rounded, eyelike marking, as on the tail of a peacock.
eye·stalk (ī'stôk') *n.* A movable, stalklike structure bearing at its tip one of the eyes of a crab or similar crustacean.
eye·strain (ī'strān') *n.* Fatigue of the ciliary muscle or of the extrinsic muscles of the eyeball caused by refractive errors or imbalance of the ocular muscles and characterized by pain in the eyes, lacrimation, headache, nausea, dizziness, or other reflex symptoms.
eye·tooth (ī'to͞oth') *n.* A canine of the upper jaw.
eye·wash (ī'wŏsh', ī'wôsh') *n.* **1.** A medicated solution applied as a wash for the eyes. **2.** Misleading or meaningless language.
eye·wink (ī'wĭngk') *n.* **1.** A wink of the eye. **2.** An instant. **3.** *Obs.* A glance.
eye·wit·ness (ī'wĭt'nəs) *n.* A person who has personally seen someone or something and can bear witness to the fact.
ey·ing (ī'ĭng) *v.* A present participle of **eye**.
ey·ra (âr'ə) *n.* A reddish-brown color phase of the jaguarondi, a wild cat of tropical America. [Am. Sp. (South America) *eirá,* a kind of fox < Guarani *eirara.*]
eyre (âr) *n. Obs.* **1.** A circuit; itineration. **2.** A circuit court held by itinerant royal justices in medieval England. [ME < OFr. *eire* < Lat. *iter,* journey.]
ey·rie (âr'ē, îr'ē) *n.* Variant of **aerie**.
ey·rir (ā'rîr') *n., pl.* **au·rar** (ou'rär', œ'rär'). See table at **currency**. [Icel. < ON, money, prob. < Lat. *aurum,* gold.]
E·ze·ki·el (ĭ-zē'kē-əl) *n.* **1.** A major Hebrew prophet of the 6th century B.C. **2.** See table at **Bible**. [Heb. *Yĕḥezqēl.*]
Ez·ra (ĕz'rə) *n.* **1.** A Hebrew high priest of the 5th century B.C. **2.** See table at **Bible**. [Heb. *'Ezrā.*]

F

1 2 Phoenician — 3 Greek — 4 5 6 Roman — 7 8 Medieval — 9 10 11 12 Modern

Around 1000 B.C. the Phoenicians and other Semitic peoples began to use graphic signs to represent individual speech sounds instead of syllables or words. They used a symbol (1,2) which is the ancestor of the letters U, V, W, and Y as well as F to represent the sound of the semivowel "w" and called it *wāw,* their word for "hook." The Greeks, adapting the Phoenician alphabet, retained the phonetic value of *wāw,* changed its shape (3), and called it *digamma* because it looked like one gamma on top of another. This sound was lost in Greek at an early date, and *digamma* no longer appears in the Greek alphabet. The Romans borrowed the alphabet from the Greeks via the Etruscans. They used *digamma* to represent the sound of the consonant "f" and adapted the shape for monumental inscriptions. Monumental script (6) is the prototype of modern capital letters (9,10). Medieval scribes adapted the Roman capitals to being quickly written on paper, parchment, and vellum. These uncial and cursive minuscules (7,8) are the prototypes of modern lower-case letters, both written and printed (12,11).

f

f or **F** (ĕf) *n., pl.* **f's** or **F's. 1.** The sixth letter of the modern English alphabet. **2.** Any of the speech sounds represented by the letter *f.* **3. F** A failing grade in schoolwork. **4. F** *Mus.* **a.** The fourth tone in the scale of C major or the sixth tone in the relative minor scale. **b.** The key or a scale in which F is the tonic. **c.** A written or printed note representing this tone. **d.** A string, key, or pipe tuned to the pitch of this tone. **F** The symbol for the element fluorine.

fa (fä) *n.* The fourth tone of the diatonic scale in solmization. [ME < Med. Lat. —see GAMUT.]

Fa·bi·an (fā′bē-ən) *adj.* **1.** Of or relating to the caution and avoidance of direct confrontation typical of the Roman general Quintus Fabius Maximus, who defeated Hannibal by the use of this strategy. **2.** Of, relating to, or being a member of the Fabian Society, which was committed to gradual rather than revolutionary means for spreading socialist principles. **—Fa′bi·an** *n.* **—Fa′bi·an·ism** *n.* **—Fa′bi·an·ist** *n.*

fa·ble (fā′bəl) *n.* **1.** A narrative making an edifying or cautionary point and often employing as characters animals that speak and act like human beings. **2.** A story about legendary persons and exploits. **3.** A falsehood; lie. *—v.* **-bled, -bling, -bles.** *—tr.* To recount as if true. *—intr. Archaic.* To compose fables. [ME < OFr. < Lat. *fabula* < *fari,* to speak.] **—fa′bler** *n.*

fa·bled (fā′bəld) *adj.* **1.** Made known or famous by fables; legendary. **2.** Existing only in fables; fictitious.

fab·li·au (făb′lē-ō′) *n., pl.* **-li·aux** (-lē-ō′, -ōz′). A medieval verse tale characterized by comic and ribald treatment of themes drawn from life. [Fr. < OFr. *fabliaux,* pl. of *fablel,* dim. of *fable,* fable.]

fab·ric (făb′rĭk) *n.* **1.** A material structure consisting of connected parts. **2.** A complex underlying structure: *the fabric of civilized society.* **3.** A method or style of construction. **4. a.** A cloth produced esp. by knitting, weaving, or felting fibers. **b.** The texture or quality of such cloth. [ME *fabryke* < OFr. *fabrique* < Lat. *fabrica* < *faber,* workman, artificer.]

fab·ric·a·ble (făb′rĭ-kə-bəl) *adj.* Capable of being molded: *a fabricable alloy.* **—fab′ric·a·bil′i·ty** *n.*

fab·ri·cant (făb′rĭ-kənt) *n. Archaic.* A manufacturer.

fab·ri·cate (făb′rĭ-kāt′) *tr.v.* **-cat·ed, -cat·ing, -cates. 1.** To make; create. **2.** To construct by combining or assembling. **3.** To make up in order to deceive. [ME *fabricaten* < Lat. *fabricari,* to make < *fabrica,* fabric.] **—fab′ri·ca′tion** *n.* **—fab′ri·ca′tor** *n.*

Fab·ry's disease (făb′rēz) *n.* A hereditary disease of fat metabolism characterized by impaired functioning of the kidneys. [After Johannes *Fabry* (1860–1930).]

fab·u·list (făb′yə-lĭst) *n.* **1.** A composer of fables. **2.** An inventor or teller of falsehoods. [OFr. *fabuliste* < Lat. *fabula,* fable.]

fab·u·lous (făb′yə-ləs) *adj.* **1.** Of the nature of a fable or myth; legendary. **2.** Told of or celebrated in fables or legends. **3.** Barely credible; astonishing: *the fabulous endurance of a marathon runner.* **4.** *Informal.* Extremely pleasing or successful: *a fabulous vacation.* [ME < Lat. *fabulosus* < *fabula,* fable.] **—fab′u·lous·ly** *adv.* **—fab′u·lous·ness** *n.*

fa·çade also **fa·cade** (fə-säd′) *n.* **1.** *Archit.* The face of a building, esp. the principal face. **2.** An artificial or deceptive front. [Fr. < Ital. *facciata* < *faccia,* face < Lat. *facies.*]

façade
Façade of the Alamo, San Antonio, Texas

face (fās) *n.* **1.** The surface of the front of the head from the top of the forehead to the base of the chin and from ear to ear. **2.** The arrangement or expression of the features of the face; countenance. **3.** A contorted facial expression; grimace. **4.** The outward appearance: *the face of the city.* **5.** Value or standing in the eyes of others; prestige: *lose face.* **6.** Effrontery; impudence. **7.** The most significant or prominent surface of an object, esp.: **a.** The surface presented to view; front. **b.** A façade. **c.** The outer surface: *the face of the earth.* **d.** A marked side: *the face of a clock.* **e.** The right side, as of fabric. **8.** *Geom.* A planar surface bounding a solid. **9.** Any of the surfaces of a rock or crystal. **10.** The end, as of a mine or tunnel, at which work is advancing. **11.** The appearance and geological surface features of an area of land; topography. **12.** *Printing.* Typeface. *—v.* **faced, fac·ing, fac·es.** *—tr.* **1.** To occupy a position with the face toward. **2.** To front upon: *a window facing the south.* **3. a.** To confront with complete awareness: *facing facts.* **b.** To overcome by confronting boldly or bravely: *"What this generation must do is face its problems"* (John F. Kennedy). **4.** To be certain to encounter; have in store: *The unskilled youth faces a difficult life.* **5.** To cause (troops) to change direction by giving a command. **6.** To turn (a playing card) so that the face is up. **7.** To furnish with a surface or cover of a different material: *bronze faced with gold foil.* **8.** To line or trim the edge of, esp. with contrasting material. **9.** To treat the surface of so as to smooth. *—intr.* **1.** To be turned or placed with the front toward a specified direction. **2.** To turn the face in a specified direction. **—*phrasal verbs.*** **face down.** To overcome or prevail over by a stare or a resolute manner. **face off.** To start play in hockey, lacrosse, and other games by releasing the puck or ball between two opposing players. **face out.** To endure to the end. **face up to. 1.** To recognize the existence or importance of. **2.** To confront bravely. **—*idioms.*** **face the music.** *Slang.* To accept the unpleasant consequences esp. of one's own actions. **face to face. 1.** In each other's presence; in direct communication: *spoke face to face.* **2.** Directly confronting: *face to face with death.* **in the face of.** Despite the opposition of; notwithstanding. **on the face of it.** From its appearance alone; apparently. **show (one's) face.** To make an appearance. **to (one's) face.** In the view or hearing of: *accused the offender to his face.* [ME < OFr. < Lat. *facies.*] **—face′a·ble** *adj.* **—face′less** *adj.*

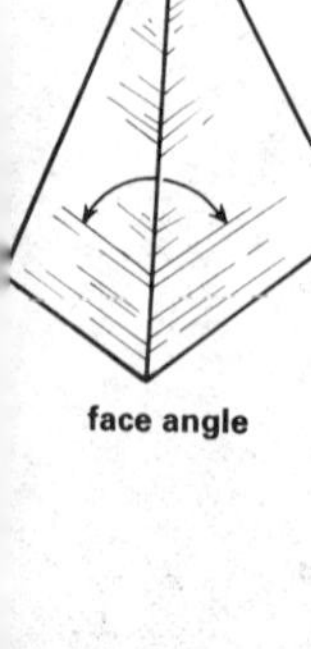

face angle

face angle *n.* The angle formed between two edges of a polyhedral angle.

face card *n.* A king, queen, or jack of a deck of playing cards.

face cloth *n.* A washcloth.

face-hard·en (fās′här′dn) *tr.v.* **-ened, -en·ing, -ens.** To harden the surface of (a metal).

face-lift·ing (fās′lĭf′tĭng) also **face-lift** (-lĭft′) *n.* **1.** Plastic surgery for tightening facial tissues and improving the appearance of facial skin. **2.** A restyling or modernization, as of a building.

face-off (fās′ôf′, -ŏf′) *n.* **1.** A method of starting play in ice hockey in which an official drops the puck between two opposing players who contend for its control. **2.** A confrontation.

face·plate (fās′plāt′) *n.* **1.** A disk attached to the mandrel of a lathe to hold flat or irregularly shaped work. **2.** The glass front of a cathode-ray tube upon which the image is projected.

fac·er (fā′sər) *n.* **1.** One that faces. **2.** A device used in smoothing or dressing a surface. **3.** *Chiefly Brit.* An unexpected blow or defeat.

face-sav·er (fās′sā′vər) *n.* Something that prevents loss of dignity or self-esteem: *The compromise was a face-saver for the boss.* **—face′-sav′ing** *n.*

fac·et (făs′ĭt) *n.* **1.** Any of the flat polished surfaces cut on a gemstone. **2.** A small planar or rounded smooth surface on a bone or tooth. **3.** One of the lenslike divisions of a compound eye, as of an insect. **4.** An aspect; phase. [Fr. *facette,* dim. of *face,* face < OFr.] **—fac′et·ed, fac′et·ted** *adj.*

fa·cete (fə-sēt′) *adj. Archaic.* Facetious; witty. [Lat. *facetus.*]

fa·ce·ti·ae (fə-sē′shē-ē′) *pl.n.* Witty or humorous writings and sayings. [Lat., pl. of *facetia,* jest < *facetus,* witty.]

fa·ce·tious (fə-sē′shəs) *adj.* Playfully jocular; humorous: *a facetious remark.* [OFr. *facetieux* < *facetie,* jest < Lat. *facetia* < *facetus,* witty.] **—fa·ce′tious·ly** *adv.* **—fa·ce′tious·ness** *n.*

face value *n.* **1.** The value printed or written on the face, as of a bill or bond. **2.** The apparent value or significance: *took their compliments at face value.*

fa·cial (fā′shəl) *adj.* Of or concerning the face. *—n.* A treatment for the face, usually consisting of a massage and the application of cosmetic creams. **—fa′cial·ly** *adv.*

facial index *n.* The ratio of facial length to facial width multiplied by 100.

facial nerve *n.* Either of the seventh pair of cranial nerves that supply motor fibers to the facial muscles and sensory fibers to the tastebuds of the anterior portion of the tongue.

-facient *suff.* **1.** Causing; bringing about: *somnifacient.* **2.** Something that causes or brings about: *abortifacient.* [< Lat. *faciēns, facient-,* p.part. of *facere,* to do.]

fa·ci·es (fā′shē-ēz′, -shēz) *n., pl.* **facies. 1.** The general aspect or outward appearance, as of a given growth of flora. **2.** *Geol.* **a.** A part differentiated from other parts in a rock by appearance or composition. **b.** A rock distinguished from related or similar rocks. **c.** A stratigraphic body distinguished from others by appearance or composition. [Lat. *facies,* form, appearance.]

fac·ile (făs′əl) *adj.* **1.** Done or achieved with little effort or difficulty; easy. **2.** Working, acting, or speaking effortlessly; fluent: *a facile speaker.* **3.** Arrived at without due care, effort, or examination; superficial. **4.** Easy and relaxed in manner. **5.** Yielding; compliant. [OFr. < Lat. *facilis* < *facere,* to do.] **—fac′ile·ly** *adv.* **—fac′ile·ness** *n.*

fa·cil·i·tate (fə-sĭl′ĭ-tāt′) *tr.v.* **-tat·ed, -tat·ing, -tates.** To make easier. [< Fr. *faciliter* < Ital. *facilitare* < *facile,* facile < Lat. *facilis.*] **—fa·cil′i·ta′tion** *n.*

fa·cil·i·ty (fə-sĭl′ĭ-tē) *n., pl.* **-ties. 1.** Ease in moving, acting, or doing; aptitude: *"an extreme facility in acquiring new dialects"* (W.H. Hudson). **2.** Readiness to be persuaded; pliability. **3.** Often **facilities.** Something that facilitates an action or process. **4.** The quality of being easy to perform. **5.** Something created to serve a particular function.

fac·ing (fā′sĭng) *n.* **1. a.** A piece of material sewn to the edge of a dress, coat, or other garment as lining or decoration. **b.** Material used for this. **2.** An outer layer or coating applied to a surface for protection or decoration.

fac·sim·i·le (făk-sĭm′ə-lē) *n.* **1.** An exact copy or reproduction, as of a document. **2. a.** A method of transmitting images or printed matter by electronic means. **b.** An image so transmitted. *—adj.* **1.** Of or used to produce facsimiles. **2.** Exactly reproduced; duplicate. [Lat. *fac simile,* make (it) similar.]

facsimile modulation *n.* A method for varying in time the physical properties of a wave in facsimile transmission.

fact (făkt) *n.* **1.** Something done: *an accessory before the fact.* **2.** Something presented as objectively real. **3.** Something that has been objectively verified. **4. a.** Something having real, demonstrable existence. **b.** The quality of being real or actual. **5.** Something that has been done or performed.

6. *Law.* The aspect of a case at law comprising events determined by evidence as distinguished from interpretation of law: *The jury made a finding of fact.* —***idiom.* in (point of) fact.** In reality or in truth; actually. [Lat. *factum,* deed < *factus,* p.part. of *facere,* to do.]

fact-find·ing (făkt′fīn′dĭng) *n.* The discovery or determination of facts or accurate information. —***modifier:*** *a fact-finding committee.* —**fact′-find′er** *n.*

fac·tion (făk′shən) *n.* **1.** A group of persons forming a cohesive, usually contentious minority within a larger group. **2.** Internal dissension; conflict within an organization or nation: *"And whereas our own beloved country . . . is now afflicted with faction and civil war"* (Lincoln). [OFr. < Lat. *factio* < *factus,* p.part. of *facere,* to do.] —**fac′tion·al** *adj.* —**fac′tion·al·ism** *n.* —**fac′tion·al·ly** *adv.*

-faction *suff.* Production; making: *petrifaction.* [ME *-faccioun* < OFr. *-faction* < Lat. *-factio.*]

fac·tious (făk′shəs) *adj.* **1.** Produced or characterized by faction. **2.** Creating or promoting faction; divisive. —**fac′tious·ly** *adv.* —**fac′tious·ness** *n.*

fac·ti·tious (făk-tĭsh′əs) *adj.* **1.** Produced artificially rather than by a natural process. **2.** Lacking authenticity or genuineness; sham: *speculators responsible for the factitious value of some stocks.* [Lat. *facticius* < *facere,* to make.] —**fac·ti′tious·ly** *adv.* —**fac·ti′tious·ness** *n.*

fac·ti·tive (făk′tĭ-tĭv) *adj.* Of or constituting a transitive verb, such as *elect,* that in some constructions takes an objective complement to modify its direct object. [NLat. *factitivus* < Lat. *facere,* to do.] —**fac′ti·tive·ly** *adv.*

fact of life *n.* **1. facts of life.** The basic physiological functions involved in sex and reproduction. **2.** Something unavoidable that must be realized or dealt with.

fac·tor (făk′tər) *n.* **1. a.** One who acts for someone else; agent. **b.** A person or firm that accepts accounts receivable as security for short-term loans. **2.** One that actively contributes to an accomplishment, result, or process. **3.** *Math.* One of two or more quantities that when multiplied together yield a given product: *2 and 3 are factors of 6.* **4.** A gene. —*tr.v.* **-tored, -tor·ing, -tors.** *Math.* To determine or indicate explicitly the factors of. [ME *factour* < OFr. *facteur* < Lat. *factor,* maker < *facere,* to make.] —**fac′tor·a·ble** *adj.* —**fac′tor·ship′** *n.*

fac·tor·age (făk′tər-ĭj) *n.* **1.** The business of a factor. **2.** The commission or fee paid to a factor.

fac·to·ri·al (făk-tôr′ē-əl, -tōr′-) *n.* The product of all the positive integers from 1 to a given number: *4 factorial, usually written 4!, is equal to 24 (1·2·3·4 = 24).* —*adj.* Of or relating to a factor or factorial.

fac·tor·ize (făk′tə-rīz′) *tr.v.* **-ized, -iz·ing, -iz·es.** To factor. —**fac′tor·i·za′tion** *n.*

fac·to·ry (făk′tə-rē) *n., pl.* **-ries. 1.** A building or group of buildings in which goods are manufactured; plant. **2.** A business establishment for commercial agents or factors in a foreign country. [Med. Lat. *factoria,* establishment for factors < Lat. *factor,* factor.]

fac·to·tum (făk-tō′təm) *n.* An employee or assistant who serves in a wide range of capacities. [Med. Lat. *factotum* : Lat. *fac,* imper. of *facere,* to do + Lat. *totum,* everything < *totus,* all.]

fac·tu·al (făk′cho͞o-əl) *adj.* **1.** Of the nature of fact; real. **2.** Of or containing facts. —**fac′tu·al′i·ty** (-ăl′ĭ-tē) *n.* —**fac′tu·al·ly** *adv.* —**fac′tu·al·ness** *n.*

fac·tu·al·ism (făk′cho͞o-ə-lĭz′əm) *n.* Devotion or adherence to fact. —**fac′tu·al·ist** *n.*

fac·u·la (făk′yə-lə) *n., pl.* **-lae** (-lē′). Any of various large bright spots or streaks on the sun's photosphere, most conspicuous at the solar edge or near sunspots. [Lat., small torch, dim. of *fax,* torch.]

fac·ul·ta·tive (făk′əl-tā′tĭv) *adj.* **1.** Of or pertaining to a mental faculty. **2. a.** Capable of occurring or not occurring; contingent. **b.** Not required or compulsory; optional. **3.** Granting permission or authority. **4.** *Biol.* Capable of adaptive response to varying environments. —**fac′ul·ta′tive·ly** *adv.*

fac·ul·ty (făk′əl-tē) *n., pl.* **-ties. 1.** An inherent power or ability. **2.** Any of the powers or capacities possessed by the human mind: *"Her strength lay in her extraordinary faculty for . . . observation"* (J.B. Priestley). **3.** The ability to perform or act. **4.** *Obs.* Occupation; trade. **5. a.** Any of the divisions or comprehensive branches of learning at a college or university: *the faculty of law.* **b.** The teachers and instructors within such a division. **c.** A body of teachers as distinguished from their students. **6.** All of the members of a learned profession: *the medical faculty.* **7.** Authorization granted by authority; conferred power. [ME *faculte* < OFr. *faculte* < Lat. *facultas* < *facilis,* facile.]

fad (făd) *n.* A fashion that is taken up with great enthusiasm for a brief period of time. [Orig. unknown.] —**fad′dism** *n.* —**fad′dist** *n.* —**fad′dy** *adj.*

fad·dish (făd′ĭsh) *adj.* **1.** Having the nature of a fad. **2.** Given to fads. —**fad′dish·ly** *adv.* —**fad′dish·ness** *n.*

fade (fād) *v.* **fad·ed, fad·ing, fades.** —*intr.* **1.** To lose brightness, loudness, or brilliance gradually; dim. **2.** To lose freshness; wither. **3.** To lose strength or vitality; wane. **4.** To disappear gradually; vanish: *a hope that faded away.* —*tr.* **1.** To cause to fade: *Time has faded her beauty.* **2.** *Football.* To move back from the scrimmage line. Used of a quarterback. **3.** *Slang.* To meet the bet of (an opposing player) in a game of dice. —***phrasal verbs.* fade in. 1.** To appear gradually. **2.** To cause to appear gradually. Used of a motion-picture or television image or of a sound. **fade out. 1.** To disappear gradually. **2.** To cause to disappear gradually. Used of a motion-picture or television image or of a sound. —*n.* **1.** A gradual diminution in the brightness or visibility of an image in motion pictures or television. **2.** A periodic reduction in the received strength of a radio transmission. [ME *faden* < OFr. *fader* < *fade,* faded < VLat. **fatidus,* prob. < Lat. *fatuus,* insipid.]

fade-in (fād′ĭn′) *n.* **1.** The gradual coming or bringing into full visibility of an image in motion pictures or television. **2.** The gradual coming or bringing into audibility of a sound, as in broadcasting.

fade·less (fād′lĭs) *adj.* Not fading or not subject to fading. —**fade′less·ly** *adv.*

fade-out (fād′out′) *n.* **1.** The gradual disappearance of a motion-picture or television image. **2.** A gradual lessening of broadcast sound.

fad·ing (fā′dĭng) *n.* **1.** A waning; decline: *"The final factor in the fading of the Renaissance was the Counter Reformation"* (Will Durant). **2.** Fluctuation in the strength of received radio signals because of variations in the transmission medium.

fa·do (fä′*th*o͞o, făth′ō) *n., pl.* **-dos.** A plaintive Portuguese folk song. [Port. < Lat. *fātum,* fate.]

fae·ces (fē′sēz) *pl.n.* Variant of **feces.**

fa·e·na (fä-ā′nä) *n.* The series of final passes performed by a matador preparatory to killing the bull. [Sp., manual labor < Catalan *feyna* < Lat. *facienda,* things to be done, neuter pl. gerund. of *facere,* to do.]

fa·er·ie also **fa·er·y** (fā′ə-rē, fâr′ē) *Archaic.* —*n., pl.* **-ies. 1.** A fairy. **2.** The land or realm of the fairies. —*adj.* **1.** Of or like a fairy or fairies. **2.** Enchanted; visionary. [ME *fairie.* —see FAIRY.]

Faer·o·ese (fâr′ō-ēz′, -ēs′) *n.* Variant of **Faroese.**

Faf·nir (fäv′nər, -nĭr′) *n.* The dragon in Norse mythology that guarded the treasure of the Nibelungs and was slain by Sigurd. [ON *Fāfnir.*]

fag¹ (făg) *n.* **1. a.** Fatiguing or tedious work; drudgery. **b.** A drudge. **2.** *Chiefly Brit.* A student at a public school who is required to perform menial tasks for a student in a higher class. —*v.* **fagged, fag·ging, fags.** —*intr.* **1.** To work to exhaustion; toil. **2.** *Chiefly Brit.* To serve as the fag of another student. —*tr.* To exhaust; weary: *was fagged out by three hours on the tennis court.* [Orig. unknown.]

fag² (făg) *n. Slang.* A cigarette. [Short for FAG END.]

fag³ (făg) *n. Offensive Slang.* Faggot².

fag end *n.* **1.** The frayed end of a length of cloth or rope. **2. a.** An inferior or worn-out remnant. **b.** The last part. [ME *fag.*]

fag·got¹ (făg′ət) *n. & v.* Variant of **fagot.**

fag·got² (făg′ət) *n. Offensive Slang.* A male homosexual. [Orig. unknown.]

fag·got·ing (făg′ə-tĭng) *n.* Variant of **fagoting.**

fag·ot also **fag·got** (făg′ət) —*n.* **1.** A bundle of twigs, sticks, or branches bound together. **2.** A bundle of pieces of iron or steel to be welded or hammered into bars. —*tr.v.* **-ot·ed, -ot·ing, -ots** also **-got·ed, -got·ing, -gots. 1.** To collect or bind into a fagot; bundle. **2.** To decorate with fagoting. [ME < OFr.]

fag·ot·ing also **fag·got·ing** (făg′ə-tĭng) *n.* **1.** A method of decorating cloth by pulling out horizontal threads and tying the remaining vertical threads into hourglass-shaped bunches. **2.** A method of joining hemmed edges by crisscrossing thread over an open seam.

Fahr·en·heit (făr′ən-hīt′) *adj.* Of or pertaining to a temperature scale that registers the freezing point of water as 32°F and the boiling point as 212°F under standard atmospheric pressure. [After Gabriel D. *Fahrenheit* (1686–1736).]

fa·ience also **fa·ïence** (fī-äns′, fā-, -äɴs′) *n.* **1.** Earthenware decorated with colorful, opaque glazes. **2.** A moderate to strong greenish blue. [Fr. < *Fayence,* Faenza, Italy.]

fail (fāl) *v.* **failed, fail·ing, fails.** —*intr.* **1.** To prove deficient or lacking; perform ineffectively or inadequately. **2.** To be unsuccessful. **3.** To receive an academic grade below the acceptable minimum. **4.** To prove insufficient in quantity or duration; give out. **5.** To decline in strength or effectiveness; fade away. **6.** To cease functioning properly. **7.** To become bankrupt or insolvent. —*tr.* **1.** To disappoint or prove undependable to: *Our sentries failed us.* **2.** To abandon; forsake: *His strength failed him.* **3.** To omit or neglect: *failed to appear.* **4. a.** To receive an academic grade below the acceptable minimum in (a course, for example). **b.** To give such a grade of failure to (a student). —*n.* **1. without fail.** Used to intensify the force esp. of a command or promise. **2.** *Commerce.* **a.** A failure to deliver securities to a purchaser within a specified time. **b.** A failure to receive the proceeds of a transaction, such as a sale of stock or securities, by a specified date. [ME *failen* < OFr. *faillir* < VLat. **fallire* < Lat. *fallere,* to deceive.]

fail·ing (fā′lĭng) *n.* **1.** The act of a person or thing that fails; failure. **2.** A minor fault or defect. —*prep.* In the absence of;

factory

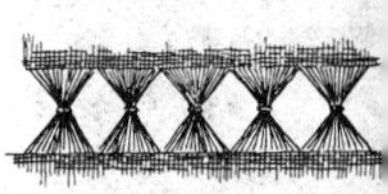

fagoting

faience

without: *Failing a rainstorm, the game will be played this afternoon.*

faille (fīl) *n.* A slightly ribbed, woven fabric of silk, cotton, or rayon. [Fr. < OFr.]

fail-safe (fāl′sāf′) *adj.* **1.** Capable of compensating automatically for a failure in a mechanical device. **2.** Acting to stop a military attack on the occurrence of any of a variety of predetermined conditions. **3.** Guaranteed not to fail. —*n.* A fail-safe mechanism. —*intr.v.* **-safed, -saf·ing, -safes.** To compensate automatically for failure.

fail-soft (fāl′sôft′, -sŏft) *adj.* Capable of compensating automatically for a partial failure. Used of an electronic device.

fair-lead

fail·ure (fāl′yər) *n.* **1.** The condition or fact of not achieving the desired end or ends: *the failure of an experiment.* **2.** One that fails. **3.** The condition or fact of being insufficient or falling short. **4.** A cessation of proper functioning or performance: *a power failure.* **5.** Nonperformance of what is requested or expected; omission: *failure to report a change of address.* **6.** The act or fact of failing to pass a course, test, or assignment. **7.** A decline in strength or effectiveness. **8.** The act or fact of becoming bankrupt or insolvent. [ME *failer,* one who fails < *failen,* to fail.]

fain (fān) *Archaic.* —*adv.* **1.** Preferably; rather. **2.** Happily; gladly. —*adj.* **1.** Ready; willing. **2.** Pleased; happy. **3.** Obliged or required. [ME < *fain,* glad < OE *fægen.*]

fai·né·ant (fā′nā-äN′) *adj.* Given to doing nothing; idle. —*n.* An irresponsible idler. [Fr., alteration of OFr. *faignant,* idler, pr.part. of *faindre,* to feign.]

faint (fānt) *adj.* **-er, -est. 1.** Lacking strength or vigor; feeble. **2.** Lacking conviction, boldness, or courage; timid. **3.** Lacking clarity and brightness; dim: *a faint recollection.* **4.** Likely to fall into a faint; dizzy and weak: *felt faint.* —*n.* An abrupt, usually brief loss of consciousness, generally associated with failure of normal blood circulation. —*intr.v.* **faint·ed, faint·ing, faints. 1.** To fall into a faint. **2.** *Archaic.* To weaken in purpose or spirit; languish. [ME < OFr., p.part. of *faindre,* to feign. —see FEIGN.] **—faint′er** *n.* **—faint′ly** *adv.* **—faint′ness** *n.*

faint·heart (fānt′härt′) *n.* A faint-hearted person.

faint-heart·ed (fānt′här′tĭd) *adj.* Deficient in conviction or courage; timid. **—faint′-heart′ed·ly** *adv.* **—faint′-heart′ed·ness** *n.*

fair¹ (fâr) *adj.* **-er, -est. 1.** Visually pleasing; lovely: *a fair maiden.* **2.** Of light color, as: **a.** Blond: *fair hair.* **b.** Not dark or ruddy: *fair skin.* **3.** Clear and sunny; free of clouds or storms: *fair skies.* **4.** Free of blemishes or stains; pure: *one's fair name.* **5.** Regular and even. **6.** Free of obstacles; open: *fair sailing.* **7.** Promising; likely: *in a fair way to succeed.* **8.** Free of favoritism or bias; impartial: *a fair judge.* **9.** Just to all parties; equitable: *a fair compromise.* **10.** Consistent with rules, logic, or ethics: *a fair tactic.* **11.** Moderately good; mildly satisfying: *a fair performance.* **12.** Superficially true or good; specious. **13.** Lawful to hunt or attack: *fair game.* —*adv.* **1.** In a proper or legal manner: *playing fair.* **2.** Directly; straight: *a blow caught fair in the stomach.* —*n.* *Archaic.* **1.** Loveliness; beauty. **2.** A beautiful or beloved woman. —*v.* **faired, fair·ing, fairs.** —*tr.* To join so as to be smooth, even, or regular. —*intr. Regional.* To become clear. —*idiom.* **fair and square.** Just and honest. [ME < OE *fæger.*] **—fair′ness** *n.*

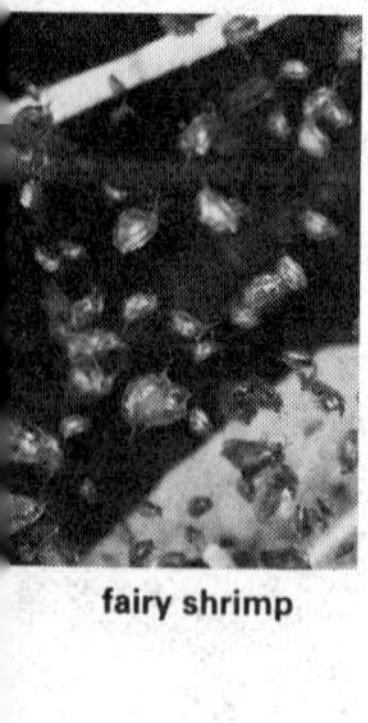

fairy shrimp

Synonyms: *fair, just, equitable, impartial, unprejudiced, unbiased, straightforward, objective, dispassionate.* These adjectives mean showing no evidence of favoritism, self-interest, or the indulgence of one's likes and dislikes. *Fair,* which has the widest range, can imply any of the foregoing senses. *Just* stresses being in accordance with a code of what is legally or ethically right and proper. *Equitable* also implies justice, but less from the standpoint of a rigid code of rules than from a sense of what is in the best interest of all concerned in a given issue. It therefore may imply justice tempered by reason or compromise. *Impartial* emphasizes lack of favoritism in deciding an issue. *Unprejudiced* means without preconceived opinions or judgments, especially those adverse to a person or thing and not soundly based. *Unbiased* implies straightness of judgment or behavior, in the absence of self-interest, prejudice, or emotionalism. *Straightforward* suggests what is frank and honest rather than devious. *Objective* implies detachment that permits a person to observe and judge without undue reference to his own experience and without indulgence of his sympathies. *Dispassionate* means free from coloring by strong personal feelings or emotions.

fair² (fâr) *n.* **1.** A gathering held at a specified time and place for the buying and selling of goods; market. **2.** An exhibition, as of farm products or manufactured goods, usually accompanied by various competitions and entertainments: *a state fair.* **3.** An exhibition intended to inform buyers and the public about a product: *a book fair.* **4.** An event, usually for the benefit of a charity or public institution, including entertainment and the sale of goods; bazaar: *a church fair.* [ME *faire* < OFr. *feire* < Med. Lat. *feria* < Lat. *feriae,* holidays.]

fair ball *n. Baseball.* A batted ball that first strikes the ground or leaves the playing field beyond first or third base within the foul lines or that is within the foul lines as it bounces past first or third base or that comes to rest or is touched by a fielder in front of first or third base within the foul lines.

fair catch *n. Football.* A catch of a punt on the fly by a defensive player who has signaled that he will not run with the ball and who therefore may not be tackled.

fair copy *n.* A copy of a document made after all corrections and revisions have been completed.

fair·ground (fâr′ground′) also **fair·grounds** (-groundz′) *n.* An open space of land where fairs or exhibitions are held.

fair-haired (fâr′hârd′) *adj.* **1.** Having blond hair. **2.** Favorite: *the fair-haired boy of the neighborhood.*

fair·ing¹ (fâr′ĭng) *n.* An auxiliary structure or the external surface of an aircraft serving to reduce drag.

fair·ing² (fâr′ĭng) *n. Chiefly Brit.* A gift, esp. one bought or given at a fair.

fair·ish (fâr′ĭsh) *adj.* Of moderately good size or quality.

fair-lead (fâr′lēd′) also **fair-lead·er** (-lē′dər) *n. Naut.* A device such as a ring or block of wood with a hole in it through which rigging is passed to hold it in place or prevent it from snagging or chafing.

fair·ly (fâr′lē) *adv.* **1. a.** In a fair or just manner; equitably. **b.** Legitimately; suitably. **2.** Clearly; distinctly. **3.** Actually; fully: *The walls fairly shook with his bellowing.* **4.** Moderately; rather: *a fairly good dinner.* **5.** *Obs.* **a.** Gently. **b.** Courteously.

fair-mind·ed (fâr′mīn′dĭd) *adj.* Just and impartial in judgment; unprejudiced. **—fair′-mind′ed·ly** *adv.* **—fair′-mind′ed·ness** *n.*

fair play *n.* Conformity to the established rules.

fair sex *n.* Women collectively.

fair shake *n. Slang.* A fair chance.

fair-spo·ken (fâr′spō′kən) *adj.* Civil, courteous, and gentle in speech.

fair trade *n.* Trade that conforms to a fair-trade agreement.

fair-trade (fâr′trād′) *tr.v.* **-trad·ed, -trad·ing, -trades.** To sell (a commodity) at a price consistent with a fair-trade agreement.

fair-trade agreement *n.* A commercial agreement under which distributors sell products of a given class at no less than a minimum price set by the manufacturer.

fair·way (fâr′wā′) *n.* **1.** A stretch of ground free of obstacles to movement. **2.** The part of a golf course covered with short grass and extending from the tee to the putting green. **3.** *Naut.* **a.** A navigable deep-water channel in a river or harbor or along a coastline. **b.** The usual course taken by vessels through a harbor or coastal waters.

fair-weath·er (fâr′wĕth′ər) *adj.* **1.** Suitable or used only during fair weather. **2.** Present and dependable only in good times: *fair-weather friends.*

fair·y (fâr′ē) *n., pl.* **-ies. 1.** A tiny imaginary being in human form, depicted as clever, mischievous, and possessing magical powers. **2.** *Slang.* A male homosexual. [ME *fairie* < OFr. *faerie* < *fae* < Lat. *fata,* the Fates < *fatum,* fate.]

fair·y·hood (fâr′ē-ho͝od′) *n.* **1.** Fairies collectively. **2.** The condition or nature of fairies.

fair·y·land (fâr′ē-lănd′) *n.* **1.** The land of the fairies. **2.** A charming, enchanting place.

fairy lily *n.* The atamasco lily.

fairy ring *n.* A circle of mushrooms in a grassy area, marking the periphery of underground mycelial growth. [From the belief that it is a dancing place for fairies.]

fairy shrimp *n.* Any of various freshwater crustaceans of the order Anostraca.

fairy tale *n.* **1.** A fanciful tale of legendary deeds and creatures, usually intended for children. **2.** A fictitious, highly fanciful story or explanation.

fait ac·com·pli (fā′tä-kôN-plē′, fĕt′ä-) *n., pl.* **faits ac·com·plis** (fā′tä-kôN-plē′, -plēz′, fĕt′ä-). An accomplished and presumably irreversible deed or fact. [Fr.]

faith (fāth) *n.* **1.** A confident belief in the truth, value, or trustworthiness of a person, idea, or thing. **2.** Belief that does not rest on logical proof or material evidence. **3.** Loyalty to a person or thing; allegiance: *keeping faith with one's supporters.* **4. a.** Belief and trust in God. **b.** Religious conviction. **5.** A system of religious beliefs. **6.** A set of principles or beliefs. —*idiom.* **in faith.** Indeed; truly. [ME < AN *fed* < OFr. *feid* < Lat. *fides* < *fidere,* to trust.]

faith·ful (fāth′fəl) *adj.* **1.** Adhering firmly and devotedly, as to a person, cause, or idea; loyal. **2.** Worthy of trust or belief; reliable. **3.** Consistent with truth or actuality: *a faithful reproduction.* **4.** Having or full of faith. —*n., pl.* **faithful** or **-fuls. 1.** The practicing members of a religious faith, esp. of Christianity or Islam. **2.** A steadfast adherent of a faith or cause. **—faith′ful·ly** *adv.* **—faith′ful·ness** *n.*

Synonyms: *faithful, loyal, true, constant, steadfast, staunch, resolute, devoted, trustworthy.* These adjectives mean firm and unchanging in attachment to a person, cause, or the like. *Faithful* and *loyal* are often interchangeable. *Faithful* in particular suggests long and undeviating attachment; *loyal* can refer to behavior over a long period or in a particular situation and is the term more often applied to allegiance to a government. *True* suggest steadiness, reliability, and in a closely related sense genuineness of friendship or the like. *Constant* stresses absence of change and thus lack of fickleness, though it lacks the emotional warmth of the preceding terms. The idea of resistance to change in ties or bonds is intensified by *steadfast* and even more so by *staunch* and *resolute,* which suggest both a strong attachment or allegiance and a readiness to lend support when the object of the allegiance is under attack. *Devoted* implies dedication to a person or cause and consequent lavishing of time or attention. *Trustworthy* refers to one who has established his right to be considered worthy of another's confidence.

faith healer *n.* One who treats disease with prayer. **—faith healing** *n.*

faith·less (fāth′lĭs) *adj.* **1.** Untrue to duty or obligation; disloyal. **2.** Without religious faith. **3.** Unworthy of faith or trust; unreliable. **—faith′less·ly** *adv.* **—faith′less·ness** *n.*

Synonyms: *faithless, unfaithful, false, disloyal, traitorous, perfidious, inconstant, fickle, undependable.* These adjectives refer to what is unworthy of trust or in violation of it. They vary considerably in specific meaning and application. *Faithless* and *unfaithful* are approximately interchangeable and imply failure to fulfill or honor promises, obligations, or allegiance. *Unfaithful* often has specific reference to failure to respect the vows of marriage. *False* differs from the two preceding terms chiefly in its greater emphasis on actual breach of a promise or pledge as distinguished from a tendency to be untrue. *Disloyal* applies to one who is false to persons or things due allegiance, especially to a nation or superior. *Traitorous* refers most often to disloyalty to a nation. *Perfidious* applies to falseness to any trust or confidence and stresses vileness of behavior. The remaining terms emphasize lack of reliability without necessarily implying violation of trust. *Inconstant* and *fickle* describe what is susceptible to change and therefore not trustworthy; *fickle* in particular implies capriciousness. *Undependable* refers broadly to that in which trust or reliance cannot be put.

fai·tour (fā′tər) *n. Obs.* A deceiver; impostor. [ME < OFr. *faiteor* < Lat. *factor,* maker < *facere,* to make.]

fake[1] (fāk) *adj.* Having a false or misleading appearance; fraudulent. *—n.* **1.** One that is not genuine or authentic; sham. **2.** *Sports.* A brief feint or aborted change of direction intended to mislead one's opponent or the opposing team. *—v.* **faked, fak·ing, fakes.** *—tr.* **1.** To contrive and present as genuine; counterfeit. **2.** To simulate; feign. **3.** To improvise (a musical passage). *—intr.* **1.** To engage in faking. **2.** *Sports.* To perform a fake. [Orig. unknown.]

fake[2] (fāk) *n.* One loop or winding of a coiled rope or cable. *—tr.v.* **faked, fak·ing, fakes.** To coil (a rope or cable). [ME *faken,* to coil a rope.]

fak·er (fā′kər) *n.* A person who fakes or who produces fakes; swindler. **—fak′er·y** (-kə-rē) *n.*

fa·kir (fə-kîr′, fä-, fā-) *n.* **1.** A Moslem religious mendicant. **2.** A Hindu ascetic or religious mendicant, esp. one who performs feats of magic or endurance. [Ar. *faqīr* < *faqura,* he was poor.]

fa·la·fel or **fe·la·fel** (fə-lä′fəl) *n.* **1.** Ground spiced chickpeas and fava beans shaped into balls and fried. **2.** A sandwich filled with falafel. [Ar. *falāfil.*]

Fa·lange (fā′lănj′, fə-lănj′) *n.* A fascist organization constituting the official ruling party of Spain after 1939. [Sp. < *falange,* phalanx < Lat. *phalanx.* —see PHALANX.] **—Fa·lan′gist** (fə-lăn′jĭst, fā′lăn′-) *n.*

fal·cate (făl′kāt′) also **fal·cat·ed** (-kā′tĭd) *adj.* Curved and tapering to a point; sickle-shaped. [Lat. *falcatus* < *falx,* sickle.]

fal·ces (făl′sēz′, fôl′-) *n.* Plural of **falx.**

fal·chion (fôl′chən) *n.* **1.** A short, broad sword with a convex cutting edge and a sharp point, used in medieval times. **2.** *Archaic.* A sword. [ME *fauchoun* < OFr. < Lat. *falx,* sickle.]

fal·ci·form (făl′sə-fôrm′) *adj.* Curved or sickle-shaped; falcate. [Lat. *falx, falc-,* sickle + -FORM.]

fal·con (făl′kən, fôl′-, fô′kən) *n.* **1. a.** Any of various birds of prey of the family Falconidae, and esp. of the genus *Falco,* having long, pointed, powerful wings adapted for swift flight. **b.** Any of several species of these birds or related birds such as hawks, trained to hunt small game. **2.** A small cannon in use from the 15th to the 17th century. [ME *faucoun* < OFr. *faucon* < LLat. *falco.*]

fal·con·er (făl′kə-nər, fôl′-, fô′kə-) *n.* **1.** A person who breeds and trains falcons. **2.** One who hunts with falcons.

fal·con·et (făl′kə-nĕt′, fôl′-, fô′kə-) *n.* **1.** A small or young falcon. **2.** Any of several small falcons of the genus *Microhierax,* chiefly of tropical Asia.

fal·con-gen·tle (făl′kən-jĕn′tl, fôl′-, fô′kən-) *n.* The female peregrine falcon. [ME *faucon gentil* < OFr. *faucon gentil,* noble falcon.]

fal·con·ry (făl′kən-rē, fôl′-, fô′kən-) *n.* **1.** The sport of hunting with falcons. **2.** The art of training falcons for hunting.

fal·cu·late (făl′kyə-lāt′) *adj.* Falcate. [< Lat. *falcula,* small sickle, dim. of *falx,* sickle.]

fal·de·ral (făl′də-răl′) *n.* Variant of **folderol.**

fald·stool (fôld′sto͞ol′) *n.* **1.** A folding or small desk stool at which worshipers kneel to pray, esp. one on which the British sovereign kneels at his coronation. **2.** A folding chair or stool, esp. one used by a bishop when not occupying his throne or when presiding away from his own cathedral. **3.** A desk at which the litany is recited. [Partial transl. of Med. Lat. *faldistolium,* folding stool, of Germanic orig.]

fall (fôl) *v.* **fell** (fĕl), **fall·en** (fô′lən), **fall·ing, falls.** *—intr.* **1.** To drop or come down without restraint under the influence of weight or gravity. **2.** To drop oneself to a lower or less erect position: *fell back in his chair.* **3. a.** To lose an upright or erect position suddenly. **b.** To drop wounded or dead, esp. in battle. **4.** To descend from or as if from the sky or atmosphere: *Night fell quickly.* **5.** To come to rest; settle: *The light fell on her book.* **6.** To hang down: *Her hair fell in ringlets.* **7.** To be cast down: *Her eyes fell.* **8.** To assume an expression of consternation or disappointment: *Her face fell when she heard the report.* **9.** To undergo conquest or capture, esp. as the result of military attack: *The city fell after a long siege.* **10.** To experience defeat or ruin. **11.** To slope downward: *The plain falls gently toward the coast.* **12.** To lessen in amount, degree, or value: *The air pressure is falling.* **13.** To diminish in pitch or volume: *His voice fell to a whisper.* **14.** To decline in rank, status, or importance. **15. a.** To give in to temptation; sin. **b.** To lose one's chastity. **16.** To pass into a particular state, condition, or situation: *fell silent; fall in love.* **17.** To occur at a specified time: *Christmas falls on a Tuesday this year.* **18.** To occur at a specified place: *The stress falls on the last syllable.* **19.** To come, as by chance. **20. a.** To be given by assignment or distribution: *The greatest task fell to him.* **b.** To be given by right or inheritance. **21.** To be included within the range or scope of something: *The specimens fall into three categories.* **22.** To come into contact; strike: *His gaze fell on a small book in the corner.* **23.** To come out; issue: *Insincere compliments fell from his lips.* **24.** To begin vigorously. **25.** To be born. Used chiefly of lambs. *—tr.* To cut down (a tree); fell. ***—phrasal verbs.*** **fall away. 1.** To decline. **2.** To withdraw friendship or support. **fall back.** To give ground; retreat. **fall back on** (or **upon**). To resort to. **fall behind. 1.** To lag behind; fail to keep up with. **2.** To be in arrears. **fall down.** *Informal.* To fail or lag in performance: *fell down on the job.* **fall for.** *Informal.* **1.** To fall suddenly in love with. **2.** To be tricked or deceived by. **fall in.** To take one's place in a military formation. **fall in with. 1.** To come to an agreement. **2.** To be in harmony with. **fall off. 1.** To become less; decrease. **2.** *Naut.* To change course to leeward. **fall on** (or **upon**). To attack suddenly. **fall out. 1.** To leave a military formation. **2.** To quarrel. **3.** To happen; occur. **fall through.** To fail; miscarry. **fall to.** To begin (an activity) energetically. *—n.* **1.** The act or an instance of falling. **2.** A sudden drop from a relatively erect to a less erect position. **3.** Something that has fallen: *a fall of hail.* **4. a.** An amount that has fallen: *a fall of two inches of rain.* **b.** The distance that something falls: *a fall of three stories.* **5.** Autumn. **6. falls** *(used with a sing. or pl. verb).* A waterfall. **7.** A downward movement or slope. **8.** Any of several pendent articles of dress, esp.: **a.** A kind of veil hung from a woman's hat and down her back. **b.** An ornamental cascade of lace or trimming attached to a dress, usually at the collar. **c.** A woman's hair piece with long, free-hanging hair. **9. a.** An overthrow or collapse: *the fall of a government.* **b.** A military capture of a place under siege. **10.** A reduction in value, amount, or degree. **11.** A decline in status, rank, or importance. **12. a.** A moral lapse. **b.** A loss of chastity. **13.** Often **Fall.** *Theol.* The loss of innocence and grace resulting from Adam's eating the forbidden fruit in the Garden of Eden. **14. a.** The act of throwing or forcing a wrestling opponent down on his back. **b.** Any of various wrestling maneuvers used for this. **15.** *Naut.* A break or rise in the level of a deck. **16. falls.** *Naut.* The apparatus used to hoist and transfer cargo or lifeboats. **17.** The end of a cable, rope, or chain that is pulled by the power source in hoisting. **18. a.** The birth of an animal, esp. a lamb. **b.** All of the animals born at one birth; litter. ***—idioms.*** **fall flat.** To fail to achieve an intended result. **fall foul** (or **afoul**). **1.** *Naut.* To collide. Used of vessels. **2.** To quarrel. **fall short. 1.** To fail to attain a specified amount, level, or degree. **2.** To prove inadequate. [ME *fallen* < OE *feallan.*]

fal·la·cious (fə-lā′shəs) *adj.* **1.** Containing or based on a fallacy. **2.** Tending to mislead; deceptive. **—fal·la′cious·ly** *adv.*

fal·la·cy (făl′ə-sē) *n., pl.* **-cies. 1.** A false notion. **2.** A statement or argument that is based on a false or invalid inference. **3.** Incorrectness of reasoning or belief; erroneousness. **4.** The quality of being deceptive. [Lat. *fallacia,* deceit < *fallax,* deceitful < *fallere,* to deceive.]

fal·lal (fă-lăl′, făl′ăl′) *n.* A trifling, showy article of dress; frippery. [Orig. unknown.] **—fal·lal′er·y** *n.*

fall·back (fôl′băk′) *n.* **1.** A mechanism for carrying forth programmed instructions despite malfunction or failure of the primary device. **2.** Something to which one can retreat or resort. **3.** A retreat. **4.** Something that falls back.

fall·en (fô′lən). Past participle of **fall.**

fall·fish (fôl′fĭsh′) *n., pl.* **fallfish** or **-fish·es.** A small, silvery freshwater fish, *Semotilus corporalis,* of streams and rivers of eastern North America.

fall guy *n. Slang.* **1.** A scapegoat. **2.** A gullible victim; dupe.

fal·li·ble (făl′ə-bəl) *adj.* **1.** Capable of making an error. **2.** Tending or likely to be erroneous. [ME < Med. Lat. *fallibilis* < Lat. *fallere,* to deceive.] **—fal′li·bil′i·ty, fal′li·ble·ness** *n.* **—fal′li·bly** *adv.*

fall·ing-out (fô′lĭng-out′) *n., pl.* **fall·ings-out** or **fall·ing-outs.** A personal disagreement; quarrel.

falcon
Peregrine falcon

falling rhythm *n.* Rhythm in which the stress regularly occurs on the first syllable of each foot.

falling star *n.* An object, such as a meteoroid, often visible as a result of being ignited by atmospheric friction.

fall line *n.* **1.** A line connecting the waterfalls of nearly parallel rivers that marks a drop in land level. **2.** The natural line of descent, as for skiing, between two points on a slope.

fallow deer

fall·off (fôl′ôf′, -ŏf′) *n.* A reduction or decrease: *a falloff in business.*

Fal·lo·pi·an tube (fə-lō′pē-ən) *n.* Either of a pair of slender ducts that connect the uterus to the region of each of the ovaries in the female reproductive system of humans and higher vertebrates. [After Gabriello *Fallopio* (1523–1562).]

Fal·lot's tetralogy (fă-lōz′) *n.* A congenital heart condition characterized by narrowing of the pulmonary artery, enlargement of the right ventricle, malpositioning of the aorta, and a defective ventricular septum. [After Étienne *Fallot* (1850–1911).]

fall·out (fôl′out′) *n.* **1. a.** The slow descent of minute particles of radioactive debris in the atmosphere following a nuclear explosion. **b.** The particles that descend in this fashion. **2.** An incidental result or side effect: *the technological fallout of the space program.*

fal·low (făl′ō) *adj.* **1.** Plowed but left unseeded during a growing season. **2.** Marked by inactivity: *abilities wasted or lying fallow.* —*n.* **1.** Land that has been left fallow. **2.** The act of plowing land and leaving it fallow. **3.** The condition or period of being fallow. —*tr.v.* **-lowed, -low·ing, -lows. 1.** To make (land) fallow by plowing. **2.** To plow and till (land), esp. to get rid of weeds. [ME *falow* < OE *fealg,* plowed land.] —**fal′low·ness** *n.*

fallow deer *n.* Either of two Eurasian deer, *Dama dama* or *D. mesopotamica,* having a yellowish coat spotted with white in summer and broad, flattened antlers in the male. [Obs. *fallow,* reddish-yellow (< ME *falwe* < OE *fealo*) + DEER.]

false (fôls) *adj.* **fals·er, fals·est. 1.** Contrary to fact or truth. **2.** Arising from mistaken ideas: *false hopes.* **3.** Deliberately untrue. **4.** Intentionally deceptive: *false promises.* **5.** Not keeping faith; treacherous: *a false friend.* **6.** Not real or natural; artificial: *false teeth.* **7.** Erected temporarily, as for support during construction. **8.** Resembling but not accurately or properly designated as such: *false indigo.* **9.** *Mus.* Of incorrect pitch. —*adv.* In a treacherous or faithless manner: *play a person false.* [ME *fals* < OFr. < Lat. *falsus,* p.part. of *fallere,* to deceive.] —**false′ly** *adv.* —**false′ness** *n.*

false alarm *n.* **1.** An emergency alarm, such as a fire alarm, that is set off unnecessarily. **2.** A signal or warning that is groundless.

false arrest *n. Law.* An unlawful or unjustifiable arrest.

false bottom *n.* A partition made so as to conceal a compartment between it and the bottom of a container, such as a trunk.

family tree
15th-century German woodcut showing bride and groom beneath family tree in which relationships are recorded in Latin

false-heart·ed (fôls′här′tĭd) *adj.* Having a deceitful nature; treacherous. —**false′-heart′ed·ness** *n.*

false·hood (fôls′ho͝od′) *n.* **1.** Lack of conformity to truth or fact; inaccuracy. **2.** The act of lying. **3.** An untrue statement; lie.

false imprisonment *n. Law.* Unlawful arrest or detention of a person.

false indigo *n.* **1.** A shrub, *Amorpha fruticosa,* of eastern North America, having compound leaves with numerous leaflets and long clusters of purplish flowers. **2.** A plant, *Baptisia australis,* of the southeastern United States, having compound leaves with three leaflets and deep-blue or purplish flowers.

false keel *n.* A protective strip fixed below a ship's main keel.

false miterwort *n.* The foamflower.

false pretense *n. Law.* Calculated misrepresentation of fact for purposes of fraud, as through forged documents.

false rib *n.* Any of the five lower pairs of ribs that do not unite directly with the sternum.

false Solomon's seal *n.* Any of several plants of the genus *Smilacina,* esp. *S. racemosa,* having a plumelike cluster of small greenish-white flowers.

fan[1]

fal·set·to (fôl-sĕt′ō) *n., pl.* **-tos. 1.** A male singing voice marked by artificially produced tones in an upper register beyond the normal range esp. of a tenor. **2.** One that sings falsetto. —*adv.* In falsetto. [Ital., dim. of *falso,* false < Lat. *falsus.*]

fals·ie (fôl′sē) *n.* Often **falsies.** *Informal.* Padding or a pad worn inside a brassiere to make the breasts appear larger.

fal·si·fy (fôl′sə-fī′) *v.* **-fied, -fy·ing, -fies.** —*tr.* **1.** To state untruthfully; misrepresent. **2. a.** To make false by altering or adding to. **b.** To counterfeit; forge. **3.** To prove to be false. —*intr.* To make untrue statements; lie. [ME *falsifien,* to show to be untrue < OFr. *falsifier,* to falsify < Med. Lat. *falsificare,* to pervert : Lat. *falsus,* false + Lat. *facere,* to make.] —**fal′si·fi·ca′tion** *n.* —**fal′si·fi′er** *n.*

fal·si·ty (fôl′sĭ-tē) *n., pl.* **-ties. 1.** The quality or condition of being false. **2.** Something false; lie.

Fal·staff·i·an (fôl-stăf′ē-ən) *adj.* Characterized by joviality and conviviality. [After John *Falstaff,* a character in *Henry IV* and *Merry Wives of Windsor* by William Shakespeare (1564–1616).]

falt·boat (fält′bōt′, fôlt′-) *n.* A foldboat. [Partial transl. of G. *Faltboot,* folding boat : *falten,* to fold (< OHG *falden*) + *Boot,* boat.]

fal·ter (fôl′tər) *intr.v.* **-tered, -ter·ing, -ters. 1.** To waver in confidence; hesitate. **2.** To speak hesitatingly; stammer. **3. a.** To move ineptly or haltingly; stumble. **b.** To operate or perform unsteadily or with a loss of effectiveness. —*n.* **1.** An unsteadiness in speech or action. **2.** A faltering sound. [ME *falteren,* to stagger.] —**fal′ter·er** *n.* —**fal′ter·ing·ly** *adv.*

falx (fălks, fôlks) *n., pl.* **fal·ces** (făl′sēz′, fôl′-) *Anat.* A sickle-shaped structure. [Lat., sickle.]

fame (fām) *n.* **1. a.** Great reputation and recognition; renown. **b.** Public esteem; reputation. **2.** *Archaic.* Rumor. —*tr.v.* **famed, fam·ing, fames. 1.** To make renowned or famous. **2.** To report to be. [ME < OFr. < Lat. *fama.*]

famed (fāmd) *adj.* Having great fame; famous.

fa·mil·ial (fə-mĭl′yəl) *adj.* **1.** Of or pertaining to a family. **2.** Passed on in a family; hereditary.

fa·mil·iar (fə-mĭl′yər) *adj.* **1.** Often encountered; common: *a familiar sight.* **2.** Having fair knowledge of something; acquainted: *was familiar with those roads.* **3.** Of established friendship; intimate: *on familiar terms.* **4.** Natural and unstudied; informal: *lectured in a familiar style.* **5.** Taking undue liberties; presumptuous. **6.** *Archaic.* Familial. **7.** Domesticated; tame. Used of animals. —*n.* **1.** A close friend or associate. **2.** An attendant spirit, often taking animal form. **3.** One who performs domestic service in the household of a high official. **4.** A person who frequents a place. [ME < OFr. *familier,* familial < Lat. *familiaris* < *familia,* family.] —**fa·mil′iar·ly** *adv.*

Synonyms: *familiar, close, intimate, fraternal, confidential, chummy.* These adjectives describe relationships involving persons favorably disposed toward one another. *Familiar* implies a friendly association based on mutual attraction, frequent contact, or common interests. *Close* intensifies the idea of nearness, especially in an emotional sense. *Intimate* suggests extremely strong ties resulting from affection or understanding and the sharing of interests, problems, and experiences. *Fraternal* implies a brotherly relationship, and *confidential* stresses trust. *Chummy,* an informal term, suggests sociableness but not necessarily great depth of feeling.

fa·mil·iar·i·ty (fə-mĭl′yăr′ĭ-tē, -mĭl′ē-ăr′-) *n., pl.* **-ties. 1.** Considerable acquaintance with or knowledge of something. **2.** Established friendship; intimacy. **3. a.** An excessively familiar or informal act; impropriety. **b.** A sexual advance. **4.** The quality or condition of being familiar.

fa·mil·iar·ize (fə-mĭl′yə-rīz′) *tr.v.* **-ized, -iz·ing, -iz·es. 1.** To make known, recognized, or familiar. **2.** To make acquainted with. —**fa·mil′iar·i·za′tion** *n.* —**fa·mil′iar·iz′er** *n.*

fam·i·ly (făm′ə-lē, făm′lē) *n., pl.* **-lies. 1.** A fundamental social group in society consisting esp. of a man and woman and their offspring. **2.** A group of persons sharing a common ancestry. **3.** Lineage, esp. distinguished lineage. **4.** All the members of a household under one roof. **5. a.** A group of like things; class. **b.** A group of individuals derived from a common stock: *the family of man.* **6.** *Biol.* A taxonomic category ranking below an order and above a genus. **7.** *Ling.* A language group whose members are derived from the same parent language. **8.** *Math.* A set of functions that can be generated by varying the parameters of a general form. —See Usage note at **collective noun.** [ME *familie* < Lat. *familia* < *famulus,* servant.]

family Bible *n.* A Bible with special pages to record births, deaths, and marriages.

family circle *n.* A section of less expensive theater seats.

family man *n.* **1.** A man having a wife and children. **2.** A man devoted to his family.

family name *n.* A surname.

family planning *n.* Planning of the number of one's children through birth-control techniques.

family room *n.* A recreation room for family members.

family tree *n.* **1.** A genealogical diagram of a family. **2.** The ancestors and descendants collectively of a family.

fam·ine (făm′ĭn) *n.* **1.** A drastic and wide-reaching shortage of food. **2.** A drastic shortage; dearth. **3.** *Archaic.* Severe hunger; starvation. **4.** *Archaic.* Extreme appetite. [ME < OFr. < Lat. *fames,* hunger.]

fam·ish (făm′ĭsh) *v.* **-ished, -ish·ing, -ish·es.** —*tr. Archaic.* **1.** To cause to endure severe hunger; starve. **2.** To cause to starve to death. —*intr. Archaic.* **1.** To endure severe deprivation, esp. of food. **2.** To starve to death. [ME *famishen,* prob. < AN < VLat. **affamare* : Lat. *ad-,* to + Lat. *fames,* hunger.] —**fam′ish·ment** *n.*

fa·mous (fā′məs) *adj.* **1.** Well or widely known. **2.** *Informal.* First-rate; excellent. **3.** *Archaic.* Infamous; notorious. [ME < AN < Lat. *famosus* < *fama,* fame.] —**fa′mous·ly** *adv.* —**fa′mous·ness** *n.*

fam·u·lus (făm′yə-ləs) *n., pl.* **-li** (-lī′). A private attendant or servant. [G. < Lat.]

fan[1] (făn) *n.* **1.** A device for creating a current of air or a breeze, esp.: **a.** A collapsible, usually wedge-shaped device made of a light material such as silk or paper. **b.** A machine using an electric motor to rotate thin, rigid vanes in order to move air, as for cooling. **2.** A machine for winnowing. **3.** Something resembling an open fan in shape. —*v.* **fanned, fan·ning, fans.** —*tr.* **1.** To move or create a current of (air) with or as if with a fan. **2.** To direct a current of air or a breeze upon, esp. in order to cool: *fan one's face.* **3.** To stir up by or as if by fanning: *fan resentment.* **4.** To open out to a fan shape. **5. a.** To fire (an automatic gun) in a continuous sweep by keeping one's finger on the trigger. **b.** To fire (a nonautomatic gun) rapidly by chopping the hammer with the palm. **6.** To winnow. **7.** *Baseball.* To strike out (a batter). *—intr.* **1.** To spread like a fan: *The group fanned out in a northerly direction.* **2.** *Baseball.* To strike out. [ME < OE *fann* < Lat. *vannus.*]

fan[2] (făn) *n. Informal.* An ardent devotee; enthusiast. [Short for FANATIC.]

fa·nat·ic (fə-năt′ĭk) *n.* A person possessed by an excessive zeal for and uncritical attachment to a cause or position. *—adj.* Fanatical. [Lat. *fanaticus,* inspired by a god < *fanum,* temple.]

Synonyms: *fanatic, extremist, zealot, enthusiast.* These nouns denote persons who show marked and usually excessive attachment to a cause, faith, activity, or the like. *Fanatic* implies the pursuit of a given interest to lengths that are considered inordinate and even irrational, and often to the exclusion of virtually all other interests. *Extremist* is not strictly limited to the basic idea that relates these terms, but frequently it is applied to one who advocates the advancement of a cause or course of action to limits far beyond those considered wise or proper by the majority, usually by means that are equally excessive. *Zealot* refers to one who is wholeheartedly devoted to a cause or goal and who typically seeks to advance it in a partisan manner. *Enthusiast* now principally implies strong interest in something such as a sport or hobby, and lacks the unfavorable connotations of the other terms.

fa·nat·i·cal (fə-năt′ĭ-kəl) *adj.* Possessed or driven by excessive or irrational zeal. **—fa·nat′i·cal·ly** *adv.* **—fa·nat′i·cal·ness** *n.*

fa·nat·i·cism (fə-năt′ĭ-sĭz′əm) *n.* Excessive, irrational zeal.

fa·nat·i·cize (fə-năt′ĭ-sīz′) *v.* **-cized, -ciz·ing, -ciz·es.** *—tr.* To make fanatical. *—intr.* To behave as a fanatic.

fan belt *n.* A taut rubber belt that transfers torque from the crankshaft to the shaft of the cooling fan on an engine.

fan·ci·er (făn′sē-ər) *n.* **1.** A person who has a special enthusiasm for or interest in something: *a fancier of antiques.* **2.** A person who breeds a plant or animal for those features held to be desirable.

fan·ci·ful (făn′sĭ-fəl) *adj.* **1.** Created in the fancy; unreal. **2.** Tending to indulge in fancy: *a fanciful mind.* **3.** Showing invention or whimsy in design; imaginative. **—fan′ci·ful·ly** *adv.* **—fan′ci·ful·ness** *n.*

fan·cy (făn′sē) *n., pl.* **-cies.** **1.** Imagination, esp. of a fantastic or whimsical nature. **2.** An image or fantastic invention created by the mind. **3.** A capricious notion; whim. **4.** A capricious liking or inclination. **5.** Critical sensibility; taste. **6.** *Obs.* Amorous or romantic attachment; love. **7. a.** The fans or enthusiasts collectively of a sport or pursuit. **b.** The sport or pursuit, such as boxing, engaging the interest of such a group. *—adj.* **-ci·er, -ci·est.** **1.** Highly decorated: *a fancy hat.* **2.** Arising in the fancy; capricious. **3.** Executed with skill; complex or intricate: *a fancy pass.* **4.** Of superior grade; fine: *fancy preserves.* **5.** Excessive or exorbitant: *paid a fancy price for his car.* **6.** Bred for unusual qualities or special points. *—tr.v.* **-cied, -cy·ing, -cies.** **1.** To visualize; imagine: *"And she tried to fancy what the flame of a candle looks like after the candle is blown out"* (Lewis Carroll). **2.** To take a fancy to; like. **3.** To suppose; guess. *—interj.* Used to express surprise: *Fancy that!* [ME *fansy.* —see FANTASY.] **—fan′ci·ly** *adv.* **—fan′ci·ness** *n.*

fancy dress *n.* A masquerade costume.

fan·cy-free (făn′sē-frē′) *adj.* **1.** Without commitment or restriction; carefree. **2.** Not in love; unattached.

fan·cy·work (făn′sē-wûrk′) *n.* Decorative needlework, such as embroidery.

fan·dan·go (făn-dăng′gō) *n., pl.* **-gos.** **1.** An animated Spanish or Spanish-American dance in triple time. **2.** A piece of music for a fandango. [Sp.]

fan·fare (făn′fâr′) *n.* **1.** A loud flourish of trumpets. **2.** *Informal.* A spectacular public display. [Fr.]

fan·far·o·nade (făn′făr-ə-nād′, -näd′) *n.* **1.** A bragging or blustering manner or behavior. **2.** A fanfare. [Fr. *fanfaronade* < Sp. *fanfarronada,* bluster < *fanfarrón,* a blusterer.]

fang (făng) *n.* **1.** A long, pointed tooth, esp.: **a.** One of the hollow, grooved teeth with which a venomous snake injects its venom. **b.** One of the teeth of a carnivorous animal, with which it seizes and tears its prey. **2.** A fanglike structure, as a chelicera of a venomous spider. **3.** The root of a tooth. [ME, capture < OE.] **—fanged** *adj.*

fan-in (făn′ĭn′) *n. Computer Sci.* The number of inputs available to a given function or logic stage.

fan·ion (făn′yən) *n.* A small flag for marking a position, used esp. by surveyors or soldiers. [Fr. < *fanon,* a vestment used at mass, of Germanic orig.]

fan-jet (făn′jĕt′) *n.* **1.** A jet engine that provides extra thrust by means of a ducted fan in its forward end that draws in extra air. **2.** An airplane with a fan-jet engine.

fan letter *n.* A piece of fan mail.

fan·light (făn′līt′) *n.* **1.** *Archit.* A half-circle window, often with sash bars arranged like the ribs of a fan. **2.** *Chiefly Brit.* A transom.

fan mail *n.* Mail sent to a public figure by admirers.

fan·ny (făn′ē) *n., pl.* **-nies.** *Slang.* The buttocks. [< *Fanny,* a nickname for *Frances.*]

fan-out (făn′out′) *n. Computer Sci.* The number of circuits fed input signals from an output terminal.

fan palm *n.* A palm tree having palmate leaves in a fanlike arrangement.

fan·tail (făn′tāl′) *n.* **1.** One of a breed of domestic pigeons having a rounded, fan-shaped tail. **2.** A goldfish of a breed having a wide, fanlike double tail fin. **3.** Any of several birds of the genus *Rhipidura,* of eastern Asia and Australia, having a long, fan-shaped tail. **4.** A fanlike tail or end. **5.** The stern overhang of a ship. **—fan′tailed′** *adj.*

fan-tan (făn′tăn′) *n.* **1.** A Chinese betting game in which the players lay wagers on the number of counters that will remain when a hidden pile of them has been divided by four. **2.** A card game in which sevens and their equivalent are played in sequence and the first player out of cards is the winner. [Chin. *fan[1] tan[1]* : *fan[1],* division + *tan[1],* to spread out.]

fan·ta·sia (făn-tā′zhə, -zhē-ə, făn′tə-zē′ə) *n. Mus.* **1.** A free composition structured according to the composer's fancy. **2.** A medley of familiar themes, with variations and interludes. [Ital. < Lat. *phantasia,* fantasy.]

fan·ta·sist (făn′tə-sĭst) *n.* One that creates a fantasy or a fantasia.

fan·ta·size (făn′tə-sīz′) *v.* **-sized, -siz·ing, -siz·es.** *—tr.* To portray in the mind; imagine. *—intr.* To indulge in fantasies.

fan·tast (făn′tăst′) *n.* A visionary; dreamer. [G. < Med. Lat. *phantasta* < *phantastes,* boaster < Gk. *phantazein,* to make visible. —see FANTASY.]

fan·tas·tic (făn-tăs′tĭk) also **fan·tas·ti·cal** (-tĭ-kəl) *adj.* **1.** Existing only in the fancy; unreal. **2. a.** Unrestrainedly fanciful; extravagant: *fantastic hopes.* **b.** Bizarre, as in form or appearance; strange. **3.** Capriciously or fancifully eccentric. **4.** *Informal.* Wonderful or superb; remarkable. *—n. Archaic.* A person who is fancifully eccentric in behavior or appearance. [ME *fantastik,* imagined < OFr. *fantastique* < Lat. *fantasticus* < Gk. *phantastikos,* creating mental images < *phantazein,* to make visible. —see FANTASY.] **—fan·tas′ti·cal′i·ty** (-tĭ-kăl′ĭ-tē) *n.* **—fan·tas′ti·cal·ly** *adv.* **—fan·tas′ti·cal·ness** *n.*

Synonyms: *fantastic, bizarre, grotesque, fanciful, exotic.* These adjectives apply to what is very strange or strikingly unusual. *Fantastic* can mean literally apart from reality, but in this comparison it more often describes what seems to have slight relation to the real world because of its strangeness or extravagance. *Bizarre* stresses oddness of character or appearance that is heightened by striking contrasts and incongruities and that shocks or fascinates. *Grotesque* refers principally to appearance or aspect in which deformity and distortion approach the point of caricature or even absurdity. *Fanciful* suggests a character, nature, or design strongly influenced by imagination, caprice, or whimsy rather than by fact, reality, reason, or experience. *Exotic* means foreign in origin or character and alluring in effect.

fan·tas·ti·cate (făn-tăs′tĭ-kāt′) *v.* **-cat·ed, -cat·ing, -cates.** To make fantastic. **—fan·tas′ti·ca′tion** *n.*

fan·ta·sy (făn′tə-sē, -zē) *n., pl.* **-sies.** **1.** The creative imagination; unrestrained fancy. **2.** Something, such as an invention, that is a creation of the fancy. **3.** A capricious or fantastic idea; conceit. **4. a.** Literary or dramatic fiction characterized by highly fanciful or supernatural elements. **b.** An example of such fiction. **5.** *Psychol.* An imagined event or condition fulfilling a wish. **6.** *Mus.* A fantasia. **7.** A coin issued esp. by a questionable authority and not intended for use as currency. **8.** *Obs.* An illusion; hallucination. *—tr.v.* **-sied, -sy·ing, -sies.** To imagine; visualize. [ME *fantasie, fansy* < OFr. *phantasie* < Lat. *phantasia* < Gk., appearance < *phantazein,* to make visible < *phainein,* to show.]

fan·toc·ci·ni (făn′tə-chē′nē) *pl.n.* **1.** Puppets animated by moving wires or mechanical means. **2.** A play or puppet show employing fantoccini. [Ital., pl. of *fantoccino,* dim. of *fantoccio,* puppet, aug. of *fante,* child, short for *infante* < Lat. *infans,* infant. —see INFANT.]

fan·tod (făn′tŏd′) *n.* **1. fantods. a.** A state of nervous irritability. **b.** Nervous movements caused by tension. **2.** An outburst of emotion; fit. [Orig. unknown.]

fan·tom (făn′təm) *n. & adj.* Variant of **phantom.**

fan vaulting *n. Archit.* An intricate style of traceried vaulting, common in late English Gothic, in which ribs arch out like a fan.

fan·wort (făn′wûrt′, -wôrt′) *n.* Any of several aquatic plants of the genus *Cabomba,* having finely divided, fanlike, submerged leaves.

far (fär) *adv.* **far·ther** (fär′*th*ər) or **fur·ther** (fûr′*th*ər), **far·thest** (fär′*th*ĭst) or **fur·thest** (fûr′*th*ĭst). **1.** To, from, or at considerable distance. **2.** To or at a specific distance, degree, or position: *Just how far are you taking this argument?* **3.** To a considerable degree; much: *felt far better yesterday.* **4.** Not at all; anything but: *seems far from content.* **5.** To an advanced point or stage: *a brilliant student who will go far.*

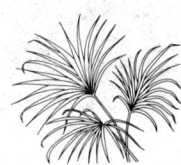

fang

fanlight

fan palm

fantail

—*adj.* **far·ther** or **fur·ther, far·thest** or **fur·thest. 1.** At considerable distance: *a far country.* **2.** More distant: *the far corner.* **3.** Extensive or lengthy: *a far trek.* **4.** Marked by political views of the most advanced or extreme nature: *the far right.* **—idioms. by far.** To a considerable or evident degree. **far and away.** By a great margin: *He's far and away the better skier.* **far and wide.** Everywhere. **so far. 1.** Up to the present moment: *So far there's been no word from him.* **2.** To a limited extent: *You can only go so far on 25 cents.* [ME (adj.) < OE *feor.*]

far·ad (făr′əd, -ăd′) *n.* A unit of capacitance equal to the capacitance of a capacitor having a charge of 1 coulomb on each plate and a potential difference of 1 volt between the plates. [After Michael *Faraday* (1791–1867).]

far·a·da·ic (făr′ə-dā′ĭk) *adj.* Variant of **faradic.**

far·a·day (făr′ə-dā′) *n.* The quantity of electricity that is capable of depositing or dissolving 1 gram equivalent weight of a substance in electrolysis, approximately 9.6494×10^4 coulombs. [After Michael *Faraday* (1791–1867).]

Far·a·day effect (făr′ə-dā′, dē) *n.* The rotation of the plane of polarization of either a plane-polarized light beam passed through a transparent isotropic medium or a plane-polarized microwave passing through a magnetic field along the lines of that field. [After Michael *Faraday* (1791–1867), its discoverer.]

Faraday rotation *n.* Faraday effect.

fa·rad·ic (fə-răd′ĭk) also **far·a·da·ic** (făr′ə-dā′ĭk) *adj.* Of, pertaining to, or using an intermittent asymmetric alternating electric current produced by an induction coil. [After Michael *Faraday* (1791–1867).]

far·a·dism (făr′ə-dĭz′əm) *n.* Faradization.

far·a·di·za·tion (făr′ə-dĭ-zā′shən) *n.* Medical therapy by the application of faradic currents.

far·a·dize (făr′ə-dīz′) *tr.v.* **-dized, -diz·ing, -diz·es.** To treat (an organ, for example) medically with faradic currents.

far·an·dole (făr′ən-dōl′) *n.* **1.** A spirited circle dance of Provençal derivation. **2.** The music for a farandole. [Fr. < Prov. *farandoulo.*]

far·a·way (fär′ə-wā′) *adj.* **1.** Very distant; remote. **2.** Abstracted; dreamy: *a faraway look.*

farce (färs) *n.* **1.** A theatrical composition in which broad improbabilities of plot and characterization are used for humorous effect. **2.** A ludicrous and empty show; mockery. **3.** A seasoned stuffing. —*tr.v.* **farced, farc·ing, farc·es. 1.** To pad or fill out (a speech, for example) with jokes or witticisms. **2.** To stuff, as for roasting. [Fr. < OFr., stuffing, interpolation, interlude < *farcir,* to stuff < Lat. *farcire.*]

far·ceur (fär-sœr′) *n.* **1.** One who acts in or writes a farce. **2.** A comic; wag. [Fr.]

far·ci also **far·cie** (fär-sē′) *adj.* Stuffed, esp. with finely ground meat: *mushrooms farci.* [Fr., p.part. of *farcir,* to stuff < OFr. < Lat. *farcire.*]

far·ci·cal (fär′sĭ-kəl) *adj.* **1.** Of or pertaining to farce. **2.** Resembling farce; ludicrous. **3.** Ridiculously clumsy; absurd. **—far′ci·cal′i·ty** (-kăl′ĭ-tē) *n.* **—far′ci·cal·ly** *adv.* **—far′ci·cal·ness** *n.*

far·cie (fär-sē′) *adj.* Variant of **farci.**

far·cy (fär′sē) *n.* Chronic cutaneous glanders. [ME *farsi* < OFr. *farcin* < LLat. *farciminum* < Lat. *farcire,* to stuff.]

farcy bud *n.* A craterlike ulcer characteristic of farcy.

far·del (fär′dl) *n. Archaic.* **1.** A pack; bundle. **2.** A burden. [ME < OFr., dim. of *farde,* package < Ar. *fardah.*]

fare (fâr) *intr.v.* **fared, far·ing, fares. 1.** To get along: *How did he fare with his project?* **2.** To turn out; go. **3.** To feed on; eat. **4.** *Archaic.* To travel; wander. —*n.* **1.** A transportation charge, as for a bus. **2.** A passenger transported for a fee. **3.** Food and drink; diet. [ME *faren* < OE *faran.*] **—far′er** *n.*

farm

fare-thee-well (fâr′*th*ē-wĕl′) *n.* **1.** A condition of perfection. **2.** The most extreme degree.

fare·well (fâr-wĕl′) *interj.* Good-by. —*n.* **1.** An acknowledgment at parting; good-by. **2.** The act of departing. ***—modifier:*** *a farewell party.* [ME *fare wel.*]

far·fel or **far·fal** (fär′fəl) *n.* Noodles in the shape of small grains or pellets. [Yiddish *farfl* < MHG *varveln.*]

far-fetched (fär′fĕcht′) *adj.* Strained or improbable: *a far-fetched alibi.*

far-flung (fär′flŭng′) *adj.* **1.** Widely distributed; wide-ranging. **2.** Remote; distant.

fa·ri·na (fə-rē′nə) *n.* Fine meal prepared from cereal grain and various other plant products and often used as a cooked cereal or in puddings. [Lat. < *far,* a kind of grain.]

far·i·na·ceous (făr′ə-nā′shəs) *adj.* **1.** Made from, rich in, or consisting of starch. **2.** Having a mealy or powdery texture. [LLat. *farinaceus,* mealy < Lat. *farina,* farina.]

farrier

far·i·nose (făr′ə-nōs′) *adj.* **1.** Similar to or yielding farina. **2.** *Biol.* Covered with mealy dust or powder. [LLat. *farinosus,* mealy < Lat. *farina,* farina.]

far·kle·ber·ry (fär′kəl-bĕr′ē) *n.* A shrub or small tree, *Vaccinium arboreum,* of the southeastern United States, having leathery leaves and hard black berries. [*Farkle,* poss. alteration of SPARKLE + BERRY.]

farm (färm) *n.* **1. a.** A tract of land cultivated for the purpose of agricultural production. **b.** The fields, buildings, animals, and personnel appurtenant to a farm. **2. a.** A tract of land devoted to the raising and breeding of domestic animals. **b.** An area of water devoted to the raising and breeding of a particular aquatic animal. **3.** *Baseball.* A minor-league club affiliated with a major-league club for the training of recruits and the maintenance of temporarily unneeded players. **4.** *Obs.* **a.** The system of leasing out the rights of collecting and retaining taxes in a certain district. **b.** A district so leased. —*v.* **farmed, farm·ing, farms.** —*tr.* **1.** To cultivate or produce a crop on. **2.** To pay a fixed sum in order to have the right to collect and retain profits from (a business, for example). **3.** To turn over (a business, for example) to another in return for the payment of a fixed sum. —*intr.* To engage in farming. ***—phrasal verb.* farm out. 1.** To send (work) from a central point to be done elsewhere. **2.** *Baseball.* To assign (a player) to a minor-league team. [ME, lease < OFr. *ferme* < Med. Lat. *firma,* fixed payments < Lat. *firmare,* to establish < *firmus,* firm.]

farm·er (fär′mər) *n.* **1.** One who operates or works on a farm. **2.** One who has paid for the right to collect and retain certain revenues or profits.

farmer cheese *n.* An unripened cheese similar to cottage cheese but drier and firmer in texture.

farmer's lung *n.* A pulmonary condition caused by continued exposure to moldy hay.

farm hand *n.* A hired farm laborer.

farm·house (färm′hous′) *n.* A dwelling on a farm.

farm·land (färm′lănd′, -lənd) *n.* An expanse of land suitable for farming.

farm·stead (färm′stĕd′) *n.* A farm, including its land and buildings.

farm·yard (färm′yärd′) *n.* An area surrounded by or adjacent to farm buildings.

far·ne·sol (fär′nĭ-sôl′, -sōl′) *n.* A compound, $C_{15}H_{26}O$, extracted from the flowers and essential oils of various plants and used in perfumery. [G. < NLat. *farnesiana,* specific epithet of *Acacia farnesiana* (whose flowers are used in making perfume), after Odoardo *Farnese* (1573–1626).]

far·o (fâr′ō) *n.* A card game in which the players lay wagers on the top card of the dealer's pack. [Var. of PHARAOH.]

Far·o·ese also **Faer·o·ese** (fâr′ō-ēz′, -ēs′) *n., pl.* **Faroese** also **Faeroese. 1.** One of the Germanic people inhabiting the Faeroe Islands. **2.** The North Germanic language spoken by the inhabitants of the Faeroe Islands. **—Fa′ro·ese′** *adj.*

far-off (fär′ôf′, -ŏf′) *adj.* Remote in space or time; distant.

far-out (fär′out′) *adj. Slang.* Extremely unconventional.

far point *n.* The farthest point at which an object can be seen distinctly by the eye at rest.

far·rag·i·nous (fə-răj′ə-nəs) *adj.* Composed of a variety of substances. [< Lat. *farrago, farragin-,* mixture < *far,* a kind of grain.]

far·ra·go (fə-rä′gō, -rā′-) *n., pl.* **-goes.** A medley; conglomeration. [Lat. *farrāgo* < *far,* a kind of grain.]

far-reach·ing (fär′rē′chĭng) *adj.* Having a wide range, influence, or effect: *far-reaching implications.*

far-red (fär′rĕd′) *adj.* **1.** Of, pertaining to, or being electromagnetic radiation with wavelengths between 30 and 1000 microns. **2.** Of, pertaining to, or being infrared light of wavelengths closest to those of visible red light, about .8 micron.

far·ri·er (făr′ē-ər) *n. Chiefly Brit.* One who shoes horses or treats them medically. [OFr. *ferrier* < Lat. *ferrārius* < *ferrum,* iron.] **—far′ri·er·y** *n.*

far·row[1] (făr′ō) *n.* A litter of pigs. —*v.* **-rowed, -row·ing, -rows.** —*tr.* To give birth to (a farrow). —*intr.* To produce a farrow. [ME **farwes* < OE *fearh,* pig.]

far·row[2] (făr′ō) *adj.* Not pregnant. Used of a cow. [ME *ferow.*]

far·see·ing (fär′sē′ĭng) *adj.* **1.** Prudent; foresighted. **2.** Able to see far; keen-sighted.

far·sight·ed (fär′sī′tĭd) *adj.* **1. a.** Able to see objects better from a distance than from short range. **b.** Hyperopic. **2.** Planning prudently for the future; foresighted. **—far′sight′ed·ly** *adv.* **—far′sight′ed·ness** *n.*

fart (färt) *intr.v.* **fart·ed, fart·ing, farts.** *Vulgar.* To expel intestinal gas through the anus; break wind. ***—phrasal verb.* fart around.** *Vulgar Slang.* To fool around; fritter time away. —*n.* **1.** *Vulgar.* A usually audible discharge of intestinal gas. **2.** *Vulgar Slang.* A mean, contemptible person. [ME *farten.*]

far·ther (fär′*th*ər) *adv.* A comparative of **far. 1.** To or at a more distant or more remote point in space or time. **2.** In addition. **3.** To a greater extent or degree. —*adj.* A comparative of **far. 1.** Remoter; more distant. **2.** Additional. [ME *ferther* < OE *furðor.*]

Usage: According to many traditional grammarians, the etymological distinction between *farther* ("more far") and *further* ("more to the fore") should be preserved. In that case *farther* should be used only for physical distance, as in *They went farther down the road. Further* should be used in most other senses, especially when referring to degree, quantity, or time: *further in debt; further steps must be taken; a further reason.* In some cases either word is acceptable to the Usage Panel; one may say either *further from the truth* or *farther from the truth.* It should be noted that writers since Shakespeare have often ignored the distinction between the two words.

far·ther·most (fär′*th*ər-mōst′) *adj.* Farthest.

far·thest (fär′*th*ĭst) *adj.* A superlative of **far.** Most remote or distant. —*adv.* A superlative of **far. 1.** To or at the most distant or remote point in space or time. **2.** To the most advanced stage or point. **3.** By the greatest extent or degree. [ME *ferthest.*]

far·thing (fär'*th*ĭng) *n.* **1.** A former British coin worth one fourth of a penny. **2.** Something of very little value. [ME *ferthing* < OE *fēorðung.*]

far·thin·gale (fär'*th*ĭn-gāl', -*th*ĭng-) *n.* A support, such as a hoop, that makes a skirt extend horizontally from the waist, worn by women in the 16th and 17th centuries. [Alteration of OFr. *verdugale* < OSp. *verdugadu* < *verdugo,* stick < *verde,* green < Lat. *viridis.* —see VERDANT.]

farthingale

fas·ces (făs'ēz') *pl.n.* A bundle of rods bound together about an ax with the blade projecting, carried before magistrates of ancient Rome as an emblem of authority. [Lat., pl. of *fascis,* bundle.]

fas·ci·a (făsh'ē-ə) *n., pl.* **-ci·ae** (-ē-ē'). **1.** *Anat.* A sheet of fibrous tissue beneath the surface of the skin, enveloping the body, enclosing muscles or muscular groups, and separating muscular layers. **2.** A broad and distinct band of color. **3.** (*also* fā'shē-ə). *Archit.* A flat horizontal band or member between moldings, esp. in a classical entablature. **4.** (fā'shə). *Chiefly Brit.* The dashboard, as of an automobile. [NLat. < Lat., band.] **—fas'ci·al** *adj.*

fas·ci·ate (făsh'ē-āt') also **fas·ci·at·ed** (-ā'tĭd) *adj.* **1.** *Bot.* Abnormally flattened or coalesced, as certain stems. **2.** *Zool.* Marked by broad bands of color, as certain insects. [Lat. *fasciatus,* p.part. of *fasciare,* to swathe < *fascia,* band.]

fas·ci·a·tion (făs'ē-ā'shən, făsh'ē-) *n.* **1.** The act of binding up or fastening, as with bandages. **2.** The manner in which something is bound up or fastened. **3.** *Bot.* An abnormal flattening or coalescence of stems or leaf stalks.

fas·ci·cle (făs'ĭ-kəl) *n.* **1.** A small bundle. **2.** Also **fas·ci·cule** (-kyo͞ol'). One of the parts of a book published in separate sections. **3.** *Bot.* A bundlelike cluster, as of stems, flowers, or leaves. **4.** *Anat.* A fasciculus. [Lat. *fasciculus,* dim. of *fascis,* bundle.] **—fas'ci·cled** *adj.*

fas·cic·u·lar (fə-sĭk'yə-lər) *adj.* Of, pertaining to, or composed of fascicles. **—fas·cic'u·lar·ly** *adv.*

fas·cic·u·late (fə-sĭk'yə-lĭt) also **fas·cic·u·lat·ed** (-lā'tĭd) *adj.* Pertaining to or resembling a fascicle; fascicular. **—fas·cic'u·late·ly** *adv.* **—fas·cic'u·la'tion** *n.*

fas·ci·cule (făs'ĭ-kyo͞ol') *n.* Variant of **fascicle** (sense 2).

fas·cic·u·lus (fə-sĭk'yə-ləs) *n., pl.* **-li** (-lī'). A bundle of anatomical fibers, esp. a bundle of nerve fibers having common functions and connections. [Lat., fascicle.]

fas·ci·nate (făs'ə-nāt') *tr.v.* **-nat·ed, -nat·ing, -nates.** —*tr.* **1.** To hold an intense interest or attraction for. **2.** To hold motionless; spellbind. **3.** *Obs.* To bewitch. —*intr.* To be irresistibly charming or attractive. [Lat. *fascinare, fascinat-,* to enchant < *fascinum,* witchcraft.]

fas·ci·nat·ing (făs'ə-nā'tĭng) *adj.* Possessing the power to charm or allure; captivating. **—fas'ci·nat'ing·ly** *adv.*

fas·ci·na·tion (făs'ə-nā'shən) *n.* **1.** The power of fascinating. **2.** The condition of being fascinated. **3.** A fascinating quality or trait.

fas·ci·na·tor (făs'ə-nā'tər) *n.* **1.** One that fascinates. **2.** A woman's head scarf made of net or lace.

fas·cine (fă-sēn', fə-) *n.* A bundle of sticks bound together for use in construction, as of fortresses and earthworks. [Fr. < Lat. *fascina* < *fascis,* bundle.]

fas·ci·o·li·a·sis (fə-sē'ə-lī'ə-sĭs, -sī'-) *n.* Infestation with a trematode worm of the genus *Fasciola.* [NLat. *Fasciola,* fluke genus + -IASIS.]

fas·cism (făsh'ĭz'əm) *n.* **1.** A philosophy or system of government that is marked by stringent social and economic control, a strong, centralized government usually headed by a dictator, and often a policy of belligerent nationalism. **2.** Oppressive or dictatorial control. [Ital. *fascismo* < *fascio,* group < Lat. *fascis,* bundle.] **—fas·cis'tic** (fə-shĭs'tĭk) *adj.*

fas·cist or **Fas·cist** (făsh'ĭst) *n.* An advocate or adherent of fascism. [Ital. *fascista* < *fascio,* group. —see FASCISM.]

Fa·scis·ti (fă-shē'stē) *pl.n.* The members of the Italian political organization led by Benito Mussolini. [Ital., pl. of *fascista,* fascist.]

fash·ion (făsh'ən) *n.* **1.** The way in which something is formed; configuration. **2.** Kind or variety; sort. **3.** A manner of performing; way: *Do it in this fashion.* **4.** The current style or custom, as in dress or behavior: *out of fashion.* **5.** A piece of clothing that is in the current mode. **6.** The manners, customs, and mode of life characteristic of the upper classes. —*tr.v.* **-ioned, -ion·ing, -ions. 1. a.** To shape or form into. **b.** To train or influence into a particular state or character. **2.** To adapt, as to a purpose or occasion. **3.** *Obs.* To contrive. ***—idiom.* after** (or **in**) **a fashion.** In some way or other, esp. to a limited extent: *She sings after a fashion.* [ME *facioun* < OFr. *faceon* < Lat. *factio* < *factus,* p.part. of *facere,* to do.] **—fash'ion·er** *n.*

Synonyms: *fashion, style, mode, vogue.* These nouns refer to the prevailing or preferrred practice in dress, manners, behavior, or the like, at a given time. *Fashion,* the broadest term, can denote custom or practice that prevails among any group of persons. Usually, however, it specifies such practice that follows the conventions of polite society or mass culture. *Style* is sometimes used interchangeably with *fashion,* but *style* can refer to what adheres to standards of elegance, the sense in which *mode* is also used. *Vogue* is applied to what prevails widely and obviously at a given time; often the term suggests enthusiastic acceptance of something for a rather short period.

fash·ion·a·ble (făsh'ə-nə-bəl) *adj.* **1.** Conforming to the current style. **2.** Of or associated with persons of fashion. —*n.* A fashionable person. **—fash'ion·a·bil'i·ty** *n.* **—fash'ion·a·ble·ness** *n.* **—fash'ion·a·bly** *adv.*

fash·ion·mon·ger (făsh'ən-mŭng'gər, -mŏng'-) *n.* A person concerned with following, spreading, or setting fashions.

fashion plate *n.* **1.** An illustration of current styles in dress. **2.** A person who consistently wears the latest fashions.

fast[1] (făst) *adj.* **-er, -est. 1.** Acting, moving, or capable of acting or moving quickly; swift. **2.** Accomplished in relatively little time: *a fast visit.* **3.** Indicating a time somewhat ahead of the actual time: *a fast wristwatch.* **4.** Adapted to or suitable for rapid movement: *a fast track.* **5. a.** Disposed to dissipation; wild: *a fast life.* **b.** Flouting conventional sexual standards. **6.** Resistant: *acid-fast.* **7.** Firmly fixed or fastened: *a fast grip.* **8.** Fixed firmly in place; secure: *shutters fast against the rain.* **9.** Loyal; firm: *fast friends.* **10.** Resisting fading: *fast dyes.* **11.** Deep; sound: *a fast sleep.* **12.** Designed for or compatible with a short exposure time: *fast film.* —*adv.* **1.** Securely; tightly. **2.** Deeply; soundly: *fast asleep.* **3.** Quickly; rapidly. **4.** Ahead of the correct or expected time. **5.** In a dissipated, immoderate way: *living fast.* **6.** *Archaic.* Close by; near. ***—idiom.* fast and loose 1.** In a deceitful manner: *played fast and loose with the facts in order to win.* **2.** In an irresponsible manner: *played fast and loose with his partner's money.* [ME < OE *fæst,* firmly fixed.]

Synonyms: *fast, rapid, swift, fleet, speedy, quick, hasty, expeditious, accelerated.* These adjectives refer to rate of activity or movement. All but the last three are often interchangeable. *Fast* is more often applied to a person or thing, and *rapid* to the activity or movement involved: *a fast runner; rapid strides. Swiftly* suggests smoothness of movement, and *fleet,* lightness of movement. *Speedy* refers to velocity or, when applied to persons, to hurry or effort to increase progress. *Quick* also can refer to velocity; more often it applies to what takes little time or to promptness of response or action in persons. *Hasty* implies hurried action and often lack of care or thought. *Expeditious* combines the senses of rapidity and efficiency as they apply to action. *Accelerated* refers to what is increased, or stepped up, in rate of progress or motion.

fast[2] (făst) *intr.v.* **fast·ed, fast·ing, fasts. 1.** To abstain from food. **2.** To eat very little or abstain from certain foods, esp. as a religious discipline. —*n.* The act or a period of fasting. [ME *fasten* < OE *fæstan.*]

fast·back (făst'băk') *n.* An automobile with a curving downward slope from roof to rear.

fast-breed·er reactor (făst'brē'dər) *n.* A breeder reactor that requires high-energy neutrons to produce fissionable material.

fas·ten (făs'ən) *v.* **-tened, -ten·ing, -tens.** —*tr.* **1.** To attach firmly to; join. **2. a.** To make fast or secure. **b.** To close, as by fixing firmly in place. **3.** To fix or direct steadily: *fastened his gaze upon the newspaper.* **4. a.** To place; attribute. **b.** To impose (oneself) without welcome. —*intr.* **1.** To become attached, fixed, or joined. **2.** To take firm hold; cling fast. **3.** To fix or focus steadily. [ME *fastnen* < OE *fæstnian.*] **—fas'ten·er** *n.*

fas·ten·ing (făs'ə-nĭng) *n.* Something, such as a hook, used to fasten.

fast food *n.* Restaurant food prepared and served quickly. ***—modifier* (fast-food):** *a fast-food restaurant.*

fas·tid·i·ous (fă-stĭd'ē-əs, fə-) *adj.* **1.** Possessing or displaying careful and meticulous attention to detail. **2.** Difficult to please; exacting. **3.** Excessively scrupulous or sensitive, esp. in matters of taste or propriety. **4.** Having complicated nutritional requirements. [ME < OFr. *fastidieux* < *Lat. fastidiosus* < *fastidium,* loathing.] **—fas·tid'i·ous·ly** *adv.* **—fas·tid'i·ous·ness** *n.*

fas·tig·i·ate (fă-stĭj'ē-ĭt) also **fas·tig·i·at·ed** (-e-ā'tĭd) *adj.* **1.** Tapering to a point. **2.** *Bot.* Erect and almost parallel, as certain branches. [Med. Lat. *fastigiatus,* high < Lat. *fastigium,* top.] **—fas·tig'i·ate·ly** *adv.*

fas·tig·i·um (fă-stĭj'ē-əm) *n.* The period of maximum development of a disease. [NLat. < Lat., extremity.]

fast·ness (făst'nĭs) *n.* **1. a.** A stronghold or fortified place. **b.** A remote and secret place. **2.** The condition or quality of being fast, esp.: **a.** Firmness; security. **b.** Rapidity; swiftness. **c.** Colorfastness.

fast-talk (făst'tôk') *tr.v.* **-talked, -talk·ing, -talks.** To affect or persuade by esp. deceptive talk or means. **—fast'-talk'er** *n.*

fat (făt) *n.* **1. a.** The glyceride ester of a fatty acid. **b.** Any of various soft solid or semisolid organic compounds comprising the glyceride esters of fatty acids and associated phosphatides, sterols, alcohols, hydrocarbons, ketones, and related compounds. **c.** A mixture of such compounds occurring widely in organic tissue, esp. in the subcutaneous connective tissue of animals and in the seeds, nuts, and fruits of plants. **d.** Organic tissue containing such substances. **e.** A solidified animal or vegetable oil. **2.** Plumpness or obesity. **3.** The best or most desirable part of something. —*adj.* **fat·ter, fat·test. 1.** Having much or too much fat or flesh; plump or obese. **2.** Full of fat or oil; greasy. **3.** Abounding in desirable elements: *Fat pine yields much resin.* **4.** Fertile or productive; rich. **5.** Having an abundant supply; well-stocked: *a fat wallet.* **6.** Yielding profit or plenty; lucrative: *a fat commission.* **7. a.** Thick; large. **b.** Puffed up; swollen. —*tr. & intr.v.* **fat·ted, fat·ting, fats.** To make or become fat. —***idiom.*** **fat chance.** *Slang.* Little or no possibility of occurrence. [ME < *fat,* plump < OE *fǣtt,* fattened.] —**fat'ly** *adv.* —**fat'ness** *n.*

Synonyms: *fat, obese, corpulent, fleshy, stout, portly, pudgy, rotund, plump, chubby.* These adjectives mean having an abundance of flesh, often to excess. *Fat* always implies excessive weight and is generally unfavorable in connotations. *Obese* is employed principally in medical usage with reference to extreme overweight, and *corpulent* is a more general term for the same condition. *Fleshy* implies an abundance of flesh that is not necessarily disfiguring. *Stout* and *portly* are sometimes used as polite terms to describe fatness. *Stout,* in stricter application, suggests a thickset, bulky person, and *portly,* one whose bulk is combined with an imposing bearing. *Pudgy* describes one who is thickset and dumpy. *Rotund* suggests roundness of figure in a squat person. *Plump* is applicable to a pleasing fullness of figure, especially in women. *Chubby* implies abundance of flesh, usually not to excess.

fa·tal (făt'l) *adj.* **1.** Causing or capable of causing death. **2.** Causing ruin or destruction; disastrous: *"Such doctrines, if true, would be absolutely fatal to my theory"* (Darwin). **3.** Most decisive; fateful. **4.** Controlling destiny. **5.** *Obs.* Destined. [ME < OFr. < Lat. *fatalis* < *fatum,* fate.]

Synonyms: *fatal, deadly, mortal, lethal.* These adjectives apply to what causes death. *Fatal* describes conditions, circumstances, or events that have produced death or are destined inevitably to cause death or dire consequences: *a fatal illness; a fatal blow. Deadly* applies to persons or things capable of killing or, in figurative usage, of producing severe hardship: *a deadly weapon; a deadly bore. Mortal* can describe a person likely to cause death, as in *a mortal enemy,* or a conditon or action that has in fact produced death: *a mortal wound. Lethal* refers to a thing that acts as a sure agent of death and may have been created solely for that purpose: *the lethal chamber.*

Usage: Although the senses of *fatal* and *fateful* have tended to merge in recent times, each has a different core of meaning. The contrast between *fatal,* in the sense of "leading to death or destruction," and *fateful,* in the sense of "affecting one's destiny or future," is illustrated by the following sentence: *The fateful decision to relax safety standards led directly to the fatal crash.*

fatigue
Fatigues

fa·tal·ism (făt'l-ĭz'əm) *n.* **1.** The doctrine that all events are predetermined by fate and therefore cannot be changed by human beings. **2.** The acceptance of the doctrine of fatalism. —**fa'tal·ist** *n.* —**fa'tal·is'tic** *adj.* —**fa'tal·is'ti·cal·ly** *adv.*

fa·tal·i·ty (fā-tăl'ĭ-tē, fə-) *n., pl.* **-ties. 1. a.** A death that results from an unexpected occurrence. **b.** One that is killed as a result of such an occurrence. **2.** The ability to cause death or disaster. **3.** The condition or quality of being governed or determined by fate. **4.** A decree made by fate; destiny. **5.** The quality or state of being doomed to disaster.

fatality rate *n.* Death rate.

fa·tal·ly (făt'l-ē) *adv.* **1. a.** So as to cause death; mortally. **b.** So as to result in disaster or ruin. **2.** According to the decree of fate; inevitably.

fa·ta mor·ga·na (fä'tə môr-gä'nə) *n.* A mirage (sense 1). [Ital., mirage, Morgan le Fay (from the belief that the mirage was caused by her witchcraft).]

fat·back (făt'băk') *n.* The strip of fat taken from the upper part of a side of pork and usually dried and salt-cured.

fat body *n.* A food reserve of fatty tissue in the larval stages of some insects.

fat cat *n. Slang.* **1.** A wealthy and highly privileged person. **2.** A rich person who is a heavy contributor to a political party.

fate (fāt) *n.* **1. a.** The supposed force, principle, or power that predetermines events. **b.** The inevitable events predestined by this force. **2.** A final result or consequence; outcome. **3.** An unfavorable destiny; doom. **4. Fates.** *Gk. & Rom. Myth.* The three goddesses who govern human destiny. [ME < OFr. or < Lat. *fatum* < neuter p.part. of *fārī,* to speak.]

fat·ed (fā'tĭd) *adj.* **1.** Governed by fate; predetermined. **2.** Condemned to death or destruction; doomed: *the fated city of Troy.*

fate·ful (fāt'fəl) *adj.* **1.** Affecting one's destiny or future: *a fateful decision.* **2.** Controlled by or as if by fate; predetermined. **3.** Bringing death or disaster; fatal. **4.** Portentous; ominous. —See Usage note at **fatal.** —**fate'ful·ly** *adv.* —**fate'ful·ness** *n.*

fat·head (făt'hĕd') *n. Slang.* A stupid person; dolt. —**fat'head'ed** *adj.* —**fat'head'ed·ly** *adv.* —**fat'head'ed·ness** *n.*

fa·ther (fä'*th*ər) *n.* **1.** The begetter of a child; male parent. **2.** One who functions in a paternal capacity with regard to another. **3.** A male ancestor; forefather. **4.** A man who creates or originates something: *a founding father.* **5. Father. a.** God. **b.** The first person of the Trinity. **6.** An elderly or venerable man. Used as a title of respect. **7.** A member of the senate in ancient Rome. **8.** Often **Father.** Any of the authoritative early writers in the Christian Church who formulated doctrines and codified religious observances. **9.** A priest or clergyman in the Roman Catholic or Anglican churches. Used as a title with or without the clergyman's name. —*v.* **-thered, -ther·ing, -thers.** —*tr.* **1.** To beget. **2.** To act or serve as a father to. **3.** To create, found, or originate. **4.** To acknowledge responsibility for. **5. a.** To attribute the paternity, creation, or origin of. **b.** To assign falsely or unjustly; foist. —*intr.* To act or serve as a father. [ME *fader* < OE *fæder.*] —**fa'ther·less** *adj.*

Usage: *Father* has lately come to be used to mean "to perform the child-rearing function of a father": *As the traditional roles of men and women have changed in our society fathering has taken on vastly greater dimensions.* A majority of the Usage Panel disapproves of this use.

Father Christmas *n. Chiefly Brit.* Santa Claus.

father confessor *n.* **1.** A priest who hears confessions. **2.** A person in whom one confides.

father figure *n.* An influential or powerful person who is the recipient of emotions usually reserved for a father.

fa·ther·hood (fä'*th*ər-ho͝od') *n.* The condition of being a father.

fa·ther-in-law (fä'*th*ər-ĭn-lô') *n., pl.* **fa·thers-in-law. 1.** The father of one's husband or wife. **2.** A stepfather.

fa·ther·land (fä'*th*ər-lănd') *n.* **1.** A person's native land. **2.** The native land of one's ancestors.

fa·ther·ly (fä'*th*ər-lē) *adj.* **1.** Of, pertaining to, or appropriate to a father. **2.** Showing the tenderness or affection of a father. —*adv.* In a fatherly manner. —**fa'ther·li·ness** *n.*

Father's Day *n.* An annual day honoring fathers and fatherhood observed on the third Sunday in June.

fath·om (făth'əm) *n., pl.* **fathom** or **-oms.** A unit of length equal to six feet and used principally in the measurement and specification of marine depths. —*tr.v.* **-omed, -om·ing, -oms. 1.** To determine the depth of; sound. **2.** To get to the bottom of and understand. [ME *fathme* < OE *fæðm,* outstretched arms.] —**fath'om·a·ble** *adj.*

Fa·thom·e·ter (fă-*th*ŏm'ĭ-tər). A trademark for a sonic depth finder.

fath·om·less (făth'əm-lĭs) *adj.* **1.** Too deep to be fathomed or measured. **2.** Too difficult to understand.

fa·tid·ic (fə-tĭd'ĭk) also **fa·tid·i·cal** (-ĭ-kəl) *adj.* Pertaining to or characterized by prophecy. [Lat. *fatidicus* : *fatum,* fate + *dicere,* to say.]

fat·i·ga·ble (făt'ĭ-gə-bəl) *adj.* Subject to weariness; easily tired. [Fr. < LLat. *fatigabilis* < Lat. *fatigare,* to fatigue.] —**fat'i·ga·bil'i·ty** *n.*

fa·tigue (fə-tēg') *n.* **1.** Physical or mental weariness resulting from exertion. **2.** Tiring effort or activity; labor. **3.** *Physiol.* The decreased capacity or complete inability of an organism, organ, or part to function normally because of excessive stimulation or prolonged exertion. **4.** Weakness in a material, such as metal or wood, resulting from prolonged stress. **5. a.** Manual or menial labor, such as barracks cleaning, assigned to soldiers. **b. fatigues.** Clothing designated or permitted for fatigue and field duty. —*v.* **-tigued, -tigu·ing, -tigues.** —*tr.* **1.** To tire out; exhaust. **2.** To create fatigue in. —*intr.* To experience fatigue. [Fr. < OFr. < *fatiguer,* to fatigue < Lat. *fatigare.*]

fat·ling (făt'lĭng) *n.* A young animal, such as a lamb or calf, fattened for slaughter.

fat·so (făt'sō) *n., pl.* **-soes.** *Slang.* A fat person.

fat-sol·u·ble (făt'sŏl'yə-bəl) *adj.* Soluble in fats or fat solvents, such as ether.

fat·ten (făt'n) *v.* **-tened, -ten·ing, -tens.** —*tr.* **1.** To make plump or fat. **2.** To fertilize (land). **3.** To increase the amount of. —*intr.* To grow fat or fatter. —**fat'ten·er** *n.*

fat·tish (făt'ĭsh) *adj.* Somewhat fat. —**fat'tish·ness** *n.*

fat·ty (făt'ē) *adj.* **-ti·er, -ti·est. 1. a.** Containing fat. **b.** Containing excessive amounts of fat. **2.** Full of fat; greasy. **3.** Derived from or chemically related to fat. —*n., pl.* **-ties.** A fat person. —**fat'ti·ly** *adv.* —**fat'ti·ness** *n.*

fatty acid *n.* Any of a large group of monobasic acids having the general formula $C_nH_{2n+1}COOH$, esp. any of a commercially important subgroup obtained from animals and plants, characteristically saturated or unsaturated aliphatic compounds with an even number of carbon atoms, the most abundant of which contain 16 or 18 carbon atoms and include palmitic, stearic, and oleic acids.

fatty alcohol *n.* Any of various alcohols derived from plant and animal oils and fats that are used in plastics and pharmaceuticals.

fa·tu·i·ty (fə-to͞o'ĭ-tē, -tyo͞o'-, fă-) *n., pl.* **-ties. 1.** Stupidity; folly. **2.** A fatuous act, remark, or sentiment. [OFr. *fatuite* < Lat. *fatuitas* < *fatuus,* fatuous.]

fat·u·ous (făch'o͞o-əs) *adj.* Complacently or foolishly stupid. [Lat. *fatuus.*] —**fat'u·ous·ly** *adv.* —**fat'u·ous·ness** *n.*

fat-wit·ted (făt'wĭt'ĭd) *adj.* Thick-headed; stupid.

fau·bourg (fō'bo͝org', fō-bo͞or') *n.* **1.** A suburb of a city. **2.** A district or quarter within a city. [ME < OFr., alteration of *forsborc* : *fors,* outside (< Lat. *foris*) + *borc,* town (< LLat. *burgus,* of Germanic orig.).]

fau·ces (fô'sēz') *pl.n. (used with a sing. or pl. verb).* The space between the mouth and pharynx, bounded by the soft palate, the base of the tongue, and the palatine arches. [Lat.] **—fau′cal** (-kəl), **fau′cial** (-shəl) *adj.*

fau·cet (fô′sĭt) *n.* A device for drawing a flow of a liquid from a pipe, drum, or other reservoir. [ME < OFr. *fausset* < *fausser,* to break in < LLat. *falsare,* to falsify < Lat. *falsus,* false.]

faugh (fô) *interj.* Used to express contempt or disgust.

fault (fôlt) *n.* **1. a.** A weakness; defect. **b.** A mistake; error. **c.** A minor offense; misdeed. **2.** Responsibility for a mistake or offense; culpability. **3.** *Geol.* A break in the continuity of a rock formation, caused by a shifting or dislodging of the earth's crust, in which adjacent surfaces are differentially displaced parallel to the plane of fracture. **4.** *Elect.* A defect in a circuit or wiring caused by imperfect connections, poor insulation, grounding, or shorting. **5.** A bad service, as in tennis. **6.** *Obs.* A lack or deficiency. *—v.* **fault·ed, fault·ing, faults.** *—tr.* **1.** To find a fault in; blame. **2.** *Geol.* To produce a fault in; fracture. *—intr.* **1.** To commit a fault or error. **2.** *Geol.* To shift so as to produce a fault. **—*idioms.* at fault. 1.** Deserving of blame; guilty. **2.** Confused and puzzled. **find fault.** To find and complain about faults; criticize. **to a fault.** Excessively. [ME *faulte* < OFr. < VLat. **fallita* < Lat. *fallere,* to fail.]

Synonyms: *fault, failing, weakness, frailty, foible, vice.* These nouns denote imperfection or deficiency of character or soundness in persons. *Fault* usually refers to a specific quality or trait that detracts in large or small measure from excellence. *Failing* more often implies a lack that keeps a person from measuring up to a high standard of behavior or performance in general or in specific circumstances. *Weakness* suggests deficiency of moral or intellectual strength. It is closely related to but stronger than *frailty,* which implies inability to withstand temptation. Even weaker in imputing censure is *foible,* which refers to a minor fault, shortcoming, or eccentricity that is easily overlooked and may even be endearing. *Vice* can refer to a moral flaw or weakness that inclines one to evil or, in a weaker sense, to any defect of character.

Usage: *Fault* as a transitive verb meaning "to criticize or find fault with" is attested as far back as the 16th century but has recently come into much wider use. A bare majority of the Usage Panel approves these examples: *One cannot fault the performance. To fault him is grossly unfair.*

fault·find·er (fôlt′fīn′dər) *n.* One who is given to petty criticism.

fault·find·ing (fôlt′fīn′dĭng) *n.* Petty criticism. *—adj.* Disposed to find trivial faults.

fault·less (fôlt′lĭs) *adj.* Without fault. **—fault′less·ly** *adv.* **—fault′less·ness** *n.*

fault plane *n.* The plane along which the break or shear of a geologic fault occurs.

fault·y (fôl′tē) *adj.* **-i·er, -i·est. 1.** Containing a fault or faults; imperfect. **2.** *Obs.* Deserving of blame; guilty. **—fault′i·ly** *adv.* **—fault′i·ness** *n.*

faun (fôn) *n. Rom. Myth.* One of a group of rural deities represented as having the body of a man and the horns, ears, tail, and sometimes legs of a goat. [ME *faun* < Lat. *Faunus,* Faunus.]

fau·na (fô′nə) *n., pl.* **-nas** or **-nae** (-nē′). Animals collectively, esp. the animals of a particular region or period. [NLat. < Lat. *Fauna,* sister of Faunus.] **—fau′nal** *adj.* **—fau′nal·ly** *adv.*

fau·nis·tic (fô-nĭs′tĭk) *adj.* Of or pertaining to the geographic distribution of fauna. **—fau·nis′ti·cal·ly** *adv.*

Fau·nus (fô′nəs) *n. Rom. Myth.* A god of nature and fertility. [Lat.]

Faust (foust) also **Faus·tus** (fou′stəs, fô′-) *n.* A magician and alchemist in German legend who sells his soul to the devil in exchange for power and worldly experience. [G.] **—Faust′i·an** (fou′stē-ən) *adj.*

fau·vism (fō′vĭz′əm) *n.* An early 20th-century movement in painting marked by the use of bold, often distorted forms and vivid colors. [Fr. *fauvisme* < *fauve,* wild beast < *fauve,* wild, of Germanic orig.]

faux pas (fō pä′) *n., pl.* **faux pas** (fō päz′). A social blunder. [Fr. : *faux,* false + *pas,* step.]

fa·va bean (fä′və) *n.* The broad bean. [Ital. *fava* (< Lat. *faba,* bean) + BEAN.]

fa·ve·o·late (fə-vē′ə-lāt′) *adj.* Pitted with cavities or cells; honeycombed. [< NLat. *faveolus,* dim. of Lat. *favus,* honeycomb.]

fa·vo·ni·an (fə-vō′nē-ən) *adj.* **1.** Of the west wind. **2.** Mild; benign. [Lat. *favonianus* < *Favonius,* the west wind.]

fa·vor (fā′vər) *n.* **1. a.** A gracious, kind, or friendly attitude. **b.** An act showing such an attitude: *Will you do me a favor?* **2. a.** Friendly regard shown esp. by a superior; partiality. **b.** A state of being held in such regard. **3.** Approval or support; sanction. **4.** Partiality; favoritism. **5. favors.** Sexual privileges, esp. as granted by a woman. **6. a.** Something given as a token of love, affection, or remembrance. **b.** A small, decorative gift, such as a paper hat, given to each guest at a party or ball. **7.** Advantage; benefit: *a balance in our favor.* **8.** *Obs.* A communication. **9.** *Obs.* **a.** Aspect or appearance. **b.** Countenance; face. **c.** A facial feature. *—tr.v.* **-vored, -vor·ing, -vors. 1.** To perform a kindness for; oblige. **2.** To treat or regard with favor. **3.** To be partial to; indulge. **4.** To be or tend to be in support of. **5.** To make easier or more possible; aid. **6.** To resemble in appearance: *favors her father.* **7.** To treat with care; be gentle with: *favored his wounded leg.* **—*idiom.* in favor of. 1.** In support of; approving. **2.** To the advantage of. **3.** Inscribed or made out to. [ME < OFr. < Lat. < *favēre,* to be favorable.] **—fa′vor·er** *n.* **—fa′vor·ing·ly** *adv.*

fa·vor·a·ble (fā′vər-ə-bəl, fāv′rə-) *adj.* **1.** Advantageous; helpful. **2.** Propitious; encouraging. **3.** Manifesting approval; commendatory. **4.** Embodying or conceding that which was desired or requested: *a favorable reply.* **5.** Indulgent or partial. **—fa′vor·a·ble·ness** *n.* **—fa′vor·a·bly** *adv.*

Synonyms: *favorable, propitious, auspicious, benign, conducive.* These adjectives describe what is beneficial or points to a successful outcome. *Favorable* is the widest in application. It can refer to persons, conditions, circumstances, or omens that contribute in some way to the attainment of a goal: *a favorable breeze; a favorable sign. Propitious* applies to persons or things that are favorably disposed toward someone or something or that give concrete assistance. Often it refers to time or circumstances considered as omens of or contributors to success: *a political climate propitious to a summit meeting. Auspicious* refers to things that by their favorable nature presage good fortune: *an auspicious start for the project. Benign* refers to persons or things favorably disposed toward one or exerting a beneficial influence. *Conducive* applies to things that lead or contribute to an end, usually a desirable result: *a neighborhood program conducive to good will in the community.*

fa·vored (fā′vərd) *adj.* **1.** Treated or thought of with special kindness or liking; privileged. **2.** Having special talents, gifts, or beauty. **3.** Having a physical appearance of a specified kind: *well-favored; ill-favored.*

fa·vor·ite (fā′vər-ĭt, fāv′rĭt) *n.* **1. a.** One that enjoys special favor or regard. **b.** One that is trusted, indulged, or preferred above all others, esp. by a superior: *a favorite of the king.* **2.** A contestant or competitor regarded as most likely to win. *—adj.* Liked or preferred above all others; regarded with special favor. [OFr. *favorit* < OItal. *favorita,* p.part. of *favorire,* to favor < *favore,* favor < Lat. *favor.*]

favorite son *n.* **1.** A person favored for presidential candidate nominee by his own state delegates at a national political convention. **2.** A person, as a celebrity, viewed with much favor by his hometown.

fa·vor·it·ism (fā′vər-ĭ-tĭz′əm, fāv′rĭ-) *n.* **1.** A display of partiality toward a favored person or group. **2.** The state of being held in special favor.

fa·vour (fā′vər) *n. & v. Chiefly Brit.* Variant of **favor.**

fa·vus (fā′vəs) *n.* A chronic fungous infection of the scalp and nails. [Lat., honeycomb.]

fawn[1] (fôn) *intr.v.* **fawned, fawn·ing, fawns. 1.** To exhibit affection, as in the manner of a dog wagging its tail and whining. **2.** To seek favor or attention by flattery and obsequious behavior. [ME *faunen* < OE *fagnian,* to rejoice.] **—fawn′er** *n.* **—fawn′ing·ly** *adv.*

fawn[2] (fôn) *n.* **1.** A young deer, esp. one less than a year old. **2.** A grayish yellowish brown to light grayish or moderate reddish brown or moderate yellowish pink. [ME < OFr. *foun,* young animal < Lat. *fetus,* offspring.]

fawn lily *n.* Any of several North American plants of the genus *Erythronium,* esp. *E. grandiflorum,* of western North America, having nodding yellow flowers.

fax (făks) *n.* A facsimile (sense 2). [Shortening and alteration of FACSIMILE.]

fay[1] (fā) *tr.v.* **fayed, fay·ing, fays.** To join or fit closely or tightly. [ME *feien* < OE *fēgan.*]

fay[2] (fā) *n.* A fairy; elf. [ME *faie* < OFr. *fae,* enchanted < Lat. *fata,* the Fates, pl. of *fatum,* fate.]

fay[3] (fā) *n. Obs.* Faith. [ME *fai.*]

fay·a·lite (fā′ə-līt′) *n.* A yellowish to black mineral, $FeSiO_4$, of the olivine group. [G. *Fayalit* < *Faial,* Faial, an island in the Azores.]

faze (fāz) *tr.v.* **fazed, faz·ing, faz·es.** To disrupt the composure of; disconcert. [Var. of FEEZE.]

fa·zen·da (fə-zĕn′də) *n., pl.* **-das.** In Brazil, a hacienda, estate, or plantation, esp. a coffee plantation. [Port.]

Fe The symbol for the element iron. [Lat. *ferrum,* iron.]

fe·al·ty (fē′əl-tē) *n., pl.* **-ties. 1. a.** The loyalty of a vassal to his feudal lord. **b.** The obligation of such loyalty. **2.** Faithfulness; allegiance. [ME *fealtye* < OFr. *fealte* < Lat. *fidelitas,* faithfulness < *fidelis,* faithful < *fides,* faith.]

fear (fîr) *n.* **1. a.** An emotion of alarm and agitation caused by the expectation or realization of danger. **b.** An instance of such a feeling. **c.** A state or condition marked by this feeling. **2.** Extreme reverence or awe, as toward a supreme power. **3.** A ground for dread or apprehension; danger. *—v.* **feared, fear·ing, fears.** *—tr.* **1.** To be afraid or frightened of. **2.** To be anxious or apprehensive about. **3.** To be in awe of; revere. **4.** To suspect: *I fear you are wrong.* **5.** *Archaic.* To feel fear within (oneself). *—intr.* **1.** To be afraid, frightened, or terrified. **2.** To feel anxious or apprehensive. [ME *fer* < OE *fǣr.*] **—fear′er** *n.*

Synonyms: *fear, fright, dread, terror, horror, panic, alarm, dismay, consternation, trepidation.* These nouns refer to emotional reaction caused by the presence or imminence of danger, evil, harm, or great misfortune. *Fear* is the most general term. *Fright* is fear suddenly aroused and character-

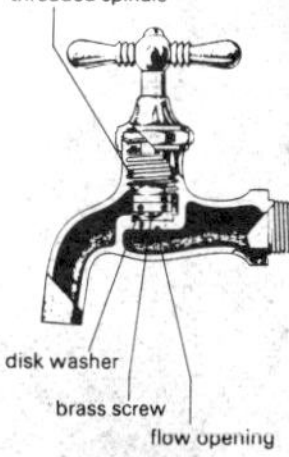

faucet
Above: Cross section
Below: Bathtub faucet

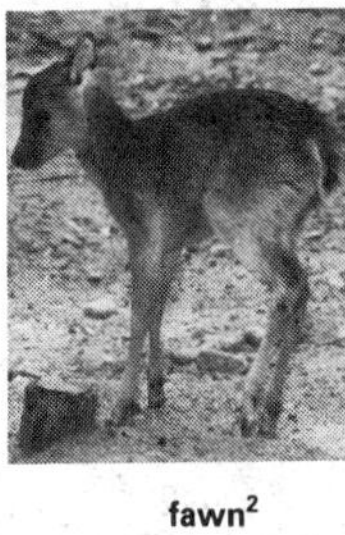

fawn[2]

ized by great agitation, usually for a short period. *Dread* is strong fear of something thought to be impending, especially of what one is powerless to avoid. *Terror* is violent, paralyzing fear, usually in the presence of great danger. *Horror* is a combination of fear and aversion or repugnance. *Panic* is strong, sudden fear, often groundless and frequently the impetus for mindless action. *Alarm* is fright aroused upon the first realization of danger. *Dismay* is strong apprehension that robs one of courage or power to act effectively. *Consternation* is the state of being confounded or made confused and helpless. *Trepidation* is apprehension or dread characteristically marked by trembling or hesitancy.

feather
With enlarged portion showing structural details

fear·ful (fîr'fəl) *adj.* **1.** Causing or capable of causing fear; frightening. **2.** Experiencing fear; frightened. **3.** Feeling anxious or apprehensive. **4.** Feeling reverence, dread, or awe. **5.** Indicating anxiety, fear, or terror. **6.** *Informal.* Extreme, as in degree or extent: *a fearful blunder.* —**fear'ful·ly** *adv.* —**fear'ful·ness** *n.*

fear·less (fîr'lĭs) *adj.* Having no fear; brave. —**fear'less·ly** *adv.* —**fear'less·ness** *n.*

fear·some (fîr'səm) *adj.* **1.** Causing or capable of causing fear. **2.** Fearful; timid. —**fear'some·ly** *adv.* —**fear'some·ness** *n.*

fea·si·ble (fē'zə-bəl) *adj.* **1.** Capable of being accomplished or brought about; possible: *a feasible project.* **2.** Capable of being utilized or dealt with successfully; suitable. **3.** Logical; likely. [ME *fesable* < OFr. *faisible* < *faire,* to do < Lat. *facere.*] —**fea'si·bil'i·ty, fea'si·ble·ness** *n.* —**fea'si·bly** *adv.*

feast (fēst) *n.* **1.** A periodic religious festival in commemoration of an event or in honor of a deity, occurrence, or person. **2.** A large, elaborately prepared meal, usually for many persons and often with entertainment; banquet. **3.** Something giving great pleasure or satisfaction: *a feast for the eyes.* —*v.* **feast·ed, feast·ing, feasts.** —*tr.* **1.** To give a feast for; entertain or feed sumptuously. **2.** To provide with pleasure; delight: *feasted his eyes on the paintings.* —*intr.* **1.** To partake of a feast. **2.** To experience something with gratification or delight. [ME *feste* < OFr. < Lat. *festum* < *festus,* joyous.] —**feast'er** *n.*

feather star

Feast of Lights *n.* Chanukah.

feat[1] (fēt) *n.* **1. a.** An act or deed. **b.** An act, esp. of courage; exploit. **2.** An act of skill, endurance, imagination, or strength; achievement. **3.** *Obs.* A specialized skill; knack. [ME *fet* < AN < OFr. *fait* < Lat. *factum* < neuter p.part. of *facere,* to do.]

feat[2] (fēt) *adj.* **-er, -est.** *Archaic.* **1.** Adroit; dexterous. **2.** Neat; trim. [ME *fete,* suitable < OFr. *fait* < Lat. *factum,* deed. —see FEAT[1].] —**feat'ly** *adv.*

feath·er (fĕth'ər) *n.* **1.** One of the light, horny structures forming the plumage of birds, consisting of numerous slender, closely arranged parallel barbs forming a vane on either side of a tapering hollow shaft. **2. feathers.** Plumage. **3. feathers.** Clothing; attire. **4.** A tuft or fringe of hair, as on the legs or tail of some dogs. **5.** Character; nature: *Birds of a feather flock together.* **6.** Something small, trivial, or inconsequential. **7. a.** A strip, wedge, or flange used as a strengthening part. **b.** A wedge or key that fits into a groove to make a joint. **8.** The vane of an arrow. **9.** A feather-shaped flaw, as in a gem or precious stone. **10.** The wake made by a submarine's periscope. **11.** The act of feathering the blade of an oar in rowing. —*v.* **-ered, -er·ing, -ers.** —*tr.* **1.** To cover, dress, or decorate with or as if with feathers. **2.** To fit (an arrow) with a feather. **3. a.** To thin, reduce, or fringe the edge of by cutting, shaving, or wearing away. **b.** To shorten and taper (hair) by cutting and thinning. **4.** To connect with a tongue-and-groove joint. **5.** To turn (an oar blade) horizontal to the surface of the water between strokes. **6.** To alter the pitch of (a propeller) so that the blade chords are parallel with the line of flight. —*intr.* **1.** To grow feathers or become feathered. **2.** To move, spread, or grow in a manner suggestive of feathers. **3.** To feather an oar. **4.** To feather a propeller. —***idioms.*** **a feather in (one's) cap.** An act or deed to one's credit. **feather (one's) nest.** To grow wealthy by making use of property or funds left in one's trust. **in fine (or good) feather.** In excellent form, health, or humor. [ME *fether* < OE *feðer.*] —**feath'er·less** *adj.*

featherstitch

feather bed *n.* **1.** A mattress stuffed with feathers. **2.** A bed having a feather mattress.

feath·er·bed (fĕth'ər-bĕd') *intr.v.* **-bed·ded, -bed·ding, -beds. 1.** To employ more workers than are actually needed for a given purpose or to limit their production. **2.** To be employed as a result of the practice of featherbedding.

feath·er·bed·ding (fĕth'ər-bĕd'ĭng) *n.* The limitation of production or the employment of more workers than needed as the result of a safety regulation or union rule.

feath·er·bone (fĕth'ər-bōn') *n.* A lightweight corset bone originally made from the quills of domestic fowl.

feath·er·brain (fĕth'ər-brān') *n.* A silly, flighty, or empty-headed person. —**feath'er·brained'** *adj.*

feath·er·edge (fĕth'ər-ĕj') *n.* A thin fragile edge, esp. a tapering edge of a board.

feather grass *n.* Any of various grasses of the genus *Stipa,* having clusters of featherlike spikelets.

feath·er·head (fĕth'ər-hĕd') *n.* A featherbrain. —**feath'er·head'ed** *adj.*

feather rot *n.* A disease of tree trunks caused by the fungus *Poria subacida* that causes the trunk to become spongy or stringy.

feather star *n.* Any of numerous crinoids of the genus *Antedon* and related genera, having a free-moving, stalkless adult stage with branched, feathery arms.

feath·er·stitch (fĕth'ər-stĭch') *n.* An embroidery stitch that produces a decorative zigzag line. —*v.* **-stitched, -stitch·ing, -stitch·es.** —*intr.* To embroider in featherstitch. —*tr.* To embroider (material) in featherstitch.

feath·er·weight (fĕth'ər-wāt') *n.* **1.** A boxer or wrestler weighing between approximately 54 and 57 kilograms or 118 and 127 pounds. **2.** A person or thing of little weight or size. **3.** An insignificant person.

feath·er·y (fĕth'ə-rē) *adj.* **1.** Covered with or consisting of feathers. **2.** Resembling or suggestive of a feather. —**feath'er·i·ness** *n.*

fea·ture (fē'chər) *n.* **1.** The make-up, shape, proportions, form, or outward appearance, esp. of a person. **2. a.** The make-up or appearance of the face or its parts. **b.** Any of the distinct parts of the face. **3.** A prominent or distinctive aspect, quality, or characteristic. **4.** The main presentation at a motion-picture theater. **5.** A prominent or extra article or story in a newspaper or periodical. **6.** Something advertised as particularly attractive or as an inducement, such as a sale item in a store. **7.** *Archaic.* Form; shape. —*tr.v.* **-tured, -tur·ing, -tures. 1.** To give special attention to; make prominent. **2.** To have as a characteristic. **3.** To draw or otherwise portray the features of. **4.** *Informal.* To resemble in features; favor. **5.** *Informal.* To imagine, picture mentally, or conceive of. [ME *feture* < OFr. < Lat. *factura* < *factus,* p.part. of *facere,* to make.]

fea·tured (fē'chərd) *adj.* **1. a.** Given particular attention or publicity; made prominent. **b.** Starring: *a featured actress.* **2.** Having a specified kind of facial features: *sharp-featured.* **3.** Formed or given a particular appearance by facial features.

fea·ture-length (fē'chər-lĕngkth', -lĕngth') *adj.* Of normal or full length: *a feature-length film.*

fe·bric·i·ty (fĭ-brĭs'ĭ-tē) *n.* The condition of having a fever. [Med. Lat. *febricitas* < Lat. *febricitare,* to have a fever < *febris,* fever.]

feb·ri·fa·cient (fĕb'rə-fā'shənt) *n.* A substance that causes a fever. —*adj.* Causing or producing fever. [Latin *febris,* fever + -FACIENT.]

fe·brif·ic (fĭ-brĭf'ĭk) *adj.* **1.** Causing fever. **2.** Having a fever; feverish. [Lat. *febris,* fever + -FIC.]

feb·ri·fuge (fĕb'rə-fyōōj') *n.* An agent that reduces a fever. —*adj.* Serving to reduce fever. [Fr. *fébrifuge* : Lat. *febris,* fever + Lat. *fugare,* to drive away.]

feb·rile (fĕb'rəl, fē'brəl) *adj.* Of, pertaining to, or characterized by fever; feverish. [Fr. *fébrile* < Lat. *febris,* fever.]

Feb·ru·ar·y (fĕb'rōō-ĕr'ē, fĕb'yōō-) *n.* The second month of the year according to the Gregorian calendar. See table at **calendar.** [ME < Lat. *Februarius* < *februa,* festival of purification, of Sabine orig.]

fe·cal (fē'kəl) *adj.* Of, pertaining to, or constituting feces.

fe·ces also **fae·ces** (fē'sēz) *pl.n.* Waste excreted from the bowels; excrement. [ME < Lat. *faeces,* pl. of *faex,* dregs.]

feck·less (fĕk'lĭs) *adj.* **1.** Lacking purpose or vitality; ineffective. **2.** Careless; irresponsible. [Sc., short for EFFECT + -LESS.] —**feck'less·ly** *adv.* —**feck'less·ness** *n.*

fec·u·lent (fĕk'yə-lənt) *adj.* Full of foul or impure matter; fecal. [ME < Lat. *faeculentus* < *faex,* dregs.] —**fec'u·lence** *n.*

fe·cund (fē'kənd, fĕk'ənd) *adj.* **1.** Capable of producing offspring or vegetation; fruitful. **2.** Marked by intellectual productivity. [ME < OFr. *fecond* < Lat. *fecundus.*] —**fe·cun'di·ty** (fĭ-kŭn'dĭ-tē) *n.*

fe·cun·date (fē'kən-dāt', fĕk'ən-) *tr.v.* **-dat·ed, -dat·ing, -dates. 1.** To make fecund or fruitful. **2.** To impregnate; fertilize. [Lat. *fecundare, fecundat-* < *fecundus,* fecund.] —**fe'cun·da'tion** *n.*

fed (fĕd) *v.* Past tense and past participle of **feed.**

Fe·da·yee (fĭ-dä'yē', -dă'ē', -dä'-) *n., pl.* **-yeen** (-yēn', -ēn'). An Arab commando operating esp. against Israel. [Ar. *fedā'yūn* < *fidā'i,* one who sacrifices himself for his country < *fidā',* redemption.]

fed·er·a·cy (fĕd'ər-ə-sē) *n., pl.* **-cies.** *Archaic.* An alliance or confederacy. [Short for CONFEDERACY.]

fed·er·al (fĕd'ər-əl, fĕd'rəl) *adj.* **1.** Of, pertaining to, or designating a form of government in which a union of states recognizes the sovereignty of a central authority while retaining certain residual powers of government. **2.** Of, constituting, or characterized by a form of government in which sovereign power is divided between a central authority and a number of constituent political units. **3.** Of or pertaining to the central government of a federation as distinct from the governments of its member units. **4.** Favorable to or advocating federation: *His federal leanings were well known.* **5.** Of or pertaining to a league, treaty, or compact. **6. Federal. a.** Of, pertaining to, or characterizing Federalism. **b.** Of, pertaining to, or supporting the Union during the American Civil War. —*n.* **Federal.** A supporter of the Union during the American Civil War, esp. a Union soldier. [< Lat. *foedus, foeder-,* league.] —**fed'er·al·ly** *adv.*

federal district *n.* An area reserved as the site of the national capital of a federation, such as the District of Columbia.

fed·er·al·ism (fĕd′ər-ə-lĭz′əm, fĕd′rə-) *n.* **1. a.** The doctrine or system of federal government. **b.** The advocacy of such a system of government. **2. Federalism.** The doctrine of the Federalist Party.

fed·er·al·ist (fĕd′ər-ə-lĭst, fĕd′rə-) *n.* **1.** An advocate of federalism. **2. Federalist.** A member or supporter of a political party that was founded in the United States in 1787 and favored a strong federal government. *—adj.* **1.** Of or pertaining to federalism or its advocates. **2. Federalist.** Of or pertaining to Federalism or Federalists.

fed·er·al·ize (fĕd′ər-ə-līz′, fĕd′rə-) *tr.v.* **-ized, -iz·ing, -iz·es. 1.** To unite in a federal union. **2.** To subject to the authority of a federal government; put under federal control. **—fed′er·al·i·za′tion** *n.*

Federal Reserve System *n.* A banking system in the United States consisting of 12 banks each serving member banks in its own district.

fed·er·ate (fĕd′ə-rāt′) *v.* **-at·ed, -at·ing, -ates.** *—tr.* To join or bring together in a league, federal union, or similar association. *—intr.* To unite in a federal union. *—adj.* (fĕd′ər-ĭt, fĕd′rĭt). United under a central government; federated. [Lat. *foederare, foederat-,* to enter into a league < *foedus,* league.]

fed·er·a·tion (fĕd′ə-rā′shən) *n.* **1.** The act of federating, esp. in order to create a federal union. **2.** A league or association formed by federating.

fed·er·a·tive (fĕd′ə-rā′tĭv, fĕd′ər-ə-, fĕd′rə-) *adj.* Forming, belonging to, or of the nature of a federation; federal. **—fed′er·a′tive·ly** *adv.*

fe·do·ra (fĭ-dôr′ə, -dōr′ə) *n.* A soft felt hat with a brim that can be turned up or down and a rather low crown creased lengthwise. [After *Fédora,* a play by Victorien Sardou (1831–1908).]

fed up *adj.* Extremely tired or disgusted: *was fed up with their indecisiveness.*

fee (fē) *n.* **1.** A fixed charge: *tuition fees.* **2.** A charge for a professional service: *a tax consultant's fee.* **3.** A tip; gratuity. **4.** *Law.* An inherited or heritable estate in land. **5. a.** In feudal law, an estate in land held from a lord on condition of homage and service. **b.** The land so held. *—tr.v.* **feed, fee·ing, fees.** To give a tip to. **—idiom. in fee.** In absolute and legal possession. [ME *fe* < AN *fee,* inherited estate < OFr. *fie,* fief, of Germanic orig.]

fee·ble (fē′bəl) *adj.* **-bler, -blest. 1. a.** Lacking strength; weak. **b.** Indicating weakness. **2. a.** Lacking vigor or force. **b.** Inadequate; ineffective: *a feeble answer.* [ME *feble* < OFr., var. of *fleible* < Lat. *flebilis,* lamentable < *flere,* to weep.] **—fee′ble·ness** *n.* **—fee′bly** *adv.*

fee·ble-mind·ed (fē′bəl-mīn′dĭd) *adj.* **1.** Mentally deficient; subnormal in intelligence. **2.** Dull-witted; stupid. **3.** *Archaic.* Weak-willed. **—fee′ble-mind′ed·ly** *adv.* **—fee′ble-mind′ed·ness** *n.*

feed (fēd) *v.* **fed** (fĕd), **feed·ing, feeds.** *—tr.* **1. a.** To give food to; supply with nourishment. **b.** To provide as food or nourishment: *feed fish to a cat.* **2. a.** To serve as food for: *The turkey is large enough to feed a dozen.* **b.** To produce food for: *The valley feeds an entire county.* **3.** To supply for consumption or utilization: *feed ammunition to a gun crew.* **4. a.** To minister to; gratify: *fed their appetite for the morbid.* **b.** To support or promote: *feed suspicions.* **5.** To supply as a cue: *feed lines to an actor.* **6.** *Sports.* To pass the ball or puck to (a teammate), esp. in order to score. *—intr.* **1.** To consume as food. **2.** To draw support or satisfaction from: *His ego feeds on flattery.* *—n.* **1. a.** Food for animals or birds; fodder. **b.** The allowance of fodder given at one time. **2.** *Informal.* A meal. **3. a.** Material or an amount of material supplied to a machine. **b.** The act of supplying this material. **4. a.** The apparatus that supplies material to a machine. **b.** The aperture through which such material enters a machine. **—idiom. off (one's) feed.** *Slang.* Temporarily without appetite for food. [ME *feden* < OE *fēdan.*]

feed·back (fēd′băk′) *n.* **1. a.** The return of a portion of the output of a process or system to the input, esp. to maintain performance or to control a system or process. **b.** The portion of the output so returned. **2.** The return of information about the result of a process. *—adj.* Of, pertaining to, or being a device or process that relies on feedback for its operation.

feedback inhibition *n.* A control mechanism in a cell in which the excessive accumulation of the end product of a series of biosynthetic reactions inhibits the action of an enzyme that occurs early in the reaction series.

feed·bag (fēd′băg′) *n.* A bag that fits over a horse's muzzle and holds feed.

feed·er (fē′dər) *n.* **1.** One that supplies food. **2.** One that feeds materials into a machine for further processing. **3.** Something that contributes to the operation, maintenance, or supply of something else, esp.: **a.** A tributary. **b.** A branch line of a transport system. **c.** An animal that is being fattened. **4.** Any of the medium-voltage lines used to distribute electric power from a substation to consumers or smaller substations.

feed·hole (fēd′hōl′) *n. Computer Sci.* One of a noninformational series of holes in a paper tape that engages a driving sprocket to carry the tape through a reading or punching device.

feed·lot (fēd′lŏt′) *n.* A lot on which livestock are fattened for market.

feed·stock (fēd′stŏk′) *n.* Raw materials required for an industrial process.

feed·stuff (fēd′stŭf′) *n.* Feed (sense 1.a.).

feed·through (fēd′thro͞o′) *n.* A conductor connecting two circuits on opposite sides of a nonconducting surface.

feel (fēl) *v.* **felt** (fĕlt), **feel·ing, feels.** *—tr.* **1. a.** To perceive through the sense of touch. **b.** To perceive as a physical sensation: *feel a sharp pain, feel the cold.* **2. a.** To touch. **b.** To examine by touching. **c.** To test or explore with caution: *feel one's way in a new job.* **3. a.** To undergo the experience of: *felt my interest rising.* **b.** To be aware of; sense: *She felt his annoyance.* **c.** To be emotionally affected by: *feel the loss of someone.* **4.** To believe; consider: *His answer was felt to be evasive.* *—intr.* **1.** To experience sensations of touch. **2.** To appear to be, esp. to the sense of touch: *The sheets felt smooth.* **3.** To be conscious of an impression or of a physical or mental state. **4.** To search or be guided by or as if by the sense of touch. **5.** To have compassion or sympathy: *feel for him in his troubles.* **6.** To have a sentiment or subjective view: *feel strongly about the election.* **—phrasal verbs. feel out.** To sound out in order to ascertain the viewpoint or opinion of. **feel up.** *Vulgar Slang.* To touch or caress the upper thighs, genitals, or posterior of. *—n.* **1. a.** Perception by touching or feeling: *the feel of a rose petal.* **b.** The act or an instance of touching or feeling: *a feel of this cloth.* **2.** The sense of touch: *rough to the feel.* **3.** The nature, condition, or quality of something perceived through or as if through the sense of touch: *the feel of a sports car.* **4.** Emotional quality; atmosphere. **5.** Intuitive awareness, knowledge, or skill. **—idiom. feel like.** *Informal.* To have an inclination or desire to or for. [ME *felen* < OE *fēlan.*]

fedora

feel·er (fē′lər) *n.* **1.** One that feels. **2.** Something, such as a hint or question, designed to elicit the attitude or intention of another. **3.** A sensory or tactile organ, such as an antenna, tentacle, or barbel.

feel·ing (fē′lĭng) *n.* **1. a.** The sensation involving perception by touch. **b.** A sensation perceived by touch. **c.** A physical sensation. **2.** An affective state of consciousness, such as that resulting from emotions, sentiments, or desires: *a feeling of excitement.* **3.** An awareness; impression: *a feeling that one is being followed.* **4. a.** An emotional state or disposition; emotion: *expressed deep feeling.* **b.** A tender emotion; fondness. **5. a.** The ability to experience and react to the emotions; sensibility: *a man of feeling.* **b. feelings.** Sensitivities: *hurt his feelings.* **6.** Opinion as distinguished from reason; sentiment. **7.** An impression produced by a person, place, thing, or event: *The guests gave the feeling of forced gaiety.* **8. a.** An appreciative regard: *a feeling for propriety.* **b.** Intuitive awareness or aptitude: *a feeling for language.* *—adj.* **1. a.** Having the ability to react or feel emotionally; sensitive. **b.** Easily moved emotionally. **2.** Having sensibility; sympathetic. **3.** Expressive of sensibility or emotion: *a feeling glance.* **—feel′ing·ly** *adv.*

Synonyms: *feeling, emotion, passion.* These nouns refer to nonintellectual or subjective human response. *Feeling* and *emotion* are often interchangeable in this sense. *Emotion,* however, is frequently considered the stronger term, especially appropriate to such response marked by excitement or agitation. *Passion,* in its broadest sense, is intense, compelling emotion.

fee simple *n., pl.* **fees simple.** *Law.* An estate in land of which the inheritor has unqualified ownership and power of disposition.

fee splitting *n.* The practice of paying commissions to professional colleagues, as doctors, on the fees received from those who have been referred by these colleagues.

feet (fēt) *n.* Plural of **foot.**

fee tail *n., pl.* **fees tail.** *Law.* An estate in land limited in inheritance to a specified individual, group, or class of heirs.

feet of clay *n.* A defect or weakness in an apparently sound character.

feeze (fēz, fāz) *n. Regional.* **1.** A heavy impact. **2.** A state of vexation. *—tr.v.* **feezed, feez·ing, feez·es. 1.** To drive off; put to flight. **2.** To faze. [ME *fese* < *fesen,* to drive away.]

Feh·ling's solution (fā′lĭngz) *n.* A solution of copper sulfate, sodium hydroxide, and Rochelle salt used in testing for the presence of sugars and aldehydes. [After Hermann *Fehling* (1812–1885).]

feign (fān) *v.* **feigned, feign·ing, feigns.** *—tr.* **1. a.** To give a false appearance of; sham: *feign sleep.* **b.** To represent falsely; pretend to: *feign authorship of a novel.* **2.** *Archaic.* **a.** To invent. **b.** To fabricate. *—intr.* To pretend; dissemble. [ME *feinen* < OFr. *feindre* < Lat. *fingere,* to form.]

feigned (fānd) *adj.* **1.** Not real; pretended. **2.** Made up; fictitious. **—feign′ed·ly** (fā′nĭd-lē) *adv.*

feint (fānt) *n.* **1.** A misleading movement or feigned attack directed toward one part to draw defensive action away from the real target or objective. **2.** A pretense; stratagem. *—intr.v.* **feint·ed, feint·ing, feints.** To make a feint. [Fr. *feinte* < OFr. < p.part. of *feindre,* to feign.]

feist (fīst) also **fice** (fīs) *n. Regional.* A small dog of mixed

feedbag

ancestry; mongrel. [Var. of obs. *fist,* short for *fisting dog* < ME *fist,* a foul smell < *fisten,* to break wind.]

feist·y (fī′stē) *adj.* **-i·er, -i·est.** *Regional.* **1.** Touchy; quarrelsome. **2.** Spirited; frisky. [< FEIST.] **—feist′i·ness** *n.*

fe·la·fel (fə-lä′fəl) *n.* Variant of **falafel.**

feld·spar (fĕld′spär′, fĕl′-) also **fel·spar** (fĕl′-) *n.* Any of a group of abundant rock-forming minerals occurring principally in igneous, plutonic, and some metamorphic rocks and consisting of silicates of aluminum with potassium, sodium, calcium, and rarely barium. [Partial transl. of obs. G. *Feldspath* : *Feld,* field (< OHG *feld*) + *Spath,* spar.]

feld·spath·ic (fĕld-spăth′ĭk, fĕl-) *adj.* Of, relating to, or containing feldspar. [< obs. G. *Feldspath,* feldspar.]

fe·li·cif·ic (fē′lĭ-sĭf′ĭk) *adj.* Producing or intended to produce happiness. [Lat. *felicificus* : *felix, felici-,* happy + *ficus,* -fic.]

fe·lic·i·tate (fĭ-lĭs′ĭ-tāt′) *tr.v.* **-tat·ed, -tat·ing, -tates. 1.** To wish happiness to; congratulate. **2.** *Archaic.* To make happy. *—adj. Obs.* Made happy. [Lat. *felicitare, felicitat-,* to make happy < *felix, felici-,* happy.] **—fe·lic′i·ta′tion** *n.* **—fe·lic′i·ta′tor** *n.*

fe·lic·i·tous (fĭ-lĭs′ĭ-təs) *adj.* **1.** Well-chosen; apt: *a felicitous comparison.* **2.** Yielding great pleasure or delight. **—fe·lic′i·tous·ly** *adv.* **—fe·lic′i·tous·ness** *n.*

fe·lic·i·ty (fĭ-lĭs′ĭ-tē) *n., pl.* **-ties. 1. a.** Great happiness; bliss. **b.** An instance of this. **2.** Something that causes or produces happiness. **3. a.** An appropriate and pleasing manner or style. **b.** An instance of this. [ME < OFr. *felicite* < Lat. *felicitas* < *felix,* happy.]

fe·lid (fē′lĭd) *adj.* Feline (sense 1). [NLat. *Felidae,* family name < *Felis,* cat genus < Lat. *felis,* cat.] **—fe′lid** *n.*

fe·line (fē′līn′) *adj.* **1.** Of or belonging to the family Felidae, which includes the lions, tigers, jaguars, and wild and domestic cats. **2.** Resembling or suggestive of a cat, as in suppleness, slyness, or stealthiness. [Lat. *felinus* < *felis,* cat.] **—fe′line′** *n.* **—fe′line′ly** *adv.* **—fe′line′ness, fe·lin′i·ty** (fĭ-lĭn′ĭ-tē) *n.*

fell[1] (fĕl) *tr.v.* **felled, fell·ing, fells. 1. a.** To cut or knock down: *fell a tree.* **b.** To kill. **2.** To sew or finish (a seam) with the raw edges flattened, turned under, and stitched down. [ME *fellen* < OE *fyllan.*] **—fell′a·ble** *adj.* **—fell′er** *n.*

fell[2] (fĕl) *adj.* **1.** Of an inhumanly cruel nature; fierce. **2.** Capable of destroying; lethal. **3.** *Scot.* Sharp and biting. **—idiom. at one fell swoop.** All at once. [ME *fel* < OFr.] **—fell′ness** *n.*

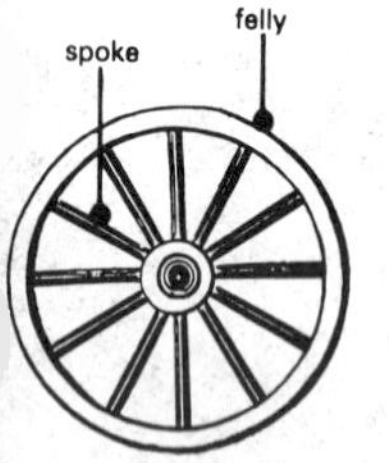

felly

fell[3] (fĕl) *n.* The hide of an animal; pelt. [ME *fel* < OE.]

fell[4] (fĕl) *v.* Past tense of **fall.**

fel·lah (fĕl′ə, fə-lä′) *n., pl.* **fel·lahs** also **fel·la·hin** or **fel·la·heen** (fĕl′ə-hēn′, fə-lä′hēn′). A peasant or agricultural laborer in Arab countries. [Ar. *fellāḥ,* dial. var. of *fallāḥ* < *falaḥa,* to cultivate.]

fel·la·ti·o (fə-lā′shē-ō′, -lä′tē-ō′, fē-) also **fel·la·tion** (-lā′shən) *n.* Oral stimulation of the penis. [NLat. < Lat. *fellatus,* p.part. of *fellare,* to suck.]

fell·mon·ger (fĕl′mŭng′gər, -mŏng′) *n. Chiefly Brit.* One who prepares hides for making leather. **—fell′mon′ger·ing, fell′mon′ger·y** *n.*

felucca

fel·low (fĕl′ō) *n.* **1. a.** A man or boy. **b.** *Informal.* A boy friend. **c.** A worthless boy or man. **2.** A comrade or associate. **3. a.** A person of equal rank, position, or background; peer. **b.** One of a pair; mate. **4.** A member of a learned society. **5.** A graduate student appointed to a position granting financial aid and providing for further study. **6.** *Chiefly Brit.* A member of an incorporated college or university. **7.** *Obs.* A person of a lower social class. *—adj.* Being of the same kind, group, occupation, society, or locality; having in common certain characteristics or interests: *fellow workers.* [ME < OE *fēolaga* < ON *fēlagi,* business partner : *fē,* money + *lag,* laying down.]

fellow creature *n.* A kindred creature, esp. another member of the human race.

fellow feeling *n.* **1.** Sympathetic awareness of others. **2.** Community of interest.

fellow man also **fel·low·man** (fĕl′ō-măn′) *n.* A kindred person or human being.

fellow servant *n. Law.* One of a group of employees working together under such circumstances that the employer cannot be expected to protect against or be liable for harm caused by the negligence of one employee to another.

fel·low·ship (fĕl′ō-shĭp′) *n.* **1. a.** The condition of being together or of sharing similar interests or experiences, as do members of a profession, religion, or nationality; companionship. **b.** The companionship of individuals in a congenial atmosphere and on equal terms. **2.** A union of friends or equals sharing similar interests; fraternity. **3.** Friendship; comradeship. **4. a.** A scholarship or grant awarded a graduate student in a college or university. **b.** The state of having been awarded such a scholarship or grant. **c.** A foundation established for the awarding of such a scholarship or grant.

fellow traveler *n.* One who sympathizes with the tenets and programs of an organized group, such as the Communist Party, without actually joining it.

fel·ly (fĕl′ē) also **fel·loe** (fĕl′ō) *n., pl.* **-lies** also **-loes.** The rim or a section of the rim of a wheel supported by spokes. [ME *felies* < OE *felg.*]

fel·o-de-se (fĕl′ō-dĭ-sā′, -sē′) *n., pl.* **fe·lo·nes-de-se** (fə-lō′nēz-) or **fel·os-de-se** (fĕl′ōz-). *Law.* **1.** The act of suicide. **2.** One who commits suicide or who dies as a result of committing an unlawful and malicious act. [Med. Lat., felon of himself.]

fel·on[1] (fĕl′ən) *n.* **1.** *Law.* A person who has committed a felony. **2.** *Archaic.* An evil person. *—adj. Archaic.* **1.** Evil. **2.** Cruel. [ME *feloun* < *feloun,* wicked < OFr. *felon* < Med. Lat. *fello,* villain.]

fel·on[2] (fĕl′ən) *n.* A purulent infection at the distal end of a finger near or around the nail or the bone. [ME *feloun,* prob. < Lat. *fel,* gall, bile.]

fe·lo·nes-de-se (fə-lō′nēz-dĭ-sā′, -sē′) *n.* A plural of **felo-de-se.**

fe·lo·ni·ous (fə-lō′nē-əs) *adj.* **1.** *Law.* **a.** Of, pertaining to, or concerning a felony. **b.** Characterized by or of the nature of a felony. **2.** *Archaic.* Evil; wicked. **—fe·lo′ni·ous·ly** *adv.* **—fe·lo′ni·ous·ness** *n.*

fel·on·ry (fĕl′ən-rē) *n.* Felons collectively.

fel·o·ny (fĕl′ə-nē) *n., pl.* **-nies.** *Law.* **1.** Any of several crimes, such as murder, rape, or burglary, considered more serious than a misdemeanor and punishable by a more stringent sentence. **2.** Any of several crimes in early English law that were punishable by forfeiture of land or goods and by possible loss of life or a bodily part.

fel·os-de-se (fĕl′ōz-dĭ-sā′, -sē′) *n.* A plural of **felo-de-se.**

fel·site (fĕl′sīt′) *n.* A fine-grained igneous rock, chiefly feldspar and quartz. [FELS(PAR) + -ITE.] **—fel·sit′ic** (-sĭt′ĭk) *adj.*

fel·spar (fĕl′spär′) *n.* Variant of **feldspar.**

felt[1] (fĕlt) *n.* **1.** A fabric of matted, compressed animal fibers, as wool or fur, sometimes mixed with vegetable or synthetic fibers. **2.** A fabric or material resembling felt. **3.** Something made of felt. *—adj.* **1.** Made of felt. **2.** Pertaining or similar to felt. *—v.* **felt·ed, felt·ing, felts.** *—tr.* **1.** To make into felt. **2.** To cover with felt. **3.** To press or mat together. *—intr.* To become like felt; mat together. [ME < OE.]

felt[2] (fĕlt) *v.* Past tense and past participle of **feel.**

felt·ing (fĕl′tĭng) *n.* **1.** The practice or process of making felt. **2.** The materials from which felt is made. **3.** Felted fabric.

fe·luc·ca (fə-lōō′kə, -lŭk′ə) *n.* A narrow, swift sailing vessel, chiefly of the Mediterranean, propelled by lateen sails. [Ital. *feluca* < Ar. *fulk,* ship.]

fel·wort (fĕl′wûrt′, -wôrt′) *n.* Any of several plants of the genus *Gentiana* or related genera, esp. *G. amarella,* having small, purplish flowers. [ME **feldwort* < OE *feldwyrt* : *feld,* field + *wyrt,* wort.]

fe·male (fē′māl′) *adj.* **1.** Of, pertaining to, or designating the sex that produces ova or bears young. **2.** Characteristic of or appropriate to the female sex; feminine. **3.** Consisting of members of the female sex. **4.** *Bot.* **a.** Pertaining to or designating an organ, such as a pistil or ovary, that functions in producing seeds or spores after fertilization. **b.** Bearing pistils but not stamens: *female flowers.* **5.** Indicating or having a part, such as a receptacle, designed to receive a complementary male part, such as a plug. *—n.* **1.** A member of the sex that produces ova or bears young. **2.** One that is female. **3.** A woman or girl as distinguished from a man or boy. **4.** *Bot.* A plant having only pistillate flowers. [ME, var. of *femelle* < OFr. < Lat. *femella,* dim. of *femina,* woman.] **—fe′male′ness** *n.*

female suffrage *n.* Woman suffrage.

fem·i·nine (fĕm′ə-nĭn) *adj.* **1.** Of or belonging to the female sex. **2.** Characterized by or possessing qualities generally attributed to a woman: *feminine tenderness.* **3.** Effeminate; womanish. **4.** *Gram.* Indicating, being, or belonging to the gender of words or grammatical forms that refer chiefly to females. *—n. Gram.* **1.** The feminine gender. **2.** A word or form belonging to the feminine gender. [ME < OFr. < Lat. *feminina* < *femina,* woman.] **—fem′i·nine·ly** *adv.* **—fem′i·nine·ness** *n.*

Synonyms: *feminine, female, womanly, womanish, effeminate, ladylike.* These adjectives describe what is of or appropriate to women. *Feminine* and *female* are essentially classifying terms. *Female,* like *male,* merely categorizes by sex: *the female population. Feminine* can be used thus narrowly: *the feminine lead in a drama.* Often, as the opposite of "masculine," it refers to things considered characteristic of women: *a well-modulated feminine voice. Womanly* describes things that become a woman: *womanly virtue. Womanish* refers to qualities distinctive to but less admirable in women or with an unfavorable implication to such qualities in men: *womanish tears. Effeminate* is largely restricted in reference to men or things and implies lack of manliness or strength: *an effeminate walk. Ladylike* is applicable to what is thought to befit women of good breeding: *ladylike behavior.*

feminine ending *n.* **1.** The termination of a line of verse in an unaccented syllable. **2.** *Gram.* A final syllable or termination that marks or forms words in the feminine gender.

feminine rhyme *n.* A rhyme in which the final syllable is unstressed.

fem·i·nin·i·ty (fĕm′ə-nĭn′ĭ-tē) *n., pl.* **-ties. 1.** The quality or condition of being feminine; womanliness. **2.** A female characteristic or trait. **3.** Womankind. **4.** Womanishness; effeminacy.

fem·i·nism (fĕm′ə-nĭz′əm) *n.* **1.** A doctrine that advocates or demands for women the same rights granted men, as in

political and economic status. **2.** The movement in support of feminism. **—fem'i·nist** *n.* **—fem'i·nis'tic** *adj.*
fe·min·i·ty (fĕ-mĭn'ĭ-tē) *n.* Femininity.
fem·i·nize (fĕm'ə-nīz') *tr. & intr.v.* **-nized, -niz·ing, -niz·es.** To make or become feminine. **—fem'i·ni·za'tion** *n.*
femme fa·tale (fĕm' fə-tăl', -täl', făm') *n., pl.* **femmes fa·tales** (fĕm' fə-tăl', -tălz', -täl', -tälz', făm'). **1.** A woman whose seductive charms may lead a man into compromising or dangerous situations. **2.** A woman of great mystery and charm. [Fr. : *femme,* woman + *fatale,* fatal.]
fem·o·ra (fĕm'ər-ə) *n.* A plural of **femur.**
fem·o·ral (fĕm'ər-əl) *adj.* Of or pertaining to the thigh or the femur. [< Lat. *femur, femor-,* femur.]
femoral artery *n.* The main artery of the thigh.
femto– *pref.* One quadrillionth (10^{-15}): *femtometer.* [Dan. or Norw. *femten,* fifteen < ON *fimmtān.*]
fem·to·joule (fĕm'tə-jo͞ol', -joul') *n.* One-quadrillionth (10^{-15}) of a joule.
fem·tom·e·ter (fĕm-tŏm'ĭ-tər) *n.* One-quadrillionth (10^{-15}) of a meter.
fem·to·sec·ond (fĕm'tə-sĕk'ənd) *n.* One-quadrillionth (10^{-15}) of a second.
fe·mur (fē'mər) *n., pl.* **fe·murs** or **fem·o·ra** (fĕm'ər-ə). **1. a.** The proximal bone of the lower or hind limb in vertebrates, situated between the pelvis and knee in humans. **b.** The thigh. **2.** The usually stout third segment of an insect's leg. [Lat.]
fen (fĕn) *n.* Low, flat, swampy land; bog. [ME < OE *fenn.*]
fence (fĕns) *n.* **1.** A structure serving as an enclosure, barrier, or boundary, usually made of posts, boards, wire, or rails. **2.** *Archaic.* A means of defense; protection. **3.** Fencing (sense 1). **4. a.** One who receives and sells stolen goods. **b.** A place where such goods are received and sold. *—v.* **fenced, fenc·ing, fenc·es.** *—tr.* **1.** To surround or close in by or as if by means of a fence. **2.** To separate or close off by or as if by means of a fence. **3.** *Archaic.* To defend or ward off. *—intr.* **1.** To practice the art of fencing. **2.** To avoid giving direct answers; hedge. **3.** To act as a fence for stolen goods. ***—idiom.* on the fence.** *Informal.* **1.** Undecided as to which of two sides to support. **2.** Neutral. [ME *fens,* short for *defense,* defense. —see DEFENSE.] **—fenc'er** *n.*
fence sitter *n.* One that takes a position of neutrality or indecision, as in a controversial matter. **—fence'-sit'ting** (fĕns'sĭt'ĭng) *n.*
fenc·ing (fĕn'sĭng) *n.* **1.** The art, practice, or sport of using a foil, épée, or saber as a means of attack or defense. **2.** A fence (sense 1). **3.** Material, such as wire, stakes, and rails, used in the construction of fences. **4.** Fences collectively.
fend (fĕnd) *v.* **fend·ed, fend·ing, fends.** *—tr.* **1.** *Archaic.* To defend. **2.** To keep or ward off: *fend off an attack.* *—intr.* **1.** *Chiefly Brit. Regional.* To make an effort to do something. **2.** To provide or earn a living: *fend for oneself.* [ME *fenden,* short for *defenden,* to defend. —see DEFEND.]
fend·er (fĕn'dər) *n.* **1.** One that fends or keeps off. **2.** A usually metal guard over the wheel of an automotive vehicle. **3.** A device at the front end of a locomotive or streetcar designed to push aside obstructions. **4.** A screen or metal framework placed in front of a fireplace to keep hot coals and debris from falling out. **5.** A device, such as a bundle of rope or a piece of timber, used on the side of a vessel or dock to absorb impact or friction.
fe·nes·tra (fə-nĕs'trə) *n., pl.* **-trae** (-trē'). **1.** *Anat.* A small opening, esp. either of two apertures in the medial wall of the middle ear. **2.** A windowlike opening. **3.** *Biol.* A transparent spot or marking, as on the wing of an insect. [Lat., window.] **—fe·nes'tral** *adj.*
fen·es·trate (fĕn'ĭ-strāt') *adj.* Fenestrated (sense 2).
fen·es·trat·ed (fĕn'ĭ-strā'tĭd) *adj.* **1.** Having windows or windowlike openings. **2.** *Biol.* Having fenestrae. [< Lat. *fenestratus,* p.part. of *fenestrare,* to furnish with windows < *fenestra,* window.]
fen·es·tra·tion (fĕn'ĭ-strā'shən) *n.* **1.** *Archit.* The design and placement of windows in a building. **2.** An opening in a structure. **3.** The surgical cutting of an artificial opening from the external auditory canal to the labyrinth of the internal ear to restore normal hearing.
Fe·ni·an (fē'nē-ən) *n.* **1.** One of a legendary group of heroic Irish warriors of the 2nd and 3rd centuries A.D. **2.** A member of a secret organization, founded in New York City in the mid-19th century, with the goal of overthrowing British rule in Ireland. [Blend of OIr. *fēinne,* pl. of *fīann,* legendary band of warriors, and *Fēne,* name of ancient inhabitants of Ireland.] **—Fe'ni·an** *adj.* **—Fe'ni·an·ism** *n.*
fen·nec (fĕn'ĭk) *n.* A small fox, *Fennecus zerda,* of desert regions of northern Africa, having fawn-colored fur and large, pointed ears. [Ar. *fenek,* furry animal.]
fen·nel (fĕn'əl) *n.* **1.** A plant, *Foeniculum vulgare,* native to Eurasia, having finely dissected leaves, clusters of small yellow flowers, and aromatic seeds used as flavoring. **2.** The seeds or edible stalks of the fennel. [ME *fenel* < OE *finul* < Med. Lat. *fenuculum* < Lat. *faeniculum,* dim. of *faenum,* hay.]
fen·ny (fĕn'ē) *adj.* **1.** Having the nature of a fen; marshy. **2.** Of, pertaining to, or found in fens.
fen·thi·on (fĕn-thī'ŏn', -ən) *n.* An organophosphorous insecticide, $C_{10}H_{15}O_3PS_2$, used for ornamental plants. [E. *fen-,* alteration of PHEN- + THI(O)- + -ON.]
fen·u·greek (fĕn'yə-grēk') *n.* **1.** A cloverlike Eurasian plant, *Trigonella foenum-graecum,* having white flowers and pungent, aromatic seeds used as flavoring. **2.** The seeds of the fenugreek. [ME *fenigrek* < OFr. *fenugrek* < Lat. *fenugraecum* < *fenum graecum,* Greek hay.]
fen·u·ron (fĕn'yə-rŏn') *n.* A white compound, $C_9H_{12}N_2O$, used as a herbicide. [*fen-,* alteration of PHEN- + U(REA) + -ON[3].]
feoff·ee (fĕ-fē', fē-) *n.* One to whom a feoffment is granted.
feoff·er also **feof·for** (fĕf'ər, fē'fər) *n.* One who grants a feoffment.
feoff·ment (fĕf'mənt, fēf'-) *n.* The action of granting a feudal estate or fee.
feof·for (fĕf'ər, fē'fər) *n.* Variant of **feoffer.**
-fer *suff.* One that bears: *aquifer.* [Lat. < *ferre,* to carry.]
fe·ral (fîr'əl, fĕr'-) *adj.* **1. a.** Existing in a wild or untamed state. **b.** Having returned to an untamed state from domestication. **2.** Of or characteristic of a wild animal; savage. [< Lat. *fera,* wild animal < *ferus,* wild.]
fer·bam (fûr'băm') *n.* A black compound, $C_9H_{18}FeN_3S_6$, used as an agricultural fungicide. [FER(RIC) (DIMETHYL-DITHIOCAR)BAM(ATE).]
fer-de-lance (fĕr'dl-ăns', -äns') *n., pl.* **fer-de-lance.** A venomous tropical American snake, *Bothrops atrox,* having brown and grayish markings. [Fr.]
fere (fîr) *n. Archaic.* **1.** A companion. **2.** A spouse. [ME < OE *fēra.*]
fe·ri·a (fîr'ē-ə, fĕr'-) *n., pl.* **-ri·as** or **-ri·ae** (-ē-ē'). A weekday on a church calendar on which no feast is observed. [Med. Lat. < LLat., festal day < Lat. *feriae.*] **—fe'ri·al** *adj.*
fe·rine (fîr'īn') *adj.* Untamed; feral. [Lat. *ferinus* < *fera,* wild animal. —see FERAL.]
fer·i·ty (fĕr'ĭ-tē) *n.* The condition or quality of being feral. [Lat. *feritas* < *ferus,* wild.]
fer·ma·ta (fĕr-mä'tə) *n. Mus.* **1.** The prolongation of a tone, chord, or rest beyond its nominal value. **2.** The sign that indicates a fermata. [Ital. < fem. p.part. of *fermare,* to stop < Lat. *firmare,* to make firm < *firmus,* firm.]
fer·ment (fûr'mĕnt') *n.* **1.** Something that causes fermentation, as a yeast, bacterium, mold, or enzyme. **2.** Fermentation. **3.** A state of agitation; turbulence. *—v.* (fər-mĕnt') **-ment·ed, -ment·ing, -ments.** *—tr.* **1.** To produce by or as if by fermentation. **2.** To cause to undergo fermentation. **3.** To make turbulent; excite. *—intr.* **1.** To undergo fermentation. **2.** To be turbulent; seethe. [ME < OFr. < Lat. *fermentum.*] **—fer·ment'a·bil'i·ty** *n.* **—fer·ment'a·ble** *adj.* **—fer·ment'er** *n.*
fer·men·ta·tion (fûr'mən-tā'shən, -mĕn-) *n.* **1.** Any of a group of chemical reactions induced by living or nonliving ferments that split complex organic compounds into relatively simple substances, esp. the anaerobic conversion of sugar to carbon dioxide and alcohol by yeast. **2.** Unrest; agitation.
fer·men·ta·tive (fər-mĕn'tə-tĭv) *adj.* **1. a.** Causing fermentation. **b.** Capable of causing or undergoing fermentation. **2.** Pertaining to or of the nature of fermentation.
fer·mi (fûr'mē, fĕr'-) *n.* A unit of length equal to 10^{-15} meter. [After Enrico *Fermi* (1901–1954).]
fer·mi·on (fûr'mē-ŏn', fĕr'-) *n.* A particle, such as an electron, proton, or neutron, having half-integral spin and obeying statistical rules requiring that not more than one in a set of identical particles may occupy a particular quantum state. [After Enrico *Fermi* (1901–1954).]
fer·mi·um (fûr'mē-əm, fĕr'-) *n. Symbol* **Fm** A synthetic transuranic metallic element having 10 isotopes with mass numbers ranging from 248 to 257 and corresponding half-lives ranging from 0.6 minute to approximately 100 days. Atomic number 100. [After Enrico *Fermi* (1901–1954).]
fern (fûrn) *n.* Any of numerous flowerless, seedless vascular plants of the class Filicinae, characteristically having fronds with divided leaflets and reproducing by means of spores. [ME < OE *fearn.*] **—fern'y** *adj.*
fern·er·y (fûr'nə-rē) *n., pl.* **-ies. 1.** A place or container in which ferns are grown. **2.** A bed or collection of ferns.
fern seed *n.* The minute spores of ferns, formerly believed to be seeds and supposed to have the power of making the possessor invisible.
fe·ro·cious (fə-rō'shəs) *adj.* **1.** Extremely savage; fierce. **2.** Marked by unrelenting intensity; extreme: *a ferocious blizzard.* [Lat. *ferox, feroci-,* fierce.] **—fe·ro'cious·ly** *adv.* **—fe·ro'cious·ness** *n.*
fe·roc·i·ty (fə-rŏs'ĭ-tē) *n.* The condition or quality of being ferocious.
-ferous *suff.* Bearing; producing; containing: *carboniferous.* [-FER + -OUS.]
ferr– *pref.* Variant of **ferro-.**
fer·rate (fĕr'āt') *n.* A ferrite (sense 1).
fer·re·dox·in (fĕr'ĭ-dŏk'sĭn) *n.* An electron-transferring iron-containing plant protein. [FER(RO)- + REDOX + -IN.]
fer·ret[1] (fĕr'ĭt) *n.* **1.** A domesticated, usually albino form of the Old World polecat, often trained to hunt rats or rabbits. **2.** A weasellike mammal, *Mustela nigripes,* of central North America, related to the ferret and having yellowish fur and dark feet. *—v.* **-ret·ed, -ret·ing, -rets.** *—tr.* **1.** To hunt with

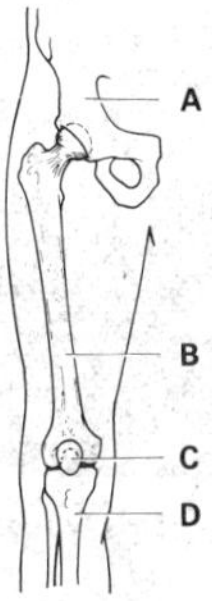

femur
A. Pelvis
B. Femur
C. Patella
D. Tibia

fencing

fender

ferret[1]

Ferris wheel

ferrets. **2.** To drive out; expel. **3.** To uncover and bring to light by searching: *ferreted out all my secrets.* —*intr.* **1.** To hunt with ferrets. **2.** To search intensively. [ME < OFr. *fuiret* < Lat. *fur,* thief.] **—fer'ret·er** *n.* **—fer'ret·y** *adj.*

fer·ret² (fĕr'ĭt) also **fer·ret·ing** (-ĭ-tĭng) *n.* A narrow piece of tape used to bind or edge fabric. [Prob. alteration of Ital. *fioretti,* floss silk, pl. of *fioretto,* dim. of *fiore,* flower < Lat. *flos,* flower.]

ferri– *pref.* Iron, esp. ferric iron: *ferricyanide.* [Lat. *ferrum,* iron.]

fer·ri·age (fĕr'ē-ĭj) *n.* **1.** The act or business of ferrying. **2.** The toll charged for ferrying.

fer·ric (fĕr'ĭk) *adj.* Of, pertaining to, or containing iron, esp. containing iron with valence 3 or with valence higher than in a corresponding ferrous compound.

ferric ammonium citrate *n.* An iron-containing salt used in the medical treatment of some forms of anemia.

ferric chloride *n.* A salt, $FeCl_3$, used as an astringent and as a hematinic.

ferric oxide *n.* A dark compound, Fe_2O_3, occurring naturally as hematite ore and rust and used in pigments, metallurgy, polishing compounds, and magnetic tapes.

fer·ri·cy·an·ic acid (fĕr'ĭ-sī-ăn'ĭk, fĕr'ī-) *n.* A reddish-brown solid compound, $H_3Fe(CN)_6$.

fer·ri·cy·a·nide (fĕr'ĭ-sī'ə-nīd', fĕr'ī-) *n.* Any of various salts derived from ferricyanic acid and used in making blue pigments.

fer·rif·er·ous (fə-rĭf'ər-əs, fĕ-) *adj.* Containing or yielding iron.

Fer·ris wheel also **fer·ris wheel** (fĕr'ĭs) *n.* A large upright, rotating wheel having suspended cars in which passengers ride for amusement. [After George W. G. *Ferris* (1859–1896).]

fer·rite (fĕr'īt') *n.* **1.** Any of a group of nonmetallic, ceramic-like, usually ferromagnetic compounds of ferric oxide with other oxides, esp. such a compound with spinel crystalline structure, characterized by extremely high electrical resistivity and used in computer memory elements, permanent magnets, and various solid-state devices. **2.** Iron having a body-centered cubic crystalline form, occurring commonly in steel, cast iron, and pig iron below 910°C.

ferrite core *n.* A magnetic core used in computer core storage.

fer·ri·tin (fĕr'ĭ-tĭn) *n.* An iron-containing protein complex that functions as a form of iron storage in the tissues.

ferro– or **ferr–** *pref.* **1.** Iron: *ferromagnetic.* **2.** Ferrous iron: *ferrocyanide.* [Lat. *ferrum,* iron.]

fer·ro·al·loy (fĕr'ō-ăl'oi', -ə-loi') *n.* Any of various alloys of iron and one or more other elements, such as manganese or silicon, used as a raw material in the production of steel.

fer·ro·con·crete (fĕr'ō-kŏn'krēt', -kŏn-krēt') *n.* Reinforced concrete.

fer·ro·cy·an·ic acid (fĕr'ō-sī-ăn'ĭk) *n.* A solid white compound, $H_4Fe(CN)_6$.

fer·ro·cy·a·nide (fĕr'ō-sī'ə-nīd') *n.* A salt derived from ferrocyanic acid, the sodium and potassium salts being used in making blue pigments, blueprint paper, and ferricyanide.

ferrotype

fer·ro·e·lec·tric (fĕr'ō-ĭ-lĕk'trĭk) *adj.* Of or pertaining to a crystalline dielectric that can be given a permanent electric polarization by application of an electric field. —*n.* A ferroelectric substance. **—fer'ro·e·lec·tric'i·ty** *n.*

fer·ro·mag·ne·sian (fĕr'ō-măg-nē'zhən, -shən) *adj.* Containing iron and magnesium.

fer·ro·mag·net (fĕr'ō-măg'nĭt) *n.* **1. a.** A ferromagnetic substance. **b.** A substance with magnetic properties resembling those of iron. **2.** A ferromagnetic magnet.

fer·ro·mag·net·ic (fĕr'ō-măg-nĕt'ĭk) *adj.* Pertaining to or characteristic of substances, such as iron, nickel, cobalt, and various alloys, that exhibit extremely high magnetic permeability, the ability to acquire high magnetization in relatively weak magnetic fields, a characteristic saturation point, and magnetic hysteresis. **—fer'ro·mag'ne·tism** *n.*

fer·ro·man·ga·nese (fĕr'ō-măng'gə-nēz', -nēs') *n.* A ferroalloy of iron and manganese, used in the production of steel.

fer·ro·sil·i·con (fĕr'ō-sĭl'ĭ-kən, -kŏn') *n.* A ferroalloy of iron and silicon used in the production of carbon steel.

fer·ro·type (fĕr'ə-tīp') *n.* **1.** A positive photograph made directly on an iron plate varnished with a thin sensitized film. **2.** The process by which ferrotypes are made.

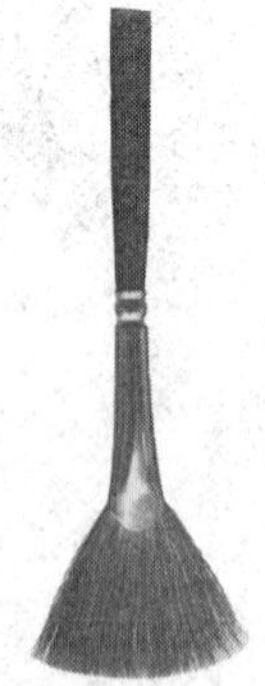
ferrule

fer·rous (fĕr'əs) *adj.* Of, pertaining to, or containing iron, esp. with valence 2.

ferrous oxide *n.* A black powdery compound, FeO, used in the manufacture of steel, green heat-absorbing glass, and enamels.

ferrous sulfate *n.* A greenish crystalline compound, $FeSO_4 \cdot 7H_2O$, used as a pigment, fertilizer, and feed additive and in sewage and water treatment.

ferrous sulfide *n.* A black to brown sulfide of iron, FeS, used in making hydrogen sulfide.

ferryboat

fer·ru·gi·nous (fə-ro͞o'jə-nəs, fĕ-) *adj.* **1.** Of, containing, or similar to iron. **2.** Having the color of iron rust. [Lat. *ferruginus* < *ferrugo,* iron rust < *ferrum,* iron.]

fer·rule (fĕr'əl) *n.* **1.** A metal ring or cap placed around a pole or shaft for reinforcement or to prevent splitting. **2.** A bushing used to secure a pipe joint. —*tr.v.* **-ruled, -rul·ing, -rules.** To furnish with a ferrule. [Var. of obs. *verrel* < ME *verrele* < OFr. *virelle* < Med. Lat. *virolla* < Lat. *viriola,* little bracelets, dim. of *viriae,* bracelets.]

fer·ry (fĕr'ē) *v.* **-ried, -ry·ing, -ries.** —*tr.* **1.** To transport by boat across a body of water. **2.** To cross. **3.** To deliver (a vehicle, esp. an aircraft) under its own power to its eventual user. **4.** To transport (people or goods) esp. by aircraft. —*intr.* To cross a body of water on or as if on a ferry. —*n., pl.* **-ries. 1. a.** A ferryboat. **b.** The place of embarkation for a ferryboat. **2.** A franchise or legal right to operate a ferrying service for a fee. **3.** A service for transporting esp. an aircraft under its own power to its eventual user. [ME *ferien* < OE *ferian.*]

fer·ry·boat (fĕr'ē-bōt') *n.* A boat used to ferry passengers or goods.

fer·ry·man (fĕr'ē-mən) *n.* A person who owns, administers, or operates a ferry.

fer·tile (fûr'tl) *adj.* **1.** *Biol.* **a.** Capable of reproducing. **b.** Capable of initiating, sustaining, or supporting reproduction. **c.** Capable of growing and developing; able to mature. **2.** *Bot.* Bearing reproductive structures or material such as spores or pollen. **3.** Rich in material needed to sustain plant growth: *fertile soil.* **4.** Highly or continuously productive; prolific: *a fertile imagination.* [ME *fertil* < OFr. *fertile* < Lat. *fertilis* < *ferre,* to bear.] **—fer'tile·ly** *adv.* **—fer'tile·ness** *n.*

fer·til·i·ty (fər-tĭl'ĭ-tē) *n.* The condition, state, or quality of being fertile.

fer·til·i·za·tion (fûr'tl-ĭ-zā'shən) *n.* **1.** The act or process of initiating biological reproduction. **2.** The process in which two gametes unite to form a zygote. **3.** The act or process of applying a fertilizer. **—fer'til·i·za'tion·al** *adj.*

fer·til·ize (fûr'tl-īz') *v.* **-ized, -iz·ing, -iz·es.** —*tr.* **1.** To cause fertilization of (an ovum, for example), esp. to provide with sperm or pollen, thereby causing fertilization. **2.** To spread fertilizer on. —*intr.* To spread fertilizer. **—fer'til·iz'a·ble** *adj.*

fer·til·iz·er (fûr'tl-ī'zər) *n.* **1.** One that fertilizes. **2.** Any of a large number of natural and synthetic materials, including manure and nitrogen, phosphorus, and potassium compounds, spread on or worked into soil to increase its fertility.

fer·ule (fĕr'əl) *n.* A baton, cane, or stick used in punishing children. [Lat. *ferula.*]

fe·ru·lic acid (fə-ro͞o'lĭk) *n.* A compound, $C_{10}H_{10}O_4$, related to vanillin and obtained from certain plants. [< NLat. *Ferula,* plant genus.]

fer·ven·cy (fûr'vən-sē) *n.* The condition or quality of being fervent.

fer·vent (fûr'vənt) *adj.* **1.** Having or showing great emotion or warmth; ardent. **2.** Extremely hot; glowing. [ME < OFr. < Lat. *fervens,* pr.part. of *fervēre,* to boil.] **—fer'vent·ly** *adv.* **—fer'vent·ness** *n.*

fer·vid (fûr'vĭd) *adj.* **1.** Intensely fervent or zealous; impassioned. **2.** Extremely hot; burning. [Lat. *fervidus* < *fervor,* passion < *fervēre,* to boil.] **—fer'vid·ly** *adv.* **—fer'vid·ness** *n.*

fer·vor (fûr'vər) *n.* **1.** Intensity of emotion; ardor. **2.** Intense heat. [ME *fervour* < OFr. < Lat. *fervor.* —see FERVID.]

fer·vour (fûr'vər) *n. Chiefly Brit.* Variant of **fervor.**

fes·cen·nine (fĕs'ə-nīn', -nēn') *adj.* Licentious; obscene. [Lat. *Fescinninus,* of Fescennia, a town in ancient Etruria noted for its licentious poetry.]

fes·cue (fĕs'kyo͞o) *n.* Any of various grasses of the genus *Festuca,* often cultivated as pasturage. [ME *festu,* stalk < OFr. < Lat. *festuca.*]

fess also **fesse** (fĕs) *n. Heraldry.* A wide horizontal band forming the middle section of an escutcheon. [ME *fesse* < OFr. < Lat. *fascia,* band.]

fess point *n. Heraldry.* The center point of an escutcheon.

-fest *suff.* A gathering or occasion characterized by a specified activity: *slugfest.* [< G. *Fest,* festival < Lat. *festum.*]

fes·tal (fĕs'təl) *adj.* Of, pertaining to, or of the nature of a feast or festival; festive. [OFr. < Lat. *festum,* feast.] **—fes'tal·ly** *adv.*

fes·ter (fĕs'tər) *v.* **-tered, -ter·ing, -ters.** —*intr.* **1.** To generate pus; suppurate. **2.** To form an ulcer. **3.** To decay; rot. **4.** To be or become a source of irritation; rankle. —*tr.* To infect, inflame, or corrupt. —*n.* A small festering sore or ulcer. [ME *festren* < *festre,* fistula < OFr. < Lat. *fistula.*]

fes·ti·nate (fĕs'tə-nĭt) *adj.* Hasty. —*v.* (-nāt') **-nat·ed, -nat·ing, -nates.** To hasten. [Lat. *festinatus,* p.part. of *festinare,* to hasten.] **—fes'ti·nate·ly** *adv.*

fes·ti·val (fĕs'tə-vəl) *n.* **1.** An occasion for feasting or celebration, esp. a day or time of religious significance that recurs at regular intervals. **2.** An often regularly recurring program of performances, exhibitions, or competitions: *a film festival.* **3.** Conviviality; revelry. —*adj.* Festive. [ME, festive < OFr. < Med. Lat. *festivalis* < Lat. *festivus* < *festus.*]

fes·tive (fĕs'tĭv) *adj.* **1.** Of, pertaining to, or appropriate to a feast or festival. **2.** Merry; joyous: *a festive occasion.* [Lat. *festivus* < *festus.*] **—fes'tive·ly** *adv.* **—fes'tive·ness** *n.*

fes·tiv·i·ty (fĕ-stĭv'ĭ-tē) *n., pl.* **-ties. 1.** A festival. **2.** The pleasure, joy, and gaiety of a festival or celebration. **3. festivities.** The proceedings or events of a festival.

fes·toon (fĕ-sto͞on') *n.* **1.** A string or garland, as of leaves or flowers, suspended in a loop or curve between two points. **2.** A representation of a festoon, as in sculpture. —*tr.v.* **-tooned, -toon·ing, -toons. 1.** To decorate with or as if with a festoon. **2.** To form or make into a festoon. [Fr. *feston* < Ital. *festone* < *festa,* feast < Lat. *festus,* festive.]

fes·toon·er·y (fĕ-sto͞o′nə-rē) *n., pl.* **-ies. 1.** An arrangement of or into festoons. **2.** Festoons collectively.

fest·schrift (fĕst′shrĭft′) *n., pl.* **-schrif·ten** (-shrĭf′tən) or **-schrifts.** A volume of learned articles or essays by colleagues and admirers, serving as a tribute or memorial esp. to a scholar. [G. : *Fest,* festival + *Schrift,* writing.]

fet– *pref.* Variant of **feto-.**

fet·a (fĕt′ə, fē′tə) *n.* A white Greek cheese made usually of goat's or ewe's milk and preserved in brine. [Mod. Gk. *(turi) pheta,* (cheese) slice < Ital. *fetta,* slice < Lat. *offa,* morsel of food.]

fe·tal also **foe·tal** (fēt′l) *adj.* Of, pertaining to, or having the nature of a fetus.

fetal alcohol syndrome *n.* A complex of birth defects including retarded growth and cardiac abnormalities that occur in infants born to alcoholic mothers.

fetal position *n.* A position of the body at rest in which the spine is curved, the head is bowed forward, and the arms and legs are drawn in toward the chest. [From its resemblance to the position of a fetus in the womb.]

fe·ta·tion (fē-tā′shən) *n.* The development of a fetus; pregnancy.

fetch[1] (fĕch) *v.* **fetched, fetch·ing, fetch·es.** *—tr.* **1.** To go or come after and return with. **2.** To cause to come. **3. a.** To draw in (breath); inhale. **b.** To bring forth (a sigh, for example). **4.** To bring in as a price: *fetched a hundred dollars at auction.* **5.** *Informal.* To strike or deal (a blow). **6.** *Naut.* To arrive at; reach. *—intr.* **1.** To go after and return with something. **2.** To retrieve game that has been killed. **3.** *Naut.* **a.** To hold a course. **b.** To turn about; veer. ***—phrasal verb.*** **fetch up. 1.** To reach a place and halt there. **2.** To make up (lost time, for example). *—n.* **1.** An act or instance of fetching. **2.** *Computer Sci.* A program routine that brings a phase of the program from storage for immediate use. **3.** A stratagem or trick. [ME *fecchen* < OE *feccean.*] **—fetch′er** *n.*

fetch[2] (fĕch) *n. Chiefly Brit.* **1.** A ghost; apparition. **2.** A doppelgänger. [Orig. unknown.]

fetch·ing (fĕch′ĭng) *adj. Informal.* Very attractive; charming. **—fetch′ing·ly** *adv.*

fete also **fête** (fāt, fĕt) *—n.* **1.** A festival or feast. **2.** An elaborate outdoor party or other entertainment, such as a fair. **3.** An elaborate party. *—tr.v.* **fet·ed, fet·ing, fetes** also **fêt·ed, fêt·ing, fêtes. 1.** To celebrate with a fete. **2.** To pay honor to. [Fr. *fête* < OFr. *feste.* —see FEAST.]

fête cham·pê·tre (fĕt′ shäN-pĕt′rə) *n.* An outdoor party or entertainment. [Fr.]

fet·er·i·ta (fĕt′ə-rē′tə) *n.* A variety of sorghum, *Sorghum vulgare caudatum,* grown in warm regions for its grain and as forage. [Ar.]

feti– *pref.* Variant of **feto-.**

fet·ich (fĕt′ĭsh, fē′tĭsh) *n.* Variant of **fetish.**

fet·ich·ism (fĕt′ĭ-shĭz′əm, fē′tĭ-) *n.* Variant of **fetishism.**

fe·ti·cide (fē′tĭ-sīd′) *n.* The intentional destruction of a human fetus. **—fe′ti·cid′al** (-sīd′l) *adj.*

fet·id (fĕt′ĭd, fē′tĭd) also **foe·tid** (fē′tĭd) *adj.* Having an offensive odor; foul-smelling. [ME < Lat. *fetidus* < *fetēre,* to stink.] **—fet′id·ly** *adv.* **—fet′id·ness** *n.*

fet·ish also **fet·ich** (fĕt′ĭsh, fē′tĭsh) *n.* **1.** An object that is superstitiously believed to have magical powers, esp. of protection. **2.** An object of unreasonably excessive attention or reverence: *made a fetish of punctuality.* **3.** Something, such as a material object or an often nonsexual part of the body, that arouses or gratifies sexual desire. [Fr. *fétiche* < Port. *feitiço,* charm < Lat. *facticus,* factitious. —see FACTITIOUS.]

fet·ish·ism also **fet·ich·ism** (fĕt′ĭ-shĭz′əm, fē′tĭ-) *n.* **1.** The worship of or belief in magical fetishes. **2.** Excessive attachment or regard. **3.** The displacement of sexual arousal or gratification to a fetish. **—fet′ish·ist** *n.* **—fet′ish·is′tic** *adj.*

fet·lock (fĕt′lŏk′) *n.* **1. a.** A projection on the lower part of the leg of a horse or related animal, above and behind the hoof. **b.** A tuft of hair on such a projection. **2.** The joint marked by the fetlock. [ME *fitlok.*]

feto– or **feti–** or **fet–** *pref.* Fetus; fetal: *fetology.* [< FETUS.]

fe·tol·o·gy (fē-tŏl′ə-jē) *n.* The medical study of a fetus. **—fe·tol′o·gist** *n.*

fe·tor (fē′tər, -tôr′) also **foe·tor** (fē′tər) *n.* An exceptionally offensive odor; stench. [ME *fetour* < Lat. *fetor* < *fetēre,* to stink.]

fe·tos·co·py (fē-tŏs′kə-pē) *n.* The examination of a fetus in the uterus by insertion of a fiber-optic device equipped with a lens into the amniotic cavity. **—fe′to·scope′** (fē′tə-skōp′) *n.*

fet·ter (fĕt′ər) *n.* **1.** A chain or shackle attached to the ankles to restrain movement. **2.** Something that serves to restrict; restraint. *—tr.v.* **-tered, -ter·ing, -ters. 1.** To put fetters on; shackle. **2.** To restrict the freedom of. [ME *feter* < OE.]

fet·ter·bush (fĕt′ər-bo͝osh′) *n.* **1.** A shrub, *Lyonia lucida,* of the southeastern United States, having evergreen leaves and clusters of white flowers. **2.** Any of several shrubs similar or related to the fetterbush, esp. one of the genus *Leucothoe.*

fet·tle (fĕt′l) *tr.v.* **-tled, -tling, -tles.** *Metallurgy.* To line (the hearth of a reverberatory furnace) with loose sand or ore preparatory to pouring molten metal. *—n.* **1.** The material used to line a furnace in fettling. **2. a.** Proper or sound condition. **b.** Mental or emotional state; spirits: *was in fine fettle.* [ME *fetlen,* to shape, prob. < OE *fetel,* girdle.]

fet·tling (fĕt′lĭng) *n.* The material, such as loose ore and sand, used to line a reverberatory furnace.

fet·tuc·ci·ne (fĕt′ə-chē′nē) *n.* **1.** Narrow strips of pasta. **2.** A dish made with fettuccine. [Ital., pl. of *fettuccina,* dim. of *fettuccia,* ribbon, dim. of *fetta,* slice. —see FETA.]

fe·tus also **foe·tus** (fē′təs) *n., pl.* **-tus·es.** The unborn young of a viviparous vertebrate; in humans, the unborn young from the end of the eighth week to the moment of birth as distinguished from the earlier embryo. [Lat., offspring.]

feud[1] (fyo͞od) *n.* A bitter, prolonged quarrel or state of enmity, as between two families, individuals, or clans. *—intr.v.* **feud·ed, feud·ing, feuds.** To carry on a feud. [ME *fede* < OFr. *faide,* of Germanic orig.]

feud[2] (fyo͞od) *n.* A fee (sense 5.a.). [Med. Lat. *feudum,* of Germanic orig.]

feu·dal (fyo͞od′l) *adj.* **1.** Of, pertaining to, or characteristic of feudalism. **2.** Of or pertaining to lands held in fee or to the holding of such lands. [Med. Lat. *feudalis* < *feudum,* feud.] **—feu′dal·ly** *adv.*

feu·dal·ism (fyo͞od′l-ĭz′əm) *n.* A political and economic system of Europe from the 9th to about the 15th century, based on the relation of lord to vassal held on condition of homage and service. **—feu′dal·ist** *n.* **—feu′dal·is′tic** *adj.*

feu·dal·i·ty (fyo͞o-dăl′ĭ-tē) *n., pl.* **-ties. 1.** The state or quality of being feudal. **2.** A feudal holding, system, or regime.

feu·dal·ize (fyo͞od′l-īz′) *tr.v.* **-ized, -iz·ing, -iz·es.** To make feudal. **—feu′dal·i·za′tion** *n.*

feu·da·to·ry (fyo͞o′də-tôr′ē, -tōr′ē) *n., pl.* **-ries. 1.** A person who holds a feudal fee; vassal. **2.** A feudal fee. *—adj.* **1.** Of, pertaining to, or characteristic of the feudal relationship between vassal and lord. **2.** Owing feudal homage or allegiance. [Med. Lat. *feudatarius,* of a feudatory < *feudare,* to enfeoff < *feudum,* feud.]

feud·ist[1] (fyo͞o′dĭst) *n.* One who participates in a feud.

feud·ist[2] (fyo͞o′dĭst) *n.* One who specializes in feudal law.

feuil·le·ton (fœ′yə-tôN′) *n.* **1.** The part of a European newspaper devoted to light fiction, reviews, and articles of general entertainment. **2.** An article appearing in a feuilleton, as an installment of a serialized novel. [Fr. < *feuillet,* dim. of *feuille,* leaf < OFr. *foille* < Lat. *folium.*] **—feuil′le·ton′ism** (-tôn′ĭz′əm, -tôN-nĭz′-) *n.* **—feuil′le·ton′ist** *n.*

Feul·gen reaction (foil′gən) *n.* A DNA-specific staining reaction based on the formation of a reddish-purple color upon contact with a reagent containing fuchsin and sulfuric acid. [After Robert *Feulgen* (1884–1955).]

fe·ver (fē′vər) *n.* **1.** Abnormally high body temperature. **2.** A disease characterized by abnormally high body temperatures. **3.** A condition of heightened activity or excitement: *a fever of anticipation.* **4.** A contagious, usually short-lived enthusiasm. [ME < OE *fefor* and OFr. *fievre,* both < Lat. *febris.*]

fever blister *n.* A cold sore.

fe·ver·few (fē′vər-fyo͞o′) *n.* An aromatic plant, *Chrysanthemum parthenium,* native to Eurasia, having clusters of buttonlike, white-rayed flowers. [ME *feverfu* < OE *feferfuge* < Lat. *febrifugia* : *febris,* fever + *fugare,* to drive away.]

feverfew

fe·ver·ish (fē′vər-ĭsh) also **fe·ver·ous** (-əs) *adj.* **1. a.** Having a fever. **b.** Of, pertaining to, or resembling a fever. **c.** Causing or tending to cause fever. **2.** Marked by intense agitation, emotion, or activity: *worked at a feverish pace.* **—fe′ver·ish·ly** *adv.* **—fe′ver·ish·ness** *n.*

fever pitch *n.* A state of extreme disturbance or excitement.

fever therapy *n.* Treatment of disease involving artificially induced fever.

fever tree *n.* Any of several trees, such as certain species of eucalyptus or *Pinckneya pubens,* of the southeastern United States, having leaves or bark used to allay fever.

fe·ver·weed (fē′vər-wēd′) *n.* Any of various plants considered to have medicinal properties.

fe·ver·wort (fē′vər-wûrt′, -wôrt′) *n.* Any of several plants considered to have medicinal properties, as the horse gentian and boneset.

few (fyo͞o) *adj.* **-er, -est.** Amounting to or consisting of a small number: *spoke for only a few minutes.* *—n. (used with a pl. verb).* **1.** An indefinitely small number of persons or things: *borrowed a few of your books.* **2.** A limited number of people: *the discerning few.* *—pron. (used with a pl. verb).* A small number of persons or things: *"Many are called, but few are chosen"* (Matthew 22:14). [ME *fewe* < OE *fēawe.*] **—few′ness** *n.*

Usage: *Few* and *fewer* are correctly used in writing only before a plural noun: *few cars; few of the books; fewer reasons. Less* is used before a mass noun: *less music; less sugar. Less than* is also used before a plural noun that denotes a measure of time, amount, or distance: *less than three weeks; less than sixty years old; less than $400.*

fey (fā) *adj.* **1.** *Scot.* **a.** Fated to die soon. **b.** Full of the sense of approaching death. **2.** Having visionary power; clairvoyant. **3.** Appearing as if under a spell; touched. [ME *feie* < OE *fǣge.*]

fez (fĕz) *n., pl.* **fez·zes.** A man's felt cap in the shape of a flat-topped cone, usually red with a black tassel hanging from the crown, worn chiefly in the eastern Mediterranean region. [Fr. < Turk. < *Fez,* a town in Morocco.]

fez

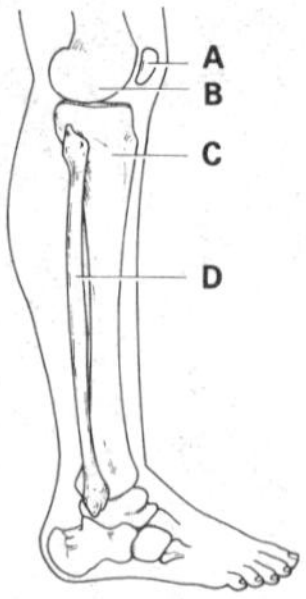

fibula
A. Patella
B. Femur
C. Tibia
D. Fibula

fichu

fiddle

fiddlehead
Fiddlehead fern

fiddler crab

fi·a·cre (fē-ä′krə) *n.* A small hackney coach. [Fr., after the Hotel de St. *Fiacre,* Paris.]
fi·an·cé (fē′än-sā′, fē-än′sā′) *n.* A man engaged to be married. [Fr., p.part. of *fiancer,* to betroth < OFr. *fiancier* < *fiance,* trust < *fier* to trust < Lat. *fidere.*]
fi·an·cée (fē′än-sā′, fē-än′sā′) *n.* A woman engaged to be married. [Fr., fem. of *fiancé,* fiancé.]
fi·as·co (fē-ăs′kō, -ä′skō) *n., pl.* **-coes** or **-cos.** A complete failure. [Fr. < Ital.]
fi·at (fē′ət, -ăt′, -ät′, fī′ăt′, -ət) *n.* **1.** An arbitrary order or decree. **2.** Authorization or sanction. [Lat., let it be done.]
fiat money *n.* Paper money decreed legal tender, not backed by gold or silver and not necessarily redeemable in coin.
fib (fĭb) *n.* An inconsequential lie. —*intr.v.* **fibbed, fib·bing, fibs.** To tell a fib. [Orig. unknown.] —**fib′ber** *n.*
fi·ber (fī′bər) *n.* **1.** A slender, elongated structure. **2.** One of the elongated, thick-walled cells that give strength and support to plant tissue. **3.** Any of the filaments constituting the intracellular matrix of connective tissue. **4.** Any of the elongated contractile cells of muscle tissue. **5.** The long threadlike process of a neuron. **6. a.** A natural or synthetic filament, as of cotton or nylon, capable of being spun into yarn. **b.** Material made of such filaments. **7.** Essential substance or character: *"stirred the deeper fibers of my nature"* (Oscar Wilde). **8.** Internal strength; toughness: *lacking in moral fiber.* [Fr. *fibre* < Lat. *fibra.*]
fi·ber·board (fī′bər-bôrd′, -bōrd′) *n.* A building material composed of wood or other plant fibers bonded together and compressed into rigid sheets.
Fi·ber·fil (fī′bər-fĭl′). A trademark for a synthetic resin used as quilt filling.
Fi·ber·glas (fī′bər-glăs′). A trademark for a type of fiber glass.
fiber glass *n.* A composite material consisting of glass fibers in resin.
fi·ber·ize (fī′bə-rīz′) *tr.v.* **-ized, -iz·ing, -iz·es.** To break into fibers. —**fi′ber·i·za′tion** *n.*
fiber optics *n.* The optics of light transmission through very fine, flexible glass rods by internal reflection. —**fi′ber-op′tic** (fī′bər-ŏp′tĭk) *adj.*
fi·ber·scope (fī′bər-skōp′) *n.* A flexible fiber-optic instrument that is used to view objects that would otherwise be inaccessible.
Fi·bo·nac·ci number (fē′bə-nä′chē) *n.* A number in the Fibonacci sequence.
Fibonacci sequence *n.* A series of numbers, 1, 1, 2, 3, 5, 8, 13, . . . , in which each successive number is equal to the sum of the two preceding numbers. [After Leonardo *Fibonacci* (d. ca. 1250).]
fibr– *pref.* Variant of **fibro-.**
fi·bre (fī′bər) *n. Chiefly Brit.* Variant of **fiber.**
fi·bri·form (fī′brə-fôrm′) *adj.* Similar in form or structure to a fiber. [FIBRE + -FORM.]
fi·bril (fī′brəl, fĭb′rəl) *n.* A small, slender fiber, as a root hair. [NLat. *fibrilla,* dim. of Lat. *fibra,* fiber.] —**fi′bril·lar** (-lər), **fi′bril·lar′y** (-lĕr′ē) *adj.*
fi·bril·late (fĭb′rə-lāt′, fī′brə-) *intr. & tr.v.* **-lat·ed, -lat·ing, -lates.** To undergo or cause to undergo fibrillation. [Back-formation < FIBRILLATION.]
fib·ril·la·tion (fĭb′rə-lā′shən, fī′brə-) *n.* **1.** The forming of fibers. **2.** Uncoordinated twitching of individual muscular fibers with little or no movement of the muscle as a whole. **3.** Fine, rapid fibrillar movements that replace the normal contraction of the ventricular muscle of the heart. [NLat. *fibrilla,* fibril + -TION.]
fi·bril·li·form (fī-brĭl′ə-fôrm′, fə-) *adj.* Having the form of a fibril.
fi·bril·lose (fī′brə-lōs′, fĭb′rə-) *adj.* Having or consisting of fibrils.
fi·brin (fī′brĭn) *n.* An elastic, insoluble protein derived from the interaction of fibrinogen with thrombin and forming a fibrous network in the coagulation of blood.
fi·brin·o·gen (fī-brĭn′ə-jən) *n.* A protein in the blood plasma that is converted to fibrin by the action of thrombin in the presence of ionized calcium.
fi·bri·nol·y·sin (fī′brə-nŏl′ĭ-sĭn) *n.* An enzyme capable of dissolving fibrin.
fi·bri·nol·y·sis (fī′brə-nôl′ĭ-sĭs) *n., pl.* **-ses** (-sēz′). The breakdown of fibrin by the action of fibrinolysin. —**fi′bri·no·lyt′ic** (-nə-lĭt′ĭk) *adj.*
fi·bri·nous (fī′brə-nəs) *adj.* Of, relating to, or having the nature of fibrin.
fibro– or **fibr–** *pref.* **1.** Fiber: *fibrous.* **2.** Fibrous tissue: *fibroma.* [Lat. *fibra,* fiber.]
fi·bro·blast (fī′brə-blăst′) *n.* A cell that gives rise to connective tissue. —**fi′bro·blast′ic** *adj.*
fi·bro·car·ti·lage (fī′brō-kär′tl-ĭj) *n.* Cartilage that contains numerous thick bundles of collagen fibers.
fi·broid (fī′broid′) *adj.* Resembling or composed of fibrous tissue. —*n.* A benign neoplasm of smooth muscle, esp. in the uterine wall.
fi·bro·in (fī′brō-ĭn) *n.* A white protein that is the essential component of raw silk and spider-web filaments. [Fr. *fibroïne* < *fibre,* fiber.]
fi·bro·ma (fī-brō′mə) *n., pl.* **-mas** or **-ma·ta** (-mə-tə). A benign neoplasm derived from fibrous tissue. —**fi·brom′a·tous** (-brŏm′ə-təs, -brō′mə-) *adj.*
fi·bro·sis (fī-brō′sĭs) *n.* The formation of fibrous tissue, as in a reparative or reactive process, in excess of amounts normally present. —**fi·brot′ic** (-brŏt′ĭk) *adj.*
fi·bro·si·tis (fī′brə-sī′tĭs) *n.* The inflammatory hyperplasia of white fibrous connective tissue. [NLat. *fibrosus,* fibrous + -ITIS.]
fi·brous (fī′brəs) *adj.* Having, consisting of, or resembling fibers. —**fi′brous·ly** *adv.* —**fi′brous·ness** *n.*
fi·bro·vas·cu·lar (fī′brō-văs′kyə-lər) *adj.* Having fibrous tissue and vascular tissue, as in the woody tissue of plants.
fib·u·la (fĭb′yə-lə) *n., pl.* **-lae** (-lē′) or **-las.** The outer and smaller of two bones of the human leg or the hind leg of an animal, between the knee and ankle. [NLat. < Lat., clasp, perh. < *figere,* to fix.]
–fic *suff.* Causing; making: *soporific.* [Lat. *-ficus* < *facere,* to do.]
–fication *suff.* Production; making: *jollification.* [ME *-ficacioun* < OFr. *-fication* < Lat. *-ficatio* < *-ficare,* to make < *-ficus,* -fic.]
fice (fīs) *n.* Variant of **feist.**
fiche (fēsh) *n.* A microfiche.
fich·u (fĭsh′ōō, fē-shōō′) *n.* A woman's triangular scarf of lightweight fabric, worn over the shoulders and crossed or tied in a loose knot at the breast. [Fr. < p.part. of *ficher,* to fix < Lat. *figere.*]
fick·le (fĭk′əl) *adj.* Characterized by erratic changeableness or instability, esp. with regard to affections or attachments; capricious. [ME *fikel* < OE *ficol,* deceitful.] —**fick′le·ness** *n.*
fic·tile (fĭk′təl, -tīl′) *adj.* **1.** Capable of being molded; plastic. **2.** Formed of a moldable substance, such as clay or earth. **3.** Of or pertaining to earthenware or pottery. [Lat. *fictilis,* made of clay < *fictus,* p.part. of *fingere,* to mold.]
fic·tion (fĭk′shən) *n.* **1.** An imaginative creation or a pretense that does not represent actuality but has been invented. **2.** The act of inventing an imaginative creation or pretense. **3.** A lie. **4. a.** A literary work whose content is produced by the imagination and is not necessarily based on fact. **b.** The category of literature comprising works of this kind, including novels, short stories, and plays. **5.** *Law.* Something accepted as fact without any real justification, merely for the sake of convenience. [ME *ficcioun* < OFr. *fiction* < Lat. *fictio* < *fictus,* p.part. of *fingere,* to form.] —**fic′tion·al** *adj.* —**fic′tion·al·ly** *adv.*
fic·tion·al·ize (fĭk′shə-nə-līz) *tr.v.* **-ized, -iz·ing, -iz·es.** To treat as or make into fiction: *fictionalized his account of the negotiations to add suspense.* —**fic′tion·al·i·za′tion** *n.*
fic·tion·eer (fĭk′shə-nîr′) *n.* One who writes fiction, esp. a prolific creator of commercial or pulp fiction.
fic·tion·ize (fĭk′shə-nīz′) *tr.v.* **-ized, -iz·ing, -iz·es.** To fictionalize. —**fic′tion·i·za′tion** *n.*
fic·ti·tious (fĭk-tĭsh′əs) *adj.* **1.** Of, pertaining to, or characterized by fiction; imaginary. **2.** Adopted or assumed in order to deceive: *a fictitious name.* **3.** Not genuinely believed or felt; sham: *greeted me with a fictitious enthusiasm.* —**fic·ti′tious·ly** *adv.* —**fic·ti′tious·ness** *n.*
fic·tive (fĭk′tĭv) *adj.* **1.** Of or pertaining to the creation of fiction. **2.** Pertaining to or characterized by fiction; fictitious. **3.** Feigned; sham. —**fic′tive·ly** *adv.*
fid (fĭd) *n. Naut.* **1.** A square bar used as a support for a topmast. **2.** A large, tapering pin used to open the strands of a rope prior to splicing. [Orig. unknown.]
–fid *suff.* Divided into parts or lobes: *pinnatifid.* [Lat. *-fidus* < *findere,* to split.]
fid·dle (fĭd′l) *n.* **1.** *Informal.* **a.** A violin. **b.** A member of the violin family. **2.** *Naut.* A guard rail used on a table during rough weather to prevent things from slipping off. **3.** *Informal.* Nonsensical trifling: *"there are things that are more/ important beyond all this fiddle"* (Marianne Moore). —*v.* **-dled, -dling, -dles.** —*intr.* **1.** *Informal.* To play a violin. **2.** To move one's fingers or hands in a nervous fashion. **3.** To putter or tamper with something in order to repair or adjust it: *always fiddling with the radio.* —*tr. Informal.* To play (a tune) on a violin. —***phrasal verb.*** **fiddle away.** To waste or squander: *fiddled away the day.* [ME *fidle* < OE *fiðele* < LLat. *vitula* < Lat. *vitulari,* to celebrate a victory < *Vitula,* goddess of victory.] —**fid′dler** *n.*
fid·dle-de-dee (fĭd′l-dē-dē′) *interj.* Used to express mild annoyance or impatience.
fid·dle-fad·dle (fĭd′l-făd′l) *interj.* Used to express mild annoyance or impatience. —*intr.v.* **-dled, -dling, -dles.** To fritter away one's time; dally. [Redup. of FIDDLE.] —**fid′dle-fad′dler** *n.*
fid·dle·head (fĭd′l-hĕd′) *n.* **1.** A curved, scroll-like ornamentation at the top of a ship's bow that resembles the neck of a violin. **2.** The coiled young frond of any of various ferns, considered a delicacy when cooked.
fiddler crab *n.* Any of various burrowing crabs of the genus *Uca,* of coastal areas, having one of the anterior claws much enlarged in the male.
fid·dle·sticks (fĭd′l-stĭks′) *interj.* Used to express mild annoyance or impatience.
fi·del·i·ty (fĭ-dĕl′ĭ-tē, fī-) *n., pl.* **-ties. 1.** Faithfulness to obligations, duties, or observances. **2.** Exact correspondence with fact or with a given quality, condition, or event; accu-

racy. **3.** The degree to which an electronic system accurately reproduces the sound or image of its input signal. [ME *fidelite* < OFr. < Lat. *fidelitas* < *fidelis*, faithful < *fides*, faith.]

Synonyms: *fidelity, allegiance, fealty, loyalty, devotion.* These nouns denote the condition of being faithful. *Fidelity* involves the unfailing fulfillment of one's duties and obligations and the keeping of one's word or vows. In a related, nonpersonal sense it refers to faithfulness to an original, as in the translation of a poem, copy of a painting, or reproduction of sound by means of a recording. *Allegiance* is faithfulness to a government or state to which one is subject, considered as a duty or as what is due in exchange for the rights of citizenship; or the term can denote adherence to a person or thing that has a legitimate claim to one's support. *Fealty,* once applied to the allegiance owed by a tenant or vassal to a feudal lord, now refers in a more general sense to faithfulness to a government, to a superior, or to persons or things in general. Whereas *allegiance* and *fealty* stress obligation on a rather impersonal level, *loyalty* more often implies a close and voluntary relationship. *Devotion* suggests virtually unlimited support for or attachment to a person or thing.

fidg·et (fĭj'ĭt) *v.* **-et·ed, -et·ing, -ets.** *—intr.* **1.** To behave or move nervously or restlessly: *fidgeted about the room, tidying everything up.* **2.** To play or fuss; fiddle: *fidgeted with his notes while lecturing.* *—tr.* To cause to behave or move nervously or restlessly. *—n.* **1.** Often **fidgets.** A condition of restlessness. **2.** One who fidgets. [Obs. *fidge,* to move restlessly, perh. < ME *fiken.*]

fidg·et·y (fĭj'ĭ-tē) *adj.* **1.** Habitually fidgeting. **2.** Unnecessarily fussy. **—fidg'et·i·ness** *n.*

fi·do (fī'dō) *n., pl.* **-dos.** A coin containing a minting error. [F(REAKS) + I(RREGULARS) + D(EFECTS) + O(DDITIES).]

fi·du·cial (fĭ-do͞o'shəl, -dyo͞o'-, fī-) *adj.* **1.** Based on or pertaining to faith or trust. **2.** Pertaining or relating to a legal trust; fiduciary. **3.** Regarded or employed as a standard of reference, as in surveying. [LLat. *fiducialis* < Lat. *fiducia,* trust < *fidere,* to trust.] **—fi·du'cial·ly** *adv.*

fi·du·ci·ar·y (fĭ-do͞o'shē-ĕr'ē, -shə-rē, -dyo͞o'-, fī-) *adj.* **1.** Of, pertaining to, or involving one who holds something in trust for another: *a fiduciary heir; a fiduciary contract.* **2. a.** Of, pertaining to, or denoting a trustee or trusteeship. **b.** Held in trust. **3.** Of, pertaining to, or consisting of fiat money. **4.** Of, pertaining to, or being a system of marking in the reticule of an optical instrument that is used as a reference point or a measuring scale. *—n., pl.* **-ies.** A person who stands in a special relation of trust, confidence, or responsibility in his obligations to others, as a company director or an agent of a principal. [Lat. *fiduciarius* < *fiducia,* trust. — see FIDUCIAL.]

fie (fī) *interj.* Used to express distaste or shock.

fief (fēf) *n.* A fee (sense 5.a.). [Fr. < OFr.]

field (fēld) *n.* **1.** A broad, level, open expanse of land. **2.** A meadow: *a field of buttercups.* **3.** A cultivated expanse of land, esp. one devoted to a particular crop. **4.** A portion of land or a geological formation containing a specified natural resource: *an oil field.* **5.** A background area, as on a flag, painting, or coin: *a blue insignia on a field of red.* **6.** *Heraldry.* The background area of a shield or one of the divisions of the background. **7.** *Sports.* **a.** An area in which a sports event takes place; ground. **b.** The portion of a playing field having specific dimensions on which the action of a game takes place: *Spectators were ordered off the field.* **c.** All the contestants or participants in an event. **d.** All the contestants except those specified: *The favorite left the field far behind.* **e.** The members of a team engaged in active play. **f.** The body of horsemen following a pack of hounds. **8. a.** An area of human activity or interest: *a field of endeavor.* **b.** A topic, subject, or area of academic interest or specialization. **c.** Profession, employment, or business. **9.** An area or setting of practical activity or application: *left her desk and went out into the field.* **10. a.** The land where a battle is or has been fought. **b.** A battle. **11.** *Math.* A set with two binary operations, designated addition and multiplication, satisfying the conditions that the set is a commutative group with respect to addition, that the set with the identity of the additive group omitted is a commutative group with respect to multiplication, and that multiplication distributes over addition for all elements in the set. **12.** *Physics.* A region of space characterized by a physical property, such as gravitational or electromagnetic force or fluid pressure, having a determinable value at every point in the region. **13.** The usually circular area in which the image is rendered by the lens system of an optical instrument. **14.** *Computer Sci.* A region, as a set of adjacent columns on a punched card, used to consistently record related information. **—modifier:** *a field hand; field experience.* *—v.* **field·ed, field·ing, fields.** *—tr.* **1.** *Sports.* To retrieve (a ball) and perform the required maneuver, esp. in baseball. **2.** To respond to adequately: *fielded the question expertly.* **3. a.** *Sports.* To place or be equipped to place in a contest: *field a team.* **b.** To put into action: *field an army of campaign workers.* *—intr. Sports.* To play as a fielder. **—idioms. play the field.** To indulge in a broad range of interests or possibilities. **take the field.** To begin or resume activity, as in military operations or in a sport. [ME < OE *feld.*]

field artillery *n.* Artillery, excluding antiaircraft artillery, light enough to be mounted for use in the field.

field capacity *n.* The maximum amount of water that a particular soil can hold.

field coil *n.* An electric coil used to generate a magnetic field, as in a motor or direct-current generator.

field corn *n.* Any of several varieties of corn used primarily as feed for livestock.

field day *n.* **1.** A day set aside for a planned activity such as athletic competition, nature study, or a public demonstration. **2.** A festive day, such as one on which a fair is held. **3.** *Informal.* An opportunity for expressing or asserting oneself with the fullest pleasure or triumph.

field effect transistor *n.* A transistor in which the output current is controlled by a variable electric field.

field emission *n.* The emission of electrons from the surface of a conductor, caused by a strong electric field.

field·er (fēl'dər) *n. Sports.* A person who plays a position in the field, esp. an outfielder in baseball.

fielder's choice *n. Baseball.* A play made by an infielder on a ground ball in which he chooses to put out an advancing base runner, thus allowing the batter to reach first base safely.

field event *n.* A throwing and jumping event of a track meet as distinguished from a running event.

field·fare (fēld'fâr') *n.* An Old World thrush, *Turdus pilaris,* having gray and brown plumage. [ME *feldfare* < OE *feldeware* : *felde,* field + *ware,* dweller.]

field glass *n.* Often **field glasses.** A portable binocular instrument used esp. outdoors for viewing distant objects.

field goal *n.* **1.** *Football.* A score worth three points made on an ordinary down by place-kicking or drop-kicking the ball over the crossbar and between the goal posts. **2.** *Basketball.* A score worth two points made by throwing the ball through the basket in regulation play.

field hand *n.* A hired laborer or worker on a farm.

field hockey *n.* Hockey (sense 2).

field hospital *n.* A hospital set up on a temporary basis to serve soldiers in a combat zone.

field house *n. Sports.* **1.** A building at an athletic field having locker rooms and storage and training facilities. **2.** A building having one or more areas for different athletic events and usually grandstands for spectators.

field ion microscope *n.* A microscope that produces an image of the atoms on a metal surface by means of ions formed in a high-voltage electric field.

field lens *n.* The lens positioned farthest from the eye in a compound eyepiece.

field magnet *n.* A magnet used to provide a magnetic field in an electrical device such as a generator or motor.

field marshal *n.* An officer in some European armies, usually ranking just below the commander-in-chief.

field mint *n.* The corn mint.

field mouse *n.* Any of various small mice, as of the genera *Apodemus* or *Microtus,* inhabiting meadows and fields and often causing damage to crops.

field officer *n.* A military officer, as a major, lieutenant colonel, or colonel, ranking above a captain and below a brigadier general.

field of force *n.* A region of space throughout which the force produced by a single agent, as an electric current, is operative.

field of honor *n.* **1.** The scene of a duel. **2.** A battlefield.

field of view *n.* A field (sense 13).

field of vision *n.* A visual field.

fields·man (fēldz'mən) *n.* A fielder in cricket.

field·stone (fēld'stōn') *n.* A stone naturally occurring in fields, often used as a building material.

field·strip (fēld'strĭp') *tr.v.* **-stripped, -strip·ping, -strips.** To disassemble (a weapon) for cleaning, repair, and inspection.

field·test (fēld'tĕst') *tr.v.* **-test·ed, -test·ing, -tests.** To test in natural operating conditions.

field trial *n.* A test for young, untried hunting dogs to determine their competence in pointing and retrieving.

field trip *n.* A group excursion for the purpose of firsthand observation, as to a museum, woods, or historical place.

field winding *n.* The electrically conducting winding of a field magnet that produces electrical excitation, esp. of a motor or generator.

field·work (fēld'wûrk') *n.* **1.** A temporary military fortification erected in the field. **2.** Work done or observations made in the field as opposed to that done or observed in a laboratory or classroom.

fiend (fēnd) *n.* **1.** An evil spirit; demon. **2.** The Devil; Satan. **3.** A diabolically evil or wicked person. **4.** *Informal.* **a.** One who is addicted to something: *a dope fiend.* **b.** One who is completely absorbed in or obsessed with a given job or pastime: *a crossword-puzzle fiend.* **5.** One who is particularly adept at something: *a fiend with computers.* [ME < OE *fēond.*]

fiend·ish (fēn'dĭsh) *adj.* **1.** Of, pertaining to, or suggestive of a fiend; diabolical. **2.** Extremely wicked or cruel. **3.** Extremely difficult or troublesome: *a fiendish problem.* **—fiend'ish·ly** *adv.* **—fiend'ish·ness** *n.*

fierce (fîrs) *adj.* **fierc·er, fierc·est.** **1.** Having a savage and violent nature; ferocious. **2.** Extremely severe or violent;

fife

fig[1]

figurehead

figure skating

figurine
18th-century English

terrible: *"the fierce thunders roar me their music"* (Ezra Pound). **3.** Extremely intense or ardent: *fierce loyalty.* **4.** *Informal.* Very difficult or unpleasant: *a fierce exam.* [ME *fiers* < OFr. < Lat. *ferus.*] **—fierce'ly** *adv.* **—fierce'ness** *n.*

fi·er·i fa·ci·as (fī'ə-rē fā'shē-əs, fā'shəs) *n. Law.* A writ of execution commanding a sheriff to lay a claim to and seize the goods and chattels of a debtor to fulfill a judgment against him. [ME < Lat., cause (it) to be done.]

fier·y (fīr'ē, fī'ə-rē) *adj.* **-i·er, -i·est. 1.** Consisting of or containing fire. **2.** Of, pertaining to, or resembling a fire: *fiery hair.* **3.** Torridly hot. **4.** Flammable. **5.** Emitting or appearing to emit sparks; glowing. **6.** Easily excited or emotionally volatile; tempestuous: *a fiery temper.* **7.** Inflamed and usually painful. [ME < *fier,* fire < OE *fȳr.*] **—fier'i·ly** *adv.* **—fier'i·ness** *n.*

fi·es·ta (fē-ĕs'tə) *n.* A festival or religious holiday, esp. a saint's day celebrated in Spanish-speaking countries. [Sp. < Lat. *festa,* neuter pl. of *festus,* joyous.]

fife (fīf) *n.* A musical instrument similar to a flute but higher in range, used primarily to accompany drums in military music. [Fr. *fifre* or G. *Pfeife* < OHG *pfīffa.*]

fife rail *n.* A rail around the lower part of a ship's mast to which the belaying pins for the rigging are secured.

fif·teen (fĭf-tēn') *n.* **1.** The cardinal number that is next after the number 14 and equal to the sum of 14 + 1. **2.** The 15th in a set or sequence. [ME *fiftene* < OE *fīftēne.*] **—fif·teen'** *adj. & pron.*

fif·teenth (fĭf-tēnth') *n.* **1.** The ordinal number that matches the number 15 in a series. **2.** One of 15 equal parts. **—fif·teenth'** *adj. & adv.*

fifth (fĭfth) *n.* **1.** The ordinal number that matches the number five in a series. **2.** One of five equal parts. **3.** One-fifth of a gallon or four-fifths of a quart of liquor. **4. a.** A musical interval encompassing five diatonic tones, such as C, D, E, F, and G. **b.** Either of the two tones constituting the extremities of such an interval. **c.** The dominant of a tonality. **5. Fifth.** The Fifth Amendment to the Constitution of the United States. [ME < OE *fīfta.*] **—fifth** *adj. & adv.*

Fifth Amendment *n.* An amendment to the Constitution of the United States, ratified in 1791, that deals with the rights of accused criminals by providing for due process of law, forbidding double jeopardy, and stating that no person may be forced to testify as a witness against himself.

fifth column *n.* A clandestine subversive organization working within a given country to further an invading enemy's military and political aims. [First applied in 1936 to rebel sympathizers inside Madrid when four columns of rebel troops were attacking that city.] **—fifth columnist** *n.*

fifth wheel *n.* **1.** A wheel or portion of a wheel placed horizontally over the forward axle of a carriage to provide support and stability during turns. **2.** An additional wheel carried on a four-wheeled vehicle as a spare. **3.** An extra and unnecessary person or thing.

fif·ti·eth (fĭf'tē-ĭth) *n.* **1.** The ordinal number that matches the number 50 in a series. **2.** One of 50 equal parts. **—fif'ti·eth** *adj. & adv.*

fif·ty (fĭf'tē) *n.* The cardinal number equal to 5 × 10. [ME *fifti* < OE *fīftig.*] **—fif'ty** *adj. & pron.*

fif·ty-fif·ty (fĭf'tē-fĭf'tē) *adj. Informal.* Divided or shared in two equal portions: *a fifty-fifty split.* **—fif'ty-fif'ty** *adv.*

fig[1] (fĭg) *n.* **1.** Any of several trees or shrubs of the genus *Ficus,* esp. *F. carica,* native to the Mediterranean region, widely cultivated for its edible fruit. **2.** The sweet, pear-shaped, many-seeded fruit of the fig tree. **3. a.** Any of several plants bearing fruit similar to the fig. **b.** The fruit of such a plant. **4.** A trivial or contemptible amount: *didn't care a fig for me.* [ME < OFr. *fige* < OProv. *figa* < Lat. *ficus.*]

fig[2] (fĭg) *n. Informal.* **1.** Dress; array: *in full fig.* **2.** Physical condition; shape: *in poor fig.* [Orig. unknown.]

fight (fīt) *v.* **fought** (fôt), **fight·ing, fights.** *—intr.* **1.** To participate in combat or battle. **2.** To participate in boxing or wrestling. **3.** To quarrel; argue. **4.** To stand up against something or assert oneself. *—tr.* **1.** To contend with physically or in battle. **2.** To box or wrestle against in a ring. **3.** To contend with or struggle against: *fight temptation.*. **4.** To try to prevent or undo the development of. **5.** To wage (a battle). **6.** To contend for by or as if by combat: *"I now resolved that Calais should be fought to the death"* (Winston Churchill). **7.** To make (one's way) by or as if by combat. **8.** To set in combat with another. ***—phrasal verb.* fight off.** To defend against or drive back (a hostile force). *—n.* **1.** A battle waged between opposing groups; combat. **2.** A quarrel or conflict. **3. a.** A physical conflict between two or more individuals. **b.** A boxing or wrestling match. **4.** A struggle to achieve an objective. **5.** The power or inclination to fight; pugnacity. [ME *fighten* < OE *feohtan.*]

fight·er (fī'tər) *n.* **1.** One engaged in fighting; combatant. **2.** *Sports.* A boxer; pugilist. **3.** A pugnacious, unyielding, or determined person. **4.** A fast, maneuverable combat aircraft used to engage enemy aircraft.

fighting chance *n.* A slight chance to win but only following a struggle.

fig leaf *n.* A stylized representation of the leaf of a fig, used esp. to conceal the genitalia of male statues.

fig marigold *n.* Any of various plants of the genus *Mesembryanthemum,* native to southern Africa, having thick, fleshy leaves and variously colored flowers.

fig·ment (fĭg'mənt) *n.* Something invented, made up, or fabricated: *a figment of her imagination.* [ME < Lat. *figmentum* < *fingere,* to form.]

fig·ur·al (fĭg'yər-əl) *adj.* Consisting of or forming a pictorial composition or design of human or animal figures.

fig·u·rant (fĭg'yə-rănt', -ränt', -räN') *n.* **1.** A member of a corps de ballet who does not perform solos. **2.** A stage performer without a speaking part. [Fr. < pr.part. of *figurer,* to represent < OFr. < Lat. *figurare,* to form < *figura,* figure.]

fig·u·ra·tion (fĭg'yə-rā'shən) *n.* **1.** The act of forming something into a particular shape. **2.** A shape, form, or outline. **3.** The act of representing with figures. **4.** A figurative representation. **5.** *Mus.* Embellishment; ornamentation.

fig·u·ra·tive (fĭg'yər-ə-tĭv) *adj.* **1. a.** Based on or making use of figures of speech; metaphorical: *figurative language.* **b.** Containing many figures of speech; ornate. **2.** Represented by a figure or figures; symbolic or emblematic. **3.** Of or relating to representation by means of animal or human figures. **—fig'u·ra·tive·ly** *adv.* **—fig'u·ra·tive·ness** *n.*

fig·ure (fĭg'yər) *n.* **1.** A written symbol representing something other than a letter, esp. a number. **2. figures.** Mathematical calculation involving the use of figures. **3.** An amount represented in numbers: *sold for a large figure.* **4.** The outline, form, or silhouette of a thing. **5.** The shape or form of a human body. **6.** An individual, esp. a well-known personage. **7.** The impression an individual makes through his behavior or appearance: *He cuts a dashing figure.* **8.** A person, animal, or object that symbolizes something. **9.** A pictorial or sculptural representation, esp. of the human body. **10. a.** A diagram. **b.** A design or pattern. **11.** An illustration printed from an engraved plate or block. **12.** A configuration or distinct group of steps in a dance. **13.** *Mus.* A brief melodic or harmonic unit often constituting the base for a larger musical phrase or structure. **14.** *Logic.* Any one of the forms that a syllogism can take, depending on the position of the middle term. **15. a.** An indistinct object: *saw figures dashing down the street.* **b.** *Obs.* An illusion; phantasm. *—v.* **-ured, -ur·ing, -ures.** *—tr.* **1.** To calculate with numbers. **2.** To make a likeness of; depict. **3.** To adorn with a design or figures. **4.** *Mus.* To indicate the chordal structure of (a bass line of single notes) with a sequence of conventionalized numbers. **5.** *Informal.* **a.** To conclude, believe, or predict: *never figured that would happen.* **b.** To interpret or regard: *figured him for a hustler.* *—intr.* **1.** To calculate; compute. **2.** To be pertinent or involved: *"the Van Winkles who figured so gallantly in the chivalrous days of Peter Stuyvesant"* (Washington Irving). ***—phrasal verbs.* figure on** (or **upon**). *Informal.* **1.** To depend on. **2.** To take into consideration; expect. **figure out.** *Informal.* To solve, decipher, or comprehend. [ME < OFr. < Lat. *figura* < *fingere,* to form.]

fig·ured (fĭg'yərd) *adj.* **1.** Shaped or fashioned. **2.** Decorated with a design; patterned: *"My dress is richly figured"* (Amy Lowell). **3.** Represented, as in graphic art or sculpture; depicted.

figured bass *n.* A continuo (sense 1).

figure eight *n.* Any of various forms or representations having the shape of the number 8, such as a knot or an ice-skating maneuver.

fig·ure·head (fĭg'yər-hĕd') *n.* **1.** A person given a position of nominal leadership but having no actual authority. **2.** A carved figure on the prow of a ship.

figure of speech *n.* An expression, such as metaphor or hyperbole, in which a nonliteral and intensive sense of a word or words is used to create a forceful, dramatic, or illuminating image.

figure skating *n.* Ice skating in which the skater traces prescribed, usually elaborate figures.

figures shift *n.* **1.** A shift in a typewriter to upper case. **2.** A data control character after which characters are interpreted as having been typed in the upper-case mode.

fig·u·rine (fĭg'yə-rēn') *n.* A small molded or sculptured figure; statuette. [Fr. < Ital. *figurina,* dim. of *figura,* figure < Lat. *figura.*]

fig wasp *n.* A small wasp of the genus *Blastophaga* that is the vehicle for caprification.

fig·wort (fĭg'wûrt', -wôrt') *n.* Any of various plants of the genus *Scrophularia,* having loose, branching clusters of small greenish or purple flowers. [FIG[1], piles (obs.) + WORT (from its use as a folk medicine).]

Fi·ji·an (fē'jē-ən) The Austronesian language of Fiji. **—Fi'ji·an** *adj.*

fil (fĭl) *n.* See table at **currency.** [Alteration of Ar. *fils.*]

fi·la (fī'lə) *n.* Plural of **filum.**

fil·a·ment (fĭl'ə-mənt) *n.* **1.** A fine or thinly spun thread, fiber, or wire. **2.** A slender, threadlike appendage, part, or structure, such as the slender stalk of a stamen on which the anther is borne or a chainlike series of cells, as in some algae. **3. a.** A fine wire heated electrically to incandescence in an electric lamp. **b.** *Electronics.* A high-resistance wire or ribbon forming the cathode in some thermionic tubes. [NLat. *filamentum* < LLat. *filare,* to spin < Lat. *filum,* thread.] **—fil'a·men'tous** (-mĕn'təs), **fil'a·men'ta·ry** (-mĕn'tə-rē, -mĕn'trē) *adj.*

fi·lar (fī′lər) *adj.* **1.** Of or pertaining to a thread. **2.** Having fine threads across the field of view for measuring small distances, as in a telescope eyepiece. [< Lat. *filum,* thread.]
fil·a·ree (fĭl′ə-rē′) *n.* The alfilaria. [Mex. Sp. *alfilerillo.* —see ALFILARIA.]
fi·lar·i·a (fə-lâr′ē-ə) *n., pl.* **-i·ae** (-ē-ē′). Any of various parasitic nematode worms of the superfamily Filarioidea that infest vertebrates and are often transmitted by biting insects. [NLat. *Filaria,* former genus name < Lat. *filum,* thread.] **—fi·lar′i·al** (-ē-əl), **fi·lar′i·an** (-ē-ən) *adj.*
fil·a·ri·a·sis (fĭl′ə-rī′ə-sĭs) *n.* Infestation of tissue, esp. with filariae. [FILAR(IA) + -IASIS.]
fil·a·ture (fĭl′ə-cho͝or′, -chər) *n.* **1.** The act or process of spinning, drawing, or twisting into threads. **2.** The act or process of reeling raw silk from cocoons. **3.** A reel used in drawing silk from cocoons. **4.** An establishment where silk is reeled. [Fr. < LLat. *filare,* to spin. —see FILAMENT.]
fil·bert (fĭl′bərt) *n.* **1.** A Eurasian shrub or tree, *Corylus maxima,* a species of hazel, cultivated for its edible nuts. **2.** The rounded, smooth-shelled nut of the filbert. [ME < AN, after St. *Philbert* (d. A.D. 684), whose feast day in late August coincides with the ripening of the nut.]
filch (fĭlch) *tr.v.* **filched, filch·ing, filch·es.** To steal (something) in a furtive manner. [ME *filchen.*] **—filch′er** *n.*
file¹ (fīl) *n.* **1.** A receptacle that keeps loose objects, esp. papers, in useful order. **2.** A collection of objects kept or arranged in or as if in a file: *the accounts-due file.* **3. a.** A line of persons, animals, or things positioned one behind another. **b.** A line of soldiers or military vehicles so positioned. **4.** Any of the rows of squares that run vertically or between players on a playing board in chess or checkers. **5.** *Obs.* A list; roll. —*v.* **filed, fil·ing, files.** —*tr.* **1.** To put or keep (papers, for example) in useful order. **2.** To enter (a legal document, for example) on public official record. **3.** To send or submit (copy) to a newspaper or other publication. —*intr.* **1.** To march or walk in a line. **2.** To apply: *file for a job.* **3.** To enter one's name in a political contest: *file for Congress.* **—idiom. on file.** Recorded and ready for reference. [< ME *filen,* to put documents on a thread < OFr. *filer* < Lat. *filum,* thread.] **—fil′er** *n.*
file² (fīl) *n.* Any of several steel tools with hardened ridged surfaces, used in smoothing, polishing, grinding down, or boring. —*tr.v.* **filed, fil·ing, files.** To smooth, polish, grind, bore, or remove with or as if with a file. [ME < OE *fīl.*] **—fil′er** *n.*
file³ (fīl) *tr.v.* **filed, fil·ing, files.** *Obs.* To sully; defile. [ME *filien* < OE *fȳlen.*]
file clerk *n.* One who is employed to maintain the files and records of an office.
file·fish (fīl′fĭsh′) *n., pl.* **filefish** or **-fish·es.** Any of various chiefly tropical marine fishes of the family Balistidae, related to and resembling the triggerfishes.
file lockout *n.* A condition that occurs when two simultaneously running computer programs request access to the same two files, with each gaining access to one file but not the other, with the result that neither program can proceed and the files block the function of the computer.
fi·let¹ (fĭ-lā′, fĭl′ā′) *n.* A net or lace with a simple pattern of squares. [Fr.]
fi·let² (fĭ-lā′, fĭl′ā′) *n. & v.* Variant of **fillet** (sense 2).
fi·let mi·gnon (fĭl′ā mēn-yôɴ′, fĭ-lā′) *n.* A small, round, very choice cut of beef from the loin. [Fr. : *filet,* fillet + *mignon,* dainty.]
fil·i·al (fĭl′ē-əl) *adj.* Of, pertaining to, or befitting a son or daughter: *filial respect.* [ME < LLat. *filialis* < Lat. *filius,* son.] **—fil′i·al·ly** *adv.*
filial generation *n. Genetics.* A set of offspring from a specific mating that follow the parental generation.
fil·i·ate (fĭl′ē-āt′) *tr.v.* **-at·ed, -at·ing, -ates. 1.** To affiliate. **2.** *Law.* To assign paternity to (a bastard child, for example). [Med. Lat. *filiare, filiat-,* to acknowledge as a son < Lat. *filius,* son.]
fil·i·a·tion (fĭl′ē-ā′shən) *n.* **1.** The condition or fact of being the child of a certain parent. **2.** A line of descent; derivation. **3. a.** The act or fact of forming a new branch, as of a society or language group. **b.** The branch thus formed. **4.** *Law.* The assignment of paternity to someone, as a bastard child.
fil·i·bus·ter (fĭl′ə-bŭs′tər) *n.* **1.** The use of obstructionist tactics, esp. prolonged speechmaking, for the purpose of delaying legislative action. **2.** An instance of the use of obstructionist tactics. **3.** An adventurer who engages in a private military action in a foreign country. —*v.* **-tered, -ter·ing, -ters.** —*intr.* **1.** To use obstructionist tactics in a legislative body. **2.** To engage in a private military action in a foreign country. —*tr.* To use obstructionist tactics against (a measure, for example). [< Sp. *filibustero,* freebooter < Fr. *flibustier* < Du. *vrijbuiter,* pirate. —see FREEBOOTER.] **—fil′i·bus′ter·er** *n.*
fil·i·form (fĭl′ə-fôrm′, fī′lə-) *adj.* Resembling or having the form of a thread. [Lat. *filum,* thread + -FORM.]
fil·i·gree (fĭl′ĭ-grē′) *n.* **1.** Delicate and intricate ornamental work made from gold, silver, or other fine twisted wire. **2.** An intricate, delicate, or fanciful ornamentation. —*tr.v.* **-greed, -gree·ing, -grees.** To decorate with or as if with filigree. [Fr. *filigrane* < Ital. *filigrana* : Lat. *filum,* thread + Lat. *granum,* grain.]
fil·ing (fī′lĭng) *n.* **1.** The act of using a file. **2.** A particle or shaving removed by a file.
Fil·i·pi·no (fĭl′ə-pē′nō) *n., pl.* **-nos.** A native, citizen, or inhabitant of the Philippines. —*adj.* **1.** Of or pertaining to the Philippines. **2.** Of or pertaining to the Filipinos. [Sp. < *(Islas) Filipinas,* Philippine (Islands).]
fill (fĭl) *v.* **filled, fill·ing, fills.** —*tr.* **1.** To put into as much as can be held. **2. a.** To stop or plug up (an opening, for example). **b.** To repair a cavity of (a tooth). **3.** To satisfy or meet; fulfill: *fill the requirements.* **4.** To supply the materials for: *fill a prescription.* **5.** To complete by insertion or addition: *fill a form out.* **6.** To supply (an empty space) with material, such as writing, an inscription, or an illustration. **7.** To put someone into: *fill a vacant post.* **8.** To discharge the duties of; hold: *fill a post.* **9.** To occupy the whole of; pervade: *Music filled the room.* **10.** To engage or occupy completely: *a mind filled with strange ideas.* **11.** To add a foreign substance to. **12. a.** To cause (a sail) to swell. **b.** To adjust (a yard) so that wind will cause a sail to swell. —*intr.* To become full. **—phrasal verbs. fill in. 1.** To provide with information that is essential or interesting: *filled her in on the most recent developments.* **2.** To act as a substitute; stand in: *an understudy filling in for the star.* **fill out.** To make or become fuller, rounder, broader, or shapelier. —*n.* **1.** An amount needed to make full, complete, or satisfied: *eat one's fill.* **2. a.** A built-up piece of land; embankment. **b.** The material, such as earth or gravel, used for this. **—idioms. fill (someone's) shoes.** To assume someone's position or duties and perform adequately. **fill the bill.** *Informal.* To serve a purpose. [ME *fillen* < OE *fyllan.*]
filled gold *n.* A relatively inexpensive metal such as brass with a relatively thick surface layer of bonded gold.
filled milk *n.* Skim milk with vegetable oils added to substitute for butter fat.
fill·er (fĭl′ər) *n.* **1.** One who fills. **2.** Something added in order to augment weight or size or to fill space. **3.** A composition, esp. a semisolid that hardens on drying, used to fill pores, cracks, or holes in a wood, plaster, or other construction surface prior to finishing. **4.** Tobacco used to form the body of a cigar. **5. a.** A short item used to fill space in a publication. **b.** Something, such as a news item, public-service message, or music, used to fill time in a radio or television presentation. **6.** A sheaf of loose papers used to fill a notebook or binder. **7.** *Archit.* An element, such as a plate, used to fill the space between two supporting members.
fil·lér (fĭl′âr′) *n., pl.* **fillér** or **-lérs.** See table at **currency.** [Hung.]
fil·let (fĭl′ĭt) *n.* **1.** A narrow strip of ribbon or similar material, often worn as a headband. **2.** Also **fi·let** (fĭ-lā′, fĭl′ā′). **a.** A strip or compact piece of boneless meat or fish. **b.** A boneless strip of meat rolled and tied, as for roasting. **3.** *Archit.* **a.** A thin, flat molding used as separation between or ornamentation for larger moldings. **b.** A ridge between the indentations of a fluted column. **4.** A narrow decorative line impressed upon the cover of a book. **5.** *Heraldry.* A narrow horizontal band placed in the lower fourth area of the chief. **6.** *Anat.* A loop-shaped band of fibers, such as the lemniscus. —*tr.v.* **-let·ed, -let·ing, -lets. 1.** To bind or decorate with or as if with a fillet. **2.** Also **fi·let** (fĭ-lā′, fĭl′ā′). To slice, bone, or make into fillets. [ME *filet* < OFr., dim. of *fil,* thread < Lat. *filum.*]
fill-in (fĭl′ĭn′) *n.* One that fills in.
fill·ing (fĭl′ĭng) *n.* **1.** Something used to fill a space, cavity, or container: *a gold filling in a tooth.* **2.** An edible mixture used to fill sandwiches, cakes, and pastries: *pie filling.* **3.** The horizontal threads that cross the warp in weaving; weft.
filling station *n.* A retail establishment at which vehicles are serviced, esp. with gasoline, oil, air, and water.
fil·lip (fĭl′əp) *n.* **1.** A snap or light blow made by pressing a fingertip against the thumb and suddenly releasing it. **2.** Something that excites or arouses; stimulus. —*tr.v.* **-liped, -lip·ing, -lips. 1.** To strike or propel with a fillip. **2.** To excite, arouse, or stimulate. [Imit.]
fil·ly (fĭl′ē) *n., pl.* **-lies. 1.** A young female horse; young mare. **2.** *Informal.* A lively and high-spirited girl. [ME *filli* < ON *fylja.*]
film (fĭlm) *n.* **1.** A thin skin or membranous coating. **2.** An abnormal thin, opaque coating on the cornea of the eye. **3. a.** A thin covering or coating: *a film of dust on the piano.* **b.** A thin, generally flexible transparent sheet, as of plastic used in wrapping or packaging. **4.** A thin sheet or strip of flexible cellulose material coated with a photosensitive emulsion, used to make photographic negatives or transparencies. **5. a.** A motion picture. **b.** Motion pictures collectively; the cinema. **6.** *Computer Sci.* A coating of magnetic alloys on glass used in manufacturing storage devices. —*v.* **filmed, film·ing, films.** —*tr.* **1.** To cover with or as if with a film. **2.** To make a motion picture of or based on. —*intr.* **1.** To become coated or obscured with or as if with a film. **2.** To make a motion picture. [ME < OE *filmen.*]
film·card (fĭlm′kärd′) *n.* A microfiche.
film·dom (fĭlm′dəm) *n.* **1.** The motion-picture industry. **2.** The people employed in the motion-picture industry.

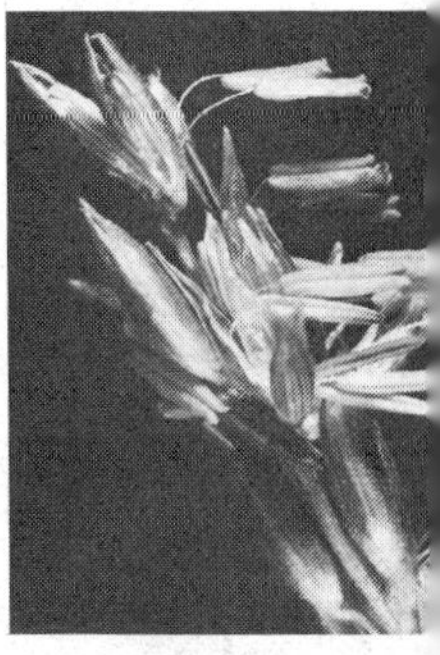
filament
Cornflower stamen

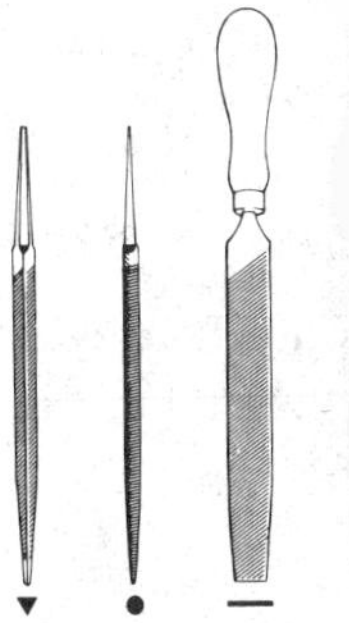
file²
Left to right: Taper file, round file, flat file, with cross sections (*below*)

filefish

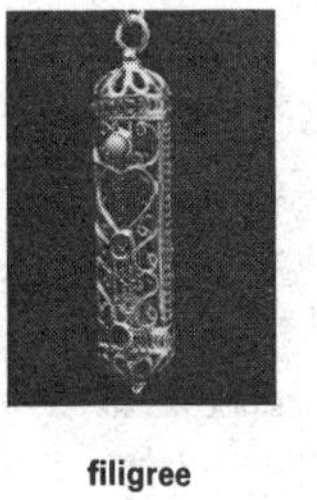
filigree

p **pop** / r **roar** / s **sauce** / sh **ship, dish** / t **tight** / th **thin, path** / *th* **this, bathe** / ŭ **cut** / ûr **urge** / v **valve** / w **with** / y **yes** / z **zebra, size** / zh **vision** / ə **about, item, edible, gallop, circus** / œ *Fr.* **feu,** *Ger.* **schön** / ü *Fr.* **tu,** *Ger.* **über** / KH *Ger.* **ich,** *Scot.* **loch** / N *Fr.* **bon.**

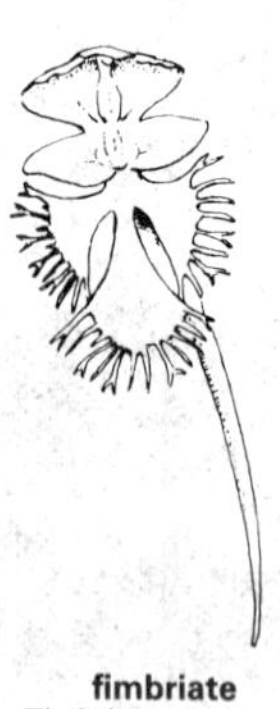

fimbriate
Fimbriate petals of a fringed orchis

fin[1]

film·go·er (fĭlm'gō'ər) *n.* One who frequently goes to see motion pictures.
film·ic (fĭl'mĭk) *adj.* Of, pertaining to, or resembling motion pictures. **—film'i·cal·ly** *adv.*
film·mak·er (fĭlm'mā'kər) *n.* One who produces motion pictures.
fil·mog·ra·phy (fĭl-mŏg'rə-fē) *n., pl.* **-phies.** Writings, as lists or books, about films or film figures.
film pack *n.* A pack of photographic sheet films that can be exposed in succession and withdrawn from the exposure position for storage at the rear of the pack.
film·set·ting (fĭlm'sĕt'ĭng) *n.* Photocomposition.
film·strip (fĭlm'strĭp') *n.* A length of film containing photographs, diagrams, or other graphic matter prepared for still projection.
film·y (fĭl'mē) *adj.* **-i·er, -i·est. 1.** Of, resembling, or consisting of film; gauzy: *filmy lingerie.* **2.** Covered by or as if by a film; hazy. **—film'i·ly** *adv.* **—film'i·ness** *n.*
fil·o·plume (fĭl'ə-plo͞om', fī'lə-) *n.* A hairlike feather having few or no barbs. [Lat. *filum,* thread + PLUME.]
fi·lose (fī'lōs') *adj.* **1.** Threadlike. **2.** Having or ending in a threadlike part. [< Lat. *filum,* thread.]
fil·ter (fĭl'tər) *n.* **1. a.** A porous substance through which a liquid or gas is passed in order to remove constituents such as suspended matter. **b.** A device containing or consisting of such a substance so used. **2.** Any of various electric, electronic, acoustic, or optical devices used to reject signals, vibrations, or radiations of certain frequencies while passing others. *—v.* **-tered, -ter·ing, -ters.** *—tr.* **1.** To pass (a liquid or gas) through a filter. **2.** To remove by passing through a filter. *—intr.* **1.** To pass through or as if through a filter: *light filtering through the blinds.* **2.** To come or go in gradually and in small groups: *an audience filtering into the theater.* [ME *filtre* < OFr. < Med. Lat. *filtrum,* of Germanic orig.] **—fil'ter·er** *n.*
fil·ter·a·ble also **fil·tra·ble** (fĭl'tər-ə-bəl, fĭl'trə-) *adj.* **1. a.** Capable of being filtered. **b.** Capable of being removed by filtering. **2.** Sufficiently minute to pass through a fine filter, thereby maintaining the infectivity of the filtrate. Used of certain viruses and bacteria. **—fil'ter·a·bil'i·ty** *n.*
filterable virus *n.* A virus sufficiently small to pass through a very fine filter, thereby maintaining the infectivity of the filtrate.
filter bed *n.* A layer of sand or gravel on the bottom of a reservoir or tank used to filter water or sewage.
filter feeder *n.* An organism that utilizes various filtering mechanisms to obtain nourishment from particulate organic material suspended in water.
filter paper *n.* Porous paper suitable for use as a filter.
filth (fĭlth) *n.* **1. a.** Foul or dirty matter. **b.** Repellent garbage or refuse. **2.** A dirty or corrupt condition; foulness. **3.** Something, as language, considered obscene, prurient, or immoral. [ME < OE *fȳlth.*]
filth·y (fĭl'thē) *adj.* **-i·er, -i·est. 1.** Covered with or full of filth; very dirty. **2.** Obscene; scatological. **3.** Vile; nasty. **—filth'i·ly** *adv.* **—filth'i·ness** *n.*
fil·tra·ble (fĭl'tər-ə-bəl, fĭl'trə-) *adj.* Variant of **filterable.**
fil·trate (fĭl'trāt') *tr. & intr.v.* **-trat·ed, -trat·ing, -trates.** To put or go through a filter. *—n.* The portion of material subjected to filtration that passes through the filter. [NLat. *filtrare, filtrat-,* to filter < Med. Lat. *filtrum,* filter.]
fil·tra·tion (fĭl-trā'shən) *n.* The act or process of filtering.
fi·lum (fī'ləm) *n., pl.* **-la** (-lə). A threadlike anatomical structure; filament. [Lat., thread.]
fim·bri·a (fĭm'brē-ə) *n., pl.* **-bri·ae** (-brē-ē'). A fringelike part or structure, as at the opening of an oviduct in mammals. [LLat., fringe < Lat. *fimbriae.*] **—fim'bri·al** *adj.*
fim·bri·ate (fĭm'brē-ĭt, -āt') also **fim·bri·at·ed** (-ā'tĭd) *adj.* Fringed, as the edge of a petal or the opening of a duct. [LLat. *fimbriatus* < *fimbria,* fringe.] **—fim'bri·a'tion** *n.*
fin[1] (fĭn) *n.* **1.** A membranous appendage extending from the body of a fish or other aquatic animal, used for locomotion, steering, or maintaining balance. **2.** Something resembling a fin in shape or function. **3.** A fixed or movable vane or airfoil used to stabilize an aircraft or missile in flight. **4.** An appendage on a boat such as a submarine. **5.** A projecting vane used for cooling, as on a radiator or engine cylinder. **6.** An ornamental projection, as on the rear fender of an automobile. *—v.* **finned, fin·ning, fins.** *—tr.* To equip with fins. *—intr.* To emerge with the fins above water. [ME < OE *finn.*]
fin[2] (fĭn) *n. Slang.* A five-dollar bill. [Yiddish *finf,* five.]
fi·na·gle (fə-nā'gəl) *v.* **-gled, -gling, -gles.** *Informal.* *—tr.* **1.** To obtain or achieve by indirect methods; wangle. **2.** To obtain by trickery or deceit. *—intr.* To use crafty, deceitful methods. [Prob. < dial. *fainaigue,* to cheat.] **—fi·na'gler** *n.*
fi·nal (fī'nəl) *adj.* **1.** Forming or occurring at the end; last. **2.** Of, pertaining to, or constituting the last element in a succession, process, or procedure: *the final movement of the concerto.* **3.** Ultimate and definitive; unalterable: *The judges' decision is final.* *—n.* Something that comes at or forms the end, esp.: **a.** The last or one of the last of a series of athletic contests. **b.** The last examination of an academic course. [ME < OFr. < Lat. *finalis* < *finis,* end.] **—fi'nal·ly** *adv.*
fi·nal·e (fə-năl'ē, -nä'lē) *n.* The concluding part of something, esp. a musical composition. [Ital. < Lat. *finalis,* final.]
fi·nal·ist (fī'nə-lĭst) *n.* A contestant in the final session of a competition.
fi·nal·i·ty (fī-năl'ĭ-tē, fə-) *n., pl.* **-ties. 1.** The condition or fact of being final. **2.** A final, conclusive, or decisive act or utterance.
fi·nal·ize (fī'nə-līz') *tr.v.* **-ized, -iz·ing, -iz·es.** To put into final form; complete. **—fi'nal·i·za'tion** *n.*
Usage: *Finalize* is frequently associated with the language of bureaucracy and so is objected to by many writers. The sentence *we will finalize plans for a class reunion* was unacceptable to the vast majority of the Usage Panel. While *finalize* has no single exact synonym, a substitute can always be found from among *complete, conclude, make final,* and *put in final form.* See also Usage note at **-ize.**
fi·nance (fə-năns', fī-, fī'năns') *n.* **1.** The science of the management of money and other assets. **2.** The management of money, banking, investments, and credit. **3. finances.** Monetary resources; funds, esp. of a government or corporate body. *—tr.v.* **-nanced, -nanc·ing, -nanc·es. 1.** To supply the funds or capital for: *financed the new car.* **2.** To supply funds to: *financing a daughter through law school.* **3.** To furnish credit to. [ME *finaunce,* money supply < OFr. *finance,* gift < *finer,* to pay ransom < *fin,* end < Lat. *finis.*]
finance bill *n.* A legislative act designed to raise public revenues.
finance company *n.* A company that makes loans to individuals.
fi·nan·cial (fə-năn'shəl, fī-) *adj.* Of, pertaining to, or involving finance, finances, or financiers. **—fi·nan'cial·ly** *adv.*
Synonyms: *financial, pecuniary, fiscal, monetary.* These adjectives refer in various senses to money. *Financial* is the broadest in application but often has reference to transactions involving money on a large scale. *Pecuniary* is more appropriate to the private, small-scale dealings of individuals. *Fiscal* applies principally to the policies and practices of a branch of government as they relate to money. *Monetary* has special reference to actual money, its coinage and printing, or its circulation.
fin·an·cier (fĭn'ən-sîr', fə-năn'-, fī'nən-) *n.* One who is occupied with or expert in large-scale financial affairs. [Fr. < OFr. < *finance,* gift. —see FINANCE.]
fin·back (fĭn'băk') *n.* The rorqual.
finch (fĭnch) *n.* Any of various relatively small birds of the family Fringillidae, as a goldfinch, bullfinch, cardinal, grosbeak, or canary, having a short, stout bill adapted for cracking seeds. [ME < OE *finc.*]
find (fīnd) *v.* **found** (found), **find·ing, finds.** *—tr.* **1.** To come upon, often by accident; meet with. **2.** To come upon after a search: *find the cause of the trouble.* **3.** To come upon through observation, experience, or study: *found the answer to the problem.* **4.** To succeed in reaching; arrive at: *The dart found the mark.* **5.** To obtain or acquire by great effort: *found the money by economizing.* **6.** To consider; regard: *I find her charm irresistible.* **7.** To recover (something lost): *found my keys.* **8.** To recover the use of; regain: *found his voice and replied.* **9.** To decide on and make a declaration about: *deliberated and found a verdict.* **10.** To furnish; supply. **11. a.** To bring (oneself) to an awareness of what one truly wishes to be and do in life. **b.** To perceive (oneself) to be in a specific condition or place. *—intr.* To come to a legal decision or verdict: *The jury found for the defendant.* ***—phrasal verb.*** **find out. 1.** To discover in a misdeed, as a crime: *The burglar was found out almost at once.* **2.** To detect the true nature or character of; expose: *Liars risk being found out.* **3.** To determine, ascertain, or corroborate something: *If you're not sure, find out.* *—n.* **1.** An act of finding. **2.** Something that is found, esp. an unexpectedly valuable discovery. [ME *finden* < OE *findan.*] **—find'a·ble** *adj.*
find·er (fīn'dər) *n.* **1.** One that finds. **2.** A device on a camera that indicates to the photographer what will appear in the field of view of the lens. **3.** *Astron.* A small telescope attached to the body of a larger one for locating an object to be observed with the larger telescope.
finder's fee *n.* A fee paid to the finder of financial backing for a venture or to a party that brings the principals together in a venture.
fin de siè·cle (făN' də sē-ĕk'lə) *adj.* Of or characteristic of the last part of the 19th century, esp. with reference to its artistic climate of effete sophistication. [Fr. : *fin,* end + *de,* of + *siècle,* century.]
find·ing (fīn'dĭng) *n.* **1.** Something that has been found. **2.** Often **findings.** A conclusion reached after examination or investigation. **3. findings.** Small tools and materials used by an artisan, as a jeweler.
fine[1] (fīn) *adj.* **fin·er, fin·est. 1.** Of superior quality, skill, or appearance: *a fine day; a fine writer.* **2.** Very small in size, weight, or bulk: *fine type.* **3. a.** Free from impurities. **b.** Containing pure metal in a specified proportion or amount. **4.** Very sharp; keen: *a blade with a fine edge.* **5.** Thin; slender: *fine hairs.* **6.** Showing workmanship of great care and delicacy: *fine china.* **7.** Consisting of extremely small particles; not coarse: *fine dust.* **8. a.** Subtle or precise: *a fine difference.* **b.** Able to make or detect effects of great subtlety or precision; sensitive: *a fine eye for color.* **9.** Trained to the highest degree of physical efficiency: *a*

fine racehorse. **10.** Characterized by refinement or elegance: *a fine lady.* **11.** In satisfactory health; quite well: *I'm fine. And you?* —*adv.* **1.** Finely. **2.** *Informal.* Very well: *doing fine.* —*tr. & intr.v.* **fined, fin·ing, fines.** To make or become finer, purer, or cleaner. [ME *fin* < OFr. < Med. Lat. *finus,* prob. < *finire,* to finish < Lat.] —**fine'ness** *n.*

fine[2] (fīn) *n.* **1.** A sum of money imposed as a penalty for an offense. **2.** *Law.* A forfeiture or penalty to be paid to the offended party in a civil action. **3.** *Law.* An amicable settlement of a suit over land ownership. **4.** *Obs.* An end; termination. —*tr.v.* **fined, fin·ing, fines.** To require the payment of a fine from; impose a fine on. —*idiom.* **in fine. 1.** In conclusion; finally. **2.** In summation; in brief. [ME *fin* < OFr. < Lat. *finis,* end.] —**fin'a·ble, fine'a·ble** *adj.*

fi·ne[3] (fē'nā) *n. Mus.* The end. [Ital. < Lat. *finis,* end.]

fine art *n.* **1. a.** Art produced or intended primarily for beauty rather than utility. **b.** Often **fine arts.** Any of such arts, including sculpture, painting, and music. **2.** Something requiring highly developed techniques and skills: *the fine art of argumentation.*

fine-drawn (fīn'drôn') *adj.* **1.** Drawn out to a slender, threadlike state, as wire. **2.** Subtly or precisely fashioned, as a theory. **3.** Delicately formed: *fine-drawn features.*

fine-grained (fīn'grānd') *adj.* Having a fine, smooth, even grain, as wood.

fine·ly (fīn'lē) *adv.* **1.** In a fine manner; splendidly. **2.** To a fine point; discriminatingly. **3.** In small pieces or parts; minutely: *finely chopped nuts.*

fine print *n.* Something, as limitations in a contract, presented in a deliberately ambiguous or cryptic manner.

fin·er·y (fī'nə-rē) *n., pl.* **-ies.** Elaborate adornment, esp. fine clothing and accessories.

fines herbes (fēn zĕrb', fēn ĕrb') *n.* Finely chopped herbs, such as parsley, chives, tarragon, and thyme, used as a seasoning. [Fr.]

fine-spun (fīn'spŭn') *adj.* **1.** Developed to extreme fineness or subtlety; elaborate. **2.** Developed to excessive fineness or subtlety; overwrought.

fi·nesse (fə-nĕs') *n.* **1.** Delicacy and refinement of performance, execution, or workmanship. **2.** Subtlety, tact, or skill in dealing with a situation. **3.** The playing of a card in a suit in which one holds a nonsequential higher card either to induce an opponent to play an intermediate card that one's partner can then top or to win the trick economically. —*v.* **-nessed, -ness·ing, -ness·es.** —*tr.* **1.** To accomplish by the use of finesse. **2.** To handle with a deceptive or evasive strategy. **3.** To play (a card) as a finesse. —*intr.* To make a finesse in a card game. [OFr., fineness < *fin,* fine.]

fine-toothed comb (fīn'to͞otht', -to͞othd') *n.* **1.** A comb with teeth set close together. **2.** A method of searching or investigating in minute detail: *examined the figures with a fine-toothed comb but found no errors.*

fin·fish (fĭn'fĭsh') *n.* An aquatic vertebrate of the superclass Pisces, as opposed to a shellfish.

fin·ger (fĭng'gər) *n.* **1.** One of the five digits of the hand, esp. one other than the thumb. **2.** The part of a glove designed to cover a finger. **3.** Something, as a peninsula, that resembles a finger. **4.** The length or width of a finger. —*v.* **-gered, -ger·ing, -gers.** —*tr.* **1.** To touch with the fingers; handle. **2.** *Mus.* **a.** To mark (a score) with indications of which fingers are to play the notes. **b.** To play (an instrument) by using the fingers in a particular order or way. **3.** *Slang.* **a.** To inform on. **b.** To designate as an intended victim. —*intr.* **1.** To handle something with the fingers. **2.** To use the fingers in playing a musical instrument. —*idiom.* **twist (or wrap) around (one's) little finger.** *Slang.* To dominate utterly and effortlessly. [ME < OE.] —**fin'ger·er** *n.*

fin·ger·board (fĭng'gər-bôrd', -bōrd') *n.* A strip of wood on the neck of a stringed instrument against which the strings are pressed in playing.

finger bowl *n.* A small bowl that holds water for rinsing the fingers at the table.

fin·ger·breadth (fĭng'gər-brĕdth') *n.* The breadth of one finger.

fin·gered (fĭng'gərd) *adj.* Having a finger or fingers, esp. of a specific number, kind, or appearance: *four-fingered; rosy-fingered.*

fin·ger·ing (fĭng'gər-ĭng) *n.* **1.** The technique used in playing a musical instrument with the fingers. **2.** The indication on a musical score of which fingers are to be used in playing.

fin·ger·ling (fĭng'gər-lĭng) *n.* A young or small fish, as a young salmon or trout.

fin·ger·nail (fĭng'gər-nāl') *n.* A thin, horny, transparent plate covering the dorsal surface of the tip of each finger.

fin·ger-paint (fĭng'gər-pānt') *tr. & intr.v.* **-paint·ed, -paint·ing, -paints.** To make by or engage in finger painting.

finger painting *n.* **1.** The technique of painting by applying color to moistened paper with the fingers. **2.** A picture made by finger painting.

finger post *n.* A guidepost in the shape of a pointing hand.

fin·ger·print (fĭng'gər-prĭnt') *n.* An ink impression of the curves formed by the system of ridges on the skin surface of the distal phalanx of a finger, esp. such an impression used as a means of identification. —*tr.v.* **-print·ed, -print·ing, -prints.** To take the fingerprints of.

finger tip also **fin·ger·tip** (fĭng'gər-tĭp') *n.* The extreme end or tip of a finger. —*idiom.* **at (one's) finger tips.** Readily or instantly available.

finger wave *n.* A wave set into dampened hair using only the fingers and a comb.

fin·i·al (fĭn'ē-əl) *n.* **1.** *Archit.* An ornament fixed to the peak of an arch or arched structure. **2.** An ornamental terminating part, such as the screw on top of a lampshade. [ME < *finial,* last, var. of *final.*]

fin·i·cal (fĭn'ĭ-kəl) *adj.* Finicky. [Prob. < FINE[1].] —**fin'i·cal·ly** *adv.* —**fin'i·cal·ness** *n.*

fin·ick·y (fĭn'ĭ-kē) *adj.* **-i·er, -i·est.** Extremely fastidious in tastes or standards; difficult to please. [< *finick,* a finical person < FINICAL.]

fin·is (fĭn'ĭs, fī'nĭs) *n.* The end. [ME < Lat.]

fin·ish (fĭn'ĭsh) *v.* **-ished, -ish·ing, -ish·es.** —*tr.* **1.** To arrive at or attain the end of: *finish a race.* **2.** To bring to an end; terminate: *finished cleaning the room.* **3.** To consume all of; use up: *finish a pie.* **4.** To bring to a desired or required state; perfect: *finish a painting.* **5.** To give (a surface) a desired or particular texture. **6.** To destroy; kill: *finish an enemy.* **7.** To bring about the ruin of: *The stock-market crash finished him.* —*intr.* **1.** To come to an end; stop. **2.** To reach the end of a task, course, or relationship. —*n.* **1. a.** The final part or conclusion; end: *a close finish in the race.* **b.** The reason for one's ruin; downfall. **2.** Something that completes, concludes, or perfects, esp.: **a.** The last treatment or coating of a surface. **b.** The surface texture produced. **c.** The material used in surfacing or finishing: *a wax finish.* **3.** Completeness, thoroughness, refinement, or smoothness of execution; perfection. [ME *finishen* < OFr. *finir, finiss-,* to complete < Lat. *finire* < *finis, end.*] —**fin'ish·er** *n.*

fin·ished (fĭn'ĭsht) *adj.* Highly accomplished or skilled; polished.

finishing school *n.* A private girls' school that stresses training in cultural subjects and preparation for life in society.

finish line *n.* A line that marks the end of a course for racing.

fi·nite (fī'nīt') *adj.* **1. a.** Having bounds; limited: *a finite list of choices.* **b.** Existing, persisting, or enduring for a limited time only; impermanent. **2.** Being neither infinite nor infinitesimal. **3.** *Math.* **a.** Bounded in an interval. Used of a quantity defined in an interval. **b.** Incapable of being put into one-to-one correspondence with a part of itself. Used of a set. **c.** Real or complex as distinguished from ideal. Used of a number. **4.** *Gram.* Limited by person, number, tense, and mood and capable of serving as a predicate. Used of verbs. —*n.* Finite entities collectively. [ME *finit* < Lat. *finitum,* p.part. of *finire,* to limit < *finis,* end.] —**fi'nite'ly** *adv.* —**fi'nite'ness** *n.*

fin·i·tude (fĭn'ĭ-to͞od', -tyo͞od', fī'nĭ-) *n.* The quality or condition of being finite.

fink (fĭngk) *Slang.* —*n.* **1.** A hired strikebreaker. **2.** An informer. **3.** An undesirable person. —*intr.v.* **finked, fink·ing, finks. 1.** To inform against another person. **2.** To withhold support or participation: *finked out on me.* [Orig. unknown.]

Finn (fĭn) *n.* **1.** A native or inhabitant of Finland. **2.** One who speaks Finnish or a Finnic language. [Swed. *Finne.*]

fin·nan had·die (fĭn'ən hăd'ē) also **finnan had·dock** (hăd'ək) *n.* Smoked haddock. [Obs. *findhorn haddock,* prob. after the *Findhorn* River, Scotland.]

finned (fĭnd) *adj.* Having a fin, fins, or finlike parts.

Fin·nic (fĭn'ĭk) *adj.* Of or pertaining to Finland or the Finns. —*n.* A branch of Finno-Ugric that includes Finnish, Estonian, and Lapp.

Finn·ish (fĭn'ĭsh) *adj.* Of or pertaining to Finland, its language, or its people. —*n.* The Finno-Ugric language of the Finns.

Fin·no-U·gric (fĭn'ō-o͞o'grĭk, -yo͞o'-) also **Fin·no-U·gri·an** (-o͞o'grē-ən, -yo͞o'-) *n.* A subfamily of the Uralic language family that includes Finnish, Hungarian, and other languages of eastern Europe and northwestern U.S.S.R. —*adj.* **1.** Pertaining to the Finns and the Ugrians. **2.** Pertaining to Finno-Ugric.

fin·ny (fĭn'ē) *adj.* **-ni·er, -ni·est. 1.** Having fins. **2.** Resembling a fin. **3.** Of, pertaining to, or characteristic of fish.

fi·no·chi·o also **fi·noc·chi·o** (fə-nō'kē-ō') *n.* A variety of fennel, *Foeniculum vulgare dulce,* whose blanched stalks are eaten as a vegetable. [Ital. *finocchio* < Lat. *feniculum,* fennel, dim. of *fenum,* hay.]

fin rot *n.* A bacterial disease of fish marked by the progressive deterioration of the fin tissue.

fiord (fyôrd, fyōrd) *n.* Variant of **fjord.**

fip·ple (fĭp'əl) *n.* **1.** A wooden block that forms a flue at the mouth end of certain musical wind instruments. **2.** An object similar to a fipple in an organ pipe. [Orig. unknown.]

fipple flute *n.* A flute, as a recorder, with a fipple.

fir (fûr) *n.* **1. a.** Any of various evergreen trees of the genus *Abies,* having flat needles and erect cones. **b.** Any of several similar or related trees, such as the Douglas fir. **2.** The wood of a fir. [ME *firre* < OE *fyrh.*] —**fir'ry** *adj.*

fire (fīr) *n.* **1. a.** A rapid, persistent chemical reaction that releases heat and light, esp. the exothermic combination of a combustible substance with oxygen. **b.** A fire distinguished by destructive power: *a forest fire.* **2. a.** Intensity, as of feel-

fingerprint

finial

firefighter

ing; ardor. **b.** Enthusiasm. **3.** Luminosity or brilliance, as of a cut and polished gemstone. **4.** Liveliness and vivacity of imagination; inspiration: *the fire of his verse.* **5.** A torment, trial, or tribulation. **6.** The discharge of firearms. —*v.* **fired, fir·ing, fires.** —*tr.* **1.** To cause to burn; ignite. **2. a.** To add fuel to (something burning). **b.** To maintain or intensify a fire in. **3.** To bake in a kiln: *fire a flowerpot.* **4.** To arouse the emotions of; make enthusiastic or ardent: *He was fired by patriotism.* **5.** To detonate or discharge (a firearm, explosives, or a projectile): *fire a rifle; fire electrons.* **6.** *Informal.* To project or hurl suddenly and forcefully: *fire a ball at a batter.* **7.** *Informal.* To discharge from a position; dismiss. —*intr.* **1.** To become ignited; flame up. **2. a.** To become excited or ardent. **b.** To become angry or annoyed. **3.** To tend a fire. **4.** To detonate or shoot a weapon: *fired at the enemy.* **5.** *Informal.* To project or hurl a missile. —**idioms. catch fire. 1.** To become ignited. **2.** To become excited or enthusiastic. **on fire. 1.** Ignited; ablaze. **2.** Filled with enthusiasm or excitement. **under fire. 1.** Exposed or subjected to enemy attack. **2.** Exposed or subjected to critical attack or censure. [ME *fir* < OE *fȳr.*] —**fir'er** *n.*

fire alarm *n.* A device, as a siren, used in announcing the outbreak of a fire.

fire ant *n.* Any of several ants of the genus *Solenopsis,* esp. *S. geminata* or *S. saevissima,* of the southern United States and tropical America, that build conspicuous mounds and are capable of inflicting a painful sting.

fire·arm (fīr'ärm') *n.* A weapon capable of firing a missile, esp. a pistol or rifle using an explosive charge as a propellant.

fire·ball (fīr'bôl') *n.* **1.** A brilliantly burning sphere. **2.** An exceptionally bright meteor. **3.** A highly luminous, intensely hot spherical cloud of dust, gas, and vapor generated by a nuclear explosion. **4.** *Informal.* A very energetic person.

fire·base (fīr'bās') *n.* A military base or site from which heavy fire is directed against the enemy.

fire beetle *n.* Any of various tropical American click beetles of the genus *Pyrophorus,* esp. *P. noctilucus,* having brightly luminous spots.

fire·bird (fīr'bûrd') *n.* Any of various birds, such as the Baltimore oriole, having bright scarlet or orange plumage.

fire blight *n.* A destructive disease of apples, pears, and related trees and plants, caused by a bacterium, *Erwinia amylovora.*

fire·boat (fīr'bōt') *n.* A boat equipped to fight fires along waterfronts and on ships.

fire bomb *n.* An incendiary bomb.

fire·box (fīr'bŏks') *n.* **1.** A chamber, as the furnace of a steam locomotive, in which fuel is burned. **2.** A box containing a device for sounding a fire alarm.

fire·brand (fīr'brănd') *n.* **1.** A piece of burning wood. **2.** A person who stirs up trouble or kindles a revolt.

fire·brat (fīr'brăt') *n.* A small, wingless insect, *Thermobia domestica,* frequenting warm areas of dwellings and often destructive to paper and other materials.

fire·break (fīr'brāk') *n.* A strip of cleared or plowed land used to stop the spread of a fire.

fire·brick (fīr'brĭk') *n.* A refractory brick, esp. of fire clay, used for lining furnaces, fireboxes, chimneys, or fireplaces.

fire brigade *n.* An organized body of firefighters.

fire·bug (fīr'bŭg') *n.* *Informal.* A person who deliberately sets fires; pyromaniac.

fire clay *n.* A type of heat-resistant clay used in the making of firebricks, crucibles, and other objects that are exposed to high temperatures.

fire control *n.* The control of the delivery of gunfire on military targets.

fire·crack·er (fīr'krăk'ər) *n.* A small explosive charge in a cylinder of heavy paper, used to make noise, as at celebrations.

fire-cure (fīr'kyŏŏr') *tr.v.* **-cured, -cur·ing, -cures.** To cure (tobacco) by exposing it to the heat and smoke of a wood fire.

fire·damp (fīr'dămp') *n.* **1.** A combustible gas, chiefly methane, occurring naturally in coal mines and forming explosive mixtures with air. **2.** The explosive mixture of firedamp and air.

fire department *n.* A department, esp. of a municipal government, whose purpose is preventing and putting out fires.

fire·dog (fīr'dôg', -dŏg') *n.* An andiron.

fire·drake (fīr'drāk') *n.* A fiery dragon of Germanic mythology. [ME *firdrake* < OE *fȳrdraca* : *fȳr,* fir + *draca,* dragon.]

fire drill *n.* A practice exercise in the use of fire-fighting equipment or the exit procedure to be followed in case of a fire.

fire-eat·er (fīr'ē'tər) *n.* **1.** A performer who pretends to swallow fire. **2.** A belligerent person. —**fire'-eat'ing** *adj.*

fire engine *n.* Any of various large motor vehicles that carry firemen and equipment to a fire and support extinguishing operations, as by pumping water.

fire escape *n.* A structure or device, as an outside stairway attached to a building, erected for emergency exit in the event of fire.

fire extinguisher *n.* A portable apparatus containing chemicals that can be discharged in a jet to extinguish a small fire.

fire irons

fire tower

firing line

fire·fight·er (fīr'fī'tər) *n.* A person employed by a fire department to fight fires.

fire·flood (fīr'flŭd') or **fire·flood·ing** (fīr'flŭd'ĭng) *n.* A procedure for extracting additional oil from producing wells by injecting compressed air into the petroleum reservoir and burning some of the oil to increase flow.

fire·fly (fīr'flī') *n.* Any of various nocturnal beetles of the family Lampyridae, characteristically having luminous abdominal organs that produce a flashing light.

fire·guard (fīr'gärd') *n.* **1.** A metal screen placed in front of an open fireplace to catch sparks. **2.** A firebreak.

fire·house (fīr'hous') *n.* A fire station.

firehouse dog *n.* A Dalmatian.

fire hydrant *n.* A hydrant.

fire irons *pl.n.* Equipment, including tongs, a shovel, and a poker, used to tend a fireplace.

fire·light (fīr'līt') *n.* The light from a fire, as in a fireplace.

fire·lock (fīr'lŏk') *n.* A flintlock (sense 2).

fire·man (fīr'mən) *n.* **1.** A firefighter. **2.** A man who tends fires; stoker. **3.** An enlisted man in the U.S. Navy engaged in the operation of the engineering machinery. **4.** *Baseball.* A relief pitcher.

fire opal *n.* An opal with brilliant flamelike yellow, orange, and red colors.

fire pink *n.* A plant, *Silene virginica,* of eastern North America, having red flowers with narrow, notched petals.

fire·place (fīr'plās') *n.* **1.** An open recess for holding a fire at the base of a chimney; hearth. **2.** A structure, usually of stone or brick, for holding an outdoor fire.

fire·plug (fīr'plŭg') *n.* A large pipe at which water may be drawn from a water main for use in extinguishing a fire; hydrant.

fire·pow·er (fīr'pou'ər) *n.* The capacity, as of a weapon, military unit, or ship, for discharging fire.

fire·proof (fīr'prōōf') *adj.* Impervious or resistant to damage by fire. —*tr.v.* **-proofed, -proof·ing, -proofs.** To make fireproof.

fire sale *n.* A sale of commodities damaged by fire.

fire screen *n.* A fireguard (sense 1).

fire ship *n.* A military vessel loaded with explosives and combustible material and set adrift among enemy ships or fortifications to destroy them.

fire·side (fīr'sīd') *n.* **1.** The area immediately surrounding a fireplace or hearth. **2.** Home.

fire station *n.* A building for fire equipment and firefighters.

fire·stone (fīr'stōn') *n.* **1.** A flint or pyrites used to strike a fire. **2.** A fire-resistant stone, as certain sandstones.

fire thorn *n.* Any of various thorny shrubs of the genus *Pyracantha,* native to Asia and often cultivated for their evergreen foliage and showy reddish or orange berries.

fire tower *n.* A tower in which a lookout for fires, esp. forest fires, is posted.

fire·trap (fīr'trăp') *n.* A building susceptible to catching fire easily or difficult to escape from in the event of fire.

fire wall *n.* A fireproof wall used as a barrier to prevent the spread of a fire.

fire·wa·ter (fīr'wô'tər, -wŏt'ər) *n.* *Slang.* Strong liquor, esp. whiskey.

fire·weed (fīr'wēd') *n.* **1.** A species of willow herb, *Epilobium angustifolium,* having terminal clusters of pinkish-purple flowers. **2.** A weedy North American plant, *Erechtites hieracifolia,* having small white or greenish flowers.

fire·wood (fīr'wŏŏd') *n.* Wood used as fuel.

fire·work (fīr'wûrk') *n.* **1. a.** A device consisting of various combinations of explosives and combustibles used to generate colored lights, smoke, and noise for amusement. **b. fireworks.** A display of such devices. **2. fireworks. a.** An exciting or spectacular display, as of musical virtuosity. **b.** A display of rage or fierce contention.

fir·ing (fīr'ĭng) *n.* **1.** The process of applying fire or heat, as in the hardening or glazing of ceramics. **2.** Fuel for fires.

firing line *n.* **1.** The line of positions from which fire is directed against a target. **2.** The vanguard of an activity or pursuit.

firing pin *n.* The part of the bolt or breech of a firearm that strikes the primer and explodes the charge of a projectile.

firing squad *n.* **1.** A detachment assigned to shoot persons condemned to death. **2.** A detachment of soldiers chosen to fire a salute at a military funeral.

fir·kin (fûr'kĭn) *n.* **1.** A small wooden barrel or keg. **2.** Any of several British units of capacity, usually equal to about 1/4 of a barrel, or 9 gallons. [ME < MDu. **verdelkijn* < *veerdel,* one-fourth.]

firm[1] (fûrm) *adj.* **-er, -est. 1.** Unyielding to pressure; solid. **2.** Marked by or indicating the tone and resiliency of healthy tissue: *firm muscles.* **3.** Securely fixed in place. **4.** Indicating or possessed of determination or resolution: *a firm voice.* **5.** Constant and steadfast: *a firm ally.* **6. a.** Not changing; fixed and definite: *a firm bargain.* **b.** Unfluctuating; steady. Used of prices. **7.** Strong and sure: *a firm grasp.* —*tr. & intr.v.* **firmed, firm·ing, firms.** To make or become firm. —*adv.* Without wavering; resolutely: *stand firm.* [ME *ferm* < OFr. < Lat. *firmus.*] —**firm'ly** *adv.* —**firm'ness** *n.*

firm[2] (fûrm) *n.* **1.** A commercial partnership of two or more persons. **2.** The name or designation under which a firm

transacts business. [Ital. *firma* < *firmare,* to ratify by signature < LLat. *firmare* < Lat., to confirm < *firmus,* firm.]
fir·ma·ment (fûr′mə-mənt) *n.* The vault or expanse of the heavens; sky. [ME < OFr. < LLat. *firmamentum* < Lat., support < *firmare,* to strengthen < *firmus,* firm.] **—fir′ma·men′tal** (-mĕn′tl) *adj.*
fir·mer chisel (fûr′mər) *n.* A chisel or gouge with a thin blade, used manually to shape and finish wood. [Fr. *fermoir* (< OFr. *formoir* < *former,* to form < Lat. *formare* < *forma,* form) + CHISEL.]
firm·ware (fûrm′wâr′) *n.* Computer programming functions implemented through a small special-purpose memory unit.
firn (fîrn) *n.* Snow that has been partially consolidated by thawing and freezing but not yet converted to glacial ice. [G. < dial. G., of last year < OHG *firni,* old.]
first (fûrst) *adj.* **1.** Corresponding in order to the number 1. **2.** Coming or located before all others. **3.** Occurring or acting prior to all others; earliest. **4.** Ranking above all others in importance or quality; foremost. **5.** Being highest in pitch or carrying the principal musical part: *first trumpet.* **6.** Of, pertaining to, or being the transmission gear or corresponding gear ratio used to produce the range of lowest drive speeds in an automotive vehicle. *—adv.* **1.** Before or above all others in time, order, rank, or importance. **2.** For the first time. **3.** Preferably; rather. *—n.* **1.** The ordinal number that matches the number 1 in a series. **2.** The one coming, occurring, or ranking before or above all others. **3.** The beginning; outset: *from the first; at first.* **4.** The voice or instrument highest in pitch or carrying the principal musical part. **5.** The transmission gear or corresponding gear ratio used to produce the range of lowest drive speeds in an automotive vehicle. **6.** The winning position in a contest. —See Usage note at **firstly.** [ME < OE *fyrst.*]
first aid *n.* Emergency treatment administered to injured or sick persons before professional medical care is available.
first base *n.* **1.** *Baseball.* **a.** The first of the bases in the infield, counterclockwise from home plate. **b.** The fielding position occupied by the first baseman. **2.** *Informal.* The first stage or step in a procedure: *The reform bill never got to first base.* **—first baseman** *n.*
first-born (fûrst′bôrn′) *adj.* First in order of birth; born first. *—n.* A first-born child.
first class *n.* **1.** The first, highest, or best group of a specified category. **2.** The most luxurious and most expensive class of accommodations on a train, passenger ship, airplane, or other conveyance. **3.** A class of mail including letters, postcards, and packages sealed against inspection.
first-class (fûrst′klăs′) *adj.* **1.** Indicating the first, highest, or best group of a specified category. **2.** Of the foremost excellence or highest quality; first-rate: *a first-class mind.* **—first′-class′** *adv.*
first cousin *n.* A cousin (sense 1).
first-de·gree burn (fûrst′dĭ-grē′) *n.* A mild burn that produces redness of the skin.
first edition *n.* **1. a.** The first published copies of a literary work printed from the same type and distributed at the same time. **b.** A single copy from a first edition. **2.** The day's first press run of a newspaper.
first floor *n.* **1.** The ground floor of a building. **2.** *Chiefly Brit.* The floor immediately above the ground floor.
first fruits *pl.n.* The first results of an undertaking.
first·hand (fûrst′hănd′) *adj.* Received from the original source: *firsthand information.* **—first′hand′** *adv.*
First International *n.* An international organization formed in 1864 by Karl Marx and Friedrich Engels to associate the trade unions of all nations.
first lady *n.* **1.** Often **First Lady.** The wife or hostess of the chief executive of a country, state, or city. **2.** The foremost woman of a specified profession or art.
first lieutenant *n.* A commissioned officer in the U.S. Army, Air Force, and Marine Corps ranking above a second lieutenant and below a captain.
first·ling (fûrst′lĭng) *n.* **1.** The first of a kind or category. **2.** A first-born offspring.
first·ly (fûrst′lē) *adv.* In the first place; to begin with.
Usage: *Firstly* may be used in a sequence: *firstly, secondly, thirdly,* and so on. However, it has fallen into disuse among many writers, who prefer this sequence: *first, secondly, thirdly.* Another alternative, since all these ordinal numbers can be used adverbially, is *first, second, third.*
first mate *n.* A ship's officer ranking immediately below the captain.
first name *n.* The name that occurs first in a person's full name.
first night *n.* **1.** The opening performance of a theatrical production. **2.** The performance presented on a first night.
first night·er (nī′tər) *n.* A member of the audience on a first night.
first offender *n.* One convicted of a legal offense for the first time.
first papers *pl.n.* The documents first filed by one applying for U.S. citizenship.
first person *n.* **1. a.** A category of linguistic forms, such as verbs or pronouns, designating the speaker or writer of the sentence in which they appear. **b.** One of the forms of this category. **2.** A discourse or literary style in which forms in the first person are used: *a novel written in the first person.*
first-rate (fûrst′rāt′) *adj.* Foremost in quality, rank, or importance. *—adv. Informal.* Excellently; very well.
first sergeant *n.* In the U.S. Army, the highest-ranking noncommissioned officer of a company or other military unit.
first-string (fûrst′strĭng′) *adj.* **1.** Being a regular member, as of a football team, rather than a substitute. **2.** First-rate.
first water *n.* **1.** The highest degree of quality or purity in diamonds or pearls. **2.** The foremost rank or quality: *a pianist of the first water.* [Prob. transl. of Ar. *mā′,* water luster.]
First World *n.* The industrialized non-Communist countries of the world.
First World War *n.* World War I.
firth (fûrth) *n. Chiefly Scot.* A long, narrow inlet of the sea; fjord. [ME *furth* < ON *fjörðr.*]
fisc (fĭsk) *n.* The treasury of a kingdom or state. [OFr. < Lat. *fiscus.*]
fis·cal (fĭs′kəl) *adj.* **1.** Of or pertaining to the treasury or finances of a nation or branch of government. **2.** Of or pertaining to finances. [OFr. < Lat. *fiscalis* < *fiscus,* treasury.] **—fis′cal·ly** *adv.*
fiscal year *n.* A 12-month period for which an organization plans the use of its funds.

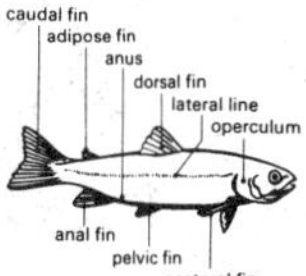

fish

fish (fĭsh) *n., pl.* **fish** or **fish·es. 1.** Any of numerous cold-blooded aquatic vertebrates of the superclass Pisces, characteristically having fins, gills, and a streamlined body and including: **a.** Any of the class Osteichthyes, having a bony skeleton. **b.** Any of the class Chondrichthyes, having a cartilaginous skeleton and including the sharks, rays, and skates. **c.** Any of the class Agnatha, lacking jaws and including the lampreys and hagfishes. **2.** Any of various unrelated aquatic animals, such as a jellyfish, cuttlefish, or crayfish. **3.** *Informal.* A person: *a cold fish; a poor fish.* **4. Fish.** Pisces (sense 2). *—v.* **fished, fish·ing, fish·es.** *—intr.* **1.** To catch or try to catch fish. **2.** To look for something by feeling one's way; grope. **3.** To seek something in a sly or indirect way: *fish for compliments.* *—tr.* **1.** To catch or try to catch fish in. **2.** To catch or pull in the manner of one who fishes: *fished the keys out of her purse.* [ME < OE *fisc.*]
fish and chips *pl.n.* Fried fillets of fish and French-fried potatoes.
fish·bowl also **fish bowl** (fĭsh′bōl′) *n.* **1.** A transparent bowl in which live fish are kept. **2.** A condition or location that is lacking in privacy.
fish cake *n.* A fried cake or patty of chopped fish, often mixed with potato or rice.
fish crow *n.* A crow, *Corvus ossifragus,* of the coast and rivers of the eastern United States.

fisher

fish·er (fĭsh′ər) *n.* **1.** One that fishes. **2. a.** A carnivorous mammal, *Martes pennanti,* of northern North America, having thick, dark-brown fur. **b.** The fur of this animal.
fish·er·man (fĭsh′ər-mən) *n.* **1.** One who fishes as an occupation or sport. **2.** A commercial fishing vessel.
fisherman's bend *n.* A knot used to secure the end of a line to a ring or spar, made by two turns with the end passing back under both.

fisherman's bend

fisherman's knot *n.* A knot used to join two lines, made by securing either end to the opposite standing part by an overhand knot.
fish·er·y (fĭsh′ə-rē) *n., pl.* **-ies. 1.** The industry or occupation of catching, processing, or selling fish, shellfish, or similar aquatic products. **2.** A place where fish can be caught. **3.** A hatchery for fish. **4.** The legal right to fish in specified waters or areas.
fish·eye (fĭsh′ī′) *adj.* Of, pertaining to, or being a wide-angle photographic lens that covers an angle of about 180 degrees, producing a circular image with barrel distortion.
fish farm *n.* A facility consisting of tanks or ponds in which food fish are raised commercially.
fish flour *n.* A flour made of dried and powdered fish.
fish fry *n.* **1.** A cookout or other meal at which fried fish is the main course. **2.** Fried fish.
fish·gig (fĭsh′gĭg′) *n.* A pronged instrument for spearing fish. [Alteration of obs. *fisgig* < Sp. *fisga,* ult. < Lat. *fixus,* fixed.]
fish hawk *n.* The osprey (sense 1).
fish·hook (fĭsh′ho͝ok′) *n.* A barbed metal hook used for catching fish.
fish·ing (fĭsh′ĭng) *n.* **1.** The act or practice of catching fish. **2.** A place for catching fish; fishery.
fishing rod *n.* A rod of wood, steel, or fiber glass used with a line for catching fish.
fish joint *n.* A joint formed by bolting fishplates to either side of two rails, timbers, or beams.
fish·meal (fĭsh′mēl′) *n.* A nutritive mealy substance produced from fish or fish parts and used as animal feed and fertilizer.
fish·mon·ger (fĭsh′mŭng′gər, -mŏng′-) *n. Chiefly Brit.* One who sells fish.
fish·net (fĭsh′nĕt′) *n.* **1.** Netting used to catch fish. **2.** A mesh fabric resembling fishnet.
fish·plate (fĭsh′plāt′) *n.* One of the connecting metal plates bolted along the side of two rails or beams placed end to end, used esp. in the laying of railroad track. [Prob. < OFr. *fiche,* peg (< *ficher,* to fix < Lat. *figere*) + PLATE.]

fisherman's knot

fish·pond (fĭsh′pŏnd′) *n.* A small body of clear water abounding in edible fish.

fish protein concentrate *n.* A flour or paste rich in protein that is prepared from ground fish and used as a nutritional additive to foods.
fish·skin disease (fĭsh′skĭn′) *n.* Ichthyosis.
fish stick *n.* An oblong piece of breaded fish fillet.
fish story *n. Informal.* An implausible and boastful story. [From the fact that fishermen traditionally exaggerate the size of their catch.]
fish·tail (fĭsh′tāl′) *adj.* Resembling or suggestive of the tail of a fish in shape or movement. *—intr.v.* **-tailed, -tail·ing, -tails.** To swing the tail of an airplane or the rear end of an automobile or other vehicle from side to side while moving forward.
fish·wife (fĭsh′wīf′) *n.* **1.** A woman who sells fish. **2.** A coarse, abusive woman; shrew.
fish·y (fĭsh′ē) *adj.* **-i·er, -i·est. 1.** Resembling or suggestive of fish, as in taste or odor. **2.** Cold or expressionless: *a fishy stare.* **3.** *Informal.* Inspiring suspicion; dubious. **—fish′i·ly** *adv.* **—fish′i·ness** *n.*
fissi– *pref.* **1.** Fission: *fissiparous.* **2.** Split; cleft: *fissipalmate.* [< Lat. *fissus,* p.part. of *findere,* to split.]
fis·sile (fĭs′əl, -īl′) *adj.* **1.** Capable of being split. **2.** *Physics.* Fissionable, esp. by neutrons of all energies. [Lat. *fissilis* < *fissus,* split. —see FISSI-.] **—fis·sil′i·ty** (fĭ-sĭl′ĭ-tē) *n.*
fis·sion (fĭsh′ən) *n.* **1.** The act or process of splitting into parts. **2.** *Physics.* A nuclear reaction in which an atomic nucleus splits into fragments, usually two fragments of comparable mass, with the evolution of approximately 100 million to several hundred million electron volts of energy. **3.** *Biol.* An asexual reproductive process in which a unicellular organism splits into two or more independently maturing daughter cells. [Lat. *fissio,* a cleaving < *fissus,* split. —see FISSI-.]
fis·sion·a·ble (fĭsh′ə-nə-bəl) *adj.* Capable of undergoing fission, esp. capable of being induced to undergo nuclear fission by slow neutrons. **—fis′sion·a·bil′i·ty** *n.*
fission bomb *n.* An atomic bomb.
fis·si·pal·mate (fĭs′ə-păl′māt′) *adj.* Having lobed or partially webbed separated toes, as the feet of certain birds.
fis·sip·a·rous (fĭ-sĭp′ər-əs) *adj.* Reproducing by biological fission. **—fis·sip′a·rous·ly** *adv.* **—fis·sip′a·rous·ness** *n.*
fis·si·ped (fĭs′ə-pĕd′) *adj.* Having the toes separated from one another, as certain carnivorous mammals. *—n.* A fissiped carnivorous mammal. [LLat. *fissipes, fissiped-,* cloven-footed : Lat. *fissus,* split + Lat. *pes,* foot.]
fis·sure (fĭsh′ər) *n.* **1.** A narrow crack or cleft, as in a rock face. **2.** The process of separation or division. **3.** A schism; split. **4.** *Anat.* A groove or furrow, as in the liver or brain, that divides an organ into lobes or separates it into areas. *—intr. & tr.v.* **-sured, -sur·ing, -sures.** To form a fissure or cause a fissure in; crack. [ME, cut < OFr. < Lat. *fissura* < *fissus,* split. —see FISSI-.]
fist (fĭst) *n.* **1.** The hand closed tightly with the fingers bent against the palm. **2.** *Informal.* A grasp; clutch. **3.** An index (sense 3). *—tr.v.* **fist·ed, fist·ing, fists. 1.** To clench into a fist. **2.** To grasp with the fist. [ME < OE *fȳst.*]
fist·fight (fĭst′fīt′) *n.* A fight with the fists.
fist·ful (fĭst′fo͝ol′) *n., pl.* **-fuls.** A handful.
fist·ic (fĭs′tĭk) *adj.* Of or pertaining to boxing; pugilistic.

fjord

fist·i·cuffs (fĭs′tĭ-kŭfs′) *pl.n.* **1.** A fistfight. **2.** Boxing. **—fist′i·cuff′er** *n.*
fis·tu·la (fĭs′chə-lə) *n., pl.* **-las** or **-lae** (-lē′). An abnormal duct or passage from an abscess, cavity, or hollow organ to the body surface or to another hollow organ. [ME < Lat.]
fis·tu·lous (fĭs′chə-ləs) *adj.* **1.** Of or resembling a fistula. **2.** Tubular and hollow; reedlike.
fit[1] (fĭt) *v.* **fit·ted** or **fit, fit·ted, fit·ting, fits.** *—tr.* **1. a.** To be the proper size and shape for. **b.** To cause to fit. **2.** To be appropriate or suitable to. **3.** To be in conformity or agreement with: *observations that fit in nicely with my theory.* **4.** To make suitable. **5.** To make ready; prepare: *Specialized training fitted her for the job.* **6.** To equip; outfit: *fit out a ship.* **7.** To provide a place or time for: *The doctor can fit you in today.* **8.** To insert or adjust so as to be properly in place: *fit a handle on a door.* *—intr.* **1.** To be the proper size and shape. **2.** To be suited; belong: *doesn't fit in with these people.* **3.** To be in harmony; agree: *Her good mood fit in with the joyful occasion.* *—adj.* **fit·ter, fit·test. 1.** Suited, adapted, or acceptable for a given circumstance or purpose: *not a fit time for discussion.* **2.** Appropriate; proper: *Do as you see fit.* **3.** Physically sound; healthy. *—n.* **1.** The state, quality, or way of being fitted. **2.** The manner in which clothing fits. **3.** The degree of precision with which surfaces are adjusted or adapted to each other in a machine or collection of parts. [ME *fitten,* to be suitable.] **—fit′ly** *adv.* **—fit′ness** *n.*
Synonyms: *fit, suitable, meet, proper, appropriate, apt, fitting, happy, felicitous.* These adjectives mean right or correct in view of the circumstances that exist. Often they are interchangeable. *Fit,* in this sense, refers to what is adapted to certain requirements or capable of measuring up to them: *tools fit for the job; fit for heavy duty. Suitable* also implies ability to meet requirements related to a particular need or to an occasion: *suitable for everyday wear. Meet* applies to what is precisely suitable or suitable in the sense of being morally right or just: *a meet reward. Proper* describes what is harmonious, either by nature or because it observes reason, custom, propriety, or the like: *a proper setting for a monument; the proper form of addressing a clergyman.* What is *appropriate* to a thing or for an occasion especially befits it, and what is *apt* is notably to the point: *appropriate remarks; an apt reply. Fitting* suggests close agreement with a prevailing mood or spirit: *a fitting observance of the holiday. Happy* and *felicitous* are applicable to what seems especially suited to an occasion by its nature or by its timeliness: *a happy turn of phrase; an unplanned but felicitous development.*
Usage: Either *fitted* or *fit* is correct as the past tense of *fit: The suit fitted* (or *fit*) *me well the last time I tried it on.* When the verb is used to mean "to cause to fit," only *fitted* is used as the past tense: *The tailor fitted* (not *fit*) *the suit in a few minutes.*
fit[2] (fĭt) *n.* **1.** *Med.* **a.** A sudden and acute attack of a disease. **b.** The sudden appearance of a symptom such as coughing. **c.** A convulsion. **2.** A sudden outburst of emotion: *a fit of jealousy.* **3.** A sudden period of vigorous activity. *—idiom.* **by (or in) fits and starts.** With irregular intervals of action and inaction; intermittently. [ME, hardship.]
fit[3] (fĭt) *n. Archaic.* A section of a poem or ballad. [ME < OE.]
fitch (fĭch) *n.* The fur of the Old World polecat. [ME *fiche.*]
fitch·ew (fĭch′o͞o) also **fitch·et** (fĭch′ĭt) *n. Archaic.* The Old World polecat or its fur. [ME *ficheux* < OFr. *ficheau* < MDu. *vitsau.*]
fit·ful (fĭt′fəl) *adj.* Occurring in or characterized by intermittent bursts of activity; irregular. **—fit′ful·ly** *adv.* **—fit′ful·ness** *n.*
fit·ting (fĭt′ĭng) *adj.* Suitable or appropriate to the circumstances. *—n.* **1.** The act of trying on clothes whose fit is being adjusted. **2.** A small, detachable part for a machine or an apparatus. **3. fittings.** *Chiefly Brit.* Furnishings or fixtures. **—fit′ting·ly** *adv.* **—fit′ting·ness** *n.*
five (fīv) *n.* **1.** The cardinal number that is next after the number 4 and equal to the sum of 4 + 1. **2.** The fifth in a set or sequence. **3.** Something having five parts, units, or members, esp. a basketball team. **4.** *Informal.* A five-dollar bill. [ME < OE *fīf;* akin to G. *fünf,* Lat. *quinque,* Gk. *pente,* and Skt. *pañca.*] **—five** *adj. & pron.*
five-and-dime (fīv′ən-dīm′) *n.* A five-and-ten.
five-and-ten (fīv′ən-tĕn′) *n.* A variety store selling inexpensive commodities.
five-fin·ger (fīv′fĭng′gər) *n.* Any of several plants having compound leaves with five leaflets, such as the cinquefoil.
five·fold (fīv′fōld′) *adj.* **1.** Consisting of five parts. **2.** Five times as many or as much. **—five′fold′** *adv.*
fiv·er (fī′vər) *n. Informal.* **1.** A five-dollar bill. **2.** *Chiefly Brit.* A five-pound note.
fix (fĭks) *v.* **fixed, fix·ing, fix·es.** *—tr.* **1. a.** To place or fasten securely. **b.** To make fast to; attach. **2.** To put into a stable or unalterable form, as: **a.** *Chem.* To make (a substance) nonvolatile or solid. **b.** *Biol.* To convert (nitrogen) into stable, biologically assimilable compounds. **c.** To kill and keep (a specimen) intact for microscopic study. **d.** To prevent discoloration of (a photographic image) by washing or coating with a chemical preservative. **3.** To direct steadily: *fixed her eyes on the page.* **4.** To establish definitely: *fix a time.* **5.** To assign: *fixing the blame.* **6.** To set right; adjust. **7.** *Computer Sci.* To convert data from floating-point notation to fixed-point notation. **8.** To restore to proper condition or working order; repair. **9.** To make ready; prepare. **10.** To spay or castrate (an animal). **11.** *Informal.* To take revenge upon; get even with. **12.** To influence or arrange the outcome of by unlawful means. *—intr.* **1.** To become concentrated, directed, or attached. **2.** To become stable or firm; harden. **3.** *Regional.* To intend: *was fixing to take the children with her.* *—n.* **1.** A difficult or embarrassing position; predicament. **2.** The position, as of a ship or aircraft, as determined by observations or radio. **3.** An instance of arranging for special consideration or exemption from a requirement, esp. by means of bribery. **4.** *Slang.* An intravenous injection of a narcotic. [ME *fixen* < *fix,* fixed in position < Lat. *fixus,* p.part. of *figere,* to fasten.] **—fix′a·ble** *adj.* **—fix′er** *n.*
fix·ate (fĭk′sāt′) *v.* **-at·ed, -at·ing, -ates.** *—tr.* **1.** To make fixed, stable, or stationary. **2.** To focus one's eyes or concentrate one's attention on. **3.** *Psychol.* To attach (oneself) to a person or thing in an immature or neurotic fashion. *—intr.* **1.** To focus or concentrate one's attention. **2.** *Psychol.* **a.** To form a fixation. **b.** To be arrested at an immature stage of psychosexual development.
fix·a·tion (fĭk-sā′shən) *n.* **1.** The act or process of fixing or fixating. **2.** *Psychol.* A strong attachment to a person or thing, esp. such an attachment formed in childhood or infancy and persisting in immature or neurotic behavior.
fix·a·tive (fĭk′sə-tĭv) *n.* Something that fixes, protects, or preserves, esp.: **a.** A liquid preservative applied to art work, such as water-color paintings or charcoal drawings. **b.** A solution used to preserve fresh tissue for microscopic examination. **c.** A liquid mixed with perfume to prevent rapid evaporation. **—fix′a·tive** *adj.*
fixed (fĭkst) *adj.* **1.** Firmly in position; stationary. **2.** *Chem.* **a.** Nonvolatile: *fixed oils.* **b.** In a stable combined form. **3.** Not subject to change or variation; constant. **4.** Firmly, often dogmatically held: *a fixed notion.* **5.** Illegally prear-

ranged as to outcome. **—fix'ed·ly** (fĭk'sĭd-lē) *adv.* **—fix'ed·ness** (-sĭd-nĭs) *n.*

fixed head *n.* A stationary device, such as a tape-recording head, that reads and imprints information on a single track of magnetic tape.

fixed oil *n.* A nonvolatile oil, esp. a fatty oil as distinguished from an essential oil.

fixed-point (fĭkst'point') *adj.* Of, pertaining to, or being a method of writing numerical quantities with a predetermined number of digits and with the decimal located at a single, unchanging position.

fixed star *n.* A star so distant from the earth that its movements can be measured only by precise observations over long periods of time.

fix·ings (fĭk'sĭngz) *pl.n. Informal.* Accessories; trimmings.

fix·i·ty (fĭk'sĭ-tē) *n., pl.* **-ties. 1.** The quality or condition of being fixed; stability. **2.** Something that is fixed or immovable.

fix·ture (fĭks'chər) *n.* **1.** Something securely fixed in place. **2.** Something attached as a permanent appendage, apparatus, or appliance: *plumbing fixtures.* **3.** *Law.* A chattel bound to realty. **4.** A person or thing long associated with, established in, or restricted to a specified place, position, or function. **5. a.** The action or process of fixing. **b.** The condition of being fixed. [Var. of obs. *fixure* < LLat. *fixura* < Lat. *fixus.* —see FIX.]

fizz (fĭz) *intr.v.* **fizzed, fizz·ing, fizz·es.** To make a hissing or bubbling sound. *—n.* **1.** A hissing or bubbling sound. **2.** Effervescence. **3.** An effervescent beverage. [Imit.]

fiz·zle (fĭz'əl) *intr.v.* **-zled, -zling, -zles. 1.** To make a hissing or sputtering sound. **2.** *Informal.* To fail or die out, esp. after a hopeful beginning. *—n. Informal.* A failure; fiasco. [Prob. < obs. *fist,* to break wind < ME *fisten.*]

fjeld (fyĕld) *n.* A high, barren plateau in the Scandinavian countries. [Dan. < ON *fjall,* mountain.]

fjord or **fiord** (fyôrd, fyōrd) *n.* A long, narrow, often deep inlet from the sea between steep cliffs and slopes. [Norw. < ON *fjörðr.*]

flab (flăb) *n.* Body tissue of a loose and flaccid nature. [Back-formation < FLABBY.]

flab·ber·gast (flăb'ər-găst') *tr.v.* **-gast·ed, -gast·ing, -gasts.** To overwhelm with astonishment. [Orig. unknown.]

flab·by (flăb'ē) *adj.* **-bi·er, -bi·est. 1.** Lacking firmness; flaccid. **2.** Lacking force or vitality; ineffectual. [Alteration of *flappy,* tending to flap < FLAP.] **—flab'bi·ly** *adv.* **—flab'bi·ness** *n.*

fla·bel·la (flə-bĕl'ə) *n.* Plural of **flabellum.**

fla·bel·late (flə-bĕl'ĭt, flăb'ə-lāt') *adj.* Fan-shaped. [< Lat. *flabellum,* small fan.]

fla·bel·li·form (flə-bĕl'ə-fôrm') *adj.* Flabellate.

fla·bel·lum (flə-bĕl'əm) *n., pl.* **-bel·la** (-bĕl'ə). A fan-shaped anatomical structure. [Lat. *flabellum,* small fan.]

flac·cid (flăk'sĭd, flăs'ĭd) *adj.* **1.** Lacking firmness or resilience: *flaccid cheeks.* **2.** Lacking vigor or energy. [Fr. *flaccide* < Lat. *flaccidus* < *flaccus,* flabby.] **—flac·cid'i·ty** (-sĭd'ĭ-tē), **flac'cid·ness** *n.* **—flac'cid·ly** *adv.*

flack (flăk) *n.* A press agent. *—intr.v.* **flacked, flack·ing, flacks.** To act as a flack. [Orig. unknown.] **—flack'er·y** *n.*

flac·on (flăk'ən, -ŏn') *n.* A small, often decorative bottle with a tight-fitting stopper or cap. [Fr. < OFr., flagon.]

flag¹ (flăg) *n.* **1.** A piece of cloth of distinctive size, color, and design, used as a symbol, standard, signal, or emblem. **2.** *Mus.* A cross stroke added to a note that is less than a quarter note in value. **3.** A ship carrying the flag of an admiral; flagship. **4.** The masthead of a newspaper. **5.** A distinctively shaped or marked tail, as of a dog or deer. *—tr.v.* **flagged, flag·ging, flags. 1.** To mark with a flag for identification or ornamentation. **2. a.** To signal with or as if with a flag. **b.** To signal to stop. **3.** *Computer Sci.* A bit or series of bits with two stable states, used in computer software to indicate a single bit of information. [Orig. unknown.] **—flag'ger** *n.*

flag² (flăg) *n.* Any of various plants having long bladelike leaves, such as an iris or cattail. [ME *flagge,* reed.]

flag³ (flăg) *intr.v.* **flagged, flag·ging, flags. 1.** To hang limply; droop. **2.** To decline in vigor or strength: *His appetite began to flag.* **3.** To decline in interest: *The conversation flagged.* [Orig. unknown.]

flag⁴ (flăg) *n.* **1.** A slab of flagstone used for paving. **2.** Flagstone. *—tr.v.* **flagged, flag·ging, flags.** To pave with flags. [ME *flagge,* piece of turf < ON *flaga,* slab of stone.]

Flag Day *n.* June 14, commemorating the adoption in 1777 of the official U.S. flag.

fla·gel·la (flə-jĕl'ə) *n.* Plural of **flagellum.**

flag·el·lant (flăj'ə-lənt, flə-jĕl'ənt) *n.* **1.** One who whips, esp. one who scourges himself by way of religious discipline or public penance. **2.** One who seeks sexual gratification in beating or being beaten by another person. [Lat. *flagellans, flagellant-,* pr.part. of *flagellare,* to flagellate.] **—flag'el·lant·ism** *n.*

fla·gel·lar (flə-jĕl'ər) *adj.* Of or pertaining to a flagellum.

flag·el·late (flăj'ə-lāt') *tr.v.* **-lat·ed, -lat·ing, -lates. 1.** To whip or flog; scourge. **2.** To punish or impel as if by whipping. *—adj.* (-lĭt, -lāt', flə-jĕl'ĭt). **1.** Having a flagellum or flagella, as unicellular organisms of the class Flagellata (or Magistophora). **2.** Resembling or having the form of a flagellum; whiplike. *—n.* (-lĭt, -lāt', flə-jĕl'ĭt). A flagellate organism. [Lat. *flagellare, flagellat-,* to whip < *flagellum,* little whip, dim. of *flagrum,* whip.]

flag·el·la·tion (flăj'ə-lā'shən) *n.* **1.** The act or practice of flagellating. **2.** The flagellar arrangement on an organism.

fla·gel·li·form (flə-jĕl'ə-fôrm') *adj.* Long, thin, and tapering; whip-shaped: *flagelliform appendages.* [Lat. *flagellum,* little whip + -FORM.]

fla·gel·lin (flə-jĕl'ĭn) *n.* A protein component of flagella.

fla·gel·lum (flə-jĕl'əm) *n., pl.* **-gel·la** (-jĕl'ə). **1.** *Biol.* A long, filamentous process, esp. one of the whiplike extensions of certain cells or unicellular organisms, usually functioning in locomotion. **2.** A whip. [Lat., little whip.]

flag·eo·let (flăj'ə-lĕt', -lā') *n.* A small flutelike instrument with a cylindrical mouthpiece, four finger holes, and two thumbholes. [Fr., dim. of OFr. *flajol,* flute.]

flag·ging¹ (flăg'ĭng) *adj.* **1.** Drooping; languid. **2.** Declining; weakening. **—flag'ging·ly** *adv.*

flag·ging² (flăg'ĭng) *n.* A pavement laid with flagstones.

fla·gi·tious (flə-jĭsh'əs) *adj.* Characterized by extremely brutal or cruel crimes; vicious. [ME *flagicious,* wicked < Lat. *flagitiosus* < *flagitium,* shameful act < *flagitare,* to incite to lewdness.] **—fla·gi'tious·ly** *adv.* **—fla·gi'tious·ness** *n.*

flag·man (flăg'mən) *n.* One who signals with or carries a flag.

flag officer *n.* An officer in the navy or coast guard holding the rank of rear admiral, vice admiral, or admiral.

flag of truce *n.* A white flag brought or displayed to an enemy as an invitation to a conference or a signal of surrender.

flag·on (flăg'ən) *n.* **1.** A large vessel for holding wine or other liquors, usually made of metal or pottery and having a handle and spout and often a lid. **2.** The quantity of liquid contained in a flagon. [ME < OFr. *flacon* < LLat. *flasco,* flask. —see FLASK.]

flag·pole (flăg'pōl') *n.* A pole on which a flag is raised.

fla·grant (flā'grənt) *adj.* **1.** Extremely or deliberately conspicuous; shocking: *a flagrant miscarriage of justice.* **2.** *Obs.* Flaming; blazing. —See Usage note at **blatant.** [Lat. *flagrans, flagrant-,* pr.part. of *flagare,* to burn.] **—fla'gran·cy, fla'grance** *n.* **—fla'grant·ly** *adv.*

Synonyms: *flagrant, glaring, gross, rank.* These adjectives refer to what is outstandingly bad, evil, erroneous, incapable, or the like. *Flagrant* and *glaring* both stress the conspicuousness of what gives cause for concern or offense. *Glaring* is somewhat more emphatic in suggesting what cannot escape notice, but *flagrant* often makes the stronger implication of wrongdoing as a moral offense rather than as an act of miscalculation or ineptitude. *Gross* and *rank* emphasize extremity or intensity. *Gross* suggests a magnitude of offense or failing that cannot be overlooked or condoned. *Rank,* like *flagrant,* sometimes implies an affront to decency. Often *rank* is used attributively as an intensifying term with the force of absolute or utter: *rank folly.*

fla·gran·te de·lic·to (flə-grăn'tē dĭ-lĭk'tō) *adv.* In the very act; red-handed. [Med. Lat., while the crime is blazing.]

flag·ship (flăg'shĭp') *n.* **1.** A ship that carries a fleet or squadron commander and bears his flag. **2.** The chief one of a related group: *the flagship of a newspaper chain.*

flag·staff (flăg'stăf') *n.* A flagpole.

flag·stone (flăg'stōn') *n.* A flat, fine-grained, hard, evenly layered stone split into slabs for use in paving; flag.

flag-wav·ing (flăg'wā'vĭng) *n.* Excessive or fanatical patriotism.

flail (flāl) *n.* A manual threshing device consisting of a long wooden handle or staff and a shorter, free-swinging stick attached to its end. *—v.* **flailed, flail·ing, flails.** *—tr.* **1.** To thresh using a flail. **2.** To beat, thrash, or strike with or as if with a flail. *—intr.* **1.** To thresh grain. **2.** To move with a flailing motion. [ME, partly < OE **flegil,* and partly < OFr. *flaiel,* both < LLat. *flagellum* < *flagrum,* whip.]

flair (flâr) *n.* **1.** A natural talent or aptitude; knack: *a flair for interior decorating.* **2.** Instinctive discernment; keenness: *a man who had a flair for the exotic.* **3.** Distinctive elegance or style: *served us with flair.* [Fr. < OFr., odor < *flairer,* to smell < LLat. *flagrare* < Lat. *fragrare,* to emit an odor.]

flak (flăk) *n.* **1. a.** Antiaircraft artillery. **b.** The bursting shells fired from such artillery. **2.** *Informal.* **a.** Excessive or abusive criticism. **b.** Dissension; opposition. [G. *Flak,* contraction of *Fliegerabwehrkanone.*]

flake¹ (flāk) *n.* **1.** A flat, thin piece or layer; chip. **2.** A small piece; bit. **3.** A small crystalline bit of snow. **4.** *Slang.* One who is somewhat eccentric; oddball. *—v.* **flaked, flak·ing, flakes.** *—tr.* **1.** To break flakes from; chip. **2.** To cover, mark, or overlay with or as if with flakes. *—intr.* To come off in flakes; chip off. ***—phrasal verb.* flake out.** *Slang.* To fall asleep or collapse from fatigue or exhaustion. [ME, of Scand. orig.] **—flak'er** *n.*

flake² (flāk) *n.* **1.** A frame or platform for drying fish or produce. **2.** A scaffold lowered over the side of a ship to support workmen or caulkers. [ME *fleke* < ON *fleki.*]

flake white *n.* A pigment made of flakes of white lead.

flak·y (flā'kē) *adj.* **-i·er, -i·est. 1.** Made of or resembling flakes. **2.** Forming or tending to form flakes or thin, crisp fragments: *a flaky crust.* **3.** *Slang.* Eccentric; crazy. **—flak'i·ly** *adv.* **—flak'i·ness** *n.*

flag¹
Rattlesnake flag from the American Revolution

flam[1] (flăm) *n. Informal.* **1.** A lie or hoax; deception. **2.** Nonsense; drivel. [Short for FLIMFLAM.]

flam[2] (flăm) *n.* A drumbeat consisting of two almost simultaneous strokes of which the first is a very rapid grace note. [Prob. imit.]

flam·bé (flām-bā′, flăɴ-) *tr.v.* **-béed, -bé·ing, -bés.** To drench with a liquor, as brandy, and ignite: *flambéed the steak at the table.* —*adj.* Served flaming in ignited liquor: *steak flambé.* [< Fr., p.part. of *flamber,* to flame < OFr. < *flambe,* flame.]

flam·beau (flăm′bō′) *n., pl.* **-beaux** (-bōz′) or **-beaus. 1.** A lighted torch. **2.** A large ornamental candlestick. [Fr. < OFr. < *flambe,* flame < Lat. *flammula,* dim. of *flamma,* flame.]

flam·boy·ant (flăm-boi′ənt) *adj.* **1.** Highly elaborate; ornate. **2.** Richly colored; resplendent. **3.** *Archit.* Pertaining to or having waved lines and flamelike forms characteristic of 15th- and 16th-century French Gothic architecture. —*n.* The royal poinciana. [Fr. < OFr., pr.part. of *flamboyer,* to blaze < *flambe,* flame.] **—flam·boy′ance, flam·boy′an·cy** *n.* **—flam·boy′ant·ly** *adv.*

flame (flām) *n.* **1.** The zone of burning gases and fine suspended matter associated with the combustion of a substance; a hot, luminous mass of burning gas or vapor. **2.** The condition of active, blazing combustion: *burst into flames.* **3.** Something like a flame in motion, brilliance, intensity, or shape. **4.** A violent or intense passion. **5.** *Informal.* A sweetheart. —*v.* **flamed, flam·ing, flames.** —*intr.* **1.** To burn brightly; blaze. **2.** To color or flash suddenly: *Her cheeks flamed with embarrassment.* —*tr.* **1.** To burn, ignite, or scorch with a flame. **2.** *Obs.* To foment; incite. [ME < AN *flaumbe* < OFr. *flambe* < Lat. *flamma.*] **—flam′er** *n.*

flame cell *n.* A hollow ciliated cell in the excretory system of some platyhelminths and rotifers.

fla·men (flā′mən) *n., pl.* **-mens** or **flam·i·nes** (flăm′ə-nēz′). A priest, esp. of a Roman deity. [ME *flamin* < Lat. *flamen.*]

fla·men·co (flə-mĕng′kō) *n.* **1.** A dance style of the Andalusian Gypsies characterized by forceful, often improvised rhythms. **2.** The music that usually accompanies a flamenco dance. [Sp., Flemish < MDu. *Vlāming,* Fleming.]

flame·out (flām′out′) *n.* Failure of a jet aircraft engine in flight.

flame·proof (flām′pro͞of′) *adj.* Flame-retardant. —*tr.v.* **-proofed, -proof·ing, -proofs.** To make flameproof. **—flame′proof′er** *n.*

flame-re·tard·ant (flām′rĭ-tär′dənt) *adj.* Resistant to catching fire. **—flame′-re·tard′ant** *n.*

flame thrower *n.* A weapon that projects ignited incendiary fuel, such as napalm, in a steady stream.

flam·i·nes (flăm′ə-nēz′) *n.* A plural of **flamen.**

flam·ing (flā′mĭng) *adj.* **1.** On fire; ablaze. **2.** Like a flame in brilliance, color, or form. **3.** Intense; ardent. **—flam′ing·ly** *adv.*

flamingo

fla·min·go (flə-mĭng′gō) *n., pl.* **-gos** or **-goes. 1.** Any of several large, gregarious wading birds of the family Phoenicopteridae, of tropical regions, having reddish or pinkish plumage, long legs, a long, flexible neck, and a bill turned downward at the tip. **2.** A moderate reddish orange. [Port. *flamengo* or Sp. *flamenco,* both prob. < OProv. *flamenc* < *flama,* flame < Lat. *flamma.*]

flam·ma·ble (flăm′ə-bəl) *adj.* Easily ignited and capable of burning with great rapidity; inflammable. [< Lat. *flammare,* to flame < *flamma,* flame.] **—flam′ma·bil′i·ty** *n.* **—flam′ma·ble** *n.*

Usage: *Flammable* and *inflammable* are identical in meaning. *Flammable* has been adopted by safety authorities for the labeling of combustible materials because the *in-* of *inflammable* was understood by some people to mean "not." *Inflammable* is nevertheless widely used by writers, even though *flammable* is well established as a substitute.

flam·y (flā′mē) *adj.* **-i·er, -i·est.** Flamelike; flaming.

flan (flăn, flän, fläɴ) *n.* **1.** A tart with a filling of custard, fruit, or cheese. **2.** A metal disk to be stamped as a coin; blank. [Fr. < OFr. *flaon* < LLat. *flado,* flat cake, of Germanic orig.]

flâ·ne·rie (flän-rē′, flä′nə-rē′) *n.* Aimless idling; dawdling. [Fr.]

flâ·neur (flä-nûr′) *n.* An aimless idler; loafer. [Fr.]

flange (flănj) *n.* A protruding rim, edge, rib, or collar, as on a wheel or a pipe shaft, used to strengthen an object, hold it in place, or attach it to another object. —*tr.v.* **flanged, flang·ing, flang·es.** To furnish with a flange. [Prob. < *flanch,* to widen out.]

flank (flăngk) *n.* **1.** The section of flesh between the last rib and the hip; side. **2.** A cut of meat from the flank of an animal. **3.** A side or lateral part. **4. a.** The right or left side of a military formation: *attack on both flanks.* **b.** The right or left side of a bastion. —*tr.v.* **flanked, flank·ing, flanks. 1.** To protect or guard the flank of. **2.** To menace or attack the flank of. **3.** To be placed or situated at the flank or side of. **4.** To put something on each side of. [ME < OFr. *flanc,* of Germanic orig.]

flank·er (flăng′kər) *n.* **1.** One that flanks. **2.** *Football.* A flankerback.

flank·er·back (flăng′kər-băk′) *n. Football.* The halfback of the offensive team stationed just behind the line of scrimmage and to the right of his team's right end.

flan·nel (flăn′əl) *n.* **1.** A soft woven cloth of wool or of a blend of wool and cotton or synthetics. **2. a. flannels.** Outer clothing, esp. trousers, made of flannel. **b.** Underclothing made of flannel. [ME, a kind of woolen cloth or garment.] **—flan′nel·ly** *adj.*

flannel bush *n.* A shrub or small tree, *Fremontia californica,* of California and northern Mexico, having downy, lobed leaves and showy yellow flowers.

flannel cake *n.* A pancake.

flan·nel·ette (flăn′ə-lĕt′) *n.* A soft cotton cloth with a nap, used chiefly for baby clothes and underclothing.

flan·nel-leaf (flăn′əl-lēf′) *n.* A mullein (sense 1).

flap (flăp) *n.* **1.** A flat, usually thin piece attached at only one side. **2.** A projecting or hanging piece usually intended to double over and protect or cover: *the flap of an envelope.* **3.** The action of waving or fluttering. **4.** The sound produced by the motion of a flap. **5.** A blow given with something flat; slap. **6.** A variable control surface on the trailing edge of an aircraft wing, used primarily to increase lift or drag. **7.** Tissue that has been partially detached and used in plastic surgery to fill an adjacent defect or to cover the cut end of a bone after amputation. **8.** *Slang.* A condition of agitation or confusion. —*v.* **flapped, flap·ping, flaps.** —*tr.* **1.** To wave (the arms, for example) up and down. **2.** To cause to move or sway with a flap. **3.** To hit with something broad and flat; slap. **4.** *Informal.* To fling down; toss. —*intr.* **1.** To move or sway while fixed at one edge or corner; flutter. **2.** To wave arms or wings up and down. **3.** To fly by beating the air with the wings. [ME *flappe,* slap < *flappen,* to beat.]

flap·doo·dle (flăp′do͞od′l) *n. Slang.* Foolish talk; nonsense. [Orig. unknown.]

flap·jack (flăp′jăk′) *n.* A pancake.

flap·pa·ble (flăp′ə-bəl) *adj. Slang.* Easily excited or upset.

flap·per (flăp′ər) *n.* **1.** One that flaps. **2.** A broad, flexible part, such as a flipper. **3.** *Informal.* A young woman, esp. one of the 1920's who showed disdain for conventional dress and behavior.

flare (flâr) *v.* **flared, flar·ing, flares.** —*intr.* **1.** To flame up with a bright, wavering light. **2.** To burst into intense, sudden flame. **3. a.** To erupt or intensify suddenly. **b.** To become suddenly angry. **4.** To expand or open outward in shape: *a flared skirt.* —*tr.* **1.** To cause to flare. **2.** To signal with a blaze of light. —*n.* **1.** A brief, wavering blaze of light. **2.** A device that produces a bright light for signaling, illumination, or identification. **3.** An outbreak, as of emotion or activity. **4.** An expanding or opening outward. **5.** A lens reflection or the resultant film fogging. **6.** A brief intense eruption from the sun's chromosphere that is associated with sunspots. **7.** *Football.* A quick pass to a back running toward the sideline. [Orig. unknown.]

flare·back (flâr′băk′) *n.* A flame produced in the breech of a gun by ignition of residual gases.

flare-up (flâr′ŭp′) *n.* **1.** A sudden outbreak of flame or light. **2.** An outburst or eruption: *a flare-up of anger.* **3.** An intensification: *a flare-up of old antagonisms.*

flash (flăsh) *v.* **flashed, flash·ing, flash·es.** —*intr.* **1.** To burst forth into or as if into flame. **2.** To appear or occur suddenly. **3.** To give off light suddenly or intermittently. **4.** To move or proceed rapidly. —*tr.* **1. a.** To cause (light) to appear suddenly or in intermittent bursts. **b.** To cause to burst into flame. **c.** To reflect (light). **d.** To cause to reflect light from (a surface). **2.** To make known or signal by flashing lights. **3.** To communicate or display at great speed. **4.** To exhibit briefly. **5.** To display ostentatiously; flaunt. **6.** To fill suddenly with water. **7.** To cover with a thin protective layer. —*n.* **1.** A sudden, brief, intense display of light. **2.** A sudden perception: *a flash of insight.* **3.** An instant: *in a flash.* **4.** A brief news dispatch or transmission. **5.** *Obs.* The language or cant of thieves, tramps, or underworld figures. **6.** A flashlight. **7. a.** Instantaneous illumination for photography. **b.** A device, such as a flash bulb, flash gun, or flash lamp, used to produce such illumination. **8.** A rush (sense 8). [ME *flashen,* to splash.]

Synonyms: *flash, gleam, glance, glint, sparkle, glitter, glisten, shimmer, glimmer, twinkle, spark, scintillate.* These verbs mean to send forth or reflect light. *Flash* refers to a sudden and brilliant but short-lived outburst of light. *Gleam* implies light of moderate brightness, either transient or constant and often appearing against a dark background. *Glance* refers most often to light reflected obliquely. *Glint* refers to emitted or reflected light in flashes. *Sparkle* suggests a rapid succession of flashes of high brilliance, and *glitter* a similar succession of even greater intensity. *Glisten* usually refers to lustrous, reflected light, and *shimmer* to the reflection of soft, undulating light. *Glimmer* is applied to emission or reflection of subdued, fleeting light. *Twinkle* refers to the intermittent emission of soft, wavering light, and *spark* to the production of brief flashes of light or fire. *Scintillate* is applied to what flashes as if throwing off sparks in a continuous stream.

flash·back (flăsh′băk′) *n.* **1.** A literary or dramatic device in which an earlier event is inserted into the normal chronological order of a narrative. **2.** The episode or scene depicted by means of a flashback.

flash·board (flăsh′bôrd′, -bōrd′) *n.* Boarding that extends above a dam to increase the depth of water held.
flash bulb *n.* A glass bulb filled with finely shredded aluminum or magnesium foil that is ignited by electricity to produce a short-duration high-intensity light flash for taking photographs.
flash burn *n.* A burn resulting from brief exposure to intense radiation.
flash card *n.* A card printed with words or numbers and briefly displayed as part of a learning drill.
flash·cube (flăsh′kyo͞ob′) *n.* A small cube that contains four flash bulbs and that rotates automatically when a picture is taken with a camera to which it is attached.
flash·er (flăsh′ər) *n.* **1.** One that flashes. **2.** A device that automatically switches an electric lamp off and on, as in a commercial display sign.
flash flood *n.* A sudden, violent flood after a heavy rain.
flash-for·ward (flăsh′fôr′wərd) *n.* A literary or dramatic device in which the chronological sequence of events is interrupted by the interjection of future events.
flash gun *n.* A dry-cell powered photographic apparatus that holds and electrically triggers a flash bulb.
flash·ing (flăsh′ĭng) *n.* Sheet metal used to reinforce and weatherproof the joints and angles of a roof.
flash lamp *n.* An electric lamp for producing a high-intensity light of very short duration for use in photography.
flash·light (flăsh′līt′) *n.* **1.** A small, portable lamp usually powered by batteries. **2.** A brief, brilliant flood of light from a photographic lamp. **3.** A bright, flashing beam or light, as of a beacon or signal lamp.
flash·o·ver (flăsh′ō′vər) *n.* An unintended electric arc, as between two pieces of apparatus.
flash photolysis *n.* A method of investigating photochemical reactions that involves the breakdown of a chemical through exposure to a very brief, intense flash of light.
flash point *n.* The lowest temperature at which the vapor of a combustible liquid can be made to ignite momentarily in air.
flash tube *n.* A gas discharge tube used in an electronic flash to produce a brief, intense flash of light.
flash unit *n.* **1.** An electronic flash system containing both power supply and flash tube in a single compact unit. **2. a.** A flash gun. **b.** A flash gun and reflector.
flash·y (flăsh′ē) *adj.* **-i·er, -i·est. 1.** Giving a momentary or superficial impression of brilliance. **2.** Cheap and showy; gaudy. **—flash′i·ly** *adv.* **—flash′i·ness** *n.*
flask (flăsk) *n.* **1.** A small bottle or other container with a narrow neck and usually a cap, esp.: **a.** A container for liquor with a flat shape. **b.** A container or case for carrying gunpowder or shot. **c.** A vial or round long-necked bottle for laboratory use. **2.** A frame for holding a sand mold in a foundry. [OFr. *flasque* < LLat. *flasco,* prob. of Germanic orig.]
flat[1] (flăt) *adj.* **flat·ter, flat·test. 1.** Having a horizontal surface without a slope, tilt, or curvature. **2.** Having a smooth, even, level surface. **3.** Having a relatively broad surface in relation to thickness or depth: *a flat board.* **4.** Stretched out or lying at full length along the ground; prone. **5.** Free of qualification; absolute: *a flat refusal.* **6.** Fixed; unvarying: *a flat rate.* **7.** Neither more nor less; exact: *ten minutes flat.* **8.** Lacking interest or excitement; dull. **9. a.** Lacking in flavor. **b.** Having lost effervescence or sparkle: *flat beer.* **10.** Deflated. Used of a tire. **11.** Commercially inactive; sluggish. **12.** Unmodulated; monotonous. **13.** Lacking variety in tint or shading; uniform. **14.** Not glossy; mat. **15.** *Mus.* **a.** Being below the correct pitch. **b.** Being one half step lower than the corresponding natural key. **16.** Designating the vowel *a* as pronounced in *bad* or *cat.* **17.** Taut. Used of a sail. *—adv.* **1. a.** Level with the ground; horizontally. **b.** Prostrate. **2.** So as to be flat. **3.** Directly; completely: *went flat against the rules.* **4.** *Mus.* Below the intended pitch. **5.** *Commerce.* Without interest charge. *—n.* **1.** A flat surface or part. **2.** Often **flats.** A stretch of level ground: *the salt flats.* **3.** A shallow frame or box for seeds or seedlings. **4.** Stage scenery on a movable wooden frame. **5.** A flatcar. **6.** A deflated tire. **7.** A shoe with a flat heel. **8.** *Mus.* **a.** A sign (♭) affixed to a note to indicate that it is to be lowered by a half step. **b.** A note that is lowered a half step. *—v.* **flat·ted, flat·ting, flats.** *—tr.* **1.** To make flat; flatten. **2.** *Mus.* To lower (a note) a semitone. *—intr. Mus.* To sing or play below the proper pitch. [ME < ON *flatr.*] **—flat′ly** *adv.* **—flat′ness** *n.*
flat[2] (flăt) *n.* **1.** An apartment on one floor of a building. **2.** *Archaic.* A story in a house. [Alteration of Sc. *flet,* inner part of a house < ME < OE.]
flat-bed press (flăt′bĕd′) *n.* A printing press in which the type, locked into a chase, is supported by a flat surface or bed and the paper is applied to the type either by a flat platen or by a cylinder against which the bed moves.
flat·boat (flăt′bōt′) *n.* A boat with a flat bottom and square ends used for transporting freight on inland waterways.
flat·car (flăt′kär′) *n.* A railroad freight car without sides or roof.
flat·fish (flăt′fĭsh′) *n., pl.* **flatfish** or **-fish·es.** Any of numerous chiefly marine fishes of the order Pleuronectiformes (or Heterosomata), which includes the flounders, soles, and other fishes having a compressed body in which, in an early stage of development, one eye moves to the same side of the body as the other and the fish swims with its eyeless side downward.
flat·foot (flăt′fo͝ot′) *n.* **1.** *pl.* **-feet** (-fēt′). A condition in which the arch of the foot is flattened down so that the entire sole makes contact with the ground. **2.** *pl.* **-foots. a.** *Informal.* A person with flat feet. **b.** *Slang.* A policeman. *—intr.v.* **-foot·ed, -foot·ing, -foots.** To walk in a flatfooted manner: *"He flatfooted along, twirling his club"* (James T. Farrell).
flat-footed (flăt′fo͝ot′ĭd) *adj.* **1.** Of or afflicted with flatfoot. **2. a.** Steady on the feet. **b.** *Informal.* Without reservation; forthright. **3.** Unable to react quickly; unprepared: *caught him flat-footed.* **—flat′-foot′ed·ly** *adv.* **—flat′-foot′ed·ness** *n.*
Flat·head (flăt′hĕd′) *n., pl.* **Flathead** or **-heads. 1. a.** One of several tribes of American Indians in the northwestern coast area who practiced head-flattening. **b.** A member of one of these tribes. **2. a.** A Salishan tribe of western Montana. **b.** One of this tribe. **3. flathead.** *Slang.* An imbecile or fool.
flat·i·ron (flăt′ī′ərn) *n.* A heated device, usually having a flat metal base, used for pressing clothes.
flat·land (flăt′lănd′, -lənd) *n.* **1.** Land that varies little in elevation. **2. flatlands.** A geographic area composed chiefly of flatland. **—flat′land′er** *n.*
flat·let (flăt′lĭt) *n. Chiefly Brit.* An efficiency apartment.
flat·ling (flăt′lĭng) also **flat·lings** (-lĭngs) *adv. Archaic.* **1.** At full length; flat. **2.** With the flat of a sword.
flat out *adv.* **1.** In a direct manner; bluntly. **2.** At top speed.
flat-out (flăt′out′) *adj.* Thoroughgoing; out-and-out.
flat silver *n.* Utensils, such as knives, forks, or spoons, made of silver or silver plate.
flat·ten (flăt′n) *v.* **-tened, -ten·ing, -tens.** *—tr.* **1.** To make flat or flatter. **2.** To knock down; lay low. *—intr.* To become flat or flatter. **—flat′ten·er** *n.*
flat·ter[1] (flăt′ər) *v.* **-tered, -ter·ing, -ters.** *—tr.* **1.** To compliment excessively and often insincerely, esp. in order to win favor. **2.** To please or gratify the vanity of: *"What really flatters a man is that you think him worth flattering"* (G.B. Shaw). **3. a.** To portray favorably. **b.** To show off becomingly or advantageously. *—intr.* To practice flattery. [ME *flateren* < OFr. *flater,* of Germanic orig.] **—flat′ter·er** *n.* **—flat·ter·ing·ly** *adv.*
flat·ter[2] (flăt′ər) *n.* **1.** A flat-faced swage or hammer used by blacksmiths. **2.** A die plate for flattening metal into strips, as in the manufacture of watch springs.
flat·ter·y (flăt′ə-rē) *n., pl.* **-ies. 1.** The act or practice of flattering. **2.** Excessive or insincere praise.
flat·tish (flăt′ĭsh) *adj.* Somewhat flat.
flat·top (flăt′tŏp′) *n. Informal.* **1.** A U.S. aircraft carrier. **2.** A man's short haircut with a flattish, brushlike crown.
flat·u·lence (flăch′ə-ləns) also **flat·u·len·cy** (-lən-sē) *n.* **1.** The presence of excessive gas in the digestive tract. **2.** Self-importance; pomposity.
flat·u·lent (flăch′ə-lənt) *adj.* **1.** Of, pertaining to, or afflicted with flatulence. **2.** Inducing flatulence. [OFr. < Lat. *flatus,* fart.] **—flat′u·lent·ly** *adv.*
fla·tus (flā′təs) *n.* Gas generated in the stomach or intestines. [Lat., fart < p.part. of *flare,* to blow.]
flat·ware (flăt′wâr′) *n.* **1.** Tableware that is fairly flat and fashioned usually of a single piece, as plates. **2.** Table utensils such as knives, forks, and spoons.
flat·wise (flăt′wīz′) also **flat·ways** (-wāz′) *adv.* With the flat side down or in contact with a surface.
flat·work (flăt′wûrk′) *n.* Laundry that can be ironed by a mangle rather than by hand.
flat·worm (flăt′wûrm′) *n.* A platyhelminth.
flaunt (flônt) *v.* **flaunt·ed, flaunt·ing, flaunts.** *—tr.* **1.** To exhibit ostentatiously; show off: *flaunts his knowledge.* **2.** *Nonstandard.* To flout. *—intr.* **1.** To parade oneself ostentatiously; show oneself off. **2.** To wave grandly: *pennants flaunting in the wind.* [Orig. unknown.] **—flaunt** *n.* **—flaunt′er** *n.* **—flaunt′ing·ly** *adv.*

Usage: *Flaunt* and *flout* are often confused. *Flaunt* as a transitive verb means "to exhibit ostentatiously": *She flaunted her diamonds.* To *flout* is "to defy openly": *She flouted the proprieties.*

flaunt·y (flôn′tē) *adj.* **-i·er, -i·est.** Inclined to flaunt; ostentatious. **—flaunt′i·ly** *adv.* **—flaunt′i·ness** *n.*
flau·tist (flô′tĭst, flou′-) *n.* A flutist. [Ital. *flautista* < *flauto,* flute < OProv. *flaut.*]
flav– *pref.* Variant of **flavo-.**
fla·va·none (flā′və-nōn′) *n.* A colorless crystalline compound, $C_{15}H_{12}O_2$, derived from flavone.
fla·ves·cent (flə-vĕs′ənt) *adj.* Turning yellow; yellowish. [Lat. *flavescens, flavescent-,* p.part. of *flavescere,* to turn yellow, inchoative of *flavere,* to be yellow < *flavus,* yellow.]
fla·vin (flā′vĭn) *n.* **1.** Any of various water-soluble yellow pigments, including riboflavin, found in plant and animal tissue as coenzymes of flavoprotein. **2.** A compound, $C_{10}H_6N_4O_2$, that is the nucleus of various natural yellow pigments.
flavin adenine di·nu·cle·o·tide (dī-no͞o′klē-ə-tīd′, -nyo͞o′-) *n.* A coenzyme, $C_{27}H_{33}N_9O_{15}P_2$, that contains riboflavin and acts as a hydrogen carrier in certain oxidative systems of the body.

flask
Above: Laboratory flask
Below: Pocket flask

flatboat

fla·vine (flā′vēn′) *n.* **1.** A brownish-red crystalline powder, $C_{14}H_{15}N_3Cl_2$, used as an antiseptic. **2.** Flavin.
flavo– or **flav–** *pref.* **1.** Yellow: *flavin.* **2.** Flavin: *flavoprotein.* [Lat. *flavus,* yellow.]
fla·vone (flā′vōn′) *n.* A crystalline compound, $C_{15}H_{10}O_2$, the parent substance of a number of important yellow pigments.
fla·vo·noid (flā′və-noid′) *n.* Any of a large group of plant substances that includes the anthocyanins, a class of flower pigments.
fla·vo·pro·tein (flā′vō-prō′tēn′, -tē-ĭn) *n.* Any of a class of enzymes containing protein-bound flavin and acting as dehydrogenation catalysts in biological reactions.
fla·vor (flā′vər) *n.* **1.** Distinctive taste; savor: *a flavor of smoke in bacon.* **2.** A distinctive yet intangible quality felt to be characteristic of a given thing: *the flavor of the Orient.* **3.** A flavoring: *contains no artificial flavors.* **4.** *Archaic.* Aroma; fragrance. —*tr.v.* **-vored, -vor·ing, -vors.** To give flavor to. [ME *flavour,* aroma < OFr. *flaor* < VLat. **flator* < Lat. *flare,* to blow.] **—fla′vor·er** *n.* **—fla′vor·less** *adj.* **—fla′vor·ous** (-əs), **fla′vor·some** (-səm) *adj.*
fla·vor·ful (flā′vər-fəl) *adj.* Full of flavor; savory. **—fla′vor·ful·ly** *adv.*
fla·vor·ing (flā′vər-ĭng) *n.* A substance, as an extract or spice, that imparts flavor.
fla·vour (flā′vər) *n. & v. Chiefly Brit.* Variant of **flavor.**
flaw¹ (flô) *n.* **1.** An imperfection, often concealed, that can cause failure: *a flaw in a pane of glass.* **2.** A defect or shortcoming in something intangible: *The flaw in her character is arrogance.* **3.** A defect in a legal document that can render it invalid. —*tr. & intr.v.* **flawed, flaw·ing, flaws.** To make or become defective. [ME *flaue,* splinter, perh. < ON *flaga,* slab of stone.] **—flaw′less** *adj.* **—flaw′less·ly** *adv.* **—flaw′less·ness** *n.*
flaw² (flô) *n.* **1. a.** A brief gust or blast of wind. **b.** A squall; passing storm. **2.** *Obs.* A burst of passion. [Prob. of Scand. orig.] **—flaw′y** *adj.*
flax (flăks) *n.* **1. a.** Any of several plants of the genus *Linum,* esp. a widely cultivated species, *L. usitatissimum,* having blue flowers, seeds that yield linseed oil, and slender stems from which a fine, light-colored textile fiber is obtained. **b.** The textile fiber obtained from this plant. **2.** Any of several plants resembling flax. **3.** A grayish yellow. [ME < OE *fleax.*]
flax·en (flăk′sən) *adj.* **1.** Made of or resembling flax. **2.** Having the pale-yellow color of flax fiber: *flaxen braids.*
flax·seed (flăks′sēd′) *n.* The seed of flax, the source of linseed oil and of emollient medicinal preparations.
flax·y (flăk′sē) *adj.* **-i·er, -i·est.** Resembling flax, as in texture.
flay (flā) *tr.v.* **flayed, flay·ing, flays.** **1.** To strip off the skin of; decorticate. **2.** To strip of money or goods; plunder. **3.** To assail with stinging criticism; excoriate. [ME *flen* < OE *flēan.*] **—flay′er** *n.*

flea

F layer *n.* **1.** The highest zone of the ionosphere, extending continuously at night from approximately 190 to 400 kilometers or 120 to 250 miles. **2.** Either of two layers into which the F layer is divided during the day, esp. in summer, usually designated F_1 and F_2 and extending respectively from approximately 145 to 240 kilometers or 90 to 150 miles and from 240 kilometers or 150 miles upward.
flea (flē) *n.* **1.** Any of various small, wingless, bloodsucking insects of the order Siphonaptera that have legs adapted for jumping and are parasitic on warm-blooded animals. **2.** Any of various small crustaceans that resemble or move like fleas. **—*idiom.* a flea in (one's) ear.** A stinging rebuke or annoying hint. [ME *fle* < OE *flēah.*]
flea·bag (flē′băg′) *n.* An inferior hotel or lodging place.
flea·bane (flē′bān′) *n.* Any of various plants of the genus *Erigeron,* having variously colored, many-rayed, daisylike flowers.
flea beetle *n.* Any of a group of small beetles from the family Chrysomelidae that have modified legs adapted for jumping.

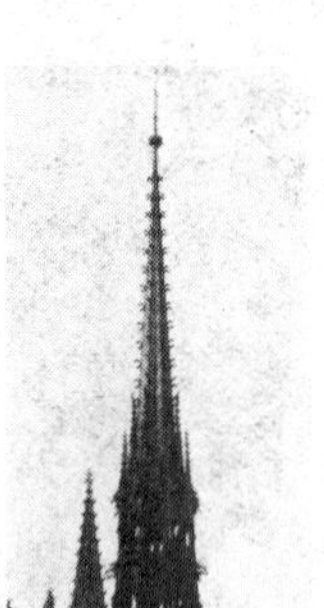
flèche

flea·bite (flē′bīt′) *n.* **1. a.** The bite of a flea. **b.** The small red mark caused by a flea's bite. **2.** A trifling loss, inconvenience, or annoyance.
flea-bit·ten (flē′bĭt′n) *adj.* **1.** Covered with fleas or fleabites. **2.** Having a pale coat with reddish-brown flecks. Used of horses.
flea collar *n.* A collar, as for a cat or dog, containing a substance for killing fleas.
flea market *n.* A market, usually in the open air, selling antiques, used household goods, and curios.
flèche (flĕsh, flāsh) *n.* A slender spire, esp. one on a church above the intersection of the nave and transepts. [Fr. < OFr., arrow.]

fleur-de-lis

flé·chette (flā-shĕt′, flĕ-) *n.* A steel missile or dart dropped from an airplane. [Fr., dim of *flèche,* arrow.]
fleck (flĕk) *n.* **1.** A tiny mark or spot. **2.** A small bit or flake. —*tr.v.* **flecked, fleck·ing, flecks.** To spot or streak: *a path flecked with sunlight.* [Prob. < ME *flekked,* spotted < ON *flekkr.*]
flec·tion (flĕk′shən) *n. Anat.* Variant of **flexion** (sense 1). **—flec′tion·al** *adj.*
fled (flĕd) *v.* Past tense and past participle of **flee.**
fledge (flĕj) *v.* **fledged, fledg·ing, fledg·es.** —*tr.* **1.** To take care of (a young bird) until it is ready to fly. **2.** To cover with or as if with feathers. **3.** To provide (an arrow) with feathers. —*intr.* To grow the plumage necessary for flight. [Prob. < obs. *fledge,* feathered < ME *flegge* < OE *flycge.*]
fledg·ling also **fledge·ling** (flĕj′lĭng) *n.* **1.** A young bird that has recently acquired its flight feathers. **2.** A young or inexperienced person.
flee (flē) *v.* **fled** (flĕd), **flee·ing, flees.** —*intr.* **1.** To run away, as from danger. **2.** To pass swiftly away; vanish. —*tr.* To run away from; shun. [ME *flen* < OE *flēon.*] **—fle′er** *n.*
fleece (flēs) *n.* **1. a.** The coat of wool of a sheep or similar animal. **b.** The yield of wool shorn from a sheep at one time. **2.** A soft, woolly covering or mass. **3.** Fabric with a soft, deep pile. —*tr.v.* **fleeced, fleec·ing, fleec·es.** **1.** To shear the fleece from. **2.** To defraud of money or property; swindle. **3.** To cover with or as if with fleece. [ME *fles* < OE *flēos.*] **—fleec′er** *n.*
fleec·y (flē′sē) *adj.* **-i·er, -i·est.** Of, like, or covered with fleece: *fleecy clouds.* **—fleec′i·ly** *adv.* **—fleec′i·ness** *n.*
fleer (flîr) *intr.v.* **fleered, fleer·ing, fleers.** To smirk or laugh in contempt or derision. —*n.* A contemptuous or derisive look or gibe. [ME *flerien,* of Scand. orig.] **—fleer′ing·ly** *adv.*
fleet¹ (flēt) *n.* **1.** A number of warships operating together under one command. **2.** A group of vehicles, such as taxicabs or fishing boats, owned or operated as a unit. [ME *flete* < OE *flēot* < *flēotan,* to float.]
fleet² (flēt) *adj.* **-er, -est.** **1.** Moving swiftly; rapid or nimble. **2.** *Archaic.* Fleeting. —*v.* **fleet·ed, fleet·ing, fleets.** —*intr.* **1.** To move or pass swiftly. **2.** To fade out; vanish. **3.** *Obs.* To drift. **4.** *Obs.* To flow. —*tr.* **1.** To cause (time) to pass quickly. **2.** *Naut.* To alter the position of; shift. [Poss. < ME *fleten,* to drift < OE *flēotan.*] **—fleet′ly** *adv.* **—fleet′ness** *n.*
Fleet Admiral *n.* The Admiral of the Fleet.
fleet·ing (flē′tĭng) *adj.* Passing quickly; ephemeral. **—fleet′ing·ly** *adv.* **—fleet′ing·ness** *n.*
Fleet Street *n.* London journalism. [After *Fleet Street,* London, England, the center of British newspaper journalism.]
flei·shig (flā′shĭk) *adj.* Consisting of, prepared with, or relating to meat or meat products. [Yiddish < MHG *vleischic,* meaty < *vleisch,* meat < OHG *fleisk,* flesh.]
Flem·ing (flĕm′ĭng) *n.* **1.** A native of Flanders. **2.** A Belgian who speaks Flemish. [ME < MDu. *Vlāming.*]
Flem·ish (flĕm′ĭsh) *adj.* Of or pertaining to Flanders, the Flemings, or their language. —*n.* **1.** The Low German language of the Flemings. **2.** The Flemings.
flense (flĕns) *tr.v.* **flensed, flens·ing, flens·es.** To strip the blubber or skin from (a whale, for example). [Dan.] **—flens′er** *n.*
flesh (flĕsh) *n.* **1. a.** The soft tissue of the body, esp. skeletal muscle distinguished from bone and viscera. **b.** Excess fat; avoirdupois. **c.** The surface or skin of the human body. **2.** The meat of animals as distinguished from the edible tissue of fish or fowl. **3.** The pulpy, usually edible part of a fruit or vegetable. **4. a.** The body as distinguished from the mind or soul. **b.** Man's physical or carnal nature. **5.** Mankind in general; humanity. **6.** One's family; kin. —*v.* **fleshed, flesh·ing, flesh·es.** —*tr.* **1.** To encourage (a falcon, for example) to participate in the chase by feeding it flesh from a kill. **2.** To fill out (a structure or framework): *fleshed out the novel with a subplot.* **3.** To clean (a hide) of adhering flesh. —*intr.* To gain weight; become plump or fleshy. **—*idiom.* in the flesh.** Alive and in person. [ME < OE *flǣsc.*]
flesh and blood *n.* **1.** Human nature or physical existence, together with its weaknesses. **2.** One's blood relatives; kin.
flesh fly *n.* Any of various flies of the genus *Sarcophaga,* whose larvae are parasitic in animal tissue.
flesh·ings (flĕsh′ĭngz) *pl.n.* **1.** Flesh-colored tights. **2.** Bits of flesh removed from a hide in cleaning.
flesh·ly (flĕsh′lē) *adj.* **-li·er, -li·est.** **1.** Of or pertaining to the body; corporeal. **2.** Of, pertaining to, or inclined to carnality; sensual. **3.** Not spiritual; worldly. **4.** Tending to plumpness; fleshy. **—flesh′li·ness** *n.*
flesh·pot (flĕsh′pŏt′) *n.* **1.** Physical well-being and gratification. **2.** Often **fleshpots.** A place in which physical comfort or gratification is obtained.
flesh wound *n.* A wound that penetrates the flesh but does not damage bones or vital organs.
flesh·y (flĕsh′ē) *adj.* **-i·er, -i·est.** **1. a.** Pertaining to, consisting of, or resembling flesh. **b.** Having much flesh; corpulent. **2.** Having a juicy or pulpy texture. **—flesh′i·ness** *n.*
fleshy fruit *n.* A fruit, such as a drupe, whose pericarp is soft and pulpy.
fletch (flĕch) *tr.v.* **fletched, fletch·ing, fletch·es.** To feather (an arrow). [Prob. back-formation < FLETCHER.]
fletch·er (flĕch′ər) *n.* One who makes arrows. [ME *fleccher* < OFr. *flechier* < *flèche,* arrow.]
fleur-de-lis or **fleur-de-lys** (flûr′də-lē′, flo͝or′-) *n., pl.* **fleurs-de-lis** or **fleurs-de-lys** (flûr′də-lēz′, flo͝or′-). **1.** An iris, esp. a white-flowered form of *Iris germanica.* **2.** A heraldic device consisting of a stylized three-petaled iris flower, used as the armorial emblem of the kings of France. [ME *flour de lice* < OFr. *flor de lis,* flower of the lily.]
flew (flo͞o) *v.* Past tense of **fly¹.**
flews (flo͞oz) *pl.n.* The pendulous corners of the upper lip of certain dogs, such as a hound. [Orig. unknown.]
flex (flĕks) *v.* **flexed, flex·ing, flex·es.** —*tr.* **1. a.** To bend

repeatedly. **b.** To bend (a joint). **c.** To bend (a joint) repeatedly. **2.** To contract (a muscle). —*intr.* To bend: *His hands flexed nervously.* —*n. Chiefly Brit.* Electric cord. [Lat. *flectere, flex-,* to bend.]
flex·a·gon (flĕk'sə-gŏn') *n.* A folded paper construction capable of being flexed along its folds to alternately reveal and conceal its faces. [FLEX + *-agon,* as in *pentagon.*]
flex·i·ble (flĕk'sə-bəl) *adj.* **1.** Capable of being bent or flexed; pliable. **2.** Susceptible to influence or persuasion; tractable. **3.** Responsive to change; adaptable: *a flexible schedule.* **—flex'i·bil'i·ty, flex'i·ble·ness** *n.* **—flex'i·bly** *adv.*
Synonyms: *flexible, malleable, ductile, plastic, pliable, pliant, supple, adaptable.* These adjectives are applied to what can readily undergo change or modification. *Flexible* refers to the ability of a thing to be bent, twisted, or turned without breaking, or the ability of persons or things to accommodate to another's wishes, changing conditions, or the like. *Malleable* is applied, literally and figuratively, to capacity for being shaped by or as if by tools. *Ductile* describes the capacity of certain metals to be drawn out or hammered thin, or of certain liquids to be channeled readily. *Plastic* refers to capacity for being molded or modeled after the fashion of plaster or clay. *Pliable* and *pliant* refer to things or materials that can be changed in shape without breaking. Applied to persons, *pliant* indicates readiness to accommodate to change or the wishes of another, and *pliable* may imply tendency to be influenced easily or to be dominated. *Supple* is applied to objects that can bend in many places without damage, or figuratively to what responds readily to change or external influence. *Adaptable* refers to the capacity of persons and things to assume modified form or to change or adjust in other respects in response to new circumstances.
flex·ile (flĕk'səl,-sīl') *adj.* Flexible.
flex·ion (flĕk'shən) *n.* **1.** Also **flec·tion.** *Anat.* **a.** The act of bending. **b.** The condition of being bent. **2.** A part that is bent. **3.** Inflection (sense 2). [Lat. *flexio,* a bending < *flectere,* to bend.]
flex·or (flĕk'sər) *n.* A muscle that acts to flex a joint. [NLat. < Lat. *flexus,* p.part. of *flectere,* to bend.]
flex·time (flĕks'tīm') *n.* An arrangement by which employees may set their own work schedules, as starting and finishing hours. [FLEX(IBLE) + TIME.]
flex·u·ous (flĕk'shōō-əs) *adj.* Bending or winding alternately from side to side. [Lat. *flexuosus* < *flexus,* p.part. of *flectere,* to bend.] **—flex'u·ous·ly** *adv.*
flex·ure (flĕk'shər) *n.* **1.** A bend, curve, or turn. **2.** The act or an instance of bending or flexing. **—flex'ur·al** *adj.*
fley (flā) *tr.v.* **fleyed, fley·ing, fleys.** *Scot.* To frighten. [ME *fleien* < OE *flēgan.*]
flib·ber·ti·gib·bet (flĭb'ər-tē-jĭb'ĭt) *n.* A silly, scatterbrained, or garrulous person. [ME *flibergebet.*]
flick[1] (flĭk) *n.* **1.** A light, quick blow, jerk, or touch. **2.** The sound accompanying a flick. **3.** A light splash, dash, or daub. —*v.* **flicked, flick·ing, flicks.** —*tr.* **1.** To touch or hit with a light, quick blow: *flicked him with his hand.* **2.** To cause to move with a light blow; snap: *flicked the light switch on.* **3.** To remove with a light, quick blow: *flicked the lint off her coat.* —*intr.* To twitch or flutter. [Imit.]
flick[2] (flĭk) *n. Informal.* A motion picture. [Back-formation < FLICKER[1].]
flick·er[1] (flĭk'ər) *v.* **-ered, -er·ing, -ers.** —*intr.* **1.** To move waveringly; flutter: *shadows flickering on the wall.* **2.** To burn unsteadily or fitfully. —*tr.* To cause to flicker. —*n.* **1.** A brief movement; tremor. **2.** An inconstant or wavering light. **3.** A brief or slight sensation. **4.** *Slang.* A motion picture. [ME *flikeren* < OE *flicerian.*]
flick·er[2] (flĭk'ər) *n.* Any of several large North American woodpeckers of the genus *Colaptes,* having a brownish back and a spotted breast. [Perh. < FLICK[1].]
flick·er·tail (flĭk'ər-tāl') *n.* A ground squirrel, *Citellus richardsoni,* of western North America.
flied (flīd) *v.* Past tense and past participle of **fly**[1] (sense 7).
fli·er also **fly·er** (flī'ər) *n.* **1.** One that flies, esp. an airplane pilot. **2.** A step in a straight stairway. **3.** *Informal.* A daring venture. **4.** A pamphlet or circular for mass distribution.
flight[1] (flīt) *n.* **1. a.** The motion of an object in or through a medium, esp. through the earth's atmosphere or through space. **b.** An instance of such motion. **c.** The distance covered in such motion. **2. a.** The act or process of flying through the air by means of wings. **b.** The ability to fly. **3.** A swift passage or movement. **4.** A scheduled airline run or trip. **5.** A group, esp. of birds or aircraft, flying together. **6.** A number of aircraft in the U.S. Air Force forming a subdivision of a squadron. **7.** A brilliant and extraordinary effort or display: *a flight of the imagination.* **8.** A series of stairs rising from one landing to another. —*intr.v.* **flight·ed, flight·ing, flights.** To migrate or fly in flocks. [ME < OE *flyht.*]
flight[2] (flīt) *n.* The act or an instance of running away. [ME < OE *flyht.*]
flight attendant *n.* An attendant who assists passengers in an airplane.
flight bag *n.* A lightweight, flexible piece of luggage with zippered outside pockets.
flight deck *n.* **1.** The upper deck of an aircraft carrier, used as a runway. **2.** An elevated compartment in certain aircraft, used by the pilot, copilot, and flight engineer.
flight engineer *n.* The crew member responsible for the mechanical performance of an aircraft flight.
flight feather *n.* One of the comparatively large, stiff feathers of a bird's wing or tail that are necessary for flight.
flight·less (flīt'lĭs) *adj.* Incapable of flying, as certain birds.
flight surgeon *n.* An air force medical officer who specializes in aviation medicine.
flight-test (flīt'tĕst') *tr.v.* **-test·ed, -test·ing, -tests.** To test (an aircraft, for example) during flight.
flight·y (flī'tē) *adj.* **-i·er, -i·est. 1. a.** Given to capricious or unstable behavior. **b.** Marked by irresponsible or silly behavior. **2.** Easily excited; skittish. **—flight'i·ly** *adv.* **—flight'i·ness** *n.*
flim·flam (flĭm'flăm') *Informal.* —*n.* **1.** Nonsense; humbug. **2.** A deception; swindle. —*tr.v.* **-flammed, -flam·ming, -flams.** To swindle. [Prob. of Scand. orig.]
flim·sy (flĭm'zē) *adj.* **-si·er, -si·est. 1.** Light, thin, and insubstantial: *a flimsy fabric.* **2.** Lacking solidity or strength: *a flimsy table.* **3.** Lacking plausibility; unconvincing: *a flimsy theory.* —*n., pl.* **-sies. 1.** Thin paper usually used to make multiple copies. **2.** Something written on flimsy. [Orig. unknown.] **—flim'si·ly** *adv.* **—flim'si·ness** *n.*
flinch (flĭnch) *intr.v.* **flinched, flinch·ing, flinch·es. 1.** To start or wince involuntarily, as from surprise or pain. **2.** To draw away; retreat. —*n.* An act or instance of flinching. [OFr. *flenchir.*] **—flinch'er** *n.* **—flinch'ing·ly** *adv.*
flin·ders (flĭn'dərz) *pl.n.* Bits, fragments, or splinters. [ME *flendris,* perh. of Scand. orig.]
fling (flĭng) *v.* **flung** (flŭng), **fling·ing, flings.** —*tr.* **1.** To throw with violence: *flung the dish against the wall.* **2.** To put or send suddenly or unexpectedly: *an army flung into battle.* **3.** To throw (oneself) into some activity with abandon and energy. **4.** To toss aside; discard: *fling propriety away.* —*intr.* To move quickly, violently, or impulsively. —*n.* **1.** An act of flinging. **2.** A brief period of indulging one's impulses; spree. **3.** *Informal.* A usually brief attempt or effort: *You take a fling at it.* [ME *flingen,* of Scand. orig.]
flink·ite (flĭng'kīt') *n.* A brownish-green mineral of manganese arsenate. [After Gustaf *Flink* (d. 1931).]
flint (flĭnt) *n.* **1.** A very hard, fine-grained quartz that sparks when struck with steel. **2.** A piece of flint used as a tool by primitive man. **3.** A small solid cylinder of a spark-producing alloy, used in lighters to ignite the fuel. **4.** Something like flint in hardness: *a jaw of flint.* [ME < OE.]
flint corn *n.* A variety of corn, *Zea mays indurata,* having small, hard seeds.
flint disease *n.* Pneumonoconiosis caused by the prolonged inhalation of stone dust.
flint glass *n.* A soft, fusible, lustrous, brilliant lead-oxide optical glass with high refraction and low dispersion.
flint·head (flĭnt'hĕd') *n.* The wood ibis.
flint·lock (flĭnt'lŏk') *n.* **1.** An obsolete gunlock in which a flint embedded in the hammer produces a spark that ignites the charge. **2.** A firearm having a flintlock.
flint·y (flĭn'tē) *adj.* **-i·er, -i·est. 1.** Containing or composed of flint. **2.** Unyielding; stern. **—flint'i·ly** *adv.* **—flint'i·ness** *n.*
flip (flĭp) *v.* **flipped, flip·ping, flips.** —*tr.* **1.** To throw with a brisk motion: *flipped me the ball.* **2.** To toss in the air, imparting a spin: *flip a coin.* **3.** To reverse or overturn quickly and effortlessly. —*intr.* **1.** To strike quickly or lightly, as with a snap of the fingers. **2.** To move suddenly or jerkily. **3.** To turn a somersault in the air. **4.** *Slang.* **a.** To go crazy. **b.** To react strongly and esp. enthusiastically: *She flipped over the new car.* —*n.* **1.** An act of flipping, esp.: **a.** A fillip or tap. **b.** A quick, jerky movement. **c.** A somersault. **2.** A mixed drink made with any of various alcoholic beverages and often including beaten eggs. —*adj. Informal.* **1.** Marked by disrespect; impertinent. **2.** Marked by unconcern; indifferent. [Perh. imit.]
flip chart *n.* A chart consisting of sheets hinged at the top that can be flipped over to present information sequentially.
flip-flop (flĭp'flŏp') *n.* **1.** The movement or sound of repeated flapping: *the flip-flop of sandals on a tile floor.* **2.** A backward somersault or handspring. **3.** *Informal.* A reversal, as of opinion. **4.** *Electronics.* An electronic circuit or mechanical device capable of assuming either of two stable states and used in computers to store a single bit of information. **—flip'-flop'** *v.* **(-flopped, -flop·ping, -flops).**
flip·pant (flĭp'ənt) *adj.* **1.** Marked by disrespectful levity or indifference. **2.** *Archaic.* Talkative; voluble. [Prob. < FLIP.] **—flip'pan·cy** *n.* **—flip'pant·ly** *adv.*
flip·per (flĭp'ər) *n.* **1.** One that flips. **2.** A wide, flat limb, as of a seal, adapted esp. for swimming. **3.** A rubber foot covering with a flat, flexible portion that widens as it extends forward from the toes, used in swimming.
flip side *n.* The reverse side, as of a phonograph record.
flirt (flûrt) *v.* **flirt·ed, flirt·ing, flirts.** —*intr.* **1.** To make playfully romantic or sexual overtures. **2.** To act so as to attract or provoke: *The bullfighter flirted with death.* **3.** To move abruptly or jerkily. —*tr.* **1.** To toss or flip suddenly. **2.** To move quickly. —*n.* **1.** One given to flirting. **2.** An abrupt, jerking movement. [Orig. unknown.]
flir·ta·tion (flûr-tā'shən) *n.* **1.** The practice of flirting. **2.** A

flicker[2]

flight deck

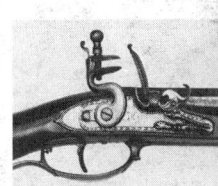

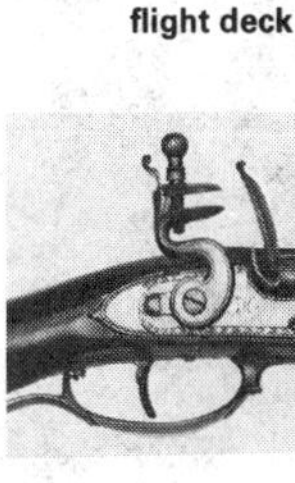
flintlock
Late 18th-century American

superficial and usually temporary romance. **3.** A brief involvement.

flir·ta·tious (flûr-tā′shəs) *adj.* **1.** Given to flirting. **2.** Full of playful allure: *a flirtatious glance.* **—flir·ta′tious·ly** *adv.* **—flir·ta′tious·ness** *n.*

flit (flĭt) *intr.v.* **flit·ted, flit·ting, flits. 1.** To move about rapidly and nimbly. **2.** To move quickly from one condition or location to another. *—n.* A fluttering or darting movement. [ME *flitten* < ON *flytja.*] **—flit′ter** *n.*

flitch (flĭch) *n.* **1.** A salted and cured side of bacon. **2.** A longitudinal cut from the trunk of a tree. **3.** One of several planks secured together to form a single beam. [ME *flicche* < OE *flicce.*]

flit·ter (flĭt′ər) *intr.v.* **-tered, -ter·ing, -ters.** To flutter. [Freq. of FLIT.]

fliv·ver (flĭv′ər) *n.* An old or cheap car. [Orig. unknown.]

float (flōt) *v.* **float·ed, float·ing, floats.** *—intr.* **1. a.** To remain suspended within or on the surface of a fluid without sinking. **b.** To be suspended in or move through space as if supported by a liquid. **2.** To move from position to position, esp. at random. **3.** *Commerce.* To find a level in relationship to other currencies solely in response to the law of supply and demand: *allowed the dollar to float.* *—tr.* **1.** To cause to remain suspended without sinking or falling. **2.** To flood (land), as for irrigation. **3.** To launch or establish (a business enterprise, for example). **4.** To release (a security) for sale. **5.** To arrange for (a loan). **6.** To make the surface of (plaster, for example) level or smooth. **7.** *Commerce.* To allow (the exchange value of a currency) to find freely its real level in relationship to other currencies. **8.** *Computer Sci.* To convert data from fixed-point notation to floating-point notation. *—n.* **1.** Something that floats, as: **a.** A raft. **b.** A buoy. **c.** A life preserver. **d.** A cork or other floating object on a fishing line. **e.** A landing platform attached to a wharf and floating on the water. **f.** A hollow ball attached to a lever to regulate the water level in a tank. **g.** An air-filled or gas-filled organ or sac that enables an organism to remain suspended in water. **2.** A large, flat vehicle bearing an exhibit in a parade. **3.** A sum of money representing checks that are outstanding. **4.** A tool for smoothing the surface of plaster or cement. **5.** A soft drink with ice cream floating in it. [ME *floten* < OE *flotian.*] **—float′a·ble** *adj.*

float·age (flō′tĭj) *n.* Variant of **flotage.**

floa·ta·tion (flō-tā′shən) *n.* Variant of **flotation.**

float·er (flō′tər) *n.* **1.** One that floats. **2.** One who wanders; drifter. **3.** An employee who is reassigned from job to job or shift to shift within an operation. **4.** One who votes illegally in different polling places. **5.** An insurance policy that protects movable property that is in transit or that is regularly subject to use in a variety of places.

float·ing (flō′tĭng) *adj.* **1.** Buoyed on or suspended in or as if in a fluid. **2.** Not secured in place; unattached. **3.** Inclined to move about. **4. a.** Available for use; in circulation. Used of capital. **b.** Short-term and usually unfunded. Used of a debt. **5.** Designed or constructed to operate smoothly and without vibration. **6.** Designating an organ of the body that is out of normal position: *a floating kidney.*

floating dock *n.* A structure that can be submerged to permit the entry and docking of a ship and then raised to lift the ship from the water for repairs.

floating island *n.* A dessert of soft custard with mounds of beaten egg whites or whipped cream floating on its surface.

float·ing-point (flō′tĭng-point′) *adj.* Of, pertaining to, or being a method of writing numeric quantities with a mantissa representing the value of the digits and a characteristic indicating the power of the number base.

floating rib *n.* One of the four lower ribs that, unlike the other ribs, are not attached at the front.

floc (flŏk) *n.* A flocculent mass as formed in certain serologic precipitin tests. [Short for FLOCCULUS.]

floc·cu·late (flŏk′yə-lāt′) *v.* **-lat·ed, -lat·ing, -lates.** *—tr.* **1.** To cause (soil) to form lumps or masses. **2.** To cause (clouds) to form fluffy masses. *—intr.* To form lumpy or fluffy masses. *—n.* Something that has flocculated. **—floc′cu·la′tion** *n.*

floc·cule (flŏk′yo͞ol) *n.* A small, loosely held mass or aggregate of fine particles suspended in or precipitated from a solution. [NLat. *flocculus,* flocculus.]

floc·cu·lent (flŏk′yə-lənt) *adj.* **1.** Having a fluffy or woolly appearance. **2.** Made up of or containing woolly masses. **3.** Flaky, waxy, and woollike, as the secretion covering some insects. **—floc′cu·lence** *n.* **—floc′cu·lent·ly** *adv.*

floc·cu·lus (flŏk′yə-ləs) *n., pl.* **-li** (-lī′). **1.** A small, fluffy mass or tuft. **2.** *Anat.* Either of two small lobes on the lower posterior border of each lobe of the cerebellum. **3.** *Astron.* Any of various masses of gases appearing as bright or dark patches on the sun's surface. [NLat., dim. of Lat. *floccus,* tuft of wool.]

flock[1]

flock[1] (flŏk) *n.* **1.** A group of animals that live, travel, or feed together. **2.** A group of people under the leadership of one person, esp. the members of a church. **3.** A large crowd or number: *had a flock of questions.* *—intr.v.* **flocked, flock·ing, flocks.** To congregate or travel in a flock or crowd. —See Usage note at **collective noun.** [ME *flok* < OE *floc.*]

Synonyms: *flock, flight, herd, drove, pack, gang, gaggle, bevy, brood.* These nouns denote a number of animals, birds, or fish considered collectively, and some have human connotations. *Flock* is applied to a congregation of animals of one kind, especially sheep or goats herded by man, and to any congregation of wild or domesticated birds, especially when on the ground. It is also applicable to people who form the membership of a church or to people under someone's care or supervision. *Flight* refers to a flock of birds in flight. *Herd* is used of a number of wild animals, especially cattle, herded by man; or of such wild animals as antelope, elephants, and zebras; or of whales and seals. Applied to people, it is used disparagingly of a crowd or of the masses, and suggests the gregarious aspect of crowd psychology. *Drove* is used of a herd or flock of cattle, sheep, geese, or the like, that are being moved or driven from one place to another; less often it refers to a crowd of people in movement. *Pack* is applicable to any body of animals, especially wolves, or of birds, especially grouse, and to a body of hounds trained to hunt as a unit. It also refers to a band or gang of persons, especially when engaged in violent or criminal pursuits. *Gang* refers to a herd, especially of buffalo or elk; to a pack of wolves or wild dogs; or to various associations of persons. *Gaggle* denotes a flock of geese or, informally, a company of women. *Bevy* is used of a company of girls, roe deer, larks, or quail. *Brood* is applicable to offspring that are still under the care of a mother, especially the offspring of domestic and game birds or, less formally, of human beings. The following related terms are used as indicated: *cast,* the number of hawks or falcons cast off at one time, usually a pair; *cete,* a company of badgers; *covert,* a flock of coots; *covey,* a family of grouse, partridges, or other game birds; *drift,* a drove or herd, especially of hogs; *exaltation,* a flight of larks; *fall,* a covey of woodcock; *gam,* a herd of whales, or a social congregation of whalers, especially at sea; *kennel,* a number of hounds or dogs housed in one place, or under the same ownership; *kindle,* a brood or litter, especially of kittens; *litter,* the total number of offspring produced at a single birth by a multiparous mammal; *muster,* a flock of peacocks; *nide,* a brood of pheasants; *pod,* a small herd of seals or whales; *pride,* a company of lions; *rout,* a company of people or animals in movement, especially knights or wolves; *school* and *shoal,* a congregation of fish, porpoises, or other aquatic mammals; *shrewdness,* a company of apes; *skein,* a flight of wildfowl; *skulk,* a congregation of vermin, especially foxes, or of thieves; *sloth,* a company of bears; *sord,* a flight of mallards; *sounder,* a herd of wild hogs; *spring,* a flock of teal; *stable,* a number of horses housed in one place, or under the same ownership; *swarm,* a colony of insects, such as ants, bees, or wasps, especially when migrating to a new nest or hive; *troop,* a number of animals, birds, or people, especially when on the move; *warren,* the inhabitants, such as rabbits, of a warren; *watch,* a flock of nightingales; *wisp,* a flock of snipe.

flock[2] (flŏk) *n.* **1.** A tuft, as of fiber or hair. **2.** Waste wool or cotton used for stuffing furniture and mattresses. **3.** An inferior grade of wool added to cloth for extra weight. **4.** Pulverized wool or felt applied to paper, cloth, or metal to produce a texture or pattern. **5.** A floccule. *—tr.v.* **flocked, flock·ing, flocks. 1.** To stuff with flock. **2.** To texture or pattern with flock. [ME *flok* < OFr. *floc* < Lat. *floccus.*]

floe (flō) *n.* **1.** A large, flat mass of ice formed on the surface of a body of water. **2.** A segment separated from an ice floe. [Prob. < Norw. *flo,* layer < ON *flō.*]

flog (flŏg, flôg) *tr.v.* **flogged, flog·ging, flogs.** To beat severely with a whip or rod. [Perh. < Lat. *flagellare.* —see FLAGELLATE.] **—flog′ger** *n.*

flood (flŭd) *n.* **1.** An overflowing of water onto land that is normally dry. **2.** Flood tide. **3.** An abundant flow or outpouring: *received a flood of applications.* **4.** A floodlight. **5. Flood.** The universal deluge recorded in the Old Testament as having occurred during the life of Noah. *—v.* **flood·ed, flood·ing, floods.** *—tr.* **1.** To cover or submerge with or as if with a flood; inundate. **2.** To fill with an abundance or an excess: *flood the market with cheap foreign goods.* *—intr.* **1.** To become inundated or submerged. **2.** To pour forth; overflow. [ME *flod* < OE *flōd.*]

flood·gate (flŭd′gāt′) *n.* **1.** A gate used to control the flow of a body of water. **2.** Something that restrains a flood or outpouring.

flood·light (flŭd′līt′) *n.* **1.** Artificial light in an intensely bright and broad beam. **2.** A unit that produces a beam of intense light. *—tr.v.* **-light·ed** or **-lit** (-lĭt′), **-light·ing, -lights.** To illuminate with a floodlight.

flood plain *n.* A plain bordering a river subject to flooding.

flood tide *n.* **1.** The incoming or rising tide. **2.** A climax or high point.

floor (flôr, flōr) *n.* **1.** The surface of a room on which one stands. **2.** The lower or supporting surface of a structure. **3.** The surface of a structure on which vehicles travel. **4.** The ground or lowermost surface, as of a forest or ocean. **5.** The lower part of a room, such as a legislative chamber, where business is conducted. **6. a.** The right to address an assembly, as granted under parliamentary procedure. **b.** The body of assembly members: *a motion from the floor.* **7. a.** A story or level of a building. **b.** The occupants of such a story. **8.** A lower limit or base. *—tr.v.* **floored, floor·ing, floors. 1.** To provide with a floor. **2.** To knock down. **3.** To press (the accelerator of a motor vehicle) to the floor. **4.** To stun; overwhelm. [ME *flor* < OE *flōr.*] **—floor'er** *n.*

floor·age (flôr'ĭj, flōr'-) *n.* Floor space.

floor·board (flôr'bôrd', flōr'bōrd') *n.* **1.** A board in a floor. **2.** The floor of a motor vehicle.

floor exercise *n. Sports.* An event in competitive gymnastics that consists of various tumbling maneuvers performed on a mat.

floor·ing (flôr'ĭng, flōr'-) *n.* **1.** A floor. **2.** Material, such as lumber or tile, used in making floors.

floor lamp *n.* A tall lamp with a base that stands on the floor.

floor leader *n.* The member of a legislature chosen by fellow party members to be in charge of the party's activities on the floor.

floor manager *n.* **1.** A floorwalker. **2.** A person who is in charge of directing something, as activities at a political convention, from the floor.

floor plan *n.* A scale diagram of a room or building drawn as if seen from above.

floor sample *n.* Merchandise sold at a reduced price because it has been a display or demonstration model.

floor show *n.* A series of entertainments presented in a nightclub.

floor·walk·er (flôr'wô'kər, flōr'-) *n.* An employee of a department store who supervises sales personnel and assists customers.

floo·zy also **floo·zie** (flo͞o'zē) *n., pl.* **-zies.** *Slang.* A slovenly or vulgar woman, esp. a prostitute. [Orig. unknown.]

flop (flŏp) *v.* **flopped, flop·ping, flops.** *—intr.* **1.** To fall down heavily and noisily. **2.** To move about in a clumsy or relaxed way. **3.** *Informal.* To fail utterly. **4.** *Slang.* To go to bed. *—tr.* To cause to fall down heavily and noisily. *—n.* **1.** The action of flopping. **2.** The sound of flopping. **3.** *Informal.* An utter failure. [Alteration of FLAP.] **—flop'per** *n.*

flop·house (flŏp'hous') *n.* A cheap hotel or boarding house.

flop·py (flŏp'ē) *adj.* **-pi·er, -pi·est.** Tending to flop; loose and flexible. **—flop'pi·ly** *adv.* **—flop'pi·ness** *n.*

floppy disk *n. Computer Sci.* A flexible plastic disk coated with magnetic material used to store computer data.

flo·ra (flôr'ə, flōr'ə) *n., pl.* **-ras** or **flo·rae** (flôr'ē', flōr'ē'). **1.** Plants collectively, esp. the plants of a particular region or time. **2.** A treatise describing the plants of a region or time. [< FLORA.]

Flo·ra (flôr'ə, flōr'ə) *n. Rom. Myth.* The goddess of flowers. [Lat. *Flora* < *flos,* flower.]

flo·rae (flôr'ē', flōr'ē') *n.* A plural of **flora.**

flo·ral (flôr'əl, flōr'-) *adj.* Of, pertaining to, or suggestive of a flower or flora. **—flo'ral·ly** *adv.*

floral envelope *n.* The perianth of a flower.

floral tube *n.* A tube in some plants that is formed by the basal fusion of the sepals, petals, and stamens.

flo·re·at·ed (flôr'ē-ā'tĭd, flōr'-) *adj.* Variant of **floriated.**

Flor·en·tine (flôr'ən-tēn', -tīn', flŏr'-) *adj.* **1.** Of or pertaining to the style of art and architecture that flourished in Florence, Italy, during the Renaissance. **2.** Often **florentine.** Having or characterizing a dull chased or rubbed finish. Used of gold. **3.** Prepared or served with spinach. [Lat. *Florentinus* < *Florentia,* Florence, Italy.]

flo·res·cence (flô-rĕs'əns, flə-) *n.* The condition, time, or period of blossoming. [NLat. *florescentia* < Lat. *florescens,* pr.part. of *florescere,* inchoative of *florere,* to bloom < *flos,* flower.] **—flo·res'cent** *adj.*

flo·ret (flôr'ĭt, flōr'-) *n.* A small flower, esp. one of the disk or ray flowers of a composite plant, such as a daisy. [ME *flouret* < OFr. *florete,* dim. of *flor,* flower. —see FLOWER.]

flo·ri·at·ed also **flo·re·at·ed** (flôr'ē-ā'tĭd, flōr'-) *adj.* Decorated with floral designs. [< Lat. *flos, flor-,* flower.]

flo·ri·bun·da (flôr'ə-bŭn'də, flōr'-) *n.* Any of several hybrid roses bearing numerous single or double flowers. [NLat., fem. of *floribundus,* blossoming freely < Lat. *flos,* flower.]

flo·ri·cul·ture (flôr'ĭ-kŭl'chər, flōr'-) *n.* The cultivation of flowering plants. [Lat. *flos, flor-,* flower + CULTURE.] **—flo'ri·cul'tur·al** *adj.* **—flo'ri·cul'tur·al·ly** *adv.* **—flo'ri·cul'tur·ist** *n.*

flor·id (flôr'ĭd, flŏr'-) *adj.* **1.** Flushed with rosy color; ruddy. **2.** Heavily decorated or embellished; ornate: *a florid prose style.* **3.** *Archaic.* Healthy; blooming. **4.** *Obs.* Abounding in or covered with flowers. [Fr. *floride* < Lat. *floridus* < *florere,* to bloom < *flos,* flower.] **—flo·rid'i·ty** (flə-rĭd'ĭ-tē, flô-), **flor'id·ness** *n.* **—flor'id·ly** *adv.*

flo·rif·er·ous (flô-rĭf'ər-əs) *adj.* Bearing flowers, esp. in abundance. [Lat. *florifer,* bearing flowers : *flos,* flower + *ferre,* to bear + -OUS.] **—flo·rif'er·ous·ly** *adv.* **—flo·rif'er·ous·ness** *n.*

flor·i·gen (flôr'ə-jən, flōr'-) *n.* A plant hormone that stimulates the flowering of buds. [Lat. *flos, flor-,* flower + -GEN.] **—flor'i·gen'ic** (-jĕn'ĭk) *adj.*

flor·in (flôr'ĭn, flŏr'-) *n.* **1.** A former British coin worth two shillings. **2.** A guilder. **3. a.** A gold coin first issued at Florence, Italy, in 1252. **b.** Any of several former European gold coins similar to the Florentine florin. [ME < OFr. < OItal. *fiorino* < *fiore,* flower < Lat. *flos,* flower.]

flo·rist (flôr'ĭst, flōr'-, flŏr'-) *n.* A person whose business is the raising or selling of flowers and ornamental plants. [Lat. *flos, flor-,* flower + -IST.]

flo·ris·tics (flô-rĭs'tĭks, flō-) *n.* The study of the numerical distribution of plants. **—flo·ris'tic** *adj.* **—flo·ris'ti·cal·ly** *adv.*

-florous *suff.* Having a specified kind or number of flowers: *tubuliflorous.* [LLat. *-florus* < Lat. *flos,* flower.]

flos·cu·lus (flŏs'kyə-ləs) *n.* A floret. [Lat., dim. of *flos,* flower.]

floss (flôs, flŏs) *n.* **1.** Short or waste silk fibers. **2.** A soft, loosely twisted thread used in embroidery. **3.** A soft, silky fibrous substance, such as corn silk. *—v.* **flossed, floss·ing, floss·es.** *—tr.* To clean between (teeth) with dental floss. *—intr.* To use dental floss. [Perh. < Fr. *floche,* down < OFr. *flosche.*]

floss·y (flô'sē, flŏs'ē) *adj.* **-i·er, -i·est.** **1.** Made of or resembling floss. **2.** *Slang.* Ostentatiously stylish; flashy.

flo·tage also **float·age** (flō'tĭj) *n.* **1.** Flotation (sense 1). **2.** Floating objects or material.

flo·ta·tion also **floa·ta·tion** (flō-tā'shən) *n.* **1.** The act or condition of floating. **2.** An act or instance of launching or financing a business venture by selling an issue of stocks or bonds. **3.** Any of several processes in which different materials, notably minerals, are separated by agitation of a pulverized mixture of the materials with water, oil, and chemicals that cause differential wetting of the suspended particles, the unwetted particles being carried by air bubbles to the surface for collection.

flo·til·la (flō-tĭl'ə) *n.* **1. a.** A fleet of small ships. **b.** A small fleet of ships. **2.** A group resembling a small fleet: *a flotilla of taxis.* [Sp., dim. of *flota,* fleet < OFr. *flote* < ON *floti.*]

flot·sam (flŏt'səm) *n.* **1.** Wreckage or cargo that remains afloat after a ship has sunk. **2. a.** Discarded odds and ends. **b.** Unemployed and vagrant people; drifters. [AN *floteson* < OFr. *floter,* to float, of Germanic orig.]

Usage: *Flotsam,* in maritime law, applies to wreckage or cargo left floating on the sea after a shipwreck. *Jetsam* applies to cargo or equipment thrown overboard (jettisoned) from a ship in distress and either sunk or washed ashore. The common phrase *flotsam and jetsam* is now used loosely to describe any objects found floating or washed ashore.

flounce[1] (flouns) *n.* A strip of gathered or pleated material attached along its upper edge to another surface, as on a garment or curtain. *—tr.v.* **flounced, flounc·ing, flounc·es.** To trim with a flounce. [Alteration of *frounce* < ME, pleat < OFr. *fronce.*]

flounce[2] (flouns) *intr.v.* **flounced, flounc·ing, flounc·es.** **1.** To move with exaggerated motions: *flounced out of the house.* **2.** To flounder or struggle. *—n.* The act or motion of flouncing. [Poss. of Scand. orig.]

floun·der[1] (floun'dər) *intr.v.* **-dered, -der·ing, -ders.** **1.** To make clumsy attempts to move or to regain one's balance. **2.** To proceed clumsily and in confusion. *—n.* The act of floundering. —See Usage note at **founder.** [Prob. alteration of FOUNDER.]

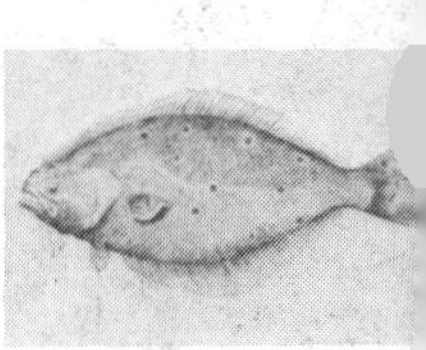
flounder[2]

floun·der[2] (floun'dər) *n.* Any of various marine flatfishes of the families Bothidae and Pleuronectidae, which include important food fishes. [ME, of Scand. orig.]

flour (flour) *n.* **1.** A soft, fine, powdery substance obtained by grinding and sifting the meal of a grain, esp. wheat. **2.** A soft, fine powder. *—tr.v.* **floured, flour·ing, flours.** **1.** To cover or coat with flour. **2.** To make into flour. [ME. —see FLOWER.] **—flour'y** *adj.*

flour·ish (flûr'ĭsh, flŭr'-) *v.* **-ished, -ish·ing, -ish·es.** *—intr.* **1.** To grow well or luxuriantly; thrive. **2.** To fare well; prosper: *"No village on the railroad failed to flourish"* (John Kenneth Galbraith). **3.** To be in one's prime. **4.** To make bold, sweeping movements. *—tr.* To wield, wave, or exhibit dramatically: *flourish a baton.* *—n.* **1.** An act or instance of waving or brandishing. **2.** An embellishment or ornamentation, esp. in writing. **3.** A dramatic action or gesture. **4.** A musical fanfare or similar passage. [ME *florishen* < OFr. *florir, floriss-,* to bloom < VLat. **florire* < Lat. *florere* < *flos,* flower.] **—flour'ish·er** *n.*

flout (flout) *v.* **flout·ed, flout·ing, flouts.** *—tr.* To show contempt for; scorn. *—intr.* To be scornful. *—n.* A contemptuous action or remark; insult. —See Usage note at **flaunt.** [Prob. < ME *flouten,* to play the flute < OFr. *flauter* < *flaute,* flute.] **—flout'er** *n.* **—flout'ing·ly** *adv.*

flow (flō) *v.* **flowed, flow·ing, flows.** *—intr.* **1.** To move or run freely in the manner characteristic of a fluid. **2.** To circulate, as the blood in the body. **3.** To discharge a stream; pour forth. **4.** To move with a continual shifting of the component particles: *Wheat flowed into the bin.* **5.** To proceed steadily and easily: *The preparations flowed smoothly.* **6.** To appear smooth, harmonious, or graceful. **7.** To rise. Used of the tide. **8.** To arise; derive: *Several conclusions flow from this hypothesis.* **9. a.** To abound or be plentiful. **b.** To overflow or flood. **10.** To hang loosely and gracefully: *The cape flowed from his shoulders.* **11.** To undergo plastic deformation without cracking or breaking. *—tr.* **1.** To release as a flow. **2.** To cause to flow. *—n.* **1. a.** The smooth motion characteristic of fluids. **b.** The act of flowing. **2.** A stream. **3. a.** A continuous output or outpouring: *a flow of ideas.* **b.** A continuous movement or circulation: *the flow of traffic.* **4.** The amount that flows in a given period of time. **5.** A rising and overflowing, esp. of dry land, of a body of water. **6.** Continuity and smoothness of appearance. **7.** Menstrual discharge. **8.** The rising of the tide. [ME *flouen* < OE *flō-wan.*] **—flow′ing·ly** *adv.*

flow·age (flō′ĭj) *n.* **1.** The act of flowing or overflowing. **2.** The state of being flooded. **3.** A liquid that flows or overflows. **4.** The gradual plastic deformation of a solid body, as by heat.

flow chart *n.* A schematic representation of a sequence of operations.

flow diagram *n.* A flow chart.

flow·er (flou′ər) *n.* **1. a.** The reproductive structure of a seed-bearing plant, characteristically having specialized male and female organs, such as stamens and a pistil, enclosed in an outer envelope of petals and sepals. **b.** Such a structure having showy or colorful parts; blossom. **c.** A reproductive organ of other plants such as mosses. **2.** A plant cultivated or conspicuous for its blossoms. **3.** The period of highest development; peak. **4.** The highest example or best representative of something: *the flower of our generation.* **5.** An embellishment. **6. flowers.** *Chem.* A fine powder produced by condensation or sublimation. *—v.* **-ered, -er·ing, -ers.** *—intr.* **1.** To produce a flower; blossom. **2.** To develop fully; peak. *—tr.* To decorate with flowers or with a floral pattern. [ME *flour* < OFr. *flor* < Lat. *flos.*] **—flow′er·er** *n.* **—flow′er·less** *adj.*

flow·er·age (flou′ər-ĭj) *n.* **1.** Flowers collectively. **2.** The process or state of flowering.

flower bug *n.* Any of a group of bugs from the family Anthocoridae that feed on insects that infest flowers.

flow·er·et (flou′ər-ĭt) *n.* A small flower.

flower girl *n.* A very young girl who carries flowers in a procession, esp. at a wedding.

flowering dogwood *n.* The dogwood.

flowering maple *n.* Any of several tropical shrubs of the genus *Abutilon,* esp. *A. hybridum,* having lobed leaves resembling those of the maple and variously colored flowers.

flowering plant *n.* An angiosperm.

flowering quince *n.* Any of several shrubs of the genus *Chaenomeles,* native to Asia, having spiny branches and red or pink flowers.

flow·er·pot (flou′ər-pŏt′) *n.* A pot in which plants are grown.

flow·er·y (flou′ə-rē) *adj.* **-i·er, -i·est. 1.** Abounding in or bedecked with flowers. **2.** Suggestive of flowers. **3.** Full of figurative and ornate expressions: *a flowery speech.* **—flow′er·i·ness** *n.*

flow meter *n.* An apparatus for monitoring, measuring, or recording fluid flow, as of a gaseous fuel.

flown[1] (flōn) *adj. Archaic.* Filled to excess. [Obs. p.part. of FLOW.]

flown[2] (flōn) *v.* Past participle of **fly**[1].

flow sheet *n.* A flow chart.

flu (flo͞o) *n. Informal.* Influenza.

flub (flŭb) *tr.v.* **flubbed, flub·bing, flubs.** To botch or bungle. *—n.* An act or instance of flubbing. **—flub′ber** *n.*

flub·dub (flŭb′dŭb′) *n. Slang.* Pretentious nonsense; bunkum. [Orig. unknown.]

fluc·tu·ant (flŭk′cho͞o-ənt) *adj.* Variable or unstable. [Lat. *fluctuans, fluctuant-,* pr.part. of *fluctuare,* to fluctuate.]

fluc·tu·ate (flŭk′cho͞o-āt′) *v.* **-at·ed, -at·ing, -ates.** *—intr.* **1.** To vary irregularly: *prices fluctuating dramatically.* **2.** To rise and fall like waves; undulate. *—tr.* To cause to fluctuate. [Lat. *fluctuare, fluctuat-* < *fluctus,* a flowing < p.part. of *fluere,* to flow.] **—fluc′tu·a′tion** *n.*

flue[1] (flo͞o) *n.* **1.** A pipe, tube, or channel through which hot air, gas, steam, or smoke may pass. **2. a.** A flue pipe. **b.** The air passage in such a pipe. [Orig. unknown.]

flue[2] (flo͞o) *n.* One of several kinds of fishing net. [ME < MDu. *vlūwe.*]

flu·ent (flo͞o′ənt) *adj.* **1.** Having facility in the use of language: *fluent in three languages.* **2. a.** Flowing effortlessly; polished. **b.** Flowing smoothly; graceful: *fluent curves.* **3.** Flowing or capable of flowing; fluid. [Lat. *fluens, fluent-,* pr.part. of *fluere,* to flow.] **—flu′en·cy** *n.* **—flu′ent·ly** *adv.*

flue pipe *n.* An organ pipe sounded by means of a current of air striking a lip in the side of the pipe and causing the air within to vibrate.

flu·er·ic (flo͞o-ĕr′ĭk) *adj.* Fluidic. [Lat. *fluere,* to flow + -IC.]

flu·er·ics (flo͞o-ĕr′ĭks) *n.* Fluidics.

fluff (flŭf) *n.* **1.** Light down or nap. **2.** Something having a light, soft, or frothy consistency or appearance. **3.** Something of little consequence. **4.** *Informal.* An error, esp. in the delivery of lines, as by an actor or announcer. *—v.* **fluffed, fluff·ing, fluffs.** *—tr.* **1.** To make light and puffy by shaking or patting into a soft, loose mass: *fluff a pillow.* **2.** *Informal.* **a.** To ruin or mar by an error. **b.** To misread or forget (one's lines). *—intr.* **1.** To become soft and puffy or feathery. **2.** *Informal.* To make an error, esp. to forget or botch one's lines. [Orig. unknown.]

fluff·y (flŭf′ē) *adj.* **-i·er, -i·est. 1.** Of, like, or covered with fluff or down. **2.** Light and airy; soft: *fluffy curls.* **—fluff′i·ly** *adv.* **—fluff′i·ness** *n.*

flü·gel·horn (flo͝o′gəl-hôrn′, flü′-) *n.* A bugle with valves, similar to the cornet but having a wider bore. [G. : *Flügel,* flank (from its use to summon flanks during a battle) + *Horn.*]

flu·id (flo͞o′ĭd) *n.* A substance that exists or is regarded as existing as a continuum characterized by low resistance to flow and the tendency to assume the shape of its container. *—adj.* **1.** Characteristic of a fluid, esp. flowing easily. **2.** Used in the measurement of fluids. **3.** Readily deformed; pliable. **4.** Smooth and effortless. **5.** Easily changed or tending to change: *a fluid situation fraught with uncertainty.* **6.** Convertible into cash: *fluid assets.* [Fr. *fluide* < Lat. *fluidus,* flowing < *fluere,* to flow.] **—flu·id′i·ty** (-ĭd′ĭ-tē), **flu′id·ness** *n.* **—flu′id·ly** *adv.*

fluid dram *n.* One-eighth of a fluid ounce.

flu·id·ex·tract (flo͞o′ĭd-ĕk′străkt′) *n.* A concentrated alcohol solution of a vegetable drug containing the equivalent of one gram in powdered form of the active principle in each milliliter.

flu·id·ic (flo͞o-ĭd′ĭk) *adj.* Of, pertaining to, or being a device operated by fluids. **—flu·id′ic** *n.*

flu·id·ics (flo͞o-ĭd′ĭks) *n. (used with a sing. verb).* The technology of fluids used as nonmoving, nonelectrical components of control and sensing systems.

fluid ounce *n.* **1.** A unit of volume or capacity in the U.S. Customary System, used in liquid measure, equal to 1.804 cubic inches. **2.** A unit of volume or capacity in the British Imperial System, used in liquid and dry measure, equal to 1.734 cubic inches.

fluke[1] (flo͞ok) *n.* **1.** *pl.* **fluke.** Any of various flatfishes, esp. a flounder of the genus *Paralichthys.* **2.** A trematode. [ME < OE *flōc.*]

fluke[2] (flo͞ok) *n.* **1.** The triangular blade at the end of either arm of an anchor, designed to catch in the ground. **2.** A barbed head, as on an arrow. **3.** One of the two horizontally flattened divisions of the tail of a whale or related animal. [Poss. < FLUKE[1].]

fluke[3] (flo͞ok) *n.* **1.** An accidentally good or successful stroke in billiards or pool. **2.** A stroke of good luck. [Orig. unknown.]

fluk·y also **fluk·ey** (flo͞o′kē) *adj.* **-i·er, -i·est. 1.** Resulting from mere chance. **2.** Constantly shifting; uncertain: *a fluky wind.* [< FLUKE[3].]

flume (flo͞om) *n.* **1.** A narrow defile or gorge, usually with a stream flowing through it. **2.** An artificial channel or chute for a stream of water. [ME *flum,* river < OFr. < Lat. *flumen* < *fluere,* to flow.]

flum·mer·y (flŭm′ə-rē) *n., pl.* **-ies. 1. a.** Any of several soft, light, bland foods, such as a custard. **b.** A soft jelly made by straining boiled, slightly fermented oatmeal or flour. **2.** Meaningless flattery or nonsense; humbug. [Welsh *llymru.*]

flum·mox (flŭm′əks) *tr.v.* **-moxed, -mox·ing, -mox·es.** *Slang.* To confuse; perplex. [Orig. unknown.]

flung (flŭng) *v.* Past tense and past participle of **fling.**

flunk (flŭngk) *Informal. —v.* **flunked, flunk·ing, flunks.** *—intr.* To fail esp. in an examination or course. *—tr.* **1.** To fail (an examination or course). **2.** To give a failing grade to. ***—phrasal verb.* flunk out.** To expel or be expelled from a school or course because of work that does not meet required standards. *—n.* A failing grade. [Orig. unknown.]

flun·ky also **flun·key** (flŭng′kē) *n., pl.* **-kies** also **-keys. 1.** A liveried manservant. **2.** An obsequious or fawning person; toady. **3.** A person who does menial or trivial work. [Sc.] **—flun′ky·ism** *n.*

flu·or (flo͞o′ôr′, -ər) *n.* Fluorite. [NLat., mineral belonging to a group used as fluxes < Lat., a flowing < *fluere,* to flow.]

fluor– *pref.* Variant of **fluoro-.**

flu·o·resce (flo͞o′ə-rĕs′, flo͞o-rĕs′) *intr.v.* **-resced, -resc·ing, -resc·es.** To undergo, produce, or show fluorescence. [Back-formation < FLUORESCENCE.]

flu·o·res·ce·in (flo͞o′ə-rĕs′ē-ĭn, flo͞o-rĕs′-) *n.* An orange-red compound, $C_{20}H_{12}O_5$, that exhibits intense fluorescence in alkaline solution and is used to dye sea water for spotting or tracing operations.

flu·o·res·cence (flo͞o′ə-rĕs′əns, flo͞o-rĕs′-) *n.* **1.** The emission of electromagnetic radiation, esp. of visible light, resulting from the absorption of incident radiation and persisting only as long as the stimulating radiation is continued. **2.** The radiation emitted by fluorescence. [FLUOR + -ESCENCE.]

fluorescence microscopy *n.* Microscopy in which the specimens are stained with a fluorescent dye and viewed by illumination with ultraviolet light.

flu·o·res·cent (flo͞o′ə-rĕs′ənt, flo͞o-rĕs′-) *adj.* Exhibiting or capable of exhibiting fluorescence.

fluorescent lamp *n.* A lamp that produces visible light by fluorescence, esp. a glass tube whose inner wall is coated with a material that fluoresces when bombarded with secondary radiation generated by a gaseous discharge within the tube.

fluor·i·date (flo͝or′ĭ-dāt′, flôr′-, flōr′-) *tr.v.* **-dat·ed, -dat·ing, -dates.** To add a fluorine compound to (a water supply, for example) for the purpose of preventing tooth decay. **—fluor′i·da′tion** *n.*

flu·o·ride (flo͞o′ə-rīd′, flo͝or′īd′, flôr′-, flōr′-) *n.* A binary compound of fluorine with another element.

fluor·i·na·tion (flo͝or′ĭ-nā′shən, flôr′-, flōr′-) *n.* The chemical introduction of fluorine into a compound.

flu·o·rine (flo͞o′ə-rēn′, -rĭn, flo͝or′ēn′, -ĭn, flôr′-, flōr′-) *n.* *Symbol* **F** A pale-yellow, highly corrosive, poisonous, gaseous halogen element, the most electronegative and most

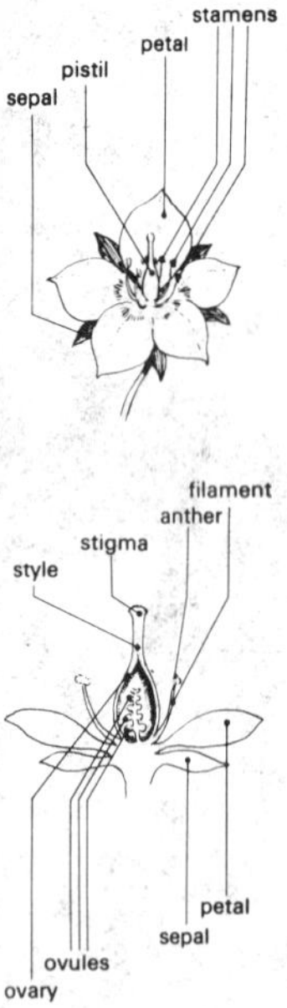

flower
Flower (*above*) and cross section showing details

reactive of all the elements, used in a wide variety of industrially important compounds. Atomic number 9; atomic weight 18.9984; freezing point -219.62°C; boiling point -188.14°C; specific gravity of liquid 1.108; valence 1. [FLUOR + -INE².]

fluor·ite (flo͝or′īt′, flôr′-, flōr′-) *n.* A generally light-colored green, blue, violet, yellow, brown, or colorless mineral, essentially CaF_2, that is often fluorescent in ultraviolet light. [Ital.]

fluoro- or **fluor-** *pref.* **1.** Fluorine: *fluorosis.* **2.** Fluorescence: *fluoroscope.*

flu·o·ro·car·bon (flo͞o′ə-rō-kär′bən, flo͝or′ō-) *n.* Any of various inert organic compounds in which fluorine replaces hydrogen, used as aerosol propellants, refrigerants, solvents, and lubricants and in making plastics and resins.

fluor·o·chrome (flo͝or′ə-krōm′, flôr′-) *n.* Any of a group of fluorescent dyes used in the staining of microorganisms to be examined by fluorescence microscopy.

flu·o·rom·e·ter (flo͞o′ə-rŏm′ĭ-tər, flo͞o-rŏm′-) *n.* An instrument for detecting and measuring fluorescence. **—flu′o·rom′e·try** *n.*

fluor·o·scope (flo͝or′ə-skōp′, flôr′-, flōr′-, flo͞o′ər-ə-) *n.* A fluorescent screen on which the internal structure of an optically opaque object, as of the human body, may be continuously viewed by transmission of x-rays through the object. *—tr.v.* **-scoped, -scop·ing, -scopes.** To examine the interior of with a fluoroscope. **—fluor′o·scop′ic** (-skŏp′ĭk) *adj.* **—fluor′o·scop′i·cal·ly** *adv.*

flu·o·ros·co·py (flo͞o′ə-rŏs′kə-pē, flo͞o-rŏs′-) *n.* Examination with the use of a fluoroscope.

flu·o·ro·sis (flo͞o′ə-rō′sĭs, flo͞o-rō′-) *n.* An abnormal condition caused by excessive intake of fluorine, characterized chiefly by mottling of the teeth. **—flu′o·rot′ic** (-rŏt′ĭk) *adj.*

flu·o·ro·u·ra·cil (flo͞o′ə-rō-yo͝or′ə-sĭl, flo͝or′ō-) *n.* A pyrimidine, $C_4H_3FN_2O_2$, used as an anticancer drug.

flu·or·spar (flo͞o′ər-spär′, flo͝or′spär′) *n.* A fluorite.

flur·ry (flûr′ē, flŭr′ē) *n., pl.* **-ries. 1.** A sudden gust of wind. **2.** A light snowfall. **3.** A sudden burst of confusion, excitement, or bustling activity. **4.** *Commerce.* A short period of active trading, as on the stock exchange. *—v.* **-ried, -ry·ing, -ries.** *—tr.* To agitate, confuse, or make nervous; fluster. *—intr.* To move or come down in a gust or flurry. [< obs. *flurr,* to scatter.]

flush¹ (flŭsh) *v.* **flushed, flush·ing, flush·es.** *—intr.* **1.** To flow and spread out suddenly and abundantly. **2.** To turn red in the face; blush. **3.** To glow, esp. with a reddish color. **4. a.** To be cleaned by a rapid, brief gush of water. **b.** To function by means of a flushing mechanism, as a toilet. *—tr.* **1.** To cause to redden or glow. **2.** To excite or elate, as with a feeling of pride or accomplishment: *flushed with victory.* **3.** To wash, empty, or purify with a sudden, rapid flow of water. *—n.* **1.** A brief but copious flow or gushing, as of water. **2.** A blush or glow. **3.** Redness of the skin, as with fever. **4.** A feeling of animation or exhilaration. **5.** A state of freshness or vigor: *the first flush of youth.* *—adj.* **-er, -est. 1.** Having a healthy reddish color. **2.** Marked by abundance; plentiful. **3.** Having an abundant supply of money; affluent. **4.** Lively and vigorous; lusty. **5. a.** Having surfaces in the same plane; even. **b.** Arranged with adjacent sides, surfaces, or edges close together: *a sofa flush against the wall.* **c.** With margins aligned with no indentations. **6.** Direct, straightforward, or solid, as a blow. *—adv.* **1.** So as to be even, in one plane, or aligned with a margin. **2.** Squarely or solidly: *The ball hit him flush on the face.* [Prob. < *flush,* to dart out.]

flush² (flŭsh) *n.* A hand in which all the cards are of the same suit, rated above a straight and below a full house in a game such as poker. [OFr. *flus* < Lat. *fluxus,* flux.]

flush³ (flŭsh) *v.* **flushed, flush·ing, flush·es.** *—tr.* To frighten (a game bird, for example) from cover. *—intr.* To dart out or fly from cover. *—n.* A bird or a flock of birds suddenly taking flight. [ME *flusshen.*]

flus·ter (flŭs′tər) *tr. & intr.v.* **-tered, -ter·ing, -ters.** To make or become nervous or upset. *—n.* A state of agitation, confusion, or excitement. [Prob. of Scand. orig.]

flute (flo͞ot) *n.* **1.** A high-pitched instrument of the woodwind family, tubular in shape and with finger holes and keys on the side and a reedless mouthpiece either at the end, as in the recorder, or on the side, as in the transverse flute. **2.** An organ stop whose flue pipe produces a flutelike tone. **3.** *Archit.* One of the rounded, parallel grooves incised on the shaft of a column as a decorative motif. **4.** A groove in cloth, as in a pleated ruffle. *—v.* **flut·ed, flut·ing, flutes.** *—tr.* **1.** To play (a tune) on a flute. **2.** To produce in a flutelike tone. **3.** To make flutes in. *—intr.* **1.** To play a flute. **2.** To sing or whistle with a flutelike tone. [ME *floute* < OFr.] **—flut′er** *n.*

flut·ing (flo͞o′tĭng) *n.* **1.** A decorative motif consisting of a series of long, rounded, parallel grooves, such as those incised in the surface of a column. **2.** The grooves formed by narrow pleats in cloth, as in a ruffle. **3.** The act of incising or making grooves.

flut·ist (flo͞o′tĭst) *n.* One who plays the flute.

flut·ter (flŭt′ər) *v.* **-tered, -ter·ing, -ters.** *—intr.* **1.** To wave or flap rapidly in an irregular manner: *curtains fluttering in the breeze.* **2. a.** To fly by a quick, light flapping of the wings. **b.** To flap the wings without flying. **3.** To vibrate or beat rapidly or erratically: *His heart fluttered wildly.* **4.** To move quickly in a nervous, restless, or excited fashion; flit. *—tr.* To cause to flutter. *—n.* **1.** An act of fluttering. **2.** A condition of nervous excitement or agitation. **3.** A commotion; flurry. **4.** *Pathol.* Abnormal pulsation, as of the heart. **5.** A distortion in reproduced sound due to frequency deviations created by faulty recording or reproduction techniques. [ME *floteren* < OE *flotorian.*] **—flut′ter·er** *n.* **—flut′ter·y** *adj.*

flutter kick *n.* A swimming kick in which the legs are held horizontally and alternately moved up and down in rapid strokes without bending the knees.

flu·vi·al (flo͞o′vē-əl) *adj.* **1.** Of, pertaining to, or inhabiting a river or stream. **2.** Produced by the action of flowing water. [ME < Lat. *fluvialis* < *fluvius,* river < *fluere,* to flow.]

flu·vi·o·ma·rine (flo͞o′vē-ō-mə-rēn′) *adj.* Pertaining to deposits, esp. near the mouth of a river, formed by the joint action of the sea and a river. [Lat. *fluvius,* river < *fluere,* to flow + MARINE.]

flux (flŭks) *n.* **1. a.** A flow or flowing. **b.** A continued flow; flood. **2.** *Physics.* **a.** A flow of matter or energy as a fluid or regarded as a fluid. **b.** Flux density. **c.** The lines of force of a magnetic field. **3.** *Med.* The discharge of large quantities of fluid material from a bodily surface or cavity. **4.** Fluctuation; change: *plans in a state of flux.* **5.** *Chem. & Metallurgy.* A substance that aids, induces, or otherwise actively participates in a flowing, as: **a.** A mineral added to a furnace charge to promote fusing of metals or to prevent the formation of oxides. **b.** A substance applied in soldering and brazing to portions of a surface to be joined, acting on application of heat to prevent oxide formation and to facilitate the flowing of solder. **c.** A readily fusible glass or enamel used as a base in ceramic work. *—v.* **fluxed, flux·ing, flux·es.** *—tr.* **1.** To melt; fuse. **2.** To apply a flux to. *—intr.* **1.** To become fluid. **2.** To flow; stream. [ME < OFr. < Lat. *fluxus* < p.part. of *fluere,* to flow.]

flux density *n. Physics.* The quantity of flux per unit area.

flux gate *n.* A detector used to indicate the direction of the terrestrial magnetic field.

flux·ion (flŭk′shən) *n.* **1.** Continual change. **2.** *Archaic.* **a.** A derivative (sense 3). **b. fluxions.** Differential calculus. [OFr. < Lat. *fluxio* < *fluxus,* flux.] **—flux′ion·al, flux′ion·ar′y** (-shə-nĕr′ē) *adj.* **—flux′ion·al·ly** *adv.*

fly¹ (flī) *v.* **flew** (flo͞o), **flown** (flōn), **fly·ing, flies.** *—intr.* **1.** To move through the air with the aid of wings or winglike parts. **2. a.** To travel by air. **b.** To pilot an aircraft. **3. a.** To rise in or be carried through the air by the wind. **b.** To float or flutter in the air: *pennants flying.* **4.** To be sent or driven through the air with great speed or force: *bullets flying.* **5. a.** To rush; hasten: *flew down the hall.* **b.** To flee; escape. **6.** To pass by swiftly, as time or youth: *a vacation flying by.* **7.** *past tense and past participle* **flied.** *Baseball.* To hit a fly ball. **8.** To react explosively; burst: *He flew into a rage.* *—tr.* **1.** To cause to float or flutter in the air: *fly a flag.* **2. a.** To pilot (an aircraft). **b.** To carry or transport in an aircraft. **c.** To pass over in an aircraft: *fly the ocean.* **d.** To perform in an aircraft: *flew 60 combat missions.* *—n., pl.* **flies. 1.** The act of flying. **2.** A fold of cloth that covers a garment fastening, esp. one on the front of trousers. **3.** A cloth flap that covers an entrance or forms a roof extension for a tent or wagon. **4.** A flyleaf. **5.** *Baseball.* A fly ball. **6. a.** The span of a flag from the staff to the outer edge. **b.** The outer edge of a flag. **7. a.** A flywheel. **b.** An analogous device, esp. one used to regulate the speed of clockwork. **8. flies.** The area directly over the stage of a theater, containing overhead lights and other equipment. **9.** *Chiefly Brit.* A one-horse carriage; hackney. **—*idioms.* fly blind.** To fly an airplane in bad visibility with the aid of instruments. **fly high.** To be elated. **fly in the face (or teeth) of.** To resist or defy openly. **fly off the handle.** To become suddenly enraged. **fly the coop.** *Slang.* To get away; escape. **on the fly. 1.** On the run; in a hurry. **2.** In flight. [ME *flien* < OE *flēogan.*]

fly² (flī) *n., pl.* **flies. 1. a.** Any of numerous winged insects of the order Diptera, esp. one of the family Muscidae, which includes the housefly and the tsetse. **b.** Any of various other flying insects, such as the caddis fly. **2.** A fishing lure simulating a fly. **—*idiom.* fly in the ointment.** Something that detracts from effectiveness; drawback. [ME *flie* < OE *flēoge.*]

fly³ (flī) *adj. Chiefly Brit. Slang.* Mentally alert; sharp. [Prob. < FLY¹.]

fly agaric *n.* A poisonous mushroom, *Amanita muscaria,* usually having a red or orange cap with white patches.

fly·a·way (flī′ə-wā′) *adj.* **1.** Blown by the wind; fluttering or streaming. **2.** Given to frivolity; flighty. **3.** Prepared for flight.

fly ball *n. Baseball.* A ball that is batted in a high arc, usually to the outfield.

fly·blow (flī′blō′) *n.* The egg or larva of a blowfly, usually deposited on food. *—tr.v.* **-blew** (-blo͞o′), **-blown** (-blōn′), **-blow·ing, -blows. 1.** To deposit (flyblows) in. **2.** To contaminate; taint.

fly·blown (flī′blōn′) *adj.* **1.** Contaminated with flyblows. **2.** Tainted; corrupt.

fly book *n.* A case in which artificial flies for fishing are carried.

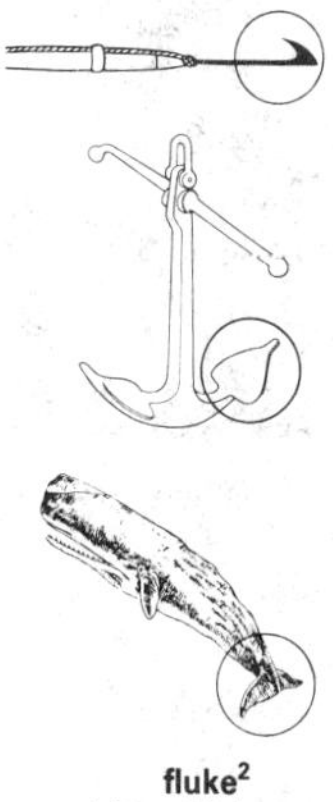

fluke²
Above: Fluke on a harpoon
Center: Fluke of an anchor
Below: Flukes of a sperm whale

flute

George Miksch Sutton
flycatcher

flying buttress

flying squirrel
Above: In a tree
Below: In flight

fly-boy (flī′boi′) *n. Slang.* An air force pilot.
fly-by (flī′bī′) *n., pl.* **-bys.** A flight passing close to a specified target or position, esp. a maneuver in which a spacecraft passes sufficiently close to a planet to make relatively detailed observations without landing.
fly-by-night (flī′bī-nīt′) *adj.* **1.** Of unreliable business character. **2.** Passing; temporary. *—n.* **1.** One who cheats his creditors, as by absconding. **2.** Something of a dubiously transitory nature.
fly·catch·er (flī′kăch′ər, -kĕch′-) *n.* Any of various birds characterized by the habit of flying suddenly from a perch to catch flying insects, esp. a member of the New World family Tyrannidae or the Old World family Muscicapidae.
fly·er (flī′ər) *n.* Variant of **flier.**
fly-fish (flī′fĭsh′) *intr.v.* **-fished, -fish·ing, -fish·es.** To angle using artificial flies for bait.
fly front *n.* A garment front that has a fly concealing the fastenings.
fly gallery *n.* A narrow platform at the side of a theater stage from which a stagehand works the ropes controlling equipment in the flies.
fly·ing (flī′ĭng) *adj.* **1.** Swiftly moving: *flying fingers.* **2.** Brief; hurried: *a flying visit.* **3.** Of, pertaining to, or concerned with aviation. *—n.* **1.** Flight in an aircraft. **2.** The piloting or navigation of an aircraft.
flying boat *n.* A large seaplane that is kept afloat by its hull rather than by pontoons.
flying bomb *n.* A robot bomb (sense 1).
flying buttress *n.* A masonry prop that springs from a solid pier and abuts against another part of the structure to receive thrust.
flying colors *n.* Complete success or victory; triumph.
flying dragon *n.* A flying lizard.
Flying Dutchman *n.* **1.** A legendary Dutch mariner condemned to sail the seas against the wind until Judgment Day. **2.** A spectral ship said to appear in storms near the Cape of Good Hope.
flying fatigue *n.* Aeroneurosis.
flying field *n.* A field graded for airplane landings and takeoffs.
flying fish *n.* Any of various marine fishes of the family Exocoetidae, having enlarged pectoral or pelvic fins capable of sustaining them in brief, gliding flight over the water.
flying fox *n.* **1.** Any of various fruit-eating bats of the genus *Pteropus,* chiefly of tropical Africa, Asia, and Australia, having a foxlike muzzle and ears. **2.** Any of several mammals similar or related to the flying fox.
flying frog *n.* An arboreal frog, *Rhacophorus reinwardtii,* of southeastern Asia, having toes connected by broad webbing and capable of gliding considerable distances.
flying gurnard *n.* Any of various chiefly tropical marine fishes of the family Dactylopteridae, having winglike, much enlarged pectoral fins.
flying head *n.* A device that is designed to read and imprint information on a moving magnetic surface while being supported above that surface by a thin film of air.
flying jib *n.* A light sail that extends beyond the jib and is attached to an extension of the jib boom.
flying lemur *n.* Either of two mammals, *Cynocephalus volans* or *C. variegatus,* of tropical Asia, that are sustained in gliding leaps by a wide, fur-covered membrane extending from each side of the body.
flying lizard *n.* Any of various small tropical Asian lizards of the genus *Draco,* capable of gliding by spreading the winglike membranes on each side of the body.
flying machine *n.* A machine designed for flight, esp. an early experimental type of aircraft.
flying mare *n.* A wrestling throw in which the attacker grabs his opponent's wrist, turns around quickly, and flips him over his shoulder onto the ground.
flying phalanger *n.* Any of several small marsupials of the family Phalangeridae, esp. one of the genus *Petaurus,* of Australia, New Guinea, and Tasmania, capable of gliding through the air sustained by large folds of skin between the forelegs and hind legs.
flying saucer *n.* Any of various unidentified flying objects typically reported and described as luminous disks.
flying squirrel *n.* Any of various squirrels of the genera *Pteromys, Glaucomys,* and related genera, having membranes between the forelegs and hind legs that enable them to glide through the air.
flying start *n.* **1.** The crossing of the starting line of a race at full speed. **2.** A quick start.
fly·leaf (flī′lēf′) *n.* A blank leaf at the beginning or end of a book.
fly net *n.* A net covering used to keep flies off or out.
fly-o·ver (flī′ō′vər) *n.* **1.** A flight of aircraft at low altitude over a specific location, usually as a military display. **2.** *Chiefly Brit.* An overpass on a highway.
fly·pa·per (flī′pā′pər) *n.* Paper coated with a sticky, sometimes poisonous substance to catch flies.
fly-poi·son (flī′poi′zən) *n.* A poisonous plant, *Amianthium muscaetoxicum,* of the southeastern United States, having narrow basal leaves and a terminal cluster of small white or greenish flowers.
fly·speck (flī′spĕk′) *n.* **1.** A small, dark speck or stain made by the excrement of a fly. **2.** A minute spot.
fly swatter *n.* A device used to kill flies or other insects, usually consisting of a flat square of plastic or wire mesh attached to a long handle.
fly·trap (flī′trăp′) *n.* **1.** A trap for catching flies. **2.** A plant, as the Venus's-flytrap, that traps insects.
fly·weight (flī′wāt′) *n.* A boxer of the lightest weight class, weighing 112 pounds or less.
fly·wheel (flī′hwēl′, -wēl′) *n.* A heavy-rimmed rotating wheel used to minimize speed variation in a machine subject to fluctuation in drive and load.
Fm The symbol for the element fermium.
f-num·ber (ĕf′nŭm′bər) *n.* The ratio of focal length to the effective aperture diameter in a lens or lens system. [F(OCAL LENGTH) + NUMBER.]
foal (fōl) *n.* The young offspring of a horse or other equine animal, esp. when under a year old. *—intr.v.* **foaled, foal·ing, foals.** To give birth to a foal. [ME *fole* < OE *fola.*]
foam (fōm) *n.* **1. a.** A mass of gas bubbles in a liquid-film matrix, esp. a light, bubbly gas and liquid mass formed by agitating a liquid containing certain soaps or detergents. **b.** A thick chemically produced froth, as shaving cream or certain firefighting substances. **2. a.** Frothy saliva from the mouth. **b.** The frothy sweat of a horse or other equine animal. **3.** The sea. **4.** Any of various light, bulky, more or less rigid materials used as thermal or mechanical insulators esp. in packaging and containers. *—intr. & tr.v.* **foamed, foam·ing, foams.** To form or cause to form foam. [ME *fom* < OE *fām.*] **—foam′ing·ly** *adv.*
foam·flow·er (fōm′flou′ər) *n.* A woodland plant, *Tiarella cordifolia,* of eastern North America, having a narrow cluster of small white flowers.
foam rubber *n.* A light, firm, spongy rubber made by beating air into latex with subsequent curing and used as an upholstery material and insulating medium.
foam·y (fō′mē) *adj.* **-i·er, -i·est. 1.** Pertaining to or resembling foam. **2.** Consisting of or covered with foam. **—foam′i·ly** *adv.* **—foam′i·ness** *n.*
fob¹ (fŏb) *n.* **1.** A small pocket at the front waistline of a man's trousers or in the front of a vest, used esp. to hold a watch. **2.** A short chain or ribbon attached to a pocket watch and worn hanging in front of the vest or waist. **3.** An ornament or seal attached to a watch chain. [Prob. of Germanic orig.]
fob² (fŏb) *tr.v.* **fobbed, fob·bing, fobs. 1.** To dispose of (goods) by fraud or deception; palm off: *fobbed off the zircon as a diamond.* **2.** To put off by deceitful or evasive means: *needed help but was fobbed off with promises.* [ME *fobben* < *fob,* trickster, prob. < *fob,* froth.]
fo·cal (fō′kəl) *adj.* **1.** Of or pertaining to a focus. **2.** Placed at or measured from a focus. **—fo′cal·ly** *adv.*
focal infection *n.* An infection localized in a specific part of the body.
fo·cal·ize (fō′kə-līz′) *tr. & intr.v.* **-ized, -iz·ing, -iz·es. 1.** To adjust or come to a focus. **2.** To bring or be brought to a focus. **3.** To localize. **—fo′cal·i·za′tion** *n.*
focal length *n.* The distance of a focal point from the surface of a lens or mirror.
focal point *n.* A point on the axis of symmetry of an optical system, as of a mirror or lens, to which parallel incident rays converge or from which they appear to diverge after passing through the system.
fo·ci (fō′sī′) *n.* A plural of **focus.**
fo'c's'le (fōk′səl) *n.* Variant of **forecastle.**
fo·cus (fō′kəs) *n., pl.* **-cus·es** or **-ci** (-sī′). **1. a.** A point in an optical system to which rays converge or from which they appear to diverge; focal point. **b.** Focal length. **c.** The distinctness or clarity with which an optical system renders an image. **d.** Adjustment for distinctness or clarity. **2.** A center of interest or activity. **3.** *Pathol.* The region of a localized bodily infection. **4.** *Geol.* The point of origin of an earthquake. **5.** *Math.* A point that together with a directrix determines a conic section. *—v.* **-cused, -cus·ing, -cus·es** or **-cussed, -cus·sing, -cus·ses.** *—tr.* **1. a.** To produce a clear image of (photographed material, for example) by adjustment of a projection lens or other optical equipment. **b.** To adjust (a lens, for example) to produce a clear image. **2.** To concentrate: *focused all his attention on finding a solution.* *—intr.* To converge at a point of focus; be focused. **—idioms. in focus.** Sharply or clearly defined; distinct. **out of focus.** Blurred or cloudy; indistinct. [NLat. < Lat., hearth.]
fod·der (fŏd′ər) *n.* **1.** Feed for livestock, often consisting of coarsely chopped stalks and leaves of corn mixed with hay. **2. a.** Raw material, as for artistic creation. **b.** Masses of people regarded as raw material for the achievement of a given end: *cannon fodder.* *—tr.v.* **-dered, -der·ing, -ders.** To feed with fodder. [ME < OE *fōdor.*]
foe (fō) *n.* **1.** A personal enemy. **2.** An enemy in war. **3.** An adversary; opponent: *a foe of tax reform.* **4.** Something that serves to oppose, injure, or impede. [ME *fo* < OE *gefā,* foe, and *fāh,* hostile.]
foehn also **föhn** (fœn, fān) *n.* A warm, dry wind coming off the lee slopes of a mountain range. [G. *Föhn* < OHG *phōno* < Lat. *favonius,* the west wind.]
foe·man (fō′mən) *n.* A foe in battle; enemy.

ă pat / ā pay / âr care / ä father / b **bib** / ch **church** / d **deed** / ĕ pet / ē be / f **fife** / g **gag** / h **hat** / hw **which** / ĭ **pit** / ī **pie** / îr **pier** / j **judge** / k **kick** / l lid, needle / m **mum** / n no, sudden / ng thing / ŏ pot / ō **toe** / ô paw, for / oi **noise** / ou **out** / o͝o **took** / o͞o **boot** /

foe·tal (fēt'l) *adj.* Variant of **fetal**.

foe·tid (fē'tĭd) *adj.* Variant of **fetid**.

foe·tor (fē'tər) *n.* Variant of **fetor**.

foe·tus (fē'təs) *n.* Variant of **fetus**.

fog[1] (fôg, fŏg) *n.* **1.** Condensed water vapor in cloudlike masses that lie close to the ground and limit visibility. **2.** A mass of floating material, such as dust or smoke, that forms an obscuring haze. **3.** A state of mental confusion or bewilderment. **4.** A dark blur on a developed photographic negative. *—v.* **fogged, fog·ging, fogs.** *—tr.* **1.** To cover or envelop with or as if with fog. **2.** To cause to be obscured; blur. **3.** To make uncertain or unclear; bewilder. **4.** To obscure or dim (a photographic negative) with a dark blur. *—intr.* **1.** To be covered with or as if with fog. **2.** To be blurred or obscured. **3.** To be dimmed or obscured with a dark blur. Used of a photographic print or negative. [Perh. of Scand. orig.]

fog[2] (fôg, fŏg) *n.* **1.** A second growth of grass appearing on a field that has been mowed or grazed. **2.** Tall, decaying grass left standing after the cutting or grazing season. [ME *fogge,* tall grass.]

fog bank *n.* An opaque mass of fog sharply defined in contrast to surrounding clearer air, esp. such a fog occurring at sea.

fog·bound (fôg'bound', fŏg'-) *adj.* **1.** Immobilized by heavy fog. **2.** Clouded or obscured by fog.

fog·bow (fôg'bō', fŏg'-) *n.* A faint white or yellowish arc-shaped light, similar to a rainbow, often seen opposite the sun in a fog bank.

fog·dog (fôg'dôg', fŏg'dŏg') *n.* A bright or clear spot in a fog bank.

fo·gey (fō'gē) *n.* Variant of **fogy**.

fog·gy (fô'gē, fŏg'ē) *adj.* **-gi·er, -gi·est. 1. a.** Full of or surrounded by fog. **b.** Resembling or suggestive of fog. **2.** Clouded or blurred as if by fog; indistinct. **3.** Bewildered; perplexed. **—fog'gi·ly** *adv.* **—fog'gi·ness** *n.*

fog·horn (fôg'hôrn', fŏg'-) *n.* **1.** A horn used, as by ships, to sound warning signals in fog or darkness. **2.** A resounding, insistent voice.

fo·gy also **fo·gey** (fō'gē) *n., pl.* **-gies** also **-geys.** A person of old-fashioned habits and outmoded attitudes: *an old fogy.* [Orig. unknown.] **—fo'gy·ish** *adj.* **—fo'gy·ism** *n.*

föhn (fœn, fān) *n.* Variant of **foehn**.

foi·ble (foi'bəl) *n.* **1.** A minor weakness or failing of character. **2.** The weaker section of a sword blade, from the middle to the tip. [Obs. Fr. < obs. *foible,* weak < OFr. *feble.* —see FEEBLE.]

foil[1] (foil) *tr.v.* **foiled, foil·ing, foils. 1.** To prevent from being successful; thwart. **2.** To obscure or confuse (a trail or scent) so as to evade pursuers. *—n.* **1.** *Archaic.* A repulse; setback. **2.** The trail or scent of an animal. [ME *foilen,* alteration of *fullen,* to trample, full, and *filen,* to pollute, defile.]

foil[2] (foil) *n.* **1.** A thin, flexible leaf or sheet of metal. **2.** A thin layer of bright metal placed under a displayed gem to lend it brilliance. **3.** One that by strong contrast underscores the distinctive characteristics of another. **4.** The metal coating applied to the back of a plate of glass to form a mirror. **5.** *Archit.* A leaflike design or space worked in stone or glass, found esp. in Gothic window tracery. **6.** *Naut.* A hydrofoil. *—tr.v.* **foiled, foil·ing, foils. 1.** To back or cover with foil. **2.** To set off by contrast. [ME < OFr. < Lat. *folium,* leaf.]

foil[3] (foil) *n.* **1.** A fencing sword with a flat guard for the hand and a thin four-sided blade tipped with a blunt point to prevent injury. **2.** Often **foils.** The art of fencing with foils. [Orig. unknown.]

foils·man (foilz'mən) *n.* One who fences with a foil; fencer.

foin (foin) *Archaic. —intr.v.* **foined, foin·ing, foins.** To thrust with a pointed weapon. *—n.* A thrust with a pointed weapon. [ME *foinen* < *foin,* a thrust < OFr. *foine,* three-pronged fish spear < Lat. *fuscina.*]

foi·son (foi'zən) *n.* **1.** *Archaic.* A plentiful harvest; good crop. **2.** *Scot.* Physical strength or power. **3. foisons.** *Obs.* Reserves of power; resources. [ME *foisoun* < OFr. *foison* < Lat. *fusio,* a pouring < *fusus,* p.part. of *fundere,* to pour.]

foist (foist) *tr.v.* **foist·ed, foist·ing, foists. 1.** To pass off as genuine, valuable, or worthy. **2.** To impose or force upon another by coercion or trickery. **3.** To insert fraudulently or deceitfully: *foisted unfair provisions into the contract.* [Dial. Du. *vuisten,* to introduce a palmed die surreptitiously < *vuist,* fist.]

fo·late (fō'lāt') *n.* Folic acid. [FOL(IC ACID) + -ATE.]

fold[1] (fōld) *v.* **fold·ed, fold·ing, folds.** *—tr.* **1.** To bend over or double up so that one part lies on another part: *fold a sheet of paper.* **2.** To make compact by successively bending over parts: *folded up the camp cot.* **3.** To bring from an extended to a closed position: *The hawk folded its wings.* **4.** To place together and intertwine: *fold one's arms.* **5.** To clasp or entwine; embrace. **6.** To mix in (a cooking ingredient) by slowly and gently turning one part over another: *folded in the beaten egg whites.* *—intr.* **1.** To become folded. **2.** *Informal.* To close for lack of funds; fail financially. **3.** *Informal.* **a.** To give in; yield. **b.** To weaken or collapse from exertion. *—n.* **1.** The act or an instance of folding. **2.** A part that has been folded over another. **3.** The space at the junction of two folded parts. **4.** A hollow or dale in hilly country. **5.** *Geol.* A bend in a stratum of rock. **6.** A coil, as of a snake. **7.** *Anat.* A crease apparently formed by folding, as of a membrane. [ME *folden* < OE *fealdan.*] **—fold'a·ble** *adj.*

fold[2] (fōld) *n.* **1. a.** A fenced enclosure for domestic animals, esp. sheep. **b.** The sheep enclosed in such a pen. **2.** A flock of sheep. **3.** A church and its members. **4.** A group of people bound together by common beliefs and aims. *—tr.v.* **fold·ed, fold·ing, folds.** To place or keep (sheep, for example) in a fold. [ME < OE *fald.*]

-fold *suff.* **1.** Divided into a specified number of parts: *five-fold.* **2.** Multiplied by a specified number: *fiftyfold.* [ME < OE *-feald.*]

fold·boat (fōld'bōt') *n.* A small boat consisting of rubberized canvas stretched over a collapsible frame. [Transl. of G. *Faltboot.*]

fold·er (fōl'dər) *n.* **1.** One that folds. **2.** A booklet or pamphlet made of one or more folded sheets of paper. **3.** A sheet of cardboard or thick paper folded in the center and used as a holder for loose paper.

fol·de·rol (fŏl'də-rŏl') also **fal·de·ral** (făl'də-răl') *n.* **1.** Foolishness; nonsense. **2.** A trifle; gewgaw. [From a refrain in some old songs.]

fold-out (fōld'out') *n.* *Printing.* A gatefold.

fo·li·a (fō'lē-ə) *n.* Plural of **folium**.

fo·li·a·ceous (fō'lē-ā'shəs) *adj.* **1.** Of, relating to, or resembling the leaf of a plant. **2.** Having leaves or leaflike structures. **3.** Consisting of thin laminated layers, as certain rocks. [Lat. *foliāceus* < *folium,* leaf.]

fo·li·age (fō'lē-ĭj, fō'lĭj) *n.* **1. a.** Plant leaves collectively. **b.** A cluster of leaves. **2.** An ornamental representation of leaves, branches, and flowers. [ME *foilage* < OFr. *foillage* < *foille,* leaf < Lat. *folium.*] **—fo'li·aged** *adj.*

foliage plant *n.* A plant cultivated chiefly for its ornamental leaves.

fo·li·ar (fō'lē-ər) *adj.* Of or pertaining to a leaf. [NLat. *foliaris* < Lat. *folium,* leaf.]

fo·li·ate (fō'lē-ĭt, -āt') *adj.* **1.** Of or pertaining to leaves. **2.** Shaped like a leaf. *—v.* (-āt') **-at·ed, -at·ing, -ates.** *—tr.* **1.** To hammer or cut (metal) into thin leaf or foil. **2. a.** To coat (glass, for example) with metal foil. **b.** To furnish or adorn with metal foil. **3.** To separate into thin layers. **4.** To decorate with foliage. **5.** To number the leaves of (a book, for example). *—intr.* **1.** To produce foliage. **2.** To split into thin layers. [Lat. *foliatus,* leafy < *folium,* leaf.]

-foliate *suff.* Having a specified kind or number of leaves: *trifoliate.* [< FOLIATE.]

fo·li·a·tion (fō'lē-ā'shən) *n.* **1.** The state of being in leaf. **2.** Decoration with foliage. **3.** *Archit.* The decoration of an opening with cusps and foils, as in Gothic tracery. **4. a.** The act or process of foliating metal. **b.** The foliating of glass. **5. a.** The process of numbering consecutively the leaves of a book. **b.** The leaves so numbered. [FOLIA(TE) + -TION.]

fo·lic acid (fō'lĭk) *n.* A yellowish-orange compound, $C_{19}H_{19}N_7O_6$, a member of the vitamin-B complex, occurring in green plants, fresh fruit, liver, and yeast and used medicinally to treat pernicious anemias. [Lat. *folium,* leaf + -IC + ACID.]

fo·lie à deux (fô-lē' ä dœ', fŏl'ē) *n.* A condition in which the same delusional ideas or beliefs are shared by two individuals who have a close relationship or association. [Fr.]

fo·li·ic·o·lous (fō'lē-ĭk'ə-ləs) *adj.* Thriving on or parasitic to leaves. [Lat. *folium,* leaf + -COLOUS.]

fo·li·o (fō'lē-ō') *n., pl.* **-os. 1. a.** A large sheet of paper folded once in the middle, making two leaves or four pages of a book or manuscript. **b.** A book or manuscript of the largest common size, usually about 15 inches in height, consisting of such folded sheets. **2.** A leaf of a book numbered only on the front side. **3.** A page number in a book. **4.** *Accounting.* A page in a ledger or two facing pages assigned a single number. **5.** *Law.* A specific number of words used as a unit for measuring the length of the text of a document. *—tr.v.* **-oed, -o·ing, -os.** To number consecutively the pages of (a book, for example). [ME < Lat., ablative of *folium,* leaf.]

-foliolate *suff.* Having a specified kind or number of leaflets: *bifoliolate.* [< *foliole,* leaflet < Fr. < NLat. *foliolum,* dim. of Lat. *folium,* leaf.]

fo·li·ose (fō'lē-ōs') *adj.* **1.** Bearing numerous leaves or leaflets; leafy. **2.** Of, like, or related to a leaf. **3.** Of or pertaining to a lichen whose thallus is flat and leafy. [Lat. *foliosus* < *folium,* leafy.]

fo·li·um (fō'lē-əm) *n., pl.* **-li·a** (-lē-ə). **1.** *Geol.* A thin layer or stratum occurring esp. in metamorphic rock. **2.** *Math.* A plane cubic curve having a single loop, a node, and two ends asymptotic to the same line. [NLat. < Lat., leaf.]

folk (fōk) *n., pl.* **folk** or **folks. 1.** A people; ethnic group. **2.** Often **folks.** People of a specified group or kind: *city folks.* **3. folks.** *Informal.* The members of one's family or childhood household; relatives. **4. folks.** *Informal.* People in general: *Folks will talk.* *—adj.* Of, occurring in, or originating among the common people: *folk art; a folk hero.* [ME < OE *folc.*]

folk dance *n.* **1. a.** A traditional dance originating among the common people of a nation or region. **b.** The music accompanying such a dance. **2.** A social gathering at which folk dances are performed. **—folk dancing** *n.*

folk etymology *n.* A change in form of a word or phrase so

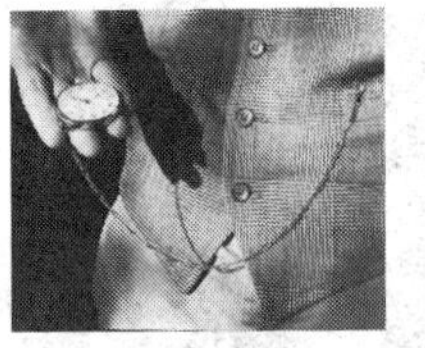

fob[1]

folium
Equation of folium is $x^3 + y^3 = 3axy$, where a is a constant

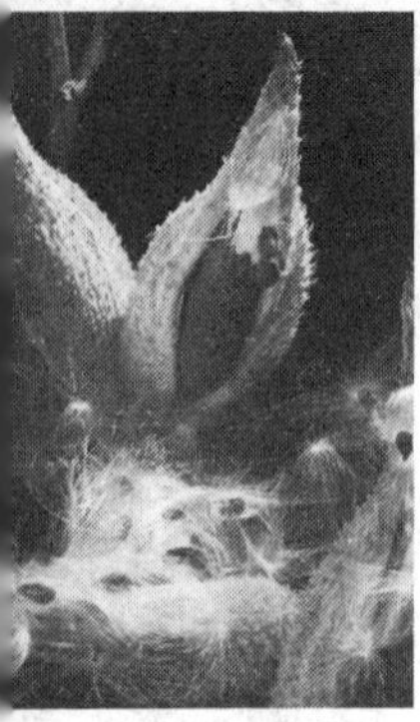

follicle
Milkweed follicles

that it resembles a more familiar term mistakenly taken to be analogous, as *sparrowgrass* for *asparagus.*

folk·lore (fōk'lôr', -lōr') *n.* **1.** The traditional beliefs, practices, legends, and tales of a people, transmitted orally. **2.** The comparative study of folk knowledge and culture. **3.** A body of widely accepted but specious notions about a place, group, or institution: *the folklore of Hollywood.* **—folk'lor'ic** *adj.* **—folk'lor'ist** *n.*

folk mass *n.* A mass in which folk music is used instead of liturgical music as part of the service.

folk medicine *n.* Traditional medicine that is practiced by people who are without access to professional medical services and that usually involves the use of natural remedies, as herbs or vegetable substances.

folk·mote (fōk'mōt') also **folk·moot** (-mo͞ot') *n.* A general assembly of the people of a town, district, or shire in medieval England. [OE *folcmōt* : *folc,* folk + *mōt,* meeting.]

folk music *n.* Music originating among the common people of a nation or region and characterized by a tradition of oral transmission.

folk rock *n.* A variety of popular music that combines elements of rock 'n' roll and folk music, often conveying themes of social protest. **—folk'-rock'** *adj.*

folk singer *n.* A singer of folk songs. **—folk singing** *n.*

folk song *n.* **1.** A song belonging to the folk music of a people or area, characterized chiefly by the directness and simplicity of the feelings expressed. **2.** A song composed in imitation of folk songs.

folk·sy (fōk'sē) *adj.* **-si·er, -si·est.** *Informal.* **1.** Simple and unpretentious in social behavior, sometimes artificially so. **2.** Characterized by congeniality and affability. **—folk'si·ly** *adv.* **—folk'si·ness** *n.*

folk·tale (fōk'tāl') *n.* A traditional, usually anonymous story handed down orally among a people.

folk·way (fōk'wā') *n.* A way of thinking or acting adopted by the members of a group as part of their shared culture.

fol·li·cle (fŏl'ĭ-kəl) *n.* **1.** *Anat.* **a.** An approximately spherical group of cells containing a cavity. **b.** A vascular body in the ovary containing ova. **2.** *Bot.* A single-chambered fruit that splits along only one seam to release its seeds. [Lat. *folliculus,* little bag, dim. of *follis,* bellows.]

fol·li·cle-stim·u·lat·ing hormone (fŏl'ĭ-kəl-stĭm'yə-lā'tĭng) *n.* A gonadotropic hormone of the anterior pituitary gland that stimulates the growth of follicles in the ovary and induces spermatogenesis in the testis.

fol·lic·u·lar (fə-lĭk'yə-lər) *adj.* **1.** Relating to, having, or resembling a follicle. **2.** Affecting or growing out of follicles.

fol·lic·u·late (fə-lĭk'yə-lĭt) also **fol·lic·u·lat·ed** (-lā'tĭd) *adj.* Having or consisting of a follicle or follicles.

fol·lic·u·li·tis (fə-lĭk'yə-lī'tĭs) *n.* Inflammation of a follicle. [Lat. *folliculus,* follicle + -ITIS.]

fol·low (fŏl'ō) *v.* **-lowed, -low·ing, -lows.** *—tr.* **1.** To come or go after: *Follow the usher.* **2.** To move behind with the intention of overtaking; pursue: *followed the suspect.* **3.** To move or go along the course of: *We followed a path to the shore.* **4.** To accept the guidance or leadership of; emulate. **5.** To be the result of: *A fight followed the argument.* **6. a.** To act in agreement with; obey: *follow the rules.* **b.** To keep to or stick to: *followed the recipe.* **7.** To come after in order, time, or position: *Night follows day.* **8.** To engage in (a trade or occupation); work at. **9.** To be evident as a consequence of: *Your conclusion does not follow your premise.* **10.** To be attentive to: listen to or watch closely: *too sleepy to follow the sermon.* **11.** To grasp the meaning or logic of; understand: *Do you follow my argument?* **12.** To inform oneself of the course or progress of: *follow the stock market.* *—intr.* **1.** To come, move, or take place after another person or thing in order or time. **2.** To occur or be evident as a consequence; result: *If you ignore your diet, trouble will follow.* **3.** To grasp the meaning or reasoning of what is said; understand. ***—phrasal verbs.*** **follow through.** **1.** *Sports.* To carry a stroke to natural completion after hitting the ball. **2.** To carry an act or project to completion; pursue fully. **follow up.** **1.** To carry to completion; follow through. **2.** To increase the effectiveness of by repetition or further action. *—n.* **1.** The act or an instance of following. **2.** A billiards shot in which the cue ball is struck in such a way that it follows the path of the object ball after impact. [ME *folowen* < OE *folgian.*]

font[1]

Synonyms: *follow, succeed, supplant, ensue, result, supervene.* These verbs mean to come after something or someone. *Follow,* which has the widest application, can refer to coming after in time or order, as a consequence or result, or by the operation of logic. *Succeed* involves coming after in time or order, especially in planned order determined by rank, inheritance, election, or the like. The term commonly is applied to the act of a person who takes the place of another or to a thing that extends continuity. *Supplant* usually refers to decisive, especially abrupt or violent, displacement or ouster. *Ensue* applies to a thing that comes after another in time, often as a consequence or logical development. *Result* refers to an event that is discernibly caused by a prior event or events. *Supervene,* in contrast, refers to the coming after of a thing that has little relation to what has preceded and that is therefore unexpected.

Usage: *As follows* (not *as follow*) is the established form of the phrase, no matter whether the noun that precedes it is singular or plural: *The regulations are as follows.*

fol·low·er (fŏl'ō-ər) *n.* **1.** One who subscribes to the teachings or methods of another; adherent. **2.** A pursuer. **3.** An attendant, servant, or subordinate. **4.** A machine element moved by another machine element.

fol·low·ing (fŏl'ō-ĭng) *adj.* **1.** Coming next in time or order: *in the following chapter.* **2.** Now to be enumerated: *The following men will report for duty.* *—adj.* A group or gathering of admirers, adherents, or disciples: *a lecturer with a large following.*

fol·low-through (fŏl'ō-thro͞o') *n.* **1.** The act or process of following through. **2.** The concluding part of a stroke, after a ball has been hit.

fol·low-up (fŏl'ō-ŭp') *n.* **1.** The act or process of following up, esp. so as to increase effectiveness. **2.** A means, as a letter or visit, used to follow up. *—adj.* Designed to follow up, esp. to reinforce previous action: *a follow-up letter.*

fol·ly (fŏl'ē) *n., pl.* **-lies.** **1.** A lack of good sense, understanding, or foresight. **2. a.** An act or instance of foolishness. **b.** A costly undertaking having an absurd or ruinous outcome. **3. follies** *(used with a sing. verb).* An elaborate theatrical revue consisting of a series of musical or dance skits. **4.** *Archaic.* Action or behavior considered immoral or criminal. **5.** *Obs.* Evil; wickedness. [ME *folie* < OFr. < *fol,* foolish < Lat. *follis,* bellows.]

Fol·som (fŏl'səm) *adj.* Of or relating to an early North American culture of the Pleistocene period flourishing east of the Rocky Mountains and notable chiefly for the use of leaf-shaped flint implements. [After *Folsom,* New Mexico.]

Fo·mal·haut (fō'məl-hôt') *n.* The brightest star in the constellation Piscis Austrinus, 24 light-years from earth. [Ar. *fum'l-hūt,* mouth of the fish.]

fo·ment (fō-mĕnt') *tr.v.* **-ment·ed, -ment·ing, -ments.** **1.** To promote the growth of; instigate. **2.** To treat (the skin, for example) by fomentation. [ME *fomenten,* to apply warm liquids to the skin < Lat. *fomentare.*] **—fo·ment'er** *n.*

fo·men·ta·tion (fō'mən-tā'shən, -mĕn-) *n.* **1.** The act of promoting discontent or strife; instigation. **2. a.** A warm, moist medicinal compress; poultice. **b.** The therapeutic application of warmth and moisture.

fo·mite (fō'mīt') *n.* An inanimate object or substance that serves to transfer infectious organisms from one individual to another. [Back-formation < NLat. *fomites,* pl. of Lat. *fomes,* tinder.]

fond[1] (fŏnd) *adj.* **-er, -est.** **1.** Having or expressing feelings of affection; tender: *a fond embrace.* **2.** Having a strong liking or affection: *fond of ballet.* **3.** Immoderately or irrationally affectionate; doting. **4.** Cherished; dear: *my fondest hopes.* **5.** *Archaic.* Naively credulous or dependent; foolish. [ME *fonned,* foolish < *fonnen,* to be foolish < *fonne,* fool.] **—fond'ly** *adv.*

fond[2] (fŏnd) *n.* **1.** A foundation; basis. **2.** The background of a design in lace. [Fr. < Lat. *fons* < Lat. *fundus,* bottom.]

fon·dant (fŏn'dənt) *n.* **1.** A sweet, creamy sugar paste used in candies and icings. **2.** A candy containing fondant. [Fr. < pr.part. of *fondre,* to melt < Lat. *fundere.*]

fon·dle (fŏn'dl) *v.* **-dled, -dling, -dles.** *—tr.* **1.** To handle, stroke, or caress lovingly. **2.** *Obs.* To treat with indulgence and solicitude; pamper. *—intr.* To show fondness or affection by caressing. [Freq. of obs. *fond,* to show fondness for.] **—fon'dler** *n.*

fond·ness (fŏnd'nĭs) *n.* **1.** Warm affection; tender liking. **2.** Strong inclination; relish. **3.** *Archaic.* Naive trustfulness; credulity.

fon·due also **fon·du** (fŏn-do͞o', -dyo͞o') *n.* A hot dish made of melted cheese and wine and eaten with bread. [Fr. < fem. p.part. of *fondre,* to melt. —see FONDANT.]

font[1] (fŏnt) *n.* **1.** A basin holding baptismal water in a church. **2.** A receptacle for holy water; stoup. **3.** The oil reservoir in an oil-burning lamp. **4.** A source of abundance; fount: *a font of knowledge.* [ME < OE < LLat. *fons,* water receptacle for baptism < Lat., fountain.] **—font'al** (fŏn'tl) *adj.*

font[2] (fŏnt) *n.* *Printing.* A complete set of type of one size and face. [OFr., casting < *fondre,* to melt. —see FONDANT.]

fon·ta·nel also **fon·ta·nelle** (fŏn'tn-ĕl') *n.* Any of the soft membranous intervals between the incompletely ossified cranial bones of fetuses and infants. [ME *fontinel* < OFr. *fontanele,* dim. of *fontaine,* fountain.]

fon·ti·na (fŏn-tē'nə) *n.* A ripened cheese of variable texture and flavor that originated in Italy. [Ital.]

food (fo͞od) *n.* **1.** Material, usually of plant or animal origin, containing or consisting of essential body nutrients, as carbohydrates, fats, proteins, vitamins, or minerals, that is taken in and assimilated by an organism to maintain life and growth. **2.** A specified kind of nourishment: *breakfast food; plant food.* **3.** Nourishment eaten in solid form as distinguished from liquid nourishment: *good food and wine.* **4.** Something that nourishes or sustains in a way suggestive of physical nourishment. [ME *fode* < OE *fōda.*]

food chain *n.* A succession of organisms in a community that constitute a feeding chain in which food energy is transferred from one organism to another as each consumes a lower member and in turn is preyed upon by a higher member.

food poisoning *n.* Poisoning caused by eating food contaminated by natural toxins or bacteria, esp. bacteria of the genus *Staphylococcus,* and characterized by vomiting, diarrhea, and prostration.
food processor *n.* An appliance consisting of a container with interchangeable blades that processes food, as by shredding or slicing, at high speed.
food stamp *n.* A stamp issued by the government and sold or given to low-income persons to be redeemed for food.
food·stuff (fo͞od′stŭf′) *n.* A substance that can be used or prepared for use as food.
food vacuole *n.* A vacuole in which phagocytized food is digested.
food web *n.* A complex of interrelated food chains in a community.
foo·fa·raw (fo͞o′fə-rô′) *n.* **1.** Excessive or flashy ornamentation. **2.** A to-do over a trifling matter. [Orig. unknown.]
fool (fo͞ol) *n.* **1.** One who is deficient in judgment, sense, or understanding. **2.** One who acts unwisely on a given occasion: *I was a fool to have refused the job.* **3.** Formerly, a member of a royal or noble household who entertained the court with jests and mimicry; jester. **4.** One who has been or can be easily deceived or imposed upon; dupe: *They made a fool of me.* **5.** *Chiefly Brit.* A dessert made of crushed, stewed fruit mixed with cream or custard and served cold. **6.** *Informal.* A person with a talent or enthusiasm for a certain activity: *a fool for stamp collecting.* **7.** *Obs.* A feebleminded person; idiot. —*v.* **fooled, fool·ing, fools.** —*tr.* **1.** To deceive or trick; dupe. **2.** To take unawares; surprise, esp. pleasantly: *We were sure he would fail, but he fooled us.* —*intr.* **1.** *Informal.* To engage in or amuse oneself with useless or trifling activity: *not working, just fooling around.* **2.** To toy or tamper with aimlessly: *shouldn't fool with matches.* **3.** To act or speak in jest; joke. **4.** To act or speak without but as if with purposeful or harmful intent: *They thought he might shoot, but he was only fooling.* —***phrasal verb.*** **fool away.** To waste (time or money) foolishly; squander. [ME *fol* < OFr. < Lat. *follis,* bellows.]
fool·er·y (fo͞o′lə-rē) *n., pl.* **-ies. 1.** Foolish behavior or speech. **2.** An instance of foolery; jest.
fool·har·dy (fo͞ol′här′dē) *adj.* **-di·er, -di·est.** Unwisely bold or venturesome; rash. [ME *folhardi* < OFr. *fol hardi,* bold fool.] **—fool′har′di·ly** *adv.* **—fool′har′di·ness** *n.*
fool·ish (fo͞o′lĭsh) *adj.* **1.** Lacking good sense or judgment; silly: *foolish remarks.* **2.** Resulting from stupidity or misinformation; unwise: *a foolish decision.* **3.** Devoid of meaning or coherence; inane: *a foolish grin.* **4.** Abashed; embarrassed: *I feel foolish telling you this.* **5.** *Archaic.* Insignificant; worthless. **—fool′ish·ly** *adv.* **—fool′ish·ness** *n.*
Synonyms: *foolish, silly, fatuous, absurd, preposterous, ridiculous, ludicrous.* These adjectives are applied to what is devoid of wisdom or good sense. *Foolish,* the least emphatic and derogatory, usually implies poor judgment in a person or general lack of wisdom or soundness in concepts or entities. *Silly* suggests what lacks point, purpose, or semblance of intellectual content. *Fatuous* intensifies the idea of emptiness or inanity and often also implies, in persons, smugness or lack of awareness of one's stupidity. *Absurd,* together with the remaining terms, implies obvious departure from truth, nature, reason, or common sense. *Preposterous* suggests what is so far from reason or sense that it seems a travesty of them and does not merit consideration. *Ridiculous* refers to what inspires derision and contempt because of its absurdity. *Ludicrous* applies to what causes scornful laughter.
fool·proof (fo͞ol′pro͞of′) *adj.* **1.** Designed so as to be proof against human incompetence, error, or misuse: *a foolproof detonator.* **2.** Always effective; infallible: *a foolproof scheme.*
fools·cap (fo͞olz′kăp′) *n.* **1.** A sheet of writing or printing paper approximately 13x16 inches. **2.** A fool's cap. [From the watermark of a fool's cap with bells orig. used for this paper.]
fool's cap *n.* **1.** A gaily decorated cap, usually with a number of loose peaks tipped with bells, formerly worn by court jesters and clowns. **2.** A dunce cap.
fool's errand *n.* A fruitless errand or undertaking.
fool's gold *n.* A mineral, such as pyrite, found in gold-colored veins or nuggets and sometimes mistaken for gold.
fool's paradise *n.* A state of delusive contentment or false hope.
fool's-pars·ley (fo͞olz′pär′slē) *n.* A poisonous plant, *Aethusa cynapium,* native to Eurasia, having finely divided leaves, clusters of small white flowers, and an unpleasant odor.
foot (fo͝ot) *n., pl.* **feet** (fēt). **1.** The lower extremity of the vertebrate leg that is in direct contact with the ground in standing or walking. **2.** A structure, such as the muscular organ extending from the ventral side of a mollusk, used for locomotion or attachment in an invertebrate animal. **3.** Something resembling or suggestive of a foot in position or function: *the foot of a mountain.* **4.** The lower end of an object or the end opposite the head, as of a bed. **5.** The lowest part or rank: *at the foot of the class.* **6.** The part of a stocking or high-topped boot that encloses the foot. **7.** A manner of moving; step: *walks with a light foot.* **8.** Foot soldiers. **9.** The attachment on a sewing machine that clamps down and guides the cloth. **10.** A metrical unit consisting of a stressed or unstressed syllable or syllables. **11.** A unit of length in the U.S. Customary and British Imperial systems equal to $^1/_3$ yard, or 12 inches. **12. foots.** Sediment that forms during the refining of oil and other liquids; dregs. —*v.* **foot·ed, foot·ing, foots.** —*intr.* **1.** To go on foot; walk. **2.** To dance. —*tr.* **1.** To go by foot over, on, or through; tread. **2.** To provide (a stocking, for example) with a foot. **3.** To add (a column of numbers) and write the total at the bottom; total: *Foot up the bill.* **4.** *Informal.* To pay: *Can you foot the monthly rent?* —***idioms.*** **at (someone's) feet.** Enchanted or fascinated by. **on foot.** Walking or standing; not riding. **put (one's) best foot forward.** *Informal.* To make a good beginning or favorable first impression. **put (one's) foot down.** *Informal.* To assert one's will emphatically; insist on one's way. **put (one's) foot in (one's) mouth.** *Informal.* To make an embarrassing or tactless blunder in speech. [ME *fot* < OE *fōt.*]

football
San Francisco '49ers

foot·age (fo͝ot′ĭj) *n.* **1.** The length or extent of something as expressed in feet. **2.** A portion of motion-picture film, esp. an amount of film depicting a specified event or kind of action: *news footage.*
foot-and-mouth disease (fo͝ot′ən-mouth′) *n.* An acute, highly contagious degenerative but usually nonfatal viral disease of cattle and other cloven-hoofed animals, characterized by fever and the eruption of vesicles around the mouth and hoofs.
foot·ball (fo͝ot′bôl′) *n.* **1. a.** A game played by two teams of 11 players each on a rectangular, 100-yard-long field with goal lines and posts at either end, the object being to gain possession of the ball and advance it in running or passing plays across the opponent's goal line. **b.** The inflated oval ball used in this game. **2.** *Chiefly Brit.* **a.** Rugby football. **b.** The ball used in Rugby football. **3.** *Chiefly Brit.* **a.** Soccer. **b.** The ball used in soccer. **4.** A problem or issue that is passed about among groups or persons without being settled: *The tax-reform issue became a political football.*
foot·board (fo͝ot′bôrd′, -bōrd′) *n.* **1.** A board or small raised platform on which to support or rest the feet, as in a carriage. **2.** An upright board across the foot of a bedstead.
foot·boy (fo͝ot′boi′) *n.* A youth employed as a servant or page.
foot brake *n.* A brake operated by pressure of the foot on a pedal, as in an automobile.
foot·bridge (fo͝ot′brĭj′) *n.* A bridge designed to carry pedestrians.

footbridge

foot-can·dle (fo͝ot′kăn′dl) *n.* *Physics.* The illumination of a surface one foot distant from a source of one candela, equal to one lumen per square foot.
foot·cloth (fo͝ot′klôth′, -klŏth′) *n.* **1.** A richly ornamented cloth draped over the back of a horse and touching the ground. **2.** *Obs.* A carpet or rug.
foot-drag·ging (fo͝ot′drăg′ĭng) *n.* Failure to take prompt or required action. **—foot′-drag′ger** *n.*
foot·ed (fo͝ot′ĭd) *adj.* **1.** Having a foot or feet. **2.** Having a specified kind or number of feet: *web-footed.*
foot·er (fo͝ot′ər) *n.* **1.** One who goes on foot; pedestrian. **2.** A person or thing measuring an indicated number of feet in height or length: *a six-footer.*
foot·fall (fo͝ot′fôl′) *n.* **1.** A footstep. **2.** The sound made by a footstep.
foot fault *n.* A fault against the server, as in tennis, called for failure to keep both feet behind the base line.
foot·gear (fo͝ot′gîr′) *n.* Footwear, as shoes or boots.
foot·hill (fo͝ot′hĭl′) *n.* A low hill near the base of a mountain or mountain range.
foot·hold (fo͝ot′hōld′) *n.* **1.** A place providing support for the foot in climbing or standing. **2.** A firm or secure position that provides a base for further advancement.
foot·ing (fo͝ot′ĭng) *n.* **1.** A secure placement of the feet in standing or moving. **2.** A surface or the condition of a surface with respect to the ease with which one may walk or run on it: *poor footing on the track.* **3.** *Archit.* The supporting base or groundwork of a structure, as for a monument or wall. **4. a.** A basis; foundation: *a business begun on a good footing.* **b.** A basis for social or business transactions with others; standing: *We're all on equal footing.* **5.** The sum of a column of figures.
foot-lam·bert (fo͝ot′lăm′bərt) *n.* *Physics.* A unit of luminance equal to $1/\pi$ candela per square foot.
foo·tle (fo͞ot′l) *Informal.* —*intr.v.* **-tled, -tling, -tles. 1.** To waste time; trifle. **2.** To talk nonsense. —*n.* Foolishness; nonsense. [Orig. unknown.] **—foo′tler** *n.*
foot·less (fo͝ot′lĭs) *adj.* **1.** Without feet. **2.** Without a firm support or basis. **3.** *Informal.* Without thought or skill; inept. **—foot′less·ly** *adv.* **—foot′less·ness** *n.*
foot·lights (fo͝ot′līts′) *pl.n.* **1.** Lights placed in a row along the front of a stage floor. **2.** The theater as a profession; the stage.
foo·tling (fo͞ot′lĭng) *adj.* *Informal.* **1.** Lacking importance or significance; trifling. **2.** Stupid; inept. [Pr.part. of FOOTLE.]
foot·lock·er (fo͝ot′lŏk′ər) *n.* A small trunk for storing personal belongings and small items, esp. one kept at the foot of a bed.
foot·loose (fo͝ot′lo͞os′) *adj.* Having no attachments or ties; free to do as one pleases.
foot·man (fo͝ot′mən) *n.* **1.** A male servant employed in a

house to wait at table, attend the door, and run various errands. **2.** *Archaic.* A foot soldier; infantryman. **3.** *Archaic.* A pedestrian.
foot·mark (fo͝ot'märk') *n.* A footprint.
foot·note (fo͝ot'nōt') *n.* **1.** A note placed at the bottom of a page of a book or manuscript that comments on or cites a reference for a designated part of the text. **2.** Something related to but of lesser importance than a larger work or occurrence. *—tr.v.* **-not·ed, -not·ing, -notes.** To furnish with or comment on in footnotes.
foot·pace (fo͝ot'pās') *n.* **1.** A walking pace. **2.** A raised platform in a room, as for a lecturer; dais.
foot·pad (fo͝ot'păd') *n. Archaic.* A highwayman or street robber who goes about on foot. [FOOT + obs. *pad,* highwayman.]

footrope
Sailors using the footrope in the furling of a sail

foot·path (fo͝ot'păth', -päth') *n.* A narrow path for persons on foot.
foot-pound (fo͝ot'pound') *n.* A unit of work equal to the work done by a force of one pound acting through a distance of one foot in the direction of the force.
foot-pound·al (fo͝ot'poun'dl) *n.* A unit of work equal to the work done by a force of one poundal acting through a distance of one foot in the direction of the force.
foot-pound-sec·ond (fo͝ot'pound'sĕk'ənd) *adj.* Of, pertaining to, or characteristic of a system of units based on the foot, the pound, and the second as the fundamental units of length, weight, and time.
foot·print (fo͝ot'prĭnt') *n.* An outline or indentation left by a foot on a surface.
foot·race (fo͝ot'rās') *n.* A race run on foot. **—foot'rac'ing** *n.*
foot·rest (fo͝ot'rĕst') *n.* A support on which to rest the feet.
foot·rope (fo͝ot'rōp') *n.* **1.** A rope attached to the lower border of a sail. **2.** A rope, rigged beneath a yard, for men to stand on during the reefing or furling of sail.
foot-rot (fo͝ot'rŏt') *n.* **1.** A degenerative infection of the feet in certain hoofed animals, esp. cattle or sheep, often resulting in loss of the hoof. **2.** A disease of plants in which the stem or trunk rots at its base.
foot soldier *n.* A soldier who fights on foot; infantryman.
foot·sore (fo͝ot'sôr', -sōr') *adj.* Having sore or tired feet from much walking. **—foot'sore'ness** *n.*
foot·stalk (fo͝ot'stôk') *n.* A supporting stalk, such as a peduncle or pedicel.
foot·stall (fo͝ot'stôl') *n.* The pedestal or plinth of a pillar.
foot·step (fo͝ot'stĕp') *n.* **1. a.** A step with the foot. **b.** The distance covered by one step: *a footstep away.* **c.** The sound of a foot stepping. **2.** A footprint. **3.** A step up or down. **—*idiom.* follow in (someone's) footsteps.** To carry on the behavior, work, or tradition of (a predecessor).
foot·stone (fo͝ot'stōn') *n.* A marking stone placed at the foot of a grave.
foot·stool (fo͝ot'sto͞ol') *n.* A low stool for supporting or resting the feet.
foot·wall (fo͝ot'wôl') *n.* The mass of rock underlying a mineral deposit in a mine.
foot·way (fo͝ot'wā') *n.* A walk or path for pedestrians.
foot·wear (fo͝ot'wâr') *n.* Covering for the feet, as shoes or slippers.
foot·work (fo͝ot'wûrk') *n.* **1.** The manner in which the feet are used or maneuvered, as in boxing. **2.** Work that involves moving around on foot; legwork.
fop (fŏp) *n.* A man who is preoccupied with and often vain about his clothes and manners; dandy. [ME, fool.]
fop·per·y (fŏp'ə-rē) *n., pl.* **-ies.** The dress or manner of a fop.
fop·pish (fŏp'ĭsh) *adj.* Of, pertaining to, or characteristic of a fop; dandified. **—fop'pish·ly** *adv.* **—fop'pish·ness** *n.*
for (fôr; fər *when unstressed*) *prep.* **1. a.** Used to indicate the object, aim, or purpose of an action or activity: *trained for the ministry; put the house up for sale; plans to run for senator.* **b.** Used to indicate a destination: *headed off for town.* **2.** Used to indicate the object of a desire, intention, or perception: *had an eye for pretty girls; eager for fame and fortune.* **3. a.** Used to indicate the recipient or beneficiary of an action: *prepared lunch for us.* **b.** On behalf of: *spoke for all the members.* **c.** In favor of: *Were they for or against the proposal?* **4. a.** Used to indicate equivalence or equality: *paid ten dollars for a ticket; repeated the conversation word for word.* **b.** Used to indicate correlation or correspondence: *took two steps back for every step forward.* **5.** Used to indicate amount, extent, or duration: *a bill for five dollars; walked for miles; held the line for several minutes.* **6.** As being: *take for granted; mistook her for the waitress.* **7.** As a result of: *crying for joy.* **8.** Used to indicate appropriateness or suitability: *It will be for the judge to decide.* **9.** Notwithstanding; despite: *was inefficient for all her experience.* **10. a.** As regards; concerning: *a gift for organization.* **b.** Considering the nature or usual character of: *was backward for his age.* *—conj.* Because; since. —See Usage note at **because.** [ME < OE.]
for– *pref.* Completely; excessively, esp. with destructive or detrimental effect: *forworn.* [ME < OE.]
fo·ra (fôr'ə, fōr'ə) *n.* A plural of **forum.**
for·age (fôr'ĭj, fŏr'-) *n.* **1.** Food for domestic animals; fodder. **2.** The act of looking or searching for forage or provisions. *—v.* **-aged, -ag·ing, -ag·es.** *—intr.* **1.** To search for forage or provisions. **2.** To make a raid, as for food. *—tr.* **1.** To wander or rummage through, esp. in search of provisions. **2.** To obtain by foraging: *foraged a snack from the refrigerator.* [ME < OFr. *fourrage* < *feurre,* fodder, of Germanic orig.] **—for'ag·er** *n.*
for·am (fôr'əm, fōr'-) *n.* A foraminiferan.
fo·ra·men (fə-rā'mən) *n., pl.* **-ram·i·na** (-răm'ə-nə) or **-ra·mens.** An opening in a bone or through a membranous anatomical structure. [Lat. *foramen, foramin-,* an opening < *forare,* to bore.] **—fo·ram'i·nal** (-răm'ə-nəl), **fo·ram'i·nous** (-nəs) *adj.*
foramen mag·num (măg'nəm) *n.* The large orifice in the base of the skull through which the spinal cord passes and becomes continuous with the medulla oblongata. [NLat.]
foramen o·val·e (ō-văl'ē, -vā'lē, -vä'-) *n.* An opening in the septum between the right and left atria in the heart of a fetus. [NLat., oval opening.]
fo·ram·i·na (fə-răm'ə-nə) *n.* A plural of **foramen.**
for·a·min·i·fer·an (fôr'ə-mĭn'ə-fər-ən, fŏr'-) also **for·a·min·i·fer** (-mĭn'ə-fər) *n.* Any of the unicellular microorganisms of the order Foraminifera, characteristically having a calcareous shell with perforations through which numerous pseudopodia protrude. [< NLat. *Foraminifera,* order name : Lat. *foramen,* an opening + Lat. *-fer,* -fer.] **—fo·ram'i·nif'er·ous** (fə-răm'ə-nĭf'ər-əs), **fo·ram'i·nif'er·al** (-əl) *adj.*
for·as·much as (fôr'əz-mŭch' əz) *conj.* Inasmuch as; since.
for·ay (fôr'ā', fŏr'ā', fŏr'ā') *n.* **1.** A sudden raid or military advance. **2.** A venture or initial attempt: *his foray into politics.* *—intr. & tr.v.* **-ayed, -ay·ing, -ays.** To make a raid or make a raid against. [ME *forrai* < *forraien,* to plunder.]
forb (fôrb) *n.* A herbaceous plant other than a grass, esp. one growing in a field or meadow. [Gk. *phorbē,* fodder < *pherbein,* to graze.]
for·bad (fər-băd', fôr-) *v.* A past tense of **forbid.**
for·bade (fər-băd', -bād', fôr-) *v.* A past tense of **forbid.**
for·bear[1] (fôr-bâr') *v.* **-bore** (-bôr', -bōr'), **-borne** (-bôrn', -bōrn'), **-bear·ing, -bears.** *—tr.* **1.** To refrain from; resist: *forbear replying.* **2.** To desist from; cease. **3.** *Obs.* To avoid; shun. *—intr.* **1.** To hold back; refrain. **2.** To be tolerant or patient in the face of provocation. [ME *forberen* < OE *forberan.*] **—for·bear'er** *n.*
for·bear[2] (fôr'bâr', fōr'-) *n.* Variant of **forebear.**
for·bear·ance (fôr-bâr'əns) *n.* **1.** An act of forbearing. **2.** Tolerance and restraint in the face of provocation; patience. **3.** *Law.* The act of a creditor who refrains from enforcing a debt when it falls due.
for·bid (fər-bĭd', fôr-) *tr.v.* **-bade** (-băd', -bād') or **-bad** (-băd'), **-bid·den** (-bĭd'n) or **-bid, -bid·ding, -bids. 1.** To command (someone) not to do something: *I forbid you to go.* **2.** To prohibit; interdict: *Smoking is forbidden.* **3.** To have the effect of preventing; preclude. [ME *forbidden* < OE *forbēodan.*] **—for·bid'dance** *n.*

Usage: *Forbid* may be used with an infinitive (*I forbid you to smoke*) or a gerund (*I forbid your smoking*) but not with *from* (*I forbid you from smoking*).

for·bid·den (fər-bĭd'n, fôr-) *v.* A past participle of **forbid.** *—adj.* Having a low probability of occurrence: *a forbidden transition.* Used of quantum phenomena.
for·bid·ding (fər-bĭd'ĭng, fôr-) *adj.* **1.** Tending or threatening to impede progress. **2.** Unfriendly; disagreeable: *a forbidding scowl.* **—for·bid'ding·ly** *adv.*
for·bore (fôr-bôr', -bōr') *v.* Past tense of **forbear.**
for·borne (fôr-bôrn',-bōrn') *v.* Past participle of **forbear.**
force (fôrs, fōrs) *n.* **1.** Capacity to do work or cause change; strength or power: *the force of an explosion; a personality of great force.* **2. a.** Power made operative against resistance; exertion: *use force in driving a nail.* **b.** The use of such power or exertion: *a confession obtained by force.* **3.** Intellectual power or vigor, as of a statement. **4. a.** A capacity for affecting, influencing, or persuading the mind or behavior; efficacy: *the force of logical argumentation.* **b.** One that possesses such capacity: *the forces of evil.* **5. a.** A body of persons or other resources organized or available for a certain purpose: *a large labor force.* **b.** A group organized for military, police, or hostile purposes: *an armed force.* **6.** *Law.* Legal validity. **7.** *Physics.* A vector quantity that tends to produce an acceleration of a body in the direction of its application. *—tr.v.* **forced, forc·ing, forc·es. 1.** To compel through pressure or necessity: *forced him to practice daily.* **2.** To obtain by the use of force or coercion: *force a confession.* **3.** To produce with effort and against one's will: *force a laugh.* **4.** To move against resistance; push: *force a square peg into a round hole.* **5.** To move, open, or clear by force: *forced his way through the crowd.* **6.** To break down or open by force: *force a lock.* **7.** To rape. **8.** To inflict or impose: *force one's will on someone.* **9.** To place undue strain on; push beyond normal capacity or use: *force one's voice.* **10.** To cause to grow by artificially accelerating the normal processes: *force flowers in a greenhouse.* **11.** *Baseball.* **a.** To put (a runner) out by tagging the base to which he must advance. **b.** To allow (a run) to be scored by walking a batter when the bases are loaded. **—*idiom.* in force. 1.** In full strength. **2.** In effect; operative: *a rule no longer in force.* [ME < OFr. < Lat. *fortis,* strong.] **—force'a·ble** *adj.* **—forc'er** *n.*

Synonyms: *force, compel, coerce, constrain, necessitate, oblige, obligate.* These verbs mean to make a person or thing follow a prescribed or dictated course. *Force* is broadly applicable to any such act and usually implies the exertion of physical strength or the operation of circumstances that permit no alternative to compliance. *Compel,* often interchangeable with *force,* stresses the power or strength of what causes compliance and is especially applicable to an act dictated by a person in authority. *Coerce* invariably implies use of strength or harsh measures in securing compliance. *Constrain* suggests binding one to a course of action, or enforced inaction, by physical or moral means or by the operation of compelling circumstances. *Necessitate* implies the operation of circumstances that create an inescapable need for the course in question. *Oblige* is applicable when compliance is caused by the operation of authority, necessity, or moral or ethical considerations, and *obligate* when compulsion is exerted by terms of a legal contract or promise, or by the dictates of one's conscience or sense of propriety.

forced (fôrst, fōrst) *adj.* **1.** Enforced or imposed; involuntary: *forced labor; a forced landing.* **2.** Produced under strain; not spontaneous; unnatural: *forced laughter.* —See Usage note at **forceful.**

force-feed (fôrs'fēd', fōrs'-) *tr.v.* **-fed** (-fĕd'), **-feed·ing, -feeds. 1.** To force to ingest food; feed forcibly. **2.** To force to assimilate: *prisoners of war being force-fed the party line.*

force field *n.* A field of force.

force·ful (fôrs'fəl, fōrs'-) *adj.* Characterized by or full of force; effective. **—force'ful·ly** *adv.* **—force'ful·ness** *n.*

Usage: *Forceful, forcible,* and *forced* have distinct, if related, meanings. *Forceful* is used to describe something that suggests strength or force: *a forceful speaker; a forceful personality. Forceful measures* may or may not involve the use of actual physical force. *Forcible,* by contrast, is most often used of actions accomplished by the application of physical force: *There had been a forcible entry. The suspect had to be restrained forcibly when she tried to escape. Forced* is used to describe a condition brought about by control or by an outside influence: *forced labor; a forced landing; a forced smile.*

force ma·jeure (fôrs' mä-zhûr', fōrs') *n.* An unexpected or uncontrollable event. [Fr. : *force,* force + *majeure,* greater.]

force·meat (fôrs'mēt', fōrs'-) *n.* Finely ground meat, fish, or poultry used in stuffing or used independently. [*Force,* variant of FARCE + MEAT.]

force of habit *n.* Automatic behavior, as from long practice or frequent repetition.

for·ceps (fôr'səps) *n., pl.* **forceps. 1.** An instrument resembling a pair of pincers or tongs, used for grasping, manipulating, or extracting. **2.** A pincerlike clasping organ at the posterior end of the abdomen in certain insects. [Lat.]

force pump *n.* A pump with a solid piston and valves used to raise a liquid or expel it under pressure.

forc·i·ble (fôr'sə-bəl, fōr'-) *adj.* **1.** Effected through the use of force: *a forcible entry.* **2.** Characterized by force; forceful. —See Usage note at **forceful. —forc'i·ble·ness** *n.* **—forc'i·bly** *adv.*

for·ci·pate (fôr'sə-pāt') *adj.* Shaped like a forceps. [Lat. *forceps, forcip-,* pincers + -ATE[1].]

ford (fôrd, fōrd) *n.* A shallow place in a body of water, such as a river, where a crossing can be made on foot. —*tr.v.* **ford·ed, ford·ing, fords.** To cross (a body of water) at a ford. [ME < OE.] **—ford'a·ble** *adj.*

for·do also **fore·do** (fôr-do͞o', fōr-) *tr.v.* **-did** (-dĭd'), **-done** (-dŭn'), **-do·ing, -does** (-dŭz'). *Archaic.* **1.** To bring to ruin; destroy. **2.** To exhaust utterly. [ME *fordon* < OE *fordōn* : *for-,* destruction + *dōn,* to do.]

fore (fôr, fōr) *adj.* Located at or toward the front; forward. —*n.* **1.** Something that is located at or toward the front. **2.** The front part. —*adv.* At, toward, or near the front; forward. —*prep.* Also **'fore.** *Archaic.* Before. —*interj.* Used by a golfer to warn those ahead that a ball is about to be driven in their direction. **—*idiom.* to the fore.** In, into, or toward a position of prominence: *A new virtuoso came to the fore.* [ME < *fore,* beforehand < OE.]

fore– *pref.* **1.** Before; earlier: *foredoom.* **2.** Front; in front of: *foredeck.* [ME < OE < *fore,* in front.]

fore and aft *adv.* **1.** From the bow of a ship to the stern; lengthwise. **2.** In, at, or toward both ends of a ship.

fore-and-aft (fôr'ən-ăft', fōr'-) *adj.* Parallel with the keel of a ship.

fore-and-aft·er (fôr'ən-ăf'tər, fōr'-) *n.* A sailing ship, such as a schooner, with a fore-and-aft rig.

fore-and-aft rig *n.* A sailing ship rig with quadrilateral and triangular sails set to the fore-and-aft line and capable of being trimmed to leeward.

fore-and-aft sail *n.* A sail set parallel with the keel of a vessel, having the foremost edge or luff attached to the mast with travelers and the upper edge set on a gaff or stay.

fore·arm[1] (fôr-ärm', fōr-) *tr.v.* **-armed, -arm·ing, -arms.** To prepare or arm in advance of a conflict.

fore·arm[2] (fôr'ärm', fōr'-) *n.* The part of the arm between the wrist and elbow.

fore·bear also **for·bear** (fôr'bâr', fōr'-) *n.* A forefather; ancestor. [ME : *fore-,* fore- + *been,* to be.]

fore·bode (fôr-bōd', fōr-) *tr.v.* **-bod·ed, -bod·ing, -bodes. 1.** To indicate the likelihood of; portend: *harsh words that foreboded estrangement.* **2.** To have a premonition of (a future misfortune).

fore·bod·ing (fôr-bō'dĭng, fōr-) *n.* **1.** A dark sense of impending evil; premonition. **2.** An evil omen; portent. —*adj.* Marked by or indicative of foreboding; ominous. **—fore·bod'ing·ly** *adv.*

fore·brain (fôr'brān', fōr'-) *n.* **1.** The anterior region of the embryonic brain from which the telencephalon and diencephalon develop. **2.** The segment of the adult brain that develops from the embryonic forebrain and includes the cerebrum, thalamus, and hypothalamus.

fore·cast (fôr'kăst', fōr'-) *v.* **-cast** or **-cast·ed, -cast·ing, -casts.** —*tr.* **1.** To estimate or calculate in advance, esp. to predict (weather conditions) by analysis of meteorological data. **2.** To serve as an advance indication of; foreshadow: *price rises that forecast inflation.* —*intr.* To make an estimation or calculation in advance. —*n.* A prediction, as of coming events or conditions. [ME *forecasten,* to plan beforehand : *fore-,* fore- + *casten,* to contrive.] **—fore'cast'er** *n.*

fore·cas·tle (fōk'səl, fôr'kăs'əl, fōr'-) also **fo'c's'le** (fōk'səl) *n.* **1.** The section of the upper deck of a ship located at the bow forward of the foremast. **2.** A superstructure at the bow of a merchant ship where the crew is housed. [ME < AN.]

fore·close (fôr-klōz', fōr-) *v.* **-closed, -clos·ing, -clos·es.** —*tr.* **1.** *Law.* **a.** To deprive (a mortgagor) of the right to redeem mortgaged property, as when he has failed in his payments. **b.** To bar an equity or right to redeem (a mortgage). **2.** To exclude or rule out; bar. **3.** To settle or resolve beforehand. —*intr.* To foreclose a mortgage. [ME *forclosen,* to exclude from an inheritance < OFr. *forclore* (p.part. *forclos*) : *fors-,* outside (< Lat. *foris*) + *clore,* to close (< Lat. *claudere*).] **—fore·clos'a·ble** *adj.*

fore·clo·sure (fôr-klō'zhər, fōr-) *n.* The act of foreclosing, esp. a legal proceeding by which a mortgage is foreclosed.

fore·court (fôr'kôrt', fōr'kōrt') *n.* **1.** A courtyard in front of a building. **2.** The part of a playing court nearest the net or wall, as in tennis or handball.

fore·deck (fôr'dĕk', fōr'-) *n.* The forward part of the deck of a ship, usually the main deck.

fore·do (fôr-do͞o', fōr-) *v.* Variant of **fordo.**

fore·doom (fôr-do͞om', fōr-) *tr.v.* **-doomed, -doom·ing, -dooms.** To doom or condemn beforehand.

fore·fa·ther (fôr'fä'*th*ər, fōr'-) *n.* **1.** An ancestor. **2.** A person from an earlier time and common tradition. [ME *forefader* : *fore-,* fore- + *fader,* father.]

fore·fend (fôr-fĕnd', fōr-) *v.* Variant of **forfend.**

fore·fin·ger (fôr'fĭng'gər, fōr'-) *n.* The index finger.

fore·foot (fôr'fo͝ot', fōr'-) *n.* **1.** One of the front feet of an animal. **2.** The part of a ship at which the prow joins the keel.

fore·front (fôr'frŭnt', fōr'-) *n.* **1.** The foremost part or area. **2.** The position of most importance, prominence, or responsibility; vanguard: *in the forefront of politics.*

fore·gath·er (fôr-găth'ər, fōr-) *v.* Variant of **forgather.**

fore·go[1] (fôr-gō', fōr-) *tr.v.* **-went** (-wĕnt'), **-gone** (-gôn', -gŏn'), **-go·ing, -goes** (-gōz'). To go before; precede, as in time or place. [ME *foregon* < OE *foregān.*] **—fore·go'er** *n.*

fore·go[2] (fôr-gō', fōr-) *v.* Variant of **forgo.**

fore·go·ing (fôr-gō'ĭng, fōr-, fôr'gō'ĭng, fōr'-) *adj.* Said, written, or encountered just before; previous: *the foregoing comment.*

fore·gone (fôr'gôn', -gŏn', fōr'-) *adj.* Past; previous. [P.part. of FOREGO[1].]

foregone conclusion *n.* An end or result regarded as inevitable.

fore·ground (fôr'ground', fōr'-) *n.* **1.** The part of a view or picture that is or is represented as nearest to the viewer. **2.** An important or prominent position; forefront.

fore·gut (fôr'gŭt', fōr'-) *n.* The anterior part of the embryonic digestive tract from which the pharynx lining, lungs, esophagus, stomach, and small intestine develop.

fore·hand (fôr'hănd', fōr'-) *adj.* **1.** Made or done with the hand moving palm forward: *a forehand tennis stroke.* **2.** *Archaic.* Taking place or done beforehand; prior. —*n.* **1.** A forehand stroke, as in tennis. **2.** The part of a horse in front of the rider. —*adv.* With a forehand stroke or motion.

fore·hand·ed (fôr'hăn'dĭd, fōr'-) *adj.* **1.** Forehand, as in tennis. **2.** Looking or planning ahead; circumspect. **3.** Having ample financial resources; well-off. **—fore'hand'ed·ly** *adv.* **—fore'hand'ed·ness** *n.*

fore·head (fôr'ĭd, fōr'-, fôr'hĕd', fōr'-) *n.* The part of the head or face between the eyebrows and the normal hairline. [ME *forhed* < OE *forhēafod.*]

for·eign (fôr'ĭn, fōr'-) *adj.* **1.** Located away from one's native country: *a foreign city.* **2.** Of, characteristic of, or from a country other than one's own: *a foreign custom.* **3.** Conducted or involved with other nations or governments; not domestic: *foreign trade.* **4.** Situated in an abnormal or improper place in the body: *a foreign object in his eye.* **5.** Not natural; alien: *Jealousy is foreign to her nature.* **6.** Not appropriate or essential; irrelevant. **7.** *Law.* Subject to the jurisdiction of another political unit. [ME *forein* < OFr. *forain* < Lat. *foras,* outside.] **—for'eign·ness** *n.*

foreign bill *n.* A draft for a sum of money to be paid in another country.

foreign correspondent *n.* A journalist who sends news re-

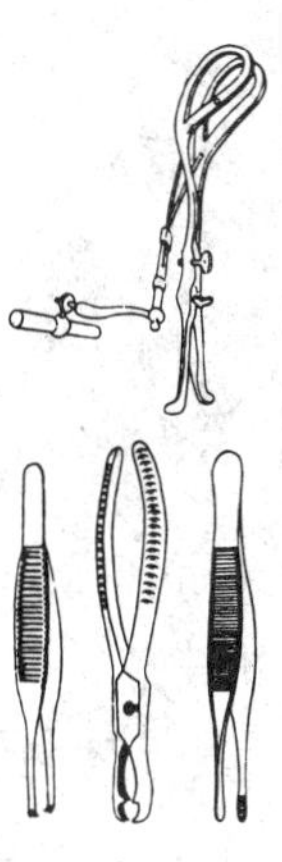

forceps
Above: Axis-traction obstetrical forceps
Below, from left: Mouse-tooth forceps; lion-jaw bone-holding forceps; thumb forceps

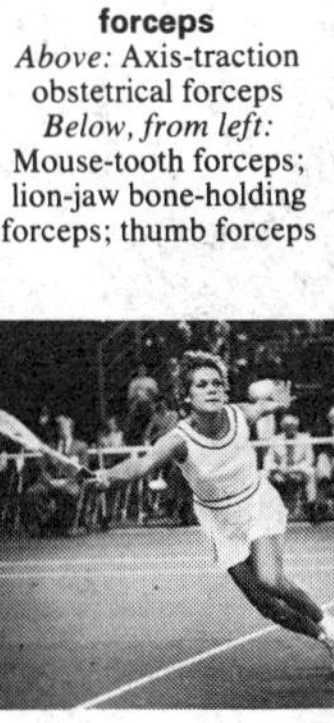

forehand

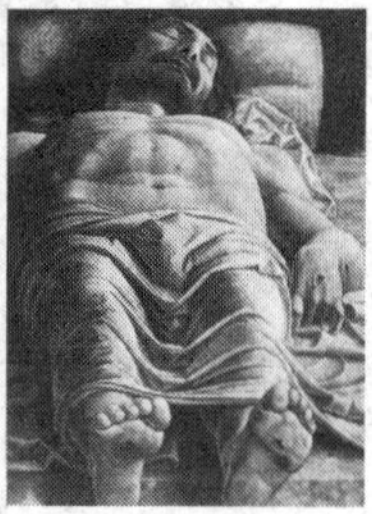

foreshorten
Foreshortened figure of the dead Christ; detail of a painting by Mantegna

ports or commentary from a foreign country for publication, as in a newspaper, or broadcasting, as on television.
for·eign·er (fôr′ə-nər, fŏr′-) *n.* A person from a foreign country.
foreign exchange *n.* **1.** The transaction of international monetary business, as between governments or businessmen of different countries. **2.** Negotiable bills drawn in one country to be paid in another country.
foreign mission *n.* **1.** A group sent to a foreign country for missionary service. **2.** A group sent to a foreign country for diplomatic service.
foreign office *n.* The official name in several countries of the governmental department in charge of foreign affairs.
foreign policy *n.* The diplomatic policy of a nation in its interactions with other nations.
foreign service *n.* The diplomatic and consular staff of a foreign office.
fore·judge also **for·judge** (fôr-jŭj′, fōr-) *tr. & intr.v.* **-judged, -judg·ing, -judg·es.** To judge beforehand; prejudge. **—fore·judg′ment** *n.*
fore·know (fôr-nō′, fōr-) *tr.v.* **-knew** (-no͞o′, -nyo͞o′), **-known** (-nōn′), **-know·ing, -knows.** To have foreknowledge of.
fore·knowl·edge (fôr-nŏl′ĭj, fōr-) *n.* Knowledge or awareness of something prior to its existence or occurrence; prescience.
fore·la·dy (fôr′lā′dē, fōr′-) *n.* A forewoman.
fore·land (fôr′lənd, fōr′-) *n.* A projecting land mass; promontory.
fore·leg (fôr′lĕg′, fōr′-) *n.* One of the front legs of an animal.
fore·limb (fôr′lĭm′, fōr′-) *n.* An anterior appendage such as a leg, wing, or flipper.
fore·lock¹ (fôr′lŏk′, fōr′-) *n.* A lock of hair that grows or falls on the forehead.
fore·lock² (fôr′lŏk′, fōr′-) *n.* A cotter pin; linchpin.
fore·man (fôr′mən, fōr′-) *n.* **1.** One that has charge of a group of workers, as at a factory. **2.** The chairman and spokesman for a jury. **—fore′man·ship′** *n.*
fore·mast (fôr′məst, -măst′, fōr′-) *n.* The forward mast on a sailing vessel.
fore·milk (fôr′mĭlk′, fōr′-) *n.* Colostrum.
fore·most (fôr′mōst′, fōr′-) *adj.* **1.** First in time or place. **2.** Ahead of all others, esp. in position or rank; paramount. *—adv.* In the front or first position. [Alteration of ME *formest* < *forme,* first < OE *forma.*]
fore·moth·er (fôr′mŭ*th*′ər, fōr′-) *n.* A female ancestor.
fore·name (fôr′nām′, fōr′-) *n.* A first name.
fore·noon (fôr′no͞on′, fōr′-, fôr-no͞on′, fōr-) *n.* The period of time between sunrise and noon.
fo·ren·sic (fə-rĕn′sĭk, -zĭk) *adj.* **1.** Pertaining to or employed in legal proceedings or argumentation: *forensic medicine.* **2.** Of, pertaining to, or employed in debate or argument; rhetorical. [Lat. *forensis* < *forum,* forum.] **—fo·ren′si·cal·ly** *adv.*
fo·ren·sics (fə-rĕn′sĭks, -zĭks) *n. (used with a sing. verb).* The study or practice of formal debate; argumentation.
fore·or·dain (fôr′ôr-dān′, fōr′-) *tr.v.* **-dained, -dain·ing, -dains.** To appoint or ordain beforehand; predestine. **—fore′or·dain′ment, fore·or′di·na′tion** (-ôr′dn-ā′shən) *n.*
fore·part (fôr′pärt′, fōr′-) *n.* **1.** The first or earliest period of time. **2.** The anterior part of something.
fore·paw (fôr′pô′, fōr′-) *n.* The paw of an animal's foreleg.
fore·peak (fôr′pēk′, fōr′-) *n.* The section of the hold of a ship that is within the angle made by the bow.
fore·play (fôr′plā′, fōr′-) *n.* Sexual stimulation preceding sexual intercourse.
fore·quar·ter (fôr′kwôr′tər, fōr′-) *n.* **1.** The front section of a side of meat. **2.** The foreleg, shoulder, and adjacent lateral parts of an animal, esp. a horse.
fore·reach (fôr-rēch′, fōr-) *v.* **-reached, -reach·ing, -reach·es.** *—tr.* To get ahead of, esp. in a sailing vessel. *—intr.* To gain ground, esp. upon a sailing vessel.
fore·run (fôr-rŭn′, fōr-) *tr.v.* **-ran** (-răn′), **-run, -run·ning, -runs.** **1.** To run in front of. **2.** To be the precursor of; foreshadow. **3.** To forestall; prevent.
fore·run·ner (fôr′rŭn′ər, fōr′-) *n.* **1.** One that precedes, as in time; predecessor. **2.** An ancestor; forebear. **3.** One that provides advance notice of the coming of others; harbinger.
fore·said (fôr′sĕd′, fōr′-) *adj.* Aforesaid.
fore·sail (fôr′səl, -sāl′, fōr′-) *n. Naut.* **1.** The principal square sail hung to the foremast of a square-rigged vessel. **2.** The principal triangular sail hung to the mast of a fore-and-aft-rigged vessel. **3.** The triangular sail hung to the forestay of a cutter or sloop.
fore·see (fôr-sē′, fōr-) *tr.v.* **-saw** (-sô′), **-seen** (-sēn′), **-see·ing, -sees.** To see or know beforehand: *foresaw the rapid jump in unemployment.* **—fore·see′a·ble** *adj.* **—fore·se′er** *n.*
fore·shad·ow (fôr-shăd′ō, fōr-) *tr.v.* **-owed, -ow·ing, -ows.** To present an indication or suggestion of beforehand; presage.
fore·sheet (fôr′shēt′, fōr′-) *n.* **1.** A rope used in trimming a foresail. **2. foresheets.** The space near the bow of an open boat.
fore·shock (fôr′shŏk′, fōr′-) *n.* A minor tremor that precedes an earthquake.
fore·shore (fôr′shôr′, fōr′shōr′) *n.* **1.** The part of a shore covered at high tide. **2.** The part of a shore between the water and occupied or cultivated land.
fore·short·en (fôr-shôr′tn, fōr-) *tr.v.* **-ened, -en·ing, -ens.** **1.** To represent the long axis of (an object) by contracting its lines so as to produce an illusion of projection or extension in space. **2.** To shorten beforehand; curtail.
fore·show (fôr-shō′, fōr-) *tr.v.* **-showed, -shown** (-shōn′) or **-showed, -show·ing, -shows.** To show or prefigure in advance.
fore·side (fôr′sīd′, fōr′-) *n.* The front or upper side.
fore·sight (fôr′sīt′, fōr′-) *n.* **1. a.** The act of foreseeing. **b.** The ability to foresee. **2.** The act of looking forward. **3.** Concern or prudence with respect to the future. **—fore′sight′ed** *adj.* **—fore′sight′ed·ly** *adv.* **—fore′sight′ed·ness** *n.*
fore·skin (fôr′skĭn′, fōr′-) *n.* The prepuce (sense 1).
fore·speak (fôr-spēk′, fōr-) *tr.v.* **-spoke** (-spōk′), **-spo·ken** (-spō′kən), **-speak·ing, speaks.** **1.** To predict. **2.** To arrange for in advance.
for·est (fôr′ĭst, fŏr′-) *n.* **1.** A dense growth of trees, together with other plants, covering a large area. **2.** Something that resembles a forest in density, quantity, or profusion: *a forest of skyscrapers.* **3.** *Law.* A defined area of land formerly set aside in England as a royal hunting ground. *—tr.v.* **-est·ed, -est·ing, -ests.** To plant trees on. [ME < OFr. < Med. Lat. *foresta* < Lat. *foris,* outside.] **—for′est·al, fo·res′tial** (fə-rĕs′chəl) *adj.* **—for′es·ta′tion** *n.*
fore·stall (fôr-stôl′, fōr-) *tr.v.* **-stalled, -stall·ing, -stalls.** **1.** To prevent, delay, or take precautionary measures against beforehand. **2.** To deal with or think of beforehand; anticipate. **3.** To prevent or hinder normal sales of by buying up merchandise, discouraging persons from bringing their goods to market, or encouraging an increase in prices of goods already on the market. [ME *forestallen,* to waylay and rob < *forestal,* highway robbery < OE *foresteall* : *fore,* in front of + *steall,* position.] **—fore·stall′er** *n.*
fore·stay (fôr′stā′, fōr′-) *n.* A stay extending from the head of the foremast to the bowsprit of a ship.
fore·stay·sail (fôr′stā′səl, -sāl′, fōr′-) *n.* A triangular sail set on the forestay.
for·est·er (fôr′ĭ-stər, fŏr′-) *n.* **1.** A person trained in forestry. **2.** One that inhabits a forest. **3.** Any of various chiefly tropical moths of the family Agaristidae.
for·est·land (fôr′ĭst-lănd′, fŏr′-) *n.* A section of land covered with forest.
forest ranger *n.* An officer in charge of protecting or managing a public forest or section of a public forest.
for·est·ry (fôr′ĭ-strē, fŏr′-) *n.* **1.** The science and art of cultivating, maintaining, and developing forests. **2.** The management of a forestland. **3.** A forestland.
fore·swear (fôr-swâr′, fōr-) *v.* Variant of **forswear.**
fore·taste (fôr′tāst′, fōr′-) *n.* An advance taste or realization. *—tr.v.* (fôr-tāst′, fōr-, fôr′tāst′, fōr′-) **-tast·ed, -tast·ing, -tastes.** To have a foretaste of; anticipate.
fore·tell (fôr-tĕl′, fōr-) *tr.v.* **-told** (-tōld′), **-tell·ing, -tells.** To tell of or indicate beforehand; predict. **—fore·tell′er** *n.*

Synonyms: *foretell, predict, forecast, prophesy, divine, augur, portend, forebode, presage, bode, betoken, foretoken.* These verbs mean to foresee or to give advance word or other indication of what is to come. *Foretell, predict, forecast,* and *prophesy* apply principally to a person's telling of something in advance of its occurrence. *Foretell* is used of any such act. *Predict* and especially *forecast* imply the giving of advance word based on study, observation, or special knowledge. *Prophesy* sometimes refers to such intellectual foretelling but can also apply to the act of a person considered to be divinely inspired or gifted with extraordinary power of foresight. To *divine* is to foresee, especially what is revealed only to one with remarkable sagacity or insight. To *augur* is to foretell from omens or signs, or the term can apply to a thing that serves as an omen or advance indication of the outcome or issue of something. *Portend* and *forebode* are chiefly used of things that serve as omens or warnings of what is evil, harmful, or unfortunate. *Presage* and *bode* are applied principally to things that give or serve as advance indications of what is to come and are not necessarily limited to evil or misfortune. *Betoken* and *foretoken* are applicable to things that foreshadow or give advance indication of something in the future, whether favorable or unfavorable.

fore·thought (fôr′thôt′, fōr′-) *n.* **1.** Deliberation, consideration, or planning beforehand. **2.** Preparation or thought for the future; anticipation. **—fore′thought′ful** *adj.* **—fore′thought′ful·ly** *adv.* **—fore′thought′ful·ness** *n.*
fore·to·ken (fôr-tō′kən, fōr-) *tr.v.* **-kened, -ken·ing, -kens.** To foreshow; presage. *—n.* (fôr′tō′kən, fōr′-). An advance warning.
fore·told (fôr-tōld′, fōr-) *v.* Past tense and past participle of **foretell.**
fore·top (fôr′tŏp′, fōr′-) *n.* **1.** (*also* -təp). A platform at the top of a ship's foremast. **2.** A forelock, esp. of a horse.
fore·top·gal·lant (fôr′tŏp-găl′ənt, fōr′-, fôr′tə-, fōr′tə-) *adj.* Of or relating to the mast directly above the foremast.
fore·top·mast (fôr′tŏp′məst, fōr′-, fôr′təp-măst′, fōr′təp-) *n.* The mast that is above the foretop.
fore·top·sail (fôr′tŏp′səl, fōr′-, fôr′təp-, fōr′təp-) *n.* The sail hung from the foretopmast.

for·ev·er (fôr-ĕv′ər, fər-) *adv.* **1.** For everlasting time; eternally. **2.** At all times; incessantly.
for·ev·er·more (fôr-ĕv′ər-môr′, -mōr′, fər-) *adv.* Forever.
fore·warn (fôr-wôrn′, fōr-) *tr.v.* **-warned, -warn·ing, -warns.** To warn in advance.
fore·went (fôr-wĕnt′) *v.* Past tense of **forego.**
fore·wing (fôr′wĭng′, fōr′-) *n.* One of a pair of anterior wings, as in certain insects.
fore·wom·an (fôr′wo͝om′ən, fōr′-) *n.* **1.** A woman who has charge of a group of workers, as at a factory. **2.** The chairwoman and spokeswoman for a jury.
fore·word (fôr′wərd, fōr′-) *n.* A preface or introductory note, esp. at the beginning of a book.
fore·worn (fôr-wôrn′, fōr-wōrn′) *adj.* Variant of **forworn.**
fore·yard (fôr′yärd′, fōr′-) *n.* The lowest yard on a foremast.
for·feit (fôr′fĭt) *n.* **1.** Something surrendered as punishment for a crime, offense, error, or breach of contract. **2.** Something placed in escrow and then redeemed after payment of a fine. **3.** A forfeiture. **4. forfeits.** A game in which forfeits are required. —*adj.* Surrendered or alienated for a crime, offense, error, or breach of contract. —*tr.v.* **-feit·ed, -feit·ing, -feits. 1.** To surrender or be forced to surrender as a forfeit. **2.** To subject to forfeiture. [ME < *forfet,* forfeited < OFr., p.part. of *forsfaire,* to commit a crime : *fors,* beyond (< Lat. *foris,* outside) + *faire,* to do (< Lat. *facere*).] **—for′feit·a·ble** *adj.* **—for′feit·er** *n.*
for·fei·ture (fôr′fĭ-cho͝or′, -chər) *n.* **1.** The act of surrendering something as a forfeit. **2.** Something that is forfeited.
for·fend also **fore·fend** (fôr-fĕnd′, fōr-) *tr.v.* **-fend·ed, -fend·ing, -fends. 1.** To keep or ward off; avert. **2.** *Archaic.* To forbid. **3.** To defend or protect. [ME *forfenden.*]
for·fi·cate (fôr′fĭ-kĭt, -kāt′) *adj.* Deeply forked or notched, as the tail of certain birds. [Lat. *forfex, forfic-,* scissors + -ATE[1].]
for·gath·er also **fore·gath·er** (fôr-găth′ər, fōr-) *intr.v.* **-ered, -er·ing, -ers. 1.** To gather together; assemble. **2.** To meet by accident. **3.** To keep company or consort. [Sc.]
for·gave (fər-gāv′, fôr-) *v.* Past tense of **forgive.**
forge[1] (fôrj, fōrj) *n.* **1.** A furnace or hearth where metals are heated or wrought; smithy. **2.** A workshop where pig iron is transformed into wrought iron. —*v.* **forged, forg·ing, forg·es.** —*tr.* **1.** To form (metal) by heating in a forge and beating or hammering into shape. **2.** To give form or shape to: *forge a treaty.* **3.** To fashion or reproduce for fraudulent purposes; counterfeit: *forge a signature.* —*intr.* **1.** To work at a forge or smithy. **2.** To make a forgery or counterfeit. [ME < OFr. < Lat. *fabrica* < *faber,* worker.] **—forge′a·bil′i·ty** *n.* **—forge′a·ble** *adj.* **—forg′er** *n.*
forge[2] (fôrj, fōrj) *intr.v.* **forged, forg·ing, forg·es. 1.** To advance gradually but firmly. **2.** To advance with an abrupt increase of speed: *forged into the lead with a strong kick.* [Orig. unknown.]
for·ger·y (fôr′jə-rē, fōr′-) *n., pl.* **-ies. 1.** The act of forging, esp. the illegal production of something counterfeit. **2.** Something counterfeit, forged, or fraudulent.
for·get (fər-gĕt′, fôr-) *v.* **-got** (-gŏt′), **-got·ten** (-gŏt′n) or **-got, -get·ting, -gets.** —*tr.* **1.** To be unable to remember. **2.** To lack concern for; neglect: *forget one's family.* **3.** To leave behind unintentionally. **4.** To fail to mention. **5.** To banish from one's thoughts: *forget a disgrace.* —*intr.* **1.** To cease remembering. **2.** To fail or neglect to become aware at the proper or specified moment: *forget about paying one's taxes.* **—idiom. forget (oneself).** To lose one's reserve or self-restraint. [ME *forgeten* < OE *forgetan.*] **—for·get′ta·ble** *adj.* **—for·get′ter** *n.*
for·get·ful (fər-gĕt′fəl, fôr-) *adj.* **1.** Tending or likely to forget. **2.** Marked by neglectful or thoughtless inattention. **—for·get′ful·ly** *adv.* **—for·get′ful·ness** *n.*
Synonyms: *forgetful, unmindful, oblivious, abstracted, absent-minded, distracted.* These adjectives refer to failure to remember or to lack of awareness or attentiveness. *Forgetful* usually implies a faulty memory or at least a tendency not to remember. Less often it is used as the equivalent of *unmindful,* which applies principally to one's failure in a specific instance to keep in mind what should be remembered, through deliberate oversight, heedlessness, or inattentiveness. *Oblivious* strictly refers to failure to remember or to be aware of something, often because one is preoccupied in another direction; less strictly the term is applied not to failure to remember a specific thing but to general unresponsiveness to or unawareness of one's surroundings. The remaining terms stress inattentiveness to immediate surroundings. *Abstracted* implies mental withdrawal as a result of preoccupation elsewhere. *Absent-minded* suggests such preoccupation, often chronic, to the point that one fails to remember or reacts haltingly or ineptly to ordinary demands on attention. *Distracted* implies diversion of attention from matters at hand and, sometimes, resultant confusion or agitation.
for·ge·tive (fôr′jĭ-tĭv, fōr′-) *adj. Archaic.* Capable of imagining or inventing. [Poss. FORGE[1] + (INVEN)TIVE.]
for·get-me-not (fər-gĕt′mē-nŏt′, fôr-) *n.* **1.** Any of various low-growing plants of the genus *Myosotis,* having clusters of small blue flowers. **2.** Any of several plants similar or related to the forget-me-not. [Transl. of OFr. *ne m'oubliez mie.*]
forg·ing (fôr′jĭng, fōr′-) *n.* **1. a.** The act of one who forges. **b.** The process used in forging. **2.** Something that is forged.
for·give (fər-gĭv′, fôr-) *v.* **-gave** (-gāv′), **-giv·en** (-gĭv′ən), **-giv·ing, -gives.** —*tr.* **1.** To excuse for a fault or offense; pardon. **2.** To renounce anger or resentment against. **3.** To absolve from payment of. —*intr.* To accord forgiveness. [ME *forgiven* < OE *forgifan.*] **—for·giv′a·ble** *adj.* **—for·giv′er** *n.*
Synonyms: *forgive, excuse, condone.* These verbs mean to pass over an offense and to free the offender from the consequences of it. To *forgive* is to grant pardon without harboring resentment. To *excuse* is to pass over a mistake or fault, usually a minor one, without demanding punishment or redress. To *condone* is to overlook an offense, usually serious, and thereby give tacit pardon.
for·give·ness (fər-gĭv′nĭs, fôr-) *n.* The act of forgiving; pardon.
for·go also **fore·go** (fôr-gō′, fōr-) *tr.v.* **-went** (-wĕnt′), **-gone** (-gôn′, -gŏn′), **-go·ing, -goes.** To abstain from; relinquish. [ME *forgon* < OE *forgān.*] **—for·go′er** *n.*
for·got (fər-gŏt′, fôr-) *v.* Past tense and a past participle of **forget.**
for·got·ten (fər-gŏt′n, fôr-) *v.* A past participle of **forget.**
fo·rint (fôr′ĭnt′) *n.* See table at **currency.** [Hung. < Ital. *fiorino,* florin. —see FLORIN.]
for·judge (fôr-jŭj′, fōr-) *v.* Variant of **forejudge.**
fork (fôrk) *n.* **1.** An implement or piece of equipment with two or more prongs used for raising, carrying, piercing, or digging. **2.** A forked utensil for serving or eating food. **3. a.** A bifurcation or separation into two or more branches or parts. **b.** The point at which such a bifurcation or separation occurs: *a fork in a road.* **c.** One of the branches of such a bifurcation or separation: *the right fork.* —*v.* **forked, fork·ing, forks.** —*tr.* **1.** To raise, carry, pitch, or pierce with a fork. **2.** To give the shape of a fork to. **3.** To launch an attack on (two chessmen). —*intr.* **1.** To divide into two or more branches. **2.** *Informal.* To hand over; pay: *forked over their entire savings as a down payment.* [ME *forke* < OE *force* < Lat. *furca.*]
forked (fôrkt, fôr′kĭd) *adj.* **1.** Containing or characterized by a fork: *a forked river.* **2.** Shaped like or similar to a fork: *a forked tail.*
fork lift *n.* A small industrial vehicle with a power-operated pronged platform that can be raised and lowered for insertion under a load to be lifted and carried.
for·lorn (fər-lôrn′, fôr-) *adj.* **1.** Appearing sad or lonely because deserted or abandoned. **2.** Suffering extreme want; destitute: *forlorn of all hope.* **3.** Wretched or pitiful in appearance or condition: *a forlorn refugee.* **4.** Nearly hopeless; desperate. [ME *forloren,* p.part. of *forlesen,* to abandon < OE *forlēosan.*] **—for·lorn′ly** *adv.* **—for·lorn′ness** *n.*
forlorn hope *n.* **1.** An advance guard of men sent on a hazardous mission. **2.** A hopeless or arduous undertaking. [By folk etymology < Du. *verloren hoop* : *verloren,* lost + *hoop,* troop.]
form (fôrm) *n.* **1.** The shape and structure of something as distinguished from its substance. **2.** The body or outward appearance of a person or animal considered separately from the face or head; figure. **3.** The essence of something as distinguished from its matter. **4.** The mode in which a thing exists, acts, or manifests itself; kind: *a form of animal life.* **5.** Procedure as determined or governed by regulation or custom. **6.** Manners or conduct as governed by etiquette, decorum, or custom. **7.** Performance considered with regard to acknowledged criteria: *a good jump shooter but with an unusual form.* **8.** Fitness, as of an athlete or animal, with regard to health or training. **9.** A fixed order of words or procedures, as in ceremony or other regulated social situation. **10.** A document with blanks for the insertion of details or information. **11.** Style or manner of presenting ideas or concepts in literary or musical composition or in organized discourse: *a treatise in the form of a dialogue.* **12.** The design, structure, or pattern of a work of art: *symphonic form.* **13.** A model for making a mold. **14.** A copy of the human figure used for modeling clothes. **15.** Linotype that has been assembled and locked up in a chase for printing. **16.** A grade in a British school or in some American private schools: *the sixth form.* **17. a.** A linguistic form. **b.** The external aspect of words with regard to their inflections, pronunciation, or spelling: *verb forms.* **18.** *Chiefly Brit.* A bench. **19.** The resting place of a hare. —*v.* **formed, form·ing, forms.** —*tr.* **1.** To give form to; shape. **2.** To shape or mold into a particular form. **3.** To fashion, train, or develop by instruction or precept: *form the mind.* **4.** To come to have; develop: *form a habit.* **5.** To constitute or compose an element, part, or characteristic of. **6.** To develop in the mind; conceive: *form an opinion.* **7. a.** To produce (a tense, for example) by assuming an inflection: *form the pluperfect.* **b.** To make (a word) by derivation or composition. **8.** To put in order; arrange. —*intr.* **1.** To become formed or shaped. **2.** To come into being; arise. **3.** To assume a specified form, shape, or pattern. [ME *forme* < Lat. *forma.*] **—form′a·bil′i·ty** *n.* **—form′a·ble** *adj.*
Synonyms: *form, figure, outline, shape, configuration, contour, profile.* These nouns refer to the distinctive appearance of a thing as determined by its visible lines. *Form,* the least specific, is that which is determined by the thing's

forge[1]

forget-me-not

fork lift

overall structure. *Figure* refers usually to identifying form as established by bounding or enclosing lines. *Outline* denotes that which marks the outer limits of a thing and gives it two-dimensional definition. *Shape* implies three-dimensional definition that indicates both outline and bulk or mass. *Configuration,* more definitely than *shape,* implies a pattern comprising an outline together with detailed indication of arrangement of parts within the outline. *Contour* refers to the bounding lines of a three-dimensional or solid figure. *Profile* denotes either the outline of the human face in side view or any distinctive outline.

-form *suff.* Having the form of: *plexiform.*

for·mal (fôr′məl) *adj.* **1.** Pertaining to the outward aspect of something as distinguished from its substance or material. **2.** Being or pertaining to the essential form or constitution of something: *a formal principle.* **3.** Following or adhering to accepted forms, conventions, or regulations: *a formal requirement.* **4.** Done in proper or regular form: *a formal reprimand.* **5.** Characterized by strict or meticulous observation of forms; methodical. **6.** Stiff or cold; ceremonious: *a formal manner.* **7.** Having the outward appearance but lacking in substance: *a purely formal greeting.* —*n.* **1.** An occasion or ceremony requiring formal attire. **2.** Formal attire. [ME < Lat. *formalis* < *forma,* shape.] **—for′mal·ly** *adv.*

for·mal·de·hyde (fôr-măl′də-hīd′) *n.* A colorless, gaseous compound, HCHO, used in manufacturing melamine and phenolic resins, fertilizers, dyes, and embalming fluids and in aqueous solution as a preservative and disinfectant. [FORM(IC ACID) + ALDEHYDE.]

for·ma·lin (fôr′mə-lĭn) *n.* A 37 per cent by weight aqueous solution of formaldehyde with some methanol. [Orig. a trademark.]

for·mal·ism (fôr′mə-lĭz′əm) *n.* **1.** Rigorous or excessive adherence to recognized forms, as in religion or art. **2.** An instance of formalism. **—for′mal·ist** *n.* **—for′mal·is′tic** *adj.*

for·mal·i·ty (fôr-măl′ĭ-tē) *n., pl.* **-ties. 1.** The quality or condition of being formal. **2.** Rigorous or ceremonious adherence to established forms, rules, or customs. **3.** An established form, rule, or custom.

for·mal·ize (fôr′mə-līz′) *tr.v.* **-ized, -iz·ing, -iz·es. 1.** To give a definite form or shape to. **2.** To make formal. **3.** To give formal endorsement to. **—for′mal·i·za′tion** *n.*

formal logic *n.* The study of the properties of propositions and deductive reasoning by abstraction and analysis of the form rather than the content of propositions under consideration.

form·am·id·ase (fôr-măm′ĭ-dās′, -dāz′) *n.* An enzyme that participates in the catabolism of the amino acid tryptophan. [FORM(IC ACID) + AMID(E) + -ASE.]

for·mant (fôr′mənt) *n.* Any of several frequency regions of relatively great intensity in a sound spectrum, which together determine the characteristic quality of a vowel sound. [G. < Lat. *formans,* pr.part. of *formare,* to form < *forma,* form.]

for·mat (fôr′măt′) *n.* **1.** A plan for the organization and arrangement of a specified production. **2.** The material form or layout of a publication. —*tr.v.* **-mat·ted, -mat·ting, -mats.** To produce (computer data, for example) in a specified form. [Fr. < G. < Lat. *formatus,* p.part. of *formare,* to form < *forma,* form.]

for·mate (fôr′māt′) *n.* A salt or ester of formic acid. [FORM(IC ACID) + -ATE[2].]

for·ma·tion (fôr-mā′shən) *n.* **1.** The process of forming or producing. **2.** Something that is formed. **3.** The manner or style in which something is formed. **4.** A specified arrangement or deployment, as of troops. **5.** *Geol.* The primary unit of lithostratigraphy, consisting of a succession of strata useful for mapping or description. **—for·ma′tion·al** *adj.*

for·ma·tive (fôr′mə-tĭv) *adj.* **1.** Forming or capable of forming. **2.** Susceptible of transformation by growth and development. **3.** Of or pertaining to formation, growth, or development: *a formative stage.* **4.** Pertaining to the formation or inflection of words. —*n.* The element of a word that is not contained in the base and that gives the word a suitable form. **—for′ma·tive·ly** *adv.*

form class *n.* A set of linguistic forms whose exact substitutability in a given construction is determined by their common embodiment of one or more morphological or syntactic features.

form·er[1] (fôr′mər) *n.* One that forms.

for·mer[2] (fôr′mər) *adj.* **1.** Occurring earlier in time. **2.** Coming before in place or order. **3.** Being the first mentioned of two. [ME, comp. of *forme,* first < OE *forma.*]

Usage: *The former* is used when referring back to the first of two persons or things mentioned. It is not used when referring to the first of three or more. For that purpose one may use *the first* or *the first-named* or repeat the name itself.

for·mer·ly (fôr′mər-lē) *adv.* At a former time; once.

form·fit·ting (fôrm′fĭt′ĭng) *adj.* Closely fitted to the body.

for·mic (fôr′mĭk) *adj.* **1.** Of or pertaining to ants. **2.** Of or pertaining to formic acid. [< Lat. *formica,* ant.]

For·mi·ca (fôr-mī′kə). A trademark for any of various high-pressure laminated plastic sheets of melamine and phenolic materials used esp. for chemical and heat-resistant surfaces.

formic acid *n.* A colorless caustic fuming liquid, HCOOH, used in dyeing and finishing textiles and paper and in the manufacture of fumigants, insecticides, and refrigerants.

for·mi·car·y (fôr′mĭ-kĕr′ē) *n., pl.* **-ies.** A nest of ants. [Med. Lat. *formicarium* < Lat. *formica,* ant.]

for·mi·civ·o·rous (fôr′mĭ-sĭv′ər-əs) *adj.* Feeding on ants. [Lat. *formica,* ant + -VOROUS.]

for·mi·da·ble (fôr′mĭ-də-bəl) *adj.* **1.** Arousing fear, dread, or alarm. **2.** Admirable or awe-inspiring: *a formidable intellect.* **3.** Difficult to surmount, defeat, or undertake; awesome. [OFr. < Lat. *formidabilis* < *formidare,* to fear < *formido,* fear.] **—for′mi·da·bil′i·ty, for′mi·da·ble·ness** *n.* **—for′mi·da·bly** *adv.*

form·less (fôrm′lĭs) *adj.* **1.** Having no specified form; shapeless. **2.** Lacking order. **—form′less·ly** *adv.* **—form′less·ness** *n.*

form letter *n.* A usually impersonal letter in a standardized format that may be sent to different people or to large numbers of people.

for·mu·la (fôr′myə-lə) *n., pl.* **-las** or **-lae** (-lē′). **1.** An established form of words or symbols for use in a ceremony or procedure. **2.** A method of doing or treating something that relies on an established, uncontroversial model or approach: *a new situation comedy that simply uses an old formula.* **3.** An utterance of conventional notions or beliefs. **4.** *Chem.* **a.** A symbolic representation of the composition or of the composition and structure of a chemical compound. **b.** The chemical compound so represented. **5.** A prescription of ingredients in fixed proportion; recipe. **6.** A liquid food prescribed for an infant and containing most required nutrients. **7.** A mathematical statement, esp. an equation, of a rule, principle, answer, or other logical relation. [Lat., dim. of *forma,* form.] **—for′mu·la′ic** (-lā′ĭk) *adj.* **—for′mu·la′i·cal·ly** *adv.*

for·mu·la·rize (fôr′myə-lə-rīz′) *tr.v.* **-rized, -riz·ing, -riz·es.** To formulate. **—for′mu·la·ri·za′tion** *n.*

for·mu·lar·y (fôr′myə-lĕr′ē) *n., pl.* **-ies. 1.** A book or other collection of formulas, such as prayers. **2.** A statement expressed in formulas. **3.** A formula. **4.** A book containing the names of pharmaceutical substances and listing their uses.

for·mu·late (fôr′myə-lāt′) *tr.v.* **-lat·ed, -lat·ing, -lates. 1.** To state as a formula. **2.** To express in systematic terms or concepts. **3.** To devise; invent: *formulate strategy.* **4.** To prepare according to a specified formula. **—for′mu·la′tion** *n.* **—for′mu·la′tor** *n.*

formula weight *n.* Molecular weight.

for·mu·lize (fôr′myə-līz′) *tr.v.* **-lized, -liz·ing, -liz·es.** To formulate. **—for′mu·li·za′tion** *n.* **—for′mu·liz′er** *n.*

for·myl (fôr′mĭl′) *n.* The univalent radical CHO. [FORM(IC ACID) + -YL.]

For·nax (fôr′năks′) *n.* A constellation in the Southern Hemisphere near Sculptor and Eridanus. [Lat. *fornax,* furnace.]

for·ni·cate (fôr′nĭ-kāt′) *intr.v.* **-cat·ed, -cat·ing, -cates.** To commit fornication. [LLat. *fornicari, fornicat-* < *fornix,* brothel.] **—for′ni·ca′tor** *n.*

for·ni·ca·tion (fôr′nĭ-kā′shən) *n.* Sexual intercourse between a man and woman not married to each other.

for·nix (fôr′nĭks) *n., pl.* **-ni·ces** (-nĭ-sēz′). *Anat.* Either of a pair of bands composed of white fibers beneath the corpus callosum of the brain. [NLat. < Lat., vault.]

for·sake (fôr-sāk′, fər-) *tr.v.* **-sook** (-so͝ok′), **-sak·en** (-sā′kən), **-sak·ing, -sakes. 1.** To give up; renounce: *forsook liquor.* **2.** To leave altogether; abandon: *forsook Hollywood and returned to the theater.* [ME *forsaken* < OE *forsacan.*]

for·sooth (fôr-so͞oth′, fər-) *adv. Archaic.* In truth; indeed. [ME *forsoth* < OE *forsōð.*]

for·spent (fôr-spĕnt′, fər-) *adj. Archaic.* Worn out with exertion; exhausted.

for·swear also **fore·swear** (fôr-swâr′, fōr-) *v.* **-swore** (fôr-swôr′, fōr-swōr′), **-sworn** (fôr-swôrn′, fōr-swōrn′), **-swear·ing, -swears.** —*tr.* **1.** To renounce or forsake unalterably. **2.** To disavow or repudiate unalterably. **3.** To perjure (oneself). —*intr.* To swear falsely; commit perjury. [ME *forsweren* < OE *forswerian.*]

for·syth·i·a (fôr-sĭth′ē-ə, fər-) *n.* Any of several shrubs of the genus *Forsythia,* native to Asia and widely cultivated for their early-blooming yellow flowers. [NLat. (genus name), after William *Forsyth* (1737–1804).]

fort
Fort Harrison in Indiana

fort (fôrt, fōrt) *n.* **1.** A fortified place or position stationed with troops. **2.** A permanent army post. [ME < OFr. < *fort,* strong < Lat. *fortis.*]

for·ta·lice (fôr′tə-lĭs) *n.* A minor defensive structure or position; small fort. [ME < Med. Lat. *fortalitia* < Lat. *fortis,* strong.]

forte[1] (fôrt, fōrt, fôr′tā′) *n.* **1.** Something in which a person excels. **2.** The strong part of a sword blade, between the middle and the hilt. [OFr. *fort* < *fort,* strong < Lat. *fortis.*]

for·te[2] (fôr′tā′) *Mus.* —*adv.* Loudly; forcefully. Used as a direction. —*n.* A note, passage, or chord played forte. —*adj.* Loud; forceful. [Ital. < *forte,* strong < Lat. *fortis.*]

for·te·pi·an·o (fôr′tā-pē-ăn′ō, -ä′nō) *Mus.* —*adv.* Loudly and then softly. Used as a direction. —*adj.* Loud and then soft. [Ital. : *forte,* loud + *piano,* soft.]

forth (fôrth, fōrth) *adv.* **1.** Forward in time, place, or order; onward: *from this time forth.* **2.** Out into view: *A stranger came forth from the crowd.* **3.** Away from a specified place;

abroad. —*prep. Archaic.* Out of; forth from. [ME < OE *forð*.]

forth·com·ing (fôrth-kŭm′ĭng, fōrth-) *adj.* **1.** About to appear or take place; approaching: *the forthcoming elections.* **2. a.** Available when required or as promised: *Federal funds were forthcoming.* **b.** Affable and outgoing: *a considerate, forthcoming lady.* —*n.* (fôrth′kŭm′ĭng, fōrth′-). An act or instance of coming forth.

forth·right (fôrth′rīt′, fōrth′-) *adj.* **1.** *Archaic.* Proceeding straight ahead. **2.** Direct and without evasion; straightforward: *a forthright appraisal.* —*adv.* **1.** Directly ahead. **2.** Directly and frankly. **3.** *Archaic.* At once. **—forth′right′ly** *adv.* **—forth′right′ness** *n.*

forth·with (fôrth-wĭth′, -wĭth′, fōrth-) *adv.* At once; immediately.

for·ti·eth (fôr′tē-ĭth) *n.* **1.** The ordinal number that matches the number 40 in a series. **2.** One of 40 equal parts. **—for′ti·eth** *adj. & adv.*

for·ti·fi·ca·tion (fôr′tə-fĭ-kā′shən) *n.* **1.** The act, science, or art of fortifying. **2.** Something, esp. a military defensive work, that serves to defend, strengthen, or fortify.

fortified wine *n.* A wine, such as sherry, to which alcohol, usually in the form of grape brandy, has been added.

for·ti·fy (fôr′tə-fī′) *v.* **-fied, -fy·ing, -fies.** —*tr.* **1.** To strengthen and secure (a position) with fortifications. **2.** To add strength to (a structure) by reinforcement; reinforce. **3.** To impart physical strength to; invigorate: *The coffee fortified him.* **4.** To give moral or mental strength to; encourage: *fortified his troubled spirit by praying.* **5.** To corroborate; support: *fortified his allegations with new evidence.* **6.** To strengthen or enrich (a substance), as by adding vitamins to food. —*intr.* To build fortifications. [ME *fortifien* < OFr. *fortifier* < LLat. *fortificare* < Lat. *fortis,* strong.] **—for′ti·fi′a·ble** *adj.* **—for′ti·fi′er** *n.*

for·tis (fôr′tĭs) *adj.* Pronounced with tension and strong articulation. Used of certain consonants such as *f* and *p.* —*n.* A fortis consonant. [NLat. < Lat., strong.]

for·tis·si·mo (fôr-tĭs′ə-mō′) *Mus.* —*adv.* Very loudly. Used as a direction. —*n., pl.* **-mos.** A note, passage, or chord played fortissimo. —*adj.* Very loud. [Ital., superl. of *forte,* strong.]

for·ti·tude (fôr′tĭ-to͞od′, -tyo͞od′) *n.* Strength of mind that allows one to endure pain or adversity with courage. [ME < Lat. *fortitudo* < *fortis,* strong.] **—for′ti·tu′di·nous** (-to͞od′n-əs, -tyo͞od′-) *adj.*

fort·night (fôrt′nīt′) *n.* Two weeks. [ME *fourtenight,* alteration of *fourtene night,* fourteen nights.]

fort·night·ly (fôrt′nīt′lē) *adj.* Happening or appearing once in or every two weeks. —*adv.* Once in two weeks; every fortnight. —*n., pl.* **-lies.** A publication issued fortnightly.

FOR·TRAN (fôr′trăn′) *n.* A computer programming language for problems that can be expressed in algebraic terms. [FOR(MULA) + TRAN(SLATION).]

for·tress (fôr′trĭs) *n.* A fortified place, esp. a large and permanent military stronghold, often including a town. [ME *forteress* < OFr. < Med. Lat. *fortalitia* < Lat. *fortis,* strong.]

for·tu·i·tous (fôr-to͞o′ĭ-təs, -tyo͞o′-) *adj.* **1.** Happening by accident or chance. **2.** Lucky or fortunate. [Lat. *fortuitus* < *forte,* by chance, ablative of *fors,* chance.] **—for·tu′i·tous·ly** *adv.* **—for·tu′i·tous·ness** *n.*

Usage: *Fortuitous* is often confused with *fortunate. Fortuitous* means "happening by chance." A *fortuitous* meeting may have either fortunate or unfortunate consequences. In common usage, it is true, some of the meaning of *fortunate* has rubbed off on *fortuitous* so that even when it is properly used, *fortuitous* often carries an implication of lucky chance rather than unlucky chance. But the word is not synonymous with *fortunate* and should not be used unless it refers to something that came about by chance or accident. The following example is termed unacceptable by a large majority of the Usage Panel: *The meeting proved fortuitous; I came away with a much better idea of my role.*

for·tu·i·ty (fôr-to͞o′ĭ-tē, -tyo͞o′-) *n., pl.* **-ties. 1.** An accidental occurrence; chance. **2.** The quality or condition of being fortuitous.

For·tu·na (fôr-to͞o′nə, -tyo͞o′-) *n.* The Roman goddess of fortune. [Lat. < *fortūna,* fortune.]

for·tu·nate (fôr′chə-nĭt) *adj.* **1.** Bringing something good and unforeseen; auspicious. **2.** Having unexpected good fortune; lucky. —See Usage note at **fortuitous. —for′tu·nate·ly** *adv.* **—for′tu·nate·ness** *n.*

for·tune (fôr′chən) *n.* **1.** Often **Fortune.** A hypothetical, often personified force or power that favorably or unfavorably governs the events of one's life: *Fortune is on our side.* **2.** The good or bad luck that is to befall someone; fate. **3.** Success, esp. when at least partially resulting from luck. **4. a.** A person's condition or standing in life determined by material possessions or financial wealth. **b.** Extensive amounts of material possessions or money; wealth. **5.** A large sum of money: *bet a fortune on the game.* —*v.* **-tuned, -tun·ing, -tunes.** —*tr. Obs.* To ascribe or give good or bad fortune to. —*intr. Archaic.* To occur by chance; happen. [ME < OFr. < Lat. *fortuna* < *fors,* chance.]

fortune cookie *n.* A cookie made from a thin layer of dough folded and baked around a slip of paper bearing a prediction of fortune or a maxim.

fortune hunter *n.* A person who seeks wealth, esp. through marriage.

for·tune·tell·er (fôr′chən-tĕl′ər) *n.* A person who professes to predict future events. **—for′tune·tell′ing** *n.*

for·ty (fôr′tē) *n., pl.* **-ties.** The cardinal number equal to 4 × 10. [ME < OE *fēowertig* : *fēower,* four + *-tig,* -ty.] **—for′ty** *adj. & pron.*

for·ty-five (fôr′tē-fīv′) *n.* **1.** A .45-caliber pistol. **2.** A phonograph record designed to be played at 45 revolutions per minute.

for·ty-nin·er (fôr′tē-nī′nər) *n.* One who took part in the 1849 California gold rush.

forty winks *n. Informal.* A short nap.

fo·rum (fôr′əm, fōr′-) *n., pl.* **fo·rums** or **fo·ra** (fôr′ə, fōr′ə). **1.** The public square or marketplace of an ancient Roman city that was the assembly place for judicial and other public activity. **2. a.** A public meeting place for open discussion. **b.** A medium for open discussion, as a radio or television program. **3.** A court of law; tribunal. **4.** A public meeting or presentation involving a discussion usually among experts and often including audience participation. [ME < Lat.]

for·ward (fôr′wərd) *adj.* **1. a.** At, near, or belonging to the front; fore. **b.** Located in advance. **2.** Going, tending, or moving toward a position in front: *a forward fall down a flight of stairs.* **3. a.** Ardently inclined; eager. **b.** Without restraint or modesty; bold. **4.** Progressive, esp. technologically, politically, or economically: *a forward concept.* **5.** Mentally, physically, socially, or biologically advanced; precocious: *a forward child.* **6.** Completed or made in advance: *bidding on forward contracts for corn.* —*adv.* **1.** Toward or tending to the front; frontward: *step forward.* **2.** In or toward the future: *looking forward to seeing you.* **3.** Into view or prominence; forth: *Come forward out of the shadows so I can see you.* —*n. Sports.* **1.** A player in certain games, such as basketball, who is part of the front line of offense or defense. **2.** The position played by a forward. —*tr.v.* **-ward·ed, -ward·ing, -wards. 1.** To send on to a subsequent destination or address. **2.** To help advance; promote. [ME < OE *foreweard.*] **—for′ward·ly** *adv.* **—for′ward·ness** *n.*

Usage: *Forwards* may be used in place of *forward* only in the adverbial sense of "toward the front": *move forward* (or *forwards*). In specific phrases the choice of one or the other is often idiomatic: *look forward; from that day forward; backwards and forwards.*

for·ward·er (fôr′wər-dər) *n.* One that forwards, esp. an agent who facilitates and assures the passage of received goods to their destination.

forward pass *n. Football.* A pass thrown in the direction of the opponent's goal.

for·wards (fôr′wərdz, fōr′-) *adv.* Forward (sense 1). —See Usage note at **forward.**

for·went (fôr-wĕnt′) *v.* Past tense of **forgo.**

for·worn also **fore·worn** (fôr-wôrn′, fōr-wōrn′) *adj. Archaic.* Worn-out.

for·zan·do (fôrt-sän′dō) *adj., adv., & n.* Variant of **sforzando.**

foss (fŏs) *n.* Variant of **fosse.**

fos·sa (fŏs′ə) *n., pl.* **fos·sae** (fŏs′ē′). A hollow or depression, as in a bone. [Lat., ditch < fem. p.part. of *fodere,* to dig.] **—fos′sate′** (fŏs′āt′) *adj.*

fosse also **foss** (fŏs) *n.* A ditch or moat. [ME < OFr. and Lat. *fossa.*]

fos·sick (fŏs′ĭk) *v.* **-sicked, -sick·ing, -sicks.** *Austral.* —*intr.* **1.** To search for gold, esp. by reworking washings or waste piles. **2.** To rummage or search, esp. for a possible profit. —*tr.* To search for by or as if by rummaging. [Orig. unknown.] **—fos′sick·er** *n.*

fos·sil (fŏs′əl) *n.* **1.** A remnant or trace of an organism of a past geologic age, such as a skeleton or leaf imprint, embedded in the earth's crust. **2.** One that is outdated or antiquated, as a rigid theory or a person with outmoded ideas. **3.** An obsolete word or word element used only in an idiom, as *fro* in *to and fro.* **—*modifier:*** *fossil ferns.* [< Lat. *fossilis,* dug up < *fossus,* p.part. of *fodere,* to dig.]

fossil
Fossilized fern fronds

fossil fuel *n.* A hydrocarbon fuel, such as petroleum, derived from living matter of a previous geologic time.

fos·sil·if·er·ous (fŏs′ə-lĭf′ər-əs) *adj.* Containing fossils.

fos·sil·ize (fŏs′ə-līz′) *v.* **-ized, -iz·ing, -iz·es.** —*tr.* **1.** To convert into a fossil. **2.** To make outmoded, rigid, or fixed. —*intr.* To become a fossil. **—fos′sil·i·za′tion** *n.*

fos·so·ri·al (fŏ-sôr′ē-əl, -sōr′-) *adj. Zool.* Adapted for or used in burrowing or digging. [Med. Lat. *fossorius* < Lat. *fossus,* p.part. of *fodere,* to dig.]

fos·ter (fô′stər, fŏs′tər) *tr.v.* **-tered, -ter·ing, -ters. 1.** To bring up; nurture. **2.** To promote the development or growth of; encourage. **3.** To nurse; cherish: *foster a secret hope.* —*adj.* Receiving, sharing, or affording parental care and nurture although not related through legal or blood ties: *a foster child.* [ME *fostren* < OE *fōstrian,* to nourish < *fōstor,* food.]

fos·ter·ling (fô′stər-lĭng, fŏs′tər-) *n.* A foster child.

Fou·cault pendulum (fo͞o-kō′) *n.* A simple pendulum suspended so that the plane of motion is not fixed, set into motion along a meridian, and appearing to turn clockwise in the Northern Hemisphere or counterclockwise in the

Southern Hemisphere, demonstrating the axial rotation of the earth. [After Jean B.L. *Foucault* (1819–1868).]
fou·droy·ant (fo͞o-droi'ənt, fo͞o'drwä-yäN') *adj.* Dazzling or stunning in effect. [Fr., pr.part of *foudroyer,* to strike with lightning < *foudre,* lightning < OFr. *fouldre* < Lat. *fulgur* < *fulgēre,* to flash.]
fought (fôt) *v.* Past tense and past participle of **fight.**
foul (foul) *adj.* **-er, -est. 1.** Offensive to the senses; revolting. **2.** Having an offensive odor; fetid. **3.** Rotten or putrid. Used esp. of food. **4.** Full of dirt or mud. **5.** Morally detestable; wicked. **6.** Of a vulgar or obscene nature: *foul language.* **7.** *Archaic.* Ugly; unattractive. **8.** *Informal.* Very disagreeable or displeasing; horrid: *a foul movie.* **9.** Bad or unfavorable. Used esp. of weather. **10.** Not according to accepted standards or rules or honor; dishonorable: *used foul means to achieve his aim.* **11.** Contrary to the rules of a game or sport. **12.** *Baseball.* Outside the foul line, as a ball. **13.** Entangled or twisted: *a foul anchor.* **14.** Clogged or obstructed; blocked: *a foul ventilator shaft.* —*n.* **1.** *Sports.* An infraction or violation of the rules of play. **2.** *Baseball.* A foul ball. **3.** An entanglement or collision. **4.** An instance of clogging or obstructing. —*adv.* In a foul manner. —*v.* **fouled, foul·ing, fouls.** —*tr.* **1.** To make dirty or foul. **2.** To bring into dishonor; besmirch. **3.** To clog or obstruct. **4.** To entangle or catch (a rope, for example). **5.** To encrust (a ship's hull) with foreign matter, such as barnacles. **6.** *Sports.* To commit a foul against. **7.** *Baseball.* To hit (a ball) outside the foul lines. —*intr.* **1.** To become foul. **2.** *Sports.* To commit a foul. **3.** *Baseball.* **a.** To hit a ball outside the foul lines. **b.** To make an out by hitting a foul ball that is caught before it touches the ground: *fouled out to the catcher.* **4.** To become entangled or twisted: *The anchor fouled on a rock.* **5.** To become clogged or obstructed. —***phrasal verbs.*** **foul out.** *Sports.* To be put out of play by exceeding the number of permissible fouls. **foul up.** *Informal.* To blunder or cause to blunder because of mistakes or poor judgment. [ME < OE *fūl.*] —**foul'ly** *adv.* —**foul'ness** *n.*

foundation

fou·lard (fo͞o-lärd') *n.* **1.** A lightweight twill or plain-woven fabric of silk or silk and cotton, usually having a small printed design. **2.** An article of clothing, esp. a necktie or scarf, made of foulard. [Fr.]
foul ball *n.* *Baseball.* A batted ball that touches the ground outside of fair territory.
foul·brood (foul'bro͝od') *n.* A disease of honeybee larvae caused by one of several types of bacteria, including *Bacillus alvei.*
foul line *n.* **1.** *Baseball.* Either of two straight lines extending from the rear of home plate to the boundary of the playing field to indicate the area in which a fair ball can be hit. **2.** *Basketball.* A line from which a player makes a foul shot. **3.** *Sports.* A boundary limiting the playing area, esp. in bowling and tennis.
foul-mouthed (foul'mouthd', -moutht') *adj.* Using obscene or scurrilous language.
foul play *n.* Unfair or treacherous action, esp. when involving violence.
foul shot *n.* *Basketball.* An unguarded throw to the basket from the foul line awarded to a fouled player and scored as one point if successful.
foul tip *n.* *Baseball.* A pitched ball that is slightly deflected off the bat into the foul zone.
foul-up (foul'ŭp') *n.* *Informal.* **1.** A condition of confusion caused by mistakes or poor judgment. **2.** Mechanical trouble.

fountain

found¹ (found) *tr.v.* **found·ed, found·ing, founds. 1.** To originate or establish (a college, for example). **2.** To establish the foundation or basis of. [ME *founden* < OFr. *fonder* < Lat. *fundare* < *fundus,* bottom.] —**found'er** *n.*
found² (found) *tr.v.* **found·ed, found·ing, founds. 1.** To melt (metal) and pour into a mold. **2.** To make (objects) by pouring molten material into a mold. [ME *founden* < OFr. *fondre* < Lat. *fundere.*] —**found'er** *n.*
found³ (found) *v.* Past tense and past participle of **find.**
foun·da·tion (foun-dā'shən) *n.* **1.** The act of founding, esp. the establishment of an institution with provisions for future maintenance. **2.** The basis on which a thing stands, is founded, or is supported. **3.** Funds for the perpetual support of an institution; endowment. **4.** An institution founded and supported by an endowment. **5.** A foundation garment. **6.** A cosmetic used as a base for facial make-up. —**foun·da'tion·al** *adj.*
foundation garment *n.* A woman's supporting undergarment, such as a corset or girdle.
foun·der (foun'dər) *v.* **-dered, -der·ing, -ders.** —*intr.* **1.** To become disabled, esp. to go lame. Used of horses. **2.** To collapse or break down; fail. **3.** *Naut.* To sink below the water. **4.** To cave in; sink. Used of ground or buildings. —*tr.* To cause to founder. —*n.* Laminitis. [ME *foundren,* to sink to the ground < OFr. *fondrer* < VLat. *fundorare* < Lat. *fundus,* bottom.]
Usage: The verbs *founder* and *flounder* are often confused. *Founder* comes from a Latin word meaning "bottom" (as in *foundation*) and originally referred to a ship's sinking; it is now used as well to mean "to fail utterly, collapse." *Flounder* means "to move clumsily, thrash about" and hence "to proceed in confusion." If John is *foundering* in Chemistry 1, he had better drop the course; if he is *floundering,* he may yet pull through.

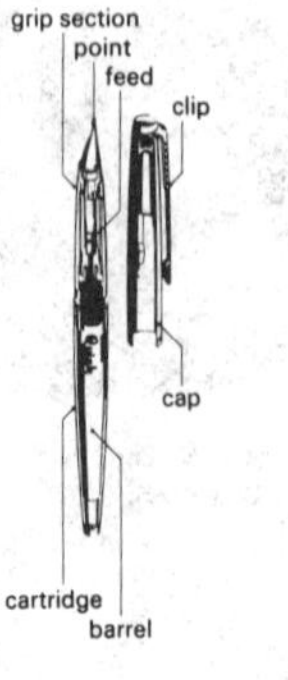

fountain pen

Found·ing Father (foun'dĭng) *n.* **1.** A member of the American Constitutional Convention of 1787. **2. founding father.** One that founds or establishes something; originator.
found·ling (found'lĭng) *n.* A child deserted by parents whose identity is not known. [ME.]
found object *n.* Any of various objects or materials picked up by chance and incorporated into a work of art. [Transl. of French *objet trouvé.*]
foun·dry (foun'drē) *n., pl.* **-dries. 1.** An establishment in which the founding of metals is done. **2. a.** The art or operation of founding. **b.** The castings made by founding.
foundry proof *n.* A proof taken from composed type for a final check before plates are made.
fount¹ (fount) *n.* **1.** A fountain. **2.** A source. [OFr. *font* < Lat. *fons,* fountain.]
fount² (fount) *n.* *Chiefly Brit.* Variant of **font².**
foun·tain (foun'tən) *n.* **1.** A spring, esp. the source of a stream. **2.** A point of origin; source. **3. a.** An artificially created jet or stream of water. **b.** A device that produces and contains such a jet or stream. **4.** A reservoir or chamber containing a supply of liquid that can be siphoned off as needed. **5.** A soda fountain. [ME < OFr. *fontaine* < LLat. *fontana* < Lat. *fontanus,* of a spring < *fons,* spring.]
foun·tain·head (foun'tən-hĕd') *n.* **1.** A spring that is the source or head of a stream. **2.** A principal source or origin.
fountain pen *n.* A pen filled from an external source and containing an ink reservoir that automatically feeds the writing point.
four (fôr, fōr) *n.* **1.** The cardinal number that is next after the number 3 and equal to the sum of 3 + 1. **2.** The fourth in a set or sequence. **3.** Something having four parts, units, or members. [ME < OE *fēower;* akin to G. *vier,* Lat. *quattuor,* Gk. *tettares,* and Skt. *catur.*] —**four** *adj. & pron.*
four-bag·ger (fôr'băg'ər, fōr'-) *n.* *Baseball. Informal.* A home run.
four·chette (fo͞or-shĕt') *n.* A narrow, forked strip of material joining the front and back sections of the fingers of gloves. [Fr. < OFr. *forchete,* fork, dim. of *forche,* pitchfork < Lat. *furca.*]
four-col·or (fôr'kŭl'ər) *adj.* Designating a color printing or photographic process in which three primary colors and black are transferred by four different plates or filters to a surface, reproducing the colors of the subject matter.
four-cy·cle (fôr'sī'kəl, fōr'-) *adj.* Designating an internal-combustion engine that requires four strokes of the piston for a cycle.
four-di·men·sion·al (fôr'dĭ-mĕn'shə-nəl, fōr'-) *adj.* Exhibiting or being specified by four dimensions, esp. the three spatial dimensions and single temporal dimension of relativity theory.
Four·drin·i·er (fo͞or-drĭn'ē-ər) *adj.* Designating a papermaking machine used to produce paper in a continuous roll or web. [After Henry *Fourdrinier* (1766–1854) and Sealy *Fourdrinier* (d. 1847).]
four-eyed fish (fôr'īd', fōr'-) *n.* Either of two freshwater fishes, *Anableps anableps* or *A. microlepis,* of tropical America, having bulging eyes divided longitudinally, with the upper part adapted for aerial vision, the lower part for underwater vision.
four flush *n.* A five-card poker hand having four cards in the same suit.
four-flush (fôr'flŭsh', fōr'-) *intr.v.* **-flushed, -flush·ing, -flush·es. 1.** To bluff in poker with a four flush. **2.** *Slang.* To make a pretense; bluff. —**four'-flush'er** *n.*
four·fold (fôr'fōld', fōr'-) *adj.* **1.** Having four units or aspects; quadruple. **2.** Being four times as much or as many. —*adv.* (fôr'fōld', fōr'-). In quadrupled measure.
four-foot·ed (fôr'fo͝ot'ĭd, fōr'-) *adj.* Having four feet.
four·gon (fo͞or-gôN') *n., pl.* **-gons** (-gôN', -gônz'). A wagon for carrying baggage. [Fr.]
four-hand·ed (fôr'hăn'dĭd, fōr'-) *adj.* **1.** Involving or requiring four players. **2.** Designed for four hands, as a piano duet.
Four-H Club (fôr'āch', fōr'-) *n.* A youth organization sponsored by the Department of Agriculture and offering instruction in agriculture and home economics. [From its four goals to improve head, heart, hands, and health.]
four hundred also **Four Hundred** *n.* The wealthiest and most exclusive social set of a community.
Fou·ri·er analysis (fo͞or'ē-ā') *n.* The approximation of a function through the application of a Fourier series to periodic data.
Fou·ri·er·ism (fo͞or'ē-ə-rĭz'əm) *n.* The system for social reform advocated by Charles Fourier in the early 19th century, proposing that society be organized into small self-sustaining communal groups. —**Fou'ri·er·ist, Fou'ri·er·ite'** (-ə-rīt') *n.*
Fourier series *n.* An infinite series of sine and cosine functions capable if uniformly convergent of approximating a wide variety of mathematical functions. [After Jean B.J. *Fourier* (1768–1830).]
four-in-hand (fôr'ĭn-hănd', fōr'-) *n.* **1.** A vehicle drawn by horses driven by one person. **2.** A team of four horses. **3.** A

necktie tied in a slipknot with the ends left hanging and overlapping.

four-leaf clover (fôr′lēf′, fōr′-) *n.* A clover leaf having four leaflets instead of the normal three, considered to be an omen of good luck.

four-let·ter word (fôr′lĕt′ər, fōr′-) *n.* Any of several short English words generally regarded as vulgar or obscene.

four-o'clock (fôr′ə-klŏk′, fōr′-) *n.* Any of several plants of the genus *Mirabilis,* esp. *M. jalapa,* native to tropical America and widely cultivated for its tubular, variously colored flowers that open in the late afternoon.

four·pence (fôr′pəns, fōr′-) *n. Chiefly Brit.* **1.** A sum of money equal to four pence. **2.** Formerly, a small silver coin worth four pence.

four-post·er (fôr′pō′stər, fōr′-) *n.* A bed having tall corner posts originally intended to support curtains or a canopy.

four·ra·gère (fo͝or′ə-zhâr′) *n.* An ornamental braided cord usually looped around the left shoulder, esp. such a cord awarded to an entire military unit. [Fr. < *fourrage,* forage < OFr. —see FORAGE.]

four·score (fôr′skôr′, fōr′skōr′) *adj.* Four times 20; 80.

four·some (fôr′səm, fōr′-) *n.* **1.** A group of four persons or things, esp. two couples. **2. a.** A game, esp. a golf match, played by four persons, two on each side. **b.** The players in such a game. [ME *four-som* < OE *fēowra sum,* one of four.]

four·square (fôr′skwâr′, fōr′-) *adj.* **1.** Having four equal sides and four right angles; square. **2.** Marked by firm or unwavering conviction. **3.** Forthright or candid. —*adv.* Squarely; forthrightly.

four-star (fôr′stär′, fōr′-) *adj.* **1.** Relating to or being a general or an admiral whose insignia carries four stars. **2.** Of superlative quality: *a four-star restaurant.*

four·teen (fôr-tēn′, fōr-) *n.* **1.** The cardinal number that is next after the number 13 and equal to the sum of 13 + 1. **2.** The fourteenth in a set or sequence. **3.** Something having fourteen parts, units, or members. [ME *fourtene* < OE *fēowertēne.*] **—four·teen′** *adj. & pron.*

four·teenth (fôr-tēnth′, fōr-) *n.* **1.** The ordinal number that matches the number 14 in a series. **2.** One of 14 equal parts. **—four·teenth′** *adj. & adv.*

fourth (fôrth, fōrth) *n.* **1.** The ordinal number that matches the number 4 in a series. **2.** One of four equal parts. **3.** *Mus.* **a.** A tone four degrees above or below a given tone in a diatonic scale. **b.** The interval between two such tones. **c.** The harmonic combination of these tones. **d.** The subdominant in a scale. **4.** The fourth forward gear of a motor vehicle. **5. Fourth.** The Fourth of July. [ME *fourthe* < OE *fēorða.*] **—fourth** *adj. & adv.*

fourth-class (fôrth′klăs′, fōrth′-) *adj.* Designating a class of mail consisting of merchandise or certain printed matter weighing over eight ounces and not sealed against inspection. —*adv.* As or by fourth-class mail.

fourth dimension *n.* Time regarded as a coordinate dimension and required by relativistic geometry, along with three spatial dimensions, to completely specify the location of any event.

fourth estate *n.* The public press.

Fourth of July *n.* Independence Day.

Fourth World *n.* The least-developed countries of the Third World, esp. in Africa and Asia.

four-wheel (fôr′hwēl′, -wēl′, fōr′-) *adj.* **1.** Having four wheels. **2.** Of, pertaining to, or designating an automotive drive mechanism in which all four wheels are connected to the source of driving power.

fo·ve·a (fō′vē-ə) *n., pl.* **-ve·ae** (-vē-ē′). A shallow cuplike depression or pit in a bone or other organ. [NLat. < Lat., small pit.] **—fo′ve·al** (-əl), **fo′ve·ate′** (-āt′) *adj.* **—fo′ve·i·form′** (-ə-fôrm′) *adj.*

fovea cen·tra·lis (sĕn-trā′lĭs) *n.* A small depression in the macula lutea of the retina, constituting the area of most distinct vision. [NLat., central fovea.]

fo·ve·ae (fō′vē-ē′) *n.* Plural of **fovea.**

fowl (foul) *n., pl.* **fowl** or **fowls. 1.** Any of various birds of the order Galliformes, esp. the common, widely domesticated chicken, *Gallus gallus.* **2. a.** A bird used as food or hunted as game. **b.** The edible flesh of such a bird. **3.** *Archaic.* A bird of any kind. —*intr.v.* **fowled, fowl·ing, fowls.** To hunt, trap, or shoot wild fowl. [ME *foul* < OE *fugol.*] **—fowl′er** *n.*

fowling piece *n.* A light shotgun for shooting birds and small animals.

fox (fŏks) *n.* **1.** Any of various carnivorous mammals of the genus *Vulpes* and related genera, related to the dogs and wolves and characteristically having upright ears, a pointed snout, and a long, bushy tail. **2.** The fur of a fox. **3.** A crafty, sly, or clever person. **4.** *Archaic.* A sword. **5.** *Naut.* Small cordage made by twisting together two or more strands of tarred yarn. —*v.* **foxed, fox·ing, fox·es.** —*tr.* **1. a.** To trick or fool by ingenuity or cunning; outwit. **b.** To baffle or confuse. **2.** *Archaic.* To intoxicate. **3.** To make (beer) sour by fermenting. **4.** To repair (a shoe) by adding a new upper. —*intr.* **1.** To act slyly or craftily. **2.** To turn sour in fermenting. Used of beer. [ME < OE.]

Fox (fŏks) *n., pl.* **Fox·es** or **Fox. 1.** A tribe of Algonquian-speaking Indians mainly of southwestern Wisconsin who merged with the Sauk in 1760. **2.** A member of the Fox.

foxed (fŏkst) *adj.* Discolored with yellowish-brown stains, as an old book or print.

fox·fire (fŏks′fīr′) *n.* A phosphorescent glow, esp. that produced by certain fungi found on rotting wood. [ME.]

fox·glove (fŏks′glŭv′) *n.* **1.** Any of several plants of the genus *Digitalis,* esp. *D. purpurea,* native to Europe, having a long cluster of large, tubular, pinkish-purple flowers and leaves that are the source of the medicinal drug digitalis. **2.** Any of several plants related to the foxglove. [ME.]

fox grape *n.* A climbing woody vine, *Vitis labrusca,* of the eastern United States, that bears purplish-black fruit and is the source of many cultivated grape varieties.

fox·hole (fŏks′hōl′) *n.* A shallow pit dug by a soldier in combat for immediate individual refuge against enemy fire.

fox·hound (fŏks′hound′) *n.* A dog developed for fox hunting, esp. a short-haired hound of either of two breeds, the English foxhound and the American foxhound.

fox squirrel *n.* A squirrel, *Sciurus niger,* of the United States, having rusty or grayish fur.

fox·tail (fŏks′tāl′) *n.* Any of several grasses of the genus *Alopecurus,* having dense, silky or bristly flowering spikes.

foxtail lily *n.* Any of several plants of the genus *Eremurus,* native to Asia, having a tall, spirelike cluster of small, bell-shaped white, yellowish, or pink flowers.

fox terrier *n.* A small dog of a breed originating in England, having a white coat with dark markings and developed in both wire-haired and smooth-coated varieties.

fox·trot (fŏks′trŏt′) *intr.v.* **-trot·ted, -trot·ting, -trots.** To dance the fox trot.

fox trot *n.* **1. a.** A ballroom dance in 2/4 or 4/4 time, composed of a variety of slow and fast steps. **b.** The music for this dance. **2.** The slow broken gait of a horse between a trot and a walk.

fox·y (fŏk′sē) *adj.* **-i·er, -i·est. 1.** Of or resembling a fox. **2.** Shrewdly clever; conniving. **3.** Having a reddish-brown color. **4.** Discolored, as by age or decay; foxed. **5.** Having the distinctive sharp flavor of some American grapes. Used of wines. **6.** *Informal.* Sensually attractive; sexy. **—fox′i·ly** *adv.* **—fox′i·ness** *n.*

foy (foi) *n. Scot.* A farewell feast, drink, or gift, as at a wedding. [Dial. Du. *fooi,* prob. < OFr. *voie,* journey < Lat. *via,* road.]

foy·er (foi′ər, foi′ā′, fwä′yā′) *n.* **1.** A lobby or anteroom, as of a theater or hotel. **2.** An entrance hall or vestibule. [Fr., hearth < Lat. *focus.*]

Fr The symbol for the element francium.

Fra (frä) *n.* Brother. The title given to a friar. [Ital., short for *frate,* brother < Lat. *frater.*]

fra·cas (frā′kəs, frăk′əs) *n.* A noisy quarrel or row; brawl. [Fr. < Ital. *fracasso* < *fracassare,* to make an uproar.]

fract·ed (frăk′tĭd) *adj. Obs.* Broken. [Lat. *fractus.* —see FRACTION.]

frac·tion (frăk′shən) *n.* **1.** A small part; bit: *moved a fraction of a step.* **2.** A disconnected piece of something; fragment. **3.** *Math.* An indicated quotient of two quantities. **4.** *Chem.* A component separated by fractionation. [ME *fraccioun,* a breaking < AN < LLat. *fractio,* a breaking of bread < Lat. *fractus,* p.part. of *frangere,* to break.]

frac·tion·al (frăk′shə-nəl) *adj.* **1.** Of, pertaining to, or constituting a fraction. **2.** Very small; insignificant. **3.** Being in fractions or pieces. **—frac′tion·al·ly** *adv.*

fractional currency *n.* **1.** A currency in a denomination less than the standard monetary unit. **2.** In the United States, a coin worth less than a dollar.

fractional distillation *n.* **1.** Distillation with rectification to obtain the purest possible product. **2.** Distillation in which the product is collected in a series of separate fractions.

frac·tion·ate (frăk′shə-nāt′) *tr.v.* **-at·ed, -at·ing, -ates.** To separate (a chemical compound) into components, as by distillation or crystallization. **—frac′tion·a′tion** *n.* **—frac′tion·a′tor** *n.*

frac·tion·ize (frăk′shə-nīz′) *tr. & intr.v.* **-ized, -iz·ing, -iz·es.** To divide into fractions. **—frac′tion·i·za′tion** *n.*

frac·tious (frăk′shəs) *adj.* **1.** Inclined to make trouble; unruly. **2.** Having a peevish nature; cranky. [< FRACTION.] **—frac′tious·ly** *adv.* **—frac′tious·ness** *n.*

frac·ture (frăk′chər) *n.* **1. a.** The act or process of breaking. **b.** The condition of being broken. **2.** A break, rupture, or crack, as in bone or cartilage. **3.** *Mineral.* **a.** The characteristic manner in which a mineral breaks. **b.** The characteristic appearance of a broken mineral. —*v.* **-tured, -tur·ing, -tures.** —*tr.* **1.** To break: *fracture a wrist.* **2.** To disrupt as if by breaking up or bursting. **3.** To break or manipulate the restrictions or rules of. —*intr.* To undergo a fracture. [ME < OFr. < Lat. *fractura* < *fractus,* p.part of *frangere,* to break.]

frae (frā) *prep. Scot.* From. [ME *fra* < ON *frā.*]

frag·ile (frăj′əl, -īl′) *adj.* **1.** Easily broken or damaged; brittle. **2.** Physically weak or delicate; frail. **3.** Tenuous or flimsy: *a fragile claim to fame.* [OFr. < Lat. *fragilis* < *frangere,* to break.] **—frag′ile·ly** *adv.* **—fra·gil′i·ty** (frə-jĭl′ĭ-tē), **frag′ile·ness** *n.*

Synonyms: *fragile, breakable, frail, delicate, brittle.* These adjectives mean susceptible to being broken or injured. *Fragile* most often describes objects whose lightness or delicacy of material requires that they be handled with great care. *Breakable* refers to what can be broken but

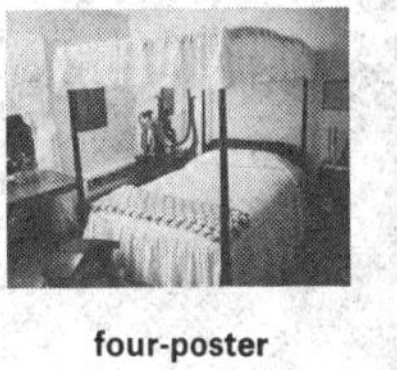

four-poster

foxglove

fox terrier

framework

makes a less strong implication of inherent weakness. *Frail,* applicable to persons and things, implies slightness of constitution, build, or structure and consequent lack of durability. *Delicate,* in this comparison, also suggests lack of durability or susceptibility to injury. *Brittle* refers to the hardness and inelasticity of some material that makes it especially subject to fracture or snapping when subjected to pressure.

frag·ment (frăg′mənt) *n.* **1.** A part broken off or detached. **2.** Something incomplete: *overheard fragments of their conversation.* —*v.* (-mĕnt′) **-ment·ed, -ment·ing, -ments.** —*tr.* To break or separate (something) into fragments. —*intr.* To break into fragments. [ME < Lat. *fragmentum* < *frangere,* to break.]

frag·men·tal (frăg-mĕn′tl) *adj.* **1.** Fragmentary. **2.** *Geol.* Consisting of broken material moved from its place of origin. —**frag·men′tal·ly** *adv.*

frag·men·tar·y (frăg′mən-tĕr′ē) *adj.* Consisting of fragments or disconnected parts. —**frag′men·tar′i·ly** (-târ′ə-lē) *adv.* —**frag′men·tar′i·ness** *n.*

frag·men·ta·tion (frăg′mən-tā′shən, -mĕn-) *n.* **1.** The act or process of breaking into fragments. **2.** The scattering of the fragments of an exploding grenade, bomb, or shell.

fragmentation bomb *n.* An aerial antipersonnel bomb that scatters shrapnel over a wide area upon explosion.

frag·men·tize (frăg′mən-tīz′) *tr. & intr.v.* **-tized, -tiz·ing, -tiz·es.** To break or become broken into fragments. —**frag′men·tiz′er** *n.*

fra·grance (frā′grəns) *n.* **1.** The state or quality of being fragrant. **2.** A sweet or pleasant odor; scent.

fra·grant (frā′grənt) *adj.* Having a pleasant odor. [ME < Lat. *fragrans,* p.part. of *fragrare,* to emit an odor.] —**fra′grant·ly** *adv.*

frail[1] (frāl) *adj.* **-er, -est. 1.** Having a delicate constitution; physically weak. **2.** Slight or unsubstantial. **3.** Easily broken or destroyed. **4.** Easily led astray or into evil. [ME < OFr. *fraile* < Lat. *fragilis* < *frangere,* to break.] —**frail′ly** *adv.* —**frail′ness** *n.*

frail[2] (frāl) *n.* **1.** A rush basket for holding fruit, esp. dried fruit. **2.** The quantity of fruit, such as raisins or figs, contained in a frail. [ME *fraiel* < OFr.]

frail·ty (frāl′tē) *n., pl.* **-ties. 1.** The condition or quality of being frail. **2.** A fault, esp. weakness of resolution, arising from the imperfections of human nature.

fraise (frāz) *n.* **1.** A barrier or defense of pointed, inclined stakes or of barbed wire. **2.** A ruff for the neck worn in the 16th century. [Fr.]

frak·tur (fräk-to͝or′) *n.* A style of letter formerly used in German manuscripts and printing. [G. < Lat. *fractura,* fracture.]

fram·be·sia (frăm-bē′zhə, -zhē-ə) *n.* Yaws. [NLat. < Fr. *framboise,* raspberry (from the appearance of the excrescence).]

frame (frām) *v.* **framed, fram·ing, frames.** —*tr.* **1.** To construct by putting together the various parts of. **2.** To conceive or design: *framed an alternate proposal.* **3.** To arrange or adjust for a purpose: *The question was framed to draw only one answer.* **4. a.** To put into words; formulate: *frame a reply.* **b.** To form (words) silently with the lips. **5.** To enclose or encircle with or as if with a frame. **6.** *Slang.* **a.** To rig evidence or events so as to incriminate (a person) falsely. **b.** To fix (a contest) so as to ensure a desired fraudulent outcome: *frame a prizefight.* —*intr.* **1.** *Archaic.* To resort; proceed. **2.** *Obs.* To manage or contrive to do something. —*n.* **1.** Something composed of parts fitted and joined together. **2.** A skeletal structure designed to give shape or support: *the frame of a house.* **3.** An open structure or rim for encasing, holding, or bordering something: *a window frame.* **4.** The human body; physique. **5.** A cold frame. **6.** A machine built upon or utilizing a frame. **7.** The general structure of something; system: *the frame of government.* **8. a.** A round or period of play in some games, such as bowling or billiards. **b.** *Baseball.* An inning. **9.** A single exposure on a roll of motion-picture film. **10.** The total area of a television picture formed by a single traverse of the scanning spot. **11.** *Slang.* A frame-up. **12.** *Obs.* Shape; form. **13.** A minimal step in a sequence of programmed instruction. [ME *framen* < *frame,* structure.] —**fram′er** *n.*

frame of reference *n.* **1.** *Physics.* A set of coordinate axes in terms of which position or movement may be specified or with reference to which physical laws may be mathematically stated. **2.** A set or system of ideas, as of philosophical or religious doctrine, in terms of which other ideas are interpreted or assigned meaning.

frame·shift (frām′shĭft′) *n.* *Genetics.* The insertion or deletion of a pair of nucleotides in a gene that causes an alteration in the codon, resulting in the incorrect reading of the codon sequence as messenger RNA is being formed.

frame-up (frām′ŭp′) *n.* *Informal.* **1.** A prearranged or fraudulent scheme. **2.** A scheme to incriminate an innocent person.

frame·work (frām′wûrk′) *n.* **1.** A structure for supporting or enclosing something, esp. a skeletal support used as the basis in something being constructed. **2.** An external work platform; rig. **3.** A basic arrangement, form, or system: *"social structure is a stronger framework for behavior than national feeling."* (Stanley Kauffman).

francolin

fram·ing (frā′mĭng) *n.* **1.** The act of providing with a framework. **2.** A frame, framework, or system of frames.

franc (frăngk) *n.* See table at **currency.** [Fr. < OFr. *franc* < Lat. *Francorum rex,* king of the Franks (from the legend on the first of these coins).]

fran·chise (frăn′chīz′) *n.* **1.** A privilege or right officially granted a person or a group by a government, esp.: **a.** The constitutional or statutory right to vote. **b.** The establishment of a corporation's existence. **c.** The grant of certain rights and powers to a corporation. **d.** Formerly, legal immunity from certain burdens, servitude, or other restrictions. **2.** Authorization granted by a manufacturer to a distributor or dealer to sell his products. **3.** The territory or limits within which a privilege, right, or immunity may be exercised. —*tr.v.* **-chised, -chis·ing, -chis·es.** To endow with a franchise. [ME *fraunchise,* freedom < OFr. *franchise* < *franche,* free.]

fran·chis·ee (frăn′chī-zē′) *n.* One who is enfranchised to run a unit of a business chain, as a restaurant.

fran·chis·er (frăn′chī′zər) *n.* One that grants a franchise.

Fran·cis·can (frăn-sĭs′kən) *n.* A member of a religious mendicant order founded by Saint Francis of Assisi in 1209 and now divided into three independent branches. —**Fran·cis′can** *adj.*

fran·ci·um (frăn′sē-əm) *n.* *Symbol* **Fr** An extremely unstable radioactive metallic element, having approximately 19 isotopes, the most stable of which is Fr 223 with a half-life of 21 minutes. Atomic number 87; valence 1. [NLat., after *France.*]

Franco– *pref.* French: *Francophone.* [< Med. Lat. *Francus,* Frenchman < LLat., Frank.]

Fran·co-A·mer·i·can (frăng′kō-ə-mĕr′ĭ-kən) *n.* An American of French descent, esp. a French-Canadian. —**Fran′co-A·mer′i·can** *adj.*

fran·co·lin (frăng′kə-lĭn) *n.* Any of various Old World birds of the genus *Francolinus,* related to and resembling the quails and partridges. [Fr. < Ital. *francolino.*]

Fran·co·phile (frăng′kə-fīl′) also **Fran·co·phil** (-fĭl′) *n.* A person who admires France, its people, and its culture.

Fran·co·phobe (frăng′kə-fōb′) *n.* A person who dislikes or fears France, its people, and its culture.

Fran·co·phone (frăng′kə-fōn′) *adj.* French-speaking. —*n.* A French-speaking person.

fran·gi·ble (frăn′jə-bəl) *adj.* Easily broken; breakable. [ME < OFr. < Med. Lat. *frangibilis* < Lat. *frangere,* to break.] —**fran′gi·bil′i·ty, fran′gi·ble·ness** *n.*

fran·gi·pan·i (frăn′jə-păn′ē, -pä′nē) *n.* **1.** Any of various tropical American shrubs of the genus *Plumeria,* having milky juice and showy, fragrant, variously colored flowers. **2.** A perfume derived from or similar in scent to the flowers of the frangipani. **3.** Also **fran·gi·pane** (frăn′jə-păn′). A creamy pastry filling flavored with almonds. [Fr. *frangipane,* after Muzio *Frangipane,* a 16th-cent. Italian marquis who prepared a perfume similar to that of the shrub.]

Fran·glais (fräɴ-glā′) *n.* French characterized by numerous borrowings from English. [Blend of Fr. *Français,* French, and *Anglais,* English.]

frank[1] (frăngk) *adj.* **-er, -est. 1.** Open and sincere in expression; straightforward. **2.** Clearly manifest; evident: *frank enjoyment.* —*tr.v.* **franked, frank·ing, franks. 1. a.** To put an official mark on (a piece of mail) so that it can be sent free of postage. **b.** To send (mail) free of charge. **2.** To place a stamp or mark on (a piece of mail) to show the payment of postage. **3.** To enable (a person) to come and go easily. —*n.* **1. a.** A mark or signature placed on a piece of mail to indicate the right to send it free of postage. **b.** The right to send mail free. **2.** A franked piece of mail. [ME, free < OFr. *franc* < Med. Lat. *francus* < LLat. *Francus,* Frank.]

Synonyms: *frank, candid, outspoken, straightforward, open, ingenuous.* These adjectives mean disposed to reveal one's thoughts honestly and without reserve. *Frank* implies forthrightness of expression, sometimes to the point of bluntness. *Candid* stresses sincerity and honesty in the sense of refusing to evade issues or to distort one's true thought. *Outspoken* usually implies boldness of speech. *Straightforward* implies directness of manner and expression. *Open* suggests freedom from all trace of secretiveness, dissembling, or reserve in manner or countenance. *Ingenuous* likewise implies freedom from disguise or deceit but can also suggest artlessness in the sense of naiveté.

frank[2] (frăngk) *n.* *Informal.* A frankfurter.

Frank (frăngk) *n.* A member of one of the Germanic tribes of the Rhine region in the early Christian era, esp. one of the Salian Franks who conquered Gaul about A.D. 500 and established an extensive empire that reached its greatest power in the ninth century. [ME < OE *Franca* and OFr. *Franc* < LLat. *Francus,* of Germanic orig.]

Frank·en·stein (frăng′kən-stīn′) *n.* **1.** An agency or creation that slips from the control of and ultimately destroys its creator. **2.** A monster having the appearance of a man. **3.** The monster created by the protagonist of Mary W. Shelley's novel *Frankenstein* (1818), which brought about the ruin of its creator.

frank·furt·er also **frank·fort·er** (frăngk′fər-tər) or **frank·furt** or **frank·fort** (-fərt) *n.* A smoked sausage of beef or beef and pork made in long, reddish links. [After *Frankfurt am Main,* West Germany.]

frank·in·cense (frăng'kĭn-sĕns') *n.* An aromatic gum resin obtained from African and Asian trees of the genus *Boswellia* and used chiefly as incense. [ME *frank encens* < OFr. *franc encens* : *franc,* superior + *encens,* incense.]

Frank·ish (frăng'kĭsh) *adj.* Of or pertaining to the Franks or their language. —*n.* The West Germanic language of the Franks.

frank·lin (frăng'klĭn) *n.* In England during the late medieval period, a freeholder of nonnoble birth but with extensive property. [ME *frankelein,* prob. < Med. Lat. *francus,* free. —see FRANK[1].]

frank·lin·ite (frăng'klĭ-nīt') *n.* A black, slightly magnetic mineral of zinc, iron, and manganese that is a valuable source of zinc. [After *Franklin,* New Jersey.]

Frank·lin stove (frăng'klĭn) *n.* A cast-iron stove shaped like a fireplace but employing metal baffles to increase its heating efficiency. [After Benjamin *Franklin* (1706–1790), its inventor.]

frank·ly (frăngk'lē) *adv.* **1.** In a frank manner; candidly. **2.** In truth; honestly: *Frankly, I don't care.*

frank·ness (frăngk'nĭs) *n.* Openness and directness of speech; candor.

frank·pledge (frăngk'plĕj') *n.* **1.** In old English law, a system in which units or tithings composed of ten households were formed, in each of which members were held responsible for one another's conduct. **2.** A member of a unit in frankpledge. [ME *frankplegge* < AN *frauncpledge* : OFr. *franc,* free, frank + OFr. *plege,* pledge. —see PLEDGE.]

fran·se·ri·a (frăn-sîr'ē-ə) *n.* Any of various herbs or shrubs of the genus *Franseria.* [NLat. *Franseria,* genus name, after Antonio *Franseri,* 18th-cent. Spanish botanist.]

fran·tic (frăn'tĭk) *adj.* **1.** Emotionally desperate or exasperated: *frantic with worry.* **2.** Characterized by rapid and disordered or nervous action: *made a frantic last-minute search.* **3.** *Archaic.* Mad; insane. [ME *frantik* < OFr. *frenetique* < Lat. *phreneticus.* —see FRENETIC.] **—fran'ti·cal·ly, fran'tic·ly** *adv.* **—fran'tic·ness** *n.*

frap (frăp) *tr.v.* **frapped, frap·ping, fraps.** *Naut.* **1.** To make secure by lashing: *frap a sail.* **2.** To take up the slack of; tighten. [ME *frapen,* to strike < OFr. *fraper.*]

frap·pé (fră-pā', frăp) *n.* **1.** A frozen, fruit-flavored mixture that is similar to sherbet and is served as a dessert or appetizer. **2.** A beverage, usually a liqueur, poured over shaved ice. **3.** A milk shake containing ice cream. [Fr., chilled < p.part. of *frapper,* to chill < OFr. *fraper,* to strike.]

frat (frăt) *n. Informal.* A college fraternity.

fra·ter·nal (frə-tûr'nəl) *adj.* **1. a.** Of or pertaining to brothers. **b.** Showing comradeship; brotherly. **2.** Pertaining to or constituting a fraternity. **3.** *Biol.* Of or pertaining to a twin or twins developed from separately fertilized ova. [ME < Med. Lat. *fraternalis* < Lat. *fraternus* < *frater,* brother.] **—fra·ter'nal·ism** *n.* **—fra·ter'nal·ly** *adv.*

fra·ter·ni·ty (frə-tûr'nĭ-tē) *n., pl.* **-ties. 1.** A body of people associated for a common purpose or interest, as a guild. **2.** A group of people linked together by similar backgrounds, predilections, or occupations: *the fraternity of bird watchers.* **3.** A chiefly social organization of male college students, usually designated by Greek letters. **4.** The quality or condition of being brothers; brotherliness. [ME *fraternite* < OFr. *fraternité* < Lat. *fraternitas* < *fraternus,* fraternal.]

frat·er·nize (frăt'ər-nīz') *intr.v.* **-nized, -niz·ing, -niz·es. 1.** To associate with others in a brotherly or congenial way. **2.** To mix intimately with the people of an enemy or alien group, often in violation of military law. [Fr. *fraterniser* < Med. Lat. *fraternizare* < Lat. *fraternus,* fraternal.] **—frat'er·ni·za'tion** *n.* **—frat'er·niz'er** *n.*

frat·ri·cide (frăt'rĭ-sīd') *n.* **1.** The killing of one's brother or sister. **2.** One who has killed his brother or sister. [Lat. *frater, fratr-,* brother + -CIDE.] **—frat'ri·cid'al** (-sīd'l) *adj.*

Frau (frou) *n., pl.* **Frau·en** (frou'ən). A married woman in a German-speaking area. Used as a title corresponding to *Mrs.* [G. < MHG *vrowe* < OHG *frouwa.*]

fraud (frôd) *n.* **1.** A deception deliberately practiced in order to secure unfair or unlawful gain. **2.** A piece of trickery. **3. a.** One who defrauds; cheat. **b.** One who assumes a false pose; impostor. [ME *fraude* < OFr. < Lat. *fraus,* deceit.]

fraud·u·lent (frô'jə-lənt) *adj.* **1.** Engaging in fraud; deceitful. **2.** Characterized by, constituting, or gained by fraud: *a fraudulent contract.* [ME < OFr. < Lat. *fraudulentus* < *fraus,* deceit.] **—fraud'u·lence** *n.* **—fraud'u·lent·ly** *adv.*

fraught (frôt) *adj.* **1.** Filled or charged with something; accompanied: *an occasion fraught with danger.* **2.** Fully laden or provided: *"A work so full with various learning fraught"* (Dryden). —*n. Obs.* Freight; cargo. [ME, p.part. of *fraughten,* to load < MDu. *vrachten* < *vracht,* freight.]

Fräu·lein (froi'līn') *n., pl.* **Fräulein. 1.** An unmarried girl or woman in a German-speaking area. Used as a title corresponding to *Miss.* **2.** *Chiefly Brit.* A German governess. [G., dim. of *Frau,* wife.]

Fraun·ho·fer lines (froun'hō'fər) *pl.n.* A set of several hundred dark lines appearing against the bright background of the continuous solar spectrum and produced by absorption of light by the cooler gases in the sun's outer atmosphere at frequencies corresponding to the atomic transition frequencies of these gases. [After Joseph von *Fraunhofer* (1787–1826).]

frax·i·nel·la (frăk'sə-nĕl'ə) *n.* The gas plant. [NLat., dim. of Lat. *fraxinus,* ash tree.]

fray[1] (frā) *n.* **1.** A scuffle or brawl. **2.** A heated dispute or contest. —*v.* **frayed, fray·ing, frays.** *Obs.* —*tr.* **1.** To alarm; frighten. **2.** To drive away. —*intr.* To fight. [ME *frai* < *affrai* < OFr. *effrei.*]

fray[2] (frā) *v.* **frayed, fray·ing, frays.** —*tr.* **1.** To wear away (the edges of fabric, for example) by rubbing. **2.** To strain; chafe: *nerves frayed by noise.* —*intr.* To become frayed or threadbare along the edges. —*n.* A frayed or threadbare spot, as on fabric. [ME *fraien* < OFr. *fraier,* to rub < Lat. *fricare.*]

fraz·zle (frăz'əl) *Informal.* —*v.* **-zled, -zling, -zles.** —*tr.* **1.** To irritate; fray. **2.** To exhaust physically or emotionally. —*intr.* To become frazzled. —*n.* **1.** A frayed or tattered condition. **2.** A condition of fatigue or nervous exhaustion: *worn to a frazzle.* [Perh. a blend of FRAY[2] and dial. *fazzle,* to tangle.]

freak[1] (frēk) *n.* **1.** A thing or occurrence that is markedly unusual or irregular: *A freak of nature produced the midsummer snow.* **2.** An abnormally formed organism, esp. a person or animal regarded as a curiosity or monstrosity. **3.** A sudden capricious turn of mind; whim: *"The freaks of the psyche can no more be explained than the Devil"* (Maurice Collis). **4.** *Slang.* **a.** A drug user or addict: *a speed freak.* **b.** A hippie. **c.** A fan or enthusiast. **—modifier:** *a freak accident.* —*intr. & tr.v.* **freaked, freak·ing, freaks.** *Slang.* **1.** To experience or cause to experience a negative reaction, as frightening hallucinations or feelings of paranoia, as a result of taking a drug, esp. a hallucinogen: *freaked out on acid.* **2.** To behave or cause to behave irrationally and uncontrollably: *freaked completely when he lost his job.* **3. a.** To become or cause to become shocked or surprised: *freaked out by the news.* **b.** To become or cause to become intensely excited or elated. [Orig. unknown.]

freak[2] (frēk) *n.* A fleck or streak of color. —*tr.v.* **freaked, freak·ing, freaks.** To speckle or streak with color: *"The white pink, and the pansy freaked with jet"* (Milton). [Orig. unknown.]

freak·ish (frē'kĭsh) *adj.* **1.** Unusual or abnormal. **2.** Pertaining to or characteristic of a freak. **3.** Capricious or whimsical. **—freak'ish·ly** *adv.* **—freak'ish·ness** *n.*

freak-out (frēk'out') *n. Slang.* **1.** An act or instance of freaking. **2.** One that freaks.

freak·y (frē'kē) *adj.* **-i·er, -i·est. 1.** Freakish. **2.** *Slang.* Frightening. **—freak'i·ly** *adv.*

freck·le (frĕk'əl) *n.* A small precipitation of pigment in the skin, often brought out by the sun. —*tr. & intr.v.* **-led, -ling, -les.** To dot or become dotted with freckles or spots of color. [ME *frakles* (pl.), alteration of *fraknes* < ON *freknur.*] **—freck'ly** *adj.*

free (frē) *adj.* **fre·er, fre·est. 1.** Not imprisoned or enslaved; at liberty. **2.** Not controlled by obligation or the will of another: *felt free to go.* **3. a.** Having political independence: *a free country.* **b.** Governed by consent and possessing civil liberties: *a free citizen.* **c.** Immune to arbitrary interference by a government: *a free press.* **4. a.** Not affected or restricted by a given condition or circumstance: *free from need; free of avarice.* **b.** Not subject to a given condition; exempt: *tax-free income.* **5.** Not subject to external restraint: *"Comment is free but facts are sacred"* (Charles Prestwich Scott). **6.** Not literal or exact: *a free translation.* **7. a.** Costing nothing; gratuitous: *a free meal.* **b.** Publicly supported: *free education.* **8. a.** Not being occupied or used: *a free shelf.* **b.** Unobstructed; clear: *a free lane.* **9.** Guileless; frank. **10.** Taking undue liberties; forward or overfamiliar. **11. a.** Liberal or lavish: *free with his money.* **b.** Making use of something unstintingly: *was free with his expense account.* **12.** Uninhibited and outspoken. **13. a.** Given, made, or done of one's own accord; spontaneous: *free advice.* **b.** Determined according to the wishes of the actor: *free choices.* **14.** *Chem. & Physics.* **a.** Unconstrained; unconfined: *free expansion.* **b.** Not fixed in position; capable of relatively unrestricted motion: *a free electron.* **c.** Not chemically bound in a molecule: *free oxygen.* **d.** Involving no collisions or interactions: *a free path.* **e.** Empty: *a free space.* **f.** Unoccupied: *a free level.* **15.** *Naut.* Favorable. Used of a wind. **16.** Not bound, fastened, or attached: *the free end of a chain.* **17.** Designating a vowel in an open syllable unchecked by a consonant, as *o* in *go.* —*adv.* **1.** In a free manner; freely. **2.** Without charge. —*tr.v.* **freed, free·ing, frees. 1.** To set at liberty. **2.** To rid or release: *a people freed from fear.* **3.** To clear or untangle. [ME *fre* < OE *frēo.*] **—free'ly** *adv.* **—free'ness** *n.*

free agent *n. Sports.* A professional player who is free to sign a contract with any team.

free alongside ship *adj. & adv.* Delivered to the pier at no extra charge.

free-as·so·ci·ate (frē'ə-sō'shē-āt', -sē-) *intr.v.* **-at·ed, -at·ing, -ates.** To engage in free association.

free association *n.* **1.** A spontaneous, logically unconstrained association of ideas and feelings. **2.** A psychoanalytic technique in which a patient's articulation of free

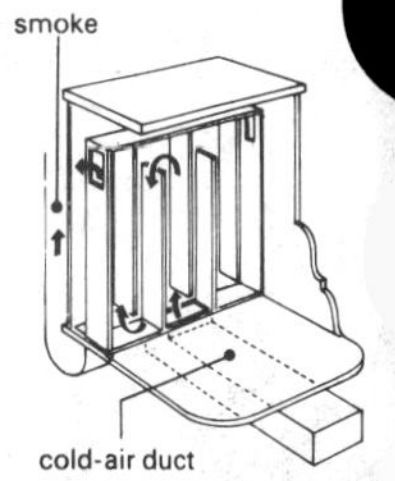

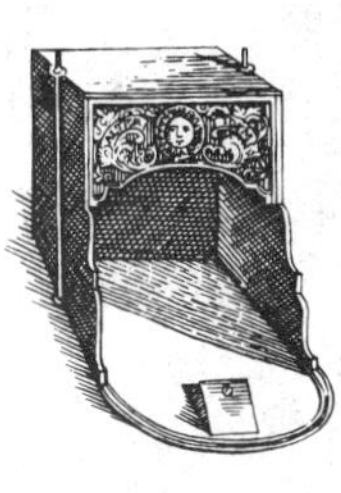

Franklin stove
Above: Diagram
Below: Franklin's design

associations is encouraged in order to elicit repressed thoughts and emotions.

free·bie also **free·bee** (frē′bē) *n. Slang.* Something given or received gratis: *"such freebies as subway and bus maps"* (New York Magazine). [< FREE.]

free·board (frē′bôrd′, -bōrd′) *n.* **1.** *Naut.* The distance between the water line and the uppermost full deck. **2.** The distance between the ground and the undercarriage of an automobile.

freeboard deck *n.* The uppermost deck that is officially considered completely watertight.

free·boot (frē′bo͞ot′) *intr.v.* **-boot·ed, -boot·ing, -boots.** To act as a freebooter; plunder. [Back-formation < FREEBOOTER.]

free·boot·er (frē′bo͞o′tər) *n.* A person who pillages and plunders, esp. a pirate. [Du. *vrijbuiter* < *vrijbuit,* plunder : *vrij,* free + *buit,* booty.]

free·born (frē′bôrn′) *adj.* **1.** Born as a free person. **2.** Pertaining to or befitting a person born free.

free city *n.* A city governed as an autonomous political unit under international auspices.

freed·man (frēd′mən) *n.* A man who has been freed from bondage.

free·dom (frē′dəm) *n.* **1.** The condition of being free of restraints. **2.** Liberty of the person from slavery, oppression, or incarceration. **3. a.** Political independence. **b.** Possession of civil rights; immunity from the arbitrary exercise of authority. **4.** Exemption from unpleasant or onerous conditions: *freedom from unfair labor practices.* **5.** The capacity to exercise choice; free will: *has the freedom to do as he wishes.* **6.** Ease or facility of movement. **7.** Frankness or boldness; lack of modesty or reserve: *the new freedom in movies and novels.* **8. a.** Unrestricted use or access: *was given the freedom of their research facilities.* **b.** The right of enjoying all of the privileges of membership or citizenship: *the freedom of the city.* [ME *fredom* < OE *frēodom.*]

Synonyms: *freedom, liberty, license.* These nouns refer to the power to act, speak, or think without the imposition of restraint. *Freedom* is the most general term and preferable when total absence of restraint or lack of restraint in general is meant. *Liberty* applies especially to individual rights defined by law and thus suggests absence of specific restrictions. However, *freedom* is sometimes also used in the narrower sense associated with individual rights. *License* in one sense denotes abuse of freedom; in another it refers to exemption from prevailing rules, granted in special cases.

freesia

freedom of the seas *n.* **1.** The doctrine that ships of any nation may travel through international waters unhampered. **2.** The right of neutral shipping in wartime to trade at will except where blockades are established.

freed·wom·an (frēd′wo͝om′ən) *n.* A woman who has been freed from bondage.

free electron *n.* An electron that is not bound to an atom, esp. an electron in a conductor that is available to move in a current.

free energy *n.* **1.** A thermodynamic quantity that is the difference between the internal energy and the product of the absolute temperature and entropy of a system. **2.** A thermodynamic quantity that is the difference between the enthalpy and the product of the absolute temperature and entropy of a system.

free enterprise *n.* The freedom of private businesses to operate competitively for profit with minimal government regulation.

free fall *n.* **1.** The fall of a body within the atmosphere without a drag-producing device such as a parachute. **2.** The unconstrained motion of a body in a gravitational field.

free flight *n.* Flight, as of an aircraft or spacecraft, after termination of powered flight.

free-float·ing (frē′flō′tĭng) *adj.* **1.** Not committed or decided. **2.** Experienced without an obvious basis or cause: *free-floating anxiety.*

free-for-all (frē′fər-ôl′) *n.* A brawl, argument, or competition in which one and all take part.

free·form (frē′fôrm′) *adj.* Designating a usually flowing asymmetric shape or outline free of formal conventions.

free form *n. Ling.* A morpheme capable of standing alone and retaining meaning.

free·hand (frē′hănd′) *adj.* Drawn by hand without the aid of tracing or drafting devices: *a freehand sketch.* **—free′hand′** *adv.*

free hand *n.* Freedom to do or decide as one sees fit.

free·hand·ed (frē′hăn′dĭd) *adj.* Openhanded; generous. **—free′hand′ed·ly** *adv.* **—free′hand′ed·ness** *n.*

free·heart·ed (frē′här′tĭd) *adj.* **1.** Unreserved; open. **2.** Generous; liberal. **—free′heart′ed·ly** *adv.* **—free′heart′ed·ness** *n.*

free·hold (frē′hōld′) *n.* **1.** *Law.* **a.** An estate held in fee or for life. **b.** The tenure by which such an estate is held. **2.** A tenure of an office or a dignity for life. [ME *frehold,* transl. of Norman Fr. *fraunc tenement.*] **—free′hold′er** *n.*

free lance *n.* **1.** A person, esp. a writer or an artist, who sells his services to employers without a long-term commitment to any one of them. **2.** One who remains uncommitted to a party and proceeds as an independent. **3.** A medieval mercenary.

free-lance (frē′lăns′) *intr. & tr.v.* **-lanced, -lanc·ing, -lanc·es.** To work as or produce and sell as a free lance. *—adj.* Of, pertaining to, or produced by a free lance. **—free′-lanc′er** *n.*

free-liv·ing (frē′lĭv′ĭng) *adj.* **1.** Given to self-indulgence. **2.** *Biol.* Living or moving independently; not part of a parasitic or symbiotic relationship.

free·load (frē′lōd′) *intr.v.* **-load·ed, -load·ing, -loads.** *Slang.* To take advantage of the charity, generosity, or hospitality of others. **—free′load′er** *n.*

free love *n.* The belief in or practice of sexual relations without marriage and without formal obligations.

free·man (frē′mən) *n.* **1.** A person not in slavery or serfdom. **2.** One who possesses the rights or privileges of a citizen.

free·mar·tin (frē′mär′tn) *n.* A sterile or otherwise sexually deficient female calf born as the twin of a bull calf. [Orig. unknown.]

free·ma·son (frē′mā′sən) *n.* **1.** A member of a guild of skilled, itinerant masons of the Middle Ages. **2. Freemason.** A member of the Free and Accepted Masons, an international secret fraternity.

free·ma·son·ry (frē′mā′sən-rē) *n.* **1.** Spontaneous fellowship and sympathy among a number of people. **2. Freemasonry.** The institutions, precepts, and rites of the Freemasons.

free on board *adj. & adv.* Without fee for delivery on board or into a carrier at a specified point or location.

free port *n.* A port or an area of a port in which imported goods can be held or processed free of customs duties before re-export.

fre·er (frē′ər) *adj.* Comparative of **free.**

free radical *n.* An atom or group of atoms having at least one unpaired electron.

free rein *n.* Unlimited freedom to act or make decisions.

free ride *n.* Something acquired without the ordinary effort or cost. **—free rider** *n.*

free·sia (frē′zhə, -zhē-ə, -zē-ə) *n.* Any of several plants of the genus *Freesia,* native to southern Africa, having one-sided clusters of fragrant, variously colored flowers. [NLat., after Friedrich H. T. *Freese* (d. 1876).]

free silver *n.* The free coinage of silver, esp. at a fixed ratio to gold.

free soil *n.* U.S. territory in which slavery was prohibited before the Civil War.

free-soil (frē′soil′) *adj.* **1.** Prohibiting slavery: *free-soil states.* **2. a.** Opposing the extension of slavery prior to the U.S. Civil War. **b. Free-Soil.** Pertaining to or designating a U.S. political party founded in 1848 to oppose the extension of slavery into U.S. Territories and the admission of slave states into the Union.

free-spo·ken (frē′spō′kən) *adj.* Candid in expression; outspoken. **—free′-spo′ken·ness** *n.*

fre·est (frē′ĭst) *adj.* Superlative of **free.**

free·stand·ing (frē′stăn′dĭng) *adj.* Standing independently free of support or attachment.

free·stone (frē′stōn′) *n.* **1.** A stone, such as limestone, soft enough to be cut easily without shattering or splitting. **2.** A fruit, esp. a peach, having a stone that does not adhere to the pulp.

free·style (frē′stīl′) *n.* A competitive event, as swimming, in which the contestant may choose his own style.

free-swim·ming (frē′swĭm′ĭng) *adj.* Able to swim freely; not sessile or attached: *the free-swimming larva of the oyster.* **—free′-swim′mer** *n.*

free·think·er (frē′thĭng′kər) *n.* One who has rejected authority and dogma, esp. in his religious thinking, in favor of rational inquiry and speculation. **—free′think′ing** *adj. & n.*

free thought *n.* Freethinking; unorthodox thought.

free throw *n. Basketball.* A foul shot.

free-throw line (frē′thrō′) *n. Basketball.* The foul line (sense 2).

free trade *n.* Trade between nations or states without protective customs tariffs. **—free trader** *n.*

free university *n.* An independent unaccredited organization set up by students within a university for the study of nontraditional subjects.

free verse *n.* Verse that does not follow a conventional metrical or stanzaic pattern and has either an irregular rhyme or no rhyme. [Trans. of Fr. *vers libre.*]

free·way (frē′wā′) *n.* **1.** A highway with several lanes and no intersections or stoplights; expressway. **2.** A highway without tolls.

free·wheel (frē′hwēl′, -wēl′) *intr.v.* **-wheeled, -wheel·ing, -wheels.** To live or move freely, aimlessly, or irresponsibly.

free wheel *n.* **1.** An automotive transmission device that allows the drive shaft to continue turning when its speed is greater than that of the engine shaft. **2.** A device in the rear-wheel hub of a bicycle that permits the wheel to turn without pedal action, as in coasting.

free·wheel·ing (frē′hwē′lĭng, -wē′-) *adj.* **1.** Pertaining to or equipped with free wheel. **2.** *Informal.* **a.** Free of restraints or rules in organization, methods, or procedure. **b.** Heedless of consequences; carefree.

free·will (frē′wĭl′) *adj.* Done of one's own accord; voluntary.

free will *n.* **1.** The ability or discretion to choose; free choice. **2.** The power, attributed esp. to human beings, of making free choices that are unconstrained by external circumstances or by necessity. [Transl. of LLat. *liberum arbitrium.*]

free world *n.* The portion of the world marked by democratic and capitalistic or socialistic systems rather than by Communist or totalitarian systems.

freeze (frēz) *v.* **froze** (frōz), **fro·zen** (frō'zən), **freez·ing, freez·es.** —*intr.* **1. a.** To pass from the liquid to the solid state by loss of heat. **b.** To acquire a surface of ice from cold. **2.** To become clogged or jammed due to the formation of ice: *The pipes froze.* **3.** To become rigid and inflexible; solidify: *opinions that froze into dogma.* **4.** To be at that degree of temperature at which ice forms: *It may freeze tonight.* **5.** To be harmed, ruined, or killed by cold or frost: *The crops froze.* **6.** To feel the cold acutely: *I'm freezing.* **7.** To become fixed, stuck, or attached by or as if by frost: *The lock had frozen.* **8.** To become incapable of acting or reacting, as from fear: *froze in front of the audience.* **9.** To become icily silent in manner: *froze at the rebuke.* —*tr.* **1. a.** To convert into ice. **b.** To cause ice to form upon. **c.** To cause to congeal or stiffen from extreme cold: *winter cold that froze the ground.* **2.** To preserve (foods, for example) by subjecting to freezing temperatures. **3.** To damage, kill, or make inoperative by cold or by the formation of ice. **4.** To make very cold; chill. **5.** To chill with an icy or formal manner. **6.** To cause to become rigid and inflexible. **7. a.** To fix (prices or wages) at a given or current level. **b.** To prohibit further manufacture or use of. **c.** To prevent or restrict the exchange, liquidation, or granting of by law: *The banks have agreed to freeze investment loans.* **8.** To anesthetize by freezing. —*n.* **1. a.** An act of freezing. **b.** The state of being frozen. **2.** A spell of cold weather; frost. —***idiom.* freeze in (one's) tracks.** To stop short and remain motionless, as with fear. [ME *fresen* < OE *frēosan.*]

freeze-dry (frēz'drī') *tr.v.* **-dried, -dry·ing, -dries.** To preserve (food, for example) by freeze-drying.

freeze-dry·ing (frēz'drī'ĭng) *n.* Preservation, as of foodstuffs, by rapid freezing and drying in a high vacuum.

freeze-etch·ing (frēz'ĕch'ĭng) *n.* A method of specimen preparation for electron microscopy in which a replica is made from a sample that has been rapidly frozen and then cut. —**freeze'-etched'** *adj.*

freez·er (frē'zər) *n.* One that freezes, esp. a thermally insulated cabinet or room that maintains a subfreezing temperature for the rapid freezing and storing of perishable food.

freezing point *n.* **1.** The temperature at which a liquid of specified composition solidifies under a specified pressure. **2.** The temperature at which the liquid and solid phases of a substance of specified composition are in equilibrium at atmospheric pressure.

free zone *n.* An area at a port or city where goods may be received and held without the payment of duty.

F region *n.* The F layer (sense 2).

freight (frāt) *n.* **1.** Goods carried by a vessel or vehicle, esp. goods transported as cargo by a commercial carrier. **2.** A burden; load. **3.** The commercial transportation of goods. **4.** The charge for transporting goods by cargo carrier. **5.** A railway train carrying goods only. —*tr.v.* **freight·ed, freight·ing, freights. 1.** To convey commercially as cargo. **2.** To load with goods to be transported. **3.** To load; charge. [ME *fraught* < MDu. *vracht.*]

freight·age (frā'tĭj) *n.* **1. a.** The commercial transportation of goods. **b.** The charge for such transportation. **2.** Cargo.

freight car *n.* A railway car designed for carrying freight.

freight·er (frā'tər) *n.* **1.** A vehicle, esp. a ship, for carrying freight. **2.** A shipper of cargo.

freight train *n.* A railroad train made up of freight cars.

frem·i·tus (frĕm'ĭ-təs) *n., pl.* **fremitus.** A palpable vibration, as felt by the hand placed on the chest during coughing or speaking. [Lat., a murmuring < *fremere,* to murmur.]

fre·na (frē'nə) *n.* A plural of **frenum.**

french (frĕnch) *tr.v.* **frenched, french·ing, french·es. 1.** To cut into thin strips before cooking. **2.** To trim fat or bone from (a chop, for example).

French (frĕnch) *adj.* Of, pertaining to, or characteristic of France or its people, language, or culture. —*n.* **1.** The Romance language of France, Switzerland, parts of Belgium, and other countries formerly under French influence or control. **2.** *(used with a pl. verb).* The people of France. [ME < OE *frencisc* < *Franca,* Frank.]

French bulldog *n.* A small, compact dog of a breed developed in France from toy English bulldogs and native breeds.

French-Ca·na·di·an also **French Canadian** (frĕnch'kə-nā'dē-ən) *n.* A Canadian of French descent. —**French'-Ca·na'di·an** *adj.*

French chalk *n.* Chalk made of a soft, white variety of talc, used by tailors for marking fabrics and by dry cleaners for removing grease spots.

French chop *n.* A rib chop with the meat and fat trimmed from the end of the rib.

French cuff *n.* A wide cuff that is folded back and fastened with a cuff link.

French curve *n.* A flat drafting instrument, usually of celluloid, with curved edges and scroll-shaped cutouts, used as a guide in connecting a set of individual points with a smooth curve.

French door *n.* A door, usually one of a pair, of light construction with glass panes often extending the full length.

French dressing *n.* **1.** A seasoned oil and vinegar salad dressing. **2.** A commercially prepared creamy dressing that is usually pinkish in color and often sweet.

French fries *pl.n.* Thin strips of potatoes fried in deep fat.

French-fry (frĕnch'frī') *tr.v.* **-fried, -fry·ing, -fries.** To fry (potato strips, for example) in deep fat.

French heel *n.* A curved, moderately high heel used on women's shoes.

French horn *n.* A valved brass wind instrument with a circular shape, tapering from a narrow mouthpiece to a flaring bell at the other end and producing a mellow tone.

French horn

French·i·fy (frĕn'chə-fī') *tr.v.* **-fied, -fy·ing, -fies.** To make French in character or quality. —**French'i·fi·ca'tion** *n.*

French kiss *n. Slang.* A kiss in which the tongue enters the partner's mouth.

French knot *n.* A decorative embroidery stitch made by looping the thread two or more times around the needle, which is then inserted into the fabric.

French leave *n.* An informal, unannounced, or abrupt departure. [From the 18th-cent. French custom of leaving without saying good-by to the host or hostess.]

French·man (frĕnch'mən) *n.* A native or citizen of France.

French marigold *n.* A widely cultivated plant, *Tagetes patula,* native to Mexico, having divided leaves and yellow flowers with reddish markings.

French pastry *n.* Any of a wide variety of rich and elaborate pastries prepared in individual portions.

French provincial *n.* A style of architecture or furniture characteristic of the provinces in 17th- and 18th-century France.

French seam *n.* A seam stitched first on the right side and then turned in and stitched on the wrong side so that the raw edges are enclosed in the seam.

French telephone *n.* A telephone with the receiver and transmitter contained in a single hand piece; handset.

French toast *n.* Sliced bread soaked in a milk and egg batter and lightly fried.

French window *n.* **1.** A window, usually one of a pair, similar to a French door. **2.** A casement window.

French·wom·an (frĕnch'wo͝om'ən) *n.* A woman who is a native or citizen of France.

fre·net·ic (frə-nĕt'ĭk) also **fre·net·i·cal** (-ĭ-kəl) *adj.* Frantic; frenzied. [ME *frenetik* < OFr. *frenetique* < Lat. *phreneticus* < Gk. *phrenitikos* < *phrenitis,* brain disease < *phrēn,* mind.] —**fre·net'i·cal·ly** *adv.*

fren·u·lum (frĕn'yə-ləm) *n., pl.* **-la** (-lə). **1.** A frenum. **2.** A spiny projection on the posterior wings of moths that joins with a process on the anterior wings to fasten the wings together. [NLat., dim. of Lat. *frenum,* bridle.]

fre·num (frē'nəm) *n., pl.* **-nums** or **-na** (-nə). A membranous structure, as the fold under the tongue, that restrains movement or supports a part. [Lat., bridle.]

fren·zied (frĕn'zēd) *adj.* Affected with or marked by frenzy; frantic. —**fren'zied·ly** *adv.*

fren·zy (frĕn'zē) *n., pl.* **-zies. 1.** A seizure of violent agitation or wild excitement, often accompanied by manic activity. **2.** Temporary madness or delirium. **3.** A mania; craze. —*tr.v.* **-zied, -zy·ing, -zies.** To drive into a frenzy. [ME *frenesie* < OFr. < Lat. *phrenesis* < Gk. < *phrēn,* mind.]

Fre·on (frē'ŏn'). A trademark for any of various nonflammable gaseous or liquid fluorocarbons that are used mainly as working fluids in refrigeration and air conditioning and as aerosol propellants.

fre·quence (frē'kwəns) *n.* Frequency. [ME, multitude < Lat. *frequentia* < *frequens,* crowded.]

fre·quen·cy (frē'kwən-sē) *n., pl.* **-cies. 1.** The property or condition of occurring frequently. **2.** *Math. & Physics.* The number of times a specified phenomenon occurs within a specified interval, as: **a.** The number of repetitions of a complete sequence of values of a periodic function per unit variation of an independent variable. **b.** The number of complete cycles of a periodic process occurring per unit time. **c.** The number of repetitions per unit time of a complete waveform, as of an electric current. **3.** *Statistics.* **a.** The number of measurements in an interval of a frequency distribution. **b.** The ratio of the number of times an event occurs in a series of trials of a chance experiment to the number of trials of the experiment performed. [Lat. *frequentia,* multitude < *frequens,* crowded.]

frequency curve *n.* A graphic approximation of the frequency polygon of a statistical distribution, usually a smooth curve with the property that its abscissa is never negative and such that the area under the curve cut off by a class is the approximate fraction of the total frequency contained in that class.

frequency distribution *n.* A set of intervals, usually adjacent and of equal width, into which the range of a statistical distribution is divided, each associated with a frequency indicating the number of measurements in that interval.

frequency modulation *n.* The encoding of a carrier wave by variation of its frequency in accordance with an input signal.

frequency polygon *n.* A graphic representation of a frequency distribution consisting of a set of points each obtained by plotting class frequency as ordinate and class mark as abscissa, together with line segments joining points of adjacent classes.

fret[3]

fre·quent (frē'kwənt) *adj.* Occurring or appearing quite often or at close intervals: *frequent errors of judgment.* —*tr.v.* (frē-kwĕnt', frē'kwənt) **-quent·ed, -quent·ing, -quents.** To pay frequent visits to; be in or at often. [ME, ample < Lat. *frequens,* numerous.] **—fre'quen·ta'tion** *n.* **—fre·quent'er** *n.* **—fre'quent·ness** *n.*

fre·quen·ta·tive (frē-kwĕn'tə-tĭv) *adj. Gram.* Expressing or denoting repeated action. —*n.* A frequentative verb or verb form.

fre·quent·ly (frē'kwənt-lē) *adv.* At frequent intervals; often.

fres·co (frĕs'kō) *n., pl.* **-coes** or **-cos. 1.** The art of painting on fresh, moist plaster with earth colors dissolved in water. **2.** A painting executed in fresco. —*tr.v.* **-coed, -co·ing, -coes.** To paint in fresco. [Ital., fresh, of Germanic orig.] **—fres'co·er, fres'co·ist** *n.*

fresh (frĕsh) *adj.* **-er, -est. 1.** New to one's experience; not encountered before. **2.** Novel; different: *a fresh slant.* **3.** Recently made, produced, or harvested; not stale or spoiled: *fresh bread.* **4.** Not preserved, as by canning, smoking, or freezing: *fresh vegetables.* **5.** Not saline or salty: *fresh water.* **6.** Not yet used or soiled; clean: *a fresh sheet of paper.* **7.** Additional; new: *fresh evidence.* **8.** Bright and clear; not dull or faded: *a fresh memory.* **9.** Having the glowing, unspoiled appearance of youth: *a fresh complexion.* **10.** Untried; inexperienced: *fresh recruits.* **11.** Having just arrived; straight: *fresh from Paris.* **12.** Revived or reinvigorated; refreshed: *fresh as a daisy after the nap.* **13.** Free from impurity or pollution; pure: *fresh air.* **14.** Fairly strong; brisk: *a fresh wind.* **15.** Having recently calved and therefore with milk: *a fresh cow.* **16.** *Informal.* Bold and saucy; impudent. —*adv.* Recently; newly: *fresh-baked bread.* —*n.* **1.** The early and fresh part: *the fresh of the day.* **2.** A freshet. [ME < OE *fersc* and < OFr. *fres,* of Germanic orig.] **—fresh'ly** *adv.* **—fresh'ness** *n.*

fresh breeze *n.* A wind whose speed is approximately 31 to 39 kilometers or 19 to 24 miles per hour.

fresh·en (frĕsh'ən) *v.* **-ened, -en·ing, -ens.** —*intr.* **1.** To become fresh, as in vigor or appearance: *freshened up after the day's work.* **2.** To become brisk; increase in strength. Used of the wind. **3.** To lose saltiness. **4.** To calve and therefore produce milk. —*tr.* To make fresh. **—fresh'en·er** *n.*

fresh·et (frĕsh'ĭt) *n.* **1.** A sudden overflow of a stream resulting from a heavy rain or a thaw. **2.** A stream of fresh water that empties into a body of salt water.

fresh gale *n.* A wind whose speed is approximately 63 to 74 kilometers or 39 to 46 miles per hour.

fresh·man (frĕsh'mən) *n.* **1.** A student in the first-year class of a high school, college, or university. **2.** A beginner; novice.

fresh·wa·ter (frĕsh'wô'tər, -wŏt'ər) *adj.* **1.** Of, pertaining to, living in, or consisting of fresh water. **2.** Situated away from the sea; inland. **3.** Accustomed to sailing on inland waters only: *a freshwater sailor.*

fret[1] (frĕt) *v.* **fret·ted, fret·ting, frets.** —*tr.* **1.** To cause to be uneasy; vex. **2. a.** To gnaw or wear away; erode. **b.** To produce a hole or worn spot in; corrode. **3.** To form (a passage or channel) by erosion. **4.** To disturb the surface of (water or a stream); agitate. —*intr.* **1.** To be vexed or troubled; worry. **2.** To be worn or eaten away; become corroded. **3.** To move agitatedly. **4.** To gnaw with the teeth in the manner of a rodent. —*n.* **1.** An act or instance of fretting. **2.** A hole or worn spot made by abrasion or erosion. **3.** Irritation of mind; agitation. [ME *freten* < OE *fretan,* to devour.]

frieze[1]

fret[2] (frĕt) *n.* One of several ridges set across the fingerboard of a stringed instrument, such as a guitar. —*tr.v.* **fret·ted, fret·ting, frets.** To provide with frets. [Orig. unknown.]

fret[3] (frĕt) *n.* **1.** An ornamental design consisting of repeated and symmetrical figures, often in relief, contained within a band or border. **2.** A headdress, worn by women of the Middle Ages, consisting of interlaced wire. —*tr.v.* **fret·ted, fret·ting, frets.** To provide with a fret. [ME < OFr. *frete.*]

fret·ful (frĕt'fəl) *adj.* Inclined to fret; peevish. **—fret'ful·ly** *adv.* **—fret'ful·ness** *n.*

fret saw *n.* A long, narrow-bladed saw with fine teeth, used in producing ornamental work in thin wood or metal.

fret·work (frĕt'wûrk') *n.* **1.** Ornamental work consisting of three-dimensional frets; geometric openwork. **2.** Fretwork represented two-dimensionally by chiaroscuro.

frigate

Freu·di·an (froi'dē-ən) *adj.* Pertaining to or in accordance with the psychoanalytic theories of Sigmund Freud. **—Freu'di·an** *n.* **—Freu'di·an·ism** *n.*

Freudian slip *n.* A verbal slip that is caused by and is indicative of an unconscious belief, thought, or emotion.

Freund's adjuvant (froindz) *n.* A substance consisting of killed microorganisms, such as mycobacteria, in an oil and water emulsion that intensifies antigenicity. [After Jules T. *Freund* (1890–1960).]

Frey (frā) also **Freyr** (frâr) *n.* The Norse god who dispenses peace, good weather, prosperity, and bountiful crops. [ON *Freyr.*]

Frey·a also **Frey·ja** (frā'ə) *n.* The Norse goddess of love and beauty and the sister of Frey. [ON *Freyja.*]

Freyr (frâr) *n.* Variant of **Frey.**

frigate bird

fri·a·ble (frī'ə-bəl) *adj.* Readily crumbled; brittle. [OFr. < Lat. *friabilis* < *friare,* to crumble.] **—fri'a·bil'i·ty, fri'a·ble·ness** *n.*

fri·ar (frī'ər) *n.* A member of a usually mendicant Roman Catholic order. [ME *frere* < OFr. < Lat. *frater,* brother.]

fri·ar·bird (frī'ər-bûrd') *n.* Any of various birds of the genus *Philemon,* of Australia and adjacent regions, having a partly naked head.

friar's lantern *n.* An ignis fatuus (sense 1).

fri·ar·y (frī'ə-rē) *n., pl.* **-ies.** A monastery of friars.

frib·ble (frĭb'əl) *v.* **-bled, -bling, -bles.** —*tr.* To waste (time, for example); fritter away. —*intr.* To waste time; trifle. —*n.* **1.** A frivolity; trifle. **2.** A frivolous person. [Orig. unknown.] **—frib'bler** *n.*

fric·an·deau (frĭk'ən-dō') *n.* A cut of veal that has been larded and braised. [Fr. < *fricasser,* to fricassee.]

fric·as·see (frĭk'ə-sē', frĭk'ə-sē') *n.* Poultry or meat cut into pieces and stewed in a gravy. —*tr.v.* **-seed, -see·ing, -sees.** To prepare as a fricassee. [Fr. *fricassée* < fem. p.part. of *fricasser,* to fricassee.]

fric·a·tive (frĭk'ə-tĭv) *n.* A consonant, such as *f* or *s* in English, produced by the forcing of breath through a constricted passage. [NLat. *fricativus* < *fricare,* to rub.] **—fric'a·tive** *adj.*

fric·tion (frĭk'shən) *n.* **1.** The rubbing of one object or surface against another. **2.** Conflict, as between persons having dissimilar ideas or interests; clash. **3.** *Physics.* A force tangential to the common boundary of two bodies in contact that resists the motion or tendency to motion of one relative to the other. [OFr. < Lat. *frictio* < *frictus,* p.part. of *fricare,* to rub.] **—fric'tion·al** *adj.* **—fric'tion·al·ly** *adv.*

friction clutch *n.* A clutch in which axial pressure with resultant friction between the clutch faces transmits torque.

friction drive *n.* An automotive transmission system in which motion is transmitted from one part to another by the surface friction of rolling contact.

friction match *n.* A match that ignites when struck on an abrasive surface.

friction tape *n.* A sturdy moisture-resistant adhesive tape used chiefly to insulate electrical conductors.

Fri·day (frī'dē, -dā') *n.* The sixth day of the week. [ME *Fridai* < OE *Frīgedæg,* Freya's day.]

fridge (frĭj) *n. Informal.* A refrigerator.

fried (frīd) *v.* Past tense and past participle of **fry**[1].

fried cake *n.* A small pastry fried in deep fat, as a doughnut.

Fried·land·er's bacillus (frēd'lĕn'dərz) *n.* A species of pathogenic bacteria, *Klebsiella pneumoniae,* that causes pneumonia. [After Karl *Friedländer* (1847–1887).]

Fried·man·ite (frēd'mə-nīt') *n. Econ.* A monetarist who supports the theory that the government should directly regulate the money supply. [After Milton *Friedman* (b. 1912).]

friend (frĕnd) *n.* **1.** A person whom one knows, likes, and trusts. **2.** An acquaintance. **3.** A person with whom one is allied in a struggle or cause; comrade. **4.** One who supports, sympathizes with, or patronizes a group, cause, or movement. **5. Friend.** A member of the Society of Friends; Quaker. —*tr.v.* **friend·ed, friend·ing, friends.** *Archaic.* To befriend. [ME < OE *frēond.*] **—friend'less** *adj.* **—friend'less·ness** *n.*

friend·ly (frĕnd'lē) *adj.* **-li·er, -li·est. 1.** Of, pertaining to, or befitting a friend. **2.** Favorably disposed; not antagonistic. **3.** Warm; comforting. —*adv.* In the manner of a friend; amicably. —*n., pl.* **-lies.** One fighting on or favorable to one's own side. **—friend'li·ness** *n.*

fri·er (frī'ər) *n.* Variant of **fryer.**

fries (frīz) *v.* Third person singular present tense of **fry**[1]. —*n.* Plural of **fry**[1].

Frie·sian (frē'zhən) *n.* Variant of **Frisian.**

frieze[1] (frēz) *n. Archit.* **1.** A plain or decorated horizontal part of an entablature between the architrave and cornice. **2.** A decorative horizontal band, as along the upper part of a wall in a room. [OFr. *frise* < Lat. *Phrygium* (*opus*), Phrygian (work), after *Phrygia,* an ancient country in Asia Minor.]

frieze[2] (frēz) *n.* A coarse, shaggy woolen cloth with an uncut nap. [ME *frise* < OFr. < MDu.]

frig (frĭg) *v.* **frigged, frig·ging, frigs.** *Vulgar Slang.* —*tr.* **1.** To have sexual intercourse with. **2.** *Chiefly Brit.* To masturbate. —*intr.* **1.** To have sexual intercourse. **2.** *Chiefly Brit.* To masturbate. [Obs. *frig,* to rub < ME, to quiver.]

frig·ate (frĭg'ĭt) *n.* **1.** A high-speed, medium-sized sailing war vessel of the 17th, 18th, and 19th centuries. **2.** A U.S. warship of approximately 5,000 to 7,000 tons, intermediate between a cruiser and a destroyer, used primarily for escort duty. **3.** *Archaic.* A fast, light vessel, as a sailboat. [Fr. *frégate* < Ital. *fregata.*]

frigate bird *n.* Any of various tropical sea birds of the genus *Fregata,* having long, powerful wings and dark plumage and characteristically snatching food from other birds in flight.

Frigg (frĭg) also **Frig·ga** (frĭg'ə) *n.* The Norse goddess of the heavens and wife of Odin. [ON.]

fright (frīt) *n.* **1.** Sudden, intense fear, as of something immediately threatening; alarm. **2.** *Informal.* Something extremely unsightly, alarming, or strange. —*tr.v.* **fright·ed, fright·ing, frights.** *Archaic.* To frighten. [ME < OE *fyrhto.*]

fright·en (frīt'n) *v.* **-ened, -en·ing, -ens.** —*tr.* **1.** To make afraid; alarm. **2.** To drive or force by arousing fear: *was* *frightened into confessing.* —*intr.* To become afraid. [ME < OE *fyrhtan.*] —**fright'en·er** *n.* —**fright'en·ing·ly** *adv.*

Synonyms: *frighten, scare, alarm, terrify, terrorize, startle, panic.* These verbs mean to cause a person to experience fear. *Frighten* and *scare* are the most general and applicable to a wide range of such experience. *Alarm* implies the sudden onset of fear or apprehension caused by awareness of danger. *Terrify* implies overwhelming, often paralyzing fear. *Terrorize* implies fear that intimidates, sometimes as a means of deliberate coercion. *Startle* suggests fear that shocks momentarily and may cause involuntary movement. *Panic* implies incapacitating terror and consequent loss of self-control and rationality.

fright·ful (frīt'fəl) *adj.* **1.** Causing disgust or shock; horrifying. **2.** Causing fright; terrifying. **3.** *Informal.* **a.** Excessive; extreme: *a frightful liar.* **b.** Disagreeable; distressing: *frightful weather.* —**fright'ful·ly** *adv.* —**fright'ful·ness** *n.*

frig·id (frĭj'ĭd) *adj.* **1.** Extremely cold. **2.** Lacking warmth of feeling. **3.** Stiff and formal in manner: *a frigid refusal to a request.* **4.** Persistently averse to sexual intercourse. [Lat. *frigidus* < *frigēre,* to be cold < *frigus,* the cold.] —**fri·gid'i·ty** (frĭ-jĭd'ĭ-tē), **frig'id·ness** *n.* —**frig'id·ly** *adv.*

Frig·i·daire (frĭj'ĭ-dâr'). A trademark for a refrigerator.

frig·i·do·re·cep·tor (frĭj'ĭ-dō-rĭ-sĕp'tər) *n.* A sensory receptor that responds to cold stimuli.

frigid zone *n.* **1.** The area within the Arctic Circle. **2.** The area within the Antarctic Circle.

frig·o·rif·ic (frĭg'ə-rĭf'ĭk) also **frig·o·rif·i·cal** (-ĭ-kəl) *adj.* Causing coldness; chilling. [Lat. *frigorificus* : *frigus,* the cold + *-ficus,* -fic.]

fri·jol (frē-hōl', frē'hōl') also **fri·jo·le** (frē-hō'lē) *n., pl.* **fri·jo·les** (frē-hō'lēz, frē'hō'-). *Southwestern U.S.* A bean cultivated and used for food. [Sp., var. of *frejol* < Catalan *fesol* < Lat. *phaseolus* < Gk. *phaselos.*]

frill (frĭl) *n.* **1.** A ruffled, gathered, or pleated border or projection, such as a fabric edge used to trim clothing or a curled paper strip for decorating the end of the bone of a piece of meat. **2.** *Zool.* A ruff of hair or feathers about the neck of an animal or bird. **3.** A wrinkling of the edge of a photographic film. **4.** *Informal.* Something superfluous. —*v.* **frilled, frill·ing, frills.** —*tr.* **1.** To make into a ruffle or frill. **2.** To add a ruffle or frill to. —*intr.* To become wrinkled along the edge, as photographic film does. [Orig. unknown.] —**frill'y** *adj.*

frilled lizard *n.* An Australian lizard, *Chlamydosaurus kingi,* having a broad, contractile membrane extending from the neck and throat.

fringe (frĭnj) *n.* **1.** A decorative border or edging of hanging threads, cords, or strips, often attached to a separate band. **2.** Something that resembles a fringe. **3.** A marginal, peripheral, or secondary part: *the fringes of the crowd.* **4.** Those members of a group or political party holding extreme views. **5.** Any of the light or dark bands produced by the diffraction or interference of light. —*tr.v.* **fringed, fring·ing, fring·es. 1.** To decorate with or as if with a fringe. **2.** To serve as a fringe to: *a pool fringed with ferns.* [ME *frenge* < OFr. < LLat. *fimbria.* —see FIMBRIA.] —**fring'y** *adj.*

fringe area *n.* A zone just outside of the range of a broadcasting station in which signals are weakened and distorted.

fringe benefit *n.* An employment benefit given in addition to one's wages or salary.

fringed gentian *n.* A plant, *Gentiana crinita,* of eastern North America, having blue, tubular flowers with fringed petals.

fringed orchis *n.* Any of various orchids of the genus *Habenaria,* having variously colored flowers with a fringed lip.

fringed polygala *n.* A plant, *Polygala paucifolia,* of eastern North America, having fringed, reddish-purple flowers.

fringe tree *n.* A shrub or small tree, *Chionanthus virginicus,* of the southeastern United States, having drooping clusters of white flowers and dark-blue fruit.

frip·per·y (frĭp'ə-rē) *n., pl.* **-ies. 1.** Pretentious or showy finery. **2.** Pretentious elegance; ostentation. **3.** Something that is trivial or nonessential. [OFr. *freperie,* old clothes < *frepe,* rag.]

Fris·bee (frĭz'bē). A trademark for a disk-shaped plastic toy that players throw and catch.

fri·sé (frē-zā') *n.* Frieze². [Fr. < p.part. of *friser,* to curl.]

fri·sette (frĭ-zĕt') *n.* Variant of **frizette.**

fri·seur (frē-zûr') *n.* A hairdresser; coiffeur. [Fr. < *friser,* to curl.]

Fri·sian (frĭzh'ən, frē'zhən) also **Frie·sian** (frē'zhən) *n.* **1.** A native or inhabitant of the Frisian Islands or Friesland. **2.** The West Germanic language of the Frisians. [< Lat. *Frisii,* the Frisians.] —**Fri'sian** *adj.*

frisk (frĭsk) *v.* **frisked, frisk·ing, frisks.** —*intr.* To move about briskly and playfully; frolic. —*tr.* To search (a person) for something concealed, esp. a weapon, by passing the hands quickly over clothes or through pockets. —*n.* **1.** An energetic, playful movement; gambol. **2.** An act of frisking. [< obs. *frisk,* lively < OFr. *frisque.*] —**frisk'er** *n.*

frisk·y (frĭs'kē) *adj.* **-i·er, -i·est.** Energetic, lively, and playful. [Obs. *frisk,* lively < OFr. *frisque.*] —**frisk'i·ly** *adv.* —**frisk'i·ness** *n.*

frit (frĭt) *n.* **1.** The fused or partially fused materials used in making glass. **2.** A vitreous substance used in making porcelain or glazes. —*tr.v.* **frit·ted, frit·ting, frits.** To make into frit. [Ital. *fritta* < fem. p.part. of *friggere,* to fry < Lat. *frigere.*]

frit fly *n.* Any of several small flies of the family Chloropidae (or Oscinidae), esp. *Oscinella frit,* having larvae that are destructive to cereal plants. [Orig. unknown.]

frith (frĭth) *n. Scot.* An estuary. [Var. of FIRTH.]

frit·il·lar·y (frĭt'l-ĕr'ē) *n., pl.* **-ies. 1.** Any of various bulbous plants of the genus *Fritillaria,* having nodding, variously colored, often spotted or checkered flowers. **2.** Any of various butterflies of the family Nymphalidae, and esp. of the genera *Speyeria* and *Boloria,* having brownish wings marked with black or silvery spots. [NLat. *Fritillaria* (genus) < Lat. *fritillus,* dice box.]

frit·ter¹ (frĭt'ər) *tr.v.* **-tered, -ter·ing, -ters. 1.** To reduce or squander little by little: *frittered away his inheritance.* **2.** To break, tear, or cut into bits; shred. [< obs. *fritter,* fragment.]

frit·ter² (frĭt'ər) *n.* A small cake made of batter, often containing fruit, vegetables, or fish, sautéed or fried in deep fat. [ME *friture* < OFr. < Lat. *frigere,* to fry.]

friv·ol (frĭv'əl) *intr.v.* **-oled, -ol·ing, -ols** or **-olled, -ol·ling, -ols.** *Informal.* To behave frivolously. [Back-formation < FRIVOLOUS.] —**friv'ol·er** *n.*

fri·vol·i·ty (frĭ-vŏl'ĭ-tē) *n., pl.* **-ties. 1.** The condition or quality of being frivolous. **2.** A frivolous act or thing.

friv·o·lous (frĭv'ə-ləs) *adj.* **1.** Unworthy of serious attention; trivial. **2.** Inappropriately silly. [ME < *frivol,* trifle < OFr. *frivole* < Lat. *frivolum.*] —**friv'o·lous·ly** *adv.* —**friv'o·lous·ness** *n.*

fri·zette also **fri·sette** (frĭ-zĕt') *n.* A curled fringe of hair, usually worn on the forehead by a woman. [Fr. *frisette* < *friser,* to curl.]

frizz¹ (frĭz) *tr. & intr.v.* **frizzed, frizz·ing, frizz·es.** To form or be formed into small, tight curls or tufts. —*n.* **1.** The condition of being frizzed. **2.** A small, tight curl or tuft. [Fr. *friser.*] —**frizz'er** *n.*

frizz² (frĭz) *v.* **frizzed, frizz·ing, frizz·es.** —*tr.* To fry or burn with a sizzling noise. —*intr.* To make a sizzling noise while frying or searing. [Prob. < FRY.]

friz·zle¹ (frĭz'əl) *v.* **-zled, -zling, -zles.** —*tr.* **1.** To fry until crisp and curled: *frizzled the bacon.* **2.** To scorch or sear with heat. —*intr.* To fry or sear with a sizzling noise. [Perh. blend of FRY and SIZZLE.]

friz·zle² (frĭz'əl) *intr. & tr.v.* **-zled, -zling, -zles.** To frizz or cause to frizz. —*n.* A small, tight curl. [Orig. unknown.]

friz·zly (frĭz'lē) *adj.* **-zli·er, -zli·est.** Tightly curled.

friz·zy (frĭz'ē) *adj.* **-zi·er, -zi·est.** Tightly curled; frizzly. —**friz'zi·ly** *adv.* —**friz'zi·ness** *n.*

fro (frō) *adv.* Away; back: *moving to and fro.* —*prep. Scot.* From. [ME < OE *fram* and ON *frā.*]

frock (frŏk) *n.* **1.** A long, loose outer garment, such as that worn by artists and craftsmen; smock. **2.** A woolen garment formerly worn by sailors; jersey. **3.** A robe worn by monks, friars, and other clerics; habit. **4.** A woman's dress. —*tr.v.* **frocked, frock·ing, frocks. 1.** To clothe in a frock. **2.** To invest with clerical office. [ME *frok* < OFr. *froc* < Med. Lat. *froccus,* of Germanic orig.]

frock coat *n.* A man's dress coat with knee-length skirts.

froe also **frow** (frō) *n.* A cleaving tool having a heavy blade set at right angles to the handle. [Orig. unknown.]

frog (frôg, frŏg) *n.* **1.** Any of numerous tailless, chiefly aquatic amphibians of the order Salientia, and esp. of the family Ranidae, characteristically having a smooth, moist skin, webbed feet, and long hind legs adapted for leaping. **2.** A wedge-shaped, horny prominence in the sole of a horse's hoof. **3.** A loop fastened to a belt to hold a tool or weapon. **4.** An ornamental looped braid or cord with a button or knot for fastening the front of a garment. **5.** A device on intersecting railroad tracks that permits wheels to cross the junction. **6.** A spiked or perforated device used to support stems in a flower arrangement. **7.** *Informal.* Hoarseness in the throat. **8.** *Offensive Slang.* A Frenchman. [ME *frogge* < OE *frogga.*]

frog·eye (frôg'ī', frŏg'ī') *n.* A plant disease caused by fungi and characterized by rounded spots on the leaves.

frog·fish (frôg'fĭsh', frŏg'-) *n., pl.* **frogfish** or **-fish·es.** Any of various anglerfishes of the family Antennariidae, of tropical and temperate seas, characteristically covered with fleshy or filamentous processes.

frog·hop·per (frôg'hŏp'ər, frŏg'-) *n.* The spittlebug.

frog kick *n.* A swimming kick in which the legs are drawn up close beneath the swimmer and then thrust outward and together vigorously.

frog·man (frôg'măn', -mən, frŏg'-) *n.* A swimmer provided with breathing apparatus and other equipment to execute underwater maneuvers, esp. military maneuvers.

frog·mouth (frôg'mouth', frŏg'-) *n.* Any of various brown or gray nocturnal birds of the genera *Podargus* and *Batrachostomus,* of southeastern Asia and Australia, having a wide mouth and a hooked bill.

frog spit also **frog spittle** *n.* **1.** Cuckoo spit. **2.** A foamlike aggregation of small aquatic plants, such as green algae, on the surface of a pond.

frol·ic (frŏl'ĭk) *n.* **1.** Gaiety; merriment. **2.** A gay, carefree time. **3.** A playful antic. —*intr.v.* **-icked, -ick·ing, -ics. 1.** To behave playfully and uninhibitedly; romp. **2.** To engage in merrymaking, joking, or teasing. —*adj. Archaic.* Merry. [Du.

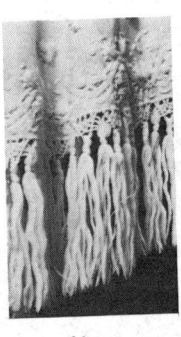

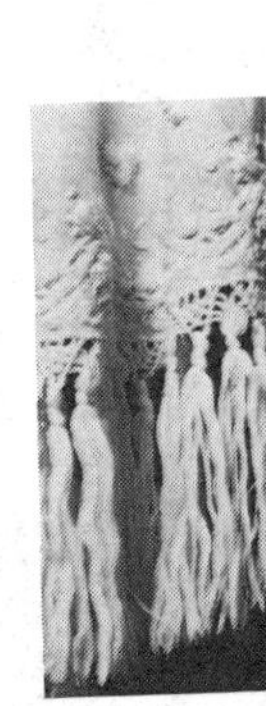

fringe

frock coat

George Miksch Sutton

frogmouth

vrolijk, merry < MDu. *vrolijc* < *vro,* happy.] **—frol'ick·er** *n.*
frol·ic·some (frŏl'ĭk-səm) *adj.* Full of high-spirited fun; playful.
from (frŭm, frŏm; frəm *when unstressed*) *prep.* **1. a.** Used to indicate a specified place or time as a starting point: *walked home from the station; from six o'clock on.* **b.** Used to indicate a specified point as the first of two limits: *from grades four to six.* **2.** Used to indicate a source, cause, agent, or instrument: *a note from the teacher; take a book from the shelf.* **3.** Used to indicate separation, removal, or exclusion: *keep someone from making a mistake; liberation from bondage.* **4.** Used to indicate differentiation: *know right from wrong.* **5.** Because of: *faint from hunger.* [ME < OE.]
frond (frŏnd) *n.* **1.** The usually compound leaf of a fern. **2.** A large compound leaf of certain other plants, such as a palm. **3.** A leaflike thallus, as of a seaweed or lichen. [Lat. *frons, frond-,* foliage.] **—frond'ed** *adj.*
fron·des·cent (frŏn-dĕs'ənt) *adj.* Bearing, resembling, or having a profusion of leaves or fronds; leafy. [Lat. *frondescens, frondescent-,* pr.part. of *frondescere,* to become leafy < *frondēre,* to put forth leaves < *frons,* foliage.] **—fron·des'cence** *n.*
fron·dose (frŏn'dōs') *adj.* **1.** Bearing fronds. **2.** Resembling a frond; frondlike. [Lat. *frondōsus* : *frons,* foliage + *-osus,* -ose.] **—fron'dose'ly** *adv.*
front (frŭnt) *n.* **1.** The forward part or surface, as of a building. **2.** The area, location, or position directly before or ahead. **3.** A position of leadership or superiority. **4.** *Archaic.* The first part; beginning. **5.** The forehead, esp. of an animal or bird. **6.** *Archaic.* The face; countenance. **7.** Demeanor or bearing, esp. in the presence of danger or difficulty: *maintain a brave front.* **8.** An outward and often feigned appearance or manner. **9.** Land bordering a lake, river, or street. **10.** A promenade along the water at a resort. **11.** Used by a desk clerk in a hotel to summon a bellboy or page. **12.** A detachable part of a man's dress shirt covering the chest; dickey. **13. a.** The most forward line of a combat force. **b.** The area of contact between opposing combat forces; battlefront. **14.** *Meteorol.* The interface between air masses at different temperatures. **15.** A group or movement uniting various individuals or organizations for the achievement of a common purpose; coalition. **16.** A nominal leader lacking in real authority; figurehead. **17.** An apparently respectable person, group, or business used as a cover for secret or illegal activities. **18.** A field of activity: *the economic front.* *—adj.* **1.** Of, pertaining to, aimed at, or located in the front. **2.** Produced at or toward the front of the oral cavity: *a front vowel.* *—v.* **front·ed, front·ing, fronts.** *—tr.* **1.** To look out upon; face. **2.** To meet in opposition; confront. **3.** To provide a front for. **4.** To serve as a front for. *—intr.* To have a front; face: *Her property fronts on the highway.* [ME < OFr. < Lat. *frons,* façade.]
front·age (frŭn'tĭj) *n.* **1.** The front part of a piece of property. **2.** The land between a building and the street. **3.** The direction in which something faces. **4.** Land adjacent to something, such as a building, street, or body of water.
fron·tal[1] (frŭn'tl) *adj.* **1.** Of, pertaining to, or situated at the front. **2.** Of or pertaining to the forehead. **3.** Of or pertaining to the frontal plane. **4.** Of or relating to a meteorological front. **—fron'tal·ly** *adv.*
fron·tal[2] (frŭn'tl) *n.* **1.** A drapery covering the front of an altar. **2.** The façade of a building. [ME *frontel* < OFr. < Med. Lat. *frontellum* < Lat. *frons,* façade.]

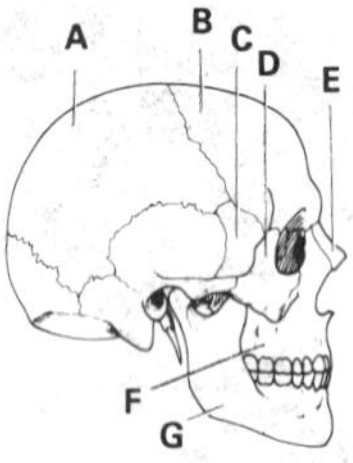

frontal bone
A. Parietal
B. Frontal
C. Sphenoid
D. Zygomatic
E. Nasal
F. Maxilla
G. Mandible

frontal bone *n.* A cranial bone consisting of a vertical portion corresponding to the forehead and an orbital or horizontal portion that enters into the formation of the roofs of the orbital and nasal cavities.
frontal lobe *n.* The largest part of the anterior portion of the cerebral cortex.
frontal lobotomy *n.* A prefrontal lobotomy.
frontal plane *n.* A plane parallel to the long axis of the body and perpendicular to the sagittal plane.
front·court (frŭnt'kôrt', -kōrt') *n.* The offensive half of the court used by a team in basketball.
front-end (frŭnt'ĕnd') *adj.* Of or pertaining to the initial phase of a project: *a front-end investment.*
front-end load *n.* The amount deducted from early payments made to a mutual fund purchase plan that covers expenses such as sales commissions.
fron·ten·is (frŭn-tĕn'ĭs, frŏn'tĕn'ĭs) *n.* A Latin-American tennis game played on a three-walled court. [Am. Sp., blend of Sp. *fronton,* gable, jai alai court (< *frenta,* forehead < Lat. *frons*) and *tenis,* tennis (< E. TENNIS).]
fron·tier (frŭn-tîr', frŏn-, frŭn'tîr', frŏn'-) *n.* **1. a.** An international border. **b.** The area along a frontier. **2.** A region just beyond or at the edge of a settled area. **3.** An undeveloped area or field for discovery or research. **—modifier:** *frontier towns.* [ME *frountier* < OFr. *frontier* < *front,* front.]
fron·tiers·man (frŭn-tîrz'mən, frŏn-) *n.* A man who lives on the frontier.
fron·tis·piece (frŭn'tĭ-spēs') *n.* **1.** An illustration that faces or immediately precedes the title page of a book, book section, or magazine. **2.** *Archaic.* A title page. **3.** *Archit.* A façade, esp. an ornamental façade. **4.** *Archit.* A small ornamental pediment, as on top of a door or window. [OFr. *frontispice,* a building's principal façade < Med. Lat. *frontispicium* : Lat. *frons,* façade + Lat. *specere,* to look at.]
front·let (frŭnt'lĭt) *n.* **1.** An ornament or band worn on the forehead, as a phylactery. **2.** The forehead of an animal or bird, esp. when distinctively marked. **3.** The ornamental border of a frontal. [ME.]
front-line (frŭnt'līn') *adj.* **1.** Located or used at a military front. **2.** Of or relating to the most advanced or important position or activity in a field or undertaking.
front man *n.* A person who serves as a nominal leader but who lacks real authority.
front matter *n.* The material, as the preface, frontispiece, and title page, preceding the text in a book.
front money *n.* Front-end money.
front office *n.* The executive or policy-making officers of an organization.
fron·to·gen·e·sis (frŭn'tō-jĕn'ĭ-sĭs) *n.* Development or intensification of a meteorological front.
fron·tol·y·sis (frŭn-tŏl'ĭ-sĭs) *n.* The disintegration of a meteorological front.
front-page (frŭnt'pāj') *adj.* Worthy of coverage on the front page of a newspaper. *—tr.v.* **-paged, -pag·ing, -pag·es.** To place or report on the front page of a newspaper.
front room *n.* A living room.
front-run·ner (frŭnt'rŭn'ər) *n.* **1.** One that is leading in a race or other competition: *the front-runner for the presidential nomination.* **2.** A competitor who performs best when in the lead. **—front'-run'ning** *adj.*
front·ward (frŭnt'wərd) *adj.* & *adv.* At or toward the front. **—front'wards** *adv.*
frore (frôr, frōr) *adj.* *Archaic.* Extremely cold; frosty. [ME, p.part. of *fresen,* to freeze < OE *frēosan.*]
frosh (frŏsh) *n., pl.* **frosh.** *Informal.* A freshman. [Shortening and alteration of FRESHMAN.]
frost (frôst, frŏst) *n.* **1.** A deposit of minute ice crystals formed from frozen water vapor. **2.** The atmospheric conditions when the temperature is below the freezing point of water. **3.** The process of freezing. **4.** A cold or icy manner; haughtiness. **5.** *Informal.* A failure. *—v.* **frost·ed, frost·ing, frosts.** *—tr.* **1.** To cover with frost. **2.** To damage or kill by frost. **3.** To cover (glass, for example) with a roughened or speckled decorative surface. **4.** To cover or decorate with icing. *—intr.* To become covered with or as if with frost. [ME < OE.]
frost·bite (frôst'bīt', frŏst'-) *n.* Local tissue destruction resulting from freezing. *—tr.v.* **-bit** (-bĭt'), **-bit·ten** (-bĭt'n), **-bit·ing, -bites.** To injure or damage with frost.
frost heave also **frost heaving** *n.* An uplifting of a surface, such as pavement or soil, caused by freezing beneath the surface.
frost·ing (frô'stĭng, frŏs'tĭng) *n.* **1.** Icing (sense 1). **2.** A roughened or speckled surface imparted to glass or metal.
frost line *n.* The limit to which frost penetrates the earth.
frost·work (frôst'wûrk', frŏst'-) *n.* **1.** The intricate patterns produced by frost, as on a windowpane. **2.** Ornamental patterns similar to frostwork, produced artificially, as on metal or glass.
frost·y (frô'stē, frŏs'tē) *adj.* **-i·er, -i·est. 1.** Producing or characterized by frost; freezing. **2.** Covered with or as if with frost. **3.** Silvery white; hoary. **4.** Cold in manner. **—frost'i·ly** *adv.* **—frost'i·ness** *n.*
froth (frôth, frŏth) *n.* **1.** A mass of bubbles in or on a liquid; foam. **2.** A salivary foam released as a result of disease or exhaustion. **3.** Something unsubstantial or trivial. *—v.* **frothed, froth·ing, froths.** *—tr.* **1.** To cover with foam. **2.** To cause to foam. *—intr.* To exude or expel froth. [ME < ON *froða.*]
froth·y (frô'thē, frŏth'ē) *adj.* **-i·er, -i·est. 1.** Made of, covered with, or resembling froth; foamy. **2.** Playfully frivolous in character or content: *a frothy French farce.* **—froth'i·ly** *adv.* **—froth'i·ness** *n.*
frot·tage (frô-täzh') *n.* **1.** A method of making a design by placing a piece of paper on top of an object and then rubbing over it, as with a pencil or charcoal. **2.** A design made by frottage. [Fr. < *frotter,* to rub.]
frou-frou (fro͞o'fro͞o) *n.* **1.** A rustling sound, as of silk. **2.** Fussy or showy dress or ornamentation. [Fr.]
frow (frō) *n.* Variant of **froe.**
fro·ward (frō'wərd, frō'ərd) *adj.* Stubbornly contrary and disobedient; obstinate. [ME : *fro,* fro + *-ward,* -ward.] **—fro'ward·ly** *adv.* **—fro'ward·ness** *n.*
frown (froun) *v.* **frowned, frown·ing, frowns.** *—intr.* **1.** To wrinkle the brow, as in thought or displeasure. **2.** To regard something with disapproval or distaste: *frowned on the use of instant coffee.* *—tr.* To express (disapproval, for example) by wrinkling the brow. *—n.* A wrinkling of the brow in thought or displeasure; scowl. [ME *frounen* < OFr. *froigner,* of Celt. orig.] **—frown'er** *n.* **—frown'ing·ly** *adv.*
frows·ty (frou'stē) *adj.* **-ti·er, -ti·est.** *Chiefly Brit.* Having a stale smell; musty. [Orig. unknown.]
frow·zy also **frow·sy** (frou'zē) *adj.* **-zi·er, -zi·est** also **-si·er, -si·est. 1.** Unkempt in appearance; slovenly. **2.** Having an unpleasant smell; musty. [Orig. unknown.] **—frow'zi·ness** *n.*
froze (frōz) *v.* Past tense of **freeze.**
fro·zen (frō'zən) *v.* Past participle of **freeze.** *—adj.* **1.** Made into, covered with, or surrounded by ice. **2.** Very cold.

3. Preserved by freezing. 4. Rendered immobile. 5. Expressive of cold unfriendliness or disdain. 6. a. Kept at a fixed level: *Rents were frozen.* b. Incapable of being withdrawn, sold, or liquidated: *frozen assets.*

frozen food *n.* Food that has undergone quick freezing and that is intended to remain frozen until used.

fruc·tif·er·ous (frŭk-tĭf′ər-əs, fro͝ok-) *adj.* Bearing fruit. [Lat. *fructifer (fructus,* fruit + *-fer,* -fer) + -OUS.]

fruc·ti·fi·ca·tion (frŭk′tə-fĭ-kā′shən, fro͝ok′-) *n.* **1.** The producing of fruit. **2.** A seed-bearing or spore-bearing structure.

fruc·ti·fy (frŭk′tə-fī′, fro͝ok′-) *v.* **-fied, -fy·ing, -fies.** —*tr.* To make fruitful or productive. —*intr.* To bear fruit. [ME *fructifien* < OFr. *fructifier* < Lat. *fructificare* : *fructus,* fruit + *facere,* to make.]

fruc·tose (frŭk′tōs′, fro͝ok′-) *n.* A very sweet sugar, $C_6H_{12}O_6$, occurring in many fruits and honey and used as a preservative for foodstuffs and as an intravenous nutrient. [Lat. *fructus,* fruit + -OSE.]

fruc·tu·ous (frŭk′cho͞o-əs, fro͝ok′-) *adj.* Fruitful; productive. [ME < OFr. < Lat. *fructuosus* < *fructus,* fruit.]

fru·gal (fro͞o′gəl) *adj.* **1.** Avoiding unnecessary expenditure of money; thrifty. **2.** Costing little; inexpensive: *a frugal lunch.* [Lat. *frugalis* < *frux,* success.] **—fru·gal′i·ty** (fro͞o-găl′ĭ-tē), **fru′gal·ness** *n.* **—fru′gal·ly** *adv.*

fru·giv·o·rous (fro͞o-jĭv′ər-əs) *adj.* Feeding on fruit; fruit-eating. [Lat. *frux, frug-,* fruit + -VOROUS.]

fruit (fro͞ot) *n., pl.* **fruit** or **fruits. 1. a.** The ripened ovary or ovaries of a seed-bearing plant, together with accessory parts, containing the seeds and occurring in a wide variety of forms. **b.** An edible, usually sweet and fleshy form of such a structure. **c.** A part or amount of such a plant product, served as food. **2.** The fertile, often spore-bearing structure of a plant that does not bear seeds. **3.** A plant crop or product. **4.** Result; outcome: *the fruit of their labor.* **5.** Offspring; progeny. **6.** *Slang.* A male homosexual. **—modifier:** *fruit trees.* —*intr. & tr.v.* **fruit·ed, fruit·ing, fruits.** To produce or cause to produce fruit. [ME < OFr. < Lat. *fructus* < p.part. of *frui,* to enjoy.]

fruit·age (fro͞o′tĭj) *n.* **1.** The process, time, or condition of bearing fruit. **2.** Fruit. **3.** A result or effect.

fruit bat *n.* Any of various fruit-eating bats of the family Pteropodidae, of tropical and subtropical regions of the Old World.

fruit·cake (fro͞ot′kāk′) *n.* A heavy, spiced cake containing nuts and candied or dried fruits.

fruit cup *n.* A mixture of fresh or preserved fruits cut into pieces and served as an appetizer or dessert.

fruit·er·er (fro͞o′tər-ər) *n.* One who grows or sells fruit.

fruit fly *n.* **1.** Any of various small flies of the family Drosophilidae, having larvae that feed on ripening or fermenting fruit, esp. a common species, *Drosophila melanogaster.* **2.** Any of various flies of the family Tripetidae (or Tephritidae), having larvae that hatch in and damage plant tissue.

fruit·ful (fro͞ot′fəl) *adj.* **1.** Producing fruit. **2.** Producing in abundance; prolific. **3.** Conducive to productivity; causing to bear in abundance. **4.** Producing results; profitable. **—fruit′ful·ly** *adv.* **—fruit′ful·ness** *n.*

fruiting body *n.* A specialized spore-producing structure, esp. of a fungus.

fru·i·tion (fro͞o-ĭsh′ən) *n.* **1.** Enjoyment derived from use or possession. **2. a.** The condition of bearing fruit. **b.** The achievement of something desired or worked for; accomplishment. [ME *fruicioun* < OFr. *fruition* < Med. Lat. *fruitio,* enjoyment < Lat. *frui,* to enjoy.]

fruit·less (fro͞ot′lĭs) *adj.* **1.** Producing no fruit. **2.** Unproductive of success: *a fruitless search.* **—fruit′less·ly** *adv.* **—fruit′less·ness** *n.*

fruit sugar *n.* Fructose.

fruit·y (fro͞o′tē) *adj.* **-i·er, -i·est. 1.** Of, containing, or relating to fruit. **2.** Tasting and smelling richly of fruit. **3.** Excessively sentimental or sweet. **4.** *Slang.* **a.** Homosexual. **b.** Crazy; odd. **—fruit′i·ness** *n.*

fru·men·ta·ceous (fro͞o′mən-tā′shəs, -mĕn-) *adj.* Resembling or consisting of grain, esp. wheat. [LLat. *frumentaceus* < Lat. *frumentum,* grain, perh. < *frui,* to enjoy.]

fru·men·ty (fro͞o′mən-tē) *n.* Hulled wheat boiled in milk and flavored with sugar and spices. [ME *frumente* < OFr. *frumentée* < *frument,* grain < Lat. *frumentum,* perh. < *frui,* to enjoy.]

frump (frŭmp) *n.* **1.** A dull, plain, unfashionable girl or woman. **2.** A colorless, primly sedate person. [Orig. unknown.] **—frump′i·ly** *adv.* **—frump′i·ness** *n.* **—frump′y** *adj.*

frump·ish (frŭm′pĭsh) *adj.* **1.** Dull or plain. **2.** Prim and sedate. **—frump′ish·ly** *adv.* **—frump′ish·ness** *n.*

frus·ta (frŭs′tə) *n.* A plural of **frustum.**

frus·trate (frŭs′trāt′) *tr.v.* **-trat·ed, -trat·ing, -trates. 1. a.** To prevent from accomplishing a purpose or fulfilling a desire; thwart. **b.** To cause feelings of discouragement or bafflement in. **2.** To make ineffectual or invalid; nullify. [ME *frustraten* < Lat. *frustrare,* to disappoint < *frustra,* in error.] **—frus′trat′er** *n.*

Synonyms: *frustrate, thwart, foil, balk.* These verbs mean to prevent the attainment or fulfillment of a goal or purpose. They are often interchangeable. *Frustrate* suggests defeating in the sense of nullifying another's accomplishment or making it ineffective. *Thwart* makes a stronger implication of direct opposition to another. *Foil* implies defeating either by direct confrontation or by outwitting, confounding, or disconcerting. *Balk* implies the placing of barriers or hindrances in another's course.

frus·tra·tion (frŭ-strā′shən) *n.* **1. a.** The act of frustrating. **b.** The condition or an instance of being frustrated. **2.** Something that frustrates.

frus·tule (frŭs′cho͞ol, -tyo͞ol) *n.* The hard, siliceous shell of a diatom. [Fr. < Lat. *frustulum,* dim. of *frustum,* piece broken off.]

frus·tum (frŭs′təm) *n., pl.* **-tums** or **-ta** (-tə). A part of a solid, such as a cone or pyramid, between two parallel planes cutting the solid, esp. the section between the base and a plane parallel to the base. [Lat., piece broken off.]

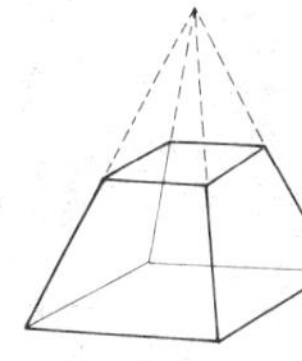

frustum

fru·tes·cent (fro͞o-tĕs′ənt) *adj.* Pertaining to, resembling, or assuming the form of a shrub; shrubby. [Lat. *frutex,* bush + -ESCENT.] **—fru·tes′cence** *n.*

fru·ti·cose (fro͞o′tĭ-kōs′) *adj.* Shrublike, esp. in form. [Lat. *fruticosus* < *frutex,* bush.]

fry[1] (frī) *v.* **fried, fry·ing, fries.** —*tr.* To cook over direct heat in hot oil or fat. —*intr.* **1.** To be cooked in a pan over direct heat in hot oil or fat. **2.** *Slang.* To undergo execution in an electric chair. —*n., pl.* **fries. 1.** A dish of a fried food. **2.** A social gathering at which food is fried and eaten: *a fish fry.* [ME *frien* < OFr. *frire* < Lat. *frigere.*]

fry[2] (frī) *n., pl.* **fry. 1.** A small fish, esp. a young, recently hatched fish. **2.** The young of certain other animals. **3.** Individuals; persons: *the young fry.* [ME *fri,* prob. < AN.]

fry·er also **fri·er** (frī′ər) *n.* **1.** One that fries. **2.** A small, young chicken suitable for frying.

frying pan *n.* A shallow, long-handled pan used for frying food.

f-stop (ĕf′stŏp′) *n.* **1.** A camera lens aperture setting that is calibrated to a corresponding f-number. **2.** An f-number. [F(OCAL LENGTH) + STOP.]

f-sys·tem (ĕf′sĭs′təm) *n.* A method of indicating the relative aperture of a camera lens based on the f-number.

fub·sy (fŭb′zē) *adj.* **-si·er, -si·est.** *Brit. Regional.* Somewhat fat and squat. [< obs. *fubs,* chubby person.]

fuch·sia (fyo͞o′shə) *n.* **1.** Any of various chiefly tropical shrubs of the genus *Fuchsia,* widely cultivated for their showy, drooping purplish, reddish, or white flowers. **2.** A strong, vivid purplish red. [NLat. *Fuchsia,* genus name, after Leonard *Fuchs* (1501–1566).]

fuchsia

fuch·sin also **fuch·sine** (fyo͞ok′sĭn, -sēn′) *n.* A dark-green synthetic aniline dyestuff, the hydrochloride of rosaniline, used to make a purple-red dye employed in coloring textiles and leather and as a bacterial stain. [FUCHS(IA) + -IN.]

fuck (fŭk) *Obscene.* —*v.* **fucked, fuck·ing, fucks.** —*tr.* To have sexual intercourse with. —*intr.* To engage in sexual intercourse. **—phrasal verbs. fuck around.** To fool around. **fuck off.** To leave at once. **fuck over.** To treat unfairly; take advantage of. **fuck up. 1.** To bungle. **2.** To act carelessly or foolishly. —*n.* **1.** An act of sexual intercourse. **2.** A partner in sexual intercourse. [Orig. unknown.]

fucked-up (fŭkt′ŭp′) *adj. Obscene.* Totally confused, mismanaged, or disordered.

fuck·er (fŭk′ər) *n. Obscene.* **1.** One that fucks. **2.** One that is offensive.

fuck·ing (fŭk′ĭng) *Obscene.* —*adj.* Damned. Used as an intensive. —*adv.* Very. Used as an intensive.

fuck·up (fŭk′ŭp′) *n. Obscene.* **1.** One who fucks up. **2.** A blunder; bungle.

fu·coid (fyo͞o′koid′) *adj.* Of or belonging to the order Fucales, which includes brown algae such as gulfweed and rockweed. —*n.* **1.** A member of the Fucales. **2.** A fossilized cast or impression of a fucoid. [Perh. < FUC(US) + -OID.]

fu·cose (fyo͞o′kōs′) *n.* An aldose, $C_6H_{12}O_5$, present in the polysaccharides associated with several blood groups. [FUC(US) + -OSE.]

fu·co·xan·thin (fyo͞o′kō-zăn′thĭn) *n.* A brown carotenoid pigment, $C_{40}H_{60}O_6$, found in brown algae. [FUC(US) + XANTH(O)- + -IN.]

fu·cus (fyo͞o′kəs) *n.* Any of various brown algae of the genus *Fucus,* which includes many of the rockweeds. [NLat. *Fucus* < Lat. *fucus,* rock lichen < Gk. *phukos.*]

fud·dle (fŭd′l) *v.* **-dled, -dling, -dles.** —*tr.* To make drunk; intoxicate. —*intr.* To drink; tipple. —*n.* A state of intoxication or confusion. [Orig. unknown.]

fud·dy-dud·dy (fŭd′ē-dŭd′ē) *n., pl.* **-dies.** One who is old-fashioned and fussy. [Orig. unknown.]

fudge (fŭj) *n.* **1.** A soft rich candy made of sugar, milk, butter, and flavoring. **2.** Nonsense; humbug. —*v.* **fudged, fudg·ing, fudg·es.** —*tr.* **1.** To fake or falsify. **2.** To evade (an issue, for example); dodge. —*intr.* **1.** To act in an indecisive manner. **2. a.** To go beyond the proper limits of something. **b.** To act dishonestly; cheat. [Orig. unknown.]

fueh·rer (fyo͝or′ər) *n.* Variant of **führer.**

fu·el (fyo͞o′əl) *n.* **1.** Something consumed to produce energy, esp.: **a.** A material such as wood, coal, gas, or oil burned to produce heat. **b.** Fissionable material used in a nuclear reactor. **c.** Nutritive material metabolized by a living organism. **2.** Something that maintains or stimulates an activity or an emotion. **—modifier:** *a fuel pump.* —*v.* **-eled, -el·ing, -els** or **-elled, -el·ling, -els.** —*tr.* **1.** To provide with fuel. **2. a.** To support the activity or existence of. **b.** To stimulate: *a passivity that fueled his irritation.* —*intr.* To take in fuel. [ME *feuel* < OFr. *fouaille* < Lat. *focus,* fire.] **—fu'el·er** *n.*

fuel cell *n.* An electrochemical cell in which the energy of a reaction between a fuel, such as liquid hydrogen, and an oxidant, such as liquid oxygen, is converted directly and continuously into electrical energy.

fuel injection *n.* Any of several methods or mechanical systems by which a fuel is vaporized and sprayed directly into the cylinders of an internal-combustion engine.

fuel oil *n.* A liquid or liquefiable petroleum product that is used to generate heat or power.

fu·ga·cious (fyōō-gā'shəs) *adj.* **1.** Passing away quickly; evanescent. **2.** *Bot.* Withering or dropping off early. [Lat. *fugax, fugac-,* swift < *fugere,* to flee.] **—fu·ga'cious·ly** *adv.* **—fu·ga'cious·ness, fu·gac'i·ty** (-găs'ĭ-tē) *n.*

-fuge *suff.* One that expels or drives away: *vermifuge.* [< Lat. *fugare,* to expel < *fuga,* flight.]

fu·gi·tive (fyōō'jĭ-tĭv) *adj.* **1.** Running away or fleeing, as from the law. **2. a.** Passing quickly; fleeting: *fugitive hours.* **b.** Difficult to comprehend or retain; elusive. **c.** Given to change or disappearance; perishable. **3.** Tending to wander; vagabond. **4.** Having to do with topics of temporary interest; ephemeral. —*n.* **1.** One who flees; refugee. **2.** Something fleeting or ephemeral. [ME *fugitif* < OFr. < Lat. *fugitivus* < *fugere,* to flee.] **—fu'gi·tive·ly** *adv.* **—fu'gi·tive·ness** *n.*

fu·gle (fyōō'gəl) *intr.v.* **-gled, -gling, -gles.** *Archaic.* **1.** To act as a fugleman. **2.** To make signals. [Back-formation < FUGLEMAN.]

fu·gle·man (fyōō'gəl-mən) *n.* **1.** *Archaic.* A soldier who formerly served as a guide and model for his company. **2.** A leader, esp. a political leader. [Alteration of G. *Flügelmann* : *Flügel,* wing + *Mann,* man.]

fugue (fyōōg) *n.* **1.** A polyphonic musical composition in which a theme or themes stated successively by a number of voices in imitation are developed contrapuntally. **2.** A pathological condition during which one is apparently conscious of his actions but has no recollection of them after returning to a normal state. [Fr. < Ital. *fuga* < Lat., flight.] **—fu'gal** (fyōō'gəl) *adj.* **—fu'gal·ly** *adv.*

füh·rer also **fueh·rer** (fyŏŏr'ər) *n.* **1.** A leader, esp. one exercising the powers of a tyrant. **2. Führer.** The title of Adolf Hitler as the leader of the German Nazis. [G. < MHG *vüerer,* bearer < *vüeren,* to bear < OHG *fuoren,* to lead.]

Fu·jian (fōō'jĕn') *n.* A dialect of Chinese spoken in Fujian Province, eastern Guangdong Province, and Taiwan.

Fu·kien (fōō'kyĕn') *n.* Fujian.

-ful *suff.* **1. a.** Full of: *playful.* **b.** Characterized by; resembling: *masterful.* **c.** Tending, given, or able to: *useful.* **2.** A quantity that fills: *armful.* [ME < OE < *full,* full.]

Usage: The plurals of nouns ending in *-ful* are usually formed by adding the letter *s: cupfuls; glassfuls; spoonfuls.*

Fu·la also **Fu·lah** (fōō'lə) *n., pl.* **Fula** or **-las** also **Fulah** or **-lahs. 1.** A mostly Moslem people of northwestern and central Africa, of mixed Hamitic and Negroid stock. **2.** A member of the Fula people.

Fu·la·ni (fōō'lä'nē, fōō-lä'-) *n., pl.* **Fulani** or **-nis. 1.** One of the Fula. **2.** The language of the Fula.

ful·crum (fŏŏl'krəm, fŭl'-) *n., pl.* **-crums** or **-cra** (-krə). **1.** The point or support on which a lever turns. **2.** An agent through which vital powers are exercised. [Lat., bedpost < *fulcire,* to support.]

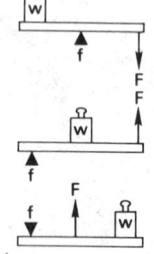

fulcrum
Black triangles represent the fulcrums of three basic levers; f is the fulcrum and F is the force needed to raise a weight W

ful·fill also **ful·fil** (fŏŏl-fĭl') *tr.v.* **-filled, -fill·ing, -fills** also **-fils. 1.** To bring into actuality; effect. **2.** To carry out (an order, for example). **3.** To measure up to; satisfy. **4.** To bring to an end; complete. [ME *fulfillen* < OE *fulfyllan* : *ful,* full + *fyllan,* to fill.] **—ful·fill'er** *n.* **—ful·fill'ment, ful·fil'ment** *n.*

ful·gent (fŏŏl'jənt, fŭl'-) *adj.* Shining brilliantly; radiant. [ME < Lat. *fulgens,* pr.part. of *fulgēre,* to shine.] **—ful'gent·ly** *adv.*

ful·gu·rant (fŏŏl'gyər-ənt, -gər-, fŭl'-) *adj.* Flashing like lightning; dazzlingly bright. [Lat. *fulgurans, fulgurant-,* pr.part. of *fulgurare,* to lighten. —see FULGURATE.]

ful·gu·rate (fŏŏl'gyə-rāt', -gə-, fŭl'-) *intr.v.* **-rat·ed, -rat·ing, -rates.** To give off or emit in flashes. [Lat. *fulgurare, fulgurat-,* to lighten < *fulgur,* lightning < *fulgēre,* to flash.] **—ful'gu·ra'tion** *n.*

ful·gu·rite (fŏŏl'gyə-rīt', -gə-, fŭl'-) *n.* A tubular body of glassy rock produced by lightning striking exposed surfaces. [Lat. *fulgur,* lightning + -ITE.]

ful·gu·rous (fŏŏl'gyər-əs, -gər-, fŭl'-) *adj.* **1.** Emitting flashes of lightning. **2.** Emitting in flashes similar to lightning. [Lat. *fulgur,* lightning + -OUS.]

fu·lig·i·nous (fyōō-lĭj'ə-nəs) *adj.* **1.** Sooty. **2.** Colored by or as if by soot. [LLat. *fuliginosus* < Lat. *fuligo,* soot.] **—fu·lig'i·nous·ly** *adv.*

full¹ (fŏŏl) *adj.* **-er, -est. 1.** Containing all that is normal or possible: *a full pail.* **2.** Complete in every particular: *a full account.* **3. a.** Of maximum or highest degree: *at full speed.* **b.** Being at the peak of development or maturity: *full bloom.* **4.** Having a great deal or many: *a book full of errors.* **5.** Totally qualified, accepted, or empowered: *a full member.* **6. a.** Rounded in shape; plump: *a full figure.* **b.** Having or made with a generous amount of fabric: *full draperies.* **7. a.** Satiated, esp. with food or drink. **b.** Providing an abundance, esp. of food. **8.** Having depth and body; rich. **9.** Completely absorbed or preoccupied. **10.** Possessing both parents in common: *full brothers.* —*adv.* **1.** To a complete extent; entirely: *full-grown; knowing full well.* **2.** Exactly; directly: *full in the path of the moon.* —*v.* **fulled, full·ing, fulls.** —*tr.* To make (a garment) full, as by pleating or gathering. —*intr.* To become full. Used of the moon. —*n.* **1.** The maximum or complete size or amount. **2.** The highest degree or state. [ME *ful* < OE.] **—full'ness, ful'ness** *n.*

full² (fŏŏl) *tr.v.* **fulled, full·ing, fulls.** To increase the weight and bulk of (cloth) by shrinking and beating or pressing. [ME *fullen* < OFr. *fuler, fouler* < Med. Lat. *fullare* < Lat. *fullo,* fuller.]

full·back (fŏŏl'băk') *n.* **1. a.** *Football.* A backfield player whose position is behind the quarterback and halfbacks and who performs offensive blocking and line plunges and defensive linebacking. **b.** A similar player in field hockey, soccer, and rugby. **2.** The position played by a fullback.

full blood *n.* **1.** Relationship established through having the same set of parents. **2.** An individual of unmixed race or breed.

full-blood·ed (fŏŏl'blŭd'ĭd) *adj.* **1. a.** Of unmixed ancestry; purebred. **b.** Related through having the same parents. **2. a.** Not pale or anemic. **b.** Vigorous and vital. **3.** Complete in all respects. **—full'-blood'ed·ness** *n.*

full-blown (fŏŏl'blōn') *adj.* **1.** Having blossomed or opened completely. **2.** Fully developed or matured. **3.** Having or displaying all the characteristics necessary for completeness.

full-bod·ied (fŏŏl'bŏd'ēd) *adj.* Having richness and intensity of flavor: *a full-bodied wine.*

full dress *n.* The attire appropriate for formal or ceremonial events.

full-dress (fŏŏl'drĕs') *adj.* **1.** Complete in every respect. **2.** Characterized by exhaustive thoroughness.

full·er¹ (fŏŏl'ər) *n.* A person who fulls cloth. [ME *fullere* < OE and < OFr. *fouleor,* both < Lat. *fullo.*]

ful·ler² (fŏŏl'ər) *n.* **1.** A hammer used by a blacksmith for grooving or spreading iron. **2.** A groove made by a fuller. [Orig. unknown.]

fuller's earth *n.* A highly absorbent claylike substance used predominantly in fulling woolen cloth, in talcum powders, as a filter, and as a catalyst.

fuller's teasel *n.* A European plant, *Dipsacus fullonum,* having bristly flower heads used by fullers to raise the nap on cloth.

full-fash·ioned (fŏŏl'făsh'ənd) *adj.* Knitted in a shape that conforms closely to body lines.

full-fledged (fŏŏl'flĕjd') *adj.* **1.** Having fully developed adult plumage. **2.** Having reached full development; mature. **3.** Having full status or rank: *a full-fledged lawyer.*

full gainer *n.* A forward dive in which the diver executes a full back somersault before entering the water.

full house *n.* A poker hand containing three of a kind and a pair.

full-length (fŏŏl'lĕngkth', -lĕngth') *adj.* **1.** Showing or fitted to the entire length, esp. of the human body: *a full-length mirror.* **2.** Of a normal or standard length: *a full-length novel.*

full moon *n.* **1.** The phase of the moon when it is visible as a fully illuminated disk. **2.** The period of the month when a full moon occurs.

full-mouthed (fŏŏl'mou*th*d', -moutht') *adj.* **1.** Having a complete set of teeth. Used of cattle and other livestock. **2.** Uttered loudly or noisily.

full nelson *n.* A wrestling hold in which both hands are first thrust under the opponent's arms from behind and then pressed against the back of the opponent's neck.

full rhyme *n.* Perfect rhyme.

full-scale (fŏŏl'skāl') *adj.* **1.** Of actual or full size; not reduced: *a full-scale model.* **2.** Employing all resources; not limited or partial: *a full-scale antiwar campaign.*

full stop *n.* A period indicating the end of a sentence.

full tilt *adv.* At high or top speed: *ran full tilt into the tree.*

full-time (fŏŏl'tīm') *adj.* Employed for or involving a standard number of hours of working time: *a full-time administrative assistant.* **—full'-time'** *adv.*

ful·ly (fŏŏl'ē) *adv.* **1.** Totally or completely. **2.** At least.

ful·mar (fŏŏl'mər, -mär') *n.* **1.** A gull-like bird, *Fulmarus glacialis,* of Arctic regions, having smoky gray plumage. **2.** Any of several birds that are similar or related to the fulmar. [Of Scand. orig.]

ful·mi·nant (fŏŏl'mə-nənt, fŭl'-) *adj.* **1.** Fulminating. **2.** *Pathol.* Occurring suddenly, rapidly, and with great intensity. [Lat. *fulminans, fulminant-,* pr.part. of *fulminare,* to strike with lightning. —see FULMINATE.]

ful·mi·nate (fŏŏl'mə-nāt', fŭl'-) *v.* **-nat·ed, -nat·ing, -nates.** —*intr.* **1.** To issue a thunderous verbal attack or denunciation: *fulminate against political chicanery.* **2.** To explode or detonate with sudden violence. —*tr.* **1.** To thunder out or issue (a denunciation, for example). **2.** To cause to explode. —*n.* An explosive salt of fulminic acid, esp. fulminate of mercury. [ME *fulminaten* < Lat. *fulminare,* to strike with lightning < *fulmen,* lightning < *fulgēre,* to flash.] **—ful'mi·na'tion** *n.* **—ful'mi·na'tor** *n.* **—ful'mi·na·to'ry** (-nə-tôr'ē, -tōr'-ē) *adj.*

fulminate of mercury *n.* A gray crystalline powder,

$Hg(CNO)_2$, that explodes when dry under the slightest friction or shock and is used as a high explosive.

ful·mine (fo͝ol'mĭn, fŭl'-) *tr. & intr.v.* **-mined, -min·ing, -mines.** *Archaic.* To fulminate. [OFr. *fulminer* < Lat. *fulminare,* to strike with lightning. —see FULMINATE.]

ful·min·ic acid (fo͝ol-mĭn'ĭk, fŭl-) *n.* An unstable acid, HONC, that forms highly explosive salts. [Lat. *fulmen, fulmin-,* lightning (see FULMINATE) + -IC.]

ful·some (fo͝ol'səm) *adj.* **1.** Offensively flattering or insincere. **2.** Offensive to the taste or sensibilities. **3.** *Archaic.* Copious or abundant in supply. [ME *fulsom,* loathsome < *ful,* full.] **—ful'some·ly** *adv.* **—ful'some·ness** *n.*

Usage: *Fulsome* is often misused, especially in the phrase *fulsome praise,* by those who think that the term is equivalent merely to *full* and *abundant.* In modern usage *full* and *abundant* are obsolete as senses of *fulsome,* which now combines the idea of fullness or abundance with that of excess or insincerity.

Fu Man·chu mustache (fo͞o' măn-cho͞o') *n.* A mustache with ends that hang downward toward the chin. [After *Fu Manchu,* character in novels by Sax Rohmer, pseudonym of A.S. Ward (1883–1959).]

fu·ma·rate (fyo͞o'mə-rāt') *n.* A salt or ester of fumaric acid. [FUMAR(IC ACID) + -ATE.]

fu·mar·ic acid (fyo͞o-măr'ĭk) *n.* An acid, $C_4H_4O_4$, found in various plants and produced synthetically, used mainly in resins, paints, and varnishes. [< NLat. *Fumaria,* genus of herbs (< LLat. *fumaria,* fumitory < Lat. *fumus,* smoke) + -IC.]

fu·ma·role (fyo͞o'mə-rōl') *n.* A hole in a volcanic area from which hot smoke and gases arise. [Ital. *fumarola* < LLat. *fumariolum* < Lat. *fumarium,* smoke chamber < *fumus,* smoke.] **—fu'ma·rol'ic** *adj.*

fu·ma·to·ri·um (fyo͞o'mə-tôr'ē-əm, -tōr'-) *n., pl.* **-to·ri·ums** or **-to·ri·a** (-tôr'ē-ə, -tōr'-). An airtight fumigation chamber in which chemical vapors are used to destroy insects and fungi on plants. [NLat. < Lat. *fūmatus,* p.part. of *fumare,* to smoke < *fumus,* smoke.]

fu·ma·to·ry (fyo͞o'mə-tôr'ē, -tōr'ē) *adj.* Of or pertaining to smoke or fumigating. *—n., pl.* **-ries.** A fumatorium. [< Lat. *fumare, fumat-,* to smoke < *fumus,* smoke.]

fum·ble (fŭm'bəl) *v.* **-bled, -bling, -bles.** *—intr.* **1.** To touch or handle nervously or idly: *fumble with a necktie.* **2.** To grope awkwardly to find or to accomplish something: *fumble for a key.* **3.** To proceed awkwardly and uncertainly; blunder: *fumble through a speech.* **4. a.** *Baseball.* To mishandle a ground ball. **b.** *Football.* To drop a ball that is in play. *—tr.* **1.** To touch or handle clumsily or idly. **2.** To make a botch of; bungle. **3.** To feel or make (one's way) awkwardly. **4. a.** *Baseball.* To mishandle (a ground ball). **b.** *Football.* To drop (a ball) while in play. *—n.* **1. a.** The act of fumbling. **b.** An instance of fumbling. **2.** *Sports.* A ball that has been fumbled. [Perh. of Scand. orig.] **—fum'bler** *n.*

fume (fyo͞om) *n.* **1.** A usually irritating or disagreeable exhalation, as of smoke, vapor, or gas. **2.** A strong or acrid odor. **3.** A state of irritation or anger. *—v.* **fumed, fum·ing, fumes.** *—tr.* **1.** To subject to or treat with fumes. **2.** To give off in or as if in fumes. *—intr.* **1.** To emit fumes. **2.** To rise in fumes. **3.** To feel or show agitation or anger. [ME < OFr. *fum* < Lat. *fumus.*]

fu·mi·gate (fyo͞o'mĭ-gāt') *v.* **-gat·ed, -gat·ing, -gates.** *—tr.* To subject to smoke or fumes, usually in order to exterminate vermin or insects or to disinfect. *—intr.* To employ smoke or fumes in order to exterminate or disinfect. [Lat. *fumigare, fumigat-,* to smoke : *fumus,* smoke + *agere,* to make.] **—fu'mi·ga'tion** *n.* **—fu'mi·ga'tor** *n.*

fu·mi·to·ry (fyo͞o'mĭ-tôr'ē, -tōr'ē) *n., pl.* **-ries.** A climbing plant, *Fumaria officinalis,* native to Europe, having finely divided leaves and spurred purplish flowers. [ME *fumetere* < OFr. *fumeterre* < Med. Lat. *fumus terre* : Lat. *fumus,* smoke + Lat. *terra,* earth.]

fun (fŭn) *n.* **1.** A source of enjoyment, amusement, or pleasure: *Clowns are fun.* **2.** Enjoyment; amusement: *have fun at the beach.* **3.** Playful and often noisy activity. *—intr.v.* **funned, fun·ning, funs.** To behave playfully; joke. **—idioms. for** (or **in**) **fun.** As a joke; playfully. **like fun.** *Slang.* Absolutely not; of course not. [Perh. < ME *fonnen,* to fool < *fon,* fool.]

fu·nam·bu·list (fyo͞o-năm'byə-lĭst) *n.* One who performs on a tightrope or a slack rope. [Lat. *funambulus* : *funis,* rope + *ambulare,* to walk.] **—fu·nam'bu·lism** *n.*

func·tion (fŭngk'shən) *n.* **1.** The action for which a person or thing is particularly fitted or employed. **2. a.** Assigned duty or activity. **b.** Specific occupation or role: *in his function as attorney.* **3.** An official ceremony or formal social occasion. **4.** Something closely related to another thing and dependent upon it for its existence, value, or significance: *Growth is a function of nutrition.* **5.** *Math.* **a.** A variable so related to another that for each value assumed by one there is a value determined for the other. **b.** A rule of correspondence between two sets such that there is a unique element in one set assigned to each element in the other. *—intr.v.* **-tioned, -tion·ing, -tions.** To have or perform a function; serve. [Lat. *functio,* performance < *fungi,* to perform.] **—func'tion·less** *adj.*

func·tion·al (fŭngk'shə-nəl) *adj.* **1.** Of or pertaining to a function. **2.** Designed for or adapted to a particular function or use: *functional architecture.* **3.** Capable of performing; operative. **4.** *Pathol.* Involving functions rather than a physiological or structural cause. **5.** *Math.* Of, relating to, or indicating a function or functions. **—func'tion·al·ly** *adv.*

functional group *n.* A distinctive reactive constituent, such as a carboxyl group, of a chemical compound.

functional illiterate *n.* A person who has had some education but does not meet a minimum standard of literacy.

func·tion·al·ism (fŭngk'shə-nə-lĭz'əm) *n.* **1.** The doctrine that the function of an object should determine its design and materials. **2.** A doctrine stressing purpose, practicality, and utility.

functional shift *n. Ling.* A shift in the syntactic function of a word, as when a noun serves as a verb.

func·tion·ar·y (fŭngk'shə-nĕr'ē) *n., pl.* **-ies.** A person who holds an office or performs a particular function; official.

function word *n.* A word, such as a preposition or a conjunction, chiefly indicating a grammatical relationship in a sentence or phrase.

fund (fŭnd) *n.* **1.** A source of supply; stock. **2. a.** A sum of money or other resources set aside for a specific purpose. **b. funds.** Available money; ready cash. **3. the funds.** The British permanent national debt, considered as securities. **4.** An organization established to administer a fund. *—tr.v.* **fund·ed, fund·ing, funds. 1.** To provide money for paying off the interest or principal of. **2.** To convert into a long-term or floating debt with fixed interest payments. **3.** To place in a fund. **4.** To furnish a fund for. [Lat. *fundus,* piece of land.]

fun·da·ment (fŭn'də-mənt) *n.* **1. a.** The buttocks. **b.** The anus. **2.** The natural features of a land surface unaltered by human beings. **3.** A foundation. **4.** An underlying theoretical basis or principle. [ME *foundement* < OFr. *fondement* < Lat. *fundamentum* < *fundare,* to lay the foundation < *fundus,* bottom.]

fun·da·men·tal (fŭn'də-mĕn'tl) *adj.* **1. a.** Forming or serving as an essential component of a system or structure; basic. **b.** Of major significance; central. **2.** *Physics.* **a.** Of or pertaining to the component of lowest frequency of a periodic wave or quantity. **b.** Of or pertaining to the lowest possible frequency of a vibrating element or system. **3.** *Mus.* Having the root in the bass. *—n.* **1.** Something that is an essential or fundamental part. **2.** *Physics.* The lowest frequency of a periodically varying quantity or of a vibrating system. **—fun'da·men'tal·ly** *adv.*

fun·da·men·tal·ism (fŭn'də-mĕn'tl-ĭz'əm) *n.* **1. a.** Often **Fundamentalism.** A Protestant movement characterized by a belief in the literal truth of the Bible. **b.** Adherence to this belief. **2.** A movement or point of view characterized by rigid adherence to fundamental or basic principles. **—fun'da·men'tal·ist** *n.* **—fun'da·men'tal·is'tic** *adj.*

fundamental particle *n. Physics.* An elementary particle.

fun·di (fŭn'dī') *n.* Plural of **fundus.**

fund raiser *n.* **1.** One who raises funds, as for an organization or a campaign. **2.** A social function, such as a dinner, for raising funds.

fund-rais·ing (fŭnd'rā'zĭng) *adj.* Intended to raise funds: *a fund-raising campaign.*

fun·dus (fŭn'dəs) *n., pl.* **-di** (-dī'). *Anat.* The inner basal surface of an organ farthest away from the opening, as in the eye or uterus. [Lat., bottom.] **—fun'dic** *adj.*

fu·ner·al (fyo͞o'nər-əl) *n.* **1.** The ceremonies held in connection with the burial or cremation of the dead. **2.** The persons accompanying a body to the grave. **3.** An end or cessation of existence. **4.** *Informal.* A source of concern or care to a person: *If he doesn't meet the deadline, that's his funeral.* [ME *funerelles* < OFr. *funerailles* < Med. Lat. *funeralia* < Lat. *funus,* death rites.]

funeral home *n.* An establishment in which the dead are prepared for burial or cremation and in which wakes and funerals may be held.

fu·ner·ar·y (fyo͞o'nə-rĕr'ē) *adj.* Of or suitable for a funeral or burial. [LLat. *funerarius* < Lat. *funus,* funeral.]

fu·ne·re·al (fyo͞o-nîr'ē-əl) *adj.* **1.** Of or pertaining to a funeral. **2.** Appropriate for or suggestive of a funeral: *funereal gloom.* [Lat. *funereus* < *funus,* funeral.] **—fu·ne're·al·ly** *adv.*

fun·gal (fŭng'gəl) *adj.* Fungous.

fun·gi (fŭn'jī') *n.* A plural of **fungus.**

fun·gi·ble (fŭn'jə-bəl) *adj. Law.* Being of such a nature or kind that one unit or part may be exchanged or substituted for another unit or equal part to discharge an obligation. *—n.* Often **fungibles.** Something fungible, as money or grain. [< Lat. *fungi,* to perform.]

fun·gi·cide (fŭn'jĭ-sīd', fŭng'gĭ-) *n.* A substance that destroys or inhibits the growth of fungi. **—fun'gi·cid'al** (-sīd'l) *adj.* **—fun'gi·cid'al·ly** *adv.*

fun·gi·form (fŭn'jə-fôrm', fŭng'gə-) *adj.* Shaped like a mushroom. [FUNG(US) + -FORM.]

fun·gi·stat (fŭn'jĭ-stăt', fŭng'gĭ-) *n.* A substance that inhibits the growth of fungi.

fun·giv·or·ous (fŭn-jĭv'ər-əs, fŭng-gĭv'-) *adj.* Feeding on fungi.

fun·go (fŭng'gō) *n., pl.* **-goes.** *Baseball.* A practice fly ball hit to a fielder with a specially designed bat. [Orig. unknown.]

fun·gous (fŭng'gəs) *adj.* **1.** Of, pertaining to, resembling, or

George Miksch Sutton

fulmar

characteristic of a fungus. **2.** Caused by a fungus. [ME, tender < Lat. *fungosus* < *fungus,* fungus.]
fun·gus (fŭng′gəs) *n., pl.* **fun·gi** (fŭn′jī′) or **fun·gus·es.** Any of numerous plants of the division or subkingdom Thallophyta, lacking chlorophyll, ranging in form from a single cell to a body mass of branched filamentous hyphae that often produce specialized fruiting bodies and including the yeasts, molds, smuts, and mushrooms. [Lat., perh. < Gk. *sphongos,* sponge.]
fun house *n.* A building or an attraction in an amusement park that features various devices intended to surprise, frighten, or amuse.
fu·ni·cle (fyo͞o′nĭ-kəl) *n.* A funiculus.
fu·nic·u·lar (fyo͞o-nĭk′yə-lər, fə-) *adj.* **1.** Of, pertaining to, or resembling a rope or cord. **2.** Operated or moved by a cable. **3.** Of, pertaining to, or constituting a funiculus. —*n.* A cable railway on a steep incline, esp. such a railway with simultaneously ascending and descending cars counterbalancing one another.
fu·nic·u·lus (fyo͞o-nĭk′yə-ləs, fə-) *n., pl.* **-li** (-lī′). **1.** *Anat.* A slender cordlike strand or band, esp.: **a.** A bundle of nerve fibers in the nerve trunk. **b.** The umbilical cord. **2.** *Bot.* A stalk connecting an ovule or seed with the placenta. [Lat. *funiculus,* slender rope, dim. of *funis,* rope.]
funk[1] (fŭngk) *Informal.* —*n.* **1. a.** A state of cowardly fright; panic. **b.** A state of depression. **2.** A cowardly, fearful person. —*v.* **funked, funk·ing, funks.** —*tr.* **1.** To take fright and shrink from. **2.** To be afraid of. —*intr.* To shrink in fright. [Prob. < obs. Flem. *fonck.*]
funk[2] (fŭngk) *n. Slang.* Funky music. [Back-formation < FUNKY.]
funk·y[1] (fŭng′kē) *adj.* **-i·er, -i·est.** Frightened; panicky.
funk·y[2] (fŭng′kē) *adj.* **-i·er, -i·est.** *Slang.* **1.** Having a moldy or musty smell. **2. a.** Having an earthy quality characteristic of the blues: *funky music.* **b.** Earthy and uncomplicated. **3.** Characterized by faddish self-expression or originality: *funky clothes.* [< *funk,* strong smell.] **—funk′i·ness** *n.*
fun·nel (fŭn′əl) *n.* **1.** A conical utensil with a small hole or narrow tube at the apex used to channel the flow of a substance into a container. **2.** Something like a funnel in shape or form. **3.** A shaft, flue, or stack for ventilation or the passage of smoke. —*v.* **-neled, -nel·ing, -nels** or **-nelled, -nel·ling, -nels.** —*intr.* **1.** To assume the shape of a funnel. **2.** To move through or as if through a funnel: *tourists funneling slowly through customs.* —*tr.* **1.** To cause to take the shape of a funnel. **2.** To cause to move through or as if through a funnel. [ME *fonel* < Prov. *fonilh* < LLat. *fundibulum* < Lat. *infundibulum* < *infundere,* to pour in. —see INFUSE.]

funnel

fun·ny (fŭn′ē) *adj.* **-ni·er, -ni·est. 1. a.** Causing laughter or amusement. **b.** Intended or designed to amuse. **2.** Strangely or suspiciously odd; curious. **3.** Tricky or deceitful. —*n., pl.* **-nies.** *Informal.* **1.** A joke or witticism. **2. funnies.** Comic strips. [< FUN.] **—fun′ni·ly** *adv.* **—fun′ni·ness** *n.*
funny bone *n. Informal.* **1.** The point near the elbow where a nerve may be pressed against bone to produce a tingling sensation. **2.** A sense of humor.
funny book *n.* A comic book.
fun·ny·man (fŭn′ē-măn′) *n.* A humorous individual, esp. a professional comedian.
funny paper *n.* A newspaper section or supplement containing comic strips.
fur (fûr) *n.* **1. a.** The thick coat of soft hair covering the body of any of various animals, such as a fox or beaver. **b.** The hair-covered, dressed pelt of such an animal, used in the making of garments and as trimming or decoration. **2.** A garment made of or lined with fur. **3.** A coating similar to fur. **—*modifier:*** *a fur coat.* —*tr.v.* **furred, fur·ring, furs. 1.** To cover or line with fur. **2.** To provide fur garments for. **3.** To cover or coat as if with fur. **4.** To line (a wall or floor) with furring. [ME *furre,* prob. short for *furrer* < OFr. *forreure,* of Germanic orig.]

furrow

fu·ran (fyo͝or′ăn′, fyo͞o-răn′) *n.* A colorless, volatile, liquid heterocyclic compound, C_4H_4O, derived from the dehydration of certain carbohydrates and used in the synthesis of organic compounds, esp. nylon. [FUR(FURAL) + -AN.]
fu·ra·nose (fyo͝or′ə-nōs′) *n.* A sugar having a cyclic structure composed of four carbon atoms and one oxygen atom.
fur·be·low (fûr′bə-lō′) *n.* **1.** A ruffle or flounce on a garment. **2.** A piece of showy ornamentation. —*tr.v.* **-lowed, -low·ing, -lows.** To decorate with a furbelow. [Alteration of *falbala.*]
fur·bish (fûr′bĭsh) *tr.v.* **-bished, -bish·ing, -bish·es. 1.** To brighten by cleaning or rubbing; polish. **2.** To restore to attractive or serviceable condition; renovate. [ME *furbishen* < OFr. *fourbir, fourbiss-,* of Germanic orig.] **—fur′bish·er** *n.*
fur·cate (fûr′kāt′) *intr.v.* **-cat·ed, -cat·ing, -cates.** To divide into branches; fork. —*adj.* Forked. [LLat. *furcatus* < Lat. *furca,* fork.] **—fur′cate′ly** *adv.* **—fur·ca′tion** *n.*
fur·cu·la (fûr′kyə-lə) *n., pl.* **-lae** (-lē′). A forked process or bone, esp. the wishbone of a bird. [NLat. < Lat., forked, prob. dim. of *furca,* fork.] **—fur′cu·lar** *adv.*
fur·fur (fûr′fər) *n., pl.* **-fu·res** (-fyə-rēz′). An epidermal scale, as in dandruff. [Lat.]
fur·fu·ra·ceous (fûr′fə-rā′shəs, -fyə-) *adj.* **1.** Made of or covered with scaly particles, as dandruff. **2.** Pertaining to or resembling bran. [LLat. *furfuraceus,* like bran < Lat. *furfur,* bran.]

fur seal
Guadalupe fur seal

fur·fu·ral (fûr′fə-răl′, -fyə-) *n.* A colorless mobile liquid, C_4H_3OCHO, used as a solvent for nitrocellulose and in the manufacture of dyes and plastics. [FURFUR + AL(DEHYDE).]
fur·fu·ran (fûr′fə-răn′, -fyə-) *n.* Furan.
fur·fu·res (fûr′fyə-rēz′) *n.* Plural of **furfur.**
fu·ri·o·so (fyo͝or′ē-ō′sō, -zō) *adj. & adv. Mus.* In a tempestuous and vigorous manner. Used esp. as a direction. [Ital. < Lat. *furiosus,* furious.]
fu·ri·ous (fyo͝or′ē-əs) *adj.* **1. a.** Full of, displaying, or characterized by extreme anger. **b.** Ragingly violent. **2.** Characterized by violent or turbulent activity. [ME < OFr. < Lat. *furiosus* < *furia,* fury.] **—fu′ri·ous·ly** *adv.*
furl (fûrl) *v.* **furled, furl·ing, furls.** —*tr.* To roll up and secure (a flag, for example) to something. —*intr.* To be rolled up. —*n.* **1.** The act of furling. **2.** A single roll or a rolled section of something furled. [OFr. *ferlier* : *fer,* firm (< Lat. *firmus*) + *lier,* to bind (< Lat. *ligare*).]
fur·long (fûr′lông′, -lŏng′) *n.* A unit for measuring distance, equal to $^1/_8$ mile or 220 yards. [ME < OE *furlang* : *furh,* furrow + *lang,* long.]
fur·lough (fûr′lō) *n.* **1.** A leave of absence from duty granted esp. to personnel of the armed services. **2.** The papers authorizing a furlough. —*tr.v.* **-loughed, -lough·ing, -loughs.** To grant a furlough to. [Du. *verlof.*]
fur·nace (fûr′nĭs) *n.* **1.** An enclosure in which energy in a nonthermal form is converted to heat. **2.** An intensely hot enclosed place. **3.** A severe test or trial. [ME < OFr. *furnais* < Lat. *furnax,* oven.]
fur·nish (fûr′nĭsh) *tr.v.* **-nished, -nish·ing, -nish·es. 1.** To equip with what is needed, esp. to provide furniture for. **2.** To supply; give: *furnish an example.* [ME *furnisshen* < OFr. *furnir, furniss-,* of Germanic orig.] **—fur′nish·er** *n.*
Synonyms: *furnish, equip, outfit, accouter.* These verbs mean to provide with what is necessary for use or operation. *Furnish* refers primarily to the provision of basic necessities. *Equip,* a narrower term, usually implies provision of more specialized items for a particular need or particular service: *equip a car with snow tires. Outfit* suggests comprehensive provision of necessary items for a larger purpose, as for an expedition or the pursuit of a line of work. *Accouter* refers most often to provisioning for military service.
fur·nish·ing (fûr′nĭ-shĭng) *n.* **1.** A piece of equipment necessary or useful for comfort or convenience. **2. furnishings.** The furniture, appliances, and other movable articles in a home or office. **3. furnishings.** Wearing apparel and accessories.
fur·ni·ture (fûr′nĭ-chər) *n.* **1.** The movable articles in a room or establishment that make it fit for use. **2.** *Archaic.* The necessary equipment for a horse. **3.** *Printing.* Blank strips of wood or metal placed between and around type on a page to hold it in place. [OFr. *fourniture* < *fournir,* to furnish.]
fu·ror (fyo͝or′ôr′, -ōr′) *n.* **1.** Violent anger; frenzy. **2.** A state of intense excitement or ecstasy. **3. a.** A general commotion. **b.** Public uproar. **4.** A fashion adopted enthusiastically by the public; fad. [Lat. < *furere,* to rage.]
fu·rore (fyo͝or′ôr′, -ōr′) *n. Chiefly Brit.* Furor (senses 3.b., 4).
fu·ro·se·mide (fyo͞o-rō′sə-mīd′) *n.* A compound, $C_{12}H_{11}ClN_2O_5S$, used as a diuretic. [FUR(FURAL) + S(ULF)- + *-emide,* alteration of AMIDE.]
furred (fûrd) *adj.* **1.** Bearing fur. **2.** Made, covered, or trimmed with fur. **3.** Wearing fur. **4.** Covered or coated as if with fur. **5.** Provided with furring, as a wall, ceiling, or floor.
fur·ri·er (fûr′ē-ər) *n.* One whose occupation is the dressing, selling, or repairing of furs. [ME *furrer* < AN.]
fur·ri·er·y (fûr′ē-ə-rē) *n., pl.* **-ies. 1.** Fur garments and trimmings collectively. **2.** The business of a furrier.
fur·ring (fûr′ĭng) *n.* **1. a.** A trimming or lining made of fur. **b.** Fur trimmings and linings collectively. **2.** A furlike coating, as on the tongue. **3. a.** The act of preparing a wall, ceiling, or floor with strips of wood or metal to provide a level surface or an air space. **b.** Strips of material used for this.
fur·row (fûr′ō, fŭr′ō) *n.* **1.** A long, narrow, shallow trench made in the ground by a plow. **2.** A rut, groove, or narrow depression. **3.** A deep wrinkle in the skin, as on the forehead. —*v.* **-rowed, -row·ing, -rows.** —*tr.* **1.** To make furrows in; plow. **2.** To form deep wrinkles in. —*intr.* To become furrowed or wrinkled. [ME *forwe* < OE *furh.*]
fur·ry (fûr′ē) *adj.* **-ri·er, -ri·est. 1.** Consisting of or similar to fur. **2.** Covered with fur or a furlike coating. **3.** Resembling fur in thickness or softness. **—fur′ri·ness** *n.*
fur seal *n.* Any of several eared seals of the genera *Callorhinus* or *Arctocephalus,* having thick, soft underfur that is valued commercially.
fur·ther (fûr′*th*ər) *adj.* Comparative of **far. 1.** More distant in degree, time, or space: *was further from the truth; the further lamppost.* **2.** Additional. —*adv.* Comparative of **far. 1.** To a greater extent; more. **2.** In addition; furthermore. **3.** At or to a more distant point in space or time. —*tr.v.* **-thered, -ther·ing, -thers.** To help the progress of; advance. —See Usage note at **farther.** [ME, earlier < OE *furðor.*] **—fur′ther·er** *n.*
fur·ther·ance (fûr′*th*ər-əns) *n.* The act of furthering, advancing, or helping forward.
fur·ther·more (fûr′*th*ər-môr′, -mōr′) *adv.* Moreover; in addition.

fur·ther·most (fûr′*th*ər-mōst′) *adj.* Most distant or remote.
fur·thest (fûr′*th*ĭst) *adj.* Superlative of **far.** Most distant in degree, time, or space. —*adv.* Superlative of **far. 1.** To the greatest extent or degree. **2.** At or to the most distant point in space or time. [ME < *further,* earlier. —see FURTHER.]
fur·tive (fûr′tĭv) *adj.* **1.** Characterized by stealth; surreptitious. **2.** Expressive of stealth; shifty. [Fr. < OFr. *furtif* < Lat. *furtivus* < *furtum,* theft < *fur,* thief.] **—fur′tive·ly** *adv.* **—fur′tive·ness** *n.*
fu·run·cle (fyo͝or′ŭng′kəl) *n.* A boil. [Lat. *furunculus,* knob on a vine, dim. of *fur,* thief.] **—fu·run′cu·lar** (fyo͞o-rŭng′kyə-lər), **fu·run′cu·lous** (-ləs) *adj.*
fu·run·cu·lo·sis (fyo͞o-rŭng′kyə-lō′sĭs) *n.* A condition characterized by the development of recurring furuncles. [Lat. *furunculus,* furuncle + -OSIS.]
fu·ry (fyo͝or′ē) *n., pl.* **-ries. 1.** Violent and intense anger; rage. **2.** Violent, uncontrolled action; turbulence. **3. Furies.** *Gk. Myth.* Three winged deities believed to pursue and punish wrongdoers. **4.** An angry or spiteful woman. [ME *furie* < OFr. < Lat. *furia* < *furere,* to rage.]
furze (fûrz) *n.* Gorse. [ME *furse* < OE *fyrs.*]
fuse[1] (fyo͞oz) *n.* **1.** A length of readily combustible material that is lighted at one end to carry a flame to and detonate an explosive at the other. **2.** Variant of **fuze.** [Ital. *fuso* < Lat. *fusus,* spindle.]
fuse[2] (fyo͞oz) *v.* **fused, fus·ing, fus·es.** —*tr.* **1.** To liquefy or reduce to a plastic state by heating; melt. **2.** To mix together by or as if by melting; blend. —*intr.* **1.** To become liquefied from heat. **2.** To become mixed or united by or as if by melting together. —*n.* A device containing an element that protects an electric circuit by melting when overloaded, thereby opening the circuit. [Lat. *fundere, fus-,* to melt.]
fu·see also **fu·zee** (fyo͞o-zē′) *n.* **1.** A friction match with a large head capable of burning in a wind. **2.** A colored flare used as a railway warning signal. **3.** A grooved, cone-shaped pulley in old-style clocks, used to equalize the force of the mainspring by maintaining a differential winding and unwinding of the cord or chain from the spring container. **4.** A fuse for detonating explosives. [Fr. *fusée,* spindleful of thread < OFr. < *fus,* spindle < Lat. *fusus.*]
fu·se·lage (fyo͞o′sə-läzh′, -zə-) *n.* The central body of an airplane that accommodates passengers, cargo, and crew and to which the wings and tail assembly are attached. [Fr. < *fuselé,* spindle-shaped < OFr. *fusel,* dim. of *fus,* spindle < Lat. *fusus.*]
fu·sel oil (fyo͞o′zəl) *n.* A clear, colorless, poisonous liquid mixture of amyl alcohols, obtained as a by-product of the fermentation of starch-containing and sugar-containing plant materials and used as a solvent for fats, oils, resins, and waxes and in the manufacture of explosives and pure amyl alcohols. [G. *Fusel,* bad liquor.]
fu·si·ble (fyo͞o′zə-bəl) *adj.* Capable of being fused or melted by heating. **—fu′si·bil′i·ty** *n.* **—fu′si·ble·ness** *n.*
fusible metal *n.* A metal alloy having a low melting point and used as solder and for safety plugs and fuses.
fu·si·form (fyo͞o′zə-fôrm′) *adj.* Tapering at each end; spindle-shaped. [Lat. *fusus,* spindle + -FORM]
fu·sil (fyo͞o′zəl) *n.* A light flintlock musket. —*adj.* Variant of **fusile.** [Fr. < OFr., steel for a tinderbox < Lat. *focus,* hearth.]
fu·sile (fyo͞o′zəl, -zīl′) also **fu·sil** (-zəl) *adj.* **1.** Formed by melting or casting. **2.** Capable of being fused. [Lat. *fusilis,* molten < *fusus,* p.part. of *fundere,* to melt.]
fu·sil·ier also **fu·sil·eer** (fyo͞o′zə-lîr′) *n.* **1.** A soldier armed with a fusil. **2.** A soldier in certain British army regiments. [Fr. < *fusil,* fusil.]
fu·sil·lade (fyo͞o′sə-läd′, -lād′, -zə-, fyo͞o′sə-läd′, -lād′, -zə-) *n.* **1.** A discharge from a number of firearms, fired simultaneously or in rapid succession. **2.** A rapid outburst or barrage. —*tr.v.* **-lad·ed, -lad·ing, -lades.** To attack or shoot down with a fusillade. [Fr. < *fusiller,* to shoot < *fusil,* fusil.]
fu·sion (fyo͞o′zhən) *n.* **1.** The act or procedure of liquefying or melting together by heat. **2.** The liquid or melted state induced by heat. **3.** A union resulting from fusing. **4.** The merging of different elements into a union. **5.** *Physics.* A nuclear reaction in which nuclei combine to form more massive nuclei with the simultaneous release of energy. [Lat. *fusio,* a melting < *fusus,* p.part. of *fundere,* to melt.]
fusion bomb *n.* An atomic bomb, esp. a hydrogen bomb, that derives its energy output principally from fusion reactions among light nuclei.
fu·sion·ism (fyo͞o′zhə-nĭz′əm) *n.* The theory or practice of forming coalitions, esp. of political groups or factions.
fuss (fŭs) *n.* **1.** Needlessly nervous or useless activity; commotion. **2. a.** A state of excessive and unwarranted concern over an unimportant matter. **b.** An objection; protest. **3.** A quarrel. —*v.* **fussed, fuss·ing, fuss·es.** —*intr.* **1.** To trouble or worry over trifles. **2.** To be excessively careful or solicitous: *fussed over their children.* **3.** To get into or be in a state of nervous or useless activity. **4.** To object; complain. —*tr. Informal.* To disturb or vex with unimportant matters. [Orig. unknown.] **—fuss′er** *n.*
fuss·budg·et (fŭs′bŭj′ĭt) *n.* A person who fusses over trifles.
fuss·pot (fŭs′pŏt′) *n.* A fussbudget.
fuss·y (fŭs′ē) *adj.* **-i·er, -i·est. 1.** Given to fussing; easily upset. **2.** Paying great attention to details; fastidious. **3.** Calling for or requiring great attention to trivial details; meticulous. **4.** Full of superfluous details. **—fuss′i·ly** *adv.* **—fuss′i·ness** *n.*
fus·tian (fŭs′chən) *n.* **1. a.** A coarse, sturdy cloth made of cotton and flax. **b.** Any of several thick, twilled cotton fabrics with a short nap. **2.** Pretentious or pompous language. [ME < OFr. *fustaigne* < Med. Lat. *fustaneum,* perh. after *Fostat,* Egypt.]
fus·tic (fŭs′tĭk) *n.* **1.** A small tropical American tree, *Chlorophora tinctoria,* having wood yielding a yellow dyestuff. **2.** The wood of the fustic. **3.** A dyestuff obtained from the wood of the fustic. [ME *fustik* < OFr. *fustoc* < Ar. *fustug* < Gk. *pistakē,* pistachio.]
fus·ti·gate (fŭs′tĭ-gāt′) *tr.v.* **-gat·ed, -gat·ing, -gates. 1.** To beat with a club; cudgel. **2.** To criticize harshly. [Lat. *fustigare, fustigat-* < *fustis,* club.] **—fus′ti·ga′tion** *n.*
fus·ty (fŭs′tē) *adj.* **-ti·er, -ti·est. 1.** Smelling of mildew or decay; moldy. **2.** Old-fashioned. [ME < OFr. *fuste,* wine cask < Lat. *fustis,* club.] **—fus′ti·ly** *adv.* **—fus′ti·ness** *n.*
fu·thark (fo͞o′thärk′) also **fu·thorc** or **fu·thork** (-thôrk′) *n.* The runic alphabet. [From the first six letters of the alphabet : *f, u, þ(th), a, r, c.*]
fu·tile (fyo͞ot′l, fyo͞o′tīl′) *adj.* **1.** Having no useful result; ineffectual. **2.** Trifling and frivolous. [Lat. *futilis.*] **—fu′tile·ly** *adv.* **—fu′tile·ness** *n.*
fu·til·i·tar·i·an (fyo͞o-tĭl′ĭ-târ′ē-ən) *n.* One who holds the view that human endeavor is futile. [Blend of FUTILE and UTILITARIAN.] **—fu·til′i·tar′i·an·ism** *n.*
fu·til·i·ty (fyo͞o-tĭl′ĭ-tē) *n., pl.* **-ties. 1.** The quality of being futile; uselessness. **2.** A futile act.
fut·tock (fŭt′ək) *n. Naut.* One of the curved timbers that form a rib in the frame of a ship. [ME *fottek.*]
futtock plate *n. Naut.* One of the iron plates attached to the top of a mast to hold the ends of the futtock shrouds.
futtock shroud *n. Naut.* One of the iron rods extending from the futtock plate, used to brace the base of a ship's mast.
fu·ture (fyo͞o′chər) *n.* **1.** The time yet to come. **2.** Something that will happen in time to come. **3.** A prospective or expected condition, esp. with regard to growth, advancement, or development: *a business with no future.* **4. futures.** Commodities or stocks bought or sold upon agreement of delivery in time to come. **5.** *Gram.* **a.** The future tense. **b.** A verb form in the future tense. —*adj.* That is to be or come in the future. [ME < OFr. *futur* and < Lat. *futurus.*] **—fu′ture·less** *adj.*
future perfect *n. Gram.* A verb tense that expresses action completed by a specified time in the future and that is formed in English by combining *will have* or *shall have* with a past participle.
future shock *n.* A condition of distress and disorientation brought on by an inability to cope with rapid societal and technological change. [From the book *Future Shock* by Alvin Toffler (b. 1928).]
future tense *n.* A verb tense expressing future time.
fu·tur·ism (fyo͞o′chə-rĭz′əm) *n.* An artistic movement originating in Italy in about 1910 and marked by an attempt to depict vividly the energetic and dynamic quality of contemporary life esp. by the motion and force of modern machinery. **—fu′tur·ist** *n.* **—fu′tur·is′tic** *adj.*
fu·tur·ist·ics (fyo͞o′chə-rĭs′tĭks) *n. (used with a sing. verb).* Futurology. **—fu′tur·ist** *n.*
fu·tu·ri·ty (fyo͞o-to͝or′ĭ-tē, -tyo͝or′-, -cho͝or′-) *n., pl.* **-ties. 1.** The future. **2.** The condition or quality of being in or of the future. **3.** A future event or possibility. **4.** A futurity race.
futurity race *n.* **1.** A race for which entries are made well in advance of the event. **2.** A race for horses entered as competitors at or before their birth.
futurity stakes *pl.n.* **1.** The stakes awarded to the winner or winners in a futurity race. **2.** A futurity race.
fu·tu·rol·o·gy (fyo͞o′chə-rŏl′ə-jē) *n.* The study or forecast of potential developments, as in science and technology, using current conditions or trends as a point of departure. **—fu′tu·rol′o·gist** *n.*
fuze also **fuse** (fyo͞oz) *n.* A mechanical or electrical mechanism used to detonate an explosive charge or device such as a bomb or grenade. [Var. of FUSE[1].]
fu·zee (fyo͞o-zē′) *n.* Variant of **fusee.**
fuzz[1] (fŭz) *n.* A mass of fine, light particles, fibers, or hairs; down: *the fuzz on a peach.* —*tr.v.* **fuzzed, fuzz·ing, fuzz·es. 1.** To cover with fuzz. **2.** To make blurred or indistinct. [Perh. back-formation < FUZZY.]
fuzz[2] (fŭz) *n. Slang.* The police. [Orig. unknown.]
fuzz·y (fŭz′ē) *adj.* **-i·er, -i·est. 1.** Covered with fuzz. **2.** Of or resembling fuzz. **3.** Not clear; indistinct. **4.** Not clearly worked out; confused. [Perh. < LG *fussig,* spongy.] **—fuzz′i·ly** *adv.* **—fuzz′i·ness** *n.*
-fy *suff.* Make; cause to become: *basify.* [ME *-fien* < OFr. *-fier* < Lat. *-ficare* < *-ficus,* -fic.]
fyke (fīk) *n.* A long, bag-shaped net held open by hoops, used for catching fish. [Du. *fuik* < MDu. *fūke.*]
fyl·fot (fĭl′fŏt′) *n.* A swastika. [ME.]

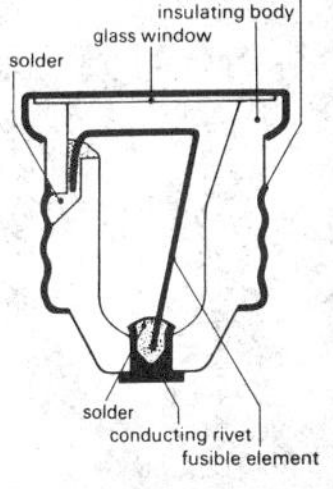

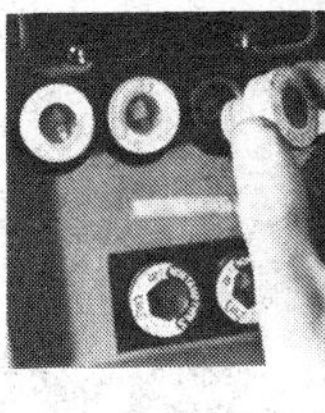

fuse[2]
Above: Diagram of a plug fuse
Below: Fuse and fuse box

G

Around 1000 B.C. the Phoenicians and other Semitic peoples began to use graphic signs to represent individual speech sounds instead of syllables or words. They used a symbol in the forms (1,2) to represent the sound of the consonant "g" and called it *gīmel,* their word for "camel." The Greeks, adapting the Phoenician alphabet, kept the phonetic value of *gīmel* but varied its shape and orientation (3,4,5,6,7) and changed its name to *gamma.* The Romans borrowed the alphabet from the Greeks via the Etruscans. Because the Etruscans did not distinguish between the sounds of the consonants "g" and "k," they used *gamma* to represent both. The Romans, who did distinguish the two sounds, added a stroke to the lower curve of the letter C (which represented "k") to identify the sound of "g" (9). They also adapted the alphabet for monumental inscriptions. Their monumental script (10) is the prototype of modern capital letters (13,14). Medieval scribes adapted the Roman capitals to being quickly written on paper, parchment, and vellum. These uncial and cursive minuscules (11,12) are the prototypes of modern lower-case letters, both written and printed (16,15). Changes in pronunciation since ancient times have given the modern letter G several different phonetic values.

g

g or **G** (jē) *n., pl.* **g's** or **G's. 1.** The seventh letter of the modern English alphabet. **2.** Any of the speech sounds represented by the letter *g.* **3.** *Mus.* **a.** The fifth tone in the scale of C major or the seventh tone in the relative minor scale. **b.** The key or a scale in which G is the tonic. **c.** A written or printed note representing this tone. **4. G.** *Slang.* One thousand dollars. **5. G.** A unit of force equal to the gravity exerted on a body at rest.

G (jē) *adj.* Indicating a motion-picture rating of such nature that all ages may be allowed admission. [Short for GENERAL.]

Ga The symbol for the element gallium.

gab (găb) *Informal.* —*intr.v.* **gabbed, gab·bing, gabs.** To talk idly or excessively about trivial matters. —*n.* Idle talk; chatter. [Perh. var. of dial. *gob* < GOB[2].] **—gab'ber** *n.*

gab·ar·dine (găb'ər-dēn', găb'ər-dēn') *n.* **1.** A worsted cotton, wool, or rayon twill. **2.** Gaberdine. [Alteration of GABERDINE.]

gab·ble (găb'əl) *v.* **-bled, -bling, -bles.** —*intr.* **1.** To speak rapidly or incoherently; jabber. **2.** To make rapid, repeated cackling noises, as a duck. —*tr.* To utter rapidly or incoherently. —*n.* **1.** Rapid, incoherent, or meaningless speech. **2.** A jumble of meaningless noises. [MDu. *gabbelen.*] **—gab'bler** *n.*

gab·bro (găb'rō) *n., pl.* **-bros.** A usually coarse-grained igneous rock composed chiefly of calcic plagioclase and pyroxene. [Ital. < Lat. *glaber,* smooth.] **—gab·bro'ic** (gă-brō'ĭk) *adj.*

gab·broid (găb'roid') *adj.* Resembling gabbro.

gab·by (găb'ē) *adj.* **-bi·er, -bi·est.** *Informal.* Tending to talk excessively; garrulous. **—gab'bi·ness** *n.*

ga·belle (gə-bĕl') *n.* A tax, esp. the salt tax imposed in France prior to 1790. [ME < OFr. < OItal. *gabella* < Ar. *qabāla,* tribute < *qabala,* he received.]

gab·er·dine (găb'ər-dēn', găb'ər-dēn') *n.* **1.** A long, coarse cloak or frock worn esp. by Jews during the Middle Ages. **2.** *Chiefly Brit.* A loose smock worn by laborers. **3.** Gabardine. [OFr. *gauvardine* < MHG *wallevart,* pilgrimage : *wallen,* to roam (< OHG *wallōn*) + *vart,* journey < OHG < *faran,* to go.]

gab·fest (găb'fĕst') *n. Slang.* A small, informal gathering for the exchange of news and gossip.

ga·bi·on (gā'bē-ən) *n.* **1.** A cylindrical wicker basket filled with earth and stones, formerly used in building fortifications. **2.** A hollow metal cylinder used esp. in constructing dams and foundations. [OFr. < OItal. *gabbione,* aug. of *gabbia,* cage < Lat. *cavea* < *cavus,* hollow.]

ga·ble (gā'bəl) *n.* **1. a.** The triangular wall section at the ends of a pitched roof, bounded by the two roof slopes and the ridge pole. **b.** An end of a building with a gable in the roof section. **2.** A triangular architectural section, usually ornamental. [ME < ON *gafl* and OFr. *gable,* of Germanic orig.] **—ga'bled** *adj.*

gable roof *n.* A pitched roof that ends in a gable.

Ga·bri·el (gā'brē-əl) *n.* In the Bible, an archangel who acts as the messenger of God. [Heb. *Gabhrī'ēl.*]

gad[1] (găd) *intr.v.* **gad·ded, gad·ding, gads.** To roam about or ramble restlessly and with little purpose; rove. [ME *gadden.*] **—gad'der** *n.*

gad[2] (găd) *n.* **1.** A spike or other pointed tool for working or breaking rock or ore. **2.** A goad, as for prodding cattle. —*tr.v.* **gad·ded, gad·ding, gads.** To break up (ore, for example) with a gad. [ME < ON *gaddr.*]

Gad (găd) *interj.* Euphemism for God. [Alteration of GOD.]

gad·a·bout (găd'ə-bout') *n.* One who gads, esp. one who goes about seeking gossip or excitement.

gad·fly (găd'flī') *n.* **1.** Any of various flies, esp. of the family Tabanidae, that bite or annoy livestock and other animals. **2.** One that acts as a constructively provocative stimulus. **3.** One habitually engaged in provocative criticism of existing institutions.

gadg·et (găj'ĭt) *n. Informal.* A small specialized mechanical device; contrivance. [Orig. unknown.] **—gadg'et·y** *adv.*

gadg·e·teer (găj'ĭ-tîr') *n. Informal.* A person who designs, builds, or delights in the use of gadgets.

gadg·et·ry (găj'ĭ-trē) *n.* **1.** Gadgets collectively. **2.** The designing or constructing of gadgets.

ga·doid (gā'doid', găd'oid') *adj.* Of or belonging to the family Gadidae, which includes fishes such as the cod and the hake. —*n.* A member of the Gadidae. [NLat. *Gadus,* fish genus (< Gk. *gados,* a kind of fish) + -OID.]

gad·o·lin·ite (găd'l-ə-nīt') *n.* A dark-colored silicate mineral containing several of the rare earths in combination with iron. [G. *Gadolinit,* after Johann *Gadolin* (1760–1852).]

gad·o·lin·i·um (găd'l-ĭn'ē-əm) *n. Symbol* **Gd** A silvery-white, malleable, ductile, metallic rare-earth element obtained from monazite and bastnaesite. It has the highest neutron-absorption cross section known and is useful in improving high-temperature characteristics of iron, chromium, and related metallic alloys. Atomic number 64; atomic weight 157.25; melting point 1,312°C; boiling point approximately 3,000°C; specific gravity from 7.8 to 7.896; valence 3. [After Johann *Gadolin* (1760–1852).]

ga·droon (gə-drōōn') *n.* **1.** *Archit.* A band of convex molding ornamentally carved with beading or reeding. **2.** An ornamental band, used esp. in silverwork, embellished with fluting, reeding, or other continuous pattern. [Fr. *godron* < OFr. *goderon.*] **—ga·droon'ing** *n.*

gad·wall (găd'wôl') *n.* A widely distributed duck, *Anas strepera,* having grayish or brown plumage. [Orig. unknown.]

Gae·a (jē'ə) *n. Gk. Myth.* The goddess of the earth and mother of the Titans. [Gk. *Gaia* < *gaia,* earth.]

Gael (gāl) *n.* **1.** A Gaelic-speaking Celt of Scotland, Ireland, or the Isle of Man. **2.** A Scottish Highlander. [Sc. Gael. *Gaidheal.*]

Gael·ic (gā'lĭk) *adj.* Of or relating to the Gaels or their languages. —*n.* **1.** Goidelic. **2.** Any of the Goidelic languages.

gaff (găf) *n.* **1.** An iron hook attached to a pole and used to land large fish. **2.** A spar used to extend the top edge of a fore-and-aft sail. **3. a.** A metal spur for the leg of a gamecock. **b.** A climbing hook used by linemen. **4.** A hoax; trick. **5.** *Slang.* Harshness of treatment; abuse. —*tr.v.* **gaffed, gaff·fing, gaffs. 1.** To hook using a gaff. **2.** To equip (a gamecock) with a gaff. **3.** *Slang.* **a.** To take in; cheat. **b.** To alter (dice, for example) in order to cheat. [ME *gaffe* < OFr., of Celt. orig.]

gaffe (găf) *n.* A clumsy social error; faux pas. [Fr.]

gaf·fer (găf'ər) *n.* **1.** *Regional.* An old man or rustic. **2.** An electrician who deals with lighting on a motion-picture or television set. [Perh. alteration of GODFATHER.]

gaff rig *n.* A rig with a fore-and-aft sail that has its upper edge supported by a gaff.

gaff-top·sail (găf'tŏp'səl, -sāl') *n.* A light triangular or quadrilateral sail set over a gaff.

gag (găg) *n.* **1.** Something forced into or put over the mouth to prevent speaking or crying out. **2.** An obstacle to or censoring of free speech. **3.** A device placed in the mouth to keep it open, as in dentistry. **4.** *Informal.* **a.** A practical joke. **b.** A comic effect or remark. —*v.* **gagged, gag·ging, gags.** —*tr.* **1.** To prevent from speech or outcry by using a gag. **2.** To repress or censor (free speech). **3.** To keep (the mouth) open by using a gag. **4.** To block off or obstruct. **5.** To cause to choke or retch. —*intr.* **1.** To choke; retch from nausea. **2.** *Informal.* To make jokes or quips. [< ME *gaggen,* to suffocate.]

ga·ga (gä'gä') *adj. Slang.* **1.** Silly; crazy. **2.** Completely absorbed, infatuated, or enthused. [Fr. < *gaga,* old fool.]

gage[1] (gāj) *n.* **1.** Something deposited or given as security against an obligation; pledge. **2.** Something, as a glove, offered or thrown down as a pledge or challenge to fight. **3.** A challenge. —*tr.v.* **gaged, gag·ing, gag·es.** *Archaic.* **1.** To pledge as security. **2.** To offer as a stake in a bet; wager. [ME < OFr., of Germanic orig.]

gage[2] (gāj) *n.* Any of several varieties of plum, as the greengage. [After Sir William *Gage* (1777–1864).]

gage[3] (gāj) *n. & v.* Variant of **gauge.** [Orig. unknown.]

gag·er (gā'jər) *n.* Variant of **gauger.**

gag·ger (găg'ər) *n.* **1.** One that gags. **2.** A piece of iron used to keep the core in position in a foundry mold.

gag·gle (găg'əl) *n.* **1.** A flock of geese. **2.** A cluster or group. [ME *gagel* < *gagelen,* to cackle.]

gag·man (găg'măn') *n.* A person who writes or uses jokes or comedy routines.

gag order *n.* A court order forbidding public reporting or commentary, as by the news media, on a case currently before the court.

gag rule *n.* A rule, as in a legislative body, limiting discussion or debate on a given issue.

gahn·ite (gä'nīt') *n.* A dark-green to brown or black mineral, $ZnAl_2O_4$. [G. *Gahnit,* after Johan G. *Gahn* (1745–1818).]

gai·e·ty also **gay·e·ty** (gā'ĭ-tē) *n., pl.* **-ties. 1.** A state of being gay or merry; cheerfulness. **2.** Festive or joyful activity; merrymaking. **3.** Gay color or showiness, as of dress; finery. [Fr. *gaieté* < OFr. *gai,* cheerful. —see GAY.]

gail·lar·di·a (gə-lär'dē-ə) *n.* Any of several plants of the genus *Gaillardia,* of western North America, having yellow or reddish rayed flowers. [NLat. *Gaillardia,* genus name, after *Gaillard* de Marentonneau, 18th-cent. French botanist.]

gai·ly also **gay·ly** (gā'lē) *adv.* In a joyful, cheerful, or happy manner; merrily.

gain[1] (gān) *v.* **gained, gain·ing, gains.** —*tr.* **1.** To become the owner of; acquire: *gained her wealth in real estate.* **2.** To acquire in competition; win: *gained a decisive victory.* **3.** To secure as profit or payment; earn: *gain a living.* **4.** To develop an increase of; build up: *a movement that gained strength; gained ten pounds.* **5.** To come to; reach: *gained the top of the mountain.* —*intr.* **1.** To become better or greater; progress: *gaining in strength.* **2.** To come nearer; get closer: *We're the best, but the other team is gaining on us.* **3.** To increase in weight: *gained as he grew older.* —*n.* **1. a.** Something gained or acquired: *territorial gains.* **b.** Progress; advancement: *economic gains.* **2.** The act of acquiring something; attainment. **3.** An increase in amount or degree: *a gain in accuracy.* **4.** *Electronics.* **a.** An increase in signal power. **b.** The ratio of output to input, as of output power to input power in an antenna or of output voltage to input voltage in an amplifier. [OFr. *gaaignier,* of Germanic orig.]

gain[2] (gān) *n.* A notch or mortise cut into a board to receive another part. —*tr.v.* **gained, gain·ing, gains. 1.** To cut out a gain in. **2.** To join by or fit into a gain. [Orig. unknown.]

gain·er (gā'nər) *n.* **1.** One that gains. **2.** A dive in which the

gable
The House of the Seven Gables, Salem, Massachusetts

gaff

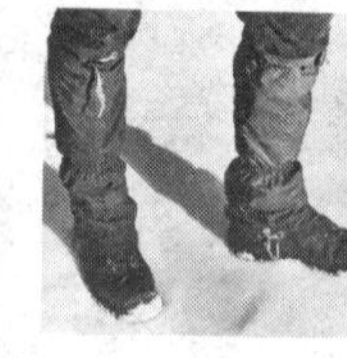

gaiter

galaxy

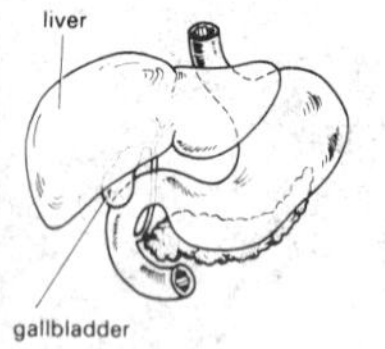

gallbladder

galleon

diver leaves the board facing forward, does a back somersault, and enters the water feet first.

gain·ful (găn′fəl) *adj.* Providing a gain; profitable: *gainful employment.* **—gain′ful·ly** *adv.* **—gain′ful·ness** *n.*

gain·less (gān′lĭs) *adj.* Providing no gain; profitless. **—gain′less·ness** *n.*

gain·ly (gān′lē) *adj.* **-li·er, -li·est.** Graceful; handsome. [ME *geinli,* gracious < *gein,* helpful < ON *gegn.*] **—gain′li·ness** *n.*

gain·say (gān-sā′) *tr.v.* **-said** (-săd′, -sĕd′), **-say·ing, -says** (-sāz′, -sĕz′). **1.** To declare false; deny. **2.** To oppose, esp. by contradiction. [ME *gainsayen* : *gain-,* against (< OE *gegn-*) + *sayen,* to say < OE *secgan.*] **—gain·say′er** *n.*

′gainst also **gainst** (gĕnst, gānst) *prep.* Against.

gait (gāt) *n.* **1.** A particular fashion or way of moving on foot. **2.** Any of the ways a horse can move by lifting the feet in different order or rhythm, as a canter, trot, or walk. *—tr.v.* **gait·ed, gait·ing, gaits.** To teach a certain gait or gaits to (a horse). [ME *gate,* path < ON *gata.*]

gait·ed (gā′tĭd) *adj.* Having a specified gait: *fast-gaited.*

gai·ter (gā′tər) *n.* **1.** A leather or heavy cloth covering for the legs extending from the instep to the ankle or knee. **2.** An ankle-high shoe with elastic sides. **3.** An overshoe with a cloth top. [Fr. *guêtre.*]

gal (găl) *n. Informal.* A girl. [Alteration of GIRL.]

ga·la (gā′lə, găl′ə, gä′lə) *n.* A festive occasion. *—adj.* Characterized by or suitable to celebration; festive. [Ital. < OSp. < OFr. *gale,* rejoicing.]

galact– *pref.* Variant of **galacto-.**

ga·lac·tic (gə-lăk′tĭk) *adj.* **1.** Of or pertaining to a galaxy, esp. the Milky Way. **2.** Very great in size; immense.

galactic equator *n.* The great circle of the celestial sphere that lies in the plane bisecting the band of the Milky Way, inclined at an angle of approximately 62 degrees to the celestial equator.

galactic nebula *n.* A nebula lying within the Milky Way.

galactic noise *n.* Radio-frequency radiation originating within the Milky Way.

galacto– or **galact–** *pref.* Milk: *galactose.* [< Gk. *gala, galakt-,* milk.]

ga·lac·to·poi·e·sis (gə-lăk′tə-poi-ē′sĭs) *n.* The secretion and continued production of milk. **—ga·lac′to·poi·et′ic** (-ĕt′ĭk) *adj.*

gal·ac·tos·am·ine (găl′ək-tō′sə-mēn′, gə-lăk-) *n.* An amino-acid derivative of galactose.

ga·lac·tose (gə-lăk′tōs′) *n.* A simple sugar, $C_6H_{12}O_6$, commonly occurring in lactose.

ga·lac·to·se·mi·a (gə-lăk′tə-sē′mē-ə) *n.* A congenital metabolic disorder caused by the inherited absence of an enzyme that catalyzes galactose and characterized by mental retardation and cataracts. **—ga·lac′to·se′mic** *adj.*

ga·lac·to·side (gə-lăk′tə-sīd′) *n.* Any of a group of glycosides that yield galactose on hydrolysis.

ga·la·go (gə-lā′gō, -lä′-) *n., pl.* **-gos.** Any of several small African primates of the genera *Galago* and *Euoticus,* having dense woolly fur, large round eyes, prominent ears, and a long tail. [NLat. *Galago,* genus name, perh. < Wolof *golokh,* monkey.]

Gal·a·had (găl′ə-hăd′) *n.* **1.** The purest of the knights of King Arthur's Round Table who alone succeeded in the quest for the Holy Grail. **2.** A man considered to be noble, pure, or chivalrous.

ga·lan·gal (gə-lăng′gəl) *n.* **1.** A plant, *Alpinia officinarum,* of eastern Asia, having pungent, aromatic roots used medicinally and as seasoning. **2.** The dried roots of the galangal. [Alteration of GALINGALE.]

gal·an·tine (găl′ən-tēn′) *n.* A dish of boned, stuffed meat or poultry cooked and served cold coated with aspic. [ME *galauntine,* a kind of sauce < OFr. *galantine,* alteration of *galatine* < Med. Lat. *galatina.*]

ga·lan·ty show (gə-lăn′tē) *n.* A shadow play performed by casting the shadows of miniature figures on a screen or wall. [Perh. < Ital. *galante,* a gallant < OFr. *galant.* —see GALLANT.]

gal·a·te·a (găl′ə-tē′ə) *n.* A durable cotton fabric, often striped, used in making clothing. [After the *Galatea,* a 19th-century English warship (from its having been used for children's sailor suits).]

Gal·a·te·a (găl′ə-tē′ə) *n. Gk. Myth.* An ivory statue of a maiden, brought to life by Aphrodite in answer to the pleas of its sculptor, Pygmalion. [Lat. < Gk. *Galateia.*]

Ga·la·tians (gə-lā′shənz) *n.* See table at **Bible.**

gal·a·vant (găl′ə-vănt′) *v.* Variant of **gallivant.**

ga·lax (gā′lăks′) *n.* A plant, *Galax aphylla,* of the southeastern United States, having glossy evergreen leaves and a cluster of small white flowers. [NLat. *Galax,* genus name.]

gal·ax·y (găl′ək-sē) *n., pl.* **-ies. 1.** *Astron.* **a.** Any of numerous large-scale aggregates of stars, gas, and dust, having one of a group of more or less definite overall structures, containing an average of 100 billion (10^{11}) solar masses, and ranging in diameter from 1,500 to 300,000 light-years. **b.** Often **Galaxy.** The Milky Way. **2.** An assembly of brilliant, beautiful, or distinguished persons or things. [ME *galaxie,* the Milky Way < LLat. *galaxias* < Gk. *galaxias,* milky < *gala,* milk.]

gal·ba·num (găl′bə-nəm, gôl-) *n.* A bitter, aromatic gum resin extracted from an Asiatic plant, *Ferula galbaniflua,* or any of several related plants, and used in incense and medicinally as a counterirritant. [ME < Lat. < Gk. *khalbanē,* of Semitic orig.]

gale[1] (gāl) *n.* **1. a.** A very strong wind. **b.** A wind having a speed between approximately 51.5 and 101.4 kilometers per hour, or 32 and 63 miles per hour. **2.** *Archaic.* A breeze. **3.** A forceful outburst, as of hilarity. [Orig. unknown.]

gale[2] (gāl) *n.* The sweet gale. [ME *gail* < OE *gagel.*]

ga·le·a (gā′lē-ə) *n., pl.* **-le·ae** (-lē-ē′). A helmet-shaped part, as the upper petal of certain plants or part of the maxilla of an insect. [NLat. < Lat., helmet.]

ga·le·ate (gā′lē-āt′) also **ga·le·at·ed** (-ā′tĭd) *adj.* **1.** *Biol.* Having a galea. **2.** Helmet-shaped. [Lat. *galeatus,* p.part. of *galeare,* to cover with a helmet < *galea,* helmet.]

ga·le·i·form (gā′lē-ə-fôrm′, gə-lē′-) *adj.* Helmet-shaped. [Lat. *galea,* helmet + -FORM.]

ga·le·na (gə-lē′nə) *n.* A gray mineral, essentially PbS, the principal ore of lead. [Lat., lead ore.]

Ga·len·ism (gā′lə-nĭz′əm) *n.* The medical theories or practices advanced by the Greek physician Galen. **—Ga·len′ic** (gā-lĕn′ĭk), **Ga·len′i·cal** *adj.*

gal Friday *n.* A girl Friday.

Ga·li·bi (gə-lē′bē) *n., pl.* **Galibi** or **-bis. 1.** A member of the Carib people of French Guiana. **2.** The language of the Galibi. [Carib.]

Ga·li·cian (gə-lĭsh′ən) *adj.* Of or pertaining to Spanish Galicia, its people, or their language. *—n.* **1.** A native or inhabitant of Spanish Galicia. **2.** The Portuguese dialect spoken in Spanish Galicia.

Gal·i·le·an[1] also **Gal·i·lae·an** (găl′ə-lē′ən) *n.* **1.** A Christian. **2.** Jesus.

Gal·i·le·an[2] (găl′ə-lē′ən, -lā′-) *adj.* Of, pertaining to, or in accordance with the work of the Italian scientist Galileo.

gal·i·lee (găl′ə-lē′) *n.* A small chapel or porch at the western end of some medieval English churches. [ME *galile* < Med. Lat. *galilaea* < Lat. *Galilea,* Galilee.]

gal·i·ma·ti·as (găl′ə-mā′shē-əs, -măt′əs) *n.* Nonsensical talk; gibberish. [Fr.]

gal·in·gale (găl′ĭn-gāl′) *n.* Any of various sedges of the genus *Cyperus,* esp. *C. longus,* of Europe, having rough-edged leaves, reddish spikelets, and aromatic roots. [ME, a kind of root < OFr. *galingal* < Ar. *khalanjān.*]

gal·i·ot also **gal·li·ot** (găl′ē-ət) *n.* **1.** A light, swift galley formerly used on the Mediterranean. **2.** A light, single-masted, flat-bottomed Dutch merchant ship. [ME < OFr. < Med. Lat. *galiota,* dim. of *galea,* galley. —see GALLEY.]

gal·i·pot (găl′ə-pŏt′, -pō′) *n.* The crude turpentine obtained from a pine tree, *Pinus pinaster,* of southern Europe.

gall[1] (gôl) *n.* **1. a.** Liver bile. **b.** The gallbladder. **2. a.** Bitterness of feeling; rancor. **b.** Something bitter to endure. **3.** Impudence; effrontery: *had the gall to try to borrow money.* [ME *galle* < OE *gealla.*]

gall[2] (gôl) *n.* **1.** A skin sore caused by friction and abrasion: *a saddle gall.* **2. a.** Exasperation; vexation. **b.** The cause of such vexation. *—v.* **galled, gall·ing, galls.** *—tr.* **1.** To make (the skin) sore by abrasion; chafe. **2.** To damage or break the surface of by or as if by friction; abrade: *the bark of saplings galled by improper staking.* **3.** To exasperate; vex. *—intr.* To become irritated, chafed, or sore. [ME *galle* < OE *gealla.*]

gall[3] (gôl) *n.* An abnormal swelling of plant tissue caused by insects, microorganisms, or external injury. [ME *galle* < Lat. *galla,* gallnut.]

Gal·la (găl′ə) *n., pl.* **Galla** or **-las. 1.** A member of a pastoral Hamitic people of southern Ethiopia and the Somali Republic. **2.** The Cushitic language of the Galla. **—Gal′la** *adj.* [Perh. < Ar. *ghalīẓ,* rough.]

gal·lant (găl′ənt) *adj.* **1.** Showy and gay in appearance, dress, or bearing; dashing: *a gallant feathered hat.* **2.** Stately; majestic. **3.** High-spirited and courageous: *gallant soldiers.* **4.** (gə-lănt′, -länt′). **a.** Attentive to women; chivalrous. **b.** Flirtatious. *—n.* (gə-lănt′, -länt′, găl′ənt). **1.** A fashionable young man. **2. a.** A man courteously attentive to women. **b.** A woman's lover; paramour. *—v.* (gə-lănt′, -länt′) **-lant·ed, -lant·ing, -lants.** *—tr.* To pay court to (a lady). *—intr.* To play the gallant. [ME *galaunt* < OFr. *galant,* pr.part. of *galer,* to rejoice < *gale,* rejoicing.] **—gal′lant·ly** *adv.*

gal·lant·ry (găl′ən-trē) *n., pl.* **-ries. 1.** Nobility of spirit or action; courage. **2.** Chivalrous attention toward women. **3.** An act or instance of gallantry in speech or behavior. **4.** *Archaic.* A bold or colorful display or appearance.

gall·blad·der also **gall bladder** (gôl′blăd′ər) *n.* A small, pear-shaped muscular sac, located under the right lobe of the liver, in which bile secreted by the liver is stored.

gal·le·ass (găl′ē-ăs′, -əs) *n.* A large, heavily armed three-masted Mediterranean galley of the 16th and 17th centuries. [OFr. *galeasse* < OItal. *galeaza,* aug. of *galea,* galley < Med. Lat. —see GALLEY.]

gal·le·on (găl′ē-ən) *n.* A large three-masted sailing ship generally having two or more decks, used during the 15th and 16th centuries esp. by Spain as a merchantman or warship. [Sp. *galeon* < OFr. *galion* < *galie,* galley. —see GALLEY.]

gal·ler·y (găl′ə-rē) *n., pl.* **-ies. 1.** A roofed promenade, esp. one extending along the wall of a building and supported by arches on the outer side. **2. a.** An enclosed narrow passageway, as a hall or corridor. **b.** A place or establishment generally resembling such a corridor in length and used for a specified purpose: *a shooting gallery.* **3.** *Regional.* A porch; verandah. **4. a.** An upper floor projecting over the rear part of the main floor of a theater and usually providing cheaper seats than those in the orchestra. **b.** The seats in such a section. **c.** The audience occupying these seats. **d.** A similar upper floor in a large building, as a church. **5. a.** A large audience or group of spectators, as at a tennis or golf match. **b.** The general public when considered as exemplifying a lack of artistic discrimination or sophistication. **6. a.** A building or hall in which artistic work is displayed. **b.** A collection of artistic work. **c.** An institution that sells works of art. **d.** A building where objects are sold at auction. **7.** An underground tunnel or other passageway, as one dug for military or mining purposes. **8.** A platform or balcony at the stern or quarters of certain early sailing ships. **9.** A decorative upright trimming or molding along the edge of a table top, tray, or shelf. **—*idiom.* play to the gallery.** To try to gain the favor or applause of the general public, esp. by crude or obvious means. [ME *galerie* < OFr., portico < OItal. *galleria* < Med. Lat. *galeria.*]

gal·ley (găl′ē) *n., pl.* **-leys. 1.** A large medieval ship of shallow draft propelled by sails and oars and used as a merchantman or warship in the Mediterranean. **2.** An ancient seagoing vessel propelled by oars. **3.** A large rowboat formerly used in England. **4.** The kitchen of a ship or airliner. **5.** *Printing.* **a.** A long tray, usually of metal, used for holding composed type. **b.** A galley proof. [ME *galei* < OFr. *galie* < Med. Lat. *galea* < Med. Gk.]

galley proof *n. Printing.* A printer's proof taken from composed type before page composition to allow for the detection and correction of errors.

galley slave *n.* **1.** A slave or convict forced to man an oar of a galley. **2.** A person forced to perform tedious or menial tasks; drudge.

galley west *adv. Informal.* Out of commission: *knocked him galley west.* [Perh. alteration of dial. *collywest,* askew.]

gall·fly (gôl′flī′) *n.* Any of various small insects of the family Cecidomyiidae that deposit their eggs on plant stems or in the bark of trees, causing the formation of galls in which their larvae grow.

gal·liard (găl′yərd) *adj. Archaic.* Spirited; lively; gay. *—n.* **1.** A spirited dance popular in France in the 16th and 17th centuries. **2.** The triple-time music for a galliard. [ME *gaillard* < OFr. *gaillart.*]

Gal·lic (găl′ĭk) *adj.* Of or pertaining to Gaul or France; French. [Lat. *Gallicus* < *Galli,* the Gauls.]

gal·lic acid (găl′ĭk, gô′lĭk) *n.* A colorless crystalline compound, $C_7H_6O_5 \cdot H_2O$, derived from tannin and used in photography, as a tanning agent, and in ink and paper manufacture.

Gal·li·can (găl′ĭ-kən) *adj.* **1.** Pertaining to or characteristic of Gallicanism. **2.** Gallic. *—n.* A supporter of Gallicanism.

Gal·li·can·ism (găl′ĭ-kə-nĭz′əm) *n.* A movement originating among the French Roman Catholic clergy that favored the restriction of papal control and the achievement by each nation of individual administrative autonomy.

Gal·li·cism (găl′ĭ-sĭz′əm) *n.* **1.** A French phrase or idiom appearing in another language. **2.** A characteristic French trait.

Gal·li·cize (găl′ĭ-sīz′) *tr. & intr.v.* **-cized, -ciz·ing, -ciz·es.** To make or become like the French, as in form, character, or custom. **—Gal′li·ci·za′tion** *n.*

gal·li·gas·kins (găl′ĭ-găs′kĭnz) *pl.n.* **1.** Full-length, loosely fitting hose or breeches worn in the 16th and 17th centuries. **2.** Loose breeches. **3.** *Regional.* Leggings. [Perh. alteration of OFr. *garguesque,* var. of *greguesque* < OItal. *grechesca,* fem. of *grechesco,* Greek < *greco* < Lat. *Graecus.* —see GREEK.]

gal·li·mau·fry (găl′ə-mô′frē) *n., pl.* **-fries.** A jumble; hodgepodge. [Fr. *galimafrée* < OFr. *calimafree.*]

gal·li·na·ceous (găl′ə-nā′shəs) *adj.* Of, belonging to, or characteristic of the order Galliformes, which includes the common domestic fowl as well as the pheasants, turkeys, and grouse. [Lat. *gallinaceus,* of poultry < *gallina,* hen, fem. of *gallus,* cock.]

gall·ing (gô′lĭng) *adj.* Causing acute irritation or exasperation; vexing: *a galling delay.* **—gall′ing·ly** *adv.*

gal·li·nip·per (găl′ə-nĭp′ər) *n.* A large mosquito or similar insect capable of inflicting a painful bite. [Orig. unknown.]

gal·li·nule (găl′ə-no͞ol′, -nyo͞ol′) *n.* Any of various wading birds of the genera *Gallinula, Porphyrio,* or *Porphyrula,* frequenting swampy regions and characteristically having dark, iridescent plumage. [NLat. *Gallinula,* genus name < Lat. *gallinula,* pullet, dim. of *gallina,* hen. —see GALLINACEUS.]

gal·li·ot (găl′ē-ət) *n.* Variant of **galliot.**

gal·li·pot (găl′ə-pŏt′) *n.* A small glazed earthenware jar formerly used by druggists for medicaments. [ME *galy pott.*]

gal·li·um (găl′ē-əm) *n. Symbol* **Ga** A rare metallic element that is liquid near room temperature, expands on solidifying, and is found as a trace element in coal, bauxite, and other minerals. It is used in semiconductor technology and as a component of various low-melting alloys. Atomic number 31; atomic weight 69.72; melting point 29.78°C; boiling point 2,403°C; specific gravity 5.907 (20°C); valences 2, 3. [< Lat. *gallus,* cock, transl. of *Lecoq* de Boisbaudran (1838–1912), its discoverer.]

gallium arsenide *n.* A dark-gray crystalline compound, GaAs, used in transistors, solar cells, and semiconducting lasers.

gal·li·vant also **gal·a·vant** (găl′ə-vănt′) *intr.v.* **-vant·ed, -vant·ing, -vants. 1.** To roam about in search of amusement; gad. **2.** To consort frivolously with members of the opposite sex; flirt. [Perh. alteration of GALLANT.]

gal·li·wasp (găl′ə-wŏsp′, -wôsp′) *n.* Any of several long-bodied lizards of the genera *Diploglossus* or *Celestus,* of Central America and the West Indies. [Orig. unknown.]

gall midge *n.* A gallfly.

gall·nut (gôl′nŭt′) *n.* The nutgall.

Gal·lo·ma·ni·a (găl′ō-mā′nē-ə, -mān′yə) *n.* A strong predilection for anything French. [Fr. *gallomanie* : *gallo-,* France (< Lat. *Gallus,* Gaul) + *-manie,* -mania.]

gal·lon (găl′ən) *n.* **1. a.** A unit of volume or capacity in the U.S. Customary System, used in liquid measure, equal to 4 quarts, or 3.785 liters. **b.** A unit of volume in the British Imperial System, used in liquid and dry measure, equal to 4.546 liters. **2.** A container with a capacity of one gallon. [ME, a liquid measure < ONFr. *galon* and < Med. Lat. *galona.*]

gal·lon·age (găl′ə-nĭj) *n.* An amount measured in gallons.

gal·loon (gə-lo͞on′) *n.* A narrow band or braid used as trimming and commonly made of lace, metallic thread, or embroidery. [Fr. *galon* < OFr. *galonner,* to decorate the hair with ribbons.] **—gal·looned′** *adj.*

gal·loot (gə-lo͞ot′) *n.* Variant of **galoot.**

gal·lop (găl′əp) *n.* **1. a.** A natural three-beat gait of a horse, faster than a canter and slower than a run. **b.** A rapid, running motion of other quadrupeds. **2.** A ride taken at the gallop. **3.** A rapid pace. *—v.* **-loped, -lop·ing, -lops.** *—tr.* **1.** To cause to gallop. **2.** To transport at or as if at a gallop. *—intr.* **1.** To ride a horse at a gallop. **2.** To move or progress rapidly. [< ME *galopen,* to go at a gallop < OFr. *galoper,* of Germanic orig.] **—gal′lop·er** *n.*

gal·lo·pade (găl′ə-pād′, -päd′) *n.* Variant of **galop.**

gal·lop·ing (găl′ə-pĭng) *adj.* **1.** Of or resembling a gallop, esp. in rhythm or rapidity. **2.** Developing at an accelerated rate and leading to death. Used of certain diseases.

gal·low·glass (găl′ō-glăs′) *n.* An armed retainer or mercenary in the service of an Irish chieftain. [Ir. Gael. *galloglach* : *gall,* foreigner + *oglach,* soldier.]

gal·lows (găl′ōz) *n., pl.* **gallows** or **-lows·es. 1. a.** A device usually consisting of two upright beams supporting a crossbeam from which a noose is suspended and used for execution by hanging. **b.** A similar structure used for supporting or suspending. **2.** Execution on a gallows or by hanging. [ME *galwes,* pl. of *galwe,* gallows < OE *galga.*]

gallows bird *n. Informal.* One who deserves to be hanged.

gallows humor *n.* Humorous treatment of a situation that is actually frightening or very grave.

gal·lows·tree (gŏl′ōz-trē′) *n.* A gallows (sense 1.a.).

gall·stone (gôl′stōn′) *n.* A small, hard, pathological concretion, chiefly of cholesterol crystals, formed in the gallbladder or in a bile duct.

gal·lus·es (găl′ə-sĭz) *pl.n. Informal.* Suspenders for trousers. [Pl. of *gallus,* suspenders, alter. of GALLOWS.]

gall wasp *n.* Any of various wasps of the family Cynipidae that produce distinctively shaped galls on oaks and other plants.

Ga·lois theory (găl-wä′) *n.* The portion of mathematical group theory concerned with the conditions under which a polynomial equation of power *n* with coefficients in a given mathematical field can be solved by repeating given operations and extracting the *n*th roots. [After Évariste *Galois* (1811–1832).]

ga·loot also **gal·loot** (gə-lo͞ot′) *n. Slang.* A clumsy, uncouth, or sloppily dressed person. [Orig. unknown.]

gal·op (găl′əp) also **gal·o·pade** (găl′ə-pād′, -päd′) *n.* **1.** A lively dance in duple rhythm, popular in the 19th century. **2.** The music for the galop. [Fr.]

ga·lore (gə-lôr′, -lōr′) *adj. Informal.* In great numbers; in abundance: *dresses galore; opportunities galore.* [Ir. Gael. *go leór,* to sufficiency.]

ga·losh (gə-lŏsh′) *n.* **1.** A waterproof overshoe. **2.** *Obs.* A sturdy heavy-soled boot or shoe. [ME *galoche,* wooden sole shoe < OFr., prob. < LLat. *gallicula,* dim. of Lat. *gallica (solea),* Gaulish (sandals) < *Galli,* Gauls.]

gal·van·ic (găl-văn′ĭk) *adj.* **1.** Of or pertaining to direct-current electricity, esp. when produced chemically. **2. a.** Having the effect of an electric shock. **b.** Produced as if by an electric shock. [GALVAN(ISM) + -IC.] **—gal·van′i·cal·ly** *adv.*

galvanic cell *n.* A primary cell.

galvanic couple *n.* A voltaic couple.

gal·va·nism (găl′və-nĭz′əm) *n.* Direct-current electricity, esp. when produced chemically. [Fr. *galvanisme* or < Ital. *galvanismo,* after Luigi *Galvani* (1737–1798).]

gal·va·nize (găl′və-nīz′) *tr.v.* **-nized, -niz·ing, -niz·es. 1.** To stimulate or shock with an electric current. **2.** To arouse to awareness or action; spur. **3.** To coat (iron or steel) with rust-resistant zinc. **—gal′va·ni·za′tion** *n.* **—gal′va·niz′er** *n.*

galvanized iron *n.* Iron coated with zinc to prevent rust.

gal·va·nom·e·ter (găl′və-nŏm′ĭ-tər) *n.* A device for detecting or measuring small electric currents by means of mechanical effects produced by the current to be measured. [GALVAN(ISM) + -METER.] **—gal′va·no·met′ric** (-nō-mĕt′rĭk), **gal′va·no·met′ri·cal** *adj.* **—gal′va·nom′e·try** *n.*

gal·van·o·scope (găl-văn′ə-skōp′, găl′və-nə-) *n.* A galvanometer used to detect the presence and direction of electric currents by the deflection of a magnetic needle. [GALVAN(ISM) + -SCOPE.] **—gal·van′o·scop′ic** (-skŏp′ĭk) *adj.* **—gal′va·nos′co·py** (găl′və-nŏs′kə-pē) *n.*

gal·yak (găl′yăk′) *n.* A flat, glossy fur made from the pelt of a stillborn lamb or kid. [Dial. R. *galyak.*]

gam[1] (găm) *n.* **1.** A school of whales. **2.** A social visit or friendly conversation, esp. between whalers. *—v.* **gammed, gam·ming, gams.** *—intr.* To visit, esp. while at sea. *—tr.* **1.** To visit with. **2.** To spend (time) in visiting. [Perh. short for GAMMON[2].]

gam[2] (găm) *n. Slang.* A person's leg. [Prob. < *gamb,* an animal leg on a coat of arms < ONFr. *gambe,* leg < LLat. *gamba,* hoof. —see GAMBOL.]

gam– *pref.* Variant of **gamo-.**

gam·ba·do[1] (găm-bā′dō) *n., pl.* **-does** or **-dos. 1.** A low leap of a horse in which all four feet are off the ground. **2.** A leaping or gamboling movement. [Sp. *gambeta* < Ital. *gambata* < OItal. —see GAMBOL.]

gam·ba·do[2] (găm-bā′dō) *n., pl.* **-does** or **-dos. 1.** Either of a pair of protective leather gaiters attached to a saddle. **2.** A rider's legging. [< Ital. *gamba,* leg < OItal. —see GAMBOL.]

gam·bier also **gam·bir** (găm′bîr) *n.* A resinous, astringent extract obtained from a woody vine, *Uncaria gambier,* of south-central Asia, used medicinally and in tanning and dyeing. [Malay.]

gam·bit (găm′bĭt) *n.* **1.** A chess opening in which one or more pawns are offered in exchange for a favorable position. **2.** A remark intended to open a conversation. **3.** A carefully considered strategy; maneuver. [Ital. *gambetto* < *gamba,* leg < OItal. —see GAMBOL.]

gam·ble (găm′bəl) *v.* **-bled, -bling, -bles.** *—intr.* **1. a.** To bet money on the outcome of a game, contest, or other event. **b.** To play a game of chance for stakes. **2.** To take a risk in the hope of gaining an advantage; speculate. *—tr.* **1.** To put up in gambling; wager. **2.** To expose to hazard; risk. *—n.* **1.** A bet, wager, or other gambling venture. **2.** An act or undertaking of uncertain outcome; risk. [Prob. < obs. *gamel,* to play games < ME *gamen,* to play < OE *gamian.*] **—gam′bler** (-blər) *n.*

gam·boge (găm-bōj′, -bo͞ozh′) *n.* **1.** A brownish or orange resin obtained from any of several trees of the genus *Garcinia,* of south-central Asia, and yielding a golden-yellow pigment. **2.** A strong yellow. [NLat. *gambogium,* alteration of *cambugium,* after *Cambodia.*] **—gam·boge′** *adj.*

gam·bol (găm′bəl) *intr.v.* **-boled, -bol·ing, -bols** or **-bolled, -bol·ling, -bols.** To leap about playfully; frolic. *—n.* A playful skipping or frolicking about. [OFr. *gambade,* horse's jump < OItal. *gambata* < *gamba,* leg < LLat., hoof, perh. < Gk. *kampē,* bend.]

gam·brel (găm′brəl) *n.* **1.** The hock of a horse or other animal. **2.** A frame used by butchers for hanging carcasses by the legs. [ONFr. *gamberel* < *gambe,* leg. —see GAM[2].]

gambrel roof

gambrel roof *n.* A ridged roof with two slopes on each side, the lower slope having the steeper pitch.

gam·bu·sia (găm-byo͞o′zhə) *n.* Any of a genus, *Gambusia,* of topminnows that feed on mosquito larvae. [NLat. *Gambusia,* genus name < Am. Sp. *gambusino,* gambusia.]

game[1] (găm) *n.* **1.** A way of amusing oneself; diversion. **2.** *Math.* A set of rules completely specifying a competition, including the permissible actions of and information available to each participant, the probabilities with which chance events may occur, the criteria for termination of the competition, and the distribution of payoffs. **3. a.** A sport or other competitive activity governed by specific rules: *the game of tennis.* **b.** A single instance of such an activity: *We lost the first game.* **4. a.** The total number of points required to win a game: *One hundred points is game in bridge.* **b.** The score accumulated at any given time in a game: *At half time the game was 14 to 12.* **5.** The equipment needed for playing certain games: *pack the children's games in the car.* **6.** A particular style or manner of playing a game: *His bridge game is only adequate.* **7.** A calculated action or approach; scheme: *You'll never see through his game.* **8. a.** Wild animals, birds, or fish hunted for food or sport. **b.** The flesh of game, eaten as food. **9. a.** Something hunted or fit to be hunted; quarry. **b.** An object of ridicule, teasing, or scorn: *They made game of him.* *—v.* **gamed, gam·ing, games.** *—tr. Archaic.* To waste or lose by gambling. *—intr.* To play for stakes, esp. for money. *—adj.* **gam·er, gam·est. 1.** Plucky and unyielding in spirit; resolute. **2.** *Informal.* Ready and willing: *Are you game for a swim?* [ME < OE *gamen.*] **—game′ly** *adv.* **—game′ness** *n.*

game[2] (găm) *adj.* **gam·er, gam·est.** Crippled; lame. [Orig. unknown.]

game·cock (găm′kŏk′) *n.* A rooster trained for cockfighting.

game fowl *n.* **1.** A bird sought after as game. **2.** Any of several breeds of domestic fowl raised esp. for cockfighting.

game·keep·er (găm′kē′pər) *n.* A person employed to protect and maintain wildlife, esp. on an estate or game preserve.

gam·e·lan (găm′ə-lăn′) *n.* A type of orchestra common to Southeast Asia, consisting mainly of tuned metal or wooden chimes and other percussion instruments. [Javanese.]

game plan *n.* **1.** The strategy devised before or used during a sports event. **2.** A strategy to reach an objective.

game show *n.* A television show in which contestants vie for prizes usually by playing a competitive game, as a quiz.

games·man·ship (gāmz′mən-shĭp′) *n.* The skill or practice of winning a game, contest, or struggle by means of dubious or unsportsmanlike methods and strategies that do not actually break the rules.

game·some (gām′səm) *adj.* Frolicsome; playful. **—game′some·ly** *adv.* **—game′some·ness** *n.*

game·ster (găm′stər) *n.* A habitual gambler.

gam·e·tan·gi·um (găm′ĭ-tăn′jē-əm) *n., pl.* **-gi·a** (-jē-ə). An organ or cell in which gametes are produced, esp. in primitive plant forms. [GAMET(E)- + Gk. *angeion,* dim. of *angos,* vessel.] **—gam′e·tan′gi·al** (-əl) *adj.*

gam·ete (găm′ēt′, gə-mēt′) *n.* A germ cell possessing the haploid number of chromosomes, esp. a mature sperm or egg capable of participating in fertilization. [NLat. *gameta* < Gk. *gametēs,* husband < *gamein,* to marry < *gamos,* marriage.] **—ga·met′ic** (-mĕt′ĭk) *adj.* **—ga·met′i·cal·ly** *adv.*

game theory *n.* The mathematical analysis of abstract models of strategic competition with the determination of best strategy as a goal, having applications in linear programming, statistical decision making, operations research, and military and economic planning.

gameto– *pref.* Gamete: *gametogenesis.* [< NLat. *gameta,* gamete.]

ga·me·to·cyte (gə-mē′tə-sīt′) *n.* A cell from which gametes are developed by division; spermatocyte or oocyte.

ga·me·to·gen·e·sis (gə-mē′tə-jĕn′ĭ-sĭs) also **gam·e·tog·e·ny** (găm′ĭ-tŏj′ə-nē) *n.* The production of gametes. **—ga·me·to·gen′ic, gam′e·tog′e·nous** (găm′ĭ-tŏj′ə-nəs) *adj.*

ga·me·to·phore (gə-mē′tə-fôr′, -fōr′) *n.* A structure, as in mosses, on which gametangia are borne. **—ga·me′to·phor′ic** (-fôr′ĭk, -fŏr′-) *adj.*

ga·me·to·phyte (gə-mē′tə-fīt′) *n.* The generation or form that reproduces sexually in a plant characterized by alternation of generations. **—ga·me′to·phyt′ic** (-fĭt′ĭk) *adj.*

gam·ic (găm′ĭk) *adj.* Of or requiring fertilization in reproduction; sexual. [< Gk. *gamos,* marriage.]

gam·in (găm′ĭn) *n.* A neglected boy who roams about the streets; urchin. [Fr.]

ga·mine (gă-mēn) *n.* **1.** A neglected girl who roams about the streets; urchin. **2.** A girl of impish appeal. [Fr., fem. of *gamin,* gamin.]

gam·ing (gā′mĭng) *n.* The playing of games of chance; gambling.

gam·ma (găm′ə) *n.* **1.** The 3rd letter of the Greek alphabet. See table at **alphabet. 2.** A gamma ray. [ME < Gk., of Phoenician orig.; akin to Heb. *gīmel,* gimel.]

gamma decay *n.* **1.** A radioactive process in which an atomic nucleus loses energy by emitting a gamma ray without a change in its atomic or mass numbers. **2.** The decay of an unstable elementary particle by photon emission.

gamma globulin *n.* Any of several globulin fractions of blood serum that are closely associated with immune bodies and used to treat infectious diseases, as measles, poliomyelitis, and infectious hepatitis.

gamma ray *n.* **1.** Electromagnetic radiation emitted by radioactive decay and having energies in a range overlapping that of the highest energy x rays, extending up to several hundred thousand electron volts. **2.** Electromagnetic radiation with energy greater than several hundred thousand electron volts. **3.** A high-energy photon.

gam·ma-ray astronomy (găm′ə-rā′) *n.* Astronomy dealing with the origin and nature of periodic gamma-ray emissions from extraterrestrial sources.

gam·mer (găm′ər) *n. Regional.* An elderly woman. [Alteration of GRANDMOTHER.]

gam·mon[1] (găm′ən) *n.* A victory in backgammon occurring before the loser has removed a single man. *—tr.v.* **-moned, -mon·ing, -mons.** To defeat in backgammon by scoring a gammon. [Prob. < ME *gamen,* game < OE.]

gam·mon[2] (găm′ən) *Chiefly Brit. Informal. —n.* Misleading or nonsensical talk. *—v.* **-moned, -mon·ing, -mons.** *—tr.* To mislead by deceptive talk. *—intr.* To talk gammon. [Orig. unknown.] **—gam′mon·er** *n.*

gam·mon[3] (găm′ən) *n.* **1.** A cured or smoked ham. **2.** The lower part of a side of bacon. [ONFr. *gambon* < *gambe,* leg. —see GAM[2].]

gam·mon[4] (găm′ən) *tr.v.* **-moned, -mon·ing, -mons.** To fasten (a bowsprit) to the stem of a ship. [Orig. unknown.]

gamo– or **gam–** *pref.* **1.** United; joined: *gamopetalous.* **2.** Sexual: *gamogenesis.* [< Gk. *gamos,* marriage.]

gam·o·gen·e·sis (găm′ə-jĕn′ə-sĭs) *n.* Sexual reproduction. **—gam′o·ge·net′ic** (-jə-nĕt′ĭk) *adj.* **—gam′o·ge·net′i·cal·ly** *adv.*

gam·o·pet·al·ous (găm′ə-pĕt′l-əs) *adj. Bot.* Having or characterizing a corolla with the petals fused or partially fused.

gam·o·phyl·lous (găm′ə-fĭl′əs) *adj. Bot.* Having or designating united leaves or leaflike parts.

gam·o·sep·al·ous (găm′ə-sĕp′ə-ləs) *adj.* Having the sepals united or partly united.

-gamous *suff.* **1. a.** Having a specified number of marriages: *monogamous.* **b.** Practicing a specified kind of marriage: *exogamous.* **2.** Having a specified kind of reproduction organs: *heterogamous.* [< Gk. *gamos,* marriage.]

gamp (gămp) *n. Chiefly Brit.* A large, baggy umbrella. Used humorously. [After Mrs. Sarah *Gamp,* a character in the novel *Martin Chuzzlewit* by Charles Dickens (1812–1870).]

gam·ut (găm′ət) *n.* **1.** A complete range; extent: *a face that expressed the gamut of emotion, from rage to peaceful contentment.* **2.** The entire series of recognized musical notes. [ME, the musical scale < Med. Lat. *gamma ut* : *gamma,* lowest note of the medieval scale (< Gk. *gamma,* gamma) + *ut,* lowest note of the ancient scale. (The notes of the scale are named after syllables in a Latin hymn to Saint John the Baptist that were sung to the notes: *Ut* queant laxis *re*sonare fibris *Mi*ra gestorum *fa*muli tuorum, *Sol*ve polluti *la*bii reatum, *S*ancte *I*ohannes.)]

gam·y (gā′mē) *adj.* **-i·er, -i·est. 1.** Having the flavor or odor of game, esp. game that is slightly spoiled. **2.** Showing an unyielding spirit; plucky. **3. a.** Disreputable. **b.** Scandalous. **—gam′i·ly** *adv.* **—gam′i·ness** *n.*

-gamy *suff.* **1.** Marriage: *exogamy.* **2.** Procreative or propagative union: *allogamy.* **3.** The possession of a specified manner of fertilization or specified reproductive organs: *apogamy.* [Gk. *-gamia* < *gamos,* marriage.]

gan·der (găn′dər) *n.* **1.** A male goose. **2.** *Informal.* A simpleton; halfwit. **3.** *Slang.* A quick look; glance: *took a gander at the paper and left.* [ME < OE *gandra.*]

gan·dy dancer (găn′dē) *n. Slang.* **1.** A railroad worker. **2.** An itinerant laborer. [Poss. after the now defunct *Gandy* Manufacturing Company of Chicago, which made tools.]

ga·nef or **ga·nof** (gä′nəf) also **gon·if** (gŏn′ĭf) *n.* A thief, scoundrel, or rascal. [Yiddish < Heb. *gannābh.*]

gang[1] (găng) *n.* **1.** A group of people who associate regularly on a social basis: *The whole gang went to a clambake.* **2.** A group of criminals or hoodlums who band together for mutual protection and profit. **3.** A group of adolescents who band together, esp. a group characterized by delinquency. **4.** A group of laborers organized together on one job or under one foreman: *a railroad gang.* **5.** A set, esp. of matched tools: *a gang of chisels.* **6. a.** A pack of wolves or wild dogs. **b.** A herd, esp. of buffalo or elk. *—v.* **ganged, gang·ing, gangs.** *—intr.* To form into or band together as a group or gang. *—tr.* **1.** To group together or arrange (pages of type, for example) into a gang. **2.** To attack as a gang. ***—phrasal verb.* gang up.** *Informal.* **1.** To make an attack as a group: *everybody ganged up on him.* **2.** To act together as a group: *ganging up against the supervisor.* [ME, band of men < OE, journey.]

gang[2] (găng) *n.* Variant of **gangue.**

gang·bus·ter (găng′bŭs′tər) *n. Slang.* A law officer who fights to break up organized criminal groups. **—*idiom.* like gangbusters.** *Slang.* With great force or zeal: *came on like gangbusters at the start of his campaign.*

gang·er (găng′ər) *n. Chiefly Brit.* A gang foreman.

gang hook *n.* A multiple fishhook consisting of two or more hooks joined shank to shank.

gan·gli·a (găng′glē-ə) *n.* A plural of **ganglion.**

gan·gli·at·ed (găng′glē-ā′tĭd) also **gan·gli·ate** (-ĭt, -āt′) *adj.* Having ganglia.

gan·gling (găng′glĭng) *adj.* Tall, thin, and ungraceful; rangy. [Perh. < dial. *gang,* to go < ME *gangen* < OE *gangan.*]

gan·gli·on (găng′glē-ən) *n., pl.* **-gli·a** (-glē-ə) or **-gli·ons. 1.** *Anat.* A group of nerve cells, as one located outside the brain or spinal cord, in vertebrates. **2.** A center of power, activity, or energy. **3.** *Pathol.* A cystic lesion resembling a tumor, occurring in a tendon sheath or joint capsule. [Gk., cystlike tumor.] **—gan′gli·on′ic** (-ŏn′ĭk) *adj.*

gan·gli·on·at·ed (găng′-glē-ə-nā′tĭd) *adj.* Gangliated.

gan·gli·o·side (găng′glē-ə-sīd′) *n.* Any of a group of glycosphingolipids found in ganglionic cells. [GANGLI(ON) + -OS(E) + -IDE.]

gan·gly (găng′glē) *adj.* **-gli·er, -gli·est.** Gangling.

gang·plank (găng′plăngk′) *n.* A board or ramp used as a removable footway between a ship and a pier.

gang·plow (găng′plou′) *n.* A plow equipped with several blades that make parallel furrows.

gang·punch (găng′pŭnch′) *tr.v.* **-punched, -punch·ing, -punch·es.** To duplicate information from a punched card onto succeeding cards.

gan·grel (găng′rəl) *n. Scot.* A vagabond; drifter. [ME.]

gan·grene (găng′grēn′, găng-grēn′) *n.* Death and decay of tissue in a part of the body, usually a limb, due to failure of blood supply, injury, or disease. *—tr. & intr.v.* **-grened, -gren·ing, -grenes.** To affect or become affected with gangrene. [Lat. *gangraena* < Gk. *gangraina.*] **—gan′gre·nous** (găng′grə-nəs) *adj.*

gang·ster (găng′stər) *n.* A member of an organized group of criminals; racketeer. **—gang′ster·ism** (-stə-rĭz′əm) *n.*

gangue also **gang** (găng) *n.* The worthless rock or other material in which valuable minerals are found. [Fr. < G. *Gang,* lode < OHG, a going.]

gang·way (găng′wā′) *n.* **1.** A passageway, as through a crowd or an obstructed area. Often used as an interjection. **2.** *Naut.* **a.** A passage along either side of a ship's upper deck. **b.** A gangplank. **c.** An opening in the bulwark of a ship through which passengers may board. **3.** *Chiefly Brit.* **a.** The aisle that divides the front and rear seating sections of the House of Commons. **b.** An aisle between seating sections, as in a theater. **4.** The main level of a mine.

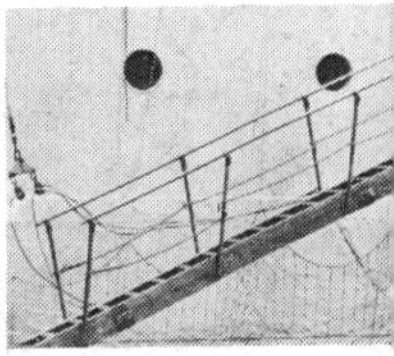

gangplank

gan·is·ter also **gan·nis·ter** (găn′ĭ-stər) *n.* **1.** A silicon-rich sedimentary rock used for refractory furnace linings. **2.** A mixture of fire clay and ground quartz, used to line furnaces. [Orig. unknown.]

gan·ja (gän′jə) *n.* A highly resinous form of marijuana, prepared by collecting only the flowering tops and leaves of carefully selected and cultivated plants. [Hindi *gājā* < Skt. *ganjā.*]

gan·net (găn′ĭt) *n.* Any of several large sea birds of the family Sulidae, esp. *Morus bassanus,* of northern coastal regions, having white plumage with black wing tips. [ME *ganet* < OE *ganot.*]

gan·nis·ter (găn′ĭ-stər) *n.* Variant of **ganister.**

ga·nof (gä′nəf) *n.* Variant of **ganef.**

gan·oid (găn′oid′) *adj.* Of, pertaining to, or characteristic of certain bony fishes, as the sturgeon and the gar, having armorlike scales consisting of bony plates covered with layers of dentine and enamel. *—n.* A ganoid fish. [< Gk. *ganos,* brightness.]

gant·let[1] (gônt′lĭt, gänt′-) *n.* A section of overlapping but independent railroad track where two sets of tracks are overlapped to afford passage at a narrow place without switching. *—tr.v.* **-let·ed, -let·ing, -lets.** To overlap (railroad tracks) to form a gantlet. [< GAUNTLET[2].]

gant·let[2] (gônt′lĭt, gänt′-) *n.* **1.** Variant of **gauntlet**[1]. **2.** Variant of **gauntlet**[2].

gant·line (gănt′līn′, -lĭn) *n.* A rope passed through a single block at the top of a mast or stackpole and used for hoisting. [Alteration of *girtline,* gantline.]

gan·try (găn′trē) *n., pl.* **-tries. 1.** A support for a barrel lying on its side. **2. a.** A bridgelike frame over which a traveling crane moves. **b.** A similar spanning frame supporting a group of railway signals over several tracks. **3.** *Aerospace.* A massive vertical frame structure used in assembling or servicing rockets. [Prob. dial. *gawn,* gallon + TREE.]

Gantt chart (gănt) *n.* A chart designed for comparing rates, as of planned production versus actual production. [After Henry Laurence *Gantt* (1861–1919).]

Gan·y·mede (găn′ə-mēd′) *n. Gk. Myth.* **1.** A Trojan boy of great beauty whom Zeus carried away to be cupbearer to the gods. **2.** A young man who serves liquors. **3.** The fourth moon of Jupiter, one of the largest planetary satellites in the solar system. [Gk. *Ganumēdēs.*]

Ganymede
Ganymede and Hebe

gaol (jāl) *n. & v. Chiefly Brit.* Variant of **jail.**

gap (găp) *n.* **1.** An opening, as in a wall; cleft. **2.** A break or pass through mountains. **3.** A suspension of continuity; hiatus: *a gap in his report.* **4.** A conspicuous difference; disparity: *a gap between expenses and receipts.* **5.** *Elect.* A space traversed by an electric spark; spark gap. **6.** *Computer Sci.* An absence of information on a recording medium, often used to signal the end of a segment of information. **7.** *Electronics.* The distance between the head of a recording device and the surface of the recording medium. *—v.* **gapped, gap·ping, gaps.** *—tr.* To make an opening or gap in. *—intr.* To be or become open. [ME < ON, chasm.]

gape (gāp, găp) *intr.v.* **gaped, gap·ing, gapes. 1.** To open the mouth wide; yawn. **2.** To stare wonderingly, as with the mouth open. **3.** To become widely open or separated: *The curtains gaped when the wind blew.* *—n.* **1.** An act or instance of gaping. **2.** A large opening. **3.** *Zool.* The width of the space between the open jaws or mandibles of a vertebrate. **4. gapes** *(used with a sing. verb).* A disease of birds, esp. young domesticated chickens and turkeys, caused by gapeworms and resulting in obstructed breathing. **5. gapes.** A fit of yawning. [ME *gapen* < ON *gapa.*] **—gap′er** *n.*

gape·worm (gāp′wûrm′, găp′-) *n.* Any of several nematode worms of the genus *Syngamus,* esp. *S. trachea,* infecting the trachea of certain birds and causing gapes.

gap·ing (gā′pĭng) *adj.* Deep and wide open; cavernous: *a gaping wound.* **—gap′ing·ly** *adv.*

gar[1] (gär) *n.* **1.** Any of several ganoid fishes of the genus *Lepisosteus,* of fresh and brackish waters of North and Central America, having an elongated body and a long snout. **2.** A fish similar to or related to the gar, as the needlefish. [Short for GARFISH.]

gar[1]

gar[2] (gär) *tr.v.* **garred, gar·ring, gars.** *Scot.* To cause or compel. [ME *geren* < ON *gera,* to make.]

ga·rage (gə-räzh′, -räj′) *n.* **1.** A building or wing of a building in which to park a car. **2.** A commercial establishment where cars are repaired, serviced, or parked. *—tr.v.* **-raged, -rag·ing, -rag·es.** To put in or take to a garage. [Fr. < *garer,* to shelter < OFr., to protect, of Germanic orig.]

garage sale *n.* A sale of used household items or clothing held at the home of the seller.

garb (gärb) *n.* **1.** Clothing, esp. a distinctive way of dressing: *sailors' garb.* **2.** An outward appearance; guise. *—tr.v.* **garbed, garb·ing, garbs.** To cover with or as if with clothing; dress. [OFr. *garbe,* grace, or OItal. *garbo,* grace, both of Germanic orig.]

gardenia

gar·bage (gär′bĭj) *n.* **1. a.** Food wastes, as from a kitchen. **b.** Refuse. **2.** Worthless matter; trash: *rhetorical garbage.* **3.** *Computer Sci.* Unwanted or incorrect information in a device's input, output, or storage. —***idiom.* garbage in, garbage out.** *Computer Sci.* A phrase describing the observation that the output of a data system can be no more correct than data it receives as input. [ME, refuse of fowls.]

gar·ban·zo (gär-bän′zō) *n., pl.* **-zos.** A seed of the chickpea. [Sp.]

gar·ble (gär′bəl) *tr.v.* **-bled, -bling, -bles. 1.** To distort or scramble so as to be unintelligible: *The radio operator garbled the message completely.* **2.** To sort out; cull. —*n.* The act or an instance of garbling. [ME *garbelen,* to inspect and remove refuse from spices < OItal. *garbellare* < Ar. *gharbala,* he selected, poss. ult. < LLat. *cribellum,* dim. of Lat. *cribrum,* sieve.] **—gar′bler** (-blər) *n.*

gar·board (gär′bôrd′, -bōrd′) *n.* The first range or strake of planks laid next to a ship's keel. [Obs. Du. *gaarboord.*]

gar·boil (gär′boil′) *n. Archaic.* Confusion; uproar. [OFr. *garbouil* < OItal. *garbuglio* < Lat. *bullire,* to boil.]

gar·çon (gär-sôɴ′) *n., pl.* **-çons** (-sôɴ′). A waiter. [Fr. < OFr. *garçun,* servant.]

gar·dant (gär′dnt) *adj.* Variant of **guardant.**

gar·den (gär′dn) *n.* **1.** A plot of land used for the cultivation of flowers, vegetables, or fruit. **2. gardens.** Grounds adorned with flowers, shrubs, and trees for public enjoyment. **3.** A yard; lawn. **4.** A fertile, well-cultivated region. —*v.* **-dened, -den·ing, -dens.** —*tr.* **1.** To cultivate (a plot of ground) as a garden. **2.** To furnish with a garden. —*intr.* To work as a gardener. —*adj.* **1.** Of, pertaining to, intended for, or found in a garden. **2.** Provided with open areas and greenery: *garden apartments.* **3.** Ordinary; usual. [ME *gardin* < ONFr., of Germanic orig.]

garden cress *n.* An annual herb, *Lepidium sativum,* of the mustard family.

gar·den·er (gärd′nər, gär′dn-ər) *n.* A person who works in or tends a garden for pleasure or profit.

garden heliotrope *n.* A widely cultivated species of valerian, *Valeriana officinalis,* having clusters of small purplish, pink, or white flowers.

gar·de·nia (gär-dēn′yə) *n.* **1.** Any of various shrubs and trees of the genus *Gardenia,* esp. *G. jasminoides,* native to China, having glossy evergreen leaves and large, fragrant, usually white flowers. **2.** The flower of the gardenia. [NLat., genus name, after Alexander *Garden* (1731–1790).]

gar·den-va·ri·e·ty (gär′dn-və-rī′ə-tē) *adj.* Common; unremarkable.

garde·robe (gärd′rōb′) *n. Archaic.* **1. a.** A chamber for storing clothes; wardrobe. **b.** The contents of a wardrobe. **2.** A private chamber. [ME < OFr. : *garder,* to keep + *robe,* robe.]

Gar·eth (găr′ĭth) *n.* A nephew of King Arthur and one of the Knights of the Round Table.

gar·fish (gär′fĭsh′) *n., pl.* **garfish** or **-fish·es.** Gar[1]. [ME.]

gar·ga·ney (gär′gə-nē) *n., pl.* **-neys.** An Old World duck, *Anas querquedula,* having the head conspicuously striped with white in the male. [Dial. Ital. *gargenei.*]

Gar·gan·tu·a (gär-găn′cho͞o-ə) *n.* A giant king noted for his enormous physical and intellectual appetites, the hero of Rabelais' satire *Gargantua and Pantagruel.*

gar·gan·tu·an also **Gar·gan·tu·an** (gär-găn′cho͞o-ən) *adj.* Of immense size or volume; colossal; huge.

gar·get (gär′gĭt) *n.* Mastitis of domestic animals, esp. cattle. [Perh. < ME, throat < OFr. *garguette.*]

gargoyle

gar·gle (gär′gəl) *v.* **-gled, -gling, -gles.** —*intr.* **1.** To force exhaled air through a liquid held in the back of the mouth in order to cleanse or medicate the mouth or throat. **2.** To produce the sound of gargling when speaking or singing. —*tr.* **1.** To rinse or medicate. **2.** To circulate or apply (a medicine, for example) by gargling. **3.** To utter with a gargling sound. —*n.* **1.** A medicated solution for gargling. **2.** A gargling sound. [OFr. *gargouiller.*]

gar·goyle (gär′goil′) *n.* **1.** A roof spout carved to represent a grotesque human or animal figure and projected from a gutter to carry rainwater clear of the wall. **2.** A grotesque ornamental figure or projection. [ME *gargoile* < OFr. *gargole.*]

gar·i·bal·di (găr′ə-bôl′dē) *n.* A loose high-necked blouse styled after the red shirts worn by the Italian nationalist leader Garibaldi and his soldiers.

gar·ish (gâr′ĭsh) *adj.* **1. a.** Marred by strident color or excessive ornamentation; gaudy. **b.** Loud and flashy: *garish make-up.* **2.** Glaring; dazzling. [Orig. unknown.] **—gar′ish·ly** *adv.* **—gar′ish·ness** *n.*

garland

gar·land (gär′lənd) *n.* **1. a.** A wreath, circlet, or festoon, esp. one of flowers or leaves. **b.** A wreath worked in metal for ornamentation or as a heraldic device. **2.** *Naut.* A ring or collar of rope used to hoist spars or prevent fraying. **3.** An anthology, as of ballads or poems. —*tr.v.* **-land·ed, -land·ing, -lands. 1.** To embellish or deck with a garland. **2.** To form into a garland. [ME < OFr. *garlande.*]

gar·lic (gär′lĭk) *n.* **1.** A plant, *Allium sativum,* related to the onion, having a bulb with a strong, distinctive odor and flavor. **2.** The bulb of the garlic, divisible into separate cloves and used as a seasoning. [ME < OE *gārlēac* : *gār,* spear + *lēac,* leek.]

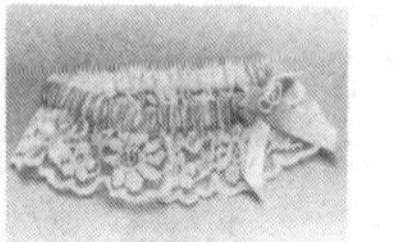

garter

gar·lick·y (gär′lĭ-kē) *adj.* Containing, tasting of, or smelling of garlic.

garlic mustard *n.* A weedy plant, *Alliaria officinalis,* native to Europe, having small white flowers and an odor of garlic.

gar·ment (gär′mənt) *n.* An article of clothing, esp. of outer clothing. —*tr.v.* **-ment·ed, -ment·ing, -ments.** To clothe; dress. [ME < OFr. *garnement* < *garnir,* to equip, of Germanic orig.]

garment bag *n.* A long bag used for holding hanging clothes, as suits or dresses, when traveling and that often folds in half and has a center handle to facilitate carrying.

gar·ner (gär′nər) *tr.v.* **-nered, -ner·ing, -ners. 1.** To gather and store in or as if in a granary. **2.** To amass; acquire. —*n.* A granary. [< ME, granary < OFr. *gernier* < Lat. *granarium* < *granum,* grain.]

gar·net[1] (gär′nĭt) *n.* **1.** Any of several common, widespread silicate minerals, occurring in two internally isomorphic series, generally crystallized, often imbedded in igneous and metamorphic rocks, colored red, brown, black, green, yellow, or white, and used both as gemstones and as abrasives. **2.** A dark to very dark red. [ME < OFr. *grenate* < *grenat,* pomegranate-red < *pome grenate,* pomegranate. —see POMEGRANATE.]

gar·net[2] (gär′nĭt) *n. Naut.* A tackle for hoisting light cargo. [ME *garnett,* prob. < MDu. *garnaat.*]

gar·net·if·er·ous (gär′nə-tĭf′ər-əs) *adj.* Containing garnets.

gar·ni·er·ite (gär′nē-ə-rīt′) *n.* An earthy, apple-green mineral, $(Ni,Mg)_6(OH)_6Si_4O_{11}\cdot H_2O$, an important nickel ore. [After Jules *Garnier* (1839?–1904).]

gar·nish (gär′nĭsh) *tr.v.* **-nished, -nish·ing, -nish·es. 1. a.** To furnish with beautifying details; embellish. **b.** To provide (food) with a garnish. **2.** *Law.* To garnishee. —*n.* **1. a.** Ornamentation; embellishment. **b.** An embellishment added to a food or drink for extra flavor or color. **2.** *Slang.* An unwarranted fee, as one extorted from a new prisoner by a jailer. [ME *garnishen* < OFr. *garnir, garniss-,* of Germanic orig.]

gar·nish·ee (gär′nĭ-shē′) *Law.* —*n.* **1.** A debtor against whom a plaintiff has instituted a process of garnishment. **2.** A third party who has been warned that money or property in his control but due or belonging to a defendant has been attached. —*tr.v.* **-eed, -ee·ing, -ees. 1.** To attach (a debtor's pay, for example) by garnishment. **2.** To serve with a garnishment.

gar·nish·ment (gär′nĭsh-mənt) *n.* **1.** *Law.* **a.** A legal proceeding whereby money or property due or belonging to a debtor but in the possession of another is applied to the payment of the debt to the plaintiff. **b.** A court order directing a third party who owes a defendant money or holds property belonging to him to withhold such money or property and to appear in court to answer inquiries. **2.** Ornamentation; embellishment.

gar·ni·ture (gär′nĭ-chər) *n.* Something that garnishes; embellishment. [OFr. < *garnir,* to garnish, of Germanic orig.]

gar·pike (gär′pīk′) *n.* **1.** Gar[1]. **2.** A marine fish, *Belone belone,* of European waters, having green bones.

gar·ret (găr′ĭt) *n.* A room on the top floor of a house, typically right under a sloping roof; attic. [ME < OFr. *garite,* watchtower < *garir,* to protect, of Germanic orig.]

gar·ri·son (găr′ĭ-sən) *n.* **1.** A military post, esp. one permanently established. **2.** The troops stationed at a garrison. —*tr.v.* **-soned, -son·ing, -sons. 1.** To assign (troops) to a military post. **2.** To supply (a post) with troops. **3.** To occupy as or convert into a garrison. [ME *garison,* fortified place < OFr. < *garir,* to protect, of Germanic orig.]

garrison cap *n.* A soft cloth cap without a visor, worn as a dress headgear chiefly by Army and Air Force personnel.

Garrison finish *n.* A finish in a contest or race in which the winner comes from behind at the last moment. [After Edward H. *Garrison* (1868–1930).]

gar·rote or **gar·rotte** (gə-rŏt′, -rōt′) —*n.* **1. a.** A method of execution by strangulation or by breaking the neck with an iron collar screwed tight. **b.** A collar used for this. **2.** Strangulation, esp. in order to rob. —*tr.v.* **-rot·ed, -rot·ing, -rots** or **-rot·ted, -rot·ting, -rottes. 1.** To execute by garrote. **2.** To strangle or throttle in order to rob. [Sp. *garrote,* cudgel, instrument of torture < OFr. *garrot.*] **—gar·rot′er** *n.*

gar·ru·li·ty (gə-ro͞o′lĭ-tē) *n.* The state or quality of being talkative; chattiness.

gar·ru·lous (găr′ə-ləs, găr′yə-) *adj.* Habitually talkative, esp. excessively so. [Lat. *garrulus* < *garrire,* to chatter.] **—gar′ru·lous·ly** *adv.* **—gar′ru·lous·ness** *n.*

gar·ter (gär′tər) *n.* **1. a.** An elasticized band worn around the leg to support hose. **b.** A suspender strap with a fastener attached to a girdle or belt for supporting hose. **c.** An elasticized band worn around the arm to keep the sleeve pushed up. **2. Garter. a.** The badge of the Order of the Garter. **b.** The order itself. **c.** Membership in this order. —*tr.v.* **-tered, -ter·ing, -ters. 1.** To fasten and hold with a garter. **2.** To put a garter upon. [ME, band to support socks < OFr. < *garet,* bend of knee, prob. of Celt. orig.]

garter snake *n.* Any of various nonvenomous North American snakes of the genus *Thamnophis,* having longitudinal stripes.

garth (gärth) *n.* **1.** A grassy quadrangle surrounded by cloisters. **2.** *Archaic.* A yard, garden, or paddock. [ME, enclosed yard < ON *garðr.*]

gas (găs) *n., pl.* **gas·es** or **gas·ses. 1. a.** The state of matter distinguished from the solid and liquid states by very low density and viscosity, relatively great expansion and contraction with changes in pressure and temperature, the ability to diffuse readily, and the spontaneous tendency to become distributed uniformly throughout any container. **b.** A substance in the gaseous state. **2.** A gaseous fuel such as natural gas. **3. a.** Gasoline. **b.** The speed control of a gasoline engine: *step on the gas.* **4.** A gaseous asphyxiant, irritant, or poison. **5.** A gaseous anesthetic. **6.** *Slang.* Idle or boastful talk. **7.** *Slang.* One that provides great fun and excitement: *thought that the idea was a gas.* **—modifier:** *a gas tank; gas stove.* —*v.* **gassed, gas·sing, gas·es** or **gass·es.** —*tr.* **1.** To supply with gas or gasoline. **2.** To treat chemically with gas. **3.** To poison with gas. —*intr.* **1.** To give off gas. **2.** *Slang.* To talk excessively. **3.** *Informal.* To fill the tank of a vehicle with gas: *gassed up before the trip.* [Du., an occult physical principle < Gk. *khaos,* chaos, coined by J.B. van Helmont, (1577–1644).]

gas·bag (găs'băg') *n.* **1.** An expansible bag for holding gas. **2.** *Slang.* One given to idle or boastful talk.

gas burner *n.* A nozzle or jet on a fitting through which combustible gas is released to burn.

gas chamber *n.* A sealed enclosure in which prisoners are executed by a poisonous gas.

gas chromatograph *n.* A device used to separate a sample into its components for analysis in gas chromatography.

gas chromatography *n.* Chromatography in which the substance to be analyzed is vaporized and diffused along with a carrier gas through a liquid or solid adsorbent for differential adsorption.

Gas·con (găs'kən) *n.* **1. a.** A native of Gascony. **b. gascon.** A boastful person; braggart. **2.** The French dialect of the Gascons. —*adj.* Of or pertaining to Gascony or the Gascons.

gas·con·ade (găs'kə-nād') *n.* Boastfulness; bravado. **—gas'con·ade'** *v.* **(-ad·ed, -ad·ing, -ades).** **—gas'con·ad'er** *n.*

gas·dy·nam·ics (găs'dī-năm'ĭks) *n. (used with a sing. verb).* The branch of dynamics that deals with thermal gaseous fluids. **—gas'dy·nam'ic** *adj.* **—gas'dy·nam'i·cist** *n.*

gas·e·ous (găs'ē-əs, găsh'əs) *adj.* **1.** Of, pertaining to, or existing as a gas. **2.** Lacking concreteness; tenuous. **—gas'e·ous·ness** *n.*

gas fitter *n.* A worker who installs or repairs gas pipes, fixtures, or appliances.

gas gangrene *n.* Gangrene occurring in a wound infected with bacteria of the genus *Clostridium,* esp. with *C. welchi* or *C. oedematiens,* and characterized by the presence of gas in the affected tissue and constitutional septic symptoms.

gas-guz·zler (găs'gŭz'lər) *n. Informal.* An automobile that consumes an excessive amount of gasoline.

gas-guz·zling (găs'gŭz'lĭng) *adj. Informal.* Using excessive amounts of gasoline: *a gas-guzzling automobile.*

gash (găsh) *tr.v.* **gashed, gash·ing, gash·es.** To make a long, deep cut in; slash deeply. —*n.* A long, deep cut or wound. [ME *garsen,* to cut < ONFr. *garser,* prob. LLat. *charaxare* < Gk. *kharassein.*]

gas·hold·er (găs'hōl'dər) *n.* A storage container for fuel gas, esp. a large, telescoping, cylindrical tank.

gas·house (găs'hous') *n.* A gasworks.

gas·i·form (găs'ə-fôrm') *adj.* In the form of gas; gaseous.

gas·i·fy (găs'ə-fī') *tr. & intr.v.* **-fied, -fy·ing, -fies.** To convert into or become gas. **—gas'i·fi'a·ble** *adj.* **—gas'i·fi·ca'tion** *n.* **—gas'i·fi'er** *n.*

gas jet *n.* **1.** A gas burner. **2.** The flame of burning gas from a gas burner.

gas·ket (găs'kĭt) *n.* **1.** Any of a wide variety of seals or packings used between matched machine parts or around pipe joints to prevent the escape of a gas or fluid. **2.** A cord or canvas strap used to secure a furled sail to a yard boom or gaff. **—idioms. blow a gasket.** *Slang.* To explode with anger. [Fr. *garcette,* dim. of *garce,* girl.]

gas·kin (găs'kĭn) *n.* **1.** The part of the hind leg of a horse or related animal between the stifle and the hock. **2. gaskins.** *Obs.* Galligaskins. [Prob. short for GALLIGASKINS.]

gas·light (găs'līt') *n.* **1.** Light produced by burning illuminating gas. **2.** A gas burner or lamp.

gas log *n.* A gas heater designed to look like a log for use in a fireplace.

gas main *n.* A major pipeline conveying gas to smaller pipes for distribution to consumers.

gas mask *n.* A respirator covering the face and having a chemical air filter to protect against poisonous gases.

gas·o·hol (găs'ə-hôl) *n.* A fuel consisting of a blend of ethanol and unleaded gasoline, esp. a blend of 10 per cent ethanol and 90 per cent gasoline. [GAS(OLINE) + (ALC)OHOL.]

gas·o·line also **gas·o·lene** (găs'ə-lēn', găs'ə-lēn') *n.* A volatile mixture of flammable liquid hydrocarbons derived chiefly from crude petroleum and used principally as a fuel for internal-combustion engines and as a solvent, illuminant, and thinner.

gas·om·e·ter (gă-sŏm'ĭ-tər) *n.* **1.** An apparatus for measuring gases. **2.** A gasholder. [Fr. *gazomètre* : *gaz,* gas + *-mètre,* -meter.]

gasp (găsp) *v.* **gasped, gasp·ing, gasps.** —*intr.* **1.** To draw in or catch the breath sharply, as from shock. **2.** To breathe convulsively or laboriously. —*tr.* To say in a breathless manner. —*n.* A short convulsive intake or catching of the breath. [ME *gaspen,* to gape < ON *geispa,* to yawn.]

gasp·er (găs'pər) *n. Chiefly Brit. Slang.* A cigarette.

gas plant *n.* A plant, *Dictamnus albus,* native to Eurasia, having aromatic foliage and white flowers and emitting a vapor capable of being ignited.

gas·ser (găs'ər) *n.* **1.** A well or drilling that yields natural gas. **2.** *Slang.* Something unusually entertaining.

gas station *n.* A filling station.

gas·sy (găs'ē) *adj.* **-si·er, -si·est. 1.** Containing, full of, or resembling gas. **2.** *Slang.* Bombastic; boastful. **—gas'si·ness** *n.*

gast (găst) *tr.v.* **gast·ed, gast·ing, gasts.** *Obs.* To frighten; scare. [ME *gasten* < OE *gǣstan.*]

gas·tight (găs'tīt') *adj.* Not permitting the escape or entry of gas. **—gas'tight'ness** *n.*

gastr– *pref.* Variant of **gastro-.**

gas·trec·to·my (gă-strĕk'tə-mē) *n., pl.* **-mies.** Surgical excision of part or all of the stomach.

gas·tric (găs'trĭk) *adj.* Of or pertaining to the stomach.

gastric juice *n.* The colorless, watery, acidic digestive fluid secreted by the stomach glands and containing hydrochloric acid, pepsin, rennin, and mucin.

gas·trin (găs'trĭn) *n.* A secretion of the gastric mucosa that stimulates production of gastric juice.

gas·tri·tis (gă-strī'tĭs) *n.* Chronic or acute inflammation of the stomach.

gastro– or **gastr–** *pref.* **1. a.** Belly: *gastropod.* **b.** Stomach: *gastritis.* **2.** Gastric: *gastrin.* [< Gk. *gastēr, gastr-,* belly.]

gas·tro·en·ter·i·tis (găs'trō-ĕn'tə-rī'tĭs) *n.* Inflammation of the mucous membrane of the stomach and intestine.

gas·tro·en·ter·ol·o·gy (găs'trō-ĕn'tə-rŏl'ə-jē) *n.* The medical study and specialty of the stomach and the intestines. **—gas'tro·en·ter'ic** (-ĕn-tĕr'ĭk) *adj.* **—gas'tro·en'ter·o·log'i·cal** *adj.* **—gas'tro·en'ter·ol'o·gist** *n.*

gas·tro·in·tes·ti·nal (găs'trō-ĭn-tĕs'tə-nəl) *adj.* Of or pertaining to the stomach and intestines.

gas·tro·lith (găs'trə-lĭth') *n.* A pathological small stony mass formed in the stomach; gastric calculus.

gas·trol·o·gy (gă-strŏl'ə-jē) *n.* The medical study of the stomach and its diseases. **—gas·trol'o·gist** *n.*

gas·tro·nome (găs'trə-nōm') also **gas·tron·o·mer** (gă-strŏn'ə-mər) *n.* A connoisseur of good food and drink; gourmet. [Fr., back-formation < *gastronomie,* gastronomy.]

gas·tro·nom·ic (găs'trə-nŏm'ĭk) also **gas·tro·nom·i·cal** (-ĭ-kəl) *adj.* Of or pertaining to gastronomy. **—gas'tro·nom'i·cal·ly** *adv.*

gas·tron·o·mist (gă-strŏn'ə-mĭst) *n.* A gastronome.

gas·tron·o·my (gă-strŏn'ə-mē) *n.* **1.** The art or science of good eating. **2.** Cooking, as of a particular region. [Fr. *gastronomie.*]

gas·tro·pod (găs'trə-pŏd') *n.* A mollusk of the class Gastropoda, as a snail, slug, cowry, or limpet, characteristically having a single, usually coiled shell and a ventral muscular mass serving as an organ of locomotion. —*adj.* Of or belonging to the Gastropoda. [NLat. *Gastropoda,* class name : GASTRO- + Gk. *pous,* foot.] **—gas·trop'o·dan** (gă-strŏp'ə-dən), **gas·trop'o·dous** (-dəs) *adj.*

gas·tro·scope (găs'trə-skōp') *n.* An instrument used for examining the interior of the stomach. **—gas'tro·scop'ic** (-skŏp'ĭk) *adj.* **—gas·tros'co·pist** (gă-strŏs'kə-pĭst) *n.* **—gas·tros'co·py** (-strŏs'kə-pē) *n.*

gas·tros·to·my (gă-strŏs'tə-mē) *n., pl.* **-mies.** The surgical construction of a permanent opening from the external surface of the body into the stomach, usually for inserting a feeding tube.

gas·trot·o·my (gă-strŏt'ə-mē) *n., pl.* **-mies.** A surgical incision into the stomach.

gas·tro·vas·cu·lar (găs'trō-văs'kyə-lər) *adj.* Having both a digestive and a circulatory function.

gas·tru·la (găs'trə-lə) *n., pl.* **-las** or **-lae** (-lē'). An embryo at the stage following the blastula and consisting of ectoderm, endoderm, and archenteron. [NLat. < Gk. *gastēr,* belly.] **—gas'tru·lar** (-lər) *adj.*

gas·tru·late (găs'trə-lāt') *intr.v.* **-lat·ed, -lat·ing, -lates.** To form or become a gastrula. **—gas'tru·la'tion** *n.*

gas turbine *n.* An air-breathing internal-combustion engine consisting essentially of an air compressor, a combustion chamber, and a turbine wheel, used esp. for propulsion rather than fixed power generation.

gas·works (găs'wûrks') *n. (used with a sing. verb).* A factory where gas for heating and lighting is produced.

gat¹ (găt) *n.* A narrow passage extending inland from a shore; channel. [Prob. < Du.]

gat² (găt) *n. Slang.* A pistol. [GAT(LING GUN).]

gat³ (gĭt) *v. Archaic.* Past tense of **get.**

gate¹ (gāt) *n.* **1.** A structure that can be swung, drawn, or lowered to block an entrance or passageway. **2. a.** An opening in a wall or fence for entrance or exit. **b.** The structure surrounding such an opening, as the monumental or fortified entrance to a palace. **3.** Something that gives access: *the gate to fortune.* **4.** A device for controlling the passage of water or gas through a dam or conduit. **5.** The total admission receipts or attendance at a public spectacle. **6.** The

gas mask

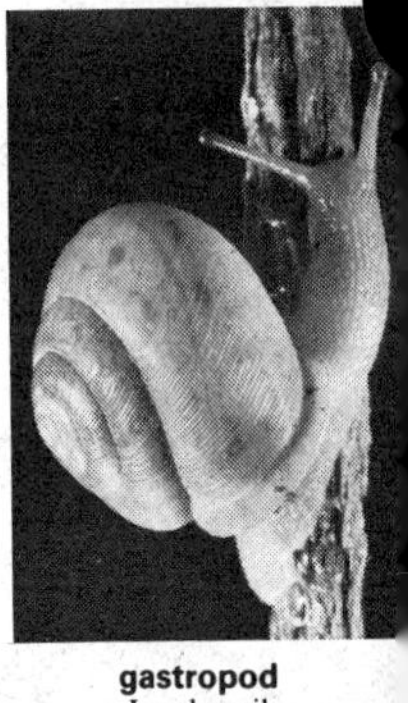

gastropod
Land snail

gateway

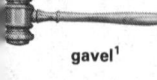

channel through which molten metal flows into the shaped cavity of a mold. **7.** *Electronics.* **a.** A circuit extensively used in computers that has an output dependent on some function of its input. **b.** Such a circuit having an output when any or all of a designated set of inputs are received within a specified time interval. —*tr.v.* **gat·ed, gat·ing, gates. 1.** *Chiefly Brit.* To punish (a student) by confinement within the college gates after a certain hour. **2.** *Electronics.* To select part of a wave for transmission, reception, or processing by magnitude or time interval. ***—idioms.*** **get the gate.** *Slang.* To be dismissed or ejected. **give (someone) the gate.** *Slang.* To dismiss or eject. [ME < OE *geat.*]

gate[2] (gāt) *n.* **1.** *Archaic.* A path or road; way. **2.** *Regional.* A particular way of acting or doing; manner. [ME < ON *gata.*]

gate·crash·er (gāt′krăsh′ər) *n.* *Slang.* A person who gains admittance without being invited or enters without paying admission.

gate·fold (gāt′fōld′) *n.* A folded insert in a book or other publication whose full size exceeds that of the regular page.

gate·keep·er (gāt′kē′pər) *n.* A person in charge of a gate.

gate-leg table (gāt′lĕg′) *n.* A drop-leaf table with movable legs arranged in pairs.

gate·post (gāt′pōst′) *n.* An upright post on which a gate is hung or against which a gate is closed.

gate·way (gāt′wā′) *n.* **1.** An opening or a structure framing an opening that may be closed by a gate. **2.** Something that serves as an entrance or means of access: *a gateway to success.*

gath·er (găth′ər) *v.* **-ered, -er·ing, -ers.** —*tr.* **1.** To cause to come together; convene. **2. a.** To accumulate gradually; amass. **b.** To harvest or pick: *gather flowers.* **c.** To gain or increase by degrees: *gather velocity.* **3. a.** To collect into one place; assemble. **b.** To arrange (signatures) in sequence for bookbinding. **4.** To run a thread through (cloth) so as to draw it up into small folds or puckers. **5.** To draw (a garment, for example) about or closer to something. **6.** To conclude; infer: *I gather that a decision has not been reached.* **7. a.** To summon up; muster: *gather courage.* **b.** To collect (one's wits or powers). **8.** To attract or be a center of attraction for. —*intr.* **1.** To come together in a group; assemble. **2.** To accumulate. **3.** To grow or increase by degrees. **4.** To come to a head, as a boil does; fester. —*n.* **1. a.** An act or instance of gathering. **b.** The quantity gathered. **2.** A small fold or pucker made in cloth by gathering it. [ME *getheren* < OE *gadrian.*] —**gath′er·er** *n.*

Synonyms: *gather, collect, assemble, congregate, accumulate, amass, marshal, rally.* These verbs mean to bring together or come together in a group or mass. *Gather,* in both transitive and intransitive use, is the most general term and therefore the most widely applicable. *Collect* is sometimes interchangeable with *gather.* Frequently, in transitive usage, *collect* refers to the careful selection of like or related things which become part of an organized whole: *collect antiques; collect stamps.* Intransitively, *collect* suggests the gradual coming together, or steady increase of things or persons. *Assemble* in all of its senses implies that the persons or things involved have a definite and usually close relationship. With respect to persons, the term suggests convening out of common interest or purpose; with respect to things, *assemble* implies fitting together component parts of a structure or machine. *Congregate* refers chiefly to the coming together of a large number of persons or animals, usually for a specific purpose. *Accumulate* is applied to the gradual increase of like or related things over an extended period. *Amass* refers to the collection or accumulation of things, especially valuable ones, to form an imposing quantity. *Marshal* implies the assembling and ordering of persons, things, or intangibles, such as thoughts or facts, so as to have them readily available for anticipated use. *Rally,* in this comparison, implies the gathering together of persons united in a common cause.

gauntlet[1]

gath·er·ing (găth′ər-ĭng) *n.* **1.** Something gathered or amassed; collection. **2.** An assembly of persons; meeting. **3.** A gather in cloth. **4.** A suppurated swelling; boil or abscess.

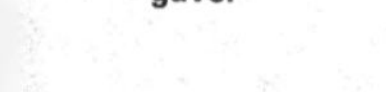

gavel[1]

Gat·ling gun (găt′lĭng) *n.* A machine gun with a cluster of barrels that are fired as the cluster is turned. [After Richard J. *Gatling* (1818–1903), its inventor.]

Gat·or·ade (gā′tər-ād′). A trademark for a thirst-quenching beverage used esp. by athletes.

gauche (gōsh) *adj.* Lacking social grace; tactless. [Fr. < OFr. *gauchir,* to turn aside, of Germanic orig.] —**gauche′ly** *adv.* —**gauche′ness** *n.*

gau·che·rie (gō′shə-rē′) *n.* **1.** An awkward or tactless action, manner, or expression. **2.** Tactlessness; awkwardness. [Fr. < *gauche,* gauche.]

gau·cho (gou′chō) *n., pl.* **-chos.** A cowboy of the South American pampas. [Am. Sp. (South America), prob. < Quechua *wáhcha,* vagabond.]

gaud (gôd) *n.* A gaudy or showy ornament. [ME *gaude,* trinket.]

gaud·er·y (gô′də-rē) *n., pl.* **-ies.** Showy things; finery.

gaud·y[1] (gô′dē) *adj.* **-i·er, -i·est.** Characterized by tasteless or showy ornaments; garish. —**gaud′i·ly** *adv.* —**gaud′i·ness** *n.*

gaud·y[2] (gô′dē) *n., pl.* **-ies.** *Chiefly Brit.* A feast, esp. an annual university dinner. [ME, ornamental rosary bead < Lat. *gaudium,* joy < *gaudēre,* to rejoice.]

gauf·fer (gŏf′ər, gô′fər) *v.* & *n.* Variant of **goffer.**

gauge also **gage** (gāj) —*n.* **1. a.** A standard or scale of measurement. **b.** A standard dimension, quantity, or capacity. **2.** An instrument for measuring or testing. **3.** A means of estimating or evaluating; test: *a gauge of character.* **4.** The position of a vessel in relation to another vessel and the wind. **5. a.** The distance between the two rails of a railroad. **b.** The distance between two wheels on an axle. **6.** The diameter of a shotgun barrel as measured by the number of lead balls of a size exactly fitting the barrel that can be made from a pound of lead. **7.** The amount of plaster of paris mixed with common plaster to speed its setting. **8.** Thickness or diameter, as of sheet metal or wire. **9.** The fineness of knitted cloth as determined by the number of loops per 1½ inches. —*tr.v.* **gauged, gaug·ing, gaug·es** also **gaged, gag·ing, gag·es. 1.** To measure precisely. **2.** To determine the capacity, volume, or contents of. **3.** To evaluate or judge: *gauge a person's ability.* **4.** To adapt to a specified measurement. **5.** To mix (plaster) in specific proportions. **6.** To chip or rub (bricks, for example) to size. [ME < ONFr.] —**gauge′a·ble** *adj.*

gaug·er also **gag·er** (gā′jər) *n.* **1.** One that gauges. **2.** *Chiefly Brit.* A revenue officer who inspects bulk goods subject to duty.

Gaul (gôl) *n.* **1.** A Celt of ancient Gaul. **2.** A Frenchman.

Gaul·ish (gô′lĭsh) *n.* The Celtic language of ancient Gaul.

Gaull·ism (gō′lĭz′əm, gô′-) *n.* **1.** The political movement supporting General Charles de Gaulle as leader of the French government in exile during World War II. **2. a.** A political movement headed by de Gaulle after World War II. **b.** The political principles and goals of de Gaulle. —**Gaull′ist** *n.*

gaum (gôm) *tr.v.* **gaumed, gaum·ing, gaums.** *Regional.* To smudge or smear. [Alteration of GUM[1].]

gaunt (gônt) *adj.* **-er, -est. 1.** Thin and bony; angular. **2.** Emaciated and haggard; drawn. **3.** Bleak and desolate; barren. [ME.] —**gaunt′ly** *adv.* —**gaunt′ness** *n.*

gaunt·let[1] also **gant·let** (gônt′lĭt, gänt′-) *n.* **1.** A protective glove worn with medieval armor. **2.** A protective glove with a flaring cuff used in manual labor. **3.** A challenge: *fling down the gauntlet.* **4.** A dress glove cuffed above the wrist. [ME < OFr. *gantelet,* dim. of *gant,* glove, of Germanic orig.]

Usage: Although *gauntlet[1]* and *gauntlet[2]* are spelled the same in modern English, they are nevertheless entered as two separate words because of their different origins. At one time, however, different spellings distinguished one term from the other. One *threw down the gauntlet.* One *ran the gantlet.* Because of their mutual influence on each other, the spellings of the two words and of their variants have fallen together and are interchangeable.

gaunt·let[2] also **gant·let** (gônt′lĭt, gänt′-) *n.* **1.** Two lines of men facing each other and armed with sticks or other weapons with which they beat a person forced to run between them. **2.** A severe trial; ordeal: *The candidate ran the gauntlet of questions from the press.* —See Usage note at **gauntlet[1].** [Alteration of *gantelope* < Sw. *gatlopp* : *gata,* lane + *lopp,* course.]

gaur (gour) *n.* A large, dark-coated bovine mammal, *Bos gaurus,* of hilly areas of southeastern Asia. [Hindi < Skt. *gaurah.*]

gauss (gous) *n., pl.* **gauss** or **gauss·es.** The centimeter-gram-second electromagnetic unit of magnetic flux density, equal to one maxwell per square centimeter. [After Karl F. *Gauss* (1777–1855).]

Gauss·i·an distribution (gou′sē-ən) *n.* Normal distribution. [After Karl F. *Gauss* (1777–1855).]

gauze (gôz) *n.* **1. a.** A thin, transparent fabric with a loose open weave, used for curtains or clothing. **b.** A cotton surgical dressing. **c.** A thin plastic or metal woven mesh. **2.** A mist or haze. [OFr. *gaze.*] —**gauz′i·ly** *adv.* —**gauz′i·ness** *n.* —**gauz′y** *adj.*

ga·vage (gə-väzh′) *n.* The introduction of material into the stomach by means of a tube. [Fr.]

gave (gāv) *v.* Past tense of **give.**

gav·el[1] (găv′əl) *n.* **1.** The mallet or hammer used by a presiding officer or auctioneer to signal for attention or order. **2.** A maul used by masons in fitting stones. —*tr.v.* **-eled, -el·ing, -els** also **-elled, -el·ling, -els.** To cause or compel by using a gavel. [Orig. unknown.]

Usage: The use of *gavel* as a verb is unacceptable to a bare majority of the Usage Panel.

gav·el[2] (găv′əl) *n.* Tribute or rent in ancient and medieval England. [ME < OE *gafol.*]

gav·el·kind (găv′əl-kīnd′) *n.* An English system of land tenure from Anglo-Saxon times to 1926 that provided for the equal division of an intestate's estate among all the sons or other heirs. [ME *gavelkinde* : OE *gafol,* gavel + OE *gecynd,* kind.]

gav·el-to-gav·el (găv′əl tə-găv′əl) *adj.* Extending from beginning to end: *gavel-to-gavel coverage of the trial.*

ga·vi·al (gā′vē-əl) *n.* A large reptile, *Gavialis gangeticus,* of southern Asia, related to and resembling the crocodiles and having a long, slender snout. [Fr. < Hindi *ghariyāl.*]

ga·votte (gə-vŏt′) *n.* **1.** A French peasant dance resembling the minuet. **2.** Music for the gavotte in moderately quick

4/4 time. [Fr. < Prov. *gavoto* < *Gavot,* native of the Alps.]

Ga·wain (gə-wān′, gä′wān′, gou′ən) *n.* A nephew of King Arthur and a knight of the Round Table.

gawk (gôk) *n.* An awkward, loutish person; oaf. —*intr.v.* **gawked, gawk·ing, gawks.** *Informal.* To stare or gape stupidly. [Perh. alteration of obs. *gaw,* to gape < ME *gawen* < ON *gā,* to heed.] —**gawk′er** *n.*

gawk·y (gô′kē) *adj.* **-i·er, -i·est.** Awkward; clumsy.

gay (gā) *adj.* **-er, -est. 1.** Showing or characterized by exuberance or happy excitement; merry. **2.** Bright or lively, esp. in color. **3.** Full of or given to social pleasures. **4.** Dissolute; licentious. **5.** Homosexual. —*n.* A homosexual. [ME *gai* < OFr., of Germanic orig.] —**gay** *adv.* —**gay′ness** *n.*

ga·yal (gə-yäl′) *n.* A domesticated bovine mammal, *Bos frontalis,* of India and Burma, having thick, pointed horns, a dark coat, and a tufted tail. [Bengali *gayāl,* prob. < Skt. *gauḥ,* ox.]

gay·e·ty (gā′ĭ-tē) *n.* Variant of **gaiety.**

gay·ly (gā′lē) *adv.* Variant of **gaily.**

gaze (gāz) *intr.v.* **gazed, gaz·ing, gaz·es.** To look intently or with fixed attention. —*n.* A steady, fixed look. [ME *gasen,* prob. of Scand. orig.] —**gaz′er** *n.*

Synonyms: *gaze, stare, gape, glare, peer, ogle.* These verbs mean to look long and fixedly. *Gaze* usually refers to prolonged and studied looking, often indicative of wonder, fascination, awe, or admiration. *Stare* stresses fixity of one's look and usually indicates marked curiosity, boldness, or insolence of manner. Both *gaze* and *stare* also can refer to a prolonged, vacant look. *Gape* suggests a prolonged, open-mouthed look reflecting amazement, awe, or stupidity. To *glare* is to fix another with a hard, hostile look, and to *peer* is to look narrowly and searchingly and seemingly with difficulty. To *ogle* is to stare impertinently in a way that indicates improper interest.

ga·ze·bo (gə-zā′bō, -zē′bō) *n., pl.* **-bos** or **-boes. 1.** A freestanding, roofed, usually open-sided structure providing a shady resting place. **2.** A belvedere. [Orig. unknown.]

gaze·hound (gāz′hound′) *n.* A dog that hunts its prey by sight rather than scent.

ga·zelle (gə-zĕl′) *n.* Any of various hoofed mammals of the genus *Gazella* and related genera, of Africa and Asia, characteristically having a slender neck, and ringed, lyrate horns. [Fr. < OFr., prob. < Sp. *gacela* < Ar. *ghazāl.*]

ga·zette (gə-zĕt′) *n.* **1.** A newspaper. **2.** An official journal. **3.** *Chiefly Brit.* An announcement in an official journal. —*tr.v.* **-zet·ted, -zet·ting, -zettes.** *Chiefly Brit.* To announce or publish in a gazette. [Fr. < Ital. *gazetta,* prob. < *gazeta,* a coin for which such a newspaper sold.]

gaz·et·teer (găz′ĭ-tîr′) *n.* **1.** A geographic dictionary or index. **2.** *Archaic.* A journalist.

gaz·pa·cho (gə-spä′chō, gəz-pä′-) *n.* A chilled soup made with tomatoes, onions, green peppers, and herbs. [Sp.]

G clef *n.* The treble clef.

Gd The symbol for the element gadolinium.

Ge The symbol for the element germanium.

ge– *pref.* Variant of **geo-.**

ge·an·ti·cline (jē-ăn′tĭ-klīn′) *n.* A large upward fold of the earth's crust. —**ge·an′ti·cli′nal** *adj.*

gear (gîr) *n.* **1. a.** A toothed wheel, cylinder, or other machine element that meshes with another toothed element to transmit motion or to change speed or direction. **b.** A complete assembly that performs a specific function in a larger machine. **c.** A transmission configuration for a specific ratio of engine to axle torque in a motor vehicle. **2.** Equipment, as tools or clothing, required for a particular activity; paraphernalia. **3.** The harness for a horse. **4.** The rigging of a ship. **5.** A sailor's personal effects. —*v.* **geared, gear·ing, gears.** —*tr.* **1. a.** To provide with gears. **b.** To connect by gears. **c.** To put into gear. **2. a.** To adjust or adapt: *geared the speech to the conservative audience.* **b.** To prepare for action: *gearing themselves up for the big game.* **3.** To provide with gear. —*intr.* **1.** To be or become in gear. **2.** To adjust so as to fit or blend. [ME *gere,* equipment < ON *gervi.*]

gear·box (gîr′bŏks′) *n.* An automotive transmission.

gear·ing (gîr′ĭng) *n.* **1.** A system of gears and associated elements by which motion is transferred within a machine. **2.** The act or technique of providing with gears.

gear·shift (gîr′shĭft′) *n.* A mechanism for changing from one gear to another in a transmission.

gear train *n.* A system of interconnected gears.

gear·wheel also **gear wheel** (gîr′hwēl′) *n.* A wheel with a toothed rim.

geck·o (gĕk′ō) *n., pl.* **-os** or **-oes.** Any of various usually small lizards of the family Gekkonidae, of warm regions, having toes with adhesive pads that enable them to climb on vertical surfaces. [Malay *ge′kok.*]

gee[1] (jē) *n.* The letter *g.*

gee[2] (jē) *interj.* Used to express a command, as to a horse or ox, to turn to the right or to go forward. —*intr.v.* **geed, gee·ing, gees.** To turn to the right.

gee[3] (jē) *interj.* Used as a mild expletive or exclamation of surprise. [Alteration of JESUS.]

gee[4] (jē) *n. Slang.* A thousand dollars. [< GEE[1], from the first letter of GRAND.]

geek (gēk) *n. Slang.* A carnival performer whose act usually consists of biting the head off a live chicken or snake. [Perh. < dial. *geek,* fool < MLG *geck.*]

gee·pound (jē′pound′) *n.* Slug[1] (sense 6). [GEE[1] (from the first letter of GRAVITY) + POUND[1].]

geese (gēs) *n.* Plural of **goose.**

gee whiz *interj.* Gee[3].

gee-whiz (jē′hwĭz′, -wĭz′) *adj. Slang.* **1.** Having a sensational aspect or quality: *The aerospace industry was once in the gee-whiz stage of development.* **2.** Characterized by wide-eyed amazement or enthusiasm: *a gee-whiz attitude about big-city life.*

gee·zer (gē′zər) *n. Slang.* An eccentric old man. [Prob. alteration of dial. *guiser,* masquerader < GUISE.]

ge·fil·te fish (gə-fĭl′tə) *n.* Chopped fish mixed with crumbs, eggs, and seasonings, cooked in a broth and usually served chilled in the form of balls or oval-shaped cakes. [Yiddish, filled fish.]

ge·gen·schein (gā′gən-shīn′) *n.* A faint, glowing spot in the sky, exactly opposite the position of the sun. [G. : *gegen,* against (< OHG *gegin*) + *Schein,* light < *scheinen,* to shine < OHG *scīnan.*]

Ge·hen·na (gĭ-hĕn′ə) *n.* **1.** A place or state of torment or suffering. **2.** Hell. [LLat. < Gk. *Geenna* < Heb. *Gê′ Hinnōm,* Valley of Hinnom, a valley south of Jerusalem.]

Gei·ger counter (gī′gər) *n.* An instrument consisting of a Geiger tube and associated electronic equipment, used to detect, measure, and record nuclear emanations, cosmic rays, and artificially produced subatomic particles.

Geiger tube *n.* A gas-filled tube containing coaxial cylindrical electrodes between which a potential difference slightly below the breakdown voltage is maintained, so that production of a pair of ions in the gas by passage of a charged particle or by ionizing radiation causes a breakdown throughout the volume of the tube. [After Hans *Geiger* (1882–1945).]

gei·sha (gā′shə) *n., pl.* **geisha** or **-shas.** A Japanese girl trained to provide entertainment, as singing, dancing, or amusing talk, esp. for men. [J. : *gei,* art + *sha,* person.]

gel (jĕl) *n.* A colloid in which the disperse phase has combined with the continuous phase to produce a semisolid material, as a jelly. —*intr.v.* **gelled, gel·ling, gels.** To become a gel. [Short for GELATIN.] —**gel′a·ble** *adj.*

ge·län·de·sprung (gə-lĕn′də-shpro͝ong′) *n.* A jump in skiing made from a crouching position with the use of both poles. [G.: *Gelände,* ground (< *Land,* land < OHG *lant*) + *Sprung,* jump < *springan,* to jump < OHG.]

gel·ate (jĕl′āt′) *intr.v.* **-at·ed, -at·ing, -ates.** To gel.

gel·a·tin also **gel·a·tine** (jĕl′ə-tən) *n.* **1.** A colorless or slightly yellow, transparent, brittle protein formed by boiling the specially prepared skin, bones, and connective tissue of animals, used in foods, drugs, and photographic film. **2.** Any of various substances similar to gelatin. **3.** A jelly made with gelatin, popular as a dessert or salad base. **4.** A thin membrane used over a theatrical light to color it. [Fr. *gélatine* < Ital. *gelatina,* dim. of *gelata,* jelly < Lat., p.part of *gelare,* to freeze < *gelu,* frost.]

ge·lat·i·nize (jə-lăt′n-īz′, jĕl′ə-tə-nīz′) *v.* **-nized, -niz·ing, -niz·es.** —*tr.* **1.** To convert to gelatin or jelly. **2.** To coat with gelatin. —*intr.* To become gelatinous. —**ge·lat′i·ni·za′tion** *n.*

ge·lat·i·nous (jə-lăt′n-əs) *adj.* **1.** Resembling gelatin; viscous. **2.** Of, pertaining to, containing, or similar to gelatin. —**ge·lat′i·nous·ly** *adv.* —**ge·lat′i·nous·ness** *n.*

ge·la·tion (jĕ-lā′shən) *n.* **1.** Solidification by cooling or freezing. **2.** The process of forming a gel. [Lat. *gelatio* < *gelare,* to freeze < *gelu,* frost.]

geld[1] (gĕld) *tr.v.* **geld·ed** or **gelt** (gĕlt), **geld·ing, gelds.** To castrate (a horse, for example). [ME *gelden* < ON *gelda.*]

geld[2] (gĕld) *n.* A tax paid to the crown by English landholders under Anglo-Saxon and Norman kings. [Med. Lat. *geldum* < OE *gield.*]

geld·ing (gĕl′dĭng) *n.* A castrated animal, esp. a male horse. [ME < ON *geldingr* < *gelda,* to geld.]

gel·id (jĕl′ĭd) *adj.* Very cold; icy: *gelid ocean waters.* [Lat. *gelidus* < *gelu,* frost.] —**ge·lid′i·ty** (jə-lĭd′ĭ-tē), **gel′id·ness** *n.* —**gel′id·ly** *adv.*

gel·ig·nite (jĕl′ĭg-nīt′) *n.* An explosive mixture, comprised of nitroglycerine, guncotton, wood pulp, and potassium nitrate. [GEL(ATIN) + Lat. *ignis,* fire + -ITE.]

gelt[1] (gĕlt) *n. Slang.* Money. [Yiddish < OHG, recompense.]

gelt[2] (gĕlt) *v.* A past tense and past participle of **geld**[1].

gem (jĕm) *n.* **1.** A precious or semiprecious stone, esp. one that has been cut and polished. **2. a.** Something that is valued for its beauty or perfection. **b.** A beloved or highly prized person. **3.** A kind of muffin. —*tr.v.* **gemmed, gem·ming, gems.** To adorn with or as if with gems. [ME *gemme* < Lat. *gemma.*]

Ge·ma·ra (gə-mär′ə, -môr′ə) *n.* The second part of the Talmud, consisting primarily of commentary on the Mishnah. [Aram. *gəmārā,* completion < *gəmār,* he finished.] —**Ge·ma′ric** *adj.* —**Ge·ma′rist** *n.*

gem·i·nate (jĕm′ə-nāt′) *v.* **-nat·ed, -nat·ing, -nates.** —*tr.* To arrange in pairs or to double. —*intr.* To occur in pairs. —*adj.* (jĕm′ə-nĭt, -nāt′). Forming a pair; doubled. [Lat. *geminare, geminat-* < *geminus,* twin.] —**gem′i·na′tion** *n.*

Gem·i·ni (jĕm′ə-nī′, -nē′) *n.* **1.** *Astron.* A constellation in the Northern Hemisphere containing the stars Castor and Pol-

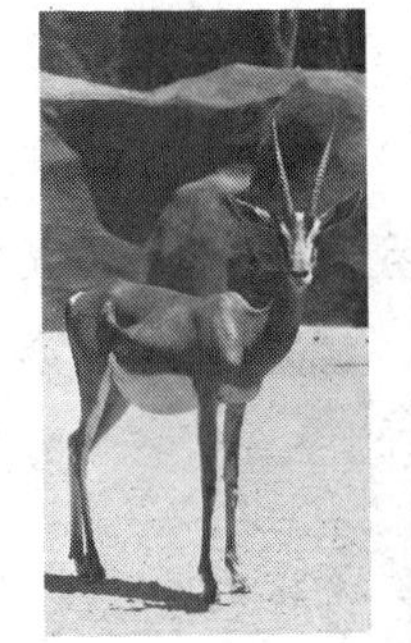

gazelle

gear

gecko

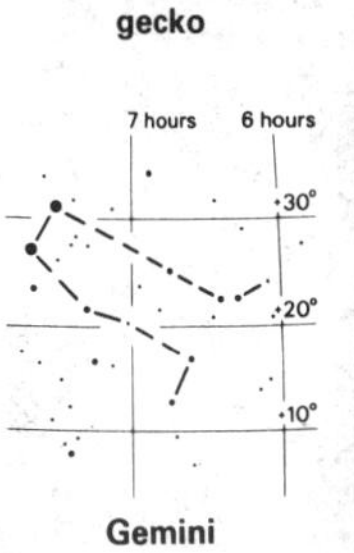

Gemini

lux. **2.** The third sign of the zodiac. [Lat. < pl. of *geminus,* twin.]

gem·ma (jĕm′ə) *n., pl.* **gem·mae** (jĕm′ē′). An asexual reproductive structure, as in liverworts or the hydra, consisting of a cell or group of cells capable of developing into a new individual; bud. [NLat. < Lat., bud.]

gem·mate (jĕm′āt′) *adj.* Having or reproducing by gemmae. —*intr.v.* **-mat·ed, -mat·ing, -mates.** To produce gemmae or reproduce by means of gemmae. [< Lat. *gemmare, gemmat-,* to bud < *gemma,* bud.] **—gem·ma′ceous** (jĕ-mā′shəs) *adj.* **—gem·ma′tion** (jĕ-mā′shən) *n.*

gem·mip·a·rous (jĕ-mĭp′ər-əs) *adj.* Reproducing by buds or gemmae. [NLat. *gemmiparus* : Lat. *gemma,* bud + Lat. *parere,* to bring forth.] **—gem·mip′a·rous·ly** *adv.*

gem·mol·o·gy (jĕ-mŏl′ə-jē) *n.* Variant of **gemology.**

gem·mu·la·tion (jĕm′yə-lā′shən) *n.* Production of or reproduction by gemmules.

gem·mule (jĕm′yo͞ol) *n.* **1.** A small gemma or similar structure, esp. a reproductive structure in some sponges that remains dormant through the winter and later develops into a new individual. **2.** A hypothetical particle of heredity postulated in the theory of pangenesis. [Fr. < Lat. *gemmula,* dim. of *gemma,* bud.] **—gem′mu·lif′er·ous** (-yo͞o-lĭf′ər-əs) *adj.*

gem·my (jĕm′ē) *adj.* **1.** Full of or set with gems. **2.** Like a gem; glittering.

gem·ol·o·gy or **gem·mol·o·gy** (jĕ-mŏl′ə-jē) *n.* The study of gems. **—gem′o·log′i·cal** (jĕm′ə-lŏj′ĭ-kəl) *adj.* **—gem·ol′o·gist** *n.*

ge·mot also **ge·mote** (gə-mōt′) *n.* A public meeting or local judicial assembly in England prior to the Norman Conquest. [OE *gemōt* : *ge-,* together + *mōt,* assembly.]

gems·bok (gĕmz′bŏk′) *n.* An antelope, *Oryx gazella,* of arid regions of southern Africa, having long, sharp, straight horns. [Afr. < Du. < G. *Gemsbock* : *Gemse,* chamois + *Bock,* buck < OHG *boc.*]

gem·stone (jĕm′stōn′) *n.* A precious or semiprecious stone that may be used as a jewel when cut and polished.

ge·müt·lich (gə-müt′lĭKH) *adj.* Having a feeling of warmth or congeniality; friendly. [G. < *gemüt,* spirit.]

ge·müt·lich·keit (gə-mo͞ot′lĭKH-kīt′) *n.* Cordial regard; amicability. [G. < *gemütlich,* gemütlich.]

–gen or **–gene** *suff.* **1.** Producer: *androgen.* **2.** One that is produced: *phosgene.* [Fr. *-gène* < Gk. *-genēs,* born.]

gen·darme (zhän′därm′) *n.* **1.** A member of a French national police organization constituting a branch of the armed forces with responsibility for general law enforcement. **2.** A policeman. [Fr. < *gens d'armes,* men of arms.]

gen·dar·me·rie also **gen·dar·mer·y** (zhän-där′mə-rē) *n.* A body of gendarmes. [Fr. < *gendarme,* gendarme.]

gen·der (jĕn′dər) *n.* **1.** *Gram.* **a.** A set of two or more categories, as masculine, feminine, and neuter, into which words are divided according to sex, animation, psychological associations, or some other characteristic, and that determine agreement with or the selection of modifiers, referents, or grammatical forms. **b.** One category of such a set. **c.** The classification of a word or grammatical form in such a category. **d.** The distinguishing form or forms used. **2.** Classification of sex. —*tr.v.* **-dered, -der·ing, -ders.** *Archaic.* To engender. [ME *gendre* < OFr., kind < Lat. *genus.*]

gene (jēn) *n.* A functional hereditary unit that occupies a fixed location on a chromosome, has a specific influence on phenotype, and is capable of mutation to various allelic forms. [G. *Gen,* short for *Pangen* : Gk. *pan,* all + Gk. *-genēs,* born.]

–gene *suff.* Variant of **-gen.**

ge·ne·al·o·gy (jē′nē-ŏl′ə-jē, -ăl′ə-jē, jĕn′ē-) *n., pl.* **-gies. 1.** A record or table of the descent of a family, group, or person from an ancestor or ancestors. **2.** Direct descent from an ancestor; lineage. **3.** The study of family histories. [ME *genealogie* < OFr. < LLat. *genealogia* < Gk. : *genea,* family + *-logia,* -logy.] **—ge′ne·a·log′i·cal** (-ə-lŏj′ĭ-kəl) *adj.* **—ge′ne·a·log′i·cal·ly** *adv.* **—ge′ne·al′o·gist** *n.*

gen·er·a (jĕn′ər-ə) *n.* Plural of **genus.**

gen·er·a·ble (jĕn′ər-ə-bəl) *adj.* Capable of being generated. [ME *generabill* < Lat. *generabilis* < *generare,* to produce < *genus,* birth.]

gen·er·al (jĕn′ər-əl) *adj.* **1.** Relating to, concerned with, or applicable to the whole or every member of a class or category. **2.** Affecting or characteristic of the majority of those involved; prevalent: *a general discontent.* **3.** Being usually the case; true or applicable in most instances but not all. **4. a.** Not limited in scope, area, or application: *as a general rule.* **b.** Not limited to one class of things: *general studies.* **5.** Involving only the main features of something rather than details or particulars. **6.** Highest or superior in rank: *the general manager.* —*n.* **1. a.** An officer in the U.S. Army, Air Force, or Marine Corps holding a rank above colonel. **b.** In England, Canada, and certain other countries, a military officer holding a rank just below field marshal. **2.** Something, as a condition, principle, or fact, that embraces or is applicable to the whole. **3.** *Archaic.* The public: *"'twas caviare to the general"* (Shakespeare). **—idiom. in general.** Generally. [ME < Lat. *generalis* < *genus,* kind.] **—gen′er·al·ness** *n.*

general anesthetic *n.* An anesthetic that anesthetizes the entire body and induces unconsciousness.

general assembly *n.* **1.** A legislative body, esp. a U.S. state legislature. **2. General Assembly.** The principal deliberative body of the United Nations. **3.** The supreme governing body of some religious denominations.

General Court *n.* **1.** A Colonial legislative body with judicial powers. **2.** The state legislature of Massachusetts and New Hampshire.

general court-martial *n.* A court-martial consisting of at least five officers for trying major offenses.

gen·er·al·cy (jĕn′ər-əl-sē) *n., pl.* **-cies.** The rank, appointment, authority, or tenure of a general.

general delivery *n.* **1.** A department of a post office which holds mail for addressees until it is called for. **2.** Mail sent to general delivery.

general election *n.* An election involving most or all constituencies of a state or nation in the choice of candidates.

gen·er·al·is·si·mo (jĕn′ər-ə-lĭs′ə-mō′) *n., pl.* **-mos.** The commander in chief of all the armed forces in certain countries. [Ital., superl. of *generale,* a general < Lat. *generalis,* general < *genus,* kind.]

gen·er·al·ist (jĕn′ər-ə-lĭst) *n.* A person with broad general knowledge and skills in several fields.

gen·er·al·i·ty (jĕn′ə-răl′ĭ-tē) *n., pl.* **-ties. 1.** The condition or quality of being general. **2.** A generalization (sense 2). **3.** A statement or idea that is imprecise or vague. **4.** The greater portion or number; majority.

gen·er·al·i·za·tion (jĕn′ər-ə-lə-zā′shən) *n.* **1.** An act or instance of generalizing. **2.** A principle, statement or idea having general application.

gen·er·al·ize (jĕn′ər-ə-līz′) *v.* **-ized, -iz·ing, -iz·es.** —*tr.* **1. a.** To reduce to a general form, class, or law. **b.** To render indefinite or unspecific. **2. a.** To infer from many particulars. **b.** To draw inferences or a general conclusion from. **3. a.** To make generally or universally applicable. **b.** To popularize. —*intr.* **1. a.** To form a concept inductively. **b.** To form general notions or conclusions. **2.** To speak or think in generalities; speak vaguely. **3.** *Med.* To spread through the body. Used of a usually localized disease.

gen·er·al·ized (jĕn′ər-ə-līzd′) *adj.* Not well-adapted to a specific environment or function; undifferentiated.

gen·er·al·ly (jĕn′ər-ə-lē) *adv.* **1.** For the most part; widely: *generally known.* **2.** As a rule; usually. **3.** In disregard of particular instances and details: *generally speaking.*

general officer *n.* A military officer ranking above colonel.

General of the Air Force *n.* A general having the highest rank in the U.S. Air Force and having an insignia of five stars.

General of the Army *n.* A general having the highest rank in the U.S. Army and having an insignia of five stars.

general paresis *n.* A brain disease of syphilitic origin, characterized by mental deterioration, speech disturbances, and progressive muscular weakness.

general practitioner *n.* A physician who does not specialize in a particular area but treats a variety of medical problems.

gen·er·al-pur·pose (jĕn′ər-əl-pûr′pəs) *adj.* Having more than one use.

general relativity *n.* The geometric theory of gravitation developed by Albert Einstein, incorporating and extending the special theory of relativity to accelerated frames of reference, and introducing the principle that gravitational and inertial forces are equivalent.

general semantics *n. (used with a sing. or pl. verb).* A doctrine proposed by Alfred Korzybski (1879–1950) that presents a method of improving human behavior through a more critical use of words and symbols.

gen·er·al·ship (jĕn′ər-əl-shĭp′) *n.* **1.** The rank, office, or tenure of a general. **2.** Leadership or skill in the conduct of a war. **3.** Skillful management or leadership.

general staff *n.* A group of military officers who are charged with assisting the commander of a division or higher unit in planning and supervising operations.

general store *n.* A retail store, usually located in a small community, that sells a wide variety of merchandise but is not subdivided into departments.

general term *n.* A mathematical expression that represents the successive terms of a sequence or series by some combination of variables and constants which, when successive integers are substituted for one of the variables, yields back the sequence or series.

gen·er·ate (jĕn′ə-rāt′) *tr.v.* **-at·ed, -at·ing, -ates. 1.** To bring into existence; produce. **2.** To engender (offspring); beget. **3.** To form (a geometric figure) by describing a curve or surface. **4.** *Computer Sci.* To produce a program by instructing a computer to follow given parameters with a skeleton program. [Lat. *generare, generat-,* to produce < *genus,* birth.] **—gen′er·a′tive** (jĕn′ə-rā′tĭv, -ər-ə-tĭv) *adj.*

gen·er·a·tion (jĕn′ə-rā′shən) *n.* **1.** The act or process of generating, esp. origination, production, or procreation. **2.** Offspring having a common parent or parents and constituting a single stage of descent. **3.** A class of objects derived from a preceding class: *the new generation of miniature computers.* **4. a.** A group of contemporaneous individuals. **b.** A group of individuals regarded as having a common, more or less contemporaneous cultural or social attribute. **5.** The average time interval between the birth of parents and the birth of their offspring. **6.** *Computer Sci.* The technique of generating programs. **—gen·er·a'tion·al** *adj.*

generation gap *n.* The differences in values and attitudes between one generation and the next, esp. a generation of adolescents and that of their parents.

generative grammar *n.* A system of rules intended to produce all the well-formed sentences of a language when applied to its lexicon, esp. such a system whose syntactic component is generated successively by rules for the construction of phrases containing a semantic component (deep structure) and by rules for the production of a phonological component (surface structure) by transforming one grammatical structure into another that is semantically equivalent.

gen·er·a·tor (jĕn'ə-rā'tər) *n.* **1.** One that generates. **2.** A machine that converts mechanical energy into electrical energy. **3.** An apparatus that generates vapor or gas. **4.** A generatrix. **5.** *Computer Sci.* A routine that performs a generating function.

gen·er·a·trix (jĕn'ə-rā'trĭks) *n., pl.* **-er·a·tri·ces** (-ə-rā'trĭ-sēz', -ər-ə-trī'sēz). A geometric element that generates a geometric figure, esp. a straight line that generates a surface by moving in a specified fashion.

ge·ner·ic (jə-nĕr'ĭk) *adj.* **1.** Relating to or descriptive of an entire group or class; general. **2.** *Biol.* Of or relating to a genus. **3.** Not having a trademark or trade name. [Fr. *générique* < Lat. *genus,* kind.] **—ge·ner'i·cal·ly** *adv.*

gen·er·os·i·ty (jĕn'ə-rŏs'ĭ-tē) *n., pl.* **-ties.** **1.** The quality of being generous, esp. liberality in giving; munificence. **2.** Nobility of thought or behavior; magnanimity. **3.** Amplitude or abundance. **4.** A generous act.

gen·er·ous (jĕn'ər-əs) *adj.* **1.** Characterized by nobility and forbearance in thought or behavior; magnanimous. **2.** Liberal in giving or sharing. **3.** Characterized by abundance; ample. **4.** Rich-flavored, as wine. **5.** *Obs.* Of noble lineage. [OFr. *genereux,* of noble birth < Lat. *generosus* < *genus,* birth.] **—gen'er·ous·ly** *adv.* **—gen'er·ous·ness** *n.*

gen·e·sis (jĕn'ĭ-sĭs) *n., pl.* **-ses** (-sēz'). **1.** The coming into being of something; origin. **2. Genesis.** See table at **Bible.** [Lat. < Gk.]

-genesis *suff.* Origin; production: *abiogenesis.* [NLat. < Lat. < Gk., birth, origin.]

gene-splic·ing (jēn'splī'sĭng) *n.* The process in which DNA fragments from one or more different organisms are combined and made to function within the cells of a host organism.

gen·et[1] (jĕn'ĭt, jə-nĕt') *n.* Any of several Old World carnivorous mammals of the genus *Genetta,* having grayish or yellowish fur with dark spots, and a long, ringed tail. [ME *genete* < OFr. < Ar. *jarnayt.*]

gen·et[2] (jĕn'ĭt) *n.* Variant of **jennet.**

ge·net·ic (jə-nĕt'ĭk) also **ge·net·i·cal** (-ĭ-kəl) *adj.* **1.** Of or pertaining to the origin or development of something. **2. a.** Of or pertaining to genetics. **b.** Affecting or affected by genes. [< GENESIS.] **—ge·net'i·cal·ly** *adv.*

genetic code *n.* The information coded within the nucleotide sequences of RNA and DNA that specifies the amino acid sequence in the synthesis of proteins, and upon which heredity is based. **—genetic coding** *n.*

genetic counseling *n.* The counseling of prospective parents on the probabilities of inherited diseases occurring in offspring and on the diagnosis and treatment of such diseases. **—genetic counselor** *n.*

genetic engineering *n.* The intentional alteration of genetic material or gene-controlled processes to prevent or ameliorate hereditary defects.

ge·net·i·cist (jə-nĕt'ĭ-sĭst) *n.* One who specializes in genetics.

ge·net·ics (jə-nĕt'ĭks) *n.* **1.** *(used with a sing. verb).* The biology of heredity, esp. the study of mechanisms of hereditary transmission and variation of organismal characteristics. **2.** *(used with a pl. verb).* The genetic constitution of an individual, group, or class.

Ge·ne·va bands (jə-nē'və) *n.* Two strips of white cloth hanging from the collar of some clerical or academic robes. [After *Geneva,* Switzerland.]

Geneva Convention *n.* An agreement first formulated at an international convention held in Geneva, Switzerland, in 1864, establishing rules for the wartime treatment of prisoners and the sick or wounded.

Geneva cross *n.* A red Greek or St. George's cross on a white ground used as a symbol by the Red Cross and as a sign of neutrality.

Geneva gown *n.* A loose black academic or clerical gown with wide sleeves. [After *Geneva,* Switzerland.]

Ge·ne·van (jə-nē'vən) also **Gen·e·vese** (jĕn'ə-vēz', -vēs') *—adj.* **1.** Of or relating to Geneva, Switzerland. **2.** Of or relating to Geneva during the time of Calvin; Calvinist. *—n.* **1.** A native or inhabitant of Geneva, Switzerland. **2.** A Calvinist.

gen·ial[1] (jēn'yəl) *adj.* **1.** Having a pleasant or friendly disposition or manner; kindly. **2.** Conducive to life, growth, or comfort; mild: *"the genial sunshine . . . saturating his miserable body with its warmth"* (Jack London). **3.** *Obs.* Characteristic of or relating to genius. **4.** *Obs.* Of or relating to marriage; nuptial. [Lat. *genialis,* festive < *genius,* spirit of festivity.] **—gen'ial·ly** *adv.* **—ge'ni·al'i·ty** (jē'nē-ăl'ĭ-tē), **gen'ial·ness** *n.*

ge·ni·al[2] (jĭ-nī'əl) *n.* Of or pertaining to the chin. [< Gk. *geneion,* chin < *genus,* jaw.]

gen·ic (jē'nĭk, jĕn'ĭk) *adj.* Of, relating to, produced by, or being a gene. **—gen'ic·al·ly** *adv.*

-genic *suff.* **1.** Producing; generating: *dysgenic.* **2.** Produced or generated by: *cryptogenic.* **3.** Suitable for production or reproduction by a specified medium: *telegenic.* [-GEN + -IC.]

ge·nic·u·late (jə-nĭk'yə-lĭt) also **ge·nic·u·lat·ed** (-lā'tĭd) *adj.* **1.** Bent at an abrupt angle like that of a bent knee. **2.** Jointed so as to be capable of bending at an abrupt angle. [Lat. *geniculatus,* with bended knee < *geniculum,* dim. of *genu,* knee.] **—ge·nic'u·late·ly** *adv.* **—ge·nic'u·la'tion** *n.*

ge·nie (jē'nē) *n.* **1.** A supernatural creature who does one's bidding. **2.** Variant of **jinni.** [Fr. *génie,* spirit < Lat. *genius,* guardian spirit.]

gen·ip (jĕn'əp) *n.* **1.** A tropical American tree, *Melicocca bijuga,* having small greenish-white flowers and small yellow fruit. **2.** The sweet, edible fruit of the genip. **3.** The genipap. [Sp. *genipa,* a kind of palm, prob. of Carib orig.]

gen·i·pap (jĕn'ə-păp') *n.* **1.** An evergreen tree, *Genipa americana,* of the West Indies, having yellowish-white flowers and edible fruit. **2.** The reddish-brown fruit of the genipap. [Portuguese *genipapo,* from Tupi.]

gen·i·tal (jĕn'ĭ-təl) *adj.* **1.** Of or relating to biological reproduction. **2.** Of or pertaining to the genitalia. *—pl.n.* **genitals.** The genitalia. [ME < Lat. *genitalis* < *gignere,* to beget.] **—gen'i·tal·ly** *adv.*

gen·i·ta·li·a (jĕn'ĭ-tā'lē-ə, -tāl'yə) *pl.n.* The reproductive organs, esp. the external sex organs. [Lat., neuter pl. of *genitalis,* generative < *gignere,* to beget.]

gen·i·ti·val (jĕn'ĭ-tī'vəl) *adj. Gram.* Of, relating to, or in the genitive case. **—gen'i·ti'val·ly** *adv.*

gen·i·tive (jĕn'ĭ-tĭv) *Gram. —adj.* **1.** Of, pertaining to, or designating a case that expresses possession, measurement, or source. **2.** Of or pertaining to an affix or a construction, as a prepositional phrase, characteristic of the genitive case. *—n.* **1.** The genitive case. **2.** A genitive form or construction. [ME *genetif* < Lat. *genetivus* < *gignere,* to beget.]

gen·i·tor (jĕn'ĭ-tər) *n.* **1.** One who begets or creates. **2.** *Anthropol.* A natural father as distinguished from the socially responsible foster father in certain cultures. [ME *genitour* < OFr. *genitor* < Lat. < *gignere,* to beget.]

gen·i·to·u·ri·nar·y (jĕn'ĭ-tō-yo͝or'ə-nĕr'ē) *adj.* Of or pertaining to the genital and urinary organs or their functions. [GENIT(AL) + URINARY.]

gen·ius (jēn'yəs) *n., pl.* **-ius·es.** **1. a.** Exceptional intellectual and creative power. **b.** One who possesses such power. **2. a.** A natural talent or inclination: *She has a genius for acting.* **b.** One who has such a talent or inclination: *He is a genius at diplomacy.* **3.** The prevailing spirit or character, as of a place, person, time, or group: *the genius of the Elizabethan poets.* **4.** *pl.* **ge·ni·i** (jē'nē-ī'). *Rom. Myth.* A tutelary deity or guardian spirit of a person or place. **5.** A person who has great influence over another. **6.** A jinni or demon. [Lat., guardian spirit.]

ge·ni·us lo·ci (jē'nē-əs lō'sī') *n.* **1.** A guardian deity of a particular locality. **2.** The distinctive atmosphere or particular character of a place. [Lat.]

gen·o·cide (jĕn'ə-sīd') *n.* The systematic, planned annihilation of a racial, political, or cultural group. [Gk. *genos,* race + -CIDE.] **—gen'o·cid'al** (-sīd'l) *adj.* **—gen'o·cid'al·ly** *adv.*

ge·nome (jē'nōm') also **ge·nom** (-nŏm) *n.* A complete haploid set of chromosomes. [G. *Genom* : *Gen,* gene + *(Chromos)om,* chromosome.] **—ge·nom'ic** (-nōm'ĭk) *adj.*

gen·o·type (jĕn'ə-tīp', jē'nə-) *n.* **1.** The genetic constitution of an organism, esp. as distinguished from its physical appearance. **2.** A group or class of organisms having the same genetic constitution. **3.** The type species of a genus. [Gk. *genos,* race + -TYPE.] **—gen'o·typ'ic** (-tĭp'ĭk), **gen'o·typ'i·cal** *adj.* **—gen'o·typ'i·cal·ly** *adv.* **—gen'o·ty·pic'i·ty** (-tī-pĭs'ĭ-tē) *n.*

-genous *suff.* **1.** Producing; generating: *hematogenous.* **2.** Produced by or in a specified manner: *hypogenous.* [-GEN + -OUS.]

gen·re (zhän'rə) *n.* **1.** Type; class. **2. a.** A category of artistic composition marked by a distinctive style, form, or content, esp. a style of painting concerned with depicting scenes and subjects of common everyday life. **b.** A distinctive class or category of literary composition. [Fr. < OFr., kind < Lat. *genus.*]

gen·ro (gĕn'rō') *n., pl.* **-ros.** In Japan, a group of elder statesmen, formerly advisers to the emperor. [J. *genrō* : Chin. *yuan*[2], first + Chin. *lao*[3], elder.]

gens (jĕnz) *n., pl.* **gen·tes** (jĕn'tēz'). **1.** The patrilinear clan forming the basic unit of the Roman tribe and having originally a common name, land, cult, and burial ground. **2.** *Anthropol.* An exogamous patrilineal clan. [Lat.]

gent[1] (jĕnt) *adj. Obs.* Graceful or neat; elegant. [ME < OFr. < Lat. *genitus,* p.part. of *gignere,* to beget.]

gent[2] (jĕnt) *n. Informal.* A man; fellow. [Short for GENTLEMAN.]

gen·ta·mi·cin (jĕn'tə-mī'sĭn) *n.* A broad-spectrum antibiotic derived from an actinomycete of the genus *Micromonospora.*

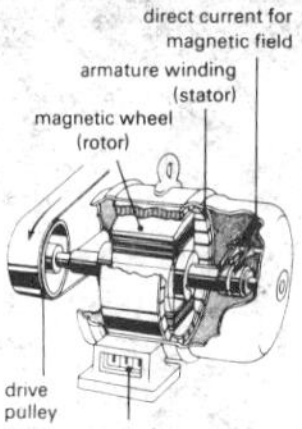

generator
Above: Electricity generator
Below: Diagram

Geneva cross

[Alteration of *gentamycin* : GENT(I)A(N VIOLET) + MYCIN.]

gen·teel (jĕn-tēl′) *adj.* **1.** Refined in manner; polite. **2.** Free from vulgarity or rudeness. **3.** Elegantly fashionable or stylish in manner or appearance. **4. a.** Striving to convey a manner or appearance of refinement and respectability. **b.** Marked by affected and somewhat prudish refinement. [OFr. *gentil.* —see GENTLE.] **—gen·teel′ly** *adv.* **—gen·teel′ness** *n.*

gen·teel·ism (jĕn-tē′lĭz′əm) *n.* A word or expression thought by its user to be genteel.

gen·tes (jĕn′tēz′) *n.* Plural of **gens.**

gen·tian (jĕn′shən) *n.* **1.** Any of numerous plants of the genus *Gentiana,* characteristically having showy blue flowers. **2.** The dried rhizome and roots of a yellow-flowered European gentian, *G. lutea,* sometimes used as a tonic. [ME *gencian* < Lat. *gentiana.*]

gentian violet *n.* A purple dye used chiefly as a biological stain and bactericide.

gen·tile (jĕn′tīl′) *n.* **1. Gentile.** One who is not of the Jewish faith or is of a non-Jewish nation. **2. Gentile.** A Christian as distinguished from a Jew. **3.** A pagan or heathen. **4. Gentile.** Among Mormons, a person who is not a Mormon. **5.** A member of a gens. —*adj.* **1.** Of or relating to a Gentile. **2.** Of or relating to tribal society, esp. of the gens. [ME *gentil* < LLat. *gentilis,* pagan < Lat., of the same clan < *gens,* clan.]

gen·ti·lesse (jĕn′tə-lĕs′) *n. Archaic.* Refinement and courtesy developed by good breeding. [ME < OFr. < *gentil,* noble. —see GENTLE.]

gen·til·i·ty (jĕn-tĭl′ĭ-tē) *n.* **1.** The condition of being genteel. **2.** The condition of being born to the gentry. **3.** Persons of the upper class collectively; gentry. **4.** The usually obsessive attempt to convey or maintain the appearance of refinement and respectability. [ME *gentilete,* nobility of birth < OFr. < *gentil,* noble. —see GENTLE.]

gen·tle (jĕn′tl) *adj.* **-tler, -tlest. 1.** Considerate or kindly in disposition; amiable. **2.** Not harsh, severe, or violent: *a gentle breeze.* **3.** Easily managed or handled; docile: *a gentle horse.* **4.** Not steep or sudden; gradual: *a gentle incline.* **5.** Of good family; well-born. **6.** *Archaic.* Noble; chivalrous: *a gentle knight.* —*n.* **1.** *Archaic.* One of gentle birth or station. **2.** The larva of a bluebottle fly. —*tr.v.* **-tled, -tling, -tles. 1.** To make gentle; mollify. **2.** To tame or break (a horse). **3.** *Obs.* To raise to the status of a noble. [ME *gentil,* noble < OFr. < Lat. *gentilis,* of the same clan < *gens,* clan.] **—gen′tle·ness** *n.* **—gen′tly** *adv.*

gentle breeze *n.* A wind having a speed between 12.9 and 19.3 kilometers per hour, or 8 and 12 miles per hour.

gen·tle·folk (jĕn′tl-fōk′) also **gen·tle·folks** (-fōks′) *pl.n.* Persons of good family and breeding.

gen·tle·man (jĕn′tl-mən) *n.* **1.** A man of gentle or noble birth or superior social position. **2.** A polite, gracious, or considerate man with high standards of propriety or correct behavior. **3.** A man of independent means who does not or need not work to support himself. **4.** A man who considers manual labor to be beneath him. **5. a.** A man. **b. gentlemen.** A form of address for a group of men used both in speech and writing. **6.** A manservant; valet. **—gen′tle·man·ly** *adj.*

geode

gen·tle·man-at-arms (jĕn′tl-mən-ət-ärmz′) *n., pl.* **gentlemen-at-arms** (-mĭn-ət-ärmz′). Any of a military corps of 40 gentlemen who attend the British sovereign as a ceremonial guard on state occasions.

gentleman farmer *n., pl.* **gentlemen farmers.** A man who farms chiefly for pleasure rather than income.

gentleman of fortune *n.* An adventurer.

gentleman's agreement *n.* An agreement guaranteed only by the honor of the participants.

gentleman's gentleman *n.* A manservant; valet.

gen·tle·wom·an (jĕn′tl-wo͝om′ən) *n.* **1.** A woman of gentle or noble birth or superior social position. **2.** A polite, gracious, or considerate woman. **3.** A woman acting as a personal attendant to a lady of rank.

Gen·too (jĕn-to͞o′) *n., pl.* **-toos.** *Archaic.* A Hindu. [Port. *gentio* < *gentio,* pagan < LLat. *gentilis.* —see GENTILE.]

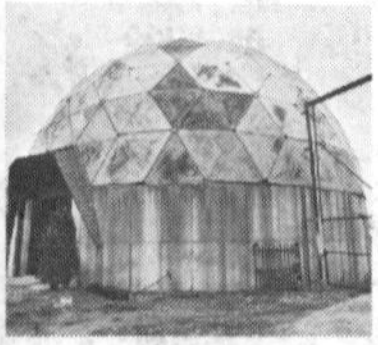
geodesic dome

gen·tri·fi·ca·tion (jĕn′trə-fĭ-kā′shən) *n.* Restoration of deteriorated urban property esp. in working-class neighborhoods by the middle and upper classes. **—gen′tri·fy** *v.* **(-fied, -fy·ing, -fies).** [GENTRY + -FICATION.]

gen·try (jĕn′trē) *n.* **1.** People of gentle birth, good breeding, or high social position. **2.** The upper middle classes in England. **3.** People of a particular class or group: *another commuter from the suburban gentry.* [ME *gentri,* nobility of birth < OFr. *genterie* < *gentil,* noble. —see GENTLE.]

gen·u·flect (jĕn′yə-flĕkt′) *intr.v.* **-flect·ed, -flect·ing, -flects. 1.** To bend the knee in a kneeling or half-kneeling position, as in worship. **2.** To exhibit a deferential or obsequious attitude or manner. [LLat. *genuflectere* : Lat. *genu,* knee + Lat. *flectere,* to bend.] **—gen′u·flec′tion** (-flĕk′shən) *n.*

gen·u·ine (jĕn′yo͞o-ĭn) *adj.* **1.** Actually possessing or produced by the alleged or apparent attribute, character, or source: *genuine sorrow.* **2.** Not spurious or counterfeit; authentic. **3.** Free from hypocrisy or dishonesty; sincere: *a genuine affection.* **4.** Being of pure or original stock: *a genuine Hawaiian.* [Lat. *genuinus,* natural.] **—gen′u·ine·ly** *adv.* **—gen′u·ine·ness** *n.*

ge·nus (jē′nəs) *n., pl.* **gen·er·a** (jĕn′ər-ə). **1.** *Biol.* A taxonomic category ranking below a family and above a species, used in taxonomic nomenclature, either alone or followed by a Latin adjective or epithet, to form the name of a species. **2.** *Logic.* A class of objects divided into subordinate species having certain common attributes. **3.** A class, group, or kind with common attributes: *"his temperament, formed by a modern genus of solitude"* (Wallace Fowlie). [Lat., kind.]

-geny *suff.* Production; generation; origin: *ontogeny.* [Gk. *-geneia* < *-genēs,* born.]

geo– or **ge–** *pref.* **1.** Earth: *geocentric.* **2.** Geography: *geopolitical.* [Gk. *geō-* < *gē,* earth.]

ge·o·bot·a·ny (jē′ō-bŏt′n-ē) *n.* Phytogeography. **—ge′o·bo·tan′ic** (-bə-tăn′ĭk), **ge′o·bo·tan′i·cal** *adj.* **—ge′o·bo·tan′ic·al·ly** *adv.* **—ge′o·bot′a·nist** (-bŏt′n-ĭst) *n.*

ge·o·cen·tric (jē′ō-sĕn′trĭk) *adj.* **1.** Pertaining to, measured from, or observed from the center of the earth. **2.** Having the earth as a center. **—ge′o·cen′tri·cal·ly** *adv.*

ge·o·chem·is·try (jē′ō-kĕm′ĭ-strē) *n.* The chemistry of the composition and alterations of the earth's crust. **—ge′o·chem′i·cal** *adj.* **—ge′o·chem′i·cal·ly** *adv.* **—ge′o·chem′ist** *n.*

ge·o·chro·nol·o·gy (jē′ō-krə-nŏl′ə-jē) *n.* The chronology of the earth's history as determined by geological events. **—ge′o·chron′o·log′ic** (-krŏn′ə-lŏj′ĭk), **ge′o·chron′o·log′i·cal** (-ĭ-kəl) *adj.* **—ge′o·chron′o·log′i·cal·ly** *adv.* **—ge′o·chro·nol′o·gist** *n.*

ge·o·chro·nom·e·try (jē′ō-krə-nŏm′ə-trē) *n.* The measurement of geologic time, as through isotopic radioactive decay. **—ge′o·chron′o·met′ric** (-krŏn′ə-mĕt′rĭk) *adj.*

ge·o·co·ro·na (jē′ō-kə-rō′nə) *n.* The outermost part of the earth's atmosphere, consisting chiefly of ionized hydrogen.

ge·ode (jē′ōd′) *n.* A small, hollow, usually spheroidal rock with crystals lining the inside wall. [Lat. *geodes,* a precious stone < Gk. *geōdēs,* earthlike : *gē,* earth + *eidos,* shape.]

ge·o·des·ic (jē′ə-dĕs′ĭk) *adj.* **1.** *Math.* Of or pertaining to the geometry of geodesics. **2.** Geodetic. —*n. Math.* In three-dimensional Euclidean space, a curve whose principal normal at any point is the normal to the surface on which the curve occurs; the shortest line between two points on any mathematically derived surface.

geodesic dome *n.* A domed or vaulted structure of lightweight straight elements that form interlocking polygons.

ge·od·e·sy (jē-ŏd′ĭ-sē) *n.* The geologic science of the size and shape of the earth. [Ult. < Gk. *geōdaisia* : *gē,* earth + *daiesthai,* to divide.] **—ge·od′e·sist** *n.*

ge·o·det·ic (jē′ə-dĕt′ĭk) also **ge·o·det·i·cal** (-ĭ-kəl) *adj.* **1.** Of or pertaining to geodesy. **2.** Geodesic. **—ge′o·det′i·cal·ly** *adv.*

geo·duck (go͞o′ē-dŭk′) *n.* A very large, edible clam, *Panope generosa,* of the Pacific coast of northwestern North America. [Chinook Jargon *go-duck.*]

ge·og·no·sy (jē-ŏg′nə-sē) *n.* The scientific study of the organization and structure of the earth and its materials. [GEO- + Gk. *-gnōsia,* knowledge < *gnōsis* < *gignōskein,* to know.]

ge·o·graph·ic (jē′ə-grăf′ĭk) also **ge·o·graph·i·cal** (-ĭ-kəl) *adj.* **1.** Of or pertaining to geography. **2.** Concerning the topography of a specific region. **—ge′o·graph′i·cal·ly** *adv.*

geographic mile *n.* A nautical mile.

ge·og·ra·phy (jē-ŏg′rə-fē) *n., pl.* **-phies. 1.** The study of the earth and its features and of the distribution of life on the earth, including human life and the effects of human activity. **2.** The geographic characteristics of an area. **3.** A book on geography. **4.** An ordered arrangement of constituent elements: *charting a geography of the mind.* [Lat. *geographia* < Gk. *geōgraphia* : *gē,* earth + *graphein,* to write.] **—ge·og′ra·pher** *n.*

ge·oid (jē′oid′) *n.* The hypothetical surface of the earth that coincides everywhere with mean sea level. [G. < Gk. *geoeidēs,* earthlike : *gē,* earth + *-eidēs,* -oid.] **—ge·oid′al** (-oid′l) *adj.*

geologic time *n.* The period of time covering the earth's geologic history.

ge·ol·o·gize (jē-ŏl′ə-jīz′) *intr.v.* **-gized, -giz·ing, -giz·es.** To study geology or make geologic investigations.

ge·ol·o·gy (jē-ŏl′ə-jē) *n., pl.* **-gies. 1.** The scientific study of the origin, history, and structure of the earth. **2.** The structure of a specific region of the earth's surface. **3.** A book on geology. **4.** The scientific study of the origin, history, and structure of the solid matter of a celestial body. **—ge·o·log′ic** (je′ə-lŏj′ĭk), **ge′o·log′i·cal** *adj.* **—ge′o·log′i·cal·ly** *adv.* **—ge·ol′o·gist, ge·ol′o·ger** *n.*

ge·o·mag·net·ic equator (jē′ō-măg-nĕt′ĭk) *n.* The great circle on the earth's surface formed by the intersection of a plane passing through the earth's center perpendicular to the axis connecting the north and south magnetic poles. It is the geometric rationalization of the empirically defined magnetic equator.

geomagnetic storm *n.* Magnetic storm.

ge·o·mag·ne·tism (jē′ō-măg′nĭ-tĭz′əm) *n.* **1.** The magnetism of the earth. **2.** The study of the earth's magnetic field. **—ge′o·mag·net′ic** (-nĕt′ĭk) *adj.* **—ge′o·mag·net′i·cal·ly** *adv.*

ge·o·man·cy (jē′ə-măn′sē) *n.* Divination by means of lines and figures. [ME *geomancie* < OFr. < Med. Lat. *geomantia* < LGk. *geōmanteia,* divination by signs from the earth : Gk.

gē, earth + Gk. *manteia,* divination. —see -MANCY.] **—ge′o·man′cer** *n.* **—ge′o·man′tic** *adj.*

ge·o·met·ric (jē′ə-mĕt′rĭk) also **ge·o·met·ri·cal** (-rĭ-kəl) *adj.* **1.** Of or pertaining to geometry and its methods and principles. **2.** Using simple geometric forms in design and decoration. **3.** Increasing or decreasing in a geometric progression. **—ge′o·met′ri·cal·ly** *adv.*

geometric isomer *n.* An isomer (sense 1.e.).

geometric mean *n.* The *n*th root, usually the positive *n*th root, of a product of *n* factors.

geometric pace *n.* Pace[1] (sense 2.d.).

geometric progression *n.* A sequence of terms, as 1, 3, 9, 27, 81, each of which is a constant multiple of the immediately preceding term.

ge·om·e·trid (jē-ŏm′ĭ-trĭd) *n.* Any of various moths of the family Geometridae, having caterpillars that move by looping the body in alternate contractions and expansions. *—adj.* Of or belonging to the Geometridae. [NLat. *Geometridae,* family name < Lat. *geometres,* geometer < Gk. *geōmetrēs* < *geōmetrein,* to measure land. —see GEOMETRY.]

ge·om·e·trize (jē-ŏm′ĭ-trīz′) *intr.v.* **-trized, -triz·ing, -triz·es. 1.** To study geometry. **2.** To apply the methods of geometry.

ge·om·e·try (jē-ŏm′ĭ-trē) *n., pl.* **-tries. 1. a.** The mathematics of the properties, measurement, and relationships of points, lines, angles, surfaces, and solids. **b.** A system of geometry: *Euclidean geometry.* **c.** A geometry restricted to a class of problems or objects: *solid geometry.* **2.** Configuration; arrangement. **3.** A surface shape. **4.** A physical arrangement suggesting geometric forms or lines. [ME *geometrie* < OFr. < Lat. *geometria* < Gk. *geōmetria* < *geōmetrein,* to measure land : *gē,* earth + *metron,* measure.] **—ge·om′e·tri′cian** (jē-ŏm′ĭ-trĭsh′ən, jē′ə-mĭ-), **ge·om′e·ter** *n.*

ge·o·mor·phic (jē′ə-môr′fĭk) *adj.* Of or like the earth, its shape, or surface configuration.

ge·o·mor·phol·o·gy (jē′ō-môr-fŏl′ə-jē) *n.* The geologic study of the configuration and evolution of land forms. **—ge′o·mor′pho·log′ic** (-môr′fə-lŏj′ĭk), **ge′o·mor′pho·log′i·cal** *adj.* **—ge′o·mor′pho·log′i·cal·ly** *adv.* **—ge′o·mor·phol′o·gist** *n.*

ge·oph·a·gy (jē-ŏf′ə-jē) *n.* The practice of eating earthy substances, as clay. **—ge·oph′a·gism** *n.* **—ge·oph′a·gist** *n.*

ge·o·phone (jē′ə-fōn′) *n.* An electronic receiver designed to pick up seismic vibrations.

ge·o·phys·ics (jē′ō-fĭz′ĭks) *n. (used with a sing. verb).* The physics of geologic phenomena, including fields such as meteorology, oceanography, geodesy, and seismology. **—ge′o·phys′i·cal** *adj.* **—ge′o·phys′i·cal·ly** *adv.* **—ge′o·phys′i·cist** *n.*

ge·o·phyte (jē′ə-fīt′) *n.* A perennial plant propagated by underground buds.

ge·o·pol·i·tics (jē′ō-pŏl′ĭ-tĭks) *n. (used with a sing. verb).* **1.** The study of the relationship between politics and geography. **2.** A Nazi doctrine of expansion that concentrated on the reallocation of geographic, economical, and political boundaries. **—ge′o·po·lit′i·cal** (-pə-lĭt′ĭ-kəl) *adj.*

ge·o·pon·ic (jē′ə-pŏn′ĭk) *adj.* Of or relating to agriculture or farming. [Gk. *geōponikos* < *geōponein,* to till : *gē,* earth + *ponein,* to toil.]

ge·o·pon·ics (jē′ə-pŏn′ĭks) *n. (used with a sing. verb).* The study or science of agriculture.

ge·o·pres·sured (je′ō-prĕsh′ərd) *adj.* Under high pressure within the earth.

ge·o·pres·sur·ized (jē′ō-prĕsh′ə-rīzd′) *adj.* Geopressured.

ge·o·probe (jē′ō-prōb′) *n.* A spacecraft designed for exploration of space near the earth.

Geor·die (jôr′dē) *n. Scot.* A guinea (sense 1.a.). [After St. *George,* whose image was once stamped on it.]

George (jôrj) *n.* **1.** A jeweled figure of Saint George killing the dragon, used as an insignia of the Knights of the Garter. **2.** An English coin during the reign of Henry VIII, imprinted with a figure of Saint George.

Geor·gette crepe (jôr-jĕt′) *n.* A sheer, strong silk or silklike fabric with a dull, creped surface. [Orig. a trademark.]

Geor·gian (jôr′jən) *adj.* **1.** Of, pertaining to, or characteristic of the reigns of the four Georges who ruled Great Britain from 1714 to 1830. **2.** Of or pertaining to the U.S. state of Georgia or to its inhabitants. **3.** Of or pertaining to the Georgian SSR, or to its people or their language. *—n.* **1.** A native or inhabitant of the state of Georgia. **2. a.** A native or inhabitant of the Georgian SSR. **b.** The language of the Soviet Georgians. **3.** A person belonging to or whose style is imitative of the period of the first four Georges of England.

geor·gic (jôr′jĭk) also **geor·gi·cal** (-jĭ-kəl) *adj.* Of or pertaining to agriculture or rural life. *—n.* A poem concerning farming or rural life. [Lat. *georgicus* < Gk. *geōrgikos* < *geōrgos,* farmer : *gē,* earth + *ergon,* work.]

ge·o·sci·ence (jē′ō-sī′əns) *n.* Any of the sciences, as geology or geochemistry, dealing with the earth. **—ge′o·sci′en·tist** *n.*

ge·o·sta·tion·ar·y (jē′ō-stā′shə-nĕr′ē) *adj.* Of or pertaining to a satellite that travels about the earth's equator at an altitude of at least 35,000 kilometers at a speed matching that of the earth's rotation, thus maintaining a constant relation to points on the earth.

ge·o·stroph·ic (jē′ə-strŏf′ĭk) *adj.* Of or pertaining to force caused by the earth's rotation. [GEO- + Gk. *strophē,* a turning < *strephein,* to turn.] **—ge′o·stroph′i·cal·ly** *adv.*

GEOLOGIC TIME SCALE

ERA	PERIOD	EPOCH	YEARS BEFORE THE PRESENT
Cenozoic	Quaternary	Holocene (Recent)	11,000
		Pleistocene (Glacial)	500,000 to 2,000,000
	Tertiary	Pliocene	13,000,000
		Miocene	25,000,000
		Oligocene	36,000,000
		Eocene	58,000,000
		Paleocene	63,000,000
Mesozoic	Cretaceous		135,000,000
	Jurassic		180,000,000
	Triassic		230,000,000
Paleozoic	Permian		280,000,000
	Carboniferous: Pennsylvanian (Upper Carboniferous)		310,000,000
	Carboniferous: Mississippian (Lower Carboniferous)		345,000,000
	Devonian		405,000,000
	Silurian		425,000,000
	Ordovician		500,000,000
	Cambrian		600,000,000
Precambrian			

ge·o·syn·chro·nous (jē′ō-sĭng′krə-nəs, -sĭn′-) *adj.* Geostationary. **—ge′o·syn′chro·nous·ly** *adv.*

ge·o·syn·cline (jē′ō-sĭn′klīn′) *n.* An extensive, usually linear depression in the earth's crust in which a succession of sedimentary strata has accumulated. **—ge′o·syn·cli′nal** (-sĭn-klī′nəl) *adj.*

ge·o·tax·is (jē′ō-tăk′sĭs) *n. Biol.* The movement of an organism in response to the forces of gravity. **—ge′o·tac′tic** (-tĭk) *adj.* **—ge′o·tac′ti·cal·ly** *adv.*

ge·o·tec·ton·ic (jē′ō-tĕk-tŏn′ĭk) *adj.* Of or relating to the shape, structure, and arrangement of the rock masses constituting the earth's crust.

ge·o·ther·mal (jē′ō-thûr′məl) also **ge·o·ther·mic** (-mĭk) *adj.* Of or pertaining to the internal heat of the earth. **—ge′o·ther′mal·ly** *adv.*

ge·ot·ro·pism (jē-ŏt′rə-pĭz′əm) *n. Biol.* The response of a living organism to gravity, as the downward growth of plant roots. **—ge′o·tro′pic** (jē′ə-trō′pĭk, -trŏp′ĭk) *adj.* **—ge′o·tro′pi·cal·ly** *adv.*

ge·rah (gîr′ə) *n.* An ancient Hebrew coin and unit of weight. [Heb. *gērāh.*]

geranium

Ge·raint (jə-rānt′) *n.* In Arthurian legend, a knight of the Round Table and husband of Enid.

ge·ra·ni·ol (jə-rā′nē-ôl′, -ōl′) *n.* A fragrant pale-yellow liquid, $C_{10}H_{18}O$, derived chiefly from the oils of geranium and citronella, and used in cosmetics and flavorings. [GERANI(UM) + -OL[1].]

ge·ra·ni·um (jə-rā′nē-əm) *n.* **1.** Any of various plants of the genus *Geranium,* having divided leaves and pink or purplish flowers. **2.** Any of various plants of the genus *Pelargonium,* native chiefly to southern Africa, esp. *P. domesticum,* widely cultivated for its rounded, often variegated leaves and showy clusters of red, pink, or white flowers. **3.** A strong to vivid red. [NLat. *Geranium,* genus name < Lat. *geranium,* stork's-bill < Gk. *geranion* < *geranos,* crane.]

ger·bil (jûr′bəl) *n.* Any of various small, mouselike rodents of the genus *Gerbillus* and related genera, of arid regions of Africa and Asia Minor, having long hind legs and a long tail. [NLat. *Gerbillus,* genus name < Fr. *gerbo,* jerboa < Ar. *yerbō′*.]

ge·rent (jĭr′ənt) *n. Archaic.* A ruler or manager; overseer. [< Lat. *gerens, gerent-,* pr.part. of *gerere,* to manage.]

ger·e·nuk (gĕr′ə-no͝ok′) *n.* An African gazelle, *Litocranius walleri,* having long legs, a long, slender neck, and backward curving horns in the male. [Somali *garanūg.*]

ger·fal·con (jûr′făl′kən, -fôl′-, -fô′-) *n.* Variant of **gyrfalcon.**

ger·i·at·ric (jĕr′ē-ăt′rĭk) *adj.* **1.** Of or pertaining to geriatrics. **2.** Of or pertaining to the aged or their characteristic afflictions. —*n.* An aged person viewed as an object of geriatrics or geriatric care. [Gk. *gēras,* old age + -IATRIC.]

ger·i·at·rics (jĕr′ē-ăt′rĭks) *n. (used with a sing. verb).* The medical study of the physiology and pathology of old age. **—ger′i·a·tri′cian** (-ə-trĭsh′ən), **ger′i·at′rist** (-rĭst, jə-rī′ə-trĭst) *n.*

germ (jûrm) *n.* **1.** *Biol.* A small organic structure or cell from which a new organism may develop. **2.** Something that may serve as the basis of further growth or development: *the germ of a program.* **3.** *Med.* A microorganism, esp. a pathogen. [Fr. *germe* < Lat. *germen,* bud.]

ger·man[1] (jûr′mən) *n.* **1.** An intricate dance for many couples. **2.** A party for dancing at which the german is featured. [Short for *German cotillion.*]

ger·man[2] (jûr′mən) *adj.* Having the same parents, or having the same grandparents on one side: *cousin-german.* [ME *germain* < OFr. < Lat. *germanus* < *germen,* offshoot.]

Ger·man (jûr′mən) *adj.* Of, pertaining to, or characteristic of Germany, its people, or their language. —*n.* **1. a.** A native or inhabitant of Germany. **b.** A person of German descent. **2.** The West Germanic language of Germany, Austria, and part of Switzerland. [Med. Lat. *Germanus* < Lat., perh. of Celt. orig.]

German cockroach *n.* The Croton bug.

ger·man·der (jər-măn′dər) *n.* Any of various usually aromatic plants of the genus *Teucrium,* with purplish or reddish flowers. [ME *germandre* < OFr. *germandree* < Med. Lat. *germandra,* alteration of *gamandrea* < LGk. *khamandrua* < Gk. *khamaidrus* : *khamai,* on the ground + *drus,* oak.]

ger·mane (jər-mān′) *adj.* Having a significant bearing upon a point at hand; pertinent: *an issue not germane to the present situation.* [ME *germain,* having the same parents. —see GERMAN[2].]

Ger·man·ic (jər-măn′ĭk) *adj.* **1. a.** Of, pertaining to, or characteristic of Germany or of the German people or their culture. **b.** Of or pertaining to Teutons. **c.** Of or pertaining to people who speak a Germanic language. **2.** Of, pertaining to, or constituting the Germanic languages. —*n.* A branch of the Indo-European language family that comprises North Germanic, West Germanic, and East Germanic.

Ger·man·ism (jûr′mə-nĭz′əm) *n.* **1.** An attitude, custom, or feature that seems characteristically German. **2.** A German idiom or phrasing appearing in another language. **3.** Esteem for Germany and emulation of German ways.

gerbil

ger·ma·ni·um (jər-mā′nē-əm) *n. Symbol* **Ge** A brittle, crystalline, gray-white metalloid element, widely used as a semiconductor, as an alloying agent and catalyst, and in certain optical glasses. Atomic number 32; atomic weight 72.59; melting point 937.4°C; boiling point 2,830°C; specific gravity 5.323 (25°C); valences 2, 4. [< Lat. *Germanus,* German.]

Ger·man·ize (jûr′mə-nīz′) *v.* **-ized, -iz·ing, -iz·es.** —*tr.* **1.** To give a German quality to. **2.** *Archaic.* To translate into German. —*intr.* To adopt German customs or attitudes. **—Ger′man·i·za′tion** *n.* **—Ger′man·iz′er** *n.*

German shepherd

German measles *n.* A mild, contagious, eruptive disease caused by a virus and capable of causing congenital defects in infants born to mothers infected during the first three months of pregnancy.

Ger·man·o·phile (jər-măn′ə-fīl′) *n.* One who loves Germany and German things.

Ger·man·o·phobe (jər-măn′ə-fōb′) *n.* One who hates or has an obsessive fear of Germany and German things.

German shepherd *n.* A large dog of a breed developed in Germany, having a dense brownish or black coat, and often trained to assist the police and the blind.

German silver *n.* Nickel silver.

germ cell *n.* A cell having reproduction as its principal function, esp. an egg or sperm cell.

gerrymander
Contemporary political cartoon showing a gerrymandered Massachusetts election district in the shape of a monster

ger·mi·cide (jûr′mĭ-sīd′) *n.* An agent that kills germs. **—ger′mi·ci′dal** (-sīd′l) *adj.*

ger·mi·nal (jûr′mə-nəl) *adj.* **1.** Of, pertaining to, or having the nature of a germ cell. **2.** Of, in, or pertaining to the earliest stage of development: *was active in the germinal stages of the space program.* [Fr. < Lat. *germen,* seed.] **—ger′mi·nal·ly** *adv.*

germinal disc *n.* A disklike region from which the embryo begins to develop in certain ova.

germinal vesicle *n.* The nucleus of an oocyte.

ger·mi·nate (jûr′mə-nāt′) *intr. & tr.v.* **-nat·ed, -nat·ing, -nates.** To begin to or cause to grow; sprout. [Lat. *germinare, germinat-,* to sprout < *germen,* seed.] **—ger′mi·na·ble** (-nə-bəl), **ger′mi·na′tive** *adj.* **—ger′mi·na′tion** *n.* **—ger′mi·na′tor** *n.*

germ layer *n.* Any of three cellular layers, the ectoderm, endoderm, or mesoderm, into which most animal embryos differentiate.

germ plasm *n.* **1.** The cytoplasm of a germ cell. **2.** Germ cells collectively. **3.** Hereditary material; genes.

germ theory *n.* The doctrine that infectious diseases are caused by the activity of microorganisms within the body.

germ warfare *n.* The use of disease germs as weapons in warfare.

geronto– or **geront–** *pref.* Old age; aged one: *gerontology.* [Fr. *géronto-* < Gk. *gerōn,* old man.]

ger·on·toc·ra·cy (jĕr′ən-tŏk′rə-sē) *n., pl.* **-cies. 1.** Government based on rule by the elders. **2.** A governing group of elders. **—ge·ron′to·crat′ic** (jə-rŏn′tə-krăt′ĭk) *adj.*

ger·on·tol·o·gy (jĕr′ən-tŏl′ə-jē) *n.* The scientific study of the physiological and pathological phenomena associated with aging. **—ge·ron′to·log′i·cal** (jə-rŏn′tə-lŏj′ĭ-kəl), **ge·ron′to·log′ic** (-lŏj′ĭk) *adj.* **—ger′on·tol′o·gist** *n.*

ger·ry·man·der (jĕr′ē-măn′dər, gĕr′-) *tr.v.* **-dered, -der·ing, -ders.** To divide (a geographic area) into voting districts to give unfair advantage to one party in elections. —*n.* An act, process, or instance of gerrymandering. [After Elbridge *Gerry* (1744–1814) + (SALA)MANDER (from the shape of an election district created while Gerry was governor of Massachusetts).]

ger·und (jĕr′ənd) *n.* **1.** A verbal form in Latin that functions as a noun. **2.** A form, such as English *cooking,* that is analogous to the gerund in languages other than Latin. [LLat. *gerundium* < Lat. *gerundum,* var. of *gerendum,* gerund of *gerere,* to carry on.] **—ge·run′di·al** (jə-rŭn′dē-əl) *adj.*

ge·run·dive (jə-rŭn′dĭv) *n.* **1.** The future passive participle that functions adjectivally and expresses the notion of fitness or necessity. **2.** A verbal adjective analogous to the gerundive in a language other than Latin. [ME *gerundif* < LLat. *gerundivus* < *gerundium.* —see GERUND.]

Ge·ry·on (jîr′ē-ən, gĕr′-) *n. Gk. Myth.* A winged monster with three bodies who was slain by Hercules. [Lat. < Gk. *Gēruōn.*]

ges·so (jĕs′ō) *n.* **1.** A preparation of plaster of paris and glue used as a base for low relief or as a surface for painting. **2.** A surface of gesso. [Ital. < *gesso,* gypsum < Lat. *gypsum.* —see GYPSUM.]

gest or **geste** (jĕst) *n. Archaic.* **1.** A notable feat or exploit. **2. a.** A verse romance or tale. **b.** A prose romance. [ME *geste.* —see JEST.]

ge·stalt or **Ge·stalt** (gə-shtält′, -shtôlt′) *n., pl.* **-stalts** or **-stalt·en** (-shtält′n, -shtôlt′n). A physical, psychological, or symbolic configuration or pattern so unified as a whole that its properties cannot be derived from its parts. [G., shape < MHG, shaped, p.part. of *stellen,* to place < OHG.]

Gestalt psychology *n.* A psychological school or doctrine holding that psychological phenomena are irreducible gestalts.

Ge·sta·po (gə-stä′pō, -shtä′-) *n.* The German internal security police as organized under the Nazi regime, known for its terrorist methods directed against those suspected of treason or questionable loyalty. [G. *Ge(heime) Sta(ats)po(lizei),* secret state police.]

ges·tate (jĕs′tāt′) *tr.v.* **-tat·ed, -tat·ing, -tates. 1.** To carry (unborn young) within the uterus for a period following conception. **2.** To conceive and develop in the mind. [Back-formation < GESTATION.]

ges·ta·tion (jĕ-stā′shən) *n.* **1.** The period of carrying developing offspring in the uterus after conception; pregnancy. **2.** The conception and development of a plan or idea in the mind. [Lat. *gestatio,* a carrying < *gestare,* freq. of *gerere,* to carry.] **—ges′ta·to′ry** (jĕs′tə-tôr′ē, -tōr′ē), **ges·ta′tion·al** *adj.*

geste (jĕst) *n.* Variant of **gest.**

ges·tic (jĕs′tĭk) *adj.* Pertaining to movement of the body, esp. in dancing. [< obs. *gest,* bearing < Fr. *geste* < Lat. *gestus* < *gerere,* to bear.]

ges·tic·u·late (jĕ-stĭk′yə-lāt′) *v.* **-lat·ed, -lat·ing, -lates.** —*intr.* To make gestures, esp. to do so to add force or emphasis during speech. —*tr.* To say or express by gestures. [Lat. *gesticulari, gesticulat-* < *gesticulus,* gesticulation, dim. of *gestus,* gesture < p.part. of *gerere,* to behave.] **—ges·tic′u·la′tive** *adj.* **—ges·tic′u·la′tor** *n.*

ges·tic·u·la·tion (jĕ-stĭk′yə-lā′shən) *n.* **1.** The act of gesticulating. **2.** A deliberate and vigorous motion or gesture. **—ges·tic′u·la·to′ry** (-lə-tôr′ē, -tōr′ē) *adj.*

ges·ture (jĕs′chər) *n.* **1.** A motion of the limbs or body made to express or help express thought or to emphasize speech. **2.** The act of moving the limbs or body as an expression of thought or emphasis. **3.** An act or expression made as a sign, often formal, of intention or attitude. *—v.* **-tured, -tur·ing, -tures.** *—intr.* To make gestures. *—tr.* To show, express, or direct by gestures. [ME < Med. Lat. *gestura,* bearing < Lat. *gestus* < p.part. of *gerere,* to behave.] **—ges'tur·er** *n.*

Ge·sund·heit (gə-zo͝ont'hīt') *interj.* Used to wish good health to a person who has just sneezed. [G.]

get (gĕt) *v.* **got** (gŏt), **got** or **got·ten** (gŏt'n), **get·ting, gets.** *—tr.* **1.** To obtain or come into possession of. **2.** To go after and obtain: *got a book from the library.* **3.** To take esp. by force; seize. **4.** To acquire as a result of action or effort: *got a prize for high achievement.* **5.** To acquire involuntarily; catch: *get the mumps.* **6.** To have current possession of. Used in the present perfect with the meaning of the present: *has got a large collection of English porcelain.* **7.** To beget. **8. a.** To cause to assume or be in a specified state or condition: *got the children tired and cross.* **b.** To make ready; prepare: *get lunch for a crowd.* **9.** To cause to come or go. **10.** To cause to undertake or perform: *got the guide to give us the complete tour.* **11.** To have as an obligation. Used in the present perfect with the meaning of the present: *We have got to leave early.* **12. a.** To evoke an emotional response or reaction in: *Romantic music really gets him.* **b.** To annoy; irritate. **13. a.** To take revenge on: *swore to get him for his betrayal.* **b.** To kill in revenge for a wrong. **14. a.** To hit; strike: *got him on the chin.* **b.** To receive as retribution or punishment. **c.** To inflict ruin or destruction upon. **15. a.** To gain or have understanding of. **b.** To learn by heart; memorize. **c.** To find or reach by calculating: *get a total.* **16.** To present a difficult problem to; puzzle: *What gets me is how so many people can believe his lies.* **17.** To perceive by hearing: *didn't get his name when we were introduced.* **18.** To make contact with, as by telephone. **19.** *Baseball.* To put out. *—intr. Informal.* **1.** To reach a certain state or condition: *got well.* **2.** To arrive: *When will we get to New York?* **3.** To start or come to be doing something: *Get going!* **4.** (gĭt). *Regional & Informal.* To depart immediately. **5.** To work for gain or profit; make money. ***—phrasal verbs.*** **get across. 1.** To make understandable or clear. **2.** To be convincing or understandable. **get along. 1.** To be in harmony. **2.** To manage or fare with reasonable success. **3.** To advance, esp. in years. **get around. 1.** To evade; circumvent. **2.** *Informal.* To convince or win over by flattering or cajoling. **get away with.** *Informal.* To be successful in avoiding retribution or criticism for. **get back at.** *Informal.* To take revenge on. **get by. 1.** To succeed with the minimum amount of effort. **2.** To manage; survive: *We'll get by if we economize.* **get off. 1.** To write and send, as a letter. **2.** To escape, as from punishment or danger: *He got off scot-free.* **3.** To obtain a release or lesser penalty for. **4.** *Slang.* To have an orgasm. **5.** *Slang.* To get high, as from a drug. **6.** *Slang.* To feel great pleasure or gratification. **get on. 1.** To get along. **2.** To advance: *is getting on in years.* **get on the stick.** *Slang.* To begin working, esp. immediately or energetically. **get to.** *Informal.* To happen to start; begin: *got to remembering good times.* **get up.** To act as the creator or organizer of: *got up a petition against rezoning.* *—n.* **1.** The act of begetting. **2.** Progeny; offspring. **3.** A return in tennis on a shot that seems impossible to reach. ***—idioms.*** **get it.** *Informal.* To be punished or scolded. **get nowhere.** To make no progress; have no success. **get there.** To achieve success. [ME *geten* < ON *geta.*] **—get'a·ble, get'ta·ble** *adj.*

Usage: *Get* has a great number of uses, some of which are acceptable at all levels and some of which are generally felt to be informal (though never incorrect). Some uses better avoided in writing are: (1) The use of *get* in place of *be* or *become* in sentences such as *He got arrested.* (2) The use of *get* or *get to* in place of *start* or *begin,* as in *When he gets* (or *gets to*) *reminiscing, he can't stop.* (3) The use of *have got to* in place of *must* in sentences like *I have got to go now.*

get·a·way (gĕt'ə-wā') *n.* **1.** The act or instance of escaping. **2.** The start, as of a race; takeoff. ***—modifier:*** *a getaway car.*

Geth·sem·a·ne (gĕth-sĕm'ə-nē) *n.* **1.** In the New Testament, the garden outside Jerusalem that was the scene of the agony and arrest of Jesus. **2. gethsemane.** An instance or place of great suffering. [Gk. *Gethsēmanē.*]

get·ter (gĕt'ər) *n.* **1.** One that gets. **2.** A material added in small amounts during a chemical or metallurgical process to absorb impurities.

get-to·geth·er (gĕt'tə-gĕth'ər) *n. Informal.* A small party.

get-up (gĕt'ŭp') *n.* **1.** An outfit or costume. **2.** The arrangement and production style, as of a magazine or book. **3.** Also **get-up-and-go.** Energy and ambition; spunk.

gew·gaw (gyo͞o'gô') *n.* A decorative trinket; bauble. [Orig. unknown.]

gey·ser (gī'zər) *n.* **1.** A natural hot spring that intermittently ejects a column of water and steam into the air. **2.** (gē'zər). *Chiefly Brit.* A gas-operated hot-water heater. [Icel. *Geysir,* name of a hot spring in Iceland < *geysa,* to gush < ON.]

gey·ser·ite (gī'zə-rīt') *n.* An opaline siliceous deposit formed around natural hot springs.

ghast·ly (găst'lē) *adj.* **-li·er, -li·est. 1.** Causing or arousing terror or dread; frightening or repellent: *a ghastly accident.* **2.** Suggestive of ghosts or death. **3.** Extremely unpleasant or bad: *"in the most abominable passage of his ghastly little book"* (Conor Cruise O'Brien). **4.** Very serious or great: *a ghastly error.* [ME *gastli* < *gasten,* to terrify < OE *gæstan.*] **—ghast'li·ness** *n.*

Synonyms: *ghastly, grim, gruesome, grisly, macabre, lurid.* These adjectives describe what is extremely forbidding in apsect. *Ghastly* implies having an appearance that suggests death or otherwise inspires shock or horror. *Grim* refers to what repels because of its stern or fierce aspect or its harsh, relentless nature. *Gruesome* and *grisly* describe what horrifies or revolts because of its crudity or utter inhumanity. *Macabre* implies an aspect that suggests or represents death in a bizarre or grotesque way rather than in naturalistic terms. *Lurid* sometimes describes physical appearance that suggests death or destruction, but more often refers to what shocks because of the vividness of its sensationalism or unsavoriness.

ghat also **ghaut** (gôt, gät) *n.* A broad flight of steps down to the bank of a river. [Hindi *ghāt* < Skt. *ghattah.*]

gha·zi (gä'zē) *n., pl.* **-zies.** A Moslem warrior who has fought successfully against infidels, often used as a title of honor. [Ar. *ghāzī,* pr.part. of *ghazā,* he fought.]

ghee (gē) *n.* A semifluid clarified butter used esp. in India. [Hindi *ghī* < Skt. *ghṛtam.*]

gher·kin (gûr'kĭn) *n.* **1. a.** A tropical American vine, *Cucumis anguria,* bearing prickly, edible fruit. **b.** The fruit of the gherkin. **2.** A small cucumber, esp. one used for pickling. [Du. *agurkje,* pickled gherkin, ult. < LGk. *angourion.*]

ghet·to (gĕt'ō) *n., pl.* **-tos** or **-toes. 1.** A slum section of a city occupied by a minority group who live there because of social or economic pressure. **2.** A section or quarter in a European city to which Jews are or were restricted. **3.** Something that resembles the isolation or restriction of a ghetto. ***—modifier:*** *ghetto children.* [Ital.]

ghet·to·ize (gĕt'ō-īz') *tr.v.* **-ized, -iz·ing, -iz·es.** To set apart in or as if in a ghetto; isolate. **—ghet'to·i·za'tion** *n.*

Ghib·el·line (gĭb'ə-lēn', -līn', -lĭn) *n.* A member of the aristocratic political faction who fought during the Middle Ages for German imperial control of Italy. [Ital. *Ghibellino.*]

ghil·lie also **gil·lie** (gĭl'ē) *n., pl.* **-lies.** A low-cut sports shoe with fringed laces. [Sc. Gael. *gille,* servant.]

ghost (gōst) *n.* **1.** The spirit of a dead person, thought to haunt living persons or former habitats. **2.** *Archaic.* The animus or soul, as opposed to the body. **3.** A demon or spirit. **4.** A returning or haunting memory or image. **5.** A slight trace or bit: *a ghost of a chance.* **6.** A faint, false, sometimes secondary, photographic or television image. **7.** One who ghostwrites. **8.** A nonexistent publication listed in bibliographies. *—v.* **ghost·ed, ghost·ing, ghosts.** *—intr. Informal.* To work as a ghostwriter. *—tr.* **1.** To haunt. **2.** *Informal.* To write (something) as a ghostwriter. [ME *gost* < OE *gāst.*]

ghost crab *n.* Any of several light-colored burrowing crabs of the genus *Ocypoda,* frequenting the tide line along sandy shores.

ghost dance *n.* Either of two religious dances practiced by certain North American Indians during the latter half of the 19th century to invoke a return of their former condition.

ghost·ly (gōst'lē) *adj.* **-li·er, -li·est. 1.** Pertaining to or resembling a ghost, wraith, or apparition; spectral. **2.** Pertaining to the spirit or to religion; spiritual. **—ghost'li·ness** *n.*

ghost town *n.* A town, esp. a boom town of the West, that has been completely abandoned.

ghost word *n.* A word that has come into a language through the perpetuation of a misreading of a manuscript, a typographical error, or a misunderstanding.

ghost·write (gōst'rīt') *v.* **-wrote** (-rōt'), **-writ·ten** (-rĭt'n), **-writ·ing, -writes.** *—intr.* To work as a ghostwriter. *—tr.* To write (something) as a ghostwriter.

ghost·writ·er (gōst'rī'tər) *n.* A person who writes for and gives credit of authorship to another person.

ghoul (go͞ol) *n.* **1.** An evil spirit or demon in Moslem folklore believed to plunder graves and feed on corpses. **2.** A grave robber. **3.** One who delights in the revolting or loathsome. [Ar. *ghūl* < *ghāla,* he took suddenly.] **—ghoul'ish** *adj.* **—ghoul'ish·ly** *adv.* **—ghoul'ish·ness** *n.*

GI (jē'ī') *n., pl.* **GIs** or **GI's.** An enlisted person in or veteran of any of the U.S. armed forces. *—adj.* **1.** Pertaining to or characteristic of a GI. **2.** In conformity to or accordance with U.S. military regulations or procedures. **3.** Issued by an official U.S. military supply department. [Abbrev. for *government issue.*]

gi·ant (jī'ənt) *n.* **1. a.** A person or thing of extraordinary size. **b.** A person of extraordinary power, significance, or importance: *He is a giant in his field.* **2.** *Gk. Myth.* One of a race of manlike beings of enormous strength and stature who warred with the Olympians and by whom they were finally destroyed. **3.** A being in folklore or myth similar to a giant. [ME *geaunt* < OFr. *geant* < VLat. **gagante* < Lat. *gigas* < Gk.]

gi·ant·ism (jī'ən-tĭz'əm) *n.* **1.** The condition of being a giant. **2.** Gigantism (sense 1.).

giant panda *n.* A panda (sense 1.).

giant sequoia *n.* A very tall evergreen tree, *Sequoia gigantea,* of mountainous regions of southern California, having a massive trunk and light-colored, reddish wood.

geyser

ghost town
Virginia City, Montana

gibbon

giant star *n.* Any of a class of highly luminous, exceptionally massive stars.

giaour (jour) *n. Islam.* A nonbeliever, esp. a Christian; infidel. [Ult. < Pers. *gaur,* infidel, var. of *gebr,* fire worshipper.]

gib (gĭb) *n.* A plain or notched, often wedge-shaped, piece of wood or metal designed to hold parts of a machine or structure in place or to provide a bearing surface, usually adjusted by a screw or key. [Orig. unknown.]

gib·ber (jĭb′ər) *intr.v.* **-bered, -ber·ing, -bers.** To prattle and chatter unintelligibly. —*n.* Senseless talk or prate. [Imit.]

gib·ber·el·lic acid (jĭb′ə-rĕl′ĭk) *n.* A substance, $C_{19}H_{22}O_6$, produced from a fungus, *Gibberella fujikuroi,* and used to promote the growth of plants, esp. seedlings. [< GIBBEREL-LIN.]

gib·ber·el·lin (jĭb′ə-rĕl′ĭn) *n.* Any of several substances of plant origin, as gibberellic acid, used to promote stem growth of plants. [< NLat. *Gibberella (fujikoroi),* the fungus from which gibberellin was first isolated.]

gib·ber·ish (jĭb′ər-ĭsh) *n.* Nonsensical, rapid talk; prattle.

gib·bet (jĭb′ĭt) *n.* **1.** A gallows. **2.** An upright post with a crosspiece, forming a T-shaped structure from which executed criminals were hung for public viewing. —*tr.v.* **-bet·ed, -bet·ing, -bets** or **-bet·ted, -bet·ting, -bets. 1.** To execute by hanging. **2.** To hang on a gibbet for public viewing. **3.** To expose to infamy or public ridicule. [ME *gibet* < OFr., dim. of *gibe,* staff, perh. of Germanic orig.]

gib·bon (gĭb′ən) *n.* Any of several arboreal apes of the genera *Hylobates* or *Symphalangus,* of tropical Asia, having a slender body and long arms. [Fr.]

gib·bos·i·ty (gĭ-bŏs′ĭ-tē) *n., pl.* **-ties. 1.** The condition of being gibbous. **2.** A rounded hump or protuberance.

gib·bous (gĭb′əs) *adj.* **1.** Characterized by convexity; protuberant. **2.** More than half but less than fully illuminated. Used of the moon or a planet: *"the gibbous moon, its light reflecting whitely"* (John Barth). **3.** Having a hump; humpbacked. [ME, bulging < Lat. *gibbus,* hump.] —**gib′bous·ly** *adv.* —**gib′bous·ness** *n.*

gibe (jīb) *v.* **gibed, gib·ing, gibes.** —*intr.* To make heckling or mocking remarks. —*tr.* To reproach by taunting; scoff. —*n.* A derisive remark. [Poss. < OFr. *giber,* to handle roughly.] —**gib′er** *n.* —**gib′ing·ly** *adv.*

gib·let (jĭb′lĭt) *n.* The heart, liver, or gizzard of a fowl, esp. when considered as a kind of meat. [ME *gibelet* < OFr.]

Gib·son (gĭb′sən) *n.* A dry martini having a small pickled onion in place of an olive or a twist of lemon peel. [< the name *Gibson.*]

Gibson girl *n.* The American girl of the 1890's as idealized in sketches by Charles Dana Gibson.

Gila monster

gid (gĭd) *n.* A disease of sheep caused by the presence of the larva of a tapeworm, *Taenia caenurus,* in the brain, and resulting in a staggering gait. [Back-formation < GIDDY.]

gid·dy (gĭd′ē) *adj.* **-di·er, -di·est. 1. a.** Having a reeling, lightheaded sensation; dizzy. **b.** Causing or capable of causing dizziness: *a giddy climb to the topmast.* **2.** Frivolous and lighthearted; flighty. —*intr. & tr.v.* **-died, -dy·ing, -dies.** To become or make giddy. [ME *gidi,* crazy < OE *gidig.*] —**gid′di·ly** *adv.* —**gid′di·ness** *n.*

Gid·e·on (gĭd′ē-ən) *n.* In the Old Testament, a judge of Israel and conqueror of the Midianites. [Heb. *Gidh'ōn* < *gādha,* he hewed.]

gie (gē) *v. Scot.* Variant of **give.**

gift (gĭft) *n.* **1.** Something that is bestowed voluntarily and without compensation. **2.** The act, right, or power of giving: *Your request is not in my gift.* **3.** A talent, endowment, aptitude, or bent. —*tr.v.* **gift·ed, gift·ing, gifts. 1.** To present with a gift. **2.** To endow with; invest. [ME < ON.]

Usage: *Gift* (verb) has a long history of use in the sense "to present as a gift, to endow": *He gifted her with a necklace.* In current use, however, *gift* in this sense is sometimes regarded as affected and is unacceptable to a large majority of the Usage Panel.

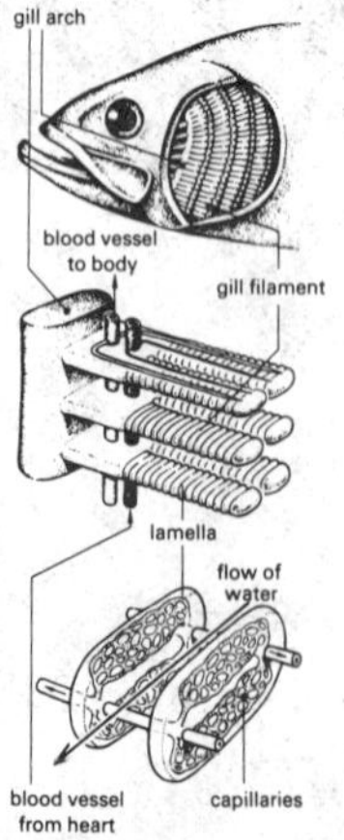

gill[1]
Gill of a fish with operculum removed and enlarged portions showing structural details

gift·ed (gĭf′tĭd) *adj.* **1.** Endowed with natural ability, talent, or other assets: *a gifted child.* **2.** Revealing talent: *a gifted rendition of an aria.* —**gift′ed·ly** *adv.* —**gift′ed·ness** *n.*

gift of tongues *n.* An ecstatic utterance that is partly or wholly unintelligible to hearers, esp. such an utterance as practiced liturgically in certain Christian congregations.

gig[1] (gĭg) *n.* **1.** A light, two-wheeled carriage drawn by one horse. **2. a.** A long, light ship's boat having oars, sails, or a motor, and usually reserved for use by the ship's captain. **b.** A fast, light rowboat. —*intr.v.* **gigged, gig·ging, gigs.** To ride in a gig. [< obs. *gig,* spinning top.]

gig[2] (gĭg) *n.* **1.** An arrangement of barbless hooks that is dragged through a school of fish to hook them in the bodies. **2.** A pronged spear for fishing. —*v.* **gigged, gig·ging, gigs.** —*tr.* **1.** To catch with a gig. **2.** *Regional.* To goad; prod. —*intr.* To fish with a gig. [Short for FISHGIG.]

gig[3] (gĭg) *Slang.* —*n.* A demerit, esp. one in the military that is assigned as a punishment. —*tr.v.* **gigged, gig·ging, gigs.** To give a demerit to. [Orig. unknown.]

gig[4] (gĭg) *n. Slang.* A job, esp. a booking for musicians. [Orig. unknown.]

giga- *pref.* One billion (10^9): *gigahertz.* [< Gk. *gigas,* giant.]

gig·a·bit (jĭg′ə-bĭt′, gĭg′-) *n. Computer Sci.* One billion (10^9) bits.

gig·a·cy·cle (jĭg′ə-sī′kəl, gĭg′-) *n.* One billion (10^9) cycles.

gig·a·hertz (jĭg′ə-hûrtz, gĭg′-) *n.* One billion (10^9) hertz.

gi·gan·tesque (jī′găn-tĕsk′) *adj.* Pertaining to or suggestive of a giant; huge. [Fr. < Ital. *gigantesco* < Gk. *gigas,* giant.]

gi·gan·tic (jī-găn′tĭk) *adj.* **1.** Pertaining to or suggestive of a giant. **2. a.** Exceedingly large of its kind. **b.** Very large or extensive: *a gigantic radio network.* [< Lat. *gigas, gigant-,* giant < Gk.] —**gi·gan′ti·cal·ly** *adv.*

gi·gan·tism (jī-găn′tĭz′əm) *n.* **1.** Excessive growth of the body or any of its parts as a result of oversecretion of the pituitary growth hormone. **2.** Abnormal size.

gig·gle (gĭg′əl) *intr.v.* **-gled, -gling, -gles.** To laugh with repeated short, high-pitched sounds. —*n.* A high-pitched, spasmodic laugh. [Imit.] —**gig′gler** *n.* —**gig′gling·ly** *adv.* —**gig′gly** *adj.*

gig·o·lo (jĭg′ə-lō′, zhĭg′-) *n., pl.* **-los. 1.** A man who is kept as a lover and supported by a woman. **2.** A man who is hired as an escort or dancing partner for a woman. [Fr.]

gig·ot (jĭg′ət, zhē-gō′) *n.* **1.** A leg of mutton, lamb, or veal for cooking. **2.** A leg-of-mutton sleeve. [OFr., dim. of *gigue,* leg, of Germanic orig.]

gigue (zhēg) *n. Mus.* **1.** The jig (sense 1.). **2. a.** A lively dance form in 6/8, 9/8, or 12/8 time, often forming the final movement of a suite. **b.** The music for this dance. [Fr. < E. JIG.]

Gi·la monster (hē′lə) *n.* A venomous lizard, *Heloderma suspectum,* of the southwestern United States, covered with black and pinkish or yellowish scales. [After *Gila* River, Arizona.]

gil·bert (gĭl′bərt) *n.* The centimeter-gram-second electromagnetic unit of magnetomotive force, equal to $10/4\pi$ ampere-turn. [After William *Gilbert* (1836–1911).]

gild[1] (gĭld) *tr.v.* **gild·ed** or **gilt** (gĭlt), **gild·ing, gilds. 1.** To cover with or as if with a thin layer of gold. **2.** To give an often deceptively attractive or improved appearance to. **3.** *Archaic.* To smear with blood. —***idiom.* gild the lily.** To adorn unnecessarily something already beautiful. [ME *gilden* < OE *gyldan.*] —**gild′er** *n.*

gild[2] (gĭld) *n.* Variant of **guild.**

gild·ing (gĭl′dĭng) *n.* **1.** The art or process of applying gilt to a surface. **2.** Gold leaf or a paint containing or simulating gold; gilt. **3.** Something employed to give a superficially attractive appearance.

Gil·ga·mesh (gĭl′gə-mĕsh′) *n. Babylonian Myth.* The semidivine king of Erech and hero of an epic collection of mythic tales, one of which tells of a flood that covered the earth. [Of Sumerian orig.]

gill[1] (gĭl) *n.* **1.** *Zool.* The respiratory organ of fishes, larval amphibians, and numerous aquatic invertebrates. **2.** Often **gills.** The wattle of a bird. **3.** Often **gills.** *Informal.* The area around the chin and neck. **4.** *Bot.* One of the thin, platelike structures on the underside of the cap of a mushroom or similar fungus. —*tr.v.* **gilled, gill·ing, gills. 1.** To catch (fish) in a gill net. **2.** To gut or clean (fish). [ME *gile,* of Scand. orig.]

gill[2] (jĭl) *n.* **1.** A unit of volume or capacity in the U.S. Customary System, used in liquid measure, equal to 4 fluid ounces (1/4 pint) or 23.656 milliliters. **2.** A unit of volume or capacity in the British Imperial System, used in dry and liquid measure, equal to 5 fluid ounces (1/4 pint) or 28.423 milliliters. [ME *gille* < Med. Lat. *gillo,* a pot.]

gill[3] (gĭl) *n. Chiefly Brit.* **1.** A ravine. **2.** A narrow stream. [ME *gille* < ON *gil.*]

gill[4] also **Gill** (jĭl) *n.* A girl; sweetheart. [ME *gille* < *Gille,* a woman's name.]

gill fungus (gĭl) *n.* A fleshy fungus having a cap with gills on the underside.

gil·lie also **gil·ly** (gĭl′ē) *n., pl.* **-lies. 1.** *Scot.* A professional guide for fishing and deerstalking. **2.** Variant of **ghillie.** [Sc. Gael. *gille.*]

gill net (gĭl) *n.* A fishing net set vertically in the water so that fish swimming into it are entangled by the gills in its mesh.

gill slit (gĭl) *n.* One of several narrow external openings connecting with the pharynx, present in all vertebrates during embryonic development, and characteristic of sharks and related fishes.

gil·ly·flow·er (gĭl′ē-flou′ər) *n.* **1.** The carnation or a similar plant of the genus *Dianthus.* **2.** Any of several plants having fragrant flowers, as the stock or wallflower. [By folk etymology < ME *gilofre* < OFr. *girofle* < Med. Lat. *corophylum,* clove < Gk. *karuophullon* : *karuon,* nut + *phullon,* leaf.]

Gil·son·ite (gĭl′sə-nīt′). A trademark for a natural black bitumen found in Utah and Colorado, used in the manufacture of acid, alkali, and waterproof coatings.

gilt[1] (gĭlt) *v.* A past tense and past participle of **gild[1]**. —*adj.* **1.** Covered with gold or something simulating gold. **2.** Having the appearance of gold. —*n.* **1.** A thin layer of gold or something simulating it that is applied in gilding. **2. a.** Shining brilliance; glitter. **b.** Superficial brilliance or gloss.

gilt[2] (gĭlt) *n.* A young sow that has not farrowed. [ME, young sow < ON *gyltr.*]

gilt-edged (gĭlt′ĕjd′) also **gilt-edge** (-ĕj′) *adj.* **1.** Having gilded edges, as the pages of a book. **2.** Of the highest quality or value: *gilt-edged securities.*

gim·bal (gĭm′bəl, jĭm′-) *n.* Often **gimbals.** A device consisting of two rings mounted on axes at right angles to each other so that an object, as a ship's compass, will remain suspended in a horizontal plane between them regardless of any motion of its support. [OFr. *gemel.* —see GIMMAL.]

gim·crack (jĭm'krăk') *n.* A cheap and showy object of little or no use; gewgaw. —*adj.* Cheap and shoddy; flimsy. [Orig. unknown.] **—gim'crack'er·y** *n.*

gim·el (gĭm'əl) *n.* The 3rd letter of the Hebrew alphabet. See table at **alphabet**. [Heb. *gīmel.*]

gim·let (gĭm'lĭt) *n.* **1.** A small hand tool for boring holes, having a spiraled shank, a screw tip, and a cross handle. **2.** A cocktail made with vodka or gin and lime juice, garnished with a slice of lime. —*tr.v.* **-let·ed, -let·ing, -lets.** To penetrate with or as if with a gimlet. —*adj.* Having a penetrating or piercing quality: *gimlet eyes.* [ME < AN *guimblet.*]

gim·mal (gĭm'əl, jĭm'-) *n.* A ring made of two narrower rings interlocked. [OFr. *gemel* < Lat. *gemelus,* dim. of *geminus,* twin.]

gim·mick (gĭm'ĭk) *n.* **1.** A device employed, often illegally, to cheat, deceive, or trick, esp. a mechanism for the secret control of a gambling wheel or other apparatus. **2.** A stratagem or scheme employed to promote a project: *an advertising gimmick.* **3.** A significant feature that is obscured or misrepresented; catch. **4.** A trivial or unnecessary innovation, as a gadget, added to enhance appeal. **5.** A small object whose name eludes one. —*tr.v.* **-micked, -mick·ing, -micks.** To add gimmicks to; clutter with gadgets or catchy details: *gimmick up a dress.* [Orig. unknown.] **—gim'mick·ry** *n.* **—gim'mick·y** *adj.*

gimp[1] (gĭmp) *n.* A narrow braid or cord of fabric, sometimes stiffened, used for trimmings. [Prob. < Du.]

gimp[2] (gĭmp) *Slang.* —*n.* **1.** A limp or limping gait. **2.** A person who limps. —*intr.v.* **gimped, gimp·ing, gimps.** To limp. [Orig. unknown.] **—gimp'y** *adj.*

gimp[3] (gĭmp) *n.* Spirit; pep. [Orig. unknown.]

gin[1] (jĭn) *n.* **1.** A strong alcoholic beverage made by distilling rye or other grains with juniper berries. **2.** A liquor similar to gin but flavored with some other aromatic substance, as aniseed. [Short for *geneva* < MDu. *genever* < OFr. *geneivre* < Lat. *juniperus,* juniper.]

gin[2] (jĭn) *n.* **1.** Any of several machines or devices, esp.: **a.** A machine for hoisting or moving heavy objects. **b.** A pile driver. **c.** A snare or trap for game. **d.** A pump operated by a windmill. **2.** A cotton gin. —*tr.v.* **ginned, gin·ning, gins.** **1.** To remove the seeds from (cotton) with a gin. **2.** To trap in a gin. [ME, short for OFr. *engin* < Lat. *ingenium,* skill.]

gin[3] (jĭn) *n.* Gin rummy.

gin·ger (jĭn'jər) *n.* **1. a.** A plant, *Zingiber officinale,* of tropical Asia, having yellowish-green flowers and a pungent, aromatic rootstock. **b.** The rootstock of the ginger, often dried and powdered and used as a spice. **2. a.** Any of various plants of the family Zingiberaceae, having variously colored, often fragrant flowers. **b.** The wild ginger. **3.** A strong brown. **4.** *Informal.* Liveliness; vigor. —*tr.v.* **-gered, -ger·ing, -gers.** **1.** To spice with ginger. **2.** *Informal.* To make more lively: *gingered up the party.* [ME *gingivere* < OE *gingifer* and OFr. *gingivre,* both < Med. Lat. *gingiber* < Lat. *zinziberi* < Gk. *zingiberis.*] **—gin'ger·y** *adj.*

ginger ale *n.* An effervescent soft drink flavored with ginger.

ginger beer *n.* A nonalcoholic drink, popular in England, that is similar to ginger ale but flavored with fermented ginger.

gin·ger·bread (jĭn'jər-brĕd') *n.* **1. a.** A dark molasses cake flavored with ginger. **b.** A soft molasses and ginger cookie cut in various shapes, sometimes elaborately decorated. **2. a.** Elaborate ornamentation. **b.** Superfluous or tasteless embellishment, esp. in architecture.

gingerbread palm *n.* The doom palm.

gin·ger·ly (jĭn'jər-lē) *adv.* With great care or delicacy; cautiously. —*adj.* Cautious; careful. [Poss. < OFr. *gensor,* comp. of *gent,* gentle. —see GENT[1].] **—gin'ger·li·ness** *n.*

gin·ger·snap (jĭn'jər-snăp') *n.* A flat, brittle cookie spiced with ginger and sweetened with molasses.

ging·ham (gĭng'əm) *n.* A yarn-dyed cotton fabric woven in stripes, checks, plaids, or solid colors. [Malay *ginggang* < *ginggang,* striped.]

gin·gi·va (jĭn'jə-və, jĭn-jī'-) *n., pl.* **-vae** (-vē'). The gum[2].

gin·gi·val (jĭn'jə-vəl, jĭn-jī'-) *adj.* **1.** Of or pertaining to the gums. **2.** *Ling.* Alveolar. [< Lat. *gingiva,* gum.]

gin·gi·vi·tis (jĭn'jə-vī'tĭs) *n.* Inflammation of the gums. [Lat. *gingiva,* gum + -ITIS.]

ging·ko (gĭng'kō) *n.* Variant of **ginkgo**.

gink (gĭnk) *n. Slang.* A man or boy. [Orig. unknown.]

gink·go also **ging·ko** (gĭng'kō) *n., pl.* **-goes** also **-koes**. A tree, *Ginkgo biloba,* native to China, having fan-shaped leaves and fleshy yellowish fruit and often used as an ornamental street tree. [J. *ginkyō,* of Chin. orig.]

gin mill *n. Slang.* A saloon.

gin rummy *n.* A variety of rummy for two or more persons in which a person may win by matching all his cards or may end the game by melding when his unmatched cards add up to ten points or less.

gin·seng (jĭn'sĕng') *n.* **1.** Any of several plants of the genus *Panax,* esp. *P. schinseng,* of eastern Asia, or *P. quinquefolium,* of North America, having small greenish flowers and a forked root believed to have medicinal properties. **2.** The root of a ginseng plant. [Chin. (Mandarin) *ren[2] shen[1]* : *ren[2],* man + *shen[1],* ginseng.]

gip (jĭp) *v. & n.* Variant of **gyp**.

Gip·sy (jĭp'sē) *n.* Variant of **Gypsy**.

gi·raffe (jə-răf') *n., pl.* **-raffes** or **giraffe**. An African ruminant mammal, *Giraffa camelopardis,* having a very long neck and legs, a tan coat with brown blotches, and short horns. [NLat. *Giraffa,* genus name < Ital. *giraffa* < Ar. *zirāfah.*]

gir·an·dole (jĭr'ən-dōl') *n.* **1.** A composition or structure in radiating form or arrangement, as a rotating display of fireworks. **2.** A branched candleholder, sometimes backed by a mirror. [Fr. < Ital. *girandola* < *girare,* to turn < Lat. *gyrare.* —see GYRATE.]

gir·a·sol also **gir·o·sol** (jĭr'ə-sôl', -sōl', -sŏl') *n.* A fire opal. [Ital. *girasole* : *girare,* to turn (< Lat. *gyrare* < *gyrus,* circle < Gk. *guros*) + *sole,* sun < Lat. *sol.*]

gird[1] (gûrd) *tr.v.* **gird·ed** or **girt** (gûrt), **gird·ing, girds.** **1. a.** To encircle with a belt or band. **b.** To fasten or secure with a belt or band. **c.** To surround. **2.** To equip or endow. **3.** To prepare (oneself) for action. [ME *girden* < OE *gyrdan.*]

gird[2] (gûrd) *intr. & tr.v.* **gird·ed, gird·ing, girds.** To jeer or jeer at. —*n.* A sarcastic remark. [ME *girden,* to strike.] **—gird'er** *n.*

gird·er (gûr'dər) *n.* A horizontal beam, as of steel or wood, used as a main support for a building or other structure.

gir·dle (gûr'dl) *n.* **1. a.** A belt or sash worn around the waist. **b.** Something that encircles like a belt. **2.** An elasticized, flexible undergarment worn over the waist and hips. **3.** A band made around the trunk of a tree by the removal of a strip of bark. **4.** The edge of a cut gem held by the setting. **5.** *Anat.* The pelvic or pectoral arch. —*tr.v.* **-dled, -dling, -dles.** **1.** To encircle with or as if with a belt. **2.** To put a girdle on. **3.** To remove a band of bark completely from the circumference of (a tree), usually to kill it. [ME *girdel* < OE *gyrdel.*]

gird·ler (gûrd'lər) *n.* **1.** One that makes girdles. **2.** Any of various insects that chew circular bands around twigs or stems in preparing nesting sites.

girl (gûrl) *n.* **1.** A female who has not yet attained womanhood. **2.** A female child. **3.** An unmarried young woman. **4.** A daughter. **5.** A sweetheart. **6.** A female servant, employee, or clerk. [ME *girle.*]

girl Friday *n. Informal.* A female employee, esp. one having a great variety of responsibilities. [GIRL + (MAN) FRIDAY.]

girl·friend also **girl friend** (gûrl'frĕnd') *n.* **1.** A female friend. **2.** A close female friend of a boy or man, esp. one seen on a romantic basis.

Girl Guide *n.* A member of the Girl Guides, a British youth organization founded in 1910.

girl·hood (gûrl'ho͝od') *n.* The state or time of being a girl.

girl·ie also **girl·y** (gûr'lē) *adj. Informal.* Featuring minimally clothed girls: *girlie magazines.*

girl·ish (gûr'lĭsh) *adj.* Pertaining to, characteristic of, or suitable for a girl. **—girl'ish·ly** *adv.* **—girl'ish·ness** *n.*

Girl Scout *n.* A member of the Girl Scouts, a youth organization founded in the United States in 1912 on the plan of the Girl Guides.

girl·y (gûr'lē) *adj.* Variant of **girlie**.

Gi·ronde (jə-rŏnd', zhĭ-) *n.* A moderate republican political party of revolutionary France (1791–93). [After *Gironde,* a department in France.] **—Gi·rond'ist** *n.*

gir·o·sol (jĭr'ə-sôl', -sōl', -sŏl') *n.* Variant of **girasol**.

girt[1] (gûrt) *v.* **girt·ed, girt·ing, girts.** —*tr.* **1.** To gird. **2.** To measure the girth of. —*intr.* To measure in girth. [Var. of GIRD.]

girt[2] (gûrt) *v.* A past tense and past participle of **gird[1]**.

girth (gûrth) *n.* **1.** The distance around something; circumference. **2.** The size of something; bulk. **3.** A strap encircling an animal's body to secure a load or saddle on its back; cinch. —*tr.v.* **girthed, girth·ing, girths.** **1.** To measure the circumference of. **2.** To encircle. **3.** To secure with a girth. [ME *gerth,* strap passing under a horse's belly to secure a load < ON *györð,* girdle.]

gi·sarme (gĭ-zärm') *n.* A halberd with a long shaft and a two-sided blade, carried by medieval foot soldiers. [ME < OFr.]

gis·mo also **giz·mo** (gĭz'mō) *n., pl.* **-mos.** *Slang.* A mechanical device or part whose name is forgotten or unknown. [Orig. unknown.]

gist (jĭst) *n.* **1.** The central idea of a matter; essence. **2.** *Law.* The grounds for action in a suit. [< OFr., it lies < *gesir,* to lie < Lat. *jacēre.*]

give (gĭv) *v.* **gave** (gāv), **giv·en** (gĭv'ən), **giv·ing, gives.** —*tr.* **1. a.** To make a present of: *gave her flowers for her birthday.* **b.** To deliver in exchange or in recompense; pay: *will give five dollars for the book.* **c.** To put temporarily at the disposal of; entrust to: *gave them the cottage for a week.* **d.** To place in the hands of; pass: *Give me the scissors.* **2. a.** To convey or offer for conveyance: *Give him my best wishes.* **b.** To bestow, esp. officially; confer: *give authority.* **c.** To accord or tender to another: *give him your confidence.* **3.** To contribute; donate: *give one's time.* **4. a.** To be a source of; afford: *His remark gave offense.* **b.** To cause to have or be subject to: *She gave him the measles.* **5.** To produce; bring forth: *a cow that gives three gallons of milk a day.* **6.** To

ginseng

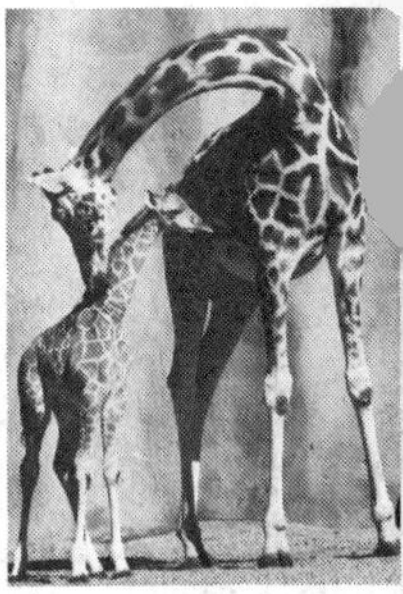
giraffe

girandole
18th-century American mirror

girder

provide (something required or expected): *Give your name and address.* **7. a.** To inflict as punishment: *gave her a spanking.* **b.** To administer: *gave him cough syrup.* **8.** To relinquish; yield: *give ground.* **9.** To emit or utter: *give a sigh.* **10. a.** To allot; assign: *give her five minutes to finish.* **b.** To designate; specify: *give a departure date.* **11.** To award as due: *gave him first prize.* **12.** To ascribe; attribute: *give him the blame.* **13. a.** To cause to take place, esp. for entertainment: *give a dinner party.* **b.** To offer or proffer: *give a toast.* **c.** To manifest; show: *give promise of brilliance.* **d.** To perform for an audience: *give a concert.* **14.** To submit for consideration or acceptance: *give an opinion.* **15.** To allow or lead: *gave me to think she loved me.* **16.** To devote; apply: *giving herself to her work.* **17.** To sacrifice: *gave a son to the war.* **18.** To take an interest to the extent of: *don't give a hoot.* —*intr.* **1.** To make gifts or donations: *give generously to charity.* **2.** To yield, as to pressure; collapse. **3.** To afford a view of or access to; open: *The doors give onto a terrace.* **4.** *Slang.* To be in progress; happen: *What gives?* —***phrasal verbs.*** **give away. 1.** To make a gift of. **2.** To present (a bride) to the bridegroom at a wedding ceremony. **3.** To reveal or make known, often accidentally. **give back.** To return: *gave him back his book.* **give in. 1.** To hand in; submit: *gave in her report.* **2.** To cease opposition; yield. **give off.** To send forth; emit: *chemical changes that give off energy.* **give out. 1.** To let (something) be known: *gave out the bad news.* **2.** To distribute; issue: *gave out surplus food to the needy.* **3.** To stop functioning; fail. **4.** To become used up; run out: *Her supply of gloves gave out.* **give over. 1.** To hand over; entrust. **2.** To make available for a particular purpose; devote. **3.** To surrender completely and unrestrainedly; abandon: *gave herself over to her grief.* **give up. 1.** To surrender: *gave himself up to the police.* **2.** To leave off; stop: *gave up smoking.* **3.** To part with; relinquish: *gave up all hope.* **4.** To abandon hope for: *gave her up as lost.* **5.** To admit defeat. **6.** To abandon what one is doing or planning to do. —*n. Informal.* Resilient springiness: *a mattress with give.* —***idioms.*** **give a good account of (oneself).** To behave or perform creditably. **give way. 1. a.** To withdraw; retreat. **b.** To make room for: *give way to an oncoming car.* **2.** To collapse from or as if from physical pressure: *The ladder gave way.* **3.** To abandon oneself: *give way to hysteria.* [ME *given* < OE *giefan.*]

give-and-take (gĭv′ən-tāk′) *n.* **1.** The practice of compromise. **2.** Lively exchange of ideas or conversation.

give·a·way (gĭv′ə-wā′) *n. Informal.* **1.** Something given away at no charge. **2.** Something that betrays or exposes, often accidentally.

giv·en (gĭv′ən) *adj.* **1. a.** Specified: *a given date.* **b.** Issued on a specified date. Used of legal documents. **2.** Granted as a supposition; acknowledged: *Given their superiority, we can't expect to win.* **3.** Having a tendency; inclined: *given to brooding.* **4.** Bestowed; presented. —**giv′en** *n.*

given name *n.* A name given to a person at birth or at baptism.

giz·mo (gĭz′mō) *n.* Variant of **gismo.**

giz·zard (gĭz′ərd) *n.* **1.** An enlargement of the alimentary canal in birds, often having dense muscular walls and containing fine grit eaten to aid in the digestion of seeds. **2.** A digestive organ similar to the gizzard in certain invertebrates, as the earthworm. [ME *giser* < OFr. *gisier* < VLat. **gicerium* < Lat. *gigeria,* cooked entrails of poultry.]

glacier

gla·bel·la (glə-bĕl′ə) *n., pl.* **-bel·lae** (-bĕl′ē′). The smooth area between the eyebrows just above the nose. [NLat. < Lat. *glabellus,* hairless < *glaber.*] —**gla·bel′lar** *adj.*

gla·brous (glā′brəs) *adj.* Having no hairs or pubescence; smooth. [Lat. *glaber,* bald.] —**gla′brous·ness** *n.*

gla·cé (glă-sā′) *adj.* **1.** Having a glazed, glossy surface. **2.** Coated with a sugar glaze; candied. —*tr.v.* **-céed, -cé·ing, -cés. 1.** To glaze. **2.** To candy. [Fr. < p.part. of *glacer,* to glaze < *glace,* ice < Lat. *glacies.*]

gla·cial (glā′shəl) *adj.* **1. a.** Of, pertaining to, or derived from a glacier. **b.** Often **Glacial.** Characterized or dominated by the existence of glaciers. Used esp. of the Pleistocene. **2.** Extremely cold; icy: *glacial waters.* **3.** Having the appearance of ice. **4.** Lacking warmth and friendliness: *a glacial stare.* [Lat. *glacialis,* icy < *glacies,* ice.] —**gla′cial·ly** *adv.*

glacial acetic acid *n.* Acetic acid that is at least 99.8 per cent pure.

glacial epoch *n.* **1.** Any of several periods during the Pleistocene epoch up to 1,000,000 years ago when much of the earth's surface was covered by glaciers. **2.** The Pleistocene epoch.

gladiolus

gla·ci·ate (glā′shē-āt′, -sē-) *tr.v.* **-at·ed, -at·ing, -ates. 1.** To subject to glacial action. **2.** To freeze. [Lat. *glaciare, glaciat-,* to freeze < *glacies,* ice.] —**gla′ci·a′tion** *n.*

gla·cier (glā′shər) *n.* A huge mass of laterally limited, moving ice originating from compacted snow. [Fr. < *glace,* ice < Lat. *glacies.*]

glacier lily *n.* The fawn lily.

gla·ci·ol·o·gy (glā′shē-ŏl′ə-jē, -sē-) *n.* The scientific study of glaciers. [GLACI(ER) + -LOGY.] —**gla′ci·o·log′ic** (-ə-lŏj′ĭk), **gla′ci·o·log′i·cal** *adj.* —**gla′ci·ol′o·gist** *n.*

gla·cis (glă-sē′, glăs′ē, glā′sĭs) *n.* **1.** A gentle slope; incline. **2.** A slope extending down from a fortification. [Fr. < OFr. *glacier,* to slide < *glace,* ice < Lat. *glacies.*]

glad (glăd) *adj.* **glad·der, glad·dest. 1.** Experiencing or exhibiting joy and pleasure. **2.** Providing joy and pleasure: *a glad occasion.* **3.** Pleased; willing: *glad to help.* **4.** *Archaic.* Of a cheerful disposition. —*tr. & intr.v.* **glad·ded, glad·ding, glads.** *Obs.* To gladden. [ME < OE *glæd.*] —**glad′ly** *adv.* —**glad′ness** *n.*

Synonyms: *glad, happy, cheerful, lighthearted, joyful, joyous.* These adjectives mean in good spirits. *Glad* often has reference to the strong feeling that results from gratification of a wish or from satisfaction with immediate circumstances. *Happy,* a more general term, can describe almost any condition of good spirits, temporary or sustained. *Cheerful* suggests good spirits made obvious by an outgoing nature, and *lighthearted* makes more explicit the absence of care. *Joyful* and *joyous,* the strongest of these terms, suggest extremely high spirits or a strong sense of fulfillment or satisfaction.

glad·den (glăd′n) *v.* **-dened, -den·ing, -dens.** —*tr.* To make glad. —*intr. Archaic.* To be glad.

glade (glād) *n.* An open space in a forest. [Perh. < GLAD, shining (obs.).]

glad hand *n. Informal.* A hearty, often insincere and offensively familiar welcome or greeting.

glad-hand (glăd′hănd′) *v.* **-hand·ed, -hand·ing, -hands.** *Informal.* —*tr.* To extend a glad hand to. —*intr.* To extend a glad hand. —**glad′-hand′er** *n.*

glad·i·ate (glăd′ē-āt′, -ĭt, glā′dē-) *adj.* Sword-shaped, as a leaf. [NLat. *gladiatus* < Lat. *gladius,* sword.]

glad·i·a·tor (glăd′ē-ā′tər) *n.* **1.** A person trained to entertain the public by engaging in mortal combat in the ancient Roman arena. **2.** A person engaged in a controversy or dispute, esp. in public; combatant. **3.** A prizefighter. [ME < Lat. < *gladius,* sword.] —**glad′i·a·to′ri·al** (-ə-tôr′ē-əl, -tōr′-) *adj.*

glad·i·o·lus (glăd′ē-ō′ləs) *n., pl.* **-li** (-lī′, -lē′) or **-lus·es. 1.** Also **glad·i·o·la** (glăd′ē-ō′lə). Any of various plants of the genus *Gladiolus,* native to tropical regions but widely cultivated elsewhere, having sword-shaped leaves and a spike of showy, variously colored flowers. **2.** *Anat.* The large middle section of the sternum. [Lat., dim. of *gladius,* sword.]

glad rags *pl.n. Informal.* One's best or most elegant clothes.

glad·some (glăd′səm) *adj.* **1.** Glad; joyful. **2.** Causing gladness. —**glad′some·ly** *adv.* —**glad′some·ness** *n.*

Glad·stone (glăd′stōn′, -stən) *n.* **1.** A light four-wheeled convertible carriage with two interior seats and places outside for a driver and footman. **2.** A Gladstone bag. [After William E. *Gladstone* (1809–1898).]

Gladstone bag *n.* A piece of light hand luggage consisting of two hinged compartments. [After William E. *Gladstone* (1809–1898).]

glair also **glaire** (glâr) *n.* **1.** Raw egg white used in sizing or glazing. **2.** A sizing or glaze made of egg white. [ME *glaire* < OFr. < Lat. *clarus,* clear.]

glair·y (glâr′ē) *adj.* **-i·er, -i·est. 1.** Resembling glair. **2.** Coated with glair. —**glair′i·ness** *n.*

glaive (glāv) *n. Archaic.* A sword, esp. a broadsword. [ME < OFr. < Lat. *gladius.*]

glam·or (glăm′ər) *n.* Variant of **glamour.**

glam·or·ize also **glam·our·ize** (glăm′ə-rīz′) *tr.v.* **-ized, -iz·ing, -iz·es. 1.** To make glamorous. **2.** To treat or portray in a romantic manner; romanticize, idealize, or glorify. —**glam′or·i·za′tion** *n.* —**glam′or·iz′er** *n.*

glam·or·ous also **glam·our·ous** (glăm′ər-əs) *adj.* Characterized by glamour. —**glam′or·ous·ly** *adv.* —**glam′or·ous·ness** *n.*

glam·our also **glam·or** (glăm′ər) *n.* **1.** An air of compelling charm, romance, and excitement, esp. when delusively alluring. **2.** *Archaic.* Magic; enchantment. [Sc., alteration of GRAMMAR (from the association of learning with magic).]

Usage: Many words, such as *honor, vapor,* and *labor,* are usually spelled with an *-or* ending in American English but with an *-our* ending in British English. The preferred spelling of *glamour,* however, is *-our,* making it an exception to the usual American practice. The adjective is more often spelled *glamorous* in both American and British usage.

glam·our·ize (glăm′ə-rīz′) *v.* Variant of **glamorize.**

glam·our·ous (glăm′ər-əs) *adj.* Variant of **glamorous.**

glance[1] (glăns) *v.* **glanced, glanc·ing, glanc·es.** —*intr.* **1.** To strike a surface at such an angle as to be deflected: *A pebble glanced off the windshield.* **2.** To direct the gaze briefly: *glance at the menu.* **3.** To shine briefly; glint. **4.** To make a passing reference; touch briefly. —*tr.* **1.** To strike (a surface) at an angle; graze: *The baseball glanced the fence.* **2.** To cause to strike a surface at an angle: *glance a stone over the stream.* —*n.* **1.** An oblique movement following impact; deflection. **2.** A brief or cursory look. **3.** A quick flash of light; gleam. [ME *glenchen, glansen,* to strike obliquely.]

glance[2] (glăns) *n.* Any of various minerals that have a brilliant luster: *silver glance.* [G. *Glanz* < OHG *glanz,* bright.]

gland (glănd) *n.* **1. a.** An organ that extracts specific substances from the blood and concentrates or alters them for subsequent secretion. **b.** Any of various nonsecretory or excretory organs that resemble such organs. **2.** *Bot.* An organ or structure that secretes a substance. **3.** A sliding machine part that is designed to hold something in place. [Fr. *glande* < OFr., gland, acorn < Lat. *glans,* acorn.]

glan·ders (glăn′dərz) *n.* *(used with a sing. or pl. verb).* A contagious, often chronic, sometimes fatal disease of horses and other animals, caused by a bacillus, *Actinobacillus mallei,* and characterized by a nasal discharge and ulcers in the lungs, respiratory tract, and skin. [< OFr. *glandre,* glandular swelling < Lat. *glandula,* dim. of *glans,* acorn.] **—glan′der·ous** *adj.*

glan·des (glăn′dēz′) *n.* Plural of **glans**.

glan·du·lar (glăn′jə-lər) *adj.* **1.** Of, pertaining to, affecting, or resembling a gland or its secretion. **2.** Functioning as a gland. **3.** Having glands. **4.** Resulting from abnormal gland function. **5.** Innate; instinctive: *a glandular hatred of flabbiness.* [Fr. *glandulaire* < *glandule,* small gland < Lat. *glandula,* glandular swelling. —see GLANDERS.] **—glan′du·lar·ly** *adv.*

glandular fever *n.* Infectious mononucleosis.

glans (glănz) *n., pl.* **glan·des** (glăn′dēz′). **1.** The glans penis. **2.** The glans clitoridis. [Lat. < *glans,* acorn (from its shape).]

glans cli·tor·i·dis (klī-tôr′ĭ-dĭs, klī-) *n.* The small mass of erectile tissue at the tip of the clitoris.

glans penis *n.* The head or tip of the penis.

glare[1] (glâr) *v.* **glared, glar·ing, glares.** *—intr.* **1.** To stare fixedly and angrily. **2.** To shine intensely and blindingly: *a searing sun glaring down on the desert.* **3.** To be conspicuous; stand out obtrusively. *—tr.* To express by staring fixedly and angrily: *glared his disapproval.* *—n.* **1.** A fixed, angry stare. **2.** An intense and blinding light. **3.** Showy brilliance; gaudiness: *the pomp and glare of rhetoric.* [ME *glaren,* to shine brightly.]

glare[2] (glâr) *n.* A sheet or surface of ice. [Prob. < GLARE[1].]

glar·ing (glâr′ĭng) *adj.* **1.** Staring fixedly and angrily: *glaring eyes.* **2.** Shining intensely and blindingly. **3.** Gaudy; garish. **4.** Painfully conspicuous: *a glaring error.* **—glar′ing·ly** *adv.*

glar·y (glâr′ē) *adj.* **-i·er, -i·est.** Dazzlingly bright; glaring.

glass (glăs) *n.* **1.** Any of a large class of materials with highly variable mechanical and optical properties that solidify from the molten state without crystallization, that are typically based on silicon dioxide, boric oxide, aluminum oxide, or phosphorus pentoxide, that are generally transparent or translucent, and that are regarded physically as supercooled liquids rather than true solids. **2.** Objects made of glass; glassware. **3.** Something made of glass, esp.: **a.** A drinking vessel. **b.** A mirror. **c.** A barometer. **d.** A windowpane. **4. a.** A device containing a lens or lenses and used as an aid to vision. **b. glasses.** A pair of lenses mounted in a light frame, used to correct faulty vision or to protect the eyes. **5.** The quantity contained by a drinking vessel; glassful. *—v.* **glassed, glass·ing, glass·es.** *—tr.* **1.** To place within glass or a glass container. **2.** To provide with glass or glass parts. **3.** To make glassy; glaze. **4. a.** To see reflected, as in a mirror. **b.** To mirror; reflect. *—intr.* To become glassy. [ME *glas* < OE *glæs.*]

glass blowing *n.* The art or process of shaping an object from molten glass by blowing air into it through a tube. **—glass blower** *n.*

glass eel *n.* An eel in its transparent, postlarval stage.

glass·ful (glăs′fo͝ol′) *n.* The quantity contained in a glass.

glass harmonica *n.* A musical instrument consisting of a set of graduated glass bowls that produce tones when a moistened finger is passed over their rims.

glass·house (glăs′hous′) *n.* **1.** A glassworks. **2.** *Chiefly Brit.* A greenhouse.

glass·ine (glă-sēn′) *n.* A nearly transparent, resilient glazed paper resistant to the passage of air and grease.

glass·mak·er (glăs′mā′kər) *n.* One who makes glass. **—glass′mak′ing** *n.*

glass·man (glăs′mən, -măn′) *n.* **1.** One who sells glass. **2.** A glassmaker.

glass snake *n.* Any of several slender, limbless, snakelike lizards of the genus *Ophisaurus,* having a tail that breaks or snaps off readily. [From the brittleness of its tail.]

glass·ware (glăs′wâr′) *n.* Objects, esp. containers, made of glass.

glass wool *n.* Fine-spun fibers of glass used esp. for insulation and in air filters.

glass·work (glăs′wûrk′) *n.* **1. a.** The manufacture of glassware or glass. **b.** The cutting and fitting of glass panes; glaziery. **2.** Glassware. **3. glassworks** *(used with a sing. verb).* An establishment where glass is manufactured.

glass·wort (glăs′wûrt′, -wôrt′) *n.* Any of various plants of the genus *Salicornia,* growing in salt marshes and having fleshy stems and rudimentary, scalelike leaves. [From its former use in making glass.]

glass·y (glăs′ē) *adj.* **-i·er, -i·est. 1.** Resembling or characterizing glass. **2.** Lifeless; expressionless: *"the face changing to a demon's face with a fixed glassy grin"* (Katherine Anne Porter). **—glass′i·ly** *adv.* **—glass′i·ness** *n.*

Glau·ber's salts also **Glau·ber's salt** (glou′bərz) *n.* A hydrated sodium sulfate, $Na_2SO_4 \cdot 10H_2O$, used in paper and glass manufacturing and as a cathartic. [After Johann R. *Glauber* (1604–1668).]

glau·co·ma (glou-kō′mə, glô-) *n.* A disease of the eye characterized by high intraocular pressure, damaged optic disk, hardening of the eyeball, and partial or complete loss of vision. [Lat., cataract < Gk. *glaukōma* < *glaukos,* gray.] **—glau·co′ma·tous** (-kō′mə-təs) *adj.*

glau·co·nite (glô′kə-nīt′) *n.* A hydrous silicate of potassium, iron, aluminum, or magnesium, $K_2(Mg,Fe)_2Al_6(Si_4O_{10})_3(OH)_{12}$, found in greensand and used as a water softener and fertilizer. [Gk. *glaukon,* neuter of gray + -ITE.] **—glau′co·nit′ic** (-nĭt′ĭk) *adj.*

glau·cous (glô′kəs) *adj.* *Bot.* Grayish green or bluish green due to a fine, whitish, powdery coating: *glaucous leaves.* [Lat. *glaucus* < Gk. *glaukos.*] **—glau′cous·ness** *n.*

glaze (glāz) *n.* **1.** A thin, smooth, shiny coating. **2.** A thin, glassy coating of ice. **3. a.** A coating of colored, opaque, or transparent material applied to ceramics before firing. **b.** A coating, as of syrup, applied to food. **c.** A transparent coating applied to the surface of a painting to modify the color tones. **4.** A glassy film, as over the eyes. *—v.* **glazed, glaz·ing, glaz·es.** *—tr.* **1.** To fit or furnish with glass: *glaze a window.* **2.** To apply a glaze to: *glaze a doughnut; glaze pottery.* **3.** To give a smooth, lustrous surface to. *—intr.* **1.** To be or become glazed or glassy: *eyes glazing over from boredom.* **2.** To form a glaze. [ME *glasen* < *glas,* glass < OE *glæs.*] **—glaz′er** *n.*

gla·zier (glā′zhər) *n.* One who cuts and fits window glass. [ME *glasier* < *glas,* glass < OE *glæs.*] **—gla′zier·y** (-zhə-rē) *n.*

glaz·ing (glā′zĭng) *n.* **1. a.** Glasswork. **b.** Glass set or made to be set in frames. **2. a.** A glaze. **b.** The act or process of applying a glaze.

gleam (glēm) *n.* **1.** A brief beam or flash of light: *saw gleams of daylight through the cracks.* **2.** A steady but subdued shining; glow: *the gleam of a steel blade.* **3.** A brief or dim indication; trace: *a gleam of intelligence.* *—v.* **gleamed, gleam·ing, gleams.** *—intr.* **1.** To emit a gleam; flash or glow: *"It shone with gold and gleamed with ivory"* (Edith Hamilton). **2.** To be manifested or indicated briefly or faintly. *—tr.* To cause to emit a gleam. [ME *glem* < OE *glæm.*]

gleam·er (glē′mər) *n.* **1.** One that gleams. **2.** Make-up applied to the face or lips to give a glossy appearance.

glean (glēn) *v.* **gleaned, glean·ing, gleans.** *—intr.* To gather grain left behind by reapers. *—tr.* **1.** To gather (grain) left behind by reapers. **2.** To collect bit by bit: *"records from which historians glean their knowledge"* (Kemp Malone). [ME *glenen* < OFr. *glener* < LLat. *glennare.*] **—glean′er** *n.*

glean·ings (glē′nĭngz) *pl.n.* Things that have been gleaned or collected bit by bit: *the gleanings of patient scholars.*

gle·ba (glē′bə) *n., pl.* **-bae** (-bē′). The inner, spore-bearing mass of a puffball. [NLat. < Lat., clod.]

glebe (glēb) *n.* **1.** *Chiefly Brit.* A plot of land granted to a clergyman as part of his benefice during his tenure of office. **2.** *Archaic.* The soil or earth; land. [Lat. *gleba,* clod.]

glede (glēd) *n.* A predatory bird, as the kite. [ME < OE *glida.*]

glee (glē) *n.* **1.** Jubilant gaiety; joy. **2.** An unaccompanied part song scored for three or more male voices that was popular in the 18th century. [ME *gle,* entertainment < OE *glēo.*]

glee club *n.* A group of singers who perform usually short pieces of choral music.

gleed (glēd) *n.* *Chiefly Brit. Regional.* A glowing coal; ember. [ME *glede* < OE *glēd.*]

glee·ful (glē′fəl) *adj.* Full of glee; joyful. **—glee′ful·ly** *adv.* **—glee′ful·ness** *n.*

glee·man (glē′mən) *n.* *Archaic.* A medieval itinerant singer; minstrel. [ME *gleman* < OE *glēoman* : *glēo,* minstrelsy + *mann,* man.]

glee·some (glē′səm) *adj.* *Archaic.* Gleeful.

gleet (glēt) *n.* **1.** Chronic inflammation of the urethra, characterized by mucopurulent discharge. **2.** The discharge characterizing gleet. [ME *glet,* slime < OFr. *glete* < Lat. *glittus,* sticky.] **—gleet′y** *adj.*

gleg (glĕg) *adj.* *Scot.* Alert and quick to respond. [ME, clear-sighted < ON *glöggr.*]

glen (glĕn) *n.* A valley. [ME < Sc. Gael. *gleann* < OIr. *glend.*]

Glen·gar·ry (glĕn-găr′ē) *n., pl.* **-ries.** A woolen cap, originating in Scotland, that is creased lengthwise and often has short ribbons at the back. [After *Glengarry,* a valley in Scotland.]

gley (glā) *n.* A sticky, bluish-gray soil layer formed under the influence of excessive moisture. [R. *glei,* clay.]

gli·a·din (glī′ə-dĭn) *n.* Any of several simple proteins derived from rye or wheat gluten. [Ital. *gliadina* < Med. Gk. *glia,* glue.]

glib (glĭb) *adj.* **glib·ber, glib·best. 1. a.** Performed with a natural, offhand ease: *a glib conversationalist.* **b.** Showing little thought, preparation, or concern: *glib replies.* **2.** Marked by a quickness or fluency that often suggests or stems from insincerity or deception: *glib politicians, promising the moon.* [Poss. of Low German orig.] **—glib′ly** *adv.* **—glib′ness** *n.*

glide (glīd) *v.* **glid·ed, glid·ing, glides.** *—intr.* **1.** To move in a smooth, effortless manner: *a submarine gliding through the water.* **2.** To move silently and furtively. **3.** To occur or pass imperceptibly. **4.** To fly without propulsion. Used of an aircraft. **5.** *Mus.* To blend one tone into the next; slur. **6.** To articulate a glide in speech. *—tr.* To cause to glide. *—n.* **1.** The act of gliding. **2.** *Mus.* A slur. **3. a.** The transitional

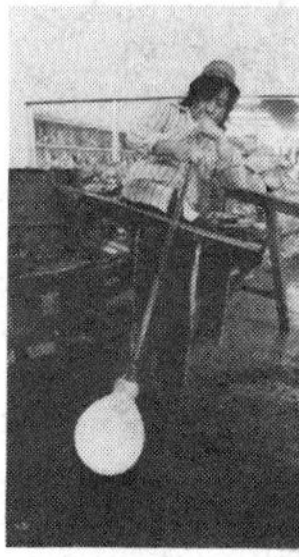

glass blowing

sound produced by passing from the articulatory position of one speech sound to that of another. **b.** A semivowel. [ME *gliden* < OE *glīdan.*]

glid·er (glī′dər) *n.* **1.** One that glides. **2.** A light, engineless aircraft designed to glide after being towed aloft or launched from a catapult. **3.** A swinging couch suspended from a vertical frame. **4.** A device that aids gliding.

glim (glĭm) *n.* A source of light, as a candle. [Perh. short. for GLIMMER.]

glim·mer (glĭm′ər) *n.* **1.** A dim or intermittent light; flicker. **2.** A faint manifestation or indication; trace: *a glimmer of her old sense of humor.* —*intr.v.* **-mered, -mer·ing, -mers. 1.** To emit a dim or intermittent light. **2.** To appear or be indicated faintly: *Hope still glimmered.* [< ME *glimeren,* to shine.]

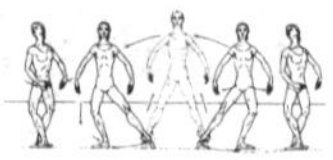

glissade

glimpse (glĭmps) *n.* **1.** A brief, incomplete view or look. **2.** *Archaic.* A brief flash of light. —*v.* **glimpsed, glimps·ing, glimps·es.** —*tr.* To obtain a brief, incomplete view of. —*intr.* To look briefly; glance: *glimpsed at the headlines.* [< ME *glimsen,* to glance.] —**glimps′er** *n.*

glint (glĭnt) *n.* **1.** A momentary flash of light; sparkle. **2.** A faint or fleeting indication; trace. —*v.* **glint·ed, glint·ing, glints.** —*intr.* **1.** To gleam or flash. **2.** *Archaic.* To move abruptly; dart. —*tr.* To cause to gleam or flash. [ME *glent,* of Scand. orig.]

glis·sade (glĭ-säd′, -săd′) *n.* **1.** A gliding ballet step. **2.** A controlled slide, in either a standing or a sitting position, used in descending a steep icy or snowy incline. —*intr.v.* **-sad·ed, -sad·ing, -sades.** To perform a glissade. [Fr. < *glisser,* to slide < OFr. *glier,* to glide, of Germanic orig.] —**glis·sad′er** *n.*

glis·san·do (glĭ-sän′dō) *n., pl.* **-di** (-dē) or **-dos.** *Mus.* A rapid slide through a series of consecutive tones in a scalelike passage. [Prob. alteration of Fr. *glissade,* sliding motion. — see GLISSADE.]

glis·ten (glĭs′ən) *intr.v.* **-tened, -ten·ing, -tens.** To shine by reflection; reflect lustrously. —*n.* A shine or sparkle; glitter. [ME *glisnen* < OE *glisnian.*]

glis·ter (glĭs′tər) *intr.v.* **-tered, -ter·ing, -ters.** To glisten. —*n.* Glitter; brilliance. [ME *glisteren* < MDu. *glinsteren* and MLG *glisteren.*]

glitch (glĭch) *n.* **1.** A minor malfunction, mishap, or technical problem. **2.** *Electronics.* A false or spurious electronic signal caused by a brief, unwanted surge of electric power. **3.** *Astron.* A sudden change in the period of rotation of a neutron star. [Prob. < Yiddish *glitsh,* slippery area < *glitshn,* to slide < G. *glitschen* < MHG *glīten,* to glide < OHG *glitan.*] —**glitch′y** *adj.*

glit·ter (glĭt′ər) *n.* **1.** A sparkling light or brightness. **2.** Brilliant or showy attractiveness. **3.** Small pieces of light-reflecting decorative material. —*intr.v.* **-tered, -ter·ing, -ters. 1. a.** To sparkle brilliantly; glisten. **b.** To sparkle malevolently or coldly: *eyes glittering at the prospect of revenge.* **2.** To be brilliantly, often deceptively attractive. [ME *gliteren* < ON *glitra.*] —**glit′ter·ing·ly** *adv.* —**glit′ter·y** *adj.*

globe

glitz (glĭts) *n. Slang.* Excessive showiness; flashiness. —**glitz′y** *adj.* [Yiddish, glitter.]

gloam (glōm) *n. Archaic.* Twilight; gloaming.

gloam·ing (glō′mĭng) *n.* Twilight; dusk. [ME *gloming* < OE *glōmung* < *glōm,* dusk.]

gloat (glōt) *intr.v.* **gloat·ed, gloat·ing, gloats.** To feel or express great, often malicious pleasure or self-satisfaction: *gloating over his opponent's defeat.* —*n.* **1.** The act of gloating. **2.** A feeling of great, often malicious pleasure or self-satisfaction. [Perh. of Scand. orig.] —**gloat′er** *n.*

glob (glŏb) *n.* **1.** A small drop; globule. **2.** A rounded, usually large lump or mass: *a glob of mashed potatoes.* [ME *globbe,* large mass < Lat. *globus,* globular mass.]

glob·al (glō′bəl) *adj.* **1.** Having the shape of a globe; spherical. **2.** Of, relating to, or involving the entire earth; worldwide: *a global disarmament treaty.* **3.** Comprehensive; total. —**glob′al·ly** *adv.*

glob·al·ism (glō′bə-lĭz′əm) *n.* **1.** Globalization. **2.** A policy promoting globalization. —**glob′al·ist** *n.*

glob·al·i·za·tion (glō′bə-lĭ-zā′shən) *n.* The act, process, or policy of making something worldwide in scope or application.

glob·al·ize (glō′bə-līz′) *tr.v.* **-ized, -iz·ing, -iz·es.** To make global; make worldwide. —**glob′al·iz′er** *n.*

glockenspiel

glo·bate (glō′bāt′) also **glo·bat·ed** (-bā′tĭd) *adj.* Having the shape of a globe; globular. [Lat. *globatus,* p.part. of *globare,* to form into a ball < *globus,* ball.]

globe (glōb) *n.* **1.** A body with the shape of a sphere, esp. a representation of the earth or heavens in the form of a hollow ball. **2. a.** The earth. **b.** A planet. **3.** An object resembling a globe, esp. a rounded container, as a glass sphere covering a light bulb. **4.** A sphere emblematic of sovereignty; orb. —*intr. & tr.v.* **globed, glob·ing, globes.** To assume the shape of or form into a globe. [ME < Lat. *globus.*]

globe·fish (glōb′fĭsh′) *n., pl.* **globefish** or **-fish·es.** Any of various fishes, as the ocean sunfish, having or capable of assuming a globular shape.

globe·flow·er (glōb′flou′ər) *n.* Any of several plants of the genus *Trollius,* having globe-shaped, usually yellow flowers.

globe·trot·ter (glōb′trŏt′ər) *n.* One who travels often and widely, esp. for sightseeing. —**globe′trot′ting** *n.*

glo·bin (glō′bĭn) *n.* A simple protein obtained from hemoglobin. [Back-formation < HEMOGLOBIN.]

glo·boid (glō′boid′) *adj.* Having a globelike shape; spheroid. —*n.* A globe-shaped object.

glo·bose (glō′bōs′) also **glo·bous** (-bəs) *adj.* Spherical; globular. [Lat. *globosus* < *globus,* sphere.] —**glo′bose′ly** *adv.* —**glo′bose′ness, glo·bos′i·ty** (-bŏs′ĭ-tē) *n.*

glob·u·lar (glŏb′yə-lər) *adj.* **1.** Having the shape of a globe or globule; spherical. **2.** Consisting of globules. **3.** Worldwide; global. —**glob′u·lar·ly** *adv.* —**glob′u·lar·ness** *n.*

globular cluster *n.* A system of stars, generally smaller in size than a galaxy, that is more or less globular in conformation.

glob·ule (glŏb′yo͞ol) *n.* A small, often minute spherical mass, esp. a small drop of liquid. [Lat. *globulus,* dim. of *globus,* sphere.]

glob·u·lif·er·ous (glŏb′yə-lĭf′ər-əs) *adj.* Composed of or producing globules.

glob·u·lin (glŏb′yə-lĭn) *n.* Any of a class of simple proteins that are found extensively in blood, milk, muscle, and plant seeds and that are insoluble in pure water, soluble in dilute salt solution, and coagulable by heat. [GLOBULE + -IN.]

glo·chid·i·um (glō-kĭd′ē-əm) *n., pl.* **-i·a** (-ē-ə). **1.** *Zool.* A parasitic larva of certain freshwater mussels of the family Unionidae, having hooks for attaching to a host fish. **2.** Also **glo·chid** (glō′kĭd). *Bot.* One of the barbed hairs or bristles on certain plants, as the prickly pear. [NLat. < Gk. *glōkhis,* barb of an arrow.] —**glo·chid′i·ate** (-ĭt, -āt′) *adj.*

glock·en·spiel (glŏk′ən-spēl′, -shpēl′) *n.* A percussion musical instrument with a series of metal bars tuned to the chromatic scale and played with two light hammers. [G. : *Glocke,* bell (< OHG *glocka*) + *Spiel,* play.]

glogg (glŏg) also **glögg** (glœg) *n.* A hot punch made of red wine, brandy, and sherry flavored with almonds, raisins, and orange peel. [Sw. *glögg* < *glödga,* to mull < OSw.]

glom·er·ate (glŏm′ər-ĭt) *adj.* Formed into a compact, rounded mass; tightly clustered; conglomerate. [Lat. *glomeratus,* p.part. of *glomerare,* to wind into a ball < *glomus,* ball.]

glom·er·ule (glŏm′ə-ro͞ol′, glŏm′yə-) *n.* **1.** *Bot.* A compact cluster of flowers. **2.** *Anat.* A glomerulus. [NLat. *glomerulus* < Lat. *glomus,* ball.] —**glo·mer′u·late** (glō-mĕr′yə-lĭt) *adj.*

glo·mer·u·lus (glō-mĕr′yə-ləs) *n., pl.* **-li** (-lī′). **1.** A tuft of capillaries situated at the origin of a vertebrate kidney. **2.** The twisted secretory portion of a sweat gland. [NLat. < Lat. *glomus,* ball.]

gloom (glo͞om) *n.* **1. a.** Partial or total darkness; dimness. **b.** A partially or totally dark place, area, or location. **2. a.** An atmosphere of melancholy or depression: *Gloom pervaded the office.* **b.** A state of melancholy or depression; despondency. —*v.* **gloomed, gloom·ing, glooms.** —*intr.* **1.** To be or become dark, shaded, or obscure. **2.** To feel, appear, or act despondent, sad, or mournful. —*tr.* **1.** To make dark, shaded, or obscure. **2.** *Archaic.* To make despondent; sadden. [Prob. < ME *gloumen,* to become dark.]

gloom·y (glo͞o′mē) *adj.* **-i·er, -i·est. 1.** Partially or totally dark, esp. dismal and dreary: *a damp, gloomy, day.* **2.** Showing or filled with gloom: *gloomy faces.* **3. a.** Causing or producing gloom; depressing: *gloomy news.* **b.** Marked by hopelessness; pessimistic: *gloomy predictions.* —**gloom′i·ly** *adv.* —**gloom′i·ness** *n.*

glop (glŏp) *Slang.* —*n.* **1.** A messy mixture, as of food. **2.** Something, as writing, that is worthless. —*tr.v.* **glopped, glop·ping, glops. 1.** To cover with glop. **2.** To put glop on. [Imit. of the sound of food being mixed.] —**glop′py** *adj.*

Glo·ri·a (glôr′ē-ə, glōr′-) *n.* **1. a.** A Christian hymn of praise to God that begins with the word *Gloria.* **b.** The music to which such a hymn is set. **2. gloria.** A halo or nimbus. [ME < Lat. *gloria,* glory.]

Gloria in ex·cel·sis De·o (ĭn ĕk-sĕl′sĭs dā′ō, dē′ō) *n.* A Latin doxology forming part of the Ordinary of the Mass, beginning with the words *Gloria in excelsis Deo.* [LLat., Glory to God in the highest.]

Gloria Pa·tri (păt′rē, pä′trē) *n.* A Latin doxology beginning with the words *Gloria Patri.* [LLat., Glory to the Father.]

glo·ri·fy (glôr′ə-fī′, glōr′-) *tr.v.* **-fied, -fy·ing, -fies. 1.** To give glory, honor, or high praise to; exalt. **2.** To cause to be or seem more glorious or excellent than is actually the case: *His descriptions glorified the house into a mansion.* **3.** To give glory to, esp. through worship. [ME *glorifien* < OFr. *glorefiier* < LLat. *glorificare* : Lat. *gloria,* glory + Lat. *facere,* to make.] —**glo′ri·fi·ca′tion** *n.* —**glo′ri·fi′er** *n.*

glo·ri·ole (glôr′ē-ōl′, glōr′-) *n.* A halo, aureole, or nimbus. [Fr. < Lat. *gloriola,* dim. of *gloria,* glory.]

glo·ri·ous (glôr′ē-əs, glōr′-) *adj.* **1.** Having or deserving glory; famous. **2.** Conferring or advancing glory: *a glorious achievement.* **3.** Characterized by great beauty and splendor; magnificent: *a glorious sunset.* **4.** *Informal.* Delightful; wonderful: *had a glorious visit.* —**glo′ri·ous·ly** *adv.* —**glo′ri·ous·ness** *n.*

glo·ry (glôr′ē, glōr′ē) *n., pl.* **-ries. 1.** Great honor, praise, or distinction accorded by common consent; renown. **2.** Something that brings honor or renown. **3.** A highly praiseworthy asset: *Her hair is her crowning glory.* **4.** Adoration, praise, and thanksgiving offered in worship: *We sing Thy glory.* **5.** Majestic beauty and splendor; resplendence: *The sun set* *in a blaze of glory.* **6.** The splendor and bliss of heaven; perfect happiness. **7.** A height of achievement, enjoyment, or prosperity: *Paris in its greatest glory.* **8.** A halo, nimbus, or aureole. —*intr.v.* **-ried, -ry·ing, -ries.** To rejoice triumphantly; exult: *petty generals who gloried in war.* [ME *glorie* < OFr. < Lat. *gloria.*]

glo·ry-of-the-snow (glôr′ē-əv-*th*ə-snō′, glōr′-) *n.* A small bulbous plant, *Chionodoxa luciliae,* native to Asia Minor, cultivated for its early-blooming blue flowers.

gloss¹ (glôs, glŏs) *n.* **1.** A surface shininess or luster. **2.** A deceptively or superficially attractive appearance. —*tr.v.* **glossed, gloss·ing, gloss·es. 1.** To give a bright sheen or luster to. **2.** To make attractive or acceptable by deception or superficial treatment: *She praised the candidate, glossing over his weaknesses.* —*intr.* To become shiny or lustrous. [Perh. of Scand. orig.]

gloss² (glôs, glŏs) *n.* **1. a.** A brief explanatory note or translation of a difficult or technical expression usually inserted in the margin or between lines of a text or manuscript. **b.** A collection of such notes; glossary. **2.** A purposefully misleading interpretation or explanation. **3.** An extensive commentary, often accompanying a text or publication. —*tr.v.* **glossed, gloss·ing, gloss·es. 1.** To provide (a text) with glosses. **2.** To give a false interpretation to. [ME *glose* < Med. Lat. *glosa* < Lat. *glossa,* word requiring explanation < Gk. *glōssa.*] **—gloss′er** *n.*

glos·sal (glô′səl, glŏs′əl) *adj.* Of or pertaining to the tongue. [< Gk. *glōssa,* tongue.]

glos·sa·ry (glô′sə-rē, glŏs′ə-) *n., pl.* **-ries.** A list of difficult or specialized words with their definitions, often placed at the back of a book. [Lat. *glossarium* < Lat. *glossa,* word requiring explanation. < Gk. *glōssa.*] **—glos·sar′i·al** (glô-sâr′ē-əl, glŏ-) *adj.* **—glos′sa·rist** *n.*

glos·sog·ra·phy (glô-sŏg′rə-fē, glŏ-) *n.* The writing and compilation of glosses or glossaries. **—glos·sog′ra·pher** *n.*

glos·so·la·li·a (glô′sə-lā′lē-ə, glŏs′ə-) *n.* **1.** Fabricated and nonmeaningful speech, esp. such speech associated with certain schizophrenic syndromes. **2.** The gift of tongues. [Gk. *glōssa,* tongue + Gk. *lalein,* to babble.]

glos·sol·o·gy (glô-sŏl′ə-jē, glŏ-) *n. Obs.* Linguistics. [Gk. *glōssa,* language + -LOGY.] **—glos·sol′o·gist** *n.*

gloss·y (glô′sē, glŏs′ē) *adj.* **-i·er, -i·est. 1.** Having a smooth, shiny, lustrous surface: *glossy satin.* **2.** Superficially and often speciously attractive; showy. —*n., pl.* **-ies.** A photographic print on smooth, shiny paper. **—gloss′i·ly** *adv.* **—gloss′i·ness** *n.*

glost (glôst, glŏst) *n.* **1.** A lead glaze used for pottery. **2.** Glazed pottery. [Var. of GLOSS¹.]

glot·tal (glŏt′l) *adj.* Relating to or articulating in the glottis.

glottal stop *n.* A speech sound produced by a momentary complete closure of the glottis, followed by an explosive release.

glot·tis (glŏt′ĭs) *n., pl.* **-tis·es** or **-ti·des** (-ĭ-dēz′) **1.** The space between the vocal cords at the upper part of the larynx. **2.** The vocal structures of the larynx. [Gk. *glōttis* < *glōtta, glōssa,* tongue.]

glove (glŭv) *n.* **1. a.** A fitted covering for the hand with a separate sheath for each finger and the thumb. **b.** A gauntlet. **2. a.** *Baseball.* An oversized padded leather covering for the hand, used in catching balls, esp. one with more finger sheaths than the catcher's or first baseman's mitt. **b.** A boxing glove. —*tr.v.* **gloved, glov·ing, gloves. 1.** To furnish with gloves. **2.** To cover with or as if with a glove. [ME < OE *glōf.*]

glove compartment *n.* A small storage container in the dashboard of an automobile.

glov·er (glŭv′ər) *n.* One who makes or sells gloves.

glow (glō) *intr.v.* **glowed, glow·ing, glows. 1.** To shine brightly and steadily, esp. without a flame: *embers glowing in the furnace.* **2. a.** To have a bright, warm, usually reddish color: *cheeks glowing from the cold.* **b.** To flush; blush. **3.** To be exuberant or radiant: *glowing with pride.* —*n.* **1.** A light produced by a body heated to luminosity; incandescence. **2.** Brilliance or warmth of color, esp. redness: *"the evening glow of the city streets when the sun has gone behind the tallest houses"* (Sean O'Faolain). **3.** A sensation of physical warmth. **4.** A warm feeling of passion or emotion; ardor. [ME *glouen* < OE *glōwan.*]

glow·er (glou′ər) *intr.v.* **-ered, -er·ing, -ers.** To look or stare angrily or sullenly. —*n.* An angry look or sullen stare. [ME *gloren.*] **—glow′er·ing·ly** *adv.*

glow plug *n.* A small heating element in a diesel engine cylinder used to facilitate starting.

glow·worm (glō′wûrm′) *n.* A firefly, esp. the luminous larva or wingless, grublike female of a firefly.

glox·in·i·a (glŏk-sĭn′ē-ə) *n.* Any of several tropical South American plants of the genus *Sinningia,* esp. *S. speciosa,* cultivated as a house plant for its showy, variously colored flowers. [NLat., after Benjamin P. *Gloxin,* 18th-cent. German botanist.]

gloze (glōz) *v.* **glozed, gloz·ing, gloz·es.** —*tr.* To minimize or underplay; gloss: *glozed over the embarrassing part.* —*intr. Archaic.* To use flattery or cajolery. [ME *glosen,* to interpret < OFr. *gloser* < *glose,* gloss < Med. Lat. *glosa.* —see GLOSS².]

gluc– *pref.* Variant of **gluco-.**

glu·ca·gon (glo͞o′kə-gŏn′) *n.* A proteinaceous pancreatic hormone that increases blood sugar. [GLUC(O)- + Gk. *agōn,* pr. part. of *agein,* to lead, drive.]

gluco– or **gluc–** *pref.* Glucose: *glucagon.* [< GLUCOSE.]

glu·cose (glo͞o′kōs′) *n.* **1.** Dextrose. **2.** A colorless to yellowish syrupy mixture of dextrose, maltose, and dextrins with about 20 per cent water, used in confectionery, alcoholic fermentation, tanning, and treating tobacco. [Fr. < Gk. *gleukos,* sweet wine.]

glu·co·side (glo͞o′kə-sīd′) *n.* A glycoside, the sugar component of which is glucose. **—glu′co·sid′ic** (-sĭd′ĭk) *adj.* **—glu′co·sid′i·cal·ly** *adv.*

glue (glo͞o) *n.* **1.** Any of various thick, sticky liquids used to hold things together. **2.** An adhesive obtained by boiling certain animal proteins. —*tr.v.* **glued, glu·ing, glues. 1.** To stick or fasten with glue. **2.** To fasten on something attentively: *Our eyes were glued to the stage.* [ME *gleu* < OFr. *glu* < LLat. *glus* < Lat. *gluten.*] **—glu′ey** *adj.*

glum (glŭm) *adj.* **glum·mer, glum·mest. 1.** In low spirits; dejected. **2.** Gloomy; dismal. [Orig. unknown.] **—glum′ly** *adv.* **—glum′ness** *n.*

Synonyms: *glum, gloomy, morose, dour, saturnine.* These adjectives mean having a cheerless or repugnant aspect or disposition. *Glum* implies dejection and silence, and more often than the other terms refers to a mood or temporary condition rather than to a person's characteristic state. *Gloomy* differs little except in being more applicable to a person given to somberness or depression by nature. *Morose* implies sourness of temper and a tendency to be uncommunicative. *Dour* especially suggests a grim or humorless exterior and sometimes an unyielding nature. *Saturnine* suggests severity of aspect, extreme gravity of nature, and often a tendency to be bitter or sardonic.

glu·ma·ceous (glo͞o-mā′shəs) *adj.* Having or resembling a glume or glumes.

glume (glo͞om) *n.* A chaffy basal bract on the spikelet of a grass. [NLat. *gluma* < Lat., husk.]

glu·on (glo͞o′ŏn) *n.* A massless, neutral elementary particle held to mediate the strong interaction that binds quarks together. [GLU(E) + -ON¹.]

glut (glŭt) *v.* **glut·ted, glut·ting, gluts.** —*tr.* **1.** To fill beyond capacity, esp. with food; satiate. **2.** To flood (a market) with an excess of goods so that supply exceeds demand. —*intr.* To eat or indulge in something excessively. —*n.* An oversupply. [ME *glotten* < OFr. *glotoiier,* to eat greedily < Lat. *gluttire.*]

glu·tam·ic acid (glo͞o-tăm′ĭk) *n.* An amino acid present in all complete proteins, found widely in plant and animal tissue, and having a salt, sodium glutamate, that is used as a flavor-intensifying seasoning. [GLUT(EN) + AM(IDE) + -IC.]

glu·ta·mine (glo͞o′tə-mēn′) *n.* A white crystalline amino acid, $C_5H_{10}N_2O_3$, occurring in plant and animal tissue and produced commercially for use in medicine and biochemical research. [GLUT(EN) + AMINE.]

glu·tar·al·de·hyde (glo͞o′tə-răl′də-hīd′) *n.* A water-soluble oily liquid, $C_5H_8O_2$, containing two aldehyde groups, used in tanning leather and as a fixative for biological tissues. [Blend of *glutaric acid* (< GLUTEN) and ALDEHYDE.]

glu·te·i (glo͞o′tē-ī′, glo͞o-tē′ī′) *n.* Plural of **gluteus.**

glu·ten (glo͞ot′n) *n.* A mixture of plant proteins occurring in cereal grains, chiefly corn and wheat, and used as an adhesive and as a flour substitute. [Lat., glue.] **—glu′ten·ous** *adj.*

gluten bread *n.* Bread made from flour with a high gluten content and low starch content.

glu·te·us (glo͞o′tē-əs, glo͞o-tē′-) *n., pl.* **glu·te·i** (glo͞o′tē-ī′, glo͞o-tē′ī′). Any of three large muscles of the buttocks. [NLat. < Gk. *gloutos,* buttock.] **—glu′te·al** *adj.*

glu·ti·nous (glo͞ot′n-əs) *adj.* Resembling or of the nature of glue; sticky. [Lat. *glutinosus* < *gluten,* glue.] **—glu′ti·nous·ly** *adv.* **—glu′ti·nous·ness, glu′ti·nos′i·ty** (-ŏs′ĭ-tē) *n.*

glut·ton (glŭt′n) *n.* **1.** A person who eats or consumes immoderate amounts of food and drink. **2.** A person with an inordinate capacity to receive or withstand something: *a glutton for punishment.* **3.** The wolverine. [ME *glotoun* < OFr. *gloton* < Lat. *glutto.*] **—glut′ton·ous** *adj.* **—glut′ton·ous·ly** *adv.*

glut·ton·y (glŭt′n-ē) *n.* Excess in eating or drinking.

glyc– *pref.* Variant of **glyco-.**

glyc·er·al·de·hyde (glĭs′ə-răl′də-hīd′) *n.* A sweet colorless solid, $C_3H_6O_3$, that is an intermediate compound in carbohydrate metabolism. [GLYCER(IN) + ALDEHYDE.]

gly·cer·ic acid (glĭ-sĕr′ĭk) *n.* A syrupy, colorless compound, $C_3H_6O_4$. [< GLYCERIN.]

glyc·er·ide (glĭs′ə-rīd′) *n.* An ester of glycerol and fatty acids. [GLYCER(IN) + -IDE.]

glyc·er·in (glĭs′ər-ĭn) *n.* Glycerol. [Fr. < Gk. *glukeros,* sweet.]

glyc·er·ol (glĭs′ə-rôl′, -rōl′, -rŏl′) *n.* A syrupy, sweet, colorless or yellowish liquid, $C_3H_8O_3$, obtained from fats and oils as a by-product of the manufacture of soaps and fatty acids and used as a solvent, antifreeze and antifrost fluid, plasticizer, and sweetener, and in the manufacture of dynamite, cosmetics, liquid soaps, inks, and lubricants. [GLYCER(IN) + -OL.]

glyc·er·yl (glĭs′ər-əl) *n.* The trivalent glycerol radical CH_2CHCH_2. [GLYCER(IN) + -YL.]

gly·cin (glī′sĭn) also **gly·cine** (-sēn′, -sĭn) *n.* A poisonous

glove
Baseball glove

gloxinia

glyph

compound, $C_8H_9NO_3$, used as a photographic developer. [< GLYCINE.]

gly·cine (glī'sēn', -sĭn) *n.* **1.** A white, very sweet crystalline amino acid, $C_2H_5NO_2$, the principal amino acid occurring in sugar cane, derived by alkaline hydrolysis of gelatin and used in biochemical research and medicine. **2.** Variant of **glycin.**

glyco– or **glyc–** *pref.* **1.** Sugar: *glycoprotein.* **2.** Glycogen: *glycogenesis.* [< Gk. *glukus,* sweet.]

gly·co·gen (glī'kə-jən) *n.* A white, sweet-tasting powder, $(C_6H_{10}O_5)_n$, occurring as the chief animal storage carbohydrate, primarily in the liver. **—gly'co·gen'ic** *adj.*

gly·co·gen·e·sis (glī'kə-jĕn'ĭ-sĭs) *n.* **1.** The formation of glycogen. **2.** The formation of sugar from glycogen. **—gly'co·ge·net'ic** (-jə-nĕt'ĭk) *adj.*

gly·col (glī'kôl', -kōl', -kŏl') *n.* **1.** Ethylene glycol. **2.** Any of various dihydric alcohols.

gly·col·ic acid (glī-kŏl'ĭk) *n.* A colorless crystalline compound, $C_2H_4O_3$, found in sugar beets, cane sugar, and unripe grapes, used in leather dyeing and tanning and in pharmaceuticals, pesticides, adhesives, and plasticizers.

gly·co·pro·tein (glī'kō-prō'tēn', -tē-ĭn) *n.* Any of several conjugated proteins that contain carbohydrates as prosthetic groups.

gly·co·side (glī'kə-sīd') *n.* Any of a group of organic compounds, occurring abundantly in plants, that produce sugars and related substances on hydrolysis. [*Glycose* (var. of GLUCOSE) + -IDE.] **—gly'co·sid'ic** (-sĭd'ĭk) *adj.*

gly·co·su·ri·a (glī'kə-sŏŏr'ē-ə, -shŏŏr'-) *n.* The excretion of abnormal quantities of sugar in the urine. [*Glycose* (var. of GLUCOSE) + -URIA.] **—gly'co·su'ric** *adj.*

gly·ox·a·line (glī-ŏk'sə-lēn', -lĭn) *n.* Imidazole. [GLY(COL) + OXAL(IC ACID) + -INE.]

glyph (glĭf) *n.* **1.** *Archit.* A vertical groove, esp. in a Doric column or frieze. **2.** A symbolic figure that is usually engraved or incised. **3.** A symbol, as figures of people on a road sign, that imparts information nonverbally. [Gk. *gluphē,* carving < *gluphein,* to carve.] **—glyph'ic** *adj.*

glyp·tic (glĭp'tĭk) *adj.* Of or relating to engraving or carving, esp. on precious stones. [Gk. *gluptikos* < *gluphein,* to carve.]

glyp·tics (glĭp'tĭks) *n.* *(used with a sing. verb).* The art of engraving or carving, esp. on precious stones; glyptography.

glyp·to·graph (glĭp'tə-grăf') *n.* An engraved inscription on a precious stone. [Gk. *gluptos,* carved (< *gluphein,* to carve) + -GRAPH.]

glyp·tog·ra·phy (glĭp-tŏg'rə-fē) *n.* The art or process of carving or engraving on precious stones. **—glyp·tog'ra·pher** *n.* **—glyp'to·graph'ic** (-tə-grăf'ĭk), **glyp'to·graph'i·cal** *adj.*

G-man (jē'măn') *n.* An agent of the Federal Bureau of Investigation. [G(OVERNMENT) + MAN.]

gnar also **gnarr** (när) *intr.v.* **gnarred, gnar·ring, gnars.** To snarl; growl. [Imit.]

gnarl[1] (närl) *intr.v.* **gnarled, gnarl·ing, gnarls.** To snarl; growl. [Freq. of GNAR.]

gnarl[2] (närl) *n.* A protruding knot on a tree. *—tr.v.* **gnarled, gnarl·ing, gnarls.** To make knotted; twist. [Back-formation < GNARLED.]

gnarled (närld) *adj.* **1.** Having gnarls; knotty or misshapen: *gnarled branches.* **2.** Crabbed in temperament. **3.** Rugged and roughened, as from old age or work: *the gnarled hands of a carpenter.* [Prob. var. of KNURLED.]

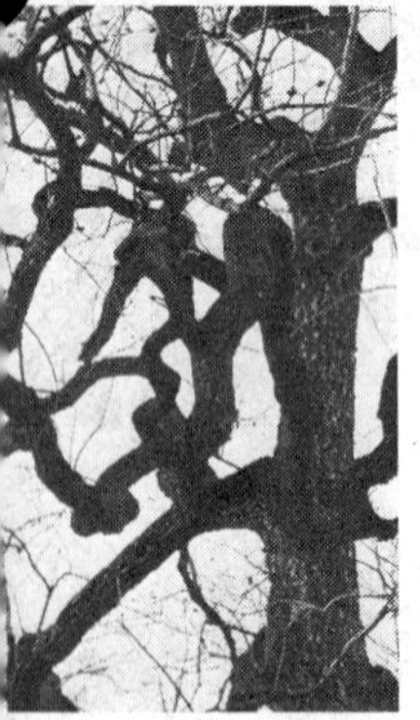
gnarled
Gnarled branches

gnarr (när) *v.* Variant of **gnar.**

gnash (năsh) *tr.v.* **gnashed, gnash·ing, gnash·es.** *—tr.* **1.** To grind or strike (the teeth, for example) together. **2.** To bite by grinding the teeth. [Alteration of ME *gnasten, gnaisten,* of Scand. orig.] **—gnash** *n.*

gnat (năt) *n.* Any of numerous small, winged insects, esp. one that bites. [ME < OE *gnæt.*]

gnat·catch·er (năt'kăch'ər, -kĕch'-) *n.* Any of several small New World birds of the genus *Polioptila,* having grayish and white plumage and a long tail.

gna·thal (nā'thəl, năth'əl) *adj.* Gnathic. [< Gk. *gnathos,* jaw.]

gnath·ic (năth'ĭk) *adj.* Of or relating to the jaw. [< Gk. *gnathos,* jaw.]

gna·thite (nā'thīt', năth'īt') *n.* A jaw or jawlike appendage of an insect or other arthropod. [Gk. *gnathos,* jaw + -ITE.]

–gnathous *suff.* Having a specified kind of jaw: *metagnathous.* [NLat. *-gnathus,* < Gk. *gnathos,* jaw.]

gnaw (nô) *v.* **gnawed, gnaw·ing, gnaws.** *—tr.* **1. a.** To bite, chew on, or erode with the teeth. **b.** To produce by gnawing: *gnaw a hole.* **c.** To erode or diminish gradually as if by gnawing: *waves gnawing the rocky shore.* **2.** To afflict or trouble persistently: *fear gnawing her.* *—intr.* **1.** To bite or chew persistently: *The dog gnawed at the bone.* **2.** To cause erosion or gradual diminishment. [ME *gnauen* < OE *gnagan.*] **—gnaw'er** *n.*

gneiss (nīs) *n.* A banded or foliated metamorphic rock, usually of the same composition as granite, in which the minerals are arranged in layers. [G. *Gneis.*] **—gneiss'ic** (nī'sĭk), **gneiss'oid'** (nī'soid'), **gneiss'ose'** (nī'sōs') *adj.*

gnu
White-bearded gnu

gnoc·chi (nyô'kē) *pl.n.* Dumplings made of flour, semolina, or potatoes, boiled or baked and served with grated cheese or sauces. [Ital., pl. of *gnocco,* alteration of *nocchio,* knot in wood.]

gnome[1] (nōm) *n.* **1.** One of a fabled race of dwarflike creatures who live underground and guard treasure hoards. **2.** A shriveled old man. [Fr. < NLat. *gnomus.*] **—gnom'ish** *adj.*

gnome[2] (nōm) *n.* A pithy saying that expresses a general truth or fundamental principle; aphorism. [Gk. *gnōmē* < *gignōskein,* to know.]

gno·mic (nō'mĭk) *adj.* Marked by aphorisms; aphoristic: *gnomic poetry.* [< GNOME[2].]

gno·mon (nō'mŏn', -mən) *n.* **1.** An object, as the style of a sundial, that projects a shadow used as an indicator. **2.** The figure that remains after a parallelogram has been removed from a similar but larger parallelogram with which it has a common corner. [Lat. < Gk. *gnōmōn* < *gignōskein,* to know.] **—gno·mon'ic, gno·mon'i·cal** *adj.*

gno·sis (nō'sĭs) *n.* Intuitive apprehension of spiritual truths, an esoteric form of knowledge sought by the Gnostics. [Gk. *gnōsis,* knowledge < *gignōskein,* to know.]

gnos·tic (nŏs'tĭk) *adj.* **1.** Of, relating to, or possessing intellectual or spiritual knowledge. **2. Gnostic.** Of or pertaining to Gnosticism. *—n.* **Gnostic.** A believer in Gnosticism. [Lat. *Gnosticus,* a Gnostic < Gk. *Gnōstikos* < *gignōskein,* to know.]

Gnos·ti·cism (nŏs'tĭ-sĭz'əm) *n.* The doctrines of certain early Christian sects that valued inquiry into spiritual truth above faith, considered salvation attainable only by the few whose faith enabled them to transcend matter, and viewed Christ as noncorporeal.

gnu (nōō, nyōō) *n.* Either of two large African antelopes, *Connochaetes gnou* or *C. taurinus,* having a drooping beard, a long, tufted tail, and curved horns in both sexes. [Xhosa *i-gnu.*]

go[1] (gō) *v.* **went** (wĕnt), **gone** (gôn, gŏn), **go·ing, goes.** *—intr.* **1.** To move along; proceed: *going by bus.* **2.** To move away from a place; depart: *Go before I really get mad.* **3. a.** To pursue a certain course. **b.** To resort to someone, as for aid: *went directly to the voters of her district.* **4. a.** To extend between two points or in a certain direction; run: *curtains going from the ceiling to the floor.* **b.** To give entry; lead: *a bulkhead going to the basement.* **5.** To move or function properly: *The car won't go.* **6. a.** To have currency. **b.** To pass from one person to another; circulate: *a story that went around the office.* **7.** To pass as the result of a sale: *went to the highest bidder.* **8.** *Informal.* Used as an intensifier when joined by *and* to a coordinate verb: *He went and meddled in our affairs.* **9.** Used in the progressive tense with an infinitive to indicate future intent or expectation: *is going to learn how to dance.* **10. a.** To be in a certain state or condition: *The vote went against him.* **b.** To come to be in a certain state or condition: *go mad; go to sleep.* **c.** To continue in a certain state or maintain an activity: *going strong with his piano studies.* **d.** To carry out as action to a certain point or extent: *went to great expense.* **11. a.** To be customarily located; belong: *The fork goes to the left of the plate.* **b.** To be capable of entering or being held: *Will the bike go into the trunk of your car?* **12. a.** To pass into someone's possession: *Her jewelry went to a granddaughter.* **b.** To be allotted or awarded: *How much of your salary goes for rent?* **13.** To be a factor that contributes or leads to: *It all goes to show us that it can be done.* **14.** To have a particular form: *as the saying goes.* **15. a.** To pass by; elapse. **b.** To be consumed or used up. **c.** To be discarded or abolished: *Luxuries will have to go.* **16. a.** To become weak; fail: *His hearing started to go.* **b.** To come apart or break up. **17.** To die. **18. a.** To get along; fare: *How are things going?* **b.** To have a successful outcome: *energy that made the advertising campaign really go.* **19. a.** To be suitable or appropriate as an accessory or accompaniment: *a color that went beautifully with her complexion.* **b.** To be as a general rule: *was well-behaved as cats go.* **20. a.** To have authority: *Whatever he says goes.* **b.** To be valid, acceptable, or adequate. **21.** *Informal.* To excrete waste from the bladder or bowels. **22.** *Obs.* To walk. *—tr.* *Informal.* To say. Used chiefly in verbal narration: *First I go "thank you," then he goes, "what for?"* **—*phrasal verbs.* go about.** To undertake. **go after.** To seek; pursue. **go along.** To cooperate: *got along by going along.* **go around.** To satisfy a demand or requirement: *just enough food to go around.* **go at.** To attack, esp. with energy. **go back on. 1.** To fail to keep: *go back on a promise.* **2.** To betray. **go down. 1.** To sink below the horizon; set. **2.** To experience defeat or ruin. **3.** *Chiefly Brit.* To leave a university. **4.** *Slang.* To occur; happen. **go down on.** *Vulgar Slang.* To perform an oral sex act upon. **go for. 1.** To have a special liking for: *really goes for progressive jazz.* **2.** To attack: *go for the jugular in an argument.* **go in.** To take part in a cooperative venture: *went in with the others to buy a present.* **go in for. 1.** To have an interest in. **2.** To take part in: *go in for skiing.* **go off. 1.** To undergo detonation; explode. **2.** To make a noise; sound. **go on.** To take place; happen: *didn't know what was going on.* **go out.** To become extinguished. **go out for.** To seek to become a participant in. **go over. 1.** To gain acceptance or approval. **2.** To examine. **go straight.** To reform after having been a criminal. **go under. 1.** To suffer defeat or destruction; fail. **2.** To lose consciousness. **go with.** To date regularly. *—n., pl.* **goes. 1.** The act or an instance of going. **2.** An attempt; effort: *had a go at acting.* **3.** The time or period of an activity. **4.** *Informal.* Energy; vitality: *had lots of go.* **5.** A go-ahead. *—adj. Informal.* Functioning correctly and ready for action: *All systems are go.* **—*idioms.* go one**

better. To surpass or outdo by one degree. **go places.** To be on the road to success. **go steady.** To date exclusively. **go the distance.** To carry a course of action through to completion. **go to (one's) head. 1.** To make one excited or dizzy. **2.** To make one vain or overconfident. **go to pieces. 1.** To lose one's self-control. **2.** To suffer the loss of one's health. **no go.** *Informal.* Ineffective; useless. **on the go.** Constantly busy or active. **to go.** To be taken out, as restaurant food or drink: *coffee to go.* [ME *gon* < OE *gān.*]

go[2] (gō) *n.* A Japanese game for two, played with counters on a board that is ruled with 19 vertical and 19 horizontal lines. [J.]

go·a (gō′ə) *n.* A gazelle, *Procapra picticaudata,* of eastern Asia, the male of which has backward-curving horns. [Tibetan *dgoba.*]

goad (gōd) *n.* **1.** A long stick with a pointed end used for prodding animals. **2.** Something that prods or urges; stimulus. —*tr.v.* **goad·ed, goad·ing, goads. 1.** To prod with a goad. **2.** To give impetus to as if with a goad; incite. [ME *gode* < OE *gād.*]

go-a·head (gō′ə-hĕd′) *n. Informal.* Permission to proceed.

goal (gōl) *n.* **1.** The purpose toward which an endeavor is directed; objective. **2.** The finish line of a race. **3.** *Sports.* **a.** A specified structure or area into or over which players endeavor to advance a ball or puck. **b.** The score awarded for such an act. [ME *gol,* boundary.]

goal·ie (gō′lē) *n.* A goalkeeper.

goal·keep·er (gōl′kē′pər) *n.* A player assigned to protect the goal in various sports.

goal post *n.* One of a pair of posts joined with a crossbar and set at each end of a football or soccer field, forming the goal.

goal·tend·er (gōl′tĕn′dər) *n.* A goalkeeper.

goal·tend·ing (gōl′tĕn′dĭng) *n.* **1.** The act of protecting the goal in various sports, as hockey. **2.** *Basketball.* An illegal play in which a player deflects a ball that is on the downward path to the basket or has already broken the plane of the cylinder, carrying the penalty of an automatic score for the offensive team.

go-a·round (gō′ə-round′) *n.* **1.** An argument. **2.** A run-around (sense 1).

goat (gōt) *n.* **1.** Any of various horned, bearded ruminant mammals of the genus *Capra,* originally of mountainous regions of the Old World, esp. one of the domesticated forms of *C. hircus.* **2. Goat.** *Astron.* Capricorn. **3.** A lecherous man. **4.** A scapegoat. ***—idiom.*** **get (someone's) goat.** *Informal.* To make angry or annoyed. [ME *got* < OE *gāt.*] **—goat′ish** *adj.*

goat antelope *n.* Any of various ruminant mammals, as the mountain goat or the chamois, having characteristics of both goats and antelopes.

goat·ee (gō-tē′) *n.* A small chin beard often trimmed into a point and resembling that of a goat.

goat·fish (gōt′fĭsh′) *n., pl.* **goatfish** or **-fish·es.** Any of various brightly colored fishes of the family Mullidae, of warm seas, having two sensory barbels on the chin.

goats·beard also **goat's-beard** (gōts′bîrd′) *n.* **1.** A plant, *Tragopogon pratensis,* native to Europe, having grasslike leaves and yellow, dandelionlike flowers. **2.** A tall plant, *Aruncus dioicus,* having compound leaves and branching clusters of small white flowers.

goat·skin (gōt′skĭn′) *n.* **1.** The skin of a goat. **2.** Leather made from a goatskin. **3.** A container, as for wine, made from a goatskin.

goat's-rue (gōts′rōō′) *n.* **1.** A North American plant, *Tephrosia virginiana,* having yellow and pink flowers. **2.** A Eurasian plant, *Galega officinalis,* cultivated for its showy, variously colored flowers.

goat·suck·er (gōt′sŭk′ər) *n.* Any of various chiefly nocturnal birds of the family Caprimulgidae, which includes the nighthawk and the whippoorwill. [From the belief that the bird sucked milk from goats]

gob[1] (gŏb) *n.* **1.** A small piece or lump. **2.** Often **gobs.** *Informal.* A large quantity, as of money. [ME *gobbe* < *gobet.* — see GOBBET.]

gob[2] (gŏb) *n. Slang.* The mouth. [Sc. and Ir. Gael.]

gob[3] (gŏb) *n. Slang.* A sailor. [Orig. unknown.]

gob·bet (gŏb′ĭt) *n.* A piece or chunk, esp. of raw meat. [ME *gobet* < OFr.]

gob·ble[1] (gŏb′əl) *v.* **-bled, -bling, -bles.** —*tr.* **1.** To devour in large, greedy gulps. **2.** To take greedily; grab: *gobbled up the few remaining tickets.* —*intr.* To eat greedily or rapidly. [Perh. < GOB[1].]

gob·ble[2] (gŏb′əl) *n.* The guttural, chortling sound of a male turkey. —*intr.v.* **-bled, -bling, -bles.** To make a gobble. [Imit.]

gob·ble·dy·gook also **gob·ble·de·gook.** (gŏb′əl-dē-gŏŏk′) *n.* Unclear, wordy jargon. [Coined by Maury Maverick (1895–1954).]

gob·bler (gŏb′lər) *n.* A male turkey.

Go·be·lin (gō′bə-lĭn, gŏb′ə-) *n.* A tapestry of a kind woven at the Gobelin works in Paris, France, noted for rich pictorial design.

go-be·tween (gō′bĭ-twēn′) *n.* One who acts as an intermediary or messenger between two sides.

gob·let (gŏb′lĭt) *n.* **1.** A drinking glass or similar vessel with a stem and base. **2.** *Archaic.* A drinking bowl without handles. [ME *gobelet* < OFr., dim. of *gobel,* cup.]

gob·lin (gŏb′lĭn) *n.* A grotesque, elfin creature of folklore, thought to work mischief or evil. [ME *gobelin* < OFr. < Med. Lat. *gobelinus.*]

go·by (gō′bē) *n., pl.* **goby** or **-bies.** Any of numerous usually small freshwater and marine fishes of the family Gobiidae, having the pelvic fins united to form a sucking disk. [Lat. *gobius* gudgeon < Gk. *kōbios.*]

go-by (gō′bī′) *n. Informal.* An intentional slight; snub.

go-cart (gō′kärt′) *n.* **1.** A small wagon for children to ride in, drive, or pull. **2.** A small frame on casters designed to help support a child learning to walk. **3.** A handcart. **4.** A stroller.

god (gŏd) *n.* **1. God. a.** A being conceived as the perfect, omnipotent, omniscient originator and ruler of the universe, the principal object of faith and worship in monotheistic religions. **b.** The force, effect, or a manifestation or aspect of this being. **c.** *Christian Science.* "Infinite Mind; Spirit; Soul; Principle; Life; Truth; Love" (Mary Baker Eddy). **2.** A being of supernatural powers or attributes, believed in and worshiped by a people, esp. a male deity thought to control some part of nature or reality. **3.** An image of a supernatural being; idol. **4.** Something that is worshiped or idealized: *money was his god.* **5.** A man of great beauty. [ME < OE.]

God-aw·ful (gŏd′ô′fəl) *adj. Slang.* Extremely trying; atrocious.

god·child (gŏd′chīld′) *n.* A person for whom another serves as sponsor at baptism.

god·daugh·ter (gŏd′dô′tər) *n.* A female godchild.

god·dess (gŏd′ĭs) *n.* **1.** A being of supernatural powers or attributes, believed in and worshiped by a people. **2.** An image of a supernatural being; idol. **3.** Something that is worshiped or idealized. **4.** A woman of great beauty or grace.

go-dev·il (gō′dĕv′əl) *n.* **1.** A logging sled. **2.** A railway hand-car. **3.** A jointed tool for cleaning an oil pipeline and disengaging obstructions. **4.** An iron dart dropped into an oil well to explode a charge of dynamite.

god·fa·ther (gŏd′fä′*th*ər) *n.* A man who sponsors a person at baptism.

god·for·sak·en also **God·for·sak·en** (gŏd′fər-sā′kən) *adj.* **1.** Located in a dismal or remote area. **2.** Desolate; forlorn.

god·head (gŏd′hĕd′) *n.* **1.** Divinity; godhood. **2. Godhead. a.** God. **b.** The essential and divine nature of God, regarded abstractly. [ME *godhede* : *god,* god (< OE) + *-hede,* -hood.]

god·hood (gŏd′hŏŏd′) *n.* The quality or state of being a god; divinity. [ME *godhode* : *god,* god (< OE) + *-hode,* -hood.]

god·less (gŏd′lĭs) *adj.* Recognizing or worshiping no god. **—god′less·ly** *adv.* **—god′less·ness** *n.*

god·like (gŏd′līk′) *adj.* Resembling or of the nature of a god or God; divine. **—god′like′ness** *n.*

god·ling (gŏd′lĭng) *n.* A minor god.

god·ly (gŏd′lē) *adj.* **-li·er, -li·est. 1.** Having great reverence for God; pious. **2.** Divine. **—god′li·ness** *n.*

god·moth·er (gŏd′mŭ*th*′ər) *n.* A woman who sponsors a person at baptism.

god·par·ent (gŏd′pâr′ənt, păr′-) *n.* A godfather or godmother.

God's acre *n.* A churchyard or burial ground. [Transl. of G. *Gottesacker.*]

god·send (gŏd′sĕnd′) *n.* Something wanted or needed that comes or happens unexpectedly. [ME *goddes sand,* God's message : *god,* God + *sand,* message < OE.]

god·son (gŏd′sŭn′) *n.* A male godchild.

God·speed (gŏd′spēd′) *n.* Success or good fortune. [From the phrase *God speed you.*]

god·wit (gŏd′wĭt′) *n.* Any of various wading birds of the genus *Limosa,* having a long, slender, slightly upturned bill. [Orig. unknown.]

goe·thite (gō′thīt′, gœ′tīt′) *n.* A brown mineral, essentially $HFeO_2$, used as an iron ore. [After Johann W. *von Goethe* (1749–1832).]

go·fer also **go-fer** (gō′fər) *n. Slang.* An employee who runs errands in addition to regular duties. [Alteration of *go for,* from that person's having to go for or after things.]

gof·fer also **gauf·fer** (gŏf′ər, gô′fər) —*tr.v.* **-fered, -fer·ing, -fers.** To press ridges or narrow pleats into (a frill, for example). —*n.* **1.** An iron used for goffering. **2.** Ridged or pleated ornamentation produced by goffering. [Fr. *gaufrer,* to emboss < OFr. *gaufre,* honeycomb < MLG *wāfel.*]

go-get·ter (gō′gĕt′ər) *n. Informal.* An enterprising, hustling person.

gog·gle (gŏg′əl) *v.* **-gled, -gling, -gles.** —*intr.* **1.** To stare with wide and bulging eyes. **2.** To roll or bulge. Used of the eyes. —*tr.* To roll or bulge (the eyes). —*n.* **1.** A stare or leer. **2. goggles.** A pair of large, usually tinted spectacles with shielding side pieces worn as a protection against wind, dust, or glare. [ME *gogelen,* to squint.] **—gog′gly** *adj.*

gog·gle-eyed (gŏg′əl-īd′) *adj.* Having prominent or rolling eyes.

go-go also **go·go** (gō′gō′) *adj. Informal.* **1. a.** Of or pertaining to discotheques or to the energetic music and dancing performed at discotheques. **b.** Engaged to perform at a discotheque: *a go-go dancer.* **2.** Energetic; lively. **3.** Of, pertain-

goat

goatee

goblet

golden eagle

goldenrod

goldfinch
American goldfinch

ing to, or engaging in a type of speculative and therefore risky stock-market operation: *a go-go fund.* [< À GOGO.]

Goi·del·ic (goi-dĕl′ĭk) *n.* A branch of the Celtic languages that includes Irish Gaelic, Scottish Gaelic, and Manx. —*adj.* **1.** Of or pertaining to the Gaels. **2.** Of, pertaining to, or characteristic of Goidelic. [< OIr. *Goidel,* Gael.]

go·ing (gō′ĭng) *n.* **1.** Departure: *comings and goings.* **2.** The condition underfoot as it affects one's headway in walking or riding. **3.** *Informal.* Progress toward a goal; heading. —*adj.* **1.** Working; running: *in going order.* **2.** In full operation; flourishing: *a going business.* **3.** Current; prevailing: *The going rates are high.* **4.** Available; to be found: *the best products going.*

go·ing-o·ver (gō′ĭng-ō′vər) *n., pl.* **go·ings-o·ver.** *Informal.* **1.** An examination; inspection. **2. a.** A severe beating. **b.** A severe reprimand.

go·ings-on (gō′ĭngz-ŏn′) *pl.n. Informal.* Proceedings or behavior, esp. when regarded with disapproval.

goi·ter also **goi·tre** (goi′tər) *n.* A chronic, noncancerous enlargement of the thyroid gland, visible as a swelling at the front of the neck, occurring without hyperthyroidism and associated with iodine deficiency. [Fr. *goitre* < Prov. *goitron* < Lat. *guttur,* throat.] —**goi′trous** (-trəs) *adj.*

Gol·con·da (gŏl-kŏn′də) *n.* A source of great riches, as a mine. [After *Golconda,* India.]

gold (gōld) *n.* **1.** *Symbol* **Au** A soft, yellow, corrosion-resistant element, the most malleable and ductile metal, occurring in veins and alluvial deposits and recovered by mining or by panning or sluicing. It is a good thermal and electrical conductor, is generally alloyed to increase its strength, and is used as an international monetary standard, in jewelry, for decoration, and as a plated coating on a wide variety of electrical and mechanical components. Atomic number 79; atomic weight 196.967; melting point 1,063.0°C; boiling point 2,966.0°C; specific gravity 19.32; valences 1, 3. **2. a.** Coinage made of gold. **b.** A gold standard. **3.** Money; riches. **4.** A light olive-brown to dark yellow or moderate, strong, to vivid yellow. **5.** Something regarded as having great value or goodness: *a heart of gold.* —*adj.* Having the color of gold. [ME < OE.]

gold·beat·er's skin (gōld′bē′tərz) *n.* Treated animal membrane used to separate sheets of gold being hammered into gold leaf.

gold·beat·ing (gōld′bē′tĭng) *n.* The act, art, or process of beating sheets of gold into gold leaf. —**gold′beat′er** *n.*

gold brick *n.* **1.** A bar of gilded cheap metal that appears to be genuine gold. **2.** A fraudulent and worthless substitute.

gold·brick (gōld′brĭk′) *Slang.* —*n.* A person, esp. a soldier, who avoids assigned duties or work; shirker. —*v.* **-bricked, -brick·ing, -bricks.** —*intr.* To shirk one's assigned duties or responsibilities. —*tr.* To cheat; swindle. —**gold′brick′er** *n.*

gold bug *n.* **1.** A North American beetle, *Metriona bicolor,* with a metallic luster. **2.** A supporter of the gold standard.

gold certificate *n.* A monetary note formerly issued to the public by the U.S. Treasury and redeemable in gold but now issued to Federal Reserve Banks to certify conformity with their legal reserve requirements.

gold digger *n. Slang.* A woman who seeks money and expensive gifts from men.

gold dust *n.* Gold in powder form.

gold·en (gōl′dən) *adj.* **1.** Of, pertaining to, made of, or containing gold. **2. a.** Having the color of gold or a yellow color suggestive of gold. **b.** Lustrous; radiant: *the golden sun.* **c.** Suggestive of gold, as in richness or splendor: *a golden voice.* **3.** Of the greatest value or importance; precious. **4.** Marked by peace, prosperity, and often creativeness: *a golden era.* **5.** Very favorable or advantageous; excellent: *a golden opportunity.* **6.** Having a promising future; seemingly assured of success: *a golden boy.* **7.** Of or pertaining to a 50th anniversary. —**gold′en·ly** *adv.* —**gold′en·ness** *n.*

golden age *n.* **1.** *Gk. & Rom. Myth.* The first age of the world, an untroubled and prosperous era during which people lived in ideal happiness. **2.** A period of peace, prosperity, and happiness.

golden ager *n.* An elderly person, esp. one of retirement age.

golden Al·ex·an·ders (ăl′ĭg-zăn′dərz) *n. (used with a sing. or pl. verb).* A plant, *Zizia aurea,* of eastern North America, having clusters of small yellow flowers.

golden aster *n.* Any of various North American plants of the genus *Chrysopsis,* having yellow, rayed flowers.

golden bantam *n.* A variety of corn having large, bright-yellow kernels on a relatively small ear.

golden calf *n.* **1.** A golden image of a sacrificial calf fashioned by Aaron and worshiped by the Israelites. **2.** Money as an object of worship; mammon.

golden club *n.* An aquatic plant, *Orontium aquaticum,* of the eastern United States, having small golden-yellow flowers covering a clublike spadix.

golden eagle *n.* An eagle, *Aquila chrysaetos,* of mountainous areas of the Northern Hemisphere, having dark plumage with yellowish feathers on the head and neck.

gol·den·eye (gōl′dən-ī′) *n.* Either of two ducks, *Bucephala clangula* or *B. islandica,* of northern regions, having a short black bill, a rounded head, and black and white plumage. [From their golden-yellow eyes.]

Golden Fleece *n. Gk. Myth.* The fleece of the golden ram, stolen by Jason and the Argonauts from the king of Colchis.

golden glow *n.* A tall plant, *Rudbeckia laciniata hortensis,* cultivated for its yellow, many-rayed, double flowers.

Golden Horde *n.* The Mongol army that swept over eastern Europe in the 13th century and established a suzerain in Russia. [From the golden tent of their commander.]

golden mean *n.* The course between extremes.

golden oldie *n.* A recording, motion picture, or other form of entertainment that was very popular in the past.

golden pheasant *n.* A pheasant, *Chrysolophus pictus,* of China and Tibet, having a long tail and brilliantly colored plumage.

gold·en·rod (gōl′dən-rŏd′) *n.* Any of numerous chiefly North American plants of the genus *Solidago,* having clusters of small yellow flowers that bloom in late summer or fall.

golden rule *n.* The biblical teaching that one should behave toward others as one would have others behave toward oneself.

gold·en·seal (gōl′dən-sēl′) *n.* A woodland plant, *Hydrastis canadensis,* of eastern North America, having small greenish-white flowers and a yellow root formerly used medicinally.

golden section *n.* A ratio, observed esp. in the fine arts, between the two dimensions of a plane figure or the two divisions of a line such that the smaller is to the larger as the larger is to the sum of the two, roughly a ratio of three to five.

gold-filled (gōld′fĭld′) *adj.* Made of a hard base metal with an outer layer of gold.

gold·finch (gōld′fĭnch′) *n.* **1.** Any of several small New World birds of the genus *Spinus,* esp. *S. tristis,* of which the male has yellow plumage with a black forehead, wings, and tail. **2.** A small Old World bird, *Carduelis carduelis,* having brownish plumage with red, yellow, and black markings.

gold·fish (gōld′fĭsh′) *n., pl.* **goldfish** or **-fish·es.** A freshwater fish, *Carassius auratus,* native to eastern Asia, characteristically having brassy or reddish coloring and bred in many ornamental forms as an aquarium fish.

gold foil *n.* Gold rolled or beaten into thin sheets thicker than gold leaf.

gold·i·locks (gōl′dē-lŏks′) *n.* A European plant, *Linosyrus vulgaris,* having narrow leaves and clusters of small yellow flowers. [Obs. *goldy,* golden (< GOLD) + LOCKS.]

gold leaf *n.* Gold beaten into extremely thin sheets used esp. for gilding.

gold mine *n. Informal.* A source of something, as information, that is wanted.

gold-of-pleas·ure (gōld′əv-plĕzh′ər) *n.* A plant, *Camelina sativa,* native to the Old World, having small yellow flowers and seeds rich in oil.

gold point *n.* **1.** The point in foreign-exchange rates at which it is no more expensive to import or export gold bullion in settling international accounts than to buy or sell bills of exchange. **2.** A fixed point on the international temperature scale equivalent to the melting point of gold, 1064.43°C, at a pressure of one atmosphere.

gold reserve *n.* The reserve of gold bullion held by a government or central bank to redeem its notes.

gold rush *n.* A rush of migrants to an area where gold has been discovered.

gold·smith (gōld′smĭth′) *n.* **1.** An artisan who fashions objects of gold. **2.** A tradesman who deals in gold articles.

goldsmith beetle *n.* Either of two scarabaeid beetles, *Cotalpa lanigera* or *Cetonia aurata,* having metallic greenish-yellow coloring.

gold standard *n.* A monetary standard under which the basic unit of currency is equal in value to and exchangeable for a specified amount of gold.

gold·stone (gōld′stōn′) *n.* An aventurine with gold-colored inclusions.

gold·thread (gōld′thrĕd′) *n.* A low-growing woodland plant, *Coptis trifolia,* having white flowers and slender yellow roots.

go·lem (gō′ləm) *n.* In Jewish folklore, an artificially created human being endowed with life by supernatural means. [Yiddish *goylem* < Heb. *gōlem* < *gālam,* he wrapped up.]

golf (gŏlf, gôlf) *n.* A game played on a large outdoor course with a series of 9 or 18 holes spaced far apart, the object being to propel a small ball with the use of various clubs into each hole with as few strokes as possible. —*intr.v.* **golfed, golf·ing, golfs.** To play golf. [ME.] —**golf′er** *n.*

golf club *n.* **1.** One of a set of clubs having a slender shaft and a head of wood or iron, used in golf. **2.** An organization of golfers.

golf course *n.* A large tract of land laid out for golf.

golf·links (gŏlf′lĭngks′) *pl.n.* A golf course.

Gol·gi apparatus also **Gol·gi complex** (gôl′jē) *n.* A network of fibrils, granules, and membranous structures present in living cells and believed to function in the formation of secretions within the cell. [After Camillo *Golgi* (1844–1926).]

gol·go·tha (gŏl′gə-thə) *n.* A place or occasion of great suffering. [After *Golgotha,* the hill near Jerusalem where Jesus was crucified.]

gol·iard (gŏl′yərd, -yär′) *n.* A wandering student in medieval Europe disposed to conviviality, license, and the making of ribald and satirical Latin songs. [OFr., glutton < *gole,* throat < Lat. *gula.*] —**gol·iar′dic** (gōl-yär′dĭk) *adj.*

Go·li·ath (gə-lī′əth) *n.* **1.** The giant Philistine warrior in the Old Testament who was slain by David with a stone and sling. **2.** A person of colossal power or achievement. [Heb. *Golyath.*]

gol·li·wog or **gol·li·wogg** (gŏl′ē-wŏg′) *n.* **1.** A black male doll of grotesque appearance. **2.** A grotesque person. [After *Golliwog,* a character in books by Bertha Upton (d. 1912).]

gol·ly (gŏl′ē) *interj.* Used to express mild surprise or wonder. [Alteration of GOD.]

gom·pho·sis (gŏm-fō′sĭs) *n., pl.* **-ses** (-sēz). An immovable peg and rigid socket articulation, as of a tooth and its bony socket. [Gk. *gomphōsis* < *gomphoun,* to fasten with bolts < *gomphos,* bolt.]

gon– *pref.* Variant of **gono-**.

–gon *suff.* A figure having a specified kind or number of angles: *isogon.* [Gk. *-gōnon* < *gōnia,* angle.]

go·nad (gō′năd′) *n.* The organ that produces gametes; a testis or ovary. [NLat. < Gk. *gonos,* procreation.] —**go·nad′al** (gō-năd′l), **go·nad′ic** *adj.*

go·nad·o·trop·ic (gō-năd′ə-trŏp′ĭk, -trō′pĭk) also **go·nad·o·troph·ic** (-trŏf′ĭk, -trō′fĭk) *adj.* Acting on or stimulating the gonads, as a hormone.

go·nad·o·tro·pin (gō-năd′ə-trō′pĭn, -trŏp′ĭn) also **go·nad·o·tro·phin** (-trō′fĭn, -trō′pĭn) *n.* A gonadotropic substance.

Gond (gŏnd) *n.* One of a people of Dravidian stock of central India.

Gon·di (gŏn′dē) *n.* The Dravidian language of the Gonds.

gon·do·la (gŏn′dl-ə, gŏn-dō′lə) *n.* **1.** A narrow, lightweight barge with ends that curve up into a point and often a small cabin in the middle, propelled with a single oar from the stern, used on the canals of Venice. **2.** A flat-bottomed river boat. **3.** A gondola car. **4.** A basket, enclosure, or instrument sling suspended from and carried aloft by a balloon. **5.** An enclosed car suspended from a cable, used for conveying passengers, as to and from a ski slope. [Ital.]

gondola car *n.* An open, shallow freight car.

gon·do·lier (gŏn′dl-îr′) *n.* The boatman of a gondola. [Fr. < Ital. *gondoliere* < *gondola,* gondola.]

gone (gôn, gŏn) *v.* Past participle of **go¹**. —*adj.* **1.** Past; bygone. **2.** Advanced beyond hope or recall. **3.** Dying or dead. **4.** Ruined; lost: *a gone cause.* **5.** Carried away; absorbed. **6.** Used up; exhausted. **7.** *Slang.* Infatuated: *gone on the girl.*

gon·er (gô′nər, gŏn′ər) *n. Slang.* One who is ruined or doomed. [< GONE.]

gon·fa·lon (gŏn′fə-lŏn′, -lən) *n.* A banner suspended from a crosspiece, esp. as a standard in an ecclesiastical procession or as the ensign of a medieval Italian republic. [Ital. *gonfalone,* of Germanic orig.]

gon·fa·lon·ier (gŏn′fə-lə-nîr′) *n.* The bearer of a gonfalon. [Fr. < Ital. *gonfaloniere* < *gonfalon,* gonfalon.]

gong (gông, gŏng) *n.* **1.** A rimmed metal disk that produces a loud, sonorous tone when struck with a padded mallet. **2.** A usually saucer-shaped bell that is struck with a mechanically operated hammer. —*intr.v.* **gonged, gong·ing, gongs.** To make the sound of a gong. [Malay *gŏng.*]

Gon·gor·ism (gŏng′gə-rĭz′əm) *n.* A florid, cluttered literary style. [After Luis de *Góngora* y Argote (1561–1627).] —**Gon′gor·is′tic** (gŏng′gə-rĭs′tĭk) *adj.*

go·nid·i·um (gō-nĭd′ē-əm) *n., pl.* **-i·a** (-ē-ə). **1.** An asexually produced reproductive cell that separates from the parent body, as in certain colonial microorganisms. **2.** An algal cell in the thallus of a lichen. [NLat. < Gk. *gonos,* birth.]

gon·if (gŏn′ĭf) *n.* Variant of **ganef**.

go·ni·om·e·ter (gō′nē-ŏm′ĭ-tər) *n.* **1.** An optical instrument for measuring crystal angles. **2.** A radio receiver and directional antenna used as a system to determine the angular direction of incoming radio signals. [Gk. *gōnia,* angle + -METER.] —**go′ni·o·met′ric** (-nē-ə-mĕt′rĭk), **go′ni·o·met′ri·cal** *adj.* —**go′ni·om′e·try** *n.*

go·ni·on (gō′nē-ŏn′) *n.* The point of the angle on either side of the lower jaw. [< Gk. *gonia,* angle.]

gono– or **gon–** *pref.* Sexual; reproductive: *gonophore.* [NLat. < Gk. < *gonos,* seed, procreation.]

gon·o·coc·cus (gŏn′ə-kŏk′əs) *n., pl.* **-coc·ci** (-kŏk′sī′, -kŏk′ī′). A bacterium, *Neisseria gonorrhoeae,* that causes gonorrhea. —**gon′o·coc′cal** (-kŏk′əl), **gon′o·coc′cic** (-kŏk′ĭk, -kŏk′sĭk) *adj.*

go-no-go (gō-nō′gō) *adj.* Of, pertaining to, or requiring the outcome of a parameter in order to stop or continue a course of action: *a go-no-go launch.*

gon·o·phore (gŏn′ə-fôr′, -fōr′) *n.* A structure bearing or consisting of a reproductive organ or part, as a reproductive cell or bud in a hydroid colony. —**gon′o·pho′ric** (-fôr′ĭk, -fōr′-), **go·noph′o·rous** (gə-nŏf′ər-əs) *adj.*

gon·o·pore (gŏn′ə-pôr′, -pōr′) *n.* A reproductive aperture or pore.

gon·or·rhe·a (gŏn′ə-rē′ə) *n.* An infectious disease of the genitourinary tract, rectum, and cervix, caused by the gonococcus, transmitted chiefly by sexual intercourse, and characterized by acute purulent urethritis with dysuria. [LLat., spermatorrhea < Gk. *gonorrhoia* : *gonos,* semen + *rhoia,* flow.] —**gon′or·rhe′al, gon′or·rhe′ic** *adj.*

–gony *suff.* Generation; reproduction; manners of origin: *heterogony.* [Lat. *-gonia* < Gk. < *gonos,* offspring.]

goo (go͞o) *n. Informal.* **1.** A sticky, wet substance. **2.** Sentimental drivel. [Orig. unknown.] —**goo′ey** *adj.*

goo·ber (go͞o′bər) *n. Regional.* A peanut. [Kongo *nguba.*]

good (go͝od) *adj.* **bet·ter** (bĕt′ər), **best** (bĕst). **1.** Having positive or desirable qualities; not bad or poor. **2.** Serving the end desired; suitable: *a good outdoor paint.* **3. a.** Not spoiled or ruined: *The milk is still good.* **b.** In excellent condition; sound: *a good tooth.* **4. a.** Superior to the average; satisfactory: *a good student.* **b.** Designating the U.S. Government grade of meat higher than standard and lower than choice. **5. a.** Of high quality: *good books.* **b.** Discriminating: *good taste.* **6.** Attractive; handsome: *good looks.* **7.** Beneficial; salutary: *a good night's rest.* **8.** Competent; skilled: *a good machinist.* **9.** Complete; thorough: *a good workout.* **10. a.** Safe; sure: *a good investment.* **b.** Valid or true: *a good reason.* **c.** Genuine; real: *a good dollar bill.* **11. a.** Ample; substantial: *a good income.* **b.** Bountiful: *a good table.* **12.** Full: *a good mile from here.* **13. a.** Pleasant; enjoyable: *having a good time at the party.* **b.** Propitious; favorable: *good weather; a good omen.* **14. a.** Of moral excellence; upright: *a good man.* **b.** Benevolent; kind: *a good soul.* **c.** Loyal; staunch: *a good Republican.* **15. a.** Well-behaved; obedient: *a good child.* **b.** Socially correct; proper: *good manners.* —*n.* **1. a.** Something that is good. **b.** A good, valuable, or useful part or aspect. **2.** Welfare; benefit: *for the common good.* **3.** Goodness; virtue: *There is much good in him.* **4. goods. a.** Commodities; wares: *frozen goods.* **b.** Portable personal property. **c.** *(used with a sing. or pl. verb).* Fabric; material. **5. goods.** *Slang.* Incriminating information or evidence: *tried to get the goods on him.* —*adv. Informal.* Well. —***idioms.* as good as.** Practically; nearly: *as good as new.* **for good.** Permanently; forever. **good and.** *Informal.* Very; thoroughly: *I'll do it when I'm good and ready.* **no good.** *Informal.* **1.** Worthless. **2.** Futile; useless: *It's no good arguing with him.* **to the good. 1.** Advantageous; for the best. **2.** In an advantageous financial position: *ended up to the good.* [ME *god* < OE *gōd.*]

Usage: *Good* is properly used as an adjective with linking verbs such as *be, seem, appear: The future looks good. The soup tastes good.* It should not be used as an adverb with other verbs: *The car runs well* (not *good*). Thus: *The dress fits well and looks good.* See also Usage note at **bad**.

good book also **Good Book** *n.* The Bible.

good-by or **good-bye** (go͝od-bī′) *interj.* Used to express farewell. —*n., pl.* **-bys** or **-byes.** An expression of farewell. [Alteration of *God be with you.*]

good-fel·low·ship (go͝od′fĕl′ō-shĭp′) *n.* Pleasant sociability; comradeship.

good-for-noth·ing (go͝od′fər-nŭth′ĭng) *n.* A person of little worth or usefulness. —*adj.* Having little worth; useless.

Good Friday *n.* The Friday before Easter, observed by Christians in commemoration of the crucifixion of Jesus.

good·heart·ed (go͝od′här′tĭd) *adj.* Kind and generous. —**good′heart′ed·ly** *adv.* —**good′heart′ed·ness** *n.*

good-hu·mored (go͝od′hyo͞o′mərd) *adj.* Cheerful; amiable. —**good′-hu′mored·ly** *adv.* —**good′-hu′mored·ness** *n.*

good·ish (go͝od′ĭsh) *adj.* **1.** Somewhat good. **2.** Somewhat large or big; goodly.

good-look·ing (go͝od′lo͝ok′ĭng) *adj.* Of a pleasing or attractive appearance; handsome.

good·ly (go͝od′lē) *adj.* **-li·er, -li·est. 1.** Of pleasing appearance; comely. **2.** Somewhat large; considerable: *a goodly sum.* —**good′li·ness** *n.*

good·man (go͝od′mən) *n. Archaic.* **1. a.** The male head of a household; master. **b.** A husband. **2.** A courteous title of address for a man not of noble birth.

good nature *n.* A cheerful, obliging disposition.

good-na·tured (go͝od′nā′chərd) *adj.* Having an easygoing, cheerful disposition. —**good′-na′tured·ly** *adv.* —**good′-na′tured·ness** *n.*

good·ness (go͝od′nĭs) *n.* **1.** The state or quality of being good. **2.** The good part of something; essence. —*interj.* Used to express surprise.

Good Samaritan *n.* **1.** In a New Testament parable, the only passer-by to aid a man who had been beaten and robbed. **2.** A compassionate person who unselfishly helps others.

good-sized (go͝od′sīzd′) *adj.* Of a fairly large size.

good-tem·pered (go͝od′tĕm′pərd) *adj.* Having an even temper; not easily irritated. —**good′-tem′pered·ly** *adv.* —**good′-tem′pered·ness** *n.*

good·wife (go͝od′wīf′) *n. Archaic.* **1.** The female head of a household; mistress. **2.** A courteous title of address for a woman not of noble birth.

good will also **good·will** (go͝od′wĭl′) *n.* **1.** An attitude of kindness or friendliness; benevolence. **2.** Cheerful acquiescence or willingness. **3.** A good relationship, as of a business enterprise with its customers or a nation with other nations.

good·y¹ (go͝od′ē) *Informal.* —*n., pl.* **-ies.** Something attractive or delectable, esp. something sweet to eat. —*interj.* Used esp. by children to express delight.

good·y² (go͝od′ē) *n., pl.* **-ies.** *Archaic.* A polite title usually

gondola
Above: Cable gondola
Below: Venetian gondola

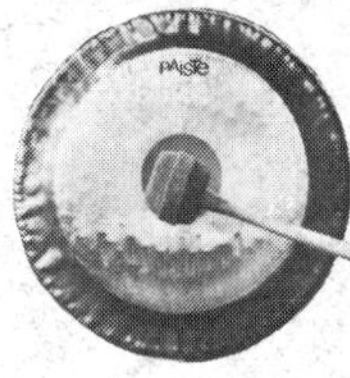

gong

p **pop** / r **roar** / s **sauce** / sh **ship, dish** / t **tight** / th **thin, path** / *th* **this, bathe** / ŭ **cut** / ûr **urge** / v **valve** / w **with** / y **yes** / z **zebra, size** / zh **vision** / ə **about, item, edible, gallop, circus** / œ *Fr.* **feu,** *Ger.* **schön** / ü *Fr.* **tu,** *Ger.* **über** / KH *Ger.* **ich,** *Scot.* **loch** / N *Fr.* **bon.**

goose[1]
Canada goose

gooseberry

gopher

Gorgon
Athena holding head of Medusa

gorilla

used with the surname of a married woman of humble rank. [Short for GOODWIFE.]
good·y-good·y (go͝od'ē-go͝od'ē) *adj.* Affectedly sweet, good, or virtuous. *—n., pl.* **-ies.** One who is goody-goody.
goof (go͞of) *Slang. —n.* **1.** An incompetent, foolish, or stupid person. **2.** A careless mistake; slip. *—v.* **goofed, goof·ing, goofs.** *—intr.* **1.** To make a silly mistake; blunder. **2.** To waste or kill time: *just goofing off.* *—tr.* To spoil; bungle: *goof up a job.* [Poss. alteration of obs. *goff,* fool.]
goof-off (go͞of'ôf', -ŏf) *n.* One who shirks work or responsibility.
goof·y (go͞o'fē) *adj.* **-i·er, -i·est.** *Slang.* Silly; ridiculous: *a goofy hat.* **—goof'i·ly** *adv.* **—goof'i·ness** *n.*
goo·gol (go͞o'gôl') *n.* The number 10 raised to the power 100 (10^{100}); the number 1 followed by 100 zeros. [Coined by Milton Sirotta, nephew of Edward Kasner (1878–1955).]
goo·gol·plex (go͞o'gôl-plĕks') *n.* The number 10 raised to the power googol; the number 1 followed by 10^{100} zeros. [GOOGOL + (DU)PLEX.]
goo-goo (go͞o'go͞o') *adj. Slang.* Amorous, often humorously so: *making goo-goo eyes at her.*
gook[1] (go͝ok, go͞ok) *n. Slang.* A dirty, sludgy, or slimy substance. [Poss. alteration of GOO.]
gook[2] (go͞ok) *n.* **1.** *Offensive Slang.* An Oriental. **2.** A North Vietnamese soldier or guerrilla in the Vietnam War. [Orig. unknown.]
goon (go͞on) *n.* **1.** *Informal.* A thug hired to intimidate or harm opponents. **2.** *Slang.* A stupid or oafish person. [Perh. alteration of dial. *gooney,* fool.]
goo·ney bird also **goo·ny bird** (go͞o'nē) *n.* An albatross, esp. *Diomedea nigripes,* common on islands of the Pacific. [< dial. *gooney,* fool.]
goos·an·der (go͞os-ăn'dər) *n. Chiefly Brit.* A bird, the common merganser, *Mergus merganser.* [Orig. unknown.]
goose[1] (go͞os) *n., pl.* **geese** (gēs). **1. a.** Any of various wild or domesticated water birds of the family Anatidae, and esp. of the genera *Anser* and *Branta,* characteristically having a shorter neck than that of a swan and a shorter, more pointed bill than that of a duck. **b.** The female of the goose, as distinguished from a gander. **c.** The flesh of the goose used as food. **2.** *Informal.* A silly person. **3.** *pl.* **goos·es.** A tailor's pressing iron with a long curved handle. **—*idiom.* cook one's goose.** *Informal.* To ruin one's chances. [ME *goos* < OE *gōs.*]
goose[2] (go͞os) *tr.v.* **goosed, goos·ing, goos·es.** *Slang.* To poke (a person) between the buttocks. [Orig. unknown.]
goose·ber·ry (go͞os'bĕr'ē, -bə-rē, go͞oz'-) *n.* **1. a.** A spiny shrub, *Ribes grossularia,* native to Eurasia, having lobed leaves, greenish flowers, and edible greenish berries. **b.** The fruit of the gooseberry plant. **2.** Any of several plants bearing fruit similar to the gooseberry.
goose bumps *pl.n.* Goose flesh.
goose egg *n. Slang.* Zero, esp. when written as a numeral to indicate that no points have been scored.
goose·fish (go͞os'fĭsh') *n., pl.* **goosefish** or **-fish·es.** Any of several anglerfishes of the genus *Lophius,* such as *L. americanus,* of North American Atlantic waters.
goose flesh *n.* Momentary roughness of skin caused by erection of the papillae in response to cold or fear.
goose·foot (go͞os'fo͝ot') *n., pl.* **-foots.** Any of various usually weedy plants of the genus *Chenopodium,* having small greenish flowers. [From the shape of its leaves.]
goose grass *n.* Cleavers.
goose·neck (go͞os'nĕk') *n.* A slender, curved object or part, as the flexible shaft of a type of desk lamp. **—goose'-necked'** *adj.*
goose pimples *pl.n.* Goose flesh.
goose step *n.* A military parade step done by swinging the legs sharply from the hips and keeping the knees locked.
goose-step (go͞os'stĕp') *intr.v.* **-stepped, -step·ping, -steps.** To execute or march in a goose step.
goos·y also **goos·ey** (go͞o'sē) *adj.* **-i·er, -i·est.** **1.** Pertaining to or resembling a goose. **2.** Foolish or scatterbrained.
go·pher (gō'fər) *n.* **1.** Any of various short-tailed, burrowing mammals of the family Geomyidae, of North America, having fur-lined external cheek pouches. **2.** A ground squirrel. **3.** Any of several burrowing tortoises of the genus *Gopherus,* esp. *G. polyphemus,* of the southeastern United States. [Orig. unknown.]
gopher ball *n. Baseball.* A pitched ball that is hit for a home run.
gopher snake *n.* A bull snake.
go·pher·wood (gō'fər-wo͝od') *n.* Yellowwood (sense 1).
Gor·di·an knot (gôr'dē-ən) *n.* **1.** An intricate knot tied by King Gordius of Phrygia and cut by Alexander the Great with his sword after hearing an oracle promise that whoever could undo it would be the next ruler of Asia. **2.** An exceedingly complicated problem or deadlock.
Gordon setter *n.* A hunting dog of a breed originating in Scotland, having a silky black and tan coat. [After Alexander, 4th Duke of *Gordon* (d. 1827).]
gore[1] (gôr) *tr.v.* **gored, gor·ing, gores.** To pierce or stab with a horn or tusk. [ME *goren* < *gore,* spear < OE *gār.*]
gore[2] (gôr) *n.* **1.** A triangular or tapering piece of cloth forming a part of something, as in a skirt or sail. **2.** A small triangular piece of land. *—tr.v.* **gored, gor·ing, gores. 1.** To provide with a gore. **2.** To cut into a gore. [ME < OE *gāra,* triangular piece of land.]
gore[3] (gôr) *n.* Blood, esp. coagulated blood from a wound. [ME, filth < OE *gor.*]
gorge (gôrj) *n.* **1.** A deep, narrow passage with steep rocky sides, and enclosed between mountains. **2.** A narrow entrance into the outwork of a fortification. **3.** The throat; gullet. **4.** An instance of gluttonous eating. **5.** A mass obstructing a narrow passage: *a shipping lane blocked by an ice gorge.* *—v.* **gorged, gorg·ing, gorg·es.** *—tr.* **1.** To stuff; glut. **2.** To devour greedily. *—intr.* To eat gluttonously. [ME, throat < OFr. < Lat. *gurges,* gulf.] **—gorg'er** *n.*
gor·geous (gôr'jəs) *adj.* **1. a.** Dazzlingly beautiful or magnificent: *wore a gorgeous Victorian gown.* **b.** Characterized by magnificence or brilliance: *pianism that revealed a gorgeous technique.* **2.** *Informal.* Wonderful or delightful. [ME *gorgeouse,* prob. < OFr. *gorrias,* elegant.] **—gor'geous·ly** *adv.* **—gor'geous·ness** *n.*
gor·ger·in (gôr'jər-ĭn) *n. Archit.* The necking of a column. [Fr. < *gorge,* throat < OFr. —see GORGE.]
gor·get (gôr'jĭt) *n.* **1.** A piece of armor protecting the throat. **2.** An ornamental collar. **3.** The scarflike part of a wimple covering the neck and shoulders. **4.** A band or patch of distinctive color on the throat esp. of a bird. [ME < OFr. *gorgete,* dim. of *gorge,* throat < Lat. *gurges,* gulf.]
Gor·gon (gôr'gən) *n.* **1.** *Gk. Myth.* Any of the three sisters Stheno, Euryale, and the mortal Medusa who had snakes for hair and eyes that if looked into turned the beholder into stone. **2. gorgon.** A repulsively ugly or terrifying woman. [ME < Lat. *Gorgo* < Gk. *Gorgō* < *gorgos,* terrible.] **—Gor·go'ni·an** (-gō'nē-ən) *adj.*
gor·go·ni·an (gôr-gō'nē-ən) *n.* Any of various corals of the order Gorgonacea, having a flexible, often branching skeleton of horny material. *—adj.* Of or belonging to the Gorgonacea. [Lat. *gorgonia,* coral < *Gorgo,* Gorgon. —see GORGON.]
gor·gon·ize (gôr'gə-nīz') *tr.v.* **-ized, -iz·ing, -iz·es.** To have a paralyzing or stupefying effect upon. [< GORGON.]
Gor·gon·zo·la (gôr'gən-zō'lə) *n.* A pungent, blue-veined, cream-colored Italian cheese made of pressed cow's milk. [After *Gorgonzola,* Italy.]
go·ril·la (gə-rĭl'ə) *n.* **1.** A large anthropoid ape, *Gorilla gorilla,* of forests of equatorial Africa, having a stocky body and coarse, dark hair. **2.** A brutish or thuglike man. [< Gk. *Gorillai,* a tribe of hairy women.]
gor·man·dize (gôr'mən-dīz') *v.* **-dized, -diz·ing, -diz·es.** *—intr.* To eat gluttonously; gorge. *—tr.* To devour (food) gluttonously. [< obs. *gormandise,* gluttony < Fr. *gourmandise* < *gourmand,* glutton.] **—gor'man·diz'er** *n.*
go-round (gō'round') *n.* A go-around.
gorp (gôrp) *n.* A mixture of high-energy foods, as dried fruit, nuts, and seeds, eaten esp. as a snack. [Perh. < slang *gorp,* to eat greedily.]
gorse (gôrs) *n.* Any of several spiny, thickset shrubs of the genus *Ulex,* esp. *U. europeaus,* native to Europe, having fragrant yellow flowers. [ME *gorst* < OE.]
go·ry (gôr'ē, gōr'ē) *adj.* **-ri·er, -ri·est.** **1.** Covered or stained with gore; bloody. **2.** Full of or characterized by bloodshed and violence. **—gor'i·ly** *adv.* **—gor'i·ness** *n.*
gosh (gŏsh) *interj.* Used to express mild surprise or delight. [Alteration of GOD.]
gos·hawk (gŏs'hôk') *n.* **1.** A large hawk, *Accipiter gentilis,* having broad, rounded wings and gray or brownish plumage. **2.** Any of several hawks similar or related to the goshawk. [ME *goshauk* < OE *goshafoc* : *gos,* goose + *hafoc,* hawk.]
gos·ling (gŏz'lĭng) *n.* **1.** A young goose. **2.** A naive or inexperienced young person. [ME < ON *gæslingr.*]
gos·pel (gŏs'pəl) *n.* **1.** Often **Gospel.** The teachings of Jesus and the Apostles. **2. a. Gospel.** One of the first four books of the New Testament, describing the life, death, and resurrection of Jesus Christ. **b.** A similar narrative. **3.** Often **Gospel.** A lection from any of the Gospels included as part of a religious service. **4.** A teaching or doctrine of a religious teacher. **5.** Gospel music. **6.** Something, as an idea or principle, accepted as unquestionably true. **—*modifier:*** *a gospel meeting; a gospel singer.* [ME < OE *gōdspel* : *gōd,* good + *spel,* tale.]
gos·pel·er also **gos·pel·ler** (gŏs'pə-lər) *n.* **1.** One who teaches or professes faith in a gospel. **2.** One who reads or sings the Gospel as part of a church service.
gospel music *n.* A kind of native American religious music that is associated with evangelism and is based on the simple melodies of folk music blended with melodic and rhythmic elements of spirituals and jazz.
gospel side also **Gospel side** *n.* The left side of an altar or chancel. [So called from the practice in some churches of reading the Gospel and the Epistle from different sides.]
gos·port (gŏs'pôrt', -pōrt') *n.* A flexible speaking tube used for communication between individual compartments or cockpits of an airplane. [After *Gosport,* England.]
gos·sa·mer (gŏs'ə-mər) *n.* **1.** A fine film of cobwebs often seen floating in the air or caught on bushes or grass. **2.** A soft, sheer, gauzy fabric. **3.** Something delicate, light, or flimsy. [ME *gossomer* : *gos,* goose (< OE gōs) + *somer,* summer < OE *sumor.*] **—gos'sa·mer·y** (-mə-rē) *adj.*

gos·sip (gŏs′əp) *n.* **1.** Rumor or talk of a personal, sensational, or intimate nature. **2.** A person who habitually spreads intimate or private rumors or facts. **3.** Trivial, chatty talk or writing. **4.** *Archaic.* A close friend or companion. **5.** *Archaic.* A godparent. —*intr.v.* **-siped, -sip·ing, -sips.** To engage in or spread gossip. [ME *godsib,* godparent < OE *godsibb* : *god,* god + *sibb,* kinsman.] **—gos′sip·er** *n.* **—gos′sip·ry** *n.* **—gos′sip·y** *adj.*

gos·sip·mong·er (gŏs′əp-mŭng′gər, -mŏng′-) *n.* A person who relates gossip.

got (gŏt) *v.* Past tense and a past participle of **get.**

Goth (gŏth) *n.* A member of a Germanic people that invaded the Roman Empire in the early centuries of the Christian era. [< ME *Gothes,* Goths < LLat. *Gothi,* of Goth. orig.]

Goth·ic (gŏth′ĭk) *adj.* **1. a.** Of or pertaining to the Goths or their language. **b.** Germanic; Teutonic. **2.** Of or pertaining to the Middle Ages; medieval. **3. a.** Of or pertaining to an architectural style prevalent in western Europe from the 12th through the 15th century and characterized by pointed arches, rib vaulting, and flying buttresses. **b.** Of or pertaining to painting, sculpture, or other art forms prevalent in northern Europe from the 12th through the 15th century. **c.** Of or relating to an architectural style derived from medieval Gothic. **4.** Often **gothic.** Of or pertaining to a style of fiction that emphasizes the grotesque, mysterious, and desolate. **5. gothic.** Barbarous; crude. —*n.* **1.** The extinct East Germanic language of the Goths. **2.** Gothic art or architecture. **3.** Often **gothic.** *Printing.* **a.** Black letter. **b.** Sans serif. **4.** A novel in the Gothic style. **—Goth′i·cal·ly** *adv.*

Gothic arch *n.* A pointed arch, esp. one with a jointed apex.

Goth·i·cism (gŏth′ĭ-sĭz′əm) *n.* **1.** The use of or imitation of Gothic style, as in architecture. **2.** A barbarous or crude manner or style.

Goth·i·cize (gŏth′ĭ-sīz′) *tr.v.* **-cized, -ciz·ing, -ciz·es.** To make Gothic.

GO TO *n.* An instruction in programming language for the computer to leave the current sequence of instructions for another sequence at another point in the program.

got·ten (gŏt′n) *v.* A past participle of **get.**

gouache (gwäsh) *n.* **1.** A method of painting with opaque water colors mixed with a preparation of gum. **2.** An opaque pigment used in gouache. **3.** A painting executed by gouache. [Fr. < Ital. *guazzo* < Lat. *aquatio,* watering < *aquari,* to fetch water < *aqua,* water.]

Gou·da (gou′də, go͞o′-) *n.* A mild, close-textured, pale-yellow cheese made from whole or partially skimmed milk. [After *Gouda,* The Netherlands.]

gouge (gouj) *n.* **1.** A chisel with a rounded, troughlike blade. **2.** A scooping or digging action, as with a gouge. **3.** A groove or hole scooped with or as if with a gouge. **4.** *Informal.* A large amount exacted or extorted. —*tr.v.* **gouged, goug·ing, goug·es. 1.** To cut or scoop out with or as if with a gouge: *"He began to gouge a small pattern in the sand with his cane"* (Vladimir Nabokov). **2.** To force out: *gouged out his eyes.* **3.** To exact exorbitantly or extort from. **4.** *Slang.* To swindle. [ME < OFr. *goi* < LLat. *gubia,* of Celt. orig.] **—goug′er** *n.*

gou·lash (go͞o′läsh′, -lăsh) *n.* A stew of beef or veal and vegetables, seasoned mainly with paprika. [Hung. *gulyás* (*hus*), herdsman's (meat) < *gulya,* herd.]

gou·ra·mi (go͝o-rä′mē, go͝or′ə-) *n., pl.* **-mis.** Any of various freshwater fishes of the family Anabantidae, of southeastern Asia, many species of which are brightly colored and popular in home aquariums. [Malay *gurami.*]

gourd (gôrd, gōrd, go͝ord) *n.* **1.** Any of several vines of the family Cucurbitaceae, related to the pumpkin, squash, and cucumber and bearing fruits with a hard rind. **2. a.** The fruit of a gourd, as a calabash, often of irregular and unusual shape. **b.** The dried and hollowed-out shell of one of these fruits, used as a drinking utensil. [ME *gourde* < AN, ult. < Lat. *cucurbita.*]

gourde (go͝ord) *n.* See table at **currency.** [Haitian < Fr. *gourd,* dull < Lat. *gurdus.*]

gour·mand (go͝or-mänd′, go͝or′mənd) *n.* A person who delights in eating well and heartily. [ME *gourmant,* glutton < OFr. *gormant.*]

Usage: A *gourmand* loves good food and drink and partakes of it heartily, and sometimes excessively or gluttonously. The *gourmet* and the *epicure,* on the other hand, possess a discriminating and cultivated taste in food and wine.

gour·man·dise (go͝or′mən-dēz′) *n.* A taste and relish for good food: *"You could see the gourmandise shining on his rosy lips"* (Glenway Wescott). [ME *gromandise,* gluttony < OFr. *gormandise* < *gormant,* glutton.]

gour·met (go͝or-mā′, go͝or′mā′) *n.* A connoisseur of fine food and drink. —See Usage note at **gourmand.** [Fr. < OFr., wine merchant's servant.]

gout (gout) *n.* **1.** A disturbance of the uric-acid metabolism occurring predominantly in males, characterized by painful inflammation of the joints, esp. of the feet and hands, and arthritic attacks and capable of becoming chronic and producing deformity. **2.** A large blob or clot: *"and makes it bleed great gouts of blood"* (Oscar Wilde). [ME *goute* < OFr. *goute,* gout, drop < Lat. *gutta,* drop (from the belief that gout was caused by drops of morbid humors).] **—gout′i·ness** *n.* **—gout′y** *adj.*

gov·ern (gŭv′ərn) *v.* **-erned, -ern·ing, -erns.** —*tr.* **1.** To make and administer the public policy and affairs of; exercise sovereign authority in. **2.** To control the speed or magnitude of; regulate: *a valve governing fuel intake.* **3.** To control the actions or behavior of. **4.** To keep under control; restrain. **5.** To exercise a deciding or determining influence on: *Chance usually governs the outcome of the game.* **6.** *Gram.* **a.** To require (a noun or verb) to be in a particular case or mood. **b.** To require the use of (a particular case or mood). —*intr.* **1.** To exercise political authority. **2.** To have or exercise a determining influence. [ME *governen* < OFr. *governer* < Lat. *gubernare* < Gk. *kubernan.*] **—gov′ern·a·ble** *adj.*

gov·er·nance (gŭv′ər-nəns) *n.* **1.** The act, process, or power of governing; government. **2.** The state of being governed.

gov·ern·ess (gŭv′ər-nĭs) *n.* A woman employed to educate and train the children of a private household.

gov·ern·ment (gŭv′ərn-mənt) *n.* **1.** The act or process of governing, esp. the control and administration of public policy in a political unit. **2.** The office, function, or authority of one who governs or of a governing body. **3.** The exercise of authority in a political unit; rule. **4.** The agency or apparatus through which an individual or body that governs exercises its authority and performs its functions. **5. a.** A governing body or organization. **b.** Those persons who comprise a governing body. **6.** A system or policy by which a political unit is governed. **7.** The management or administration of an organization, business, or institution. **8.** Political science. **—gov′ern·men′tal** (-mĕn′tl) *adj.* **—gov′ern·men′tal·ly** *adv.*

Usage: In American usage *government* always takes a singular verb. In British usage *government,* in the sense of a governing group of officials, is usually construed as a plural collective and therefore takes a plural verb: *The government are determined to follow this course.*

Government Issue *n.* Something issued by the government, as U.S. Army equipment.

gov·er·nor (gŭv′ər-nər) *n.* **1.** A person who governs, esp.: **a.** The chief executive of a state in the United States. **b.** An official appointed to govern a colony or territory. **c.** A member of a governing body. **2.** The manager or administrative head of an organization, business, or institution. **3.** A military commandant. **4.** *Chiefly Brit. Informal.* Mister; sir. Used in direct address. **5.** A feedback device on a machine or engine that is used to provide automatic control, as of speed, pressure, or temperature. [ME *governour* < OFr. *governeor* < Lat. *gubernator,* < *gubernare,* to govern. —see GOVERN.]

gov·er·nor-gen·er·al (gŭv′ər-nər-jĕn′ər-əl) *n., pl.* **gov·er·nors-gen·er·al** or **gov·er·nor-gen·er·als.** A governor of a large territory who has other, subordinate governors under his jurisdiction. **—gov′er·nor-gen′er·al·ship′** *n.*

gov·er·nor·ship (gŭv′ər-nər-shĭp′) *n.* The office, term, or jurisdiction of a governor.

gow·an (gou′ən) *n. Scot.* A yellow or white wildflower, esp. the Old World daisy. [Prob. alteration of ME *gollan* < ON *gullinn,* golden < *gull,* gold.]

gown (goun) *n.* **1.** A long, loose, flowing garment, as a robe or nightgown. **2.** A long, usually formal woman's dress. **3.** A distinctive outer robe worn on ceremonial occasions, as by scholars or clergymen. **4.** The faculty and student body of a university: *perfect accord between town and gown.* —*tr.v.* **gowned, gown·ing, gowns.** To dress in or invest with a gown. [ME *goune* < OFr. < Med. Lat. *gunna,* fur robe.]

gowns·man (gounz′mən) *n.* One who wears a distinctive gown as a mark of his profession or office.

goy (goi) *n., pl.* **goy·im** (goi′ĭm) or **goys.** *Offensive.* One who is not Jewish; Gentile. [Yiddish < Heb. *gōy,* people.] **—goy′ish** *adj.*

Graaf·i·an follicle (grä′fē-ən, grăf′ē-) *n.* Any of the follicles in the mammalian ovary containing a maturing ovum. [After Regnier de *Graaf* (1641–1673).]

grab[1] (grăb) *v.* **grabbed, grab·bing, grabs.** —*tr.* **1.** To take or grasp suddenly. **2.** To capture or restrain; arrest. **3.** To obtain or appropriate unscrupulously or forcibly. **4.** To take hurriedly. **5.** *Slang.* To capture the attention of: *an author who knows how to grab the reader.* —*intr.* To make a snatch: *He grabbed for the gun.* —*n.* **1.** A sudden seizure. **2.** Something grabbed. **3.** A mechanical device for gripping an object. **—*idiom.* up for grabs.** *Informal.* Available for anyone to take or win. [MLG *grabben.*] **—grab′ber** *n.*

grab[2] (grăb) *n.* An Oriental coastal vessel with two or three masts. [Ar. *ghurāb.*]

grab bag *n.* **1.** A container filled with articles, such as party gifts, to be drawn sight unseen. **2.** A miscellaneous collection of often valuable items.

grab·ble (grăb′əl) *intr.v.* **-bled, -bling, -bles. 1.** To feel around with the hands; grope. **2.** To fall down; sprawl. [Du. *grabbelen* < MDu., freq. of *grabben,* to grab.]

grab·by (grăb′ē) *adj.* **-bi·er, -bi·est.** Inclined to grab; greedy. **—grab′bi·ness** *n.*

gra·ben (grä′bən) *n.* A usually elongated depression of the earth's crust between two parallel faults. [G., trench < OHG *grabo* < *graban,* to dig.]

grace (grās) *n.* **1.** Seemingly effortless beauty or charm of movement, form, or proportion. **2.** A characteristic or quality pleasing for its charm or refinement. **3.** A sense of fitness

Gothic
A Gothic church

gourd

Graces

grackle
Common purple grackle

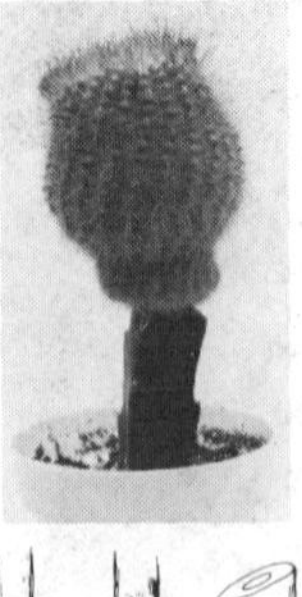

graft[1]
Above: Two kinds of cactus grafted together
Below: (*Left to right*) Cleft graft, whip graft, bud graft

or propriety. **4. a.** A disposition to be generous or helpful; good will. **b.** Mercy; clemency. **5.** A favor rendered by one who need not do so; indulgence. **6.** A temporary immunity or exemption; reprieve. **7.** *Theol.* **a.** Divine love and protection bestowed freely upon mankind. **b.** The state of being protected or sanctified by the favor of God. **c.** An excellence or power granted by God. **8.** A short prayer of blessing or thanksgiving said before or after a meal. **9.** Used with *his, her,* or *your* as a title of courtesy for a duke, duchess, or archbishop. **10.** *Mus.* An embellishment such as an appoggiatura or trill. —*tr.v.* **graced, grac·ing, grac·es. 1.** To honor or favor. **2.** To give beauty, elegance, or charm to. **3.** *Mus.* To embellish with grace notes. —***idioms.*** **in the good (**or **bad) graces of.** In (or out of) favor with. **with good (**or **bad) grace.** In a willing (or grudging) manner. [ME, divine love < OFr. < Lat. *gratia,* good will < *gratus,* pleasing.]

grace cup *n.* **1.** A cup used at the end of a meal, usually after grace, for the final toast. **2.** The final toast of a meal.

grace·ful (grās′fəl) *adj.* Showing grace of movement, form, or proportion. **—grace′ful·ly** *adv.* **—grace′ful·ness** *n.*

grace·less (grās′lĭs) *adj.* **1.** Lacking grace; clumsy. **2.** Having no sense of propriety or decency. **3.** Inferior or clumsy in treatment or performance: *a graceless production of* Richard III. **—grace′less·ly** *adv.* **—grace′less·ness** *n.*

grace note *n. Mus.* A note, esp. an appoggiatura, added as an embellishment.

Grac·es (grā′sĭz) *pl.n. Gk. Myth.* Three sister goddesses, Aglaia, Euphrosyne, and Thalia, who dispense charm and beauty.

grac·ile (grăs′əl, -īl′) *adj.* **1.** Gracefully slender. **2.** Graceful. [Lat. *gracilis.*] **—gra·cil′i·ty** (grə-sĭl′ĭ-tē) *n.*

gra·ci·o·so (grä′sē-ō′sō, -zō) *n., pl.* **-sos.** A clown or buffoon in Spanish comedies. [Sp. < Lat. *gratiosus,* agreeable. —see GRACIOUS.]

gra·cious (grā′shəs) *adj.* **1.** Characterized by kindness and warm courtesy. **2.** Characterized by tact and propriety: *responded to the insult with gracious humor.* **3.** Of a merciful or compassionate nature. **4.** Condescendingly courteous; indulgent. **5.** Characterized by charm or beauty; graceful. **6.** Characterized by elegance and good taste: *a gracious dinner.* **7.** *Obs.* Fortunate or prosperous. —*interj.* Used to express surprise or mild emotion. [ME < OFr. *gracieus* < Lat. *gratiosus,* agreeable < *gratia,* good will < *gratus,* pleasing.] **—gra′cious·ly** *adv.* **—gra′cious·ness** *n.*

grack·le (grăk′əl) *n.* **1.** Any of several New World blackbirds of the family Icteridae, esp. of the genera *Quiscalus* or *Cassidix,* having iridescent blackish plumage. **2.** Any of several Asian mynas of the genus *Gracula.* [Lat. *graculus,* jackdaw.]

grad (grăd) *n. Informal.* A graduate of a school or college.

gra·date (grā′dāt′) *v.* **-dat·ed, -dat·ing, -dates.** —*intr.* To pass imperceptibly from one degree, shade, or tone to another. —*tr.* **1.** To cause to pass imperceptibly from one degree, shade, or tone to another. **2.** To arrange according to or in grades. [Back-formation < GRADATION.]

gra·da·tion (grā-dā′shən) *n.* **1. a.** A series of gradual, successive stages; a systematic progression. **b.** A degree or stage in such a progression. **2.** Advancement by successive stages, tones, or shades, as from one color to another. **3.** The act of gradating or arranging in grades. **4.** An ablaut. [Lat. *gradatio* < *gradus,* step.] **—gra·da′tion·al** *adj.* **—gra·da′tion·al·ly** *adv.*

grade (grād) *n.* **1.** A stage or degree in a process. **2.** A position in a scale of size or quality, as of eggs or beef. **3.** A group of persons or things all falling in the same specified limits; class. **4. a.** A class at an elementary school or the pupils in it. **b. grades.** Elementary school. **5.** A mark indicating a student's level of accomplishment. **6.** A military, naval, or civil-service rank. **7.** The degree of inclination of a slope, road, or other surface. **8.** A slope or gradual inclination, esp. of a road or railroad track. **9.** A domestic animal produced by crossbreeding one of purebred stock with one of ordinary stock. —*v.* **grad·ed, grad·ing, grades.** —*tr.* **1.** To arrange in steps or degrees. **2.** To arrange in a series or according to a scale. **3. a.** To determine the quality of (academic work, for example); evaluate. **b.** To give a grade to (a student, for example). **4.** To level or smooth to a desired or horizontal gradient. **5.** To gradate. **6.** To improve the quality of (livestock) by crossbreeding with purebred stock. —*intr.* **1.** To hold a certain rank or position. **2.** To change or progress gradually. —***idiom.*** **make the grade. 1.** To reach the highest point of an inclination. **2.** To reach a goal or standard; succeed. [Fr. < Lat. *gradus,* step.]

grade crossing *n.* An intersection of roads, railroad tracks, or a road and a railroad track at the same level.

grade point also **grade index** *n.* A point assigned to a course credit, as in a university, that corresponds to the letter grade made in a course.

grade point average also **grade point index** *n.* The average grade earned, as by a student, figured by dividing the grade points earned by the number of credits attempted.

grade school *n.* An elementary school.

gra·di·ent (grā′dē-ənt) *n.* **1.** A rate of inclination; slope. **2.** An ascending or descending part; incline. **3.** *Physics.* The maximum rate at which a variable physical quantity changes in value per unit change in position. **4.** *Math.* A vector having coordinate components that are the partial derivatives of a function with respect to its variables. [Perh. < GRADE.]

gra·din (grăd′n) also **gra·dine** (grā′dēn′, grə-dēn′) *n.* One of a series of steps or tiered seats, as in an amphitheater. [Fr. < Ital. *gradino,* dim. of *grado,* step < Lat. *gradus.*]

grad·u·al (grăj′o͞o-əl) *adj.* Advancing or progressing by regular or continuous degrees: *gradual erosion; a gradual slope.* —*n. Rom. Cath. Ch.* **1.** A book containing the choral portions of the Mass. **2.** The antiphon sung between the Epistle and the Gospel of the Mass. [Med. Lat. *gradualis* < Lat. *gradus,* step.] **—grad′u·al·ly** *adv.* **—grad′u·al·ness** *n.*

grad·u·al·ism (grăj′o͞o-ə-lĭz′əm) *n.* The belief in or policy of advancing toward a goal by gradual, often slow stages. **—grad′u·al·ist** *n.* **—grad′u·al·is′tic** *adj.*

grad·u·ate (grăj′o͞o-āt′) *v.* **-at·ed, -at·ing, -ates.** —*intr.* **1. a.** To be granted an academic degree or diploma. **b.** *Nonstandard.* To receive an academic degree from. **2.** To change gradually or by degrees. —*tr.* **1.** To grant an academic degree or diploma to. **2.** To arrange or divide into categories, steps, or grades. **3.** To divide into marked intervals, esp. for use in measurement. —*n.* (-ĭt). **1.** One who has received an academic degree or diploma. **2.** A graduated container, such as a beaker or flask. —*adj.* (-ĭt). **1.** Possessing an academic degree or diploma. **2.** Of, for, or relating to studies beyond a bachelor's degree: *graduate courses.* [ME *graduaten,* to confer a degree < Med. Lat. *graduare* < Lat. *gradus,* degree.] **—grad′u·a′tor** *n.*

Usage: A strict traditionalist would insist that *she was graduated from college* is the only correct usage. But the usage *she graduated from college* is by now entirely acceptable, and the variant without a preposition, as in *she graduated college,* is rapidly gaining ground.

grad·u·a·tion (grăj′o͞o-ā′shən) *n.* **1. a.** The conferring or receipt of an academic degree or diploma marking completion of studies. **b.** A ceremony at which degrees or diplomas are conferred; commencement. **2. a.** A division or interval on a graduated scale. **b.** A mark indicating the boundary of such an interval. **3.** An arrangement in or division into stages or degrees.

Graeco– *pref.* Variant of **Greco-**.

graf·fi·to (grə-fē′tō, gră-, grä-) *n., pl.* **-ti** (-tē). A crude drawing or inscription scratched on a wall or other surface, usually so as to be seen by the public. [Ital., dim. of *graffio,* a scratching < *graffiare,* to scratch.]

graft[1] (grăft) *v.* **graft·ed, graft·ing, grafts.** —*tr.* **1. a.** To unite (a shoot or bud) with a growing plant by insertion or placing in close contact. **b.** To join (a plant or plants) by such union. **2.** To transplant or implant (tissue, for example) surgically into a bodily part to compensate for a defect. **3.** To join or unite closely. —*intr.* **1.** To make a graft. **2.** To be or become grafted. —*n.* **1. a.** A detached shoot or bud united or to be united with a growing plant. **b.** The union or point of union of a detached shoot or bud with a growing plant by insertion or attachment. **c.** A plant produced by such union. **2. a.** Material, esp. tissue or an organ, surgically attached to or inserted into a bodily part to compensate for a defect. **b.** The procedure of implanting or transplanting such material. **c.** The configuration or condition resulting from such a procedure. [ME *graffen* < *graffe,* graft < OFr. *graife,* stylus (from its shape) < Lat. *graphium* < Gk. *graphion* < *graphein,* to write.] **—graft′er** *n.*

graft[2] (grăft) *n.* **1.** The unscrupulous use of one's position to derive profit or advantages; extortion. **2.** Money or an advantage gained or yielded by unscrupulous means. —*tr. & intr.v.* **graft·ed, graft·ing, grafts.** To gain by or practice graft. [Perh. < GRAFT (to unite).] **—graft′er** *n.*

graft·age (grăf′tĭj) *n.* The process of making a graft in horticulture.

gra·ham (grā′əm) *n.* Whole-wheat flour. [After Sylvester *Graham* (1794–1851).]

graham cracker *n.* A slightly sweet, usually rectangular cracker made of whole-wheat flour.

grail also **Grail** (grāl) *n.* **1.** The cup or chalice in medieval legend used by Christ at the Last Supper and subsequently the object of many chivalrous quests. **2.** The object of a prolonged endeavor. [ME *gral* < OFr. *graal* < Med. Lat. *gradalis,* dish.]

grain (grān) *n.* **1. a.** A small, hard seed or fruit, esp. that produced by a cereal grass. **b.** The seeds of such plants collectively, esp. after having been harvested. **2.** Cereal grasses collectively: *a field of grain.* **3. a.** A relatively small discrete particulate or crystalline mass: *a grain of sand.* **b.** A small amount or the smallest amount possible: *hasn't a grain of sense in his whole body.* **4.** *Aerospace.* A mass of solid propellant formed from a number of smaller pieces. **5.** A unit of weight in the U.S. Customary System, an avoirdupois unit equal to 0.002285 ounce, or .065 gram. **6.** The arrangement, direction, or pattern of the fibrous tissue in wood. **7. a.** The side of a hide or piece of leather from which the hair or fur is removed. **b.** The pattern or markings on this side of leather. **8.** The pattern produced, as in stone, by the arrangement of particulate constituents. **9.** The relative size of the particles composing a substance or pattern: *a coarse grain.* **10.** A painted, stamped, or printed design that imitates the pattern found in wood, leather, or stone. **11.** The direction or texture of fibers in a woven fabric. **12.** A state of fine crystallization. **13. a.** Basic temperament or nature; disposition. **b.** An essential quality or characteristic. **14.** *Archaic.* Color; tint. **15.** *Obs.* **a.** Cochineal or kermes. **b.** Red dye made from cochineal or kermes. **c.** A fast dye. —*v.* **grained, grain·ing, grains.** —*tr.* **1.** To cause to form into grains; granulate. **2.** To paint, stamp, or print with a design imitating the grain of wood, leather, or stone. **3.** To give a granular or rough texture to. **4.** To remove the hair or fur from (hides) in preparation for tanning. —*intr.* To form grains. —***idioms.*** **against the (or one's) grain.** In contradiction to one's natural disposition or character. **with a grain of salt.** With reservations; skeptically. [ME < OFr. *graine* < Lat. *granum.*] —**grain'er** *n.*

grain alcohol *n.* Alcohol.

grain elevator *n.* A building equipped with mechanical lifting devices and used for storing grain.

grains of paradise *pl.n.* **1.** The pungent, aromatic seeds of a tropical African plant, *Aframomum melegueta,* used medicinally. **2.** The seeds of cardamom.

grain·y (grā'nē) *adj.* **-i·er, -i·est. 1.** Made of or resembling grain; granular. **2.** Resembling the grain of wood. —**grain'i·ness** *n.*

gram[1] (grăm) *n.* A metric unit of mass and weight, equal to one-thousandth (10^{-3}) of a kilogram. [Fr. *gramme* < LLat. *gramma,* a small weight < Gk.]

gram[2] (grăm) *n.* **1.** Any of several plants, such as the chickpea, bearing seeds widely used as food in tropical Asia. **2.** The seeds of a gram. [Obs. Port. < Lat. *granum,* seed.]

-gram *suff.* Something written or drawn; a record: *cardiogram.* [Lat. *-gramma* < Gk. < *gramma,* letter.]

gra·ma (grä'mə, grăm'ə) *n.* Any of various grasses of the genus *Bouteloua,* of western North America and South America, forming dense tufts or mats and often used as pasturage. [Sp. *grama* < Lat. *gramen,* grass.]

gram·a·rye (grăm'ə-rē) *n.* Occult learning; magic. [ME *gramarie* < OFr. *gramaire,* grammar. —see GRAMMAR.]

gram atom (grăm'ăt'əm) *n.* The mass in grams of an element numerically equal to the atomic weight.

gram calorie *n.* A calorie (sense 1).

gra·mer·cy (grə-mûr'sē, grăm'ər-) *interj. Archaic.* Used to express surprise or gratitude. [ME *gramerci* < OFr. *grand merci,* great thanks.]

gram·i·ci·din (grăm'ĭ-sīd'n) *n.* An antibiotic produced by a bacterium, *Bacillus brevis,* and used against most Gram-positive pathogenic bacteria. [GRAM(-POSITIVE) + -CID(E) + -IN.]

gra·min·e·ous (grə-mĭn'ē-əs) *adj.* **1.** Of, pertaining to, or characteristic of grasses. **2.** Of or belonging to the family Gramineae, which includes the grasses. [Lat. *gramineus,* grassy < *gramen,* grass.] —**gra·min'e·ous·ness** *n.*

gram·i·niv·o·rous (grăm'ə-nĭv'ər-əs) *adj.* Feeding on grasses, grain, or seeds. [Lat. *gramen,* grass + -VOROUS.]

gram·mar (grăm'ər) *n.* **1.** The study of language as a systematically composed body of words that exhibit discernible regularity of structure and arrangement into sentences and sometimes including such aspects of language as the pronunciation of words, the meanings of words, and the history of words. **2. a.** The phenomena with which grammar deals as exhibited by a specific language at a specific time. **b.** The system of rules implicit in a language, viewed as a mechanism for generating all sentences possible in that language. **3.** A normative or prescriptive system of rules setting forth the current standard of usage for pedagogical or reference purposes. **4.** Writing or speech judged with regard to the rules or practice of grammar: *bad grammar.* **5.** A book containing the morphologic, syntactic, and semantic rules for a specific language. **6. a.** The basic principles of an area of knowledge: *the grammar of music.* **b.** A book dealing with such principles. [ME *gramere* < OFr. *gramaire* < Lat. *grammatica* < Gk. *grammatikē* < *grammatikos,* of letters < *gramma,* letter.]

gram·mar·i·an (grə-mâr'ē-ən) *n.* A specialist in grammar.

grammar school *n.* **1.** An elementary school (sense 1). **2.** *Chiefly Brit.* A secondary or preparatory school. **3.** A school stressing the study of classical languages.

gram·mat·i·cal (grə-măt'ĭ-kəl) *adj.* **1.** Of or relating to grammar. **2.** Conforming to the rules of grammar. [LLat. *grammaticalis* < Lat. *grammaticus* < Gk. *grammatikos,* of letters < *gramma,* letter.] —**gram·mat'i·cal'i·ty** (-kăl'ĭ-tē) *n.* —**gram·mat'i·cal·ly** *adv.*

grammatical gender *n.* The gender assigned to a word in the grammar of a language as distinct from natural gender or sex.

gram·ma·tol·o·gy (grăm'ə-tŏl'ə-jē) *n.* The study and science of systems of graphic script. [Gk. *gramma, grammat-,* letter + -LOGY.] —**gram'ma·to·log'ic** (-tə-lŏj'ĭk), **gram'ma·to·log'i·cal** *adj.* —**gram'ma·tol'o·gist** *n.*

gramme (grăm) *n. Chiefly Brit.* Variant of **gram**[1].

gram-mo·lec·u·lar weight (grăm'mə-lĕk'yə-lər) *n.* A mole[5].

gram molecule *n.* A mole[5].

Gram-neg·a·tive (grăm'nĕg'ə-tĭv) *adj.* Of, pertaining to, or being a microorganism that does not retain the purple dye used in Gram's method.

gram·o·phone (grăm'ə-fōn') *n.* A record player; phonograph. [Orig. a trademark.]

Gram-pos·i·tive (grăm'pŏz'ĭ-tĭv) *adj.* Of, pertaining to, or being a microorganism that retains the purple dye used in Gram's method.

gram·pus (grăm'pəs) *n.* **1.** A marine mammal, *Grampus griseus,* related to and resembling the dolphins but lacking a beaklike snout. **2.** Any of several cetaceans, such as the killer whale, similar to the grampus. [Alteration of ME *graspeis* < OFr. *craspois* : *cras,* fat (< Lat. *crassus*) + *pois,* fish < Lat. *piscis.*]

Gram's method (grămz) *n.* A differential staining technique using the retention or lack of retention of a purple dye to classify bacteria. [After Hans C.J. *Gram* (1855–1938).]

gran·a·dil·la (grăn'ə-dĭl'ə, -dē'yə) *n.* **1.** Any of various tropical American passionflowers, esp. *Passiflora quadrangularis,* bearing edible fruit. **2.** The egg-shaped, fleshy fruit of the granadilla. [Sp., dim of *granada,* pomegranate < Lat. *granatus,* seedy < *granum,* grain.]

gran·a·ry (grăn'ə-rē, grā'nə-) *n., pl.* **-ries. 1.** A building for storing threshed grain. **2.** A region yielding a copious quantity of grain. [Lat. *granarium* < *granum,* seed.]

grand (grănd) *adj.* **-er, -est. 1.** Having higher rank than others of the same category: *a grand admiral.* **2.** Having more importance than others; principal: *the grand ballroom.* **3.** Including or covering all units or aspects: *the grand total.* **4.** Large and impressive in size, scope, or extent; magnificent. **5. a.** Of a rich and sumptuous nature: *A grand meal was laid before them.* **b.** Of a solemn, stately, or splendid nature, as certain kinds of public ceremonies. **6. a.** Dignified or noble in appearance or effect: *a grand old face that bespeaks suffering but not defeat.* **b.** Noble or admirable in conception or intent: *a grand purpose.* **c.** Lofty or sublime in character: *a mock-epic written in the grand style.* **7.** Wonderful or terrific: *had a grand time.* —*n.* **1.** A grand piano. **2.** *Slang.* A thousand dollars. [Fr. < OFr. < Lat. *grandis.*] —**grand'ly** *adv.* —**grand'ness** *n.*

Synonyms: *grand, magnificent, imposing, stately, majestic, august, grandiose.* These adjectives mean extremely impressive in some respect. Both *grand* and *magnificent* apply to what is on a large or otherwise impressive scale, physically or aesthetically. *Grand* also can imply dignity, sweep, or eminence, and *magnificent* suggests sumptuousness and excellence of quality. *Imposing* describes what is impressive with respect to size, bearing, power, or general excellence. *Stately* refers principally to dignified and lofty appearance or manner. *Majestic* is applicable to appearance, bearing, manner, or artistic quality, and suggests dignity, nobility, or grandeur. *August* describes persons or things that inspire reverence or awe because of exalted rank or character or because of impressive aspect. *Grandiose* refers principally to things that are on an exceedingly large scale, often with the implication of false pretension to greatness or of affectation or pompousness on the part of their creators.

gran·dad·dy (grăn'dăd'ē) *n.* Variant of **granddaddy.**

gran·dam (grăn'dăm', -dəm) also **gran·dame** (-dăm', -dəm) *n.* **1.** A grandmother. **2.** An old woman. [ME *graundame* < OFr. *grand dame,* great lady.]

grand·aunt (grănd'ănt', -änt') *n.* A sister of one's grandparent.

grand·child (grănd'chīld', grăn'-) *n.* A child of one's son or daughter.

grand·dad (grăn'dăd') *n. Informal.* A grandfather.

grand·dad·dy also **gran·dad·dy** (grăn'dăd'ē) *n.* **1.** A grandfather (sense 1). **2.** One that is the first, oldest, or most respected of its kind: *the granddaddy of the modern computer.*

grand·daugh·ter (grăn'dô'tər) *n.* The daughter of one's son or daughter.

grand duchess *n.* **1.** The wife or widow of a grand duke. **2.** A woman who is sovereign of a grand duchy. **3.** The daughter of a czar or of one of his male descendants.

grand duchy *n.* A territory ruled by a grand duke or a grand duchess.

grand duke *n.* **1.** A nobleman who is below a king in rank and is sovereign of a grand duchy. **2.** A son or grandson of a czar.

gran·dee (grăn-dē') *n.* **1.** A nobleman of the highest rank in Spain or Portugal. **2.** A person of eminence or high rank. [Sp. *grande* < Lat. *grandis,* great.]

gran·deur (grăn'jər, -jŏŏr') *n.* **1.** The quality or condition of being grand; magnificence: *"The world is charged with the grandeur of God"* (Gerard Manley Hopkins). **2.** Nobility or greatness of character. [OFr. < *grand,* great < Lat. *grandis*]

grand·fa·ther (grănd'fä'*th*ər, grăn'-) *n.* **1.** The father of one's mother or father. **2.** A forefather; ancestor.

grandfather clause *n.* A clause in the constitutions of several southern states prior to 1915 designed to disfranchise blacks by exempting from stringent voting requirements all lineal descendants of persons who were registered voters before 1867.

grandfather clock *n.* A pendulum clock enclosed in a tall, narrow cabinet. [From the song *My Grandfather's Clock* by Henry C. Work (1832–1884).]

grandfather file *n. Computer Sci.* A magnetic tape or disk containing the original information for a programming system.

grain elevator

grampus

grandfather clock

grand piano

grand·fa·ther·ly (grănd′fä′*th*ər-lē, grăn′-) *adj.* **1.** Characteristic of or befitting a grandfather. **2.** Having the qualities of a grandfather; benevolent.
grandfather tape *n.* A grandfather file.
gran·dil·o·quence (grăn-dĭl′ə-kwəns) *n.* Pompous or bombastic speech or expression. [< Lat. *grandiloquus,* speaking loftily : *grandis,* great + *loqui,* to speak.] **—gran·dil′o·quent** *adj.* **—gran·dil′o·quent·ly** *adv.*
gran·di·ose (grăn′dē-ōs′, grăn′dē-ōs′) *adj.* **1.** Characterized by greatness of scope or intent; grand. **2.** Characterized by feigned or affected grandeur; pompous. [Fr. < Ital. *grandioso* < *grande,* great < Lat. *grandis.*] **—gran′di·ose′ly** *adv.* **—gran′di·os′i·ty** (-ŏs′ĭ-tē), **gran′di·ose′ness** *n.*
gran·di·o·so (grän′dē-ō′sō, -zō, grăn′) *Mus.* —*adv.* In a grand and noble style. Used as a direction. —*adj.* Grand and noble in style. [Ital. —see GRANDIOSE.]
grand jury *n.* A jury of 12 to 23 persons convened in private session to evaluate accusations against persons charged with crime and to determine whether the evidence warrants a bill of indictment.
Grand La·ma (grănd′ lä′mə) *n.* The Dalai Lama.
grand larceny *n.* The theft of property of a value exceeding the amount constituting petit larceny.
grand·ma (grănd′mä′, grăn′mä′, grăm′mä′, grăm′ə) *n. Informal.* A grandmother.
grand mal (gräɴ mäl′, grän, grănd′ măl′) *n.* A form of epilepsy characterized by severe seizures involving spasms and loss of consciousness. [Fr. : *grand,* great + *mal,* illness.]
grand·moth·er (grănd′mŭ*th*′ər, grăn′-) *n.* **1.** The mother of one's father or mother. **2.** A female ancestor.
grand·moth·er·ly (grănd′mŭ*th*′ər-lē, grăn′-) *adj.* **1.** Characteristic of or befitting a grandmother. **2.** Having the qualities of a grandmother; solicitous.
grand·neph·ew (grănd′nĕf′yo͞o, grăn′-) *n.* A son of one's nephew or niece.
grand·niece (grănd′nēs′, grăn′-) *n.* A daughter of one's nephew or niece.
grand opera *n.* A serious or melodramatic drama having the entire text set to music.
grand·pa (grănd′pä′, grăn′pä′, grăm′pä′, grăm′pə) *n. Informal.* A grandfather.
grand·par·ent (grănd′pâr′ənt, -păr′-, grăn′-) *n.* A parent of one's mother or father; grandmother or grandfather.
grand piano *n.* A piano having the strings strung in a horizontal harp-shaped frame supported usually on three legs.
Grand Prix (gräɴ′ prē′) *n., pl.* **Grand Prix** (prēz′, prē′). Any of several competitive international road races for sports cars of specific engine size over an exacting and usually risky course. [Fr., short for *Grand Prix de Paris,* great prize of Paris.]
grand·sire (grănd′sīr′, grăn′-) also **grand·sir** (-sər) *n. Archaic.* **1.** A grandfather. **2.** A male ancestor; forefather. **3.** An old man.
grand slam *n.* **1.** A slam[2]. **2.** The winning of all the major or specified events in a contest, esp. sporting events on a professional circuit. **3.** *Baseball.* A home run hit when three runners are on base.
grand·son (grănd′sŭn′, grăn′-) *n.* The son of one's son or daughter.
grand·stand (grănd′stănd′, grăn′-) *n.* **1.** A roofed stand for spectators at a stadium or racetrack. **2.** The spectators or audience at an event. —*intr.v.* **-stand·ed, -stand·ing, -stands.** To perform ostentatiously so as to impress an audience. **—grand′stand′er** *n.*
grand tour *n.* **1.** An extended tour of continental Europe formerly considered a finishing course in the education of young men of the English upper class. **2.** A comprehensive tour or survey.
grand·un·cle (grănd′ŭng′kəl) *n.* The uncle of one's father or mother.
grange (grānj) *n.* **1. Grange a.** An association of farmers founded in the United States in 1867. **b.** One of the branch lodges of this association. **2.** *Chiefly Brit.* A farm, esp. the residence and outbuildings of a gentleman farmer. **3.** *Archaic.* A granary. [ME *graunge,* granary < OFr. *grange* < Med. Lat. *granica* < Lat. *granum,* seed.] **—grang′er** *n.*
grang·er·ize (grān′jə-rīz′) *tr.v.* **-ized, -iz·ing, -iz·es. 1.** To illustrate (a book) with drawings, prints, or engravings taken from other books. **2.** To mutilate (a book) by clipping out its illustrative material for similar use in another book. [After James *Granger* (1723–1776).] **—grang′er·ism** *n.* **—grang′er·i·za′tion** *n.* **—grang′er·iz′er** *n.*
grani– *pref.* Grain; seed: *granivorous.* [Lat. < *granum,* seed.]
gran·ite (grăn′ĭt) *n.* **1.** A common, coarse-grained, light-colored, hard igneous rock consisting chiefly of quartz, orthoclase or microcline, and mica, used in monuments and for building. **2.** Unyielding endurance; steadfastness: *a will of granite.* [Ital. *granito* < *granito,* grained, p.part. of *granire,* to make grainy < *grano,* grain < Lat. *granum.*] **—gra·nit′ic** (gră-nĭt′ĭk), **gran′it·oid′** (grăn′ĭ-toid′) *adj.*
granite paper *n.* A paper containing a low proportion of colored mottling fibers.
gran·ite·ware (grăn′ĭt-wâr′) *n.* **1.** Enameled iron utensils. **2.** Earthenware with a speckled glaze resembling granite.
gra·niv·o·rous (grə-nĭv′ər-əs) *adj.* Feeding on grain and seeds.

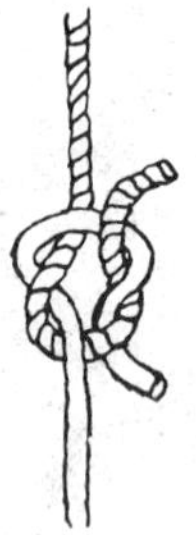
granny knot

grape

grapefruit

gran·ny or **gran·nie** (grăn′ē) *n., pl.* **-nies. 1.** A grandmother. **2.** A fussy person. **3.** *Southern U.S.* A midwife. [Short for GRANDMOTHER.]
granny knot *n.* A knot resembling a square knot but with the second tie crossed incorrectly.
grano– *pref.* Granite: *granolith.* [G. < *Granit,* granite < Ital. *granito.* —see GRANITE.]
gra·no·la (grə-nō′lə) *n.* Rolled oats mixed with various ingredients, as dried fruit, brown sugar, and nuts, used esp. as a breakfast cereal. [Orig. a trademark.]
gran·o·lith (grăn′ə-lĭth′) *n.* A paving stone of crushed granite and cement. **—gran′o·lith′ic** *adj.*
gran·o·phyre (grăn′ə-fīr′) *n.* A fine-grained granite porphyry having a groundmass with irregular intergrowths of quartz and feldspar. [G. *Granophyr* : *grano-,* grano- + *Porphyr,* porphyry < Med. Lat. *porphyrium.* —see PORPHYRY.] **—gran′o·phyr′ic** (-fîr′ĭk) *adj.*
grant (grănt) *tr.v.* **grant·ed, grant·ing, grants. 1.** To allow or consent to the fulfillment of: *grant a request.* **2.** To permit or accord, as a favor or privilege: *civil rights granted to all citizens.* **3. a.** To bestow; confer: *grant aid.* **b.** To transfer (property) by a deed. **4.** To concede; acknowledge: *Granting the genius of your plan, you still won't find backers.* —*n.* **1.** The act of granting. **2.** Something granted. **3.** *Law.* **a.** A transfer of property by deed. **b.** The property transferred. **c.** The deed by which the property is transferred. **4.** One of several tracts of land in New Hampshire, Maine, and Vermont originally granted to an individual or group. [ME *graunter* < OFr. *granter,* var. of *creanter,* to assure < VLat. **credentare* < Lat. *credens,* pr.part. of *credere,* to believe.] **—grant′a·ble** *adj.* **—grant′er** *n.*

Synonyms: *grant, vouchsafe, concede.* These verbs refer to giving. *Grant* usually implies that the giver is in a favored position with respect to the receiver, sometimes in a position of authority, and that he acts out of justice, mercy, or generosity. *Vouchsafe* emphasizes more strongly the giver's superior position and suggests that he acts from generosity or courtesy, often condescendingly. *Concede* usually implies giving reluctantly in response to a strong claim. In another related sense, *grant* and *concede* mean to admit something to be true. *Grant* refers to voluntary admission, and *concede* to a more reluctant act. *Grant* often suggests that one does not insist on establishment of proof before yielding; *concede* usually implies that one yields to an adversary's superior claim.

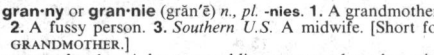

grant·ee (grăn-tē′) *n. Law.* One to whom a grant is made. —See Usage note at **-ee**[1].
grant-in-aid (grănt′ĭn-ād′) *n., pl.* **grants-in-aid. 1.** A federal grant of funds to a state or local government to subsidize a public project. **2.** A grant of funds to an institution or an individual to subsidize a project or program.
gran·tor (grăn′tər, -tôr′) *n. Law.* One who makes a grant.
grants·man·ship (grănts′mən-shĭp′) *n.* The art of obtaining grants-in-aid. [GRANT + (GAME)SMANSHIP).]
gran·u·lar (grăn′yə-lər) *adj.* **1.** Composed or appearing to be composed of granules or grains. **2.** Having a grainy texture. **—gran′u·lar′i·ty** (-lăr′ĭ-tē) *n.* **—gran′u·lar·ly** *adv.*
gran·u·late (grăn′yə-lāt′) *v.* **-lat·ed, -lat·ing, -lates.** —*tr.* **1.** To form into grains or granules. **2.** To make rough and grainy. —*intr.* To become granular or grainy. **—gran′u·la′tive** *adj.* **—gran′u·la′tor** *n.*
gran·u·la·tion (grăn′yə-lā′shən) *n.* **1. a.** The act or process of granulating. **b.** The condition or appearance of being granulated. **2.** *Physiol.* **a.** The formation of small, fleshy, beadlike protuberances on the surface of a wound that is healing. **b.** One of these protuberances.
gran·ule (grăn′yo͞ol) *n.* **1.** A small grain or pellet; particle. **2.** *Astron.* Any of the smallest transient, brilliant markings visible in the photosphere of the sun. [LLat. *granulum,* dim. of *granum,* grain.]
gran·u·lite (grăn′yə-līt′) *n.* A granular metamorphic rock often banded in appearance and composed chiefly of feldspar, quartz, and garnet. **—gran′u·lit′ic** (-lĭt′ĭk) *adj.*
gran·u·lo·cyte (grăn′yə-lō-sīt′) *n.* A granular leukocyte. **—gran′u·lo·cyt′ic** (-sĭt′ĭk) *adj.*
gran·u·lo·ma (grăn′yə-lō′mə) *n., pl.* **-mas** or **-ma·ta** (-mə-tə). One of numerous granulated nodules of inflamed tissue, usually occurring with ulcerated infections. **—gran′u·lo′ma·tous** (-mə-təs) *adj.*
gran·u·lose (grăn′yə-lōs′) *adj.* Having a surface covered with granules.
grape (grāp) *n.* **1.** Any of numerous woody vines of the genus *Vitis,* bearing clusters of edible fruit and widely cultivated in many species and varieties. **2.** The fleshy, smooth-skinned, purple, red, or green fruit of a grape, eaten raw or dried and widely used in winemaking. **3.** A dark violet to dark grayish purple. **4.** Grapeshot. [ME < OFr., bunch of grapes.]
grape fern *n.* Any of various ferns of the genus *Botrychium,* having a fertile frond bearing small, grapelike clusters of spore cases.
grape·fruit (grāp′fro͞ot′) *n.* **1.** An evergreen tropical or semitropical tree, *Citrus paradisi,* cultivated for its edible fruit. **2.** The large, round fruit of the grapefruit, having a yellow rind and juicy, somewhat acid pulp. [So called because the fruit grows in clusters.]

grape hyacinth *n.* Any of various plants of the genus *Muscari,* native to Eurasia, having narrow leaves and dense terminal clusters of rounded, usually blue flowers.

grape·shot (grăp′shŏt′) *n.* A cluster of small iron balls formerly used as a cannon charge. [From its resemblance to a cluster of grapes.]

grape sugar *n.* Dextrose.

grape·vine (grāp′vīn′) *n.* **1.** A vine on which grapes grow. **2. a.** The informal transmission of information, gossip, or rumor from person to person. **b.** A secret information source.

graph (grăf) *n.* **1.** A drawing that exhibits a relationship, often functional, between two sets of numbers as a set of points having coordinates determined by the relationship. **2.** A pictorial device, as a pie chart or bar graph, used to display numerical relationships. **3.** A representation of a quantity, as of a complex number, by a geometric object such as a point in a plane. —*tr.v.* **graphed, graph·ing, graphs. 1.** To represent by a graph. **2.** To plot (a function) on a graph. [Short for *graphic formula.*]

-graph *suff.* **1.** Something written or drawn: *monograph.* **2.** An instrument for writing, drawing, or recording: *seismograph.* [Fr. *-graphe* < Lat. *-graphum* < Gk. *-graphon* < *graphein,* to write.]

graph·eme (grăf′ēm′) *n.* **1.** A letter of an alphabet. **2.** The sum of letters and letter combinations that represent a single phoneme. [Gk. *graphein,* to write + -EME.] **—gra·phe′mic** (gră-fē′mĭk) *adj.* **—gra·phe′mi·cal·ly** *adv.*

-grapher *suff.* One who writes about a specified subject or in a specified manner: *stenographer.* [< LLat. *-graphus* < Gk. *-graphos* < *graphein,* to write.]

graph·ic (grăf′ĭk) also **graph·i·cal** (-ĭ-kəl) *adj.* **1. a.** Of or pertaining to written representation. **b.** Of or pertaining to pictorial representation. **2.** Of, pertaining to, or represented by or as if by a graph. **3. a.** Described in vivid detail. **b.** Clearly outlined or set forth. **4.** Of or pertaining to the graphic arts. **5.** Of or pertaining to graphics. **6.** *Geol.* Having crystals resembling printed characters. —*n.* **1.** A work of graphic art. **2.** A picture, chart, or other pictorial device used for illustration, as in a lecture. **3.** A graphic display generated by a computer or imaging device. [Lat. *graphicus* < Gk. *graphikos* < *graphē,* writing < *graphein,* to write.] **—graph′i·cal·ly** *adv.* **—graph′ic·ness** *n.*

graphic arts *pl.n.* **1.** Any of the fine or applied visual arts that involves the application of lines and strokes to a two-dimensional surface. **2.** Reproductions made from blocks, plates, or type, as engravings and lithographs.

graph·ics (grăf′ĭks) *n. (used with a sing. or pl. verb).* **1. a.** The making of drawings in accordance with the rules of mathematics, as in engineering or architecture. **b.** Calculations, as of structural stress, from such drawings. **2.** The process by which a computer displays graphics for operator manipulation.

graph·ite (grăf′īt′) *n.* The soft, steel-gray to black, hexagonally crystallized allotrope of carbon, used in lead pencils, lubricants, paints and coatings, and various fabricated forms including molds, bricks, electrodes, crucibles, and rocket nozzles. [Gk. *graphein,* to write + -ITE[1].] **—gra·phit′ic** (gră-fĭt′ĭk) *adj.*

graph·i·tize (grăf′ĭ-tīz′) *tr.v.* **-tized, -tiz·ing, -tiz·es. 1.** To convert into graphite by a heating process. **2.** To coat or impregnate with graphite. **—graph′i·ti·za′tion** *n.*

gra·phol·o·gy (gră-fŏl′ə-jē) *n.* The study of handwriting, esp. when employed as a means of analyzing character. [Gk. *graphē,* writing (< *graphein,* to write) + -LOGY.] **—graph′o·log′i·cal** (grăf′ə-lŏj′ĭ-kəl) *adj.* **—gra·phol′o·gist** *n.*

graph paper *n.* Paper ruled into small squares of equal size for use in drawing charts, graphs, or diagrams.

-graphy *suff.* **1.** A writing or representation produced in a specified manner or by a specified process: *photography.* **2. a.** A writing about a specified subject: *oceanography.* **b.** A representation of a specified object: *phonography.* [Lat. *-graphia* < Gk. < *graphein,* to write.]

grap·nel (grăp′nəl) *n.* A small anchor with three or more flukes, esp. one used for anchoring a vessel. [ME *grapenel,* prob. ult. < OFr. *grapin,* hook, of Germanic orig.]

grap·pa (grä′pə) *n.* An Italian brandy distilled from the residue of pressed wine. [Ital.]

grap·ple (grăp′əl) *n.* **1. a.** An iron shaft with claws at one end for grasping and holding, esp. one for drawing and holding an enemy ship alongside. **b.** A grapnel. **2.** The act of grappling. **3. a.** A contest in which the participants attempt to clutch or grip each other. **b.** A grasp or grip in such a contest. —*v.* **-pled, -pling, -ples.** —*tr.* **1.** To seize and hold with a grapple. **2.** To seize firmly with the hands. —*intr.* **1.** To hold on to something with or as if with a grapple. **2.** To use a grapple, as for dragging. **3.** To struggle, as in wrestling: *grappled with his conscience.* **4.** To attempt to cope: *grapple with the political realities of our time.* [ME *grapel* < OFr. *grape,* hook.] **—grap′pler** *n.*

grap·pling (grăp′lĭng) *n.* **1.** A grappling iron. **2.** A grapnel.

grappling iron also **grappling hook** *n.* An iron bar with claws at one end, used to raise sunken objects or secure a ship alongside.

grap·to·lite (grăp′tə-līt′) *n.* Any of numerous extinct colonial marine animals chiefly of the orders Dendroidea and Graptoloidea, of the Cambrian to the Mississippian periods. [Gk. *graptos,* written (< *graphein,* to write) + -LITE (from the resemblance of the fossils' impressions on shale to markings on a slate).]

grap·y (grā′pē) *adj.* **-i·er, -i·est.** Of, like, or suggestive of grapes.

grasp (grăsp) *v.* **grasped, grasp·ing, grasps.** —*tr.* **1.** To take hold of or seize firmly with or as if with the hand. **2.** To clasp firmly with or as if with the hand. **3.** To take hold of intellectually; comprehend. —*intr.* **1.** To make a motion of seizing, snatching, or clutching. **2.** To show eager and prompt willingness or acceptance: *grasps at any opportunity.* —*n.* **1.** The act of grasping. **2. a.** A firm hold or grip. **b.** An embrace. **3.** The ability or power to seize or attain; reach: *The presidency was within his grasp.* **4.** Understanding; comprehension: *"only a vague intuitive grasp of the meaning of greatness in literature"* (Gilbert Highet). [ME *graspen.*]

grasp·ing (grăs′pĭng) *adj.* Exceedingly eager for material gain; avaricious. **—grasp′ing·ly** *adv.* **—grasp′ing·ness** *n.*

grass (grăs) *n.* **1. a.** Any of numerous plants of the family Gramineae, characteristically having narrow leaves, hollow, jointed stems, and spikes or clusters of membranous flowers borne in smaller spikelets. **b.** Such plants collectively. **2.** Any of various plants having slender leaves like those of the true grasses. **3.** An expanse of ground, as a lawn, covered with grass or similar plants. **4.** Grazing land; pasture. **5.** *Slang.* Marijuana. **6.** *Electronics.* The small variations in amplitude of an oscilloscope display due to electrical noise. —*v.* **grassed, grass·ing, grass·es.** —*tr.* **1. a.** To cover with grass. **b.** To grow grass on. **2.** To feed (livestock) with grass. —*intr.* **1.** To become covered with grass. **2.** To graze. [ME *gras* < OE *græs.*]

grass green *n.* A moderate yellow-green to strong or dark yellowish-green. **—grass′-green′** *adj.*

grass·hop·per (grăs′hŏp′ər) *n.* **1.** Any of numerous insects of the families Locustidae (or Acrididae) and Tettigoniidae, often destructive to plants and characteristically having long hind legs adapted for jumping. **2.** A light, usually unarmed airplane used for liaison and scouting. **3.** A cocktail consisting of crème de menthe, crème de cacao, and cream.

grass·land (grăs′lănd′) *n.* An area, such as a prairie or meadow, of grass or grasslike vegetation.

grass·roots (grăs′ro͞ots′, -ro͝ots′) *pl.n. (used with a sing. or pl. verb).* **1.** People or society at a local level rather than at the center of major political activity. **2.** The groundwork or source of something.

grass snake *n.* Any of several greenish snakes, esp. *Opheodrys vernalis,* of eastern North America.

grass snipe *n.* The pectoral sandpiper.

grass tree *n.* Any of several woody-stemmed Australian plants of the genus *Xanthorrhoea,* having stiff, grasslike leaves and a spike of small white flowers.

grass widow *n.* **1.** A woman who is divorced or separated from her husband. **2.** A woman whose husband is temporarily absent. **3.** An abandoned mistress. **4.** The mother of an illegitimate child.

grass·y (grăs′ē) *adj.* **-i·er, -i·est. 1.** Covered with or abounding in grass. **2.** Resembling or suggestive of grass, as in color or odor.

grate[1] (grāt) *v.* **grat·ed, grat·ing, grates.** —*tr.* **1.** To reduce to fragments, shreds, or powder by rubbing against an abrasive surface. **2.** To cause to make a harsh grinding or rasping sound through friction: *grating her teeth.* **3.** To irritate or annoy persistently. **4.** *Archaic.* To rub or wear away. —*intr.* **1.** To make a harsh rasping sound by or as if by scraping or grinding. **2.** To cause irritation or annoyance: *grates on my nerves.* —*n.* A harsh, rasping sound made by scraping or rubbing: *the grate of a key in a lock.* [ME *graten* < OFr. *grater,* to scrape, of Germanic orig.]

grate[2] (grāt) *n.* **1.** A framework of parallel or latticed bars for blocking an opening. **2.** A framework of metal bars used to hold the fuel in a stove, furnace, or fireplace. **3.** A fireplace. **4.** A perforated iron plate or screen for sieving and grading crushed ore. —*tr.v.* **grat·ed, grat·ing, grates.** To equip with a grate. [ME < Med. Lat. *grata* < Lat. *cratis,* wickerwork.]

grate·ful (grāt′fəl) *adj.* **1.** Appreciative of benefits received; thankful. **2.** Expressing gratitude. **3.** Affording pleasure or comfort; agreeable. [< obs. *grate,* pleasing < Lat. *gratus.*] **—grate′ful·ly** *adv.* **—grate′ful·ness** *n.*

grat·er (grā′tər) *n.* **1.** One that grates. **2.** An implement with sharp-edged slits and perforations on which to grate foods.

grat·i·fi·ca·tion (grăt′ə-fĭ-kā′shən) *n.* **1.** The act of gratifying. **2.** The condition of being gratified. **3.** An instance or cause of gratification. **4.** *Archaic.* A reward.

grat·i·fy (grăt′ə-fī′) *tr.v.* **-fied, -fy·ing, -fies. 1.** To please or satisfy: *His achievement gratified his father.* **2.** To give what is desired to; indulge: *gratified her curiosity.* **3.** *Archaic.* To reward. [ME *gratifien,* to favor < Lat. *gratificare,* to oblige : *gratus,* pleasing + *facere,* to make.] **—grat′i·fi′er** *n.*

gra·tin (grät′n, grăt′n) *n.* A crust consisting of browned crumbs and butter, often with grated cheese. [Fr. < OFr. < *grater,* to scrape, of Germanic orig.]

grat·ing (grā′tĭng) *n.* **1.** A grill or network of bars set in a window or door or used as a partition; grate. **2.** *Physics.* Diffraction grating.

grappling iron

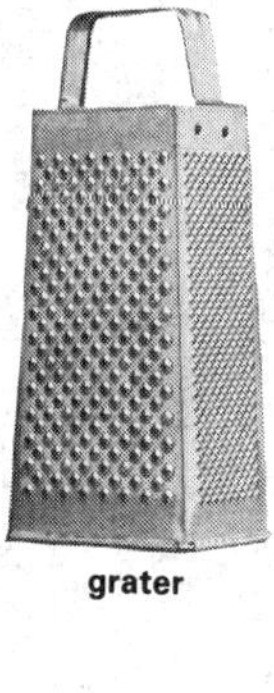
grater

grat·is (grăt′ĭs, grā′tĭs) *adv. & adj.* Without charge. [ME < Lat., alteration of *gratiis,* out of kindness, ablative pl. of *gratia,* kindness < *gratus,* pleasing.]

grat·i·tude (grăt′ĭ-to͞od′, -tyo͞od′) *n.* The state of being grateful; thankfulness. [ME < Med. Lat. *gratitudo* < Lat. *gratus,* pleasing.]

gra·tu·i·tous (grə-to͞o′ĭ-təs, -tyo͞o′-) *adj.* **1.** Given or granted without return or recompense; unearned. **2.** Given or received without cost or obligation; free. **3.** Unnecessary or unwarranted; unjustified: *gratuitous criticism.* [Lat. *gratuitus,* voluntary < *gratia,* favor < *gratus,* pleasing.] **—gra·tu′i·tous·ly** *adv.* **—gra·tu′i·tous·ness** *n.*

gra·tu·i·ty (grə-to͞o′ĭ-tē, -tyo͞o′-) *n., pl.* **-ties.** A favor or gift, usually in the form of money, given in return for service. [OFr. *gratuite* < Med. Lat. *gratuitas,* gift < Lat. *gratia, favor* < *gratus,* pleasing.]

grat·u·late (grăch′ə-lāt′) *tr.v.* **-lat·ed, -lat·ing, -lates.** *Archaic.* To congratulate. [Lat. *gratulari, gratulat-* < *gratus,* pleasing.] **—grat′u·la′tion** *n.* **—grat′u·la·to′ry** (-lə-tôr′ē, -tōr′ē) *adj.*

grau·pel (grou′pəl) *n.* Precipitation consisting of pellets of snow. [G., dim. of *Graupe,* barley.]

gra·va·men (grə-vā′mən) *n., pl.* **-va·mens** or **-vam·i·na** (-văm′ə-nə). *Law.* The part of a charge or accusation that weighs most substantially against the accused. [LLat. *gravamen* < Lat. *gravare,* to burden < *gravis,* heavy.]

grave[1] (grāv) *n.* **1.** An excavation for the interment of a corpse. **2.** A place of burial. **3.** Death or extinction. [ME < OE *græf.*]

grave[2] (grāv) *adj.* **grav·er, grav·est. 1.** Of an extremely serious nature; important: *a grave decision in a time of crisis.* **2.** Fraught with danger or harm: *a grave wound.* **3.** Dignified in conduct or character: *a grave procession.* **4.** Somber; dark. Used of colors. **5.** (*also* gräv). **a.** Written with or modified by the mark ˋ, as the è in *Sèvres.* **b.** *Ling.* Articulated toward the back of the oral cavity. *—n.* (*also* gräv). The grave accent, ˋ, indicating a pronounced *e* for the sake of meter in the usually nonsyllabic ending *-ed* in English poetry. [OFr. < Lat. *gravis.*] **—grave′ly** *adv.* **—grave′ness** *n.*

grave[3] (grāv) *tr.v.* **graved, grav·en** (grā′vən) or **graved, grav·ing, graves. 1.** To sculpt or carve; engrave. **2.** To stamp or impress deeply, as words or ideas. [ME *graven* < OE *grafan.*]

grave[4] (grāv) *tr.v.* **graved, grav·ing, graves.** To clean and coat with pitch (the bottom of a wooden ship). [ME *graven.*]

gra·ve[5] (grä′vā) *Mus. —adv.* Slowly and solemnly. Used as a direction to the performer. *—adj.* Slow and solemn. [Ital. < Lat. *gravis,* ponderous.]

grave·dig·ger (grāv′dĭg′ər) *n.* One that digs graves.

grav·el (grăv′əl) *n.* **1.** An unconsolidated mixture of rock fragments or pebbles. **2.** *Pathol.* The sandlike granular material of urinary calculi. *—tr.v.* **-eled, -el·ing, -els** or **-elled, -el·ling, -els. 1.** To apply a surface of gravel to. **2.** To confuse; perplex. **3.** *Informal.* To irritate. [ME < OFr. *gravele,* dim. of *grave,* coarse sand, of Celt. orig.]

grav·el-blind (grăv′əl-blīnd′) *adj.* Having minimal vision.

grav·el·ly (grăv′ə-lē) *adj.* **1.** Of, full of, or covered with gravel. **2.** Having a harsh rasping sound: *a gravelly voice.*

grav·en (grā′vən) *v.* A past participle of **grave[3]**.

graven image *n.* An idol or fetish carved in wood or stone.

grav·er (grā′vər) *n.* **1.** A person who carves or engraves. **2.** An engraver's cutting tool.

grave robber *n.* A person who plunders valuables from tombs or graves or who steals corpses, as for illicit dissection.

Graves' disease (grāvz) *n.* Exophthalmic goiter. [After Robert J. *Graves* (1796–1853).]

grave·stone (grāv′stōn′) *n.* A stone placed over a grave as a marker.

gravestone

grave·yard (grāv′yärd′) *n.* A burial ground; cemetery.

graveyard shift *n.* **1.** A work shift that runs during the early morning hours, as from midnight to 8:00 A.M. **2.** The workers on an early-morning shift.

grav·id (grăv′ĭd) *adj.* Pregnant. [Lat. *gravidus* < *gravis,* heavy.] **—gra·vid′i·ty** (grə-vĭd′ĭ-tē), **grav′id·ness** *n.* **—grav′id·ly** *adv.*

gra·vim·e·ter (grə-vĭm′ĭ-tər, grăv′ə-mē-) *n.* An instrument used to determine specific gravity. [Fr. *gravimètre* : Lat. *gravis,* heavy + *-mètre,* -meter.] **—gra·vim′e·try** (grə-vĭm′ĭ-trē) *n.*

grav·i·met·ric (grăv′ə-mĕt′rĭk) also **grav·i·met·ri·cal** (-rĭ-kəl) *adj.* Of or pertaining to measurement by weight. [Lat. *gravis,* heavy + METRIC.] **—grav′i·met′ri·cal·ly** *adv.*

graving dock *n.* A dry dock where ships are repaired and their hulks are cleaned.

grav·i·sphere (grăv′ĭ-sfîr′) *n.* The spherical region of space dominated by the gravitational influence of a celestial body. [GRAVI(TY) + SPHERE.]

grayling

grav·i·tate (grăv′ĭ-tāt′) *intr.v.* **-tat·ed, -tat·ing, -tates. 1.** To move in response to the force of gravity. **2.** To move downward. **3.** To be attracted by or as if by an irresistible force: *"My excuse must be that all Celts gravitate towards each other"* (Oscar Wilde). **—grav′i·tat′er** *n.*

grav·i·ta·tion (grăv′ĭ-tā′shən) *n.* **1.** *Physics.* **a.** The natural phenomenon of attraction between massive bodies. **b.** The degree of such attraction. **c.** The action or process of moving under the influence of this attraction. **2.** A movement toward a source of attraction: *the gravitation of the middle classes to the suburbs.* **—grav′i·ta′tion·al** *adj.* **—grav′i·ta′tion·al·ly** *adv.* **—grav′i·ta′tive** *adj.*

gravitational collapse *n.* The process by which stars, star clusters, and galaxies form from dilute interstellar gas under the influence of gravity.

gravitational interaction *n.* A hypothesized weak, fundamental interaction between elementary particles.

gravitational wave *n.* A wave hypothesized to propagate the force of gravity and to travel at the speed of light.

grav·i·ton (grăv′ĭ-tŏn′) *n.* A particle postulated to be the quantum of gravitational interaction and presumed to have zero electric charge, zero rest mass, and spin 2. [GRAVIT(ATION) + -ON[1].]

grav·i·ty (grăv′ĭ-tē) *n.* **1.** *Physics.* **a.** The force of gravitation, which for any two sufficiently massive bodies is directly proportional to the product of their masses and inversely proportional to the square of the distance between them, esp. the attractive central gravitational force exerted by a celestial body such as the earth. **b.** Gravitation. **c.** Weight. **2.** Grave consequence; seriousness or importance: *the gravity of their problem.* **3.** Solemnity or dignity of manner. [OFr. *gravite,* heaviness < Lat. *gravitas* < *gravis,* heavy.]

gravity wave *n.* A gravitational wave.

gra·vure (grə-vyo͝or′) *n.* **1. a.** A method of printing with etched plates or cylinders; intaglio printing. **b.** Photogravure. **2.** A plate or reproduction produced by or used in the process of gravure. [Fr. < *graver,* to engrave < OFr., of Germanic orig.]

gra·vy (grā′vē) *n., pl.* **-vies. 1. a.** The juices that drip from cooking meat. **b.** A sauce made by thickening and seasoning these juices. **2.** *Slang.* Money, profit, or benefit easily or unexpectedly gained. [ME *grave* < OFr.]

gravy boat *n.* An elongated dish or pitcher for serving gravy.

gravy train *n. Slang.* An occupation or job that requires little effort while yielding considerable profit.

gray (grā) also **grey** *—adj.* **-er, -est. 1.** Of or pertaining to an achromatic color of any lightness between the extremes of black and white. **2. a.** Dull or dark, as from lack of light: *a gray, rainy afternoon.* **b.** Lacking in cheer; gloomy. **3. a.** Having gray hair; hoary. **b.** Old, venerable, or ancient. **4.** Intermediate in character or position, esp. in the area of morality or propriety. *—n.* **1.** An achromatic color of any lightness between the extremes of black and white. **2.** An object or animal of the color gray. **3.** Often **Gray. a.** A member of the Confederate Army in the Civil War. **b.** The Confederate Army itself. *—tr. & intr. v.* **grayed, gray·ing, grays** also **greyed, grey·ing, greys.** To make or become gray. [ME *grei* < OE *græg.*]

gray·beard (grā′bîrd′) *n.* An old man.

gray·fish (grā′fĭsh′) *n., pl.* **grayfish** or **-fish·es.** A dogfish (sense 1).

gray·ish (grā′ĭsh) *adj.* Having a perceptible quality of grayness.

gray·lag goose (grā′lăg′) *n.* A gray goose, *Anser anser,* of marshy areas of the Old World. [Poss. GRAY + dial. *lag,* last.]

gray·ling (grā′lĭng) *n., pl.* **grayling** or **-lings.** Any of several freshwater food fishes of the genus *Thymallus,* of the Northern Hemisphere, having a small mouth and a large dorsal fin.

gray matter *n.* **1.** The brownish-gray nerve tissue of the brain and spinal cord, composed of nerve cells and fibers and some supportive tissue. **2.** *Informal.* Brains; intellect.

gray mullet *n.* The mullet.

gray panther *n.* A member of a militant organization of elderly individuals. [GRAY + (BLACK) PANTHER.]

gray squirrel *n.* A common squirrel, *Sciurus carolinensis,* of eastern North America, having gray or blackish fur.

gray·wacke (grā′wăk′, -wăk′ə) *n.* Any of various shale-containing dark-gray sandstones. [Partial transl. of G. *Grauwacke* : *grau,* gray + *Wacke,* boulder.]

gray whale *n.* A whalebone whale, *Eschrichtius glaucus,* of Pacific waters, having grayish coloring with white blotches.

gray wolf *n.* The timber wolf.

graze[1] (grāz) *v.* **grazed, graz·ing, graz·es.** *—intr.* To feed on growing grasses and herbage. *—tr.* **1.** To feed on (herbage) in a field or on pasture land. **2.** To feed on the herbage of (land). **3.** To put (livestock) out to feed. **4.** To afford sufficient herbage for: *This field will graze 30 head of cattle.* **5.** To tend (feeding livestock) in a pasture. [ME *grasen* < OE *grasian* < *græs,* grass.] **—graz′er** *n.*

graze[2] (grāz) *v.* **grazed, graz·ing, graz·es.** *—tr.* **1.** To touch lightly in passing; brush. **2.** To scrape or scratch slightly; abrade. *—intr.* To scrape or touch something lightly in passing. *—n.* **1.** An act of brushing or scraping along a surface. **2.** A minor scratch or abrasion. [Perh. < GRAZE[1].] **—graz′ing·ly** *adv.*

gra·zier (grā′zhər) *n.* A person who grazes cattle.

gra·zi·o·so (grät′sē-ō′sō, -zō) *Mus. —adv.* Gracefully; smoothly. Used as a direction. *—adj.* Graceful; smooth. [Ital. < Lat. *gratiosus,* agreeable. —see GRACIOUS.]

grease (grēs) *n.* **1.** Animal fat when melted or soft. **2.** A thick oil or viscous substance, esp. when used as a lubricant. **3. a.** The oily substance present in raw wool; suint. **b.** Raw wool that has not been cleansed of this. *—tr.v.* (grēs, grēz) **greased, greas·ing, greas·es. 1.** To coat, smear, or soil with grease or lard. **2.** To lubricate with grease. ***—idiom.* grease (someone's) palm.** *Slang.* To bribe. [ME *grese* < AN *grece* < OFr. *graisse* < Lat. *crassus,* fat.]

grease monkey *n. Slang.* A mechanic, esp. a garage attendant, who lubricates machinery.

grease paint *n.* Theatrical make-up.

greas·er (grē'sər, -zər) *n.* **1.** *Offensive Slang.* A native of Mexico or of Latin America. **2.** *Slang.* A young white male of working-class background who is tough and esp. aggressive.

grease·wood (grēs'wo͝od') *n.* **1.** A spiny shrub, *Sarcobatus vermiculatus,* of western North America, having small alternate leaves, white stems, and small greenish flowers. **2.** Any of various plants similar or related to the greasewood, as the creosote bush.

greas·y (grē'sē, -zē) *adj.* **-i·er, -i·est. 1.** Coated or soiled with grease. **2.** Containing grease, esp. too much grease. **3.** Suggestive of grease in slickness or slipperiness: *a greasy character.* **—greas'i·ly** *adv.* **—greas'i·ness** *n.*

great (grāt) *adj.* **-er, -est. 1.** Extremely large in size; big. **2.** Larger than others of the same kind: *the great auk.* **3.** Large in quantity or number: *A great throng awaited him.* **4.** Extensive in time or distance. **5.** Remarkable or outstanding in magnitude, degree, or extent: *a great crisis.* **6.** Of outstanding significance or importance: *a great work of art.* **7.** Chief or principal: *the great house on the estate.* **8.** Superior in quality or character; noble: *"For he was great, ere fortune made him so"* (Dryden). **9.** Powerful; influential: *one of the great nations of the West.* **10.** Eminent; distinguished: *a great leader.* **11.** Grand; aristocratic. **12.** *Archaic.* Pregnant: *great with child.* **13.** *Informal.* Enthusiastic: *a great boxing fan.* **14.** *Informal.* Very skillful: *great at algebra.* **15.** *Informal.* Very good; first-rate: *a great book.* **16.** Being one generation removed from the relative specified: *a great-grandfather.* *—n.* One that is great. *—adv. Informal.* Very well. [ME *grete* < OE *grēat,* thick, coarse.] **—great'ly** *adv.* **—great'ness** *n.*

great auk *n.* A large, flightless sea bird, *Pinguinus impennis,* formerly common on northern Atlantic coasts but extinct since the middle of the 19th century.

great-aunt (grāt'ănt', -änt') *n.* A grandaunt.

Great Bear *n.* Ursa Major.

great circle *n.* A circle that is the intersection of the surface of a sphere with a plane passing through the center of the sphere.

great·coat (grāt'kōt') *n.* A heavy overcoat.

Great Dane *n.* A large and powerful dog of a breed developed in Germany, having a smooth, short coat and a narrow head.

great divide *n.* **1.** A large or major watershed. **2.** A major point of change, esp. death.

great·en (grāt'n) *tr. & intr.v.* **-ened, -en·ing, -ens.** *Archaic.* To make or become great or greater.

great·er also **Great·er** (grā'tər) *adj.* Designating a city and its populous suburbs: *Greater Los Angeles.*

great·heart·ed (grāt'här'tĭd) *adj.* **1.** Noble or courageous in spirit. **2.** Generous; magnanimous. **—great'heart'ed·ly** *adv.* **—great'heart'ed·ness** *n.*

great horned owl *n.* A large North American owl, *Bubo virginianus,* having brownish plumage.

great laurel *n.* The rosebay (sense 1).

Great Powers *pl.n.* Those nations having the greatest social, political, and economic influence in international affairs.

Great Pyr·e·nees (pîr'ə-nēz') *n.* A large, heavy-boned dog of an ancient breed, having a thick white coat.

Great Russian *n.* A member of the Russian-speaking people inhabiting the central and northeastern U.S.S.R.

great seal *n.* The principal seal of a government or state, with which official documents are stamped.

Great Spirit *n.* The principal deity in the religion of many North American Indian tribes.

great-un·cle (grāt'ŭng'kəl) *n.* A granduncle.

Great War *n.* World War I.

greave (grēv) *n.* Often **greaves.** Leg armor worn below the knee. [ME *greve* < OFr.]

greaves (grēvz) *pl.n.* The unmelted residue left after animal fat or tallow has been rendered. [LG *greven.*]

grebe (grēb) *n.* Any of various diving birds of the family Podicipedidae, having lobed, fleshy membranes along each toe and a pointed bill. [Fr. *grèbe.*]

Gre·cian (grē'shən) *adj.* Greek. *—n.* A native of Greece. [< Lat. *Graecia,* Greece < *Graecus,* Greek. —see GREEK.]

Gre·cism (grē'sĭz'əm) *n.* **1.** The style or spirit of Greek culture, art, or thought. **2.** Something done in imitation of Greek style or spirit. **3.** An idiom of the Greek language.

Gre·cize (grē'sīz') *tr.v.* **-cized, -ciz·ing, -ciz·es.** To make Greek or Hellenic in form or style. [Lat. *graecizare* < *Graecus,* Greek. —see GREEK.]

Greco– or **Graeco–** *pref.* Greece; Greek: *Greco-Roman.* [Lat. *Graeco-* < *Graecus,* Greek.]

Grec·o-Ro·man (grĕk'ō-rō'mən, grē'kō-) *adj.* Of or pertaining to both Greece and Rome: *Greco-Roman mythology.*

gree (grē) *n. Scot.* Superiority. [ME *gre* < OFr., step < Lat. *gradus.*]

greed (grēd) *n.* An excessive desire to acquire or possess, as wealth or power, beyond what one needs or deserves. [Back-formation < GREEDY.]

greed·y (grē'dē) *adj.* **-i·er, -i·est. 1.** Excessively desirous of acquiring or possessing something, esp. in quantity. **2.** Wanting to eat or drink more than one can reasonably consume; gluttonous. **3.** Extremely eager or desirous: *greedy for the opportunity to prove her ability.* [ME *gredi* < OE *grǣdig.*] **—greed'i·ly** *adv.* **—greed'i·ness** *n.*

Greek (grēk) *n.* **1.** The Indo-European language of the Greeks. **2. a.** An indigenous inhabitant of Greece. **b.** A descendant of an indigenous inhabitant of Greece. **3.** *Slang.* A member of a fraternity or sorority having a name composed of Greek letters. **4.** Something that is unintelligible: *It's Greek to me.* *—adj.* **1.** Of, pertaining to, or designating Greece, the Hellenes, their language, or their culture. **2.** Of, pertaining to, or designating the Greek Orthodox Church. [ME *Grek* < OE *Grecas,* the Greeks < Lat. *Graecus,* Greek < Gk. *Graikos,* tribal name.]

Greek Catholic *n.* **1.** A member of the Eastern Orthodox Church. **2.** A member of a Uniat Church.

Greek cross *n.* A cross formed by two bars of equal length crossing in the middle at right angles to each other.

Greek fire *n.* An incendiary composition used by the Byzantine Greeks to set fire to enemy ships.

green (grēn) *n.* **1.** Any of a group of colors that may vary in lightness and saturation and whose hue is that of the emerald or somewhat less yellow than that of growing grass; the hue of that portion of the spectrum lying between yellow and blue; one of the additive or light primaries; one of the psychological primary hues, evoked in the normal observer by radiant energy having a wavelength of approximately 530 nanometers. **2.** Something green in color. **3. greens.** Green growth or foliage, esp.: **a.** The branches and leaves of plants used for decoration. **b.** Leafy plants or plant parts eaten as vegetables. **4. a.** A grassy lawn or plot. **b.** A putting green. *—adj.* **-er, -est. 1.** Of the color green. **2.** Abounding in or covered with green growth or foliage. **3.** Made with green or leafy vegetables: *a green salad.* **4.** Mild or temperate in climate. **5.** Youthful; vigorous. **6.** Brand-new; fresh. **7.** Not mature or ripe; young: *green persimmons.* **8.** Pale and sickly in appearance; wan. **9.** Not yet fully processed, esp.: **a.** Not aged: *green wood.* **b.** Not cured or tanned: *green pelts.* **10.** Lacking training or experience. **11. a.** Lacking sophistication or worldly experience; naive. **b.** Easily duped or deceived; gullible. *—tr. & intr.v.* **greened, green·ing, greens.** To make or become green. [ME *grene* < OE *grēne.*] **—green'ly** *adv.* **—green'ness** *n.*

green alga *n.* Any of the numerous algae of the division Chlorophyta, having pronounced green coloring, as spirogyra and sea lettuce.

green·back (grēn'băk') *n.* A legal-tender note of U.S. currency.

Greenback Party *n.* A former U.S. political party, organized in 1874, that advocated the use of inconvertible paper money.

green bean *n.* The string bean (sense 2).

green·belt (grēn'bĕlt') *n.* A belt of recreational parks, farmland, or uncultivated land surrounding a community.

Green Beret *n.* A member of the U.S. Army Special Forces. [From the green beret that is part of the uniform.]

green·bri·er (grēn'brī'ər) *n.* The catbrier.

green corn *n.* Young, tender ears of sweet corn.

green dragon *n.* A plant, *Arisaema dracontium,* of eastern North America, having divided leaves and minute flowers at the base of a long, slender spadix projecting from a narrow green spathe.

green·er·y (grē'nə-rē) *n., pl.* **-ies. 1. a.** Green foliage; verdure. **b.** Such foliage used for decoration. **2.** A place where plants are grown.

green-eyed (grēn'īd') *adj.* Jealous.

green·finch (grēn'fĭnch') *n.* A Eurasian bird, *Carduelis chloris* (or *Chloris chloris*), having green and yellow plumage.

green·fly (grēn'flī') *n.* Any of several greenish insects, esp. an aphid.

green·gage (grēn'gāj') *n.* A variety of plum having yellowish-green skin and sweet flesh.

green·gro·cer (grēn'grō'sər) *n. Chiefly Brit.* A retailer of fresh fruit and vegetables. **—green'gro'cer·y** *n.*

green·head (grēn'hĕd') *n.* A male mallard duck.

green·heart (grēn'härt') *n.* **1.** A tropical American tree, *Ocotea rodioei* (or *Nectandra rodioei*), having dark, greenish, durable wood. **2.** Any of various trees similar to the greenheart. **3.** The wood of the greenheart.

green·horn (grēn'hôrn') *n.* **1.** An inexperienced or immature person. **2.** A newcomer, esp. an immigrant who is unfamiliar with local ways. **3.** A gullible person. [Obs. *greynhorne,* animal with immature horns.]

green·house (grēn'hous') *n.* **1.** A usually glass-enclosed structure used for cultivating plants that require controlled temperature and humidity. **2.** *Slang.* A part of an aircraft covered with a clear plastic bubble or shell.

greenhouse effect *n.* The sequence of phenomena comprising the absorption of solar radiation by the earth, its conversion and re-emission in the infrared, and the absorption of this radiation, esp. in the wavelength region from 5 to 17 microns, by atmospheric ozone, water vapor, and carbon

great horned owl

great seal
The great seal of the United States

greenhouse

dioxide, preventing its dissipation into space and resulting in a steady, gradual rise in the temperature of the atmosphere.

green·ing (grē′nĭng) *n.* Any of several varieties of green-skinned apples.

green·ish (grē′nĭsh) *adj.* Somewhat green.

Green·land spar (grēn′lənd) *n.* Cryolite.

green·let (grēn′lĭt) *n.* Any of various greenish birds of the genus *Hylophilus,* of Central and South America, related to the vireos.

green light *n.* **1.** The green-colored light that signals traffic to proceed. **2.** Permission to proceed.

green·ling (grēn′lĭng) *n.* Any of various food fishes of the family Hexagrammidae, of the northern Pacific.

green manure *n.* A growing crop, such as a clover or grass, that is plowed under the soil to improve fertility.

green monkey *n.* Any of several African monkeys of the genus *Cercopithecus,* esp. *C. aethiops sabaeus,* having yellowish-gray fur with a greenish tinge.

gree·nock·ite (grē′nə-kīt′) *n.* A yellow to brown or red mineral, essentially CdS, used as a cadmium ore. [After Charles Cathcart, Lord *Greenock* (d. 1859).]

green pepper *n.* The unripened green fruit of various pepper plants.

green plover *n.* The lapwing.

green revolution *n.* The significant increase in agricultural productivity resulting from the introduction of high-yield varieties of grains and improved management techniques.

green·room (grēn′ro͞om′, -ro͝om′) *n.* A waiting room or lounge in a theater or concert hall for the use of performers when off-stage. [So called because such rooms were originally painted green.]

green·sand (grēn′sănd′) *n.* A sand or sediment given a dark greenish color by grains of glauconite.

green·shank (grēn′shăngk′) *n.* An Old World wading bird, *Tringa nebularia,* having greenish legs and a long bill.

green·sick·ness (grēn′sĭk′nĭs) *n.* Chlorosis (sense 2). **—green′sick′** *adj.*

green snake *n.* Any of several nonvenomous North American snakes of the genus *Opheodrys,* having a slender yellow-green body.

green soap *n.* A translucent, yellowish-green soft or liquid soap made chiefly from vegetable oils and used in the treatment of chronic skin disorders.

green·stone (grēn′stōn′) *n.* Any of various altered basic igneous rocks colored green by chlorite, hornblende, and epidote.

green·sward (grēn′swôrd′) *n.* Turf on which the grass is green.

green tea *n.* Tea made from leaves that are not fermented before being dried.

green thumb *n.* A knack for making plants grow well.

green turtle *n.* A large marine turtle, *Chelonia mydas,* having greenish flesh esteemed as food.

Green·wich time also **Greenwich mean time** (grĭn′ĭj, -ĭch, grĕn′-) *n.* Mean solar time for the meridian at Greenwich, England, used as a basis for calculating time throughout most of the world.

green·wood (grēn′wo͝od′) *n.* A wood or forest when the foliage is green.

greet (grēt) *tr.v.* **greet·ed, greet·ing, greets. 1.** To address in a friendly and respectful way; welcome or salute. **2.** To receive with a specified reaction: *greet a joke with laughter.* **3.** To be perceived by: *A din greeted our ears.* [ME *greten* < OE *grētan.*] **—greet′er** *n.*

greet·ing (grē′tĭng) *n.* A gesture or word of welcome or salutation.

greeting card *n.* A card that is imprinted with a greeting and often a suitable illustration and that is sent or given on a special occasion or holiday.

greg·a·rine (grĕg′ə-rīn′) *n.* Any of various sporozoan protozoans of the order Gregarinida that are parasitic within invertebrates such as arthropods and annelids. *—adj.* Of or belonging to the Gregarinida. [NLat. *Gregarina,* genus name < Lat. *gregarius,* belonging to a flock < *grex,* flock.] **—greg′a·rin′i·an** (-rĭn′ē-ən) *adj.*

gre·gar·i·ous (grĭ-gâr′ē-əs) *adj.* **1.** Tending to move in or form a group, as a herd, pack, or flock, with others of the same kind. **2.** Seeking and enjoying the company of others; sociable. **3.** *Bot.* Growing in groups that are close together but not densely clustered or matted. [Lat. *gregarius,* belonging to a flock < *grex,* flock.] **—gre·gar′i·ous·ly** *adv.* **—gre·gar′i·ous·ness** *n.*

Gre·go·ri·an calendar (grĭ-gôr′ē-ən, -gōr′-) *n.* The calendar in use throughout most of the world, sponsored by Pope Gregory XIII in 1582.

Gregorian chant *n.* The monodic liturgical plainsong of the Roman Catholic Church. [After Pope Gregory I (540?–604).]

grei·sen (grī′zən) *n.* A granitic rock composed chiefly of quartz and mica. [G. < *greissen,* to split.]

grem·lin (grĕm′lĭn) *n.* **1.** An imaginary gnomelike creature to whom mechanical problems in aircraft are often attributed. **2.** A mischief-maker. [Orig. unknown.]

gre·nade (grə-nād′) *n.* **1.** A missile containing priming and bursting charges, designed to be thrown by hand or fired from a launcher-equipped rifle. **2.** A glass container filled with a volatile chemical or a liquid that is dispersed when the glass is thrown and smashed. [Fr. < OFr. *grenate,* pomegranate (from its shape), ult. < Lat. *granatum* < *granatus,* having many seeds < *granum,* seed.]

grenade
Hand grenade

gren·a·dier (grĕn′ə-dîr′) *n.* **1. a.** A member of the British Grenadier Guards, the first regiment of the royal household infantry. **b.** A soldier formerly bearing grenades. **2.** Any of various fishes of the family Macrouridae, chiefly of the deep ocean, having a long tapering tail and lacking a tail fin. [Fr. < *grenade,* grenade.]

gren·a·dine (grĕn′ə-dēn′, grĕn′ə-dēn′) *n.* **1.** A thick, sweet syrup made from pomegranates or red currants and used as flavoring, esp. in beverages. **2.** A thin openwork fabric of silk, cotton, or a synthetic. [Fr. < *grenade,* pomegranate < OFr. *grenate.* —see GRENADE.]

Gresh·am's law (grĕsh′əmz) *n.* The theory that if two kinds of money in circulation have the same denominational value but different intrinsic values, the money with higher intrinsic value will be hoarded and eventually driven out of circulation by the money with lesser intrinsic value. [After Sir Thomas *Gresham* (1519?–1579).]

gres·so·ri·al (grĕ-sôr′ē-əl, -sōr′-) *adj.* **1.** Adapted for walking. **2.** Having legs adapted for walking. [NLat. *gressorius* < Lat. *gradi,* to walk.]

grew (gro͞o) *v.* Past tense of **grow.**

grew·some (gro͞o′səm) *adj.* Variant of **gruesome.**

grey (grā) *adj., n., & v.* Variant of **gray.**

grey·hen (grā′hĕn′) *n.* The female of the black grouse.

grey·hound (grā′hound′) *n.* A large, slender dog of an ancient breed, having a smooth coat, a narrow head, and long legs and capable of running swiftly. [ME *grehound* < OE *grīghund.*]

greyhound

grey·lag (grā′lăg′) *n.* The graylag goose.

grib·ble (grĭb′əl) *n.* Any of several small, wood-boring marine crustaceans of the genus *Limnoria,* esp. *L. lignorum,* often damaging underwater wooden structures. [Poss. dim. of GRUB.]

grid (grĭd) *n.* **1.** A framework of parallel or crisscrossed bars; gridiron. **2.** A pattern of horizontal and vertical lines forming squares of uniform size on a map, chart, aerial photograph, or optical device, used as a reference for locating points. **3.** A football field. **4.** *Elect.* **a.** An interconnected system of electric cables and power stations that distributes electricity over a large area. **b.** A corrugated or perforated conducting plate in a storage battery. **c.** A network or coil of fine wires located between the plate and the filament in an electron tube. **5.** The starting positions of cars on a racecourse. **6.** *Printing.* A device in a phototypesetting machine upon which are etched the characters used in composition. [Short for GRIDIRON.]

grid·dle (grĭd′l) *n.* A flat pan or other flat metal surface used for cooking by dry heat. *—tr.v.* **-dled, -dling, -dles.** To cook on a griddle. [ME *gridel,* gridiron < OFr. *gridil* < Lat. *craticula,* dim. of *cratis,* wickerwork.]

grid·dle·cake (grĭd′l-kāk′) *n.* A pancake.

grid·i·ron (grĭd′ī′ərn) *n.* **1.** A flat framework of parallel metal bars used for broiling meat or fish. **2.** A framework or network suggestive of a gridiron. **3.** A football field. **4.** A metal structure high above the stage of a theater from which ropes or cables are strung to scenery and lights. [ME *gridere,* alteration of *gridel.* —see GRIDDLE.]

grief (grēf) *n.* **1.** Deep mental anguish, as over a loss; sorrow. **2.** A source of grief. **3.** *Obs.* A grievance. ***—idiom.*** **come to grief.** To meet with disaster; fail. [ME < OFr. < *grever,* to grieve. —see GRIEVE.]

griev·ance (grē′vəns) *n.* **1. a.** An actual or supposed circumstance regarded as just cause for protest. **b.** A complaint or protest based on such a circumstance. **2.** Indignation or resentment stemming from a feeling of having been wronged. **3.** *Obs.* **a.** The act of inflicting hardship or harm. **b.** The cause of harm or hardship. [ME *grevaunce* < OFr. *grevance* < *grever,* to harm. —see GRIEVE.]

grieve (grēv) *v.* **grieved, griev·ing, grieves.** *—tr.* **1.** To cause to be sorrowful; distress. **2.** *Archaic.* To hurt or harm. *—intr.* To experience grief; mourn. [ME *grevan* < OFr. *grever,* to harm < Lat. *gravare,* to burden < *gravis,* heavy.] **—griev′ing·ly** *adv.*

griev·ous (grē′vəs) *adj.* **1.** Causing grief, pain, or anguish: *a grievous loss.* **2.** Serious or dire; grave: *a grievous crime.* **—griev′ous·ly** *adv.* **—griev′ous·ness** *n.*

grif·fin also **grif·fon** or **gryph·on** (grĭf′ən) *n.* A fabulous beast with the head and wings of an eagle and the body of a lion. [ME *griffoun* < OFr. *griffon* < Lat. *gryphus* < Gk. *grups.*]

griffin
1st-century B.C.
Roman frieze

grif·fon (grĭf′ən) *n.* **1.** Any of several breeds of dog having a wiry coat, esp. a small dog of a breed originating in Belgium, having a short, bearded muzzle. **2.** Variant of **griffin.** [Alteration of GRIFFIN.]

grift (grĭft) *Slang. —n.* **1.** Money made dishonestly, as in a swindle. **2.** A swindle or confidence game. *—intr.v.* **grift·ed, grift·ing, grifts.** To practice swindling or cheating. [Var. of GRAFT[2].] **—grift′er** *n.*

grig (grĭg) *n. Archaic.* A lively, bright person. [ME, dwarf.]

gri·gri also **gris-gris** (grē′grē) *n.* An African charm, fetish, or amulet. [Of African orig.]

grill (grĭl) *tr.v.* **grilled, grill·ing, grills. 1.** To broil on a gridiron. **2.** To torture as if by broiling. **3.** *Informal.* To question relentlessly; cross-examine. **4.** To mark or emboss with a gridiron. —*n.* **1.** A cooking utensil with parallel metal bars; gridiron. **2.** Food cooked by broiling or grilling. **3.** A grillroom. **4.** A series of marks grilled or embossed on a surface. **5.** Variant of **grille.** [Fr. *griller* < *gril,* gridiron < OFr. *greille* < Lat. *craticula,* dim. of *cratis,* wickerwork.] **—grill'er** *n.*

gril·lage (grĭl'ĭj) *n.* A network or frame of crossed timbers serving as a foundation, usually on treacherous soil. [Fr. < *grille,* gridiron < OFr. *greille.* —see GRILL.]

grille also **grill** (grĭl) *n.* **1.** A metal grating used as a screen, divider, barrier, or decorative element, as in a window or gateway. **2.** A square opening at the back of the hazard side of a court-tennis court. [Fr. —see GRILLAGE.]

grill·room (grĭl'ro͞om', -ro͝om') *n.* A restaurant or room in a restaurant where grilled foods are served.

grilse (grĭls) *n., pl.* **grilse.** A young salmon on its first return from the sea to fresh or brackish waters. [ME *grills.*]

grim (grĭm) *adj.* **grim·mer, grim·mest. 1.** Unrelenting; rigid: *a grim insistence on continuing.* **2.** Uninviting or unnerving in aspect; forbidding: *"undoubtedly the grimmest part of him was his iron claw"* (J.M. Barrie). **3.** Ghastly; sinister: *"he made a grim jest at the horrifying nature of his wound"* (Reginald Pound). **4.** Dismal; gloomy. **5.** Ferocious; savage. [ME < OE, fierce.] **—grim'ly** *adv.* **—grim'ness** *n.*

grim·ace (grĭm'ĭs, grĭ-mās') *n.* A sharp contortion of the face expressive of pain, contempt, or disgust. —*intr.v.* **-aced, -ac·ing, -ac·es.** To make a grimace. [Fr. < OFr., of Germanic orig.] **—grim'ac·er** *n.*

gri·mal·kin (grĭ-môl'kĭn, -măl'-) *n.* **1.** A cat, esp. an old female cat. **2.** A shrewish old woman. [Var. of *graymalkin* : GRAY + obs. *Malkin,* a woman's name.]

grime (grīm) *n.* Black dirt or soot, esp. such dirt clinging to or ingrained in a surface. —*tr.v.* **grimed, grim·ing, grimes.** To cover with grime; begrime. [ME < MLG.]

Grimm's Law (grĭmz) *n.* A formula describing the regular changes undergone by Indo-European stop consonants represented in Germanic, essentially stating that Indo-European *p, t,* and *k* became Germanic *f, th,* and *h;* Indo-European *b, d,* and *g,* Germanic *p, t,* and *k;* and Indo-European *bh, dh,* and *gh,* Germanic *b, d,* and *g.* [After Jakob *Grimm* (1785–1863).]

grim·y (grī'mē) *adj.* **-i·er, -i·est.** Covered or ingrained with grime. **—grim'i·ly** *adv.* **—grim'i·ness** *n.*

grin (grĭn) *v.* **grinned, grin·ning, grins.** —*intr.* To smile broadly, showing the teeth. —*tr.* To express with a grin. —*n.* **1.** The act of grinning. **2.** The expression of the face produced by grinning. [ME *grennan,* to grimace < OE *grennian.*] **—grin'ner** *n.* **—grin'ning·ly** *adv.*

grind (grīnd) *v.* **ground** (ground), **grind·ing, grinds.** —*tr.* **1. a.** To crush, pulverize, or powder by friction, esp. by rubbing between two hard surfaces: *grind wheat into flour.* **b.** To shape, sharpen, or refine with friction: *grind a lens.* **2.** To rub (two surfaces) together; gnash: *grind the teeth.* **3.** To bear down on harshly; crush. **4. a.** To operate by turning a crank. **b.** To produce by turning a crank. **5.** To produce mechanically or without inspiration: *"The production line grinds out a uniform product"* (Dwight Macdonald). **6.** To instill or teach by persistent repetition: *grind the truth into their heads.* —*intr.* **1.** To perform the operation of grinding. **2.** To become crushed, pulverized, or powdered by friction. **3.** To move with noisy friction; grate: *a train grinding along rusty rails.* **4.** *Informal.* To devote oneself to study or work. **5.** *Slang.* To rotate the pelvis in the manner of a stripteaser. —*n.* **1.** The act of grinding. **2.** A crunching or grinding noise. **3.** A specific grade or degree of pulverization, as of coffee beans: *drip grind.* **4.** *Informal.* A laborious task, routine, or study: *the daily grind.* **5.** *Informal.* A student who works or studies excessively. **6.** *Slang.* A single erotic rotation of the pelvis. [ME *grinden* < OE *grindan.*] **—grind'ing·ly** *adv.*

grind·er (grīn'dər) *n.* **1.** One that grinds, esp.: **a.** A person who sharpens cutting edges. **b.** A machine that grinds: *a meat grinder.* **2.** A molar. **3. grinders.** *Informal.* The teeth. **4.** *Slang.* A hero (sense 6).

grind·stone (grīnd'stōn') *n.* **1.** A stone disk turned on an axle for grinding, polishing, or sharpening tools. **2.** A millstone.

grin·go (grĭng'gō) *n., pl.* **-gos.** *Offensive.* In Latin America, a foreigner, esp. an American or Englishman. [Sp., gibberish.]

grip¹ (grĭp) *n.* **1. a.** A tight hold; firm grasp. **b.** The pressure or strength of such a grasp. **c.** A manner of grasping and holding. **2.** Mastery; command: *a good grip on French grammar.* **3. a.** A mechanical device that grasps and holds. **b.** A part designed to be grasped and held; handle. **4.** A suitcase or valise. **5. a.** A stagehand who helps in shifting scenery. **b.** A member of a film production crew who adjusts sets and props and sometimes assists the cameraman. —*v.* **gripped, grip·ping, grips.** —*tr.* **1.** To secure and maintain a tight hold on; seize firmly. **2.** To hold the interest or attention of: *a scene that gripped the entire audience.* —*intr.* To hold securely. [ME < OE *gripe,* grasp.] **—grip'ping·ly** *adv.*

grip² (grĭp) *n.* Variant of **grippe.**

gripe (grīp) *v.* **griped, grip·ing, gripes.** —*tr.* **1.** To cause sharp pain in the bowels of. **2.** *Informal.* To irritate; annoy. **3.** To grasp; seize. **4.** *Archaic.* To oppress or afflict. —*intr.* **1.** *Informal.* To complain naggingly or petulantly; grumble. **2.** To have sharp pains in the bowels. —*n.* **1.** *Informal.* A complaint. **2. gripes.** Sharp, repeated pains in the bowels. **3.** A grip; grasp. **4.** A handle. [ME *gripen,* to seize < OE *gripan.*] **—grip'er** *n.*

grippe also **grip** (grĭp) *n.* Influenza. [Fr. < *gripper,* to seize < OFr., of Germanic orig.] **—grip'py** *adj.*

grip·sack (grĭp'săk') *n.* A small suitcase.

gri·saille (grĭ-zī', -zāl') *n.* **1.** A style of monochromatic painting in shades of gray. **2.** A painting or design in grisaille. [Fr. < *gris,* gray < OFr., of Germanic orig.]

gris·e·ous (grĭz'ē-əs, grĭs'-) *adj.* Mottled or grizzled with gray. [Med. Lat. *griseus,* of Germanic orig.]

gri·sette (grĭ-zĕt') *n.* A French working-class girl. [Fr. < *grisette,* a cheap gray dress fabric < *gris,* gray. —see GRISAILLE.]

gris-gris (grē'grē) *n.* Variant of **grigri.**

gris·ly (grĭz'lē) *adj.* **-li·er, -li·est.** Inspiring repugnance; gruesome. [ME *grisli* < OE *grislīc.*] **—gris'li·ness** *n.*

gri·son (grī'sən, grĭz'ən) *n.* Either of two carnivorous mammals, *Grison vittatus* or *G. cuja,* of Central and South America, having grizzled fur, a slender body, and short legs. [Fr. < OFr., gray animal < *gris,* gray. —see GRISAILLE.]

grist (grĭst) *n.* **1.** Grain or a quantity of grain for grinding. **2.** Ground grain. **—*idiom.* grist for (or to) the mill.** Something that can be turned to one's advantage. [ME < OE.]

gris·tle (grĭs'əl) *n.* Cartilage, esp. when present in meat. [ME *gristel* < OE *gristle.*]

gris·tly (grĭs'lē) *adj.* **-tli·er, -tli·est. 1.** Composed of or containing gristle. **2.** Resembling gristle. **—gris'tli·ness** *n.*

grist·mill (grĭst'mĭl') *n.* A mill for grinding grain.

grit (grĭt) *n.* **1.** Minute rough granules, as of sand or stone. **2.** The texture or structure of stone to be used in grinding. **3.** A coarse hard sandstone used for making grindstones and millstones. **4.** *Informal.* Indomitable spirit; pluck. —*v.* **grit·ted, grit·ting, grits.** —*tr.* **1.** To clamp (the teeth) together. **2.** To cover or treat with grit. —*intr.* To make a grinding noise. [ME *gret,* sand < OE *grēot.*]

grith (grĭth) *n.* Protection or sanctuary provided persons by Old English law in certain circumstances, as when in a church or traveling on the king's highway. [ME < OE *grið.*]

grits (grĭts) *pl.n.* Coarsely ground grain, esp. corn. [< ME *grutla,* coarse meal < OE *grytla.*]

grit·ty (grĭt'ē) *adj.* **-ti·er, -ti·est. 1.** Containing or resembling grit. **2.** Showing resolution and fortitude; plucky. **—grit'ti·ly** *adv.* **—grit'ti·ness** *n.*

griv·et (grĭv'ĭt) *n.* A long-tailed African monkey, *Cercopithecus aethiops,* having a greenish-gray coat. [Fr.]

griz·zle (grĭz'əl) *tr. & intr.v.* **-zled, -zling, -zles.** To make or become gray. —*n.* **1.** *Archaic.* Gray hair. **2. a.** The color of a roan animal. **b.** A roan animal. —*adj.* **1.** Gray. **2.** Roan. [ME *grisel,* gray < OFr. < *gris,* gray, of Germanic orig.]

griz·zly (grĭz'lē) *adj.* **-zli·er, -zli·est.** Grayish or flecked with gray. —*n., pl.* **-zlies.** A grizzly bear.

grizzly bear *n.* The grayish form of the brown bear, *Ursus arctos,* of northwestern North America, often considered a separate species, *U. horribilis.*

groan (grōn) *v.* **groaned, groan·ing, groans.** —*intr.* **1.** To voice a deep, wordless, prolonged sound expressive of pain, grief, annoyance, or disapproval. **2.** To make a sound expressive of stress or strain: *mattress springs groaning.* —*tr.* To utter or convey with groaning. —*n.* The sound made in groaning. [ME *gronen* < OE *grānian.*] **—groan'er** *n.* **—groan'ing·ly** *adv.*

groat (grōt) *n.* A British silver fourpence piece used from the 14th to the 17th century. [ME *grot* < MDu. *groot,* a small coin.]

groats (grōts) *pl.n.* Hulled, usually crushed grain, esp. oats. [ME *grotes* < OE *grotan.*]

gro·cer (grō'sər) *n.* A storekeeper who sells foodstuffs and various household supplies. [ME, wholesaler < AN *grasser* < OFr. *grossier* < Med. Lat. *grossarius* < *grossus,* gross < LLat., thick.]

gro·cer·y (grō'sə-rē) *n., pl.* **-ies. 1.** A store selling foodstuffs and various household supplies. **2. groceries.** Commodities sold by a grocer.

grog (grŏg) *n.* Alcoholic liquor, esp. rum diluted with water. [After Old *Grog,* nickname of Admiral Edward Vernon (1684–1757), who ordered that diluted rum be served to his sailors.]

grog·gy (grŏg'ē) *adj.* **-gi·er, -gi·est.** Unsteady and dazed; shaky. [< GROG.] **—grog'gi·ly** *adv.* **—grog'gi·ness** *n.*

grog·ram (grŏg'rəm, grō'grəm) *n.* A coarse, often stiffened fabric of silk, mohair, or wool, or a blend of these. [Alteration of GROSGRAIN.]

groin (groin) *n.* **1. a.** *Anat.* The crease at the junction of the thigh and the trunk, together with the adjacent region. **b.** The external genital organs. **2.** *Archit.* The curved edge at the junction of two intersecting vaults. —*tr.v.* **groined, groin·ing, groins.** To provide or build with groins. [ME *grinde,* perh. < OE *grynde,* abyss.]

grom·met (grŏm'ĭt) also **grum·met** (grŭm'-) *n.* **1. a.** A reinforced eyelet, as in cloth or leather, through which a fastener may be passed. **b.** A small metal or plastic ring used to reinforce such an eyelet. **2.** *Naut.* A rope or metal ring used

grille

gristmill

groin
Above: Groin vaulting in the Abbey of Notre-Dame-de-Pontaut
Below: Groins in early 12th-century vaulting

for securing the edge of a sail. [Prob. < obs. Fr. *gormette,* chain joining the ends of a bit < *gourmer,* bridle.]

grom·well (grŏm′wəl, -wĕl′) *n.* **1.** Any of several plants of the genus *Lithospermum,* having small yellow or white flowers. **2.** Any of several plants similar or related to the gromwell. [ME *gromil* < OFr.]

groom (gro͞om, gro͝om) *n.* **1.** A man or boy employed to take care of horses. **2.** A bridegroom. **3.** One of several officers in an English royal household. **4.** *Archaic.* **a.** A man. **b.** A manservant. —*tr.v.* **groomed, groom·ing, grooms. 1.** To make neat and trim: *groomed himself carefully in front of the mirror.* **2.** To clean and brush (an animal). **3.** To train, as for a specific position; prepare: *groom a candidate for Congress.* [ME *grom.*]

grooms·man (gro͞omz′mən, gro͝omz′-) *n.* The best man or an usher at a wedding.

groove (gro͞ov) *n.* **1.** A long, narrow furrow or channel. **2.** *Slang.* A situation or activity to which one is esp. well suited. **3.** *Slang.* A settled, humdrum routine; rut. **4.** *Slang.* A very pleasurable experience. —*v.* **grooved, groov·ing, grooves.** —*tr.* To cut a groove in. —*intr. Slang.* **1.** To take great pleasure or satisfaction; enjoy oneself: *just sitting around, grooving on the music.* **2.** To react or come together harmoniously. [ME *groof,* mining shaft, prob. < MDu. *groove,* ditch.]

groov·y (gro͞o′vē) *adj.* **-i·er, -i·est.** *Slang.* Pleasing; deeply satisfying. **—groov′i·ness** *n.*

grope (grōp) *v.* **groped, grop·ing, gropes.** —*intr.* **1.** To reach about uncertainly; feel one's way: *groped for the telephone.* **2.** To search blindly or uncertainly: *grope for an answer.* —*tr.* To make (one's way) by groping. —*n.* The act of groping. [ME *gropen* < OE *grāpian.*] **—grop′er** *n.* **—grop′ing·ly** *adv.*

gros·beak (grōs′bēk′) *n.* Any of various finches of the genera *Hesperiphona, Pinicola,* and related genera, having a thick, rounded bill. [Partial transl. of Fr. *grosbec* : *gros,* thick + *bec,* beak.]

gro·schen (grō′shən) *n., pl.* **groschen.** See table at **currency.** [G. < MHG *grosse* < Med. Lat. (*denarius*) *grossus,* thick (denarius) < LLat. *grossus,* thick.]

gros·grain (grō′grān′) *n.* **1.** A heavy silk or rayon fabric with narrow horizontal ribs. **2.** A ribbon made of grosgrain. [Fr. *gros grain,* coarse grain.]

gros point (grō) *n.* **1.** A large needlepoint stitch covering two vertical and two horizontal threads. **2.** Work done in gros point. [Fr. : *gros,* large + *point,* point.]

gross (grōs) *adj.* **-er, -est. 1. a.** Exclusive of deductions; total: *gross profits.* **b.** Unmitigated in any way; utter. **2.** Glaringly obvious; flagrant: *gross injustice.* **3. a.** Coarse; vulgar. **b.** Offensive; disgusting. **c.** Lacking sensitivity or discernment; unrefined. **d.** Carnal; sensual. **4. a.** Overweight; corpulent. **b.** Dense; profuse. **5.** Broad; general: *the gross outlines of a plan.* **6.** *Pathol.* Visible to the naked eye: *a gross lesion.* —*n.* **1.** *pl.* **gross·es.** The entire body or amount; total. **2.** *pl.* **gross.** A group of 144 or 12 dozen items. —*tr.v.* **grossed, gross·ing, gross·es.** To earn as a total income or profit before deductions. —***phrasal verb.*** **gross out.** *Slang.* To fill with disgust; nauseate. [ME *gros,* large < OFr. < LLat. *grossus,* thick.] **—gross′ly** *adv.* **—gross′ness** *n.*

gross index *n. Computer Sci.* The general index first consulted in locating particular records.

gross national product *n.* The total market value of all the goods and services produced by a nation during a specified period.

gros·su·la·rite (grŏs′yə-lə-rīt′) *n.* A light-green, pink, gray, or brown garnet with composition $Ca_3Al_2(SiO_4)_3$, found alone or as a constituent part of the common garnet. [G. *Grossularit* < NLat. *Grossularia,* a former genus of gooseberry (from the color of some garnets) < Fr. *groseille,* gooseberry < OFr. *grosele.*]

grosz (grôsh) *n., pl.* **gro·szy** (grô′shē). See table at **currency.** [Pol. < Czech *gros* < Med. Lat. (*denarius*) *grossus,* thick (denarius) < LLat. *grossus,* thick.]

grot (grŏt) *n.* A grotto.

gro·tesque (grō-tĕsk′) *adj.* **1.** Characterized by ludicrous or incongruous distortion. **2.** Outlandish; bizarre. **3.** Of or designating the grotesque in art or a work executed in this style. —*n.* **1.** One that is grotesque. **2. a.** An artistic and decorative art style developed in 16th-century Italy and characterized by incongruous combinations of monstrous or natural forms. **b.** A work of art executed in this style. [< Fr., a fanciful style of decorative art < Ital. *grottesca* < *grottesco,* of a grotto < *grotta,* grotto.] **—gro·tesque′ly** *adv.* **—gro·tesque′ness** *n.*

gro·tes·que·ry also **gro·tes·que·rie** (grō-tĕs′kə-rē) *n., pl.* **-ries. 1.** The state of being grotesque; grotesqueness. **2.** Something that is grotesque.

grot·to (grŏt′ō) *n., pl.* **-toes** or **-tos. 1.** A small cave or cavern. **2.** An artificial structure or excavation made to resemble a cave or cavern. [Ital. *grotta* < OItal. < VLat. **grupta* < Lat. *crypta,* vault. —see CRYPT.]

grot·ty (grŏt′ē) *adj.* **-ti·er, -ti·est.** *Chiefly Brit. Slang.* Wretched; miserable. [Alteration of GROTESQUE.]

grouch (grouch) *intr.v.* **grouched, grouch·ing, grouch·es.** To grumble or sulk. —*n.* **1.** A grumbling or sulky mood. **2.** A complaint; grudge. **3.** A habitually complaining or irritable person. [Prob. alteration of obs. *grutch,* to complain < ME *grucchen* < OFr. *grouchier.*]

grouch·y (grou′chē) *adj.* **-i·er, -i·est.** Tending to complain and grumble; peevish; grumpy. **—grouch′i·ly** *adv.* **—grouch′i·ness** *n.*

ground[1] (ground) *n.* **1. a.** The solid surface of the earth. **b.** The floor of a body of water, esp. the sea. **2.** Soil; earth: *level the ground for a lawn.* **3.** Often **grounds.** An area of land designated for a particular purpose: *burial grounds.* **4. grounds.** The land surrounding or forming part of a house or other building: *The embassy has beautiful grounds.* **5.** Often **grounds.** The foundation for an argument, belief, or action; basis. **6.** Often **grounds.** The underlying condition prompting an action; cause: *grounds for suspicion; a ground for divorce.* **7.** An area of reference; subject. **8.** A surrounding area; background. **9.** The preparatory coat of paint on which a picture is to be painted. **10. grounds.** The sediment at the bottom of a liquid, esp. coffee. **11.** *Elect.* **a.** The position or portion of an electric circuit that is at zero potential with respect to the earth. **b.** A conducting connection to such a position or to the earth. **c.** A large conducting body, such as the earth, used as a return for electric currents and as an arbitrary zero of potential. —*v.* **ground·ed, ground·ing, grounds.** —*tr.* **1.** To place or set on the ground. **2.** To provide a basis for (a theory, for example); justify. **3.** To supply with basic information; instruct in fundamentals. **4. a.** To prevent (an aircraft or pilot) from flying. **b.** *Informal.* To restrict esp. to a certain place as a punishment. **5.** *Elect.* To connect (an electric circuit) to a ground. **6.** *Naut.* To run (a vessel) aground. **7.** *Baseball.* To hit (a ball) on the ground. **8.** *Football.* To throw a ball to the ground to stop play and avoid being tackled behind the line of scrimmage. —*intr.* **1.** To hit or reach the ground. **2.** *Baseball.* To hit a ground ball. **3.** *Naut.* To run aground. —***phrasal verb.*** **ground out.** *Baseball.* To make an out by hitting a ground ball that is fielded and thrown to first base in advance of the batter. —***idioms.*** **break ground. 1.** To cut or dig into the soil, as in plowing or excavating. **2.** To begin on an undertaking. **cover ground. 1.** To move about or travel, esp. over a considerable distance and at a satisfactory rate of speed. **2.** To accomplish a great deal. **from the ground up.** Leaving out nothing; thoroughly. **gain ground. 1.** To make progress. **2.** To gain favor or popularity. **give ground.** To give way; yield an advantage. **hold** (or **stand**) **(one's) ground.** To maintain one's position in the face of attack or opposition. [ME < OE *grund.*]

ground[2] (ground) *v.* Past tense and past participle of **grind.**

ground ball *n. Baseball.* A batted ball that rolls or bounces along the ground.

ground bass *n.* A short musical passage that is continually repeated in the bass under the changing harmonies and melodies of the upper range.

ground beetle *n.* Any of numerous chiefly black or brown beetles of the family Carabidae that often crawl under stones, logs, or debris.

ground cherry *n.* Any of various chiefly New World plants of the genus *Physalis,* having round, fleshy fruit enclosed in a papery, bladderlike husk.

ground cloth *n.* A ground sheet.

ground cover *n.* Low-growing plants that form a dense, extensive growth and tend to prevent soil erosion.

ground crew *n.* A team of mechanics and technicians who maintain and service aircraft on the ground.

ground-ef·fect machine (ground′ĭ-fĕkt′) *n.* A vehicle designed for traveling over land or water by means of an air cushion.

ground·er (groun′dər) *n. Baseball.* A ground ball.

ground floor *n.* The floor of a building at or nearly at ground level.

ground glass *n.* Glass that has been subjected to grinding or etching to create a roughened, nontransparent surface.

ground hemlock *n.* A low-growing yew, *Taxus canadensis,* of northeastern North America.

ground hog *n.* The woodchuck.

ground-hog day (ground′hôg′, -hŏg′) *n.* February 2, traditionally the point that indicates an early or late spring. [From the legend that the ground hog emerges from hibernation on this day and returns to its burrow if it sees its shadow, presaging prolonged winter weather.]

ground ivy *n.* A creeping or trailing aromatic plant, *Glechoma hederacea,* native to Eurasia, having rounded, scalloped leaves and small purplish flowers.

ground·less (ground′lĭs) *adj.* Having no ground or foundation; unsubstantiated: *groundless optimism.* **—ground′less·ly** *adv.* **—ground′less·ness** *n.*

ground·ling (ground′lĭng) *n.* **1. a.** A plant or animal living on or close to the ground. **b.** A fish that lives at the bottom of the water. **2.** A person with uncultivated tastes. **3.** A spectator in the cheaper part of an Elizabethan theater; commoner.

ground loop *n.* A sharp, uncontrollable turn of an aircraft in taxiing, landing, or taking off.

ground·mass (ground′măs′) *n.* The fine-grained crystalline base of porphyritic rock in which phenocrysts are embedded.

ground·nut (ground′nŭt′) *n.* **1. a.** A climbing vine, *Apios* *tuberosa,* of eastern North America, having compound leaves, clusters of fragrant brownish flowers, and small edible tubers. **b.** Any of several plants having underground tubers or nutlike parts. **c.** The tuber or nutlike part of such a plant. **2.** *Chiefly Brit.* The peanut (senses 1 and 2).

ground pine *n.* **1.** A club moss, esp. *Lycopodium obscurum* or a similar species. **2.** A low-growing plant, *Ajuga chamaepitys,* native to the Old World, having narrow leaves, yellow flowers, and a resinous odor.

ground plan *n.* **1.** A plan of a floor of a building as if seen from overhead. **2.** A preliminary plan or strategy.

ground plum *n.* **1.** A plant, *Astragalus crassicarpus,* of the central and western United States, having compound leaves, purple or white flowers, and green, plumlike, edible fruit. **2.** The fruit of the ground plum.

ground rent *n. Chiefly Brit.* Rent paid for land to be used chiefly for building.

ground robin *n.* The towhee.

ground rule *n.* **1.** A rule governing the playing of a game on a particular field, course, or court. **2.** A basic rule of procedure or behavior.

ground·sel[1] (ground'səl, groun'-) *n.* Any of various plants of the genus *Senecio,* having rayed, usually yellow flowers. [ME *groundeswille* < OE *grundeswylige,* perh. : *gund,* pus + *swelgan,* to swallow (from its use in reducing abscesses).]

ground·sel[2] (ground'səl, groun'-) *n.* Variant of **groundsill.**

ground sheet *n.* **1.** A waterproof cover used to protect an area of ground, as a baseball field. **2.** A waterproof sheet placed under camp bedding as a protection against dampness.

ground·sill (ground'sĭl') also **ground·sel** (ground'səl, groun'-) *n.* The horizontal timber nearest the ground in the frame of a building.

ground speed also **ground·speed** (ground'spēd') *n.* The speed of an airborne aircraft computed in terms of the ground distance traversed in a given period of time.

ground squirrel *n.* Any of various rodents of the genus *Citellus* (or *Spermophilus*) and related genera, related to and resembling the chipmunks.

ground state *n. Physics.* The state of least energy in a physical system.

ground swell *n.* **1.** An undulation of the ocean with deep rolling waves, often caused by a distant storm or earthquake. **2.** An unexpected, sudden gathering of force, as of public opinion.

ground water also **ground·wa·ter** (ground'wô'tər, -wŏt'ər) *n.* Water beneath the earth's surface between saturated soil and rock that supplies wells and springs.

ground wave *n.* A radio wave that travels along the earth's surface.

ground·work (ground'wûrk') *n.* Preliminary work; foundation or basis.

ground zero *n.* **1.** The target of a missile, bomb, or other projectile. **2.** The site of a nuclear explosion.

group (gro͞op) *n.* **1.** An assemblage of persons or objects gathered or located together; aggregation: *a group of dinner guests; a group of Chinese porcelains.* **2.** Two or more figures that make up a unit or a design, as in sculpture. **3.** A number of individuals or things considered together because of similarities. **4.** *Ling.* A subdivision of a linguistic family, less inclusive than a branch. **5. a.** A military unit consisting of two or more battalions and a headquarters. **b.** A unit of two or more U.S. Air Force squadrons, smaller than a wing. **6.** A class or collection of related objects or entities, as: **a.** Two or more atoms behaving or regarded as behaving as a single chemical unit. **b.** A vertical column in the periodic table of elements. **c.** A geologic stratigraphic unit, esp. a unit consisting of two or more formations. **7.** *Math.* A set together with a binary operation under which the set is closed and associative and for which the set contains an identity element and an inverse for every element in the set. ***—modifier:*** *a group discussion.* *—v.* **grouped, group·ing, groups.** *—tr.* To place or arrange in a group. *—intr.* To form or belong to a group. [Fr. *groupe* < Ital. *gruppo,* of Germanic orig.]

Usage: *Group* as a collective noun can be followed by a singular or plural verb. It takes a singular verb when the persons or things that make up the group are considered collectively: *The dance group is ready for rehearsal. Group* takes a plural verb when the persons or things that make it up are considered individually: *The group were divided in their sympathies.* See also Usage note at **collective noun.**

grou·per[1] (gro͞o'pər) *n., pl.* **grouper** or **-pers.** Any of various often large fishes of the genera *Epinephelus, Mycteroperca,* and related genera, of warm seas. [Port. *garoupa.*]

group·er[2] (gro͞o'pər) *n.* A groupie (sense 2).

group·ie (gro͞o'pē) *n. Slang.* **1.** A female fan, esp. a fan of a rock group, who follows the group around on tours, often in the hope of achieving sexual intimacy. **2.** A member of a group sharing the same weekend house, usually in a beach or ski resort.

group·ing (gro͞o'pĭng) *n.* **1.** The act or process of arranging in groups. **2.** A collection of people or things arranged in a group.

group insurance *n.* Insurance covering members of a group under a single contract or under individual contracts.

group theory *n.* The branch of mathematics concerned with the properties of groups.

group therapy *n.* A form of psychotherapy that involves sessions guided by a therapist and attended by several patients who discuss their emotional problems with each other.

group·think (gro͞op'thĭngk') *n.* **1.** The act or practice of decision- and policy-making by a group, as a board of directors or a research team. **2.** The practice of conforming to group values or ethical standards.

grouse[1] (grous) *n., pl.* **grouse** or **grous·es.** Any of various plump birds of the family Tetraonidae, chiefly of the Northern Hemisphere, having mottled brown or grayish plumage. [Orig. unknown.]

grouse[2] (grous) *Informal.* *—intr.v.* **groused, grous·ing, grous·es.** To complain; grumble. *—n.* A cause for complaint; grievance. [Orig. unknown.] **—grous'er** *n.*

grout (grout) *n.* **1. a.** A thin mortar used to fill cracks and crevices in masonry. **b.** A thin plaster for finishing walls and ceilings. **2.** Often **grouts.** *Chiefly Brit.* Sediment; lees. *—tr.v.* **grout·ed, grout·ing, grouts.** To fill or finish with grout. [ME, grain used for making malt, mud < OE *grūt,* coarse meal.] **—grout'er** *n.*

grove (grōv) *n.* A small wood or stand of trees lacking dense undergrowth. [ME < OE *grāf.*]

grov·el (grŏv'əl, grŭv'-) *intr.v.* **-eled, -el·ing, -els** also **-elled, -el·ling, -els.** **1.** To behave in a servile or demeaning manner; cringe. **2.** To lie or creep in a prostrate position, often as a token of subservience or humility. **3.** To give oneself over to base pleasures. [Back-formation < obs. *groveling,* prone, face downward < ME < *grufe* < ON *ā grūfu* < *grūfa,* to lie face down.] **—grov'el·er** *n.* **—grov'el·ing·ly** *adv.*

grow (grō) *v.* **grew** (gro͞o), **grown** (grōn), **grow·ing, grows.** *—intr.* **1.** To increase in size by a natural process. **2. a.** To expand; gain: *The business grew under new management.* **b.** To increase in amount or degree; intensify: *Her anxiety grew.* **3.** To develop and reach maturity. **4.** To be capable of growth; thrive: *plants that will grow in deep shade.* **5.** To become attached by or as if by the process of growth: *tree trunks that had grown together.* **6.** To come into existence from a source; spring up: *love that grew out of friendship.* **7.** To come to be by a gradual process or by degrees; become: *grow angry; grow cold; grow rich.* *—tr.* **1.** To cause to grow; raise: *grow tulips.* **2.** To let grow: *grow a beard.* ***—phrasal verbs.*** **grow on** (or **upon**). **1.** To become gradually more pleasurable to: *a style that grows on a person.* **2.** To become gradually more acceptable to: *At first he hated the new method, but it grew on him.* **grow up.** To become an adult. [ME *growen* < OE *grōwan.*] **—grow'er** *n.*

growing pains *pl.n.* **1.** Pains in the limbs and joints of children, often mistakenly attributed to rapid growth. **2.** Problems arising in the initial stages of an enterprise.

growl (groul) *n.* **1.** The low, guttural, menacing sound made by a dog or other animal. **2.** A gruff, surly utterance. *—v.* **growled, growl·ing, growls.** *—intr.* **1.** To utter a growl. **2.** To make a sound suggestive of a growl: *The wind growled.* **3.** To speak in an angry or surly manner. *—tr.* To utter by growling: *growl orders.* [Prob. imit.]

growl·er (grou'lər) *n.* **1.** One that growls. **2.** A small iceberg. **3.** *Elect.* An electromagnetic device with two poles, used for magnetizing, demagnetizing, and finding short-circuited coils.

grown (grōn) *v.* Past participle of **grow.** *—adj.* **1.** Having full growth; mature: *a grown woman.* **2.** Produced or cultivated in a certain way or place: *home-grown vegetables.*

grown-up (grōn'ŭp') *adj.* Not immature or infantile; mature and adult: *a grown-up attitude toward work.* *—n.* An adult.

growth (grōth) *n.* **1. a.** The process of growing. **b.** A stage in the process of growing; size. **c.** Full development; maturity. **2.** Development from a lower or simpler to a higher or more complex form; evolution. **3.** An increase, as in size, number, value, or strength; extension or expansion: *population growth.* **4.** Something that grows or has grown: *a new growth of grass.* **5.** An abnormal mass of tissue growing in or on a living organism. **6.** The result of growth; production.

growth company *n.* A company whose rate of growth significantly exceeds that of the average in its field or the overall rate of economic growth.

growth fund *n.* A mutual fund whose goal is capital appreciation.

grub (grŭb) *v.* **grubbed, grub·bing, grubs.** *—tr.* **1.** To clear of roots and stumps by digging. **2.** To dig up by the roots. **3.** *Slang.* To obtain by importunity: *grub a cigarette.* *—intr.* **1.** To dig in the earth: *grub for potatoes.* **2. a.** To search laboriously; rummage. **b.** To toil arduously; drudge: *grub for a living.* *—n.* **1.** The thick, wormlike larva of certain beetles and other insects. **2.** A drudge. **3.** *Slang.* Food. [ME *grubben.*] **—grub'ber** *n.*

grub·by (grŭb'ē) *adj.* **-bi·er, -bi·est.** **1.** Dirty; unkempt: *grubby old work clothes.* **2.** Infested with grubs. **3.** Contemptible; despicable. **—grub'bi·ly** *adv.* **—grub'bi·ness** *n.*

grub·stake (grŭb'stāk') *n.* Supplies or funds advanced to a mining prospector or a person starting a business in return for a promised share of the profits. *—tr.v.* **-staked, -stak·ing, -stakes.** To supply with a grubstake. **—grub'stak'er** *n.*

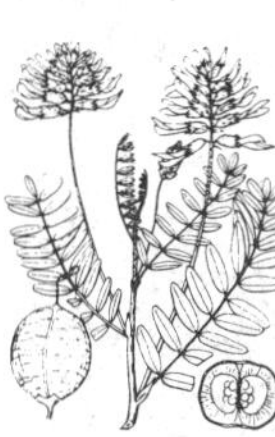
ground plum

grouse[1]

grove

Grub Street (grŭb) *n.* The world of impoverished writers and literary hacks. [After *Grub Street,* London.]
grudge (grŭj) *tr.v.* **grudged, grudg·ing, grudg·es.** To be reluctant to give or admit; begrudge: *even grudged the tuition money.* —*n.* A deep-seated feeling of resentment or rancor. [ME *grucchen,* to complain < OFr. *grouchier.*] —**grudg'er** *n.* —**grudg'ing·ly** *adv.*
gru·el (gro͞o'əl) *n.* **1.** A thin, watery porridge. **2.** *Chiefly Brit.* Severe punishment. [ME < OFr. < *gru,* groats, of Germanic orig.]
gru·el·ing also **gru·el·ling** (gro͞o'ə-lĭng) *adj.* Demanding and exhausting: *a grueling hike.* —**gru'el·ing·ly** *adv.*
grue·some also **grew·some** (gro͞o'səm) *adj.* Causing horror and repugnance; frightful and shocking: *a gruesome murder.* [Obs. *grue,* to shudder (< ME *gruen*) + -SOME[1].] —**grue'some·ly** *adv.* —**grue'some·ness** *n.*
gruff (grŭf) *adj.* **-er, -est. 1.** Brusque and unfriendly; stern: *a gruff reply.* **2.** Hoarse; harsh: *a gruff voice.* [Du. *grof* < MDu.] —**gruff'ly** *adv.* —**gruff'ness** *n.*
grum (grŭm) *adj.* **grum·mer, grum·mest.** Morose; glum. [Perh. blend of GRIM and GLUM.]
grum·ble (grŭm'bəl) *v.* **-bled, -bling, -bles.** —*intr.* **1.** To complain in a surly manner; mutter discontentedly: *"The governed will always find something to grumble about"* (Crane Brinton). **2.** To rumble or growl. —*tr.* To express in a grumbling, discontented manner. —*n.* **1.** A muttered complaint. **2.** A rumble. [Freq. of ME *grummen,* to grumble.] —**grum'bler** *n.* —**grum'bling·ly** *adv.* —**grum'bly** *adj.*
grum·met (grŭm'ĭt) *n.* Variant of **grommet.**
grump (grŭmp) *n.* **1. grumps.** A fit of ill temper. **2.** A cranky, complaining person. —*intr.v.* **grumped, grump·ing, grumps. 1.** To complain and mutter. **2.** To behave in a grumpy manner. [Perh. imit of discontented muttering.]
grump·y (grŭm'pē) *adj.* **-i·er, -i·est.** Fretful and peevish; cranky. —**grump'i·ly** *adv.* —**grump'i·ness** *n.*
grun·gy (grŭn'jē) *adj.* **-gi·er, -gi·est.** *Slang.* Being in a dirty, run-down, or inferior condition: *grungy old jeans.* [Orig. unknown.]
grun·ion (grŭn'yən) *n.* A small fish, *Leuresthes tenuis,* of coastal waters of California and Mexico, that spawns along beaches during high spring tides at the time of the full moon. [Perh. < Sp. *gruñón,* grumbler < *gruñir,* to grumble < Lat. *grunnire,* to grunt.]
grunt (grŭnt) *v.* **grunt·ed, grunt·ing, grunts.** —*intr.* **1.** To utter a deep, guttural sound, as a hog does. **2.** To utter a sound similar to a grunt, as in disgust. —*tr.* To utter or express with a grunt: *grunted approval.* —*n.* **1.** A deep, guttural sound. **2.** Any of various chiefly tropical marine fishes of the genus *Haemulon* and related genera that produce grunting sounds. **3.** *Slang.* An infantryman in the U.S. military, esp. in the Vietnam War. **4.** *Slang.* One who performs routine or mundane tasks. [ME *grunten* < OE *grunnettan.*] —**grunt'er** *n.* —**grunt'ing·ly** *adv.*
Grus (grŭs) *n.* A constellation in the Southern Hemisphere near Indus and Phoenix. [Lat., crane.]
Gru·yère (gro͞o-yâr', grē-) *n.* A pale-yellow, firm-textured cheese, with or without holes, made from whole milk. [After *Gruyère,* a district in Switzerland.]
gryph·on (grĭf'ən) *n.* Variant of **griffin.**
G-string (jē'strĭng') *n.* **1.** A narrow loincloth supported by a waistband; breechcloth. **2.** A garment similar to a G-string that is worn esp. by stripteasers. [Orig. unknown.]
G-suit (jē'so͞ot') *n.* A flight garment designed to counteract the effects of high acceleration by exerting pressure on parts of the body below the chest. [G(RAVITY) + SUIT.]
gua·ca·mo·le (gwä'kə-mō'lē) *n.* A spread of mashed avocado, tomato pulp, mayonnaise, and seasonings. [Mex. Sp. < Nahuatl *ahuacamolli* : *ahuacatl,* avocado + *molli,* sauce.]
gua·cha·ro (gwä'chə-rō') *n., pl.* **-ros.** A nocturnal bird, *Steatornis caripensis,* of tropical America, whose young have a layer of fat that yields an oil used in cooking and for lighting. [Sp. (South America) < Quechua *guacho,* orphan.]
gua·co (gwä'kō) *n., pl.* **-cos.** Any of several tropical American plants used as an antidote against snakebite, esp. *Mikania guaco* or *Aristolochia serpentina.* [Am. Sp.]
guai·ac (gwī'ăk') *n.* Guaiacum (sense 3).
guai·a·col (gwī'ə-kôl', -kōl') *n.* A yellowish, oily, aromatic liquid, $C_7H_8O_2$, used chiefly as an expectorant and a local anesthetic. [GUAIAC(UM) + -OL[2].]
guai·a·cum (gwī'ə-kəm) *n.* **1.** A tree of the genus *Guaiacum;* a lignum vitae. **2.** The wood of a guaiacum. **3.** A greenish-brown resin obtained from the lignum vitae and used medicinally and in varnishes. [NLat. < Sp. *guayacan* < Taino.]
guan (gwän) *n.* Any of several birds of the genus *Penelope* and related genera, of the jungles of tropical America, related to and resembling the curassows. [South American Sp.]
gua·na·co (gwə-nä'kō) *n., pl.* **-cos** or **guanaco.** A brownish South American mammal, *Lama guanicoe,* related to and resembling the domesticated llama. [Sp. < Quechua *huanaco.*]
gua·neth·i·dine (gwä-nĕth'ĭ-dēn') *n.* A drug, $C_{10}H_{22}N_4$, used in the treatment of hypertension. [Blend of GUANIDINE and ETHYL.]
gua·ni·dine (gwä'nĭ-dēn') *n.* A strong crystalline base, CH_5N_3, found in plant and animal tissues and used for organic syntheses. [GUAN(INE) + -ID(E) + -INE.]

guava

gua·nine (gwä'nēn') *n.* A purine, $C_5H_5N_5O$, that is a constituent of both ribonucleic and deoxyribonucleic acids. [< GUANO, in which it is found.]
gua·no (gwä'nō) *n., pl.* **-nos.** A substance composed chiefly of the dung of sea birds or bats, accumulated along certain coastal areas or in caves and used as fertilizer. [Sp. < Quechua *huanu,* dung.]
gua·no·sine monophosphate (gwä'nə-sēn') *n.* Cyclic GMP. [GUAN(INE) + (RIB)OSE + -INE + MONOPHOSPHATE.]
guar (gwär) *n.* A legume, *Cyamopsis tetragonoloba,* adapted to semiarid regions and grown for its seeds and as forage. [Hindi *guār.*]
gua·ra·ni (gwä'rə-nē') *n., pl.* **guarani** or **-nis.** See table at **currency.** [Sp. *guaraní,* Guarani.]
Gua·ra·ni (gwä'rə-nē') *n., pl.* **-nis** or **Guarani. 1. a.** A Tupi-Guaranian group of South American Indians of Paraguay, Bolivia, and southern Brazil. **b.** A member of one of these tribes. **2.** The language of the Guaranis. [Sp. *guaraní.*]
guar·an·tee (găr'ən-tē') *n.* **1.** Something that ensures a particular outcome or condition: *Money is not a guarantee of happiness.* **2.** A promise or assurance, esp. as to the quality or durability of a product or service. **3.** A guaranty. **4.** Something given or held as security; pledge. **5.** A guarantor. —*tr.v.* **-teed, -tee·ing, -tees. 1.** To assume responsibility for the debt, default, or miscarriage of. **2.** To assume responsibility for the quality or execution of. **3.** To undertake to accomplish or secure something: *guaranteed to free the captives.* **4.** To furnish security for. **5.** To give a guarantee for: *The manufacturer guaranteed his product.* **6.** To make certain; ensure. [Perh. alteration of GUARANTY.]
guar·an·tor (găr'ən-tôr', găr'ən-tər) *n.* **1.** One that makes or gives a guarantee. **2.** One that makes or gives a guaranty.
guar·an·ty (găr'ən-tē) *n., pl.* **-ties. 1.** An agreement by which one person assumes the responsibility of assuring payment or fulfillment of another's debts or obligations. **2.** Something that guarantees: *His record is a guaranty of his honesty.* **3. a.** Something held or provided as security for the execution, completion, or existence of something else. **b.** The act of providing such security. **4.** A guarantor. —*tr.v.* **-tied, -ty·ing, -ties.** To guarantee. [OFr. *garantie* < *garant,* warrant, of Germanic orig.]
guard (gärd) *v.* **guard·ed, guard·ing, guards.** —*tr.* **1.** To protect from harm or danger, esp. by careful watching; keep secure: *guard a bank; guarding the President.* **2.** To watch over to prevent escape, violence, or indiscretion: *guarded the prisoner.* **3.** To keep watch at (a door, for example) to supervise entries and exits. **4.** To furnish (a device or object) with a protective piece. **5.** *Archaic.* To escort. —*intr.* To take precautions: *guard against infection.* —*n.* **1. a.** An individual or a group that stands watch or acts as a sentinel. **b.** One who supervises prisoners. **c.** A body of persons who form an escort or perform drill exhibitions on ceremonial occasions: *an honor guard.* **2.** *Chiefly Brit.* A railway employee in charge of a train. **3.** *Football.* One of the two players on either side of the center. **4.** *Basketball.* Either of the two players who initiate plays from the center of the court. **5.** A defensive position or stance in certain sports such as boxing or fencing. **6. a.** The act or duty of guarding. **b.** Protection; watch: *a prisoner under close guard.* **7.** Something that gives protection; safeguard: *a guard against tooth decay.* **8.** A device or apparatus that prevents injury, damage, or loss, esp.: **a.** An attachment or covering put on a machine to protect the operator. **b.** A chain or band used to help safeguard something, such as a bracelet, from loss. **c.** A ring used to prevent a more valuable ring from sliding off the finger. **9.** *Electronics.* A signal that prevents accidental activation of a device or ambiguous interpretation of data. —*Idioms.* **off (one's) guard.** Not alert; unprepared. **on (one's) guard.** Alert and watchful; cautious. [Ult. < OFr. *garden,* of Germanic orig.] —**guard'er** *n.*
guar·dant also **gar·dant** (gär'dnt) *adj. Heraldry.* Indicating an animal shown in full face, turned toward the viewer. [OFr. *gardant,* pr.part. of *garder,* to guard, of Germanic orig.]
guard cell *n.* One of the paired epidermal cells that control the opening and closing of a stoma in plant tissue.
guard·ed (gär'dĭd) *adj.* Cautious; restrained: *guarded optimism.* —**guard'ed·ly** *adv.* —**guard'ed·ness** *n.*
guard hair *n.* Any of the coarse hairs covering the underfur of certain mammals.
guard·house (gärd'hous') *n.* **1.** A building that accommodates a military guard. **2.** A military jail for the detention of those guilty of minor offenses.
guard·i·an (gär'dē-ən) *n.* **1.** One that guards. **2.** A person who is legally responsible for the care and management of the person or property of one who is considered by law to be incompetent to manage his own affairs, as a child who is a minor. **3.** A superior in a Franciscan monastery. [ME *gardein* < OFr. < *garder,* to guard, of Germanic orig.] —**guard'i·an·ship'** *n.*
guard·rail (gärd'rāl') *n.* A protective rail, as on a footpath or highway.
guard·room (gärd'ro͞om', -ro͝om') *n.* **1.** A room used by

ă **pat** / ā **pay** / âr **care** / ä **father** / b **bib** / ch **church** / d **deed** / ĕ **pet** / ē **be** / f **fife** / g **gag** / h **hat** / hw **which** / ĭ **pit** / ī **pie** / îr **pier** / j **judge** / k **kick** / l **lid, needle** / m **mum** / n **no, sudden** / ng **thing** / ŏ **pot** / ō **toe** / ô **paw, for** / oi **noise** / ou **out** / o͝o **took** / o͞o **boot** /

guards on duty. **2.** A room in which military prisoners are confined.

guards·man (gärdz'mən) *n.*, **1.** A member of the U.S. National Guard. **2.** *Chiefly Brit.* A soldier in a regiment of household guards.

Guar·ne·ri·us (gwär-nâr'ē-əs, -nîr'-) *n.* A violin made by a member of the Guarneri family of Italian violinmakers in the 17th and 18th centuries.

gua·va (gwä'və) *n.* **1.** Any of various tropical American shrubs and trees of the genus *Psidium,* esp. *P. guajava,* having white flowers and edible fruit. **2.** The fruit of a guava. [Sp. *guayaba* < a native word in the Caribbean islands.]

gua·yu·le (gwī-ōō'lē) *n.* A woody plant or shrub, *Parthenium argentatum,* of the southwestern United States and Mexico, having sap sometimes used as a source of rubber. [Am. Sp. < Nahuatl *cuauhuli* : *cuahuitl,* tree + *uli,* latex gum.]

gu·ber·na·to·ri·al (gōō'bər-nə-tôr'ē-əl, -tōr'-, gyōō'-) *adj.* Of or pertaining to a governor. [< Lat. *gubernator,* governor.]

guck (gŭk, gŏŏk) *n. Slang.* A messy substance such as sludge. [Poss. G(OO) + (M)UCK.]

gudg·eon[1] (gŭj'ən) *n.* **1. a.** A small Eurasian freshwater fish, *Gobio gobio.* **b.** Any of various similar fishes. **2.** *Slang.* Someone who is easily duped. [ME *gojoun* < OFr. *goujon* < Lat. *gobius* < Gk. *kōbios.*]

gudg·eon[2] (gŭj'ən) *n.* **1.** A metal pivot or journal at the end of a shaft or axle, around which a wheel or other device turns. **2.** The socket of a hinge into which the pin fits. **3.** *Naut.* The socket for the pintle of a rudder. **4.** A metal pin that joins two pieces of stone. [ME *gojoun* < OFr. *gojon,* peg < *goi,* gouge. —see GOUGE.]

gudgeon pin *n.* A wrist pin.

Gud·run (gŏŏd'rōōn') also **Guth·run** (gŏŏ*th*'-) *n.* The daughter of the king of the Nibelungs and wife of Sigurd in the *Volsunga Saga.* [ON *Guðrun.*]

guel·der rose (gĕl'dər) *n.* A shrub, *Viburnum opulus,* native to Eurasia, having clusters of white flowers and small red fruit. [After *Guelderland,* a province in the Netherlands.]

Guelph also **Guelf** (gwĕlf) *n.* A member of a strong faction in medieval Italy that supported the power of the pope and the city-states in a struggle against the German emperors and the Ghibellines. [Ital. *Guelf.*]

Guen·e·vere (gwĕn'ə-vîr) *n.* Variant of **Guinevere.**

gue·non (gə-nōn') *n.* Any of various African monkeys of the genus *Cercopithecus,* having long hind legs and a long tail. [Fr.]

guer·don (gûr'dn) *n.* A reward; requital. —*tr.v.* **-doned, -don·ing, -dons.** To reward. [ME < OFr. < Med. Lat. *widerdonum,* alteration of OHG *widarlōn* : *widar,* back + *lōn,* reward.]

gue·ril·la (gə-rĭl'ə) *n.* Variant of **guerrilla.**

Guern·sey (gûrn'zē) *n., pl.* **-seys.** One of a breed of brown and white dairy cattle originally developed on the Isle of Guernsey.

guer·ril·la or **gue·ril·la** (gə-rĭl'ə) *n.* **1.** A member of an irregular military force operating usually in small, independent groups capable of great speed and mobility. **2.** *Archaic.* Warfare carried out by guerrillas. [Sp. *guerilla,* dim. of *guerra,* war, of Germanic orig.]

guerrilla theater *n.* Street theater.

guess (gĕs) *v.* **guessed, guess·ing, guess·es.** —*tr.* **1.** To make a judgment about without sufficient information. **2.** To find the correct answer to by inference or surmise. **3.** To suppose; consider. —*intr.* To make a conjecture: *could only guess at his motives.* —*n.* An act or instance of guessing; conjecture. [ME *gessen,* to infer.] **—guess'er** *n.*

guess·ti·mate (gĕs'tə-mĭt) *n. Informal.* An approximate estimate. [Blend of GUESS and ESTIMATE.] **—guess'ti·mate'** (-māt') *v.* **(-mat·ed, -mat·ing, -mates).**

guess·work (gĕs'wûrk') *n.* **1.** The process of making guesses. **2.** An answer or the result obtained by guessing.

guest (gĕst) *n.* **1.** A person who is a recipient of hospitality at the home or table of another. **2.** A person to whom entertainment or hospitality has been extended. **3.** One who is a customer of an establishment such as a restaurant or hotel. **4.** A person who is a visiting participant in a program. **5.** *Zool.* A commensal organism, esp. an insect that lives in the nest or burrow of another species. —*tr. & intr.v.* **guest·ed, guest·ing, guests.** To entertain as or be a guest. [ME *gest* < ON *gestr.*]

guff (gŭf) *n. Slang.* Foolish talk; nonsense. [< obs. *guff,* puff.]

guf·faw (gə-fô') *n.* A hearty or coarse burst of laughter. —*intr.v.* **-fawed, -faw·ing, -faws.** To produce or emit a guffaw. [Imit.]

guid·ance (gīd'ns) *n.* **1.** An act or instance of guiding. **2.** Counseling, as on vocational, educational, or marital problems. **3.** Any of various processes for guiding the path of a missile by means of built-in equipment.

guide (gīd) *n.* **1.** One who shows the way by leading, directing, or advising. **2.** A person employed to point out and give information about objects of interest. **3.** A guidebook. **4. a.** Something that serves to direct or indicate. **b.** A device that acts to regulate or direct a motion or operation. **5.** A soldier stationed at the right or left of a column to control the alignment of the marchers, show the direction, or mark the point of pivot. —*v.* **guid·ed, guid·ing, guides.** —*tr.* **1.** To serve as a guide for; conduct. **2.** To direct the course of. **3.** To exert control or influence over. —*intr.* To serve as a guide. [ME < OFr. < OProv. *guida,* of Germanic orig.] **—guid'a·ble** *adj.* **—guid'er** *n.*

guide·book (gīd'bŏŏk') *n.* A handbook of information, esp. for travelers.

guided missile *n.* A missile capable of being guided while it is in flight.

guided wave *n.* An electromagnetic or acoustic wave transmitted by a process that limits its physical dispersion along the length of its transmission.

guide·line (gīd'līn') *n.* A statement of policy or procedure.

guide·post (gīd'pōst') *n.* **1.** A post with a directional sign. **2.** One that gives direction.

guide rope *n.* A rope fastened to another rope that is lifting a load, to guide the rope and steady the load.

guide·word (gīd'wûrd') *n.* A word or term that appears at the top of a page of a reference book, such as a dictionary, to indicate the first or last entry on the page.

gui·don (gī'dŏn', gīd'n) *n.* **1.** A small flag or pennant carried as a standard by a military unit. **2.** A soldier bearing a guidon. [Fr. < Ital. *guidone* < *guida,* guide < OProv., of Germanic orig.]

guild also **gild** (gĭld) *n.* **1. a.** An association of persons of the same trade or pursuits. **b.** A medieval association or society of merchants, craftsmen, or artisans. **2.** *Ecol.* One of four groups of plants, the lianas, epiphytes, saprophytes, and parasites, having a characteristic mode of existence that involves some dependence upon other plant life. [ME < ON *gildi.*]

guil·der (gĭl'dər) *n.* See table at **currency.** [Alteration of Du. *gulden.* —see GULDEN.]

guild·hall (gĭld'hôl') *n.* **1.** The meeting hall of a guild. **2.** A town hall.

guilds·man (gĭldz'mən) *n.* **1.** A member of a guild. **2.** An adherent or advocate of guild socialism.

guild socialism *n.* An English socialist doctrine of the early 20th century in which industry was to be owned by the state but managed by a council of workers.

guile (gīl) *n.* **1.** Insidious, treacherous cunning; deceit. **2.** *Obs.* A trick; stratagem. —*tr.v.* **guiled, guil·ing, guiles.** *Archaic.* To beguile; deceive. [ME < OFr., of Germanic orig.] **—guile'ful** *adj.* **—guile'ful·ly** *adv.* **—guile'ful·ness** *n.*

guile·less (gīl'lĭs) *adj.* Free of guile; artless. **—guile'less·ly** *adv.* **—guile'less·ness** *n.*

guil·le·mot (gĭl'ə-mŏt') *n.* Any of several small sea birds of the genus *Cepphus,* of northern regions, having black plumage with white markings. [Fr. < *Guillaume,* William.]

guil·loche (gĭ-lōsh', gē-yōsh') *n. Archit.* An ornamental border formed of two or more bands interlaced in such a way as to repeat a rounded design. [Fr. *guillochis.*]

guil·lo·tine (gĭl'ə-tēn', gē'ə-) *n.* **1.** A machine with a heavy blade that falls freely between upright guides to behead a condemned prisoner. **2.** A cutting instrument, such as a paper cutter, similar to a guillotine. **3.** A method of limiting debate in a legislative body by fixing beforehand a time for voting. —*tr.v.* **-tined, -tin·ing, -tines.** To behead with a guillotine. [After Joseph I. *Guillotin* (1738–1814).]

guilt (gĭlt) *n.* **1.** The fact of being responsible for an offense or wrongdoing. **2.** *Law.* **a.** Culpability for a crime or lesser breach of regulations. **b.** The disposition to break the law. **3.** Guilty behavior. **4.** Remorseful awareness of having done something wrong. [ME *gilt* < OE *gylt.*]

guilt·less (gĭlt'lĭs) *adj.* Free from guilt; innocent. **—guilt'less·ly** *adv.* **—guilt'less·ness** *n.*

guilt·y (gĭl'tē) *adj.* **-i·er, -i·est.** **1.** Responsible for or chargeable with a reprehensible act: *guilty of cheating.* **2.** *Law.* Having committed a crime: *plead guilty.* **3.** At fault; culpable: *the guilty party.* **4.** Laden with, prompted by, or showing a sense of guilt: *a guilty conscience.* **—guilt'i·ly** *adv.* **—guilt'i·ness** *n.*

guimpe (gămp, gĭmp) *n.* **1.** A short, sleeved blouse worn with a jumper. **2.** A yoke insert for a low-necked dress. **3.** A starched cloth covering the neck and shoulders as part of a nun's habit. **4.** Gimp[1]. [Fr. < OFr. *guimple,* of Germanic orig.]

guin·ea (gĭn'ē) *n.* **1. a.** A former British gold coin worth one pound and five pence. **b.** The sum of one pound and five pence. **2.** *Offensive.* An Italian or a person of Italian descent. [After the *Guinea* coast of Africa, the source of the gold from which it was first made.]

guinea fowl *n.* Any of several pheasantlike birds of the family Numididae, native to Africa, esp. a widely domesticated species, *Numida meleagris,* having blackish plumage marked with many small white spots. [After the *Guinea* coast of Africa.]

guinea hen *n.* **1.** A female guinea fowl. **2.** The guinea fowl.

guinea pig *n.* **1.** Any of various South American burrowing rodents of the genus *Cavia,* having variously colored hair and no visible tail and widely domesticated as pets and as experimental animals. **2.** A person who is used as a subject for experimentation. [Prob. alteration of *Guiana.*]

guinea worm *n.* A long, threadlike nematode worm, *Dracunculus medinensis,* of tropical Asia and Africa, that is a subcutaneous parasite of man and other animals. [Prob. after the *Guinea* coast of Africa.]

Guin·e·vere (gwĭn'ə-vîr') also **Guen·e·vere** (gwĕn'-) *n.* The

Guernsey

George Miksch Sutton

guillemot

guilloche

George Miksch Sutton

guinea fowl

guitar

George Miksch Sutton
gull[1]

wife of King Arthur and the mistress of Lancelot according to Arthurian legend.

gui·pure (gĭ-po͝or′, -pyo͝or′) *n.* A kind of coarse, large-patterned lace without a net ground. [Fr. < OFr. < *guiper,* to cover with silk, of Germanic orig.]

guise (gīz) *n.* **1.** Outward appearance; aspect. **2.** Mode of dress; garb. **3.** *Obs.* Custom; habit. [ME, fashion < OFr., of Germanic orig.]

gui·tar (gĭ-tär′) *n.* A musical instrument having a large flat-backed sound box similar in shape to a violin, a long fretted neck, and usually six strings, played by strumming or plucking. [Fr. *guitare* < Sp. *guitarra* < Ar. *gītār* < Gk. *kithara,* cithara.] **—gui·tar′ist** *n.*

gui·tar·fish (gĭ-tär′fĭsh′) *n., pl.* **guitarfish** or **-fish·es.** Any of several marine fishes of the family Rhinobatidae, related to the skates and rays and having a guitar-shaped body.

Gu·ja·ra·ti (go͞o′jə-rä′tē, go͞oj′ə-) *n., pl.* **Gujarati. 1.** The Indic language of Gujarat. **2.** A native or inhabitant of Gujarat.

gul (go͞ol) *n.* A stylized rose motif in an oriental rug. [Pers., rose.]

gu·lar (go͞o′lər, gyo͞o′-) *adj.* Of, pertaining to, or located on the throat. [< Lat. *gula,* throat.]

gulch (gŭlch) *n.* A small shallow canyon with smoothly inclined slopes and steep sides; ravine. [Orig. unknown.]

gul·den (go͞ol′dən, go͞ol′-) *n., pl.* **-dens** or **gulden.** A guilder. [ME < MDu. *gulden (florijn),* golden (florin).]

gules (gyo͞olz) *n. Heraldry.* The color red, indicated on a blazon by engraved vertical lines. [ME *goules* < OFr., pl. of *gole,* throat < Lat. *gula.*]

gulf (gŭlf) *n.* **1.** A large area of a sea or ocean partially enclosed by land, esp. a long landlocked portion of sea opening through a strait. **2.** A deep, wide chasm; abyss. **3.** A distance that separates; gap: *"the gulf between the Victorian sensibility and our own"* (Babette Deutsch). **4.** A whirlpool; eddy. *—tr.v.* **gulfed, gulf·ing, gulfs.** To engulf. [ME *goulf* < OFr. *golf* < OItal. *golfa,* ult. < Gk. *kolpos.*]

gulf·weed (gŭlf′wēd′) *n.* Any of several brownish seaweeds of the genus *Sargassum,* of tropical Atlantic waters, that have rounded air bladders and often form dense, floating masses. [After the *Gulf* of Mexico, where it is found.]

gull[1] (gŭl) *n.* Any of various chiefly coastal aquatic birds of the subfamily Larinae, having long wings, webbed feet, and usually gray and white plumage. [ME *gull,* of Celt. orig.]

gull[2] (gŭl) *n.* A gullible person; dupe. *—tr.v.* **gulled, gull·ing, gulls.** To take advantage of; cheat. [Orig. unknown.]

Gul·lah (gŭl′ə) *n.* **1.** One of a group of blacks inhabiting the Sea Islands and coastal area of South Carolina, Georgia, and northern Florida. **2.** The language of the Gullahs, which is based on English but includes vocabulary elements and grammatical features from several African languages.

gul·let (gŭl′ĭt) *n.* **1.** *Anat.* The esophagus. **2.** The throat. [ME *golet* < OFr., dim. of *gole,* throat < Lat. *gula.*]

gul·li·ble (gŭl′ə-bəl) *adj.* Easily deceived or duped. [< GULL[2].] **—gul′li·bil′i·ty** *n.* **—gul′li·bly** *adv.*

Gul·li·ver (gŭl′ə-vər) *n.* In Jonathan Swift's satire *Gulliver's Travels* (1726), the Englishman who travels to the imaginary lands of Lilliput, Brobdingnag, and Laputa, and the land of the Houyhnhnms.

gul·ly[1] (gŭl′ē) *n., pl.* **-lies.** A deep ditch or channel cut in the earth by running water after a downpour. *—v.* **-lied, -ly·ing, -lies.** *—tr.* To wear a gully in. *—intr.* To form a gully. [Prob. alteration of GULLET.]

gul·ly[2] (gŭl′ē) *n., pl.* **-lies.** *Chiefly Brit. Regional.* A large knife. [Short for dial. *gully knife,* a large knife.]

gulp (gŭlp) *v.* **gulped, gulp·ing, gulps.** *—tr.* **1.** To swallow greedily or rapidly in large amounts. **2.** To stifle by or as if by swallowing. *—intr.* To choke or gasp, as in swallowing. *—n.* **1.** The act of gulping. **2.** A large mouthful. **3.** *Computer Sci.* A small group of bytes that may be either data or instruction. [ME *gulpen.*] **—gulp′er** *n.* **—gulp′ing·ly** *adv.*

gum[1] (gŭm) *n.* **1. a.** Any of various viscous substances that are exuded by certain plants and trees and that dry into water-soluble, noncrystalline, brittle solids. **b.** A similar plant exudate, such as a resin. **2.** A substance that resembles a plant gum. **3. a.** Any of various trees, such as one of the genera *Eucalyptus, Liquidambar,* or *Nyssa,* that are a source of gum. **b.** The wood of such a tree. **4.** Chewing gum. *—v.* **gummed, gum·ming, gums.** *—tr.* To cover, smear, seal, fill, or fix in place with or as if with gum. *—intr.* **1.** To exude or form gum. **2.** To become sticky or clogged with or as if with gum. ***—phrasal verb.* gum up.** *Slang.* To ruin; bungle: *gum up the works.* [ME *gomme* < OFr. *gome* < Lat. *gummi* < Gk. *kommi* of Egypt. orig.]

gum[2] (gŭm) *n.* The firm connective tissue that is covered by mucous membrane and that envelops the alveolar arches of the jaw and surrounds the bases of the teeth. [ME *goma* < OE *gōma,* palate.]

gum ammoniac *n.* Ammoniac.

gum arabic *n.* A gum exuded by various African trees of the genus *Acacia,* esp. *A. senegal,* used in the preparation of pills and emulsions, the manufacture of mucilage and candies, and in general as a thickener and colloidal stabilizer.

gum benjamin *n.* Benzoin.

gum benzoin *n.* Benzoin.

gum·bo (gŭm′bō) *n., pl.* **-bos. 1.** Okra (senses 1 and 2). **2.** A soup or stew thickened with okra. **3.** A fine silty soil, common in the southern and western United States, that forms an unusually sticky mud when wet. **4. Gumbo.** A patois spoken by some blacks and Creoles in Louisiana and the French West Indies. [Louisiana Fr. *gombo,* of African orig.]

gum·boil (gŭm′boil′) *n.* A small boil or abscess on the gum.

gum·bo-lim·bo (gŭm′bō-lĭm′bō) *n., pl.* **-bos.** An aromatic tree, *Bursera simaruba,* of Florida and the West Indies, having compound leaves and small white flowers. [GUMBO + *limbo,* of unknown orig.]

gum·drop (gŭm′drŏp′) *n.* A small candy made of sweetened, colored, and flavored gum arabic or gelatin and coated with coarse granulated sugar.

gum·ma (gŭm′ə) *n., pl.* **-mas** or **-ma·ta** (-ə-tə). A small, rubbery tumor formed in an advanced stage of syphilis. [NLat. < Lat. *gummi,* gum. —see GUM.] **—gum′ma·tous** *adj.*

gum·mo·sis (gŭ-mō′sĭs) *n.* The pathological formation of patches of gum on certain plants, such as sugar cane and certain fruit trees, resulting from attack by insects, microorganisms, or adverse weather conditions. [Lat. *gummi,* gum + -OSIS.]

gum·mous (gŭm′əs) also **gum·mose** (gŭm′ōs′) *adj.* Made of or resembling gum.

gum·my (gŭm′ē) *adj.* **-mi·er, -mi·est. 1.** Consisting of or containing gum. **2.** Suffused with or yielding gum. **3.** Sticky; viscid. **—gum′mi·ness** *n.*

gum plant *n.* Any of several North American plants of the genus *Grindelia,* esp. *G. squarosa,* having sticky leaves and bracts and yellow, rayed flowers.

gump·tion (gŭmp′shən) *n. Informal.* **1.** Common sense. **2.** Boldness of enterprise; initiative. [Orig. unknown.]

gum resin *n.* A mixture of gum and resin that exudes from some plants or trees.

gum·shoe (gŭm′sho͞o′) *Slang.* *—n.* A detective. *—intr.v.* **-shoed, -shoe·ing, -shoes.** To perform or engage in the work of a detective.

gum tree *n.* Gum[1] (sense 3.a.).

gum·wood (gŭm′wo͝od′) *n.* Gum[1] (sense 3.b.).

gun (gŭn) *n.* **1.** A weapon consisting essentially of a metal tube from which a projectile is fired at high velocity into a flat trajectory. **2.** A cannon as distinguished from a small firearm. **3.** A portable firearm. **4.** A device that shoots a projectile. **5.** A discharge of a gun as a signal or salute. **6.** One who carries or uses a gun, esp.: **a.** A hunter. **b.** A person skilled in the use of a gun. **7.** A mechanism controlling the flow of fuel to an engine; throttle. *—v.* **gunned, gun·ning, guns.** *—tr.* **1.** To fire upon; shoot. **2.** To open the throttle of so as to accelerate: *gun an engine.* *—intr.* To hunt or shoot with a gun. ***—phrasal verb.* gun for. 1.** To seek to catch, overcome, or destroy. **2.** To seek with tenacity: *gun for high office.* [ME *gonne,* cannon, perh. < ON *gunnr,* battle.]

gun·boat (gŭn′bōt′) *n.* A small armed vessel.

gun carriage *n.* A frame or structure upon which a gun is mounted for firing or maneuvering.

gun·cot·ton (gŭn′kŏt′n) *n.* Nitrocellulose.

gun dog *n.* A dog trained to assist hunters, as in flushing or retrieving game.

gun·fight (gŭn′fīt′) *n.* A duel or battle with guns. **—gun′fight′er** *n.*

gun·fire (gŭn′fīr′) *n.* The firing of guns.

gun·flint (gŭn′flĭnt′) *n.* The piece of flint used to strike the igniting spark in a flintlock.

gung ho (gŭng′ hō′) *adj. Slang.* **1.** Unswervingly dedicated and loyal. **2.** Extremely enthusiastic. [Pidgin E., prob. < Chin. (Mandarin) *gong[1] he[2],* to work together : *gong[1],* work + *he[2],* together.]

gunk (gŭngk) *n. Informal.* A filthy, slimy, or greasy substance. [< *Gunk,* a trademark for liquid soap.]

gun·lock (gŭn′lŏk′) *n.* A device for igniting the charge of a firearm.

gun·man (gŭn′mən) *n.* **1. a.** A man who is armed with a gun. **b.** A professional killer. **2.** A man of great skill in the use of a gun.

gun·met·al (gŭn′mĕt′l) *n.* **1.** An alloy of copper with ten per cent tin. **2.** Metal used for guns. **3.** A dark gray. **—gun′met′al** *adj.*

gun moll *n. Slang.* The girl friend of a gangster.

Gun·nar (go͝on′är′, -ər) *n.* The husband of Brynhild, the brother-in-law of Sigurd, and the brother of Gudrun according to Germanic legend.

Gunn effect (gŭn) *n. Electronics.* The production of high-speed current fluctuations when voltage in excess of a critical level is applied to a semiconductor device, resulting in microwave generation. [After J. B. *Gunn* (b. 1928).]

gun·nel[1] (gŭn′əl) *n.* Any of various long, eellike fishes of the family Pholidae, of northern seas. [Orig. unknown.]

gun·nel[2] (gŭn′əl) *n.* Variant of **gunwale.**

gun·ner (gŭn′ər) *n.* **1.** A soldier, sailor, or airman who aims or fires a gun. **2.** One who hunts with a gun. **3.** A warrant officer having charge of ordnance.

gun·ner·y (gŭn′ə-rē) *n.* **1.** The art and science of constructing and operating guns. **2.** The use of guns.

gun·ny (gŭn′ē) *n.* A coarse fabric made of jute or hemp. [Hindi *gōnī* < Skt. *goṇī,* sack.]

gun·ny·sack (gŭn′ē-săk′) *n.* A sack made of gunny.

gun·pow·der (gŭn′pou′dər) *n.* Any of various explosive

powders used to propel projectiles from guns, esp. a black explosive mixture of potassium nitrate, charcoal, and sulfur.
gunpowder tea *n.* A green tea whose leaves are rolled into pellets.
gun·room (gŭn′ro͝om′, -ro͞om′) *n.* The quarters of midshipmen and junior officers on a British warship.
gun·run·ner (gŭn′rŭn′ər) *n.* One that smuggles firearms and ammunition. —**gun′run′ning** *n.*
gun·shot (gŭn′shŏt′) *n.* **1.** Shot fired from a gun. **2.** The range of a gun.
gun-shy (gŭn′shī′) *adj.* **1.** Afraid of loud noise, as that made by gunfire. **2.** Extremely distrustful or wary.
gun·sling·er (gŭn′slĭng′ər) *n.* A gunman. —**gun′sling′ing** *n.*
gun·smith (gŭn′smĭth′) *n.* One who makes or repairs firearms.
gun·stock (gŭn′stŏk′) *n.* A handle on a gun; stock.
Gun·ter's chain (gŭn′tərz) *n.* A chain (sense 9). [After Edmund *Gunter* (1581–1626).]
Gun·ther (go͝on′tər) *n.* In the *Nibelungenlied,* a king of Burgundy and husband of Brunhild. [G.]
gun·wale also **gun·nel** (gŭn′əl) *n.* The upper edge of a ship's side.
Guo·yu (ko͞o′yo͞o′) *n.* Mandarin (sense 3). [Chin. : *guo*², nation + *yu*³, language.]
gup·py (gŭp′ē) *n., pl.* **-pies.** A small, brightly colored freshwater fish, *Poecilia reticulata* or *Lebistes reticulatus,* of northern South America and adjacent islands of the West Indies, that is popular in home aquariums. [After R.J.L. *Guppy* (1836–1916).]
gur·gi·ta·tion (gûr′jĭ-tā′shən) *n.* A whirling motion; ebullition. [< LLat. *gurgitare,* to engulf < *gurges,* whirlpool.]
gur·gle (gûr′gəl) *v.* **-gled, -gling, -gles.** —*intr.* **1.** To flow in a broken, uneven current making intermittent low sounds. **2.** To make a gurgling sound. —*tr.* To express or pronounce with a gurgling sound. —*n.* The act or sound of gurgling. [Prob. imit.] —**gur′gling·ly** *adv.*
Gur·kha (go͝or′kə) *n.* **1.** A member of a Rajput ethnic group predominant in Nepal. **2.** A soldier from Nepal serving in the British or Indian armies.
gur·nard (gûr′nərd) *n., pl.* **-nards** or **gurnard. 1.** Any of various marine fishes of the family Triglidae, and esp. of the Old World genus *Trigla,* having large, fanlike pectoral fins. **2.** The flying gurnard. [ME < OFr. *gornart.*]
gur·ney (gûr′nē) *n., pl.* **-neys.** A wheeled stretcher or litter.
gu·ru (go͞or′o͞o, go͞o-ro͞o′) *n., pl.* **-rus. 1.** *Hinduism.* A personal spiritual teacher. **2. a.** A recognized leader or guide. **b.** An acknowledged advocate, as of a movement or idea. [Hindi *gurū* < Skt. *guru-,* venerable.]
gush (gŭsh) *v.* **gushed, gush·ing, gush·es.** —*intr.* **1.** To flow forth suddenly and violently. **2.** To issue or emit an abundant flow. **3.** To make an excessive display of sentiment or enthusiasm. —*tr.* To emit abundantly. —*n.* **1.** A sudden, violent, or copious outflow: *a gush of tears.* **2.** Something emitted by gushing. **3.** An excessive display of sentiment. [ME *gushen,* prob. of Scand. orig.]
gush·er (gŭsh′ər) *n.* **1.** One that gushes. **2.** A gas or oil well with an abundant natural flow.
gush·y (gŭsh′ē) *adj.* **-i·er, -i·est.** Characterized by excessive displays of sentiment or enthusiasm. —**gush′i·ly** *adv.* —**gush′i·ness** *n.*
gus·set (gŭs′ĭt) *n.* A triangular insert, as in a garment, for strengthening or enlarging. [ME < OFr. *gosset.*]
gus·sy (gŭs′ē) *tr.v.* **-sied, -sy·ing, -sies.** To dress up; decorate: *all gussied up in sequins and feathers.* [Orig. unknown.]
gust¹ (gŭst) *n.* **1.** A violent, abrupt rush of wind. **2.** An abrupt or sudden outburst. —*intr.v.* **gust·ed, gust·ing, gusts.** To blow in gusts. [Prob. < ON *gustr.*] —**gust′i·ly** *adv.* —**gust′i·ness** *n.* —**gust′y** *adj.*
gust² (gŭst) *n.* **1.** *Archaic.* Relish; gusto. **2.** *Obs.* Personal taste or inclination; liking. [ME *guste,* taste < Lat. *gustus.*]
gus·ta·tion (gŭ-stā′shən) *n.* The act or faculty of tasting. [Lat. *gustatio,* a tasting < *gustare,* to taste < *gustus,* taste.]
gus·ta·tive (gŭs′tə-tĭv) *adj.* Gustatory.
gus·ta·to·ry (gŭs′tə-tôr′ē, -tōr′ē) *adj.* Of or pertaining to the sense of taste. —**gus′ta·to′ri·ly** *adv.*
gus·to (gŭs′tō) *n., pl.* **-toes. 1.** A specialized or individual taste. **2.** Vigorous enjoyment; zest. **3.** *Archaic.* Artistic style. [Ital. < Lat. *gustus,* taste.]
gut (gŭt) *n.* **1.** The alimentary canal or a portion thereof, esp. the intestine or stomach. **2. guts.** The bowels; entrails. **3. guts.** The essential contents of something: *the guts of an old television set.* **4.** The intestines of some animals used as strings for musical instruments or as surgical sutures. **5. guts.** *Slang.* Courage; fortitude. **6.** A narrow passage or channel. **7.** Fibrous material taken from the silk gland of a silkworm before it spins a cocoon, used for fishing tackle. —*tr.v.* **gut·ted, gut·ting, guts. 1.** To remove the intestines or entrails of; eviscerate. **2.** To destroy the interior of: *gut a house.* —*adj. Slang.* **1.** Arousing or involving basic emotions; visceral: *a gut issue; a gut response.* **2.** Easy: *gut courses.* [< ME *guttes,* entrails < OE *guttas.*] —**gut′ty** *adj.*
Guth·run (go͞oth′ro͞on′). *n.* Variant of **Gudrun.**
gut·less (gŭt′lĭs) *adj.* Lacking courage. —**gut′less·ness** *n.*
guts·y (gŭt′sē) *adj.* **-i·er, -i·est.** *Slang.* Full of courage; plucky. —**guts′i·ly** *adv.* —**guts′i·ness** *n.*
gut·ta (gŭt′ə) *n., pl.* **gut·tae** (gŭt′ē′). **1.** *Archit.* One of a group of small, droplike ornaments on a Doric entablature. **2.** *Med.* A drop. [Lat., drop.]
gut·ta-per·cha (gŭt′ə-pûr′chə) *n.* A rubbery substance derived from the latex of any of several tropical trees of the genera *Palaquium* and *Payena* and used as electrical insulation and for waterproofing. [Malay *gĕtah percha* : *gĕtah,* sap + *percha,* strip of cloth.]
gut·tate (gŭt′āt′) also **gut·tat·ed** (-ā′tĭd) *adj.* **1. a.** In the form of drops. **b.** Having drops. **2.** Spotted as if by drops. [Lat. *guttatus,* speckled < *gutta,* drop.]
gut·ter (gŭt′ər) *n.* **1.** A channel for draining off water at the edge of a street or road. **2.** A pipe or trough for draining off water under the border of a roof. **3.** A furrow or groove formed by running water. **4.** The trough on either side of a bowling alley. **5.** *Printing.* The white space between the facing pages of a book. **6.** The lowest class or state of human existence. —*v.* **-tered, -ter·ing, -ters.** —*tr.* To form gutters or furrows in. —*intr.* **1.** To flow in channels or rivulets. **2.** To melt away through the channel in the side of the hollow formed by a burning wick. Used of a candle. **3.** To burn with a low flame; flicker. [ME *goter* < OFr. *gotier* < VLat. **guttarie* < Lat. *gutta,* drop.]
gut·ter·snipe (gŭt′ər-snīp′) *n.* **1.** A street urchin. **2.** A person of the lowest class.
gut·tur·al (gŭt′ər-əl) *adj.* **1.** Of or pertaining to the throat. **2.** Produced in the throat. **3.** Velar. [OFr. < Lat. *guttur,* throat.] —**gut′tur·al** *n.* —**gut′tur·al·ism** *n.* —**gut′tur·al′i·ty** (-ə-răl′ĭ-tē) *n.* —**gut′tur·al·ly** *adv.* —**gut′tur·al·ness** *n.*
gut·tur·al·ize (gŭt′ər-ə-līz′) *tr.v.* **-ized, -iz·ing, -iz·es. 1.** To pronounce gutturally. **2.** To velarize. —**gut′tur·al·i·za′tion** *n.*
guy¹ (gī) *n.* A rope, cord, or cable used for steadying, guiding, or holding something. —*tr.v.* **guyed, guy·ing, guys.** To steady, guide, or hold with a guy. [Prob. of LG orig.]
guy² (gī) *n.* **1.** *Informal.* A man; fellow. **2.** *Informal.* **guys.** Persons of either sex: *What are you guys doing?* **3.** *Chiefly Brit.* A person of odd or grotesque appearance or dress. **4.** Often **Guy.** An effigy of Guy Fawkes paraded through the streets of English towns and burned on Guy Fawkes Day. —*tr.v.* **guyed, guy·ing, guys.** To make fun of; mock. [After *Guy* Fawkes (1570–1606).]
Guy Fawkes Day (gī′ fôks′) *n.* November 5 celebrated in commemoration of the 1605 attempt led by Guy Fawkes to assassinate the king and assembled parliament in retaliation for increasing repression of Roman Catholics in England.
guy·ot (gē′ō) *n.* A flat-topped seamount. [After Arnold H. *Guyot* (1807–1884).]
guz·zle (gŭz′əl) *v.* **-zled, -zling, -zles.** —*tr.* To drink greedily or habitually: *guzzle whisky.* —*intr.* To drink esp. alcoholic beverages greedily or habitually. [Orig. unknown.] —**guz′zler** *n.*
gybe (jīb) *v. & n.* Variant of **jibe¹.**
gym (jĭm) *n. Informal.* **1.** A gymnasium. **2.** Physical education. **3.** A frame supporting structures used in outdoor play.
gym·kha·na (jĭm-kä′nə) *n. Chiefly Brit.* A display of athletic or equestrian contests. [Prob. alteration of Hindi *gendkhānā,* racket court.]
gym·na·si·um (jĭm-nā′zē-əm) *n., pl.* **-si·ums** or **-si·a** (-zē-ə). **1.** A room or building equipped for gymnastics and sports. **2.** (gĭm-nä′zē-o͝om′). An academic high school in various European countries, esp. Germany, that prepares students for studies at a university. [Lat., school < Gk. *gumnasion* < *gumnazein,* to exercise naked < *gumnos,* naked.]
gym·nast (jĭm′năst′) *n.* One skilled in gymnastic exercises. [Gk. *gumnastēs* < *gumnazein,* to exercise naked < *gumnos,* naked.]
gym·nas·tic (jĭm-năs′tĭk) *adj.* Of or pertaining to gymnastics. —**gym·nas′ti·cal·ly** *adv.*
gym·nas·tics (jĭm-năs′tĭks) *n. (used with a sing. or pl. verb).* Body-building exercises, esp. those performed with special apparatus in a gymnasium.
gym·nos·o·phist (jĭm-nŏs′ə-fĭst) *n.* One of an ancient sect of naked Hindu ascetics, as reported in classical antiquity. [Lat. *gymnosophista* < Gk. *gumnosophistēs* : *gumnos,* naked + *sophistēs,* expert. —see SOPHIST.]
gym·no·sperm (jĭm′nə-spûrm′) *n.* A plant of the class Gymnospermae, which includes the coniferous trees and other plants having seeds not enclosed within an ovary. [NLat. *Gymnospermae,* class name : Gk. *gumnos,* naked + Gk. *sperma,* seed.] —**gym′no·sper′mous** *adj.* —**gym′no·sper′my** *n.*
gyn- *pref.* Variant of **gyno-.**
gynaec- or **gynaeco-** *pref.* Variants of **gyneco-.**
gy·nan·dro·morph (jī-năn′drə-môrf′, gī-) *n.* An individual having male and female characteristics. —**gy·nan′dro·mor′phic, gy·nan′dro·mor′phous** *adj.* —**gy·nan′dro·mor′phism, gy·nan′dro·mor′phy** *n.*
gy·nan·drous (jī-năn′drəs, gī-) *adj.* **1.** Having the stamens and pistil united to form a column. **2.** Hermaphroditic.
gyn·ar·chy (jĭn′är′kē, jī′när′-, gī′-) *n., pl.* **-chies.** Government by women. —**gyn·ar′chic** *adj.*
-gyne *suff.* Female reproductive organ: *trichogyne.* [< Gk. *gunē,* woman.]
gyneco- or **gynec-** or **gynaeco-** or **gynaec-** *pref.* Woman: *gynecology.* [Gk. *gunaiko-* < *gunē,* woman.]
gyn·e·coc·ra·cy (jĭn′ĭ-kŏk′rə-sē, gī′nĭ-) *n., pl.* **-cies.** Political

ascendancy of women. [Gk. *gunaikokratia* : *gunē,* woman + *-kratia,* -cracy.]

gy·ne·col·o·gy (gī′nĭ-kŏl′ə-jē, jĭn′ĭ-) *n.* The medical science of disease, reproductive physiology, and endocrinology in women. **—gy′ne·co·log′i·cal** (-kə-lŏj′ĭ-kəl), **gy′ne·co·log′ic** *adj.* **—gy′ne·col′o·gist** *n.*

gyn·e·cop·a·thy (jĭn′ĭ-kŏp′ə-thē, gī′nĭ-) *n.* Any of various diseases peculiar to women.

gyn·i·at·rics (jĭn′ē-ăt′rĭks, gī′nē-) *n.* *(used with sing. verb).* The treatment of diseases peculiar to women.

gyno– or **gyn–** *pref.* **1.** Woman: *gyniatrics.* **2.** Female reproductive organ; pistil: *gynophore.* [Gk. *guno-* < *gunē,* woman.]

gy·noc·ra·cy (gī-nŏk′rə-cē) *n., pl.* **-cies.** A gynecocracy.

gy·noe·ci·um (jĭ-nē′sē-əm, gī-) *n., pl.* **-ci·a** (-sē-ə). The female reproductive organs of a flower; the pistil or pistils collectively. [NLat., alteration of Lat. *gynaeceum,* women's apartments < Gk. *gunaikeion* < *gunē,* woman.]

gyn·o·phore (jĭn′ə-fôr′, -fōr′, gī′nə-) *n.* The stalk of a pistil. **—gyn′o·phor′ic** (-fôr′ĭk, -fōr′-) *adj.*

–gynous *suff.* **1.** Of, pertaining to, or having a specified number of females: *heterogynous.* **2. a.** Of, pertaining to, or situated in a specified place with respect to female organs of a plant: *epigynous.* **b.** Having a specified number or kind of female organs of a plant: *tetragynous.* [NLat. *-gynus* < Gk. *-gunos* < *gunē, woman.*]

–gyny *suff.* **1.** The state or condition of having a specified number of women or females: *monogyny.* **2.** The condition of being situated in a specified place with respect to female plant organs: *epigyny.* [< Gk. *gunē,* woman.]

gyp also **gip** (jĭp) *Informal.* *—tr.v.* **gypped, gyp·ping, gyps** also **gipped, gip·ping, gips.** To swindle, cheat, or defraud. *—n.* **1.** The act or an instance of gypping; swindle. **2.** One who gyps; swindler. [Poss. short for GYPSY.] **—gyp′per** *n.*

gyp joint *n. Slang.* An establishment that makes a practice of overcharging or defrauding its clientele.

gyp·lure (jĭp′lo͝or′) *n.* A synthetic form of the sex attractant of the female gypsy moth used to trap male gypsy moths. [GYP(SY MOTH) + LURE.]

gyp·soph·i·la (jĭp-sŏf′ə-lə) *n.* Any of various plants of the genus *Gypsophila,* having small white or pink flowers and including the baby's-breath. [NLat. *Gypsophila,* genus name : Gk. *gupsos,* chalk + Gk. *philos,* loving.]

gyp·sum (jĭp′səm) *n.* A white mineral, $CaSO_4 \cdot 2H_2O$, used in the manufacture of plaster of Paris, gypsum plaster and plasterboard, Portland cement, wallboards, and fertilizers. [Lat. < Gk. *gupsos,* of Semitic orig.] **—gyp′se·ous** (-sē-əs), **gyp·sif′er·ous** (-sĭf′ər-əs) *adj.*

gypsum board *n.* Plasterboard.

Gyp·sy also **Gip·sy** (jĭp′sē) *—n., pl.* **-sies. 1.** One of a nomadic Caucasoid people originally migrating from the border region between Iran and India to Europe in the 14th or 15th century and now living principally in Europe and the United States. **2.** Romany (sense 2). **3. gypsy.** One that resembles a Gypsy in appearance or behavior. [Shortening and alteration of EGYPTIAN.]

gypsy cab *n.* A taxicab that is licensed only to respond to calls but that cruises the streets for passengers.

gypsy moth *n.* A moth, *Porthetria dispar,* native to the Old World, having hairy caterpillars that feed on foliage and are very destructive to trees.

gy·ral (jī′rəl) *adj.* **1.** Moving in a circular or spiral path; gyratory. **2.** Pertaining to a gyrus. **—gy′ral·ly** *adv.*

gy·rate (jī′rāt′) *intr.v.* **-rat·ed, -rat·ing, -rates. 1.** To revolve on or around a center or axis. **2.** To circle or spiral. *—adj. Biol.* In rings; coiled. [Lat. *gyrare, gyrat-* < *gyrus,* circle < Gk. *guros.*] **—gy·ra′tion** *n.* **—gy′ra′tor** *n.* **—gy′ra·to′ry** (-rə-tôr′ē, -tōr′ē) *adj.*

gyre (jīr) *n.* **1. a.** A ring or circle. **b.** A spiral. **2.** A circular or spiral motion. [Lat. *gyrus* < Gk. *guros.*]

gy·rene (jī-rēn′) *n. Slang.* A U.S. Marine. [Prob. alteration of MARINE.]

gyr·fal·con also **ger·fal·con** (jûr′făl′kən, -fôl′-, -fô′-) *n.* A large falcon, *Falco rusticolus,* of northern regions, having various color phases ranging from black to white. [ME *gerfaucoun* < OFr. *girfaut,* of Germanic orig.]

gy·ri (jī′rī′) *n.* Plural of **gyrus.**

gy·ro[1] (jī′rō) *n., pl.* **-ros. 1.** A gyroscope. **2.** A gyrocompass.

gy·ro[2] (jī′rō) *n.* A sandwich of pita bread filled with roasted meat, esp. lamb, and often vegetables, as onions and tomatoes. [Mod. Gk. *gurō* < Gk. *guros,* turn.]

gyro– *pref.* **1.** Spinning: *gyromagnetic.* **2.** Circle; spiral: *gyroplane.* **3.** Gyroscope: *gyrostabilizer.* [Lat. *guro-,* circle < Gk. *guro-* < *guros.*]

gy·ro·com·pass (jī′rō-kŭm′pəs, -kŏm′-) *n.* A navigational device in which the interaction of a gyroscope's angular momentum with the force produced by the earth's rotation is used to maintain a north-south orientation of the gyroscopic spin axis, thereby providing a stable directional reference.

gy·ro·cop·ter (jī′rō-kŏp′tər) *n.* A rotary-wing aircraft that is driven forward by a conventional propeller. [GYRO- + (HELI)COPTER.]

gy·ro·mag·net·ic (jī′rō-măg-nĕt′ĭk) *adj.* Of, pertaining to, or resulting from the magnetic properties of a spinning, electrically charged particle.

gyromagnetic ratio *n.* The ratio of the magnetic moment to the intrinsic angular momentum of a spinning particle.

gyro pilot *n.* An automatic pilot incorporating a gyroscope to initiate corrections to aircraft control surfaces and thus maintain a preset course and altitude.

gy·ro·plane (jī′rə-plăn′) *n.* An aircraft such as a helicopter or autogyro that is equipped with wings that rotate about an approximately vertical axis.

gy·ro·scope (jī′rə-skōp′) *n.* **1.** A device consisting essentially of a spinning mass, typically a disk or wheel, the spin axis of which turns between two low-friction supports and maintains its angular orientation with respect to inertial coordinates when not subjected to external torques. **2.** A spinning mass. **—gy′ro·scop′ic** (-skŏp′ĭk) *adj.* **—gy′ro·scop′i·cal·ly** *adv.*

gy·ro·sta·bi·liz·er (jī′rō-stā′bə-lī′zər) *n.* A device having a heavy gyroscope whose axis spins in a vertical plane to reduce the side-to-side rolling of a ship or airplane.

gy·ro·stat (jī′rə-stăt′) *n.* A gyrostabilizer. **—gy′ro·stat′ic** *adj.* **—gy′ro·stat′i·cal·ly** *adv.*

gy·rus (jī′rəs) *n., pl.* **-ri** (-rī′). Any of the prominent, rounded, elevated convolutions at the surfaces of the cerebral hemispheres. [Lat., circle < Gk. *guros.*]

gyve (jīv) *Archaic. n.* A shackle or fetter, esp. for the leg. *—tr.v.* **gyved, gyv·ing, gyves.** To shackle or fetter. [ME *give.*]

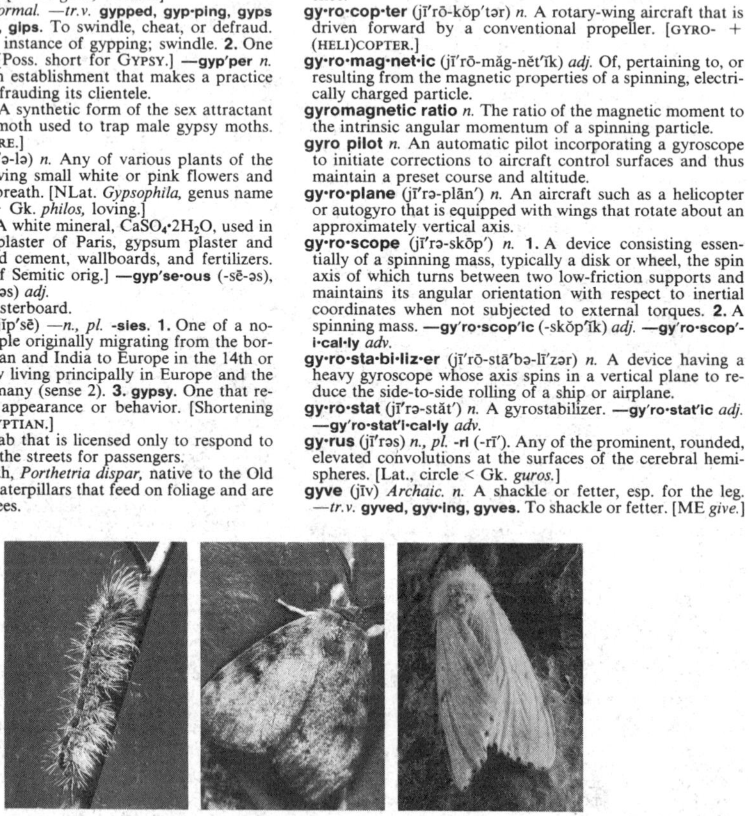

gypsy moth
Left: Larva
Center: Adult male
Right: Adult female

H

Around 1000 B.C. the Phoenicians and other Semitic peoples began to use graphic signs to represent individual speech sounds instead of syllables or words. They used a symbol in the forms (1,2) to represent a laryngeal consonant that is not found in English or any other Indo-European language and called it *hēth.* The Greeks, adapting the Phoenician alphabet, varied the shape of *hēth* (3,4) and changed its name to *ēta.* They first used it to represent the sound of the aspirate "h" but later to represent the vowel "ē." The Romans borrowed the alphabet from the Greeks via the Etruscans and adapted it for monumental inscriptions. Monumental script (7) is the prototype of modern capital letters (10,11). Medieval scribes adapted the Roman capitals to being quickly written on paper, parchment, and vellum. These uncial and cursive minuscules (8,9) are the prototypes of modern lower-case letters, both written and printed (13,12).

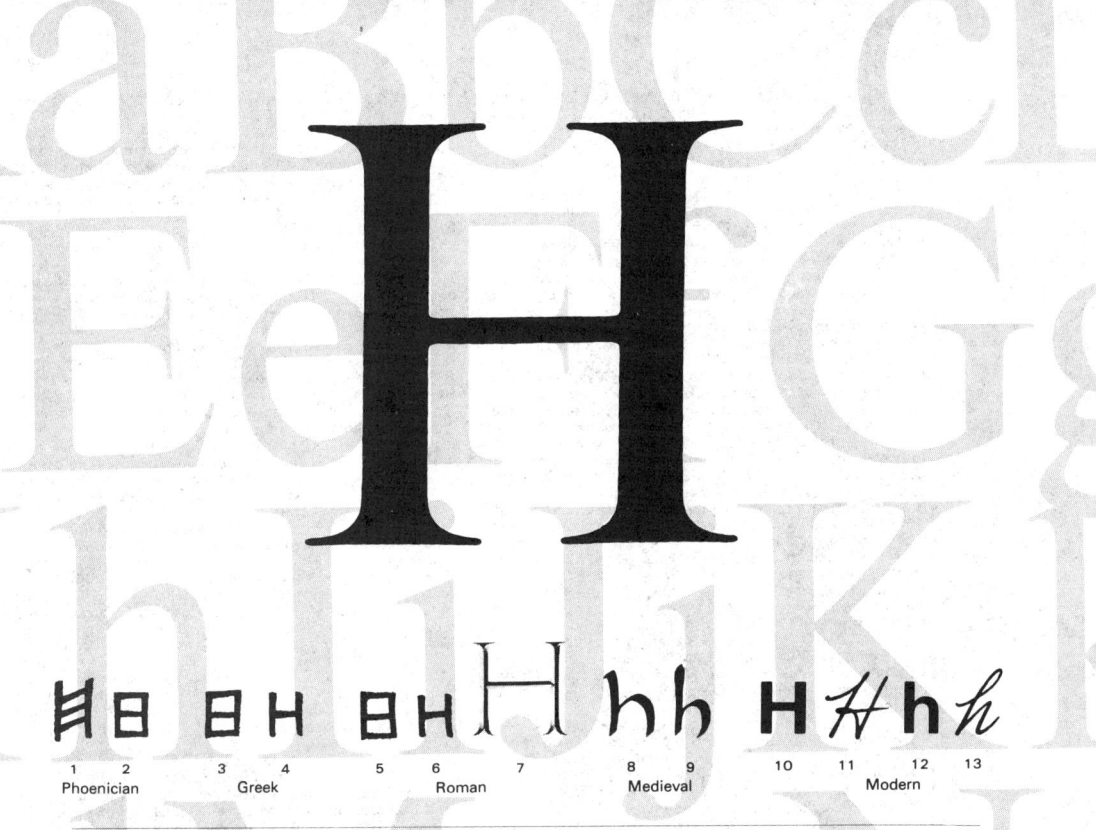

h

h or **H** (āch) *n., pl.* **h's** or **H's.** **1.** The eighth letter of the modern English alphabet. **2.** Any of the speech sounds represented by the letter *h.* **3.** The eighth in a series.

H The symbol for the element hydrogen.

ha also **hah** (hä) *interj.* Used to express surprise, wonder, triumph, puzzlement, or pique.

Ha·bak·kuk (hăb'ə-kŭk', hə-băk'ək) *n.* **1.** A Hebrew prophet of the late 7th century B.C. **2.** See table at **Bible.** [Heb. *Ḥăbhaqqūq,* prob. < *ḥābhaq,* he embraced.]

ha·ba·ne·ra (hä'bə-nâr'ə, ä'bə-) *n.* **1.** A slow Cuban dance. **2.** The music for a habanera, in duple time, with a repetitive rhythmic pattern of a dotted eighth and sixteenth note pair followed by a pair of eighth notes. [Sp. *(danza) habanera,* Havanan (dance) < *la Habana,* Havana, Cuba.]

hab·da·lah also **Hab·da·lah** (häv'dä-lä') *n.* A Jewish religious ceremony observed at the close of a Sabbath or holy day. [Heb. *habdālāh,* separation.]

ha·be·as corpus (hā'bē-əs) *n. Law.* One of a variety of writs that may be issued to bring a party before a court or judge, having as its function the release of a party from unlawful restraint. [ME < Med. Lat., you should have the body (from the first words of the writ).]

hab·er·dash·er (hăb'ər-dăsh'ər) *n.* **1.** A dealer in men's furnishings. **2.** *Chiefly Brit.* A dealer in sewing notions and small wares. [ME < AN *haberdassher.*]

hab·er·dash·er·y (hăb'ər-dăsh'ə-rē) *n., pl.* **-ies.** **1.** The goods and wares sold by a haberdasher. **2.** A haberdasher's shop.

hab·er·geon (hăb'ər-jən) *n.* **1.** A short, sleeveless coat of mail. **2.** A hauberk. [ME < OFr. *hauberjon* < *hauberc,* hauberk. —see HAUBERK.]

hab·ile (hăb'ĭl) *adj.* Generally adroit or handy. [Fr. < Lat. *habilis* < *habēre,* to handle.]

ha·bil·i·ment (hə-bĭl'ə-mənt) *n.* **1.** Often **habiliments. a.** The dress or garb associated with an office or occasion. **b.** Clothes. **2. habiliments.** Characteristic equipment or furnishings; trappings: *surrounded by the habiliments of the theater.* [ME *habylement* < OFr. *habillement* < *habiller,* to clothe < *habile,* habile.]

ha·bil·i·tate (hə-bĭl'ĭ-tāt') *v.* **-tat·ed, -tat·ing, -tates.** —*tr.* **1.** To clothe. **2.** To fit out or equip (a mine) for operation. **3.** *Obs.* To impart an ability or capacity to; qualify. —*intr.* To qualify oneself for a post or office. [LLat. *habilitare, habilitat-,* to enable < Lat. *habilitas,* ability < *habilis,* able < *habēre,* to handle.] **—ha·bil'i·ta'tion** *n.*

hab·it (hăb'ĭt) *n.* **1. a.** A constant, often unconscious inclination to perform an act, acquired through its frequent repetition. **b.** An established disposition of the mind or character. **2.** Customary manner or practice: *a man of ascetic habits.* **3.** An addiction. **4.** Physical constitution. **5.** Characteristic appearance, form, or manner of growth, esp. of a plant. **6. a.** A distinctive dress or costume, esp. of a religious order. **b.** A riding habit. —*tr.v.* **-it·ed, -it·ing, -its.** To clothe; dress. [ME, clothing < OFr., custom < Lat. *habitus,* condition < p.part. of *habēre,* to have.]

Synonyms: *habit, practice, custom, usage, use, wont, habitude, fashion.* These nouns refer to patterns of behavior set by continual repetition. *Habit* applies to any activity so well established that it occurs without thought on the part of an individual. *Practice* denotes any chosen pattern of individual or group behavior. *Custom* is either individual or group behavior, especially as established by long practice and accepted conventions. *Usage* refers to customary practice that has become an accepted standard for a group, and thus regulates individual behavior. *Use* and *wont* are terms for customary and distinctive practice of an individual or a group. *Habitude* refers to an individual's habitual inclination to follow a set course; unlike *habit,* it applies to a disposition to behave in a certain way, rather than to a specific act. *Fashion* implies behavior based on prevailing customs of a group or, in a contrasting sense, on individual tendencies: *in his own characteristic fashion.*

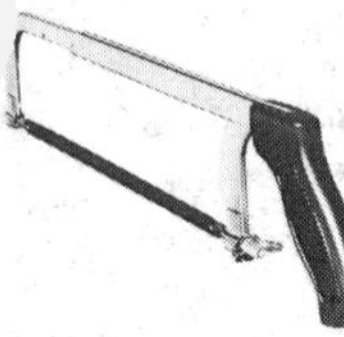

hacksaw

hab·it·a·ble (hăb'ĭ-tə-bəl) *adj.* Suitable to live in; inhabitable. [ME < OFr. < Lat. *habitabilis* < *habitare,* to dwell, freq. of *habēre,* to have.] **—hab'it·a·bil'i·ty, hab'it·a·ble·ness** *n.* **—hab'it·a·bly** *adv.*

hab·i·tant (hăb'ĭ-tənt) *n.* **1.** An inhabitant. **2.** Also **ha·bi·tan** (ă'bē-täɴ'). An inhabitant of French descent in Canada or Louisiana belonging to the small farmer class. [OFr. < pr.part. of *habiter,* to dwell < Lat. *habitare.* —see HABITABLE.]

hab·i·tat (hăb'ĭ-tăt') *n.* **1.** The area or type of environment in which an organism or biological population normally lives or occurs. **2.** The place where a person or thing is most likely to be found. [Lat., it dwells < *habitare,* to dwell. —see HABITABLE.]

hab·i·ta·tion (hăb'ĭ-tā'shən) *n.* **1.** The act of inhabiting. **2.** The state of being inhabited. **3. a.** Natural environment or locality. **b.** Place of abode; residence. [ME *habitacioun* < Lat. *habitatio* < *habitatus,* p.part. of *habitare,* to dwell. —see HABITABLE.]

hab·it-form·ing (hăb'ĭt-fôr'mĭng) *adj.* **1.** Leading to physiological addiction: *a habit-forming drug.* **2.** Tending to become habitual.

ha·bit·u·al (hə-bĭch'o͞o-əl) *adj.* **1.** Of the nature of a habit. **2.** Behaving or performing in a certain manner by habit; inveterate: *a habitual smoker.* **3.** Established by long use; usual: *his habitual place.* **—ha·bit'u·al·ly** *adv.* **—ha·bit'u·al·ness** *n.*

ha·bit·u·ate (hə-bĭch'o͞o-āt') *v.* **-at·ed, -at·ing, -ates.** —*tr.* To accustom by frequent repetition or prolonged exposure. —*intr.* To develop a tolerance or psychological dependence through continued use. [LLat. *habituare, habituat-,* to bring into a condition < Lat. *habitus,* condition. —see HABIT.] **—ha·bit'u·a'tion** *n.*

hab·i·tude (hăb'ĭ-to͞od', -tyo͞od') *n.* A customary behavior or manner. [ME < Lat. *habitudo,* condition < *habitus.* —see HABIT.]

ha·bit·u·é (hə-bĭch'o͞o-ā') *n.* A frequenter of a particular place or kind of place, esp. a place of entertainment. [Fr. < p.part. of *habituer,* to frequent < LLat. *habituare,* to be in a condition. —see HABITUATE.]

hab·i·tus (hăb'ĭ-təs) *n., pl.* **habitus.** Physical and constitutional characteristics, esp. as related to susceptibility to a disease. [Lat., condition. —see HABIT.]

ha·ček (hä'chĕk') *n.* A diacritical mark (ˇ) that resembles an inverted circumflex and is used over certain letters, as *č,* to indicate quality of pronunciation. [Czech *háček.*]

ha·chure (hă-sho͝or', hăsh'o͝or) *n.* One of the short lines used to shade or to indicate slopes on maps and also their degree and direction. —*tr.v.* (hă-sho͝or') **-chured, -chur·ing, -chures.** To make hatching on (a map). [Fr. < *hacher,* to cross-hatch. —see HASH[1].]

ha·ci·en·da (hä'sē-ĕn'də) *n.* **1.** In Spanish-speaking countries, a large estate or a plantation. **2.** The house of the owner of the hacienda. [Sp. < Lat. *facienda,* things to be done, neuter pl. gerund. of *facere,* to do.]

hack[1] (hăk) *v.* **hacked, hack·ing, hacks.** —*tr.* **1.** To cut or chop with repeated and irregular blows. **2.** To break up the surface of (soil). **3.** To cut or mutilate as if by hacking: *hacked millions off the budget.* **4.** *Informal.* To cope with successfully; manage: *couldn't hack a second job.* —*intr.* **1.** To chop or cut by hacking. **2.** To cough roughly or harshly. —*n.* **1.** A rough, irregular cut made by hacking. **2.** A tool, such as a hoe, used for hacking. **3.** A blow made by hacking. **4.** A rough, dry cough. [ME *hakken* < OE *haccian.*] **—hack'er** *n.*

hack[2] (hăk) *n.* **1.** A horse used for riding or driving; hackney. **2.** A worn-out horse for hire; jade. **3. a.** One who undertakes unpleasant or distasteful tasks for money or reward; hireling. **b.** A writer hired to produce routine or commercial writing. **4.** A carriage or hackney for hire. **5.** *Informal.* **a.** A taxicab. **b.** The driver of a taxicab. —*v.* **hacked, hack·ing, hacks.** —*tr.* **1.** To let out (a horse) for hire. **2.** To make banal or hackneyed with indiscriminate use. —*intr.* **1.** *Informal.* To work as the driver of a taxicab. **2.** *Informal.* To work for hire as a writer. **3.** To ride on horseback at an ordinary pace. —*adj.* **1.** By, characteristic of, or designating a hack: *hack journalism.* **2.** Hackneyed; banal. [Short for HACKNEY.]

hack·a·more (hăk'ə-môr', -mōr') *n.* A rope or rawhide halter with a wide band that can be lowered over a horse's eyes, used in breaking horses to a bridle. [Alteration of Sp. *jaquima,* halter < OSp. *xaquima* < Ar. *shakīmah,* bit of a bridle.]

hack·ber·ry (hăk'bĕr'ē) *n.* **1.** Any of various trees or shrubs of the genus *Celtis,* having inconspicuous flowers and berrylike, often edible fruit. **2.** The fruit of a hackberry. **3.** The soft, yellowish wood of a hackberry. [Alteration of obs. *hagberry,* of Scandinavian orig.]

hack·but (hăk'bŭt') also **hag·but** (hăg'-) *n.* A harquebus. [OFr. *haquebute* < MLG *hakebusse.* —see HARQUEBUS.] **—hack'but·eer'** (-bə-tîr'), **hack'but'ter** *n.*

hack·ie (hăk'ē) *n. Slang.* A taxicab driver.

hack·le[1] (hăk'əl) *n.* **1.** One of the long, slender, often glossy feathers on the neck of a bird, esp. a male domestic fowl. **2. hackles.** The erectile hairs at the back of the neck, esp. of a dog or similar animal. **3.** A tuft of cock feathers trimming an artificial fishing fly. —*tr.v.* **-led, -ling, -les.** To trim (a fly) with a hackle. ***—idiom.* get one's hackles up.** To be ready to fight. [ME *hakell,* of OE orig.]

hack·le[2] (hăk'əl) *v.* **-led, -ling, -les.** —*tr.* To chop roughly; mangle by hacking. —*intr.* To hack. [Freq. of HACK[1].]

hack·ly (hăk'lē) *adj.* Nicked or notched; jagged. [< HACKLE[2].]

hack·man (hăk'mən) *n.* The driver of a hack or hired carriage.

hack·ma·tack (hăk'mə-tăk') *n.* The tamarack. [Of Algonquian orig.]

hack·ney (hăk'nē) *n., pl.* **-neys.** **1.** Often **Hackney.** A horse of a breed developed in England, having a gait characterized by pronounced flexion of the knee. **2.** A horse suited for routine riding or driving. **3.** A coach or carriage for hire. —*tr.v.* **-neyed, -ney·ing, -neys.** **1.** To cause to become banal and trite through overuse. **2.** To hire out; let. —*adj.* **1.** Banal; trite. **2.** Hired. [ME *hakenei,* prob. after *Hakenei,* Hackney, a borough in England where such horses were raised.]

hack·neyed (hăk'nēd) *adj.* Overused and thus cheapened; trite.

hack·saw (hăk'sô') *n.* A saw consisting of a tough, fine-toothed blade stretched taut in a frame, used for cutting metal.

hack·work (hăk'wûrk') *n.* Commissioned work, as writing,

done usually by formula and in conformance with commercial standards.
had (hăd) *v.* Past tense and past participle of **have.**
ha·dal (hād′l) *adj.* Of or relating to the ocean depths below 6,000 meters. [Fr. < *Hadès,* Hades.]
had·dock (hăd′ək) *n., pl.* **haddock** or **-docks.** A food fish, *Melanogrammus aeglefinus,* of northern Atlantic waters, related to and resembling the cod. [ME *haddok.*]
hade (hād) *n.* The angle of inclination from the vertical of a vein, fault, or lode. [Orig. unknown.]
Ha·des (hā′dēz) *n. Gk. Myth.* **1.** The god of the netherworld and dispenser of earthly riches. **2.** The netherworld kingdom of Hades, the abode of the shades of the dead. **3.** Also **hades.** Hell. [Gk. *Haidēs.*]
hadj (hăj) *n.* Variant of **haj.**
hadj·i (hăj′ē) *n.* Variant of **haji.**
had·n't (hăd′nt). Had not.
had·ron (hăd′rŏn′) *n.* Any of a class of elementary particles that take part in the strong interaction. **—had·ron′ic** *adj.* [Gk. *hadros,* thick + -ON[1].]
hadst (hădst) *v. Archaic.* Second person singular past tense of **have.**
hae (hā, hă) *tr.v.* **haed, haen** (hān, hăn), **hae·ing, haes.** *Scot.* To have.
-haemia *suff.* Variant of **-emia.**
haet (hāt) *n. Scot.* A minute amount; jot. [Sc., short for *hae it,* take it.]
ha·fiz (hä′fĭz) *n.* **1.** A Moslem who has memorized the Koran. **2.** A title of respect used with the name of a Moslem who has memorized the Koran. [Pers. < Ar. *hāfiz* < *hafiza,* he memorized.]
haf·ni·um (hăf′nē-əm) *n. Symbol* **Hf** A brilliant, silvery, metallic element separated from ores of zirconium and used in nuclear reactor control rods, as a getter for oxygen and nitrogen, and in the manufacture of tungsten filaments. Atomic number 72; atomic weight 178.49; melting point 2,150°C; boiling point 5,400°C; specific gravity 13.29; valence 4. [NLat. < *Hafnia,* Lat. name for Copenhagen, Denmark.]
haft (hăft) *n.* A handle or hilt, esp. a handle of a tool or weapon. *—tr.v.* **haft·ed, haft·ing, hafts.** To fit into or equip with a hilt or handle. [ME < OE *hæft.*]
haf·ta·rah or **haf·to·rah** (häf′tə-rä′, häf-tôr′ə) *n.* Variants of **haphtarah.**
hag[1] (hăg) *n.* **1.** An ugly, frightful old woman. **2.** A witch; sorceress. **3.** *Obs.* A female demon. [ME *hagge,* perh. short for OE *hægtesse,* witch.]
hag[2] (hăg) *n. Chiefly Brit.* **1.** A boggy area; quagmire. **2.** A spot in boggy land that is softer or more solid than the surrounding area. **3.** A cutting in a peat bog. [Of Scandinavian orig.]
Ha·gar (hā′gər) *n.* In the Old Testament, the concubine of Abraham and mother of his bastard son Ishmael who was turned out of Abraham's household by Sarah because of her jealousy for her own son Isaac. [Heb. *Hāghār.*]
hag·born (hăg′bôrn′) *adj.* Born of a witch or hag.
hag·but (hăg′bŭt′) *n.* Variant of **hackbut.**
hag·fish (hăg′fĭsh′) *n., pl.* **hagfish** or **-fish·es.** Any of various primitive, eel-shaped marine fishes of the family Myxinidae, having a jawless sucking mouth with rasping teeth with which they bore into and feed on other fishes. [HAG[1] + FISH.]
Hag·ga·dah also **Hag·ga·da** (hə-gä′də, -gô′də) *n., pl.* **-doth** (-dōt′, -dōth′). **1.** Traditional Jewish literature, esp. the nonlegal part of the Talmud. **2.** The book containing the story of the Exodus and the ritual of the Seder, read at the Passover Seder. [Heb. *haggādāh* < *higgidh,* he narrated.] **—hag·gad′ic** (-găd′ĭk, -gä′dĭk, -gô′dĭk) *adj.*
hag·ga·dist (hə-gä′dĭst, -gô′-) *n.* **1.** A haggadic writer. **2.** A student of haggadic literature. **—hag′ga·dis′tic** (hăg′ə-dĭs′tĭk) *adj.*
Hag·ga·i (hăg′ē-ī′, hăg′ī′) *n.* **1.** A Hebrew prophet of the 6th century B.C. **2.** See table at **Bible.** [Heb.]
hag·gard (hăg′ərd) *adj.* **1. a.** Appearing worn and exhausted; gaunt. **b.** Wild and unruly; uncontrolled. **2.** Wild and intractable. Used of a hawk in falconry. *—n.* An adult hawk captured for training. [OFr. *hagard,* wild.] **—hag′gard·ly** *adv.* **—hag′gard·ness** *n.*

Synonyms: *haggard, wasted, worn, careworn.* These adjectives mean showing the effects of anxiety, disease, hunger, or fatigue. *Haggard* refers particularly to facial appearance and implies thinness, tiredness, and often the expression of one seemingly distraught or harried. *Wasted* stresses emaciation, or marked loss of flesh, with consequent frailness or enfeeblement; the term is most often associated with illness or extreme physical hardship. *Worn* can refer to emaciation or to the effects of overwork or worry. *Careworn* is applicable to one whose physical appearance reveals the effects of worry, anxiety, or burdensome responsibility.

hag·gis (hăg′ĭs) *n.* A Scottish dish consisting of a mixture of the minced heart, lungs, and liver of a sheep or calf mixed with suet, onions, oatmeal, and seasonings, and boiled in the stomach of the animal. [ME *hagese.*]
hag·gish (hăg′ĭsh) *adj.* Of or characteristic of a hag. **—hag′gish·ly** *adv.* **—hag′gish·ness** *n.*
hag·gle (hăg′əl) *v.* **-gled, -gling, -gles.** *—intr.* **1.** To bargain, as over the price of something; dicker. **2.** To argue in an attempt to come to terms. *—tr.* **1.** To cut in a crude, unskillful manner; hack. **2.** *Archaic.* To harass or worry by wrangling. *—n.* An instance of haggling. [Freq. of dial. *hag,* to cut < ME *haggen* < ON *höggva.*] **—hag′gler** *n.*
hagi- *pref.* Variant of **hagio-.**
hag·i·ar·chy (hăg′ē-är′kē, hā′jē-) also **hag·i·oc·ra·cy** (hăg′ē-ŏk′rə-sē, hā′jē-) *n., pl.* **-chies** also **-cies.** Government by holy men, such as priests or saints.
hagio- or **hagi-** *pref.* **1.** Saint: *hagiography.* **2.** Holy: *hagioscope.* [LLat. < Gk. < *hagios,* holy.]
hag·i·oc·ra·cy (hăg′ē-ŏk′rə-sē, hā′jē-) *n.* Variant of **hagiarchy.**
Hag·i·og·ra·pha (hăg′ē-ŏg′rə-fə, hā′jē-) *pl.n. (used with a sing. or pl. verb).* The third of the three ancient Jewish divisions of the Old Testament, containing those books not in the Law (Torah) or the Prophets, and comprising usually the Psalms, Proverbs, Job, the Song of Solomon, Ruth, Lamentations, Ecclesiastes, Esther, Daniel, Ezra, Nehemiah, and Chronicles. See table at **Bible.** [LLat. < Gk. : *hagio-,* sacred + *-graphos,* written.]
hag·i·og·ra·phy (hăg′ē-ŏg′rə-fē, hā′jē-) *n., pl.* **-phies. 1.** Biography of saints. **2.** A worshipful or idealizing biography. **—hag′i·og′raph·er** *n.* **—hag′i·o·graph′ic** (-ə-grăf′ĭk), **hag′i·o·graph′i·cal** *adj.*
hag·i·ol·o·gy (hăg′ē-ŏl′ə-jē, hā′jē-) *n., pl.* **-gies. 1.** Literature dealing with the lives of saints. **2.** A collection of sacred writings. **3.** An authoritative list of saints. **—hag′i·o·log′ic** (-ə-lŏj′ĭk), **hag′i·o·log′i·cal** *adj.* **—hag′i·ol′o·gist** *n.*
hag·i·o·scope (hăg′ē-ə-skōp′, hā′jē-) *n.* A small opening provided in an interior wall of a church to enable those in the transept to have a view of the main altar. **—hag′i·o·scop′ic** (-skŏp′ĭk) *adj.*
hag·rid·den (hăg′rĭd′n) *adj.* **1.** Harassed by or as if by a witch. **2.** Tormented or harassed, as by unreasoning fears.
hah (hä) *interj.* Variant of **ha.**
ha-ha[1] (hä′hä′) *n.* A sound made in imitation of laughter.
ha-ha[2] (hä′hä′) also **haw-haw** (hô′hô′) *n.* A moat, walled ditch, or hedge sunk in the ground to serve as a fence without impairing the view or scenic appeal. [Fr.]
Hai·da (hī′də) *n., pl.* **Haida** or **-das. 1.** Any of the North American Indian tribes inhabiting the Queen Charlotte Islands, British Columbia, and Prince of Wales Island, Alaska. **2.** A member of the Haida. **3. a.** A language family of the Na-dene phylum. **b.** The language of the Haida and the only surviving language of the Haida language family. **—Hai′dan** *adj.*
haik (hīk, hāk) *n.* A large piece of cotton, silk, or wool cloth worn as an outer garment by Arabs. [Ar. *ḥā'ik* < *ḥāka,* he wove.]

haik

hai·ku (hī′ko͞o) *n., pl.* **haiku.** An unrhymed Japanese lyric poem having a fixed three-line form consisting of 5, 7, and 5 syllables respectively. [J. : *hai,* amusement (< Chin. *pai*[2], parallel) + *ku,* sentence (< Chin. *ju*[4]).]
hail[1] (hāl) *n.* **1.** Precipitation in the form of pellets of ice and hard snow. **2.** Something that falls with the force and quantity of a shower of hail: *a hail of criticism.* *—v.* **hailed, hail·ing, hails.** *—intr.* **1.** To precipitate. **2.** To fall like hail. *—tr.* To pour down or forth: *hail oaths at someone.* [ME < OE *hægel.*]
hail[2] (hāl) *v.* **hailed, hail·ing, hails.** *—tr.* **1. a.** To salute or greet. **b.** To greet or acclaim enthusiastically. **2.** To call out to in order to catch the attention of: *hail a cab.* *—intr.* To signal or call to a passing ship as a greeting or an identification of oneself. ***—phrasal verb.*** **hail from.** To come or originate from. *—n.* **1.** The act of hailing. **2.** A shout made to greet or catch the attention of someone. **3.** Hailing distance: *told me to stay within hail.* *—interj.* Used to express a greeting or tribute. [ME *heilen* < *(wæs) hæil,* (be) healthy. —see WASSAIL.]
hail·er (hā′lər) *n.* **1.** One that hails. **2.** A bullhorn.
hail-fel·low (hāl′fĕl′ō) also **hail-fel·low-well-met** (hāl′fĕl′ō-wĕl′mĕt′) *adj.* Heartily friendly and congenial. [From the obs. greeting *hail, fellow!*] **—hail′-fel·low** *n.*

Usage: The first word of the phrase *hail-fellow-well-met* is often misspelled *hale* in the mistaken belief that it means "sound," as in *hale and hearty.* It was originally part of a greeting, *Hail, fellow!*

Hail Mary *n.* A Roman Catholic prayer based on the greetings of Gabriel and Saint Elizabeth to the Virgin Mary.
hail·stone (hāl′stōn′) *n.* A hard pellet of snow and ice.
hail·storm (hāl′stôrm′) *n.* A storm with hail.
hair (hâr) *n.* **1. a.** One of the cylindrical, often pigmented filaments characteristically growing from the epidermis of a mammal. **b.** A growth of such filaments, as that forming the coat of an animal or covering the scalp of a human being. **2.** A filamentous projection or bristle similar to a hair, such as a seta of an arthropod or an epidermal process of a plant. **3.** Fabric made from the hair of certain animals: *a coat of camel's hair.* **4.** A minute distance or narrow margin: *win by a hair.* **5.** A precise or exact degree: *calibrated to a hair.* ***—idioms.*** **let one's hair down.** To drop one's reserve or inhibitions. **split hairs.** To make petty and fine distinctions. [ME *her* < OE *hær.*]

hair·ball (hâr′bôl′) *n.* A small mass of hair swallowed by an animal, often causing indigestion or convulsions.
hair·breadth (hâr′brĕdth′) *adj.* Extremely close: *a hairbreadth escape.* —*n.* Variant of **hairsbreadth.**
hair·brush (hâr′brŭsh′) *n.* A brush for the hair.
hair·cloth (hâr′klôth′, -klŏth′) *n.* A wiry fabric woven esp. from horsehair or camel's hair, used for upholstering and for stiffening garments.
hair·cut (hâr′kŭt′) *n.* **1.** An act or instance of cutting the hair. **2.** The style in which hair is cut.
hair·do (hâr′dōō′) *n., pl.* **-dos.** The style in which hair is arranged.
hair·dress·er (hâr′drĕs′ər) *n.* A person who cuts or arranges hair.
hair·dress·ing (hâr′drĕs′ĭng) *n.* **1.** The occupation of a hairdresser. **2.** The act of dressing or arranging the hair. **3.** A cosmetic or medicinal preparation for dressing the hair.
haired (hârd) *adj.* Having a specified kind of hair: *a long-haired cat.*
hair·less (hâr′lĭs) *adj.* Having little or no hair.
hair·line (hâr′līn′) *n.* **1.** The outline of the growth of hair on the head, esp. across the front. **2.** A very slender line. **3.** *Printing.* **a.** A very fine line on a typeface. **b.** A style of type using such lines. **4. a.** A textile design having thin, threadlike stripes. **b.** A fabric, usually a worsted, with such stripes.
hair piece *n.* A covering or bunch of human or artificial hair used to cover baldness or give shape to a coiffure.
hair·pin (hâr′pĭn′) *n.* **1.** A thin, cylindrical strip of metal or other material bent in a long U shape, used by women to secure a hairdo or a headdress. **2.** Something shaped like a hairpin, esp. a sharp turn in a road.
hair-rais·er (hâr′rā′zər) *n.* Something that causes wild excitement, terror, or thrills.
hair-rais·ing (hâr′rā′zĭng) *adj.* Causing excitement, terror, or thrills.
hairs·breadth or **hair's-breadth** (hârz′brĕdth′) also **hair·breadth** (hâr′brĕdth′) *n.* A small space, distance, or margin: *win by a hairsbreadth.*
hair seal *n.* Any of various seals of the family Phocidae, having a stiff, hairlike coat in the adult and ears visible only as small indentations.
hair shirt *n.* A coarse haircloth garment worn next to the skin by religious ascetics as penance.
hair space *n. Printing.* The narrowest of the metal spaces used for separating words or letters.
hair·split·ting (hâr′splĭt′ĭng) *n.* The making of unreasonably fine distinctions. **—hair′split′ter** *n.*
hair spray *n.* A commercial product sprayed on the hair and esp. on a hairdo to keep it in place.
hair·spring (hâr′sprĭng′) *n.* A fine coiled spring that regulates the movement of the balance wheel in a watch or clock.
hair·streak (hâr′strēk′) *n.* Any of numerous butterflies of the subfamily Theclinae, having transverse streaks on the underwings and fine, hairlike projections on the hind wings.
hair stroke *n.* A very fine line in writing or printing.
hair style *n.* The design of a coiffure. **—hair stylist** *n.*
hair trigger *n.* A gun trigger adjusted to respond to a very slight pressure.
hair-trig·ger (hâr′trĭg′ər) *adj.* Responding to the slightest provocation: *a hair-trigger temper.*
hair·weav·ing (hâr′wē′vĭng) *n.* The process of interweaving a hair piece of human hair with a balding person's own hair. **—hair′weave′** *n.*
hair·worm (hâr′wûrm′) *n.* **1.** Any of various slender, parasitic nematode worms of the genus *Trichostrongylus,* that infest the stomach and small intestine of cattle, sheep, and related animals. **2.** A horsehair worm.
hair·y (hâr′ē) *adj.* **-i·er, -i·est. 1.** Covered with hair or hairlike projections. **2.** Of or like hair: *a hairy coat.* **3.** *Slang.* Fraught with difficulties; hazardous: *a hairy escape; a hairy problem.* **—hair′i·ness** *n.*
Hai·tian (hā′shən, -tē-ən) *adj.* Of or pertaining to Haiti, its people, or its dialect. —*n.* **1.** A native or inhabitant of Haiti. **2.** Haitian Creole.
Haitian Creole *n.* A language spoken by the majority of Haitians that is based on French and various African languages.
haj or **hajj** also **hadj** (hăj) *n.* A pilgrimage to Mecca made during Ramadan as an objective of the religious life of a Moslem. [Ar. *ḥajj* < *ḥajja,* he went on a pilgrimage.]
haj·i or **haj·ji** also **hadj·i** (hăj′ē) *n.* One who has made a pilgrimage to Mecca during Ramadan. Often used as a title of address. [Ar. *ḥājjī* < *ḥajj,* pilgrimage. —see HAJ.]
hake (hāk) *n., pl.* **hake** or **hakes.** Any of various marine food fishes of the genera *Merluccius* and *Urophycis,* related to and resembling the cod. [ME, poss. < OE *haca,* hook (from the shape of its lower jaw).]
Ha·ken·kreuz (hä′kən-kroits′) *n.* The swastika used as a symbol of Nazi Germany or of anti-Semitism. [G. : *Haken,* hook + *Kreuz,* cross.]
ha·kim[1] (hä′kēm) *n.* A Moslem physician. [Ar. *ḥakīm* < *ḥakama,* he was wise.]
ha·kim[2] (hä′kĭm) *n. pl.* **hakim** or **-kims.** A Moslem ruler, provincial governor, or judge. [Ar. *ḥākim* < *ḥakama,* to exercise authority.]
hal– *pref.* Variant of **halo-.**
Ha·la·kah also **Hal·la·cha** (hä′lä-KHä′, hä-lä′KHə) *n. Judaism.* The legal part of Talmudic literature, an interpretation of the laws of the Scriptures. [Heb. *halākhāh,* tradition < *hālakh,* he went.] **—Ha·lak′ic** (hə-lăk′ĭk) *adj.*
ha·la·tion (hā-lā′shən) *n.* **1.** A blurring or spreading of light around bright areas on a photographic image. **2.** A ring of light appearing around a bright object on a television screen. [HAL(O) + -ATION.]
ha·la·vah (hä′lə-vä′) *n.* Variant of **halvah.**
hal·berd (hăl′bərd, hôl′-) also **hal·bert** (-bərt) *n.* A weapon of the 15th and 16th centuries having an axlike blade and a steel spike mounted on the end of a long shaft. [OFr. *hallebarde* < MHG *helmbarde* : *helm,* handle + *barte,* ax < OHG *barta.*] **—hal′ber·dier′** (-bər-dîr′) *n.*
hal·cy·on (hăl′sē-ən) *n.* **1.** A fabled bird, identified with the kingfisher, that was supposed to have had the power to calm the wind and the waves during the winter solstice while it nested on the sea. **2.** A kingfisher. —*adj.* **1.** Calm and peaceful; tranquil. **2.** Prosperous; golden: *halcyon years.* [ME *alcioun* < Lat. *alcyon* < Gk. *alkuōn,* a mythical bird.]
Hal·cy·o·ne (hăl-sī′ə-nē′) *n.* Variant of **Alcyone.**
hale[1] (hāl) *adj.* **hal·er, hal·est.** Sound in health; not infirm. [ME < OE *hāl.*] **—hale′ness** *n.*
hale[2] (hāl) *tr.v.* **haled, hal·ing, hales. 1.** To compel to go. **2.** *Archaic.* To pull, drag, draw, or hoist. [ME *halen* < OFr. *haler,* of Germanic orig.]
ha·ler (hä′lər, -lĕr′) *n., pl.* **-lers** or **-le·ru** (-lə-rōō′). See table at **currency.** [Czech < MHG *haller,* a coin < *Hall,* a town in Germany where it was once minted.]
half (hăf, häf) *n., pl.* **halves** (hăvz, hävz). **1. a.** One of two equal parts that together constitute a whole. **b.** A part of something approximately equal to the remainder. **2.** *Informal.* A fifty-cent piece. **3.** *Sports.* One of the two playing periods into which certain games are divided. **4.** *Chiefly Brit.* A school term; semester. **5.** Half an hour: *a half past one.* —*adj.* **1.** Being one of two equal parts. **2.** Being approximately a half. **3.** Partial or incomplete: *a half smile.* **4.** Having only one parent in common with another person. —*adv.* **1.** To the extent of exactly or nearly 50 per cent: *a half-empty tank.* **2.** Not completely or sufficiently; partly: *only half-prepared.* **—*idioms.* by half.** By a considerable extent. **by halves.** Reluctantly; unenthusiastically. **in half.** Into halves. **not the half of.** Only a fraction or a small part of. [ME < OE *healf.*]

Usage: The phrases *a half, half of,* and *half a* are all correct, though they may differ slightly in meaning. For example, *a half day* is used when *day* has the special sense "a working day," and the phrase then means "four hours." *Half of a day* and *half a day* are not restricted in this way and can mean either four or twelve hours. When the accompanying word is a pronoun, however, the phrase with *of* must be used: *half of them.* The phrase *a half a,* though frequently heard, is held by some to be unacceptable.

half-and-half (hăf′ənd-hăf′, häf′ənd-häf′) *adj.* Being half one thing and half another. —*adv.* In equal portions. —*n.* **1.** A mixture of two things in equal portions, esp. a mixture of equal parts of milk and cream. **2.** *Chiefly Brit.* A blend of malt liquors, esp. porter and ale.
half·back (hăf′băk′, häf′-) *n.* **1.** *Football.* One of the two players positioned near the flanks behind the line of scrimmage. **2.** One of several players in various sports stationed behind the forward line. **3.** The position played by a halfback.
half-baked (hăf′bākt′, häf′-) *adj.* **1.** Only partly baked. **2.** *Informal.* Not sufficiently thought out; ill-conceived: *a half-baked scheme.* **3.** *Informal.* Lacking good judgment or common sense: *a half-baked visionary.*
half binding *n.* A bookbinding in which the back and often the corners of the volume are bound in a material differing from the rest of the cover.
half blood also **half-blood** (hăf′blŭd′, häf′-) *n.* **1. a.** The relationship existing between persons having only one parent in common. **b.** A person existing in such a relationship. **2.** A half-breed. **3.** A half-blooded domestic animal.
half-blood·ed (hăf′blŭd′ĭd, häf′-) *adj.* **1.** Having only one parent in common. **2.** Having parents of different ethnic types. **3.** Having one parent of pedigreed stock and the other of unknown or mixed ancestry. Used of animals.
half boot *n.* A low boot extending just above the ankle.
half-bound (hăf′bound′, häf′-) *adj.* Having a half binding.
half-bred (hăf′brĕd′, häf′-) *adj.* Having only one parent that is purebred.
half-breed (hăf′brēd′, häf′-) *n. Offensive Slang.* A person having parents of different ethnic types. —*adj.* Half-blooded; hybrid.
half brother *n.* A brother related through one parent only.
half-caste (hăf′kăst′, häf′-) *n.* A person of mixed racial descent. —*adj.* Of mixed racial descent.
half cock *n.* The position of the hammer of a firearm when it is raised halfway and locked by a catch so that the trigger cannot be pulled.
half·cocked (hăf′kŏkt′, häf′-) *adj.* **1.** At the position of half cock. **2.** *Informal.* Inadequately prepared or conceived.

half-crown (hăf′kroun′, häf′-) *n.* A former British coin worth two shillings and sixpence.
half dime *n.* An obsolete five-cent silver coin minted in the United States between 1792 and 1873.
half dollar *n.* A U.S. silver coin worth 50 cents.
half eagle *n.* An obsolete U.S. gold coin worth five dollars, last issued in 1929.
half gainer *n.* A dive in which the diver springs from the board facing forward, rotates backward in the air in a half backward somersault, and enters the water headfirst, facing the board.
half·heart·ed (hăf′här′tĭd, häf′-) *adj.* Done with or possessing little interest, enthusiasm, or heart; uninspired: *made a halfhearted attempt at painting.* **—half′heart′ed·ly** *adv.* **—half′heart′ed·ness** *n.*
half hitch *n.* A hitch made by looping a rope or strap around an object, and then back around itself, bringing the end of the rope through the loop.
half-hour (hăf′our′, häf′-) *n.* **1.** A period of 30 minutes. **2.** The middle point of an hour. **—half′-hour′ly** *adj. & adv.*
half-in·te·gral (hăf′ĭn′tĭ-grəl, häf′-) *adj.* Having an integer as a numerator and 2 as a denominator. Used of a fraction.
half-length (hăf′lĕngkth, -lĕngth′, häf′-) *n.* A portrait that shows only the upper half and hands of a person. *—adj.* **1.** Of or denoting a half-length portrait. **2.** Of half the full length.
half-life (hăf′līf′, häf′-) *n.* **1.** *Physics.* The time required for half the nuclei in a sample of a specific isotopic species to undergo radioactive decay. **2.** *Biol.* **a.** The time required by living tissue, an organ, or an organism to eliminate by biological processes half the quantity of a substance taken in. **b.** The time required for the radioactivity of material taken in by a living organism to be reduced to half its initial value by a combination of biological elimination processes and radioactive decay.
half-light (hăf′līt′, häf′-) *n.* The soft, subdued light found at dusk or dawn or in dimly lit interiors.
half-line (hăf′līn′, häf′-) *n.* A straight line extending in just one direction from a given point.
half-mast (hăf′măst′, häf′-) *n.* The position about halfway up a mast or pole at which a flag is flown as a symbol of mourning for the dead or as a signal of distress. *—tr.v.* **-mast·ed, -mast·ing, -masts.** To place (a flag) at half-mast.
half-moon (hăf′mo͞on′, häf′-) *n.* **1.** The moon when only half its disk is illuminated. **2.** Something shaped like a crescent, as the lunula of the fingernail.
half nelson *n.* A wrestling hold in which one arm is passed under the opponent's arm from behind to the back of his neck.
half note *n. Mus.* A note having one half the value of a whole note.
half·pen·ny (hā′pə-nē, hāp′nē) *n.* **1.** *pl.* **half·pence** (hā′pəns) or **half·pen·nies.** A British coin worth one half of a penny. **2.** The sum of one half of a penny.
half pint *n. Slang.* A small person or animal.
half relief *n.* Sculptural relief composed of modeled forms that project approximately halfway from the background.
half sister *n.* A sister related through one parent only.
half-slip (hăf′slĭp′, häf′-) *n.* A woman's underskirt that extends from the waist to the hem of the outer garment.
half sole *n.* A shoe sole extending from the shank to the toe.
half-sole (hăf′sōl′, häf′-) *tr.v.* **-soled, -sol·ing, -soles.** To fit or repair with a half sole.
half sovereign *n.* An obsolete gold coin of Britain worth ten shillings.
half-staff (hăf′stăf′, häf′-) *n.* Half-mast.
half step *n.* **1.** A semitone. **2.** A marching step of 15 inches at quick time and 18 at double time.
half-tim·bered (hăf′tĭm′bərd, häf′-) also **half-tim·ber** (-bər) *adj.* Having a wooden framework with plaster or masonry filling the spaces.
half time *n. Sports.* The intermission between halves in certain games.
half title *n.* The title of a book printed at the top of the first page of the text or on a full page preceding the main title page.
half·tone (hăf′tōn′, häf′-) *n.* **1.** A tone or value halfway between a highlight and a dark shadow. **2. a.** A picture in which the gradations of light are obtained by the relative darkness and density of tiny dots produced by photographing the subject through a fine screen. **b.** A picture made by such a process.
half tone *n.* A semitone.
half-track (hăf′trăk′, häf′-) *n.* A military motor vehicle, often lightly armored, with caterpillar treads in place of wheels. **—half′-track′, half′-tracked′** *adj.*
half-truth (hăf′tro͞oth′, häf′-) *n.* A statement, esp. one intended to deceive, that omits some of the facts necessary for a truthful description or account.
half volley *n. Sports.* A stroke in certain games, such as tennis, in which the ball is hit immediately after it bounces off the ground.
half·way (hăf′wā′, häf′-) *adj.* **1.** Midway between two points or conditions. **2.** Reaching or including only half or a portion; partial: *halfway measures.* **—half′way′** *adv.*
halfway house *n.* **1.** An inn or other stopping place that marks the midpoint of a journey. **2.** A rehabilitation center where people who have left an institution, such as a hospital or prison, are helped to readjust to the outside world.
half-wit (hăf′wĭt′, häf′-) *n.* **1.** A mentally deficient person. **2.** A stupid, foolish, or frivolous person. **—half′-wit′ted** *adj.* **—half′-wit′ted·ly** *adv.* **—half′-wit′ted·ness** *n.*
hal·i·but (hăl′ə-bət, hŏl′-) *n., pl.* **halibut** or **-buts.** Any of several large, edible flatfishes of the genus *Hippoglossus* and related genera, of northern Atlantic or Pacific waters. [ME : *hali,* holy (from its being eaten on holy days) + *butte,* flatfish < MDu.]

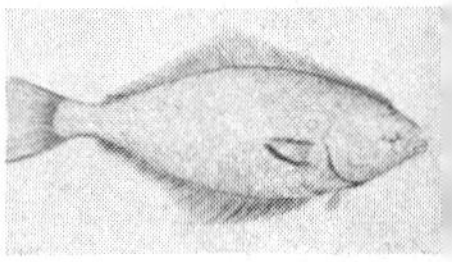

halibut

hal·ide (hăl′īd′, hā′līd′) *n.* A binary chemical compound of a halogen with a more electropositive element or group.
hal·i·dom (hăl′ĭ-dəm) *n. Obs.* **1.** Something considered holy. **2.** A sanctuary. [ME < OE *haligdom* : *halig,* holy + *-dom,* -dom.]
hal·ite (hăl′īt′, hā′līt′) *n.* Rock salt.
hal·i·to·sis (hăl′ĭ-tō′sĭs) *n.* A condition characterized by stale or foul-smelling breath. [Lat. *halitus,* breath (< *halare,* to breathe) + -OSIS.]
hall (hôl) *n.* **1.** A corridor or passageway in a building. **2.** A large entrance room or vestibule in a building; lobby. **3. a.** A building for public gatherings or entertainments. **b.** The large room in which such events are held. **4.** A building used for the meetings, entertainments, or living quarters of a fraternity or other social or religious organization. **5. a.** A building belonging to a school, college, or university that provides classroom, dormitory, or dining facilities. **b.** A large room in such a building. **c.** The group of students occupying such a building. **d.** *Chiefly Brit.* A meal served in such a building. **6.** The main house on a landed estate. **7. a.** The house or castle of a medieval king or nobleman. **b.** The large principal room in such a house or castle, used for dining, entertaining, and sleeping. [ME *halle* < OE *heall.*]
hal·lah (KHä′lə, hä′-) *n.* Variant of **challah.**
Hall effect *n.* The generation of an electric potential perpendicular to both an electric current flowing along a thin conducting material and an external magnetic field applied at right angles to the current upon application of the magnetic field. [After Edwin H. *Hall* (1855–1938).]
hal·lel (hä-lāl′) *n. Judaism.* A chant of praise consisting of Psalms 113 through 118, used during Passover and on certain other holidays. [Heb. *hallēl* < *hĕllēl,* he praised.]
hal·le·lu·jah (hăl′ə-lo͞o′yə) *interj.* Used to express praise or joy. *—n.* **1.** The exclamation of "hallelujah." **2.** A musical composition expressing praise and based on the word "hallelujah." [Heb. *hallelūyāh,* praise God : *hallelū,* pl. imper. of *hĕllēl,* he praised + *Yāh,* God.]
Hal·ley's comet (hăl′ēz) *n.* A comet with a period of approximately 76 years, the first for which a return was successfully predicted. It last appeared in 1910. [After Edmund *Halley* (1656–1742), from his prediction of its return after observing it in 1682.]
hal·liard (hăl′yərd) *n.* Variant of **halyard.**
hall·mark (hôl′märk′) *n.* **1.** A mark used in England to stamp gold and silver articles that meet established standards of purity. **2.** A mark indicating quality or excellence. **3.** A conspicuous feature or characteristic: *"The sense of guilt is the hallmark of civilized humanity"* (Theodor Reik). *—tr.v.* **-marked, -mark·ing, -marks.** To mark with a hallmark. [After Goldsmith's *Hall* in London, England, where gold and silver articles were appraised and stamped.]
hall of fame also **Hall of Fame** *n.* **1.** A building housing memorial items honoring illustrious persons. **2.** A group of persons judged outstanding in a sport, profession, or other category.
hal·loo (hə-lo͞o′) also **hal·loa** (hə-lō′) *—interj.* **1.** Used to gain someone's attention. **2.** Used to urge on hounds in a hunt. *—n.* A shout or call of "halloo." *—v.* **-looed, -loo·ing, -loos** also **-loaed, -loa·ing, -loas.** *—intr.* To shout "halloo." *—tr.* **1.** To urge on or pursue by calling "halloo" or shouting. **2.** To call out to. **3.** To shout or yell. [Alteration of obs. *holla,* stop! —see HELLO.]
hal·low (hăl′ō) *tr.v.* **-lowed, -low·ing, -lows. 1.** To make or set apart as holy. **2.** To respect or honor greatly; revere. [ME *halwen* < OE *hālgian.*]
hal·lowed (hăl′ōd) *adj.* **1.** Sanctified; consecrated. **2.** Highly venerated; sacrosanct.
Hal·low·een also **Hal·low·e'en** (hăl′ə-wēn′, hŏl′-) *n.* The eve of All Saints' Day, falling on October 31 and celebrated by children who beg treats or play pranks. [Short for *All Hallow Even.*]
Hal·low·mas also **Hal·low·mass** (hăl′ō-məs, -măs′) *n. Archaic.* The feast of All Saints' Day or Allhallowmas on November 1. [Short for ALLHALLOWMAS.]
Hall·statt (hôl′stăt′, häl′shtät′) *adj.* Of or pertaining to a dominant Iron Age culture of central and western Europe, probably chiefly Celtic, that flourished from the 9th century B.C. to the 5th. [After the type-site at *Hallstatt,* Austria.]
hal·lu·ces (hăl′yə-sēz′, hăl′ə-) *n.* Plural of **hallux.**
hal·lu·ci·nate (hə-lo͞o′sə-nāt′) *v.* **-nat·ed, -nat·ing, -nates.** *—intr.* To undergo hallucination. *—tr.* To cause to have hallucinations. [Lat. *hallucinari, hallucinat-,* to dream.]
hal·lu·ci·na·tion (hə-lo͞o′sə-nā′shən) *n.* **1. a.** False or distorted perception of objects or events with a compelling

halo
Detail of embroidered medallion of St. Francis, late 16th- to 17th-century Italian

halter[1]

hammer

George Miksch Sutton
hammerhead
Above: Sphyrna zygaena
Below: Scopus umbretta

hammock[1]

sense of their reality, usually as a product of mental disorder or as a response to a drug. **b.** The complex of material so perceived. **2.** A false or mistaken idea; delusion. **—hal·lu'ci·na'tion·al** *adj.* **—hal·lu'ci·na'tive** *adj.*

hal·lu·ci·na·to·ry (hə-lo͞o'sə-nə-tôr'ē, -tōr'ē) *adj.* **1.** Characterizing or characterized by hallucination. **2.** Inducing hallucination.

hal·lu·cin·o·gen (hə-lo͞o'sə-nə-jən) *n.* A drug that induces hallucination. [HALLUCIN(ATION) + -GEN.] **—hal·lu'cin·o·gen'ic** (-jĕn'ĭk) *adj.*

hal·lu·ci·no·sis (hə-lo͞o'sə-nō'sĭs) *n.* An abnormal condition or mental state characterized by hallucination. [HALLUCI-N(ATION) + -OSIS.]

hal·lux (hăl'əks) *n., pl.* **hal·lu·ces** (hăl'yə-sēz', hăl'ə-). **1.** The inner or first digit on the hind foot of a mammal; in man, the big toe. **2.** The often backward-directed toe of a bird. [Lat.]

hall·way (hôl'wā') *n.* **1.** A corridor in a building. **2.** An entrance hall.

halm (hôm) *n.* Variant of **haulm.**

ha·lo (hā'lō) *n., pl.* **-los** or **-loes. 1.** A circular band of colored light around a light source, as around the sun or moon, caused by the refraction and reflection of light by ice particles suspended in the intervening atmosphere. **2. a.** Something resembling a halo. **b.** A nimbus. **3.** The aura of majesty or glory surrounding a person, thing, or event that is regarded with reverence, awe, or sentiment. *—tr.v.* **-loed, -lo·ing, -los** or **-loes.** To encircle with a halo. [Med. Lat. < Lat. *halos* < Gk. *halōs.*]

halo- or **hal-** *pref.* **1.** Salt: *halophyte.* **2.** Halogen: *halocarbon.* [Fr. < Gk. < *hals,* sea, salt.]

hal·o·bi·ont (hăl'ō-bī'ŏnt') *n.* An organism that lives or grows in a saline environment.

hal·o·car·bon (hăl'ə-kär'bən) *n.* A compound consisting of carbon and a halogen.

hal·o·cline (hăl'ə-klīn') *n.* A vertical gradient in ocean salinity.

hal·o·gen (hăl'ə-jən) *n.* Any of a group of five chemically related nonmetallic elements that includes fluorine, chlorine, bromine, iodine, and astatine. **—ha·log'e·nous** (hă-lŏj'ə-nəs) *adj.*

hal·o·ge·nate (hăl'ə-jə-nāt') *tr.v.* **-nat·ed, -nat·ing, -nates.** To treat or combine with a halogen. **—hal'o·ge·na'tion** *n.*

hal·o·phile (hăl'ə-fīl') *n.* An organism that requires a salty environment. **—hal'o·phil'ic** (hăl'ə-fĭl'ĭk), **ha·loph'i·lous** (hă-lŏf'ə-ləs) *adj.*

hal·o·phyte (hăl'ə-fīt') *n.* A plant that grows in saline soil. **—hal'o·phyt'ic** (-fĭt'ĭk) *adj.*

hal·o·thane (hăl'ə-thān') *n.* A colorless, nonflammable liquid, $C_2HBrClF_3$, used as an inhalational anesthetic. [HALO- + (E)THANE.]

halt[1] (hôlt) *n.* A suspension of movement or progress, esp. a temporary one. *—v.* **halt·ed, halt·ing, halts.** *—tr.* To cause to stop; arrest. *—intr.* To stop; pause. [G. < MHG < imper. of *halten,* to stop < OHG *haltan.*]

halt[2] (hôlt) *intr.v.* **halt·ed, halt·ing, halts. 1.** To be defective or to proceed poorly, as in the development of an argument in logic or in the rhythmical structure of a verse. **2.** To proceed or act with uncertainty or indecision; waver. **3.** To limp or hobble. *—adj. Archaic.* Lame; crippled. [ME *halten,* to limp < OE *healtian.*]

hal·ter[1] (hôl'tər) *n.* **1.** A device made of rope or leather straps that fits around the head or neck of an animal and can be used to lead or secure it. **2.** A rope with a noose used for execution by hanging. **3.** Death or execution by hanging. **4.** A bodice for women that ties behind the neck and across the back, leaving the arms, shoulders, and back bare. *—tr.v.* **-tered, -ter·ing, -ters. 1. a.** To put a halter on. **b.** To control with or as if with a halter. **2.** To hang (someone). [ME < OE *hælftre.*]

hal·ter[2] (hôl'tər, hăl'-) also **hal·tere** (-tîr') *n., pl.* **hal·ter·es** (hôl-tîr'ēz, hăl-). Either of the small, clublike balancing organs that are the rudimentary hind wings of dipterous insects such as flies or mosquitoes. [Lat., lead weights used in leaping exercises < Gk. < *hallesthai,* to jump.]

halt·ing (hôl'tĭng) *adj.* **1.** Limping; lame. **2.** Imperfect; defective: *a halting verse.* **3.** Hesitant or wavering: *a halting voice.*

hal·vah or **hal·va** (häl-vä', häl'vä) also **ha·la·vah** (hä'lə-vä') *n.* A confection of Turkish origin consisting of crushed sesame seeds in a binder of honey. [Yiddish *halva* < Rum. < Turk. *helva* < Ar. *ḥalwā.*]

halve (hăv, häv) *tr.v.* **halved, halv·ing, halves. 1.** To divide into two equal portions or parts. **2.** To lessen or reduce by half. **3.** *Informal.* To share equally. **4.** In golf, to play (a game or hole) using the same number of strokes as one's opponent. [ME *halven* < *half,* half. —see HALF.]

halves (hăvz, hävz) *n.* Plural of **half.**

hal·yard also **hal·liard** (hăl'yərd) *n.* A rope used to raise or lower a sail, flag, or yard. [Alteration of ME *halier* < *halen,* to pull. —see HALE[2].]

ham (hăm) *n.* **1.** The thigh of the hind leg of certain animals, esp. a hog. **2.** The meat of the thigh of a hog. **3.** The back of the knee. **4.** The back of the thigh. **5. hams.** The buttocks. **6.** *Slang.* An actor who overacts or a performer who exaggerates excessively. **7.** *Informal.* A licensed amateur radio operator. *—v.* **hammed, ham·ming, hams.** *—intr.* To overact. *—tr.* To exaggerate or overdo (a role or line, for example). [ME *hamme* < OE *hamm.*]

Ham (hăm) *n.* In the Old Testament, the second of the three sons of Noah, often considered the ancestor of the Egyptians. [Heb. *Ḥam.*]

ham·a·dry·ad (hăm'ə-drī'əd) *n., pl.* **-ads** or **-a·des** (-ə-dēz'). **1.** *Gk. & Rom. Myth.* A wood nymph who lives only as long as the tree of which she is the spirit lives. **2.** The king cobra. [Lat. *hamadryas, hamadryad-,* < Gk. *Hamadruas* : *hama,* together with + *druas,* dryad < *drus,* tree.]

ham·a·dry·as (hăm'ə-drī'əs) *n.* A baboon, *Comopithecus hamadryas,* of northern Africa and Arabia, the adult male of which has a heavy mane. [Lat., hamadryad. —see HAMADRYAD.]

ha·mal also **ham·mal** (hə-mäl') *n.* A porter or bearer in certain Moslem countries. [Ar. *ḥammāl* < *ḥamala,* he carried.]

Ha·man (hā'mən) *n.* In the Old Testament, a Persian minister who was hanged from his own gallows when his plot against the Jews was revealed by Esther. [Heb. *Hāmān.*]

ha·mate (hā'māt') *adj.* Hooked at the tip. [Lat. *hamatus* < *hamus,* hook.]

ham·burg·er (hăm'bûr'gər) also **ham·burg** (-bûrg') *n.* **1. a.** Ground meat, usually beef. **b.** A patty of such meat. **2.** A sandwich made with a hamburger patty, usually in a roll or bun. [Short for *Hamburger steak,* after *Hamburg,* Germany.]

hame (hām) *n.* One of the two curved wooden or metal pieces of a harness that fit around the neck of a draft animal and to which the traces are attached. [ME < MDu.]

Ham·il·to·ni·an (hăm'əl-tō'nē-ən) *n.* A mathematical function that can be used systematically and with great generality to generate the equations of motion of a dynamic system, equal for many such systems to the sum of the kinetic and potential energies of the system expressed in terms of the system's coordinates and momenta treated as independent variables. [After William R. *Hamilton* (1805–1865).]

Ham·ite (hăm'īt') *n.* A member of a group of related peoples inhabiting northern and northeastern Africa, including the Berbers and the descendants of the ancient Egyptians. [After HAM.]

Ha·mit·ic (hă-mĭt'ĭk) *adj.* Of or relating to the Hamites or the language of the Hamites. *—n.* A subfamily of the Afro-Asiatic language family that includes Berber, Egyptian, Coptic, and the Cushitic languages of Ethiopia.

Ham·i·to-Se·mit·ic (hăm'ĭ-tō-sə-mĭt'ĭk) *n.* Afro-Asiatic. [HAMIT(IC) + SEMITIC.]

ham·let (hăm'lĭt) *n.* A small village. [ME *hamelet* < OFr., dim. of *ham,* village, of Germanic orig.]

ham·mal (hə-mäl') *n.* Variant of **hamal.**

ham·mer (hăm'ər) *n.* **1.** A hand tool used to exert an impulsive force by striking, consisting of a handle with a perpendicularly attached head of a relatively heavy, rigid material. **2.** A tool or device similar to a hammer in function or action, as: **a.** The part of a gunlock that hits the primer or firing pin or explodes the percussion cap causing the gun to go off. **b.** One of the padded wooden pieces of a piano that strike the strings. **c.** A part of an apparatus that strikes a gong or bell, as in a clock. **3.** *Anat.* The malleus. **4.** *Sports.* A metal ball weighing 16 pounds and having a long wire or wooden handle by which it is thrown in track-and-field competition. **5.** A small mallet used by auctioneers. *—v.* **-mered, -mer·ing, -mers.** *—tr.* **1.** To hit once or repeatedly with or as if with a hammer; pound. **2.** To beat into a shape with or as if with a hammer: *hammered out the dents in the fender; hammered out a contract acceptable to both sides.* **3.** To put together, fasten, or seal, particularly with nails, by hammering. **4.** To force upon by constant repetition. *—intr.* **1.** To deal repeated blows with or as if with a hammer; pummel: *"wind hammered at us violently in gusts"* (Thor Heyerdahl). **2.** To beat in the manner of a hammer: *His pulse hammered.* **3.** *Informal.* To keep at something continuously: *hammered away at the problem.* **—idioms. go** (or **come) under the hammer.** To be put up for auction. **hammer and tongs.** With tremendous energy or effort; vigorously. [ME *hamer* < OE *hamor.*] **—ham'mer·er** *n.*

hammer and sickle *n.* An emblem of the Communist movement, consisting of a crossed hammer and sickle signifying the alliance of workers and peasants.

ham·mered (hăm'ərd) *adj.* Shaped or worked with a metalworker's hammer and often showing the marks of these tools: *hammered gold.*

ham·mer·head (hăm'ər-hĕd') *n.* **1.** The head of a hammer. **2.** Any of several large, predatory sharks of the genus *Sphyrna,* having the sides of the head elongated into large, fleshy extensions with the eyes at the ends. **3.** A bird, *Scopus umbretta,* of Africa and southwestern Asia, having brown plumage, a large, bladelike bill, and a long, backward-pointing crest.

hammer lock *n.* A wrestling hold in which the opponent's arm is pulled behind his back and twisted upward.

ham·mer·toe (hăm'ər-tō') *n.* A toe, usually the second, that is congenitally bent downward.

ham·mock[1] (hăm'ək) *n.* A hanging, easily swung cot or lounge of canvas or netting suspended between two trees or other supports. [Sp. *hamaca* < Taino.]

ham·mock² (hăm′ək) *n.* Variant of **hummock**.

ham·my (hăm′ē) *adj.* **-mi·er, -mi·est.** Marked or characterized by overacting; affectedly humorous or dramatic. **—ham′mi·ly** *adv.* **—ham′mi·ness** *n.*

ham·per¹ (hăm′pər) *tr.v.* **-pered, -per·ing, -pers.** To prevent the free movement, action, or progress of. *—n. Naut.* Necessary but encumbering equipment on a ship. [ME *hamperen.*]

ham·per² (hăm′pər) *n.* A large basket, usually with a cover. [ME < OFr. *hanapier,* a case for holding goblets < *hanap,* goblet, of Germanic orig.]

Hamp·shire (hămp′shîr, -shər) *n.* **1.** A large sheep of a breed originating in England. **2.** A pig of a breed developed in the United States, having a black body with a white, beltlike band. [After *Hampshire,* England.]

ham·ster (hăm′stər) *n.* Any of several Eurasian rodents of the family Cricetidae, esp. *Mesocricetus auratus,* having large cheek pouches and a short tail, popular as a pet and used in laboratory research. [G. < OHG *haumstro,* of Slavic orig.]

ham·string (hăm′strĭng′) *n.* **1.** Either of two tendons at the rear hollow of the human knee. **2.** The large sinew in the back of the hock of a quadruped. *—tr.v.* **-strung** (-strŭng′), **-string·ing, -strings. 1.** To cut the hamstring of (an animal or person) and thereby cripple. **2.** To destroy or hinder the efficiency of; frustrate.

ham·u·lus (hăm′yə-ləs) *n., pl.* **-li** (-lī′). A small hooklike projection or process, as at the end of a bone. [Lat., dim. of *hamus,* hook.]

ham·za also **ham·zah** (hăm′zə) *n.* A sign in Arabic orthography used to represent the sound of a glottal stop, transliterated in English as an apostrophe. [Ar. < *hamaza,* he compressed.]

hand (hănd) *n.* **1. a.** The terminal part of the human arm below the wrist, consisting of the palm, four fingers, and an opposable thumb, used for grasping and holding. **b.** A homologous or similar part in other animals. **2.** A unit of length equal to four inches or 10.16 cm, used esp. to specify the height of a horse. **3.** Something suggesting the shape or function of the human hand. **4. a.** Any of the rotating pointers used as indexes on the face of a mechanical clock. **b.** A pointer, as on a gauge or dial. **5.** *Printing.* An index (sense 3). **6.** Lateral direction indicated according to the way in which one is facing: *at my right hand.* **7.** A style or individual sample of writing; penmanship. **8.** A round of applause to signify approval. **9.** Physical assistance; help: *gave me a hand with the bags.* **10. a.** In card games, the cards held by a given player at any time. **b.** The number of cards dealt each player; deal. **c.** A player or participant: *a fourth hand for bridge.* **d.** A portion or section of a game during which all the cards dealt out are played: *a hand of poker.* **11. a.** One who performs manual labor: *a factory hand.* **b.** One who is part of a group or crew. **12. a.** A participant in an activity. **b.** One who specializes in a particular activity or pursuit: *an old hand at labor negotiations.* **13. a.** The immediacy of a source of information; degree of reliability: *at first hand.* **b.** The strength or force of one's position: *negotiated from a strong hand.* **14. a.** Often **hands.** Possession, ownership, or keeping: *The books should be in her hands by noon.* **b.** Often **hands.** Power; jurisdiction; care: *in good hands.* **15. a.** Involvement or participation: *"In all this was evident the hand of the counterrevolutionaries"* (John Reed). **b.** An influence or effect: *she had a hand in all the major decisions.* **16.** An aptitude or ability: *tried his hand at decorating.* **17.** Evidence of craftsmanship or artistic skill: *can see the hand of a master even in the lighter poems.* **18.** A manner or way of performing something: *a light hand with make-up.* **19. a.** Permission or a promise, esp. a pledge to wed. **b.** A commitment or agreement, esp. when sealed by a handshake; word: *You have my hand on that.* *—tr.v.* **hand·ed, hand·ing, hands. 1.** To give or pass with or as if with the hands; transmit: *Hand me your keys.* **2.** To aid, direct, or conduct with the hands: *The usher handed the patron to her seat.* **3.** *Naut.* To roll up and secure (a sail); furl. ***—phrasal verbs.* hand down. 1.** To bequeath as an inheritance to one's heirs. **2.** To make and pronounce an official decision, esp. a court verdict. **hand on.** To turn over to another. **hand out. 1.** To distribute freely; disseminate. **2.** To administer or deal out. **hand over.** To release or relinquish to another. ***—idioms.* at hand. 1.** Close by; near. **2.** Soon in time; imminent. **at the hand (or hands) of.** Performed by someone or through the agency of someone. **bite the hand that feeds one.** To repay kindness with malice. **by hand.** Performed manually. **come to hand.** To become apparent. **force one's hand.** To force one to act prematurely or unwillingly in a given situation. **hand and foot.** With absolute effort or fidelity: *waited on him hand and foot.* **hand in (or and) glove.** On intimate terms or in close association. **hand in hand.** In cooperation; jointly. **hand it to.** *Slang.* To give credit to. **hand over fist.** *Slang.* At a tremendous rate: *making money hand over fist.* **hands down.** With no trouble; easily. **in hand. 1.** Under control. **2.** Presently accessible. **3.** In preparation. **off one's hands.** Out of one's jurisdiction, responsibility, or care. **on hand.** Available. **on (or upon) one's hands.** In one's possession, often as an imposed responsibility or burden. **on (the) one hand.** As one point of view or side of an issue; in one respect. **on the other hand.** As another, or opposite, point of view; from another standpoint. **out of hand. 1.** Out of control. **2.** At once; immediately. **3.** Over and done with; finished. **4.** Uncalled for or improper; indiscreet. **show one's hand.** To reveal something previously hidden, such as a plan or intention. **throw up one's hands.** To give up in hopelessness; concede. **tip one's hand.** To reveal something unwittingly. **to hand. 1.** Nearby. **2.** In one's possession. **with a heavy hand. 1.** In a clumsy or awkward manner. **2.** With great severity or emphasis. **with a high hand.** In a presumptuous or cavalier fashion; overbearingly. [ME < OE.]

hand·bag (hănd′băg′) *n.* **1.** A woman's bag for carrying personal articles. **2.** A piece of small hand luggage.

hand·ball (hănd′bôl′) *n.* **1.** A game, similar in scoring to volleyball, played by two or more players batting a ball against a wall with their hands, usually with a special glove. **2.** The small rubber ball used in handball.

hand·bar·row (hănd′băr′ō) *n.* A flat framework or litter having carrying poles at each end.

hand·bill (hănd′bĭl′) *n.* A printed sheet or pamphlet distributed by hand.

hand·book (hănd′bo͝ok′) *n.* **1.** A concise manual or reference book providing specific information or instruction about a subject. **2. a.** A book in which off-track bets are recorded. **b.** A place where off-track bets are taken.

hand·breadth (hănd′brĕdth′) also **hand's-breadth** or **hand's breadth** (hăndz′-) *n.* A linear measurement approximating the width of the palm of the hand, from 6.25 to 10 centimeters, or 2½ to 4 inches.

hand·car (hănd′kär′) *n.* A small open railroad car propelled by a hand pump or a small motor.

hand·cart (hănd′kärt′) *n.* A small, usually two-wheeled cart pulled or pushed by hand.

hand·clasp (hănd′klăsp′) *n.* The act of clasping the hand of another, esp. in friendship.

hand·craft (hănd′krăft′) *n.* Variant of **handicraft.** *—tr.v.* (hănd-krăft′) **-craft·ed, -craft·ing, -crafts.** To fashion or make by hand. **—hand′crafts′man, hand′craft′man** *n.*

hand·cuff (hănd′kŭf′) *n.* A restraining device consisting of a pair of strong, connected hoops that can be tightened and locked about the wrists and used on one or both arms of a prisoner in custody; manacle. *—tr.v.* **-cuffed, -cuff·ing, -cuffs. 1.** To restrain with handcuffs. **2.** To render ineffective or impotent.

hand·ed (hăn′dĭd) *adj.* **1.** Of or pertaining to dexterity or preference as regards a hand or hands: *one-handed; left-handed.* **2.** Pertaining to a specified number of people: *a four-handed card game.*

hand·ed·ness (hăn′dĭd-nĭs) *n.* A tendency to use one hand as opposed to the other.

hand·fast (hănd′făst′) *n. Archaic.* A handclasp used to signify a pledge, as a marriage.

hand·ful (hănd′fo͝ol′) *n., pl.* **-fuls. 1.** The quantity or number that can be held in the hand. **2.** A small but undefined quantity or number: *a handful of requests.* **3.** *Informal.* A person or thing too difficult to control or handle easily.

hand glass *n.* **1.** A small magnifying glass held in the hand. **2.** A mirror with a handle.

hand·grip (hănd′grĭp′) *n.* **1.** A grip by the hand. **2.** Something suited to a grip by the hand, as a handle. **3. handgrips.** Hand-to-hand combat.

hand·gun (hănd′gŭn′) *n.* A firearm that can be used with one hand; pistol.

hand·hold (hănd′hōld′) *n.* **1.** A grip by the hand. **2.** Something that one can hold on to for support.

hand·i·cap (hăn′dē-kăp′) *n.* **1. a.** A race or contest in which advantages or compensations are given different contestants to equalize the chances of winning. **b.** Such an advantage or penalty. **2.** A disadvantage or deficiency, esp. a physical or mental disability that prevents or restricts normal achievement. **3.** A hindrance. *—tr.v.* **-capped, -cap·ping, -caps. 1.** To assign a handicap or handicaps to (a contestant). **2.** To cause to be at a disadvantage; impede. [< obs. *hand in cap,* a game in which forfeits were held in a cap.]

hand·i·cap·per (hăn′dē-kăp′ər) *n.* **1.** One who assigns handicaps. **2.** One who predicts the winners in a horse race, esp. one who publishes such predictions as a guide for bettors.

hand·i·craft (hăn′dē-krăft′) also **hand·craft** (hănd′krăft′) *n.* **1.** Skill and facility with the hands; workmanship. **2.** A craft or occupation requiring skilled use of the hands. **3.** Work produced by skilled hands. [ME *handiecraft,* var. of *handcraft.*]

hand·i·crafts·man (hăn′dē-krăfts′mən) *n.* A person skilled in handicraft; craftsman.

hand·i·ly (hăn′dĭ-lē) *adv.* **1.** In a handy or easy manner. **2.** Conveniently.

hand·i·work (hăn′dē-wûrk′) *n.* **1.** Work performed by hand. **2.** Something that is accomplished by a single person's efforts. **3.** The product of a person's actions. [ME *handiwerk* < OE *handgeweorc* : *hand,* hand + *geweorc,* work.]

hand·ker·chief (hăng′kər-chĭf) *n.* **1.** A small square of cloth used esp. for wiping the nose or mouth. **2.** A large piece of cloth worn as a decorative article; scarf.

hamper²

hamster

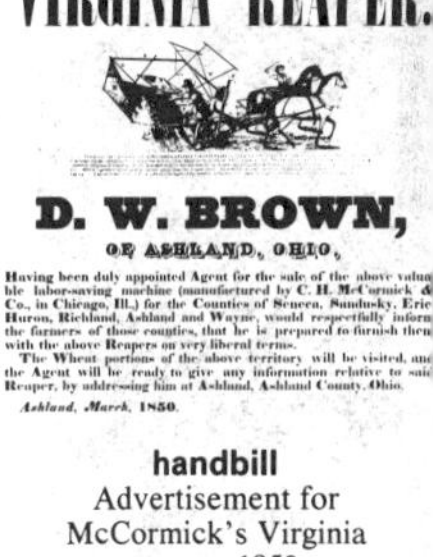

handbill
Advertisement for McCormick's Virginia reaper, 1850

handcart

handcuff

han·dle (hăn′dl) *v.* **-dled, -dling, -dles.** —*tr.* **1.** To touch, lift, or hold with the hands. **2.** To operate with the hands; manipulate. **3.** To deal with or have responsibility for; conduct: *handle corporation law.* **4. a.** To direct, execute, or dispose of: *handle an investment.* **b.** To manage, administer to, or represent: *handle a boxer.* **5.** To confront or cope with: *handle a crowd; handle a problem.* **6.** To deal or trade in the purchase or sale of: *the branch office that handles grain exports.* —*intr.* To act or function under operation: *a car that handles well in the snow.* —*n.* **1.** A part that is designed to be held or operated with the hand. **2.** An opportunity or means for achieving a purpose. **3.** *Slang.* A person's name. **4.** The total amount of money bet on an event or over a set period of time. [ME *handelen* < OE *handlian.*]

han·dle·bar (hăn′dl-bär′) *n.* Often **handlebars.** A curved metal steering bar, as on a bicycle.

handlebar mustache

handlebar mustache *n.* A long, curved mustache resembling a handlebar.

han·dler (hănd′lər) *n.* **1.** One that handles something. **2.** *Sports.* **a.** A person who trains or exhibits an animal, such as a dog. **b.** A person who acts as the trainer or second of a boxer.

han·dling (hănd′lĭng) *n.* **1.** The act or an instance of one that handles something. **2.** The way in which a matter, esp. a delicate one, is taken care of. **3.** The way in which a presentation, esp. an artistic or theatrical work, is treated.

hand·made (hănd′mād′) *adj.* Made or prepared by hand rather than by machine.

hand·maid (hănd′mād′) also **hand·maid·en** (-mād′n) *n.* **1.** A female servant or attendant. **2.** Something that serves as an aid.

hand-me-down (hănd′mē-doun′) *adj.* **1.** Handed down to one person after being used and discarded by another. **2.** Of inferior quality; shabby. —*n.* Something passed on from one person to another.

hand-off (hănd′ôf′, -ŏf′) *n. Football.* A play in which one player hands the ball to another.

hand organ *n.* A barrel organ operated by turning a crank.

hand·out (hănd′out′) *n.* **1.** Food, clothing, or money given to a beggar. **2.** A folder or leaflet circulated free of charge. **3.** A prepared news or publicity release.

hand-pick (hănd′pĭk′) *tr.v.* **-picked, -pick·ing, -picks. 1.** To gather or pick by hand. **2.** To select personally. **—hand′-picked′** *adj.*

hand·print (hănd′prĭnt′) *n.* An outline or an indentation left by a hand on a surface.

hand puppet *n.* A puppet (sense 2).

hand organ

hand·rail (hănd′rāl′) *n.* A narrow rail to be grasped with the hand for support.

hand·saw (hănd′sô′) *n.* A small saw operated by hand.

hand's-breadth or **hand's breadth** (hăndz′brĕdth′) *n.* Variant of **handbreadth.**

hand·sel (hănd′səl) also **han·sel** (hăn′-) *Chiefly Brit.* —*n.* **1.** A gift to express good wishes at the beginning of a new year or enterprise. **2.** The first money or barter taken in, as by a new business or on the opening day of business, esp. when considered a token of good luck. **3. a.** A first payment; earnest money. **b.** A specimen or foretaste of what is to come. —*tr.v.* **-seled, -sel·ing, -sels** or **-selled, -sel·ling, -sels. 1.** To give a handsel to. **2.** To launch with a ceremonial gesture or gift. **3.** To do or use for the first time. [ME *hanselle* < OE *handselen* and ON *handsal,* transfer.]

hand·set (hănd′sĕt′) *n.* A portable telephone transmitter and receiver module.

hand·shake (hănd′shāk′) *n.* The grasping of right hands by two people as in greeting or leave-taking.

hands-off (hăndz′ôf′, -ŏf′) *adj.* Characterized by nonintervention: *a hands-off foreign policy.*

hand·some (hăn′səm) *adj.* **-som·er, -som·est. 1.** Pleasing and dignified in form or appearance. **2.** Generous or copious: *a handsome reward.* **3.** Marked by or requiring skill or dexterity: *did some handsome maneuvers on the skating rink.* **4.** Appropriate or fitting. **5.** Moderately large. [ME *handsom,* handy.] **—hand′some·ly** *adv.* **—hand′some·ness** *n.*

hands-on (hăndz′ŏn′, -ôn′) *adj.* Involving active participation; applied, as opposed to theoretical: *"We're involved in hands-on operations, pulling levers, pushing buttons"* (Arthur R. Taylor).

handstand

hand·spike (hănd′spīk′) *n.* A bar used as a lever.

hand·spring (hănd′sprĭng′) *n.* A gymnastic feat in which the body is flipped completely forward or backward from an upright position, landing first on the hands, then on the feet.

hand·stand (hănd′stănd′) *n.* The act of balancing on the hands with one's feet in the air.

hand-to-hand (hănd′tə-hănd′) *adj.* Being at close quarters.

hand-to-mouth (hănd′tə-mouth′) *adj.* Having or providing only the bare essentials.

hand·work (hănd′wûrk′) *n.* Work done by hand rather than by machine.

hand·wo·ven (hănd′wō′vən) *adj.* **1.** Woven on a hand-operated loom: *handwoven rugs.* **2.** Woven by hand: *handwoven baskets.*

hang glider

hand·writ·ing (hănd′rī′tĭng) *n.* **1.** Writing done with the hand. **2.** The writing characteristic of a particular person.

hand·y (hăn′dē) *adj.* **-i·er, -i·est. 1.** Skillful in using one's hands, esp. in a variety of ways. **2.** Readily accessible. **3.** Useful; convenient: *a handy gadget.* **4.** Easy to use or handle: *a handy reference book.* [< HAND.] **—hand′i·ness** *n.*

hand·y·man also **handy man** (hăn′dē-măn′) *n.* One who does odd jobs or various small tasks.

hang (hăng) *v.* **hung** (hŭng), **hang·ing, hangs.** —*tr.* **1.** To fasten from above with no support from below; suspend. **2.** To suspend or fasten so as to allow free movement at or about the point of suspension: *hang a door.* **3.** *past tense & past participle* **hanged** or **hung.** To execute by suspending by the neck. **4.** To fix or attach at an appropriate angle: *hang a scythe to its handle.* **5.** To alter the hem of (a garment) so as to fall evenly at a specified height. **6.** To furnish, decorate, or appoint by suspending objects around or about: *hang a room with curtains.* **7.** To hold or incline downward; let droop: *hang one's head in sorrow.* **8.** To attach to a wall: *hang wallpaper.* **9.** To deadlock (a jury) by failing to render a unanimous verdict. **10.** *Baseball.* To throw (a pitch) in such a manner so as to fail to break. —*intr.* **1.** To be attached from above with no support from below. **2.** To die as a result of hanging. **3.** To remain suspended or poised over a place or object; hover. **4.** To attach oneself as an impediment or dependent; cling. **5.** To incline downward; droop. **6.** To depend: *everything hangs on the committee's decision.* **7.** To pay strict attention: *hang on every word.* **8.** To remain unresolved or uncertain: *Her future hung in the balance.* **9.** To fit the body in loose lines: *a dress that hangs well.* **10.** To be on display, as in a gallery. **11.** *Baseball.* To fail to break or move in the intended way, as a curve ball. **—*phrasal verbs.* hang around.** *Informal.* **1.** To spend time idly; loiter. **2.** To keep company; consort. **hang back.** To be averse; hold back. **hang off.** To hold back; be averse. **hang on. 1.** To cling tightly to something. **2.** To continue persistently; persevere. **3.** To keep a telephone connection open. **hang onto.** To hold or cling tightly to. **hang out.** *Slang.* To spend one's free time in a certain place. **hang together. 1.** To stand united; stick together. **2.** To constitute a coherent totality. **hang up. 1.** To suspend on a hook or hanger. **2.** To replace (a telephone receiver) on its cradle. **3.** To retard or impede; hinder: *hang up a project.* **4.** To halt the movement or action of. **5.** To end a telephone conversation. **6.** To become halted or snagged. —*n.* **1.** The way in which something hangs. **2.** A downward inclination or slope. **3.** Particular meaning or significance. **4.** *Informal.* The proper method for doing, using, or handling something: *get the hang of it.* **5.** A suspension of motion; slackening. **—*idioms.* give** (or **care) a hang.** To be concerned or anxious. **hang fire. 1.** To be slow in firing, as a gun. **2.** To delay. **hang in there.** *Informal.* To persevere despite difficulties; persist. **hang loose.** *Slang.* To stay calm or relaxed. **hang tough.** *Informal.* To remain firmly resolved: *"We are going to hang tough on this"* (Donald T. Regan). **let it all hang out.** *Slang.* **1.** To be completely relaxed. **2.** To be completely candid. [ME *hongen,* partly < OE *hangian,* to hang, and partly < OE *hōn,* to hang.]

Usage: *Hanged,* as the past tense and past participle of *hang,* is used in the sense of "put to death by hanging." In the following example *hung* would be unacceptable to a majority of the Usage Panel: *Frontier courts hanged many a prisoner after a summary trial.* In all other senses of the word, *hung* is the preferred form as past tense and past participle.

han·gar (hăng′ər, hăng′gər) *n.* A structure esp. for housing or repairing aircraft. [Fr. < OFr., prob. < Med. Lat. *angarium,* shed for shoeing horses.]

hang·dog (hăng′dôg′, -dŏg′) *adj.* **1.** Shamefaced or guilty. **2.** Downcast; intimidated. —*n.* A sneaky or despicable person.

hang·er (hăng′ər) *n.* **1.** One that hangs. **2.** A contrivance to which something hangs or by which something is hung. **3.** A device around which a garment is draped for hanging from a hook or rod. **4.** A loop or strap by which something is hung. **5.** A bracket on an automobile's spring shackle designed to hold it to the chassis. **6.** A decorative strip of cloth hung on a garment or wall.

hang·er-on (hăng′ər-ŏn′, -ôn′) *n., pl.* **hang·ers-on** (hăng′ərz-). A sycophant; parasite.

hang glider *n.* A device resembling a kite from which a harnessed rider hangs while gliding from a height.

hang·ing (hăng′ĭng) *n.* **1.** An execution on a gallows. **2.** Something hung, as draperies or a tapestry. **3.** A descending slope or inclination. —*adj.* **1.** Situated on a sharp declivity. **2.** Projecting downward; overhanging. **3.** Suited for holding something that hangs. **4. a.** Deserving death by hanging: *a hanging crime.* **b.** Disposed to inflict the sentence of death by hanging: *a hanging judge.*

hanging indention *n.* The indention of every line in a paragraph except the first.

hang·man (hăng′mən) *n.* One employed to execute condemned prisoners by hanging.

hang·nail (hăng′nāl′) *n.* A small piece of dead skin at the side or the base of a fingernail that is partly detached from the rest of the skin. [Alteration of AGNAIL.]

hang·out (hăng′out′) *n.* A frequently visited place.

hang·o·ver (hăng′ō′vər) *n.* **1.** Unpleasant physical effects following the heavy use of alcohol. **2.** A letdown, as after a period of excitement. **3.** A vestige; holdover: *hangovers from prewar legislation.*

hang·tag (hăng′tăg′) *n.* A tag attached to a piece of merchandise giving information about its composition and proper care and use.

hang-up (hăng′ŭp′) *n. Informal.* **1.** A psychological or emotional difficulty or inhibition. **2.** An obstacle to smooth progress or development.

hank (hăngk) *n.* **1.** A coil or loop. **2.** A ring on a stay attached to the head of a jib or staysail. **3.** A looped bundle, as of yarn. [ME < ON *hönk.*]

han·ker (hăng′kər) *intr.v.* **-kered, -ker·ing, -kers.** To have a longing; crave. [Perh. < dial. Du. *hankeren.*] **—hank′er·er** *n.*

han·kie also **han·ky** (hăng′kē) *n., pl.* **-kies.** A handkerchief.

han·ky-pan·ky (hăng′kē-păng′kē) *n. Slang.* **1.** Devious or mischievous activity. **2.** Foolish talk or action. [Perh. alteration of HOCUS-POCUS.]

Han·o·ve·ri·an (hăn′ō-vîr′ē-ən) *adj.* Of or pertaining to the kingdom or province of Hanover, the electoral house of Hanover, or the royal family of Hanover.

Han·sard (hăn′sərd) *n.* The official report of the proceedings and debates of the British or Canadian Parliament. [After Luke *Hansard* (1752–1828).]

hanse (hăns) *n.* A medieval merchant guild or trade association. [ME < OFr. < MLG < OHG *hansa,* military troop.] **—han′se·at′ic** (hăn′sē-ăt′ĭk) *adj.*

Hanseatic League *n.* A protective and commercial association of free towns in northern Germany and neighboring areas, formally organized in 1358 and dissolved in the 17th century.

han·sel (hăn′səl) *n. & v.* Variant of **handsel.**

Han·sen's disease (hăn′sənz) *n.* Leprosy. [After A. G. H. *Hansen* (1841–1912).]

han·som (hăn′səm) *n.* A two-wheeled covered carriage with the driver's seat above and behind. [After Joseph A. *Hansom* (1803–1882).]

Ha·nuk·kah or **Ha·nu·kah** (KHä′nə-kə, hä′-) *n.* Variant of **Chanukah.**

han·u·man (hŭn′o͝o-män′) *n., pl.* **-mans.** A monkey, *Presbytis entellus,* of southern Asia, having bristly hairs on the crown and the sides of the face. [Skt. < *hanu,* jaw.]

hao·le (hou′lē, -lā) *n.* An individual, esp. a Caucasian, who is not a native Hawaiian. [Hawaiian.]

hap (hăp) *n.* **1.** Fortune; chance. **2.** A happening; occurrence. *—intr.v.* **happed, hap·ping, haps.** To happen. [ME < ON *happ.*]

ha·pax le·go·me·non (hā′păks′ lĭ-gŏm′ə-nŏn′) *n., pl.* **ha·pax le·go·me·na** (-gŏm′ə-nə). A word or form that occurs only once in the recorded corpus of a given language. [Gk., once said.]

hap·haz·ard (hăp-hăz′ərd) *adj.* Dependent upon or characterized by mere chance. *—n.* Mere chance; fortuity. *—adv.* Casually; by chance. **—hap·haz′ard·ly** *adv.* **—hap·haz′ard·ness** *n.*

haph·ta·rah also **haf·ta·rah** or **haf·to·rah** (häf′tə-rä′, häf-tôr′ə) *n., pl.* **-ta·roth** (-tə-rōt′, -rōs′, -tôr′ōt′, -ōs′). A reading selected from the Prophets, read in the synagogue service on the Sabbath following each lesson from the Torah. [Heb. *haphṭārāh* < *haphṭēr,* he concluded < *pāṭar,* he separated.]

hap·less (hăp′lĭs) *adj.* Luckless; unfortunate.

hap·lite (hăp′līt′) *n.* Variant of **aplite.**

hap·loid (hăp′loid′) *adj. Genetics.* Having the number of chromosomes present in the normal germ cell, equal to half the number in the normal somatic cell. *—n.* A haploid individual. [Gk. *haploeidēs,* single : *haplous,* single + *-eidēs,* -oid.]

hap·loi·dy (hăp′loi′dē) *n. Genetics.* The state or condition of being haploid.

hap·lol·o·gy (hăp-lŏl′ə-jē) *n.* The shortening of a word by contraction of similar sounds or syllables in its pronunciation. [Gk. *haplous,* single, simple + *logos,* speech < *legein,* to speak.]

hap·lo·sis (hăp-lō′sĭs) *n. Genetics.* Reduction of the diploid number of chromosomes by one half to the haploid number by meiosis. [Gk. *haplous,* single + -OSIS.]

hap·ly (hăp′lē) *adv.* By chance or accident.

hap·pen (hăp′ən) *intr.v.* **-pened, -pen·ing, -pens. 1. a.** To come to pass. **b.** To come into being; take place. **2.** To take place or occur by chance. **3.** To come upon something by chance. **4.** To appear by chance; turn up. [ME *happenen* < *hap,* hap.]

hap·pen·chance (hăp′ən-chăns′) *n.* Variant of **happenstance.**

hap·pen·ing (hăp′ə-nĭng) *n.* **1.** An event, esp. one of special significance. **2.** An improvised, often spontaneous spectacle or performance, esp. one involving audience participation.

hap·pen·stance (hăp′ən-stăns′) also **hap·pen·chance** (-chăns′) *n.* A chance circumstance. [HAPPEN + (CIRCUM)STANCE.]

hap·py (hăp′ē) *adj.* **-pi·er, -pi·est. 1.** Characterized by good luck; fortunate. **2.** Enjoying, showing, or marked by pleasure or joy. **3.** Well-adapted; appropriate; felicitous: *a happy turn of phrase.* **4.** Cheerful; willing: *happy to help.* **5. a.** Characterized by a spontaneous or obsessive inclination to use something. **b.** Enthusiastic about or involved with to a disproportionate degree: *money-happy.* [ME < *hap,* hap.] **—hap′pi·ly** *adv.* **—hap′pi·ness** *n.*

hap·py-go-luck·y (hăp′ē-gō-lŭk′ē) *adj.* Taking things easily; carefree.

happy hour *n.* A period of time, usually in late afternoon and early evening, during which a bar or lounge features drinks at reduced prices.

hap·ten (hăp′tĕn′) also **hap·tene** (-tēn′) *n.* An antigen that is incomplete and cannot by itself cause antibody formation but can neutralize specific antibodies in an artificial environment outside the body. [G. : Gk. *haptein,* to fasten + G. *-en,* -ene.]

hap·tic (hăp′tĭk) or **hap·ti·cal** (-tĭ-kəl) *adj.* Of or relating to the sense of touch. [< Gk. *haptesthai,* to touch.]

ha·ra-ki·ri (hăr′ĭ-kîr′ē) *n.* Ritual suicide by disembowelment formerly practiced by the Japanese samurai and upper classes. [J.]

ha·rangue (hə-răng′) *n.* **1.** A long, pompous speech, esp. one delivered before a gathering. **2.** A speech or piece of writing characterized by strong feeling or expression; tirade. *—v.* **-rangued, -rangu·ing, -rangues.** *—tr.* To deliver a harangue to. *—intr.* To deliver a harangue. [ME *arang,* a speech to an assembly < OFr. *arenge* < Med. Lat. *harenga.*] **—ha·rangu′er** *n.*

hansom

ha·rass (hə-răs′, hăr′əs) *tr.v.* **-rassed, -rass·ing, -rass·es. 1.** To irritate or torment persistently. **2.** To wear out; exhaust. **3.** To impede and exhaust (an enemy) by repeated attacks or raids. [Fr. *harasser,* prob. < OFr. *harer,* to set a dog on < *hare,* interjection used to set a dog on, of Germanic orig.] **—ha·rass′er** *n.* **—ha·rass′ment** *n.*

Synonyms: *harass, hound, badger, pester, plague, bait, torment.* These verbs are closely related when they mean to trouble or disturb persons. *Harass* implies systematic persecution by besetting with annoyances, threats, or demands. *Hound* suggests unrelentingly pursuing or dunning in order to gain a desired end. *Badger* refers to persistent nagging or teasing, *pester* to the inflicting of a succession of petty annoyances or distractions, and *plague* to the inflicting of worry, vexation, or other mental tribulation over an extended period. *Bait* implies deliberate persecution by taunting, insulting, or heckling. *Torment,* the most general of these terms, is applicable to any action that inflicts distress, vexation, or the like.

har·bin·ger (här′bĭn-jər) *n.* One that indicates or foreshadows what is to come; forerunner. *—tr.v.* **-gered, -ger·ing, -gers.** To signal the approach of; presage. [ME *herbengar,* person sent ahead to prepare lodging < OFr. *herbergeor* < *herbergier,* to provide lodgings for < *herberge,* lodgings, of Germanic orig.]

har·bor (här′bər) *n.* **1.** A sheltered part of a body of water deep enough to provide anchorage for ships. **2.** A place of shelter; refuge. *—tr.v.* **-bored, -bor·ing, -bors. 1.** To give shelter to. **2.** To provide with often temporary quarters. **3.** To entertain or nourish (a specified thought or feeling): *harbor a grudge.* [ME *herberwe.*] **—har′bor·er** *n.*

har·bor·age (här′bər-ĭj) *n.* **1.** Shelter and anchorage for ships. **2.** Shelter; refuge.

har·bor·mas·ter (här′bər-măs′tər) *n.* An officer who oversees and enforces the regulations of a harbor.

harbor seal *n.* A hair seal, *Phoca vitulina,* of coastal waters of the Northern Hemisphere, having a spotted coat.

har·bour (här′bər) *n. & v. Chiefly Brit.* Variant of **harbor.**

hard (härd) *adj.* **-er, -est. 1.** Resistant to pressure; not readily penetrated; firm. **2. a.** Physically toughened; rugged. **b.** Mentally toughened; strong-minded. **3. a.** Requiring great effort or endurance: *a project that took years of hard work.* **b.** Performed with or marked by great diligence or energy. **4. a.** Intense in force or degree: *a hard blow.* **b.** Inclement: *a long, hard winter.* **5. a.** Stern or strict in nature or comportment: *a hard taskmaster.* **b.** Resistant to persuasion or appeal; obdurate. **c.** Making few concessions: *drives a hard bargain.* **6. a.** Difficult to endure: *a hard life.* **b.** Oppressive or unjust in nature or effect: *restrictions that were hard on welfare applicants.* **c.** Lacking compassion or sympathy; callous. **7. a.** Harsh or severe in intention or effect: *said some hard things that I won't forget.* **b.** Bitter; resentful: *No hard feelings, I hope.* **8. a.** Causing damage or premature wear: *Snow and ice are hard on a car's finish.* **b.** Bad; adverse: *hard luck.* **9.** Difficult to resolve or complete; troublesome: *ran into some hard problems.* **10.** Difficult to understand or convey: *Physics was the hardest course for me.* **11. a.** Real and unassailable: *hard evidence.* **b.** Definite; firm: *a hard commitment.* **c.** Close; penetrating: *need to take a hard look at the situation.* **d.** Free from illusion or bias; practical: *brought some hard common sense to the discussion.* **12. a.** Marked by sharp outline or definition; stark. **b.** Lacking in delicacy, shading, or nuance. **13. a.** Metallic as opposed to paper: *hard money.* **b.** Backed by bullion rather than by credit. Used of money. **c.** *Commerce.* High and stable. Used of prices. **14.** Durable; lasting: *hard merchandise.* **15.** Erect; tumid. Used of a penis. **16.** Having high alcoholic content; intoxicating. **17.** Containing dissolved substances, as salts, that interfere with the lathering action of soap. Used of water. **18.** Pronounced as a stop, as the *c* in *cake* and the *g* in *log.* **19.** *Physics.* Of relatively high energy; penetrating: *hard x-rays.* **20.** High in gluten content: *hard wheat.* **21.** Not subject to biodegradation, as certain chemicals: *a hard detergent.* **22.** Physically addictive and harmful: *hard drugs.* *—adv.* **1.** With strenuous effort; intently: *worked hard all day.* **2.** With great force, vigor, or energy: *pressed hard on the lever.* **3.** In such a way as to cause great damage or hardship: *industrial cities hit hard by unemployment.* **4.** With great distress, grief, or bitterness: *took the divorce hard.* **5.** Firmly; securely: *held hard to the railing.* **6.** Toward or into a solid condition: *cement that sets hard within a day.* **7.** Near in space or time; close: *The factory stands hard by the railroad tracks.* **8.** *Naut.* Completely; fully: *hard alee.* **—idioms. hard and fast.** Defined, fixed, and invariable: *hard and fast rules.* **hard up.** *Informal.* In need; poor. [ME < OE *heard.*]

Synonyms: *hard, difficult, arduous, intricate, troublesome.* These adjectives are closely related when they mean requiring great physical or mental effort. *Hard* and *difficult,* the most general terms, are interchangeable in many examples, but *difficult* is often the more appropriate where a challenge requiring special skills or ingenuity is involved. *Arduous* refers to what involves burdensome labor or persistent effort, especially physical. *Intricate* describes what is difficult because its complexity makes great mental demands. *Troublesome* implies demands that cause vexation, worry, or anxiety.

hard·back (härd′băk′) *adj.* Bound in cloth, cardboard, or leather rather than paper. Used of books. *—n.* A hardback book.

hard·ball (härd′bôl′) *n.* **1.** Baseball. **2.** *Informal.* The use of any means, however ruthless, to attain an objective.

hard-bit·ten (härd′bĭt′n) *adj.* Toughened by experience.

hard·board (härd′bôrd′, -bōrd′) *n.* A construction board made by compressing fibers of wood chips usually with a binder at a high temperature.

hard-boiled (härd′boild′) *adj.* **1.** Cooked by boiling in the shell to a solid consistency. Used of eggs. **2.** *Informal.* Callous; unfeeling. **3.** *Informal.* Unsentimental and practical; tough.

hard·bound (härd′bound′) *adj.* & *n.* Hardback.

hard cider *n.* Fermented cider.

hard coal *n.* Anthracite.

hard copy *n.* Readable printed copy of the output of a machine, as a computer.

hard core *n.* The durable and resistant central part of a given entity, esp. the most intractable or die-hard nucleus of a specified group or organization: *the hard core of the separatist movement.*

hard-core also **hard·core** (härd′kôr′, -kōr′) *adj.* **1.** Stubbornly resistant or inveterate: *the hard-core criminal element.* **2.** Held to constitute an intractable social problem: *hard-core poverty.* **3.** Extremely graphic or explicit. Used esp. of pornography.

hard·cov·er (härd′kŭv′ər) *adj.* & *n.* Hardback.

hard·edge (härd′ĕj′) *n.* A form of abstract painting characterized by clearly defined geometric shapes and often bright colors.

hard·en (här′dn) *v.* **-ened, -en·ing, -ens.** *—tr.* **1.** To make hard or harder. **2.** To toughen mentally or physically; inure. **3.** To make unfeeling, unsympathetic, or callous: *"To love love and not its meaning hardens the heart in monstrous ways"* (Archibald MacLeish). **4.** To make sharp, as in outline. *—intr.* **1.** To become hard or harder. **2. a.** To rise. Used of prices. **b.** To become stable. **3.** To become inured.

hard·en·er (här′dn-ər) *n.* **1.** One that hardens. **2.** A substance added to varnish or paint to give a harder surface or finish.

hard·en·ing (här′dn-ĭng) *n.* **1.** The act or process of becoming hard or harder. **2.** Something that hardens, as a substance added to iron to yield steel.

hard-fist·ed (härd′fĭs′tĭd) *adj.* Tightfisted; stingy.

hard·hack (härd′hăk′) *n.* A woody plant, *Spiraea tomentosa,* of eastern North America, having leaves with rusty down on the undersides and spirelike clusters of small, rose-pink flowers.

hard-hand·ed (härd′hăn′dĭd) *adj.* **1.** Having hands calloused or hardened by work. **2.** Oppressive; tyrannical. **—hard′-hand′ed·ness** *n.*

hard·hat (härd′hat′) *adj.* **1.** Pertaining to construction work or demolition. **2.** *Informal.* Of, relating to, or characterized by extreme conservatism. **3.** *Slang.* Extremely patriotic.

hard hat *n.* **1.** A lightweight protective helmet, usually of metal or reinforced plastic, worn by construction workers. **2.** *Informal.* A construction worker. **3.** *Slang.* An extremely patriotic person with a conventional, usually unquestioning sense of morality. **4.** *Informal.* An ultraconservative.

hard·head (härd′hĕd′) *n.* **1.** A shrewd and tough person. **2.** A stubborn, unmovable person. **3.** *pl.* **hardhead** or **-heads.** Any of several fishes having a bony head, esp. a common croaker, *Micropogon undulatus,* of Atlantic waters.

hard·head·ed (härd′hĕd′ĭd) *adj.* **1.** Stubborn; willful. **2.** Realistic; pragmatic. **—hard′head′ed·ly** *adv.* **—hard′-head′ed·ness** *n.*

hard·heart·ed (härd′här′tĭd) *adj.* Lacking in feeling or compassion; pitiless and cold. **—hard′heart′ed·ly** *adv.* **—hard′-heart′ed·ness** *n.*

hard-hit·ting (härd′hĭt′ĭng) *adj.* Effective; forceful.

har·di·hood (här′dē-ho͝od′) *n.* **1.** Boldness and daring. **2.** Self-assured impudence or insolence.

hard labor *n.* Compulsory physical labor coincident with a prison term imposed as a legal punishment for a crime.

hard landing *n.* The landing by impact of a spacecraft that lacks devices, such as retrorockets, to slow it down.

hard line *n.* A firm, uncompromising policy, position, or stance.

hard-line also **hard·line** (härd′līn′) *adj.* Characterized by a firm, uncompromising policy, position, or stance: *a hard-line foreign policy.* **—hard′-lin′er** *n.*

hard liquor *n.* Distilled liquor.

hard·ly (härd′lē) *adv.* **1.** Barely; just. **2.** To almost no degree; almost not. **3.** Probably or almost surely not: *"Easily was a man made an infidel, but hardly might he be converted to another faith"* (T.E. Lawrence). **4.** With severity; harshly **5.** With great difficulty; painfully. [ME *hardli,* hardily < OE *heardlīce.*]

Synonyms: *hardly, scarcely, barely.* These adverbs are frequently interchangeable as they refer to sufficiency in quantity, capacity, or ability. *Hardly* and *scarcely* imply either scant sufficiency or, less often, possible insufficiency: *hardly enough; scarcely sufficient to go around; hardly able to see; scarcely large enough to be visible.* In both senses *scarcely* is the stronger term. *Barely* usually suggests no doubt as to sufficiency but implies a narrowness of margin that leaves nothing or virtually nothing to spare: *barely enough; barely on time; barely able to hear.*

Usage: *Hardly* has the force of a negative; therefore it is not used with another negative: *I could hardly see* (not *couldn't hardly see*). *She listened with hardly a smile* (not *without hardly a smile*). • A clause following *hardly* is introduced by *when* or, less often, by *before: We were hardly seated when* (or *before*) *the fire broke out.* Such a clause is not introduced by *than* in formal style: *Hardly had he finished raising the tent when* (not *than*) *the storm broke.*

hard maple *n.* The sugar maple.

hard·ness (härd′nĭs) *n.* **1.** The quality or condition of being hard. **2.** *Mineral.* The relative resistance of a mineral to scratching, as measured by the Mohs scale. **3.** The relative resistance of a metal to denting, scratching, or bending.

hard news *n.* News, as in a newspaper or television report, that deals with formal or serious topics and events. **—hard′-news′** (härd′no͞oz′, -nyo͞oz′) *adj.*

hard-nosed (härd′nōzd′) *adj.* Hardheaded.

hard-on (härd′ŏn′, -ôn′) *n.* *Vulgar Slang.* An erection of the penis.

hard palate *n.* The relatively hard, bony anterior portion of the palate.

hard·pan (härd′păn′) *n.* **1.** A layer of hard subsoil or clay. **2.** Hard, unbroken ground. **3.** A foundation; bedrock.

hard rock *n.* A style of rock'n'roll characterized by a harsh, amplified sound and frequently employing distortion, feedback, and other electronic modulations.

hard rubber *n.* A relatively inelastic rubber made with 30 to 50 per cent sulfur and usually some lime or magnesia as a filler.

hards (härdz) *pl.n.* *(used with a sing. verb).* The coarse refuse of flax or similar fiber. [ME < OE *heordan.*]

hard sauce *n.* A creamy sauce of butter and sugar with rum, brandy, or vanilla flavoring, served chilled with puddings, gingerbread, or fruitcakes.

hard·scrab·ble (härd′skrăb′əl) *adj.* Earning a bare subsistence, as on the land; marginal: *the sharecropper's hardscrabble life.* *—n.* Barren or marginal farmland.

hard sell *n.* *Informal.* Aggressive, high-pressure selling or promotion.

hard·set (härd′sĕt′) *adj.* **1.** In a difficult or ticklish position. **2.** Rigid; fixed. **3.** Obstinate.

hard-shell (härd′shĕl′) also **hard-shelled** (-shĕld′) *adj.* **1.** Having a thick, heavy, or hardened shell. **2.** Uncompromising; confirmed. *—n.* A hard-shell clam or crab.

hard-shell clam *n.* The quahog.

hard-shell crab *n.* A marine crab with a fully hardened shell, esp. the edible species *Callinectes sapidus,* of eastern North America, in this stage.

hard·ship (härd′shĭp′) *n.* **1.** Extreme privation; suffering. **2.** Something that causes privation or suffering.

hard-spun (härd′spŭn′) *adj.* Twisted tightly in spinning, often to the point of curling and looping. Used of yarn.

hard·stand (härd′stănd′) *n.* A hard-surfaced area for parking planes or ground vehicles.

hard·tack (härd′tăk′) *n.* A hard biscuit or bread made only with flour and water; sea biscuit.

hard·top (härd′tŏp′) *n.* An automobile designed to look like a convertible but having a rigidly fixed, hard top.

hard·ware (härd′wâr′) *n.* **1.** Metal goods and utensils such as locks, tools, and cutlery. **2. a.** A computer and the associated physical equipment directly involved in the performance of communications or data-processing functions. **b.** Machines and other physical equipment directly involved in performing an industrial, technological, or military function. **3.** *Informal.* Weapons, esp. military weapons.

hard water *n.* Water containing dissolved salts of calcium and magnesium.

hard-wired (härd′wīrd′) *adj.* Of, relating to, or implemented through logic circuitry permanently connected within a computer or calculator. —**hard'wire'** *v.* (**-wired, -wir·ing, -wires**).

hard·wood (härd'wŏŏd') *n.* **1.** The wood of a broad-leaved flowering tree as distinguished from that of a conifer. **2.** A broad-leaved flowering tree.

har·dy[1] (här'dē) *adj.* **-di·er, -di·est. 1.** Stalwart and rugged; strong. **2.** Courageous; intrepid. **3.** Brazenly daring; audacious. **4.** Capable of surviving unfavorable conditions such as cold weather or lack of moisture. Used esp. of cultivated plants. [ME < OFr. *hardi* < *hardir,* to harden, of Germanic orig.] —**har'di·ly** *adv.* —**har'di·ness** *n.*

har·dy[2] (här'dē) *n., pl.* **-dies.** A square-shanked chisel that fits into a square hole in an anvil. [Prob. < HARD.]

hare (hâr) *n.* Any of various mammals of the family Leporidae, and esp. of the genus *Lepus,* related to and resembling the rabbits but characteristically having longer ears, large hind feet, and long legs adapted for jumping. [ME < OE *hara.*]

hare and hounds *n.* A game in which one group of players leaves a trail of paper scraps for a pursuing group to follow.

hare·bell (hâr'bĕl') *n.* A plant, *Campanula rotundifolia,* having slender stems and leaves and bell-shaped blue flowers. [ME *harebelle* : *hare,* hare + *belle,* bell.]

hare·brained (hâr'brānd') *adj.* Giddy; flighty: *a harebrained scheme.*

Usage: The first part of the compound *harebrained* is often misspelled "hair" in the belief that the meaning of the word is "with a hair-sized brain" rather than "with no more sense than a hare." Though *hairbrained* has a long history, this spelling is not established usage.

Ha·re Krish·na (hä'rē krĭsh'nə) *n., pl.* **Ha·re Krish·nas.** A member of a religious group devoted to the Hindu god Krishna. [Hindi *hare,* invocation of God + *Krishna,* Krishna.]

hare·lip (hâr'lĭp') *n.* A congenital fissure or pair of fissures in the upper lip. —**hare'lipped'** *adj.*

har·em (hâr'əm, hăr'-) *n.* **1.** A house or a section of a house reserved for women members of a Moslem household. **2.** The wives, concubines, female relatives, and servants occupying a harem. [Ar. *ḥarīm.*]

har·i·cot (hăr'ĭ-kō') *n.* **1.** The edible pod or seed of any of several beans, esp. the string bean. **2.** A highly seasoned mutton or lamb stew with vegetables. [Fr.]

hark (härk) *intr.v.* **harked, hark·ing, harks.** To listen attentively. —***idiom.*** **hark back.** To return to a previous point, as in a narrative. [ME *herken* < *herkenen,* to hark < OE *hercnian.*]

har·ken (här'kən) *v.* Variant of **hearken.**

harl (härl) *n.* Filaments or fibers, as of hemp or flax. [ME, fiber, filament, perh. of MLG orig.]

har·le·quin (här'lĭ-kwĭn, -kĭn) *n.* **1. Harlequin.** A conventional buffoon of the commedia dell'arte, traditionally presented in a mask and parti-colored tights. **2.** A clown; buffoon. —*adj.* Having a pattern of brightly colored diamond shapes. [Obs. Fr. < OItal. *arlecchino* < OFr. *Helquin,* a demon, poss. of Germanic orig.]

har·le·quin·ade (här'lĭ-kwə-nād') *n.* **1.** A comedy or pantomime in which Harlequin is the main attraction. **2.** Farcical clownings or buffoonery.

harlequin bug *n.* A flat-bodied, brightly colored insect, *Murgantia histrionica,* that is destructive to cabbage and other plants.

har·lot (här'lət) *n.* A prostitute. [ME < OFr. *arlot,* vagabond.] —**har'lot·ry** (här'lə-trē) *n.*

harm (härm) *n.* **1.** Physical or psychological injury or damage. **2.** Wrong; evil. —*tr.v.* **harmed, harm·ing, harms.** To damage or injure. [ME < OE *hearm.*]

har·mat·tan (här'mə-tăn', här-măt'n) *n.* A dry, dusty wind that blows along the northwestern coast of Africa. [Twi *haramata.*]

harm·ful (härm'fəl) *adj.* Causing or capable of causing harm; injurious. —**harm'ful·ly** *adv.* —**harm'ful·ness** *n.*

harm·less (härm'lĭs) *adj.* Not capable of harming. —**harm'less·ly** *adv.* —**harm'less·ness** *n.*

har·mon·ic (här-mŏn'ĭk) *adj.* **1. a.** Of or pertaining to musical harmony as distinguished from melody or rhythm. **b.** Of or pertaining to harmonics. **2.** Characterized by harmony; concordant. —*n.* **1.** A tone in the harmonic series of overtones produced by a fundamental tone. **2.** A tone produced on a stringed instrument by lightly touching an open or stopped vibrating string at a given fraction of its length so that both segments vibrate. **3.** A wave whose frequency is a whole-number multiple of that of another. **4. harmonics.** *(used with a sing. verb).* The theory or study of the physical properties and characteristics of musical sound. [Lat. *harmonicus* < Gk. *harmonikos* < *harmonia,* harmony.] —**har·mon'i·cal·ly** *adv.*

har·mon·i·ca (här-mŏn'ĭ-kə) *n.* **1.** A small, rectangular musical instrument consisting of a row of free reeds set back in air holes, played by exhaling or inhaling. **2.** A musical instrument consisting of a series of glass bowls of varying sizes played by rubbing the finger along the wet rims. **3.** A musical instrument consisting of tuned strips of metal or glass fixed to a frame and struck with a hammer. [Obs. *armonica,* glass bowl instrument < Ital. *armonica,* harmonious < Lat. *harmonicus,* harmonic. —see HARMONIC.]

harmonic analysis *n.* The representation of mathematical functions by means of linear operations such as summation or integration on characteristic sets of functions, esp. such representation by Fourier series.

harmonic mean *n.* The reciprocal of the arithmetic mean of the reciprocals of a specified set of numbers.

harmonic progression *n.* A sequence of quantities the reciprocals of which form an arithmetic progression, as 1, $1/3$, $1/5$, $1/7$, ...

harmonic series *n.* **1.** *Math.* A series whose terms are in harmonic progression, as $1 + 1/3 + 1/5 + 1/7 + \ldots$. **2.** A series of tones consisting of a fundamental tone and the overtones produced by it, whose frequencies are consecutive integral multiples of the frequency of the fundamental.

har·mo·ni·ous (här-mō'nē-əs) *adj.* **1.** Exhibiting accord in feeling or action: *a harmonious relationship.* **2.** Having component elements pleasingly or appropriately combined: *a harmonious structure.* **3.** Characterized by harmony of sound; melodious. —**har·mo'ni·ous·ly** *adv.* —**har·mo'ni·ous·ness** *n.*

har·mo·nist (här'mə-nĭst) *n.* One skilled in musical harmony. —**har'mo·nis'tic** *adj.* —**har'mo·nis'ti·cal·ly** *adv.*

har·mo·ni·um (här-mō'nē-əm) *n.* An organlike keyboard instrument that produces tones with free metal reeds actuated by air forced from a bellows. [Fr. < *harmonie,* harmony < OFr. *armonie* < Lat. *harmonia.* —see HARMONY.]

har·mo·nize (här'mə-nīz') *v.* **-nized, -niz·ing, -niz·es.** —*tr.* **1.** To bring into agreement or harmony; make harmonious. **2.** To provide harmony for (a melody). —*intr.* **1.** To be in agreement; be harmonious. **2.** To sing or play in harmony. —**har'mo·ni·za'tion** *n.* —**har'mo·niz'er** *n.*

har·mo·ny (här'mə-nē) *n., pl.* **-nies. 1.** Agreement in feeling or opinion; accord: *live in harmony.* **2.** A pleasing combination of the elements that form a whole: *color harmony; the order and harmony of the universe.* **3.** *Mus.* **a.** The study of the structure, progression, and relation of chords. **b.** The simultaneous combination of notes in a chord. **c.** The structure of a musical work or passage as considered from the point of view of its chordal characteristics and relationships. **4.** A combination of musical sounds considered to be pleasing. **5.** A collation of parallel passages, esp. from the Gospels, with a commentary demonstrating their consonance and explaining their discrepancies. —***modifier:*** *a harmony class; a harmony book.* [ME *armonie* < Lat. *harmonia* < Gk. < *harmos,* joint.]

har·ness (här'nĭs) *n.* **1.** The gear or tackle, other than a yoke, with which a draft animal pulls a vehicle or implement. **2.** Something resembling a harness, as the arrangement of straps used to hold a parachute to the body. **3.** A device that raises and lowers the warp threads on a loom. **4.** *Archaic.* Armor for a man or a horse. —*tr.v.* **-nessed, -ness·ing, -ness·es. 1. a.** To put a harness on (a draft animal). **b.** To fasten by the use of a harness. **2.** To bring under control and direct the force of: *If he can harness his energy, he will accomplish a great deal.* —***idiom.*** **in harness.** On duty. [ME *harnes* < OFr., poss. of Germanic orig.] —**har'ness·er** *n.*

harness race *n.* A horse race between pacers or trotters harnessed to sulkies.

harp (härp) *n.* **1.** A musical instrument consisting of an upright, open triangular frame with 46 strings of graded lengths played by plucking with the fingers. **2.** Something similar to a harp. —*intr.v.* **harped, harp·ing, harps.** To play a harp. —***phrasal verb.*** **harp on (or upon).** To talk or write about to an excessive and tedious degree; dwell on. [ME < OE *hearpe* and < OFr. *harpe* (of Germanic orig).] —**harp'er** *n.* —**harp'ist** *n.*

har·pins (här'pĭnz) also **har·pings** (-pĭngz) *pl.n.* Extensions of the ribbands of a ship under construction. [Perh. < HARP.]

har·poon (här-pōōn') *n.* A spearlike weapon with a barbed head used in hunting whales and large fish. —*tr.v.* **-pooned, -poon·ing, -poons.** To strike, kill, or capture with or as if with a harpoon. [Prob. < Du. *harpoen* < OFr. *harpon* < *harper,* to seize.] —**har·poon'er** *n.*

harpoon gun *n.* A small cannonlike apparatus used to fire harpoons.

harp·si·chord (härp'sĭ-kôrd', -kōrd') *n.* A keyboard instrument whose strings are plucked by means of quills or leather plectrums. [Ital. *arpicordo* : *arpi,* harp + *corda,* string < Lat. *chorda* < Gk. *khordē.*] —**harp'si·chord'ist** *n.*

Har·py (här'pē) *n., pl.* **-pies. 1.** *Gk. Myth.* One of several loathsome, voracious monsters with the head and trunk of a woman and the tail, wings, and talons of a bird. **2. harpy.** A predatory person. **3. harpy.** A shrewish woman. [Lat. *Harpyia* < Gk. *Harpuiai.*]

har·que·bus (här'kwə-bəs, -kə-) *n.* A heavy, portable matchlock gun invented during the 15th century. [OFr. *harquebuse* < MLG *hakebusse* : *hake,* hook + *busse,* gun.]

har·ri·dan (hăr'ĭ-dn) *n.* A vicious, scolding woman. [Poss. < Fr. *haridelle,* gaunt woman.]

har·ri·er[1] (hăr'ē-ər) *n.* **1.** One that harries. **2.** Any of various slender, narrow-winged hawks of the genus *Circus,* which prey on small animals.

har·ri·er[2] (hăr'ē-ər) *n.* **1.** One of a breed of small hounds

hare
Lepus townsendii

harmonica

harness

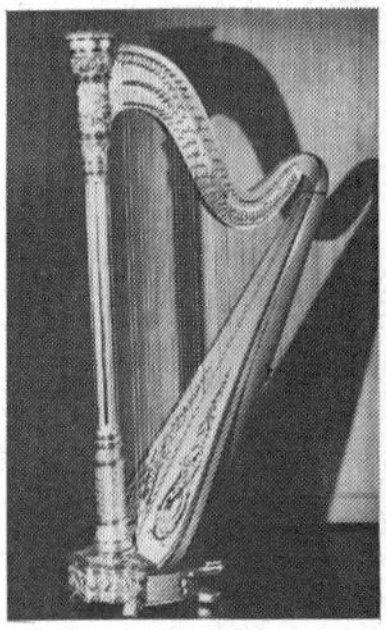

harp

harpsichord

harrow[1]

hartebeest

harvester

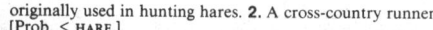

hastate
A hastate leaf

hatchet

originally used in hunting hares. **2.** A cross-country runner. [Prob. < HARE.]

har·row[1] (hăr′ō) *n.* A farm instrument consisting of a heavy frame with sharp teeth or upright disks, used to break up and even off plowed ground. *—tr.v.* **-rowed, -row·ing, -rows. 1.** To break up and level (soil or land) with a harrow. **2.** To inflict great distress or torment on. [ME *harwe.*] **—har′row·er** *n.*

har·row[2] (hăr′ō) *tr.v.* **-rowed, -row·ing, -rows.** *Archaic.* To plunder; sack. [ME *herwen,* var. of *harien,* to harry.]

har·row·ing (hăr′ō-ĭng) *adj.* Extremely distressing; agonizing: *a harrowing experience.*

har·ry (hăr′ē) *tr.v.* **-ried, -ry·ing, -ries. 1.** To raid, as in war; sack or pillage. **2.** To disturb or annoy by or as if by constant attacks; harass. [ME *harien* < OE *hergian.*]

harsh (härsh) *adj.* **-er, -est. 1.** Unpleasant to the senses, esp. to the sense of hearing. **2.** Extremely severe or exacting; stern. [ME *harsk,* of Scand. orig.] **—harsh′ly** *adv.* **—harsh′ness** *n.*

harsh·en (här′shən) *tr. & intr.v.* **-ened, -en·ing, -ens.** To make or become harsh.

hars·let (här′slĭt) *n.* Variant of **haslet.**

hart (härt) *n., pl.* **harts** or **hart.** A male deer, esp. a male red deer over five years old. [ME < OE *heorot.*]

har·te·beest (här′tə-bēst′, härt′bēst′) *n., pl.* **-beests** or **hartebeest.** Either of two African antelopes, *Alcelaphus buselaphus* or *A. lichtensteini,* with a brownish coat and ridged, outward-curving horns. [Obs. Afr. < Du. : *hart,* deer + *beest,* beast.]

hart's-tongue (härts′tŭng′) *n.* An evergreen fern, *Phyllitis scolopendrium,* with narrow, undivided fronds. [So called from the shape of its fronds.]

har·um-scar·um (hâr′əm-skâr′əm, hăr′əm-skăr′əm) *adj.* Lacking a sense of responsibility; reckless. *—adv.* With abandon; recklessly. [Perh. < HARE + SCARE.]

ha·rus·pex (hə-rŭs′pĕks′, hăr′ə-spĕks′) *n., pl.* **ha·rus·pi·ces** (hə-rŭs′pĭ-sēz′). A Roman priest who practiced divination by the inspection of the entrails of animals. [Lat.]

har·vest (här′vĭst) *n.* **1.** The act or process of gathering a crop. **2.** The crop that ripens or is gathered in a season. **3. a.** The amount or measure of the crop gathered in one season. **b.** The time or season of such gathering. **4.** The result or consequence of an action. **—*modifier:*** *a harvest festival.* *—v.* **-vest·ed, -vest·ing, -vests.** *—tr.* **1.** To gather (a crop). **2.** To gather a crop from. **3.** To receive (the benefits or consequences of an action). *—intr.* To gather a crop. [ME < OE *hærfest.*]

harvest bug *n.* The chigger.

har·vest·er (här′vĭ-stər) *n.* **1.** A person who gathers a crop. **2.** A machine for harvesting crops; reaper.

harvest fly *n.* Any of several cicadas of the genus *Tibicen* that produce a shrill sound heard late in summer.

harvest home *n.* **1.** The completion of a harvest. **2. a.** The time of completing a harvest. **b.** A festival held at this time. **c.** A song sung at this time.

har·vest·man (här′vĭst-mən) *n.* **1.** One who harvests. **2.** The daddy longlegs.

harvest mite *n.* The chigger.

harvest moon *n.* The full moon that occurs nearest the autumnal equinox.

has (hăz) *v.* Third person singular present tense of **have.**

has-been (hăz′bĭn′) *n. Informal.* One that is no longer famous, popular, successful, or useful.

ha·sen·pfef·fer (hä′zən-fĕf′ər) *n.* A highly seasoned stew of marinated rabbit meat. [G. : *Hase,* rabbit (< MHG < OHG *haso*) + *Pfeffer,* pepper (< OHG *pfeffar* < Lat. *piper*).]

hash[1] (hăsh) *n.* **1.** A dish of chopped meat, potatoes, and sometimes vegetables, usually browned. **2.** A jumble or hodgepodge. **3.** A reworking or restatement of material already familiar. *—tr.v.* **hashed, hash·ing, hash·es. 1.** To chop into pieces; mince. **2.** *Informal.* To make a mess of; mangle. **3.** *Informal.* To discuss carefully; review: *hash over future plans.* **—*idioms.* make a hash of. 1.** To make a mess of; botch. **2.** To defeat soundly. **settle (someone's) hash.** To silence or subdue. [Fr. *hachis* < *hacher,* to chop up < OFr. *hachier* < *hache,* ax, of Germanic orig.]

hash[2] (hăsh) *n. Slang.* Hashish.

hash·eesh (hăsh′ēsh′) *n.* Variant of **hashish.**

hash house *n. Slang.* A cheap restaurant.

hash·ish (hăsh′ēsh′, -ĭsh) also **hash·eesh** (-ēsh′) *n.* A purified extract prepared from the dried flowers of the hemp plant, smoked or chewed as a mild narcotic. [Ar. *ḥashīsh.*]

hash mark *n. Slang.* A service stripe on the sleeve of an enlisted person's uniform.

Ha·sid (KHä′sĭd) *n.* Variant of **Chassid.**

has·let (hăs′lĭt, hăz′-) also **hars·let** (här′slĭt) *n.* The heart, liver, and other edible viscera of an animal, esp. hog viscera. [ME *hastelet* < OFr., dim. of *haste,* roast meat, spit, perh. < Lat. *hasta,* spear.]

has·n't (hăz′ənt). Has not.

hasp (hăsp) *n.* A metal fastener with a hinged, slotted part that fits over a staple and is secured by a pin, bolt, or padlock. *—tr.v.* **hasped, hasp·ing, hasps.** To fasten or lock with a hasp. [ME < OE *hæpse.*]

Has·sid (KHä′sĭd) *n.* Variant of **Chassid.**

has·sle (hăs′əl) *Informal.* *—n.* **1.** An argument or fight. **2.** Trouble; bother. *—v.* **-sled, -sling, -sles.** *—intr.* To argue or fight. *—tr.* To bother or harass: *street gangs hassling passers-by.* [Poss. HA(GGLE) + (TU)SSLE.]

has·sock (hăs′ək) *n.* **1.** A thick cushion used as a footstool or for kneeling. **2.** A dense clump of grass. [ME *hassok,* clump of grass < OE *hassuc.*]

hast (hăst) *v. Archaic.* Second person singular present tense of **have.**

has·tate (hăs′tāt′) *adj.* Shaped like the head of an arrow or spear: *a hastate leaf.* [NLat. *hastatus* < Lat. *hasta,* spear.] **—has′tate′ly** *adv.*

haste (hāst) *n.* **1.** Swiftness; rapidity. **2.** Overeagerness to act. **3.** Rash or headlong action; precipitateness. *—intr. & tr.v.* **hast·ed, hast·ing, hastes.** To hasten or cause to hasten. **—*idiom.* make haste.** To move or act swiftly; hurry. [ME < OFr., of Germanic orig.]

has·ten (hā′sən) *v.* **-tened, -ten·ing, -tens.** *—intr.* To move or act swiftly. *—tr.* **1.** To hurry. **2.** To speed the progress of; expedite.

hast·y (hā′stē) *adj.* **-i·er, -i·est. 1.** Characterized by speed; rapid. **2.** Done or made too quickly to be accurate or wise; rash: *a hasty decision.* **3.** Easily angered; irritable. **—hast′i·ly** *adv.* **—hast′i·ness** *n.*

hasty pudding *n.* **1.** Cornmeal mush served with maple syrup, brown sugar, or other sweetening. **2.** *Chiefly Brit.* A mush made with flour or oatmeal.

hat (hăt) *n.* **1.** A covering for the head, esp. one with a shaped crown and brim. **2. a.** A hat of distinctive color and shape worn as a symbol of office. **b.** The office symbolized by the wearing of such a hat. **3.** A role or office symbolized by or as if by the wearing of special hats: *wore different hats as homemaker and executive.* *—tr.v.* **hat·ted, hat·ting, hats.** To supply or cover with a hat. **—*idioms.* at the drop of a hat.** At the slightest pretext or provocation. **pass the hat.** To take up a collection of money. **take (one's) hat off to.** To respect, admire, or congratulate. **talk through (one's) hat. 1.** To talk nonsense. **2.** To bluff. **throw (or toss) (one's) hat into the ring.** To enter a political race as a candidate for office. **under (one's) hat.** As a secret or in confidence. [ME < OE *hæt.*]

hat·band (hăt′bănd′) *n.* A band of ribbon or cloth worn on a hat just above the brim.

hat·box (hăt′bŏks′) *n.* A usually round box or case for a hat.

hatch[1] (hăch) *n.* **1. a.** An opening, as in the deck of a ship, in the roof or floor of a building, or in an airplane. **b.** The cover for such an opening. **c.** A hatchway. **d.** A ship's compartment. **2.** A floodgate. [ME, small door < OE *hæc.*]

hatch[2] (hăch) *v.* **hatched, hatch·ing, hatch·es.** *—intr.* To emerge from or break out of an egg. *—tr.* **1.** To produce (young) from an egg. **2.** To cause (an egg) to produce young. **3.** To devise or originate, esp. in secret. *—n.* **1.** The act or an instance of hatching. **2.** The young hatched at one time; brood. [ME *hacchen.*] **—hatch′er** *n.*

hatch[3] (hăch) *tr.v.* **hatched, hatch·ing, hatch·es.** To shade by drawing or etching fine parallel or crossed lines on. *—n.* A fine line used in hatching. [ME *hachen,* to inlay < OFr. *hachier,* to draw lines, to cut < *hache,* ax, of Germanic orig.]

hatch·back (hăch′băk′) *n.* An automobile, as a coupe, having a hatch in a sloping back that opens upward.

hatch·el (hăch′əl) *n.* A comb for separating flax fibers. *—tr.v.* **-eled, -el·ing, -els** also **-elled, -el·ling, els.** To separate (flax fibers) with a hatchel. [ME *hechele.*]

hatch·er·y (hăch′ə-rē) *n., pl.* **-ies.** A place where eggs, esp. those of fish or poultry, are hatched.

hatch·et (hăch′ĭt) *n.* **1.** A small, short-handled ax for use in one hand. **2.** A tomahawk. **—*idiom.* bury the hatchet.** To stop fighting; make peace. [ME *hachet* < OFr. *hachete,* dim. of *hache,* ax, of Germanic orig.]

hatchet face *n.* A long, gaunt face with sharp features. **—hatch′et-faced′** *adj.*

hatchet man *n. Slang.* **1.** One hired to commit murder. **2.** One hired or assigned to carry out a disagreeable task or an unscrupulous order.

hatch·ing (hăch′ĭng) *n.* **1.** The fine lines used in graphic arts to give the impression of shading. **2.** The process of decorating with hatching.

hatch·ment (hăch′mənt) *n.* A panel bearing the coat of arms of a dead person. [Prob. alteration of ACHIEVEMENT.]

hatch·way (hăch′wā′) *n.* **1.** A hatch leading to a hold, compartment, or cellar. **2.** A ladder or stairway within a hatchway.

hate (hāt) *v.* **hat·ed, hat·ing, hates.** *—tr.* **1.** To feel animosity or hostility toward. **2.** To detest. **3.** To feel dislike or distaste for: *hates washing dishes.* *—intr.* To feel hatred. *—n.* **1.** Intense dislike or animosity; hatred. **2.** An object of detestation or hatred: *a pet hate.* [ME *haten* < OE *hatian.*] **—hat′er** *n.*

hate·ful (hāt′fəl) *adj.* **1.** Arousing hatred; detestable. **2.** Feeling or showing hatred; malevolent. **—hate′ful·ly** *adv.* **—hate′ful·ness** *n.*

Synonyms: *hateful, detestable, odious, obnoxious, offensive, repellent.* These adjectives, closely related and often interchangeable, describe what causes strong dislike or distaste. *Hateful* refers to what stirs up hatred, enmity, or animosity, and *detestable* to what arouses intense hatred or scorn. *Odious* suggests being the object of one's disgust or aversion. *Obnoxious* is applied to what causes irritation, resentment, or even stronger feeling, and often has reference to rude or insulting behavior. *Offensive* has wide application to what offends or arouses displeasure and is the least forceful of these terms unless qualified by an adverb. *Repellent* implies having a character or nature that drives people away or causes the possessor to be shunned.

hath (hăth) *v. Archaic.* Third person singular present tense of **have.**

ha·tred (hā′trĭd) *n.* Violent hostility or animosity. [ME : *hate,* hate + OE *rǣden,* condition.]

hat·ter (hăt′ər) *n.* One whose occupation is the manufacture, selling, or repair of hats.

hat trick *n.* **1.** Three wickets taken in cricket by a bowler in three consecutive balls. **2.** Three consecutive wins, hits, or goals made by one player in one game, as in ice hockey. [From the hat that was a reward for the feat.]

hau·ber·geon (hô′bər-jən) *n.* Variant of **habergeon.**

hau·berk (hô′bərk) *n.* A long tunic made of chain mail. [ME < OFr. *hauberc,* of Germanic orig.]

haugh (hôKH) *n. Scot.* A low-lying meadow in a river valley. [ME *hawch* < OE *healh,* corner of land.]

haugh·ty (hô′tē) *adj.* **-ti·er, -ti·est.** Proud and vain to the point of arrogance. [< ME *haut* < OFr. < Lat. *altus,* high.] **—haugh′ti·ly** *adv.* **—haugh′ti·ness** *n.*

haul (hôl) *v.* **hauled, haul·ing, hauls.** *—tr.* **1.** To pull or drag forcibly; tug. **2.** To transport, as with a truck or cart. **3.** To change the course of (a ship), esp. in order to sail closer into the wind. *—intr.* **1.** To pull; tug. **2.** To provide transportation; cart. **3. a.** To shift direction: *The wind hauled to the east.* **b.** To change one's mind. **4.** To change the course of a ship. **—*phrasal verbs.* haul off.** To draw back slightly, as in preparation for initiating an action: *hauled off and socked him.* **haul up.** To come to a halt. *—n.* **1.** The act of pulling or dragging. **2.** The act of transporting or carting. **3.** A distance, esp. the distance over which something is pulled or transported. **4.** Something that is pulled or transported; load. **5.** Everything collected or acquired by a single effort; the take: *a haul of fish.* **—*idiom.* for (or over) the long haul.** For a long time. [ME *haulen* < OFr. *haler,* of Germanic orig.] **—haul′er** *n.*

haul·age (hô′lĭj) *n.* **1.** The act or process of hauling. **2.** A charge made for hauling.

haulm also **halm** (hôm) *n. Chiefly Brit.* The stems of peas, beans, potatoes, or grasses. [ME *halm,* straw < OE.]

haunch (hônch, hŏnch) *n.* **1.** The hip, buttock, and upper thigh in humans and animals. **2.** The loin and leg of a four-footed animal, esp. as used for food: *a haunch of venison.* **3.** Either of the sides of an arch, curving down from the apex to an impost. [ME *haunche* < OFr. *hanche* < Med. Lat. *hancha,* of Germanic orig.]

haunt (hônt, hŏnt) *v.* **haunt·ed, haunt·ing, haunts.** *—tr.* **1.** To inhabit, visit, or appear to in the form of a ghost or other supernatural being. **2.** To visit often; frequent. **3.** To come to mind continually; obsess: *was haunted by the riddle.* **4.** To be continually present in; pervade: *the melancholy that haunts his music.* *—intr.* To recur or visit often, esp. as a ghost or other supernatural being. *—n.* **1.** A place much frequented. **2.** (hănt). *Regional.* A ghost or other supernatural being. [ME *haunten,* to frequent < OFr. *hanter.*]

haunt·ing (hôn′tĭng, hŏn′-) *adj.* Continually recurring to the mind; unforgettable: *a haunting melody.* **—haunt′ing·ly** *adv.*

Hau·sa (hou′sə, -zə) *n., pl.* **Hausa** or **Hau·sas. 1.** One of a Negroid people of Niger and northern Nigeria. **2.** The language of the Hausa, which is widely used as a trade language in western Africa.

haus·frau (hous′frou′) *n.* A housewife. [G.]

haus·tel·lum (hô-stĕl′əm) *n., pl.* **-tel·la** (-stĕl′ə). A mouth part prolonged into a proboscis and adapted as a sucking organ, as in many insects. [NLat. < Lat. *haustus,* p.part. of *haurire,* to draw up.] **—haus·tel′late** (hô-stĕl′ĭt, hô′stə-lāt′) *adj.*

haus·to·ri·um (hô-stôr′ē-əm, -stōr′-) *n., pl.* **-to·ri·a** (-stôr′ē-ə, -stōr′-). *Bot.* A specialized branch of hyphae or a similar structure by which parasitic plants such as fungi obtain food from a host plant. [NLat. < Lat. *haustus,* p.part. of *haurire,* to draw up.] **—haus·to′ri·al** *adj.*

haut·boy also **haut·bois** (hō′boi′, ō′boi′) *n., pl.* **-boys** also **-bois** (-boiz′). An oboe. [Fr. *hautbois* : *haut,* high (< Lat. *altus*) + *bois,* wood, of Germanic orig.]

haute cou·ture (ōt′ ko͞o-to͞or′) *n.* **1.** The leading establishments or designers for the creation of exclusive fashions for women. **2. a.** The creation of exclusive fashions for women. **b.** The fashions created. [Fr. : *haute,* high + *couture,* sewing.]

haute cui·sine (ōt′ kwĭ-zēn′) *n.* **1.** Elaborate or skillfully prepared cuisine. **2.** The food prepared in the style of haute cuisine. [Fr. : *haute,* high + *cuisine,* cooking.]

haute é·cole (ōt′ ā-kôl′) *n.* The art, techniques, or practice of expert horsemanship. [Fr. : *haute,* high + *école,* school.]

hau·teur (hō-tûr′, ō-tûr′) *n.* Haughtiness in bearing and attitude; arrogance. [Fr. < *haut,* high < Lat. *altus.*]

have (hăv) *v.* **had** (hăd), **hav·ing** (hăv′ĭng), **has** (hăz). **1. a.** To be in possession of: *already had a car.* **b.** To possess as a characteristic, quality, or function: *has a beard; had a great deal of energy.* **c.** To possess or contain as a constituent part: *a car that has an automatic choke.* **2.** To occupy a particular relation to: *had a great many disciples.* **3.** To possess knowledge of or facility in: *has very little Spanish.* **4.** To hold in the mind; entertain: *had doubts about his loyalty.* **5.** To use or exhibit in action: *have compassion.* **6. a.** To come into possession of; acquire: *Not one copy was to be had in the entire town.* **b.** To receive; get: *had a letter from my aunt.* **c.** To accept; take: *I'll have the blue one.* **7. a.** To suffer from: *have defective vision.* **b.** To be subject to the experience of: *had a difficult time last winter.* **8. a.** To cause to be done or performed: *have the clothes cleaned.* **b.** To cause to, as by persuasion or compulsion: *had him run an errand.* **c.** To cause to be: *had everyone fascinated.* **9.** To permit; allow: *won't have that kind of behavior in his house.* **10.** To carry on, perform, or execute: *have an argument.* **11. a.** To place at a disadvantage: *She has you on every point.* **b.** *Informal.* To get the better of, esp. by trickery or deception: *realized too late that they'd been had by a confidence man.* **12. a.** To procreate; beget: *wanted to have a son.* **b.** To bear: *She's going to have a baby.* **c.** To give birth to: *had twins.* **13.** To partake of: *have lunch.* **14.** To be obliged to; must: *simply have to get there on time.* **15.** To engage in sexual intercourse with. **16.** To influence by dishonest means; bribe: *an incorruptible official who could not be had.* *—aux.* Used with a past participle to form the following tenses indicating completed action: **a.** Present perfect: *has gone for good.* **b.** Past perfect: *regretted that he had lost his temper.* **c.** Future perfect: *will have finished by the time we arrive.* **—*phrasal verbs.* have at.** To attack. **have on. 1.** To wear: *had on red shoes.* **2.** To be scheduled: *have a dinner party on for tomorrow evening.* *—n.* One that possesses esp. material wealth. **—*idioms.* had better (**or **best).** Ought to: *You had better go now.* **have done with.** To stop; cease: *Have done with your foolish quibbling!* **have had it. 1.** To have done everything that is possible or that will be permitted. **2.** To have endured all that one can. **3.** To be in a state beyond remedy, repair, or salvage. **have it in for (someone).** To intend to harm, esp. because of a grudge. **have it out.** To settle decisively, esp. by means of an argument or discussion. **have (one's) eye on. 1.** To look at, esp. attentively and continuously. **2.** To have as one's objective. **have (something) coming.** To deserve whatever one receives: *He had that coming to him.* **have to do with.** To be concerned or associated with. [ME *haven* < OE *habban.*]

have·lock (hăv′lŏk′, -lək) *n.* A cloth covering for a cap, having a flap to cover and protect the back of the neck. [After Henry *Havelock* (1795–1857).]

ha·ven (hā′vən) *n.* **1.** A harbor or anchorage; port. **2.** A place of refuge or rest; sanctuary. *—tr.v.* **-vened, -ven·ing, -vens.** To put into or provide with a haven. [ME < OE *hæfen.*]

have-not (hăv′nŏt′) *n.* One enjoying little or no material wealth.

have·n't (hăv′ənt). Have not.

hav·er·sack (hăv′ər-săk′) *n.* A bag worn over one shoulder to carry supplies, as on a hike. [Fr. *havresac* < G. *Habersack* : *Haber,* oats (< OHG *habaro*) + *Sack,* sack (< OHG *sac* < Lat. *saccus*).]

hav·oc (hăv′ək) *n.* **1.** Widespread destruction; devastation. **2.** Disorder or chaos: *a wild party that created havoc in the house.* *—tr.v.* **-ocked, -ock·ing, -ocs.** To destroy or pillage. **—*idiom.* cry havoc.** To sound an alarm. [ME *havok* < AN.]

haw[1] (hô) *n.* An utterance used by a speaker who is fumbling for words. *—intr.v.* **hawed, haw·ing, haws.** To fumble in speaking. [Imit.]

haw[2] (hô) *n.* **1.** The fruit of a hawthorn. **2.** A hawthorn or similar tree or shrub. [ME < OE *haga.*]

haw[3] (hô) *n.* A nictitating membrane, esp. of a domesticated animal. [Orig. unknown.]

haw[4] (hô) *interj.* Used to command an animal to turn left. *—intr.v.* **hawed, haw·ing, haws.** To turn left.

Ha·wai·ian (hə-wä′yən) *n.* **1.** A native or resident of Hawaii. **2.** The Polynesian language of Hawaii. **—Ha·wai′ian** *adj.*

Hawaiian guitar *n.* An electric guitar consisting of a long sounding board and six to eight steel strings that are plucked while being pressed with a steel bar.

haw·finch (hô′fĭnch′) *n.* **1.** An Old World bird, *Coccothraustes coccothraustes,* having a thick bill, brown, white, and black plumage, and a short tail. **2.** Any of various birds similar or related to the hawfinch. [HAW[2] + FINCH.]

haw-haw (hô′hô′) *n.* Variant of **ha-ha[2].**

hawk[1] (hôk) *n.* **1. a.** Any of various birds of prey of the order Falconiformes, and esp. of the genera *Accipiter* and *Buteo,* characteristically having a short, hooked bill and strong claws adapted for seizing. **b.** Any of various similar birds. **2.** A person who preys on others; shark. **3. a.** *Informal.* A person who favors military force or action in order to carry out foreign policy. **b.** One who demonstrates an actively aggressive or combative attitude, as in an argument. *—intr.v.* **hawked, hawk·ing, hawks. 1.** To hunt with trained hawks. **2.** To swoop and strike in the manner of a hawk. [ME *hauk* < OE *hafoc.*] **—hawk′ish** *adj.* **—hawk′ish·ly** *adv.* **—hawk′ish·ness** *n.*

hawk[2] (hôk) *v.* **hawked, hawk·ing, hawks.** *—intr.* To peddle goods by calling out. *—tr.* To peddle (goods) by calling out. [Back-formation < HAWKER.]

hauberk

hawk[1]
Red-tailed hawk

hawksbill

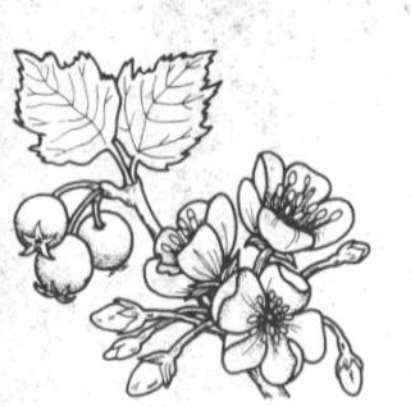

hawthorn

haystack

hazel

hawk³ (hôk) *v.* **hawked, hawk·ing, hawks.** *—intr.* To clear or attempt to clear the throat by or as if by coughing up phlegm. *—tr.* To clear the throat of (phlegm). *—n.* An audible effort to clear the throat by expelling phlegm. [Imit.]
hawk·er (hô'kər) *n.* A person who hawks goods; peddler. [Prob. < LG *höker* < MLG *hōker* < *hōken,* to peddle.]
hawk-eyed (hôk'īd') *adj.* Having very sharp eyesight.
hawk moth *n.* Any of various moths of the family Sphingidae, having a large body, long, narrow forewings, and characteristically feeding while in flight on nectar from flowers.
hawk's-beard (hôks'bîrd') *n.* Any of various plants of the genus *Crepis,* related to and resembling the dandelion.
hawks·bill (hôks'bĭl') *n.* A tropical sea turtle, *Eretmochelys imbricata,* valued as a source of tortoiseshell.
hawk·weed (hôk'wēd') *n.* Any of various often hairy plants of the genus *Hieracium,* having yellow or orange dandelion-like flowers.
hawse (hôz) *n.* **1.** The part of a ship where the hawseholes are located. **2.** A hawsehole. **3.** The space between the bows and anchors of an anchored ship. **4.** The arrangement of a ship's anchor cables when both starboard and port anchors are secured. [ME *hals,* bow strake < ON, bow.]
hawse·hole (hôz'hōl') *n.* An opening in the bow of a ship through which a cable or hawser is passed.
haw·ser (hô'zər) *n.* A cable or rope used in mooring or towing a ship. [ME < AN *hauceur* < OFr. *haucier,* to hoist < Lat. *altus,* high.]
haw·thorn (hô'thôrn') *n.* Any of various thorny trees or shrubs of the genus *Crataegus,* having white or pinkish flowers and reddish fruit. [ME < OE *hagaðorn* : *haga,* haw + *ðorn,* thorn.]
hay (hā) *n.* **1.** Grass or other plants, such as clover or alfalfa, cut and dried for fodder. **2.** *Slang.* A trifling amount of money: *gets $100 an hour, which isn't hay.* *—v.* **hayed, hay·ing, hays.** *—intr.* To mow and cure grass and herbage for hay. *—tr.* **1.** To make (grass) into hay. **2.** To feed with hay. [ME < OE *hīeg.*] **—hay'er** *n.*
hay·cock (hā'kŏk') *n.* *Chiefly Brit.* A conical mound of hay.
hay fever *n.* An acute allergic condition of the mucous membranes of the upper respiratory tract and the eyes, characterized by a running nose and sneezing, conjunctivitis, and headaches and often caused by an abnormal sensitivity to certain airborne pollens, esp. of the ragweed and related plants.
hay·fork (hā'fôrk') *n.* **1.** A hand tool for pitching hay. **2.** A machine-operated fork for moving hay.
hay·loft (hā'lôft', -lŏft') *n.* A loft for storing hay.
hay·mak·er (hā'mā'kər) *n.* **1.** One that hays. **2.** *Slang.* A powerful blow with the fist.
hay·mow (hā'mou') *n.* **1.** A hayloft. **2.** The hay stored in a hayloft. **3.** *Archaic.* A haystack.
hay·rack (hā'răk') *n.* **1.** A rack from which livestock feed. **2. a.** A rack fitted to a wagon for carrying hay. **b.** A wagon fitted with such a rack.
hay·seed (hā'sēd') *n.* **1.** Grass seed shaken out of hay. **2.** Pieces of chaff or straw that fall from hay. **3.** *Slang.* A country bumpkin; yokel.
hay·stack (hā'stăk') *n.* A large stack of hay for winter storage in the open.
hay·wire (hā'wīr') *n.* Wire used in baling hay. *—adj. Informal.* **1.** Not functioning properly; broken. **2.** Mentally or emotionally upset; crazy: *went haywire when his wife died.*
haz·ard (hăz'ərd) *n.* **1.** A chance; accident. **2.** A chance of being injured or harmed; danger: *Space travel is full of hazards.* **3.** A possible source of danger: *a fire hazard.* **4.** A dice game similar to craps. **5.** A sandtrap or other obstacle on a golf course. *—tr.v.* **-ard·ed, -ard·ing, -ards. 1.** To expose to danger or harm. **2.** To venture (something); dare: *hazard a guess.* [ME, dice game < OFr. *hasard* < OSp. *azar* < Ar. *azzahr,* gaming die.]
haz·ard·ous (hăz'ər-dəs) *adj.* **1.** Marked by danger; perilous. **2.** Depending on chance; risky. **—haz'ard·ous·ly** *adv.* **—haz'ard·ous·ness** *n.*
haze¹ (hāz) *n.* **1. a.** Atmospheric moisture, dust, smoke, and vapor suspended to form a partially opaque condition. **b.** The atmospheric condition so formed. **2.** A vague or confused state of mind. *—intr.v.* **hazed, haz·ing, haz·es.** To become misty or hazy; blur. [Prob. back-formation < HAZY.]
haze² (hāz) *tr.v.* **hazed, haz·ing, haz·es. 1.** *Naut.* To persecute or harass with meaningless, difficult, or humiliating tasks. **2.** To initiate, as into a college fraternity, by exacting humiliating performances from or playing rough practical jokes upon. **3.** *Regional.* To drive (cattle or horses) with saddle horses. [Orig. unknown.] **—haz'er** *n.*
ha·zel (hā'zəl) *n.* **1. a.** Any of various shrubs or small trees of the genus *Corylus,* esp. *C. avellana,* of Europe, or *C. americana,* of North America, bearing edible nuts enclosed in a leafy husk. **b.** The nut of such a shrub or tree, having a smooth brown shell. **2.** A light to strong brown or yellowish brown. [ME *hasel* < OE *hæsel.*] **—ha'zel** *adj.*
ha·zel·nut (hā'zəl-nŭt') *n.* The hard-shelled, edible nut of a hazel.
haz·y (hā'zē) *adj.* **-i·er, -i·est. 1.** Marked by the presence of haze; misty. **2.** Not clearly defined; vague. [Orig. unknown.] **—haz'i·ly** *adv.* **—haz'i·ness** *n.*
haz·zan (KHä'zən) *n.* Variant of **chazan.**
H-bomb (āch'bŏm') *n.* A hydrogen bomb.
he¹ (hē) *pron.* **1.** The male that is neither the speaker nor the hearer. **2.** Used to refer to any person whose sex is not specified: *He who hesitates is lost.* *—n.* A male animal or person: *Is the cat a he?* —See Usage notes at **be, everyone,** and **I.** [ME < OE *hē.*]
he² (hā) *n.* The 5th letter of the Hebrew alphabet. See table at **alphabet.** [Heb. *hē.*]
He The symbol for the element helium.
head (hĕd) *n.* **1. a.** The uppermost or forwardmost part of the body of a vertebrate, containing the brain or principal ganglia and the eyes, ears, nose, mouth, and jaws. **b.** The analogous part of an invertebrate organism. **2.** The seat of the faculty of reason; intelligence, intellect, or mind: *did the figuring in his head.* **3.** A mental ability or aptitude: *a good head for mathematics.* **4.** Freedom of choice or of action: *gave him his head.* **5.** *Slang.* A habitual drug user: *an acid head.* **6.** A portrait or representation of a person's head. **7.** Often **heads** *(used with a sing. verb).* The side of a coin having the principal design and the date. **8.** *Informal.* A headache. **9. a.** An individual; person: *count heads.* **b.** *pl.* **head.** A single animal: *20 head of cattle.* **10.** A person who leads, rules, or is in charge of something; leader, chief, or director: *heads of state.* **11.** The foremost or leading position: *marched at the head of the parade.* **12.** A headwater. **13. a.** The difference in depth of a liquid at two given points. **b.** The measure of pressure at the lower point expressed in terms of this difference. **c.** The pressure exerted by a liquid or gas: *a head of steam.* **14.** The froth or foam that rises to the top in pouring an effervescent liquid, such as beer. **15.** The tip of an abscess, boil, or pimple, in which pus forms. **16.** A turning point; crisis: *bring matters to a head.* **17. a.** A projection, weight, or fixture at the end of an elongated object: *the head of a pin.* **b.** The working end of a tool or implement: *the head of a hammer.* **c.** The part of an explosive device that carries the explosive; warhead. **18.** An attachment to or part of a machine that holds or contains the operative device: *the recording head of a tape recorder.* **19.** A rounded, compact mass of leaves, buds, or flowers: *a head of cabbage.* **20.** *Bot.* A dense, compact cluster of flowers, as of composite plants or clover. **21.** The uppermost part of something; top: *Place the appropriate name at the head of each column.* **22.** The end considered the most important: *The host usually sits at the head of the table.* **23.** Either end of an object whose two ends are interchangeable, as a drum. **24.** *Naut.* **a.** The forward part of a vessel. **b.** The toilet on a ship. **c.** The top part or upper edge of a sail. **25.** A passage or gallery in a coal mine. **26. a.** The top of a book or of a page. **b.** *Informal.* A headline or heading. **c.** A distinct topic or category. **27.** Headway; progress. **28.** *Gram.* A word in a construction that has the same grammatical function as the construction as a whole, as *boy* in *a lazy young boy.* ***—modifier:*** *a head covering; the head librarian.* *—v.* **head·ed, head·ing, heads.** *—tr.* **1.** To be in charge of; lead: *The minister headed the committee.* **2.** To be in the first or foremost position of: *Collins heads the list of job candidates.* **3.** To aim, point, or turn in a certain direction: *headed the team of horses up the hill.* **4.** To remove the head or top of. **5.** To hit (a soccer ball) in the air with one's head. **6.** To place a heading on: *head each column with a number.* *—intr.* **1.** To proceed or go in a certain direction: *head for town.* **2.** To form a head, as lettuce or cabbage. **3.** To originate, as a stream or river; rise. ***—phrasal verb.*** **head off.** To block the progress or completion of; intercept: *Try to head him off before he gets home.* ***—idioms.*** **go to (one's) head. 1.** To make one lightheaded or drunk: *Wine goes to her head.* **2.** To make conceited: *Success went to his head.* **head and shoulders above.** Far superior to: *head and shoulders above her colleagues in analytical capability.* **head over heels. 1.** Rolling, as in a somersault: *tripped and fell head over heels.* **2.** Completely; hopelessly: *head over heels in love.* **keep (one's) head.** To remain calm; remain in control of oneself. **lose (one's) head.** To lose one's poise or self-control. **off** (or **out of**) **(one's) head.** Insane; crazy. **over (one's) head. 1.** Beyond one's ability to understand or deal with: *a subject that is completely over her head.* **2.** To a higher-ranking person: *went over his boss's head and spoke to the manager.* **put heads together.** To consult and plan together. [ME < OE *hēafod.*]

Usage: The phrase *head up* is sometimes used in place of the verb *head: She heads up the committee.* The use of *head up* is unacceptable to a large majority of the Usage Panel.

head·ache (hĕd'āk') *n.* **1.** A pain in the head. **2.** *Informal.* Something, such as a problem, that causes annoyance or trouble. **—head'ach'y** (-ā'kē) *adj.*
head·band (hĕd'bănd') *n.* **1.** A band worn around the head. **2.** An ornamental strip at the top of a page or beginning of a chapter or paragraph. **3.** A cloth band attached to the top of the spine of a book.
head·board (hĕd'bôrd', -bōrd') *n.* A board or panel that forms the head, as of a bed.
head·cheese (hĕd'chēz') *n.* A jellied loaf or sausage made from chopped and boiled parts of the feet, head, and sometimes the tongue and heart of an animal, usually a hog.
head cold *n.* Coryza.

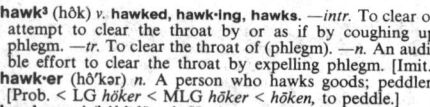

ă pat / ā pay / âr care / ä father / b **bib** / ch **church** / d **deed** / ĕ pet / ē be / f **fife** / g **gag** / h **hat** / hw **which** / ĭ pit / ī **pie** / îr **pier** /
j **judge** / k **kick** / l **lid,** needle / m **mum** / n **no,** sudden / ng **thing** / ŏ pot / ō **toe** / ô **paw, for** / oi **noise** / ou **out** / o͝o **took** / o͞o **boot** /

head·count·er (hĕd′koun′tər) *n.* A pollster.
head·dress (hĕd′drĕs′) *n.* **1.** A covering or ornament for the head. **2.** A hairdo; coiffure.
head·ed (hĕd′ĭd) *adj.* **1.** Growing or grown into a head. **2.** Having a head or heading. **3.** Having a specified kind or number of heads: *a two-headed eagle.*
head·er (hĕd′ər) *n.* **1.** One that fits a head on an object. **2.** One that removes a head from an object, esp. a machine that reaps the heads of grain and passes them into a wagon or receptacle. **3.** A pipe that serves as a central connection for two or more smaller pipes. **4.** A floor or roof beam placed between two long beams that supports the ends of the tailpieces. **5.** A brick laid across rather than parallel with a wall. **6.** *Informal.* A headlong dive or fall.
head·first (hĕd′fûrst′) also **head·fore·most** (hĕd′fôr′mōst′, -məst, -fōr′-) *adv.* **1.** With the head leading; headlong: *went headfirst down the stairs.* **2.** Impetuously; brashly.
head gate *n.* **1.** A control gate upstream of a lock or canal. **2.** A floodgate that controls the flow of water in a ditch, sluice, race, or channel.
head·gear (hĕd′gîr′) *n.* **1.** A covering, such as a hat or helmet, for the head. **2.** The part of a harness that fits about a horse's head. **3.** The rigging for hauling or lifting located at the head of a mine shaft.
head-hunt·ing (hĕd′hŭn′tĭng) *n.* **1.** The custom of cutting off and preserving the heads of enemies as trophies. **2.** *Slang.* The process of attempting to remove influence and position from enemies, esp. political enemies. **3.** *Slang.* The attempt to recruit personnel, esp. executive personnel, as for a corporation. **—head′-hunt′er** *n.*
head·ing (hĕd′ĭng) *n.* **1.** The title, subtitle, or topic that stands at the top or beginning, as of a text. **2.** The course or direction in which a ship or aircraft is moving. **3.** A gallery or drift in a mine.
head·lamp (hĕd′lămp′) *n.* A headlight.
head·land (hĕd′lənd, -lănd′) *n.* **1.** A point of land, usually high and with a sheer drop, extending out into a body of water; promontory. **2.** The unplowed land at the end of a plowed furrow.
head·less (hĕd′lĭs) *adj.* **1. a.** Without a head. **b.** Decapitated. **2.** Lacking a leader or director. **3.** Brainless; foolish. **—head′less·ness** *n.*
head·light (hĕd′līt′) *n.* A lamp mounted on the front of a vehicle.
head·line (hĕd′līn′) *n.* **1.** The title or caption of a newspaper article, usually set in large type. **2.** A line at the head of a page or passage giving information such as the title, author, and page number. *—tr.v.* **-lined, -lin·ing, -lines. 1.** To supply (a page or passage) with a headline. **2. a.** To present as a headliner: *The Palace Theater headlines a magician.* **b.** To serve as the headliner of: *He headlines the bill.*
head·lin·er (hĕd′lī′nər) *n.* A performer who receives prominent billing; star.
head·lock (hĕd′lŏk′) *n.* A wrestling hold in which the head of one wrestler is locked under the arm of the other.
head·long (hĕd′lông′, -lŏng′) *adv.* **1.** With the head leading; headfirst. **2.** Impetuously; rashly. *—adj.* (hĕd′lông′, -lŏng′). **1.** Done with the head leading; headfirst: *a headlong dive.* **2.** Impetuous; rash. **3.** *Archaic.* Steep; sheer. [ME *hedling* < *hed,* head.]
head·mas·ter also **head master** (hĕd′măs′tər) *n.* A man who is principal of a school, usually a private school.
head·mis·tress also **head mistress** (hĕd′mĭs′trĭs) *n.* A woman who is principal of a school, usually a private girls' school.
head·most (hĕd′mōst′, -məst) *adj.* Leading; foremost.
head-on (hĕd′ŏn′, -ôn′) *adj.* **1.** Facing forward; frontal. **2.** With the front end foremost: *a head-on collision.* **—head′-on′** *adv.*
head·phone (hĕd′fōn′) *n.* A receiver, as for a radio, held to the ear by a headband.
head·piece (hĕd′pēs′) *n.* **1.** A protective covering for the head. **2.** A set of headphones; headset. **3.** A headstall. **4.** An ornamental design, esp. at the top of a page.
head pin *n.* A kingpin (sense 1).
head·quar·ter (hĕd′kwôr′tər) *tr. & intr.v.* **-tered, -ter·ing, -ters.** *Informal.* To provide with or establish headquarters.
Usage: The verb *headquarter* is used informally in both transitive and intransitive senses: *The European correspondent will headquarter in Paris. The magazine has headquartered him in a building that houses many foreign journalists.* Both these examples are unacceptable in formal writing to a large majority of the Usage Panel.
head·quar·ters (hĕd′kwôr′tərz) *pl.n. (used with a sing. or pl. verb).* **1.** The offices of a commander, as of a military unit, from which official orders are issued. **2.** A center of operations or administration: *The company has its headquarters in the suburbs.*
Usage: The noun *headquarters* is used with either a singular or a plural verb. The plural is more common: *The headquarters are in Boston.* But the singular is sometimes preferred when reference is to authority rather than to physical location: *Battalion headquarters has approved the retreat.*
head·race (hĕd′rās′) *n.* A watercourse that feeds water into a mill, water wheel, or turbine.
head·rest (hĕd′rĕst′) *n.* **1.** A support for the head, as at the back of a chair. **2.** A cushion attached to the top of the back of an automobile seat, esp. to prevent whiplash injury.
head restraint *n.* A headrest (sense 2).
head·sail (hĕd′səl, -sāl′) *n.* A sail, such as a jib, set forward of a foremast.
head·set (hĕd′sĕt′) *n.* A pair of headphones.
head·ship (hĕd′shĭp′) *n.* The position or office of a head or leader.
head shop *n. Slang.* A specialty shop that sells paraphernalia for drug users.
head shrinker *n. Slang.* A psychiatrist, esp. a psychoanalyst.
heads·man (hĕdz′mən) *n.* A public executioner who beheads condemned prisoners.
head·spring (hĕd′sprĭng′) *n.* A fountainhead; source.
head·stall (hĕd′stôl′) *n.* The section of a bridle that fits over a horse's head.
head start *n.* **1.** A start before other contestants in a race. **2.** An early start that confers an advantage.
head·stock (hĕd′stŏk′) *n.* A nonmoving part of a machine or powered tool that supports a revolving part, such as the spindle of a lathe.
head·stone (hĕd′stōn′) *n.* **1.** A memorial stone set at the head of a grave. **2.** Also **head stone.** A keystone.
head·strong (hĕd′strông′, -strŏng′) *adj.* **1.** Inclined to insist on having one's own way; willful and obstinate. **2.** Resulting from willfulness and obstinacy.
heads up *interj.* Used as a warning to watch out for a potential source of danger, as at a construction site.
head-trip (hĕd′trĭp′) *n. Slang.* **1.** An experience that stimulates the mind. **2.** An exploration of one's own perceptions or emotions.
head·wait·er (hĕd′wā′tər) *n.* A waiter who is in charge of the other waiters in a restaurant and is often responsible for taking reservations and seating guests.
head·wa·ter (hĕd′wô′tər, -wŏt′ər) *n.* Often **headwaters.** The water from which a river rises.
head·way (hĕd′wā′) *n.* **1.** Movement forward; advance. **2.** Progress toward a goal. **3.** The clear vertical space beneath a ceiling or archway; clearance. **4.** The amount of distance or time that separates two vehicles traveling the same route.
head wind *n.* A wind blowing directly opposite to the course of a plane or ship.
head·work (hĕd′wûrk′) *n.* Mental activity or work. **—head′work′er** *n.*
head·y (hĕd′ē) *adj.* **-i·er, -i·est. 1.** Tending to make dizzy; intoxicating: *a heady success; heady perfume.* **2.** Headstrong; obstinate. **—head′i·ly** *adv.* **—head′i·ness** *n.*
heal (hēl) *v.* **healed, heal·ing, heals.** *—tr.* **1.** To restore to health or soundness; cure. **2.** To set right; repair: *healed the rift between us.* **3.** To restore (a person) to spiritual wholeness. *—intr.* To become whole and sound; return to health. [ME *helen* < OE *hǣlan.*] **—heal′a·ble** *adj.* **—heal′er** *n.*
heal-all (hēl′ôl′) *n.* The self-heal.
health (hĕlth) *n.* **1.** The overall condition of an organism at a given time: *was in poor health.* **2.** Soundness, esp. of body or mind; freedom from disease or abnormality. **3.** A condition of optimal well-being: *concerned about the ecological health of the area.* **4.** A wish for someone's good health, often expressed as a toast. [ME *helthe* < OE *hǣlð.*]
health food *n.* A food believed to be highly beneficial to health.
health·ful (hĕlth′fəl) *adj.* **1.** Conducive to good health; salutary. **2.** Healthy. —See Usage note at **healthy. —health′ful·ly** *adv.* **—health′ful·ness** *n.*
health insurance *n.* Insurance against expenses incurred through illness of the insured.
health spa *n.* A business establishment with equipment and facilities to help customers lose weight.
health·y (hĕl′thē) *adj.* **-i·er, -i·est. 1.** Possessing good health. **2.** Conducive to good health; healthful: *healthy air.* **3.** Indicative of good health; sound: *a healthy attitude.* **4.** Sizable; considerable: *a healthy portion.* **—health′i·ly** *adv.* **—health′i·ness** *n.*
Synonyms: *healthy, sound, wholesome, hale, robust, well, hardy, vigorous, well-preserved.* These adjectives are compared in the sense of being in good physical or mental condition. *Healthy* stresses the absence of disease and often implies energetic activity. *Sound* emphasizes freedom from imperfection or impairment of function. *Wholesome* suggests appealing healthiness and moral fitness. *Hale* stresses absence of infirmity, especially in elderly persons. *Robust* emphasizes physical strength and ruggedness. *Well* merely specifies absence of sickness. *Hardy* is applicable to one capable of withstanding physical hardship, and *vigorous* to one whose energy and activity are indicative of a sound mind and body. *Well-preserved* refers to lack of outward evidence of bodily deterioration.
Usage: One can expect to be *healthy* ("full of health") if the regimen one follows is *healthful* ("conducive to health"). However, the distinction is breaking down. *Healthful* is largely restricted to the meaning "conducive to health," but *healthy* is commonly used in both senses: *a healthy person; a healthy climate.*
heap (hēp) *n.* **1.** A group of things piled haphazardly or in

disorder. **2.** *Informal.* A great deal; a lot. **3.** *Slang.* An old or run-down car; rattletrap. —*tr.v.* **heaped, heap·ing, heaps. 1.** To put or throw in a heap; pile up. **2.** To fill to overflowing: *heap a plate with vegetables.* **3.** To bestow in abundance or lavishly. [ME < OE *hēap.*]

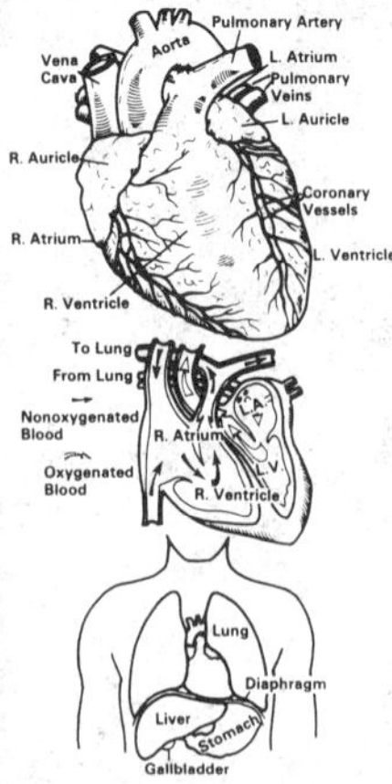

heart

hear (hîr) *v.* **heard** (hûrd), **hear·ing, hears.** —*tr.* **1.** To perceive by the ear. **2.** To listen to attentively. **3. a.** To learn by hearing. **b.** To acquire, as news or information. **4.** To listen to in an official, professional, or formal capacity: *heard the last witness in the afternoon.* **5.** To attend. —*intr.* **1.** To be capable of perceiving sound. **2.** To receive news or information; learn: *I heard about your accident.* **3.** To refuse to consider something: *I won't hear of your going!* [ME *hearen* < OE *hīeran.*] **—hear'er** *n.*

hear·ing (hîr'ĭng) *n.* **1.** The sense by which sound is perceived; the capacity to hear. **2.** The range of audibility; earshot. **3.** An opportunity to be heard. **4.** *Law.* **a.** A preliminary examination of an accused person. **b.** The trial of an equity case. **5.** A session, as of an investigatory committee, at which testimony is taken from witnesses.

hearing aid *n.* An electronic apparatus that amplifies sound and is worn to compensate for poor hearing.

hear·ken also **har·ken** (här'kən) *v.* **-kened, -ken·ing, -kens.** —*intr.* To listen attentively; give heed. —*tr. Archaic.* To listen to; hear. [ME *herknen* < OE *hercnian.*]

hear·say (hîr'sā') *n.* **1.** Information heard from another. **2.** *Law.* Evidence based on the reports of others rather than on the personal knowledge of a witness and therefore generally not admissible as testimony.

hearse (hûrs) *n.* **1.** A vehicle for conveying a dead person to a church or cemetery. **2.** A triangular candelabrum used at Tenebrae during Holy Week in the Roman Catholic Church. **3.** A framelike structure over a coffin or tomb on which to hang epitaphs. [ME *herse,* a harrow-shaped structure for holding candles over a coffin < OFr. *herce* < Med. Lat. *hercia* < Lat. *hirpex,* harrow.]

heart (härt) *n.* **1. a.** *Anat.* The hollow, muscular organ in vertebrates that pumps blood received from the veins into the arteries, thereby supplying the entire circulatory system. **b.** A similarly functioning structure in invertebrates. **2.** The area that is the approximate location of the heart in the body; breast. **3.** The vital center of one's being, emotions, and sensibilities. **4. a.** Emotional constitution, disposition, or mood: *had a change of heart.* **b.** Capacity for sympathy or concern; compassion: *He has no heart.* **c.** Love; affection: *The child won his heart.* **5.** Courage; fortitude. **6. a.** The central or innermost physical part: *the heart of the financial district.* **b.** The most important or essential part: *the heart of the problem.* **7.** A conventionalized two-lobed representation of the heart. **8. a.** A playing card bearing a red, heart-shaped symbol. **b. hearts.** The suit of cards marked with this symbol. **9. hearts** *(used with a sing. verb).* A card game in which the object is either to avoid hearts when taking tricks or to take all the hearts. —*tr.v.* **heart·ed, heart·ing, hearts.** *Archaic.* To encourage; hearten. **—idioms. by heart.** By memory or rote. **heart and soul.** Completely; entirely. **to (one's) heart's content.** To one's entire satisfaction, without limitation. **with all (one's) heart. 1.** With great willingness or pleasure. **2.** With the deepest feeling or devotion. [ME *hert* < OE *heorte.*]

heart·ache (härt'āk') *n.* Emotional anguish; sorrow.

heart attack *n.* **1.** The condition or an instance of heart failure. **2.** A seizure of abnormal heart functioning, as a coronary thrombosis.

heart·beat (härt'bēt') *n.* **1.** A single complete pulsation of the heart. **2.** The vital force or driving impulse.

heart block *n.* Reduction or complete lack of coordination in the beating of the atria and ventricles of the heart.

heart·break (härt'brāk') *n.* Intense sorrow or grief.

heart·break·ing (härt'brā'kĭng) *adj.* **1.** Causing heartbreak. **2.** Causing great distress or difficulty. **—heart'break'ing·ly** *adv.*

heart·bro·ken (härt'brō'kən) *adj.* Suffering from or exhibiting great grief or despair. **—heart'bro'ken·ly** *adv.* **—heart'bro'ken·ness** *n.*

hearth
Lawrence House, Medford, Massachusetts

heart·burn (härt'bûrn') *n.* A burning sensation in the stomach and esophagus, often accompanied by the eructation of small quantities of a highly acid fluid, caused by excess acidity of stomach fluids; pyrosis.

heart disease *n.* Organic or functional abnormality of the heart.

heart·en (här'tn) *tr.v.* **-ened, -en·ing, -ens.** To give strength or hope to; encourage.

heart failure *n.* The inability of the heart to pump blood at an adequate rate, resulting in congestion in the tissues, shortness and wheezing of breath, pitting edema, and enlarged and tender liver.

heart·felt (härt'fĕlt') *adj.* Deeply or sincerely felt; earnest.

hearth (härth) *n.* **1.** The floor of a fireplace, usually extending into a room and paved with brick, flagstone, or cement. **2.** The fireside as a symbol of home or family life. **3.** *Metallurgy.* **a.** The lowest part of a blast furnace or cupola, from which the molten metal flows. **b.** The bottom of a reverberatory furnace, where ore is exposed to the flame. **4.** The fireplace of a blacksmith's forge. [ME *herth* < OE *heorth.*]

hearth money *n.* Peter's pence (sense 2).

heather

hearth·stone (härth'stōn') *n.* **1.** Stone used in the construction of a hearth. **2.** The fireside; home. **3.** A soft stone or powder used for scouring and whitening hearths or doorsteps.

heart·i·ly (här'tl-ē) *adv.* **1.** In a hearty manner. **2.** With sincere good will; warmly. **3.** Thoroughly; completely: *wished heartily that they would leave.* **4.** With great appetite or enjoyment: *eat heartily.*

heart·land (härt'lănd') *n.* A central region, esp. one held in geopolitical theory to be strategically, economically, or militarily vital to a nation.

heart·less (härt'lĭs) *adj.* **1.** Devoid of compassion or feeling. **2.** *Archaic.* Devoid of enthusiasm; spiritless. **—heart'less·ly** *adv.* **—heart'less·ness** *n.*

heart-rend·ing (härt'rĕn'dĭng) *adj.* Evoking anguish or deep distress.

hearts·ease also **heart's-ease** (härts'ēz') *n.* **1.** Peace of mind. **2.** A plant, *Viola tricolor,* native to Eurasia, having small, spurred, variously colored flowers. [ME *herts ease.*]

heart·sick (härt'sĭk') *adj.* Profoundly disappointed; despondent. **—heart'sick'ness** *n.*

heart-strick·en (härt'strĭk'ən) also **heart-struck** (-strŭk') *adj.* Overwhelmed with grief, dismay, or remorse.

heart·string (härt'strĭng') *n.* **1. heartstrings.** The deepest feelings or affections: *a tug at the heartstrings.* **2.** One of the nerves or tendons formerly believed to brace and sustain the heart.

heart-struck (härt'strŭk') *adj.* Variant of **heart-stricken.**

heart·throb (härt'thrŏb') *n.* **1.** A heartbeat. **2. a.** Sentimental or tender emotion. **b.** A sweetheart.

heart-to-heart (härt'tə-härt') *adj.* Candid; frank.

heart·wood (härt'wo͝od') *n.* The older, inactive central wood of a tree or woody plant, usually darker and harder than the sapwood.

heart·worm (härt'wûrm') *n.* A nematode worm, *Dirofilaria immitis,* parasitic in the heart and bloodstream of dogs and other mammals.

heart·y (här'tē) *adj.* **-i·er, -i·est. 1.** Marked by unrestrained warmth of feeling: *a hearty welcome.* **2.** Complete or thorough; unequivocal. **3.** Vigorous; robust. **4. a.** Enjoying or requiring much food: *a hearty appetite.* **b.** Providing abundant nourishment. **c.** Satisfying; substantial: *a hearty meal.* —*n., pl.* **-ies. 1.** A good fellow; comrade. **2.** A sailor.

heat (hēt) *n.* **1.** A form of energy associated with the motion of atoms or molecules in solids and capable of being transmitted through solid and fluid media by conduction, through fluid media by convection, and through empty space by radiation. **2.** The physiological sensation of being hot. **3. a.** A pathologically intense body temperature. **b.** Intense or excessive warmth. **4.** The condition of being hot. **5. a.** Intensity, as of emotion. **b.** The most intense or active stage: *the heat of battle.* **6.** Estrus. **7.** One of a series of efforts or attempts. **8. a.** One round of several in a competition, such as a race. **b.** A preliminary contest held to determine finalists. **9.** *Informal.* Pressure; stress. **10.** *Slang.* **a.** An intensification esp. of police activity in pursuing criminals. **b.** The police. —*v.* **heat·ed, heat·ing, heats.** —*tr.* **1.** To make warm or hot. **2.** To excite the feelings of; inflame. —*intr.* **1.** To become warm or hot. **2.** To become excited emotionally or intellectually. [ME *hete* < OE *hǣtu.*]

heat capacity *n.* The amount of heat required to raise the temperature of a body by one degree, either at constant pressure or at constant volume and without inducing chemical changes or change of phase.

heat·er (hē'tər) *n.* **1.** An apparatus that heats or provides heat. **2.** One who heats something or tends a heating apparatus. **3.** *Slang.* A pistol.

heat exchanger *n.* A device used to transfer heat from a fluid flowing on one side of a barrier to a fluid or fluids flowing on the other.

heat exhaustion *n.* A reaction to excessive heat, marked by prostration, weakness, and collapse resulting from dehydration.

heath (hēth) *n.* **1.** Any of various usually low-growing shrubs of the genus *Erica* and related genera, native to the Old World, having small evergreen leaves and small, urn-shaped pink or purplish flowers. **2.** An extensive tract of open, uncultivated land covered with herbage and low shrubs. [ME, uncultivated land < OE *hǣð.*]

hea·then (hē'*th*ən) *n., pl.* **-thens** or **heathen. 1. a.** One who belongs to a tribe or nation that does not acknowledge the God of Judaism, Christianity, or Islam. **b.** Such persons collectively; the unconverted. **2. a.** One who is regarded as irreligious or uncivilized. **b.** Such persons collectively. [ME *hethen* < OE *hǣðen.*] **—hea'then** *adj.* **—hea'then·dom** (-dəm), **hea'then·ism, hea'then·ry** *n.*

hea·then·ish (hē'*th*ə-nĭsh) *adj.* **1.** Of or having to do with the heathen. **2.** Uncouth; barbarous. **—hea'then·ish·ly** *adv.* **—hea'then·ish·ness** *n.*

heath·er (hĕ*th*'ər) *n.* **1.** A low-growing shrub, *Calluna vulgaris,* native to Eurasia, growing in dense masses and having small evergreen leaves and clusters of small, urn-shaped pinkish-purple flowers. **2.** Heath (sense 1). **3.** A grayish purple to purplish red. [ME *hathir.*] **—heath'er** *adj.*

heath·er·y (hĕ*th*'ə-rē) *adj.* **1.** Of, relating to, or like heather. **2.** Flecked with various colors.

heath hen *n.* A prairie chicken, *Tympanuchus cupido,* that became extinct in eastern North America during the first part of the 20th century.
heat island *n.* An industrial or urban area in which a greater amount of heat is retained, as by buildings and streets, than in areas nearby, as the suburbs.
heat lightning *n.* Intermittent flashes of light across the horizon on a hot summer evening, unaccompanied by thunder and thought to be cloud reflections of distant lightning.
heat of fusion *n.* The quantity of heat required to melt a unit mass of a solid at a specified temperature.
heat of vaporization *n.* The amount of heat required to convert a unit liquid mass at a specified temperature into vapor.
heat prostration *n.* Heat exhaustion.
heat pump *n.* An engine that transfers heat from a relatively low-temperature reservoir to one at a higher temperature.
heat rash *n.* Miliaria.
heat shield *n.* A barrier that prevents the heating of a space by absorbing, reflecting, or dissipating external heat, esp. a protective structure on a spacecraft or missile that dissipates heat on atmospheric re-entry by melting and vaporizing.
heat sink *n.* **1.** An environment having a much greater heat capacity and at a lower temperature than an object with which it is in thermal contact. **2.** A device by means of which heat is absorbed or stored in or removed from a thermal system.
heat stroke *n.* A severe illness caused by exposure to excessively high temperatures and characterized by severe headache, high fever with a dry hot skin, tachycardia, and in serious cases collapse and coma.
heat-treat (hēt′trēt′) *tr.v.* **-treat·ed, -treat·ing, -treats.** To treat (metal, for example) by alternate heating and cooling in order to produce desired characteristics, as increased hardness. **—heat treater** *n.* **—heat treatment** *n.*
heat wave *n.* A period of unusually hot weather.
heave (hēv) *v.* **heaved, heav·ing, heaves.** *—tr.* **1.** To raise or lift with great force or effort; hoist. **2.** To throw with great effort; hurl: *heave the shot put.* **3.** To utter painfully or with effort: *heaved a sigh.* **4.** *past tense & past participle* **hove** (hōv). *Naut.* To raise or haul by means of a rope. **5. a.** To cause to rise. **b.** To displace or move (a stratum, for example). *—intr.* **1.** To rise up or swell; bulge. **2.** *Informal.* To retch. **3.** *past tense & past participle* **hove** (hōv). *Naut.* **a.** To move to a specified position. **b.** To move a ship in a particular manner or direction. ***—phrasal verb.* heave to.** To bring or come to a stop. *—n.* **1.** The effort of heaving. **2.** An act of hurling; throw. **3.** A horizontal dislocation, as of a rock stratum, at a fault. **4. a.** An upward movement. **b. heaves.** *Informal.* The act or an instance of retching. **5. heaves** *(used with a sing. or pl. verb).* A pulmonary disease of horses characterized by respiratory irregularities, such as coughing, and noticeable esp. after exercise or in cold weather. [ME *heven* < OE *hebban.*] **—heav′er** *n.*
heav·en (hĕv′ən) *n.* **1.** Often **heavens.** The sky or universe as seen from the earth; firmament. **2.** The abode of God, the angels, and the souls of those who are granted salvation. **3. Heaven.** God. **4.** A condition or place of supreme happiness: *The lake was heaven.* [ME *heven* < OE *heofan.*]
heav·en·ly (hĕv′ən-lē) *adj.* **1.** Sublime; delightful. **2.** Of or having to do with heaven; celestial. **3.** Of or pertaining to the abode of God. **—heav′en·li·ness** *n.*
heav·en·ward (hĕv′ən-wərd) *adj. & adv.* Toward heaven. **—heav′en·wards** (-wərdz) *adv.*
heav·i·er-than-air (hĕv′ē-ər-thən-âr′) *adj.* Being an aircraft that is heavier than the air it displaces.
heav·i·ly (hĕv-ə-lē) *adv.* **1.** In a heavy manner. **2.** Very slowly and with difficulty; laboriously. **3.** Greatly or severely: *heavily in debt.*
Heav·i·side layer (hĕv′ĭ-sīd′) *n.* E layer. [After Oliver *Heaviside* (1850–1925).]
heav·y (hĕv′ē) *adj.* **-i·er, -i·est. 1.** Having relatively great weight. **2.** Having relatively high density; having a high specific gravity: *a heavy metal.* **3. a.** Large, as in number or quantity: *heavy rainfall.* **b.** Large in capacity, yield, or output. **4. a.** Dense or thick: *heavy fog.* **b.** Of great intensity or depth: *a heavy silence.* **5. a.** Having great power or force: *heavy seas.* **b.** Difficult to move; unwieldy, esp. due to great weight. **c.** Stocky and compact; stoutly built. **6. a.** Indulging to a great degree: *a heavy drinker.* **b.** Involved or participating on a large scale: *a heavy investor.* **7. a.** Of great import or seriousness; grave: *heavy matters of state.* **b.** Sad or painful: *heavy news.* **8. a.** Hard to do or accomplish; arduous. **b.** Not easily borne; oppressive: *heavy taxes.* **9.** Too rich to digest easily or quickly: *a heavy meal.* **10.** Having large or marked physical features; coarse. **11.** Weighed down with concern or sadness: *a heavy heart.* **12.** Lacking vitality. **13.** Deficient in vivacity or grace. **14.** Strong and pervasive; pungent: *a heavy scent.* **15. a.** Weighed down: burdened: *trees heavy with plums.* **b.** Showing or marked by weariness: *heavy eyes.* **16.** Of, relating to, or involving the production of basic products, such as steel: *heavy industry.* **17.** Pregnant. **18.** Of or pertaining to a serious dramatic role. **19.** *Physics.* **a.** Designating an isotope with a mass greater than that of others found in the same element. **b.** Designating an atomic particle having a mass between that of pi mesons and protons. **20.** Bearing weighty arms or armor. **21.** *Slang.* Of great significance or profundity. **22.** *Slang.* Very popular or important: *a rock star who is really heavy.* *—adv.* Heavily. *—n., pl.* **-ies. 1.** A villain in a story or play. **2.** A villain. **3. a.** A serious or tragic role in a play. **b.** An actor playing such a role. **4.** *Slang.* One that is very important or influential. [ME *hevy* < OE *hefig.*] **—heav′i·ness** *n.*
Synonyms: *heavy, weighty, hefty, massive, ponderous, cumbersome, unwieldy.* These adjectives are applied to persons or things with respect to weight, size, or shape, especially as these qualities affect their movement or management. Some also have related figurative application. *Heavy,* in careful usage, refers to great weight or high density. Figuratively, *heavy* applies to what is burdensome or oppressive to the spirit. *Weighty* literally denotes having great weight, without reference to an implied comparison; figuratively, it describes what is very serious or important. *Hefty* refers principally, and less formally, to heaviness or brawniness of physique. *Massive* describes what is imposing in size or bulk and in solidity and strength. *Ponderous* refers to what has great mass and weight and usually implies heaviness of movement. Figuratively, *ponderous* describes what is complicated, involved, or lacking in grace or lightness of spirit. *Cumbersome* stresses difficulty of movement or operation caused by heaviness or bulkiness. *Unwieldy* refers less to sheer weight than to peculiarity of construction that causes a thing to be unmanageable or clumsy in operation.
heav·y-dut·y (hĕv′ē-do͞o′tē, -dyo͞o′-) *adj.* Made to withstand hard use or wear.
heav·y-foot·ed (hĕv′ē-fo͝ot′ĭd) *adj.* Having a heavy, lumbering gait.
heav·y-hand·ed (hĕv′ē-hăn′dĭd) *adj.* **1.** Clumsy; awkward. **2.** Oppressive; harsh. **—heav′y-hand′ed·ness** *n.*
heav·y-heart·ed (hĕv′ē-här′tĭd) *adj.* Melancholy; depressed. **—heav′y-heart′ed·ly** *adv.* **—heav′y-heart′ed·ness** *n.*
heavy hydrogen *n.* An isotope of hydrogen with mass number greater than 1; deuterium.
heav·y·set (hĕv′ē-sĕt′) *adj.* Having a heavy, compact build.
heavy spar *n.* Barite.
heavy water *n.* Any of several isotopic varieties of water, esp. deuterium oxide, consisting chiefly or exclusively of molecules containing hydrogen with mass number greater than 1 and used as a moderator in certain nuclear reactors.
heav·y·weight (hĕv′ē-wāt′) *n.* **1.** One of above average weight. **2.** One that competes in the heaviest class, esp. a boxer weighing more than 81 kilograms or 175 pounds. **3.** *Informal.* A person of great importance or influence.
heb·do·mad (hĕb′də-măd′) *n.* **1.** A group of seven. **2.** A period of seven days; week. [Lat. *hebdomas, hebdomad-,* the number seven < Gk. < *hepta,* seven.]
heb·dom·a·dal (hĕb-dŏm′ə-dəl) *adj.* Weekly. **—heb·dom′a·dal·ly** *adv.*
He·be (hē′bē) *n. Gk. Myth.* The goddess of youth and spring. [Gk. *Hēbē* < *hēbē,* youthful.]
he·be·phre·ni·a (hē′bə-frē′nē-ə, -frĕn′ē-) *n.* A schizophrenia characterized by foolish mannerisms, delusions, hallucinations, and regressive behavior. [Gk. *hēbē,* youth + -PHRENIA.] **—he′be·phren′ic** (-frĕn′ĭk, -frē′nĭk) *adj.*
heb·e·tate (hĕb′ĭ-tāt′) *tr.v.* **-tat·ed, -tat·ing, -tates.** To make obtuse or dull. [Lat. *hebetare, hebetat-* < *hebes,* blunt.] **—heb′e·ta′tion** *n.* **—heb′e·ta′tive** *adj.*
heb·e·tude (hĕb′ĭ-to͞od′, -tyo͞od′) *n.* Dullness of mind; mental lethargy. [LLat. *hebetudo* < Lat. *hebes,* dull.] **—heb′e·tu′di·nous** (-to͞od′n-əs, -tyo͞od′-) *adj.*
He·bra·ic (hĭ-brā′ĭk) also **He·bra·i·cal** (-ĭ-kəl) *adj.* Of, pertaining to, or characteristic of the Hebrews or their language or culture. [ME *Ebraik* < LLat. *Hebraicus* < Gk. *Hebraikos* < *Hebraios.* —see HEBREW.] **—He·bra′i·cal·ly** *adv.*
He·bra·ism (hē′brā-ĭz′əm) *n.* **1.** A manner or custom characteristic of the Hebrews. **2.** A linguistic feature typical of Hebrew occurring esp. in another language. **3.** The culture, spirit, or character of the Hebrew people. **4.** Judaism. [< HEBRAIC.]
He·bra·ist (hē′brā′ĭst) *n.* A scholar who specializes in the study of Hebrew. **—He′bra·is′tic, He′bra·is′ti·cal** *adj.* **—He′bra·is′ti·cal·ly** *adv.*
He·bra·ize (hē′brā-īz′) *v.* **-ized, -iz·ing, -iz·es.** *—tr.* To make Hebraic in form or idiom. *—intr.* To use or adopt Hebraisms. **—He′bra·i·za′tion** *n.*
He·brew (hē′bro͞o) *n.* **1.** A member or descendant of a northern Semitic people; Israelite. **2. a.** The Semitic language of the ancient Hebrews. **b.** Any of the various later forms of this language, esp. the language of the Israelis. **3. Hebrews** *(used with a sing. verb).* See table at **Bible.** [ME *Ebreu* < OFr. < Lat. *Hebraeus,* Hebraic < Gk. *Hebraios* < Aram. *'ibhray* < Heb. *'ibhrī* < *'ēbher,* region across < *ābhar,* he crossed over.] **—He′brew** *adj.*
Hebrew Scriptures *pl.n.* The Pentateuch, the Prophets, and the Hagiographa, forming the covenant between God and the Jewish people that is the foundation and Bible of Judaism while constituting for Christians the Old Testament.
Hec·a·te (hĕk′ə-tē) *n. Gk. Myth.* An ancient fertility goddess and protectress of witches. [Lat. < Gk. *Hekatē.*]
hec·a·tomb (hĕk′ə-tōm′) *n.* **1.** In ancient Greece and Rome,

heath hen

Hebe
Ganymede and Hebe

hector
Hector being dragged around the walls of Troy by Achilles

a sacrifice to the gods consisting originally of 100 oxen. **2.** A large-scale sacrifice or slaughter. [Lat. *hecatombe* < Gk. *hekatombē* : *hekaton,* hundred + *bous,* ox.]
heck (hĕk) *interj. & n.* Hell.
heck·le (hĕk′əl) *tr.v.* **-led, -ling, -les. 1.** To try to embarrass and annoy by questions, gibes, or objections; badger. **2.** To comb (flax or hemp) with a hatchel. [ME *hekelen,* to comb with a hatchel < *hekel,* hatchel < MDu.] **—heck′ler** *n.*
hect– *pref.* Variant of **hecto-.**
hec·tare (hĕk′târ′) *n.* A metric unit of area equal to 100 ares or 2.471 acres.
hec·tic (hĕk′tĭk) *adj.* **1.** Characterized by feverish activity, confusion, or haste. **2.** Of, relating to, or having an undulating fever, as in diseases such as tuberculosis or septicemia. **3.** Consumptive; feverish. **4.** Flushed. [ME *etik,* recurring, consumptive < OFr. *etique* < LLat. *hecticus* < Gk. *hektikos* < *hexis,* habit.]
hecto– or **hect–** *pref.* One hundred (10^2): *hectare.* [Fr. < Gk. *hekaton,* hundred.]
hec·to·cot·y·lus (hĕk′tō-kŏt′l-əs) *n., pl.* **-cot·y·li** (-kŏt′l-ī′). A modified arm of the male of certain cephalopods, such as the octopus, containing sperm and functioning as a reproductive organ. [NLat. : HECTO- + Gk. *kotulē,* small cup.]
hec·to·gram also **hec·to·gramme** (hĕk′tə-grăm′) *n.* A metric unit of mass equal to 100 grams or 3.527 avoirdupois ounces.
hec·to·graph (hĕk′tə-grăf′) *n.* A machine using a glycerin-coated layer of gelatin to make copies of typed or written material. *—tr.v.* **-graphed, -graph·ing, -graphs.** To copy by means of a hectograph. [G. *Hektograph* : *hekto-,* hecto- + *-graph,* -graph.] **—hec′to·graph′ic** *adj.* **—hec′to·graph′i·cal·ly** *adv.*
hec·to·li·ter also **hec·to·li·tre** (hĕk′tə-lē′tər) *n.* **1.** A metric unit of capacity or volume, used in liquid measure, equal to 100 liters or 105.7 liquid quarts. **2.** A metric unit of capacity or volume, used in dry measure, equal to 100 liters or 90.8 dry quarts.
hec·to·me·ter also **hec·to·me·tre** (hĕk′tə-mē′tər, hĕk-tŏm′ĭ-tər) *n.* A metric unit of length equal to 100 meters or 328 feet.
hec·tor (hĕk′tər) *n.* **1. Hector.** *Gk. Myth.* A Trojan prince killed by Achilles in Homer's *Iliad.* **2.** A bully. *—v.* **-tored, -tor·ing, -tors.** *—tr.* To intimidate or dominate in a blustering way. *—intr.* To behave like a bully; swagger. [Gk. *Hektōr.*]
Hec·u·ba (hĕk′yə-bə) *n.* The wife of Priam in Homer's *Iliad.* [Lat. < Gk. *Hekabē.*]
he'd (hēd). **1.** He had. **2.** He would.
hed·dle (hĕd′l) *n.* One of a set of parallel cords or wires in a loom used to separate and guide the warp threads and make a path for the shuttle. [Prob. alteration of ME *helde* < OE *hefeld.*]
hedge (hĕj) *n.* **1.** A row of closely planted shrubs or low-growing trees forming a fence or boundary. **2.** A means of protection or defense, esp. against financial loss. **3.** An intentionally noncommittal or ambiguous statement. *—v.* **hedged, hedg·ing, hedg·es.** *—tr.* **1.** To enclose or bound with or as if with hedges. **2.** To hem in or hinder with or as if with a hedge. **3.** To minimize or protect against the loss of by counterbalancing one transaction, such as a bet, against another. *—intr.* **1.** To plant or cultivate hedges. **2.** To take compensatory measures so as to counterbalance possible loss. **3.** To avoid making a clear, direct response or statement. [ME < OE *hecg.*] **—hedg′er** *n.* **—hedg′y** *adj.*
hedge fund *n.* A limited-partnership fund that invests private capital speculatively to maximize capital appreciation.
hedge·hog (hĕj′hôg′, -hŏg′) *n.* **1.** Any of several small Old World mammals of the family Erinaceidae, and esp. of the genus *Erinaceus,* having the back covered with dense, erectile spines and characteristically rolling into a ball for protection. **2.** Any of several spiny animals similar to the hedgehog. [ME *hedge hogge.*]
hedge·hop (hĕj′hŏp′) *intr.v.* **-hopped, -hop·ping, -hops.** To fly an airplane close to the ground, rising above objects as they appear, as in spraying crops. **—hedge′hop′per** *n.*
hedge hyssop *n.* Any of various plants of the genus *Gratiola,* growing in damp places and having small yellow or whitish flowers.
hedge·row (hĕj′rō′) *n.* A row of bushes, shrubs, or trees forming a hedge.
he·don·ic (hĭ-dŏn′ĭk) *adj.* **1.** Of, pertaining to, or marked by pleasure. **2.** Of or relating to hedonism or hedonists. [Gk. *hēdonikos* < *hēdonē,* pleasure.] **—he·don′i·cal·ly** *adv.*
he·don·ics (hĭ-dŏn′ĭks) *n.* *(used with a sing. verb).* **1.** *Psychol.* The study of pleasant and unpleasant sensations. **2.** *Philos.* A branch of ethics that deals with the relation of pleasure to duty.
he·don·ism (hēd′n-ĭz′əm) *n.* **1.** Pursuit of or devotion to pleasure. **2.** The ethical doctrine that only that which is pleasant or has pleasant consequences is intrinsically good. **3.** *Psychol.* The doctrine that behavior is motivated by the desire for pleasure and the avoidance of pain. [Gk. *hēdonē,* pleasure + -ISM.]
he·don·ist (hēd′n-ĭst) *n.* One who holds that pleasure is the chief good. **—he′don·is′tic** *adj.* **—he′don·is′ti·cal·ly** *adv.*

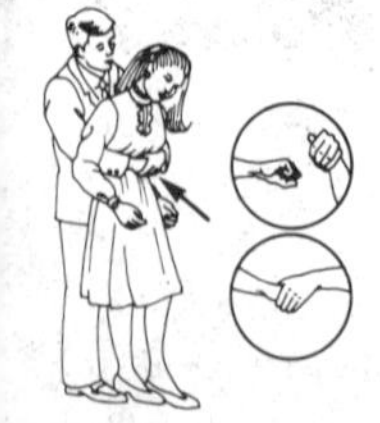

Heimlich maneuver
1. Stand behind victim and wrap arms around waist
2. Grasp hands as shown, with thumb of fist against victim's abdomen above navel but below ribs
3. Press your fists into victim's abdomen with quick upper thrust

–hedral *suff.* Having a specified kind or number of surfaces: *dihedral.* [< -HEDRON.]
–hedron *suff.* A crystal or geometric figure having a specified kind or number of surfaces: *heptahedron.* [Gk. *-edron* < *hedra,* base.]
hee·bie-jee·bies (hē′bē-jē′bēz) *pl.n. Slang.* A feeling of uneasiness or nervousness; jitters. [Coined by Billy De Beck (1890–1942), American cartoonist, in his comic strip *Barney Google.*]
heed (hēd) *v.* **heed·ed, heed·ing, heeds.** *—tr.* To pay attention to. *—intr.* To pay attention. *—n.* Close attention; notice. [ME *heden* < OE *hēdan.*]
heed·ful (hēd′fəl) *adj.* Paying close attention; taking heed. **—heed′ful·ly** *adv.* **—heed′ful·ness** *n.*
heed·less (hēd′lĭs) *adj.* Paying little heed; thoughtless. **—heed′less·ly** *adv.* **—heed′less·ness** *n.*
hee·haw (hē′hô′) *n.* **1.** The braying sound made by a donkey. **2.** A noisy laugh; guffaw. *—intr.v.* **-hawed, -haw·ing, -haws. 1.** To bray. **2.** To guffaw. [Imit.]
heel[1] (hēl) *n.* **1. a.** The rounded posterior portion of the human foot under and behind the ankle. **b.** The corresponding part of the hind foot of other vertebrates. **c.** A similar anatomical part, such as the fleshy rounded base of the human palm or the hind toe of a bird. **2. a.** The part, as of a sock, shoe, or stocking, that covers the heel. **b.** The built-up portion of a shoe or boot, supporting the heel. **3.** One of the crusty ends of a loaf of bread. **4.** *Naut.* **a.** The lower end of a mast. **b.** The after end of a ship's keel. **5.** The basal end of a plant cutting or tuber used in propagation. **6.** *Slang.* A dishonorable man; cad. *—v.* **heeled, heel·ing, heels.** *—tr.* **1.** To furnish with a heel or heels. **2.** *Slang.* To furnish esp. with money. *—intr.* To follow at one's heels. ***—idioms.*** **on (or upon) the heels of. 1.** Directly behind. **2.** Immediately following. **take to (one's) heels.** To run away. **to heel. 1.** Close behind. **2.** Under discipline or control. [ME < OE *hēla.*] **—heel′less** *adj.*
heel[2] (hēl) *v.* **heeled, heel·ing, heels.** *—intr.* To tilt to one side; list. *—tr.* To cause (a ship) to list. *—n.* An inclination or tilt, as of a boat, to one side; list. [Alteration of ME *helden* < OE *hieldan.*]
heel-and-toe (hēl′ən-tō′) *adj.* Characterized by a stride in which the heel of one foot touches ground before the toe of the other foot is lifted.
heel bone *n.* The calcaneus.
heel·er (hē′lər) *n.* **1.** One who heels shoes. **2.** *Informal.* A ward heeler.
heel·piece (hēl′pēs′) *n.* A piece made for or serving as the heel of a shoe or stocking.
heel·post (hēl′pōst′) *n.* The post to which a door or gate is hinged.
heel·tap (hēl′tăp′) *n.* A small amount of liquor remaining in a container or drinking vessel.
heft (hĕft) *n.* Weight; heaviness. *—v.* **heft·ed, heft·ing, hefts.** *—tr.* **1.** To lift in order to judge the weight of. **2.** To hoist up; heave. *—intr.* To weigh. [Alteration of HEAVE.]
heft·y (hĕf′tē) *adj.* **-i·er, -i·est. 1.** Weighty; heavy. **2.** Rugged; powerful. **3.** Of considerable size. **—heft′i·ly** *adv.* **—heft′i·ness** *n.*
He·ge·li·an·ism (hā-gā′lē-ə-nĭz′əm) *n.* The idealist philosophy of Georg Wilhelm Friedrich Hegel in which the dialectic is used as an analytic tool in order to approach a higher unity. **—He·ge′li·an** *adj. & n.*
he·gem·o·ny (hĭ-jĕm′ə-nē, hĕj′ə-mō′nē) *n., pl.* **-nies.** The predominant influence of one state over others. [Gk. *hēgemonia* < *hēgemōn,* leader < *hēgeisthai,* to lead.] **—heg′e·mon′ic** (hĕj′ə-mŏn′ĭk) *adj.*
he·gi·ra (hĭ-jī′rə, hĕj′ər-ə) *n.* **1. Hegira.** The flight of Mohammed from Mecca to Medina in A.D. 622. **2.** A flight to escape danger. [Med. Lat. < Ar. *alhijrat* < *hajara,* he left.]
Hei·del·berg man (hīd′l-bûrg′) *n.* An extinct early member of the human species, a form of *Homo erectus,* known primarily from a fossil jawbone found near Heidelberg, West Germany, in 1907.
heif·er (hĕf′ər) *n.* A young cow, esp. one that has not yet given birth to a calf. [ME < OE *hēahfore.*]
heigh-ho (hī′hō′, hā′-) *interj.* Used to express fatigue, mild surprise, boredom, or disappointment.
height (hīt) *n.* **1.** The highest or uppermost point; summit. **2. a.** The highest or most advanced degree; zenith: *at the height of her career.* **b.** The point of highest intensity; climax: *the height of a storm.* **3. a.** The distance from the base to the top of something. **b.** The elevation of something above a given level; altitude. **4. a.** The condition or attribute of being high or tall. **b.** Stature, esp. of the human body. **5. a.** An eminence, as a hill or mountain. **b.** A high point, position, or degree. **6.** *Obs.* High rank, estate, or degree. [ME < OE *hēahðu.*]
height·en (hīt′n) *tr. & intr.v.* **-ened, -en·ing, -ens. 1.** To increase or cause to increase in quantity or degree. **2.** To make or become high or higher. **—height′en·er** *n.*
height-to-pa·per (hīt′tə-pā′pər) *n. Printing.* The height of type from foot to face, standardized at 0.9186 inch or 2.296 centimeters.
Heim·lich maneuver (hīm′lĭkʜ′, -lĭk′) *n.* A maneuver that is designed to dislodge an object, as food, from a choking person's windpipe and in which the victim is clasped from be-

hind, a closed fist is placed below the rib cage, and air is forced out of the lungs with a hard upward thrust. [After Henry J. *Heimlich,* 20th-cent. American surgeon.]

hei·nous (hā′nəs) *adj.* Grossly wicked or reprehensible; abominable: *a heinous crime.* [ME < OFr. *hainos* < *haine,* hatred < *hair,* to hate, of Germanic orig.] **—hei′nous·ly** *adv.* **—hei′nous·ness** *n.*

heir (âr) *n.* **1.** *Law.* A person who inherits or is entitled by law or by the terms of a will to inherit the estate of another. **2.** A person who succeeds or is in line to succeed to a hereditary rank, title, or office. **3.** One who receives or is expected to receive a heritage, as of ideas, from a predecessor. [ME < AN < Lat. *heres.*]

heir apparent *n., pl.* **heirs apparent.** *Law.* An heir whose right to inheritance is indefeasible by law provided he survives his ancestor.

heir·dom (âr′dəm) *n.* **1.** Succession by right of blood. **2.** An inheritance.

heir·ess (âr′ĭs) *n.* A woman who is an heir, esp. to great wealth.

heir·loom (âr′lo͞om′) *n.* **1.** A valued possession passed down in a family through succeeding generations. **2.** *Law.* An article of personal property included in an inherited estate. [ME *heirlome* : *heir,* heir + *lome,* implement.]

heir presumptive *n., pl.* **heirs presumptive.** *Law.* An heir whose claim can be defeated by the birth of a closer relative before the death of the ancestor.

heir·ship (âr′shĭp′) *n.* **1.** The condition of being an heir. **2.** The right to inheritance; heirdom.

Hei·sen·berg uncertainty principle (hī′zən-bûrg′) *n.* The uncertainty principle. [After Werner K. *Heisenberg* (1901–1976).]

heist (hīst) *Slang.* —*tr.v.* **heist·ed, heist·ing, heists.** To rob; steal. —*n.* A robbery; burglary. [Alteration of HOIST.]

Hel (hĕl) *n. Norse Myth.* **1.** The daughter of Loki and the goddess of death. **2.** The underworld of the dead not killed in battle. [ON.]

He·La cell (hĕl′ə) *n.* Any of the human cancer cells of a continuously cultured strain used in biomedical research. [After *He(len) La(ne),* who donated such cells in 1951.]

held (hĕld) *v.* Past tense and past participle of **hold.**

hel·den·te·nor also **Hel·den·te·nor** (hĕl′dən-tə-nôr′, -nōr′) *n.* **1.** A tenor voice with a striking dramatic or brilliant quality that is well suited for heroic roles, as those in Wagnerian opera. **2.** A person with a heldentenor. [G. : *Held,* hero + *Tenor,* tenor.]

Hel·en of Troy (hĕl′ən) *n. Gk. Myth.* The daughter of Zeus and Leda and wife of Menelaus whose abduction by Paris caused the Trojan War. [Gk. *Helenē.*]

heli–¹ *pref.* Helicopter: *heliport.* [< HELICOPTER.]

heli–² *pref.* Variant of **helio-.**

he·li·a·cal (hĭ-lī′ə-kəl) *adj.* Of or pertaining to the sun, esp. rising and setting with the sun. [LLat. *heliacus* < Gk. *hēliakos* < *hēlios,* sun.] **—he·li′a·cal·ly** *adv.*

helic– *pref.* Variant of **helico-.**

hel·i·cal (hĕl′ĭ-kəl, hē′lĭ-) *adj.* **1.** Of or having the shape of a helix. **2.** Having a shape approximating that of a helix. **—hel′i·cal·ly** *adv.*

hel·i·ces (hĕl′ĭ-sēz′, hē′lĭ-) *n.* A plural of **helix.**

he·lic·i·ty (hē-lĭs′ĭ-tē, hĕ-) *n.* The component of the spin of a particle along its direction of motion.

helico– or **helic–** *pref.* Helix; spiral: *helicity.* [Gk. *heliko-* < *helix,* spiral.]

hel·i·coid (hĕl′ĭ-koid′, hē′lĭ-) *adj.* Arranged in or having the approximate shape of a flattened spiral. —*n. Math.* A surface generated by a plane curve or a twisted curve that is rotated about a linear axis and at the same time is translated in the direction of the axis so that the two rates have a constant ratio. [Gk. *helikoeidēs* : *helix,* spiral + *-oeidēs,* -oid.]

hel·i·con (hĕl′ĭ-kŏn′, -kən) *n.* A large circular brass tuba that fits around the player's shoulder. [Prob. < Gk. *helix, helik-,* spiral.]

hel·i·cop·ter (hĕl′ĭ-kŏp′tər) *n.* An aircraft that derives its lift from blades that rotate about an approximately vertical central axis. —*intr. & tr.v.* **-tered, -ter·ing, -ters.** To go or carry by helicopter. [Fr. *hélicoptère* : Gk. *helix,* spiral + Gk. *pteron,* wing.]

helio– or **heli–** *pref.* Sun: *heliogram.* [< Gk. *hēlios,* sun.]

he·li·o·cen·tric (hē′lē-ō-sĕn′trĭk) also **he·li·o·cen·tri·cal** (-trĭ-kəl) *adj.* **1.** Referred or relative to the sun. **2.** Having the sun as a center. **—he′li·o·cen·tric′i·ty** (-sĕn-trĭs′ĭ-tē) *n.*

he·li·o·gram (hē′lē-ə-grăm′) *n.* A message sent by heliograph.

he·li·o·graph (hē′lē-ə-grăf′) *n.* **1.** An apparatus once used to photograph the sun. **2.** A signaling apparatus that reflects sunlight with a movable mirror to flash coded messages. —*tr. & intr.v.* **-graphed, -graph·ing, -graphs.** To communicate or signal by heliograph. **—he′li·og′raph·er** (-ŏg′rə-fər) *n.* **—he′li·o·graph′ic** *adj.* **—he′li·og′raph·y** *n.*

he·li·o·gra·vure (hē′lē-ō-grə-vyo͝or′) *n. Printing.* Photogravure.

he·li·om·e·ter (hē′lē-ŏm′ĭ-tər) *n.* A telescope equipped to measure small angular distances between celestial bodies. **—he′li·o·met′ric** (-ə-mĕt′rĭk), **he′li·o·met′ri·cal** *adj.* **—he′li·o·met′ri·cal·ly** *adv.* **—he′li·om′e·try** *n.*

He·li·os (hē′lē-ŏs′) *n. Gk. Myth.* The sun god, son of Hyperion, depicted as driving his chariot across the sky from east to west daily. [Gk. *Hēlios* < *hēlios,* sun.]

he·li·o·stat (hē′lē-ə-stăt′) *n.* An instrument in which a mirror is automatically moved so that it reflects sunlight in a constant direction.

he·li·o·tax·is (hē′lē-ō-tăk′sĭs) *n. Biol.* The movement of an organism in response to the light of the sun.

he·li·o·ther·a·py (hē′lē-ō-thĕr′ə-pē) *n.* Medical therapy involving exposure to sunlight.

he·lio·trope (hēl′yə-trōp′) *n.* **1.** Any of several plants of the genus *Heliotropium,* esp. *H. arborescens,* native to South America, having small, highly fragrant purplish flowers. **2.** The garden heliotrope. **3.** Any of various plants that turn toward the sun. **4.** Bloodstone. **5.** A moderate, light, or brilliant violet to moderate or deep reddish purple. [Lat. *heliotropium* < Gk. *hēliotropion* : *hēlios,* sun + *tropos,* turn.] **—he′lio·trope′** *adj.*

he·lio·tro·pin (hēl′yə-trō′pĭn, hē′lē-ŏt′rə-pĭn) *n.* Piperonal.

he·li·ot·ro·pism (hē′lē-ŏt′rə-pĭz′əm) *n.* Growth or movement of an organism toward or away from the light of the sun. **—he′li·o·trop′ic** (-ə-trŏp′ĭk) *adj.* **—he′li·o·trop′i·cal·ly** *adv.*

he·li·o·type (hē′lē-ə-tīp′) *n. Printing.* **1.** A photomechanically produced plate for pictures or type made by exposing a gelatin film under a negative, hardening it with chrome alum, and printing directly from it. **2.** Also **he·li·o·typ·y** (hē′lē-ə-tī′pē). The process of producing a heliotype. —*tr.v.* **-typed, -typ·ing, -types.** To produce a heliotype of. **—he′li·o·typ′ic** (-tĭp′ĭk) *adj.*

he·li·o·zo·an (hē′lē-ə-zō′ən) *n.* Any of various aquatic protozoans of the order Heliozoa, having numerous stiff, radiating pseudopodia. **—he′li·o·zo′ic** (-zō′ĭk) *adj.*

hel·i·pad (hĕl′ə-păd′) *n.* A heliport.

hel·i·port (hĕl′ə-pôrt′, -pōrt′) *n.* A place for helicopters to land and take off.

hel·i·stop (hĕl′ĭ-stŏp′) *n.* A heliport.

he·li·um (hē′lē-əm) *n. Symbol* **He** A colorless, odorless, tasteless inert gaseous element used to inflate and so provide lift for balloons, as an inert component of various artificial atmospheres, in gaseous laser media, and as a superfluid in the form of helium II for extensive cryogenic research. Atomic number 2; atomic weight 4.0026; boiling point –268.6°C; liquid density at boiling point 7.62 pounds per cubic foot. [NLat. < Gk. *hēlios,* sun (so called because its existence was deduced from the solar spectrum).]

helium I *n. Symbol* **He I** Liquid helium existing as a normal fluid between the superfluid transition point of approximately 2.178°K at 1 atmosphere pressure and its boiling point of 4.2°K.

helium II *n. Symbol* **He II** Liquid helium existing as a superfluid below the transition point of approximately 2.178°K at 1 atmosphere and having extremely low viscosity and extremely high thermal conductivity.

he·lix (hē′lĭks) *n., pl.* **-lix·es** or **hel·i·ces** (hĕl′ĭ-sēz′, hē′lĭ-). **1.** *Math.* A three-dimensional curve that lies on a cylinder or cone and cuts the elements at a constant angle. **2.** A spiral form or structure. **3.** *Anat.* The folded rim of skin and cartilage around the outer ear. **4.** *Archit.* A volute on a Corinthian or Ionic capital. [Lat. < Gk.]

hell (hĕl) *n.* **1.** The abode of the dead in ancient traditions; underworld. **2.** Often **Hell.** In many religions, the abode of condemned souls and devils; the place of punishment for the wicked after death. **3.** A place or situation of evil, misery, discord, or destruction: *into the hell of battle.* **4. a.** Torment; anguish: *went through hell on the job.* **b.** Someone or something that causes trouble, agony, or annoyance: *He's hell when a job is poorly done.* **5. Hell.** *Christian Science.* Mortal belief; sin or error. **6.** A sharp scolding: *gave him hell for cheating.* **7. a.** A tailor's receptacle for discarded material. **b.** A hellbox. **8.** Used as an intensive: *How the hell can I go? You did one hell of a job.* —*intr. v.* **helled, hell·ing, hells.** *Informal.* To behave riotously; carouse: *out all night helling around.* —*interj. Slang.* Used to express anger, disgust, or impatience. —***idioms.*** **hell or (or and) high water.** *Informal.* Troubles or difficulties of whatever magnitude: *We're staying, come hell or high water.* **hell to pay.** *Informal.* Bad trouble to be faced: *If he's wrong, there'll be hell to pay.* [ME *helle* < OE.]

he'll (hēl). **1.** He will. **2.** He shall.

hell·bend·er (hĕl′bĕn′dər) *n.* A large aquatic salamander, *Cryptobranchus alleganiensis,* of eastern and central North America.

hell-bent (hĕl′bĕnt′) *adj.* Impetuously or recklessly determined to do or achieve something: *was hell-bent on winning.*

hell·box (hĕl′bŏks′) *n.* A printer's receptacle for broken or discarded type.

hell·cat (hĕl′kăt′) *n.* **1.** A bad-tempered and evil woman; vixen. **2.** A person who torments others.

hell·div·er (hĕl′dī′vər) *n. Informal.* A New World grebe, *Podilymbus podiceps.*

Hel·le (hĕl′ē) *n. Gk. Myth.* The daughter of a Greek king who, while fleeing with her brother from their stepmother, drowned in the Hellespont, thereafter named for her. [Gk. *Hellē.*]

hel·le·bore (hĕl′ə-bôr′, -bōr′) *n.* **1.** Any of various plants of the genus *Helleborus,* native to Eurasia, most species of

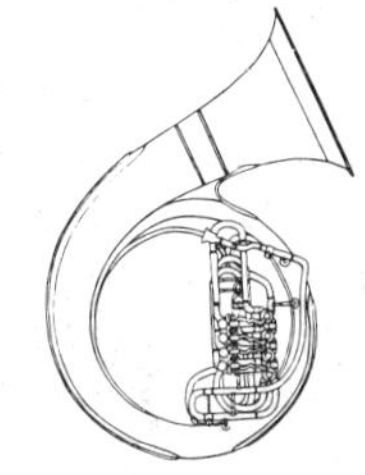

helicon

helicopter

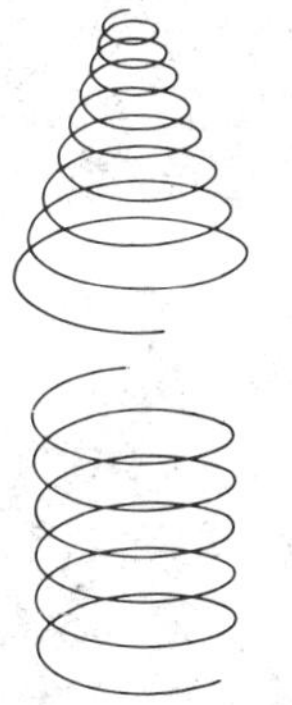

helix
Above: Conical helix
Below: Cylindrical helix

hellebore

which are poisonous. **2.** Any of various plants of the genus *Veratrum,* esp. *V. viride,* of North America, having large leaves and greenish flowers and yielding a toxic alkaloid used medicinally. [ME *ellebre* < OFr. < Lat. *elleborus* < Gk. *helleboros,* perh. : *hellos,* fawn + *-boros,* eaten < *bibrōskein,* to eat.]

hel·le·bo·rin (hĕl′ə-bôr′ĭn, -bōr′-) *n.* A poisonous compound, $C_{28}H_{36}O_6$, extracted from *Helleborus viridis,* a species of hellebore.

Hel·lene (hĕl′ēn′) also **Hel·le·ni·an** (hĕ-lē′nē-ən) *n.* A Greek. [Gk. *Hellēn.*]

Hel·len·ic (hĕ-lĕn′ĭk) *adj.* Of or relating to the ancient Greeks or their language. *—n.* The branch of the Indo-European language family that consists only of Greek.

Hel·le·nism (hĕl′ə-nĭz′əm) *n.* **1.** An idiom peculiar to the Greeks. **2.** The civilization and culture of ancient Greece. **3.** The adoption of Greek ideas, style, or culture.

Hel·le·nist (hĕl′ə-nĭst) *n.* **1.** One in classical times who adopted the Greek language and culture, esp. a Jew of the Diaspora. **2.** A devotee or student of Greek civilization, language, or literature.

Hel·le·nis·tic (hĕl′ə-nĭs′tĭk) also **Hel·le·nis·ti·cal** (-tĭ-kəl) *adj.* **1.** Relating to the Hellenists. **2. a.** Of or relating to Greek history and culture from the time of Alexander the Great into the first century B.C. **b.** Pertaining to or in the style of the Greek art or architecture of this period.

Hel·le·nize (hĕl′ə-nīz′) *v.* **-nized, -niz·ing, -niz·es.** *—intr.* To adopt Greek ways and speech; become Greek or Hellenistic. *—tr.* To make Greek or Hellenistic; Grecize. **—Hel′le·ni·za′tion** *n.* **—Hel′le·niz′er** *n.*

hell·er (hĕl′ər) *n. Regional.* A person who behaves recklessly or wildly. [< HELL.]

hell-for-leath·er (hĕl′fər-lĕth′ər) *adv. & adj. Informal.* At breakneck speed.

hell·gram·mite (hĕl′grə-mīt′) *n.* The large, brownish aquatic larva of the dobson fly, often used as fishing bait. [Orig. unknown.]

hell·hole (hĕl′hōl′) *n.* **1.** A hellish place, esp. one of extreme wretchedness and squalor. **2.** *Obs.* The pit of hell.

hell·hound (hĕl′hound′) *n.* **1.** Cerberus, the watchdog of Hades. **2.** A devilish person; fiend.

hel·lion (hĕl′yən) *n. Informal.* A mischievous, troublesome person. [Prob. alteration of dial. *hallion,* worthless person.]

hell·ish (hĕl′ĭsh) *adj.* Of, like, or worthy of hell; fiendish. **—hell′ish·ly** *adv.* **—hell′ish·ness** *n.*

hel·lo (hĕ-lō′, hə-) also **hul·lo** (hə-) *—interj.* Used to greet someone, answer the telephone, or express surprise. *—n., pl.* **-los.** A calling or greeting of "hello." *—intr.v.* **-loed, -lo·ing, -loes.** To call "hello." [Alteration of obs *holla,* stop!, prob. < OFr. *hola* : *ho,* ho! + *la,* there.]

helm[1] (hĕlm) *n.* **1.** The steering gear of a ship, esp. the tiller or wheel. **2.** A position of leadership or control. *—tr.v.* **helmed, helm·ing, helms.** To take the helm of; steer. [ME < OE *helma.*]

helm[2] (hĕlm) *n. Archaic.* A helmet. *—tr.v.* **helmed, helm·ing, helms.** To cover or furnish with a helmet. [ME < OE and < ON *hjālmr.*]

helmet

hel·met (hĕl′mĭt) *n.* **1.** A piece of armor, usually of metal, designed to protect the head. **2. a.** A head covering of hard material, such as leather, metal, or plastic, worn to protect the head. **b.** The headgear with a glass mask worn by deep-sea divers. **c.** A pith helmet; topi. **d.** A hat having the shape of a helmet. **3.** *Bot.* The hood-shaped sepal or corolla of some flowers. *—tr. & intr.v.* **-met·ed, -met·ing, -mets.** To provide with or put on a helmet. [ME.] **—hel′met·ed** *adj.*

hel·minth (hĕl′mĭnth′) *n.* A worm, esp. a parasitic intestinal nematode or trematode worm. [Gk. *helmins, helminth-.*]

hel·min·thi·a·sis (hĕl′mĭn-thī′ə-sĭs) *n.* A disease caused by an infestation of parasitic worms.

hel·min·thic (hĕl-mĭn′thĭk) *adj.* **1.** Of or pertaining to worms, esp. parasitic intestinal worms. **2.** Tending to expel worms; anthelmintic. *—n.* A vermifuge or anthelmintic.

hel·min·thol·o·gy (hĕl′mĭn-thŏl′ə-jē) *n.* The scientific study of worms, esp. parasitic worms. **—hel′min·thol′o·gist** *n.*

helmsman

helms·man (hĕlmz′mən) *n.* A person who steers a ship. **—helms′man·ship′** *n.*

hel·ot (hĕl′ət) *n.* **1. Helot.** One of a class of serfs in ancient Sparta. **2.** A serf; bondsman. [Lat. *Helotes,* Helots < Gk. *Heilōtes.*] **—hel′ot·ry** (-ə-trē) *n.*

hel·ot·ism (hĕl′ə-tĭz′əm) *n.* A system under which a nominally free social class or a religious, national, or racial minority is permanently oppressed and degraded.

help (hĕlp) *v.* **helped, help·ing, helps.** *—tr.* **1.** To give assistance to; aid: *I helped her find the book. He helped her into her coat.* **2.** To contribute to; further the progress or advancement of. **3.** To give relief to: *help the poor.* **4.** To ease; relieve: *medication to help your cold.* **5.** To be able to prevent, change, or rectify: *I cannot help her laziness.* **6.** To refrain from; avoid: *couldn't help laughing.* **7.** To wait on, as in a store or restaurant. *—intr.* To be of service; give assistance. ***—phrasal verb.* help out.** To aid with a problem or difficulty. *—n.* **1. a.** The act or an instance of helping. **b.** Aid; assistance. **2.** Relief; remedy. **3.** One that helps. **4. a.** A person employed to help, esp. a farm worker or a domestic servant. **b.** Such employees collectively. ***—idioms.* cannot help but.** To be unable to avoid or resist: *He cannot help but do what they ask.* **help (oneself) to. 1.** To serve oneself: *Help yourself to the cookies.* **2.** To take (something) without asking permission. [ME *helpen* < OE *helpan* and < ON *hjalpa.*] **—help′er** *n.*

Synonyms: *help, aid, assist, succor.* These verbs mean to contribute to the fulfillment of a need or to the achievement of a purpose or end. *Help* and *aid,* the most general, are frequently interchangeable, though *help* sometimes conveys a stronger suggestion of effectual action. *Assist* usually implies making a secondary contribution or acting as a subordinate. *Succor* refers to going to the relief of one in want or distress.

Usage: *Help* in the sense "avoid" or "refrain from" is frequently used in an expression such as *I cannot help but think.* For formal writing the Usage Panel prefers either *I cannot help thinking* or *I cannot but think.* • Another common use of *help* is exemplified by the sentence *Don't change it any more than you can help* (that is, "any more than you have to"). Some grammarians condemn this usage on the ground that *help* in this sense means "avoid" and logically requires a negative. But the expression is a well-established idiom.

help·ful (hĕlp′fəl) *adj.* Providing help; useful. **—help′ful·ly** *adv.* **—help′ful·ness** *n.*

help·ing (hĕl′pĭng) *n.* A portion of food for one person.

help·less (hĕlp′lĭs) *adj.* **1.** Unable to manage by oneself; dependent. **2.** Lacking power or strength. **3.** Incapable of being remedied. **—help′less·ly** *adv.* **—help′less·ness** *n.*

help·mate (hĕlp′māt′) *n.* A helper and companion, esp. a spouse. —See Usage note at **helpmeet.**

help·meet (hĕlp′mēt′) *n.* A helpmate. [HELP + MEET[2].]

Usage: The existence of the two words *helpmeet* and *helpmate,* meaning exactly the same thing, is a comedy of errors. God's promise to Adam, as rendered in the King James version of the Bible, was to give him "an help meet for him" (that is, a helper fit for him). In the 17th century the two words *help* and *meet* in this passage were mistaken for one word, applying to Eve, and thus *helpmeet* came to mean "a wife." Then in the 18th century, in a misguided attempt to make sense of the word, the spelling *helpmate* was introduced. Both errors are now beyond recall, and both spellings are acceptable.

hel·ter-skel·ter (hĕl′tər-skĕl′tər) *adv.* **1.** In disorderly haste; pell-mell. **2.** Haphazardly. *—adj.* **1.** Carelessly hurried and confused. **2.** Haphazard. *—n.* Turmoil; confusion. [Orig. unknown.]

helve (hĕlv) *n.* A handle of a tool, such as an ax, chisel, or hammer. [ME < OE *hielfe.*]

Hel·ve·tian (hĕl-vē′shən) *adj.* **1.** Of or relating to the Helvetii. **2.** Swiss. *—n.* **1.** One of the Helvetii. **2.** A Swiss. [Lat. *Helvetius.*]

Hel·ve·ti·i (hĕl-vē′shē-ī′) *pl.n.* A Celtic people inhabiting Helvetia during the time of Julius Caesar. [Lat.]

hem[1] (hĕm) *n.* An edge or border of a piece of cloth, esp. a finished edge, as for a garment, made by folding the selvage or raw edge under and stitching it down. *—tr.v.* **hemmed, hem·ming, hems. 1.** To fold back and stitch down the edge of. **2.** To surround and shut in; enclose: *a valley hemmed in by mountains.* [ME < OE.] **—hem′mer** *n.*

hem[2] (hĕm) *n.* A short cough or clearing of the throat made esp. to gain attention, hide embarrassment, or fill a pause in speech. *—intr.v.* **hemmed, hem·ming, hems. 1.** To utter a hem. **2.** To hesitate in speech. ***—idiom.* hem and haw.** To be hesitant and indecisive; equivocate: *hemmed and hawed about answering.* [Imit.]

hem- or **hema-** *pref.* Variant of **hemo-.**

he·ma·cy·tom·e·ter (hē′mə-sī-tŏm′ĭ-tər) *n.* An instrument for estimating the number of blood cells in a measured volume of blood.

he·mag·glu·ti·nate (hē′mə-glōōt′n-āt′) *tr.v.* **-nat·ed, -nat·ing, -nates.** To cause agglutination of red blood cells. **—he′mag·glu′tin·a′tion** *n.*

he·mag·glu·ti·nin (hē′mə-glōōt′n-ĭn) *n.* An antibody that causes agglutination of red blood cells containing or coated with the corresponding antigen.

he·mal (hē′məl) *adj.* **1.** Of or pertaining to the blood or blood vessels. **2.** Relating to or located on or in the side of the body that contains the heart.

he-man (hē′măn′) *n. Informal.* A strong, muscular, virile man.

hemat- *pref.* Variant of **hemato-.**

he·ma·te·in (hē′mə-tē′ĭn, hē′mə-tēn′) *n.* A dark-purple crystalline compound, $C_{16}H_{12}O_6$, used as an indicator and as a biological stain.

he·mat·ic (hĭ-măt′ĭk) *adj.* Of, pertaining to, resembling, containing, or acting on blood. *—n. Med.* A remedy for anemia or other blood diseases. [Gk. *haimatikos* < *haima,* blood.]

he·ma·tin (hē′mə-tĭn) *n.* A blue to blackish-brown powder, $C_{34}H_{32}N_4O_4{\cdot}FeOH$, that is the hydroxide of heme, containing ferric iron.

he·ma·tin·ic (hē′mə-tĭn′ĭk) *adj.* Acting to improve the blood. *—n.* A hematinic drug.

he·ma·tite (hē′mə-tīt′) *n.* A blackish-red to brick-red mineral, essentially Fe_2O_3, the chief ore of iron. [Lat. *haemites* < Gk. (*lithos*) *haimatitēs,* bloodlike (stone) < *haima,* blood.] **—he′ma·tit′ic** (-tĭt′ĭk) *adj.*

hemato– or **hemat–** *pref.* Blood: *hematology.* [Gk. *haimato-* < *haima,* blood.]

he·ma·to·blast (hē'mə-tə-blăst', hĭ-măt'ə-) *n.* **1.** A platelet of the blood. **2.** An immature blood cell. **—he'ma·to·blas'tic** *adj.*

he·mat·o·crit (hĭ-măt'ə-krĭt') *n.* A centrifuge used to separate the cellular and other particulate matter of blood from the plasma. [HEMATO- + Gk. *kritēs,* judge < *krinein,* to judge.]

he·ma·to·gen·e·sis (hē'mə-tə-jĕn'ĭ-sĭs, hĭ-măt'ə-) *n.* Hematopoiesis. **—he'ma·to·gen'ic** (-jĕn'ĭk), **he'ma·to·ge·net'ic** (-jə-nĕt'ĭk) *adj.*

he·ma·tog·e·nous (hē'mə-tŏj'ə-nəs) *adj.* **1.** Producing blood. **2.** Originating in the blood.

he·ma·toid (hē'mə-toid') *adj.* **1.** Bloody. **2.** Like blood.

he·ma·tol·o·gy (hē'mə-tŏl'ə-jē) *n.* The science encompassing the generation, anatomy, physiology, pathology, and therapeutics of blood. **—he'ma·to·log'ic** (-tə-lŏj'ĭk), **he'ma·to·log'i·cal** *adj.* **—he'ma·to·log'i·cal·ly** *adv.* **—he'ma·tol'o·gist** *n.*

he·ma·tol·y·sis (hē'mə-tŏl'ĭ-sĭs) *n.* Hemolysis.

he·ma·to·ma (hē'mə-tō'mə) *n., pl.* **-mas** or **-ma·ta** (-mə-tə). A localized swelling filled with blood.

he·ma·to·poi·e·sis (hē'mə-tō-poi-ē'sĭs, hĭ-măt'ə-) *n.* The formation of blood in the body. **—he'ma·to·poi·et'ic** (-ĕt'ĭk) *adj.*

he·ma·to·sis (hē'mə-tō'sĭs) *n.* Oxygenation of venous blood in the lungs.

he·ma·tox·y·lin (hē'mə-tŏk'sə-lĭn) *n.* A yellow or red crystalline compound, $C_{16}H_{14}O_6 \cdot 3H_2O$, the coloring principle of logwood, used in dyes, inks, and stains. [< NLat. *Haematoxylon,* a genus of plants.]

he·ma·to·zo·on (hē'mə-tō-zō'ŏn', hĭ-măt'ə-) *n., pl.* **-zo·a** (-zō'ə). A parasitic protozoan or similar organism that lives in the blood. **—he'ma·to·zo'al, he'ma·to·zo'ic** *adj.*

he·ma·tu·ri·a (hē'mə-tŏŏr'ē-ə, -tyŏŏr'-) *n.* A condition in which there is blood or red blood cells in the urine.

heme (hēm) *n.* The nonprotein, ferrous-iron-containing component of hemoglobin, having composition $C_{34}H_{32}FeN_4O_4$. [< HEMATIN.]

he·mel·y·tron (hĕ-mĕl'ĭ-trŏn') *n., pl.* **-tra** (-trə). An insect forewing that is thickened at the base and membranous at the apex, characteristic of the true bugs.

hem·er·a·lo·pi·a (hĕm'ər-ə-lō'pē-ə) *n.* A visual defect manifested as the inability to see as clearly in bright light as in dim light. [NLat. < Gk. *hēmeralōps* : *hēmera,* day + *alaos,* blind + *ōps,* eye.]

hemi– *pref.* **1.** Half: *hemihedral.* **2.** Partial; partially: *hemiparasite.* [Lat. *hemi-* < Gk. *hēmi-*.]

-hemia *suff.* Variant of **-emia.**

hem·i·al·gi·a (hĕm'ē-ăl'jē-ə) *n.* Pain affecting one entire half of the body.

he·mic (hē'mĭk) *adj.* Of or pertaining to blood.

hem·i·cel·lu·lose (hĕm'ĭ-sĕl'yə-lōs', -lōz') *n.* Any of several polysaccharides that are more complex than a sugar and less complex than cellulose, derived from plants and produced commercially from corn grain hulls.

hem·i·chor·date (hĕm'ĭ-kôr'dāt', -dĭt) *n.* Any of various wormlike marine animals of the phylum or subphylum Hemichordata, having a primitive notochord and gill slits. *—adj.* Of or belonging to the Hemichordata.

hem·i·cy·cle (hĕm'ĭ-sī'kəl) *n.* A semicircular structure or arrangement. [Fr. *hémicycle* < Lat. *hemicyclium* < Gk. *hēmikuklion* : *hēmi-,* half + *kuklos,* circle.]

hem·i·dem·i·sem·i·qua·ver (hĕm'ē-dĕm'ē-sĕm'ē-kwā'vər) *n. Chiefly Brit.* A sixty-fourth note.

hem·i·he·dral (hĕm'ĭ-hē'drəl) *adj.* Exhibiting only half the faces required for complete symmetry. Used of a crystal. [HEMI- + -HEDR(ON) + -AL.]

hem·i·hy·drate (hĕm'ĭ-hī'drāt') *n.* A hydrate in which the molecular ratio of water molecules to anhydrous compound is 1:2. **—hem'i·hy'drat'ed** *adj.*

hem·i·mor·phic (hĕm'ĭ-môr'fĭk) *adj.* Asymmetric at the axial ends.

hem·i·mor·phite (hĕm'ĭ-môr'fīt') *n.* Calamine (sense 1). [HEMIMORPH(IC) + -ITE.]

he·min (hē'mĭn) *n.* A brown or blue crystalline compound, $C_{34}H_{32}N_4O_4FeCl$, that is the chloride of heme and is used in identifying blood stains.

hem·i·par·a·site (hĕm'ĭ-păr'ə-sīt') *n.* An organism that is partially parasitic. **—hem'i·par'a·sit'ic** (-sĭt'ĭk) *adj.*

hem·i·ple·gia (hĕm'ĭ-plē'jə, -jē-ə) *n.* Paralysis of one side of the body only. [MGk. *hēmiplēgia* : Gk. *hēmi-,* half + Gk. *plēgē,* stroke.] **—hem'i·ple'gic** (-plē'jĭk) *adj.*

he·mip·ter·an (hĭ-mĭp'tər-ən) *adj.* Of or belonging to the Hemiptera; hemipterous. *—n.* A hemipterous insect. **—he·mip'ter·on'** (-tə-rŏn') *n.*

he·mip·ter·ous (hĭ-mĭp'tər-əs) *adj.* Of or belonging to the Hemiptera, a large group of insects that includes the true bugs of the order Heteroptera and their allies of the order Homoptera.

hem·i·sphere (hĕm'ĭ-sfîr') *n.* **1. a.** A half of a sphere bounded by a great circle. **b.** A half of a symmetric, approximately spherical object as divided by a plane of symmetry: *a cerebral hemisphere.* **2.** Either half of the celestial sphere as divided by the ecliptic, the celestial equator, or the horizon. **3.** Either the northern or southern half of the earth as divided by the equator or the eastern or western half as divided by a meridian. **—hem'i·spher'ic** (-sfîr'ĭk, -sfĕr'-), **hem'i·spher'i·cal** *adj.* **—hem'i·spher'i·cal·ly** *adv.*

hem·i·stich (hĕm'ĭ-stĭk') *n.* Half a line of verse, esp. when separated rhythmically from the rest of the line by a caesura. [Lat. *hemistichium* < Gk. *hēmistikhion* : *hēmi-,* half + *stikhos,* line.]

hem·line (hĕm'līn') *n.* The line that is formed by the hem of a garment, as a dress.

hem·lock (hĕm'lŏk') *n.* **1. a.** Any of various evergreen trees of the genus *Tsuga,* of North America and eastern Asia, having short, flat needles and small cones. **b.** The wood of such a tree, used as a source of lumber, wood pulp, and tannic acid. **2. a.** Any of several poisonous plants of the genera *Conium* and *Cicuta,* such as the poison hemlock. **b.** A poison obtained from the poison hemlock. [ME *hemlok,* poisonous hemlock < OE *hymlīc.*]

hemlock
Genus *Tsuga*

hemo– or **hema–** or **hem–** *pref.* Blood: *hemacytometer.* [< Gk. *haima,* blood.]

he·mo·chro·ma·to·sis (hē'mə-krō'mə-tō'sĭs) *n.* A disease of iron metabolism characterized by accumulation of iron-containing pigments in the skin, liver enlargement, and diabetes.

he·mo·cy·a·nin (hē'mō-sī'ə-nĭn) *n.* A bluish, oxygen-bearing, copper-containing substance similar to hemoglobin, present in the blood of certain insects, crustaceans, and other invertebrates.

he·mo·cyte (hē'mə-sīt') *n.* A cell or similar formation in the blood.

he·mo·di·al·y·sis (hē'mō-dī-ăl'ĭ-sĭs) *n.* Dialysis of the blood.

he·mo·flag·el·late (hē'mō-flăj'ə-lāt', -lĭt, flə-jĕl'ĭt) *n.* A flagellate protozoan, such as a trypanosome, that is parasitic in the blood.

he·mo·glo·bin (hē'mə-glō'bĭn) *n.* The oxygen-bearing, iron-containing conjugated protein in vertebrate red blood cells, consisting of about 6 per cent heme and 94 per cent globin and having as a typical formula $(C_{738}H_{1166}FeN_{203}O_{208}S_2)_4$. [Short for obs. *hematoglobulin.*]

he·mo·leu·ko·cyte (hē'mə-lōō'kə-sīt') *n.* A white blood cell; leukocyte.

he·mo·ly·sin (hē'mə-lī'sĭn) *n.* An agent or substance that initiates lysis of red blood cells, thereby liberating hemoglobin.

he·mol·y·sis (hĭ-mŏl'ĭ-sĭs, hē'mə-lī'sĭs) *n.* The lysis of red blood cells. **—he'mo·lyt'ic** (hē'mə-lĭt'ĭk) *adj.*

he·mo·phil·i·a (hē'mə-fĭl'ē-ə) *n.* A hereditary plasma-coagulation disorder principally affecting males but transmitted by females and characterized by excessive, sometimes spontaneous bleeding.

he·mo·phil·i·ac (hē'mə-fĭl'ē-ăk') *n.* A person who suffers from hemophilia.

he·mo·phil·ic (hē'mə-fĭl'ĭk) *adj.* **1.** Of or pertaining to hemophilia. **2.** Growing well in blood or in a culture containing blood, as certain bacteria.

he·mo·pho·bi·a (hē'mə-fō'bē-ə) *n.* A morbid fear of blood. **—he'mo·pho'bic** *adj.*

he·mo·poi·e·sis (hē'mə-poi-ē'sĭs) *n.* Hematopoiesis. **—he'mo·poi·et'ic** (-ĕt'ĭk) *adj.*

he·mop·ty·sis (hĭ-mŏp'tĭ-sĭs) *n.* The spitting up of blood from the lungs or bronchial tubes. [HEMO- + Gk. *ptusis,* a spitting < *ptuein,* to spit.]

hem·or·rhage (hĕm'ər-ĭj) *n.* Bleeding, esp. copious discharge of blood from the blood vessels. *—intr.v.* **-rhaged, -rhag·ing, -rhag·es.** To bleed copiously in or as if in a hemorrhage. [Obs. *hemoragie* < OFr. *hemorragie* < Lat. *haemorrhagia* < Gk. *haimorrhagia* : *haimo,* hemo- + *rhēgnunai,* to break.] **—hem'or·rhag'ic** (hĕm'ə-răj'ĭk) *adj.*

hem·or·rhoid (hĕm'ə-roid') *n.* **1.** An itching or painful mass of dilated veins in swollen anal tissue. **2. hemorrhoids.** The pathological condition in which such swollen masses occur. [ME *emoroides,* hemorrhoids < Lat. *haemorrhoidae* < Gk. *haimorrhoides* < *haimorrhos,* flowing with blood : *haima,* blood + *rhein,* to flow.]

hem·or·rhoid·al (hĕm'ə-roid'l) *adj.* **1.** Of or pertaining to hemorrhoids. **2.** *Anat.* Supplying the region of the rectum and anus. Used of certain arteries.

hem·or·rhoid·ec·to·my (hĕm'ə-roi-dĕk'tə-mē) *n., pl.* **-mies.** The removal of hemorrhoids by surgery.

he·mo·sta·sis (hē'mə-stā'sĭs) also **he·mo·sta·sia** (-zhə, -zhē-ə, -zē-ə) *n.* The stopping of a flow or circulation of blood.

he·mo·stat (hē'mə-stăt') *n.* **1.** An agent, as a chemical, that stops bleeding. **2.** A clamplike instrument used in surgery to reduce or prevent bleeding.

he·mo·stat·ic (hē'mə-stăt'ĭk) *adj.* Acting to stop the flow of blood. *—n.* A hemostatic agent.

hemp (hĕmp) *n.* **1. a.** A tall plant, *Cannabis sativa,* native to Asia, having stems that yield a coarse fiber used in cordage. **b.** The fiber of this plant. **c.** A narcotic, such as hashish, derived from this plant. **2. a.** Any of various plants similar or related to hemp, esp. one yielding a fiber similar to that of *Cannabis sativa.* **b.** The fiber of such a plant. [ME < OE *hænep.*]

hemp agrimony *n.* A Eurasian plant, *Eupatorium cannabinum,* having clusters of small reddish-purple flowers.

hemp

hemp·en (hĕm′pən) *adj.* Of, pertaining to, or resembling hemp.

hemp nettle *n.* Any of various plants of the genus *Galeopsis,* esp. *G. tetrahit,* native to Eurasia, having bristly stems and white or reddish flowers.

hemp·weed (hĕmp′wēd′) *n.* Climbing hempweed.

hem·stitch (hĕm′stĭch′) *n.* **1.** A decorative stitch usually bordering a hem, as on a handkerchief, made by drawing out several parallel threads and catching together the cross threads in uniform groups. **2.** Needlework in which the hemstitch is used. —*tr.v.* **-stitched, -stitch·ing, -stitch·es.** To ornament or embroider with hemstitch. **—hem′stitch′er** *n.*

hen (hĕn) *n.* **1.** A female bird, esp. the adult female of the domestic fowl. **2.** The female of certain aquatic animals, such as an octopus or a lobster. **3.** *Slang.* A woman, esp. a fussy old woman. [ME < OE.]

henbane

hen-and-chick·ens (hĕn′ən-chĭk′ənz) *n., pl.* **hens-and-chick·ens** (hĕnz′-). Any of several plants having many runners or offshoots, esp. the houseleek.

hen·bane (hĕn′bān′) *n.* A poisonous plant, *Hyoscyamus niger,* native to the Mediterranean region, having an unpleasant odor, clammy leaves, and funnel-shaped greenish-yellow flowers and yielding a juice used medicinally.

hen·bit (hĕn′bĭt′) *n.* A plant, *Lamium amplexicaule,* native to Europe, having toothed leaves and small white or purplish-red flowers. [HEN + BIT¹.]

hence (hĕns) *adv.* **1. a.** For this reason; therefore: *handmade and hence expensive.* **b.** From this source: *She grew up in the Sudan; hence her interest in Nubian art.* **2.** From this time; from now: *A year hence he will have forgotten.* **3. a.** From this place; away from here. **b.** From this life. [ME, from this place < *henne* < OE *heonon.*]

hence·forth (hĕns′fôrth′) also **hence·for·ward** (hĕns-fôr′wərd) *adv.* From this time forth; from now on.

hench·man (hĕnch′mən) *n.* **1. a.** A loyal and trusted follower or subordinate. **b.** A person who supports a political figure chiefly out of self-seeking interests. **2.** A member of a criminal gang. **3.** *Obs.* A page to a prince or other person of high rank. [ME *hencheman,* servant to a person of rank < *hengest,* horse < OE + *man,* man.]

hen·dec·a·syl·lab·ic (hĕn-dĕk′ə-sĭ-lăb′ĭk) *adj.* Containing 11 syllables. —*n.* A verse of 11 syllables. [< Lat. *hendecasyllabus,* a line of eleven syllables : Gk. *hendeka,* eleven (*hen,* one + *deka,* ten) + Gk. *sullabē,* syllable. —see SYLLABLE.] **—hen·dec′a·syl′la·ble** (-sĭl′ə-bəl) *n.*

hen·di·a·dys (hĕn-dī′ə-dĭs) *n.* A figure of speech in which two words connected by a conjunction are used to express a single notion that would normally be expressed by an adjective and a substantive, as *grace and favor* instead of *gracious favor.* [Med. Lat. < Gk. *hen dia duoin,* one by means of two.]

hen·e·quen also **hen·e·quin** (hĕn′ĭ-kwĭn) *n.* **1.** A tropical American plant, *Agave fourcroydes,* having large, thick leaves that yield a coarse reddish fiber used in making rope and twine. **2.** The fiber obtained from the henequen. [Sp. *henequén,* perh. of Taino orig.]

hen harrier *n.* The marsh hawk.

henna

hen·na (hĕn′ə) *n.* **1. a.** A tree or shrub, *Lawsonia inermis,* of Asia and northern Africa, having fragrant white or reddish flowers. **b.** A reddish dyestuff obtained from the leaves of this plant, used as a cosmetic dye and for coloring leather. **2.** A moderate or strong reddish brown to strong brown. —*tr.v.* **-naed, -na·ing, -nas.** To dye (hair, for example) with henna. [Ar. *ḥinnā′.*] **—hen′na** *adj.*

hen·ner·y (hĕn′ə-rē) *n., pl.* **-ies. 1.** A poultry farm. **2.** A pen for domestic fowl.

hen·o·the·ism (hĕn′ə-thē-ĭz′əm) *n.* Belief in one god without denying the existence of others. [G. *Henotheismus* : Gk. *heis,* one + Gk. *theos,* god.] **—hen′o·the′ist** *n.* **—hen′o·the·is′tic** *adj.*

hepatica

hen·peck (hĕn′pĕk′) *tr.v.* **-pecked, -peck·ing, -pecks.** *Informal.* To dominate or harass (one's husband) with persistent nagging.

hen·ry (hĕn′rē) *n., pl.* **-ries** or **-rys.** The unit of inductance in which an induced electromotive force of one volt is produced when the current is varied at the rate of one ampere per second. [After Joseph *Henry* (1797–1878).]

hent (hĕnt) *tr.v.* **hent·ed, hent·ing, hents.** *Obs.* To take hold of; seize. [ME *henten* < OE *hentan.*]

hep (hĕp) *adj.* Variant of **hip².**

hep·a·rin (hĕp′ər-ĭn) *n.* A complex organic acid found esp. in lung and liver tissue and having the ability in certain circumstances to prevent the clotting of blood. [Gk. *hēpar,* liver + -IN.]

hepat– *pref.* Variant of **hepato–.**

he·pat·ic (hĭ-păt′ĭk) *adj.* **1.** Of, pertaining to, or resembling the liver. **2.** Acting on or occurring in the liver. **3.** Of or belonging to the Hepaticae, a class of mosslike plants that includes the liverworts. —*n.* **1.** A drug used in liver diseases. **2.** A plant of the class Hepaticae. [ME *epatic* < Lat. *hepaticus* < Gk. *hēpatikos* < *hēpar,* liver.]

Hepplewhite
18th-century American Hepplewhite chair

he·pat·i·ca (hĭ-păt′ĭ-kə) *n.* Any of several woodland plants of the genus *Hepatica,* esp. *H. americana,* of eastern North America, having three-lobed leaves and white or lavender flowers. [NLat. *Hepatica,* genus name < Med. Lat., liverwort < Lat. *hepaticus,* hepatic.]

hep·a·ti·tis (hĕp′ə-tī′tĭs) *n.* Inflammation of the liver, caused by infectious or toxic agents, characterized by jaundice, and usually accompanied by fever and other systemic manifestations.

hepato– or **hepat–** *pref.* Liver: *hepatitis.* [< Gk. *hēpar, hēpat-,* liver.]

hep·a·to·gen·ic (hĕp′ə-tō-jĕn′ĭk) also **hep·a·tog·e·nous** (-tŏj′ə-nəs) *adj.* Produced by or originating in the liver.

hep·a·to·tox·ic·i·ty (hĕp′ə-tō-tŏk-sĭs′ĭ-tē) *n.* **1.** The quality or condition of being toxic to the liver. **2.** The degree to which a substance causes hepatotoxicity. **—hep′a·to·tox′ic** (-tŏk′sĭk) *adj.*

hep·a·to·tox·in (hĕp′ə-tō-tŏk′sĭn) *n.* A substance causing hepatotoxicity.

hep·cat (hĕp′kăt′) *n. Slang.* A performer or devotee of swing and jazz during the 1940's.

He·phaes·tus (hĭ-fĕs′təs) *n. Gk. Myth.* The god of fire and metalworking. [Lat. < Gk. *Hēphaistos.*]

Hep·ple·white (hĕp′əl-hwīt′, -wīt′) *adj.* Of or designating an English style of furniture of the late 18th century. [After George *Hepplewhite* (d. 1786).]

hepta– or **hept–** *pref.* Seven: *heptarchy.* [< Gk. *hepta,* seven.]

hep·tad (hĕp′tăd′) *n.* A group or series of seven. [Gk. *heptas, heptad-,* the number seven < *hepta,* seven.]

hep·ta·gon (hĕp′tə-gŏn′) *n.* A seven-sided polygon. [Gk. *heptagōnos,* having seven angles : *hepta,* seven + *gōnos,* -gon.] **—hep·tag′o·nal** (-tăg′ə-nəl) *adj.*

hep·ta·he·dron (hĕp′tə-hē′drən) *n.* A polyhedron with seven faces. **—hep′ta·he′dral** (-drəl) *adj.*

hep·tam·e·ter (hĕp-tăm′ĭ-tər) *n.* **1.** A unit of verse consisting of seven feet. **2.** A line of verse written in heptameter.

hep·tane (hĕp′tān′) *n.* A volatile, colorless, highly flammable liquid hydrocarbon, $CH_3(CH_2)_5CH_3$, obtained in the fractional distillation of petroleum and used as a standard in determining octane ratings, as an anesthetic, and as a solvent.

hep·tar·chy (hĕp′tär′kē) *n., pl.* **-chies. 1. a.** Government by seven persons. **b.** A state so governed. **2.** Often **Heptarchy.** The informal confederation of the Anglo-Saxon kingdoms from the 5th to the 9th century, consisting of Kent, Sussex, Wessex, Essex, Northumbria, East Anglia, and Mercia.

hep·ta·stich (hĕp′tə-stĭk′) *n.* A stanza or strophe consisting of seven lines.

Hep·ta·teuch (hĕp′tə-to͞ok′, -tyo͞ok′) *n.* The first seven books of the Old Testament. [Gk. *heptateukhos,* volume containing seven books : *hepta,* seven + *teukhos,* book.]

her (hər, ər; hûr *when stressed*) *pron.* **1.** The objective case of **she.** Used: **a.** As the direct object of a verb: *They saw her in the library.* **b.** As the indirect object of a verb: *They gave her a book.* **c.** As the object of a preposition: *This letter is addressed to her.* **2.** The possessive form of **she.** Used as a modifier before a noun: *her purse; her accomplishments; her first rebuff.* —See Usage notes at **be, everyone,** and **I.** [ME < OE *hire.*]

He·ra (hîr′ə) *n. Gk. Myth.* The sister and wife of Zeus, identified by the Romans with Juno. [Gk. *Hēra.*]

Her·a·cles or **Her·a·kles** (hĕr′ə-klēz′) *n.* Variants of **Hercules** (sense 1).

her·ald (hĕr′əld) *n.* **1.** A person who carries or proclaims important news; messenger. **2.** One that gives a sign or indication of something to come; harbinger: *The crocus is the herald of spring.* **3.** *Chiefly Brit.* An official whose specialty is heraldry. **4. a.** An official formerly charged with making royal proclamations and bearing messages of state between sovereigns. **b.** An official who formerly made proclamations and conveyed challenges at a tournament. —*tr.v.* **-ald·ed, -ald·ing, -alds.** To proclaim; announce: *heard the cheers that heralded their arrival.* [ME < AN, of Germanic orig.]

he·ral·dic (hə-răl′dĭk) *adj.* Of or pertaining to heralds or heraldry. **—he·ral′di·cal·ly** *adv.*

her·ald·ry (hĕr′əl-drē) *n., pl.* **-ries. 1.** The study or art of tracing genealogies, of determining, designing, and granting coats of arms, and of ruling on questions of rank or protocol. **2.** Armorial ensigns or devices. **3.** Pageantry.

herb (ûrb, hûrb) *n.* **1.** A plant that has a fleshy stem as distinguished from the woody tissue of shrubs and trees and that generally dies back at the end of each growing season. **2.** Any of various often aromatic plants used esp. in medicine or as seasoning. [ME *herbe* < OFr. *erbe* < Lat. *herba.*]

her·ba·ceous (hûr-bā′shəs, ûr-) *adj.* **1.** Pertaining to or characteristic of an herb as distinguished from a woody plant. **2.** Green and leaflike in appearance or texture. [Lat. *herbaceus* < *herba,* herb.]

herb·age (ûr′bĭj, hûr′-) *n.* **1.** Herbaceous plant growth, esp. grass or similar vegetation used for pasturage. **2.** The fleshy, often edible parts of plants. [ME < OFr. *erbage* < Med. Lat. *herbagium* < Lat. *herba.*]

herb·al (hûr′bəl, ûr′-) *adj.* Of, relating to, or containing herbs. —*n.* A book about plants and herbs, esp. those that are useful to man.

herb·al·ist (hûr′bə-lĭst, ûr′-) *n.* One who grows, collects, or specializes in the use of herbs, esp. medicinal herbs.

her·bar·i·um (hûr-bâr′ē-əm, ûr-) *n., pl.* **-i·ums** or **-i·a** (-ē-ə). **1.** A collection of dried plants mounted and labeled for use in scientific study. **2.** A place or institution where a herbarium is kept. [LLat. < Lat. *herba,* vegetation.]

herb bennet *n.* A hairy Eurasian plant, *Geum urbanum,* having small yellow flowers and an astringent root formerly used medicinally. [ME *herbe benet* < AN < Med. Lat. *herba benedicta.*]

her·bi·cide (hûr′bĭ-sīd′, ûr′-) *n.* A substance used to destroy plants, esp. weeds. **—her′bi·cid′al** (-sīd′l) *adj.*

her·bi·vore (hûr′bə-vôr′, -vōr′, ûr′-) *n.* A herbivorous animal. [NLat. *Herbivora,* former mammalian group < *herbivorus,* herbivorous.]

her·biv·o·rous (hûr-bĭv′ər-əs, ûr-) *adj.* Feeding on plants; plant-eating. [NLat. *herbivorus* : Lat. *herba,* vegetation + *vorare,* to swallow up.] **—her·biv′o·rous·ly** *adv.*

herb Par·is (păr′ĭs) *n.* A European plant, *Paris quadrifolia,* having a whorl of four leaves and a solitary yellow or greenish flower. [Prob. Med. Lat. *herba paris.*]

herb Rob·ert (rŏb′ərt) *n.* A low-growing plant, *Geranium robertianum,* having divided leaves and small reddish-purple flowers. [ME *herbe Robert* < OFr. *erbe Robert* < Med. Lat. *herba Roberti.*]

her·cu·le·an (hûr′kyə-lē′ən, hûr-kyo͞o′lē-) *adj.* **1.** Of unusual size, power, or difficulty. **2.** Often **Herculean.** Of or resembling Hercules: *Herculean strength.* **3. Herculean.** Of or relating to Hercules.

Her·cu·les (hûr′kyə-lēz′) *n.* **1.** Also **Her·a·cles** or **Her·a·kles** (hĕr′ə-klēz′). *Gk. & Rom. Myth.* The son of Zeus and Alcmene, a hero of extraordinary strength who won immortality by performing 12 labors demanded by Hera. **2.** *Astron.* A constellation in the Northern Hemisphere near Lyra and Corona Borealis that contains the star Ras Algheti and the globular cluster M13. [Lat. < Gk. *Hēraklēs.*]

Her·cu·les′-club (hûr′kyə-lēz-klŭb′) *n.* **1.** A tree or shrub, *Aralia spinosa,* of the southeastern United States, having prickly compound leaves and large clusters of small white flowers. **2.** A spiny tree, *Zanthoxylum clava-herculis,* of the southeastern United States, having clusters of small greenish-yellow flowers.

herd (hûrd) *n.* **1. a.** A group of cattle or other domestic animals of a single kind kept together for a specific use. **b.** A number of wild animals of one species that remain together as a group: *a herd of elephants.* **2. a.** A large number of people; crowd: *a herd of stranded passengers.* **b.** The multitude of common people regarded as a mass: *"It is the luxurious and dissipated who set the fashions which the herd so diligently follow"* (Henry David Thoreau). *—v.* **herd·ed, herd·ing, herds.** *—intr.* **1.** To come together in a herd. **2.** To keep company; associate. *—tr.* **1.** To gather, keep, or drive (animals) in a herd. **2.** To gather and lead in a group: *herded the children into the auditorium.* **3.** To tend (sheep or cattle). [ME < OE *heord.*]

herd·er (hûr′dər) *n.* **1.** A person who tends or drives a herd. **2.** A herdsman.

her·dic (hûr′dĭk) *n.* A small horse-drawn cab with two wheels, side seats, and an entrance at the back. [After Peter *Herdic* (1824–1888).]

herds·man (hûrdz′mən) *n.* A person who owns or breeds livestock.

here (hîr) *adv.* **1.** At or in this place: *Stop here.* **2.** At this time; now: *We'll adjourn the meeting here.* **3.** At or on this point, detail, or item: *Here I must disagree.* **4.** In the present life or condition. **5.** To this place; hither: *Come here.* *—adj.* **1.** Used for emphasis after a demonstrative pronoun: *Which word? This one here.* **2.** Used for emphasis after a noun modified by a demonstrative pronoun: *this word here.* **3.** *Nonstandard.* Used for emphasis between a demonstrative pronoun and a noun: *this here word.* *—interj.* Used to respond to a roll call, attract attention, command an animal, or rebuke or admonish. **—idiom. neither here nor there.** Unimportant and irrelevant. [ME < OE *hēr.*]

Usage: In formal usage *here* is not properly placed before a noun in a phrase such as *this here house,* though some dialects do allow such a construction. In constructions introduced by *here is* and *here are* the number of the verb is governed by the subject, which appears after the verb: *Here is the zebra. Here are the zebras. Here are Pat and Jim.*

here·a·bout (hîr′ə-bout′) also **here·a·bouts** (-bouts′) *adv.* In this general vicinity; around here.

here·af·ter (hîr-ăf′tər) *adv.* **1.** Immediately following this in time, order, or place; after this. **2.** In a future time or state: *win salvation hereafter.* *—n.* The afterlife: *belief in a hereafter.*

here·by (hîr-bī′) *adv.* By this means.

her·e·dit·a·ment (hĕr′ĭ-dĭt′ə-mənt) *n.* *Law.* Property that can be inherited. [Med. Lat. *hereditamentum* < LLat. *hereditare,* to inherit. —see HERITAGE.]

he·red·i·tar·y (hə-rĕd′ĭ-tĕr′ē) *adj.* **1.** *Law.* **a.** Descending from an ancestor to a legal heir; passing down by inheritance. **b.** Having title or possession through inheritance. **2.** Genetically transmitted or transmissible. **3. a.** Appearing in or characteristic of successive generations. **b.** Derived from or fostered by one's ancestors: *a hereditary prejudice.* **4.** Ancestral; traditional: *their hereditary home.* **5.** Of or relating to heredity or inheritance. [Lat. *hereditarius* < *hereditas,* inheritance < *heres,* heir.] **—he·red′i·tar′i·ly** (-târ′ə-lē) *adv.* **—he·red′i·tar′i·ness** *n.*

he·red·i·tist (hə-rĕd′ĭ-tĭst) *n.* One who supports the theory that heredity rather than environment determines personality.

he·red·i·ty (hə-rĕd′ĭ-tē) *n., pl.* **-ties. 1.** The genetic transmission of characteristics from parents to offspring. **2.** The totality of characteristics and associated potentialities transmitted to an individual organism by heredity. [OFr. *heredite,* inheritance < Lat. *hereditas* < *heres,* heir.]

Here·ford (hûr′fərd, hĕr′ə-fərd) *n.* Any of a breed of beef cattle developed in Herefordshire, England, having a reddish coat with white markings.

here·in (hîr-ĭn′) *adv.* In or into this.

here·in·af·ter (hîr′ĭn-ăf′tər) *adv.* In a following part of this document, statement, or book.

here·in·be·fore (hîr′ĭn-bĭ-fôr′, -fōr′) *adv.* In a preceding part of this document, statement, or book.

here·in·to (hîr-ĭn′to͞o) *adv.* Into this matter, circumstance, situation, or place.

here·of (hîr-ŭv′, -ŏv′) *adv.* Pertaining to or concerning this.

here·on (hîr-ŏn′, -ôn′) *adv.* Hereupon.

he·re·si·arch (hə-rē′zē-ärk′, hĕr′ĭ-sē-) *n.* The founder or chief proponent of a heresy. [LLat. *haeresiarcha* < LGk. *hairesiarkhēs* : Gk. *hairesis,* sect + Gk. *-arkhēs,* -arch.]

her·e·sy (hĕr′ĭ-sē) *n., pl.* **-sies. 1. a.** An opinion or doctrine at variance with established religious beliefs, esp. dissension from or denial of Roman Catholic dogma by a professed believer or baptized church member. **b.** Adherence to such dissenting opinion or doctrine. **2. a.** A controversial or unorthodox opinion or doctrine, as in politics, philosophy, or science. **b.** Adherence to such controversial or unorthodox opinion. [ME *heresie* < OFr. < LLat. *haeresis* < LGk. *hairesis* < Gk., faction < *haireisthai,* to choose.]

her·e·tic (hĕr′ĭ-tĭk) *n.* A person who holds controversial opinions, esp. one who publicly dissents from the officially accepted dogma of the Roman Catholic Church. [ME *heretik* < OFr. *eretique* < LLat. *haereticus* < Gk. *hairetikos,* factious < *hairesthai,* to choose.]

he·ret·i·cal (hə-rĕt′ĭ-kəl) *adj.* **1.** Of or pertaining to heresy or heretics. **2.** Characterized by, revealing, or approaching departure from established beliefs or standards. **—he·ret′i·cal·ly** *adv.* **—he·ret′i·cal·ness** *n.*

here·to (hîr-to͞o′) *adv.* To this document, matter, or proposition.

here·to·fore (hîr′tə-fôr′, -fōr′) *adv.* Up to the present time; previously. [ME : *here,* here (< OE *hēr*) + *to fore,* previously (< OE *toforan*).]

here·un·to (hîr-ŭn′to͞o) *adv.* Hereto.

here·up·on (hîr′ə-pŏn′, -pôn′) *adv.* Immediately after this; at this.

here·with (hîr-wĭth′, -wĭth′) *adv.* **1.** Along with this. **2.** By this means; hereby.

her·i·ot (hĕr′ē-ət) *n.* A tribute or service rendered to a feudal lord on the death of a tenant. [ME < OE *heregeatu* : *here,* army + *geatwe,* equipment.]

her·i·ta·ble (hĕr′ĭ-tə-bəl) *adj.* **1.** Capable of being inherited; hereditary. **2.** Capable of inheriting or of taking by inheritance. [ME < OFr. < *heriter,* to inherit. —see HERITAGE.] **—her′i·ta·bil′i·ty** *n.*

her·i·tage (hĕr′ĭ-tĭj) *n.* **1.** Property that can be inherited; inheritance. **2.** Something passed down from preceding generations; tradition. **3.** The status acquired by a person through birth; birthright: *a heritage of affluence and social position.* [ME < OFr. < *heriter,* to inherit < LLat. *hereditare* < Lat. *heres,* heir.]

her·i·tor (hĕr′ĭ-tər) *n.* An inheritor. [ME *heriter* < AN < Lat. *hereditarius,* hereditary. —see HEREDITARY.]

her·i·tress (hĕr′ĭ-trĭs) *n.* A woman who inherits; inheritor.

her·ma (hûr′mə) also **herm** (hûrm) *n.* A statue consisting of the head of the Greek god Hermes mounted on a square stone post. [Lat. < Gk. *hermēs* (after *Hermēs,* Hermes).]

her·maph·ro·dite (hər-măf′rə-dīt′) *n.* **1.** One having the sex organs and many of the secondary sex characteristics of both male and female. **2.** *Biol.* An organism, such as an earthworm or a monoclinous plant, having male and female reproductive organs in the same individual. **3.** Something composed of a combination of diverse or contradictory elements. [ME *hermofrodite* < Med. Lat. *hermofroditus* < Lat. *hermaphroditus* < Gk. *hermaphroditos* < *Hermaphroditos,* Hermaphroditus.] **—her·maph′ro·dit′ic** (-dĭt′ĭk) *adj.* **—her·maph′ro·dit′i·cal·ly** *adv.*

hermaphrodite brig *n.* A two-masted vessel with a square-rigged foremast and a schooner-rigged mainmast.

her·maph·ro·dit·ism (hər-măf′rə-dī-tĭz′əm) also **her·maph·ro·dism** (-rə-dĭz′əm) *n.* The condition of being a hermaphrodite.

Her·maph·ro·di·tus (hər-măf′rə-dī′təs) *n.* *Gk. Myth.* The son of Hermes and Aphrodite, who became united in one body with the nymph Salmacis. [Gk. *Hermaphroditos* : *Hermēs,* Hermes + *Aphroditē,* Aphrodite.]

her·me·neu·tic (hûr′mə-no͞o′tĭk, -nyo͞o′-) also **her·me·neu·ti·cal** (-tĭ-kəl) *adj.* Interpretive; explanatory. [Gk. *hermeneutikos* < *hermēneutēs,* interpreter < *hermēnuenein,* to interpret < *hermēneus,* interpreter.] **—her′me·neu′ti·cal·ly** *adv.*

her·me·neu·tics (hûr′mə-no͞o′tĭks, -nyo͞o′-) *n.* *(used with a sing. verb).* The science and methodology of interpretation, esp. of the Bible. [< HERMENEUTIC.]

Her·mes (hûr′mēz) *n.* *Gk. Myth.* The god of commerce, invention, cunning, and theft, who also served as messenger and herald for the other gods. [Gk. *Hermēs.*]

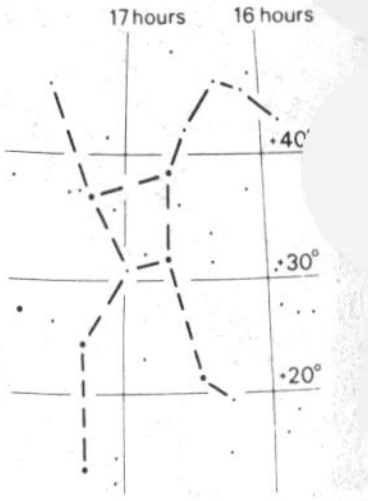

Hercules
Above: Mythological figure
Below: Constellation

hermaphrodite brig

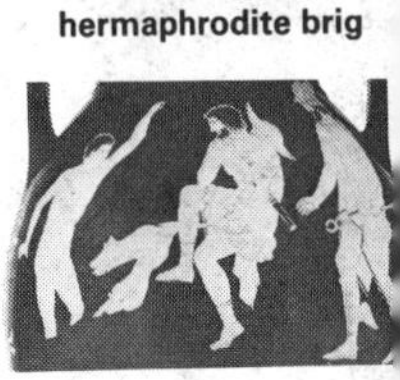

Hermes
On a 5th-century B.C. Greek vase

hermit crab

heron
Great White Heron

Hermes Tris·me·gis·tus (trĭs′mə-jĭs′təs) *n.* The Egyptian god Thoth, the legendary author of works on alchemy, astrology, and magic. [Lat. < Gk. *Hermēs trismegistos.*]

her·met·ic (hər-mĕt′ĭk) also **her·met·i·cal** (-ĭ-kəl) *adj.* **1. a.** Completely sealed, esp. against the escape or entry of air. **b.** Impervious to outside interference or influence: *the hermetic confines of his isolated existence.* **2.** Often **Hermetic. a.** Of or pertaining to Hermes Trismegistus or to the works ascribed to him. **b.** Having to do with the occult sciences, esp. alchemy; magical. [NLat. *hermeticus,* after *Hermes* Trismegistus.] **—her·met′i·cal·ly** *adv.*

her·mit (hûr′mĭt) *n.* **1.** A person who has withdrawn from society and lives a solitary existence; recluse. **2.** A spiced cookie made with molasses, raisins, and nuts. [ME *heremite* < Med. Lat. *heremita* < LLat. *eremita* < Gk. *erēmitēs* < *erēmia,* desert < *erēmos,* solitary.] **—her·mit′ic, her·mit′i·cal** *adj.* **—her·mit′i·cal·ly** *adv.*

her·mit·age (hûr′mĭ-tĭj) *n.* **1. a.** The habitation of a hermit or group of hermits. **b.** A monastery or abbey. **2.** A place where one can live in seclusion; retreat. **3.** The condition or way of life of a hermit. [ME < OFr. *hermitaige* < Med. Lat. *heremita,* hermit. —see HERMIT.]

Her·mi·tage (ĕr′mĭ-täzh′) *n.* A rich, full-bodied, usually red wine produced in southeastern France. [After Tain *l'Ermitage,* a commune in France.]

hermit crab *n.* Any of various crustaceans of the section Anomura within the order Decapoda, having a soft, unarmored abdomen and occupying and carrying about the empty shell of a snail or other univalve mollusk.

hermit thrush *n.* A North American bird, *Hylocichla guttata,* having brownish plumage, a spotted breast, and a distinctive melodious song.

hern (hûrn) *n. Archaic & Regional.* A heron. [Var. of HERON.]

her·ni·a (hûr′nē-ə) *n., pl.* **-ni·as** or **-ni·ae** (-nē-ē′). The protrusion of an organ, organic part, or other bodily structure through the wall that normally contains it. [ME < Lat.] **—her′ni·al** *adj.*

her·ni·ate (hûr′nē-āt′) *intr.v.* **-at·ed, -at·ing, -ates.** To protrude through an abnormal bodily opening. [HERNI(A) + -ATE.] **—her′ni·a′tion** *n.*

he·ro (hîr′ō) *n., pl.* **-roes. 1.** In mythology and legend, a man, often of divine ancestry, who is endowed with great courage and strength, celebrated for his bold exploits, and favored by the gods. **2.** A man noted for feats of courage or nobility of purpose, esp. one who has risked or sacrificed his life: *a war hero.* **3.** A man noted for his special achievements in a particular field: *the heroes of medicine.* **4.** The principal male character in a novel, poem, or dramatic presentation. **5.** *Slang.* A large sandwich consisting of a roll that is split lengthwise and contains a variety of fillings, as lettuce, tomatoes, onions, meats, and cheese. [Lat. *heros* < Gk. *hērōs.*]

He·ro (hîr′ō) *n. Gk. Myth.* A priestess of Aphrodite beloved by Leander. [Lat. < Gk. *Hērō.*]

he·ro·ic (hĭ-rō′ĭk) also **he·ro·i·cal** (-ĭ-kəl) *adj.* **1.** Of, relating to, or resembling the heroes of literature, legend, or myth. **2.** Having, displaying, or marked by the qualities appropriate to a hero; courageous: *heroic deeds.* **3. a.** Impressive in size or scope; grand: *a heroic undertaking.* **b.** Of a size or scale that is larger than life: *heroic sculpture.* —*n.* **1.** A heroic verse or poem. **2. heroics.** Melodramatic behavior or language: *"We trust the House . . . will come up with answers without all the political heroics"* (Atlanta Constitution). **—he·ro′i·cal·ly** *adv.* **—he·ro′i·cal·ness** *n.*

heroic couplet *n.* A verse unit consisting of two rhymed lines in iambic pentameter.

heroic meter *n.* Heroic verse.

heroic play *n.* A Restoration tragedy written in rhymed couplets and generally characterized by extravagant declamatory rhetoric.

heroic verse *n.* One of several verse forms suitable for and traditionally used in epic and dramatic poetry, esp.: **a.** The dactylic hexameter in Greek and Latin. **b.** The iambic pentameter in English.

her·o·in (hĕr′ō-ĭn) *n.* A white, odorless, bitter crystalline compound, $C_{17}H_{17}NO(C_2H_3O_2)_2$, that is derived from morphine and is a highly addictive narcotic. [G. < Gk. *hērōs,* hero (from the feeling of omnipotence experienced while taking the drug).] **—her′o·in·ism** *n.*

her·o·ine (hĕr′ō-ĭn) *n.* **1.** A woman noted for her courage and daring acts. **2.** A woman noted for her special achievements in a particular field. **3.** The principal female character in a novel, poem, or dramatic presentation. [Lat. *heroina* < Gk. *hērōinē,* fem. of *hērōs,* hero.]

her·o·ism (hĕr′ō-ĭz′əm) *n.* **1.** Heroic conduct or behavior. **2.** Heroic characteristics or qualities; courage.

her·on (hĕr′ən) *n.* Any of various wading birds of the family Ardeidae, having a long neck, long legs, and a long, pointed bill. [ME < OFr., of Germanic orig.]

her·on·ry (hĕr′ən-rē) *n., pl.* **-ries.** A place frequented by herons.

hero worship *n.* Intense or excessive admiration for a hero or a person regarded as a hero.

he·ro-wor·ship (hîr′ō-wûr′shĭp) *tr.v.* **-shiped, -ship·ing, -ships** or **-shipped, -ship·ping, -ships.** To feel hero worship for. **—he′ro-wor′ship·er** *n.*

her·pes (hûr′pēz) *n.* Any of several viral diseases causing eruptions of the skin or mucous membrane, esp. herpes simplex or herpes zoster. [Lat. < Gk. *herpēs* < *herpein,* to creep.] **—her·pet′ic** (hər-pĕt′ĭk) *adj.*

herpes la·bi·a·lis (lā′bē-ā′lĭs) *n.* A cold sore. [NLat., herpes of the lip.]

herpes sim·plex (sĭm′plĕks′) *n.* A viral infection with blistering of the lips, external nares, glans, prepuce, or vulva. [NLat., simple herpes.]

her·pes·vi·rus (hûr′pēz-vī′rəs) *n.* Any of various DNA-containing animal viruses that produce herpes.

herpes zos·ter (zŏs′tər, zō′stər) *n.* A viral infection with eruption of vesicles along a nerve path on one side of the body, often accompanied or followed by severe neuralgia. [NLat., girdle herpes.]

her·pe·tol·o·gy (hûr′pĭ-tŏl′ə-jē) *n.* The scientific study of reptiles and amphibians as a branch of zoology. [Gk. *herpeton,* reptile < *herpein,* to creep.] **—her′pe·to·log′ic** (-tə-lŏj′ĭk), **her′pe·to·log′i·cal** *adj.* **—her′pe·to·log′i·cal·ly** *adv.* **—her′pe·tol′o·gist** *n.*

Herr (hĕr) *n., pl.* **Her·ren** (hĕr′ən). A title of courtesy prefixed to the name or professional title of a German, equivalent to English *Mister.* [G.]

Her·ren·volk (hĕr′ən-fōk′, -fôlk′) *n.* A people assertedly endowed with the right to dominate and exploit other peoples. [G.]

her·ring (hĕr′ĭng) *n., pl.* **herring** or **-rings.** Any of various fishes of the family Clupeidae, esp. *Clupea harengus,* a commercially important food fish of Atlantic and Pacific waters. [ME < OE *hǣring.*]

her·ring·bone (hĕr′ĭng-bōn′) *n.* **1.** A pattern consisting of rows of short, slanted parallel lines, with the direction of the slant alternating row by row. **2.** A twilled fabric woven in a herringbone pattern. **3.** A method of climbing a ski slope with the tips of the skis pointed outward. **—modifier:** *a herringbone tweed.* —*v.* **-boned, -bon·ing, -bones.** —*tr.* To arrange or decorate with a herringbone pattern. —*intr.* **1.** To produce a herringbone pattern. **2.** To ascend a ski slope by executing a herringbone.

herring gull *n.* A common, widely distributed gull, *Larus argentatus,* having gray and white plumage with black wing tips.

hers (hûrz) *pron.* Used to indicate the one or ones belonging to her: *If you can't find your hat, take hers.* [ME < *hire,* her.]

her·self (hûr-sĕlf′) *pron.* **1.** That one identical with her. Used: **a.** Reflexively as the direct or indirect object of a verb or as the object of a preposition: *She hurt herself.* **b.** For emphasis: *She herself wasn't certain.* **c.** In an absolute construction: *In difficulties herself, she was unable to help.* **2.** Her normal or healthy condition or state: *She isn't herself today.* —See Usage note at **myself.** [ME *hire selfe* < OE *hire selfre.*]

hertz (hûrts) *n.* A unit of frequency equal to one cycle per second. [After Heinrich R. *Hertz* (1857-1894).]

Hertz·i·an wave (hûrt′sē-ən, hĕrt′-) *n.* An electromagnetic wave, usually of radio frequency, produced by the oscillation of electricity in a conductor. [After Heinrich R. *Hertz* (1857–1894).]

Hertz·sprung-Rus·sell diagram (hĕrts′sprŭng-rŭs′əl) *n.* A graph of the logarithms of the luminosities of stars plotted against the logarithms of their surface temperatures. [After Ejnar *Hertzsprung* (1873–1967) and Henry N. *Russell* (1877–1957).]

he's (hēz). **1.** He is. **2.** He has.

Hesh·van also **Hesh·wan** (KHĕsh′vən) *n.* The second month of the Hebrew calendar. See table at **calendar.** [Heb. *heshwān.*]

hes·i·tan·cy (hĕz′ĭ-tən-sē) *n., pl.* **-cies. 1.** The state or quality of being hesitant. **2.** An instance of hesitating.

hes·i·tant (hĕz′ĭ-tənt) *adj.* Inclined or tending to hesitate. **—hes′i·tant·ly** *adv.*

hes·i·tate (hĕz′ĭ-tāt′) *intr.v.* **-tat·ed, -tat·ing, -tates. 1. a.** To be slow to act, speak, or decide. **b.** To pause in uncertainty; waver. **2.** To be reluctant: *He hesitated to ask for help.* **3.** To speak haltingly; falter. [Lat. *haesitare, haesitat-,* to hesitate, freq. of *haerēre,* to hold fast.] **—hes′i·tat′er** *n.* **—hes′i·tat′ing·ly** *adv.*

Synonyms: *hesitate, vacillate, waver, falter.* These verbs mean to express uncertainty or indecision. *Hesitate* implies inaction caused by uncertainty about what to do or say. *Vacillate* implies prolonged inaction during which one weighs alternative and usually conflicting courses without making a decisive choice. *Waver* suggests either inability to act, resulting from indecision, or tentative and ineffectual action once a choice has been made. *Falter* refers to acting indecisively or ineffectually and implies retreat from a course decided on or inability to carry it out.

hes·i·ta·tion (hĕz′ĭ-tā′shən) *n.* **1.** The act or an instance of hesitating. **2.** The state of being hesitant. **3.** A pause or faltering in speech.

Hes·pe·ri·an (hĕ-spîr′ē-ən) *adj.* Of or pertaining to the west. [< Lat. *Hesperius* < Gk. *hesperios* < *hesperos,* evening.]

Hes·per·i·des (hĕ-spĕr′ĭ-dēz′) *pl.n. Gk. Myth.* **1.** The nymphs who together with a dragon watch over a garden in which golden apples grow. **2.** *(used with a sing. verb).* A garden, situated at the western end of the earth, in which golden apples grow. [Lat. *Hesperides* < Gk., pl. of *hesperis,*

western < *hesperios* < *hesperos,* evening.] **—Hes'per·id'i·an, Hes'per·id'e·an** (hĕs'pə-rĭd'ē-ən) *adj.*
hes·per·id·i·a (hĕs'pə-rĭd'ē-ə) *n.* Plural of **hesperidium.**
hes·per·i·din (hĕ-spĕr'ĭ-dĭn) *n.* A white or colorless crystalline compound, $C_{28}H_{34}O_{15}$, occurring in citrus fruit. [HESPERID(IUM) + -IN.]
hes·per·id·i·um (hĕs'pə-rĭd'ē-əm) *n., pl.* **-i·a** (-ē-ə). A form of berry having a thickened, leathery rind and juicy pulp divided into segments, as an orange or other citrus fruit. [NLat., after the *Hesperides,* where golden apples grow.]
Hes·per·us (hĕs'pər-əs) *n.* The planet Venus in its appearance as the evening star. [Lat. < Gk. *Hesperos.*]
Hes·sian (hĕsh'ən) *n.* **1.** An inhabitant of Hesse. **2.** A German mercenary in the British army in America during the Revolutionary War. **3.** A mercenary.
Hessian boot *n.* A high, tasseled man's boot.
Hessian fly *n.* A small fly, *Mayetiola destructor,* having larvae that infest and destroy wheat and other grain plants.
hes·so·nite (hĕs'ə-nīt') *n.* Variant of **essonite.**
hest (hĕst) *n. Archaic.* Command; behest. [ME < OE *hǣs.*]
Hes·ti·a (hĕs'tē-ə) *n. Gk. Myth.* The goddess of the hearth, daughter of Cronus and Rhea. [Gk.]
he·tae·ra (hĭ-tîr'ə) also **he·tai·ra** (-tīr'ə) *n., pl.* **-tae·rae** (-tîr'ē) or **-tae·ras** also **-tai·rai** (-tīr'ī') or **-tai·ras. 1.** In ancient Greece, a courtesan or concubine, esp. one of a special class of cultivated female companions. **2.** An adventuress. [Gk. *hetaira,* fem. of *hetairos,* companion.]
heter– *pref.* Variant of **hetero-.**
het·er·e·cious (hĕt'ə-rē'shəs) *adj.* Variant of **heteroecious.**
het·er·o (hĕt'ə-rō') *n., pl.* **-os.** A heterosexual. **—het'er·o** *adj.*
hetero– or **heter–** *pref.* **1.** Other; different: *heterochromatic.* **2.** Containing different kinds of atoms: *heterocyclic.* [< Gk. *heteros,* other.]
het·er·o·cer·cal (hĕt'ə-rō-sûr'kəl) *adj.* Pertaining to, designating, or characterized by a tail fin having two unequal lobes, with the vertebral column extending into the upper, usually larger lobe, as in sharks. [HETERO- + Gk. *kerkos,* tail + -AL.]
het·er·o·chro·mat·ic (hĕt'ə-rō-krō-măt'ĭk) *adj.* **1.** Of, pertaining to, or having different colors; varicolored. **2.** Consisting of different wavelengths or frequencies. **3.** Of or pertaining to heterochromatin. **—het'er·o·chro'ma·tism** (-krō'mə-tĭz'əm) *n.*
het·er·o·chro·ma·tin (hĕt'ə-rō-krō'mə-tĭn) *n.* Chromosomal material exhibiting maximal staining in the nuclear meiotic interphase and lacking specific genetic activity.
het·er·o·chro·mo·some (hĕt'ə-rō-krō'mə-sōm') *n.* A chromosome composed primarily of heterochromatin.
het·er·o·cy·clic (hĕt'ə-rō-sī'klĭk, -sĭk'lĭk) *adj.* Containing more than one kind of atom joined in a ring. **—het'er·o·cy'cle** (-sī'kəl) *n.* **—het'er·o·cy'clic** *n.*
het·er·o·dox (hĕt'ər-ə-dŏks') *adj.* **1.** Not in agreement with accepted beliefs, esp. departing from church doctrine or dogma. **2.** Holding unorthodox opinions. [LLat. *heterodoxus* < Gk. *heterodoxos* : *heteros,* other + *doxa,* opinion < *dokein,* to think.]
het·er·o·dox·y (hĕt'ər-ə-dŏk'sē) *n., pl.* **-ies. 1.** The condition or quality of being heterodox. **2.** A heterodox opinion or doctrine.
het·er·o·dyne (hĕt'ər-ə-dīn') *adj.* Having alternating currents of two different frequencies that are combined to generate a current that has sum and difference frequencies, either of which may be used in radio or television receivers by proper tuning or filtering. *—tr.v.* **-dyned, -dyn·ing, -dynes.** To combine (a radio-frequency wave) with a locally generated wave of different frequency in order to produce a new frequency equal to the sum or difference of the two.
het·er·oe·cious also **het·er·e·cious** (hĕt'ə-rē'shəs) *adj.* Spending alternate stages of a life cycle on different unrelated hosts. Used of parasites such as rusts and tapeworms. [HETERO- + Gk. *oikos,* house + -OUS.] **—het'er·oe'cism** (-sĭz'əm) *n.*
het·er·o·gam·ete (hĕt'ə-rō-găm'ēt', -gə-mēt') *n.* Either of two conjugating gametes, such as the small, motile male spermatozoon and the larger, nonmotile female ovum, that differ in size, form, or behavior.
het·er·o·ga·met·ic (hĕt'ə-rō-gə-mĕt'ĭk) *adj.* Having a dissimilar pair of sex chromosomes, as in human males, or one unpaired sex chromosome, as in some male insects.
het·er·og·a·mous (hĕt'ə-rŏg'ə-məs) *adj.* **1.** *Biol.* Characterized by the fusion of unlike gametes in the reproductive process. **2.** *Bot.* Bearing flowers of different kinds, esp. both male and female flowers.
het·er·og·a·my (hĕt'ə-rŏg'ə-mē) *n.* **1.** Alternation of generations, one sexual, the other parthenogenetic, as in some aphids. **2.** A state in which uniting gametes are dissimilar in structure and size as well as in function. **—het'er·o·gam'ic** (-rō-găm'ĭk) *adj.*
het·er·o·ge·ne·i·ty (hĕt'ə-rō'jə-nē'ĭ-tē) *n.* The quality or state of being heterogeneous.
het·er·o·ge·ne·ous (hĕt'ər-ə-jē'nē-əs, -jēn'yəs) *adj.* **1.** Consisting of or involving dissimilar elements or parts; not homogeneous: *a heterogeneous collection.* **2.** Completely different; incongruous. [Gk. *heterogenēs* (*heteros,* other + *genos,* kind) + -OUS.] **—het'er·o·ge'ne·ous·ly** *adv.* **—het'er·o·ge'ne·ous·ness** *n.*
het·er·o·gen·e·sis (hĕt'ə-rō-jĕn'ĭ-sĭs) *n.* Metagenesis. **—het'er·o·ge·net'ic** (-jə-nĕt'ĭk) *adj.*
het·er·o·gen·ic (hĕt'ə-rō-jĕn'ĭk) *adj.* Heterogenous[1].
het·er·og·e·nous[1] (hĕt'ə-rŏj'ə-nəs) *adj.* Originating outside the body. **—het'er·og'e·ny** *n.*
het·er·og·e·nous[2] (hĕt'ə-rŏj'ə-nəs) *adj.* Heterogeneous (sense 1).
het·er·og·o·nous (hĕt'ə-rŏg'ə-nəs) *adj.* Characterized by the alternation of sexual and asexual generations. [HETERO- + -GON(Y) + -OUS.] **—het'er·og'o·ny** *n.*
het·er·o·graft (hĕt'ə-rō-grăft') *n.* Tissue taken from one species and grafted onto another.
het·er·og·y·nous (hĕt'ə-rŏj'ə-nəs) *adj.* Having two types of females, one able to reproduce sexually, the other infertile, as in ants.
het·er·o·lec·i·thal (hĕt'ə-rō-lĕs'ə-thəl) *adj.* Having nonhomogeneous nutrient distribution in an ovum. [HETERO- + Gk. *lekithos,* yolk + -AL.]
het·er·ol·o·gous (hĕt'ə-rŏl'ə-gəs) *adj.* **1.** Derived from a different species: *a heterologous graft.* **2.** Of or pertaining to cytologic or histological elements not normally occurring in a designated part of the body. [HETERO- + Gk. *logos,* word + -OUS.] **—het'er·ol'o·gous·ly** *adv.*
het·er·ol·o·gy (hĕt'ə-rŏl'ə-jē) *n.* Lack of correspondence between bodily parts, as in structure, arrangement, or development, arising from differences in origin. [HETERO- + (ANA)LOGY.]
het·er·ol·y·sis (hĕt'ə-rŏl'ĭ-sĭs, -ə-rō-lī'sĭs) *n., pl.* **-ses** (-sēz'). **1.** *Biol.* Dissolution of cells or protein components in one species by lytic agents of another. **2.** *Chem.* An organic reaction in which the breaking of bonds leads to the formation of ion pairs. **—het'er·o·lyt'ic** (-rō-lĭt'ĭk) *adj.*
het·er·om·er·ous (hĕt'ə-rŏm'ər-əs) *adj.* Having unequal or differing parts within the same structure or similar structures.
het·er·o·mor·phic (hĕt'ə-rō-môr'fĭk) *adj.* **1.** Having different forms at different periods of the life cycle. **2.** Heteromorphous. **—het'er·o·mor'phism** *n.*
het·er·o·mor·phous (hĕt'ə-rō-môr'fəs) *adj.* Having an irregular or atypical form or forms, as in stages of insect metamorphosis.
het·er·on·o·mous (hĕt'ə-rŏn'ə-məs) *adj.* **1.** Subject to external or foreign laws or domination; not autonomous. **2.** Differing in development or manner of specialization, as the dissimilar segments of certain arthropods. [HETERO- + Gk. *nomos,* law + -OUS.] **—het'er·on'o·mous·ly** *adv.*
het·er·o·nym (hĕt'ər-ə-nĭm') *n.* One of two or more words that have identical spelling but different meanings and pronunciations, as *row* (a line) and *row* (a fight). [Back-formation < HETERONYMOUS.]
het·er·on·y·mous (hĕt'ə-rŏn'ə-məs) *adj.* **1.** Pertaining to, being, or of the nature of a heteronym. **2.** Being different names or terms but having correspondence or interrelationship, as *master* and *mistress.* [LGk. *heterōnumos* : Gk. *hetero-,* different (< *heteros,* other) + Gk. *onoma,* name.]
het·er·o·phyl·lous (hĕt'ə-rō-fĭl'əs) *adj. Bot.* Having unlike leaves on one plant. **—het'er·o·phyl'ly** *n.*
het·er·o·phyte (hĕt'ər-ə-fīt') *n.* A plant, such as a parasite or saprophyte, that obtains its nourishment from living or dead organic sources. **—het'er·o·phyt'ic** (-fĭt'ĭk) *adj.*
het·er·o·plas·ty (hĕt'ər-ə-plăs'tē) *n., pl.* **-ties.** The surgical grafting of tissue obtained from another person or from a lower animal. **—het'er·o·plas'tic** *adj.*
het·er·o·ploid (hĕt'ə-rə-ploid') *adj.* Having a chromosome number that is not a whole-number multiple of the haploid chromosome number. **—het'er·o·ploid'** *n.* **—het'er·o·ploi'dy** (-ploi'dē) *n.*
het·er·op·ter·ous (hĕt'ə-rŏp'tər-əs) *adj.* Of or belonging to the insect order Heteroptera, which includes the true bugs, characterized by forewings and hind wings that differ from one another.
het·er·o·sex (hĕt'ə-rō-sĕks') *n.* Heterosexuality.
het·er·o·sex·u·al (hĕt'ə-rō-sĕk'shōō-əl) *adj.* **1.** Characterized by attraction to the opposite sex. **2.** Of or pertaining to different sexes. *—n.* A heterosexual person. **—het'er·o·sex'u·al'i·ty** (-ăl'ĭ-tē) *n.* **—het'er·o·sex'u·al·ly** *adv.*
het·er·o·sis (hĕt'ə-rō'sĭs) *n.* Increased vigor or other superior qualities arising from the crossbreeding of genetically different plants or animals. [Gk. *heteroiōsis,* alternation < *heteroioun,* to alter < *heteroios,* different in kind < *heteros,* other.] **—het'er·ot'ic** (-rŏt'ĭk) *adj.*
het·er·o·spo·rous (hĕt'ər-ə-spôr'əs, -spōr'-, hĕt'ə-rŏs'pər-əs) *adj.* Producing microspores and megaspores. **—het'er·o·spo'ry** *n.*
het·er·o·tax·is (hĕt'ə-rō-tăk'sĭs) also **het·er·o·tax·y** (hĕt'ər-ə-tăk'sē) or **het·er·o·tax·i·a** (hĕt'ə-rō-tăk'sē-ə) *n.* Abnormal structural arrangement. **—het'er·o·tac'tic** (-tăk'tĭk), **het'er·o·tac'tous** (-tăk'təs) *adj.*
het·er·o·thal·lic (hĕt'ə-rō-thăl'ĭk) *adj.* Producing male gametangia in one structure or plant and female gametangia in a different structure or plant, as in some algae and fungi. [HETERO- + THALL(US) + -IC.] **—het'er·o·thal'lism** *n.*
het·er·o·tro·phic (hĕt'ər-ə-trō'fĭk, -trŏf'ĭk) *adj.* Obtaining nourishment from organic substances, as all animals and some plants do. **—het'er·o·tro'phi·cal·ly** *adv.* **—het'er·ot'ro·phy** (-ə-rŏt'rə-fē) *n.*

heterocercal
Heterocercal tail fin of tiger shark

het·er·o·typ·ic (hĕt′ə-rō-tĭp′ĭk) also **het·er·o·typ·i·cal** (-ĭ-kəl) *adj.* **1.** *Biol.* Relating to or designating the first reduction division of meiosis. **2.** Of a different type or form. [HETERO- + TYPIC(AL).]

het·er·o·zy·go·sis (hĕt′ə-rō-zī-gō′sĭs) *n.* **1.** Derivation from or union between genetically different gametes. **2.** The condition of being a heterozygote.

het·er·o·zy·gote (hĕt′ə-rō-zī′gōt′) *n.* A zygote that has inherited different alleles at one or more loci. **—het′er·o·zy′gous** *adj.*

heth (KHăt, KHăth, KHĕt, KHĕth) *n.* The 8th letter of the Hebrew alphabet. See table at **alphabet.** [Heb. *hēth.*]

heu·land·ite (hyo͞o′lən-dīt′) *n.* A white, red, or yellow zeolite mineral with composition $(Ca,Na,K)_6Al_{10}(Al,Si)_4\ Si_{29}O_{80}\cdot 25H_2O$. [After Henry *Heuland* (1777–1856).]

heu·ris·tic (hyo͞o-rĭs′tĭk) *adj.* **1.** Of or relating to a usually speculative formulation serving as a guide in the investigation or solution of a problem: *"the historian discovers the past by the judicious use of such a heuristic device as the 'ideal type'"* (Karl J. Weintraub). **2.** Of, relating to, or constituting an educational method in which learning takes place through discoveries that result from investigations made by the student. **3.** *Computer Sci.* Relating to or using a problem-solving technique in which the most appropriate solution of several found by alternative methods is selected at successive stages of a program for use in the next step of the program. *—n.* A heuristic method or process. [< Gk. *heuriskein,* to find.] **—heu·ris′ti·cal·ly** *adv.*

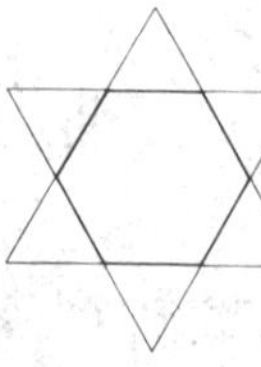

hexagram

hew (hyo͞o) *v.* **hewed, hewn** (hyo͞on) or **hewed, hew·ing, hews.** *—tr.* **1.** To make or shape with or as if with an ax: *hew a path through the underbrush.* **2.** To cut down with an ax; fell: *hew an oak.* **3.** To strike or cut; cleave. *—intr.* **1.** To cut by repeated blows, as of an ax. **2.** To adhere or conform strictly; hold: *hew to the line.* [ME *hewen* < OE *hēawan.*] **—hew′er** *n.*

hex¹ (hĕks) *n.* **1.** An evil spell; curse. **2.** One that brings bad luck. *—tr.v.* **hexed, hex·ing, hex·es. 1.** To put a hex on. **2.** To wish or bring bad luck to. [Pennsylvania Du. < G. *Hexe,* witch < MHG *hecse.*] **—hex′er** *n.*

hex² (hĕks) *adj.* Hexagonal. Used of hardware.

hexa– or **hex–** *pref.* **1.** Six: *hexachord.* **2.** Containing six atoms, molecules, or groups: *hexose.* [Gk. < *hex,* six.]

hex·a·chlo·ro·eth·ane (hĕk′sə-klôr′ō-ĕth′ān′, -klōr′-) also **hex·a·chlor·eth·ane** (-klôr-ĕth′ān′, -klōr-) *n.* A colorless crystalline compound, Cl_3CCCl_3, that is used as a camphor substitute and in pyrotechnics, explosives, and veterinary medicine.

hibachi

hex·a·chlo·ro·phene (hĕk′sə-klôr′ə-fēn′, -klōr′-) *n.* An almost odorless white powder, $(C_6HCl_3OH)_2CH_2$, used as a bactericidal agent in soaps, cosmetics, and skin medications. [HEXA- + CHLORO- + PHEN(OL).]

hex·a·chord (hĕk′sə-kôrd′) *n.* In medieval music, a sequence of six tones with a semitone in the middle, the others being whole tones. [HEXA- + Gk. *khordē,* string.]

hex·ad (hĕk′săd′) *n.* A group or series of six. [LLat. *hexas, hexad-,* the number six < Gk. < *hex,* six.] **—hex·ad′ic** (-săd′ĭk) *adj.*

hex·a·gon (hĕk′sə-gŏn′) *n.* A polygon having six sides. [Gk. *hexagōnon* < *hexagōnos,* having six angles : *hexa-,* six + *gōnos,* -gon.]

hex·ag·o·nal (hĕk-săg′ə-nəl) *adj.* **1.** Having six sides. **2.** Containing or shaped like a hexagon. **3.** *Mineral.* Having three equal axes intersecting at 60 degrees in one plane and one axis of variable length that is at right angles to the others. **—hex·ag′o·nal·ly** *adv.*

hibiscus

hex·a·gram (hĕk′sə-grăm′) *n.* **1.** A six-pointed star formed by extending each of the sides of a regular hexagon into equilateral triangles. **2.** A figure of six lines or sides.

hex·a·he·dron (hĕk′sə-hē′drən) *n., pl.* **-drons** or **-dra** (-drə). A polyhedron with six faces. [Gk. *hexaedron* < *hexaedros,* having six sides : *hexa-,* six + *hedra,* side.] **—hex′a·he′dral** (-drəl) *adj.*

hex·am·er·ous (hĕk-săm′ər-əs) *adj.* **1.** Having six similar parts or divisions. **2.** *Bot.* Having flower parts, such as petals, sepals, and stamens, in sets of six. **—hex·am′er·ism** *n.*

hickory

hex·am·e·ter (hĕk-săm′ĭ-tər) *n.* A dactylic line consisting of five dactyls and a trochee or spondee. [Lat. < Gk. *hexametron* : *hexa-,* six (< *hex*) + *metron,* meter.] **—hex′a·met′ric** (-sə-mĕt′rĭk), **hex′a·met′ri·cal** *adj.*

hex·a·meth·yl·ene·tet·ra·mine (hĕk′sə-mĕth′ə-lēn-tĕt′-rə-mēn′) *n.* Methenamine.

hex·ane (hĕk′sān′) *n.* A colorless, flammable liquid, $CH_3(CH_2)_4CH_3$, derived from the fractional distillation of petroleum and used as a solvent and as the working fluid in low-temperature thermometers.

hex·a·pod (hĕk′sə-pŏd′) *n.* A member of the class Insecta (or Hexapoda); an insect. *—adj.* **1.** Of or belonging to the Hexapoda. **2.** Having six legs or feet. [NLat. *Hexapoda,* class name : Gk. *hexa-,* six + Gk. *pous,* foot.] **—hex·ap′o·dous** (hĕk-săp′ə-dəs) *adj.*

Hex·a·teuch (hĕk′sə-to͞ok′, -tyo͞ok′) *n.* The first six books of the Old Testament. [HEXA- + Gk. *teukos,* book.]

hex·o·san (hĕk′sə-săn′) *n.* Any of several polysaccharides that form a hexose on hydrolysis.

hex·ose (hĕk′sōs′) *n.* Any of various simple sugars that have six carbon atoms per molecule.

hex·yl (hĕk′səl) *n.* The hydrocarbon radical C_6H_{13}, having a valence of 1.

hex·yl·re·sor·ci·nol (hĕk′səl-rĭ-zôr′sə-nôl′, -nōl′) *n.* A yellowish-white crystalline phenol, $C_{12}H_{18}O_2$, used as an antiseptic and anthelminthic.

hey (hā) *interj.* Used to attract attention or to express surprise, appreciation, wonder, or pleasure. [ME.]

hey·day (hā′dā′) *n.* The period of greatest popularity, success, or power; prime. [Orig. unknown.]

Hf The symbol for the element hafnium.

Hg The symbol for the element mercury. [NLat. *hydrargyrum,* mercury < Lat. *hydrargyrus,* artificial mercury < Gk. *hudrarguros* : *hudr-,* hydro- + *arguros,* silver.]

hi (hī) *interj. Informal.* Used to express greeting.

hi·a·tus (hī-ā′təs) *n., pl.* **-tus·es** or **hiatus. 1.** A gap or interruption in space, time, or continuity; break: *a hiatus in their narrative.* **2.** A slight pause that occurs when two immediately adjacent vowels in consecutive syllables are pronounced, as in *reality* and *naive.* **3.** *Anat.* A separation, aperture, or fissure. [Lat. < *hiare,* to gape.]

Hi·a·wath·a (hī′ə-wŏth′ə, -wô′thə, hē′ə-) *n.* The Indian hero of Longfellow's narrative poem *The Song of Hiawatha.*

hi·ba·chi (hĭ-bä′chē) *n., pl.* **-chis.** A portable charcoal-burning brazier with a grill, often used for cooking. [J. : *hi,* fire + *bachi,* bowl.]

hi·ber·nac·u·lum (hī′bər-năk′yə-ləm) *n., pl.* **-la** (-lə). *Biol.* **1.** A case, covering, or structure in which an organism remains dormant for the winter. **2.** The shelter of a hibernating animal. [Lat., winter residence < *hibernare,* to winter < *hibernus,* wintry.]

hi·ber·nal (hī-bûr′nəl) *adj.* Of or pertaining to winter. [Lat. *hibernalis* < *hibernus,* wintry.]

hi·ber·nate (hī′bər-nāt′) *intr.v.* **-nat·ed, -nat·ing, -nates. 1.** To pass the winter in a dormant or torpid state. **2.** To be in an inactive or dormant state or period. [Lat. *hibernare, hibernat-,* to winter < *hibernus,* wintry.] **—hi′ber·na′tion** *n.* **—hi′ber·na′tor** *n.*

Hi·ber·ni·an (hī-bûr′nē-ən) *n.* A native or inhabitant of Ireland. [< Lat. *Hibernia,* Ireland.] **—Hi·ber′ni·an** *adj.*

hi·bis·cus (hī-bĭs′kəs) *n.* Any of various chiefly tropical plants, shrubs, or trees of the genus *Hibiscus,* having large, showy, variously colored flowers. [NLat., genus name < Lat., marsh mallow < Gk. *hibiskos.*]

hic·cup also **hic·cough** (hĭk′əp) *—n.* **1.** A spasm of the diaphragm resulting in a sudden, abortive inhalation that is stopped by a spasmodic glottal closure. **2. hiccups.** An attack of hiccups. *—intr.v.* **-cupped, -cup·ping, -cups** also **-coughed, -cough·ing, -coughs. 1.** To make a hiccup. **2.** To have an attack of hiccups. [Imit.]

hick (hĭk) *Informal. —n.* A gullible, provincial person; yokel. *—adj.* Provincial; unsophisticated: *a hick town.* [After *Hick,* a nickname for Richard.]

hick·ey (hĭk′ē) *n., pl.* **-eys.** *Informal.* **1.** A device or contrivance; gadget. **2. a.** A pimple. **b.** A reddish mark on the skin caused by kissing, biting, or sucking, as in lovemaking. **3.** A pipe-bending apparatus. **4.** A threaded electrical fitting to connect a fixture to an outlet box. [Orig. unknown.]

hick·o·ry (hĭk′ə-rē) *n., pl.* **-ries. 1.** Any of several chiefly North American deciduous trees of the genus *Carya,* having smooth or shaggy bark, compound leaves, and hard, smooth nuts with an edible kernel. **2. a.** The hard, tough, heavy wood of a hickory tree. **b.** A walking stick or switch made from such wood. [Earlier *pohickery* < *pawcohiccora,* food prepared from crushed hickory nuts, of Algonquian orig.]

hid (hĭd) *v.* Past tense and a past participle of **hide¹.**

hi·dal·go (hĭ-dăl′gō, ē-thäl′-) *n., pl.* **-gos.** A member of the minor nobility in Spain. [Sp. < OSp. *hijo dalgo* : *hijo,* son (< Lat. *filius*) + *de,* of (< Lat.) + *algo,* something < Lat. *aliquid* (*alius,* some + *quid,* something).]

hid·den (hĭd′n) *v.* A past participle of **hide¹.**

hid·den·ite (hĭd′n-īt′) *n.* A transparent emerald-green variety of spodumene, used as a gemstone. [After William E. *Hidden* (1853–1918).]

hide¹ (hīd) *v.* **hid** (hĭd), **hid·den** (hĭd′n) or **hid, hid·ing, hides.** *—tr.* **1.** To put or keep out of sight; secrete. **2.** To prevent the disclosure or recognition of; conceal: *tried to hide the facts.* **3.** To cut off from sight; cover up: *Clouds hid the stars.* **4.** To avert (one's gaze), esp. in shame or grief. *—intr.* **1.** To keep oneself out of sight. **2.** To seek refuge. [ME *hiden* < OE *hȳdan.*] **—hid′er** *n.*

Synonyms: *hide, conceal, secrete, cache, screen, bury, cloak.* These verbs mean to keep from the sight or knowledge of others. *Hide* and *conceal* refer both to putting physical things out of sight and to withholding information or disguising one's feelings or thoughts. *Conceal* often implies deliberate intent to keep from sight or knowledge, whereas *hide* also can refer to natural phenomena: *The thief hid* (or *concealed*) *the stolen money. Night hides the city's ugliness. Secrete, cache, screen,* and *bury* refer chiefly to removing physical objects from sight. *Secrete* and *cache* involve concealment in a place unknown to others, and *cache* also implies storing protectively for later use. To *screen* is to shield or block from view by interposing another object, and to *bury* is to cover. *Cloak* usually refers to concealing thoughts, plans, or the like by secrecy or by masking or disguising them.

hide² (hīd) *n.* The skin of an animal, esp. the thick, tough skin of a large animal. *—tr.v.* **hid·ed, hid·ing, hides.** To beat severely; flog. ***—idiom.*** **hide nor (or or) hair.** A trace; vestige: *haven't seen hide nor hair of him since our argument.* [ME < OE *hȳd.*]

hide³ (hīd) *n.* An old English measure of land, usually the amount held adequate for one free family and its dependents. [ME < OE *hīd.*]

hide-and-seek (hīd′n-sēk′) *n.* **1.** A children's game in which one player tries to find and catch others who are hiding. **2.** A game or action involving evasion.

hide·a·way (hīd′ə-wā′) *n.* **1.** A hide-out. **2.** A secluded or isolated place.

hide·bound (hīd′bound′) *adj.* **1.** Having abnormally dry, stiff skin that adheres closely to the underlying flesh. Used of domestic animals such as cattle. **2.** Having the bark so contracted and unyielding as to hinder growth. Used of trees. **3.** Stubbornly prejudiced, narrow-minded, or inflexible.

hid·e·ous (hĭd′ē-əs) *adj.* **1.** Repulsive, esp. to the sight; revoltingly ugly. **2.** Repugnant to the moral sense; despicable. [ME < AN *hidous* < OFr. *hide,* fear.] **—hid′e·ous·ly** *adv.* **—hid′e·ous·ness** *n.*

hide-out (hīd′out′) *n.* A place of shelter or concealment.

hid·ey-hole (hī′dē-hōl′) *n.* A hideaway.

hi·dro·sis (hī-drō′sĭs) *n.* Perspiration, esp. in excessive or abnormal amounts. [Gk. *hidrōsis,* sweating < *hidros,* sweat.] **—hi·drot′ic** (-drŏt′ĭk) *adj.*

hie (hī) *intr.v.* **hied, hie·ing** or **hy·ing, hies.** To go quickly; hasten. [ME *hien* < OE *hīgian.*]

hi·e·mal (hī′ə-məl) *adj.* Of or pertaining to winter. [Lat. *hiemalis* < *hiems,* winter.]

hier– *pref.* Variant of **hiero–.**

hi·er·arch (hī′ə-rärk′, hī′rärk′) *n.* **1.** One who occupies a position of authority in an ecclesiastical hierarchy. **2.** One who occupies a high position in a hierarchy. [OFr. *hierarche* < Med. Lat. *hierarcha* < Gk. *hierarkhēs,* high priest : *hieros,* sacred + *arkhos,* leader.] **—hi′er·ar′chal** *adj.*

hi·er·ar·chy (hī′ə-rär′kē, hī′rär′-) *n., pl.* **-chies. 1. a.** A body of persons organized or classified according to rank or authority. **b.** A body of entities arranged in a graded series. **2. a.** A body of clergy organized into successive ranks or grades with each level subordinate to the one above. **b.** Ecclesiastical rule by a hierarchy. [ME *iherarchie* < OFr. *jerarchie* < Med. Lat. *hierarchia* < Gk. *hierarkhia,* rule of a high priest < *hierarkhēs,* high priest. —see HIERARCH.] **—hi′er·ar′chi·cal, hi′er·ar′chic** *adj.* **—hi′er·ar′chi·cal·ly** *adv.*

hi·er·at·ic (hī′ə-răt′ĭk, hī-răt′-) *adj.* **1.** Of or associated with sacred persons or offices; sacerdotal. **2.** Constituting or pertaining to a simplified cursive style of Egyptian hieroglyphics. [Lat. *hieraticus* < Gk. *hieratikos* < *hierasthai,* to be a priest < *hieros,* sacred.] **—hi′er·at′i·cal·ly** *adv.*

hiero– or **hier–** *pref.* Sacred; holy: *hierology.* [Gk. < *hieros,* holy.]

hi·er·oc·ra·cy (hī′ə-rŏk′rə-sē, hī-rŏk′-) *n., pl.* **-cies.** Government by the clergy; ecclesiastical rule. **—hi′er·o·crat′ic** (hī′ər-ə-krăt′ĭk, hī′rə-krăt′-), **hi′er·o·crat′i·cal** *adj.*

hi·er·o·dule (hī′ər-ə-do͞ol′, -dyo͞ol′) *n.* A temple slave in the service of a specified deity. [LLat. *hierodulus* < Gk. *hierodoulos* : *hieron,* temple + *doulos,* slave.] **—hi′er·o·du′lic** (-do͞o′lĭk, -dyo͞o′-) *adj.*

hi·er·o·glyph (hī′ər-ə-glĭf′, hī′rə-) *n.* A hieroglyphic.

hi·er·o·glyph·ic (hī′ər-ə-glĭf′ĭk, hī′rə-) also **hi·er·o·glyph·i·cal** (-ĭ-kəl) *adj.* **1.** Of or pertaining to a system of writing, as that of ancient Egypt, in which pictorial symbols are used to represent words or sounds. **2.** Written with hieroglyphic symbols. **3.** Difficult to read or decipher. *—n.* **hieroglyphic. 1.** A picture or symbol used in hieroglyphic writing. **2. hieroglyphics. a.** Hieroglyphic writing. **b.** Illegible or undecipherable writing. **3.** Something that resembles a hieroglyphic. [Fr. *hiéroglyphique* < LLat. *hieroglyphicus* < Gk. *hierogluphikos* : *hieros,* sacred + *gluphē,* carving < *gluphein,* to carve.] **—hi′er·o·glyph′i·cal·ly** *adv.*

hi·er·ol·o·gy (hī′ə-rŏl′ə-jē, hī-rŏl′-) *n., pl.* **-gies.** The sacred literature of a given people.

hi·er·o·phant (hī′ər-ə-fănt′, hī′rə-, hī-ĕr′ə-fənt) *n.* **1.** An expounder of Eleusinian mysteries. **2.** An interpreter of sacred mysteries or arcane knowledge. [LLat. *hierophanta* < Gk. *hierophantēs* : *hieros,* sacred + *phainein,* to reveal.] **—hi′er·o·phan′tic** *adj.*

hi·fa·lu·tin (hī′fə-lo͞ot′n) *adj.* Variant of **highfalutin.**

hi-fi (hī′fī′) *n.* **1.** High fidelity. **2.** An electronic system for reproducing high-fidelity sound from radio, records, or magnetic tape. [HI(GH) FI(DELITY).]

hig·gle (hĭg′əl) *intr.v.* **-gled, -gling, -gles.** To haggle. [Prob. alteration of HAGGLE.] **—hig′gler** *n.*

hig·gle·dy-pig·gle·dy (hĭg′əl-dē-pĭg′əl-dē) *adv.* In utter disorder or confusion. *—adj.* Topsy-turvy; jumbled. [Orig. unknown.]

high (hī) *adj.* **-er, -est. 1. a.** Having a relatively great elevation; extending far upward: *a high mountain; a high stool.* **b.** Extending a specified distance upward: *a cabinet ten feet high.* **2.** Being at or near its peak: *high noon.* **3.** Beginning to decompose, as meat; gamy. **4.** Far removed in time; remote: *high antiquity.* **5. a.** Having a musical pitch that corresponds to a relatively great number of cycles per second: *the high tones of a flute.* **b.** Not soft or hushed; piercing: *a high voice.* **6.** Situated far from the equator: *a high latitude.* **7.** Of great importance: *a high priority.* **8.** Eminent in rank or status: *a high official.* **9.** Serious; grave: *high treason.* **10.** Lofty or exalted in quality or character: *a person of high morals.* **11. a.** Greater than usual or expected, as in quantity, magnitude, cost, or degree: *a high temperature; high prices.* **b.** Favorable: *a high opinion of himself.* **12.** Of great force or violence: *high winds.* **13.** Excited; elated: *high spirits.* **14.** *Informal.* Intoxicated by or as if by alcohol or a narcotic. **15.** Advanced in development or complexity: *higher forms of animal life.* **16.** Luxurious; extravagant: *high living.* **17.** Pronounced with part of the tongue close to the palate: *a high vowel.* *—adv.* **-er, -est.** At, in, or to a high position, price, or level: *flying high in the sky.* *—n.* **1.** A high place or region. **2.** A high level or degree: *Prices reached a new high.* **3.** The transmission gear of an automotive vehicle producing maximum speed. **4.** A center of high atmospheric pressure; anticyclone. **5.** *Informal.* Intoxication or euphoria induced by or as if by a stimulant or narcotic. ***—idioms.*** **high and dry. 1.** Helpless; alone: *left me high and dry.* **2.** Out of water, as a ship. **high and low.** Here and there; everywhere. **high and mighty.** Arrogant; domineering. [ME < OE *hēah.*] **—high′ly** *adv.*

high·ball (hī′bôl′) *n.* **1.** A beverage consisting of alcoholic liquor and water or a carbonated liquid served in a tall glass. **2.** A railroad signal indicating full speed ahead. *—intr.v.* **-balled, -ball·ing, -balls.** To move ahead at full speed.

high beam *n.* A high-intensity headlight on a vehicle.

high·bind·er (hī′bīn′dər) *n.* **1.** A member of a Chinese-American secret society of paid assassins and blackmailers. **2.** A corrupt politician. [After the *Highbinders,* a group of ruffians in New York City ca. 1806.]

high blood pressure *n.* Hypertension (sense 1).

high·born (hī′bôrn′) *adj.* Of noble birth.

high·boy (hī′boi′) *n.* A tall chest of drawers divided into two sections and supported on four legs.

high·bred (hī′brĕd′) *adj.* Of superior breed or stock.

high·brow (hī′brou′) *n.* *Informal.* One who has or affects superior learning or culture. **—high′brow′, high′browed′** *adj.* **—high′brow′ism** *n.*

high-bush cranberry (hī′bo͝osh′) *n.* A North American shrub, *Viburnum trilobum,* having broad clusters of white flowers and scarlet fruit.

high·chair (hī′châr′) *n.* A baby's feeding chair that usually has a detachable tray and is mounted on tall legs.

High-Church (hī′chûrch′) *adj.* Favoring or marked by the incorporation of elements, such as the liturgy, usually associated with Roman Catholicism into the forms of worship of the Anglican Church. **—High′-Church′man** *n.*

high-class (hī′klăs′) *adj.* First-class.

high comedy *n.* Comedy marked by sophisticated characterizations and clever dialogue.

high court *n.* A supreme court.

high-en·er·gy (hī′ĕn′ər-jē) *adj.* **1.** Of or relating to elementary particles with energies exceeding hundreds of thousands of electron volts. **2.** Yielding a large amount of energy upon undergoing chemical reaction. **3.** Vigorous; dynamic.

higher criticism *n.* Critical study of biblical texts with regard to questions of their character, composition, editing, and collection.

higher education *n.* Education beyond the secondary level, esp. at the college level.

higher learning *n.* Education or scholastic attainment at the college or university level.

high·er-up (hī′ər-ŭp′) *n.* *Informal.* One who has a superior rank, position, or status.

high explosive *n.* A powerful, fast-acting explosive.

high·fa·lu·tin or **hi·fa·lu·tin** (hī′fə-lo͞ot′n) also **high·fa·lu·ting** (-lo͞ot′n, -lo͞o′tĭng) *adj.* *Informal.* Pompous or pretentious. [Orig. unknown.]

high fashion *n.* The latest in trend-setting fashion or design.

high fidelity *n.* The electronic reproduction of sound, esp. from broadcast, recorded, or taped sources, with minimal distortion. **—high′-fi·del′i·ty** *adj.*

high-flown (hī′flōn′) *adj.* **1.** Lofty; exalted. **2.** Pretentious; inflated.

high·fly·ing (hī′flī′ĭng) *adj.* **1.** Rising to a great height. **2.** Lofty in form or ambitions.

high frequency *n.* A radio frequency in the range between 3 and 30 megahertz.

high gear *n.* **1.** High (sense 3). **2.** A state of maximum activity, energy, or force.

High German *n.* **1.** German as indigenously spoken and written in central and southern Germany. **2.** German (sense 2).

high-grade (hī′grād′) *adj.* Of superior quality.

high·hand·ed (hī′hăn′dĭd) *adj.* Arrogant or overbearing in manner. **—high′hand′ed·ly** *adv.* **—high′hand′ed·ness** *n.*

high-hat (hī′hăt′) *tr.v.* **-hat·ted, -hat·ting, -hats.** *Slang.* To treat in a condescending or supercilious manner. **—high′-hat′** *adj.*

High Holiday *n.* **1.** Rosh Hashanah. **2.** Yom Kippur.

high·jack (hī′jăk′) *v. & n.* Variant of **hijack.**

high jinks *pl.n.* Mischievous pranks.

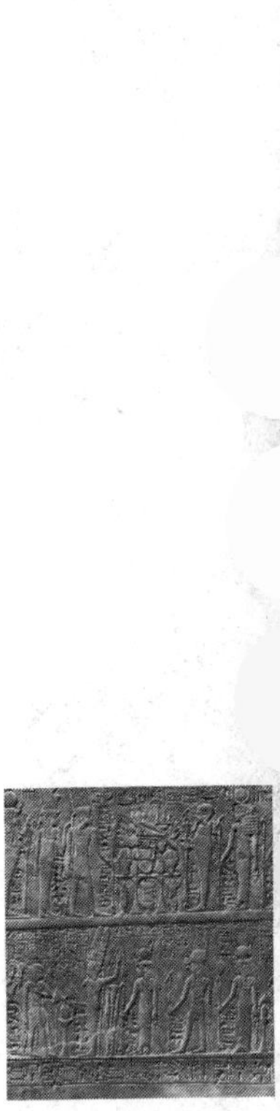

hieroglyphic
16th- to 14th-century B.C. Egyptian hieroglyphics

highboy
American Chippendale bonnet-top highboy

high jump

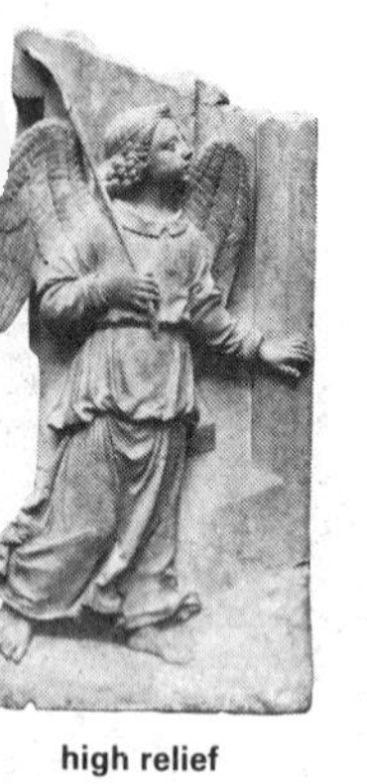

high relief

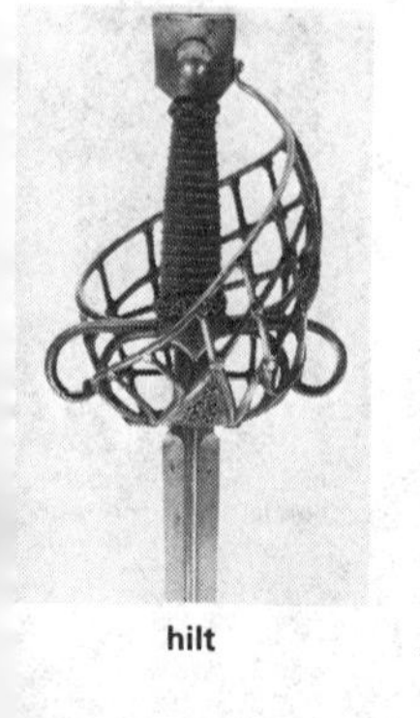

hilt

high jump *n.* **1.** A jump for height in a field contest. **2.** A contest in which high jumps are made.

high·land (hī′lənd) *n.* **1.** Elevated land. **2. highlands.** A mountainous region or part of a country. —*adj.* **1.** Of, relating to, or characteristic of a highland. **2. Highland.** Of or relating to the Highlands of Scotland.

high·land·er (hī′lən-dər) *n.* **1.** One who lives in a highland area. **2. Highlander.** An inhabitant of the Highlands of Scotland.

Highland fling *n.* A folk dance of the Highlands of Scotland.

high-lev·el (hī′lĕv′əl) *adj.* **1.** Occurring, carried out, or situated at a high level. **2.** Being at a high level of importance: *a high-level official.*

high·light (hī′līt′) *n.* **1.** A light or brilliantly lighted area, as in a painting or photograph. **2.** An outstanding event or occurrence. —*tr.v.* **-light·ed, -light·ing, -lights. 1.** To give a highlight to. **2.** To make prominent; emphasize. **3.** To be the highlight of.

high·light·er (hī′lī′tər) *n.* **1.** One that highlights. **2.** A cosmetic for emphasizing facial features.

High Mass *n.* A sung mass celebrated by a priest or prelate, often assisted by a deacon and a subdeacon.

high-mind·ed (hī′mīn′dĭd) *adj.* **1.** Characterized by elevated ideals or conduct; noble. **2.** *Archaic.* Disdainfully proud; haughty. **—high′-mind′ed·ly** *adv.* **—high′-mind′ed·ness** *n.*

high muckamuck *n. Slang.* A muckamuck. [Chinook Jargon *hiu muckamuck.*]

high·ness (hī′nĭs) *n.* **1.** Tallness; height. **2. Highness.** A title of honor for royalty: *His Royal Highness.*

high noon *n.* **1.** Exactly noon. **2.** The highest or most advanced stage or period: *was at the high noon of her creativity.*

high-oc·tane (hī′ŏk′tān′) *adj.* Having a high octane number.

high-pitched (hī′pĭcht′) *adj.* **1.** High in pitch, as a voice or musical tone. **2.** Steeply sloped, as a roof.

high place *n.* In early Semitic religions, a place of worship on top of a hill.

high-pow·ered (hī′pou′ərd) also **high-pow·er** (-pou′ər) *adj.* Having great power or energy; dynamic.

high-pres·sure (hī′prĕsh′ər) *adj.* **1.** Of or pertaining to pressures higher than normal, esp. higher than atmospheric pressure. **2.** *Informal.* Using aggressive and persistent methods of persuasion. —*tr.v.* **-sured, -sur·ing, -sures.** *Informal.* To convince or influence by using high-pressure methods.

high priest *n.* **1.** *Judaism.* A chief priest, esp. of the ancient Levitical priesthood. **2.** *Mormon Ch.* A priest of the Melchizedek order. **3.** The head or chief proponent, as of a movement or doctrine: *the high priest of modern art.* **—high priesthood** *n.*

high priestess *n.* A woman who functions or is regarded as a high priest.

high relief *n.* Sculptural relief in which the modeled forms project from the background by at least half their depth.

high-rise (hī′rīz′) *adj.* **1.** Designating or being a multistoried building equipped with elevators. **2.** Of, relating to, or being a bicycle with handlebars that are longer than average —*n.* **1.** A high-rise building. **2.** A high-rise bicycle.

high-ris·er (hī′rī′zər) *n.* **1.** A high-rise building. **2.** A high-rise bicycle.

high-risk (hī′rĭsk′) *adj.* **1.** Of, relating to, or characterized by risk: *"Retailing has always been a high-risk business, subject to whim and even weather"* (Newsweek). **2.** Being particularly subject to potential danger or hazard: *a high-risk pregnancy.*

high·road (hī′rōd′) *n.* **1.** *Chiefly Brit.* A main road; highway. **2.** A simple, direct, or sure path: *the highroad to happiness.*

high roller *n. Informal.* **1.** A big spender. **2.** One who gambles, esp. for high stakes. **—high′-roll′ing** (hī′rō′lĭng) *adj.*

high school *n.* A secondary school that includes grades 9 or 10 through 12 or grades 7 through 12. ***—modifier* (high-school):** *a high-school teacher.*

high seas *n.* The open waters of an ocean or sea beyond the limits of the territorial jurisdiction of a country.

high-sound·ing (hī′soun′dĭng) *adj.* Pretentious; pompous.

high-spir·it·ed (hī′spĭr′ĭ-tĭd) *adj.* **1.** Having a proud or unbroken spirit; brave. **2.** Vivacious; lively. **—high′-spir′it·ed·ly** *adv.* **—high′-spir′it·ed·ness** *n.*

high street *n. Chiefly Brit.* A main street.

high-strung (hī′strŭng′) *adj.* Tending to be extremely nervous and sensitive.

high style *n.* High fashion.

high·tail (hī′tāl′) *intr.v.* **-tailed, -tail·ing, -tails.** *Slang.* To go or clear out in a great hurry. [From those animals who raise their tails before fleeing.]

high tea *n. Chiefly Brit.* A substantial meal served in the late afternoon or early evening.

high tech *n.* **1.** A style of interior decoration marked by the use of industrial materials, equipment, or design. **2.** High technology.

high technology *n.* Technology involving highly advanced or specialized systems or devices.

high-ten·sion (hī′tĕn′shən) *adj.* Having a high voltage.

high-test (hī′tĕst′) *adj.* **1.** Meeting the most exacting requirements. **2.** Of or pertaining to highly volatile high-octane gasoline.

high tide *n.* **1. a.** The tide at its full, when the water reaches its highest level. **b.** The time at which this occurs. **2.** A point of culmination; climax.

high-toned (hī′tōnd′) *adj.* **1.** Intellectually, morally, or socially superior: *a high-toned lecture.* **2.** *Informal.* Pretentiously elegant or fashionable: *a high-toned country club.*

high treason *n.* Treason against one's state or sovereign.

high water *n.* **1.** High tide. **2.** The state of a body of water that has reached its highest level.

high-wa·ter mark (hī′wô′tər, -wŏt′ər) *n.* **1.** A mark indicating the highest level reached by a body of water. **2.** The highest point, as of achievement; apex.

high·way (hī′wā′) *n.* A main public road, esp. one connecting towns and cities.

high·way·man (hī′wā′mən) *n.* A robber who holds up travelers on a highway.

hi·jack also **high·jack** (hī′jăk′) *Informal.* —*tr.v.* **-jacked, -jack·ing, -jacks. 1.** To stop and rob (a vehicle in transit). **2.** To steal (goods) from a vehicle in transit. **3.** To seize control of (a moving vehicle, such as an aircraft), esp. in order to go to a place other than the scheduled destination. **4.** To steal from (a person). **5.** To force or coerce (someone). —*n.* An act or instance of hijacking. [Orig. unknown.] **—hi′jack′er** *n.*

hike (hīk) *v.* **hiked, hik·ing, hikes.** —*intr.* **1.** To go on an extended walk for pleasure or exercise. **2.** To go up, esp. to be raised or caught up: *Her coat hiked up in back.* —*tr.* **1.** To increase or raise in amount: *Shopkeepers had hiked their prices for the tourist trade.* **2.** To pull up or raise with a sudden motion; hitch: *He hiked up his pants.* —*n.* **1.** A long walk or march. **2.** An upward movement; rise. [Orig. unknown.] **—hik′er** *n.*

hi·la (hī′lə) *n.* Plural of **hilum.**

hi·lar·i·ous (hĭ-lâr′ē-əs, -lăr′-, hī-) *adj.* Boisterously funny; causing merriment. [Lat. *hilarus,* cheerful + -IOUS. —see HILARITY.] **—hi·lar′i·ous·ly** *adv.* **—hi·lar′i·ous·ness** *n.*

hi·lar·i·ty (hĭ-lăr′ĭ-tē, -lâr′-, hī-) *n.* Boisterous merriment. [OFr. *hilarite,* cheerfulness < Lat. *hilaritas* < *hilarus,* cheerful < Gk. *hilaros.*]

hill (hĭl) *n.* **1.** A well-defined natural elevation that is smaller than a mountain. **2.** A small heap, pile, or mound. **3. a.** A mound of earth piled around and over a plant. **b.** A plant thus covered. **4.** An incline, esp. in a road; slope. —*tr.v.* **hilled, hill·ing, hills. 1.** To form into a hill, pile, or heap. **2.** To cover (a plant) with a mound of soil. [ME *hille* < OE *hyl.*] **—hill′er** *n.*

hill·bil·ly (hĭl′bĭl′ē) *n., pl.* **-lies.** *Informal.* A person from the backwoods or a remote mountain area. ***—modifier:*** *hillbilly music.* [HILL + *Billy,* a nickname for William.]

hill·ock (hĭl′ək) *n.* A small hill. [ME *hillok* < *hille,* hill.] **—hill′ock·y** *adj.*

hill·side (hĭl′sīd′) *n.* The side or slope of a hill.

hill·top (hĭl′tŏp′) *n.* The crest or top of a hill.

hill·y (hĭl′ē) *adj.* **-i·er, -i·est. 1.** Having many hills. **2.** Similar to a hill; steep. **—hill′i·ness** *n.*

hilt (hĭlt) *n.* The handle of a weapon or tool, esp. of a sword or dagger. ***—idiom.* to the hilt.** To the limit; completely. [ME < OE.]

hi·lum (hī′ləm) *n., pl.* **-la** (-lə). **1.** *Bot.* **a.** The scarlike mark on a seed, such as a bean, formed at the point where it was joined to the stalk connecting it to the placenta. **b.** The nucleus of a starch grain. **2.** *Anat.* A small opening or notch through which ducts, nerves, or vessels enter or leave an organ. [Lat., trifle.]

him (hĭm) *pron.* The objective case of **he.** Used: **1.** As the direct object of a verb: *They assisted him.* **2.** As the indirect object of a verb: *They offered him a ride.* **3.** As the object of a preposition: *This letter is addressed to him.* —See Usage notes at **be, everyone,** and **I.** [ME < OE.]

hi·mat·i·on (hĭ-măt′ē-ŏn′) *n., pl.* **-i·a** (-ē-ə). A long loose outer garment worn by men and women in ancient Greece. [Gk., dim. of *hima,* garment < *hennunai,* to clothe.]

him·self (hĭm-sĕlf′) *pron.* **1.** That one identical with him. Used: **a.** Reflexively as the direct or indirect object of a verb or the object of a preposition: *He blamed himself.* **b.** For emphasis: *He himself lacked the courage.* **c.** In an absolute construction: *In debt himself, he could offer no financial assistance.* **2.** His normal or healthy condition or state: *He hasn't been himself lately.* —See Usage note at **myself.** [ME < OE *himselfum.*]

Him·yar·ite (hĭm′yə-rīt′) *n.* **1.** A member of an ancient tribe of southwestern Arabia. **2.** The Semitic language of the ancient Himyarites. —*adj.* Of, relating to, or characteristic of the Himyarite people, their language, or their culture. [After *Himyar,* a legendary king in Yemen.] **—Him′yar·it′ic** (-rĭt′ĭk) *adj.*

hin (hĭn) *n.* A unit of liquid measure used by the ancient Hebrews, equal to about a half gallon. [Heb. *hīn,* of Egyptian orig.]

Hi·na·ya·na (hē′nə-yä′nə) *n.* A small, conservative branch of Buddhism following the Pali scriptures and the nontheistic ideal of self-purification to nirvana. [Skt. *hīnayāna,* lesser vehicle.] **—Hi′na·ya′nist** *n.* **—Hi′na·ya·nis′tic** (-yä-nĭs′tĭk) *adj.*

hind[1] (hīnd) also **hind·er** (hīn′dər) *adj.* Located at or forming the back or rear; posterior: *hind legs.* [ME *hinde,* short for *bihinde* < OE *bihindan.*]

hind[2] (hīnd) *n.* **1.** A female red deer. **2.** Any of several fishes of the genus *Epinephelus,* of Atlantic waters, related to and resembling the groupers. [ME < OE.]

hind[3] (hīnd) *n.* **1.** *Chiefly Brit.* A farm laborer, esp. a skilled worker. **2.** *Archaic.* A rustic or country bumpkin. [ME < OE *hīwan.*]

hind·brain (hīnd′brān′) *n.* The rhombencephalon.

hin·der[1] (hĭn′dər) *tr.v.* **-dered, -der·ing, -ders. 1.** To get in the way of; hamper. **2.** To obstruct or delay the progress of. [ME *hindren* < OE *hindrian.*] **—hin′der·er** *n.*

Synonyms: *hinder, hamper, impede, retard, encumber, obstruct, block, dam, bar, balk.* These verbs mean to slow or prevent progress, movement, or other desired action. *Hinder* and *hamper* are applied to any restraining influence, physical or otherwise, intentional or accidental. *Impede* usually implies slowing by making movement difficult. To *retard* is to delay or hold back, and to *encumber* is to weigh down or burden, physically or figuratively. *Obstruct* implies interference that brings progress to a virtual halt or prevents a desired action. *Block* refers to preventing progress, passage, or other action, and *dam* to restraining the progress or release of something, such as water or emotion, by interposing a barrier. To *bar* is to prevent entry or exit or to rule out a course of action, and to *balk* is to frustrate a course by putting obstacles in one's path.

hind·er[2] (hīn′dər) *adj.* Variant of **hind**[1].

hind·er·most (hīn′dər-mōst′) *adj.* Variant of **hindmost.**

hind·gut (hīnd′gŭt′) *n.* The posterior portion of the embryonic alimentary canal.

Hin·di (hĭn′dē) *n.* **1. a.** A group of vernacular Indic dialects spoken in northern India. **b.** The literary and official language of northern India that is based on these dialects. **2.** A member of a cultural group of northern India speaking a Hindi dialect. [Hindi *Hindī* < *Hind,* India < Pers. < OPers. *Hindu,* the Indus River.] **—Hin′di** *adj.*

hind·most (hīnd′mōst′) also **hind·er·most** (hīn′dər-) *adj.* Farthest to the rear; last.

Hin·doo (hĭn′do͞o) *n. & adj. Archaic.* Variant of **Hindu.**

Hin·doo·ism (hĭn′do͞o-ĭz′əm) *n. Archaic.* Variant of **Hinduism.**

hind·quar·ter (hīnd′kwôr′tər) *n.* **1.** The posterior portion of a side of beef, lamb, veal, or mutton, including a hind leg and one or two ribs. **2. hindquarters.** The posterior part of a quadruped, adjacent to the hind legs.

hin·drance (hĭn′drəns) *n.* **1. a.** The act of hindering. **b.** The condition of being hindered. **2.** One that hinders; impediment. [ME *hindraunce,* harm < *hindren,* to hinder.]

hind·sight (hīnd′sīt′) *n.* **1.** The rear sight of a firearm. **2.** Perception of the significance and nature of events after they have occurred.

Hin·du (hĭn′do͞o) *n.* **1.** A native of India, esp. northern India. **2.** A believer in Hinduism. *—adj.* **1.** Of or pertaining to the Hindus and their culture. **2.** Of or pertaining to Hinduism. [Pers. *Hindū* < *Hind,* India. —see HINDI.]

Hindu calendar *n.* The lunisolar calendar of the Hindus.

Hin·du·ism (hĭn′do͞o-ĭz′əm) *n.* A diverse body of religion, philosophy, and cultural practice native to and predominant in India, characterized by a belief in reincarnation and a supreme being of many forms and natures, by the view that opposing theories are aspects of one eternal truth, and by a desire for liberation from earthly evils.

Hin·du·sta·ni (hĭn′do͞o-stä′nē, -stăn′ē) *n.* **1.** A native of Hindustan. **2.** A group of Indic dialects that includes Urdu and Hindi. *—adj.* Of or pertaining to Hindustani or Hindustan.

hinge (hĭnj) *n.* **1.** A jointed or flexible device that allows the turning or pivoting of a part, such as a door or lid, on a stationary frame. **2.** A structure or part similar to a hinge, such as that enabling the valves of a bivalve mollusk to open and close. **3.** A small folded paper rectangle gummed on one side, used esp. to fasten stamps in an album. **4.** A point or circumstance upon which subsequent events depend. *—v.* **hinged, hing·ing, hing·es.** *—tr.* To attach by or equip with a hinge. *—intr.* To depend; be contingent: *plans hinging on her approval.* [ME.]

hin·ny (hĭn′ē) *n., pl.* **-nies.** The hybrid offspring of a male horse and a female ass. [Lat. *hinnus* < Gk. *innos.*]

hint (hĭnt) *n.* **1.** A slight indication or intimation. **2. a.** A brief or indirect suggestion; tip. **b.** A statement conveying information in an indirect fashion. **3.** A barely perceptible amount: *just a hint of color.* **4.** *Obs.* An occasion; opportunity. *—v.* **hint·ed, hint·ing, hints.** *—tr.* To make known by a hint; intimate. *—intr.* To give a hint or hints: *wouldn't hint at the true purpose of the meeting.* [Poss. < obs. *hent,* the act of seizing < obs. *hent,* to seize < ME *henten* < OE *hentan.*] **—hint′er** *n.*

hin·ter·land (hĭn′tər-lănd′) *n.* **1.** The land directly adjacent to and inland from a coast. **2.** A region remote from urban areas; back country. [G. : *hinter-,* behind + *Land,* land.]

hip[1] (hĭp) *n.* **1. a.** The laterally projecting prominence of the pelvis or pelvic region from the waist to the thigh. **b.** A homologous posterior region in quadrupeds. **2.** The hip joint. **3.** *Archit.* The external angle formed by the meeting of two adjacent sloping sides of a roof. [ME < OE *hype.*]

hip[2] (hĭp) *adj.* **hip·per, hip·pest.** *Slang.* **1.** Aware of and interested in the newest tastes and attitudes. **2. a.** Cognizant; wise: *hip to what's going on.* **b.** Comprehending. *—n.* The quality or state of being hip. [Orig. unknown.] **—hip′ness** *n.*

hip[3] (hĭp) *n.* The fleshy, berrylike, often brightly colored seed receptacle of a rose. [ME *hipe* < OE *hēopa.*]

hip[3]

hip[4] (hĭp) *interj.* Used as a cheer or a signal for a cheer: *Hip, hip, hurrah!*

hip·bone (hĭp′bōn′) *n.* The innominate bone.

hip-hug·gers (hĭp′hŭg′ərz) *pl.n.* Tight-fitting pants whose waistline rests at hip level.

hip joint *n.* The joint between the innominate bone and the femur.

hipped (hĭpt) *adj. Chiefly Brit.* Melancholy; depressed. [Shortening and alteration of HYPOCHONDRIAC.]

hip·pie also **hip·py** (hĭp′ē) *n., pl.* **-pies.** A person who opposes and rejects many of the conventional standards and customs of society, esp. one who advocates extreme liberalism in sociopolitical attitudes and lifestyles. [< HIP[2].] **—hip′pie·dom** (-dəm) *n.*

hip·po (hĭp′ō) *n., pl.* **-pos.** *Informal.* A hippopotamus.

hip·po·cam·pus (hĭp′ə-kăm′pəs) *n., pl.* **-pi** (-pī′). *Anat.* One of two ridges along each lateral ventricle of the brain. [LLat., a sea horse with a horse's forelegs and a dolphin's tail < Gk. *hippokampos* : *hippos,* horse + *kampos,* sea monster.] **—hip′po·cam′pal** *adj.*

hip·po·cras (hĭp′ə-krăs′) *n.* A cordial made from wine and flavored with spices, formerly used as a medicine. [ME *ipocras* < OFr. < *Ypocras,* Hippocrates (460?–377? B.C.).]

Hip·po·crat·ic oath (hĭp′ə-krăt′ĭk) *n.* An oath of ethical professional behavior sworn by new physicians, attributed to Hippocrates.

Hip·po·crene (hĭp′ə-krēn′, hĭp′ə-krē′nē) *n. Gk. Myth.* A fountain on Mount Helicon, Greece, held sacred to the Muses and regarded as a source of poetic inspiration. [Lat. < Gk. *Hippokrēnē* : *hippos,* horse (from the myth that Pegasus' hoof created it) + *krēnē,* fountain.]

hip·po·drome (hĭp′ə-drōm′) *n.* **1.** An open-air stadium with an oval course for horse and chariot races in ancient Greece and Rome. **2.** An arena for horse shows. [OFr. < Lat. *hippodromos* < Gk. : *hippos,* horse + *dromos,* race.]

hip·po·griff also **hip·po·gryph** (hĭp′ə-grĭf′) *n.* A mythological monster having the wings, claws, and head of a griffin and the body and hindquarters of a horse. [Fr. *hippogriffe* < Ital. *ippogrifo* : *ippo-,* horse (< Lat. *hippos* < Gk.) + *grifo,* griffin (< LLat. *gryphus*).]

Hip·pol·y·ta (hĭ-pŏl′ĭ-tə) *n. Gk. Myth.* A queen of the Amazons slain by Hercules in completion of his labors. [Lat. < Gk. *Hippolutē.*]

Hip·pol·y·tus (hĭ-pŏl′ĭ-təs) *n. Gk. Myth.* A son of Theseus who spurned the advances of his stepmother, Phaedra, and was killed by Poseidon. [Lat. < Gk. *Hippolutos.*]

hip·po·pot·a·mus (hĭp′ə-pŏt′ə-məs) *n., pl.* **-mus·es** or **-mi** (-mī′). **1.** A large, chiefly aquatic African mammal, *Hippopotamus amphibius,* having dark, thick, almost hairless skin, short legs, and a broad, wide-mouthed muzzle. **2.** An animal similar to but smaller than the hippopotamus, *Choeropsis liberiensis.* [Lat. < LGk. *hippopotamos* : Gk. *hippos,* horse + Gk. *potamos,* river.]

hippopotamus

hip·py (hĭp′ē) *n.* Variant of **hippie.**

hip roof *n.* A roof having sloping edges and sides.

hip·ster (hĭp′stər) *n. Slang.* One who is aware of or in accordance with the latest trends and tastes. **—hip′ster·ism** *n.*

hi·ra·ga·na (hîr′ə-gä′nə) *n.* One of two sets of Japanese syllabaries, having a cursive form. [J. : *hira,* flat + *kana,* kana.]

hir·cine (hûr′sīn′, -sĭn) *adj.* Of or characteristic of a goat, esp. in strong odor. [Lat. *hircinus* < *hircus,* goat.]

hire (hīr) *tr.v.* **hired, hir·ing, hires. 1.** To engage the services of (a person) for a fee. **2.** To engage the temporary use of (something) for a fee; rent: *hire a car for the day.* **—*phrasal verb.* hire out. 1.** To grant one's services for a fee: *hires out as a free-lance photographer.* **2.** To allow the use of for a fee: *hired out the cottage for the summer.* *—n.* **1.** Payment for services or for the use of something. **2.** The act of hiring. **3.** The condition or fact of being hired. [ME *hiren* < OE *hȳrian.*] **—hir′a·ble, hire′a·ble** *adj.* **—hir′er** *n.*

hire·ling (hīr′lĭng) *n.* One who offers his services solely for compensation, esp. a person willing to perform offensive or menial tasks for a fee.

hiring hall *n.* A union-operated placement center where jobs from various employers are allotted to registered applicants according to a set order based usually on rotation or seniority.

hir·sute (hûr′so͞ot′, hîr′-, hər-so͞ot′) *adj.* Covered with hair; hairy. [Lat. *hirsutus.*] **—hir′sute′ness** *n.*

hir·sut·ism (hûr′so͞o-tĭz′əm, hîr′-, hər-so͞o′-) *n.* Heavy growth of hair, often in abnormal distribution.

hir·u·din (hîr-o͝od′n, hîr′ə-dən, -yə-) *n.* A substance extracted from the salivary glands of leeches and used as an anticoagulant. [Lat. *hirudo, hirudin-,* leech.]

his (hĭz) *adj.* The possessive form of **he.** Used to indicate that the male previously referred to is the possessor or the agent or recipient of an action: *his wallet; his accomplishments; his first rebuff.* *—pron. (used with a sing. or pl. verb).* That or those belonging to him: *The brown boots are his. If you can't find your hat, take his.* —See Usage note at **everyone.** [ME < OE.]

His·pan·ic (hĭ-spăn′ĭk) *adj.* Of or pertaining to the language, people, and culture of Spain, Portugal, or Latin America.

—*n.* An American of Spanish or Latin-American origin or descent. [Lat. *Hispanicus,* after *Hispania* (Spain).] **—His·pan'i·cism** (-ĭ-sĭz'əm) *n.* **—His·pan'i·cist** (-ĭ-sĭst) *n.*

his·pid (hĭs'pĭd) *adj.* Covered with stiff or rough hairs; bristly: *hispid stems.* [Lat. *hispidus.*] **—his·pid'i·ty** (hĭ-spĭd'ĭ-tē) *n.*

hiss (hĭs) *n.* **1.** A sharp, sibilant sound similar to a sustained *s.* **2.** An expression of disapproval, contempt, or dissatisfaction conveyed by a hiss. —*v.* **hissed, hiss·ing, hiss·es.** —*intr.* To utter a hiss. —*tr.* **1.** To utter with a hiss. **2.** To express (disapproval, contempt, or dissatisfaction) by hissing. [ME *hissen.*] **—hiss'er** *n.*

hist– *pref.* Variant of **histo-.**

his·tam·i·nase (hĭ-stăm'ə-nās', -nāz', hĭs'tə-mə-) *n.* An enzyme that occurs in the digestive system and converts histidine to histamine.

his·ta·mine (hĭs'tə-mēn', -mĭn) *n.* A white crystalline compound, $C_5H_9N_3$, found in plant and animal tissue, that is formed from histidine by the action of putrefactive bacteria, is a stimulant of gastric secretion, and is used medicinally as a vasodilator. **—his'ta·min'ic** (-mĭn'ĭk) *adj.*

his·ti·dine (hĭs'tĭ-dēn', -dĭn) *n.* A colorless, crystalline amino acid, $C_6H_9N_3O_2$, used as a feed additive and dietary supplement. [HIST(O)- + -ID(E) + -INE.]

his·ti·o·cyte (hĭs'tē-ə-sīt') *n.* A fixed phagocyte that is part of the reticuloendothelial system and that functions as a protective mechanism by ingesting foreign particles in the blood. [Gk. *histion,* web (dim. of *histos* < *histanai,* to cause to stand) + -CYTE.] **—his'ti·o·cyt'ic** (-sĭt'ĭk) *adj.*

histo– or **hist–** *pref.* Body tissue: *histogenesis.* [< Gk. *histos,* web < *histanai,* to cause to stand.]

his·to·chem·is·try (hĭs'tō-kĕm'ĭ-strē) *n.* The chemistry of cells and tissues. **—his'to·chem'i·cal** *adj.* **—his'to·chem'i·cal·ly** *adv.*

his·to·com·pat·i·bil·i·ty (hĭs'tō-kəm-păt'ə-bĭl'ĭ-tē) *n.* A state or condition in which the absence of immunological interference permits the grafting of tissue or the transfusion of blood. **—his'to·com·pat'i·ble** *adj.*

his·to·gen·e·sis (hĭs'tō-jĕn'ĭ-sĭs) *n.* The formation and development of bodily tissues. **—his'to·ge·net'ic** (-jə-nĕt'ĭk), **his'to·gen'ic** *adj.* **—his'to·ge·net'i·cal·ly, his'to·gen'i·cal·ly** *adv.*

his·to·gram (hĭs'tə-grăm') *n.* A graphic representation of a frequency distribution in which the widths of contiguous vertical bars are proportional to the class widths of the variable and the heights of the bars are proportional to the class frequencies. [Gk. *histos,* beam, mast + -GRAM.]

his·tol·o·gy (hĭ-stŏl'ə-jē) *n.* **1.** The anatomical study of the microscopic structure of animal and plant tissues. **2.** The microscopic structure of tissue. [Fr. *histologie* : *histo-,* histo- + *-logie,* -logy.] **—his'to·log'i·cal** (hĭs'tə-lŏj'ĭ-kəl) *adj.* **—his'to·log'i·cal·ly** *adv.* **—his·tol'o·gist** *n.*

his·tol·y·sis (hĭ-stŏl'ĭ-sĭs) *n.* The breakdown and disintegration of organic tissue. **—his'to·lyt'ic** (hĭs'tə-lĭt'ĭk) *adj.* **—his'to·lyt'i·cal·ly** *adv.*

his·tone (hĭs'tōn') *n.* Any of several simple water-soluble proteins, found esp. in glandular tissues, that can release on hydrolysis a high proportion of basic amino acids.

his·to·pa·thol·o·gy (hĭs'tō-pə-thŏl'ə-jē, -pă-) *n.* The pathology of changes in diseased tissue. **—his'to·path'o·log'ic** (-păth'ə-lŏj'ĭk), **his'to·path'o·log'i·cal** *adj.* **—his'to·path'o·log'i·cal·ly** *adv.* **—his'to·pa·thol'o·gist** *n.*

his·to·phys·i·ol·o·gy (hĭs'tō-fĭz'ē-ŏl'ə-jē) *n.* The physiology of the microscopic functioning of bodily tissues. **—his'to·phys'i·o·log'ic** (-ē-ə-lŏj'ĭk), **his'to·phys'i·o·log'i·cal** *adj.*

his·to·ri·an (hĭ-stôr'ē-ən, -stōr'-, -stŏr'-) *n.* **1.** A writer, student, or scholar of history. **2.** A person who makes a record of proceedings.

his·tor·ic (hĭ-stôr'ĭk, -stŏr'-) *adj.* **1.** Having importance in or influence on history. **2.** Historical.

Usage: *Historic* and *historical* are differentiated in usage, although their senses overlap. *Historic* refers to what is important in history: *the historic first voyage to outer space.* It is also used of what is famous or interesting because of its association with persons or events in history: *a historic house. Historical* refers to whatever existed in the past, whether regarded as important or not: *a historical character.* Events are *historical* if they happened, *historic* only if they are regarded as important. *Historical* refers also to anything concerned with history or the study of the past: *a historical novel; historical discoveries.* The differentiation between the words is not complete. They are often used interchangeably: *historic times* or *historical times.*

his·tor·i·cal (hĭ-stôr'ĭ-kəl, -stŏr'-) *adj.* **1.** Of, relating to, or of the character of history. **2.** Based on or concerned with events in history. **3.** Having considerable importance or influence in history; historic. **4.** Diachronic. —See Usage note at **historic. —his·tor'i·cal·ly** *adv.* **—his·tor'i·cal·ness** *n.*

historical linguistics *n.* The study of language development chronologically with emphasis on evolutionary development.

historical materialism *n.* A major tenet in the Marxist theory of history that regards material economic forces as the base upon which sociopolitical institutions and ideas are built.

historical present *n.* The present tense used in the narration of events set in the past.

historical school *n.* A school of theorists, as in law or economics, stressing the influence of historical conditions.

his·tor·i·cism (hĭ-stôr'ĭ-sĭz'əm, -stŏr'-) *n.* A theory of history that holds that events are determined or influenced by conditions and inherent processes beyond the control of human beings. **—his·tor'i·cist** *adj. & n.*

his·to·ric·i·ty (hĭs'tə-rĭs'ĭ-tē) *n.* Historical authenticity.

his·tor·i·cize (hĭ-stôr'ĭ-sīz', -stŏr'-) *v.* **-cized, -ciz·ing, -ciz·es.** —*tr.* To make or make appear historical. —*intr.* To use historical details or materials.

his·to·ri·og·ra·pher (hĭ-stôr'ē-ŏg'rə-fər, -stōr'-) *n.* **1.** One specializing in historiography. **2.** A historian, esp. one designated by a group or public institution.

his·to·ri·og·ra·phy (hĭ-stôr'ē-ŏg'rə-fē, -stōr'-) *n.* **1.** The principles or methodology of historical study. **2.** The writing of history. **3.** Historical literature. [OFr. *historiographie* < Gk. *historiographia* : *historia,* history + *-graphia,* writing.] **—his·to'ri·o·graph'ic** (-ē-ə-grăf'ĭk), **his·to'ri·o·graph'i·cal** *adj.* **—his·to'ri·o·graph'i·cal·ly** *adv.*

his·to·ry (hĭs'tə-rē) *n., pl.* **-ries. 1.** A narrative of events; story. **2.** A chronological record of events, as of the life or development of a people or institution, often including an explanation of or commentary on those events. **3.** The branch of knowledge that records and analyzes past events. **4.** The events forming the subject matter of history. **5.** An interesting past: *a house with a history.* **6.** Something that is not of current concern: *My youth is now history.* **7.** A drama based on historical events. **8.** A record of a patient's medical background. [Lat. *historia* < Gk. < *histōr,* learned man.]

his·tri·on·ic (hĭs'trē-ŏn'ĭk) also **his·tri·on·i·cal** (-ĭ-kəl) *adj.* **1.** Of or pertaining to actors or acting. **2.** Excessively dramatic or emotional; affected. [LLat. *histrionicus* < Lat. *histrio,* actor, of Etruscan orig.] **—his'tri·on'i·cal·ly** *adv.*

his·tri·on·ics (hĭs'trē-ŏn'ĭks) *n.* **1.** *(used with a sing. verb).* Theatrical arts. **2.** *(used with a pl. verb).* Exaggerated emotional behavior calculated for effect.

hit (hĭt) *v.* **hit, hit·ting, hits.** —*tr.* **1.** To come in contact with forcefully; strike. **2.** To cause to come into contact with: *hit her hand against the wall.* **3.** To deal a blow to. **4.** To strike with a missile: *He fired and hit the target.* **5.** *Sports.* **a.** To reach with a propelled object: *hit the open man with a perfect pass.* **b.** To score in this way: *hit the winning basket.* **c.** To perform (a shot or maneuver) successfully: *couldn't hit the jump shot.* **6.** *Baseball.* **a.** To make (a base hit): *hit a single.* **b.** To bat against (a pitcher or kind of pitch) successfully: *can't hit a slider.* **7.** To reach and affect adversely: *hit hard by the recession.* **8.** To come upon or discover, often by chance. **9.** To attain or reach: *Monthly sales hit a new high.* **10.** To accord with; suit: *The idea hit his fancy.* **11.** To propel with a blow. **12.** *Informal.* To request or obtain from: *He's always hitting me for a loan.* **13.** *Informal.* To resort to excessively: *hitting the bottle.* —*intr.* **1.** To strike or deal a blow. **2.** To come in contact; collide. **3. a.** To attack. **b.** To happen or occur. **4.** To achieve or find something desired or sought: *finally hit on the answer.* **5.** *Baseball.* To bat. —*n.* **1.** A collision or impact. **2.** A successfully executed shot, blow, thrust, or throw. **3.** A successful or popular venture: *a Broadway hit.* **4.** An apt or effective remark. **5.** *Baseball.* A base hit. **6.** *Slang.* A dose of a narcotic drug. **7.** *Slang.* A murder planned and carried out usually by a member of an underworld syndicate. **—*idioms.* hit it off.** To get along well together. **hit the books.** To study, esp. hard. **hit the hay** (or **sack**). To go to bed. **hit the nail on the head.** To be absolutely right. **hit the road.** To set out, as on a trip; leave. **hit the roof** (or **ceiling**). To express anger, esp. vehemently. **hit the spot.** To give total or desired satisfaction, as food or drink. [ME *hitten* < OE *hyttan* < ON *hitta.*]

hit-and-run (hĭt'n-rŭn') *adj.* **1.** Designating or involving the driver of a motor vehicle who drives on after striking a pedestrian or another vehicle. **2.** *Baseball.* Pertaining to or designating a play in which a man on base runs on the pitch and the batter attempts to hit the ball.

hitch (hĭch) *v.* **hitched, hitch·ing, hitch·es.** —*tr.* **1.** To fasten or catch temporarily with or as if with a loop, hook, or noose. **2.** To connect or attach, as to a vehicle: *hitched the horses to the buggy.* **3.** *Informal.* To join in marriage. **4.** To raise by pulling or jerking: *hitch up one's trousers.* **5.** *Informal.* To hitchhike. —*intr.* **1.** To move haltingly; hobble. **2.** To become entangled, snarled, or fastened. **3.** *Slang.* To be united in marriage. **4.** *Informal.* To hitchhike. —*n.* **1.** Any of various knots used as a temporary fastening. **2.** A device used to connect one thing to another. **3.** A short jerking motion; tug. **4.** A hobble or limp. **5.** An impediment or delay: *a hitch in our plans.* **6.** A term of service, esp. of military service. [Orig. unknown.]

hitch·hike (hĭch'hīk') *v.* **-hiked, -hik·ing, -hikes.** —*intr.* To travel by soliciting free rides along a road. —*tr.* To solicit or get (a free ride) along a road. **—hitch'hik'er** *n.*

hitching post *n.* A post for temporarily tying up an animal, esp. a horse.

hith·er (hĭth'ər) *adv.* To or toward this place: *Come hither.* —*adj.* Located on the near side. [ME < OE *hider.*]

hith·er·most (hĭth'ər-mōst') *adj.* Nearest to this place or side.

hith·er·to (hĭth'ər-to͞o', hĭth'ər-to͞o') *adv.* Until this time.

hith·er·ward (hĭth′ər-wərd) also **hith·er·wards** (-wərdz) *adv.* Hither.

Hit·ler·i·an (hĭt-lîr′ē-ən) *adj.* Of, pertaining to, or characteristic of Adolf Hitler, his beliefs, or his regime in Germany.

Hit·ler·ism (hĭt′lə-rĭz′əm) *n.* The fascistic and nationalistic theories and methods of Adolf Hitler and the Nazis. **—Hit′ler·ite′** (-lə-rīt′) *n.*

hit list *n. Slang.* **1.** A list of potential murder victims as drawn up by a crime syndicate. **2.** A list designating a target, as for attack, coercion, or elimination: *"had a hit list of executives he wanted fired"* (New York Magazine).

hit man *n. Slang.* A hatchet man (sense 1).

hit-or-miss (hĭt′ər-mĭs′) *adj.* Lacking care or accuracy; random.

hit·ter (hĭt′ər) *n.* **1.** One who hits or strikes something. **2.** *Baseball.* A batter.

Hit·tite (hĭt′īt′) *n.* **1.** A member of an ancient people living in Asia Minor and northern Syria about 2000–1200 B.C. **2.** The Indo-European language of the Hittites. *—adj.* Of or pertaining to the Hittites, their culture, or their language. [Heb. *Ḥittī* < Hittite *Hatti.*]

hive (hīv) *n.* **1.** A structure for housing bees, esp. honeybees. **2.** A colony of bees living in a hive. **3.** A place swarming with active people. *—v.* **hived, hiv·ing, hives.** *—tr.* **1.** To collect (bees) into a hive. **2.** To store (honey) in a hive. **3.** To store up; accumulate. *—intr.* **1.** To enter a hive. **2.** To live with many others in close association. [ME < OE *hȳf.*]

hives (hīvz) *pl.n. (used with a sing. or pl. verb).* Urticaria. [Orig. unknown.]

ho (hō) *interj.* Used to express surprise or joy, to attract attention to something sighted, or to urge onward: *Land ho! Westward ho!* [ME < OFr. and < ON *hō.*]

Ho The symbol for the element holmium.

hoa·gie (hō′gē) *n.* A hero (sense 5). [Orig. unknown.]

hoar (hôr, hōr) *adj.* Hoary. *—n.* Hoarfrost. [ME *hor* < OE *hār.*]

hoard (hôrd, hōrd) *n.* A hidden fund or supply stored for future use; cache. *—v.* **hoard·ed, hoard·ing, hoards.** *—intr.* To gather or accumulate a hoard. *—tr.* To accumulate or gather by saving or hiding. [ME *hord* < OE.] **—hoard′er** *n.*

hoard·ing (hôr′dĭng, hōr′-) *n. Chiefly Brit.* **1.** A temporary wooden fence around a building or structure under construction or repair. **2.** A billboard. [Obs. *hoard* < AN *hurdis* < OFr. *hourd,* scaffold, of Germanic orig.]

hoar·frost (hôr′frôst′, -frŏst′, hōr′-) *n.* Frozen dew that forms a white coating on a surface.

hoarse (hôrs, hōrs) *adj.* **hoars·er, hoars·est. 1.** Low and grating in sound. **2.** Having a husky, grating voice. [ME *hors* < OE *hās.*] **—hoarse′ly** *adv.* **—hoarse′ness** *n.*

hoars·en (hôr′sən, hōr′-) *tr. & intr.v.* **-ened, -en·ing, -ens.** To make or become hoarse.

hoar·y (hôr′ē, hōr′ē) *adj.* **-i·er, -i·est. 1.** Gray or white with or as if with age. **2.** Covered with grayish hair or pubescence: *hoary leaves.* **3.** Very old; ancient. **—hoar′i·ness** *n.*

hoat·zin (wät-sēn′) *n.* A brownish, crested bird, *Opisthocomus hoazin,* of tropical South America, whose young have claws on the first and second digits of the wings. [Am. Sp. < Nahuatl *uatzin,* pheasant.]

hoax (hōks) *n.* **1.** An act intended to deceive or trick. **2.** Something that has been established or accepted by fraudulent means. *—tr.v.* **hoaxed, hoax·ing, hoax·es.** To deceive or cheat by using a hoax. [Perh. alteration of HOCUS.] **—hoax′er** *n.*

hob¹ (hŏb) *n.* **1.** A shelf or projection at the back or side of the inside of a fireplace, used for keeping things warm. **2.** A tool used for cutting the teeth of machine parts, as of a gearwheel. [Orig. unknown.]

hob² (hŏb) *n.* A hobgoblin, sprite, or elf. [After ME *Hobbe,* a nickname for Robert.]

Hobb·ism (hŏb′ĭz′əm) *n.* A political theory promulgated by Thomas Hobbes, advocating powerful government as the only means of adequately controlling the inevitable problems created by the inherent selfish, aggrandizing nature of human beings.

hob·ble (hŏb′əl) *v.* **-bled, -bling, -bles.** *—intr.* To walk or move along haltingly or with difficulty; limp. *—tr.* **1.** To put a device around the legs of (an animal) so as to hamper but not prevent movement. **2.** To cause to limp. **3.** To hamper the action or progress of; impede. *—n.* **1.** An awkward, clumsy, or irregular walk or gait. **2.** A device, such as a rope or strap, used to hobble an animal. **3.** *Archaic.* An awkward situation. [ME *hobblen* < MDu. *hobbelen.*] **—hob′bler** *n.*

hob·ble·bush (hŏb′əl-bo͝osh′) *n.* A shrub, *Viburnum alnifolium,* of northeastern North America, having flat clusters of white flowers with the marginal flowers larger than the others.

hob·ble·de·hoy (hŏb′əl-dē-hoi′) *n., pl.* **-hoys.** A gawky adolescent boy. [Orig. unknown.]

hobble skirt *n.* A type of long skirt, popular between 1910 and 1914, that was so narrow below the knees that it restricted normal stride.

hob·by¹ (hŏb′ē) *n., pl.* **-bies.** An activity or interest pursued outside of one's regular work and engaged in primarily for pleasure. [ME *hobi,* small horse < *Hobyn,* nickname for Robert.] **—hob′by·ist** *n.*

hob·by² (hŏb′ē) *n., pl.* **-bies.** Any of several small falcons of the genus *Falco,* formerly used for hawking. [ME *hobi* < OFr. *hobe.*]

hob·by·horse (hŏb′ē-hôrs′) *n.* **1.** A child's toy consisting of a long stick with an imitation horse's head on one end. **2.** A rocking horse. **3. a.** A figure of a horse worn around the waist of a mummer pretending to ride a horse. **b.** A person wearing such a figure. **4. a.** A favorite topic or hobby. **b.** Something with which one is obsessed; fixation.

hob·gob·lin (hŏb′gŏb′lĭn) *n.* **1.** An ugly, mischievous elf or goblin. **2.** A bugbear.

hob·nail (hŏb′nāl′) *n.* A short nail with a thick head used to protect the soles of shoes or boots.

hobnail

hob·nob (hŏb′nŏb′) *intr.v.* **-nobbed, -nob·bing, -nobs.** To associate familiarly: *hobnobs with some pretty influential politicians.* [< the phrase *(drink) hob or nob,* (toast) one another alternately.]

ho·bo (hō′bō) *n., pl.* **-boes** or **-bos. 1.** A tramp; vagrant. **2.** A migratory, usually unskilled worker. [Orig. unknown.] **—ho′bo·ism** *n.*

Hob·son's choice (hŏb′sənz) *n.* An apparently free choice that offers no real alternative. [After Thomas *Hobson* (1544–1631), English liveryman, from his requirement that customers take either the horse nearest the stable door or none.]

hock¹ (hŏk) *n.* **1.** The tarsal joint of the hind leg of a digitigrade quadruped, such as a horse, corresponding to the human ankle. **2.** A joint in the leg of a domestic fowl similar to the hock of a quadruped. *—tr.v.* **hocked, hock·ing, hocks.** To disable by cutting the tendons of the hock; hamstring. [ME *hoche* < OE *hōh,* heel.]

hock² (hŏk) *n. Chiefly Brit.* White Rhine wine. [Alteration of G. *Hochheimer,* after *Hochheim,* West Germany.]

hock³ (hŏk) *Informal. —tr.v.* **hocked, hock·ing, hocks.** To pawn. *—n.* The state of being pawned. ***—idiom.* in hock.** In debt. [< Du. *hok,* prison.]

hock·ey (hŏk′ē) *n.* **1.** A game played on ice in which two opposing teams of skaters, using curved sticks, try to drive a puck into the opponents' goal. **2.** A form of hockey played on foot on a turf field and using a ball rather than a puck. [Orig. unknown.]

hockey
Field hockey

hockey stick *n.* A long-handled stick with one curved end, used in hockey.

hock·shop (hŏk′shŏp′) *n. Informal.* A pawnshop.

ho·cus (hō′kəs) *tr.v.* **-cused, -cus·ing, -cus·es** or **-cussed, -cus·sing, -cus·ses. 1.** To fool or deceive; hoax. **2.** To infuse (food or drink) with a drug. [Short for HOCUS-POCUS.]

ho·cus-po·cus (hō′kəs-pō′kəs) *n.* **1.** Nonsense words or phrases used as a formula by conjurers. **2.** A trick performed by a magician or juggler. **3.** A deception or chicanery. *—v.* **-cused, -cus·ing, -cus·es** or **-cussed, -cus·sing, -cus·ses.** *—tr.* To deceive; trick. *—intr.* To be deceptive. [Poss. < an alteration of Lat. *hoc est corpus,* this is the body (from its use in the Eucharist at the time of transubstantiation).]

hod (hŏd) *n.* **1.** A trough carried over the shoulder for transporting loads, such as bricks. **2.** A coal scuttle. [Perh. alteration of dial. *hot* < ME *hotte,* pannier < OFr., of Germanic orig.]

ho·dad (hō′dăd′) also **ho·dad·dy** (-dăd′ē) *n.* A person who does not surf but who spends time at surfing beaches pretending to be a surfer. [Orig. unknown.]

hodge·podge (hŏj′pŏj′) *n.* A mixture of dissimilar ingredients; jumble. [ME *hochepot* < OFr. —see HOTCHPOT.]

Hodg·kin's disease (hŏj′kĭnz) *n.* A usually chronic, progressive, sometimes fatal disease of unknown etiology, marked by inflammatory enlargement of the lymph nodes, spleen, and often liver and kidneys. [After Thomas *Hodgkin* (1798–1866).]

hoe (hō) *n.* A tool with a flat blade attached approximately at right angles to a long handle, used for weeding, cultivating, and gardening. *—v.* **hoed, hoe·ing, hoes.** *—tr.* To weed, cultivate, or dig up with a hoe. *—intr.* To work with a hoe. [ME *houe* < OFr., of Germanic orig.] **—ho′er** *n.*

hoe·cake (hō′kāk′) *n.* A thin cake made of cornmeal.

hoe-down (hō′doun′) *n.* **1.** A square dance. **2.** The music for a hoe-down. **3.** A party at which hoe-downs are danced.

hog (hôg, hŏg) *n.* **1.** Any of various mammals of the family Suidae, which includes the domesticated pig as well as wild species, such as the boar and the wart hog. **2.** A domesticated pig, esp. one weighing over 120 pounds. **3.** A self-indulgent, gluttonous, or filthy person. **4.** Also **hogg.** *Chiefly Brit.* A young sheep before its second shearing. *—v.* **hogged, hog·ging, hogs.** *—tr.* **1.** To take more than one's share of. **2.** To cause (the back) to arch like that of a hog. **3.** To shorten (a horse's mane). *—intr. Naut.* To arch upward in the middle. Used of a ship's keel. ***—idioms.* go hog wild.** To react in an excited, immoderate, or irrational manner. **high off (or on) the hog.** In a lavish or extravagant manner. [ME < OE *hogg,* poss. of Celtic orig.]

ho·gan (hō′găn′, -gən) *n.* An earth-covered Navaho dwelling. [Navaho.]

hog·back (hôg′băk′, hŏg′-) *n.* A sharp ridge with steeply sloping sides, produced by the erosion of the broken edges of highly tilted strata.

hog cholera *n.* A highly infectious, often fatal viral disease

hogfish

of swine, characterized by fever, loss of appetite, diarrhea, and exhaustion.

hog·fish (hôg′fĭsh′, hŏg′-) *n., pl.* **hogfish** or **-fish·es. 1.** A colorful fish, *Lachnolaimus maximus,* of warm Atlantic waters, having a long snout in the adult male. **2.** The pigfish.

hogg (hôg, hŏg) *n.* Variant of **hog** (sense 4).

hog·gish (hô′gĭsh, hŏg′ĭsh) *adj.* **1.** Coarsely self-indulgent or gluttonous. **2.** Filthy. **—hog′gish·ly** *adv.* **—hog′gish·ness** *n.*

Hog·ma·nay (hŏg′mə-nā′) *n. Scot.* New Year's Eve, when children traditionally go from house to house asking for presents. [Orig. unknown.]

hog·nose snake (hôg′nōz′, hŏg′-) *n.* Any of several thick-bodied, nonvenomous North American snakes of the genus *Heterodon,* having an upturned snout.

hog peanut *n.* A twining North American vine, *Amphicarpa bracteata,* having clusters of pinkish or white flowers and bearing curving pods as well as basal or underground fleshy one-seeded fruit.

hogs·head (hôgz′hĕd′, hŏgz′-) *n.* **1.** Any of various units of volume or capacity ranging from 62.5 to 140 gallons, or from approximately 237 to 529 liters, esp. a unit of capacity used in liquid measure in the United States, equal to 63 gallons, or approximately 239 liters. **2.** A large barrel or cask with the capacity to hold a hogshead.

hog-tie also **hog·tie** (hôg′tī′, hŏg′-) *tr.v.* **-tied, -ty·ing** or **-tie·ing, -ties. 1.** To tie together the legs of. **2.** To impede or disrupt in movement or action.

hog·wash (hôg′wŏsh′, hŏg′wŏsh′) *n.* **1.** Garbage fed to hogs; swill. **2.** Worthless, false, or ridiculous speech or writing.

hog·weed (hôg′wēd′, hŏg′-) *n.* Any of various coarse, weedy plants.

ho hum *interj.* Used to express boredom or weariness.

ho-hum (hō′hŭm′) *adj.* Boring and conventional: *"a ho-hum speaker who couldn't capture the attention of the conventioneers"* (Chicago Tribune).

hoicks (hoiks) *interj.* Variant of **yoicks.**

hoi pol·loi (hoi′ pə-loi′) *n.* The common people; masses. [Gk., the many.]

hoist (hoist) *tr.v.* **hoist·ed, hoist·ing, hoists.** To raise or haul up with or as if with the help of a mechanical apparatus. *—n.* **1.** An apparatus for lifting heavy or cumbersome objects. **2.** The act of hoisting; lift. **3.** *Naut.* **a.** The height or vertical dimension of a flag or of any square sail other than a course. **b.** A group of flags raised together as a signal. [Alteration of dial. *hoise.*] **—hoist′er** *n.*

hoi·ty-toi·ty (hoi′tē-toi′tē) *adj.* **1.** Pretentiously self-important; pompous. **2.** Lightheaded; flighty. **3.** Tending to take offense easily. *—n., pl.* **-ties. 1.** Pretentiousness; arrogance. **2.** Giddiness. [Redup. of dial. *hoit,* to romp.]

hoke (hōk) *tr.v.* **hoked, hok·ing, hokes.** *Slang.* To give an artificial, false, or misleading quality to. [< HOKUM.]

hok·ey (hō′kē) *adj.* **-i·er, -i·est.** *Slang.* **1.** Corny; trite. **2.** Artificial; phony. **—hok′i·ly** *adv.* **—hok′i·ness** *n.*

ho·key-po·key (hō′kē-pō′kē) *n.* **1.** Chicanery; hocus-pocus. **2.** Ice cream formerly sold by street venders.

hok·ku (hō′ko͞o) *n., pl.* **hokku.** Haiku.

ho·kum (hō′kəm) *n.* **1.** Something that may seem impressive but is untrue or insincere; nonsense. **2.** A stock technique for eliciting a desired response from an audience. [Perh. HO(CUS-POCUS) + (BUN)KUM.]

hoist

hol– *pref.* Variant of **holo-.**

Hol·arc·tic (hō-lärk′tĭk, -lär′tĭk, hŏ-) *adj.* Of or designating the zoogeographic region that includes the northern areas of the earth and is divided into Nearctic and Palearctic regions.

hold[1] (hōld) *v.* **held** (hĕld), **hold·ing, holds.** *—tr.* **1. a.** To have and keep in one's grasp. **b.** To keep up; support: *a nail too small to hold the mirror.* **c.** To maintain in a certain position or relationship: *held my assistant at arm's length.* **d.** To keep in reserve or custody: *holding him for questioning.* **2. a.** To receive or be able to receive as contents; contain: *The car holds six people.* **b.** To have in store: *can only wait and see what the future holds.* **3. a.** To have and maintain in one's possession. **b.** To maintain control over: *The dam held the flood waters.* **c.** To retain or defend by force or coercion: *soldiers who held the village for a week; held the stolen Picasso for ransom.* **4. a.** To impose control or restraint upon; check: *held her temper.* **b.** To stall or delay: *Hold him till I get there.* **c.** To stop the movement or progress of; arrest: *Hold the presses!* **5. a.** To maintain in a given condition or action: *a plane holding course.* **b.** To retain the attention or interest of: *a second-rate comic who can't hold an audience.* **6. a.** To be the legal possessor of. **b.** To bind by a contract. **c.** To adjudge or decree. **d.** To cause to keep; obligate: *held her to her promise.* **7.** To comport; carry: *held himself as a gentleman at all times.* **8. a.** To keep in the mind or heart; harbor: *hold a grudge.* **b.** To consider or believe; judge: *holds it a point of honor not to respond to attacks by the press.* **c.** To assert; affirm: *holds that his economic program is the only answer to high prices and increased unemployment.* **9. a.** To have or occupy (a position): *held the governorship for six years.* **b.** To have or gain through merit or consensus: *holds the utmost respect of his peers.* **10. a.** To cause to take place; put on: *held the race in Florida.* **b.** To convene or assemble: *held a meeting of the board.* *—intr.* **1.** To maintain a grasp or grip. **2.** To maintain a desired or accustomed position or condition. **3.** To adhere closely; keep: *held to a southwesterly course.* **4.** To stand up under stress, pressure, or opposition; last. **5.** To be valid, applicable, or true: *His theory holds.* **6.** *Slang.* To have illicit or illegally obtained material or goods, esp. narcotics, in one's possession. **—*phrasal verbs.* hold back. 1.** To retain in one's possession or control. **2.** To impede the progress of. **hold down.** To work at and keep (a job). **hold off.** To stop or delay doing something. **hold on. 1.** To maintain one's grip; cling. **2.** To keep at; continue. **3.** To stop or wait for someone or something. **hold out. 1.** To last; endure. **2.** To continue to resist. **3.** To refuse to reach or satisfy an agreement. **hold over. 1.** To postpone or delay. **2.** To continue or prolong the term or engagement of. **hold to.** To remain loyal or faithful to. **hold up. 1.** To offer or present as an example: *held her paintings up as beautiful.* **2.** To obstruct or delay. **3.** To rob. **hold with.** To agree with; support. *—n.* **1.** The act or a means of grasping; grip. **2.** Something held onto, as for support. **3. a.** A bond or force that restrains, dominates, or affects something: *a writer with a strong hold on the reading public.* **b.** Complete control: *has to get a hold on himself; took hold of the situation.* **4.** A prison cell. **5.** *Archaic.* A fortified place; stronghold. **6.** *Mus.* **a.** The sustaining of a note longer than its indicated time value. **b.** The symbol designating this pause; fermata. **7. a.** A temporary halt, as in a countdown. **b.** A condition or period of waiting: *put the caller on hold.* **c.** A state of delay or suspended activity: *put the romance on hold.* **—*idioms.* hold forth.** To talk at great length. **hold the fort. 1.** To maintain a secure position. **2.** To assume responsibility esp. in another's absence. **hold the line.** To keep something at an acceptable level by regulation or aggressive action: *holding the line on salary increases.* **hold water.** To stand up to critical examination. [ME *holden* < OE *healdon.*]

hold[2] (hōld) *n.* The lower interior part of a ship or airplane in which cargo is stored. [Alteration of ME *hole* < OE *hulu,* hull.]

hold·all (hōld′ôl′) *n.* A case or bag for carrying miscellaneous items, as when traveling.

hold·back (hōld′băk′) *n.* A strap or iron between the shaft and the harness on a drawn wagon, allowing the horse to stop or back up.

hold·en (hōl′dən) *v. Archaic.* Past participle of **hold[1].**

hold·er (hōl′dər) *n.* **1.** A person who holds something. **2.** A device for holding something. **3. a.** One who possesses something; owner. **b.** One who occupies or controls something. **4.** *Law.* One who legally possesses and is entitled to the payment of a check, bill, or promissory note.

hold·fast (hōld′făst′) *n.* **1.** Any of various devices used to fasten something securely. **2.** *Biol.* An organ or structure of attachment, esp. the basal, rootlike formation by which certain seaweeds or other algae are attached to a surface.

hold·ing (hōl′dĭng) *n.* **1.** Land rented or leased from another. **2.** Often **holdings.** Legally owned property, such as land, capital, or stocks. **3.** A court ruling, esp. a ruling on a point of law raised in an official proceeding.

holding company *n.* A company controlling partial or complete interest in other companies.

holding pattern *n.* **1.** A usually circular pattern flown by aircraft awaiting clearance to land at an airport. **2.** A state of waiting or delay; static situation.

hold·out (hōld′out′) *n. Informal.* A person who withholds or delays cooperation or agreement.

hold·o·ver (hōld′ō′vər) *n.* One that remains from an earlier time, esp. an officeholder kept in his position after his term is over.

hold·up (hōld′ŭp′) *n.* **1.** A delay; interruption. **2.** A robbery, esp. an armed robbery.

hole (hōl) *n.* **1.** A cavity in a solid. **2.** An opening or perforation through something: *a hole in the clouds.* **3.** A deep place in a body of water. **4.** An animal's hollowed-out habitation, such as a burrow. **5.** An ugly, squalid, or depressing dwelling. **6.** A deep or isolated place of confinement; dungeon. **7.** A fault or flaw: *holes in his argument.* **8.** An awkward situation; predicament. **9. a.** In golf, the small pit lined with a cup into which the ball must be hit. **b.** One of the divisions of a golf course, from tee to cup. **10.** *Electronics.* A vacant electron energy state that is manifested as a charge defect in a crystalline solid, the defect behaving as a positive charge carrier with charge magnitude equal to that of the electron. *—v.* **holed, hol·ing, holes.** *—tr.* **1.** To put a hole in. **2.** To put or propel into a hole. *—intr.* To make a hole. **—*phrasal verbs.* hole out.** In golf, to hit one's ball into the hole. **hole up. 1.** To hibernate in or as if in a hole. **2.** To hide out or shut oneself up. **—*idioms.* hole in one.** In golf, the driving of the ball from the tee into the hole in only one stroke. **in the hole.** *Informal.* In debt. [ME < OE *hol.*] **—hole′y** *adj.*

Synonyms: *hole, hollow, cavity, excavation, cave, grotto, pit, pocket, crater.* These nouns refer to unfilled space in an otherwise solid body. *Hole* is applicable to any opening in or through such an object. *Hollow* denotes either an unfilled area in a solid body or a surface depression in such a body; examples of the second sense are valleys and ravines. *Cavity* refers to any unfilled space in a solid object, and *excavation* to a manmade cavity. A *cave* is a hollow, or empty chamber, in the earth, and a *grotto* is a cave or an artificially created area made to resemble a cave. A *pit* is a cavity or hole in the earth, often one that descends to a considerable depth from an opening on the surface. *Pocket* is applied principally to a cavity in the earth that contains water or a mineral deposit or to any cavity in a solid body that contains foreign matter. *Crater* refers to a bowl-shaped surface depression found naturally around the mouth of a volcano or geyser or created in warfare by the action of bombs or land mines.

hol·i·day (hŏl′ĭ-dā′) *n.* **1.** A day on which custom or the law dictates a halting of general business activity to commemorate or celebrate a particular event. **2.** A religious feast day; holy day. **3.** A day free from work that one may spend at leisure; day off. **4.** Often **holidays.** *Chiefly Brit.* A vacation. —*intr.v.* **-dayed, -day·ing, -days.** *Chiefly Brit.* To pass a holiday or vacation: *holidaying in the Bahamas.* [ME *holidai,* holy day < OE *hālig dæg.*]

ho·li·er-than-thou (hō′lē-ər-*th*ən-*th*ou′) *adj.* Showing an attitude of superior virtue; self-righteously pious.

ho·li·ness (hō′lē-nĭs) *n.* **1.** The state or quality of being holy; sanctity. **2. Holiness.** A title of address used for various high ecclesiastical dignitaries and esp. for the pope.

ho·lism (hō′lĭz′əm) *n.* The theory that reality is made up of organic or unified wholes that are greater than the simple sum of their parts. **—ho′list** *n.*

ho·lis·tic (hō-lĭs′tĭk) *adj.* **1.** Of or pertaining to holism. **2. a.** Emphasizing the importance of the whole and the interdependence of its parts. **b.** Concerned with wholes rather than analysis or dissection into parts: *holistic medicine; holistic ecology.* **—ho·lis′ti·cal·ly** *adv.*

hol·land (hŏl′ənd) *n.* A cotton or linen fabric, often glazed, that is used esp. for window shades and upholstery. [ME *holand,* after *Holand,* a county in the Netherlands < MDu.]

hol·lan·daise sauce (hŏl′ən-dāz′) *n.* A creamy sauce of butter, egg yolks, and lemon or vinegar. [Fr. *sauce Hollandaise.*]

Hol·lands (hŏl′əndz) *n.* Gin made in the Netherlands. [Du. *Hollandsch* < *hollandsch genever,* Dutch gin.]

hol·ler[1] (hŏl′ər) *v.* **-lered, -ler·ing, -lers.** —*intr.* **1.** To yell or shout. **2.** *Informal.* To complain. —*tr.* To yell or shout (an utterance). —*n.* A yell or shout; call. [< OFr. *holà,* stop! — see HELLO.]

hol·ler[2] (hŏl′ər) *adj., n., & v. Regional.* Variant of **hollow.**

Hol·ler·ith (hŏl′ə-rĭth′) also **Hollerith code** *n.* A code used for recording alphanumeric information on punch cards. [After Herman *Hollerith* (1860–1929).]

Hollerith card *n.* A punch card.

hol·low (hŏl′ō) *adj.* **-er, -est. 1.** Having a cavity, gap, or space within: *a hollow wall.* **2.** Being deeply indented or concave; depressed: *a hollow basin.* **3.** Without substance or character: *a hollow person.* **4.** Without truth or validity; specious: *hollow arguments.* **5.** Having a reverberating, sepulchral sound: *hollow footsteps.* —*n.* **1.** A cavity, gap, or space within something: *the hollow behind a wall.* **2.** An indented or concave surface or area. **3.** A void; emptiness: *a hollow in one's life.* —*v.* **-lowed, -low·ing, -lows.** —*tr.* **1.** To make hollow: *hollow out a pumpkin.* **2.** To scoop or form by making concave: *hollow out a nest in the sand.* —*intr.* To become hollow. [ME *holwe* < *holgh,* hole < OE *holh.*] **—hol′low·ly** *adv.* **—hol′low·ness** *n.*

hol·low·ware (hŏl′ō-wâr′) *n.* Tableware, such as bowls, pitchers, or knife handles, that are tubular or bowl-shaped.

hol·ly (hŏl′ē) *n., pl.* **-lies. 1. a.** Any of numerous trees or shrubs of the genus *Ilex,* often having bright-red berries and glossy, evergreen leaves with spiny margins. **b.** Branches or leaves of the holly, traditionally used for Christmas decoration. **2.** Any of various trees or plants similar or related to the holly. [ME *holi* < OE *holen.*]

hol·ly·hock (hŏl′ē-hŏk′) *n.* A tall plant, *Althaea rosea,* native to China and widely cultivated for its showy spike of large, variously colored flowers. [ME *holihocke,* marsh mallow : *holi,* holy (< OE *halig*) + *hoc,* mallow (< OE).]

Hol·ly·wood (hŏl′ē-wo͝od′) *n.* The U.S. motion-picture industry or the somewhat meretriciously glamorous atmosphere often attributed to it. [After *Hollywood,* California.]

hollywood bed *n.* A mattress on a box spring supported by a metal frame or attached low legs, often with an upholstered headboard.

holm (hōm, hōlm) *n. Chiefly Brit.* An island in a river. [ME < ON *holmr.*]

hol·mic (hōl′mĭk) *adj.* Pertaining to holmium in its trivalent state.

hol·mi·um (hōl′mē-əm) *n. Symbol* **Ho** A relatively soft, malleable, stable rare-earth element occurring in gadolinite, monazite, and other rare-earth minerals. Atomic number 67; atomic weight 164.930; melting point 1,461°C; boiling point 2,600°C; specific gravity 8.803; valence 3. [NLat. < *Holmia* (Stockholm), Sweden.]

holm oak (hōm, hōlm) *n.* A tree, *Quercus ilex,* native to the Mediterranean region, having prickly evergreen leaves. [Poss. ME *holm* < *holm,* holly < *holi.*]

holo- or **hol-** *pref.* Whole; entire; entirely: **holoblastic.** [< Gk. *holos,* whole.]

ho·lo·blas·tic (hō′lə-blăs′tĭk, hŏl′ə-) *adj.* Exhibiting cleavage in which the entire egg separates into individual blastomeres. **—hol′o·blas′ti·cal·ly** *adv.*

ho·lo·caust (hō′lə-kôst′, hŏl′ə-) *n.* **1.** Great or total destruction, esp. by fire. **2. a.** Widespread destruction **b.** A disaster. **3.** Often **Holocaust.** A massive slaughter, esp. the genocide of European Jews by the Nazis during World War II. **4.** A sacrificial offering that is consumed entirely by flames. [ME < Lat. *holocaustum* < Gk. *holokauston* < *holokaustos,* burnt whole : *holo-,* whole + *kaustos,* burnt < *kaein,* to burn.] **—ho′lo·caus′tal, ho′lo·caus′tic** *adj.*

Ho·lo·cene (hō′lə-sēn′, hŏl′ə-) *adj.* Of, belonging to, or designating the geologic time, rock series, or sedimentary deposits of the more recent of the two epochs of the Quaternary period, extending from the end of the Pleistocene to the present. —*n.* The Holocene epoch or system of deposits.

ho·lo·crine (hō′lə-krĭn, -krīn′, -krēn′, hŏl′ə-) *adj.* Pertaining to a gland whose secretion is formed by the degeneration of the gland's cells, as sebaceous glands. [HOLO- + Gk. *krinein,* to separate.]

ho·lo·en·zyme (hō′lō-ĕn′zīm′, hŏl′ō-) *n.* A complete enzyme consisting of an apoenzyme and a coenzyme.

Hol·o·fer·nes (hŏl′ə-fûr′nēz, hō′lə-) *n.* In the Apocrypha, an Assyrian general of Nebuchadnezzar's army killed by Judith. [LLat. < Gk. *Holophernēs.*]

ho·lo·gram (hō′lə-grăm′, hŏl′ə-) *n.* **1.** The pattern produced on a photosensitive medium that has been exposed by holography and then photographically developed. **2.** The photosensitive medium so exposed and so developed.

ho·lo·graph (hō′lə-grăf′, hŏl′ə-) *n.* **1.** A document written wholly in the handwriting of the person whose signature it bears. **2.** A hologram. [< LLat. *holographus,* entirely written by the signer < Gk. *holographos* : *holos,* whole + *-graphos,* written.] **—ho′lo·graph′ic, ho′lo·graph′i·cal** *adj.* **—ho′lo·graph′i·cal·ly** *adv.*

ho·log·raph·y (hō-lŏg′rə-fē) *n.* The technique of producing images by wave-front reconstruction, esp. by using lasers to record on a photographic plate the diffraction pattern from which a three-dimensional image can be projected.

ho·lo·he·dral (hō′lə-hē′drəl, hŏl′ə-) *adj.* Having as many planes as required for complete symmetry in a given crystal system.

ho·lo·me·tab·o·lism (hō′lō-mə-tăb′ə-lĭz′əm, hŏl′ō-) *n.* Complete metamorphosis of a developing insect. **—ho′lo·me·tab′o·lous** *adj.*

ho·lo·phras·tic (hō′lə-frăs′tĭk, hŏl′ə-) *adj.* Polysynthetic. [HOLO- + Gk. *phrastikos,* expressive < *phrazein,* to show.]

ho·lo·thu·ri·an (hō′lə-tho͝or′ē-ən, -thyo͝or′-, hŏl′ə-) *n.* Any of various echinoderms of the class Holothuroidea, which includes the sea cucumbers. [NLat. *Holothuria,* genus name < Gk. *holothourion,* water polyp.] **—hol′o·thu′ri·an** *adj.*

ho·lo·type (hō′lə-tīp′, hŏl′ə-) *n.* The single specimen used as the basis of the original published description of a taxonomic species and later designated as the type specimen. **—ho′lo·typ′ic** (-tĭp′ĭk) *adj.*

ho·lo·zo·ic (hō′lə-zō′ĭk, hŏl′ə-) *adj.* Obtaining nourishment by the ingestion of organic material, as animals do.

holp (hōlp) *v. Archaic.* Past tense of **help.**

hol·pen (hōl′pən) *v. Archaic.* Past participle of **help.**

Hol·stein (hōl′stīn′) *n.* Any of a breed of large black and white dairy cattle originally developed in Friesland. [After *Holstein,* a region in West Germany.]

hol·ster (hōl′stər) *n.* **1.** A leather case shaped to hold a pistol. **2.** A belt with loops or slots for carrying small tools or other equipment. [Du.] **—hol′stered** *adj.*

holt (hōlt) *n. Archaic.* A wood or grove; copse. [ME < OE.]

ho·lus-bo·lus (hō′ləs-bō′ləs) *adv.* All at once.

ho·ly (hō′lē) *adj.* **-li·er, -li·est. 1.** Belonging to, derived from, or associated with a divine power; sacred. **2.** Regarded with or worthy of worship or veneration; revered: *a holy book.* **3.** Living according to a strict or highly moral religious or spiritual system; saintly: *a holy man.* **4.** Specified or set apart for a religious purpose: *a holy hour.* **5.** Solemnly undertaken; sacrosanct: *a holy pledge.* **6.** Regarded or deserving special respect or reverence: *The pursuit of peace is man's holiest quest.* [ME < OE *hālig.*] **—ho′li·ly** *adv.* **—ho′li·ness** *n.*

Holy Communion *n.* The Eucharist.

holy day also **ho·ly·day** (hō′lē-dā′) *n.* A day specified for religious observance.

Holy Father *n.* One of the titles of the pope.

Holy Ghost *n.* The third person of the Christian Trinity.

Holy Grail *n.* The Grail.

Holy Office *n.* A congregation of the Roman Catholic Church that deals with the protection of the faith and morals.

holy of holies *n.* **1.** The innermost shrine of a Jewish tabernacle and temple. **2.** A particularly sacrosanct place.

holy orders *n. Eccles.* **1.** The sacrament or rite of ordination. **2.** The rank of an ordained Christian minister or priest. **3.** The principal orders of the clergy in the Roman Catholic Church, Eastern Orthodox Church, and Anglican Church.

Holy Roller *n. Offensive.* A member of any of various religious sects in which spiritual fervor is expressed by shouts and violent bodily movements.

holly

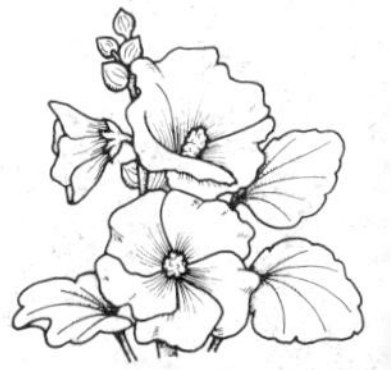

hollyhock

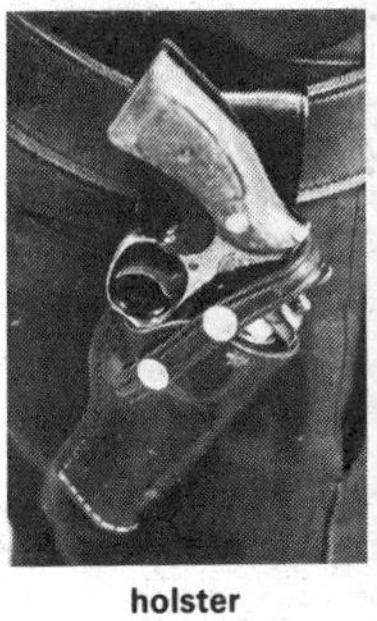

holster

Holy Saturday *n.* The Saturday before Easter.
Holy See *n. Rom. Cath. Ch.* The court, office, or jurisdiction of the pope.
Holy Spirit *n.* The Holy Ghost.
ho·ly·stone (hō′lē-stōn′) *n.* A piece of soft sandstone used for scouring the wooden decks of a ship. —*tr.v.* **-stoned, -ston·ing, -stones.** To scrub or scour with a holystone. [Perh. from its being used while kneeling.]
Holy Synod *n.* The governing body of any of the Eastern Orthodox churches.
Holy Thursday *n.* **1.** Maundy Thursday. **2.** Ascension Day.
holy water *n.* Water blessed by a priest.
Holy Week *n.* The week before Easter.
hom– *pref.* Variant of **homo-**.
hom·age (hŏm′ĭj, ŏm′-) *n.* **1.** Under feudal law, ceremonial acknowledgment by a vassal of allegiance to his lord. **2.** Special honor or respect shown or expressed publicly. [ME < OFr. < Med. Lat. *hominaticum* < Lat. *homo,* man.]
hom·bre[1] (ŏm′brā′, -brē) *n. Slang.* A man; fellow. [Sp. < Lat. *homo.*]
hom·bre[2] (hŏm′bər) *n.* Variant of **ombre**.
Hom·burg also **hom·burg** (hŏm′bûrg′) *n.* A man's felt hat having a soft, dented crown and a shallow, slightly rolled brim. [After *Homburg,* West Germany.]
home (hōm) *n.* **1.** A place where one lives; residence. **2.** The physical structure within which one lives, as a house or apartment. **3.** A dwelling place together with the family or social unit that occupies it; household. **4. a.** An environment offering security and happiness. **b.** A valued place regarded as a refuge or place of origin. **5.** The place, as a country or town, where one was born or lived for a long period. **6.** The native habitat, as of a plant or animal. **7.** The place where something is discovered, founded, developed, or promoted; source. **8.** A headquarters or base of operations; home base. **9. a.** *Baseball.* Home plate. **b.** Home base (sense 3). **10.** An institution where people are cared for: *a home for the elderly.* —*adj.* **1.** Of or pertaining to a home, esp. to one's household or house: *home cooking; home furnishings.* **2.** Of, pertaining to, or being a place of origin or headquarters: *the home office.* **3.** Taking place in the city where a team is franchised: *a home game.* —*adv.* **1.** At, to, or toward the direction of home. **2.** To the point at which something is directed: *The arrow struck home.* **3.** To the center or heart of something; deeply: *His comments struck home.* —*v.* **homed, hom·ing, homes.** —*intr.* **1.** To go or return home. **2.** To be guided to a target automatically, as by means of radio waves. **3.** To move or lead toward a goal: *The investigators were homing in on the truth.* —*tr.* To guide (a missile or aircraft) to a target automatically. —***idioms.* at home. 1.** Available to receive visitors: *at home Thursdays.* **2.** Comfortable and relaxed; at ease. **3.** Feeling an easy competence and familiarity: *at home in French.* **home free.** Free of tension or stress, usually after expending considerable effort: *closed the deal successfully and was home free.* [ME < OE *hām.*]
home base *n.* **1.** *Baseball.* Home plate. **2.** A base of operations; headquarters. **3.** An objective toward which players of a game, such as baseball or backgammon, progress; home.
home·bod·y (hōm′bŏd′ē) *n. pl.* **-ies.** One whose interests center on the home.
home·bound[1] (hōm′bound′) *adj.* Heading homeward. [HOME + BOUND[4].]
home·bound[2] (hōm′bound′) *adj.* Restricted or confined to home: *homebound invalids.* [HOME + BOUND[3].]
home·bred (hōm′brĕd′) *adj.* Raised, bred, or reared at home; domestic.
home-brew (hōm′br o͞o′) *n.* An alcoholic beverage, esp. beer, that is made at home. **—home′-brewed′** *adj.*
home·com·ing (hōm′kŭm′ĭng) *n.* **1.** A coming to or returning home. **2.** In colleges and universities, an annual event for visiting alumni.
home economics *n.* The science and art of home management. **—home economist** *n.*
home front *n.* The civilian population of a country at war.
home·grown (hōm′grōn′) *adj.* **1.** Made or grown at home. **2.** Originating in or characteristic of a place of origin: *a homegrown singing star.*
home·land (hōm′lănd′) *n.* One's native land.
home·less (hōm′lĭs) *adj.* Having no home or haven.
home·ly (hōm′lē) *adj.* **-li·er, -li·est. 1.** Characteristic of the home or of home life. **2.** Of a simple or unpretentious nature; plain: *homely truths.* **3.** Lacking elegance or refinement. **4.** Not attractive or good-looking. **—home′li·ness** *n.*
home·made (hōm′mād′) *adj.* **1.** Made or prepared in the home: *homemade pie.* **2.** Made by oneself. **3.** Crudely or simply made.
home·mak·er (hōm′mā′kər) *n.* A person who manages a household.
homeo– or **homoio–** *pref.* Like; similar: *homeostasis.* [Lat. *homoeo-* < Gk. *homoio-* < *homoios,* similar < *homos,* same.]
ho·me·o·mor·phism (hō′mē-ə-môr′fĭz′əm) *n.* **1.** *Chem.* A close similarity in the crystal forms of unlike chemical compounds. **2.** *Math.* A one-to-one correspondence between the points of two geometric figures that is continuous in both directions. [HOMEO- + Gk. *morphē,* form + -ISM.] **—ho′me·o·mor′phous** *adj.*
ho·me·op·a·thy (hō′mē-ŏp′ə-thē) *n.* A system of medical treatment based on the use of minute quantities of remedies that in massive doses produce effects similar to those of the disease being treated. [G. *Homöopathie* : *homöo-,* homeo- + *-pathie,* -pathy.] **—ho′me·o·path′** (-ə-păth′), **ho′me·op′a·thist** *n.* **—ho′me·o·path′ic** *adj.* **—ho′me·o·path′i·cal·ly** *adv.*
ho·me·o·sta·sis (hō′mē-ō-stā′sĭs) *n.* A state of physiological equilibrium produced by a balance of functions and of chemical composition within an organism. **—ho′me·o·stat′ic** (-stăt′ĭk) *adj.*
ho·me·o·therm (hō′mē-ə-thûrm′) *n.* Variant of **homoiotherm.**
ho·me·o·ther·mous (hō′mē-ə-thûr′məs) *adj.* Homoiothermic.
home plate *n. Baseball.* A base, usually consisting of a hard rubber slab, at one of the corners of a diamond at which a batter stands when hitting and which a base runner must finally touch in order to score.
hom·er[1] (hō′mər) *n.* **1.** *Baseball.* A home run. **2.** A homing pigeon.
ho·mer[2] (hō′mər) *n.* An ancient Hebrew measure of capacity containing 10 ephahs, or about 10 or 11 bushels, in dry measure, or 10 baths, or about 100 gallons, in liquid measure. [Heb. *ḥomer.*]
Ho·mer·ic (hō-mĕr′ĭk) *adj.* **1.** Of, pertaining to, or characteristic of the poet Homer, his works, or the legends and age of which he wrote. **2.** Heroic in proportion, degree, or character; epic. **—Ho·mer′i·cal·ly** *adv.*
home·room (hōm′ro͞om′, -ro͝om′) *n.* A school classroom to which a group of pupils of the same grade are required to report before morning and afternoon classes.
home rule *n.* The principle or practice of self-government in the internal affairs of a dependent country or other political unit.
home run *n. Baseball.* A hit that allows the batter to make a complete circuit of the diamond and score a run.
home screen *n.* Television.
home·sick (hōm′sĭk′) *adj.* Acutely longing for one's family and home. **—home′sick′ness** *n.*
home·spun (hōm′spŭn′) *adj.* **1.** Spun or woven in the home. **2. a.** Made of a homespun fabric. **b.** Homemade. **3.** Simple and homely in character; unpretentious. —*n.* **1.** A plain coarse woolen cloth made of homespun yarn. **2.** A sturdy fabric similar to homespun made on a power loom.
home·stead (hōm′stĕd′) *n.* **1.** A house, esp. a farmhouse, with adjoining buildings and land. **2.** *Law.* Property designated by a householder as his home and protected by law from forced sale to meet debts. **3.** Land claimed by a settler or a squatter, esp. under the Homestead Act. **4.** The place where one's home is. —*v.* **-stead·ed, -stead·ing, -steads.** —*intr.* To settle and farm land, esp. under the Homestead Act. —*tr.* To claim and settle (land) as a homestead. **—home′stead′er** *n.*
Homestead Act *n.* An act passed by Congress in 1862 promising ownership of a 160-acre tract of public land to a head of a family after he had cleared and improved the land and lived on it for five years.
homestead law *n.* Any of several laws passed in most states exempting a householder's homestead from attachment or forced sale to meet general debts.
home·stretch (hōm′strĕch′) *n.* **1.** The portion of a racetrack from the last turn to the finish line. **2.** The final stages of an undertaking.
home·town (hōm′toun′) *n.* The town or city of one's birth or main residence.
home·ward (hōm′wərd) *adj. & adv.* At or toward home. **—home′wards** (-wərdz) *adv.*
home·work (hōm′wûrk′) *n.* **1.** Work, such as schoolwork or piecework, that is to be done at home. **2.** Work of a preparatory or preliminary nature.
hom·ey also **hom·y** (hō′mē) *adj.* **-i·er, -i·est.** *Informal.* Having a feeling of home; homelike. **—hom′ey·ness** *n.*
hom·i·cid·al (hŏm′ĭ-sīd′l, hō′mĭ-) *adj.* **1.** Of or pertaining to homicide. **2.** Tending to homicide. **—hom′i·cid′al·ly** *adv.*
hom·i·cide (hŏm′ĭ-sīd′, hō′mĭ-) *n.* **1.** The killing of one person by another. **2.** A person who kills another person. [ME < OFr. < Lat. *homicidum* < *homicida,* murderer : *homo,* man + *caedere,* to kill.]
hom·i·let·ic (hŏm′ə-lĕt′ĭk) also **hom·i·let·i·cal** (-ĭ-kəl) *adj.* **1.** Pertaining to or of the nature of a homily. **2.** Pertaining to homiletics. **—hom′i·let′i·cal·ly** *adv.*
hom·i·let·ics (hŏm′ə-lĕt′ĭks) *n. (used with a sing. verb).* The art of preaching. [Gk. *homilētikē,* art of conversation < *homilētikos,* of conversation < *homilētos,* conversation < *homilein,* to converse with < *homilos,* crowd.]
hom·i·ly (hŏm′ə-lē) *n., pl.* **-lies. 1.** A sermon, esp. one intended to edify a congregation on a practical matter. **2.** A tedious moralizing lecture or admonition. [ME *omelie* < OFr. < LLat. *homilia* < Gk., discourse < *homilos,* crowd.] **—hom′i·list** *n.*
homing pigeon *n.* A domestic pigeon trained to return to its home roost.
hom·i·nid (hŏm′ə-nĭd) *n.* A primate of the family Hominidae, of which modern man, *Homo sapiens,* is the only extant

species. —*adj.* Of the Hominidae. [NLat. *Hominidae,* family name : < *Homo,* genus name < Lat. *homo,* man.]

hom·i·noid (hŏm′ə-noid′) *adj.* **1.** Of or belonging to the superfamily Hominoidea, which includes the apes and man. **2.** Resembling a human being; manlike. —*n.* A member of the Hominoidea. [NLat. *Hominoidea,* superfamily name < *Homo,* genus name < Lat. *homo,* man.]

hom·i·ny (hŏm′ə-nē) *n.* Hulled and dried kernels of corn, prepared as food by boiling. [Perh. of Algonquian orig.]

hominy grits *pl.n.* Hominy ground into a coarse white meal.

hom·mos (hŭm′əs, hŏm′-) *n.* Variant of **hummus.**

ho·mo[1] (hō′mō) *n.* A member of the genus *Homo,* which includes the extinct and extant species of man. [NLat. *Homo,* genus name < Lat. *homo,* man.]

ho·mo[2] (hō′mō) *n., pl.* **-mos.** *Slang.* A homosexual.

homo– or **hom–** *pref.* Same; like: *homophone.* [Lat. < Gk. < *homos,* same.]

ho·mo·cen·tric (hō′mə-sĕn′trĭk, hŏm′ə-) *adj.* Having the same center. [NLat. *homocentricus* : Gk. *homos,* same + Gk. *kentron,* center.]

ho·mo·cer·cal (hō′mə-sûr′kəl, hŏm′ə-) *adj.* Pertaining to, designating, or characterized by a tail fin having two symmetrical lobes extending from the end of the vertebral column, as in most bony fishes. [HOMO- + Gk. *kerkos,* tail + -AL.]

ho·mo·chro·mat·ic (hō′mə-krō-măt′ĭk, hŏm′ə-) *adj.* Of or characterized by one color; monochromatic. **—ho′mo·chro′ma·tism** (-krō′mə-tĭz′əm) *n.*

ho·mo·e·rot·i·cism (hō′mō-ĭ-rŏt′ĭ-sĭz′əm) also **ho·mo·er·o·tism** (-ĕr′ə-tĭz′əm) *n.* Sexual attraction for one's own sex; homosexuality. **—ho′mo·e·rot′ic** (-ĭ-rŏt′ĭk) *adj.*

ho·mog·a·mous (hō-mŏg′ə-məs) *adj. Bot.* **1.** Having flowers that are sexually alike in the same plant or inflorescence. **2.** Having stamens and pistils that mature simultaneously.

ho·mo·ge·ne·i·ty (hō′mə-jə-nē′ĭ-tē, -nā′-, hŏm′ə-) *n.* The state or quality of being homogeneous.

ho·mo·ge·ne·ous (hō′mə-jē′nē-əs, -jēn′yəs) *adj.* **1.** Of the same or similar nature or kind: *an intellectually homogeneous class.* **2.** Uniform in structure or composition throughout. **3.** *Math.* Consisting of terms of the same degree or elements of the same dimension. [Med. Lat. *homogeneus* < Gk. *homogenēs* : *homos,* same + *genos,* kind.] **—ho′mo·ge′ne·ous·ly** *adv.* **—ho′mo·ge′ne·ous·ness** *n.*

ho·mog·e·nize (hō-mŏj′ə-nīz′, hə-) *tr.v.* **-nized, -niz·ing, -niz·es. 1.** To make homogeneous. **2. a.** To reduce to particles and disperse throughout a fluid. **b.** To make uniform in consistency, esp. to render (milk) uniform in consistency by emulsifying the fat content. [< HOMOGENEOUS.] **—ho·mog′e·ni·za′tion** *n.* **—ho·mog′e·niz′er** *n.*

ho·mog·e·nous (hō-mŏj′ə-nəs, hə-) *adj.* **1.** *Biol.* Of or exhibiting homogeny. **2.** Homogeneous.

ho·mog·e·ny (hō-mŏj′ə-nē, hə-) *n. Biol.* Correspondence between organs or parts, possibly of dissimilar function, related by common descent. [Gk. *homogenia,* homogeneity < *homogenēs,* homogeneous.]

ho·mo·graft (hō′mə-grăft′, hŏm′ə-) *n.* A graft of tissue obtained from a member of the same species as the individual receiving it.

hom·o·graph (hŏm′ə-grăf′, hō′mə-) *n.* One of two or more words that have the same spelling but differ in origin, meaning, and sometimes pronunciation. **—hom′o·graph′ic** *adj.*

homoio– *pref.* Variant of **homeo-.**

ho·moi·o·therm (hō-moi′ə-thûrm′) also **ho·me·o·therm** (hō′mē-ə-thûrm′) *n.* A homoiothermous organism, such as a bird or mammal.

ho·moi·o·ther·mic (hō-moi′ə-thûr′mĭk) or **ho·moi·o·ther·mal** (-məl) also **ho·moi·o·ther·mous** (-məs) *adj.* Maintaining a relatively constant and warm body temperature that is independent of environmental temperature; warm-blooded.

Ho·moi·ou·si·an (hō′moi-o͞o′zē-ən, -sē-) *n.* A member of an Arian party in the fourth century that held that Jesus the Son and God the Father were of similar but not of the same substance. [< Gk. *homoiousios,* of similar substance : *homoios,* similar + *ousia,* substance.]

ho·mol·o·gate (hō-mŏl′ə-gāt′, hə-) *tr.v.* **-gat·ed, -gat·ing, -gates.** *Scot.* To approve, esp. to confirm officially. [Med. Lat. *homologare, homologat-* < Gk. *homologein,* to agree < *homologos,* agreeing. —see HOMOLOGOUS.]

ho·mo·log·i·cal (hō′mə-lŏj′ĭ-kəl, hŏm′ə-) also **ho·mo·log·ic** (-lŏj′ĭk) *adj.* Homologous. **—ho′mo·log′i·cal·ly** *adv.*

ho·mol·o·gize (hō-mŏl′ə-jīz′, hə-) *tr.v.* **-gized, -giz·ing, -giz·es. 1.** To make homologous. **2.** To show to be homologous. **—ho·mol′o·giz′er** *n.*

ho·mol·o·gous (hō-mŏl′ə-gəs, hə-) *adj.* **1.** Corresponding or similar in position, value, structure, or function. **2.** *Biol.* Corresponding in structure and evolutionary origin, as the flippers of a seal and the arms of a human being. **3.** *Genetics.* Having the same linear sequence of genes as another chromosome. **4.** *Chem.* Belonging to or being a series of organic compounds each successive member of which differs from the preceding member by a constant increment, esp. by an added CH_2 group. [Gk. *homologos,* agreeing : *homos,* same + *logos,* proportion.]

hom·o·lo·graph·ic (hŏm′ə-lə-grăf′ĭk) *adj.* Maintaining the ratio of parts. [Gk. *homalos,* even + GRAPHIC.]

homolographic projection *n.* An equal-area projection reproducing the ratios of areas as they exist on the earth's surface.

hom·o·logue also **hom·o·log** (hŏm′ə-lôg′, -lŏg′, hō′mə-) *n.* Something homologous; a homologous organ or part.

ho·mol·o·gy (hō-mŏl′ə-jē, hə-) *n., pl.* **-gies. 1.** The quality or condition of being homologous. **2.** A homologous relationship or correspondence. **3.** *Math.* A topologic classification of configurations into distinct types that imposes an algebraic structure or hierarchy on families of geometric figures. [Gk. *homologia,* agreement < *homologos,* agreeing. —see HOMOLOGOUS.]

ho·mol·o·sine projection (hō-mŏl′ə-sīn′) *n.* An equal-area map of the earth's surface laid out on the basis of sinusoidal curves, with the interruptions over ocean areas so that the continents may appear with minimal distortion. [Gk. *homalos,* even + -INE.]

ho·mo·mor·phism (hō′mə-môr′fĭz′əm, hŏm′ə-) *n.* Similarity of external form, appearance, or size. **—ho′mo·mor′phic, ho′mo·mor′phous** *adj.*

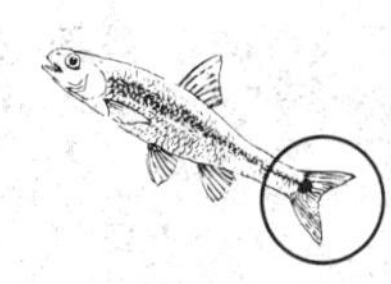

homocercal
Homocercal tail fin of spotted shiner

hom·o·nym (hŏm′ə-nĭm′, hō′mə-) *n.* **1.** One of two or more words that have the same sound and often the same spelling but differ in meaning. **2. a.** A word that is used to designate several different things. **b.** A namesake. **3.** *Biol.* One of two or more identical but conflicting taxonomic designations independently proposed for members of different categories. [Lat. *homonymum* < Gk. *homōnumon* < *homōnumos,* homonymous.] **—hom′o·nym′ic** *adj.*

ho·mon·y·mous (hō-mŏn′ə-məs) *adj.* **1.** Having the same name. **2.** Of the nature of a homonym; homonymic. [Lat. *homonymus* < Gk. *homōnumos* : *homos,* same + *onoma,* name.] **—ho·mon′y·mous·ly** *adv.*

ho·mon·y·my (hō-mŏn′ə-mē) *n.* The quality or condition of being homonymous.

Ho·mo·ou·si·an (hō′mō-o͞o′sē-ən, -zē-, hŏm′ō-) *n.* A Christian supporting the Council of Nicaea's Trinitarian definition of Jesus the Son of God as consubstantial with God the Father. [LLat. *homousianus* < *homousius,* of same substance < Gk. *homoousios* : *homos,* same + *ousia,* substance.]

ho·mo·phile (hō′mə-fīl′) *adj.* **1.** Homosexual. **2.** Being actively concerned with the rights and welfare of homosexuals. **—ho′mo·phile′** *n.*

ho·mo·pho·bi·a (hō′mə-fō′bē-ə) *n.* Fear of homosexuals or homosexuality. **—ho′mo·pho′bic** (-fō′bĭk) *adj.*

hom·o·phone (hŏm′ə-fōn′, hō′mə-) *n.* One of two or more words that have the same sound but differ in spelling, origin, and meaning. **—ho·moph′o·nous** (hō-mŏf′ə-nəs) *adj.*

hom·o·phon·ic (hŏm′ə-fŏn′ĭk, hō′mə-) *adj.* **1.** Having the same sound. **2.** *Mus.* Having or characterized by a single melodic line with accompaniment. [Gk. *homophōnos* : *homos,* same + *phōnē,* sound.]

ho·moph·o·ny (hō-mŏf′ə-nē) *n.* **1.** The quality or condition of being homophonic. **2.** Homophonic music.

ho·mo·phy·ly (hō′mə-fī′lē, hŏm′ə-, hō-mŏf′ə-lē) *n.* Resemblance arising from common ancestry. [HOMO- + PHYL(UM) + -Y.] **—ho′mo·phyl′ic** (-fĭl′ĭk) *adj.*

ho·mo·plas·tic (hō′mə-plăs′tĭk, hŏm′ə-) *adj.* **1.** Of, pertaining to, or exhibiting homoplasy. **2.** Of, pertaining to, or derived from a different individual of the same species: *a homoplastic graft.* **—ho′mo·plas′ti·cal·ly** *adv.*

ho·mo·pla·sy (hō′mə-plā′sē, -plăs′ē, hŏm′ə-) *n.* Superficial structural similarity arising from convergence or parallel evolution.

ho·mop·ter·an (hō-mŏp′tər-ən) *n.* A homopterous insect. —*adj.* Of or belonging to the order Homoptera; homopterous. [NLat. *Homoptera,* order name : Gk. *homos,* same + Gk. *pteron,* wing.]

ho·mop·ter·ous (hō-mŏp′tər-əs) *adj.* Of or belonging to the order Homoptera, which includes insects such as the cicadas, aphids, and scale insects. [< NLat. *Homoptera,* order name. —see HOMOPTERAN.]

Ho·mo sa·pi·ens (hō′mō sā′pē-ənz, -ĕnz′) *n.* Modern man, the only extant species of the genus *Homo.* [NLat. *Homo sapiens,* specific name : *Homo,* genus name (< Lat. *homo,* man) + Lat. *sapiens,* pr.part. of *sapere,* to be wise.]

ho·mo·sex (hō′mə-sĕks′) *n.* Homosexuality.

ho·mo·sex·u·al (hō′mō-sĕk′sho͞o-əl) *adj.* Pertaining to, characteristic of, or exhibiting homosexuality. —*n.* A homosexual person.

ho·mo·sex·u·al·i·ty (hō′mō-sĕk′sho͞o-ăl′ĭ-tē) *n.* **1.** Sexual desire for others of one's own sex. **2.** Sexual activity with another of the same sex.

ho·mo·spo·rous (hō′mə-spôr′əs, -spōr′-, hŏm′ə-, hō-mŏs′pər-əs) *adj. Bot.* Producing spores of one kind only. **—ho′mo·spo′ry** *n.*

ho·mo·tax·is (hō′mō-tăk′sĭs, hŏm′ō-) *n.* Similarity of arrangement and fossils in noncontemporaneous or widely separated geologic deposits. **—ho′mo·tax′ic** (-tăk′sĭk), **ho′mo·tax′i·al** (-tăk′sē-əl) *adj.*

ho·mo·thal·lic (hō′mō-thăl′ĭk, hŏm′ō-) *adj. Bot.* Having male and female reproductive structures in the same thallus, as in some fungi and algae.

ho·mo·zy·go·sis (hō′mō-zī-gō′sĭs, hŏm′ō-) *n.* The union of genetically identical gametes, resulting in the formation of a homozygote. **—ho′mo·zy·got′ic** (-gŏt′ĭk) *adj.*

ho·mo·zy·gote (hō′mō-zī′gōt′, hŏm′ō-) *n.* A zygote derived from the union of genetically identical gametes.

ho·mo·zy·gous (hō′mō-zī′gəs, hŏm′ō-) *adj.* Having identical alleles at corresponding chromosomal loci. **—ho′mo·zy′gous·ly** *adv.*

ho·mun·cu·lus (hō-mŭng′kyə-ləs) *n., pl.* **-li** (-lī′). A diminutive man; manikin. [Lat., dim. of *homo,* man.]

hom·y (hō′mē) *adj.* Variant of **homey.**

ho·nan also **Ho·nan** (hō′năn′) *n.* A pongee fabric of even color made originally from silk produced by the silkworms of Honan.

hon·cho (hŏn′chō) *Slang.* —*n., pl.* **-chos.** One who is in charge; manager or leader: *"Some of the big-name honchos . . . featured in the glossy . . . magazines"* (New Yorker). —*tr.v.* **-choed, -cho·ing, -chos.** To direct and manage (personnel and projects): *"He . . . is honchoing preparations for the forthcoming . . . economic summit"* (Newsweek). [J., squad leader : *han,* squad + *chō,* chief.]

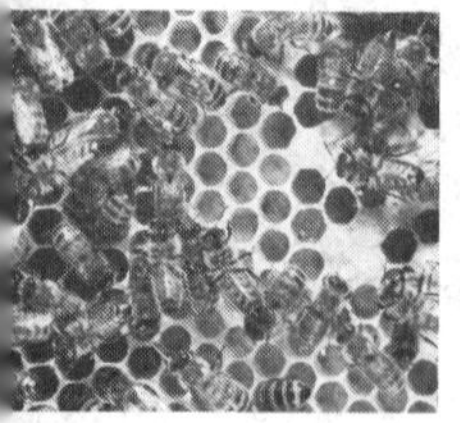

honeycomb

hone[1] (hōn) *n.* **1.** A fine-grained whetstone for giving a keen edge to a cutting tool. **2.** A tool with a rotating abrasive tip for enlarging holes to precise dimensions. —*tr.v.* **honed, hon·ing, hones. 1.** To sharpen on a hone. **2.** To perfect or make more intense or effective: *hone a writing style.* [ME < OE *hān.*]

hone[2] (hōn) *intr.v.* **honed, hon·ing, hones.** *Informal.* **1.** To whine or moan. **2.** To hanker; yearn. [OFr. *hoigner* < *hon,* cry of discontent.]

hon·est (ŏn′ĭst) *adj.* **1.** Marked by or displaying truthfulness and integrity; upright. **2.** Not deceptive or fraudulent; genuine: *honest weight.* **3.** Equitable; fair: *honest wages for an honest day's work.* **4. a.** Characterized by integrity and truth; not false: *honest reporting.* **b.** Sincere; frank: *an honest critique.* **5. a.** Of good repute; respectable. **b.** Without affectation; plain: *honest folk.* **6.** Virtuous; chaste. [ME < OFr. *honeste* < Lat. *honestus* < *honos,* honor.] **—hon′est·ly** *adv.*

honest broker *n.* A neutral agent, as in mediation.

hon·es·ty (ŏn′ĭ-stē) *n., pl.* **-ties. 1.** The quality or condition of being honest; integrity. **2.** Truthfulness; sincerity: *in all honesty.* **3.** *Archaic.* Chastity. **4.** A plant, *Lunaria annua,* native to Eurasia, cultivated for its fragrant purplish flowers and round, flat, papery, silver-white seed pods.

Synonyms: *honesty, veracity, honor, integrity, probity.* These nouns denote qualities closely associated with moral excellence. *Honesty* implies truthfulness, fairness in dealing, and absence of fraud, deceit, and dissembling. *Veracity* is truthfulness in expression. *Honor* implies close adherence to a strict moral or ethical code. *Integrity* is moral soundness, especially as it is revealed in dealings that test steadfastness to truth, purpose, responsibility, or trust. *Probity* is proven integrity.

hone·wort (hōn′wûrt′, -wôrt′) *n.* Any of several plants of the genus *Cryptotaenia,* esp. *C. canadensis,* of eastern North America, having clusters of small whitish flowers. [*Hone-* (of unknown orig.) + WORT.]

George Miksch Sutton

honeyeater

hon·ey (hŭn′ē) *n., pl.* **-eys. 1. a.** A sweet yellowish or brownish viscid fluid produced by various bees from the nectar of flowers and used as food. **b.** A similar substance made by certain other insects. **2.** Sweetness; pleasantness. **3.** *Informal.* Sweetheart; dear. Used as a term of endearment. **4.** *Informal.* Something remarkably fine: *a honey of a car.* —*tr.v.* **-eyed** or **-ied, -ey·ing, -eys. 1.** To sweeten with or as if with honey. **2.** To cajole with sweet talk. [ME *honi* < OE *hunig.*]

honey bear *n.* The kinkajou.

hon·ey·bee (hŭn′ē-bē′) *n.* Any of several social bees of the genus *Apis* that produce honey, esp. *A. mellifera,* widely domesticated as a source of honey and beeswax.

hon·ey·comb (hŭn′ē-kōm′) *n.* **1.** A structure of hexagonal, thin-walled cells constructed from beeswax by honeybees to hold honey and eggs. **2.** Something resembling a honeycomb in structure or pattern. —*tr.v.* **-combed, -comb·ing, -combs. 1.** To fill with holes; riddle: *Her alibi was honeycombed with lies.* **2.** To form in or cover with a honeycomb pattern.

George Miksch Sutton

honey guide

hon·ey·creep·er (hŭn′ē-krē′pər) *n.* **1.** Any of various small, often brightly colored tropical American birds of the subfamily Dacninae, having a curved bill adapted for sucking nectar from flowers. **2.** Any of several birds of the family Drepanididae, of Hawaii, that are similar to the honeycreepers.

hon·ey·dew (hŭn′ē-do͞o′, -dyo͞o′) *n.* **1.** A sweet, sticky substance excreted by various insects, esp. aphids, on the leaves of plants. **2.** A sweet exudate similar to honeydew on the leaves of plants. **3.** A honeydew melon.

honeydew melon *n.* A melon, a variety of *Cucumis melo,* having a smooth, whitish rind and green flesh.

hon·ey·eat·er (hŭn′ē-ē′tər) *n.* Any of various birds of the family Meliphagidae, of Australia and adjacent regions, having a long, extensible tongue adapted for sucking nectar from flowers.

honeysuckle

hon·eyed also **hon·ied** (hŭn′ēd) *adj.* **1.** Containing, full of, or sweetened with honey. **2.** Ingratiating; sugary: *honeyed words.* **3.** Sweet; dulcet: *a honeyed voice.*

honey guide *n.* Any of various tropical Old World birds of the family Indicatoridae, some species of which lead animals or people to the nests of wild honeybees, where they eat the wax that remains after the honey has been removed.

honey locust *n.* Mesquite.

hon·ey·moon (hŭn′ē-mo͞on′) *n.* **1.** A holiday or trip taken by a newly married couple. **2.** The early harmonious period of a relationship. —*intr.v.* **-mooned, -moon·ing, -moons.** To spend a honeymoon. [From the notion that the first month of marriage is sweet.] **—hon′ey·moon′er** *n.*

hon·ey·suck·le (hŭn′ē-sŭk′əl) *n.* **1.** Any of various shrubs or vines of the genus *Lonicera,* having tubular, often very fragrant yellowish, white, or pink flowers. **2.** Any of various plants similar or related to the honeysuckle. [ME *honisouke* < OE *hunisūce* : *hunig,* honey + *sūcan,* to suck.]

hong (hông, hŏng) *n.* A factory, warehouse, or foreign trading house in China. [Cantonese, a business establishment.]

hon·ied (hŭn′ēd) *adj.* Variant of **honeyed.**

honk (hôngk, hŏngk) *n.* **1.** The raucous, resonant sound characteristic of a wild goose. **2.** A sound similar to a goose's honk. —*v.* **honked, honk·ing, honks.** —*intr.* To emit a honk. —*tr.* To cause (a horn) to produce a honk. [Imit.] **—honk′er** *n.*

hon·ky or **hon·kie** (hông′kē, hŏng′-) *n., pl.* **-kies.** *Offensive Slang.* A white person. [Orig. unknown.]

hon·ky-tonk (hŏng′kē-tŏngk′, hŏng′kē-tŏngk′) *n. Slang.* A cheap, noisy bar or dance hall. —*adj. Mus.* Of or designating a type of ragtime usually played on a tinny old piano. —*intr.v.* **-tonked, -tonk·ing, -tonks.** *Slang.* To make the rounds of cheap, noisy bars or dance halls. [Orig. unknown.]

hon·or (ŏn′ər) *n.* **1.** Special esteem or respect; reverence: *the honor shown to him.* **2. a.** Reputation; good name. **b.** A source or cause of credit: *was an honor to the profession.* **3. a.** Glory or recognition; distinction. **b.** A mark, token, or gesture of respect or distinction: *the place of honor at the table.* **c.** A military decoration. **d.** A title conferred for achievement, as a knighthood. **4.** Nobility of mind; probity. **5.** High rank. **6.** The dignity accorded to position: *awed by the honor of his office.* **7.** Great privilege: *I have the honor to present the governor.* **8. Honor.** A title of address often accorded to mayors and judges: *Your Honor.* **9. a.** A code of principally male dignity, integrity, and pride, maintained in some societies, as in feudal Europe, by force of arms. **b.** Personal integrity maintained without legal or other obligation. **c.** A woman's chastity or reputation for chastity. **10. honors.** Social courtesies offered to guests: *did the honors at tea.* **11. honors. a.** Special recognition for unusual academic achievement: *graduate with honors.* **b.** A program of individual advanced study for exceptional students. **12.** The right of being first at the tee in golf. **13.** Often **honors.** The four or five highest cards in trump or in all suits, esp. in bridge. —*tr.v.* **-ored, -or·ing, -ors. 1. a.** To hold in respect; esteem. **b.** To show respect for. **2.** To confer distinction upon: *honored us with his presence.* **3.** To accept or pay (a check, for example) as valid. [ME < OFr. < Lat.] **—hon′or·er** *n.*

Synonyms: *honor, homage, reverence, veneration, deference.* These nouns refer to the feeling or expression of admiration, respect, or esteem. *Honor,* the most general term, is applicable both to the feeling and to the expression. *Homage* is an expression of high regard, often a ceremonial tribute that conveys allegiance or professional respect. *Reverence* is a feeling of deep respect and devotion. *Veneration* is both the feeling and worshipful expression of respect, love, and awe, especially for one whose wisdom, dignity, sacredness, rank, or age merits such attention. *Deference* is respect or courteous regard for one that takes the form of yielding to his judgment or wishes.

hon·or·a·ble (ŏn′ər-ə-bəl) *adj.* **1.** Deserving or winning honor and respect. **2.** Bringing distinction or recognition: *honorable service.* **3.** Possessing and characterized by honor: *an honorable man.* **4.** Consistent with honor or good name: *the only honorable course.* **5.** Distinguished; illustrious: *an honorable gathering.* **6.** Attended by marks of recognition and honor: *an honorable burial.* **7. Honorable. a.** Used as a title of respect for certain high officials. **b. Honorable.** *Chiefly Brit.* Used as a courtesy title of the children of barons and viscounts and the younger sons of earls. **—hon′or·a·ble·ness** *n.* **—hon′or·a·bly** *adv.*

honorable mention *n.* A citation to one who has performed well in a competition but has not been awarded a prize.

hon·o·rar·i·um (ŏn′ə-râr′ē-əm) *n., pl.* **-i·ums** or **-i·a** (-ē-ə). A payment given to a professional person for services for which fees are not legally or traditionally required. [Lat. < *honorarius,* honorary.]

hon·or·ar·y (ŏn′ə-rĕr′ē) *adj.* **1.** Held or given as a mark of honor, esp. conferred as an honor without the usual adjuncts: *an honorary degree.* **2. a.** Holding an office or title given as an honor, without payment: *the honorary secretary of the association.* **b.** Voluntary. **3.** Relying upon honor; not legally enforceable, as a duty or obligation. [Lat. *honorarius* < *honor,* honor.]

hon·or·ee (ŏn′ə-rē′) *n.* One who receives an honor.

hon·or·if·ic (ŏn′ə-rĭf′ĭk) *adj.* Conferring or showing respect or honor. —*n.* A title, phrase, or grammatical form conveying respect, used esp. when addressing a social superior. [Lat. *honorificus* : *honor,* honor + *-ficus,* -fic.] **—hon′or·if′i·cal·ly** *adv.*

honors of war *pl.n.* Certain courtesies granted a surrendering foe, as the privilege of marching out bearing arms and colors.

hon·our (ŏn′ər) *n. & v. Chiefly Brit.* Variant of **honor.**

hooch¹ also **hootch** (ho͞och) *n. Slang.* **1.** Alcoholic liquor, esp. inferior or bootleg liquor. **2.** Marijuana. [Short for *hoochino,* after *Hoochino,* an Alaskan tribe that made a kind of distilled liquor.]
hooch² (ho͞och) *n. Slang.* A dwelling, esp. a thatched hut. [Alteration of J. *uchi,* house.]
hood¹ (ho͝od) *n.* **1.** A loose pliable covering for the head and neck, either attached to a robe or jacket or separate. **2.** An ornamental draping of cloth hung from the shoulders of an academic or ecclesiastical robe. **3.** A sack used to cover a falcon's head to keep it quiet. **4.** Something resembling a hood in shape or function, as: **a.** A metal cover or cowl for a hearth or stove. **b.** A carriage top. **c.** The hinged metal lid over an automobile engine. **d.** An expanded part, crest, or marking on or near the head of an animal. *—tr.v.* **hood·ed, hood·ing, hoods.** To supply or cover with a hood. [ME *hod* < OE *hōd.*]
hood² (ho͞od) *n. Slang.* **1.** A hoodlum; thug. **2.** A tough-looking youth. [Short for HOODLUM.]
-hood *suff.* **1. a.** Condition; state; quality: *manhood.* **b.** An instance of a specified state or quality: *falsehood.* **2.** A group sharing a specified state or quality: *sisterhood.* [ME *-hode* < OE *-hād.*]
hood·ed (ho͝od'ĭd) *adj.* **1.** Covered with or having a hood. **2.** Shaped like a hood, cowl, or similar covering. **3.** *Zool.* Having a crest, coloration, or skin formation suggesting a hood.
hooded seal *n.* A seal, *Cystophora cristata,* of northern seas, having a grayish, spotted coat and an inflatable hoodlike or bladderlike pouch in the region of the nose.
hood·lum (ho͞od'ləm, ho͝od'-) *n.* **1.** A gangster; thug. **2.** A tough, destructive young man. [Orig. unknown.] **—hood'lum·ism** *n.*
hoo·doo (ho͞o'do͞o) *n., pl.* **-doos. 1.** Voodoo. **2. a.** Bad luck. **b.** One that brings bad luck. *—tr.v.* **-dooed, -doo·ing, -doos.** To bring bad luck to. [Of African orig.] **—hoo'doo·ism** *n.*
hood·wink (ho͝od'wĭngk') *tr.v.* **-winked, -wink·ing, -winks. 1.** To deceive; trick. **2.** *Archaic.* To blindfold. **3.** *Obs.* To conceal. **—hood'wink'er** *n.*
hoo·ey (ho͞o'ē) *n. Slang.* Nonsense. [Orig. unknown.]
hoof (ho͝of, ho͞of) *n., pl.* **hoofs** or **hooves** (ho͞ovz, ho͝ovz). **1. a.** The horny sheath covering the toes or lower part of the foot of a mammal of the orders Perissodactyla and Artiodactyla, such as a horse, ox, or deer. **b.** The foot of such an animal, esp. a horse. **2.** *Slang.* The human foot. *—v.* **hoofed, hoof·ing, hoofs.** *—tr.* **1.** To trample with the hoofs. **2.** *Informal.* To walk. *—intr. Slang.* **1.** To dance. **2.** To go on foot; walk. ***—idiom.*** **on the hoof.** Alive; not yet butchered. Used esp. of cattle. [ME *hof* < OE *hōf.*]
hoof-and-mouth disease (ho͝of'ən-mouth', ho͞of'-) *n.* Foot-and-mouth disease.
hoof·bound (ho͝of'bound', ho͞of'-) *adj.* Afflicted with drying and contraction of the hoof, resulting in lameness. Used of a horse.
hoofed (ho͝oft, ho͞oft) *adj.* Having hoofs; ungulate.
hoof·er (ho͝of'ər, ho͞o'fər) *n. Slang.* A professional dancer, esp. a tap dancer.
hook (ho͝ok) *n.* **1.** A curved or sharply bent device, usually of metal, used to catch, drag, suspend, or fasten something. **2.** A fishhook. **3.** A catch; snag. **4.** Something shaped like a hook, esp.: **a.** A curved or barbed plant or animal part. **b.** A short angled or curved line on a letter. **c.** In surfing, the lip of a breaking wave. **d.** A sickle. **5.** *Baseball.* A curve ball. **6.** A short swinging blow in boxing delivered with a crooked arm. **7.** A golf stroke that sends the ball to the left of the player. *—v.* **hooked, hook·ing, hooks.** *—tr.* **1. a.** To catch or connect with or as if with a hook. **b.** *Informal.* To snare. **c.** *Informal.* To please and make a fan of. **d.** *Slang.* To cause to become addicted. **e.** *Slang.* To steal; snatch. **2.** To fasten by means of a hook. **3.** To pierce or gore as if with a hook. **4.** To make (a rug) by looping yarn through canvas with a type of crochet hook. **5.** *Baseball.* To pitch (a ball) with a curve. **6.** To hit with a hook in boxing. **7.** To hit (a golfball) in a hook. *—intr.* **1.** To bend like a hook. **2.** To fasten by means of a hook or a hook and eye. ***—phrasal verb.*** **hook up. 1.** To assemble or wire (a mechanism). **2.** To connect a mechanism and a source of power. **3.** *Slang.* To form a tie or connection. ***—idioms.*** **by hook or (by) crook.** By whatever means possible, fair or unfair. **get the hook.** *Slang.* To be dismissed or thrown out. **hook, line, and sinker.** *Slang.* Without reservation; completely. **off the hook. 1.** *Slang.* Freed, as from blame or a vexatious obligation. **2.** Left off the cradle. Used of a telephone receiver. **on (one's) own hook.** *Informal.* By one's own efforts. [ME *hok* < OE *hōc.*]
hook·ah (ho͝ok'ə) *n.* An Eastern smoking pipe designed with a long tube passing through an urn of water that cools the smoke as it is drawn through. [Urdu < Ar. *ḥuqqah,* the hookah's water urn.]
hook and eye *n.* A clothes fastener consisting of a small blunt metal hook with a corresponding loop.
hook-and-lad·der truck (ho͝ok'ən-lăd'ər) *n.* A fire engine equipped with extension ladders and hooked poles.
hooked (ho͝okt) *adj.* **1.** Bent or angled like a hook. **2.** Having a hook. **3.** Made by hooking yarn. **4.** *Slang.* **a.** Addicted to a narcotic. **b.** Entrapped by a custom or thing. **—hook'ed·ness** (ho͝ok'ĭd-nĭs) *n.*
hook·er¹ (ho͝ok'ər) *n.* **1.** A single-masted fishing smack used off the coast of Ireland. **2.** An old worn-out or clumsy ship. [Du., alteration of MDu. *hoeckboot* : *hoec,* fishhook + *boat,* boat.]
hook·er² (ho͝ok'ər) *n.* **1.** One that hooks. **2.** *Slang.* A prostitute.
hook·nose (ho͝ok'nōz') *n.* An aquiline nose. **—hook'nosed'** *adj.*
hook shot *n. Basketball.* A shot made by arcing the far hand upward while being positioned or moving sideways to the basket.
hook·up (ho͝ok'ŭp') *n.* **1.** A system of electric circuits and electrically powered equipment designed to operate together. **2. a.** A configuration of mechanical parts or devices acting as an integrated unit. **b.** A plan or schematic drawing of such a system or such a configuration. **3.** *Informal.* A connection, often between unlikely associates or factors.
hook·worm (ho͝ok'wûrm') *n.* Any of numerous small, parasitic nematode worms of the family Ancylostomatidae, having hooked mouth parts with which they fasten themselves to the intestinal walls of various hosts, including man, causing the disease ancylostomiasis.
hookworm disease *n.* Ancylostomiasis.
hook·y (ho͝ok'ē) *n. Informal.* Absence without leave; truancy: *play hooky.* [Orig. unknown.]
hoo·li·gan (ho͞o'lĭ-gən) *n. Informal.* A young ruffian; hoodlum. [Orig. unknown.] **—hoo'li·gan·ism** *n.*
hoop (ho͞op, ho͝op) *n.* **1.** A circular band of metal or wood put around a cask or barrel to bind the staves together. **2.** A large wooden, plastic, or metal ring used as a plaything. **3.** One of the lightweight circular supports for a hoop skirt. **4.** A circular, ringlike earring. **5.** One of a pair of circular wooden or metal frames used to hold material taut for embroidery or similar needlework. **6.** *Basketball. Informal.* **a.** The basket. **b.** The game of basketball. **7.** A croquet wicket. *—tr.v.* **hooped, hoop·ing, hoops. 1.** To hold together or support with or as if with a hoop. **2.** To encircle. [ME *hop.*]
hoop·er (ho͞o'pər, ho͝op'ər) *n.* A cooper.
hoop·la (ho͞op'lä', ho͝op'-) *n. Slang.* **1.** Boisterous jovial commotion or excitement. **2.** Talk intended to mislead or confuse. [Fr. *houp-là,* oops!]
hoo·poe (ho͞o'po͞o, -pō) *n.* An Old World bird, *Upupa epops,* having distinctively patterned plumage, a fanlike crest, and a slender, downward-curving bill. [Alteration of obs. *hoop* < OFr. *huppe* < Lat. *upupa.*]
hoop skirt *n.* A long full skirt belled out with a series of connected hoops.
hoop snake *n.* Any of several snakes, such as the mud snake, that supposedly grasp the tail in the mouth and move with a rolling, hooplike motion.
hoo·ray (ho͞o-rā') *interj., n., & v.* Variant of **hurrah.**
hoose·gow (ho͞os'gou') *n. Slang.* A jail. [Sp. *juzgado,* courtroom < p.part. of *juzgar,* to judge < Lat. *judicare* < *judex,* judge.]
Hoo·sier (ho͞o'zhər) *n.* A nickname for a native or resident of Indiana. [Orig. unknown.]
hoot¹ (ho͞ot) *v.* **hoot·ed, hoot·ing, hoots.** *—intr.* **1.** To utter the characteristic cry of an owl. **2.** To make a loud raucous cry, esp. of derision or contempt. *—tr.* **1.** To shout down or drive off with jeering cries: *hoot a speaker off a platform.* **2.** To express or convey by hooting: *hooted their disgust.* *—n.* **1. a.** The characteristic cry of an owl. **b.** A sound suggesting an owl's cry, esp. the sound of an automobile horn. **2.** A cry of scorn or derision. **3.** *Chiefly Brit. Slang.* Someone or something that is hilariously funny. ***—idiom.*** **not give (or care) a hoot.** To be completely indifferent to: *I don't give a hoot what you think.* [ME *houten.*] **—hoot'er** *n.*
hoot² (ho͞ot, o͞ot) also **hoots** (ho͞ots, o͞ots) *interj. Chiefly Scot.* Used to express annoyance or objection.
hootch (ho͞och) *n.* Variant of **hooch¹.**
hoot·en·an·ny (ho͞ot'n-ăn'ē) *n., pl.* **-nies. 1.** An informal performance by folk singers, typically with participation by the audience. **2.** *Informal.* An unidentified or unidentifiable gadget. [Orig. unknown.]
hoot owl *n.* Any of various owls having a hooting cry.
hoots (ho͞ots, o͞ots) *interj. Chiefly Scot.* Variant of **hoot².**
hooves (ho͞ovz, ho͝ovz) *n.* A plural of **hoof.**
hop¹ (hŏp) *v.* **hopped, hop·ping, hops.** *—intr.* **1.** To move with light bounding skips or leaps. **2.** To jump on one foot. **3.** To make a quick trip, esp. in an airplane. *—tr.* **1.** To move over by hopping. **2.** To jump aboard: *hop a freight.* *—n.* **1. a.** A light springy jump or leap, esp. on one foot. **b.** A rebound. **2.** *Informal.* A dance; ball. **3.** A short distance. **4.** A short trip, esp. by air. **5.** A free ride; lift. ***—idiom.*** **hop, skip, and (a) jump.** A short distance. [ME *hoppen* < OE *hoppian.*]
hop² (hŏp) *n.* **1.** Any of several twining vines of the genus *Humulus,* esp. *H. lupulus,* having lobed leaves and green, conelike flowers. **2. hops.** The dried, ripe flowers of the hop plant, containing a bitter, aromatic oil and used in brewing beer. **3.** *Slang.* Opium. *—tr.v.* **hopped, hop·ping, hops.** To flavor with hops. ***—phrasal verb.*** **hop up.** *Slang.* **1.** To increase the power or energy of. **2.** To stimulate with or as if with a narcotic. [ME *hoppe* < MDu.]
hop clover *n.* A clover, *Trifolium agrarium,* or one of a simi-

hookah

George Miksch Sutton
hoopoe

hoop skirt
19th-century woodcut

hop²

horn
Above: (*Left*) Horns of the kudu and (*right*) the springbok
Below: (*Left*) Horns of the mouflon and (*right*) the gnu

George Miksch Sutton
hornbill

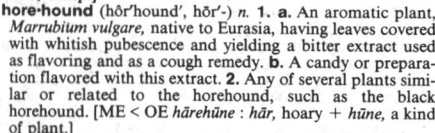

horned toad

hornet

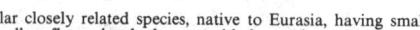

lar closely related species, native to Eurasia, having small yellow flower heads that resemble hops when withered.

hope (hōp) *v.* **hoped, hop·ing, hopes.** —*intr.* **1.** To wish for something with expectation of its fulfillment. **2.** *Archaic.* To have confidence; trust. —*tr.* **1.** To look forward to with confidence or expectation: *hoped his daughter would carry on the tradition.* **2.** To expect and desire. —*n.* **1.** A wish or desire accompanied by confident expectation of its fulfillment. **2.** Something that is hoped for or desired. **3.** One that is a source of or reason for hope: *the team's only hope for victory.* **4.** *Archaic.* Trust; confidence. —**idiom. hope against hope.** To hope with little reason or justification. [ME *hopen* < OE *hopian.*] —**hop'er** *n.*

hope chest *n.* A chest used by a young woman for clothing and household goods, such as linens and silver, in anticipation of marriage.

hope·ful (hōp'fəl) *adj.* **1.** Having or manifesting hope. **2.** Inspiring hope; promising. —*n.* A person who aspires to success or who shows promise of succeeding, esp. as a political candidate. —**hope'ful·ness** *n.*

hope·ful·ly (hōp'fə-lē) *adv.* **1.** In a hopeful manner. **2.** It is to be hoped.

Usage: The use of *hopefully* to mean "it is to be hoped," as in *hopefully we'll get there before dark,* is grammatically justified by analogy to the similar uses of *happily* and *mercifully.* However, this usage is by now such a bugbear to traditionalists that it is best avoided on grounds of civility, if not logic.

hope·less (hōp'lĭs) *adj.* **1.** Having no hope; despairing. **2.** Offering no hope; bleak. **3.** Incurable. **4.** Having no possibility of solution; impossible. —**hope'less·ly** *adv.* —**hope'less·ness** *n.*

hop·head (hŏp'hĕd') *n. Slang.* A drug addict.

hop hornbeam *n.* Any of several trees of the genus *Ostrya,* esp. *O. virginiana,* of eastern North America, having fruit resembling hops.

Ho·pi (hō'pē) *n., pl.* **Hopi** or **-pis. 1.** A tribe of North American Indians now inhabiting a reservation in northeastern Arizona. **2.** A member of the Hopi. **3.** The Uto-Aztecan language of the Hopi. [Hopi *hópi,* peaceful.]

hop·lite (hŏp'līt') *n.* A heavily armed foot soldier of ancient Greece. [Gk. *hoplitēs* < *hoplon,* weapon.] —**hop·lit'ic** (-lĭt'ĭk) *adj.*

hop-o'-my-thumb (hŏp'ə-mī-thŭm') *n.* A tiny person; dwarf. [Alteration of *hop on my thumb.*]

hop·per (hŏp'ər) *n.* **1.** One that hops. **2. a.** A funnel-shaped container in which materials such as grain or fuel are stored in readiness for dispensation. **b.** Any of various other receptacles in which something is held in readiness prior to usage or consideration. **c.** A freight car with a door in the floor through which materials are unloaded.

hop·sack·ing (hŏp'săk'ĭng) also **hop·sack** (-săk') *n.* A loosely woven, coarse fabric of cotton or wool used in clothing. [From its being used for bags by hop growers.]

hop·scotch (hŏp'skŏch') *n.* A children's game in which players toss a small object into the numbered spaces of a pattern of rectangles outlined on the ground and then hop or jump through the spaces to retrieve the object.

ho·ra also **ho·rah** (hôr'ə, hōr'ə) *n.* A traditional round dance of Rumania and Israel. [Heb. *hōrāh* < Rum. *horă.*]

ho·ra·ry (hôr'ə-rē, hōr'-) *adj.* **1.** Of an hour or hours. **2.** Occurring once an hour; hourly. [Med. Lat. *horarius* < Lat. *hora,* hour.]

Ho·ra·tian (hə-rā'shən) *adj.* Of, relating to, or characteristic of the Latin poet Horace or his works.

horde (hôrd, hōrd) *n.* **1.** A large group or crowd; swarm: *a horde of mosquitoes.* **2. a.** A nomadic Mongol tribe. **b.** Any nomadic tribe or group. [OFr. < G. < Pol. *horda* < Turk. *ordū,* camp.]

hore·hound (hôr'hound', hōr'-) *n.* **1. a.** An aromatic plant, *Marrubium vulgare,* native to Eurasia, having leaves covered with whitish pubescence and yielding a bitter extract used as flavoring and as a cough remedy. **b.** A candy or preparation flavored with this extract. **2.** Any of several plants similar or related to the horehound, such as the black horehound. [ME < OE *hārehūne* : *hār,* hoary + *hūne,* a kind of plant.]

ho·ri·zon (hə-rī'zən) *n.* **1.** The apparent intersection of the earth and sky as seen by an observer. **2.** *Astron.* **a.** The circular intersection of a plane tangent to the earth at the observer's station with the celestial sphere. **b.** The intersection with the celestial sphere of a plane through the center of the earth and perpendicular to the line connecting the zenith and the nadir. **c.** The great circle of the celestial sphere at the intersection of the sensible and rational horizons at infinity, its plane passing through the center of the earth. **3.** The range of a person's knowledge, experience, or interest. **4.** *Geol.* **a.** A specific position in a stratigraphic column, as the location of one or more fossils, that serves to identify the stratum with a particular period. **b.** A specific layer of soil in a cross section of land. [ME *orizon* < OFr. *orizonte* < LLat. *horizon* < Gk. *horizōn* (*kuklos*), limiting (circle) < *horizein,* to limit < *horos,* boundary.]

hor·i·zon·tal (hôr'ĭ-zŏn'tl, hŏr'-) *adj.* **1. a.** Of, relating to, or near the horizon. **b.** Parallel to or in the plane of the horizon. **2.** Occupying or restricted to the same level in a hierarchy: *a horizontal study of verbal ability.* —*n.* Something, as a line, plane, or object, that is horizontal. [< LLat. *horizon,* horizon.] —**hor'i·zon'tal·ly** *adv.*

horizontal union *n.* A craft union.

hor·mone (hôr'mōn') *n.* A substance formed by one organ and conveyed, as by the blood stream, to another, which it stimulates to function by means of its chemical activity. [Gk. *hormōn,* pr.part. of *horman,* to urge on < *hormē,* impulse.] —**hor·mon'al** (-mō'nəl), **hor·mon'ic** (-mŏn'ĭk) *adj.* —**hor·mon'al·ly** *adv.*

horn (hôrn) *n.* **1.** One of the hard, usually permanent structures projecting from the head of certain mammals, such as cattle, sheep, goats, or antelopes, consisting of a bony core covered with a sheath of keratinous material. **2.** A hard protuberance, such as an antler or a projection on the head of a giraffe or rhinoceros, that is similar to or suggestive of a horn. **3. a.** The hard, smooth keratinous material forming the outer covering of the horns of cattle or related animals. **b.** A natural or synthetic substance resembling this. **4.** A container made from a horn: *a powder horn.* **5.** Something having the shape of a horn, esp.: **a.** A cornucopia. **b.** Either of the ends of a new moon. **c.** The point of an anvil. **d.** The pommel of a saddle. **e.** An ear trumpet. **f.** A device for projecting sound waves, as in a loudspeaker. **g.** A hollow, metallic electromagnetic transmission antenna with a characteristically rectangular cross section. **6.** *Mus.* **a.** A wind instrument made of an animal horn. **b.** A wind instrument made of brass. **c.** A French horn. **d.** *Informal.* A trumpet. **7.** A signaling device, usually electrical, that produces a sound similar to that of a horn: *a fog horn.* **8.** *Slang.* A telephone. —*v.* **horned, horn·ing, horns. —horn in.** *Slang.* To join without being invited; intrude. —*adj.* Made of horn. —**idioms. blow** (or **toot**) **(one's) own horn.** To brag or boast about oneself. **on the horns of a dilemma.** Faced with two equally undesirable alternatives. [ME < OE.]

horn·beam (hôrn'bēm') *n.* **1.** Any of various trees of the genus *Carpinus,* having smooth, grayish bark and hard, whitish wood. **2.** The wood of a hornbeam.

horn·bill (hôrn'bĭl') *n.* Any of various tropical Old World birds of the family Bucerotidae, having a very large bill, often surmounted by an enlarged protuberance at the base.

horn·blende (hôrn'blĕnd') *n.* An amphibole mineral, $CaNa(Mg,Fe)_4(Al,Fe,Ti)_3Si_6O_{22}(O,OH)_2$, commonly green or bluish-green to black in color, formed in the late stages of cooling in igneous rock. [G. : *Horn,* horn + *Blende,* blende.]

horn·book (hôrn'bo͝ok') *n.* **1.** An early primer consisting of a single page protected by a transparent sheet of horn, formerly used in teaching children to read. **2.** A text that instructs in the basic skills or rudiments of a subject.

horned (hôrnd) *adj.* Having a horn.

horned pout *n.* A hornpout.

horned toad *n.* Any of several lizards of the genus *Phrynosoma,* of western North America and Central America, having hornlike projections on the head, a flattened, spiny body, and a short tail.

horned viper *n.* A venomous African snake, *Cerastes cornutus,* having a hornlike projection above each eye.

hor·net (hôr'nĭt) *n.* Any of various large stinging wasps, chiefly of the genera *Vespa* and *Vespula,* characteristically building a large papery nest. [ME < OE *hyrnet.*]

hor·ni·to (hôr-nē'tō) *n., pl.* **-tos.** A low mound of volcanic origin, sometimes emitting smoke or vapor. [Sp., dim. of *horno,* oven < Lat. *furnus.*]

horn-mad (hôrn'măd') *adj.* Extremely angry; enraged.

horn of plenty *n.* A cornucopia.

horn·pipe (hôrn'pīp') *n.* **1.** A musical instrument with a single reed, finger holes, and a bell and mouthpiece made of horn. **2. a.** A spirited British folk dance originally accompanied by a hornpipe. **b.** The music accompanying such a dance.

horn·pout (hôrn'pout') *n.* A freshwater catfish, *Ictalurus nebulosus* (or *Ameiurus nebulosus*), native to eastern North America, having a large head with barbels.

horn·swog·gle (hôrn'swŏg'əl) *tr.v.* **-gled, -gling, -gles.** *Regional Slang.* To deceive; bamboozle. [Orig. unknown.]

horn·tail (hôrn'tāl') *n.* Any of various sawflies of the family Siricidae, the female of which has a long, stout ovipositor.

horn·worm (hôrn'wûrm') *n.* The larva of the hawk moth, having a hornlike posterior segment.

horn·wort (hôrn'wûrt', -wôrt') *n.* Any of several aquatic plants of the genus *Ceratophyllum,* forming submerged branching masses in quiet water.

horn·y (hôr'nē) *adj.* **-i·er, -i·est. 1.** Having horns or hornlike projections. **2.** Made of horn or a similar substance. **3.** Tough and calloused: *horny skin.* **4.** *Vulgar Slang.* Sexually aroused. —**horn'i·ness** *n.*

hor·o·loge (hôr'ə-lōj', hŏr'-) *n.* A timepiece. [ME *orloge* < OFr. < Lat. *horologium* < Gk. *hōrologion* : *hōra,* hour + *legein,* to speak.]

ho·rol·o·ger (hô-rŏl'ə-jər) *n.* Variant of **horologist.**

hor·o·log·ic (hôr'ə-lŏj'ĭk, hŏr'-) also **hor·o·log·i·cal** (-ĭ-kəl) *adj.* Of or relating to a horologe or horology.

ho·rol·o·gist (hô-rŏl'ə-jĭst) also **ho·rol·o·ger** (-jər) *n.* One who practices or is skilled in horology.

Hor·o·lo·gi·um (hôr'ə-lō'jē-əm, hŏr'-) *n.* A constellation in

the Southern Hemisphere near Hydrus, Eridanus, and Reticulum. [Lat. *horologium,* horologe.]
ho·rol·o·gy (hô-rŏl′ə-jē) *n.* **1.** The science of measuring time. **2.** The art of making timepieces. [Gk. *hōra,* hour + -LOGY.]
hor·o·scope (hôr′ə-skōp′, hŏr′-) *n.* **1. a.** The aspect of the planets and stars at a given moment, such as the moment of a person's birth, used by astrologers. **b.** A diagram of the signs of the zodiac based on such an aspect. **2.** A forecast, as of a person's future, based on a horoscope. [OFr. < Lat. *horoscopus* < Gk. *hōroskopos* : *hōra,* hour + *skopos,* observer.]
hor·ren·dous (hô-rĕn′dəs, hə-) *adj.* Hideous; dreadful. [Lat. *horrendus* < gerund. of *horrēre,* to tremble.] **—hor·ren′dous·ly** *adv.*
hor·rent (hôr′ənt, hŏr′-) *adj. Archaic.* Covered with bristles; bristling. [Lat. *horrens, horrent-,* pr.part. of *horrēre,* to tremble.]
hor·ri·ble (hôr′ə-bəl, hŏr′-) *adj.* **1.** Arousing or tending to arouse horror; dreadful: *"War is beyond all words horrible"* (Winston Churchill). **2.** Very unpleasant; disagreeable. [ME < OFr. < Lat. *horribilis* < *horrēre,* to tremble.] **—hor′ri·ble·ness** *n.* **—hor′ri·bly** *adv.*
hor·rid (hôr′ĭd, hŏr′-) *adj.* **1.** Causing horror; dreadful. **2.** Extremely disagreeable; offensive. **3.** *Archaic.* Bristling; rough. [Lat. *horridus* < *horrēre,* to tremble.] **—hor′rid·ly** *adv.* **—hor′rid·ness** *n.*
hor·rif·ic (hô-rĭf′ĭk, hŏ-) *adj.* Causing horror; terrifying. [OFr. *horrifique* < Lat. *horrificus* : *horrēre,* to tremble + *-ficus,* -fic.] **—hor·rif′i·cal·ly** *adv.*
hor·ri·fy (hôr′ə-fī′, hŏr′-) *tr.v.* **-fied, -fy·ing, -fies. 1.** To cause to feel horror. **2.** To cause unpleasant surprise to; shock. [Lat. *horrificare* < *horrificus,* horrific.] **—hor′ri·fi·ca′tion** *n.* **—hor′ri·fy′ing·ly** *adv.*
hor·rip·i·la·tion (hô-rĭp′ə-lā′shən, hŏ-) *n.* The bristling of the body hair, as from fear or cold; goose flesh. [LLat. *horripilatio* < Lat. *horripilare,* to bristle with hairs : *horrēre,* to tremble + *pilus,* hair.] **—hor·rip′i·late′** *v.* **(-lat·ed, -lat·ing, -lates).**
hor·ror (hôr′ər, hŏr′-) *n.* **1.** An intense and painful feeling of repugnance and fear. **2.** Intense dislike; abhorrence. **3.** One that causes horror. **4.** *Informal.* Something unpleasant, ugly, or disagreeable: *That hat is a horror.* **5.** *Slang.* Intense nervous depression or anxiety: *a bad case of the horrors.* [ME *horrour* < OFr. *horreur* < Lat. *horror* < *horrēre,* to tremble.]
hors de com·bat (ôr′ də kôN-bä′) *adj. & adv.* Out of action; disabled. [Fr.]
hors d'oeuvre (ôr dûrv′) *n., pl.* **hors d'oeuvres** (ôr dûrvz′) or **hors d'oeuvre.** An appetizer served before a meal. [Fr. : *hors,* outside + *de,* of + *oeuvre,* work.]
horse (hôrs) *n.* **1. a.** A large hoofed mammal, *Equus caballus,* having a short-haired coat, a long mane, and a long tail, domesticated since ancient times and used for riding and for drawing or carrying loads. **b.** An adult male horse; stallion. **c.** Any of various equine mammals, such as the wild Asian species, *E. przewalskii,* or certain extinct forms related ancestrally to the modern horse. **2.** Mounted soldiers; cavalry: *a squadron of horse.* **3.** A frame or device, usually with four legs, used for supporting or holding. **4.** A piece of gymnastic equipment with an upholstered body used esp. for vaulting. **5.** *Slang.* Heroin. **6.** Often **horses.** Horsepower. **7.** *Geol.* **a.** A block of rock interrupting a vein and containing no minerals. **b.** A large block of displaced rock that is caught along a fault. *—v.* **horsed, hors·ing, hors·es.** *—tr.* **1.** To provide with a horse. **2.** To haul or hoist energetically. *—intr.* To be in heat. Used of mares. ***—phrasal verb.*** **horse around.** To indulge in horseplay. *—adj.* **1.** Of or pertaining to a horse. **2.** Mounted on horses. **3.** Drawn or operated by a horse. **4.** Larger or cruder than others that are similar. ***—idioms.*** **a horse of another** (or **a different**) **color.** Another matter entirely; something else. **be** (or **get**) **on (one's) high horse.** To be or become disdainful, superior, or conceited. **hold (one's) horses.** To restrain oneself. **the horse's mouth.** A source of information regarded as original or unimpeachable. [ME < OE *hors.*]
horse·back (hôrs′băk′) *n.* **1.** The back of a horse. **2.** A natural ridge; hogback. ***—modifier:*** *horseback riding.* *—adv.* On the back of a horse.
horse balm *n.* A plant, *Collinsonia canadensis,* of eastern North America, having clusters of yellow, lemon-scented flowers. [From its former use for treating ailments of horses.]
horse bean *n.* The broad bean.
horse·car (hôrs′kär′) *n.* **1.** A streetcar drawn by horses. **2.** A car for transporting horses.
horse chestnut *n.* **1.** Any of several trees of the genus *Aesculus,* esp. *A. hippocastanum,* native to Eurasia, having palmate leaves, erect clusters of white flowers tinged with red, and brown, shiny nuts enclosed in a spiny bur. **2.** The nut of a horse chestnut.
horse·flesh (hôrs′flĕsh′) *n.* **1.** The flesh of a horse. **2.** Horses collectively, esp. for driving, riding, or racing.
horse·fly also **horse fly** (hôrs′flī′) *n.* Any of numerous large flies of the family Tabanidae, the females of which suck the blood of various mammals.
horse gentian *n.* Any of various plants of the genus *Triosteum,* having small purplish-brown flowers and leathery orange-yellow fruit.
horse·hair (hôrs′hâr′) *n.* **1.** The hair of a horse, esp. from the mane or tail. **2.** Cloth made of horsehair. ***—modifier:*** *a horsehair sofa.*
horsehair worm *n.* Any of various slender aquatic worms of the phylum Nematomorpha, the larvae of which are parasitic within insects.
horse·hide (hôrs′hīd′) *n.* **1. a.** The hide of a horse. **b.** Leather made from this hide. **2.** *Informal.* A baseball.
horse latitudes *pl.n.* Either of two belts of latitudes located over the oceans at about 30 to 35 degrees north and south, having high barometric pressure, calms, and light, changeable winds.
horse·laugh (hôrs′lăf′, -läf′) *n.* A loud, coarse laugh; guffaw.
horse·leech (hôrs′lēch′) *n.* Any of several large leeches of the genus *Haemopis.*
horse·less carriage (hôrs′lĭs) *n.* An automobile.
horse mackerel *n.* **1.** Any of several marine fishes of the genus *Trachurus.* **2.** Any of several tunas or related fishes.
horse·man (hôrs′mən) *n.* **1. a.** A man who rides a horse. **b.** One skilled at horsemanship. **2.** A man who breeds and raises horses.
horse·man·ship (hôrs′mən-shĭp′) *n.* The art of equitation.
horse marine *n.* **1.** A marine assigned to the cavalry. **2.** A cavalryman assigned to a ship.
horse·mint (hôrs′mĭnt′) *n.* Any of several coarse, aromatic plants such as *Monarda punctata* or *Mentha longifolia.*
horse nettle *n.* A prickly-stemmed plant, *Solanum carolinense,* of eastern and central North America, having purplish or white star-shaped flowers and yellowish berries.
horse opera *n.* A film or other theatrical work about the American West.
horse·play (hôrs′plā′) *n.* Rowdy, rough play.
horse·pow·er (hôrs′pou′ər) *n.* **1.** A unit of power in the U.S. Customary System, equal to 745.7 watts or 33,000 foot-pounds per minute. **2.** The power exerted by a horse in pulling.
horse·rad·ish (hôrs′răd′ĭsh) *n.* **1.** A coarse plant, *Armoracia rusticana* (or *A. lapathifolia*), native to Eurasia, having a thick, whitish, pungent root. **2.** The shredded or grated root of the horseradish, often used as a condiment.
horse sense *n. Informal.* Common sense.
horse·shit (hôrs′shĭt′, hôrsh′-) *n.* **1.** *Vulgar.* Excrement of a horse. **2.** *Vulgar Slang.* Nonessential or insincere talk or action; nonsense.
horse·shoe (hôrs′sho͞o′, hôrsh′-) *n.* **1.** A narrow U-shaped iron plate fitted and nailed to a horse's hoof. **2.** Something shaped like a horseshoe. **3. horseshoes** *(used with a sing. verb).* A game in which players try to toss horseshoes so that they encircle a stake. *—tr.v.* **-shoed, -shoe·ing, -shoes.** To shoe (a horse).
horseshoe crab *n.* Any of various marine arthropods of the class Merostomata, esp. *Limulus polyphemus* (or *Xiphosura polyphemus*), of eastern North America, having a large, rounded body and a stiff, pointed tail.
horse·tail (hôrs′tāl′) *n.* Any of various nonflowering plants of the genus *Equisetum,* having a jointed, hollow stem and narrow, sometimes much reduced leaves.
horse trade *n.* A transaction characterized by shrewd and vigorous bargaining. **—horse trader** *n.*
horse·weed (hôrs′wēd′) *n.* A weedy North American plant, *Erigeron canadensis,* having narrow leaves and numerous small white or greenish flowers.
horse·whip (hôrs′hwĭp′, -wĭp′) *n.* A whip used to control a horse. *—tr.v.* **-whipped, -whip·ping, -whips.** To beat with or as if with a horsewhip.
horse·wom·an (hôrs′wo͝om′ən) *n.* **1. a.** A woman who rides a horse. **b.** A woman skilled at horsemanship. **2.** A woman who breeds and raises horses.
hors·ey (hôr′sē) *adj.* Variant of **horsy.**
horst (hôrst) *n.* A massive block of the earth's crust that lies between two faults and is higher than the surrounding land. [G. < MHG < OHG *hurst,* hill.]
hors·y also **hors·ey** (hôr′sē) *adj.* **-i·er, -i·est. 1.** Of, pertaining to, or characteristic of a horse. **2.** Devoted to horses and horsemanship: *the horsy crowd.* **3.** Large and clumsy. **—hors′i·ly** *adv.* **—hors′i·ness** *n.*
hor·ta·tive (hôr′tə-tĭv) *adj.* Hortatory. [LLat. *hortativus* < Lat. *hortari,* to exhort.] **—hor′ta·tive·ly** *adv.*
hor·ta·to·ry (hôr′tə-tôr′ē, -tōr′ē) *adj.* Characterized by or given to exhortation or strong urging. [LLat. *hortatorius* < *hortari,* to exhort.]
hor·ti·cul·ture (hôr′tĭ-kŭl′chər) *n.* **1.** The science or art of cultivating fruits, vegetables, flowers, and plants. **2.** The cultivation of a garden. [Lat. *hortus,* garden + (AGRI)CULTURE.] **—hor′ti·cul′tur·al** *adj.* **—hor′ti·cul′tur·al·ly** *adv.* **—hor′ti·cul′tur·ist** *n.*
Ho·rus (hôr′əs, hōr′-) *n.* The ancient Egyptian god of the sun, represented as having the head of a hawk. [LLat. < Gk. *Hōros,* of Egyptian orig.]
ho·san·na (hō-zăn′ə) *interj.* Used to express praise or adoration to God. *—n.* A cry of "hosanna." [ME *osanna* < Lat. < Gk. *hōsanna* < Heb. *hosha'nā,* short for *hosh' āhanna,* save (us).]

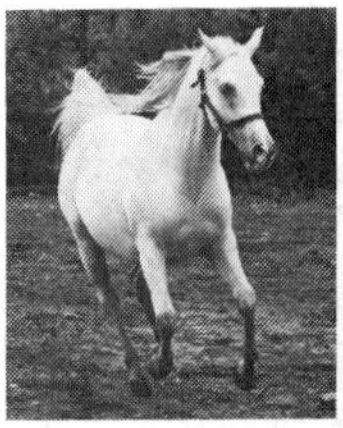

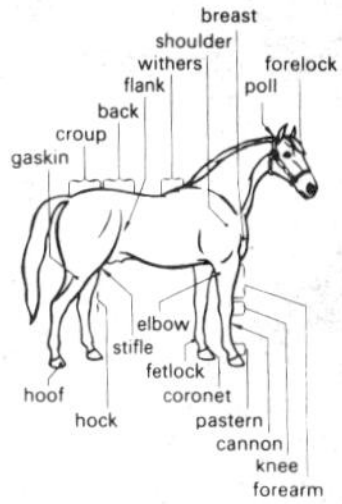

horse
Above: Arabian horse
Below: Anatomical diagram

horse chestnut

horseshoe crab

hose (hōz) *n., pl.* **hose. 1. a.** Stockings. **b.** Socks. **2. a.** A man's garment that covers the legs and hips and fastens to a doublet by points. **b.** Short full breeches reaching to the knees. **3.** *pl.* **hos·es.** A flexible tube for conveying liquids or gases under pressure. —*tr.v.* **hosed, hos·ing, hos·es.** To water, drench, or wash with a hose. [ME, a stocking < OE.]
Ho·se·a (hō-zē'ə, -zā'ə) *n.* **1.** A Hebrew minor prophet of the 8th century B.C. **2.** See table at **Bible.** [Heb. *Hōshēa'.*]
ho·sier (hō'zhər) *n.* A maker of or dealer in hosiery. [ME < *hose,* a stocking < OE.]
ho·sier·y (hō'zhə-rē) *n.* **1. a.** Stockings and socks; hose. **b.** *Chiefly Brit.* Stockings, socks, and underclothing. **2.** The business of a hosier.
hos·pice (hŏs'pĭs) *n.* **1.** A shelter or lodging for travelers, children, or the destitute, often maintained by monks. **2.** An establishment or a program that provides for the physical and emotional needs of terminally ill patients. [Fr. < OFr. < Lat. *hospitium,* hospitality < *hospes,* host.]
hos·pi·ta·ble (hŏs'pĭ-tə-bəl, hŏ-spĭt'ə-bəl) *adj.* **1.** Cordial and generous to guests. **2.** Having an open mind; receptive. **3.** Favorable to growth and development: *a hospitable environment.* [NLat. *hospitabilis* < Med. Lat. *hospitare,* to receive as a guest < Lat. *hospes,* host.] —**hos'pi·ta·bly** *adv.*
hos·pi·tal (hŏs'pĭ-tl, -pĭt'l) *n.* **1.** An institution that provides medical or surgical care and treatment for the sick and the injured. **2.** A home, often charitable, for old people, the infirm, or foundlings. **3.** A repair shop for specified items: *a doll hospital.* [ME, hospice < OFr. *ospital* < Med. Lat. *hospitale* < Lat. *hospitalis,* of a guest < *hospes,* guest.]
Hos·pi·tal·er also **Hos·pi·tal·ler** (hŏs'pĭt'l-ər) *n.* A member of a military religious order founded among European crusaders in 12th-century Palestine. [ME *Hospiteler* < OFr. *hospitalier* < Med. Lat. *hospitale,* hospice. —see HOSPITAL.]
hos·pi·tal·i·ty (hŏs'pĭ-tăl'ĭ-tē) *n., pl.* **-ties. 1.** Cordial and generous reception of guests. **2.** An instance of being hospitable. [ME *hospitalite* < OFr. < Lat. *hospitalitas* < *hospitalis,* of a guest. —see HOSPITAL.]
hos·pi·tal·ize (hŏs'pĭt'l-īz') *tr.v.* **-ized, -iz·ing, -iz·es.** To put into a hospital for treatment. —**hos'pi·tal·i·za'tion** *n.*
host[1] (hōst) *n.* **1. a.** One who entertains guests in a social or business capacity. **b.** One that furnishes facilities for a function or event. **c.** One who serves as master of ceremonies on a radio or television program. **2.** *Biol.* An organism that harbors and provides nourishment for a parasite. —*tr.v.* **host·ed, host·ing, hosts.** *Informal.* To serve as host for or at: *"the garden party he had hosted last spring"* (Saturday Review). [ME < OFr. < Lat. *hospes.*] —**host'ly** *adj.*
host[2] (hōst) *n.* **1.** An army. **2.** A great number; multitude. [ME < OFr. < LLat. *hostis* < Lat., enemy.]
host[3] also **Host** (hōst) *n. Eccles.* The consecrated bread or wafer of the Eucharist. [ME < Lat. *hostia,* sacrifice.]
hos·tage (hŏs'tĭj) *n.* **1.** A person held as a pledge that certain terms will be fulfilled. **2.** The state of being held as a hostage. [ME < OFr. < *host,* guest, host. —see HOST[1].]
hos·tel (hŏs'təl) *n.* **1.** A supervised, inexpensive lodging, esp. for youthful travelers. **2.** An inn. —*intr.v.* **-teled, -tel·ing, -tels.** To stay at hostels while traveling, as by bicycle. [ME, lodging < OFr. < Med. Lat. *hospitale,* hospice. —see HOSPITAL.]
hos·tel·er (hŏs'tə-lər) *n.* **1.** *Archaic.* An innkeeper. **2.** A youthful traveler who stops at hostels.
hos·tel·ry (hŏs'təl-rē) *n., pl.* **-ries.** An inn; hotel.
host·ess (hō'stĭs) *n.* **1.** A woman who acts as a host. **2.** A woman whose occupation is to greet and serve patrons, as in a restaurant or on an airplane.
hos·tile (hŏs'təl, -tīl') *adj.* **1.** Of or pertaining to an enemy. **2.** Feeling or showing enmity; antagonistic. **3.** Not hospitable. —*n.* One that is hostile. [OFr. < Lat. *hostilis* < *hostis,* enemy.] —**hos'tile·ly** *adv.*
hos·til·i·ty (hŏ-stĭl'ĭ-tē) *n., pl.* **-ties. 1.** The state of being hostile; antagonism or enmity. **2. a.** A hostile act. **b. hostilities.** Overt warfare.
hos·tler (hŏs'lər, ŏs'-) *n.* **1.** A person who takes charge of horses, as at an inn; stableman. **2.** A worker who services a large vehicle or engine, such as a locomotive. [ME < AN *hostiler* < OFr. *hostel,* lodging. —see HOSTEL.]
hot (hŏt) *adj.* **hot·ter, hot·test. 1. a.** Possessing great heat. **b.** Yielding much heat. **c.** Being at a high temperature. **2.** Higher in temperature than is normal or desirable: *a hot forehead.* **3.** Highly spiced: *hot mustard.* **4. a.** Charged or energized with electricity: *a hot wire.* **b.** Radioactive, esp. to a dangerous degree. **5. a.** Marked by intensity or warmth of emotion; fiery: *a hot temper.* **b.** Having or displaying desire or enthusiasm. **c.** Arousing excited interest and attention: *a hot issue.* **6.** *Slang.* Arousing or experiencing sexual excitement. **7.** *Slang.* **a.** Obtained by stealing: *a hot car.* **b.** Wanted by the police. **8.** Close to a successful solution or conclusion: *hot on the trail.* **9.** *Informal.* **a.** New; fresh: *hot off the press.* **b.** Extremely popular: *a hot sales item.* **10.** *Slang.* Very good or impressive. **11.** *Slang.* **a.** Possessing or showing unusual skill: *a hot pilot.* **b.** Unusually lucky. **12.** *Mus.* Marked by strong rhythms and improvisation: *hot jazz.* —*n.* **the hots.** *Slang.* Strong sexual attraction or desire. —**idioms. hot under the collar.** *Informal.* Angry. **in hot water.** *Informal.* In trouble. **make it hot for.** *Informal.* To make things uncomfortable or dangerous for. [ME < OE *hāt.*] —**hot'ness** *n.*
hot air *n. Slang.* Empty, often boastful talk.
hot·bed (hŏt'bĕd') *n.* **1.** A glass-covered bed of soil heated with fermenting manure or by electricity, used for the germination of seeds or for protecting tender plants. **2.** An environment conducive to rapid, vigorous growth and development, esp. of something bad: *a hotbed of intrigue.*
hot-blood·ed (hŏt'blŭd'ĭd) *adj.* Easily excited or aroused. —**hot'-blood'ed·ness** *n.*
hot·box (hŏt'bŏks') *n.* An overheated axle or journal box, as on a railway car, caused by excessive friction.
hot cake *n.* A pancake. —**idiom. go (or sell) like hot cakes.** To be in great demand.
hotch (hŏch) *intr.v.* **hotched, hotch·ing, hotch·es.** *Scot.* To fidget. [Perh. < OFr. *hocher,* to shake.]
hotch·pot (hŏch'pŏt') *n. Law.* The gathering together of properties to secure an equal division of the total for distribution among the heirs of an intestate parent. [AN < OFr., mixture, stew: *hocher,* to shake together + *pot,* pot.]
hotch·potch (hŏch'pŏch') *n.* **1.** A hodgepodge. **2.** A hotchpot. [Alteration of HOTCHPOT.]
hot cross bun *n.* A sweet bun often made with raisins and marked on top with a cross of frosting, traditionally eaten during Lent.
hot dog *n.* A hot frankfurter, usually served in a long soft roll. —*interj. Informal.* Used to express satisfaction or enthusiasm.
hot-dog (hŏt'dôg', -dŏg') *intr.v.* **-dogged, -dog·ging, -dogs.** *Slang.* To do stunts or acrobatic feats, esp. while skiing or surfing. —**hot'-dog'ger** *n.*
ho·tel (hō-tĕl') *n.* A public house that provides lodging and usually meals and other services. [Fr. *hôtel* < OFr. *hostel,* hostel.]
hot flash *n.* A transient vasomotor symptom of menopause that involves dilation of the skin capillaries and the sensation of heat over the whole body.
hot·foot (hŏt'fŏŏt') *intr.v.* **-foot·ed, -foot·ing, -foots.** To go in haste: *hotfoot it out of town.* —*adv.* In haste. —*n., pl.* **-foots.** A trick or joke in which a match is stealthily inserted into the side of someone's shoe and lit.
hot·head (hŏt'hĕd') *n.* A hotheaded person.
hot·head·ed (hŏt'hĕd'ĭd) *adj.* **1.** Easily angered or excited. **2.** Impetuous; rash. —**hot'head'ed·ly** *adv.* —**hot'head'ed·ness** *n.*
hot·house (hŏt'hous') *n.* A heated greenhouse for plants requiring an even, relatively warm temperature. —*adj.* Resembling or having qualities like those of a plant grown in a hothouse; delicate and sensitive: *Her mother, a hothouse creature, cried easily and often.*
hot line *n.* **1.** A direct communications link, as a telephone line, esp. one between heads of government, for use in a crisis or emergency. **2.** A telephone facility that enables a caller to talk confidentially with a sympathetic listener about a personal problem or crisis.
hot·ly (hŏt'lē) *adv.* In an intense or fiery fashion: *answered hotly that he was innocent.*
hot pants *pl.n.* **1.** *Vulgar Slang.* Anxious sexual desire. **2.** Very short shorts worn by women as an outer garment.
hot pepper *n.* **1.** The pungent fruit of any of several varieties of *Capsicum frutescens.* **2.** A pepper (sense 6).
hot plate *n.* **1.** An electrically heated plate for cooking or warming food. **2.** A table-top cooking device with one or two burners.
hot rod also **hot·rod** or **hot-rod** (hŏt'rŏd') *n. Slang.* An automobile rebuilt or modified for increased speed and power. —**hot rodder** *n.*
hot seat *n.* **1.** *Slang.* The electric chair. **2.** *Informal.* A situation or position that is a source of stress, embarrassment, or disquiet.
hot·shot (hŏt'shŏt') *n.* **1.** *Slang.* An ostentatiously skillful person. **2.** A nonstop freight train.
hot spring *n.* A natural spring discharging water that is above body temperature, or over 98°F.
Hot·ten·tot (hŏt'n-tŏt') *n., pl.* **Hottentot** or **-tots. 1. a.** A people of southern Africa held to be related to the Bantu and Bushmen. **b.** A member of this people. **2.** The language of the Hottentot. [Afr.]
hot toddy *n.* A toddy (sense 1).
hot tub *n.* A very large usually wooden tub in which a group of people may soak.
hou·dah (hou'də) *n.* Variant of **howdah.**
Hou·dan (hōō'dăn') *n.* A domesticated fowl having black and white plumage and a V-shaped comb. [Fr., after *Houdan,* France.]
hound (hound) *n.* **1. a.** A dog of any of various breeds used for hunting, characteristically having drooping ears, a short coat, and a deep, resonant voice. **b.** A dog. **2.** A contemptible person; scoundrel. **3.** An enthusiast or addict: *a coffee hound.* —*tr.v.* **hound·ed, hound·ing, hounds. 1.** To pursue relentlessly and tenaciously. **2.** To urge insistently; nag. [ME < OE *hund.*] —**hound'er** *n.*
hound's-tongue (houndz'tŭng') *n.* Any of several plants of the genus *Cynoglossum,* esp. *C. officinale,* native to Eurasia, having hairy leaves, small reddish-purple flowers, and prickly, clinging fruit.

of man or mankind: *the course of human events.* **2.** Having or manifesting the form, nature, or qualities characteristic of man. **3.** Prone to or marked by the frailties and weaknesses associated with man as an imperfect being: *Forgive me—I'm only human.* **4.** Made up of people: *formed a human bridge.* —*n.* A human being; person. [ME *humain* < OFr. < Lat. *humanus.*] —**hu'man·ness** *n.*

human being *n.* A member of the genus *Homo* and esp. of the species *Homo sapiens.*

hu·mane (hyo͞o-mān') *adj.* **1.** Characterized by kindness, mercy, or compassion: *a humane judge.* **2.** Marked by an emphasis on humanistic values and concerns: *a humane education.* [ME *humain,* human.] —**hu·mane'ly** *adv.* —**hu·mane'ness** *n.*

human engineering *n.* **1.** The industrial management of labor. **2.** The technology of the efficient use of machines by human beings.

hu·man·ism (hyo͞o'mə-nĭz'əm) *n.* **1.** A doctrine or attitude that is concerned primarily with human beings and their values, capacities, and achievements. **2.** Absorption in or study of the humanities. **3.** Often **Humanism.** A cultural and intellectual movement of the Renaissance that emphasized secular concerns as a result of the study of the literature, art, and civilization of ancient Greece and Rome. —**hu'man·ist** *n.* —**hu'man·is'tic** *adj.* —**hu'man·is'ti·cal·ly** *adv.*

hu·man·i·tar·i·an (hyo͞o-măn'ĭ-târ'ē-ən) *n.* A person who is devoted to the promotion of human welfare and the advancement of social reforms; philanthropist. —***modifier:*** *humanitarian concerns.*

hu·man·i·tar·i·an·ism (hyo͞o-măn'ĭ-târ'ē-ə-nĭz'əm) *n.* Concern for human welfare, esp. as manifested through philanthropy.

hu·man·i·ty (hyo͞o-măn'ĭ-tē) *n., pl.* **-ties. 1.** Human beings collectively; the human race. **2.** The condition, quality, or fact of being human; humanness. **3.** The quality of being humane; benevolence. **4.** A humane quality or action. **5. humanities.** Those subjects, such as philosophy, literature, and the fine arts, that are concerned with man and his culture as distinguished from the sciences. [ME *humanite* < OFr. < Lat. *humanitas* < *humanus,* human.]

hu·man·ize (hyo͞o'mə-nīz') *tr.v.* **-ized, -iz·ing, -iz·es. 1.** To portray or endow with human characteristics or attributes. **2.** To make humane. —**hu'man·i·za'tion** *n.* —**hu'man·iz'er** *n.*

hu·man·kind (hyo͞o'mən-kīnd') *n.* The human race; mankind.

hu·man·ly (hyo͞o'mən-lē) *adv.* **1.** In a human way. **2.** Within the scope of human means, capabilities, or powers. **3.** According to human experience or knowledge.

hu·man·oid (hyo͞o'mə-noid') *adj.* Resembling a human being in appearance. —*n.* An android.

hum·ble (hŭm'bəl) *adj.* **-bler, -blest. 1.** Marked by meekness or modesty in behavior, attitude, or spirit. **2.** Showing deferential or submissive respect. **3.** Of low rank or station; unpretentious: *a humble cottage.* —*tr.v.* **-bled, -bling, -bles. 1.** To humiliate. **2.** To make lower in condition or station. [ME < OFr. < Lat. *humilis* < *humus,* ground.] —**hum'ble·ness** *n.* —**hum'bler** *n.* —**hum'bly** *adv.*

hum·ble·bee (hŭm'bəl-bē') *n.* A bumblebee. [ME *humbulbe.*]

humble pie *n.* A pie formerly made from the edible organs of a deer or hog. —***idiom.* eat humble pie.** To apologize abjectly in humiliating circumstances. [Obs. *humble,* edible animal organs (< ME *hombuls* < OFr. *nombles* < Lat. *lumbulus* < *lumbus,* loin) + PIE.]

Hum·boldt Current (hŭm'bōlt') *n.* A cold ocean current of the South Pacific, flowing north along the northern coast of Chile and Peru to southern Ecuador. [After F. H. Alexander von *Humboldt* (1769–1859).]

hum·bug (hŭm'bŭg') *n.* **1.** Something intended to deceive; hoax. **2.** One who tries to trick or deceive. **3.** Nonsense; rubbish. —*v.* **-bugged, -bug·ging, -bugs.** —*tr.* To deceive or trick. —*intr.* To practice deception or trickery. [Orig. unknown.] —**hum'bug'ger** *n.* —**hum'bug'ger·y** *n.*

hum·ding·er (hŭm'dĭng'ər) *n. Slang.* Someone or something that is extraordinary or superior. [Orig. unknown.]

hum·drum (hŭm'drŭm') *adj.* Without change, variety, or excitement; monotonous. —*n.* One that is dull or unexciting. [Orig. unknown.]

hu·mec·tant (hyo͞o-mĕk'tənt) *n.* A substance that promotes retention of moisture. —*adj.* Promoting moisture retention. [< Lat. *humectans, humectant-,* pr.part. of *humectare,* to moisten < *humectus,* moist < *humēre,* to be moist.]

hu·mer·al (hyo͞o'mər-əl) *adj.* **1.** Of, pertaining to, or located in the region of the humerus or the shoulder. **2.** Pertaining to or being a body part analogous to the humerus. —**hu'mer·al** *n.*

humeral veil *n. Rom. Cath. Ch.* A silk veil covering the shoulders that is worn at a High Mass by a subdeacon or priest.

hu·mer·us (hyo͞o'mər-əs) *n., pl.* **-mer·i** (-mə-rī'). The long bone of the upper part of the arm, extending from the shoulder to the elbow. [NLat. < Lat., upper arm.]

hu·mic (hyo͞o'mĭk) *adj.* Of, pertaining to, or derived from humus.

hu·mid (hyo͞o'mĭd) *adj.* Containing a large amount of water or water vapor. Used esp. of air. [OFr. *humide* < Lat. *humidus* < *humēre,* to be moist.] —**hu'mid·ly** *adv.*

hu·mid·i·fi·er (hyo͞o-mĭd'ə-fī'ər) *n.* An apparatus for increasing the humidity in a room, greenhouse, or other enclosure.

hu·mid·i·fy (hyo͞o-mĭd'ə-fī') *tr.v.* **-fied, -fy·ing, -fies.** To make humid. —**hu·mid'i·fi·ca'tion** *n.*

hu·mid·i·stat (hyo͞o-mĭd'ĭ-stăt') *n.* An instrument designed to indicate or control the relative humidity of the air.

hu·mid·i·ty (hyo͞o-mĭd'ĭ-tē) *n.* Dampness, esp. of the air. [ME *humidite* < OFr. < Med. Lat. *humiditas* < Lat. *humidus,* humid.]

hu·mi·dor (hyo͞o'mĭ-dôr') *n.* A container for the storage of cigars that has a device for keeping the humidity level constant. [< HUMID.]

hu·mil·i·ate (hyo͞o-mĭl'ē-āt') *tr.v.* **-at·ed, -at·ing, -ates.** To lower the pride or dignity of; mortify. [LLat. *humiliare, humiliat-,* to humble < *humilis,* humble.] —**hu·mil'i·a·to'ry** (-ē-ə-tôr'ē, -tōr'ē) *adj.*

hu·mil·i·a·tion (hyo͞o-mĭl'ē-ā'shən) *n.* **1.** The act of humiliating; degradation. **2.** The state or condition of being humiliated; disgrace.

hu·mil·i·ty (hyo͞o-mĭl'ĭ-tē) *n., pl.* **-ties.** The quality or condition of being humble; lack of pride. [ME *humilite* < OFr. < LLat. *humilitas* < *humilis,* humble. —see HUMBLE.]

hum·ming·bird (hŭm'ĭng-bûrd') *n.* Any of numerous chiefly tropical New World birds of the family Trochilidae, usually very small in size and having a long, slender bill, wings capable of beating very rapidly, and often brilliantly colored plumage.

hummingbird

hum·mock (hŭm'ək) also **ham·mock** (hăm'-) *n.* **1.** A low mound or ridge of earth; knoll. **2.** A ridge or hill of ice in an ice field. [Orig. unknown.] —**hum'mock·y** *adj.*

hum·mus (hŭm'əs) also **hom·mos** (hŭm'əs, hŏm'-) *n.* A smooth, thick mixture of pureed chickpeas and tahini used esp. as a sandwich spread or a dip. [Ar. *ḥummuṣ,* chickpea.]

hu·mon·gous (hyo͞o-mŏng'gəs, -mŭng'-) or **hu·mun·gous** (-mŭng'-) *adj. Slang.* Extremely large in size or scope; enormous. [Perh. alteration of HUGE + TREMENDOUS.]

hu·mor (hyo͞o'mər) *n.* **1.** The quality of being amusing or comical: *He saw the humor of the situation.* **2.** The ability to perceive, enjoy, or express what is comical or funny: *a sense of humor.* **3.** In medieval physiology, one of the four fluids of the body, blood, phlegm, choler, and black bile, the dominance of which was thought to determine a person's character and general health. **4. a.** A state of mind; mood: *in a good humor.* **b.** Characteristic disposition; temperament: *a girl of sullen humor.* **5.** A sudden, unanticipated whim. **6.** *Physiol.* **a.** A clear or hyaline body fluid, such as blood, lymph, or bile. **b.** Aqueous humor. —*tr.v.* **-mored, -mor·ing, -mors. 1.** To comply with the wishes or ideas of; indulge. **2.** To adapt or accommodate oneself to. —***idiom.* out of humor.** In a bad mood; irritable. [ME, fluid < OFr. *umor* < Lat. *humor.*]

hu·mor·al (hyo͞o'mər-əl) *adj.* Of, pertaining to, or arising from any of the bodily humors.

hu·mor·esque (hyo͞o'mə-rĕsk') *n.* A whimsical or light-spirited musical composition. [G. *Humoreske* < *Humor,* humor < E. HUMOR.]

hu·mor·ist (hyo͞o'mər-ĭst) *n.* **1.** A person with a good sense of humor. **2.** A performer or writer who specializes in humor.

hu·mor·less (hyo͞o'mər-lĭs) *adj.* **1.** Devoid of a sense of humor. **2.** Devoid of humor: *"She winked at me, but it was humorless; a wink of warning"* (Truman Capote). —**hu'mor·less·ly** *adv.* —**hu'mor·less·ness** *n.*

hu·mor·ous (hyo͞o'mər-əs) *adj.* **1.** Possessing or characterized by humor: *a humorous story.* **2.** Employing or expressing humor: *a humorous writer.* **3.** *Obs.* Damp and moist. —**hu'mor·ous·ly** *adv.* —**hu'mor·ous·ness** *n.*

hu·mour (hyo͞o'mər) *n.* & *v. Chiefly Brit.* Variant of **humor.**

hump (hŭmp) *n.* **1.** A rounded mass or protuberance, such as the fleshy structure on the back of a camel or of some cattle. **2.** A deformity of the back, due in human beings to an abnormal curvature of the spine. **3.** A low mound of earth; hummock. **4.** *Chiefly Brit. Slang.* A feeling of depression; an emotional slump. —*v.* **humped, hump·ing, humps.** —*tr.* **1.** To bend or make into a hump. **2.** *Slang.* To exert (oneself). **3.** *Vulgar Slang.* To engage in sexual intercourse with. —*intr.* **1.** To arch so as to become a hump. **2.** *Slang.* To exert oneself. —***idiom.* over the hump.** Past the worst or most difficult part of something. [Orig. unknown.]

hump·back (hŭmp'băk') *n.* **1.** A hunchback (senses 1, 3). **2.** Kyphosis. **3.** A whalebone whale, *Megaptera novaeangliae,* having a rounded back and long, knobby flippers. —**hump'backed'** *adj.*

humped (hŭmpt) *adj.* Having a hump.

humph (hŭmf) *interj.* Used to express doubt, displeasure, or contempt.

hump·y (hŭm'pē) *adj.* **-i·er, -i·est. 1.** Covered with or containing humps. **2.** Resembling a hump.

hu·mun·gous (hyo͞o-mŭng'gəs) *adj.* Variant of **humongous.**

hu·mus (hyo͞o'məs) *n.* A brown or black organic substance consisting of partially or wholly decayed vegetable matter that provides nutrients for plants and increases the ability of soil to retain water. [Lat., soil.]

hurdle

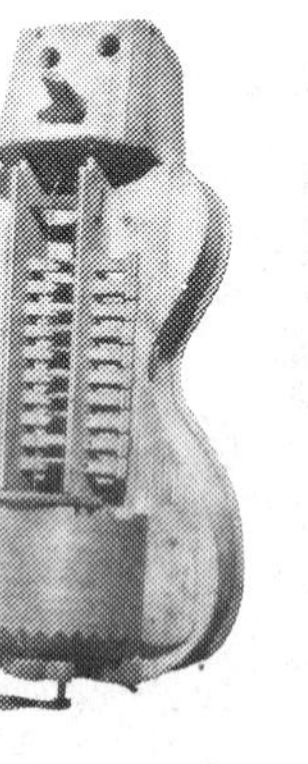

hurdy-gurdy

Hun (hŭn) *n.* **1.** One of a fierce barbaric race of Asiatic nomads who, led by Attila, ravaged Europe in the 4th and 5th centuries A.D. **2.** Often **hun.** A savage, uncivilized, or destructive person. **3.** *Offensive Slang.* A German. [LLat. *Hunni,* the Huns < Turki *Hunyü.*]

hunch (hŭnch) *n.* **1.** An intuitive feeling or guess: *trusted his hunches.* **2.** A hump. **3.** A lump or chunk. *—v.* **hunched, hunch·ing, hunch·es.** *—tr.* **1.** To bend or draw up into a hump: *hunched his shoulders against the wind.* **2.** To push or shove. *—intr.* **1.** To draw oneself up closely into a crouched or cramped posture: *The scared child hunched in a corner.* **2.** To thrust oneself forward. [Orig. unknown.]

hunch·back (hŭnch′băk′) *n.* **1.** An individual afflicted with an abnormally curved or hunched back; humpback. **2.** Kyphosis. **3.** An abnormally curved or hunched back. **—hunch′backed′** *adj.*

hun·dred (hŭn′drĭd) *n., pl.* **hundred** or **-dreds. 1.** The cardinal number equal to 10 x 10, or 10^2. **2.** A currency note worth 100 dollars. **3.** The number in the third position left of the decimal point in an Arabic numeral. **4. hundreds.** The numbers between 100 and 999. **5.** An administrative division of some English and American counties. [ME < OE.] **—hun′dred** *adj. & pron.*

hun·dredth (hŭn′drĭdth) *n.* **1.** The ordinal number that matches the number 100 in a series. **2.** One of 100 equal parts. **—hun′dredth** *adj. & adv.*

hun·dred·weight (hŭn′drĭd-wāt′) *n., pl.* **hundredweight** or **-weights. 1.** A unit of weight in the U.S. Customary System equal to 100 pounds or approximately 45.36 kilograms. **2.** A unit of weight in the British Imperial System equal to 112 pounds or approximately 50.80 kilograms.

hung (hŭng) *v.* A past tense and past participle of **hang.**

Hun·gar·i·an (hŭng-gâr′ē-ən) *adj.* Of or relating to Hungary or its people, language, or culture. *—n.* **1.** A native or inhabitant of Hungary. **2.** Magyar (sense 2).

hun·ger (hŭng′gər) *n.* **1. a.** A strong desire for food. **b.** The discomfort, weakness, or pain caused by a lack of food. **2.** A strong desire or craving: *a hunger for affection.* *—v.* **-gered, -ger·ing, -gers.** *—intr.* **1.** To have a need or desire for food. **2.** To have a strong desire or craving: *Reduced to poverty, he hungered for his old life.* *—tr.* To cause to experience hunger; make hungry. ***—idiom.* (strictly) from hunger.** *Slang.* Very bad; wretched: *a comedy act that is strictly from hunger.* [ME < OE *hungor.*]

hunger strike *n.* A voluntary fast undertaken as a method of protest. **—hunger striker** *n.*

hung jury *n.* A jury unable to agree on a verdict.

hung over *adj.* Suffering from a hangover.

hun·gry (hŭng′grē) *adj.* **-gri·er, -gri·est. 1.** Experiencing hunger. **2.** Extremely desirous; avid: *hungry for recognition.* **3.** Characterized by or expressing hunger or craving: *hungry eyes.* **4.** Lacking richness or fertility: *hungry soil.* [ME *hungri* < OE *hungrig.*] **—hun′gri·ly** *adv.* **—hun′gri·ness** *n.*

hung up *adj. Informal.* **1.** Delayed: *got hung up in traffic.* **2.** Having a hang-up; distressed: *can't understand why he's hung up about his job.* **3.** Being very much involved or preoccupied: *teen-agers hung up on their appearance; hung up on soap operas.*

hunk (hŭngk) *n. Informal.* A large piece; chunk: *grabbed two hunks of freshly baked bread.* [Perh. < Flem. *hunke,* a piece of food.]

hun·ker (hŭng′kər) *intr.v.* **-kered, -ker·ing, -kers.** To squat close to the ground; crouch. *—n.* **hunkers.** *Regional.* The haunches. [Prob. of Scand. orig.]

hunks (hŭngks) *n., pl.* **hunks. 1.** An irritable or disagreeable old person; grouch. **2.** A stingy man; miser. [Orig. unknown.]

hun·ky-do·ry (hŭng′kē-dôr′ē, -dōr′ē) *adj. Slang.* Perfectly satisfactory; fine. [Obs. *hunk,* goal + *-dory,* of unknown orig.]

Hun·nish (hŭn′ĭsh) *adj.* **1.** Of, pertaining to, or resembling the Huns. **2.** Barbarous. **—Hun′nish·ness** *n.*

hunt (hŭnt) *v.* **hunt·ed, hunt·ing, hunts.** *—tr.* **1. a.** To pursue (game) for food or sport. **b.** To seek out; search for. **2.** To search through, as for game or prey. **3.** To make use of (hounds, for example) in pursuing game. **4.** To drive out forcibly; chase away, esp. by harassing. *—intr.* **1.** To pursue game or other animals in order to capture or kill them. **2.** To make a search; seek. **3.** *Aerospace.* **a.** To yaw back and forth about a flight path, as if seeking a new direction or another angle of attack. Used of aircraft, rockets, and space vehicles. **b.** To rotate up and down or back and forth without being deflected by the pilot. Used of a control surface or a rocket motor in gimbals. **4. a.** To oscillate about a selected value. Used of a control system. **b.** To swing back and forth or to oscillate. Used of an indicator on a display or instrument panel. *—n.* **1.** The act or sport of hunting. **2. a.** A hunting expedition or outing, usually with horses and hounds. **b.** Those taking part in a hunt. **3.** A diligent and thorough search or pursuit: *the hunt for the escaped prisoner.* [ME *hunten* < OE *huntian.*]

hunt·er (hŭn′tər) *n.* **1.** A person who hunts. **2.** A dog bred or trained for use in hunting. **3.** A horse, esp. a fast, strong jumper, bred or trained for use in hunting.

hunt·ing (hŭn′tĭng) *n.* **1.** The sport or activity of pursuing game. **2.** *Elect.* The periodic variation in speed of a synchronous motor with respect to the current.

hunt·ress (hŭn′trĭs) *n.* A woman who hunts; hunter.

hunts·man (hŭnts′mən) *n.* **1.** A man who hunts; hunter. **2.** A man who manages the hounds in the hunting field.

hur·dle (hûr′dl) *n.* **1. a.** A light, portable barrier used in obstacle races that usually consists of two uprights between which a horizontal bar may be hung at varying heights. **b.** Often **hurdles.** A race in which hurdles must be jumped. **2.** An obstacle or difficulty. **3.** *Chiefly Brit.* A portable section of fencing used chiefly for folding sheep. **4.** *Chiefly Brit.* A frame or sledge formerly used to carry condemned persons to their executions. *—v.* **-dled, -dling, -dles.** *—tr.* **1.** To jump or leap over (a barrier) in or as if in a race. **2.** To overcome or deal with successfully. *—intr.* To jump or leap over a barrier in or as if in a race. [ME *hurdel,* portable panel for temporary fences < OE *hyrdel.*] **—hur′dler** *n.*

hur·dy-gur·dy (hûr′dē-gûr′dē, hûr′dē-gûr′dē) *n., pl.* **-dies.** A musical instrument, such as a barrel organ, played by turning a crank. [Prob. imit.]

hurl (hûrl) *v.* **hurled, hurl·ing, hurls.** *—tr.* **1.** To throw with or as if with great force: *hurl a javelin; hurling insults at each other.* **2.** To send with great vigor; thrust: *hurled the army against the enemy.* **3.** To throw down; overthrow. *—intr.* **1.** To move with great speed, force, or violence; hurtle. **2.** To pitch a baseball. *—n.* An act or instance of hurling. [ME *hurlen.*] **—hurl′er** *n.*

hurl·ing (hûr′lĭng) *n.* An Irish game resembling lacrosse but played with a broad-bladed, netless stick.

hur·ly-bur·ly (hûr′lē-bûr′lē) *n., pl.* **-lies.** Tumultuous commotion; uproar. [Alteration and redup. of *hurling,* gerund of HURL.]

Hu·ron (hyo͝or′ən, -ŏn′) *n., pl.* **Huron** or **-rons. 1.** A confederation of four tribes of North American Indians formerly inhabiting the region east of Lake Huron and the St. Lawrence Valley. **2.** A member of any of the Huron. **3.** The Iroquoian language of the Huron. [Fr. < OFr. *hure,* fur.] **—Hu′ron** *adj.*

hur·rah (ho͝o-rä′, -rô′) also **hoo·ray** or **hur·ray** (-rā′). *—interj.* Used as an exclamation of pleasure, approval, elation, or victory. *—n.* A shout of "hurrah." *—v.* **-rahed, -rah·ing, -rahs** also **-rayed, -ray·ing, -rays.** *—tr.* To applaud, cheer, or approve by shouting "hurrah." *—intr.* To shout "hurrah." [Alteration of HUZZAH.]

hur·ri·cane (hûr′ĭ-kān′) *n.* A severe tropical cyclone with winds exceeding approximately 119 kilometers per hour, or 74 miles per hour, originating in the tropical regions of the Atlantic Ocean or Caribbean Sea, traveling north, northwest, or northeast from its point of origin, and usually involving heavy rains. [Sp. *huracan* < Carib.]

hurricane deck *n.* The upper deck on a passenger steamship.

hurricane lamp *n.* A lamp that consists of a candle or electric bulb covered by a glass chimney.

hur·ried (hûr′ēd, hŭr′-) *adj.* **1.** Moving or acting rapidly; rushed. **2.** Done in great haste: *a hurried tour.* **—hur′ried·ly** *adv.* **—hur′ried·ness** *n.*

hur·ry (hûr′ē, hŭr′-) *v.* **-ried, -ry·ing, -ries.** *—intr.* To move or act with haste or speed: *hurried to the store.* *—tr.* **1.** To cause to move or act more rapidly; hasten. **2.** To cause to move or act too quickly; rush: *Don't hurry the cook or dinner will be spoiled.* **3.** To speed the progress or completion of; expedite. *—n., pl.* **-ries. 1.** The act of hurrying. **2.** The need or wish to hurry; a condition of urgency: *Are you in a hurry to leave?* [Perh. ME *horien.*] **—hur′ri·er** *n.*

hur·ry-scur·ry also **hur·ry-skur·ry** (hûr′ē-skûr′ē, hŭr′ē-skŭr′ē) *—intr.v.* **-ried, -ry·ing, -ries.** To move or act with undue hurry and confusion. *—n., pl.* **-ries.** Confused haste; agitation. [Redup. of HURRY.] **—hur′ry-scur′ry** *adj. & adv.*

hurt (hûrt) *v.* **hurt, hurt·ing, hurts.** *—tr.* **1.** To cause physical damage or pain to; injure. **2.** To cause mental or emotional suffering to; distress. **3.** To damage or impair: *hurt his chances for victory.* *—intr.* **1.** To have a feeling of pain or discomfort: *My leg hurts.* **2.** To cause suffering, distress, or damage: *The tax bill hurts.* *—n.* **1.** Something that hurts; a pain, injury, or wound. **2.** Mental suffering; anguish. **3.** A wrong; harm. [ME *hurten,* perh. < OFr. *hurter,* to bang into, of Germanic orig.] **—hurt′er** *n.*

hurt·ful (hûrt′fəl) *adj.* Causing hurt or injury; damaging. **—hurt′ful·ly** *adv.* **—hurt′ful·ness** *n.*

hur·tle (hûr′tl) *v.* **-tled, -tling, -tles.** *—intr.* To move with or as if with great speed and a rushing noise. *—tr.* To throw or fling with great force; hurl. [ME *hurtlen,* to collide, freq. of *hurten,* to hurt.]

hurt·less (hûrt′lĭs) *adj.* **1.** Causing no hurt; harmless. **2.** Having no hurt; unhurt.

hus·band (hŭz′bənd) *n.* **1.** A married man. **2.** *Archaic.* A manager or steward, as of a household. **3.** A prudent and thrifty manager. *—tr.v.* **-band·ed, -band·ing, -bands. 1.** To manage or use economically; conserve: *husbanded her energy.* **2.** *Archaic.* To find a husband for. [ME *huseband* < OE *hūsbōnda* < ON *hūsbōndi* : *hūs,* house + *bōndi,* dwelling < *būa,* to dwell.]

hus·band·man (hŭz′bənd-mən) *n.* A person whose occupation is husbandry; farmer. [ME *husbondman.*]

hus·band·ry (hŭz′bən-drē) *n.* **1. a.** The cultivation of crops and the breeding and raising of livestock; agriculture. **b.** The application of scientific principles, esp. to animal breeding. **2.** Good, careful management of resources; economy. [ME *husbondri* < *huseband,* husband.]

hush (hŭsh) *v.* **hushed, hush·ing, hush·es.** —*tr.* **1.** To make silent or quiet. **2.** To calm; soothe. **3.** To keep from the knowledge of the public; suppress. —*intr.* To be or become silent or still. —*n.* A silence or stillness, esp. after noise. —*adj. Archaic.* Silent; quiet. [Prob. back-formation < ME *husht,* silent.]

hush-hush (hŭsh′hŭsh′) *adj. Informal.* Secret; confidential.

hush money *n. Informal.* A bribe or payment made to keep something secret.

hush·pup·py (hŭsh′pŭp′ē) *n.* A fried cornmeal fritter. [From its use as food for dogs.]

husk (hŭsk) *n.* **1.** The membranous or green outer envelope of many fruits and seeds, as of an ear of corn or a nut. **2.** A shell or outer layer that is often worthless. **3.** A framework that serves as a support. —*tr.v.* **husked, husk·ing, husks.** To remove the husk from. [ME.] **—husk′er** *n.*

husking bee *n.* A cornhusking (sense 2).

husk·y[1] (hŭs′kē) *adj.* **-i·er, -i·est. 1.** Hoarse or deep, as from emotion: *a husky voice.* **2. a.** Resembling a husk. **b.** Containing husks. [< HUSK.] **—husk′i·ly** *adv.* **—husk′i·ness** *n.*

husk·y[2] (hŭs′kē) *adj.* **-i·er, -i·est.** *Informal.* Rugged and strong; burly. —*n., pl.* **-ies.** A husky person. [Perh. < HUSK.] **—husk′i·ness** *n.*

hus·ky[3] (hŭs′kē) *n., pl.* **-kies. 1.** Often **Husky.** A dog of a breed developed in Siberia for pulling sleds, having a dense, furry, variously colored coat. **2.** A dog similar to a husky of a breed of Arctic origin. [Prob. shortening and alteration of ESKIMO.]

hus·sar (hə-zär′, -sär′) *n.* **1.** A horseman of the Hungarian light cavalry organized during the 15th century. **2.** A member of any of various European units of light cavalry. [Hung. *huszár* < Serbian *husar* < OItal. *corsaro.* —see CORSAIR.]

Huss·ite (hŭs′īt′, ho͝os′-) *n.* A follower of the Bohemian religious reformer John Huss. —*adj.* Of or pertaining to John Huss or his religious theories. **—Huss′it′ism** *n.*

hus·sy (hŭz′ē, hŭs′ē) *n., pl.* **-sies. 1.** A saucy or mischievous girl. **2.** An immoral woman. [Alteration of HOUSEWIFE.]

hust·ings (hŭs′tĭngz) *pl.n. (used with a sing. or pl. verb).* **1.** *Chiefly Brit.* A court formerly held in some English cities and still held infrequently in London. **2.** *Chiefly Brit.* **a.** A platform on which candidates for Parliament formerly stood to address the electors. **b.** The proceedings at a parliamentary election. **3. a.** A place where political speeches are made. **b.** An act or instance of political campaigning. [ME *husting,* court of common pleas < OE *hūsting,* meeting < ON *hūsðing* : *hūs,* house + *ðing,* assembly.]

hus·tle (hŭs′əl) *v.* **-tled, -tling, -tles.** —*tr.* **1.** To jostle or shove roughly. **2.** *Informal.* To move hurriedly or urgently: *hustle the prisoner onto a plane.* **3.** *Informal.* To urge forward; hurry along. **4.** *Slang.* **a.** To gain by energetic effort. **b.** To sell or obtain by questionable means. —*intr.* **1.** To jostle; push. **2.** *Informal.* To perform or move energetically and rapidly. **3.** *Slang.* To obtain something by deceitful and underhand methods. **4.** *Slang.* To solicit customers for or as a prostitute. —*n. Informal.* **1.** An act or instance of hustling. **2.** Busy activity. [Du. *husselen,* to shake < MDu. *hustelen,* freq. of *hutsen.*] **—hus′tler** *n.*

hut (hŭt) *n.* **1.** A makeshift or crude dwelling or shelter; shack. **2.** A temporary structure for sheltering troops. —*tr. & intr.v.* **hut·ted, hut·ting, huts.** To shelter or take shelter in a hut. [Fr. *hutte,* of Germanic orig.]

hutch (hŭch) *n.* **1.** A pen or coop for small animals, esp. rabbits. **2.** A cupboard with drawers for storage and usually open shelves above. **3.** A chest or bin for storage. **4.** A hut. [ME *huche* < OFr., fishpond < Med. Lat.]

hut·ment (hŭt′mənt) *n.* An encampment of huts.

hutz·pah (ho͝ot′spə, KHo͝ot′-) *n.* Variant of **chutzpah.**

Huy·gens' principle (hī′gənz) *n.* The principle that any point on a wave front may be regarded as the source of a secondary wave and that the position of the wave front at any time is determined by the envelope at that time of the secondary waves arising from a previous wave front. [After Christiaan *Huygens* (1629–1695).]

huz·za also **huz·zah** (hə-zä′) *Archaic.* —*n.* A shout of encouragement or triumph; cheer. —*interj.* Used to express joy, encouragement, or triumph. [Orig. unknown.]

hy·a·cinth (hī′ə-sĭnth) *n.* **1. a.** Any of several bulbous plants of the genus *Hyacinthus,* native to the Mediterranean region, having narrow leaves and a terminal cluster of variously colored, usually very fragrant flowers, esp. the widely cultivated species *H. orientalis.* **b.** Any of several similar or related plants. **2.** A plant, perhaps a lily, gladiolus, or iris, that, according to Greek mythology, sprang from the blood of the slain Hyacinthus. **3.** A deep purplish blue to vivid violet. **4. a.** A reddish or cinnamon-colored variety of transparent zircon, used as a gemstone. **b.** A blue precious stone, perhaps a sapphire, known in antiquity. [Lat. *hyacinthus* < Gk. *huakinthos,* wild hyacinth.] **—hy′a·cin′thine** (-sĭn′thĭn, -thīn′) *adj.*

hyacinth bean *n.* A twining vine, *Dolichos lablab,* of the Old World tropics, having purple or white flowers and edible pods and seeds.

Hy·a·cin·thus (hī′ə-sĭn′thəs) *n. Gk. Myth.* A beautiful youth, loved but accidentally killed by Apollo, from whose blood Apollo caused the hyacinth to grow. [Lat. < Gk. *Huakinthos.*]

Hy·a·des (hī′ə-dēz′) *pl.n.* **1.** *Gk. Myth.* The five daughters of Atlas and sisters of the Pleiades, placed by Zeus in the heavens. **2.** *Astron.* An asterism of five stars in the constellation Taurus, supposed by ancient astronomers to indicate rain when they rose with the sun. [Lat. < Gk. *Huades.*]

hy·ae·na (hī-ē′nə) *n.* Variant of **hyena.**

hy·a·lin (hī′ə-lĭn) also **hy·a·line** (-lĭn, -līn′) *n.* **1.** *Physiol.* The uniform matrix of hyaline cartilage. **2.** *Pathol.* A transparent substance occurring in certain degenerative skin conditions. [Gk. *hualos,* glass + -IN.]

hy·a·line (hī′ə-lĭn, -līn′) *adj.* Translucent or transparent like glass. —*n.* **1.** A glassy or transparent appearance. **2.** Something that is translucent or transparent. **3.** Variant of **hyalin.** [LLat. *hyalinus* < Gk. *hualinos* < *hualos,* glass.]

hyaline cartilage *n.* Cartilage that has a glassy, translucent appearance and a bluish color, which in the adult is composed of cells in a seemingly homogeneous, translucent matrix, as in joints, and which in the fetus forms most of the skeleton.

hy·a·lite (hī′ə-līt′) *n.* A clear, colorless opal. [G. *Hyalit* < Gk. *hualos,* glass.]

hy·a·loid (hī′ə-loid′) *adj.* Glassy or transparent in appearance; hyaline. [Gk. *hualoeidēs* : *hualos,* glass + *-eidēs,* -oid.]

hy·a·lo·plasm (hī′ə-lō-plăz′əm) *n.* The clear, fluid portion of cytoplasm as distinguished from included granular and netlike components. [G. *Hyaloplasma* : Gk. *hualos,* glass + G. *-plasma,* -plasm.]

hy·brid (hī′brĭd) *n.* **1.** *Genetics.* The offspring of genetically dissimilar parents or stock, esp. the offspring produced by breeding plants or animals of different varieties, species, or races. **2.** Something of mixed origin or composition. **3.** A word whose elements are derived from different languages. ***—modifier:** a hybrid tulip.* [Lat. *hybrida.*] **—hy′brid·ism** *n.* **—hy·brid′i·ty** (hī-brĭd′ĭ-tē) *n.*

hy·brid·ize (hī′brĭ-dīz′) *intr. & tr.v.* **-ized, -iz·ing, -iz·es.** To produce or cause to produce hybrids; crossbreed. **—hy′brid·i·za′tion** *n.* **—hy′brid·iz′er** *n.*

hy·brid·o·ma (hī′brĭ-dō′mə) *n.* A cell resulting from the hybridization of a lymphocyte and tumor cell that is used to produce a specific antibody.

hybrid vigor *n.* Heterosis.

hy·da·thode (hī′də-thōd′) *n.* A microscopic epidermal structure in many plants through which water is excreted. [Gk. *hudōr, hydat-,* water + *hodos,* road.]

hy·da·tid (hī′də-tĭd) *n.* **1.** A cyst formed as a result of infestation by a tapeworm, *Echinococcus granulosus,* in a larval stage. **2.** The encysted larva of *E. granulosus.* [Gk. *hudatis, hudatid-,* watery vesicle < *hudōr,* water.]

hydr– *pref.* Variant of **hydro-.**

Hy·dra (hī′drə) *n.* **1.** *Gk. Myth.* A many-headed monster that was slain by Hercules. **2.** A constellation in the equatorial region of the southern sky near Cancer, Libra, and Centaurus. **3. hydra** *pl.* **-dras** or **-drae** (-drē). Any of various small, freshwater polyps of the genus *Hydra* and related genera, having a naked, cylindrical body and an oral opening surrounded by tentacles. **4. hydra** A multifarious source of destruction that cannot be eradicated by a single attempt. [ME *Idra* < Lat. *Hydra* < Gk. *Hudra.*]

hy·dral·a·zine (hī-drăl′ə-zēn′) *n.* An antihypertensive drug, $C_8H_8N_4$. [HYDR(O)- + (PHTH)AL(IC ACID) + AZINE.]

hy·dran·gea (hī-drān′jə, -drăn′-) *n.* Any of various shrubs or trees of the genus *Hydrangea,* having large, flat-topped or rounded clusters of white, pink, or blue flowers. [NLat. *Hydrangea,* genus name : Gk. *hudōr,* water + Gk. *angos,* vessel.]

hy·drant (hī′drənt) *n.* An upright pipe with a nozzle or spout for drawing water from a water main.

hy·dranth (hī′drănth′) *n.* The oral opening and tentacles of a feeding polyp in a hydroid colony. [HYDR(O)- + Gk. *anthos,* flower.]

hy·drase (hī′drās′, -drāz′) *n.* An enzyme that catalyzes the addition or removal of water from a substrate.

hy·dras·tine (hī-drăs′tēn′, -tĭn) *n.* A poisonous white alkaloid, $C_{21}H_{21}NO_6$, obtained from the root of the goldenseal, *Hydrastis canadensis,* and used locally to treat catarrhal inflammation of mucous membranes. [NLat. *Hydrastis,* plant genus + -INE[2].]

hy·drate (hī′drāt′) *n.* A compound containing water combined in a definite ratio, the water being retained or regarded as being retained in its molecular state. —*v.* **-drat·ed, -drat·ing, -drates.** —*tr.* To combine with water, esp. to form a hydrate. —*intr.* To become a hydrate. **—hy·dra′tion** *n.* **—hy′dra′tor** *n.*

hy·drat·ed (hī′drā′tĭd) *adj.* Chemically combined with water, esp. existing in the form of a hydrate.

hy·drau·lic (hī-drô′lĭk) *adj.* **1.** Of, involving, moved, or operated by a fluid, esp. water, under pressure. **2.** Setting and hardening under water, as Portland cement. **3.** Of or pertaining to hydraulics. [Lat. *hydraulicus* < Gk. *hudraulis,* wa-

hyacinth

Hydra
A hydra budding

hydrangea

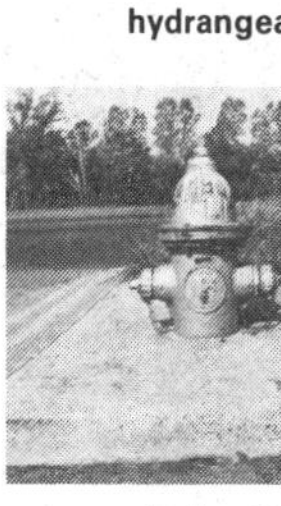

hydrant

ter organ : *hudor,* water + *aulos,* pipe.] **—hy·drau'li·cal·ly** *adv.*

hydraulic brake *n.* A brake in which the braking force is transmitted to the braking surface by a compressed fluid.

hydraulic cement *n.* A cement capable of solidifying under water.

hydraulic press *n.* A machine in which a large force is exerted on the larger of two pistons in a pair of hydraulically coupled cylinders by means of a relatively small force applied to the smaller piston.

hydraulic ram *n.* **1.** A water pump in which the downward flow of naturally running water is intermittently halted by a valve so that the flow is forced upward through an open pipe into a reservoir. **2.** The large output piston of a hydraulic press.

hy·drau·lics (hī-drô'lĭks) *n. (used with a sing. verb).* The physical science and technology of the static and dynamic behavior of fluids.

hy·dra·zine (hī'drə-zēn', -zĭn) *n.* A colorless, fuming, corrosive hygroscopic liquid, H_2NNH_2, used in jet and rocket fuels.

hy·dric (hī'drĭk) *adj.* **1.** Of, containing, or pertaining to hydrogen. **2.** Pertaining to, characterized by, or requiring considerable moisture.

hy·dride (hī'drīd') *n.* A compound of hydrogen with another, more electropositive element or group.

hy·dri·od·ic acid (hī'drē-ŏd'ĭk) *n.* A clear colorless or pale-yellow aqueous solution of hydrogen iodide, HI, that is a strong acid and reducing agent.

hydro– or **hydr–** *pref.* **1. a.** Water: *hydroelectric.* **b.** Liquid: *hydrodynamics.* **2.** Hydrogen: *hydrochloride.* [< Gk. *hudōr,* water.]

hy·dro·bi·ol·o·gy (hī'drō-bī-ŏl'ə-jē) *n.* Limnology. **—hy'dro·bi'o·log'i·cal** (-bī'ə-lŏj'ĭ-kəl) *adj.* **—hy'dro·bi·ol'o·gist** *n.*

hy·dro·bro·mic acid (hī'drə-brō'mĭk) *n.* A clear colorless or faintly yellow highly acidic and corrosive aqueous solution of hydrogen bromide, HBr, used in the manufacture of bromides.

hy·dro·car·bon (hī'drə-kär'bən) *n.* Any of numerous organic compounds, such as benzene and methane, that contain only carbon and hydrogen. **—hy'dro·car'bo·na'ceous** (-bə-nā'shəs), **hy'dro·car·bon'ic** (-bŏn'ĭk), **hy'dro·car'bon·ous** (-bə-nəs) *adj.*

hy·dro·cele (hī'drə-sēl') *n.* A pathological accumulation of serous fluid in a bodily cavity, esp. in the testes. [Lat. < Gk. *hudrokēle* : *hudōr,* water + *kēlē,* tumor.]

hy·dro·ceph·a·lus (hī'drō-sĕf'ə-ləs) also **hy·dro·ceph·a·ly** (-lē) *n.* A usually congenital condition in which an abnormal accumulation of fluid in the cerebral ventricles causes enlargement of the skull and compression of the brain. [NLat. < Gk. *hudrokephalon* : *hudōr,* water + *kephalē,* head.] **—hy'dro·ce·phal'ic** (-sə-făl'ĭk), **hy'dro·ceph'a·loid', hy'dro·ceph'a·lous** *adj.*

hy·dro·chlo·ric acid (hī'drə-klôr'ĭk, -klōr'-) *n.* A clear, colorless, fuming, poisonous, highly acidic aqueous solution of hydrogen chloride, HCl, used in petroleum production, as a chemical intermediate, and in ore reduction, food processing, pickling, and metal cleaning.

hy·dro·chlo·ride (hī'drə-klôr'īd', -klōr'-) *n.* A compound resulting or regarded as resulting from the reaction of hydrochloric acid with an organic base.

hy·dro·col·loid (hī'drə-kŏl'oid') *n.* A substance that forms a gel with water. **—hy'dro·col·loid'al** (-kə-loid'l) *adj.*

hy·dro·cor·al (hī'drə-kôr'əl, -kŏr'-) *n.* Any of various colonial marine hydrozoans of the order Hydrocorallinae, having a limestone skeleton and thus resembling the true corals.

hy·dro·cor·ti·sone (hī'drə-kôr'tĭ-sōn', -zōn') *n.* A bitter crystalline hormone, $C_{21}H_{30}O_5$, derived from the adrenal cortex and having activity and medical uses similar to those of cortisone.

hy·dro·cy·an·ic acid (hī'drō-sī-ăn'ĭk) *n.* A colorless, volatile, extremely toxic, flammable aqueous solution of hydrogen cyanide, HCN, used in the manufacture of dyes, fumigants, and plastics.

hy·dro·dy·nam·ic (hī'drō-dī-năm'ĭk) also **hy·dro·dy·nam·i·cal** (-ĭ-kəl) *adj.* **1.** Of or pertaining to hydrodynamics. **2.** Of, pertaining to, or operated by the force of liquid in motion. **—hy'dro·dy·nam'i·cal·ly** *adv.*

hy·dro·dy·nam·ics (hī'drō-dī-năm'ĭks) *n. (used with a sing. verb).* The dynamics of fluids, esp. incompressible fluids, in motion. **—hy'dro·dy·nam'i·cist** *n.*

hy·dro·e·lec·tric (hī'drō-ĭ-lĕk'trĭk) *adj.* **1.** Generating electricity by conversion of the energy of running water. **2.** Of, pertaining to, or using electricity so generated. **—hy'dro·e·lec'tri·cal·ly** *adv.* **—hy'dro·e·lec·tric'i·ty** (-ĭ-lĕk-trĭs'ĭ-tē) *n.*

hy·dro·flu·or·ic acid (hī'drō-flōō-ôr'ĭk, -ŏr'-, -flōōr'ĭk) *n.* A colorless, fuming, corrosive, dangerously poisonous aqueous solution of hydrogen fluoride, HF, used to etch or polish glass, pickle certain metals, and clean masonry.

hydrofoil

hy·dro·foil (hī'drə-foil') *n.* **1.** One of a set of blades attached to the hull of a boat and aligned in the water at a small angle to the horizontal so that when the boat is in motion the fluid striking each blade's underside creates a high-pressure region below the blade, low pressure above it, and a resultant lift that raises the craft out of the water for efficient high-speed operation. **2.** A boat equipped with hydrofoils.

hy·dro·form·ing (hī'drə-fôr'mĭng) *n.* A process in which naphthas are converted to high-octane aromatics in the presence of hydrogen and a catalyst under pressure and heat. **—hy'dro·form'er** *n.*

hy·dro·gen (hī'drə-jən) *n. Symbol* **H** A colorless, highly flammable gaseous element, the lightest of all gases and the most abundant element in the universe, used in the production of synthetic ammonia and methanol, in petroleum refining, in the hydrogenation of organic materials, as a reducing atmosphere, in oxyhydrogen torches, and in rocket fuels. Atomic number 1; atomic weight 1.00797; melting point –259.14°C; boiling point –252.5°C; density 0.08988 gram per liter; valence 1. [Fr. *hydrogène* : Gk. *hudōr,* water + *-gène,* -gen.] **—hy·drog'e·nous** (-drŏj'ə-nəs) *adj.*

hy·drog·e·nase (hī-drŏj'ə-nās', -nāz') *n.* An enzyme that catalyzes the formation of hydrogen in certain microorganisms.

hy·dro·gen·ate (hī'drə-jə-nāt', hī-drŏj'ə-) *tr.v.* **-at·ed, -at·ing, -ates.** To combine with or subject to the action of hydrogen, esp. to combine (an unsaturated compound) with hydrogen. **—hy'dro·gen·a'tion** *n.* **—hy'dro·gen·a'tor** *n.*

hydrogen bomb *n.* An explosive weapon of great destructive power derived from the fusion of nuclei of various hydrogen isotopes in the formation of helium nuclei.

hydrogen bond *n.* An essentially ionic chemical bond between a strongly electronegative atom and a hydrogen atom already bonded to another strongly electronegative atom.

hydrogen bromide *n.* An irritating colorless gas, HBr, used in the manufacture of barbiturates and synthetic hormones.

hydrogen chloride *n.* A colorless, fuming, corrosive, suffocating gas, HCl, used in the manufacture of plastics.

hydrogen cyanide *n.* Hydrocyanic acid.

hydrogen fluoride *n.* A colorless, fuming, mobile, corrosive liquid, or a highly soluble corrosive gas, HF, used in the manufacture of hydrofluoric acid, as a reagent, catalyst, and fluorinating agent, and in the refining of uranium and the preparation of many fluorine compounds.

hydrogen iodide *n.* A corrosive, colorless, suffocating gas, HI, used to manufacture hydriodic acid.

hydrogen ion *n.* The positively charged ion of hydrogen, H^+, formed by removal of the electron from atomic hydrogen.

hy·dro·gen·ol·y·sis (hī'drō-jə-nŏl'ĭ-sĭs) *n.* The breaking of a chemical bond in an organic molecule with the simultaneous addition of a hydrogen atom to each of the resulting molecular fragments.

hydrogen peroxide *n.* A colorless, heavy, strongly oxidizing liquid, H_2O_2, an essentially unstable compound, capable of reacting explosively with combustibles and used principally in aqueous solution as an antiseptic, bleaching agent, oxidizing agent, and laboratory reagent.

hydrogen sulfide *n.* A colorless, flammable, poisonous compound, H_2S, having a characteristic rotten-egg odor and used as a precipitator, purifier, and reagent.

hy·drog·ra·phy (hī-drŏg'rə-fē) *n., pl.* **-phies. 1.** The scientific description and analysis of the physical conditions, boundaries, flow, and related characteristics of oceans, lakes, rivers, and other surface waters. **2.** The mapping of bodies of water. **3.** A book on hydrography. [OFr. *hydrographie* : *hydro-,* hydro- + *-graphie,* -graphy.] **—hy·drog'ra·pher** *n.* **—hy'dro·graph'ic** (hī'drə-grăf'ĭk) *adj.* **—hy'dro·graph'i·cal·ly** *adv.*

hy·droid (hī'droid') *n.* **1.** Any of numerous characteristically colonial hydrozoan coelenterates having a polyp rather than a medusoid form as the dominant stage of the life cycle. **2.** The asexual polyp in the life cycle of a hydrozoan. *—adj.* Of, pertaining to, or characteristic of a hydroid. [NLat. *Hydra,* hydra genus + -OID.]

hy·dro·ki·net·ic (hī'drō-kĭ-nĕt'ĭk, -kī-) also **hy·dro·ki·net·i·cal** (-ĭ-kəl) *adj.* **1.** Of or pertaining to hydrokinetics. **2.** Of or pertaining to the kinetic energy and motion of fluids.

hy·dro·ki·net·ics (hī'drō-kĭ-nĕt'ĭks, -kī-) *n. (used with a sing. verb).* The kinetics of fluids, esp. incompressible fluids, in motion.

hy·drol·o·gy (hī-drŏl'ə-jē) *n.* The scientific study of the properties, distribution, and effects of water on the earth's surface, in the soil and underlying rocks, and in the atmosphere. **—hy'dro·log'ic** (-drə-lŏj'ĭk), **hy'dro·log'i·cal** *adj.* **—hy'dro·log'i·cal·ly** *adv.* **—hy·drol'o·gist** *n.*

hy·drol·y·sate (hī-drŏl'ĭ-sāt', hī'drə-lī'-) also **hy·drol·y·zate** (-zāt') *n.* A product of hydrolysis. [HYDROLYS(IS) + -ATE.]

hy·drol·y·sis (hī-drŏl'ĭ-sĭs) *n.* Decomposition of a chemical compound by reaction with water, such as the dissociation of a dissolved salt or the catalytic conversion of glucose to starch. **—hy'dro·lyte'** (-līt') *n.* **—hy'dro·lyt'ic** (-drə-lĭt'ĭk) *adj.*

hy·dro·lyze (hī'drə-līz') *tr. & intr.v.* **-lyzed, -lyz·ing, -lyz·es.** To subject to or undergo hydrolysis. **—hy'dro·lyz'a·ble** *adj.* **—hy'dro·ly·za'tion** *n.*

hy·dro·mag·net·ics (hī'drō-măg-nĕt'ĭks) *n.* Magnetohydrodynamics. **—hy'dro·mag·net'ic** *adj.*

hy·dro·man·cy (hī'drə-măn'sē) *n.* Divination by water. [ME *ydromancy* < OFr. *hydromancie* < Lat. *hydromantia* < Gk. *hudromanteia* : *hudōr,* water + *manteia,* divination. —see -MANCY.]

hy·dro·me·chan·ics (hī'drō-mĭ-kăn'ĭks) *n. (used with a sing. verb).* Mechanics dealing with the motion and equilibrium states of fluids. —**hy'dro·me·chan'i·cal** *adj.*

hy·dro·me·du·sa (hī'drō-mĭ-do͞o'sə, -dyo͞o'-) *n., pl.* **-sas** or **-sae** (-sē). A hydrozoan in its medusoid stage. [HYDRO(ID) + MEDUSA.]

hy·dro·mel (hī'drə-mĕl') *n.* Mead[1]. [ME *ydromel* < OFr. < Lat. *hydromel* < Gk. *hudromeli* : *hudōr,* water + *meli,* honey.]

hy·dro·met·al·lur·gy (hī'drō-mĕt'l-ûr'jē) *n.* The separation of metal from ores and ore concentrates by chemical reactions in aqueous solution, as leaching, extraction, and precipitation. —**hy'dro·met'al·lur'gi·cal** *adj.*

hy·dro·me·te·or (hī'drō-mē'tē-ər, -ôr') *n.* A precipitation body, such as rain, snow, sleet, or hail, derived from the condensation of water in the atmosphere.

hy·dro·me·te·or·ol·o·gy (hī'drō-mē'tē-ə-rŏl'ə-jē) *n.* The meteorology of the occurrence, motion, and changes of state of atmospheric water. —**hy'dro·me'te·or'o·log'i·cal** (-ôr'ə-lŏj'ĭ-kəl, -ŏr'-) *adj.* —**hy'dro·me'te·or·ol'o·gist** *n.*

hy·drom·e·ter (hī-drŏm'ĭ-tər) *n.* An instrument used to determine specific gravity, esp. a sealed, graduated tube, weighted at one end, that sinks in a fluid to a depth used as a measure of the fluid's specific gravity. —**hy'dro·met'ric** (hī'drə-mĕt'rĭk), **hy'dro·met'ri·cal** *adj.* —**hy'dro·met'ri·cal·ly** *adv.* —**hy·drom'e·try** *n.*

hy·dro·ni·um (hī-drō'nē-əm) *n.* A hydrated hydrogen ion, H_3O^+. [HYDR(O)- + (AMM)ONIUM.]

hy·drop·a·thy (hī-drŏp'ə-thē) *n.* The therapeutic use of water. —**hy'dro·path'ic** (hī'drə-păth'ĭk), **hy'dro·path'i·cal** *adj.* —**hy·drop'a·thist, hy'dro·path'** *n.*

hy·dro·phane (hī'drə-fān') *n.* An opal that is almost opaque when dry but transparent when wet. —**hy·droph'a·nous** (hī-drŏf'ə-nəs) *adj.*

hy·dro·phil·ic (hī'drə-fĭl'ĭk) *adj.* Having an affinity for, absorbing, wetting smoothly with, tending to combine with, or capable of dissolving in water. [NLat. *hydrophilus,* hydrophilous + -IC.] —**hy'dro·phile'** (hī'drə-fĭl') *n.* —**hy'dro·phi·lic'i·ty** (-fə-lĭs'ĭ-tē) *n.*

hy·droph·i·lous (hī-drŏf'ə-ləs) *adj. Bot.* Growing or thriving in water. —**hy·droph'i·ly** *n.*

hy·dro·pho·bi·a (hī'drə-fō'bē-ə) *n.* **1.** Fear of water. **2.** Rabies.

hy·dro·pho·bic (hī'drə-fō'bĭk, -fŏb'ĭk) *adj.* **1.** Antagonistic to, shedding, tending not to combine with, or incapable of dissolving in water. **2.** Of or exhibiting hydrophobia. —**hy'dro·pho·bic'i·ty** (-bĭs'ĭ-tē) *n.*

hy·dro·phone (hī'drə-fōn') *n.* An electrical instrument for detecting or monitoring sound under water.

hy·dro·phyte (hī'drə-fīt') *n.* A plant that grows in and is adapted to an aquatic or very wet environment. —**hy'dro·phyt'ic** (-fĭt'ĭk) *adj.*

hy·dro·plane (hī'drə-plān') *n.* **1.** A seaplane. **2.** A motorboat designed so that the prow and much of the hull lift out of the water and skim the surface at high speeds. **3.** A hydrofoil (sense 2). **4.** A horizontal rudder on a submarine. —*intr.v.* **-planed, -plan·ing, -planes. 1.** To drive or ride in a hydroplane. **2. a.** To skim along on the surface of the water. **b.** To be or go out of control by skimming along the surface of a wet road. Used of a car.

hy·dro·pon·ics (hī'drə-pŏn'ĭks) *n. (used with a sing. verb).* The cultivation of plants in water containing dissolved inorganic nutrients, rather than in soil. [HYDRO- + (GEO)PONICS.] —**hy'dro·pon'ic** *adj.* —**hy'dro·pon'i·cal·ly** *adv.* —**hy'dro·pon'i·cist, hy'dro·pon'ist** *n.*

hy·dro·qui·none (hī'drō-kwĭ-nōn', -kwĭn'ōn') also **hy·dro·quin·ol** (-kwĭn'ôl', -ōl') *n.* A white crystalline compound, $C_6H_4(OH)_2$, used as a photographic developer, antioxidant, stabilizer, and reagent.

hy·dro·scope (hī'drə-skōp') *n.* An optical device used for viewing objects much below the surface of water. —**hy'dro·scop'ic** (-skŏp'ĭk) *adj.*

hy·dro·sol (hī'drə-sôl', -sōl') *n.* A sol with water as the dispersing medium. [HYDRO- + SOL(UTION).] —**hy'dro·sol'ic** (-sŏl'ĭk) *adj.*

hy·dro·sphere (hī'drə-sfîr') *n.* The waters of the earth distinguished from the lithosphere and the atmosphere. —**hy'dro·spher'ic** (-sfîr'ĭk, -sfĕr'-) *adj.*

hy·dro·stat·ic (hī'drə-stăt'ĭk) also **hy·dro·stat·i·cal** (-ĭ-kəl) *adj.* Of or pertaining to hydrostatics. —**hy'dro·stat'i·cal·ly** *adv.*

hy·dro·stat·ics (hī'drə-stăt'ĭks) *n. (used with a sing. verb).* The statics of fluids, esp. incompressible fluids.

hy·dro·sul·fate (hī'drə-sŭl'fāt') *n.* A salt formed by the union of sulfuric acid with an alkaloid or other organic base.

hy·dro·sul·fide (hī'drə-sŭl'fīd') *n.* A chemical compound derived from hydrogen sulfide by replacement of one of the hydrogen atoms with a basic radical or base.

hy·dro·sul·fite (hī'drə-sŭl'fīt') *n.* **1.** A salt of hyposulfurous acid. **2.** Sodium hydrosulfite.

hy·dro·sul·fu·rous acid (hī'drō-sŭl-fyo͝or'əs, -sŭl'fər-əs) *n.* Hyposulfurous acid.

hy·dro·tax·is (hī'drə-tăk'sĭs) *n. Biol.* Movement of an organism in response to moisture. —**hy'dro·tac'tic** (-tăk'tĭk) *adj.*

hy·dro·ther·a·peu·tics (hī'drə-thĕr'ə-pyo͞o'tĭks) *n. (used with a sing. verb).* Hydrotherapy. —**hy'dro·ther'a·peu'tic** *adj.*

hy·dro·ther·a·py (hī'drə-thĕr'ə-pē) *n., pl.* **-pies.** The medical use of water in the treatment of certain diseases.

hy·dro·ther·mal (hī'drə-thûr'məl) *adj.* **1.** Of or relating to hot water. **2.** *Geol.* **a.** Of or relating to hot magmatic emanations that are rich in water. **b.** Of or relating to the rocks, ore deposits, and springs produced by such emanations. —**hy'dro·ther'mal·ly** *adv.*

hy·dro·tho·rax (hī'drə-thôr'ăks', -thōr'-) *n.* The presence of serous fluid from the blood in one or both pleural cavities, often associated with cardiac failure.

hy·drot·ro·pism (hī-drŏt'rə-pĭz'əm) *n.* Growth or movement of an organism in response to water. —**hy'dro·tro'pic** (hī'drə-trō'pĭk, -trŏp'ĭk) *adj.* —**hy'dro·tro'pi·cal·ly** *adv.*

hy·drous (hī'drəs) *adj.* Containing water, esp. that of crystallization or hydration.

hy·drox·ide (hī-drŏk'sīd') *n.* A chemical compound containing the hydroxyl group.

hydroxide ion *n.* The ion OH^-, characteristic of basic hydroxides.

hy·drox·y (hī-drŏk'sē) *adj.* Containing the hydroxyl group, as an acid. [< HYDROXYL.]

hy·drox·yl (hī-drŏk'sĭl) *n.* The univalent radical or group OH, characteristic of bases, certain acids, phenols, alcohols, carboxylic and sulfonic acids, and amphoteric compounds. [HYDR(O)- + OX(YGEN) + -YL.] —**hy'drox·yl'ic** (hī'drŏk-sĭl'ĭk) *adj.*

hy·drox·yl·a·mine (hī-drŏk'sə-lə-mēn', hī'drŏk-sĭl'ə-mēn') *n.* A colorless crystalline compound, NH_2OH, explosive when heated above 130°C, that is used as a reducing agent and in organic synthesis.

hy·drox·yl·ate (hī-drŏk'sə-lāt') *tr.v.* **-at·ed, -at·ing, -ates.** To introduce the hydroxyl radical into. —**hy·drox'y·la'tion** *n.*

hydroxyl ion *n.* A hydroxide ion.

hy·dro·zo·an (hī'drə-zō'ən) *n.* Any of numerous coelenterates of the class Hydrozoa, which includes the hydroids, hydrocorals, and siphonophores. —*adj.* Of, pertaining to, or belonging to the class Hydrozoa. [< NLat. *Hydrozoa,* class name : HYDRO- + Gk. *zōia,* pl. of *zōion,* animal.]

Hy·drus (hī'drəs) *n.* A constellation in the Southern Hemisphere near Tucana and Mensa. [Lat. < Gk. *hudros,* water serpent.]

hy·e·na also **hy·ae·na** (hī-ē'nə) *n.* Any of several carnivorous mammals of the genera *Hyaena* or *Crocuta,* of Africa and Asia, having powerful jaws, relatively short hind limbs, and coarse hair. [ME *hiena* < Med. Lat. < Lat. *hyaena* < Gk. *huaina* < *hys,* hog.]

hyena

hy·e·tal (hī'ĭ-tl) *adj.* Of or relating to rain or to rainy regions. [< Gk. *huetos,* rain.]

Hy·ge·ia (hī-jē'ə) *n. Gk. Myth.* The goddess of health. [Gk. *Hugieia* < *hugiēs,* healthy.]

hy·giene (hī'jēn') *n.* **1.** The science of health and the prevention of disease. **2.** Conditions and practices that serve to promote or preserve health. [Fr. *hygiène* and NLat. *hygiena,* both < Gk. *hugieinos,* healthful < *hugiēs,* healthy.] —**hy·gien'ist** (hī-jē'nĭst, hī'jē'-, hī-jĕn'ĭst) *n.*

hy·gi·en·ic (hī'jē-ĕn'ĭk, hī-jĕn'-) *adj.* **1.** Of or pertaining to hygiene. **2.** Tending to promote or preserve health. **3.** Sanitary. —**hy'gi·en'i·cal·ly** *adv.*

hy·gi·en·ics (hī'jē-ĕn'ĭks, hī-jĕn'-) *n. (used with a sing. verb).* Hygiene (sense 1).

hygro– *pref.* Moisture; humidity: *hygroscope.* [< Gk. *hugros,* moist.]

hy·gro·graph (hī'grə-grăf') *n.* An automatic hygrometer that records variations in atmospheric humidity.

hy·grom·e·ter (hī-grŏm'ĭ-tər) *n.* Any of several instruments that measure atmospheric humidity. —**hy'gro·met'ric** (hī'grə-mĕt'rĭk) *adj.* —**hy·grom'e·try** *n.*

hy·gro·scope (hī'grə-skōp') *n.* An instrument that measures changes in atmospheric moisture.

hy·gro·scop·ic (hī'grə-skŏp'ĭk) *adj.* Readily absorbing moisture, as from the atmosphere. —**hy'gro·scop'i·cal·ly** *adv.* —**hy'gro·sco·pic'i·ty** (-skō-pĭs'ĭ-tē) *n.*

hy·ing (hī'ĭng) *v.* A present participle of **hie.**

hy·lo·zo·ism (hī'lə-zō'ĭz'əm) *n.* The philosophical doctrine that life is a property or derivative of matter, that life and matter are inseparable, or that matter possesses a spiritual component. [Gk. *hulē,* matter + Gk. *zoē,* life + -ISM.] —**hy'lo·zo'ic** *adj.* —**hy'lo·zo'ist** *n.* —**hy'lo·zo·is'tic** (-zō-ĭs'tĭk) *adj.*

hy·men (hī'mən) *n.* A membranous fold of tissue partly or completely occluding the external vaginal orifice. [LLat. < Gk. *humēn,* membrane.] —**hy'men·al** *adj.*

Hy·men (hī'mən) *n. Gk. Myth.* The god of marriage. [Lat. < Gk. *Humēn.*]

hy·me·ne·al (hī'mə-nē'əl) *adj.* Of or pertaining to a wedding or marriage. —*n.* A wedding song or poem. [Lat. *hymenaeus* < Gk. *humenaios* < *Humēn,* Hymen.] —**hy'me·ne'al·ly** *adv.*

hy·me·ni·um (hī-mē'nē-əm) *n., pl.* **-ni·a** (-nē-ə) or **-ni·ums.** The spore-bearing layer of the fruiting body of certain fungi, containing asci or basidia. [NLat. < Gk. *humēn,* membrane.] —**hy·me'ni·al** (-əl) *adj.*

hy·me·nop·ter·an (hī'mə-nŏp'tər-ən) also **hy·me·nop·ter·on** (-tə-rŏn') *n.* An insect of the order Hymenoptera, characteristically having two pairs of membranous wings and including the bees, wasps, and ants. *—adj.* **hymenopteran.** Of or belonging to the Hymenoptera. [NLat. *Hymenoptera,* order name : Gk. *humēn,* membrane + Gk. *pteron,* wing.] **—hy'me·nop'ter·ous** (-tər əs) *adj.*

hymn (hĭm) *n.* **1.** A song of praise or thanksgiving, esp. to God. **2.** A song of praise or joy; paean. *—v.* **hymned, hymn·ing, hymns.** *—tr.* To praise, glorify, or worship in or as if in a hymn. *—intr.* To sing hymns. [ME *imne* < OFr. *ymne* < Lat. *hymnus,* song of praise < Gk. *humnos.*]

hym·nal (hĭm'nəl) *n.* A book or collection of church hymns. [ME *hymnale* < Med. Lat. *hymnale* < Lat. *hymnus,* hymn.]

hymn·book (hĭm'bo͝ok') *n.* A hymnal.

hym·no·dy (hĭm'nə-dē) *n., pl.* **-dies. 1.** The singing of hymns. **2.** The composing or writing of hymns. **3.** The hymns of a particular period or church. [Med. Lat. *hymnodia* < Gk. *humnōidia* : *humnos,* hymn + *ōidē,* song.] **—hym'no·dist** (-dĭst) *n.*

hym·nol·o·gy (hĭm-nŏl'ə-jē) *n.* Hymnody. [Gk. *humnologia,* singing of hymns : *humnos,* hymn + *-logia,* -logy.] **—hym'no·log'ic** (hĭm'nə-lŏj'ĭk), **hym'no·log'i·cal** *adj.* **—hym·nol'o·gist** *n.*

hy·oid (hī'oid') *adj.* Of or pertaining to the hyoid bone. *—n.* The hyoid bone. [NLat. *hyoides,* the hyoid bone < Gk. *huoeidēs* : *hu,* name of the letter upsilon + *-eidēs,* -oid.]

hyoid bone *n.* A U-shaped bone between the mandible and the larynx at the base of the tongue.

hy·o·scine (hī'ə-sēn') *n.* Scopolamine. [G. *Hyoscin* < NLat. *Hyoscyamus,* henbane genus < Gk. *huoskuamus,* henbane : *hus,* pig + *kuamos,* bean.]

hy·o·scy·a·mine (hī'ə-sī'ə-mēn') *n.* A poisonous, white crystalline alkaloid, $C_{17}H_{23}NO_3$, isometric with atropine and used as an antispasmodic, analgesic, and sedative. [< NLat. *Hyoscyamus,* henbane genus. —see HYOSCINE.]

hyp– *pref.* Variant of **hypo-.**

hyp·a·bys·sal (hĭp'ə-bĭs'əl, hī'pə-) *adj.* Solidifying chiefly as a minor intrusion, esp. as a dike or sill, before reaching the earth's surface. Used of rocks. **—hyp'a·bys'sal·ly** *adv.*

hy·pae·thral (hī-pē'thrəl) *adj.* **1.** Open to the sky. **2.** Lacking a roof; roofless: *an ancient hypaethral temple.* [Lat. *hypaethrus* < Gk. *hupaithros* : *hupo,* under + *aithēr,* sky.]

hy·pan·thi·um (hī-păn'thē-əm) *n., pl.* **-thi·a** (-thē-ə). The modified, often enlarged floral receptacle of various plants, having a cup-shaped or tubular form. **—hy·pan'thi·al** *adj.*

hype¹ (hīp) *Slang.* *—n.* **1.** A hypodermic injection, syringe, or needle. **2.** A drug addict. *—tr.v.* **hyped, hyp·ing, hypes.** To stimulate with or as if with a hypodermic injection. [Shortening and alteration of HYPODERMIC.]

hype² (hīp) *Slang.* *—n.* **1.** Something deliberately misleading; deception. **2.** Exaggerated or extravagant claims made esp. in advertising or promotional material: *"The Christmas hype starts at Thanksgiving"* (Vogue). *—tr.v.* **hyped, hyp·ing, hypes.** To publicize or promote by inflated or misleading claims: *"The most dazzling dancers don't get hyped into stardom until their late teens"* (New York Times). [Orig. unknown.]

hyped-up (hīpt'ŭp') *adj. Slang.* Stimulated with or as if with a hypodermic injection.

hy·per (hī'pər) *adj. Slang.* **1.** Having a very excitable or nervous temperament; high-strung. **2.** Being emotionally stimulated or overexcited. [Short for HYPERACTIVE.]

hyper– *pref.* **1.** Over; above; beyond: *hypercharge.* **2.** Excessive; excessively: *hypercritical.* [< Gk. *huper,* over, beyond.]

hy·per·ac·id (hī'pər-ăs'ĭd) *adj.* Containing excessive acid; excessively acidic. **—hy'per·a·cid'i·ty** (-ə-sĭd'ĭ-tē) *n.*

hy·per·ac·tive (hī'pər-ăk'tĭv) *adj.* Excessively or abnormally active. **—hy'per·ac·tiv'i·ty** (-ăk-tĭv'ĭ-tē) *n.*

hy·per·ae·mi·a (hī'pə-rē'mē-ə) *n.* Variant of **hyperemia.**

hy·per·aes·the·sia (hī'pər-ĭs-thē'zhə) *n.* Variant of **hyperesthesia.**

hy·per·bar·ic (hī'pər-băr'ĭk) *adj.* Of, pertaining to, producing, operating, or occurring at pressures higher than normal atmospheric pressure: *a hyperbaric chamber; hyperbaric therapy.* **—hy'per·bar'i·cal·ly** *adv.*

hy·per·bo·la (hī-pûr'bə-lə) *n., pl.* **-las** or **-lae** (-lē). A plane curve having two branches, formed by: **a.** A conic section intersecting both halves of a right circular cone. **b.** The locus of points related to two given points such that the difference in the distances of each point from the two given points is a constant. [NLat. < Gk. *huperbolē.* —see HYPERBOLE.]

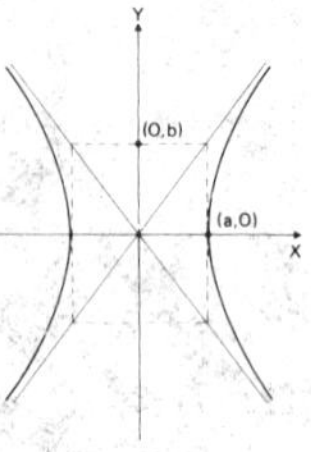

hyperbola
The equation of the hyperbola shown is
$$\frac{x^2}{a^2} - \frac{y^2}{b^2} = 1$$

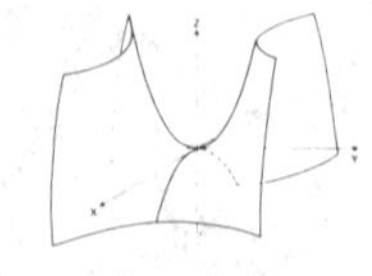
hyperbolic paraboloid

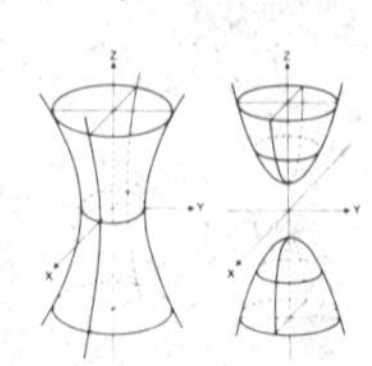
hyperboloid

hy·per·bo·le (hī-pûr'bə-lē) *n.* An exaggeration or extravagant statement used as a figure of speech, as *I could sleep for a year* or *This book weighs a ton.* [Lat. *hyperbole* < Gk. *huperbolē* < *huperballein,* to exceed : *huper,* beyond + *ballein,* to throw.]

hy·per·bol·ic (hī'pər-bŏl'ĭk) also **hy·per·bol·i·cal** (-ĭ-kəl) *adj.* **1.** Of, pertaining to, or employing hyperbole. **2.** *Math.* **a.** Of, pertaining to, or having the form of a hyperbola. **b.** Based on or having a metric that is a hyperbola: *hyperbolic geometry.* **c.** Of or pertaining to a hyperbolic function: *hyperbolic cosine.* **—hy'per·bol'i·cal·ly** *adv.*

hyperbolic function *n.* Any of a set of six functions related, for a real variable *z,* to the hyperbola in a manner analogous to the relationship of the trigonometric functions to a circle, including: **a.** The hyperbolic sine, defined by the equation $\sinh z = \frac{1}{2}(e^z - e^{-z})$. **b.** The hyperbolic cosine, defined by the equation $\cosh z = \frac{1}{2}(e^z + e^{-z})$. **c.** The hyperbolic tangent, defined by the equation $\tanh z = \sinh z/\cosh z$. **d.** The hyperbolic cotangent, defined by the equation $\coth z = \cosh z/\sinh z$. **e.** The hyperbolic secant, defined by the equation $\operatorname{sech} z = 1/\cosh z$. **f.** The hyperbolic cosecant, defined by the equation $\operatorname{csch} z = 1/\sinh z$.

hyperbolic paraboloid *n.* A surface of which all sections parallel to one coordinate plane are hyperbolas and all sections parallel to another coordinate plane are parabolas.

hy·per·bo·lism (hī-pûr'bə-lĭz'əm) *n.* **1.** The use of hyperbole. **2.** A hyperbole.

hy·per·bo·lize (hī-pûr'bə-līz') *intr. & tr.v.* **-lized, -liz·ing, -liz·es.** To use or express with hyperbole; exaggerate.

hy·per·bo·loid (hī-pûr'bə-loid') *n.* Either of two quadric surfaces having a finite center with certain plane sections that are hyperbolas and others that are ellipses or circles. **—hy·per'bo·loid'al** (-loid'l) *adv.*

Hy·per·bo·re·an (hī'pər-bôr'ē-ən, -bōr'-, -bə-rē'ən) *n. Gk. Myth.* One of a people known to the ancient Greeks from the earliest times, living in an unidentified country in the far north. *—adj.* **1.** Of or pertaining to the Hyperboreans. **2. hyperborean. a.** Of or pertaining to the far north; arctic. **b.** Very cold; frigid. [Lat. *Hyperborei,* the Hyperboreans < Gk. *Huperboreoi* : *huper,* extreme + *boreios,* northern < *Boreas,* Boreas.]

hy·per·cat·a·lex·is (hī'pər-kăt'l-ĕk'sĭs) *n.* The addition of one or more syllables in excess of the normal number in a verse or metric line. [HYPER- + NLat. *catalexis,* omission in the last foot of a line < Gk. *katalēxis,* ending < *katalēgein,* to leave off.] **—hy'per·cat'a·lec'tic** (-ĕk'tĭk) *adj.*

hy·per·charge (hī'pər-chärj') *n.* A quantum number numerically equal to twice the average electric charge of a particle multiplet or, equivalently, to the sum of the strangeness and the baryon number.

hy·per·crit·ic (hī'pər-krĭt'ĭk) *n.* A person who is excessively critical.

hy·per·crit·i·cal (hī'pər-krĭt'ĭ-kəl) *adj.* Excessively critical; captious. **—hy'per·crit'i·cal·ly** *adv.* **—hy'per·crit'i·cism** *n.*

hy·per·e·mi·a also **hy·per·ae·mi·a** (hī'pə-rē'mē-ə) *n.* The presence of an abnormally large blood supply. **—hy'per·e'mic** (-mĭk) *adj.*

hy·per·es·the·sia also **hy·per·aes·the·sia** (hī'pər-ĭs-thē'zhə) *n.* Abnormal sensitivity of the senses. **—hy'per·es·thet'ic** (-thĕt'ĭk) *adj.*

hy·per·eu·tec·tic (hī'pər-yo͞o-tĕk'tĭk) *adj.* Having the minor component present in a larger amount than in the eutectic composition of the same components.

hy·per·ex·ten·sion (hī'pər-ĭk-stĕn'shən) *n.* Extension of a bodily limb beyond normal limits.

hy·per·fine structure (hī'pər-fīn') *n.* The splitting of a spectral line into two or more components as a result of the spin or magnetic moment of the atomic nucleus.

hy·per·gly·ce·mi·a (hī'pər-glī-sē'mē-ə) *n.* The presence of an abnormally high concentration of glucose in the blood. **—hy'per·gly·ce'mic** *adj.*

hy·per·gol·ic (hī'pər-gŏl'ĭk) *adj.* Igniting spontaneously on contact of its components. Used of a rocket fuel. [G. *Hypergol,* a hypergolic fluid propellant (*hyp-,* hyper- + Gk. *ergon,* work + *-ol,* -ole) + -IC.] **—hy'per·gol'** (hī'pər-gôl', -gōl') *n.* **—hy'per·gol'i·cal·ly** *adv.*

hy·per·in·fla·tion (hī'pər-ĭn-flā'shən) *n.* Extremely high inflation.

hy·per·in·su·lin·ism (hī'pər-ĭn'sə-lə-nĭz'əm) *n.* The presence of abnormally great quantities of insulin in the blood, resulting in hypoglycemia.

Hy·pe·ri·on (hī-pîr'ē-ən) *n. Gk. Myth.* A Titan, the son of Gaea and Uranus and father of Helios, the sun god. [Lat. < Gk. *Huperiōn.*]

hy·per·ir·ri·ta·bil·i·ty (hī'pər-ĭr'ĭ-tə-bĭl'ĭ-tē) *n.* Excessive sensitivity to irritation. **—hy'per·ir'ri·ta·ble** *adj.*

hy·per·ker·a·to·sis (hī'pər-kĕr'ə-tō'sĭs) *n.* Hypertrophy of the horny layer of the skin. [HYPER- + Gk. *keras, kerat-,* horn + -OSIS.] **—hy'per·ker'a·tot'ic** (-tŏt'ĭk) *adj.*

hy·per·ki·ne·sia (hī'pər-kĭ-nē'zhə) also **hy·per·ki·ne·sis** (-sĭs) *n.* Pathologically excessive motion. [HYPER- + Gk. *kinēsis,* movement + -IA.] **—hy'per·ki·net'ic** (-nĕt'ĭk) *adj.*

hy·per·mar·ket (hī'pər-mär'kĭt) *n. Chiefly Brit.* A very large commercial establishment that combines a department store and a supermarket.

hy·per·me·ter (hī-pûr'mĭ-tər) *n.* Hypercatalexis. **—hy'per·met'ric** (hī'pər-mĕt'rĭk), **hy'per·met'ri·cal** *adj.*

hy·per·me·tro·pi·a (hī'pər-mĭ-trō'pē-ə) *n.* Hyperopia. [Gk. *hupermetros,* beyond measure (*huper,* beyond + *metron,* measure) + -OPIA.] **—hy'per·me·tro'pic** (-trō'pĭk, -trŏp'ĭk), **hy'per·me·tro'pi·cal** *adj.* **—hy'per·met'ro·py** (-mĕt'rə-pē) *n.*

hy·perm·ne·sia (hī'pərm-nē'zhə) *n.* Unusually exact or vivid memory. [HYPER- + (A)MNESIA.] **—hy'perm·ne'sic** (-zĭk, -sĭk) *adj.*

hy·per·on (hī'pə-rŏn') *n.* A subatomic particle with mass greater than the nucleon, decaying into a nucleon or another hyperon and lighter particles and having $2I + 1$ charge states, where I is the isospin of the particle multiplet.

hy·per·o·pi·a (hī'pə-rō'pē-ə) *n.* A pathological condition of the eye in which parallel rays are focused behind the retina because of a refractive error or because of flattening of the globe of the eye, so that vision is better for distant than near objects. **—hy′per·ope′** (hī′pə-rōp′) *n.* **—hy′per·o′pic** (-ō′pĭk, -ŏp′ĭk) *adj.*

hy·per·os·to·sis (hī′pər-ŏ-stō′sĭs) *n.* Excessive or abnormal thickening or growth of bone tissue. [HYPER- + OST(EO) + -OSIS.] **—hy′per·os·tot′ic** (-stŏt′ĭk) *adj.*

hy·per·pi·tu·i·ta·rism (hī′pər-pĭ-to͞o′ĭ-tə-rĭz′əm, -tyo͞o′-) *n.* Pathologically excessive production of anterior pituitary hormones, esp. growth hormones, resulting in acromegaly or gigantism. **—hy′per·pi·tu′i·tar′y** (-tĕr′ē) *adj.*

hy·per·pla·sia (hī′pər-plā′zhə) *n.* A nontumorous increase in the number of cells in an organ or tissue with consequent enlargement of the affected part. **—hy′per·plas′tic** (-plăs′tĭk) *adj.*

hy·per·ploid (hī′pər-ploid′) *adj.* Having a chromosome number in excess of but not an exact multiple of the normal diploid number. **—hy′per·ploid′** *n.* **—hy′per·ploi′dy** *n.*

hy·perp·ne·a (hī′pərp-nē′ə, hī′pər-nē′ə) *n.* Abnormally deep and rapid breathing. [HYPER- + Gk. *pnoē*, breath < *pnein*, to breathe.] **—hy′perp·ne′ic** (-ĭk) *adj.*

hy·per·py·rex·i·a (hī′pər-pī-rĕk′sē-ə) *n.* Abnormally high fever; hyperthermia. **—hy′per·py·rex′i·al, hy′per·py·ret′ic** (-rĕt′ĭk) *adj.*

hy·per·sen·si·tive (hī′pər-sĕn′sĭ-tĭv) *adj.* Abnormally or excessively sensitive. **—hy′per·sen′si·tive·ness, hy′per·sen′si·tiv′i·ty** (-tĭv′ĭ-tē) *n.*

hy·per·sex·u·al (hī′pər-sĕk′sho͞o-əl) *adj.* Being excessively interested or involved in sexual activity. **—hy′per·sex′u·al′i·ty** (-sĕk′sho͞o-ăl′ĭ-tē) *n.*

hy·per·son·ic (hī′pər-sŏn′ĭk) *adj.* Of, pertaining to, or relating to speed equal to or exceeding five times the speed of sound. **—hy′per·son′i·cal·ly** *adv.*

hy·per·sthene (hī′pərs-thēn′) *n.* A green, brown, or black splintery, cleavable pyroxene mineral, essentially $(Fe,Mg)_2Si_2O_6$. [Fr. *hypersthène* : *hyper-*, hyper- + Gk. *sthenos*, strength.] **—hy′per·sthen′ic** (-thĕn′ĭk) *adj.*

hy·per·ten·sion (hī′pər-tĕn′shən) *n.* Abnormally high arterial blood pressure. **—hy′per·ten′sive** *adj. & n.*

hy·per·ther·mi·a (hī′pər-thûr′mē-ə) *n.* Unusually high fever; hyperpyrexia. **—hy′per·ther′mal** *adj.*

hy·per·thy·roid (hī′pər-thī′roid′) *adj.* Of, pertaining to, or afflicted with hyperthyroidism.

hy·per·thy·roid·ism (hī′pər-thī′roi-dĭz′əm) *n.* Pathologically excessive production of thyroid hormones.

hy·per·to·ni·a (hī′pər-tō′nē-ə) also **hy·per·to·nic·i·ty** (-tō-nĭs′ĭ-tē) *n.* The state of being hypertonic.

hy·per·ton·ic (hī′pər-tŏn′ĭk) *adj.* **1.** *Pathol.* Having extreme muscular or arterial tension. **2.** *Chem.* Having the higher osmotic pressure of two solutions.

hy·per·tro·phy (hī-pûr′trə-fē) *n.* A nontumorous increase in the size of an organ or part as a result of the enlargement without increase in number of constituent cells. *—intr. & tr.v.* **-phied, -phy·ing, -phies.** To grow or cause to grow abnormally large. **—hy′per·tro′phic** (-trō′fĭk) *adj.*

hy·per·ven·ti·la·tion (hī′pər-vĕn′tl-ā′shən) *n.* Abnormally fast or deep respiration in which excessive quantities of air are taken in, causing buzzing in the ears, tingling of extremities, and sometimes fainting.

hy·per·vi·ta·min·o·sis (hī′pər-vī′tə-mə-nō′sĭs) *n.* Any of various abnormal conditions in which the physiological effect of a vitamin is produced to a pathological degree by excessive use of the vitamin.

hy·pes·the·sia (hī′pĭs-thē′zhə) *n.* Variant of **hypoesthesia.**

hy·pha (hī′fə) *n., pl.* **-phae** (-fē). Any of the threadlike filaments forming the mycelium of a fungus. [NLat. < Gk. *huphē*, web.] **—hy′phal** *adj.*

hy·phen (hī′fən) *n.* A punctuation mark (-) used to connect the parts of a compound word or between syllables of a word, esp. of a word divided at the end of a line. *—tr.v.* **-phened, -phen·ing, -phens.** To hyphenate. [LLat. < LGk. *huphen*, a sign indicating a compound < Gk., together : *hupo*, under + *hen*, one.]

hy·phen·ate (hī′fə-nāt′) *tr.v.* **-at·ed, -at·ing, -ates.** To divide or connect (syllables or word elements) with a hyphen. **—hy′phen·a′tion** *n.*

hypn– *pref.* Variant of **hypno-.**

hyp·na·gog·ic also **hyp·no·gog·ic** (hĭp′nə-gŏj′ĭk, -gō′jĭk) *adj.* **1.** Inducing sleep. **2.** Of or pertaining to the state of drowsiness preceding sleep. [Fr. *hypnagogique* : Gk. *hupnos*, sleep + Gk. *agōgos*, leading < *agein*, to lead.]

hypno– or **hypn–** *pref.* **1.** Sleep: *hypnophobia.* **2.** Hypnosis: *hypnoanalysis.* [< Gk. *hupnos*, sleep.]

hyp·no·a·nal·y·sis (hĭp′nō-ə-năl′ĭ-sĭs) *n.* A psychoanalytic technique in which hypnosis is used to elicit unconscious material from a patient.

hyp·no·gen·e·sis (hĭp′nō-jĕn′ĭ-sĭs) *n.* The process of inducing or entering a hypnotic state. **—hyp′no·ge·net′ic** (-jə-nĕt′ĭk) *adj.* **—hyp′no·ge·net′i·cal·ly** *adv.*

hyp·no·gog·ic (hĭp′nə-gŏj′ĭk, gō′jĭk) *adj.* Variant of **hypnagogic.**

hyp·noid (hĭp′noid′) also **hyp·noi·dal** (hĭp-noid′l) *adj.* Of or resembling hypnosis or sleep.

hyp·no·pho·bi·a (hĭp′nə-fō′bē-ə) *n.* Abnormal fear of sleep. **—hyp′no·pho′bic** *adj.*

hyp·no·pom·pic (hĭp′nə-pŏm′pĭk) *adj.* Of or pertaining to the partially conscious state preceding complete awakening. [HYPNO- + Gk. *pompē*, a sending away + -IC.]

Hyp·nos (hĭp′nŏs′) *n. Gk. Myth.* The god of sleep. [Gk.]

hyp·no·sis (hĭp-nō′sĭs) *n., pl.* **-ses** (-sēz′). **1.** An artificially induced sleeplike condition in which an individual is extremely responsive to suggestions made by the hypnotist. **2.** Hypnotism. **3.** A sleeplike condition.

hyp·no·ther·a·py (hĭp′nō-thĕr′ə-pē) *n.* Therapy based on or using hypnosis.

hyp·not·ic (hĭp-nŏt′ĭk) *adj.* **1. a.** Of or pertaining to hypnosis. **b.** Of or pertaining to hypnotism. **2.** Inducing or tending to induce sleep; soporific. *—n.* **1. a.** A person who is hypnotized. **b.** A person who can be hypnotized. **2.** An agent that causes sleep; soporific. [Fr. *hypnotique* < LLat. *hypnoticus* < Gk. *hupnōtikos* < *hupnoun*, to put to sleep < *hupnos*, sleep.] **—hyp·not′i·cal·ly** *adv.*

hyp·no·tism (hĭp′nə-tĭz′əm) *n.* **1.** The theory or practice of inducing hypnosis. **2.** An act of inducing hypnosis. **—hyp′no·tist** *n.*

hyp·no·tize (hĭp′nə-tīz′) *tr.v.* **-tized, -tiz·ing, -tiz·es. 1.** To put in a state of hypnosis. **2.** To fascinate by or as if by hypnosis. **—hyp′no·tiz′a·ble** *adj.* **—hyp′no·ti·za′tion** *n.* **—hyp′no·tiz′er** *n.*

hy·po¹ (hī′pō) *n.* Sodium thiosulfate. [Short for HYPOSULFITE.]

hy·po² (hī′pō) *n., pl.* **-pos.** *Informal.* **1.** A hypodermic syringe. **2.** A hypodermic injection.

hypo– or **hyp–** *pref.* **1.** Below; beneath; under: *hypodermic.* **2.** Less than normal; deficient: *hypoesthesia.* **3.** In the lowest state of oxidation: *hypoxanthine.* [Gk. *hupo-* < *hupo*, under, beneath.]

hy·po·a·cid·i·ty (hī′pō-ə-sĭd′ĭ-tē) *n.* **1.** *Chem.* Slight acidity. **2.** *Med.* Below normal acidity.

hy·po·bar·ic (hī′pə-băr′ĭk) *adj.* Below normal pressure. **—hy′po·bar′ism** *n.*

hy·po·blast (hī′pə-blăst′) *n.* The endoblast. **—hy′po·blas′tic** *adj.*

hy·po·caust (hī′pə-kôst′) *n.* In ancient Rome, a space under the floor where heat from a furnace was accumulated to heat a room or a bath. [Lat. *hypocaustum* < Gk. *hupokauston* < *hupokaiein*, to light a fire beneath : *hupo*, beneath + *kaiein*, to burn.]

hy·po·cen·ter (hī′pə-sĕn′tər) *n.* The surface position directly beneath the center of a nuclear explosion. **—hy′po·cen′tral** *adj.*

hy·po·chlo·rite (hī′pə-klôr′īt′, -klōr′-) *n.* A salt or ester of hypochlorous acid.

hy·po·chlo·rous acid (hī′pə-klôr′əs, -klōr′-) *n.* A weak, unstable acid, HOCl, occurring only in solution and used as a bleach, oxidizer, deodorant, and disinfectant.

hy·po·chon·dri·a (hī′pə-kŏn′drē-ə) *n.* **1.** The persistent neurotic conviction that one is or is likely to become ill, often involving experiences of real pain, when illness is neither present nor likely. **2.** Plural of **hypochondrium.** [LLat., abdomen (the seat of melancholy) < Gk. *hupokhondria*, pl. of *hupokhondrion*, abdomen < *hupokhondrios*, under the cartilage of the breastbone : *hupo*, under + *khondros*, cartilage.]

hy·po·chon·dri·ac (hī′pə-kŏn′drē-ăk′) *n.* A person afflicted with hypochondria. *—adj.* **1.** Pertaining to or afflicted with hypochondria. **2.** *Anat.* Pertaining to or located in the hypochondrium. **—hy′po·chon·dri′a·cal** (-kŏn-drī′ə-kəl) *adj.* **—hy′po·chon·dri′a·cal·ly** *adv.*

hy·po·chon·dri·a·sis (hī′pə-kən-drī′ə-sĭs) *n.* Hypochondria. [HYPOCHONDR(IA) + -IASIS.]

hy·po·chon·dri·um (hī′pə-kŏn′drē-əm) *n., pl.* **-dri·a** (-drē-ə). The upper lateral region of the abdomen, below the lowest ribs. [NLat. < Gk. *hupokhondrion*, abdomen. —see HYPOCHONDRIA.]

hy·poc·o·rism (hī-pŏk′ə-rĭz′əm, hī′pə-kôr′ĭz′əm, -kōr′-) *n.* **1.** A name of endearment; pet name. **2.** The use of hypocorisms. [LLat. *hypocorisma* < Gk. *hupokorisma* < *hupokorizesthai*, to call by endearing names : *hypo*, below + *korizesthai*, to caress < *koros*, boy, and *korē*, girl.] **—hy′po·co·ris′tic** (hī′pə-kə-rĭs′tĭk), **hy′po·co·ris′ti·cal** *adj.* **—hy′po·co·ris′ti·cal·ly** *adv.*

hy·po·cot·yl (hī′pə-kŏt′l) *n.* The part of the axis of a plant embryo or seedling plant that is below the cotyledons. [HYPO- + COTYL(EDON).]

hy·poc·ri·sy (hĭ-pŏk′rĭ-sē) *n., pl.* **-sies. 1.** The practice of professing beliefs, feelings, or virtues that one does not hold or possess; insincerity. **2.** An instance or act of hypocrisy. [ME *ipocrisie* < OFr. < LLat. *hypocrisis* < Gk. *hupokrisis*, pretense < *hupokrinesthai*, to pretend : *hupo-*, from under + *krinesthai*, to explain.]

hyp·o·crite (hĭp′ə-krĭt′) *n.* A person given to hypocrisy. [ME *ipocrite* < OFr. < LLat. *hypocrita* < Gk. *hupocritēs*, actor < *hupokrinein*, to play a part. —see HYPOCRISY.]

hyp·o·crit·i·cal (hĭp′ə-krĭt′ĭ-kəl) *adj.* **1.** Characterized by hypocrisy: *hypocritical praise.* **2.** Being a hypocrite: *a hypocritical rogue.* **—hyp′o·crit′i·cal·ly** *adv.*

hy·po·cy·cloid (hī′pō-sī′kloid′) *n.* The plane locus of a point fixed on a circle that rolls on the inside circumference of a fixed circle.

hy·po·derm (hī′pə-dûrm′) *n.* Variant of **hypodermis.**

hy·po·der·mal (hī′pə-dûr′məl) *adj.* **1.** Of or pertaining to the hypodermis. **2.** Lying below the epidermis.

hy·po·der·mic (hī′pə-dûr′mĭk) *adj.* **1.** Of or pertaining to the layer just beneath the epidermis. **2.** Pertaining to the

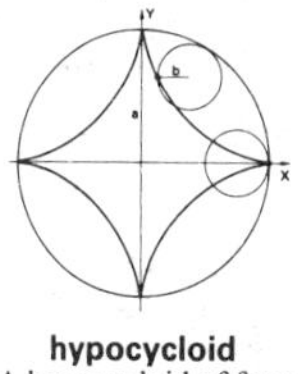

hypocycloid
A hypocycloid of four cusps; $a = 4b$

hypodermis. **3.** Injected beneath the skin. —*n.* **1.** A hypodermic injection. **2.** A hypodermic needle. **3.** A hypodermic syringe. [HYPO- + DERM(ATO)- + -IC.] —**hy'po·der'mi·cal·ly** *adv.*

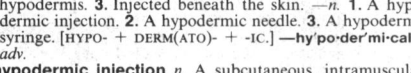

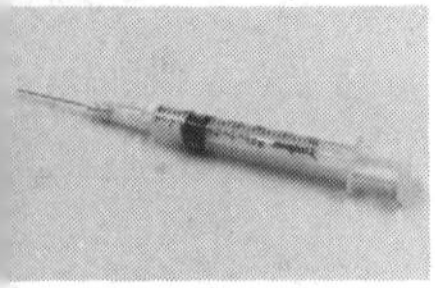

hypodermic syringe

hypodermic injection *n.* A subcutaneous, intramuscular, or intravenous injection by means of a hypodermic syringe and needle.

hypodermic needle *n.* **1.** A hollow needle used with a hypodermic syringe. **2.** A hypodermic syringe complete with needle.

hypodermic syringe *n.* A syringe fitted with a hypodermic needle for hypodermic injections.

hy·po·der·mis (hī'pə-dûr'mĭs) also **hy·po·derm** (hī'pə-dûrm') *n.* **1.** *Zool.* An epidermal layer of cells that secretes an overlying chitinous cuticle, as in arthropods. **2.** *Bot.* A layer of cells lying immediately below the epidermis.

hy·po·es·the·sia (hī'pō-ĭs-thē'zhə) also **hy·pes·the·sia** (hī'pĭs-) *n. Pathol.* Partial loss of sensation; diminished sensibility. [HYPO- + (AN)ESTHESIA.]

hy·po·eu·tec·tic (hī'pō-yōō-tĕk'tĭk) *adj. Chem.* Having the minor component present in a smaller amount than in the eutectic composition of the same components.

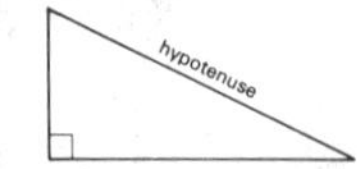

hypotenuse

hy·po·gas·tri·um (hī'pə-găs'trē-əm) *n., pl.* **-tri·a** (-trē-ə). The lowest of the three median regions of the abdomen. [NLat. < Gk. *hypogastrion* : *hupo,* below + *gastēr,* belly.] —**hy'po·gas'tric** *adj.*

hy·po·ge·a (hī'pə-jē'ə) *n.* Plural of **hypogeum.**

hy·po·ge·al (hī'pə-jē'əl) also **hy·po·ge·an** (-ən) or **hy·po·ge·ous** (-əs) *adj.* **1.** Located under the earth's surface; underground. **2.** *Bot.* Designating or characterized by cotyledons that remain below the surface of the ground. [< LLat. *hypogeus* < Gk. *hupogaios* : *hupo,* below + *gaia,* earth.] —**hy'po·ge'al·ly** *adv.*

hy·po·gene (hī'pə-jēn') *adj.* Formed or situated below the earth's surface. Used of rocks. [HYPO- + (EPI)GENE.]

hy·pog·e·nous (hī-pŏj'ə-nəs) *adj. Bot.* Developing or growing on a lower surface, as fungi on leaves.

hy·po·ge·ous (hī'pə-jē'əs) *adj.* Variant of **hypogeal.**

hy·po·ge·um (hī'pə-jē'əm) *n., pl.* **-ge·a** (-jē'ə). **1.** A subterranean chamber of an ancient building. **2.** An ancient subterranean burial chamber, such as a catacomb. [Lat. < Gk. *hupogaion* < *hupogaios,* hypogeal.]

hy·po·glos·sal (hī'pə-glŏs'əl) *adj. Anat.* Of or pertaining to the hypoglossal nerve. —*n.* The hypoglossal nerve. [< NLat. *hypoglossus,* hypoglossal nerve : HYPO- + Gk. *glōssa,* tongue.]

hypoglossal nerve *n.* A motor nerve attached to the medulla oblongata and innervating the muscles of the tongue.

hy·po·gly·ce·mi·a (hī'pō-glī-sē'mē-ə) *n.* An abnormally low level of sugar in the blood. —**hy'po·gly·ce'mic** *adj.*

hy·pog·y·nous (hī-pŏj'ə-nəs) *adj. Bot.* Having or characterizing floral parts or organs that are below and not in contact with the ovary. —**hy·pog'y·ny** (-nē) *n.*

hy·po·ma·ni·a (hī'pə-mā'nē-ə, -măn'yə) *n.* A mild state of mania involving slightly abnormal elation and overactivity. —**hy'po·man'ic** (-măn'ĭk) *adj.*

hy·po·nas·ty (hī'pə-năs'tē) *n.* An upward bending of leaves or other plant parts, resulting from growth of the lower side. —**hy'po·nas'tic** *adj.*

hy·po·phos·phite (hī'pō-fŏs'fīt') *n.* A salt of hypophosphorous acid.

hy·po·phos·pho·rous acid (hī'pō-fŏs'fər-əs, -fŏs-fôr'əs, -fōr'-) *n.* A clear, colorless or slightly yellow liquid, H_3PO_2, used in the preparation of hypophosphites.

hy·poph·y·sis (hī-pŏf'ĭ-sĭs) *n., pl.* **-ses** (-sēz'). The pituitary gland. [NLat. < Gk. *hupophusis,* attachment underneath < *hupophein,* to grow beneath : *hupo,* beneath + *phuein,* to grow.] —**hy·poph'y·se'al** (hī-pŏf'ĭ-sē'əl), **hy'po·phys'i·al** (hī'pə-fĭz'ē-əl) *adj.*

hy·po·pi·tu·i·ta·rism (hī'pō-pĭ-tōō'ĭ-tə-rĭz'əm, -tyōō'-) *n.* Deficient or diminished production of pituitary hormones. —**hy'po·pi·tu'i·tar'y** (-tĕr'ē) *adj.*

hy·po·pla·sia (hī'pō-plā'zhə) *n. Pathol.* Incomplete or arrested development of an organ or part. —**hy'po·plas'tic** (-plăs'tĭk) *adj.*

hy·po·ploid (hī'pō-ploid') *adj. Genetics.* Having a chromosome number less by only a few chromosomes than the normal diploid number. —**hy'po·ploi'dy** *n.*

hy·po·pne·a (hī'pō-nē'ə) *n.* Abnormally slow and shallow breathing. [HYPO- + Gk. *pnoē,* breath < *pnein,* to breathe.]

hy·po·sen·si·tiv·i·ty (hī'pō-sĕn'sĭ-tĭv'ĭ-tē) *n.* Less than normal sensitivity. —**hy'po·sen'si·tive** *adj.*

hy·po·sen·si·tize (hī'pō-sĕn'sĭ-tīz') *tr.v.* **-tized, -tiz·ing, -tiz·es.** To make less sensitive; desensitize. —**hy'po·sen'si·ti·za'tion** *n.*

hy·pos·ta·sis (hī-pŏs'tə-sĭs) *n., pl.* **-ses** (-sēz'). **1.** *Philos.* The substance or essence of something. **2.** *Theol.* **a.** Any of the persons of the Trinity. **b.** The essential person of Christ in which his human and divine natures are united. **3.** An entity that has been hypostatized. **4. a.** A settling of solid particles in a fluid. **b.** Something that settles to the bottom of a fluid; sediment. **5.** A condition in which the action of one gene conceals or suppresses the action of another gene that is not its allele but that affects the same organ, part, or state of the body. [LLat. < Gk. *hupostasis* : *hupo,* beneath + *stasis,* a standing.] —**hy'po·stat'ic** (hī'pə-stăt'ĭk), **hy'po·stat'i·cal** *adj.* —**hy'po·stat'i·cal·ly** *adv.*

hy·pos·ta·tize (hī-pŏs'tə-tīz') *tr.v.* **-tized, -tiz·ing, -tiz·es.** **1.** To symbolize (a concept) in a concrete form. **2.** To ascribe material existence to. [< Gk. *hupostatos,* standing under < *hyphistasthai,* to stand under : *hupo,* beneath + *histasthai,* to stand.] —**hy·pos'ta·ti·za'tion** *n.*

hy·po·sthe·ni·a (hī'pəs-thē'nē-ə) *n.* Abnormal lack of strength; weakness. [HYPO- + Greek *sthenos,* strength.] —**hy'po·sthen'ic** (-thĕn'ĭk) *adj.*

hy·po·style (hī'pə-stīl') *n.* A building with a roof or ceiling supported by rows of columns. [< Gk. *hupostulos,* resting upon pillars : *hupo,* beneath + *stulos,* pillar.] —**hy'po·style'** *adj.*

hy·po·sul·fite (hī'pō-sŭl'fīt') *n.* Sodium thiosulfate.

hy·po·sul·fu·rous acid (hī'pō-sŭl-fyŏŏr'əs, -sŭl'fər-əs) *n.* An unstable acid, $H_2S_2O_4$, known only in aqueous solution and used as a bleaching and reducing agent.

hy·po·tax·is (hī'pə-tăk'sĭs) *n.* The dependent or subordinate relationship of clauses with connectives. [Gk. *hupotaxis,* subjection < *hupotassein,* to arrange under : *hupo,* under + *tattein,* to arrange.] —**hy'po·tac'tic** (-tăk'tĭk) *adj.*

hy·pot·e·nuse (hī-pŏt'n-ōōs', -yōōs') also **hy·poth·e·nuse** (-pŏth'ə-nōōs', -nyōōs') *n.* The side of a right triangle opposite the right angle. [Lat. *hypotenusa* < Gk. *hupoteinousa* < *hupoteinein,* to stretch under : *hupo,* under + *teinein,* to stretch.]

hy·po·thal·a·mus (hī'pō-thăl'ə-məs) *n.* The part of the brain that lies below the thalamus, forming the major portion of the ventral region of the diencephalon and functioning to regulate bodily temperature, certain metabolic processes, and other autonomic activities. —**hy'po·tha·lam'ic** (-thə-lăm'ĭk) *adj.*

hy·poth·e·cate (hī-pŏth'ĭ-kāt') *tr.v.* **-cat·ed, -cat·ing, -cates.** To pledge (property) as security or collateral for a debt without transfer of title or possession. [Med. Lat. *hypothecare, hypothecat-* < LLat. *hypotheca,* pledge < Gk. *hupothēkē* < *hupotithenai,* to give as a pledge : *hupo,* beneath + *tithenai,* to place.] —**hy·poth'e·ca'tion** *n.* —**hy·poth'e·ca'tor** (-kā'tər) *n.*

hy·poth·e·nuse (hī-pŏth'ə-nōōs', -nyōōs') *n.* Variant of **hypotenuse.**

hy·po·ther·mal (hī'pō-thûr'məl) *adj. Geol.* Of, pertaining to, or being high-temperature deposits derived from magmatic emanations forced under pressure into place in pre-existing rock openings.

hy·po·ther·mi·a (hī'pō-thûr'mē-ə) *n.* A condition of abnormally low body temperature. [NLat. : HYPO- + Gk. *thermē,* heat.] —**hy'po·ther'mic** *adj.*

hy·poth·e·sis (hī-pŏth'ĭ-sĭs) *n., pl.* **-ses** (-sēz'). **1.** An explanation that accounts for a set of facts and that can be tested by further investigation; theory. **2.** Something that is taken to be true for the purpose of argument or investigation; assumption. [Gk. *hupothesis* < *hupotithenai,* to suppose : *hupo,* beneath + *tithenai,* to place.]

hy·poth·e·size (hī-pŏth'ĭ-sīz') *tr. & intr.v.* **-sized, -siz·ing, -siz·es.** To assert as or form a hypothesis.

hy·po·thet·i·cal (hī'pə-thĕt'ĭ-kəl) also **hy·po·thet·ic** (-thĕt'ĭk) *adj.* **1.** Of, pertaining to, or based on a hypothesis. **2. a.** Suppositional; conjectural. **b.** Conditional; contingent. [Gk. *hupothetikos* < *hupothesis,* hypothesis.] —**hy'po·thet'i·cal·ly** *adv.*

hy·po·thy·roid (hī'pō-thī'roid') *adj.* Affected by or manifesting hypothyroidism.

hy·po·thy·roid·ism (hī'pō-thī'roi-dĭz'əm) *n.* **1.** Insufficient production of thyroid hormones. **2.** A pathological condition resulting from severe thyroid insufficiency, esp. myxedema or cretinism.

hy·po·ton·ic (hī'pō-tŏn'ĭk) *adj.* **1.** *Pathol.* Having less than normal tone or tension. **2.** *Chem.* Having the lower osmotic pressure of two fluids. —**hy'po·to·nic'i·ty** (-tə-nĭs'ĭ-tē) *n.*

hy·pot·ro·phy (hī-pŏt'rə-fē) *n.* Less than normal growth. —**hy'po·tro'phic** (hī'pə-trō'fĭk) *adj.*

hy·po·xan·thine (hī'pō-zăn'thēn') *n.* A white powder, $C_5H_4N_4O$, that is an intermediate in the metabolism of animal purines.

hy·pox·i·a (hī-pŏk'sē-ə, hĭ-) *n.* Deficiency in the amount of oxygen reaching bodily tissues.

hypso– or **hyps–** *Pref.* Height: *hypsometer.* [< Gk. *hupsos,* height.]

hyp·sog·ra·phy (hĭp-sŏg'rə-fē) *n., pl.* **-phies. 1. a.** The scientific study of the earth's topologic configuration above sea level, esp. the measurement and mapping of land elevations. **b.** A representation or description of such features, as on a map. **2.** Hypsometry. —**hyp'so·graph'ic** (hĭp'sə-grăf'ĭk), **hyp'so·graph'i·cal** *adj.*

hyp·som·e·ter (hĭp-sŏm'ĭ-tər) *n.* An instrument using the altitude-pressure dependence of boiling points to determine land elevations.

hyp·som·e·try (hĭp-sŏm'ĭ-trē) *n.* The measurement of elevation relative to sea level. —**hyp'so·met'ric** (hĭp'sə-mĕt'rĭk), **hyp'so·met'ri·cal** *adj.* —**hyp'so·met'ri·cal·ly** *adv.* —**hyp·som'e·trist** *n.*

hy·rax (hī'răks') *n., pl.* **-rax·es** or **-ra·ces** (-rə-sēz'). Any of several herbivorous mammals of the family Procaviidae within the order Hyraoidea, of Africa and adjacent Asia, resembling woodchucks or similar rodents but more closely related to the hoofed mammals. [Gk. *hurax,* shrew mouse.]

hy·son (hī′sən) *n.* A type of Chinese green tea whose leaves are twisted or curled. [Chin. (Mandarin) *xi[1] chun[1]* : *xi[1],* warm, sunny + *chun[1],* springlike.]

hys·sop (hĭs′əp) *n.* **1. a.** A woody plant, *Hyssopus officinalis,* native to Asia, having spikes of small blue flowers and aromatic leaves used in perfumery and as a condiment. **b.** Any of several similar or related plants. **2.** An unidentified plant mentioned in the Bible as the source of twigs used for sprinkling in certain Hebraic purificatory rites. [ME *ysop* < OE *hysope* and OFr. *ysope,* both < Lat. *hyssōpus* < Gk. *hussōpos,* of Semitic orig.]

hyster– *pref.* Variant of **hystero-.**

hys·ter·ec·to·my (hĭs′tə-rĕk′tə-mē) *n., pl.* **-mies.** Total or partial surgical removal of the uterus.

hys·ter·e·sis (hĭs′tə-rē′sĭs) *n., pl.* **-ses** (-sēz′). The failure of a property that has been changed by an external agent to return to its original value when the cause of the change is removed. [Gk. *husterēsis,* a shortcoming < *husterein,* to come late < *husteros,* late.] **—hys′ter·et′ic** (-rĕt′ĭk) *adj.*

hys·ter·i·a (hĭ-stĕr′ē-ə, -stîr′-) *n.* **1.** A neurosis characterized by conversion symptoms, a calm mental attitude, and episodes of hallucination, somnambulism, amnesia, and other mental aberrations. **2.** Excessive or uncontrollable emotion, such as fear or panic. [NLat. < HYSTERIC.]

hys·ter·ic (hĭ-stĕr′ĭk) *n.* **1.** A person suffering from hysteria. **2. hysterics** *(used with a sing. or pl. verb).* **a.** A fit of uncontrollable laughing and crying. **b.** An attack of hysteria. *—adj.* Hysterical. [Lat. *hystericus,* hysterical < Gk. *husterikos* < *hustera,* womb (from the former idea that disturbances in the womb caused hysteria).]

hys·ter·i·cal (hĭ-stĕr′ĭ-kəl) *adj.* **1.** Of, characterized by, or arising from hysteria. **2.** Having or prone to having hysterics. **—hys·ter′i·cal·ly** *adv.*

hystero– or **hyster–** *pref.* **1.** Uterus: *hysterectomy.* **2.** Hysteria: *hysteroid.* [< Gk. *hustera,* womb.]

hys·ter·o·gen·ic (hĭs′tə-rō-jĕn′ĭk) *adj.* Causing hysteria.

hys·ter·oid (hĭs′tə-roid′) *adj.* Resembling hysteria.

hys·ter·on prot·er·on (hĭs′tə-rŏn prŏt′ə-rŏn′) *n.* **1.** A figure of speech in which the natural or rational order of its terms is reversed, as *bred and born* instead of *born and bred.* **2.** The logical fallacy of assuming as a premise a proposition following something yet to be proved. [LLat. < Gk. *husteron proteron,* latter first.]

hys·ter·ot·o·my (hĭs′tə-rŏt′ə-mē) *n., pl.* **-mies.** Surgical incision of the uterus.

I

1 2 Phoenician · 3 4 5 6 Greek · 7 8 Roman · 9 10 Medieval · 11 12 13 14 Modern

Around 1000 B.C. the Phoenicians and other Semitic peoples began to use graphic signs to represent individual speech sounds instead of syllables or words. They used a symbol in the forms (1,2) to represent the sound of the semivowel "y" and called it *yōdh,* their word for "hand." The Greeks, adapting the Phoenician alphabet, varied the shape of *yōdh* (3,4,5,6) and altered its name to *iōta.* They used *iōta* to represent the sound of the vowel "i". The Romans borrowed the alphabet from the Greeks via the Etruscans and used *iōta* to represent both the vowel "i" and the semivowel "y." In time they added a hook to I to identify the semivowel, and the new symbol became the letter J. They continued to use the letter I to represent the vowel and adapted it for monumental inscriptions. Monumental script (8) is the prototype of modern capital letters (11,12). Medieval scribes adapted the Roman capitals to being quickly written on paper, parchment, and vellum, adding the dot to I to distinguish it from other similarly shaped letters. These uncial and cursive minuscules (9,10) are the prototypes of modern lower-case letters, both written and printed (14,13).

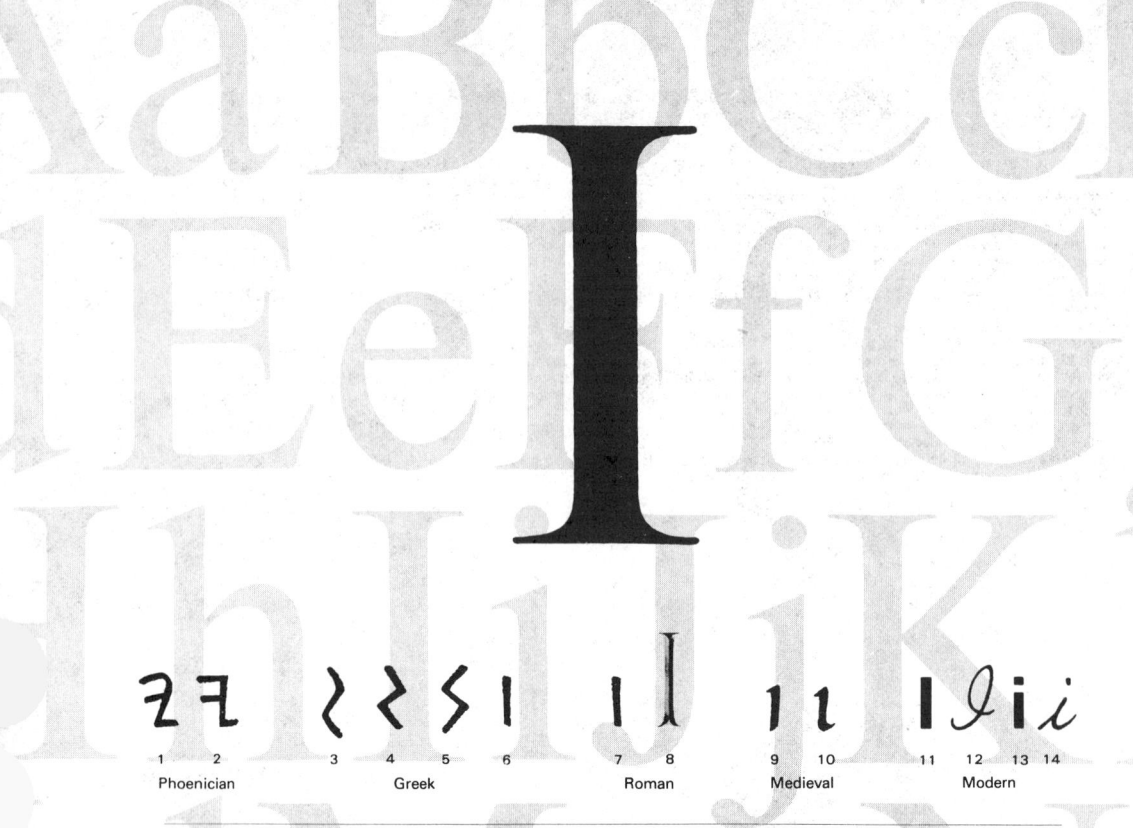

i

i or **I** (ī) *n., pl.* **i's** or **I's.** **1.** The ninth letter of the modern English alphabet. **2.** Any of the speech sounds represented by the letter *i.* **3.** Something shaped like the letter I. **4.** The ninth in a series.

I[1] (ī) *pron.* The one that is the speaker or writer. *—n., pl.* **I's.** The self; ego. [ME < OE *ic.*]

Usage: The question as to when to use the nominative pronouns *I, he, she, we,* and *they* and when to use the objective pronouns *me, him, her, us,* and *them* has always been a source of controversy among grammarians and uncertainty among speakers. When the subject of a sentence is a complex phrase in which a pronoun is joined to other elements by *and* or *or,* grammarians are unanimous in considering it a part of the subject proper, so that the nominative form must be used: *Pat and I* (not *me*) *will be there to greet you. Either Kim or he* (not *him*) *will come in first.* Some grammarians have gone so far as to extend this rule to cover the use of pronouns as one-word answers to questions that ask about the identity of the subject of a verb; that is, as an answer to "Who cut down the cherry tree?" we are supposed to say *"I"* (as in *"I did*) rather than *"Me."* But such sentences are likely to occur only in informal speech or in written dialogue; in either case, the use here of a nominative, such as *I,* can only be felt as pedantic. • Mistakes in pronoun choice come in two varieties. There is a natural tendency to use objective forms like *me* and *him* where nominatives like *I* and *he* would strictly be required: *He has more money than me* instead of the correct *than I. In the end, it turned out to have been them all along* instead of the technically correct *turned out to have been they.* Strict grammarians are likely to regard such mistakes as the result of a carelessness that no one ever manages entirely to avoid. But in an effort to get the pronouns right, some err in the opposite direction, substituting nominatives like *I* where the objective *him* would be correct. The result is constructions like *between you and I* (properly *between you and me*) or *it surprised Mary more than Kim or I* (properly, *Kim or me*). Mistakes of this second sort are likely to be regarded as overcorrections that betray a fundamental linguistic insecurity on the part of the speaker. While there is no entirely safe course for the speaker in doubt as to which form to use, this difference between the risks in incorrect use of the nominative and the objective should be borne in mind. See also Usage note at **be.**

I[2] The symbol for the element iodine.

-i- Used as a connective to join word elements: *brutify.* [ME < OFr. < Lat., stem vowel of nouns and adjectives used in combination.]

-ia[1] *suff.* **1.** Disease; pathological condition: *anoxia.* **2.** Territory; country: *Manchuria.* [NLat. < Lat. and Gk., n. suffix.]

-ia[2] *suff.* Things derived from, relating to, or belonging to: *personalia.* [Partly < Lat., neuter pl. of *-ius,* and partly < Gk., neuter pl. of *-ios,* n. and adj. suffixes.]

-ial *suff.* Of, relating to, or characterized by: *baronial.* [ME < OFr. < Lat. *-ialis.*]

i·amb (ī'ămb', -ăm') also **i·am·bus** (ī-ăm'bəs) *n., pl.* **i·ambs** also **-bus·es** or **-bi** (-bī'). A metric foot consisting of a short syllable followed by a long syllable or an unstressed syllable followed by a stressed syllable. [Fr. *iambe* < Lat. *iambus* < Gk. *iambos.*]

i·am·bic (ī-ăm'bĭk) *adj.* **1.** Consisting of iambs or characterized by their predominance: *iambic pentameter.* **2.** Employing iambic rhythm, esp. in the various genres associated with its use: *the iambic poetry of antiquity.* *—n.* **1.** An iamb. **2.** Often **iambics.** A verse, stanza, or poem written in iambs: *the lethal iambics of Archilochus.*

i·am·bus (ī-ăm'bəs) *n.* Variant of **iamb.**

-ian *suff.* **1.** Of, relating to, or resembling: *Bostonian.* **2.** One relating to, belonging to, or resembling: *academician.* [OFr. *-ien* < Lat. *-ianus,* adj. and n. suffix.]

-iana *suff.* Variant of **-ana.**

-iasis *suff.* A pathological condition characterized or produced by: *teniasis.* [NLat. < Gk., n. suffix.]

-iatric *suff.* Of or pertaining to a specified kind of medical treatment or healing: *geriatric.* [< Gk. *iatrikos,* medical < *iatros,* physician < *iasthai,* to heal.]

-iatrics *suff.* Medical treatment: *bariatrics.* [< -IATRIC.]

i·at·ro·gen·ic (ī-ăt'rə-jĕn'ĭk) *adj.* Induced in a patient by a physician's words or actions. Used esp. of imagined illnesses. [Gk. *iatros,* physician (< *iasthai,* to heal) + -GENIC.] **—i·at'ro·gen'i·cal·ly** *adv.*

-iatry *suff.* Medical treatment: *psychiatry.* [Fr. *-iatrie* < NLat. *-iatria* < Gk. *-iatreia,* art of healing < *iatros,* physician < *iasthai,* to heal.]

I-beam (ī'bēm') *n.* A steel beam or girder with a cross section formed like the capital letter I.

I·be·ri·an (ī-bîr'ē-ən) *adj.* **1. a.** Of or pertaining to the ancient ethnologic group or groups that inhabited the Iberian Peninsula. **b.** Of or pertaining to the language or culture of these groups. **2.** Of or pertaining to the Iberian Peninsula. **3.** Of or pertaining to ancient Iberia in the Caucasus, its inhabitants, their language, or their culture. *—n.* **1. a.** A member of the ancient Caucasoid people that inhabited the Iberian Peninsula. **b.** Any of the languages spoken by the ancient peoples of the Iberian Penninsula. **2.** An inhabitant of the Iberian Peninsula. **3.** An inhabitant of ancient Iberia in the Caucasus.

i·bex (ī'bĕks') *n.* Any of several wild goats of the genus *Capra,* of mountainous regions of the Old World, esp. *C. ibex,* having long, ridged, backward-curving horns. [Lat.]

ibex

I·bib·i·o (ī-bĭb'ē-ō) *n., pl.* **Ibibio** or **-os.** **1.** A people of southeastern Nigeria. **2.** A member of the Ibibio. **3.** The Niger-Congo language of the Ibibio.

i·bi·dem (ĭb'ĭ-dĕm', ī-bī'dəm) *adv.* In the same place. Used in footnotes and bibliographies to refer to the book, chapter, article, or page cited just before. [Lat.]

-ibility *suff.* Variant of **-ability.**

i·bis (ī'bĭs) *n.* **1.** Any of various long-billed wading birds of the family Threskiornithidae. **2.** The wood ibis. [Lat. < Gk., of Egypt. orig.]

-ible *suff.* Variant of **-able.**

I·bo (ē'bō) *n., pl.* **Ibo** or **I·bos.** **1.** A member of one of various Negroid tribes of Nigeria. **2.** The Kwa language of the Ibo.

-ic *suff.* **1.** Of, pertaining to, or characterized by: *seismic.* **2.** Having a valence higher than that of a specified element in compounds or ions named with adjectives ending in *-ous: sulfuric acid.* **3.** One pertaining to or characterized by: *academic.* [ME < Lat. *-icus.*]

Ic·a·rus (ĭk'ər-əs) *n.* **1.** *Gk. Myth.* The son of Daedalus, who, in escaping from Crete on artificial wings made for him by his father, flew so close to the sun that the wax with which his wings were fastened melted, and he fell into the Aegean Sea. **2.** An asteroid with an eccentric orbit that passes closest to the sun at a distance of within 30 million kilometers. [Lat. < Gk. *Ikaros.*]

ice (īs) *n.* **1.** Water frozen solid. **2.** A surface, layer, or mass of frozen water. **3.** Something resembling frozen water. **4.** A dessert consisting of sweetened and flavored crushed ice. **5.** Cake frosting; icing. **6.** *Slang.* Diamonds. **7.** The playing field in ice hockey; rink. **8.** *Informal.* Extreme unfriendliness or reserve. *—v.* **iced, ic·ing, ic·es.** *—tr.* **1.** To coat or slick with ice. **2.** To cause to become ice; freeze. **3.** To chill by setting in or as if in ice. **4.** To cover or decorate (a cake, for example) with a sugar coating. **5.** *Slang.* To insure of victory, as in a game; clinch. **6.** To shoot (the puck) far out of defensive territory in ice hockey. *—intr.* To turn into or become coated with ice; freeze: *The pond iced over in November.* **—*idioms.* break the ice.** **1.** To relax a tense or unduly formal atmosphere or social situation. **2.** To make a start; begin something. **on ice.** **1.** *Informal.* **a.** In reserve or readiness. **b.** Held incommunicado. **2.** Certain to be won. [ME *ise* < OE *īs.*]

ice age *n.* **1.** Any of a series of cold periods marked by extensive glaciation alternating with periods of relative warmth, together constituting the Pleistocene or glacial epoch. **2. Ice Age.** The Pleistocene or glacial epoch.

ice ax *n.* An ax used by mountaineers for cutting steps in ice.

ice bag *n.* A small waterproof bag used as an ice pack.

ice·berg (īs'bûrg') *n.* **1.** A massive floating body of ice broken away from a glacier. **2.** *Informal.* A cold or aloof person. [Partial transl. of Dan. and Norw. *isberg* : *is,* ice + *berg,* mountain.]

George Miksch Sutton

ibis

ice·blink (īs'blĭngk') *n.* **1.** A yellowish glare in the sky over an ice field. **2.** A coastal ice cliff.

ice·boat (īs'bōt') *n.* **1.** A boatlike vehicle set on runners that sails on ice. **2.** An icebreaker (sense 1). **—ice'boat'ing** *n.*

ice·bound (īs'bound') *adj.* Locked in or covered over by ice.

ice·box (īs'bŏks') *n.* **1.** An insulated chest or box in which ice is put to cool and preserve food. **2.** A refrigerator.

ice·break·er (īs'brā'kər) *n.* **1.** A sturdy ship built for breaking a passage through icebound waters. **2.** A protective pier or dock apron used as a buffer against floating ice.

ice cap *n.* An extensive perennial cover of ice and snow.

ice cream *n.* A smooth, sweet, cold food prepared from a frozen mixture of milk products, usually containing 10 to 14 per cent butterfat and an average of 10.5 per cent nonfat milk solids, approximately 15 per cent cane or beet sugar, flavoring, and sometimes small amounts of colloidal materials and emulsifiers.

ice-cream cone (īs'krēm') *n.* **1.** A conical wafer used to hold a scoop of ice cream. **2.** An ice-cream cone with ice cream in it.

ice-cream soda *n.* A refreshment consisting of ice cream scoops in a mixture of soda water and flavoring syrup.

icebreaker

iced (īst) *adj.* **1.** Covered over with ice. **2.** Chilled with ice. **3.** Decorated or coated with icing.

ice·fall (īs'fôl') *n.* **1.** The face or sheer side of a glacier, resembling a frozen waterfall. **2.** An avalanche of ice.

ice field *n.* A large, level expanse of floating ice.

ice floe *n.* A flat expanse of floating ice, smaller than an ice field.

ice fog *n.* Pogonip.

ice foot *n.* A belt or ledge of ice that forms along the shoreline in Arctic regions.

ice hockey *n.* Hockey (sense 1).

ice·house (īs'hous') *n.* A place where ice is made, stored, or sold.

Ice·land·er (īs'lən-dər) *n.* A native or inhabitant of Iceland.

Ice·land·ic (īs-lăn'dĭk) *adj.* Of or pertaining to Iceland, its

inhabitants, their language, or culture. —*n.* The North Germanic language of the Icelanders.
Iceland moss *n.* A brittle, grayish-brown, edible lichen, *Cetraria islandica,* of northern regions.
Iceland spar *n.* A doubly refracting transparent calcite used in optical instruments.
ice milk *n.* A smooth, sweet, cold food prepared from a frozen mixture of milk products, usually containing 3 to 6 per cent butterfat, 11 to 14 per cent nonfat milk solids, and 12 to 15 per cent sugar.
ice needle *n.* Any of the thin ice crystals that float high in the atmosphere in certain conditions of clear, cold weather.
ice-out (īs'out') *n.* The thawing of ice on the surface of a body of water, as a lake.
ice pack *n.* **1.** A floating mass of compacted ice fragments. **2.** A folded cloth or sac filled with crushed ice and applied to sore or swollen parts of the body.
ice pick *n.* A pointed awl for chipping or breaking ice.

ice pick

ice plant *n.* A plant, *Mesembryanthemum crystallinum,* native to southern Africa, having white or pink flowers and fleshy leaves and stems covered with glistening encrustations.
ice point *n.* The temperature at which pure water and ice are in equilibrium in a mixture at 1 atmosphere of pressure.
ice show *n.* An entertainment consisting of dance routines, stunts, and buffoonery performed by ice skaters.
ice skate *n.* **1.** A metal runner or blade that is fitted to the sole of a shoe for skating on ice. **2.** A shoe or light boot with a runner for skating on ice permanently fixed to it.
ice-skate (īs'skāt') *intr.v.* **-skat·ed, -skat·ing, -skates.** To skate on ice. **—ice skater** *n.*

ice-skate

ice storm *n.* A storm in which snow or rain freezes on contact.
ice water *n.* Very cold or chilled water, esp. for drinking and often with ice in it.
ich (ĭk) *n.* A contagious disease of tropical aquarium fishes, caused by a protozoan, *Ichthyophthirius multifiliis,* and characterized by small white pustules on the body. [Short for NLat. *Ichthyophthirius,* genus name : ICHTHYO- + Gk. *phtheir,* louse.]
ich·neu·mon (ĭk-no͞o'mən, -nyo͞o'-) *n.* A mongoose of the genus *Herpestes,* esp. *H. ichneumon,* of Africa. [Lat. < Gk. *ikhneumōn,* weasel < *ikhneuein,* to track < *ikhnos,* track.]

ichneumon

ichneumon fly *n.* Any of various wasplike insects of the family Ichneumonidae, having larvae that are parasitic on the larvae of other insects.

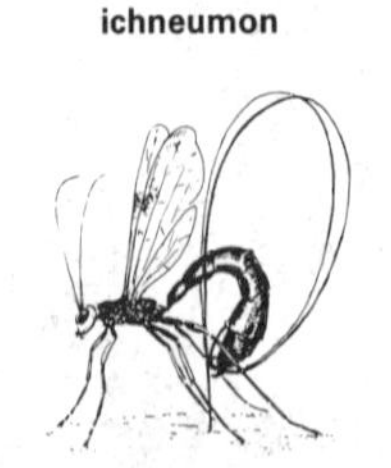
ichneumon fly

ichneumon wasp *n.* An ichneumon fly.
ich·nite (ĭk'nīt') *n.* A fossilized footprint. [Gk. *iknos,* track + -ITE.]
i·chor (ī'kôr', ī'kər) *n.* **1.** *Gk. Myth.* The rarefied fluid said to run in the veins of the gods. **2.** *Pathol.* A watery, acrid discharge from a wound or ulcer. [Gk. *ikhōr.*] **—i'chor·ous** (ī'kər-əs) *adj.*
ichthy– *pref.* Variant of **ichthyo-.**
ich·thy·ic (ĭk'thē-ĭk) *adj.* Of, pertaining to, or characteristic of fishes.
ichthyo– or **ichthy–** *pref.* Fish: *ichthyophagous.* [Lat. < Gk. *ikhthuo-* < *ikhthus,* fish.]
ich·thy·o·fau·na (ĭk'thē-ə-fô'nə) *n.* The fish of a particular region.
ich·thy·oid (ĭk'thē-oid') also **ich·thy·oi·dal** (ĭk'thē-oid'l) *adj.* Characteristic of or resembling a fish. —*n.* A fish or fishlike vertebrate.
ich·thy·ol·o·gy (ĭk'thē-ŏl'ə-jē) *n.* Zoology specializing in the study of fishes. **—ich'thy·o·log'ic** (-ə-lŏj'ĭk), **ich'thy·o·log'i·cal** *adj.* **—ich'thy·ol'o·gist** *n.*
ich·thy·oph·a·gous (ĭk'thē-ŏf'ə-gəs) *adj.* Feeding on fish; fish-eating.
ich·thy·or·nis (ĭk'thē-ôr'nĭs) *n.* Any of various extinct, toothed, fish-eating birds of the genus *Ichthyornis* that existed during the Cretaceous period. [NLat. *Ichthyornis,* genus name : ICHTHY(O) + Gk. *ornis,* bird.]
ich·thy·o·saur (ĭk'thē-ə-sôr') also **ich·thy·o·sau·rus** (ĭk'thē-ə-sôr'əs) *n., pl.* **-saurs** also **-sau·ri** (-sôr'ī'). Any of various extinct fishlike marine reptiles of the order Ichthyosauria, of the Triassic to the Cretaceous periods. [ICHTHYO- + Gk. *sauros,* lizard.]

ichthyosaur

ich·thy·o·sis (ĭk'thē-ō'sĭs) *n.* A congenital skin disease, characterized by dry, thickened, scaly skin.
–ician *suff.* One who practices; specialist: *technician.* [ME < OFr. *-icien.*]
i·ci·cle (ī'sĭ-kəl) *n.* **1.** A tapering spike of ice formed by the freezing of dripping or falling water. **2.** *Informal.* An aloof or emotionally unresponsive person. [ME *isikel* : *is,* ice + *ikel,* icicle < OE *gicel.*]
i·ci·ly (ī'sə-lē) *adv.* In an icy or chilling manner.
i·ci·ness (ī'sē-nĭs) *n.* The condition or quality of being icy.
ic·ing (ī'sĭng) *n.* **1.** A sweet glaze made of sugar, butter, water, egg whites or milk, and often flavored and cooked, used to cover or decorate cakes, cookies, and other baked goods. **2.** The act of intentionally shooting the puck far out of defensive territory in ice hockey.
ick·y (ĭk'ē) *adj.* **-i·er, -i·est.** *Informal.* **1.** Disagreeably sticky: *icky candy.* **2.** Offensive; distasteful: *icky sentimentality.* [Perh. alteration of STICKY.]
i·con also **i·kon** (ī'kŏn') *n.* **1. a.** An image; representation. **b.** A simile or symbol. **2.** A representation or picture of a sacred Christian personage, itself regarded as sacred, esp. in the tradition of the Eastern Churches. [Lat. < Gk. *eikōn,* likeness, image.]
icon– *pref.* Variant of **icono-.**
i·con·ic (ī-kŏn'ĭk) *adj.* **1.** Pertaining to or having the character of an icon. **2.** Having a conventional formulaic style. Used of certain memorial statues and busts.
icono– or **icon–** *pref.* Image; icon: *iconolatry.* [Gk. *eikono-* < *eikōn,* image.]
i·con·o·clasm (ī-kŏn'ə-klăz'əm) *n.* **1.** The action or doctrine of destroying religious images. **2.** The attacking of established institutions, practices, or attitudes. [< ICONOCLAST.]
i·con·o·clast (ī-kŏn'ə-klăst') *n.* **1.** One who destroys sacred images. **2.** One who attacks and seeks to overthrow traditional or popular ideas or institutions. [Med. Lat. *iconoclastes* < Med. Gk. *eikonoklastēs* : Gk. *eikōn,* image + *-klastēs,* breaker < Gk. *klan,* to break.] **—i·con'o·clas'tic** (-klăs'tĭk) *adj.*
i·co·nog·ra·phy (ī'kə-nŏg'rə-fē) *n., pl.* **-phies. 1. a.** Pictorial illustration of a given subject. **b.** The collected representations illustrating a subject. **2. a.** A set of specified or traditional symbolic forms associated with the subject or theme of a stylized work of art. **b.** The conventions defining them and governing their interrelationship. **3.** A treatise or book dealing with iconography. [Gk. *eikonographia,* description, sketch : *eikōn,* image, likeness + *-graphia,* -graphy.] **—i'co·nog'ra·pher** *n.* **—i·con'o·graph'ic** (ī-kŏn'ə-grăf'ĭk), **i·con'o·graph'i·cal** *adj.*
i·co·nol·a·try (ī'kə-nŏl'ə-trē) *n.* The worship of images or icons. **—i'co·nol'a·ter** *n.*
i·co·nol·o·gy (ī'kə-nŏl'ə-jē) *n.* The branch of art history dealing with the description, analysis, and interpretations of icons or iconic representations. **—i·con'o·log'i·cal** (ī-kŏn'ə-lŏj'ĭ-kəl) *adj.* **—i'co·nol'o·gist** *n.*
i·con·o·scope (ī-kŏn'ə-skōp') *n.* A television-camera tube equipped for rapid scanning of an information-storing, photoactive mosaic.
i·co·nos·ta·sis (ī'kə-nŏs'tə-sĭs) *n., pl.* **-ses** (-sēz'). The screen dividing the sanctuary from the main body of an Eastern Orthodox church. [< LGk. *eikonostasion,* shrine : *eikōn,* image + Gk. *stasis,* a standing.]
i·co·sa·he·dron (ī-kō'sə-hē'drən) *n., pl.* **-dra** (-drə) or **-drons.** A polyhedron having 20 faces. [Gk. *eikosaedron* : *eikosi,* twenty + *-edron,* -hedron.] **—i·co'sa·he'dral** *adj.*
–ics *suff.* **1.** Science; art; study; knowledge; skill: *graphics.* **2.** Actions, activities, or practices of: *athletics.* **3.** Qualities or operations of: *mechanics.* [-IC + -S (n.pl. suffix), transl. of Gk. *-ika* < neuter pl. of *-ikos,* adj. suffix.]
ic·ter·ic (ĭk-tĕr'ĭk) *adj.* **1.** Pertaining to or having jaundice. **2.** Used to treat jaundice. —*n.* A remedy for jaundice. [IC-TER(US) + -IC.]
ic·ter·o·gen·ic (ĭk'tər-ə-jĕn'ĭk) *adj.* Causing jaundice. [IC-TER(US) + -GENIC.]
ic·ter·us (ĭk'tər-əs) *n.* Jaundice. [NLat. < Gk. *ikteros.*]
ic·tus (ĭk'təs) *n., pl.* **-tus·es** or **ictus.** *Pathol.* A sudden attack. [Lat., stroke < p.part. of *icere,* to strike.]
i·cy (ī'sē) *adj.* **i·ci·er, i·ci·est. 1.** Containing or covered with ice. **2.** Resembling ice: *icy fingers.* **3.** Bitterly cold; freezing: *an icy day.* **4.** Chilling in manner: *an icy smile.*
id (ĭd) *n.* The division of the psyche associated with instinctual impulses and demands for immediate satisfaction of primitive needs. [NLat. < Lat., it.]
I'd (īd). **1.** I had. **2.** I would. **3.** I should.
–id *suff.* Body; particle: *chromatid.* [< Lat. *-is, -id-,* fem. patronymic suffix.]
ID card (ī'dē') *n.* A card often bearing a photograph that gives identifying data, as name, age, or organizational membership, about an individual.
–ide *suff.* Chemical compound: *cyanide.* [G. *-id* < Fr. *-ide* (as in *oxide*) < *acide,* acid.]
i·de·a (ī-dē'ə) *n.* **1.** Something that exists in the mind, potentially or actually, as a product of mental activity, such as a thought, image, or conception. **2.** An opinion, conviction, or principle: *has some strange political ideas.* **3.** A plan, scheme, or method. **4.** The gist of a specific action or situation; significance. **5.** A notion; fancy. **6.** *Obs.* A mental image of something remembered. **7.** *Mus.* A theme or motif. **8.** *Philos.* **a.** In the philosophy of Plato, an archetype of which a corresponding being in phenomenal reality is an imperfect replica. **b.** In the philosophy of Kant, a concept of reason that is transcendent but nonempirical. **c.** In the philosophy of Hegel, absolute truth; the complete and ultimate product of reason. —See Usage note at **concept.** [Lat. < Gk., form, class, notion.]
i·de·al (ī-dē'əl, ī-dēl') *n.* **1.** A conception of something in its absolute perfection. **2.** One that is regarded as a standard or model of perfection or excellence. **3.** An ultimate object of endeavor; goal. **4.** An honorable or worthy principle or aim. —*adj.* **1. a.** Of, pertaining to, or embodying an ideal. **b.** Conforming to an ultimate form or standard of perfection or excellence. **2.** Considered the best of its kind. **3.** Completely or highly satisfactory: *The location is ideal.* **4. a.** Existing only in the mind; imaginary. **b.** Lacking practicality or the possibility of realization. **5.** Of, pertaining to, or consisting of ideas or mental images. **6.** *Philos.* **a.** Exist-

ing as an archetype or pattern, esp. as a Platonic idea or perception. **b.** Of or pertaining to idealism. [Fr. < LLat. *idealis* < Lat. *idea,* idea.]

Synonyms: *ideal, model, exemplar, standard, prototype, archetype.* These nouns refer to things or, less often, to persons that serve as the basis of direction or guidance in work or behavior. An *ideal* is a goal of perfection in the form of a person or thing, sometimes imaginary. A *model* is a pattern or a person who serves as a pattern in the creation of something; in a related sense the term refers to a person or thing worthy of imitation. The latter sense approaches that of *exemplar,* a person or thing that serves as an ideal example by reason of being either very worthy or truly representative of a type, admirable or otherwise. A *standard* is an established criterion or recognized level of excellence used as a measure of achievement. *Prototype* and *archetype* both denote original models of things subsequently reproduced. What develops from a *prototype* may represent significant modifications from the original. An *archetype,* in contrast, is usually construed as an ideal form that establishes an unchanging pattern for all things of its kind.

i·de·al·ism (ī-dē′ə-lĭz′əm) *n.* **1.** The action or practice of envisioning things in an ideal form. **2.** Pursuit of one's ideals. **3.** An idealizing treatment of a subject in literature or art. **4.** The philosophical theory that the object of external perception, in itself or as perceived, consists of ideas.

i·de·al·ist (ī-dē′ə-lĭst) *n.* **1.** One whose conduct is influenced by ideals, esp. when they conflict with practical considerations. **2.** One who is unrealistic and impractical. **3.** An artist or writer whose work is imbued with idealism. **4.** An adherent of any system of philosophical idealism.

i·de·al·is·tic (ī-dē′ə-lĭs′tĭk) *adj.* Pertaining to or having the nature of an idealist or idealism. **—i′de·al·is′ti·cal·ly** *adv.*

i·de·al·i·ty (ī′dē-ăl′ĭ-tē) *n., pl.* **-ties. 1.** The state or quality of being ideal. **2.** Existence in idea only.

i·de·al·ize (ī-dē′ə-līz′) *v.* **-ized, -iz·ing, -iz·es.** *—tr.* **1.** To regard as ideal. **2.** To make or envision as ideal. *—intr.* **1.** To render something as an ideal. **2.** To conceive an ideal or ideals. **—i·de′al·i·za′tion** *n.* **—i·de′al·iz′er** *n.*

i·de·al·ly (ī-dē′ə-lē) *adv.* **1.** In conformity with an ideal; perfectly. **2.** In theory or imagination; theoretically.

i·de·ate (ī′dē-āt′) *v.* **-at·ed, -at·ing, -ates.** *—tr.* To form an idea of; imagine; conceive. *—intr.* To conceive mental images; think. **—i′de·a′tion** *n.* **—i′de·a′tion·al** *adj.*

i·dée fixe (ē-dā fēks′) *n., pl.* **i·dées fixes** (ē-dā fēks′). A fixed idea; obsession. [Fr.]

i·dem (ī′dĕm′) *pron.* Used to indicate a reference previously mentioned. [Lat., the same < *id,* it.]

i·den·tic (ī-dĕn′tĭk) *adj.* **1.** Designating diplomatic action or language in which two or more governments agree to use the same forms in their relations with other governments. **2.** *Archaic.* Identical. [Med. Lat. *identicus,* identical.]

i·den·ti·cal (ī-dĕn′tĭ-kəl) *adj.* **1.** Being the same: *used the senator's identical words.* **2.** Being exactly equal and alike. **3.** Having such a near similarity or resemblance as to be essentially equal or interchangeable. **4.** *Biol.* Of or pertaining to a twin or twins developed from the same ovum. [Med. Lat. *identicus* < LLat. *identitas,* identity.] **—i·den′ti·cal·ly** *adv.* **—i·den′ti·cal·ness** *n.*

Usage: Some authorities on usage specify *with* as the preferred preposition after *identical.* But either *with* or *to* is now acceptable.

i·den·ti·fi·ca·tion (ī-dĕn′tə-fĭ-kā′shən) *n.* **1.** The act of identifying. **2.** The state of being identified. **3.** Proof or evidence of identity. **4.** *Psychol.* **a.** An individual's recognition of a personal or group identity. **b.** The transferal of response to an object considered identical to another.

identification card *n.* An ID card.

i·den·ti·fi·er (ī-dĕn′tə-fī′ər) *n.* **1.** One that identifies. **2.** *Computer Sci.* A symbol that serves to identify, indicate, or name a body of data.

i·den·ti·fy (ī-dĕn′tə-fī′) *v.* **-fied, -fy·ing, -fies.** *—tr.* **1. a.** To establish the identity of. **b.** To ascertain the origin, nature, or definitive characteristics of. **2.** To determine the taxonomic classification of. **3.** To consider as identical or united; equate. **4.** *Psychol.* To associate or affiliate (oneself) closely with a person or group. *—intr.* To establish an identification with another or others. [Med. Lat. *identificare* : LLat. *identitas,* identity + Lat. *facere,* to make.] **—i·den′ti·fi′a·ble** *adj.* **—i·den′ti·fi′er** *n.*

Usage: *Identify* is well established in the sense, popularized by psychology, of "to see oneself as one with." A majority of the Usage Panel accepts this example: *He identified himself with the hero of a new novel.* A majority also accepts the same example without the reflexive pronoun: *He identified with the hero of a new novel.*

i·den·ti·ty (ī-dĕn′tĭ-tē) *n., pl.* **-ties. 1.** The collective aspect of the set of characteristics by which a thing is definitively recognizable or known. **2.** The set of behavioral or personal characteristics by which an individual is recognizable as a member of a group. **3.** The quality or condition of being the same as something else. **4.** The distinct personality of an individual regarded as a persisting entity; individuality. **5.** *Math.* **a.** An equality satisfied by all values of the variables for which the expressions involved in the equality are defined. **b.** A unity. [LLat. *identitas* < Lat. *idem,* the same < *id,* it.]

identity crisis *n.* **1.** A psychosocial state or condition of disorientation and role confusion occurring esp. in adolescents as a result of conflicting pressures and expectations. **2.** An analogous state of confusion occurring in a social structure, as an institution or a corporation.

identity element *n.* The element of a set of numbers that when combined with another number in an operation leaves that number unchanged. For example, 0 is the identity element under addition for the real numbers, since if a is any real number, $a + 0 = 0 + a = a$. Similarly, 1 is the identity element under multiplication for the real numbers, since $a \times 1 = 1 \times a = a$.

identity matrix *n.* A square matrix with numeral 1's along the diagonal from upper left to lower right and 0's in all other positions.

identity sign *n.* A mathematical symbol ($\equiv$), used to denote identity rather than equality.

ideo– *pref.* Idea: *ideography.* [Fr. *idéo-* < Gk. *idea,* form, idea.]

id·e·o·gram (ĭd′ē-ə-grăm′, ī′dē-) also **id·e·o·graph** (-grăf′) *n.* **1.** A character or symbol representing an idea or thing without expressing a particular word or phrase for it, as Chinese characters. **2.** A graphic symbol, as &, $, or @.

id·e·og·ra·phy (ĭd′ē-ŏg′rə-fē, ī′dē-) *n.* **1.** The representation of ideas by graphic symbols. **2.** The use of ideograms to express ideas. **—id′e·o·graph′ic** (-ə-grăf′ĭk) *adj.*

i·de·o·log·i·cal (ī′dē-ə-lŏj′ĭ-kəl, ĭd′ē-) also **i·de·o·log·ic** (-lŏj′ĭk) *adj.* **1.** Of or relating to ideology. **2.** Of or concerned with ideas.

i·de·ol·o·gist (ī′dē-ŏl′ə-jĭst, ĭd′ē-) *n.* **1.** An advocate or adherent of a given ideology. **2.** *Archaic.* A visionary; theorist.

i·de·o·logue (ī′dē-ə-lŏg, ĭd′ē-) *n.* An advocate of a given ideology, esp. one of its official exponents. [Fr. *idéologue,* back-formation < *idéologie,* ideology.]

i·de·ol·o·gy (ī′dē-ŏl′ə-jē, ĭd′ē-) *n., pl.* **-gies.** The body of ideas reflecting the social needs and aspirations of an individual, group, class, or culture. [Fr. *idéologie* : *idéo-,* ideo- + *-logie,* -logy.]

i·de·o·mo·tor (ī′dē-ə-mō′tər, ĭd′ē-) *adj.* Of or being a motor response to an ideational rather than a sensory stimulus.

ides (īdz) *n. (used with a sing. verb).* In the ancient Roman calendar, the 15th day of March, May, July, or October or the 13th day of the other months. [ME *idus* < OFr. *ides* < Lat. *idus.*]

idio– *pref.* **1.** Private; personal; one's own: *idiolect.* **2.** Distinct; separate: *idioplasm.* [Gk. < *idios,* personal, private.]

id·i·o·blast (ĭd′ē-ə-blăst′) *n.* A plant cell that differs noticeably in form from neighboring cells. **—id′i·o·blas′tic** *adj.*

id·i·o·cy (ĭd′ē-ə-sē) *n., pl.* **-cies. 1.** *Psychol.* A condition of subnormal intellectual development or ability, characterized by intelligence in the lowest measurable range. **2.** Extreme folly or stupidity. **3.** A foolish or stupid utterance or deed. [< IDIOT.]

id·i·o·lect (ĭd′ē-ə-lĕkt′) *n.* The speech of an individual, considered as a linguistic pattern unique among speakers of his language or dialect. [IDIO- + (DIA)LECT.] **—id′i·o·lec′tal, id′i·o·lec′tic** *adj.*

id·i·om (ĭd′ē-əm) *n.* **1.** A speech form or expression of a given language that is peculiar to itself grammatically or that cannot be understood from the individual meanings of its elements. **2.** The specific grammatical, syntactic, and structural character of a given language. **3.** A regional speech or dialect. **4.** A specialized vocabulary used by a group of people; jargon: *legal idiom.* **5.** A style of artistic expression characteristic of a given individual, school, period, or medium: *the idiom of the French impressionists.* [OFr. *idiome* < LLat. *idioma* < Gk. < *idiousthai,* to make one's own < *idios,* own, personal, private.]

id·i·o·mat·ic (ĭd′ē-ə-măt′ĭk) *adj.* **1.** Peculiar to or characteristic of a given language. **2.** Resembling or having the nature of an idiom. **3.** Using many idioms. **—id′i·o·mat′i·cal·ly** *adv.*

id·i·o·mor·phic (ĭd′ē-ə-môr′fĭk) *adj.* Having a characteristic shape. Used of well-crystallized minerals. [< Gk. *idiomorphos,* having one's own form : *idios,* own + *morphē,* shape.] **—id′i·o·mor′phi·cal·ly** *adv.*

id·i·op·a·thy (ĭd′ē-ŏp′ə-thē) *n. Med.* **1.** A disease of unknown origin or cause; primary disease. **2.** A disease for which no cause is known. [Gk. *idiopathia,* disease having its own origin : *idios,* own + *pathos,* suffering.] **—id′i·o·path′ic** (-ō-păth′ĭk) *adj.* **—id′i·o·path′i·cal·ly** *adv.*

id·i·o·plasm (ĭd′ē-ə-plăz′əm) *n.* A hypothetical structural unit of germ plasm. **—id′i·o·plas′mic, id′i·o·plas·mat′ic** (-ō-plăz-măt′ĭk) *adj.*

id·i·o·syn·cra·sy (ĭd′ē-ō-sĭng′krə-sē) *n., pl.* **-sies. 1.** A structural or behavioral characteristic peculiar to an individual or group. **2.** A physiological or temperamental peculiarity. **3.** Hypersensitivity to a drug. [Gk. *idiosunkrasia* : *idios,* own + *sunkrasis,* mixture, temperament (*sun,* together + *krasis,* mixture).] **—id′i·o·syn·crat′ic** (-sĭn-krăt′ĭk) *adj.* **—id′i·o·syn·crat′i·cal·ly** *adv.*

id·i·ot (ĭd′ē-ət) *n.* **1.** *Psychol.* A mentally deficient person, having intelligence in the lowest measurable range, being unable to guard against common dangers and incapable of learning connected speech. **2.** A foolish or stupid person.

ideogram
Chinese characters

idol
15th- to 14th-century B.C. Egyptian sculpture of the goddess Sechmet

[ME, ignorant person < OFr. *idiote* < Lat. *idiota* < Gk. *idiōtēs,* private person, layman < *idios,* own, private.]

idiot box *n. Slang.* Television.

id·i·ot·ic (ĭd'ē-ŏt'ĭk) *adj.* **1.** Exhibiting idiocy. **2.** Showing foolishness or stupidity. **—id'i·ot'i·cal·ly** *adv.*

idiot light *n.* A light on the instrument panel of an automobile that gives forewarning, as of an overheated engine.

i·dle (īd'l) *adj.* **i·dler, i·dlest. 1. a.** Not in use. **b.** Without a job; unemployed. **c.** Not scheduled to compete, as a sports team. **2.** Lazy; shiftless. **3.** Lacking foundation in fact. *—v.* **i·dled, i·dling, i·dles.** *—intr.* **1.** To pass time without working or in avoiding work. **2.** To move lazily and without purpose. **3.** To run at a slow speed or out of gear. *—tr.* **1.** To pass (time) without working or in avoiding work; waste: *idle the afternoon away.* **2.** To make or cause to be unemployed or inactive. **3.** To cause (a motor, for example) to idle. [ME *idel* < OE *īdel.*] **—i'dle·ness** *n.* **—i'dler** (-īd'lər) *n.* **—i'dly** *adv.*

Usage: *Idle* is now accepted in the transitive sense of "to make idle." The following example is accepted on all levels of speech and writing by the Usage Panel: *The dock strike had idled many crews and their ships.*

idle character *n.* An alphanumeric or digital character that is transmitted over a communications line but does not appear in the output of the receiving terminal.

idle pulley also **idler pulley** *n.* A pulley on a shaft that rests on or presses against a drive belt to guide it or take up slack.

idle wheel *n.* **1.** A gear, wheel, or roller interposed between two similar parts to convey motion from one to the other without change in speed or direction of motion. **2.** An idle pulley.

i·do·crase (ī'də-krās', -krāz', ĭd'ə-) *n.* A green, brown, yellow, or blue mineral that is essentially $Ca_{10}Al_4(Mg,Fe)_2Si_9O_{34}(OH)_4$. [Fr. : Gk. *eidos,* form + *krasis,* mixture.]

i·dol (īd'l) *n.* **1. a.** An image used as an object of worship. **b.** A false god. **2.** A person or thing that is blindly or excessively adored. **3.** *Archaic.* Something visible but without substance. [ME < OFr. *idole* < LLat. *idolum* < Gk. *eidōlon,* image < *eidos,* form.]

i·dol·a·ter (ī-dŏl'ə-tər) *n.* **1.** One who worships idols. **2.** One who blindly or excessively adores a person or thing. [ME *idolatrer* < OFr. *idolatre* < LLat. *idololatres* < Gk. *eidōlolatrēs* : *eidōlon,* idol + *-latrēs,* worshiper.]

i·dol·a·trous (ī-dŏl'ə-trəs) *adj.* **1.** Of or pertaining to idolatry. **2.** Given to idolatry. **3.** Constituting idolatry. **—i·dol'a·trous·ly** *adv.* **—i·dol'a·trous·ness** *n.*

i·dol·a·try (ī-dŏl'ə-trē) *n., pl.* **-tries. 1.** The worship of idols. **2.** Blind or excessive adoration or devotion. [ME *idolatrie* < OFr. < Med. Lat. *idolatria* < LLat. *idololatria* < Gk. *eidōlolatria* : *eidolōn,* idol + *latreia,* service.]

i·dol·ize (īd'l-īz') *tr.v.* **-ized, -iz·ing, -iz·es. 1.** To regard with blind admiration or devotion. **2.** To worship as an idol. **—i'dol·i·za'tion** *n.* **—i'dol·iz'er** *n.*

igloo
Above: Summer igloo
Below: Winter igloo

i·dyll also **i·dyl** (īd'l) *n.* **1.** A short poem or prose piece describing a picturesque episode or scene of rustic life. **2.** A scene or event of rural simplicity. **3.** A narrative poem treating a tragic, epic, or romantic theme. **4. a.** A carefree episode or experience. **b.** A romantic interlude. [Lat. *idyllium* < Gk. *eidullion,* dim. of *eidos,* form, figure.]

i·dyl·list (īd'l-ĭst) *n.* A writer of idylls.

i·dyl·lic (ī-dĭl'ĭk) *adj.* **1.** Of, pertaining to, or having the nature of an idyll. **2.** Having a natural charm and picturesqueness. **—i·dyl'li·cal·ly** *adv.*

-ie *suff.* Variant of **-y³.**

if (ĭf) *conj.* **1. a.** In the event that: *If I were to go, I would be late.* **b.** Granting that: *If that's true, what should we do?* **c.** On condition that: *She will sing only if she is paid.* **2.** Although possibly; even though: *a handsome if useless trinket.* **3.** Whether: *Ask if he will come.* **4.** Used to introduce an exclamatory clause, indicating a wish: *If she had only come earlier! —n.* A possibility, condition, or stipulation: *no ifs, ands, or buts.* [ME < OE *gif.*]

Usage: Either *if* or *whether* may be used to introduce a clause indicating uncertainty after a verb such as *ask, doubt, know, learn, see: We shall soon learn whether* (or *if*) *it is true. If* should be avoided when it may be ambiguous, as in the following: *Let her know if she is invited.* Depending on the meaning, that could be better phrased: *Let her know whether she is invited. Let her know in the event that she is invited.* Often the phrase *if not* is also ambiguous: *The discovery offered persuasive, if not conclusive, evidence.* This could mean "persuasive and perhaps conclusive" or "persuasive but not conclusive." A clause introduced by *if* may contain either a past subjunctive verb (*if I were going*) or an indicative verb (*if I was going*) depending on the meaning intended. Traditionally, the subjunctive is used to describe a situation that is known to be contrary to fact, as in *if America were still a British colony* or *if Napoleon had been an Englishman.* The main clause of such a sentence must then contain the modal verb *would* or (less frequently) *should: If America were still a British colony, we would drink more tea than we do. If I were the President, I should* (or *would*) *make June 1 a national holiday.* When the situation described by the *if* clause is not known to be false, however, that clause must contain an indicative verb, and the choice of verb in the main clause will depend upon the intended meaning: *If Hamlet was really written by Marlowe, as many have claimed, then we have underestimated Marlowe's genius. If Kim was out all day, as you say, then I understand why she didn't answer the phone.* The indicative is also required when the situation described by the *if* clause is assumed to be true: *If I was short with you a moment ago, it is only because I wasn't paying attention. If Rome is the liveliest city in Italy, Milan is the most elegant.* When an *if* clause is preceded by *ask* or *wonder,* only the indicative should be used: *He asked if Napoleon was* (not *were*) *a great general. I wonder if she was* (not *were*) serious. There is a growing tendency to use *would have* in place of the subjunctive in contrary-to-fact *if* clauses, but this usage is still considered incorrect. Instead of *if I would have been born in the 12th century,* write *if I had been born;* instead of *if I would of been the President,* write *if I were.*

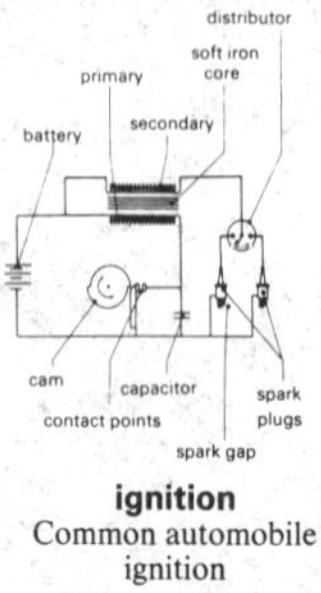

ignition
Common automobile ignition

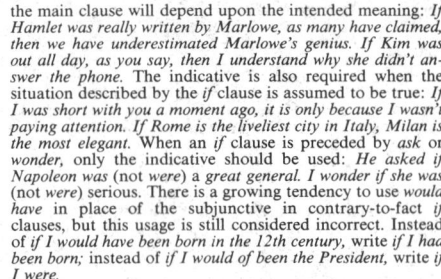

if·fy (ĭf'ē) *adj. Informal.* Characterized by doubt, uncertainty, or chance. [< IF.]

I formation *n. Football.* An alignment of the offensive team in which all the backs line up in single file behind the center.

ig·loo (ĭg'lo͞o) *n., pl.* **-loos. 1.** An Eskimo dwelling, sometimes built of blocks of ice or hard snow. **2.** A dome-shaped structure or building. [Eskimo *iglu,* house.]

ig·ne·ous (ĭg'nē-əs) *adj.* **1.** Of, relating to, or characteristic of fire. **2.** *Geol.* **a.** Formed by solidification from a molten or partially molten state. Used of rocks. **b.** Of or pertaining to rock so formed. [Lat. *igneus* < *ignis,* fire.]

ig·nis fat·u·us (ĭg'nĭs făch'o͞o-əs) *n., pl.* **ig·nes fat·u·i** (ĭg'nēz făch'o͞o-ī'). **1.** A phosphorescent light that hovers or flits over swampy ground at night, possibly caused by spontaneous combustion of gases emitted by rotting organic matter. **2.** Something that misleads or deludes; illusion. [Med. Lat., foolish fire.]

ig·nite (ĭg-nīt') *v.* **-nit·ed, -nit·ing, -nites.** *—tr.* **1. a.** To cause to burn. **b.** To set fire to. **2.** To subject to great heat, esp. to make luminous by heat. **3.** To arouse the passions of; excite: *Her insults ignited my anger. —intr.* **1.** To begin to burn. **2.** To begin to glow. [LLat. *ignire, ignit-* < *ignis,* fire.] **—ig·nit'a·ble, ig·nit'i·ble** *adj.* **—ig·nit'er, ig·ni'tor** *n.*

ig·ni·tion (ĭg-nĭsh'ən) *n.* **1.** The raising of a substance to its ignition point, as by electric current, friction, or mechanical shock. **2. a.** An electrical system, typically powered by a battery or magneto, that provides the spark to ignite the fuel mixture in an internal-combustion engine. **b.** A switch that activates this system.

ignition point *n.* The minimum temperature at which a substance will continue to burn without additional application of external heat.

ig·ni·tron (ĭg-nī'trŏn', ĭg'nĭ-) *n.* A single-anode, mercury-vapor rectifier in which current passes as an arc between the anode and a mercury-pool cathode, used in power rectification. [Lat. *ignis,* fire + -TRON.]

ig·no·ble (ĭg-nō'bəl) *adj.* **1.** Not having a noble character or purpose; dishonorable. **2.** Not of the nobility; common. [Lat. *ignobilis* : *in-,* not + *nobilis,* noble.] **—ig'no·bil'i·ty** (-bĭl'ĭ-tē), **ig·no'ble·ness** *n.* **—ig·no'bly** *adv.*

ig·no·min·i·ous (ĭg'nə-mĭn'ē-əs) *adj.* **1.** Characterized by shame or disgrace. **2.** Deserving disgrace or shame; despicable. **3.** Degrading; debasing: *an ignominious defeat at the polls.* **—ig'no·min'i·ous·ly** *adv.* **—ig'no·min'i·ous·ness** *n.*

ig·no·min·y (ĭg'nə-mĭn'ē, -mə-nē) *n., pl.* **-ies. 1.** Great personal dishonor or humiliation. **2.** Shameful or disgraceful action, conduct, or character. [Lat. *ignominia* : *in-,* not + *nomen,* name, reputation.]

ig·no·ra·mus (ĭg'nə-rā'məs) *n.* An ignorant person. [NLat. < Lat., we do not know < *ignorare,* to be ignorant.]

ig·no·rance (ĭg'nər-əns) *n.* The condition of being ignorant.

ig·no·rant (ĭg'nər-ənt) *adj.* **1.** Without education or knowledge. **2.** Exhibiting lack of education or knowledge: *an ignorant mistake.* **3.** Unaware or uninformed: *ignorant of what had happened.* [ME *ignoraunt* < OFr. *ignorant* < Lat. *ignorans,* pr.part. of *ignorare,* to be ignorant.] **—ig'no·rant·ly** *adv.*

Synonyms: *ignorant, uneducated, untaught, unlearned, untutored, unlettered, illiterate.* These adjectives mean lacking in knowledge or education. *Ignorant* can refer to a person's low level of knowledge in general or, in a narrower sense, to his being uninformed or unaware of a specific thing. *Uneducated, untaught, unlearned,* and *untutored* imply lack of schooling. *Unlettered* describes one deficient in book learning or in the ability to read and write. *Illiterate* refers most often to inability to meet an established minimum level of achievement in reading and writing.

ig·nore (ĭg-nôr', -nōr') *tr.v.* **-nored, -nor·ing, -nores.** To refuse to pay attention to; disregard. [Fr. *ignorer* < Lat. *ignorare,* not to know, to be ignorant.] **—ig·nor'a·ble** *adj.* **—ig·nor'er** *n.*

I·go·rot (ĭg'ə-rōt', ē'gə-) *n., pl.* **Igorot** or **-rots. 1.** A member of any of several related tribes of mountainous northern Luzon, Philippines. **2.** The Austronesian language of the Igorot.

i·gua·na (ĭ-gwä'nə) *n.* Any of various large tropical American lizards of the family Iguanidae, often having spiny projections along the back. [Sp. < Arawak *iwana.*]

i·guan·o·don (ĭ-gwä'nə-dŏn') *n.* Any of various large dinosaurs of the genus *Iguanodon,* of the Jurassic and Cretaceous periods. [NLat. *Iguanodon,* genus name : IGUANA + Gk. *odōn,* tooth.]
ih·ram (ē-räm') *n.* **1.** The sacred dress of Moslem pilgrims, consisting of two lengths of white cotton. **2.** The sacred state in which Moslem pilgrims exist while wearing the ihram. [Ar. *iḥrām,* prohibition < *ḥarama,* he prohibited.]
IHS *n.* A graphic symbol for Jesus. [Short for Gk. *IHSOUS,* Jesus.]
i·ke·ba·na (ē'kä-bä'nä, ĭk'ə-) *n.* The Japanese art of arranging flowers with special regard to balance, harmony, and form. [J. : *ikeru,* to arrange + *hana,* flower.]
i·kon (ī'kŏn') *n.* Variant of **icon.**
il–[1] *pref.* Variant of **in-**[1]. Used before *l.*
il–[2] *pref.* Variant of **in-**[2]. Used before *l.*
i·lang-i·lang (ē'läng'ē'läng') *n.* Variant of **ylang-ylang.**
–ile[1] *suff.* Of, pertaining to, or capable of: *audile.* [ME < OFr. < Lat. *-ilis.*]
–ile[2] *suff.* A division of a specified size in the range of a statistic: *percentile.* [Perh. < Lat. *-ilis,* adj. suffix.]
il·e·a (ĭl'ē-ə) *n.* Plural of **ileum.**
il·e·ac (ĭl'ē-ăk') *adj.* **1.** Of or pertaining to ileus. **2.** Of or pertaining to the ileum.
il·e·i·tis (ĭl'ē-ī'tĭs) *n.* Inflammation of the ileum. [ILE(UM) + -ITIS.]
il·e·o·ce·cal (ĭl'ē-ō-sē'kəl) *adj.* Of or pertaining to the ileum and the cecum. [ILE(UM) + CECUM.]
il·e·os·to·my (ĭl'ē-ŏs'tə-mē) *n., pl.* **-mies.** The surgical construction of an artificial excretory opening through the abdominal wall into the ileum. [ILE(UM) + -STOMY.]
il·e·um (ĭl'ē-əm) *n., pl.* **-e·a** (-ē-ə). The portion of the small intestine extending from the jejunum to the cecum. [NLat. < Lat., groin, flank.] **—il'e·al** *adj.*
il·e·us (ĭl'ē-əs) *n.* Intestinal obstruction causing colic, vomiting, and toxemia. [Lat. *ileos* < Gk. *eileos,* intestinal obstruction < *eilein,* to squeeze, turn.]
i·lex (ī'lĕks') *n.* **1.** Any of various trees or shrubs of the genus *Ilex;* holly. **2.** The holm oak. [Lat., holm oak.]
il·i·um (ĭl'ē-əm) *n., pl.* **-i·a** (-ē-ə). The uppermost and widest of three bones comprising one of the lateral halves of the pelvis. [NLat. < Lat. *ileum,* groin, flank.]
ilk (ĭlk) *n.* Type or kind: *can't trust men of his ilk.* *—pron. Scot.* The same. Used following a name to indicate that the one named resides in an area bearing the same name: *Duncan of that ilk.* *—adj.* Variant of **ilka.** [ME, same < OE *ilca.*]
il·ka (ĭl'kə) also **ilk** (ĭlk) *adj. Scot.* Each; every. [ME *ilk a,* each one : *ilk,* var. of *ech,* each + *a,* one, a.]
ill (ĭl) *adj.* **worse** (wûrs), **worst** (wûrst). **1.** Not healthy; sick: *began to feel ill.* **2.** Not normal; unsound: *ill health.* **3.** Resulting in suffering; distressing: *ill effects.* **4.** Having evil intentions; hostile: *did her an ill turn.* **5.** Not favorable; unpropitious: *ill luck.* **6.** Not up to recognized standards of excellence or conduct. **7.** Harmful; cruel. *—idiom.* **ill at ease.** Nervous and uncomfortable. *—adv.* **worse, worst. 1.** In an ill manner; not well. **2.** Scarcely or with difficulty. *—n.* **1.** Evil; sin. **2.** Disaster, distress, or harm. **3.** Something that causes suffering; trouble: *no easy cure for social ills.* [ME < ON *illr,* bad.]
I'll (īl). **1.** I will. **2.** I shall.
ill-ad·vised (ĭl'əd-vīzd') *adj.* Done without wise counsel or careful deliberation. **—ill'-ad·vis'ed·ly** (-vī'zĭd-lē) *adv.*
il·la·tion (ĭ-lā'shən) *n.* **1.** The act of inferring or drawing conclusions. **2.** A conclusion; deduction. [LLat. *illatio* < Lat. *illatus,* p.part. of *inferre,* to carry in, infer : *in-,* in + *ferre,* to carry.]
il·la·tive (ĭl'ə-tĭv, ĭ-lā'-) *adj.* **1.** Of, pertaining to, or of the nature of an illation. **2.** Expressing or preceding an inference. Used of a word. *—n.* **1.** An illative word or phrase as *hence* or *for that reason.* **2.** Illation (sense 2).
ill-being (ĭl'bē'ĭng) *n.* A condition of being lacking in prosperity, happiness, or health.
ill-bod·ing (ĭl'bō'dĭng) *adj.* Portending evil; inauspicious.
ill-bred (ĭl'brĕd') *adj.* **1.** Badly brought up; impolite. **2.** Not thoroughbred.
il·le·gal (ĭ-lē'gəl) *adj.* **1.** Prohibited by law. **2.** Prohibited by official rules. **3.** *Computer Sci.* Unacceptable to or not performable by a computer: *an illegal operation.* *—n.* An illegal emigrant. **—il·le'gal·ly** *adv.*
il·le·gal·i·ty (ĭl'ē-găl'ĭ-tē) *n., pl.* **-ties. 1.** The state or quality of being illegal. **2.** An illegal act.
il·leg·i·ble (ĭ-lĕj'ə-bəl) *adj.* Not legible or decipherable. **—il·leg'i·bil'i·ty, il·leg'i·ble·ness** *n.* **—il·leg'i·bly** *adv.*
il·le·git·i·ma·cy (ĭl'ĭ-jĭt'ə-mə-sē) *n.* **1.** The quality or condition of being illegitimate. **2.** Bastardy.
il·le·git·i·mate (ĭl'ĭ-jĭt'ə-mĭt) *adj.* **1.** Against the law; illegal. **2.** Born out of wedlock. **3.** Not in correct grammatical usage. **4.** Incorrectly deduced; illogical. **—il'le·git'i·mate·ly** *adv.*
ill-fat·ed (ĭl'fā'tĭd) *adj.* **1.** Destined for misfortune; doomed. **2.** Marked by or causing misfortune; unlucky.
ill-fa·vored (ĭl'fā'vərd) *adj.* **1.** Having an ugly or unattractive face. **2.** Objectionable; offensive. **3.** Doomed; ill-fated.
ill-got·ten (ĭl'gŏt'n) *adj.* Obtained in an evil or dishonest manner.
ill humor *n.* An irritable state of mind; surliness.
ill-hu·mored (ĭl'hyōō'mərd) *adj.* Irritable and surly. **—ill'-hu·mored·ly** *adv.*
il·lib·er·al (ĭ-lĭb'ər-əl) *adj.* **1.** Narrow-minded; bigoted. **2.** *Archaic.* Ungenerous, mean, or stingy. **3.** *Archaic.* **a.** Lacking liberal culture. **b.** Ill-bred; vulgar. [Lat. *illiberalis* : *in-,* not + *liberalis,* liberal.] **—il·lib'er·al'i·ty, il·lib'er·al·ness** *n.* **—il·lib'er·al·ly** *adv.*
il·lic·it (ĭ-lĭs'ĭt) *adj.* Not sanctioned by custom or law; unlawful. [Lat. *illicitus* : *in-,* not + *licitus,* lawful. —see LICIT.] **—il·lic'it·ly** *adv.* **—il·lic'it·ness** *n.*
il·lim·it·a·ble (ĭ-lĭm'ĭ-tə-bəl) *adj.* Incapable of being limited or circumscribed; limitless. **—il·lim'it·a·bil'i·ty, il·lim'it·a·ble·ness** *n.* **—il·lim'it·a·bly** *adv.*
Il·li·noi·an (ĭl'ə-noi'ən) *adj.* Of or pertaining to the third glacial stage in North America. [After the state of *Illinois.*]
Il·li·nois (ĭl'ə-noi', -noiz') *n., pl.* **Illinois. 1. a.** A confederacy of Indian tribes that inhabited Illinois and parts of Iowa, Wisconsin, and Missouri. **b.** A member of this confederacy or one of the member tribes. **2.** An Algonquian language of the Illinois and Miami peoples. [Fr., of Algonquian orig.]
il·liq·uid (ĭ-lĭk'wĭd) *adj.* **1.** Incapable of being readily converted into cash: *illiquid assets.* **2.** Lacking in cash or liquid assets: *not bankrupt but just illiquid.* **—il'li·quid'i·ty** (ĭl'ĭ-kwĭd'ĭ-tē) *n.*
il·lit·er·a·cy (ĭ-lĭt'ər-ə-sē) *n., pl.* **-cies. 1.** The quality or condition of being unable to read and write. **2.** An error caused by or thought characteristic of illiteracy.
il·lit·er·ate (ĭ-lĭt'ər-ĭt) *adj.* **1. a.** Unable to read and write. **b.** Having little or no formal education. **2. a.** Marked by inferiority to an expected standard of familiarity with language and literature. **b.** Violating prescribed standards of speech or writing. **3.** Ignorant of the fundamentals of a given art or branch of knowledge: *musically illiterate.* *—n.* One who is illiterate. [Lat. *illiteratus* : *in-,* not + *literatus,* literate.] **—il·lit'er·ate·ly** *adv.* **—il·lit'er·ate·ness** *n.*
ill-man·nered (ĭl'măn'ərd) *adj.* Lacking or indicating a lack of good manners; rude. **—ill'-man'nered·ly** *adv.*
ill-na·tured (ĭl'nā'chərd) *adj.* **1.** Having or showing a disagreeable disposition; surly. **2.** Spiteful; nasty. **—ill'-na'tured·ly** *adv.* **—ill'-na'tured·ness** *n.*
ill·ness (ĭl'nĭs) *n.* **1. a.** Sickness of body or mind. **b.** A sickness. **2.** *Obs.* Evil; wickedness.
il·log·ic (ĭ-lŏj'ĭk) *n.* The lack of logic.
il·log·i·cal (ĭ-lŏj'ĭ-kəl) *adj.* **1.** Contradicting or disregarding the principles of logic. **2.** Without logic; senseless. **—il·log'i·cal'i·ty** (-kăl'ĭ-tē), **il·log'i·cal·ness** *n.* **—il·log'i·cal·ly** *adv.*
ill-sort·ed (ĭl'sôr'tĭd) *adj.* Badly matched.
ill-starred (ĭl'stärd') *adj.* Ill-fated; unlucky.
ill-tem·pered (ĭl'tĕm'pərd) *adj.* Having a bad temper; irritable. **—ill'-tem'pered·ly** *adv.*
ill-timed (ĭl'tīmd') *adj.* Done or occurring at an inappropriate time; untimely.
ill-treat (ĭl'trēt') *tr.v.* **-treat·ed, -treat·ing, -treats.** To maltreat. **—ill'-treat'ment** *n.*
il·lume (ĭ-lōōm') *tr.v.* **-lumed, -lum·ing, -lumes.** To illuminate. [Short for ILLUMINE.]
il·lu·mi·nance (ĭ-lōō'mə-nəns) *n.* Illumination (sense 8).
il·lu·mi·nant (ĭ-lōō'mə-nənt) *n.* Something that gives off light.
il·lu·mi·nate (ĭ-lōō'mə-nāt') *v.* **-nat·ed, -nat·ing, -nates.** *—tr.* **1.** To provide or brighten with light. **2.** To decorate or hang with lights. **3.** To make understandable; clarify. **4.** To enlighten intellectually or spiritually; enable to understand. **5.** To endow with fame or splendor; celebrate. **6.** To adorn (a page of a book, for example) with ornamental designs, miniatures, or lettering in brilliant colors or precious metals. **7.** To expose to or reveal by radiation. *—intr.* **1.** To become lighted; glow. **2.** To be exposed to or revealed by radiation. *—n.* (-nĭt). One who has or professes to have an unusual degree of enlightenment. [Lat. *illuminare, illuminat-* : *in-,* in + *luminare,* to light up < *lumen,* light.]
il·lu·mi·na·ti (ĭ-lōō'mə-nä'tē) *pl.n.* **1.** Persons claiming to be unusually enlightened with regard to some subject. **2. Illuminati.** Any of various groups that claimed special religious enlightenment. [Lat., pl. of *illuminatus,* p.part. of *illuminare,* to illuminate.]
il·lu·mi·na·tion (ĭ-lōō'mə-nā'shən) *n.* **1.** The act of illuminating. **2.** The state of being illuminated. **3.** A light source. **4.** Lighting used as decoration. **5.** Spiritual or intellectual enlightenment. **6.** Clarification; elucidation. **7. a.** The art or act of decorating a text, page, or initial letter with ornamental designs, miniatures, or lettering. **b.** An example of this art. **8.** *Physics.* The luminous flux per unit area at any point on a surface exposed to incident light.
il·lu·mi·na·tive (ĭ-lōō'mə-nā'tĭv) *adj.* Of, causing, or capable of causing illumination.
il·lu·mi·na·tor (ĭ-lōō'mə-nā'tər) *n.* **1.** One that illuminates. **2.** A device for producing, concentrating, or reflecting light. **3.** A person who illuminates manuscripts or other objects.
il·lu·mine (ĭ-lōō'mĭn) *tr.v.* **-mined, -min·ing, -mines.** To give light to; illuminate. [ME *illuminen* < Lat. *illuminare,* to illuminate.] **—il·lu'mi·na·ble** *adj.*
il·lu·mi·nism (ĭ-lōō'mə-nĭz'əm) *n.* **1.** Belief in or proclamation of a special personal enlightenment. **2. Illuminism.** The ideas and principles of various groups of Illuminati. [ILLUMIN(ATI) + -ISM.] **—il·lu'mi·nist** *n.*

illuminate
The Empire State Building in New York City illuminated at night

illumination
15th-century French book of hours

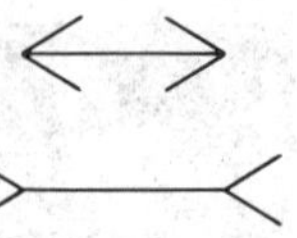

illusion
Müller-Lyer illusion: an optical illusion in which two lines of the same length appear unequal

ill-use (ĭl'yo͞oz') *tr.v.* **-used, -us·ing, -us·es.** To maltreat. —*n.* (ĭl'yo͞os'). Also **ill-us·age** (-yo͞o'sĭj, -zĭj). Bad or unjust treatment.

il·lu·sion (ĭ-lo͞o'zhən) *n.* **1. a.** An erroneous perception of reality. **b.** An erroneous concept or belief. **2.** The condition of being deceived by a false perception or belief. **3.** Something, as a fantastic plan or desire, that causes an erroneous belief or perception. **4.** Illusionism (sense 2). **5.** A fine transparent cloth, used for dresses or trimmings. [ME < OFr. < LLat. *illusio* < Lat., a mocking, irony < *illusus,* p.part. of *illudere,* to mock : *in-*, against + *ludere,* to play.] —**il·lu'sion·al, il·lu'sion·ar'y** *adj.*

il·lu·sion·ism (ĭ-lo͞o'zhə-nĭz'əm) *n.* **1.** The doctrine that the material world is an immaterial product of the senses. **2.** The use of illusionary techniques and devices in art or decoration. —**il·lu'sion·is'tic** *adj.*

il·lu·sion·ist (ĭ-lo͞o'zhə-nĭst) *n.* **1.** An adherent of the doctrine of illusionism. **2.** A magician or ventriloquist. **3.** An artist whose work is marked by illusionism.

il·lu·sive (ĭ-lo͞o'sĭv) *adj.* Of, pertaining to, or of the nature of an illusion; illusory. —**il·lu'sive·ly** *adv.* —**il·lu'sive·ness** *n.*

il·lu·so·ry (ĭ-lo͞o'sə-rē, -zə-rē) *adj.* Produced by, based on, or having the nature of an illusion; deceptive.

il·lus·trate (ĭl'ə-strāt', ĭ-lŭs'trāt') *v.* **-trat·ed, -trat·ing, -trates.** —*tr.* **1. a.** To clarify, as by use of examples or comparisons. **b.** To clarify by serving as an example or comparison. **2.** To provide (a publication) with explanatory or decorative features. **3.** *Obs.* To illuminate. —*intr.* To present a clarification, example, or explanation. [Lat. *illustrare, illustrat-* : *in-*, in + *lustrare,* to make bright < *lustrum,* purification.] —**il'lus·tra'tor** *n.*

il·lus·tra·tion (ĭl'ə-strā'shən) *n.* **1. a.** The action of clarifying or explaining. **b.** The state of being clarified or explained. **2.** Something used to clarify or explain. **3.** Visual matter used to clarify or to decorate a text. **4.** *Obs.* Illumination. —**il'lus·tra'tion·al** *adj.*

il·lus·tra·tive (ĭ-lŭs'trə-tĭv, ĭl'ə-strā'tĭv) *adj.* Acting as an illustration. —**il·lus'tra·tive·ly** *adv.*

il·lus·tri·ous (ĭ-lŭs'trē-əs) *adj.* **1.** Famous or celebrated. **2.** *Obs.* Shining brightly. [< Lat. *illustris,* distinguished, bright < *illustrare,* to illustrate.] —**il·lus'tri·ous·ly** *adv.* —**il·lus'tri·ous·ness** *n.*

il·lu·vi·ate (ĭ-lo͞o'vē-āt') *intr.v.* **-at·ed, -at·ing, -ates.** To undergo illuviation. [Back-formation < ILLUVIATION.]

il·lu·vi·a·tion (ĭ-lo͞o'vē-ā'shən) *n.* The deposition in an underlying soil layer of colloids, soluble salts, and mineral particles leached out of an overlying soil layer. [IL-[2] + (AL)LUVI(UM) + -ATION.] —**il·lu'vi·al** *adj.*

ill will *n.* Unfriendly feeling; enmity.

il·ly (ĭl'lē) *adv.* Badly; ill: *"Beauty is jealous, and illy bears the presence of a rival."* (Jefferson).

Il·lyr·i·an (ĭ-lĭr'ē-ən) *n.* **1.** One of a people inhabiting ancient Illyria. **2.** The Indo-European language of the Illyrians. —*adj.* Of, pertaining to, or characteristic of the Illyrians or their language.

il·men·ite (ĭl'mə-nīt') *n.* A lustrous black-to-brownish titanium ore, essentially $FeTiO_3$. [G. *Ilmenit,* after Ilmen, a range in the Ural Mountains, where it was first found.]

I·lo·ca·no also **I·lo·ka·no** (ē'lō-kä'nō) *n., pl.* **Ilocano** also **Ilokano** or **-nos. 1.** One of a people inhabiting northwestern Luzon, Philippines. **2.** The Austronesian language of the Ilocano. —*adj.* Of, pertaining to, or characteristic of the Ilocano or their language. [Sp. *Ilócano* < *Iloko,* a Malayan people in the Philippines.]

I'm (īm). I am.

im-[1] *pref.* Variant of **in-[1]**. Used before *b, m,* and *p.*

im-[2] *pref.* Variant of **in-[2]**. Used before *b, m,* and *p.*

im·age (ĭm'ĭj) *n.* **1.** A reproduction of the form of someone or something, esp. a sculptured likeness. **2.** An optically formed duplicate, counterpart, or other representative reproduction of an object, esp. an optical reproduction of an object formed by a lens or mirror. **3.** A close or exact resemblance to another; double: *He is the image of his uncle.* **4. a.** The concept of someone or something that is held by the public. **b.** The character projected by someone or something to the public, esp by the mass media. **5.** A personification of something specified: *He is the image of health.* **6.** A mental picture of something not real or present. **7. a.** A vivid description or representation of something. **b.** A figure of speech. **8.** *Obs.* An apparition. **9.** *Math.* A set of values of a function corresponding to a particular subset of a domain. **10.** *Computer Sci.* An exact duplication of data in a file onto another medium. —*tr.v.* **-aged, -ag·ing, -ag·es. 1.** To make or produce a likeness of. **2.** To mirror or reflect. **3.** To symbolize or typify. **4.** To picture mentally; imagine. **5.** To describe, esp. to describe so vividly as to call up a mental picture of. [ME < OFr. < Lat. *imago.*]

image orthicon *n.* An orthicon.

im·age·ry (ĭm'ĭj-rē) *n., pl.* **-ries. 1.** Mental pictures or images. **2. a.** The use of figures of speech or vivid descriptions in writing or speaking to produce mental images. **b.** A metaphoric representation, as in music, art, or motion pictures. **3. a.** Representative images, particularly statues or icons. **b.** The art of making such images. [ME *imagerie* < OFr. < *image,* image.]

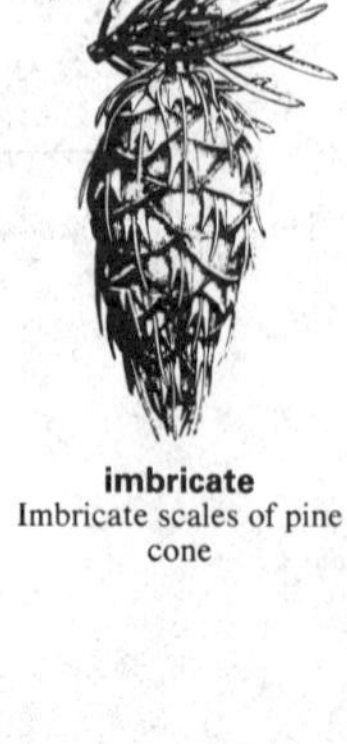

imbricate
Imbricate scales of pine cone

i·mag·i·na·ble (ĭ-măj'ə-nə-bəl) *adj.* Capable of being conceived of by the imagination. —**i·mag'i·na·bly** *adv.*

i·ma·gi·nal (ĭ-mā'gə-nəl, ĭ-mä'-) *adj.* Of or relating to an insect imago. [< NLat. *imago, imagin-*, imago.]

i·mag·i·nar·y (ĭ-măj'ə-nĕr'ē) *adj.* **1.** Having existence only in the imagination; unreal. **2.** *Math.* **a.** Of, pertaining to, or being the coefficient of the imaginary unit in a complex number. **b.** Of, pertaining to, involving, or being an imaginary number. **c.** Involving only a complex number of which the real part is zero. —*n., pl.* **-ies.** *Math.* An imaginary number. —**i·mag'i·nar'i·ly** *adv.* —**i·mag'i·nar'i·ness** *n.*

imaginary number *n.* A complex number in which the real part is zero and the coefficient of the imaginary unit is not zero.

imaginary unit *n.* The positive square root of −1.

i·mag·i·na·tion (ĭ-măj'ə-nā'shən) *n.* **1. a.** The power of the mind to form a mental image or concept of something that is not real or present. **b.** Such power of the mind used creatively. **2.** The ability to confront and deal with reality by using the creative power of the mind; resourcefulness. **3.** *Archaic.* **a.** An unrealistic idea or notion; fancy. **b.** A plan or scheme. **4.** A traditional or widely held belief or opinion. —**i·mag'i·na'tion·al** *adj.*

Synonyms: *imagination, fancy, fantasy.* These nouns refer to the power of the mind to form images of things not present to the senses or within the actual experience of the person involved. *Imagination* is broadly applicable to all such functions. *Fancy* suggests mental invention that is capricious, whimsical, or playful, and characteristically well removed from reality. *Fantasy* is applied principally to the product of imagination given free rein, especially to elaborate mental representation having little similarity to the real world.

i·mag·i·na·tive (ĭ-măj'ə-nə-tĭv, -nā'tĭv) *adj.* **1.** Having a lively imagination, esp. a creative imagination. **2.** Tending to indulge in the fanciful or in make-believe. **3. a.** Created by, indicative of, or characterized by imagination or creativity. **b.** Having no truth; false. —**i·mag'i·na·tive·ly** *adv.* —**i·mag'i·na·tive·ness** *n.*

i·mag·ine (ĭ-măj'ĭn) *v.* **-ined, -in·ing, -ines.** —*tr.* **1.** To form a mental picture or image of. **2.** To think; conjecture: *I imagine you're right.* **3.** To have a notion without adequate foundation; fancy: *imagines himself to be an artist.* —*intr.* **1.** To employ the imagination. **2.** To make a guess; conjecture. [ME *imaginen* < OFr. *imaginer* < Lat. *imaginari* < *imago,* image.] —**i·mag'in·er** *n.*

im·a·gism (ĭm'ə-jĭz'əm) *n.* A literary movement, launched early in the 20th century in revolt against romanticism, to promote free verse and precise imagery. —**im'a·gist** *n.* —**im'a·gis'tic** *adj.*

i·ma·go (ĭ-mā'gō, ĭ-mä'-) *n., pl.* **-goes** or **-gi·nes** (-gə-nēz'). **1.** An insect in its sexually mature adult stage after metamorphosis. **2.** *Psychoanal.* An often idealized image of a person, usually a parent, formed in childhood and persisting into adulthood. [NLat. *imago, imagin-* < Lat. *imago,* image.]

i·mam (ĭ-mäm') *n.* **1.** A prayer leader of Islam. **2.** A Moslem scholar, esp. an authority on Islamic law. **3. Imam. a.** A title accorded to Mohammed and his four immediate successors. **b.** One of the leaders regarded by the Shiites as successors of Mohammed. **c.** Any of various religious and temporal leaders claiming descent from Mohammed. [Ar. *imām,* leader < *amma,* he led.]

i·mam·ate (ĭ-mä'māt') *n.* **1.** The office of an Imam. **2.** A country or region governed by an Imam.

i·ma·ret (ĭ-mä'rĕt) *n.* An inn or hostel for pilgrims in Turkey. [Turk. < Ar. *imārah,* hospice < *amara,* he built.]

im·bal·ance (ĭm-băl'əns) *n.* A lack of balance, as in distribution or functioning.

im·be·cile (ĭm'bə-sĭl, -səl) *n.* **1.** A feeble-minded person. **2.** A dolt. —*adj.* Also **im·be·cil·ic** (ĭm'bə-sĭl'ĭk). **1.** Deficient in mental ability. **2.** Stupid. [OFr. *imbecille,* feeble < Lat. *imbecillus* : *in-*, not + *bacillum,* staff, dim. of *baculum,* rod.] —**im'be·cile·ly** *adv.*

im·be·cil·i·ty (ĭm'bə-sĭl'ĭ-tē) *n., pl.* **-ties. 1.** The quality or condition of being an imbecile. **2. a.** Great foolishness or stupidity. **b.** Something, as action or conduct, that is imbecilic.

im·bed (ĭm-bĕd') *v.* Variant of **embed.**

im·bibe (ĭm-bīb') *v.* **-bibed, -bib·ing, -bibes.** —*tr.* **1.** To drink. **2.** To absorb or take in as if by drinking: *"the whole body . . . imbibes delight through every pore"* (Thoreau). **3.** To receive and absorb into the mind: *"Gladstone had . . . imbibed a strong prejudice against Americans"* (Philip Magnus). **4.** *Obs.* To permeate; saturate. —*intr.* To drink. [ME *embiben,* to soak, saturate < OFr. *embiber* < Lat. *imbibere,* to drink in : *in-*, in + *bibere,* to drink.] —**im·bib'er** *n.*

im·bi·bi·tion (ĭm'bə-bĭsh'ən) *n.* **1.** The act of imbibing. **2.** The absorption of fluid by a solid or colloid that results in swelling.

im·bri·cate (ĭm'brĭ-kāt') *adj.* Having the edges overlapping in a regular arrangement, as roof tiles or the scales of a fish. —*v.* **-cat·ed, -cat·ing, -cates.** —*tr.* To overlap in a regular pattern. —*intr.* To be arranged with regular overlapping edges. [Lat. *imbricatus,* p.part. of *imbricare,* to cover with roof tiles < *imbrex,* roof tile < *imber,* rain.]

im·bri·ca·tion (ĭm'brĭ-kā'shən) *n.* **1.** A regular overlapping of edges. **2.** A pattern or design having overlapping edges.

im·bro·glio (ĭm-brōl′yō) *n., pl.* **-glios. 1. a.** A difficult or intricate situation; entanglement. **b.** A confused or complicated disagreement or quarrel. **2.** A confused heap; tangle. [Ital., prob. < Fr. *embrouiller,* to confuse. —see EMBROIL.]

im·brue (ĭm-bro͞o′) *tr.v.* **-brued, -bru·ing, -brues.** To stain or saturate. [ME *enbrewen* < OFr. *embreuver,* to moisten : *en-,* in + *breu,* broth, of Germanic orig.]

im·brute (ĭm-bro͞ot′) *tr. & intr.v.* **-brut·ed, -brut·ing, -brutes.** To make or become brutal.

im·bue (ĭm-byo͞o′) *tr.v.* **-bued, -bu·ing, -bues. 1.** To saturate, as with stain or dye. **2.** To inspire, permeate, or pervade: *work imbued with the revolutionary spirit.* [Lat. *imbuere,* to moisten, stain.]

im·id·az·ole (ĭm′ĭd-ăz′ōl′) *n.* Any of a group of heterocyclic compounds, esp. the white crystalline base $C_3H_4N_2$. [IMID(E) + AZOLE.]

im·ide (ĭm′īd′) *n.* A compound derived from ammonia containing the divalent NH group combined with two acid radicals. [Alteration of AMIDE.]

im·ine (ĭm′ēn′, ĭ-mēn′) *n.* A compound derived from ammonia containing the divalent NH group combined with alkyl or other nonacid radicals. [Alteration of AMINE.]

i·mip·ra·mine (ĭ-mĭp′rə-mēn′, ĭm′ə-prăm′ēn) *n.* A water-soluble compound, $C_{19}H_{24}N_2$, used medically as an antidepressant. [IM(IDE) + PR(OPYL) + AMINE.]

im·i·ta·ble (ĭm′ĭ-tə-bəl) *adj.* Capable or worthy of being imitated.

im·i·tate (ĭm′ĭ-tāt′) *tr.v.* **-tat·ed, -tat·ing, -tates. 1.** To model oneself after the behavior or actions of. **2. a.** To copy or mimic the actions, appearance, mannerisms, or speech of. **b.** To copy or use the literary, artistic, or musical style of. **3.** To copy exactly; reproduce. **4.** To appear like; resemble. [Lat. *imitari, imitat-.*] **—im′i·ta′tor** *n.*

Synonyms: *imitate, copy, mimic, ape, parody, simulate.* These verbs mean to follow something or someone taken as a model. To *imitate* is to act like another person or to follow a pattern or style set by another. To *copy* is to duplicate an original as precisely as possible. To *mimic* is to copy another's actions, speech, or mannerisms closely, either seriously or with intent to ridicule. To *ape* is to ridicule by mimicry or to follow another's lead slavishly. To *parody* is either to make fun of another's style by imitating it with comic effect or to attempt a serious imitation and fail. To *simulate* is to feign or assume the appearance of something falsely by imitating its identifying signs or characteristics.

im·i·ta·tion (ĭm′ĭ-tā′shən) *n.* **1.** An act of imitating. **2.** Something derived or copied from an original. **3.** *Mus.* The repetition of a phrase or sequence often with variations in key, rhythm, and voice. **—*modifier:*** *imitation fur.* **—im′i·ta′tion·al** *adj.*

im·i·ta·tive (ĭm′ĭ-tā′tĭv) *adj.* **1.** Of or involving imitation. **2.** Not original; derivative. **3.** Tending to imitate. **4.** Onomatopoeic. **—im′i·ta′tive·ly** *adv.* **—im′i·ta′tive·ness** *n.*

im·mac·u·la·cy (ĭ-măk′yə-lə-sē) *n.* The quality or condition of being immaculate.

im·mac·u·late (ĭ-măk′yə-lĭt) *adj.* **1.** Free from stain or blemish; pure. **2.** Free from fault or error: *an immaculate record.* **3.** Impeccably clean; spotless. **4.** Having no markings. [ME *immaculat* < Lat. *immaculatus* : *in-,* not + *maculatus,* p.part. of *maculare,* to blemish < *macula,* spot.] **—im·mac′u·late·ly** *adv.* **—im·mac′u·late·ness** *n.*

Immaculate Conception *n. Rom. Cath. Ch.* The doctrine that the Virgin Mary was conceived in her mother's womb free from all stain of original sin.

im·ma·nent (ĭm′ə-nənt) *adj.* **1.** Existing or remaining within; inherent: *believed in a God immanent in human beings.* **2.** Restricted entirely to the mind; subjective. [LLat. *immanens, immanent-,* pr.part. of *immanēre,* to remain in : Lat. *in-,* in + Lat. *manēre,* to remain.] **—im′ma·nence, im′ma·nen·cy** *n.* **—im′ma·nent·ly** *adv.*

im·ma·nent·ism (ĭm′ə-nən-tĭz′əm) *n.* Any of various religious theories postulating that a deity or abstract spirit is immanent in the world.

im·ma·te·ri·al (ĭm′ə-tîr′ē-əl) *adj.* **1.** Having no material body or form. **2.** Of no importance or relevance; inconsequential. **—im′ma·te′ri·al·ly** *adv.* **—im′ma·te′ri·al·ness** *n.*

im·ma·te·ri·al·ism (ĭm′ə-tîr′ē-ə-lĭz′əm) *n. Philos.* A metaphysical doctrine asserting the nonexistence of corporeal reality. **—im′ma·te′ri·al·ist** *n.*

im·ma·te·ri·al·i·ty (ĭm′ə-tîr′ē-ăl′ĭ-tē) *n., pl.* **-ties. 1.** The state or quality of being immaterial. **2.** Something immaterial.

im·ma·te·ri·al·ize (ĭm′ə-tîr′ē-ə-līz′) *tr.v.* **-ized, -iz·ing, -iz·es.** To render immaterial.

im·ma·ture (ĭm′ə-tyo͝or′, -to͝or′, -cho͝or′) *adj.* **1.** Not fully grown or developed; unripe. **2.** Marked by or suggesting a lack of normal maturity. [Lat. *immaturus* : *in-,* not + *maturus,* mature.] **—im′ma·ture′ly** *adv.* **—im′ma·tur′i·ty, im′ma·ture′ness** *n.*

im·meas·ur·a·ble (ĭ-mĕzh′ər-ə-bəl) *adj.* **1.** Incapable of being measured. **2.** Vast; limitless. **—im·meas′ur·a·bil′i·ty, im·meas′ur·a·ble·ness** *n.* **—im·meas′ur·a·bly** *adv.*

im·me·di·a·cy (ĭ-mē′dē-ə-sē) *n., pl.* **-cies. 1.** The condition or quality of being immediate. **2.** Something immediate, as in importance.

im·me·di·ate (ĭ-mē′dē-ĭt) *adj.* **1.** Acting or occurring without the interposition of another agency or object; direct: *an immediate result.* **2.** Directly apprehended or perceived: *immediate awareness.* **3.** Next in line or relation: *the immediate successor.* **4.** Occurring at once: *an immediate response.* **5. a.** Of or near the present time: *the immediate future.* **b.** Of or pertaining to the present: *dealing first with the immediate problem.* **6.** Close at hand; near: *the immediate vicinity.* **7.** Directly affecting someone or something: *her immediate sphere of influence.* [LLat. *immediatus* : Lat. *in-,* not + *mediatus,* p.part. of *mediare,* to be in the middle < Lat. *medius,* middle.] **—im·me′di·ate·ness** *n.*

immediate constituent *n.* A meaningful constituent, such as a word, that enters directly into the formation of a linguistic construction, such as a phrase.

im·me·di·ate·ly (ĭ-mē′dē-ĭt-lē) *adv.* **1.** Without intermediary; directly: *met with the parties immediately involved in the suit.* **2.** Without delay. *—conj.* As soon as: *He phoned immediately he reached home.*

Synonyms: *immediately, instantly, forthwith, directly, promptly, presently.* These adverbs mean with little or no delay. They are arranged in approximate order of intensity. *Immediately* and *instantly* imply no delay whatever, as between request and response. *Forthwith, directly,* and *promptly* all stress readiness of response but with a brief interval prior to fulfillment of the action involved. *Presently* has the mere force of soon.

im·med·i·ca·ble (ĭ-mĕd′ĭ-kə-bəl) *adj.* Incurable.

Im·mel·mann turn (ĭm′əl-mən) *n.* A maneuver in which an airplane first completes half a loop and then half a roll in order to simultaneously gain altitude and change direction in flight. [After Max *Immelmann* (1890–1916).]

im·me·mo·ri·al (ĭm′ə-môr′ē-əl, -mōr′-) *adj.* Reaching beyond the limits of memory, tradition, or recorded history. [Med. Lat. *immemorialis* : Lat. *in-,* not + Lat. *memorialis,* memorial < *memoria,* memory < *memor,* mindful.] **—im′me·mo′ri·al·ly** *adv.*

im·mense (ĭ-mĕns′) *adj.* **1.** Extremely large; huge: *immense icebergs; an immense span of time.* **2.** Immeasurably vast; boundless. **3.** *Slang.* Surpassingly good; excellent. [OFr. < Lat. *immensus* : *in-,* not + *mensus,* p.part. of *metiri,* to measure.] **—im·mense′ly** *adv.* **—im·mense′ness** *n.*

im·men·si·ty (ĭ-mĕn′sĭ-tē) *n., pl.* **-ties. 1.** The quality or state of being immense. **2.** Something immense.

im·men·sur·a·ble (ĭ-mĕn′shər-ə-bəl) *adj.* Immeasurable. [LLat. *immensurabilis* : Lat. *in,* not + *mensurabilis,* measurable < *mensura,* measure.]

im·merge (ĭ-mûrj′) *intr.v.* **-merged, -merg·ing, -merg·es.** To submerge or disappear in or as if in a liquid. [Lat. *immergere.* —see IMMERSE.] **—im·mer′gence** *n.*

im·merse (ĭ-mûrs′) *tr.v.* **-mersed, -mers·ing, -mers·es. 1.** To cover completely in a liquid; submerge. **2.** To baptize by submerging in water. **3.** To involve profoundly; absorb. [< Lat. *immersus,* p.part. of *immergere,* to immerse : *in-,* in + *mergere,* to dip.]

im·mers·i·ble (ĭ-mûr′sə-bəl) *adj.* Capable of being completely immersed in water without suffering damage: *an immersible coffee pot.*

im·mer·sion (ĭ-mûr′zhən, -shən) *n.* **1.** An act of immersing. **2.** The condition of being immersed. **3.** Baptism performed by totally submerging a person in water. **4.** *Astron.* The obscuring of a celestial body by another or by the shadow of another.

im·mesh (ĭ-mĕsh′) *v.* Variant of **enmesh**.

im·me·thod·i·cal (ĭm′ə-thŏd′ĭ-kəl) *adj.* Not methodical. **—im′me·thod′i·cal·ly** *adv.*

im·mi·grant (ĭm′ĭ-grənt) *n.* **1.** One who leaves a country to settle permanently in another. **2.** An organism that appears where it was formerly unknown.

im·mi·grate (ĭm′ĭ-grāt′) *v.* **-grat·ed, -grat·ing, -grates.** *—intr.* To enter and settle in a country or region to which one is not native. *—tr.* To send or introduce as immigrants —See Usage note at **migrate**. [Lat. *immigrare, immigrat-,* to go into : *in-,* in + *migrare,* to depart.] **—im′mi·gra′tion** *n.*

im·mi·nence (ĭm′ə-nəns) *n.* **1.** The quality or condition of being imminent. **2.** Something imminent.

im·mi·nen·cy (ĭm′ə-nən-sē) *n, pl.* **-cies.** Imminence.

im·mi·nent (ĭm′ə-nənt) *adj.* About to occur; impending. [Lat. *imminens,* pr.part. of *imminēre,* to overhang.] **—im′mi·nent·ly** *adv.* **—im′mi·nent·ness** *n.*

im·min·gle (ĭ-mĭng′gəl) *intr. & tr.v.* **-gled, -gling, -gles.** To intermingle; blend.

im·mis·ci·ble (ĭ-mĭs′ə-bəl) *adj.* Incapable of mixing or blending. **—im·mis′ci·bil′i·ty** *n.* **—im·mis′ci·bly** *adv.*

im·mit·i·ga·ble (ĭ-mĭt′ĭ-gə-bəl) *adj.* Not capable of being mitigated. **—im·mit′i·ga·bly** *adv.*

im·mit·tance (ĭ-mĭt′ns) *n.* Electrical impedance or admittance. [IM(PEDANCE) + (AD)MITTANCE.]

im·mix (ĭ-mĭks′) *tr.v.* **-mixed, -mix·ing, -mix·es.** To commingle; blend. [Back-formation < ME *immixte,* mixed in < Lat. *immixtus,* p.part. of *immiscere,* to blend : *in-,* in + *miscere,* to mix.] **—im·mix′ture** *n.*

im·mo·bile (ĭ-mō′bəl, -bēl′, -bīl′) *adj.* **1.** Incapable of being moved; fixed. **2.** Not moving; motionless. [ME *immobil* < OFr. *immobile* < Lat. *immobilis* : *in-,* not + *mobilis,* mobile.] **—im′mo·bil′i·ty** *n.*

im·mo·bi·lize (ĭ-mō′bə-līz′) *tr.v.* **-lized, -liz·ing, -liz·es. 1.** To

immigrant
Immigrant family arrives in New York in the 1920's

render immobile. **2.** To impede movement or use of: *immobilize troops.* **3. a.** To withdraw (specie) from circulation and reserve as security for other money. **b.** To convert (floating capital) into fixed capital. —**im·mo'bi·li·za'tion** *n.* —**im·mo'bi·liz'er** *n.*

im·mod·er·a·cy (ĭ-mŏd'ər-ə-sē) *n.* **1.** The quality or condition of being immoderate. **2.** Something immoderate.

im·mod·er·ate (ĭ-mŏd'ər-ĭt) *adj.* Exceeding normal or appropriate bounds; extreme: *immoderate spending; immoderate resentment.* [ME < Lat. *immoderatus* : *in-,* not + *moderatus,* moderate.] —**im·mod'er·ate·ly** *adv.* —**im·mod'er·ate·ness, im·mod'er·a'tion** *n.*

im·mod·est (ĭ-mŏd'ĭst) *adj.* **1.** Lacking modesty. **2.** Morally offensive. **3.** Arrogant. [Lat. *immodestus* : *in-,* not + *modestus,* modest.] —**im·mod'est·ly** *adv.* —**im·mod'es·ty** *n.*

im·mo·late (ĭm'ə-lāt') *tr.v.* **-lat·ed, -lat·ing, -lates. 1.** To kill as a sacrifice. **2.** To destroy. [Lat. *immolare, immolat-,* to sacrifice, sprinkle with sacrificial meal : *in-,* on + *mola,* meal.] —**im'mo·la'tion** *n.* —**im'mo·la'tor** *n.*

im·mor·al (ĭ-môr'əl, ĭ-mŏr'-) *adj.* Contrary to established moral principles. —**im·mor'al·ly** *adv.*

im·mor·al·ist (ĭ-môr'ə-lĭst, -mŏr'-) *n.* One who advocates immorality.

im·mor·al·i·ty (ĭm'ô-răl'ĭ-tē, ĭm'ə-) *n., pl.* **-ties. 1.** The quality or condition of being immoral. **2.** An immoral act or practice.

im·mor·tal (ĭ-môr'tl) *adj.* **1.** Not subject to death. **2.** Having eternal fame; imperishable. **3.** Of or pertaining to immortality. —*n.* **1.** One not subject to death. **2.** One whose fame is enduring. **3. Immortals.** The gods of ancient Greece and Rome. [ME < OFr. *immortel* < Lat. *immortalis* : *in-,* not + *mortalis,* mortal.] —**im·mor'tal·ly** *adv.*

im·mor·tal·i·ty (ĭm'ôr-tăl'ĭ-tē) *n.* **1.** The quality or condition of being immortal. **2.** Endless life. **3.** Enduring fame.

im·mor·tal·ize (ĭ-môr'tl-īz') *tr.v.* **-ized, -iz·ing, -iz·es.** To make immortal.

im·mor·telle (ĭm'ôr-tĕl') *n.* A plant with flowers that retain their color when dried. [Fr. < fem. of *immortel,* immortal < OFr.]

im·mo·tile (ĭ-mōt'l, ĭ-mō'tīl') *adj.* Not moving or not having the power to move. —**im'mo·til'i·ty** *n.*

im·mov·a·ble (ĭ-mo͞o'və-bəl) *adj.* **1. a.** Incapable of being moved. **b.** Incapable of movement. **2.** Not capable of alteration. **3.** Unyielding in principle, purpose, or adherence; steadfast. **4.** Incapable of being moved emotionally. **5.** *Law.* Not liable to be removed: *immovable property.* —*n.* **1.** One that is incapable of movement. **2.** Often **immovables.** Property, as real estate, that cannot be moved. —**im·mov'a·ble·ness, im·mov'a·bil'i·ty** *n.* —**im·mov'a·bly** *adv.*

im·mune (ĭ-myo͞on') *adj.* **1. a.** Exempt: *immune from taxation.* **b.** Not affected or responsive: *immune to persuasion.* **2.** *Med.* Having immunity. [Lat. *immunis,* exempt from service : *in-,* not + *munia,* duties.] —**im·mune'** *n.*

im·mu·ni·ty (ĭ-myo͞o'nĭ-tē) *n., pl.* **-ties. 1.** The quality or condition of being immune. **2.** An inherited, acquired, or induced resistance to a specific pathogen.

im·mu·nize (ĭm'yə-nīz') *tr.v.* **-nized, -niz·ing, -niz·es.** To render immune. —**im'mu·ni·za'tion** *n.*

immuno– *pref.* Immunity: *immunoelectrophoresis.* [< IMMUNE.]

im·mu·no·as·say (ĭm'yə-nō-ăs'ā, ĭm-yo͞o'-) *n.* The analysis and identification of a substance on the basis of its antigenic actions.

im·mu·no·chem·is·try (ĭm'yə-nō-kĕm'ĭ-strē) *n.* The chemistry of immunologic phenomena, as of antigen stimulation of tissue or of antigen-antibody reactions.

im·mu·no·e·lec·tro·pho·re·sis (ĭm'yə-nō-ĭ-lĕk'trə-fə-rē'sĭs, ĭm-yo͞o'-) *n.* The separation of antigens by electrophoresis with identification through specific immunological reactions.

im·mu·no·ge·net·ics (ĭm'yə-nō-jə-nĕt'ĭks) *n.* *(used with a sing. verb).* The study of the interrelation between immunity to disease and genetic make-up.

im·mu·no·gen·ic (ĭm'yə-nō-jĕn'ĭk) *adj.* Producing immunity.

im·mu·no·glob·u·lin (ĭm'yə-nō-glŏb'yə-lĭn, ĭm-yo͞o'-) *n.* One of a group of blood serum proteins capable of acting as an antibody.

im·mu·nol·o·gy (ĭm'yə-nŏl'ə-jē) *n.* The medical study of immunity. —**im'mu·no·log'ic** (-nə-lŏj'ĭk), **im'mu·no·log'i·cal** *adj.* —**im'mu·no·log'i·cal·ly** *adv.*

im·mu·no·sup·pres·sive (ĭm'yə-nō-sə-prĕs'ĭv) *adj.* Tending to suppress a natural immune response of an organism to an antigen: *an immunosuppressive drug.*

im·mu·no·ther·a·py (ĭm'yə-nō-thĕr'ə-pē, ĭm-yo͞o'-) *n.* **1.** The treatment of disease by use of antigenic preparations. **2.** The treatment of disease or infection by immunosuppressive techniques. —**im'mu·no·ther'a·pist** *n.*

im·mure (ĭ-myo͝or') *tr.v.* **-mured, -mur·ing, -mures. 1.** To confine within or as if within walls; imprison. **2.** To build into a wall; entomb in a wall. [Med. Lat. *immurare* : Lat. *in-,* in + Lat. *murus,* wall.] —**im·mure'ment** *n.*

im·mu·ta·ble (ĭ-myo͞o'tə-bəl) *adj.* Not subject or susceptible to change. [ME < Lat. *immutabilis* : *in-,* not + *mutabilis,* mutable.] —**im·mu'ta·bil'i·ty, im·mu'ta·ble·ness** *n.* —**im·mu'ta·bly** *adv.*

impatiens

imp (ĭmp) *n.* **1.** A mischievous child. **2.** A small demon. **3.** *Archaic.* A graft. —*tr.v.* **imped, imp·ing, imps. 1.** In falconry, to graft (new feathers) onto the wing of a bird to repair damage or to increase flying capacity. **2.** *Archaic.* To furnish with wings. [ME *impe,* scion, sprig, offspring < OE *impa,* young shoot < *impian,* to graft, ult. < Gk. *emphuein,* to implant : *en-,* in + *phuein,* to grow.]

im·pact (ĭm'păkt') *n.* **1.** The striking of one body against another; collision. **2.** The force or impetus transmitted by a collision. **3.** The effect or impression of one thing upon another: *still gauging the impact of automation on labor.* —*v.* (ĭm-păkt') **-pact·ed, -pact·ing, -pacts.** —*tr.* **1.** To pack firmly together. **2.** To strike forcefully. **3.** *Informal.* To have an effect or impact on. —*intr.* To have an effect or impact. [Lat. *impactus,* p.part. of *impingere,* to push against. —see IMPINGE.] —**im·pac'tion** *n.*

Usage: *Impact* (verb) had been used principally in the sense of "to pack together": *Traffic impacts the area during rush hour.* Recently it has come into more general use in the sense of "to have an impact on." Sometimes it is used transitively: *These taxes impact small business.* Sometimes it is used intransitively (with *on*): *social pathologies, common to the inner city, that impact most heavily on such a community.* The preceding example is unacceptable to a large majority of the Usage Panel.

im·pact·ed (ĭm-păk'tĭd) *adj.* **1.** Wedged together at the broken ends. Used of a fractured bone. **2. a.** Placed in the alveolus in a manner prohibiting eruption into a normal position. Used of a tooth. **b.** Driven upward into the alveolar process or surrounding tissue. Used of a tooth.

im·pair (ĭm-pâr') *tr.v.* **-paired, -pair·ing, -pairs.** To diminish in strength, value, quantity, or quality: *a severe storm impairing communications.* [ME *empairen* < OFr. *empeirer* < VLat. **impejorare* : Lat. *in-* (intensive) + LLat. *pejorare,* to worsen < Lat. *pejor,* worse.] —**im·pair'ment** *n.*

im·pa·la (ĭm-pä'lə) *n.* An African antelope, *Aepyceros melampus,* having a reddish coat, and ridged, curved horns in the male. [Zulu *im-pala.*]

im·pale (ĭm-pāl') *tr.v.* **-paled, -pal·ing, -pales. 1. a.** To pierce with a sharp stake or point. **b.** To torture or kill by impaling. **2.** To render helpless as if by impaling: *impaled by grief.* [Med. Lat. *impalare* : Lat. *in-,* in + Lat. *palus,* stake.] —**im·pale'ment** *n.* —**im·pal'er** *n.*

im·pal·pa·ble (ĭm-păl'pə-bəl) *adj.* **1.** Not perceptible to the touch; intangible. **2.** Not easily perceived or grasped by the mind. —**im·pal'pa·bil'i·ty** *n.* —**im·pal'pa·bly** *adv.*

im·pan·el (ĭm-păn'əl) *tr.v.* **-eled, -el·ing, -els** or **-elled, -el·ling, -els.** To enroll (a jury) upon a panel or list. —**im·pan'el·ment** *n.*

im·par·i·ty (ĭm-păr'ĭ-tē) *n., pl.* **-ties.** Inequality; disparity. [LLat. *imparitas* < Lat. *impar,* not equal : *in-,* not + *par,* equal.]

im·part (ĭm-pärt') *tr.v.* **-part·ed, -part·ing, -parts. 1.** To grant a share of; bestow: *impart advice.* **2.** To make known; disclose. [Lat. *impartire* : *in-,* in + *partire,* to share < *pars,* part.]

im·par·tial (ĭm-pär'shəl) *adj.* Not partial or biased; unprejudiced. —**im'par·ti·al'i·ty** (-shē-ăl'ə-tē), **im·par'tial·ness** *n.* —**im·par'tial·ly** *adv.*

im·part·i·ble (ĭm-pär'tə-bəl) *adj.* Not partible; indivisible. [LLat. *impartibilis* : Lat. *in-,* not + Lat. *partibilis,* partible.] —**im·part'i·bil'i·ty** *n.* —**im·part'i·bly** *adv.*

im·pass·a·ble (ĭm-păs'ə-bəl) *adj.* Impossible to traverse or surmount. —**im·pass'a·bil'i·ty, im·pass'a·ble·ness** *n.* —**im·pass'a·bly** *adv.*

im·passe (ĭm'păs') *n.* **1.** A road or passage having no exit; cul-de-sac. **2. a.** A difficult situation offering no workable escape. **b.** A deadlock, as in negotiations; stalemate. [Fr. : *in-,* not (< Lat. *in-*) + *passer,* to pass < OFr.]

im·pas·si·ble (ĭm-păs'ə-bəl) *adj.* **1.** Not subject to suffering or pain. **2.** Impassive. [ME < OFr. < LLat. *impassibilis* : *in-,* not + *passibilis,* passible.] —**im·pas'si·bil'i·ty, im·pas'si·ble·ness** *n.* —**im·pas'si·bly** *adv.*

im·pas·sion (ĭm-păsh'ən) *tr.v.* **-sioned, -sion·ing, -sions.** To arouse the passions of. [Ital. *impassionare* : *in-,* in (< Lat.) + *passione,* passion < LLat. *passio,* suffering. —see PASSION.]

im·pas·sioned (ĭm-păsh'ənd) *adj.* Filled with passion; ardent.

im·pas·sive (ĭm-păs'ĭv) *adj.* **1.** Devoid of or not subject to emotion. **2.** Revealing no emotion; expressionless. **3.** Incapable of physical sensation. **4.** Motionless; still. [IN[1] + Lat. *passivus,* capable of feeling. —see PASSIVE.] —**im·pas'sive·ly** *adv.* —**im·pas'sive·ness, im'pas·siv'i·ty** *n.*

im·paste (ĭm-pāst') *tr.v.* **-past·ed, -past·ing, -pastes. 1.** To make into a paste. **2.** To apply pigment thickly to. [Ital. *impastare* : *in-,* in (< Lat.) + *pasta,* paste < LLat.]

im·pas·to (ĭm-păs'tō, -päs'-) *n.* The application of thick layers of pigment to a canvas or other surface in painting. [Ital. < *impastare,* to impaste.]

im·pa·tience (ĭm-pā'shəns) *n.* The quality or condition of being impatient.

im·pa·tiens (ĭm-pā'shənz, -shəns) *n.* A plant of the genus *Impatiens,* which includes the jewelweed. [NLat. *Impatiens,* genus name < Lat. *impatiens,* impatient.]

im·pa·tient (ĭm-pā'shənt) *adj.* **1.** Unable to wait patiently or tolerate delay; restless. **2.** Unable to endure irritation or opposition; intolerant. **3.** Expressing or produced by impatience: *shot me an impatient stare.* **4.** Restively eager or desirous: *impatient to begin.* [ME *impacient* < OFr. *impatient* < Lat. *impatiens* : *in-*, not + *patiens,* pr.part. of *pati,* to suffer, endure.] **—im·pa'tient·ly** *adv.*

im·peach (ĭm-pēch') *tr.v.* **-peached, -peach·ing, -peach·es. 1. a.** To make an accusation against. **b.** To charge with malfeasance in office before a proper tribunal. **2.** To challenge or discredit; attack. [ME *empechen,* to impede, molest, accuse < AN *empecher* < LLat. *impedicare,* to entangle : Lat. *in-*, in + Lat. *pedica,* fetter.] **—im·peach'a·ble** *adj.* **—im·peach'er** *n.* **—im·peach'ment** *n.*

im·pearl (ĭm-pûrl') *tr.v.* **-pearled, -pearl·ing, -pearls. 1.** To form into pearls. **2.** To adorn with or as if with pearls.

im·pec·ca·ble (ĭm-pĕk'ə-bəl) *adj.* **1.** Without flaw; perfect. **2.** Not capable of sin or wrongdoing. [Lat. *impeccabilis* : *in-*, not + *peccare,* to sin.] **—im·pec'ca·bil'i·ty** *n.* **—im·pec'ca·bly** *adv.*

im·pe·cu·ni·ous (ĭm'pĭ-kyo͞o'nē-əs) *adj.* Lacking money; penniless. [IM-[1] + obs. *pecunious,* rich < ME < Lat. *pecuniosus* < *pecunia,* money, wealth.] **—im'pe·cu'ni·ous·ly** *adv.* **—im'pe·cu'ni·ous·ness, im'pe·cu'ni·os'i·ty** (-ŏs'ĭ-tē) *n.*

im·pe·dance (ĭm-pēd'ns) *n.* A measure of the total opposition to current flow in an alternating-current circuit, equal to the ratio of the rms electromotive force in the circuit to the rms current produced by it, and usually represented in complex notation as $Z = R + iX$, where R is the ohmic resistance and X is the reactance. [< IMPEDE.]

impedance matching *n.* The use of electric circuits, transmission lines, and other devices to make the impedance of a load equal to the internal impedance of the source of power, thereby making possible the most efficient transfer of power.

im·pede (ĭm-pēd') *tr.v.* **-ped·ed, -ped·ing, -pedes.** To retard or obstruct the progress of; block. [Lat. *impedire* : *in-*, in + *pes,* foot.] **—im·ped'er** *n.*

im·ped·i·ment (ĭm-pĕd'ə-mənt) *n.* **1.** A hindrance or obstruction. **2.** Something that impedes, esp.: **a.** An organic defect preventing clear articulation: *a speech impediment.* **b.** *Law.* Something that obstructs the making of a legal contract. [Lat. *impedimentum* < *impedire,* to impede.] **—im·ped'i·men'tal** (-mĕn'tl), **im·ped'i·men'ta·ry** *adj.*

im·ped·i·men·ta (ĭm-pĕd'ə-mĕn'tə) *pl.n.* Objects, as provisions or baggage, that impede or encumber. [Lat. *impedimenta,* pl. of *impedimentum,* impediment.]

im·pel (ĭm-pĕl') *tr.v.* **-pelled, -pel·ling, -pels. 1.** To urge to action through moral pressure; compel. **2.** To drive forward; propel. [Lat. *impellere* : *in-*, against + *pellere,* to drive.]

im·pel·ler (ĭm-pĕl'ər) *n.* **1.** One that impels. **2. a.** A rotor or rotor blade. **b.** A rotating device used to force a gas in a given direction under pressure.

im·pend (ĭm-pĕnd') *intr.v.* **-pend·ed, -pend·ing, -pends. 1.** To hang or hover menacingly. **2.** To be about to take place. **3.** *Archaic.* To overhang. [Lat. *impendēre* : *in-*, against + *pendēre,* to hang.]

im·pen·dent (ĭm-pĕn'dənt) *adj.* Being close at hand; impending.

im·pen·e·tra·bil·i·ty (ĭm-pĕn'ĭ-trə-bĭl'ĭ-tē) *n.* **1.** The quality or condition of being impenetrable. **2.** The inability of two bodies to occupy the same space at the same time.

im·pen·e·tra·ble (ĭm-pĕn'ĭ-trə-bəl) *adj.* **1.** Not capable of being penetrated or entered. **2.** Incapable of being understood; incomprehensible. **3.** Impervious to argument or sentiment. [ME < OFr. < Lat. *impenetrabilis* : *in-*, not + *penetrabilis,* penetrable.] **—im·pen'e·tra·ble·ness** *n.* **—im·pen'e·tra·bly** *adv.*

im·pen·i·tent (ĭm-pĕn'ĭ-tənt) *adj.* Not penitent; unrepentant. [LLat. *impaenitens* : Lat. *in-*, not + Lat. *paenitens,* penitent.] **—im·pen'i·tence** *n.* **—im·pen'i·tent** *n.* **—im·pen'i·tent·ly** *adv.*

im·per·a·tive (ĭm-pĕr'ə-tĭv) *adj.* **1.** Expressing a command or plea; peremptory. **2.** Having the power or authority to command or control. **3.** *Gram.* Of, pertaining to, or constituting the mood that expresses a command or request. **4.** Obligatory; mandatory. *—n.* **1.** *Gram.* **a.** The imperative mood. **b.** A verb form of the imperative mood. **2. a.** A command; order. **b.** An obligation. [LLat. *imperativus* < Lat. *imperare,* to command. —see EMPEROR.] **—im·per'a·tive·ly** *adv.* **—im·per'a·tive·ness** *n.*

im·pe·ra·tor (ĭm'pə-rä'tôr', -tər) *n.* **1.** A supreme commander in ancient Rome. **2.** An emperor. [Lat. —see EMPEROR.] **—im'pe·ra·to'ri·al** *adj.*

im·per·cep·ti·ble (ĭm'pər-sĕp'tə-bəl) *adj.* **1.** Not perceptible by the mind or senses. **2.** So subtle, slight, or gradual as to be barely perceptible. **—im'per·cep'ti·bil'i·ty, im'per·cep'ti·ble·ness** *n.* **—im'per·cep'ti·bly** *adv.*

im·per·cep·tive (ĭm'pər-sĕp'tĭv) *adj.* Not perceptive; lacking perception. **—im'per·cep·tiv'i·ty, im'per·cep'tive·ness** *n.*

im·per·fect (ĭm-pûr'fĭkt) *adj.* **1.** Not perfect. **2.** *Gram.* Of or being the tense of a verb that shows, usually in the past, an action or condition as incomplete, continuous, or coincident with another action. **3.** Having either stamens or a pistil only: *imperfect flowers.* **4.** Not legally enforceable. *—n.* **1.** *Gram.* The imperfect tense. **2.** *Gram.* A verb in the imperfect tense. **3.** A piece of merchandise, esp. clothing, having a minor flaw that does not impair its use, usually sold at a discount. [ME *imparfit* < OFr. *imparfait* < Lat. *imperfectus* : *in-*, not + *perfectus,* perfect.] **—im·per'fect·ly** *adv.* **—im·per'fect·ness** *n.*

imperfect fungus *n.* Any of various fungi of the order Fungi Imperfecti, which reproduce only by asexual means.

im·per·fec·tion (ĭm'pər-fĕk'shən) *n.* **1.** The quality or condition of being imperfect. **2.** A defect; flaw.

im·per·fec·tive (ĭm'pər-fĕk'tĭv) *adj.* Denoting a verb aspect or form that expresses action without regard to its beginning or completion.

im·per·fo·rate (ĭm-pûr'fər-ĭt) *adj.* **1.** Not perforated; having no opening. **2.** Not perforated into perforated rows. Used of stamps and sheets of stamps. *—n.* An imperforate stamp.

im·pe·ri·al[1] (ĭm-pîr'ē-əl) *adj.* **1.** Of or pertaining to an empire or emperor. **2.** Designating a nation or government having sovereign rights over colonies or dependencies. **3. a.** *Obs.* Having supreme authority; sovereign. **b.** Regal; majestic. **4.** Outstanding in size or quality. **5.** Of or relating to the British Imperial System of weights and measures. *—n.* **1. Imperial.** A supporter or a soldier of the Holy Roman Empire. **2.** An emperor or empress. **3.** The top of a carriage. **4.** Something outstanding in size or quality. **5.** A variable size of paper, usually 23 by 33 inches. [ME < OFr. < LLat. *imperialis* < Lat. *imperium,* command. —see EMPIRE.] **—im·pe'ri·al·ly** *adv.*

im·pe·ri·al[2] (ĭm-pîr'ē-əl) *n.* A pointed beard grown from the lower lip and chin. [Fr. *impériale,* imperial, after Emperor Napoleon III of France.]

imperial[2]

im·pe·ri·al·ism (ĭm-pîr'ē-ə-lĭz'əm) *n.* **1.** The policy of extending a nation's authority by territorial acquisition or by the establishment of economic and political hegemony over other nations. **2.** The system, policies, or practices of an imperial government. **—im·pe'ri·al·ist** *n.* **—im·pe'ri·al·is'tic** *adj.* **—im·pe'ri·al·is'ti·cal·ly** *adv.*

imperial moth *n.* A large New World moth, *Eacles imperialis,* having yellow wings with purplish or brownish markings.

im·per·il (ĭm-pĕr'əl) *tr.v.* **-iled, -il·ing, -ils** or **-illed, -il·ling, -ils.** To put in peril; endanger. **—im·per'il·ment** *n.*

im·pe·ri·ous (ĭm-pîr'ē-əs) *adj.* **1.** Arrogantly domineering or overbearing. **2.** *Obs.* Regal; imperial. **3.** Urgent; pressing. [Lat. *imperiosus* < *imperium,* imperium.] **—im·pe'ri·ous·ly** *adv.* **—im·pe'ri·ous·ness** *n.*

im·per·ish·a·ble (ĭm-pĕr'ĭ-shə-bəl) *adj.* Not perishable. **—im·per'ish·a·bil'i·ty, im·per'ish·a·ble·ness** *n.* **—im·per'ish·a·bly** *adv.*

im·pe·ri·um (ĭm-pîr'ē-əm) *n., pl.* **-ri·a** (-ē-ə). **1.** Absolute rule; supreme power. **2.** A sphere of power or dominion; empire. **3.** *Law.* The right or power of a state to enforce the law. [Lat. —see EMPIRE.]

im·per·ma·nent (ĭm-pûr'mə-nənt) *adj.* Not permanent; not lasting or durable. **—im·per'ma·nence, im·per'ma·nen·cy** *n.*

im·per·me·a·ble (ĭm-pûr'mē-ə-bəl) *adj.* Not permeable. [LLat. *impermeabilis* : Lat. *in-*, not + *permeabilis,* permeable.] **—im·per'me·a·bil'i·ty, im·per'me·a·ble·ness** *n.* **—im·per'me·a·bly** *adv.*

im·per·mis·si·ble (ĭm'pər-mĭs'ə-bəl) *adj.* Not permissible. **—im'per·mis'si·bil'i·ty** *n.* **—im'per·mis'si·bly** *adv.*

im·per·son·al (ĭm-pûr'sə-nəl) *adj.* **1. a.** Having no personal reference or connection: *an impersonal remark.* **b.** Showing no emotion or personality: *an aloof, impersonal manner.* **c.** Not responsive to or expressive of human personalities: *a large, impersonal corporation.* **2.** *Gram.* **a.** Denoting a verb that expresses the action of an unspecified agent and is used in the third person singular with no subject expressed, as *meseems,* or with a formal subject, as in *it snowed.* **b.** Indefinite. Used of pronouns. **—im·per'son·al'i·ty** *n.* **—im·per'son·al·ly** *adv.*

im·per·son·al·ize (ĭm-pûr'sə-nə-līz') *tr.v.* **-ized, -iz·ing, -iz·es.** To make impersonal.

im·per·son·ate (ĭm-pûr'sə-nāt') *tr.v.* **-at·ed, -at·ing, -ates. 1.** To act the character or part of. **2.** *Archaic.* To embody; personify. **—im·per'son·a'tion** *n.* **—im·per'son·a'tor** *n.*

im·per·ti·nence (ĭm-pûr'tn-əns) *n.* **1.** The quality or condition of being impertinent, as: **a.** Insolence. **b.** Irrelevance. **2.** An impertinent act or statement.

im·per·ti·nen·cy (ĭm-pûr'tn-ən-sē) *n., pl.* **-cies.** Impertinence.

im·per·ti·nent (ĭm-pûr'tn-ənt) *adj.* **1.** Not constrained within proper or established limits, esp. of manners or good taste; insolent: *an impertinent request.* **2.** Not pertinent; irrelevant. [ME, irrelevant < OFr. < LLat. *impertinens* : Lat. *in-*, not + *pertinens,* pertinent.] **—im·per'ti·nent·ly** *adv.*

im·per·turb·a·ble (ĭm'pər-tûr'bə-bəl) *adj.* Unshakably calm and collected. **—im'per·turb'a·bil'i·ty, im'per·turb'a·ble·ness** *n.* **—im'per·turb'a·bly** *adv.*

im·per·vi·ous (ĭm-pûr'vē-əs) *adj.* **1.** Incapable of being penetrated: *a material impervious to water.* **2.** Incapable of being affected: *impervious to fear.* [Lat. *impervius* : *in-*, not + *pervius,* pervious.] **—im·per'vi·ous·ly** *adv.* **—im·per'vi·ous·ness** *n.*

im·pe·ti·go (ĭm'pĭ-tī'gō) *n.* A contagious skin disease characterized by superficial pustules that burst and form characteristic thick yellow crusts. [Lat. < *impetere,* to attack. —see IMPETUS.]

im·pe·trate (ĭm′pĭ-trāt′) *tr.v.* **-trat·ed, -trat·ing, -trates. 1.** To obtain by entreaty or petition. **2.** To beseech. [Lat. *impetrare, impetrat-,* to obtain : *in-* (intensive) + *patrare,* to bring about.] **—im′pe·tra′tion** *n.* **—im′pe·tra′tor** *n.*

im·pet·u·os·i·ty (ĭm-pĕch′o͞o-ŏs′ĭ-tē) *n., pl.* **-ties. 1.** The quality or condition of being impetuous. **2.** An impetuous act.

im·pet·u·ous (ĭm-pĕch′o͞o-əs) *adj.* **1.** Characterized by sudden energy, action, or emotion; impulsive: *an impetuous decision he'll come to regret.* **2.** Having or marked by violent force: *impetuous, heaving waves.* [ME < OFr. *impetueux* < Lat. *impetuosus* < *impetus,* impetus.] **—im·pet′u·ous·ly** *adv.* **—im·pet′u·ous·ness** *n.*

Synonyms: *impetuous, heedless, hasty, headlong, sudden.* These adjectives describe persons and their actions and decisions when marked by abruptness or lack of deliberation. *Impetuous* suggests impulsiveness, impatience, or lack of thoughtfulness. *Heedless* implies carelessness or lack of a sense of responsibility or proper regard for the consequences of action. *Hasty* and *headlong* both stress hurried action, and the latter especially implies recklessness. *Sudden* is applied to action or to personal attributes, such as moods, that make themselves apparent abruptly or unexpectedly.

im·pe·tus (ĭm′pĭ-təs) *n., pl.* **-tus·es. 1. a.** An impelling force; impulse. **b.** Something that incites; stimulus. **2.** The force or energy associated with a moving body. [Lat., attack < *impetere,* to attack : *in-,* against + *petere,* to go towards, seek.]

im·pi·e·ty (ĭm-pī′ĭ-tē) *n., pl.* **-ties. 1.** The quality or state of being impious. **2.** An impious act. **3.** Undutifulness.

im·pinge (ĭm-pĭnj′) *intr.v.* **-pinged, -ping·ing, -ping·es. 1.** To collide or strike: *Sound waves impinge on the eardrum.* **2.** To encroach; trespass: *impinging on my privacy.* [Lat. *impingere,* to push against : *in-,* against + *pangere,* to fasten.] **—im·pinge′ment** *n.* **—im·ping′er** *n.*

im·pi·ous (ĭm′pē-əs, ĭm-pī′-) *adj.* **1.** Not pious; lacking reverence. **2.** Lacking due respect or dutifulness. [Lat. *impius,* irreverent, undutiful : *in-,* not + *pius,* reverent, dutiful.] **—im′pi·ous·ly** *adv.* **—im′pi·ous·ness** *n.*

imp·ish (ĭm′pĭsh) *adj.* Of or befitting an imp; mischievous. **—imp′ish·ly** *adv.* **—imp′ish·ness** *n.*

im·plac·a·ble (ĭm-plăk′ə-bəl, -plā′kə-) *adj.* Incapable of appeasement or mitigation; inexorable: *implacable foes.* [Lat. *implacabilis* : *in-,* not + *placabilis,* placable.] **—im·plac′a·bil′i·ty, im·plac′a·ble·ness** *n.* **—im·plac′a·bly** *adv.*

im·plant (ĭm-plănt′) *tr.v.* **-plant·ed, -plant·ing, -plants. 1.** To entrench or set in firmly, as in the ground. **2.** To establish permanently, as in the mind or consciousness; instill. **3.** *Med.* To insert or embed surgically, as in grafting. *—n.* (ĭm′plănt′). Something implanted, esp. surgically implanted tissue. **—im′plan·ta′tion** *n.*

im·plau·si·ble (ĭm-plô′zə-bəl) *adj.* Not plausible; difficult to believe. **—im·plau′si·bil′i·ty, im·plau′si·ble·ness** *n.* **—im·plau′si·bly** *adv.*

im·plead (ĭm-plēd′) *tr.v.* **-plead·ed, -plead·ing, -pleads.** To sue in a court of law. [ME *empleden* < AN *empleder* : *en-* (intensive < Lat. *in-*) + *pleder,* to plead. —see PLEAD.]

im·ple·ment (ĭm′plə-mənt) *n.* **1.** A tool, utensil, or instrument. **2.** An article used to outfit or equip. **3.** A means employed to achieve a given end; agent. *—tr.v.* (ĭm′plə-mĕnt′) **-ment·ed, -ment·ing, -ments. 1.** To put into practical effect; carry out: *implement the new procedures.* **2.** To supply with implements. [ME < LLat. *implementum,* a filling up < Lat. *implēre,* to fill up : *in-* (intensive) + *plēre,* to fill.] **—im′ple·men·ta′tion** (ĭm′plə-mən-tā′shən, -mĕn-) *n.*

im·pli·cate (ĭm′plĭ-kāt′) *tr.v.* **-cat·ed, -cat·ing, -cates. 1.** To involve or connect intimately or incriminatingly. **2.** To imply. **3.** *Archaic.* To interweave or entangle; entwine. [Lat. *implicare, implicat-,* to entangle, unite : *in-,* in + *plicare,* to fold.]

im·pli·ca·tion (ĭm′plĭ-kā′shən) *n.* **1.** The act of implicating or the condition of being implicated. **2.** The act of implying or the condition of being implied. **3.** Something that is implied, esp.: **a.** An indirect indication. **b.** An inference. **—im′pli·ca′tive** *adj.* **—im′pli·ca′tive·ly** *adv.*

im·plic·it (ĭm-plĭs′ĭt) *adj.* **1.** Implied or understood although not directly expressed: *thought we had an implicit understanding.* **2.** Contained in the nature of something although not readily apparent: *could see a great pianist implicit in the talented but unpolished young musician.* **3.** Having no doubts or reservations; unquestioning: *implicit trust.* [Lat. *implicitus,* var. of *implicatus,* p.part. of *implicare,* to entangle. —see IMPLICATE.] **—im·plic′it·ly** *adv.* **—im·plic′it·ness** *n.*

implicit differentiation *n.* The process of isolating the derivative of a dependent variable of an implicit function by differentiating each term of the function separately, expressing the desired derivative as a symbol, and solving the resulting expression for the symbol.

implicit function *n.* A mathematical expression in which the function of concern is not directly expressed but must be arrived at by manipulation of the expression.

im·plode (ĭm-plōd′) *v.* **-plod·ed, -plod·ing, -plodes.** *—intr.* To undergo implosion. *—tr.* **1.** To pronounce by implosion. **2.** To cause to undergo implosion. [IN-² + (EX)PLODE.]

im·plore (ĭm-plôr′, -plōr′) *tr.v.* **-plored, -plor·ing, -plores. 1.** To appeal to in supplication; beseech. **2.** To plead or beg for urgently; entreat. [Lat. *implorare* : *in-,* in + *plorare,* to weep.] **—im′plo·ra′tion** *n.* **—im·plor′er** *n.* **—im·plor′ing·ly** *adv.*

im·plo·sion (ĭm-plō′zhən) *n.* **1.** A violent collapse inward, as of a highly evacuated glass vessel. **2.** Violent compression. **3.** The stopping of the breath in the formation of a stop consonant. [IN-² + (EX)PLOSION.]

im·plo·sive (ĭm-plō′sĭv) *adj.* Pronounced by implosion. *—n.* A consonant pronounced by implosion.

im·ply (ĭm-plī′) *tr.v.* **-plied, -ply·ing, -plies. 1.** To involve or suggest by logical necessity; entail: *His goals imply a good deal of hard work.* **2.** To say or express indirectly: *His tone implied a malicious purpose.* **3.** *Obs.* To entangle. —See Usage note at **infer.** [ME *implien,* to enfold < OFr. *emplier* < Lat. *implicare.* —see IMPLICATE.]

im·po·lite (ĭm′pə-līt′) *adj.* Not polite; discourteous. [Lat. *impolitus,* unpolished, inelegant : *in-,* not + *politus,* polished, p.part. of *polire,* to polish.] **—im′po·lite′ly** *adv.* **—im′po·lite′ness** *n.*

im·pol·i·tic (ĭm-pŏl′ĭ-tĭk) *adj.* Not wise or expedient; not politic. **—im·pol′i·tic·ly** *adv.*

im·pon·der·a·ble (ĭm-pŏn′dər-ə-bəl) *adj.* Incapable of being evaluated or weighed with precision. **—im·pon′der·a·bil′i·ty, im·pon′der·a·ble·ness** *n.* **—im·pon′der·a·bly** *adv.*

im·pone (ĭm-pōn′) *tr.v.* **-poned, -pon·ing, -pones.** *Obs.* To wager or stake. [Lat. *imponere,* to place upon : *in-,* on + *ponere,* to place.]

im·port (ĭm-pôrt′, -pōrt′, ĭm′pôrt′, -pōrt′) *v.* **-port·ed, -port·ing, -ports.** *—tr.* **1.** To bring or carry in from an outside source, esp. to bring in (goods) from a foreign country for trade or sale. **2.** To carry or hold the meaning of; signify: *a high inflation rate importing hard times for the consumer.* **3.** To imply. **4.** *Archaic.* To have meaning for. *—intr.* To be significant. *—n.* (ĭm′pôrt′, -pōrt′). **1.** Something imported. **2.** The occupation of importing. **3.** Meaning; signification. **4.** Importance; significance: *a Supreme Court decision with a far-reaching import on the issue of criminal rights.* [ME *importen* < Lat. *importare* : *in-,* in + *portare,* to carry.] **—im·port′a·bil′i·ty** *n.* **—im·port′a·ble** *adj.* **—im·port′er** *n.*

im·por·tance (ĭm-pôr′tns) *n.* **1.** The condition or quality of being important; significance. **2.** Personal status; standing. **3.** *Obs.* An important matter. **4.** *Obs.* Meaning; import. **5.** *Obs.* Importunity.

Synonyms: *importance, consequence, moment, significance, import, weight.* These nouns refer to the quality of a thing that makes it influential or worthy of note, esteem, or the like. *Importance,* the most general term, usually can be substituted for any of the others, although it lacks their special implications. *Consequence* is especially applicable to persons or things of notable rank or position and to things that are important with respect to what follows them as an outcome or development. *Moment* implies importance or consequence that is readily apparent. *Significance* and *import* refer to the quality of a thing, often not readily apparent, that gives the thing special meaning or value. *Weight* is frequently used when a personal evaluation or judgment of importance is suggested.

im·por·tant (ĭm-pôr′tnt) *adj.* **1.** Marked by or having great value, significance, or consequence. **2.** Suggesting or having an air of great weight or moment; authoritative. **3.** *Obs.* Importunate. [OFr. < OItal. *importante* < Med. Lat. *importans,* pr.part. of *importare,* to mean < Lat., to import.] **—im·por′tant·ly** *adv.*

Usage: The following sentence may be written with the adjective *important: The truth is evident; more important, it will prevail.* It may also be written with an adverb: *The truth is evident; more importantly, it will prevail.* Most grammarians prescribe the adjective form, in which *important* stands for "what is important." But half the members of the Usage Panel accept the adverbial form.

im·por·ta·tion (ĭm′pôr-tā′shən, -pōr-) *n.* **1.** The act or business of importing. **2.** Something imported.

im·por·tu·nate (ĭm-pôr′chə-nĭt) *adj.* Stubbornly or unreasonably persistent in request or demand. **—im·por′tu·nate·ly** *adv.* **—im·por′tu·nate·ness** *n.*

im·por·tune (ĭm′pôr-to͞on′, -tyo͞on′, ĭm-pôr′chən) *tr.v.* **-tuned, -tun·ing, -tunes. 1.** To beset with repeated and insistent requests. **2.** *Obs.* To ask for insistently and repeatedly. **3.** *Obs.* To annoy; vex. *—adj.* Importunate. [Med. Lat. *importunari,* to be troublesome < Lat. *importunus,* inconvenient: *in-,* not + *portus,* harbor.] **—im′por·tune′ly** *adv.* **—im′por·tun′er** *n.*

im·por·tu·ni·ty (ĭm′pôr-to͞o′nĭ-tē, -tyo͞o′-) *n., pl.* **-ties. 1.** The act of importuning. **2.** The state or quality of being importunate.

im·pose (ĭm-pōz′) *v.* **-posed, -pos·ing, -pos·es.** *—tr.* **1.** To establish or apply as compulsory; levy: *impose a tax.* **2.** To apply or make prevail by or as if by authority: *impose a peace settlement.* **3.** To obtrude or force (oneself, for example) upon another or others. **4.** *Printing.* To arrange (type or plates) on an imposing stone. **5.** To pass off on others: *He imposed a fraud on his company.* *—intr.* To take unfair advantage of something or someone: *always imposing on her generosity.* [OFr. < Lat. *impositus,* p.part. of *imponere,* to place upon: *in-,* on + *ponere,* to place.] **—im·pos′er** *n.*

im·pos·ing (ĭm-pō′zĭng) *adj.* Impressive or awesome.

imposing stone *n. Printing.* A stone or metal slab on which material to be printed is arranged.

im·po·si·tion (ĭm′pə-zĭsh′ən) *n.* **1.** The act of imposing. **2.** Something imposed, as a tax, undue burden, or fraud. **3.** A burdensome or unfair demand, as upon someone's time. **4.** *Printing.* The arrangement of printed matter to form a sequence of pages.

im·pos·si·bil·i·ty (ĭm-pŏs′ə-bĭl′ĭ-tē) *n., pl.* **-ties. 1.** The condition or quality of being impossible. **2.** Something impossible.

im·pos·si·ble (ĭm-pŏs′ə-bəl) *adj.* **1.** Not capable of existing or happening. **2.** Having little likelihood of happening or being accomplished. **3.** Unacceptable. **4.** Extremely difficult to deal with or tolerate: *an impossible child; an impossible situation.* [ME < OFr. < Lat. *impossibilis* : *in-*, not + *possibilis,* possible.] **—im·pos′si·bly** *adv.*

im·post[1] (ĭm′pōst′) *n.* **1.** Something imposed or levied, as a tax or duty. **2.** The weight a horse must carry in a handicap race. [OFr. < Med. Lat. *impostum* < Lat. *impostus,* p.part. of *imponere,* to place upon. —see IMPOSE.]

im·post[2] (ĭm′pōst′) *n. Archit.* The uppermost part of a column or pillar supporting an arch. [Fr. *imposte* < Ital. *imposta* < Lat., fem. p.part. of *imponere,* to place upon. —see IMPOSE.]

im·pos·tor (ĭm-pŏs′tər) *n.* A person who deceives under an assumed identity. [OFr. *imposteur* < LLat. *impositor* < Lat. *impositus,* p.part. of *imponere,* to place upon. —see IMPOSE.]

Synonyms: *impostor, quack, faker, humbug, mountebank, charlatan.* These nouns denote persons who pretend to be other than what they are or who otherwise practice deception for gain. An *impostor* assumes the identity of another for the purpose of deceiving. A *quack* usually practices medicine without being properly qualified. *Faker,* informal, refers broadly to one who perpetrates fraud. A *humbug* is a self-important or self-deluded cheat who misrepresents himself. A *mountebank* is either a dealer in quack medicines or any flamboyant, unscrupulous dealer or promoter. A *charlatan* makes false claim to skill or knowledge, using a deceitful display to hide his deficiency.

im·pos·ture (ĭm-pŏs′chər) *n.* The act or practice of deceiving by the assumption of a false identity. [LLat. *impostura* < Lat. *impositus,* p.part. of *imponere,* to place upon. —see IMPOSE.]

im·po·tence (ĭm′pə-təns) also **im·po·ten·cy** (-tən-sē) *n.* The quality or condition of being impotent.

im·po·tent (ĭm′pə-tənt) *adj.* **1.** Lacking physical strength or vigor; weak. **2.** Powerless; ineffectual. **3. a.** Incapable of sexual intercourse. **b.** Sterile. Used of males. **4.** *Obs.* Lacking self-restraint. [ME < OFr. < Lat. *impotens* : *in-*, not + *potens,* potent.] **—im′po·tent·ly** *adv.*

im·pound (ĭm-pound′) *tr.v.* **-pound·ed, -pound·ing, -pounds. 1.** To confine in or as if in a pound. **2.** To seize and retain in legal custody. **3.** To accumulate (water) in a reservoir. **—im·pound′age, im·pound′ment** *n.* **—im·pound′er** *n.*

im·pov·er·ish (ĭm-pŏv′ər-ĭsh) *tr.v.* **-ished, -ish·ing, -ish·es. 1.** To reduce to poverty; make poor. **2.** To deprive of natural richness or strength: *impoverish the soil.* [ME *empoverishen* < OFr. *empovrir, empovriss-* : *en-* (causative) + *povre,* poor < Lat. *pauper.*] **—im·pov′er·ish·ment** *n.*

im·prac·ti·ca·ble (ĭm-prăk′tĭ-kə-bəl) *adj.* **1.** Not capable of being done or carried out. **2.** Unfit for passage, as a road. **3.** *Archaic.* Unmanageable; intractable. **—im·prac′ti·ca·bil′i·ty, im·prac′ti·ca·ble·ness** *n.* **—im·prac′ti·ca·bly** *adv.*

Usage: *Impracticable* applies to that which is not capable of being carried out or put into practice. *Impractical* refers to that which is not sensible or prudent. A plan may be *impractical* if it involves undue cost or effort and still not be *impracticable.* The distinction between these words is subtle, and *impractical* is often used where *impracticable* would be more precise. See also Usage note at **possible.**

im·prac·ti·cal (ĭm-prăk′tĭ-kəl) *adj.* **1.** Unwise to implement or maintain in practice. **2.** Incapable of dealing efficiently with practical matters, esp. financial matters. **3.** Not a part of experience, fact, or practice; theoretical. **4.** Impracticable. —See Usage note at **impracticable. —im·prac′ti·cal′i·ty, im·prac′ti·cal·ness** *n.*

im·pre·cate (ĭm′prĭ-kāt′) *tr.v.* **-cat·ed, -cat·ing, -cates.** To invoke evil upon; curse. [Lat. *imprecari, imprecat-* : *in-*, on + *precari,* to pray, ask.] **—im′pre·ca′tor** *n.* **—im′pre·ca·to′ry** (-kə-tôr′ē, -tōr′ē) *adj.*

im·pre·ca·tion (ĭm′prĭ-kā′shən) *n.* **1.** The act of imprecating. **2.** A curse.

im·pre·cise (ĭm′prĭ-sīs′) *adj.* Not precise. **—im′pre·cise′ly** *adv.* **—im′pre·ci′sion** (-sĭzh′ən) *n.*

im·preg·na·ble[1] (ĭm-prĕg′nə-bəl) *adj.* **1.** Incapable of being captured or entered by force: *an impregnable castle.* **2.** Unable to be shaken or criticized, as a conviction. [ME < OFr. : *in-*, not (< Lat. *in-*) + *pregnable,* pregnable.]

im·preg·na·ble[2] (ĭm-prĕg′nə-bəl) *adj.* Capable of being impregnated.

im·preg·nate (ĭm-prĕg′nāt′) *tr.v.* **-nat·ed, -nat·ing, -nates. 1.** To make pregnant; inseminate. **2.** To fertilize (an ovum, for example). **3.** To fill throughout or saturate. **4.** To permeate or imbue. *—adj.* Being saturated or filled. [LLat. *impregnare, impregnat-* : Lat. *in-*, in + *praegnans,* pregnant.] **—im′preg·na′tion** *n.* **—im·preg′na′tor** *n.*

im·pre·sa (ĭm-prā′zə) *n.* An emblem or device with a motto. [Ital., undertaking. —see IMPRESARIO.]

im·pre·sa·ri·o (ĭm′prĭ-sär′ē-ō′, -sâr′-) *n., pl.* **-os. 1.** One who sponsors or produces entertainment, esp. the director of an opera company. **2.** A manager; producer. [Ital. < *impresa,* undertaking < *impreso,* p.part.of *imprendere,* to undertake < VLat. —see EMPRISE.]

im·press[1] (ĭm-prĕs′) *tr.v.* **-pressed, -press·ing, -press·es. 1.** To produce or apply with pressure. **2.** To mark or stamp with or as if with pressure. **3.** To produce a vivid perception or image of. **4.** To affect or influence deeply or forcibly. **5.** To transmit a force or motion to. *—n.* (ĭm′prĕs′). **1.** The act of impressing. **2.** A mark or pattern produced by impressing. **3.** A stamp or seal meant to be impressed. [ME *impressen* < Lat. *impressus,* p.part. of *imprimere* : *in-*, in + *premere,* to press.]

impost[2]
Abbey of
Notre-Dame-de-Pontaut

im·press[2] (ĭm-prĕs′) *tr.v.* **-pressed, -press·ing, -press·es. 1.** To compel (a person) to serve in a military force. **2.** To confiscate (property). *—n.* Impressment.

im·press·i·ble (ĭm-prĕs′ə-bəl) *adj.* Susceptible to being impressed. **—im·press′i·bil′i·ty** *n.* **—im·press′i·bly** *adv.*

im·pres·sion (ĭm-prĕsh′ən) *n.* **1.** The act or process of impressing. **2.** The effect, mark, or imprint made on a surface by pressure. **3.** An effect, feeling, or image retained as a consequence of experience. **4.** A vague notion, remembrance, or belief. **5.** *Printing.* **a.** All the copies of a publication printed at one time from the same set of type. **b.** A single copy of this printing. **6.** An imitation or caricature of a famous personality done esp. by a professional entertainer. **7.** An initial or single coat of color or paint. **8.** An imprint of the teeth and surrounding tissue, used in dentistry as a mold in making dentures or inlays.

im·pres·sion·a·ble (ĭm-prĕsh′ə-nə-bəl) *adj.* **1.** Capable of receiving an impression; plastic. **2.** Readily or easily influenced; suggestible. **—im·pres′sion·a·bil′i·ty, im·pres′sion·a·ble·ness** *n.*

im·pres·sion·ism (ĭm-prĕsh′ə-nĭz′əm) *n.* **1.** Often **Impressionism.** A theory or style of painting originating and developed in France during the 1870's, characterized chiefly by concentration on the general impression produced by a scene or object and by the use of unmixed primary colors and small strokes to simulate actual reflected light. **2.** A literary style characterized generally by the use of details and mental associations to evoke subjective and sensory impressions rather than the re-creation of objective reality. **3.** A musical style of the late 19th and early 20th centuries, using lush and somewhat vague harmony and rhythm to evoke suggestions of mood, place, and natural phenomena. **4.** The practice or habit of expressing or developing one's subjective response to a work of art or actual experience.

im·pres·sion·ist (ĭm-prĕsh′ə-nĭst) *n.* **1.** One, esp. an artist or a composer, who practices or upholds the theories of impressionism. **2.** An entertainer who does impressions.

im·pres·sion·is·tic (ĭm-prĕsh′ə-nĭs′tĭk) *adj.* **1.** Of, pertaining to, or comprising impressionism. **2.** Of, pertaining to, involving, or based on impression as opposed to reason or fact. **3.** Impressionable. **—im·pres′sion·is′ti·cal·ly** *adv.*

im·pres·sive (ĭm-prĕs′ĭv) *adj.* Making a strong or vivid impression; commanding attention: *an impressive ceremony.* **—im·pres′sive·ly** *adv.* **—im·pres′sive·ness** *n.*

im·press·ment (ĭm-prĕs′mənt) *n.* The act or policy of seizing people or property for public service or use.

im·pres·sure (ĭm-prĕsh′ər) *n. Archaic.* Impression.

im·prest[1] (ĭm-prĕst′) *n.* An advance or loan of government funds for some service to the government. [< Ital. *impresto,* lent, advanced < *imprestare,* to lend : *in-*, toward (< Lat.) + *prestare,* to lend < Lat. *praestare,* to give < *praesto,* at hand.]

im·prest[2] (ĭm-prĕst′) *v. Archaic.* Past tense and past participle of **impress.**

im·pri·ma·tur (ĭm′prə-mä′tər, -mā′tər) *n.* **1.** Official approval or license to print or publish, esp. under conditions of censorship. **2.** Official sanction. [NLat., let it be printed.]

im·pri·mis (ĭm-prī′mĭs) *adv.* In the first place. [ME < Lat. *in primis,* among the first (things).]

im·print (ĭm-prĭnt′) *tr.v.* **-print·ed, -print·ing, -prints. 1.** To produce or impress (a mark or pattern) on a surface. **2.** To stamp or produce a mark on. **3. a.** To produce a vivid, often favorable effect on the mind or emotions. **b.** To establish firmly in the mind. *—n.* (ĭm′prĭnt′). **1.** A mark or pattern produced by imprinting. **2.** A distinguishing influence or effect: *architecture that shows the imprint of Spanish colonization.* **3.** A publisher's name, often with the date, address, and edition of a publication, printed at the bottom of a title page. [ME *emprenten* < OFr. *empreinter* < *empreinte,* impression < *empreindre,* to print < Lat. *imprimere,* to impress.]

im·print·ing (ĭm′prĭn′tĭng) *n.* A learning process occurring early in the life of a social animal in which a behavior pattern is established through association with a parent or other role model.

im·pris·on (ĭm-prĭz′ən) *tr.v.* **-oned, -on·ing, -ons.** To put in or as if in prison; confine. [ME *emprisonen* < OFr. *emprisoner* : *en-*, in (< Lat. *in-*) + *prison,* prison.] **—im·pris′on·ment** *n.*

im·prob·a·bil·i·ty (ĭm-prŏb′ə-bĭl′ĭ-tē) *n., pl.* **-ties. 1.** The quality or condition of being improbable. **2.** Something improbable.

im·prob·a·ble (ĭm-prŏb′ə-bəl) *adj.* Unlikely to take place or to be true; doubtful. [Lat. *improbabilis* : *in-*, not + *probabilis*, probable.] **—im·prob′a·ble·ness** *n.* **—im·prob′a·bly** *adv.*

im·pro·bi·ty (ĭm-prō′bĭ-tē) *n.* Lack of probity; dishonesty. [ME *improbite* < Lat. *improbitas* < *improbus*, dishonest : *in-*, not + *probus*, honest, good.]

im·promp·tu (ĭm-prŏmp′to͞o, -tyo͞o) *adj.* Performed or conceived without rehearsal or preparation: *an impromptu speech.* *—adv.* Spontaneously. *—n.* **1.** Something made or done impromptu, as a speech. **2.** *Mus.* A short lyrical composition esp. for the piano. [Fr. < Lat. *in promptu*, at hand : *in*, in + *promptus*, ready. —see PROMPT.]

im·prop·er (ĭm-prŏp′ər) *adj.* **1.** Not suited to circumstances or needs; unsuitable: *received improper care.* **2.** Not in keeping with conventional mores; indecorous. **3.** Not consistent with truth, fact, or rule; incorrect. **4.** Irregular or abnormal, as in form. [OFr. *impropre* < Lat. *improprius* : *in-*, not + *proprius*, proper.] **—im·prop′er·ly** *adv.* **—im·prop′er·ness** *n.*

Synonyms: *improper, unbecoming, unseemly, indelicate, indecent, indecorous.* These adjectives mean in violation of accepted standards of what is right or proper. *Improper* can apply to any act or statement contrary to such standards, but often refers to unethical conduct, violation of etiquette, or morally offensive behavior. *Unbecoming* suggests what is beneath the standard implied by one's character or position. What is *unseemly* or *indelicate* violates good taste; *indelicate* suggests immodesty, coarseness, or tactlessness. *Indecorous,* the weakest of these terms, implies violation of the manners of polite society.

improper fraction *n.* A fraction in which the numerator is larger than or equal to the denominator.

improper integral *n.* An integral having at least one nonfinite limit or having an integrand that becomes infinite between the limits of integration.

im·pro·pri·e·ty (ĭm′prə-prī′ĭ-tē) *n., pl.* **-ties. 1.** The quality or condition of being improper. **2.** An improper act. **3.** An improper or unacceptable usage in speech or writing.

im·prove (ĭm-pro͞ov′) *v.* **-proved, -prov·ing, -proves.** *—tr.* **1.** To advance to a better state or quality; make better. **2.** To increase the productivity or value of (land). *—intr.* **1.** To become or get better. **2.** To make beneficial additions or changes: *improve on the translation.* [ME *improven,* to enclose land for cultivation < AN *emprouwer* : OFr. *en-* (causative) + *prou,* profit < LLat. *prode,* advantageous. —see PROUD.]

Synonyms: *improve, better, help, ameliorate, enhance.* These verbs mean to make more attractive or desirable in some respect. *Improve,* the most general term, refers to an act of raising in quality or value or of relieving an undesirable situation. *Better* is often interchangeable with *improve* in the preceding senses; used reflexively, *better* implies worldly gain: *better himself by changing jobs. Help* usually implies limited relief or change for the better: *medicine that helped her. Ameliorate* refers to improving or bettering conditions that cry out for change. *Enhance,* in contrast, suggests adding to something already attractive or worthy and thus increasing its value.

im·prove·ment (ĭm-pro͞ov′mənt) *n.* **1.** The act or procedure of improving. **2.** The state of being improved. **3.** A change or addition that improves.

im·prov·i·dent (ĭm-prŏv′ĭ-dənt) *adj.* **1.** Not providing for the future; thriftless. **2.** Rash; incautious. **—im·prov′i·dence** *n.* **—im·prov′i·dent·ly** *adv.*

im·pro·vi·sa·tion (ĭm-prŏv′ĭ-zā′shən, ĭm′prə-vĭ-) *n.* **1.** The act of improvising. **2.** Something improvised, esp. a dramatic skit.

im·prov·i·sa·tor (ĭm-prŏv′ĭ-zā′tər) *n.* One who improvises.

im·prov·i·sa·to·ry (ĭm-prŏv′ĭ-zə-tôr′ē, ĭm′prə-vĭ′zə-tôr′ē, -tōr′ē) also **im·prov·i·sa·to·ri·al** (ĭm-prŏv′ĭ-zə-tôr′ē-əl, -tōr′ē-əl) *adj.* **1.** Of or pertaining to improvisation. **2.** Of or pertaining to an improviser.

im·pro·vise (ĭm′prə-vīz′) *v.* **-vised, -vis·ing, -vis·es.** *—tr.* **1.** To invent, compose, or recite without preparation. **2.** To make or provide from available materials. *—intr.* To invent, compose, recite, or execute something offhand. [Fr. *improviser* < Ital. *improvvisare* < *improvviso,* unforeseen < Lat. *improvisus* : *in-*, not + *provisus,* p.part. of *providere,* to foresee. —see PROVIDE.] **—im′pro·vis′er** *n.*

im·pru·dence (ĭm-pro͞od′ns) *n.* **1.** The quality or condition of being imprudent. **2.** An imprudent act.

im·pru·dent (ĭm-pro͞od′ənt) *adj.* Not prudent; unwise or indiscreet. [ME < Lat. *imprudens* : *in-*, not + *prudens,* prudent.]

im·pu·dence (ĭm′pyə-dəns) also **im·pu·den·cy** (-dən-sē) *n.* **1.** The quality of being impudent. **2.** Impudent behavior.

im·pu·dent (ĭm′pyə-dənt) *adj.* **1.** Characterized by brash behavior or impertinent disrespect. **2.** *Obs.* Immodest. [ME < Lat. *impudens* : *in-*, not + *pudens,* pr.part. of *pudēre,* to be ashamed.] **—im′pu·dent·ly** *adv.*

im·pu·dic·i·ty (ĭm′pyo͞o-dĭs′ĭ-tē) *n.* Immodesty; shamelessness. [OFr. *impudicite* < Lat. *impudicus,* immodest : *in-*, not + *pudicus,* modest < *pudēre,* to be ashamed.]

im·pugn (ĭm-pyo͞on′) *tr.v.* **-pugned, -pugn·ing, -pugns.** To oppose or attack as false, esp. to criticize or refute by argumentation. [ME *impugnen* < OFr. *impugner* < Lat. *impugnare,* to fight against : *in-*, against + *pugnare,* to fight.] **—im·pugn′a·ble** *adj.* **—im·pugn′er** *n.*

im·pu·is·sance (ĭm-pyo͞o′ĭ-səns, ĭm-pwĭs′əns) *n.* Lack of power or effectiveness; weakness. **—im·pu′is·sant** *adj.*

im·pulse (ĭm′pŭls′) *n.* **1. a.** An impelling force. **b.** The motion produced by such a force. **2. a.** A sudden spontaneous inclination or urge: *had an impulse to tell him off.* **b.** A motivating force; incentive: *questioned the impulse behind the reorganization plan.* **3. a.** An inherent propensity, usually of a nonrational nature: *"Respect for the liberty of others is not a natural impulse in most men"* (Bertrand Russell). **b.** A general tendency or spirit; current: *can hear the romantic impulse in all his music.* **4.** *Electronics.* A short-term change in the intensity of a medium. **5.** *Physics.* The product of the average value of a force with the time during which it acts, equal in general to the change in momentum produced by the force in this time interval. **6.** *Physiol.* An instance of the transmission of energy from one neuron to another. [Lat. *impulsus* < p.part. of *impellere,* to impel. —see IMPEL.]

im·pul·sion (ĭm-pŭl′shən) *n.* **1.** The act of impelling or the condition of being impelled. **2.** An impelling force; thrust. **3.** Motion produced by an impelling force; momentum. **4.** An urging; compulsion: *"I do not move . . . unless it be under the impulsion of a third party"* (Samuel Beckett).

im·pul·sive (ĭm-pŭl′sĭv) *adj.* **1.** Inclined to act on impulse rather than thought. **2.** Produced as a result of impulse; precipitate: *an impulsive act.* **3.** Having force or power to impel or incite; forceful. **4.** *Physics.* Acting within brief time intervals. Used esp. of a force. **—im·pul′sive·ly** *adv.* **—im·pul′sive·ness** *n.*

im·pu·ni·ty (ĭm-pyo͞o′nĭ-tē) *n., pl.* **-ties.** Exemption from punishment, penalty, or harm. [Lat. *impunitas* < *impunis,* not punished : *in-*, not + *poena,* penalty < Gk. *poinē.*]

im·pure (ĭm-pyo͝or′) *adj.* **1.** Not pure or clean; contaminated. **2.** Not purified by religious rite; defiled. **3.** Immoral or obscene. **4.** Mixed with another and usually inferior substance; adulterated. **5.** Being a composite of more than one color or mixed with black or white. Used of color. **6.** Deriving from more than one source, style, or convention; bastardized. Used esp. of the arts. **7.** Not proper or consistent in grammar, vocabulary, idiom, or other usage. **—im·pure′ly** *adv.* **—im·pure′ness** *n.*

im·pu·ri·ty (ĭm-pyo͝or′ĭ-tē) *n., pl.* **-ties. 1.** The quality or condition of being impure, esp.: **a.** Contamination or pollution. **b.** Lack of consistency or homogeneity; adulteration. **c.** A state of immorality; sin. **2.** Something that renders something else impure; contaminant.

im·put·a·ble (ĭm-pyo͞o′tə-bəl) *adj.* Capable of being ascribed or imputed; attributable. **—im·put′a·bly** *adv.*

im·pu·ta·tion (ĭm′pyo͞o-tā′shən) *n.* **1.** The act of imputing. **2.** Something imputed or ascribed. **—im·pu′ta·tive** (ĭm-pyo͞o′tə-tĭv) *adj.* **—im·pu′ta·tive·ly** *adv.*

im·pute (ĭm-pyo͞ot′) *tr.v.* **-put·ed, -put·ing, -putes. 1.** To ascribe (a crime or fault) to another. **2.** To attribute to a cause or source. **3.** To attribute (wickedness or merit) to a person as transmitted by another. [ME *imputen* < OFr. *emputer* < Lat. *imputare,* to charge : *in-*, in + *putare,* to reckon, compute.]

in (ĭn) *prep.* **1. a.** Within the limits, bounds, or area of: *was hit in the face; in the spring; in the garden.* **b.** From the outside to a point within; into: *threw the letter in the garbage can.* **2.** To or at a situation or condition of: *was split in two; in debt; in love.* **3. a.** Having the activity, occupation, or function of: *in politics; in command.* **b.** During the act or process of: *tripped in racing for the bus.* **4. a.** With the arrangement or order of: *fell in luxuriant folds; in equal payments.* **b.** After the style or form of: *in iambic pentameter.* **5. a.** With the characteristic, attribute, or property of: *a tall man in an afro.* **b.** Used to indicate a material or element from which something is made: *a statue in bronze.* **6.** With the aim or purpose of: *went in search of a dictionary.* **7.** By the instrumentality or means of: *paneled the library in walnut.* **8.** With reference to: *six inches in depth.* **9.** Used to indicate the second and larger term of a ratio or proportion: *saved only one in ten.* *—adv.* **1.** To or toward the inside: *He stepped in.* **2.** To or toward a destination or goal: *The group closed in.* **3.** Into a usual place, as of business or residence: *He's not in.* **4. a.** In a position of success or favor. **b.** In a particular relationship: *in bad with her supervisor.* **5. a.** In fashion. **b.** In season. *—adj.* **1.** Very fashionable: *the in thing to wear.* **2.** Extremely concerned with or aware of the latest fashion: *a member of the in crowd.* **3.** Incoming; entering. **4.** Having power; incumbent. *—n.* **1.** One that has position, influence, or power. **2.** *Informal.* Influence; power. ***—idioms.*** **in for.** Guaranteed to get or have: *in for a shock.* **ins and outs. 1.** The twists and turns, as of a roadway. **2.** The characteristic features and difficulties. **in that.** For the reason that. [ME < OE.]

In The symbol for the element indium.

in-[1] or **il-** or **im-** or **ir-** *pref.* Not: *inarticulate.* [ME < OFr. < Lat.]

in-[2] or **il-** or **im-** or **ir-** *pref.* **1.** In, into, within: *intubation.* **2.** En-[1]. [ME < OFr. < Lat. < *in,* in, within.]

-in *suff.* **1.** or **-ine.** A neutral chemical compound: *globulin.* **2.** Enzyme: *pancreatin.* **3. a.** A pharmaceutical: *niacin.*

b. An antibiotic: *penicillin.* **4.** Variant of **-ine**[2] (sense 3). [Fr. *-ine.* —see -INE[2].]

in·a·bil·i·ty (ĭn′ə-bĭl′ĭ-tē) *n.* Lack of ability or means.

in ab·sen·tia (ĭn ăb-sĕn′shə, -shē-ə) *adv.* In absence; while or although not present. [Lat.]

in·ac·ces·si·ble (ĭn′ăk-sĕs′ə-bəl) *adj.* Not accessible; unapproachable. **—in′ac·ces′si·bil′i·ty** *n.* **—in′ac·ces′si·bly** *adv.*

in·ac·cu·ra·cy (ĭn-ăk′yər-ə-sē) *n., pl.* **-cies. 1.** The quality or condition of being inaccurate. **2.** An error.

in·ac·cu·rate (ĭn-ăk′yər-ĭt) *adj.* **1.** Not accurate. **2.** Mistaken or incorrect. **—in·ac′cu·rate·ly** *adv.* **—in·ac′cu·rate·ness** *n.*

in·ac·tion (ĭn-ăk′shən) *n.* Lack or absence of action.

in·ac·ti·vate (ĭn-ăk′tə-vāt′) *tr.v.* **-vat·ed, -vat·ing, -vates.** To render inactive. **—in·ac′ti·va′tion** *n.*

in·ac·tive (ĭn-ăk′tĭv) *adj.* **1.** Not active or not tending to be active. **2. a.** Being out of use. **b.** Retired from duty or service. **3. a.** *Chem.* Not readily participating in chemical reactions. **b.** *Biol.* Having no significant effect on or interaction with living organisms. **c.** *Med.* Quiescent. Used esp. of a disease. **d.** *Physics.* Displaying little or no radioactivity. **4.** Not functioning or operating. **—in·ac′tive·ly** *adv.* **—in·ac′tive·ness, in′ac·tiv′i·ty** *n.*

Synonyms: *inactive, idle, inert, passive, dormant, torpid, supine.* These adjectives mean not involved in, or disposed to, activity. *Inactive* merely indicates absence of activity in a person or thing. *Idle* refers to inactivity of persons, whether through unemployment, choice, laziness, or any other cause. *Inert* describes things powerless to move themselves, to resist motion impressed on them, or to produce a desired effect. Applied to persons, *inert* implies lethargy or unreceptiveness, especially of mind or spirit. *Passive* is applied to persons and things that are acted upon by external force or provocation but do not themselves react positively, as by resisting or showing emotion. *Dormant* refers principally to things in a state of suspended activity, such as volcanoes long inactive but not extinct. *Torpid* suggests the inactivity of a hibernating animal. *Supine* implies abjectness in persons, made manifest by lack of will or stamina, especially in situations that test courage or resolution.

in·ad·e·qua·cy (ĭn-ăd′ĭ-kwə-sē) *n., pl.* **-cies. 1.** The quality or condition of being inadequate. **2.** A failing or lack.

in·ad·e·quate (ĭn-ăd′ĭ-kwĭt) *adj.* **1.** Not adequate; insufficient. **2.** Not able; incapable: *He's inadequate to the job.* **—in·ad′e·quate·ly** *adv.*

in·ad·mis·si·ble (ĭn′əd-mĭs′ə-bəl) *adj.* Not admissible. **—in′ad·mis′si·bil′i·ty** *n.* **—in′ad·mis′si·bly** *adv.*

in·ad·ver·tence (ĭn′əd-vûr′tns) *n.* **1.** The quality of being inadvertent. **2.** An instance of being inadvertent; mistake; oversight. [Med. Lat. *inadvertentia* : Lat. *in-,* not + Lat. *advertens,* pr.part. of *advertere,* to turn toward. —see ADVERSE.]

in·ad·ver·ten·cy (ĭn′əd-vûr′tn-sē) *n., pl.* **-cies.** Inadvertence.

in·ad·ver·tent (ĭn′əd-vûr′tnt) *adj.* **1.** Not duly attentive. **2.** Accidental; unintentional. **—in′ad·ver′tent·ly** *adv.*

in·ad·vis·a·ble (ĭn′əd-vī′zə-bəl) *adj.* Unwise; not recommended. **—in′ad·vis′a·bil′i·ty** *n.*

in ae·ter·num (ĭn ē-tûr′nəm) *adv.* Forever; to eternity. [Lat.]

in·al·ien·a·ble (ĭn-āl′yə-nə-bəl, -ā′lē-ə-nə-) *adj.* Not capable of being transferred to another: *inalienable rights.* **—in·al′ien·a·bil′i·ty** *n.* **—in·al′ien·a·bly** *adv.*

in·al·ter·a·ble (ĭn-ôl′tər-ə-bəl) *adj.* Not alterable; unchangeable. **—in·al′ter·a·bil′i·ty** *n.* **—in·al′ter·a·bly** *adv.*

in·am·o·ra·ta (ĭn-ăm′ə-rä′tə) *n., pl.* **-tas.** A woman with whom one is in love or has an intimate relationship. [Ital., fem. of *inamorato,* inamorato.]

in·am·o·ra·to (ĭn-ăm′ə-rä′tō) *n., pl.* **-tos.** A male with whom one is in love or has an intimate relationship. [Ital. < p.part. of *inammore,* to enamor : *in-,* in (< Lat.) + *amore,* love < Lat. *amor* < *amore,* to love.]

in-and-in (ĭn′ənd-ĭn′) *adv.* Repeatedly within the same or closely related stocks: *to breed pigs in-and-in.* **—in′-and-in′** *adj.*

in-and-out (ĭn′ənd-out′) *adj.* Involving the purchase and sale of a single security within a short period of time.

in·ane (ĭn-ān′) *adj.* Lacking sense or substance; empty: *an inane comment.* —*n.* Empty space; the void. [Lat. *inanis,* empty, vain.] **—in·ane′ly** *adv.*

in·an·i·mate (ĭn-ăn′ə-mĭt) *adj.* **1.** Not having the qualities associated with active, living organisms; not animate. **2.** Not exhibiting life; appearing lifeless or dead. **3.** Not animated or energetic; dull. **—in·an′i·mate·ly** *adv.* **—in·an′i·mate·ness** *n.*

in·a·ni·tion (ĭn′ə-nĭsh′ən) *n.* **1.** Exhaustion, as from lack of nourishment. **2.** The condition or quality of being empty. [ME *inanisioun* < LLat. *inanitio* < *inanire,* to make empty < *inanis,* empty.]

in·an·i·ty (ĭn-ăn′ĭ-tē) *n., pl.* **-ties. 1.** The condition or quality of being inane. **2.** Something fatuous or absurd: *"His mind was steeled against the inanities she uttered"* (Henry James).

in·ap·peas·a·ble (ĭn′ə-pē′zə-bəl) *adj.* Incapable of being appeased.

in·ap·pe·tence (ĭn-ăp′ĭ-təns) also **in·ap·pe·ten·cy** (-tən-sē) *n.* Lack of appetite. **—in·ap′pe·tent** *adj.*

in·ap·pli·ca·ble (ĭn-ăp′lĭ-kə-bəl) *adj.* Not applicable. **—in·ap′pli·ca·bil′i·ty** *n.* **—in·ap′pli·ca·bly** *adv.*

in·ap·po·site (ĭn-ăp′ə-zĭt) *adj.* Not pertinent; unsuitable. **—in·ap′po·site·ly** *adv.*

in·ap·pre·cia·ble (ĭn′ə-prē′shə-bəl) *adj.* Too small to be noticed or to constitute a significant difference; negligible. **—in′ap·pre′cia·bly** *adv.*

in·ap·pre·cia·tive (ĭn′ə-prē′shə-tĭv, -shē-ā′tĭv) *adj.* Feeling or showing no appreciation; unappreciative. **—in′ap·pre′cia·tive·ly** *adv.* **—in′ap·pre′cia·tive·ness** *n.*

in·ap·proach·a·ble (ĭn′ə-prō′chə-bəl) *adj.* Not approachable. **—in′ap·proach′a·bil′i·ty** *n.* **—in′ap·proach′a·bly** *adv.*

in·ap·pro·pri·ate (ĭn′ə-prō′prē-ĭt) *adj.* Not appropriate; unsuitable or improper. **—in′ap·pro′pri·ate·ly** *adv.* **—in′ap·pro′pri·ate·ness** *n.*

in·apt (ĭn-ăpt′) *adj.* **1.** Inappropriate. **2.** Inept. **—in·apt′ly** *adv.* **—in·apt′ness** *n.*

in·ap·ti·tude (ĭn-ăp′tĭ-to͞od′, -tyo͞od′) *n.* **1.** Inappropriateness. **2.** Lack of skill; ineptitude.

in·ar·tic·u·late (ĭn′är-tĭk′yə-lĭt) *adj.* **1.** Uttered without the use of normal words or syllables; incomprehensible as speech or language: *"a cry . . . that . . . sank down into an inarticulate whine"* (Jack London). **2.** Unable to speak; speechless: *inarticulate with astonishment.* **3.** Unable to speak with clarity or eloquence. **4.** Unexpressed: *inarticulate sorrow.* **5.** *Biol.* Not having joints or segments. **—in′ar·tic′u·late·ly** *adv.* **—in′ar·tic′u·late·ness** *n.*

inauguration
Inauguration of Ronald Reagan as President of the United States, 1981

in·ar·tis·tic (ĭn′är-tĭs′tĭk) *adj.* **1.** Not conforming to the principles or criteria of art. **2.** Lacking taste or interest in art. **—in·ar·tis′tic·al·ly** *adv.*

in·as·much as (ĭn′əz-mŭch′) *conj.* **1.** Because of the fact that; since. **2.** To the extent that; insofar as.

in·at·ten·tion (ĭn′ə-tĕn′shən) *n.* Lack of attention, notice, or regard; neglect.

in·at·ten·tive (ĭn′ə-tĕn′tĭv) *adj.* Showing a lack of attention; negligent. **—in′at·ten′tive·ly** *adv.* **—in′at·ten′tive·ness** *n.*

in·au·di·ble (ĭn-ô′də-bəl) *adj.* Incapable of being heard. **—in·au′di·bly** *adv.*

in·au·gu·ral (ĭn-ô′gyər-əl) *adj.* **1.** Of, relating to, or characteristic of an inauguration. **2.** Initial; first: *the inaugural issue of a magazine.* —*n.* **1.** An inaugural speech. **2.** An inauguration.

in·au·gu·rate (ĭn-ô′gyə-rāt′) *tr.v.* **-rat·ed, -rat·ing, -rates. 1.** To induct into office by a formal ceremony. **2.** To begin or start officially. **3.** To open or begin use of formally with a ceremony; dedicate. [Lat. *inaugurare, inaugurat-* : *in-,* in + *augurare,* to auger < *augur,* soothsayer.] **—in·au′gu·ra′tor** *n.*

in·au·gu·ra·tion (ĭn-ô′gyə-rā′shən) *n.* **1.** A formal beginning or introduction. **2.** Formal introduction to an office.

in·aus·pi·cious (ĭn′ô-spĭsh′əs) *adj.* Not auspicious; unfavorable. **—in′aus·pi′cious·ly** *adv.* **—in′aus·pi′cious·ness** *n.*

in between *prep.* Between two things.

in-be·tween (ĭn′bĭ-twēn′) *adj.* Intermediate: *Adolescence is an awkward in-between age.* —*n.* An intermediate or intermediary: *conservatives, radicals, and in-betweens.*

in·board (ĭn′bôrd′, -bōrd′) *adj.* **1.** Within the hull or toward the center of a ship. **2.** Relatively close to the fuselage of an aircraft: *the inboard engines.* **3.** Toward the center of a machine. —*n.* A motor attached to the inside of the hull of a boat. **—in′board′** *adv.*

in·born (ĭn′bôrn′) *adj.* **1.** Possessed by an organism at birth. **2.** Inherited or hereditary.

in·bound (ĭn′bound′) *adj.* Homeward bound or incoming.

in·bounds (ĭn′boundz′) *adj. Basketball.* Of or pertaining to a means of putting the ball in play by having one player standing out of bounds pass it to another player on the court.

in·breathe (ĭn′brēth′) *tr.v.* **-breathed, -breath·ing, -breathes.** To breathe (something) in; inhale.

in·bred (ĭn′brĕd′) *adj.* **1.** Produced by inbreeding. **2.** Innate; deep-seated: *an inbred hatred of communism.*

in·breed (ĭn′brēd′) *tr.v.* **-bred** (-brĕd′), **-breed·ing, -breeds. 1.** To produce by the continued breeding of closely related individuals. **2.** To breed or develop within; engender. **—in·breed′er** *n.*

in·breed·ing (ĭn′brē′dĭng) *n.* The breeding of closely related individuals.

In·ca (ĭng′kə) *n., pl.* **Inca** or **-cas. 1.** An Indian of the group of Quechuan peoples who ruled Peru before the Spanish conquest. **2.** A king or other member of the royal family of the Inca. [Sp. < Quechua *inka,* ruler.]

In·ca·ic (ĭn-kā′ĭk) *adj. & n.* Incan.

in·cal·cu·la·ble (ĭn-kăl′kyə-lə-bəl) *adj.* **1.** Not capable of being calculated; indeterminate. **2.** Unpredictable; uncertain: *"The motions of her mind were as incalculable as the flit of a bird"* (Edith Wharton). **—in·cal′cu·la·bil′i·ty, in·cal′cu·la·ble·ness** *n.* **—in·cal′cu·la·bly** *adv.*

Incan
An Incan city in Peru

in·ca·les·cent (ĭn′kə-lĕs′ənt) *adj.* Growing hotter or more ardent. [Lat. *incalescens, incalescent-,* pr.part. of *incalescere,* to grow warm : *in-* (intensive) + *calescere,* to grow warm, inceptive of *calēre,* to be warm.] **—in·ca·les′cence** *n.*

in cam·er·a (ĭn kăm′ər-ə) *adv.* **1.** In secret; privately. **2.** *Law.* In private with a judge rather than in open court. [Lat., in the chamber.]

In·can (ĭng′kən) *adj.* Of or relating to the Incas, their civilization, or their language. —*n.* **1.** An Inca. **2.** Quechua.

in·can·desce (ĭn′kən-dĕs′) *v.* **-desced, -desc·ing, -desc·es.** —*intr.* To become incandescent. —*tr.* To cause to become

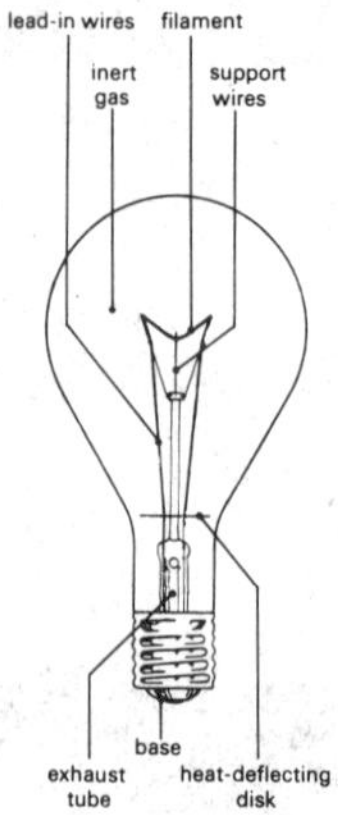

incandescent lamp

incandescent. [Lat. *incandescere,* to glow : *in-* (intensive) + *candescere,* to glow, inceptive of *candēre,* to shine.]
in·can·des·cence (ĭn′kən-dĕs′əns) *n.* **1.** The emission of visible light by a hot object. **2.** The light emitted by an incandescent object. **3.** A high degree of emotion, intensity, or brilliance.
in·can·des·cent (ĭn′kən-dĕs′ənt) *adj.* **1.** Emitting visible light as a result of being heated. **2.** Shining brilliantly; very bright. **3.** Characterized by ardent emotion, intensity, or brilliance: *an incandescent devotion.* **—in′can·des′cent·ly** *adv.*
incandescent lamp *n.* An electric lamp in which a filament is heated to incandescence by an electric current.
in·can·ta·tion (ĭn′kăn-tā′shən) *n.* **1.** Ritual recitation of verbal charms or spells to produce a magical effect. **2. a.** The formulaic words, phrases, or sounds used in an incantation. **b.** Conventionalized words and slogans used and repeated in a manner likened to the utterance of spells: *the pious incantations of the administration.* **3.** The casting of spells. [ME *incantacioun* < OFr. *incantation* < LLat. *incantatio,* spell < Lat. *incantore,* to enchant. —see ENCHANT.] **—in′can·ta′tion·al** *adj.* **—in·can′ta·to′ry** (-tə-tôr′ē, -tōr′ē) *adj.*
in·ca·pa·ble (ĭn-kā′pə-bəl) *adj.* **1. a.** Lacking the requisite ability or power: *incapable of carrying a tune.* **b.** Lacking the capacity to realize: *incapable of love.* **c.** Unable to do or perform; incompetent. **2.** *Law.* Lacking legal qualifications or requirements; ineligible. **—in·ca′pa·bil′i·ty, in·ca′pa·ble·ness** *n.* **—in·ca′pa·bly** *adv.*
in·ca·pac·i·tate (ĭn′kə-păs′ĭ-tāt′) *tr.v.* **-tat·ed, -tat·ing, -tates. 1.** To deprive of strength or ability; disable. **2.** To make legally ineligible; disqualify. **—in′ca·pac′i·ta′tion** *n.*
in·ca·pac·i·ty (ĭn′kə-păs′ĭ-tē) *n., pl.* **-ties. 1.** Lack of capacity; inadequate strength or ability. **2.** A defect or handicap; disability. **3.** *Law.* Something that renders legally ineligible; disqualification.
in·cap·su·late (ĭn-kăp′sə-lāt′) *v.* Variant of **encapsulate.**
in·car·cer·ate (ĭn-kär′sə-rāt′) *tr.v.* **-at·ed, -at·ing, -ates. 1.** To put in jail. **2.** To shut in; confine. [Lat. *incarcerare, incarcerat-* : *in-,* in + *carcer,* prison.] **—in·car′cer·a′tion** *n.* **—in·car′cer·a′tor** *n.*
in·car·na·dine (ĭn-kär′nə-dīn′, -dēn′, -dĭn) *adj.* **1.** Flesh-colored. **2.** Blood-red. *—tr.v.* **-dined, -din·ing, -dines.** To make incarnadine, esp. to redden. [OFr. *incarnadin* < OItal. *incarnatino* < *incarnato,* flesh-colored < Lat. *incarnatus,* incarnate.]
in·car·nate (ĭn-kär′nĭt) *adj.* **1. a.** Invested with bodily nature and form. **b.** Embodied in human form; personified: *He is evil incarnate.* **2.** Incarnadine. *—tr.v.* (ĭn-kär′nāt′) **-nat·ed, -nat·ing, -nates. 1. a.** To give bodily, esp. human, form to. **b.** To personify. **2.** To realize in action or fact; actualize. [LLat. *incarnatus,* p.part. of *incarnare,* to make flesh : *in-,* in + *caro,* flesh.]
in·car·na·tion (ĭn′kär-nā′shən) *n.* **1. a.** The act of incarnating. **b.** The condition of being incarnated. **2. a. Incarnation.** *Theol.* The embodiment of God in the human form of Jesus. **b.** A bodily manifestation of a supernatural being. **4.** One held to personify a given abstract quality or idea. **5.** The fact or an instance of occupying a given condition: *hopes for a better life in another incarnation.*
in·case (ĭn-kās′) *v.* Variant of **encase.**
in·cau·tious (ĭn-kô′shəs) *adj.* Not cautious; rash. **—in·cau′tious·ly** *adv.* **—in·cau′tious·ness** *n.*
in·cen·di·ar·y (ĭn-sĕn′dē-ĕr′ē) *adj.* **1. a.** Causing or capable of causing fire. **b.** Of or designating a device, esp. a military missile, containing chemicals that produce intensely hot fire when exploded. **c.** Of or involving arson. **2.** Tending to inflame; inflammatory. *—n., pl.* **-ies. 1.** An arsonist. **2.** An incendiary device. **3.** One who creates or stirs up factionism or sedition; agitator. [Lat. *incendiarius* < *incendium,* fire < *incendere,* to set on fire.] **—in·cen′di·a·rism** (-ə-rĭz′əm) *n.*
incendiary bomb *n.* A bomb used to start a fire.
in·cense[1] (ĭn-sĕns′) *tr.v.* **-censed, -cens·ing, -cens·es.** To cause to be angry; infuriate. [ME *encensen* < OFr. *incenser* < Lat. *incensus,* p.part. of *incendere,* to set on fire.]
in·cense[2] (ĭn′sĕns′) *n.* **1.** An aromatic substance, as a gum or wood, that burns with a pleasant odor. **2.** The smoke or odor produced by the burning of incense. **3.** A pleasant smell. **4.** Flattery or adulation. *—tr.v.* **-censed, -cens·ing, -cens·es. 1.** To perfume with incense. **2.** To burn incense to, as a ritual offering. [ME *encens* < OFr. < LLat. *incensum* < Lat., neuter p.part. of *incendere,* to set on fire.]
in·cen·tive (ĭn-sĕn′tĭv) *n.* Something, as the fear of punishment or the expectation of reward, that incites to action or effort. *—adj.* Inciting; motivating. [ME < Lat. *incentivum* < *incentivus,* inciting < *incentus,* p.part. of *incinere,* to sound : *in-* (intensive) + *canere,* to sing.]
in·cep·tion (ĭn-sĕp′shən) *n.* The beginning of something; commencement. [Lat. *inceptio* < *incipere,* to begin : *in-,* in + *capere,* to take.]
in·cep·tive (ĭn-sĕp′tĭv) *adj.* **1.** Incipient; beginning. **2.** *Gram.* Inchoative. *—n.* An inchoative verb.
in·cer·ti·tude (ĭn-sûr′tĭ-to͞od′, -tyo͞od′) *n.* **1.** Uncertainty. **2.** Absence of confidence; doubt. **3.** Insecurity or instability. [OFr. < LLat. *incertitudo* : *in-,* not + *certitudo,* certitude.]
in·ces·sant (ĭn-sĕs′ənt) *adj.* Continuing without respite or interruption; continuous. [LLat. *incessans, incessant-* : *in-,* not + *cessans,* pr.part. of *cessare,* to stop. —see CEASE.] **—in·ces′san·cy** *n.* **—in·ces′sant·ly** *adv.*
in·cest (ĭn′sĕst′) *n.* **1.** Sexual intercourse between persons who are so closely related that their marriage is illegal or forbidden by custom. **2.** The statutory crime of participating in an incestuous relationship. [ME < Lat. *incestum,* neuter of *incestus,* impure : *in-,* not + *castus,* pure, chaste.]
in·ces·tu·ous (ĭn-sĕs′cho͞o-əs) *adj.* **1.** Of, involving, or suggestive of incest. **2.** Having committed incest. **—in·ces′tu·ous·ly** *adv.* **—in·ces′tu·ous·ness** *n.*
inch[1] (ĭnch) *n.* **1.** A unit of length in the U.S. Customary and British Imperial systems, equal to $^1/_{12}$ of a foot or 2.54 centimeters. **2. a.** A fall, as of rain or snow, sufficient to cover a surface to the depth of one inch. **b.** A unit or degree of atmospheric or other pressure as measured by a barometer or manometer that is equal to the pressure balanced by a one-inch column of liquid, usually mercury, in the measuring device. **3.** A very small degree or amount: *He won't budge an inch.* *—intr. & tr.v.* **inched, inch·ing, inch·es.** To move or cause to move slowly or by small degrees. ***—idioms.*** **every inch.** In every respect; entirely: *"Ay, every inch a king!"* (Shakespeare). **inch by inch.** Very gradually or slowly. **within an inch of.** Almost to the point of. [ME < OE *ynce* < Lat. *uncia,* twelfth part < *unus,* one.]
inch[2] (ĭnch) *n. Scot.* A small island. [ME < Sc. Gael. *innis.*]
inch·meal (ĭnch′mēl′) *adv.* Little by little; gradually. [INCH + (PIECE)MEAL.]
in·cho·ate (ĭn-kō′ĭt) *adj.* **1.** In an initial or early stage; incipient. **2.** Imperfectly formed or developed: *an inchoate idea.* [Lat. *inchoatus,* p.part. of *inchoare, incohare,* to begin : *in-,* in + *colum,* part of a yoke harness.] **—in·cho′ate·ly** *adv.* **—in·cho′ate·ness** *n.*
in·cho·a·tive (ĭn-kō′ə-tĭv) *adj.* **1.** Beginning; initial. **2.** *Gram.* Of or relating to a verb or verbal form that denotes the beginning of an action, state, or event. **—in·cho′a·tive** *n.* **—in·cho′a·tive·ly** *adv.*
inch·worm (ĭnch′wûrm′) *n.* A measuring worm.
in·ci·dence (ĭn′sĭ-dəns) *n.* **1.** An act, instance, or manner of affecting; occurrence. **2.** The extent or frequency of occurrence: *the high incidence of malaria in the tropics.* **3.** *Physics.* The arrival of incident radiation or of an incident projectile at a surface.
in·ci·dent (ĭn′sĭ-dənt) *n.* **1.** A definite and separate occurrence; event. **2.** A usually minor event or condition that is subordinate to another. **3.** Something contingent upon or related to something else. **4.** An occurrence or event that interrupts normal procedure or precipitates a crisis: *an international incident.* *—adj.* **1.** Tending to arise or occur as a concomitant: *delays and confusion incident to heavy holiday air traffic.* **2.** Related to or dependent on another thing. **3.** *Law.* Contingent upon or related to something else. **4.** *Physics.* Falling upon; striking: *incident radiation.* [ME < OFr. < Lat. *incidens,* pr.part. of *incidere,* to happen : *in-,* on + *cadere,* to fall.]
in·ci·den·tal (ĭn′sĭ-dĕn′tl) *adj.* **1.** Occurring or likely to occur as an unpredictable or minor concomitant: *the snags incidental to a changeover in upper management.* **2.** Of a minor, casual, or subordinate nature: *incidental expenses.* *—n.* Often **incidentals.** A minor concomitant circumstance, event, item, or expense.
in·ci·den·tal·ly (ĭn′sĭ-dĕn′tl-ē) *adv.* **1.** By chance; casually. **2.** (*also* ĭn′sĭ-dĕnt′lē). Apart from the main subject; parenthetically.
incidental music *n.* Music used in connection with a drama and intended to project a mood, played as background behind action or dialogue or as an interlude before and after each act.
in·cin·er·ate (ĭn-sĭn′ə-rāt′) *v.* **-at·ed, -at·ing, -ates.** *—tr.* To consume by burning. *—intr.* To burn or burn up. [Med. Lat. *incinerare, incinerat-* : Lat. *in-,* in + *cinis,* ashes.] **—in·cin′er·a′tion** *n.*
in·cin·er·a·tor (ĭn-sĭn′ə-rā′tər) *n.* One that incinerates, esp. a furnace or other apparatus for burning waste.
in·cip·i·ent (ĭn-sĭp′ē-ənt) *adj.* Beginning to exist or appear: *refuses to recognize the company's incipient financial problems.* [Lat. *incipiens, incipient-,* pr.part. of *incipere,* to begin. —see INCEPTION.] **—in·cip′i·en·cy, in·cip′i·ence** *n.* **—in·cip′i·ent·ly** *adv.*
in·cise (ĭn-sīz′) *tr.v.* **-cised, -cis·ing, -cis·es. 1.** To cut into or mark with a sharp instrument. **2. a.** To engrave (designs or writing, for example) into a surface; carve. **b.** To engrave designs, writing, or other pattern into. [OFr. *inciser* < Lat. *incisus,* p.part. of Lat. *incidere* : *in-,* in + *caedere,* to cut.]
in·cised (ĭn-sīzd′) *adj.* **1.** Cut into; engraved. **2.** Made with or as if with a sharp instrument. **3.** Deeply notched: *the incised margin of a leaf.*
in·ci·sion (ĭn-sĭzh′ən) *n.* **1.** The act of incising. **2. a.** A surgical cut into soft tissue. **b.** The scar resulting from such a cut. **3.** A notch, as in the edge of a leaf. **4.** Incisiveness.
in·ci·sive (ĭn-sī′sĭv) *adj.* **1.** Having or suggesting sharp mental perception. **2.** Direct and effective; telling: *incisive comments.* **—in·ci′sive·ly** *adv.* **—in·ci′sive·ness** *n.*
Synonyms: *incisive, trenchant, biting, cutting, crisp, clear-cut.* These adjectives are synonymous when they refer to thought or expression marked by keenness and forceful-

ness. *Incisive* and *trenchant* are applicable both to sharp mental perception and to its expression. They suggest the ability of the mind to penetrate to the heart of a subject and the power to express the thought thus formed clearly, usually succinctly, and very forcefully. *Biting* and *cutting* apply to expression capable of penetrating or making a sharp impression on another person, as through sarcasm. *Crisp,* in this comparison, refers to a style of expression that is clear, concise, and invigorating. *Clear-cut* specifies distinctness of outline and thus sharpness of definition of what is formed in the mind and then expressed.

in·ci·sor (ĭn-sī′zər) *n.* A tooth adapted for cutting, located at the apex of the dental arch.

in·ci·ta·tion (ĭn′sī-tā′shən) *n.* **1.** An act or instance of inciting; stimulation. **2.** Something that incites; incentive.

in·cite (ĭn-sīt′) *tr.v.* **-cit·ed, -cit·ing, -cites.** To provoke to action; stir up or urge on. [OFr. *inciter* < Lat. *incitare,* to urge forward : *in-* (intensive) + *citare,* to stimulate, freq. of *ciēre,* to put in motion.] **—in·cite′ment** *n.* **—in·cit′er** *n.*

Synonyms: *incite, instigate, foment, abet.* These verbs mean to stir a group of persons to action or to give support to such action. *Incite* primarily is applied to arousing the will and spirit to act, as by forceful oratory. *Instigate* refers to conceiving a plan of action, often one involving drastic change, and making it operative. *Foment* usually refers to the systematic arousing of feelings of discord, rebellion, or the like, which produce violent action. *Abet* implies either active aid or tacit approval of actions, especially acts in violation of what is right or proper.

in·ci·vil·i·ty (ĭn′sĭ-vĭl′ĭ-tē) *n., pl.* **-ties. 1.** The quality or condition of being uncivil. **2.** An uncivil or discourteous act.

in·clasp (ĭn-klăsp′) *v.* Variant of **enclasp.**

in·clem·ent (ĭn-klĕm′ənt) *adj.* **1.** Stormy. **2.** Severe or unmerciful. [Lat. *inclemens, inclement-,* harsh, severe : *in-,* not + *clemens,* mild.] **—in·clem′en·cy** *n.* **—in·clem′ent·ly** *adv.*

in·clin·a·ble (ĭn-klī′nə-bəl) *adj.* **1.** Favorably disposed; amenable. **2.** *Archaic.* Disposed or inclined to do something.

in·cli·na·tion (ĭn′klə-nā′shən) *n.* **1.** An attitude or disposition toward something. **2.** A trend or general tendency toward a particular aspect, condition, or character. **3.** Something for which one has a preference or leaning: *"I shall indulge the inclination so natural in old men, to be talking of themselves"* (Franklin). **4.** The act of inclining, as a bow. **5.** The state of being inclined; tilt. **6. a.** A deviation from a definite direction, esp. from a horizontal or vertical. **b.** The degree of deviation from a horizontal or vertical.

in·cline (ĭn-klīn′) *v.* **-clined, -clin·ing, -clines.** *—intr.* **1.** To deviate from a horizontal or vertical; slant. **2.** To be disposed to a certain preference, opinion, or disposition. **3.** To lower or bend the head or body, as in a nod or bow. *—tr.* **1.** To cause to lean, slant, or slope. **2.** To influence to have a certain tendency; dispose: *Recent events inclined him to distrust all politicians.* **3.** To bend or lower in a nod or bow. *—n.* (ĭn′klīn′). An inclined surface; slope or gradient. [ME *enclinen* < OFr. *encliner* < Lat. *inclinare* : *in-,* toward + *clinare,* to lean.] **—in·clin′er** *n.*

in·clined (ĭn-klīnd′) *adj.* **1.** Having a preference, disposition, or tendency. **2.** Sloping, slanting, or leaning.

inclined plane *n.* A plane inclined to the horizontal, a simple machine used to raise or lower a load by rolling or sliding.

in·cli·nom·e·ter (ĭn′klə-nŏm′ĭ-tər) *n.* **1.** An instrument used to determine magnetic dip. **2.** An instrument for showing the inclination of an airplane or ship relative to the horizontal. **3.** A clinometer.

in·close (ĭn-klōz′) *v.* Variant of **enclose.**

in·clude (ĭn-klo͞od′) *tr.v.* **-clud·ed, -clud·ing, -cludes. 1.** To have or take in as a part or member; contain. **2.** To put into a group, class, or total. [ME *includen* < Lat. *includere,* to enclose : *in-,* in + *claudere,* to close.] **—in·clud′a·ble, in·clud′i·ble** *adj.*

Synonyms: *include, comprise, comprehend, embrace, involve.* These verbs mean to take in or contain one or more things as part of something larger. *Include* and *comprise* both take as their objects things or persons that are constituent parts. *Comprise* usually implies that all of the components are stated: *The track meet comprises 15 events* (that is, consists of or is composed of). *Include* can be so used, but, like the remaining terms, more often implies an incomplete listing: *The meet includes among its high points a return match between leading sprinters. Comprehend* and *embrace* usually refer to the taking in of intangibles as part of a broader subject: *Law and order comprehend much more than exercise of police power. A person's tastes in reading need not embrace every subject fashionable at the moment. Involve* usually suggests the relationship of a thing that is a logical consequence or required condition of something more inclusive: *A heavy scholastic schedule involves extra effort.*

Usage: *Include* is used most appropriately before an incomplete list of components: *The ingredients of the cake include butter and egg yolk.* If all the components are named, it is generally clearer to write: *The ingredients are. . . .*

in·clud·ed (ĭn-klo͞o′dĭd) *adj.* **1.** *Bot.* Not protruding beyond a surrounding part, as stamens that do not project from a corolla. **2.** Formed by and between two intersecting straight lines: *an included angle.*

in·clu·sion (ĭn-klo͞o′zhən) *n.* **1.** The act of including or the state of being included. **2.** Something included. **3.** A solid, liquid, or gaseous foreign body enclosed in a mineral or rock. **4.** *Biol.* A nonliving mass in cytoplasm. **5.** *Computer Sci.* A logical operation that assumes the second statement of a pair is true if the first one is true. [Lat. *inclusio* < *inclusus,* p.part. of *includere,* to enclose. —see INCLUDE.]

inclusion body *n.* An abnormal structure in a cell nucleus or cytoplasm having characteristic staining properties and associated esp. with the presence of filterable viruses.

in·clu·sive (ĭn-klo͞o′sĭv) *adj.* **1.** Taking a great deal or everything within its scope; comprehensive. **2.** Including the specified extremes or limits as well as the area between them: *the numbers one to ten, inclusive.* **—in·clu′sive·ly** *adv.* **—in·clu′sive·ness** *n.*

inclusive of *prep.* Taking into consideration or account; including.

in·co·er·ci·ble (ĭn′kō-ûr′sə-bəl) *adj.* Incapable of coercion.

in·cog·i·tant (ĭn-kŏj′ĭ-tənt) *adj.* Thoughtless; inconsiderate. [Lat. *incogitans, incogitant-* : *in-,* not + *cogitans,* pr.part. of *cogitare,* to think. —see COGITATE.]

in·cog·ni·ta (ĭn-kŏg′nĭ-tə, ĭn′kŏg-nē′tə) *adj. & adv.* With one's identity disguised or concealed. Used of a woman. [Ital., fem. of *incognito,* incognito.] **—in·cog′ni·ta** *n.*

in·cog·ni·to (ĭn-kŏg′nĭ-tō′, ĭn′kŏg-nē′tō) *adj. & adv.* With one's identity disguised or concealed. *—n.* **1.** One who is incognito. **2.** The condition of being incognito. [Ital. < Lat. *incognitus,* unknown : *in-,* not + *cognitus,* p.part. of *cognoscere,* to learn. —see COGNITION.]

in·cog·ni·zant (ĭn-kŏg′nĭ-zənt) *adj.* Lacking knowledge or awareness of something; unaware.

in·co·her·ence (ĭn′kō-hîr′əns) *n.* **1.** The condition or quality of being incoherent. **2.** Something incoherent.

in·co·her·en·cy (ĭn′kō-hîr′ən-sē) *n., pl.* **-cies.** Incoherence.

in·co·her·ent (ĭn′kō-hîr′ənt) *adj.* **1.** Not coherent; lacking order, connection, or harmony. **2.** Unable to think or express one's thoughts in a clear or orderly manner: *incoherent with grief.* **—in′co·her′ent·ly** *adv.* **—in′co·her′ent·ness** *n.*

in·com·bus·ti·ble (ĭn′kəm-bŭs′tə-bəl) *adj.* Incapable of burning. *—n.* An incombustible object or material. [ME < Med. Lat. *incombustibilis* : Lat. *in-,* not + Lat. *combustus,* p.part. of *comburere,* to burn up. —see COMBUSTION.] **—in′com·bus′ti·bil′i·ty** *n.* **—in′com·bus′ti·bly** *adv.*

in·come (ĭn′kŭm′) *n.* **1.** The amount of money or its equivalent received during a period of time in exchange for labor or services, from the sale of goods or property, or as profit from financial investments. **2.** *Archaic.* An influx. [ME, enhance, arrival : *in,* in + *comen,* to come.]

income tax *n.* A tax levied on annual income.

in·com·ing (ĭn′kŭm′ĭng) *adj.* **1.** Coming in; entering. **2.** About to come in: *the incoming president.* *—n.* **1.** The act of coming in; arrival. **2.** Often **incomings.** Income; revenue.

in·com·men·su·ra·ble (ĭn′kə-mĕn′sər-ə-bəl, -shər-) *adj.* **1. a.** Incapable of being measured. **b.** Lacking a common quality upon which to make a comparison. **2.** *Math.* Having no common measure. *—n.* Something that is incommensurable. **—in′com·men′su·ra·bil′i·ty** *n.* **—in′com·men′su·ra·bly** *adv.*

in·com·men·su·rate (ĭn′kə-mĕn′sər-ĭt, -shər-) *adj.* **1. a.** Not commensurate; disproportionate: *a reward incommensurate with his efforts.* **b.** Inadequate. **2.** Incommensurable. **—in′com·men′su·rate·ly** *adv.* **—in′com·men′su·rate·ness** *n.*

in·com·mode (ĭn′kə-mōd′) *tr.v.* **-mod·ed, -mod·ing, -modes.** To cause to be inconvenienced; disturb. [Fr. *incommoder* < OFr. < Lat. *incommodare* < *incommodus,* inconvenient : *in-,* not + *commodus,* convenient. —see COMMODIOUS.]

in·com·mo·di·ous (ĭn′kə-mō′dē-əs) *adj.* Inconvenient or uncomfortable, as by not affording sufficient space. **—in′com·mo′di·ous·ly** *adv.* **—in′com·mo′di·ous·ness** *n.*

in·com·mod·i·ty (ĭn′kə-mŏd′ĭ-tē) *n., pl.* **-ties. 1.** Inconvenience. **2.** Something that is inconvenient.

in·com·mu·ni·ca·ble (ĭn′kə-myo͞o′nĭ-kə-bəl) *adj.* **1.** Not communicable. **2.** *Rare.* Incommunicative. **—in′com·mu′ni·ca·bil′i·ty** *n.* **—in′com·mu′ni·ca·bly** *adv.*

in·com·mu·ni·ca·do (ĭn′kə-myo͞o′nĭ-kä′dō) *adj.* Without the means or right of communicating with others, as one held in solitary confinement. [Sp., p.part. of *incomunicar,* to deny communication : *in-,* not (< Lat.) + *comunicar,* to communicate < Lat. *communicare* < *communis,* common.] **—in′com·mu′ni·ca′do** *adv.*

in·com·mu·ni·ca·tive (ĭn′kə-myo͞o′nĭ-kā′tĭv, -kə-tĭv) *adj.* Not communicative; uncommunicative. **—in′com·mu′ni·ca′tive·ly** *adv.* **—in′com·mu′ni·ca′tive·ness** *n.*

in·com·mut·a·ble (ĭn′kə-myo͞o′tə-bəl) *adj.* **1.** Incapable of being exchanged. **2.** Not changeable; unalterable. **—in′com·mut′a·bil′i·ty, in′com·mut′a·ble·ness** *n.* **—in′com·mut′a·bly** *adv.*

in·com·pa·ra·ble (ĭn-kŏm′pər-ə-bəl) *adj.* **1.** Incapable of being compared; incommensurable. **2.** So outstanding as to be beyond comparison; unsurpassed. **—in·com′pa·ra·bil′i·ty, in·com′pa·ra·ble·ness** *n.* **—in·com′pa·ra·bly** *adv.*

in·com·pat·i·bil·i·ty (ĭn′kəm-păt′ə-bĭl′ĭ-tē) *n., pl.* **-ties. 1.** The state or quality of being incompatible. **2. incompati-**

bilities. Mutually exclusive or antagonistic qualities or things.

in·com·pat·i·ble (ĭn′kəm-păt′ə-bəl) *adj.* **1.** Incapable of blending or associating due to disharmony, incongruity, or antagonism. **2.** Incapable of being held simultaneously by one person, as offices. **3.** *Logic.* Incapable of being simultaneously true; mutually exclusive. —*n.* Often **incompatibles**. Incompatible elements, persons, or objects. [Med. Lat. *incompatibilis* : *in-*, not (< Lat.) + *compatibilis,* compatible.] **—in′com·pat′i·ble·ness** *n.* **—in′com·pat′i·bly** *adv.*

in·com·pe·tent (ĭn-kŏm′pĭ-tənt) *adj.* Not competent. —*n.* An incompetent person. **—in·com′pe·tence, in·com′pe·ten·cy** *n.* **—in·com′pe·tent·ly** *adv.*

in·com·plete (ĭn′kəm-plēt′) *adj.* **1.** Not complete. **2.** *Football.* Not caught or not caught in bounds. Used of a forward pass. **—in′com·plete′ly** *adv.* **—in′com·plete′ness, in′com·ple′tion** *n.*

in·com·pli·ant (ĭn′kəm-plī′ənt) *adj.* Not compliant; unyielding. **—in′com·pli′ance, in′com·pli′an·cy** *n.* **—in′com·pli′ant·ly** *adv.*

in·com·pre·hen·si·ble (ĭn′kŏm-prĭ-hĕn′sə-bəl, ĭn-kŏm′-) *adj.* **1.** Incapable of being understood or comprehended, as: **a.** Unintelligible. **b.** Unknowable; unfathomable. **2.** *Archaic.* Without limits; boundless. **—in′com·pre·hen′si·bil′i·ty, in′com·pre·hen′si·ble·ness** *n.* **—in′com·pre·hen′si·bly** *adv.*

in·com·pre·hen·sion (ĭn′kŏm-prĭ-hĕn′shən, ĭn-kŏm′-) *n.* Lack of comprehension or understanding.

in·com·pre·hen·sive (ĭn′kŏm-prĭ-hĕn′sĭv, ĭn-kŏm′-) *adj.* Not comprehensive or all-inclusive; limited in range or scope. **—in′com·pre·hen′sive·ly** *adv.* **—in′com·pre·hen′sive·ness** *n.*

in·com·press·i·ble (ĭn′kəm-prĕs′ə-bəl) *adj.* Incapable of being compressed. **—in′com·press′i·bil′i·ty** *n.*

in·com·put·a·ble (ĭn′kəm-pyōō′tə-bəl) *adj.* Incapable of being computed or calculated. **—in′com·put′a·bil′i·ty** *n.*

in·con·ceiv·a·ble (ĭn′kən-sē′və-bəl) *adj.* **1.** Incapable of being comprehended or fully grasped. **2.** So unlikely or surprising as to have been thought impossible; unbelieveable. **—in′con·ceiv′a·bil′i·ty, in′con·ceiv′a·ble·ness** *n.* **—in′con·ceiv′a·bly** *adv.*

in·con·cin·ni·ty (ĭn′kən-sĭn′ĭ-tē) *n.* Lack of congruity or harmony; unsuitability. [Lat. *inconcinnitas,* awkwardness < *inconcinnus,* awkward : *in-*, not + *concinnus,* skillfully put together.]

in·con·clu·sive (ĭn′kən-klōō′sĭv) *adj.* Not conclusive. **—in′con·clu′sive·ly** *adv.* **—in′con·clu′sive·ness** *n.*

in·con·den·sa·ble also **in·con·den·si·ble** (ĭn′kən-dĕn′sə-bəl) *adj.* Incapable of being condensed. **—in′con·den′sa·bil′i·ty** *n.*

in·con·dite (ĭn-kŏn′dĭt, -dīt′) *adj.* Badly constructed; crude. [Lat. *inconditus* : *in-*, not + *conditus,* p.part. of *condere,* to put together.] **—in·con′dite·ly** *adv.*

in·con·form·i·ty (ĭn′kən-fôr′mĭ-tē) *n.* Nonconformity.

in·con·gru·ent (ĭn-kŏng′grōō-ənt, ĭn′kŏn-grōō′ənt) *adj.* **1.** Not congruent. **2.** Incongruous. **—in·con′gru·ence** *n.* **—in·con′gru·ent·ly** *adv.*

in·con·gru·i·ty (ĭn′kŏn-grōō′ĭ-tē) *n., pl.* **-ties. 1.** Lack of congruence. **2.** The state or quality of being incongruous. **3.** Something that is incongruous.

in·con·gru·ous (ĭn-kŏng′grōō-əs) *adj.* **1.** Not corresponding; disagreeing: *a plan incongruous with good sense.* **2.** Made up of disparate, inconsistent, or discordant parts or qualities: *an incongruous group of people.* **3.** Not consistent with what is logical, customary, or correct; inappropriate: *an incongruous cheerfulness for such a somber occasion.* [Lat. *incongruus* : *in-*, not + *congruus,* congruous.] **—in·con′gru·ous·ly** *adv.* **—in·con′gru·ous·ness** *n.*

in·con·nec·tor (ĭn′kə-nĕk′tər) *n.* A flow-chart symbol that indicates continuation of a broken line of flow.

in·con·se·quent (ĭn-kŏn′sĭ-kwənt) *adj.* **1.** Not obtained as a result. **2.** Not derived from the premises or obtained by logic or reason; irrelevant. **3.** Proceeding without logical sequence; haphazard. **4.** Out of character with the nature or style of something. **5.** Unimportant; insignificant. [LLat. *inconsequens, inconsequent-* : Lat. *in-*, not + *consequens,* consequent.] **—in·con′se·quence** *n.* **—in·con′se·quent·ly** *adv.*

in·con·se·quen·tial (ĭn-kŏn′sĭ-kwĕn′shəl) *adj.* **1.** Without consequence; lacking importance; petty. **2.** Inconsequent. —*n.* A triviality. **—in·con′se·quen′ti·al′i·ty** (-kwĕn′shē-ăl′ĭ-tē), **in·con′se·quen′tial·ness** *n.* **—in·con′se·quen′tial·ly** *adv.*

in·con·sid·er·a·ble (ĭn′kən-sĭd′ər-ə-bəl) *adj.* Too small or unimportant to merit attention or consideration; trivial. **—in′con·sid′er·a·ble·ness** *n.* **—in′con·sid′er·a·bly** *adv.*

in·con·sid·er·ate (ĭn′kən-sĭd′ər-ĭt) *adj.* Not considerate; thoughtless of others. [Lat. *inconsideratus* : *in-*, not + *consideratus,* considerate.] **—in′con·sid′er·ate·ly** *adv.* **—in′con·sid′er·ate·ness, in′con·sid′er·a′tion** *n.*

in·con·sis·tence (ĭn′kən-sĭs′təns) *n.* Inconsistency.

in·con·sis·ten·cy (ĭn′kən-sĭs′tən-sē) *n., pl.* **-cies. 1.** The state or quality of being inconsistent. **2.** Something that is inconsistent.

in·con·sis·tent (ĭn′kən-sĭs′tənt) *adj.* **1.** Not consistent, esp.: **a.** Not regular or predictable; erratic. **b.** Lacking in correct logical relation; contradictory: *inconsistent statements.* **c.** Not in agreement or harmony; incompatible: *an intersection inconsistent with the road map.* **2.** *Math.* Not solvable for the unknowns by the same set of values. **—in′con·sis′tent·ly** *adv.*

Synonyms: *inconsistent, incongruous, incompatible, discordant, uncongenial.* These adjectives mean in marked disagreement. *Inconsistent* describes what reveals lack of uniformity in overall purpose, design, procedure, or content. Human thought or behavior is *inconsistent* when a succession of individual acts reveals basic disagreement or contradiction; two or more accounts of a single occurrence are *inconsistent* when they differ in important details. *Incongruous* implies disagreement that shows up noticeably or even glaringly. The term is frequently applied to human behavior or speech at odds with a person's character or temperament, or improper under the circumstances, and to things that reveal lack of harmony in design or that clash with surroundings. *Incompatible* refers to what is unsuited to coexistence, to persons of differing temperaments, and to things that have fundamental differences or contradictions. *Discordant* implies a relationship of persons or things marked by clash of termperaments, opinions, or principles. *Uncongenial* suggests a less stridently unharmonious relationship involving persons or persons and their environments.

in·con·sol·a·ble (ĭn′kən-sō′lə-bəl) *adj.* Incapable of being consoled or comforted; despondent. **—in′con·sol′a·bil′i·ty, in′con·sol′a·ble·ness** *n.* **—in′con·sol′a·bly** *adv.*

in·con·so·nant (ĭn-kŏn′sə-nənt) *adj.* Lacking harmony, agreement, or compatibility; discordant. **—in·con′so·nance** *n.* **—in·con′so·nant·ly** *adv.*

in·con·spic·u·ous (ĭn′kən-spĭk′yōō-əs) *adj.* Not readily noticeable. **—in′con·spic′u·ous·ly** *adv.* **—in′con·spic′u·ous·ness** *n.*

in·con·stan·cy (ĭn-kŏn′stən-sē) *n., pl.* **-cies.** The state or quality of being inconstant.

in·con·stant (ĭn-kŏn′stənt) *adj.* **1.** Not remaining the same; likely to change, esp. often and without discernible pattern or reason. **2.** Fickle; faithless. **—in·con′stant·ly** *adv.*

in·con·sum·a·ble (ĭn′kən-sōō′mə-bəl) *adj.* Incapable of being consumed. **—in′con·sum′a·bly** *adv.*

in·con·test·a·ble (ĭn′kən-tĕs′tə-bəl) *adj.* Incapable of being contested; unquestionable: *incontestable proof.* **—in′con·test′a·bil′i·ty, in′con·test′a·ble·ness** *n.* **—in′con·test′a·bly** *adv.*

in·con·ti·nence (ĭn-kŏn′tə-nəns) *n.* The quality or state of being incontinent.

in·con·ti·nent (ĭn-kŏn′tə-nənt) *adj.* Not continent, esp.: **a.** Not restrained; uncontrolled. **b.** Incapable of controlling the excretory functions. [ME < OFr. < Lat. *incontinens,* unrestrained : *in-*, not + *continens,* restrained. —see CONTINENT[2].] **—in·con′ti·nent·ly** *adv.*

in·con·trol·la·ble (ĭn′kən-trō′lə-bəl) *adj.* Not controllable.

in·con·tro·vert·i·ble (ĭn-kŏn′trə-vûr′tə-bəl) *adj.* Incapable of being disputed; unquestionable. **—in·con′tro·vert′i·bil′i·ty, in·con′tro·vert′i·ble·ness** *n.* **—in·con′tro·vert′i·bly** *adv.*

in·con·ven·ience (ĭn′kən-vēn′yəns) *n.* **1.** The state or quality of being inconvenient. **2.** Something that is inconvenient. —*tr.v.* **-ienced, -ienc·ing, -ienc·es.** To cause inconvenience to or for; trouble.

in·con·ven·ient (ĭn′kən-vēn′yənt) *adj.* Not convenient, esp.: **a.** Not accessible or handy. **b.** Difficult or awkward to perform. **c.** Inopportune; untimely. [ME < OFr. < Lat. *inconveniens* : *in-*, not + *conveniens,* convenient.] **—in′con·ven′ient·ly** *adv.*

in·con·vert·i·ble (ĭn′kən-vûr′tə-bəl) *adj.* **1.** Incapable of being converted or exchanged. **2.** Not redeemable for money in coin: *inconvertible paper currency.* **—in′con·vert′i·bil′i·ty, in′con·vert′i·ble·ness** *n.* **—in′con·vert′i·bly** *adv.*

in·con·vinc·i·ble (ĭn′kən-vĭn′sə-bəl) *adj.* Incapable of being convinced.

in·co·or·di·nate (ĭn′kō-ôr′dn-ĭt, -āt′) *adj.* Lacking coordination; uncoordinated. **—in′co·or′di·nate·ly** *adv.*

in·co·or·di·na·tion (ĭn′kō-ôr′dn-ā′shən) *n.* Lack of coordination, esp. lack of the ability to exercise normal voluntary control of relatively complex muscular movement.

in·cor·po·rate (ĭn-kôr′pə-rāt′) *v.* **-rat·ed, -rat·ing, -rates.** —*tr.* **1.** To unite with or blend indistinguishably into something already in existence. **2.** To admit as a member to a corporation or similar organization. **3.** To cause to merge or combine together into a united whole. **4.** To cause to form into a legal corporation. **5.** To give substance or material form to; embody. —*intr.* **1.** To become united or combined into an organized body. **2.** To form a legal corporation. —*adj.* (-pər-ĭt). **1.** Combined into one united body; merged. **2.** Formed into a legal corporation. [ME *incorporaten* < LLat. *incorporare,* to form into a body : Lat. *in-*, in + Lat. *corpus,* body.] **—in·cor′po·ra·ble** (-pə-rə-bəl) *adj.* **—in·cor′po·ra′tion** *n.* **—in·cor′po·ra′tive** *adj.* **—in·cor′po·ra′tor** *n.*

in·cor·po·rat·ed (ĭn-kôr′pə-rā′tĭd) *adj.* **1.** United into one body; combined. **2.** Formed into or organized and maintained as a legal business corporation.

in·cor·po·rat·ing (ĭn-kôr′pə-rā′tĭng) *adj.* Polysynthetic.

in·cor·po·re·al (ĭn′kôr-pôr′ē-əl, -pōr′-) *adj.* **1.** Lacking material form or substance. **2.** *Law.* Intangible, as a right or patent. [< Lat. *incorporeus* : *in-*, not + *corpus*, body.] **—in′cor·po′re·al·ly** *adv.*

in·cor·po·re·i·ty (ĭn-kôr′pə-rē′ĭ-tē) *n.* The state or quality of being incorporeal; immateriality. [< Lat. *incorporeus*, incorporeal.]

in·cor·rect (ĭn′kə-rĕkt′) *adj.* Not correct, esp.: **a.** Erroneous; wrong. **b.** Defective; faulty. **c.** Improper; inappropriate. **—in′cor·rect′ly** *adv.* **—in′cor·rect′ness** *n.*

in·cor·ri·gi·ble (ĭn-kôr′ĭ-jə-bəl, -kŏr′-) *adj.* **1.** Incapable of being corrected or reformed: *an incorrigible criminal.* **2.** Firmly rooted; ineradicable. **3.** Not manageable or controllable. *—n.* One that will not be corrected or reformed. [ME < LLat. *incorrigibilis* : Lat. *in-*, not + Lat. *corrigere*, to correct. —see CORRECT.] **—in·cor′ri·gi·bil′i·ty, in·cor′ri·gi·ble·ness** *n.* **—in·cor′ri·gi·bly** *adv.*

in·cor·rupt (ĭn′kə-rŭpt′) *adj.* **1.** Not corrupt or immoral. **2.** Not decayed; unspoiled. **3.** Not marred by errors or faults. [ME < Lat. *incorruptus* : *in-*, not + *corruptus*, corrupt.] **—in′cor·rupt′ly** *adv.* **—in′cor·rupt′ness** *n.*

in·cor·rupt·i·ble (ĭn′kə-rŭp′tə-bəl) *adj.* **1.** Incapable of being corrupted morally. **2.** Not subject to corruption or decay. **—in′cor·rupt′i·bil′i·ty** *n.* **—in′cor·rupt′i·bly** *adv.*

in·crease (ĭn-krēs′) *v.* **-creased, -creas·ing, -creas·es.** *—intr.* **1.** To become greater or larger. **2.** To multiply; reproduce. *—tr.* To make greater or larger. *—n.* (ĭn′krēs′). **1.** The act of increasing. **2.** The amount or rate by which something is increased: *a tax increase of ten per cent.* **3.** *Archaic.* Reproduction and spread; propagation. [ME *encresen* < OFr. *encreistre, encreiss-* < Lat. *increscere* : *in-*, in + *crescere*, to grow.] **—in·creas′a·ble** *adj.* **—in·creas′er** *n.* **—in·creas′ing·ly** *adv.*

Synonyms: *increase, magnify, enlarge, expand, extend, augment, grow.* These verbs mean to become greater or to make greater. They vary considerably with respect to areas of application. *Increase* has a broad range, since it pertains to greatness in quality, physical dimensions, rate, as of productivity, degree, or intensity. *Magnify* refers principally to making larger physically, in appearance or actuality, or figuratively by exaggeration. *Enlarge* refers to increase in size, volume, or range. To *extend* is to lengthen in space or time or to broaden, figuratively, in range of application. To *augment* is to add to something so as to increase it in amount or degree. To *grow* is to increase in size, amount, strength, scope, or influence, usually by progressive stages.

in·cre·ate (ĭn′krē-āt′, ĭn-krē′ĭt) *adj.* Existing without having been created. **—in′cre·ate′ly** *adv.*

in·cred·i·ble (ĭn-krĕd′ə-bəl) *adj.* **1.** Too implausible to be believed; unbelievable. **2.** Hard to believe; astonishing. [ME < Lat. *incredibilis* : *in-*, not + *credibilis*, credible.] **—in·cred′i·ble·ness** *n.* **—in·cred′i·bly** *adv.*

in·cre·du·li·ty (ĭn′krĭ-do͞o′lĭ-tē, -dyo͞o′-) *n.* The state or quality of being incredulous; disbelief.

in·cred·u·lous (ĭn-krĕj′ə-ləs) *adj.* **1.** Disbelieving; skeptical: *incredulous of flying-saucer stories.* **2.** Expressing disbelief: *an incredulous stare.* [Lat. *incredulus* : *in-*, not + *credulus*, credulous.] **—in·cred′u·lous·ly** *adv.* **—in·cred′u·lous·ness** *n.*

in·cre·ment (ĭn′krə-mənt, ĭng′-) *n.* **1.** An increase in number, size, or extent. **2.** Something added or gained. **3.** A small increase in quantity. **4.** One of a series of regular additions or contributions. **5.** *Math.* A small positive or negative change in a variable. [ME < Lat. *incrementum* < neuter p.part. of *increscere*, to increase.] **—in′cre·men′tal** (-mĕn′tl) *adj.* **—in′cre·men′tal·ly** *adv.*

in·cre·men·tal·ism (ĭn′krə-mĕn′tl-ĭz′əm) *n.* Social or political gradualism. **—in′cre·men′tal·ist** *n.*

in·cres·cent (ĭn-krĕs′ənt) *adj.* Showing a progressively larger lighted surface; waxing. Used of the moon. [Lat. *increscens, increscent-*, pr.part. of *increscere*, to increase.]

in·cre·tion (ĭn-krē′shən) *n.* **1.** The process of internal secretion characteristic of endocrine glands. **2.** The product of incretion; hormone. [IN-² + (SE)CRETION.]

in·crim·i·nate (ĭn-krĭm′ə-nāt′) *tr.v.* **-nat·ed, -nat·ing, -nates.** To charge with or involve in a crime or other wrongful act. [LLat. *incriminare, incriminat-* : Lat. *in-*, in + Lat. *crimen*, crime.] **—in·crim′i·na′tion** *n.* **—in·crim′i·na·to′ry** (-nə-tôr′ē, -tōr′ē) *adj.*

in·crust (ĭn-krŭst′) *v.* Variant of **encrust.**

in·cu·bate (ĭn′kyə-bāt′, ĭng′-) *v.* **-bat·ed, -bat·ing, -bates.** *—tr.* **1.** To warm (eggs), as by bodily heat, so as to promote embryonic development and the hatching of young; brood. **2.** To maintain (a bacterial culture, for example) at optimum environmental conditions for development. **3.** To cause to develop; foment. *—intr.* **1.** To brood eggs. **2.** To develop and hatch. **3.** To undergo incubation. [Lat. *incubare, incubat-*, to lie down on : *in-*, on + *cubare*, to lie down.] **—in′cu·ba′tive** *adj.*

in·cu·ba·tion (ĭn′kyə-bā′shən, ĭng′-) *n.* **1. a.** The act of incubating. **b.** The state of being incubated. **2.** *Med.* The development of an infection from the time of its entry into or initiation within an organism up to the time of the first appearance of signs or symptoms. **—*modifier:*** *an incubation period.* **—in′cu·ba′tion·al** *adj.* **—in′cu·ba′tive** *adj.*

in·cu·ba·tor (ĭn′kyə-bā′tər, ĭng′-) *n.* One that incubates, esp.: **a.** A cabinet in which a uniform temperature can be maintained, used in growing bacterial cultures. **b.** An apparatus for maintaining an infant, esp. a premature infant, in an environment of controlled temperature, humidity, and oxygen. **c.** A temperature-controlled enclosure for hatching eggs artificially.

in·cu·bus (ĭn′kyə-bəs, ĭng′-) *n., pl.* **-bus·es** or **-bi** (-bī′). **1.** An evil spirit believed to descend upon and have sexual intercourse with sleeping women. **2.** A nightmare. **3.** Something that is oppressively or nightmarishly burdensome. [ME < LLat. < Lat. *incubare*, to lie down on. —see INCUBATE.]

in·cu·des (ĭng-kyo͞o′dēz) *n.* Plural of **incus.**

in·cul·cate (ĭn-kŭl′kāt′, ĭn′kŭl-) *tr.v.* **-cat·ed, -cat·ing, -cates.** To teach or impress by urging or frequent repetition; instill. [Lat. *inculcare, inculcat-*, to force upon : *in-*, in + *calcare*, to trample < *calx*, heel.] **—in′cul·ca′tion** *n.* **—in·cul′ca′tor** *n.*

in·cul·pa·ble (ĭn-kŭl′pə-bəl) *adj.* Free from guilt; blameless.

in·cul·pate (ĭn-kŭl′pāt′, ĭn′kŭl-) *tr.v.* **-pat·ed, -pat·ing, -pates.** To incriminate. [LLat. *inculpare, inculpat-* : Lat. *in-*, on + Lat. *culpare*, to blame < *culpa*, fault.] **—in′cul·pa′tion** *n.* **—in·cul′pa·to′ry** (-pə-tôr′ē, -tōr′ē) *adj.*

in·cult (ĭn-kŭlt′) *adj.* Not cultured; coarse. [Lat. *incultus* : *in-*, not + *cultus*, p.part. of *colere*, to till.]

in·cum·ben·cy (ĭn-kŭm′bən-sē) *n., pl.* **-cies. 1.** The condition or quality of being incumbent. **2.** Something that is incumbent. **3. a.** The holding and administering of an office or ecclesiastical benefice. **b.** The term of such an office or benefice.

in·cum·bent (ĭn-kŭm′bənt) *adj.* **1.** Lying, leaning, or resting on something else. **2.** Imposed as an obligation or duty; obligatory. **3.** Currently holding a specified office: *the incumbent mayor.* *—n.* A person who holds an office or ecclesiastical benefice. [ME < Lat. *incumbens*, pr.part. of *incumbere*, to lean upon : *in-*, on + *cumbere*, to recline.] **—in·cum′bent·ly** *adv.*

in·cu·nab·u·lum (ĭn′kyə-năb′yə-ləm, ĭng′-) *n., pl.* **-la** (-lə). **1.** A book printed before 1501. **2.** An artifact of an early period. [< Lat. *incunabula* (pl.), swaddling clothes, cradle : *in-*, in + *cunabula*, cradle, infancy < *cunae*, cradle.] **—in′cu·nab′u·lar** (-lər) *adj.*

in·cur (ĭn-kûr′) *tr.v.* **-curred, -cur·ring, -curs.** To become liable or subject to, esp. as a result of one's own actions; bring upon oneself: *incur heavy expenses.* [Lat. *incurrere*, to run upon : *in-*, in + *currere*, to run.]

in·cur·a·ble (ĭn-kyo͝or′ə-bəl) *adj.* **1.** Not curable: *an incurable disease.* **2.** Not capable of being reformed or dissuaded; stubborn: *an incurable optimist.* **—in·cur′a·bil′i·ty, in·cur′a·ble·ness** *n.* **—in·cur′a·bly** *adv.*

in·cu·ri·ous (ĭn-kyo͝or′ē-əs) *adj.* Not curious; uninterested. [Lat. *incuriosus*, careless : *in-*, not + *curiosus*, careful < *cura*, care.] **—in·cu′ri·os′i·ty** (-ŏs′ĭ-tē), **in·cu′ri·ous·ness** *n.* **—in·cu′ri·ous·ly** *adv.*

in·cur·rent (ĭn-kûr′ənt) *adj.* Affording passage to an inflowing current. [Lat. *incurrens, incurrent-*, pr.part. of *incurrere*, to run upon. —see INCUR.]

in·cur·sion (ĭn-kûr′zhən, -shən) *n.* **1.** A sudden attack on or invasion of hostile territory; raid. **2.** An act of entering or raiding another's territory or domain. [ME < OFr. < Lat. *incursio* < *incursus*, p.part. of *incurrere*, to run upon. —see INCUR.]

in·cur·vate (ĭn-kûr′vāt′, ĭn′kûr-vāt′) *tr.v.* **-vat·ed, -vat·ing, -vates.** To cause to bend into an inward curve. *—adj.* (-kûr′vāt′, -vĭt). Curved inward. **—in′cur·va′tion** *n.* **—in·cur′va·ture′** (-cho͝or′, -chər) *n.*

in·curve (ĭn-kûrv′, ĭn′kûrv′) *tr. & intr.v.* **-curved, -curv·ing, -curves.** To bend into an inward curve. *—n.* (ĭn′kûrv′). An inward curve. [Lat. *incurvare* : *in-*, in + *curvus*, curve.]

in·cus (ĭng′kəs) *n., pl.* **in·cu·des** (ĭng-kyo͞o′dēz). An anvil-shaped bone in the mammalian middle ear. [Lat. *incus*, anvil < *incusus*, p.part. of *incudere*, to forge with a hammer : *in-*, in + *cudere*, to beat, forge.]

in·cuse (ĭn-kyo͞oz′, -kyo͞os′) *adj.* Formed by hammering, stamping, or pressing: *an incuse design on a coin.* [Lat. *incusus*, p.part. of *incudere*, to forge with a hammer. —see INCUS.]

in·da·ba (ĭn-dä′bə) *n.* A conference of indigenous tribes in southern Africa. [Zulu *in-daba*, matter for discussion.]

in·da·mine (ĭn′də-mēn′) *n.* Any of a group of organic bases that form unstable bluish or greenish salts used as dyes. [IND(IGO) + AMINE.]

in·debt·ed (ĭn-dĕt′ĭd) *adj.* Morally, socially, or legally obligated to another; beholden. [ME *endetted* < OFr. *endette* < p.part. of *endetter*, to oblige : *en-*, in (< Lat. *in-*) + *dette*, debt. —see DEBT.]

in·debt·ed·ness (ĭn-dĕt′ĭd-nĭs) *n.* **1.** The state of being indebted. **2.** Something that is owed to another.

in·de·cen·cy (ĭn-dē′sən-sē) *n., pl.* **-cies. 1.** The state or quality of being indecent. **2.** Something that is indecent.

in·de·cent (ĭn-dē′sənt) *adj.* **1.** Offensive to good taste; unseemly. **2.** Offensive to public moral values; immodest. **—in·de′cent·ly** *adv.*

in·de·ci·pher·a·ble (ĭn′dĭ-sī′fər-ə-bəl) *adj.* Incapable of being deciphered. **—in′de·ci′pher·a·bil′i·ty, in′de·ci′pher·a·ble·ness** *n.*

in·de·ci·sion (ĭn′dĭ-sĭzh′ən) *n.* Inability or reluctance to make up one's mind; irresolution.

in·de·ci·sive (ĭn′dĭ-sī′sĭv) *adj.* **1.** Not decisive; inconclusive. **2.** Prone to or characterized by indecision; irresolute.

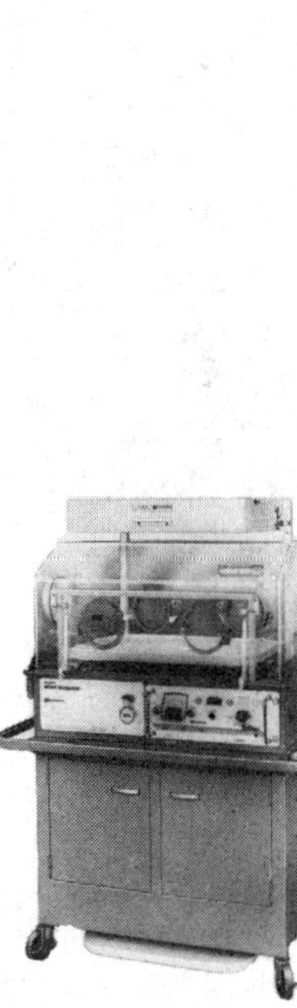

incubator
Incubator for an infant

3. Not clearly defined; indefinite. **—in'de·ci'sive·ly** *adv.* **—in'de·ci'sive·ness** *n.*

in·de·clin·a·ble (ĭn'dĭ-klī'nə-bəl) *adj.* Having no set of grammatical inflections.

in·de·com·pos·a·ble (ĭn-dē'kəm-pō'zə-bəl) *adj.* Not capable of being split into component parts.

in·dec·o·rous (ĭn-dĕk'ər-əs) *adj.* Lacking propriety or good taste. **—in·dec'o·rous·ly** *adv.* **—in·dec'o·rous·ness** *n.*

in·de·cor·um (ĭn'dĭ-kôr'əm, -kōr'-) *n.* **1.** Lack of decorum; impropriety. **2.** An instance of indecorous behavior or action.

in·deed (ĭn-dēd') *adv.* **1.** Without a doubt; certainly; truly. **2.** In fact; in reality. **3.** Admittedly; unquestionably. *—interj.* Used to express surprise, skepticism, or irony. [ME *indede,* in fact : *in,* in + *dede,* deed.]

in·de·fat·i·ga·ble (ĭn'dĭ-făt'ĭ-gə-bəl) *adj.* Incapable of being fatigued; tireless. [Lat. *indefatigabilis* : *in-,* not + *defatigare* to tire out (*de-,* thoroughly + *fatigare,* to weary).] **—in'de·fat'i·ga·bil'i·ty, in'de·fat'i·ga·ble·ness** *n.* **—in'de·fat'i·ga·bly** *adv.*

in·de·fea·si·ble (ĭn'dĭ-fē'zə-bəl) *adj.* Not capable of being annulled or made void. **—in'de·fea'si·bil'i·ty** *n.* **—in'de·fea'si·bly** *adv.*

in·de·fec·ti·ble (ĭn'dĭ-fĕk'tə-bəl) *adj.* **1.** Having the ability to resist defect or failure; lasting. **2.** Without flaw or defect; perfect. **—in'de·fec'ti·bil'i·ty** *n.* **—in'de·fec'ti·bly** *adv.*

in·de·fen·si·ble (ĭn'dĭ-fĕn'sə-bəl) *adj.* Not capable of being defended, esp.: **a.** Inexcusable; unpardonable. **b.** Invalid; untenable. **c.** Vulnerable to physical attack. **—in'de·fen'si·bil'i·ty, in'de·fen'si·ble·ness** *n.* **—in'de·fen'si·bly** *adv.*

in·de·fin·a·ble (ĭn'dĭ-fī'nə-bəl) *adj.* Not capable of being defined, described, or analyzed. *—n.* One that is indefinable. **—in'de·fin'a·ble·ness** *n.* **—in'de·fin'a·bly** *adv.*

in·def·i·nite (ĭn-dĕf'ə-nĭt) *adj.* Not definite, esp.: **a.** Unclear; vague. **b.** Lacking precise limits. **c.** Uncertain; undecided. [Lat. *indefinitus* : *in-,* not + *definitus,* definite.] **—in·def'i·nite·ly** *adv.* **—in·def'i·nite·ness** *n.*

indefinite article *n. Gram.* An article, as English *a* or *an,* that does not fix the identity of the noun modified.

indefinite integral *n. Math.* The set of all functions of which a given function is the derivative, usually represented by $\int f(x)dx + C$, where $\int f(x)dx$ is any member of the set and C is an arbitrary constant.

indefinite pronoun *n. Gram.* A pronoun, as English *any* or *some,* that does not specify the identity of its object.

in·de·his·cent (ĭn'dĭ-hĭs'ənt) *adj.* Not splitting open at maturity: *indehiscent fruit.* **—in'de·his'cence** *n.*

in·del·i·ble (ĭn-dĕl'ə-bəl) *adj.* **1.** Incapable of being removed, erased, or washed away; permanent. **2.** Making a mark not easily erased or washed away: *an indelible laundry pencil.* [Lat. *indelebilis* : *in-,* not + *delebilis,* capable of being destroyed < *delēre,* to destroy.] **—in·del'i·bil'i·ty, in·del'i·ble·ness** *n.* **—in·del'i·bly** *adv.*

in·del·i·ca·cy (ĭn-dĕl'ĭ-kə-sē) *n., pl.* **-cies. 1.** The quality or condition of being indelicate. **2.** Something that is indelicate.

in·del·i·cate (ĭn-dĕl'ĭ-kĭt) *adj.* **1. a.** Offensive to or lacking in propriety. **b.** Bordering on vulgarity; coarse. **2.** Prone to or marked by lack of sensitivity to the feelings of others; tactless. **—in·del'i·cate·ly** *adv.* **—in·del'i·cate·ness** *n.*

in·dem·ni·fi·ca·tion (ĭn-dĕm'nə-fĭ-kā'shən) *n.* **1. a.** The act of indemnifying. **b.** The condition of being indemnified. **2.** Something that indemnifies; indemnity.

in·dem·ni·fy (ĭn-dĕm'nə-fī') *tr.v.* **-fied, -fy·ing, -fies. 1.** To protect against damage, loss, or injury; insure. **2.** To make compensation to for damage, loss, or injury suffered. [< Lat. *indemnis,* uninjured : *in-,* not + *damnum,* harm.] **—in·dem'ni·fi'er** *n.*

in·dem·ni·ty (ĭn-dĕm'nĭ-tē) *n., pl.* **-ties. 1.** Security against damage, loss, or injury. **2.** A legal exemption from liability for damages. **3.** Compensation for damage, loss, or injury suffered. [ME *indempnite* < AN < LLat. *indemnitas* < Lat. *indemnis,* uninjured. —see INDEMNIFY.]

in·de·mon·stra·ble (ĭn'dĭ-mŏn'strə-bəl) *adj.* Incapable of being proved or demonstrated. **—in'de·mon'stra·ble·ness, in'de·mon'stra·bil'i·ty** *n.* **—in'de·mon'stra·bly** *adv.*

in·dene (ĭn'dēn') *n.* A colorless organic liquid, C_9H_8, obtained from coal tar and used in preparing synthetic resins. [IND(OLE) + -ENE.]

in·dent¹ (ĭn-dĕnt') *v.* **-dent·ed, -dent·ing, -dents.** *—tr.* **1. a.** To cut or tear (a document with two or more copies) along an irregular line so that the parts can later be matched for establishing authenticity. **b.** To draw up (a document) in duplicate or triplicate. **2. a.** To notch or serrate the edge of; make jagged. **b.** To make notches, grooves, or holes in (wood, for example) for the purpose of mortising. **c.** To fit or join together by or as if by mortising. **3.** To set (the first line of a paragraph, for example) in from the margin. **4.** *Chiefly Brit.* To order (goods) by purchase order or official requisition. *—intr.* **1.** To form an indentation. **2.** *Chiefly Brit.* To draw up or order an indent. *—n.* (ĭn-dĕnt', ĭn'dĕnt'). **1.** An indenture. **2.** A U.S. certificate issued at the close of the Revolutionary War for interest due on the public debt. **3.** *Chiefly Brit.* An official requisition or purchase order for goods. **4.** An indention. [ME *endenten,* to notch < OFr. *endenter* < Med. Lat. *indentare* : Lat. *in-,* in + Lat. *dens,* tooth.] **—in·dent'er** *n.*

in·dent² (ĭn-dĕnt') *tr.v.* **-dent·ed, -dent·ing, -dents. 1.** To make a dent in. **2.** To impress (a design, for example); stamp. *—n.* (ĭn-dĕnt', ĭn'dĕnt'). An indentation.

in·den·ta·tion (ĭn'dĕn-tā'shən) *n.* **1. a.** The act of indenting. **b.** The condition of being indented. **2.** A notch or jagged cut in an edge. **3.** A recess in a border, coastline, or other boundary. **4.** The blank space between a margin and the beginning of an indented line.

in·den·tion (ĭn-dĕn'shən) *n.* **1. a.** The act of indenting. **b.** The condition of being indented. **2.** The blank space between a margin and the beginning of an indented line. **3.** *Archaic.* An indentation or dent.

in·den·ture (ĭn-dĕn'chər) *n.* **1. a.** A document in duplicate having indented edges. **b.** A legal deed or contract executed between two or more parties. **c.** Often **indentures.** A contract binding one party into the service of another for a specified term. **d.** An official or authenticated inventory, list, or voucher. **2.** Indentation. *—tr.v.* **-tured, -tur·ing, -tures. 1.** To bind into the service of another by indenture. **2.** *Archaic.* To form an indentation in. [ME *endenture,* a written agreement < AN < OFr. *endenter,* to indent.]

in·de·pend·ence (ĭn'dĭ-pĕn'dəns) *n.* **1.** The state or quality of being independent. **2.** *Archaic.* Sufficient income for self-support; competence.

Independence Day *n.* July 4, a U.S. legal holiday celebrating the anniversary of the adoption of the Declaration of Independence in 1776.

in·de·pend·en·cy (ĭn'dĭ-pĕn'dən-sē) *n., pl.* **-cies. 1.** Independence. **2.** An independent territory or state. **3. Independency.** The Independent movement in 17th-century England.

in·de·pend·ent (ĭn'dĭ-pĕn'dənt) *adj.* **1.** Politically autonomous; self-governing. **2.** Free from the influence, guidance, or control of another or others; self-reliant: *an independent mind.* **3.** Not determined or influenced by someone or something else; not contingent: *an independent study of air pollution.* **4.** Affiliated with or loyal to no one political party or organization: *an independent voter.* **5.** Not dependent on or affiliated with a larger or controlling group or system: *an independent food store.* **6. a.** Financially self-sufficient; self-supporting. **b.** Providing or being sufficient income to enable one to live without working: *a person of independent means.* **7.** *Math.* **a.** Not dependent on other variables: *an independent variable.* **b.** Of or pertaining to a system of equations no one of which is necessarily satisfied by a set of values of the independent variables that satisfy all the others. **c.** Of, pertaining to, describing, or being an outcome of a trial of a chance experiment the probability of which does not depend on the outcome of any other trial of the chance experiment. *—n.* **1.** One that is independent, esp. a voter who does not pledge allegiance to any one political party. **2. Independent.** A member of a movement in England in the 17th century advocating the political and religious independence of individual congregations. **3. Independent.** *Chiefly Brit.* A Congregationalist.

independent clause *n. Gram.* A clause that contains a subject, a verb, and sometimes an object and modifiers, and that is capable of standing alone as a complete sentence.

in-depth (ĭn'dĕpth') *adj.* Detailed; thorough: *an in-depth study.*

in·de·scrib·a·ble (ĭn'dĭ-skrī'bə-bəl) *adj.* **1.** Incapable of being described. **2.** Exceeding description: *indescribable delight.* **—in'de·scrib'a·bil'i·ty, in'de·scrib'a·ble·ness** *n.* **—in'de·scrib'a·bly** *adv.*

in·de·struc·ti·ble (ĭn'dĭ-strŭk'tə-bəl) *adj.* Incapable of being destroyed; unbreakable. **—in'de·struc'ti·bil'i·ty, in'de·struc'ti·ble·ness** *n.* **—in'de·struc'ti·bly** *adv.*

in·de·ter·min·a·ble (ĭn'dĭ-tûr'mə-nə-bəl) *adj.* **1.** Incapable of being fixed or measured; not ascertainable. **2.** Incapable of being finally settled or decided. **—in'de·ter'min·a·bly** *adv.*

in·de·ter·mi·na·cy (ĭn'dĭ-tûr'mə-nə-sē) *n.* The state or quality of being indeterminate.

in·de·ter·mi·nate (ĭn'dĭ-tûr'mə-nĭt) *adj.* **1. a.** Not precisely determined: *a person of indeterminate age.* **b.** Incapable of being determined. **c.** Lacking clarity or precision; vague. **d.** Not known in advance. **2.** *Bot.* Not terminating in a flower and continuing to grow at the apex: *an indeterminate inflorescence.* [ME *determinat* < LLat. *indeterminatus* : Lat. *in-,* not + *determinatus,* determinate.] **—in'de·ter'mi·nate·ly** *adv.* **—in'de·ter'mi·nate·ness, in'de·ter'mi·na'tion** *n.*

in·de·ter·min·ism (ĭn'dĭ-tûr'mə-nĭz'əm) *n.* **1.** Indeterminacy; unpredictability. **2.** The philosophical doctrine that in some circumstances volition occurs independent of physiological and psychological antecedents. **—in'de·ter'min·ist** *n.* **—in'de·ter'min·is'tic** *adj.*

in·dex (ĭn'dĕks') *n., pl.* **-dex·es** or **-di·ces** (-dĭ-sēz'). **1.** Something that serves to guide, point out, or otherwise facilitate reference, esp.: **a.** An alphabetized listing of names, places, and subjects included in a printed work that gives for each item the page on which it is mentioned. **b.** A series of notches cut into the edge of a book for easy access to chapters or other divisions. **c.** A table, file, or catalogue. **2.** Something that reveals or indicates; sign: *"Her face . . . was a fair index to her disposition"* (Samuel Butler).

3. A character (☞) used in printing to call attention to a particular paragraph or section. **4.** An indicator or pointer, as in a scientific instrument. **5.** *Math.* **a.** A number or symbol, often written as a subscript or superscript to a mathematical expression, that indicates an operation to be performed on, an ordering relation involving, or a use of the associated expression. **b.** A number derived from a formula used to characterize a set of data: *cost-of-living index.* **6. Index.** A list formerly published by Church authority for Roman Catholics restricting or forbidding the reading of certain books. —*tr.v.* **-dexed, -dex·ing, -dex·es. 1.** To furnish with an index: *index a book.* **2.** To enter in an index. **3.** To indicate or signal. **4.** To adjust through indexation. [Lat. *index, indic-,* forefinger, pointer < *indicare,* to indicate.] **—in'dex'er** *n.*

in·dex·a·tion (ĭn'dĕk-sā'shən) *n.* The linkage of economic factors, as wages, interest, or prices, to a cost-of-living index so they rise and fall within the rate of inflation.

index finger *n.* The finger next to the thumb.

index number *n.* A number indicating change in magnitude, as of price, wage, employment, or production shifts, relative to the magnitude at some specified point usually taken as 100.

index of refraction *n.* The ratio of the speed of light in a vacuum to the speed of light in a medium under consideration.

India ink *n.* **1.** A black pigment made from lampblack mixed with a binding agent and molded into cakes or sticks. **2.** A liquid ink made from India ink.

In·di·a·man (ĭn'dē-ə-mən) *n.* A large merchant ship formerly used on trade routes to India.

In·di·an (ĭn'dē-ən) *n.* **1.** A native or inhabitant of India or of the East Indies. **2.** A member of any of the aboriginal peoples of North America, South America, or the West Indies. **3.** Any of the native languages of the American Indians. **4.** The constellation Indus. —*adj.* **1.** Of or pertaining to India or the East Indies, their culture, or their people. **2.** Of or pertaining to the aboriginal people of North America, South America, or the West Indies. —See Usage note at **Native American.**

Indian agent *n.* An official representing the United States government in dealings with American Indians, esp. on reservations.

Indian almond *n.* A tree, *Terminalia catappa,* of tropical Asia, having fruit with edible seeds.

Indian bread *n.* Any of various plants, as the breadroot, having edible parts used by American Indians for food.

Indian club *n.* A bottle-shaped wooden club swung in the hand for gymnastic exercise.

Indian corn *n.* Corn (sense 1.c.).

Indian file *n.* Single file.

Indian giver *n. Informal.* One who gives something as a gift to another and then takes or demands it back.

Indian hemp *n.* Hemp.

Indian licorice *n.* The rosary pea.

Indian meal *n.* Cornmeal (sense 1).

Indian paintbrush *n.* Any of various plants of the genus *Castilleja,* having spikes of flowers surrounded by showy, brightly colored bracts.

Indian pipe *n.* A waxy white or sometimes pinkish saprophytic woodland plant, *Monotropa uniflora,* having scalelike leaves and a solitary, nodding flower.

Indian pudding *n.* A pudding made of cornmeal and milk and sweetened with molasses.

Indian red *n.* An iron oxide used as a paint and cosmetic pigment.

Indian summer *n.* **1.** A period of mild weather occurring in late autumn or early winter. **2.** A pleasant, tranquil, or flourishing period occurring at the end of something.

Indian tobacco *n.* A poisonous North American plant, *Lobelia inflata,* having light-blue flowers and rounded seed pods.

Indian turnip *n.* The jack-in-the pulpit.

Indian wrestling *n.* **1.** Arm wrestling. **2.** A form of wrestling in which two opponents lie supine in reversed position with their near arms and near raised legs locked and attempt to force each other's leg down. **3.** A form of wrestling in which two opponents stand facing each other with usually right hands interlocked and the outsides of their near feet set together and attempt to unbalance each other.

India paper *n.* **1.** A thin, uncoated, delicate paper made of vegetable fiber, used esp. for taking impressions of engravings. **2.** Bible paper.

India rubber *n.* Rubber (sense 1).

In·dic (ĭn'dĭk) *adj.* **1.** Of or pertaining to India, its people, or their culture. **2.** Of, pertaining to, or constituting the Indic languages. —*n.* A branch of the Indo-European language family that comprises the languages of the Indian subcontinent and Sri Lanka.

in·di·can (ĭn'dĭ-kăn') *n.* **1.** A potassium salt, C_8H_6NOSOK, found in sweat and urine that results from the conversion of tryptophan to indole by intestinal bacteria. **2.** A glucoside, $C_{14}H_{17}NO_6$, occurring in the indigo plant. [< Lat. *indicum,* indigo.]

in·di·cant (ĭn'dĭ-kənt) *n.* Something that serves to indicate.

in·di·cate (ĭn'dĭ-kāt') *tr.v.* **-cat·ed, -cat·ing, -cates. 1.** To demonstrate or point out: *indicate a route.* **2.** To serve as a sign, symptom, or token of; signify: *"The cracking and booming of the ice indicate a change of temperature"* (Thoreau). **3.** To suggest or demonstrate the necessity, expedience, or advisability of: *The symptoms indicate immediate surgery.* **4.** To state or express briefly: *indicated his wishes.* [Lat. *indicare, indicat-,* to show : *in-,* in + *dicare,* to proclaim.] **—in'di·ca·to'ry** (-kə-tôr'ē, -tōr'ē) *adj.*

in·di·ca·tion (ĭn'dĭ-kā'shən) *n.* **1.** The action of indicating. **2. a.** Something that indicates; sign. **b.** Something indicated as necessary or expedient. **3.** The degree indicated by a measuring instrument.

in·dic·a·tive (ĭn-dĭk'ə-tĭv) *adj.* **1.** Serving to indicate: *behavior indicative of anger.* **2.** *Gram.* Pertaining to, designating, or being a verb mood used to indicate that the denoted act or condition is an objective fact. —*n. Gram.* **1.** The indicative mood. **2.** A verb in the indicative mood. **—in·dic'a·tive·ly** *adv.*

in·di·ca·tor (ĭn'dĭ-kā'tər) *n.* **1.** One that indicates, as: **a.** A pointer or index. **b.** Any of various meters, gauges, or other instruments that are used to monitor the operation or condition of an engine, furnace, electrical network, reservoir, or other physical system. **c.** The needle, dial, or other registering device on such an instrument. **2.** *Chem.* Any of various substances, as litmus or phenolphthalein, that indicate the presence, absence, or concentration of a substance or the degree of reaction between two or more substances by means of a characteristic change, esp. in color. **3.** Any of various statistical values that collectively provide an indication of the stability of an economic system.

in·di·ces (ĭn'dĭ-sēz') *n.* A plural of **index.**

in·di·cia (ĭn-dĭsh'ə, -dĭsh'ē-ə) *pl.n.* **1.** Identifying marks; indications. **2.** Markings on bulk mailings used as a substitute for stamps or cancellations. [Lat., pl. of *indicium,* sign < *index,* index.]

in·dict (ĭn-dīt') *tr.v.* **-dict·ed, -dict·ing, -dicts. 1.** To accuse of a crime or other offense; charge. **2.** *Law.* To make a formal accusation or indictment against by the findings of a jury, esp. a grand jury. [Alteration of ME *enditen,* to accuse, write a document < AN *enditer,* to indite.] **—in·dict'a·ble** *adj.* **—in'dict·ee'** (ĭn'dī-tē') *n.* **—in·dict'er, in·dict'or** *n.*

in·dic·tion (ĭn-dĭk'shən) *n.* A 15-year cycle used as a chronological unit in ancient Rome and incorporated in some medieval systems. [ME *indiccioun* < LLat. *indictio,* proclamation, period of 15 years < *indicere,* to proclaim. —see INDITE.]

in·dict·ment (ĭn-dīt'mənt) *n.* **1. a.** The act of indicting. **b.** The state of being indicted. **2.** *Law.* A written statement charging a party with the commission of a crime or other offense, drawn up by a prosecuting attorney and found and presented by a grand jury.

in·dif·fer·ence (ĭn-dĭf'ər-əns, -dĭf'rəns) *n.* The state or quality of being indifferent.

in·dif·fer·en·cy (ĭn-dĭf'ər-ən-sē, -dĭf'rən-) *n. Archaic.* Indifference.

in·dif·fer·ent (ĭn-dĭf'ər-ənt, -dĭf'rənt) *adj.* **1.** Characterized by a lack of partiality or bias. **2.** Not mattering one way or the other; of no great importance. **3.** Having no marked feeling one way or the other; without a preference. **4.** Having no particular interest or concern; apathetic. **5.** Being neither too much nor too little; moderate. **6.** Being neither good nor bad; mediocre. **7.** Being neither right nor wrong. **8.** Not active or involved; neutral. **9.** *Biol.* Undifferentiated, as cells or tissue. [ME < OFr. < Lat. *indifferens* : *in-,* not + *differens,* different.] **—in·dif'fer·ent·ly** *adv.*

Synonyms: *indifferent, unconcerned, apathetic, incurious, detached, disinterested.* These adjectives mean marked by absence of interest or of self-interest. *Indifferent* and *unconcerned* can imply nothing beyond that, but sometimes they suggest that a person has a tendency to be aloof or unfeeling when a display of interest would be in order. *Apathetic* implies listlessness and lack of concern where interest would be expected or proper. *Incurious* stresses absence of intellectual interest or curiosity. *Detached* suggests absence of close involvement with the matter at hand, together with a striving for an objective, impersonal point of view, but not lack of interest. *Disinterested* implies impartiality and freedom from self-interest or desire for gain rather than lack of concern.

in·dif·fer·ent·ism (ĭn-dĭf'ər-ən-tĭz'əm, -dĭf'rən-) *n.* The belief that religions are all of like validity. **—in·dif'fer·ent·ist** *n.*

in·di·gen (ĭn'dĭ-jən, -jĕn') also **in·di·gene** (-jēn') *n.* One that is native or indigenous to an area. [Lat. *indigena.*]

in·di·gence (ĭn'dĭ-jəns) *n.* Neediness; poverty.

in·dig·e·nous (ĭn-dĭj'ə-nəs) *adj.* **1.** Occurring or living naturally in a particular area or environment; native. **2.** Intrinsic; innate. [LLat. *indigenus* < *indigena,* a native.] **—in·dig'e·nous·ly** *adv.* **—in·dig'e·nous·ness** *n.*

in·di·gent (ĭn'dĭ-jənt) *adj.* **1.** Lacking the means of subsistence; impoverished. **2.** *Archaic.* Lacking or deficient. —*n.* A destitute or needy person. [ME < OFr. < Lat. *indigens,* pr.part. of *indigēre,* to need : *indu,* in + *egēre,* to lack.] **—in'di·gent·ly** *adv.*

in·di·gest·ed (ĭn'dĭ-jĕs'tĭd, -dī-) *adj. Archaic.* **1. a.** Not carefully thought over or considered. **b.** Shapeless or chaotic. **2.** Not digested.

Indian corn

Indian paintbrush

Indian tobacco

in·di·gest·i·ble (ĭn'dĭ-jĕs'tə-bəl, -dī-) *adj.* Difficult or impossible to digest. **—in'di·gest'i·bil'i·ty** *n.* **—in'di·gest'i·bly** *adv.*
in·di·ges·tion (ĭn'dĭ-jĕs'chən, -dī-) *n.* **1.** Inability to digest something, esp. food. **2.** Discomfort or illness resulting from indigestion.
in·dign (ĭn-dīn') *adj. Obs.* **1.** Unworthy. **2.** Shameful; disgraceful. [ME *indigne* < OFr. < Lat. *indignus* : *in-*, not + *dignus,* worthy.]
in·dig·nant (ĭn-dĭg'nənt) *adj.* Characterized by or filled with indignation. **—in·dig'nant·ly** *adv.*
in·dig·na·tion (ĭn'dĭg-nā'shən) *n.* Anger aroused by something unjust, mean, or unworthy. [ME *indignacioun* < Lat. *indignatio* < *indignari,* to regard as unworthy : *in-*, not + *dignus,* worthy.]
in·dig·ni·ty (ĭn-dĭg'nĭ-tē) *n., pl.* **-ties. 1. a.** Humiliating, degrading, or abusive treatment. **b.** Something that offends a person's pride or sense of dignity; affront. **2.** *Obs.* The lack of dignity or honor. [Lat. *indignitas* < *indignus,* unworthy. — see INDIGN.]

indigo

in·di·go (ĭn'dĭ-gō') *n., pl.* **-gos** or **-goes. 1. a.** Any of various plants of the genus *Indigofera,* some of which yield a blue dyestuff. **b.** Any of several plants similar or related to the indigo. **2.** A blue dye obtained from indigo or other plants or produced synthetically. **3.** A dark blue to grayish purplish blue. [Sp. *indigo* < Lat. *indicum* < Gk. *indikon (pharmakon),* Indian (dye) < *India,* India.]
indigo bunting *n.* A small bird, *Passerina cyanea,* of North and Central America, the male of which has deep-blue plumage.
indigo snake *n.* A nonvenomous bluish-black snake, *Drymarchon corais,* of the southern United States and northern Mexico.
in·dig·o·tin (ĭn-dĭg'ə-tĭn, ĭn'dĭ-gō'-) *n.* A dark-blue crystalline compound, $C_{16}H_{10}N_2O_2$, the principal coloring matter of indigo. [INDIGO + -IN.]
in·di·rect (ĭn'dĭ-rĕkt', -dī-) *adj.* **1.** Diverging from a direct course; roundabout. **2. a.** Not straight to the point, as in speaking; circumlocutory. **b.** Not forthright and candid; devious. **3.** Not directly planned for; secondary: *indirect benefits.* **—in'di·rect'ly** *adv.* **—in'di·rect'ness** *n.*

Synonyms: *indirect, circuitous, roundabout.* These adjectives mean not leading directly to a destination. *Indirect* refers to any deviation from the shortest route between starting point and destination. *Circuitous* and *roundabout* are stronger in their suggestion of time-consuming deviation from a straight path; *circuitous* implies a twisting or winding course, and *roundabout* one that circles or winds. Figuratively, the terms are applied to procedure or discourse that is not straightforward. In this sense they can imply an effort to deceive or evade.

indirect discourse *n.* Discourse reporting the words of another with consequent grammatical changes to conform the reported statement to the sentence in which it is included.
in·di·rec·tion (ĭn'dĭ-rĕk'shən, -dī-) *n.* **1.** The quality or state of being indirect. **2.** Lack of direction; aimlessness. **3.** Lack of straightforwardness; deviousness.
indirect lighting *n.* Illumination by reflected or diffused light.
indirect object *n.* A grammatical object indirectly affected by the action of a verb, as *me* in *Sing me a song* and *the turtle* in *He feeds the turtle lettuce.*
indirect tax *n.* A tax demanded of persons who ultimately pass on the burden of the tax to others, esp. a tax on goods passed on to the consumer in the form of higher prices.
in·dis·creet (ĭn'dĭ-skrēt') *adj.* Lacking discretion; injudicious. **—in'dis·creet'ly** *adv.* **—in'dis·creet'ness** *n.*
in·dis·crete (ĭn'dĭ-skrēt') *adj.* Not divided or divisible into separate parts; unified.
in·dis·cre·tion (ĭn'dĭ-skrĕsh'ən) *n.* **1.** Lack of discretion; injudiciousness. **2.** An indiscreet act or remark.
in·dis·crim·i·nate (ĭn'dĭ-skrĭm'ə-nĭt) *adj.* **1.** Lacking in discrimination: *indiscriminate admiration of power.* **2.** Random; haphazard. **3.** Confused; motley. **4.** Not properly restrained; promiscuous. **—in'dis·crim'i·nate·ly** *adv.* **—in'dis·crim'i·nate·ness** *n.*
in·dis·crim·i·na·tion (ĭn'dĭ-skrĭm'ə-nā'shən) *n.* The condition or quality of being indiscriminate. **—in'dis·crim'i·na'tive** *adj.*
in·dis·pen·sa·ble (ĭn'dĭ-spĕn'sə-bəl) *adj.* **1.** Incapable of being dispensed with; essential. **2.** Incapable of being set aside or escaped; inevitable. *—n.* One that is indispensable. **—in'dis·pen'sa·bil'i·ty, in'dis·pen'sa·ble·ness** *n.* **—in'dis·pen'sa·bly** *adv.*
in·dis·pose (ĭn'dĭ-spōz') *tr.v.* **-posed, -pos·ing, -pos·es. 1.** To make averse; disincline. **2.** To render unfit; disqualify. **3.** To cause to be or feel ill; sicken.
in·dis·posed (ĭn'dĭ-spōzd') *adj.* **1.** Mildly ill. **2.** Averse; disinclined.
in·dis·po·si·tion (ĭn-dĭs'pə-zĭsh'ən) *n.* **1.** Aversion; disinclination. **2.** A minor ailment.
in·dis·put·a·ble (ĭn'dĭ-spyōō'tə-bəl) *adj.* Incapable of being disputed; undeniable. **—in'dis·put'a·ble·ness** *n.* **—in'dis·put'a·bly** *adv.*
in·dis·sol·u·ble (ĭn'dĭ-sŏl'yə-bəl) *adj.* **1.** Impossible to break or undo; binding: *an indissoluble contract.* **2.** Incapable of being dissolved, disintegrated, or decomposed. **—in'dis·sol'u·bil'i·ty, in'dis·sol'u·ble·ness** *n.* **—in'dis·sol'u·bly** *adv.*
in·dis·tinct (ĭn'dĭ-stĭngkt') *adj.* **1.** Not clearly delineated. **2. a.** Faint; dim. **b.** Vague; unclear. **—in'dis·tinct'ly** *adv.* **—in'dis·tinct'ness** *n.*
in·dis·tinc·tive (ĭn'dĭ-stĭngk'tĭv) *adj.* Lacking distinctive qualities; not distinctive. **—in'dis·tinc'tive·ly** *adv.* **—in'dis·tinc'tive·ness** *n.*
in·dis·tin·guish·a·ble (ĭn'dĭ-stĭng'gwĭ-shə-bəl) *adj.* Not distinguishable, esp.: **a.** Not readily perceptible. **b.** Without distinctive qualities. **—in'dis·tin'guish·a·ble·ness, in'dis·tin'guish·a·bil'i·ty** *n.* **—in'dis·tin'guish·a·bly** *adv.*
in·dite (ĭn-dīt') *tr.v.* **-dit·ed, -dit·ing, -dites. 1.** To write; compose. **2.** To set down in writing. **3.** *Obs.* To dictate. [ME *enditen,* to write a document < AN *enditer* < VLat. **indictare* < Lat. *indicere,* to proclaim : *in-*, toward + *dicere,* to say.] **—in·dite'ment** *n.* **—in·dit'er** *n.*
in·di·um (ĭn'dē-əm) *n. Symbol* **In** A soft, malleable, silvery-white metallic element found primarily in ores of zinc and tin, used as a plating over silver in making mirrors, in plating aircraft bearings, and in compounds for making transistors. Atomic number 49; atomic weight 114.82; melting point 156.61°C; boiling point 2,000°C; specific gravity 7.31; valences 1, 2, 3. [IND(IGO) + -IUM.]
in·di·vid·u·al (ĭn'də-vĭj'ōō-əl) *adj.* **1. a.** Of or relating to a single human being. **b.** By or for one person: *an individual portion.* **2.** Existing as a distinct entity; separate: *individual words.* **3.** Distinguished by particular attributes or identifying traits; distinctive: *an individual way of dressing.* **4.** Indivisible as an entity; inseparable. *—n.* **1. a.** A single human being considered separately from a group or from society. **b.** A single organism as distinguished from a group or colony. **2.** A particular person: *a disagreeable individual.* [ME, single, indivisible < Med. Lat. *individualis* < Lat. *individuus* : *in-*, not + *dividuus,* divisible < *dividere,* to divide.] **—in'di·vid'u·al·ly** *adv.*

Usage: *Individual* (noun) in the sense of "a person" is fittingly used when a single human being is distinguished from a group or mass, by contrast or by stress on a special quality: *the individual's right to dissent from a majority view; an individual to the core.* It is not acceptably used, according to a majority of the Usage Panel, when it is simply a substitute for *person: Two individuals were arrested for the crime.*

in·di·vid·u·al·ism (ĭn'də-vĭj'ōō-ə-lĭz'əm) *n.* **1.** Individuality. **2.** The assertion of one's own will and personality; personal independence. **3.** *Econ.* **a.** The theory that a citizen should have freedom in his economic pursuits and should succeed by his own initiative. **b.** The practice of this theory. **4.** The doctrine that the interests of the individual should take precedence over the interests of the state or social group.
in·di·vid·u·al·ist (ĭn'də-vĭj'ōō-ə-lĭst) *n.* **1.** One who asserts individuality by independence of thought and action. **2.** One who advocates individualism. **—in'di·vid'u·al·is'tic** *adj.* **—in'di·vid'u·al·is'ti·cal·ly** *adv.*
in·di·vid·u·al·i·ty (ĭn'də-vĭj'ōō-ăl'ĭ-tē) *n., pl.* **-ties. 1.** The quality of being individual; distinctness. **2.** The aggregate of qualities and characteristics that distinguish one person or thing from others. **3.** A single, distinct entity. **4.** *Archaic.* Indivisibility.
in·di·vid·u·al·ize (ĭn'də-vĭj'ōō-ə-līz') *tr.v.* **-ized, -iz·ing, -iz·es. 1.** To give individuality to. **2.** To consider or treat individually; particularize. **3.** To modify to suit the wishes or needs of a particular individual. **—in'di·vid'u·al·i·za'tion** *n.*
in·di·vid·u·ate (ĭn'də-vĭj'ōō-āt') *tr.v.* **-at·ed, -at·ing, -ates. 1.** To individualize. **2.** To form into a separate and distinct entity.
in·di·vid·u·a·tion (ĭn'də-vĭj'ōō-ā'shən) *n.* **1.** The act or process of individuating, esp. the process by which social individuals become differentiated one from the other. **2.** The condition of being individuated; individuality.
in·di·vis·i·ble (ĭn'də-vĭz'ə-bəl) *adj.* **1.** Incapable of being divided. **2.** *Math.* Incapable of being divided exactly. **—in'di·vis'i·ble·ness, in'di·vis'i·bil'i·ty** *n.* **—in'di·vis'i·bly** *adv.*
Indo– *pref.* **1.** India; East Indies: *Indochina.* **2.** Indo-European: *Indo-Hittite.* [Gk. < *Indos,* India.]
In·do-Ar·y·an (ĭn'dō-âr'ē-ən, -ăr'-) *adj.* **1.** Belonging to or characteristic of any of the Indo-European-speaking peoples of the Indian subcontinent. **2.** Indo-Iranian. *—n.* **1.** One of the Indo-Aryan peoples. **2.** Indo-Iranian.
in·doc·ile (ĭn-dŏs'əl) *adj.* Difficult to control or instruct; not docile. **—in'do·cil'i·ty** (ĭn'dō-sĭl'ĭ-tē, -dŏ-) *n.*
in·doc·tri·nate (ĭn-dŏk'trə-nāt') *tr.v.* **-nat·ed, -nat·ing, -nates. 1.** To instruct in a body of doctrine. **2.** To teach to accept a system of thought uncritically: *indoctrinating the workers with an incessant stream of propaganda.* **—in·doc'tri·na'tion** *n.*
In·do-Eu·ro·pe·an (ĭn'dō-yŏŏr'ə-pē'ən) *n.* **1. a.** A family of languages consisting of most of the languages of Europe as well as those of Iran, the Indian subcontinent, and other parts of Asia. **b.** Proto-Indo-European. **2.** A member of a people speaking an Indo-European language. **—In'do-Eu'ro·pe'an** *adj.*
In·do-Ger·man·ic (ĭn'dō-jər-măn'ĭk) *n.* Indo-European. **—In'do-Ger·man'ic** *adj.*
In·do-Hit·tite (ĭn'dō-hĭt'īt') *n.* **1.** A language family that in-

cludes Indo-European and Anatolian. **2.** The hypothetical parent language of Indo-European and Anatolian.
In·do-I·ra·ni·an (ĭn′dō-ĭ-rā′nē-ən) *n.* A subfamily of the Indo-European language family that comprises the Indic and Iranian branches. **—In′do-I·ra′ni·an** *adj.*
in·dole (ĭn′dōl′) *n.* A white crystalline compound, C_8H_7N, obtained from coal tar and used in perfumery and medicine and as a flavoring. [IND(IGO) + -OLE.]
in·dole·a·ce·tic acid (ĭn′dō-lə-sē′tĭk) *n.* A plant hormone, $C_{10}H_9NO_2$, that stimulates growth.
in·dole·am·ine (ĭn′dō-lăm′ēn, ĭn′dō-lə-mēn′) *n.* Any of various derivatives of indole containing an amine group.
in·do·lence (ĭn′də-ləns) *n.* Disinclination to exert oneself.
in·do·lent (ĭn′də-lənt) *adj.* **1. a.** Disinclined to exert oneself; habitually lazy. **b.** Conducive to inactivity or laziness; languorous. **c.** Marked by indolence: *an indolent yawn.* **2.** *Pathol.* Causing little or no pain: *an indolent tumor.* [LLat. *indolens, indolent-,* painless : Lat. *in-,* not + Lat. *dolens,* pr.part. of *dolēre,* to feel pain.] **—in′do·lent·ly** *adv.*
in·do·meth·a·cin (ĭn′dō-mĕth′ə-sĭn) *n.* An anti-inflammatory and analgesic drug, $C_{19}H_{16}ClNO_4$, used in the treatment of rheumatoid arthritis. [INDO(LE) + METH- + AC(ETIC ACID) + -IN.]
in·dom·i·ta·ble (ĭn-dŏm′ĭ-tə-bəl) *adj.* Incapable of being overcome, subdued, or vanquished; unconquerable. [LLat. *indomitabilis,* untameable : Lat. *in-,* not + *domitare,* to tame, freq. of *domare,* to subdue.] **—in·dom′i·ta·ble·ness** *n.* **—in·dom′i·ta·bly** *adv.*
In·do·ne·sian (ĭn′də-nē′zhən, -shən) *n.* **1.** A native or inhabitant of the Republic of Indonesia. **2.** A member of a hypothetical non-Malay race of Indonesia, Malaysia, and the Philippines, having both Mongoloid and Polynesian characteristics. **3. a.** A subfamily of Austronesian that includes Malay, Tagalog, and the languages of Indonesia. **b.** Bahasa Indonesia. *—adj.* Of or pertaining to Indonesia, its people, or their language.
in·door (ĭn′dôr′, -dōr′) *adj.* **1.** Of, pertaining to, or situated in the interior of a house or other building: *an indoor pool.* **2.** Carried on within doors: *an indoor party.*
in·doors (ĭn-dôrz′, -dōrz′) *adv.* In or into a house or other building.
in·dorse (ĭn-dôrs′) *v.* Variant of **endorse.**
In·dra (ĭn′drə) *n. Hinduism.* A principal Vedic deity associated with rain and thunder. [Skt. *Indraḥ.*]
in·draft (ĭn′drăft′, -dräft′) *n.* **1.** A pulling or drawing inward. **2.** An inward flow or current, as of air.
in·drawn (ĭn′drôn′) *adj.* **1.** Drawn in. **2.** Characterized by reserve.
in·du·bi·ta·ble (ĭn-dōō′bĭ-tə-bəl, -dyōō′-) *adj.* Too apparent to be doubted; unquestionable. **—in·du′bi·ta·bly** *adv.*
in·duce (ĭn-dōōs′, -dyōōs′) *tr.v.* **-duced, -duc·ing, -duc·es. 1.** To lead or move by influence or persuasion: *finally induced him to give up smoking.* **2. a.** To bring about the occurrence of; cause. **b.** To arouse by stimulating. **3.** To infer by inductive reasoning. **4.** *Physics.* To produce (an electric current or magnetic effect) by induction. [ME *inducen* < Lat. *inducere,* to bring in : *in-,* in + *ducere,* to lead.] **—in·duc′er** *n.* **—in·duc′i·ble** *adj.*
in·duce·ment (ĭn-dōōs′mənt, -dyōōs′-) *n.* **1.** The act or process of inducing. **2.** Something that induces or leads to action; motive. **3.** An introductory or background statement explaining the main allegations in a legal proceeding.
in·duct (ĭn-dŭkt′) *tr.v.* **-duct·ed, -duct·ing, -ducts. 1. a.** To place ceremoniously or formally in an office or position; install. **b.** To admit as a member; initiate. **c.** To admit to military service. **2.** *Physics.* To induce. [ME *inducten* < Lat. *inductus,* p.part. of *inducere,* to bring in. —see INDUCE.] **—in′duc·tee′** *n.*
in·duc·tance (ĭn-dŭk′təns) *n.* A circuit element, typically a conducting coil, in which electromotive force is generated by electromagnetic induction.
in·duc·tion (ĭn-dŭk′shən) *n.* **1.** The act of inducting or of being inducted. **2.** *Elect.* **a.** The generation of electromotive force in a closed circuit by a varying magnetic flux through the circuit. **b.** The charging of an isolated conducting object by momentarily grounding it while a charged body is nearby. **3. a.** The act or process of deriving general principles from particular facts or instances. **b.** *Math.* A deductive method of proof in which verification of a proposition consists of proving the first case and the case immediately following an arbitrary case for which the proposition is assumed to be correct. **4.** The act of adducing. **5.** *Archaic.* A preface or prologue esp. to a literary composition.
induction coil *n.* A transformer, often used in automotive ignition systems, in which an interrupted, low-voltage direct current in the primary is converted into an intermittent, high-voltage current in the secondary.
in·duc·tive (ĭn-dŭk′tĭv) *adj.* **1.** Of, relating to, or utilizing induction: *the inductive method.* **2.** *Elect.* Of or arising from inductance: *inductive reactance.* **3.** Causing or influencing; inducing. **4.** Introductory. **—in·duc′tive·ly** *adv.* **—in·duc′tive·ness** *n.*
inductive statistics *n.* The branch of statistics involving generalizations, predictions, estimations, and decisions from data initially presented.
in·duc·tor (ĭn-dŭk′tər) *n.* **1.** One that inducts. **2.** *Elect.* A device that functions by or introduces inductance into a circuit.
in·due (ĭn-dōō′, -dyōō′) *v.* Variant of **endue.**
in·dulge (ĭn-dŭlj′) *v.* **-dulged, -dulg·ing, -dulg·es.** *—tr.* **1.** To yield to the desires and whims of, esp. to an excessive degree; humor. **2. a.** To yield to; gratify: *indulge a craving for chocolate.* **b.** To allow (oneself) unrestrained gratification: *indulged herself with idle daydreams.* **3.** To grant an ecclesiastical indulgence or dispensation to. *—intr.* To indulge oneself. [Lat. *indulgēre,* to be kind.] **—in·dulg′er** *n.*
in·dul·gence (ĭn-dŭl′jəns) *n.* **1.** The act of indulging or the state of being indulgent. **2.** Something indulged in: *Sports cars are an expensive indulgence.* **3. a.** Something granted as a favor or privilege. **b.** Permission to extend the time of payment or performance. **4.** Liberal or lenient treatment; tolerance. **5.** *Rom. Cath. Ch.* The remission of punishment still due for a sin that has been sacramentally absolved. *—tr.v.* **-genced, -genc·ing, -genc·es.** *Rom. Cath. Ch.* To attach an indulgence to.
in·dul·gent (ĭn-dŭl′jənt) *adj.* Showing, characterized by, or given to indulgence; lenient. **—in·dul′gent·ly** *adv.*
in·dult (ĭn-dŭlt′) *n.* A usually temporary dispensation granted in the Roman Catholic Church. [ME < Med. Lat. *indultum* < Lat. *indultus,* p.part. of *indulgēre,* to be kind.]
in·du·pli·cate (ĭn-dōō′plĭ-kĭt, -dyōō′-) *adj. Bot.* Having the edges folded or turned inward. [IN- + Lat. *duplicatus,* doubled. —see DUPLICATE.]
in·du·rate (ĭn′də-rāt′, -dyə-) *v.* **-rat·ed, -rat·ing, -rates.** *—tr.* **1.** To make hard. **2.** To make hardy. **3.** To make callous. *—intr.* **1.** To harden. **2.** To become firmly fixed or established. *—adj.* (ĭn′dōō-rĭt, -dyə-). Hardened; obstinate; unfeeling. [Lat. *indurare, indurat-* : *in-* (intensive) + *durus,* hard.] **—in′du·ra′tion** *n.* **—in′du·ra′tive** *adj.*
In·dus (ĭn′dəs) *n.* A constellation in the Southern Hemisphere.
in·du·si·um (ĭn-dōō′zē-əm, -zhē-, -dyōō′-) *n., pl.* **-si·a** (-zē-ə, -zhē-ə). An enclosing membrane, as that covering the sorus of a fern. [Lat., tunic < *induere,* to put on.]
in·dus·tri·al (ĭn-dŭs′trē-əl) *adj.* **1.** Of, pertaining to, or derived from industry. **2.** Having highly developed industries: *an industrial nation.* **3.** Employed, required, or used in industry: *industrial manpower.* *—n.* **1.** A person employed in industry. **2.** An industrial firm. **3.** A stock or bond issued by an industrial enterprise.
industrial arts *pl.n. (used with a sing. verb).* A subject of study in schools aimed at developing the manual and technical skills required to work with tools and machinery.
in·dus·tri·al·ism (ĭn-dŭs′trē-ə-lĭz′əm) *n.* A system in which industries are dominant. **—in·dus′tri·al·ist** *n.*
in·dus·tri·al·ize (ĭn-dŭs′trē-ə-līz′) *v.* **-ized, -iz·ing, -iz·es.** *—tr.* To cause to be or become industrial. *—intr.* To become industrial. **—in·dus′tri·al·i·za′tion** *n.*
industrial park *n.* An area usually located on the outskirts of a city and zoned for a group of industries and businesses.
industrial psychology *n.* Psychology applied to such problems of industry as personnel selection, training, and efficiency. **—industrial psychologist** *n.*
industrial revolution *n.* Often **Industrial Revolution.** Radical social and economic changes, as those that took place in England in the late 18th century, brought about when extensive mechanization of production systems results in a shift from home manufacturing to large-scale factory production.
industrial union *n.* A labor union to which all the workers of a particular industry can belong regardless of their trade.
in·dus·tri·ous (ĭn-dŭs′trē-əs) *adj.* **1.** Diligently active; assiduous in work or study. **2.** *Obs.* Skillful; clever. **—in·dus′tri·ous·ly** *adv.* **—in·dus′tri·ous·ness** *n.*
in·dus·try (ĭn′də-strē) *n., pl.* **-tries. 1.** The commercial production and sale of goods and services. **2.** A specific branch of manufacture and trade: *the textile industry.* **3.** Industrial management as distinguished from labor. **4.** Diligence; assiduity. [ME *industrie,* skill < OFr. < Lat. *industria,* diligence.]
in·dwell (ĭn-dwĕl′) *v.* **-dwelt** (-dwĕlt′), **-dwell·ing, -dwells.** *—intr.* To exist as an energizing inner spirit, force, or principle. *—tr.* To exist or reside within as an energizing spirit, force, or principle. **—in′dwell′er** *n.*
-ine[1] *suff.* **1.** Of or pertaining to: *Benedictine.* **2.** Made of; resembling: *opaline.* [ME < OFr. *-in,* partly < Lat. *-īnus,* adj. suffix, and partly < Lat. *-inus* < Gk. *-inos,* adj. suffix.]
-ine[2] *suff.* **1.** A chemical substance: *azine.* **2.** Halogen: *bromine.* **3.** or **-in.** Alkaloid: *quinine.* **4.** A mixture of compounds: *gasoline.* **5.** Commercial material: *glassine.* **6.** Variant of **-in** (sense 1). [Fr. < Lat. *-ina,* fem. of *-inus,* of or belonging to.]
in·e·bri·ant (ĭn-ē′brē-ənt) *adj.* Intoxicating. *—n.* An intoxicant.
in·e·bri·ate (ĭn-ē′brē-āt′) *tr.v.* **-at·ed, -at·ing, -ates. 1.** To make drunk; intoxicate. **2.** To exhilarate or stupefy as if with alcohol. *—adj.* (ĭn-ē′brē-ĭt). Intoxicated. *—n.* (ĭn-ē′brē-ĭt). An intoxicated person, esp. a drunkard. [Lat. *inebriare, inebriat-* : *in-* (intensive) + *ebriare,* to intoxicate < *ebrius,* drunk.] **—in·e′bri·a′tion** *n.*
in·e·bri·at·ed (ĭn-ē′brē-ā′tĭd) *adj.* Exhilarated or stupefied by or as if by alcohol; intoxicated.
in·e·bri·e·ty (ĭn′ĭ-brī′ĭ-tē) *n.* Drunkenness; intoxication.

in·ed·i·ble (ĭn-ĕd′ə-bəl) *adj.* Not suitable for food; not edible.

in·ed·it·ed (ĭn-ĕd′ĭ-tĭd) *adj.* **1.** Not edited. **2.** Not published.

in·ef·fa·ble (ĭn-ĕf′ə-bəl) *adj.* **1.** Beyond expression; indescribable or unspeakable: *ineffable delight.* **2.** Not to be uttered; taboo: *the ineffable name of the Deity.* [ME < OFr. < Lat. *ineffabilis* : *in-*, not + *effabilis*, utterable < *effari*, to utter (*ex-*, out + *fari*, to speak).] **—in·ef′fa·bil′i·ty, in·ef′fa·ble·ness** *n.* **—in·ef′fa·bly** *adv.*

in·ef·face·a·ble (ĭn′ĭ-fā′sə-bəl) *adj.* Not effaceable; indelible. **—in′ef·face′a·bil′i·ty** *n.* **—in′ef·face′a·bly** *adv.*

in·ef·fec·tive (ĭn′ĭ-fĕk′tĭv) *adj.* **1.** Not producing an intended effect; ineffectual: *an ineffective plea.* **2.** Incapable of performing or accomplishing efficiently: *an ineffective teacher.* **—in′ef·fec′tive·ly** *adv.* **—in′ef·fec′tive·ness** *n.*

in·ef·fec·tu·al (ĭn′ĭ-fĕk′cho͞o-əl) *adj.* **1.** Not yielding an intended effect; vain. **2.** Lacking the ability to do or perform effectively: *an ineffectual ruler.* **—in′ef·fec′tu·al′i·ty, in′ef·fec′tu·al·ness** *n.* **—in′ef·fec′tu·al·ly** *adv.*

in·ef·fi·ca·cious (ĭn-ĕf′ĭ-kā′shəs) *adj.* Not capable of producing a desired effect or result; ineffective. **—in·ef′fi·ca′cious·ly** *adv.* **—in·ef′fi·ca′cious·ness** *n.*

in·ef·fi·ca·cy (ĭn-ĕf′ĭ-kə-sē) *n.* The state or quality of being inefficacious.

in·ef·fi·cien·cy (ĭn′ĭ-fĭsh′ən-sē) *n., pl.* **-cies. 1.** The quality, condition, or fact of being inefficient. **2.** Something inefficient.

in·ef·fi·cient (ĭn′ĭ-fĭsh′ənt) *adj.* **1.** Not efficient. **2.** Lacking in ability; incompetent. **3.** Wasteful of time, energy, or materials. **4.** Not producing the intended result. **—in′ef·fi′cient·ly** *adv.*

in·e·las·tic (ĭn′ĭ-lăs′tĭk) *adj.* **1.** Not elastic; unyielding. **2.** Not responding or adapting readily to change. **—in′e·las·tic′i·ty** (-ĭ-lă-stĭs′ĭ-tē) *n.*

in·el·e·gant (ĭn-ĕl′ĭ-gənt) *adj.* **1.** Lacking elegance. **2.** Lacking refinement or polish; coarse. [OFr. < Lat. *inelegans* : *in-*, not + *elegans*, elegant.] **—in·el′e·gant·ly** *adv.* **—in·el′e·gance** *n.*

in·el·i·gi·ble (ĭn-ĕl′ĭ-jə-bəl) *adj.* **1.** Not qualified for election to an office or position. **2.** Not worthy of being chosen. *—n.* A person who is not eligible. **—in·el′i·gi·bil′i·ty** *n.* **—in·el′i·gi·bly** *adv.*

in·el·o·quent (ĭn-ĕl′ə-kwənt) *adj.* Not eloquent. **—in·el′o·quence** *n.* **—in·el′o·quent·ly** *adv.*

in·e·luc·ta·ble (ĭn′ĭ-lŭk′tə-bəl) *adj.* Not to be avoided or overcome; inevitable. [Lat. *ineluctabilis* : *in-*, not + *eluctari*, to struggle out of (*ex-*, out + *luctari*, to struggle).] **—in′e·luc′ta·bil′i·ty** *n.* **—in′e·luc′ta·bly** *adv.*

in·ept (ĭn-ĕpt′) *adj.* **1.** Not suitable to the circumstances or occasion; inappropriate. **2.** Lacking in judgment, sense, or reason; foolish. **3.** Awkward or clumsy; incompetent. [Lat. *ineptus* : *in-*, not + *aptus*, suitable. —see APT.] **—in·ept′ly** *adv.* **—in·ept′ness, in·ep′ti·tude** *n.*

in·e·qual·i·ty (ĭn′ĭ-kwŏl′ĭ-tē) *n., pl.* **-ties. 1.** The condition of being unequal. **2.** Social or economic disparity. **3.** Unevenness; lack of smoothness or regularity. **4.** Variability; changeability. **5.** An instance of being unequal. **6.** *Math.* An algebraic statement that a quantity is greater than or is less than another quantity.

in·eq·ui·ta·ble (ĭn-ĕk′wĭ-tə-bəl) *adj.* Not equitable; unfair. **—in·eq′ui·ta·bly** *adv.*

in·eq·ui·ty (ĭn-ĕk′wĭ-tē) *n., pl.* **-ties. 1.** Injustice; unfairness. **2.** An instance of injustice or unfairness.

in·e·rad·i·ca·ble (ĭn′ĭ-răd′ĭ-kə-bəl) *adj.* Incapable of being eradicated. **—in′e·rad′i·ca·bly** *adv.*

in·er·rant (ĭn-ĕr′ənt) *adj.* Free from errors. **—in·er′ran·cy** *n.*

in·ert (ĭn-ûrt′) *adj.* **1.** Unable to move or act. **2.** Moving or acting very slowly; sluggish. **3.** *Chem.* **a.** Exhibiting no chemical activity; totally unreactive. **b.** Exhibiting chemical activity under special or extreme conditions only. [Lat. *iners, inert-*, inactive : *in-*, not + *ars*, skill.] **—in·ert′ly** *adv.* **—in·ert′ness** *n.*

in·er·tia (ĭn-ûr′shə) *n.* **1.** *Physics.* The tendency of a body to resist acceleration; the tendency of a body at rest to remain at rest or of a body in motion to stay in motion in a straight line unless disturbed by an external force. **2.** Resistance to motion, action, or change. [NLat. < Lat., idleness < *iners*, inert.] **—in·er′tial** *adj.* **—in·er′tial·ly** *adv.*

inertial frame *n.* A frame of reference relative to which the Newtonian law of motion, that a mass m subjected to a force F moves in accordance with the equation $F = ma$, where a is the acceleration, is valid.

inertial guidance *n.* Guidance in which gyroscopic and accelerometer data are used by a computer to maintain a predetermined course.

inertial platform *n.* The devices used in inertial guidance and their mounting platform.

inertia welding *n.* A welding of metals caused by the heat of friction from pressing a spinning metallic piece against a stationary one.

in·es·cap·a·ble (ĭn′ĭ-skā′pə-bəl) *adj.* Incapable of being escaped or avoided; inevitable. **—in′es·cap′a·bly** *adv.*

in·es·sen·tial (ĭn′ĭ-sĕn′shəl) *adj.* **1.** Not essential; unessential. **2.** Without essence. **—in·es·sen′tial** *n.* **—in′es·sen′ti·al′i·ty** *n.*

in·es·ti·ma·ble (ĭn-ĕs′tə-mə-bəl) *adj.* **1.** Incapable of being estimated or computed; indeterminable: *inestimable damage.* **2.** Of incalculable value. **—in·es′ti·ma·bly** *adv.*

infanta
Detail from "The Maids of Honor" by Diego Velázquez

in·ev·i·ta·ble (ĭn-ĕv′ĭ-tə-bəl) *adj.* Incapable of being avoided or prevented. **—in·ev′i·ta·bil′i·ty** *n.* **—in·ev′i·ta·bly** *adv.*

in·ex·act (ĭn′ĭg-zăkt′) *adj.* **1.** Not true, accurate, or precise. **2.** Not rigorous. **—in′ex·act′ly** *adv.* **—in′ex·act′ness** *n.*

in·ex·act·i·tude (ĭn′ĭg-zăk′tĭ-to͞od′, -tyo͞od′) *n.* Lack of exactitude; inexactness.

in·ex·cus·a·ble (ĭn′ĭk-skyo͞o′zə-bəl) *adj.* Not capable of being excused or justified; unpardonable. **—in′ex·cus′a·ble·ness** *n.* **—in′ex·cus′a·bly** *adv.*

in·ex·haust·i·ble (ĭn′ĭg-zô′stə-bəl) *adj.* **1.** Incapable of being entirely consumed or used up. **2.** Incapable of being tired out. **—in′ex·haust′i·bil′i·ty, in′ex·haust′i·ble·ness** *n.* **—in′ex·haust′i·bly** *adv.*

in·ex·is·tent (ĭn′ĭg-zĭs′tənt) *adj.* Having no existence; nonexistent. **—in′ex·is′tence** *n.*

in·ex·o·ra·ble (ĭn-ĕk′sər-ə-bəl) *adj.* Not capable of being persuaded by entreaty; unyielding. [Lat. *inexorabilis* : *in*, not + *exorabilis*, pliant < *exorare*, to prevail upon (ex- (intensive) + *orare*, to argue.] **—in·ex′o·ra·bil′i·ty** *n.* **—in·ex′o·ra·ble·ness** *n.* **—in·ex′o·ra·bly** *adv.*

in·ex·pe·di·ent (ĭn′ĭk-spē′dē-ənt) *adj.* Not expedient; inadvisable. **—in′ex·pe′di·ence, in′ex·pe′di·en·cy** *n.* **—in′ex·pe′di·ent·ly** *adv.*

in·ex·pen·sive (ĭn′ĭk-spĕn′sĭv) *adj.* Not high in price; cheap. **—in′ex·pen′sive·ly** *adv.* **—in′ex·pen′sive·ness** *n.*

in·ex·pe·ri·ence (ĭn′ĭk-spîr′ē-əns) *n.* **1.** Lack of experience. **2.** Lack of the knowledge gained from experience. **—in′ex·pe′ri·enced** *adj.*

in·ex·pert (ĭn-ĕk′spûrt′) *adj.* Not expert; unskilled. **—in·ex′pert′ly** *adv.* **—in·ex′pert′ness** *n.*

in·ex·pi·a·ble (ĭn-ĕk′spē-ə-bəl) *adj.* **1.** Not capable of being expiated or atoned for. **2.** *Obs.* Implacable. **—in·ex′pi·a·bly** *adv.*

in·ex·plain·a·ble (ĭn′ĭk-splā′nə-bəl) *adj.* Not explainable; inexplicable. **—in′ex·plain′a·bly** *adv.*

in·ex·pli·ca·ble (ĭn-ĕk′splĭ-kə-bəl, ĭn′ĭk-splĭk′ə-bəl) *adj.* Incapable of being explained or interpreted. **—in·ex′pli·ca·bil′i·ty, in·ex′pli·ca·ble·ness** *n.* **—in·ex′pli·ca·bly** *adv.*

in·ex·plic·it (ĭn′ĭk-splĭs′ĭt) *adj.* Not explicit; indefinite.

in·ex·press·i·ble (ĭn′ĭk-sprĕs′ə-bəl) *adj.* Incapable of being expressed; indescribable. **—in′ex·press′i·bil′i·ty, in′ex·press′i·ble·ness** *n.* **—in′ex·press′i·bly** *adv.*

in·ex·pug·na·ble (ĭn′ĭk-spŭg′nə-bəl, -spyo͞o′nə-) *adj.* Not capable of being overcome or overthrown; impregnable. **—in′ex·pug·na·bil′i·ty** *n.* **—in′ex·pug′na·bly** *adv.*

in·ex·ten·si·ble (ĭn′ĭk-stĕn′sə-bəl) *adj.* Not extensible.

in ex·ten·so (ĭn ĕk-stĕn′sō) *adv.* At full length. [Lat.]

in·ex·tin·guish·a·ble (ĭn′ĭk-stĭng′gwĭ-shə-bəl) *adj.* Not capable of being extinguished. **—in′ex·tin′guish·a·bly** *adv.*

in·ex·tir·pa·ble (ĭn′ĭk-stûr′pə-bəl) *adj.* Incapable of being eradicated or destroyed.

in ex·tre·mis (ĭn ĕk-strē′mĭs) *adv.* At the point of death. [Lat., in extreme (circumstances).]

in·ex·tri·ca·ble (ĭn-ĕk′strĭ-kə-bəl) *adj.* **1. a.** Incapable of being disentangled or untied. **b.** Too intricate or complicated to solve. **2.** Impossible to escape or get free of: *an inextricable bond.* **—in·ex′tri·ca·bil′i·ty, in·ex′tri·ca·ble·ness** *n.* **—in·ex′tri·ca·bly** *adv.*

in·fal·li·ble (ĭn-făl′ə-bəl) *adj.* **1.** Incapable of erring: *an infallible guide.* **2.** Incapable of failing; certain: *an infallible antidote.* **3.** *Rom. Cath. Ch.* Incapable of error in expounding doctrine on faith or morals. [Fr. < Med. Lat. *infallibilis* : Lat. *in-*, not + *fallibilis*, fallible.] **—in·fal′li·bil′i·ty, in·fal′li·ble·ness** *n.* **—in·fal′li·bly** *adv.*

in·fa·mous (ĭn′fə-məs) *adj.* **1.** Having an exceedingly bad reputation; notorious. **2.** Causing or deserving infamy. **3.** *Law.* Convicted of a crime, as treason or felony, that brings infamy. [ME < Med. Lat. *infamosus* < Lat. *infamis* : *in-*, not + *fama*, renown, fame.] **—in′fa·mous·ly** *adv.* **—in′fa·mous·ness** *n.*

in·fa·my (ĭn′fə-mē) *n., pl.* **-mies. 1.** Evil fame or reputation. **2.** The condition of being infamous. **3.** An evil or criminal act that is publicly known. [ME *infamie*, dishonor < OFr. < Lat. *infamia* < *infamis*, infamous.]

in·fan·cy (ĭn′fən-sē) *n., pl.* **-cies. 1.** The state or period of being an infant. **2.** An early stage of existence. **3.** *Law.* The state or period of being a minor.

in·fant (ĭn′fənt) *n.* **1.** A child in the earliest period of its life. **2.** *Law.* A person under the legal age of majority; minor. [ME < OFr. *enfant* < Lat. *infans* : *in-*, not + *fans*, pr.part. of *fari*, to speak.]

in·fan·ta (ĭn-făn′tə, -fän′-) *n.* A daughter of a Spanish or Portuguese king. [Sp. and Port., fem. of *infante*, infante.]

in·fan·te (ĭn-făn′tē, -fän′tā) *n.* A son of a Spanish or Portuguese king other than the heir to the throne. [Sp. and Port. < Lat. *infans*, infant.]

in·fan·ti·cide (ĭn-făn′tĭ-sīd′) *n.* **1.** The killing of an infant. **2.** A person who kills an infant. [LLat. *infanticidium*, the killing of a child, and *infanticida*, killer of a child : Lat. *infans*, infant + Lat. *caedere*, to kill.]

in·fan·tile (ĭn′fən-tīl′, -tĭl) *adj.* **1.** Of or relating to infants or infancy. **2.** Lacking in maturity; childish. [Fr. < Lat. *infantilis* < *infans*, infant.]

infantile autism *n.* Autism (sense 2).

infantile paralysis *n.* Poliomyelitis.

in·fan·til·ism (ĭn′fən-tə-lĭz′əm, ĭn-făn′tə-) *n.* A state of arrested development in an adult, characterized by a retention of infantile mentality accompanied by stunted growth and sexual immaturity.

in·fan·try (ĭn′fən-trē) *n., pl.* **-tries.** The branch of an army made up of units trained to fight on foot. [Fr. *infanterie* < Ital. *infanteria* < *infante,* youth, foot soldier < Lat. *infans,* infant.]

in·fan·try·man (ĭn′fən-trē-mən) *n.* A soldier in the infantry.

infant school *n. Chiefly Brit.* A kindergarten.

in·farct (ĭn′färkt′, ĭn-färkt′) *n.* A necrotic area of tissue resulting from failure of local blood supply. [Lat. *infarctus,* p.part. of *infarcire,* to cram : *in-,* in + *farcire,* to stuff.] **—in·farct′ed** *adj.* **—in·farc′tion** *n.*

in·fat·u·ate (ĭn-făch′o͞o-āt′) *tr.v.* **-at·ed, -at·ing, -ates. 1.** To cause to behave foolishly. **2.** To inspire with foolish and unreasoning love or attachment. *—adj.* (ĭn-făch′o͞o-ĭt, -āt′). Infatuated. [Lat. *infatuare, infatuat-* : *in-* (causative) + *fatuus,* foolish.] **—in·fat′u·a′tion** *n.*

in·fat·u·at·ed (ĭn-făch′o͞o-ā′tĭd) *adj.* Possessed by an unreasoning passion or attraction. **—in·fat′u·at′ed·ly** *adv.*

in·fau·na (ĭn′fô′nə) *n.* Aquatic animals that live on the substrate of a body of water. [IN-[2] + FAUNA.]

in·fea·si·ble (ĭn-fē′zə-bəl) *adj.* Not feasible; impracticable.

in·fect (ĭn-fĕkt′) *tr.v.* **-fect·ed, -fect·ing, -fects. 1.** To contaminate with pathogenic microorganisms. **2.** To communicate a disease to. **3.** To invade and produce infection in. **4.** To corrupt. **5.** To affect as if by contagion: *an enthusiasm that infected all of us.* [ME *infecten* < Lat. *infectus,* p.part. of *inficere,* to stain : *in-,* in + *facere,* to do.]

in·fec·tion (ĭn-fĕk′shən) *n.* **1. a.** Invasion by pathogenic microorganisms of a bodily part in which conditions are favorable for growth, production of toxins, and subsequent injury to tissue. **b.** An instance of such invasion. **c.** The pathological state resulting from such invasion. **d.** An agent or contaminated substance responsible for such invasion. **2.** An infectious disease. **3.** Ready communication of an emotion or attitude by contact or example.

in·fec·tious (ĭn-fĕk′shəs) *adj.* **1.** Capable of causing infection. **2.** Capable of being transmitted by infection without actual contact. **3.** Caused by a microorganism. **4.** Easily or readily communicated: *an infectious chuckle.* **—in·fec′tious·ly** *adv.* **—in·fec′tious·ness** *n.*

infectious mononucleosis *n.* Mononucleosis (sense 2).

in·fec·tive (ĭn-fĕk′tĭv) *adj.* Capable of producing infection; infectious. **—in·fec′tive·ness, in′fec·tiv′i·ty** *n.*

in·fe·lic·i·tous (ĭn′fĭ-lĭs′ĭ-təs) *adj.* **1.** Not happy; unfortunate; sad. **2.** Inappropriate; inopportune. **—in′fe·lic′i·tous·ly** *adv.*

in·fe·lic·i·ty (ĭn′fĭ-lĭs′ĭ-tē) *n., pl.* **-ties. 1.** The quality or condition of being infelicitous. **2.** Something inappropriate or unpleasing. [ME *infelicite,* unhappiness < Lat. *infelicitas* < *infelix,* unhappy : *in-,* not + *felix,* happy.]

in·fer (ĭn-fûr′) *v.* **-ferred, -fer·ring, -fers.** *—tr.* **1.** To conclude from evidence or premises. **2.** To have as a logical consequence. **3.** To lead to as a consequence or conclusion. *—intr.* To draw inferences. [OFr. *inferer* < Lat. *inferre,* to bring in, deduce : *in-,* in- + *ferre,* to bear.] **—in·fer′a·ble** *adj.* **—in·fer′a·bly** *adv.* **—in·fer′rer** *n.*

Usage: *Infer* is sometimes confused with *imply,* but the distinction is a useful one. To *imply* is "to state indirectly." To *infer* is "to draw a conclusion." The use of *infer* to mean *imply* is unacceptable to a large majority of the Usage Panel. One should write: *The report implies* (not *infers*) *that we were to blame but doesn't come right out and say it.*

in·fer·ence (ĭn′fər-əns) *n.* **1. a.** The act or process of inferring or deriving a conclusion from facts or premises. **b.** The premises and conclusions of a particular act of inferring. **2.** Something inferred, esp. a conclusion derived by inference.

in·fer·en·tial (ĭn′fə-rĕn′shəl) *adj.* **1.** Of, relating to, or involving inference. **2.** Derived or capable of being derived by inference. **—in′fer·en′tial·ly** *adv.*

in·fe·ri·or (ĭn-fîr′ē-ər) *adj.* **1.** Situated under or beneath. **2.** Low or lower in order, degree, or rank. **3.** Low or lower in quality, value, or estimation. **4.** *Bot.* Located below the perianth and other floral parts. Used of an ovary. **5.** *Printing.* Set below the normal line of type. [ME < Lat., comp. of *inferus,* low.] **—in·fe′ri·or** *n.* **—in·fe′ri·or′i·ty** (-ôr′ĭ-tē, -ŏr′-) *n.*

inferiority complex *n.* A persistent sense of inadequacy or a tendency to self-diminishment.

in·fer·nal (ĭn-fûr′nəl) *adj.* **1.** Of or relating to a lower world of the dead. **2.** Of or relating to hell. **3. a.** Fiendish; devilish. **b.** Abominable; damnable. [ME < OFr. < LLat. *infernalis* < *infernus,* hell < Lat., lower, underground.] **—in·fer′nal·ly** *adv.*

infernal machine *n.* An explosive device maliciously designed to harm or destroy.

in·fer·no (ĭn-fûr′nō) *n., pl.* **-nos. 1.** A place or condition resembling or suggestive of hell, esp. with respect to extreme suffering or intolerable heat. **2.** A place likened to hell. [Ital., hell < LLat. *infernus.* —see INFERNAL.]

in·fer·tile (ĭn-fûr′tl) *adj.* Not fertile; unproductive. **—in′fer·til′i·ty** (ĭn′fər-tĭl′ĭ-tē) *n.*

in·fest (ĭn-fĕst′) *tr.v.* **-fest·ed, -fest·ing, -fests.** To spread in or overrun in large numbers so as to be harmful or unpleasant. [ME *infesten,* to distress < OFr. *infester* < Lat. *infestare,* to attack < *infestus,* hostile.] **—in′fes·ta′tion** *n.* **—in·fest′er** *n.*

in·fi·del (ĭn′fĭ-dəl, -dĕl′) *n.* **1.** One who has no religious beliefs. **2.** One who is an unbeliever with respect to some religion, esp. Christianity or Islam. [ME *infidele,* heathen < OFr. < Lat. *infidelis,* unbelieving : *in-,* not + *fides,* faith.]

in·fi·del·i·ty (ĭn′fĭ-dĕl′ĭ-tē) *n., pl.* **-ties. 1.** Lack of religious belief. **2.** Lack of fidelity or loyalty; unfaithfulness. **3. a.** Marital unfaithfulness. **b.** An act of marital unfaithfulness.

in·field (ĭn′fēld′) *n.* **1.** A field located near a farmhouse. **2.** *Baseball.* **a.** The area of a baseball field bounded by home plate and first, second, and third bases. **b.** The defensive positions of first base, second base, third base, and shortstop considered as a unit. **3.** The area inside a racetrack or running track.

in·field·er (ĭn′fēl′dər) *n. Baseball.* A player who plays in the infield.

in·fight·ing (ĭn′fī′tĭng) *n.* **1.** Fighting or boxing at close range. **2.** Contention among associates in a group or organization. **—in′fight′er** *n.*

in·fil·trate (ĭn-fĭl′trāt′, ĭn′fĭl-) *v.* **-trat·ed, -trat·ing, -trates.** *—tr.* **1.** To cause (a liquid, for example) to permeate a substance by passing through its interstices or pores. **2.** To permeate by passing a liquid or gas through the interstices of. **3.** To pass (troops, for example) surreptitiously into enemy-held territory. **4.** To enter or take up positions in gradually or surreptitiously. *—intr.* To gain entrance gradually or surreptitiously. *—n.* A substance that accumulates gradually in bodily tissues.

in·fil·tra·tion (ĭn′fĭl-trā′shən) *n.* **1.** The act or process of infiltrating. **2.** The state of being infiltrated. **3.** Something that infiltrates. **—in·fil′tra·tive** (-trə-tĭv) *adj.*

in·fi·nite (ĭn′fə-nĭt) *adj.* **1.** Having no boundaries or limits. **2.** Immeasurably great, as in duration or extent. **3.** *Math.* **a.** Existing beyond or being greater than any arbitrarily large value. **b.** Unlimited in spatial extent. **c.** Of or pertaining to a set capable of being put into one-to-one correspondence with a proper subset of itself. *—n.* Something infinite. [ME *infinit* < OFr. < Lat. *infinitus* : *in-,* not + *finitus,* finite.] **—in′fi·nite·ly** *adv.* **—in′fi·nite·ness** *n.*

Synonyms: *infinite, limitless, illimitable, boundless, measureless, eternal, innumerable, numberless, countless.* These adjectives are applicable to what does not have known limits or boundaries. *Infinite,* the most inclusive, refers to what has no limits with respect to quantity, extent, time, or degree and is therefore indeterminate. In usage it is applied most often to what is large beyond measure. *Limitless, illimitable, boundless* and *measureless* refer principally to what, either physically or figuratively, has no known limits in extent, size, or quantity: *the limitless reaches of outer space; boundless opportunity. Eternal* indicates the absence of limits in time; it applies to what has no known beginning and presumably no end, and is thus everlasting. *Innumerable, numberless,* and *countless* refer to quantity beyond reckoning.

in·fin·i·tes·i·mal (ĭn′fĭn-ĭ-tĕs′ə-məl) *adj.* **1.** Immeasurably or incalculably minute. **2.** *Math.* Capable of having values arbitrarily close to zero. *—n.* **1.** An infinitesimal amount or quantity. **2.** *Math.* A function having values arbitrarily close to zero. [< NLat. *infinitesimus,* infinite in rank < Lat. *infinitus,* infinite.] **—in′fin·i·tes′i·mal·ly** *adv.*

infinitesimal calculus *n.* Differential and integral calculus.

in·fin·i·ti·val (ĭn′fĭn-ĭ-tī′vəl) *adj.* Relating to the infinitive.

in·fin·i·tive (ĭn-fĭn′ĭ-tĭv) *n.* A verb form that functions as a substantive while retaining certain verbal characteristics, such as modification by adverbs and that in English may be preceded by *to,* as in: *To go willingly is to show strength* or *We want him to work harder,* or may also occur without *to,* as in *She had them read the letter.* —See Usage note at **split infinitive.** [LLat. *infinitivus,* unlimited, indefinite < Lat. *infinitus,* infinite.]

in·fin·i·tude (ĭn-fĭn′ĭ-to͞od′, -tyo͞od′) *n.* **1.** The state or quality of being infinite. **2.** An infinite quantity, number, or extent.

in·fin·i·ty (ĭn-fĭn′ĭ-tē) *n., pl.* **-ties. 1.** The quality or condition of being infinite. **2.** Unbounded space, time, or quantity. **3.** An indefinitely large number. **4.** *Math.* The limit that a function f is said to approach at $x = a$ when for x close to a, $f(x)$ is larger than any preassigned number.

in·firm (ĭn-fûrm′) *adj.* **1.** Weak in body, esp. from old age; feeble. **2.** Lacking moral firmness; irresolute. **3.** Not sound or valid; insecure. [ME *infirme* < Lat. *infirmus* : *in-,* not + *firmus,* strong, firm.] **—in·firm′ly** *adv.*

in·fir·ma·ry (ĭn-fûr′mə-rē) *n., pl.* **-ries.** A place for the care of the sick or injured, esp. a small hospital or dispensary in an institution. [Med. Lat. *infirmaria* < Lat. *infirmus,* infirm.]

in·fir·mi·ty (ĭn-fûr′mĭ-tē) *n., pl.* **-ties. 1.** Lack of power; disability. **2.** Bodily debilitation; frailty. **3.** Moral weakness. **4.** A failing or defect in a person's character.

in·fix (ĭn-fĭks′) *tr.v.* **-fixed, -fix·ing, -fix·es. 1.** To fix into another. **2.** To fix in the mind; instill. **3.** *Gram.* To insert (a morphological element) into the body of a word. *—n.* (ĭn′fĭks′). An inflectional or derivational element appearing in the body of a word, as Tagalog *sinulat,* "written," in which the infix *-in-* appears as the marker of a passive form that contrasts with the active form *sulat,* "write." [Lat. *infigere, infix-* : *in-,* in + *figere,* to fasten.]

in·flame (ĭn-flām′) *v.* **-flamed, -flam·ing, -flames.** —*tr.* **1.** To set on fire; kindle. **2.** To arouse to strong emotion. **3.** To make more violent; intensify: *"inflamed to madness an already savage nature"* (Robert Graves). **4.** To produce inflammation in. —*intr.* **1.** To catch fire. **2.** To become excited or aroused. **3.** To be affected by inflammation. [ME *inflaumen* < OFr. *enflammer* < Lat. *inflammare* : *in-* (intensive) + *flammare,* to set on fire < *flamma,* flame.]

in·flam·ma·ble (ĭn-flăm′ə-bəl) *adj.* **1.** Tending to ignite easily and burn rapidly; flammable. **2.** Quickly or easily aroused to strong emotion; passionate. —See Usage note at **flammable.** [Fr. < Med. Lat. *inflammabilis* < Lat. *inflammare,* to inflame.] **—in·flam′ma·bil′i·ty** *n.* **—in·flam′ma·ble** *n.* **—in·flam′ma·bly** *adv.*

in·flam·ma·tion (ĭn′flə-mā′shən) *n.* **1.** The act of inflaming or the state of being inflamed. **2.** Localized heat, redness, swelling, and pain as a result of irritation, injury, or infection.

in·flam·ma·to·ry (ĭn-flăm′ə-tôr′ē, -tōr′ē) *adj.* **1. a.** Tending to arouse passion or desire. **b.** Tending to arouse or excite anger or violence. **2.** Characterized or caused by inflammation. **—in·flam′ma·to′ri·ly** *adv.*

in·flate (ĭn-flāt′) *v.* **-flat·ed, -flat·ing, -flates.** —*tr.* **1.** To fill and swell with a gas. **2.** To cause to puff up. **3.** To raise or expand abnormally. —*intr.* To become inflated. [Lat. *inflare, inflat-* : *in-,* in + *flare,* to blow.]

in·flat·ed (ĭn-flā′tĭd) *adj.* **1.** Distended or expanded by or as if by gas or air. **2.** Unduly increased or puffed up: *an inflated ego.* **3.** Full of empty or pretentious language; bombastic. **4.** Increased or raised to abnormal levels: *inflated wages.* **5.** Hollow and enlarged: *an inflated calyx.*

in·fla·tion (ĭn-flā′shən) *n.* **1.** The act of inflating or the state of being inflated. **2.** *Econ.* An abnormal increase in available currency and credit beyond the proportion of available goods, resulting in a sharp and continuing rise in price levels. **—in·fla′tion·ar′y** (-shə-nĕr′ē) *adj.*

in·fla·tion·ist (ĭn-flā′shə-nĭst) *n.* One who advocates a policy of economic inflation. **—in·fla′tion·ism′** *n.*

in·flect (ĭn-flĕkt′) *v.* **-flect·ed, -flect·ing, -flects.** —*tr.* **1.** To turn from a course or alignment; bend. **2.** To alter (the voice) in tone or pitch; modulate. **3.** *Gram.* To alter (a word) by inflection. —*intr. Gram.* To be modified by inflection. [ME *inflecten,* to bend < Lat. *inflectere* : *in-,* intensive + *flectere,* to blend.] **—in·flec′tive** *adj.* **—in·flec′tor** *n.*

in·flec·tion (ĭn-flĕk′shən) *n.* **1.** The act of inflecting or a state of being inflected. **2.** An alteration in pitch or tone of the voice. **3.** *Gram.* **a.** An alteration of the form of a word indicating grammatical features, such as number, person, or tense. **b.** A word element involved in such an alteration. **c.** An inflected form of a word. **—in·flec′tion·al** *adj.* **—in·flec′tion·al·ly** *adv.*

in·flexed (ĭn-flĕkst′) *adj.* Bent or curved inward or downward, as petals or sepals. [< Lat. *inflexus,* p.part. of *inflectere,* to bend. —see INFLECT.]

in·flex·i·ble (ĭn-flĕk′sə-bəl) *adj.* **1.** Not flexible; rigid. **2.** Incapable of being changed; unalterable: *inflexible standards.* **3.** Adhering firmly to an intention or purpose; unyielding. **—in·flex′i·bil′i·ty, in·flex′i·ble·ness** *n.* **—in·flex′i·bly** *adv.*

Synonyms: *inflexible, inexorable, adamant, obdurate.* These adjectives mean not capable of being swayed or diverted from a course. *Inflexible* is applicable to things not capable of change or to persons whose conduct is governed by principles that do not permit alteration of a course. *Inexorable* implies lack of sensitivity to persuasion or entreaty. The term describes things, such as fate or law, that are inevitable in operation and uncompromising in effect. *Adamant* refers to personal conduct and implies adherence to a determined course, despite pleas to the contrary. *Obdurate* adds to *adamant* the implication of hard-heartedness.

in·flex·ion (ĭn-flĕk′shən) *n. Chiefly Brit.* Inflection.

in·flict (ĭn-flĭkt′) *tr.v.* **-flict·ed, -flict·ing, -flicts. 1.** To cause or carry out by physical assault or other aggressive action. **2.** To impose: *"malignant Nature, who reserves the right to inflict upon her children the most terrifying jests"* (Thornton Wilder). **3.** To afflict. [Lat. *infligere, inflitc-* : *in-,* on + *fligere,* to strike.] **—in·flict′er, in·flic′tor** *n.* **—in·flic′tive** *adj.*

in·flic·tion (ĭn-flĭk′shən) *n.* **1.** The act or process of inflicting. **2.** Something, as punishment, that is inflicted.

in·flight (ĭn′flīt′) *adj.* **1.** Carried out or made while in flight. **2.** Provided for use or enjoyment while in flight.

in·flo·res·cence (ĭn′flə-rĕs′əns) *n.* **1.** *Bot.* A characteristic arrangement of flowers on a stalk or in a cluster. **2.** A flowering. [NLat. *inflorescentia* < LLat. *inflorescere,* to begin to flower : *in-* (intensive) + *florescere,* to begin to blossom, inceptive of *florēre,* to blossom < *flos,* flower.] **—in′flo·res′cent** *adj.*

in·flow (ĭn′flō′) *n.* **1.** The act or process of flowing in or into. **2.** Something that flows in or into.

in·flu·ence (ĭn′flo͞o-əns) *n.* **1.** A power indirectly or intangibly affecting a person or a course of events. **2. a.** Power to sway or affect based on prestige, wealth, ability, or position. **b.** One exercising such power. **c.** An effect or change produced by such power. **3. a.** An occult ethereal fluid believed to flow from the stars and to affect the fate of men. **b.** An occult power believed to emanate from the stars. —*tr.v.* **-enced, -enc·ing, -enc·es. 1.** To have power over; affect. **2.** To cause a change in the character, thought, or action of; have an effect upon. [ME < OFr. < Med. Lat. *influentia* < Lat. *influens,* pr.part. of *influere,* to flow in : *in-,* in + *fluere,* to flow.] **—in′flu·enc·er** *n.*

in·flu·ent (ĭn′flo͞o-ənt, ĭn-flo͞o′-) *adj.* Flowing in or into. —*n.* Something that flows in or into, esp. a tributary. [ME < Lat. *influens,* flowing in. —see INFLUENCE.]

in·flu·en·tial (ĭn′flo͞o-ĕn′shəl) *adj.* Having or exercising influence. **—in′flu·en′tial·ly** *adv.*

in·flu·en·za (ĭn′flo͞o-ĕn′zə) *n.* An acute infectious viral disease characterized by inflammation of the respiratory tract, fever, muscular pain, and irritation in the intestinal tract. [Ital. < Med. Lat. *influentia,* influence.]

in·flux (ĭn′flŭks′) *n.* A flowing in. [LLat. *influxus* < Lat., p.part. of *influere,* to flow in. —see INFLUENCE.]

in·fold (ĭn-fōld′) *v.* **-fold·ed, -fold·ing, -folds.** —*intr.* To fold inward. —*tr.* To enfold. **—in·fold′er** *n.* **—in·fold′ment** *n.*

in·form (ĭn-fôrm′) *v.* **-formed, -form·ing, -forms.** —*tr.* **1.** To give form or character to; be the formative principle of. **2.** To animate or inspire with a particular quality or character; imbue. **3.** To form or shape (the mind or character) by teaching or training. **4.** To impart information to. —*intr.* To disclose or give information, esp. incriminating information. [ME *enfourmen* < OFr. *enfourmer* < Lat. *informare* : *in-,* in + *forma,* form.]

in·for·mal (ĭn-fôr′məl) *adj.* **1.** Not according to prescribed regulations or forms: *an informal agreement.* **2.** Of, for, or pertaining to ordinary everyday use; casual: *informal clothes.* **3.** More appropriate for use in the spoken language than in the written language esp. of business, technical, or official communications. **—in·for′mal·ly** *adv.*

in·for·mal·i·ty (ĭn′fôr-măl′ĭ-tē) *n., pl.* **-ties. 1.** The state or quality of being informal. **2.** An informal act.

in·form·ant (ĭn-fôr′mənt) *n.* **1.** One who discloses information; informer. **2.** One who furnishes linguistic or cultural information to a researcher.

in·for·mat·ics (ĭn′fər-măt′ĭks) *n. (used with a sing. verb).* Information science. [INFORMAT(ION) + -ICS.]

in·for·ma·tion (ĭn′fər-mā′shən) *n.* **1.** The act of informing or the condition of being informed; communication of knowledge. **2.** Knowledge derived from study, experience, or instruction. **3.** Knowledge of a specific event or situation; news. **4.** *Law.* A formal accusation of a crime made by a public officer rather than by indictment by a grand jury. **5.** A nonaccidental signal used as an input to a computer or communications system. **6.** A numerical measure of the uncertainty of an experimental outcome. **—in′for·ma′tion·al** *adj.*

information science *n.* The science concerned with the gathering, manipulation, classification, storage, and retrieval of recorded knowledge.

information theory *n.* The theory of the probability of transmission of messages with specified accuracy when the bits of information constituting the messages are subject, with certain probabilities, to transmission failure, distortion, and accidental additions.

in·form·a·tive (ĭn-fôr′mə-tĭv) *adj.* Providing or disclosing information; instructive. **—in·form′a·tive·ly** *adv.* **—in·form′a·tive·ness** *n.*

in·form·a·to·ry (ĭn-fôr′mə-tôr′ē, -tōr′ē) *adj.* Informative.

in·formed (ĭn-fôrmd′) *adj.* **1.** Possessing, displaying, or making use of information: *the informed consumer.* **2.** Based on factual knowledge: *an informed appraisal.*

in·form·er (ĭn-fôr′mər) *n.* **1.** An informant. **2.** One who informs against others, often for compensation.

infra– *pref.* Below; beneath; inferior to: *infrasonic.* [Lat. *infra,* below.]

in·fract (ĭn-frăkt′) *tr.v.* **-fract·ed, -fract·ing, -fracts.** To infringe; violate. [Lat. *infractus,* p.part. of *infringere,* to destroy. —see INFRINGE.] **—in·frac′tor** *n.*

in·frac·tion (ĭn-frăk′shən) *n.* The act or an instance of violating; infringement.

in·fra dig (ĭn′frə dĭg′) *adj.* Beneath one's dignity. [Short for Lat. *infra dignitatem.*]

in·fran·gi·ble (ĭn-frăn′jə-bəl) *adj.* **1.** Not capable of being broken. **2.** Inviolable. [OFr. < LLat. *infrangibilis* : Lat. *in-,* not + Lat. *frangere,* to break.] **—in·fran′gi·bil′i·ty** *n.* **—in·fran′gi·bly** *adv.*

in·fra·or·bit·al (ĭn′frə-ôr′bĭ-təl) *adj. Anat.* Located or occurring beneath the orbit.

in·fra·red (ĭn′frə-rĕd′) *adj.* **1.** Of, pertaining to, or being electromagnetic radiation having wavelengths greater than those of visible light and shorter than those of microwaves. **2.** Generating, using, or sensitive to infrared radiation.

in·fra·son·ic (ĭn′frə-sŏn′ĭk) *adj.* **1.** Generating or using waves or vibrations with frequencies below that of audible sound. **2.** Subsonic (sense 1).

in·fra·sound (ĭn′frə-sound′) *n.* A wave phenomenon sharing the physical nature of sound but with a range of frequencies below that of human hearing.

in·fra·struc·ture (ĭn′frə-strŭk′chər) *n.* **1.** An underlying base or foundation esp. for an organization. **2.** The basic facilities, equipment, and installations needed for the functioning of a system or organization.

in·fre·quent (ĭn-frē′kwənt) *adj.* **1.** Not frequent; rare. **2.** Not occurring regularly; occasional: *an infrequent guest.* —**in·fre′quence, in·fre′quen·cy** *n.* —**in·fre′quent·ly** *adv.*

in·fringe (ĭn-frĭnj′) *v.* **-fringed, -fring·ing, -fring·es.** —*tr.* **1.** To violate or go beyond the limits of (a law, for example). **2.** *Obs.* To defeat; invalidate. —*intr.* To encroach upon something: *a law that infringed upon the rights of property owners.* [Lat. *infringere* : *in-* (intensive) + *frangere,* to break.] —**in·fring′er** *n.*

in·fringe·ment (ĭn-frĭnj′mənt) *n.* **1.** A violation, as of a law or agreement. **2.** An encroachment, as of a right or privilege.

in·fun·dib·u·li·form (ĭn′fən-dĭb′yə-lə-fôrm′) *adj.* Funnel-shaped.

in·fun·dib·u·lum (ĭn′fən-dĭb′yə-ləm) *n., pl.* **-la** (-lə). Any of various funnel-shaped bodily passages or parts. [Lat., funnel < *infundere,* to pour in. —see INFUSE.] —**in′fun·dib′u·lar** (-lər), **in′fun·dib′u·late′** (-lāt′, -lĭt) *adj.*

in·fu·ri·ate (ĭn-fyo͝or′ē-āt′) *tr.v.* **-at·ed, -at·ing, -ates.** To make furious; enrage. —*adj.* (ĭn-fyo͝or′ē-ĭt). *Archaic.* Furious. [Med. Lat. *infuriare, infuriat-* : Lat. *in-* (intensive) + *furia,* fury < *furere,* to be mad.] —**in·fu′ri·at′ing·ly** *adv.* —**in·fu′ri·a′tion** *n.*

in·fuse (ĭn-fyo͞oz′) *tr.v.* **-fused, -fus·ing, -fus·es. 1.** To put into; introduce: *infused new vigor into the movement.* **2.** To cause to pervade; imbue: *infused them with a feeling of urgency.* **3.** To give an animating or motivating impulse to. **4.** To steep or soak without boiling in order to extract soluble elements or active principles. [ME *infusen* < OFr. *infuser* < Lat. *infusus,* p.part. of *infundere,* to pour in : *in-,* in + *fundere,* to pour.] —**in·fus′er** *n.*

in·fus·i·ble (ĭn-fyo͞o′zə-bəl) *adj.* Incapable of being fused or melted. —**in·fus′i·bil′i·ty, in·fus′i·ble·ness** *n.*

in·fu·sion (ĭn-fyo͞o′zhən) *n.* **1.** The act or process of infusing. **2.** An admixture. **3.** The liquid product obtained by infusing. **4.** The introduction of a solution into a vein.

in·fu·so·ri·al (ĭn′fyo͞o-sôr′ē-əl, -sōr′-, -zôr′-, -zōr′-) *adj.* **1.** Of or pertaining to infusorians. **2.** Containing or consisting of infusorians.

in·fu·so·ri·an (ĭn′fyo͞o-sôr′ē-ən, -sōr′-, -zôr′-, -zōr′-) *n.* Any of numerous microscopic organisms, esp. of the phylum Protozoa or the order Rotifera, occurring in stagnant water or in infusions containing organic material. —*adj.* Of or pertaining to infusorians. [NLat. *Infusoria,* class of protozoan < Lat. *infusus,* p.part. of *infundere,* to pour in. —see INFUSE.]

-ing[1] *suff.* **1.** Used to form the present participle of verbs: *seeing.* **2.** Used to form adjectives resembling present participles but not derived from verbs: *swashbuckling.* [ME, alteration of *-end, -ind* < OE *-ende,* pr.part. suffix.]

-ing[2] *suff.* **1. a.** Action, process, or art: *dancing.* **b.** An instance of an action, process, or art: *a gathering.* **2.** An action or process connected with a specified thing: *berrying.* **3. a.** Something necessary to perform an action or process: *mooring.* **b.** The result of an action or process: *a drawing.* **c.** Something connected with a specified thing or concept: *siding, offing.* [ME < OE *-ung.*]

-ing[3] *suff.* One having a specified quality or nature: *wilding.* [ME < OE, belonging to, descended from.]

in·gen·ious (ĭn-jēn′yəs) *adj.* **1.** Possessing or showing great skill in creating or devising. **2.** Original and imaginative in design, construction, or execution: *an ingenious scheme.* **3.** *Obs.* Having genius; brilliant. [Fr. *ingénieux* < Lat. *ingeniosus* < *ingenium,* inborn talent : *in-,* in + *gignere,* to beget.] —**in·gen′ious·ly** *adv.* —**in·gen′ious·ness** *n.*

in·gé·nue (ăn′zhə-no͞o′) *n.* **1.** An artless girl or young woman. **2. a.** The role of an ingénue in a dramatic production. **b.** An actress playing an ingénue. [Fr., fem. of *ingénu,* guileless < Lat. *ingenuus,* ingenuous.]

in·ge·nu·i·ty (ĭn′jə-no͞o′ĭ-tē, -nyo͞o′-) *n., pl.* **-ties. 1.** Inventive skill or imagination; cleverness. **2.** Imaginative and clever design or construction. **3.** An ingenious or imaginative device. **4.** *Archaic.* Ingenuousness. [Lat. *ingenuitas,* frankness < *ingenuus,* ingenuous.]

in·gen·u·ous (ĭn-jĕn′yo͞o-əs) *adj.* **1.** Without sophistication or worldliness; artless. **2.** Openly straightforward or frank; candid. **3.** *Obs.* Ingenious. [Lat. *ingenuus,* honest, freeborn : *in-,* in + *gignere,* to beget.] —**in·gen′u·ous·ly** *adv.* —**in·gen′u·ous·ness** *n.*

in·gest (ĭn-jĕst′) *tr.v.* **-gest·ed, -gest·ing, -gests.** To take in by or as if by swallowing. [Lat. *ingerere, ingest-,* to carry in : *in-,* in + *gerere,* to carry.] —**in·ges′tion** *n.* —**in·ges′tive** *adj.*

in·ges·ta (ĭn-jĕs′tə) *pl.n.* Ingested matter, esp. food. [NLat., neuter pl. of Lat. *ingestus,* p.part. of *ingerere,* to carry in. —see INGEST.]

in·gle (ĭng′gəl) *n.* **1.** A fire upon a hearth. **2.** A fireplace.

in·gle·nook (ĭng′gəl-no͝ok′) *n.* **1.** A nook or corner beside an open fireplace. **2.** A bench placed in an inglenook. [Sc. Gael. *aingeal.*]

in·glo·ri·ous (ĭn-glôr′ē-əs, -glōr′-) *adj.* **1.** Not glorious. **2.** Ignominious; dishonorable. [Lat. *inglorius* : *in-,* not + *gloria,* fame.] —**in·glo′ri·ous·ly** *adv.* —**in·glo′ri·ous·ness** *n.*

in·got (ĭng′gət) *n.* **1.** A mass of metal shaped for convenience in storage or transportation. **2.** A casting mold for metal. [ME, mold for casting metal, alteration of OFr. *lingot,* metal ingot.]

in·grain (ĭn-grān′) *tr.v.* **-grained, -grain·ing, -grains. 1.** To impress indelibly on the mind or nature; infuse. **2.** *Archaic.* To dye or stain into the fiber of. —*adj.* **1.** Deeply rooted; instilled. **2.** Dyed in the yarn before weaving or knitting. **3.** Made of fiber or yarn dyed before weaving. Used esp. of rugs. —*n.* **1.** Yarn or fiber dyed before manufacture. **2.** An article made of ingrained yarns, as carpets.

in·grained (ĭn-grānd′) *adj.* **1.** Worked deeply into the texture or fiber. **2.** Firmly established; deep-seated.

in·grate (ĭn′grāt′) *n.* An ungrateful person. [ME *ingrat,* ungrateful < Lat. *ingratus* : *in-,* not + *gratus,* pleasing, thankful.]

in·gra·ti·ate (ĭn-grā′shē-āt′) *tr.v.* **-at·ed, -at·ing, -ates.** To make an effort to insinuate (oneself) into the good graces or favor of another. [IN- (in) + Lat. *gratia,* favor < *gratus,* pleasing.] —**in·gra′ti·at′ing·ly** *adv.* —**in·gra′ti·a′tion** *n.* —**in·gra′ti·a·to′ry** (-shē-ə-tôr′ē, -tōr′ē) *adj.*

in·grat·i·tude (ĭn-grăt′ĭ-to͞od′, -tyo͞od′) *n.* Lack of gratitude; ungratefulness. [ME < OFr. < LLat. *ingratitudo* < *ingratus,* ungrateful. —see INGRATE.]

in·gre·di·ent (ĭn-grē′dē-ənt) *n.* Something that is an element in a mixture or compound; constituent. [ME < Lat. *ingrediens,* pr.part. of *ingredi,* to enter : *in-,* in + *gradi,* to step.]

in·gress (ĭn′grĕs′) *n.* **1.** Also **in·gres·sion** (ĭn-grĕsh′ən). A going in or entering. **2.** The right or permission to enter. [ME *ingresse* < Lat. *ingressus* < p.part. of *ingredi,* to enter. —see INGREDIENT.]

in·gres·sive (ĭn-grĕs′ĭv) *adj.* **1.** Of, pertaining to, or involving ingress. **2.** Inchoative (sense 2). —**in·gres′sive** *n.* —**in·gres′sive·ness** *n.*

in-group (ĭn′gro͞op′) *n. Informal.* A group united by common beliefs, attitudes, and interests and characteristically excluding outsiders.

in·grow·ing (ĭn′grō′ĭng) *adj.* Growing inward.

in·grown (ĭn′grōn′) *adj.* **1.** Grown abnormally into the flesh: *an ingrown toenail.* **2.** Grown within; innate.

in·growth (ĭn′grōth′) *n.* **1.** The act of growing inward. **2.** Something that grows inward.

in·gui·nal (ĭng′gwə-nəl) *adj.* Of, relating to, or located in the groin. [Lat. *inguinalis* < *inguen,* groin.]

in·gur·gi·tate (ĭn-gûr′jĭ-tāt′) *tr.v.* **-tat·ed, -tat·ing, -tates.** To swallow greedily or in excessive amounts; guzzle. [Lat. *ingurgitare, ingurgitat-* : *in-,* in + *gurges,* whirlpool.] —**in·gur′gi·ta′tion** *n.*

in·hab·it (ĭn-hăb′ĭt) *v.* **-it·ed, -it·ing, -its.** —*tr.* **1.** To reside in. **2.** To be present in: *an old stadium inhabited with the spirits of great stars of bygone days.* —*intr. Archaic.* To dwell. [ME *enhabiten* < OFr. *enhabiter* < Lat. *inhabitare* : *in-,* in + *habitare,* to dwell, freq. of *habēre,* to have.] —**in·hab′it·a·bil′i·ty** *n.* —**in·hab′it·a·ble** *adj.* —**in·hab′i·ta′tion** *n.* —**in·hab′it·er** *n.*

in·hab·i·tan·cy (ĭn-hăb′ĭ-tən-sē) *n., pl.* **-cies.** Occupancy.

in·hab·i·tant (ĭn-hăb′ĭ-tənt) *n.* A permanent resident.

in·hab·it·ed (ĭn-hăb′ĭ-tĭd) *adj.* Having inhabitants; populated.

in·ha·lant (ĭn-hā′lənt) *adj.* Used in or for inhaling. —*n.* Something that is inhaled, as a medicine.

in·ha·la·tion (ĭn′hə-lā′shən) *n.* The act or an instance of inhaling.

in·ha·la·tor (ĭn′hə-lā′tər) *n.* A device that produces a vapor to ease breathing or to medicate by inspiration.

in·hale (ĭn-hāl′) *v.* **-haled, -hal·ing, -hales.** —*tr.* To draw in by breathing. —*intr.* To breathe in. [Lat. *inhalare* : *in-,* in + *halare,* to breath.]

in·hal·er (ĭn-hā′lər) *n.* **1.** One that inhales. **2.** An inhalator. **3.** A respirator.

in·har·mon·ic (ĭn′här-mŏn′ĭk) *adj.* Not harmonic; discordant.

in·har·mo·ni·ous (ĭn′här-mō′nē-əs) *adj.* **1.** Not in harmony; discordant. **2.** Not in accord or agreement. —**in′har·mo′ni·ous·ly** *adv.* —**in′har·mo′ni·ous·ness** *n.*

in·here (ĭn-hîr′) *intr.v.* **-hered, -her·ing, -heres.** To be inherent or innate. [Lat. *inhaerēre* : *in,* in + *haerēre,* to stick.] —**in·her′ence** (-hîr′əns, -hĕr′-), **in·her′en·cy** *n.*

in·her·ent (ĭn-hîr′ənt, -hĕr′-) *adj.* Existing as an essential constituent or characteristic; intrinsic. [Lat. *inhaerens, inhaerent-,* pr.part. of *inhaerēre,* to inhere.] —**in·her′ent·ly** *adv.*

in·her·it (ĭn-hĕr′ĭt) *v.* **-it·ed, -it·ing, -its.** —*tr.* **1.** To come into possession of; possess. **2.** To receive (property) from an ancestor or another person by legal succession or will. **3.** *Biol.* To receive genetically from an ancestor. —*intr.* To hold or take possession of an inheritance. [ME *enheriten,* to make (someone) an heir < OFr. *enheriter* < LLat. *inhereditare* : Lat. *in-,* in + Lat. *heres,* heir.] —**in·her′i·tor** *n.* —**in·her′i·trix** (-ĭ-trĭks) *n.*

in·her·it·a·ble (ĭn-hĕr′ĭ-tə-bəl) *adj.* **1.** Capable of inheriting; having the right to inherit. **2.** Capable of being inherited.

in·her·i·tance (ĭn-hĕr′ĭ-təns) *n.* **1.** The act of inheriting. **2.** Something that is inherited or is to be inherited. **3.** Something regarded as a heritage: *the cultural inheritance of Rome.* **4.** *Biol.* **a.** The process of genetic transmission of characteristics. **b.** A characteristic so inherited.

inheritance tax *n.* A tax on inherited property.

in·hib·it (ĭn-hĭb′ĭt) *tr.v.* **-it·ed, -it·ing, -its. 1.** To restrain or hold back; prevent. **2.** To prohibit; forbid. [ME *inhibiten,* to forbid < Lat. *inhibitus,* p.part. of *inhibēre,* to restrain : *in-,* in

ingot
Steel ingots

+ *habēre,* to have.] **—in·hib'it·a·ble** *adj.* **—in·hib'it·er** *n.* **—in·hib'i·tive, in·hib'i·to'ry** (-tôr'ē, -tōr'ē) *adj.*

in·hi·bi·tion (ĭn'hə-bĭsh'ən, ĭn'ə-) *n.* **1.** The act of inhibiting or the state of being inhibited. **2. a.** Restraint of a behavioral process or the condition inducing such restraint. **b.** The process by which the superego prevents conscious expression of an instinct.

in·hib·i·tor (ĭn-hĭb'ĭ-tər) *n.* **1.** A substance used to retard or halt an undesirable reaction, as rusting. **2.** One that inhibits.

in·hos·pi·ta·ble (ĭn-hŏs'pĭ-tə-bəl, ĭn'hŏ-spĭt'ə-bəl) *adj.* **1.** Displaying no hospitality; unfriendly. **2.** Not affording shelter or sustenance; barren. **—in·hos'pi·ta·ble·ness, in·hos'pi·tal'i·ty** *n.* **—in·hos'pi·ta·bly** *adv.*

in-house (ĭn'hous') *adj.* Being or coming from within an organization: *in-house counsel.*

in·hu·man (ĭn-hyo͞o'mən) *adj.* **1. a.** Lacking kindness or pity; brutal. **b.** Deficient in emotional warmth; cold. **2.** Not in accord with human needs: *an inhuman environment.* **3.** Not of ordinary human form; monstrous. [Lat. *inhumanus* : *in-,* not + *humanus,* human.] **—in·hu'man·ly** *adv.* **—in·hu'man·ness** *n.*

in·hu·mane (ĭn'hyo͞o-mān') *adj.* Lacking in pity or compassion. **—in'hu·mane'ly** *adv.*

in·hu·man·i·ty (ĭn'hyo͞o-măn'ĭ-tē) *n., pl.* **-ties. 1.** Lack of pity or compassion. **2.** An inhuman or cruel act.

in·hume (ĭn-hyo͞om') *tr.v.* **-humed, -hum·ing, -humes.** To place in a grave; inter. [Lat. *inhumare* : *in-,* in + *humus,* earth.] **—in'hu·ma'tion** *n.* **—in·hum'er** *n.*

in·im·i·cal (ĭn-ĭm'ĭ-kəl) *adj.* **1.** Injurious or harmful in effect; adverse: *habits inimical to good health.* **2.** Unfriendly; hostile: *a cold and inimical voice.* [LLat. *inimicalis* < Lat. *inimicus,* enemy. —see ENEMY.]

in·im·i·ta·ble (ĭn-ĭm'ĭ-tə-bəl) *adj.* Defying imitation; matchless. **—in·im'i·ta·bil'i·ty** *n.* **—in·im'i·ta·bly** *adv.*

in·iq·ui·tous (ĭ-nĭk'wĭ-təs) *adj.* Of or characterized by iniquity; wicked. **—in·iq'ui·tous·ly** *adv.* **—in·iq'ui·tous·ness** *n.*

in·iq·ui·ty (ĭ-nĭk'wĭ-tē) *n., pl.* **-ties. 1.** Wickedness; sinfulness. **2.** A grossly immoral act; sin. [ME *iniquite* < OFr. < Lat. *iniquitas* < *iniquus,* unjust, harmful : *in-,* not + *aequus,* equal.]

in·i·tial (ĭ-nĭsh'əl) *adj.* **1.** Occurring at the very beginning; first. **2.** Denoting the first letter or letters of a word. *—n.* **1.** Often **initials.** The first letter or letters of a person's name or names, used as a shortened signature or for identification. **2.** The first letter of a word. **3.** A large, often highly decorated letter set at the beginning of a chapter, verse, paragraph. *—tr.v.* **-tialed, -tial·ing, -tials** also **-tialled, -tial·ling, -tails.** To mark or sign with initials. [Lat. *initialis* < *initium,* beginning < *initus,* p.part. of *inire,* to enter : *in-,* in + *ire,* to go.] **—in·i'tial·ly** *adv.*

in·i·tial·ize (ĭ-nĭsh'ə-līz') *tr.v.* **-ized, iz·ing, -iz·es.** *Computer Sci.* To set to a starting position or value. **—in·i'tial·i·za'tion** *n.* **—in·i'tial·iz'er** *n.*

initial teaching alphabet *n.* An alphabet with 44 symbols each of which represents a single sound that is used to teach beginning reading of English.

in·i·ti·ate (ĭ-nĭsh'ē-āt') *tr.v.* **-at·ed, -at·ing, -ates. 1.** To cause to begin: *initiated an advertising campaign.* **2.** To introduce (a person) to a new field, interest, skill, or activity. **3.** To admit into membership, as with ceremonies or ritual. *—adj.* (-ĭt). Initiated. *—n.* (-ĭt). **1.** One who has been initiated. **2.** A novice; beginner. [Lat. *initiare, initiat-* < *initium,* beginning. —see INITIAL.] **—in·i'ti·a'tor** *n.*

in·i·ti·a·tion (ĭ-nĭsh'ē-ā'shən) *n.* **1. a.** The act or an instance of initiating. **b.** The condition of being initiated. **2.** A ceremony, ritual, test, or period of instruction with which a new member is admitted to an organization or office or to knowledge.

inkstand
18th-century English

in·i·tia·tive (ĭ-nĭsh'ə-tĭv) *n.* **1.** The power, ability, or instinct to begin or to follow through energetically with a plan or task; enterprise and determination. **2.** The first step; opening move: *take the initiative.* **3. a.** The power or right to introduce a new legislative measure. **b.** The right and procedure by which citizens can propose a law by petition and ensure its submission to the electorate. *—adj.* **1.** Of or pertaining to initiation. **2.** Used to initiate; initiatory. **—*idiom.* on (one's) own initiative.** Without prompting or direction from others; on one's own. **—in·i'tia·tive·ly** *adv.*

in·i·ti·a·to·ry (ĭ-nĭsh'ē-ə-tôr'ē, -tōr'ē) *adj.* **1.** Introductory; initial. **2.** Used to initiate; initiative.

in·ject (ĭn-jĕkt') *tr.v.* **-ject·ed, -ject·ing, -jects. 1.** To force or drive (a fluid) into something: *inject fuel into an engine cylinder.* **2. a.** *Med.* To introduce (a fluid) into the skin, subcutaneous tissue, muscle, blood vessels, or a bodily cavity. **b.** To introduce a fluid into: *injected the patient with digitalis.* **3.** To introduce into conversation or consideration: *inject a note of humor into the negotiations.* **4.** To place into an orbit, trajectory, or stream. [< Lat. *injectus,* p.part. of *inicere,* to put in : *in-,* in + *jacere,* to throw.] **—in·jec'tor** *n.*

inlay
1st-century B.C. Roman mosaic

in·jec·tion (ĭn-jĕk'shən) *n.* **1.** The act of injecting. **2.** A fluid that is injected, esp. a dose of liquid medicine.

in·ju·di·cious (ĭn'jo͞o-dĭsh'əs) *adj.* Lacking or showing a lack of judgment or discretion; unwise. **—in'ju·di'cious·ly** *adv.* **—in'ju·di'cious·ness** *n.*

in·junc·tion (ĭn-jŭngk'shən) *n.* **1.** The act or an instance of enjoining; a command, directive, or order. **2.** *Law.* A court order enjoining or prohibiting a party from a specific course of action. [LLat. *injunctio,* command < Lat. *injunctus,* p.part. of *injungere,* to enjoin : *in-,* in + *jungere,* to join.] **—in·junc'tive** *adj.*

in·jure (ĭn'jər) *tr.v.* **-jured, -jur·ing, -jures. 1.** To cause physical harm to; hurt. **2.** To cause damage to; impair. **3.** To cause distress to; wound: *injured his feelings.* **4.** To commit an injustice or offense against; wrong. [Back-formation < INJURY.] **—in'jur·er** *n.*

Synonyms: *injure, harm, hurt, damage, impair, mar, spoil, wound.* These verbs refer to acts causing loss in some respect. *Injure* has the widest range. With respect to persons, it can refer to acts that adversely affect health, appearance, feelings, or reputation or that do injustice according to law. Applied to things, it implies an act that lowers value. *Harm* and *hurt* refer principally to what causes physical or mental distress to living things or diminishes the worth of inanimate objects. *Damage* usually implies injury to reputation or status or injury that decreases the value of property. *Impair* refers to what diminishes the quality of health or the strength or utility of things. *Mar* applies principally to acts that injure things, either physically by disfiguring or figuratively by depriving them of highest quality. *Spoil* refers both to destroying the usefulness or value of things and to causing harm to human character or personality through overindulgence. *Wound* refers to causing either physical injury to persons or animals or mental distress to persons.

in·ju·ri·ous (ĭn-jo͝or'ē-əs) *adj.* **1.** Causing or tending to cause injury; harmful. **2.** Slanderous; libelous. **—in·ju'ri·ous·ly** *adv.* **—in·ju'ri·ous·ness** *n.*

in·ju·ry (ĭn'jə-rē) *n., pl.* **-ries. 1.** Damage of or to a person, property, reputation, or thing. **2.** A wound or other specific damage. **3.** *Law.* A wrong or damage done to another person or to his property, reputation, or rights when caused by the wrongful act of another. **4.** *Obs.* An insult. [ME *injurie* < AN < Lat. *injuria,* a wrong < *injurius,* unjust : *in-,* not < *jus,* law.]

in·jus·tice (ĭn-jŭs'tĭs) *n.* **1.** Lack of justice; violation of another's rights or of what is right. **2.** A specific unjust act; wrong. [ME < OFr. < Lat. *injustitia* < *injustus,* unjust : *in-,* not + *justus,* just.]

Synonyms: *injustice, injury, wrong, grievance.* These nouns denote acts or conditions that cause persons to suffer hardship or loss undeservedly. *Injustice* refers to violation of a person's rights. *Injury* is damage or hurt, suffered through violation of one's rights, for which he can seek legal redress. *Wrong,* in a legal sense, refers to what violates the rights of an individual or adversely affects the public welfare. In the general sense, *wrong* is an intensification of *injustice. Grievance* refers to an act or condition that is regarded as a wrong and gives rise to a complaint.

ink (ĭngk) *n.* **1.** A pigmented liquid or paste used esp. for writing or printing. **2.** A dark liquid secreted by cuttlefish and other cephalopods. *—tr.v.* **inked, ink·ing, inks.** To mark or stain with ink. [ME *inke* < OFr. *enque* < LLat. *encaustum,* purple ink < Gk. *enkauston* < *enkaiein,* to paint in encaustic. —see ENCAUSTIC.] **—ink'i·ness** *n.* **—ink'y** *adj.*

ink·ber·ry (ĭngk'bĕr'ē) *n.,* **1.** A shrub, *Ilex glabra,* of eastern North America, having black, berrylike fruit. **2.** Pokeweed. **3.** The fruit of an inkberry.

ink·blot (ĭngk'blŏt') *n.* **1.** A blotted pattern of spilled ink. **2.** A pattern resembling an inkblot and used in the Rorschach test.

ink·horn (ĭngk'hôrn') *n.* A small container made of horn or similar material, formerly used to hold writing ink. *—adj.* Pedantic; recondite: *inkhorn words.*

ink·ling (ĭngk'lĭng) *n.* **1.** A hint or intimation. **2.** A vague idea or notion. [Perh. < ME *inklen,* to mention.]

ink sac *n. Biol.* An organ, containing ink, located near the rectum in some cephalopods.

ink·stand (ĭngk'stănd') *n.* **1.** A tray or rack for bottles of ink, pens, and other writing implements. **2.** An inkwell.

ink·well (ĭngk'wĕl') *n.* A small reservoir for ink.

inky cap (ĭngk'ē) *n.* Any of various mushrooms of the genus *Coprinus,* having gills that dissolve into a dark liquid on maturing.

in·lace (ĭn-lās') *v.* Variant of **enlace.**

in·laid (ĭn'lād') *adj.* **1.** Set into a surface in a decorative pattern. **2.** Decorated with a pattern set into a surface.

in·land (ĭn'lənd) *adj.* **1.** Of, pertaining to, or located in the interior part of a country or region. **2.** Operating or applying within the borders of a country or region; domestic: *inland tariffs.* *—adv.* In, toward, or into the interior of a country or region. *—n.* (-lănd', -lənd). The interior of a country or region. **—in'land'er** *n.*

in-law (ĭn'lô') *n.* A relative by marriage. [Back-formation < such compounds as *mother-in-law.*]

in·lay (ĭn-lā', ĭn'lā') *tr.v.* **-laid, -lay·ing, -lays. 1. a.** To set (pieces of ivory, for example) into a surface, usually at the same level, to form a design. **b.** To decorate by setting in such designs. **2.** To insert (a photograph, for example) within a mat in a book. *—n.* (ĭn'lā'). **1.** Contrasting material set into a surface in pieces to form a design. **2.** A design, pattern, or decoration made by inlaying. **3.** A solid filling, as of gold or porcelain, fitted to a cavity in a tooth and cemented in place. **—in·lay'er** *n.*

in·let (ĭn′lĕt′, -lĭt) *n.* **1.** A bay, cove, or other recess along a coast. **2.** A stream or bay leading inland, as from the ocean; estuary. **3.** A narrow passage of water, as between two islands. **4.** A drainage passage, as to a culvert. **5.** An opening providing a means of entrance.

in·li·er (ĭn′lī′ər) *n.* An older rock formation completely surrounded by newer strata.

in-line (ĭn′līn′) *adj.* Having the parts arranged in a straight line. —*adv.* Being arranged in an in-line manner.

in lo·co pa·ren·tis (ĭn lō′kō pə-rĕn′tĭs) *adv.* In the position or place of a parent. [Lat.]

in·ly (ĭn′lē) *adv.* Inwardly.

in·mate (ĭn′māt′) *n.* **1.** A resident in a building or dwelling. **2.** A person confined to an institution, as a prison or hospital.

in me·di·as res (ĭn mē′dē-əs rās′) *adv.* In or into the middle of a sequence of events. [Lat., in the middle of things.]

in me·mo·ri·am (ĭn′ mə-môr′ē-əm, -mōr′-). *prep.* In memory of; as a memorial to. Used in epitaphs. [Lat.]

in·most (ĭn′mōst′) *adj.* Innermost.

inn (ĭn) *n.* **1.** A public lodging house serving food and drink to travelers; hotel. **2.** A tavern or restaurant. **3.** *Chiefly Brit.* Formerly, a residence hall for students. [ME < OE.]

in·nards (ĭn′ərdz) *pl.n.* *Informal.* **1.** Internal bodily organs; viscera. **2.** The inner parts, as of a machine. [Alteration of INWARDS.]

in·nate (ĭ-nāt′, ĭn′āt′) *adj.* **1.** Possessed at birth; inborn. **2.** Possessed as an essential characteristic; inherent. **3.** Of or produced by thought as distinguished from experience. [ME *innat* < Lat. *innatus,* p.part. of *innasci,* to be born in : *in-,* in + *nasci,* to be born.] **—in·nate′ly** *adv.* **—in·nate′ness** *n.*

Synonyms: *innate, inborn, inbred, congenital, hereditary.* These adjectives mean belonging by nature or from birth rather than through acquisition at a later time. *Innate, inborn,* and *inbred* are often used interchangeably with reference to persons. *Inborn* is strongest in implying possession of something from birth. What is *inbred* is either present from birth or developed through one's earliest training or associations, and what is *innate* seems essential to the nature or make-up of the person or thing in question. *Congenital* is applied principally to physical characteristics, especially to defects acquired during fetal development. *Hereditary* refers to what is genetically transmitted, or the term can describe what is handed down by right of inheritance.

in·ner (ĭn′ər) *adj.* **1.** Located or occurring farther inside: *an inner room.* **2.** Less apparent; deeper: *the inner meaning of a poem.* **3.** Of or pertaining to the spirit or mind: *"Beethoven's manuscript looks like a bloody record of a tremendous inner battle"* (Leonard Bernstein). **4.** More exclusive, influential, or important: *the inner circles of government.* [ME < OE *innera.*]

inner city *n.* The older, central part of a city, esp. when characterized by crowded low-income neighborhoods.

in·ner-di·rect·ed (ĭn′ər-dĭ-rĕk′tĭd, -dī-) *adj.* Guided, as in thought and behavior, by one's own set of values rather than by societal standards or norms.

inner ear *n.* The internal ear.

in·ner·most (ĭn′ər-mōst′) *adj.* **1.** Situated or occurring farthest within. **2.** Most intimate: *innermost feelings.*

inner product *n.* *Math.* Scalar product.

inner space *n.* **1.** Space at or near the earth's surface, esp. space beneath the sea. **2.** The inner, esp. the subconscious or spiritual, part of the self.

in·ner·vate (ĭ-nûr′vāt′, ĭn′ər-) *tr.v.* **-vat·ed, -vat·ing, -vates.** **1.** To supply (a bodily part) with nerves. **2.** To stimulate (a nerve or bodily part). **—in′ner·va′tion** *n.*

in·nerve (ĭ-nûrv′) *tr.v.* **-nerved, -nerv·ing, -nerves.** To give nervous energy to; stimulate.

in·ning (ĭn′ĭng) *n.* **1. a.** *Baseball.* One of nine divisions or periods of a regulation game, in which each team has a turn at bat as limited by three outs. **b. innings.** *(used with a sing. verb).* The division or period of a cricket game during which one team is at bat. **2.** Often **innings.** An opportunity to act or speak out; turn. **3.** *Archaic.* The reclamation of flooded or marshy land. [< IN.]

inn·keep·er (ĭn′kē′pər) *n.* One who owns or manages an inn.

in·no·cence (ĭn′ə-səns) *n.* **1.** The state, quality, or virtue of being innocent. **2.** Bluets.

in·no·cent (ĭn′ə-sənt) *adj.* **1.** Uncorrupted by evil, malice, or wrongdoing; sinless: *an innocent child.* **2.** Not guilty of a specific crime; legally blameless: *found innocent of all charges.* **3.** Not dangerous or harmful; innocuous: *an innocent prank.* **4.** Not experienced or worldly; naive: *innocent tourists.* **5.** Not exposed to or familiar with something specified; unaware or ignorant. **6.** Betraying or suggesting no deception or guile; artless: *an innocent smile.* —*n.* **1.** A person, esp. a child, who is free of evil or sin. **2.** A simple, guileless, inexperienced, or unsophisticated person. **3.** A very young child. [ME < OFr. < Lat. *innocens* : *in-,* not + *nocens,* pr.part. of *nocēre,* to harm.] **—in′no·cent·ly** *adv.*

in·noc·u·ous (ĭ-nŏk′yo͞o-əs) *adj.* **1.** Having no adverse effect; harmless. **2.** Lacking significance or impact; insipid: *an innocuous speech.* [Lat. *innocuus* : *in-,* not + *nocuus,* harmful < *nocēre,* to harm.] **—in·noc′u·ous·ly** *adv.* **—in·noc′u·ous·ness** *n.*

in·nom·i·nate (ĭ-nŏm′ə-nĭt) *adj.* **1.** Having no name. **2.** Anonymous. [LLat. *innominatus* : Lat. *in-,* not + *nominatus,* p.part. of *nominare,* to name < *nomen,* name.]

innominate artery *n.* An artery that arises from the aortic arch and divides into the right subclavian and right carotid arteries.

innominate bone *n.* A large flat bone forming the lateral half of the pelvis.

innominate vein *n.* One of a pair of veins each formed by the union of the internal jugular and subclavian veins that join to form the superior vena cava.

in·no·vate (ĭn′ə-vāt′) *v.* **-vat·ed, -vat·ing, -vates.** —*tr.* To begin or introduce (something new). —*intr.* To begin or introduce something new; be creative. [Lat. *innovare, innovat,* to renew : *in-* (intensive) + *novus,* new.] **—in′no·va′tive** *adj.* **—in′no·va′tor** *n.*

in·no·va·tion (ĭn′ə-vā′shən) *n.* **1.** The act of innovating. **2.** Something newly introduced. **—in′no·va′tion·al** *adj.*

Inns of Court *pl.n.* **1.** The four legal societies in England founded about the beginning of the 14th century and having the exclusive right to confer the degree of barrister on law students. **2.** The buildings housing the Inns of Court.

in·nu·en·do (ĭn′yo͞o-ĕn′dō) *n., pl.* **-does.** **1.** An indirect or subtle and usually derogatory implication in expression; insinuation. **2.** *Law.* **a.** A plaintiff's interpretation, in a libel suit, of allegedly libelous or slanderous material. **b.** An explanation of a word or charge. [Lat. *innuendo,* by hunting < *innuendum,* gerund of *innuere,* to nod to.]

In·nu·it (ĭn′yo͞o-ĭt) *n., pl.* **Innuit** or **-its.** **1.** An Eskimo of North America and Greenland as distinguished from one of Asia and the Aleutian Islands. **2.** The language of the Innuits. [Eskimo, people, pl. of *innuk,* person.]

in·nu·mer·a·ble (ĭ-no͞o′mər-ə-bəl, ĭ-nyo͞o′-) *adj.* Too many to be counted or numbered. **—in·nu′mer·a·ble·ness** *n.* **—in·nu′mer·a·bly** *adv.*

in·nu·mer·ous (ĭ-no͞o′mər-əs) *adj.* Innumerable.

in·nu·tri·tion (ĭn′no͞o-trĭsh′ən, -nyo͞o-) *n.* Lack of nutrition; poor nourishment. **—in′nu·tri′tious** *adj.*

in·ob·ser·vance (ĭn′əb-zûr′vəns) *n.* **1.** Lack of heed or attention; disregard. **2.** Nonobservance, as of a law or custom. **—in′ob·ser′vant** *adj.*

in·ob·tru·sive (ĭn′əb-tro͞o′sĭv) *adj.* Not noticeable; unobtrusive.

in·oc·u·la·ble (ĭ-nŏk′yə-lə-bəl) *adj.* **1.** Transmissible by inoculation. **2.** Susceptible to a disease transmitted by inoculation. **—in·oc′u·la·bil′i·ty** *n.*

in·oc·u·lant (ĭ-nŏk′yə-lənt) *n.* Inoculum.

in·oc·u·late (ĭ-nŏk′yə-lāt′) *tr.v.* **-lat·ed, -lat·ing, -lates.** **1.** To communicate a disease to by transferring its virus or other causative agent into the body. **2.** To introduce the virus of a disease or other antigenic material into in order to immunize, cure, or experiment. **3.** To implant microorganisms or infectious material into (a culture medium). [ME *inoculaten,* to graft a scion < Lat. *inoculare* : *in-,* in + *oculus,* eye, bud.] **—in·oc′u·la′tive** *adj.* **—in·oc′u·la′tor** *n.*

in·oc·u·la·tion (ĭ-nŏk′yə-lā′shən) *n.* **1.** The act or process or an instance of inoculating. **2.** Inoculum.

in·oc·u·lum (ĭ-nŏk′yə-ləm) *n.* The material used in an inoculation. [NLat. < Lat. *inoculare,* to graft a scion. —see INOCULATE.]

in·o·dor·ous (ĭn-ō′dər-əs) *adj.* Having no odor.

in·of·fen·sive (ĭn′ə-fĕn′sĭv) *adj.* **1.** Giving no offense; unobjectionable. **2.** Causing no harm; harmless. **—in′of·fen′sive·ly** *adv.* **—in′of·fen′sive·ness** *n.*

in·of·fi·cious (ĭn′ə-fĭsh′əs) *adj.* *Law.* Contrary to natural affection or moral duty. Used of a will in which the testator disinherits his rightful heirs without sufficient reason. [Lat. *inofficiosus,* undutiful : *in-,* not + *officiosus,* dutiful < *officium,* duty.]

in·op·er·a·ble (ĭn-ŏp′ər-ə-bəl, -ŏp′rə-) *adj.* **1.** Not operable. **2.** Not susceptible to surgery. **—in·op′er·a·bly** *adv.*

in·op·er·a·tive (ĭn-ŏp′ər-ə-tĭv, -ŏp′rə-) *adj.* Not working or functioning. **—in·op′er·a·tive·ness** *n.*

in·o·per·cu·late (ĭn′ō-pûr′kyə-lĭt) *adj.* *Biol.* Lacking an operculum. **—in′o·per′cu·late** *n.*

in·op·por·tune (ĭn-ŏp′ər-to͞on′, -tyo͞on′) *adj.* Not opportune; ill-timed. **—in·op′por·tune′ly** *adv.* **—in·op′por·tune′ness** *n.*

in·or·di·nate (ĭn-ôr′dn-ĭt) *adj.* **1.** Exceeding reasonable limits; immoderate. **2.** Not regulated; disorderly. [ME *inordinat* < Lat. *inordinatus* : *in-,* not + *ordinatus,* p.part. of *ordinare,* to set in order < *ordo,* order.] **—in·or′di·na·cy, in·or′di·nate·ness** *n.* **—in·or′di·nate·ly** *adv.*

in·or·gan·ic (ĭn′ôr-găn′ĭk) *adj.* **1. a.** Involving neither organic life nor the products of organic life. **b.** Not composed of organic matter. **2.** Of or relating to the chemistry of compounds not usually classified as organic. **3.** Not arising in normal growth; artificial. **4.** Lacking system or structure. **—in′or·gan′i·cal·ly** *adv.*

in·os·cu·late (ĭn-ŏs′kyə-lāt′) *v.* **-lat·ed, -lat·ing, -lates.** —*tr.* **1.** To unite (blood vessels, for example) by small openings. **2.** To make continuous; blend. —*intr.* **1.** To open into one another. **2.** To unite so as to be continuous; blend. [IN-[2] + Lat. *osculare, osculat-,* to provide with an opening < *osculum,* dim. of *os,* mouth.] **—in·os′cu·la′tion** *n.*

in·o·si·tol (ĭ-nō′sĭ-tôl′, -tōl′) *n.* Any of nine isomeric alcohols, $C_6H_6(OH)_6$, esp. one found in plant and animal tissue and classified as a member of the vitamin B complex. [Gk. *is, in-,* sinew + -IT(E) + -OL.]

in·o·tro·pic (ē'nə-trō'pĭk, -trŏp'ĭk, ī'nə-) *adj.* Influencing muscular contractility. [Gk. *is, in-,* tendon, sinew + -TROPIC.]

in·pa·tient (ĭn'pā'shənt) *n.* A patient staying in a hospital for treatment.

in per·so·nam (ĭn' pər-sō'nəm) *adj. & adv. Law.* Against a person. Used of a proceeding. [Lat.]

in pet·to (ĭn pĕt'ō) *adj. & adv.* In secret or private. Used of appointments of cardinals by the pope undisclosed in consistory. [Ital., in the breast.]

in·phase (ĭn'fāz') *adj. Elect.* Having the same phase.

in pos·se (ĭn pŏs'ē) *adj. & adv.* In potential but not in actuality. [Lat., in possibility.]

in pro·pri·a per·so·na (ĭn prō'prē-ə pər-sō'nə) *adv.* In one's own person or self; personally. [Lat.]

inscription

in·put (ĭn'po͝ot') *n.* **1.** Something put into a system or expended in its operation to achieve a result or output, esp.: **a.** Energy, work, or power used to drive a machine. **b.** Current, electromotive force, or power supplied to an electric circuit, network, or device. **c.** Information put into a communications system for transmission or into a data-processing system for processing. **d.** The entirety of basic resources, including materials, equipment, and funds, required to complete a project. **e.** A position, terminal, or station at which input enters a system. **2. a.** The act of putting in; infusion: *a steady input of fuel.* **b.** An amount put in. **3.** Contribution to or participation in a common effort: *a discussion with input from all members of the group.* **4.** Information in general. **—in'put'** *v.* **(-put·ted** or **-put, -put·ting, -puts).**

Usage: *Input* has gained currency in senses not related to physics or computer technology. Example: *The report questioned whether, in such a closed administration, a president thus shielded had access to a sufficiently varied input to have a realistic picture of the nation* (*input* here meaning "a flow of information"). Example: *The nominee declared that he had no input, so far as he knew, in the adoption of the plank on abortion* (*input* here meaning "an active role, a voice in policy making"). These newer uses are unacceptable to a majority of the Usage Panel.

in·quest (ĭn'kwĕst') *n.* **1. a.** A judicial inquiry of some matter usually held before a jury, esp. an inquiry into the cause of a death. **b.** A jury making such an inquiry. **2.** An investigation; inquiry. [ME *enqueste* < OFr., of Lat. orig.]

in·qui·e·tude (ĭn-kwī'ĭ-to͞od', -tyo͞od') *n.* **1.** Restlessness. **2.** A state of uneasiness; disquietude. [ME, disturbance < LLat. *inquietudo,* restlessness < Lat. *inquies,* restless : *in-,* not + *quietus,* quiet.]

in·qui·line (ĭn'kwə-līn', -lĭn, ĭng'-) *n.* An animal that characteristically lives commensally in the burrow or dwelling place of an animal of another kind. *—adj.* Being or living as an inquiline. [Lat. *inquilinus,* lodger, tenant : *in-,* in + *colere,* to dwell.] **—in'qui·lin·ism** (-lə-nĭz'əm), **in'qui·lin'i·ty** (-lĭn'ĭ-tē) *n.* **—in'qui·lin'ous** (-lī'nəs) *adj.*

in·quire (ĭn-kwīr') *v.* **-quired, -quir·ing, -quires.** *—intr.* **1. a.** To put a question. **b.** To request information: *inquire about departure times; inquire after another's health.* **2.** To make a search or study; investigate: *inquire into a case.* *—tr.* To ask about: *"I am free to inquire what a work of art means to me"* (Bernard Berenson). [ME *enquiren* < OFr. *enquerrer* < Med. Lat. *inquerere* < Lat. *inquirere* : *in-* (intensive) + *quaerere,* to seek.] **—in·quir'er** *n.* **—in·quir'ing·ly** *adv.*

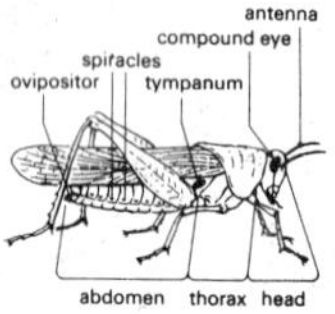

insect
Grasshopper

in·quir·y (ĭn-kwīr'ē, ĭn'kwīr'ē, ĭn'kwə-rē, ĭng'-) *n., pl.* **-ies.** **1.** The act of inquiring. **2.** A question; query. **3.** A close examination of some matter in a quest for information or truth.

in·qui·si·tion (ĭn'kwĭ-zĭsh'ən, ĭng'-) *n.* **1.** The act of inquiring into a matter; investigation. **2. a.** An inquest. **b.** The verdict of a judicial inquiry. **3. a. Inquisition.** A former tribunal in the Roman Catholic Church directed at the suppression of heresy. **b.** An investigation that violates the privacy or rights of individuals. **c.** A rigorous or harsh interrogation. [ME *inquisicioun* < OFr. *inquisicion* < Lat. *inquisitio* < *inquirere,* to inquire.] **—in'qui·si'tion·al** *adj.*

in·quis·i·tive (ĭn-kwĭz'ə-tĭv) *adj.* **1.** Unduly curious and inquiring. **2.** Eager to learn. **—in·quis'i·tive·ly** *adv.* **—in·quis'i·tive·ness** *n.*

in·quis·i·tor (ĭn-kwĭz'ĭ-tər) *n.* One who inquires, esp. a questioner who is excessively rigorous or harsh.

in·quis·i·to·ri·al (ĭn-kwĭz'ĭ-tôr'ē-əl, -tōr'-) *adj.* **1.** Of, pertaining to, characteristic of, or having the function of an inquisitor. **2.** *Law.* **a.** Pertaining to a trial in which one party acts as both prosecutor and judge. **b.** Pertaining to a criminal proceeding conducted in secrecy. **—in·quis'i·to'ri·al·ly** *adv.*

in re (ĭn rā', rē') *prep. Law.* In the matter or case of; in regard to. [Lat.]

in rem (ĭn rĕm') *adj. & adv. Law.* Against a thing, as property, status, or a right. [Lat.]

in·road (ĭn'rōd') *n.* **1.** A hostile invasion; raid. **2.** An advance, esp. at another's expense; encroachment: *Japanese products have made inroads into the American economy.* [IN + ROAD, raid (obs.).]

in·rush (ĭn'rŭsh') *n.* A sudden rushing in; influx.

in·sal·i·vate (ĭn-săl'ə-vāt') *tr.v.* **-vat·ed, -vat·ing, -vates.** To mix (food) with saliva in chewing. **—in·sal'i·va'tion** *n.*

in·sa·lu·bri·ous (ĭn'sə-lo͞o'brē-əs) *adj.* Not salubrious; unhealthful.

in·sane (ĭn-sān') *adj.* **1.** Of, exhibiting, or afflicted with insanity. **2.** Characteristic of, used by, or for the insane: *an insane asylum.* **3.** Very foolish; absurd. [Lat. *insanus* : *in-,* not + *sanus,* sane, healthy.] **—in·sane'ly** *adv.* **—in·sane'·ness** *n.*

in·san·i·tar·y (ĭn-săn'ĭ-tĕr'ē) *adj.* Not sanitary; unhygienic.

in·san·i·ty (ĭn-săn'ĭ-tē) *n., pl.* **-ties.** **1.** Persistent mental disorder or derangement. **2. a.** *Law.* Unsoundness of mind sufficient in the judgment of a civil court to render a person unfit to maintain a contractual or other legal relationship or to warrant commitment to a mental hospital. **b.** *Law.* In most criminal jurisdictions, a degree of mental malfunctioning sufficient to prevent the accused from knowing right from wrong in regard to the act he is charged with, or to render him unaware of the nature of the act when committing it. **3. a.** Extreme foolishness; folly. **b.** Something that is extremely foolish.

Synonyms: *insanity, lunacy, madness, mania, dementia.* These nouns denote conditions of mental disability. *Insanity* is a pronounced and usually prolonged condition of mental disorder that legally renders a person not responsible for his actions. *Lunacy* is sometimes used interchangeably with *insanity,* or it can denote derangement relieved intermittently by periods of clear-mindedness. *Madness,* a more general term, often stresses the violent side of mental ilness. *Mania* refers principally to the excited phase of manic-depressive psychosis. *Dementia* implies mental deterioration brought on by organic disorders.

in·sa·tia·ble (ĭn-sā'shə-bəl, -shē-ə-) *adj.* Incapable of being satiated; never satisfied: *an insatiable appetite.* [ME *insaciable* < OFr. < Lat. *insatiabilis* : *in-,* not + *satiare,* to fill < *satis,* enough.] **—in·sa'tia·bil'i·ty, in·sa'tia·ble·ness** *n.* **—in·sa'tia·bly** *adv.*

in·sa·ti·ate (ĭn-sā'shē-ĭt) *adj.* Not satisfied; insatiable. **—in·sa'ti·ate·ly** *adv.* **—in·sa'ti·ate·ness** *n.*

in·scribe (ĭn-skrīb') *tr.v.* **-scribed, -scrib·ing, -scribes.** **1. a.** To write, print, carve, or engrave (words or letters) on or in a surface. **b.** To mark or engrave (a surface) with words or letters. **2.** To enter (a name) on a list or in a register. **3.** To sign one's name or write a brief message in or on (a book or picture) when giving it as a gift. **4.** *Math.* To enclose (a polygon or polyhedron) within a closed configuration of lines, curves, or surfaces so that every vertex of the enclosed figure is incident on the enclosing configuration. [Lat. *inscribere* : *in-,* in + *scribere,* to write.] **—in·scrib'er** *n.*

in·scrip·tion (ĭn-skrĭp'shən) *n.* **1.** The act or an instance of inscribing. **2.** Something that is inscribed, as the wording on a coin, gravestone, or label. **3.** An enrollment or registration of names. **4.** A short, signed message in a book or on a picture given as a gift. [ME *inscripcioun* < Lat. *inscriptio* < *inscribere,* to inscribe.] **—in·scrip'tion·al, in·scrip'tive** *adj.* **—in·scrip'tive·ly** *adv.*

in·scru·ta·ble (ĭn-skro͞o'tə-bəl) *adj.* Difficult to understand or fathom; enigmatic: *an inscrutable face.* **—in·scru'ta·bil'i·ty, in·scru'ta·ble·ness** *n.* **—in·scru'ta·bly** *adv.*

in·sect (ĭn'sĕkt') *n.* **1. a.** Any of numerous usually small invertebrate animals of the class Insecta (or Hexapoda), having an adult stage characterized by three pairs of legs, a segmented body with three major divisions, and usually two pairs of wings. **b.** Any of various similar invertebrate animals, as a spider, centipede, or tick. **2.** A small or contemptible person. [Lat. *insectum* < *insectus,* segmented, p.part. of *insecare,* to cut up : *in-,* in + *secare,* to cut.]

in·sec·ta·ry (ĭn'sĕk'tə-rē, ĭn-sĕk'-) *n., pl.* **-ries.** A place in which living insects are kept or bred.

in·sec·ti·cide (ĭn-sĕk'tĭ-sīd') *n.* An agent used to kill insects. **—in·sec'ti·cid'al** (-sīd'l) *adj.* **—in·sec'ti·cid'al·ly** *adv.*

in·sec·ti·vore (ĭn-sĕk'tə-vôr', -vōr') *n.* **1.** Any of various mammals of the order Insectivora, characteristically feeding on insects and including the shrews, moles, and hedgehogs. **2.** An organism that feeds on insects. [NLat. *Insectivora,* order name : Lat. *insectum,* insect + Lat. *vorare,* to devour.]

in·sec·tiv·o·rous (ĭn'sĕk-tĭv'ər-əs) *adj.* **1.** Feeding on insects. **2.** *Bot.* Capable of trapping and absorbing insects, as the pitcher plant.

in·se·cure (ĭn'sĭ-kyo͝or') *adj.* **1.** Not secure or safe; inadequately guarded or protected: *an insecure fortress.* **2.** Unsure; unstable; shaky: *an insecure hold.* **3.** Lacking self-confidence; uncertain: *feeling insecure about the interview.* **—in'se·cure'ly** *adv.* **—in'se·cu'ri·ty** (-kyo͝or'ĭ-tē), **in'se·cure'ness** *n.*

in·sem·i·nate (ĭn-sĕm'ə-nāt') *tr.v.* **-nat·ed, -nat·ing, -nates.** **1.** To sow seed in. **2.** To introduce semen into the uterus of. [Lat. *inseminare, inseminat-* : *in-,* in + *seminare,* to plant < *semen,* seed.] **—in·sem'i·na'tion** *n.* **—in·sem'i·na'tor** *n.*

in·sen·sate (ĭn-sĕn'sāt', -sĭt) *adj.* **1. a.** Lacking sensation; inanimate. **b.** Unconscious. **2.** Lacking sensibility; unfeeling. **3.** Lacking sense; foolish. **—in·sen'sate'ly** *adv.* **—in·sen'sate'ness** *n.*

in·sen·si·ble (ĭn-sĕn'sə-bəl) *adj.* **1.** Imperceptible; inappreciable: *an insensible change.* **2.** Deprived of the power of feeling; unconscious: *lay insensible where he had fallen.*

3. a. Unsusceptible; unaffected: *insensible to the cold.* **b.** Unheeding; unmindful: *I am not insensible of your concern.* **c.** Unfeeling; callous; cold. **4.** Lacking intelligence; irrational. **—in·sen'si·bil'i·ty, insen'si·ble·ness** *n.* **—in·sen'si·bly** *adv.*

in·sen·si·tive (ĭn-sĕn'sĭ-tĭv) *adj.* **1.** Not physically sensitive; numb. **2. a.** Lacking in sensitivity to the feelings or circumstances of others; unfeeling. **b.** Lacking in responsiveness: *insensitive to the needs of the customers.* **—in·sen'si·tiv'i·ty, in·sen'si·tive·ness** *n.* **—in·sen'si·tive·ly** *adv.*

in·sen·tient (ĭn-sĕn'shənt) *adj.* Without sensation or consciousness; inanimate. **—in·sen'tience** *n.*

in·sep·a·ra·ble (ĭn-sĕp'ər-ə-bəl, -sĕp'rə-) *adj.* Incapable of being separated. **—in·sep'a·ra·bil'i·ty, in·sep'a·ra·ble·ness** *n.* **—in·sep'a·ra·bly** *adv.*

in·sert (ĭn-sûrt') *tr.v.* **-sert·ed, -sert·ing, -serts. 1.** To put or set into, between, or among: *inserted the key in the lock.* **2.** To introduce into the body of something; interpolate: *insert an illustration into the text.* **3.** To place into an orbit, trajectory, or stream. *—n.* (ĭn'sûrt'). Something inserted or intended for insertion, as a picture or chart into written material. [Lat. *inserere, insert-* : *in-*, in + *serere,* to join.] **—in·sert'er** *n.*

in·ser·tion (ĭn-sûr'shən) *n.* **1.** The act of inserting. **2.** Something inserted, as a strip of lace, embroidery, or other trim inserted in a piece of fabric. **3.** A point or mode of attachment. **—in·ser'tion·al** *adj.*

in-serv·ice (ĭn'sûr'vĭs) *adj.* **1.** Of, relating to, or being a full-time employee: *in-service teachers.* **2.** Taking place or continuing while one is a full-time employee: *in-service training workshops.*

in·ses·so·ri·al (ĭn'sĕ-sôr'ē-əl, -sōr'-) *adj.* Perching or adapted for perching. [LLat. *insessor,* occupant < Lat. *insessus,* p.part. of *insidēre,* to sit upon —see INSIDIOUS.]

in·set (ĭn'sĕt', ĭn-sĕt') *tr.v.* **-set, -set·ting, -sets.** To insert; set in. *—n.* (ĭn'sĕt'). **1.** Something set in, as: **a.** A small map or illustration set within a larger one. **b.** A leaf or group of pages inserted in a publication. **c.** A piece of material set into a garment as trim. **2. a.** An inflow, as of water. **b.** A channel.

in·shore (ĭn'shôr', -shōr') *adj.* **1.** Close to a shore. **2.** Coming toward a shore. **—in'shore'** *adv.*

in·shrine (ĭn-shrīn') *v.* Variant of **enshrine.**

in·side (ĭn-sīd', ĭn'sīd') *n.* **1.** An inner or interior part. **2.** An inner side or surface. **3.** The middle part; the part away from the edge. **4. insides.** *Informal.* **a.** The inner organs; entrails. **b.** The inner parts or workings. **5.** *Slang.* Confidential information; tip. *—adj.* **1.** Inner; interior. **2.** For the interior. **3.** Pertaining to or coming from those in authority: *the inside office.* **4.** *Baseball.* Passing too near the body of the batter. Used of a pitch. *—adv.* Into or in the interior; within. *—prep.* **1.** Within: *inside an hour.* **2.** Into: *going inside the house.* **—idioms. inside of.** *Informal.* Within: *inside of the cave; inside of an hour.* **inside out. 1.** With the inner surface turned out; reversed. **2.** *Informal.* Thoroughly. **on the inside.** In a position of confidence or influence.

Usage: *Inside* and *inside of* have the same meaning. *Inside* is generally preferred, especially in writing, when the reference is to position or location: *inside the stadium. Inside of* is used more acceptably when the reference is to time: *inside of* (or *inside*) *an hour.*

in·sid·er (ĭn-sī'dər) *n.* **1.** An accepted member of a group. **2.** Someone who has special knowledge or access to confidential information.

inside track *n.* **1.** The path next to the inner rail in a curved race track. **2.** An advantageous position in a competition.

in·sid·i·ous (ĭn-sĭd'ē-əs) *adj.* **1.** Working or spreading harmfully in a subtle or stealthy manner. **2.** Intended to entrap; treacherous. **3.** Beguiling but harmful; alluring. [Lat. *insidiosus* < *insidiae,* ambush < *insidēre,* to sit upon : *in-*, on + *sedēre,* to sit.] **—in·sid'i·ous·ly** *adv.* **—in·sid'i·ous·ness** *n.*

in·sight (ĭn'sīt') *n.* **1.** The capacity to discern the true nature of a situation; penetration. **2.** An elucidating glimpse.

in·sight·ful (ĭn'sīt'fəl, ĭn-sīt'-) *adj.* Showing or having insight; perceptive. **—in'sight'ful·ly** *adv.*

in·sig·ni·a (ĭn-sĭg'nē-ə) also **in·sig·ne** (-nē) *n., pl.* **insignia** or **-ni·as. 1.** A badge of office, rank, membership, or nationality; emblem. **2.** A distinguishing sign. [Lat., pl. of *insigne,* badge of office < *insignis,* remarkable : *in-*, in + *signum,* sign.]

Usage: *Insignia,* a Latin plural form, may be used with either a singular or a plural verb: *The insignia was* (or *were*) *displayed.* The traditional English plural is *insignia,* but *insignias* is now acceptable and is standard in the U.S. Army.

in·sig·nif·i·cance (ĭn'sĭg-nĭf'ĭ-kəns) *n.* The quality or state of being insignificant.

in·sig·nif·i·can·cy (ĭn'sĭg-nĭf'ĭ-kən-sē) *n., pl.* **-cies. 1.** Insignificance. **2.** One that is insignificant.

in·sig·nif·i·cant (ĭn'sĭg-nĭf'ĭ-kənt) *adj.* Not significant, esp.: **a.** Lacking in importance; trivial. **b.** Small in size, power, or value. **c.** Lacking in meaning; meaningless. **—in'sig·nif'i·cant·ly** *adv.*

in·sin·cere (ĭn'sĭn-sîr') *adj.* Not sincere; hypocritical. **—in'sin·cere'ly** *adv.* **—in'sin·cer'i·ty** (-sĕr'ĭ-tē) *n.*

in·sin·u·ate (ĭn-sĭn'yo͞o-āt') *v.* **-at·ed, -at·ing, -ates.** *—tr.* **1. a.** To introduce (a thought, for example) gradually and insidiously. **b.** To introduce (oneself) by subtle and artful means. **2.** To convey with oblique allusions; hint at. *—intr.* To make insinuations. [Lat. *insinuare, insinuat-* : *in-*, in + *sinuare,* to curve < *sinus,* curve.] **—in·sin'u·a'tive** *adj.* **—in·sin'u·a'tor** *n.*

in·sin·u·at·ing (ĭn-sĭn'yo͞o-ā'tĭng) *adj.* **1.** Provoking gradual doubt or suspicion; suggestive: *insinuating remarks.* **2.** Ingratiating: *a silky, insinuating voice.* **—in·sin'u·at'ing·ly** *adv.*

in·sin·u·a·tion (ĭn-sĭn'yo͞o-ā'shən) *n.* **1.** The act or practice of insinuating. **2.** Something that is insinuated, esp. an artfully indirect suggestion.

in·sip·id (ĭn-sĭp'ĭd) *adj.* **1.** Lacking flavor or zest; unpalatable. **2.** Lacking excitement, stimulation, or interest; dull. [LLat. *insipidus*: Lat. *in-*, not + *sapidus,* savory < Lat. *sapere,* to taste.] **—in'si·pid'i·ty** (ĭn'sĭ-pĭd'ĭ-tē), **in·sip'id·ness** *n.* **—in·sip'id·ly** *adv.*

in·sip·i·ence (ĭn-sĭp'ē-əns) *n. Archaic.* Lack of wisdom. [ME < OFr. < Lat. *insipientia* < *insipiens,* unwise : *in-*, not + *sapiens,* wise, pr.part. of *sapere,* to taste, have sense.]

in·sist (ĭn-sĭst') *v.* **-sist·ed, -sist·ing, -sists.** *—intr.* To be firm in a demand or course; refuse to yield: *He insisted on giving me a second helping.* *—tr.* To assert or demand vehemently and persistently: *We insist that you accept these gifts.* [Lat. *insistere,* to persist : *in-*, on + *sistere,* to stand.] **—in·sis'tence, in·sis'ten·cy** *n.*

in·sis·tent (ĭn-sĭs'tənt) *adj.* **1.** Firm in asserting a demand or opinion; unyielding. **2.** Demanding notice: *insistent hunger.* **3.** Repetitive and persistent: *the wren's insistent note.* **—in·sis'tent·ly** *adv.*

in si·tu (ĭn sī'to͞o) *adj. & adv.* In the original place. [Lat.]

in·snare (ĭn-snâr') *v.* Variant of **ensnare.**

in·so·bri·e·ty (ĭn'sə-brī'ĭ-tē) *n.* Lack of sobriety; intemperance.

in·so·far (ĭn'sō-fär') *adv.* To such an extent.

insofar as *conj.* To the extent that.

in·so·late (ĭn'sō-lāt', ĭn-sō'-) *tr.v.* **-lat·ed, -lat·ing, -lates.** To expose to sunlight, as for bleaching. [Lat. *insolare, insolat-* : *in-*, in + *sol,* sun.]

in·so·la·tion (ĭn'sō-lā'shən) *n.* **1. a.** Exposure to sunlight. **b.** Therapeutic exposure to sunlight. **2.** Sunstroke. **3. a.** The solar radiation incident on the earth or another planet. **b.** The rate of delivery of such radiation per unit area surface.

in·sole (ĭn'sōl') *n.* **1.** The inner sole of a shoe or boot. **2.** An extra strip of material put inside a shoe for comfort or protection.

in·so·lence (ĭn'sə-ləns) *n.* **1.** The quality of being insolent. **2.** An instance of insolent behavior.

in·so·lent (ĭn'sə-lənt) *adj.* **1.** Presumptuous and insulting in manner or speech; arrogant. **2.** Audaciously impudent; impertinent. [ME < Lat. *insolens* : *in-*, not + *solens,* pr.part. of *solēre,* to be accustomed.] **—in'so·lent·ly** *adv.*

in·sol·u·ble (ĭn-sŏl'yə-bəl) *adj.* **1.** Incapable of being dissolved. **2.** Incapable of being solved or explained. [ME *insoluble,* unanswerable < Lat. *insolubilis,* irrefutable : *in-*, not + *solvere,* to loosen.] **—in·sol'u·bil'i·ty, in·sol'u·ble·ness** *n.* **—in·sol'u·bly** *adv.*

in·solv·a·ble (ĭn-sŏl'və-bəl) *adj.* Incapable of being solved. **—in·solv'a·bly** *adv.*

in·sol·ven·cy (ĭn-sŏl'vən-sē) *n.* The condition of being insolvent.

in·sol·vent (ĭn-sŏl'vənt) *adj.* **1.** Unable to meet debts or discharge liabilities; bankrupt. **2.** Of or pertaining to insolvent or bankrupt persons. *—n.* One who is insolvent.

in·som·ni·a (ĭn-sŏm'nē-ə) *n.* Chronic inability to sleep. [Lat. < *insomnis,* sleepless : *in-*, not + *somnus,* sleep.] **—in·som'ni·ac** (-ăk') *adj. & n.*

in·so·much as (ĭn'sō-mŭch') *conj.* **1.** To such extent or degree as. **2.** Since; inasmuch as.

in·sou·ci·ance (ĭn-so͞o'sē-əns, ăɴ'so͞o-syäɴs') *n.* Blithe lack of concern; nonchalance.

in·sou·ci·ant (ĭn-so͞o'sē-ənt, ăɴ'so͞o-syäɴ') *adj.* Blithely unconcerned; nonchalant. [Fr. : *in-*, not (< Lat.) + *souciant,* pr.part. of *soucier,* to trouble < Lat. *sollicitare,* to vex. —see SOLICIT.] **—in·sou'ci·ant·ly** *adv.*

in·soul (ĭn-sōl') *v.* Variant of **ensoul.**

in·spect (ĭn-spĕkt') *tr.v.* **-spect·ed, -spect·ing, -spects. 1.** To examine carefully and critically, esp. for flaws. **2.** To review or examine officially: *The barracks were inspected weekly.* [Lat. *inspectare,* freq. of *inspicere,* to look into : *in-*, in + *specere,* to look.] **—in·spec'tive** *adj.*

in·spec·tion (ĭn-spĕk'shən) *n.* **1.** The act of inspecting. **2.** Official examination or review. **—in·spec'tion·al** *adj.*

in·spec·tor (ĭn-spĕk'tər) *n.* **1.** A person, esp. an official, who inspects. **2.** A police officer of the rank next below superintendent. **—in·spec'to·ral, in'spec·to'ri·al** (-tôr'ē-əl, -tōr'-) *adj.* **—in·spec'tor·ship'** *n.*

in·spec·tor·ate (ĭn-spĕk'tər-ĭt) *n.* **1.** The office or duties of an inspector. **2.** A staff of inspectors. **3.** An inspector's district.

inspector general *n., pl.* **inspectors general.** An officer with general investigative powers within a civil, military, or other organization.

in·sphere (ĭn-sfîr') *v.* Variant of **ensphere.**

in·spi·ra·tion (ĭn'spə-rā'shən) *n.* **1. a.** Stimulation of the mind or emotions to a high level of feeling or activity.

insignia

b. The condition of being so stimulated. **2.** An agency, as a person or a work of art, that moves the intellect or emotions or that prompts action or invention. **3.** Something that is inspired; a sudden creative act or idea. **4.** The quality of inspiring or exalting: *a painting full of inspiration.* **5.** *Theol.* Divine guidance or influence exerted directly upon the mind and soul of man. **6.** The act of breathing in; inhalation.

in·spi·ra·tion·al (ĭn'spə-rā'shə-nəl) *adj.* **1.** Of or pertaining to inspiration. **2.** Providing or intended to convey inspiration. **3.** Resulting from inspiration. **—in'spi·ra'tion·al·ly** *adv.*

in·spi·ra·tor (ĭn'spə-rā'tər) *n.* **1.** An inhaler. **2.** A respirator.

in·spir·a·to·ry (ĭn-spīr'ə-tôr'ē, -tōr'ē) *adj.* Of, pertaining to, or used for the drawing in of air.

in·spire (ĭn-spīr') *v.* **-spired, -spir·ing, -spires.** *—tr.* **1.** To affect, guide, or arouse by divine influence. **2.** To fill with noble or reverent emotion; exalt: *hymns that inspire the congregation.* **3.** To stimulate to creativity or action. **4.** To elicit; arouse: *a woman capable of inspiring a man's devotion.* **5.** To be the cause or source of; bring about: *an invention that inspired many imitations.* **6.** To inhale (air). **7.** *Archaic.* **a.** To breathe upon. **b.** To breathe life into. *—intr.* **1.** To stimulate energies, ideals, or reverence. **2.** To inhale. [ME *enspiren* < OFr. *enspirer* < Lat. *inspirare* : *in-*, into + *spirare,* to breathe.] **—in·spir'er** *n.* **—in·spir'ing·ly** *adv.*

in·spir·it (ĭn-spĭr'ĭt) *tr.v.* **-it·ed, -it·ing, -its.** To instill courage or life into; animate.

in·spis·sate (ĭn-spĭs'āt', ĭn'spĭ-sāt') *intr. & tr.v.* **-sat·ed, -sat·ing, -sates.** To thicken or cause to thicken, as by boiling or evaporation; condense. [< LLat. *inspissatus,* thickened : Lat. *in-* (intensive) + *spissus,* thick.] **—in'spis·sa'tion** *n.* **—in·spis'sa'tor** *n.*

in·sta·bil·i·ty (ĭn'stə-bĭl'ĭ-tē) *n., pl.* **-ties.** Lack of stability.

in·stall also **in·stal** (ĭn-stôl') *tr.v.* **-stalled, -stall·ing, -stalls** also **-stals. 1.** To set in position and connect or adjust for use. **2.** To induct into an office, rank, or position: *a ceremony to install the new prime minister.* **3.** To settle in an indicated place or condition; establish: *installed herself in the spare room.* [ME *installen* < OFr. *installer* < Med. Lat. *installare* : *in-*, in + *stallum,* place.] **—in·stall'er** *n.*

in·stal·la·tion (ĭn'stə-lā'shən) *n.* **1. a.** The act of installing. **b.** The state of being installed. **2.** A system of machinery or other apparatus set up for use. **3.** A military base or camp.

in·stall·ment[1] also **in·stal·ment** (ĭn-stôl'mənt) *n.* **1.** One of several successive payments in settlement of a debt. **2.** A portion of something issued at intervals. **3.** A chapter or part of a literary work presented serially. **—modifier:** *the installment plan.* [Alteration of obs. *estallment* < OFr. *estaler,* to place, fix < *estal,* place, of Germanic orig.]

in·stall·ment[2] also **in·stal·ment** (ĭn-stôl'mənt) *n.* Installation.

in·stance (ĭn'stəns) *n.* **1.** Something that is representative of a group or class; example. **2.** A legal proceeding or process; suit. **3.** A step in a process. **4. a.** Prompting; request: *called at the instance of his wife.* **b.** *Archaic.* Urgent solicitation. **5.** *Obs.* An impelling motive. *—tr.v.* **-stanced, -stanc·ing, -stanc·es. 1.** To offer as an example; cite. **2.** To demonstrate or show by being an example; exemplify. [ME *instaunce* < OFr. *instance* < Lat. *instantia,* presence < *instans,* present. —see INSTANT.]

in·stan·cy (ĭn'stən-sē) *n.* **1.** Urgency. **2.** Immediateness; instantaneousness.

in·stant (ĭn'stənt) *n.* **1.** A very brief time; moment. **2.** A particular point in time: *the instant he arrives.* **3.** The current month: *your letter of the 15th instant.* *—adj.* **1.** Immediate: *instant attention.* **2.** Imperative; urgent: *an instant need.* **3.** Now under consideration; present. **4. a.** Designed for quick preparation with minimal effort: *instant mashed potatoes.* **b.** Appearing, done, or taking place with or as if with maximum quickness and ease. *—adv.* Instantly. [ME < OFr. < Lat. *instans,* present, pr.part. of *instare,* to approach : *in-*, on + *stare,* to stand.]

in·stan·ta·ne·ous (ĭn'stən-tā'nē-əs) *adj.* **1.** Occurring or completed without perceptible delay. **2.** Present or occurring at a specific instant: *instantaneous velocity.* [Med. Lat. *instantaneus* < Lat. *instans,* present. —see INSTANT.] **—in'stan·ta'ne·ous·ly** *adv.* **—in'stan·ta'ne·ous·ness** *n.*

in·stan·ter (ĭn-stăn'tər) *adv.* Without delay; instantly. [Med. Lat. < Lat., urgently < *instans,* present. —see INSTANT.]

in·stant·ly (ĭn'stənt-lē) *adv.* **1.** At once; immediately. **2.** *Archaic.* Urgently. *—conj.* As soon as.

instant replay *n.* A recording of an event on videotape for playback immediately upon completion of the event.

in·star[1] (ĭn-stär') *tr.v.* **-starred, -star·ring, -stars.** To stud with or as if with stars.

in·star[2] (ĭn'stär') *n.* An insect or other arthropod between molts, as during metamorphosis. [NLat. < Lat., image, form.]

in·state (ĭn-stāt') *tr.v.* **-stat·ed, -stat·ing, -states.** To establish in office; install.

in·stau·ra·tion (ĭn'stô-rā'shən) *n.* *Archaic.* **1.** Renovation; restoration. **2.** Institution; establishment. [Lat. *instauratio* < *instaurare,* to renew.]

in·stead (ĭn-stĕd') *adv.* In the place of something previously mentioned; as an alternative or substitute: *Planning to drive, he walked instead.* [ME *in sted of,* in place of.]

instead of *prep.* In place of; rather than.

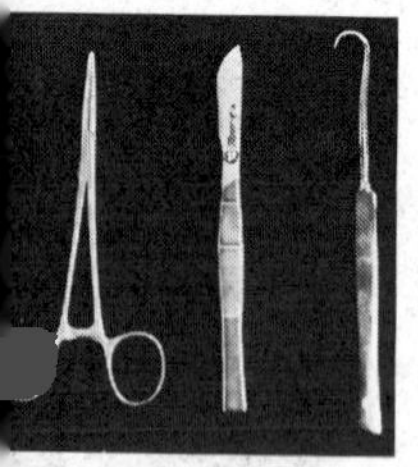

instrument

in·step (ĭn'stĕp') *n.* **1.** The arched middle part of the human foot. **2.** The part of a shoe or stocking covering the instep.

in·sti·gate (ĭn'stĭ-gāt') *tr.v.* **-gat·ed, -gat·ing, -gates. 1.** To urge on; goad. **2.** To foment; stir up. [Lat. *instigare, instigat-.*] **—in'sti·ga'tion** *n.* **—in'sti·ga'tive** *adj.* **—in'sti·ga'tor** *n.*

in·still also **in·stil** (ĭn-stĭl') *tr.v.* **-stilled, -still·ing, -stills** also **-stils. 1.** To introduce by gradual, persistent efforts; implant: *"morality . . . may be instilled into their minds"* (Jefferson). **2.** To pour in drop by drop. [Lat. *instillare,* to drip in : *in-*, in + *stillare,* to drip < *stilla,* drop.] **—in'stil·la'tion** (ĭn'stə-lā'shən) *n.* **—in·still'er** *n.*

in·stinct (ĭn'stĭngkt') *n.* **1. a.** The innate aspect of behavior that is unlearned, complex, and normally adaptive. **b.** A powerful motivation or impulse. **2.** An innate capability or aptitude. *—adj.* (ĭn-stĭngkt'). **1.** *Obs.* Impelled from within. **2.** Imbued; filled: *words instinct with love.* [ME < Lat. *instinctus,* impulse < p.part. of *instinguere,* to incite : *in-*, on + *stinguere,* to prick.]

in·stinc·tive (ĭn-stĭngk'tĭv) *adj.* **1.** Of, pertaining to, or arising from instinct. **2.** Arising from a natural impulse; spontaneous and unthinking: *an instinctive dislike of spiders.* **—in·stinc'tive·ly** *adv.*

in·sti·tute (ĭn'stĭ-to͞ot', -tyo͞ot') *tr.v.* **-tut·ed, -tut·ing, -tutes. 1. a.** To establish, organize, and set in operation. **b.** To initiate; begin. **2.** To establish or invest in an office or position. *—n.* **1.** *Obs.* The act of instituting. **2.** Something instituted, esp. an authoritative rule or precedent. **3.** An organization founded to promote some cause: *an institute for the deaf.* **4. a.** An educational institution. **b.** The building or buildings housing such an institution. **5.** A short, intensive workshop or seminar on one specific subject. **6. institutes.** A digest of the principles or rudiments of some subject, esp. a legal abstract. [ME *instituten* < Lat. *institutus,* p.part. of *instituere,* to establish : *in-*, in + *statuere,* to set up < *stare,* to stand.] **—in'sti·tut'er, in'sti·tu'tor** *n.*

in·sti·tu·tion (ĭn'stĭ-to͞o'shən, -tyo͞o'shən) *n.* **1.** The act of instituting. **2. a.** A custom, practice, relationship, or behavioral pattern of importance in the life of a community or society. **b.** *Informal.* An ever-present feature; fixture. **3. a.** An established organization or foundation, esp. one dedicated to public service or to culture. **b.** The building or buildings housing such an organization. **4.** A place of confinement, as a mental asylum. **—in'sti·tu'tion·al** *adj.* **—in'sti·tu'tion·al·ly** *adv.*

in·sti·tu·tion·al·ism (ĭn'stĭ-to͞o'shə-nə-lĭz'əm, -tyo͞o'-) *n.* **1.** Adherence to or belief in established forms, esp. belief in organized religion. **2.** Use of institutions for those incapable of self-maintenance. **—in'sti·tu'tion·al·ist** *n.*

in·sti·tu·tion·al·ize (ĭn'stĭ-to͞o'shə-nə-līz', -tyo͞o'-) *tr.v.* **-ized, -iz·ing, -iz·es. 1.** To make into, treat as, or give the character of an institution to. **2.** To commit (a person) to an institution. **—in'sti·tu'tion·al·i·za'tion** *n.*

in·stroke (ĭn'strōk') *n.* An inward stroke, esp. a piston stroke moving away from the crankshaft.

in·struct (ĭn-strŭkt') *v.* **-struct·ed, -struct·ing, -structs.** *—tr.* **1.** To furnish with knowledge; teach. **2.** To give orders to; direct. *—intr.* To serve as an instructor. [ME *instructen* < Lat. *instructus,* p.part. of *instruere,* to prepare : *in-*, in + *struere,* to build.]

in·struc·tion (ĭn-strŭk'shən) *n.* **1.** The act, practice, or profession of instructing. **2. a.** Imparted knowledge. **b.** An imparted or acquired item of knowledge; lesson. **3.** *Computer Sci.* A machine code telling a computer to perform a particular operation. **4.** Often **instructions.** A direction; order. **—in·struc'tion·al** *adj.*

in·struc·tive (ĭn-strŭk'tĭv) *adj.* Conveying knowledge or information; enlightening. **—in·struc'tive·ly** *adv.* **—in·struc'tive·ness** *n.*

in·struc·tor (ĭn-strŭk'tər) *n.* **1.** One who instructs; teacher. **2. a.** An academic rank below assistant professor. **b.** One who holds such a rank. **—in·struc'tor·ship'** *n.*

in·stru·ment (ĭn'strə-mənt) *n.* **1.** A means by which something is done; agency. **2. a.** One used to accomplish some purpose. **b.** A person used and controlled by another; dupe. **3.** A mechanical implement. **4.** A device for recording or measuring, esp. such a device functioning as part of a control system. **5.** A device for producing music. **6.** A legal document. *—tr.v.* (-mĕnt') **-ment·ed, -ment·ing, -ments. 1.** To provide or equip with instruments. **2.** To address a legal document to. [ME < Lat. *instrumentum,* tool < *instruere,* to prepare. —see INSTRUCT.]

in·stru·men·tal (ĭn'strə-mĕn'tl) *adj.* **1.** Serving as a means or agency; implemental. **2.** Of, pertaining to, or accomplished with an instrument or tool. **3.** Performed on or written for a musical instrument. **4.** *Gram.* Of or designating a case used typically to express means, agency, or accompaniment. *—n.* *Gram.* **1.** The instrumental case. **2.** A word in the instrumental case. **—in'stru·men'tal·ly** *adv.*

in·stru·men·tal·ism (ĭn'strə-mĕn'tl-ĭz'əm) *n.* A pragmatic theory that ideas are instruments that function as guides of action, their validity being determined by the success of the action.

in·stru·men·tal·ist (ĭn-strə-mĕn'tl-ĭst) *n.* **1.** One who plays a musical instrument. **2.** An advocate or student of instrumentalism.

in·stru·men·tal·i·ty (ĭn'strə-mĕn-tăl'ĭ-tē) *n., pl.* **-ties. 1.** The state or quality of being instrumental. **2.** Agency; means. **3.** A subsidiary branch, as of a government, by means of which functions or policies are carried out.

in·stru·men·ta·tion (ĭn′strə-mĕn-tā′shən) *n.* **1.** The application or use of instruments. **2. a.** The study and practice of arranging music for instruments. **b.** The arrangement or orchestration resulting from such practice. **3.** The study, development, and manufacture of instruments, as for scientific use. **4.** Instrumentality.

instrument panel *n.* A mounted array of instruments used to operate a machine.

in·sub·or·di·nate (ĭn′sə-bôr′dn-ĭt) *adj.* Not submissive to authority: *has a history of insubordinate behavior.* **—in′sub·or′di·na′tion** *n.* **—in′sub·or′di·nate·ly** *adv.*

Synonyms: *insubordinate, rebellious, mutinous, factious, seditious.* These adjectives are applied to persons or their actions and mean in opposition to, and usually in defiance of, established authority. *Insubordinate* implies failure to recognize or accept the authority of a superior. *Rebellious* implies open defiance of authority to which one is subject. *Mutinous,* a still stronger term, pertains to uprising against lawful authority, especially that of a naval or military command. *Factious* describes what promotes divisiveness, dissension, or disunity within a group or organization. *Seditious* applies principally to the stirring up of resistance against a government.

in·sub·stan·tial (ĭn′səb-stăn′shəl) *adj.* **1.** Lacking substance or reality; imaginary. **2. a.** Not firm; flimsy. **b.** Delicate; fine. **—in′sub·stan′ti·al′i·ty** (-shē-ăl′ĭ-tē) *n.*

in·suf·fer·a·ble (ĭn-sŭf′ər-ə-bəl, -sŭf′rə-) *adj.* Incapable of being endured; intolerable. **—in·suf′fer·a·ble·ness** *n.* **—in·suf′fer·a·bly** *adv.*

in·suf·fi·cien·cy (ĭn′sə-fĭsh′ən-sē) *n., pl.* **-cies. 1.** The quality or state of being insufficient. **2.** Something insufficient.

in·suf·fi·cient (ĭn′sə-fĭsh′ənt) *adj.* Not sufficient; inadequate. **—in′suf·fi′cient·ly** *adv.*

in·suf·flate (ĭn′sə-flāt′, ĭn-sŭf′lāt′) *tr.v.* **-flat·ed, -flat·ing, -flates. 1.** To blow or breathe into or on. **2.** To treat medically by blowing a powder, gas, or vapor into a bodily cavity. [LLat. *insufflare, insufflat-* : Lat. *in-,* on + Lat. *sufflare,* to inflate.] **—in′suf·fla′tor** *n.*

in·suf·fla·tion (ĭn′sə-flā′shən) *n.* **1.** The act or an instance of insufflating. **2.** *Eccles.* A ritual act of breathing on baptismal water or upon one being baptized.

in·su·lar (ĭn′sə-lər, ĭns′yə-) *adj.* **1.** Of, pertaining to, or constituting an island. **2. a.** Characteristic or suggestive of the isolated life of an island. **b.** Circumscribed and detached in outlook and experience. **3.** *Anat.* Designating isolated tissue or an island of tissue. [LLat. *insularis* < Lat. *insula,* island.] **—in′su·lar·ism, in′su·lar′i·ty** (-lăr′ĭ-tē) *n.* **—in′su·lar·ly** *adv.*

insular sclerosis *n.* Multiple sclerosis.

in·su·late (ĭn′sə-lāt′, ĭns′yə-) *tr.v.* **-lat·ed, -lat·ing, -lates. 1.** To cause to be in a detached or isolated position. **2.** *Physics.* To prevent the passage of heat or electricity or sound into or out of, esp. by interposition of an appropriate insulator. [< LLat. *insulatus,* made into an island < Lat. *insula,* island.]

in·su·la·tion (ĭn′sə-lā′shən, ĭns′yə-) *n.* **1.** The act of insulating or the state of being insulated. **2.** Material used in insulating.

in·su·la·tor (ĭn′sə-lā′tər, ĭns′yə-) *n.* **1.** A material that insulates, esp. a nonconductor of sound, heat, or electricity. **2.** A device that insulates.

in·su·lin (ĭn′sə-lĭn) *n.* **1.** A polypeptide hormone secreted by the islands of Langerhans and functioning to regulate carbohydrate metabolism by controlling blood glucose levels. **2.** A preparation derived from the pancreas of the pig or the ox for use in the medical treatment of diabetes. [NLat. *insula,* islet (of Langerhans) < Lat., island + -IN.]

insulin shock *n.* Hypoglycemia resulting from excessive insulin in the blood.

in·sult (ĭn-sŭlt′) *v.* **-sult·ed, -sult·ing, -sults.** *—tr.* **1. a.** To speak to or treat in an insolent or contemptuous way. **b.** To cause damage or offense to: *a speech that insulted the intelligence of the audience.* **2.** *Obs.* To make an attack upon. *—intr. Obs.* To behave arrogantly. *—n.* (ĭn′sŭlt′). **1.** An offensive action or remark. **2.** *Med.* An injury, irritation, or trauma. [OFr. *insulter,* to triumph over < Lat. *insultare,* to revile : *in-,* on + *saltare,* to dance, freq. of *salire,* to jump.] **—in·sult′er** *n.* **—in·sult′ing·ly** *adv.*

in·su·per·a·ble (ĭn-so͞o′pər-ə-bəl) *adj.* Incapable of being overcome; insurmountable: *an insuperable barrier.* **—in·su′per·a·bil′i·ty, in·su′per·a·ble·ness** *n.* **—in·su′per·a·bly** *adv.*

in·sup·port·a·ble (ĭn′sə-pôr′tə-bəl, -pōr′-) *adj.* **1.** Unbearable; intolerable. **2.** Lacking grounds or defense; unjustifiable: *an insupportable claim.* **—in′sup·port′a·ble·ness** *n.* **—in′sup·port′a·bly** *adv.*

in·sup·press·i·ble (ĭn′sə-prĕs′ə-bəl) *adj.* Irrepressible. **—in′sup·press′i·bly** *adv.*

in·sur·ance (ĭn-sho͝or′əns) *n.* **1. a.** The act, business, or system of insuring. **b.** The state of being insured. **c.** A means of being insured. **2. a.** Coverage by a contract binding a party to indemnify another against specified loss in return for premiums paid. **b.** The sum for which such a contract insures something. **c.** The periodical premium paid for this coverage.

in·sure (ĭn-sho͝or′) *v.* **-sured, -sur·ing, -sures.** *—tr.* **1.** To cover with insurance. **2.** To make sure, certain, or secure. *—intr.* To buy or sell insurance. —See Usage note at **assure.** [ME *ensuren,* to assure < OFr. *enseurer,* perh. var. of *assurer,* to assure. —see ASSURE.] **—in·sur′a·bil′i·ty** *n.* **—in·sur′a·ble** *adj.*

in·sured (ĭn-sho͝ord′) *n.* One covered by insurance.

in·sur·er (ĭn-sho͝or′ər) *n.* One that insures, esp. an underwriter.

instrument panel

in·sur·gence (ĭn-sûr′jəns) *n.* Uprising; revolt.

in·sur·gen·cy (ĭn-sûr′jən-sē) *n.* **1.** The quality or circumstance of being insurgent. **2.** Insurgence.

in·sur·gent (ĭn-sûr′jənt) *adj.* Rising in revolt against civil authority or a government in power. *—n.* **1.** One who revolts against civil authority. **2.** A member of a political party who rebels against its leadership. [Lat. *insurgens, insurgent-,* pr.part. of *insurgere,* to rise up : *in-* (intensive) + *surgere,* to rise.] **—in·sur′gent·ly** *adv.*

in·sur·mount·a·ble (ĭn′sər-moun′tə-bəl) *adj.* Incapable of being surmounted; insuperable: *insurmountable odds.* **—in′sur·mount′a·bly** *adv.*

in·sur·rec·tion (ĭn′sə-rĕk′shən) *n.* An act or instance of open revolt against civil authority or a constituted government. [ME *insurrecion* <OFr. < Lat. *insurrectio* < *insurgere,* to rise up. —see INSURGENT.] **—in′sur·rec′tion·al** *adj.* **—in′sur·rec′tion·ar′y** *adj. & n.* **—in′sur·rec′tion·ism** *n.* **—in′sur·rec′tion·ist** *n.*

in·sus·cep·ti·ble (ĭn′sə-sĕp′tə-bəl) *adj.* Not susceptible. **—in·sus·cep′ti·bil′i·ty** *n.* **—in′sus·cep′ti·bly** *adv.*

insulation

in·tact (ĭn-tăkt′) *adj.* **1.** Not impaired in any way. **2.** Having all parts; whole. [ME *intacte* < Lat. *intactus* : *in-,* not + *tactus,* p.part. of *tangere,* to touch.] **—in·tact′ness** *n.*

in·ta·glio (ĭn-tăl′yō, -täl′-) *n., pl.* **-glios. 1. a.** A figure or design incised beneath the surface of hard metal or stone. **b.** The art or process of carving a design in this manner. **2.** A gemstone carved in intaglio. **3.** Printing done with a plate bearing an image in intaglio. **4.** A die incised so as to produce a design in relief. [Ital. < *intagliare,* to engrave : *in-,* in (< Lat.) + *tagliare,* to cut < VLat. **talliare.*—see TAILOR.]

in·take (ĭn′tāk′) *n.* **1.** An opening by which a fluid is admitted into a container or conduit. **2. a.** The act of taking in. **b.** Something, esp. energy, taken in.

in·tan·gi·ble (ĭn-tăn′jə-bəl) *adj.* **1.** Incapable of being perceived by the senses. **2.** Incapable of being realized or defined. *—n.* Something intangible, esp. an asset that cannot be perceived by the senses. **—in·tan′gi·bil′i·ty, in·tan′gi·ble·ness** *n.* **—in·tan′gi·bly** *adv.*

in·tar·si·a (ĭn-tär′sē-ə) *n.* **1.** A mosaic worked in wood. **2.** The art or practice of making intarsia. [Ital. *intarsio* < *tarsia,* inlaid mosaic work < Ar. *tarṣi.*]

in·te·ger (ĭn′tĭ-jər) *n.* **1.** A member of the set of positive whole numbers (1, 2, 3, . . .), negative whole numbers (−1, −2, −3, . . .), and zero (0). **2.** A complete unit or entity. [< Lat., whole, complete.]

in·te·gra·ble (ĭn′tĭ-grə-bəl) *adj.* Capable of being integrated. **—in′te·gra·bil′i·ty** *n.*

insulator

in·te·gral (ĭn′tĭ-grəl, ĭn-tĕg′rəl) *adj.* **1.** Essential or necessary for completeness; constituent. **2.** Possessing everything essential; entire. **3.** (ĭn′tĭ-grəl). *Math.* **a.** Expressed or expressible as or in terms of integers. **b.** Expressed as or involving integrals. *—n.* **1.** A complete unit; whole. **2.** (ĭn′tĭ-grəl). *Math.* **a.** A definite integral. **b.** An indefinite integral. [LLat. *integralis,* making up a whole < Lat. *integer,* complete.] **—in′te·gral′i·ty** *n.* **—in′te·gral·ly** *adv.*

integral calculus *n.* The mathematical study of integration, the properties of integrals, and their applications.

integral domain *n.* A commutative ring with unity having no proper divisors of zero, that is, having no nonzero elements *a, b* such that $a \cdot b = 0$, where 0 is the additive identity.

in·te·grand (ĭn′tĭ-grănd′) *n.* A function or equation to be integrated. [< Lat. *integrandus,* gerund. of *integrare,* to integrate.]

in·te·grant (ĭn′tĭ-grənt) *adj.* Integral.

in·te·grate (ĭn′tĭ-grāt′) *v.* **-grat·ed, -grat·ing, -grates.** *—tr.* **1.** To make into a whole by bringing all parts together; unify. **2.** To join with something else; unite. **3.** To open to people of all races or ethnic groups without restriction; desegregate. **4.** *Math.* **a.** To calculate the integral of. **b.** To perform integration upon. **5.** To bring about the integration of (personality traits). *—intr.* To become integrated or undergo integration. [Lat. *integrare, integrat-,* to make whole < *integer,* complete.] **—in′te·gra′tive** *adj.*

integrated circuit *n.* A tiny wafer of substrate material upon which is etched or imprinted a complex of electronic components and their interconnections. **—integrated circuitry** *n.*

in·te·gra·tion (ĭn′tĭ-grā′shən) *n.* **1. a.** An act or the process of integrating. **b.** The state of becoming integrated. **c.** Desegregation. **2.** The organization of organic, psychological, or social traits and tendencies of a personality into a harmonious whole. **—in′te·gra′tion·ist** *n.*

in·te·gra·tor (ĭn′tĭ-grā′tər) *n.* **1.** One that integrates. **2.** An instrument for mechanically calculating definite integrals.

in·teg·ri·ty (ĭn-tĕg′rĭ-tē) *n.* **1.** Rigid adherence to a code or

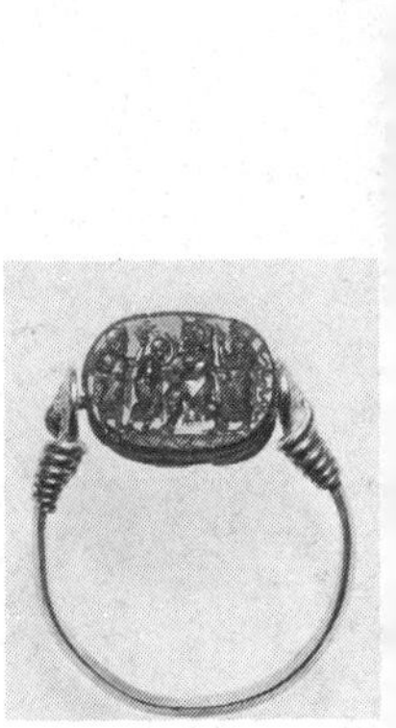

intaglio
6th-century B.C.
Etruscan gem

standard of values; probity. **2.** The state of being unimpaired; soundness. **3.** The quality or condition of being whole or undivided; completeness. [ME *integrite* < OFr. < Lat. *integritas,* soundness < *integer,* whole, complete.]

in·te·gro·dif·fer·en·tial (ĭn'tĭ-grō-dĭf'ə-rĕn'shəl, ĭn-tĕg'rō-) *adj.* Involving both mathematical differentiation and integration. [INTEGR(ATION) + DIFFERENTIAL.]

in·teg·u·ment (ĭn-tĕg'yo͞o-mənt) *n.* An outer covering or coat, as the skin of an animal, the coat of a seed, or the membrane enclosing an organ. [Lat. *integumentum* < *integere,* to cover : *in-,* on + *tegere,* to cover.] **—in·teg'u·men'ta·ry** (-mĕn'tə-rē, -mĕn'trē) *adj.*

in·tel·lect (ĭn'tl-ĕkt') *n.* **1. a.** The ability to learn and reason as distinguished from the ability to feel or will; capacity for knowledge and understanding. **b.** The ability to think abstractly or profoundly. **2.** A person of great intellectual ability. [ME < OFr. < Lat. *intellectus,* perception < p.part. of *intellegere,* to perceive. —see INTELLIGENT.]

in·tel·lec·tion (ĭn'tl-ĕk'shən) *n.* **1.** The act or process of exercising the intellect. **2.** A thought or idea. [ME *intelleccioun,* understanding < OFr. < Lat. *intellectio* < *intellectus,* intellect.]

in·tel·lec·tive (ĭn'tl-ĕk'tĭv) *adj.* Of, pertaining to, or generated by the intellect. **—in'tel·lec'tive·ly** *adv.*

in·tel·lec·tron·ics (ĭn'tl-ĕk-trŏn'ĭks) *n. (used with a sing. verb).* The use of electronic devices to extend human intellect. [Blend of INTELLECT and ELECTRONICS.]

in·tel·lec·tu·al (ĭn'tl-ĕk'cho͞o-əl) *adj.* **1. a.** Of or pertaining to the intellect. **b.** Rational rather than emotional. **2.** Appealing to or engaging the intellect. **3. a.** Intelligent. **b.** Given to exercise of the intellect. *—n.* An intellectual person. **—in'tel·lec'tu·al'i·ty** (-ăl'ĭ-tē) *n.* **—in'tel·lec'tu·al·ly** *adv.*

in·tel·lec·tu·al·ism (ĭn'tl-ĕk'cho͞o-ə-lĭz'əm) *n.* **1.** The exercise or application of the intellect. **2.** Devotion to exercise or development of the intellect. **—in'tel·lec'tu·al·ist** *n.* **—in'tel·lec'tu·al·is'tic** *adj.*

in·tel·lec·tu·al·ize (ĭn'tl-ĕk'cho͞o-ə-līz') *tr.v.* **-ized, -iz·ing, -iz·es.** To furnish a rational structure or meaning for. **—in'tel·lec'tu·al·i·za'tion** *n.* **—in'tel·lec'tu·al·iz'er** *n.*

in·tel·li·gence (ĭn-tĕl'ə-jəns) *n.* **1. a.** The capacity to acquire and apply knowledge. **b.** The faculty of thought and reason. **c.** Superior powers of mind. **2. a.** An intelligent, incorporeal being, esp. an angel. **b. Intelligence.** *Christian Science.* The primal, eternal quality of God. **3.** Received information; news. **4. a.** Secret information, esp. about an actual or potential enemy. **b.** An agency, staff, or office employed in gathering such information.

intelligence quotient *n.* The ratio of tested mental age to chronological age, usually expressed as a quotient multiplied by 100.

in·tel·li·genc·er (ĭn-tĕl'ə-jən-sər, -jĕn'-) *n.* **1.** One who conveys news; informant. **2.** A secret agent, informer, or spy.

intelligence test *n.* A standardized test used to establish an intelligence level rating by measuring an individual's ability to form concepts, solve problems, acquire information, reason, and perform other intellectual operations.

in·tel·li·gent (ĭn-tĕl'ə-jənt) *adj.* **1.** Having intelligence. **2.** Having a high degree of intelligence; mentally acute. **3.** Showing sound judgment and rationality. **4.** Guided or motivated by the intellect; rational. **5.** Capable of performing certain functions of a computer: *an intelligent terminal.* [Lat. *intellegens, intellegent-,* pr.part. of *intellegere,* to perceive : *inter-,* between + *legere,* to choose.] **—in·tel'li·gen'tial** (ĭn-tĕl'ə-jĕn'shəl) *adj.* **—in·tel'li·gent·ly** *adv.*

Synonyms: *intelligent, bright, brilliant, knowing, quick-witted, smart, intellectual.* These adjectives are applied to persons and their behavior when they give evidence of mental keeness. *Intelligent* usually implies the ability to cope with demands created by novel situations and new problems, to apply what is learned from experience, and to use the power of reasoning and inference effectively as a guide to behavior. *Bright,* sometimes used interchangeably with *intelligent,* implies mental acuteness in general, and *brilliant* suggests the same quality, especially when it is displayed impressively. *Knowing* implies discernment and shrewdness, and *quick-witted,* alertness and adroitness of mental function. *Smart* is often a general term implying mental keeness; more specifically it can refer to practical knowledge, ability to learn quickly, or to sharpness or shrewdness, sometimes considered unfavorably. *Intellectual* activities stress the working of the intellect, and *intellectual* persons are those who show mental capacity well beyond the ordinary.

in·tel·li·gent·si·a (in-tĕl'ə-jĕnt'sē-ə, -gĕnt'-) *n.* The intellectual elite of a society. [R. *intelligentsiya* < Lat. *intellegentia,* intelligence < *intelligens,* intelligent.]

in·tel·li·gi·ble (ĭn-tĕl'ĭ-jə-bəl) *adj.* **1.** Capable of being understood. **2.** Capable of being apprehended by the intellect alone. [ME < Lat. *intellegibilis* < *intellegere,* to perceive. —see INTELLIGENT.] **—in·tel'li·gi·bil'i·ty, in·tel'li·gi·ble·ness** *n.* **—in·tel'li·gi·bly** *adv.*

in·tem·per·ance (ĭn-tĕm'pər-əns, -prəns) *n.* Lack of temperance, as in the indulgence of an appetite or passion.

in·tem·per·ate (ĭn-tĕm'pər-ĭt, -tĕm'prĭt) *adj.* Not temperate or moderate; excessive. **—in·tem'per·ate·ly** *adv.* **—in·tem'per·ate·ness** *n.*

in·tend (ĭn-tĕnd') *v.* **-tend·ed, -tend·ing, -tends.** *—tr.* **1.** To have in mind; plan. **2. a.** To design for a specific purpose. **b.** To have in mind for a particular use. **3.** To signify; mean. *—intr.* To have in mind some purpose or design. [ME *entenden* < OFr. *entendre* < Lat. *intendere* : *in-,* into + *tendere,* to stretch.]

Usage: *Intend* may be followed by an infinitive (*intended to go*) or a gerund (*intended going*), by a *that* clause with a subjunctive verb (*intended that he be present*), or by a noun and an infinitive (*intended him to receive the prize*).

in·ten·dance (ĭn-tĕn'dəns) *n.* **1.** The function of an intendant; management. **2.** An intendancy.

in·ten·dan·cy (ĭn-tĕn'dən-sē) *n., pl.* **-cies. 1.** The position or function of an intendant. **2.** Intendants collectively. **3.** The district supervised by an intendant, as in Latin America.

in·ten·dant (ĭn-tĕn'dənt) *n.* **1.** An administrative official serving a French, Spanish, or Portuguese monarch. **2.** A district administrator in some countries of Latin America. [Fr. < OFr., administrator < Lat. *intendens,* pr.part. of *intendere,* to intend.]

in·tend·ed (ĭn-tĕn'dĭd) *adj.* **1.** Deliberate; intentional. **2.** Prospective; future. *—n. Informal.* An engaged person.

in·tend·ment (ĭn-tĕnd'mənt) *n.* The true meaning or intention of something, esp. a law.

in·ten·er·ate (ĭn-tĕn'ə-rāt') *tr.v.* **-at·ed, -at·ing, -ates.** To make tender; soften. [IN-[2] + Lat. *tener,* tender + -ATE[1].] **—in·ten'er·a'tion** *n.*

in·tense (ĭn-tĕns') *adj.* **1.** Possessing or displaying a distinctive feature to an extreme degree: *the intense sun of the tropics.* **2.** Extreme in degree, strength, or size. **3.** Involving or showing strain or extreme effort: *intense concentration.* **4. a.** Deeply felt; profound. **b.** Tending to feel deeply. —See Usage note at **intensive.** [ME < OFr. < Lat. *intensus,* stretched, p.part. of *intendere,* to intend.] **—in·tense'ly** *adv.* **—in·tense'ness** *n.*

in·ten·si·fi·er (ĭn-tĕn'sə-fī'ər) *n.* **1.** One that intensifies. **2.** An intensive.

in·ten·si·fy (ĭn-tĕn'sə-fī') *v.* **-fied, -fy·ing, -fies.** *—tr.* **1.** To make intense or more intense. **2.** To increase the contrast of (a photographic image). *—intr.* To become intense or more intense. **—in·ten'si·fi·ca'tion** *n.*

in·ten·sion (ĭn-tĕn'shən) *n.* **1.** *Logic.* The properties connoted by a term. **2.** Intensity. [Lat. *intensio,* an intensifying < *intensus,* stretched. —see INTENSE.]

in·ten·si·ty (ĭn-tĕn'sĭ-tē) *n., pl.* **-ties. 1.** Exceptionally great concentration, power, or force. **2.** *Physics.* **a.** The measure of effectiveness of a force field given by the force per unit test element. **b.** The energy transferred by a wave per unit time across a unit area perpendicular to the direction of propagation.

in·ten·sive (ĭn-tĕn'sĭv) *adj.* **1.** Of, pertaining to, or characterized by intensity. **2.** Tending to emphasize or intensify. **3.** Extremely or highly concentrated. **4.** Constituting or relating to a method esp. of land cultivation that aims to increase the productivity of a fixed area by means of an increase in the capital and labor. **5.** *Physics.* Having the same value for any subdivision of a thermodynamic system. Used of pressure, for example. *—n.* A linguistic element, as the adverbs *extremely* or *awfully,* that provide force or emphasis.

Usage: *Intensive* is often used interchangeably with *intense.* However, it has the special meaning of "concentrated" (the opposite of *extensive*). Thus, one speaks of *intense heat* but *intensive study.*

intensive care *n.* **1.** Special medical equipment and services provided for seriously ill patients. **2.** A hospital unit that specializes in intensive care.

in·tent (ĭn-tĕnt') *n.* **1.** That which is intended; purpose. **2.** The state of mind operative at the time of an action. **3. a.** Meaning; purport. **b.** Connotation. *—adj.* **1.** Firmly fixed; concentrated. **2.** Having the attention applied; engrossed. **3.** Having the mind fastened upon some purpose. [ME *entente* < OFr. < Med. Lat. *intentus* < Lat., attentive to, p.part. of *intendere,* to intend.]

in·ten·tion (ĭn-tĕn'shən) *n.* **1.** A plan of action; design. **2. a.** An aim that guides action; object. **b. intentions.** Purpose in regard to marriage: *honorable intentions.* **3.** The general connotation or concept of something; what something is meant to convey. **4.** *Med.* The course or manner of healing of a surgical wound. **5.** The import; meaning. [ME *entencioun* < OFr. < Lat. *intentio,* attention < *intendere,* to intend.]

Synonyms: *intention, intent, purpose, object, goal, end, aim, objective.* These nouns refer to what one hopes to achieve or attain. *Intention* signifies a course of action that one proposes to follow. *Intent,* often a legal term, more strongly implies a fixed course pursued deliberately, and *purpose* adds to this the idea of resolution or determination to carry out what one proposes. *Object* and *goal* are sometimes interchangeable in referring to the proposed attainment. *Object,* however, often implies something clearcut and attainable by practical means, and *goal* something more idealistic or remote. *End* suggests an ultimate attainment, viewed from long range, and *aim,* the direction one's efforts take in pursuit of the end. *Objective* refers to an end or goal with the implication that it can be reached.

in·ten·tion·al (ĭn-tĕn′shə-nəl) *adj.* **1.** Done deliberately; intended: *an intentional slight.* **2.** Having to do with logical intention or connotation. **—in·ten′tion·al′i·ty** (-năl′ĭ-tē) *n.* **—in·ten′tion·al·ly** *adv.*

in·ter (ĭn-tûr′) *tr.v.* **-terred, -ter·ring, -ters.** To place in a grave or tomb. [ME *enteren* < OFr. *enterrer* < Med. Lat. *interrare* : Lat. *in-*, in + Lat. *terra*, earth.]

inter– *pref.* **1.** Between; among: *international.* **2.** Within; in the midst of: *intertropical.* **3.** Mutual; mutually: *interrelate.* **4.** Reciprocal; reciprocally: *intermingle.* [ME < OFr. < Lat. < *inter*, between, among.]

in·ter·a·bang (ĭn-tĕr′ə-băng′) *n.* Variant of **interrobang.**

in·ter·act (ĭn′tər-ăkt′) *intr.v.* **-act·ed, -act·ing, -acts.** To act on each other. **—in′ter·ac′tion** *n.* **—in′ter·ac′tive** *adj.*

in·ter·ac·tive terminal (ĭn′tər-ăk′tĭv) *n.* A computer or data-processing terminal capable of providing a source of both input and output for the computer system to which it is connected.

in·ter a·li·a (ĭn′tər ā′lē-ə, ä′lē-ə) *adv.* Among other things. [Lat.]

in·ter a·li·os (ĭn′tər ā′lē-ōs′, ä′lē-ōs′) *adv.* Among other persons. [Lat.]

in·ter·brain (ĭn′tər-brān′) *n.* The diencephalon.

in·ter·breed (ĭn′tər-brēd′) *v.* **-bred** (-brĕd′), **-breed·ing, -breeds.** *—intr.* **1.** To breed with another kind or species. **2.** To breed within a narrow range or with closely related types or individuals; inbreed. *—tr.* To cause to interbreed.

in·ter·ca·lar·y (ĭn-tûr′kə-lĕr′ē, ĭn′tər-kăl′ə-rē) *adj.* **1. a.** Inserted in the calendar to make the calendar year correspond to the solar year. Used of a day or a month. **b.** Having such a day or month inserted. Used of a year. **2.** Interpolated. [Lat. *intercalarius* < *intercalare*, to intercalate.]

in·ter·ca·late (ĭn-tûr′kə-lāt′) *tr.v.* **-lat·ed, -lat·ing, -lates.** **1.** To insert (a day or month) in a calendar. **2.** To insert, interpose, or interpolate. [Lat. *intercalare, intercalat-* : *inter-*, among + *calare*, to proclaim.] **—in·ter′ca·la′tion** *n.* **—in·ter′ca·la′tive** *adj.*

in·ter·cede (ĭn′tər-sēd′) *intr.v.* **-ced·ed, -ced·ing, -cedes.** **1.** To plead on another's behalf. **2.** To act as mediator in a dispute. [Lat. *intercedere*, to intervene : *inter-*, between + *cedere*, to go.] **—in′ter·ced′er** *n.*

in·ter·cel·lu·lar (ĭn′tər-sĕl′yə-lər) *adj.* Among or between cells.

in·ter·cept (ĭn′tər-sĕpt′) *tr.v.* **-cept·ed, -cept·ing, -cepts.** **1. a.** To stop, deflect, or interrupt the progress or intended course of. **b.** *Sports.* To take possession of by catching (an opponent's ball), esp. in football. **2.** To intersect. **3.** *Obs.* To cut off from access or communication. **4.** To prevent. *—n.* (ĭn′tər-sĕpt′) **1.** *Math.* The distance from the origin of coordinates along a coordinate axis to the point at which a line, curve, or surface intersects the axis. **2.** Interception. [Lat. *intercipere, intercept-* : *inter-*, between + *capere*, to seize.] **—in′ter·cep′tive** *adj.*

in·ter·cep·tion (ĭn′tər-sĕp′shən) *n.* **1.** The act of intercepting or the state of being intercepted. **2. a.** Something that is intercepted. **b.** *Sports.* A pass that is intercepted, esp. a forward pass in football.

in·ter·cep·tor also **in·ter·cept·er** (ĭn′tər-sĕp′tər) *n.* **1.** One that intercepts. **2.** A fast-climbing, highly maneuverable fighter plane designed to intercept enemy aircraft.

in·ter·ces·sion (ĭn′tər-sĕsh′ən) *n.* **1.** Entreaty in favor of another. **2.** Mediation in a dispute. [ME < OFr. < Lat. *intercessio*, intervention < *intercessus*, p.part. of *intercedere*, to intervene. —see INTERCEDE.] **—in′ter·ces′sion·al** *adj.* **—in′ter·ces′sor** *n.* **—in′ter·ces′so·ry** *adj.*

in·ter·change (ĭn′tər-chānj′) *v.* **-changed, -chang·ing, -chang·es.** *—tr.* **1.** To switch each of (two things) into the place of the other. **2.** To give and receive mutually; exchange. *—intr.* To change places with each other. *—n.* (ĭn′tər-chānj′). **1.** The act or process or an instance of interchanging; exchange. **2.** A highway intersection designed to permit traffic to move freely from one road to another without crossing another line of traffic. [ME *enterchaungen* < OFr. *entrechangier* : *inter-*, between (< Lat.) + *changier*, to change.] **—in′ter·chang′er** *n.*

in·ter·change·a·ble (ĭn′tər-chān′jə-bəl) *adj.* Capable of mutual interchange. **—in′ter·change′a·bil′i·ty, in′ter·change′a·ble·ness** *n.* **—in′ter·change′a·bly** *adv.*

in·ter·clav·i·cle (ĭn′tər-klăv′ĭ-kəl) *n.* A bone located in front of the sternum and between the clavicles in most reptiles.

in·ter·col·le·giate (ĭn′tər-kə-lē′jĭt, -jē-ĭt) *adj.* Involving or representing two or more colleges.

in·ter·co·lum·ni·a·tion (ĭn′tər-kə-lŭm′nē-ā′shən) *n.* **1.** The open spaces between the columns in a colonnade. **2.** The system by which the columns of a colonnade are spaced.

in·ter·com (ĭn′tər-kŏm′) *n.* An intercommunication system, as between two rooms. [Short for INTERCOMMUNICATION.]

in·ter·com·mu·ni·cate (ĭn′tər-kə-myōō′nĭ-kāt′) *intr.v.* **-cat·ed, -cat·ing, -cates.** **1.** To communicate with each other. **2.** To be connected or adjoined, as rooms. **—in′ter·com·mu′ni·ca′tion** *n.* **—in′ter·com·mu′ni·ca′tive** (-kā′tĭv, -kə-tĭv) *adj.*

in·ter·con·nect (ĭn′tər-kə-nĕkt′) *v.* **-nect·ed, -nect·ing, -nects.** *—intr.* To be connected one to the other. *—tr.* To connect reciprocally. **—in′ter·con·nec′tion** *n.*

in·ter·con·ti·nen·tal (ĭn′tər-kŏn′tə-nĕn′tl) *adj.* **1.** Extending or taking place among or between continents: *intercontinental warfare.* **2.** Capable of traveling from one continent to another: *an intercontinental ballistic missile.*

in·ter·con·ver·sion (ĭn′tər-kən-vûr′zhən, -shən) *n.* Mutual conversion. **—in′ter·con·vert′i·ble** *adj.* **—in·ter·con·vert′a·bil′i·ty** *n.*

in·ter·cos·tal (ĭn′tər-kŏs′təl) *adj.* Located or occurring between the ribs. [NLat. *intercostalis* : INTER- + Lat. *costa*, rib.]

in·ter·course (ĭn′tər-kôrs′, -kōrs′) *n.* **1.** Dealings or communications between persons or groups. **2.** Sexual intercourse. [ME *entercours* < OFr. *entrecours* < Lat. *intercursus*, p.part. of *intercurrere*, to mingle with : *inter-*, between + *currere*, to run.]

in·ter·crop (ĭn′tər-krŏp′) *v.* **-cropped, -crop·ping, -crops.** *—intr.* To grow a second crop between the rows of another. *—tr.* To plant a crop between the rows of (another). **—in′ter·crop′** *n.*

in·ter·cur·rent (ĭn′tər-kûr′ənt) *adj.* **1.** Occurring as an interruption in a process. **2.** *Pathol.* Occurring during the course of an existing disease. [Lat. *intercurrens, intercurrent-*, pr.part. of *intercurrere*, to mingle with. —see INTERCOURSE.]

in·ter·den·tal (ĭn′tər-dĕn′tl) *adj.* **1.** Located between the teeth. **2.** Pronounced with the tip of the tongue between the teeth, as (*th*) in *that* or (th) in *thumb.* *—n.* An interdental consonant.

in·ter·de·pend·ent (ĭn′tər-dĭ-pĕn′dənt) *adj.* Mutually dependent. **—in′ter·de·pend′ence** *n.*

in·ter·dict (ĭn′tər-dĭkt′) *tr.v.* **-dict·ed, -dict·ing, -dicts.** **1.** To prohibit or place under an ecclesiastical or legal sanction. **2.** To cut or destroy (an enemy line of communication) by firepower so as to halt an enemy's advance. *—n.* (ĭn′tər-dĭkt′) **1.** A prohibition by court order. **2.** *Rom. Cath. Ch.* An ecclesiastical censure excluding a person or district from participation in most sacraments and from Christian burial. [Alteration of ME *enterditen*, to place under a church ban < OFr. *entredit*, an interdict < p.part. of *entredire*, to forbid < Lat. *interdicere* : *inter-*, between + *dicere*, to say.] **—in′ter·dic′tion** *n.* **—in′ter·dic′tive, in′ter·dic′to·ry** *adj.* **—in′ter·dic′tive·ly** *adv.* **—in′ter·dic′tor** *n.*

in·ter·est (ĭn′trĭst, -tər-ĭst, -trĕst′) *n.* **1. a.** A feeling of curiosity or concern about something. **b.** Something, as a quality or feature, that is the cause of such a feeling. **2.** Regard for one's benefit or advantage; self-interest. **3. a.** A right, claim, or legal share in something. **b.** Something in which such a right, claim, or share is held. **c.** Involvement with or participation in something. **4. a.** A charge for a loan, usually a percentage of the amount loaned. **b.** An excess or bonus beyond what is expected or due. **5.** A group of persons sharing esp. a financial interest in an enterprise or industry. *—tr.v.* **-est·ed, -est·ing, -ests.** **1.** To arouse the curiosity or hold the attention of. **2.** To cause to become involved or concerned with. **3.** *Obs.* To concern or affect. [ME, legal claim < OFr. < Lat., it is of importance, 3rd sing. indicative of *interesse*, to be between : *inter-*, between + *esse*, to be.]

in·ter·est·ed (ĭn′trĭ-stĭd, -tər-ĭ-stĭd, -tə-rĕs′tĭd) *adj.* **1.** Having or showing curiosity, fascination, or concern. **2.** Possessing a right, claim, or share. **—in′ter·est·ed·ly** *adv.* **—in′ter·est·ed·ness** *n.*

in·ter·est·ing (ĭn′trĭ-stĭng, -tər-ĭ-stĭng, -tə-rĕs′tĭng) *adj.* Arousing or holding attention; absorbing. **—in′ter·est·ing·ly** *adv.*

in·ter·face (ĭn′tər-fās′) *n.* **1.** A surface forming a common boundary between adjacent regions. **2. a.** A point at which independent systems or diverse groups interact. **b.** The device or system by which interaction at an interface is effected. *—v.* **-faced, -fac·ing, -fac·es.** *—tr.* **1.** To join by means of an interface. **2.** To serve as an interface for. *—intr.* **1.** To serve as an interface or to become interfaced. **2.** To interact or coordinate smoothly. **—in′ter·fa′cial** *adj.*

in·ter·fere (ĭn′tər-fîr′) *intr.v.* **-fered, -fer·ing, -feres.** **1.** To come between so as to be a hindrance or obstacle; impede. **2.** *Sports.* To illegally obstruct the movement of the ball or of an opposing player, esp. to impede illegally the catching of a pass in football. **3.** To intervene or intrude in the affairs of others; meddle. **4.** To strike one hoof against the opposite hoof or leg while moving. Used of a horse. **5.** *Physics.* To produce interference with (another wave). **6.** *Electronics.* To inhibit or prevent clear reception of (broadcast signals). [ME *enterferen*, to meddle < OFr. *entreferer.*] **—in′ter·fer′er** *n.* **—in′ter·fer′ing·ly** *adv.*

Synonyms: *interfere, meddle, tamper.* These verbs are compared in the sense of concerning oneself in the affairs of other persons. *Interfere* and *meddle* are sometimes interchangeable. *Meddle* is the stronger in implying unwanted, unwarranted, or unnecessary intrusion. It is somewhat weaker than *interfere* in implying action that seriously hampers, hinders, or frustrates. *Tamper* refers to intervention in the form of making unauthorized alterations or changes, especially ones that corrupt.

in·ter·fer·ence (ĭn′tər-fîr′əns) *n.* **1. a.** The act, process, or an instance of interfering. **b.** Something that interferes. **2. a.** *Football.* The blocking of defensive tacklers to protect the ball carrier. **b.** *Sports.* The illegal obstruction or hindrance of the ball or of an opposing player. **3.** *Physics.* The

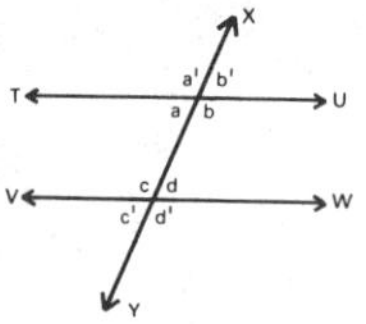

interior angle
Interior angles of parallel lines (angles a, b, c, and d)

phenomenon of two or more waves of the same frequency combining to form a wave in which the disturbance at any point is the algebraic or vector sum of the disturbances due to the interfering waves at that point. **4.** *Electronics.* **a.** The inhibition or prevention of clear reception of broadcast signals. **b.** The distorted portion of a received signal. **—in'ter·fer·en'tial** (-fə-rĕn'shəl) *adj.*

in·ter·fe·rom·e·ter (ĭn'tər-fə-rŏm'ĭ-tər) *n.* Any of several optical, acoustical, or radio-frequency instruments that use interference phenomena between a reference wave and an experimental wave, or between two parts of an experimental wave, to determine wavelengths, wave velocities, distances, and directions. **—in'ter·fer'o·met'ric** *adj.* **—in'ter·fer'o·met'ri·cal·ly** *adv.* **—in'ter·fer·om'e·try** *n.*

in·ter·fer·on (ĭn'tər-fîr'ŏn') *n.* A cellular protein produced in response to and acting to prevent replication of an infectious viral form within an infected cell. [INTERFER(E) + -ON[3].]

in·ter·fer·tile (ĭn'tər-fûr'tl) *adj.* Having the ability to interbreed.

in·ter·ga·lac·tic (ĭn'tər-gə-lăk'tĭk) *adj.* Between galaxies.

in·ter·gen·er·a·tion·al (ĭn'tər-jĕn'ə-rā'shə-nəl) *adj.* Being or occurring between generations: *intergenerational misunderstandings.*

in·ter·gla·cial (ĭn'tər-glā'shəl) *adj.* Between glacial epochs.

in·ter·gov·ern·men·tal (ĭn'tər-gŭv'ərn-mĕn'tl) *adj.* Being or occurring between two or more governments or divisions of government.

in·ter·grade (ĭn'tər-grād') *intr.v.* **-grad·ed, -grad·ing, -grades.** To merge into each other in a series of stages, forms, or types. *—n.* (ĭn'tər-grād'). A transitional step, grade, or form. **—in'ter·gra·da'tion** (-grā-dā'shən) *n.*

in·ter·group (ĭn'tər-gro͞op') *adj.* Being or occurring between two or more social groups.

in·ter·im (ĭn'tər-ĭm) *n.* An interval of time between one event, process, or period and another. *—adj.* Belonging to or taking place during an interim; temporary: *an interim agreement.* [< Lat., in the meantime < *inter,* at intervals, between.]

in·ter·i·on·ic (ĭn'tər-ī-ŏn'ĭk) *adj.* Located or occurring between ions.

in·te·ri·or (ĭn-tîr'ē-ər) *adj.* **1.** Of, relating to, or located in the inside; inner. **2.** Of or relating to the mental or spiritual life. **3.** Situated away from a coast or border; inland. *—n.* **1.** The internal portion or area of something. **2.** One's mental or spiritual being. **3.** A representation of the inside of a building or room, as in a painting. **4.** The inland part of a given political or geographic entity. [Lat., comp. of *inter,* within.] **—in·te'ri·or'i·ty** (-ôr'ĭ-tē, -ŏr'-) *n.* **—in·te'ri·or·ly** *adv.*

interior angle *n.* **1. a.** Any of four angles formed between two straight lines cut by a transversal. **b.** A vertex angle measured wholly within a polygon. **2.** The angle formed inside a polygon by two adjacent sides.

interior decoration *n.* The planning and execution of the layout, decoration, and furnishing of an architectural interior.

interior decorator *n.* One who practices or specializes in interior decoration.

interior design *n.* Interior decoration.

interior monologue *n.* An often lengthy representation in monologue form of a fictional character's thoughts and emotions.

in·ter·ject (ĭn'tər-jĕkt') *tr.v.* **-ject·ed, -ject·ing, -jects.** To insert between other elements; interpose. [Lat. *interjicere, interject-,* to put between : *inter-,* between + *jacere,* to throw.] **—in·ter·jec'tor** *n.* **—in'ter·jec'to·ry** *adj.*

in·ter·jec·tion (ĭn'tər-jĕk'shən) *n.* **1.** An exclamation; ejaculation. **2. a.** A part of speech consisting of exclamatory terms, such as words, capable of standing alone. **b.** A word, phrase, or utterance used exclamatorily to express emotion, as *Heavens!* or *Oh!* **—in'ter·jec'tion·al** *adj.* **—in'ter·jec'tion·al·ly** *adv.*

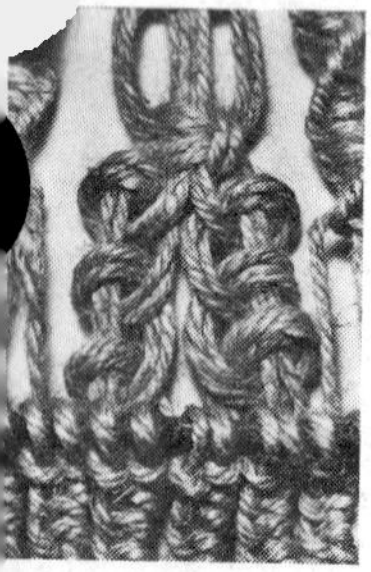

interlace
Interlaced cords

in·ter·lace (ĭn'tər-lās') *v.* **-laced, -lac·ing, -lac·es.** *—tr.* **1.** To connect by or as if by lacing together; interweave. **2.** To intersperse; intermix. *—intr.* To intertwine. **—in'ter·lace'ment** *n.*

in·ter·lam·i·nate (ĭn'tər-lăm'ə-nāt') *tr.v.* **-nat·ed, -nat·ing, -nates. 1.** To insert between layers. **2.** To arrange in alternating layers. **—in'ter·lam'i·nar** (-nər) *adj.* **—in'ter·lam'i·na'tion** *n.*

in·ter·lard (ĭn'tər-lärd') *tr.v.* **-lard·ed, -lard·ing, -lards.** To insert something foreign into: *interlarded his narrative with witty remarks.* [ME *interlarden,* to mix fat into < OFr. *entrelarder* : *entre-,* between (< Lat. *inter-*) + *lard,* lard < Lat. *laridum.*]

in·ter·leaf (ĭn'tər-lēf') *n.* A blank leaf inserted between two leaves of a book.

in·ter·leave (ĭn'tər-lēv') *tr.v.* **-leaved, -leav·ing, -leaves.** To provide with an interleaf.

in·ter·line[1] (ĭn'tər-līn') *tr.v.* **-lined, -lin·ing, -lines.** To insert between printed or written lines. **—in'ter·lin'e·a'tion** (-lĭn'ē-ā'shən) *n.*

in·ter·line[2] (ĭn'tər-līn') *tr.v.* **-lined, -lin·ing, -lines.** To fit (a garment) with an interlining.

in·ter·lin·e·ar (ĭn'tər-lĭn'ē-ər) *adj.* **1.** Inserted between the lines of a text. **2.** Written or printed with different languages or versions in alternating lines.

interlock
Interlocking logs

in·ter·lin·ing (ĭn'tər-lī'nĭng) *n.* An extra lining between the outer fabric and the regular lining of a garment.

in·ter·lock (ĭn'tər-lŏk') *intr.v.* **-locked, -lock·ing, -locks. 1.** To unite firmly or join closely, as by hooking or dovetailing. **2.** *Computer Sci.* To prevent initiation of new operations until current operations are completed.

in·ter·lo·cu·tion (ĭn'tər-lō-kyo͞o'shən) *n.* Speech between two or more persons; conversation. [Lat. *interlocutio* < *interlocutus,* p.part. of *interloqui,* to interrupt : *inter-,* between + *loqui,* to speak.]

in·ter·loc·u·tor (ĭn'tər-lŏk'yə-tər) *n.* **1.** Someone who takes part in a conversation. **2.** The performer in a minstrel show who is placed midway between the end men and engages in banter with them.

in·ter·loc·u·to·ry (ĭn'tər-lŏk'yə-tôr'ē, -tōr'ē) *adj.* Pronounced or decided during the course of a legal action or suit and merely temporary or provisional in nature.

in·ter·lope (ĭn'tər-lōp', ĭn'tər-lōp') *intr.v.* **-loped, -lop·ing, -lopes. 1.** To violate the legal rights, esp. the trading rights, of others. **2.** To interfere in the affairs of others. [Back-formation < E. *interloper* : INTER- + Du. *loper,* running < MDu. < *loopen,* to run.] **—in'ter·lop'er** *n.*

in·ter·lude (ĭn'tər-lo͞od') *n.* **1.** An intervening episode, feature, or period of time. **2. a.** A short farcical entertainment performed between the acts of a medieval mystery or morality play. **b.** A 16th-century genre of comedy derived from this. **c.** An entertainment between the acts of a play. **3.** A short musical piece inserted between the parts of a longer composition. [ME *enterlude,* a dramatic entertainment < OFr. *entrelude* < Med. Lat. *interludium* : Lat. *inter-,* between + Lat. *ludus,* play.]

in·ter·lu·nar (ĭn'tər-lo͞o'nər) *adj.* Of or relating to the period between the old and new moon when the moon is not visible.

in·ter·mar·ry (ĭn'tər-măr'ē) *intr.v.* **-ried, -ry·ing, -ries. 1.** To marry a member of another group. **2.** To be bound together by the marriages of members. **3.** To marry within one's family, tribe, or clan. **—in'ter·mar'riage** *n.*

in·ter·med·dle (ĭn'tər-mĕd'l) *intr.v.* **-dled, -dling, -dles.** To interfere in the affairs of others; meddle. [ME *entermedlen* < OFr. *entremedler* : *entre-,* between (< Lat. *inter-*) + *medler,* to mix. —see MEDDLE.] **—in'ter·med'dler** *n.*

in·ter·me·di·a·cy (ĭn'tər-mē'dē-ə-sē) *n.* The state of being intermediate.

in·ter·me·di·ar·y (ĭn'tər-mē'dē-ĕr'ē) *n., pl.* **-ies. 1.** One who acts as a mediator. **2.** One that acts as an agent between persons or things; means. **3.** An intermediate state or stage.

in·ter·me·di·ate (ĭn'tər-mē'dē-ĭt) *adj.* Lying or occurring between two extremes or in a middle position or state. *—n.* **1.** One that is intermediate. **2.** An intermediary. **3.** *Chem.* A substance formed as a necessary stage in the manufacture of a desired end-product. **4.** An automobile that is smaller than a full-sized model but larger than a compact. *—intr.v.* (ĭn'tər-mē'dē-āt') **-at·ed, -at·ing, -ates. 1.** To act as an intermediary; mediate. **2.** To intervene. [ME < Med. Lat. *intermediatus* < Lat. *intermedius* : *inter-,* between + *medius,* middle.] **—in'ter·me'di·ate·ly** *adv.* **—in'ter·me'di·ate·ness** *n.* **—in'ter·me'di·a'tion** *n.* **—in'ter·me'di·a'tor** *n.*

in·ter·ment (ĭn-tûr'mənt) *n.* The act or ritual of interring.

in·ter·mez·zo (ĭn'tər-mĕt'sō, -mĕd'zō) *n., pl.* **-zos** or **-zi** (-sē, -zē). **1.** A brief entr'acte. **2. a.** A short movement separating the major sections of a lengthy musical composition or work. **b.** An independent instrumental composition having the character of such a movement. [Ital. < Lat. *intermedius,* intermediate.]

in·ter·mi·na·ble (ĭn-tûr'mə-nə-bəl) *adj.* Tiresomely protracted. **—in·ter'mi·na·bly** *adv.*

in·ter·min·gle (ĭn'tər-mĭng'gəl) *tr. & intr.v.* **-gled, -gling, -gles.** To mix or become mixed together.

in·ter·mis·sion (ĭn'tər-mĭsh'ən) *n.* **1. a.** The act of intermitting. **b.** The state of being intermitted. **2.** A respite or recess. **3.** The period between the acts of a theatrical performance. [Lat. *intermissio* < *intermissus,* p.part. of *intermittere,* to intermit.]

in·ter·mit (ĭn'tər-mĭt') *tr. & intr.v.* **-mit·ted, -mit·ting, -mits.** To suspend or cause to suspend activity temporarily or periodically. [Lat. *intermittere* : *inter-,* at intervals + *mittere,* to let go.] **—in'ter·mit'ter** *n.*

in·ter·mit·tent (ĭn'tər-mĭt'nt) *adj.* Stopping and starting at intervals. **—in'ter·mit'tence** *n.* **—in'ter·mit'tent·ly** *adv.*

intermittent current *n.* A periodically interrupted unidirectional electric current.

in·ter·mix (ĭn'tər-mĭks') *tr. & intr.v.* **-mixed, -mix·ing, -mix·es.** To mix or become mixed together. [Back-formation < *intermixt,* intermixed < Lat. *intermixtus,* p.part. of *intermiscēre,* to mix together : *inter-,* among + *miscēre,* to mix.]

in·tern (ĭn'tûrn') *n.* Also **in·terne. 1.** An advanced student or recent graduate undergoing supervised practical training. **2.** One who is interned; internee. *—v.* **-terned, -tern·ing, -terns.** *—intr.* (ĭn'tûrn'). To train or serve as an intern. *—tr.* (ĭn-tûrn'). To confine, esp. in wartime. *—adj.* (ĭn-tûrn'). *Archaic.* Internal. [Fr. *interne,* house physician < OFr., internal < Lat. *internus.*] **—in'tern·ship'** *n.*

in·ter·nal (ĭn-tûr'nəl) *adj.* **1.** Of, relating to, or located within the limits or surface of something; inner. **2.** Residing in or dependent on the essential nature of something; intrinsic. **3.** Located, acting, or effective within the body. **4.** Of or relating to the domestic affairs of a nation. [NLat. *internalis* < Lat. *internus* < *inter,* within.] **—in·ter'nal'i·ty** *n.* **—in·ter'nal·ly** *adv.*

in·ter·nal-com·bus·tion engine (ĭn-tûr'nəl-kəm-bŭs'chən) *n.* An engine, as an automotive gasoline piston engine or a diesel, in which fuel is burned within the engine proper rather than in an external furnace, as in a steam engine.

internal ear *n.* The portion of the ear that includes the semicircular canals, the vestibule, and the cochlea.

in·ter·nal·ize (ĭn-tûr'nə-līz') *tr.v.* **-ized, -iz·ing, -iz·es. 1.** To make internal. **2.** To take in (cultural values, for example) and make an integral part of one's attitudes or beliefs. **—in·ter'nal·i·za'tion** *n.*

internal medicine *n.* The medical study and treatment of nonsurgical constitutional diseases in adults.

internal rhyme *n.* Rhyme between a word within a line and another word at the end of that line or between two words within two different lines.

internal secretion *n.* A secretion of an endocrine gland discharged directly into the blood.

in·ter·na·tion·al (ĭn'tər-năsh'ə-nəl) *adj.* **1.** Of, relating to, or involving two or more nations. **2.** Extending across the boundaries of two or more nations. *—n.* **International.** Any of several socialist organizations of international scope formed during the late 19th and early 20th centuries. **—in'ter·na'tion·al'i·ty** *n.* **—in'ter·na'tion·al·ly** *adv.*

International Date Line *n.* The date line.

in·ter·na·tion·al·ism (ĭn'tər-năsh'ə-nə-lĭz'əm) *n.* **1.** The state or quality of being international in character, principles, concern, or attitude. **2.** A policy or practice of cooperation among nations, esp. in politics and economy. **—in'ter·na'tion·al·ist** *n.*

in·ter·na·tion·al·ize (ĭn'tər-năsh'ə-nə-līz') *tr.v.* **-ized, -iz·ing, -iz·es. 1.** To make international. **2.** To put under international control. **—in'ter·na'tion·al·i·za'tion** *n.*

international law *n.* A set of rules generally regarded and accepted as binding in relations between states and nations.

international Morse code *n.* The continental code.

International Phonetic Alphabet *n.* A phonetic alphabet sponsored by the International Phonetic Association to provide a unique symbol for each speech sound.

international pitch *n.* A standard of tuning of 440 vibrations per second for A above middle C.

International System *n.* A complete, coherent system of units used for scientific work, based on the metric system with the addition of units of time, electric current, temperature, and luminous intensity.

international unit *n.* An internationally accepted quantity of a biological, as a vitamin or antibiotic, that produces a specific biological effect.

in·terne (ĭn'tûrn', ĭn-tûrn') *n., v., & adj.* Variant of **intern.**

in·ter·nec·ine (ĭn'tər-nĕs'ēn', -ĭn-, -nē'sīn') *adj.* **1.** Mutually destructive; ruinous or fatal to both sides. **2.** Characterized by bloodshed or carnage. **3.** Of or relating to struggle within a group. [Lat. *internecinus* < *internecio,* massacre < *internecare,* to slaughter : *inter-* (intensive) + *necare,* to kill.]

in·tern·ee (ĭn'tûr-nē') *n.* One who is interned.

in·ter·neu·ron (ĭn'tər-no͝or'ŏn', -nyo͝or'-) *n.* An internuncial neuron. **—in'ter·neu'ro·nal** (-no͝or'ə-nəl, -nyo͝or'-, -no͞o-rō'-, -nyo͞o-) *adj.*

in·ter·nist (ĭn-tûr'nĭst) *n.* A physician who specializes in internal medicine. [INTERN(AL MEDICINE) + -IST.]

in·tern·ment (ĭn-tûrn'mənt) *n.* The act of interning or the state of being interned.

in·ter·node (ĭn'tər-nōd') *n.* A section or part between two nodes, as of a nerve or stem. **—in'ter·nod'al** (-nōd'l) *adj.*

in·ter·nu·cle·ar (ĭn'tər-no͞o'klē-ər, -nyo͞o'-) *adj.* Located or occurring between nuclei.

in·ter·nun·cial (ĭn'tər-nŭn'shəl, -sē-əl) *adj.* Linking two neurons in a neuronal pathway. [INTERNUNCI(O) + -AL.] **—in'ter·nun'cial·ly** *adv.*

in·ter·nun·ci·o (ĭn'tər-nŭn'sē-ō', -no͞on'-) *n., pl.* **-os. 1.** A Vatican diplomatic envoy or representative ranking just beneath a nuncio. **2.** A messenger or agent; go-between. [Ital. *internunzio* < Lat. *internuntius,* mediator : *inter-,* between + *nuntius,* messenger.]

in·ter·o·cep·tor (ĭn'tər-ō-sĕp'tər) *n.* A specialized sensory nerve receptor responding to stimuli originating in internal organs. [INTER(IOR) + (RE)CEPTOR.] **—in'ter·o·cep'tive** *adj.*

in·ter·of·fice (ĭn'tər-ô'fĭs, -ŏf'ĭs) *adj.* Taking place between offices, esp. of an organization.

in·ter·pel·late (ĭn'tər-pĕl'āt', ĭn'tər-pə-lāt') *tr.v.* **-lat·ed, -lat·ing, -lates.** To question (a government official) formally about government policy or action or about personal behavior. [Lat. *interpellare, interpellat-,* to interrupt, disturb.] **—in'ter·pel·la'tion** *n.* **—in'ter·pel'la'tor** *n.*

in·ter·pen·e·trate (ĭn'tər-pĕn'ĭ-trāt') *v.* **-trat·ed, -trat·ing, -trates.** *—tr.* To penetrate between or throughout. *—intr.* To penetrate mutually. **—in'ter·pen'e·tra'tion** *n.* **—in'ter·pen'e·tra'tive** *adj.*

in·ter·per·son·al (ĭn'tər-pûr'sə-nəl) *adj.* Of, relating to, involving, or being relations between persons. **—in'ter·per'son·al·ly** *adv.*

in·ter·phase (ĭn'tər-fāz') *n.* A period or stage between two successive mitotic divisions of a cell nucleus. **—in'ter·phase'** *v.* **(-phased, -phas·ing, -phas·es).**

in·ter·plan·e·tar·y (ĭn'tər-plăn'ĭ-tĕr'ē) *adj.* Between planets.

in·ter·play (ĭn'tər-plā') *n.* Reciprocal action and reaction; interaction. *—intr.v.* **-played, -play·ing, -plays.** To act or react on each other; interact.

in·ter·plead (ĭn'tər-plēd') *intr.v.* **-plead·ed, -plead·ing, -pleads.** *Law.* To go to court together to establish a dispute involving a third party. [ME *enterpleden* < AN *enterpleder* : *enter-,* between (< Lat. *inter-*) + *pleder,* to plead < OFr. *plaidier.* —see PLEAD.]

in·ter·plead·er (ĭn'tər-plē'dər) *n. Law.* A legal procedure to determine which of two persons bringing the same suit against a third person is the rightful claimant.

in·ter·po·late (ĭn-tûr'pə-lāt') *v.* **-lat·ed, -lat·ing, -lates.** *—tr.* **1.** To insert or introduce between other elements or parts. **2. a.** To insert (material) into a text. **b.** To insert into a conversation. **3.** To change or falsify (a text) by introducing new or false material. **4.** *Math.* To determine a value of (a function) between known values by a procedure or algorithm different from that specified by the function itself. *—intr.* To make insertions or additions. [Lat. *interpolare, interpolat-* : *inter-,* between + *polire,* to embellish.] **—in·ter'po·la'tion** *n.* **—in·ter'po·la'tive** *adj.* **—in·ter'po·la'tor** *n.*

in·ter·pose (ĭn'tər-pōz') *v.* **-posed, -pos·ing, -pos·es.** *—tr.* **1. a.** To insert or introduce between parts. **b.** To place (oneself) between. **2.** To introduce or interject (a comment, for example) during a conversation or discourse. **3.** To exert (influence or authority) in order to interfere or intervene. *—intr.* **1.** To come between. **2.** To come between the parties in a dispute; intervene. **3.** To insert a remark, question, or argument. [OFr. *interposer* < Lat. *interpositus,* p.part. of *interponere,* to put between : *inter-,* between + *ponere,* to put.] **—in'ter·po'sal** *n.* **—in'ter·pos'er** *n.* **—in'ter·po·si'tion** (-pə-zĭsh'ən) *n.*

in·ter·pret (ĭn-tûr'prĭt) *v.* **-pret·ed, -pret·ing, -prets.** *—tr.* **1.** To explain to oneself the meaning of; elucidate. **2.** To expound the significance of. **3.** To represent or render the meaning of, esp. through artistic performance. *—intr.* **1.** To offer an explanation. **2.** To serve as an interpreter for speakers of different languages. [ME *interpreten* < OFr. *interpreter* < Lat. *interpretari* < *interpres,* negotiator, explainer.] **—in·ter'pret·a·bil'i·ty, in·ter'pret·a·ble·ness** *n.* **—in·ter'pret·a·ble** *adj.*

in·ter·pre·ta·tion (ĭn-tûr'prĭ-tā'shən) *n.* **1.** The act, process, or result of interpreting; explanation. **2.** A representation of the meaning of a work of art as expressed esp. in representation or performance. **—in·ter'pre·ta'tion·al** *adj.*

in·ter·pre·ta·tive (ĭn-tûr'prĭ-tā'tĭv) *adj.* Expository; explanatory. **—in·ter'pre·ta'tive·ly** *adv.*

in·ter·pret·er (ĭn-tûr'prĭ-tər) *n.* **1.** One who translates orally from one language into another. **2.** One who gives or expounds an interpretation. **3.** *Computer Sci.* A program that translates an instruction into a machine language and executes it before proceeding to the next one.

in·ter·pre·tive (ĭn-tûr'prĭ-tĭv) *adj.* Interpretative. **—in·ter'pre·tive·ly** *adv.*

in·ter·pu·pil·lar·y (ĭn'tər-pyo͞o'pə-lĕr'ē) *adj.* Located or occurring between the pupils of the eyes.

in·ter·reg·num (ĭn'tər-rĕg'nəm) *n., pl.* **-nums** or **-na** (-nə). **1.** The interval of time between the end of a sovereign's reign and the accession of a successor. **2.** A period of temporary suspension of the usual functions of government or control. **3.** A gap in continuity. [Lat. : *inter-,* between + *regnum,* reign < *rex,* king.] **—in'ter·reg'nal** *adj.*

in·ter·re·late (ĭn'tər-rĭ-lāt') *v.* **-lat·ed, -lat·ing, -lates.** *—tr.* To place in mutual relationship. *—intr.* To come into mutual relationship. **—in'ter·re·la'tion** *n.* **—in'ter·re·la'tion·ship'** *n.*

in·ter·ro·bang also **in·ter·a·bang** (ĭn-tĕr'ə-băng') *n.* A punctuation mark used esp. to end a simultaneous question and exclamation. [INTERRO(GATION POINT) + BANG, (printers' slang) exclamation point.]

in·ter·ro·gate (ĭn-tĕr'ə-gāt') *tr.v.* **-gat·ed, -gat·ing, -gates. 1.** To question formally. **2.** *Computer Sci.* To send out or give a signal to for setting off an appropriate response. [Lat. *interrogare, interrogat-* : *inter-,* between + *rogare,* to ask.] **—in·ter'ro·ga'tion** *n.* **—in·ter'ro·ga'tion·al** *adj.*

interrogation point *n.* A question mark.

in·ter·rog·a·tive (ĭn'tə-rŏg'ə-tĭv) *adj.* **1.** Of the nature of a question; asking a question. **2.** Used to ask a question. *—n.* **1.** A word or form used to ask a question. **2.** An interrogative sentence or expression. **—in'ter·rog'a·tive·ly** *adv.*

in·ter·ro·ga·tor (ĭn-tĕr'ə-gā'tər) *n.* One that interrogates.

in·ter·rog·a·to·ry (ĭn'tə-rŏg'ə-tôr'ē, -tōr'ē) *adj.* Interrogative. *—n., pl.* **-ries.** *Law.* A written question, as to a witness, usually answered under oath. **—in'ter·rog'a·to'ri·ly** *adv.*

in·ter·rupt (ĭn'tə-rŭpt') *v.* **-rupt·ed, -rupt·ing, -rupts.** *—tr.* **1.** To break the continuity or uniformity of. **2.** To hinder or stop by breaking in upon. *—intr.* To break in upon an action or discourse. *—n. Computer Sci.* **1.** A signal to a computer that stops the execution of a running program in order to run a program of higher priority. **2.** A circuit that conveys an interrupt signal. [ME *interrupten* < OFr. *interrupte,* interrupted < Lat. *interruptus,* p.part. of *interrumpere,* to break off : *inter-*, between + *rumpere*, to break.] **—in'ter·rup'tion** *n.* **—in'ter·rup'tive** *adj.*

in·ter·rupt·er (ĭn'tə-rŭp'tər) *n.* **1.** One that interrupts. **2.** *Elect.* A device for periodically and automatically opening or closing an electric circuit.

in·ter·scho·las·tic (ĭn'tər-skə-lăs'tĭk) *adj.* Existing or conducted between or among schools.

in·ter se (ĭn'tər sē', sā') *adv. & adj.* Between or among themselves. [Lat.]

in·ter·sect (ĭn'tər-sĕkt') *v.* **-sect·ed, -sect·ing, -sects.** *—tr.* **1.** To cut across or through. **2.** To form an intersection with. *—intr.* **1.** To cut across or overlap each other. **2.** To form an intersection. [Lat. *intersecare, intersect-* : *inter-*, between + *secare,* to cut.]

in·ter·sec·tion (ĭn'tər-sĕk'shən) *n.* **1. a.** The act or process of intersecting. **b.** (*also* ĭn'tər-sĕk'-). A place where things intersect, esp. a place where two or more roads cross. **2.** *Math.* **a.** The point or locus of points common to two or more geometric figures. **b.** A set every member of which is an element of each of two or more given sets.

in·ter·ses·sion (ĭn'tər-sĕsh'ən) *n.* The time between two academic sessions or semesters. **—in'ter·ses'sion·al** *adj.*

in·ter·sex (ĭn'tər-sĕks') *n.* An intersexual individual.

in·ter·sex·u·al (ĭn'tər-sĕk'shōō-əl) *adj.* **1.** Existing or occurring between the sexes. **2.** Having sexual characteristics intermediate between those of a typical male and a typical female. **—in'ter·sex'u·al'i·ty** (-ăl'ĭ-tē) *n.* **—in'ter·sex'u·al·ly** *adv.*

in·ter·space (ĭn'tər-spās') *tr.v.* **-spaced, -spac·ing, -spac·es.** To make or occupy a space between. *—n.* (ĭn'tər-spās'). A space between two things; interval. **—in'ter·spa'tial** (-spā'shəl) *adj.*

in·ter·spe·cif·ic (ĭn'tər-spĭ-sĭf'ĭk) *adj.* Arising between species.

in·ter·sperse (ĭn'tər-spûrs') *tr.v.* **-spersed, -spers·ing, -spers·es. 1.** To distribute among other things at intervals. **2.** To supply or diversify with things distributed at intervals. [< Lat. *interspersus,* interspersed : *inter-*, between + *sparsus,* p.part. of *spargere,* to scatter.] **—in'ter·spers'ed·ly** (-spûr'sĭd-lē) *adv.* **—in'ter·sper'sion** (-spûr'zhən, -shən) *n.*

in·ter·state (ĭn'tər-stāt') *adj.* Pertaining to, existing between, or connecting two or more states. *—n.* One of a system of highways extending between or connecting U.S. cities or states.

in·ter·stel·lar (ĭn'tər-stĕl'ər) *adj.* Between or among the stars.

in·ter·stice (ĭn-tûr'stĭs) *n., pl.* **-sti·ces** (-stĭ-sēz', -sĭz). A space, esp. a small or narrow one, between things or parts. [Fr. < LLat. *interstitium* < Lat. *interstitus,* p.part. of *intersistere,* to stand in the middle : *inter-*, between + *sistere,* to stand.]

in·ter·sti·tial (ĭn'tər-stĭsh'əl) *adj.* **1.** Of, pertaining to, or occurring in interstices. **2.** Affecting or based on interstices. **—in'ter·sti'tial·ly** *adv.*

in·ter·tex·ture (ĭn'tər-tĕks'chər) *n.* **1. a.** The act of interweaving. **b.** The state of being interwoven. **2.** Something that is interwoven.

in·ter·tid·al (ĭn'tər-tīd'l) *adj.* Of, pertaining to, or being the region between the extremes of high and low tide. **—in'ter·tid'al·ly** *adv.*

in·ter·tri·bal (ĭn'tər-trī'bəl) *adj.* Existing between tribes.

in·ter·trop·i·cal (ĭn'tər-trŏp'ĭ-kəl) *adj.* **1.** Between or within the tropics. **2.** Of or pertaining to the tropics.

in·ter·twine (ĭn'tər-twīn') *tr. & intr.v.* **-twined, -twin·ing, -twines.** To join by twining together. **—in'ter·twine'ment** *n.*

intertwine
A 19th-century valentine showing the delicately intertwined bands of a love knot

in·ter·twist (ĭn'tər-twĭst') *tr. & intr.v.* **-twist·ed, -twist·ing, -twists.** To intertwine.

in·ter·ur·ban (ĭn'tər-ûr'bən) *adj.* Pertaining to or connecting urban areas: *an interurban railroad.*

in·ter·val (ĭn'tər-vəl) *n.* **1.** A space between two objects, points, or units. **2.** The temporal duration between two specified instants, events, or states. **3.** *Math.* **a.** A set consisting of all the numbers between a pair of given numbers. **b.** Such a set including the endpoints. **c.** Such a set not including the endpoints. **d.** A line segment representing such a set. **e.** A set of numbers greater than or less than a given number and including or excluding the given number. **4.** *Chiefly Brit.* An intermission, as between acts of a play. **5.** The difference in pitch between two musical tones. [ME *intervalle* < OFr. < Lat. *intervallum* : *inter-*, between + *vallum,* rampart.]

in·ter·vale (ĭn'tər-vāl') *n. Regional.* A tract of low-lying land, esp. along a river. [Obs. *intervale,* alteration of INTERVAL.]

in·ter·vene (ĭn'tər-vēn') *intr.v.* **-vened, -ven·ing, -venes. 1.** To enter or occur as an extraneous condition or characteristic. **2.** To come, appear, or lie between two things. **3.** To occur or come between periods or points of time. **4.** To come in or between so as to hinder or modify: *intervened to prevent a fight.* **5.** To interfere, usually through force or threat of force, in the affairs of another nation. **6.** *Law.* To enter into a suit as a third party for the protection of an alleged interest. [Lat. *intervenire* : *inter-*, between + *venire,* to come.] **—in'ter·ven'er** *n.* **—in'ter·ven'tion** (-vĕn'shən) *n.*

in·ter·ven·tion·ism (ĭn'tər-vĕn'shə-nĭz'əm) *n.* The policy or practice of intervening in the affairs of another sovereign state. **—in'ter·ven'tion·ist** *n.*

in·ter·ver·te·bral (ĭn'tər-vûr'tə-brəl, -vûr-tē'-) *adj.* Located between vertebrae. **—in'ter·ver'te·bral·ly** *adv.*

intervertebral disk *n.* A broad disk of fibrocartilage situated between adjoining vertebrae of the spinal column.

in·ter·view (ĭn'tər-vyōō') *n.* **1.** A formal face-to-face meeting, esp. one arranged for the assessment of the qualifications of an applicant, as for employment or admission. **2. a.** A conversation, as one conducted by a reporter, in which facts or statements are elicited from another. **b.** An account or reproduction of such a conversation. *—v.* **-viewed, -view·ing, -views.** *—tr.* To obtain an interview from. *—intr.* To have an interview: *interviewed with a publishing company.* [Fr. *entrevue* < *entrevu,* p.part. of *entrevoir,* to see : *entre-*, between (< Lat. *inter-*) + *voir,* to see < Lat. *vidēre.*] **—in'ter·view·ee'** *n.* **—in'ter·view'er** *n.*

in·ter vi·vos (ĭn'tər vē'vōs', vī'-) *adj.* Between living persons: *an inter vivos gift.* [Lat.]

in·ter·vo·cal·ic (ĭn'tər-vō-kăl'ĭk) *adj.* Immediately followed and immediately preceded by a vowel.

in·ter·volve (ĭn'tər-vŏlv') *tr. & intr.v.* **-volved, -volv·ing, -volves.** To intertwine.

in·ter·weave (ĭn'tər-wēv') *v.* **-wove** (-wōv'), **-wo·ven** (-wō'vən), **-weav·ing, -weaves.** *—tr.* **1.** To weave together. **2.** To blend together; intermix. *—intr.* To intertwine.

in·tes·tate (ĭn-tĕs'tāt', -tĭt) *adj.* **1.** Having made no legal will. **2.** Not disposed of by a legal will. *—n.* One who dies without a legal will. [ME < OFr. *intestat* < Lat. *intestatus* : *in-*, not + *testatus,* testate.] **—in·tes'ta·cy** (-tə-sē) *n.*

in·tes·ti·nal (ĭn-tĕs'tə-nəl) *adj.* Of, pertaining to, or constituting the intestine. **—in·tes'ti·nal·ly** *adv.*

intestinal fortitude *n.* Courage; endurance.

in·tes·tine (ĭn-tĕs'tĭn) *n.* The portion of the alimentary canal extending from the stomach to the anus. [Lat. *intestinum* < *intestinus,* internal < *intus,* within.]

in·thrall (ĭn-thrôl') *v.* Variant of **enthrall.**

in·throne (ĭn-thrōn') *v.* Variant of **enthrone.**

in·ti·ma (ĭn'tə-mə) *n., pl.* **-mae** (-mē') or **-mas.** *Anat.* The innermost layer of an organ or part, esp. the wall of a lymphatic vessel, artery, or vein. [NLat. < Lat., fem. of *intimus,* innermost.] **—in'ti·mal** *adj.*

in·ti·ma·cy (ĭn'tə-mə-sē) *n., pl.* **-cies.** The condition of being intimate.

in·ti·mate[1] (ĭn'tə-mĭt) *adj.* **1.** Marked by close acquaintance, association, or familiarity: *an intimate understanding of the rules.* **2.** Pertaining to or indicative of one's deepest nature. **3.** Essential; innermost. **4.** Characterized by informality and privacy: *an intimate nightclub.* **5. a.** Very personal; private. **b.** Of or having sexual relations. *—n.* A close friend or confidant. [LLat. *intimatus,* p.part. of *intimare,* to intimate.] **—in'ti·mate·ly** *adv.* **—in'ti·mate·ness** *n.*

in·ti·mate[2] (ĭn'tə-māt') *tr.v.* **-mat·ed, -mat·ing, -mates. 1.** To communicate with a hint or other indirect sign; imply subtly. **2.** To announce; proclaim. [LLat. *intimare, intimate-,* to make known < Lat. *intimus,* innermost.] **—in'ti·mat'er** *n.* **—in'ti·ma'tion** *n.*

in·tim·i·date (ĭn-tĭm'ĭ-dāt') *tr.v.* **-dat·ed, -dat·ing, -dates. 1.** To make timid; threaten. **2.** To discourage or inhibit by or as if by threats. [Med. Lat. *intimidare, intimidat-* : Lat. *in-* (intensive) + *timidus,* timid.] **—in·tim'i·da'tion** *n.* **—in·tim'i·da'tor** *n.*

in·tinc·tion (ĭn-tĭngk'shən) *n. Eccles.* The administration of the Eucharist by dipping the host into the wine and offering both simultaneously to the communicant. [LLat. *intinctio,* a dipping in < Lat. *intingere,* to dip in : *in-*, in + *tingere,* to moisten.]

in·tine (ĭn'tēn') *n.* The inner wall layer of a spore or pollen grain. [G. < Lat. *intus,* within.]

in·tit·ule (ĭn-tĭch'ōōl) *tr.v.* **-uled, -ul·ing, -ules.** *Chiefly Brit.* To give a designation or title to (a legislative act, for example). [OFr. *intituler* < LLat. *intitulare* : Lat. *in-*, in + Lat. *titulus,* title.]

in·to (ĭn'tōō) *prep.* **1.** To the inside or interior of. **2.** To the activity or occupation of: *go into banking.* **3.** To the condition or form of: *break into pieces.* **4.** So as to be in or be included in: *enter into an agreement.* **5.** To a point within the limits of a period of time or extent of space: *well into the week.* **6.** Against: *ram into a tree.* **7.** Toward; in the direction of: *look into the distance.* **8.** *Informal.* Interested in or involved with: *They are into vegetarianism.* [ME < OE : *in,* in + *to,* to.]

in·tol·er·a·ble (ĭn-tŏl'ər-ə-bəl) *adj.* **1.** Incapable of being tolerated; unbearable: *intolerable agony.* **2.** Inordinate; extravagant. **—in·tol'er·a·bil'i·ty, in·tol'er·a·ble·ness** *n.* **—in·tol'er·a·bly** *adv.*

in·tol·er·ance (ĭn-tŏl'ər-əns) *n.* **1.** The quality or condition of being intolerant. **2.** Inability to tolerate.

in·tol·er·ant (ĭn-tŏl'ər-ənt) *adj.* Not tolerant, esp.: **a.** Unwilling to tolerate differences in opinions or beliefs, esp. religious beliefs. **b.** Unable or unwilling to endure: *intolerant of interruptions.* **—in·tol'er·ant·ly** *adv.*

in·to·nate (ĭn'tə-nāt') *tr.v.* **-nat·ed, -nat·ing, -nates. 1.** To intone. **2.** To utter with a particular tone of voice.

in·to·na·tion (ĭn'tə-nā'shən, -tō-) *n.* **1. a.** The act of intoning. **b.** An intoned utterance. **2.** A manner of producing or uttering tones, esp. with regard to accuracy of pitch. **3. a.** The use of pitch as an element of meaning in language.

b. A use of pitch characteristic of a speaker or dialect. —**in′to·na′tion·al** *adj.*
in·tone (ĭn-tōn′) *v.* **-toned, -ton·ing, -tones.** —*tr.* **1.** To recite in a singing tone. **2.** To utter in a monotone. —*intr.* To speak with a singing tone or with a given intonation. [ME *entonen* < OFr. *entoner* < Med. Lat. *intonare* : Lat. *in-*, in + Lat. *tonus*, tone.] —**in·ton′er** *n.*
in to·to (ĭn tō′tō) *adv.* Totally; altogether. [Lat.]
in·tox·i·cant (ĭn-tŏk′sĭ-kənt) *n.* An agent that intoxicates, esp. an alcoholic beverage. —*adj.* Intoxicating.
in·tox·i·cate (ĭn-tŏk′sĭ-kāt′) *tr.v.* **-cat·ed, -cat·ing, -cates.** **1.** To induce, esp. by the effect of ingested alcohol, any of a series of progressively deteriorating states ranging from exhilaration to stupefaction. **2.** To stimulate or excite: *"a man whom life intoxicates, who has no need of wine"* (Anaïs Nin). **3.** To poison. [Med. Lat. *intoxicare, intoxicat-*, to poison : Lat. *in-*, in + Lat. *toxicum*, poison. —see TOXIC.] —**in·tox′i·ca′tion** *n.* —**in·tox′i·ca′tive** *adj.* —**in·tox′i·ca′tor** *n.*
intra– *pref.* Within: *intraocular.* [LLat. < Lat. *intra*, within.]
in·tra·ar·te·ri·al (ĭn′trə-är-tîr′ē-əl) *adj.* Within an artery. —**in′tra·ar·te′ri·al·ly** *adv.*
in·tra·a·tom·ic (ĭn′trə-ə-tŏm′ĭk) *adj.* Within an atom.
in·tra·car·di·ac (ĭn′trə-kär′dē-ăk′) *adj.* Within a chamber of the heart.
in·tra·car·ti·lag·i·nous (ĭn′trə-kär′tl-ăj′ə-nəs) *adj.* Within cartilage.
in·tra·cel·lu·lar (ĭn′trə-sĕl′yə-lər) *adj.* Within a cell or cells. —**in′tra·cel′lu·lar·ly** *adv.*
in·tra·cos·tal (ĭn′trə-kŏs′tl) *adj.* On the inner surface of a rib or ribs. [INTRA- + Lat. *costa*, rib + -AL.]
in·tra·cra·ni·al (ĭn′trə-krā′nē-əl) *adj.* Within the skull. —**in′tra·cra′ni·al·ly** *adv.*
in·trac·ta·ble (ĭn-trăk′tə-bəl) *adj.* **1.** Difficult to manage or govern; stubborn. **2.** Difficult to mold or manipulate. **3.** Difficult to alleviate, remedy, or cure: *intractable pain.* —**in·trac′ta·bil′i·ty, in·trac′ta·ble·ness** *n.* —**in·trac′ta·bly** *adv.*
in·tra·cu·ta·ne·ous (ĭn′trə-kyo͞o-tā′nē-əs) *adj.* Within the skin. —**in′tra·cu·ta′ne·ous·ly** *adv.*
in·tra·day (ĭn′trə-dā′) *adj.* Occurring in the course of a single day.
in·tra·der·mal (ĭn′trə-dûr′məl) *adj.* Within the dermis of the skin.
in·tra·dos (ĭn′trə-dŏs′, -dō′, -ĭn-trā′dŏs′, -dōs′) *n., pl.* **-dos** (-dōz′) or **-dos·es** (-dŏs′ĭz). *Archit.* The inner curve of an arch. [Fr. : *intra-*, within (< Lat.) + *dos*, back < Lat. *dorsum.*]
in·tra·ga·lac·tic (ĭn′trə-gə-lăk′tĭk) *adj.* Occurring or situated within the space of a galaxy.
in·tra·mo·lec·u·lar (ĭn′trə-mə-lĕk′yə-lər) *adj.* Within a molecule. —**in′tra·mo·lec′u·lar·ly** *adv.*
in·tra·mu·ral (ĭn′trə-myo͝or′əl) *adj.* **1.** Existing or carried on within the bounds of an institution, esp. a school: *intramural athletics.* **2.** *Anat.* Within the wall of a cavity or organ. —**in′tra·mu′ral·ly** *adv.*
in·tra·mus·cu·lar (ĭn′trə-mŭs′kyə-lər) *adj.* Within a muscle. —**in′tra·mus′cu·lar·ly** *adv.*
in·tran·si·gent also **in·tran·si·geant** (ĭn-trăn′sə-jənt) *adj.* Refusing to moderate an esp. extreme position; uncompromising. [Fr. *intransigeant* < Sp. *intransigente* : *in-*, not (< Lat.) + *transigente*, pr.part. of *transigir*, to compromise < Lat. *transigere*, to come to an agreement (*trans-*, through + *agere*, to drive).] —**in·tran′si·gence, in·tran′si·gen·cy** *n.* —**in·tran′si·gent** *n.* —**in·tran′si·gent·ly** *adv.*
in·tran·si·tive (ĭn-trăn′sĭ-tĭv) *Gram.* —*adj.* Designating a verb or verb construction that does not require a direct object to complete its meaning. —*n.* An intransitive verb. [LLat. *intransitivus* : *in-*, not + *transitivus*, transitive.] —**in·tran′si·tive·ly** *adv.* —**in·tran′si·tive·ness** *n.*
in·tra·nu·cle·ar (ĭn′trə-no͞o′klē-ər, -nyo͞o′-) *adj.* Within a nucleus.
in·tra·oc·u·lar (ĭn′trə-ŏk′yə-lər) *adj.* Within the eyeball.
in·tra·per·son·al (ĭn′trə-pûr′sə-nəl) *adj.* Occurring within one's own mind or self. —**in′tra·per′son·al·ly** *adv.*
in·tra·psy·chic (ĭn′trə-sī′kĭk) *adj.* Existing or taking place within the psyche. —**in′tra·psy′chi·cal·ly** *adv.*
in·tra·spe·cif·ic (ĭn′trə-spĭ-sĭf′ĭk) *adj.* Occurring among members of the same species.
in·tra·state (ĭn′trə-stāt′) *adj.* Pertaining to or existing within the boundaries of a state.
in·tra·u·ter·ine (ĭn′trə-yo͞o′tər-ĭn, -tə-rīn′) *adj.* Within the uterus.
intrauterine device *n.* A stainless steel or plastic loop, ring, or spiral inserted into the uterus as a contraceptive.
in·trav·a·sa·tion (ĭn-trăv′ə-sā′shən) *n.* The entry of foreign matter into a blood vessel.
in·tra·vas·cu·lar (ĭn′trə-văs′kyə-lər) *adj.* Within the blood vessels or lymphatics. —**in′tra·vas′cu·lar·ly** *adv.*
in·tra·ve·na·tion (ĭn′trə-vē-nā′shən) *n.* The entry of foreign matter into a vein.
in·tra·ve·nous (ĭn′trə-vē′nəs) *adj.* Within a vein or veins. —**in′tra·ve′nous·ly** *adv.*
in·treat (ĭn-trēt′) *v.* Variant of **entreat.**
in·trench (ĭn-trĕnch′) *v.* Variant of **entrench.**
in·trench·ment (ĭn-trĕnch′mənt) *n.* Variant of **entrenchment.**
in·trep·id (ĭn-trĕp′ĭd) *adj.* Marked by resolute courage; fearless and bold: *an intrepid mountaineer.* [Fr. *intrépide* < Lat. *intrepidus* : *in-*, not + *trepidus*, alarmed.] —**in′tre·pid′i·ty** (-trə-pĭd′ĭ-tē), **in·trep′id·ness** *n.* —**in·trep′id·ly** *adv.*
in·tri·ca·cy (ĭn′trĭ-kə-sē) *n., pl.* **-cies.** **1.** The condition or quality of being intricate. **2.** Something intricate.
in·tri·cate (ĭn′trĭ-kĭt) *adj.* **1.** Having many complexly arranged elements; elaborate. **2.** Solvable or comprehensible only with painstaking effort. [ME < Lat. *intricatus*, p.part. of *intricare*, to entangle, perplex : *in-*, in + *tricae*, perplexities.] —**in′tri·cate·ly** *adv.* —**in′tri·cate·ness** *n.*
in·tri·gant also **in·tri·guant** (ĭn′trē-gänt′, ăn′trē-gäɴ′) *n.* One who intrigues; intriguer. [Fr. < Ital. *intrigante*, pr.part. of *intrigare*, to perplex. —see INTRIGUE.]
in·trigue (ĭn′trēg′, ĭn-trēg′) *n.* **1. a.** A secret or underhand scheme; plot. **b.** The practice of or involvement in such schemes. **2.** A clandestine love affair. —*v.* (ĭn-trēg′) **-trigued, -trigu·ing, -trigues.** —*intr.* To engage in intrigue; plot. —*tr.* **1.** To effect by intriguing. **2.** To arouse the interest or curiosity of: *Hibernation has long intrigued biologists.* [Fr. < Ital. *intrigo* < *intrigare*, to perplex < Lat. *intricare.* —see INTRICATE.] —**in·trigu′er** *n.*

Usage: *Intrigue* is fully established as a noun and as a verb in all meanings except that of "to arouse the interest or curiosity of." In that sense it has been resisted by writers on usage, who regard it as an unneeded French substitute for available English words such as *interest, fascinate, pique, puzzle.* Nevertheless, it has gained increasing acceptance because no single English word has precisely the same meaning. The following example is acceptable to a majority of the Usage Panel: *The announcement of a special press conference intrigued the correspondents in the manner of a good suspense novel.*

in·trin·sic (ĭn-trĭn′zĭk, -sĭk) *adj.* **1.** Of or pertaining to the essential nature of a thing; inherent. **2.** *Anat.* Situated within or belonging solely to a body part, as certain nerves and muscles. [OFr. *intrinseque*, inner < LLat. *intrinsecus*, inward < Lat., inwardly : *intra*, within + *secus*, alongside.] —**in·trin′si·cal·ly** *adv.*
in·trin·si·cal (ĭn-trĭn′zĭ-kəl, -sĭ-) *adj. Archaic.* Intrinsic.
intrinsic factor *n.* A substance produced by the gastric mucosa that combines with vitamin B_{12} and promotes its absorption by the stomach.
intro– *pref.* **1.** In; inward: *introjection.* **2.** Inward: *introvert.* [Lat. < *intro*, to the inside.]
in·tro·duce (ĭn′trə-do͞os′, -dyo͞os′) *tr.v.* **-duced, -duc·ing, -duc·es.** **1. a.** To present (a person) by name to another in order to establish an acquaintance. **b.** To present (a performer, for example) to the public for the first time. **2.** To propose, create, or bring into use or acceptance for the first time: *introduce legislation.* **3.** To provide with a beginning knowledge or first experience of something. **4. a.** To bring or put in something new or different; add. **b.** To bring in and establish in a new place or surroundings. **5.** To put inside or into; insert or inject. **6.** To open or begin; preface. [Lat. *introducere*, to bring in : *intro*, within + *ducere*, to lead.] —**in′tro·duc′er** *n.* —**in′tro·duc′i·ble** *adj.*
in·tro·duc·tion (ĭn′trə-dŭk′shən) *n.* **1. a.** The act or process of introducing. **b.** The fact of being introduced. **2.** A means of presenting one person to another, as a personal letter. **3.** Something recently introduced: *"He loathed a fork; it is a modern introduction which has still scarcely reached common people"* (D.H. Lawrence). **4.** Something spoken, written, or otherwise presented in introducing, esp.: **a.** A preface, as to a book. **b.** A short preliminary movement in a musical work. **c.** A basic introductory text or course of study. [ME *introduccioun* < OFr. *introduction* < Lat. *introductio* < *introducere*, to bring in. —see INTRODUCE.]
in·tro·duc·to·ry (ĭn′trə-dŭk′tə-rē) *adj.* **1.** Of, pertaining to, or constituting an introduction. **2.** Serving to introduce. —**in′tro·duc′to·ri·ly** *adv.*
in·tro·it also **In·tro·it** (ĭn′trō′ĭt, -troit′, ĭn-trō′ĭt) *n.* **1.** A hymn or psalm sung at the opening of a service, esp. in the Anglican Church. **2.** The beginning of the proper of the Mass in the Roman Catholic Church, usually consisting of a psalm verse, antiphon, and the Gloria Patri. [ME, entrance < OFr. *introït* < Lat. *introitus* < p.part. of *introire*, to enter : *intro*, in + *ire*, to go.]
in·tro·jec·tion (ĭn′trə-jĕk′shən) *n.* **1.** The ascription of living characteristics to inanimate objects. **2.** The unconscious incorporation into one's personality of the characteristics of another person or of an inanimate object. [INTRO- + (PRO)JECTION.]
in·tro·mis·sion (ĭn′trə-mĭsh′ən) *n.* The act or process of intromitting; introduction or admission. [Med. Lat. *intromissio* < Lat. *intromissus*, p.part. of *intromittere*, to intromit.] —**in′tro·mis′sive** *adj.*
in·tro·mit (ĭn′trə-mĭt′) *tr.v.* **-mit·ted, -mit·ting, -mits.** To cause or permit to enter; introduce or admit. [Lat. *intromittere*, to send in : *intro*, in + *mittere*, to send.] —**in′tro·mit′tent** *adj.* —**in′tro·mit′ter** *n.*
in·trorse (ĭn′trôrs′) *adj. Bot.* Facing inward; turned toward the axis. Used esp. of anthers. [Lat. *introrsus*, contraction of *introversus*, inwards : *intro*, to the inside + *versus*, p.part. of *vertere*, to turn.]
in·tro·spect (ĭn′trə-spĕkt′, ĭn′trə-spĕkt′) *intr.v.* **-spect·ed, -spect·ing, -spects.** To engage in introspection. [Lat. *intro-*

spicere, introspect-, to look into : *intro,* within + *specere,* to look.] —**in'tro·spec'tive** *adj.* —**in'tro·spec'tive·ly** *adv.* —**in'tro·spec'tive·ness** *n.*

in·tro·spec·tion (ĭn'trə-spĕk'shən) *n.* Contemplation of one's own thoughts, feelings, and sensations; self-examination. —**in'tro·spec'tion·al** *adj.*

in·tro·ver·sion (ĭn'trə-vûr'zhən, -shən) *n.* **1. a.** The act of introverting. **b.** The condition of being introverted. **2.** The direction of or tendency to direct one's thoughts and interests inward. **3.** *Med.* The turning of one part within another. —**in'tro·ver'sive** *adj.*

in·tro·vert (ĭn'trə-vûrt', ĭn'trə-vûrt') *v.* **-vert·ed, -vert·ing, -verts.** —*tr.* **1.** To turn or direct inward. **2.** To concentrate (one's interests) upon oneself. **3.** To turn (a tubular organ or part) inward upon itself. —*intr.* To exhibit introversion. —*n.* (ĭn'trə-vûrt'). **1.** A person whose thoughts and interests are directed inward. **2.** An anatomic structure, as the intestine, that is turned inward upon itself. [INTRO- + Lat. *vertere,* to turn.]

in·trude (ĭn-tro͞od') *v.* **-trud·ed, -trud·ing, -trudes.** —*tr.* **1.** To put or force in, esp. without invitation, fitness, or leave: *intruded opinion into a factual report.* **2.** *Geol.* To thrust (molten rock) into a stratum. —*intr.* To come in rudely or inappropriately; enter as an improper or unwanted element: *"The flute would be intruding here like a delicate lady at a club smoker"* (Leonard Bernstein). [Lat. *intrudere,* to thrust in : *in-* in + *trudere,* to thrust.] —**in·trud'er** *n.*

Synonyms: *intrude, obtrude, interlope.* These verbs mean to force oneself or something upon other persons without their consent or approval. *Intrude* is more often found in the sense of violating another's privacy, and *obtrude* in the transitive sense of forcing opinions, ideas, or the like on another's attention. *Interlope* implies intermeddling in another's affairs; sometimes it also implies depriving another of what is his by right.

in·tru·sion (ĭn-tro͞o'zhən) *n.* **1. a.** The act of intruding. **b.** The fact of being intruded upon. **2.** An inappropriate or unwelcome addition. **3.** *Law.* Illegal entry upon or appropriation of the property of another. **4.** *Geol.* **a.** The forcing of molten rock into an earlier formation. **b.** The intrusive mass so produced.

in·tru·sive (ĭn-tro͞o'sĭv, -zĭv) *adj.* **1.** Intruding or tending to intrude. **2.** *Geol.* Designating igneous rock that is forced into another stratum while in molten state; irruptive. **3.** *Ling.* Constituting an epenthesis. —**in·tru'sive·ly** *adv.* —**in·tru'sive·ness** *n.*

in·trust (ĭn-trŭst') *v.* Variant of **entrust.**

in·tu·bate (ĭn'to͞o-bāt', -tyo͞o-) *tr.v.* **-bat·ed, -bat·ing, -bates.** To insert a tube into (an organ or passage). —**in'tu·ba'tion** *n.* —**in'tur·ba'tion·al** *adj.*

in·tu·it (ĭn-to͞o'ĭt, -tyo͞o'-) *tr.v.* **-it·ed, -it·ing, -its.** To know or sense by intuition. [Back-formation < INTUITION.]

in·tu·i·tion (ĭn'to͞o-ĭsh'ən, -tyo͞o-) *n.* **1. a.** The act or faculty of knowing without the use of rational processes; immediate cognition. **b.** Knowledge gained by the use of this faculty. **2.** Sharp insight. [ME *intuicioun,* insight < Med. Lat. *intuitio* < LLat., view < Lat. *intueri,* to look at : *in-,* on + *tueri,* to look at.] —**in'tu·i'tion·al** *adj.* —**in'tu·i'tion·al·ly** *adv.*

in·tu·i·tion·al·ism (ĭn'to͞o-ĭsh'ə-nə-lĭz'əm, -tyo͞o-) *n.* Intuitionism. —**in'tu·i'tion·al·ist** *n.*

in·tu·i·tion·ism (ĭn'to͞o-ĭsh'ə-nĭz'əm, -tyo͞o-) *n.* **1.** The theory that basic truths are known by intuition rather than reason. **2.** The theory that objects of perception are known to be real by intuition. **3.** The theory that ethical principles are known to be valid and universal through intuition. —**in'tu·i'tion·ist** *n.*

in·tu·i·tive (ĭn-to͞o'ĭ-tĭv, -tyo͞o'-) *adj.* **1.** Of, pertaining to, or arising from intuition. **2.** Known or perceived through intuition. **3.** Possessing or demonstrating intuition. —**in·tu'i·tive·ly** *adv.* —**in·tu'i·tive·ness** *n.*

in·tu·mesce (ĭn'to͞o-mĕs', -tyo͞o-) *intr.v.* **-mesced, -mesc·ing, -mesc·es.** To swell or expand; enlarge. [Lat. *intumescere,* to swell up : *in-* (intensive) + *tumescere,* to begin to swell < *tumere,* to swell.]

in·tu·mes·cence (ĭn'to͞o-mĕs'əns, -tyo͞o-) *n.* **1. a.** The process of swelling. **b.** The condition of being swollen. **2.** A swollen organ or part. —**in'tu·mes'cent** *adj.*

in·tus·sus·cept (ĭn'tə-sə-sĕpt') *intr. & tr.v.* **-cept·ed, -cept·ing, -cepts.** To undergo or cause to undergo intussusception; invaginate. [Prob. back-formation < INTUSSUSCEPTION.] —**in'tus·sus·cep'tive** *adj.*

in·tus·sus·cep·tion (ĭn'tə-sə-sĕp'shən) *n.* Invagination, esp. an infolding of one part of the intestine into another. [NLat. *intussusceptio* : Lat. *intus,* within + Lat. *susceptio,* a taking up < *suscipere,* to take up (*sub-,* under + *capere,* to take).]

in·twine (ĭn-twīn') *v.* Variant of **entwine.**

in·twist (ĭn-twĭst') *v.* Variant of **entwist.**

in·u·lase (ĭn'yə-lās') *n.* An enzyme that catalyzes the conversion of inulin to levulose. [INUL(IN) + -ASE.]

in·u·lin (ĭn'yə-lĭn) *n.* A carbohydrate, $(C_6H_{10}O_5)_3$ or $(C_6H_{10}O_5)_4$, found in the roots of many plants and used to manufacture fructose. [Prob. < G. *Inulin* < NLat. *Inula,* plant genus < Lat. *inula,* elecampane < Gk. *helenion.*]

in·unc·tion (ĭn-ŭngk'shən) *n.* **1.** The process of applying and rubbing in an ointment. **2.** The act of anointing, as in a religious ceremony. [Lat. *inunctio,* an anointing < *inunguere,* to anoint : *in-,* on + *unguere,* to smear.]

in·un·date (ĭn'ŭn-dāt') *tr.v.* **-dat·ed, -dat·ing, -dates.** **1.** To cover with water, esp. flood water; overflow. **2.** To overwhelm as if with a flood; swamp: *inundated with requests.* [Lat. *inundare, inundat-* : *in-,* in + *undare,* to flow < *unda,* wave.] —**in'un·da'tion** *n.* —**in'un·da'tor** *n.* —**in·un'da·to'ry** (ĭ-nŭn'də-tôr'ē, -tōr'ē) *adj.*

in·ure (ĭn-yo͝or') *tr.v.* **-ured, -ur·ing, -ures.** To make used to something undesirable, esp. by prolonged subjection; accustom: *"Though the food became no more palatable, he soon became sufficiently inured to it"* (John Barth). [Back-formation < ME *enured,* accustomed < the phrase *in ure,* customary : *in,* in + *ure,* use < AN **eure* < Lat. *opera,* pl. of *opus,* work.] —**in·ure'ment** *n.*

in·urn (ĭn-ûrn') *tr.v.* **-urned, -urn·ing, -urns.** **1.** To put in an urn, as the ashes of the dead. **2.** To bury or entomb; inter.

in·u·tile (ĭn-yo͞ot'l, -yo͞o'tīl') *adj.* Lacking in utility; useless. [ME < OFr. < Lat. *inutilis* : *in-,* not + *utilis,* useful < *uti,* to use.] —**in·u'tile·ly** *adv.* —**in'u·til'i·ty** (ĭn'yo͞o-tĭl'ĭ-tē) *n.*

in·vade (ĭn-vād') *v.* **-vad·ed, -vad·ing, -vades.** —*tr.* **1.** To enter by force in order to conquer or pillage. **2.** To encroach or intrude upon; violate. **3.** To overrun as if by invading; pervade. **4.** To enter and spread harm through. —*intr.* To make an invasion. [Lat. *invadere* : *in-,* in + *vadere,* to go.] —**in·vad'er** *n.*

in·vag·i·nate (ĭn-văj'ə-nāt') *v.* **-nat·ed, -nat·ing, -nates.** —*tr.* **1.** To enclose in or as if in a sheath. **2.** To infold so as to form a hollow space within a previously solid structure; introvert. —*intr.* To become enclosed or turned within. [Med. Lat. *invaginare, invaginat-* : Lat. *in-,* in + Lat. *vagina,* sheath.]

in·vag·i·na·tion (ĭn-văj'ə-nā'shən) *n.* **1. a.** The act or process of invaginating. **b.** The condition of being invaginated. **2.** Something invaginated, as an organ or part. **3.** The infolding of a blastula to form a gastrula.

in·va·lid[1] (ĭn'və-lĭd) *n.* A chronically ill or disabled person. —*adj.* **1.** Disabled by illness or injury. **2.** Of, pertaining to, or for invalids. —*tr.v.* **-lid·ed, -lid·ing, -lids.** **1.** To make an invalid of; disable physically. **2.** *Chiefly Brit.* To release or exempt from duty because of ill health. [Fr. *invalide,* sickly, infirm < Lat. *invalidus,* weak : *in-,* not + *validus,* strong < *valēre,* to be strong.]

in·val·id[2] (ĭn-văl'ĭd) *adj.* **1.** Not legally or factually valid; null. **2.** Falsely based or reasoned; faulty. [Lat. *invalidus,* weak. —see INVALID[1].] —**in'va·lid'i·ty** (-və-lĭd'ĭ-tē) *n.* —**in·val'id·ly** *adv.*

in·val·i·date (ĭn-văl'ĭ-dāt') *tr.v.* **-dat·ed, -dat·ing, -dates.** To make invalid; nullify. —**in·val'i·da'tion** *n.* —**in·val'i·da'tor** *n.*

in·va·lid·ism (ĭn'və-lĭ-dĭz'əm) *n.* The condition of being chronically ill or disabled.

in·val·u·a·ble (ĭn-văl'yo͞o-ə-bəl) *adj.* **1.** Of inestimable value; priceless: *invaluable paintings.* **2.** Of inestimable use or help; indispensable: *an invaluable service.* —**in·val'u·a·bly** *adv.* —**in·val'u·a·ble·ness** *n.*

in·var·i·a·ble (ĭn-vâr'ē-ə-bəl) *adj.* Not changing or subject to change; constant. —**in·var'i·a·bil'i·ty, in·var'i·a·ble·ness** *n.* —**in·var'i·a·bly** *adv.*

in·var·i·ant (ĭn-vâr'ē-ənt) *adj.* **1.** Not varying; constant. **2.** Unaffected by a designated mathematical operation, as a transformation of coordinates. —*n.* An invariant quantity, function, configuration, or system. —**in·var'i·ance** *n.*

in·va·sion (ĭn-vā'zhən) *n.* **1.** The act of invading, esp. entrance of an army to conquer or pillage. **2.** The onset of something injurious or harmful, as a disease. [ME *invasioun* < OFr. *invasion* < LLat. *invasio* < Lat. *invadere,* to invade.]

in·va·sive (ĭn-vā'sĭv) *adj.* **1.** Tending to spread, esp. tending to invade healthy tissue. **2.** Of, pertaining to, or given to armed aggression. —**in·va'sive·ness** *n.*

in·vec·tive (ĭn-vĕk'tĭv) *n.* **1.** A denunciatory or abusive expression. **2.** Denunciatory or abusive language; vituperation. —*adj.* Of, pertaining to, or characterized by invective. [< ME *invectif,* denunciatory < OFr. < Lat. *invectivus,* reproachful < *invehere,* to inveigh.] —**in·vec'tive·ly** *adv.* —**in·vec'tive·ness** *n.*

in·veigh (ĭn-vā') *intr.v.* **-veighed, -veigh·ing, -veighs.** To give vent to angry disapproval; protest vehemently. [Lat. *invehi,* to attack, inveigh, passive of *invehere,* to carry in : *in-,* in + *vehere,* to carry.] —**in·veigh'er** *n.*

in·vei·gle (ĭn-vā'gəl, ĭn-vē'-) *tr.v.* **-gled, -gling, -gles.** **1.** To lead astray or win over by deceitful flattery or persuasion. **2.** To obtain by cajolery. [Alteration of OFr. *aveugler,* to blind < *aveugle,* blind < Med. Lat. *ab oculis,* without eyes.] —**in·vei'gle·ment** *n.* —**in·vei'gler** *n.*

in·vent (ĭn-vĕnt') *tr.v.* **-vent·ed, -vent·ing, -vents.** **1.** To produce or contrive (something previously unknown) by the use of ingenuity or imagination. **2.** To fabricate; make up. [Lat. *invenire, invent-,* to find : *in-,* on + *venire,* to come.] —**in·vent'i·ble** *adj.* —**in·ven'tor** *n.*

in·ven·tion (ĭn-vĕn'shən) *n.* **1.** The act or process of inventing. **2.** A new device, method, or process developed from study and experimentation. **3.** A mental fabrication, esp. a falsehood. **4.** Skill in inventing; inventiveness. **5.** *Mus.* A short composition developing a single theme contrapuntally. **6.** *Archaic.* A discovery; finding. —**in·ven'tion·al** *adj.*

in·ven·tive (ĭn-vĕn′tĭv) *adj.* **1.** Of, pertaining to, or characterized by invention. **2.** Adept or skillful at inventing; creative. **—in·ven′tive·ly** *adv.* **—in·ven′tive·ness** *n.*

in·ven·to·ry (ĭn′vən-tôr′ē, -tōr′ē) *n., pl.* **-ries. 1. a.** A detailed list of things in one's view or possession, esp. a periodic survey of all goods and materials in stock. **b.** The process of making such a survey. **c.** The items listed in such a survey. **d.** The quantity of goods and materials on hand; stock. **2.** An evaluation or survey, as of personal characteristics or abilities. *—tr.v.* **-ried, -ry·ing, -ries. 1.** To make an inventory of. **2.** To include in an inventory. [Med. Lat. *inventorium,* list, alteration of LLat. *inventarium* < Lat. *invenire,* to find. —see INVENT.] **—in′ven·to′ri·al** *adj.* **—in′ven·to′ri·al·ly** *adv.*

in·ve·rac·i·ty (ĭn′və-răs′ĭ-tē) *n., pl.* **-ties. 1.** Lack of veracity; untruthfulness. **2.** An untruth; falsehood.

in·ver·ness also **In·ver·ness** (ĭn′vər-nĕs′) *n.* **1.** A loose overcoat with a detachable cape. **2.** The cape of an inverness. [After *Inverness,* a city and former county of Scotland.]

in·verse (ĭn-vûrs′, ĭn′vûrs′) *adj.* **1.** Reversed in order, nature, or effect. **2.** Turned upside down; inverted. *—n.* (ĭn′vûrs′, ĭn-vûrs′). **1.** Something that is opposite, as in sequence or character; reverse. **2.** *Math.* An element x^* in a set S related to a designated element x in S such that $x^* \cdot x = x \cdot x^* = I$, where $\cdot$ is a binary operation defined in S and I is the identity element, esp.: **a.** The reciprocal of a designated quantity. **b.** The negative of a designated quantity. [Lat. *inversus,* p.part. of *invertere,* to invert.] **—in·verse′ly** *adv.*

in·ver·sion (ĭn-vûr′zhən, -shən) *n.* **1. a.** The act of inverting. **b.** The state of being inverted. **2.** An interchange of position, esp. of adjacent objects in a sequence, as: **a.** A change in normal word order, as the placement of a verb before its subject. **b.** *Mus.* A rearrangement or result of the rearrangement of tones in which upper and lower voices are transposed, as in counterpoint, or in which each interval in a single melody is applied in the opposite direction. **3.** Homosexuality. **4.** *Chem.* Conversion from the dextrorotatory to the levorotatory or from the levorotatory to the dextrorotatory form. **5.** A state in which the air temperature increases with increasing altitude, holding surface air down along with its pollutants. [Lat. *inversio* < *invertere,* to invert.]

in·vert (ĭn-vûrt′) *v.* **-vert·ed, -vert·ing, -verts.** *—tr.* **1.** To turn inside out or upside down. **2.** To reverse the position, order, or condition of. **3.** To subject to inversion. *—intr.* To be subjected to inversion. *—n.* (ĭn′vûrt′). **1.** Something inverted. **2.** A homosexual. [Lat. *invertere* : *in-,* in + *vertere,* to turn.] **—in·vert′i·ble** *adj.*

in·ver·tase (ĭn-vûr′tās′, ĭn′vər-tās′, -tāz′) *n.* A plant and animal enzyme that catalyzes the conversion of sucrose to glucose and fructose.

in·ver·te·brate (ĭn-vûr′tə-brĭt, -brāt′) *adj.* Lacking a backbone or spinal column; not vertebrate. *—n.* An invertebrate animal. [NLat. *invertebratus* : Lat. *in-,* not + NLat. *vertebratus,* vertebrate.]

inverted comma *n. Chiefly Brit.* A quotation mark.

inverted mordent *n. Mus.* A pralltriller.

in·vert·er (ĭn-vûr′tər) *n.* **1.** One that inverts. **2.** A device used to convert direct current into alternating current. **3.** A circuit that takes in a positive pulse and puts out a negative one.

invert sugar *n.* A hygroscopic mixture of equal parts of glucose and fructose resulting from the hydrolysis of sucrose and used chiefly in brewing and in medicine.

in·vest (ĭn-vĕst′) *v.* **-vest·ed, -vest·ing, -vests.** *—tr.* **1.** To commit (money or capital) in order to gain profit or interest. **2.** To spend or utilize for future advantage or benefit: *invested energy in the research program.* **3.** To endow with authority or power. **4.** To inaugurate with ceremony; install in office. **5.** To endow with an enveloping or pervasive quality. **6.** To clothe; adorn. **7.** To cover completely; envelop. **8.** To surround with troops or ships; besiege. *—intr.* To make an investment. [Ital. *investire* < Lat., to clothe, surround : *in-,* in + *vestis,* clothes.] **—in·ves′tor** *n.*

in·ves·ti·gate (ĭn-vĕs′tĭ-gāt′) *v.* **-gat·ed, -gat·ing, -gates.** *—tr.* To observe or inquire into in detail; examine systematically. *—intr.* To make a detailed inquiry or systematic examination. [Lat. *investigare, investigat-* : *in-,* in + *vestigare,* to track < *vestigium,* footprint.] **—in·ves′ti·ga·ble** (-gə-bəl), **in·ves′ti·ga′tive, in·ves′ti·ga·to′ry** (-gə-tôr′ē, -tōr′ē) *adj.* **—in·ves′ti·ga′tion** *n.*

in·ves·ti·ga·tor (ĭn-vĕs′tĭ-gā′tər) *n.* One who investigates, esp. a detective. **—in·ves′ti·ga·to′ri·al** (-gə-tôr′ē-əl, -tōr′-) *adj.*

in·ves·ti·ture (ĭn-vĕs′tə-chŏŏr′, -chər) *n.* **1.** The act or formal ceremony of conferring the authority and symbols of a high office. **2.** Something that covers or adorns. [ME < Med. Lat. *investitura* < Lat. *investire,* to clothe. —see INVEST.]

in·vest·ment (ĭn-vĕst′mənt) *n.* **1.** The act of investing. **2.** An amount invested. **3.** Property or another possession acquired for future income or benefit. **4.** Investiture. **5.** *Archaic.* A garment; vestment. **6.** An outer covering or layer. **7.** A military siege.

in·vet·er·ate (ĭn-vĕt′ər-ĭt) *adj.* **1.** Firmly established by long standing; deep-rooted. **2.** Persisting in an ingrained habit; habitual: *an inveterate liar.* [ME, obstinate, long-established < Lat. *inveteratus,* p.part. of *inveterare,* to make old : *in-,* in, into + *vetus,* old.] **—in·vet′er·a·cy** (-ər-ə-sē), **in·vet′er·ate·ness** *n.* **—in·vet′er·ate·ly** *adv.*

in·vid·i·ous (ĭn-vĭd′ē-əs) *adj.* **1.** Tending to rouse ill will, animosity, or resentment; offensive. **2.** Containing or implying a slight; discriminatory. **3.** *Obs.* Envious. [Lat. *invidiosus,* envious, hostile < *invidia,* envy. —see ENVY.] **—in·vid′i·ous·ly** *adv.* **—in·vid′i·ous·ness** *n.*

in·vig·or·ate (ĭn-vĭg′ə-rāt′) *tr.v.* **-at·ed, -at·ing, -ates.** To impart vigor, strength, or vitality to; animate. **—in·vig′or·at′ing·ly** *adv.* **—in·vig′or·a′tion** *n.* **—in·vig′or·a′tor** *n.*

in·vin·ci·ble (ĭn-vĭn′sə-bəl) *adj.* Incapable of being defeated or overcome; unconquerable. [ME < OFr. < Lat. *invincibilis* : *in-,* not + *vincibilis,* vincible.] **—in·vin′ci·bil′i·ty, in·vin′ci·ble·ness** *n.* **—in·vin′ci·bly** *adv.*

in·vi·o·la·ble (ĭn-vī′ə-lə-bəl) *adj.* **1.** Secure from violation or profanation. **2.** Impregnable to assault or trespass. **—in·vi′o·la·bil′i·ty, in·vi′o·la·ble·ness** *n.* **—in·vi′o·la·bly** *adv.*

in·vi·o·late (ĭn-vī′ə-lĭt) *adj.* Not violated or profaned; intact. [ME < Lat. *inviolatus* : *in-,* not + *violatus,* p.part. of *violare,* to violate.] **—in·vi′o·la·cy** (-lə-sē), **in·vi′o·late·ness** *n.* **—in·vi′o·late·ly** *adv.*

in·vis·cid (ĭn-vĭs′ĭd) *adj.* **1.** Having no viscosity. **2.** Of or pertaining to an inviscid fluid.

in·vis·i·ble (ĭn-vĭz′ə-bəl) *adj.* **1.** Incapable of being seen; not visible. **2.** Not accessible to view; hidden. **3.** Not easily noticed or detected; inconspicuous. **4.** Not published in financial statements: *an invisible asset.* *—n.* One that is invisible. **—in·vis′i·bil′i·ty, in·vis′i·ble·ness** *n.* **—in·vis′i·bly** *adv.*

invisible ink *n.* Ink that is colorless and invisible until treated by a chemical, heat, or special light.

in·vi·ta·tion (ĭn′vĭ-tā′shən) *n.* **1.** The act of inviting. **2.** A spoken or written request for one's presence or participation. **3.** An allurement, enticement, or attraction.

in·vi·ta·tion·al (ĭn′vĭ-tā′shə-nəl) *adj.* Restricted to invited participants: *an invitational golf tournament.*

in·vi·ta·to·ry (ĭn-vī′tə-tôr′ē, -tōr′ē) *n., pl.* **-ries.** A psalm or other piece sung as an invitation to prayer in church services. *—adj.* Constituting or containing an invitation. [ME *invitiatorie* < Med. Lat. *invitiatorium* < LLat. *invitiatorius,* inviting < Lat. *invitare,* to invite.]

in·vite (ĭn-vīt′) *tr.v.* **-vit·ed, -vit·ing, -vites. 1.** To request the presence or participation of. **2.** To request formally. **3.** To welcome; encourage: *invite questions from the audience.* **4.** To tend to bring on; provoke. **5.** To entice; tempt. *—n.* (ĭn′vīt′). *Informal.* An invitation. [OFr. *inviter* < Lat. *invitare.*]

in·vit·ing (ĭn-vī′tĭng) *adj.* Attractive; tempting: *an inviting dessert.* **—in·vit′ing·ly** *adv.*

in vi·tro (ĭn vē′trō) *adj. & adv.* In an artificial environment outside the living organism. [NLat., in glass.]

in vi·vo (ĭn vē′vō) *adj. & adv.* Within a living organism. [NLat., in a living body.]

in·vo·cate (ĭn′və-kāt′) *tr.v.* **-cat·ed, -cat·ing, -cates.** *Archaic.* To invoke. [Lat. *invocare, invocat-,* to invoke.]

in·vo·ca·tion (ĭn′və-kā′shən) *n.* **1.** The act or process of invoking, esp. an appeal to a higher power for assistance. **2.** A prayer or other formula used in invoking, as at the opening of a religious service. **3. a.** An act of conjuring up a spirit by incantation. **b.** An incantation used in conjuring. [ME < OFr. < Lat. *invocatio* < *invocare,* to invoke.]

in·voc·a·to·ry (ĭn-vŏk′ə-tôr′ē, -tōr′ē) *adj.* Of, pertaining to, or having the nature of an invocation.

in·voice (ĭn′vois′) *n.* **1.** A detailed list of goods shipped or services rendered, with an account of all costs; bill. **2.** The goods or services itemized in an invoice. *—tr.v.* **-voiced, -voic·ing, -voic·es.** To make an invoice of or tender an invoice to; bill. [Alteration of obs. *invoyes,* pl. of *invoy,* invoice < Fr. *envoy* < *envoyer,* to send. —see ENVOY.]

in·voke (ĭn-vōk′) *tr.v.* **-voked, -vok·ing, -vokes. 1.** To call upon for assistance, support, or inspiration. **2.** To appeal to or cite in support or justification. **3.** To call for earnestly; solicit. **4.** To summon with incantations; conjure. **5.** To resort to; use or apply: *The governor invoked his veto power.* [OFr. *invoquer* < Lat. *invocare* : *in-,* in + *vocare,* to call.] **—in·vok′er** *n.*

in·vol·u·cel (ĭn-vŏl′yə-sĕl′) *n. Bot.* A secondary involucre, as at the base of an umbellule in a compound umbel. [NLat. *involucellum,* dim. of *involucrum,* involucre.]

in·vo·lu·cra (ĭn′və-lōō′krə) *n.* Plural of **involucrum.**

in·vo·lu·cre (ĭn′və-lōō′kər) *n.* A whorl or series of leaflike scales or bracts beneath or around a flower or flower cluster. [NLat. *involucrum,* involucrum.] **—in′vo·lu′cral** (-krəl), **in′vo·lu′crate** (-krĭt, -krāt′) *adj.*

in·vo·lu·crum (ĭn′və-lōō′krəm) *n., pl.* **-cra** (-krə). An enveloping sheath or envelope. [NLat. < Lat., wrapper, envelope < *involvere,* to enwrap. —see INVOLVE.]

in·vol·un·tar·y (ĭn-vŏl′ən-tĕr′ē) *adj.* **1.** Not performed willingly or deliberately. **2.** Not subject to control; automatic. **—in·vol′un·tar′i·ly** (-târ′ə-lē) *adv.* **—in·vol′un·tar′i·ness** *n.*

in·vo·lute (ĭn′və-lōōt′) *adj.* **1.** Intricate; complex. **2.** *Bot.* **a.** Having the margins rolled inward. **b.** Having whorls that obscure the axis or other volutions, as the shell of a cowry. *—n. Math.* **1.** The locus of a fixed point on a taut, inextensible string as it unwinds from a fixed plane curve. **2.** The locus of any point on a tangent line as it rolls but does not

involucel
Compound umbel

slide around a fixed curve. [Lat. *involutus,* p.part. of *involvere,* to enwrap. —see INVOLVE.] **—in'vo·lute'ly** *adv.*

in·vo·lu·tion (ĭn'və-lo͞o'shən) *n.* **1. a.** The act of involving. **b.** The state of being involved. **2. a.** Intricacy; complexity. **b.** Something that is intricate or complex, as a complicated grammatical construction. **3.** *Math.* The multiplying of a quantity by itself a specified number of times; raising to a power. **4.** *Biol.* The formation of a gastrula from a blastula by the ingrowth of blastomeres at the dorsal lip. [Lat. *involutio* < *involvere,* to enwrap. —see INVOLVE.] **—in'vo·lu'tion·al** *adj.*

in·volve (ĭn-vŏlv') *tr.v.* **-volved, -volv·ing, -volves. 1.** To contain or include as a part. **2.** To have as a necessary feature or consequence; entail. **3.** To draw in as a participant; embroil. **4.** To occupy or engross; absorb: *completely involved with his work.* **5.** To make complex or intricate; complicate. **6.** To wrap; envelop. **7.** *Archaic.* To wind or coil about. **8.** *Math.* To raise (a number) to a specified degree. [ME *involven* < OFr. *involver* < Lat. *involvere,* to enwrap : *in-,* in + *volvere,* to roll, turn.] **—in·volve'ment** *n.* **—in·volv'er** *n.*

in·volved (ĭn-vŏlvd') *adj.* **1.** Complicated; intricate. **2.** Involute; twisted. **3.** Confused; tangled. **—in·volv'ed·ly** (-vŏl'vĭd-lē) *adv.*

in·vul·ner·a·ble (ĭn-vŭl'nər-ə-bəl) *adj.* **1.** Immune to attack; impregnable. **2.** Incapable of being damaged, injured, or wounded. [Lat. *invulnerabilis* : *in-,* not + *vulnerare,* to wound < *vulnus,* wound.] **—in·vul'ner·a·bil'i·ty, in·vul'ner·a·ble·ness** *n.* **—in·vul'ner·a·bly** *adv.*

in·ward (ĭn'wərd) *adj.* **1.** Located inside; inner. **2.** Directed or moving toward the interior. **3.** Of, pertaining to, or existing in the thoughts or mind. **4.** Intimate; familiar. *—adv.* **1.** Toward the inside, center, or interior. **2.** Toward the mind or the self: *thoughts turned inward.* *—n.* **1.** An inner or central part. **2.** An inner essence or spirit. **3. inwards.** Entrails; innards. [ME < OE *inweard.*] **—in'wards** *adv.*

in·ward·ly (ĭn'wərd-lē) *adv.* **1.** On or in the inside; within. **2.** Privately; to oneself: *"kept his lips closed with the expression of a man inwardly laughing"* (T.S. Stribling).

in·ward·ness (ĭn'wərd-nĭs) *n.* **1.** Intimacy; familiarity. **2.** Preoccupation with one's own thoughts or feelings; introspection. **3.** Essential or fundamental nature. **4.** Internal quality or essence.

in·weave (ĭn-wēv') *tr.v.* **-wove** (-wōv'), **-wo·ven** (-wō'vən), **-weav·ing, -weaves.** To weave into a fabric or design.

in·wind (ĭn-wīnd') *v.* Variant of **enwind.**

in·wrap (ĭn-răp') *v.* Variant of **enwrap.**

in·wreathe (ĭn-rēth') *v.* Variant of **enwreathe.**

in·wrought (ĭn-rôt', ĭn'rôt') *adj.* **1.** Worked or woven in. **2.** Having a decorative pattern worked or woven in.

I·o (ī'ō) *n. Gk. Myth.* A maiden who was loved by Zeus and transformed by Hera into a heifer. [Lat. < Gk. *Īō.*]

iod– *pref.* Variant of **iodo-.**

i·o·date (ī'ə-dāt') *tr.v.* **-dat·ed, -dat·ing, -dates.** To iodize. *—n.* (ī'ə-dāt', -dĭt). A salt of iodic acid. **—i'o·da'tion** *n.*

i·od·ic acid (ī-ŏd'ĭk) *n.* A colorless or white crystalline powder, HIO_3, used as an antiseptic and deodorant. [Fr. *iodique* < *iode,* iodine.]

i·o·dide (ī'ə-dīd') *n.* A binary compound of iodine with a more electropositive atom or group.

i·o·dine (ī'ə-dīn', -dĭn, -dēn') *n. Symbol* **I 1.** A lustrous, grayish-black, corrosive, poisonous halogen element having radioactive isotopes, esp. I 131, used as tracers and in thyroid disease diagnosis and therapy, and compounds used as germicides, antiseptics, and dyes. Atomic number 53; atomic weight 126.9044; melting point 113.5°C; boiling point 184.35°C; specific gravity (solid, 20°C) 4.93; valences 1, 3, 5, 7. **2.** A tincture of iodine and sodium iodide, NaI, or potassium iodide, KI, used as an antiseptic for wounds. [Fr. *iode,* iodine (< Gk. *iōdēs,* violet-colored < *ion,* violet) + -INE.]

io moth

i·o·dize (ī'ə-dīz') *tr.v.* **-dized, -diz·ing, -diz·es.** To treat or combine with iodine or an iodide.

iodo– or **iod–** *pref.* Iodine: *iodoform.* [Fr. *iode,* iodine.]

i·o·do·form (ī-ō'də-fôrm', ī-ŏd'ə-) *n.* A yellowish iodine compound, CHI_3, used as an antiseptic. [IODO- + FORM(YL).]

i·o·do·phor (ī-ō'də-fôr') *n.* A substance consisting of iodine and a solubilizing agent that releases free iodine when in solution. [IODO- + -PHOR(E).]

i·o·dop·sin (ī'ə-dŏp'sĭn) *n.* A light-sensitive pigment in the retinal cones of the eye.

i·o moth (ī'ō) *n.* A large yellowish moth, *Automeris io,* of North America, with prominent eyelike spots on the hind wings. [After *Io,* who was tormented by gadflies sent by Hera as a punishment.]

Ionic
An Ionic capital

i·on (ī'ən, ī'ŏn') *n.* An atom, group of atoms, or molecule that has acquired or is regarded as having acquired a net electric charge by gaining electrons in or losing electrons from an initially electrically neutral configuration. [< Gk. *ion,* something that goes, neuter pr.part. of *ienai,* to go.]

–ion *suff.* **1. a.** Action or process: *oxidization.* **b.** Result of an action or process: *indention.* **2.** State or condition: *hydration.* [ME < OFr. < Lat. *-io,* n. suffix.]

ion engine *n.* A rocket engine that develops thrust by expelling ions rather than gaseous combustion products.

ion exchange *n.* A reversible chemical reaction between a solid and a fluid mixture by means of which ions may be interchanged, used in water softening and separation of radioactive isotopes.

I·o·ni·an (ī-ō'nē-ən) *adj.* Of or pertaining to Ionia or its inhabitants. **—I·o'ni·an** *n.*

i·on·ic (ī-ŏn'ĭk) *adj.* Of, containing, or involving ions.

I·on·ic (ī-ŏn'ĭk) *adj.* **1.** Of or pertaining to Ionia or the Ionians. **2.** Pertaining to or designating the Ionic order of architecture. *—n.* The ancient Greek dialect of Ionia.

ionic bond *n.* A chemical bond characteristic of salts and formed by the complete transfer of one or more electrons from one kind of atom to another.

Ionic order *n.* An order of classical Greek architecture characterized by two opposed volutes in the capital.

ionic propulsion *n.* Propulsion by the reactive thrust of a high-speed beam of similarly charged ions ejected by an ion engine.

i·on·i·za·tion (ī'ə-nĭ-zā'shən) *n.* **1.** The formation of one or more ions by the addition of electrons to or the removal of electrons from an electrically neutral atomic or molecular configuration by heat, electrical discharge, radiation, or chemical reaction. **2.** The state or condition of being ionized.

ionization chamber *n.* A gas-filled enclosure fitted with electrodes between which electric current flows upon ionization of the gas by incident radiation, the electrodes being maintained at a potential difference just sufficient to collect ions thus produced without causing further ionization.

ionization potential *n.* The energy required to remove completely the weakest bound electron from its ground state in an atom or molecule so that the resulting ion is also in its ground state.

i·on·ize (ī'ə-nīz') *tr. & intr.v.* **-ized, -iz·ing, -iz·es.** To convert totally or partially into ions.

ionizing radiation *n.* Radiation capable of producing ionization, including energetic charged particles such as alpha and beta rays, nonparticulate radiation such as x-rays, and neutrons.

i·o·none (ī'ə-nōn') *n.* Either of two yellowish to colorless liquid isomers, $C_{13}H_{20}O$, having a strong odor of violets and used in perfumes. [Gk. *ion,* violet + -ONE.]

i·on·o·sphere (ī-ŏn'ə-sfîr') *n.* An electrically conducting set of layers of the earth's atmosphere, extending from altitudes of approximately 50 kilometers to more than 400 kilometers, or 30 to 250 miles, caused by ionization of rarefied atmospheric gases by incident solar radiation. [ION + -SPHERE.] **—i·on'o·spher'ic** (-sfîr'ĭk, -sfĕr'-) *adj.*

ion propulsion *n.* Ionic propulsion.

ion rocket *n.* **1.** A rocket using ionic propulsion. **2.** An ion engine.

ion trap *n.* A magnet mounted to the neck of a kinescope to prevent ions from striking the kinescope screen.

i·o·ta (ī-ō'tə) *n.* **1.** The 9th letter of the Greek alphabet. See table at **alphabet. 2.** A very small amount; bit. [Gk. *iōta,* of Phoenician orig.; akin to Hebrew *yōdh,* yod.]

i·o·ta·cism (ī-ō'tə-sĭz'əm) *n.* The conversion of other vowel sounds in Greek to the sound of iota. [LLat. *iotacismus* < Gk. *iōtakismos* < *iōta,* iota.]

IOU (ī'ō-yo͞o') *n., pl.* **IOU's** or **IOUs.** A promise to pay a debt. [< the pronunciation of *I owe you.*]

–ious *suff.* Having; having the qualities of; full of: *bilious.* [ME, partly < Lat. *-ius,* and partly < OFr. *-ieus, -ieux* < Lat. *-iosus.*]

I·o·wa (ī'ə-wə) *n., pl.* **Iowa** or **-was. 1.** A tribe of North American Indians formerly inhabiting the region of Minnesota, Iowa, and Missouri. **2.** A member of the Iowa. **3.** The Siouan language of the Iowa. [Dakota *Ayuhwa.*] **—I'o·wa** *adj.*

ip·e·cac (ĭp'ĭ-kăk') also **ip·e·cac·u·an·ha** (ĭp'ĭ-kăk'yo͞o-ăn'ə) *n.* **1.** A low-growing South American shrub, *Cephaelis ipecacuanha,* having roots used medicinally. **2.** The dried roots of the ipecac. [< Port. *ipecacuanha* < Tupi *ipekaaguéne.*]

Iph·i·ge·ni·a (ĭf'ə-jə-nī'ə) *n. Gk. Myth.* The daughter of Clytemnestra and Agamemnon, offered as a sacrifice to Artemis to enable the Greek fleet to sail for Troy. [Lat. < Gk. *Iphigeneia.*]

ip·se dix·it (ĭp'sē dĭk'sĭt) *n.* **1.** An unsupported assertion, usually by a person of standing. **2.** An arbitrary statement; dictum. [Lat., he himself said (it).]

ip·si·lat·er·al (ĭp'sə-lăt'ər-əl) *adj.* Affecting or located on the same side of the body. [Alteration of Lat. *ipse,* self + LATERAL.] **—ip'si·lat'er·al·ly** *adv.*

ip·sis·si·ma ver·ba (ĭp-sĭs'ə-mə vûr'bə) *pl.n.* The very words. [Lat.]

ip·so fac·to (ĭp'sō făk'tō) *adv.* By the fact itself; by that very fact: *An alien, ipso facto, has no right to a U.S. passport.* [Lat.]

ip·so ju·re (ĭp'sō jo͝or'ē) *adv.* By the law itself. [Lat.]

IQ or **I.Q.** (ī'kyo͞o') *n.* Intelligence quotient.

Ir The symbol for the element iridium.

ir–¹ *pref.* Variant of **in-¹.** Used before *r.*

ir–² *pref.* Variant of **in-².** Used before *r.*

I·ra·ni·an (ĭ-rā'nē-ən) *adj.* Of or pertaining to Iran, its inhabitants, or their language. *—n.* **1.** A native or inhabitant of Iran. **2.** A branch of the Indo-European language family that includes Persian, Kurdish, Pashto, and other languages of Iran, Afghanistan, and western Pakistan.

I·ra·qi (ĭ-rä′kē) *adj.* Of or pertaining to Iraq, its inhabitants, or their language. —*n., pl.* **Iraqi** or **-qis. 1.** A native or inhabitant of Iraq. **2.** The modern dialect of Arabic spoken in Iraq.

i·ras·ci·ble (ĭ-răs′ə-bəl, ī-răs′-) *adj.* **1.** Prone to outbursts of temper; easily angered. **2.** Characterized by or resulting from anger. [ME *irascible* < OFr. < LLat. *irascibilis* < Lat. *irasci,* to be angry < *ira,* anger.] **—i·ras′ci·bil′i·ty, i·ras′ci·ble·ness** *n.* **—i·ras′ci·bly** *adv.*

i·rate (ī-rāt′, ī′rāt′) *adj.* **1.** Extremely angry; enraged. **2.** Characterized or occasioned by anger: *an irate phone call.* [Lat. *iratus,* p.part. of *irasci,* to be angry < *ira,* anger.] **—i·rate′ly** *adv.*

ire (īr) *n.* Wrath; anger. [ME < OFr. < Lat. *ira.*]

ire·ful (īr′fəl) *adj.* Full of ire; wrathful. **—ire′ful·ly** *adv.*

i·ren·ic (ī-rĕn′ĭk, ī-rē′nĭk) also **i·ren·i·cal** (-ĭ-kəl, -nĭ-kəl) *adj.* Promoting peace; conciliatory. [Gk. *eirēnikos* < *eirēnē,* peace.] **—i·ren′i·cal·ly** *adv.*

irid– *pref.* Variant of **irido-.**

ir·i·da·ceous (ĭr′ĭ-dā′shəs) *adj.* Of or pertaining to the iris family. [< NLat. *Iridacea,* iris family < *Iris,* type genus < Lat., iris.]

ir·i·dec·to·my (ĭr′ĭ-dĕk′tə-mē, ī′rĭ-) *n., pl.* **-mies.** The surgical removal of part of the iris of the eye.

ir·i·des·cence (ĭr′ĭ-dĕs′əns) *n.* The state or quality of being iridescent.

ir·i·des·cent (ĭr′ĭ-dĕs′ənt) *adj.* **1.** Producing a display of lustrous, rainbowlike colors. **2.** Brilliant, lustrous, or colorful in effect or appearance: *an iridescent smile.*

i·rid·ic (ĭ-rĭd′ĭk, ī-rĭd′-) *adj.* Pertaining to the iris of the eye.

i·rid·i·um (ĭ-rĭd′ē-əm) *n. Symbol* **Ir** A very hard and brittle, exceptionally corrosion-resistant, whitish-yellow metallic element occurring in platinum ores and used principally to harden platinum and in high-temperature materials, electrical contacts, and wear-resistant bearings. Atomic number 77; atomic weight 192.2; melting point 2,410°C; boiling point 4,527°C; specific gravity 22.42 (17°C); valences 3, 4. [Gk. *iris, irid-,* rainbow + -IUM (from the colors produced by dissolving it in hydrochloric acid).]

irido– or **irid–** *pref.* **1.** Rainbow: *iridescent.* **2.** Iris of the eye: *iridectomy.* **3.** Iridium: *iridosmine.* [Lat. *iris, irid-,* rainbow.]

ir·i·dos·mine (ĭr′ĭ-dŏz′mĭn′) *n.* Osmiridium. [G. *Iridosmin.*]

i·ris (ī′rĭs) *n., pl.* **i·ris·es** or **i·ri·des** (ī′rĭ-dēz′, ĭr′ĭ-). **1.** The pigmented, round, contractile membrane of the eye, situated between the cornea and lens, and perforated by the pupil. **2.** Any of numerous plants of the genus *Iris,* having narrow sword-shaped leaves and showy, variously colored flowers. **3.** A rainbow or rainbowlike display of colors. [ME, rainbow < Lat. < Gk., rainbow, iris of the eye.]

I·ris (ī′rĭs) *n. Gk. Myth.* The goddess of the rainbow and messenger of the gods. [Lat. < Gk.]

iris diaphragm *n.* A metallic diaphragm adjustable to vary the diameter of a central aperture, commonly used on cameras to regulate the amount of light admitted to a lens.

I·rish (ī′rĭsh) *adj.* Of or relating to Ireland, its people, or their language. —*n.* **1. a.** The inhabitants of Ireland. **b.** People of immediate Irish descent. **2. a.** Irish Gaelic. **b.** Irish English. **3.** *Informal.* Fieriness of temper or passion; high spirit. [ME < OE *Iras,* the Irish.]

Irish bull *n.* An apparently consistent but actually illogical or inconsistent statement.

Irish coffee *n.* A beverage of sweetened hot coffee and Irish whiskey, topped with whipped cream.

Irish elk *n.* A large extinct European deer of the genus *Megaceros,* of the Pliocene and Pleistocene epochs, having very large palmate antlers.

Irish English *n.* English as spoken by the Irish.

Irish Gaelic *n.* The Goidelic language of Ireland.

I·rish·ism (ī′rĭsh-ĭz′əm) *n.* An Irish idiom or custom.

I·rish·man (ī′rĭsh-mən) *n.* A man of Irish birth or descent.

Irish moss *n.* An edible North Atlantic seaweed, *Chondrus crispus,* that yields a mucilaginous substance used medicinally and in preparing jellies.

Irish setter *n.* A setter having a silky reddish-brown coat.

Irish stew *n.* A stew of meat and vegetables.

Irish terrier *n.* A terrier having a wiry brown coat.

Irish whiskey *n.* Whiskey made by the distillation of barley.

Irish wolfhound *n.* A large dog of an ancient breed, having a rough, shaggy coat.

I·rish·wom·an (ī′rĭsh-wo͝om′ən) *n.* A woman of Irish birth or descent.

i·ri·tis (ī-rī′tĭs) *n.* Inflammation of the iris of the eye. [IR(IS) + -ITIS.]

irk (ûrk) *tr.v.* **irked, irk·ing, irks.** To vex or irritate. [ME *irken,* to weary, prob. of Celt. orig.]

irk·some (ûrk′səm) *adj.* Causing annoyance or bother; tedious: *irksome restrictions.* **—irk′some·ly** *adv.* **—irk′some·ness** *n.*

i·ron (ī′ərn) *n.* **1.** *Symbol* **Fe** A silvery-white, lustrous, malleable, ductile, magnetic or magnetizable, metallic element occurring abundantly in combined forms, notably in hematite, limonite, magnetite, and taconite, and used alloyed in a wide range of important structural materials. Atomic number 26; atomic weight 55.847; melting point 1,535°C; boiling point 3,000°C; specific gravity 7.874 (20°C); valences 2, 3, 4, 6. **2.** Great hardness or strength; firmness: *a will of iron.* **3.** An implement made of iron alloy or similar metal, esp. a bar heated for use in branding, curling hair, or cauterizing. **4.** A golf club with a metal head, numbered from one to nine according to the degree of slant of the face of the club. **5.** A metal appliance with a handle and a weighted flat bottom, used when heated to press wrinkles from fabric. **6.** A harpoon. **7. irons.** Fetters; shackles. **8.** A tonic, pill, or other medication containing iron as a dietary supplement. ***—modifier:*** *an iron fist; an iron constitution; an iron will.* —*v.* **i·roned, i·ron·ing, i·rons.** —*tr.* **1. a.** To press and smooth with a heated iron. **b.** To remove (creases) by pressing. **2.** To put in irons; fetter. **3.** To fit or clad with iron. —*intr.* To iron clothes. ***—phrasal verb.*** **iron out.** To settle through discussion or compromise; work out. ***—idiom.*** **an iron in the fire.** An undertaking or project. [ME *iren* < OE *īren.*]

Iron Age *n.* The generally prehistoric period succeeding the Bronze Age, characterized by the introduction of iron metallurgy, in Europe beginning around the eighth century B.C.

iron blue *n.* Any of various light- and heat-resistant, semitransparent blue pigments of powerful tinctorial strength, used chiefly in permanent industrial finishes, printing inks, and artists' colors.

i·ron·bound (ī′ərn-bound′) *adj.* **1.** Bound with iron. **2.** Rigid and unyielding. **3.** Bound with rocks and cliffs, as a coast.

i·ron·clad (ī′ərn-klăd′) *adj.* **1.** Sheathed with iron plates for protection. **2.** Rigid; fixed: *an ironclad rule.* —*n.* A 19th-century warship having sides armored with metal plates.

Iron Curtain *n.* A social, political, or military barrier that prevents free exchange or communication, esp. the political and ideological barrier between the Soviet bloc and western Europe after World War II.

iron gray *n.* A dark gray with a slightly greenish tinge.

iron hand *n.* Rigorous or despotic control: *ruling with an iron hand.* **—i′ron-hand′ed** (ī′ərn-hăn′dĭd) *adj.* **—i′ron·hand′ed·ness** *n.*

iron horse *n. Informal.* A railroad locomotive.

i·ron·ic (ī-rŏn′ĭk) also **i·ron·i·cal** (ī-rŏn′ĭ-kəl) *adj.* **1.** Characterized by or constituting irony. **2.** Given to the use of irony. **—i·ron′i·cal·ly** *adv.* **—i·ron′i·cal·ness** *n.*

i·ron·ing (ī′ər-nĭng) *n.* **1.** The act or process of pressing clothes with a heated iron. **2.** The clothing pressed or to be pressed with a heated iron.

ironing board *n.* A long narrow padded board on a collapsible support, used as a working surface for ironing.

i·ro·nist (ī′rə-nĭst) *n.* A notable user of irony, esp. a writer.

iron lung *n.* A tank in which the entire body except the head is enclosed and by means of which pressure is regularly increased and decreased to provide artificial respiration.

iron maiden *n.* A medieval instrument of torture consisting of an iron frame in the form of a person in which a victim was enclosed and impaled on interior spikes.

i·ron·mas·ter (ī′ərn-măs′tər) *n. Chiefly Brit.* A manufacturer of iron.

i·ron·mon·ger (ī′ərn-mŭng′gər, -mŏng′-) *n. Chiefly Brit.* A hardware merchant.

i·ron·mon·ger·y (ī′ərn-mŭng′gə-rē, -mŏng′-) *n., pl.* **-ies.** *Chiefly Brit.* **1.** Ironware. **2.** The shop or business of an ironmonger.

iron oxide *n.* Any of various oxides of iron, such as ferrous oxide.

iron pyrites *n.* Pyrite.

i·ron·smith (ī′ərn-smĭth′) *n.* One who works in iron; blacksmith.

i·ron·stone (ī′ərn-stōn′) *n.* **1.** One of several kinds of iron ore with admixtures of silica and clay. **2.** A hard white pottery.

i·ron·ware (ī′ərn-wâr′) *n.* Iron utensils and other products made of iron.

i·ron·weed (ī′ərn-wēd′) *n.* Any plant of the genus *Vernonia,* having clusters of purplish flowers.

i·ron·wood (ī′ərn-wo͝od′) *n.* **1.** Any of various trees having very hard wood. **2.** The wood of an ironwood.

i·ron·work (ī′ərn-wûrk′) *n.* Work in iron, as gratings and rails.

i·ron·works (ī′ərn-wûrks′) *pl.n. (used with a sing. or pl. verb).* A building or establishment where iron is smelted or where heavy iron products are made.

i·ro·ny (ī′rə-nē) *n., pl.* **-nies. 1. a.** The use of words to convey the opposite of their literal meaning. **b.** An expression or utterance marked by such a deliberate contrast between apparent and intended meaning. **c.** A literary style employing ironic contrasts for humorous or rhetorical effect. **2. a.** Incongruity between what might be expected and what actually occurs: *"Hyde noted the irony of Ireland's copying the nation she most hated"* (Richard Kain). **b.** An occurrence, result, or circumstance notable for such incongruity. **3.** The dramatic effect achieved by leading an audience to understand an incongruity between a situation and the accompanying speeches, while the characters in the play remain unaware of the incongruity. **4.** Feigned ignorance, as in the Socratic method of instruction. [Lat. *ironia* < Gk. *eirōneia,* feigned ignorance < *eirōn,* dissembler < *eirein,* to say.]

Ir·o·quoi·an (ĭr′ə-kwoi′ən) *n.* **1.** A family of North American Indian languages of the eastern part of Canada and the

iris

Irish setter

Irish terrier

Irish wolfhound

ironwork

ironworks

United States that includes Iroquois, Cherokee, Conestoga, Erie, and Wyandot. **2.** A member of a tribe using a language of the Iroquoian family. —*adj.* Of or constituting the Iroquoian language family.

Ir·o·quois (ĭr′ə-kwoi′) *n., pl.* **Iroquois** (-kwoi′, -kwoiz′). **1.** Any of several North American Indian tribes formerly inhabiting New York State and forming the confederacy known as the Five Nations, including the Cayuga, Mohawk, Oneida, Onondaga, and Seneca peoples. After 1722 the confederacy was joined by the Tuscaroras to form the Six Nations. **2.** A member of any of the Iroquois tribes. **3.** Any of the languages of the Iroquois. [Fr. < Algonquin *Irinakhoiw.*] —**Ir′o·quois′** *adj.*

ir·ra·di·ant (ĭ-rā′dē-ənt) *adj.* Sending forth radiant light. [Lat. *irradians, irradiant-,* pr.part. of *irradiare,* to irradiate.] —**ir·ra′di·ance, ir·ra′di·an·cy** *n.*

ir·ra·di·ate (ĭ-rā′dē-āt′) *v.* **-at·ed, -at·ing, -ates.** —*tr.* **1. a.** To expose to radiation. **b.** To treat with radiation. **2.** To emit in a manner analogous to the emission of light. —*intr. Archaic.* **1.** To send forth rays; radiate. **2.** To become radiant. [Lat. *irradiare, irradiat-,* to illuminate : *in-,* on + *radiare,* to shine < *radius,* ray.] —**ir·ra′di·a′tive** *adj.* —**ir·ra′di·a′tor** *n.*

ir·ra·di·a·tion (ĭ-rā′dē-ā′shən) *n.* **1.** The act of irradiating or the condition of being irradiated. **2.** Therapy or treatment by exposure to radiation.

ir·rad·i·ca·ble (ĭ-răd′ĭ-kə-bel) *adj.* Incapable of being destroyed or uprooted. [Med. Lat. *irradicabilis* : Lat. *in-,* not + Lat. *radix,* root.] —**ir·rad′i·ca·bly** *adv.*

ir·ra·tion·al (ĭ-răsh′ə-nəl) *adj.* **1. a.** Not endowed with reason. **b.** Affected by loss of usual or normal mental clarity; incoherent, as from shock. **c.** Contrary to reason; illogical: *an irrational dislike.* **2. a.** Designating a syllable in Greek and Latin prosody whose length does not fit the metric pattern. **b.** Designating a metric foot containing such a syllable. **3.** *Math.* Incapable of being expressed as an integer or a quotient of integers. —**ir·ra′tion·al·ly** *adv.* —**ir·ra′tion·al·ness** *n.*

ir·ra·tion·al·ism (ĭ-răsh′ə-nə-lĭz′əm) *n.* Irrational thought, expression, or behavior.

ir·ra·tion·al·i·ty (ĭ-răsh′ə-năl′ĭ-tē) *n., pl.* **-ties. 1.** The state or quality of being irrational. **2.** An irrational idea or action.

irrational number *n.* A member of the set of real numbers that is not a member of the set of rational numbers.

ir·re·claim·a·ble (ĭr′ĭ-klā′mə-bəl) *adj.* Incapable of being reclaimed: *irreclaimable wasteland.* —**ir′re·claim′a·bil′i·ty, ir′re·claim′a·ble·ness** *n.* —**ir′re·claim′a·bly** *adv.*

ir·rec·on·cil·a·ble (ĭ-rĕk′ən-sī′lə-bəl, ĭ-rĕk′ən-sī′-) *adj.* Not capable of being reconciled. —*n.* **1.** A person, esp. a member of a group, who will not compromise, adjust, or submit. **2. irreconcilables.** Conflicting ideas or beliefs that cannot be brought into harmony. —**ir·rec′on·cil′a·bil′i·ty** *n.* —**ir·rec′on·cil′a·bly** *adv.*

ir·re·cov·er·a·ble (ĭr′ĭ-kŭv′ər-ə-bəl) *adj.* Incapable of being recovered; irreparable: *irrecoverable losses.* —**ir′re·cov′er·a·ble·ness** *n.* —**ir′re·cov′er·a·bly** *adv.*

ir·re·cu·sa·ble (ĭr′ĭ-kyo͞o′zə-bəl) *adj.* Not subject to challenge or objection. [Fr. *irrécusable* < LLat. *irrecusabilis* : Lat. *in-,* not + *recusabilis,* deserving of rejection < Lat. *recusare,* to refuse. —see RECUSANT.] —**ir′re·cu′sa·bly** *adv.*

ir·re·deem·a·ble (ĭr′ĭ-dē′mə-bəl) *adj.* **1.** Incapable of being bought back or paid off: *an irredeemable annuity.* **2.** Not convertible into coin. **3.** Incapable of being remedied. **4.** Incapable of being redeemed or reformed. —**ir′re·deem′a·bly** *adv.*

ir·re·den·tist (ĭr′ĭ-dĕn′tĭst) *n.* One who advocates the recovery of lands of which his nation has been deprived or of territory culturally or historically related to his nation but now subject to a foreign government. [Ital. *irredentista* < *(Italia) irredenta,* unredeemed (Italy), Italian-speaking areas subject to other countries.] —**ir′re·den′tism** *n.* —**ir′re·den′tist** *adj.*

ir·re·duc·i·ble (ĭr′ĭ-do͞o′sə-bəl, -dyo͞o′-) *adj.* Incapable of being reduced to a desired, simpler, or smaller form or amount. —**ir′re·duc′i·bil′i·ty, ir′re·duc′i·ble·ness** *n.* —**ir′re·duc′i·bly** *adv.*

ir·ref·ra·ga·ble (ĭ-rĕf′rə-gə-bəl) *adj.* Incapable of being refuted or controverted; indisputable. [LLat. *irrefragabilis* : Lat. *in-,* not + Lat. *refragari,* to oppose.] —**ir·ref′ra·ga·bil′i·ty** *n.* —**ir·ref′ra·ga·bly** *adv.*

ir·re·fran·gi·ble (ĭr′ĭ-frăn′jə-bəl) *adj.* **1.** Incapable of being broken; indestructible. **2.** *Physics.* Incapable of being refracted. —**ir′re·fran′gi·bly** *adv.*

ir·ref·u·ta·ble (ĭ-rĕf′yə-tə-bəl, ĭr′ĭ-fyo͞o′-) *adj.* Incapable of being refuted or disproved; incontrovertible: *irrefutable arguments.* —**ir·ref′u·ta·bil′i·ty** *n.* —**ir·ref′u·ta·bly** *adv.*

ir·re·gard·less (ĭr′ĭ-gärd′lĭs) *adv. Nonstandard.* Regardless.

ir·reg·u·lar (ĭ-rĕg′yə-lər) *adj.* **1.** Not according to rule, accepted order, or general practice: *irregular hiring practices.* **2.** Not conforming to legality, moral law, or social convention: *an irregular marriage.* **3.** Not straight, uniform, or symmetrical: *irregular facial features.* **4.** Of uneven rate, occurrence, or duration: *an irregular heartbeat.* **5.** Deviating from type; asymmetrically arranged or atypical. **6.** *Bot.* Having differing floral parts, esp. petals. **7.** Falling below the manufacturer's standard or usual specifications; imperfect. **8.** *Gram.* Departing from the usual set of inflectional forms. An example of an irregular verb is *be.* **9.** Not belonging to a permanent, organized military force: *irregular troops.* —*n.* **1.** One that is irregular. **2.** A soldier, such as a guerrilla, who is not a member of a regular military force. —**ir·reg′u·lar·ly** *adv.*

ir·reg·u·lar·i·ty (ĭ-rĕg′yə-lăr′ĭ-tē) *n., pl.* **-ties. 1.** The quality or state of being irregular. **2.** Something that is irregular: *found the firm's books riddled with irregularities.* **3.** Constipation.

ir·rel·a·tive (ĭ-rĕl′ə-tĭv) *adj.* **1.** Having no correlative relationship; unconnected. **2.** Irrelevant. —**ir·rel′a·tive·ly** *adv.*

ir·rel·e·vance (ĭ-rĕl′ə-vəns) *n.* **1.** The quality or state of being irrelevant. **2.** Something that is irrelevant.

ir·rel·e·van·cy (ĭ-rĕl′ə-vən-sē) *n., pl.* **-cies.** Irrelevance.

ir·rel·e·vant (ĭ-rĕl′ə-vənt) *adj.* Having no applications or effects in a specified circumstance. —**ir·rel′e·vant·ly** *adv.*

ir·re·lig·ion (ĭr′ĭ-lĭj′ən) *n.* Hostility or indifference to religion.

ir·re·lig·ious (ĭr′ĭ-lĭj′əs) *adj.* Hostile or indifferent to religion; ungodly. —**ir′re·lig′ious·ly** *adv.* —**ir′re·lig′ious·ness** *n.*

ir·re·me·a·ble (ĭ-rē′mē-ə-bəl) *adj. Archaic.* Affording no possibility of return. [Lat. *irremeabilis* : *in-,* not + *remeare,* to return (*re-,* back + *meare,* to go).]

ir·re·me·di·a·ble (ĭr′ĭ-mē′dē-ə-bəl) *adj.* Impossible to remedy, correct, or repair; incurable. —**ir′re·me′di·a·bly** *adv.*

ir·re·mis·si·ble (ĭr′ĭ-mĭs′ə-bəl) *adj.* Not remissible; unpardonable. —**ir′re·mis′si·bil′i·ty** *n.* —**ir′re·mis′si·bly** *adv.*

ir·re·mov·a·ble (ĭr′ĭ-mo͞o′və-bəl) *adj.* Not removable. —**ir′re·mov′a·bil′i·ty** *n.* —**ir′re·mov′a·bly** *adv.*

ir·rep·a·ra·ble (ĭ-rĕp′ər-ə-bəl) *adj.* Incapable of being repaired, rectified, or amended: *irreparable harm.* —**ir·rep′a·ra·bil′i·ty, ir·rep′a·ra·ble·ness** *n.* —**ir·rep′a·ra·bly** *adv.*

ir·re·peal·a·ble (ĭr′ĭ-pē′lə-bəl) *adj.* Not repealable.

ir·re·place·a·ble (ĭr′ĭ-plā′sə-bəl) *adj.* Incapable of being replaced. —**ir′re·place′a·bly** *adv.*

ir·re·pres·si·ble (ĭr′ĭ-prĕs′ə-bəl) *adj.* Impossible to control or restrain: *irrepressible laughter.* —**ir′re·pres′si·bil′i·ty, ir′re·pres′si·ble·ness** *n.* —**ir′re·pres′si·bly** *adv.*

ir·re·proach·a·ble (ĭr′ĭ-prō′chə-bəl) *adj.* Beyond reproach; faultless. —**ir′re·proach′a·ble·ness** *n.* —**ir′re·proach′a·bly** *adv.*

ir·re·sis·ti·ble (ĭr′ĭ-zĭs′tə-bəl) *adj.* **1.** Impossible to resist: *an irresistible impulse.* **2.** Having an overpowering appeal: *irresistible beauty.* —**ir′re·sis′ti·bil′i·ty, ir′re·sis′ti·ble·ness** *n.* —**ir′re·sis′ti·bly** *adv.*

ir·re·sol·u·ble (ĭr′ĭ-zŏl′yə-bəl) *adj.* Not capable of being solved.

ir·res·o·lute (ĭ-rĕz′ə-lo͞ot′) *adj.* **1.** Unresolved as to action or procedure. **2.** Lacking in resolution; indecisive. —**ir·res′o·lute′ly** *adv.* —**ir·res′o·lute′ness, ir·res′o·lu′tion** *n.*

ir·re·solv·a·ble (ĭr′ĭ-zŏl′və-bəl) *adj.* **1.** Incapable of being resolved. **2.** Not capable of being separated into component parts; irreducible.

ir·re·spec·tive (ĭr′ĭ-spĕk′tĭv) *adj. Archaic.* Characterized by disregard; heedless. —**ir′re·spec′tive·ly** *adv.*

irrespective of *prep.* Without consideration of; regardless of.

ir·res·pi·ra·ble (ĭ-rĕs′pər-ə-bəl, ĭr′ĭ-spīr′-) *adj.* Not fit for breathing; not respirable.

ir·re·spon·si·ble (ĭr′ĭ-spŏn′sə-bəl) *adj.* **1.** Not liable to be called to account by a higher authority. **2.** Not mentally or financially fit to assume responsibility. **3.** Lacking a sense of responsibility. **4.** Marked by a lack of responsibility: *irresponsible accusations.* —*n.* An irresponsible person. —**ir′re·spon′si·bil′i·ty, ir′re·spon′si·ble·ness** *n.* —**ir′re·spon′si·bly** *adv.*

ir·re·spon·sive (ĭr′ĭ-spŏn′sĭv) *adj.* **1.** Not responsive, as to treatment or stimuli. **2.** Not responding or answering readily. —**ir′re·spon′sive·ly** *adv.* —**ir′re·spon′sive·ness** *n.*

ir·re·triev·a·ble (ĭr′ĭ-trē′və-bəl) *adj.* Not capable of being retrieved or recovered. —**ir′re·triev′a·ble·ness, ir′re·triev′a·bil′i·ty** *n.* —**ir′re·triev′a·bly** *adv.*

ir·rev·er·ence (ĭ-rĕv′ər-əns) *n.* **1.** Lack of reverence or due respect. **2.** A disrespectful act or remark.

ir·rev·er·ent (ĭ-rĕv′ər-ənt) *adj.* **1. a.** Lacking in reverence; disrespectful. **b.** Gently or humorously sardonic in manner. **2.** Proceeding from irreverence: *an irreverent act.* —**ir·rev′er·ent·ly** *adv.*

ir·re·vers·i·ble (ĭr′ĭ-vûr′sə-bəl) *adj.* Incapable of being reversed. —**ir′re·vers′i·bil′i·ty, ir′re·vers′i·ble·ness** *n.* —**ir′re·vers′i·bly** *adv.*

ir·rev·o·ca·ble (ĭ-rĕv′ə-kə-bəl) *adj.* Incapable of being retracted or revoked; irreversible: *an irrevocable decision.* —**ir·rev′o·ca·bil′i·ty, ir·rev′o·ca·ble·ness** *n.* —**ir·rev′o·ca·bly** *adv.*

ir·ri·ga·ble (ĭr′ĭ-gə-bəl) *adj.* Capable of being irrigated.

ir·ri·gate (ĭr′ĭ-gāt′) *tr.v.* **-gat·ed, -gat·ing, -gates. 1.** To supply (dry land) with water by means of ditches, pipes, or streams. **2.** To wash out (a canal or wound) with water or a medicated fluid. **3.** To vitalize or make fertile. [Lat. *irrigare, irrigat-* : *in-,* in + *rigare,* to water.] —**ir′ri·ga′tion** *n.* —**ir′ri·ga′tion·al** *adj.* —**ir′ri·ga′tor** *n.*

ir·ri·ta·bil·i·ty (ĭr′ĭ-tə-bĭl′ĭ-tē) *n.* **1.** The quality or state of being irritable; testiness; petulance. **2.** *Pathol.* Excessive sensitivity. **3.** *Biol.* The capacity to respond to stimuli.

ir·ri·ta·ble (ĭr′ĭ-tə-bəl) *adj.* **1.** Easily irritated or annoyed. **2.** *Pathol.* Abnormally sensitive. **3.** *Biol.* Responsive to stimuli. [Lat. *irritabilis* < *irritare,* to irritate.] **—ir′ri·ta·ble·ness** *n.* **—ir′ri·ta·bly** *adv.*

ir·ri·tant (ĭr′ĭ-tənt) *adj.* Causing irritation, esp. physical irritation. *—n.* Something that causes irritation. [Lat. *irritans, irritant-,* pr.part. of *irritare,* to irritate.]

ir·ri·tate (ĭr′ĭ-tāt′) *tr.v.* **-tat·ed, -tat·ing, -tates. 1. a.** To exasperate; vex. **b.** To provoke. **2.** To chafe or inflame. [Lat. *irritare.*] **—ir′ri·tat′ing·ly** *adv.* **—ir′ri·ta′tor** *n.*

ir·ri·ta·tion (ĭr′ĭ-tā′shən) *n.* **1.** The act of irritating. **2.** Something that irritates. **3.** The condition of being irritated; vexation. **4.** *Pathol.* Incipient inflammation, soreness, roughness, or irritability of a bodily part.

ir·ri·ta·tive (ĭr′ĭ-tā′tĭv) *adj.* Involving irritation.

ir·ro·ta·tion·al (ĭr′ō-tā′shə-nəl) *adj.* Not rotating or involving rotation.

ir·rupt (ĭ-rŭpt′) *intr.v.* **-rupt·ed, -rupt·ing, -rupts. 1.** To break or burst in. **2.** *Ecol.* To increase irregularly in number. Used of a population. [Lat. *irrumpere, irrupt-* : *in-,* in + *rumpere,* to burst.] **—ir·rup′tion** *n.*

ir·rup·tive (ĭ-rŭp′tĭv) *adj.* **1.** Irrupting or tending to irrupt. **2.** *Geol.* Intrusive.

is (ĭz) *v.* The third person singular present tense of **be.** [ME < OE.]

is– *pref.* Variant of **iso-.**

I·saac (ī′zək) *n.* A Hebrew patriarch, the son of Abraham and Sarah and the father of Jacob. [LLat. *Isaacus* < Gk. *Isaak* < Heb. *Yiṣḥāq* < *yiṣḥāq,* he laughs.]

I·sa·iah (ī-zā′ə, ī-zī′ə) *n.* **1.** A Hebrew prophet of the 8th century B.C. **2.** See table at **Bible.** [Heb. *Yĕsha'yāhu.*]

i·sal·lo·bar (ī-săl′ə-bär′) *n.* A line on a weather map connecting places exhibiting equal changes in barometric pressure within a given period of time. [IS(O)- + ALLO- + Gk. *baros,* weight.]

–isation *suff.* Variant of **-ization.**

is·che·mi·a (ĭ-skē′mē-ə) *n.* A local anemia caused by mechanical obstruction of the blood supply. [NLat. *ischaemia* < Gk. *iskhaimos,* a stopping of the blood : *iskhein,* to restrain + *haima,* blood.] **—i·sche′mic** *adj.*

is·chi·um (ĭs′kē-əm) *n., pl.* **-chi·a** (-kē-ə). The lowest of three major bones comprising each half of the pelvis. [Lat., hip joint < Gk. *iskhion.*] **—is′chi·al** *adj.*

–ise *suff.* Variant of **-ize.**

is·en·tro·pic (ī′sən-trō′pĭk, -trŏp′ĭk) *adj.* Without change in entropy; at constant entropy. [IS(O)- + ENTROP(Y) + -IC.] **—is′en·tro′pi·cal·ly** *adv.*

I·seult (ĭ-so͞olt′) also **I·sol·de** (ĭ-sōl′də, ĭ-zōl′-) *n.* A legendary Irish princess of Arthurian times who married the king of Cornwall and had a hopeless love affair with his knight Tristan.

–ish *suff.* **1.** Of, pertaining to, or being: *Swedish.* **2. a.** Characteristic of: *girlish.* **b.** Having the esp. undesirable qualities of: *childish.* **3.** Approximately; somewhat: *greenish.* **4.** Tending toward; preoccupied with: *selfish.* [ME < OE *-isc.*]

Ish·ma·el (ĭsh′mē-əl) *n.* **1.** In the Old Testament, the son of Abraham by Sarah's handmaid, Hagar. **2.** An outcast. [LLat. *Ismaēl* < Heb. *Yishmā'ēl* : *yishma',* he will hear + *Ēl,* God.]

Ish·ma·el·ite (ĭsh′mē-ə-līt′) *n.* **1.** One of a group of desert-dwelling people believed by the ancient Hebrews to be descended from Ishmael. **2.** One at odds with society. **—Ish′ma·el·it′ism** *n.*

Ish·tar (ĭsh′tär′) *n.* The ancient Assyrian and Babylonian goddess of love and fertility, and also of war. [Akkadian.]

i·sin·glass (ī′zən-glăs′, ī′zĭng-) *n.* **1.** A transparent, almost pure gelatin prepared from the air bladder of certain fishes, as the sturgeon. **2.** Muscovite. [By folk ety. < obs. Du. *huizenblas* < MDu. *huusblase* : *huus,* sturgeon + *blase,* bladder.]

I·sis (ī′sĭs) *n.* An ancient Egyptian goddess of fertility and sister and wife of Osiris. [Lat. < Gk.]

Is·lam (ĭs-läm′, ĭz-, ĭs′läm′, ĭz′-) *n.* **1.** A religion based upon the teachings of the prophet Mohammed, believing in one God (Allah) and in Paradise and Hell, and having a body of law put forth in the Koran and the Sunna. **2. a.** All those nations of the world whose dominant populations and religion are Moslem. **b.** Islamic civilization. **3.** Moslems collectively. [Ar. *islām,* submission (to God) < *aslama,* he surrendered < *salama,* he was safe.] **—Is·lam′ic** *adj.*

Is·lam·ism (ĭs′lə-mĭz′əm, ĭz′-) *n.* The religious faith, principles, or cause of Islam. **—Is·lam′ist** (-lä′mĭst) *n.*

Is·lam·ize (ĭs′lə-mīz′, ĭz′-) *tr.v.* **-ized, -iz·ing, -iz·es.** To convert to Islam.

is·land (ī′lənd) *n.* **1.** A land mass, esp. one smaller than a continent, entirely surrounded by water. **2.** Something regarded as resembling an island, esp. in being completely isolated. **3.** *Anat.* A tissue or cluster of cells separated from surrounding tissue by a groove or differing from surrounding tissue in structure. *—tr.v.* **-land·ed, -land·ing, -lands.** To make into or as if into an island; insulate. [ME *ilond* < OE *īegland.*]

is·land·er (ī′lən-dər) *n.* An inhabitant of an island.

islands of Lang·er·hans (läng′ər-häns′) *pl.n.* Irregular masses of small cells that lie in the interstitial tissue of the pancreas and secrete insulin. [After Paul *Langerhans* (1847–1888).]

isle (īl) *n.* An island, esp. a small one. [ME *ile* < OFr. *isle* < Lat. *insula.*]

is·let (ī′lĭt) *n.* A little island.

islets of Lang·er·hans (läng′ər-häns′) *pl.n.* Islands of Langerhans.

ism (ĭz′əm) *n. Informal.* A distinctive doctrine, system, or theory. [< -ISM.]

–ism *suff.* **1.** Action, process; practice: *terrorism.* **2.** Characteristic behavior or quality: *heroism.* **3. a.** State; condition; quality: *pauperism.* **b.** State or condition resulting from an excess of something specified: *strychninism.* **4.** Distinctive or characteristic trait: *Latinism.* **5.** Doctrine; theory; system of principles: *pacifism.* [ME *-isme* < OFr. < Lat. *-ismus* < Gk. *-ismos,* n. suffix.]

Is·ma·i·li (ĭs′mä-ē′lē) also **Is·ma·i·li·an** (-ē′lē-ən) *n.* A Moslem of a Shiah sect. [Ar. *Isma'īlīy,* after *Isma'īl* (d. A.D. 760), son of the sixth Imam Jafar.]

is·n't (ĭz′ənt). Is not.

iso– or **is–** *pref.* **1.** Equal; uniform: *isobar.* **2.** Isomeric: *isopropyl.* [Gk. < *isos,* equal.]

i·so·ag·glu·ti·na·tion (ī′sō-ə-glo͞ot′n-ā′shən) *n.* The agglutination of an agglutinogen by the serum of another individual of the same species.

i·so·ag·glu·ti·nin (ī′sō-ə-glo͞ot′n-ĭn) *n.* An isoantibody that causes agglutination of cells.

i·so·ag·glu·tin·o·gen (ī′sō-ăg′lo͞o-tĭn′ə-jən) *n.* An isoantigen that on exposure to its isoantibody induces agglutination of cells to which it is attached. [ISOAGGLUTIN(IN) + -GEN.]

i·so·an·ti·bod·y (ī′sō-ăn′tē-bŏd′ē) *n., pl.* **-ies.** An antibody that occurs in only some individuals of a species and reacts specifically with the corresponding isoantigen.

i·so·an·ti·gen (ī′sō-ăn′tĭ-jən) *n.* An antigen that occurs in only some individuals of a species and never in those having cells that contain the corresponding isoantibody. **—i′so·an′ti·gen′ic** *adj.* **—i′so·an′ti·ge·nic′i·ty** *n.*

i·so·bar (ī′sə-bär′) *n.* **1.** A line on a map connecting points of equal pressure. **2.** Any of two or more nuclides having the same mass number but different atomic numbers. [ISO- + Gk. *baros,* weight.] **—i′so·bar′ic** (-bär′ĭk, -băr′-) *adj.*

i·so·chro·mat·ic (ī′sə-krō-măt′ĭk) *adj.* Orthochromatic (sense 2).

i·soch·ro·nal (ī-sŏk′rə-nəl) *adj.* **1.** Equal in duration. **2.** Characterized by or occurring at equal intervals of time. [< Gk. *isokhronos* : *isos,* equal + *khronos,* time.] **—i·soch′ro·nal·ly** *adv.* **—i·soch′ro·nism** *n.*

i·soch·ro·nize (ī-sŏk′rə-nīz′) *tr.v.* **-nized, -niz·ing, -niz·es.** To make isochronal.

i·soch·ro·nous (ī-sŏk′rə-nəs) *adj.* Isochronal. **—i·soch′ro·nous·ly** *adv.*

i·soch·ro·ous (ī-sŏk′rō-əs) *adj.* Having the same color throughout. [ISO- + Gk. *khrōs,* flesh, color.]

i·so·cli·nal (ī′sə-klī′nəl) *adj.* Having the same inclination or dip. *—n.* An isoclinic line. **—i′so·cli′nal·ly** *adv.*

i·so·cline (ī′sə-klīn′) *n.* An anticline or syncline with strata so tightly folded as to have the same dip.

i·so·clin·ic (ī′sə-klĭn′ĭk) *adj. & n.* Isoclinal. **—i′so·clin′i·cal·ly** *adv.*

isoclinic line *n.* A line on a map connecting points of equal magnetic dip.

i·so·di·a·met·ric (ī′sō-dī′ə-mĕt′rĭk) *adj.* Having equal diameters.

i·so·di·mor·phism (ī′sō-dī-môr′fĭz′əm) *n.* Isomorphism between crystalline forms of two dimorphic substances.

i·so·dy·nam·ic (ī′sō-dī-năm′ĭk) *adj.* Having equal force or strength.

i·so·e·lec·tric (ī′sō-ĭ-lĕk′trĭk) *adj.* Having equal electric potential.

i·so·e·lec·tron·ic (ī′sō-ĭ-lĕk-trŏn′ĭk) *adj.* Having equal numbers of electrons or the same electronic configuration.

i·so·en·zyme (ī′sō-ĕn′zīm′) *n.* Any of the chemically distinct forms of an enzyme that remain functionally the same. **—i′so·en·zy′mic** *adj.*

i·so·ga·mete (ī′sō-gə-mēt′, -găm′ēt′) *n.* A gamete that is morphologically indistinguishable from one with which it unites.

i·sog·a·my (ī-sŏg′ə-mē) *n.* Conjugation of isogametes or of identical cells. **—i·sog′a·mous** *adj.*

i·so·gloss (ī′sə-glôs′, -glŏs′) *n.* A geographical boundary line delimiting the area in which a given linguistic feature occurs. [ISO- + Gk. *glossa,* language.] **—i′so·gloss′al** *adj.*

i·so·gon (ī′sə-gŏn′) *n.* An equiangular polygon.

i·so·gon·ic (ī′sə-gŏn′ĭk) also **i·sog·o·nal** (ī-sŏg′ə-nəl) *adj.* Having equal angles. *—n.* An isogonic line.

isogonic line *n.* A line on a map connecting points of equal magnetic declination.

i·so·gram (ī′sə-grăm′) *n.* A line on a map, chart, or graph connecting points of equal value.

i·so·hel (ī′sō-hĕl′) *n.* A line drawn on a map connecting points receiving equal sunlight. [ISO- + Gk. *helios,* sun.]

i·so·he·mo·ly·sin (ī′sō-hē′mə-lī′sən, -hĕm′ə-, -hĭ-mŏl′ĭ-sĭn) *n.* Hemolysin obtained from the serum of an individual injected with red blood cells from another individual of the same species.

i·so·he·mol·y·sis (ī′sō-hə-mŏl′ĭ-sĭs) *n.* Hemolysis resulting from the action of isohemolysin.

i·so·hy·et (ī′sō-hī′ĭt) *n.* A line drawn on a map connecting

Isis

points receiving equal rainfall. [ISO- + Gk. *huetos,* rain.]
i·so·la·ble (ī'sə-lə-bəl) also **i·so·lat·a·ble** (-lāt'ə-bəl) *adj.* Capable of being isolated.
i·so·late (ī'sə-lāt') *tr.v.* **-lat·ed, -lat·ing, -lates. 1.** To separate from a group or whole and set apart. **2.** To place in quarantine. **3.** *Chem.* To obtain (a substance) in an uncombined form. **4.** To render free of external influence; insulate. —*adj.* (-lĭt, -lāt'). Solitary; alone. [Back-formation < *isolated,* set apart < Fr. *isolé* < Ital. *isolato* < LLat. *insulatus,* made into an island < *insula,* island.] **—i'so·la'tor** *n.*
i·so·la·tion (ī'sə-lā'shən) *n.* **1.** The act of isolating. **2.** The condition of being isolated.
i·so·la·tion·ism (ī'sə-lā'shə-nĭz'əm) *n.* A national policy of abstaining from political or economic entanglements with other countries. **—i'so·la'tion·ist** *n.*
I·sol·de (ĭ-sōl'də, ĭ-zōl'-) *n.* Variant of **Iseult.**
i·so·lec·i·thal (ī'sə-lĕs'ə-thəl) *adj.* Having the yolk evenly distributed throughout the egg. [ISO- + LECITH(IN) + -AL.]
i·so·leu·cine (ī'sə-lo͞o'sēn') *n.* An essential amino acid, $C_6H_{13}NO_2$, isomeric with leucine.
i·so·mag·net·ic (ī'sō-măg-nĕt'ĭk) *adj.* Designating or pertaining to points of equal magnetic induction.
i·so·mer (ī'sə-mər) *n.* **1.** *Chem.* **a.** A compound having the same percentage composition and molecular weight as another compound but differing in chemical or physical properties. **b.** Such a compound so differing because of the manner of linkage of its constituent atoms. **c.** Such a compound so differing because of the manner of arrangement of its constituent atoms in space. **d.** A stereoisomer manifesting one of two structures that rotate the plane of polarization of polarized light either to the left or to the right. **e.** A stereoisomer having no effect on polarized light but exhibiting isomerism because of a structural asymmetry about a double bond in the molecule. **2.** *Physics.* An atom the nucleus of which can exist in any of several bound excited states for a measurable period of time. **—i'so·mer'ic** (-mĕr'ĭk) *adj.*
i·som·er·ase (ī-sŏm'ə-rās') *n.* An enzyme that catalyzes isomerization reactions.
i·som·er·ism (ī-sŏm'ə-rĭz'əm) *n.* **1.** The phenomenon of the existence of isomers. **2.** The complex of chemical and physical phenomena characteristic of or attributable to isomers. **3.** The state or condition of being an isomer.
i·som·er·ize (ī-sŏm'ə-rīz') *v.* **-ized, -iz·ing, -iz·es.** —*tr.* To cause to change into an isomeric form. —*intr.* To become changed into an isomeric form. **—i·som'er·i·za'tion** *n.*
i·som·er·ous (ī-sŏm'ər-əs) *adj.* **1.** Having an equal number of parts, as organs or markings. **2.** Having or designating floral whorls with equal numbers of parts.
i·so·met·ric (ī'sə-mĕt'rĭk) also **i·so·met·ri·cal** (-rĭ-kəl) *adj.* **1.** Of or exhibiting equality in dimensions or measurements. **2.** Of or being a crystal system of three equal and mutually orthogonal axes. **3.** *Physiol.* Of or involving muscular contraction occurring when the ends of the muscle are fixed in place so that significant increases in tension occur without appreciable increases in length. —*n.* **isometric. 1.** A line connecting isometric points. **2. isometrics.** *(used with a sing. verb).* Isometric exercise. [< Gk. *isometros,* of equal measure : *isos,* equal + *metron,* measure.]
isometric exercise *n.* Exercise involving isometric contraction.
i·so·me·tro·pi·a (ī'sō-mĭ-trō'pē-ə) *n.* Equality of refraction in both eyes. [Gk. *isometros,* isometric + -OPIA.]
i·som·e·try (ī-sŏm'ĭ-trē) *n.* **1.** Equality of measure. **2.** Equality of elevation above sea level.
i·so·morph (ī'sə-môrf') *n.* An object, organism, or group exhibiting isomorphism.
i·so·mor·phic (ī'sə-môr'fĭk) *adj.* Related by an isomorphism.
i·so·mor·phism (ī'sə-môr'fĭz'əm) *n.* **1.** *Biol.* Similarity in form, as in different kinds of organisms. **2.** *Math.* **a.** A one-to-one correspondence between the elements of two sets such that the result of an operation on elements of one set corresponds to the result of the analogous operation on their images in the other set. **b.** A mapping * of a group G onto another group H such that $(ab)^* = (a^*)(b^*)$ for all a, b in G. **3.** The existence or an instance of the existence of two or more different substances having closely similar crystalline structure, crystalline dimensions, and chemical composition. **—i'so·mor'phous** *adj.*

issuant
A lion issuant

i·so·ni·a·zid (ī'sə-nī'ə-zĭd) *n.* A crystalline compound, $C_6H_7N_3O$, used in the treatment of tuberculosis. [ISONI(COTINIC ACID) + (HYDR)AZID(E).]
i·so·oc·tane (ī'sō-ŏk'tān') *n.* A highly flammable liquid, C_8H_{18}, used to determine the octane numbers of fuels.
i·so·pi·es·tic (ī'sō-pī-ĕs'tĭk, -pē-) *adj.* Marked by or indicating equal pressure; isobaric. —*n.* An isobar. [ISO- + Gk. *piestos,* able to be compressed < *piezein,* to press tight.]
i·so·pod (ī'sə-pŏd') *n.* Any of numerous crustaceans of the order Isopoda, which includes the sow bugs and gribbles. [NLat. *Isopoda,* order name : ISO- + Gk. *pous,* foot.] **—i'so·pod'** *adj.*
i·so·prene (ī'sə-prēn') *n.* A colorless volatile liquid, C_5H_8, used chiefly to make synthetic rubber. [ISO- + PR(OPYL) + -ENE.]
i·so·pro·pyl alcohol (ī'sə-prō'pəl) *n.* A clear, colorless, flammable, mobile liquid, C_3H_8O, used in antifreeze compounds, lotions and cosmetics, and as a solvent for gums, shellac, and essential oils.
i·sos·ce·les (ī-sŏs'ə-lēz') *adj.* Having two equal sides: *an isosceles triangle.* [LLat. *isosceles* < Gk. *isoskelēs* : *isos,* equal + *skelos,* leg.]
i·so·seis·mic (ī'sə-sīz'mĭk) also **i·so·seis·mal** (-məl) *adj.* Of, pertaining to, or exhibiting equal seismic intensities.
i·sos·mot·ic (ī'sŏz-mŏt'ĭk, -sŏs-) *adj.* Of or exhibiting equal osmotic pressure.
i·so·spin (ī'sə-spĭn') *n.* A quantum number related to the number of charge states of a subatomic particle by the equation $2I + 1 = M$, where M is the number of such states. [ISO(TOPIC) + SPIN.]
i·sos·ta·sy (ī-sŏs'tə-sē) *n.* An equilibrium condition resulting from isotropic equalization of pressure. [ISO- + Gk. *stasis,* a standstill.]
i·so·therm (ī'sə-thûrm') *n.* A line drawn on a weather map or chart linking all points having identical mean temperature for a given period or identical temperature at a given time. [Fr. *isotherme,* having the same temperature : Gk. *isos,* equal + Gk. *thermē,* heat.]
i·so·ther·mal (ī'sə-thûr'məl) *adj.* **1.** Of, pertaining to, or indicating equal temperatures. **2.** Of or designating changes of pressure and volume at constant temperature. **3.** Of or pertaining to an isotherm. —*n.* An isotherm.
i·so·tone (ī'sə-tōn') *n.* One of two or more atoms whose nuclei have the same number of neutrons but different numbers of protons. [ISO- + Gk. *tonos,* tension, stretching.]
i·so·ton·ic (ī'sə-tŏn'ĭk) *adj.* **1.** Of equal tension. **2.** Isosmotic. [ISO- + Gk. *tonos,* tension.] **—i'so·ton'i·cal·ly** *adv.* **—i'so·to·nic'i·ty** (-tə-nĭs'ĭ-tē) *n.*
i·so·tope (ī'sə-tōp') *n.* One of two or more atoms whose nuclei have the same number of protons but different numbers of neutrons. [ISO- + Gk. *topos,* place.] **—i'so·top'ic** (-tŏp'ĭk) *adj.* **—i'so·top'i·cal·ly** *adv.*
isotopic spin *n.* Isospin.
i·so·tro·pic (ī'sə-trō'pĭk, -trŏp'ĭk) *adj.* Identical in all directions; invariant with respect to direction. **—i·sot'ro·py** (ī-sŏt'rə-pē), **i·sot'ro·pism** (-pĭz'əm) *n.*
i·so·zyme (ī'sə-zīm') *n.* Isoenzyme. [ISO- + (EN)ZYME.] **—i'so·zy'mic** *adj.*
Is·ra·el (ĭz'rē-əl) *n.* **1. a.** In the Old Testament, Jacob. **b.** The descendants of Jacob. **2.** The whole Hebrew people, past, present, and future, regarded as the chosen people of Jehovah by virtue of the covenant of Jacob. [Lat. < Gk. *Israēl* < Heb. *Yisrā'ēl.*]
Is·rae·li (ĭz-rā'lē) *adj.* Of or relating to the state of Israel or its people. —*n., pl.* **Israeli** or **-lis.** A native or inhabitant of the state of Israel.
Is·ra·el·ite (ĭz'rē-ə-līt') *n.* A Hebrew, esp. a descendant of Jacob. —*adj.* Also **Is·ra·el·it·ic** (ĭz'rē-ə-lĭt'ĭk). Of or relating to Israel or the Israelites.
Is·sa·char (ĭs'ə-kär') *n.* **1.** In the Old Testament, one of the patriarchs of Israel, son of Jacob and Leah. **2.** The tribe descended from Issachar. [LLat. < Gk. < Heb. *Yissākhār.*]
Is·sei (ēs'sā') *n., pl.* **Issei** or **-seis.** A Japanese immigrant to the United States or Canada. [J., first generation < Chin. (Mandarin) *yi¹ shi⁴* : *yi¹,* first + *shi⁴,* generation.]
is·su·a·ble (ĭsh'o͞o-ə-bəl) *adj.* **1.** Capable of issuing or being issued. **2.** Capable of being established as an issue; open to debate or litigation. **3.** Authorized for issue.
is·su·ance (ĭsh'o͞o-əns) *n.* An act of issuing; issue.
is·su·ant (ĭsh'o͞o-ənt) *adj.* **1.** *Archaic.* Emerging. **2.** In heraldry, designating an animal with only the upper part depicted.
is·sue (ĭsh'o͞o) *n.* **1. a.** An act or instance of flowing, passing, or giving out. **b.** An act of circulating, distributing, or publishing by an office or official group: *government issue of new bonds.* **2.** Something produced, published, or offered, as: **a.** An item or set of items, as stamps or coins, made available at one time by an office or bureau. **b.** A single copy of a periodical. **c.** A distinct set of copies of an edition of a book distinguished from others of that edition by variations in the printed matter. **d.** A final result or conclusion, as a solution to a problem. **e.** Proceeds from estates or fines. **f.** Something proceeding from a specified source: *suspicions that were the issue of a deranged mind.* **3.** Offspring; progeny. **4. a.** A point or matter of discussion, debate, or dispute. **b.** A matter of public concern. **c.** The essential point; crux: *the real issue.* **d.** A culminating point leading to a decision: *bring a case to an issue.* **5.** A place of egress; outlet: *a lake with no issue to the sea.* **6.** *Pathol.* **a.** A discharge, as of blood. **b.** A suppurating sore. **7.** *Archaic.* Termination; close. —*v.* **-sued, -su·ing, -sues.** —*intr.* **1.** To go or come out. **2.** To accrue as proceeds or profit: *Little money issued from the stocks.* **3.** To be born or be descended. **4.** To be circulated or published. **5.** To spring or result from. **6.** To terminate or result in. —*tr.* **1.** To cause to flow out; emit. **2.** To circulate or distribute in an official capacity: *issued uniforms to the players.* **3.** To publish. **—*idioms.* at issue. 1.** In question; in dispute. **2.** At variance; in disagreement. **join issue. 1.** To enter into controversy. **2.** *Law.* To submit an issue jointly for decision. **take issue.** To take an opposing point of view; disagree. [ME, exit, act of going out <

OFr. < VLat. *exuta* < Lat. *exitus,* p.part. of *exire,* to go out : *ex-,* out + *ire,* to go.] **—is'su·er** *n.*

–ist *suff.* **1. a.** One that performs a specified action: *lobbyist.* **b.** One that produces, makes, operates, plays, or is connected with a specified thing: *novelist.* **2.** A specialist in a specified art, science, or skill: *biologist.* **3.** An adherent or advocate of a specified doctrine, theory, or school of thought: *anarchist.* **4.** One that is characterized by a specified trait or quality: *romanticist.* [ME *-iste* < OFr. < Lat. *-ista, istes* < Gk. *-istēs,* agent n. suffix.]

isth·mi (ĭs'mī') *n.* A plural of **isthmus.**

isth·mi·an (ĭs'mē-ən) *adj.* **1.** Of, pertaining to, or forming an isthmus. **2. Isthmian.** Of or pertaining to the Isthmus of Corinth, esp. with regard to the biennial pan-Hellenic games held there in antiquity.

isth·mus (ĭs'məs) *n., pl.* **-mus·es** or **-mi** (-mī'). **1.** A narrow strip of land connecting two larger masses of land. **2.** *Anat.* **a.** A narrow strip of tissue joining two larger organs or parts of an organ. **b.** A narrow passage connecting two larger cavities. [Lat. < Gk. *isthmos.*]

is·tle also **ix·tle** (ĭs'lē, ĭst'-) *n.* A plant, pita, or its fiber. [Mex. Sp. *ixtle* < Nahuatl *ixtli,* fibrous stem.]

it (ĭt) *pron.* **1.** That one previously mentioned. Used as the subject, the direct object, the indirect object, or the object of a preposition for a nonhuman entity, an animate being, as a person or animal whose sex is unknown, unspecified, or irrelevant, a group of objects or individuals, or an abstraction: *polished the table until it shone; couldn't find out who it was; opened the meeting by calling it to order; gave it a good cleaning.* **2.** Used as the subject of an impersonal verb: *It is snowing.* **3. a.** Used as an anticipatory subject: *Is it certain that he'll win?* **b.** Used as an anticipatory subject to emphasize a term that is not itself a subject: *It was on Friday that he left.* **4.** Used to refer to a general condition or state of affairs: *He couldn't stand it.* **5.** *Informal.* Used to refer to something that is the best, the most desirable, or without equal: *That steak was really it!* —*n.* A player in a game, as tag, who attempts to find or catch the other players. [ME < OE *hit.*]

it·a·col·u·mite (ĭt'ə-kŏl'yə-mīt') *n.* A variety of sandstone that is flexible when cut into thin slabs. [After *Itacolumi,* a mountain in Brazil where it is found.]

I·tal·ian (ĭ-tăl'yən) *adj.* Pertaining to Italy, its people, or their language. —*n.* **1.** A native or citizen of Italy, or a person of Italian descent. **2.** The Romance language of the Italians and one of the three official languages of Switzerland. [ME < Lat. *Italianus* < *Italia,* Italy.]

I·tal·ian·ate (ĭ-tăl'yə-nāt', -nĭt) *adj.* Italian in character.

I·tal·ian·ism (ĭ-tăl'yə-nĭz'əm) *n.* **1.** An Italian custom, trait, or expression. **2.** A quality characteristic of Italy or its people.

I·tal·ian·ize (ĭ-tăl'yə-nīz') *v.* **-ized, -iz·ing, -iz·es.** —*tr.* To give an Italian aspect to. —*intr.* To adopt Italian speech, manners, or customs. **—I·tal'ian·i·za'tion** *n.*

Italian sandwich *n.* A hero (sense 5).

Italian sonnet *n.* A Petrarchan sonnet.

I·tal·ic (ĭ-tăl'ĭk, ī-tăl'-) *adj.* **1.** Of or pertaining to ancient Italy or its peoples. **2.** Of or pertaining to Italic. **3. italic.** Of or being a style of printing type patterned upon a Renaissance script with the letters slanting to the right: *This sentence is printed in italic type.* —*n.* **1.** A branch of the Indo-European language family that includes Latin, Oscan, and Umbrian. **2.** Often **italics.** Italic print or typeface. [Lat. *Italicus* < Gk. *Italikos* < *Italia,* Italy < Lat.]

I·tal·i·cism (ĭ-tăl'ĭ-sĭz'əm) *n.* An Italianism, esp. a word or idiom borrowed from or suggestive of the Italian language.

i·tal·i·cize (ĭ-tăl'ĭ-sīz', ī-tăl'-) *tr.v.* **-cized, -ciz·ing, -ciz·es. 1.** To print in italic type. **2.** To underscore (written matter) with a single line to indicate italics. **—i·tal'i·ci·za'tion** *n.*

itch (ĭch) *n.* **1.** A skin sensation causing a desire to scratch. **2.** Any of various contagious skin diseases marked by intense irritation, eruptions, and itching. **3.** A restless desire or craving for something: *an itch to travel.* —*v.* **itched, itch·ing, itch·es.** —*intr.* **1. a.** To feel, have, or produce an itch. **b.** To have a desire to scratch. **2.** To have a persistent restless craving. —*tr.* **1.** To cause to itch. **2.** To scratch an itch. [ME *icchen* < OE *giccan.*]

itch mite *n.* A parasitic mite, *Sarcoptes scabiei,* that causes scabies.

itch·y (ĭch'ē) *adj.* **-i·er, -i·est. 1.** Having or causing an itching sensation. **2.** Restless or nervous. **—itch'i·ness** *n.*

–ite[1] *suff.* **1.** Native or resident of: *New Jerseyite.* **2. a.** Descendant of: *Levite.* **b.** Adherent or follower of: *Luddite.* **3.** A part of an organ, body, or bodily part: *somite.* **4.** Rock; mineral: *graphite.* **5.** A commercial product: *ebonite.* [ME < OFr. < Lat. *-ita, -ites* < Gk. *-itēs.*]

–ite[2] *suff.* A salt or ester of an acid named with an adjective ending in *-ous: sulfite.* [Fr., alteration of *-ate,* -ate < NLat. *-atum.* —see -ATE[2].]

i·tem (ī'təm) *n.* **1.** A single article or unit included in a collection, enumeration, or series and that is specified separately. **2.** A clause of a bill, charter, or other document. **3.** An entry in an account. **4. a.** A bit of information; detail. **b.** A short piece in a newspaper or magazine. —*tr.v.* **i·temed, i·tem·ing, i·tems.** *Archaic.* To compute. —*adv.* Also; likewise. Used to introduce each article in an enumeration or list. [< ME, also, moreover < Lat. < *ita,* so.]

i·tem·ize (ī'tə-mīz') *tr.v.* **-ized, -iz·ing, -iz·es.** To set down item by item; list. **—i'tem·i·za'tion** *n.* **—i'tem·iz'er** *n.*

it·er·ance (ĭt'ər-əns) *n.* Iteration.

it·er·ant (ĭt'ər-ənt) *adj.* Marked by iteration; repeating.

it·er·ate (ĭt'ə-rāt') *tr.v.* **-at·ed, -at·ing, -ates.** To say or perform again; repeat. [Lat. *iterare, iterat-* < *iterum,* again.] **—it'er·a'tion** *n.*

it·er·a·tive (ĭt'ə-rā'tĭv, -ər-ə-tĭv) *adj.* **1.** Characterized by or involving repetition, recurrence, reiteration, or repetitiousness. **2.** *Gram.* Frequentative. **3.** *Math.* Of, pertaining to, or being a computational procedure to produce a desired result by replication of a series of operations that successively better approximates the desired result.

ith·y·phal·lic (ĭth'ə-făl'ĭk) *adj.* **1.** Of or pertaining to the phallus carried in the ancient festival of Bacchus. **2.** Having the penis erect. Used of graphic and sculptural representations. **3.** Lascivious; salacious. [LLat. *ithyphallicus* < Gk. *ithuphallikos* < *ithuphallos,* erect phallus : *ithus,* straight + *phallos,* phallus.]

ivory
Carved ivory bracelet

i·tin·er·an·cy (ī-tĭn'ər-ən-sē, ĭ-tĭn'-) also **i·tin·er·a·cy** (-ə-sē) *n.* A state or system of itinerating, esp. in the role or office of public speaker, minister, or judge.

i·tin·er·ant (ī-tĭn'ər-ənt, ĭ-tĭn'-) *adj.* Traveling from place to place, esp. to perform some duty or work: *an itinerant judge; itinerant labor.* —*n.* One who itinerates. [LLat. *itinerans, itinerant-,* pr.part. of *itinerari,* to travel < Lat. *iter,* journey.]

i·tin·er·ar·y (ī-tĭn'ə-rĕr'ē, ĭ-tĭn'-) *n., pl.* **-ies. 1.** A route or proposed route of a journey. **2.** An account or record of a journey. **3.** A travelers' guidebook. —*adj.* **1.** Of or pertaining to a journey or to a route. **2.** Traveling from place to place; itinerant. [ME *itinerarie* < LLat. *itinerarium,* course of travel < *itinerarius,* of traveling < Lat. *iter,* journey.]

i·tin·er·ate (ī-tĭn'ə-rāt', ĭ-tĭn'-) *intr.v.* **-at·ed, -at·ing, -ates.** To travel from place to place. [LLat. *itinerari, itinerat-* < Lat. *iter,* journey.] **—i·tin'er·a'tion** *n.*

–itis *suff.* **1.** Inflammation or disease of: *laryngitis.* **2.** Excessive preoccupation with, indulgence in, reliance on, or possession of the qualities of: *televisionitis.* [NLat. < Gk., n. suffix.]

it'll (ĭt'l). **1.** It will. **2.** It shall.

–itol *suff.* An alcohol containing more than one hydroxyl group: *mannitol.* [-IT(E) + -OL.]

its (ĭts) *adj.* The possessive form of **it.** Used to indicate possession or the agent or recipient of an action: *a cat cleaning its paws; a committee that failed to publish its findings; a manuscript that has undergone its third revision.* [Alteration of *it's* : IT + -'S[1].]

Usage: *Its,* the possessive form of the pronoun *it,* is never written with an apostrophe. The contraction *it's* (for *it is* or *it has*) is always written with an apostrophe.

it's (ĭts). **1.** It is. **2.** It has.

it·self (ĭt-sĕlf') *pron.* **1.** That one identical with it. Used: **a.** Reflexively as the direct or indirect object of a verb or the object of a preposition: *This record player turns itself off.* **b.** For emphasis: *The trouble is in the machine itself.* **c.** In an absolute construction: *Itself no great painting, it still reveals talent.* **2.** Its normal or healthy condition: *The computer is acting itself again since the program was corrected.*

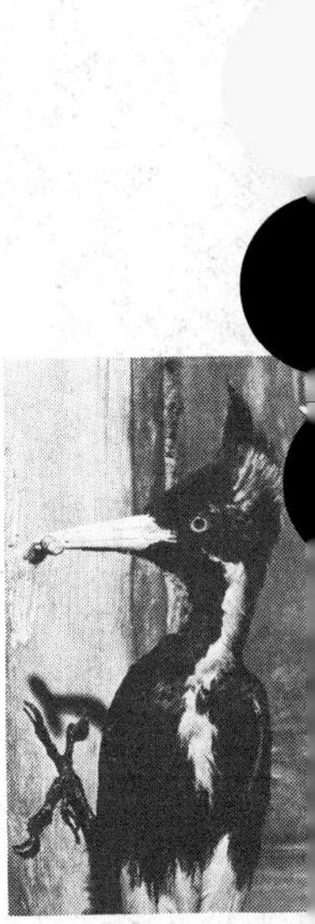

ivory-billed woodpecker
Male of the species

it·ty-bit·ty (ĭt'ē-bĭt'ē) also **it·sy-bit·sy** (ĭt'sē-bĭt'sē) *adj. Informal.* Very small. [Prob. alteration of *little bit.*]

–ity *suff.* State; quality: *abnormality.* [ME *-itie* < OFr. *-ite* < Lat. *-itas.*]

–ium *suff.* Chemical element or group: *californium.* [NLat. < Lat. < Gk. *-ion,* dim. suffix.]

I've (īv). I have.

–ive *suff.* Performing or tending toward a specified action: *demonstrative.* [ME < OFr. *-if, -ive* < Lat. *-ivus,* adj. suffix.]

i·vied (ī'vēd) *adj.* Overgrown or cloaked with ivy.

i·vo·ry (ī'və-rē, īv'rē) *n., pl.* **-ries. 1. a.** The hard, smooth, yellowish-white dentine forming the main part of the tusks of the elephant, used as an ornamental material. **b.** A similar substance forming the tusks or teeth of certain other animals, as the walrus. **2.** A tusk, esp. an elephant's tusk. **3.** A substance resembling ivory. **4.** A pale or grayish yellow to yellowish white. **5.** An article made of ivory. **6.** Often **ivories. a.** Piano keys. **b.** Dice. **c.** The teeth. ***—modifier:*** *an ivory statue.* —*adj.* Of the color ivory. [ME *ivorie* < OFr. *ivoire* < Lat. *eboreus,* of ivory < *ebur,* ivory, of Egypt. orig.]

i·vo·ry·bill (ī'və-rē-bĭl', īv'rē-) *n.* Ivory-billed woodpecker.

i·vo·ry-billed woodpecker (ī'və-rē-bĭld', īv'rē-) *n.* A large, probably extinct North American woodpecker, *Campephilus principalis,* having a white bill.

ivory black *n.* A black pigment prepared from charred ivory.

ivory nut *n.* The hard seed of an American palm, *Phytelephas macrocarpa,* yielding an ivorylike substance.

ivory tower *n.* A place or attitude of retreat, esp. preoccupation with lofty, remote, or intellectual considerations rather than with practical everyday life. [Transl. of Fr. *tour d'ivoire.*]

i·vy (ī'vē) *n., pl.* **i·vies. 1.** Any of several woody, climbing or trailing plants of the genus *Hedera,* native to the Old World,

ivy

esp. *H. helix,* having lobed, evergreen leaves and berrylike black fruit. **2.** Any of various climbing or creeping plants similar to the ivy. [ME *ivi* < OE *ifig.*]

Ivy League *n.* An association of eight colleges in the northeastern United States, comprising Brown, Columbia, Cornell, Dartmouth, Harvard, Princeton, the University of Pennsylvania, and Yale. [So called because of the ivy that covers the older college buildings.] **—Ivy Leaguer** *n.*

I·wis (ĭ-wĭs′) *adv. Archaic.* Certainly; assuredly. [ME < OE *gewis,* certain.]

Ix·i·on (ĭk-sī′ən) *n. Gk. Myth.* A Thessalian king whom Zeus punished for his temerity in seeking Hera's love by having him bound to a perpetually revolving wheel in Hades. [Lat. < Gk. *Ixīōn.*]

Ix·tle (ĭs′lē, ĭst′-) *n.* Variant of **istle.**

I·yar also **Iy·yar** (ē-yär′, ē′yär′) *n.* The eighth month of the year of the Hebrew calendar. See table at **calendar.** [Heb. *iyyār.*]

Iz·ar (ĭ-zär′) *n.* A long cotton outer garment, usually white, worn by women in many Moslem countries. [Ar. *'izār,* veil.]

-ization or **-isation** *suff.* Action, process, or result of doing or making: *colonization.* [-IZ(E) + -ATION.]

-ize or **-ise** *suff.* **1. a.** To cause to be or to become: *dramatize.* **b.** To cause to conform to or resemble: *Hellenize.* **c.** To treat as: *idolize.* **2. a.** To treat or affect with: *anesthetize.* **b.** To subject to: *tyrannize.* **3.** To treat according to or practice the method of: *pasteurize.* **4.** To become; become like: *materialize.* **5.** To perform, engage in, or produce: *botanize.* [ME *-isen* < OFr. *-iser* < LLat. *-izare* < Gk. *-izein,* v. suffix.]

Usage: The practice of turning nouns or adjectives into verbs by adding *-ize* is an ancient and useful one. It has created many standard words, such as *Americanize, criticize, formalize, nationalize, specialize,* though some of these were met with resistance when they were first introduced. But this practice has also given us such words as *finalize* and *concretize,* which still bother many people, and a great many linguistic experiments of questionable value, such as *envisionize* and *reprivatize.* New coinages of this sort should be used with great caution until they have passed the tests of utility, permanence, and acceptance by good writers.

J

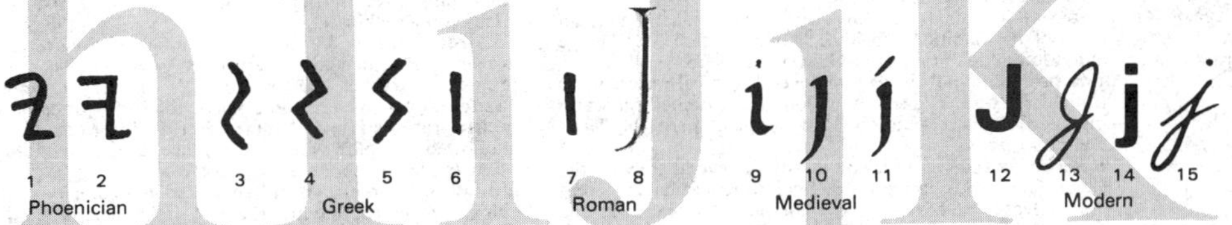

Around 1000 B.C. the Phoenicians and other Semitic peoples began to use graphic signs to represent individual speech sounds instead of syllables or words. They used a symbol in the forms (1,2) to represent the sound of the semivowel "y" and called it *yōdh,* their word for "hand." The Greeks, adapting the Phoenician alphabet, varied the shape of *yōdh* (3,4,5,6) and altered its name to *iōta.* They used *iōta* to represent the sound of the vowel "i." The Romans borrowed the alphabet from the Greeks via the Etruscans and used *iōta* to represent both the vowel "i" and the semivowel "y." In time, they added a hook to *iōta* to identify the semivowel, and the new symbol became the letter J. They also adapted the alphabet for monumental inscriptions, and their monumental script (8) is the prototype of modern capital letters (12,13). Medieval scribes adapted the Roman capitals to being quickly written on paper, parchment, and vellum, retaining the dot from the letter I to distinguish J (and I) from other similarly shaped letters. These uncial and cursive minuscules (9,10,11) are the prototypes of modern lower-case letters, both written and printed (15,14). During the medieval period and well into modern times the letters I and J were interchangeable. In the 17th century they were finally distinguished and assigned their modern phonetic values.

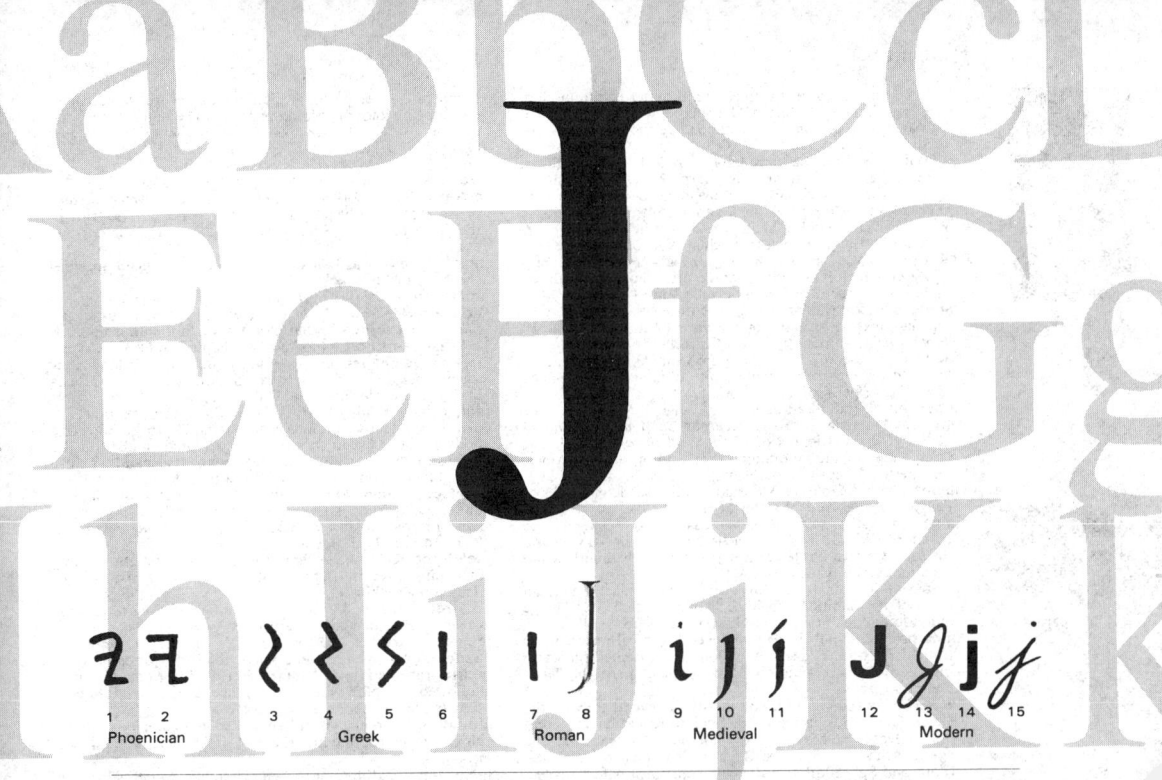

j

jabot

jack

jackal

jackhammer

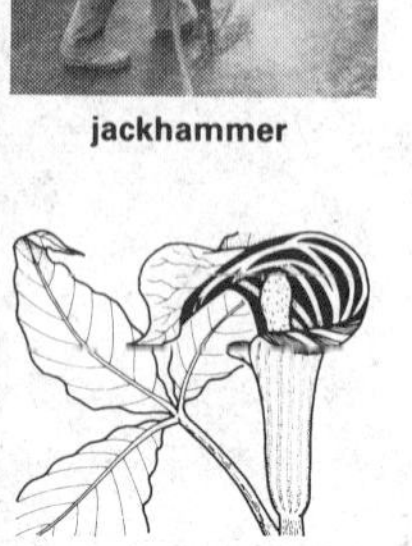

jack-in-the-pulpit

j or **J** (jā) *n., pl.* **j's** or **J's 1.** The tenth letter of the modern English alphabet. **2.** Any of the speech sounds represented by the letter *j*. **3.** Something shaped like the letter J. **4.** The tenth in a series.

jab (jăb) *v.* **jabbed, jab·bing, jabs.** *—tr.* **1.** To poke or thrust abruptly, esp. with something sharp. **2.** To thrust into or against with a rough, abrupt movement. **3.** To punch with short blows. *—intr.* **1.** To make an abrupt jabbing motion. **2.** To deliver a quick punch. *—n.* **1.** A quick stab or blow. **2.** A short straight punch in boxing. [Var. of JOB[2].]

jab·ber (jăb′ər) *v.* **-bered, -ber·ing, -bers.** *—intr.* To talk rapidly, unintelligibly, or idly. *—tr.* To utter rapidly or unintelligibly. *—n.* Rapid or babbling talk. [Imit.] **—jab′ber·er** *n.*

jab·ber·wock·y (jăb′ər-wŏk′ē) *n.* Nonsense speech or writing designed to give the appearance of making sense. [< *Jabberwocky,* a poem by Lewis Carroll (1832–1898).]

jab·i·ru (jăb′ə-ro͞o′) *n.* A large tropical American wading bird, *Jabiru mycteria,* having white plumage and a naked neck. [Port., perh. of Tupian orig.]

jab·o·ran·di (jăb′ə-răn-dē′) *n., pl.* **-dis. 1.** Either of two tropical American shrubs, *Pilocarpus jaborandi* or *P. microphyllus,* the dried leaves of which yield pilocarpine. **2.** The dried leaves of the jaborandi. [Port. and Sp. (South America), perh. of Tupi-Guarani orig.]

ja·bot (zhă-bō′, jăb′ō) *n.* An ornamental cascade of ruffles or frills down the front of a shirt. [Fr.]

ja·cal (hä-käl′) *n., pl.* **ja·ca·les** (hä-kä′lās) or **ja·cals.** A thatch-roofed hut made of wattle and daub in Mexico and the southwestern United States. [Mex. Sp. < Nahuatl *xacalli* : *xamitl,* adobe + *calli,* house.]

jac·a·mar (jăk′ə-mär′) *n.* Any of various tropical American birds of the family Galbulidae, having iridescent plumage and a long bill. [Fr. < Tupi-Guarani *jacamaciri.*]

ja·ca·na (zhä′sə-nä′) *n.* Any of several tropical marsh birds of the family Jacanidae, having long toes adapted for walking on floating vegetation. [Port. *jaçaná,* perh. of Tupi-Guarani orig.]

jac·a·ran·da (jăk′ə-răn′də) *n.* **1.** Any of several trees of the genus *Jacaranda,* native to tropical America, having compound leaves and clusters of pale-purple flowers. **2.** The wood of the jacaranda tree. **3.** A wood similar to jacaranda. [Port. and Sp. (South America) < Tupi *yacarandá.*]

ja·cinth (jā′sĭnth, jăs′ĭnth) *n.* Hyacinth (sense 4.a.). [ME *jacinte* < OFr. *jacinte* or Med. Lat. *jacintus,* both < Lat. *hyacinthus,* a blue precious stone. —see HYACINTH.]

jack (jăk) *n.* **1.** Often **Jack. a.** A man; fellow. **b.** One who does odd or heavy jobs. **c.** A lumberjack. **d.** A sailor; tar. **2.** A playing card showing the figure of a knave and ranking below a queen. **3. a.** A usually portable device for raising heavy objects by means of force applied with a lever, screw, or hydraulic press. **b.** A wooden wedge for cleaving rock. **c.** A support or brace, esp. the iron crosstree on a topgallant masthead. **4.** The male of certain animals, esp. the ass. **5.** Any of several food and game fishes chiefly of the genus *Caranx,* of Atlantic and Pacific waters. **6.** A pin in some bowling games. **7. a. jacks.** *(used with a sing. or pl. verb).* A game played with a set of small six-pointed metal pieces and a small ball, the object being to pick up the pieces in various combinations. **b.** One of the metal pieces used. **8.** A socket that accepts a plug at one end and attaches to electric circuitry at the other. **9.** A small flag flown at the bow of a ship, usually to indicate nationality. **10.** *Slang.* Money. **11.** Applejack. *—v.* **jacked, jack·ing, jacks.** *—tr.* **1.** To hunt or fish for with a jacklight. **2.** To hoist with or as if with a jack. **3.** To raise: *jack prices up.* **4.** To bolster confidence in; support. *—intr.* To jacklight. ***—phrasal verb.* jack off.** *Vulgar Slang.* To masturbate. ***—idiom.* every man jack.** Every single person of a group. [< the name JACK.]

jack·al (jăk′əl, -ôl′) *n.* **1.** Any of several doglike carnivorous mammals of the genus *Canis,* of Africa and Asia. **2. a.** An accomplice or lackey who aids in the commission of base or disreputable acts. **b.** One who performs menial tasks for another. [Turk. *chakāl* < Pers. *shagāl.*]

jack·a·napes (jăk′ə-nāps′) *n.* **1.** A conceited or impudent person. **2.** A mischievous child. **3.** *Archaic.* A monkey or ape. [ME *Jack Napis,* nickname of William de la Pole, first Duke of Suffolk (d. 1450).]

jack·ass (jăk′ăs′) *n.* **1.** A male ass or donkey. **2.** A foolish or stupid person; blockhead.

jackass rig *n. Naut.* A nonstandard combination of square rig and fore-and-aft rig on a sailing ship having two or more masts.

jack bean *n.* A tropical American plant, *Canavalia ensiformis,* having clusters of purple flowers and long pods.

jack·boot (jăk′bo͞ot′) *n.* **1.** A stout military boot extending above the knee. **2.** One that uses bullying tactics, esp. to force compliance. **3.** An aggressive or totalitarian, esp. military, policy or regime.

jack·boot·ed (jăk′bo͞o′tĭd) *adj.* **1.** Wearing jackboots. **2.** Cruelly and violently oppressive.

jack·daw (jăk′dô′) *n.* A Eurasian bird, *Corvus monedula,* related to and resembling the crow.

jack·et (jăk′ĭt) *n.* **1.** A short coat, usually extending to the hip. **2.** An outer covering or casing, esp.: **a.** The skin of a potato. **b.** The dust jacket of a book. **c.** Insulation covering a steam pipe, wire, boiler, or similar part. **d.** A paper or thin cardboard envelope for a phonograph record. **e.** An open envelope or folder for filing papers. **f.** The outer metal shell or case of a bullet. *—tr.v.* **-et·ed, -et·ing, -ets.** To supply or cover with a jacket. [ME *jaket,* dim. of OFr. *jaque,* short jacket.]

Jack Frost *n.* Frost or cold weather personified.

jack·fruit (jăk′fro͞ot′) *n.* **1.** A tree, *Artocarpus heterophyllus,* of tropical Asia, bearing large, edible fruit. **2.** The fruit of the jackfruit tree. [Port. *jaca* (< Malayalam *chakka*) + FRUIT.]

jack·ham·mer (jăk′hăm′ər) *n.* A hand-held pneumatic machine for drilling rock.

jack-in-the-box (jăk′ĭn-*thə*-bŏks′) *n., pl.* **jack-in-the-box·es** or **jacks-in-the-box.** A toy consisting of a usually grotesque puppet that springs up out of a box when the lid is opened.

jack-in-the-pul·pit (jăk′ĭn-*thə*-po͝ol′pĭt, -pŭl′-) *n., pl.* **jack-in-the-pul·pits** or **jacks-in-the-pul·pit.** A plant, *Arisaema triphyllum,* of eastern North America, having a leaflike spathe enclosing a clublike spadix.

jack·knife (jăk′nīf′) *n.* **1.** A large clasp pocketknife. **2.** A dive executed by jumping headfirst and then bending the body at the waist to form a 90-degree angle and, with the legs straight, touching the feet with the hands before straightening out to enter the water, hands first. *—v.* **-knifed, -knif·ing, -knifes.** *—tr.* **1.** To cut or stab with a jackknife. **2.** To fold or double like a jackknife. *—intr.* **1.** To bend or fold up like a jackknife: *a truck that jackknifed.* **2.** To form a 90-degree angle.

jack·light (jăk′līt′) *n.* A light used as a lure in night hunting or fishing. *—intr.v.* **-light·ed, -light·ing, -lights.** To hunt or fish with a jacklight.

jack mackerel *n.* A food and game fish, *Trachurus symmetricus,* of Pacific coastal waters.

jack-of-all-trades (jăk′əv-ôl′trādz′) *n., pl.* **jacks-of-all-trades.** A person who can do many different kinds of work.

jack-o'-lan·tern (jăk′ə-lăn′tərn) *n.* **1.** A lantern made from a hollowed pumpkin with a carved face. **2.** An ignis fatuus or similar phenomenon.

jack pine *n.* An evergreen tree, *Pinus banksiana,* of northern North America, having short, twisted needles and soft wood.

jack·plane (jăk′plān′) *n.* A bench plane for rough surfacing.

jack·pot (jăk′pŏt′) *n.* **1. a.** The accumulated stakes in a kind of poker that requires one to hold a pair of jacks or better in order to open the betting. **b.** A cumulative pool or kitty in various games and competitions. **2.** A top prize or reward. ***—idiom.* hit the jackpot.** *Informal.* To experience great success or sudden good fortune.

jack rabbit *n.* Any of several large long-eared, long-legged hares of the genus *Lepus,* of western North America. [JACK(ASS) + RABBIT.]

jack·screw (jăk′skro͞o′) *n.* A jack for lifting, operated by a screw.

jack·shaft (jăk′shăft′) *n.* A short shaft that transmits motion from a motor to a machine, esp. in an automobile.

jack·snipe (jăk′snīp′) *n., pl.* **jacksnipe** or **-snipes. 1.** An Old World wading bird, *Limnocryptes minima,* having brownish plumage and a long bill. **2.** Any of several birds similar to the jacksnipe.

Jack·so·ni·an (jăk-sō′nē-ən) *adj.* Of or pertaining to Andrew Jackson, his concepts of popular government, or his Presidency. *—n.* A supporter of Andrew Jackson.

jack·stay (jăk′stā′) *n. Naut.* **1.** A stay for racing or cruising vessels used to steady the mast against the strain of the gaff. **2.** A rope, rod, or batten along the upper side of a yard, gaff, or boom to which a sail is fastened. **3.** A rope or rod running vertically on the forward side of the mast on which the yard moves.

jack·straw (jăk′strô′) *n.* **1. jackstraws.** *(used with a sing. verb).* A game played with a pile of straws or thin sticks, with the players attempting in turn to remove a single stick without disturbing the others. **2.** One of the straws or sticks used in jackstraws.

jack-tar also **Jack-tar** (jăk′tär′) *n.* A sailor.

Ja·cob (jā′kəb) *n.* In the Old Testament, a Hebrew patriarch, son of Isaac and grandson of Abraham, and the father of 12 sons, the ancestors of the 12 tribes of Israel. [Heb. *Ya'aqōbh* < *'aqēbh,* heel.]

Jac·o·be·an (jăk′ə-bē′ən) *adj.* Of or pertaining to the reign of James I of England or his times. *—n.* A prominent figure of the Jacobean period. [NLat. *Jacobaeus* < *Jacobus,* James.]

Jac·o·bin (jăk′ə-bĭn) *n.* **1.** A radical republican during the French Revolution. **2.** A radical or extreme leftist. **3.** A Dominican friar. [Fr., after the *Jacobin* friars, in whose convent the Jacobins first met.] **—Jac′o·bin·ic, Jac′o·bin′i·cal** *adj.* **—Jac′o·bin·ism** *n.* **—Jac′o·bin·ize′**(-bĭ-nīz′) *v.* **(-ized, -iz·ing, -iz·es).**

Jac·o·bite (jăk′ə-bīt′) *n.* A supporter of James II of England or of the Stuart pretenders following 1688. [< NLat. *Jacobus,* James.] **—Jac′o·bit′i·cal** (-bĭt′ĭ-kəl) *adj.* **—Jac′o·bit·ism** (-bī-tĭz′əm) *n.*

Jacob's ladder *n.* **1.** *Naut.* A rope or chain ladder with rigid rungs. **2.** A plant of the genus *Polemonium,* having blue flowers and numerous paired leaflets. [From the ladder seen by the patriarch Jacob in a dream.]

jac·o·net (jăk′ə-nĕt′) *n.* A lightweight cotton cloth resem-

ă pat / ā pay / âr care / ä father / b **bib** / ch **church** / d **deed** / ĕ pet / ē be / f **fife** / g **gag** / h **hat** / hw **which** / ĭ pit / ī **pie** / îr **pier** / j **judge** / k **kick** / l **lid, needle** / m **mum** / n **no, sudden** / ng **thing** / ŏ **pot** / ō **toe** / ô **paw, for** / oi **noise** / ou **out** / o͝o **took** / o͞o **boot** /

bling lawn used for clothing and bandages. [Urdu *jagannāthī,* after *Jagannath,* India.]
jac·quard also **Jac·quard** (jăk′ärd′, jə-kärd′) *adj.* **1.** A special loom or other apparatus or the method employed in the weaving of a figured fabric. **2.** A fabric with an intricately woven pattern made on a jacquard loom. [After Joseph M. *Jacquard* (1752–1834).]
Jac·que·rie (zhä-krē′) *n.* **1.** The uprising of the French peasants against the nobility in 1358. **2. jacquerie.** A peasant revolt, esp. a very bloody one. [Fr. < OFr. *jacqerie,* peasantry < *jacques,* peasant < the name *Jacques.*]
jac·ti·ta·tion (jăk′tĭ-tā′shən) *n.* **1.** A false boasting or claim, esp. one detrimental to the interests of another. **2.** *Pathol.* Extreme restlessness or tossing in bed. [Med. Lat. *jactitatio, jactitation-,* false declaration < *jactitare,* to utter, freq. of *jactare,* to boast, freq. of *jacere,* to throw.]
Ja·cuz·zi (jə-ko͞o′zē, jă-). A trademark for a device that swirls water in a bath.
jade[1] (jād) *n.* Either of two distinct minerals, nephrite and jadeite, that are generally pale green or white and are used mainly as gemstones or in carving. [Fr. < Sp. *ijada* < *(piedra de) ijada,* (stone of the) flank (from the belief that it cured renal colic) < VLat. **iliata* < Lat. *ilia,* pl. of *ilium,* flank.]
jade[2] (jād) *n.* **1.** A broken-down or useless horse; nag. **2. a.** A shrewish or disreputable woman. **b.** A willful or coquettish girl. —*v.* **jad·ed, jad·ing, jades.** —*tr.* To exhaust or wear out. —*intr.* To become weary or spiritless. [ME.]
jad·ed (jā′dĭd) *adj.* **1.** Wearied with fatigue; worn-out. **2. a.** Rendered dull or insensitive as or as if by excess or by surfeit; sated: *"the sickeningly sweet life of the amoral, jaded, bored upper classes"* (John Simon). **b.** Cynically or pretentiously callous. —**jad′ed·ly** *adv.* —**jad′ed·ness** *n.*
jade·ite (jā′dīt′) *n.* A rare, emerald to light-green, white, red-brown, yellow-brown, or violet jade, $NaAlSi_2O_6$, used as a gem and for ornamental carvings.
jae·ger (yā′gər) *n.* **1.** *(also* jā′gər). Any of several sea birds of the genus *Stercorarius,* that snatch food from other birds. **2.** A huntsman or hunting attendant. [G. *Jäger,* jaeger, hunter < OHG *jagāri* < *jagōn,* to hunt.]
jag[1] (jăg) *n.* **1.** A sharp projection; barb. **2. a.** A hanging flap along the edge of a garment. **b.** A slash or slit in a garment exposing material of a different color. —*tr.v.* **jagged, jag·ging, jags. 1.** To cut jags in; notch. **2.** To cut unevenly. **3.** *Scot.* To prick; jab sharply. [ME *jagge.*]
jag[2] (jăg) *n.* **1.** *Slang.* A bout or spree: *a shopping jag.* **2.** A small load or portion. —*Idiom.* **have a jag on.** Be high, as on alcohol or drugs. [Orig. unknown.]
jag·ged (jăg′ĭd) *adj.* **1. a.** Having a rough surface or edge. **b.** Having sharp pieces or projections on a surface or edge. **2.** Having a rough or harsh quality. —**jag′ged·ly** *adv.* —**jag′ged·ness** *n.*
jag·ger·y (jăg′ə-rē) *n.* Unrefined sugar made from palm sap. [Port. *jagara* < Kanarese *sharkare* < Skt. *śarkarā,* sugar.]
jag·gy (jăg′ē) *adj.* **-gi·er, -gi·est.** Jagged; serrated.
jag·uar (jăg′wär′, jăg′yo͞o-är′) *n.* A large feline mammal, *Panthera onca,* of tropical America, having a tawny coat spotted with black rosettelike markings. [Sp. and Port. < Guarani *jaguá,* dog.]
jag·ua·ron·di also **jag·ua·run·di** (jăg′wə-rŭn′dē) *n.* A long-tailed grayish-brown wild cat, *Felis jaguarundi,* of tropical America. [Sp. and Port. < Guarani *jaguarundi,* var. of *jaguá,* dog.]
Jah·veh (yä′vā) or **Jah·weh** (yä′wā, -vā) *n.* Variants of **Yahweh.**
jai a·lai (hī′ lī′, hī′ ə-lī′, hī′ ə-lī′) *n.* An extremely fast court game in which players use a long hand-shaped basket strapped to the wrist to propel the ball against a wall. [Sp. < Basque : *jai,* festival + *alai,* joyous.]
jail (jāl) *n.* **1.** A place for the confinement of persons in lawful detention; prison. **2.** Detention in a jail. —*tr.v.* **jailed, jail·ing, jails.** To detain in custody; imprison. [ME *jaiole* < OFr., ult. < Lat. *cavea,* cage.]
jail·bait (jāl′bāt′) *n.* *Slang.* A girl below the age of consent with whom sexual intercourse can constitute statutory rape.
jail·bird (jāl′bûrd′) *n.* *Informal.* A prisoner or ex-convict.
jail·break (jāl′brāk′) *n.* An escape from jail.
jail delivery *n.* **1.** *Chiefly Brit.* The clearing of a jail by bringing all the prisoners to trial. **2.** A mass escape or forcible freeing of prisoners from a jail.
jail·er also **jail·or** (jā′lər) *n.* The keeper of a jail.
Jain (jīn) also **Jai·na** (jī′nə) *n.* A believer or follower of Jainism. [Hindi *jaina* < Skt. *jaina-,* relating to the saints < *jinaḥ,* saint, victor < *jayati,* he conquers.]
Jain·ism (jī′nĭz′əm) *n.* An ascetic religion of India, founded in the 6th century B.C., that teaches the immortality and transmigration of the soul and denies the existence of a perfect or supreme being.
jakes (jāks) *n.* *(used with a sing. verb). Regional.* A privy. [Orig. unknown.]
jal·ap (jăl′əp, jä′ləp) *n.* **1.** A Mexican plant, *Exogonium purga,* having a tuberous rootstock that is dried, powdered, and used medicinally as a cathartic. **2.** Any of several plants similar to or related to the jalap. **3.** The dried rootstock of the jalap or a related plant. [Fr. < Mex. Sp. *jalapa,* short for *(purga de) Jalapa,* (purgative of) Jalapa, after *Jalapa,* Mexico.]
ja·lop·y (jə-lŏp′ē) *n., pl.* **-ies.** *Informal.* An old, dilapidated vehicle, esp. an automobile. [Orig. unknown.]
jal·ou·sie (jăl′ə-sē) *n.* A blind or shutter having adjustable horizontal slats for regulating the passage of air and light. [Fr. < *jalousie,* jealousy < OFr. *gelosie* < *gelos,* jealous. —see JEALOUS.]
jam[1] (jăm) *v.* **jammed, jam·ming, jams.** —*tr.* **1.** To drive or wedge forcibly into a tight position: *jammed the cork in the bottle.* **2.** To activate or apply suddenly: *jam the brakes on.* **3.** To cause to lock in an unworkable position: *jam the typewriter keys.* **4.** To fill or pack to excess; cram. **5.** To block, congest, or clog: *The drain was jammed by debris.* **6.** To crush or bruise: *jam a finger.* **7.** *Electronics.* To interfere with or prevent the clear reception of (broadcast signals) by electronic means. —*intr.* **1.** To become wedged; stick. **2.** To become inoperable because of jammed parts. **3.** To force into or through a limited space. **4.** *Mus.* To play jazz improvisations. —*n.* **1.** The act of jamming or the condition of being jammed. **2.** A crush or congestion of people or things in a limited space. **3.** *Informal.* A difficult situation; predicament. [Orig. unknown.]
jam[2] (jăm) *n.* A preserve made from whole fruit boiled to a pulp with sugar. [Poss. < JAM[1] (to crush).]
jamb (jăm) *n.* **1.** The vertical posts or pieces of a door or window frame. **2.** A jambeau. [ME *jambe* < OFr. < LLat. *gamba,* hoof. —see GAMBOL.]
jam·ba·lay·a (jŭm′bə-lī′ə) *n.* A Creole dish consisting of rice that has been cooked with shrimp, oysters, ham, or chicken and seasoned with spices and herbs. [Louisiana Fr.]
jam·beau (jăm′bō) *n., pl.* **-beaux** (-bōz). A piece of armor for the leg below the knee. [ME.]
jam·bo·ree (jăm′bə-rē′) *n.* **1.** A noisy celebration. **2.** A large assembly, often international, as of Boy Scouts. **3.** A mass gathering or assembly, as of a political party or association. [Orig. unknown.]
James (jāmz) *n.* **1.** The reputed author of the Epistle of James in the New Testament. **2.** See table at **Bible.**
James·i·an (jām′zē-ən) *adj.* **1.** Pertaining to or characteristic of William James, his philosophy, or his teachings. **2.** Pertaining to or characteristic of Henry James or his writings.
jam session *n.* **1.** An impromptu gathering of jazz musicians to play improvisations together. **2.** An impromptu or highly informal discussion.
jan·gle (jăng′gəl) *v.* **-gled, -gling, -gles.** —*intr.* To make a harsh, metallic sound. —*tr.* **1.** To cause to make a harsh, discordant sound. **2.** To grate on or jar (the nerves). —*n.* A harsh, metallic sound. [ME *janglen,* to chatter < OFr. *jangler,* prob. of Germanic orig.] —**jan′gler** *n.*
jan·is·sar·y (jăn′ĭ-sĕr′ē) also **jan·i·zar·y** (-zĕr′ē) *n., pl.* **-ies.** A soldier in an elite guard of Turkish troops organized in the 14th century and abolished in 1826. [Fr. *janissaire* < Turk. *yeniçeri* : *yeni,* new + *çeri,* soldier.]
jan·i·tor (jăn′ĭ-tər) *n.* **1.** One who attends to the maintenance or cleaning of a building. **2.** A doorman. [Lat., doorkeeper < *janua,* door < *janus,* arch.] —**jan′i·to′ri·al** (-tôr′ē-əl, -tōr′-) *adj.*
jan·i·zar·y (jăn′ĭ-zĕr′ē) *n.* Variant of **janissary.**
Jan·sen·ism (jăn′sə-nĭz′əm) *n.* The theological principles of Cornelis Jansen, condemned as heretical by the Roman Catholic Church, which emphasize predestination, deny free will, and maintain that human nature is incapable of good. —**Jan′sen·ist** *n.* —**Jan′sen·is′tic** *adj.*
Jan·u·ar·y (jăn′yo͞o-ĕr′ē) *n., pl.* **-ies.** The first month of the year in the Gregorian calendar. See table at **calendar.** [ME *januarie* < Lat. *Januarius (mensis),* (month of) Janus < *Janus,* Janus.]
Ja·nus (jā′nəs) *n.* *Rom. Myth.* An ancient Roman god of gates and doorways, depicted with two faces looking in opposite directions. [Lat.]
Ja·nus-faced (jā′nəs-fāst′) *adj.* Hypocritical.
Jap (jăp) *n.* *Offensive Slang.* Japanese.
ja·pan (jə-păn′) *n.* **1.** A black enamel or lacquer used to produce a durable glossy finish. **2.** An object decorated and varnished in the Japanese manner. —*tr.v.* **-panned, -pan·ning, -pans. 1.** To enamel with japan. **2.** To coat with a glossy finish. [After *Japan.*]
Ja·pan clover (jə-păn) *n.* A leguminous plant, *Lespedeza striata,* native to Asia, cultivated as a forage plant and for soil improvement.
Japan Current *n.* A warm ocean current flowing northeast from the Philippine Sea past southeastern Japan to the North Pacific.
Jap·a·nese (jăp′ə-nēz′, -nēs′) *n., pl.* **Japanese. 1.** A native or inhabitant of Japan. **2.** The language of the Japanese. —**Jap′a·nese′** *adj.*
Japanese andromeda *n.* A shrub, *Pieris japonica,* native to Japan, having small, early-blooming white flowers.
Japanese beetle *n.* A metallic-green and brownish beetle, *Popillia japonica,* native to eastern Asia, the larvae and adults of which are serious plant pests in North America.
Japanese cedar *n.* A tree, the cryptomeria, or its wood.
Japanese iris *n.* A plant, *Iris kaempferi,* native to Asia, and cultivated in many horticultural varieties for its large, flat, showy flowers.
Japanese ivy *n.* Boston ivy.
Japanese leaf *n.* Chinese evergreen.

George Miksch Sutton
jaeger

jaguar

jalousie

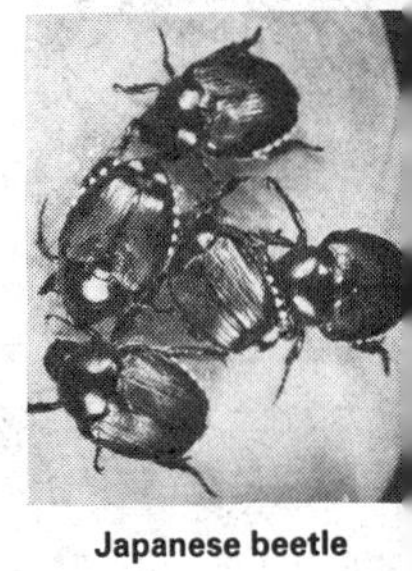
Japanese beetle

Japanese maple *n.* A shrub or small tree, *Acer palmatum,* native to eastern Asia and widely cultivated for its decorative, deeply lobed, often reddish foliage.
Japanese quince *n.* Japonica.
Japanese river fever *n.* Scrub typhus.
Japanese spurge *n.* Pachysandra.
Japan wax *n.* A pale-yellow solid wax obtained from the berries of certain plants of the genus *Rhus* and used in wax matches, soaps, food packaging, and as a substitute for beeswax.
jape (jāp) *v.* **japed, jap·ing, japes.** —*intr.* To joke or quip. —*tr.* To make sport of. —*n.* A joke or quip. [ME *japen,* prob. < OFr. *japer,* to chatter.] —**jap'er** *n.* —**jap'er·y** *n.*
Ja·pheth (jā'fĭth) *n.* In the Old Testament, the youngest of Noah's three sons. [Gk. *Iapheth* < Heb. *Yepeth.*]
Jap·lish (jăp'lĭsh) *n.* Japanese with many words borrowed from English. [JAP(ANESE) + (ENG)LISH.]
ja·pon·i·ca (jə-pŏn'ĭ-kə) *n.* **1.** A shrub, *Chaenomeles japonica,* native to Japan, cultivated for its red flowers. **2.** The camellia. [NLat., specific epithet of the species *Chaenomeles japonica* < *Japonia,* Japan.]
jar[1] (jär) *n.* **1.** A cylindrical glass or earthenware vessel with a wide mouth and usually without handles. **2.** The contents of a jar. [Fr. *jarre* < Prov. *jarra* < Ar. *jarrah,* earthen vessel.] —**jar'ful** *n.*
jar[2] (jär) *v.* **jarred, jar·ring, jars.** —*intr.* **1.** To make or utter a harsh sound. **2.** To disturb or irritate; grate: *His voice jarred on her nerves.* **3.** To shake or shiver from impact. **4.** To clash or conflict: *"We ourselves . . . often jar with the landscape"* (Isak Dinesen). —*tr.* **1.** To bump or cause to move or shake from impact. **2.** To startle or unsettle; shock. —*n.* **1.** A jolt; shock. **2.** A harsh or grating sound; discord. [Perh. of imit. orig.]
jar·di·nière (järd'n-îr', zhär-dē-nyâr') *n.* **1.** A large, decorative stand or pot for plants. **2.** Diced, cooked vegetables served as a garnish with meat. [Fr., fem. of *jardinier,* gardener < *jardin,* garden, of Germanic orig.]
jar·gon[1] (jär'gən) *n.* **1.** Nonsensical, incoherent, or meaningless talk. **2.** A hybrid language or dialect; pidgin. **3.** The specialized or technical language of a trade, profession, or similar group. —*intr.v.* **-goned, -gon·ing, -gons.** To speak in or use jargon. [ME *jargoun* < OFr. *jargon.*]
jar·gon[2] (jär-gŏn') also **jar·goon** (jär-go͞on') *n.* A smoky, yellow, or colorless variety of zircon. [Fr.]
jar·gon·ize (jär'gə-nīz') *v.* **-ized, -iz·ing, -iz·es.** —*tr.* To debase or translate into jargon. —*intr.* To talk in jargon.
jar·goon (jär-go͞on') *n.* Variant of **jargon**[2].
jarl (yärl) *n.* A great chieftain or nobleman of the medieval Scandinavians. [ON.]
jas·mine (jăz'mĭn) also **jes·sa·mine** (jĕs'ə-mĭn) *n.* **1.** Any of several vines or shrubs of the genus *Jasminum,* esp. *J. officinalis,* native to Asia, having fragrant white flowers used in making perfume. **2.** Any of several woody vines of the genus *Gelsemium,* esp. *G. sempervirens,* of the southeastern United States, having fragrant yellow flowers. **3.** Any of several plants or shrubs having fragrant flowers. **4.** A light to brilliant yellow. [Fr. *jasmin* < Ar. *yāsamīn* < Pers. *yasmīn.*]

jasmine

Ja·son (jā'sən) *n. Gk. Myth.* The leader of the Argonauts in quest of the Golden Fleece and the husband of Medea. [Gk. *Iasōn.*]
jas·per (jăs'pər) *n.* **1.** An opaque variety of quartz, reddish, brown, or yellow in color. **2.** Chalcedony, esp. green chalcedony. [ME *jaspre* < AN < OFr. < Lat. *jaspis* < Gk. *iaspis,* of Semitic orig.]
jasper ware *n.* A fine white porcelain or stoneware invented by Josiah Wedgwood, often colored by metallic oxides with raised designs remaining white.
Jat (jät) *n.* A member of an Indo-Aryan people of the Punjab and Uttar Pradesh. [Hindi *jāṭ.*]
ja·to (jā'tō) *n.* **1.** A takeoff aided by an auxiliary jet or rocket. **2.** An auxiliary unit providing thrust for a jato. [< *JATO,* acronym for *jet-assisted takeoff.*]
jaun·dice (jôn'dĭs, jän'-) *n.* Yellowish discoloration of tissues and bodily fluids with bile pigment caused by any of several pathological conditions in which normal processing of bile is interrupted. [ME *jaunis* < OFr. *jaunice* < *jaune,* yellow < Lat. *galbinus,* yellowish < *galbus,* yellow.]
jaun·diced (jôn'dĭst, jän'-) *adj.* **1.** Affected with jaundice. **2.** Yellow or yellowish. **3.** Affected by or exhibiting envy, prejudice, or hostility.

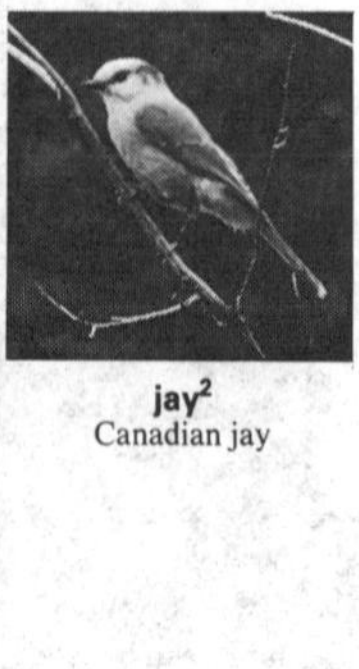

jay[2]
Canadian jay

jaunt (jônt, jänt) *n.* A short trip or excursion, usually for pleasure. —*intr.v.* **jaunt·ed, jaunt·ing, jaunts.** To make a short journey. [Orig. unknown.]
jaunting car *n.* A light, open cart with seats hung back to back over its two wheels, used in Ireland.
jaun·ty (jôn'tē, jän'-) *adj.* **-ti·er, -ti·est.** **1.** Crisp and dapper in appearance; natty. **2.** Having a buoyant or self-confident air; brisk. **3.** Well-bred. [Fr. *gentil,* noble < OFr. —see GENTLE.] —**jaun'ti·ly** *adv.* —**jaun'ti·ness** *n.*
ja·va (jăv'ə, jä'və) *n. Informal.* Brewed coffee. [After *Java.*]
Ja·va man (jä'və, jăv'ə) *n.* Pithecanthropus.
Jav·a·nese (jăv'ə-nēz', -nēs', jä'və-) *adj.* Of or pertaining to Java or to the people, language, or culture of Java. —*n., pl.* **Javanese.** **1.** A native or inhabitant of Java. **2.** The Indonesian language of Java. [*Java* + *-nese,* as in *Japanese.*]
Java sparrow *n.* A small grayish bird, *Padda oryzivora,* native to tropical Asia and often kept as a cage bird.
jave·lin (jăv'lĭn, jăv'ə-) *n.* **1.** A light spear thrown with the hand and used as a weapon. **2. a.** A metal or metal-tipped spear, generally not less than 8 1/2 feet in length, used in contests of distance throwing. **b.** The athletic field event in which a javelin is thrown. [OFr. *javeline,* var. of *javelot,* of Celtic orig.]
Ja·velle water also **Ja·vel water** (zhə-vĕl') *n.* An aqueous solution of potassium or sodium hypochlorite, used as a disinfectant and bleaching agent. [After *Javel,* a former town in France.]
jaw (jô) *n.* **1.** Either of two bony or cartilaginous structures in most vertebrates forming the framework of the mouth and holding the teeth. **2.** The anatomical parts forming the wall of the mouth and serving to open and close it. **3.** Either of two opposed hinged parts in a mechanical device. **4. jaws.** The walls of a pass, canyon, or cavern. **5. jaws.** A dangerous situation or confrontation: *the jaws of death.* **6.** *Slang.* **a.** Impudent argument or back talk. **b.** Chatter. —*intr.v.* **jawed, jaw·ing, jaws.** *Slang.* **1.** To talk vociferously; jabber. **2.** To talk; converse. [ME *jowe.*]
jaw·bone (jô'bōn') *n.* A bone of the jaw, esp. the bone of the lower jaw. —*v.* **-boned, -bon·ing, -bones.** *Informal.* —*tr.* To try to influence or pressure through strong persuasion, esp. to urge to comply voluntarily. —*intr.* To urge voluntary compliance with official wishes or guidelines. —**jaw'bon·er** *n.* —**jaw'bon·ing** *n.*
jaw·break·er (jô'brā'kər) *n.* **1.** A kind of very hard candy. **2.** *Slang.* A word that is difficult to pronounce.
Jaws of Life. A trademark for a pneumatic tool consisting of a pincerlike metal device that is inserted into the body of a severely damaged vehicle to provide access to persons trapped inside.
jay[1] (jā) *n.* The letter *j.*
jay[2] (jā) *n.* **1.** Any of various often crested birds of the genera *Garrulus, Cyanocitta, Aphelocoma,* and related genera within the family Corvidae, often having a loud, harsh call. **2.** An overly talkative person; chatterbox. **3.** *Slang.* A newcomer or inexperienced person. [ME *jai* < OFr. < LLat. *gaius.*]
jay·bird (jā'bûrd') *n.* A jay[2] (sense 1).
Jay·cee (jā'sē') *n.* A member of a junior chamber of commerce. [Pronunciation of the initial letters in *junior chamber* (*of commerce*).]
jay·hawk·er (jā'hô'kər) *n.* **1.** One of the free-soil guerrillas in Kansas or Missouri during the border disputes of 1857–59. **2.** A robber; bandit. [< *jayhawk,* a fictitious bird.]
jay·vee (jā'vē') *n. Informal.* **1.** A junior varsity. **2.** A member of a junior varsity. [Pronunciation of the initial letters in JUNIOR VARSITY.]
jay·walk (jā'wôk') *intr.v.* **-walked, -walk·ing, -walks.** To cross a street illegally or recklessly. [< JAY[2] (newcomer).] —**jay'walk'er** *n.*
jazz (jăz) *n.* **1.** A kind of native American music first played extemporaneously by black bands in Southern towns at the turn of the century, characterized by a strong but flexible rhythmic understructure with solo and ensemble improvisations on basic tunes and chord patterns and, in more recent styles, a highly sophisticated harmonic idiom. **2.** Big-band dance music, popular esp. in the 1920's and 1930's. **3.** *Slang.* Animation; enthusiasm. **4.** *Slang.* **a.** Extreme exaggeration: *all that jazz about his big deals.* **b.** Nonsense. **5.** *Slang.* Miscellaneous and unspecified things: *brought the food and all the jazz to go with it.* —*v.* **jazzed, jazz·ing, jazz·es.** —*tr.* **1.** To play in a jazz style. **2.** *Slang.* To lie or exaggerate to: *Don't jazz me.* —*intr. Slang.* To lie or exaggerate. —***phrasal verb.* jazz up.** *Informal.* To make more interesting; enliven. [Orig. unknown.] —**jazz'er** *n.*
jazz·man (jăz'măn', -mən) *n.* A jazz musician or composer.
jazz·y (jăz'ē) *adj.* **-i·er, -i·est.** **1.** Resembling jazz; rhythmical. **2.** *Slang.* Showy; flashy. —**jazz'i·ly** *adv.* —**jazz'i·ness** *n.*
jeal·ous (jĕl'əs) *adj.* **1.** Fearful or wary of being supplanted, esp. apprehensive of the loss of another's affection. **2. a.** Resentful or bitter in rivalry; envious: *jealous of her success.* **b.** Inclined to suspect rivalry. **3.** Vigilant in guarding something: *jealous of his good name.* **4.** Concerning or arising from feelings of envy, apprehension, or bitterness: *jealous thoughts.* **5.** Intolerant of disloyalty or infidelity; autocratic: *a jealous God.* [ME *jelous* < OFr. *gelos,* jealous, zealous < Med. Lat. *zelosus* < LLat. *zelos,* zeal < Gk. *zēlos.*] —**jeal'ous·ly** *adv.* —**jeal'ous·ness** *n.*
jeal·ous·y (jĕl'ə-sē) *n., pl.* **-ies.** **1.** A jealous attitude or disposition. **2.** Close vigilance.
jean (jēn) *n.* **1.** A heavy, strong, twilled cotton, used in making uniforms and work clothes. **2. jeans.** Clothes, esp. pants, made of jean. [Short for obs. *jene fustian,* Genoan fustian < ME *Jene,* Genoa.]
Jeep (jēp). A trademark for a civilian motor vehicle.
jeer (jîr) *v.* **jeered, jeer·ing, jeers.** —*intr.* To speak or shout derisively; mock. —*tr.* To abuse openly; taunt. —*n.* A scoffing or taunting remark or shout. [Origin unknown.] —**jeer'er** *n.* —**jeer'ing·ly** *adv.*
Jef·fer·so·ni·an (jĕf'ər-sō'nē-ən) *adj.* Of, pertaining to, or typical of Thomas Jefferson or his political attitudes and theories. —*n.* A follower of Jefferson or a proponent of his politics. —**Jef'fer·so'ni·an·ism** *n.*

Je·ho·vah (jĭ-hō′və) *n.* God, esp. in Christian translations of the Old Testament. [Alteration of Heb. *Yahweh,* Yahweh.]
Jehovah's Witnesses *n.* A religious sect founded in the United States during the late 19th century, whose followers practice active evangelism, preach the imminent approach of the millennium, and are strongly opposed to war and to the authority of organized government in matters of conscience.
je·june (jə-jo͞on′) *adj.* **1.** Lacking in nutrition; insubstantial. **2.** Not interesting; dull: *jejune words and useless empty phrases.* **3.** Lacking maturity; puerile: *surprised by his jejune response to the problem.* [< Lat. *jejunus,* hungry.] **—je·june′ly** *adv.* **—je·june′ness** *n.*
je·ju·num (jə-jo͞o′nəm) *n., pl.* **-na** (-nə). The section of the small intestine between the duodenum and the ileum. [Med. Lat. < Lat. *jejunus,* fasting (so called because in dissection it was always found empty).]
Je·kyll and Hyde (jĕk′əl-ən-hīd′, jē′kəl-) *n. Informal.* One who has quasi-schizophrenic alternating phases of pleasantness and unpleasantness. [After *The Strange Case of Dr. Jekyll and Mr. Hyde* by Robert L. Stevenson (1850–1894).]
jell (jĕl) *v.* **jelled, jell·ing, jells.** *—intr.* **1.** To become firm or gelatinous; congeal. **2.** *Informal.* To take shape or fall into place; crystallize: *My ideas on the subject haven't jelled yet. —tr.* **1.** To cause to become firm or gelatinous; jelly. **2.** To cause to take shape; make clear and definite; crystallize. [Back-formation < JELLY.]
Jell-O (jĕl′ō). A trademark for a gelatin dessert.
jel·ly (jĕl′ē) *n., pl.* **-lies. 1.** A soft, semisolid food substance with a resilient consistency, made by the setting of a liquid containing pectin or gelatin, or by the addition of gelatin to a liquid, esp. such a substance made of fruit juice containing pectin boiled with sugar. **2.** A substance with the consistency of jelly, such as a petroleum ointment. **3.** Something similar or likened to jelly. *—v.* **-lied, -ly·ing, -lies.** *—tr.* To make or cause to become jelly. *—intr.* To become jelly; set. [ME *gele* < OFr. *gelee* < Lat. *gelata,* p.part. of *gelare,* to freeze < *gelu,* frost.]
jel·ly·bean (jĕl′ē-bēn′) *n.* A small ovoid candy with a hardened sugar coating over a chewy center.
jel·ly·fish (jĕl′ē-fĭsh′) *n., pl.* **jellyfish** or **-fish·es. 1.** Any of numerous usually free-swimming marine coelenterates of the class Scyphozoa, characteristically having a gelatinous, tentacled, often bell-shaped medusoid stage as the dominant or only phase of its life cycle. **2.** Any of various coelenterates similar or related to the jellyfish. **3.** *Informal.* A person who lacks force of character; weakling.
jel·ly·roll (jĕl′ē-rōl′) *n.* A thin sheet of sponge cake layered with jelly and then rolled up.
je·ne·sais·quoi (zhə′nə-sā-kwä′, -sĕ-) *n.* Something that is difficult to describe or express. [Fr., I know not what.]
jen·net (jĕn′ĭt) *n.* A small Spanish saddle horse. [ME *genet* < OFr. < Sp. *jinete,* light horseman < Ar. *Zeneti,* a Berber tribe famed for horsemanship.]
jen·ny (jĕn′ē) *n., pl.* **-nies. 1.** A female donkey. **2.** A female wren. **3.** A spinning jenny. [< the name *Jenny.*]
jeop·ard·ize (jĕp′ər-dīz′) *tr.v.* **-ized, -iz·ing, -izes.** To expose to loss or injury; imperil.
jeop·ard·y (jĕp′ər-dē) *n., pl.* **-ies. 1.** Danger or risk of loss or injury; peril. **2.** *Law.* The defendant's risk or danger of conviction when put on trial. [ME *jupartie* < OFr. *jeu parti,* even game, uncertainty : *jeu,* game (< Lat. *jocus*) + *parti,* p.part. of *partir,* to divide < Lat. *partire* < *pars,* part.]
Jeph·thah (jĕf′thə, jĕp′-) *n.* In the Old Testament, a judge of Israel who sacrificed his daughter to fulfill a rash vow. [Gk. *Iephthe* < Heb. *yiphtaḥ.*]
je·quir·i·ty bean (jĭ-kwĭr′ĭ-tē) *n.* Rosary pea. [Ult. < Tupi-Guarani *jekirtí.*]
jer·bo·a (jər-bō′ə) *n.* Any of various small, leaping rodents of the family Dipodidae, of Asia and northern Africa, having long hind legs and a long, tufted tail. [Med. Lat. < Ar. *yerbō'.*]
jer·e·mi·ad (jĕr′ə-mī′əd) *n.* An elaborate and prolonged lamentation or tale of woe. [Fr. *jérémiade,* after *Jérémie,* Jeremiah.]
Jer·e·mi·ah (jĕr′ə-mī′ə) *n.* **1.** A Hebrew prophet of the 7th and 6th centuries B.C. **2.** See table at **Bible.** [Heb. *Yirmayāhū.*]
jerk¹ (jûrk) *v.* **jerked, jerk·ing, jerks.** *—tr.* **1.** To give an abrupt thrust, push, pull, or twist to. **2.** To throw or toss with a quick abrupt motion. **3.** To utter abruptly or sharply. **4.** To make and serve (ice cream sodas, for example) at a soda fountain. *—intr.* **1.** To move in sudden abrupt motions; jolt. **2.** To make spasmodic motions: *His legs jerked from fatigue.* **—phrasal verb. jerk off.** *Offensive Slang.* To masturbate. *—n.* **1.** A sudden, abrupt motion, as a yank or twist. **2.** A jolting or lurching motion. **3.** *Physiol.* A sudden spasmodic, muscular movement. **4. jerks.** Involuntary convulsive twitching often resulting from excitement. **5. jerks.** *Slang.* Chorea. **6.** *Slang.* A dull, stupid, or fatuous person. [Orig. unknown.] **—jerk′er** *n.*
jerk² (jûrk) *tr.v.* **jerked, jerk·ing, jerks.** To cut (meat) into long strips and dry in the sun or cure by exposing to smoke. [Back-formation < JERKY².]
jer·kin (jûr′kĭn) *n.* A short, close-fitting, often sleeveless coat or jacket, usually of leather. [Orig. unknown.]
jerk·wa·ter (jûrk′wô′tər, -wŏt′ər) *adj.* **1.** *Informal.* Remote, small, and insignificant: *a jerkwater town.* **2.** Contemptibly trivial. [< *jerkwater,* a branch-line train, so called because its small boiler had to be refilled often, requiring train crews to "jerk" or draw water from streams.]
jerk·y¹ (jûr′kē) *adj.* **-i·er, -i·est. 1.** Characterized by jerks or jerking. **2.** *Slang.* Foolish. **—jerk′i·ly** *adv.* **—jerk′i·ness** *n.*
jerk·y² (jûr′kē) *n.* Meat cured by jerking. [Alteration of CHARQUI.]
jer·o·bo·am (jĕr′ə-bō′əm) *n.* A wine bottle holding about 4/5 of a gallon or 3.028 liters. [After *Jeroboam I* (d. ?912 B.C.), king of northern Israel.]
Jer·ry (jĕr′ē) *n., pl.* **-ries.** *Chiefly Brit. Slang.* A German, esp. a German soldier. [Alteration of GERMAN.]
jer·ry·build (jĕr′ē-bĭld′) *tr.v.* **-built** (-bĭlt′), **-build·ing, -builds.** To build shoddily, flimsily, and cheaply. [Orig. unknown.] **—jer′ry·build′er** *n.*
jer·sey (jûr′zē) *n., pl.* **-seys. 1.** A soft, plain-knitted fabric used for clothing. **2.** A close-fitting knitted pullover shirt, jacket, or sweater. **3.** Often **Jersey.** Any of a breed of fawn-colored dairy cattle developed on the island of Jersey and yielding milk rich in butterfat. [After *Jersey,* England.]
Je·ru·sa·lem artichoke (jə-ro͞o′sə-ləm, -zə-ləm) *n.* **1.** A North American sunflower, *Helianthus tuberosus,* having yellow, rayed flowers and edible tuberous roots. **2.** The tuber of the Jerusalem artichoke, eaten as a vegetable. [By folk ety. < Ital. *girasole,* sunflower. —see GIRASOL.]
Jerusalem cherry *n.* A small shrub, *Solanum pseudocapsicum,* native to the Old World, bearing inedible reddish fruit and used as a house plant.
Jerusalem cross *n.* A cross with four arms, each terminating in a crossbar.
Jerusalem oak *n.* A weedy North American plant, *Chenopodium botrys,* having lobed leaves and a characteristic odor suggestive of turpentine.
Jerusalem thorn *n.* A spiny tropical American tree, *Parkinsonia aculeata,* having clusters of yellow flowers.
jess (jĕs) *n.* A short strap fastened around the leg of a hawk or other bird used in falconry, to which a leash may be fastened. *—tr.v.* **jessed, jess·ing, jess·es.** To put jesses on (a bird). [ME *ges* < OFr., pl. of *jet,* throw < VLat. **jectus* < Lat. *jacere,* to throw.]
jes·sa·mine (jĕs′ə-mĭn) *n.* Variant of **jasmine.**
jest (jĕst) *n.* **1.** Something said or done to provoke amusement and laughter. **2.** A frolicsome attitude or mood: *spoken in jest.* **3.** A jeering remark; taunt. **4.** An object of ridicule; laughingstock. *—v.* **jest·ed, jest·ing, jests.** *—intr.* **1.** To act or speak playfully. **2.** To make witty or amusing remarks. **3.** To utter scoffs; gibe. *—tr.* To make fun of; ridicule. [ME *geste,* tale < OFr. < Lat. *gesta,* deeds < *gerere,* to perform.]
jest·er (jĕs′tər) *n.* One given to jesting, esp. a fool or buffoon at medieval courts.
Jes·u·it (jĕzh′o͞o-ĭt, jĕz′yo͞o-) *n.* **1.** A member of the Society of Jesus, a Roman Catholic order founded by Saint Ignatius Loyola in 1534. **2.** Often **jesuit.** One given to subtle casuistry. [Fr. *Jésuite* < *Jésus,* Jesus < LLat. *Jesus.* —see JESUS.] **—Jes′u·it′i·cal** *adj.* **—Jes′u·it′i·cal·ly** *adv.*
Je·sus (jē′zəs) *n.* **1.** The founder of Christianity, regarded by Christians as the son of God and the Messiah. **2.** *Christian Science.* "The highest human corporeal concept of the divine idea" (Mary Baker Eddy). [LLat. < Gk. *Iēsous* < Heb. *Yēshua'* < *Yĕhōshūa',* Joshua.]
Jesus freak *n. Slang.* A member of a fundamentalist evangelical group, esp. of young people, devoted to the teachings of Jesus.
jet¹ (jĕt) *n.* **1.** A dense black coal that takes a high polish and is used for jewelry. **2.** A deep black. *—adj.* **1.** Made of or resembling jet. **2.** Black as jet. [ME *get* < AN < OFr. *jayet* < Lat. *gagates* < Gk. *gagatēs,* after *Gagai,* a town in Asia Minor.]
jet² (jĕt) *n.* **1. a.** A high-velocity fluid stream forced under pressure out of a small-diameter opening or nozzle. **b.** A nozzle or other outlet for emitting such a stream. **2.** Something emitted in or as if in such a stream: *"such myriad and such vivid jets of images."* (Henry Roth). **3. a.** A jet-propelled vehicle, esp. a jet-propelled aircraft. **b.** A jet engine. *—v.* **jet·ted, jet·ting, jets.** *—intr.* **1.** To move quickly. **2.** To travel by jet plane. *—tr.* To propel outward or squirt, as under pressure. [OFr. < *jeter,* to spout forth < VLat. **jectare* < Lat. *jactare,* freq. of *jacere,* to throw.]
jet·a·va·tor (jĕt′ə-vā′tər) *n.* A surface that deflects a rocket's propulsion stream in order to change the direction of thrust. [JET² + (ELE)VATOR.]
jet boat *n.* A boat propelled by a powerful jet of water created by a specially designed engine.
je·té (zhə-tā′) *n.* A leap in ballet with one leg extending forward and the other backward. [Fr. < p.part. of *jeter,* to throw.]
jet engine *n.* **1.** An engine that develops thrust by ejecting a jet, esp. a jet of gaseous combustion products. **2.** A jet engine equipped to consume atmospheric oxygen, used esp. in aircraft, and distinguished from rocket engines with self-contained fuel-oxidizer systems.
jet lag *n.* The psychological dislocation and disruption of

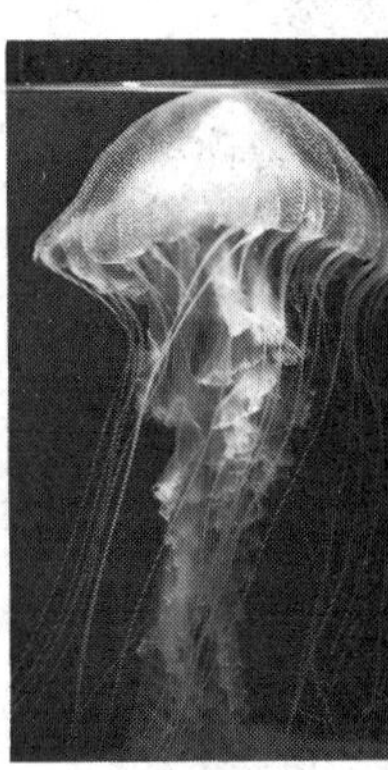
jellyfish

jerkin

jet²
Lear jet

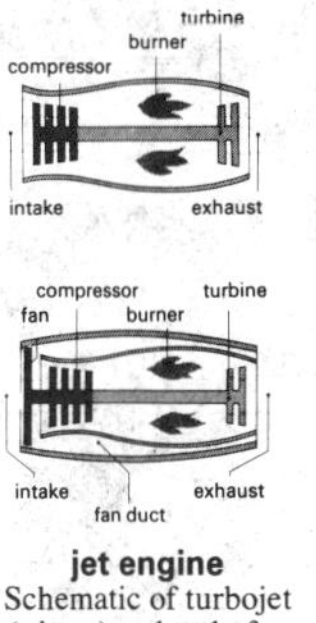

jet engine
Schematic of turbojet (*above*) and turbofan (*below*) jet engines

jetty[1]

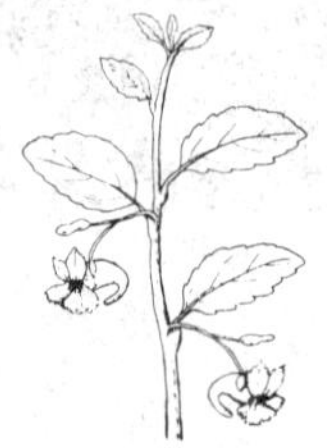
jewelweed

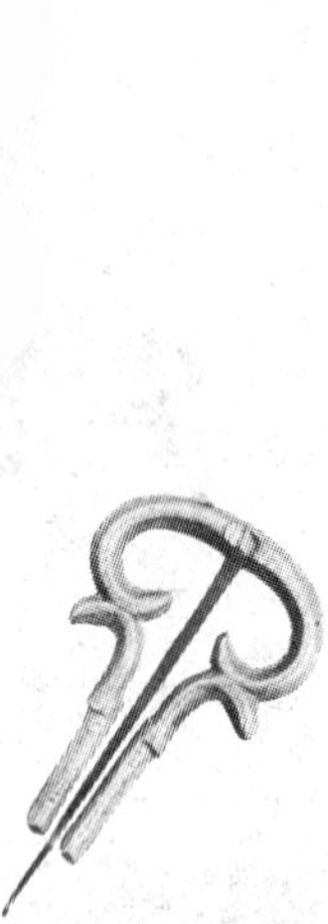
jew's-harp

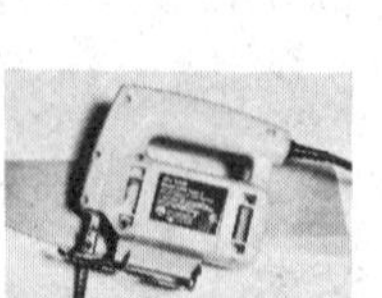
jigsaw

jimsonweed

bodily rhythms caused by high-speed travel across several time zones in a jet airplane.

jet·lin·er (jĕt'lī'nər) *n.* A large passenger-carrying jet airplane.

jet·port (jĕt'pôrt', -pōrt') *n.* An airport equipped for jet aircraft.

jet-pro·pelled (jĕt'prə-pĕld') *adj.* Driven by jet propulsion.

jet propulsion *n.* Propulsion derived from the rearward expulsion of matter in a jet stream, esp. propulsion by jet engines.

jet·sam (jĕt'səm) *n.* **1.** Cargo or equipment thrown overboard to lighten a ship in distress. **2.** Discarded cargo or equipment found washed ashore. **3.** Discarded odds and ends. —See Usage note at **flotsam.** [Alteration of JETTISON.]

jet set *n.* An international social set made up of wealthy people who travel from one fashionable place to another. **—jet setter** *n.*

jet stream *n.* **1.** A high-speed wind near the troposphere, generally moving from a westerly direction at speeds often exceeding 400 kilometers per hour, or 250 miles an hour. **2.** A high-speed stream; jet.

jet·ti·son (jĕt'ĭ-sən, -zən) *tr.v.* **-soned, -son·ing, -sons. 1.** To cast off or overboard. **2.** To discard as unwanted or burdensome: *jettisoned the whole marketing plan.* —*n.* **1.** The act of jettisoning. **2.** Jetsam. [< ME *jetteson,* a throwing overboard < AN *gettesone* < Lat. *jactatio* < *jactare,* freq. of *jacere,* to throw.]

jet·ty[1] (jĕt'ē) *n., pl.* **-ties. 1.** A pier or other structure projecting into a body of water to influence the current or tide or protect a harbor or shoreline. **2.** A wharf. [ME *gete* < OFr. *jete,* p.part. of *jeter,* to project. —see JET[2].]

jet·ty[2] (jĕt'ē) *adj.* **1.** Resembling jet. **2.** Having the color of jet. **—jet'ti·ness** *n.*

Jet·way (jĕt'wā'). A trademark for a telescoping bridge ramp for loading and unloading passengers between an aircraft and a terminal building.

jeu·nesse do·rée (zhœ-nĕs' dô-rā') *n.* Fashionable and wealthy young people. [Fr., gilded youth.]

Jew (jo͞o) *n.* **1.** An adherent of Judaism. **2.** A descendant of the Hebrew people. [ME *Jeu* < OFr. *giu* < Lat. *Judaeus* < Gk. *Ioudaios* < Aram. *Yəhūdāy* < Heb. *Yĕhūdī,* after *Yĕhūdāh,* Judah, son of Jacob and Leah.]

jew·el (jo͞o'əl) *n.* **1.** A costly ornament of precious metal or gems used as adornment. **2.** A precious stone; gem. **3.** A small gem or gem substitute used as a bearing in a watch. **4.** One that is treasured or esteemed. —*tr.v.* **-eled, -el·ing, -els** or **-elled, -el·ling, -els. 1.** To adorn with jewels. **2.** To fit with jewels, as a watch. [ME *juel* < OFr. *jöel* < perh. < *jeu,* game < Lat. *jocus,* joke.]

jew·el·er also **jew·el·ler** (jo͞o'ə-lər) *n.* A person who makes, repairs, or deals in jewelry.

jew·el·fish (jo͞o'əl-fĭsh') *n., pl.* **jewelfish** or **-fish·es.** A small, brilliantly colored freshwater fish, *Hemichromis bimaculatus,* of tropical Africa, popular in home aquariums.

jew·el·ry (jo͞o'əl-rē) *n.* Jewels, esp. ornaments made of precious metals set with gems or from imitation materials.

jew·el·weed (jo͞o'əl-wēd') *n.* Any of several plants of the genus *Impatiens,* having yellowish, spurred flowers and seed pods that burst open at a touch when ripe.

Jew·ess (jo͞o'ĭs) *n.* A Jewish woman.

jew·fish (jo͞o'fĭsh') *n., pl.* **jewfish** or **-fish·es.** Any of several large marine fishes of the family Serranidae, esp. *Epinephelus itajara,* of tropical Atlantic waters.

Jew·ish (jo͞o'ĭsh) *adj.* Of, concerning, or characteristic of the Jews, their customs, or their religion. **—Jew'ish·ly** *adv.* **—Jew'ish·ness** *n.*

Jewish calendar *n.* A calendar used by the Jewish people that dates the creation of the world at 3761 B.C. See table at **calendar.**

Jew·ry (jo͞o'rē) *n.* **1.** The Jewish people. **2.** A section of a medieval city inhabited by Jews; ghetto.

jew's-harp also **jews'-harp** (jo͞oz'härp') *n.* A small musical instrument with a lyre-shaped metal frame and a projecting steel tongue that is held between the teeth when played.

Jez·e·bel (jĕz'ə-bĕl', -bəl) *n.* **1.** A Phoenician princess of the 9th century B.C., and a queen of Israel as the wife of Ahab. **2. jezebel.** A scheming, evil woman. [Heb. *Izebhel.*]

JHVH or **JHWH** *n.* Variants of **YHWH.**

jib[1] (jĭb) *n.* **1.** *Naut.* A triangular sail stretching from the foretopmast head to the jib boom and in small craft to the bowsprit or the bow. **2. a.** The arm of a mechanical crane. **b.** The boom of a derrick. —*v.* **jibbed, jib·bing, jibs.** *Naut.* —*intr.* To jibe. —*tr.* To cause (a sail) to jibe. [Orig. unknown.]

jib[2] (jĭb) *intr.v.* **jibbed, jib·bing, jibs. 1.** To stop short and turn restively from side to side; balk. Used of an animal. **2.** To draw back, balk, or shy. —*n.* Also **jib·ber** (jĭb'ər). An animal that jibs. [Orig. unknown.]

jib boom *n.* *Naut.* A spar forming a continuation of the bowsprit.

jibe[1] (jīb) *v.* **jibed, jib·ing, jibes.** —*intr.* To shift a fore-and-aft sail from one side of a vessel to the other while sailing before the wind. —*tr.* To cause to jibe. [Perh. < obs. Du. *gijben.*]

jibe[2] (jīb) *intr.v.* **jibed, jib·ing, jibes.** *Informal.* To be in accord; agree. [Orig. unknown.]

jibe[3] (jīb) *v. & n.* Variant of **gibe.**

jif·fy (jĭf'ē) also **jiff** (jĭf) *n.* *Informal.* An indeterminately short period of time: *I'll be there in a jiffy.* [Orig. unknown.]

jig (jĭg) *n.* **1. a.** Any of various lively dances in triple time. **b.** The music for such a dance. **2.** A joke or trick. **3.** A typically metal fishing lure with one or more hooks, usually fished on or near the bottom with a jiggling retrieve. **4.** An apparatus for cleaning or separating ore by agitation in water. **5.** A device for guiding a tool or for holding machine work in place. —*v.* **jigged, jig·ging, jigs.** —*intr.* **1.** To dance or play a jig. **2.** To move or bob up and down jerkily and rapidly. **3.** To operate a jig. —*tr.* **1.** To bob or jerk up and down or to and fro. **2.** To machine with the aid of a jig. **3.** To separate or clean (ore) by shaking a jig. [Orig. unknown.]

jig·ger[1] (jĭg'ər) *n.* **1.** A person who jigs or operates a jig. **2. a.** A small measure for liquor, usually holding 1½ ounces. **b.** This amount of liquor. **3.** A device that operates with a jerking or jolting motion, as a drill. **4.** *Naut.* **a.** A light all-purpose tackle. **b.** A small sail set in the stern of a yawl or similar boat. **5.** A trivial article or device whose name eludes one; gadget.

jig·ger[2] (jĭg'ər) *n.* **1.** The chigger (sense 1). **2.** The chigoe (sense 1). [Var. of CHIGOE.]

jigger mast *n.* **1.** The short after mast from which the jigger sail is set on a ketch or yawl. **2.** The fourth mast aft on a four-masted ship.

jig·gle (jĭg'əl) *v.* **-gled, -gling, -gles.** —*intr.* To move or rock lightly up and down or to and fro in an unsteady, jerky manner. —*tr.* To cause to jiggle. —*n.* A jiggling motion. [Freq. of JIG.]

jig·saw (jĭg'sô') *n.* A usually power-driven saw with a narrow vertical reciprocating blade, used to cut sharp curves.

jigsaw puzzle *n.* A puzzle consisting of a mass of irregularly shaped pieces of cardboard, plastic, or wood that form a picture when fitted together.

ji·had (jĭ-häd') *n.* **1.** A Moslem holy war against infidels. **2.** A crusade. [Ar. *jihād.*]

jill (jĭl) *n.* Variant of **gill[4].**

jil·lion (jĭl'yən) *n.* An indeterminately large number. [Alteration of MILLION.]

jilt (jĭlt) *tr.v.* **jilt·ed, jilt·ing, jilts.** To deceive or drop (a lover) suddenly or callously. —*n.* A woman who discards a lover. [Orig. unknown.]

jim-crow also **Jim-Crow** (jĭm'krō') *adj.* *Slang.* **1.** Favoring or promoting the segregation of blacks: *jim-crow policies.* **2.** For blacks only: *a jim-crow waiting room.* [< *Jim Crow.*]

Jim Crow or **jim crow** *n.* *Slang.* The systematic practice of discriminating against and suppressing black people. [< *Jim Crow,* derogatory term for a black person, ult. < the title of a 19th-century song.] **—Jim'-Crow'ism** *n.*

jim-dan·dy (jĭm'dăn'dē) *adj.* *Informal.* One that is very pleasing or excellent of its kind. [*Jim,* nickname for *James* + DANDY.]

jim-jams (jĭm'jămz') *pl.n.* *Slang.* **1.** The jitters. **2.** Delirium tremens. [Orig. unknown.]

Jim·mies (jĭm'ēz). A trademark for chocolate sprinkles for ice cream.

jim·my (jĭm'ē) *n., pl.* **-mies.** A short crowbar with curved ends. —*tr.v.* **-mied, -my·ing, -mies.** To pry open with or as if with a jimmy. [< the name *Jimmy,* nickname for *James.*]

jim·son·weed (jĭm'sən-wēd') *n.* A coarse, poisonous plant, *Datura stramonium,* having large, trumpet-shaped white or purplish flowers and prickly fruit. [Alteration of E. *Jamestown weed,* after *Jamestown,* Virginia.]

jin·gle (jĭng'gəl) *v.* **-gled, -gling, -gles.** —*intr.* **1.** To make a tinkling or ringing metallic sound. **2.** To have the catchy sound of a poetic jingle. —*tr.* To cause to jingle. —*n.* **1. a.** The sound produced by bits of metal striking together. **b.** Something resembling or suggesting this. **2.** A simple, repetitious, catchy rhyme or doggerel. [ME *ginglen.*]

jingle shell *n.* The thin, translucent, rounded, yellowish or grayish shell of any of several marine bivalve mollusks of the genus *Anomia.*

jin·go (jĭng'gō) *n., pl.* **-goes.** One who vociferously supports his country, esp. one who supports a belligerent foreign policy; blatant patriot; chauvinist. —*adj.* **1.** Of or pertaining to a jingo. **2.** Characterized by jingoism. —*interj.* **by jingo.** Used to express surprise or for emphasis. [From the phrase *by jingo,* used in the refrain of a bellicose English song.] **—jin'go·ish** *adj.*

jin·go·ism (jĭng'gō-ĭz'əm) *n.* Extreme nationalism or chauvinism characterized esp. by a belligerent foreign policy. **—jin'go·ist** *n.* **—jin'go·is'tic** *adj.* **—jin'go·is'ti·cal·ly** *adv.*

jink (jĭngk) *intr.v.* **jinked, jink·ing, jinks.** To make a quick, evasive turn. —*n.* **1.** A sudden evasive turn. **2. jinks.** Rambunctious play; frolic. [Orig. unknown.]

jin·ni also **jin·nee** (jĭn'ē, jĭ-nē') *n., pl.* **jinn** (jĭn). In Moslem legend, a spirit capable of assuming human or animal form and exercising supernatural influence over men. [Ar. *jinnīy.*]

jin·rik·sha or **jin·rick·sha** also **jin·rik·i·sha** (jĭn-rĭk'shô') *n.* A small, two-wheeled, oriental carriage drawn by one or two men. [J. *jinrikisha* : *jin,* man + *riki,* strength + *sha,* vehicle (of Chin. orig.).]

jinx (jĭngks) *Informal.* —*n.* **1.** One believed to bring bad luck. **2.** A condition or period of bad luck caused by a jinx.

—tr.v. **jinxed, jinx·ing, jinx·es.** To bring bad luck or misfortune to. [Poss. < E. *jynx,* wryneck (from the use of the bird in witchcraft) < Lat. *iynx* < Gk. *iunx* < *iuzein,* to call.]

ji·pi·ja·pa (hē'pē-hä'pə) *n.* A palmlike plant, *Carludovica palmata,* of Central and South America, having long-stalked, fanlike leaves that are used to make Panama hats. [Sp. (South America) after *Jipijapa,* Ecuador.]

jit·ney (jĭt'nē) *n., pl.* **-neys. 1.** *Informal.* A small bus or automobile that transports passengers on a route for a small fare. **2.** *Archaic.* A nickel. [Orig. unknown.]

jit·ter (jĭt'ər) *intr.v.* **-tered, -ter·ing, -ters.** To be nervous or uneasy; fidget. *—n.* **1.** A jittering movement; tic. **2. jitters.** A fit of nervousness. [Orig. unknown.]

jit·ter·bug (jĭt'ər-bŭg') *n.* **1.** A strenuous dance performed to quick-tempo jazz or swing music and consisting of various two-step patterns embellished with twirls and sometimes acrobatic maneuvers, esp. popular in the 1940's. **2.** A person who dances the jitterbug. *—intr.v.* **-bugged, -bug·ging, -bugs.** To dance the jitterbug.

jit·ter·y (jĭt'ə-rē) *adj.* **-i·er, -i·est. 1.** Having or feeling the jitters. **2.** Marked by jittering movements.

jiu·jit·su or **jiu·jut·su** (jo͞o-jĭt'so͞o) *n.* Variants of **jujitsu.**

jive (jīv) *Slang. —n.* **1.** Jazz or swing music. **2.** The jargon of jazz musicians and enthusiasts. **3.** Deceptive, nonsensical, or glib talk. *—v.* **jived, jiv·ing, jives.** *—intr.* **1.** To play or dance to jive music. **2.** To talk nonsense; kid. *—tr.* To cajole or mislead. *—adj.* Misleading; phony. [Orig. unknown.] **—jiv'er** *n.*

job[1] (jŏb) *n.* **1.** An action that needs to be done; task. **2.** A regular activity performed in exchange for payment, esp. a trade, occupation, or profession. **3. a.** A specific piece of work to be done for a set fee: *an expensive repair job.* **b.** The object to be worked on. **c.** Something resulting from or produced by work. **4.** A position in which one is employed. **5.** A specified duty or responsibility: *It was her job to clean the yard.* **6.** *Computer Sci.* A program application to be performed as a single logical unit. **7.** *Informal.* A difficult or strenuous task: *It was a rough job to convince her to come to the game.* **8.** *Informal.* A bad or unsatisfactory piece of work: *Boy, he did a job on her hair.* **9.** *Informal.* A state of affairs: *Their marriage turned out to be a bad job.* **10.** *Informal.* A criminal act, esp. a robbery: *a bank job.* **11.** Something done ostensibly for the public welfare, but actually for improper private gain. *—v.* **jobbed, job·bing, jobs.** *—intr.* **1.** To work at odd jobs. **2.** To work by the piece. **3.** To act as a middleman or jobber. **4.** To exploit one's position for private profits. *—tr.* **1.** To purchase (merchandise) from manufacturers and sell it to retailers. **2.** To arrange for (contracted work) to be done in portions by others; subcontract. **3.** To transact (official business) dishonestly for private profit. **—*idiom.* on the job.** Paying close attention; on the alert. [Perh. < obs. *job,* piece.]

job[2] (jŏb) *Archaic. —tr. & intr.v.* **jobbed, job·bing, jobs.** To jab or make a jab. *—n.* A jab. [ME *jobben.*]

Job (jōb) *n.* **1.** In the Old Testament, an upright man whose faith in God survived the test of repeated calamities. **2.** See table at **Bible.** [LLat. < Gk. *Iōb* < Heb. *Iyyōbh.*]

job action *n.* A temporary action, as a strike or slowdown, by workers to exact demands or to protest a company decision.

job·ber (jŏb'ər) *n.* **1.** One who buys merchandise from manufacturers and sells it to retailers. **2.** One who works by the piece or at odd jobs. **3.** *Chiefly Brit.* A middleman in the exchange of stocks and securities among brokers.

job·ber·y (jŏb'ə-rē) *n.* Corruption among public officials. [< JOB[1] (to seek graft).]

job control language *n.* A computer language used for communication with a computer's operating system.

job·hold·er (jŏb'hōl'dər) *n.* One who has a regular job.

job-hop (jŏb'hŏp') *intr.v.* **-hopped, -hop·ping, -hops.** To engage in job-hopping. **—job'-hop'per** *n.*

job-hop·ping (jŏb'hŏp'ĭng) *n.* The practice of changing jobs frequently, esp. as a means of quick financial gain.

job·less (jŏb'lĭs) *adj.* **1.** Being without a job. **2.** Of or relating to those who are without jobs. **—job'less·ness** *n.*

job lot *n.* **1.** Miscellaneous merchandise sold in one lot. **2.** A collection of cheap items.

job·name (jŏb'nām') *n.* *Computer Sci.* A code assigned to a specific job instruction in a computer program for user reference.

Job's comforter *n.* One who discourages or saddens while seemingly offering sympathy or comfort. [After *Job,* who was given false sympathy by his friends.]

Job's-tears (jōbz'tîrz') *n. (used with a sing. or pl. verb).* **1.** A grass, *Coix lacryma-jobi,* of tropical Asia, having white, beadlike seeds. **2.** The edible seeds of the Job's-tears.

job stick *n. Printing.* A composing stick.

Jo·cas·ta (jō-kăs'tə) *n. Gk. Myth.* A Theban queen who unknowingly married her own son, Oedipus. [Gk. *Iokastē.*]

jock[1] (jŏk) *n.* **1.** A jockey. **2.** A disc jockey. [Short for JOCKEY.]

jock[2] (jŏk) *n.* **1.** A jockstrap. **2.** *Slang.* **a.** A male athlete, esp. in college. **b.** One characterized by excessive concern for machismo. [Short for JOCKSTRAP.]

jock·ey (jŏk'ē) *n., pl.* **-eys. 1.** One who rides horses in races, esp. as a profession. **2.** *Slang.* One who operates a specified vehicle, machine, or device: *a bus jockey.* *—v.* **-eyed, -ey·ing, -eys.** *—tr.* **1.** To ride (a horse) as jockey. **2.** To direct or maneuver by cleverness or skill: *jockeyed the car into a tight space.* **3.** To trick; cheat. *—intr.* **1.** To ride a horse in a race. **2.** To maneuver for a certain position or advantage. **3.** To employ trickery. [Dim. of Sc. *Jock,* var. of *Jack,* nickname for *John.*]

Jock·ey (jŏk'ē). A trademark for briefs for men.

jock·strap also **jock strap** (jŏk'străp') *n.* An athletic supporter. [Slang *jock,* penis + STRAP.]

jo·cose (jō-kōs') *adj.* **1.** Given to joking; merry. **2.** Characterized by joking; humorous. [Lat. *jocosus* < *jocus,* joke.] **—jo·cose'ly** *adv.* **—jo·cose'ness, jo·cos'i·ty** (-ĭ-tē) *n.*

joc·u·lar (jŏk'yə-lər) *adj.* **1.** Given to or characterized by joking. **2.** Meant in jest; facetious. [Lat. *jocularis,* droll < *joculus,* dim. of *jocus,* joke.] **—joc'u·lar'i·ty** (-lăr'ĭ-tē) *n.* **—joc'u·lar·ly** *adv.*

joc·und (jŏk'ənd, jō'kənd) *adj.* Having a cheerful disposition or quality; merry. [ME *jocound* < OFr. *jocond* < LLat. *jocundus* < Lat. *jucundus* < *juvare,* to delight.] **—jo·cun'di·ty** (jō-kŭn'dĭ-tē) *n.* **—joc'und·ly** *adv.*

jodh·pur boots (jŏd'pər) *n.* Short ankle-height leather boots worn with jodhpurs for riding.

jodh·purs (jŏd'pərz) *pl.n.* Wide-hipped riding breeches of heavy cloth, fitting tightly at the knees and ankles. [After *Jodhpur,* a region in India.]

Jo·el (jō'əl) *n.* **1.** A Hebrew Minor Prophet. **2.** See table at **Bible.** [Heb. *Yō'ēl.*]

joe-pye weed (jō'pī') *n.* Any of several tall North American plants of the genus *Eupatorium,* having whorled leaves and terminal clusters of small pinkish or purplish flowers. [Orig. unknown.]

jo·ey (jō'ē) *n., pl.* **-eys.** *Austral.* A young animal, esp. a kangaroo. [Native word in Australia.]

jog[1] (jŏg) *v.* **jogged, jog·ging, jogs.** *—tr.* **1.** To jar or move by shoving, bumping, or jerking. **2.** To give a slight push or shake to; nudge. **3.** To stimulate (one's memory, for example); stir. *—intr.* **1. a.** To run or ride at a steady slow trot. **b.** To run in such a way for sport or exercise. **2.** To proceed in a leisurely manner with or as if with occasional bumps: *"while his life was thus jogging easily along"* (Duff Cooper). *—n.* **1.** A slight jolt or shake. **2.** A nudge. **3.** A slow steady pace. [Orig. unknown.] **—jog'ger** *n.*

jog[2] (jŏg) *n.* **1.** A protruding or receding part in a surface or line. **2.** An abrupt change in direction. *—intr.v.* **jogged, jog·ing, jogs.** To turn sharply; veer. [Perh. var. of JAG[1].]

jog·ging *n.* Exercise that consists of running at a slow, regular pace or alternately running and walking.

jog·gle[1] (jŏg'əl) *v.* **-gled, -gling, -gles.** *—tr.* To shake or jar slightly. *—intr.* To move with a shaking or jolting motion. *—n.* A shaking or jolting motion. [Freq. of JOG[1].]

jog·gle[2] (jŏg'əl) *n.* **1.** A joint between two pieces of building material formed by a notch and a fitted projection. **2.** The notch or the projecting piece used in a joggle. *—tr.v.* **-gled, -gling, -gles.** To join or attach by means of a joggle. [< JOG[2].]

jog trot *n.* **1.** A slow, steady, jolting pace. **2.** A regular, humdrum way of living or of doing something.

john (jŏn) *n. Slang.* **1.** A toilet. **2.** A prostitute's customer. [< the name *John.*]

John (jŏn) *n.* **1.** One of the Twelve Apostles, and the reputed author of the 4th Gospel, three epistles, and Book of Revelation. **2.** See table at **Bible.**

John Bar·ley·corn (jŏn' bär'lē-kôrn') *n.* A personification of malt liquor or of alcoholic beverages in general.

John Birch Society (jŏn' bûrch') *n.* An ultraconservative anticommunist organization established by Robert Welch in 1958. [After *John Birch* (d. 1945).] **—John Bircher** *n.*

John Bull (jŏn' bo͝ol') *n.* **1.** A personification of England or the English. **2.** A typical Englishman. [After *John Bull,* a character in *Law is a Bottomless Pit* by John Arbuthnot (1667–1735).]

John Doe (jŏn' dō') *n.* **1.** A name used in legal proceedings to designate a fictitious or unidentified person. **2.** An average, undistinguished man.

John Do·ry (jŏn' dôr'ē, dōr'ē) *n.* Either of two fishes, *Zenopsis ocellata,* of the western Atlantic, or *Zeus faber,* of the eastern Atlantic, having spiny fins and a laterally compressed body.

John Han·cock (jŏn' hăn'kŏk') *n. Informal.* A person's signature. [After *John Hancock* (1737–1793), from the prominence of his signature on the Declaration of Independence.]

john·ny·cake (jŏn'ē-kāk') *n.* A corncake.

John·ny-come-late·ly (jŏn'ē-kŭm-lāt'lē) *n., pl.* **-lies.** *Informal.* A newcomer or latecomer, esp. a recent adherent to a cause or fashion.

John·ny-jump-up (jŏn'ē-jŭmp'ŭp') *n.* The heartsease (sense 2). [From its quick growth.]

John·ny-on-the-spot (jŏn'ē-ŏn'*th*ə-spŏt', -ôn'-) *n. Informal.* A person who is available and ready to act when necessary.

John·ny Reb (jŏn'ē rĕb') *n. Informal.* A Confederate soldier.

John·son grass (jŏn'sən) *n.* A coarse grass, *Sorghum halepense,* native to the Mediterranean area, cultivated for forage, but often a troublesome weed. [After William Johnson (d. 1859).]

John·so·ni·an (jŏn-sō'nē-ən) *adj.* Of, resembling, or relating

jockey

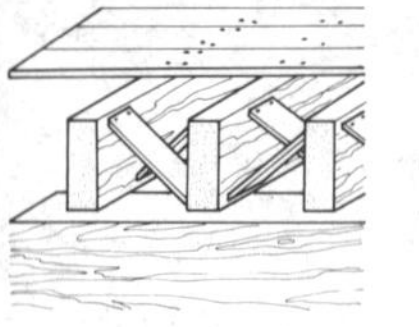

joist

joker
Playing card

jonquil

to Samuel Johnson or his writings. —*n.* An admirer or student of Samuel Johnson or his work.

John·son noise (jŏn′sən) *n.* Thermal noise. [After John B. *Johnson* (1887–1970).]

joie de vi·vre (zhwä′ də vē′vrə) *n.* Hearty or carefree enjoyment of life. [Fr., joy of living.]

join (join) *v.* **joined, join·ing, joins.** —*tr.* **1.** To put or bring together so as to make continuous or form a unit: *joined hands in a circle.* **2.** To put or bring into close association or relationship: *joined by marriage; join forces.* **3.** *Math.* To connect (points), as with a straight line. **4.** To form a junction with: *where the stream joins the river.* **5.** To become a part or member of. **6.** To take a place among, in, or with: *I'll join you later.* **7.** *Informal.* To adjoin. —*intr.* **1.** To come or act together so as to form a connection: *Many townspeople joined in the search.* **2.** To become a member of a group. **3.** To take part; participate: *He joined in the singing.* —*n.* A joint; junction. [ME *joinen* < OFr. *joindre* < Lat. *jungere.*]

Synonyms: *join, combine, unite, consolidate, link, connect, relate, associate.* These verbs refer to the bringing or coming together of persons or things. *Join* is applied to the physical attachment of things and to the coming together of persons, usually in a close relationship. *Combine* suggests mixing or merging of related components to effect a specific purpose. *Unite* stresses the coherence or oneness of persons or things joined. *Consolidate* implies a particular compactness or closeness of merged components. *Link* and especially *connect* imply a looser relationship in which individual units retain their identities while coming together at some point, either through physical contact or mental association. *Relate* refers to attachment of persons through kinship or to connection of things through logical association. *Associate* implies a relationship of persons having common aims, interests, or the like or a relationship of things that are similar, complementary, or have connection in one's thoughts.

join·der (join′dər) *n.* **1.** The act of joining. **2.** *Law.* **a.** A joining of causes of action or defense in a suit. **b.** A joining of parties in a suit. **c.** The formal acceptance of an issue offered. [< Fr. *joindre,* to join < Lat. *jungere.*]

join·er (joi′nər) *n.* **1.** One that joins. **2.** *Chiefly Brit.* A carpenter, esp. a cabinetmaker. **3.** *Informal.* A person given to joining groups, organizations, or causes.

joint (joint) *n.* **1. a.** A point or position at which two or more things are joined. **b.** A configuration in or by which two or more things are joined. **2.** The manner of joining. **3.** *Anat.* A point of connection or articulation between more or less movable parts, as between bones or between segments in the leg of an arthropod. **4.** *Bot.* A point on a stem from which a leaf or branch may grow; node. **5.** *Geol.* A fracture or crack in a rock mass along which no appreciable movement has occurred. **6.** A large cut of meat for roasting. **7.** *Slang.* **a.** A cheap or disreputable gathering place, such as a sleazy bar. **b.** A public establishment or dwelling. **8.** *Slang.* A marijuana cigarette. **9.** *Vulgar Slang.* A penis. —*adj.* **1.** Shared by or common to two or more: *a joint income-tax return.* **2.** Sharing with another or others. **3.** Formed or characterized by cooperation or united action. **4.** Involving both houses of a legislature: *a joint session.* **5.** *Law.* Regarded as one legal body; united in identity of interest or liability. **6.** *Math.* Involving two or more variables. —*tr.v.* **joint·ed, joint·ing, joints. 1.** To combine or attach at a joint or joints. **2.** To provide or construct with joints. **3.** To cut (meat) into joints. —***idiom.*** **out of joint. 1.** Dislocated, as a bone. **2.** Not harmonious; inconsistent. **3.** Out of order; unsatisfactory. **4.** In bad spirits or humor; out of sorts. —See Usage note at **mutual.** [ME < OFr. < p.part. of *joindre,* to join < Lat. *jungere.*] —**joint′ed** *adj.*

Joint Chiefs of Staff *n.* The principal military advisory group to the President of the United States, composed of the chiefs of the Army, Navy, and Air Force, and sometimes the commandant of the Marines.

joint·er (join′tər) *n.* One that joints, esp. a machine or tool used in making joints.

joint·ly (joint′lē) *adv.* Together; in common.

joint probability *n.* The probability that two or more specific outcomes will occur in an event.

joint resolution *n.* A resolution passed by both houses of a bicameral legislature and eligible to become a law if signed by the chief executive or passed over the chief executive's veto.

joint stock *n.* Stock or capital funds of a company held jointly or in common by its owners.

joint-stock company (joint′stŏk′) *n.* A business whose capital is held in transferable shares of stock by its joint owners.

join·ture (join′chər) *n.* **1.** *Law.* **a.** An arrangement by which a man may set aside property to be used for the support of his wife after his death. **b.** The property so designated. **2.** *Obs.* The act of joining or the state of being joined. [ME < OFr., a joining < Lat. *junctura* < *junctus,* p.part. of *jungere,* to join.]

joint·worm (joint′wûrm′) *n.* The larva of certain wasps of the family Eurytomidae, esp. of *Harmolita tritici,* infesting wheat and causing hard swellings in the stems.

joist (joist) *n.* Any of the parallel horizontal beams set from wall to wall to support the boards of a floor or ceiling. —*tr.v.* **joist·ed, joist·ing, joists.** To construct with joists. [ME. *giste* < OFr., ult. < Lat. *jacēre,* to lie.]

jo·jo·ba (hə-hō′bə) *n.* A shrub, *Simmondsia Californica,* of southwestern North America with edible seeds that contain a valuable oil. [Mex. Sp.]

joke (jōk) *n.* **1.** A brief, amusing story, esp. one with a punch line. **2.** An amusing or jesting remark; pun. **3.** A mischievous trick; prank. **4.** An amusing or ludicrous incident or situation. **5.** Something not to be taken seriously; triviality: *His accident was no joke.* **6.** An object of amusement or laughter; laughingstock. —*v.* **joked, jok·ing, jokes.** —*intr.* **1.** To tell or play jokes; jest. **2.** To speak in fun; be facetious. —*tr.* To make fun of; tease. [Lat. *jocus.*] —**jok′ing·ly** *adv.*

Synonyms: *joke, jest, witticism, quip, sally, crack, wisecrack, gag.* These nouns refer to forms of humorous sayings or actions. *Joke* and *jest,* which can denote something said or done, are approximately interchangeable, though *jest* now occurs infrequently in this sense. *Witticism* refers to verbal humor, usually with an intellectual flavor and neatly phrased. *Quip* suggests a light, pointed, bantering remark, and *sally* a sudden, clever, or witty statement. *Crack* and *wisecrack* refer less formally to flippant or mocking retorts or to impromptu remarks in response to a specific situation. *Gag* is principally applicable to a broadly comic remark or, less often, to comic by-play in a theatrical routine.

jok·er (jō′kər) *n.* **1. a.** A person who tells or plays jokes. **b.** An insolent person who seeks to make a show of cleverness. **2.** A playing card, usually printed with a picture of a jester, used in certain games as the highest ranking card or as a wild card. **3.** A minor clause in a document such as a legislative bill that voids or changes its original or intended purpose. **4.** An unseen or unpredicted difficulty, fact, or circumstance. **5.** A deceptive means of getting the better of someone.

jol·li·fi·ca·tion (jŏl′ə-fĭ-kā′shən) *n.* Festivity; revelry. [< JOLLY.]

jol·li·ty (jŏl′ĭ-tē) *n.* Gaiety; merriment.

jol·ly (jŏl′ē) *adj.* **-li·er, -li·est. 1.** Full of merriment and good spirits; fun-loving. **2.** Exhibiting or occasioning happiness or mirth; cheerful. **3.** Greatly pleasing; enjoyable. —*adv. Chiefly Brit. Informal.* Very; extremely: *a jolly good cook.* —*v.* **-lied, -ly·ing, -lies.** —*tr.* To keep amused or diverted for one's own purposes; humor. —*intr.* To amuse oneself with humorous or teasing banter. —*n., pl.* **-lies. 1.** *Chiefly Brit.* A good or festive time. **2. jollies.** *Slang.* Amusement; kicks: *However you get your jollies is fine with me.* [ME *joli* < OFr.] —**jol′li·ly** *adv.* —**jol′li·ness** *n.*

Synonyms: *jolly, jovial, merry, blithe, jocular, convivial.* These adjectives describe persons who show good humor or high spirits or who are companionable in general. *Jolly* and *jovial* are especially associated with outward display of good cheer that invites friendship and promotes camaraderie. *Merry* suggests love of fun and laughter, and *blithe* implies buoyancy and freedom from care. *Jocular* refers to one who is sportive or given to joking and *convivial* to one who derives great pleasure from the cheerful companionship of others.

jol·ly·boat (jŏl′ē-bōt′) *n.* A medium-sized ship's boat used for rough work and minor tasks. [Perh. alteration of obs. *jolywat.*]

Jolly Rog·er (rŏj′ər) *n.* A black flag bearing the emblematic white skull and crossbones of a pirate ship.

jolt (jōlt) *v.* **jolt·ed, jolt·ing, jolts.** —*tr.* **1.** To bump into. **2.** To shake or knock about. **3.** To jar with or as if with a sudden, sharp blow. **4.** To put into a specified condition by or as if by a blow: *"now and then he jolted a nodding reader awake by inserting a witty paragraph"* (Walter Blair). —*intr.* To proceed in an irregular, bumpy, or jerky fashion. —*n.* **1.** A sudden jarring or jerking, as from a blow. **2.** An abrupt or unexpected shock or reversal: *The news came as a jolt.* [Orig. unknown.] —**jolt′er** *n.* —**jolt′i·ly** *adv.* —**jolt′i·ness** *n.* —**jolt′y** *adj.*

Jo·ma·da (jə-mä′dä) *n.* Variant of **Jumada.**

Jo·nah (jō′nə) *n.* **1.** An Old Testament prophet who was thrown overboard during a storm at sea caused by his disobedience to God, swallowed by a great fish, and disgorged unharmed three days later. **2.** See table at **Bible. 3.** One thought to bring bad luck. [Heb. *Yōnāh.*]

Jon·a·than[1] (jŏn′ə-thən) *n.* In the Old Testament, the eldest son of King Saul of Israel and friend of David. [Heb. *Yōnāthān.*]

Jon·a·than[2] (jŏn′ə-thən) *n.* A variety of red, late-ripening apple. [After *Jonathan* Hasbrouck (d. 1846).]

jones (jōnz) *n. Slang.* **1.** An addiction to heroin. **2.** Heroin. [Perh. < the name *Jones.*]

jon·gleur (zhôN-glœr′) *n.* A wandering minstrel and storyteller in medieval England and France. [Fr. < OFr., var. of *joglere.* —see JUGGLER.]

jon·quil (jŏng′kwəl, jŏn′-) *n.* A widely cultivated plant, *Narcissus jonquilla,* having long, narrow leaves and short-tubed, fragrant yellow flowers. [NLat. *Jonquilla,* species name < Sp. *junquillo,* dim. of *junco,* reed < Lat. *juncus.*]

Jor·dan almond (jôr′dn) *n.* **1.** A large variety of almond from Málaga, Spain, used widely in confections. **2.** An almond covered with a hard, colored and flavored sugar coating. [By folk ety. < ME *jardin almaund* : OFr. *jardin,* garden (of Germanic orig.) + ME *almaund,* almond. —see ALMOND.]

Jor·dan curve (jôr'dn) *n.* A curve, as a circle, that is closed and does not intersect itself. [After Camille *Jordan* (1838–1922).]

Jordan curve theorem *n.* A basic theorem of topology that states that every simple closed curve divides a plane into two regions and acts as the common boundary between them.

jo·rum (jôr'əm, jōr'-) *n.* **1.** A large drinking bowl. **2.** The amount contained by a jorum. [Perh. after *Joram,* who brought vessels of silver, gold, and brass to King David.]

Jo·seph (jō'zəf, -səf) *n.* **1.** In the Old Testament, son of Jacob and Rachel, sold into slavery in Egypt. **2.** In the New Testament, the husband of Mary the mother of Jesus. **3. joseph.** A long riding coat with a small cape, worn by women in the 18th century. [Heb. *Yōsēph.*]

Joseph of Ar·i·ma·the·a (ăr'ə-mə-thē'ə) *n.* In the New Testament, an Israelite who provided a tomb for Jesus and who is the subject of many legends.

Jo·seph·son effect (jō'zəf-sən, -səf-) *n.* The radiative effect associated with the passage of electron pairs across an insulating barrier separating two superconductors. [After B. D. *Josephson,* (b. 1940).]

Josephson junction *n.* An insulating barrier producing the Josephson effect.

josh (jŏsh) *v.* **joshed, josh·ing, josh·es.** *—tr.* To tease (someone) good-humoredly. *—intr.* To banter; joke. *—n.* A teasing or joking remark. [Orig. unknown.]

Josh·u·a (jŏsh'o͞o-ə) *n.* **1.** Successor of Moses in the Exodus. **2.** See table at **Bible.** [Heb. *Yĕhōshūa.*]

Joshua tree *n.* A treelike plant, *Yucca brevifolia,* of the southwestern United States, having sword-shaped leaves and greenish-white flowers. [Prob. after JOSHUA, from the resemblance of the tree's greatly extended branches to Joshua's outstretched arm as he pointed with his spear to the city of Ai.]

joss (jŏs) *n.* A Chinese idol or image. [Pidgin E. < Port. *deos,* god < Lat. *deus.*]

joss house *n.* A Chinese temple or shrine.

joss stick *n.* A stick of incense burned before a joss.

jos·tle (jŏs'əl) *v.* **-tled, -tling, -tles.** *—intr.* **1.** To come in contact or collide. **2.** To make one's way by pushing or elbowing. **3.** To vie for an advantage or position. **4.** To be in close proximity. *—tr.* **1.** To come into contact or collision with. **2.** To force by pushing or elbowing. **3.** To vie with for an advantage or position. **4.** To be in close proximity with: *"books written in all languages by men and women of all tempers, races, and ages jostle each other on the shelf"* (Virginia Woolf). *—n.* **1.** A rough shove or push. **2.** The state of being crowded together. [Obs. *justle,* freq. of *just,* to joust < ME *justen* < OFr. *juster.* —see JOUST.]

jot (jŏt) *n.* The smallest bit; iota. *—tr.v.* **jot·ted, jot·ting, jots.** To write down briefly or hastily: *jot down an address.* [Lat. *iota* < Gk. *iōta,* iota.]

jot·ting (jŏt'ĭng) *n.* A brief note or memorandum.

Jo·tun·heim (yô'to͝on-hām') also **Jö·tunn·heim** (yœ'-) *n. Myth.* Utgard. [ON *jötunheimar* : *jötunn,* giant + *heimr,* home.]

joule (jo͞ol, joul) *n.* **1.** The International System unit of energy, equal to the work done when a current of 1 ampere is passed through a resistance of 1 ohm for 1 second. **2.** A unit of energy, equal to the work done when the point of application of a force of 1 newton is displaced 1 meter in the direction of the force. [After James P. *Joule* (1818–1889).]

jounce (jouns) *intr. & tr.v.* **jounced, jounc·ing, jounc·es.** To move or cause to move with bumps and jolts; bounce. *—n.* A rough, jolting bounce. [ME *jouncen.*]

jour·nal (jûr'nəl) *n.* **1. a.** A personal record of occurrences, experiences, and reflections kept on a regular basis; a diary. **b.** A record or account of daily events. **c.** An official record of daily proceedings, as of a legislative body. **d.** A ship's log. **2.** *Accounting.* **a.** A daybook. **b.** A book of original entry in a double-entry system, listing all transactions and indicating the accounts to which they belong. **3.** A newspaper. **4.** A periodical presenting news in a particular area: *a medical journal.* **5.** The part of a machine shaft or axle supported by a bearing. [ME < OFr. *jornel* < *jornel,* daily < LLat. *diurnalis.* —see DIURNAL.]

journal box *n.* A housing in a machine enclosing a journal and its bearings.

jour·nal·ese (jûr'nə-lēz', -lēs') *n.* The slick, superficial style of writing often held to be characteristic of newspapers and magazines.

jour·nal·ism (jûr'nə-lĭz'əm) *n.* **1.** The collecting, writing, editing, and publishing of news or news articles through newspapers or magazines. **2.** Material written for publication in a newspaper or magazine. **3.** The style of writing characteristic of material in newspapers and magazines, consisting of the direct presentation of facts or occurrences with little attempt at analysis or interpretation. **4.** Newspapers and magazines. **5.** An academic course training one in journalism. **6.** Written material of current interest or wide popular appeal.

jour·nal·ist (jûr'nə-lĭst) *n.* **1.** One whose occupation is journalism. **2.** One who keeps a journal.

jour·nal·is·tic (jûr'nə-lĭs'tĭk) *adj.* Of, pertaining to, or characteristic of journalism or journalists. **—jour'nal·is'ti·cal·ly** *adv.*

jour·nal·ize (jûr'nə-līz') *v.* **-ized, -iz·ing, -iz·es.** *—tr.* To record in a journal. *—intr.* To keep a personal or financial journal. **—jour'nal·iz'er** *n.*

jour·ney (jûr'nē) *n., pl.* **-neys. 1. a.** Travel from one place to another; trip. **b.** The distance to be traveled or the time required for such a trip. **2.** Something suggestive of passage or movement from one place to another: *the journey of life.* *—v.* **-neyed, -ney·ing, -neys.** *—intr.* To make a journey; travel. *—tr.* To travel over or through. [ME *journei,* day, day's travel, journey < OFr. *jornee* < VLat. **diurnata* < Lat. *diurnus,* of a day < *dies,* day.] **—jour'ney·er** *n.*

Joshua tree

jour·ney·man (jûr'nē-mən) *n.* **1.** One who has fully served an apprenticeship in a trade or craft and is a qualified worker in another's employ. **2.** A competent but undistinguished worker. [ME *journeiman* < *journei,* a day's work. —see JOURNEY.]

jour·ney·work (jûr'nē-wûrk') *n.* The work of a journeyman.

joust (joust, jŭst, jo͞ost) also **just** (jŭst) *—n.* **1. a.** A combat with lances between two mounted knights or men-at-arms; a tilting match. **b. jousts.** A series of these matches; tournament. **2.** Personal combat or competition suggestive of a joust. *—intr.v.* **joust·ed, joust·ing, jousts** also **just·ed, just·ing, justs. 1.** To engage in combat on horseback, esp. with lances. **2.** To engage in personal combat or competition. [ME < OFr. *juste* < *juster,* to joust < VLat. **juxtare* < Lat. *juxta,* close together.]

Jove (jōv) *n.* Jupiter (sense 1). *—interj.* **by Jove.** Used to express surprise or emphasis. [ME < Lat. *Jovis.*]

jo·vi·al (jō'vē-əl) *adj.* Marked by hearty conviviality. [Fr. < Ital. *giovale,* born under the planet Jupiter < *Giove,* Jupiter.] **—jo'vi·al'i·ty** *n.* **—jo'vi·al·ly** *adv.*

Jo·vi·an (jō'vē-ən) *adj.* Of, pertaining to, or resembling Jove.

jowl[1] (joul) *n.* **1.** The jaw, esp. the lower jaw. **2.** The cheek. [ME *chaule* < OE *ceafl.*]

jowl[2] (joul) *n.* **1.** The flesh under the lower jaw, esp. when plump or flaccid. **2.** A fleshy part similar to a jowl, as a dewlap or a wattle. [ME *cholle.*]

joy (joi) *n.* **1. a.** A condition or feeling of great pleasure or happiness; delight. **b.** The expression or manifestation of such feeling. **2.** A source or object of pleasure or satisfaction. *—v.* **joyed, joy·ing, joys.** *—intr.* To take great pleasure; rejoice. *—tr. Archaic.* **1.** To fill with joy. **2.** To enjoy. [ME *joi* < OFr. < Lat. *gaudia,* pl. of *gaudium,* joy < *gaudere,* to *rejoice.*]

joy·ance (joi'əns) *n.* Enjoyment; delight.

joy·ful (joi'fəl) *adj.* Feeling, causing, or indicating joy. **—joy'ful·ly** *adv.* **—joy'ful·ness** *n.*

joy·less (joi'lĭs) *adj.* Cheerless; dismal. **—joy'less·ly** *adv.* **—joy'less·ness** *n.*

joy·ous (joi'əs) *adj.* Feeling or causing joy; joyful. **—joy'ous·ly** *adv.* **—joy'ous·ness** *n.*

joy·pop (joi'pŏp') *intr.v.* **-popped, -pop·ping, -pops.** *Slang.* To use narcotic drugs infrequently without becoming addicted. **—joy'pop'per** *n.*

joy ride *n.* **1.** A ride taken for fun and often for the thrills provided by reckless driving. **2.** A hazardous, reckless, and often costly venture.

joy·stick (joi'stĭk') *n. Slang.* **1.** The control stick of an airplane. **2.** A manual control device that resembles an airplane's joystick.

J particle *n.* A neutral meson having an unusually long lifetime.

ju·ba (jo͞o'bə) *n.* A group dance probably of West African origin characterized by complex rhythmic clapping and body movements and practiced on plantations in the South during the 18th and 19th centuries. [Orig. unknown.]

Ju·bal (jo͞o'bəl) *n.* A descendant of Cain who by Biblical account is the inventor of musical instruments.

ju·bi·lant (jo͞o'bə-lənt) *adj.* **1.** Exultingly joyful. **2.** Expressing joy. [Lat. *jubilans, jubilant-,* pr.part. of *jubilare,* to raise a shout of joy.] **—ju'bi·lance, ju'bi·lan·cy** *n.* **—ju'bi·lant·ly** *adv.*

ju·bi·late (jo͞o'bə-lāt') *intr.v.* **-lat·ed, -lat·ing, -lates.** To rejoice; exult. [Lat. *jubilare, jubilat-,* to raise a shout of joy.]

Ju·bi·la·te (yo͞o'bə-lä'tā, -tē, jo͞o'-) *n.* **1. a.** The 100th Psalm in the King James Bible and in most modern Catholic versions or the 99th in the Vulgate. **b.** A musical setting of the Jubilate. **2.** The third Sunday after Easter. **3.** A song or outburst of joy and triumph. [Lat., imper. of *jubilare,* to raise a shout of joy (the first word of the psalm).]

ju·bi·la·tion (jo͞o'bə-lā'shən) *n.* **1. a.** The act of rejoicing. **b.** The state of being jubilant. **2.** A celebration or other expression of joy.

ju·bi·lee (jo͞o'bə-lē, jo͞o'bə-lē') *n.* **1. a.** A special anniversary, esp. a 50th anniversary. **b.** The celebration of such an anniversary. **2.** A season or occasion of joyful celebration. **3.** Jubilation; rejoicing. **4.** Often **Jubilee.** In the Old Testament, a year of rest to be observed by the Israelites every 50th year, during which slaves were to be set free, alienated property restored to the former owners, and the lands left untilled. **5.** *Rom. Cath. Ch.* A year during which plenary indulgence may be obtained by the performance of certain pious acts. [ME *jubile* < OFr. < LLat. *jubilaeus,* the Jewish year of jubilee < LGk. *iōbēlaios* < Heb. *yōbhēl.*]

Ju·dah (jo͞o'də) *n.* **1.** Son of Jacob and Leah and ancestor of one of the twelve tribes of Israel. **2.** The tribe of Israel descended from Judah. [Heb. *Yĕhūdāh.*]

Ju·da·ic (jo͞o-dā'ĭk) also **Ju·da·i·cal** (-ĭ-kəl) *adj.* Of, pertaining to, or characteristic of Jews or Judaism. [Lat. *Judaicus* < Gk. *Ioudaikos* < Gk. *Ioudaios,* Jew.] **—Ju·da'i·cal·ly** *adv.*

Ju·da·ism (jo͞o'dē-ĭz'əm) *n.* **1.** The monotheistic religion of the Jewish people, tracing its origins to Abraham and having its spiritual and ethical principles embodied chiefly in the Bible and the Talmud. **2.** Conformity to the traditional ceremonies and rites of the Jewish religion. **3.** The cultural, spiritual, and social way of life of the Jewish people. **4.** The Jewish people. [LLat. *Judaismus* < Gk. *Ioudaismos* < *Ioudaios,* Jew. —see JEW.]

Ju·da·ize (jo͞o'dē-īz') *v.* **-ized, -iz·ing, -iz·es.** *—tr.* To bring into conformity with Judaism. *—intr.* To adopt Jewish customs and beliefs. **—Ju'da·i·za'tion** *n.* **—Ju'da·iz'er** *n.*

Ju·das (jo͞o'dəs) *n.* **1.** The Apostle who betrayed Jesus. **2.** One of the Twelve Apostles, known as Saint Jude to distinguish him from Judas Iscariot. **3.** One who betrays under the appearance of friendship. **4. judas.** A one-way peephole in a door. [LLat. < Gk. *Ioudas* < Heb. *Yĕhūdāh,* Judah.]

judo

Judas tree *n.* The redbud. [From the belief that Judas Iscariot hanged himself on such a tree.]

Jude (jo͞od) *n.* **1.** The author of the Epistle of Jude in the New Testament. **2.** See table at **Bible.** [Alteration of JUDAS.]

Ju·de·o-Span·ish (jo͞o-dā'ō-spăn'ĭsh) *n.* Ladino. [Lat. *Judaeus,* Jewish + SPANISH.]

judge (jŭj) *v.* **judged, judg·ing, judg·es.** *—tr.* **1. a.** To pass judgment upon in a court of law. **b.** To sit in judgment upon; try. **c.** *Obs.* To pass sentence upon; condemn. **2. a.** To determine or decide authoritatively after deliberation. **b.** To appraise discriminatingly as an expert. **c.** To declare after determination: *They judged her a witch.* **3.** To form an opinion about: *judge character.* **4.** To arrive at or draw a conclusion. **5.** *Informal.* To have as an opinion or assumption; suppose. **6.** *Obs.* To govern; rule. *—intr.* **1.** To act or decide as a judge. **2.** To form an opinion or evaluation. *—n.* **1. a.** A public official who hears and decides cases brought before a court of law. **b.** An appointed arbiter in a contest or competition. **c.** One whose critical judgment or opinion is sought; connoisseur. **2. a.** A leader of the Israelites during a period of about 400 years between the death of Joshua and the accession of Saul. **b. Judges.** See table at **Bible.** [ME *jugen* < AN *juger* < OFr. *jugier* < Lat. *judicare* < *judex,* judge.]

Synonyms: *judge, arbitrator, arbiter, referee, umpire.* These nouns denote persons empowered to make decisions that determine points at issue. A *judge* is either the presiding officer in a court of justice or, in a nonlegal sense, anyone in a position to make such decisions because he has authority or knowledge recognized as authoritative. An *arbitrator* usually works, singly or with associates, to settle disputes, especially in labor-management relations, and derives his authority by advance consent of the disputants, who choose him or approve his selection for the job. An *arbiter* is usually one who has no official status but is recognized as pre-eminent in a given nonlegal area, such as fashion or literature. Less often *arbiter* is used interchangeably with *arbitrator.* In legal terminology, a *referee* is an attorney appointed by a court to make a determination of a case or to investigate and report on it, and an *umpire* is a person called upon to settle an issue that arbitrators are unable to resolve. In sports, *referee* and *umpire* refer to officials who enforce the rules and settle points at issue.

judge advocate *n., pl.* **judge advocates. 1.** A commissioned officer in the U.S. Army or Air Force assigned to the Judge Advocate General's Corps. **2.** A staff officer serving as legal adviser to a commander. **3.** An officer acting as prosecutor at a court-martial.

juggler

Judge Advocate General *n., pl.* **Judge Advocates General** or **Judge Advocate Generals.** A major general in the U.S. Army or Air Force who serves as senior legal officer.

judge·ment (jŭj'mənt) *n.* Variant of **judgment.**

judge·ship (jŭj'shĭp') *n.* The office or jurisdiction of a judge.

judg·mat·ic (jŭj-măt'ĭk) also **judg·mat·i·cal** (-ĭ-kəl) *adj. Informal.* Judicious. [< JUDGE.] **—judg·mat'i·cal·ly** *adv.*

judg·ment also **judge·ment** (jŭj'mənt) *n.* **1. a.** The mental ability to perceive and distinguish the relation between two objects. **b.** The capacity to form an opinion by distinguishing and evaluating. **c.** The capacity to make sound and reasonable decisions; good sense; discernment. **d.** The exercise of making sound and reasonable decisions. **e.** Something, as an opinion or estimate, formed by sound and reasonable evaluation. **2.** A discriminating or authoritative appraisal or opinion. **3.** A rough guess or estimation: *make a judgment of the distance.* **4.** An assertion of something believed. **5.** A formal decision, as of an arbiter in a contest. **6.** *Law.* **a.** A determination of a court of law; a judicial decision. **b.** A court act creating or affirming an obligation, such as a debt. **c.** A writ in witness of such an act. **7. Judgment.** The final judgment of mankind by a divine being. [ME *jugement* < OFr. < *jugier,* judge. —see JUDGE.] **—judg·men'tal** *adj.*

Judgment Day *n.* **1.** In the teleology of Judaism, Christianity, and Islam, the day of God's final judgment. **2.** A day of reckoning or final judgment.

ju·di·ca·ble (jo͞o'dĭ-kə-bəl) *adj.* **1.** Capable of being judged. **2.** Liable to be judged. [LLat. *judicabilis* < Lat. *judicare,* to judge < *judex,* judge.]

ju·di·ca·tor (jo͞o'dĭ-kā'tər) *n.* One that acts as judge. [LLat. < Lat. *judicare,* to judge < *judex,* judge.]

ju·di·ca·to·ry (jo͞o'dĭ-kə-tôr'ē, -tōr'ē) *n., pl.* **-ries. 1.** A court of justice. **2.** A judiciary (sense 2). *—adj.* Of or pertaining to the administration of justice. [Med. Lat. *judicatorium* < Lat. *judicare,* to judge < *judex,* judge.]

ju·di·ca·ture (jo͞o'dĭ-kə-cho͝or') *n.* **1.** The administering of justice. **2.** The position, function, or authority of a judge. **3.** The jurisdiction of a law court or a judge. **4.** A court of law. **5.** A judiciary (sense 2). [Med. Lat. *judicatura* < Lat. *judicare,* to judge < *judex,* judge.]

ju·di·cial (jo͞o-dĭsh'əl) *adj.* **1.** Of, pertaining to, or proper to courts of law or to the administration of justice. **2.** Decreed by or proceeding from a court of justice. **3.** Pertaining or appropriate to the office of a judge. **4.** Relative to, characterized by, or expressing judgment. **5.** *Theol.* Proceeding from a divine judgment. [ME < Lat. *judicialis* < *judicium,* judgment < *judex,* judge.] **—ju·di'cial·ly** *adv.*

ju·di·ci·ar·y (jo͞o-dĭsh'ē-ĕr'ē) *n., pl.* **-ies. 1.** The judicial branch of government. **2. a.** A system of courts of law for the administration of justice. **b.** The judges of these courts. [Lat. *judiciarius* < *judicium,* judgment < *judex,* judge.]

ju·di·cious (jo͞o-dĭsh'əs) *adj.* Having or exhibiting sound judgment. [Fr. *judicieux* < OFr. < Lat. *judicium,* judgment < *judex,* judge.] **—ju·di'cious·ly** *adv.* **—ju·di'cious·ness** *n.*

Ju·dith (jo͞o'dĭth) *n.* **1.** In the Apocrypha, a Jewish woman who rescued her people by slaying the Assyrian general Holofernes. **2.** See table at **Bible.** [Heb. *Yĕhūdīth.*]

ju·do (jo͞o'dō) *n.* A modern form of jujitsu applying principles of balance and leverage, often used as a method of physical training. [J. *jūdō* : *jū,* soft (< Chin. *rou*[2]) + *dō,* way.] **—ju'do·ist** *n.*

jug (jŭg) *n.* **1.** A small pitcher. **2. a.** A tall, often rounded vessel of earthenware, glass, or metal with a small mouth, a handle, and usually a stopper or cap. **b.** The contents of a jug. **3.** *Slang.* A jail. *—tr.v.* **jugged, jug·ging, jugs. 1.** To stew (a hare, for example) in an earthenware jug or jar. **2.** *Slang.* To put in jail. [Poss. < *Jug,* nickname for *Joan.*]

ju·ga (jo͞o'gə) *n.* A plural of **jugum.**

ju·gate (jo͞o'gāt', -gĭt) *adj.* Joined in or forming a pair or pairs. [< Lat. *jugum,* yoke.]

jug band *n.* A musical group that uses unconventional or improvised instruments, such as jugs, kazoos, and washboards.

Jug·ger·naut (jŭg'ər-nôt') *n.* **1.** A title of the Hindu deity Krishna, whose idol is drawn in an annual procession on a huge car or wagon under the wheels of which worshipers are said to have thrown themselves to be crushed. **2. juggernaut.** Something, as a belief or institution, that elicits blind and destructive devotion, or to which people are ruthlessly sacrificed. **3. juggernaut.** An overwhelming and irresistible force or movement. [Hindi *jagannath* < Skt. *jaganāthaḥ,* lord of the world : *jagat,* the world (< *gacchati,* it goes) + *nathaḥ,* lord.]

jug·gle (jŭg'əl) *v.* **-gled, -gling, -gles.** *—tr.* **1.** To keep (two or more objects) in the air at one time by alternately tossing and catching them. **2.** To keep (more than two activities, for example) in motion or progress at one time. **3.** To attempt to balance or otherwise cope with. **4.** To manipulate in order to deceive: *juggle figures in a ledger.* *—intr.* **1.** To perform tricks with sleight of hand. **2.** To make juggling motions. **3.** To use trickery to deceive. *—n.* **1.** An act of juggling. **2.** A piece of trickery for a dishonest purpose. [ME *jogelen,* to entertain by performing tricks < OFr. *jogler* < Lat. *joculari,* to jest < *joculus,* dim. of *jocus,* joke.]

jug·gler (jŭg'lər) *n.* **1.** One who performs tricks of dexterity. **2.** One who uses tricks, deception, or fraud. [ME *jogelour,* jester < OFr. *joglere* < Lat. *joculator* < *joculari,* to jest. —see JUGGLE.]

jug·gler·y (jŭg'lə-rē) *n., pl.* **-ies. 1.** The art or performance of a juggler. **2.** Trickery; deception.

jug·head (jŭg'hĕd') *n. Slang.* A dull, slow-witted person.

jug·u·lar (jŭg'yə-lər) *adj.* Of, pertaining to, or located in the region of the neck or throat. *—n.* A jugular vein. ***—idiom.* go for the jugular.** To attempt to administer a fatal or final blow. [LLat. *jugularis* < Lat. *jugulum,* collarbone, dim. of *jugum,* yoke.]

jugular vein *n.* Any of various large veins of the neck.

ju·gum (jo͞o'gəm) *n., pl.* **-ga** (-gə) or **-gums.** A paired or yokelike structure, such as a pair of opposite leaflets or a lobe joining the bases of the forewings and hind wings of certain insects. [Lat., yoke.]

juice (jo͞os) *n.* **1. a.** A fluid naturally contained in plant or animal tissue. **b.** A bodily secretion. **2.** *Slang.* **a.** Vigorous life and vitality. **b.** Power; clout. **3.** *Slang.* **a.** Electric current. **b.** Fuel for an engine. **4.** *Slang.* Liquor. **5.** *Slang.* An interesting fact or development, esp. of a private or scandalous nature. *—tr.v.* **juiced, juic·ing, juic·es.** To extract the juice from. ***—phrasal verb.* juice up.** *Informal.* To give energy, spirit, or interest to. [ME *jus* < OFr. < Lat.]

juic·er (jo͞o'sər) *n.* **1.** An appliance for extracting juice from fruits and vegetables. **2.** *Slang.* One who drinks liquor habitually or excessively.

juic·y (jo͞o'sē) *adj.* **-i·er, -i·est. 1.** Full of juice; succulent. **2. a.** Richly interesting: *a juicy mystery novel.* **b.** Racy; titillating: *a juicy bit of gossip.* **3.** Yielding wealth; lucrative. **—juic'i·ly** *adv.* **—juic'i·ness** *n.*

ju·jit·su also **ju·jut·su** or **jiu·jit·su** or **jiu·jut·su** (jo͞o-jĭt'so͞o) *n.* A Japanese art of self-defense or hand-to-hand combat based on set maneuvers that force an opponent to use his weight and strength against himself. [J. *jūjitsu* : *jū,* soft (< Chin. *rou*[2]) + *jitsu,* art (< Chin. *shu*[4]).]

ju·ju (jo͞o'jo͞o) *n.* **1.** An object used as a fetish, charm, or amulet in West Africa. **2.** Supernatural power ascribed to a juju. [Perh. < Hausa *jūju,* evil spirit.] **—ju'ju·ism'** *n.*

ju·jube (jo͞o'jo͞ob') *n.* **1. a.** Any of several spiny trees of the genus *Ziziphus,* esp. *Z. jujuba,* native to the Old World, having small yellowish flowers and dark-red fruit. **b.** The fleshy, edible fruit of this tree. **2.** (*also* jo͞o'jo͞o-bē'). A fruit-flavored, usually chewy candy or lozenge. [ME < Med. Lat. *jujuba* < Lat. *zizyphum* < Gk. *zizuphon.*]

ju·jut·su (jo͞o-jĭt'so͞o) *n.* Variant of **jujitsu.**

juke box (jo͞ok) *n.* A coin-operated phonograph, equipped with push buttons for the selection of records. [< E. *jukehouse,* roadhouse with music and dancing, prob. < dial. E. *juke,* disorderly, poss. of African orig.]

ju·lep (jo͞o'lĭp) *n.* **1.** A mint julep. **2.** A sweet syrupy drink, esp. one to which medicine may be added. [ME, a sugar syrup < OFr. < Ar. *julāb* < Pers. *gulāb* : *gul,* rose + *āb,* water.]

Jul·ian calendar (jo͞ol'yən) *n.* The calendar introduced by Julius Caesar in Rome in 46 B.C., eventually replaced by the Gregorian calendar.

ju·li·enne (jo͞o'lē-ĕn', zhü-lyĕn') *adj.* Cut into long, thin strips: *julienne potatoes.* —*n.* Consommé or broth garnished with strips of julienne vegetables. [Fr.]

Ju·ly (jo͞o-lī') *n.* The seventh month of the year according to the Gregorian calendar. See table at **calendar.** [ME *juil* < OFr. < Lat. *Julius,* after *Julius* Caesar.]

Ju·ma (jo͞o'mä) *n.* The Islamic Sabbath, falling on Friday.

Ju·ma·da (jo͞o-mä'dä) also **Jo·ma·da** (jə-) *n.* **1.** The fifth month of the year in the Moslem calendar, having 30 days. **2.** The sixth month of the year in the Moslem calendar, having 29 days. See table at **calendar.** [Ar. *Jumādā.*]

jum·ble (jŭm'bəl) *v.* **-bled, -bling, -bles.** —*intr.* To move, mix, or mingle in a confused, disordered manner. —*tr.* **1.** To stir or mix in a disordered mass. **2.** To muddle; confuse: *The rapid-fire questioning jumbled his thoughts.* —*n.* **1.** A confused or disordered mass: *a jumble of sales goods.* **2.** A disordered state; muddle. [Orig. unknown.]

jum·bo (jŭm'bō) *n., pl.* **-bos.** An unusually large person, animal, or thing. —*adj.* Larger than average: *jumbo shrimp.* [After *Jumbo,* a large elephant exhibited by P.T. Barnum (1810–1891).]

jum·buck (jŭm'bŭk') *n. Austral.* A sheep. [A native word in Australia.]

jump (jŭmp) *v.* **jumped, jump·ing, jumps.** —*intr.* **1. a.** To spring off the ground or other base by a muscular effort of the legs and feet. **b.** To move suddenly and in one motion: *jumped out of bed.* **c.** To move involuntarily, as in surprise: *jumped at the knock on the door.* **d.** To respond or act quickly: *Jump when I give you an order.* **2.** To spring at with the intent to assail or censure: *jumped at me for criticizing her.* **3. a.** To join with or show eagerness: *jumped into the race for the nomination.* **b.** To grab at readily: *jump at a bargain.* **c.** To arrive at hastily or haphazardly: *jump to conclusions.* **4.** To move randomly or aimlessly: *jumps from job to job.* **5. a.** To undergo a sudden and pronounced increase: *Prices jumped.* **b.** To rise suddenly in position or rank: *jumped over two others with more seniority.* **6. a.** To skip over space or material, leaving a break in continuity: *The lecture kept jumping from one subject to another.* **b.** To be displaced by a sudden jerk: *The phonograph needle jumped.* **c.** To be displaced vertically or laterally due to improper alignment: *The film jumped during projection.* **d.** *Computer Sci.* To move from one set of instructions in a program to another farther ahead or behind rather than moving sequentially. **7.** To move over an opponent's playing piece in checkers. **8.** To make a jump bid in bridge. **9.** To show enterprise and quickness. **10.** To have a lively, pulsating quality: *a disco that really jumps.* —*tr.* **1.** To leap over or across: *jump a fence.* **2.** To leap upon: *jump a bus.* **3.** To spring upon in sudden attack: *Muggers jumped him in the park.* **4.** To move or start prematurely: *jumped the starter's gun.* **5.** To cause to leap: *jump a horse over a fence.* **6.** To cause to increase suddenly and pronouncedly: *Unexpected shortages jumped prices.* **7.** To skip: *The typewriter jumped a space.* **8.** To promote, esp. by more than one level: *jumped him to head foreman.* **9.** To take (an opponent's piece) in checkers by moving over it with one's own. **10.** To raise (a partner's bid) in bridge by more than is necessary. **11.** To leave (a course) through mishap: *The train jumped the rail.* **12.** *Slang.* **a.** To leave hastily; skip: *jumped town before I could catch up with him.* **b.** To leave (a position) in violation of a contract: *jumped the team.* —*n.* **1.** The act of jumping; leap. **2.** The space or distance covered by a leap: *a jump of seven feet.* **3.** A hurdle, barrier, or span to be jumped. **4.** A track sport featuring skill in jumping: *the high jump.* **5. a.** A sudden, pronounced rise, as in price or salary. **b.** An impressive promotion. **6.** A step or level: *managed to stay a jump ahead of the others.* **7.** A sudden or major transition, as from one career or subject to another. **8. a.** A short trip. **b.** One in a series of moves and stopovers, as with a circus or road show. **9.** In checkers, a move made by jumping. **10.** *Computer Sci.* A movement from one set of instructions to another. **11. a.** An involuntary nervous movement, as when startled. **b. jumps.** The fidgets. —***idioms.*** **get** (or **have**) **a jump on** (**someone**). *Informal.* To have a head start over another. **jump a claim.** To take land or rights from another by violence or fraud. **jump bail.** To forfeit one's bail by absconding. **jump ship.** To desert. **jump the gun.** To start something too soon. [Perh. of imit. orig.]

jump ball *n. Basketball.* A method of starting play or determining possession in which an official tosses the ball up between two opposing players who must then jump and try to tap the ball to a teammate.

jump bid *n.* A bridge bid at a higher level than that required to exceed the preceding bid.

jump·er[1] (jŭm'pər) *n.* **1.** One that jumps. **2.** A type of coasting sled. **3.** *Elect.* A short length of wire used temporarily to complete or by-pass a circuit. **4.** *Basketball.* A jump shot.

jum·per[2] (jŭm'pər) *n.* **1.** A sleeveless dress worn over a blouse or sweater. **2.** A loose, protective garment worn over other clothes. **3.** Often **jumpers.** A child's garment consisting of straight-legged pants attached to a biblike bodice. [Prob. < E. dial. *jump,* loose jacket.]

jumper cable *n.* A booster cable.

jumping bean *n.* A seed, as of certain Mexican shrubs or plants of the genera *Sebastiana* and *Sapium,* containing the larva of a moth, *Laspeyresia saltitans,* the movements of which cause the seed to jerk or roll.

jumping jack *n.* **1.** A toy figure with jointed limbs that can be made to dance by pulling an attached string. **2.** A physical exercise performed by jumping to a position with legs spread wide and hands touching overhead and then returning to a standing position with arms at the sides.

jumping mouse *n.* Any of various small rodents of the family Zapodidae, having a long tail and long hind legs.

jump·ing-off place (jŭm'pĭng-ôf', -ŏf') *n.* **1.** A very remote spot. **2.** A beginning point for an enterprise.

jump-off (jŭmp'ôf', -ŏf') *n.* The commencement of a race or of a planned military attack.

jump rope *n.* A sturdy rope usually with handles that is twirled and jumped over in children's games or in conditioning exercises.

jump seat *n.* **1.** A portable or collapsible seat in the flight deck of an airplane or in an automobile between the front and rear seats. **2.** A small rear seat in a sports car.

jump shot *n. Basketball.* A ball shot made by a player at the highest point of his jump.

jump-start (jŭmp'stärt') *tr.v.* **-start·ed, -start·ing, -starts.** To start (an automobile engine) by pushing or rolling the automobile and suddenly releasing the clutch or by using a booster cable connected to the battery of another automobile. —*n.* The process or an instance of jump-starting.

jump suit *n.* **1.** A parachutist's uniform. **2.** Also **jump·suit** (jŭmp'so͞ot'). A one-piece garment consisting of a blouse or shirt with attached slacks or shorts.

jump·y (jŭm'pē) *adj.* **-i·er, -i·est. 1.** Characterized by fitful, jerky movements. **2.** Nervous or on edge, as with apprehension. **—jump'i·ness** *n.*

jun (jo͝on) *n., pl.* **jun.** See table at **currency.** [Korean.]

jun·co (jŭng'kō) *n., pl.* **-cos** or **-coes.** Any of various North American birds of the genus *Junco,* having predominantly gray plumage. [NLat. *Junco,* genus name < Sp. < Lat. *juncus,* reed.]

junc·tion (jŭngk'shən) *n.* **1.** The act or process of joining or the condition of being joined. **2.** The place where two things join or meet, esp. the place where two roads or railway routes join or cross paths. **3.** A transition layer or boundary between two different materials or between physically different regions in a single material, esp.: **a.** A connection between conductors or sections of a transmission line. **b.** The interface between a region of predominantly positive charge carriers and another of predominantly negative charge carriers in a semiconductor. **c.** A mechanical or alloyed contact between different metals or other materials, as in a thermocouple. [Lat. *junctio* < *junctus,* p.part. of *jungere,* to join.] **—junc'tion·al** *adj.*

junction box *n.* An enclosed panel used to connect or branch electric circuits without making permanent splices.

junc·ture (jŭngk'chər) *n.* **1.** The act of joining or the condition of being joined. **2.** The line or point where two things are joined; joint; hinge. **3.** A point or interval in time, esp. a crisis or similar turning point. **4.** The transition or mode of transition from one sound to another in speech. [ME < Lat. *junctura* < *junctus,* p.part. of *jungere,* to join.]

June (jo͞on) *n.* The sixth month of the year according to the Gregorian calendar. See table at **calendar.** [ME *juin* < OFr. < Lat. *Junius,* after *Juno.*]

June beetle or **June bug** *n.* Any of various North American beetles of the subfamily Melolonthinae, having larvae that are often destructive to crops.

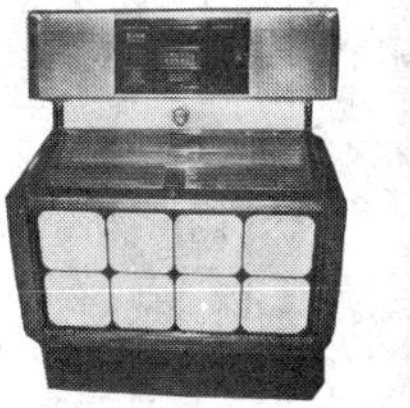

juke box

June·ber·ry (jo͞on′bĕr′ē) *n.* The shadbush.
June bug *n.* A June beetle.
Jung·i·an (yo͝ong′ē-ən) *adj.* Of, pertaining to, or characteristic of Carl G. Jung or his theories of psychology. —**Jung′i·an** *n.*
jun·gle (jŭng′gəl) *n.* **1.** Land densely overgrown with tropical vegetation and trees. **2.** A dense thicket or growth. **3.** *Slang.* A hobo camp or place of rendezvous. **4.** A place or milieu characterized by intense, often ruthless competition or struggle for survival. **5.** A maze, entanglement, or confusion that causes frustration and leads nowhere. [Hindi *jaṅgal,* wasteland < Skt. *jāṅgala-,* wild, arid.] —**jun′gly** (-glē) *adj.*
jungle fowl *n.* Any of several birds of the genus *Gallus,* of southeastern Asia, esp. *G. gallus,* considered to be the ancestor of the common domestic fowl.
jungle gym *n.* A structure of poles and bars on which children can play. [Orig. a trademark.]
jun·ior (jo͞on′yər) *adj.* **1.** Younger. Used to distinguish the son from the father of the same name. **2.** Designed for or including youthful persons. **3.** Lower in rank or shorter in length of tenure: *the junior senator.* **4.** Designating the third year of a U.S. high school or college. **5.** Lesser in scale than the usual. —*n.* **1.** A person who is younger than another. **2.** A person lesser in rank or time of participation or service; subordinate. **3.** A student in the third year of a U.S. high school or college. **4.** A clothing size for girls and women with slender figures. [Lat., compar. of *juvenis,* young.]
junior college *n.* An educational institution offering a two-year course that is generally the equivalent of the first two years of a four-year undergraduate course.
junior high school *n.* A school in the U.S. system generally including the seventh, eighth, and sometimes ninth grades.
jun·ior·i·ty (jo͞on-yôr′ĭ-tē, -yŏr′-) *n.* The rank or condition of being a junior.
junior miss *n.* **1.** A teenage girl. **2.** Junior (sense 4).
junior varsity *n.* A high-school or college team that competes in interschool sports on the level below varsity.
ju·ni·per (jo͞o′nə-pər) *n.* Any of various evergreen trees or shrubs of the genus *Juniperus,* having scalelike, often prickly foliage and aromatic, bluish-gray, berrylike fruit. [ME < Lat. *juniperus.*]
juniper oil *n.* An essential oil obtained from the fruit of the common juniper, most commonly used for flavoring gin and liqueurs.
junk[1] (jŭngk) *n.* **1.** Scrapped materials such as glass, rags, paper, or metals that can be converted into usable stock. **2.** *Informal.* **a.** Something worn-out or fit to be discarded. **b.** Something cheap or shoddy. **c.** Something meaningless, fatuous, or unbelievable; nonsense. **3.** *Slang.* Heroin. **4.** *Naut.* **a.** Hard salt beef. **b.** Old cordage, reused for gaskets, oakum, and mats. —*tr.v.* **junked, junk·ing, junks.** To throw away or discard as useless; scrap. [ME *jonk,* an old cable or rope.]
junk[2] (jŭngk) *n.* A Chinese flat-bottomed ship with a high poop and battened sails. [Port. *junco* < Javanese *djong.*]
junk art also **junk sculpture** *n.* Three-dimensional art made from junked materials, as metal, glass, or wood.
junk·er (jŭng′kər) *n.* Something, esp. a motor vehicle, that is so old and broken-down as to be beyond or unworthy of repair.
Jun·ker (yo͝ong′kər) *n.* A member of the Prussian landed aristocracy. [G. < OHG *junchērro* : *jung,* young + *hērro,* compar. of *hēr,* worthy.] —**Jun′ker·dom** *n.*
jun·ket (jŭng′kĭt) *n.* **1.** A sweet food made from flavored milk and rennet. **2.** A party, banquet, or outing. **3.** A trip, esp. one taken by an official and underwritten with public funds. **4.** A tour, esp. a trip covering a professional circuit. —*v.* **-ket·ed, -ket·ing, -kets.** —*intr.* **1.** To hold a party or banquet. **2.** To make an excursion. —*tr.* To fete at a party or banquet. [ME *jonket,* a kind of food served on rushes < *jonket,* rush basket, ult. < Lat. *juncus,* rush.] —**jun′ket·er, jun′ket·eer′** *n.*
junk food *n.* Any of various fast-service restaurant foods or prepackaged snack foods of low nutritional value.
junk·ie also **junk·y** (jŭng′kē) *n., pl.* **-ies.** *Slang.* **1.** A narcotics addict, esp. one using heroin. **2.** One who has an avid interest or devotion: *a sports junkie.*
junk mail *n.* Third-class mail, such as advertisements, mailed indiscriminately in large quantities.
junk sculpture *n.* Variant of **junk art.**
junk·y (jŭng′kē) *n.* Variant of **junkie.**
junk·yard (jŭngk′yärd′) *n.* A yard or lot that is used to store junk, such as scrap metal or old cars that can be resold.
Ju·no (jo͞o′nō) *n. Rom. Myth.* The principal goddess of the Pantheon, wife and sister of Jupiter, patroness primarily of marriage and the well-being of women. [Lat.]
Ju·no·esque (jo͞o′nō-ĕsk′) *adj.* Having the stately bearing and imposing beauty of the goddess Juno.
jun·ta (ho͝on′tə, jŭn′-) *n.* **1.** A group of military officers holding state power in a country after a coup d'état. **2.** A council or small legislative body in a government, esp. in Central and South American countries. **3.** A junto. [Sp. and Port., conference < Lat. *juncta,* p.part. of *jungere,* to join.]

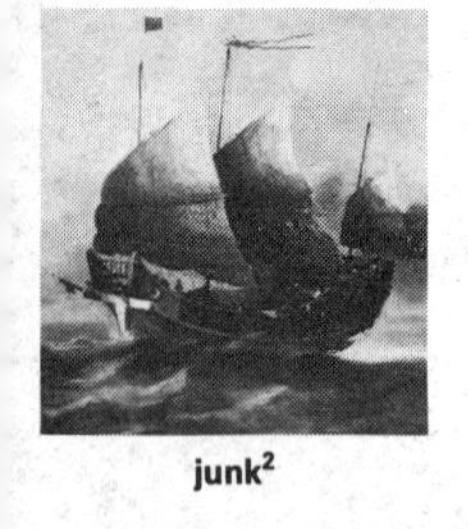

junk[2]

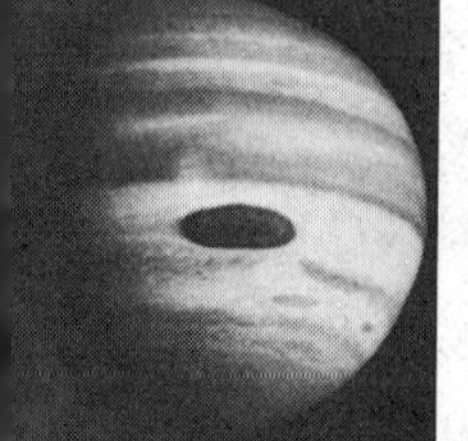

Jupiter

jun·to (jŭn′tō) *n., pl.* **-tos.** A small, usually secret group united for a common interest. [Var. of JUNTA.]
Ju·pi·ter (jo͞o′pĭ-tər) *n.* **1.** *Rom. Myth.* The supreme god, patron of the Roman state, brother and husband of Juno. **2.** *Astron.* The fifth planet from the sun, the largest and most massive in the solar system, having a diameter of approximately 138,000 kilometers, or 86,000 miles, a mass approximately 318 times that of Earth, and a sidereal period of revolution about the sun of 11.86 years at a mean distance of 777 million kilometers, or 483 million miles. [Lat.]
ju·ral (jo͝or′əl) *adj.* **1.** Of or pertaining to law. **2.** Of or pertaining to rights and obligations. [< Lat. *jus, jur-,* law.] —**ju′ral·ly** *adv.*
Ju·ras·sic (jo͝o-răs′ĭk) *adj.* Of, belonging to, or designating the time and deposits of the second period of the Mesozoic era, characterized by the existence of dinosaurs and the appearance of primitive mammals and birds. —*n.* The Jurassic period. [Fr. *jurassique,* after the *Jura* Mountains.]
ju·rat (jo͝or′ăt′) *n.* A certification on an affidavit declaring when, where, and before whom it was sworn. [< Lat. *juratum,* p.part. of *jurare,* to swear < *jus,* law.]
ju·rid·i·cal (jo͝o-rĭd′ĭ-kəl) also **ju·rid·ic** (-ĭk) *adj.* Of or pertaining to the law and its administration. [Lat. *juridicus* : *jus,* law + *dicere,* to say.] —**ju·rid′i·cal·ly** *adv.*
ju·ris·con·sult (jo͝or′ĭs-kŏn′sŭlt′) *n.* A person learned in law; jurist. [Lat. *jurisconsultus* : *jus,* law + *consultus,* skilled, p.part. of *consulere,* to take counsel.]
ju·ris·dic·tion (jo͝or′ĭs-dĭk′shən) *n.* **1.** The right and power to interpret and apply the law. **2. a.** Authority or control. **b.** The extent of authority or control. **3.** The territorial range of authority or control. [ME *jurisdiccioun* < Med. Lat. *jurisdictio* < Lat. : *jus,* law + *dictio,* declaration. —see DICTION.] —**ju′ris·dic′tion·al** *adj.* —**ju′ris·dic′tion·al·ly** *adv.*
ju·ris doctor (jo͝or′ĭs) *n.* An academic degree that is the equivalent of a bachelor of laws. [NLat. < Lat., doctor of law.]
ju·ris·pru·dence (jo͝or′ĭs-pro͞od′ns) *n.* **1.** The philosophy or the formal science of law. **2.** A division or department of law. [LLat. *jurisprudentia* : *jus,* law + *prudentia,* knowledge < *prudens,* knowing. —see PRUDENT.] —**ju′ris·pru·den′tial** (-pro͞o-dĕn′shəl) *adj.* —**ju′ris·pru·den′tial·ly** *adv.*
ju·ris·pru·dent (jo͝or′ĭs-pro͞od′nt) *adj.* Versed in jurisprudence. —*n.* A jurist.
ju·rist (jo͝or′ĭst) *n.* One who is skilled in the law, esp. an eminent judge, lawyer, or legal scholar. [OFr. *juriste* < Med. Lat. *jurista* < Lat. *jus,* law.]
ju·ris·tic (jo͝o-rĭs′tĭk) also **ju·ris·ti·cal** (-tĭ-kəl) *adj.* **1.** Of or pertaining to a jurist or to jurisprudence. **2.** Of or pertaining to law or legality. —**ju·ris′ti·cal·ly** *adv.*
ju·ror (jo͝or′ər, -ôr′) *n.* **1. a.** A person serving as a member of a jury. **b.** A person called or designated for jury duty. **2.** A person who serves on any body acting in a capacity analogous to that of a jury. [ME *jurour* < AN < Lat. *jurator,* swearer < *jurare,* to swear.]
ju·ry[1] (jo͝or′ē) *n., pl.* **-ries.** **1.** A body of persons sworn to judge and give a verdict on a given matter, esp. a body of persons summoned by law and sworn to hear and hand down a verdict upon a case presented in court. **2.** A group of persons forming a committee to judge, as at a competition. [ME *jure* < AN, ult. < Lat. *jurare,* to swear < *jus,* law.]
ju·ry[2] (jo͝or′ē) *adj. Naut.* Intended or designed for temporary use; makeshift: *a jury rig.* [Orig. unknown.]
jus gen·ti·um (yo͞os gĕn′tē-əm) *n.* The law of nations; international law. [Lat.]
jus·sive (jŭs′ĭv) *n. Gram.* A word, mood, or form used to express command. [< Lat. *jussus,* p.part. of *jubēre,* to command.] —**jus′sive** *adj.*
just[1] (jŭst) *adj.* **1.** Honorable and fair in one's dealings and actions: *a just ruler.* **2.** Consistent with moral right; righteous: *a just cause.* **3.** Properly due or merited: *just deserts.* **4.** Valid within the law; legitimate. **5.** Suitable or proper in nature; fitting: *a just touch of solemnity.* **6.** Based on fact or sound reason; well-founded: *a just appraisal.* —*adv.* (jəst, jĭst; jŭst *when stressed*). **1.** Precisely; exactly: *just enough salt.* **2.** At the exact moment of: *It's just six.* **3.** Only a moment ago: *He just arrived.* **4.** By a narrow margin; barely: *You just missed her.* **5.** At a little distance: *saw him just down the road.* **6.** Merely; only: *I just meant that I agree.* **7.** Simply; certainly: *It's just beautiful!* **8.** Perhaps; possibly: *I just may go.* —***idiom.*** **just about.** Almost; very nearly: *I've just about had enough.* [ME *juste* < Lat. *justus.*] —**just′ly** *adv.* —**just′ness** *n.*
just[2] (jŭst) *n.* & *v.* Variant of **joust.**
jus·tice (jŭs′tĭs) *n.* **1. a.** The principle of moral rightness; equity. **b.** Conformity to moral rightness in action or attitude; righteousness. **2.** The upholding of what is just, esp. fair treatment and due reward in accordance to honor, standards, or law; fairness. **3.** Something that is just or due: *Justice was served by his downfall.* **4.** The quality of being just, fair, or impartial. **5.** Conformity to truth, fact, or sound reason: *He's angry, and with justice.* **6.** The administration and procedure of law. **7. a.** A judge. **b.** A justice of the peace. —***idiom.*** **do justice to. 1.** To approach with proper appreciation; enjoy fully. **2.** To show to full advantage. [ME < OFr. < Lat. *justitia* < *justus,* just.]

justice of the peace *n.* A magistrate of the lowest level of certain state court systems, having authority to act upon minor offenses, commit cases to a higher court for trial, perform marriages, and administer oaths.

jus·ti·ci·a·ble (jŭ-stĭsh'ə-bəl) *adj.* **1.** Appropriate for or subject to court trial. **2.** Liable for court decision. [OFr. < *justicier,* to try < Med. Lat. *justitiare* < Lat. *justitia,* justice < *justus,* just.] **—jus·ti'cia·bil'i·ty** *n.*

jus·ti·ci·ar·y (jŭ-stĭsh'ē-ĕr'ē) also **jus·ti·ci·ar** (jŭ-stĭsh'ē-ər) *n., pl.* **-ies** also **-ars.** A high judicial officer in medieval England. [Med. Lat. *justitiarius* < Lat. *justitia,* justice < *justus,* law.]

jus·ti·fi·a·ble (jŭs'tə-fī'ə-bəl, jŭs'tə-fī'-) *adj.* Capable of being justified. **—jus'ti·fi'a·bil'i·ty, jus'ti·fi'a·ble·ness** *n.* **—jus'ti·fi'a·bly** *adv.*

jus·ti·fi·ca·tion (jŭs'tə-fĭ-kā'shən) *n.* **1.** The act of justifying. **2.** The condition or fact of being justified. **3.** Something that justifies: *"There are few justifications for a revolution"* (Burke).

jus·ti·fi·ca·tive (jŭs'tə-fĭ-kā'tĭv) also **jus·tif·i·ca·to·ry** (jŭ-stĭf'ĭ-kə-tôr'ē, -tōr'ē) *adj.* Serving as justification.

jus·ti·fy (jŭs'tə-fī') *v.* **-fied, -fy·ing, -fies.** *—tr.* **1.** To demonstrate or prove to be just, right, or valid. **2.** To declare free of blame; absolve. **3.** *Theol.* To free (man) of the guilt and penalty attached to grievous sin. Used only of God. **4.** *Law.* **a.** To demonstrate good reason for (an action taken). **b.** To prove to be qualified as a bondsman. **5.** *Printing.* To adjust or space (lines) to the proper length. *—intr. Printing.* To be or become properly spaced and of the correct length. Used of a line of type. [ME *justifien* < OFr. *justifier,* to administer justice < LLat. *justificare,* to act justly toward : Lat. *justus,* just + Lat. *facere,* to do.]

jut (jŭt) *intr.v.* **jut·ted, jut·ting, juts.** To project, usually sharply, beyond the limits of the main body; protrude: *"He had a sharp crooked nose jutting out of a lean dancer's face"* (Graham Greene). *—n.* Something that protrudes; projection. [Var. of JET².]

jute (jo͞ot) *n.* **1.** Either of two Asian plants, *Corchorus capsularis* or *C. olitorius,* yielding a fiber used for sacking and cordage. **2.** The fiber obtained from the jute plant. [Bengali *jhuṭo* < Skt. *jūṭaḥ,* twisted hair.]

Jute (jo͞ot) *n.* A member of any of several Germanic tribes, some of whom invaded Britain and settled in Kent in the 5th century A.D. [< ME *Iutes,* the Jutes < OE *Iotas.*]

ju·ve·nes·cent (jo͞o'və-nĕs'ənt) *adj.* Becoming young or youthful. [Lat. *juvenescens, juvenescent-,* pr.part. of *juvenescere,* to reach the age of youth < *juvenis,* young.] **—ju've·nes'cence** *n.*

ju·ve·nile (jo͞o'və-nīl', -nəl) *adj.* **1.** Not fully developed; not yet adult. **2.** Characteristic of youth or children; immature. **3.** Intended for or appropriate to children or young persons: *juvenile fashions.* *—n.* **1. a.** A young person; child. **b.** A young animal that has not reached sexual maturity. **2.** An actor who plays roles of children or young persons. **3.** A children's book. [Lat. *juvenilis* < *juvenis,* young.] **—ju've·nile'ly** *adv.* **—ju've·nile'ness** *n.*

jute

juvenile court *n.* A court with jurisdiction over all cases involving children under a specified age, usually 18 years.

juvenile delinquency *n.* Antisocial or criminal behavior by children or adolescents. **—juvenile delinquent** *n.*

juvenile hormone *n.* A hormone secreted by the corpus allatum of athropod larvae that controls metamorphosis.

ju·ve·nil·i·a (jo͞o'və-nĭl'ē-ə) *pl.n.* Works, particularly written or artistic works, produced in childhood or youth. [Lat., neuter pl. of *juvenilis,* juvenile < *juvenis,* young.]

ju·ve·nil·i·ty (jo͞o'və-nĭl'ĭ-tē) *n., pl.* **-ties.** **1.** The quality or condition of being foolishly juvenile; immaturity. **2.** The quality or condition of being young or youthful. **3.** An instance of juvenility. **4.** Young persons collectively.

ju·ve·noc·ra·cy (jo͞o'və-nŏk'rə-sē) *n.* Rule or influence by young people. [Lat. *juvenis,* a young person + -CRACY.]

jux·ta·pose (jŭk'stə-pōz') *tr.v.* **-posed, -pos·ing, -pos·es.** To place side by side, esp. for comparison or contrast. [Fr. *juxtaposer* : Lat. *juxta,* close together + Fr. *poser,* to place. — see POSE.]

jux·ta·po·si·tion (jŭk'stə-pə-zĭsh'ən) *n.* The act of juxtaposing or the state of being juxtaposed. **—jux'ta·po·si'tion·al** *adj.*

K

Around 1000 B.C. the Phoencians and other Semitic peoples began to use graphic signs to represent individual speech sounds instead of syllables or words. They used a symbol in the forms (1,2,3) to represent the sound of the consonant "k" and called it *kaph,* their word for "hollow of the hand." The Greeks, adapting the Phoenician alphabet, kept the phonetic value of *kaph* but reversed its orientation (5,6) and changed its name to *kappa.* The Romans borrowed the alphabet from the Greeks via the Etruscans and adapted it for monumental inscriptions. Monumental script (8) is the prototype of modern capital letters (11,12). Medieval scribes adapted the Roman capitals to being quickly written on paper, parchment, and vellum. These uncial and cursive minuscules (9,10) are the prototypes of modern lower-case letters, both written and printed (14,13).

k

k or **K** (kā) *n., pl.* **k's** or **K's. 1.** The 11th letter of the modern English alphabet. **2.** A speech sound represented by the letter *k.* **3.** The 11th in a series. **4.** *Informal.* Thousand: *a job that pays $40k.* **5.** A unit of computer storage capacity equal to 1024 bytes.

K The symbol for the element potassium. [NLat. *kalium*].

Kaa·ba (kä'bə) *n.* A Moslem shrine in Mecca, the goal of pilgrims, toward which Moslems turn to pray. [Ar. *ka'bah* < *ka'b,* cube.]

kab (kăb) *n.* Variant of **cab**[2].

kab·a·la or **kab·ba·la** (kăb'ə-lə, kə-bä'lə) *n.* Variants of **cabala.**

ka·bob (kə-bŏb') *n.* Shish kebab.

ka·bu·ki (kə-bōō'kē) *n.* A Japanese popular drama in which gestures, dances, and songs are performed in a formal and stylized manner. [J., art of singing and dancing : *kabu,* singing and dancing (< Chin. *ge*[1] *wu*[3]) + *ki,* art, artist (< Chin. *ji*[4]).]

Ka·byle (kə-bīl') *n., pl.* **Kabyle** or **-byles. 1.** A Berber of Tunisia or Algeria. **2.** The Berber language of the Kabyle. [Fr. < Ar. *qabā'il,* pl. of *qabīlah,* tribe.]

ka·chi·na (kə-chē'nə) *n.* A doll that represents one of the rain-bringing ancestral spirits of the Hopi. [Hopi *qacina,* supernatural.]

Kad·dish (kä'dĭsh) *n. Judaism.* A prayer recited in the daily synagogue services and by mourners after the death of a close relative. [Aram. *qaddīsh,* holy.]

kaf·fee klatsch (kô'fē klăch', kä'fē klăch') *n.* Variant of **coffee klatch.**

Kaf·fir also **Kaf·ir** (kăf'ər) *n., pl.* **Kaffir** or **-firs** also **Kafir** or **-firs. 1. a.** A member of a Bantu-speaking tribe of South Africa; Xhosa. **b.** Xhosa (sense 2). **2.** A non-Moslem. **3.** *Offensive.* A black South African. **4. kaffir** or **kafir.** A sorghum, *Sorghum vulgare caffrorum,* cultivated in dry regions for grain and fodder. [Ar. *kāfir,* infidel.]

kaf·fi·yeh (kä-fē'ə, kă-) *n.* A cloth headdress fastened by a band around the crown and usually worn by Arab men. [Ar. *kaffīyah.*]

Kaf·ir (kăf'ər) *n., pl.* **Kafir** or **-firs. 1. a.** An Iranian people of northeastern Afghanistan. **b.** A member of the Kafir people. **2.** Variant of **Kaffir.** [Ar. *kāfir,* infidel.]

Kaf·i·ri (kăf'ə-rē) *n.* The Indic language of the Iranian Kafir.

Kaf·ka·esque (käf'kə-ĕsk', kăf'-) *adj.* **1.** Of or characteristic of Franz Kafka or his writings. **2.** Characterized by surreal distortion and usually by a sense of impending danger.

kaf·tan (kăf'tən, käf'-) *n.* Variant of **caftan.**

Kail·yard School (kāl'yärd') *n.* A group of writers who make considerable use of Scots dialect in their works about Scottish life. [Sc. *kailyard,* kitchen garden : *kail,* kale + YARD.]

kain (kān) *n.* Tax or rent payments made in kind. [ME *cain* < Sc. Gael. *cāin.*]

kai·nite (kī'nīt', kā'-) *n.* A mineral, $KCL \cdot MgSO_4 \cdot 3H_2O$, used as fertilizer and as a source of potassium compounds. [G. *Kainit* : Gk. *kainos,* new + *-it,* -ite.]

Kai·ser (kī'zər) *n.* An emperor of the Holy Roman Empire (A.D. 962–1806), of Austria (1804–1918), or of Germany (1871–1918). [ME < OE *cāsere,* ult. < Lat. *Caesar,* Caesar. —see CAESAR.]

Kai·ser·in (kī'zər-ĭn) *n.* The wife of a Kaiser. [G., fem. of *Kaiser,* Kaiser < OHG *Keisur* < Lat. *Caesar,* Caesar. —see CAESAR.]

ka·ka (kä'kə) *n.* A brownish-green New Zealand parrot, *Nestor meridionalis.* [Maori.]

ka·ka·po (kä'kə-pō') *n., pl.* **-pos.** A ground-dwelling New Zealand parrot, *Strigops habroptilus,* with greenish plumage. [Maori : *kaka,* parrot + *po,* night.]

ka·ke·mo·no (kä'kə-mō'nō) *n., pl.* **-nos.** A vertical Japanese scroll painting. [J. : *kake,* hanging + *mono,* object.]

kak·is·toc·ra·cy (kăk'ĭ-stŏk'rə-sē, kä'kĭ-) *n.* Government by the least qualified or most unprincipled citizens. [Gk. *kakistos,* worst + -CRACY.]

ka·la-a·zar (kä'lə-ə-zär') *n.* A chronic, usually fatal disease occurring chiefly in Asia, caused by a protozoan parasite, *Leishmania donovani,* and characterized by irregular fever, enlargement of the spleen and liver, hemorrhages, and extreme emaciation. [Hindi *kālā-āzār* : *kālā,* black (< Skt. *kālā* , of Dravidian orig.) + *āzār,* disease < Pers.]

kale (kāl) *n.* **1.** A variety of cabbage, *Brassica oleracea acephala,* with crinkled leaves that do not form a tight head. **2.** *Slang.* Money. [ME < OE *cāl,* cole < Lat. *caulis,* cabbage.]

ka·lei·do·scope (kə-lī'də-skōp') *n.* **1.** A tube-shaped optical instrument that is rotated to produce a succession of symmetrical designs by means of mirrors reflecting the constantly changing patterns made by bits of colored glass at one end of the tube. **2.** A constantly changing set of colors. **3.** A series of changing phases or events. [Gk. *kalos,* beautiful + *eidos,* form + -SCOPE.] **—ka·lei'do·scop'ic** (-skŏp'ĭk), **ka·lei'do·scop'i·cal** *adj.* **—ka·lei'do·scop'i·cal·ly** *adv.*

kal·ends (kăl'əndz, kā'ləndz) *n.* Variant of **calends.**

ka·lim·ba (kə-lĭm'bə) *n.* An African musical instrument in the shape of a wooden box set with metal bars that are plucked with the fingers. [Of African orig.]

Kal·muck also **Kal·muk** (kăl'mŭk', kăl-mŭk') or **Kal·myk** (kăl'mĭk, kăl-mĭk') *n.* **1.** A member of a Buddhist Mongol people originally of northwestern China. **2.** The Mongolian language of the Kalmucks. [R. *Kalmyk.*]

kal·so·mine (kăl'sə-mīn') *n.* Variant of **calcimine.**

Ka·ma (kä'mə) *n.* The Hindu god of love. [Skt. *kāmaḥ.*]

ka·ma·la (kä'mə-lə, kăm'ə-) *n.* **1.** An Asian tree, *Mallotus philippinensis,* that bears a hairy, capsular fruit. **2.** A vermifugal powder obtained from the capsules of the kamala. [Skt. *kamalam,* lotus, prob. of Dravidian orig.]

Ka·ma·su·tra (kä'mə-sōō'trə) *n.* A Sanskrit treatise setting forth rules for love and marriage in accordance with Hindu law. [Skt. *kāmasūtram* : *kāmaḥ,* love + *sūtram,* manual.]

kame (kām) *n.* A short ridge or mound of sand and gravel deposited during the melting of glacial ice. [Sc. < ME *camb,* comb < OE.]

ka·mi·ka·ze (kä'mĭ-kä'zē) *n.* **1.** In World War II, a Japanese pilot trained to make a suicidal crash attack. **2.** An airplane loaded with explosives to be piloted in a suicide attack. —*adj.* Suicidal: *kamikaze hot rodders.* [J. : *kami,* god + *kaze,* wind.]

ka·na (kä'nə) *n.* **1.** Hiragana. **2.** Katakana. [J., pseudo-characters : *ka,* false (< Chin. *jia*[3])+ *na,* name (< Chin. *ming*[2]).]

kan·a·my·cin (kăn'ə-mī'sĭn) *n.* A water-soluble broad-spectrum antibiotic, $C_{18}H_{36}O_{11}N_4$, from a soil actinomycete. [NLat. *kanamyceticus* (specific epithet of a species of actinomycete) + -IN.]

Kan·a·rese (kăn'ə-rēz', -rēs') *n., pl.* **Kanarese. 1.** One of the Kannada-speaking peoples of Mysore, Republic of India. **2.** Kannada. [After *Kanara,* an area of southwest India.] **—Kan'ar·ese'** *adj.*

kan·ga·roo (kăng'gə-rōō') *n.* Any of various herbivorous marsupials of the family Macropodidae, of Australia and adjacent areas, with short forelimbs, large hind limbs adapted for leaping, and a long, tapered tail. [Prob. < a native word in Australia.]

kangaroo court *n.* **1.** A mock court set up in violation of established legal procedure. **2.** A court characterized by dishonesty or incompetence.

kangaroo rat *n.* Any of various long-tailed rodents of the genera *Dipodomys* and *Microdipodops,* of arid areas of western North America, with long hind legs adapted for jumping.

kangaroo vine *n.* A climbing or trailing vine, *Cissus antarctica,* native to Australia and often grown as a house plant for its glossy green foliage.

Kan·na·da (kä'nə-də) *n.* The principal Dravidian language of Mysore, a state in southern India.

ka·o·lin also **ka·o·line** (kā'ə-lĭn) *n.* A fine clay used in ceramics and refractories and as a filler or coating for paper and textiles. [Fr. < Chin. (Mandarin) *gao*[1] *ling*[3], an area of Jiangxi Province where it was first obtained.]

ka·o·lin·ite (kā'ə-lĭ-nīt') *n.* A mineral, $Al_2O_3 \cdot 2SiO_2 \cdot 2H_2O$, the principal constituent of kaolin. **—ka'o·lin·i'tic** *adj.*

ka·on (kā'ŏn') *n.* An unstable meson produced in either an electrically charged form or a neutral form as the result of a high-energy particle collision. [*Ka,* pronunciation of the letter *k* + -ON.]

Ka·pell·meis·ter (kə-pĕl'mī'stər, kä-) *n., pl.* **Kapellmeister.** The leader of a choir or orchestra. [G. : *kapell,* choir + *Meister,* master.]

kaph (käf, kôf) *n.* The 11th letter of the Hebrew alphabet. See table at **alphabet.** [Heb. *kāph.*]

ka·pok (kā'pŏk') *n.* A silky fiber obtained from the fruit of the silk-cotton tree and used for insulation and as padding in pillows, mattresses, and life preservers. [Malay.]

kap·pa (kăp'ə) *n.* The 10th letter of the Greek alphabet. See table at **alphabet.** [Gk., of Phoenician orig., akin to Heb. *kāph.*]

ka·put also **ka·putt** (kä-pŏŏt', -pōōt', kə-) *adj. Informal.* **1.** Destroyed; wrecked. **2.** Incapacitated. [G. *kaputt* < Fr. *capot,* not having won a trick at piquet.]

kar·a·bi·ner (kăr'ə-bē'nər) *n.* An oblong steel ring that is snapped to the eye of a piton and through which a rope is run, used in mountaineering. [G.]

kar·a·kul (kăr'ə-kəl) *n.* **1.** One of a breed of Central Asian sheep with a pelt that is curled and glossy in the young but wiry and coarse in the adult. **2.** Fur made from the pelt of a karakul lamb. [After *Karakul,* a lake in central Asian USSR.]

kar·at (kăr'ət) *n.* A unit of measure for the fineness of gold, equal to 1/24 of the total amount of pure gold in an alloy. [OFr. *carat,* unit of weight for precious stones. —see CARAT.]

ka·ra·te (kə-rä'tē) *n.* A Japanese art of self-defense in which sharp blows and kicks are administered to pressure-sensitive points on the body of an opponent. [J. : *kara,* empty + *te,* hand.] **—ka·ra'te·ist** *n.*

kar·ma (kär'mə, kûr'-) *n.* **1.** *Hinduism & Buddhism.* The total effect of a person's actions and conduct during the successive phases of his existence, regarded as determining his destiny. **2.** Fate; destiny. **3.** *Informal.* A distinctive aura, atmosphere, or feeling: *There's bad karma around this place today.* [Skt. *karman,* deed < *karoti,* he does.] **—kar'mic** (-mĭk) *adj.*

ka·roo also **kar·roo** (kə-rōō') *n.* An arid plateau of southern Africa. [Afr. *karo,* of Hottentot orig.]

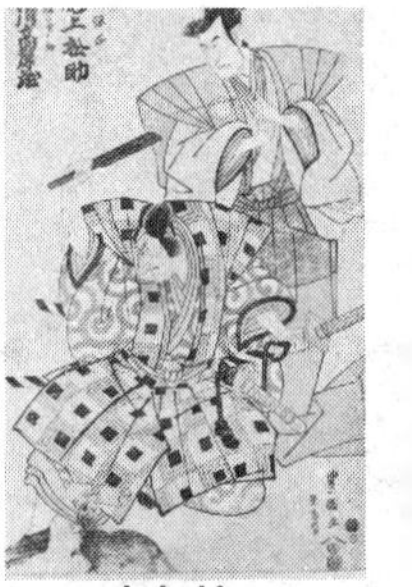

kabuki
Japanese print of kabuki actors

kangaroo

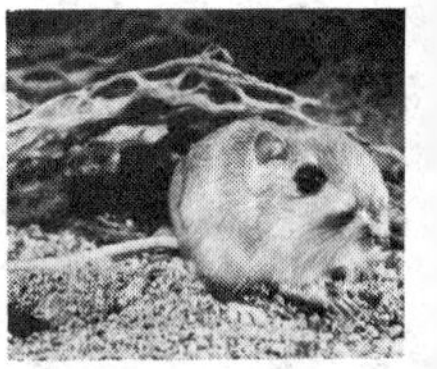

kangaroo rat

kapok

karate

karst (kärst) *n.* An area of irregular limestone in which erosion has produced fissures, sinkholes, underground streams, and caverns. [G.] **—karst'ic** *adj.*
kart (kärt) *n.* A miniature car used in racing. [Prob. < *Go-Kart,* a trademark.]
kart·ing (kär'tĭng) *n.* The sport of racing miniature cars.
karyo– also **caryo–** *pref.* **1.** Cell nucleus: *karyogamy.* **2.** Nut; kernel: *caryopsis.* [NLat. < Gk. *karuon,* nut.]
kar·y·og·a·my (kăr'ē-ŏg'ə-mē) *n.* The coming together and fusing of gamete nuclei.
kar·y·o·ki·ne·sis (kăr'ē-ō-kə-nē'sĭs) *n.* Mitosis.
kar·y·o·lymph (kăr'ē-ə-lĭmf') *n.* The clear homogeneous liquid portion of nuclear protoplasm.
kar·y·o·plasm (kăr'ē-ə-plăz'əm) *n.* Nucleoplasm. **—kar'y·o·plas'mic** (-mĭk) *adj.*
kar·y·o·some (kăr'ē-ə-sōm') *n.* A spherical aggregation of chromatin in a resting nucleus during mitosis.
kar·y·o·type (kăr'ē-ə-tīp') *n.* **1.** The chromosomal complement of an individual or of a species. **2.** A photomicrograph of metaphase chromosomes in a standard array. **—kar'y·o·typ'ic** (-tĭp'ĭk), **kar'y·o·typ'i·cal** *adj.*
ka·sha (kä'shə) *n.* Buckwheat groats. [R.]
Kash·mir goat (kăsh'mîr', kăzh'-) *n.* Variant of **Cashmere goat.**
Kash·mir·i (kăsh-mîr'ē, kăzh-) *n.* An Indic language of Jammu and Kashmir.
ka·ta·ka·na (kä'tä-kä'nä) *n.* A phonetic Japanese syllabary used for writing foreign words or documents, such as telegrams. [J. : *kata,* one + *kana,* kana.]
Ka·tha·rev·u·sa (kä'thə-rĕv'ə-sä'). The official form of Modern Greek, which contains morphological and lexical features borrowed from classical Greek. [Mod. Gk. *kathareuousa* < Gk. < *kathareuein,* to be pure < *katharos,* pure.]
ka·thar·sis (kə-thär'sĭs) *n.* Variant of **catharsis.**
ka·ty·did (kā'tē-dĭd') *n.* Any of various green insects related to the grasshoppers and the crickets, with specialized organs on the wings of the male that produce a shrill sound when rubbed together. [Imit. of its sound.]
katz·en·jam·mer (kăt'sən-jăm'ər) *n.* **1.** A loud, discordant noise. **2.** A hangover. **3.** A state of depression or bewilderment. [G. : *Katzen,* cats + *Jammer,* misery.]
kau·ri (kou'rē) *n.* **1. a.** Any of several coniferous trees of the genus *Agathis,* esp. *A. australis,* of New Zealand. **b.** The white, close-grained wood of this tree. **2.** A resin that is obtained directly from the kauri or from deposits of its fossilized resin and used in varnishes and enamels. [Maori *kawri.*]
ka·va (kä'və) *n.* **1.** An Australasian shrub, *Piper methysticum,* whose roots are used to make an intoxicating beverage. **2.** The beverage made from kava. [Tongan, kava, bitter.]
kay (kā) *n.* The letter *k.*
Kay (kā) *n.* In Arthurian legend, the foster brother and steward of King Arthur.

kayak

kay·ak (kī'ăk') *n.* **1.** A watertight Eskimo canoe consisting of a light wooden frame completely covered with skins except for an opening in the center. **2.** A lightweight canoe similar in construction to a kayak. [Eskimo *qajaq.*]
kay·o (kā-ō', kā'ō') *Slang.* *—n., pl.* **-os.** A knockout in boxing. *—tr.v.* **-oed, -o·ing, -os.** To knock out; put out of commission. [Pronunciation of *K.O.,* abbreviation of *knock out.*]

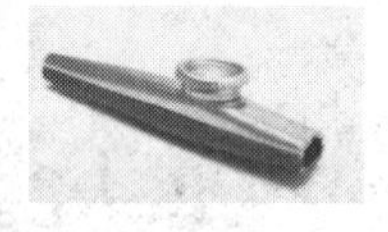
kazoo

ka·zoo (kə-zōō') *n., pl.* **-zoos.** A toy musical instrument with a membrane that produces a sound when a player hums or sings into the mouthpiece. [Imit. of its sound.]
ke·a (kē'ə) *n.* A brownish-green New Zealand parrot, *Nestor notabilis,* that normally eats insects but sometimes kills sheep by slashing them and eating their fat and flesh. [Maori.]
ke·bab also **ke·bob** (kə-bŏb') *n.* Shish kebab.
Kech·ua (kĕch'wə, -wä') *n.* Variant of **Quechua.**
kedge (kĕj) *Naut.* *—n.* A light anchor used for warping a vessel. *—v.* **kedged, kedg·ing, kedg·es.** *—tr.* To warp (a vessel) by means of a kedge. *—intr.* To move by means of a kedge. [< *kedge,* to warp a vessel, poss. < ME *caggen,* to tie.]
kedg·er·ee (kĕj'ə-rē', kĕj'ə-rē') *n.* A dish consisting of flaked fish, boiled rice, and eggs. [Hindi *khichṛī* < Skt. *khiccā.*]

keel[1]

keel[1] (kēl) *n.* **1. a.** The principal structural member of a ship, running lengthwise along the center line from bow to stern, to which the frames are attached. **b.** A corresponding structure on an aircraft. **2.** A ship. **3.** A structure, as the breastbone of a bird, that resembles a ship's keel in function or shape. **4.** A pair of united petals in certain flowers, as those of the pea. *—tr.v. & intr.v.* **keeled, keel·ing, keels.** To capsize. ***—phrasal verb.*** **keel over.** To collapse or fall in or as if in a faint: *keeled over when he heard the terrible news.* [ME *kele* < ON *kjölr.*]

keg

keel[2] (kēl) *n.* **1. a.** A freight barge, esp. one for carrying coal on the Tyne in England. **b.** The amount of coal this barge can hold. **2.** A British unit of weight formerly used for coal, equal to 21.2 long tons. [ME *kele* < MDu. *kiel.*]
keel[3] (kēl) *tr.v.* **keeled, keel·ing, keels.** *Archaic & Regional.* To make cool. [ME *kelen* < OE *cēlan,* to become cool.]
keel·boat (kēl'bōt') *n.* A river boat with a keel but without sails, used for carrying freight.
keel·haul (kēl'hôl') *tr.v.* **-hauled, -haul·ing, -hauls. 1.** To punish by dragging under the keel of a ship. **2.** To rebuke harshly. [Du. *kielhalen* : *kiel,* keel of a ship + *halen,* to haul.]
keel·son (kēl'sən, kĕl'-) *n. Naut.* A timber or girder fastened above and parallel to the keel for additional strength. [Poss. < LG *kielswin.*]
keen[1] (kēn) *adj.* **-er, -est. 1.** Having a fine, sharp cutting edge or point. **2.** Intellectually acute. **3.** Acutely sensitive. **4.** Sharp; vivid; strong: *"His entire body hungered for keen sensation, something exciting"* (Richard Wright). **5.** Intense; piercing: *a keen wind.* **6.** Pungent; acrid. **7. a.** Ardent; enthusiastic. **b.** Eagerly desirous: *keen on going.* **8.** *Slang.* Great; splendid; fine. [ME *kene* < OE *cēne,* brave.] **—keen'ly** *adv.* **—keen'ness** *n.*
keen[2] (kēn) *n.* A loud, wailing lament for the dead. *—intr.v.* **keened, keen·ing, keens.** To wail or lament loudly. [Ir. Gael. *caoine* < *caoninim,* I lament.] **—keen'er** *n.*
keep (kēp) *v.* **kept** (kĕpt), **keep·ing, keeps.** *—tr.* **1.** To retain possession of. **2.** To have as a supply. **3.** To provide with maintenance and support: *kept a wife and many children on a small salary.* **4.** To store; put customarily: *Where do you keep your saw?* **5. a.** To supply with room and board for a charge: *keep boarders.* **b.** To raise: *keep chickens.* **6.** To maintain for use or service: *a city dweller who didn't keep a car.* **7.** To manage, tend, or have charge of: *keep shop.* **8.** To preserve (food). **9.** To cause to continue in a state, condition, or course of action: *attempted to keep the patient calm.* **10. a.** To maintain records in: *keep a yearly diary.* **b.** To enter (data) in a book: *keep financial records.* **11. a.** To detain: *was kept after school.* **b.** To restrain: *kept the child away from the hot stove.* **c.** To refrain from divulging: *keep a secret.* **d.** To save; reserve: *keep extra money for emergencies.* **12.** To maintain: *keep late hours.* **13.** To adhere to; fulfill: *keep one's word.* **14.** To celebrate; observe. *—intr.* **1.** To remain in a state or condition; stay: *keep in line; keep quiet.* **2.** To continue to do: *keep on talking; keep guessing.* **3.** To remain fresh or unspoiled: *The dessert won't keep.* ***—phrasal verbs.*** **keep down.** To prevent from accomplishing or succeeding. **keep off.** To stay away from. **keep up. 1.** To maintain in good condition. **2.** To persevere in; carry on. **3.** To continue at the same level or pace. **4.** To match one's competitors, colleagues, or neighbors in success or lifestyle: *unsuccessfully tried to keep up with his associates.* *—n.* **1.** Care; charge: *The child is in my keep for the day.* **2.** The means by which one is supported: *earn one's keep.* **3. a.** The stronghold of a castle. **b.** A jail. ***—idioms.*** **for keeps. 1.** For an indefinitely long period: *gave it to me for keeps.* **2.** Seriously and permanently: *We're separating for keeps.* **keep at it.** To persevere in an action or work. **keep (one's) eyes open** or **peeled.** To be on the lookout. **keep (one's) nose clean.** To stay out of trouble. **keep pace.** To stay even. **keep to.** To adhere to: *keep to the original purpose.* **keep to (oneself). 1.** To shun the company of others. **2.** To refrain from divulging: *kept the news to herself.* [ME *kepen* < OE *cēpan,* to observe.]

Synonyms: *keep, retain, withhold, reserve, grasp, clutch.* These verbs mean to have something in one's possession or control. *Keep* is the most general and imprecise. *Retain* sometimes indicates mere possession but often in the face of loss: *what the mind retains; seeking to retain control. Withhold* implies a deliberate holding back of something in one's possession. *Reserve* refers to a holding back for the future or for a special purpose. In a related sense *reserve* refers to keeping for oneself the right to act in a certain way. *Grasp* and *clutch* apply to securing firm physical possession.

keep·er (kē'pər) *n.* **1.** One that keeps, esp.: **a.** An attendant, guard, or warden. **b.** One who has the charge or care of something. **2.** A device for keeping something in place.
keep·ing (kē'pĭng) *n.* **1.** The action of holding, guarding, or supporting. **2.** Custody; care; guardianship. **3.** Harmony; conformity.
keep·sake (kēp'sāk') *n.* Something given or kept; memento.
kees·hond (kās'hônt') *n., pl.* **-hon·den** (-hôn'dən) or **-honds.** A dog of a breed originating in the Netherlands, with a thick grayish-black coat. [Du., prob. : *kees,* nickname for *Cornelis,* Cornelius + *hond,* dog < MDu.]
kef (kēf, kĕf, käf) *n.* Variant of **kif.**
ke·fir (kĕ-fîr') *n.* A creamy drink made of fermented cow's milk. [R., of Caucasian orig.]
keg (kĕg) *n.* A small cask or barrel. [ME *kag* < ON *kaggi.*]
keg·ler (kĕg'lər) *n.* A person who bowls; bowler. [G. < *kegeln,* to bowl < *Kegel,* bowling pin < OHG *kegil,* peg.]
keis·ter (kē'stər) *n. Slang.* **1.** The buttocks. **2.** The anus. [Orig. unknown.]
kel·ly green (kĕl'ē) *n.* A strong yellowish green. [< the name *Kelly.*]
ke·loid (kē'loid') *n.* Tissue scarring that is caused by trauma or surgical incision. [Fr. *kéloïde* : Gk. *khēlē,* claw + *-oïde,* -oid.] **—ke·loid'al** *adj.*
kelp (kĕlp) *n.* **1.** Any of various brown, often very large seaweeds of the order Laminariales. **2.** The ash of kelp, used as a source of potash and iodine. [ME *culp.*]
kel·pie[1] also **kel·py** (kĕl'pē) *n., pl.* **-pies.** A malevolent water spirit of Scottish legend. [Prob. of Celt. orig.]
kel·pie[2] (kĕl'pē) *n.* A sheep dog of a breed originating in Australia. [< *Kelpie,* the name of an early specimen of the breed.]

ă pat / ā pay / âr care / ä father / b bib / ch church / d deed / ĕ pet / ē be / f fife / g gag / h hat / hw which / ĭ pit / ī pie / îr pier / j judge / k kick / l lid, needle / m mum / n no, sudden / ng thing / ŏ pot / ō toe / ô paw, for / oi noise / ou out / ŏŏ took / ōō boot /

kel·py (kĕl′pē) *n.* Variant of **kelpie[1]**.
Kelt (kĕlt) *n.* Variant of **Celt.**
Kelt·ic (kĕl′tĭk) *n. & adj.* Variant of **Celtic.**
kel·vin (kĕl′vĭn) *n.* The unit of thermodynamic temperature equal to 1/273.16 of the thermodynamic temperature of the triple point of water. [After William Thompson (1824–1907), first Baron *Kelvin.*]
Kel·vin (kĕl′vĭn) *adj.* Of or pertaining to an absolute scale of temperature whose zero point is approximately −273.16°C.
kempt (kĕmpt) *adj.* Tidy; trim: *a nicely kempt beard.* [Prob. back-formation < UNKEMPT.]
ken (kĕn) *v.* **kenned** or **kent** (kĕnt), **ken·ning, kens.** —*tr.* **1.** *Scot.* To know (a person or thing). **2.** *Regional.* To recognize. **3.** *Archaic.* To descry. —*intr. Scot.* To have an understanding of something. —*n.* **1.** Perception; understanding. **2. a.** Range of vision. **b.** View; sight. [ME *kennen* < OE *cennan,* to declare.]
Ken·dal green (kĕn′dl) *n.* **1.** A coarse green woolen fabric similar to tweed. **2.** The color of Kendal green. [After *Kendal,* England, where it was orig. made.]
ken·do (kĕn′dō) *n.* The Japanese art of fencing with bamboo sticks. [J.]
Ken·il·worth ivy (kĕn′əl-wûrth′) *n.* A trailing or climbing vine, *Cymbalaria muralis,* with lobed leaves and pale-purple flowers. [After *Kenilworth* Castle, Warwickshire, England.]
ken·nel[1] (kĕn′əl) *n.* **1.** A shelter for a dog. **2.** A pack of dogs, esp. hounds. **3.** An establishment where dogs are bred, trained, or boarded. **4.** The lair of a fox or other wild animal. —*v.* **-neled, -nel·ing, -nels** or **-nelled, -nel·ling, -nells.** —*tr.* To place or keep in or as if in a kennel. —*intr.* To take cover or lie in or as if in a kennel. [ME *kenel* < OFr. *chenil* < VLat. **canile* < Lat. *canis,* dog.]
ken·nel[2] (kĕn′əl) *n.* A gutter along a street. [ME *cannel* < ONFr. *canel,* channel < Lat. *canalis.*]
Ken·nel·ly-Heav·i·side layer (kĕn′ə-lē-hĕv′ē-sīd′) *n.* The E layer of the ionosphere. [After Arthur E. *Kennelly* (1861–1939) and Oliver *Heaviside* (1850–1925).]
ken·ning (kĕn′ĭng) *n.* A metaphorical, usually compound expression used as a name, esp. in Old English and Old Norse poetry. [ON < *kenna,* to name with a kenning, to know.]
ke·no (kē′nō) *n.* A game of chance, similar to lotto, that uses balls rather than counters. [Orig. unknown.]
ke·no·sis (kĭ-nō′sĭs) *n. Theol.* The relinquishment of the form of God by Christ in becoming man and suffering death. [LGk. *kenōsis* < Gk., an emptying < *kenoun,* to empty < *kenos,* empty.] —**ke·not′ic** (-nŏt′ĭk) *adj.*
kent (kĕnt) *v.* A past tense and past participle of **ken.**
kent·ledge (kĕnt′lĭj) *n.* Pig iron used as permanent ballast. [Orig. unknown.]
Ken·tuck·y bluegrass (kən-tŭk′ē) *n.* Bluegrass (sense 1).
Kentucky coffee tree *n.* A deciduous North American tree, *Gymnocladus dioica,* with flat, pulpy pods containing seeds formerly used as a coffee substitute.
Ke·ogh plan (kē′ō) *n.* A retirement plan for the self-employed and their employees. [After Eugene J. *Keogh* (b. 1907).]
ke·pi (kā′pē, kĕp′ē) *n.* A French military cap with a flat, circular top and a visor. [Fr. *képi* < dial. G. *käppi,* dim. of G. *Kappe,* cap < OHG *kappa,* cloak, prob. < LLat. *cappa,* cloak.]
kept (kĕpt) *v.* Past tense and past participle of **keep.**
kerat– *pref.* Variant of **kerato-.**
ker·a·tec·to·my (kĕr′ə-tĕk′tə-mē) *n., pl.* **-mies.** Surgical removal of all or part of the cornea.
ker·a·tin (kĕr′ə-tĭn) *n.* A tough, fibrous protein substance that forms the outer layer of epidermal structures such as hair, nails, horns, and hoofs. [Gk. *keras, kerat-,* horn + -IN.] —**ke·rat′i·nous** (kə-răt′n-əs) *adj.*
ker·a·tin·ize (kĕr′ə-tə-nīz′) *tr. & intr.v.* **-ized, -iz·ing, -iz·es.** To convert into keratin. —**ker′a·tin·i·za′tion** *n.*
ker·a·ti·tis (kĕr′ə-tī′tĭs) *n., pl.* **-tit·i·des** (-tĭt′ĭ-dēz′). Inflammation of the cornea.
kerato– or **kerat–** *pref.* **1.** Horn; horny: *keratosis.* **2.** Cornea: *keratectomy.* [Gk. *kerato-* < *keras,* horn.]
ker·a·to·sis (kĕr′ə-tō′sĭs) *n., pl.* **-ses** (-sēz′). A condition of the skin characterized by excessive growth of horny tissue. —**ker′a·tot′ic** (-tŏt′ĭk) *adj.*
kerb (kûrb) *n. Chiefly Brit.* Variant of **curb** (sense 2).
ker·chief (kûr′chĭf, -chēf′) *n.* **1.** A woman's square scarf, often worn as a head covering. **2.** A handkerchief. [ME *courchef* < OFr. *couvrechef* : *covrir,* to cover (< Lat. *cooperire* : *co(m)-,* completely + *operire,* to cover) + *chef,* head < Lat. *caput.*]
kerf (kûrf) *n.* **1.** A groove or notch made by a cutting tool such as a saw or an ax. **2.** The width of a groove made by a cutting tool. [ME < OE *cyrf,* act of cutting.]
ker·mes (kûr′mēz) *n.* The dried bodies of the females of various scale insects of the genus *Kermes,* used as a red dyestuff. [Fr. *kermès* < Ar. *qirmiz.*]
ker·mis also **ker·mess** or **kir·mess** (kûr′mĭs) *n.* **1.** An outdoor fair in the Low Countries. **2.** A fund-raising fair or carnival. [Du. *kermis* < MDu. *kercmisse* : *kerc,* church + *misse,* mass < LLat. *missa* < Lat. *mittere,* to send.]
kern[1] also **kerne** (kûrn) *n.* **1.** A medieval Scottish or Irish foot soldier. **2.** A loutish person. [ME *kerne* < OIr. *ceithern,* band of foot soldiers, poss. < *cath,* battle.]
kern[2] (kûrn) *Printing.* —*n.* The portion of a typeface that projects beyond the body or shank of a character. —*tr.v.* **kerned, kern·ing, kerns.** To provide (type) with a kern. [Fr. *carne,* corner < Lat. *cardo,* hinge.]
kerne (kûrn) *n.* Variant of **kern[1]**.
ker·nel (kûr′nəl) *n.* **1.** A grain or seed, as of a cereal grass, enclosed in a hard husk. **2.** The inner, usually edible part of a nut or fruit stone. **3.** The most material and central part; core. [ME *kirnel* < OE *cyrnel,* dim. of *corn,* seed.]
kern·ite (kûr′nīt′) *n.* A colorless to white crystalline compound, $Na_2B_4O_7 \cdot 4H_2O$, that is a major source of borax and boron compounds. [After *Kern* County, California.]
ker·o·gen (kĕr′ə-jən) *n.* A bituminous material in shale that yields oil upon heating. [Gk. *kēros,* wax + -GEN.]
ker·o·sene or **ker·o·sine** (kĕr′ə-sēn′, kĕr′ə-sēn′, kăr′ə-sēn′, kăr′ə-sēn′) *n.* A thin oil that is distilled from petroleum or shale oil, used as a fuel and alcohol denaturant. [Orig. a trademark.]
Ker·ry (kĕr′ē) *n., pl.* **-ries.** One of a breed of small, black dairy cattle of Irish origin. [After County *Kerry,* Ireland.]
Kerry blue terrier *n.* One of a breed of terriers of Irish origin, with a dense, wavy bluish-gray coat. [After County *Kerry,* Ireland.]
ker·sey (kûr′zē) *n., pl.* **-seys. 1.** A woolen, often ribbed fabric formerly used for hose and trousers. **2.** A twilled woolen fabric, sometimes with a cotton warp, used for coats. **3.** Often **kerseys.** A garment made of kersey. [ME, prob. after *Kersey,* a village in Suffolk, England.]
ker·sey·mere (kûr′zē-mîr′) *n.* A fine woolen cloth with a fancy twill weave. [Alteration of CASSIMERE.]
kes·trel (kĕs′trəl) *n.* **1.** A small Old World falcon, *Falco tinnunculus,* with brown and gray plumage. **2.** Any of several Old World falcons. [ME *castrel,* prob. < OFr. *cresserelle.*]
ket– *pref.* Variant of **keto-.**
ketch (kĕch) *n.* A two-masted fore-and-aft-rigged sailing vessel with a mizzen or jigger mast stepped aft of a taller mainmast but forward of the rudder. [ME *cache.*]
ketch·up (kĕch′əp, kăch′-) *n.* A condiment consisting of a thick, smooth-textured, spicy sauce usually made from tomatoes. [Chin. (Amoy) *ketsiap,* a kind of sauce.]
ke·tene (kē′tēn′) *n.* A pungent, toxic, colorless gas, H_2C_2O, used chiefly as an acetylation agent.
keto– or **ket–** *pref.* Ketone: *ketosis.* [< KETONE.]
ke·to·gen·e·sis (kē′tō-jĕn′ĭ-sĭs) *n.* The formation of ketone bodies, as in diabetes. —**ke′to·gen′ic** *adj.*
ke·tone (kē′tōn′) *n.* Any of a class of organic compounds having a carbonyl group linked to a carbon atom in each of two hydrocarbon radicals and having the general formula $R_1(CO)R_2$, where R_1 may be the same as R_2. [G. < *Aketon,* acetone.] —**ke·ton′ic** (kē-tŏn′ĭk) *adj.*
ketone body *n.* Any of several substances, such as acetoacetic acid, increasing in the blood in certain diabetic and other pathological conditions.
ke·tose (kē′tōs′) *n.* Any of various carbohydrates containing a ketone group in each molecule.
ke·to·sis (kē-tō′sĭs) *n.* A pathological accumulation of ketone bodies in the body. —**ke·tot′ic** (-tŏt′ĭk) *adj.*
ke·to·ste·roid (kē′tō-stîr′oid′, -stĕr′-) *n.* A steroid containing a ketone group.
ket·tle (kĕt′l) *n.* **1.** A metal pot, usually with a lid, for boiling or stewing. **2.** A teakettle. **3.** A kettledrum. **4.** A depression left in a mass of glacial drift, apparently formed by the melting of an isolated block of glacial ice. **5.** A pothole. —*idiom.* **kettle of fish. 1.** A troublesomely awkward or embarrassing situation. **2.** A matter to be reckoned with: *Making money and keeping it are two quite different kettles of fish.* [ME *ketel* < ON *ketill*]
ket·tle·drum (kĕt′l-drŭm′) *n.* A large copper or brass hemispherical drum with a parchment head that can be tuned by adjusting the tension.
kev·el (kĕv′əl) *n.* A sturdy belaying pin for the heavier cables of a ship. [ME *kevile,* peg < ONFr. *keville* < Lat. *clavicula,* dim. of *clavis,* key.]
kew·pie (kyōō′pē) *n.* A small, fat-cheeked, wide-eyed doll with a curl of hair on top of the head. [Orig. a trademark.]
key[1] (kē) *n., pl.* **keys. 1. a.** A usually metal notched and grooved implement that is turned to open or close a lock. **b.** A device that functions like a key: *the key of a clock; opened the can with a key.* **2.** Something that is a means of access, control, or possession. **3. a.** A vital, crucial element. **b.** A set of answers to a test. **c.** A table, gloss, or cipher for decoding or interpreting. **4.** A device, as a wedge or pin, inserted to lock together mechanical or structural parts. **5.** The keystone in the crown of an arch. **6. a.** A button or lever that is pressed with the finger to operate a machine. **b.** A button or lever that is pressed with the finger to produce or modulate the sound of a musical instrument, as a clarinet or a piano. **7.** *Mus.* **a.** A tonal system consisting of seven tones in fixed relationship to a tonic, having a characteristic key signature and being since the Renaissance the structural foundation of the bulk of Western music; tonality. **b.** The principal tonality of a musical work: *an etude in the key of E.* **8.** The pitch of a voice or other sound: *She spoke in a high key.* **9.** A characteristic tone or level of intensity, as of a speech, theatrical performance, or sales campaign. **10.** A samara. **11.** *Slang.* A kilogram of marijuana or

kepi

kerf

Kerry blue terrier

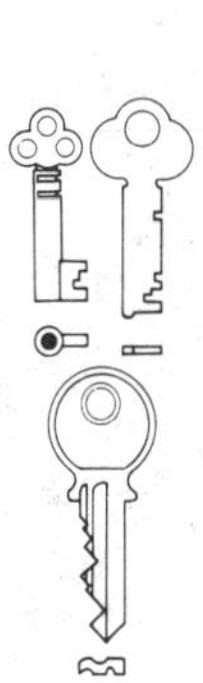
key[1]
A variety of keys

heroin. ***—modifier:*** *key decisions; the key element; a key chain.* *—tr.v.* **keyed, key·ing, keys. 1.** To lock with or as if with a key. **2.** To furnish (an arch) with a keystone. **3.** To regulate the musical pitch of. **4.** To bring into harmony; adjust; adapt. **5.** To supply an explanatory key for. ***—phrasal verb.*** **key up.** To make intense or nervous. ***—idiom.*** **in** (or **out of**) **key.** In (or out of) tune with other factors. [ME < OE *cæg.*]

key[2] (kē) *n., pl.* **keys.** A low offshore island or reef, esp. in the Gulf of Mexico. [Sp. *cayo,* prob. < OFr. *quai,* quay, of Celtic orig.]

key·board (kē′bôrd′, -bōrd′) *n.* A set of keys, as on a piano, an organ, or a typewriter. *—tr.v.* **-board·ed, -board·ing, -boards.** To set (copy) by means of a keyed typesetting machine. **—key′board′er** *n.*

key·card (kē′kärd′) *n.* A coded, usually plastic card that is scanned in order to operate a mechanism such as a door or a cash-dispensing machine.

key club *n.* A private club featuring liquor and entertainment. [From the key to the premises given to each member.]

keyed (kēd) *adj.* **1.** Equipped with keys. **2.** Strengthened or secured with a key. **3.** Built with a keystone: *a keyed arch.*

key fruit *n.* A samara. [From its shape.]

key·hole (kē′hōl′) *n.* The hole in a lock into which a key fits.

key money *n.* Payment made to a landlord as an inducement to assure a rental.

keystone

Keynes·i·an (kān′zē-ən) *adj.* Of or pertaining to the economic theories of John M. Keynes, esp. those theories advocating government monetary and fiscal programs designed to increase employment. *—n.* A supporter of Keynes's economic views. **—Keynes′i·an·ism** *n.*

key·note (kē′nōt′) *n.* **1.** The tonic of a musical key. **2.** A prime underlying element or theme: *"the keynote of the revolution settlement was personal freedom under the law"* (G.M. Trevelyan). *—tr.v.* **-not·ed, -not·ing, -notes. 1.** To give or set the keynote of. **2.** To give a keynote address at.

keynote address *n.* An opening address, as at a political convention, that outlines the issues to be considered.

key·not·er (kē′nō′tər) *n.* One who gives a keynote address.

keynote speech *n.* A keynote address.

key·punch (kē′pŭnch′) *n.* A keyboard machine that is used to punch holes in cards or tapes for data-processing systems. *—tr.v. & intr.v.* **-punched, -punch·ing, -punch·es.** To process on a keypunch. **—key′punch′er** *n.*

key signature *n.* The group of sharps or flats placed to the right of the clef on a musical staff to identify the key.

key·stone (kē′stōn′) *n.* **1.** *Archit.* The central wedge-shaped stone of an arch that locks its parts together. **2.** Something that is the central supporting element of a whole.

key·stroke (kē′strōk′) *n.* A stroke of a key, as of a typewriter or word processor.

key·way (kē′wā′) *n.* **1.** A slot in a wheel hub or shaft for a key. **2.** The keyhole of a cylinder lock.

khak·i (kăk′ē, kä′kē) *n.* **1.** A color ranging from light olive brown to yellowish brown. **2.** A sturdy cloth of the color khaki. **3. khakis.** A uniform of khaki cloth. *—adj.* Of the color khaki. [Urdu < *khāk,* dust < Pers.]

kham·sin (kăm-sēn′) *n.* A generally southerly hot wind from the Sahara that blows across Egypt from late March to early May. [Ar. *rīḥ al-khamsīn,* wind of the 50 days.]

khan[1] (kän, kăn) *n.* **1.** A ruler, an official, or an important person in India and some central Asian countries. **2.** A medieval ruler of a Mongol, Tatar, or Turkish tribe. [ME *caan* < OFr. < Turk. *khān,* ruler.]

khan[2] (kän, kăn) *n.* A caravansary in certain countries of Asia. [Ar. *khān.*]

khan·ate (kä′nāt′, kăn′āt′) *n.* **1.** The realm of a khan. **2.** The position of a khan.

khe·dive (kə-dēv′) *n.* A Turkish viceroy ruling Egypt from 1867 to 1914. [Fr. *khédive* < Turk. *hidiv* < Pers. *khidīw,* prince.]

khi (kī) *n.* Variant of **chi.**

Khmer (kə-mâr) *n., pl.* **Khmer** or **Khmers. 1. a.** A people of Cambodia. **b.** A member of this people. **2.** The Mon-Khmer language of the Khmer that is the official language of Cambodia. **—Khmer′i·an** *adj.*

Khoi·san (koi′sän′) *n.* A family of languages of southwestern Africa, including those of the Bushmen and the Hottentots.

khoum (ko͞om, ko͝om) *n.* See table at **currency.** [Native word in Mauritania.]

ki·ang (kē-äng′) *n.* A wild ass, *Equus hemionus kiang,* of the mountains of eastern Asia. [Tibetan *rkyan.*]

klaugh (kyäKH) *n. Scot.* Trouble; anxiety. [Prob. < Sc. Gael. *cabhag.*]

kib·butz (kĭ-bo͞ots′, -bo͝ots′) *n., pl.* **kib·but·zim** (kĭb′o͞ot-sēm′, -o͝ot-). A collective farm or settlement in modern Israel. [Mod. Heb. *qibbūṣ* < Heb., gathering < *qibbēṣ,* he gathered.]

kibe (kīb) *n.* An ulcerated chilblain, esp. one on the heel. [ME *kybe,* poss. < Welsh *cibi.*]

kib·itz (kĭb′ĭts, kĭ-bĭts′) *intr.v.* **-itzed, -itz·ing, -itz·es.** *Informal.* **1.** To look on and offer unwanted and usually meddlesome advice to others. **2.** To chat; converse. [Yiddish *kibitsen* < G. *kiebitzen,* to look on < *Kiebitz,* kibitzer, lapwing.] **—kib′itz·er** *n.*

kib·lah (kĭb′lə) *n.* The direction toward which Moslems face when they pray. [Ar. *qiblah.*]

ki·bosh (kī′bŏsh′, kī-bŏsh′) *n. Informal.* Something that checks or stops: *put the kibosh on that stupid plan.* [Orig. unknown.]

kick (kĭk) *v.* **kicked, kick·ing, kicks.** *—intr.* **1.** To strike out with the foot or feet. **2. a.** To score or gain ground by kicking a ball. **b.** *Football.* To punt. **3.** To recoil, as a gun when fired. **4.** *Informal.* **a.** To express negative feelings vigorously; complain. **b.** To oppose by argument; protest. *—tr.* **1.** To strike with the foot. **2.** To propel by striking with the foot. **3.** To spring back against suddenly, as a gun when fired. **4.** *Sports.* To score (a goal or point) by kicking a ball. ***—phrasal verbs.*** **kick around.** *Informal.* **1.** To treat badly; abuse. **2.** To move from place to place. **3.** To give consideration or thought to (an idea). **kick back. 1.** To recoil unexpectedly and violently. **2.** *Slang.* To return (stolen items). **3.** *Slang.* To pay a kickback. **kick in.** *Slang.* **1.** To contribute (one's share). **2.** To die. **kick off. 1.** *Sports.* To begin or resume play with a kickoff. **2.** To begin; start. **3.** *Slang.* To die. **kick out.** *Slang.* To throw out; dismiss. **kick up. 1.** To cause to be propelled upward with force: *tires kicking up gravel.* **2.** To stir up (trouble): *kicked up a row.* **3.** To show signs of disorder: *His ulcer kicked up.* *—n.* **1. a.** A vigorous blow with the foot. **b.** The thrusting motion of the legs in swimming. **2.** The jolting recoil of a gun. **3.** *Slang.* Complaint; protest. **4.** *Slang.* Power; force: *still a lot of kick in that engine.* **5.** *Slang.* **a.** A feeling of pleasurable stimulation: *got a kick out of the show.* **b. kicks.** Fun; thrills: *just for kicks.* **6.** *Slang.* Temporary, often obsessive interest: *He's on a science-fiction kick.* **7.** *Slang.* A sudden, striking surprise; twist. **8. a.** An act or instance of kicking a ball. **b.** A kicked ball. **c.** The distance spanned by a kicked ball. ***—idioms.*** **kick the bucket.** *Slang.* To die. **kick the habit.** *Slang.* To free oneself of an addiction, as to narcotics or cigarettes. **kick up (one's) heels.** *Slang.* To cast off one's inhibitions and have a good time. **kick upstairs.** To promote to a higher yet less desirable position. [ME *kiken.*]

Kick·a·poo (kĭk′ə-po͞o′) *n., pl.* **Kickapoo** or **-poos. 1. a.** A tribe of Indians formerly of northern Illinois and southern Wisconsin. **b.** A member of this tribe. **2.** The Algonquian language of the Kickapoo. [Kickapoo *kiwĕgapawa.*]

kick·back (kĭk′băk′) *n.* **1.** A sharp reaction; repercussion. **2.** *Slang.* A percentage payment to a person able to influence or control a source of income, as by confidential arrangement or coercion.

kick·er (kĭk′ər) *n.* **1.** One that kicks. **2.** *Informal.* A sudden, surprising turn of events; twist. **3.** A tricky or concealed condition; pitfall. **4.** A condition that imposes an automatic increase, as in a pension plan.

kick·off (kĭk′ôf′, -ŏf′) *n.* **1.** *Sports.* A place kick in football or soccer with which play is begun. **2.** A beginning.

kick plate *n.* A protective sheet of metal attached to the bottom of a door.

kick·shaw (kĭk′shô′) *n.* **1.** A fancy food; delicacy. **2.** A trinket; gewgaw. [Alteration of Fr. *quelque chose,* something.]

kick·stand (kĭk′stănd′) *n.* A swiveling metal bar for holding a two-wheeled vehicle, as a motorcycle, upright when not being ridden.

kick·y (kĭk′ē) *adj.* **-i·er, -i·est.** *Slang.* Providing a kick by being unusual or unconventional.

kid (kĭd) *n.* **1. a.** A young goat. **b.** The young of a similar animal, such as an antelope. **2.** The flesh of a young goat. **3.** Leather made from the skin of a young goat. **4.** An article made of kidskin. **5.** *Informal.* **a.** A child. **b.** A young person. **6.** *Slang.* Pal. Used as a term of familiar address, esp. for a young person: *Hi, kid! What's up?* ***—modifier:*** *a kid belt; a kid brother who is four years younger.* *—v.* **kid·ded, kid·ding, kids.** *—tr. Informal.* **1.** To mock playfully; tease. **2.** To deceive in fun; fool. *—intr.* **1.** *Informal.* To engage in teasing or good-humored fooling. **2.** To bear young, as a goat or an antelope. [ME < ON *kið.*] **—kid′der** *n.* **—kid′ding·ly** *adv.*

Kid·der·min·ster (kĭd′ər-mĭn′stər) *n.* An ingrain carpet. [After *Kidderminster,* England, where it was originally made.]

kid·die (kĭd′ē) *n.* Variant of **kiddy.**

kid·do (kĭd′ō) *n., pl.* **-os.** *Slang.* Pal. Used as a term of familiar address: *I'm a detective, kiddo; watch it!*

Kid·dush (kĭd′əsh, kĭ-do͞osh′) *n. Judaism.* The traditional blessing and prayer recited over bread or a cup of wine on the eve of the Sabbath or a festival. [Heb. *qiddūsh* < *qiddesh,* he sanctified.]

kid·dy also **kid·die** (kĭd′ē) *n., pl.* **-dies.** *Slang.* A small child.

kid glove *n.* A glove made of fine, soft leather, esp. kidskin. ***—idiom.*** **with kid gloves.** Tactfully and cautiously.

kid·nap (kĭd′năp′) *tr.v.* **-napped, -nap·ping, -naps** or **-naped, -nap·ing, -naps.** To seize and detain unlawfully and usually for ransom. [Prob. back-formation < *kidnapper* : KID + obs. *napper,* thief.] **—kid′nap′per, kid′nap′er** *n.*

kid·ney (kĭd′nē) *n., pl.* **-neys. 1.** *Anat.* Either of a pair of structures in the dorsal region of the vertebrate abdominal cavity, functioning to maintain proper water balance, regulate acid-base concentration, and excrete metabolic wastes as urine. **2.** The kidney of certain animals, eaten as food. **3.** An excretory organ of certain invertebrates. **4.** Kind; sort. [ME *kidenei.*]

kidney bean *n.* **1.** A bean, *Phaseolus vulgaris,* cultivated in many forms for its edible seeds. **2.** The reddish seed of the kidney bean.

kidney stone *n.* A small hard mass, usually of mineral salts from urine, that forms in a kidney.

kid·skin (kĭd'skĭn') *n.* Soft leather made from the skin of a young goat.

kid stuff *n. Informal.* **1.** Something suitable only for children. **2.** Something very easy or uncomplicated.

kid·vid (kĭd'vĭd') *n. Slang.* Television programs for children. [KID + VID(EO).]

kiel·ba·sa (kĕl-bä'sə, kĭl-, kē1-) *n.* A smoked Polish sausage. [Pol.]

kie·sel·guhr (kē'zəl-go͝or') *n.* Diatomite. [G. : *Kiesel,* pebble + *Guhr,* earthy deposit from water.]

kie·ser·ite (kē'zə-rīt') *n.* A whitish to yellowish hydrous magnesium sulfate mineral. [G. *Kieserit,* after Dietrich G. *Kieser* (1779–1862).]

kif (kĭf, kēf) also **kef** (kĕf, kēf, kăf) *n.* **1.** A smoking material, as Indian hemp, used esp. in the Maghreb. **2.** The euphoria caused by smoking kif. [Ar. *kayf,* pleasure.]

Ki·ku·yu (kĭ-ko͞o'yo͞o) *n., pl.* **Kikuyu** or **-yus. 1.** A member of a Bantu people of Kenya. **2.** The Bantu language of the Kikuyu.

kil·der·kin (kĭl'dər-kĭn) *n.* **1.** A cask. **2.** An English measure of capacity equal to about 68 liters, or 18 gallons. [ME < MDu. *kindekijn,* dim. of *kintal,* hundredweight < Med. Lat. *quintale* < Ar. *qinṭār,* ult. < Lat. *centum,* hundred.]

ki·lim (kē-lēm') *n.* An oriental tapestry-woven rug or other textile piece. [Turk. < Pers. *kilīm.*]

kill (kĭl) *v.* **killed, kill·ing, kills.** —*tr.* **1. a.** To put to death. **b.** To deprive of life: *The Black Plague was a disease that killed millions.* **2.** To put an end to; extinguish. **3. a.** To destroy a vitally essential quality in: *Too much garlic killed the taste of the meat.* **b.** To cause to cease operating: *killed the motor.* **4.** To pass (time) in aimless activity. **5.** To consume entirely; finish off: *kill a bottle of whiskey.* **6.** To cause extreme pain or discomfort to: *My shoes are killing me.* **7.** To mark for deletion; rule out. **8.** To thwart passage of; veto: *kill a congressional bill.* **9.** To cause to stop; turn off. **10. a.** To hit (a ball) with great force. **b.** To hit (a ball) with such force in a racket game as to make a return impossible. —*intr.* **1.** To be fatal; cause death or extinction. **2.** To commit murder. —***phrasal verb.* kill off.** To destroy in such large numbers as to render extinct. —*n.* **1.** The act of killing. **2.** An animal killed, esp. in hunting. —***idiom.* in at the kill.** Present at the moment of triumph. [ME *killen.*]

kill·deer (kĭl'dîr') *n., pl.* **killdeer** or **-deers.** A New World bird, *Charadrius vociferus,* that is indigenous to inland waters and fields and has a distinctive cry. [Imit.]

kill·er (kĭl'ər) *n.* **1.** One that kills. **2.** The killer whale.

killer whale *n.* A black and white predatory whale, *Orcinus orca,* that inhabits cold seas.

kil·lick (kĭl'ĭk) *n.* A small anchor, esp. one made of a stone in a wooden frame. [Orig. unknown.]

kil·li·fish (kĭl'ĭ-fĭsh') *n., pl.* **killifish** or **-fish·es.** Any of numerous small fishes of the family Cyprinodontidae, inhabiting chiefly fresh and brackish waters in warm regions. [Orig. unknown.]

kill·ing (kĭl'ĭng) *n.* **1.** Murder; homicide. **2.** Quarry; kill. **3.** A sudden large profit. —*adj.* **1.** Designed or apt to kill; fatal. **2.** Exhausting: *a killing pace.* **3.** *Informal.* Hilarious. —**kill'ing·ly** *adv.*

kill·joy (kĭl'joi') *n.* A person who spoils the enthusiasm or fun of others.

kill shot *n. Sports.* A shot in various games, esp. racquet games, that is so forcefully hit or perfectly placed that it cannot be returned.

kiln (kĭln, kĭl) *n.* Any of various ovens for hardening, burning, or drying substances such as grain, meal, or clay, esp. a brick-lined oven used to bake or fire ceramics. —*tr.v.* **kilned, kiln·ing, kilns.** To process in a kiln. [ME *kilne* < OE *cyln* < Lat. *culina,* kitchen < *coquere,* to cook.]

ki·lo (kē'lō) *n., pl.* **-los.** A kilogram.

kilo- *pref.* One thousand (10^3): *kilowatt.* [Fr. < Gk. *khilioi,* thousand.]

kil·o·baud (kĭl'ə-bôd') *n.* One thousand baud.

kil·o·bit (kĭl'ə-bĭt') *n.* One thousand binary digits.

kil·o·cal·o·rie (kĭl'ə-kăl'ə-rē) *n.* A kilogram calorie.

kil·o·cy·cle (kĭl'ə-sī'kəl) *n.* **1.** A unit equal to 1,000 cycles. **2.** One thousand cycles per second.

kil·o·gram (kĭl'ə-grăm') *n.* **1.** The fundamental unit of mass in the International System, about 2.2046 pounds. **2.** A force equal to a kilogram weight, or the product of a kilogram mass with the acceleration of gravity.

kilogram calorie *n.* A calorie (sense 3).

kil·o·gram-me·ter (kĭl'ə-grăm-mē'tər) *n.* A meter-kilogram-second unit of work equal to the work performed by a one-kilogram force acting through a distance of one meter.

kil·o·hertz (kĭl'ə-hûrts') *n.* One thousand hertz.

kil·o·li·ter (kĭl'ə-lē'tər) *n.* One thousand liters.

kil·o·me·ter (kĭl'ə-mē'tər, kĭ-lŏm'ĭ-tər) *n.* One thousand meters, about 0.62137 mile. —**kil'o·met'ric** (-mĕt'rĭk) *adj.*

kil·o·par·sec (kĭl'ə-pär'sĕk') *n.* One thousand parsecs.

kil·o·rad (kĭl'ə-răd') *n.* One thousand rads.

kil·o·ton (kĭl'ə-tŭn') *n.* **1.** One thousand tons. **2.** An explosive force equivalent to that of 1,000 tons of TNT.

kil·o·volt (kĭl'ə-vōlt') *n.* One thousand volts.

kil·o·watt (kĭl'ə-wŏt') *n.* One thousand watts.

kil·o·watt-hour (kĭl'ə-wŏt-our') *n.* A unit of electric power consumption indicating the total energy developed by a power of one kilowatt acting for one hour.

kilt (kĭlt) *n.* A knee-length skirt with deep pleats, usually of a tartan wool, worn esp. as part of the dress for men in the Scottish Highlands. —*tr.v.* **kilt·ed, kilt·ing, kilts.** To tuck up around the body. [< *kilt,* to tuck up < ME *kilten,* of Scand. orig.]

kil·ter (kĭl'tər) *n.* Good condition; proper form: *The radio was out of kilter.* [Orig. unknown.]

Kim·bun·du (kĭm-bo͝on'do͞o) *n.* A Bantu language of Angola.

ki·mo·no (kə-mō'nə, -nō) *n., pl.* **-nos. 1.** A long, loose, wide-sleeved Japanese robe worn with a broad sash. **2.** A loose robe worn mainly by women. [J. : *ki,* to wear + *mono,* object.]

kin (kĭn) *n.* One's relatives; family; kindred; kinfolk. —***idiom.* next of kin.** The person or persons closest in blood relationship. [ME < OE *cyn.*]

-kin or **-kins** *suff.* Little one: *devilkin.* [ME < MDu.]

ki·na (kē'nə) *n., pl.* **kina** or **-nas.** See table at **currency.** [Native word in Papua, New Guinea.]

ki·nase (kī'nās') *n.* An enzyme that catalyzes the transfer of phosphate from ADP or ATP to an acceptor. [KIN(ETIC) + -ASE.]

kind[1] (kīnd) *adj.* **-er, -est. 1.** Of a friendly, generous, or warmhearted nature. **2.** Showing sympathy or understanding; charitable: *a kind word.* **3.** Humane; considerate: *kind to animals.* **4.** Forbearing; tolerant: *very kind about the broken window.* **5.** Generous; liberal: *kind words of praise.* **6.** Agreeable; beneficial: *a dry climate kind to asthmatics.* [ME < OE *(ge)cynde,* natural.]

Synonyms: *kind, kindly, kindhearted, benign, benevolent, gracious, compassionate.* These adjectives apply to persons and their actions when they show evidence of concern or sympathy for others. *Kind* and *kindly* are approximately interchangeable in describing persons and their natures; with reference to acts that reflect consideration or sympathy, *kindly* is more common. *Kindhearted* especially suggests an innate tendency to behave in such manner. *Benign* implies gentleness by nature; *benevolent,* charitableness and desire to promote others' welfare; *gracious,* courtesy and warmth, especially to those at a disadvantage; and *compassionate,* a tendency to be easily moved to pity.

kind[2] (kīnd) *n.* **1.** A class of similar or related individuals. **2.** A specific type: *What kind of airplane is that?* **3.** *Archaic.* Manner. **4.** A doubtful or borderline member of a given category: *a kind of shelter; a kind of bluish color.* —***idioms.* all kinds of.** *Informal.* Plenty of; ample: *We have all kinds of time to finish the job.* **in kind. 1.** With produce or commodities rather than with money: *pay in kind.* **2.** In the same manner or with something equivalent: *returned the slight in kind.* **kind of.** *Informal.* Rather; somewhat: *I'm kind of hungry.* [ME < OE *(ge)cynd,* nature.]

Usage: The use of the plurals *these* and *those* with *kind,* as in *these kind of films,* has respectable literary antecedents and has often been defended as a sensible idiom by British grammarians. But the usage will raise the hackles of those who go strictly by the rules and is probably best avoided in writing, if only to avoid offending the sensibilities of traditionalists. It is easy enough to substitute *this* (or *that*) *kind of* or *these* (or *those*) *kinds of* and to see that the following noun and verb agree in number with *kind: This kind of film has had a lot of success in foreign markets. Those are the kinds of books that capture the public imagination.* • When *kind of* is used to mean "more or less," it is properly preceded by the indefinite article *a* in formal writing: *a kind of genius* (not *kind of a genius*) • The use of *kind of* to mean "somewhat," as in *he was kind of sleepy,* is generally regarded as informal.

kin·der·gar·ten (kĭn'dər-gär'tn) *n.* A program or class for four- to six-year-old children that serves as an introduction to school. [G. : *Kinder,* pl. of *Kind,* child (< OHG *kind*) + *Garten,* garden < MHG *garte* < OHG *garto.*]

kin·der·gart·ner (kĭn'dər-gärt'nər) *n.* **1.** A child who attends kindergarten. **2.** A teacher in a kindergarten. [G. *Kindergärtner* < *Kindergarten,* kindergarten.]

kind·heart·ed (kīnd'här'tĭd) *adj.* Having or proceeding from a kind heart. —**kind'heart'ed·ly** *adv.* —**kind'heart'ed·ness** *n.*

kin·dle[1] (kĭn'dl) *v.* **-dled, -dling, -dles.** —*tr.* **1. a.** To build or fuel (a fire). **b.** To set fire to; ignite. **2.** To cause to glow; light up: *The sunset kindled the skies.* **3. a.** To inflame; make ardent. **b.** To arouse; inspire: *"No spark had yet kindled in him an intellectual passion"* (George Eliot). —*intr.* **1.** To catch fire; burst into flame. **2.** To become bright; glow. **3. a.** To become inflamed. **b.** To be stirred up; rise. [ME *kindelen* < ON *kynda.*] —**kin'dler** *n.*

kin·dle[2] (kĭn'dl) *tr. & intr.v.* **-dled, -dling, -dles.** To give birth to young. Used esp. of rabbits. [ME.] —**kin'dle** *n.*

kind·less (kīnd'lĭs) *adj.* **1.** Heartless. **2.** *Obs.* Inhuman.

kind·li·ness (kīnd'lē-nĭs) *n.* **1.** The quality or state of being kindly. **2.** A kindly deed.

kin·dling (kĭnd'lĭng) *n.* Easily ignited material, such as dry sticks of wood, used to start a fire.

killdeer

kiln

kilt

kimono

king
Playing card

King Charles spaniel

kingfisher

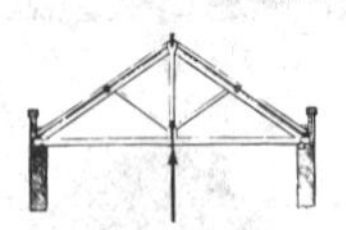
king post

kiosk

kind·ly (kīnd′lē) *adj.* **-li·er, -li·est. 1.** Of a sympathetic, helpful, or benevolent nature: *a kindly interest; a gentle, kindly soul.* **2.** Agreeable; pleasant: *a kindly breeze.* **3.** *Archaic.* Natural to its kind. *—adv.* **1.** Out of kindness: *kindly overlooked their mistake.* **2.** In a kind manner: *spoke kindly to us.* **3.** Pleasantly; agreeably: *The sun shone kindly.* **4.** In an accommodating manner: *Would you kindly fill in your name and address?* **5.** *Obs.* In a way or course that is natural; fittingly. **—*idiom.* take kindly to. 1.** To be receptive to: *take kindly to new methods.* **2.** To be naturally attracted or fitted to; thrive on.
kind·ness (kīnd′nĭs) *n.* **1.** The quality or state of being kind. **2.** An instance of kind behavior.
kin·dred (kĭn′drĭd) *n.* **1.** A group of related persons, as a clan or tribe. **2.** A person's relatives; kinfolk. *—adj.* **1.** Of the same ancestry or family: *kindred clans.* **2.** Having a similar or related origin, nature, or character: *kindred emotions.* [ME : *kin,* kin + OE *ræden,* condition < *rædan,* to advise.] **—kin′dred·ness** *n.*
kine (kīn) *n. Archaic.* Plural of **cow**[1]. [ME *kyn.*]
kin·e·mat·ics (kĭn′ə-măt′ĭks) *n. (used with a sing. verb).* The study of motion exclusive of the influences of mass and force. [< Gk. *kinēma, kinēmat-,* motion < *kinein,* to move.] **—kin′e·mat′ic, kin′e·mat′i·cal** *adj.* **—kin′e·mat′i·cal·ly** *adv.*
kin·e·scope (kĭn′ĭ-skōp′, kī′nĭ-) *n.* **1.** A cathode-ray tube in a television receiver that translates received electrical signals into a visible picture on a luminescent screen. **2.** A film of a transmitted television program. *—tr.v.* **-scoped, -scop·ing, -scopes.** To make a kinescope of (a transmitted television program). [Orig. a trademark.]
ki·ne·si·ol·o·gy (kə-nē′sē-ŏl′ə-jē, -zē-) *n.* The study of muscles and their movements, esp. as applied to physical conditioning. [Gk. *kinēsis,* movement (< *kinein,* to move) + -LOGY.] **—ki·ne′si·ol′o·gist** *n.*
-kinesis *suff.* **1.** Motion: *photokinesis.* **2.** Division: *cytokinesis.* [NLat. < Gk. *kinēsis,* movement < *kinein,* to move.]
kin·es·the·sia (kĭn′ĭs-thē′zhə, kī′nĭs-) *n.* The sensation of bodily position, presence, or movement resulting chiefly from stimulation of sensory nerve endings in muscles, tendons, and joints. [Gk. *kinein,* to move + ESTHESIA.] **—kin′es·thet′ic** (-thĕt′ĭk) *adj.* **—kin′es·thet′i·cal·ly** *adv.*
ki·net·ic (kĭ-nĕt′ĭk, kī-) *adj.* Of, relating to, or produced by motion. [Gk. *kinētikos* < *kinētos,* moving < *kinein,* to move.]
kinetic art *n.* An art form, such as an assemblage or sculpture, comprised of parts designed to be set in motion by an internal mechanism or an external stimulus, such as light or air. **—kinetic artist** *n.*
kinetic energy *n.* Energy associated with motion, equal for a body in pure translational motion at nonrelativistic speeds to one half the product of its mass and the square of its speed.
ki·net·i·cism (kə-nĕt′ĭ-sĭz′əm) *n.* The theory or practice of kinetic art. **—ki·net′i·cist** *n.*
ki·net·ics (kĭ-nĕt′ĭks, kī-) *n. (used with a sing. verb).* **1.** The study of all aspects of motion, comprising both kinematics and dynamics. **2.** The study of the relationship between motion and the forces affecting motion.
kinetic theory *n.* A theory of the thermodynamic behavior of matter, esp. of pressure-volume-temperature relationships in gases, based in its simplest form on the identification of heat with the kinetic energy of a substance's rapid, randomly moving molecules and on a classical dynamic analysis of molecular motion under simplifying assumptions, including the conservation of energy and momentum in all collisions and the applicability of statistical analysis for large numbers of molecules.
ki·ne·tin (kī′nə-tĭn) *n.* A plant growth substance that promotes cell division.
kin·folk (kĭn′fōk′) also **kins·folk** (kĭnz′fōk′) or **kin·folks** (kĭn′fōks′) *pl.n.* Members of one's family; kindred.
king (kĭng) *n.* **1.** A male monarch. **2.** One that is the most powerful or eminent of a particular group, category, or place. **3. King.** God; Christ. **4.** A playing card bearing a picture of a king. **5. a.** The principal chess piece, capable of being moved one square in any direction. **b.** A piece in checkers that has reached the opponent's side of the board and been crowned. [ME < OE *cyning.*]
king·bolt (kĭng′bōlt′) *n.* A vertical bolt used for such purposes as joining the body of a wagon to the front axle and usually acting as a pivot.
King Charles spaniel (chärlz) *n.* A variety of toy spaniel with a curly black and tan coat and long ears. [After *King Charles* II of England (1630–1685).]
king cobra *n.* A large, venomous snake, *Ophiophagus hannah,* of tropical Asia.
king crab *n.* **1.** A large crab, *Paralithodes camtschatica,* inhabiting the coastal waters of Alaska, Japan, and Siberia and valued commercially for its edible flesh. **2.** The horseshoe crab.
king·craft (kĭng′krăft′) *n.* A king's manner of ruling.
king·cup (kĭng′kŭp′) *n. Chiefly Brit.* **1.** Any of several plants with yellow flowers. **2.** The marsh marigold.
king·dom (kĭng′dəm) *n.* **1.** A political or territorial unit that is ruled by a king or queen. **2. a.** The eternal spiritual sovereignty of God. **b.** The realm over which this sovereignty extends. **3.** An area, province, or realm in which one thing is dominant: *the kingdom of the imagination.* **4.** One of the three main taxonomic divisions into which natural organisms and objects are classified: *the animal kingdom; the mineral kingdom.* [ME < OE *cyningdom.*]
kingdom come *n.* The next world: *a bomb that could blow us to kingdom come.* [From the phrase *thy kingdom come* in the Lord's Prayer.]
king·fish (kĭng′fĭsh′) *n., pl.* **kingfish** or **-fish·es. 1. a.** Any of several food and game fishes of the genus *Menticirrhus,* indigenous to warm Atlantic waters. **b.** Any of several similar or related fishes. **2.** *Informal.* A pre-eminent or powerful person, esp. a prominent political leader.
king·fish·er (kĭng′fĭsh′ər) *n.* Any of various birds of the family Alcedinidae, characteristically having a crested head. [ME *kyngys fischare,* king's fisher.]
King James Bible *n.* See table at **Bible.**
king·let (kĭng′lĭt) *n.* Either of two small, grayish North American birds, *Regulus satrapa* or *R. calendula,* with a yellowish or reddish patch on the crown of the head.
king·ly (kĭng′lē) *adj.* **-li·er, -li·est. 1.** Having the status or rank of king. **2.** Relating to or suitable for a king; majestic; regal. *—adv.* As a king; royally. **—king′li·ness** *n.*
king mackerel *n.* A food and game fish, *Scomberomorus cavalla,* of warm Atlantic waters.
king·mak·er (kĭng′mā′kər) *n.* A person with sufficient political power to influence the selection of a candidate for office.
king-of-arms (kĭng′əv-ärmz′) *n., pl.* **kings-of-arms.** A high-ranking heraldic officer in England.
king·pin (kĭng′pĭn′) *n.* **1.** The foremost or central pin in an arrangement of bowling pins. **2.** The most important or essential one. **3.** A kingbolt.
king post *n.* A supporting post extending vertically from a crossbeam to the apex of a triangular truss.
Kings (kĭngz) *n.* See table at **Bible.**
King's bench *n.* A division of the British superior courts system that hears criminal and civil cases. Used when the monarch is a male.
King's Counsel *n.* A barrister appointed as counsel to the British crown. Used when the monarch is a male.
King's English *n.* Spoken or written English that is considered a standard of good usage.
king·ship (kĭng′shĭp′) *n.* **1.** The position, power, province, or prerogative of a king. **2.** The domain ruled by a king; kingdom. **3.** The period or tenure of a king; reign. **4.** The style of a king; majesty. **5.** A monarchy.
king-size (kĭng′sīz′) also **king-sized** (-sīzd′) *adj.* Larger than the usual or standard size: *a king-size bed; king-size cigarettes.*
king snake *n.* Any of various nonvenomous New World snakes of the genus *Lampropeltis,* with yellow or reddish markings.
king·wood (kĭng′wŏŏd′) *n.* **1.** A South American tree, *Dalbergia cearensis,* with hard, fine-textured, purplish-brown wood used in cabinetmaking. **2.** The wood of the kingwood tree.
ki·nin (kī′nĕn) *n.* Any of various polypeptides that act in the contraction of smooth muscle. [Gk. *kinein,* to move + -IN.]
kink (kĭngk) *n.* **1.** A tight curl or a sharp twist in a wirelike material, typically caused by the tensing of a looped section. **2.** A painful muscle spasm, as in the neck or back; crick. **3.** A slight difficulty or flaw, as in a plan or system. **4.** A physical or mental quirk. **5.** A clever idea for doing something. *—tr. & intr.v.* **kinked, kink·ing, kinks.** To form kinks. [LG *kinke* < MLG.]
kink·a·jou (kĭng′kə-jōō′) *n.* An arboreal mammal, *Potos flavus,* of tropical America, with brownish fur and a long, prehensile tail. [Fr. *quincajou,* of Algonquian orig.]
kink·y (kĭng′kē) *adj.* **-i·er, -i·est. 1.** Tightly curled; frizzy: *kinky hair.* **2.** *Informal.* **a.** Marked by or making use of a perverted eroticism. **b.** Marked by sexual perversion. **—kink′i·ly** *adv.* **—kink′i·ness** *n.*
kin·ni·kin·nick also **kin·ni·kin·nic** (kĭn′ĭ-kĭ-nĭk′) *n.* **1.** A preparation made from dried leaves, bark, and sometimes tobacco and smoked esp. by American Indians. **2.** A plant, such as the bearberry, with leaves or bark used in kinnikinnick. [Of Algonquian orig.]
ki·no (kē′nō) *n., pl.* **-nos.** A reddish resin obtained from several Old World tropical trees of the genera *Pterocarpus* and *Butea.* [Prob. < Mandingo *keno.*]
-kins *suff.* Variant of **-kin.**
kins·folk (kĭnz′fōk′) *pl.n.* Variant of **kinfolk.**
kin·ship (kĭn′shĭp′) *n.* The state of being related by common ancestry.
kins·man (kĭnz′mən) *n.* **1.** A male relative. **2.** A man sharing the same racial, cultural, or national background as another.
kins·wom·an (kĭnz′wŏŏm′ən) *n.* **1.** A female relative. **2.** A woman sharing the same racial, cultural, or national background as another.
ki·osk (kē′ŏsk′, kē-ŏsk′) *n.* **1.** An open gazebo or pavilion. **2.** A small structure used as a newsstand or refreshment booth. **3.** A cylindrical structure on which advertisements are posted. [Fr. *kiosque* < Turk. *köshk* < Pers. *kūshk,* portico.]
Ki·o·wa (kī′ə-wô′, -wä′, -wā′) also **Ki·o·way** (-wā′) *n., pl.* **Ki·owa** or **-was** also **Kioway** or **-ways. 1. a.** A tribe of Plains Indians formerly of Colorado, Oklahoma, Kansas, New

Mexico, and Texas. **b.** A member of this tribe. **2.** The Uto-Aztecan language of the Kiowa. [Kiowa *Kâ-i-gwŭ.*]

kip[1] (kĭp) *n., pl.* **kip.** See table at **currency.** [Thai.]

kip[2] (kĭp) *n.* The untanned hide of a small or young animal, such as a calf. [Obs. Du.]

kip[3] (kĭp) *Chiefly Brit. Slang.* —*n.* **1.** A rooming house. **2.** A room or bed in a rooming house. **3.** A bed. **4.** Sleep. —*intr.v.* **kipped, kip·ping, kips.** To sleep. [Poss. < Dan. *kippe,* cheap inn.]

kip[4] (kĭp) *n.* A 1,000-pound unit of weight. [KI(LO)- + P(OUND).]

kip·per (kĭp′ər) *n.* **1.** A male salmon or sea trout in the spawning season. **2.** A split, salted, and smoked herring. —*tr.v.* **-pered, -per·ing, -pers.** To cure (fish) by splitting, salting, and smoking. [ME *kypre* < OE *cypera.*]

Kir·ghiz (kîr-gēz′) *n., pl.* **Kirghiz** or **-ghiz·es. 1.** A member of a Turkic people living principally in the Kirghiz SSR of the Soviet Union. **2.** The Turkic language of the Kirghiz.

kir·i·ga·mi (kîr′ĭ-gä′mē) *n.* The Japanese art of making ornamental designs by cutting and folding paper. [J. : *kiri,* to cut + *kami,* paper.]

kirk (kûrk) *n.* **1.** *Scot.* A church. **2. Kirk.** *Chiefly Brit.* The Presbyterian Church of Scotland. [ME < ON *kirkja* < OE *cirice,* church. —see CHURCH.]

kir·mess (kûr′mĭs) *n.* Variant of **kermis.**

kirsch (kîrsh) *n.* A colorless brandy made from the fermented juice of cherries. [G. *Kirsch(wasser),* cherry (water).]

kir·tle (kûr′tl) *n.* **1.** A knee-length tunic or coat formerly worn by men. **2.** A woman's long dress or skirt. [ME < OE *cyrtel,* prob. ult. < Lat. *curtus,* shortened.]

kish·ke (kĭsh′kə) *n.* Derma[2]. [Yiddish, of Slav. orig.]

Kis·lev (kĭs′ləf) *n.* The third month of the Hebrew year. See table at **calendar.** [Heb. *kislēw.*]

kis·met (kĭz′mĕt′, -mĭt) *n.* Fate; fortune. [Turk. < Ar. *qismah,* portion < *qasama,* he allotted.]

kiss (kĭs) *v.* **kissed, kiss·ing, kiss·es.** —*tr.* **1.** To touch or caress with the lips as a sign of sexual passion, affection, greeting, or respect. **2.** To touch lightly; brush against. —*intr.* To engage in mutual touching or caressing with the lips. ***—phrasal verb.* kiss off.** *Informal.* To get rid of; dismiss. —*n.* **1. a.** A caress or touch with the lips. **b.** A slight or gentle touch. **2. a.** A small piece of candy, esp. of chocolate. **b.** A baked confection made of meringue. [ME *kissen* < OE *cyssan.*]

kiss·er (kĭs′ər) *n.* **1.** A person who kisses. **2.** *Slang.* The mouth. **3.** *Slang.* The face.

kissing bug *n.* An assassin bug, *Melanolestes picipes,* that inflicts a painful bite on a sleeping person, often on the lips.

kissing cousin *n.* A distant relative known well enough to be kissed when greeted.

kissing disease *n. Informal.* Mononucleosis.

kiss of death *n.* Something, as an action, that is ultimately ruinous. [From the kiss by which Judas betrayed Jesus.]

kiss-off (kĭs′ôf′, -ŏf′) *n. Informal.* A dismissal.

kiss of life *n. Chiefly Brit.* Mouth-to-mouth resuscitation.

kiss of peace *n.* A ceremonial gesture, as a kiss or a handclasp, used as a sign of brotherhood in Christian liturgies.

kist (kĭst) *n.* Variant of **cist[2].**

kit[1] (kĭt) *n.* **1. a.** A set of articles used for a specific purpose: *a survival kit; a travel kit.* **b.** A container for such a set. **2.** A set of parts or materials to be assembled: *a model airplane kit.* **3.** A packaged set of related materials: *a sales kit.* **4.** A container such as a box, bag, valise, or knapsack. **5.** *Chiefly Brit. Regional.* A tub. ***—idiom.* the (whole) kit and caboodle.** *Informal.* The entire collection or lot. [ME *kitt,* wooden tub.]

kit[2] (kĭt) *n.* **1.** A kitten. **2.** A young, often undersized furbearing animal. [Short for KITTEN.]

kit[3] (kĭt) *n.* A small three-stringed violin. [Orig. unknown.]

kitch·en (kĭch′ən) *n.* **1.** A place where food is cooked or prepared. **2.** The facilities and equipment used in the preparation and serving of food. **3.** A department that prepares, cooks, and serves food. ***—modifier:*** *kitchen utensils.* [ME *kichene* < OE *cycene,* ult. < LLat. *coquina* < fem. of Lat. *coquinus,* of cooking < *coquere,* to cook.]

kitchen cabinet *n.* **1.** A cabinet or cupboard for use in the kitchen. **2.** An informal group who advise the head of a government.

kitch·en·er (kĭch′ə-nər) *n.* **1.** A person who manages a kitchen, esp. in a monastery. **2.** *Chiefly Brit.* A large cooking stove.

kitch·en·ette (kĭch′ə-nĕt′) *n.* A small kitchen.

kitchen garden *n.* A garden in which vegetables and fruits are grown for household consumption.

kitchen midden *n.* A refuse heap or mound with artifacts, shells, and often bones indicating the site of a primitive human settlement. [Transl. of Dan. *køkkenmødding.*]

kitchen police *n.* **1.** Enlisted military personnel assigned to work in the kitchen. **2.** The work of the kitchen police.

kitch·en·ware (kĭch′ən-wâr′) *n.* Utensils, as pots and pans, for use in the kitchen.

kite (kīt) *n.* **1.** A light framework covered with cloth, plastic, or paper, designed to climb and fly in a steady breeze at the end of a long string. **2.** Any of the light sails of a ship, used in a light wind. **3.** Any of various predatory birds of the subfamilies Milvinae and Elaninae, with a long, often forked tail. **4.** A negotiable paper, as a check, representing a fictitious financial transaction and used temporarily to sustain credit or raise money. —*v.* **kit·ed, kit·ing, kites.** —*intr.* **1.** To fly like a kite; soar or glide. **2.** To get money or credit with a kite. —*tr.* To use a kite to sustain credit or raise money. [ME, bird of prey < OE *cyta.*]

kith and kin (kĭth′ən kĭn′) *n.* Friends and neighbors. [ME *kyth* < OE *cyð.*]

kitsch (kĭch) *n.* **1.** Pretentious bad taste, esp. in the arts. **2.** Something that exemplifies kitsch. [G. < *kitschen,* to put together sloppily.] **—kitsch′y** *adj.*

kit·ten (kĭt′n) *n.* A young cat. —*intr.v.* **-tened, -ten·ing, -tens.** To bear kittens. [ME *kitoun,* prob. < ONFr. **caton,* dim. of *cat,* cat < LLat. *cattus.*]

kit·ten·ish (kĭt′n-ĭsh) *adj.* Playful; coy. **—kit′ten·ish·ly** *adv.* **—kit′ten·ish·ness** *n.*

kit·ti·wake (kĭt′ē-wāk′) *n.* Either of two gulls, *Rissa tridactyla* or *R. brevirostris,* of northern regions. [Imit. of its cry.]

kit·tle (kĭt′l) *adj. Scot.* **1.** Unpredictable; capricious. **2.** Touchy. [< Sc., to tickle < ME *kytyllen,* prob. of ON orig.]

kit·ty[1] (kĭt′ē) *n.* **1. a.** An extra hand or part of a hand in some card games, to be used by the highest bidder. **b.** A fund made up of a portion of each player's winnings in a card game, used to pay the game expenses. **2.** A pool of money. [< KIT[1].]

kit·ty[2] (kĭt′ē) *n., pl.* **-ties.** *Informal.* A cat, esp. a kitten. [Shortening and alteration of KITTEN.]

kit·ty-cor·nered (kĭt′ē-kôr′nərd) *adj.* Cater-cornered.

Kitty Litter. A trademark for absorbent material used in a box or pan for the waste of small domestic pets, esp. cats.

ki·va (kē′və) *n.* An underground or partly underground room in a Pueblo Indian village, used by the men esp. for ceremonies or councils. [Hopi.]

ki·wi (kē′wē) *n.* **1.** Any of several flightless birds of the genus *Apteryx,* native to New Zealand, with vestigial wings and a long, slender bill. **2.** A vine, *Actinidia chinensis,* native to Asia, bearing fuzzy, edible fruit. [Maori.]

kiwi

Klan (klăn) *n.* The Ku Klux Klan.

Klans·man (klănz′mən) *n.* A member of the Ku Klux Klan.

klav·ern (klăv′ərn) *n.* A local organizational unit of the Ku Klux Klan. [KL(AN) + (C)AVERN.]

Klax·on (klăk′sən). A trademark for a loud horn formerly used on automobiles.

Kleen·ex (klē′nĕks′). A trademark for a soft cleansing tissue.

Klein bottle (klīn) *n.* A one-sided topologic surface having no inside or outside, formed by inserting the small open end of a tapered tube through the side of the tube and making it contiguous with the larger open end. [After Felix *Klein* (1849–1925).]

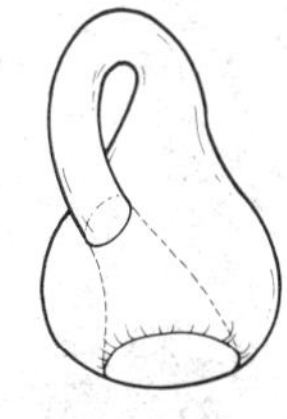

Klein bottle

klep·to·ma·ni·a (klĕp′tə-mā′nē-ə, -mān′yə) *n.* An obsessive impulse to steal in spite of the absence of economic necessity or personal desire. [Gk. *kleptein,* to steal + -MANIA.] **—klep′to·ma′ni·ac′** (-nē-ăk′) *n.*

klieg light (klēg) *n.* A powerful carbon-arc lamp producing an intense light and used esp. in making movies. [After John H. *Kliegl* (1869–1959) and Anton T. *Kliegl* (1872–1927).]

klip·spring·er (klĭp′sprĭng′ər) *n.* A small, hoofed African mammal, *Oreotragus oreotragus,* with large ears. [Afr. : Du. *klip,* cliff + Du. *springer,* jumper < *springen,* to leap.]

kloof (klo͞of) *n.* A deep ravine in South Africa. [Afr. < Du. < MDu. *clove.*]

klutz (klŭts) *n. Slang.* **1.** A clumsy, dull-witted person. **2.** A bungler. [Yiddish < G. *Klotz,* wooden block < MHG *kloz.*] **—klutz′i·ness** *n.* **—klutz′y** *adj.*

kly·stron (klī′strŏn′) *n.* An electron tube used to amplify or generate radio waves of microwave range frequencies by means of velocity modulation. [Orig. a trademark.]

knack (năk) *n.* **1.** A clever, expedient, and specific way of doing something. **2.** A specific talent for doing something. **3.** *Archaic.* **a.** A cleverly designed device. **b.** A knickknack. [ME *knak.*]

knack·er (năk′ər) *n. Chiefly Brit.* **1.** A person who buys worn-out or old livestock and sells the meat or hides. **2.** A person who buys discarded structures and dismantles them to sell the materials. [< Obs. *knacker,* saddler.] **—knack′er·y** (-ə-rē) *n.*

knack·wurst also **knock·wurst** (nŏk′wûrst′, -wo͝orst′) *n.* A short, thick, highly seasoned sausage resembling a frankfurter. [G. : *knacken,* to crack (< MHG) + *Wurst,* sausage.]

knap[1] (năp) *tr.v.* **knapped, knap·ping, knaps. 1.** *Chiefly Brit. Regional.* To strike sharply; rap. **2.** To break or chip flints with a sharp blow. **3.** *Chiefly Brit. Regional.* To snap at or bite. [ME *knappen.*] **—knap′per** *n.*

knap[2] (năp) *n. Regional.* The crest of a hill; summit. [ME < OE *cnæp.*]

knap·sack (năp′săk′) *n.* A bag, as of canvas or nylon, worn on the back to carry supplies and equipment. [LG *knappsack* : *knappen,* to bite + *sack,* bag.]

knap·weed (năp′wēd′) *n.* Any of various plants of the genus *Centaurea,* with purplish, thistlelike flowers. [ME *knopwed* : *knop,* knob + *wed,* weed.]

knar also **knaur** (när) *n.* A knot or burl on a tree or in wood. [ME *knarre.*]

knave (nāv) *n.* **1.** An unprincipled, crafty person. **2.** *Archaic.*

klieg light

A male servant. **3.** The jack in card games. [ME < OE *cnafa,* boy.]

knav·er·y (nā′və-rē) *n.* **1.** Dishonest, crafty dealing. **2.** A piece of mischief or trickery.

knav·ish (nā′vĭsh) *adj.* Relating to or characteristic of a knave; roguish. **—knav′ish·ly** *adv.* **—knav′ish·ness** *n.*

knawel (nôl) *n.* A low-growing, weedy plant, *Scleranthus annuus,* native to Eurasia, with narrow leaves and inconspicuous green flowers. [G. *Knäuel,* ball of yarn < MHG *kliuwel,* dim. of *kliuwe,* ball of yarn < OHG *kliuwa.*]

knead (nēd) *tr.v.* **knead·ed, knead·ing, kneads. 1.** To mix and work (a substance) into a uniform mass, esp. to fold, press, and stretch dough with the hands. **2.** To make or shape by or as if by kneading. [ME *kneden* < OE *cnedan.*] **—knead′er** *n.*

knee (nē) *n.* **1. a.** *Anat.* The joint or region of the human leg that is the articulation for the tibia, fibula, and patella. **b.** A joint of a leg of a vertebrate, as in the forelimb of a hoofed animal. **2.** One of the woody projections arising from the roots of some swamp-growing trees: *cypress knees.* —*tr.v.* **kneed, knee·ing, knees.** To push or strike with the knee. [ME < OE *cnēo.*]

knee action *n.* An automotive front-wheel suspension that permits independent vertical motion of each wheel.

knee breeches *pl.n.* Breeches extending to just below the knee.

knee·cap (nē′kăp′) *n.* **1.** The patella (sense 1.a.). **2.** A kneepad.

knee-deep (nē′dēp′) *adj.* **1.** Reaching to the knees. **2.** Submerged to the knees. **3.** Deeply occupied or engaged.

knee-high (nē′hī′) *adj.* Knee-deep. —*n.* (nē′hī′). A stocking that extends to just below the knee.

knee·hole (nē′hōl′) *n.* A space or opening for the knees, as under a desk or counter.

knee jerk *n.* A sudden involuntary kick forward produced by a smart tap to the tendon below the patella.

knee-jerk (nē′jûrk′) *adj.* **1.** Automatic: *Unrest is often a knee-jerk reaction to authoritarianism.* **2.** Marked by or reacting with unthinking predictability: *knee-jerk pessimism.*

kneel (nēl) *intr.v.* **knelt** (nĕlt) or **kneeled, kneel·ing, kneels.** To fall or rest on bent knees. [ME *knelen* < OE *cnēowlian.*]

kneel·er (nē′lər) *n.* **1.** One who kneels. **2.** Something, as a stool, cushion, or board, to kneel on.

knee·pad (nē′păd′) *n.* A protective covering for the knee.

knell (nĕl) *v.* **knelled, knell·ing, knells.** —*intr.* **1.** To sound a bell, esp. for a funeral; toll. **2.** To sound mournfully or ominously. —*tr.* To signal, summon, or proclaim by tolling. —*n.* **1.** An act or instance of knelling; toll. **2.** A signal of disaster or destruction. [ME *knellen* < OE *cnyllan.*]

knelt (nĕlt) *v.* A past tense and past participle of **kneel.**

Knes·set (knĕs′ĕt′) *n.* The Israeli parliament. [Heb. *Kĕneseth,* assembly < *kanas,* he gathered.]

knew (no͞o, nyo͞o) *v.* Past tense of **know.**

Knick·er·bock·er (nĭk′ər-bŏk′ər) *n.* **1. a.** A descendant of the Dutch settlers of New York. **b.** A New Yorker. **2. knickerbockers.** Full breeches gathered and banded just below the knee. [After Diedrich *Knickerbocker,* fictitious author of *History of New York,* by Washington Irving.]

Knickerbocker
Hiking knickerbockers

knick·ers (nĭk′ərz) *pl.n.* **1.** Long bloomers formerly worn as underwear by women and girls. **2.** Knickerbockers. [Short for KNICKERBOCKERS.]

knick·knack (nĭk′năk′) *n.* A small, ornamental article; trinket. [Redup. of KNACK.]

knife (nīf) *n., pl.* **knives** (nīvz). **1.** A cutting instrument consisting of a sharp blade with a handle. **2.** A cutting edge; blade. —*v.* **knifed, knif·ing, knifes.** —*tr.* **1.** To use a knife on, esp. to cut, stab, or wound. **2.** *Informal.* To hurt, defeat, or betray by underhand means. —*intr.* To cut or slash a way through with or as if with a knife. [ME *knif* < OE *cnīf.*] **—knif′er** *n.*

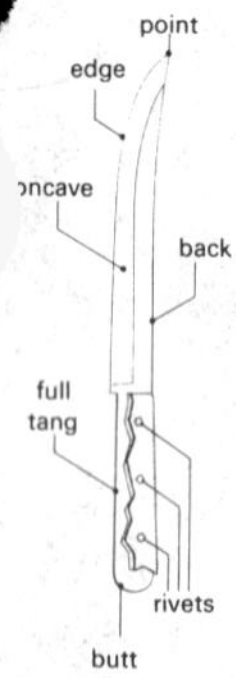

knife

knife-edge (nīf′ĕj′) *n.* **1.** The cutting edge of a blade. **2.** A sharp, knifelike edge: *the knife-edge of criticism.* **3.** A wedge of metal used as a low-friction fulcrum for a balancing beam or lever.

knight (nīt) *n.* **1.** A medieval tenant giving military service as a mounted man-at-arms to a feudal landholder. **2.** A medieval gentleman-soldier, usually high-born, raised by a sovereign to privileged military status after training as a page and squire. **3.** The holder of a nonhereditary dignity conferred by a sovereign in recognition of personal merit or services to the country. **4.** A member of an order or brotherhood that calls its members knights. **5. a.** A defender, champion, or zealous upholder of a cause or principle. **b.** The devoted champion of a lady. **6.** A chess piece that can be moved two squares horizontally and one vertically or two vertically and one horizontally. —*tr.v.* **knight·ed, knight·ing, knights.** To raise (a person) to knighthood. [ME < OE *cniht.*]

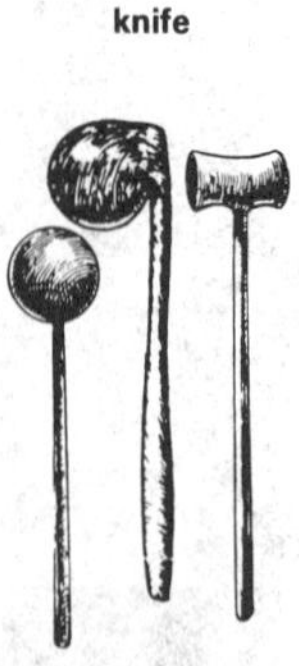

knobkerrie
Three types of knobkerries

knight er·rant (ĕr′ənt) *n., pl.* **knights errant. 1.** A knight of medieval romance who wandered in search of adventure. **2.** One given to adventurous or quixotic conduct. **—knight′-er′rant·ry** (nīt′ĕr′ən-trē) *n.*

knight·head (nīt′hĕd′) *n.* Either of two timbers rising from the keel of a sailing ship to support the inner end of the bowsprit. [From the fact that it was sometimes decorated with a carving of a human head.]

knight·hood (nīt′ho͝od′) *n.* **1.** The rank, profession, or dignity of a knight. **2.** The behavior of or qualities befitting a knight; chivalry. **3.** Knights as a body or class.

knight·ly (nīt′lē) *adj.* Of, pertaining to, or befitting a knight. **—knight′li·ness** *n.*

Knight of Pythias *n.* A member of a secret, philanthropic fraternal order.

Knights of the Round Table *pl.n.* In Arthurian legend, the knights of the court of King Arthur.

Knight Templar *n., pl.* **Knights Templars.** A member of an order of knights founded in 1119 to protect pilgrims in the Holy Land during the Second Crusade and suppressed in 1312.

knish (kə-nĭsh′) *n.* A piece of dough stuffed with potato, meat, or cheese and baked or fried. [Yiddish < R.]

knit (nĭt) *v.* **knit** or **knit·ted, knit·ting, knits.** —*tr.* **1.** To make or fashion by intertwining yarn or thread in a series of connected loops either on a machine or by hand. **2.** To join closely; unite securely. **3.** To draw (the brows) together in wrinkles; furrow. —*intr.* **1.** To make, as a fabric or garment, by knitting. **2.** To come or grow together securely. **3.** To come together in wrinkles or furrows. —*n.* A fabric or garment made by knitting. [ME *knitten* < OE *cnyttan,* to tie in a knot.] **—knit′ter** *n.*

knit·ting (nĭt′ĭng) *n.* **1.** The process of producing something knitted. **2.** Knitted work.

knitting needle *n.* A long, thin, pointed rod used in knitting.

knit·wear (nĭt′wâr′) *n.* Knitted garments.

knives (nīvz) *n.* Plural of **knife.**

knob (nŏb) *n.* **1. a.** A rounded protuberance on a surface or extremity. **b.** A rounded dial. **2.** A prominent rounded hill or mountain. [ME *knobbe,* prob. < MLG.] **—knobbed** *adj.* **—knob′by** *adj.*

knob·ker·rie (nŏb′kĕr′ē) *n.* A short club with one knobbed end, used as a weapon by South African tribesmen. [Afr. *knopkierie* : *knop,* knob (< MDu. *cnoppe*) + *kieri,* club < Hottentot *kirri.*]

knock (nŏk) *v.* **knocked, knock·ing, knocks.** —*tr.* **1.** To strike with a hard blow. **2.** To cause to collide. **3.** To produce by hitting or striking: *knocked a hole in the wall.* **4.** To instill with or as if with blows: *tried to knock some sense into his head.* **5.** *Slang.* To criticize adversely; disparage. —*intr.* **1.** To strike a blow or series of blows. **2.** To collide. **3. a.** To make a pounding or clanking noise. **b.** To undergo engine knock. **—*phrasal verbs.* knock around** (or **about**). *Informal.* **1.** To be rough or brutal with; maltreat. **2.** To wander from place to place. **3.** To discuss or consider. **knock back.** *Informal.* To gulp (an alcoholic drink). **knock down. 1.** To disassemble into parts, as for storage or shipping. **2.** To declare sold at an auction, as by striking a blow with a gavel. **3.** *Informal.* To reduce, as in price. **4.** *Slang.* To receive as wages; earn. **knock off. 1.** *Informal.* **a.** To take a break or rest from; stop. **b.** To cease work. **2.** *Informal.* To make, accomplish, or consume hastily or easily. **3.** *Informal.* To eliminate; deduct: *The grocer knocked off a little from the bill.* **4.** *Slang.* To kill. **5.** *Slang.* To hold up or rob. **6.** *Informal.* To copy the production or design of. **knock out. 1.** To render unconscious. **2.** In boxing, to defeat by knocking down to the canvas for a count of ten. **3.** *Informal.* To render useless or inoperative: *electricity knocked out by a storm.* **4.** *Informal.* To exert or exhaust (oneself or another) to the utmost. **knock together.** To make or assemble quickly or carelessly. **knock up. 1.** *Chiefly Brit. Informal.* To gain the attention of or wake up by knocking at the door. **2.** To exhaust; wear out. **3.** *Slang.* To make pregnant. —*n.* **1.** An instance of knocking; blow. **2.** The sound of a sharp tap on a hard surface; rap. **3.** A pounding, clanking noise made by an engine, esp. one in poor operating condition. **4.** *Slang.* A cutting, often petty criticism. **—*idioms.* knock cold.** To knock out. **knock dead.** *Slang.* To affect strongly, usually positively: *a virtuoso performance that knocked the audience dead.* **knock for a loop.** *Slang.* To surprise tremendously; astonish. **knock out of the box.** *Baseball.* To force the removal of (an opposing pitcher) by heavy hitting. [ME *knokken* < OE *cnocian.*]

knock·a·bout (nŏk′ə-bout′) *n.* A small sloop with a mainsail, a jib, and a keel but no bowsprit. —*adj.* **1.** Boisterous; rowdy. **2.** Appropriate for rough wear or use.

knock·down (nŏk′doun′) *adj.* **1.** Strong enough to knock down or overwhelm; powerful: *a knockdown blow.* **2.** Designed to be assembled and disassembled quickly and easily: *knockdown furniture.* —*n.* **1.** The act of knocking down. **2.** An overwhelming blow or shock. **3.** An apparatus designed to be assembled and disassembled quickly and easily.

knock·down-drag·out (nŏk′doun-drăg′out′) *adj.* Marked by roughness, violence, and acrimony: *a knockdown-dragout quarrel.*

knock·er (nŏk′ər) *n.* **1.** One that knocks. **2.** A fixture used for knocking on a door.

knocker

knock-knee (nŏk′nē′) *n.* An abnormal condition in which one knee is turned toward the other or in which each is turned toward the other. **—knock′-kneed′** *adj.*

knock·off (nŏk′ôf′, -ŏf′) *n.* *Informal.* A usually less expensive copy, as of a garment.

knock·out (nŏk′out′) *n.* **1. a.** The act of knocking out. **b.** The state of being knocked out. **2.** In boxing, the knock-

ing out of an opponent. **3.** *Slang.* One that is very impressive or attractive. **—*modifier:*** *a knockout punch.*
knockout drops *pl.n. Slang.* A solution, as of chloral hydrate, put into a drink to make the drinker unconscious.
knock·wurst (nŏk′wûrst′, -wo͝orst′) *n.* Variant of **knackwurst.**
knoll¹ (nōl) *n.* A small rounded hill or mound; hillock. [ME *knolle* < OE *cnoll.*]
knoll² (nōl) *Archaic.* *—tr. & intr.v.* **knolled, knoll·ing, knolls.** To ring or sound mournfully. *—n.* A knell. [ME *knollen,* prob. alteration of *knellen,* to knell < OE *cnyllan.*]
knop (nŏp) *n.* A decorative knob. [ME *knoppe* < OE *cnop.*]
knot¹ (nŏt) *n.* **1. a.** A compact intersection of interlaced material, as cord, ribbon, or rope. **b.** A fastening made by tying together lengths of material, as rope, in a prescribed way. **2.** A decorative bow of ribbon, fabric, or braid. **3.** A unifying bond, esp. a marriage bond. **4.** A tight cluster of persons or things. **5.** A difficult problem. **6. a.** A hard place or node, esp. on a tree, at a point from which a stem or branch grows. **b.** The circular, often darker cross section of such a node as it appears cross-grained on a piece of cut lumber. **7.** A protuberant growth in living tissue: *a knot in a gland.* **8.** *Naut.* **a.** A division on a log line used to measure the speed of a ship. **b.** A unit of speed, one nautical mile per hour, about 1.15 statute miles per hour. **c.** A distance of one nautical mile. *—v.* **knot·ted, knot·ting, knots.** *—tr.* **1.** To tie in or fasten with a knot. **2.** To entangle. **3.** To cause to form knots. *—intr.* **1.** To become snarled or entangled. **2.** To form a knot. [ME < OE *cnotta.*] **—knot′ted** *adj.*
Usage: In nautical usage *knot* is a unit of speed, not of distance, and has a built-in meaning of "per hour." Therefore, a ship would strictly be said to travel at ten knots (not ten knots per hour).
knot² (nŏt) *n.* Either of two shore birds, *Calidris canutus* or *C. tenvirostris,* related to the sandpipers. [Orig. unknown.]
knot·grass (nŏt′grăs′) *n.* **1.** A low-growing, weedy plant, *Polygonum aviculare,* with very small greenish flowers. **2.** Any of several grasses with jointed stems.
knot·hole (nŏt′hōl′) *n.* A hole in a piece of lumber where a knot once was.
knot·ty (nŏt′ē) *adj.* **-ti·er, -ti·est. 1.** Tied or snarled in knots. **2.** Covered with knots or knobs; gnarled. **3.** Hard to understand or solve; puzzling: *a knotty problem.* **—knot′ti·ness** *n.*
knotty pine *n.* Pine wood with a large number of knots, used esp. for paneling and furniture.
knot·weed (nŏt′wēd′) *n.* Any of several plants of the genus *Polygonum,* with jointed stems and inconspicuous flowers.
knout (nout) *n.* A leather scourge used for flogging criminals. *—tr.v.* **knout·ed, knout·ing, knouts.** To flog with a knout. [Fr. < R. *knut,* prob. < *knūtr,* knot.]
know (nō) *v.* **knew** (no͞o, nyo͞o), **known** (nōn), **know·ing, knows.** *—tr.* **1.** To perceive directly with the senses or mind; apprehend with clarity or certainty. **2.** To be certain of; regard as true beyond doubt. **3.** To have a practical understanding of or thorough experience with: *know how to swim.* **4.** To be subjected to; experience: *"a black stubble that had known no razor"* (Faulkner). **5. a.** To recognize (something) as being the same as something else previously known. **b.** To be acquainted or familiar with. **6.** To be able to distinguish; recognize: *Do you know him from his twin brother?* **7.** *Archaic.* To have sexual intercourse with: *"And Adam knew Eve his wife; and she conceived"* (Genesis 4:1). *—intr.* **1.** To possess knowledge. **2.** To be cognizant or aware. **—*idiom.* in the know.** Possessing correct or secret information. [ME *knowen* < OE *(ge)cnāwan.*] **—know′a·ble** *adj.* **—know′er** *n.*
know-how (nō′hou′) *n. Informal.* The knowledge and skill required to do something correctly.
know·ing (nō′ĭng) *adj.* **1.** Possessing knowledge, intelligence, or understanding. **2.** Having or showing clever awareness and resourcefulness; shrewd. **3.** Deliberate: *knowing complicity in the plot.* **—know′ing·ly** *adv.* **—know′ing·ness** *n.*
know-it-all (nō′ĭt-ôl′) *n. Informal.* A person who claims to know everything.
knowl·edge (nŏl′ĭj) *n.* **1.** The state or fact of knowing. **2.** Familiarity, awareness, or understanding gained through experience or study. **3.** The sum or range of what has been perceived, discovered, or learned. **4.** Learning; erudition: *men of knowledge.* **5.** Specific information about something. **6.** *Archaic.* Sexual intercourse. [ME *knowlech* < *knowlechen,* to acknowledge < *knowen,* to know < OE *(ge)cnāwan.*]
Synonyms: *knowledge, information, learning, erudition, lore, scholarship, wisdom, enlightenment.* These nouns refer to cognitive or intellective mental components acquired and retained through study and experience. *Knowledge* includes both empirical material and that derived by inference or interpretation. *Information* is usually construed as narrower in scope and implies a random collection of material rather than orderly synthesis. *Learning* usually refers to what is gained by schooling and study, and *erudition* adds to this the idea of profound knowledge often in a specialized area. *Lore* is knowledge gained by tradition or intuition rather than formally. The remaining terms refer to qualities possessed by persons rather than directly to what is stored in their minds. *Scholarship* is the distinctive mark of one who has mastered some area of learning, as reflected in the quality of his work, especially with respect to scope, thoroughness, and care. *Wisdom* involves sound judgment and the ability to apply what has been acquired mentally to the conduct of one's affairs. *Enlightenment* is the state of possessing knowledge and truth.
knowl·edge·a·ble (nŏl′ĭ-jə-bəl) *adj.* Possessing or showing knowledge.
known (nōn) *v.* Past participle of **know.** *—adj.* Proved, satisfactorily specified, or completely understood. *—n.* Something that is known.
know-noth·ing (nō′nŭth′ĭng) *n.* **1. Know-Nothing.** A member of a mid-19th-century American political movement that was antagonistic toward immigrants and Roman Catholics. **2.** An ignoramus. **3.** An agnostic. **4.** An anti-intellectual.
knuck·le (nŭk′əl) *n.* **1.** *Anat.* **a.** The prominence of the dorsal aspect of a joint of a finger, esp. one of the joints connecting the fingers to the hand. **b.** A rounded protuberance formed by the bones in a joint. **2.** A cut of meat centering on the carpal joint, as of a pig. **3.** The part of a hinge through which the pin passes. **4. knuckles.** Brass knuckles. *—tr.v.* **-led, -ling, -les. 1.** To press, rub, or hit with the knuckles. **2.** To shoot (a marble) with the thumb over the bent forefinger. **—*phrasal verbs.* knuckle down.** To apply oneself earnestly to a task. **knuckle under.** To yield to pressure; give in. [ME *knokel.*]
knuckle ball *n. Baseball.* A typically slow, randomly fluttering pitch thrown by gripping the ball with the knuckles of two or three fingers.
knuck·le·bone (nŭk′əl-bōn′) *n.* A knobbed bone, as of a knuckle or joint.
knuck·le·dust·ers (nŭk′əl-dŭs′tərz) *pl.n. Slang.* Brass knuckles.
knuck·le·head (nŭk′əl-hĕd′) *n.* A stupid person; blockhead.
knuckle joint *n.* A hinged joint in which a pin fastens together two rods, one of which has an eye that fits between the two projections of the other.
knuckle sandwich *n. Slang.* A punch in the mouth.
knur (nûr) *n.* A gnarl. [ME *knor,* a swelling.]
knurl (nûrl) *n.* **1.** A protuberance, as a knob or knot. **2.** One of a series of small ridges, as along the edge of an object such as a thumbscrew. *—tr.v.* **knurled, knurl·ing, knurls.** To provide with knurls; mill. [Prob. < KNUR.] **—knurl′y** *adj.*
KO (kā′ō′) *Slang.* *—tr.v.* **KO'd, KO'ing, KO's.** To knock out, as in boxing. *—n.* (kā-ō′, kā′ō′) *pl.* **KO's.** A knockout in boxing.
ko·a·la (kō-ä′lə) *n.* An Australian arboreal marsupial, *Phascolarctos cinereus,* that has dense grayish fur and that feeds chiefly on the leaves and bark of eucalyptus trees. [Native word in Australia.]
ko·an (kō′än′) *n.* A riddle in the form of a paradox used in Zen Buddhism as an aid to meditation and a means of gaining intuitive knowledge. [J. : *ko,* public + *an,* matter.]
ko·bo (kô′bô′) *n., pl.* **kobo.** See table at **currency.** [Alteration of COPPER.]
ko·bold (kō′bôld′) *n.* **1.** A mischievous household elf in German folklore. **2.** A gnome that haunts underground places in German folklore. [G. < MHG *kobolt.*]
Ko·dak (kō′dăk′). A trademark for a small hand camera and camera film.
Ko·di·ak bear (kō′dē-ăk′) *n.* A brown bear, *Ursus arctos,* inhabiting islands and coastal areas of Alaska and sometimes considered a separate species (*U. middendorffi*). [After *Kodiak* island, Alaska.]
kohl (kōl) *n.* A preparation used esp. by women as eye make-up. [Ar. *koḥl.*]
kohl·ra·bi (kōl-rä′bē, -răb′ē) *n.* A plant, *Brassica caulorapa,* with a thickened basal part that is eaten as a vegetable. [G. < Ital. *cavolo rapa* : *cavolo,* cabbage (< Lat. *caulis*) + *rapa,* turnip < Lat.]
Koi·ne (koi-nā′, koi′nā′) *n.* **1.** A dialect of Greek that developed primarily from Attic and became the common language of the Hellenistic world from which later stages of Greek are descended. **2. koine.** A lingua franca. [Gk. *koinē (dialektos),* common (language) < *koinos,* common.]
kok-sa·ghyz (kōk′sə-gēz′) *n.* A central Asian dandelion, *Taraxacum koksaghyz,* with fleshy roots that yield a form of rubber. [R. < Turk. *kok-sagĭz* : *kok,* root + *sagĭz,* rubber.]
ko·la (kō′lə) *n.* Either of two African trees, *Cola nitida* or *C. acuminata,* that bear nuts used in the manufacture of beverages and medicines. [Of African orig.]
ko·lac·ky (kə-lä′kē, -lăk′ē) *n., pl.* **kolacky.** A pastry consisting of a rich, sweet bun with a fruit or poppyseed filling. [Czech *koláč.*]
kola nut *n.* The nut of a kola tree, containing caffeine and theobromine and yielding an extract used in carbonated beverages and in pharmaceutical products.
ko·lin·sky (kə-lĭn′skē) *n.* **1.** Any of several northern Eurasian minks, esp. *Mustela siberica.* **2.** The fur of the kolinsky. [R. *kolinskiĭ,* of Kola < *Kola,* peninsula in northwestern USSR.]
kol·khoz (kŏl-kôz′) *n.* A Soviet collective farm. [R. < *kollektivnoe khozyaistvo,* collective farm.]
Kol Nid·re (kōl nĭd′rā, -rə, kôl) *n. Judaism.* The opening prayer recited on the eve of Yom Kippur. [Aram. *kol nidhrē,* all the vows (the opening words of the prayer).]

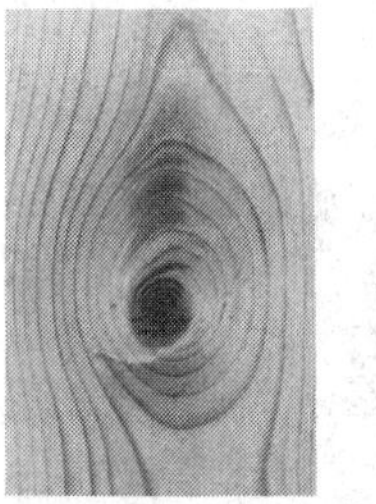
knot¹
Lumber knot

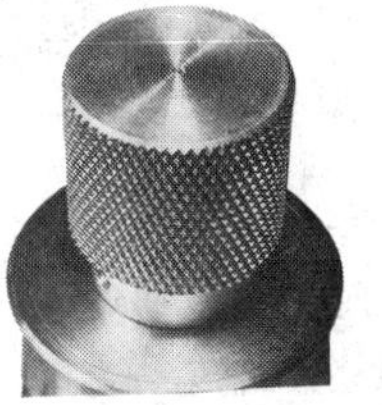
knurl

koala

p **pop** / r **roar** / s **sauce** / sh **ship, dish** / t **tight** / th **thin, path** / *th* **this, bathe** / ŭ **cut** / ûr **urge** / v **valve** / w **with** / y **yes** / z **zebra, size** / zh **vision** / ə **about, item, edible, gallop, circus** / œ *Fr.* **feu,** *Ger.* **schön** / ü *Fr.* **tu,** *Ger.* **über** / KH *Ger.* **ich,** *Scot.* **loch** / N *Fr.* **bon.**

Komodo dragon

George Miksch Sutton

kookaburra

kraken
Attacking a ship

Krishna
15th-century Indian statue of Krishna dancing

Ko·mo·do dragon (kə-mō'dō) *n.* A large monitor lizard, *Varanus komodoensis,* native to the Indonesian islands of Komodo and Flores.

Kon·go (kŏng'gō) *n.* A Bantu language spoken in the region of the lower Congo River.

koo·doo (ko͝o'do͞o) *n.* Variant of **kudu.**

kook (ko͞ok) *n. Slang.* An eccentric, zany person. [Poss. < CUCKOO.] **—kook'i·ness** *n.* **—kook'y** *adj.*

kook·a·bur·ra (ko͝ok'ə-bûr'ə, -bŭr'ə) *n.* A large kingfisher, *Dacelo novaeguineae* or *D. gigas,* native to Australia, with a call that resembles raucous laughter. [Native word in Australia.]

ko·peck (kō'pĕk') *n.* See table at **currency.** [R. *kopeĭka.*]

kor (kôr, kōr) *n.* A homer[2]. [Heb. *kōr.*]

Ko·ran (kə-răn', -rän', kô-, kō-) *n.* The sacred text of Islam, believed to contain the revelations made by Allah to Mohammed. [Ar. *qur'ān* < *qara'a,* he read.] **—Ko·ran'ic** (-răn'ĭk) *adj.*

Ko·re·an (kə-rē'ən, kô-, kō-) *n.* The language of the Koreans, which is of no known linguistic affiliation. **—Ko·re'an** *adj.*

ko·sher (kō'shər) *adj.* **1.** Conforming to or prepared in accordance with Jewish dietary laws, as: **a.** Slaughtered or prepared for eating according to rabbinic law; ritually pure: *kosher meat.* **b.** Specializing in the preparation or sale of such food: *a kosher delicatessen.* **2.** *Slang.* **a.** Proper; correct; permissible. **b.** Genuine; legitimate. *—tr.v.* **-shered, -sher·ing, -shers.** To make kosher. [Yiddish < Heb. *kāshēr,* proper.]

ko·to (kō'tō) *n., pl.* **-tos.** A Japanese musical instrument that has 13 strings stretched over an oblong box. [J.]

kou·miss (ko͞o-mĭs', ko͞o'mĭs) *n.* Variant of **kumiss.**

kow·tow (kou-tou', kou'tou') *n.* **1.** A Chinese salutation in which one touches the forehead to the ground as an expression of respect or submission. **2.** An obsequious act. *—intr.v.* **-towed, -tow·ing, -tows. 1.** To perform a kowtow. **2.** To show servile deference; fawn. [Chin. (Mandarin) *ke[1] tou[2]* : *ke[1],* to knock + *tou[2],* head.]

Kr The symbol for the element krypton.

kraal (krôl, kräl) *n.* **1.** A village of southern African natives, typically consisting of huts surrounded by a stockade. **2.** An enclosure for livestock in southern Africa. [Afr. < Port. *curral,* pen.]

kraft (krăft) *n.* A tough wrapping paper made from sulfate wood pulp. [G., strength < OHG.]

krait (krīt) *n.* Any of several venomous snakes of the genus *Bungarus,* of southeastern Asia. [Hindi *karait.*]

kra·ken (krä'kən) *n.* A sea monster in Norwegian legend. [Dial. Norw.]

K ration *n.* A U.S. Army emergency field ration used in World War II and consisting of a single packaged meal.

kraut (krout) *n.* **1.** Sauerkraut. **2.** Often **Kraut.** *Offensive Slang.* A German. [G. —see SAUERKRAUT.]

Krebs cycle (krĕbz) *n.* A series of enzymatic reactions in aerobic organisms involving oxidative metabolism of acetyl units, esp. during respiration, to provide the main source of cellular energy in the form of phosphate-rich ATP. [After Sir Hans Adolf *Krebs* (1900–1981).]

Krem·lin (krĕm'lĭn) *n.* **1. a.** The citadel of an ancient Russian city. **b.** The citadel of Moscow, housing the offices of the Soviet government. **2.** The Soviet government. [Fr. < R. *kreml',* citadel.]

Krem·lin·ol·o·gy (krĕm'lə-nŏl'ə-jē) *n.* The study of the policies of the Soviet government. **—Krem'lin·o·log'i·cal** (-nə-lŏj'ĭ-kəl) *adj.* **—Krem'lin·ol'o·gist** *n.*

kreu·zer (kroit'sər) *n.* Any of several small coins of low value formerly used in Austria and Germany. [G. < MHG *kriuzer* < *kriuze,* cross < OHG *kruzi* < Lat. *crux.*]

krieg·spiel (krēg'spēl', -shpēl') *n.* A war game played with miniature figures or markers on a large map or terrain model. [G. : *Krieg,* war + *Spiel,* game.]

Kriem·hild (krēm'hĭld', -hĭlt') also **Kriem·hil·de** (krēm-hĭl'-də) *n.* The wife of Siegfried and avenger of his murder in Germanic legend.

krill (krĭl) *pl.n.* Small marine crustaceans of the order Euphausiacea that are the principal food of whalebone whales. [Norw., young of fish.]

krim·mer (krĭm'ər) *n.* Gray, curly fur made from the pelts of lambs of the Crimean region. [G. < *Krim,* Crimea.]

kris (krēs) *n.* A Malayan sword with a wavy double-edged blade. [Malay *kĕris.*]

Krish·na (krĭsh'nə) *n. Hinduism.* The eighth and principal avatar of Vishnu, often depicted as a handsome young man playing a flute. [Hindi < Skt. *krsnah* < *krsna-,* black.] **—Krish'na·ism** *n.*

Kriss Krin·gle (krĭs krĭng'gəl) *n.* Santa Claus. [G. *Christkindl,* Santa Claus, the Christ child : *Christ,* Christ + *Kindl,* dim. of *Kind,* child < OHG.]

kro·na[1] (krō'nə) *n., pl.* **-nur** (-nər). See table at **currency.** [Icel. *krōna,* prob. < Lat. *corona,* wreath. —see CROWN.]

kro·na[2] (krō'nə) *n.,pl.* **-nor** (-nôr', -nər). See table at **currency.** [Swed., prob. ult. < Lat. *corona,* wreath. —see CROWN.]

kro·ne (krō'nə) *n., pl.* **-ner** (-nər). See table at **currency.** [Norw., prob. ult. < Lat. *corona,* wreath. —see CROWN.]

kro·ner (krō'nər) *n.* **1.** See table at **currency. 2.** Plural of **krone.** [Dan., prob. ult. < Lat. *corona,* wreath. —see CROWN.]

kro·nor (krō'nôr', -nər) *n.* Plural of **krona[2].**

kro·nur (krō'nər) *n.* Plural of **krona[1].**

Kru·ger·rand (kro͞o'gə-rănd', -ränd') *n.* A gold coin of the Republic of South Africa. [Afr., after S. J. P. *Kruger* (1825–1904) + *rand,* rand.]

kryp·ton (krĭp'tŏn') *n. Symbol* **Kr** A whitish, inert gaseous element used chiefly in gas-discharge lamps and fluorescent lamps. Atomic number 36; atomic weight 83.80; melting point −156.6°C; boiling point −152.30°C; density 3.73 grams per liter (0°C). [Gk. *krupton,* neut. of *kruptos,* hidden < *kruptein,* to hide.]

Ksha·tri·ya (kə-shăt'rē-ə, -chăt'-) *n.* **1.** A major Hindu caste, including the professional, governing, and military occupations. **2.** A member of the Kshatriya. [Skt. *kṣatriyaḥ* < *kṣatram,* rule, power < *kṣayati,* he rules.]

ku·chen (ko͞o'kən, -KHən) *n.* A yeast-raised coffee cake. [G. *Kuchen* < MHG *kuoche,* cake < OHG *kuocho.*]

ku·dos (kyo͞o'dŏs', -dōs', ko͞o'-) *n.* Acclaim or prestige as a result of achievement or position: *"the kudos of the Presidency of the United States"* (Eric F. Goldman). [Gk.]

Usage: *Kudos* is one of those words, like *congeries,* that look like plurals but are etymologically singular, and so it is correctly used with a singular verb: *Kudos is due her.*

ku·du also **koo·doo** (ko͞o'do͞o) *n., pl.* **kudu** or **-dus** also **koodoo** or **-doos.** Either of two African hoofed mammals, *Tragelaphus strepsiceros* or *T. imberbis,* having a brownish coat with narrow, white vertical stripes and long, spirally curved horns in the male. [Afr. *koedoe,* of Xhosa orig.]

kud·zu (ko͝od'zo͞o) *n.* A vine, *Pueraria lobata,* native to Japan, that has compound leaves and clusters of reddish-purple flowers and is grown for fodder and forage. [J. *kuzu.*]

Ku Klux·er (ko͞o klŭk'sər, kyo͞o) *n.* A person who belongs to the Ku Klux Klan. **—Ku Klux'ism** *n.*

Ku Klux Klan (ko͞o' klŭks klăn', kyo͞o') *n.* **1.** A secret society organized in the South after the Civil War to reassert white supremacy with terroristic methods. **2.** A secret fraternal organization founded in Georgia in 1915 and dedicated to maintaining legal and de facto segregation of blacks. [Orig. unknown.]

ku·lak (ko͞o-lăk', ko͞o'lăk', -läk') *n.* A prosperous or landed peasant in Czarist Russia and during the October Revolution. [R.]

Kul·tur (ko͝ol-to͝or') *n.* **1.** Culture. **2.** An idealized view of German culture and civilization. [G. < Lat. *cultura,* culture. —see CULTURE.]

Kul·tur·kampf (ko͝ol-to͝or'kämpf') *n.* A conflict between secular and religious authorities: *"The 1920's proved to be the focal decade in the Kulturkampf of American Protestantism"* (Richard Hofstadter). [G. : *Kultur,* Kultur + *Kampf,* struggle < OHG *kamph,* prob. ult. < Lat. *campus,* field.]

ku·miss also **kou·miss** (ko͞o-mĭs', ko͞o'mĭs) *n.* A drink of western and central Asia made from the fermented milk of a mare or camel. [R. *kumys,* of Tatar orig.]

küm·mel (kĭm'əl, kü'məl) *n.* A colorless liqueur flavored chiefly with caraway. [G., cumin seed < OHG *kumīn,* ult. < Lat. *cuminum,* —see CUMIN.]

kum·quat (kŭm'kwŏt') *n.* **1.** Any of several trees or shrubs of the genus *Fortunella* that bears an edible, small, orangelike fruit. **2.** The citrus fruit of the kumquat, with an acid pulp and a thin, edible rind. [Cantonese *kam kwat,* golden orange.]

kun·da·li·ni (ko͞on'də-lē'nē) *n.* In Yogic tradition, spiritual energy that lies dormant at the base of the spine until it is activated and channeled upward to the brain to produce enlightenment. [Skt. *kuṇḍalinī* < *kuṇḍalin-,* coiled < *kundalam,* ring.]

kung fu (ko͝ong' fo͞o', go͝ong'-) *n.* A Chinese art of self-defense similar to karate. [Chin. (Mandarin) *gong[1] fu[5]* : *gong[1],* skill + *fu[5],* distinguished person, artisan.]

kunz·ite (ko͝ont'sīt') *n.* A lilac-colored spodumene used as a gemstone. [After George F. *Kunz* (1856–1932).]

Kuo·yu (kwo͞o'yo͞o') *n.* Variant of **Guoyu.**

Kurd·ish (kûr'dĭsh, ko͝or'-) *n.* The Iranian language of the Kurds.

kur·ra·jong (kûr'ə-jông', -jŏng', kŭr'-) *n.* An Australian tree, *Brachychiton populneum,* with evergreen leaves and yellowish or reddish flowers. [Native word in Australia.]

kur·to·sis (kər-tō'sĭs) *n.* The general form or a quantity indicative of the general form of a statistical frequency curve near the distribution's mean. [Gk. *kurtōsis,* curvature < *kurtos,* convex.]

ku·ru[1] (ko͞o'ro͞o) *n.* See table at **currency.** [Turk. *kuruş.*]

ku·ru[2] (ko͝or'o͞o) *n.* A fatal neurological disease caused by a slow-acting virus, found in New Guinea. [Native word in New Guinea.]

kvass (kə-väs') *n.* A fermented Russian beverage similar to beer, made from rye or barley. [R. *kvas.*]

kvetch (kə-vĕch') *Slang.* *—intr.v.* **kvetched, kvetch·ing, kvetch·es.** To complain or find fault persistently and querulously. *—n.* A chronic and annoying complainer. [Yiddish *kvetchen* < G. *quetschen,* to squeeze.]

Kwa (kwä) *n.* A branch of the Niger-Congo language family

ă pat / ā pay / âr care / ä father / b bib / ch church / d deed / ĕ pet / ē be / f fife / g gag / h hat / hw which / ĭ pit / ī pie / îr pier / j judge / k kick / l lid, needle / m mum / n no, sudden / ng thing / ŏ pot / ō toe / ô paw, for / oi noise / ou out / o͝o took / o͞o boot /

that includes Ibo, Yoruba, and other languages of West Africa. **—Kwa** *adj.*
kwa·cha (kwä'chə) *n.* See table at **currency**. [Native word in Zambia.]
kwan·za (kwän'zə) *n., pl.* **kwanza** or **-zas**. See table at **currency**. [Swahili.]
kwa·shi·or·kor (kwä'shē-ôr'kôr') *n.* Severe malnutrition, esp. in children, characterized by anemia, edema, potbelly, depigmentation of the skin, and loss of hair or change in hair color. [Native word in Ghana.]
ky·ack (kī'ăk') *n.* A packsack that hangs on either side of a packsaddle. [Orig. unknown.]
ky·a·nite (kī'ə-nīt') *n.* A usually blue mineral, Al_2SiO_5, used as a refractory. [G. *Zyanit* : Gk. *kyanos,* dark blue enamel *-it,* -ite.]
kyat (chät) *n.* See table at **currency**. [Burmese.]
ky·lix (kī'lĭks, kĭl'ĭks) *n., pl.* **ky·li·kes** (kī'lĭ-kēz', kĭl'ĭ-). A shallow, typically tall-stemmed drinking cup used in ancient Greece. [Gk. *kulix.*]
ky·mo·graph (kī'mə-grăf') *n.* An instrument for recording variations in pressure, as of the blood. [Gk. *kuma,* something swollen (< *kuein,* to swell) + GRAPH.] **—ky'mo·graph'ic** *adj.*
Kym·ric (kĭm'rĭk) *adj. & n.* Variant of **Cymric**.
Kym·ry (kĭm'rē) *n.* Variant of **Cymry**.
ky·pho·sis (kī-fō'sĭs) *n.* Abnormal rearward curvature of the spine. [Gk. *kuphōsis* < *kuphos,* bent.] **—ky·phot'ic** (-fŏt'ĭk) *adj.*
Kyr·i·e (kîr'ē-ā') *n.* A liturgical prayer in the Christian church beginning with or composed of the words "Lord, have mercy." [LLat. < Gk. *Kurie eleēson,* Lord, have mercy.]
Kyrie e·le·i·son (ī-lā'ĭ-sŏn', -sən) *n.* Kyrie.

Ku Klux Klan

kumquat

L

1 2 Phoenician — 3 4 5 6 7 Greek — 8 9 10 Roman — 11 12 Medieval — 13 14 15 16 Modern

Around 1000 B.C. the Phoenicians and other Semitic peoples began to use graphic signs to represent individual speech sounds instead of syllables or words. They used a symbol in the forms (1,2) to represent the sound of the consonant "l" and called it *lāmedh*. The Greeks, adapting the Phoenician alphabet, kept the phonetic value of *lāmedh* but varied its orientation and changed its name to *lambda* (3,4,5,6,7). The Romans borrowed the alphabet from the Greeks via the Etruscans and adapted it for monumental inscriptions. Monumental script (10) is the prototype of modern capital letters (13,14). Medieval scribes adapted the Roman capitals to being quickly written on paper, parchment, and vellum. These uncial and cursive minuscules (11,12) are the prototypes of modern lower-case letters, both written and printed (16,15).

l

l or **L** (ĕl) *n., pl.* **l's** or **L's. 1.** The 12th letter of the modern English alphabet. **2.** Any of the speech sounds represented by the letter *l.* **3.** Something shaped like the letter L. **4.** The Roman numeral for 50. **5.** The 12th in a series.

la[1] (lä) *n. Mus.* **1.** The syllable used to represent the sixth tone of the diatonic scale. **2.** The tone A. [ME < Med. Lat. —see GAMUT.]

la[2] (lä) *interj. Chiefly Regional.* Used to express emphasis or to indicate surprise.

La The symbol for the element lanthanum.

laa·ger (läʹgər) *n.* A defensive encampment encircled by wagons or armored vehicles. *—intr.v.* **-gered, -ger·ing, -gers.** To camp in a laager. [Obs. Afr. *lager.*]

lab (lăb) *n.* A laboratory.

lab·a·rum (lăbʹər-əm) *n., pl.* **-a·ra** (-ər-ə). **1.** An ecclesiastical banner, esp. one for carrying in processions. **2.** The banner adopted by Constantine the Great after his conversion to Christianity. [LLat.]

lab·da·num (lăbʹdə-nəm) also **lad·a·num** (lădʹn-əm) *n.* A resinous exudation of certain Old World plants of the genus *Cistus,* yielding a fragrant essential oil used in flavorings and perfumes. [Med. Lat.]

la·bel (lāʹbəl) *n.* **1.** Something functioning as a means of identification, esp. a small piece of paper or cloth attached to an article to designate its origin, owner, contents, use, or destination. **2.** A descriptive term; epithet. **3.** *Computer Sci.* A symbol or set of symbols identifying the contents of a file, memory, tape, or record. **4.** A molding over a door or window; dripstone. **5.** A figure in a heraldic field consisting of a narrow horizontal bar with several pendants. **6.** A distinctive name identifying a product or manufacturer. *—tr.v.* **-beled, -bel·ing, -bels** or **-belled, -bel·ling, -bels. 1.** To attach a label to. **2.** To identify or designate with a label. **3.** To describe or classify as. [ME, ornamental strip of cloth < OFr., poss. of Germanic orig.] **—laʹbel·er, laʹbel·ler** *n.*

la·bel·lum (lə-bĕlʹəm) *n., pl.* **-bel·la** (-bĕlʹə). The often enlarged lip of an orchid. [NLat. < Lat., little lip, dim. of *labrum,* lip.] **—la·belʹlate** (-ĭt) *adj.*

la·bi·a (lāʹbē-ə) *n.* Plural of **labium.**

la·bi·al (lāʹbē-əl) *adj.* **1.** Of or pertaining to the lips or labia. **2.** Articulated with one lip or both lips, as the sound *b, m, v, w,* or *ü.* *—n.* A labial consonant. [Med. Lat. *labialis* < Lat. *labium,* lip.] **—laʹbi·al·ly** *adv.*

la·bi·al·ize (lāʹbē-ə-līzʹ) *tr.v.* **-ized, -iz·ing, -iz·es.** To make labial; round. **—laʹbi·al·i·zaʹtion** *n.*

labia ma·jo·ra (mə-jôrʹə, -jōrʹə) *pl. n.* Two rounded folds of tissue that form the external lateral boundaries of the vulva. [NLat. : Lat. *labia,* lips + Lat. *majora,* larger.]

labia mi·no·ra (mə-nôrʹə, -nōrʹə) *pl.n.* Two narrow folds of tissue enclosed within the cleft of the labia majora. [NLat. : Lat. *labia,* lips + Lat. *minora,* smaller.]

la·bi·ate (lāʹbē-ĭt, -ātʹ) *adj.* **1.** Having lips or liplike parts. **2.** *Bot.* **a.** Having or characterizing flowers with the corolla divided into two liplike parts. **b.** Of or belonging to the family Labiatae, which includes the mints. *—n.* A labiate plant. [NLat. *labiatus* < Lat. *labium,* lip.]

la·bile (lāʹbīlʹ, -bəl) *adj.* **1.** Open to change; adaptable. **2.** Constantly undergoing or likely to undergo chemical change; unstable: *a labile compound.* [ME *labil,* forgetful, wandering < Lat. *labilis,* liable to slip < *labi,* to slip.] **—la·bilʹi·ty** (-bĭlʹĭ-tē) *n.*

labio– *pref.* Labial: *labiovelar.* [< Lat. *labium,* lip.]

la·bi·o·den·tal (lāʹbē-ō-dĕnʹtl) *adj.* Articulated with the lip and teeth, as the sound *f.* *—n.* A labiodental sound.

la·bi·o·ve·lar (lāʹbē-ō-vēʹlər) *adj.* Simultaneously labial and velar, as *kw* in *quick.* *—n.* A labiovelar sound.

la·bi·um (lāʹbē-əm) *n., pl.* **-bi·a** (-bē-ə). **1.** *Anat.* Any of four folds of tissue of the female external genitalia. **2.** *Zool.* A liplike structure, such as that forming the floor of the mouth in insects. **3.** *Bot.* One of the liplike divisions of a labiate corolla. [NLat. < Lat., lip.]

la·bor (lāʹbər) *n.* **1.** Physical or mental exertion, esp. when difficult or exhausting; work. **2.** A specific task. **3.** A particular form of work or method of working: *manual labor.* **4.** Work for wages as distinguished from work for profit. **5. a.** Workers collectively; the laboring class. **b.** The trade-union movement, esp. its officials. **6. Labor.** A political party representing the interests of workers, esp. in Great Britain. **7.** Something produced by labor. **8.** The physical efforts of childbirth; parturition. *—v.* **-bored, -bor·ing, -bors.** *—intr.* **1.** To work; toil. **2.** To strive painstakingly. **3. a.** To proceed with great effort; plod. **b.** To pitch and roll, as a ship. **4.** To suffer from a burden or disadvantage: *labor under a misconception.* **5.** To undergo the efforts of childbirth. *—tr.* **1.** To deal with in exhaustive or excessive detail: *labor a point.* **2.** To distress; burden. *—adj.* **1.** Of or pertaining to labor. **2. Labor.** Of or pertaining to a political party representing the interests of the working class. [ME < OFr. < Lat.] **—laʹbor·er** *n.*

lab·o·ra·to·ry (lăbʹrə-tôrʹē, -tōrʹē, lə-bŏrʹə-trē, -tə-rē) *n., pl.* **-ries. 1.** A room or building equipped for scientific experimentation or research. **2.** A place where drugs and chemicals are manufactured. **3.** A place for practice, observation, or testing. **4.** An academic period devoted to work or study in a laboratory. [Med. Lat. *laboratorium* < Lat. *laborare,* to labor < *labor,* labor.]

Labor Day *n.* The first Monday in September, a legal holiday observed in the United States and Canada in honor of working people.

la·bored (lāʹbərd) *adj.* **1.** Done or produced with effort. **2.** Lacking natural ease; strained.

la·bor-in·ten·sive (lāʹbər-ĭn-tĕnʹsĭv) *adj.* Requiring or having a large expenditure of labor in comparison to capital.

la·bo·ri·ous (lə-bôrʹē-əs, -bōrʹ-) *adj.* **1.** Requiring or marked by long, hard work; labored. **2.** Hard-working; industrious. [ME < OFr. *laborieux* < Lat. *laboriosus* < *labor,* labor.] **—la·boʹri·ous·ly** *adv.* **—la·boʹri·ous·ness** *n.*

la·bor·ite (lāʹbə-rītʹ) *n.* **1.** A member or supporter of a labor movement or union. **2. Laborite.** A member of a political party representing labor.

la·bor·sav·ing (lāʹbər-sāʹvĭng) *adj.* Designed to conserve or decrease the amount of human labor needed.

labor union *n.* An organization of wage earners formed for the purpose of serving the members' interests with respect to wages and working conditions.

Labrador retriever

la·bour (lāʹbər) *n., v., & adj. Chiefly Brit.* Variant of **labor.**

la·bour·ite (lāʹbə-rītʹ) *n. Chiefly Brit.* Variant of **laborite.**

la·bra (lāʹbrə) *n.* Plural of **labrum.**

Lab·ra·dor Current (lăbʹrə-dôrʹ) *n.* A cold ocean current flowing southward from Baffin Bay along the coast of Labrador and turning east after intersecting with the Gulf Stream.

lab·ra·dor·ite (lăbʹrə-dôrʹītʹ, -dô-rītʹ) *n.* A plagioclase feldspar found in igneous rocks and characterized by brilliant colors in some specimens. [After *Labrador* peninsula, Canada.]

Labrador retriever *n.* A dog of a breed originating in Newfoundland and having a short, dense coat and a tapering tail. [After *Labrador,* a region of Canada.]

labyrinth

la·bret (lāʹbrĭt) *n.* An ornament inserted in a perforation in the lip. [Lat. *labrum,* lip + -ET.]

la·brum (lāʹbrəm) *n., pl.* **-bra** (-brə). A lip or liplike structure, such as that forming the roof of the mouth in insects. [NLat. < Lat., lip.]

la·bur·num (lə-bûrʹnəm) *n.* Any of several trees or shrubs of the genus *Laburnum,* esp. *L. anagyroides,* cultivated for its drooping clusters of yellow flowers. [NLat. *Laburnum,* genus name < Lat. *laburnum,* broad-leaved bean-trefoil.]

lab·y·rinth (lăbʹə-rĭnthʹ) *n.* **1.** An intricate structure of interconnecting passages through which it is difficult to find one's way; maze. **2.** Something highly intricate or convoluted in character, composition, or construction. **3.** *Anat.* **a.** A group of communicating anatomical cavities. **b.** The internal ear, comprising the semicircular canals, vestibule, and cochlea. [Lat. *labyrinthus* < Gk. *laburinthos.*]

lab·y·rin·thi·an (lăbʹə-rĭnʹthē-ən) *adj.* Labyrinthine.

lab·y·rin·thine (lăbʹə-rĭnʹthĭn, -thēnʹ) *adj.* Of, pertaining to, resembling, or constituting a labyrinth.

lac[1] (lăk) *n.* A resinous secretion of the lac insect used in making shellac. [Du. *lac* or Fr. *laque* both < Hindi *lākh* < Skt. *lākṣā,* red dye, resin.]

lac[2] also **lakh** (läk) *n.* **1.** In India, the sum of 100,000: *12 lacs of rupees.* **2.** A very large number. [Hindi *lākh* < Skt. *lakṣam,* mark, sign.]

lac·co·lith (lăkʹə-lĭthʹ) *n.* A mass of igneous rock intruded between layers of sedimentary rock, resulting in uplift. [Gk. *lakkos,* cistern + -LITH.]

lace (lās) *n.* **1.** A cord or ribbon used to draw and tie together two opposite edges, as of a shoe. **2.** A delicate fabric made of yarn or thread in an open weblike pattern. **3.** Gold or silver braid ornamenting an officer's uniform. *—v.* **laced, lac·ing, lac·es.** *—tr.* **1.** To thread a cord through the eyelets or around the hooks of. **2. a.** To draw together and tie the laces of. **b.** To restrain or constrict by tightening laces, esp. of a corset. **3.** To pull or pass through; intertwine: *lace garlands through a trellis.* **4.** To trim or decorate with or as if with lace. **5.** To add a touch of liquor to. **6.** To streak with color. **7.** To give a beating to; thrash. **8.** *Computer Sci.* To punch holes in all the rows of (a punchcard column). *—intr.* To be fastened or tied with a lace. [ME < OFr. < Lat. *laqueus,* noose.] **—lacʹer** *n.*

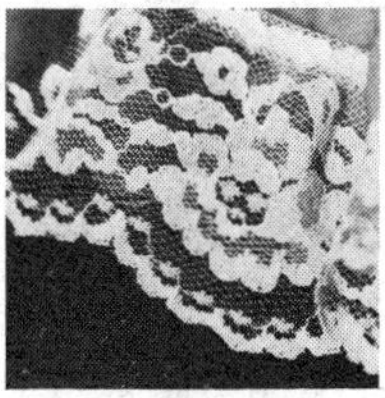
lace

lace-cur·tain (lāsʹkûrʹtn) *adj.* Emulating or aspiring to the middle class.

lac·er·ate (lăsʹə-rātʹ) *tr.v.* **-at·ed, -at·ing, -ates. 1.** To rip, cut, or tear. **2.** To cause deep emotional pain to; distress. *—adj.* (-rĭt, -rātʹ). **1.** Torn; mangled. **2.** Wounded. **3.** Having jagged, deeply cut edges: *lacerate leaves.* [Lat. *lacerare, lacerat-* < *lacer,* lacerated.] **—lacʹer·aʹtive** *adj.*

lac·er·a·tion (lăsʹə-rāʹshən) *n.* **1.** The act of lacerating. **2.** A jagged wound or cut.

La·cer·ta (lə-sûrʹtə) *n.* A constellation in the Northern Hemisphere near Cygnus and Andromeda. [NLat. < Lat. *lacerta,* lizard.]

lace·wing (lāsʹwĭngʹ) *n.* Any of various greenish or brownish insects of the families Chrysopidae and Hemerobiidae, having four gauzy wings, threadlike antennae, and larvae that feed on insect pests such as aphids and scale insects.

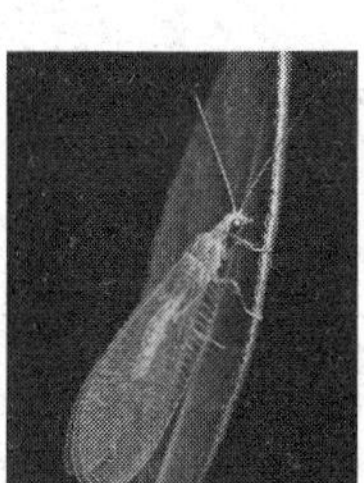
lacewing

lach·es (lăchʹĭz, lāʹchĭz) *n., pl.* **laches.** *Law.* Negligence, esp. delay in asserting a right or a claim. [ME, negligence < AN < OFr. *lasche,* lax < Lat. *laxus.*]

Lach·e·sis (lăkʹĭ-sĭs) *n. Gk. Myth.* One of the three Fates. [Gk. *Lakhesis* < *lankhanein,* to obtain by lot.]

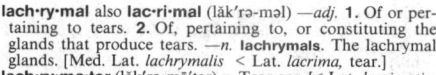

laciniate
Laciniate leaf

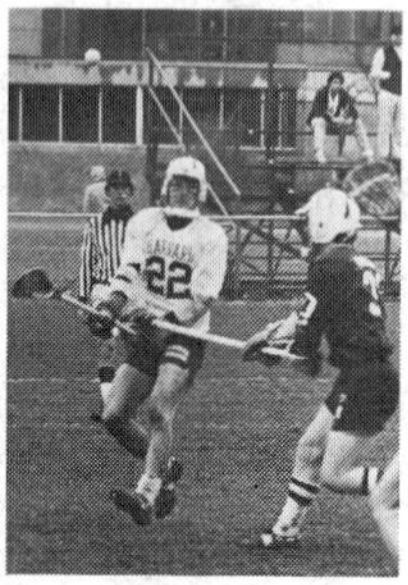
lacrosse

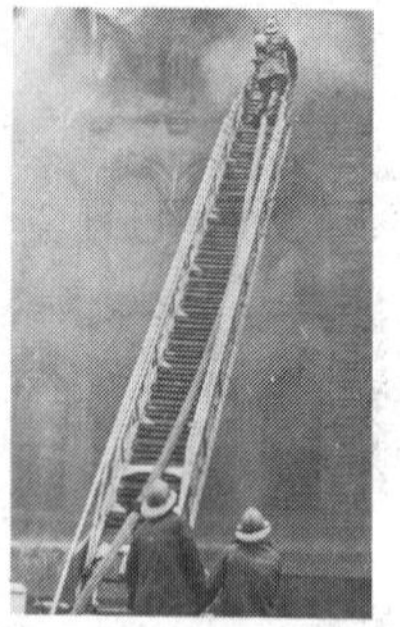
ladder

ladle
18th-century American ladle made by Paul Revere

lach·ry·mal also **lac·ri·mal** (lăk′rə-məl) —*adj.* **1.** Of or pertaining to tears. **2.** Of, pertaining to, or constituting the glands that produce tears. —*n.* **lachrymals.** The lachrymal glands. [Med. Lat. *lachrymalis* < Lat. *lacrima,* tear.]
lach·ry·ma·tor (lăk′rə-mā′tər) *n.* Tear gas. [< Lat. *lacrimatio,* a weeping < *lacrimare,* to cry < *lacrima,* tear.]
lach·ry·mose (lăk′rə-mōs′) *adj.* **1.** Weeping or inclined to weep; tearful. **2.** Causing or tending to cause tears; sorrowful. [Lat. *lacrimosus* < *lacrima,* tear.] —**lach′ry·mose′ly** *adv.*
lac·ing (lā′sĭng) *n.* **1.** Something that laces; lace. **2.** A beating or thrashing. **3.** A touch of liquor added to a beverage or food. **4.** *Computer Sci.* A set of multiple holes in a punchcard signifying to a device the end of a card run.
la·cin·i·ate (lə-sĭn′ē-ĭt, -āt′) *adj.* **1.** Fringed. **2.** Having edges cut into narrow, fringelike segments or lobes: *laciniate petals.* [< Lat. *lacinia,* edge.] —**la·cin′i·a′tion** *n.*
lac insect *n.* Any of various insects of the subfamily Lacciferinae, esp. *Laccifer lacca,* of southern Asia, the female of which secretes the resinous substance lac.
lack (lăk) *n.* **1.** A deficiency or absence; want: *a lack of money.* **2.** Something that is needed. —*v.* **lacked, lack·ing, lacks.** —*tr.* **1.** To be entirely without or have very little of. **2.** To be in need of. —*intr.* **1.** To be wanting or deficient. **2.** To be in need of something. [ME.]
Synonyms: *lack, want, need.* These verbs mean to be without, or deficient in, something necessary or highly desirable. *Lack* emphasizes the void or deficiency that results from the absence of the thing in question or from the inadequacy of its supply. *Want* and *need* put the stress on the urgent necessity for filling the void or remedying the inadequacy.
Usage: As an intransitive verb *lack* is used chiefly in the present participle with *in: You will not be lacking in support from me.* As a transitive verb it requires no preposition but is sometimes used with *for: You will not lack* (or *lack for*) *support from me.* In that example the Usage Panel prefers *lack* to *lack for.* In some cases, however, the two phrasings can convey different meanings: *He lacks nothing* ("he has everything"). *He lacks for nothing* ("he has everything he needs").
lack·a·dai·si·cal (lăk′ə-dā′zĭ-kəl) *adj.* Lacking spirit, liveliness, or interest; languid. [*Lackadaisy,* alteration of LACKADAY + -IC + -AL.] —**lack′a·dai′si·cal·ly** *adv.* —**lack′a·dai′si·cal·ness** *n.*
lack·a·day (lăk′ə-dā′) *interj. Archaic.* Used to express regret or disapproval. [Alteration of *alack the day.*]
lack·ey (lăk′ē) *n., pl.* **-eys. 1.** A liveried male servant; footman. **2.** A servile follower; toady. —*v.* **-eyed, -ey·ing, -eys.** —*tr.* To wait on as a lackey; attend. —*intr. Obs.* To act in a servile manner; toady. [OFr. *laquais* < Catalan *alacay.*]
lack·lus·ter (lăk′lŭs′tər) *adj.* Lacking luster, brightness, or vitality; dull.
la·con·ic (lə-kŏn′ĭk) *adj.* Using or marked by the use of few words; terse; concise. [Lat. *Laconicus,* Spartan < Gk. *Lakōnikos* (from the reputation of the Spartans for brevity of speech).] —**la·con′i·cal·ly** *adv.*
lac·o·nism (lăk′ə-nĭz′əm) *n.* Terseness or succinctness of style or expression.
lac·quer (lăk′ər) *n.* **1.** Any of various clear or colored synthetic coatings made by dissolving nitrocellulose or other cellulose derivatives together with plasticizers and pigments in a mixture of volatile solvents and used to give surfaces a high gloss. **2.** A glossy, often resinous material, such as the exudation of the lacquer tree, used as a surface coating. **3.** A baked-on finish on the inside of food and beverage cans. —*tr.v.* **-quered, -quer·ing, -quers. 1.** To coat with lacquer. **2.** To give a sleek, glossy finish to. [Obs. Fr. *lacre,* sealing wax < Port. < *laca,* resin of the lac insect < Hindi *lākh.* —see LAC[1].] —**lac′quer·er** *n.*
lacquer tree *n.* A tree, *Rhus verniciflua,* of eastern Asia, having a toxic exudation from which a black lacquer is obtained.
lac·ri·mal (lăk′rə-məl) *adj. & n.* Variant of **lachrymal.**
lac·ri·ma·tion (lăk′rə-mā′shən) *n.* The secretion of tears, esp. in excess.
la·crosse (lə-krôs′, -krŏs′) *n.* A game, played on a field by two teams of ten players each, in which participants use a long-handled stick with a webbed pouch to maneuver a ball into the opposing team's goal. [Canadian Fr. *la crosse* < Fr. (*le jeu de*) *la crosse,* (the game of) the hooked stick < OFr., crosier, of Germanic orig.]
lact- *pref.* Variant of **lacto-.**
lac·tal·bu·min (lăk′tăl-byōō′mĭn) *n.* The albumin contained in milk.
lac·tase (lăk′tās′) *n.* An enzyme occurring in certain yeasts and in the intestinal juices of mammals that catalyzes the conversion of lactose into glucose and galactose.
lac·tate (lăk′tāt′) *intr.v.* **-tat·ed, -tat·ing, -tates.** To secrete or produce milk. —*n.* A salt or ester of lactic acid. —**lac·ta′tion** *n.* —**lac·ta′tion·al** *adj.*
lac·te·al (lăk′tē-əl) *adj.* **1.** Of, pertaining to, or resembling milk. **2.** *Anat.* Of or pertaining to any of numerous minute lymph-carrying vessels that convey chyle from the intestine to the thoracic duct. —*n. Anat.* A lacteal vessel. [< Lat. *lacteus* < *lac,* milk.] —**lac′te·al·ly** *adv.*
lac·tes·cent (lăk-tĕs′ənt) *adj.* **1.** Becoming milky. **2.** Milky. **3.** *Biol.* Secreting or yielding a milky juice, as certain plants and insects. [Lat. *lactescens, lactescent-,* pr.part. of *lactescere,* inchoative of *lactēre,* to be milky < *lac,* milk.] —**lac·tes′cence** *n.*
lac·tic (lăk′tĭk) *adj.* Of, pertaining to, or derived from milk.
lactic acid *n.* A hygroscopic syrupy liquid, $C_3H_6O_3$, present in sour milk, molasses, various fruits, and wines and used in foods and beverages as an acidulant, flavoring, and preservative and in adhesives, plasticizers, and pharmaceuticals.
lac·tif·er·ous (lăk-tĭf′ər-əs) *adj.* **1.** Producing, secreting, or conveying milk. **2.** *Bot.* Yielding latex or a similar milky juice. [LLat. *lactifer,* bearing milk (*lac,* milk + *-fer,* -fer) + -OUS.] —**lac·tif′er·ous·ness** *n.*
lacto- or **lact-** *pref.* **1.** Milk: *lactoprotein.* **2.** Lactose: *lactase.* **3.** Lactic acid: *lactate.* [Fr. < LLat. < Lat. *lac,* milk.]
lac·to·ba·cil·lus (lăk′tō-bə-sĭl′əs) *n.* Any of various bacilli of the genus *Lactobacillus* that ferment lactic acid from carbohydrates.
lac·to·fla·vin (lăk′tə-flā′vĭn, lăk′tə-flā′-) *n.* Riboflavin.
lac·to·gen·ic (lăk′tə-jĕn′ĭk) *adj.* Inducing lactation.
lac·tone (lăk′tōn′) *n.* A cyclic ester of a hydroxyl acid, formed by removing the constituents of water from a molecule of the acid. —**lac·ton′ic** (-tŏn′ĭk) *adj.*
lac·to·pro·tein (lăk′tō-prō′tēn′, -tē-ən) *n.* A protein normally present in milk.
lac·tose (lăk′tōs′) *n.* A white crystalline disaccharide, $C_{12}H_{22}O_{11}$, made from whey and used in pharmaceuticals, infant foods, bakery products, and confections.
la·cu·na (lə-kyōō′nə) *n., pl.* **-nae** (-nē) or **-nas. 1.** An empty space or missing part; gap. **2.** *Anat.* A cavity or depression. [Lat. —see LAGOON.] —**la·cu′nal, la·cu′nar, la·cu′na·ry** *adj.*
la·cu·nar (lə-kyōō′nər) *n. Archit.* **1.** A ceiling with recessed panels. **2.** *pl.* **lac·u·nar·i·a** (lăk′yə-nâr′ē-ə). A panel in a lacunar ceiling. [Lat. < *lacuna,* hole. —see LAGOON.]
la·cus·trine (lə-kŭs′trĭn) *adj.* **1.** Of or pertaining to lakes. **2.** Living or growing in lakes. [< Fr. *lacustre* < Lat. *lacus,* lake.]
lac·y (lā′sē) *adj.* **-i·er, -i·est.** Of, pertaining to, or resembling lace. —**lac′i·ness** *n.*
lad (lăd) *n.* **1.** A young man; youth. **2.** *Informal.* A man of any age; fellow. [ME.]
lad·a·num (lăd′n-əm) *n.* Variant of **labdanum.**
lad·der (lăd′ər) *n.* **1.** A device consisting of two long structural members crossed by parallel rungs, used to climb or descend. **2.** Something resembling a ladder, esp. a run in a stocking. **3. a.** A means of ascent and descent: *ascending the social ladder.* **b.** A series of ranked stages or levels: *high on the executive ladder.* —*intr.v.* **-dered, -der·ing, -ders.** To run, as a stocking does. [ME < OE *hlǣder.*]
lad·der-back (lăd′ər-băk′) *n.* **1.** A chair back consisting of two upright posts connected by horizontal slats. **2.** A chair with a ladder-back. —**lad′der-back′** *adj.*
lad·die (lăd′ē) *n.* A young lad.
la-de-da (lä′dē-dä′) *adj.* Variant of **la-di-da.**
lade (lād) *v.* **lad·ed, lad·en** (lād′n) or **lad·ed, lad·ing, lades.** —*tr.* **1. a.** To load with or as if with cargo. **b.** To place as a load for or as if for shipment. **2.** To weigh down; burden or oppress. **3.** To take up or remove (water) with a ladle or dipper; bale. —*intr.* **1.** To take on cargo. **2.** To ladle a liquid. [ME *laden* < OE *hladan.*]
lad·en (lād′n) *v.* A past participle of **lade.** —*adj.* **1.** Weighed down with a load; heavy. **2.** Oppressed; burdened.
la-di-da also **la-de-da** (lä′dē-dä′) *adj. Informal.* Affectedly genteel; pretentious. [Perh. imit. of affected speech.]
ladies' man *n.* Variant of **lady's man.**
la·dies'-tress·es also **la·dy's-tress·es** (lā′dēz-trĕs′ĭz) *n.* (*used with a sing. or pl. verb*). Any of various orchids of the genus *Spiranthes,* having a spike of small white flowers usually in a twisted or spiral arrangement.
La·din (lə-dēn′) *n.* **1.** Romansch. **2.** A person who is a native speaker of Ladin. [Rhaeto-Romanic < Lat. *Latinus,* Latin.]
lad·ing (lā′dĭng) *n.* **1.** An act of loading. **2.** Cargo; freight.
La·di·no (lə-dē′nō) *n.* A Romance language with elements borrowed from Hebrew that is spoken by Sephardic Jews esp. in the Balkans. [Sp., Latin < Lat. *Latinus.*]
la·dle (lād′l) *n.* A long-handled spoon with a deep bowl for serving liquids. —*tr.v.* **-dled, -dling, -dles.** To lift out or convey with a ladle. [ME < OE *hlædel* < *hladan,* to lade.]
la·dy (lā′dē) *n., pl.* **-dies. 1.** A woman having the refined habits and gentle manners often associated with breeding and culture. **2. a.** A woman regarded as proper and virtuous. **b.** A well-behaved young girl: *She's a perfect little lady.* **3.** The female head of a household. **4.** A woman, esp. when spoken of or to in a polite way. **5. a.** A woman to whom a man is romantically attached. **b.** *Informal.* A wife. **6. Lady.** *Chiefly Brit.* The general feminine title of nobility and of other rank, used: **a.** For the wife of a knight or baronet. **b.** Semiformally for a marchioness, countess, or viscountess. **c.** As the usual style for the wife of a baron. **d.** Semiformally for a baroness in her own right. **e.** As a courtesy title for the daughter of a duke, marquis, or earl. **f.** As a courtesy title for the wife of a younger son of a duke or marquis. **7.** Often **Our Lady.** The Virgin Mary. [ME, female head of a household < OE *hlǣfdige.*]
lady beetle *n.* A ladybug.
la·dy·bird (lā′dē-bûrd′) *n.* A ladybug.

la·dy·bug (lā′dē-bŭg′) *n.* Any of numerous small beetles of the family Coccinellidae, often reddish with black spots, feeding on insect pests such as aphids and scale insects. [LADY, title of Mary, the mother of Jesus + BUG.]

Lady Chapel also **lady chapel** *n.* A chapel in a cathedral, usually located behind the sanctuary, dedicated to the Virgin Mary.

la·dy·fin·ger (lā′dē-fĭng′gər) also **la·dys·fin·ger** (lā′dēz-) *n.* A small, oval sponge cake suggestive in shape of a finger.

lady in waiting *n., pl.* **ladies in waiting.** A lady of a court appointed to serve or attend a queen or princess.

la·dy·kill·er (lā′dē-kĭl′ər) *n. Slang.* A man reputed to be exceptionally successful and often ruthless with women.

la·dy·like (lā′dē-līk′) *adj.* **1.** Characteristic of a lady; well-bred. **2.** Appropriate for or becoming a lady. **3.** Unduly sensitive to matters of propriety or decorum. **4.** Lacking virility or strength.

la·dy·love (lā′dē-lŭv′) *n.* A sweetheart.

la·dys·fin·ger (lā′dēz-fĭng′gər) *n.* Variant of **ladyfinger.**

la·dy·ship (lā′dē-shĭp′) *n.* Often **Ladyship.** A form of address employed in speaking or referring to a woman holding the rank of lady: *if it please your ladyship.*

lady's man also **ladies' man** *n.* A man who enjoys and attracts the company of women.

la·dy's-slip·per (lā′dēz-slĭp′ər) *n.* Any of various orchids of the genus *Cypripedium,* having variously colored flowers with an inflated, pouchlike lip.

la·dy's-smock (lā′dēz-smŏk′) *n.* The cuckooflower.

la·dy's-thumb (lā′dēz-thŭm′) *n.* A plant, *Polygonum persicaria,* native to Europe, having clusters of very small pinkish flowers.

la·dy's-tress·es (lā′dēz-trĕs′ĭz) *n.* Variant of **ladies'-tresses.**

La·er·tes (lā-ûr′tēz) *n. Gk. Myth.* The father of Odysseus. [Lat. < Gk. *Laertēs.*]

La·e·trile (lā′ĭ-trĭl′, -trəl). A trademark for an anti-cancer drug obtained by hydrolyzing amygdalin and oxidizing the resulting glycoside.

lag[1] (lăg) *v.* **lagged, lag·ging, lags.** *—intr.* **1.** To fail to keep up a pace; straggle. **2.** To proceed or develop slowly or abnormally slowly. **3.** To fail, weaken, or slacken gradually; flag. **4.** To determine the order of play in billiards by successively hitting the cue ball against the end rail, the ball rebounding closest to the head rail indicating the player to shoot first. *—tr.* **1.** To cause to fall or lag behind. **2.** To shoot, throw, or pitch (a coin, for example) at a mark. *—n.* **1.** One that lags. **2.** The act, process, or condition of lagging. **3.** A condition of slowness or retardation. **4. a.** An extent or duration of lagging. **b.** An interval between events or phenomena. [Orig. unknown.] **—lag′ger** *n.*

lag[2] (lăg) *n.* **1.** A barrel stave. **2.** A strip, as of wood, that forms a part of the covering for a cylindrical object. *—tr.v.* **lagged, lag·ging, lags.** To furnish or cover with lags. [Prob. of Scand. orig.]

lag[3] (lăg) *Slang. —tr.v.* **lagged, lag·ging, lags. 1.** To arrest. **2.** To send to prison. *—n.* **1. a.** A convict. **b.** An ex-convict. **2.** A period of imprisonment; sentence. [Orig. unknown.]

lag·an (lăg′ən) also **li·gan** (lī′gən) or **lag·end** (lăg′ənd) *n.* Cargo or equipment thrown into the sea but attached to a float or buoy so that it can be recovered. [OFr., perh. of Scand. orig.]

Lag b'O·mer (läg′ bō′mər, läg′bə ō′mər) *n.* A Jewish holiday celebrated on the 33rd day after the 2nd day of Passover, on the 18th day of Iyar. [Heb.]

la·ger (lä′gər) *n.* A type of beer, originally brewed in Germany, that contains a relatively small amount of hops and is aged from six weeks to six months to allow sedimentation. [G. *Lagerbier* : *Lager,* stone + *bier,* beer.]

lag·gard (lăg′ərd) *n.* One that lags; straggler. *—adj.* Lagging or apt to lag. **—lag′gard·ly** *adv.* **—lag′gard·ness** *n.*

lag·ging (lăg′ĭng) *n.* **1.** Insulation used to prevent heat diffusion, as from a steam pipe. **2.** A wooden frame built esp. to support the sides of an arch until the keystone is positioned. [< LAG[2].]

la·gniappe (lăn-yăp′, lăn′yăp′) *n.* **1.** A small gift presented by a store owner to a customer with his purchase. **2.** *Informal.* An extra or unexpected gift or benefit. [Louisiana Fr. < Am. Sp. *la ñapa,* the lagniappe < Quechua *yapay,* to give more.]

lag·o·morph (lăg′ə-môrf′) *n.* Any of various gnawing mammals of the order Lagomorpha, which includes the rabbits, hares, and pikas. [NLat. *Lagomorpha,* order name : Gk. *lagōs,* hare + Gk. *morphē,* shape.] **—lag′o·mor′phic** (-môr′fĭk), **lag′o·mor′phous** (-fəs) *adj.*

la·goon (lə-go͞on′) *n.* A shallow body of water, esp. one separated from the sea by sandbars or coral reefs. [Fr. *lagune* and Ital. *laguna,* both < Lat. *lacuna,* pool < *lacus,* lake.]

lag screw *n.* A heavy wood screw having a square bolt head. [From its orig. use for securing barrel staves.]

la·ic (lā′ĭk) also **la·i·cal** (-ĭ-kəl) *adj.* Of or pertaining to the laity; secular. *—n.* A layman. [LLat. *laicus.*] **—la′i·cal·ly** *adv.*

la·i·cize (lā′ĭ-sīz′) *tr.v.* **-cized, -ciz·ing, -ciz·es. 1.** To free from ecclesiastical control; give over to laymen. **2.** To change to lay status; secularize. **—la′i·ci·za′tion** *n.*

laid (lād) *v.* Past tense and past participle of **lay[1].**

laid-back (lād′băk′) *adj. Informal.* Having a relaxed or casual atmosphere or character; easygoing.

laid paper *n.* A paper made on wire molds that give it a characteristic watermark of close thin lines.

lain (lān) *v.* Past participle of **lie[1].**

lair (lâr) *n.* **1.** The den or dwelling of a wild animal. **2.** A den or hideaway. **3.** *Obs.* A resting place; couch. [ME < OE *leger.*]

laird (lârd) *n. Scot.* The owner of a landed estate. [Sc., alteration of LORD.]

lais·sez faire also **lais·ser faire** (lĕs′ā fâr′) *n.* **1.** An economic doctrine that opposes governmental regulation of or interference in commerce beyond the minimum necessary for a free-enterprise system to operate according to its own economic laws. **2.** *Informal.* Noninterference in the affairs of others. [Fr. < imper. of *laisser faire,* to let (people) do (as they choose).] **—lais′sez-faire′** *adj.*

lais·sez-pas·ser (lĕs′ā-pä-sā′) *n.* A pass, esp. one used in lieu of a passport. [Fr. : *laissez,* imper. of *laisser,* to let + *passer,* to pass.]

la·i·ty (lā′ĭ-tē) *n., pl.* **-ties. 1.** Laymen collectively as distinguished from the clergy. **2.** All those persons who are not members of a given profession or other specialization. [< LAY[2].]

La·ius (lā′əs) *n. Gk. Myth.* The king of Thebes who was mistakenly killed by his own son, Oedipus. [Lat. < Gk. *Laios.*]

lake[1] (lāk) *n.* **1.** A large inland body of fresh or salt water. **2.** A large pool of any liquid. [ME < OFr. *lac* < Lat. *lacus.*]

lake[2] (lāk) *n.* **1.** A pigment consisting of organic coloring matter with an inorganic base or carrier. **2.** A deep red. *—tr.v.* **laked, lak·ing, lakes.** To cause (blood plasma) to become red by releasing hemoglobin from erythrocytes, as by suspending the erythrocytes in water. [Var. of LAC[1].]

lake dwelling *n.* A dwelling, esp. a prehistoric dwelling, built on piles in a shallow lake.

lake herring *n.* A food fish, *Coregonus artedii* (or *Leucichthys artedi*), of the Great Lakes region, related to the whitefishes.

lak·er (lā′kər) *n.* **1.** A fish, such as the lake trout, living in a lake. **2.** A ship used on lakes.

lake trout *n.* A freshwater food fish, *Salvelinus namaycush,* of the Great Lakes.

lakh (läk) *n.* Variant of **lac[2].**

lal·a·pa·loo·za or **lal·la·pa·loo·za** (lŏl′ə-pə-lo͞o′zə) *n.* Variants of **lollapalooza.**

Lal·lan (lăl′ən) also **Lal·lans** (lăl′ənz) *n. Scot.* **1.** The Lowlands of Scotland. **2.** Scots as spoken in southern and eastern Scotland. [Sc., alteration of LOWLAND.] **—Lal′lan** *adj.*

Lal·ly (lă′lē). A trademark for a concrete-filled steel cylinder used as a supporting member in a building.

lal·ly·gag (lăl′ē-găg′) *v.* Variant of **lollygag.**

lam[1] (lăm) *v.* **lammed, lam·ming, lams.** *Slang. —tr.* To give a thorough beating to; thrash. *—intr.* To strike; wallop. [Prob. of Scand. orig.]

lam[2] (lăm) *Slang. —intr.v.* **lammed, lam·ming, lams.** To escape, as from prison. *—n.* Flight, esp. from the law: *on the lam.* [Orig. unknown.]

la·ma (lä′mə) *n.* A Buddhist monk of Tibet or Mongolia. [Tibetan *blama.*]

La·marck·i·an (lə-mär′kē-ən) *adj.* Of or pertaining to Lamarckism. *—n.* A supporter of Lamarckism.

La·marck·ism (lə-mär′kĭz′əm) *n.* The theory that adaptive responses to environment cause structural changes capable of being inherited. [After Chevalier de *Lamarck* (1744–1829), its formulator.]

la·ma·ser·y (lä′mə-sĕr′ē) *n., pl.* **-ies.** A monastery of lamas. [Fr. *lamaserie* < *lama,* lama < Tibetan *blama.*]

La·maze (lə-mäz′) *adj.* Relating to or being a method of childbirth in which the mother is prepared physically and psychologically to give birth without the use of drugs. [After Fernand *Lamaze* (1890–1957).]

lamb (lăm) *n.* **1. a.** A young sheep, esp. one not yet weaned. **b.** The flesh of a young sheep used as meat. **c.** Lambskin. **2.** A sweet, mild-mannered person; dear. **3.** One who can be fleeced, esp. in financial matters; dupe. *—intr.v.* **lambed, lamb·ing, lambs.** To give birth to a lamb. [ME < OE.]

lam·baste (lăm-bāst′) *tr.v.* **-bast·ed, -bast·ing, -bastes.** *Slang.* **1.** To give a thrashing to; beat. **2.** To scold sharply; berate. [Perh. LAM[1] + BASTE[3].]

lamb·da (lăm′də) *n.* **1.** The 11th letter of the Greek alphabet. See table at **alphabet. 2.** An electrically neutral subatomic particle in the baryon family, having a mass 2,183 times that of the electron and a mean lifetime of approximately 2.5×10^{-10} second. [Gk., of Phoenician orig.; akin to Heb. *lāmedh,* lamed.]

lambda point *n.* **1.** The temperature at which the transition from helium I to superfluid helium II occurs, approximately 2.19°K. **2.** The temperature of any phase transition in which the specific heat regarded as a function of temperature has a logarithmic singularity.

lam·bent (lăm′bənt) *adj.* **1.** Flickering lightly over or on a surface. **2.** Characterized by effortless brilliance or lightness: *a lambent wit.* **3.** Having a gentle glow; luminous. [Lat. *lambens, lambent-,* pr.part. of *lambere,* to lick.] **—lam′ben·cy** *n.* **—lam′bent·ly** *adv.*

lam·bert (lăm′bərt) *n.* A unit of brightness equal to $1/\pi$ can-

ladybug

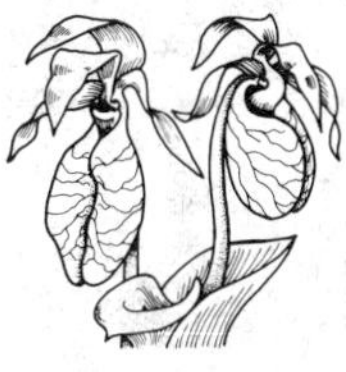

lady's-slipper

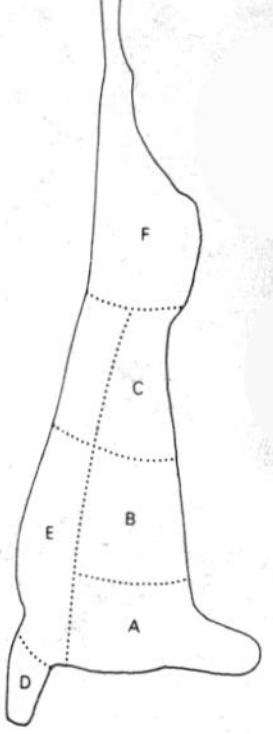

lamb
Above: Newborn lamb
Below: Cuts of lamb
A. Shoulder
B. Ribs
C. Loin
D. Shank
E. Breast
F. Leg

dle per square centimeter. [After Johann H. *Lambert* (1728–1777).]

lamb·kill (lăm′kĭl′) *n.* Sheep laurel.

lam·bre·quin (lăm′bər-kĭn, -brə-kĭn) *n.* **1.** A short ornamental drapery for the top of a window or door or the edge of a shelf. **2.** A heavy, protective cloth or other material worn over a helmet in medieval times. [Fr. < Du. **lamperkin* < *lamper,* veil.]

lamb·skin (lăm′skĭn′) *n.* **1.** The hide of a lamb, esp. when dressed without removing the fleece, as for a garment. **2.** Leather made from the dressed hide of a lamb.

lamb's-let·tuce (lămz′lĕt′əs) *n.* Corn salad.

lamb's-quar·ters also **lamb's quarters** (lămz′kwôr′tərz) *n.* *(used with a sing. or pl. verb).* Pigweed (sense 1).

lamb's wool *n.* **1.** Wool shorn from a lamb. **2.** A fabric or yarn made from lamb's wool.

lame[1] (lām) *adj.* **lam·er, lam·est. 1.** Disabled in one or more limbs, esp. in a leg or foot, so that the ability to walk or move freely is impaired. **2.** Marked by pain or rigidness: *a lame elbow.* **3.** Weak and ineffectual; unsatisfactory: *a lame attempt to apologize.* —*tr.v.* **lamed, lam·ing, lames.** To cause to become lame; cripple. [ME < OE *lama.*] **—lame′ly** *adv.* **—lame′ness** *n.*

lamp
Kerosene lamp

lame[2] (lām) *n.* A thin metal plate, esp. one of the overlapping steel plates in medieval armor. [OFr. < Lat. *lamina,* thin plate.]

la·mé (lă-mā′) *n.* A brocaded fabric having metallic threads in the warp or in the filling. [Fr. < *lamé,* spangled < OFr. *lame,* lame, thin metal plate.]

lame·brain (lām′brān′) *n.* A thick-witted person; ninny. **—lame′brained′** (-brānd′) *adj.*

la·med also **la·medh** (lä′mĕd′) *n.* The 12th letter of the Hebrew alphabet. See table at **alphabet.** [Heb. *lāmedh.*]

lame duck *n.* **1.** An elected officeholder or group continuing in office during the period between failure to win an election and the inauguration of a successor. **2.** An ineffective person; weakling.

lamell– *pref.* Variant of **lamelli–.**

la·mel·la (lə-mĕl′ə) *n., pl.* **-mel·lae** (-mĕl′ē′) or **-mel·las.** A thin scale, plate, or layer, as in the gills of a bivalve mollusk or forming one of the gills of a mushroom. [NLat. < Lat., small thin plate < *lamina,* thin plate.] **—la·mel′lar** *adj.* **—la·mel′lar·ly** *adv.*

la·mel·late (lə-mĕl′āt′, lăm′ə-lāt′) *adj.* **1.** Having, composed of, or arranged in thin layers or lamellae. **2.** Resembling a lamella. **—lam′el·la′ted** *adj.* **—lam′el·la′tion** *n.*

lamelli– or **lamell–** *pref.* Lamella: *lamelliform.* [< LAMELLA.]

la·mel·li·branch (lə-mĕl′ə-brănk′) *n.* Any of the mollusks of the class Pelecypoda (or Lamellibranchia), having a hinged bivalve shell and including the clams, mussels, and oysters. —*adj.* Of or pertaining to lamellibranchs. [NLat. *Lamellibranchia,* class name : LAMELLI– + Lat. *branchia,* gill < Gk. *brankhia,* gills.]

la·mel·li·corn (lə-mĕl′ĭ-kôrn′) *adj.* Of or belonging to the superfamily Lamellicornia (or Scarabaeoidea), which includes the scarabs and other beetles having antennae tipped with movable leaflike plates. —*n.* A lamellicorn beetle. [NLat. *Lamellicornia,* superfamily name : LAMELLI– + Lat. *cornu,* horn.]

la·mel·li·form (lə-mĕl′ə-fôrm′) *adj.* Having the form of a thin plate or lamella.

lamprey
Above: Detail of mouth
Below: Petromyzon marinus

la·ment (lə-mĕnt′) *v.* **-ment·ed, -ment·ing, -ments.** —*tr.* **1.** To express grief for or about; mourn: *lament a death.* **2.** To regret deeply; deplore. —*intr.* To wail; complain: " *'Doesn't she know,' she lamented, 'that black's bad luck for weddings?'* " (Mary McCarthy). —*n.* **1.** A feeling or expression of grief; lamentation. **2.** A song or poem expressing grief; elegy. [OFr. *lamenter* < Lat. *lamentari* < *lamentum,* lament.] **—la·ment′er** *n.*

la·men·ta·ble (lə-mĕn′tə-bəl, lăm′ən-) *adj.* **1.** To be lamented; deplorable. **2.** Exhibiting sorrow or grief; mournful. **—lam′en·ta·bly** *adv.*

lam·en·ta·tion (lăm′ən-tā′shən) *n.* An act or instance of lamenting.

Lam·en·ta·tions (lăm′ən-tā′shənz) *n.* *(used with a sing. verb).* See table at **Bible.**

la·ment·ed (lə-mĕn′tĭd) *adj.* Mourned for. **—la·ment′ed·ly** *adv.*

la·mi·a (lā′mē-ə) *n., pl.* **-as** or **-ae** (-ē′). **1.** *Gk. Myth.* A monster represented as a serpent with the head and breasts of a woman, reputed to prey upon humans and suck the blood of children. **2.** A female vampire. [ME < Lat. < Gk.]

lam·i·na (lăm′ə-nə) *n., pl.* **-nae** (-nē′) or **-nas. 1.** A thin plate, sheet, or layer. **2.** *Bot.* The expanded area of a leaf. **3.** *Zool.* A scalelike or platelike structure, as one of the thin layers of sensitive tissue in the hoof of a horse. [Lat.] **—lam′i·nar, lam′i·nal** *adj.*

lam·i·nar flow (lăm′ə-nər) *n.* Nonturbulent flow of a viscous fluid in layers near a boundary, as of lubricating oil in bearings.

lanceolate
Lanceolate leaves

lam·i·nate (lăm′ə-nāt′) *v.* **-nat·ed, -nat·ing, -nates.** —*tr.* **1.** To beat or compress into a thin plate or sheet. **2.** To divide into thin layers. **3.** To make by uniting several layers. **4.** To cover with thin sheets. —*intr.* To split into thin layers or sheets. —*adj.* (-nĭt, -nāt′). Consisting of, arranged in, or covered with laminae. —*n.* A laminated product, as plywood. [LAMIN(A) + -ATE[1].] **—lam′i·na′tor** *n.*

lam·i·nat·ed (lăm′ə-nā′tĭd) *adj.* **1.** Composed of layers bonded together. **2.** Arranged in laminae; laminate.

lam·i·na·tion (lăm′ə-nā′shən) *n.* **1. a.** The process of laminating. **b.** The state of being laminated. **2.** Something laminated. **3.** A lamina.

lam·i·ni·tis (lăm′ə-nī′tĭs) *n.* Inflammation of the sensitive laminae in the hoof of a horse.

Lam·mas (lăm′əs) *n.* A harvest festival formerly held in England on August 1. [ME < OE *hlāfmæss* : *hlāf,* loaf + *mæsse,* Mass.]

lam·mer·gei·er also **lam·mer·gey·er** (lăm′ər-gī′ər) *n.* A large predatory bird, *Gypaetus barbatus,* of mountainous regions of the Old World. [G. *Lämmergeier* : *Lamm,* lamb + *Geier,* vulture.]

lamp (lămp) *n.* **1. a.** A device that generates light, heat, or therapeutic radiation. **b.** A vessel containing oil or alcohol burned through a wick for illumination. **2.** A star, planet, meteor, or other celestial body. **3.** Something that illumines the mind or soul. [ME < OFr. *lampe* < Lat. *lampas* < Gk. < *lampein,* to shine.]

lamp·black (lămp′blăk′) *n.* A gray or black pigment made from the soot collected from incompletely burned carbonaceous materials, used as a pigment and in matches, explosives, lubricants, and fertilizers.

lam·pi·on (lăm′pē-ən) *n.* An oil-burning lamp, often of colored glass, for outdoor use. [Fr. < Ital. *lampione,* aug. of *lampa,* lamp < OFr. *lampe.* —see LAMP.]

lamp·light (lămp′līt′) *n.* The light shed by a lamp.

lamp·light·er (lămp′lī′tər) *n.* One that lights lamps.

lam·poon (lăm-po͞on′) *n.* **1.** A broad satirical piece that uses ridicule to attack a person, group, or institution. **2.** A light, good-humored satire. —*tr.v.* **-pooned, -poon·ing, -poons.** To ridicule or satirize in a lampoon. [Fr. *lampon* < *lampons,* let us drink (from the refrain of a drinking song) < *lamper,* to gulp down.] **—lam·poon′er, lam·poon′ist** *n.* **—lam·poon′er·y** *n.*

lamp·post (lămp′pōst′) *n.* A post supporting a street lamp.

lam·prey (lăm′prē) *n., pl.* **-preys.** Any of various primitive elongated freshwater or anadromous fishes of the family Petromyzontidae, characteristically having a jawless sucking mouth with a rasping tongue. [ME *lamprei* < OFr. *lampreie* < Med. Lat. *lampreda.*]

lamp shell *n.* A brachiopod.

la·nai (lə-nī′, lä-) *n., pl.* **-nais.** A verandah or roofed patio. [Hawaiian.]

la·nate (lā′nāt′) *adj.* Having or consisting of woolly hairs. [Lat. *lanatus* < *lana,* wool.]

Lan·cas·tri·an (lăng-kăs′trē-ən) *adj.* Of or pertaining to the royal house of Lancaster that ruled in England from 1399 to 1461.

lance (lăns) *n.* **1.** A thrusting weapon with a long wooden shaft and a sharp metal head. **2.** An implement similar to a lance for spearing fish. **3.** A lancer. **4.** A lancet. —*tr.v.* **lanced, lanc·ing, lanc·es. 1.** To pierce with a lance. **2.** To make a surgical incision in; cut into; *lance a boil.* [ME < OFr. < Lat. *lancea.*]

lance corporal *n.* **1.** In the U.S. Marine Corps, an enlisted person ranking above a private first class and below a corporal. **2.** In the British Army, a private acting as a corporal.

lance·let (lăns′lĭt) *n.* Any of various small, flattened marine organisms of the subphylum Cephalochordata, allied to the vertebrates but having a notochord rather than a true vertebral column.

Lan·ce·lot (lăn′sə-lət, -lŏt′, län′-) *n.* In Arthurian legend, a knight of the Round Table whose love affair with Queen Guinevere resulted in a war with King Arthur.

lan·ce·o·late (lăn′sē-ə-lāt′) *adj.* Narrow and tapering at each end: *lanceolate leaves.* [LLat. *lanceolatus* < Lat. *lanceola,* little lance, dim. of *lancea,* lance.] **—lan′ce·o·late′ly** *adv.*

lanc·er (lăn′sər) *n.* **1.** A cavalryman armed with lances. **2.** A member of a regiment originally armed with lances. **3. lancers** *(used with a sing. verb).* **a.** A form of quadrille. **b.** The music for this dance. [OFr. *lancier* < *lance,* lance.]

lan·cet (lăn′sĭt) *n.* **1.** A surgical knife with a short, wide, double-edged blade. **2. a.** A lancet arch. **b.** A lancet window. [ME < OFr., dim. of *lance,* lance.]

lancet arch *n.* An arch that is narrow and pointed like the head of a spear.

lancet fish *n.* Either of two large marine fishes, *Alepisaurus ferox,* of the Atlantic, or *A. richardsoni,* of the Pacific, having long, sharp teeth and a large dorsal fin.

lancet window *n.* A tall narrow window set in a lancet arch.

lance·wood (lăns′wo͝od′) *n.* **1.** Any of several tropical American trees, such as one of the genera *Calycophyllum* or *Mimusops,* having hard, durable, uniformly grained wood. **2.** The wood of a lancewood.

land (lănd) *n.* **1.** The solid ground of the earth, esp. as distinguished from the sea. **2. a.** The ground or soil; earth: *till the land.* **b.** A topographically or functionally distinct tract: *desert land.* **3. a.** A nation; country. **b.** The people of a nation, district, or region. **c. lands.** Territorial possessions or property. **4.** Public or private landed property; real estate. **5.** An area or realm: *the land of make-believe.* **6.** *Law.* **a.** A tract of land that may be owned, together with everything growing or constructed upon it. **b.** A landed estate. **7.** The raised portion of a grooved surface. —*v.* **land·ed, land·ing, lands.** —*tr.* **1. a.** To bring to and unload on land: *land cargo.* **b.** To set down on land or another surface: *land an airplane.* **2.** To cause to arrive in a place or condition: *His activities landed him in jail.* **3. a.** To catch and pull in (a fish). **b.** To win; secure: *land a big contract.* **4.** To deliver: *land a blow on the head.* —*intr.* **1. a.** To come to shore. **b.** To disembark. **2.** To descend toward and settle on the ground or another surface. **3.** To arrive in a place or condition: *landed at the theater too late.* **4.** To come to rest in a certain way or place: *land on one's feet.* [ME < OE.]

lan·dau (lăn'dô', -dou') *n.* **1.** A four-wheeled closed carriage with front and back passenger seats that face each other and a roof in two sections that can be lowered or detached. **2.** A style of automobile with a roof similar to that of a landau. [After *Landau,* Bavaria, Germany.]

lan·dau·let or **lan·dau·lette** (lăn'dl-ĕt') *n.* **1.** A small landau. **2.** An automobile with a collapsible roof over the back seat and an open driver's seat.

land bank *n.* A bank that issues long-term loans on real estate in return for mortgages.

land·ed (lăn'dĭd) *adj.* **1.** Owning land: *landed gentry.* **2.** Consisting of land or real estate: *a landed estate.*

land·er (lăn'dər) *n.* **1.** One that lands. **2.** A space vehicle designed to land on a celestial body.

land·fall (lănd'fôl') *n.* **1.** The act or an instance of sighting or reaching land after a voyage or flight. **2.** The land sighted or reached after a voyage or flight.

land·fill (lănd'fĭl') *n.* **1.** A method of rehabilitating land in which garbage and trash are buried in low-lying ground to build it up. **2.** Land that has been rehabilitated by landfill.

land grant *n.* A government grant of public land for a railroad, highway, or state college.

land·hold·er (lănd'hōl'dər) *n.* A person who owns land. —**land'hold'ing** *n.*

land·ing (lăn'dĭng) *n.* **1. a.** The act or process of coming to land or rest, esp. after a voyage or flight. **b.** A termination, esp. of a voyage or flight. **2.** A site for loading and unloading passengers and cargo. **3. a.** An intermediate platform on a flight of stairs. **b.** The area at the top or bottom of a staircase.

landing craft *n.* A naval craft designed to convey troops and equipment from ship to shore.

landing field *n.* A tract of land used by aircraft for landing and taking off.

landing gear *n.* The undercarriage of an aircraft, designed to support the weight of the craft and its load on the ground.

landing strip *n.* An aircraft runway without airport facilities.

land·la·dy (lănd'lā'dē) *n.* **1.** A woman who owns and rents land, buildings, or dwelling units. **2.** A woman who runs a rooming house or inn; innkeeper.

land·less (lănd'lĭs) *adj.* Owning or having no land.

land·locked (lănd'lŏkt') *adj.* **1.** Entirely or almost entirely surrounded by land. **2.** Confined to inland waters, as certain salmon.

land·lord (lănd'lôrd') *n.* **1.** A person who owns and rents land, buildings, or dwelling units. **2.** A man who runs a rooming house or inn; innkeeper.

land·lord·ism (lănd'lôr-dĭz'əm) *n.* Land management in which ownership of land is vested in a private individual or group that leases it to tenants, esp. tenants who cultivate it.

land·lub·ber (lănd'lŭb'ər) *n.* A person unfamiliar with the sea or seamanship. —**land'lub'ber·ly** *adj.*

land·mark (lănd'märk') *n.* **1.** A fixed marker, as a concrete block, indicating a boundary line. **2.** A prominent and identifying feature of a landscape. **3.** An event marking an important stage of development or a turning point in history. **4.** A building or site that has historical significance, esp. one that is marked for preservation by a municipal or national government.

land·mass (lănd'măs') *n.* A large area of land.

land mine *n.* An explosive mine laid usually just below the surface of the ground.

land office *n.* A government office that handles and keeps records of the sale or transfer of public land.

land-of·fice business (lănd'ô'fĭs, -ŏf'ĭs) *n.* A thriving, extensive, or rapidly moving volume of trade.

land·own·er (lănd'ō'nər) *n.* One who owns land. —**land'own'er·ship'** *n.* —**land'own'ing** *n. & adj.*

land-poor (lănd'po͝or') *adj.* Owning much unprofitable land but lacking the capital to improve or maintain it.

land reform *n.* Measures, as the division of large properties into smaller ones, taken to bring about a more equitable apportionment of agricultural land.

land·scape (lănd'skāp') *n.* **1.** A view or vista of scenery on land: *a desert landscape.* **2.** A picture depicting a landscape. **3.** The branch of art dealing with the representation of natural scenery. —*v.* **-scaped, -scap·ing, -scapes.** —*tr.* To adorn or improve (a section of ground) by contouring the land and planting flowers, shrubs, or trees. —*intr.* To arrange grounds artistically as a profession. [Du. *landschap* : *land,* land + *-schap,* -ship.]

landscape architect *n.* One whose professional skill is the decorative and functional alteration and planting of grounds, esp. at or around a building site. —**landscape architecture** *n.*

landscape gardener *n.* One whose occupation is the decoration of land by planting trees and shrubs and designing gardens. —**landscape gardening** *n.*

land·scap·ist (lănd'skā'pĭst) *n.* A painter of landscapes.

land·side (lănd'sīd') *n.* The flat side of a plow opposite the furrow.

lands·leit (länts'līt') *n.* Plural of **landsman[2]**. [Yiddish *landslayt,* pl. of *landsman,* landsman. —see LANDSMAN[2].]

land·slide (lănd'slīd') *n.* **1.** Also **land·slip** (-slĭp'). **a.** The dislodging and fall of a mass of earth and rock. **b.** The dislodged mass. **2. a.** An overwhelming majority of votes for a political party or candidate. **b.** An election that sweeps a party or candidate into office. **c.** A great victory.

Lands·mål (länts'môl') *n.* An official and literary form of Norwegian based on the spoken dialects of Norway. [Norw. : *land,* country + *mål,* speech.]

lands·man[1] (lăndz'mən) *n.* One who lives and works on land as distinguished from a seaman.

lands·man[2] (länts'mən) *n., pl.* **lands·leit** (länts'līt'). A fellow Jew who comes from the same district or town, esp. in Eastern Europe. [Yiddish < MHG *lantsman* : OHG *lant,* land + MHG *man,* man.]

land·ward (lănd'wərd) *adj. & adv.* To or toward land. —**land'wards** *adv.*

lane (lān) *n.* **1. a.** A narrow way or passage between walls, hedges, or fences. **b.** A narrow country road. **2.** A narrow passage, course, or track, as: **a.** A prescribed course for ships or aircraft. **b.** A strip delineated on a street or highway to accommodate a single line of automobiles. **c.** One of a set of parallel courses marking the bounds for contestants in a race. **d.** A wood-surfaced passageway along which a bowling ball is rolled. [ME < OE.]

lang (lăng) *adj. Scot.* Long.

lang·lauf (läng'louf') *n.* A cross-country ski run. [G. : *lang,* long + *lauf,* race.] —**lang'lauf'er** *n.*

lang·ley (lăng'lē) *n.* A unit of illumination used to measure temperature, as of a star, equal to one gram calorie per square centimeter of irradiated surface. [After Samuel *Langley* (1834–1906).]

Lan·go·bard (lăng'gə-bärd') *n.* A Lombard (sense 1). [Lat. *Langobardus.*] —**Lan'go·bar'dic** *adj.*

lan·gouste (läɴ-go͞ost') *n.* The spiny lobster. [Fr. < OFr. < OProv. *langosta.*]

lang·syne also **lang syne** (lăng-zīn') —*adv. Scot.* Long ago; long since. —*n.* Time long past; times past. [ME *lang sine.*]

lan·guage (lăng'gwĭj) *n.* **1. a.** The use by human beings of voice sounds, and often of written symbols that represent these sounds, in organized combinations and patterns to express and communicate thoughts and feelings. **b.** A system of words formed from such combinations and patterns, used by the people of a particular country or by a group of people with a shared history or set of traditions. **2.** A nonverbal method of communicating ideas, as by a system of signs, symbols, or gestures: *the language of algebra.* **3.** Body language. **4.** The special vocabulary and usages of a scientific, professional, or other group. **5.** A characteristic style of speech or writing: *ribald language.* **6. a.** Abusive, violent, or profane utterance: *"language that would make your hair curl"* (W.S. Gilbert). **b.** A particular manner of utterance: *gentle language.* **7.** The manner or means of communication between living creatures other than humans: *the language of dolphins.* **8.** Language as a subject of study. **9.** The wording of a legal document or statute as distinct from the spirit. **10.** *Computer Sci.* Machine language. [ME < OFr. < Lat. *lingua.*]

langue d'oc (läng dôk', läɴg) *n.* Provençal. [Fr. < OFr., language of *oc,* from the use of the word *oc* for "yes" in Provençal.]

langue d'o·ïl (läng doil', doi', läɴg' dô-ēl') *n.* French (sense 1). [Fr. < OFr., language of *oïl,* from the use of the word *oïl* for "yes" in French.]

lan·guet (lăng'gwĭt, lăng-gwĕt') *n.* A thing or part resembling a tongue in shape or function. [ME < OFr. *languette,* dim. of *langue,* tongue < Lat. *lingua.*]

lan·guid (lăng'gwĭd) *adj.* **1.** Lacking energy or vitality; weak. **2.** Showing little or no spirit or animation. **3.** Lacking vigor or force; slow. [OFr. *languide* < Lat. *languidus* < *languere,* to be languid.] —**lan'guid·ly** *adv.* —**lan'guid·ness** *n.*

lan·guish (lăng'gwĭsh) *intr.v.* **-guished, -guish·ing, -guish·es. 1. a.** To be or become weak or feeble; lose strength or vigor. **b.** To exist or continue in miserable or disheartening conditions. **2.** To remain unattended or be neglected: *legislation languishing in committee.* **3.** To become downcast; pine. **4.** To affect a wistful or languid air, esp. in order to gain sympathy. [ME *languishen* < OFr. *languir, languiss-* < Lat. *languēre,* to be languid.] —**lan'guish·er** *n.* —**lan'guish·ing·ly** *adv.* —**lan'guish·ment** *n.*

lan·guor (lăng'gər, lăng'ər) *n.* **1.** Lack of physical or mental energy; listlessness. **2.** A dreamy, lazy mood or quality. **3.** Oppressive quiet or stillness. [ME < OFr. *langor* < Lat. *languor* < *languēre,* to be languid.] —**lan'guor·ous** *adj.* —**lan'guor·ous·ly** *adv.* —**lan'guor·ous·ness** *n.*

lan·gur (läng-go͝or') *n.* Any of various slender, long-tailed

landing strip

Asian monkeys of the genus *Presbytis* and related genera. [Hindi *langūr,* perh. < Skt. *lāṅgūlam,* a hairy tail.]

lan·iard (lăn′yərd) *n.* Variant of **lanyard.**

la·nif·er·ous (lə-nĭf′ər-əs) *adj.* Having wool or woollike hair. [Lat. *lanifer* (*lana,* wool + *-fer,* -fer) + -OUS.]

lank (lăngk) *adj.* **-er, -est. 1.** Long and lean; gaunt. **2.** Long, straight, and limp: *lank hair.* [ME **lank* < OE *hlanc.*] **—lank′ly** *adv.* **—lank′ness** *n.*

lank·y (lăng′kē) *adj.* **-i·er, -i·est.** Tall, thin, and ungainly. **—lank′i·ly** *adv.* **—lank′i·ness** *n.*

lan·ner (lăn′ər) *n.* **1.** A falcon, *Falco biarmicus,* of Africa and the Mediterranean region. **2.** A female lanner, used in falconry. [ME *laner* < AN < Med. Lat. *lanarius.*]

lan·ner·et (lăn′ə-rĕt′) *n.* A male lanner, smaller than the female, used in falconry. [ME *laneret* < OFr., dim. of *lanier,* lanner < Med. Lat. *lanarius.*]

lan·o·lin (lăn′ə-lĭn) *n.* A yellowish-white fatty substance obtained from wool and used in soaps, cosmetics, and ointments. [G. < Lat. *lana,* wool.]

lan·ta·na (lăn-tä′nə, -tăn′ə) *n.* Any of various aromatic, chiefly tropical shrubs of the genus *Lantana,* having dense clusters of small, variously colored flowers. [NLat. *Lantana,* genus name < dial. Ital. *lantana,* viburnum.]

lan·tern (lăn′tərn) *n.* **1. a.** An often portable case with transparent or translucent sides for holding and protecting a light. **b.** A decorative casing for a light, often of paper. **2. a.** *Obs.* A lighthouse. **b.** The room at the top of a lighthouse where the light is located. **3.** A structure built on top of a roof with open or windowed walls to let in light and air. **4.** A slide projector. [ME < OFr. *lanterne* < Lat. *lanterna* < Gk. *lamptēr* < *lampein,* to shine.]

lantern fish *n.* Any of numerous small deep-sea fishes of the family Myctophidae, having phosphorescent light organs.

lantern fly *n.* Any of various chiefly tropical insects of the subfamily Fulgorinae, having an enlarged, elongated head.

lantern jaw *n.* A lower jaw that protrudes beyond the upper jaw. **—lan′tern-jawed′** *adj.*

lantern pinion *n.* A lantern wheel.

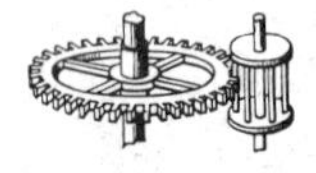

lantern wheel

lantern wheel *n.* A small pinion consisting of circular disks connected by cylindrical bars that serve as teeth, now used chiefly in inexpensive clocks.

lan·tha·nide (lăn′thə-nīd′) *n.* A rare-earth element. [LANTHAN(UM) + -IDE.]

lanthanide series *n.* The set of chemically related elements with atomic numbers from 57 to 71; the rare-earth elements.

lan·tha·num (lăn′thə-nəm) *n. Symbol* **La** A soft, silvery-white, malleable, ductile, metallic rare-earth element, obtained chiefly from monazite and bastnaesite, used in glass manufacture and with other rare earths in carbon lights for motion-picture and television studio lighting. Atomic number 57; atomic weight 138.91; melting point 920°C; boiling point 3,469°C; specific gravity 5.98 to 6.186; valence 3. [NLat. < Gk. *lanthanein,* to escape notice.]

lant·horn (lănt′hôrn′, lăn′tərn) *n. Chiefly Brit.* A lantern. [Var. of LANTERN.]

la·nu·gi·nous (lə-no͞o′jə-nəs, -nyo͞o′-) *adj.* Covered with soft, short hair; downy. [Lat. *lanuginosus* < *lanugo,* lanugo.] **—la·nu′gi·nous·ness** *n.*

la·nu·go (lə-no͞o′gō, -nyo͞o′-) *n., pl.* **-gos.** Fine, soft hair. [Lat.]

lan·yard also **lan·iard** (lăn′yərd) *n.* **1.** A short rope or gasket used on a ship for fastening something or for securing rigging. **2.** A cord worn around the neck for carrying something, as a knife. **3.** A cord with a hook at one end used to fire a cannon. [ME *langer,* strap < OFr. *laniere,* of Germanic orig.]

lap joint

Lao (lou) *n., pl.* **Lao** or **Laos. 1. a.** One of a Buddhist people of Thai stock living in the area of the Mekong River in Laos and Thailand. **b.** The Lao people. **2.** The Tai language of the Lao. *—adj.* Of the Lao or their language.

La·oc·o·on (lā-ŏk′ō-ŏn′) *n. Gk. Myth.* A Trojan priest of Apollo who was killed with his two sons by two serpents for having warned his people against the Trojan horse. [Lat. < Gk. *Laokoōn.*]

La·od·i·ce·an (lā-ŏd′ĭ-sē′ən) *adj.* Indifferent or lukewarm esp. in religion. [After *Laodicea,* an ancient city in Asia Minor.] **—La·od′i·ce′an** *n.*

La·om·e·don (lā-ŏm′ĭ-dŏn′) *n. Gk. Myth.* The founder and king of Troy and father of Priam. [Lat. < Gk. *Laomedōn.*]

La·o·tian (lā-ō′shən, lou′shen) *n. & adj.* Lao. [Fr. *Laotien* < *Lao,* Lao.]

lap[1] (lăp) *n.* **1.** The front region or area from the lower trunk to the knees of a seated person. **2.** The portion of a garment that covers the lower trunk to the knees. [ME < OE *læppa,* lappet.] **—lap′ful′** (-fo͝ol′) *n.*

larch

lap[2] (lăp) *v.* **lapped, lap·ping, laps.** *—tr.* **1.** To fold, wrap, or wind over or around something. **2.** To envelop in something; swathe. **3.** To place or lay (a thing) so as to cover part of another; overlap. **4.** In cabinetwork, to join by or as if by scarfing. **5.** To get ahead of (an opponent) in a race by one or more complete circuits of the course. **6.** To polish until smooth. *—intr.* **1.** To fold or wind around something. **2.** To extend beyond or project onto an edge; overlap. *—n.* **1. a.** A part that overlaps. **b.** The amount by which a part overlaps another. **2. a.** One complete turn or circuit, esp. of a racetrack. **b.** One complete length of a straight course, as of a swimming pool. **c.** A segment or stage, as of a trip. **d.** A length, as of rope, required to make one complete turn, as around a wheel. **3.** A continuous band or layer of cotton, flax, or other fiber. **4.** A wheel, disk, or slab of leather or metal, either stationary or rotating, for polishing and smoothing. [ME *lappen* < *lap,* lap, flap of a garment.]

lap[3] (lăp) *v.* **lapped, lap·ping, laps.** *—tr.* **1.** To take in (a liquid or food) with the tongue. **2.** To wash against with a gentle intermittent slapping sound: *waves lapping the shore.* *—intr.* **1.** To take in a liquid or food with the tongue. **2.** To wash against a shore with a gentle intermittent slapping sound. ***—phrasal verb.* lap up.** *Informal.* To receive eagerly or greedily: *lapping up praise.* *—n.* **1. a.** The act or process of lapping. **b.** The amount ingested by lapping. **2.** A watery food or drink. **3.** The sound of lapping water. [ME *lappen* < OE *lapian.*] **—lap′per** *n.*

lap·a·rot·o·my (lăp′ə-rŏt′ə-mē) *n., pl.* **-mies.** Surgical incision into the abdominal wall. [Gk. *lapara,* flank (< *laparos,* soft) + -TOMY.]

lap belt *n.* An automobile seat belt that fastens across the lap.

lap·board (lăp′bôrd′, -bōrd′) *n.* A flat board held on the lap as a substitute for a table or desk.

lap dog *n.* A small, easily held dog kept as a pet.

la·pel (lə-pĕl′) *n.* The part of a garment that is an extension of the collar and folds back against the breast. [< LAP[1].]

lap·i·dar·i·an (lăp′ĭ-dâr′ē-ən) *adj.* Cut in or inscribed on stone. [Lat. *lapidarius* < *lapis,* stone.]

lap·i·dar·y (lăp′ĭ-dĕr′ē) *n., pl.* **-ies. 1.** A person who cuts, polishes, or engraves gems. **2.** A dealer in precious or semiprecious stones. *—adj.* **1.** Of or relating to precious stones or the art of working with them. **2. a.** Engraved in stone. **b.** Suitable for inscription in stone: *lapidary prose.* [Lat. *lapidarius* < *lapis,* stone.]

la·pil·lus (lə-pĭl′əs) *n., pl.* **-pil·li** (-pĭl′ī′). A small solidified fragment of lava. [Lat., small stone, dim. of *lapis,* stone.]

lap·in (lăp′ĭn, lä-păN′) *n.* **1.** A rabbit. **2.** Rabbit fur, esp. when sheared and dyed. [Fr.]

lap·is laz·u·li (lăp′ĭs lăz′yə-lē, lăzh′ə-) *n.* **1.** An opaque azure-blue to deep-blue gemstone of lazurite. **2.** Lazurite. [ME < Med. Lat. : Lat. *lapis,* stone + *lazulum,* lapis lazuli < Ar. *lāzaward* < Pers. *lājwārd.*]

Lap·ith (lăp′ĭth) *n. Gk. Myth.* One of a Thessalonian tribe who at the disastrous wedding of their king defeated the drunken centaurs. [< Lat. *Lapithae,* Lapiths < Gk. *Lapithai.*]

lap joint *n.* A joint in which the ends or edges are overlapped and fastened together.

Lapp (lăp) *n.* **1.** One of a people of nomadic tradition who inhabit Lapland. **2.** The Finno-Ugric language of the Lapps. [Swed.]

lap·pet (lăp′ĭt) *n.* **1.** A decorative flap or loose fold on a garment or headdress. **2.** A flaplike structure, such as the wattle of a bird. [< LAP[1].]

lap robe *n.* A small blanket to cover the lap, legs, and feet, as of a passenger in an automobile.

lapse (lăps) *v.* **lapsed, laps·ing, laps·es.** *—intr.* **1. a.** To fall away from a level, as of morality, to a different and usually less desirable one; backslide. **b.** To slip gradually; drift: *lapse into dreaminess.* **2.** To pass; elapse: *Years had lapsed since we last met.* **3. a.** *Law.* To pass to another through neglect or omission. Used of a right or privilege, a benefice, or an estate. **b.** To be no longer in force because of neglect, disuse, or the passage of time: *The guarantee lapsed.* *—tr.* To allow to lapse. *—n.* **1. a.** A slip, error, or failure, esp. a slight or unimportant one: *a lapse of memory.* **b.** A fall from rectitude; moral error. **2.** A slipping into a less desirable condition; decline: *a lapse into barbarism.* **3. a.** The passage of time. **b.** An interval or period of passing time. **4.** *Law.* The termination of a right or privilege through disuse, neglect, or death. [Lat. *labi, laps-,* to lapse.] **—laps′er** *n.*

lap·strake (lăp′strāk′) also **lap·streak** (-strēk′) *adj. Naut.* Built with each strake overlapping the one below; clinker-built. *—n.* A clinker-built boat.

La·pu·ta (lə-pyo͞o′tə) *n.* In Swift's *Gulliver's Travels,* a flying island inhabited by philosophers engaged in absurdly impractical enterprises. **—La·pu′tan** (-pyo͞ot′n) *n. & adj.*

lap·wing (lăp′wĭng′) *n.* Any of several Old World birds of the genus *Vanellus,* related to the plovers, esp. *V. vanellus,* having a narrow crest. [ME < OE *hlēapewince.*]

Lar (lär) *n., pl.* **Lar·es** (lâr′ēz) A tutelary deity or spirit of an ancient Roman household. [Lat.]

lar·board (lär′bərd) *Naut.* *—n.* Port[2]. *—adj.* On the port side. [ME *laddebord.*]

lar·ce·nist (lär′sə-nĭst) also **lar·ce·ner** (-nər) *n.* One who commits larceny.

lar·ce·ny (lär′sə-nē) *n., pl.* **-nies.** The felonious taking and removing of another's personal property with the intent of permanently depriving the owner; theft. [ME < OFr. *larcin,* theft < Lat. *latrocinium,* robbery < *latro,* robber.] **—lar′ce·nous** *adj.*

larch (lärch) *n.* **1.** Any of several coniferous trees of the genus *Larix,* having deciduous needles and heavy, durable wood. **2.** The wood of a larch. [MHG *larche* < Lat. *larix.*]

lard (lärd) *n.* The white solid or semisolid rendered fat of a hog. *—tr.v.* **lard·ed, lard·ing, lards. 1.** To cover or coat with lard or a similar fat. **2.** To insert strips of fat in (meat) before cooking. **3. a.** To make richer with or as if with fat. **b.** To enrich with additions; embellish: *larded his report with quotations.* [ME < OFr. *larde* < Lat. *lardum.*] **—lard'y** *adj.*

lar·der (lär'dər) *n.* **1.** A place where meat and other foods are kept. **2.** A supply of food. [ME < AN < Med. Lat. *lardarium* < Lat. *lardum,* lard.]

lar·don (lär'dŏn') also **lar·doon** (lär-do͞on') *n.* A strip of fat for larding meat. [Fr. < OFr. < *larde,* lard.]

lar·ee (lâr'ē) *n.* See table at **currency.** [Ult. < Pers. *Lārī.*]

Lar·es (lâr'ēz) *n.* Plural of **Lar.**

lares and penates *pl.n.* Household possessions.

large (lärj) *adj.* **larg·er, larg·est. 1.** Of greater than average size, extent, quantity, or amount; big. **2.** Of greater than average scope, breadth, or capacity; comprehensive. **3.** Understanding and tolerant: *a large and generous spirit.* **4. a.** Pretentious; boastful. Used of speech or manners. **b.** *Obs.* Gross; coarse. Used of speech or language. **5.** *Naut.* Designating a favorable wind. ***—idiom.*** **at large. 1.** Not in confinement or captivity; at liberty: *a convict still at large.* **2.** At length; copiously. **3.** As a whole; in general: *the country at large.* **4.** Representing a nation, state, or district as a whole. **5.** Not assigned to a particular country: *ambassador at large.* [ME < OFr. < Lat. *largus.*] **—large'ness** *n.*

Synonyms: *large, big, great.* These adjectives are applied to what is notably above the average of its kind in size, degree, or the like. *Large* and *big* are interchangeable in many contexts. However, *large* is more often found in references to physical dimensions, quantity, and capacity: *a large building; a large estate; a large sum; a large glass. Big* is especially applicable to physical bulk or mass, volume of sound, and figurative magnitude: *big ears; a big noise; a big heart; big problems. Great* implies impressiveness or distinctiveness in references involving physical size: *a great ocean liner.* Often the term is used figuratively to express degree: *great sorrow.*

large calorie *n.* A calorie (sense 3).

large-heart·ed (lärj'här'tĭd) *adj.* Having a generous disposition; sympathetic. **—large'-heart'ed·ness** *n.*

large intestine *n.* The portion of the intestine that extends from the ileum to the anus, forming an arch around the convolutions of the small intestine and including the cecum, colon, rectum, and anal canal.

large·ly (lärj'lē) *adv.* **1.** For the most part; mainly. **2.** On a large scale; amply.

large-mind·ed (lärj'mīn'dĭd) *adj.* Marked by breadth or liberality of views; open-minded. **—large'-mind'ed·ly** *adv.* **—large'-mind'ed·ness** *n.*

large·mouth bass (lärj'mouth') *n.* A North American freshwater food and game fish, *Micropterus salmoides.*

large-scale (lärj'skāl') *adj.* **1.** Of large scope; extensive. **2.** Drawn or made large to show detail, as a map or model.

lar·gess also **lar·gesse** (lär-zhĕs', -jĕs', lär'jĕs') *n.* **1. a.** Liberality in giving, esp. when attended by condescension. **b.** Money or gifts bestowed. **2.** Generosity of spirit or attitude. [ME *largesse* < OFr. *largece* < *large,* generous < Lat. *largus,* abundant.]

lar·ghet·to (lär-gĕt'ō) *Mus.* —*adv.* Moderately slow in tempo. Used as a direction. —*n., pl.* **-tos.** A movement or passage played larghetto. —*adj.* Of a moderately slow tempo. [Ital. < *largo,* largo.]

larg·ish (lär'jĭsh) *adj.* Fairly large.

lar·go (lär'gō) *Mus.* —*adv.* In a slow, solemn manner. Used as a direction. —*adj.* Slow and solemn. —*n., pl.* **-gos.** A largo movement or passage. [Ital. < Lat. *largus,* large.]

lar·i·at (lăr'ē-ət) *n.* **1.** A long rope with a running noose for catching livestock; lasso. **2.** A rope for picketing grazing horses or mules. [Sp. *la reata* : *la,* the + *reatar,* to tie again (*re-,* again + *atar,* to tie).]

lark[1] (lärk) *n.* **1.** Any of various chiefly Old World birds of the family Alaudidae, having a sustained, melodious song. **2.** Any of several birds similar to the lark, as the meadowlark. [ME < OE *lāwerce.*]

lark[2] (lärk) *n.* **1.** A carefree adventure. **2.** A harmless prank. —*intr.v.* **larked, lark·ing, larks.** To engage in fun or merry pranks. [Prob. < alteration of dial. *lake,* to play < ME *laken* < ON *leika.*]

lark·spur (lärk'spûr') *n.* Any of various plants of the genus *Delphinium,* having spurred, variously colored flowers.

lar·ri·gan also **Lar·ri·gan** (lăr'ĭ-gən) *n.* A moccasin with knee-high leggings made of oiled leather. [Orig. unknown.]

lar·rup (lăr'əp) *Regional.* —*tr.v.* **-ruped, -rup·ing, -rups.** To beat; flog; thrash. —*n.* A blow. [Orig. unknown.]

lar·um (lăr'əm) *n. Archaic.* An alarm. [Short for ALARUM.]

lar·va (lär'və) *n., pl.* **-vae** (-vē). **1.** The wingless, often wormlike form of a newly hatched insect before undergoing metamorphosis. **2.** The newly hatched, earliest stage of any of various animals that undergo metamorphosis, differing markedly in form and appearance from the adult. [NLat. < Lat., ghost.] **—lar'val** *adj.*

lar·vi·cide (lär'vĭ-sīd') *n.* An insecticide designed to kill larval pests. **—lar'vi·cid'al** (-sīd'l) *adj.*

laryng– *pref.* Variant of **laryngo-.**

la·ryn·ge·al (lə-rĭn'jē-əl, -jəl, lăr'ən-jē'əl) also **la·ryn·gal** (lə-rĭng'gəl) *adj.* **1.** Of, pertaining to, affecting, or near the larynx. **2.** Produced in or with the larynx; glottal. —*n.* **1.** A part of the larynx. **2.** A laryngeal sound. **3.** Any of a set of sounds of uncertain character reconstructed for Proto-Indo-European from indirect evidence. [NLat. *laryngeus* < *larynx,* larynx.]

lar·yn·gec·to·my (lăr'ən-jĕk'tə-mē) *n., pl.* **-mies.** Surgical removal of part or all of the larynx.

la·ryn·ges (lə-rĭn'jēz) *n.* A plural of **larynx.**

lar·yn·gi·tis (lăr'ən-jī'tĭs) *n.* Inflammation of the larynx. **—lar'yn·git'ic** (-jĭt'ĭk) *adj.*

laryngo– or **laryng–** *pref.* Larynx: *laryngitis.* [NLat. < Gk. *larungo-* < *larunx,* larynx.]

lar·yn·gol·o·gy (lăr'ən-gŏl'ə-jē) *n.* The branch of medicine concerned with the study and treatment of the larynx. **—lar'yn·gol'o·gist** *n.*

la·ryn·go·scope (lə-rĭng'gə-skōp', -rĭn'jə-) *n.* A tubular instrument or apparatus used to observe the interior of the larynx. **—la·ryn'go·scop'ic** (-skŏp'ĭk), **la·ryn'go·scop'i·cal** *adj.* **—la·ryn'go·scop'i·cal·ly** *adv.* **—lar'yn·gos'co·py** (lăr'ən-gŏs'kə-pē) *n.*

lar·ynx (lăr'ĭngks) *n., pl.* **la·ryn·ges** (lə-rĭn'jēz) or **lar·ynx·es.** The upper part of the respiratory tract between the pharynx and the trachea, having cartilaginous walls and containing the vocal cords enveloped in folds of mucous membrane attached to the sides. [NLat. < Gk. *larunx.*]

la·sa·gna also **la·sa·gne** (lə-zän'yə) *n.* **1.** Flat, wide noodles. **2.** A dish made by baking lasagna with layers of ground meat, tomato sauce, and cheese. [Ital. < Lat. *lasanum,* cooking pot < Gk. *lasanon,* chamber pot.]

las·car (lăs'kər) *n.* An East Indian sailor. [Hindi *lashkari* < *lashkar,* army < Pers. < Ar. *al-'askar,* the army.]

las·civ·i·ous (lə-sĭv'ē-əs) *adj.* **1.** Of or characterized by lust; lewd. **2.** Exciting sexual desires. [ME < LLat. *lasciviosus* < Lat. *lascivia,* lasciviousness < *lascivus,* lascivious.] **—las·civ'i·ous·ly** *adv.* **—las·civ'i·ous·ness** *n.*

lase (lāz) *intr.v.* **lased, las·ing, las·es.** To function as a laser; emit coherent radiation by the action of a laser. [Back-formation < LASER.]

la·ser (lā'zər) *n.* **1.** Any of several devices that convert incident electromagnetic radiation of mixed frequencies to one or more discrete frequencies of highly amplified and coherent visible radiation. **2.** A device whose output is in an invisible region of the electromagnetic spectrum. [L(IGHT) A(MPLIFICATION BY) S(TIMULATED) E(MISSION OF) R(ADIATION).]

lash[1] (lăsh) *n.* **1. a.** A stroke or blow with or as if with a whip. **b.** A whip. **c.** The thongs of a whip. **2.** A remark that insults, reprimands, or ridicules. **3.** An eyelash. —*v.* **lashed, lash·ing, lash·es.** —*tr.* **1.** To strike with or as if with a whip. **2.** To strike against with force or violence: *sleet lashing the roof.* **3.** To move or wave rapidly: *an angry lion lashing his tail to and fro.* **4.** To make a scathing verbal or written attack against. **5.** To incite or goad: *words that lashed them into action.* —*intr.* **1.** To move rapidly or violently; dash. **2.** To strike with or as if with a whip. **3.** To make a scathing verbal or written attack. [ME, prob. < *lashen,* to deal a blow.] **—lash'er** *n.*

lash[2] (lăsh) *tr.v.* **lashed, lash·ing, lash·es.** To secure or bind, as with a rope, cord, or chain. [ME *lashen,* to lace < OFr. *lachier* < Lat. *laqueare,* to ensnare < *laqueus,* snare.] **—lash'er** *n.*

lash·ing (lăsh'ĭng) *n.* Something used for securing or binding.

lash·ings (lăsh'ĭngz) *pl.n. Chiefly Brit.* Lavish quantities. [< LASH[1], to lavish (obs.).]

lass (lăs) *n.* **1.** A girl or young woman. **2.** A sweetheart. [ME *las.*]

Las·sa fever (lä'sə, lăs'ə) *n.* An acute viral disease characterized by high fever, headache, ulcers of the mucous membranes, and high mortality. [After *Lassa,* a village in Nigeria.]

las·sie (lăs'ē) *n.* A lass.

las·si·tude (lăs'ĭ-to͞od', -tyo͞od') *n.* A state of listless weakness, exhaustion, or torpor. [Lat. *lassitudo* < *lassus,* weary.]

las·so (lăs'ō, lă-so͞o') *n., pl.* **-sos** or **-soes.** A long rope or leather thong with a running noose at one end used esp. to catch horses and cattle; lariat. —*tr.v.* **-soed, -so·ing, -sos** or **-soes.** To catch with or as if with a lasso; rope. [Sp. < Lat. *laqueus,* snare.] **—las'so·er** *n.*

last[1] (lăst) *adj.* **1.** Being, coming, or placed after all others; final: *the last game of the season.* **2.** Being the only one left: *his last nickel.* **3.** Just past; most recent: *last year.* **4.** Most up-to-date; newest: *the last thing in evening clothes.* **5.** Highest in extent or degree; utmost. **6.** Most valid, authoritative, or conclusive. **7.** Least likely or expected: *the last man we would have suspected.* **8.** Being the latest possible: *waited until the very last minute.* **9.** Lowest in rank, size, or importance. **10. a.** Of or pertaining to a terminal period or stage, as of life: *her last days.* **b.** Administered just before death: *the last sacraments.* —*adv.* **1.** After all others in chronology or sequence: *arrived last.* **2.** At a time just previous to the present; most recently: *wrote last from Paris.* **3.** At the end; finally: *And last add the butter.* —*n.* **1.** One that is last: *ate all the chocolates but the last.* **2.** The end: *held out until the last.* **3.** The final mention or appearance of something: *haven't seen the last of her.* ***—idioms.*** **at last.** After a considerable length of time; finally. **at long last.** After a long time or wait. [ME < OE *latost,* superl. of *læt,* late.] **—last'ly** *adv.*

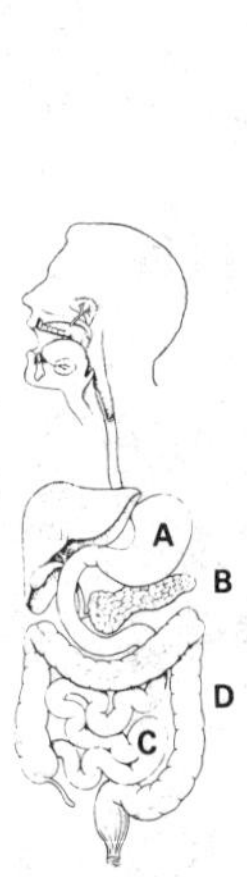

large intestine
A. Stomach
B. Pancreas
C. Small intestine
D. Large intestine

George Miksch Sutton
lark[1]

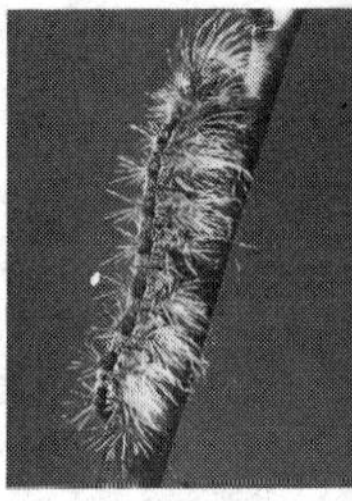

larva
Gypsy moth larva

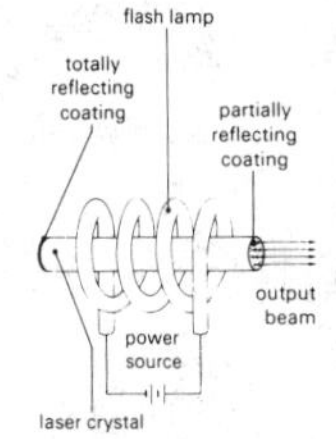

laser
Simplified diagram of a crystal laser

Synonyms: *last, final, terminal, eventual, ultimate.* These adjectives refer to that which brings a series, sequence, or any collection of like things to an end: *the last day of the month; the last piece of candy. Final* refers to the end of a progression or process, and stresses the definiteness of the conclusion: *his final remark; our final offer. Terminal* is applied to that which marks a limit or boundary in space, time, development, or operativeness: *the terminal point of enemy penetration; the terminal stage of tuberculosis. Eventual* refers to an outcome or issue: *eventual date of publication;* sometimes it implies a foreseeable or inevitable result: *the eventual downfall of a corrupt government. Ultimate* is applied to that which marks the termination of a lengthy progression and beyond which there exists no other: *our ultimate fate; an ultimate goal; the ultimate authority.*

last[2] (lăst) *v.* **last·ed, last·ing, lasts.** *—intr.* **1. a.** To continue in existence; go on: *The war lasted four years.* **b.** To continue to live; survive: *wasn't expected to last.* **2.** To remain in good condition; endure: *Clay lasts longer than paper.* **3.** To remain in adequate supply: *Will our water last? —tr.* To supply adequately: *left enough milk to last the family for the weekend.* [ME *lasten* < OE *lǣsten.*] **—last'er** *n.*

last[3] (lăst) *n.* A block or form shaped like a human foot and used in making or repairing shoes. *—tr.v.* **last·ed, last·ing, lasts.** To mold or shape on a last. [ME < OE *lǣste* < *lǣst,* sole of the foot.]

last[4] (lăst) *n. Chiefly Brit.* A unit of weight or volume varying for different commodities and in different districts and approximating 80 bushels, 640 gallons, or 2 tons. [ME, a kind of measure < OE *hlæst.*]

last-ditch (lăst'dĭch') *adj.* Done or made as a final measure, esp. to prevent a crisis or disaster: *a last-ditch effort to avert the threatened strike.*

Last Supper
12th-century illustration of the Last Supper

Las·tex (lăs'tĕks'). A trademark for a yarn having a core of elastic rubber wound with rayon, nylon, silk, or cotton threads.

last hurrah *n.* A last appearance or effort, esp. at the end of a career.

last·ing (lăs'tĭng) *adj.* Continuing or remaining for a long time; enduring. *—n.* A durable twilled fabric. **—last'ing·ly** *adv.* **—last'ing·ness** *n.*

Last Judgment *n.* The final judgment by God of all mankind.

last-min·ute (lăst'mĭn'ĭt) *adj.* Relating to or being the moment just before a climactic, conclusive, or calamitous event: *last-minute decisions; a last-minute emergency.*

last straw *n.* The last of a series of annoyances or disappointments that leads one to a final loss of patience, temper, trust, or hope.

Last Supper *n.* Christ's supper with his disciples on the night before his Crucifixion.

last word *n.* **1.** The final statement in a verbal argument. **2. a.** A conclusive or authoritative statement or treatment: *the last word in automobile safety.* **b.** The power or authority of ultimate decision. **3.** *Informal.* The newest or most up-to-date example of a category, as of fashion; the latest thing: *a food processor that is the last word in kitchen equipment.*

lat·a·ki·a (lăt'ə-kē'ə) *n.* A grade of Turkish tobacco. [After *Latakia,* Syria.]

latch (lăch) *n.* A fastening or lock, usually consisting of a bar that fits into a notch, slot, or cavity. *—tr.v.* **latched, latch·ing, latch·es.** To close or lock with or as if with a latch. ***—phrasal verb.* latch on to** (or **onto**). *Informal.* **1.** To attach oneself to; cling to. **2.** To get possession of; obtain. [ME *latche* < *lacchen,* to seize < OE *læccan.*]

latch·et (lăch'ĭt) *n.* A leather thong or strap used to fasten a shoe or sandal on the foot. [ME *lachet* < OFr., var. of *lacet,* shoestring < *lace,* lace. —see LACE.]

latch·key (lăch'kē') *n.* A key for opening a latch, esp. one on an outside door or gate.

latchkey child *n.* A young child who returns from school and remains at home unsupervised for an indefinite period until the parents arrive from work.

latch·string (lăch'strĭng') *n.* A cord attached to a latch and often passed through a hole in the door to allow lifting of the latch from the outside.

late (lāt) *adj.* **lat·er, lat·est. 1.** Coming, occurring, or remaining after the usual or proper time: *The bus is late.* **2. a.** Beginning at or lasting until an advanced hour: *a late supper.* **b.** Occurring, being, or continuing toward the end or more advanced part, as of a time period: *the late 19th century.* **3.** Having begun or occurred just previous to the present time; recent: *a late development.* **4. a.** Having recently occupied a position or place: *the company's late president.* **b.** Dead, esp. if only recently deceased: *the late Mr. Foster. —adv.* **lat·er, lat·est. 1.** After the expected, usual, or proper time: *a train that arrived late.* **2.** At or into an advanced period or point of time: *a project undertaken late in his career.* **3.** Recently: *As late as last week he was still in town.* ***—idiom.* of late.** In the near past; lately. [ME < OE *læt.*] **—late'ness** *n.*

Usage: From the standpoint of usage, it is perfectly correct to refer to a former official as *our late president.* But if the official is still alive, *former* should be used.

lat·ed (lā'tĭd) *adj.* Belated. [< LATE.]

la·teen (lə-tēn', lă-) *adj.* Being, pertaining to, or rigged with a triangular sail hung on a long yard attached at an angle to a short mast. *—n.* **1.** A lateen-rigged boat. **2.** A lateen sail. [Fr. *(voile) latine,* lateen (sail).]

Late Greek *n.* The Greek language as used from the 4th to the 9th century.

Late Latin *n.* The Latin language as used from the 3rd to the 7th century.

late·ly (lāt'lē) *adv.* Not long ago; recently.

la·ten·cy (lāt'n-sē) *n.* **1.** The state or quality of being latent. **2.** *Computer Sci.* The time required for a device to begin physical output of a desired piece of data once processing is complete.

la·tent (lāt'nt) *adj.* Present or potential but not evident or active: *latent talent. —n.* A fingerprint that is difficult to see but that can be made visible for scrutiny. [Lat. *latens, latent-,* pr.part. of *latēre,* to lie hidden.] **—la'tent·ly** *adv.*

Synonyms: *latent, dormant, quiescent.* These adjectives describe what is existent or capable of existence but is not manifesting itself. What is *latent* is not clearly visible: *latent energy.* What is *dormant* is inactive, as if sleeping or in suspended animation: *a dormant volcano; dormant legislative proposals.* Persons or things are *quiescent* when they cease to be active or marked by activity; sometimes the term suggests termporary inactivity: *a quiescent interlude between school terms.*

latent heat *n.* The quantity of heat absorbed or released by a substance undergoing a change of state, as by ice changing to water or water to steam.

latent period *n.* **1.** The incubation period of an infectious disease. **2.** The interval between stimulus and response.

lat·er·al (lăt'ər-əl) *adj.* **1.** Of, relating to, or situated at or on the side. **2.** Designating a sound produced by breath passing along one or both sides of the tongue. *—n.* **1.** A lateral part, projection, passage, or appendage. **2.** *Football.* A lateral pass. **3.** A lateral sound, such as *l.* [Lat. *lateralis* < *latus,* side.] **—lat'er·al·ly** *adv.*

lateral line *n.* A linear series of sensory pores and tubes extending along the side of a fish or certain other aquatic animals.

lateral pass *n. Football.* A usually underhand pass that is thrown sideways or backward.

lat·er·ite (lăt'ə-rīt') *n.* A red residual soil in humid tropical and subtropical regions, containing concentrations of iron and aluminum hydroxides and sometimes used as an ore of iron, aluminum, manganese, or nickel. [Lat. *later,* brick + -ITE.] **—lat'er·it'ic** (-rĭt'ĭk) *adj.*

la·tex (lā'tĕks') *n., pl.* **la·ti·ces** (lā'tĭ-sēz', lăt'ĭ-) or **la·tex·es. 1.** The usually milky, viscous sap of certain trees and plants, such as the rubber tree, that coagulates on exposure to air. **2.** An emulsion of rubber or plastic globules in water, used in paints, adhesives, and various synthetic rubber products. **3.** A latex paint. [NLat. *Latex, Latic-* < Lat., fluid.]

latex paint *n.* A paint having a binder that is a latex.

lath (lăth) *n., pl.* **laths** (lă*th*z, lăths). **1. a.** A narrow, thin strip of wood or metal, used esp. in making a supporting structure for plaster, shingles, slates, or tiles. **b.** A building material, such as a sheet of metal mesh, used for similar purposes. **2. a.** Lathing. **b.** Work made with or from lathing. *—tr.v.* **lathed, lath·ing, laths.** To build, cover, or line with laths. [ME.]

lathe (lā*th*) *n.* A machine on which a piece of wood, metal, or other material is spun and shaped by a fixed cutting or abrading tool. *—tr.v.* **lathed, lath·ing, lathes.** To cut or shape on a lathe. [Prob. < ME, supporting structure.]

lath·er (lă*th*'ər) *n.* **1.** A light foam formed by soap or detergent agitated in water. **2.** Froth formed by profuse sweating, as on a horse. **3.** *Informal.* A condition of impatient or troubled excitement; agitation. *—v.* **-ered, -er·ing, -ers.** *—tr.* **1.** To coat with lather. **2.** *Informal.* To give a beating to; whip. *—intr.* **1.** To produce lather; foam. **2.** To become coated with lather, as a horse. [Ult. < OE *lēaðor.*] **—lath'er·er** *n.* **—lath'er·y** *adj.*

lath·ing (lăth'ĭng, lă*th*'-) *n.* **1.** The act or process of building with laths. **2.** Work made of laths. **3.** A quantity of laths.

la·ti·ces (lā'tĭ-sēz', lăt'ĭ-) *n.* A plural of **latex.**

la·tic·i·fer (lā-tĭs'ə-fər) *n.* A plant duct containing latex.

lat·i·cif·er·ous (lăt'ĭ-sĭf'ər-əs) *adj.* Secreting or exuding latex.

lat·i·fun·di·um (lăt'ə-fŭn'dē-əm) *n., pl.* **-di·a** (-dē-ə). A great landed estate, esp. of the ancient Romans. [Lat. : *latus,* broad + *fundus,* estate.]

Lat·in (lăt'n) *adj.* **1.** Of or relating to Latium, its people, or its culture. **2.** Of or relating to ancient Rome, its people, or its culture. **3.** Of, relating to, or composed in the language of ancient Rome and Latium. **4.** Of or relating to those countries or peoples using Romance languages, esp. the countries of Latin America. **5.** Of or relating to the Roman Catholic Church as distinguished from the Eastern Orthodox Church. *—n.* **1.** The Italic language of ancient Latium and Rome which overspread western Europe and until modern times was the dominant language of church, school, and state. **2.** A native or resident of ancient Latium. **3.** A member of a Latin people, esp. of Latin America. **4.** A Roman Catholic. [ME < OFr. < Lat. *Latinus* < *Latium,* an ancient country in Italy.]

Latin alphabet *n.* The Roman alphabet adopted from the Greek by way of the Etruscan alphabet, consisting of 23 letters upon which the modern western European alphabets are founded.

Lat·in-A·mer·i·can (lăt′n-ə-mĕr′ĭ-kən) *adj.* Of, pertaining to, or designating the countries of the Western Hemisphere south of the United States having Spanish, Portuguese, or French as their official languages. **—Latin American** *n.*

Lat·in·ate (lăt′n-āt′) *adj.* Of, pertaining to, or derived from Latin.

Latin Church *n.* The Roman Catholic Church.

Latin cross *n.* A cross with the horizontal bar shorter than the vertical bar.

Latin cross

Lat·in·ism (lăt′n-ĭz′əm) *n.* An idiom, structure, or word derived from or imitative of Latin.

Lat·in·ist (lăt′n-ĭst) *n.* A scholar of Latin.

La·tin·i·ty (lə-tĭn′ĭ-tē) *n.* The manner in which Latin is used in speaking or writing.

Lat·in·ize (lăt′n-īz′) *v.* **-ized, -iz·ing, -iz·es.** *—tr.* **1. a.** To translate into Latin. **b.** To transliterate into the characters of the Latin alphabet; Romanize. **2.** To cause to adopt or acquire Latin characteristics or customs. **3.** To cause to follow or resemble the Roman Catholic Church in dogma or practices. *—intr.* To use Latinisms. **—Lat′in·i·za′tion** *n.* **—Lat′in·iz′er** *n.*

La·ti·no (lə-tē′nō, lă-) *n.* A native or inhabitant of Latin America.

lat·ish (lā′tĭsh) *adj & adv. Informal.* Fairly late.

lat·i·tude (lăt′ĭ-to͞od′, -tyo͞od′) *n.* **1.** Extent; breadth. **2.** Freedom from normal restraints, limitations, or regulations. **3. a.** The angular distance north or south of the equator, measured in degrees along a meridian, as on a map or globe. **b.** A region of the earth considered in relation to its distance from the equator: *temperate latitudes.* **4.** *Astron.* The angular distance of a celestial body north or south of the ecliptic. [ME < OFr. < Lat. *latitudo* < *latus,* wide.] **—lat′i·tu′di·nal** (-to͞od′n-əl, -tyood′-) *adj.* **—lat′i·tu′di·nal·ly** *adv.*

lat·i·tu·di·nar·i·an (lăt′ĭ-to͞od′n-âr′ē-ən, -tyo͞od′-) *adj.* Favoring freedom of thought and behavior, esp. in religion. *—n.* A latitudinarian person. [Lat. *latitudo, latitudin-,* latitude + -ARIAN.] **—lat′i·tu′di·nar′i·an·ism** *n.*

la·trine (lə-trēn′) *n.* A communal toilet of a type often used in a barracks, esp. one without plumbing. [Fr. < Lat. *latrina* < *lavatrina* < *lavare,* to wash.]

-latry *suff.* Worship: *bibliolatry.* [< Gk. *latreia,* service, worship.]

lat·ten (lăt′n) *n.* **1.** An alloy formerly made of or made to resemble brass, hammered thin and used in the manufacture of church vessels. **2.** A thin sheet of metal, esp. of tin. [ME *latton* < OFr. *laton.*]

lat·ter (lăt′ər) *adj.* **1.** Designating the second of two persons or things mentioned. **2.** Further advanced in time or sequence; later. **3.** Closer to the end: *the latter part of the book.* *—n.* The second of two persons or things mentioned. [ME < OE *lattre.*] **—lat′ter·ly** *adv.*

Usage: *Latter,* as used in contrast to *former,* refers to the second of two: *Jones and Smith have been nominated, but the latter may decline the post. Latter* is not appropriate when more than two are named: *Jones, Smith, and Kowalski have been nominated.* Kowalski should then be referred to as *the last, the last of these,* or *the last-named,* or else the name should be repeated.

lat·ter-day (lăt′ər-dā′) *adj.* Belonging to present or recent times; modern.

Latter-day Saint *n.* A Mormon.

lat·tice (lăt′ĭs) *n.* **1. a.** An open framework made of strips of metal, wood, or similar material interwoven to form regular, patterned spaces. **b.** A screen, window, gate, or similar structure made of such a framework. **2.** Something, such as a decorative motif or heraldic bearing, that resembles an open, patterned framework. **3.** *Physics.* A regular, periodic configuration of points, particles, or objects throughout an area or space, esp. the arrangement of ions or molecules in a crystalline solid. *—tr.v.* **-ticed, -tic·ing, -tic·es.** To construct or furnish with a lattice or latticework. [ME *latice* < OFr. *latiz.*] **—lat′ticed** *adj.*

lattice

lat·tice·work (lăt′ĭs-wûrk′) *n.* **1.** A lattice or something resembling a lattice; trelliswork. **2.** A structure made of lattices.

Lat·vi·an (lăt′vē-ən) *n.* **1.** A native or resident of Latvia. **2.** The Baltic language of the Latvians. **—Lat′vi·an** *adj.*

laud (lôd) *tr.v.* **laud·ed, laud·ing, lauds.** To give praise to; glorify. *—n.* **1.** Praise; glorification. **2.** A hymn or song of praise. **3.** Often **Lauds.** *(used with a sing. or pl. verb).* The service of prayers following the matins and constituting with them the first of the seven canonical hours. [Lat. *laudare* < *laus,* praise.] **—laud′er** *n.*

laud·a·ble (lô′də-bəl) *adj.* Deserving approbation; praiseworthy. **—laud′a·bil′i·ty, laud′a·ble·ness** *n.* **—laud′a·bly** *adv.*

lau·da·num (lôd′n-əm) *n.* A tincture of opium. [NLat.]

laud·a·tion (lô-dā′shən) *n.* The act of lauding; praise.

laud·a·tive (lô′də-tĭv) *adj.* Laudatory.

laud·a·to·ry (lô′də-tôr′ē, -tōr′ē) *adj.* Of, relating to, or giving praise. [LLat. *laudatorius* < Lat. *laudare,* to laud. —see LAUD.]

laugh (lăf, läf) *v.* **laughed, laugh·ing, laughs.** *—intr.* **1.** To express esp. mirth or derision usually by a series of inarticulate sounds, with the mouth open in a wide smile. **2.** To show amusement at someone or something: *laughed at our jokes.* **3.** To feel derision or scorn for someone or something: *laughed at his theories.* **4.** To produce sounds resembling laughter. *—tr.* **1.** To effect by laughter: *laughed him off the stage.* **2.** To say with a laugh. ***—phrasal verb.*** **laugh away (or off).** To treat as ridiculously or laughably trivial. *—n.* **1. a.** The act of laughing. **b.** The sound of laughing. **2.** *Informal.* Something amusing, improbable, or ridiculous; joke: *That's a laugh.* [ME *laughen* < OE *hliehan.*] **—laugh′er** *n.* **—laugh′ing·ly** *adv.*

laugh·a·ble (lăf′ə-bəl, läf′-) *adj.* Causing or deserving laughter or derision. **—laugh′a·ble·ness** *n.* **—laugh′a·bly** *adv.*

laughing gas *n.* Nitrous oxide.

laughing jackass *n.* The kookaburra.

laugh·ing·stock (lăf′ĭng-stŏk′, läf′-) *n.* An object of jokes or ridicule; butt.

laugh·ter (lăf′tər, läf′-) *n.* **1.** The act of laughing. **2.** The sound produced by laughing. **3.** *Archaic.* A cause or subject for laughter. [ME < OE *hleahtor.*]

launce (lăns, läns, lôns) *n.* The sand lance. [Perh. alteration of LANCE.]

launch[1] (lônch, länch) *v.* **launched, launch·ing, launch·es.** *—tr.* **1.** To send off or discharge with force; propel: *launch a missile.* **2.** To put or lower (a boat) into the water, esp. for the first time. **3.** To put into action; initiate. **4.** To give a start to (someone). *—intr.* **1.** To rush or spring forward; plunge. **2.** To make a beginning. **3.** To move out to sea. *—n.* An act of launching. [ME *launchen* < ONFr. *lancher,* var. of OFr. *lancier* < LLat. *lanceare,* to wield a lance < *lancea,* lance.]

launch[2] (lônch, länch) *n.* **1.** A large ship's boat. **2.** A large, open motorboat. [Sp. and Port. *lancha,* both prob. of Malay orig.]

launch·er (lôn′chər, län′-) *n.* One that launches, as: **a.** A device for firing grenades. **b.** A device for firing rockets.

launch pad also **launching pad** *n.* The base or platform from which a rocket or space vehicle is launched.

launch vehicle *n.* A booster (sense 4).

laun·der (lôn′dər, län′-) *v.* **-dered, -der·ing, -ders.** *—tr.* **1. a.** To wash (clothes, for example). **b.** To wash and iron: *launders his shirts himself.* **2.** To clean up as if by laundering. **3.** To channel through an intermediate party in order to conceal the source: *laundered the money via offshore banks.* *—intr.* **1.** To undergo washing in a specified way: *This material launders well.* **2.** To wash or wash and iron clothes or linens. *—n.* A wooden trough for water, used for washing ore. [< obs. *launder,* launderer < ME, alteration of *lavender* < OFr. *lavandier* < Lat. *lavanda,* things to be washed < *lavare,* to wash.] **—laun′der·er** *n.*

laun·der·ette (lôn′də-rĕt′, län′-) *n.* A self-service laundry. [Orig. a trademark.]

laun·dress (lôn′drĭs, län′-) *n.* A woman employed to wash and iron clothes or linens.

Laun·dro·mat (lôn′drə-măt′, län′-). A trademark for a commercial establishment equipped with washing machines and dryers, usually coin-operated and self-service.

laun·dry (lôn′drē, län′-) *n., pl.* **-dries. 1.** Soiled or laundered clothes and linens; wash. **2.** A place where laundering is done. [< obs. *launder,* launderer. —see LAUNDER.]

lau·re·ate (lôr′ē-ĭt, lŏr′-) *adj.* **1.** Worthy of honor or distinction. **2.** Crowned or decked with laurel as a mark of honor. **3.** *Archaic.* Made of laurel sprigs, as a wreath or crown. *—n.* **1.** One honored for achievements esp. in the arts or sciences. **2.** A poet laureate. [ME < Lat. *laureatus* < *laurea,* crown of laurel < *laureus,* of laurel < *laurus,* laurel.] **—lau′re·ate·ship′** *n.*

lau·rel (lôr′əl, lŏr′-) *n.* **1.** A shrub or tree, *Laurus nobilis,* native to the Mediterranean region, having aromatic evergreen leaves and small blackish berries. **2.** Any of several shrubs or trees, such as the mountain laurel, that are related or similar to the laurel. **3.** Often **laurels. a.** A wreath of laurel conferred as a mark of honor in ancient times upon poets, heroes, and victors in athletic contests. **b.** Honor and glory won for achievement. *—tr.v.* **-reled, -rel·ing, -rels** or **-relled, -rel·ling, -rels.** To crown with laurel. [ME < Lat. *laureola,* dim. of *laurea,* laurel tree. —see LAUREATE.]

laurel
Mountain laurel

Lau·ren·tian (lô-rĕn′shən) *adj.* **1.** Of, pertaining to, or being in the vicinity of the St. Lawrence River. **2.** *Geol.* Of or relating to the gneissic granite of the early Precambrian (Archeozoic).

lau·ric acid (lôr′ĭk, lŏr′-) *n.* A fatty acid, $C_{12}H_{24}O_2$, obtained chiefly from coconut oil, and used in making soaps, cosmetics, insecticides, and alkyd resins. [Lat. *laurus,* laurel + -IC.]

lau·ryl alcohol (lôr′əl, lŏr′-) *n.* A colorless solid alcohol, $C_{12}H_{26}O$, used in synthetic detergents. [LAUR(EL) + -YL + ALCOHOL.]

la·va (lä′və, lăv′ə) *n.* **1.** Molten rock that issues from a volcano or a fissure in the earth's surface. **2.** The rock formed by the cooling and solidifying of lava. [Ital. < Lat. *labes,* fall.]

la·va·bo (lə-vā′bō, -vä′bō) *n., pl.* **-boes. 1.** Often **Lavabo.** In the Roman Catholic and Anglican churches, the ceremonial washing of the hands and recitation from the Psalms by the celebrant before the Eucharist. **2.** A washbowl and water tank with a spout that are fastened to a wall. [Lat., I shall wash < *lavare,* to wash.]

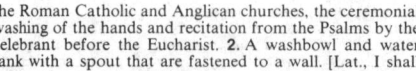

lav·age (lăv′ĭj, lä-väzh′) *n.* A washing, esp. of a hollow organ, such as the stomach or lower bowel, with repeated injections of water. [Fr. < OFr. < *laver,* to wash < Lat. *lavare.*]

la·va-la·va (lä′və-lä′və) *n.* A draped, kiltlike garment of cotton print worn by Polynesians and esp. Samoans. [Samoan.]

lav·a·liere (lăv′ə-lîr′) also **la·val·lière** (lä′vä-lyâr′) *n.* A pendant worn on a chain around the neck. [Fr. *lavallière,* after Louise de *la Vallière* (1644–1710).]

la·va·tion (lă-vā′shən, lā-) *n.* The process or an instance of washing; cleansing. [Lat. *lavatio* < *lavare,* to wash.]

lav·a·to·ry (lăv′ə-tôr′ē, -tōr′ē) *n., pl.* **-ries. 1.** A room equipped with washing and often toilet facilities. **2.** A basin or bowl, esp. one permanently installed with running water, for washing. **3.** A toilet. [ME *lavatorie,* piscina < Med. Lat. *lavatorium* < Lat. *lavare,* to wash.]

lave (lāv) *v.* **laved, lav·ing, laves.** —*tr.* **1.** To wash; bathe. **2. a.** To lap or wash against. **b.** To flow along or against: *"The quiet and the cool laved her"* (Edna Ferber). —*intr. Archaic.* To wash oneself. [ME *laven* < OE *lafian* < Lat. *lavare.*]

lavender

lav·en·der (lăv′ən-dər) *n.* **1. a.** Any of various aromatic Old World plants of the genus *Lavandula,* esp. *L. officinalis,* having clusters of small purplish flowers and yielding an oil used in perfumery. **b.** The fragrant dried leaves, stems, and flowers of the lavender. **2.** A pale to light or moderate purple to very light or very pale violet. [ME < AN *lavendre* < Med. Lat. *lavendula.*] —**lav′en·der** *adj.*

la·ver[1] (lā′vər) *n.* **1.** *Judaism.* A large basin used in ancient times by the priest for ablutions before making a sacrificial offering. **2.** *Archaic.* A vessel, stone basin, or trough used for washing. [ME, water pitcher < OFr. *laveoir.*]

la·ver[2] (lā′vər) *n.* Any of several edible seaweeds of the genus *Porphyra.* [NLat. < Lat., a water plant.]

lav·er·ock (lăv′ər-ək) *n. Chiefly Scot.* A skylark. [ME < OE *lāwerce.*]

lav·ish (lăv′ĭsh) *adj.* **1.** Spending or giving with liberality or abundance; prodigal. **2.** Characterized by or produced with extravagance and profusion: *a lavish buffet.* —*tr.v.* **-ished, -ish·ing, -ish·es.** To give or expend unstintingly. [< ME *lavas* < OFr. *lavasse,* downpour < *laver,* to wash < Lat. *lavare.*] —**lav′ish·er** *n.* —**lav′ish·ly** *adv.* —**lav′ish·ness** *n.*

law (lô) *n.* **1. a.** A rule established by authority, society, or custom. **b.** The body or system of such rules. **c.** The control or authority imposed by such a system of rules. **2.** The common law. **3. a.** The actions or processes by which the laws of a society are enforced and through which redress for grievances is obtained. **b.** An agency of the law. **c.** An agent of the law. **4. a.** The science and study of law; jurisprudence. **b.** Knowledge of law. **c.** The profession of a lawyer. **5. Law.** The body of principles or precepts held to express the divine will, esp. as revealed in the Bible: *Mosaic Law.* **6.** A rule or principle that must be obeyed. **7.** A rule or procedural principle applicable in a particular domain: *the law of harmony.* **8.** A code of principles and regulations. **9.** A formulation describing a relationship that is presumed to hold between or among phenomena for all cases in which the specified conditions are met: *Newton's third law.* **10.** *Math.* A general principle or rule that holds in all cases to which it is applicable. —*intr.v.* **lawed, law·ing, laws.** To go to law; litigate. [ME < OE *lagu.*]

law-a·bid·ing (lô′ə-bī′dĭng) *adj.* Abiding by the law.

law·break·er (lô′brā′kər) *n.* One that breaks the law.

law·ful (lô′fəl) *adj.* **1.** Within the law; allowed by law: *lawful methods.* **2.** Established, sanctioned, or recognized by the law: *the lawful heir.* **3.** Obeying the law; law-abiding. —**law′ful·ly** *adv.* —**law′ful·ness** *n.*

law·giv·er (lô′gĭv′ər) *n.* **1.** One who gives a code of laws to a people. **2.** A lawmaker; legislator.

law·less (lô′lĭs) *adj.* **1.** Unrestrained by law; disobedient: *a lawless person.* **2.** Heedless of or contrary to the law: *a lawless act.* **3.** Not governed by law: *the lawless frontier.* —**law′less·ly** *adv.* —**law′less·ness** *n.*

law·mak·er (lô′mā′kər) *n.* One who makes laws; legislator. —**law′mak′ing** *n.*

lawn mower

law merchant *n., pl.* **laws merchant.** The rules and regulations applied to trade and commerce, drawn from the customs of merchants in the past.

lawn[1] (lôn) *n.* A usually closely mown plot or area planted with grass or similar plants. [ME *laund,* glade < OFr. *lande,* prob. of Celt. orig.] —**lawn′y** *adj.*

lawn[2] (lôn) *n.* A very fine, thin fabric of cotton or linen. [ME *laun,* after *Laon,* France.] —**lawn′y** *adj.*

lawn mower *n.* A rotary-blade machine for cutting grass.

lawn tennis *n.* Tennis played on a grass court.

law of large numbers *n.* Bernoulli's law.

Law of Moses *n.* The Pentateuch.

law of nations *n.* International law.

law of parsimony *n.* Ockham's razor.

law·ren·ci·um (lô-rĕn′sē-əm, lō-) *n. Symbol* **Lw** A synthetic transuranic element having a single isotope with mass number 257 and a half-life of 8 seconds. Atomic number 103. [After Ernest O. *Lawrence* (1901–1958).]

law·suit (lô′so͞ot′) *n.* A case brought before a court.

law·yer (lô′yər) *n.* One whose profession is to give legal advice and assistance to clients and represent them in court or in other legal matters. [ME *lauier* < *law,* law.] —**law′yer·ly** *adv.*

Synonyms: *lawyer, attorney, counselor, counsel, barrister, solicitor, advocate.* These nouns denote persons who practice law. *Lawyer* is the general and most comprehensive term for one authorized to manage the legal affairs of a client, give legal advice, and plead cases in court. *Attorney* is often used interchangeably with *lawyer* but in a narrower sense refers to a legal agent for a client in the transaction of business. In a still narrower sense, *attorney* denotes anyone legally appointed to transact another's business. *Counselor* and *counsel* are terms for persons who give legal advice and serve as trial lawyers; *counsel* is also applied to a team of lawyers employed in conducting a case. *Barrister* refers principally to an English trial lawyer, and *solicitor* to an English lawyer whose practice is devoted largely to serving as a legal agent, representing clients in minor courts, and preparing cases for trial in superior courts. *Advocate* is largely restricted to military usage; in Scotland and France, it has the approximate sense of trial lawyer.

lax (lăks) *adj.* **-er, -est. 1.** Lacking in rigor, strictness, or firmness. **2.** Not taut, firm, or compact; slack. **3.** Loose and not easily retained or controlled. Used of bowel movements. **4.** Pronounced with the muscles of the tongue and jaw partially relaxed, as the vowel *e* in *let.* [ME < Lat. *laxus,* loose.] —**lax′ly** *adv.* —**lax′ness** *n.*

lax·a·tive (lăk′sə-tĭv) *n. Med.* A drug that stimulates evacuation of the bowels. —*adj.* **1.** Stimulating evacuation of the bowels. **2.** Causing looseness or relaxation, esp. of the bowels. [ME < OFr. *laxatif* < Med. Lat. *laxativus,* preventing constipation < Lat. *laxare* to relax < *laxus,* loose.]

lax·i·ty (lăk′sĭ-tē) *n.* The state or quality of being lax.

lay[1] (lā) *v.* **laid** (lād), **lay·ing, lays.** —*tr.* **1.** To cause to lie down: *lay a child in its crib.* **2. a.** To place in or bring to a particular state or position. **b.** To bury. **3.** To put or set down; deposit. **4.** To produce and deposit: *lay eggs.* **5.** To cause to subside. **6.** To put up to or against: *lay an ear to the door.* **7.** To put forward as a reproach or accusation: *laid the blame on him.* **8.** To put in order or readiness for use: *lay the table for lunch.* **9.** To devise; make: *lay plans.* **10.** To spread over a surface: *lay paint on a canvas.* **11.** To place or give (importance): *lay stress on clarity of expression.* **12.** To impose as a burden or punishment: *lay a penalty upon him.* **13.** To present for examination: *lay a case before a committee.* **14.** To put forward as a demand or assertion: *laid claim to the estate.* **15.** To place (a bet); wager. **16.** To aim (a gun or cannon). **17. a.** To place together (strands) to be twisted into rope. **b.** To make in this manner: *lay up cable.* **18.** *Vulgar Slang.* To have sexual intercourse with. —*intr.* **1.** To produce and deposit eggs. **2.** To bet; wager. **3.** *Nonstandard.* To lie. **4.** To engage energetically in an action. —***phrasal verbs.*** **lay aside. 1.** To give up; abandon: *lay aside hope of rescue.* **2.** To put aside for the future; save. **lay away. 1.** To reserve for the future; save. **2.** To put aside and hold for future delivery. **lay by.** To save. **lay down. 1.** To store for the future. **2.** To specify as a guide or rule. **lay in.** To store for future use. **lay into.** To scold sharply. **lay off. 1.** To terminate the employment of (a worker), esp. temporarily. **2.** To mark off. **3.** To give up; quit. **4.** To refrain from annoying or criticizing. **5.** To stop; cease. **lay out. 1.** To make a detailed plan for. **2.** *Informal.* To speak. **3.** To clothe and prepare (a corpse) for burial. **4.** *Informal.* To knock to the ground or unconscious. **lay over.** To make a stopover in the course of a journey. **lay to.** *Naut.* **1.** To bring (a ship) to a stop in open water. **2.** To remain stationary and face into the wind. **lay up. 1.** To stock for future use. **2.** *Informal.* To confine with an illness or injury. **3.** To put (a ship) in dock, as for repairs. —*n.* **1. a.** The direction the strands of a rope or cable are twisted in: *a left lay.* **b.** The amount of such twist. **2.** The state of one that lays eggs: *a hen coming into lay.* **3. a.** *Chiefly Brit. Slang.* A line of activity. **b.** An occupation. **4.** *Vulgar Slang.* **a.** Sexual intercourse. **b.** A partner in sexual intercourse. —***idioms.*** **lay down the law.** To assert positively and often arrogantly. **lay it on thick. 1.** To exaggerate; overstate. **2.** To flatter effusively. **lay of the land.** The nature, arrangement, or disposition of something. [ME *laien* < OE *lecgan.*]

Usage: *Lay* ("to put, place, or prepare") and *lie* ("to recline or be situated") are frequently confused. *Lay* is a transitive verb and takes an object. *Lay* and its principal parts (*laid, laying*) are correctly used in the following examples: *He laid* (not *lay*) *the newspaper on the table. The table was laid for four. Lie* is an intransitive verb and does not take an object. *Lie* and its principal parts (*lay, lain, lying*) are correctly used in the following examples: *She often lies* (not *lays*) *down after lunch. When I lay* (not *laid*) *down, I fell asleep. The rubbish had lain* (not *laid*) *there a week. I was lying* (not *laying*) *in bed when he called. The valley lies to the east.* There are a few exceptions to these rules. The idioms *lay low, lay for,* and the nautical use of *lay,* as in *lay at anchor,* though intransitive, are well established.

lay[2] (lā) *adj.* **1.** Of or pertaining to the laity; secular. **2.** Not of or coming from a particular profession: *lay opinion.* [ME < OFr. *lai* < LLat. *laicus* < Gk. *laikos* < *laos,* the people.]

lay[3] (lā) *n.* A ballad. [ME < OFr. *lai.*]

lay[4] (lā) *v.* Past tense of **lie**[1].

lay·a·bout (lā'ə-bout') *n. Chiefly Brit.* A lazy person.

lay day *n. Commerce.* One of a certain number of days in port allowed the lessee of a ship without charge. [Prob. < LAY[1].]

lay·er (lā'ər) *n.* **1.** A single thickness, coating, or stratum spread out or covering a surface. **2.** One that lays, esp. a hen. **3.** A stem that is covered with soil for rooting while still part of a living plant. —*v.* **-ered, -er·ing, -ers.** —*tr.* To propagate (a plant) by means of a layer. —*intr.* **1.** To separate or split into layers. **2.** To take root as a result of layering. [ME *leier,* one who lays stones < *laien,* to lay. —see LAY[1].]

lay·er·ing (lā'ər-ĭng) also **lay·er·age** (-ĭj) *n.* The process of rooting branches, twigs, or stems that are still attached to a parent plant, as by placing a specially treated part in moist soil.

lay·ette (lā-ĕt') *n.* Clothing and other equipment for a newborn child. [Fr. < OFr., dim. of *laie,* box < MDu. *laege.*]

lay figure *n.* **1.** A mannequin (sense 2). **2.** A subservient person.

lay·man (lā'mən) *n.* **1.** One who is not a member of the clergy. **2.** One who does not belong to a particular profession or who does not have special or advanced training or skill.

lay·off (lā'ôf', -ŏf') *n.* **1.** The suspension or dismissal of employees. **2.** A period of temporary inactivity or rest.

lay·out (lā'out') *n.* **1.** The act of laying out or planning. **2.** The arrangement or plan of something laid out; overall picture or form: *the layout of a factory.* **3. a.** The spread and juxtaposition of printed matter, as of a newspaper or magazine page. **b.** A dummy, sketch, or paste-up for matter to be printed. **4.** *Informal.* Establishment or quarters for a specific purpose.

lay·o·ver (lā'ō'vər) *n.* A usually short stop or break in a journey.

lay·per·son (lā'pûr'sən) *n.* A layman or a laywoman.

lay reader *n.* A layman in the Anglican or Roman Catholic church authorized by a bishop to read some parts of the service.

lay-up (lā'ŭp') *n. Basketball.* A usually one-handed, banked shot made close to the basket after driving in.

lay·wom·an (lā'wŏŏm'ən) *n.* A woman who is not a member of the clergy.

la·zar (lā'zər, lăz'ər) *n. Archaic.* A person afflicted with a loathsome disease, esp. leprosy; leper. [ME < Med. Lat. *lazarus* < LLat. *Lazarus,* Lazarus, a beggar in the New Testament < Gk. *Lazaros.*]

laz·a·ret·to (lăz'ə-rĕt'ō) also **laz·a·ret** or **laz·a·rette** (lăz'ə-rĕt') *n., pl.* **-tos. 1.** A hospital treating contagious diseases. **2.** A building or ship used as a quarantine station. **3.** Often **lazaret.** A storage space between the decks of a ship. [Ital. < *lazzaro,* lazar < Med. Lat. *lazarus.* —see LAZAR.]

Laz·a·rus (lăz'ər-əs) *n.* In the New Testament: **1.** The brother of Mary and Martha whom Jesus raised from the dead. **2.** The diseased beggar in the parable of the rich man and the beggar. [LLat. < Gk. *Lazaros.*]

laze (lāz) *v.* **lazed, laz·ing, laz·es.** —*intr.* To be lazy; loaf. —*tr.* To spend (time) in loafing. [Back-formation < LAZY.]

laz·u·li (lăz'yŏŏ-lē, -ŏŏ-, lăzh'ŏŏ-) *n.* Lapis lazuli.

laz·u·lite (lăz'yŏŏ-līt', lăz'ə-, lăzh'ə-) *n.* A relatively rare, light- to deep-blue mineral, essentially (Mg, Fe)$Al_2(PO_4)_2(OH)_2$. [Med. Lat. *lazulum,* lapis lazuli + -ITE.]

laz·u·rite (lăz'yŏŏ-rīt', lăz'ə-, lăzh'ə-) *n.* A relatively rare, blue, violet-blue, or greenish-blue mineral, $Na_{4.5}Al_3Si_3O_{12}S$. [G. *Lazurit* < Med. Lat. *lazur* < Ar. *lāzaward,* lapis lazuli. —see LAPIS LAZULI.]

la·zy (lā'zē) *adj.* **-zi·er, -zi·est. 1.** Resistant to work or exertion; disposed to idleness. **2.** Slow-moving; sluggish: *a lazy river.* **3.** Conducive to idleness or indolence: *a lazy summer day.* **4.** Depicted as reclining or lying on its side. Used of a livestock brand. [Prob. of LG orig.] **—la'zi·ly** *adv.* **—la'zi·ness** *n.*

la·zy·bones (lā'zē-bōnz') *pl.n. (used with a sing. or pl. verb). Slang.* A lazy person.

lazy eye *n.* Amblyopia.

lazy Susan *n.* A revolving tray for condiments or food.

lazy tongs *pl.n.* Tongs having a jointed extensible framework operated by scissorslike handles, used for grasping an object at a distance.

LCD (ĕl'sē-dē') *n.* A digital display consisting of a liquid crystal material between sheets of glass that becomes readable in the presence of an applied voltage. [L(IQUID) C(RYSTAL) D(ISPLAY).]

L-do·pa (ĕl-dō'pə) *n.* A drug used in the treatment of Parkinson's disease. [L(EVOROTATORY) + DOPA.]

lea (lē, lā) also **ley** (lā, lē) *n.* Grassland; meadow. [ME < OE *lēah.*]

leach (lēch) *v.* **leached, leach·ing, leach·es.** —*tr.* **1.** To remove soluble constituents from by the action of a percolating liquid. **2.** To remove from a substance by the action of a percolating liquid. —*intr.* **1.** To be dissolved and washed out by a percolating liquid. **2.** To lose or yield soluble matter to a percolating liquid. —*n.* **1.** The act or process of leaching. **2.** A porous, perforated, or sievelike vessel that holds material to be leached. **3. a.** The substance through which a liquid is leached. **b.** The solution thus leached. [Orig. unknown.] **—leach'a·bil'i·ty** *n.* **—leach'a·ble** *adj.* **—leach'er** *n.*

lead[1] (lēd) *v.* **led** (lĕd), **lead·ing, leads.** —*tr.* **1.** To show the way to by going in advance. **2.** To guide or direct in a course: *lead a horse.* **3.** To serve as a route for: *The path led him to a cemetery.* **4.** To guide the action or opinion of: *led him to believe otherwise.* **5.** To direct the performance or activities of: *lead an orchestra.* **6.** To play a principal or guiding role: *lead a discussion.* **7.** To go or be at the head of: *His name led the list.* **8.** To be ahead of: *led the runner-up by three strides.* **9.** To pass or go through; live: *lead an independent life.* **10.** To begin or open with against an opponent: *led an ace.* **11.** To aim in front of (a moving target). —*intr.* **1.** To be first; be ahead. **2.** To go first as a guide. **3.** To act as commander, director, or guide. **4.** To afford a passage, course, or route. **5.** To tend toward a certain goal or result. **6.** To make the initial play, as in a game or contest. **7.** *Baseball.* To advance a few paces away from one's base toward the next while the pitcher is in his delivery. Used of a base runner. ***—phrasal verbs.*** **lead off.** *Baseball.* To be the first batter in an inning. **lead on. 1.** To lure along a particular course. **2.** To make an approach to a subject by gradual or indirect means. —*n.* **1.** The first or foremost position. **2.** The margin by which one holds a position of advantage or superiority. **3.** A piece of information of possible use in a search; clue. **4.** The ability to lead; leadership. **5.** An example; precedent. **6. a.** The principal role in a dramatic production. **b.** The person playing such a role. **7. a.** The introductory portion of a news story. **b.** An important and usually prominently displayed news story. **8.** *Games.* **a.** The first play. **b.** The prerogative or turn to make the first play. **c.** The card played. **9.** *Baseball.* A position taken by a base runner away from his base toward the next. **10.** A leash. **11. a.** A deposit of gold ore in an old riverbed. **b.** A lode (sense 1). **12.** *Elect.* A conductor by which one circuit element is electrically connected to another or to the circuit. [ME *leaden* < OE *lǣdan.*]

lead[2] (lĕd) *n.* **1.** *Symbol* **Pb** A soft, malleable, ductile, bluish-white, dense metallic element, extracted chiefly from galena and used in containers and pipes for corrosives, in solder and type metal, bullets, radiation shielding, paints, and antiknock compounds. Atomic number 82; atomic weight 207.19; melting point 327.5°C; boiling point 1,744°C; specific gravity 11.35; valences 2, 4. **2.** A plumb bob suspended by a line, used to make soundings. **3. leads.** *Chiefly Brit.* A flat roof covered with sheets of lead. **4.** Bullets from or for firearms; shot. **5. leads.** Strips of lead used to hold the panes of a window. **6.** *Printing.* A thin strip of metal used to separate lines of type. **7. a.** Any of various, often graphitic compositions used as the writing substance in pencils. **b.** A thin stick of such material. —*tr.v.* **lead·ed, lead·ing, leads. 1.** To cover, line, weight, fill, or treat with lead. **2.** *Printing.* To provide space between (lines of type) with leads. **3.** To secure (window glass) with leads. [ME < OE *lēad.*]

lead acetate (lĕd) *n.* A poisonous white crystalline compound, $Pb(C_2H_3O_2)_2{\cdot}3H_2O$, used in dyes, waterproofing compounds, and varnishes.

lead arsenate (lĕd) *n.* A poisonous white crystalline compound, $Pb_3(AsO_4)_2$, used in insecticides and herbicides.

lead carbonate (lĕd) *n.* A poisonous white amorphous powder, $PbCO_3$, used as a paint pigment.

lead chromate (lĕd) *n.* A poisonous yellow crystalline compound, $PbCrO_4$, used as a paint pigment.

lead colic (lĕd) *n.* Painter's colic.

lead·en (lĕd'n) *adj.* **1.** Made of or containing lead. **2. a.** Heavy and inert. **b.** Listless; sluggish. **3.** Lacking liveliness or sparkle. **4.** Low in spirits; depressed: *a leaden heart.* **5.** Dull, dark gray. **—lead'en·ly** *adv.* **—lead'en·ness** *n.*

lead·er (lē'dər) *n.* **1.** One that leads or guides. **2.** One in charge or in command of others. **3. a.** The head of a political party or organization. **b.** One who has influence or power, esp. of a political nature. **4. a.** A conductor, esp. a conductor of an orchestra, band, or choral group. **b.** The principal performer of an orchestral section or a group. **5.** The foremost horse in a harnessed team. **6.** A loss leader. **7.** *Chiefly Brit.* The main newspaper editorial. **8. leaders.** *Printing.* Dots or dashes in a row leading the eye across a page, as in an index entry. **9.** A pipe for conducting liquid. **10.** A short length of gut, wire, or similar material by which the hook is attached to a fishing line. **11.** *Bot.* The growing apex or main shoot of a shrub or tree. **12.** An economic indicator that tends to predict a change in the economy. [ME *ledere* < OE *lǣdere.*]

lazy tongs

lead·er·ship (lē'dər-shĭp') *n.* **1.** The position or office of a leader. **2.** The capacity or ability to lead.

lead glass *n.* Flint glass.

lead-in (lēd'ĭn') *n.* **1.** An introduction. **2.** A program, as on television, that precedes another. **3.** The part of an antenna or aerial that leads to an electronic transmitter or receiver.

lead·ing[1] (lē'dĭng) *adj.* **1.** Having a position in the lead; foremost: *the leading candidate.* **2.** Playing a lead in a theatrical production: *a leading lady.* **3.** Formulated so as to direct or control a response: *a leading question.* **—lead'ing·ly** *adv.*

lead·ing[2] (lĕd'ĭng) *n.* **1.** A border or rim of lead, as around a windowpane. **2.** *Printing.* The spacing between lines.

lead·ing edge (lē'dĭng) *n.* **1.** The edge of a sail that faces the wind. **2.** The front edge of an airplane propeller blade or wing.

lead·ing tone (lē'dĭng) *n. Mus.* The seventh tone, or degree, of a scale, a half tone below the tonic; a subtonic.

lead line (lĕd) *n.* A sounding line.

lead monoxide (lĕd) *n.* Litharge.

lead·off (lēd'ôf', -ŏf') *n.* **1.** An opening play or move. **2.** One that leads off.

lead pencil (lĕd) *n.* A pencil that uses graphite as its marking substance.

lead·plant (lĕd'plănt') *n.* A shrub, *Amorpha canescens,* of central North America, having leaves covered with whitish hairs.

lead poisoning (lĕd) *n.* Acute or chronic poisoning by lead or any of its salts, the acute form causing severe gastroenteritis, and the chronic form anemia, abdominal pain, constipation, partial paralysis, and convulsions.

leads·man (lĕdz'mən) *n.* The man who uses the lead line in taking soundings.

lead tetraethyl (lĕd) *n.* Tetraethyl lead.

lead-time (lēd'tīm') *n.* The time between the decision to start a project and the completion of the work.

lead·wort (lĕd'wûrt', -wôrt') *n.* **1.** Any of various chiefly tropical plants of the genus *Plumbago,* having clusters of variously colored flowers. **2.** Any of several plants similar to the leadwort.

leaf (lēf) *n., pl.* **leaves** (lēvz). **1.** A usually green, flattened structure of vascular plants, characteristically consisting of a bladelike expansion attached to a stem, and functioning as a principal organ of photosynthesis and transpiration. **2.** A leaflike organ or structure. **3.** Leaves collectively; foliage. **4.** The leaves of a plant used or processed for a specific purpose: *tobacco leaf.* **5.** One of the folded sheets, as bound in a volume, each side of which constitutes a page. **6.** A very thin sheet of material: *gold leaf.* **7.** A hinged or removable section for a table top. **8.** A hinged or otherwise movable section of a folding door, shutter, or gate. **9.** One of several metal strips forming a leaf spring. *—v.* **leafed, leaf·ing, leafs.** *—intr.* **1.** To produce leaves; put forth foliage. **2.** To turn through pages: *leafed through the catalogue.* *—tr.* To turn through the pages of. [ME < OE *lēaf.*] **—leaf'less** *adj.* **—leaf'like** *adj.*

leaf·age (lē'fĭj) *n.* Leaves; foliage.

leaf fat *n.* Fat that encloses the kidneys of a hog, used in making lard.

leaf·hop·per (lēf'hŏp'ər) *n.* Any of numerous insects of the family Cicadellidae that suck juices from plants.

leaf insect *n.* Any of various chiefly Asiatic insects of the genus *Phyllium* and related genera that resemble leaves.

leaf lard *n.* High-grade lard made from the leaf fat of a hog.

leaf·let (lē'flĭt) *n.* **1.** One of the segments of a compound leaf. **2.** A small leaf or leaflike part. **3.** A printed, usually folded handbill or flier, such as an advertising circular. *—v.* **-let·ed, -let·ing, -lets** or **-let·ted, -let·ting, -lets.** *—intr.* To hand out leaflets. *—tr.* To hand out leaflets to.

leaf miner *n.* Any of numerous small flies and moths that in the larval state dig into and feed on leaf tissue.

leaf mold *n.* Humus or compost consisting of decomposed leaves and other organic material.

leaf spot *n.* Any of various plant diseases resulting in well-defined necrotic areas on the leaves.

leaf spring

leaf spring *n.* A composite spring, used esp. in automotive suspensions, consisting of several layers of flexible metallic strips joined to act as a single unit.

leaf·stalk (lēf'stôk') *n.* The stalk by which a leaf is attached to a stem; petiole.

leaf·y (lē'fē) *adj.* **-i·er, -i·est. 1.** Having or covered with leaves. **2.** Consisting of leaves. **3.** Resembling or similar to a leaf. **—leaf'i·ness** *n.*

league[1] (lēg) *n.* **1.** An association of states, organizations, or individuals for common action; alliance. **2.** An association of sports teams or clubs that compete chiefly among themselves. **3.** A class of competition: *out of his league.* *—v.* **leagued, leagu·ing, leagues.** *—intr.* To come together in or as if in a league. *—tr.* To bring together in or as if in a league. [ME *ligg* < OFr. *ligue* < Ital. *liga* < *legare,* to bind < Lat. *ligare.*]

league[2] (lēg) *n.* **1. a.** A unit of distance equal to 3 statute miles or about 4.83 kilometers. **b.** Any of various other units of about the same length. **2.** A square league. [ME *leuge* < Med. Lat. *leuga,* a measure of distance, of Celt. orig.]

lea·guer[1] (lē'gər) *n.* **1.** A siege. **2.** The camp esp. of a besieging army. *—tr.v.* **-guered, -guer·ing, -guers.** *Archaic.* To besiege; beleaguer. [Du. *leger.*]

leagu·er[2] (lē'gər) *n.* One that belongs to a league.

Le·ah (lē'ə) *n.* In the Old Testament, the elder daughter of Laban and first wife of Jacob. [Heb.]

leak (lēk) *v.* **leaked, leak·ing, leaks.** *—intr.* **1.** To permit the escape or passage of something through a breach or flaw. **2.** To escape or pass through a breach or flaw. **3.** To become publicly known through a breach of secrecy: *The news leaked out.* *—tr.* **1.** To permit (a substance) to escape or pass through a breach or flaw. **2.** To disclose (information) without authorization or official sanction. *—n.* **1.** A crack or opening that permits something to escape from or enter a container or conduit. **2. a.** Loss of electric current as a result of faulty insulation. **b.** The path or place at which this loss takes place. **3.** An unauthorized or deliberate disclosure of confidential information: *"Sometimes we can't respond to stories based on leaks"* (Ronald Reagan). **4.** An act or instance of leaking. **5.** *Slang.* An act of urinating. [ME *leke,* prob. of MLG orig.] **—leak'er** *n.*

leak·age (lē'kĭj) *n.* **1.** The process or an instance of leaking. **2.** Something that escapes by leaking. **3.** An amount lost as the result of leaking.

leak·y (lē'kē) *adj.* **-i·er, -i·est.** Permitting leakage.

lean[1] (lēn) *v.* **leaned** or **leant** (lĕnt), **lean·ing, leans.** *—intr.* **1.** To bend or slant away from the vertical. **2.** To incline the weight of the body so as to be supported: *leaning against the railing.* **3.** To rely for assistance or support: *Lean on me for help.* **4.** To have a tendency or preference: *a government that leans toward fascism.* **5.** *Informal.* To exert pressure: *Their boss is leaning on them.* *—tr.* **1.** To set or place so as to be resting or supported. **2.** To cause to incline. *—n.* A tilt or inclination away from the vertical. [ME *lenen* < OE *hleonian.*]

lean[2] (lēn) *adj.* **-er, -est. 1.** Not fleshy or fat; thin. **2.** Containing little or no fat. **3. a.** Not productive or prosperous: *lean years.* **b.** Severely curtailed or reduced: *a lean budget.* **4. a.** Lacking mineral value: *lean ore.* **b.** Lacking in combustible material: *lean fuel.* *—n.* Meat with little or no fat. [ME *lene* < OE *hlǣne.*] **—lean'ly** *adv.* **—lean'ness** *n.*

Synonyms: *lean, spare, skinny, scrawny, lank, lanky, rawboned, gaunt.* These adjectives describe persons who are thin of body. *Lean* and *spare* often suggest desirable absence of flesh in one who is athletic and vigorous; sometimes, however, they have no particular connotation. *Skinny* and *scrawny* imply unattractive thinness associated with underdevelopment or undernourishment. *Lank* describes one who is thin in proportion to height, and *lanky* one who is thin, tall, and loose-jointed. *Rawboned* suggests the lankiness or spareness of an outdoorsman. *Gaunt* implies thinness that gives undue prominence to the bones and may suggest illness or hardship.

Le·an·der (lē-ăn'dər) *n. Gk. Myth.* A youth who loved Hero and drowned during one of his nightly swims across the Hellespont to be with her. [Lat. < Gk. *Leandros.*]

lean·ing (lē'nĭng) *n.* A tendency; proclivity; inclination.

leant (lĕnt) *v.* A past tense and past participle of **lean[1]**.

lean-to (lēn'to͞o') *n., pl.* **-tos. 1.** A structure with a single-pitch roof attached to the side of a building. **2.** A shelter or shed having a roof with only one slope.

leap (lēp) *v.* **leaped** or **leapt** (lĕpt, lēpt), **leap·ing, leaps.** *—intr.* **1.** To jump off the ground with a spring of the legs. **2.** To move quickly, abruptly, or impulsively: *leaps at every chance to advance himself.* *—tr.* To jump over: *couldn't leap the brook.* *—n.* **1.** The act of leaping. **2.** The distance cleared in a leap. **3.** An abrupt or precipitous passage, shift, or transition. [ME *lepen* < OE *hlēapan.*] **—leap'er** *n.*

leap·frog (lēp'frôg', -frŏg') *n.* A game in which one player kneels or bends over while the next in line leaps over him. *—v.* **-frogged, -frog·ging, -frogs.** *—tr.* **1.** To jump over in or as if in leapfrog. **2.** To advance (two military units) by engaging one with the enemy while moving the other to a position forward of the first unit. *—intr.* To move forward or progress in or as if in leapfrog.

leapfrog test *n.* A method of checking the internal operations of a computer by performing arithmetic or logical operations on one section of storage, transferring the new information to another section, repeating the operations, and crosschecking the results.

leapt (lĕpt, lēpt) *v.* A past tense and past participle of **leap**.

leap year *n.* **1.** A year in the Gregorian calendar having 366 days, with the extra day, February 29, intercalated to compensate for the quarter-day difference between an ordinary year and the astronomical year. **2.** An intercalary year in a calendar.

Lear (lîr) *n.* The protagonist in Shakespeare's tragedy *King Lear.*

learn (lûrn) *v.* **learned** or **learnt** (lûrnt), **learn·ing, learns.** *—tr.* **1.** To gain knowledge, comprehension, or mastery of through experience or study. **2.** To fix in the mind or memory; memorize: *learned the speech in a few hours.* **3.** To acquire experience of or an ability or skill in: *learned how to whistle.* **4.** To become informed of; find out. **5.** *Nonstandard.* To cause to acquire knowledge; teach. **6.** *Obs.* To give information of. *—intr.* To gain knowledge, comprehension, or skill: *learned of the job through the grapevine.* [ME *lernen* < OE *leornian.*] **—learn'er** *n.*

Usage: *Learn* in modern usage is nonstandard in the sense of "to teach": *She taught* (not *learned*) *him English.*

learn·ed (lûr'nĭd) *adj.* **1.** Having or demonstrating profound knowledge or scholarship; erudite; scholarly. **2.** Directed toward scholars: *a learned journal.*

learn·ing (lûr'nĭng) *n.* **1.** Instruction; education. **2.** Acquired wisdom, knowledge, or skill.

learning disability *n.* A condition held to be associated with neurological dysfunction that is characterized by inability to master a skill, as reading or numerical calculation.

learn·ing-dis·a·bled (lûr′nĭng-dĭs-ā′bəld) *adj.* Having a learning disability.

learnt (lûrnt) *v.* A past tense and past participle of **learn**.

lease (lēs) *n.* **1.** A contract granting use or occupation of property during a specified period in exchange for a specified rent. **2.** The term or duration of a lease. **3.** Property used or occupied under the terms of a lease. *—tr.v.* **leased, leas·ing, leas·es. 1.** To grant use or occupation of under the terms of a lease. **2.** To use or occupy under a lease. ***—idiom.* a new lease on life.** An opportunity to continue under improved circumstances. [ME *les* < AN < *lesser,* to lease < OFr. *laissier,* to let go < Lat. *laxare,* to loosen < *laxus,* loose.] **—leas′a·ble** *adj.*

lease·hold (lēs′hōld′) *n.* **1.** Possession by lease. **2.** Property held by lease. **—lease′hold′er** *n.*

leash (lēsh) *n.* **1.** A chain, rope, or strap attached to the collar or harness of an animal and used to lead it or hold it in check. **2.** Control; check: *emotions kept in leash.* **3.** A set of three animals, such as hounds. **4.** A set of three. *—tr.v.* **leashed, leash·ing, leash·es.** To restrain with or as if with a leash. [ME *lesh* < OFr. *laisse* < *laissier,* to let go. —see LEASE.]

leash law *n.* An ordinance requiring that dogs be kept on a leash when not restricted to their owners' property.

leas·ing (lē′sĭng) *n. Archaic.* **1.** The act of lying. **2.** A lie; falsehood. [ME *lesing* < OE *lēasung* < *lēasian,* to lie < *lēas,* false.]

least (lēst) *adj.* **1.** Lowest in importance or rank. **2.** Smallest in magnitude or degree. *—adv.* To or in the smallest degree. *—n.* One that is least. ***—idioms.* at least. 1.** According to the lowest possible assessment; not less than. **2.** In any event; anyway: *You might at least answer.* **in the least.** At all: *I don't mind in the least.* [ME < OE *lǣst.*]

least common denominator *n.* Lowest common denominator.

least common multiple *n.* The least quantity that is exactly divisible by each of two or more designated quantities; for example, 12 is the least common multiple of 2, 3, 4, and 6.

least flycatcher *n.* A small grayish North American bird, *Empidonax minimus.*

least squares *pl.n.* A method of determining the line or curve that best fits a relation between two experimental sets of data, using the criterion that the sums of the squares of deviations of experimental points from curve ordinates be a minimum.

least·ways (lēst′wāz′) *adv. Regional.* At least.

least·wise (lēst′wīz′) *adv. Informal.* Anyway; at least.

leath·er (lĕth′ər) *n.* **1.** The dressed or tanned hide of an animal, usually with the hair removed. **2.** Any of various articles or parts made of leather, as a strap or boot. **3.** The flap of a dog's ear. *—tr.v.* **-ered, -er·ing, -ers. 1.** To cover wholly or in part with leather. **2.** *Informal.* To beat with a leather strap. [ME *lether* < OE *leðer.*]

leath·er·back (lĕth′ər-băk′) *n.* A large, chiefly tropical marine turtle, *Dermochelys coriacea,* with a leathery, longitudinally ridged carapace.

leatherback

leath·er·ette (lĕth′ə-rĕt′) *n.* An imitation leather. [Orig. a trademark.]

leath·er·jack·et (lĕth′ər-jăk′ĭt) *n.* A fish, *Oligoplites saurus,* of Atlantic and Pacific waters, having tough, leathery skin and venomous spines on the anal fin.

leath·ern (lĕth′ərn) *adj. Archaic.* Made of, covered with, or resembling leather.

leath·er·neck (lĕth′ər-nĕk′) *n. Slang.* A member of the United States Marine Corps. [From the leather neckband that was once part of the uniform.]

leath·er·wood (lĕth′ər-wo͝od′) *n.* **1.** A shrub, *Dirca palustris,* of eastern North America, having tough, pliable bark and small yellow flowers. **2.** The titi.

leath·er·y (lĕth′ə-rē) *adj.* Having the texture or appearance of leather; tough or weathered: *a leathery face.*

leave[1] (lēv) *v.* **left** (lĕft), **leav·ing, leaves.** *—tr.* **1.** To go out of or away from. **2.** To go without taking or removing: *left his book on the subway.* **3.** To have as a result, consequence, or remainder: *left a trail of smoke.* **4.** To cause or allow to be or remain in a specified state: *left the lights on.* **5.** To have remaining after death: *left a son.* **6.** To bequeath. **7.** To give over to another to control or act upon: *Leave all the details to him.* **8. a.** To abandon; forsake: *leave home.* **b.** To remove oneself from association with or participation in: *left the navy for civilian life.* **9.** To give or deposit, as for use or information, upon one's departure or in one's absence: *left a note for you; leave one's name and address.* *—intr.* To depart; go. ***—phrasal verb.* leave off. 1.** To stop; cease. **2.** To stop doing or using. [ME *leven* < OE *lǣfan.*]

Usage: *Leave alone* is acceptable as a substitute for *let alone* in the sense of "to refrain from disturbing or interfering." The following examples are approved by a majority of the Usage Panel: *Leave him alone and he will produce. Left alone, he was quite productive.* Those who do not accept these examples generally feel that *leave alone* should be restricted to the sense of "to depart and leave one in solitude": *They were left alone in the wilderness.* • In formal writing *leave* is not an acceptable substitute for *let* in the sense of "to allow or permit." Only *let* is acceptable in the following examples: *Let me be. Let him go. Let us not quarrel. Let it lie.*

leave[2] (lēv) *n.* **1.** Permission. **2. a.** Official permission to be absent from work or duty, esp. that granted to military personnel. **b.** The absence granted by such permission. **3.** Formal or verbal farewell: *took leave of her with a heavy heart.* [ME < OE *lēaf.*]

leave[3] (lēv) *intr.v.* **leaved, leav·ing, leaves.** To put forth foliage; leaf. [ME *leven* < *leaf,* leaf.]

leaved (lēvd) *adj.* **1.** Having or bearing a leaf or leaves. **2.** Having a specified number or kind of leaves: *three-leaved; wide-leaved.*

leav·en (lĕv′ən) *n.* **1.** A substance, such as yeast or cream of tartar, used as an ingredient in batters and doughs to produce fermentation. **2.** An element or influence that works subtly to lighten or enliven a whole. *—tr.v.* **-ened, -en·ing, -ens. 1.** To add leavening to. **2.** To produce fermentation in. **3.** To pervade with a lightening or enlivening influence. [ME < OFr. *levain* < VLat. **levamen* < Lat. *levare,* to raise.]

leav·en·ing (lĕv′ə-nĭng) *n.* An agent that produces fermentation; leaven.

leaves (lēvz) *n.* Plural of **leaf**.

leave-tak·ing (lēv′tā′kĭng) *n.* A departure or farewell.

leav·ings (lē′vĭngz) *pl.n.* Scraps or remains; residue.

Leb·a·nese (lĕb′ə-nēz′, -nēs′) *adj.* Of or pertaining to Lebanon, its people, or their culture. *—n., pl.* **Lebanese.** A native or inhabitant of Lebanon.

le·bens·raum (lā′bəns-roum′) *n.* Additional territory deemed necessary to a nation for its continued existence or economic well-being. [G.]

lech[1] (lĕch) *n. Slang.* **1.** A lecher. **2.** A lecherous desire. *—intr.v.* **leched, lech·ing, lech·es.** To behave in a lecherous manner. [Short for LECHER.]

lech[2] (lĕch) *n.* Variant of **letch**.

lech·er (lĕch′ər) *n.* A man given to lechery. [ME < OFr. < *lechier,* to live in debauchery, of Germanic orig.]

lech·er·ous (lĕch′ər-əs) *adj.* Given to, characterized by, or inciting lechery. **—lech′er·ous·ly** *adv.* **—lech′er·ous·ness** *n.*

lech·er·y (lĕch′ə-rē) *n., pl.* **-ies. 1.** Excessive indulgence in sexual activity. **2.** Prurience; lasciviousness.

lec·i·thin (lĕs′ə-thĭn) *n.* Any of a group of phosphatides found in all plant and animal tissues, produced commercially from egg yolks, soybeans, and corn and used in the processing of foods, pharmaceuticals, cosmetics, paints and inks, and rubber and plastics. [Gk. *lekithos,* egg yolk + -IN.]

lec·i·thin·ase (lĕs′ə-thə-nās′, -nāz′) *n.* Any of several enzymes that hydrolyze lecithin.

lec·tern (lĕk′tərn) *n.* **1.** A reading desk with a slanted top holding the books from which Scriptural passages are read during a church service. **2.** A stand that serves as a support for the notes or books of a speaker. [ME *lectorn* < OFr. *lettrun* < Med. Lat. *lecternum* < Lat. *legere,* to read.]

lec·tion (lĕk′shən) *n.* **1.** A variant reading or transcription of a text or copy. **2.** A reading from Scripture that forms a part of a church service. [Lat. *lectio,* a reading < *legere,* to read.]

lec·tion·ar·y (lĕk′shə-nĕr′ē) *n., pl.* **-ies.** A book containing lections or a list of lections to be read at church services. [LLat. *lectionarium* < Lat. *lectio,* a reading. —see LECTION.]

lec·tor (lĕk′tər) *n.* **1.** A person who reads aloud certain of the Scriptural passages used in a church service; reader. **2.** A public lecturer or reader in certain universities. [ME < LLat. < Lat., reader < *legere,* to read.]

lec·ture (lĕk′chər) *n.* **1.** An exposition of a given subject delivered before an audience or class, esp. for the purpose of instruction. **2.** A sober admonition or reproof; reprimand. *—v.* **-tured, -tur·ing, -tures.** *—intr.* To deliver a lecture. *—tr.* **1.** To deliver a lecture to (a class or audience). **2.** To admonish or reprove soberly and often at length: *always lecturing me about my manners.* [ME, a reading < OFr. < Med. Lat. *lectura* < *legere,* to read.] **—lec′tur·er** *n.*

led (lĕd) *v.* Past tense and past participle of **lead[1]**.

LED (ĕl′ē-dē′, lĕd) *n.* A semiconductor diode that converts applied voltage to light and that is used in digital displays, as of a calculator. [L(IGHT) E(MITTING) D(IODE).]

Le·da (lē′də) *n. Gk. Myth.* A queen of Sparta and the mother, by Zeus in the form of a swan, of Helen and Pollux and by her husband of Castor and Clytemnestra. [Lat. < Gk. *Lēda.*]

le·der·ho·sen (lā′dər-hō′zən) *pl.n.* Leather shorts worn by men and boys, esp. in Bavaria. [G. < MHG *lederhose* : *leder,* leather + *hose,* trousers.]

ledge (lĕj) *n.* **1.** A horizontal projection forming a narrow shelf on a wall. **2.** A cut or projection forming a shelf on a cliff or rock wall. **3.** An underwater ridge or rock shelf. **4.** A level of rock-bearing ore; vein. [ME, piece of wood used for bracing, prob. < *leggen,* to lay < OE *lecgan.*] **—ledg′y** *adj.*

ledg·er (lĕj′ər) *n.* **1. a.** A book in which the monetary transactions of a business are posted in the form of debits and credits. **b.** A book to which the record of accounts is transferred as final entry from original postings. **2.** A slab of stone laid flat over a grave. **3.** A horizontal timber in a scaffold, attached to the uprights and supporting the putlogs. [ME *legger,* breviary, prob. < *leggen,* to lay. —see LEDGE.]

leeboard
Sailing vessel with leeboard

leek

ledger board *n.* The top railing of a fence or balustrade.
ledger line *n. Mus.* A short line placed above or below a staff to accommodate notes higher or lower than the staff's range.
lee (lē) *n.* **1.** The side away from the direction from which the wind blows; the side sheltered from the wind. **2.** Cover; shelter. *—adj.* Of or pertaining to the side, as of a ship, that is sheltered from the wind. [ME *le* < OE *hleo,* shelter.]
lee·board (lē′bôrd′, -bōrd′) *n.* One of a pair of movable boards or plates attached to the hull of sailing vessels to prevent slippage downwind.
leech[1] (lēch) *n.* **1.** Any of various chiefly aquatic bloodsucking or carnivorous annelid worms of the class Hirudinea, of which one species, *Hirudo medicinalis,* was formerly used by physicians to bleed their patients. **2.** One who preys on or clings to another; parasite. **3.** *Archaic.* A physician. *—v.* **leeched, leech·ing, leech·es.** *—tr.* To bleed with leeches. *—intr.* To attach oneself to another in the manner of a leech. [ME *leche,* physician, leech < OE *lǣce.*]
leech[2] (lēch) *n.* **1.** Either vertical edge of a square sail. **2.** The after edge of a fore-and-aft sail. [ME *leche,* prob. < MLG *līk,* leech line.]
leek (lēk) *n.* A plant, *Allium porrum,* related to the onion and having a white, slender bulb and dark-green leaves. [ME *lek* < OE *lēac.*]
leer (lîr) *intr.v.* **leered, leer·ing, leers.** To look obliquely or suggestively, as with prurient interest, malicious intent, or insidious triumph. *—n.* A sly, suggestive, or cunning look. [Prob. < obs. *leer,* cheek < ME *ler* < OE *hlēor.*]
leer·y (lîr′ē) *adj.* **-i·er, -i·est.** *Informal.* Suspicious or distrustful; wary. **—leer′i·ly** *adv.* **—leer′i·ness** *n.*
lees (lēz) *pl.n.* Sediment settling during fermentation, esp. in wine; dregs. [Pl. of obs. *lee,* sediment < ME *lie* < OFr. < Med. Lat. *lia.*]
lee shore *n.* A shore toward which the wind is blowing and toward which a ship is likely to be driven.
lee·ward (lē′wərd, lo͞o′ərd) *adj.* Located on or moving toward the side toward which the wind is blowing. *—n.* The lee side or quarter. **—lee′ward** *adv.*
lee·way (lē′wā′) *n.* **1.** The drift of a ship or plane to leeward of true course. **2.** A margin of freedom or variation, as of activity, time, or expenditure; latitude.
left[1] (lĕft) *adj.* **1. a.** Of, designating, belonging to, or located on the side of the body to the north when the subject is facing east. **b.** Of, designating, directed toward, or located on the left side. **2.** Often **Left.** Of or belonging to the political or intellectual Left. *—n.* **1. a.** The direction or position on the left side. **b.** The left side. **c.** The left hand. **d.** A turn in the direction of the left hand or side. **2.** Often **Left. a.** The individuals and groups who advocate the adoption of sometimes extreme measures in order to achieve the equality, freedom, and well-being of the citizens of a state. **b.** The opinion of those advocating such measures as opposed to conservative opinion. *—adv.* Toward or on the left. [ME.]
left[2] (lĕft) *v.* Past tense and past participle of **leave**[1].
left field *n.* **1.** *Baseball.* **a.** The third of the outfield that is to the left, looking from home plate. **b.** The position played by the left fielder. **2.** A position far from the center or mainstream, as of opinion or reason: *out in left field.*
left fielder *n. Baseball.* The player who defends left field.
left-hand (lĕft′hănd′) *adj.* **1.** Of, pertaining to, or located on the left. **2.** Intended for the left hand or for use by a left-handed person.
left-hand·ed (lĕft′hăn′dĭd) *adj.* **1.** Having more dexterity in or using the left hand more easily than the right. **2.** Executed with the left hand. **3.** Designed for wear on or use by the left hand. **4.** Awkward; maladroit. **5.** Of doubtful sincerity; dubious: *left-handed flattery.* **6.** Of, pertaining to, or born of a morganatic marriage. **7.** Turning or spiraling from right to left; counterclockwise. *—adv.* With the left hand. **—left′-hand′ed·ly** *adv.* **—left′-hand′ed·ness** *n.*
left-hand·er (lĕft′hăn′dər) *n.* One who is left-handed.
left·ism also **Left·ism** (lĕf′tĭz′əm) *n.* The ideology of the political Left. **—left′ist** *n. & adj.*
left·o·ver (lĕft′ō′vər) *adj.* Being unused or uneaten. *—n.* Often **leftovers. 1.** An unused portion or remnant of something, esp. of food. **2.** A dish made out of leftovers.
left wing also **Left Wing** *n.* The leftist faction of a group. **—left′-wing′** *adj.* **—left′-wing′er** *n.*
left·y (lĕf′tē) *n., pl.* **-ies.** *Slang.* **1.** A left-handed person. **2.** An advocate or member of the political Left.
leg (lĕg) *n.* **1. a.** A limb or appendage of an animal, used for locomotion or support. **b.** The lower or hind limb in humans and primates. **c.** The part of the limb between the knee and foot in vertebrates. **d.** The back part of the hindquarter of a food animal. **2.** A supporting part resembling a leg in shape or function. **3.** One of the branches of a forked or jointed object. **4.** The part of a garment, esp. of a pair of trousers, that covers all or part of the leg. **5.** Either side of a right triangle that is not the hypotenuse. **6.** A stage of a journey or course, esp.: **a.** The distance traveled by a sailing vessel on a single tack. **b.** The part of an air route or flight pattern that is between two successive stops, positions, or changes in direction. *—intr.v.* **legged, leg·ging, legs.** *Informal.* To go on foot; walk or run. **—idioms. a leg to stand on.** A justifiable or logical basis for defense; support: *He doesn't have a leg to stand on in this debate.* **a leg up.** An act or instance of assisting; boost. **on (one's) last legs.** At the end of one's strength or health; ready to collapse, fail, or die. **pull (someone's) leg.** *Informal.* To tease, make fun of, or fool. **stretch (one's) legs.** To stand or walk, esp. after sitting for a long time. [ME < ON *leggr.*]
leg·a·cy (lĕg′ə-sē) *n., pl.* **-cies. 1.** Money or property bequeathed to someone by will. **2.** Something handed down from an ancestor or predecessor or from the past: *a legacy of religious freedom.* [ME *legat* < OFr. < Med. Lat. *legantia* < Lat. *legare,* to bequeath as a legacy.]
le·gal (lē′gəl) *adj.* **1.** Of, relating to, or concerned with law: *legal papers.* **2. a.** Authorized by or based on law: *a legal right.* **b.** Established by law; statutory: *the legal owner.* **3.** In conformity with or permitted by law. **4.** Recognized or enforced by law rather than by equity. **5.** Created by the law: *a legal offense.* **6.** Applicable to or characteristic of lawyers or their profession. [ME < OFr. < Lat. *legalis* < *lex,* law.] **—le′gal·ly** *adv.*
legal age *n.* The age at which a person may by law assume the rights and responsibilities of an adult.
legal cap *n.* A white writing paper, often ruled, measuring $8^{1}/_{2}$ by 13 to 16 inches and generally used by lawyers.
le·gal·ese (lē′gə-lēz′, -lēs′) *n.* The specialized vocabulary of the legal profession.
legal holiday *n.* A holiday authorized by law and characterized by a limit or ban on work or official business.
le·gal·ism (lē′gə-lĭz′əm) *n.* Strict and literal adherence to the law. **—le′gal·ist** *n.* **—le′gal·is′tic** *adj.* **—le′gal·is′ti·cal·ly** *adv.*
le·gal·i·ty (lē-găl′ĭ-tē) *n., pl.* **-ties. 1.** The state or quality of being legal; lawfulness. **2.** Adherence to or observance of the law. **3. legalities.** Requirements enjoined by law.
le·gal·ize (lē′gə-līz′) *tr.v.* **-ized, -iz·ing, -iz·es.** To make legal or lawful. **—le′gal·i·za′tion** *n.*
legal pad *n.* A ruled pad of writing paper that measures $8^{1}/_{2}$ by 14 inches.
legal reserve *n.* The sum of money that a bank or insurance company is required by law to set aside as security.
legal tender *n.* Currency that may be offered in payment of a debt and that a creditor must accept.
leg·ate (lĕg′ĭt) *n.* An official emissary, esp. an official representative of the pope. [ME < OFr. *legat* < Med. Lat. *legatus* < Lat. *legare,* to send as ambassador.] **—leg′ate·ship′** *n.*
leg·a·tee (lĕg′ə-tē′) *n.* The inheritor of a legacy.
le·ga·tion (lĭ-gā′shən) *n.* **1.** The sending of a legate. **2. a.** A diplomatic mission in a foreign country ranking below an embassy. **b.** The legate and staff of such a mission. **c.** The premises occupied by a legation. [ME *legacious* < OFr. < Lat. *legatio* < *legare,* to send as an ambassador.]
le·ga·to (lĭ-gä′tō) *Mus. —adv.* In a smooth, even style. Used as a direction. *—adj.* Smooth and even. *—n., pl.* **-tos.** A smooth, even style, performance, or passage. [Ital. < *legare,* to bind < Lat. *ligare.*]
le·ga·tor (lĭ-gā′tər) *n.* A person who makes a will; testator. [Lat. < *legare,* to bequeath.]
leg·end (lĕj′ənd) *n.* **1. a.** An unverified popular story handed down from earlier times. **b.** A body or collection of such stories. **c.** A romanticized or popularized myth of modern times. **2.** A person who achieves legendary fame. **3. a.** An inscription or title on an object, such as a coin. **b.** An explanatory caption accompanying a map, chart, or illustration. [ME < OFr. *legende* < Med. Lat. *legenda* < Lat. neuter pl. gerund. of *legere,* to read.]
leg·en·dar·y (lĕj′ən-dĕr′ē) *adj.* Of, constituting, based on, or of the nature of a legend.
leg·er·de·main (lĕj′ər-də-mān′) *n.* **1.** Sleight of hand. **2.** Deception or trickery; hocus-pocus. [ME < OFr. *leger de main.*]
le·ges (lē′jēz′) *n.* Plural of **lex.**
leg·gings (lĕg′ĭngz) *pl.n.* A leg covering of material such as canvas or leather.
leg·gy (lĕg′ē) *adj.* **-gi·er, -gi·est. 1.** Having disproportionately long legs: *a leggy colt.* **2.** *Informal.* Having attractively long and slender legs. **3.** Having long, spindly, often leafless stems. **—leg′gi·ness** *n.*
leg·horn (lĕg′hôrn′, -ərn) *n.* **1. a.** The dried and bleached straw of an Italian variety of wheat. **b.** A plaited fabric made from this straw. **c.** A hat made from this fabric. **2.** Often **Leghorn.** One of a breed of domestic fowl of Mediterranean origin, noted for prolific production of eggs. [After *Leghorn,* Italy.]
leg·i·ble (lĕj′ə-bəl) *adj.* Capable of being read or deciphered. [ME < LLat. *legibilis* < Lat. *legere,* to read.] **—leg′i·bil′i·ty, leg′i·ble·ness** *n.* **—leg′i·bly** *adv.*
le·gion (lē′jən) *n.* **1.** The major unit of the Roman army consisting of 3,000 to 6,000 infantry troops and 100 to 200 cavalrymen. **2.** A large number; multitude. **3.** Often **Legion.** A national organization of former servicemen. *—adj.* Constituting a large number; multitudinous: *Her admirers were legion.* [ME *legioun* < OFr. *legion* < Lat. *legio* < *legere,* to gather.]
le·gion·ar·y (lē′jə-nĕr′ē) *adj.* Of, relating to, or constituting a legion. *—n., pl.* **-ies.** A soldier of a legion.
legionary ant *n.* An army ant.
le·gion·naire (lē′jə-nâr′) *n.* A member of a legion. [Fr. *légionnaire* < *legion,* legion < OFr. —see LEGION.]

Legionnaires' disease *n.* A severe disease caused by the bacterium *Legionella premophilia* and characterized by pneumonia, dry cough, and muscular pain. [So called because it was first recognized when an outbreak occurred during the American Legion Convention in 1976.]

Legion of Honor *n.* A high French civilian and military decoration, instituted in 1802.

Legion of Merit *n.* A U.S. military decoration awarded for exceptionally meritorious conduct in the performance of outstanding services.

leg·is·late (lĕj'ĭ-slāt') *v.* **-lat·ed, -lat·ing, -lates.** —*intr.* To pass a law or laws. —*tr.* To create or bring about by legislation; enact into law. [Back-formation < LEGISLATOR.]

leg·is·la·tion (lĕj'ĭ-slā'shən) *n.* **1.** The act or process of legislating; lawmaking. **2.** A proposed or enacted law or group of laws.

leg·is·la·tive (lĕj'ĭ-slā'tĭv) *adj.* **1.** Of or relating to legislation. **2.** Resulting from or decided by legislation. **3.** Having the power to create laws; designed to legislate. **4.** Of or relating to a legislature. —*n.* The legislative body of a government; legislature. **—leg'is·la'tive·ly** *adv.*

leg·is·la·tor (lĕj'ĭ-slā'tər) *n.* A person who creates or enacts laws, esp. a member of a legislative body. [Lat. : *lex,* law + *lator,* proposer < *latus,* p.part. of *ferre,* to propose.]

leg·is·la·ture (lĕj'ĭ-slā'chər) *n.* An officially selected body of persons vested with the responsibility and the power to make laws for a political unit, such as a nation.

le·gist (lē'jĭst) *n.* A specialist in law. [ME *legiste* < OFr. < Med.Lat. *legista* < Lat. *lex,* law.]

le·git (lə-jĭt') *adj. Slang.* Legitimate.

le·git·i·ma·cy (lə-jĭt'ə-mə-sē) *n.* The quality or fact of being legitimate.

le·git·i·mate (lə-jĭt'ə-mĭt) *adj.* **1.** In compliance with the law; lawful: *a legitimate business.* **2.** In accordance with established or accepted patterns and standards: *legitimate advertising.* **3.** Based on logical reasoning; reasonable: *a legitimate solution.* **4.** Authentic; genuine: *had a legitimate complaint.* **5.** Born of legally married parents. **6.** Of, relating to, or ruling by hereditary right. **7.** Of or pertaining to drama of high professional quality that excludes burlesque, vaudeville, and some forms of musical comedy: *the legitimate theater.* —*tr.v.* (-māt') **-mat·ed, -mat·ing, -mates. 1.** To justify as legitimate; authorize. **2.** To make, establish, or declare legitimate. [ME, born in wedlock < OFr. *legitimer,* to be legitimate < Med. Lat. *legitimare* < Lat. *legitimus,* legitimate < *lex,* law.] **—le·git'i·mate·ly** *adv.* **—le·git'i·ma'tion** *n.*

le·git·i·ma·tize (lə-jĭt'ə-mə-tīz') *tr.v.* **-tized, -tiz·ing, -tiz·es.** To legitimate.

le·git·i·mist (lə-jĭt'ə-mĭst) *n.* A person who believes in or supports rule by hereditary right. **—le·git'i·mism** *n.*

le·git·i·mize (lə-jĭt'ə-mīz') *tr.v.* **-mized, -miz·ing, -miz·es.** To legitimate. **—le·git'i·mi·za'tion** *n.* **—le·git'i·miz'er** *n.*

leg-of-mut·ton (lĕg'ə-mŭt'n, lĕg'əv-) *adj.* Resembling a leg of mutton in shape; tapering sharply from one large end to a point or smaller end, as a sleeve.

leg·room (lĕg'ro͞om', -ro͝om') *n.* Room in which to stretch the legs while seated.

leg·ume (lĕg'yo͞om', lə-gyo͞om') *n.* **1. a.** A pod, such as that of a pea or bean, that splits into two valves with the seeds attached to the lower edge of one of the valves. **b.** Such a pod or seed used as food. **2.** A plant of the family Leguminosae, characteristically bearing legumes. [Fr. *légume* < Lat. *legumen,* bean.]

le·gu·mi·nous (lə-gyo͞o'mə-nəs) *adj.* **1.** Of, belonging to, or characteristic of the family Leguminosae, which includes peas, beans, clover, alfalfa, and other plants. **2.** Resembling or having the nature of a legume. [NLat. *Leguminosae,* family name < Lat. *lugumen,* bean.]

leg·work (lĕg'wûrk') *n. Informal.* Work, such as collecting information, that involves walking or traveling about.

le·hu·a (lā-ho͞o'ə) *n.* A tree, *Metrosideros collina,* of Hawaii and other Pacific islands, having showy red flowers. [Hawaiian.]

lei[1] (lā, lā'ē) *n., pl.* **leis.** A garland of flowers, esp. one worn around the neck. [Hawaiian.]

lei[2] (lā) *n.* Plural of **leu.**

Leices·ter (lĕs'tər) *n.* A sheep of a breed developed in Leicestershire, England, having long, fine wool.

leish·man·i·a·sis (lēsh'mə-nī'ə-sĭs) *n.* **1.** An infection with flagellate protozoans of the genus *Leishmania.* **2.** A disease, such as kala-azar or either of two clinically distinct, ulcerative skin diseases, caused by protozoans of the genus *Leishmania.* [< NLat. *Leishmania,* genus of protozoans, after Sir William B. *Leishman* (1865–1926).]

leis·ter (lē'stər) *n.* A three-pronged spear used for fishing. —*tr.v.* **-tered, -ter·ing, -ters.** To spear (a fish) with a leister. [Of Scand. orig.]

lei·sure (lē'zhər, lĕzh'ər) *n.* Freedom from time-consuming duties, responsibilities, or activities. **—*modifier:*** *leisure time.* **—*idioms.* at leisure. 1.** Having free time. **2.** Not employed, occupied, or engaged. **at (one's) leisure.** When one has free time; at one's convenience. [ME < OFr. *leisir* < Lat. *licēre,* to be permitted.]

lei·sured (lē'zhərd, lĕzh'ərd) *adj.* Characterized by leisure.

lei·sure·ly (lē'zhər-lē, lĕzh'ər-) *adj.* Without haste; unhurried: *a leisurely meal.* —*adv.* In an unhurried manner; slowly. **—lei'sure·li·ness** *n.*

leisure suit *n.* A suit for informal wear consisting of a shirt-like jacket and matching slacks.

leit·mo·tif also **leit·mo·tiv** (līt'mō-tēf') *n.* **1.** A melodic passage or phrase, esp. in Wagnerian opera, associated with a specific character, thing, or element. **2.** A dominant and recurring theme, as in a novel. [G. *Leitmotiv* : *leiten,* to lead (< OHG) + *motiv,* motive (< Fr. *motif).*]

lek (lĕk) *n.* See table at **currency.** [Albanian.]

LEM (lĕm) *n.* A lunar excursion module.

lem·an (lĕm'ən, lē'mən) *n. Archaic.* **1.** A lover. **2.** A mistress. [ME : *leof,* dear (< OE *lēof*) + *man,* man (< OE).]

lem·ma[1] (lĕm'ə) *n., pl.* **-mas** or **-ma·ta** (-ə-tə). **1.** A subsidiary proposition assumed to be valid and used to demonstrate a principal proposition. **2.** A theme, argument, or subject indicated in a title. **3.** A glossed word or phrase in a glossary or other listing. [Lat. < Gk. *lēmma* < *lambanein,* to take.]

lem·ma[2] (lĕm'ə) *n. Bot.* The outer, lower bract enclosing the flower in a grass spikelet. [Gk., husk < *lepein,* to peel.]

lem·ming (lĕm'ĭng) *n.* Any of various rodents of the genus *Lemmus* and related genera, of northern regions, such as the European species *L. lemmus,* noted for its mass migrations into the sea. [Norw.]

lem·nis·cus (lĕm-nĭs'kəs) *n., pl.* **-nis·ci** (-nĭs'ī', -nĭs'kī', -nĭs'kē). A bundle of nerve fibers located in the brain. [NLat. < Lat., ribbon < Gk. *lēmniskos.*]

lem·on (lĕm'ən) *n.* **1. a.** A spiny evergreen tree, *Citrus limonia,* native to Asia, widely cultivated for its yellow, egg-shaped fruit. **b.** The fruit of the lemon, having an aromatic rind and acid, juicy pulp. **2.** Lemon yellow. **3.** *Informal.* One that is or proves to be unsatisfactory; washout. —*adj.* Brilliant, vivid yellow to greenish yellow. [ME *limon* < OFr. < Ar. *laymūn* < Pers. *līmūn.*]

lem·on·ade (lĕm'ə-nād') *n.* A drink made of lemon juice, water, and sugar.

lemon balm *n.* Balm (sense 3).

lem·on·grass (lĕm'ən-grăs') *n.* Any of several tropical grasses of the genus *Cymbopogon,* esp. *C. citratus,* yielding an aromatic oil used in perfumery and as flavoring.

lemon verbena *n.* An aromatic plant, *Lippia citriodora,* native to South America, cultivated for its fragrant foliage and flowers.

lem·on·y (lĕm'ə-nē) *adj.* Having the characteristic odor, flavor, or color of lemons.

lemon yellow *n.* A brilliant, vivid yellow to greenish yellow. **—lem'on-yel'low** *adj.*

lem·pi·ra (lĕm-pîr'ə) *n.* See table at **currency.** [Am. Sp., after *Lempira,* a 16th-cent. Indian leader who resisted the Spanish.]

le·mur (lē'mər) *n.* Any of several arboreal primates chiefly of the family Lemuridae, of Madagascar and adjacent islands, having large eyes, soft fur, and a long tail. [Lat. *lemures,* lemures.]

lem·u·res (lĕm'ə-rās', lĕm'yə-rēz') *pl.n.* In ancient Rome, the spirits of the dead considered as frightening specters. [Lat.]

Len·a·pe (lĕn'ə-pē) also **Len·i-Len·a·pe** or **Len·ni-Len·a·pe** (lĕn'ē-) *n.* The Delaware (senses 1, 2). **—Len'a·pe** *adj.*

lend (lĕnd) *v.* **lent** (lĕnt), **lend·ing, lends.** —*tr.* **1. a.** To give or allow the use of (something) temporarily on the condition that it or its equivalent will be returned. **b.** To provide (money) temporarily on the condition that the amount borrowed be returned, usually with an interest fee. **2.** To contribute; impart: *Books lent a feeling of warmth to the room.* **3.** To accommodate or offer (oneself) to; be suitable for: *laws that lend themselves to various interpretations.* —*intr.* To make a loan. —See Usage note at **loan.** [ME *lenden* < OE *lǣnan* < *lǣn,* loan.] **—lend'er** *n.*

lending library *n.* A library from which books may be borrowed or rented for a minimal fee.

length (lĕngkth, lĕngth) *n.* **1.** The state, quality, or fact of being long. **2.** The measurement of the extent of something along its greatest dimension: *the length of the boat.* **3.** A piece of something, often of a standard size, that is normally measured along the greatest dimension: *a length of cloth.* **4.** A measure of something used as a unit to estimate distances: *an arm's length.* **5.** The extent or distance of something from beginning to end as measured in space. **6.** The amount of time between specified moments; duration: *the length of a meeting.* **7.** An extent to which an action or policy is carried: *went to great lengths to prove him wrong.* **8. a.** The quantity of a vowel. **b.** The quantity of a syllable. **—*idiom.* at length. 1.** After some time; eventually. **2.** For a considerable time; fully. [ME < OE *lengðu.*]

length·en (lĕngk'thən, lĕng'-) *tr. & intr.v.* **-ened, -en·ing, -ens.** To make or become longer. **—length'en·er** *n.*

length·wise (lĕngkth'wīz', lĕngth'-) *adv. & adj.* Of, along, or referred to the direction of length.

length·y (lĕngk'thē, lĕng'-) *adj.* **-i·er, -i·est. 1.** Of considerable length, esp. in time. **2.** Excessively long; drawn-out. **—length'i·ly** *adv.* **—length'i·ness** *n.*

le·ni·ence (lē'nē-əns, lēn'yəns) *n.* Leniency.

le·ni·en·cy (lē'nē-ən-sē, lēn'yən-) *n., pl.* **-cies. 1.** The condition or quality of being lenient. **2.** A lenient act.

le·ni·ent (lē'nē-ənt, lēn'yənt) *adj.* **1.** Inclined not to be harsh; merciful or indulgent. **2.** Not austere or strict; generous:

leg-of-mutton
Leg-of-mutton sleeves

lei[1]

lemon

lemur

lens

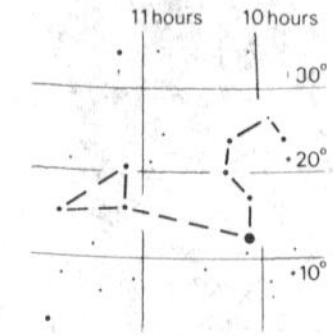

Leo

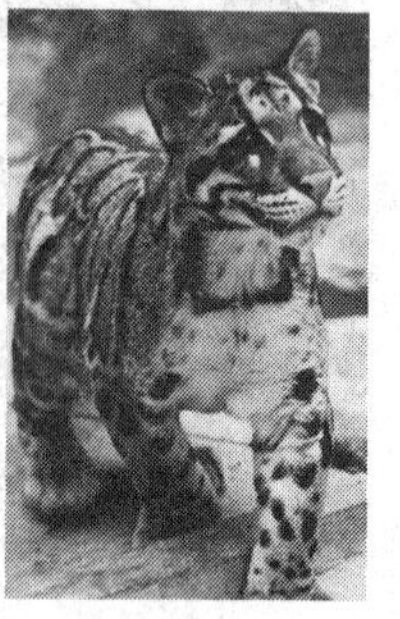
leopard
Clouded leopard

lenient rules. [Lat. *leniens, lenient-*, pr.part. of *lenire,* to pacify < *lenis,* soft.] —**le'ni·ent·ly** *adv.*

Len·i-Len·a·pe or **Len·ni-Len·a·pe** (lĕn'ē-lĕn'ə-pē) *n.* Variants of **Lenape.**

Len·in·ism (lĕn'ə-nĭz'əm) *n.* The theory and practice of proletarian revolution as developed by Lenin. —**Len'in·ist** *n.*

le·nis (lē'nĭs, lā'-) *adj.* Articulated with little or no aspiration, as the consonants *b* and *d* compared with *p* and *t.* [Lat., soft.]

len·i·tive (lĕn'ĭ-tĭv) *adj.* Easing or capable of easing pain or discomfort. —*n.* A lenitive medicine. [OFr. *lenitif* < Med. Lat. *lenitivus* < Lat. *lenire,* to soothe < *lenis,* soft.] —**len'i·tive·ly** *adv.*

len·i·ty (lĕn'ĭ-tē) *n.* The condition or quality of being lenient; leniency. [Lat. *lenitas* < *lenis,* soft.]

lens (lĕnz) *n.* **1. a.** A carefully ground or molded piece of glass, plastic, or other transparent material with opposite surfaces either or both of which are curved, by means of which light rays are refracted so that they converge or diverge to form an image. **b.** A combination of two or more such pieces, sometimes with other optical devices such as prisms, used to form an image for viewing or photographing. **2.** A device that causes radiation other than light to converge or diverge by an action analogous to that of an optical lens. **3.** A transparent, biconvex body of the eye between the iris and the vitreous humor that focuses light rays entering through the pupil to form an image on the retina. [NLat. < Lat., lentil (from a double convex lens's resemblance to a lentil).]

lent (lĕnt) *v.* Past tense and past participle of **lend.**

Lent (lĕnt) *n.* The 40 weekdays from Ash Wednesday until Easter observed by Christians as a season of fasting and penitence. [ME *lente,* spring, lent < OE *lencten.*]

Lent·en (lĕn'tən) *adj.* **1.** Of or pertaining to Lent. **2.** Characteristic of or appropriate to Lent; meager; somber.

len·ti·cel (lĕn'tĭ-sĕl') *n.* One of the small pores on the surface of the stems of woody plants that allows the passage of gases to and from the interior tissue. [NLat. *lenticella,* dim. of Lat. *lens,* lentil.] —**len'ti·cel'late** (-sĕl'ĭt) *adj.*

len·tic·u·lar (lĕn-tĭk'yə-lər) *adj.* **1.** Shaped like a biconvex lens. **2.** Of or pertaining to a lens. [Lat. *lenticularis,* like a lentil < *lenticula,* lentil, dim. of *lens,* lentil.]

len·ti·go (lĕn-tī'gō) *n., pl.* **-tig·i·nes** (-tĭj'ə-nēz'). **1.** A freckle. **2.** A nevus. [Lat. < *lens,* lentil.] —**len·tig'i·nous** (-tĭj'ə-nəs), **len·tig'i·nose'** (-nōs') *adj.*

len·til (lĕn'təl) *n.* **1.** A leguminous plant, *Lens esculenta* (or *L. culinaris*), native to the Old World, having pods containing edible seeds. **2.** The round, flattened seed of the lentil. [ME < OFr. *lentille* < Lat. *lenticula,* dim. of *lens,* lentil.]

len·tisk (lĕn'tĭsk') *n.* The mastic tree. [ME *lentiske* < Lat. *lentiscus.*]

len·to (lĕn'tō) *Mus.* —*adv.* Slowly. Used as a direction. —*adj.* Slow. —*n., pl.* **-tos.** A lento movement or passage. [Ital. < Lat. *lentus,* slow.]

Le·o (lē'ō) *n.* **1.** A constellation in the Northern Hemisphere near Cancer and Virgo, containing the bright stars Regulus and Denebola. **2.** The fifth sign of the zodiac. [Lat.]

Leo Minor *n.* A constellation in the Northern Hemisphere near Leo and Ursa Major.

le·one (lē-ōn') *n.* See table at **currency.** [After Sierra *Leone.*]

Le·o·nid (lē'ə-nĭd) *n., pl.* **Le·o·nids** or **Le·on·i·des** (lē-ŏn'ĭ-dēz'). A falling star of the meteor shower that annually recurs in mid-November. [< Lat. *Leo, Leon-,* the constellation Leo.]

le·o·nine (lē'ə-nīn') *adj.* Of, pertaining to, or characteristic of a lion. [ME < OFr. < Lat. *leoninus* < *leo,* lion.]

leop·ard (lĕp'ərd) *n.* **1. a.** A large feline mammal, *Panthera pardus,* of Africa and Asia, having a tawny coat with dark rosettelike markings and also a black color phase. **b.** Any of several felines, such as the cheetah or the snow leopard. **c.** The pelt or fur of a leopard. **2.** In heraldry, a lion in side view, having one forepaw raised and the head facing the observer. [ME < OFr. < LLat. *leopardus* < LGk. *leopardos* : Gk. *leōn,* lion + Gk. *pardos,* pard.]

leop·ard·ess (lĕp'ər-dĭs) *n.* A female leopard.

leopard lily *n.* A tall plant, *Lilium pardalinum,* of the western United States, having orange-red, dark-spotted flowers.

leopard moth *n.* A moth, *Zeuzera pyrina,* having spotted wings and larvae that damage trees by boring into the wood.

leop·ard's-bane (lĕp'ərdz-bān') *n.* **1.** Any of several widely cultivated plants of the genus *Doronicum,* having rayed yellow flowers. **2.** Any of several plants similar or related to a leopard's-bane.

le·o·tard (lē'ə-tärd') *n.* **1.** Often **leotards.** A snugly fitting, elastic one-piece garment that covers the torso, worn esp. by dancers or acrobats. **2. leotards.** Tights. [After Jules *Léotard* (1830–1870).]

Lep·cha (lĕp'chə) *n., pl.* **Lepcha** or **-chas. 1.** Any of a Mongoloid people living in Sikkim, India. **2.** The Tibeto-Burman language of the Lepcha.

lep·er (lĕp'ər) *n.* **1.** A person afflicted with leprosy. **2.** A person who is avoided by others; pariah. [ME < *lepre,* leprosy < OFr. < LLat. *lepra* < Gk. < *lepros,* scaly < *lepos, lepis,* scale.]

lepido- *pref.* Scale; flake: *lepidopteran.* [< Gk. *lepis, lepid-,* scale.]

le·pid·o·lite (lĭ-pĭd'l-īt') *n.* A lilac or pink to gray mica, $K_2Li_3Al_4Si_7O_2(OH, F)_3$, used as lithium ore and in ceramic production. [G. *Lepidolith* : *Lepido-,* lepido- + *-lith,* -lith.]

lep·i·dop·ter·a (lĕp'ĭ-dŏp'tər-ə) *n.* Plural of **lepidopteron.**

lep·i·dop·ter·an (lĕp'ĭ-dŏp'tər-ən) *n.* A lepidopterous insect. [NLat. *Lepidoptera,* order name : LEPIDO- + *pteron,* wing.]

lep·i·dop·ter·ist (lĕp'ĭ-dŏp'tər-ĭst) *n.* An entomologist specializing in the study of butterflies and moths.

lep·i·dop·ter·on (lĕp'ĭ-dŏp'tə-rŏn', -tər-ən) *n., pl.* **-ter·a** (-tər-ə). A lepidopteran.

lep·i·dop·ter·ous (lĕp'ĭ-dŏp'tər-əs) *adj.* Of or belonging to the order Lepidoptera, which includes insects such as the butterflies and moths having four wings covered with small scales.

lep·i·dote (lĕp'ĭ-dōt') *adj.* Covered with small, scurfy scales. [Gk. *lepidōtos* < *lepis,* scale.]

lep·o·rine (lĕp'ə-rīn', -ər-ĭn) *adj.* Of or characteristic of rabbits or hares. [Lat. *leporinus* < *lepus,* hare.]

lep·re·chaun (lĕp'rĭ-kŏn', -kôn') *n.* One of a race of elves in Irish folklore who can reveal hidden treasure to someone who catches him. [Ir. Gael. *lupracán* < MIr. *luchrupán* < OIr. *luchorpán* : *lū,* small + *corp,* body < Lat. *corpus.*]

lep·ro·sar·i·um (lĕp'rə-sâr'ē-əm) *n., pl.* **-i·ums** or **-i·a** (-ē-ə). A hospital for the treatment of lepers. [Med. Lat. < LLat. *leprosus,* leprous. —see LEPROUS.]

lep·rose (lĕp'rōs') *adj.* Scurfy or scaly; leprous. [LLat. *leprosus.* —see LEPROUS.]

lep·ro·sy (lĕp'rə-sē) *n.* A chronic, infectious, granulomatous disease occurring almost exclusively in tropical and subtropical regions, caused by a bacillus, *Mycobacterium leprae,* and ranging in severity from noncontagious and spontaneously remitting forms to contagious, malignant forms with progressive anesthesia, paralysis, ulceration, nutritive disturbances, gangrene, and mutilation. [< LEPROUS.] —**lep·rot'ic** (lĕ-prŏt'ĭk) *adj.*

lep·rous (lĕp'rəs) *adj.* **1.** Having leprosy. **2.** Of, relating to, or resembling leprosy. **3.** *Biol.* Having or consisting of loose, scurfy scales. [ME < OFr. *lepros* < LLat. *leprosus* < *lepra,* leprosy. —see LEPER.] —**lep'rous·ly** *adv.*

-lepsy *suff.* Fit; seizure: *narcolepsy.* [Gk. *-lēpsia* < *lēpsis,* seizure < *lambanein,* to take.]

lep·ta (lĕp'tə) *n.* Plural of **lepton**[1].

lepto- or **lept-** *pref.* Slender; thin; fine: *leptocephalus.* [< Gk. *leptos,* fine, thin < *lepein,* to peel.]

lep·to·ceph·a·lus (lĕp'tə-sĕf'ə-ləs) *n., pl.* **-li** (-lī'). One of the slender, transparent larvae of eels and certain other fishes.

lep·ton[1] (lĕp'tŏn') *n., pl.* **-ta** (-tə). See table at **currency.** [Mod. Gk. < Gk., small coin < *leptos,* fine, small < *lepein,* to peel.]

lep·ton[2] (lĕp'tŏn') *n.* Any of a family of subatomic particles including the electron, the muon, and their associated neutrinos, all having spin equal to $^1/_2$ and masses less than those of the mesons. —**lep·ton'ic** (-tŏn'ĭk) *adj.*

lepton number *n.* A number calculated by subtracting the number of antileptons from the number of leptons in a system of elementary particles.

lep·to·some (lĕp'tə-sōm') *n.* A person with a slender, thin, or frail body. [G. *Leptosom* : Gk. *leptos,* slender + Gk. *sōma,* body.] —**lep'to·so·mat'ic** (-sō-măt'ĭk) *adj.*

Le·pus (lē'pəs) *n.* A constellation in the Southern Hemisphere near Orion and Columba. [Lat. *lepus,* hare.]

Les·bi·an (lĕz'bē-ən) *n.* **1.** A native or resident of Lesbos. **2. lesbian.** A woman who is a homosexual. **3.** The ancient Greek dialect of Lesbos. —**Les'bi·an** *adj.*

lese maj·es·ty also **lèse ma·jes·té** (lēz' măj'ĭ-stē) *n.* **1.** An offense or crime committed against the ruler or supreme power of a state. **2.** An affront to another's dignity. [OFr. *lese majeste* < Lat. *laesa majestas* : *laesa,* p.part. of *laedere,* to injure + *majestas,* majesty. —see MAJESTY.]

le·sion (lē'zhən) *n.* **1.** A wound or injury. **2.** A circumscribed pathological alteration of tissue. **3.** A point or patch of a skin disease. [ME *lesioun* < OFr. *lesion* < Lat. *laesio* < *laedere,* to injure.]

les·pe·de·za (lĕs'pĭ-dē'zə) *n.* A plant of the genus *Lespedeza,* which includes the bush clovers. [NLat. *Lespedeza,* genus name, after V.M. *Lespedez* (fl. 1785), Spanish governor of East Florida.]

less (lĕs) *adj.* **1.** Not as great in amount or quantity: *less time to spare.* **2.** Lower in importance, esteem, or rank: *no less a person than the First Lady.* **3.** Consisting of a smaller number: *less than ten.* —*prep.* Minus; subtracting: *Five less two is three.* —*adv.* Comparative of **little.** To a smaller extent, degree, or frequency: *less happy.* —*n.* A smaller amount: *received less than she asked for.* —*pron.* Fewer things or persons: *Many things begin badly; less end well.* —*idioms.* **less than.** Not at all: *a less than favorable outlook.* **much** (or **still**) **less.** Certainly not: *I'm not blaming anyone, much less you.* —See Usage note at **few.** [ME *lesse* < OE *lǣssa.*]

-less *suff.* **1.** Without; lacking: *blameless.* **2.** Unable to act or be acted upon in a specified way: *dauntless.* [ME *-lesse* < OE *-lēas* < *lēas,* without.]

les·see (lĕ-sē') *n.* One that holds a lease. [ME < AN < OFr. *lesser,* to lease.]

less·en (lĕs'ən) *v.* **-ened, -en·ing, -ens.** —*tr.* **1.** To cause to decrease; make less. **2.** To make little of; belittle. —*intr.* To

leotard

become less; decrease. [ME *lessenen* < *lessen,* to lessen < *lesse,* less.]

less·er (lĕs′ər) *adj.* **1.** Smaller in amount, value, or importance, esp. in a comparison between two things: *a lesser evil.* **2.** Of a smaller size than other similar forms: *the lesser anteater.* [ME < *lesse,* less.]

lesser celandine *n.* A plant, *Ranunculus ficaria,* having heart-shaped leaves and yellow flowers.

les·son (lĕs′ən) *n.* **1.** Something to be learned. **2. a.** A period of instruction; class. **b.** An assignment or exercise in which something is to be learned. **c.** An act or instance of instructing; teaching. **3. a.** An experience, example, or observation that imparts beneficial new knowledge or wisdom. **b.** The knowledge or wisdom acquired. **4.** A rebuke or reprimand. **5.** A reading from the Bible or other sacred writing as part of a religious service. *—tr.v.* **-soned, -son·ing, -sons. 1.** To teach a lesson to; instruct. **2.** To rebuke; reprimand. [ME *lessoun* < OFr. *leson* < Lat. *lectio,* a reading. —see LECTION.]

les·sor (lĕs′ôr′, lĕ-sôr′) *n.* One who lets property under a lease. [ME *lessour* < AN < OFr. *lesser,* to lease.]

lest (lĕst) *conj.* For fear that: *tiptoed lest the guard should hear him; anxious lest she should become ill.* [ME < OE *ðȳ lǣs ðe.*]

let¹ (lĕt) *v.* **let, let·ting, lets.** *—tr.* **1.** To grant permission to; allow: *She let him continue.* **2.** To cause to; make: *let the news be known.* **3.** Used as an auxiliary in the imperative: **a.** In order to express a command, request, or proposal: *Let's finish the job! Let x equal y.* **b.** In order to express a warning or threat: *Just let her try!* **4.** To permit to enter, proceed, or depart: *let the dog in.* **5.** To release from or as if from confinement: *let the air out of the balloon.* **6.** To rent or lease: *let rooms.* **7.** To award, esp. after bids have been submitted: *let the construction job to a new firm.* *—intr.* **1.** To become rented or leased. **2.** To be or become assigned, as to a contractor. ***—phrasal verbs.*** **let down. 1.** To withdraw support from; forsake. **2.** To fail to meet the expectations of; disappoint. **let on. 1.** To allow it to be known: *Don't let on that you know me.* **2.** To pretend. **let up. 1.** To make less; diminish. **2.** To stop; cease. **3.** To be or become more lenient to. ***—idiom.*** **let it all hang out.** *Slang.* To speak or act openly and candidly. [ME *leten* < OE *lǣtan.*]

Usage: In colloquial speech *let's* has come increasingly to be used as a mere indicator that a suggestion is being proffered, and its connection with the more formal *let us* has become correspondingly attenuated, so that one hears usages like *let's us go, don't let's get all excited,* and *let's get yourself ready for the doctor.* These usages are best avoided in formal writing. See also Usage note at **leave.**

let² (lĕt) *n.* **1.** Something that hinders; obstacle: *free to investigate without let or hindrance.* **2.** A stroke in tennis and other net games that is invalid and must be repeated. *—tr.v.* **let·ted** or **let, let·ting, lets.** *Archaic.* To hinder or obstruct. [ME < *letten,* to hinder < OE *lettan.*]

-let *suff.* **1.** Small one: *craterlet.* **2.** Something worn on: *armlet.* [ME *-lette* < OFr. *-elet.*]

letch also **lech** (lĕch) *n.* A strong desire or craving, esp. one of a sexual nature. [Perh. back-formation < obs. *letcher,* var. of LECHER.]

let·down (lĕt′doun′) *n.* **1.** A decrease, decline, or relaxation, as of effort or energy. **2.** A disappointment. **3.** The descent made by an airplane in order to land.

le·thal (lē′thəl) *adj.* **1.** Capable of causing death. **2.** Of, pertaining to, or causing death. **3.** Extremely harmful; devastating: *a lethal slur on his honesty.* [Lat. *lethalis* < *lethum,* death.] **—le·thal′i·ty** (lē-thăl′ĭ-tē) *n.* **—le′thal·ly** *adv.*

le·thar·gic (lə-thär′jĭk) *adj.* Of, causing, or characterized by lethargy. **—le·thar′gi·cal·ly** *adv.*

leth·ar·gy (lĕth′ər-jē) *n., pl.* **-gies. 1.** Sluggish indifference; apathy. **2.** A state of unconsciousness resembling deep sleep. [ME *letargie* < OFr. *letargie* < Med. Lat. *litargia* < Lat. *lethargia* < Gk. *lēthargia* < *lethargos,* forgetful < *lēthē,* forgetfulness.]

Synonyms: *lethargy, lassitude, sluggishness, torpor, stupor, languor.* These nouns refer to conditions in which a person is unable or disinclined to be active, physically or mentally. *Lethargy* often implies the operation of physically disabling factors, such as illness or overwork, or it can reflect apathy or indifference. *Lassitude* implies inactivity or loss of vigor resulting from physical or mental strain. *Sluggishness* is slowness of body or mind, produced by ailments or indolence. *Torpor* suggests the suspension of physical and mental activity characteristic of an animal in hibernation. *Stupor* is marked by cessation or great decrease of mental activity or feeling, often produced by sleepiness, illness, or the effect of alcohol or narcotics. *Languor* is lack of vigor or spirit characteristic of one who is indolent or satiated by overindulgence in luxury or pleasure.

le·the (lē′thē) *n.* **1. Lethe.** *Gk. Myth.* The river of forgetfulness in Hades. **2.** Oblivion; loss of memory. [Gk. *lēthē.*] **—le′the·an** (lē′thē-ən) *adj.*

Le·to (lē′tō′) *n.* *Gk. Myth.* A consort of Zeus and the mother of Apollo and Artemis. [Gk. *Lētō.*]

let's (lĕts). Let us.

Lett (lĕt) *n.* A native or inhabitant of Latvia; Latvian. [G. *Lette* < Latvian *Latvi.*]

let·ter (lĕt′ər) *n.* **1.** A written symbol or character representing a speech sound and being a component of an alphabet. **2.** A written or printed communication directed to an individual or organization. **3.** Often **letters.** A certified document granting rights to its bearer. **4.** The literal meaning of something: *the letter of the law.* **5. letters.** *(used with a sing. verb).* Literary culture or learning. **6. a.** A piece of type that prints a single character. **b.** A specific style of type. **c.** The characters in one style of type. **7.** An emblem in the shape of the initial of a school awarded to athletes. *—v.* **-tered, -ter·ing, -ters.** *—tr.* **1.** To write letters on. **2.** To write in letters. *—intr.* **1.** To write or form letters. **2.** To earn an athletic letter: *She lettered in three sports in college.* [ME < OFr. *lettre* < Lat. *littera.*] **—let′ter·er** *n.*

letter bomb *n.* An explosive mailed in an envelope to a designated victim.

let·ter·box (lĕt′ər-bŏks′) *n.* A mailbox.

letter carrier *n.* A mailman.

let·tered (lĕt′ərd) *adj.* **1. a.** Educated to read and write; literate. **b.** Erudite; learned. **2.** Of or relating to literacy or learning. **3.** Inscribed or marked with or as if with letters.

let·ter·form (lĕt′ər-fôrm′) *n.* The development or design of the shape of an alphabet letter.

let·ter·head (lĕt′ər-hĕd′) *n.* **1.** The heading at the top of a sheet of letter paper, usually consisting of a name and address. **2.** Stationery imprinted with a letterhead.

let·ter·ing (lĕt′ər-ĭng) *n.* **1.** The act, process, or art of forming letters. **2.** Letters inscribed, as on a sign.

letter of credit *n.* A letter issued by a bank authorizing the bearer to draw a stated amount of money from the issuing bank, its branches, or other associated banks or agencies.

let·ter-per·fect (lĕt′ər-pûr′fĭkt) *adj.* Correct to the last detail.

let·ter·press (lĕt′ər-prĕs′) *n.* **1. a.** The process of printing from a raised inked surface. **b.** Something printed in this fashion. **2.** The text, as of a book, distinct from illustrations or other ornamentation.

letters of administration *n.* A legal document entrusting an individual with the administration of the estate of a decedent.

letters of credence also **letter of credence** *n.* An official document conveying the credentials of a diplomatic envoy to a foreign government.

letters of marque also **letter of marque** (märk) *n.* **1.** A document issued by a nation allowing a private citizen to seize citizens or goods of another nation. **2.** A document issued by a nation allowing a private citizen to equip a ship with arms in order to attack enemy ships. [ME *lettres of marque* < OFr. *marque,* reprisal, of Germanic orig.]

letters patent *pl.n.* A document issued by a government to a patentee granting an exclusive right to the enjoyment or possession of an invention.

letters testamentary *pl.n.* A document issued by a probate court or officer informing an executor of a will of his appointment and empowering him to discharge his responsibilities.

Let·tish (lĕt′ĭsh) *adj.* Of or relating to the Latvians or their language. *—n.* Latvian (sense 2).

let·tuce (lĕt′əs) *n.* **1. a.** Any of various plants of the genus *Lactuca,* esp. *L. sativa,* cultivated for its edible leaves. **b.** The leaves of *L. sativa,* eaten as salad. **2.** *Slang.* Paper money. [ME *lettuse* < OFr. *letues,* pl. of *laitue* < Lat. *lactuca* < *lac,* milk (from its milky juice).]

lettuce

let·up (lĕt′ŭp′) *n.* **1.** A reduction in pace, force, or intensity; slowdown. **2.** A temporary stop; pause.

le·u (lĕ′o͞o) *n., pl.* **lei** (lā). See table at **currency.** [Rum. < Lat. *leo,* lion.]

leuc- *pref.* Variant of **leuko-.**

leu·cine (lo͞o′sēn′) *n.* An essential amino acid, $C_6H_{13}NO_2$, derived from the hydrolysis of protein by pancreatic enzymes and used as a nutrient. [LEUC(O)- + -INE.]

leu·cite (lo͞o′sīt′) *n.* A white or gray mineral, essentially $KAl(SiO_3)_2$. [G. *Leucit* : *leuc-,* leuko- + *-it,* -ite.] **—leu·cit′ic** (-sĭt′ĭk) *adj.*

leu·co- *pref.* Variant of **leuko-.**

leu·co·plast (lo͞o′kə-plăst′) also **leu·co·plas·tid** (lo͞o′kə-plăs′tĭd) *n.* A colorless plastid in the cytoplasm of plant cells around which starch collects. [LEUCO- + PLAST(ID).]

leuk- *pref.* Variant of **leuko-.**

leu·ke·mi·a (lo͞o-kē′mē-ə) *n.* Any of a group of usually fatal diseases of the reticuloendothelial system involving uncontrolled proliferation of leukocytes. **—leu·ke′mic** (-kē′mĭk) *adj.* & *n.*

leuko- or **leuk-** also **leuco-** or **leuc-** *pref.* **1.** White; colorless: *leukoderma.* **2.** Leukocyte: *leukopenia.* [NLat. < Gk. *leukos,* clear, white.]

leu·ko·cyte also **leu·co·cyte** (lo͞o′kə-sīt′) *n.* Any of the white or colorless nucleated cells occurring in blood. **—leu′ko·cyt′ic** (-sĭt′ĭk) *adj.* **—leu′ko·cy′toid′** *adj.*

leu·ko·cy·to·sis also **leu·co·cy·to·sis** (lo͞o′kə-sī-tō′sĭs) *n., pl.* **-ses** (-sēz′). A large increase in the number of leukocytes in the blood. **—leu′ko·cy·tot′ic** (-tŏt′ĭk) *adj.*

leu·ko·der·ma also **leu·co·der·ma** (lo͞o′kə-dûr′mə) *n.* Partial or total lack of skin pigmentation. **—leu′ko·der′mal, leu′ko·der′mic** *adj.*

leu·ko·ma also **leu·co·ma** (lo͞o-kō′mə) *n.* A dense, white

opacity of the cornea of the eye. [Gk. *leukōma* < *leukoun,* to make white < *leukos,* white.]
leu·ko·pe·ni·a also **leu·co·pe·ni·a** (lo͞o'kə-pē'nē-ə) *n.* An abnormally low number of leukocytes in the circulating blood. **—leu'ko·pe'nic** (-pē'nĭk) *adj.*
leu·ko·poi·e·sis also **leu·co·poi·e·sis** (lo͞o'kə-poi-ē'sĭs) *n.* The formation and development of leukocytes. **—leu'ko·poi·et'ic** (-ĕt'ĭk) *adj.*
leu·kor·rhe·a also **leu·cor·rhe·a** (lo͞o'kə-rē'ə) *n.* A vaginal discharge containing mucus and pus cells. **—leu'kor·rhe'al** (-rē'əl) *adj.*
lev (lĕf) *n., pl.* **lev·a** (lĕv'ə). See table at **currency.** [Bulgarian.]
lev– *pref.* Variant of **levo-.**
lev·a (lĕv'ə) *n.* Plural of **lev.**
Lev·al·loi·si·an (lĕv'ə-loi'zē-ən) *adj.* Of or relating to a western European stage in lower Paleolithic culture, known from the method of striking off flake tools from pieces of flint. [After *Levallois*-Perret, a district of France.]
lev·al·lor·phan (lĕv'ə-lôr'făn', -fən) *n.* A morphine-related drug used to counteract morphine poisoning. [LEV(OROTATORY) + ALL(IUM) + (M)ORPH(INE) + -AN.]
le·vant (lə-vănt') *n.* A type of heavy, coarse-grained morocco leather often used in bookbinding. [After *Levant,* countries bordering the eastern Mediterranean.]
le·vant·er (lə-văn'tər) *n.* **1.** A strong easterly wind of the Mediterranean area. **2. Levanter.** A native of the Levant.
le·va·tor (lə-vā'tər) *n., pl.* **lev·a·to·res** (lĕv'ə-tôr'ēz, -tōr'-). **1.** *Anat.* A muscle that raises a bodily part. **2.** A surgical instrument for lifting the depressed part of a fractured skull. [< Lat. *levare, levat-,* to raise. —see LEVER.]

levee[1]

lev·ee[1] (lĕv'ē) *n.* **1.** An embankment raised to prevent a river from overflowing. **2.** A small ridge or raised area bordering an irrigated field. **3.** A landing place on a river; pier. [Fr. *levée* < OFr. *levee* < *lever,* to raise. —see LEVER.]
lev·ee[2] (lĕv'ē, lə-vē', -vā') *n.* **1.** A reception held by a monarch or other high-ranking person on arising from bed. **2.** A formal reception, as at a court. [Fr. *levé,* var. of *lever,* a rising < *lever,* to rise < OFr. —see LEVER.]

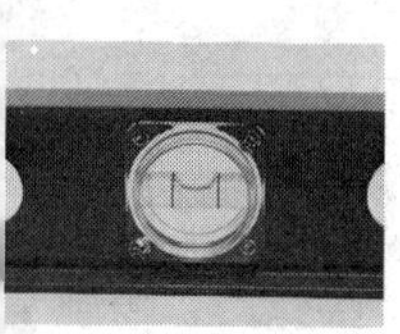
level

lev·el (lĕv'əl) *n.* **1.** Relative position or rank on a scale: *a high level of achievement.* **2.** A natural or proper position, place, or stage: *finally found his own level.* **3.** Position along a vertical axis; height or depth: *a platform at knee level.* **4. a.** A horizontal line or plane at right angles to the plumb. **b.** The position or height of such a line or plane. **5.** A flat, horizontal surface. **6.** A land area of uniform elevation. **7. a.** An instrument for ascertaining whether a surface is horizontal, consisting essentially of an encased, liquid-filled tube containing an air bubble that moves to a center window when the instrument is set on a horizontal plane. **b.** Such a device combined with a telescope and used in surveying. **c.** A computation of the difference in elevation between two points by using such a device. **8.** *Computer Sci.* A bit, element, channel, or row of information. *—adj.* **1.** Having a flat, smooth surface. **2.** On a horizontal plane. **3.** Being at the same height or position as another; even. **4.** Being at the same degree of rank, standing, or advantage as another; equal. **5.** Without abrupt variations; steady: *spoke in a level tone.* **6.** Rational and measured: *came to a level appraisal of the situation.* *—v.* **-eled, -el·ing, -els** or **-elled, -el·ling, -els.** *—tr.* **1.** To make horizontal, flat, or even: *leveled the lawn with a roller.* **2.** To tear down; raze. **3.** To knock down with or as if with a blow. **4.** To place on the same level; equalize. **5.** To aim along a horizontal plane: *leveled the gun at the target.* **6.** To direct emphatically or forcefully toward someone: *leveled charges of dishonesty.* **7.** To measure the different elevations of (a tract of land) with a level. *—intr.* **1.** To render persons or things equal; equalize. **2.** To aim a weapon horizontally. **3.** *Informal.* To be frank and open. ***—phrasal verb.* level off. 1.** To move toward stability or consistency. **2.** To maneuver an aircraft into flight that is parallel to the surface of the earth after gaining or losing altitude. *—adv.* Along a flat or even line or plane. ***—idioms.* (one's) level best.** The best one can do in an earnest attempt. **on the level.** *Informal.* Without deception; honest. [ME, an instrument to check that a surface is horizontal < OFr. *livel* < Lat. *libella,* dim. of *libra,* balance.] **—lev'el·ly** *adv.* **—lev'el·ness** *n.*

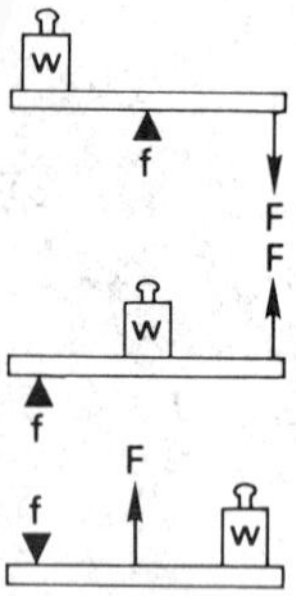

lever
Three basic types of lever; **f** is the fulcrum and **F** is the force needed to raise a weight **W**

Synonyms: *level, flat, plane, even, smooth, flush.* These adjectives are applicable to surfaces in which there are no variations, or no significant variations, in the form of elevations or depressions. *Level* implies being horizontal or parallel with the line of the horizon. *Flat* often refers to such a horizontal surface, but can also be applied to one that is oblique or even vertical. *Plane* and *even* refer to flat surfaces that are wholly without elevations or depressions and demonstrably so either by the application of scientific principles, in the case of *plane,* or by observation, in the case of *even. Smooth* describes a surface in which the absence of even slight irregularities can be established by sight or touch. *Flush* is applied to a surface that is on an exact level with an adjoining one, forming a continuous surface.
level compensator *n.* An automatic gain control device used in the receiving equipment of telegraphic circuits.
level crossing *n. Chiefly Brit.* A grade crossing.
lev·el·er also **lev·el·ler** (lĕv'ə-lər) *n.* **1.** One that levels. **2. a.** One who advocates the abolition of social inequities. **b. Leveller.** A member of an English radical political movement active in the 1640's that advocated universal male suffrage, parliamentary democracy, and religious tolerance.
lev·el·head·ed (lĕv'əl-hĕd'ĭd) *adj.* Characteristically self-composed and sensible. **—lev'el·head'ed·ness** *n.*
leveling rod *n.* A graduated pole or stick with a movable marker, used with a surveyor's level to measure differences in elevation.
level of significance *n.* The probability of a false rejection of the null hypothesis in a statistical test.
lev·er (lĕv'ər, lē'vər) *n.* **1.** A simple machine consisting of a rigid body, typically a metal bar, pivoted on a fixed fulcrum. **2.** A projecting handle used to adjust or operate a mechanism. **3.** A means of accomplishing; tool: *used his friendship as a lever to obtain advancement.* *—tr.v.* **-ered, -er·ing, -ers.** To move or lift with or as if with a lever. [ME < OFr. *levier* < *lever,* to raise < Lat. *levare* < *levis,* light.]
lev·er·age (lĕv'ər-ĭj, lē'vər-) *n.* **1. a.** The action of a lever. **b.** The mechanical advantage of a lever. **2.** Power to act effectively: *Being on two committees gave him leverage.* **3.** The use of credit in order to improve one's speculative capacity. *—tr.v.* **-aged, -ag·ing, -ag·es. 1. a.** To provide (a company) with leverage. **b.** To supplement (money, for example) with leverage. **2.** To affect, as if by leverage: *a lifestyle leveraged by business responsibilities.*
lev·er·et (lĕv'ər-ĭt) *n.* A young hare, esp. one less than a year old. [ME < AN, dim. of *levre,* hare, var. of OFr. *lievre* < Lat. *lepus.*]
Le·vi (lē'vī') *n.* **1.** In the Old Testament, a son of Jacob and Leah. **2.** A tribe of Israel descended from Levi. [Heb.]
lev·i·a·ble (lĕv'ē-ə-bəl) *adj.* Capable of being levied or levied on.
le·vi·a·than (lə-vī'ə-thən) *n.* **1.** A monstrous sea creature mentioned in the Old Testament. **2.** A very large animal. **3.** Something unusually large of its kind. [ME < LLat. < Heb. *libhyēthĕn.*]
lev·i·gate (lĕv'ĭ-gāt') *tr.v.* **-gat·ed, -gat·ing, -gates. 1.** To make into a smooth, fine powder, as by grinding when moist. **2.** To suspend in a liquid. **3.** To make smooth; polish. *—adj.* (-gāt', -gĭt). Smooth. [Lat. *levigare, levigat-* : *levis,* smooth + *agere,* to make.] **—lev'i·ga'tion** *n.*
lev·in (lĕv'ĭn) *n. Archaic.* Lightning. [ME.]
lev·i·rate (lĕv'ər-ĭt, -ə-rāt', lē'vər-ĭt, -və-rāt') *n.* The practice of marrying the widow of one's brother, as required by ancient Hebrew law. [< Lat. *levir,* husband's brother.] **—lev'i·rat'ic** (-răt'ĭk), **lev'i·rat'i·cal** *adj.*
Le·vi's (lē'vīz'). A trademark for close-fitting trousers of heavy denim.
lev·i·tate (lĕv'ĭ-tāt') *intr. & tr.v.* **-tat·ed, -tat·ing, -tates.** To rise or cause to rise into the air and float in apparent defiance of gravity. [< LEVITY.] **—lev'i·ta'tion** *n.* **—lev'i·ta'tion·al** *adj.* **—lev'i·ta'tor** *n.*
Le·vite (lē'vīt') *n.* One of the tribe of Levi, assistants to the Temple priests. [ME < LLat. *Levites* < Gk. *Leuitēs* < *Leui,* Levi < Heb. *Lēwī.*]
Le·vit·i·cal (lə-vĭt'ĭ-kəl) also **Le·vit·ic** (-vĭt'ĭk) *adj.* **1.** Of or relating to the Levites. **2.** Of or relating to Leviticus.
Le·vit·i·cus (lə-vĭt'ĭ-kəs) *n.* See table at **Bible.**
lev·i·ty (lĕv'ĭ-tē) *n., pl.* **-ties. 1.** The state or quality of being light; buoyancy. **2.** A light manner or attitude, esp. when inappropriate; frivolity. **3.** Changeableness; inconstancy. [Lat. *levitas* < *levis,* light.]
le·vo (lē'vō) *adj.* Levorotatory.
levo– or **lev–** *pref.* **1.** To the left: *levorotatory.* **2.** Levorotatory: *levulose.* [Fr. *lévo-* < Lat. *laevus,* left.]
le·vo·ro·ta·tion (lē'və-rō-tā'shən) *n.* A counterclockwise rotation, esp. of the plane of polarized light.
le·vo·ro·ta·to·ry (lē'və-rō'tə-tôr'ē, -tōr'ē) also **le·vo·ro·ta·ry** (-rō'tə-rē) *adj.* **1.** Turning or rotating the plane of polarization of light to the left or counterclockwise. **2.** *Chem.* Of or pertaining to a chemical solution that rotates the plane of polarized light to the left or counterclockwise.
lev·u·lose (lĕv'yə-lōs', -lōz') *n.* Fructose. [LEV- + *-ul* (of unknown orig.) + -OSE.]
lev·y (lĕv'ē) *v.* **-ied, -y·ing, -ies.** *—tr.* **1.** To impose or collect (a tax, for example). **2.** To draft into military service. **3.** To declare and carry on (a war). *—intr.* To confiscate property, esp. in accordance with a legal judgment. *—n., pl.* **-ies. 1.** The act or process of levying. **2.** Money, property, or troops levied. [< ME *leve,* levy, tax < OFr. *levee* < *lever,* to raise. —see LEVER.] **—lev'i·er** *n.*
lewd (lo͞od) *adj.* **-er, -est. 1. a.** Preoccupied with sex and sexual desire; lustful. **b.** Obscene; indecent. **2.** *Obs.* Wicked. [ME *leued,* unlearned, lascivious < OE *lǣwede,* ignorant.] **—lewd'ly** *adv.* **—lewd'ness** *n.*

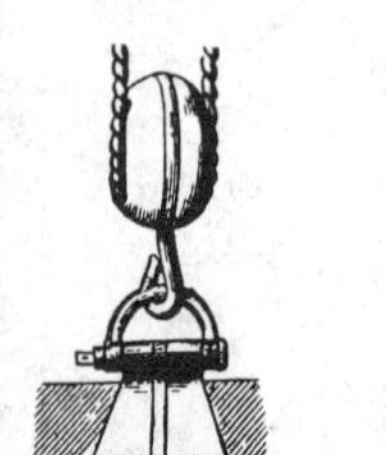
lewis

lew·is (lo͞o'ĭs) *n.* A dovetailed iron tenon made of several parts and designed to fit into a dovetail mortise in a large stone so that it can be lifted by a hoisting apparatus. [Perh. from the name *Lewis.*]
lew·is·ite (lo͞o'ĭ-sīt') *n.* An oily, colorless to violet or brown liquid, $C_2H_2AsCl_3$, used to make a highly toxic military gas. [After Winford Lee *Lewis* (1878–1943).]
lew·is·son (lo͞o'ĭ-sən) *n.* A lewis.
lex (lĕks) *n., pl.* **le·ges** (lē'jēz'). Law. [Lat.]
lex·eme (lĕk'sēm') *n.* A meaningful speech form that is one of the vocabulary items of a language.

lex·i·cal (lĕk′sĭ-kəl) *adj.* **1.** Of or relating to the vocabulary, words, or morphemes of a language. **2.** Of or relating to lexicography or a lexicon. [LEXIC(ON) + -AL.] **—lex′·i·cal′i·ty** (-kăl′ĭ-tē) *n.* **—lex′i·cal·ly** *adv.*

lex·i·cog·ra·phy (lĕk′sĭ-kŏg′rə-fē) *n.* The process or work of writing or compiling a dictionary. **—lex′i·cog′ra·pher** *n.* **—lex′i·co·graph′ic** (-kə-grăf′ĭk), **lex′i·co·graph′i·cal** *adj.* **—lex′i·co·graph′i·cal·ly** *adv.*

lex·i·col·o·gy (lĕk′sĭ-kŏl′ə-jē) *n.* A branch of linguistics that deals with the lexical component of language. **—lex′i·co·log′i·cal** (-kə-lŏj′ĭ-kəl) *adj.* **—lex′i·co·log′i·cal·ly** *adv.* **—lex′i·col′o·gist** *n.*

lex·i·con (lĕk′sĭ-kŏn′) *n.* **1.** A dictionary. **2.** A stock of terms used in a particular profession, subject, or style; vocabulary. **3.** *Ling.* The morphemes of a language. [LGk. *lexikon* < Gk. *lexikos,* of words < *lexis,* word < *legein,* to speak.]

ley (lā, lē) *n.* Variant of **lea.**

Ley·den jar (līd′n) *n.* An early form of capacitor consisting of a glass jar lined inside and out with tinfoil and having a conducting rod connected to the inner foil lining and passing out of the jar through an insulated stopper. [After *Leyden,* Netherlands.]

Lha·sa ap·so (lä′sə ăp′sō, lăs′ə) *n.* A small dog of a Tibetan breed, having a long, straight coat. [After *Lhasa,* Tibet + Tibetan *apso,* Lhasa apso.]

li (lē) *n., pl.* **li.** A Chinese measure of distance measuring about 1/3 of a mile or 0.52 kilometers. [Chin. (Mandarin) *li*^{3}.]

Li The symbol for the element lithium.

li·a·bil·i·ty (lī′ə-bĭl′ĭ-tē) *n., pl.* **-ties. 1.** The state of being liable. **2. a.** Something for which one is liable; an obligation or debt. **b. liabilities.** The financial obligations entered in the balance sheet of a business enterprise. **3.** Something that holds one back; handicap. **4.** Likelihood.

li·a·ble (lī′ə-bəl) *adj.* **1.** Legally obligated; responsible: *liable for military service.* **2.** Susceptible; subject: *liable to criminal charges.* **3.** Likely: *It is liable to rain today.* [Prob. AN **liable* < OFr. *lier,* to bind < Lat. *ligare.*]

li·ai·son (lē′ā-zŏn′, lē-ā′-) *n.* **1. a.** Communication between different groups or units of an organization. **b.** A channel or means of communication: *served as the President's liaison with Congress.* **2. a.** A close relationship, connection, or link. **b.** An adulterous relationship; affair. **3.** The pronunciation of the usually silent final consonant of a word when followed by a word beginning with a vowel. [Fr. < OFr. < *lier,* to bind. —see LIABLE.]

li·an·a (lē-ä′nə, -ăn′ə) also **li·ane** (-än′, -ăn′) *n.* Any of various high-climbing, usually woody vines common in the tropics. [Fr. *liane.*]

li·ang (lē-äng′) *n., pl.* **liang** or **li·angs.** A former Chinese unit of weight, equivalent to 1/16 of the catty, approximately 1 1/3 ounces or 37.24 grams. [Chin. (Mandarin) *liang*^{3}.]

li·ar (lī′ər) *n.* One who tells lies.

lib (lĭb) *n. Informal.* Liberation (sense 2).

li·ba·tion (lī-bā′shən) *n.* **1. a.** The pouring of a liquid offering as a religious ritual. **b.** The liquid poured. **2.** *Informal.* A beverage, esp. an intoxicating beverage. [ME *libacioun* < Lat. *libatio* < *libare,* to pour out as an offering.] **—li·ba′tion·ar′y** (-shə-nĕr′ē) *adj.*

lib·ber (lĭb′ər) *n. Informal.* One who is a proponent of liberation: *a women's libber.*

li·bec·cio (lĭ-bĕch′ē-ō′, -bĕch′ō) *n.* A southwest wind in Italy. [Ital. < Lat. *Libs,* the southwest wind < Gk. *Lips.*]

li·bel (lī′bəl) *n.* **1.** *Law.* **a.** A written, printed, or pictorial statement that damages a person by defaming his character or reputation, damaging him in his occupation, or exposing him to public ridicule. **b.** The act or tort of presenting such a statement to the public. **2.** The written claims presented by a plaintiff in an action at admiralty law or to an ecclesiastical court. *—tr.v.* **-beled, -bel·ing, -bels** or **-belled, -bel·ling, -bels.** To make or publish a libel about. [ME, litigant's written complaint < OFr. *libelle* < Lat. *libellus,* petition, dim. of *liber,* book.] **—li′bel·er, li′bel·ist** *n.*

li·bel·ant also **li·bel·lant** (lī′bə-lənt) *n.* The plaintiff in a case of ecclesiastical or admiralty libel.

li·bel·ee also **li·bel·lee** (lī′bə-lē′) *n.* The defendant in a case of ecclesiastical or admiralty libel.

li·bel·ous also **li·bel·lous** (lī′bə-ləs) *adj.* Involving or constituting a libel; defamatory. **—li′bel·ous·ly** *adv.*

lib·er·al (lĭb′ər-əl, lĭb′rəl) *adj.* **1.** Having, expressing, or following political views or policies that favor civil liberties, democratic reforms, and the use of governmental power to promote social progress. **2.** Having, expressing, or following views or policies that favor the freedom of individuals to act or express themselves in a manner of their own choosing. **3. Liberal.** Of, designating, or belonging to a political party that advocates liberal social or political views, esp. in the United States, Great Britain, and Canada. **4.** Of, relating to, or characteristic of representational forms of government. **5.** Tolerant of the ideas or behavior of others; broad-minded. **6. a.** Tending to give freely; generous: *a liberal benefactor.* **b.** Generous in amount; ample: *a liberal serving.* **7.** Not literal; loose or approximate: *a liberal translation.* **8.** *Obs.* **a.** Permissible or appropriate for a freeborn man. **b.** Morally unrestrained. **9.** Of, relating to, or based on the liberal arts. *—n.* **1.** A person with liberal ideas or opinions. **2. Liberal.** A member of a Liberal political party. [ME, generous < OFr. < Lat. *liberalis* < *liber,* free.] **—lib′er·al·ly** *adv.* **—lib′er·al·ness** *n.*

liberal arts *pl.n.* Academic disciplines, such as languages, history, and philosophy, that provide information of general cultural concern, as distinguished from more narrowly practical training, as for a vocation or profession.

lib·er·al·ism (lĭb′ər-ə-lĭz′əm, lĭb′rə-) *n.* **1.** The state or quality of being liberal. **2.** Liberal views and policies, esp. in regard to social or political questions. **3.** A liberalizing movement within Protestantism. **—lib′er·al·ist** (-lĭst) *n.* **—lib′er·al·is′tic** (-lĭs′tĭk) *adj.*

lib·er·al·i·ty (lĭb′ə-răl′ĭ-tē) *n., pl.* **-ties. 1.** The quality or state of being liberal. **2.** An instance of being liberal.

lib·er·al·ize (lĭb′ər-ə-līz′, lĭb′rə-) *tr.* & *intr.v.* **-ized, -iz·ing, -iz·es.** To make or become liberal or more liberal. **—lib′er·al·i·za′tion** *n.* **—lib′er·al·iz′er** *n.*

lib·er·ate (lĭb′ə-rāt′) *tr.v.* **-at·ed, -at·ing, -ates. 1.** To set free, as from oppression, confinement, or foreign control. **2.** *Chem.* To release from combination, as a gas. **3.** *Slang.* To obtain by illegal means, as by looting: *some fine brandy we had liberated from the Germans.* [Lat. *liberare, liberat-* < *liber,* free.] **—lib′er·a′tor** *n.*

Lhasa apso

lib·er·a·tion (lĭb′ə-rā′shən) *n.* **1.** The act of liberating or the state of being liberated. **2.** The action or process of trying to achieve equal rights and status: *women's liberation; gay liberation.* **—lib′er·a′tion·ist** *n.*

lib·er·tar·i·an (lĭb′ər-târ′ē-ən) *n.* **1.** One who believes in freedom of action and thought. **2.** One who believes in free will. [< LIBERTY.] **—lib′er·tar′i·an·ism** *n.*

lib·er·tin·age (lĭb′ər-tē′nĭj) *n.* Libertinism.

lib·er·tine (lĭb′ər-tēn′) *n.* **1.** One who acts without moral restraint; a dissolute person. **2.** One who defies established religious precepts. *—adj.* Morally unrestrained; dissolute. [ME, freedman < Lat. *libertinus* < *libertus* < *liberare,* to liberate.]

lib·er·tin·ism (lĭb′ər-tē-nĭz′əm) *n.* **1.** The state or quality of being libertine. **2.** The behavior characteristic of a libertine; promiscuity.

lib·er·ty (lĭb′ər-tē) *n., pl.* **-ties. 1. a.** The condition of being free from restriction or control. **b.** The right to act, believe, or express oneself in a manner of one's own choosing. **c.** The condition of being free from confinement, servitude, or forced labor. **2.** Freedom from unjust or undue governmental control. **3.** A right to engage in certain actions without control or interference: *the liberties protected by the Bill of Rights.* **4.** Often **liberties. a.** A breach or overstepping of propriety or social convention. **b.** A statement, attitude, or action not warranted by conditions or actualities: *a historical novel that takes liberties with chronology.* **c.** An unwarranted risk; chance: *took foolish liberties on the ski slopes.* **5.** A period, usually short, during which a sailor is authorized to go ashore. ***—idiom.* at liberty. 1.** Not in confinement or under constraint; free. **2.** Not employed, occupied, or in use. [ME *liberte* < OFr. < Lat. *libertas* < *liber,* free.]

liberty cap *n.* A brimless, conical cap that fit snugly around the head and that was used as a symbol of liberty by the French revolutionaries and was also worn in the United States before 1800.

li·bid·i·nous (lĭ-bĭd′n-əs) *adj.* Characterized by or having lustful desires; lascivious. [ME < Lat. *libidinosus* < *libido,* lust.] **—li·bid′i·nous·ly** *adv.* **—li·bid′i·nous·ness** *n.*

li·bi·do (lĭ-bē′dō, -bī′-) *n., pl.* **-dos. 1.** The psychic and emotional energy associated with instinctual biological drives. **2. a.** Sexual desire. **b.** Manifestation of the sexual drive. [Lat., desire.] **—li·bid′i·nal** (-bĭd′n-əl) *adj.* **—li·bid′i·nal·ly** *adv.*

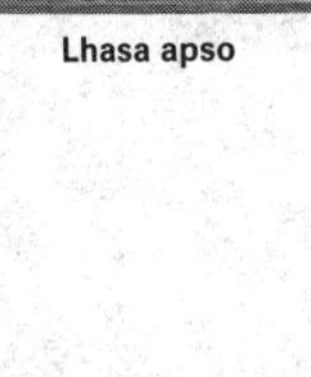

Libra

Li·bra (lī′brə, lē′-) *n.* **1.** A constellation in the Southern Hemisphere near Scorpius and Virgo. **2.** The seventh sign of the zodiac. **3. libra.** *pl.* **-brae** (-brē′). A unit of weight in ancient Rome corresponding to a pound and equivalent to approximately 12 ounces. [Lat. < *libra,* balance.]

li·brar·i·an (lī-brâr′ē-ən) *n.* **1.** A person who is a specialist in library work. **2.** *Computer Sci.* A computer program that originates, stores, and distributes the programs that make up an operating system. **—li·brar′i·an·ship′** *n.*

li·brar·y (lī′brĕr′ē) *n., pl.* **-ies. 1. a.** A place in which literary and artistic materials, such as books, periodicals, newspapers, pamphlets, and prints, are kept for reading or reference. **b.** A collection of such materials, esp. when systematically arranged for reference. **c.** An institution or foundation maintaining such a collection. **2.** A commercial establishment that lends books for a fee. **3.** A series or set of books issued by a publisher. **4.** An organized collection of recorded data arranged for ease of use. [ME *librarie* < AN < Lat. *libraria,* bookseller's shop < *liber,* book.]

library science *n.* The principles, practice, or study of library administration and care.

library tape *n.* **1.** A magnetic tape stored separately from the computer from which it was generated. **2.** A magnetic tape containing a listing of library tapes.

li·bra·tion (lī-brā′shən) *n.* A very slow oscillation, real or apparent, of a satellite as viewed from the larger celestial body around which it revolves. [Lat. *libratio,* oscillation < *librare,* to balance < *libra,* balance.] **—li·bra′tion·al** *adj.* **—li′bra·to′ry** (-brə-tôr′ē, -tōr′ē) *adj.*

li·bret·tist (lĭ-brĕt′ĭst) *n.* The author of a libretto.

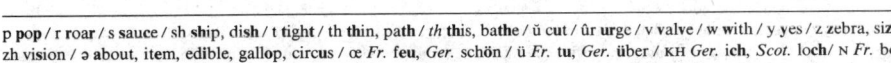

li·bret·to (lĭ-brĕt′ō) *n., pl.* **-bret·tos** or **-bret·ti** (-brĕt′ē). **1.** The text of an opera or other dramatic musical work. **2.** A book containing a libretto. [Ital., dim. of *libro,* book < Lat. *liber.*]

Lib·y·an (lĭb′ē-ən) *adj.* Of or relating to Libya, its people, or its language. —*n.* **1.** A native or inhabitant of Libya. **2.** A Berber language of ancient northern Africa.

lice (līs) *n.* Plural of **louse** (sense 1).

li·cence (lī′səns) *n. Chiefly Brit.* Variant of **license.**

li·cense (lī′səns) *n.* **1. a.** Official or legal permission to do or own a specified thing. **b.** Proof of permission granted, usually in the form of a document, card, plate, or tag: *a driver's license.* **2.** Deviation from normal rules, practices, or methods in order to achieve a certain end or effect: *poetic license.* **3.** Latitude of action, esp. in behavior or speech. **4.** Lack of due restraint; excessive freedom. **5.** Heedlessness for the precepts of proper behavior; licentiousness. —*tr.v.* **-censed, -cens·ing, -cens·es. 1.** To give or yield permission to or for. **2.** To grant a license to or for; authorize. [ME *licence* < OFr. < Lat. *licentia* < *licēre,* to be permitted.] **—li′cens·a·ble** *adj.* **—li′cens·er, li′cen·sor′** (-sən-sôr′) *n.*

lichen

licensed practical nurse *n.* A nurse who has completed a practical nursing program and who is licensed by a state to provide routine patient care under the direction of a registered nurse or a physician.

licensed vocational nurse *n.* A licensed practical nurse who is permitted by license to practice in California or Texas.

li·cens·ee (lī′sən-sē′) *n.* One to whom a license is granted.

li·cen·ti·ate (lī-sĕn′shē-ĭt) *n.* **1.** A person who is granted a license by an authorized body to practice a specified profession. **2. a.** A degree from certain European universities ranking just below that of a doctor. **b.** One holding such a degree. [Med. Lat. *licentiatus* < *licentiare,* to allow < Lat. *licentia,* freedom. —see LICENSE.]

li·cen·tious (lī-sĕn′shəs) *adj.* **1.** Lacking moral discipline or sexual restraint. **2.** Having no regard for accepted rules or standards. [Lat. *licentiosus* < *licentia,* freedom. —see LICENSE.] **—li·cen′tious·ly** *adv.* **—li·cen′tious·ness** *n.*

li·chee (lē′chē) *n.* Variant of **litchi.**

li·chen (lī′kən) *n.* **1.** Any of numerous plants consisting of a fungus, usually of the class Ascomycetes, in close combination with certain of the green or blue-green algae, characteristically forming a crustlike, scaly, or branching growth on rocks or tree trunks. **2.** *Pathol.* Any of various skin eruptions occurring primarily in lichenlike patches. —*tr.v.* **-chened, -chen·ing, -chens.** To cover with lichens. [Lat. < Gk. *leikhēn.*] **—li′chen·ous** *adj.*

li·chen·in (lī′kə-nĭn) *n.* A white, starchlike, gelatinous compound, $C_6H_{10}O_5$, obtained from the lichen Iceland moss.

lich gate also **lych gate** (lĭch) *n.* A roofed gateway to a churchyard used originally as a resting place for a bier before burial. [ME *lich,* corpse (< OE *lic*) + GATE.]

lic·it (lĭs′ĭt) *adj.* Permitted by law; legal. [ME < Lat. *licēre,* to be permitted.] **—lic′it·ly** *adv.* **—lic′it·ness** *n.*

lick (lĭk) *v.* **licked, lick·ing, licks.** —*tr.* **1.** To pass the tongue over or along. **2.** To lap up. **3.** To move over or flicker at like a tongue: *The waves licked the rocks lining the shore.* **4.** *Slang.* To punish with a beating; thrash. **5.** *Slang.* To get the better of; defeat: *licked her weight problem.* —*intr.* To pass or move quickly and rapidly: *The flames licked at our feet.* —*n.* **1.** The act or process of licking. **2.** A small quantity; bit. **3.** A deposit of exposed natural salt that is licked by passing animals. **4.** A sudden hard stroke; blow. ***—idioms.*** **lick and a promise.** A superficial effort made without care or enthusiasm. **lick into shape.** To bring into satisfactory condition or appearance. **lick (one's) chops.** To anticipate delightedly. **lick (one's) wounds.** To recuperate after a defeat. [ME *licken* < OE *liccian.*] **—lick′er** *n.*

lick·er·ish (lĭk′ər-ĭsh) *adj.* **1.** Lascivious; lecherous. **2.** *Archaic.* Relishing good food. **3.** Greedy; gluttonous. **4.** *Obs.* Arousing hunger; appetizing. [ME *likerous,* perh. < AN **likerous,* var. of OFr. *lechereus* < *lecher,* lecher. —see LECHER.] **—lick′er·ish·ness** *n.*

lick·e·ty-split (lĭk′ĭ-tē-splĭt′) *adv. Informal.* With great speed. [Prob. alteration of LICK + SPLIT.]

lick·ing (lĭk′ĭng) *n. Slang.* **1.** A beating; thrashing. **2.** A severe loss or defeat.

lick·spit·tle (lĭk′spĭt′l) *n.* A fawning underling; toady.

lic·o·rice (lĭk′ər-ĭs, -ĭsh) *n.* **1. a.** A plant, *Glycyrrhiza glabra,* of the Mediterranean region, having blue flowers and a sweet, distinctively flavored root. **b.** The root of this plant, used as a flavoring in candy, liquors, tobacco, and medicines. **c.** A confection made from or flavored with the licorice root. **2.** Any of various plants resembling licorice. [ME < AN < LLat. *liquiritia,* alteration of Lat. *glycyrrhiza,* root of licorice < Gk. *glukurrhiza* : *glukus,* sweet + *rhiza,* root.]

lic·tor (lĭk′tər) *n.* A Roman functionary who carried fasces when attending a magistrate in public appearances. [ME *littoures,* lictors < Lat. *lictores.*]

lid (lĭd) *n.* **1.** A removable or hinged cover for a hollow receptacle. **2.** An eyelid. **3.** *Biol.* A flaplike covering such as an operculum. **4.** A curb or restraint: *put a lid on government spending.* **5.** *Slang.* A hat. **6.** *Slang.* An ounce, or 28 grams, of marijuana. —*tr.v.* **lid·ded, lid·ding, lids.** To cover with or as if with a lid. ***—idiom.*** **flip (one's) lid.** *Slang.* To lose one's composure or sanity. [ME < OE *hlid.*]

lid·less (lĭd′lĭs) *adj.* **1.** Having no lid. **2.** *Archaic.* Sleepless; watchful.

lie[1] (lī) *intr.v.* **lay** (lā), **lain** (lān), **ly·ing, lies. 1.** To be or place oneself in a flat, horizontal, or recumbent position; recline: *lay under a tree to sleep.* **2.** To be placed on or supported by a surface that is usually horizontal: *Dirty dishes lay on the table.* **3.** To be or remain in a specific condition: *The dust has lain undisturbed for years.* **4.** To exist; be inherent: *The solution lies in research.* **5.** To occupy a position or place: *The spring lies beyond this hill.* **6.** To extend: *Our land lies between these trees and the river.* **7.** *Archaic.* To stay for a night or short while. **8.** *Law.* To be admissible or maintainable. ***—phrasal verbs.*** **lie down. 1.** To submit meekly to defeat, disappointment, or insults: *refused to take the snub lying down.* **2.** To fail to do or perform: *He's lying down on the job.* **lie in.** To be in confinement for childbirth. **lie to.** *Naut.* To remain stationary while facing the wind. **lie with. 1.** To be decided by, dependent upon, or up to: *The choice lies with you.* **2.** *Archaic.* To have sexual intercourse with. —*n.* **1.** The manner or position in which something is situated. **2.** A haunt or hiding place of an animal. **3.** The position of a golf ball that has come to a stop. ***—idiom.*** **lie low. 1.** To keep oneself or one's plans hidden. **2.** To bide one's time but remain ready for action. —See Usage note at **lay[1]**. [ME *lien* < OE *licgan.*]

lie[2] (lī) *n.* **1.** A false statement deliberately presented as being true; falsehood. **2.** Something meant to deceive or give a wrong impression. —*v.* **lied, ly·ing, lies.** —*intr.* **1.** To present false information with the intention of deceiving. **2.** To convey a false image or impression: *Appearances often lie.* —*tr.* To cause to be in a specific condition or affect in a specific way by telling lies: *lied himself into trouble.* ***—idiom.*** **give the lie to. 1.** To accuse of lying. **2.** To prove to be untrue. [ME < OE *lyge.*]

lied (lēt) *n., pl.* **lie·der** (lē′dər). A German art song. [G. < OHG *liod.*]

Lie·der·kranz (lē′dər-kränts′, -kränts′). A trademark for a soft cheese resembling a mild Limburger.

lie detector *n.* A polygraph used to detect lying.

lief (lēf) *adv.* Readily; willingly: *I would as lief go now as later.* —*adj. Archaic.* **1.** Beloved; dear. **2.** Ready or willing. [ME < OE *lēof,* dear.]

liege (lēj) *n.* **1.** A lord or sovereign in feudal law. **2.** A vassal or subject owing allegiance and services to a lord or sovereign under feudal law. **3.** A loyal subject to a monarch. —*adj.* **1. a.** Entitled to the loyalty and services of vassals or subjects: *a liege lord.* **b.** Bound to give such allegiance and services to a lord or monarch. **2.** Loyal; faithful. [ME *lege* < OFr. *lige* < LLat. *leticus* < *letus,* serf, of Germanic orig.]

liege·man (lēj′mən) *n.* **1.** A feudal vassal or subject. **2.** A loyal supporter, follower, or subject.

lien (lēn, lē′ən) *n. Law.* The right to take and hold or sell the property of a debtor as security or payment for a debt. [OFr. < Lat. *ligamen,* bond < *ligare,* to bind.]

li·e·nal (lī-ē′nəl) *adj.* Of or relating to the spleen. [Lat. *lien,* spleen + -AL.]

li·erne (lē-ûrn′) *n.* A reinforcing rib used in Gothic vaulting to connect the intersections and bosses of the primary ribs. [Fr.]

lieu (lo͞o) *n. Archaic.* Place; stead. ***—idiom.*** **in lieu of.** In place of; instead of. [OFr. < Lat. *locus.*]

lieu·ten·ant (lo͞o-tĕn′ənt) *n.* **1. a.** An officer in the U.S. Army, Air Force, or Marine Corps ranking below a captain. **b.** An officer in the U.S. Navy ranking above an ensign and below a lieutenant commander. **2.** (lĕf-tĕn′ənt). A commissioned officer in the British and Canadian navies ranking just below a lieutenant commander. **3.** An officer in a police or fire department ranking below a captain. **4.** One who acts in place of his superior; deputy. [ME, deputy < OFr. : *lieu,* lieu + *tenir,* to hold < Lat. *tenēre.*] **—lieu·ten′an·cy** *n.*

lieutenant colonel *n.* An officer in the U.S. Army, Air Force, or Marine Corps ranking above a major and below a colonel.

lieutenant commander *n.* An officer in the U.S. Navy or Coast Guard ranking above a lieutenant and below a commander.

lieutenant general *n.* An officer in the U.S. Army, Air Force, or Marine Corps ranking above a major general and below a general.

lieutenant governor *n.* **1.** An elected official ranking just below the governor of an American state. **2.** The nonelective chief of government of a Canadian province. **—lieutenant governorship** *n.*

life (līf) *n., pl.* **lives** (līvz). **1.** The property or quality that distinguishes living organisms from dead organisms and inanimate matter, manifested in functions such as metabolism, growth, response to stimuli, and reproduction. **2.** Living organisms collectively: *plant life; marine life.* **3.** A living being, esp. a person: *an earthquake that claimed hundreds of lives.* **4.** The physical, mental, and spiritual experiences that constitute a person's existence. **5. a.** The interval of time between birth and death; lifetime: *lived there all his life.* **b.** A particular segment of this period: *her adolescent life.* **c.** The period from an occurrence until death: *elected for life.* **6.** The time for which something exists or functions: *the useful life of a car.* **7.** A spiritual state regarded as a transcending of death. **8.** An account of a person's life; biography. **9.** Human existence or activity in general: *real life; everyday life.* **10. a.** A manner of living: *led a good life.* **b.** The activities and interests of a particular area or realm: *musical life in New York.* **11.** A source of vitality; animating force: *She's the life of the show.* **12.** Liveliness or vitality; animation: *a face that is full of life.* **13.** Something that actually exists regarded as a subject for an artist: *painted from life.* **14.** Actual environment or reality; nature. **15. Life.** *Christian Science.* God. ***—modifier:*** *life imprisonment; a life story.* ***—idioms.*** **come to life.** To become animated; grow lively. **for dear life.** Desperately or urgently. **for the life of (one).** *Informal.* Though trying hard: *For the life of me I couldn't remember his name.* [ME < OE *līf.*]

life belt *n.* A life preserver worn like a belt.

life·blood (līf′blŭd′) *n.* **1.** Blood regarded as essential for life. **2.** An indispensable or vital part of something: *Capable workers are the lifeblood of the business.*

life·boat (līf′bōt′) *n.* **1.** A boat carried on a ship for use if the ship has to be abandoned. **2.** A boat used for rescue service.

life buoy *n.* Buoy (sense 2).

life cycle *n.* **1.** The course of developmental changes through which an organism passes from its inception as a fertilized zygote to the mature state in which another zygote may be produced. **2.** A progression through a series of differing stages of development, as in insect metamorphosis.

life expectancy *n.* The number of years that an individual is expected to live as determined by statistics.

life·guard (līf′gärd′) *n.* An expert swimmer employed to safeguard swimmers, as at a beach.

life history *n.* **1.** The history of changes undergone by an organism from inception or conception to death. **2.** The developmental history of an individual or group in society.

life insurance *n.* Insurance that guarantees a specific sum of money to a designated beneficiary upon the death of the insured.

life jacket *n.* A life preserver in the form of a jacket or vest.

life·less (līf′lĭs) *adj.* **1.** Having no life; inanimate. **2.** Not inhabited by living beings. **3.** Having lost life; dead. **4.** Lacking vitality or animation; dull. **—life′less·ly** *adv.* **—life′less·ness** *n.*

life·like (līf′līk′) *adj.* Accurately representing real life: *a lifelike statue.* **—life′like′ness** *n.*

life line *n.* **1. a.** An anchored line thrown as a support to someone falling or drowning. **b.** A line shot to a ship in distress. **c.** A line used to raise and lower deep-sea divers. **2.** A means or route by which necessary supplies are transported. **3.** One that is or is regarded as a source of salvation in a crisis.

life·long (līf′lông′, -lŏng′) *adj.* Continuing for a lifetime.

life preserver *n.* **1.** A buoyant device, usually in the shape of a ring, belt, or jacket, designed to keep a person afloat in the water. **2.** *Chiefly Brit.* A weapon such as a blackjack.

lif·er (lī′fər) *n. Slang.* **1.** A prisoner serving a life sentence. **2.** A right-to-lifer.

life raft *n.* A raft usually made of wood or inflatable material and used by people who have been forced into water.

life·sav·er (līf′sā′vər) *n.* **1.** One that saves a life. **2.** A lifeguard. **3.** One that provides help in a crisis or emergency. **4.** A life preserver shaped like a ring. **—life′sav′ing** *n.*

life-size (līf′sīz′) also **life-sized** (-sīzd′) *adj.* Being of the same size as an original: *a life-size statue.*

life span *n.* The period of time during which an organism remains alive under normal or optimum conditions.

life·style also **life-style** or **life style** (līf′stīl′) *n.* A way of life or style of living that reflects the attitudes and values of an individual or a group.

life-sup·port system (līf′sə-pôrt′, -pōrt′) *n.* **1.** The equipment that provides a viable environment for persons in a spacecraft. **2.** Hospital equipment that enables a patient who might be unable to survive independently to continue to live.

life·time (līf′tīm′) *n.* **1.** The period of time during which an individual is alive. **2.** The period of time during which an object, property, process, or phenomenon exists or functions. ***—modifier:*** *a lifetime guarantee.*

life·way (līf′wā′) *n.* A way or manner of living.

life·work (līf′wûrk′) *n.* The chief or entire work of a person's lifetime.

lift (lĭft) *v.* **lift·ed, lift·ing, lifts.** *—tr.* **1.** To direct or carry from a lower to a higher position; raise: *lift one's eyes; lifted the child up on his shoulders.* **2. a.** To revoke by taking back; rescind: *lift a ban.* **b.** To bring an end to (a blockade or siege) by removing forces. **c.** To cease (artillery fire) in an area. **3.** To raise in condition, rank, or esteem. **4.** To remove (plants) from the ground for transplanting. **5.** To project or sound in loud, clear tones: *lifted their voices in song.* **6.** *Informal.* To steal; pilfer: *lifted his wallet.* **7.** *Informal.* To copy from something already published; plagiarize. **8.** To pay off or clear (a debt, for example). **9.** To perform cosmetic surgery on (the face), esp. in order to remove wrinkles. **10.** To hit (a golf ball) very high into the air. *—intr.* **1.** To rise; ascend. **2.** To disappear or disperse by or as if by rising: *By afternoon the clouds had lifted.* **3.** To become elevated; soar: *Their spirits lifted when help came.* ***—phrasal verb.*** **lift off.** To begin flight, as a rocket or spacecraft. *—n.* **1. a.** The act or process of lifting. **b.** The act or process of rising. **2.** Power or force available for raising: *the lift of a pump.* **3.** An amount or weight lifted or capable of being lifted at one time; load. **4. a.** The extent or height to which something is raised. **b.** The distance or space through which something is raised. **5.** A rise or elevation in the level of the ground. **6.** An elevation of the spirit. **7.** A raised, high, or erect position, as of a part of the body: *the lift of his chin.* **8.** A machine or device designed to pick up, raise, or carry something. **9.** One of the layers of leather, rubber, or other material making up the heel of a shoe. **10.** *Chiefly Brit.* An elevator. **11.** A ride in a vehicle given to help someone reach a destination. **12.** Assistance or help. **13.** A set of pumps used in a mine. **14.** The component of the total aerodynamic force acting on an airfoil or on an entire aircraft or winged missile perpendicular to the relative wind and normally exerted in an upward direction, opposing the pull of gravity. [ME *liften* < ON *lypta.*] **—lift′a·ble** *adj.* **—lift′er** *n.*

Synonyms: *lift, raise, rear, elevate, hoist, heave, boost.* These verbs mean to move or bring something from a lower level to a higher one. *Lift* stresses the expenditure of effort thus involved. *Raise* often implies movement to a position that is approximately vertical, or figurative movement to a higher plane or level. *Rear* is interchangeable with *raise* in the sense of bringing to an upright position, though it is now infrequently so used. *Elevate* refers to movement to a markedly higher level; figuratively it often suggests exalting, ennobling, or increasing in rank. *Hoist* is applied principally to the lifting of heavy objects by mechanical means, and *heave* to lifting or raising that requires great exertion. *Boost* refers informally to upward movement effected by pushing from below; figuratively it is applied to increase or advance in amount, degree, status, or favor.

lift·off (lĭft′ôf′, -ŏf′) *n.* The initial movement by which or instant in which a rocket or other craft commences flight.

lig·a·ment (lĭg′ə-mənt) *n.* **1.** *Anat.* A sheet or band of tough, fibrous tissue connecting two or more bones or cartilages or supporting an organ, fascia, or muscle. **2.** A unifying or connecting tie or bond. [ME < Lat. *ligamentum,* bond < *ligare,* to bind.] **—lig′a·ment′al** (-mĕn′tl), **lig′a·men′ta·ry** (-mĕn′tə-rē, -mĕn′trē), **lig′a·men′tous** *adj.*

li·gan (lī′gən) *n.* Variant of **lagan.**

li·gase (lī′gās′) *n.* An enzyme that catalyzes molecule linkage, generally splitting off a pyrophosphate group from ATP concurrently. [Lat. *ligare,* to bind + -ASE.]

li·gate (lī′gāt′) *tr.v.* **-gat·ed, -gat·ing, -gates.** To tie or bind with a ligature. [Lat. *ligare, ligat-.*]

li·ga·tion (lī-gā′shən) *n.* **1. a.** The act of binding. **b.** The state of being bound. **2.** Something that binds; ligature.

lig·a·ture (lĭg′ə-chŏŏr′, -chər) *n.* **1.** The act of tying or binding. **2. a.** A cord, wire, or bandage used for tying or binding. **b.** A thread, wire, or cord used in surgery to close vessels or tie off ducts. **3.** Something that unites; bond. **4.** A character or type, such as *fi,* combining two or more letters. **5.** *Mus.* **a.** A group of notes intended to be played or sung as one phrase. **b.** A curved line indicating such a phrase; slur. *—tr.v.* **-tured, -tur·ing, -tures.** To ligate. [ME < Lat. *ligatura* < *ligare,* to bind.]

light¹ (līt) *n.* **1.** *Physics.* **a.** Electromagnetic radiation that has a wavelength in the range from about 3,900 to about 7,700 angstroms and that may be perceived by the unaided, normal human eye. **b.** Electromagnetic radiation. **2.** The sensation of perceiving light: *a sudden light that made him blink.* **3. a.** A source of light, esp. an electric lamp: *left a light burning in the hall.* **b.** The illumination derived from such a source. **4.** A mechanical device that uses light as a signal or warning, esp. a beacon or a traffic signal. **5. a.** Daylight. **b.** Dawn; daybreak. **6.** Something that admits light, as a window. **7.** A source of fire, as a match or cigarette lighter. **8. a.** Spiritual awareness; illumination. **b.** Something that provides information or enlightens: *threw some light on the question.* **9.** Public attention; general knowledge: *brought the scandal to light.* **10.** A way of looking at or considering a matter; aspect: *saw the situation in a different light.* **11.** *Archaic.* Eyesight. **12. lights.** One's individual opinions, choices, or standards: *acted according to their own lights.* **13. a.** Visible light considered necessary for seeing: *enough light to read by.* **b.** A particular kind of illumination: *poor light for reading.* **14.** A prominent or distinguished person; luminary: *one of the leading lights of the theater.* **15.** An expression of the eyes. **16. Light.** In Quaker doctrine, the guiding spirit or divine presence in each person. **17.** The representation of light in art. *—v.* **light·ed** or **lit** (lĭt), **light·ing, lights.** *—tr.* **1.** To set on fire; ignite. **2.** To cause to give out light; make luminous: *lit a lamp.* **3.** To provide, cover, or fill with light; illuminate: *fireworks lighting the sky.* **4.** To signal, direct, or guide with or as if with lights. **5.** To enliven or animate: *A smile lit his face.* *—intr.* To start to burn; be ignited or kindled. *—adj.* **-er, -est.** **1.** Having a greater rather than lesser degree of lightness. Used of a color. **2.** Characterized by or filled with light; bright: *a room that is light when the shutters are open.* **3.** Not dark in color; fair: *light hair and skin.* **4.** Served with milk or cream. Used of coffee. ***—idioms.*** **in (the) light of.** In consideration of; in relationship to. **see the light.** To comprehend

lifeboat

life jacket

life preserver

or perceive the meaning of something for the first time. [ME < OE *lēoht.*]

Usage: *Lighted* and *lit* are equally acceptable as past tense and past participle of *light.* When used as an adjective, *lighted* is usual: *a lighted window.* But *lit* is the regular combining form: *a moonlit sky; starlit.*

lighthouse

light meter

light[2] (līt) *adj.* **-er, -est. 1. a.** Of relatively little weight; not heavy. **b.** Of relatively little weight for its size or bulk: *Titanium is a light metal.* **c.** Of less than the correct, standard, or legal weight: *a light pound.* **2.** Exerting little force or impact; gentle: *a light pat.* **3. a.** Of little quantity; scanty: *light snow.* **b.** Consuming or using relatively moderate amounts; abstemious: *a light eater; a light smoker.* **4.** Requiring little effort or exertion: *light household tasks.* **5.** Having little importance; insignificant: *light chatter.* **6.** Intended primarily as entertainment; not serious or profound: *a light comedy.* **7.** Free from worries or troubles; blithe: *a light heart.* **8.** Characterized by frivolity. **9.** Liable to change; fickle. **10.** Mildly dizzy: *felt light in the head.* **11.** Lacking in sexual discrimination; wanton. **12.** Moving easily and quickly; nimble: *light and graceful on her feet.* **13.** Designed for ease and quickness of movement: *a light airplane.* **14.** Carrying little weight. **15.** Carrying little equipment or arms: *light cavalry.* **16.** Requiring relatively little equipment and utilizing relatively simple processes: *light industry.* **17.** Easily awakened or disturbed: *a light sleeper.* **18. a.** Easily digested: *a light supper.* **b.** Having a spongy or flaky texture; well-leavened: *light pastries.* **19.** Having a loose, porous consistency: *light earth.* **20.** Containing a relatively small amount of alcohol: *a light wine.* **21.** Designating a vowel or syllable pronounced with little or no stress. *—adv.* **-er, -est. 1.** Lightly. **2.** With little weight and few burdens: *traveling light.* *—intr.v.* **light·ed** or **lit** (lĭt), **light·ing, lights. 1.** To get down, as from a horse; dismount. **2.** To come to rest; alight. **3.** To come upon unexpectedly: *Misfortune lighted upon him.* **4.** To come upon by chance or accident. ***—phrasal verbs.*** **light into.** To attack verbally or physically; assail. **light out.** To leave hastily; run off. ***—idiom.*** **make light of.** To regard or treat as insignificant or petty. [ME < OE *lēoht.*]

light adaptation *n.* The process in which the eye adapts to increased illumination. **—light'-a·dapt'ed** (līt'ə-dăp'tĭd) *adj.*

light·en[1] (līt'n) *v.* **-ened, -en·ing, -ens.** *—tr.* **1. a.** To make light or lighter; illuminate. **b.** To make (a color) lighter. **2.** *Archaic.* To enlighten. *—intr.* **1.** To become lighter; brighten. **2.** To be luminous; shine. **3.** To give off flashes of lightning.

light·en[2] (līt'n) *v.* **-ened, -en·ing, -ens.** *—tr.* **1.** To make less heavy. **2.** To lessen the oppressiveness, trouble, or severity of. **3.** To relieve of cares or worries; gladden. *—intr.* **1.** To become lighter. **2.** To become less oppressive, troublesome, or severe. **3.** To become cheerful.

light·er[1] (lī'tər) *n.* **1.** One that ignites something. **2.** A mechanical device for lighting a cigarette, cigar, or pipe.

light·er[2] (lī'tər) *n.* A large barge, esp. one used to deliver or unload goods to or from a cargo ship. *—tr.v.* **-ered, -er·ing, -ers.** To convey (cargo) in a lighter. [ME < *lighten,* to make less heavy < OE *līhtan.*]

light·er·age (lī'tər-ĭj) *n.* **1.** The transportation of goods on a lighter. **2.** The fee charged for lightering.

light·er-than-air (lī'tər-*th*ən-âr') *adj.* Having a weight less than that of the air displaced. Used of certain aircraft.

light·face (līt'fās') *n. Printing.* A typeface or font of characters having relatively thin, light lines. **—light'faced'** *adj.*

light-fin·gered (līt'fĭng'gərd) *adj.* **1.** Having quick and nimble fingers. **2.** Skilled at petty thievery. **—light'-fin'gered·ness** *n.*

light-foot·ed (līt'fo͝ot'ĭd) also **light·foot** (-fo͝ot') *adj.* Treading with light and nimble ease. **—light'-foot'ed·ly** *adv.* **—light'-foot'ed·ness** *n.*

light-hand·ed (līt'hăn'dĭd) *adj.* Having a light, delicate touch. **—light'-hand'ed·ly** *adv.* **—light'-hand'ed·ness** *n.*

light·head·ed (līt'hĕd'ĭd) *adj.* **1.** Delirious, giddy, or faint: *lightheaded with wine.* **2.** Given to frivolity; silly. **—light'head'ed·ly** *adv.* **—light'head'ed·ness** *n.*

light·heart·ed (līt'här'tĭd) *adj.* Free from care or trouble; cheerful. **—light'heart'ed·ly** *adv.* **—light'heart'ed·ness** *n.*

light heavyweight *n.* A boxer or wrestler weighing between 161 and 175 pounds.

light·house (līt'hous') *n.* A tall structure topped by a powerful light used as a beacon or signal to aid marine navigation.

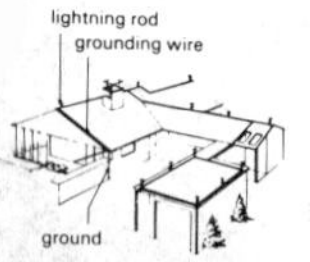

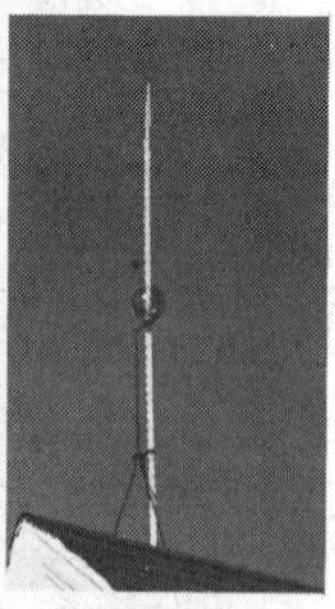

lightning rod
Above: Diagram
Below: Rod

light·ing (lī'tĭng) *n.* **1.** The state of being lighted; illumination. **2. a.** The method or equipment used to provide artificial illumination. **b.** The illumination so provided. **3.** The act or process of igniting.

light·ly (līt'lē) *adv.* **1.** With little weight or force; gently. **2.** To a slight extent or amount: *apply paint lightly.* **3. a.** With little difficulty; easily. **b.** With agility and grace; nimbly. **4. a.** In a carefree manner; cheerfully: *took the news lightly.* **b.** Without sufficient care or consideration; indifferently: *treated the situation much too lightly.*

light meter *n.* An exposure meter.

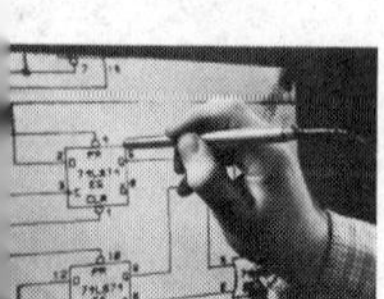

light pen

light-mind·ed (līt'mīn'dĭd) *adj.* Frivolous, silly, or inanely giddy. **—light'-mind'ed·ly** *adv.* **—light'-mind'ed·ness** *n.*

light·ness[1] (līt'nĭs) *n.* **1.** The quality or condition of being illuminated. **2.** The dimension of the color of an object by which the object appears to reflect or transmit more or less of the incident light, varying from black to white for surface colors, and from black to colorless for transparent volume colors.

light·ness[2] (līt'nĭs) *n.* **1.** The state or quality of having little weight or force. **2.** Ease or quickness of movement; agility. **3.** Ease or cheerfulness in manner or style. **4.** Freedom from worry or trouble. **5.** Lack of appropriate seriousness; levity. **6.** Delicacy or subtlety in workmanship, performance, or effect.

light·ning (līt'nĭng) *n.* **1. a.** A large-scale high-tension natural electric discharge in the atmosphere. **b.** The visible flash of light accompanying such a discharge. **2.** *Informal.* A sudden, usually improbable stroke of fortune. *—intr.v.* **-ninged** (-nĭngd), **-ning, -nings.** To discharge a flash of lightning. *—adj.* Moving with remarkable speed or suddenness. [ME < *lightenen,* to illuminate < *lighten* < *light,* illumination.]

lightning arrester *n.* A protective device for electrical equipment that reduces excessive voltage resulting from lightning to a safe level by grounding the discharge.

lightning bug *n.* A firefly.

lightning rod *n.* A grounded metal rod placed high on a structure to prevent damage by conducting lightning to the ground.

light opera *n.* An operetta.

light pen *n.* A small photosensitive device connected to a computer and moved by hand over an output display in order to manipulate information in the computer.

lights (līts) *pl.n.* The lungs, esp. the lungs of an animal used for food. [ME *lightes* < *light,* light in weight.]

light·ship (līt'shĭp') *n.* A ship with a powerful light or warning signals that is anchored in dangerous waters to alert other vessels.

light show *n.* A display of colored lights in kaleidoscopic patterns, often accompanied by slides and film loops.

light·some[1] (līt'səm) *adj.* **1.** Providing light; luminous. **2.** Covered with or full of light; bright. **—light'some·ly** *adv.* **—light'some·ness** *n.*

light·some[2] (līt'səm) *adj.* **1.** Light, nimble, or graceful in movement. **2.** Free from worry or care; cheerful. **3.** Frivolous; silly. **—light'some·ly** *adv.* **—light'some·ness** *n.*

lights out *n.* **1.** A signal to extinguish lights for the night. **2.** Bedtime.

light-struck (līt'strŭk') *adj.* Fogged by accidental exposure. Used of photosensitive materials.

light stylus *n.* A light pen.

light water *n.* Ordinary water as distinguished from heavy water.

light·weight (līt'wāt') *n.* **1.** One that weighs relatively little. **2.** A boxer or wrestler weighing between 127 and 135 pounds. **3.** A person of little ability, intelligence, influence, or importance.

light·wood (līt'wo͝od') *n.* Dry, easily ignited, often resinous wood, used for kindling or fuel.

light-year also **light year** (līt'yîr') *n.* The distance that light covers traveling in a vacuum for a period of one year, approximately 9.46 trillion kilometers or 5.878 trillion (5.878×10^{12}) miles.

lign– *pref.* Variant of **ligni-.**

lig·ne·ous (lĭg'nē-əs) *adj.* Consisting of or having the texture or appearance of wood; woody. [Lat. *ligneus* < *lignum,* wood.]

ligni– or **ligno–** or **lign–** *pref.* Wood: *lignocellulose.* [< Lat. *lignum,* wood.]

lig·ni·fy (lĭg'nə-fī') *v.* **-fied, -fy·ing, -fies.** *—intr.* To form or turn into wood through the formation and deposit of lignin in cell walls. *—tr.* To make woody or woodlike by the deposit of lignin. [Fr. *lignifier* < Lat. *lignum,* wood.] **—lig'ni·fi·ca'tion** *n.*

lig·nin (lĭg'nĭn) *n.* The chief noncarbohydrate constituent of wood, a polymer that functions as a natural binder and support for the cellulose fibers of woody plants.

lig·nite (lĭg'nīt') *n.* A low-grade, brownish-black coal. [Fr. < Lat. *lignum,* wood.] **—lig·nit'ic** (-nĭt'ĭk) *adj.*

ligno– *pref.* Variant of **ligni-.**

lig·no·cel·lu·lose (lĭg'nō-sĕl'yə-lōs') *n.* A combination of lignin and cellulose that strengthens woody cells.

lig·num vi·tae (lĭg'nəm vī'tē) *n., pl.* **lignum vi·taes. 1. a.** Either of two tropical American trees, *Guaiacum officinale* or *G. sanctum,* having evergreen leaves and heavy, durable, resinous wood. **b.** The wood of either of these trees. **2.** Any of several trees similar or related to the lignum vitae. [Lat. *lignum,* wood + Lat. *vitae,* genitive of *vita,* life.]

lig·ro·in (lĭg'rō-ən) *n.* A volatile, flammable fraction of petroleum, obtained by distillation and used as a solvent. [Orig. unknown.]

lig·u·la (lĭg'yə-lə) *n., pl.* **-lae** (-lē') or **-las.** A strap-shaped structure, esp. a mouth part in certain insects. [NLat., ligule. —see LIGULE.]

lig·u·late (lĭg'yə-lĭt, -lāt') *adj.* **1.** Strap-shaped. **2.** Having a ligule.

lig·ule (lĭg'yo͞ol) *n.* A straplike structure, such as a ray flower of a daisy or a sheathlike organ at the base of a grass leaf. [NLat. *ligula* < Lat., dim. of *lingua,* tongue.]

lig·ure (lĭg'yo͝or') *n.* A precious stone of ancient Israel. [ME < LLat. *ligurius* < Gk. *ligurion.*]

lik·a·ble also **like·a·ble** (lī′kə-bəl) *adj.* Pleasing; attractive. **—lik′a·ble·ness, like′a·ble·ness** *n.*

like[1] (līk) *v.* **liked, lik·ing, likes.** *—tr.* **1.** To find pleasant or attractive; enjoy. **2.** To want to have: *would like some coffee.* **3.** To feel about; regard: *How do you like her nerve!* **4.** *Regional.* To be pleasing to. *—intr.* **1.** To have an inclination or preference: *If you like, we can meet you there.* **2.** *Scot.* To be pleased. *—n.* Something that is liked; preference: *made a list of his likes and dislikes.* [ME *liken* < OE *līcian.*]

Synonyms: *like, love, enjoy, relish, fancy, dote.* These verbs mean to be attracted to or to take pleasure in. *Like,* the least forceful, usually suggests only mild interest or regard. *Love,* in careful use, implies much stronger attachment or affection and deeper involvement on an emotional or, less often, intellectual level. *Enjoy* is applied to what gives personal satisfaction or fulfillment; *relish,* to what moves one to keen or zestful appreciation and thus brings great personal gratification; and *fancy,* to what appeals to one's taste, inclination, or caprice. *Dote* implies infatuation or foolish and extravagant attachment.

like[2] (līk) *prep.* **1.** Possessing the characteristics of; similar to. **2.** In the typical manner of: *It's not like you to take offense.* **3.** Inclined or disposed to: *felt like running away.* **4.** As if the probability exists for: *looks like a bad year for farmers.* **5.** Such as: *saved things like old newspapers and pieces of string.* *—adj.* **1.** Possessing the same or almost the same characteristics; similar: *on this and like occasions.* **2.** Alike: *They are as like as two brothers.* *—adv.* **1.** Used as an intensifier of action: *worked like hell.* **2.** *Informal.* Probably; likely: *Like as not she'll change her mind.* **3.** *Nonstandard.* Used to provide emphasis: *Like let's get going.* *—n.* One similar to or like another: *was subject to coughs, asthma, and the like.* *—conj.* **1.** In the same way that; as: *To dance like she does requires great discipline.* **2.** As if: *It looks like we'll finish on time.* ***—idiom.*** **the like** (or **likes**) **of.** Such a one as: *wouldn't put ourselves out for the likes of her.* [ME < *like,* similar (< OE *gelīc*), and *like,* similarly (< OE *gelīce*).]

Usage: *Like* has been used as a conjunction since Shakespeare's time by the best writers. But the usage has been so vehemently attacked by purists in recent times that the sensible writer will avoid it lest his readers pay more attention to his words than their content. Prudence requires *The engine responds as* (not *like*) *it should.* Constructions like *looks like, sounds like,* and *tastes like* are less likely to offend, but *as if* is better used in formal style: *It looks as if* (not *like*) *there will be another drought.* There can be no objection to the use of *like* as a conjunction when the following verb is not expressed: *He took to politics like a duck to water.* This usage is acceptable to a majority of the Usage Panel.

like[3] (līk) also **liked** (līkt) *aux.v. Nonstandard.* To be just on the point of; be or come near to: *I like to have killed him when he said that.* [ME *liken,* to compare < *like,* similar < OE *gelīc.*]

-like *suff.* Resembling or characteristic of: *ladylike.* [< LIKE[2].]

like·a·ble (lī′kə-bəl) *adj.* Variant of **likable.**

like·li·hood (līk′lē-ho͝od′) *n.* **1.** The state of being likely or probable; probability. **2.** Something that is probable.

like·ly (līk′lē) *adj.* **-li·er, -li·est. 1.** Possessing or displaying the qualities or characteristics that make something probable: *They are likely to become angry with him.* **2.** Within the realm of credibility; plausible: *a likely excuse.* **3.** Apparently appropriate; suitable: *a likely place.* **4.** Apt to achieve success or yield a desired outcome; promising: *a likely topic for investigation.* **5.** Attractive; pleasant. *—adv.* Probably. [ME < both OE *gelīclic* (< *gēlic,* similar) and ON *līkligr* (< *līkr,* similar).]

Usage: *Likely* as an adverb is preferably preceded by a qualifying word such as *quite, very,* or *most: He will very likely arrive on Friday. The new government quite likely will be more receptive to change.* Without qualifiers, the preceding examples are unacceptable to a majority of the Usage Panel. No qualifier is needed when *likely* is used as an adjective: *She called it a likely story.* See also Usage note at **apt.**

like-mind·ed (līk′mīn′dĭd) *adj.* Of the same turn of mind.

lik·en (lī′kən) *tr.v.* **-ened, -en·ing, -ens.** To see, mention, or show as like or similar; compare. [ME *liknen* < *liken,* to compare. —see LIKE[3].]

like·ness (līk′nĭs) *n.* **1.** The state or quality of resembling or being like something. **2.** An imitative appearance; semblance. **3.** A pictorial, graphic, or sculptured representation of something; image.

Synonyms: *likeness, similarity, similitude, resemblance, analogy, affinity.* These nouns are applied to the relationship between persons or things that are in agreement or conformity in some respect. *Likeness* can refer to any degree of correspondence, but in the absence of a qualifying term usually implies close agreement. *Similarity* and *similitude* suggest agreement in certain details, but not close overall correspondence. *Resemblance* refers to correspondence in appearance or in some other external, or surface, detail. *Analogy* is correspondence between unlike things that are otherwise not comparable. The correspondence consists not in the fundamental nature or appearance of the things involved but in the similarity of certain of their properties or functions: *the analogy between the working of the human heart and the distribution of goods and services under an economic system. Affinity* is correspondence based on kinship or on the possession of properties, characteristics, or sympathies that cause persons or things to be compatible or to have attraction for one another.

like·wise (līk′wīz′) *adv.* **1.** In the same way; similarly: *"Some have little power to do good, and have likewise little strength to resist evil"* (Samuel Johnson). **2.** As well; also; too.

Usage: *Likewise,* not being a conjunction, cannot take the place of a connective such as *and* or *together with,* as in *He risked his fortune, likewise his honor.* Properly, *He risked his fortune and* (or *and likewise*) *his honor.*

lik·ing (lī′kĭng) *n.* **1.** A feeling of attraction or love; fondness. **2.** Preference or taste.

li·ku·ta (lē-ko͞o′tä) *n., pl.* **ma·ku·ta** (mä-ko͞o′tä). See table at **currency.** [Native word in Zaire.]

li·lac (lī′lək, -lŏk′, -lăk′) *n.* **1.** Any of various shrubs of the genus *Syringa,* esp. *S. vulgaris,* widely cultivated for its clusters of fragrant purplish or white flowers. **2.** A pale to light or moderate purple. [Obs. Fr. < Sp. < Ar. *līlak* < Pers., var. of *nīlak* < *nīl,* blue.] **—li′lac** *adj.*

li·lan·ge·ni (lĭ-läng′gē-nē) *n.* See table at **currency.** [Native word in Swaziland.]

Lil·ith (lĭl′ĭth) *n.* **1.** In ancient Semitic legend, an evil female spirit alleged to haunt deserted places and attack children. **2.** In Hebrew folklore, the first wife of Adam, believed to have been in existence before the creation of Eve. [Heb. *līlīth.*]

Lil·li·pu·tian also **lil·li·pu·tian** (lĭl′ə-pyo͞o′shən) *n.* A very small person or being. *—adj.* **1.** Very small; diminutive. **2.** Trivial; petty. [After the *Lilliputians,* a people in *Gulliver's Travels* by Jonathan Swift (1667–1745).]

lilt (lĭlt) *n.* **1.** A light, happy tune or song. **2.** A cheerful or lively manner of speaking, in which the pitch of the voice varies pleasantly. **3.** A light or resilient manner of moving or walking. *—v.* **lilt·ed, lilt·ing, lilts.** *—tr.* To say, sing, or play in a cheerful, rhythmic manner. *—intr.* **1.** To speak, sing, or play with liveliness or rhythm. **2.** To move with lightness and buoyancy. [< ME *lilten,* to sound an alarm.]

lil·y (lĭl′ē) *n., pl.* **-ies. 1.** Any of various plants of the genus *Lilium,* having showy, variously colored, often trumpet-shaped flowers. **2. a.** Any of various plants similar or related to the lily, such as the day lily or the water lily. **b.** The flower of such a plant. [ME *lilie* < OE < Lat. *lilium.*]

lil·y-liv·ered (lĭl′ē-lĭv′ərd) *adj.* Cowardly; timid.

lily of the valley *n., pl.* **lilies of the valley.** A widely cultivated plant, *Convallaria majalis,* having a cluster of fragrant, bell-shaped white flowers.

lily pad *n.* One of the floating leaves of a water lily.

lil·y-white (lĭl′ē-hwīt′, -wīt′) *adj.* **1.** White as a lily. **2.** Beyond reproach; blameless. **3.** *Informal.* Excluding or seeking to exclude blacks.

li·ma bean (lī′mə) *n.* **1.** Any of several varieties of a tropical American plant, *Phaseolus limensis,* having flat pods containing large, light-green, edible seeds. **2.** The seed of the lima bean. [After *Lima,* Peru.]

lim·a·cine (lĭm′ə-sēn′, lī′mə-) *adj.* Of, pertaining to, or resembling a slug. [< Lat. *limax, limac-,* slug < *limus,* slime.]

limb[1] (lĭm) *n.* **1.** One of the larger branches of a tree. **2.** One of the jointed appendages of an animal, used for locomotion or grasping, as an arm, leg, wing, or flipper. **3.** An extension or projecting part. **4.** One that is considered to be an extension, member, or representative of a larger body or group. **5.** *Informal.* An impish child. *—tr.v.* **limbed, limb·ing, limbs.** To dismember. ***—idiom.*** **out on a limb.** *Informal.* In a difficult, awkward, or vulnerable position. [ME *lim* < OE.]

limb[2] (lĭm) *n.* **1.** *Astron.* The circumferential edge of the apparent disk of a celestial body. **2.** The edge of a graduated arc or circle used in an instrument to measure angles. **3.** *Bot.* The expanded tip of a petal or the expanded upper part of a united corolla. [Lat. *limbus,* border.]

lim·bate (lĭm′bāt′) *adj. Bot.* Having an edge or margin of a different color. [LLat. *limbatus,* bordered < Lat. *limbus,* border.]

lim·ber[1] (lĭm′bər) *adj.* **1.** Bending or flexing readily; pliable. **2.** Capable of moving, bending, or contorting easily; supple. *—v.* **-bered, -ber·ing, -bers.** *—tr.* To make limber: *limbered up his legs.* *—intr.* To make oneself limber: *players limbering up before the game.* [Orig. unknown.] **—lim′ber·ly** *adv.* **—lim′ber·ness** *n.*

lim·ber[2] (lĭm′bər) *n.* A two-wheeled, horse-drawn vehicle used to tow a field gun. [ME *limour,* the shaft of a cart.]

lim·bers (lĭm′bərz) *pl.n. Naut.* Gutters or channels on each side of a ship's keelson that drain bilge water into the pump well. [Alteration of Fr. *lumière* < OFr. *lumiere,* opening < LLat. *luminare,* light. —see LUMINARY.]

lim·bi (lĭm′bī′) *n.* Plural of **limbus.**

lim·bo[1] (lĭm′bō) *n., pl.* **-bos. 1.** Often **Limbo.** *Theol.* The abode of souls kept from Heaven through circumstance, such as lack of baptism. **2.** A region or condition of oblivion or neglect: *kept his promotion in limbo for months.* **3.** A state or place of confinement. **4.** An intermediate place or state. [ME < Med. Lat. *limbus* < Lat., border.]

lim·bo[2] (lĭm′bō) *n.* A West Indian dance in which the danc-

lilac

lily

lily of the valley

lily pad

ers keep bending over backward and passing under a pole that is lowered slightly each time. [Native word in the West Indies.]

lime[1]

Lim·burg·er (lĭm′bûr′gər) *n.* A soft white cheese with a very strong odor and flavor. [After *Limburg,* Belgium.]

lim·bus (lĭm′bəs) *n., pl.* **-bi** (-bī′). *Biol.* A distinctive border or edge. [Lat., border.]

lime[1] (līm) *n.* **1.** A spiny tree, *Citrus aurantifolia,* native to Asia, having evergreen leaves, fragrant white flowers, and edible fruit. **2.** The egg-shaped fruit of the lime tree, having a green rind and acid juice used as flavoring. [Fr. < Prov. *limo* < Ar. *līmah.*]

lime[2] (līm) *n.* Any of several Old World linden trees. [Alteration of obs. *line,* linden < ME *lind* < OE.]

lime[3] (līm) *n.* **1. a.** Calcium oxide. **b.** Any of various mineral and industrial forms of calcium oxide differing chiefly in water content and percentage of such constituents as silica, alumina, and iron. **2.** A sticky substance smeared on twigs and used to catch small birds; birdlime. —*tr.v.* **limed, lim·ing, limes. 1.** To treat with lime. **2.** To smear with birdlime. **3.** To catch or snare with or as if with birdlime. [ME < OE *līm.*] —**lim′y** *adj.*

lime·ade (lī-mād′) *n.* A sweetened beverage of lime juice and plain or carbonated water.

lime·kiln (līm′kĭl′, -kĭln′) *n.* A furnace used to reduce naturally occurring forms of calcium carbonate to lime.

lime·light (līm′līt′) *n.* **1. a.** A stage light in which lime is heated to incandescence producing brilliant illumination. **b.** The brilliant light so produced. **2.** A focus of public attention.

li·men (lī′mən) *n., pl.* **li·mens** or **lim·i·na** (lĭm′ə-nə). The threshold of a physiological or psychological response. [Lat., threshold.] —**lim′i·nal** (lĭm′ə-nəl) *adj.*

lim·er·ick (lĭm′ər-ĭk) *n.* A light humorous or nonsensical verse of five anapestic lines usually with the rhyme scheme *aabba.* [After *Limerick,* a county of the Republic of Ireland.]

lime·stone (līm′stōn′) *n.* A shaly or sandy sedimentary rock, chiefly $CaCO_3$, containing variable quantities of magnesium carbonate and quartz, used as a building stone, and in the manufacture of lime, carbon dioxide, and cement.

lime-twig (līm′twĭg′) *n.* **1.** A twig covered with birdlime to catch birds. **2.** A snare.

lime·wa·ter (līm′wô′tər, -wŏt′ər) *n.* A clear colorless alkaline aqueous solution of calcium hydroxide, used in calamine lotion and other skin preparations and sometimes as an antacid.

lim·ey (lī′mē) *n., pl.* **-eys.** *Slang.* **1.** A British seaman. **2.** An Englishman.

li·mic·o·line (lī-mĭk′ə-līn′, -lĭn) *adj.* Of or pertaining to shore birds, such as sandpipers, of the suborder Charadrii. [< NLat. *Limicolae,* former order name : Lat. *limus,* mud + *colere,* to inhabit.]

lim·it (lĭm′ĭt) *n.* **1.** The point, edge, or line beyond which something cannot or may not proceed. **2. limits.** The boundary surrounding a specific area; bounds: *within the city limits.* **3.** Something that confines or restricts. **4.** The greatest amount or number allowed. **5.** In games of chance, the largest amount which may be bet at one time. **6.** *Math.* A number or point k that is approached by a function $f(x)$ as x approaches a if, for every positive number ε, there exists a number δ such that $|f(x)-k|<\varepsilon$ if $0<|x-a|<\delta$. **7.** *Informal.* One that approaches or exceeds certain limits, as of credibility, forbearance, or acceptability. —*tr.v.* **-it·ed, -it·ing, -its.** To confine or restrict within limits. [ME *limite* < OFr. < Lat. *limes.*] —**lim′it·a·ble** *adj.* —**lim′it·er** *n.*

Synonyms: *limit, restrict, confine, circumscribe, bound.* These verbs mean to keep or contain within a specified area. *Limit* refers principally to establishing a maximum, as in quantity, degree, space, or time, beyond which a person or thing cannot or may not go. It is sometimes interchangeable with *restrict* and *confine,* but *restrict* and *confine* more often refer to keeping persons, things, or activities within a prescribed area: *messages limited to 50 words; a sale limited* (or *confined*) *to two days; a soldier restricted* (or *confined*) *to his quarters; wiretapping restricted* (or *confined*) *to cases involving national security. Circumscribe* is applied to encircling in a literal sense or, more often, to keeping something intangible, such as power, law, or influence, within specified and often narrow limits. *Bound* refers largely to setting geographical limits.

lim·i·tar·y (lĭm′ĭ-tĕr′ē) *adj. Archaic.* **1. a.** Of or relating to a limit or boundary. **b.** Limiting; restrictive. **2.** Limited.

lim·i·ta·tion (lĭm′ĭ-tā′shən) *n.* **1.** The act of limiting or the state of being limited. **2.** A restriction. **3.** *Law.* A limited period during which, by statute, an action may be brought.

lim·it·ed (lĭm′ĭ-tĭd) *adj.* **1.** Confined or restricted within certain limits: *has only limited experience.* **2.** Not attaining the highest goals or achievement: *a limited success.* **3.** Having governmental or ruling powers restricted by enforceable limitations, as a constitution or legislative body. **4.** Designating transportation facilities, such as trains or buses, that make few stops and carry relatively few passengers. —*n.* A limited train or bus. —**lim′i·ted·ly** *adv.* —**lim′i·ted·ness** *n.*

limited edition *n.* An edition, as of a book, limited to a specified number of copies.

limited war *n.* A war whose objective is of smaller scope than the total defeat of the enemy.

lim·i·ting (lĭm′ĭ-tĭng) *adj.* **1.** Acting as a limit. **2.** *Gram.* Restricting the range of application of the noun that is modified.

lim·it·less (lĭm′ĭt-lĭs) *adj.* **1.** Having no limit. **2.** Unconfined or unrestricted. —**lim′it·less·ly** *adv.* —**lim′it·less·ness** *n.*

limit point *n. Math.* A limit (sense 6).

limn (lĭm) *tr.v.* **limned, limn·ing** (lĭm′nĭng), **limns. 1.** To describe. **2.** To depict by painting or drawing. [ME *limnen,* to illuminate (a manuscript), prob. < *limnour,* an illuminator < AN *lymnour* < OFr. *enluminer,* to illuminate (a manuscript) < Lat. *illuminare,* to adorn < *lumen,* light.] —**limn′er** (lĭm′nər) *n.*

lim·net·ic (lĭm-nĕt′ĭk) *adj.* Of or occurring in the deeper, open waters of lakes or ponds. [< Gk. *limnē,* lake.]

lim·nol·o·gy (lĭm-nŏl′ə-jē) *n.* The scientific study of the life and phenomena of lakes, ponds, and streams. [Gk. *limnē,* lake + -LOGY.] —**lim′no·log′i·cal** (-nə-lŏj′ĭ-kəl) *adj.* —**lim′no·log′i·cal·ly** *adv.* —**lim·nol′o·gist** *n.*

lim·o (lĭm′ō) *n., pl.* **lim·os.** A limousine.

lim·o·nene (lĭm′ə-nēn′) *n.* A liquid, $C_{10}H_{16}$, with a characteristic lemonlike fragrance, used as a solvent, wetting agent, and dispersing agent, and in the manufacture of resins. [Fr. *limonène* < obs. Fr. *limon,* lemon < OFr. —see LEMON.]

li·mo·nite (lī′mə-nīt′) *n.* A widely occurring yellowish-brown to black natural iron oxide, essentially $FeO(OH){\cdot}nH_2O$, used as an ore of iron. [G. *Limonit* < Gk. *leimōn,* meadow.] —**li′mo·nit′ic** (-nĭt′ĭk) *adj.*

lim·ou·sine (lĭm′ə-zēn′, lĭm′ə-zēn′) *n.* Any of various large passenger vehicles, esp. a luxurious automobile usually driven by a chauffeur and sometimes having a glass partition separating the passenger compartment from the driver's seat. [After *Limousin,* a region of France.]

limp (lĭmp) *intr.v.* **limped, limp·ing, limps. 1.** To walk lamely, esp. with irregularity, as if favoring one leg. **2.** To move or proceed haltingly or unsteadily. —*n.* An irregular, jerky, or awkward gait. —*adj.* **-er, -est. 1.** Lacking or having lost rigidity, stiffness, or the ability to support itself: *a limp leaf.* **2.** Lacking strength or firmness; weak: *a limp handshake.* [Prob. < obs. *limphalt,* lame.] —**limp′ly** *adv.* —**limp′ness** *n.*

lim·pet (lĭm′pĭt) *n.* **1.** Any of numerous marine gastropod mollusks, as of the families Acmaeidae and Patellidae, characteristically having a tent-shaped shell and adhering to rocks of tidal areas. **2.** One who clings persistently. **3.** A type of explosive designed to cling to the hull of a ship and detonate on contact or signal. [Poss. < ME *lempet.*]

lim·pid (lĭm′pĭd) *adj.* **1.** Characterized by transparent clearness; pellucid: *a limpid pool.* **2.** Easily intelligible; clear: *writes in a limpid style.* **3.** Calm and untroubled; serene. [Fr. *limpide* < Lat. *limpidus.*] —**lim·pid′i·ty, lim′pid·ness** *n.* —**lim′pid·ly** *adv.*

limp·kin (lĭmp′kĭn) *n.* A brownish wading bird, *Aramus guarauna,* of warm, swampy regions of the New World, having a distinctive, wailing call.

lin·ac (lĭn′ăk′) *n.* A linear accelerator. [LIN(EAR) AC(CELERATOR).]

lin·age also **line·age** (lī′nĭj) *n.* **1.** The number of lines of printed or written material. **2.** Payment for written work at a specified amount per line.

lin·al·o·ol (lĭ-năl′ō-ôl′, -ōl′) *n.* A colorless, fragrant liquid, $C_{10}H_{18}O$, distilled from the oils of rosewood, bergamot, and other plants and trees, and used in perfume manufacture. [Sp. *linaloe,* fragrant wood of a Mexican tree (< LLat. *lignum aloes,* wood of the aloe) + -OL[2].]

linch·pin (lĭnch′pĭn′) *n.* **1.** A locking pin inserted in the end of a shaft, as in an axle, to prevent a wheel from slipping off. **2.** A central and cohesive element: *Reduced spending is the linchpin of his economic program.* [ME *linspin* : *lins,* linchpin (< OE *lynis*) + *pin,* pin (< OE *pinn).*]

Lin·coln (lĭng′kən) *n.* Any of a breed of sheep with long wool, developed in Lincoln, England.

Lin·coln·esque (lĭng′kə-nĕsk′) *adj.* Suggestive of Abraham Lincoln.

lin·den (lĭn′dən) *n.* Any of various trees of the genus *Tilia,* having heart-shaped leaves and yellowish, often fragrant flowers, and often planted for shade. [ME, made of linden wood < OE < *lind,* linden.]

line[1] (līn) *n.* **1. a.** The locus of a point having one degree of freedom; curve. **b.** A set of points (x, y) that satisfy the linear equation $ax + by + c = 0$, where a and b are not both zero. **2. a.** A thin, continuous mark, as that made by a pen, pencil, or brush applied to a surface. **b.** A similar mark cut or scratched into a surface. **c.** A crease in the skin, esp. on the face; wrinkle. **3.** A real or imaginary straight line positioned in relation to fixed points of reference. **4. a.** A border or boundary: *the county line.* **b.** A limit or constraint: *drew the line at armed intervention.* **c.** A demarcation. **d.** A contour or outline. **5. a.** A mark used to define a shape or represent a contour. **b.** Any of the marks that make up the formal design of a picture. **6. a.** A cable, rope, string, cord, or wire. **b.** A rope used aboard a ship. **c.** A fishing line. **d.** A clothesline. **7.** A pipe or system of pipes for conveying a fluid. **8.** An electric-power transmission cable. **9. a.** A wire or system of wires connecting telephone or telegraph systems. **b.** An open or functioning telephone connection. **10. a.** A passenger or cargo system of transportation, usually over a definite route. **b.** A company owning or managing such a system. **11.** A railway track or system of tracks. **12.** A course of progress or movement; route: *the line of flight.* **13.** A general method, manner, or course of procedure: *different lines of thought.* **14.** An official or prescribed policy: *the party line.* **15.** A condition of agreement; alignment: *brought the front wheels into line.* **16. a.** One's trade, occupation, or field of interest. **b.** The range of one's competence: *out of my line.* **17.** *Archaic.* One's lot or position in life. **18.** Merchandise or services of a similar or related nature: *carries a complete line of small tools.* **19.** A group of persons or things arranged in a row or series. **20. a.** A chronological series of persons or things who succeed each other: *a line of kings.* **b.** Ancestry or lineage. **c.** A strain, as of livestock or plants, developed by selective breeding. **21. a.** A sequence of related things that leads to a certain ending: *a line of argument.* **b.** An ordered system of operations that allows a sequential manufacture or assembly of goods at all or various stages of production. **22. a.** A horizontal row of printed or written words or symbols. **b.** A unit of verse made up of a certain number of metrical feet characteristic of the verse. **23.** A brief letter; note. **24.** Often **lines.** The dialogue of a play or other theatrical presentation. **25.** A calculated or glib way of speaking, usually to obtain an undeclared end. **26. lines.** *Chiefly Brit. Informal.* A marriage certificate. **27.** In bridge, a horizontal demarcation dividing categories of points scored. **28. a.** A source of information. **b.** The information itself. **29.** *Mus.* One of the five parallel marks composing a staff. **30. a.** A military formation in which elements, such as troops, tanks, or ships, are arranged abreast of each other. **b.** The battle area closest to the enemy. **c.** The troops in this area. **d.** Combatant troops. **e.** The officers in direct command of warships. **f.** A bulwark or trench. **g.** An extended system of such fortifications or defenses. **31.** *Sports.* **a.** A foul line. **b.** A real or imaginary mark demarcating a specified section of a playing area or field. **c.** A real or imaginary mark or point at which a race begins or ends. **32.** *Football.* **a.** A line of scrimmage. **b.** The linemen. —*v.* **lined, lin·ing, lines.** —*tr.* **1.** To mark or incise with a line or lines. **2.** To represent with lines. **3.** To place in a series or row. **4.** To form a bordering line along: *Small stalls lined the alley.* **5.** *Baseball.* To hit (a ball) sharply in usually a straight line. —*intr. Baseball.* To hit a line drive: *lined out to shortstop.* **—phrasal verb. line up. 1.** To arrange in a line; align. **2.** To organize and make ready: *lined up considerable support for the bill.* **—idioms. between the lines.** By inference; in an indirect manner. **down the line. 1.** All the way; completely. **2.** At a point or end in the future. **in line for.** Next in order for: *in line for the presidency.* **on the line.** *Informal.* **1.** Ready or available for immediate payment. **2.** In jeopardy; so as to be risked: *put his reputation on the line.* **out of line.** Uncalled-for; improper; unruly. [ME < OE, cord, and OFr. *ligne,* line, both < Lat. *linea,* string < *linum,* thread.]

line^{2} (līn) *tr.v.* **lined, lin·ing, lines. 1.** To fit a covering to the inside surface of: *a coat lined with fur.* **2.** To cover the inner surface of: *Moisture lined the cave's walls.* **3.** To fill plentifully, as with money or food. [ME *linen* < *line,* flax < OE *līn* < Lat. *linum.*]

lin·e·age^{1} (lĭn'ē-ĭj) *n.* **1. a.** Direct descent from a particular ancestor; ancestry. **b.** Derivation. **2.** The descendants of a common ancestor considered to be the founder of the line. [ME < OFr. *lignage* < *ligne,* line. —see LINE^{1}.]

line·age^{2} (lī'nĭj) *n.* Variant of **linage.**

lin·e·al (lĭn'ē-əl) *adj.* **1.** Belonging to or being in the direct line of descent from an ancestor. **2.** Derived from or relating to a particular line of descent. **3.** Linear. [ME < AN *lineale* < Med. Lat. *linealis* < LLat. < Lat. *linea,* line < *linum,* thread.] **—lin'e·al·ly** *adv.*

lin·e·a·ment (lĭn'ē-ə-mənt) *n.* **1.** A distinctive shape, contour, or line, esp. of the face. **2.** Often **lineaments.** A definitive or characteristic feature. [ME *liniament* < Lat. *lineamentum* < *linea,* line < *linum,* thread.]

lin·e·ar (lĭn'ē-ər) *adj.* **1.** Of, relating to, or resembling a line; straight. **2. a.** In, of, describing, described by, or related to a straight line. **b.** Having only one dimension. **3.** Characterized by, composed of, or emphasizing drawn lines rather than painterly effects. **4.** *Bot.* Narrow and elongated: *a linear leaf.* [Lat. *linearis* < *linea,* line < *linum,* thread.] **—lin'e·ar·ly** *adv.*

Linear A *n.* An undeciphered writing system used on Crete from the 18th to the 15th century B.C.

linear accelerator *n.* An electron, proton, or heavy-ion accelerator in which the paths of the particles accelerated are essentially straight lines rather than circles or spirals.

linear algebra *n.* **1.** A branch of mathematics dealing with the theory of systems of linear equations, matrices, vector spaces, determinants, and linear transformations. **2.** A mathematical ring and vector space with scalars from an associated field, the multiplication of which is of the form $(aA)\ (bB) = (ab)\ (AB)$, where a and b are scalars and A and B are vectors.

linear al·kyl·ate sulfonate (ăl'kə-lāt') *n.* A biodegradable surfactant that is used in detergents and is a salt of sulfonic acid.

Linear B *n.* A syllabic script used in Mycenaean Greek documents of Crete and Pylos from the 14th to the 12th century B.C.

linear combination *n.* A mathematical expression of first order, composed of the sums and differences of elements with non-zero coefficients.

linear dependence *n.* The property of a mathematical set, with its coefficients taken from another, of having at least one linear combination equal to zero when at least one of the coefficients is not equal to zero.

linear equation *n.* An algebraic equation, such as $x + y + 5 = 0$, in which the highest degree term in the variable or variables is of the first degree.

linear independence *n.* The property of a mathematical set, with its coefficients taken from another, of having no linear combinations equal to zero unless all of the coefficients are equal to zero.

lin·e·ar·ize (lĭn'ē-ə-rīz') *tr.v.* **-ized, -iz·ing, -iz·es.** To put or project in linear form. **—lin'e·ar·i·za'tion** *n.*

linear measure *n.* **1.** Measurement of length. **2.** A unit or system of units for measuring length.

linear momentum *n.* Momentum (sense 1).

linear perspective *n.* A form of perspective in drawing or painting in which parallel lines are represented as converging so as to give the illusion of depth and distance.

lin·e·a·tion (lĭn'ē-ā'shən) *n.* **1.** The action of marking or outlining with lines. **2.** An outline. **3.** An arrangement of lines.

line·back·er (līn'băk'ər) *n.* *Football.* Any of the defensive players forming a second line of defense behind the ends and tackles. **—line'back'ing** *n.*

line breeding *n.* Selective breeding to perpetuate certain qualities or characteristics in a strain of livestock.

line cut *n.* A letterpress printing plate made from a line drawing by a photoengraving process.

line drawing *n.* A drawing made with lines only, esp. one used as copy for a line cut.

line drive *n.* *Baseball.* A batted ball hit sharply so that its path roughly describes a straight line.

line engraving *n.* **1. a.** A metal plate, used in intaglio printing, on the surface of which design lines have been hand engraved. **b.** The process of making such an engraving. **c.** A print made from such an engraving. **2.** A line cut.

line·man (līn'mən) *n.* **1.** One employed to install or repair telephone, telegraph, or electric power lines. **2.** One employed to inspect and repair railroad tracks. **3.** *Football.* A player positioned on the forward line.

lin·en (lĭn'ən) *n.* **1. a.** Thread made from fibers of the flax plant. **b.** Cloth woven from this thread. **2.** Garments or articles made from linen or similar material. **3.** Paper made from flax fibers, or given a linenlike luster. —*adj.* **1.** Made of flax or linen. **2.** Resembling linen. [ME < *linen,* of cloth < OE *līnen* < Lat. *linum,* thread.]

line of credit *n.* A credit line (sense 2).

line of force *n.* A theoretical line in a field of force, any tangent to which gives the direction of the field at the point of tangency.

line of scrimmage *n.* *Football.* An imaginary line across the field on which the ball rests and at which the teams line up for a new play.

line of sight *n.* **1.** An imaginary line from the eye to the object being looked at. **2.** An unobstructed path between electronic sending and receiving antennas.

lin·e·o·late (lĭn'ē-ə-lāt') *adj.* Marked with fine lines. [NLat. *lineolatus* < Lat. *lineola,* little line, dim. of *linea,* line < *linum,* thread.]

line printer *n.* A high-speed printing device, primarily used in data processing, that prints an entire line of type as a unit rather than printing each character individually.

lin·er^{1} (lī'nər) *n.* **1.** One that draws or makes lines. **2.** A commercial ship or airplane, esp. one carrying passengers on a regular route. **3.** *Baseball.* A line drive.

lin·er^{2} (lī'nər) *n.* **1.** One who makes or puts in linings. **2.** Something used as a lining.

line score *n.* *Sports.* A summary of the scoring by period in a game printed in the form of a horizontal table, esp. an inning-by-inning record of the runs scored in a baseball game plus the total of each team's hits, runs, and errors.

lines·man (līnz'mən) *n.* **1. a.** *Football.* An official who marks the downs and the position of the ball and watches for certain violations from the sidelines. **b.** *Sports.* An official in various court games whose chief duty is to call shots that fall out of bounds. **2.** A lineman (sense 1).

line spectrum *n.* A spectrum consisting of a set of discrete, fairly narrow lines.

line squall *n.* *Naut.* A squall or squalls occurring along a narrow band of thunderstorms.

line storm *n.* A violent storm or series of storms of rain and wind popularly supposed to take place during the equinoxes.

line-up also **line·up** (līn'ŭp') *n.* **1.** A line of persons formed for inspection or identification. **2. a.** The members of a team chosen to start a game. **b.** A list of such players. **3.** A group of persons, organizations, or things enlisted or arrayed for a specific purpose.

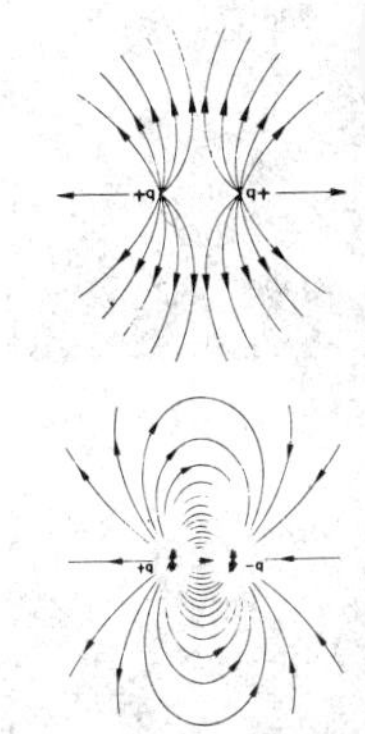

line of force
Electric lines of force
Above: Equal and similar charges
$(+q,\ q+)$
Below: Equal but opposite charges
$(+q,\ -q)$

p **pop** / r **roar** / s **sauce** / sh **ship, dish** / t **tight** / th **thin, path** / *th* **this, bathe** / ŭ **cut** / ûr **urge** / v **valve** / w **with** / y **yes** / z **zebra, size** / zh **vision** / ə **about, item, edible, gallop, circus** / œ *Fr.* **feu,** *Ger.* **schön** / ü *Fr.* **tu,** *Ger.* **über** / KH *Ger.* **ich,** *Scot.* **loch** / N *Fr.* **bon.**

ling¹ (lĭng) *n., pl.* **ling** or **lings.** Any of various marine food fishes related to or resembling the cod, such as a burbot or hake. [ME.]

ling² (lĭng) *n.* Heather (sense 1). [ME < ON *lyng.*]

–ling¹ *suff.* **1.** One connected with: *worldling.* **2.** One having a specified quality: *underling.* **3.** One that is young, small, or inferior: *duckling.* [ME < OE.]

–ling² *suff.* In a specified direction, manner, or condition: *darkling.* [ME < OE.]

lin·gam (lĭng'gəm) also **lin·ga** (-gə) *n.* A stylized phallus worshiped as a symbol of the Hindu god Shiva. [Skt. *liṅgam,* penis.]

ling·cod (lĭng'kŏd') *n., pl.* **lingcod** or **-cods.** A food fish, *Ophiodon elongatus,* of northern Pacific waters.

lin·ger (lĭng'gər) *v.* **-gered, -ger·ing, -gers.** —*intr.* **1.** To delay in departing or leaving something; tarry. **2.** To hover between life and death for some time before dying. **3.** To persist: *The memory still lingers.* **4.** To proceed slowly; saunter. **5.** To be tardy in acting; procrastinate. —*tr.* To pass (a period of time) in a leisurely or aimless manner. [ME *lengeren* < *lenger,* longer < OE *lengra.*] **—lin'ger·er** *n.* **—lin'ger·ing·ly** *adv.*

lin·ge·rie (län'zhə-rā', län'zhə-rē) *n.* **1.** Women's underwear. **2.** *Archaic.* Linen articles, esp. garments. [Fr. < *linge,* linen < Lat. *linea,* made of linen < *linum,* thread.]

lin·go (lĭng'gō) *n., pl.* **-goes.** Language that is unintelligible or unfamiliar, esp.: **a.** A foreign language. **b.** The specialized vocabulary of a particular field or discipline. [Prob. Port. *lingoa* < Lat. *lingua,* language.]

lin·gon·ber·ry (lĭng'ən-bĕr'ē) *n.* The cowberry (sense 2). [Swed. *lingon,* a kind of berry + BERRY.]

lin·gua (lĭng'gwə) *n., pl.* **-guae** (-gwē'). A tongue or tonguelike organ. [Lat.]

lingua fran·ca (frăng'kə) *n., pl.* **lingua fran·cas** (-kəz) also **lin·guae fran·cae** (lĭng'gwē frăng'kē). **1.** A mixture of Italian with French, Spanish, Arabic, Greek, and Turkish, spoken in the Mediterranean area, esp. in the Levant. **2.** A language used as a medium of communication between peoples of different languages. **3.** Something that is similar to a common language. [Ital.]

link¹

lin·gual (lĭng'gwəl) *adj.* **1.** Of, pertaining to, or resembling the tongue or a tonguelike organ. **2.** Pronounced with the tongue in conjunction with other organs of speech. **3.** Linguistic. —*n.* A sound that is pronounced with the tongue in conjunction with other organs of speech, as the sounds (t), (l), and (n). **—lin'gual·ly** *adv.*

lin·gui·ne also **lin·gui·ni** (lĭng-gwē'nē) *n. (used with a sing. verb).* Pasta in the form of long, flat, thin strands. [Ital. < *lingua,* tongue < Lat.]

lin·guist (lĭng'gwĭst) *n.* **1.** A person who speaks several languages fluently. **2.** A specialist in linguistics. [Lat. *lingua,* language + -IST.]

lin·guis·tic (lĭng-gwĭs'tĭk) *adj.* Of or relating to language or linguistics. **—lin·guis'ti·cal·ly** *adv.*

linguistic atlas *n.* A set of maps recording the geographical distribution of variations in speech.

linguistic form *n.* A meaningful unit of speech, such as an affix, word, phrase, or sentence.

linguistic geography *n.* The branch of linguistics that involves the study of regional variations of speech forms. **—linguistic geographer** *n.*

lin·guis·tics (lĭng-gwĭs'tĭks) *n. (used with a sing. verb).* The study of the nature and structure of human speech.

lin·gu·late (lĭng'gyə-lāt') *adj.* Tongue-shaped. [Lat. *lingulatus* < *lingula,* little tongue, dim. of *lingua.*]

lin·i·ment (lĭn'ə-mənt) *n.* A medicinal fluid applied to the skin as an anodyne or counterirritant. [ME < LLat. *linimentum* < Lat. *linere,* to rub over.]

li·nin (lī'nĭn) *n.* The filamentous, achromatic material in the nucleus of a cell that interconnects the chromatin granules. [Lat. *linum,* thread.]

lin·ing (lī'nĭng) *n.* **1. a.** An interior covering or coating. **b.** Material that may be used for such covering or coating. **2.** The act or process of applying a lining to something.

Linotype

link¹ (lĭngk) *n.* **1.** One of the rings or loops forming a chain. **2.** Something resembling a chain link in its physical arrangement or its connecting function, esp.: **a.** One of several sausages strung together. **b.** A unit in a transportation or communications system. **c.** A single connecting element. **3.** A cuff link. **4.** A unit of length used in surveying, equal to 0.01 chain, 7.92 inches, or about 20.12 centimeters. **5.** A rod or lever transmitting motion in a machine. **6.** *Computer Sci.* An identifying term attached to an element in a system to facilitate connection to other identified elements. —*tr. & intr.v.* **linked, link·ing, links.** To connect or become connected with or as if with links. [ME *linke,* of Scand. orig.] **—link'er** *n.*

link² (lĭngk) *n.* A torch formerly used for lighting one's way in the streets. [Poss. < Med. Lat. *linchinus,* candle < Lat. *lynchnus* < Gk. *lukhnos.*]

lion

link·age (lĭng'kĭj) *n.* **1.** The act or process of linking. **2.** The state or condition of being linked. **3.** A system of interconnected machine elements, such as rods, springs, and pivots, used to transmit power or motion. **4.** A measure of the induced voltage in a circuit caused by a magnetic flux and equal to the flux times the number of turns in the coil that surrounds it. **5.** *Genetics.* A relationship between two or more nonallelic genes occupying the same chromosome that causes them to have closely associated inherited effects. **6.** A diplomatic negotiating strategy holding that progress on one issue is an essential element for progress on other issues: "*We saw linkage . . . as synonymous with an overall strategic and geopolitical view*" (Henry Kissinger).

link·boy (lĭngk'boi') *n.* A boy formerly hired to carry a torch to guide persons along dark streets.

linked (lĭngkt) *adj.* **1.** Connected, esp. by or as if by links. **2.** *Genetics.* Exhibiting linkage. **3.** *Computer Sci.* Provided with links.

linking verb *n.* A copula (sense 1).

links (lĭngks) *pl.n.* **1.** A golf course. **2.** *Scot.* Relatively flat or undulating sandy turf-covered ground usually along a seashore. [ME < OE *hlincas,* pl. of *hlinc,* ridge.]

link·up (lĭngk'ŭp') *n.* **1.** An instance of meeting or contact, as of two spacecraft. **2. a.** Something that serves to link or join. **b.** A functional unit derived from the linking up of separate elements.

linn (lĭn) *n. Scot.* **1.** A waterfall. **2.** A steep ravine. [Sc. Gael. *linne.*]

Lin·nae·an also **Lin·ne·an** (lĭ-nē'ən) *adj.* Of or pertaining to Linnaeus or to the system of taxonomic classification and nomenclature originated by him.

lin·net (lĭn'ĭt) *n.* A small Old World songbird, *Acanthis cannabina,* having brownish plumage. [OFr. *linette* < *lin,* flax < Lat. *linum.*]

lin·o·le·ic acid (lĭn'ə-lē'ĭk) *n.* A colorless to straw-colored liquid, $C_{18}H_{32}O_2$, an important component of drying oils and an essential fatty acid in the human diet. [Gk. *linon,* flax + OLEIC ACID.]

lin·o·len·ic acid (lĭn'ə-lĕn'ĭk) *n.* A colorless liquid, $C_{18}H_{30}O_2$, an important component of natural drying oils and an essential fatty acid in the human diet. [Alteration of LINOLEIC ACID.]

li·no·le·um (lĭ-nō'lē-əm) *n.* A durable, washable material made in sheets by pressing a mixture of heated linseed oil, rosin, powdered cork, and pigments onto a burlap or canvas backing, used as a floor and counter-top covering. [Orig. a trademark.]

Li·no·type (lī'nə-tīp'). A trademark for a machine that sets type on a metal slug, operated by a keyboard.

lin·sang (lĭn'săng') *n.* Any of several Asian or African carnivorous mammals of the genera *Poiana* and *Prionodon,* having a spotted coat and a long banded tail. [Malay.]

lin·seed (lĭn'sēd') *n.* The seed of flax, esp. when used as the source of linseed oil; flaxseed. [ME *linsed* < OE *līnsǣd* : *līn,* flax (< Lat. *linum*) + *sǣd,* seed.]

linseed oil *n.* A yellowish oil extracted from the seeds of flax and used as a drying oil in paints and varnishes and in linoleum, printing inks, and synthetic resins.

lin·sey-wool·sey (lĭn'zē-wo͝ol'zē) *n., pl.* **-seys.** A coarse fabric of cotton or linen woven with wool. [ME *linsiwolsie.*]

lin·stock (lĭn'stŏk') *n.* A long forked stick for holding a match, formerly used to fire cannon. [Du. *lontstok* : *lont,* match + *stok,* stick.]

lint (lĭnt) *n.* **1.** Clinging bits of fiber and fluff; fuzz. **2.** Downy material obtained by scraping linen cloth and used for dressing wounds. **3.** The mass of soft fibers surrounding the seeds of unginned cotton. [ME < Med. Lat. *linteum* < Lat., linen cloth < *linum,* flax.]

lin·tel (lĭn'tl) *n.* The horizontal beam that forms the upper member of a window or door frame and supports part of the structure above it. [ME < OFr. < Lat. *limitaris,* of a threshold < *limes,* boundary.]

lint·er (lĭn'tər) *n.* **1. linters.** The short fibers that cling to cotton seeds after the first ginning. **2.** A machine that removes linters from the seeds of cotton.

lint·white (lĭnt'hwīt', -wīt') *n.* A linnet. [ME *linkwhitte,* alteration of OE *līnetwige.*]

lin·u·ron (lĭn'yə-rŏn') *n.* A herbicide, $C_9H_{10}O_2Cl_2N_2$, used to selectively kill weeds. [Orig. unknown.]

li·on (lī'ən) *n.* **1.** A large, carnivorous feline mammal, *Panthera leo,* of Africa and India, having a short tawny coat and a long, heavy mane around the neck and shoulders in the male. **2.** Any of several large wildcats, esp. the cougar. **3.** A person thought to resemble a lion, as in bravery or ferocity. **4.** A person of great eminence or prestige. **5. Lion.** Leo (sense 2). **—*idiom.* lion's share.** The greatest or best part of a whole. [ME < OFr. < Lat. *leo* < Gk. *leōn.*]

li·on·ess (lī'ə-nĭs) *n.* A female lion.

li·on·heart·ed (lī'ən-här'tĭd) *adj.* Extraordinarily courageous.

li·on·ize (lī'ə-nīz') *tr.v.* **-ized, -iz·ing, -iz·es.** To look upon or treat (a person) as a celebrity. **—li'on·iz'er** *n.*

lip (lĭp) *n.* **1.** *Anat.* Either of two fleshy, muscular folds that together surround the opening of the mouth. **2.** A structure or part that encircles or bounds an orifice, esp.: **a.** *Anat.* A labium. **b.** The margin of flesh around a wound. **c.** Either of the margins of the aperture of a gastropod shell. **d.** The rim, as of a vessel, bell, or crater. **3.** *Bot.* One of the protruding divisions of an irregular corolla or calyx, either paired as in the snapdragon or single as in an orchid. **4.** The tip of a pouring spout. **5.** *Slang.* Insolent talk. —*tr.v.* **lipped, lip·ping, lips. 1. a.** To touch the lips to. **b.** To kiss. **2.** To utter.

3. To lap or splash against. **4.** To hit a golf ball so that it stops just at the edge of (the hole). *—adj.* Formed or uttered with the help of the lips; labial. [ME < OE *lippa.*]

lip– *pref.* Variant of **lipo-.**

lip·ase (lĭp′ās′, lī′pās′) *n.* An enzyme that hydrolyzes fats to form glycerol and fatty acids.

lip-gloss (lĭp′glôs′, -glŏs′) *n.* A cosmetic that gives shine or gloss to the lips.

lip·id (lĭp′ĭd, lī′pĭd) also **lip·ide** (lĭp′īd′, lī′pīd′) *n.* Any of numerous fats and fatlike materials that are generally insoluble in water but soluble in common organic solvents, are related to the fatty acid esters, and together with carbohydrates and proteins constitute the principal structural material of living cells. **—lip·id′ic** *adj.*

lipo– or **lip–** *pref.* Fat; fatty; fatty tissue: *lipolysis.* [NLat. < Gk. *lipos,* fat.]

lip·oid (lĭp′oid′, lī′poid′) also **li·poi·dal** (lĭ-poid′l, lī-) *adj.* Resembling fat; fatty. **—lip′oid′** *n.*

li·pol·y·sis (lĭ-pŏl′ĭ-sĭs, lī-) *n.* Hydrolysis of fat.

li·po·ma (lĭ-pō′mə, lī-) *n., pl.* **-ma·ta** (-mə-tə) or **-mas.** A benign tumor of chiefly fatty cells. **—li·pom′a·tous** (-pŏm′ə-təs) *adj.*

lip·o·pro·tein (lĭp′ō-prō′tēn′, -tē-ĭn, lī′pō-) *n.* A conjugated protein consisting of a simple protein combined with a lipid group.

lip·o·trop·ic (lĭp′ō-trŏp′ĭk, -trō′pĭk, lī′pō-) *adj.* Preventing abnormal or excessive accumulation of fat in the liver. **—li·pot′ro·py** (lĭ-pŏt′rə-pē, lī-), **li·pot′ro·pism** *n.*

lip-read (lĭp′rēd′) *v.* **-read** (-rĕd′), **-read·ing, -reads.** *—tr.* To interpret (another's utterance) by lip reading. *—intr.* To use lip reading.

lip reading *n.* A technique for understanding unheard speech by interpreting lip and facial movements. **—lip reader** *n.*

lip service *n.* Insincere agreement or payment of respect.

lip·stick (lĭp′stĭk′) *n.* A stick of waxy or pastelike lip coloring enclosed in a small cylindrical case.

lip-synch (lĭp′sĭngk′) *v.* **-synched, -synch·ing, -synchs.** *—intr.* To move the lips in synchronization with recorded sound, as lyrics to a song. *—tr.* To move the lips in synchronization with: *lip-synched the song perfectly.* [LIP + SYNCH(RONIZE).]

Lip·tau·er (lĭp′tou′ər) *n.* **1.** A soft cheese originating in Hungary. **2. a.** A cheese spread made of Liptauer and paprika. **b.** An imitation spread made with cream cheese or cottage cheese. [G., after *Liptau* (Liptow), Hungary.]

li·quate (lī′kwāt′) *tr.v.* **-quat·ed, -quat·ing, -quates.** To separate (the metals in an alloy) by melting some constituents while leaving others solid. [Lat. *liquare, liquat-,* to melt.] **—li·qua′tion** *n.*

liq·ue·fac·tion (lĭk′wə-făk′shən) *n.* **1.** The process of liquefying. **2.** The state of being liquefied. [ME < LLat. *liquifactio* < Lat. *liquefacere,* to make fluid : *liquēre,* to be fluid + *facere,* to make.]

liq·ue·fy also **liq·ui·fy** (lĭk′wə-fī′) *v.* **-fied, -fy·ing, -fies.** *—tr.* To cause to become liquid, esp.: **a.** To melt (a solid) by heating. **b.** To condense (a gas) by cooling. *—intr.* To become liquid. [OFr. *liquefier* < Lat. *liquefacere* : *liquēre,* to be liquid + *facere,* to make.] **—liq′ue·fi′er** *n.*

li·ques·cent (lĭ-kwĕs′ənt) *adj.* Becoming or tending to become liquid; melting. [Lat. *liquescens, liquescent-,* pr. part. of *liquescere,* to become liquid < *liquēre,* to be liquid.] **—li·ques′cence, li·ques′cen·cy** *n.*

li·queur (lĭ-kûr′, -kyŏor′) *n.* A sweet alcoholic beverage made with various aromatic ingredients; cordial. [Fr. < OFr. *liquor,* a liquid. —see LIQUOR.]

liq·uid (lĭk′wĭd) *n.* **1. a.** The state of matter in which a substance exhibits a characteristic readiness to flow, little or no tendency to disperse, and relatively high incompressibility. **b.** Matter or a specific body of matter in this state. **2.** The sounds of *l* and *r,* which are nonfrictional and similar to vowels. *—adj.* **1.** Of or being a liquid. **2.** Liquefied, esp.: **a.** Melted by heating: *liquid wax.* **b.** Condensed by cooling: *liquid oxygen.* **3.** Clear and shining: *liquid brown eyes.* **4. a.** Flowing and clear; limpid: *liquid prose.* **b.** Articulated without friction and capable of being prolonged like a vowel, as the speech sounds *l* and *r.* **5.** Flowing readily. **6.** Readily converted into cash: *liquid assets.* [< ME, of a liquid < OFr. *liquide* < Lat. *liquidus* < *liquēre,* to be liquid.] **—li·quid′i·ty** (lĭ-kwĭd′ĭ-tē) *n.* **—liq′uid·ly** *adv.*

liquid air *n.* Air in the liquid state, condensed from the gas by cooling and sometimes pressure.

liq·uid·am·bar (lĭk′wĭ-dăm′bər) *n.* A tree of the genus *Liquidambar,* as the sweet gum. [NLat. *Liquidambar,* genus name : Lat. *liquidus,* liquid + Med. Lat. *ambar,* amber.]

liq·ui·date (lĭk′wĭ-dāt′) *v.* **-dat·ed, -dat·ing, -dates.** *—tr.* **1. a.** To pay off or settle (a debt, claim, or obligation). **b.** To settle the affairs of (a business firm, for example) by determining the liabilities and applying the assets to their discharge. **c.** To convert (assets) into cash. **2.** To put an end to; abolish. **3.** To put to death; kill. *—intr.* To enter into or be in the process of liquidating financially. [LLat. *liquidare, liquidat-,* to melt < Lat. *liquidus,* liquid.]

liquid crystal *n.* Any of various liquids in which the atoms or molecules are regularly arrayed in either one dimension or two dimensions, the order giving rise to optical properties, such as anisotropic scattering, associated with the crystals.

liquid measure *n.* **1.** A unit or system of units of liquid capacity. **2.** A measure for liquids.

liq·ui·fy (lĭk′wə-fī′) *v.* Variant of **liquefy.**

liq·uor (lĭk′ər) *n.* **1.** An alcoholic beverage made by distillation rather than by fermentation. **2.** A liquid substance, such as broth, produced in cooking. **3.** An aqueous solution of a nonvolatile substance. **4.** A solution, emulsion, or suspension for industrial use. *—tr.v.* **-uored, -uor·ing, -uors. 1.** *Slang.* To cause to become drunk with alcoholic liquor: *was all liquored up.* **2. a.** To treat (leather) with grease. **b.** To steep (malt, for example). [ME, a liquid < OFr. < Lat. < *liquēre,* to be liquid.]

li·quo·rice (lĭk′ər-ĭs, -ĭsh) *n. Chiefly Brit.* Variant of **licorice.**

li·ra (lîr′ə, lē′rə) *n., pl.* **li·re** (lîr′ā, lē′rā) or **li·ras.** See table at **currency.** [Ital. < Lat. *libra,* a unit of weight.]

lir·i·pipe (lîr′ə-pīp′) *n.* A long scarf or cord attached to and hanging from a hood. [Med. Lat. *liripipium.*]

li·sen·te (lē-sĕn′tā) *n., pl.* **lisente.** See table at **currency.** [Sotho < E. CENT.]

lisle (līl) *n.* **1.** A fine, smooth, tightly twisted thread spun from long-stapled cotton and used esp. for hosiery and underwear. **2.** Fabric knitted of lisle. [After *Lisle* (Lille), France.]

lisp (lĭsp) *n.* **1.** A speech defect or mannerism characterized by the failure to produce normal sibilants, esp. by the substitution of the sounds (th) and (*th*) for the sibilants (s) and (z). **2.** The sound of a lisp. *—v.* **lisped, lisp·ing, lisps.** *—intr.* **1.** To speak with a lisp. **2.** To speak imperfectly, as a child does. *—tr.* To pronounce with a lisp. [ME *lispen* < OE *wlispian.*] **—lisp′er** *n.*

lis·some also **lis·som** (lĭs′əm) *adj.* **1.** Easily bent; supple. **2.** Capable of moving with ease; limber. [Alteration of LITHESOME.] **—lis′some·ly** *adv.* **—lis′some·ness** *n.*

list[1] (lĭst) *n.* An item-by-item series of numbers or words, as the names of persons or things, written or printed one after the other: *a shopping list; a guest list.* *—v.* **list·ed, list·ing, lists.** *—tr.* **1.** To make a list of; itemize. **2.** To enter in a list; register. **3.** *Archaic.* To recruit. **4.** To put (oneself) in a specific category: *lists herself as an artist.* *—intr.* **1.** *Archaic.* To enlist in the armed forces. **2.** To have a stated list price: *a radio that lists for $10 over the sale price.* [Fr. *liste* < OItal. *lista,* of Germanic orig.]

list[2] (lĭst) *n.* **1. a.** A narrow strip, esp. of wood. **b.** A listel. **c.** A border or selvage of cloth. **2.** A stripe or band of color. **3.** *Obs.* A boundary; border. **4. lists. a.** An arena for tournaments or other contests, esp. jousting. **b.** A place of combat. **c.** An area of controversy. **5.** A ridge thrown up between two furrows by a lister in plowing. *—tr.v.* **list·ed, list·ing, lists. 1.** To cover, line, or edge with list. **2.** To cut a thin strip from the edge of. **3.** To furrow or plant (land) with a lister. [ME < OE *līste.*]

list[3] (lĭst) *n.* An inclination to one side, as of a ship; tilt. *—intr. & tr.v.* **list·ed, list·ing, lists.** To lean or cause to lean to the side; heel. [Orig. unknown.]

list[4] (lĭst) *intr. & tr.v.* **list·ed, list·ing, lists.** *Archaic.* To listen or listen to. [ME *listen* < OE *hlystan.*]

list[5] (lĭst) *Archaic.* *—v.* **list·ed, list·ing, lists.** *—tr.* To be pleasing to; satisfy. *—intr.* To be disposed; choose. *—n.* A desire or inclination. [ME *listen,* to desire < OE *lystan.*]

lis·tel (lĭs′təl) *n. Archit.* A narrow border, molding, or fillet. [OFr. < OItal. *listello,* dim. of *lista,* border, of Germanic orig.]

lis·ten (lĭs′ən) *intr.v.* **-tened, -ten·ing, -tens. 1.** To make an effort to hear something. **2.** To pay attention; give heed. ***—phrasal verb.* listen in. 1.** To tune in and listen to a broadcast. **2.** To listen to a conversation between others, esp. to eavesdrop. [ME *listenen* < *listen,* to listen < *hlystan.*] **—lis′ten·er** *n.*

list·er (lĭs′tər) *n.* A plow equipped with a double moldboard that turns up the soil on each side of the furrow, often having an attached drill for seed planting. [Ult. < LIST[2].]

list·ing (lĭs′tĭng) *n.* **1.** An act or instance of making or entering in a list. **2.** An entry in a list or directory. **3.** A list.

list·less (lĭst′lĭs) *adj.* Marked by a lack of energy or by disinclination toward any effort; lethargic. [ME *listles,* prob. < *list,* ability < OE.] **—list′less·ly** *adv.* **—list′less·ness** *n.*

list price *n.* A basic published or advertised price, often subject to discount.

lit[1] (lĭt) *v.* A past tense and past participle of **light[1].**

lit[2] (lĭt) *v.* A past tense and past participle of **light[2].**

lit·a·ny (lĭt′n-ē) *n., pl.* **-nies. 1.** A liturgical prayer consisting of phrases recited by a leader alternating with responses by the congregation. **2.** A repetitive or incantatory recital: *a daily litany of complaints.* [ME *letanie* < OFr. < Med. Lat. *letania* < LLat. *litania* < LGk. *litaneia* < Gk., entreaty < *litanuein,* to entreat < *litanos,* entreating < *litē,* supplication.]

li·tchi also **li·chee** or **ly·chee** (lē′chē) *n.* **1.** A Chinese tree, *Litchi chinensis,* bearing edible fruit. **2.** Also **litchi nut.** The fruit of the litchi tree. [Chin. (Mandarin) *li[4] zhi[1].*]

-lite *suff.* Stone; mineral; fossil: *coprolite.* [Fr., alteration of *-lithe* < Gk. *lithos,* stone.]

li·ter (lē′tər) *n.* A metric unit of volume equal to a cubic decimeter, approximately 1.056 liquid quarts or 0.908 dry

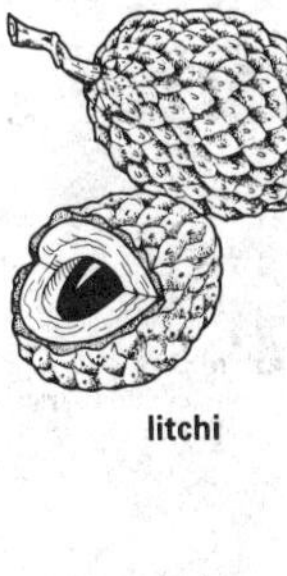

litchi

quart. [Fr. *litre* < obs. *litron,* measure of capacity < Med. Lat. *litra* < Gk., unit of weight.]

lit·er·a·cy (lĭt′ər-ə-sē) *n.* The condition or quality of being literate, esp. the ability to read and write.

lit·er·al (lĭt′ər-əl) *adj.* **1.** In accordance with, conforming to, or upholding the exact or primary meaning of a word or words. **2.** Word for word; verbatim: *a literal translation.* **3.** Concerned chiefly with facts; prosaic: *a literal mind.* **4.** Avoiding exaggeration, metaphor, or embellishment; plain: *a literal statement.* **5.** Consisting of, using, or expressed by letters: *literal notation.* —*n. Computer Sci.* A letter or symbol in data that represents itself. [ME < OFr. < LLat. *litteralis,* of letters < Lat. *littera,* letter.] —**lit′er·al·ness** *n.*

lit·er·al·ism (lĭt′ər-ə-lĭz′əm) *n.* **1.** Adherence to the explicit sense of a given text or doctrine. **2.** Literal portrayal; realism. —**lit′er·al·ist** *n.* —**lit′er·al·is′tic** *adj.*

lit·er·al·ize (lĭt′ər-ə-līz′) *tr.v.* **-ized, -iz·ing, -iz·es.** To make literal.

lit·er·al·ly (lĭt′ər-ə-lē) *adv.* **1.** In a literal or strict sense. **2.** Really; actually: *"There are people in the world who literally do not know how to boil water"* (Craig Claiborne).

Usage: *Literally* means "in a manner that accords precisely with the words." It is often used to mean "figuratively" or "in a manner of speaking," which is almost the opposite of its true meaning. Thus, it is not correct to say *he was literally breathing fire* except when speaking of a dragon.

lit·er·ar·y (lĭt′ə-rĕr′ē) *adj.* **1.** Of, relating to, or dealing with literature. **2.** Appropriate to literature rather than to everyday speech or writing. **3.** Versed in or fond of literature or learning: *a literary person.* **4.** Of or relating to writers or the profession of literature: *literary circles.* **5.** Bookish; pedantic. [Lat. *litterarius* < *littera,* letter.] —**lit′er·ar′i·ly** (-râr′ə-lē) *adv.* —**lit′er·ar′i·ness** *n.*

lit·er·ate (lĭt′ər-ĭt) *adj.* **1.** Able to read and write. **2.** Knowledgeable; educated. **3.** Familiar with literature; literary. **4.** Well-written; polished: *a literate essay.* —*n.* **1.** Someone who can read and write. **2.** A well-informed, educated person. [ME *litterate* < Lat. *litteratus* < *littera,* letter.] —**lit′er·ate·ly** *adv.* —**lit′er·ate·ness** *n.*

lit·er·a·ti (lĭt′ə-rä′tē) *pl.n.* The literary intelligentsia. [Ital. < Lat. *litteratus,* literate < *littera,* letter.]

lit·er·a·tim (lĭt′ə-rā′tĭm, -rä′-) *adv.* Letter for letter; literally. [Med. Lat. < Lat. *littera,* letter.]

lit·er·a·ture (lĭt′ər-ə-cho͝or′, -chər) *n.* **1.** A body of writings in prose or verse. **2.** Imaginative or creative writing, esp. of recognized artistic value; belles-lettres. **3.** The art or occupation of a literary writer. **4.** The body of written work produced by scholars or researchers in a given field: *medical literature.* **5.** Printed material, as for a political campaign. **6.** The aggregate of musical compositions, esp. for a specific instrument or ensemble. [ME, book learning < OFr. < LLat. *litteratura* < *litterae,* literature < *littera,* letter.]

literature search *n.* A systematic search for and investigation of published material pertaining to a given subject.

lith– *pref.* Variant of **litho-.**

–lith *suff.* **1.** Rock; stone: *xenolith.* **2.** Stone implement or structure: *megalith.* **3.** Mineral concretion; calculus: *cystolith.* [< Gk. *lithos,* stone.]

lith·arge (lĭth′ärj′, lĭ-thärj′) *n.* A yellow lead oxide, PbO, used in storage batteries, glass, and as a pigment. [ME *litarge* < OFr. < Lat. *lithargyrus* < Gk. *litharguros* : *lithos,* stone + *arguros,* silver.]

lithe (līth) *adj.* **1.** Readily bent; supple: *lithe branches.* **2.** Marked by effortless grace: *a lithe ballerina.* [ME < OE *līðe.*] —**lithe′ly** *adv.* —**lithe′ness** *n.*

lithe·some (līth′səm) *adj.* Lithe; lissome.

lith·i·a (lĭth′ē-ə) *n.* Lithium oxide. [NLat. < Gk. *lithos,* stone.]

li·thi·a·sis (lĭ-thī′ə-sĭs) *n., pl.* **-ses** (-sēz′). The pathological formation of calculi in the body.

lithia water *n.* Mineral water containing some lithium salts.

lith·ic (lĭth′ĭk) *adj.* **1.** Of or pertaining to stone. **2.** Of or pertaining to lithium.

–lithic *suff.* Pertaining to or characteristic of a specified stage in the use of stone by human beings: *Eolithic.* [< LITHIC.]

lith·i·um (lĭth′ē-əm) *n. Symbol* **Li** A soft, silvery, highly reactive metallic element that is used as a heat transfer medium, in thermonuclear weapons, and in various alloys, ceramics, and optical forms of glass. Atomic number 3; atomic weight 6.939; melting point 179°C; boiling point 1,317°C; specific gravity 0.534; valence 1.

lithium oxide *n.* A strongly alkaline white powder, Li_2O, used in ceramics and glass.

litho– or **lith–** *pref.* **1.** Stone: *lithosphere.* **2.** Lithium: *lithic.* [Lat. < Gk. < *lithos,* stone.]

lith·o·graph (lĭth′ə-grăf′) *n.* A print produced by lithography. —*tr.v.* **-graphed, -graph·ing, -graphs.** To produce by lithography. [Back-formation < LITHOGRAPHY.] —**li·thog′raph·er** (lĭ-thŏg′rə-fər) *n.* —**lith′o·graph′ic, lith′o·graph′i·cal** *adj.* —**lith′o·graph′i·cal·ly** *adv.*

li·thog·ra·phy (lĭ-thŏg′rə-fē) *n.* A printing process in which the image configuration to be printed is rendered on a flat surface, as on stone or now chiefly on sheet zinc or aluminum, and treated so that it will retain ink while the nonimage areas are treated to repel ink. [G. *Lithographie* : *litho-,* litho- + *-graphie,* -graphy.]

li·thol·o·gy (lĭ-thŏl′ə-jē) *n.* **1.** The gross physical character of a rock. **2.** The microscopic study, description, and classification of rock. —**lith′o·log′ic** (lĭth′ə-lŏj′ĭk), **lith′o·log′i·cal** *adj.* —**lith′o·log′i·cal·ly** *adv.* —**li·thol′o·gist** *n.*

lith·o·phyte (lĭth′ə-fīt′) *n.* **1.** *Bot.* A plant that grows on a rocky surface. **2.** An organism, such as coral, that has a stony structure. —**lith′o·phyt′ic** (-fĭt′ĭk) *adj.*

lith·o·pone (lĭth′ə-pōn′) *n.* A white pigment consisting of a mixture of zinc sulfide, zinc oxide, and barium sulfate. [LITHO- + Gk. *ponos,* product.]

lith·o·sphere (lĭth′ə-sfîr′) *n.* **1.** The solid part of the earth as distinguished from the hydrosphere and atmosphere. **2.** The rocky crust of the earth.

lith·o·stra·tig·ra·phy (lĭth′ō-strə-tĭg′rə-fē) *n.* **1.** Stratigraphy based on the physical and petrographic properties of rocks. **2.** The interpretation of the physical characters of sedimentary rocks. —**lith′o·strat′i·graph′ic** (-străt′ĭ-grăf′ĭk) *adj.*

li·thot·o·my (lĭ-thŏt′ə-mē) *n., pl.* **-mies.** Surgery to remove calculi. [LLat. *lithotomia* < Gk. : *lithos,* stone + *temnien,* to cut.]

li·thot·ri·ty (lĭ-thŏt′rĭ-tē) *n., pl.* **-ties.** The surgical operation of pulverizing calculi in the bladder or urethra. [LITHO- + alteration of Gk. *thruptein,* to crush.]

Lith·u·a·ni·an (lĭth′o͞o-ā′nē-ən) *adj.* Of or pertaining to Lithuania, its people, or their language. —*n.* **1.** A native or inhabitant of Lithuania. **2.** The Baltic language of the Lithuanians.

lit·i·gant (lĭt′ĭ-gənt) *n.* One who is engaged in a lawsuit. —*adj.* Engaged in a lawsuit. [Lat. *litigans, litigant-,* a disputant < pr.part. of *litigare,* to litigate. —see LITIGATE.]

lit·i·gate (lĭt′ĭ-gāt′) *v.* **-gat·ed, -gat·ing, -gates.** —*tr.* To subject to legal proceedings. —*intr.* To engage in legal proceedings. [Lat. *litigare, litigat-* : *lis,* lawsuit + *agere,* to drive.] —**lit′i·ga·ble** (-gə-bəl) *adj.* —**lit′i·ga′tion** *n.* —**lit′i·ga′tor** *n.*

li·ti·gious (lĭ-tĭj′əs) *adj.* **1.** Of, pertaining to, or characterized by litigation. **2.** Tending to engage in lawsuits. —**li·ti′gious·ly** *adv.* —**li·ti′gious·ness** *n.*

lit·mus (lĭt′məs) *n.* A blue, amorphous powder derived from certain lichens that changes to red with increasing acidity and to blue with increasing alkalinity. [Of Scand. orig.]

litmus paper *n.* An unsized white paper impregnated with litmus and used as an acid-base indicator.

litmus test *n.* **1.** A test for chemical acidity using litmus paper. **2.** A test that uses a single indicator to prompt a decision: *"The word 'hopefully' has become the litmus test to determine whether one is a language snob or a language slob"* (William Safire).

li·to·tes (lī′tə-tēz′, lĭt′ə-) *n., pl.* **litotes.** A figure of speech in which an affirmative is expressed by the negation of its opposite, as in *no small problem.* [Gk. *litotēs* < *litos,* plain.]

li·tre (lē′tər) *n. Chiefly Brit.* Variant of **liter.**

lit·ter (lĭt′ər) *n.* **1.** A conveyance typically consisting of an enclosed couch mounted on shafts and used to carry a single passenger. **2.** A stretcher for the sick or wounded. **3.** Straw or other material used as bedding for animals. **4.** The young produced at one birth by a multiparous mammal. **5.** A disorderly accumulation of objects, esp. carelessly discarded waste materials or scraps. **6.** The uppermost layer of the forest floor consisting chiefly of decaying organic matter. —*v.* **-tered, -ter·ing, -ters.** —*tr.* **1.** To give birth to (a litter). **2.** To make untidy by discarding rubbish carelessly. **3.** To scatter about. **4.** To supply (animals) with litter for bedding. —*intr.* **1.** To give birth to a litter. **2.** To scatter litter. [ME < AN *littere* < Med. Lat. *litera* < Lat. *lectus,* bed.] —**lit′ter·er** *n.*

lit·té·ra·teur also **lit·ter·a·teur** (lĭt′ər-ə-tûr′, lĭt′rə-) *n.* A man of letters. [Fr. < Lat. *litterator,* critic < *littera,* letter.]

lit·ter·bag (lĭt′ər-băg′) *n.* A bag used, as in an automobile, for disposal of trash.

lit·ter·bug (lĭt′ər-bŭg′) *n. Informal* One who litters public areas with waste materials.

lit·tle (lĭt′l) *adj.* **lit·tler** or **less** (lĕs), **lit·tlest** or **least** (lēst). **1.** Small in size: *a stout little man.* **2.** Short in extent or duration; brief: *little time.* **3.** Small in quantity or degree: *little money.* **4.** Unimportant; trivial. **5.** Narrow; petty: *mean little comments.* **6.** Without much power or influence; of minor status: *the little people of the world.* **7.** Being at an early stage of growth; young: *a little child.* **8.** Appealing; endearing: *a little rascal.* —*adv.* **less, least. 1.** Not much; scarcely: *He sleeps little.* **2.** Not at all; not in the least: *They little expected such trouble.* —*n.* **1.** A small amount or quantity: *Give me a little.* **2.** Something much less than all: *I know little of his history.* **3.** A short distance or time: *a little down the road; a little past four o'clock.* —***idiom.*** **little by little.** By small degrees or increments; gradually. [ME < OE *lȳtel.*] —**lit′tle·ness** *n.*

little auk *n.* The dovekie.

Little Bear *n.* Ursa Minor.

Little Dipper *n.* The seven brightest stars in the constellation Ursa Minor.

lit·tle·neck (lĭt′l-nĕk′) *n.* The quahog clam when small and suitable for eating raw. [After *Littleneck* Bay, New York.]

little owl *n.* A small Old World owl, *Athene noctua,* having streaked brownish plumage.

litter
Above: Ancient Roman
Below: A litter of kittens

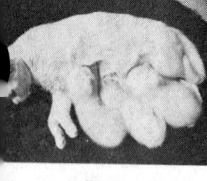

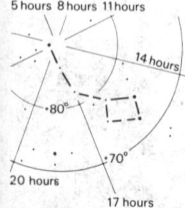

Little Dipper
In the constellation Ursa Minor

little slam *n.* The winning of all but one of the tricks during the play of one hand of bridge.
little theater *n.* A small theater usually for a community, collegiate, or experimental drama group.
little toe *n.* The smallest and outermost toe of the human foot.
lit·to·ral (lĭt′ər-əl) *adj.* Of, pertaining to, or existing on a shore. —*n.* A shore or coastal region. [Lat. *litoralis* < *litus,* shore.]
li·tur·gi·cal (lĭ-tûr′jĭ-kəl) also **li·tur·gic** (-tûr′jĭk) *adj.* **1.** Of, relating to, or characteristic of liturgy. **2.** Using or used in liturgy. —**li·tur′gi·cal·ly** *adv.*
li·tur·gics (lĭ-tûr′jĭks) *n. (used with a sing. verb).* The study of liturgies.
li·tur·gi·ol·o·gy (lĭ-tûr′jē-ŏl′ə-jē) *n.* Liturgics. —**li·tur′gi·ol′o·gist** *n.*
lit·ur·gist (lĭt′ər-jĭst) *n.* **1.** One who uses or advocates the use of liturgical forms. **2.** A scholar in liturgics.
lit·ur·gy (lĭt′ər-jē) *n., pl.* **-gies. 1.** The rite of the Eucharist. **2.** The prescribed form for a public religious service; ritual. [LLat. *liturgia* < Gk. *leitourgia,* public service < *leitourgos,* public servant : *leos,* people + *ergon,* work.]
liv·a·ble also **live·a·ble** (lĭv′ə-bəl) *adj.* **1.** Suitable to live in; habitable. **2.** Bearable; endurable. —**liv′a·ble·ness** *n.*
live[1] (lĭv) *v.* **lived, liv·ing, lives.** —*intr.* **1.** To be alive; exist. **2.** To continue to be alive. **3.** To support oneself; subsist: *living on rice and fish; lived on inherited income.* **4.** To reside; dwell: *lives on a farm.* **5.** To conduct one's life in a particular manner: *lived frugally.* **6.** To pursue a positive, satisfying existence; enjoy life to the utmost. **7.** To remain in human memory: *He lives in the minds of us all.* —*tr.* **1.** To spend or pass (one's life). **2.** To go through; experience: *lived a nightmare.* **3.** To embody in one's manner of existence: *He lived his beliefs.* —***phrasal verbs.* live down.** To overcome or reduce the shame of (a misdeed, for example) over a period of time. **live in.** To reside in the place where one is employed, as a household servant. **live out.** To live outside one's place of employment. **live up to. 1.** To live in accordance with: *lived up to their ideals.* **2.** To come up to; not disappoint: *live up to a great reputation.* **3.** To fulfill; carry out: *lived up to her end of the bargain.* **live with.** To put up with; resign oneself to: *had to live with an unpleasant situation.* —***idiom.* live it up.** *Informal.* To engage in as much pleasure as possible. [ME *liven* < OE *libban.*]
live[2] (līv) *adj.* **1.** Having life; living. **2.** Of current interest: *a live topic.* **3.** Glowing; burning: *a live coal.* **4.** Not yet exploded but capable of being fired: *live ammunition.* **5.** *Elect.* Carrying an electric current or energized with electricity: *dangerous live wires.* **6.** Not mined or quarried; native: *live ores.* **7.** Broadcast while actually being performed; not taped, filmed, or recorded: *a live television program.* **8.** *Printing.* Not yet set into type: *live copy.* **9.** *Sports.* Being or capable of being in play: *a live ball.* —*adv.* At, during, or from a live production: *The show originates live from Los Angeles.* [Short for ALIVE.]
live·a·ble (lĭv′ə-bəl) *adj.* Variant of **livable.**
live-bear·er (līv′bâr′ər) *n.* An ovoviviparous fish, such as a guppy. —**live′-bear′ing** *adj.*
live-for·ev·er (lĭv′fər-ĕv′ər) *n.* The orpine.
live-in (lĭv′ĭn′) *adj.* **1.** Residing in the place where one is employed: *a live-in cook.* **2.** Residing together with another, esp. in sexual intimacy.
live·li·hood (līv′lē-ho͝od′) *n.* Means of support; subsistence. [ME *liflode* < OE *līflād* : *līf,* life + *lād,* course.]
Synonyms: *livelihood, living, subsistence, sustenance, maintenance, support, keep.* These nouns refer to that which provides the necessities of life. *Livelihood* and *living* usually specify the occupation, work, or other means by which one earns an income. *Subsistence* refers to that which barely supports life, and *sustenance* to the means by which one exists on any economic level. *Maintenance, support,* and *keep* are usually reckoned as the equivalent in money of what is needed to provide necessities such as food, lodging, and clothing. *Support* is also applied to one that provides the means for obtaining the necessities of life.
live load (līv) *n.* A moving, variable weight added to the dead load or intrinsic weight of a structure or vehicle.
live·long (lĭv′lông′, -lŏng′) *adj.* Complete; whole: *the livelong day.* [ME *lefe long* : *lefe,* dear (< OE *lēof*) + *long,* long.]
live·ly (līv′lē) *adj.* **-li·er, -li·est. 1.** Full of life, energy, or activity; vigorous: *a lively baby.* **2.** Full of spirit; gay and animated: *a lively tune.* **3.** Characterized by animated intelligence; bright: *a lively dispute.* **4.** Inspiring spirit; refreshing. **5.** Effervescent; sparkling. **6.** Keen; brisk: *lively trade between the two countries.* **7.** Bouncing readily upon impact; resilient: *a lively tennis ball.* —*adv.* In a vigorous, energetic, or spirited manner: *Step lively!* [ME *lifli* < OE *līflīc* < *līf,* life.] —**live′li·ly** *adv.* —**live′li·ness** *n.*
li·ven (lī′vən) *intr. & tr.v.* **-vened, -ven·ing, -vens.** To become or cause to become lively.
live oak (līv) *n.* Any of several evergreen American oaks, such as *Quercus virginiana,* of the southeastern United States, or *Q. agrifolia,* of southwestern North America.
liv·er[1] (lĭv′ər) *n.* **1.** *Anat.* A large compound tubular vertebrate gland that secretes bile and that acts in the formation of blood and in the metabolism of carbohydrates, fats, proteins, minerals, and vitamins. **2.** An organ similar to the liver in invertebrates. **3.** The liver of an animal used as food. [ME < OE *lifer.*]
liv·er[2] (lĭv′ər) *n.* One who lives in a specified manner: *a high liver.*
liver extract *n.* A dry, brownish powder containing the soluble thermolabile fraction of mammalian livers that is capable of increasing the number of red blood corpuscles in persons afflicted with pernicious anemia.
liver fluke *n.* **1.** Any of several parasitic trematode worms, such as *Fasciola hepatica* or *Opisthorchis sinensis* (or *Clonorchis sinensis*), that infest the liver of various animals, including man. **2.** Infestation with liver flukes.
liv·er·ied (lĭv′ə-rēd, lĭv′rēd) *adj.* Wearing livery, esp. as a servant: *a liveried footman.*
liv·er·ish (lĭv′ər-ĭsh) *adj.* **1.** Resembling liver, esp. in color. **2.** Having a liver disorder; bilious. **3.** Having a disagreeable disposition; irritable. —**liv′er·ish·ness** *n.*
liv·er·leaf (lĭv′ər-lēf′) *n.* The hepatica.
liver starch *n.* Glycogen.
liv·er·wort (lĭv′ər-wûrt′, -wôrt′) *n.* **1.** Any of numerous green nonflowering plants of the class Hepaticae within the division Bryophyta. **2.** The hepatica.
liv·er·wurst (lĭv′ər-wûrst′, -wo͝orst′) *n.* A type of sausage made of or containing ground liver. [Partial trans. of G. *Leberwurst* : *Leber,* liver + *Wurst,* sausage.]
liv·er·y (lĭv′ə-rē, lĭv′rē) *n., pl.* **-ies. 1.** The costume or insignia worn by the retainers of a feudal lord. **2.** A distinctive uniform worn by the male servants of a household, as by footmen. **3.** The distinctive dress worn by the members of a particular group. **4. a.** The boarding and care of horses for a fee. **b.** The hiring out of horses and carriages. **c.** A livery stable. **5.** *Law.* The official delivery of property, esp. land, to a new owner. [ME < OFr. *livree,* delivery < *livrer,* to deliver < Lat. *liberare,* to free < *liber,* free.]
liv·er·y·man (lĭv′ə-rē-mən, lĭv′rē-) *n.* A keeper or employee of a livery stable.
livery stable *n.* A stable that boards horses and keeps horses and carriages for hire.
lives (līvz) *n.* Plural of **life.**
live steam *n.* Steam coming from a boiler at full pressure.
live·stock (līv′stŏk′) *n.* Domestic animals, such as cattle or horses, raised for home use or for profit.
live wire (līv) *n.* **1.** A wire carrying electric current. **2.** *Informal.* A vivacious, alert, or energetic person.
liv·id (lĭv′ĭd) *adj.* **1.** Discolored, as from a bruise; black-and-blue. **2.** Ashen or pallid, as from anger. **3.** Extremely angry; furious. [Fr. *livide* < Lat. *lividus* < *livēre,* to be livid.] —**li·vid′i·ty** (lĭ-vĭd′ĭ-tē), **liv′id·ness** *n.* —**liv′id·ly** *adv.*
liv·ing (lĭv′ĭng) *adj.* **1.** Possessing life; alive: *famous living painters.* **2.** In active function or use: *a living language.* **3.** Of or relating to persons who are alive. **4.** Suited for daily life: *a living alcove.* **5.** Full of life, interest, and vitality: *made history a living subject.* **6.** True to life; real: *the living image of her mother.* **7.** *Informal.* Definite; absolute: *a living doll.* —*n.* **1.** The condition or action of maintaining life: *the high cost of living.* **2.** A manner or style of life: *plain living.* **3.** A means of maintaining life; livelihood: *made their living by hunting.* **4.** *Chiefly Brit.* A church benefice, including the revenue attached to it.
Synonyms: *living, alive, extant.* These adjectives are applied to what has continuing existence. *Living* and *alive* refer principally to organisms that have life. *Extant* describes something in existence, often a single or limited surviving example of its kind.
living room *n.* A room in a private residence intended for general use.
living wage *n.* A wage sufficient to provide minimally satisfactory living conditions.
living will *n.* A will in which the signer requests to be allowed to die instead of being kept alive by medical life-support systems in the event of a terminal illness.
li·vre (lē′vər, lē′vrə) *n.* A former French money of account originally worth a pound of silver. [Fr. < Lat. *libra,* a unit of weight.]
lix·iv·i·ate (lĭk-sĭv′ē-āt′) *tr.v.* **-at·ed, -at·ing, -ates.** To wash or percolate the soluble matter from. [< LLat. *lixivium,* lye < Lat. *lixivius,* of lye < *lixa,* lye.] —**lix·iv′i·a′tion** *n.*
liz·ard (lĭz′ərd) *n.* **1.** Any of numerous reptiles of the suborder Sauria (or Lacertilia), characteristically having an elongated, scaly body, four legs, and a tapering tail. **2.** Leather made from the skin of a lizard. [ME < OFr. *lisarde* < Lat. *lacerta.*]
lizard fish *n.* Any of various bottom-dwelling fishes of the family Synodontidae, of warm seas, having a lizardlike head.
-'ll *suff.* Shall; will: *She'll arrive later.*
lla·ma (lä′mə) *n.* A South American ruminant mammal, *Lama peruana,* related to the camel and raised for its soft, fleecy wool and as a beast of burden. [Sp. < Quechua.]
lla·no (lä′nō, lăn′ō) *n., pl.* **-nos.** A large, grassy, almost treeless plain, esp. one in Latin America. [Sp., plain < Lat. *planum* < *planus,* level.]
lo (lō) *interj.* Used to attract attention or to show surprise. [ME < OE *lā.*]
loach (lōch) *n.* Any of various Old World freshwater fishes

live oak

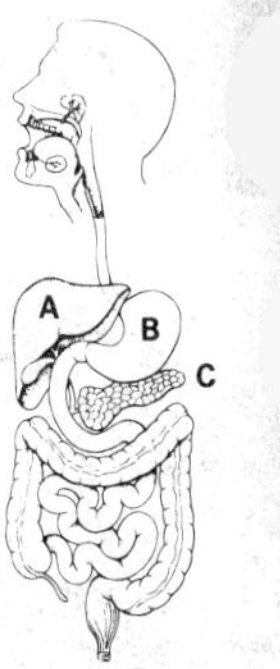

liver[1]
A. Liver
B. Stomach
C. Pancreas

llama

of the family Cobitidae, having barbels around the mouth. [ME *loche* < OFr.]

load (lōd) *n.* **1. a.** A weight or mass that is carried, lifted, or supported. **b.** The overall force to which a structure is subjected in supporting a weight or mass or in resisting externally applied forces. **2. a.** Something that is carried, as by a vehicle, person, or animal: *a load of firewood.* **b.** The quantity of such material: *a wagon with a full load of hay.* **3. a.** The share of work allocated to or required of an individual, machine, group, or organization. **b.** The demand for services or performance made on a machine or system. **4.** The amount that can be loaded into a machine or device at one time. **5.** A single charge of ammunition for a firearm. **6. a.** Mental stress regarded as a depressing weight or burden: *a load off my mind.* **b.** A responsibility regarded as an oppressive weight. **7.** The external mechanical resistance against which a machine acts. **8. a.** The power output of a generator or power plant. **b.** A device or the resistance of a device to which power is delivered. **9.** The sales charge added to the price of a share in a mutual fund. **10.** Often **loads.** *Informal.* A great number or amount: *loads of parties.* —*v.* **load·ed, load·ing, loads.** —*tr.* **1. a.** To put or place (a load) in or on a structure, device, or conveyance: *loading grain onto a train.* **b.** To put or place in or on (a structure, device, or conveyance): *load a ship.* **2.** To provide or fill nearly to overflowing: *loaded the table with food.* **3.** To weigh down; burden: *was loaded with worries.* **4.** To charge (a firearm) with ammunition. **5. a.** To insert into a holder or magazine: *loaded tape into the recorder; loaded film into the camera.* **b.** To insert film, tape, or something similar into: *loaded the camera with film.* **6.** To make (dice) heavier on one side by adding weight. **7.** To distort (a question, for example) so as to elicit a desired response. **8.** To dilute, adulterate, or doctor. **9.** To raise the power demand in (an electrical circuit), as by adding resistance. **10.** To increase (an insurance premium or a mutual-fund share price) by adding expenses or sale costs. —*intr.* **1.** To receive a load. **2.** To charge a firearm with ammunition. **3.** To put or place a load in or on a structure, device, or conveyance. —***idiom.*** **get a load of.** *Slang.* To take notice of: *Get a load of that new car.* [ME *lode* < OE *lād.*] —**load'er** *n.*

lobster

load·ed (lō'dĭd) *adj.* **1.** Intended to trick or trap: *a loaded question.* **2.** *Slang.* Intoxicated. **3.** *Slang.* Having much money.

load·er (lō'dər) *n.* A computer program that transfers data from off-line memory by means of an input or storage device.

load·ing (lō'dĭng) *n.* **1.** A weight, stress, or burden put or placed on something. **2.** A substance added to something; filler. **3.** An addition to an insurance premium to cover extra costs. **4.** *Elect.* The addition of inductance to a transmission line to improve its transmission characteristics.

loading program *n.* A sequence of computer instructions that starts the processing of a program entered by means of an automatic input device.

load line *n.* A Plimsoll mark.

load·star (lōd'stär') *n.* Variant of **lodestar.**

load·stone (lōd'stōn') *n.* Variant of **lodestone.**

loaf¹ (lōf) *n., pl.* **loaves** (lōvz). **1.** A shaped mass of bread baked in one piece. **2.** A shaped mass of food: *veal loaf.* [ME *lof* < OE *hlāf.*]

loaf² (lōf) *intr.v.* **loafed, loaf·ing, loafs.** To spend time lazily or aimlessly; idle. [Orig. unknown.] —**loaf'er** *n.*

Loaf·er (lō'fər). A trademark for a low leather step-in shoe with an upper resembling a moccasin but with a broad, flat heel.

loam (lōm) *n.* **1.** Soil consisting mainly of sand, clay, silt, and organic matter. **2.** A mixture of moist clay and sand, together with straw, used esp. in making bricks and foundry molds. —*tr.v.* **loamed, loam·ing, loams.** To fill, cover, or coat with loam. [ME *lome,* clay < OE *lām.*] —**loam'y** *adj.*

loan (lōn) *n.* **1. a.** A sum of money lent at interest. **b.** Something lent for temporary use. **2.** A temporary transfer to a duty or place away from a regular job. —*tr.v.* **loaned, loan·ing, loans.** *Informal.* To lend. [ME *lone* < ON *lān.*]

Usage: *Loan* has long been established as a verb, especially in business usage, though some hold that *lend* is the preferred form, in general as well as formal writing. A majority of the Usage Panel prefers *lend* in these examples: *If you lend* (not *loan*) *money to a friend, he may cease to be your friend. When I refused to lend* (not *loan*) *him my pen, he became very angry.* Many phrases and figurative uses require *lend: lend an ear; a moneylender; distance lends enchantment.*

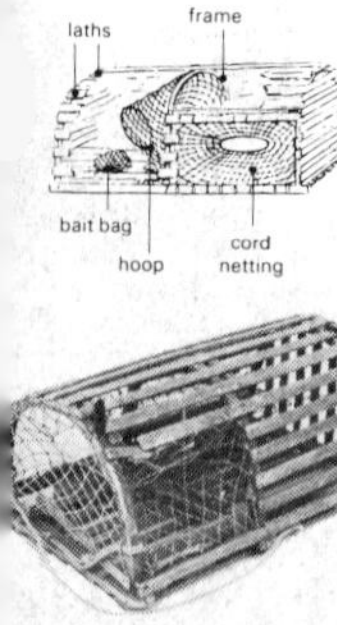

lobster pot
Above: Diagram showing trap interior
Below: Trap

loan shark *n. Informal.* A usurer, esp. one who is financed and supported by gangsters.

loan·sharking (lōn'shär'kĭng) *n. Informal.* The practice of lending money at usurious and often illegal interest rates.

loan translation *n.* A form of borrowing from one language to another whereby the semantic components of a given term are literally translated into their equivalents in the borrowing language, as *superman* from German *Übermensch.*

loan-word also **loan·word** (lōn'wûrd') *n.* A word adopted from another language and at least partly naturalized, as *hors d'oeuvre.*

loath also **loth** (lōth, lō*th*) *adj.* Unwilling or reluctant; disinclined: *loath to go.* [ME *loth* < OE *lāð,* displeasing.]

loathe (lō*th*) *tr.v.* **loathed, loath·ing, loathes.** To dislike greatly; abhor. [ME *lothen* < OE *lāthian.*] —**loath'er** *n.*

loath·ing (lō'*th*ĭng) *n.* Extreme dislike; abhorrence. —**loath'·ing·ly** *adv.*

loath·ly (lō*th*'lē, lōth'-) *adj.* Loathsome. [ME *lothly* < OE *lāðlīc.*]

loath·some (lō*th*'səm, lōth'-) *adj.* Arousing loathing; abhorrent. [ME *lothsome* < *loth* hate, and *loth,* hateful. —see LOATH.] —**loath'some·ly** *adv.* —**loath'some·ness** *n.*

loaves (lōvz) *n.* Plural of **loaf¹.**

lob (lŏb) *v.* **lobbed, lob·bing, lobs.** —*tr.* To hit, throw, or propel in a high arc. —*intr.* **1.** To hit a ball in a high arc. **2.** To move heavily or clumsily. —*n.* **1.** A ball hit, thrown, or propelled in a high arc. **2.** *Chiefly Brit. Regional.* A clumsy dull person; lout. [Prob. of LG orig.] —**lob'ber** *n.*

lo·bar (lō'bər, -bär') *adj.* Of or relating to a lobe, as one of those in the lungs.

lo·bate (lō'bāt') also **lo·bat·ed** (-bā'tĭd) *adj.* **1.** Having lobes. **2.** Resembling a lobe. —**lo'bate'ly** *adv.*

lo·ba·tion (lō-bā'shən) *n.* **1.** The state of being lobed. **2.** A lobe or part resembling a lobe.

lob·by (lŏb'ē) *n., pl.* **-bies. 1.** A hall, foyer, or waiting room at or near the entrance to a building such as a hotel or theater. **2.** A public room next to the assembly chamber of a legislative body. **3.** A group of private persons engaged in trying to influence legislators, esp. in favor of a special interest. —*v.* **-bied, -by·ing, -bies.** —*intr.* To try to influence legislators, esp. in favor of a special interest. —*tr.* **1.** To try to influence legislators to pass (legislation). **2.** To try to influence (an official) to take a desired action. [Med.Lat. *lobium,* monastic cloister, of Germanic orig.] —**lob'by·er** *n.* —**lob'by·ism** *n.* —**lob'by·ist** *n.*

lobe (lōb) *n.* **1.** A rounded projection, esp. a rounded, projecting anatomical part such as the fatty lobule of the auricle of the human ear. **2.** A subdivision of an organ or part bounded by fissures, connective tissue, or other structural boundaries. [OFr. < LLat. *lobus* < Gk. *lobos.*]

lo·bec·to·my (lō-bĕk'tə-mē) *n., pl.* **-mies.** Surgical excision of a lobe.

lobed (lōbd) *adj.* Having lobes: *lobed leaves.*

lobe·fin (lōb'fĭn') *n.* Any of various mostly extinct bony fishes of the subclass Sarcopterygii, of which the coelacanth is a living representative. —**lobe'finned'** *adj.*

lo·be·li·a (lō-bē'lē-ə, -bēl'yə) *n.* Any of numerous plants of the genus *Lobelia,* having terminal clusters of variously colored flowers. [NLat. *Lobelia,* genus name, after Matthias de *Lobel* (1538–1616).]

lob·lol·ly (lŏb'lŏl'ē) *n., pl.* **-lies.** *Regional.* **1.** A mudhole; mire. **2.** A lout. [Perh. dial. *lob,* to bubble + *lolly,* broth.]

loblolly pine *n.* A pine, *Pinus taeda,* of the southeastern United States, having strong wood used as lumber and for paper pulp.

lo·bo (lō'bō) *n., pl.* **-bos.** *Western U.S.* The gray or timber wolf, *Canis lupus.* [Sp., wolf < Lat. *lupus.*]

lo·bot·o·my (lō-bŏt'ə-mē) *n., pl.* **-mies. 1.** Surgical division of one or more cerebral nerve tracts. **2.** Surgical incision into a lobe.

lob·scouse (lŏb'skous') *n.* A seaman's stew made of meat, vegetables, and hardtack. [Perh. dial. *lob,* to bubble + *scouse,* broth.]

lob·ster (lŏb'stər) *n.* **1.** Any of several relatively large marine crustaceans of the genus *Homarus,* having five pairs of legs, the first pair modified into large claws. **2.** Any of several crustaceans related to the lobsters, as the spiny lobster. **3.** The flesh of a lobster used as food. [ME *lobstere* < OE *loppestre,* perh. < Lat. *locusta.*]

lobster pot *n.* A slatted cage with an opening covered by a funnel-shaped net used for trapping lobsters.

lobster ther·mi·dor (thûr'mĭ-dôr') *n.* A dish consisting of cooked lobster meat mixed with a cream sauce, put into a lobster shell, sprinkled with cheese, and browned. [After *Thermidor,* the 11th month of the calendar used during the French Revolution.]

lob·u·late (lŏb'yə-lāt') also **lob·u·lat·ed** (-lā'tĭd) *adj.* Having or consisting of lobules. —**lob'u·la'tion** *n.*

lob·ule (lŏb'yo͞ol) *n.* **1.** A small lobe. **2.** A section or subdivision of a lobe. [NLat. *lobulus,* dim. of LLat. *lobus,* lobe.] —**lob'u·lar** (-yə-lər), **lob'u·lose'** (-yə-lōs') *adj.* —**lob'u·lar·ly** *adv.*

lob·worm (lŏb'wûrm') *n.* A lugworm. [Dial. *lob,* lout + WORM.]

lo·cal (lō'kəl) *adj.* **1.** Of or pertaining to a particular place. **2.** Pertaining to, existing in, or serving a particular locality: *local government.* **3.** Not broad or general; not widespread; narrow-minded. **4.** Of or affecting a limited part of the body; not systemic: *a local infection.* **5.** Making all possible or scheduled stops on a route; not express: *a local train.* —*n.* **1.** A local public conveyance, as a bus. **2.** A local chapter or branch of an organization, esp. of a labor union. **3.** A person from a particular locality. [ME < LLat. *localis* < Lat. *locus,* place.] —**lo'cal·ly** *adv.*

local anesthetic *n.* An anesthetic that acts only on and around the point where it is applied or injected.

local color *n.* The interest or flavor of a locality imparted by the customs and sights peculiar to it.

lo·cale (lō-kăl') *n.* **1.** A locality, esp. with reference to a particular event. **2.** The scene or setting, as of a novel. [Fr. *local* < *local,* local < OFr. < LLat. *localis.* —see LOCAL.]

lo·cal·ism (lō'kə-lĭz'əm) *n.* **1. a.** A local idiom. **b.** A local mannerism or custom. **2.** Devotion to local interests and customs.

lo·cal·i·ty (lō-kăl'ĭ-tē) *n., pl.* **-ties. 1.** A particular neighborhood, place, or district. **2.** The fact or quality of having position in space. [Fr. *localité* < LLat. *localitas* < *localis,* local. —see LOCAL.]

lo·cal·ize (lō'kə-līz') *v.* **-ized, -iz·ing, -iz·es.** *—tr.* **1.** To make local. **2.** To confine or restrict to a particular locality. **3.** To attribute to a particular locality. *—intr.* To become local, esp. to become fixed in one area or part. **—lo'cal·i·za'tion** *n.*

local option *n.* Option granted usually by a state government to a local government on controversial issues, such as the opening of stores on Sundays and the sale of alcoholic beverages.

lo·cate (lō'kāt', lō-kāt') *v.* **-cat·ed, -cat·ing, -cates.** *—tr.* **1.** To determine or specify the position and boundaries of: *locate Albany on the map.* **2.** To find by searching, examining, or experimenting: *locate the source of error.* **3.** To station, situate, or store: *locate an agent in Rochester.* *—intr.* To become established; settle. [Lat. *locare, locat-,* to place < *locus,* place.] **—lo'cat'a·ble** *adj.* **—lo'cat'er** *n.*

lo·ca·tion (lō-kā'shən) *n.* **1.** The act or process of locating. **2.** A place where something is or could be located; site. **3.** A site away from a motion-picture studio at which a scene is shot: *make a movie on location.* **4.** A tract of land that has been surveyed and marked off. [Lat. *locatio,* a placing < *locare,* to place. —see LOCATE.] **—lo·ca'tion·al** *adj.*

loc·a·tive (lŏk'ə-tĭv) *Gram. —adj.* Being a noun case in certain Indo-European languages, such as Sanskrit, that denotes place or the place where. *—n.* **1.** The locative case. **2.** A word in the locative case. [Lat. *locus,* place + (VOC)ATIVE.]

lo·ca·tor (lō'kā'tər) *n.* One that locates, as a person who fixes the boundaries of a mining claim.

loch (lŏKH, lŏk) *n. Scot.* **1.** A lake. **2.** An arm of the sea similar to a fjord. [ME *louch* < Sc. Gael. *loch.*]

lo·chi·a (lō'kē-ə, lŏk'ē-ə) *pl.n.* The normal discharge of blood, tissue, and mucus from the vagina after childbirth. [Gk. *lokhia* < *lokhios,* of childbirth < *lokhos,* childbirth.] **—lo'chi·al** *adj.*

lo·ci (lō'sī', -kī') *n.* Plural of **locus.**

lock[1] (lŏk) *n.* **1.** A device that is used, as on a door, to hold, close, or secure and that is operated by a key, a combination, or a keycard. **2.** A section of a waterway, closed off with gates, in which a vessel may be raised or lowered by the raising or lowering of the section's water level. **3.** A mechanism in a firearm for exploding the charge. **4.** An entanglement or interlocking of elements or parts. **5.** A wrestling hold that is secured on a part of an opponent's body. *—v.* **locked, lock·ing, locks.** *—tr.* **1. a.** To fasten shut or secure with a lock, as against entry: *lock a door.* **b.** To shut or make secure by or as if by locking: *locked up the house.* **2. a.** To safeguard or confine by or as if by means of a lock: *locking the dog in for the night; locked the criminal up in his cell.* **b.** To put and keep in a particular condition or situation: *felt she had become locked into an untenable relationship.* **3.** To engage and interlock securely so as to be immobile. **4.** To clasp or link firmly; intertwine: *locked arms and walked away.* **5.** To contend in struggle or battle: *were locked in combat.* **6. a.** To equip (a waterway) with locks. **b.** To pass (a vessel) through a lock. **7.** *Printing.* **a.** To secure (letterpress type) in a chase or press bed by tightening the quoins. **b.** To fasten (a curved plate) to the cylinder of a rotary press. **8.** To invest (funds) in such a way that they cannot easily be converted into cash. **9.** *Computer Sci.* To end the processing of (a magnetic tape or disk) in such a way as to deny access to its contents. *—intr.* **1.** To become fastened by or as if by means of a lock. **2.** To become entangled; interlock. **3.** To become rigid or immobile. **4.** To pass or flow through a lock in a waterway. ***—phrasal verb.* lock out.** To withhold work from (employees) during a lockout. ***—idioms.* lock horns.** To become embroiled in conflict. **lock, stock, and barrel.** Together with everything; entirely: *sold the place lock, stock, and barrel.* [ME < OE *loc,* bolt, bar, and *loca,* enclosure.]

lock[2] (lŏk) *n.* **1. a.** A strand or curl of hair; tress. **b. locks.** The hair of the head. **2.** A small wisp or tuft, as of wool or cotton. [ME *locke* < OE *locc, loca.*]

lock·age (lŏk'ĭj) *n.* **1.** The passage of a ship through a lock. **2.** The toll paid for the use of a lock. **3.** A system of locks.

lock·er (lŏk'ər) *n.* **1.** One that locks. **2.** An enclosure that can be locked, esp. one at a gymnasium or public place for the safekeeping of clothing and valuables. **3.** A flat trunk for storage. **4.** A heavily insulated refrigerated cabinet, compartment, or room for storing frozen foods.

locker room *n.* **1.** A room, as in a gymnasium or school, with lockers in which equipment and clothing can be stored. **2.** A room for changing one's clothes, as at a public swimming place.

lock·et (lŏk'ĭt) *n.* A small ornamental case for a picture or keepsake, usually worn as a pendant. [OFr. *locquet,* latch < *loc,* lock, of Germanic orig.]

lock·jaw (lŏk'jô') *n.* **1.** Tetanus. **2.** A symptom of tetanus, in which the jaw is locked closed because of a tonic spasm of the muscles of mastication.

lock·nut also **lock nut** (lŏk'nŭt') *n.* **1.** A usually thin nut screwed down on another nut to prevent it from loosening. **2.** A self-locking nut.

lock·out (lŏk'out') *n.* The withholding of work from employees and closing down of a plant by an employer during a labor dispute.

lock·smith (lŏk'smĭth') *n.* One who makes or repairs locks.

lock step *n.* **1.** A way of marching in which the marchers follow each other as closely as possible. **2.** A standardized procedure that is closely and mindlessly followed.

lock stitch *n.* A stitch made on a sewing machine by the interlocking of the upper thread and the bobbin thread.

lock·up (lŏk'ŭp') *n.* **1.** *Informal.* A jail, esp. one in which offenders are held while awaiting a court hearing. **2. a.** The act of locking. **b.** The state of being locked.

lo·co (lō'kō) *n., pl.* **-cos. 1.** Locoweed. **2.** Loco disease. *—tr.v.* **-coed, -co·ing, -cos. 1.** To poison with locoweed. **2.** *Slang.* To make insane; craze. *—adj. Slang.* Mad; insane. [Sp., crazy.]

loco disease *n.* A disease of livestock caused by locoweed poisoning and characterized by dullness, lack of coordination, and partial paralysis.

Lo·co·fo·co (lō'kə-fō'kō) *n., pl.* **-cos.** A member of a radical faction of the New York Democratic Party organized in 1835. [Prob. LOCO(MOTIVE) + alteration of Ital. *fuoco,* fire < Lat. *focus,* hearth.]

lo·co·ism (lō'kō-ĭz'əm) *n.* Loco disease.

lo·co·mo·tion (lō'kə-mō'shən) *n.* **1.** The act of moving or the ability to move from place to place. **2.** Travel. [Lat. *locus,* place + MOTION.]

lo·co·mo·tive (lō'kə-mō'tĭv) *n.* A self-propelled engine, usually electric or diesel-powered, that pulls or pushes freight or passenger cars on railroad tracks. *—adj.* **1.** Of or involved in locomotion. **2.** Of, pertaining to, or being a locomotive. **3.** Able to move independently from place to place. **4.** Of or pertaining to travel. [Lat. *locus,* place + LLat. *motivus,* moving.]

lo·co·mo·tor (lō'kə-mō'tər) *adj.* Locomotive (sense 1). [Lat. *locus,* place + Lat. *motor,* mover < *movere,* to move.]

locomotor ataxia *n.* Tabes dorsalis.

lo·co·weed (lō'kō-wēd') *n.* Any of several plants of the genera *Oxytropis* and *Astragalus,* of the western and central United States, causing severe poisoning when eaten by livestock.

loc·u·lar (lŏk'yə-lər) also **loc·u·late** (-lāt', -lĭt) or **loc·u·lat·ed** (-lā'tĭd) *adj.* Having, formed of, or divided into small cells or cavities. [LOCUL(US) + -AR.] **—loc'u·la'tion** *n.*

loc·ule (lŏk'yōōl) *n.* A small cavity or compartment within an organ or part, such as a plant ovary. [NLat. < Lat. *loculus,* little place. —see LOCULUS.]

loc·u·lus (lŏk'yə-ləs) *n., pl.* **-li** (-lī'). A locule. [NLat. < Lat., little place, dim. of *locus,* place.]

lo·cum te·nens (lō'kəm' tē'nĕnz', -nənz) *n. Chiefly Brit.* A person, esp. a physician or clergyman, who substitutes for another. [Med. Lat., one holding a place.]

lo·cus (lō'kəs) *n., pl.* **-ci** (-sī', -kī'). **1.** A locality; place. **2.** The set or configuration of all points satisfying specified geometric conditions. **3.** The position that a gene occupies on a chromosome. [Lat.]

locus clas·si·cus (klăs'ĭ-kəs) *n., pl.* **loci clas·si·ci** (klăs'ĭ-sī'). A passage from a classic or standard work that is cited as an illustration or instance. [NLat.]

lo·cust (lō'kəst) *n.* **1.** Any of numerous grasshoppers of the family Locustidae, often traveling in swarms and causing damage to vegetation. **2.** A cicada such as the seventeen-year locust. **3. a.** A North American tree, *Robinia pseudoacacia,* having compound leaves, drooping clusters of fragrant white flowers, and hard, durable wood. **b.** Any of several similar or related trees, such as the honey locust or the carob. **4.** The wood of a locust tree. [ME < Lat. *locusta.*]

lo·cu·tion (lō-kyōō'shən) *n.* **1.** A particular word, phrase, or expression considered from the point of view of style. **2.** Style of speaking; phraseology. [ME *locucion* < Lat. *locutio* < *loqui,* to speak.]

lode (lōd) *n.* **1. a.** A fissure in a rock formation that is filled with a metalliferous ore. **b.** A vein of mineral ore deposited between clearly demarcated, nonmetallic layers of rock. **2.** A rich source or supply. [ME *lode,* way < OE *lād.*]

lode·star also **load·star** (lōd'stär') *n.* **1.** A star that is used as a point of reference, esp. the North Star. **2.** A guiding principle, interest, or ambition. [ME *lodesterre* : *lode,* way (< OE *lād*) + *sterre,* star < OE *steorra.*]

lode·stone also **load·stone** (lōd'stōn') *n.* **1.** A magnetized piece of magnetite. **2.** One that attracts strongly. [Obs. *lode,* way (< ME < OE *lād*) + STONE.]

lodge (lŏj) *n.* **1. a.** A cottage or cabin, often rustic, used as a temporary abode or shelter: *a ski lodge.* **b.** A small house on the grounds of an estate or park originally used by a caretaker or gatekeeper. **c.** An inn. **2. a.** A North American Indian living unit such as a hogan, wigwam, or long house. **b.** The group living in such a unit. **3. a.** A local chapter of certain fraternal organizations. **b.** The meeting hall of such a chapter. **c.** The members of such a chapter. **4.** The den of certain animals, as the dome-shaped structure built by bea-

locket
Above: Closed
Below: Open to show photographs

locomotive

locust
Above: Periodical cicada
Below: Black locust

vers. —*v.* **lodged, lodg·ing, lodg·es.** —*tr.* **1. a.** To provide with quarters temporarily, esp. for sleeping. **b.** To rent a room to. **c.** To place or establish in quarters: *lodge children with relatives.* **2.** To serve as a depository for; harbor. **3.** To place, leave, or deposit, as for safety. **4.** To fix, force, or implant: *lodge a bullet in a wall.* **5.** To register (a charge) in court or with an appropriate party; file: *lodge a complaint.* **6.** To vest (authority, for example). **7.** *Archaic.* To beat (crops) down flat. —*intr.* **1. a.** To live in a place temporarily. **b.** To rent accommodations, esp. for sleeping. **2.** To be or become embedded. [ME < OFr. *loge,* of Germanic orig.]

lodge·pole pine (lŏj′pōl′) *n.* A pine, *Pinus contorta,* of western North America, having light wood used in construction.

lodg·er (lŏj′ər) *n.* One that lodges, esp. one who rents and lives in a furnished room.

lodg·ing (lŏj′ĭng) *n.* **1.** A place to live. **2.** Often **lodgings.** Sleeping accommodations. **3. lodgings.** Rented rooms.

lodg·ment also **lodge·ment** (lŏj′mənt) *n.* **1. a.** The act of lodging. **b.** The state of being lodged. **2.** A place for lodging. **3.** An accumulation or deposit. **4.** A military foothold or beachhead gained in enemy or neutral territory.

lod·i·cule (lŏd′ĭ-kyo͞ol′) *n.* One of the small scales at the base of each flower in grasses. [Lat. *lodicula,* small blanket, dim. of *lodix,* blanket.]

lo·ess (lō′əs, lĕs, lŭs) *n.* A buff to gray, fine-grained, calcareous silt or clay, thought to be a deposit of wind-blown dust. [G. *Löss* < dial. G. *Lösch* < *lösch,* loose.] —**lo·es′si·al** (lō-ĕs′ē-əl, lĕs′ē-əl) *adj.*

loft (lôft, lŏft) *n.* **1.** A large, usually unpartitioned floor over a commercial or industrial space. **2.** An open space under a roof; attic. **3.** A gallery or balcony, as in a church. **4.** A hayloft. **5. a.** A coop in which pigeons are kept. **b.** A flock of pigeons kept in such a coop. **6.** A large room where full-scale plans of a vessel are laid out or where rigging is assembled. **7. a.** The backward slant of the face of a golf club head, designed to drive the ball in a high arc. **b.** A golf stroke that drives the ball in a high arc. **c.** The upward course of a ball driven in a high arc. —*tr.v.* **loft·ed, loft·ing, lofts. 1.** To put, store, or keep in a loft. **2.** To propel in a high arc. **3.** To lay out a drawing of (the parts of a ship's engine, for example). [ME, upstairs room < ON *lopt.*]

loft·y (lôf′tē, lŏf′-) *adj.* **-i·er, -i·est. 1.** Of imposing height. **2.** Elevated in character; noble. **3.** Affecting grandness; pompous. **4.** Arrogant; haughty. [ME, noble < *loft,* upstairs room. —see LOFT.] —**loft′i·ly** *adv.* —**loft′i·ness** *n.*

log[1] (lôg, lŏg) *n.* **1. a.** A usually large trunk of a fallen or felled tree. **b.** A long, thick section of trimmed but unhewn timber. **2.** A device trailed from a ship to determine its speed through the water. **3. a.** A record of a ship's speed, progress, and shipboard events of navigational importance. **b.** The book in which this record is kept. **c.** A record of performance, such as the flight record of an aircraft. —*v.* **logged, log·ging, logs.** —*tr.* **1. a.** To cut down the timber of (a section of land). **b.** To cut (trees) into logs. **2. a.** To enter in a ship's or aircraft's log. **b.** To travel (a specified distance, time, or speed). **3.** To spend (time); chalk up creditably: *logged 25 years with the company.* —*intr.* To cut down, trim, and haul timber. [ME.]

log[2] (lôg, lŏg) *n.* Logarithm.

log– *pref.* Variant of **logo-.**

–log *suff.* Variant of **-logue.**

lo·gan·ber·ry (lō′gən-bĕr′ē) *n.* **1.** A trailing, prickly plant, *Rubus loganobaccus,* cultivated for its acid, edible fruit. **2.** The red fruit of the loganberry. [After James H. *Logan* (1841–1928).]

loganberry

log·a·rithm (lô′gə-rĭ*th*′əm, lŏg′ə-) *n.* The exponent indicating the power to which a fixed number, the base, must be raised to produce a given number. For example, if $n^x = a$, the logarithm of *a,* with *n* as the base, is *x;* symbolically, $\log_n a = x$. [NLat. *logarithmus* : Gk. *logos,* reason + *arithmos,* number.] —**log′a·rith′mic** (-rĭ*th*′mĭk), **log′a·rith′mi·cal** *adj.* —**log′a·rith′mi·cal·ly** *adv.*

log·book (lôg′bo͝ok′, lŏg′-) *n.* The official record book of a ship or aircraft.

loge (lōzh) *n.* **1.** A small compartment, esp. a box in a theater. **2.** The front rows of a theater's mezzanine. [Fr. < OFr., lodge.]

log·ger (lô′gər, lŏg′ər) *n.* **1.** A lumberjack. **2.** A tractor, crane, or other machine used for hauling or loading logs.

log·ger·head (lô′gər-hĕd′, lŏg′ər-) *n.* **1.** A marine turtle, *Caretta caretta,* having a large, beaked head. **2.** An iron tool consisting of a long handle with a bulbous end, used when heated to melt tar or to warm liquids. **3.** A post on a whaleboat used to help secure a rope holding a harpooned whale. **4. a.** *Informal.* A blockhead; dolt. **b.** A disproportionately large head. —***idiom.* at loggerheads.** In a head-on dispute. [Prob. dial. *logger,* wooden block (< LOG) + HEAD.]

loggerhead shrike *n.* A North American bird, *Lanius ludovicianus,* having gray and white plumage and a hooked beak.

log·gi·a (lô′jē-ə, lŏj′ē-ə) *n.* **1.** A roofed but open gallery or arcade along the front or side of a building, often at an upper level. **2.** An open balcony in a theater. [Ital. < Fr. *loge.* —see LOGE.]

log·ging (lô′gĭng, lŏg′ĭng) *n.* The work or business of felling and trimming trees and transporting the logs to a mill.

lo·gi·a (lō′gē-ä′) *n.* Plural of **logion.**

log·ic (lŏj′ĭk) *n.* **1.** The study of the principles of reasoning, esp. of the structure of propositions as distinguished from their content and of method and validity in deductive reasoning. **2. a.** A system of reasoning. **b.** A mode of reasoning. **c.** The formal, guiding principles of a discipline, school, or science. **3.** Valid reasoning, esp. as distinguished from invalid or irrational argumentation. **4.** The relationship of element to element to whole in a set of objects, individuals, principles, or events. **5.** *Computer Sci.* **a.** The circuitry in a computer. **b.** The graphic representation of the circuitry of a computer. [ME < OFr. *logique* < Lat. *logica* < Gk. *logikē* < *logikos,* of reason < *logos,* reason.]

log·i·cal (lŏj′ĭ-kəl) *adj.* **1.** Of, pertaining to, in accordance with, or of the nature of logic. **2.** Showing consistency of reasoning. **3.** Reasonable on the basis of earlier statements or events: *a logical assumption.* **4.** Able to reason clearly: *a logical thinker.* —**log′i·cal′i·ty** (-kăl′ĭ-tē), **log′i·cal·ness** *n.* —**log′i·cal·ly** *adv.*

logical circuit *n.* A computer switching circuit that performs an arithmetic logic function.

logical positivism *n.* A philosophy asserting the primacy of observation in assessing the truth of statements of fact and holding that metaphysical and subjective arguments not based on observable data are meaningless, meaningful statements being either a priori and analytic or a posteriori and synthetic.

logic circuit *n.* A logical circuit.

lo·gi·cian (lō-jĭsh′ən) *n.* A practitioner of a system of logic.

lo·gi·on (lō′gē-ŏn′) *n., pl.* **-gi·a** (-gē-ä′). One of the sayings of Jesus not recorded in the Gospels but supposed to have belonged to the source material from which they were compiled. [Gk., oracle < *logos,* word.]

lo·gis·tic (lō-jĭs′tĭk) also **lo·gis·ti·cal** (-tĭ-kəl) *adj.* **1.** Of or pertaining to symbolic logic. **2.** Of or pertaining to logistics. [Gk. *logistikos,* of calculation < *logistēs,* calculator < *logizein,* to calculate < *logos,* reckoning.] —**lo′gis·ti′cian** (-jĭ-stĭsh′ən) *n.*

lo·gis·tics (lō-jĭs′tĭks, lə-) *n.* *(used with a sing. or pl. verb).* The procurement, distribution, maintenance, and replacement of materiel and personnel.

log·jam (lôg′jăm′, lŏg′-) *n.* **1.** A mass of floating logs crowded immovably together. **2.** A deadlock, as in negotiations; impasse.

log·nor·mal (lôg-nôr′məl, lŏg-) *adj.* Of, relating to, or being a logarithmic function with a normal distribution. —**log′nor·mal′i·ty** (-măl′ĭ-tē) *n.* —**log·nor′mal·ly** *adv.*

lo·go (lō′gō′, lô′gō′, lŏg′ō′) *n., pl.* **-gos.** A logotype.

logo– or **log–** *pref.* Word; speech: *logogram.* [Gk. < *logos,* word, speech.]

log·o·gram (lô′gə-grăm′, lŏg′ə-) *n.* A symbol or letter representing an entire word, such as ¢ for cents. —**log′o·gram·mat′ic** (-grə-măt′ĭk) *adj.* —**log′o·gram·mat′i·cal·ly** *adv.*

log·o·graph (lô′gə-grăf′, lŏg′ə-) *n.* A logogram. —**log′o·graph′ic** *adj.* —**log′o·graph′i·cal·ly** *adv.*

lo·gog·ra·phy (lō-gŏg′rə-fē) *n.* The use of logotypes in design and printing.

log·o·griph (lô′gə-grĭf′, lŏg′ə-) *n.* A word puzzle, as an anagram or one in which clues are given in a set of verses. [Fr. *logogriphe* : Gk. *logos,* word + Gk. *griphos,* fishing basket.]

Log·os (lŏg′ŏs′, lō′gŏs′) *n.* **1.** Cosmic reason, affirmed in ancient Greek philosophy as the source of world order and intelligibility. **2.** The self-revealing thought and will of God, as set forth in the Gospel of John, often associated with the second person of the Trinity. [Gk., reason.]

lo·go·type (lô′gə-tīp′, lŏg′ə-) *n.* **1.** A single piece of type bearing two or more usually separate elements. **2.** The name, symbol, or trademark of a company or publication, borne on one printing plate or piece of type.

log·roll (lôg′rōl′, lŏg′-) *v.* **-rolled, -roll·ing, -rolls.** —*tr.* To work toward the passage of (legislation) by logrolling. —*intr.* To engage in political logrolling.

log·roll·ing (lôg′rō′lĭng, lŏg′-) *n.* **1.** Birling. **2.** The exchanging of political favors, esp. the trading of influence or votes among legislators to achieve passage of projects of interest to one another. —**log′roll′er** *n.*

–logue or **–log** *suff.* Speech; discourse: *travelogue.* [Gk. *-logos* < *legein,* to speak.]

log·wood (lôg′wo͝od′, lŏg′-) *n.* **1.** A tropical American tree, *Haematoxylon campechianum,* having dark heartwood from which a dyestuff is obtained. **2.** The heartwood of the logwood. **3.** The blackish or brownish dye obtained from the heartwood of the logwood.

lo·gy (lō′gē) *adj.* **-gi·er, -gi·est.** Characterized by lethargy; sluggish. [Perh. < Du. *log,* heavy.]

–logy *suff.* **1.** Discourse; expression: *phraseology.* **2.** Science; theory; study: *dermatology.* [ME *-logie* < OFr. < Lat. *-logia* < Gk. < *logos,* word, speech.]

loin (loin) *n.* **1.** *Anat.* The part of the side and back between the ribs and the pelvis. **2.** A cut of meat taken from the loin of an animal. **3. loins. a.** The region of the thighs and groin. **b.** The reproductive organs. [ME *loine* < OFr. *loigne* < Lat. *lumbus.*]

loin·cloth (loin′klôth′, -klŏth′) *n.* A strip of cloth worn around the loins.

loi·ter (loi′tər) *intr.v.* **-tered, -ter·ing, -ters. 1.** To stand idly about; linger aimlessly. **2.** To proceed slowly or with many stops. **3.** To delay or dawdle: *loiter over a job.* [ME *loiteren.*] **—loi′ter·er** *n.*

Lo·ki (lō′kē) *n. Myth.* A Norse god who created discord, esp. among his fellow gods. [ON.]

loll (lŏl) *v.* **lolled, loll·ing, lolls.** *—intr.* **1.** To move, stand, or recline in an indolent or relaxed manner. **2.** To hang or droop laxly. *—tr.* To permit to hang or droop laxly. *—n. Archaic.* An act or attitude of lolling. [ME *lollen* < MDu., to doze.] **—loll′er** *n.* **—loll′ing·ly** *adv.*

lol·la·pa·loo·za (lŏl′ə-pə-lo͞o′zə) *n. Slang.* Something outstanding of its kind. [Orig. unknown.]

Lol·lard (lŏl′ərd) *n.* One of a sect of reformers who were followers of John Wycliffe in the 14th and 15th centuries. [ME < MDu. *Lollaert,* heretic.]

lol·li·pop also **lol·ly·pop** (lŏl′ē-pŏp′) *n.* A piece of hard candy on the end of a stick. [Perh. dial. *lolly,* tongue + POP[1].]

lol·lop (lŏl′əp) *intr.v.* **-loped, -lop·ing, -lops.** *Chiefly Brit.* **1.** To lounge about; loll. **2.** To move with a bobbing motion. [LOLL + (GALL)OP.]

lol·ly (lŏl′ē) *n., pl.* **-lies.** *Chiefly Brit.* **1.** A piece of hard candy. **2.** Money. [Short for LOLLIPOP.]

lol·ly·gag (lŏl′ĭ-găg′) *intr.v.* **-gagged, -gag·ging, -gags.** To waste time by fooling around; dawdle. [Orig. unknown.]

Lom·bard (lŏm′bərd, -bärd′, lŭm′-) *n.* **1.** One of a Germanic people that invaded northern Italy in A.D. 568 and established a kingdom in the Po Valley. **2.** A native of Lombardy. **3.** *Archaic.* A banker or pawnbroker. [ME < OFr. *lombart* < Ital. *lombardo* < Lat. *Langobardus.*] **—Lom·bar′dic** (lŏm-bär′dĭk, lŭm-) *adj.*

Lom·bar·dy poplar (lŏm′bər-dē, lŭm′-) *n.* A tree, *Populus nigra italica,* having upward-pointing branches that form a slender, columnar outline.

lo·ment (lō′mĕnt′) *n.* A pod, as of the tick trefoil or similar leguminous plants, having a series of constrictions separating the individual seeds. [NLat. *lomentum* < Lat., skin conditioner made of bean meal < *lavare,* to wash.]

Lon·don broil (lŭn′dən) *n.* Broiled flank steak, cut into thin slices.

lone (lōn) *adj.* **1. a.** Without companionship; isolated. **b.** Disposed to solitude. **2.** Being the only one of its kind; sole: *the lone doctor in the county.* **3.** Standing or located by itself. [ME, short for *alone.* —see ALONE.]

lone·ly (lōn′lē) *adj.* **-li·er, -li·est. 1. a.** Without companions; lone. **b.** Characterized by aloneness; solitary: *a lonely existence.* **2.** Unfrequented by people; desolate: *a lonely crossroads.* **3. a.** Dejected by the awareness of being alone. **b.** Producing such dejection: *the loneliest night of the week.* **—lone′li·ly** *adv.* **—lone′li·ness** *n.*

lone·ly-hearts (lōn′lē-härts′) *adj.* Of or relating to lonely individuals who are looking for companions or marriage partners: *a lonely-hearts column in the newspaper.*

lon·er (lō′nər) *n. Informal.* One who avoids the company of other people.

lone·some (lōn′səm) *adj.* **1. a.** Dejected, due to lack of companionship. **b.** Producing the sense of loneliness: *a lonesome trip.* **2.** Deserted; unfrequented: *a lonesome valley.* **3.** Lone: *a lonesome pine.* *—n. Informal.* Self: *He ate all by his lonesome.*

long[1] (lông, lŏng) *adj.* **-er, -est. 1. a.** Having great length. **b.** Tall. **2.** Of relatively great duration: *a long time.* **3.** Of a specified linear extent or duration: *a mile long; an hour long.* **4.** Extending beyond an average or a standard: *a long game.* **5.** Tediously protracted; lengthy: *a long speech.* **6.** Concerned with distant issues; far-reaching: *a long view.* **7.** Involving substantial chance; risky: *long odds.* **8.** Having an abundance or an excess of: *long on hope.* **9.** Having a large holding of a security or commodity in expectation of a rise in price: *long on steel.* **10. a.** In phonetics, having a comparatively protracted duration. **b.** Of, relating to, or being a vowel sound in English, such as the vowel sound in *mate* or *feet,* that is historically descended from a long vowel. **11. a.** In prosody, being of relatively great duration. Used of a syllable. **b.** Stressed or accented. *—adv.* **1.** During or for an extended period of time: *The promotion was long due.* **2.** At or to a considerable distance; far: *He wrote long into the night.* **3.** For or throughout a specified period: *They talked all night long.* **4.** At a point of time distant from that referred to: *long before we were born.* *—n.* **1.** A long time. **2.** A long syllable, vowel, or consonant. **3.** One who acquires large holdings of a security expecting a rise in price. **4. a.** A garment size for a tall person. **b. longs.** Full-length trousers. ***—idioms.*** **before long.** Soon. **the long and the short.** The substance; gist: *The long and the short of it is they won.* [ME < OE *lang.*]

long[2] (lông, lŏng) *intr.v.* **longed, long·ing, longs.** To yearn or desire greatly: *He longed to go home.* [ME *longen* < OE *langian.*]

lon·ga·nim·i·ty (lŏng′gə-nĭm′ĭ-tē) *n.* Equanimity in the face of suffering and adversity; forbearance. [ME *longanimite* < OFr. < LLat. *longanimitas* < *longanimis,* patient : Lat. *longus,* long + Lat. *animus,* soul.]

long·boat (lông′bōt′, lŏng′-) *n.* The longest boat carried by a sailing ship, esp. by a merchantman.

long·bow (lông′bō′, lŏng′-) *n.* **1.** A wooden bow roughly five to six feet long. **2.** A Medieval English bow, sometimes exceeding six feet in length.

long distance *n.* **1.** An operator or system that places long-distance telephone calls. **2.** A long-distance telephone call.

long-dis·tance (lông′dĭs′təns, lŏng′-) *adj.* **1.** Located at a long distance or far away. **2.** Covering a long distance. **3.** Of or involving telephone communications to a distant station. *—adv.* By long-distance telephone.

long division *n.* A process of division in arithmetic, usually used when the divisor has more than one digit, in which the remainders leading to succeeding steps of the procedure are recorded in a determinate pattern.

long dozen *n.* Thirteen; baker's dozen.

long-drawn-out (lông′drôn′out, lŏng′-) *adj.* Extended to a great length; prolonged.

lon·ge·ron (lŏn′jər-ən) *n.* A structural member that runs from front to rear of an aircraft's fuselage. [Fr. < *longer,* to go along < LLat. *longare,* to lengthen < Lat. *longus,* long.]

lon·gev·i·ty (lŏn-jĕv′ĭ-tē) *n.* **1. a.** A long duration of life. **b.** Length of life. **2.** Long duration or continuance, as in an occupation. [LLat. *longaevitas* < Lat. *longaevus,* ancient : *longus,* long + *aevum,* age.] **—lon·ge′vous** (-jē′vəs) *adj.*

long face *n.* A discontented or sullen facial expression.

long green *n. Slang.* Paper money.

long·hair (lông′hâr′, lŏng′-) *n.* **1.** One dedicated to the arts and esp. to classical music. **2.** One whose taste in the arts is held to be overrefined. **3.** A person with long hair, esp. a male whose hair length symbolizes alienation from or protest against the values of conventional society. **—long′hair′, long′haired′** *adj.*

long·hand (lông′hănd′, lŏng′-) *n.* Cursive writing.

long·head (lông′hĕd′, lŏng′-) *n.* **1.** A head having a cephalic index of less than 75.9. **2.** A person having a longhead.

long·head·ed also **long-head·ed** (lông′hĕd′ĭd, lŏng′-) *adj.* **1.** Dolichocephalic. **2.** Foresighted or wise.

long·horn (lông′hôrn′, lŏng′-) *n.* One of a breed of long-horned cattle formerly bred in the southwestern United States.

long-horned beetle (lông′hôrnd′, lŏng′-) *n.* Any of numerous beetles of the family Cerambycidae, having long legs and long antennae.

long house *n.* A long wooden dwelling, esp. of the Iroquois.

lon·gi·corn (lŏn′jĭ-kôrn′) *n.* A long-horned beetle. *—adj.* **1.** Having long antennae. **2.** Of or belonging to the family Cerambycidae, which includes the long-horned beetles. [< NLat. *Longicornia,* former group name : Lat. *longus,* long + Lat. *cornu,* horn.]

long·ing (lông′ĭng, lŏng′-) *n.* A strong persistent yearning or desire, esp. one that cannot be fulfilled. **—long′ing·ly** *adv.*

long·ish (lông′ĭsh, lŏng′-) *adj.* Fairly long.

lon·gi·tude (lŏn′jĭ-to͞od′, -tyo͞od′) *n.* **1.** The angular distance on the earth or on a globe or map, east or west of the prime meridian at Greenwich, England, to the point on the earth's surface for which the longitude is being ascertained, expressed either in degrees or in hours, minutes, and seconds. **2.** The angular distance, measured in degrees eastward along the ecliptic from the vernal equinox to the great circle passing through the pole of the ecliptic and the celestial point being measured. [ME, length < OFr. < Lat. *longitudo* < *longus,* long.]

lon·gi·tu·di·nal (lŏn′jĭ-to͞od′n-əl, -tyo͞od′-) *adj.* **1.** Of or pertaining to length. **2.** Placed or running lengthwise. **3.** Pertaining to longitude. **—lon′gi·tu′di·nal·ly** *adv.*

long johns *pl.n. Informal.* Long, warm underwear.

long jump *n. Sports.* In track and field events, a jump for distance rather than height, made either from a stationary position or a moving start.

long·leaf pine (lông′lēf′, lŏng′-) *n.* An evergreen tree, *Pinus australis* (or *P. palustris*), of the southeastern United States, having long needles and heavy, tough, resinous wood valued as timber and as a source of turpentine.

long-lived (lông′lĭvd′, -līvd′, lŏng′-) *adj.* **1.** Having a long life. **2.** Persistent: *a long-lived rumor.* **—long′-lived′ness** *n.*

long measure *n.* Linear measure.

Lon·go·bard (lŏng′gō-bärd′) *n., pl.* **-bards** or **-bar·di** (-bär′dē). Lombard (sense 3). [Lat. *Longobardus.*] **—Lon′go·bar′dic** *adj.*

long-play·ing (lông′plā′ĭng, lŏng′-) *adj.* Relating to or being a microgroove phonograph record, esp. one turning at 33 1/3 revolutions per minute.

long purples *n.* The purple loosestrife.

long-range (lông′rānj′, lŏng′-) *adj.* **1.** Requiring or involving an extended span of time: *long-range planning.* **2.** Of, suitable for, or covering long distances.

long·shore (lông′shôr′, -shōr′, lŏng′-) *adj.* Occurring, living, or working along a seacoast. [Short for ALONGSHORE.]

long·shore·man (lông′shôr′mən, -shōr′mən, lŏng′-) *n.* A dock worker who loads and unloads ships.

long shot *n.* **1.** An entry, as in a horse race, with only a slight chance of winning. **2. a.** A bet made at and against great odds. **b.** A risky venture that will pay off handsomely if successful. ***—idiom.*** **by a long shot.** By a great amount.

long-sight·ed (lông′sī′tĭd, lŏng′-) *adj.* Farsighted. **—long′-sight′ed·ness** *n.*

long·some (lông′səm, lŏng′-) *adj.* Tiresomely long.

long·spur (lông′spûr′, lŏng′-) *n.* Any of several birds of the

longbow

genera *Calcarius* and *Rhyncophanes,* of northern regions, having brownish plumage and long-clawed hind toes.

long-stand·ing (lông′stăn′dĭng, lŏng′-) *adj.* Of long duration.

loom[2]

long-suf·fer·ing (lông′sŭf′ər-ĭng, lŏng′-) *adj.* Patiently enduring wrongs or difficulties. —*n.* Also **long-suf·fer·ance** (-əns). Patient endurance. —**long′-suf′fer·ing·ly** *adv.*

long suit *n.* **1.** In certain card games, a suit containing more cards than any of the other suits in a hand. **2.** The personal quality or talent that is one's strongest asset.

long-term (lông′tûrm′, lŏng′-) *adj.* Involving, maturing, or being in effect after a number of years: *a long-term investment.*

long-time (lông′tīm′, lŏng′-) *adj.* Having existed or persisted for a long time.

long ton *n.* A ton (sense 1.a.).

long-wind·ed (lông′wĭn′dĭd, lŏng′-) *adj.* **1.** Wearisomely verbose: *a long-winded bore.* **2.** Not subject to quick loss of breath. —**long′-wind′ed·ly** *adv.* —**long′-wind′ed·ness** *n.*

long·wise (lông′wīz′, lŏng′-) *adv.* Lengthwise.

loo[1] (lo͞o) *n., pl.* **loos.** A card game in which each player contributes stakes to a pool. [Short for obs. *lanterloo* < Fr. *lanturlu.*]

loo[2] (lo͞o) *n., pl.* **loos.** *Chiefly Brit. Slang.* A toilet. [Perh. < Fr. *lieux d'aisances.*]

loo·by (lo͞o′bē) *n., pl.* **-bies.** A big, gangling, clumsy fellow; lubber. [ME *loby.*]

loo·fa or **loo·fah** (lo͞o′fə) *n.* **1. a.** Any of several Old World tropical vines of the genus *Luffa.* **b.** The fruit of such a vine, having a fibrous, spongelike interior. **2.** The dried, fibrous part of the loofa fruit, used as a washing sponge or as a filter. [Ar. *lūfah.*]

George Miksch Sutton

loon[1]

look (lo͝ok) *v.* **looked, look·ing, looks.** —*intr.* **1.** To employ one's eyes in seeing; examine. **2. a.** To turn one's glance. **b.** To turn one's attention: *looked to her for a solution.* **3.** To seem or appear to be: *look morose.* **4.** To face in a specified direction: *The cottage looks on the river.* —*tr.* **1.** To turn one's eyes on. **2.** To convey by one's expression: *She looked daggers at me.* **3.** To have an appearance in conformity with: *look one's age.* —***phrasal verbs.*** **look after.** To take care of. **look down on** (or **upon**). To regard with contempt or condescension. **look for.** To expect. **look to. 1.** To expect: *He looked to hear from her.* **2.** To attend to. **3.** To rely upon. **look up. 1.** To search for and find, as in a reference book. **2.** To visit. **3.** *Informal.* To improve: *Things are looking up for him.* **look up to.** To admire. —*n.* **1. a.** The action of looking. **b.** A gaze or glance. **2.** Appearance or aspect. **3. looks.** Physical appearance, esp. when pleasing. [ME *loken* < OE *lōcian.*]

look-a·like (lo͝ok′ə-līk′) *n.* One that closely resembles another; double.

look·down (lo͝ok′doun′) *n.* A marine fish, *Selene vomer,* of Atlantic waters, having a steep frontal profile.

look·er (lo͝ok′ər) *n.* **1.** One who looks. **2.** *Slang.* A very attractive person.

look·er-on (lo͝ok′ər-ŏn′, -ôn′) *n., pl.* **look·ers-on.** A spectator.

look-in (lo͝ok′ĭn′) *n.* **1.** A short visit. **2.** A quick glance.

looking glass *n.* A mirror.

look·out (lo͝ok′out′) *n.* **1.** The act of observing or keeping watch. **2.** A high place or structure commanding a wide view for observation. **3.** One who keeps watch. **4.** Outlook; view. **5.** A matter of concern or worry.

look-see (lo͝ok′sē′) *n. Informal.* A quick survey or glance.

look-up (lo͝ok′ŭp′) *n.* A procedure in which a table of values stored in a computer is searched for a specified value.

loosestrife

loom[1] (lo͞om) *intr.v.* **loomed, loom·ing, looms. 1.** To come into view as a massive, distorted, or indistinct image. **2.** To appear to the mind in a magnified and threatening form. **3.** To seem imminent; impend. —*n.* A distorted, threatening appearance of something, as through fog or darkness. [Orig. unknown.]

loom[2] (lo͞om) *n.* A machine or device from which cloth is produced by interweaving thread or yarn at right angles. [ME *lome* < OE *gelōma,* tool.]

loon[1] (lo͞on) *n.* Any of several diving birds of the genus *Gavia,* of northern regions, having a laughlike cry. [Of Scand. orig.]

loon[2] (lo͞on) *n.* **1.** A mad or simple-minded person. **2.** An idler. [ME *louen,* rogue.]

loon·y also **lun·y** (lo͞o′nē) *Informal.* —*adj.* **-i·er, -i·est. 1.** Extremely foolish or silly. **2.** Crazy; insane. —*n., pl.* **-ies.** A loony person.

loony bin *n. Informal.* An insane asylum; madhouse.

loquat

loop[1] (lo͞op) *n.* **1. a.** A length of line that is folded over and joined at the ends. **b.** The opening formed by such a doubled line. **2.** Something having a roughly oval, closed, or nearly closed turn or figure. **3.** *Elect.* A closed circuit. **4.** *Computer Sci.* A sequence of computer instructions that repeats until a terminal condition prevails. **5.** A flight maneuver in which an aircraft flies a circular path in a vertical plane with the lateral axis of the aircraft remaining horizontal. **6.** A league[1] (sense 2). —*v.* **looped, loop·ing, loops.** —*tr.* **1.** To form into a loop. **2.** To fasten, join, or encircle with a loop or loops. **3.** To fly (an aircraft) in a loop. **4.** To move in a loop or arc. **5.** *Elect.* To join (conductors) so as to complete a circuit. —*intr.* **1.** To form a loop. **2.** To move in a loop. **3.** To make a loop in an aircraft. [ME *loupe.*]

loop[2] (lo͞op) *n. Archaic.* A loophole (sense 1). [ME *loupe* < Med. Lat. *loupa,* of Germanic orig.]

loop·er (lo͞o′pər) *n.* **1.** One that makes loops. **2.** A measuring worm.

loop·hole (lo͞op′hōl′) *n.* **1.** A small hole or slit in a wall, esp. one through which small arms may be fired. **2.** A way of escaping a difficulty, esp. an omission or an ambiguity, as in the wording of a contract or law, that provides a means of evasion.

loose (lo͞os) *adj.* **loos·er, loos·est. 1.** Not fastened or restrained: *loose bricks in the wall.* **2.** Not taut or drawn up tightly; slack: *a loose anchor line.* **3.** Free from confinement or imprisonment; unfettered. **4.** Not tight-fitting or tightly fitted. **5.** Not bound, bundled, stapled, or gathered together. **6.** Not compact or dense in arrangement or structure. **7.** Not fast: *a loose dye.* **8.** Lacking a sense of restraint or responsibility; idle: *loose talk.* **9.** Lacking conventional moral restraint in sexual behavior. **10.** Not literal or exact: *a loose translation.* —*adv.* **1.** In a loose manner. **2.** *Slang.* In a calm or unruffled condition: *Just try to hang loose.* —*v.* **loosed, loos·ing, loos·es.** —*tr.* **1.** To let loose; release. **2.** To make loose; undo. **3.** To cast loose; detach. **4.** To let fly; discharge. **5.** To release pressure on; ease. **6.** To make less strict; relax. —*intr.* **1.** To become loose. **2.** To discharge a missile; fire. [ME *louse* < ON *lauss.*] —**loose′ly** *adv.* —**loose′ness** *n.*

loose-joint·ed (lo͞os′join′tĭd) *adj.* **1.** Having freely articulated joints. **2.** Limber or agile in movement. —**loose′-joint′ed·ness** *n.*

loose-leaf (lo͞os′lēf′) *adj.* Having leaves that can be easily removed, rearranged, or replaced: *a loose-leaf notebook.*

loos·en (lo͞o′sən) *v.* **-ened, -en·ing, -ens.** —*tr.* **1.** To untie or make looser. **2.** To free from restraint, pressure, or strictness. **3.** To free (the bowels) from constipation. —*intr.* To become loose or looser. [ME *lousnen* < *lousen* < *louse,* loose.]

loose·strife (lo͞os′strīf′) *n.* **1.** Any of various plants of the genus *Lysimachia,* having usually yellow flowers. **2.** Any of various plants of the genus *Lythrum.* [Intended as transl. of Gk. *lusimakheion* (interpreted as *lusis,* loosening + *machē,* battle), from the name *Lusimakhos.*]

loot (lo͞ot) *n.* **1.** Valuables pillaged in time of war; spoils. **2.** Stolen goods. **3.** *Informal.* Goods illicitly obtained, as by bribery. **4.** *Slang.* Money. —*v.* **loot·ed, loot·ing, loots.** —*tr.* **1.** To pillage; steal. **2.** To take as spoils. —*intr.* To engage in pillage. [Hindi *lūṭ* < Skt. *lotram,* plunder.] —**loot′er** *n.*

lop[1] (lŏp) *tr.v.* **lopped, lop·ping, lops. 1.** To cut off (a part) from; trim: *lop dead branches.* **2.** To cut off from a tree or shrub. **3.** To eliminate or excise as superfluous. [Perh. < ME *loppe,* small branches < Med. Lat. *loppa.*] —**lop′per** *n.*

lop[2] (lŏp) *intr. & tr.v.* **lopped, lop·ping, lops.** To hang or let hang loosely; droop. [Orig. unknown.]

lope (lōp) *intr.v.* **loped, lop·ing, lopes.** To run or ride with a steady, easy gait. —*n.* A steady, easy gait. [ME *lopen* < ON *hlaupa.*] —**lop′er** *n.*

lop-eared (lŏp′îrd′) *adj.* Having bent or drooping ears.

lop·py (lŏp′ē) *adj.* **-pi·er, -pi·est.** Hanging limp; pendulous.

lop·sid·ed (lŏp′sī′dĭd) *adj.* **1.** Heavier, larger, or higher on one side than on the other. **2.** Sagging or leaning to one side. —**lop′sid′ed·ly** *adv.* —**lop′sid′ed·ness** *n.*

lo·qua·cious (lō-kwā′shəs) *adj.* Very talkative; garrulous. [Lat. *loquax, loquac-,* loquacious < *loqui,* to speak.] —**lo·qua′cious·ly** *adv.* —**lo·qua′cious·ness, lo·quac′i·ty** (lō-kwăs′ĭ-tē) *n.*

lo·quat (lō′kwŏt′, -kwăt′) *n.* **1.** A small tree, *Eriobotrya japonica,* native to eastern Asia, having fragrant white flowers and yellow, pear-shaped fruit. **2.** The edible fruit of the loquat. [Cantonese *lō kwat.*]

lo·ran (lôr′ăn′, lōr′-) *n.* A long-range navigational system based on pulsed radio signals from two or more pairs of ground stations of known position, used by a navigator to establish his own position by an analysis involving the time intervals between pulses. [LO(NG-)RA(NGE) N(AVIGATION).]

lord (lôrd) *n.* **1.** A man of high rank in a feudal society or in one that retains feudal forms and institutions, esp.: **a.** A king. **b.** A territorial magnate. **c.** The proprietor of a manor. **2. Lord.** *Chiefly Brit.* The general masculine title of nobility and other rank, used: **a.** Semiformally for any peer other than a duke. **b.** As the usual style for a baron. **c.** As a courtesy title for a younger son of a duke or marquis. **d.** As part of the titles of certain high officials and dignitaries. **e.** As a nominal title for a bishop. **3. a. Lord.** God. **b.** *Archaic.* The head of a household. **c.** *Archaic.* A husband. **d.** A man of renowned power. **e.** A man who has mastery in a given field or activity. —*intr.v.* **lord·ed, lord·ing, lords.** To play the lord; domineer: *lording it over the newcomers.* [ME < OE *hlāford* : *hlāf,* bread + *weard,* guardian.]

Lord Chancellor *n., pl.* **Lords Chancellor.** The presiding officer of the House of Lords.

lord·ing (lôr′dĭng) *n.* **1.** *Archaic.* Lord; sir. **2.** *Obs.* A lordling.

lord·ling (lôrd′lĭng) *n.* An immature or insignificant lord.

lord·ly (lôrd′lē) *adj.* **-li·er, -li·est. 1.** Of, pertaining to, or characteristic of a lord. **2.** Very dignified and noble in nature: *a lordly and charitable enterprise.* **3.** Pretentiously arrogant and overbearing. —*adv.* In a lordly fashion. **—lord′li·ness** *n.*

Lord of Misrule *n.* A master of traditional Christmas revelry in England during the 15th and 16th centuries.

lor·do·sis (lôr-dō′sĭs) *n.* An abnormal forward curvature of the spine in the lumbar region. [NLat. < Gk. *lordōsis* < *lordos,* bent backward.] **—lor·dot′ic** (-dŏt′ĭk) *adj.*

Lord's Day or **Lord's day** *n.* The Sabbath; Sunday.

lord·ship (lôrd′shĭp′) *n.* **1.** Often **Lordship.** A form of address employed in speaking or referring to a man holding the title of lord: *if it please your lordship.* **2.** The position or authority of a lord. **3.** The territorial fief of a feudal lord.

Lord's Prayer *n.* The prayer taught by Jesus to his disciples.

Lord's Supper *n.* **1.** The Last Supper. **2.** The Eucharist.

Lord's Table *n.* The Communion table.

lore[1] (lôr, lōr) *n.* **1.** Accumulated fact, tradition, or belief about a particular subject. **2.** Knowledge acquired through education or experience. **3.** *Archaic.* Material taught or learned. [ME < OE *lār.*]

lore[2] (lôr, lōr) *n.* The area between a bird's eye and the base of the bill. [NLat. *lorum* < Lat., thong.]

Lo·re·lei (lôr′ə-lī′, lō′rə-lī′) *n.* A siren of Germanic legend whose singing lures sailors to shipwreck. [G.]

Lo·rentz contraction (lō′rĕnts) also **Lo·rentz-Fitz·ger·ald contraction** (lō′rĕnts-fĭts-jĕr′əld) *n.* The contraction in length of a moving body, as measured by an observer at rest with respect to the body, by the factor $(1 - v^2/c^2)^{1/2}$, where *v* is the relative speed of the moving body and *c* the speed of light. [After Hendrik A. *Lorentz* (1853–1928).]

lor·gnette (lôrn-yĕt′) *n.* Eyeglasses or opera glasses with a short handle. [Fr. < *lorgner,* to leer at < OFr. < *lorgne,* squinting.]

lor·gnon (lôrn-yŏɴ′) *n.* Lorgnette. [Fr. < *lorgner,* to leer at. —see LORGNETTE.]

lo·ri·ca (lô-rī′kə, lō-) *n., pl.* **-cae** (-sē′). A protective external shell or case, as of a rotifer, diatom, or certain protozoans. [Lat., leather cuirass < *lorum,* thong.] **—lor′i·cate′** (lôr′ĭ-kāt′, lŏr′-), **lor′i·ca′ted** (-kā′tĭd) *adj.*

lor·i·keet (lôr′ĭ-kēt′, lŏr′-) *n.* Any of several small Australasian parrots of the subfamily Loriinae. [LOR(Y) + (PARA)KEET.]

lo·ris (lôr′ĭs, lōr′-) *n.* Any of several small, nocturnal, arboreal primates of the genera *Loris* and *Nycticebus,* of tropical Asia, having dense, woolly fur, large eyes, and a vestigial tail. [Fr., poss < obs. Du. *loeris,* clown.]

lorn (lôrn) *adj.* Bereft; forlorn. [ME, p.part. of *lesen,* to suffer a loss < OE *leosan.*]

lor·ry (lôr′ē, lŏr′ē) *n., pl.* **-ries. 1.** A low, horse-drawn, four-wheeled wagon. **2.** *Chiefly Brit.* A motor truck. **3.** A flatbed freight car that runs on rails. [Orig. unknown.]

lo·ry (lôr′ē, lōr′ē) *n., pl.* **-ries.** Any of various brightly colored Australasian parrots of the subfamily Loriinae, having a tongue with a brushlike tip. [Malay *luri.*]

lose (lo͞oz) *v.* **lost** (lôst, lŏst), **los·ing, los·es.** —*tr.* **1. a.** To be unable to find; mislay. **b.** To incur the deprivation of, as by negligence or accident. **2.** To be unable to maintain, sustain, or keep: *lost his financial backers.* **3. a.** To be deprived of: *lost everything when the business failed.* **b.** To be deprived of through death: *lost her husband.* **4.** To fail to win: *lose the game.* **5.** To fail to use or take advantage of: *lose a chance.* **6.** To fail to hear, see, or understand. **7.** To remove (oneself), as from everyday reality into a fantasy world. **8.** To rid oneself of: *lose ten pounds.* **9.** To stray or wander from: *lose one's way.* **10.** To make (oneself) disappear or fade from view: *He lost himself in the crowd.* **11.** To elude or outdistance: *lose one's pursuers.* **12.** To cause or result in the loss of: *Failure to reply lost her a job.* **13.** To cause to be destroyed: *Both planes were lost in the crash.* —*intr.* **1.** To suffer loss. **2.** To be defeated. **3.** To run slow. Used of a timepiece. ***—phrasal verbs.*** **lose out.** To fail to achieve or receive an expected gain. **lose out on.** To miss (an opportunity, for example). [ME *losen* < OE *lōsian* < *los,* loss.]

lo·sel (lō′zəl, lo͞o′-, lŏz′əl) *n.* One that is worthless. [ME < *lesen,* to suffer a loss. —see LORN.]

los·er (lo͞o′zər) *n.* **1.** One that loses. **2. a.** One that fails consistently, esp. because of incompetence. **b.** Something destined to fail.

loss (lôs, lŏs) *n.* **1.** The act or an instance of losing. **2.** Something or someone that is lost. **3.** The harm or suffering caused by losing or by being lost. **4. losses. a.** Casualties. **b.** Setbacks. **5.** Destruction. **6.** *Elect.* The power decrease in a circuit, circuit element, or device caused by resistance. **7.** The amount of a claim on an insurer by an insured. ***—idiom.*** **at a loss.** Perplexed; puzzled. [ME *los,* perh. back-formation < *lost,* p.part. of *losen,* to lose.]

loss leader *n.* A commodity offered by a retail store at cost or less to attract customers.

loss ratio *n.* The ratio between the premiums paid to an insurance company and the claims settled by the company.

lost (lôst, lŏst) *v.* Past tense and past participle of **lose.** —*adj.* **1.** Unable to find one's way. **2. a.** No longer in one's possession. **b.** No longer known or practiced: *a lost art.* **3.** Unable to function, act, or make progress. **4.** Spiritually or physically destroyed. **5.** Completely involved or absorbed; rapt: *lost in thought.*

Usage: The phrase *lost to* can sometimes be ambiguous, as in *As a result of the battle, control of the Mediterranean was lost to Rome* (lost by Rome or lost by someone else to Rome?). Unless the context makes the meaning clear, the sentence should be reworded.

lot (lŏt) *n.* **1.** An object used in making a determination or choice by chance. **2. a.** The use of lots for selection. **b.** The selections made. **3.** Something that befalls an individual as a result of determination by lot. **4.** One's fortune in life; fate. **5.** A number of associated people or things. **6.** Kind, type, or sort. **7.** Miscellaneous articles sold as one unit. **8.** A large extent, amount, or number: *felt a lot better; has a lot of trouble; made lots of new friends.* **9. a.** A piece of land. **b.** A piece of land having fixed boundaries. **c.** A motion-picture studio. —*tr.v.* **lot·ted, lot·ting, lots. 1.** To apportion by lots; allot. **2.** To divide (land) into lots. [ME < OE *hlot.*]

Lot (lŏt) *n.* Abraham's nephew, whose wife was turned into a pillar of salt when she looked back as they fled from Sodom. [Heb. *lōṭ.*]

lo·tah also **lo·ta** (lō′tə) *n.* A rounded copper or brass container used in India to carry water or store food. [Hindi *loṭā.*]

loth (lōth, lōth) *adj.* Variant of **loath.**

Lo·thar·i·o (lō-thâr′ē-ō) *n., pl.* **-os.** A seducer. [After *Lothario,* a character in *The Fair Penitent,* a play by Nicholas Rowe (1674–1718).]

lo·ti (lō′tē) *n., pl.* **loti.** See table at **currency.** [Sotho < *Loti,* a range of mountains in Lesotho.]

lo·tic (lō′tĭk) *adj.* Of, pertaining to, or living in moving water. [< Lat. *lotus,* p.part. of *lavere,* to wash.]

lo·tion (lō′shən) *n.* **1.** A medicated liquid for external application. **2.** Any of various externally applied cosmetic liquids. [ME *locion* < Lat. *lotio,* a washing < *lavere,* to wash.]

lo·tos (lō′təs) *n.* Variant of **lotus.**

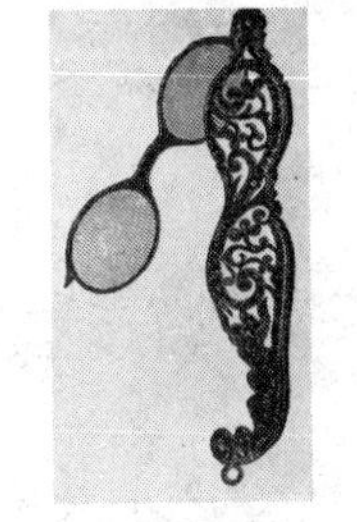

lorgnette

lot·ter·y (lŏt′ə-rē) *n., pl.* **-ies. 1.** A contest in which tokens are distributed or sold, the winning token or tokens being secretly predetermined or ultimately selected in a chance drawing. **2.** An activity or event regarded as having an outcome depending on fate. [Prob. < Du. *loterije* < *lot,* lot.]

lot·to (lŏt′ō) *n.* A game of chance played with numbered counters selected by lot to be placed upon the corresponding numbers on the players' boards. [Ital. < Fr. *lot,* lot, of Germanic orig.]

lo·tus also **lo·tos** (lō′təs) *n.* **1. a.** An aquatic plant, *Nelumbo nucifera,* native to southern Asia, having large leaves, fragrant, pinkish flowers, and a broad, rounded, perforated seed pod. **b.** Any of several plants similar or related to the lotus, as certain water lilies. **2.** A representation of any of various lotus plants in classical, usually Egyptian, sculpture, architecture, and art. **3.** Any of several leguminous plants of the genus *Lotus.* **4. a.** A small tree or shrub, *Zizyphus lotus,* of the Mediterranean region, the fruit of which is said to be that eaten by the lotus-eaters. **b.** The fruit of this tree. [Lat., name of several plants < Gk. *lōtos.*]

lo·tus-eat·er (lō′təs-ē′tər) *n.* **1.** One of a North African people described in the *Odyssey* who fed on the lotus and hence lived in a drugged, indolent state. **2.** An indolent sybarite.

loud (loud) *adj.* **-er, -est. 1.** Characterized by high volume and intensity of sound. **2.** Producing a sound of high volume and intensity. **3.** Clamorous and insistent: *loud denials.* **4. a.** Having offensively bright colors: *a loud necktie.* **b.** Having an offensively strong odor. **c.** Offensive in manner. —*adv.* **-er, -est.** In a loud manner. [ME < OE *hlūd.*] **—loud′ly** *adv.* **—loud′ness** *n.*

loud·en (loud′n) *tr. & intr.v.* **-ened, -en·ing, -ens.** To make or become louder.

loud·mouth (loud′mouth′) *n.* One given to loud and irritating or indiscreet talk. **—loud′mouthed′** (-mou*th*d′, -moutht′) *adj.*

loud·speak·er (loud′spē′kər) *n.* A device that converts electric signals to audible sound.

lough (lŏKH, lŏk) *n. Ir.* **1.** A lake. **2.** A bay or inlet of the sea. [ME < OE *luh,* of Celt. orig.]

lou·is d'or (lo͞o′ē dôr′) also **lou·is** (lo͞o′ē) *n.* **1.** A gold coin of France from 1640 until the Revolution. **2.** A 20-franc gold coin of post-Revolutionary France. [Fr. : *Louis,* Louis XIII + *d'or,* of gold.]

Lou·i·si·an·a French (lo͞o-ē′zē-ăn′ə) *n.* French as spoken by the descendants of the original French settlers of Louisiana.

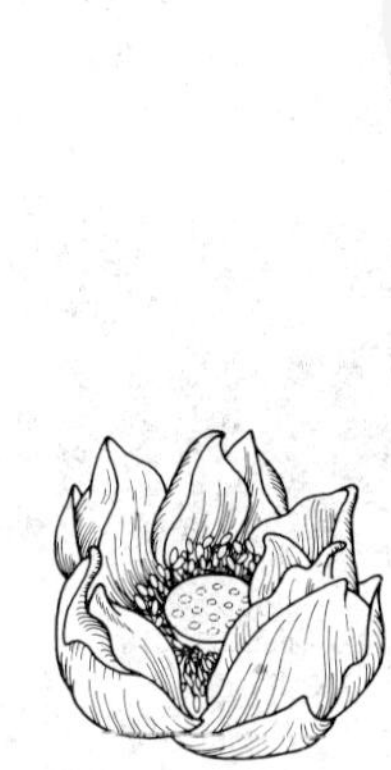

lotus

Lou·is Qua·torze (lo͞o′ē kă-tôrz′) *adj.* Of, pertaining to, or characteristic of the baroque style in architecture, furniture, and decoration of the reign of Louis XIV. [Fr., Louis XIV.]

Lou·is Quinze (lo͞o′ē kăɴz′) *adj.* Of, pertaining to, or characteristic of the rococo style in architecture, furniture, and decoration of the reign of Louis XV. [Fr., Louis XV.]

Lou·is Seize (lo͞o′ē sĕz′) *adj.* Of, pertaining to, or characteristic of the neoclassic style in architecture, furniture, and decoration of the reign of Louis XVI. [Fr., Louis XVI.]

Lou·is Treize (lo͞o′ē trĕz′) *adj.* Of, pertaining to, or characteristic of the heavy late-Renaissance style in architecture, furniture, and decoration of the reign of Louis XIII. [Fr., Louis XIII.]

lounge (lounj) *v.* **lounged, loung·ing, loung·es.** —*intr.* **1.** To move or act in a lazy, relaxed way; loll. **2.** To pass time idly. —*tr.* To pass (time) in lounging. —*n.* **1.** A public waiting room, as in a hotel or air terminal, often having smoking or

loupe

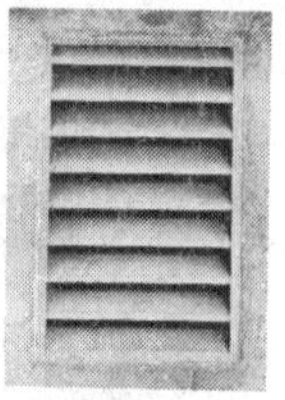
louver

love-in-a-mist

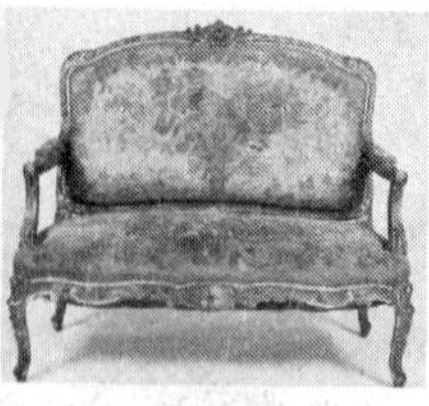
love seat
Louis XV style

lowboy
Chippendale lowboy

lavatory facilities. **2. a.** A living room. **b.** A lobby. **3.** A long couch, esp. one having no back and a headrest at one end. [Orig. unknown.] **—loung'er** *n.*
loupe (lo͞op) *n.* A small magnifying glass usually set in an eyepiece and used chiefly by watchmakers and jewelers. [Fr.]
loup-ga·rou (lo͞o'gə-ro͞o', -gä-) *n., pl.* **loups-ga·rous** (lo͞o'gə-ro͞oz', -gä-ro͞o'). A werewolf. [Fr. : *loup,* wolf (< Lat. *lupus*) + *garou,* werewolf, of Germanic orig.]
loup·ing ill (lou'pĭng, lō'-) *n.* Tremble (sense 3.a.). [< obs. *loup,* to leap < ME *loupen.*]
lour (lou'ər) *v. & n.* Variant of **lower¹**.
louse (lous) *n.* **1.** *pl.* **lice** (līs). Any of numerous small, flat-bodied, wingless, biting or sucking insects of the order Anoplura, many of which are external parasites on various animals, including man. **2.** *pl.* **lous·es.** *Slang.* A mean or despicable person. *—tr.v.* **loused, lous·ing, lous·es.** *Slang.* To bungle: *louse up a deal.* [ME < OE *lūs.*]
louse·wort (lous'wûrt', -wôrt') *n.* Any of numerous plants of the genus *Pedicularis,* having clusters of irregular, variously colored flowers.
lous·y (lou'zē) *adj.* **-i·er, -i·est. 1.** Infested with lice. **2.** Extremely contemptible; nasty: *a lousy trick.* **3.** Very painful or unpleasant: *a lousy headache.* **4.** Inferior or worthless. **5.** *Slang.* Abundantly supplied: *lousy with money.* **—lous'i·ly** *adv.* **—lous'i·ness** *n.*
lout¹ (lout) *n.* An awkward, stupid person; oaf. [Poss. < LOUT².]
lout² (lout) *intr.v.* **lout·ed, lout·ing, louts.** *Archaic.* **1.** To bow or curtsy. **2.** To bend or stoop. [ME *louten* < OE *lūtan.*]
lout·ish (lou'tĭsh) *adj.* Having the characteristics of a lout; clumsy or boorish. **—lout'ish·ly** *adv.* **—lout'ish·ness** *n.*
lou·ver also **lou·vre** (lo͞o'vər) *n.* **1. a.** A framed opening in a wall fitted with fixed or movable slanted slats. **b.** One of the slats used in a louver. **2.** A lantern-shaped cupola on the roof of many medieval buildings to admit air and provide for the escape of smoke. **3.** A slatted ventilating opening, as on an automobile hood. [ME *luver,* hole in the roof < OFr. < Med. Lat. *luvarium.*] **—lou'vered** *adj.*
lov·a·ble also **love·a·ble** (lŭv'ə-bəl) *adj.* Having characteristics that attract love or affection. **—lov'a·bil'i·ty, lov'a·ble·ness** *n.* **—lov'a·bly** *adv.*
lov·age (lŭv'ĭj) *n.* A plant, *Levisticum officinale,* having small, aromatic seeds used as seasoning. [ME < OFr. *luvesche* < LLat. *levisticum,* alteration of Lat. *ligusticum* < *ligusticus,* Ligurian.]
love (lŭv) *n.* **1. a.** An intense affection for another person based on familial or personal ties. **b.** A strong affection for or attachment to another person based on regard or shared experiences or interests. **2.** An expression of one's affection: *send him my love.* **3. a.** An intense attraction to another person based largely on sexual desire. **b.** The deep affection, tenderness, and concern felt for a person with whom one has or wishes to have a relationship based on sexual attraction. **c.** The person who is the object of such an attraction; beloved. **4. a.** Intense sexual passion. **b.** Sexual intercourse. **c.** A love affair (sense 1). **5.** An intense emotional attachment, as for a pet or treasured object. **6. a.** A strong enthusiasm: *a love of language.* **b.** The object of such an enthusiasm: *The outdoors is her greatest love.* **7. Love.** Eros or Cupid, the god of love in classical mythology. **8. a.** God's benevolence and mercy toward man. **b.** Man's devotion to or adoration of God. **c.** The feeling of benevolence, kindness, or brotherhood toward others. **9. Love.** *Christian Science.* God (sense 4). **10.** A zero score in tennis. *—v.* **loved, lov·ing, loves.** *—tr.* **1.** To feel love for. **2. a.** To embrace or caress. **b.** To have sexual intercourse with. **3.** To like or desire enthusiastically: *loves to swim.* **4.** To thrive on; need: *The cactus loves hot, dry air.* *—intr.* To experience loving tenderness or sexual desire for another. ***—idioms.*** **fall in love.** To become enamored of or sexually attracted to someone. **for love or money.** Under any circumstances: *He would not do that for love or money.* [ME < OE *lufu.*]

Synonyms: *love, affection, devotion, fondness, infatuation.* These nouns refer to feelings of attraction and attachment experienced by persons. *Love* suggests a feeling more intense and less susceptible to control than that associated with the other words of this group. *Affection* is a more unvarying feeling of warm regard for another person. *Devotion* is dedication and attachment to a person or thing; contrasted with *love,* it implies a more selfless and often a more settled feeling. *Fondness,* in its most common modern sense, is rather strong liking for a person or thing. *Infatuation* is extravagant attraction or attachment to a person or thing, usually short in duration and indicative of folly or faulty judgment.

love·a·ble (lŭv'ə-bəl) *adj.* Variant of **lovable**.
love affair *n.* **1.** An intimate sexual relationship or episode between lovers. **2.** A strong enthusiasm: *America's love affair with the automobile.*
love apple *n. Archaic.* A tomato.
love·bird (lŭv'bûrd') *n.* Any of various small Old World parrots, chiefly of the genus *Agapornis,* often kept as a cage bird.
love child *n.* An illegitimate child.
love feast *n.* **1. a.** Among early Christians, a meal eaten with others as a symbol of love. **b.** A similar symbolic meal among certain modern Christian sects. **2.** A gathering intended to promote good will among the participants.
love-in-a-mist (lŭv'ĭn-ə-mĭst') *n.* A plant, *Nigella damascena,* native to Europe, having blue or whitish flowers surrounded by numerous threadlike bracts.
love knot *n.* A stylized knot regarded as a symbol of the constancy of two lovers.
love·less (lŭv'lĭs) *adj.* **1.** Characterized by an absence of love. **2.** Feeling no love; unloving. **3.** Receiving no love; unloved.
love-lies-bleed·ing (lŭv'līz-blē'dĭng) *n.* A tropical plant, *Amaranthus caudatus,* having clusters of small red flowers.
love·lock (lŭv'lŏk') *n.* A lock of hair, often tied with ribbon, worn by courtiers during the 17th and 18th centuries.
love·lorn (lŭv'lôrn') *adj.* Bereft of love or one's lover.
love·ly (lŭv'lē) *adj.* **-li·er, -li·est. 1.** Full of love; loving. **2.** Inspiring love or affection. **3.** Having pleasing or attractive qualities. **4.** Enjoyable; delightful. *—n., pl.* **-lies.** *Informal.* **1.** A beautiful person, esp. a woman. **2.** A lovely object. **—love'li·ness** *n.* **—love'ly** *adv.*
love·mak·ing (lŭv'mā'kĭng) *n.* **1.** Sexual activity, esp. sexual intercourse. **2.** Courtship.
lov·er (lŭv'ər) *n.* **1.** Someone who loves another, esp. one who feels sexual love. **2. lovers.** A couple in love with each other. **3. a.** A paramour. **b.** A sexual partner. **4.** One who is fond of or devoted to something. **—lov'er·ly** *adj. & adv.*
lovers' knot *n.* A true lovers' knot.
love seat *n.* A small sofa or double chair that seats two people.
love·sick (lŭv'sĭk') *adj.* **1.** So deeply affected by love as to be unable to act normally. **2.** Exhibiting a lover's yearning. **—love'sick'ness** *n.*
lov·ing (lŭv'ĭng) *adj.* **1.** Feeling love; affectionate. **2.** Indicative of or exhibiting love.
loving cup *n.* **1.** A large, ornamental wine vessel, usually made of silver and having two or more handles. **2.** A loving cup given as an award in modern sporting events and similar affairs.
lov·ing-kind·ness (lŭv'ĭng-kīnd'nĭs) *n.* Affection or tenderness stemming from sincere love for someone.
low¹ (lō) *adj.* **-er, -est. 1. a.** Having little relative height; not tall. **b.** Rising only slightly above surrounding surfaces: *low relief.* **c.** Situated or placed below normal height: *a low lighting fixture.* **d.** Situated below the surrounding surfaces: *water standing in low spots.* **e.** *Archaic.* Dead and buried. **f.** Cut to show the wearer's chest, back, and neck; décolleté. **2.** Near or at the horizon: *The sun is low in the sky.* **3.** Sounded with all or part of the tongue depressed. Used of a vowel. The vowel (ä) in *large* is low. **4.** Of less than usual or average depth; shallow: *The river is low.* **5. a.** Humble in status or character. **b.** Of relatively simple structure in the scale of living organisms. **6.** Morally base: *a low stunt to pull.* **7. a.** Lacking strength or vigor; weak. **b.** Emotionally or mentally depressed. **8. a.** Below average in degree, intensity, or amount: *a low temperature.* **b.** Below an average or standard: *low wages; a low level of workmanship.* **c.** Pertaining to or designating latitudes nearest to the equator. **d.** Of relatively small price: *The cost is low.* **e.** Not flourishing or advancing. **9. a.** *Mus.* Being a sound produced by a relatively small frequency of vibrations: *a low tone.* **b.** Not loud; hushed: *a low voice.* **10.** Being almost without money: *low in funds.* **11.** Not adequately provided with or equipped for; short: *low on supplies.* **12.** Depreciatory; disparaging: *a low opinion of his qualities.* **13.** Brought down or reduced in health or wealth. *—adv.* **1. a.** In a low position, level, or space. **b.** In a low condition or rank; humbly: *You value yourself too low.* **2.** In or to a reduced, humbled, or degraded condition: *brought low by business reverses.* **3.** Softly; quietly: *speak low.* **4.** With a deep pitch. **5.** At a small price: *bought low, sold high.* *—n.* **1.** A low level, position, or degree: *The stock market fell to a new low.* **2.** A region of depressed barometric pressure. **3.** The gear configuration or setting that produces the lowest range of output speeds, as in an automotive transmission. [ME *loue* < ON *lāgr.*] **—low'ness** *n.*
low² (lō) *n.* The characteristic sound uttered by cattle; moo. *—intr.v.* **lowed, low·ing, lows.** To utter a low; moo. [ME *lowen* < OE *hlōwan.*]
low beam *n.* A low-intensity headlight on a vehicle.
low·born (lō'bôrn') *adj.* Of humble birth.
low·boy (lō'boi') *n.* A low, tablelike chest of drawers.
low·bred (lō'brĕd') *adj.* Coarse; vulgar.
low·brow (lō'brou') *n. Informal.* One having uncultivated tastes. *—adj.* Also **low·browed** (-broud'). Uncultivated; vulgar.
Low-Church (lō'chûrch') *adj.* Of or relating to a faction in the Anglican Church that is opposed to excessive ritualism and favors a more evangelical doctrine. **—Low'-Church'man** *n.*
low comedy *n.* Comedy characterized by slapstick, burlesque, and horseplay.
low·down (lō'doun') *n. Slang.* The whole truth.
low-down (lō'doun') *adj.* **1.** Despicable; base. **2.** Emotionally depressed.
low·er¹ also **lour** (lou'ər) *—intr.v.* **-ered, -er·ing, -ers** also

loured, lour·ing, lours. **1.** To look angry, sullen, or threatening. **2.** To appear dark or threatening, as the sky. *—n.* **1.** A threatening, sullen, or angry look. **2.** A dark and ominous look, as of thunderheads. [ME *louren.*] **—low'er·ing·ly** *adv.*

low·er² (lō'ər) *adj.* **1.** Below someone or something in rank, position, or authority. **2.** Below a similar or comparable thing: *a lower shelf.* **3. Lower.** *Geol. & Archaeol.* Being an earlier division of the period named. **4.** Denoting the larger and usually more representative house of a bicameral legislature. *—v.* **-ered, -er·ing, -ers.** *—tr.* **1.** To let, bring, or move down to a lower level. **2.** To reduce in value, degree, or quality. **3.** To weaken; undermine: *lower one's energy.* **4.** To reduce in standing or respect. *—intr.* **1.** To move down. **2.** To become less; diminish.

lower bound *n. Math.* A number that is not greater than any number in a set.

Lower Carboniferous *n.* Mississippian.

low·er-case (lō'ər-kās') *adj. Printing.* Of or pertaining to small letters as distinguished from capitals: *a, b, and c are lower-case letters.* *—tr.v.* **-cased, -cas·ing, -cas·es.** To set (type) in lower case. **—lower case** *n.*

lower class *n.* The class or classes of lower than middle rank in a society. **—low'er-class'** *adj.*

low·er·class·man (lō'ər-klăs'mən) *n.* An underclassman.

Lower Cretaceous *n.* Comanchean.

lower criticism *n.* Textual criticism and verbal examination of a written work, esp. of the Bible.

low·er·most (lō'ər-mōst') *adj.* Lowest.

lower world *n.* The abode of the dead, considered in ancient times to be beneath the surface of the earth.

low·er·y (lou'ə-rē) *adj.* Overcast; threatening.

lowest common denominator *n.* The least common multiple of the denominators of a set of fractions.

lowest common multiple *n.* Least common multiple.

lowest terms *pl.n.* The numerator and denominator of a fraction that have had all common factors but 1 factored out and cancelled.

low frequency *n.* A radio frequency in the range from 30 to 300 kilocycles per second.

Low German *n.* **1.** The German dialects of northern Germany, esp. as used since the beginning of the modern period. **2.** The continental West Germanic languages except High German.

low-key (lō'kē') also **low-keyed** (lō'kēd') *adj.* **1.** Having low intensity; subdued. **2.** Having or producing uniformly dark tones with little contrast.

low·land (lō'lənd) *n.* An area of land that is low in relation to the surrounding country.

low·land·er (lō'lən-dər) *n.* **1.** A native or inhabitant of a lowland. **2. Lowlander.** An inhabitant of the Scottish Lowlands.

low-lev·el (lō'lĕv'əl) *adj.* **1.** Pertaining to or being of low rank or importance. **2.** Situated in or occurring at a low level.

low·life (lō'līf') *n.* A person of low social status or moral character.

low·ly (lō'lē) *adj.* **-li·er, -li·est.** **1.** Having or suited for a low rank or position. **2.** Humble or meek in manner. **3.** Plain or prosaic in nature. *—adv.* **1.** In a low manner, condition, or position. **2.** In a meek or humble manner. **3.** Low in sound. **—low'li·ness** *n.*

Low Mass *n.* A Mass of nonelaborate ceremonial form that is recited rather than sung by the priest.

low-mind·ed (lō'mīn'dĭd) *adj.* Exhibiting a coarse, vulgar character. **—low'-mind'ed·ly** *adv.* **—low'-mind'ed·ness** *n.*

low-necked (lō'nĕkt') also **low-neck** (-nĕk') *adj.* Having a low-cut neckline; décolleté.

low-pitched (lō'pĭcht') *adj.* **1.** Low in tone or tonal range. **2.** Having a moderate slope: *a low-pitched roof.*

low-pres·sure (lō'prĕsh'ər) *adj.* **1.** Having, working under, or exerting little pressure. **2.** Relaxed; easygoing.

low profile *n.* Behavior or activity carried out in such a way as not to attract attention to itself.

low relief *n.* Sculptural relief that projects very little from the background.

low-rise (lō'rīz') *adj.* Being one or two stories high and having no elevators: *a low-rise apartment building.*

low-spir·it·ed (lō'spĭr'ĭ-tĭd) *adj.* In low spirits; depressed. **—low'-spir'it·ed·ly** *adv.* **—low'-spir'it·ed·ness** *n.*

Low Sunday *n.* The Sunday following Easter.

low-ten·sion (lō'tĕn'shən) *adj.* **1.** Of or at low potential or voltage. **2.** Operating at low voltage.

low-test (lō'tĕst') *adj.* Having low volatility and a high boiling point. Used of gasoline.

low tide *n.* **1.** The tide at its lowest ebb. **2.** The time at which low tide occurs.

low water *n.* **1.** The lowest level of water in a body of water, such as a river, lake, or reservoir. **2.** Low tide.

lox¹ (lŏks) *n.* Smoked salmon. [Yiddish *laks* < MHG *lahs,* salmon < OHG.]

lox² (lŏks) *n.* Liquid oxygen, esp. as a rocket fuel oxidizer. [L(IQUID) OX(YGEN).]

lox·o·drom·ic (lŏk'sə-drŏm'ĭk) also **lox·o·drom·i·cal** (-ĭ-kəl) *adj. Naut.* Pertaining to sailing on a rhumb line. [Gk. *loxos,* slanting + Gk. *dromos,* course.] **—lox'o·drom'i·cal·ly** *adv.*

loxodromic curve *n.* A rhumb line.

loy·al (loi'əl) *adj.* **1.** Steadfast in allegiance to one's homeland, government, or sovereign. **2.** Faithful to a person, ideal, or custom. **3.** Of or professing loyalty. [Fr. < OFr. *loial* < Lat. *legalis,* legal < *lex,* law.] **—loy'al·ly** *adv.*

loy·al·ist (loi'ə-lĭst) *n.* **1.** One who maintains loyalty to a lawful government, political party, or sovereign, esp. during war or revolutionary change. **2. Loyalist.** A Tory. **—loy'al·ism** *n.*

loy·al·ty (loi'əl-tē) *n., pl.* **-ties.** **1.** The state or quality of being loyal. **2. loyalties.** Feelings of devoted attachment and affection.

loz·enge (lŏz'ĭnj) *n.* **1.** A four-sided planar figure with a diamondlike shape; a rhombus that is not a square. **2.** A lozenge-shaped, medicated drop for local medication of the mouth or throat. [ME *losenge* < OFr.]

LP (ĕl'pē') *n.* A long-playing record. [Orig. a trademark.]

LSD (ĕl'ĕs-dē') *n.* Lysergic acid diethylamide.

Lu The symbol for the element lutetium.

lu·au (lo͞o-ou', lo͞o'ou') *n.* An elaborate Hawaiian feast. [Hawaiian *lu'au.*]

lub·ber (lŭb'ər) *n.* **1.** A clumsy fellow. **2.** An inexperienced sailor. [ME *lobur,* lazy lout.]

lubber line also **lubber's line** *n.* A line or mark on a compass or cathode-ray indicator that represents the heading of a ship or aircraft.

lubber's hole *n.* A hole through the platform surrounding the upper part of a ship's mast, through which one may climb to go aloft.

lu·bri·cant (lo͞o'brĭ-kənt) *n.* **1.** A usually oily substance, such as grease, that reduces friction, heat, and wear when applied as a surface coating to moving parts. **2.** One that helps reduce difficulty or conflict. **—lu'bri·cant** *adj.*

lu·bri·cate (lo͞o'brĭ-kāt') *v.* **-cat·ed, -cat·ing, -cates.** *—tr.* **1.** To apply a lubricant to. **2.** To make slippery or smooth. *—intr.* To act as a lubricant. [Lat. *lubricare, lubricat-* < *lubricus,* slippery.] **—lu'bri·ca'tion** *n.* **—lu'bri·ca'tive** *adj.*

lu·bri·ca·tor (lo͞o'brĭ-kā'tər) *n.* **1.** One who lubricates. **2.** A lubricant. **3.** A device for applying a lubricant.

lu·bri·cious (lo͞o-brĭsh'əs) also **lu·bri·cous** (lo͞o'brĭk-əs) *adj.* **1.** Having a slippery or smooth quality. **2. a.** Marked by lewdness; wanton. **b.** Sexually stimulating; salacious. **3.** Marked by shiftiness or trickery. [Lat. *lubricus,* slippery.] **—lu·bri'cious·ly** *adv.* **—lu·bri'cious·ness** *n.*

lu·bric·i·ty (lo͞o-brĭs'ĭ-tē) *n.* The quality or condition of being lubricious. [LLat. *lubricitas,* slipperiness < Lat. *lubricus,* slippery.]

lu·carne (lo͞o-kärn') *n.* A dormer window. [OFr. *lucane,* poss. of Germanic orig.]

lu·cent (lo͞o'sənt) *adj.* **1.** Giving off light; luminous. **2.** Translucent; clear. [Lat. *lucens, lucent-,* pr.part. of *lucēre,* to shine.] **—lu'cen·cy** *n.* **—lu'cent·ly** *adv.*

lu·cerne (lo͞o-sûrn') *n. Chiefly Brit.* Alfalfa. [Fr. *luzerne* < Prov. *luzerno.*]

lu·ces (lo͞o'sēz') *n.* A plural of **lux.**

lu·cid (lo͞o'sĭd) *adj.* **1.** Easily understood; intelligible. **2.** Mentally sound; sane. **3.** Translucent. [Lat. *lucidus* < *lux,* light < *lucēre,* to shine.] **—lu·cid'i·ty** (-sĭd'ĭ-tē), **lu'cid·ness** *n.* **—lu'cid·ly** *adv.*

Lu·ci·fer (lo͞o'sə-fər) *n.* **1.** The archangel cast from heaven for leading a revolt of the angels; Satan. **2.** The planet Venus in its appearance as the morning star. **3. lucifer.** A friction match. [ME < Lat., morning star < *lucifer,* light-bearing : *lux,* light + *ferre,* to bring.]

lu·cif·er·ase (lo͞o-sĭf'ə-rās') *n.* An enzyme that catalyzes the oxidation of luciferin.

lu·cif·er·in (lo͞o-sĭf'ər-ĭn) *n.* A pigment in bioluminescent animals, such as fireflies or certain marine crustaceans, that produces an almost heatless, bluish-green light when oxidized. [Lat. *lucifer,* light-bringing + -IN.]

Lu·ci·na (lo͞o-sī'nə) *n. Archaic.* A midwife. [Lat., goddess of childbirth < *lucinus,* light-bringing < *lux,* light < *lucēre,* to shine.]

Lu·cite (lo͞o'sīt'). A trademark for a transparent thermoplastic acrylic resin.

luck (lŭk) *n.* **1.** The chance happening of fortunate or adverse events. **2.** Good fortune or prosperity; success. *—intr.v.* **lucked, luck·ing, lucks.** To gain success or something desirable by chance: *lucked out in finding that rare book.* [ME *lucke* < MDu. *luc.*] **—luck'less** *adj.*

luck·i·ly (lŭk'ə-lē) *adv.* With or by favorable chance.

luck·y (lŭk'ē) *adj.* **-i·er, -i·est.** **1.** Having good luck. **2.** Occurring by chance; fortuitous. **3.** Believed to bring good luck: *a lucky number.* **—luck'i·ness** *n.*

lu·cra·tive (lo͞o'krə-tĭv) *adj.* Producing wealth; profitable. [ME *lucratif* < OFr. < Lat. *lucrativus* < *lucrari,* to profit < *lucrum,* profit.]

lu·cre (lo͞o'kər) *n.* Money or profits. [ME < Lat. *lucrum.*]

lu·cu·brate (lo͞o'kyo͞o-brāt') *intr.v.* **-brat·ed, -brat·ing, -brates.** To write in a scholarly fashion. [Lat. *lucubrare, lucubrat-,* to work at night by lamplight < *lux,* light < *lucēre,* to shine.]

lu·cu·bra·tion (lo͞o'kyo͞o-brā'shən) *n.* **1.** Laborious study or writing. **2.** Pedantry in speech or writing.

lu·cu·lent (lo͞o'kyo͞o-lənt) *adj.* Easily understood; lucid. [ME, shiny < Lat. *luculentus* < *lux,* light < *lucēre,* to shine.]

low relief

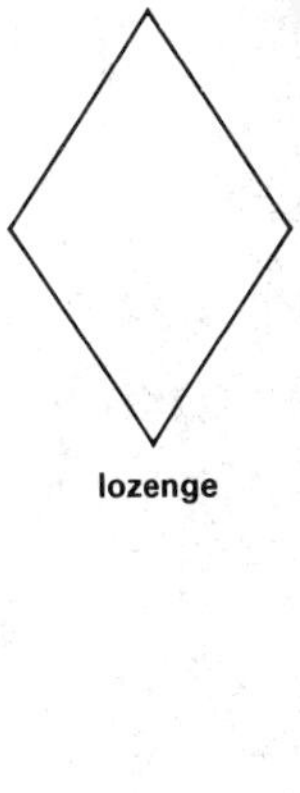

lozenge

Lu·cul·lan (lo͞o-kŭl′ən) *adj.* Lavish; luxurious: *a Lucullan banquet.* [After Lucius Licinius *Lucullus* (110?–57? B.C.), Roman patron of arts.]

Lud·dite (lŭd′īt′) *n.* Any of a group of British workmen who, between 1811 and 1816, rioted and destroyed laborsaving textile machinery in the belief that such machinery would diminish employment. [After Ned *Ludd,* a legendary leader.]

lu·di·crous (lo͞o′dĭ-krəs) *adj.* Laughable or hilarious because of obvious absurdity or incongruity. [Lat. *ludicrus,* sportive < *ludus,* game < *ludere,* to play.] **—lu′di·crous·ly** *adv.* **—lu′di·crous·ness** *n.*

lu·es (lo͞o′ēz) *n., pl.* **lues.** Syphilis. [NLat. < Lat., plague.] **—lu·et′ic** (-ĕt′ĭk) *adj.* **—lu·et′i·cal·ly** *adv.*

luff (lŭf) *n.* **1.** The act of sailing closer into the wind. **2.** The forward side of a fore-and-aft sail. **3.** The fullest part of the bow of a ship. *—intr.v.* **luffed, luff·ing, luffs. 1.** To steer a sailing vessel nearer into the wind. **2.** To flap while losing wind. Used of a sail. [ME *loffe,* spar for holding a square sail on a windward tack < OFr. *lof,* prob. of Germanic orig.]

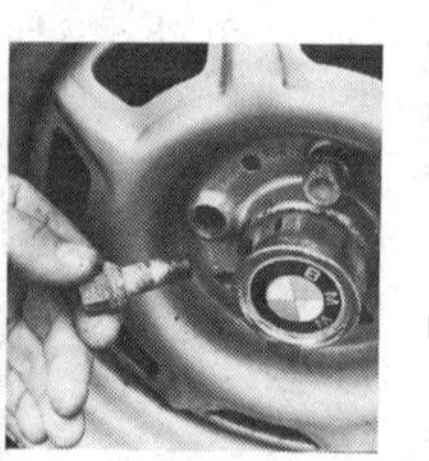

lug[1]

lug[1] (lŭg) *n.* **1.** A handle or projection on a vessel or machine that is shaped like an ear, used as a hold or support. **2.** A nut, esp. one that is closed at one end to serve as a cap. **3.** A loop, usually of leather, at the side of the saddle of a harness rig through which one of the shafts of a cart or other conveyance passes. **4.** A copper or brass fitting to which electrical wires can be soldered or otherwise connected. **5.** *Slang.* A clumsy fool; blockhead. [ME *lugge,* earflap.]

lug[2] (lŭg) *v.* **lugged, lug·ging, lugs.** *—tr.* **1.** To drag or haul (something) laboriously. **2.** To pull or drag with short jerks. *—intr.* **1.** To pull with difficulty; tug. **2.** To move by jerks or as if under a heavy burden. *—n.* **1.** *Archaic.* An act of lugging. **2.** *Archaic.* Something that is lugged. **3.** A lugsail. **4.** *Slang.* An extortion of money: *put the lug on.* [ME *luggen,* of Scand. orig.]

luge

luge (lo͞ozh) *n.* **1.** A sled, similar in design to a toboggan, that is ridden with the rider lying on his back. **2.** A competition in which luges race against a clock. [Fr.]

lug·gage (lŭg′ĭj) *n.* Something that one lugs, esp. baggage. [Probably LUG[2] + (BAG)GAGE.]

lug·ger (lŭg′ər) *n.* A small boat used for fishing, sailing, or coasting and having two or three masts, each with a lugsail, and two or three jibs set on the bowsprit. [< LUGSAIL.]

lug·sail (lŭg′səl) *n.* A quadrilateral sail lacking a boom and having the foot larger than the head, bent to a yard hanging obliquely on the mast. [Perh. < LUG[1].]

lu·gu·bri·ous (lo͞o-go͞o′brē-əs, lo͞o-gyo͞o′-) *adj.* Mournful, esp. to an exaggerated or ludicrous degree. [Lat. *lugubris* < *lugēre,* to mourn.] **—lu·gu′bri·ous·ly** *adv.* **—lu·gu′bri·ous·ness** *n.*

lug·worm (lŭg′wûrm′) *n.* Any of various segmented, burrowing marine worms of the genus *Arenicola,* esp. *A. marina,* often used as fishing bait. [Orig. unknown.]

Luke (lo͝ok) *n.* **1.** A companion of the Apostle Paul, traditionally regarded as author of the third Gospel and The Acts of the Apostles. **2.** See table at **Bible.**

luke·warm (lo͝ok′wôrm′) *adj.* **1.** Mildly warm; tepid. **2.** Lacking in enthusiasm; indifferent. [ME *leukwarm* : *leuk,* lukewarm + *warm,* warm.] **—luke′warm′ly** *adv.* **—luke′warm′ness** *n.*

lull (lŭl) *v.* **lulled, lull·ing, lulls.** *—tr.* **1.** To cause to sleep or rest; soothe. **2.** To deceive into trustfulness: *"that honeyed charm that he used so effectively to lull his victims"* (S. J. Perelman). *—intr.* To become calm. *—n.* **1.** A relatively calm interval in a storm or other turbulence. **2.** An interval of lessened activity: *a lull in sales.* [ME *lullen.*]

lull·a·by (lŭl′ə-bī′) *n., pl.* **-bies.** A soothing song with which to lull a child to sleep. *—tr.v.* **-bied, -by·ing, -bies.** To quiet with or as if with a lullaby. [Obs. *lulla,* interjection used in lullabies (< ME *lullai* < *lullen,* to lull) + (BYE)-BY(E).]

lu·lu (lo͞o′lo͞o) *n. Slang.* An object, action, or idea that is remarkable. [Perh. from *Lulu,* a nickname for *Louise.*]

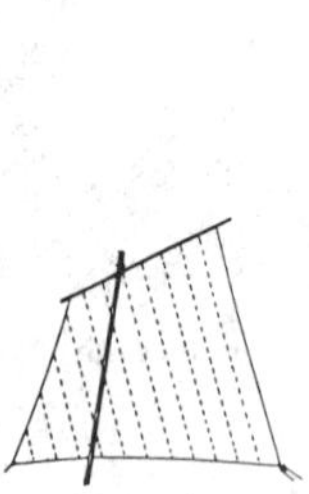

lugsail

lum·ba·go (lŭm-bā′gō) *n.* A painful, inflammatory rheumatism of the tendons and muscles of the lumbar region. [Lat. < *lumbus,* loin.]

lum·bar (lŭm′bər, -bär′) *adj.* Of or situated in the part of the back and sides between the lowest ribs and the pelvis. *—n.* A lumbar artery, nerve, vertebra, or part. [NLat. *lumbaris* < Lat. *lumbus,* loin.]

lum·ber[1] (lŭm′bər) *n.* **1.** Timber sawed into standardized boards, planks, or other structural members. **2.** *Chiefly Brit.* Miscellaneous stored articles. **3.** Something useless or cumbersome. *—v.* **-bered, -ber·ing, -bers.** *—tr.* **1. a.** To cut down (trees) and prepare as marketable timber. **b.** To cut down the timber of. **2.** *Chiefly Brit.* To clutter with or as if with unused articles. *—intr.* To cut and prepare timber for the market. [Perh. < LUMBER[2].] **—lum′ber** *adj.* **—lum′ber·er, lum′ber·man** *n.*

lum·ber[2] (lŭm′bər) *intr.v.* **-bered, -ber·ing, -bers. 1.** To walk or move with heavy clumsiness. **2.** To move with a rumbling noise. [ME *lomeren.*]

lum·ber·jack (lŭm′bər-jăk′) *n.* **1.** One who fells trees and transports the timber to a mill. **2.** A short, warm outer jacket.

lum·ber·yard (lŭm′bər-yärd′) *n.* An establishment that sells lumber and other building materials from a yard.

lum·bri·coid (lŭm′brĭ-koid′) *adj.* Resembling an earthworm. *—n.* A parasitic roundworm, *Ascaris lumbricoides,* that infests the human intestine. [Lat. *lumbricus,* earthworm + -OID.]

lu·men (lo͞o′mən) *n., pl.* **-mens** or **-mi·na** (-mə-nə). **1.** *Anat.* The inner open space of a tubular organ, as of a blood vessel or an intestine. **2.** *Physics.* The unit of luminous flux in the International System, equal to the luminous flux emitted in a solid angle of one steradian by a uniform point source having an intensity of one candle. [NLat. < Lat., an opening.] **—lu′men·al, lu′min·al** *adj.*

lu·mi·nance (lo͞o′mə-nəns) *n.* **1.** The condition or quality of being luminous. **2.** *Physics.* The luminous intensity per unit projected area of a given surface viewed from a given direction.

lu·mi·nar·y (lo͞o′mə-nĕr′ē) *n., pl.* **-ies. 1.** An object, as a celestial body, that gives light. **2.** A source of intellectual or spiritual light. **3.** A notable person in a specific field. [ME < OFr. *luminarie* and Med. Lat. *luminarium* < LLat. *luminare* < Lat. *lumen,* light.] **—lu′mi·nar′y** *adj.*

lu·mi·nesce (lo͞o′mə-nĕs′) *intr.v.* **-nesced, -nesc·ing, -nesc·es.** To be or become luminescent. [Back-formation < LUMINESCENCE.]

lu·mi·nes·cence (lo͞o′mə-nĕs′əns) *n.* **1.** The emission of light, as in phosphorescence, fluorescence, and bioluminescence, by processes that derive energy from essentially nonthermal sources such as chemical, biochemical, or crystallographic changes, the motion of subatomic particles, or the excitation of an atomic system by radiation, esp. such emission distinguished from incandescence. **2.** The light emitted by luminescence. [Lat. *lumen, lumin-,* light + -ESCENCE.]

lu·mi·nes·cent (lo͞o′mə-nĕs′ənt) *adj.* Capable of, exhibiting, or suitable for the emission of luminescence.

lu·mi·nif·er·ous (lo͞o′mə-nĭf′ər-əs) *adj.* Generating, yielding, or transmitting light. [Lat. *lumen, lumin-,* light + -FEROUS.]

lu·mi·nos·i·ty (lo͞o′mə-nŏs′ĭ-tē) *n.* **1.** The condition or quality of being luminous. **2.** Something luminous. **3.** Also **luminosity factor.** The ratio of luminous flux at a specific wavelength to the radiant flux at the same wavelength.

lu·mi·nous (lo͞o′mə-nəs) *adj.* **1.** Emitting light, esp. emitting self-generated light. **2.** Full of light; illuminated. **3. a.** Easily comprehended; clear. **b.** Enlightened and intelligent. [ME < OFr. *lumineux* < Lat. *luminosus* < *lumen,* light.] **—lu′mi·nous·ly** *adv.* **—lu′mi·nous·ness** *n.*

luminous efficiency *n.* The ratio of the total luminous flux to the total radiant flux of an emitting source.

luminous energy *n.* The radiant energy of electromagnetic waves in the visible portion of the electromagnetic spectrum.

luminous flux *n.* The rate of flow of light per unit time, esp. the flux of visible light expressed in lumens.

luminous intensity *n.* The luminous flux density per solid angle as measured in a given direction relative to the emitting source.

luminous paint *n.* A paint containing a phosphorescent or fluorescent substance that makes it glow in the dark.

lum·mox (lŭm′əks) *n.* An extremely clumsy, ungainly person. [Orig. unknown.]

lump[1] (lŭmp) *n.* **1.** An irregularly shaped mass or piece. **2.** A small cube of sugar. **3.** *Pathol.* A swelling or small, palpable mass. **4.** An aggregate; collection; totality. **5.** An ungainly or dull-witted person. **6. lumps. a.** Punishment in the form of beatings: *take one's lumps.* **b.** One's just deserts; comeuppance. *—adj.* **1.** Formed into lumps: *lump sugar.* **2.** Not broken or divided into parts: *one lump payment.* *—v.* **lumped, lump·ing, lumps.** *—tr.* **1.** To put together in a single group without discrimination. **2.** To move with heavy clumsiness. **3.** To make into lumps. *—intr.* **1.** To become lumpy. **2.** To move heavily. [ME.]

lump[2] (lŭmp) *tr.v.* **lumped, lump·ing, lumps.** *Informal.* To tolerate (what must be endured): *like it or lump it.* [Orig. unknown.]

lum·pen (lŭm′pən, lo͝om′-) *adj.* Of or pertaining to dispossessed, often displaced individuals who have been cut off from the socioeconomic class with which they would ordinarily be identified: *lumpen intellectuals.* [< G. *Lumpenproletariat,* the lowest section of the proletariat < *Lump,* contemptible person < *Lumpen,* rags.]

lump·er (lŭm′pər) *n.* A laborer employed to load and unload ships. [< LUMP[1].]

lump·fish (lŭmp′fĭsh′) *n., pl.* **lumpfish** or **-fish·es.** A fish, *Cyclopterus lumpus,* of Atlantic waters, having a body covered with tuberous excrescences. [Obs. *lump,* lumpfish + FISH.]

lump·ish (lŭm′pĭsh) *adj.* **1.** Stupid; dull. **2.** Clumsy; cumbersome. **—lump′ish·ly** *adv.* **—lump′ish·ness** *n.*

lump·y (lŭm′pē) *adj.* **-i·er, -i·est. 1.** Covered or filled with lumps. **2.** Thickset or cumbersome. **3.** Characterized by short, jumbled waves, as a tidal rip.

lumpy jaw *n.* Actinomycosis.

Lu·na (lo͞o′nə) *n.* **1.** The goddess of the moon. **2. luna.** An alchemical designation for silver. [Lat. < *luna,* moon.]

lu·na·cy (lo͞o′nə-sē) *n., pl.* **-cies. 1.** Intermittent mental derangement. **2.** Insanity. **3. a.** Great or wild foolishness. **b.** A wildly foolish act. [< LUNATIC.]

luna moth *n.* A large, pale-green North American moth,

Actias luna, having a long projection on each hind wing. [NLat. *luna,* specific epithet of *Actias luna* < Lat., moon.]
lu·nar (lo͞o'nər) *adj.* **1.** Of, involving, caused by, or affecting the moon. **2.** Measured by the revolution of the moon. **3.** Of or relating to silver. [Lat. *lunaris* < *luna,* moon.]
lunar caustic *n.* Silver nitrate used in cauterization.
lunar excursion module also **lunar module** *n.* A spacecraft designed to transport astronauts from a command module orbiting the moon to the lunar surface and back.
lunar month *n.* A month (sense 5).
lu·nar·naut (lo͞o'nər-nôt') *n.* An astronaut who explores the moon. [LUNAR + (ASTRO)NAUT.]
lunar year *n.* An interval of 12 lunar months.
lu·nate (lo͞o'nāt') also **lu·nat·ed** (-nā'tĭd) *adj.* Crescent-shaped. [Lat. *lunatus* < *lunare,* to bend like a crescent < *luna,* moon.]
lunate bone *n.* The second of three bones forming the upper row of bones in the wrist.
lu·na·tic (lo͞o'nə-tĭk) *adj.* **1.** Suffering from lunacy; insane. **2.** Of or for the insane: *a lunatic asylum.* **3.** Wildly or giddily foolish: *a lunatic decision.* [ME *lunatik* < OFr. *lunatique* < Lat. *lunaticus* < *luna,* moon.] **—lu'na·tic** *n.*
lunatic fringe *n.* The fanatical, extremist, or irrational members of a society or group, esp. such members of a political or religious group.
lu·na·tion (lo͞o-nā'shən) *n.* The time elapsing between two successive new moons, averaging 29 days, 12 hours, 44 minutes, 28 seconds. [ME *lunacioun* < Med. Lat. *lunatio* < Lat. *luna.*]
lunch (lŭnch) *n.* **1.** A meal eaten at midday. **2.** The food provided for a midday meal. *—intr.v.* **lunched, lunch·ing, lunch·es.** To eat lunch. **—*idiom.* out to lunch.** *Informal.* Not in touch with the real world; crazy. [Perh. < Sp. *lonja,* slice < OFr. *longe.*] **—lunch'er** *n.*
lunch·eon (lŭn'chən) *n.* **1.** A lunch. **2.** An afternoon party at which a light meal is served. [Prob. < LUNCH.]
lunch·eon·ette (lŭn'chə-nĕt') *n.* A small restaurant that serves simple, easily prepared meals.
lunch·room (lŭnch'ro͞om', -ro͝om') *n.* **1.** A luncheonette. **2.** A room in a facility, as a school, in which lunches may be purchased or those brought from home may be eaten.
lune (lo͞on) *n.* A portion of a sphere enclosed between two semicircles having their common end points at opposite poles. [Lat. *luna,* moon.]
lu·nette (lo͞o-nĕt') *n.* **1.** *Archit.* **a.** A small, circular or crescent-shaped opening in a vaulted roof. **b.** A crescent-shaped or semicircular space, usually over a door or window, that may contain another window, a sculpture, or a mural. **2.** A type of military fortification that has two projecting faces and two parallel flanks. [Fr. < OFr., moon-shaped object < *lune,* moon < Lat. *luna,* moon.]
lung (lŭng) *n.* **1.** Either of two spongy, saclike respiratory organs in most vertebrates, occupying the chest cavity together with the heart, and functioning to remove carbon dioxide from the blood and provide it with oxygen. **2.** An invertebrate structure, similar to the lung, as in terrestrial snails. [ME *lunge* < OE *lungen.*]
lunge (lŭnj) *n.* **1.** A sudden thrust or pass, as with a sword. **2.** A sudden forward movement or plunge. *—v.* **lunged, lung·ing, lung·es.** *—intr.* **1.** To make a thrust or pass. **2.** To move with a lunge. *—tr.* To cause (someone) to lunge. [Alteration of obs. *allonge* < Fr. *alongier,* to lunge : *à,* to + *long,* long.]
lung·er¹ (lŭn'jər) *n.* One that lunges.
lung·er² (lŭng'ər) *n.* *Informal.* One who has tuberculosis of the lungs.
lung·fish (lŭng'fĭsh') *n., pl.* **lungfish** or **-fish·es.** Any of several elongated tropical freshwater fishes of the order Dipnoi (or Dipneusti), having lungs as well as gills, and in certain species constructing a mucus-lined mud covering in which to withstand an extended drought.
lung·wort (lŭng'wûrt', -wôrt') *n.* **1.** Any of various plants of the genus *Mertensia,* having drooping clusters of tubular, usually blue flowers. **2.** Any of several plants of the genus *Pulmonaria,* native to Europe, with long-stalked leaves and coiled clusters of blue or purple flowers, formerly used in treating respiratory disorders.
lu·ni·so·lar (lo͞o'nĭ-sō'lər) *adj.* Of or caused by both the sun and the moon. [Lat. *luna,* moon + SOLAR.]
lu·ni·ti·dal (lo͞o'nĭ-tīd'l) *adj.* Of or pertaining to tidal phenomena caused by the moon. [Lat. *luna,* moon + TIDAL.]
lunitidal interval *n.* The time elapsing between the moon's transit of a particular meridian and the next high tide at that meridian.
lunk·er (lŭng'kər) *n.* *Informal.* Something unusually large of its kind, esp. a game fish. [Orig. unknown.]
lunk·head (lŭngk'hĕd') *n.* *Slang.* A stupid person. [Prob. alteration of LUMP + HEAD.] **—lunk'head'ed** *adj.*
lu·nu·la (lo͞on'yə-lə) *n., pl.* **-lae** (-lē'). A small crescent-shaped structure or marking. [Lat. < *luna,* moon.]
lu·nu·lar (lo͞on'yə-lər) *adj.* Crescent-shaped.
lu·nu·late (lo͞on'yə-lāt', -lĭt) also **lu·nu·lat·ed** (-lā'tĭd) *adj.* **1.** Small and lunular. **2.** Having crescent-shaped markings.
lu·nule (lo͞on'yo͞ol) *n.* A lunula.
lun·y (lo͞o'nē) *adj.* Variant of **loony.**
Lu·per·ca·li·a (lo͞o'pər-kā'lē-ə) *n.* A fertility festival in ancient Rome, celebrated on February 15 in honor of the pastoral god Lupercus. [Lat. < *Lupercus,* Roman god of flocks.] **—Lu'per·ca'li·an** *adj.*
lu·pine¹ also **lu·pin** (lo͞o'pən) *n.* Any of various plants of the genus *Lupinus,* having clusters of variously colored flowers. [ME < Lat. *lupinum* < *lupinus,* wolflike < *lupus,* wolf.]
lu·pine² (lo͞o'pīn') *adj.* **1.** Wolflike. **2.** Rapacious; ravenous. [Lat. *lupinus* < *lupus,* wolf.]
lu·pu·lin (lo͞op'yə-lən) *n.* Minute yellowish-brown hairs from the strobiles of the hop plant, formerly used as a sedative. [NLat. *lupulus,* specific epithet for a hop species (< Lat. *lupus,* a hop plant) + -IN.]
lu·pus (lo͞o'pəs) *n.* Any of several diseases of the skin and mucous membranes, many causing disfiguring lesions, esp.: **a.** Lupus vulgaris, characterized by ulcerating, nodular facial lesions, esp. around the nose and ears. **b.** Lupus erythematosus, characterized by eruption of atrophic scarred lesions with chronically inflamed margins. [Med. Lat. < Lat., wolf.]

lungfish

lurch¹ (lûrch) *intr.v.* **lurched, lurch·ing, lurch·es. 1.** To stagger. **2.** To roll or pitch suddenly or erratically, as a ship during a storm. *—n.* **1.** A staggering or tottering movement or gait. **2.** An abrupt rolling or pitching. [Orig. unknown.]
lurch² (lûrch) *n.* In the game of cribbage, the losing position of a player who scores 30 points or less to the winner's 61. **—*idiom.* in the lurch.** In a difficult or embarrassing position. [OFr. *lourche,* a kind of game < *lourche,* soundly defeated.]
lurch·er (lûr'chər) *n.* **1.** *Archaic.* A sneak thief. **2.** *Chiefly Brit.* A crossbred dog used by poachers. [< obs. *lurch,* to lurk < ME *lorchen,* perh. < *lurken.* —see LURK.]
lure (lo͝or) *n.* **1. a.** Something that tempts or attracts with the promise of gaining pleasure or reward. **b.** An attraction or appeal. **2.** A decoy used in catching animals, esp. an artificial bait used in catching fish. **3.** A bunch of feathers attached to a long cord, used in falconry to recall the hawk. *—tr.v.* **lured, lur·ing, lures. 1.** To attract by wiles or temptation; entice. **2.** To recall (a falcon) with a lure. [ME < OFr., of Germanic orig.]

lupine¹

Synonyms: *lure, entice, inveigle, decoy, tempt, seduce, beguile.* These verbs refer to leading or attempting to lead a person from his course, usually into harm or wrong, by exerting a strong attraction. *Lure* strongly implies capture by calculated and deliberate means. *Entice* involves drawing one on skillfully by making attractive promises; *inveigle,* winning over by coaxing, flattery, or specious talk; and *decoy,* trapping or ensnaring by false appearances or deception. *Tempt* and *seduce* both imply an effort to overcome moral resistance by means that are otherwise not explicit. Unlike *tempt, seduce* clearly connotes success in leading astray, and in one sense means causing another to surrender chastity. *Beguile* implies deluding or victimizing by craft, charm, or any device that diverts attention.
lu·rid (lo͝or'ĭd) *adj.* **1. a.** Causing shock or horror; gruesome. **b.** Stressing violence or sensationalism. **2.** Glowing or shining with the glare of fire through a haze: *lurid flames.* **3.** Sallow or pallid in color. [Lat. *luridus,* pale < *luror,* paleness.] **—lu'rid·ly** *adv.* **—lu'rid·ness** *n.*
lurk (lûrk) *intr.v.* **lurked, lurk·ing, lurks. 1.** To lie in wait, as in ambush. **2.** To move furtively; sneak. **3.** To exist unobserved or unsuspected: *dangers lurking around every bend.* [ME *lurken,* of Scand. orig.]
lus·cious (lŭsh'əs) *adj.* **1.** Sweet and pleasant to taste or smell: *a luscious melon.* **2.** Having strong sensory appeal; seductive. **3.** *Archaic.* Excessively sweet; cloying. [ME *lucius,* short for *delicious,* delicious. —see DELICIOUS.]
lush¹ (lŭsh) *adj.* **-er, -est. 1. a.** Having or characterized by luxuriant vegetation. **b.** Characterized by an abundance; plentiful. **c.** Extremely productive; thriving. **2. a.** Luxurious; opulent: *lush carpets.* **b.** Delicious; savory. **c.** Voluptuous; sensual. **3.** Overelaborate or extravagant: *lush rhetoric.* [ME *lusch,* soft.] **—lush'ly** *adv.* **—lush'ness** *n.*

lure
Fishing lure

lush² (lŭsh) *Slang.* *—n.* **1.** A drunkard. **2.** Intoxicating liquor. *—intr.v.* **lushed, lush·ing, lush·es.** To drink liquor to excess. [Orig. unknown.]
lust (lŭst) *n.* **1.** Intense or unrestrained sexual craving. **2.** An overwhelming desire or craving: *a lust for power.* **3.** *Obs.* Pleasure; relish. *—intr.v.* **lust·ed, lust·ing, lusts.** To have an intense or obsessive desire, esp. sexual desire. [ME < OE, desire.]
lus·ter (lŭs'tər) *n.* **1.** Soft reflected light; sheen. **2.** Brilliance or radiance of light; brightness. **3.** Glorious or radiant quality; splendor. **4.** A glass pendant, esp. on a chandelier. **5.** A decorative object, as a chandelier having glass pendants. **6.** Any of various substances, as wax, used to give an object a gloss or polish. **7.** A fabric, as alpaca, having a glossy surface. **8.** The appearance of a mineral surface judged by its brilliance and ability to reflect light. *—v.* **-tered, -ter·ing, -ters.** *—tr.* To give a gloss or sheen to. *—intr.* To be or become lustrous. [OFr. *lustre* < OItal. *lustro* < *lustrare,* to make bright < Lat. < *lustrum,* purification < *luere,* to set free.]
lus·ter·ware (lŭs'tər-wâr') *n.* Pottery having a metallic sheen.
lust·ful (lŭst'fəl) *adj.* Excited by lust. **—lust'ful·ly** *adv.* **—lust'ful·ness** *n.*

lust·i·hood (lŭs'tē-hŏŏd') *n.* **1.** Sexual capacity or appetite. **2.** Physical or mental vigor.
lus·tral (lŭs'trəl) *adj.* **1.** Of, pertaining to, or used in a rite of purification. **2.** Pertaining to a lustrum. [Lat. *lustralis* < *lustrium,* lustrum. —see LUSTER.]
lus·trate (lŭs'trāt') *tr.v.* **-trat·ed, -trat·ing, -trates.** To purify by means of ceremony. [Lat. *lustrare, lustrat-,* to purify, make bright. —see LUSTER.] **—lus·tra'tion** *n.* **—lus'tra·tive** (-trə-tĭv) *adj.*
lus·tre (lus'tər) *n. & v. Chiefly Brit.* Variant of **luster.**
lus·trous (lŭs'trəs) *adj.* **1.** Having an overall sheen or glow. **2.** Gleaming with or as if with brilliant light; radiant. **—lus'trous·ly** *adv.* **—lus'trous·ness** *n.*
lus·trum (lŭs'trəm) *n.* **1.** A ceremonial purification of the entire ancient Roman population after the census every five years. **2.** A period of five years. [Lat. —see LUSTER.]
lust·y (lŭs'tē) *adj.* **-i·er, -i·est. 1.** Full of vigor; robust. **2.** Powerful: *a lusty drink.* **3.** Lustful. **4.** *Archaic.* Merry; joyous. **—lust'i·ly** *adv.* **—lust'i·ness** *n.*
lu·sus na·tu·rae (lōō'səs nə-tōōr'ē, -tyōōr'ē) *n.* A freak of nature. [Lat.]
lu·ta·nist (lōōt'n-ĭst) *n.* A lutist (sense 2). [Med. Lat. *lutanista* < *lutana,* lute, poss. < OFr. *lut.* —see LUTE[1].]
lute[1] (lōōt) *n.* A musical stringed instrument having a body shaped like half a pear and usually a bent neck with a fretted fingerboard with pegs for tuning. [ME < OFr. *lut* < Ar *al-'ud.*]

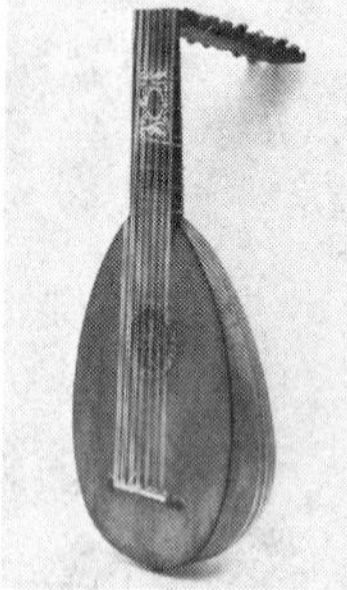

lute[1]

lute[2] (lōōt) *n.* A substance, such as dried clay or cement, used to pack and seal joints and other connections or coat a porous surface to make it tight. [ME < OFr. *lut* < Lat. *lutum,* potter's clay.]
lu·te·al (lōō'tē-əl) *adj.* Of or relating to the corpus luteum.
lu·te·ci·um (lōō-tē'shē-əm) *n.* Variant of **lutetium.**
lu·te·in (lōō'tē-ĭn, -tēn') *n.* A yellow pigment isolated from the corpus luteum and found in body fats and egg yolk. [Lat. *luteum* (< *luteus,* yellow < *lutum,* yellowweed) + -IN.]
lu·te·ous (lōō'tē-əs) *adj.* Of a light or moderate greenish yellow. [Lat. *luteus,* yellow. —see LUTEIN.]
lu·te·ti·um also **lu·te·ci·um** (lōō-tē'shē-əm) *n. Symbol* **Lu** A silvery-white rare-earth element that is exceptionally difficult to separate from the other rare-earth elements, used in nuclear technology. Atomic number 71; atomic weight 174.97; melting point 1,652°C; boiling point 3,327°C; specific gravity 9.872; valence 3. [Lat. *Lutetia,* ancient name of Paris, France + -IUM.]
Lu·ther·an (lōō'thər-ən) *adj.* **1.** Of or relating to Martin Luther or his religious teachings and esp. to the doctrine of justification by faith alone. **2.** Of or relating to the branch of the Protestant Church adhering to the views of Martin Luther. —*n.* A member of the Lutheran Church. **—Lu'ther·an·ism** *n.*
lu·tist (lōō'tĭst) *n.* **1.** A maker of lutes. **2.** A lute player.
lux (lŭks) *n., pl.* **lux·es** or **lu·ces** (lōō'sēz'). The International System unit of illumination, equal to one lumen per square meter. [Lat., light < *lucēre,* to shine.]
lux·ate (lŭk'sāt') *tr.v.* **-at·ed, -at·ing, -ates.** To put out of joint; dislocate. [Lat. *luxare, luxat-* < *luxus,* dislocated.] **—lux·a'tion** *n.*
luxe (lŏŏks, lŭks) *n.* The condition of being elegantly sumptuous. [Fr., luxury < Lat. *luxus.*]
lux·u·ri·ant (lŭg-zhŏŏr'ē-ənt, lŭk-shŏŏr'-) *adj.* **1. a.** Characterized by rich or profuse growth. **b.** Producing or yielding in abundance. **2.** Excessively florid or elaborate. **3.** Marked by or displaying luxury; luxurious. [Lat. *luxurians, luxuriant-,* pr.part. of *luxuriare,* to be luxuriant. —see LUXURIATE.] **—lux·u'ri·ance** *n.* **—lux·u'ri·ant·ly** *adv.*

Lyra

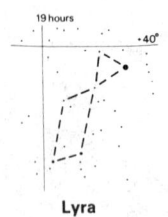

lux·u·ri·ate (lŭg-zhŏŏr'ē-āt', lŭk-shŏŏr'-) *intr.v.* **-at·ed, -at·ing, -ates. 1.** To take luxurious pleasure; indulge oneself. **2.** To proliferate. **3.** To grow profusely; thrive. [Lat. *luxuriare, luxuriat-,* to be luxuriant < *luxuria,* luxury.]
lux·u·ri·ous (lŭg-zhŏŏr'ē-əs, lŭk-shŏŏr'-) *adj.* **1.** Fond of or inclined to luxury. **2.** Of or relating to unrestrained or self-indulgent gratification of the senses. **3.** Of the most expensive and choice variety: *luxurious silks.*
lux·u·ry (lŭg'zhə-rē, lŭk'shə-) *n., pl.* **-ries. 1.** Something that is not essential but is conducive to pleasure and comfort. **2.** Something that is expensive or hard to obtain. **3.** Sumptuous living or surroundings: *lives in luxury.* [ME *luxurie,* lust < OFr. < Lat. *luxuria* < *luxus,* luxury.]
Lw The symbol for the element lawrencium.
lwei (lwā) *n., pl.* **lwei.** See table at **currency.** [Of Bantu orig.]
-ly[1] *suff.* **1.** Like; resembling; having the characteristics of: *sisterly.* **2.** Recurring at a specified interval of time: *hourly.* [ME *-li* < OE *-lic.*]
-ly[2] *suff.* **1.** In a specified manner; in the manner of: *gradually.* **2.** At a specified interval of time: *weekly.* **3.** With respect to: *partly.* [ME *-li* < OE *-lice* < *-lic,* adj. suffix.]
ly·ase (lī'ās') *n.* An enzyme that catalyzes the formation of double bonds by removing chemical groups from a substrate without hydrolysis or that adds chemical groups at double bonds. [Gk. *luein,* to loosen + -ASE.]
ly·can·thrope (lī'kən-thrōp', lī-kăn'-) *n.* A werewolf. [NLat. *lycanthropus* < Gk. *lukanthrōpos* : *lukos,* wolf + *anthrōpos,* man.]
ly·can·thro·py (lī-kăn'thrə-pē) *n.* The magical ability to assume the form and characteristics of a wolf.
ly·cée (lē-sā') *n.* A French public secondary school. [Fr. < OFr., lyceum < Lat. *Lyceum.* —see LYCEUM.]
ly·ce·um (lī-sē'əm) *n.* **1.** A hall in which public lectures, concerts, and similar programs are presented. **2.** An organization sponsoring public programs and entertainment. [Lat. < Gk. *Lukeion,* the school outside Athens, Greece, where Aristotle taught (335–323 B.C.).]
ly·chee (lē'chē) *n.* Variant of **litchi.**
lych gate (lĭch) *n.* Variant of **lich gate.**
lych·nis (lĭk'nĭs) *n.* Any of various plants of the genus *Lychnis,* which includes the campions. [NLat. *Lychnis,* genus name < Lat. *lychnis,* a red flower < Gk. *lukhnis* < *lukhinos,* lamp.]
Ly·ci·an (lĭsh'ē-ən, lĭsh'ən) *n.* **1.** An inhabitant of ancient Lycia. **2.** The Anatolian language of the Lycians. —*adj.* Of or pertaining to the Lycians or their language.
ly·co·po·di·um (lī'kə-pō'dē-əm) *n.* **1.** A plant of the genus *Lycopodium,* which includes the club mosses. **2.** The yellowish powdery spores of certain club mosses, esp. *Lycopodium clavatum,* used in fireworks and explosives and as a covering for pills. [NLat. *Lycopodium,* genus name : Gk. *lukos,* wolf + Gk. *pous,* foot.]
lyd·dite (lĭd'īt') *n.* An explosive consisting chiefly of picric acid. [After *Lydd,* England.]
Lyd·i·an (lĭd'ē-ən) *n.* **1.** One of a people of ancient Lydia. **2.** The Anatolian language of the Lydians. —*adj.* Of or pertaining to the Lydians or their language.
lye (lī) *n.* **1.** The liquid obtained by leaching wood ashes. **2.** Potassium hydroxide. **3.** Sodium hydroxide. [ME *lie* < OE *lēag.*]
ly·ing[1] (lī'ĭng) *v.* Present participle of **lie[1].** —*adj.* Reclining.
ly·ing[2] (lī'ĭng) *v.* Present participle of **lie[2].** —*adj.* Untruthful.
ly·ing-in (lī'ĭng-ĭn') *n., pl.* **ly·ings-in** or **ly·ing-ins.** The confinement of a woman in childbirth.
lymph (lĭmf) *n.* **1.** A clear, transparent, watery, sometimes faintly yellowish liquid that contains white blood cells and some red blood cells, travels through the lymphatic system to return to the venous blood stream through the thoracic duct, and acts to remove bacteria and certain proteins from the tissues, to transport fat from the intestines, and to supply lymphocytes to the blood. **2.** *Archaic.* A spring or stream of pure, clear water. [Lat. *lympha,* water, prob. < Gk. *numphē,* water spirit.]
lymph– *pref.* Variant of **lympho-.**
lym·phad·e·ni·tis (lĭm-făd'n-ī'tĭs, lĭm'fə-də-nī'-) *n.* Inflammation of the lymph nodes. [LYMPH + Gk. *adēn,* gland + -ITIS.]
lym·phat·ic (lĭm-făt'ĭk) *adj.* **1.** Of or relating to lymph, a lymph vessel, or a lymph node. **2.** Lacking energy or vitality; sluggish. —*n.* A vessel that conveys lymph. [NLat. *lymphaticus* < *lympha,* lymph.]
lymphatic system *n.* The interconnected system of spaces and vessels between tissues and organs by which lymph is circulated throughout the body.
lym·pha·tism (lĭm'fə-tĭz'əm) *n.* A pathological condition of infancy and childhood characterized by hyperplasia of the lymphatic structures, spleen, and bone marrow.
lym·pha·ti·tis (lĭm'fə-tī'tĭs) *n.* Inflammation of lymph nodes or vessels. [LYMPHAT(IC) + -ITIS.]
lymph follicle *n.* Any of the round masses of lymphocytes in the cortex of a lymph node.
lymph gland *n.* A lymph node.
lymph node *n.* Any of numerous oval or round bodies, located along the lymphatic vessels, that supply lymphocytes to the circulatory system and remove bacteria and foreign particles from the lymph.
lymph nodule *n.* A lymph follicle.
lympho– or **lymph–** *pref.* Lymph; lymphatic system: *lymphocyte.* [< LYMPH.]
lym·pho·blast (lĭm'fə-blăst') *n.* An immature lymphocyte.
lym·pho·cyte (lĭm'fə-sīt') *n.* A white blood cell formed in lymphoid tissue, as in the lymph nodes, spleen, thymus, and tonsils, constituting between 22 to 28 per cent of all leukocytes in the normal adult human's blood. **—lym'pho·cyt'ic** (-sĭt'ĭk) *adj.*
lym·pho·cy·to·sis (lĭm'fō-sī-tō'sĭs) *n.* A form of leukocytosis in which lymphocytes are greatly increased in number. **—lym'pho·cy·tot'ic** (-tŏt'ĭk) *adj.*
lym·phoid (lĭm'foid') *adj.* Of or pertaining to lymph, lymphatic tissue, or the lymphatic system.
lym·pho·ma (lĭm-fō'mə) *n., pl.* **-ma·ta** (-mə-tə) or **-mas.** Any of various abnormally proliferative diseases of lymphoid tissue. **—lym·pho'ma·toid', lym·phom'a·tous** (-fŏm'ə-təs) *adj.*
lym·pho·poi·e·sis (lĭm'fō-poi-ē'sĭs) *n., pl.* **-ses** (-sēz'). The formation of lymphocytes. **—lym'pho·poi·et'ic** (-ĕt'ĭk) *adj.*
lyn·ce·an (lĭn-sē'ən) *adj.* Sharp-sighted. [Lat. *lynceus* < Gk. *Lunkeios,* pertaining to Lynceus, an Argonaut noted for his excellent sight.]
lynch (lĭnch) *tr.v.* **lynched, lynch·ing, lynch·es.** To execute without due process of law, esp. to hang. [< LYNCH LAW.]
lynch law *n.* The punishment of persons suspected of crime without due process of law. [Perh. after Charles *Lynch* (1736–1796).]
lynx (lĭngks) *n.* Any of several wild cats of the genus *Lynx,* esp. *L. canadensis,* of northern North America, or *L. lynx,* of

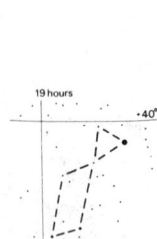

Eurasia, having thick, soft fur, a short tail, and tufted ears. [Lat. < Gk. *lunx.*]
lynx-eyed (lĭngks′īd′) *adj.* Keen of vision.
lyo– *pref.* Dispersion; dissolution: *lyophilic.* [< Gk. *luein,* to loosen, dissolve.]
ly·on·naise (lī′ə-nāz′, lē′-) *adj.* Cooked with onions: *lyonnaise potatoes.* [< Fr. *à la Lyonnaise,* in the manner of Lyon < *Lyon,* Lyon, France.]
ly·o·phil·ic (lī′ə-fĭl′ĭk) *adj.* Of, relating to, or exhibiting a strong affinity between the dispersed phase and the dispersing medium of a colloid.
ly·oph·i·liz·er (lī-ŏf′ə-lī′zər) *n.* A device for freeze-drying. [LYOPHIL(IC) + -IZE.]
ly·o·pho·bic (lī′ə-fō′bĭk) *adj.* Of, relating to, or exhibiting a lack of strong affinity between the dispersed phase and the dispersing medium of a colloid.
Ly·ra (lī′rə) *n.* A constellation in the Northern Hemisphere near Cygnus and Hercules and containing the star Vega. [Lat. *lyra,* lyre.]
ly·rate (lī′rāt′, -rĭt) *adj.* Having a form or curvature suggestive of a lyre.
lyre (līr) *n.* A stringed instrument of the harp family used to accompany a singer or reader of poetry, esp. in ancient Greece. [ME *lire* < OFr. < Lat. *lyra* < Gk. *lura.*]
lyre·bird (līr′bûrd′) *n.* Either of two Australian birds, *Menura superba* (or *M. novaehollandae*) or *M. alberti,* of which the male has a long tail spread during courtship in a lyre-shaped display.
lyr·ic (lĭr′ĭk) *adj.* **1. a.** Of or relating to a category of poetic literature that is representational of music in its sound patterns and generally characterized by subjectivity and sensuality of expression. **b.** Relating to or constituting a poem in this category, as a sonnet or ode. **c.** Being a poet of lyric verse. **2.** Highly enthusiastic; exuberant. **3. a.** Of or pertaining to the lyre or harp. **b.** Appropriate for accompaniment by the lyre. **4.** Having a singing voice of light volume and modest range. **5.** Lyrical. —*n.* **1.** A lyric poem or poet. **2.** Often **lyrics.** The words of a song. [OFr. *lyrique,* of a lyre < Lat. *lyricus* < Gk. *lurikos* < *lura,* lyre.]
lyr·i·cal (lĭr′ĭ-kəl) *adj.* **1.** Expressing feeling or emotion, esp. deep personal emotion, in a direct and affecting manner. **2.** Lyric. —**lyr′i·cal·ly** *adv.*
lyr·i·cism (lĭr′ĭ-sĭz′əm) *n.* **1. a.** The character or quality of subjectivity and sensuality of expression, esp. in the arts. **b.** Melodiousness. **2.** An intense outpouring of exuberant emotion.
lyr·i·cist (lĭr′ĭ-sĭst) *n.* A writer of song lyrics.
lyr·ism (lĭr′ĭz′əm) *n.* Lyricism. [Fr. *lyrisme* < Gk. *lurismos,* played on the lyre < *lura,* lyre.]
lyr·ist (lĭr′ĭst) *n.* **1.** A lyricist. **2.** (līr′ĭst). One who plays a lyre. [Lat. *lyristes,* lyre player < Gk. *luristēs* < *lura,* lyre.]
lys– *pref.* Variant of **lyso-.**
lyse (līs, līz) *intr. & tr.v.* **lysed, lys·ing, lys·es.** To undergo or cause to undergo lysis. [< LYSIS.]
Ly·sen·ko·ism (lĭ-sĕng′kō-ĭz′əm) *n.* The biological doctrine of Trofim Lysenko that maintains the possibility of inheriting environmentally acquired characteristics.
ly·ser·gic acid (lĭ-sûr′jĭk, lī-) *n.* A crystalline alkaloid, $C_{16}H_{16}N_2O_2$, derived from ergot and used in medical research. [LYS(O)- + ERG(OT) + -IC + ACID.]
lysergic acid di·eth·yl·am·ide (dī′ĕth-əl-ăm′īd′) *n.* A hallucinogenic drug, $C_{20}H_{25}N_3O$, derived from lysergic acid.
ly·ses (lī′sēz′) *n.* Plural of **lysis.**
lysi– *pref.* Variant of **lyso-.**
ly·sin (lī′sĭn) *n.* A specific antibody that acts to destroy blood cells, tissues, or microorganisms.
ly·sine (lī′sēn′, -sĭn) *n.* An essential, crystalline amino acid, $C_6H_{14}N_2O_2$, used in nutrition studies, in culture media, and to fortify foods and feeds.
ly·sis (lī′sĭs) *n., pl.* **-ses** (-sēz′). **1.** *Biochem.* The dissolution or destruction of red blood cells, bacteria, or other antigens by a specific lysin. **2.** *Med.* The gradual subsiding of the symptoms of an acute disease. [NLat. < Gk. *lusis,* a loosening < *luein,* to loosen.]
–lysis *suff.* Decomposition; dissolving; disintegration: *hydrolysis.* [NLat. < Gk. *lusis,* a loosening < *luein,* to unbind.]
lyso– or **lysi–** or **lys–** *pref.* **1.** Lysis: *lysin.* **2.** Lysin: *lysogenesis.* [< Gk. *lusis,* a loosening < *luein,* to unbind.]
ly·so·gen·e·sis (lī′sō-jĕn′ĭ-sĭs) *n.* The production of lysins.
Ly·sol (lī′sôl′, -sōl′, -sŏl′). A trademark for a liquid antiseptic and disinfectant.
ly·so·zyme (lī′sə-zīm′) *n.* An enzyme occurring naturally in tears, capable of destroying the cell walls of certain bacteria, and thereby acting as a mild antiseptic.
–lyte *suff.* A substance that can be decomposed by a specified process: *electrolyte.* [< Gk. *lutos,* soluble < *luein,* to unbind.]
lyt·ic (lĭt′ĭk) *adj.* **1.** Of, pertaining to, or causing lysis. **2.** Of or relating to a lysin. [Gk. *lutikos,* able to loose < *luein,* to loosen.]
–lytic *suff.* Of, pertaining to, or causing a specified kind of decomposition: *cellulolytic.* [< Gk. *lutikos,* able to loosen < *luein,* to unbind.]
lyt·ta (lĭt′ə) *n., pl.* **lyt·tae** (lĭt′ē′). A thin cartilaginous strip on the underside of the tongue of certain carnivorous mammals, such as dogs. [Lat. < Gk. *lutta, lussa,* madness.]
–lyze *suff.* To cause or undergo lysis: *pyrolyze.* [< LYSIS.]

lyre
Detail from an ancient Greek vase painting

George Miksch Sutton
lyrebird

M

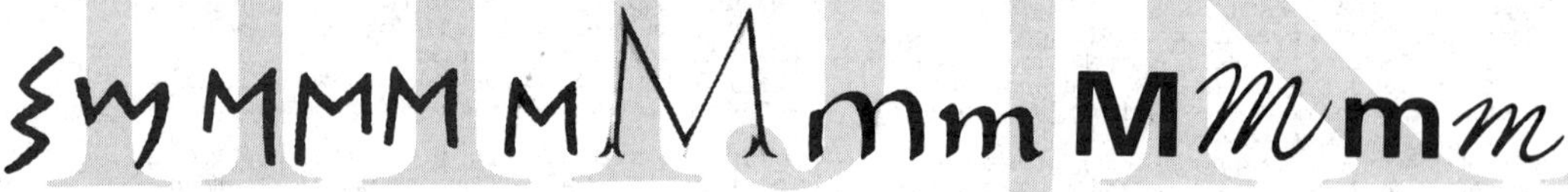

Around 1000 B.C. the Phoenicians and other Semitic peoples began to use graphic signs to represent individual speech sounds instead of syllables or words. They used a symbol in the forms (1,2) to represent the sound of the consonant "m" and called it *mēm,* their word for "water." The Greeks, adapting the Phoenician alphabet, kept the phonetic value of *mēm* but eliminated its tail and changed its name to *mu.* The Romans borrowed the alphabet from the Greeks via the Etruscans and adapted it for monumental inscriptions. Monumental script (7) is the prototype of modern capital letters (10,11). Medieval scribes adapted the Roman capitals to being quickly written on paper, parchment, and vellum. These uncial and cursive minuscules (8,9) are the prototypes of modern lower-case letters, both written and printed (13,12).

m

m or **M** (ĕm) *n., pl.* **m's** or **M's. 1.** The 13th letter of the modern English alphabet. **2.** Any of the speech sounds represented by the letter *m.* **3.** The 13th in a series. **4. M** The Roman numeral for 1,000.

-'m *suff.* Am: *I'm feeling fine.*

ma (mä, mô) *n. Informal.* Mother. [Short for MAMA.]

Ma'am (măm). Madam.

mac (măk) *n. Chiefly Brit. Informal.* A mackintosh.

Mac (măk) *n. Informal.* A fellow; guy. Used to address a man whose name is unknown. [Prob. < *Mac-*, a common prefix in Scottish and Irish surnames.]

ma·ca·bre (mə-kä'brə, -bər) *adj.* **1.** Suggesting the horror of death and decay; gruesome: *macabre tales of war and plague in the Middle Ages.* **2.** Comprising or including a representation of death. [Fr. < (*danse*) *macabre* (dance of) death < OFr. *(danse de) Macabre.*] **—ma·ca'bre·ly** *adv.*

mac·ad·am (mə-kăd'əm) *n.* A pavement of layers of compacted broken stone, now usually bound with tar or asphalt. [After John L. *McAdam* (1756–1836).]

mac·a·da·mi·a nut (măk'ə-dā'mē-ə) *n.* The round, hard-shelled, edible nut of an Australian tree, *Macadamia ternifolia,* now cultivated in Hawaii. [NLat. *Macadamia,* genus name, after John *Macadam* (1827–1865).]

mac·ad·am·ize (mə-kăd'ə-mīz') *tr.v.* **-ized, -iz·ing, -iz·es.** To construct or pave (a road) with macadam. **—mac·ad'am·i·za'tion** *n.* **—mac·ad'am·iz'er** *n.*

ma·caque (mə-kăk', -käk') *n.* Any of several short-tailed monkeys of the genus *Macaca,* of southeastern Asia, Japan, Gibraltar, and northern Africa. [Fr. < Port. *macaco,* poss. < Kongo.]

mac·a·ro·ni (măk'ə-rō'nē) *n.* **1.** *pl.* **macaroni.** A paste or pasta of wheat flour pressed into hollow tubes or other shapes, dried, and prepared for eating by boiling. **2.** *pl.* **-ni** or **-nies. a.** A member of a class of well-traveled young Englishmen of the 18th and 19th centuries who affected foreign customs and manners. **b.** A fashionable fop. [Ital. *maccheroni,* pl. of *maccherone* < dial. Ital. *maccarone,* macaroni.]

mac·a·ron·ic (măk'ə-rŏn'ĭk) *adj.* **1.** Of or pertaining to a literary composition containing a mixture of vernacular words with Latin words or with non-Latin words given Latin terminations. **2.** Of or involving a mixture of two or more languages. [NLat. *macaronicus* < dial. Ital. *maccarone,* macaroni.] **—mac'a·ron'ic** *n.*

mac·a·roon (măk'ə-ro͞on') *n.* A chewy cookie made with sugar, egg whites, and almond paste or coconut. [Fr. *macaron* < dial. Ital. *maccarone,* small cake, macaroni.]

ma·caw (mə-kô') *n.* Any of various tropical American parrots of the genera *Ara* and *Anodorhynchus,* including the largest parrots, characterized by long saber-shaped tails, curved powerful bills, and usually brilliant plumage. [Port. *macaú.*]

Mac·beth (mək-bĕth', măk-) *n.* A Scottish general, the protagonist of Shakespeare's tragedy *Macbeth.*

Mac·ca·bees (măk'ə-bēz') *n.* See table at **Bible. —Mac'ca·be'an** *adj.*

mac·ca·boy (măk'ə-boi') *n.* A perfumed snuff made in Martinique. [Fr. *macouba,* after *Macouba,* a district of Martinique.]

mace[1] (mās) *n.* **1.** A heavy medieval war club with a spiked or flanged metal head, used to crush armor. **2.** A ceremonial staff borne or displayed as the symbol of authority of a legislative body. **3.** A macebearer. [ME < OFr.]

mace[2] (mās) *n.* An aromatic spice made from the dried, waxy, scarlet or yellowish covering that partly encloses the kernel of the nutmeg. [ME < OFr. < Med. Lat. *macis* < Gk. *makir,* an Indian spice.]

Mace (mās). An alternate trademark for Chemical Mace. *—tr.v.* **mace, maced, mac·ing, mac·es.** To attack by spraying with Chemical Mace.

mace·bear·er (mās'bâr'ər) *n.* An official who carries a mace of office.

mac·é·doine (măs'ə-dwän') *n.* **1.** A mixture of finely cut vegetables or fruits, sometimes jellied, served as a salad, dessert, or appetizer. **2.** A mixture; medley. [Fr. < *Macédoine,* Macedonian (perh. from the variety of races in Macedonia).]

Mac·e·do·ni·an (măs'ĭ-dō'nē-ən) *adj.* Of or pertaining to ancient or modern Macedonia, or the people or languages of these regions. *—n.* **1.** A native or inhabitant of ancient or modern Macedonia. **2.** The language of ancient Macedonia, which is of uncertain linguistic affiliation but has features considered to be Indo-European. **3.** The Slavic language of modern Macedonia.

mac·er (mā'sər) *n.* A macebearer.

mac·er·ate (măs'ə-rāt') *v.* **-at·ed, -at·ing, -ates.** *—tr.* **1.** To make soft by soaking or steeping in a liquid. **2.** To separate into constituents by soaking. **3.** To cause to become lean, usually by starvation. *—intr.* To become macerated; undergo macerating. [Lat. *macerare, macerat-,* to macerate.] **—mac'er·a'tion** *n.* **—mac'er·a'tor, mac'er·at'er** *n.*

Mach also **mach** (măk) *n.* Mach number.

ma·chet·e (mə-shĕt'ē, -chĕt'ē) *n.* A large, heavy knife with a broad blade, used for cutting vegetation and as a weapon. [Sp., dim. of *macho,* mace.]

Mach·i·a·vel·li·an (măk'ē-ə-vĕl'ē-ən) *adj.* **1.** Of or pertaining to Machiavelli or Machiavellianism. **2.** Suggestive of or characterized by the principles of expediency, deceit, and cunning attributed to Machiavelli. **—Mach'i·a·vel'li·an, Mach'i·a·vel'list** (-vĕl'ĭst) *n.*

Mach·i·a·vel·li·an·ism (măk'ē-ə-vĕl'ē-ə-nĭz'əm) also **Mach·i·a·vel·lism** (-vĕl'ĭz'əm) *n.* The political doctrine of Machiavelli, which denies the relevance of morality in political affairs and holds that craft and deceit are justified in pursuing and maintaining political power.

ma·chic·o·late (mə-chĭk'ə-lāt') *tr.v.* **-lat·ed, -lat·ing, -lates.** To furnish with machicolations. [Med. Lat. *machicolare, machicolat-* < OFr. *machicoller* < *machicoleis,* machicolation : *macher,* to crush + *col,* neck < Lat. *collum.*]

ma·chic·o·la·tion (mə-chĭk'ə-lā'shən) *n.* **1. a.** A projecting gallery at the top of a castle wall, supported by a row of corbeled arches, having openings in the floor through which stones and boiling liquids could be dropped on attackers. **b.** One of these openings. **2.** A row of small corbeled arches used as an ornamental architectural feature.

mach·i·nate (măk'ə-nāt', măsh'-) *v.* **-nat·ed, -nat·ing, -nates.** *—tr.* To devise (a plot). *—intr.* To plot. [Lat. *machinari, machinat-,* to design, invent < *machina,* device. —see MACHINE.] **—mach'i·na'tor** *n.*

mach·i·na·tion (măk'ə-nā'shən, măsh'-) *n.* **1.** The act of plotting. **2.** A crafty plot or action, usually intended to achieve an evil purpose.

ma·chine (mə-shēn') *n.* **1. a.** A system, usually of rigid bodies, formed and connected to alter, transmit, and direct applied forces in a predetermined manner to accomplish a specific objective, such as the performance of useful work. **b.** A simple device, such as a lever, pulley, or inclined plane, that alters the magnitude or direction, or both, of an applied force. **2.** A system or device together with its power source and auxiliary equipment, such as an automobile or jackhammer. **3.** A system or device, such as an electronic computer, that performs or assists in the performance of a human task. **4. a.** An intricate natural system or organism, such as the human body. **b.** A functional unit of such a system, such as the heart or kidney. **5.** A person who acts in a rigid or mechanical manner. **6.** An organized group of persons whose members are under the control of one or more leaders. **7.** Deus ex machina. **—*modifier:*** *machine parts.* *—v.* **-chined, -chin·ing, -chines.** *—tr.* To cut, shape, or finish by machine. *—intr.* To be cut, shaped, or finished by machine. [Fr. < OFr. < Lat. *machina* < Gk. *makhana, mēkhanē* < *mēkhos,* means.] **—ma·chin'a·ble** *adj.*

macaw

machine finish *n.* Mill finish.

machine gun *n.* A gun that fires rapidly and repeatedly.

ma·chine-gun (mə-shēn'gŭn') *tr.v.* **-gunned, -gun·ning, -guns.** To fire at or kill with a machine gun.

machine language *n.* Any of various systems of symbols used to code information that is to be fed into a computer.

ma·chine-read·a·ble (mə-shēn'rē'də-bəl) *adj.* Capable of being read or used by a computer.

ma·chin·er·y (mə-shē'nə-rē, -shēn'rē) *n., pl.* **-ies. 1.** Machines or machine parts collectively. **2.** The working parts of a particular machine. **3.** A system of related elements that operates in a definable manner: *diplomatic and political machinery.* **4. a.** A device or means for achieving or effecting a result. **b.** A literary device for bringing about a calculated effect such as a happy ending.

machine shop *n.* A workshop where power-driven tools are used for making, finishing, or repairing machines or machine parts.

machine tool *n.* A power-driven tool for machining.

machine translation *n.* Automatic translation, as by computer, from one language to another.

ma·chin·ist (mə-shē'nĭst) *n.* **1.** One skilled in operating machine tools. **2.** One who makes, operates, or repairs machines. **3.** A warrant officer who assists the engineer officer in the engine room of a navy vessel. **4.** *Archaic.* A person in charge of stage machinery.

ma·chis·mo (mä-chēz'mō) *n.* An exaggerated sense of masculinity stressing such attributes as courage, virility, and domination of women. [Sp. < *macho,* male. —see MACHO.]

Mach·me·ter (mäk'mē'tər) *n.* An aircraft instrument that indicates speed in Mach numbers.

Mach number *n.* The ratio of the speed of an object to the speed of sound in the surrounding medium. For example, an aircraft moving twice as fast as sound is said to be traveling at Mach 2. [After Ernst *Mach* (1836–1916).]

mace[1]

ma·cho (mä'chō) *adj.* Characterized by machismo. *—n., pl.* **-chos. 1.** Machismo. **2.** A male characterized by machismo. [Sp., male < Lat. *masculus.*]

mac·in·tosh (măk'ĭn-tŏsh') *n.* Variant of **mackintosh.**

mack·er·el (măk'ər-əl, măk'rəl) *n., pl.* **mackerel** or **-els. 1.** Any of several marine fishes of the family Scombridae, esp. the Atlantic mackerel, *Scomber scombrus,* an important food fish having dark, wavy bars on the back and a silvery belly. **2.** Any of the smaller fishes of the suborder Scombroidea, such as the Spanish mackerel. **3.** Any of various fishes resembling mackerel. [ME *makerel* < OFr. *maquerel.*]

mackerel sky *n.* A formation of cirrocumulus or altocumulus clouds suggesting the bars on a mackerel's back.

mack·i·naw (măk'ə-nô') *n.* **1.** A short, double-breasted coat of heavy, usually plaid, woolen material. **2.** The cloth from which a mackinaw coat is made, usually of wool, often with

a heavy nap. **3.** A flat-bottomed boat with a pointed bow and square stern, once used on the upper Great Lakes. [After *Mackinaw* City, Michigan.]
Mackinaw blanket *n.* A thick blanket in solid colors or stripes, formerly used in northern and western North America by Indians, traders, and trappers.
Mackinaw trout *n.* The lake trout.
mack·in·tosh also **mac·in·tosh** (măk′ĭn-tŏsh′) *n. Chiefly Brit.* **1.** A raincoat. **2.** A lightweight, waterproof fabric that was originally of rubberized cotton. [After Charles *Macintosh* (1766–1843), its inventor.]
mack·le (măk′əl) also **mac·ule** (măk′yo͞ol) *Printing.* —*n.* A spot, esp. a blurred or double impression caused by a slipping of the type or wrinkle in the paper. —*v.* **-led, -ling, -les** also **-uled, -ul·ing, -ules.** —*tr.* To blur or double (a printed impression). —*intr.* To become blurred. [Fr. *macule* < Lat. *macula,* spot.]
mac·le (măk′əl) *n.* **1.** Chiastolite. **2.** Twin (sense 4). **3.** A spot or discoloration in a mineral. [Fr. < OFr., lozenge < Lat. *macula,* mesh.]
macr– *pref.* Variant of **macro-**.
mac·ra·mé (măk′rə-mā′) *n.* Coarse lacework made by weaving and knotting cords into a pattern. [Fr. < Ital. *macramè* < Turk. *makrama,* towel < Ar. *miqramah,* striped cloth.]

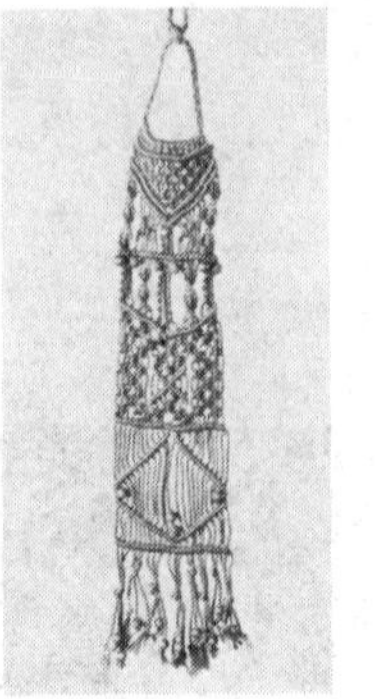
macramé

mac·ren·ceph·a·ly (măk′rĕn-sĕf′ə-lē) also **mac·ren·ce·pha·li·a** (-sə-fā′lē-ə) *n.* Abnormal enlargement of the brain.
mac·ro (măk′rō′) *n. Computer Sci.* An instruction in assembly language that is implemented by a sequence of instructions in machine language. [Short for MACROINSTRUCTION.]
macro– or **macr–** *pref.* **1.** Large: *macronucleus.* **2.** Long: *macrobiosis.* **3.** Inclusive: *macroinstruction.* [< Gk. *makros,* large.]
mac·ro·bi·o·sis (măk′rō-bī-ō′sĭs) *n.* Longevity. [LGk. *makrobiōsis* : Gk. *makros,* long + Gk. *biōsis,* way of life.]
mac·ro·bi·o·ta (măk′rō-bī-ō′tə) *n.* The macroscopic plant and animal life of a particular region.
mac·ro·bi·ot·ics (măk′rō-bī-ŏt′ĭks) *n. (used with a sing. verb).* **1.** The theory or practice of promoting longevity. **2.** A method purporting to promote longevity, principally by means of diet consisting chiefly of whole grains, vegetables, and fish. —**mac′ro·bi·ot′ic** *adj.*
mac·ro·ceph·a·ly (măk′rō-sĕf′ə-lē) also **mac·ro·ce·pha·li·a** (-sə-fā′lē-ə) *n.* Abnormally large cranial capacity. —**mac′ro·ce·phal′ic** (-sə-făl′ĭk), **mac′ro·ceph′a·lous** *adj.*
mac·ro·cli·mate (măk′rō-klī′mĭt) *n. Meteorol.* The climate of a large geographical area. —**mac′ro·cli·mat′ic** *adj.*
mac·ro·code (măk′rə-kōd′) *n.* **1.** A coding system that assembles sets of computer instructions. **2.** A single code representing a set of computer instructions.
mac·ro·con·sum·er (măk′rō-kən-so͞o′mər) *n. Ecol.* A heterotrophic organism that ingests other organisms or particulate organic matter.
mac·ro·cosm (măk′rə-kŏz′əm) *n.* **1.** The entire world; universe. **2.** A system reflecting on a large scale one of its component systems or parts. [Fr. *macrocosme* < Med. Lat. *macrocosmus* : Gk. *makros,* large + Gk. *kosmos,* world.] —**mac′ro·cos′mic** *adj.* —**mac′ro·cos′mic·al·ly** *adv.*
mac·ro·cyte (măk′rō-sīt′) *n.* An abnormally large red blood cell associated with some forms of anemia. —**mac′ro·cyt′ic** (-sĭt′ĭk) *adj.*
mac·ro·cy·to·sis (măk′rō-sī-tō′sĭs) *n.* A condition in which the blood contains macrocytes. —**mac′ro·cy·tot′ic** (-tŏt′ĭk) *adj.*
mac·ro·ec·o·nom·ics (măk′rō-ĕk′ə-nŏm′ĭks, -ē′kə-) *n. (used with a sing. verb).* The study of the overall aspects and workings of a national economy, such as income, output, and the interrelationship among diverse economic sectors. —**mac′ro·ec′o·nom′ic** *adj.*
mac·ro·ev·o·lu·tion (măk′rō-ĕv′ə-lo͞o′shən, -ē′və-) *n.* Evolution involving whole species or large groups of organisms. —**mac′ro·ev′o·lu′tion·ar′y** *adj.*
mac·ro·ga·mete (măk′rō-gə-mēt′, -găm′ēt′) *n.* The larger of two conjugating cells, usually female, in protozoans.
mac·ro·glob·u·lin (măk′rō-glŏb′yə-lĭn) *n.* A globulin of high molecular weight.
mac·ro·glob·u·lin·e·mi·a (măk′rō-glŏb′yə-lə-nē′mē-ə) *n.* The presence of an abnormally large amount of macroglobulins in the blood serum.
mac·ro·graph (măk′rō-grăf′) *n.* A representation of an object at least as large as the object.
ma·crog·ra·phy (mə-krŏg′rə-fē) *n.* **1.** Examination of objects with the unaided eye. **2.** Abnormally large handwriting, sometimes indicating a nervous disorder.
mac·ro·in·struc·tion (măk′rō-ĭn-strŭk′shən) *n.* A macro.
mac·ro·mere (măk′rə-mîr′) *n.* A large blastomere.
mac·ro·mol·e·cule (măk′rō-mŏl′ĭ-kyo͞ol′) *n.* A very large molecule, as a polymer or protein, consisting of many smaller structural units. —**mac′ro·mo·lec′u·lar** *adj.*
ma·cron (mā′krŏn′, -krən) *n.* **1.** A diacritical mark placed above a vowel to indicate a long sound or phonetic value in pronunciation, such as (ā) in the word *make.* **2.** The horizontal mark (—) used to indicate a stressed or long syllable in a foot of verse. [Gk. *makron* < *makros,* long.]
mac·ro·nu·cle·us (măk′rō-no͞o′klē-əs, -nyo͞o′-) *n., pl.* **-cle·i** (-klē-ī′). A large, trophic, nonreproductive nucleus in the cells of ciliated protozoans.
mac·ro·nu·tri·ent (măk′rō-no͞o′trē-ənt, -nyo͞o′-) *n.* An element, such as carbon, hydrogen, oxygen, or nitrogen, required in large proportion for the growth and development of plants.
mac·ro·phage (măk′rə-fāj′) *n.* A large phagocytic cell of the reticuloendothelial system. —**mac′ro·phag′ic** *adj.*
mac·ro·phys·ics (măk′rō-fĭz′ĭks) *n. (used with a sing. verb).* The physics of macroscopic phenomena.
mac·ro·phyte (măk′rə-fīt′) *n.* A macroscopic plant in an aquatic environment. —**mac′ro·phyt′ic** (-fĭt′ĭk) *adj.*
ma·crop·ter·ous (mə-krŏp′tər-əs) *adj.* Having unusually large fins or wings. [Gk. *makropteros* : *makros,* large + *pteron,* wing.]
mac·ro·scop·ic (măk′-rə-skŏp′ĭk) also **mac·ro·scop·i·cal** (-ĭ-kəl) *adj.* **1.** Large enough to be perceived or examined without instrumentation, esp. as by the unaided eye. **2.** Pertaining to observations made without magnifying instruments, esp. as by the unaided eye. [MACRO- + -SCOP(Y) + -IC.] —**mac′ro·scop′i·cal·ly** *adv.*
mac·ro·spo·ran·gi·um (măk′rō-spə-răn′jē-əm) *n., pl.* **-gi·a** (-jē-ə). A megasporangium.
mac·ro·spore (măk′rə-spôr′, -spōr′) *n. Bot.* A megaspore (sense 2).
mac·u·la (măk′yə-lə) *n., pl.* **-lae** (-lē′). **1.** A spot, stain, blemish, or pit, esp. a discoloration of the skin caused by excess or lack of pigment. **2.** A sunspot. [Lat., spot.] —**mac′u·lar** (-lər) *adj.*
macula lu·te·a (lo͞o′tē-ə) *n., pl.* **maculae lu·te·ae** (lo͞o′tē-ē′). An area in the eye near the center of the retina at which visual perception is most acute. [NLat. : Lat. *macula,* spot + Lat. *lutea,* yellow.]
mac·u·late (măk′yə-lāt′) *tr.v.* **-lat·ed, -lat·ing, -lates.** To spot, blemish, or pollute. —*adj.* (măk′yə-lĭt). **1.** Spotted or blotched. **2.** Stained; impure. [ME *maculaten* < Lat. *maculare* < *macula,* spot.]
mac·u·la·tion (măk′yə-lā′shən) *n.* **1.** The act of spotting or staining. **2.** A spotted or stained condition. **3.** The spotted markings of a plant or animal, such as the spots of the leopard.
mac·ule (măk′yo͞ol) *v.* Variant of **mackle.** —*n.* **1.** Variant of **mackle. 2.** Variant of **macula.** [ME *maculen* < OFr. *maculer* < *macule,* spot < Lat. *macula.*]
mad (măd) *adj.* **mad·der, mad·dest. 1.** Suffering from a disorder of the mind; insane. **2.** Temporarily or apparently deranged by violent sensations, emotions, or ideas: *mad with jealousy.* **3.** *Informal.* Feeling or showing strong liking or enthusiasm: *mad about sports.* **4.** *Informal.* Angry; resentful. **5.** Lacking restraint or reason; foolish: *He'd have to be mad to take up with her again.* **6.** Marked by extreme excitement, confusion, or agitation; frantic: *a mad scramble for the bus.* **7.** Boisterously gay; hilarious: *had a mad time.* **8.** Affected by rabies; rabid. —*tr. & intr.v.* **mad·ded, mad·ding, mads.** To madden. —***idioms.*** **have a mad on.** *Slang.* To sulk; be angry. **like mad.** *Slang.* Wildly; impetuously: *He drove like mad.* [ME < OE *gemǣdde* < **gemǣdan,* to madden < *gemād,* mad.]
Mad·a·gas·car periwinkle (măd′ə-găs′kər) *n.* A plant, *Vinca rosea,* native to Madagascar, having pink or white flowers.
Mad·am (măd′əm) *n.* **1.** *pl.* **Mes·dames** (mā-dăm′). **a.** Used as a title of courtesy in addressing a woman. **b.** Used formerly as a title of courtesy before a given name but now used only before a surname or a title indicating rank or office: *Madam Ambassador.* **2. madam.** The mistress of a household. **3. madam.** A woman who manages a brothel. [ME < OFr. *ma dame* : *ma,* my + *dame,* lady.]
Ma·dame (mə-dăm′, măd′əm) *n., pl.* **Mes·dames** (mā-däm′) Used as a French title of courtesy for a married woman. [Fr. < OFr. *ma dame* : *ma,* my + *dame,* lady.]
mad·cap (măd′kăp′) *n.* A rash or impulsive person. —*adj.* Impulsive; wild.
mad·den (măd′n) *v.* **-dened, -den·ing, -dens.** —*tr.* **1.** To make mad; drive insane. **2.** To make angry; irritate. —*intr.* To become infuriated.
mad·den·ing (măd′n-ĭng) *adj.* **1.** Tending to drive mad. **2.** Tending to anger or irritate: *a maddening delay at the airport.* —**mad′den·ing·ly** *adv.*
mad·der[1] (măd′ər) *n.* **1. a.** Any of various plants of the genus *Rubia,* esp. a Eurasian species, *R. tinctoria,* having small, yellow flowers and a red, fleshy root. **b.** The root of this plant, formerly an important source of dye. **2.** A red dye obtained from the madder root. **3.** A medium to strong red or reddish orange. [ME < OE *mædere.*]
mad·der[2] (măd′ər) *adj.* Comparative of **mad.**
mad·ding (măd′ĭng) *adj. Archaic.* Frenzied: *"Far from the madding crowd's ignoble strife"* (Thomas Gray).
mad·dish *adj.* Somewhat mad.
mad-dog skullcap (măd′dôg′, -dŏg′) *n.* A North American plant, *Scutellaria lateriflora,* having one-sided clusters of two-lipped blue or white flowers.
made (mād) *v.* Past tense and past participle of **make.** —*adj.* **1.** Produced or manufactured by constructing, shaping, or forming: *handmade chocolates.* **2.** Produced or created artificially. **3.** Invented; contrived. **4.** Assured of success: *a made man.* —***idiom.*** **made for.** Perfectly suited for: *made for each other.*

Ma·dei·ra (mə-dîr′ə) *n.* A fortified dessert wine, esp. from the island of Madeira.
Madeira vine *n.* A tropical American vine, *Boussingaultia baselloides,* having small, white, fragrant flowers.
mad·e·leine (măd′ə-lĕn′) *n.* A small, rich cake, baked in a shell-shaped mold. [After *Madeleine* Paulmier, a 19th-cent. French pastry cook.]
Mad·e·moi·selle (măd′ə-mə-zĕl′, mȧd-mwȧ-zĕl′) *n., pl.* **Mad·e·moi·selles** (-zĕlz) or **Mes·de·moi·selles** (măd′mwä-zĕl′). **1.** Used as a French title of courtesy for a young girl or unmarried woman. **2. mademoiselle.** A French governess. **3. mademoiselle.** Any of several marine fishes of the genus *Bairdiella,* esp. *B. chrysura,* of the U.S. Atlantic and Gulf Coasts. [Fr. < OFr. *ma demoiselle* : *ma,* my + *demoiselle,* young lady.]
made-to-or·der (mād′to͞o-ôr′dər) *adj.* **1.** Made in accordance with particular instructions or requirements; custom-made. **2.** Very suitable.
made-up (mād′ŭp′) *adj.* **1.** Fabricated; invented: *a made-up story.* **2.** Changed or adorned by the application of cosmetics or make-up: *a made-up actress.* **3. a.** Complete; finished: *a made-up package.* **b.** Put together; arranged: *a made-up page of type.*
mad·house (măd′hous′) *n.* **1.** An asylum for the mentally ill. **2.** *Informal.* A place of great disorder and confusion.
Mad·i·son Avenue (măd′ĭ-sən) *n.* The American advertising industry. [After *Madison Avenue,* New York, New York, the center of American advertising.]
mad·ly (măd′lē) *adv.* **1.** Insanely. **2.** Wildly; frantically. **3.** Foolishly; rashly.
mad·man (măd′măn′, -mən) *n.* A man who is or seems to be mentally ill.
mad money *n. Slang.* **1.** Carfare carried by a girl on a date to pay her way home in the event of a quarrel with her escort. **2.** A small sum of money kept for unlikely contingencies.
mad·ness (măd′nĭs) *n.* **1.** Insanity. **2.** Great folly. **3.** Fury; rage. **4.** Enthusiasm; excitement.
Ma·don·na (mə-dŏn′ə) *n.* **1.** The Virgin Mary. **2.** *Obs.* A married woman in Italy. [Ital. : *ma,* my (< Lat. *mea*) + *donna,* lady (< Lat. *domina*).]
Madonna lily *n.* A plant, *Lilium candidum,* native to Eurasia, having white, trumpet-shaped flowers.
ma·dras (măd′rəs, mə-drăs′, -dräs′) *n.* **1.** A cotton cloth of fine texture, usually with a plaid, striped, or checked pattern. **2.** A silk cloth, generally striped. **3. a.** A light cotton cloth used for drapery. **b.** A similar cloth of rayon. **4.** A large handkerchief of brightly colored silk or cotton, often worn as a turban. [After *Madras,* India.]
mad·re·pore (măd′rə-pôr′, -pōr′) *n.* Any of various corals of the genus *Madrepora,* including the reef builders of tropical seas. [Fr. < Ital. *madrepora* : *madre,* mother (< Lat. *mater*) + *porus,* tufa (< Gk. *pōros*).] **—mad′re·por′ic** *adj.*
mad·re·por·ite (măd′rə-pôr′īt, -pōr′-) *n.* A perforated structure in most echinoderms that forms the intake for their water-vascular system. [So called because the perforations resemble those of the madrepore.]
mad·ri·gal (măd′rĭ-gəl) *n.* **1.** An unaccompanied vocal composition for two or three voices in simple harmony, following a strict poetic form, developed in Italy in the late 13th and early 14th centuries. **2.** A polyphonic part song, developed in Italy in the 16th century and very popular in England in the 16th and early 17th centuries, that is usually unaccompanied and features parts for four to six voices, using a secular text and sometimes an accompaniment by strings that either doubles or replaces one or more of the vocal parts. **3.** A lyric poem with a pastoral, idyllic, or amatory subject, developed from the lyrics of the 13th-century Italian madrigal. **4.** A part song. [Ital. *madrigale* < Med. Lat. *matricalis,* simple < *matrix,* womb < *mater,* mother.] **—mad′ri·gal·ist** *n.*
ma·dri·lène also **ma·dri·lene** (măd′rĭ-lĕn′) *n.* A consommé flavored with tomato, generally served chilled. [Fr. (*consommé*) *madrilène,* Madrid (consommé).]
ma·dro·ña (mə-drō′nyə) also **ma·dro·ño** (mə-drō′nyō) or **ma·dro·ne** (mə-drō′nə) *n.* A tree, *Arbutus Menziesi,* of western North America, having glossy, evergreen leaves, white flowers, and red-orange fruit. [Sp. *madroño.*]
mad tom *n.* Any of several small freshwater North American catfishes of the genus *Noturus,* common in the east-central United States, having poisonous spines.
ma·du·ro (mə-do͞or′ō) *n., pl.* **-ros.** A strong-flavored cigar with a dark wrapper. [Sp. < *maduro,* mature < Lat. *maturus.*] **—ma·du′ro** *adj.*
mad·wom·an (măd′wo͝om′ən) *n.* A woman who is or seems to be mentally ill.
mad·wort (măd′wûrt′, -wôrt′) *n.* **1.** A low-growing plant, *Asperugo procumbens,* native to Eurasia, having rough stems and small blue flowers. **2.** Alyssum (sense 1).
Mae·ce·nas (mĭ-sē′nəs, mī-) *n.* A patron, esp. one generous to artists. [After Gaius *Maecenas* (70–8 B.C.).]
mael·strom (māl′strəm) *n.* **1.** A whirlpool of extraordinary size or violence. **2.** A situation that resembles a whirlpool in violence or turbulence: *caught in the maelstrom of war.* [Obs. Du. : *malen,* to whirl + *stroom,* stream.]
mae·nad (mē′năd′) *n.* **1.** *Gk. Myth.* A woman member of the orgiastic cult of Dionysus. **2.** A frenzied woman. [Lat. *maenas, maenad-,* maenad < Gk. *mainas* < *mainesthai,* to be mad.]
ma·es·to·so (mä′ĕs-tō′sō, -zō) *adj. & adv. Mus.* In a majestic and stately manner. Used as a direction. [Ital. < *maestà,* majesty < Lat. *majestas.*]
maes·tro (mīs′trō) *n., pl.* **-tros** or **-tri** (-trē). A master in any art, esp. a composer, conductor, or music teacher. [Ital. < Lat. *magister,* master.]
Mae West *n.* (mā′ wĕst′). An inflatable, vestlike life preserver. [After *Mae West* (1892–1980), so called from its resemblance to her curvaceous torso.]
maf·fick (măf′ĭk) *intr.v.* **-ficked, -fick·ing, -ficks.** *Chiefly Brit.* To rejoice or celebrate with boisterous public demonstrations. [After *Mafeking,* South Africa, from the celebrations following the relief on May 17, 1900, of a British garrison besieged there.]
Ma·fi·a (mä′fē-ə) *n.* **1.** A secret terrorist organization in Sicily, operating since the early 19th century in opposition to legal authority. **2.** An alleged international criminal organization believed active, esp. in Italy and the United States, since the late 19th century. [Ital. < dial. Ital. *mafia,* bluster, boldness, prob. < Ar. *mahyah,* boasting.]
Ma·fi·o·so (mä′fē-ō′sō) *n., pl.* **-si** (-sē). A member of the Mafia. [Ital. < *mafia,* mafia.]
mag (măg) *n. Slang.* A magazine.
mag·a·zine (măg′ə-zēn′, măg′ə-zēn′) *n.* **1. a.** A place where goods are stored, esp. a building (as in a fort) or a storeroom (as on a warship) where ammunition is stored. **b.** The contents of a storehouse, esp. a stock of ammunition. **2.** A periodical containing a collection of articles, stories, pictures, or other features. **3. a.** A compartment in some types of firearms, often a small, detachable box, in which cartridges are held to be fed into the firing chamber. **b.** A compartment in a camera in which rolls or cartridges of film are held for feeding through the exposure mechanism. **c.** Any of various other compartments attached to machines, for storing or supplying necessary material. [OFr. *magazin* < OItal. *magazzino* < Ar. *makhāzin,* pl. of *makhzan,* storehouse < *khazana,* to store.]
mag·da·len (mag′də-lən) also **mag·da·lene** (-len′) *n.* **1.** A reformed prostitute. **2.** A reformatory for prostitutes. [After *Mary Magdalene,* traditionally identified with the woman taken in adultery in the New Testament.]
Mag·da·le·ni·an (măg′də-lē′nē-ən) *adj. Archaeol.* Of or pertaining to the last upper Paleolithic culture of Europe, succeeding the Aurignacian. [Fr. *magdalénien,* after La *Madeleine,* a prehistoric site in Dordogne, France.]
Mag·el·lan·ic cloud (măj′ə-lăn′ĭk) *n.* Either of two small galaxies, the closest to the Milky Way, faintly visible near the south celestial pole. [After Ferdinand *Magellan* (1480?–1521).]
Ma·gen Da·vid also **Mo·gen Da·vid** (mô′gən dô′vĭd) *n.* A six-pointed star, formed by placing two triangles together, one upon the other or interlaced, that is a symbol of Judaism. [Heb. *māgen Dāwid.*]
ma·gen·ta (mə-jĕn′tə) *n.* **1.** Fuchsin. **2.** A moderate to vivid purplish red, or dark to strong reddish purple. [After *Magenta,* Italy.]
mag·got (măg′ət) *n.* **1.** The legless, soft-bodied larva of any of various insects of the order Diptera, esp. of the housefly and the bluebottle fly, usually found in decaying matter or as a parasite. **2.** An extravagant notion; whim. [ME *magot,* prob. of Scand. orig.] **—mag′got·y** *adj.*
ma·gi (mā′jī′) *n.* The plural of **magus.**
mag·ic (măj′ĭk) *n.* **1.** The art that purports to control or forecast natural events, effects, or forces by invoking the supernatural. **2. a.** The practice of using charms, spells, or rituals to attempt to produce supernatural effects or to control events in nature. **b.** The charms, spells, and rituals so used. **3.** The exercise of sleight of hand or conjuring for entertainment. **4.** A mysterious quality of enchantment: *the magic of the distant past.* [ME *magik* < OFr. *magique* < LLat. *magice* < Gk. *magikē* < *magos,* magician. —see MAGUS.]
Synonyms: *magic, black magic, sorcery, voodoo, witchcraft, necromancy, alchemy. Magic* is the most inclusive of these related nouns; it pertains to all supposedly supernatural powers that affect natural events, but is often used broadly in the sense of that which seems to transcend rational explanation. *Black magic,* which is practiced with intent to do harm, is the approximate equivalent of *sorcery;* these specifically involve the use of charms and spells. *Voodoo* is a form of sorcery that originated in Africa and is generally associated with fetishes. *Witchcraft* is associated with evil intent and with power derived from evil spirits; it suggests a broader set of techniques than used in *sorcery. Necromancy* signifies forecasting of the future through supposed communication with the dead. *Alchemy* is now applied figuratively to any seemingly miraculous change for the better, an extension of the original sense of transmutation.
mag·i·cal (măj′ĭ-kəl) *adj.* **1.** Pertaining to or produced by magic. **2.** Enchanting; bewitching. **—mag′i·cal·ly** *adv.*
ma·gi·cian (mə-jĭsh′ən) *n.* **1.** A sorcerer; wizard. **2.** One who performs magic for entertainment or diversion. **3.** One

Madonna
13th-century French sculpture

maenad
4th-century B.C. Greek vase painting

Magen David

magician

whose skill or art seems to be magical: *a magician with words.*

magic lantern *n.* An optical device formerly used to project the enlarged image of a picture.

magic number *n. Physics.* Any of the numbers 2, 6, 8, 14, 20, 28, 50, 82, 126, that represent the number of neutrons or protons in strongly bound, exceptionally stable, and abundant atomic nuclei.

mag·is·te·ri·al (măj′ĭ-stîr′ē-əl) *adj.* **1.** Of, pertaining to, or characteristic of a master or teacher; authoritative. **2.** Dogmatic; overbearing: *offended by his magisterial manner of giving advice.* **3.** Of or pertaining to a magistrate or his official functions. [LLat. *magisterius* < Lat. *magister,* master.] **—mag′is·te′ri·al·ly** *adv.*

mag·is·te·ri·um (măj′ĭ-stîr′ē-əm) *n.* The authority to teach religious doctrine, esp. as claimed by the Roman Catholic Church. [Lat., teaching authority.]

mag·is·tra·cy (măj′ĭs-trə-sē) also **mag·is·tra·ture** (-trə-cho͝or′) *n., pl.* **-cies** also **-tures. 1.** The position, function, or term of office of a magistrate. **2.** A body of magistrates. **3.** The district under jurisdiction of a magistrate.

mag·is·tral (măj′ĭ-strəl) *adj.* **1.** Magisterial (sense 3). **2.** Prepared as specified by a physician's prescription. Used of medicines. **3.** Principal; main: *the magistral line of fortifications.* [LLat. *magistralis,* belonging to a master < *magister,* master.]

mag·is·trate (măj′ĭ-strāt′, -strĭt) *n.* **1.** A civil officer with power to administer and enforce law. **2.** A minor official with limited judicial authority, such as a justice of the peace or the judge of a police court. [Lat. *magistratus* < *magister,* master.]

mag·is·tra·ture (măj′ĭ-strā′chər, -strə-cho͝or′) *n.* Magistracy.

Ma·gle·mo·si·an (mä′glə-mō′zē-ən) *adj. Archaeol.* Of or pertaining to a Mesolithic forest culture of northern Europe. [After *Maglemose,* Denmark.]

mag·ma (măg′mə, mäg′-) *n., pl.* **-ma·ta** (-mä′tə) or **-mas. 1.** A mixture of finely divided solids with enough liquid to produce a pasty mass. **2.** *Geol.* The molten matter under the earth's crust, from which igneous rock is formed by cooling. **3.** A pharmacological suspension of particles in a liquid, such as milk of magnesia. **4.** The residue of fruits after expressing the juice; pomace. [ME < Lat. < Gk., ungent < *massein,* to knead.] **—mag·mat′ic** (-măt′ĭk) *adj.*

Mag·na Char·ta or **Mag·na Car·ta** (măg′nə kär′tə) *n.* **1.** The charter of English political and civil liberties granted by King John at Runnymede on June 15, 1215. **2.** A document or piece of legislation that serves as a guarantee of basic rights. [Med. Lat. : Lat. *magna,* great + *charta,* charter.]

mag·na cum lau·de (mäg′nə ko͝om lou′də) *adv.* With high honors. [Lat.]

mag·na·nim·i·ty (măg′nə-nĭm′ĭ-tē) *n.* **1.** The quality of being magnanimous. **2.** A magnanimous act.

mag·nan·i·mous (măg-năn′ə-məs) *adj.* Noble of mind and heart, esp. generous in forgiving. [Lat. *magnanimus* : *magnus,* great + *animus,* soul.] **—mag·nan′i·mous·ly** *adv.* **—mag·nan′i·mous·ness** *n.*

mag·nate (măg′nāt′, -nĭt) *n.* A powerful or influential person, esp. in business or industry: *a railroad magnate.* [ME *magnat* < LLat. *magnatus* < Lat. *magnus,* great.]

mag·ne·sia (măg-nē′zhə, -shə) *n.* Magnesium oxide, esp. when processed for purity. [Med. Lat., mineral ingredient of the philosopher's stone < Gk. *Magnēsia* (*lithos*), Magnesian (stone) < *Magnēs,* of Magnesia, an ancient city in Asia Minor.] **—mag·ne′sian** *adj.*

mag·ne·site (măg′nə-sīt′) *n.* **1.** A white, yellowish, or brown, usually crystalline mineral of magnesium carbonate, $MgCO_3$, used in the manufacture of magnesium oxide and carbon dioxide. **2.** Any of several grades of magnesium oxide obtained from magnesite.

mag·ne·si·um (măg-nē′zē-əm, -zhəm) *n. Symbol* **Mg** A light, silvery, moderately hard, metallic element which in ribbon or powder form burns with a brilliant white flame. It is used in structural alloys, pyrotechnics, flash photography, and incendiary bombs. Atomic number 12; atomic weight 24.312; melting point 651°C; boiling point 1,107°C; specific gravity 1.74; valence 2. [< MAGNESIA.]

magnesium carbonate *n.* A very light, odorless, white powdery compound, $MgCO_3$, used in a wide variety of manufactured products including inks, glass, dentifrices, and cosmetics.

magnesium hydroxide *n.* A white powder, $Mg(OH)_2$, used as an antacid and laxative.

magnesium oxide *n.* A white, powdery compound, MgO, having a high melting point (2,800°C), and used in high-temperature refractories, electric insulation, food packaging, and semiconductor devices.

magnesium sulfate *n.* A colorless, crystalline compound, $MgSO_4$, used in fireproofing, ceramics, matches, explosives, and fertilizers.

mag·net (măg′nĭt) *n.* **1.** A body that attracts iron and certain other materials by virtue of a surrounding field of force produced by the motion of its atomic electrons and the alignment of its atoms. **2.** An electromagnet. **3.** A person, place, object, or situation that exerts attraction. [ME < Lat. < Gk. *magnēs* < *Magnēs lithos,* Magnesian stone < *Magnēs,* of Magnesia, an ancient city in Asia Minor.]

magnet
Magnet with iron filings showing field of magnetic force

magnet– *pref.* Variant of **magneto-**.

mag·net·ic (măg-nĕt′ĭk) *adj.* **1.** Of or relating to magnetism or magnets. **2.** Having the properties of a magnet. **3.** Relating to the magnetic poles of the earth: *a magnetic compass bearing.* **4.** Capable of being magnetized or of being attracted by a magnet. **5.** Operating by means of magnetism: *a magnetic recorder.* **6.** Having an unusual power or ability to attract: *a magnetic personality.* **—mag·net′i·cal·ly** *adv.*

magnetic bottle *n.* A magnetic field used to confine plasma, as during nuclear fusion.

magnetic bubble *n.* A small, stable, cylindrical region of magnetization in thin film or material that can be manipulated by an external magnetic field and used to represent data in a computer memory.

magnetic compass *n.* An instrument using a magnetic needle to show direction relative to the earth's magnetic field.

magnetic core *n.* Core (sense 4).

magnetic declination *n.* The angle between the geographic meridian and the local magnetic meridian, in navigation indicated as degrees plus (+) to the east, or degrees minus (–) to the west, of the geographic meridian.

magnetic dip *n.* The angle that the earth's magnetic field makes with the horizontal plane at any specific location.

magnetic equator *n.* A line connecting all points on the earth's surface where there is no magnetic dip.

magnetic field *n.* A condition in a region of space, established by the presence of a magnet, or of an electric current, and characterized by the existence of a detectable magnetic force at every point in the region.

magnetic field strength *n.* **1.** Magnetic intensity. **2.** Magnetic induction (sense 1).

magnetic flux *n.* The total number of magnetic lines of force passing through a bounded area in a magnetic field.

magnetic flux density *n.* Magnetic induction (sense 1).

magnetic force *n.* **1.** The force on a magnetic pole in a magnetic field. **2.** The force on an electrically charged particle, or on an electric current, in a magnetic field.

magnetic head *n.* A device, as in a tape recorder, that converts electric impulses into variations in the magnetism of a surface for storage and subsequent retrieval.

magnetic hysteresis *n.* The failure of the magnetization in a body to return to its original value when the external field is reduced.

magnetic inclination *n.* Magnetic dip.

magnetic induction *n.* **1.** A vector quantity that specifies the direction and magnitude of magnetic force at every point in a magnetic field. **2.** The temporary conversion of a piece of iron or of certain other materials into a magnet by a magnetic field.

magnetic intensity *n.* That part of a magnetic field related solely to external currents as a cause, without reference to the presence of matter.

magnetic line of force *n.* A curve whose tangent at any point is along the direction of magnetic force at that point. The number of lines of force per unit area in the neighborhood of a point is proportional to the magnetic induction at that point.

magnetic meridian *n.* A meridian passing through the earth's magnetic poles.

magnetic mine *n.* A marine mine detonated by a mechanism that responds to a mass of magnetic material, such as the steel hull of a ship.

magnetic moment *n.* The ratio of the maximum torque exerted on a magnet, or on an electric current loop, in a magnetic field to the magnetic induction of the field.

magnetic needle *n.* A needle-shaped bar magnet usually suspended on a low-friction mounting and used in various instruments, esp. in the magnetic compass, to indicate the alignment of a local magnetic field.

magnetic north *n.* The direction of the earth's magnetic pole, to which the north-seeking pole of a magnetic needle points when free from local magnetic influence.

magnetic permeability *n.* A measure of the ability of a medium to modify a magnetic field, equal to the ratio of magnetic induction to magnetic intensity.

magnetic pickup *n.* A type of phonograph pickup that utilizes a coil in a magnetic field to receive vibrations from the stylus and convert them into electric impulses.

magnetic pole *n.* **1.** Either of two limited regions in a magnet at which the magnet's field is most intense, each of which is designated by the approximate geographic direction to which it is attracted. **2.** Either of two variable points on the earth, close to but not coinciding with the geographic poles, where the earth's magnetic field is most intense.

magnetic pole strength *n.* A measure of the effectiveness of a magnet, equal to the quotient of the magnetic moment by the length of the magnet.

magnetic pyrites *n.* Pyrrhotite.

magnetic recording *n.* **1.** The recording of a signal, such as sound or computer instructions, in the form of a magnetic pattern on a magnetizable surface for storage and subsequent retrieval. **2.** A surface containing a magnetic recording.

magnetic storm *n.* A severe but transitory fluctuation in

the earth's magnetic field believed to be produced by currents of charged particles and gamma rays, resulting from abnormal solar activity.
magnetic susceptibility *n.* The ratio of the magnetic permeability of a medium to that of a vacuum, minus one. It is positive for a paramagnetic or ferromagnetic medium, negative for a diamagnetic medium.
magnetic tape *n.* A plastic tape coated with iron oxide for use in magnetic recording.
magnetic variation *n.* Magnetic declination.
mag·net·ism (măg′nĭ-tĭz′əm) *n.* **1.** The class of phenomena exhibited by the field of force produced by a magnet or by an electric current. **2.** The study of magnets and their effects. **3.** The force exerted by a magnetic field. **4.** Magnetic flux. **5.** Unusual power to attract, fascinate, or influence: *the magnetism of money.* **6.** Animal magnetism.
mag·net·ite (măg′nĭ-tīt′) *n.* The mineral form of black iron oxide, Fe_3O_4, often occurring with titanium or magnesium, and an important ore of iron.
mag·net·i·za·tion (măg′nĭ-tĭ-zā′shən) *n.* **1.** The process of making a substance temporarily or permanently magnetic, as by insertion in a magnetic field. **2.** The magnetic moment per unit volume induced in a body by an external field. **3.** The property of being magnetic.
mag·net·ize (măg′nĭ-tīz′) *tr.v.* **-ized, -iz·ing, -iz·es. 1.** To make magnetic. **2.** To attract, charm, or influence. **—mag′net·iz′a·ble** *adj.* **—mag′net·iz′er** *n.*
magnetizing force *n.* The magnetic intensity at any point in a substance capable of being magnetized.
mag·ne·to (măg-nē′tō) *n., pl.* **-tos.** A small generator of alternating current with permanent magnets, used in the ignition systems of some internal-combustion engines. [Short for *magnetoelectric machine.*]
magneto– or **magnet–** *pref.* **1.** Magnetism; magnetic: *magnetochemistry.* **2.** Magnetic field: *magnetometer.* [< MAGNET.]
mag·ne·to·e·lec·tric (măg-nē′tō-ĭ-lĕk′trĭk, -ē′lĕk′-) *adj.* Of or pertaining to electricity produced by magnetic means. **—mag·ne′to·e·lec·tric′i·ty** *n.*
mag·ne·to·flu·id·dy·nam·ics (măg-nē′tō-flōō′ĭd-dī-năm′ĭks, -nĕt′ō-) *n.* Magnetohydrodynamics. **—mag·ne′to·flu′id·dy·nam′ic** *adj.*
mag·ne·to·gas·dy·nam·ics (măg-nē′tō-găs′dī-năm′ĭks) *n.* *(used with a sing. or pl. verb).* Magnetohydrodynamics. **—mag·ne′to·gas′dy·nam′ic** *adj.*
mag·ne·to·graph (măg-nē′tō-grăf′) *n.* A magnetometer equipped for recording, as by photography.
mag·ne·to·hy·dro·dy·nam·ics (măg-nē′tō-hī′drō-dī-năm′ĭks) *n. (used with a sing. or pl. verb).* The study of electrically conducting fluids, such as molten metal or plasma, in electric and magnetic fields. **—mag·ne′to·hy′dro·dy·nam′ic** *adj.*
mag·ne·tom·e·ter (măg′nĭ-tŏm′ĭ-tər) *n.* An instrument for comparing the intensity and direction of magnetic fields. **—mag′ne·to·met′ric** *adj.* **—mag′ne·tom′e·try** *n.*
mag·ne·to·mo·tive force (măg-nē′tō-mō′tĭv) *n.* **1.** The agency that produces magnetic flux in a magnetic circuit. **2.** The strength of such an agency, equal to the work required to carry a hypothetical isolated magnetic pole of unit strength completely around the circuit.
mag·ne·ton (măg′nĭ-tŏn′) *n.* A unit of the magnetic moment of a subatomic particle, equal to $eh/4\pi mc$, where *e* is the particle's electric charge, *m* its mass, *h* Planck's constant, and *c* the speed of light; esp.: **a.** The *Bohr magneton,* calculated using the mass and charge of the electron. **b.** The *nuclear magneton,* calculated using the mass of the nucleon.
mag·ne·to·plas·ma·dy·nam·ics (măg-nē′tō-plăz′mə-dī-năm′ĭks, -nĕt′ō-) *n.* Magnetohydrodynamics. **—mag·ne′to·plas′ma·dy·nam′ic** *adj.*
mag·ne·to·sphere (măg-nē′tō-sfîr′) *n.* An asymmetric region surrounding the earth, extending from about five hundred to several thousand kilometers above the surface, in which charged particles are trapped and their behavior dominated by the earth's magnetic field.
mag·ne·to·stric·tion (măg-nē′tō-strĭk′shən) *n.* The deformation of a ferromagnetic material subjected to a magnetic field.
mag·ne·tron (măg′nĭ-trŏn′) *n.* A thermionic tube in which the electron beam is controlled by electromagnetic fields and generates high-power microwaves. [MAGNE(T) + -TRON.]
mag·nif·ic (măg-nĭf′ĭk) *adj.* **1.** Magnificent (sense 2). **2.** Imposingly large. **3. a.** Exalted. **b.** Pompous; grandiloquent. [ME *magnifique* < OFr. < Lat. *magnificus* : *magnus,* great + *facere,* to make.] **—mag·nif′i·cal·ly** *adv.*
Mag·nif·i·cat (măg-nĭf′ĭ-kăt′) *n.* **1. a.** The canticle beginning *Magnificat anima mea Dominum* ("My soul doth magnify the Lord"). **b.** A musical setting of this text. **2. magnificat.** A hymn or song of praise. [Lat., it magnifies.]
mag·ni·fi·ca·tion (măg′nə-fĭ-kā′shən) *n.* **1. a.** The act of magnifying or the state of being magnified. **b.** The process of enlarging the size of something, as an optical image. **c.** Something that has been magnified. **2.** The ratio of an optical image size to object size.
mag·nif·i·cence (măg-nĭf′ĭ-səns) *n.* **1.** Greatness or lavishness of surroundings; splendor. **2.** Grand or imposing beauty: *the magnificence of the scenery.*
mag·nif·i·cent (măg-nĭf′ĭ-sənt) *adj.* **1.** Splendid in appearance; grand: *a magnificent palace.* **2.** Grand or noble in thought or deed; exalted. **3.** Outstanding of its kind; superlative: *a magnificent place for sailing.* [Lat. *magnificens, magnificent-,* var. of *magnificus.* —see MAGNIFIC.] **—mag·nif′i·cent·ly** *adv.*
mag·nif·i·co (măg-nĭf′ĭ-kō′) *n., pl.* **-coes. 1.** A nobleman of the Venetian Republic. **2.** A person of distinguished rank, importance, or appearance. [Ital. < *magnifico,* magnificent < Lat. *magnificus.* —see MAGNIFIC.]
mag·ni·fi·er (măg′nə-fī′ər) *n.* **1. a.** A magnifying glass. **b.** A system of optical components that magnifies. **2.** One that magnifies.
mag·ni·fy (măg′nə-fī′) *v.* **-fied, -fy·ing, -fies.** *—tr.* **1.** To make greater in size; enlarge. **2.** To cause to appear greater or seem more important; exaggerate: *grossly magnified a trivial situation.* **3.** To increase the apparent size of, esp. by means of a lens. **4.** To glorify or praise. *—intr.* To increase or have the power to increase the size or volume of an image or sound. [ME *magnifien* < OFr. *magnifier* < Lat. *magnificare* < *magnificus,* magnificent. —see MAGNIFIC.]
magnifying glass *n.* A converging lens that enlarges the image of an object.

magnifying glass

mag·nil·o·quent (măg-nĭl′ə-kwənt) *adj.* Lofty and extravagant in speech; grandiloquent. [Lat. *magniloquus* : *magnus,* great + *loqui,* to speak.] **—mag·nil′o·quence** *n.* **—mag·nil′o·quent·ly** *adv.*
mag·ni·tude (măg′nĭ-tōōd′, -tyōōd′) *n.* **1. a.** Greatness of rank or position: *"such duties as were expected of a landowner of his magnitude"* (Anthony Powell). **b.** Greatness in size or extent. **c.** Greatness in significance or influence. **2.** *Astron.* The relative brightness of a celestial body designated on a numerical scale, originally integers from 1 (brightest) through 6 (faintest visible), now extended to include negative integers, integers above 6, and decimals, with the scale rule such that a decrease of 1 unit represents an increase in apparent brightness by a factor of 2.512. **3.** *Math.* **a.** A number assigned to a member of a set to form the basis of comparison with other members of the same set. **b.** A property that can be quantitatively described, such as the volume of a sphere or the length of a vector. [ME, great size < Lat. *magnitudo* < *magnus,* great.]
mag·no·lia (măg-nōl′yə) *n.* **1.** Any of various evergreen or deciduous trees and shrubs of the genus *Magnolia,* of the Western Hemisphere and Asia, many of which are cultivated for their showy white, pink, purple, or yellow flowers. **2.** The flower of the magnolia. [NLat. *Magnolia,* genus name, after Pierre *Magnol* (1638–1715).]

magnolia

magnolia warbler *n.* A black-and-yellow, ground-nesting songbird, *Dendroica magnolia,* of North America.
mag·num (măg′nəm) *n.* **1.** A bottle, holding about two-fifths of a gallon, for wine or liquor. **2.** The amount of liquid contained in a magnum. [Lat., neuter of *magnus,* great.]
mag·num o·pus (măg′nəm ō′pəs) *n.* **1.** A great work, esp. a literary or artistic masterpiece. **2.** The greatest single work of an artist, writer, or composer. [Lat.]
mag·nus hitch (măg′nəs) *n.* A clove hitch with one extra turn. [Orig. unknown.]
ma·got (mă-gō′, măg′ət) *n.* **1.** The Barbary ape. **2.** A fanciful, often grotesque figure in the Japanese or Chinese style. [Fr.]
mag·pie (măg′pī′) *n.* **1.** Any of various birds of the family Corvidae, found worldwide, having a long, graduated tail, and black, blue, or green coloring with white markings, noted for their chattering call. The species *Pica pica,* the black-billed magpie, is widespread in the Northern Hemisphere. **2.** Any of various birds resembling the magpie. **3.** Any of several piping crows and bell magpies of the family Cracticidae, of Australia. **4.** A person who chatters. [*Mag,* a nickname for *Margaret* + PIE[2].]
ma·guey (mə-gā′) *n.* **1.** Any of various plants of the genus *Agave,* native to tropical America. **2.** Any plant of the genus *Furcraea.* **3.** The fiber obtained from the maguey. [Sp., of Cariban orig.]
ma·gus (mā′gəs) *n., pl.* **ma·gi** (mā′jī′). **1.** A member of the Zoroastrian priestly caste of the Medes and Persians. **2. Magus.** One of the three wise men from the East who traveled to Bethlehem to pay homage to the infant Jesus. **3.** A sorcerer; magician. [ME < Lat. *magus,* sorcerer < Gk. *magos* < Pers. *maguš.*] **—ma′gi·an** (mā′jē-ən) *n.*
Mag·yar (măg′yär′, măg′-, mŭd′-) *n.* **1.** A member of the principal ethnic group of Hungary. **2.** The Finno-Ugric language of the Magyars that is the official language of Hungary. [Hung.] **—Mag′yar** *adj.*
ma·ha·ra·jah or **ma·ha·ra·ja** (mä′hə-rä′jə, -zhə) *n.* A king or prince in India ranking above a raja, esp. the sovereign of one of the former native states. [Hindi *mahārājā* < Skt. : *mahā-,* great + *rājā,* king.]
ma·ha·ra·ni or **ma·ha·ra·nee** (mä′hə-rä′nē) *n.* **1.** The wife of a maharajah. **2.** A princess in India ranking above a rani, esp. the sovereign ruler of one of the former native states. [Hindi *mahārānī* < Skt. *mahārājñī* : *mahā-,* great + *rājñī,* queen.]
ma·ha·ri·shi (mä′hə-rē′shē, mə-här′ə-shē) *n.* A Hindu teacher of mysticism and spiritual knowledge. [Skt. *mahārṣi* : *mahat-,* great + *ṛṣi,* sage.]
ma·hat·ma (mə-hät′mə, -hăt′-) *n.* **1.** In India and Tibet, one

of a class of persons venerated for great knowledge and love of humanity. **2. Mahatma.** A Hindu title of respect for a man renowned for spirituality and high-mindedness. [Skt. *mahātman* : *mahā-*, great + *ātman*, self, soul.]

Ma·ha·ya·na (mä'hə-yä'nə) *n.* One of the major schools of Buddhism, active in Japan, Korea, Nepal, Tibet, Mongolia, and China, that teaches social concern and universal salvation. [Skt. *Mahāyānam* : *mahā-*, great + *yānam*, vehicle.] **—Ma'ha·ya'nist** *n.* **—Ma'ha·ya·nis'tic** *adj.*

Mah·di (mä'dē) *n.* **1.** The Islamic messiah who, it is believed, will appear at the world's end and establish a reign of peace and righteousness. **2.** An Islamic leader who assumes the role of a messiah. [Ar. *mahdīy* < *madā*, he lead in the right way.] **—Mah'dism** *n.* **—Mah'dist** *n.*

Ma·hi·can (mə-hē'kən) also **Mo·hi·can** (mō-, mə-) *n., pl.* **Mahican** or **-cans** also **Mohican** or **-cans. 1.** A tribe or confederacy of Algonquian-speaking Indians that formerly lived between the upper Hudson River Valley and Lake Champlain. **2.** A member of the Mahican tribe or confederacy. **3.** The Algonquian language of the Mahican.

mah·jong also **mah·jongg** (mä'zhŏng', -zhông') *n.* A game of Chinese origin usually played by four persons with tiles resembling dominoes and bearing various designs, which are drawn and discarded until one player wins with a hand of four combinations of three tiles each and a pair of matching tiles. [Chin. (Mandarin) *ma*[2] *jiang*[4].]

mahl·stick (môl'stĭk') *n.* Variant of **maulstick.**

ma·hog·a·ny (mə-hŏg'ə-nē) *n., pl.* **-nies. 1. a.** Any of various tropical American trees of the genus *Swietenia*, valued for their hard, reddish-brown wood. **b.** The wood of any of these trees, esp. that of *S. mahogani*, used for making furniture. **2. a.** Any of several trees having wood resembling true mahogany. **b.** The wood of any of these trees. **3.** A moderate reddish brown. [Orig. unknown.]

ma·hout (mə-hout') *n.* The keeper and driver of an elephant. [Hindi *mahāut* < Skt. *mahāmātraḥ*, an honorific title: *mahā-*, great + *mātram*, measure, size.]

Mah·ra·ti (mə-rä'tē, mə-răt'ē) *n.* Variant of **Marathi.**

Mah·rat·ta (mə-răt'ə) *n.* Variant of **Maratha.**

Mah·rat·ti (mə-rä'tē, mə-răt'ē) *n.* Variant of **Marathi.**

ma·huang (mä-hwäng') *n.* Any of various Asiatic plants or shrubs of the genus *Ephedra*, esp. *E. sinica*, from which ephedrine is obtained. [Chin. (Mandarin) *ma*[2] *huang*[2] : *ma*[2], hemp + *huang*[2], yellow.]

mah·zor (mäkн'zôr', -zər) *n., pl.* **mah·zor·im** (mäкн-zôr'ĭm) or **-zors.** The Hebrew prayer book containing rituals prescribed for holidays. [Heb. *maḥzor.*]

Mai·a (mā'ə, mī'ə) *n.* **1.** *Gk. Myth.* A goddess, the eldest of the Pleiades. **2.** The brightest star in the Pleiades. [Lat. < Gk. < *maia*, mother.]

maid (mād) *n.* **1. a.** A girl or an unmarried woman. **b.** A virgin. **2.** A female servant. [ME < OE *mægden.*]

maid·en (mād'n) *n.* **1. a.** An unmarried girl or woman. **b.** A virgin. **2.** A machine resembling the guillotine, used to behead criminals in the 16th and 17th centuries in Scotland. **3.** A racehorse that has never won a race. **4.** *Sports.* A maiden over. **5.** A one-year-old woody plant. *—adj.* **1.** Of, pertaining to, or befitting a maiden: *a maiden blush.* **2.** Being an unmarried woman: *a maiden aunt.* **3.** Inexperienced; untried. **4.** Designating a racehorse that has never won a race. **5.** First or earliest: *a maiden voyage.* [ME < OE *mægden.*]

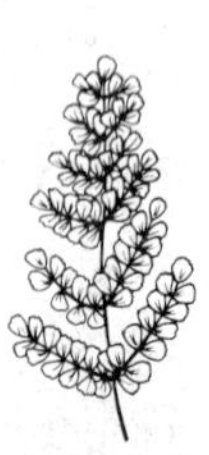

maidenhair

maid·en·hair or **maid·en·hair fern** (mād'n-hâr') *n.* Any of various ferns of the genus *Adiantum*, having dark stems and light-green, feathery fronds with fan-shaped leaflets. [From the fineness of its stems.]

maidenhair tree *n.* The ginkgo.

maid·en·head (mād'n-hĕd') *n.* **1.** The condition or quality of being a maiden; virginity. **2.** A hymen. [ME *maidenhed* : *maiden* (< OE *mægden*) + *-hed*, -hood < OE *-had.*]

maid·en·hood (mād'n-hŏŏd') *n.* The condition or time of being a maiden.

maid·en·ly (mād'n-lē) *adj.* Pertaining to or suitable for a maiden. **—maid'en·li·ness** *n.*

maiden name *n.* A woman's family name before marriage.

maiden over *n.* An over in cricket during which no runs are scored.

maid·hood (mād'hŏŏd') *n.* Maidenhood.

maid in waiting *n., pl.* **maids in waiting.** An unmarried woman attending a queen or princess.

Maid Mar·i·an (mâr'ē-ən, măr'-) *n.* Robin Hood's sweetheart in some versions of the legend.

maid of honor *n., pl.* **maids of honor. 1.** An unmarried noblewoman attendant upon a queen or princess. **2.** The chief unmarried female attendant of a bride.

maid·ser·vant (mād'sûr'vənt) *n.* A female servant.

Mai·du (mī'dōō) *n., pl.* **Maidu** or **-dus. 1. a.** An Indian tribe formerly living in the Sacramento Valley area of California. **b.** A member of this tribe. **2.** The Penutian language of the Maidu. [Maidu.] **—Mai'du** *adj.*

ma·ieu·tic (mā-yōō'tĭk, mī-) also **ma·ieu·ti·cal** (-tĭ-kəl) *adj.* Pertaining to that aspect of the Socratic method that induces a respondent to formulate latent concepts through a dialectic or logical sequence of questions. [Gk. *maieutikos* < *maieuesthai*, to act as midwife < *maia*, midwife.]

mail[1] (māl) *n.* **1. a.** Materials, such as letters and packages, handled in a postal system. **b.** Postal material for a specific person or organization. **c.** Material processed for distribution from a post office at a specified time: *the morning mail.* **2.** Often **mails.** A system by which letters, packages, and other postal materials are transported. **3.** A vehicle by which mail is transported. *—v.* **mailed, mail·ing, mails.** *—tr.* To send by mail. *—intr.* To send letters and other postal material by mail. [ME *male*, bag < OFr., of Germanic orig.] **—mail'a·ble** *adj.* **—mail'a·bil'i·ty** *n.*

mail[2] (māl) *n.* **1.** Flexible armor composed of small overlapping metal rings, loops of chain, or scales. **2.** The protective shell or covering of certain animals, such as the turtle. **3.** The full-grown breast feathers of a hawk. *—tr.v.* **mailed, mail·ing, mails.** To cover or armor with mail. [ME < OFr. *maile* < Lat. *macula*, mesh.]

mail[3] (māl) *n. Chiefly Scot.* Rent; payment; tribute. [ME *maile* < OE *māl*, agreement < ON.]

mail·bag (māl'băg') *n.* **1.** A large canvas sack used for transporting mail. **2.** A bag suspended from the shoulder, used by letter carriers for carrying mail.

mail·box (māl'bŏks') *n.* **1.** A public container for deposit of outgoing mail. **2.** A private box for incoming mail.

mail call *n.* Distribution of mail to members of a military unit.

mail carrier *n.* **1.** A vehicle or other device used for transporting mail. **2.** One who carries and delivers mail.

mail drop *n.* **1.** A receptacle or slot for the delivery of mail. **2.** An address at which a person receives mail but does not reside.

mailed (māld) *adj.* **1.** Covered with or made of plates of mail. **2.** Having a hard covering of scales, spines, or horny plate, as an armadillo or lobster.

mailed fist *n.* The threat of military force.

mail·er (mā'lər) *n.* **1.** One who uses the mails. **2. a.** A person who addresses, stamps, or otherwise prepares mail. **b.** A mailing machine. **3.** A ship that carries mail. **4.** A container, such as a cardboard tube, used to hold material to be mailed. **5.** An advertising leaflet included with a letter.

Mail·gram (māl'grăm'). A trademark for a telegram delivered by the postal service.

mail·ing (mā'lĭng) *n.* **1.** Something sent by mail. **2.** A batch of mail dispatched at one time by a sender.

mailing machine *n.* Any of various machines that stamp, address, or seal material for mailing.

mail·lot (mä-yō') *n.* **1.** A coarsely knitted, stretchable jersey fabric. **2. a.** A gymnastic suit or pair of tights made of maillot. **b.** A bathing suit, esp. one for women, of maillot, usually of one piece. [Fr. < OFr., swaddling clothes < *maille*, band of cloth < Lat. *macula*, mesh.]

mail·man (māl'măn', -mən) *n.* One who carries and delivers mail.

mail order *n.* A request for goods or services that is received, and often filled, through the mail.

mail-or·der house (māl'ôr'dər) *n.* A business establishment that is primarily organized to promote, receive, and fill requests for merchandise or services through the mail.

maim (mām) *tr.v.* **maimed, maim·ing, maims. 1.** To disable or disfigure, usually by depriving of the use of a limb or bodily member. **2.** To make imperfect or defective; impair. [ME *maimen* < OFr. *mahaignier.*] **—maim'er** *n.*

main[1] (mān) *adj.* **1.** Most important; principal. **2.** Exerted to the utmost; sheer: *by main strength.* **3.** *Obs.* Of or relating to a continuous area or stretch, as of land or water. **4.** *Naut.* Connected to or located near the mainmast: *a main skysail.* *—n.* **1.** The principal or most important part or point: *students who are, in the main, competent.* **2.** The principal pipe or conduit in a system for conveying water, gas, oil, or other utility. **3.** Physical strength: *might and main.* **4.** The mainland, as distinguished from islands. **5.** The open ocean. **6.** *Naut.* **a.** The mainsail. **b.** The mainmast. [ME < OE *mægen.*]

main[2] (mān) *n.* **1.** *Games.* In hazard, a number more than four but not exceeding nine that is called by the caster before throwing the dice. **2.** A series of cockfights consisting of an odd number of matches. [Prob. < MAIN[1].]

main chance *n.* One's most advantageous opportunity.

main clause *n. Gram.* The principal clause or predication in a complex sentence.

main deck *n.* The principal deck of a ship or other large vessel.

main drag *n. Slang.* The principal street of a city or town.

main·frame (mān'frām') *n.* The central processing unit of a computer exclusive of peripheral and remote devices.

main·land (mān'lănd', -lənd) *n.* The principal land mass of a continent, as distinguished from an island or peninsula.

main·line (mān'līn') *intr.v.* **-lined, -lin·ing, -lines.** *Slang.* To inject narcotics directly into a major vein. **—main'lin'er** *n.*

main line *n.* **1.** A principal section of a railroad line. **2.** *Slang.* A principal and easily accessible vein, usually in the arm or leg, into which narcotics can be injected.

main·ly (mān'lē) *adv.* For the most part; chiefly.

main·mast (mān'məst, -măst') *n.* **1.** The principal mast of a vessel. **2.** The taller mast, whether forward or aft, of any two-masted sailing vessel. **3.** The second mast aft of any sailing ship with three or more masts.

main roy·al·mast (roi'əl-məst, -măst') *n.* The section of the

mainmast of a square-rigged vessel above the main topgallantmast.
main·sail (mān′səl, -sāl′) *n.* **1.** The principal sail of a vessel. **2.** A quadrilateral or triangular sail set from the after part of the mainmast on a fore-and-aft rigged vessel. **3.** A square sail set from the main yard on a square-rigged vessel.
main sequence *n.* A major grouping of stars, containing the sun and 90 per cent of the known stars in the vicinity of the sun, characterized by an approximately uniform average increase of luminosity with surface temperature as represented by a single band on the Hertzsprung-Russell diagram.
main·sheet (mān′shēt′) *n.* The rope that controls the angle at which the mainsail is trimmed and set.
main·spring (mān′sprĭng′) *n.* **1.** The principal spring in a mechanical device, esp. in a watch or clock, that drives the mechanism by uncoiling. **2.** A motivating force: *He was the mainspring of the reform movement.*
main·stay (mān′stā′) *n.* **1.** A strong rope that serves to steady and support the mainmast of a sailing vessel. **2.** A principal support: *Agriculture is a mainstay of the economy.*
main stem *n.* **1.** The principal street in a town or city. **2.** Main line (sense 1).
main·stream (mān′strēm′) *n.* The prevailing current or direction of a movement or influence. *—adj.* Having, influenced by, or harmonizing with the prevalent attitudes and values of a society or group: *mainstream morality.* *—tr.v.* **-streamed, -stream·ing, -streams.** To place (a handicapped student) in regular school classes. **—main′stream′ing** *n.*
main street *n.* **1.** The principal street of an American small town or city. **2. Main Street.** The culture of smug, materialistic, and provincial small towns. [After *Main Street,* a novel by Sinclair Lewis (1885–1951).]
main·tain (mān-tān′) *tr.v.* **-tained, -tain·ing, -tains. 1.** To continue; carry on: *maintain good relations.* **2.** To preserve or keep in a given existing condition, as of efficiency or repair: *maintain two cars.* **3. a.** To provide for: *maintain a family.* **b.** To keep in existence; sustain: *food to maintain life.* **4.** To defend, as against danger or attack: *"Perhaps the Germans could not maintain the corridor"* (Winston Churchill). **5.** To declare to be true; affirm: *The defendant maintains his innocence.* [ME *maintainen* < OFr. *maintenir* < Med. Lat. *manutenēre* < Lat. *manu tenēre,* to hold in the hand.] **—main·tain′a·ble** *adj.* **—main·tain′er** *n.*
main·te·nance (mān′tə-nəns) *n.* **1. a.** The action of maintaining. **b.** The state of being maintained. **2.** The work of keeping something in proper condition. **3.** A means of maintaining or supporting: *His income barely provided maintenance.* **4.** *Law.* An unlawful meddling in a law suit by assisting either party having the means to carry it on. [ME < OFr. < *maintenir,* to maintain. —see MAINTAIN.]
main·top (mān′tŏp′) *n.* A platform at the head of the mainmast on a square-rigged vessel.
main topgallant *n.* A sail or yard set from the topgallant section of a mainmast.
main top·gal·lant·mast (tə-găl′ənt-məst, tŏp-) *n.* The section of the mainmast next above the main topmast on a square-rigged vessel.
main topmast *n.* The section of the mainmast on a square-rigged sailing vessel between the lower mast and the main topgallantmast.
main topsail *n.* The sail that is set above the mainsail.
main yard *n.* The lower yard on a mainmast.
mai tai (mī′ tī′) *n.* A cocktail made with rum, curaçao, and fruit juices. [Tahitian *maitai,* good.]
mai·tre d′ (mā′trə dē′, mā′tər) *n., pl.* **mai·tre d′s** (dēz′). *Informal.* Maitre d'hôtel.
mai·tre d′hô·tel (mā′trə dō-tĕl′) *n., pl.* **mai·tres d′hô·tel** (mā′trə dō-tĕl′). **1.** A headwaiter. **2.** A major-domo. **3.** A sauce of melted butter, chopped parsley, lemon juice, salt, and pepper. [Fr. *maître,* master + *de,* of + *hôtel,* house.]
maize (māz) *n.* **1.** Corn (sense 1). **2.** A light yellow to moderate orange yellow. [Sp. *maíz* < Carib *mahiz.*] **—maize** *adj.*
ma·jes·tic (mə-jĕs′tĭk) also **ma·jes·ti·cal** (-tĭ-kəl) *adj.* Having or exhibiting stateliness or great dignity. **—ma·jes′ti·cal·ly** *adv.*
maj·es·ty (măj′ĭ-stē) *n., pl.* **-ties. 1. a.** The greatness and dignity of a sovereign. **b.** The sovereignty and power of God. **2.** The supreme authority or power: *the majesty of the law.* **3. a.** A royal personage. **b. Majesty.** A title used in speaking of or to a sovereign monarch: *Your Majesty.* **4. a.** Royal dignity of bearing or aspect; grandeur. **b.** Stateliness, splendor, or magnificence, as of appearance, style, or character: *the Greek statue in all the majesty of its classical beauty.* [ME *majeste* < OFr. < Lat. *majestas* < *major,* greater. —see MAJOR.]
ma·jol·i·ca (mə-jŏl′ĭ-kə, -yŏl′-) *n.* **1.** Tin-glazed earthenware that is often richly colored and decorated, esp. an earthenware of this type produced in Italy. **2.** A modern pottery made in imitation of majolica. [OItal. *maiolica* < *Majolica,* Majorca.]
ma·jor (mā′jər) *adj.* **1.** Greater in importance, rank, or stature: *a major scientific discovery.* **2.** Requiring great attention or concern; serious: *a major illness.* **3.** *Law.* Having attained full legal age. **4.** Of a greater number, quantity, or extent. **5.** Designating or relating to the principal field of academic specialization chosen by students in a college or university. **6.** More inclusive in scope. **7.** *Mus.* **a.** Designating a scale or mode having half steps between the third and fourth and the seventh and eighth degrees. **b.** Equivalent to the distance between the tonic note and the second or third or sixth or seventh degrees of a major scale or mode: *a major interval.* **c.** Based on a major scale: *major key.* *—n.* **1. a.** An officer in the U.S. Army, Air Force, or Marine Corps ranking above a captain and below a lieutenant colonel. **b.** An officer of similar rank in other military or paramilitary organizations. **2.** *Law.* One who has reached full legal age. **3. a.** A subject or field chosen as an academic specialization. **b.** A student specializing in such a field: *a history major.* **4.** *Logic.* A major premise or major term. **5.** *Mus.* A major scale, key, interval, or mode. **6. majors.** *Sports.* The major leagues. *—intr.v.* **-jored, -jor·ing, -jors.** To pursue academic studies in a major field. [ME *majour* < Lat. *major,* comp. of *magnus,* great.]
major axis *n.* **1.** The line intersecting an ellipse and passing through both of its focuses. **2.** The longest axis of an ellipsoid.
ma·jor-do·mo (mā′jər-dō′mō) *n., pl.* **-mos. 1.** The head steward or butler in the household of a sovereign or great nobleman. **2.** A steward or butler. [Ital. *maggiordomo* or Sp. *mayordomo,* both < Med. Lat. *major domus* : *major,* chief + Lat. *domus,* of the house.]
ma·jor·ette (mā′jə-rĕt′) *n.* A drum majorette.
major gene *n.* Oligogene.
major general. *n.* An officer in the U.S. Army, Air Force, or Marine Corps, who ranks above a brigadier general and below a lieutenant general.
ma·jor·i·tar·i·an·ism (mə-jôr′ĭ-târ′ē-ə-nĭz′əm, -jŏr′-) *n.* The belief in or practice of decision-making in an organized group by a numerical majority of its members. **—ma·jor′i·tar′i·an** *n.*
ma·jor·i·ty (mə-jôr′ĭ-tē, -jŏr′-) *n., pl.* **-ties. 1.** The greater number or part of something. **2. a.** A number more than half of the total number of a given group. **b.** The number of votes cast in any election above the total number of all other votes cast. **3.** The status of legal age when full civil and personal rights may be exercised legally. **4.** The political party, group, or faction having the most power by virtue of its larger representation or electoral strength. **5.** The military rank, commission, or office of a major. **6.** *Obs.* The fact or state of being greater; superiority. [OFr. *majorite* < Med. Lat. *majoritas* < Lat. *major,* greater. —see MAJOR.]

Usage: When *majority* refers to a particular number of votes, it takes a singular verb: *Her majority was five votes. His majority has been growing by 5 per cent every year.* When it refers to a group of persons or things that are in the majority, it may take either a singular or plural verb, depending on whether the group is considered as a whole or as a set of people considered individually. So we say *the majority elects* (not *elect*) *the candidate it wants* (not *they want*), since the election is accomplished by the group as a whole; but *the majority of the voters live* (not *lives*) *in the city,* since living in the city is something that each voter does individually. • *Majority* is often preceded by *great* (but not by *greater*) in expressing, emphatically, the sense of "most of": *The great majority approved.* The phrase *greater majority* is appropriate only when considering two majorities: *He won by a greater majority in this election than in the last.*

majority leader *n.* The leader of the majority party in a legislature, as in the U.S. Senate or House of Representatives.
majority rule *n.* A political doctrine by which a numerical majority of the voters holds the power to make decisions binding on all the voters.
major league *n.* **1.** Either of the two principal groups of professional baseball teams in the United States. **2.** A league of principal importance in other professional sports, such as basketball, football, or ice hockey.
ma·jor-league (mā′jər-lēg′) *adj.* In a leading or significant position: *Car rental is now a major-league business.*
ma·jor-med·i·cal (mā′jər-mĕd′ĭ-kəl) *adj.* Of, relating to, or being a type of insurance plan that covers most of the medical bills of major illnesses.
major orders *pl.n.* Holy orders.
major party *n.* A political party able to gain control of a government with comparative regularity.
major premise *n.* In a syllogism, the premise containing the major term.
Major Prophets *pl.n.* The Hebrew prophets Isaiah, Jeremiah, and Ezekiel.
major scale *n.* *Mus.* A diatonic scale having half steps between the third and fourth and the seventh and eighth tones.
major suit *n.* *Games.* In bridge, a suit of superior scoring value, either spades or hearts.
major term *n.* A term of a syllogism that forms the predicate of the conclusion and the subject or predicate of the major premise.
ma·jus·cule (mə-jŭs′kyōōl, măj′ə-skyōōl′) *n.* **1.** A large letter, either capital or uncial, used in writing or printing. **2.** Writing that uses majuscule letters. [Fr. < Lat. *majuscu-*

majolica
Made in 15th century in Florence, Italy

major scale
Key of C

lus, somewhat great, dim. of *major,* greater. —see MAJOR.] **—ma·jus'cule, ma·jus'cu·lar** (mə-jŭs'kyə-lər) *adj.*

mak·ar (mä'kər, mă'-) *n. Chiefly Scot.* A poet. [ME *maker,* maker.]

make (māk) *v.* **made** (mād), **mak·ing, makes.** —*tr.v.* **1. a.** To cause to exist or happen; create. **b.** To bring into existence by forming or modifying materials: *make a coat.* **c.** To create by putting together component parts. **d.** To form by assembling individuals or constituents: *make a quorum.* **2. a.** To cause to be or become: *made our position clear.* **b.** To cause to assume a specified function or role: *made him treasurer; made Chicago his home.* **3.** To cause to be experienced by someone: *made problems for all of us.* **4. a.** To formulate or construct, esp. by the use of mental or imaginative power: *make plans.* **b.** To compose: *make verses.* **5. a.** To prepare; fix: *make breakfast.* **b.** To get ready or set in order for use: *make a bed.* **c.** To gather and light the materials for (a fire). **6. a.** To act so as to carry out or engage in. Used with a noun object indicating the nature of the action: *make war.* **b.** To perform by moving the body or a part of the body: *make a bow.* **c.** To achieve or produce by effort or action: *made peace between the two factions.* **7. a.** To institute or establish; enact: *make a rule.* **b.** To draw up and execute in a suitable form: *make a will.* **8. a.** To reach by traveling: *made Washington in two hours.* **b.** To complete or accomplish by traveling across or over: *make the rounds.* **9. a.** To attain; reach: *tried to make it to the top of the hill; didn't make the quota.* **b.** To attain the rank or position of: *made lieutenant.* **c.** To acquire a place in or on: *made the basketball team.* **10. a.** To acquire (money, for example), as by work. **b.** To gain through behavior or effort: *make friends.* **c.** To score or achieve in a game or sport. **11.** To be a sufficient guarantee for the success of: *His approval can make or break a young actor.* **12.** To compel to act: *made him leave.* **13. a.** To be capable of conversion into, esp. by a process of fabrication or manufacture: *Oak makes strong furniture.* **b.** To be capable of growing or developing into: *made a fine physician.* **14. a.** To draw a conclusion as to the significance or nature of: *don't know what to make of his decision.* **b.** To calculate, conjecture, or estimate to be. **c.** To consider as being: *wasn't the fool some people made her.* **15. a.** To amount to: *makes a great deal of difference.* **b.** To bring up to the sum of; count as: *This makes the second time that you've been late.* **c.** To constitute the essential being or nature of: *believed that clothes made the man.* **16.** To succeed in reaching and boarding; catch: *make a train.* **17.** *Slang.* To succeed in having sexual intercourse with. **18.** To appear to begin (an action). **19.** *Obs.* To act; behave. —*intr.* **1.** To act; behave. **2.** To begin or appear to begin an action: *made as if to leave.* **3.** To go; proceed: *made after the bus like greased lightning.* **4.** To have a particular effect: *small details that make for comfort.* **5.** To undergo fabrication or manufacture. ***—phrasal verbs.*** **make off. 1.** To depart in haste. **2.** To snatch; steal: *made off with the profits.* **make out. 1.** To discern or see, esp. with difficulty: *could barely make out the beacon in the fog.* **2.** To understand; comprehend: *couldn't make out what she was trying to say.* **3.** To fill in (a document, for example): *made out my income tax form.* **4.** *Informal.* To prove or imply: *He tried to make me out a liar.* **5.** *Informal.* To pretend to be true: *He made out that he was innocent.* **6.** *Slang.* **a.** To neck; pet. **b.** To have sexual intercourse. **7.** *Slang.* To get along in a given way; fare: *made out well in business.* **make over. 1.** To redo; renovate. **2.** To change or transfer the ownership of, usually by means of a legal document: *He made over the property to his son.* **make up. 1.** To construct, create, or form by collecting and fitting components, parts, or materials together. **2.** To apply cosmetics to the face. **3.** To construct falsely or fictionally; fabricate: *made up an excuse.* **4.** To come to a decision: *made up her mind to stand firm.* **5. a.** To offset a deficit: *make up the difference.* **b.** To compensate for a mistake, offense, or omission: *make up for lost time.* **6.** To resolve a quarrel: *kissed and made up.* **7.** To make ingratiating overtures to someone: *made up to his friend's sister.* **8.** To take (an examination, for example) again or at a later time because of a previous absence or failure. **9.** *Printing.* To arrange material into (columns or pages) for printing: *made up the front page.* —*n.* **1.** The act or process of making. **2.** The style or manner in which a thing is made: *I dislike the make of this coat.* **3. a.** A manufacturing style. **b.** A specific line of manufactured goods, identified by the maker's name or the registered trademark: *a famous make of shirt.* **4.** The physical or moral nature of a person: *Let's see what make of man you are.* **5.** The amount produced, esp. the output of a factory. ***—idioms.*** **make a face.** To distort the features of the face; grimace. **make a go of.** To achieve success in: *made a go of the marriage.* **make a mountain out of a molehill.** To attach undue importance to a trivial matter. **make away with. 1.** To make off with. **2.** To use up; consume. **make believe.** To pretend. **make bold.** To venture. **make book.** To accept bets on a race, game, or contest. **make do.** To manage to get along with the means available: *had to make do on a low salary.* **make ends meet.** To manage carefully so as to make one's means sufficient and adequate for one's needs. **make eyes.** To ogle. **make fun of.** To mock; ridicule. **make good. 1. a.** To carry out successfully; achieve: *He made good his career plans.* **b.** To carry out (a promise, for example): *made good his vow.* **2.** To repay; indemnify: *make good one's debts.* **3.** To succeed: *make good in the big city.* **make hay.** To take advantage of and capitalize on an opportunity: *His opponents made hay of the scandal.* **make it. 1.** *Informal.* To be successful: *finally made it as an opera singer.* **2.** *Slang.* To have sexual intercourse. **make light of.** To treat as unimportant: *made light of his handicaps.* **make love. 1.** To court; woo. **2.** To embrace and caress; pet. **3.** To engage in sexual intercourse. **make much of.** To treat as of great importance. **make no bones about.** To be forthright, unequivocal, and sure: *made no bones about his contempt for the fellow.* **make public.** To disclose to public knowledge. **make sail. 1.** To begin a voyage. **2.** To set sail. **make the grade.** To measure up to a given standard. **make the most of.** To use to the greatest advantage. **make the scene.** *Slang.* To put in an appearance: *made the scene at the party.* **make time. 1.** To move fast: *We'll have to make time if we're going to keep the appointment.* **2.** *Slang.* To make progress toward winning, esp. romantic or sexual favors: *made time with the stewardess.* **make tracks.** *Slang.* To move with haste. **make waves.** *Slang.* To cause a disturbance or controversy. **make way. 1.** To give room for passage. **2.** To make progress. **make whoopee.** *Slang.* To have an uproariously good time; raise Cain. **make with.** *Slang.* To perform; produce: *a flirt making with the big eyes; started making with the hard work.* **on the make. 1.** Eagerly and often brashly striving for financial or social improvement: *a young executive on the make.* **2.** *Slang.* Sexually adventurous or aggressive. [ME *maken* < OE *macian.*]

make-be·lieve (māk'bĭ-lēv') *n.* Playful or fanciful pretense. **—make'-be·lieve'** *adj.*

make·fast (māk'făst') *n. Naut.* An object, such as a buoy, post, or pile, to which a boat is tied.

mak·er (mā'kər) *n.* **1.** One that makes. **2.** *Law.* An individual who signs a promissory note. **3. Maker.** God (sense 1). **4.** *Archaic.* A poet.

make-read·y (māk'rĕd'ē) *n. Printing.* The operation of preparing a form for printing by adjusting and leveling the plates to insure a clear impression.

make·shift (māk'shĭft') *n.* Something used or assembled as a temporary or expedient substitute. **—make'shift'** *adj.*

make-up also **make·up** (māk'ŭp') *n.* **1.** The way in which something is composed or arranged; construction. **2.** *Printing.* The arrangement or composition, as of type or illustrations, on a page or in a book. **3.** The qualities or temperament that constitute a personality; disposition. **4.** Cosmetics applied esp. to the face. **5.** The cosmetics that an actor uses in portraying a role. **6.** A special examination prepared for a student who has been absent from or has failed a previous examination.

make·weight (māk'wāt') *n.* **1.** Something added on a scale in order to meet a required weight. **2.** A counterweight; counterbalance.

make-work (māk'wûrk') *n.* Work of little or no value done only to keep someone busy; busywork.

ma·ki·mo·no (mä'kĭ-mō'nō) *n.* A horizontal Japanese decorative scroll featuring pictures or calligraphy. [J., scroll : *maki,* roll + *mono,* thing.]

mak·ing (mā'kĭng) *n.* **1.** The act of one that makes or the process of being made. **2.** A means of gaining success: *The job will be the making of him.* **3. a.** Something made. **b.** The amount or quantity of something made at one time. **4.** Often **makings.** The materials or substances necessary for making or doing something: *We have the makings of a fine organization.* **5. makings.** *Slang.* The paper and tobacco for rolling a cigarette.

ma·ko shark (mä'kō) *n.* Either of two sharks of the genus *Isurus,* characterized by a large heavy body and a nearly symmetrical tail. [Maori *mako.*]

ma·ku·ta (mä-ko͞o'tä) *n.* Plural of **likuta.**

mal– *pref.* **1.** Bad; badly: *maladminister.* **2.** Abnormal; abnormally: *malformation.* [ME < OFr. < Lat. < *male,* badly and *malus,* bad.]

mal·ab·sorp·tion (măl'əb-sôrp'shən, -zôrp'-) *n.* Defective or inadequate absorption of nutrients from the intestinal tract.

Ma·lac·ca (mə-lăk'ə) *n.* The stem of the rattan palm of Asia, used for walking sticks. [After *Malacca,* Malaysia.]

Mal·a·chi (măl'ə-kī') *n.* **1.** A Hebrew prophet of the fifth century B.C., the last of the Minor Prophets. **2.** See table at **Bible.** [Heb. *Mal'ākhī.*]

mal·a·chite (măl'ə-kīt') *n.* A green to nearly black mineral carbonate of copper, $CuCO_3 \cdot Cu(OH)_2$, used as a source of copper and for ornamental stoneware. [ME *melochite* < Lat. *molochites* < Gk. *molokhitis* < *molokhē,* mallow.]

mal·a·col·o·gy (măl'ə-kŏl'ə-jē) *n.* The scientific study of mollusks. [Fr. *malacologie,* contraction of *malacozoologie* < NLat. *Malacozoa,* a classification that includes mollusks : Gk. *malakos* soft + Gk. *zōia,* animal.]

mal·a·dap·ta·tion (măl'ă-dăp-tā'shən) *n.* Faulty or inadequate adaptation.

mal·a·dap·ted (măl'ə-dăp'tĭd) *adj.* Not suited, as to a certain function or situation.

mal·a·dap·tive (măl'ə-dăp'tĭv) *adj.* **1.** Marked by faulty or

inadequate adaptation. **2.** Not assisting or promoting adaptation.
mal·ad·just·ment (măl′ə-jŭst′mənt) *n.* **1.** Faulty adjustment, as in a machine. **2.** *Psychol.* Inability to adjust personality needs to the demands of the environment. **3.** Imbalance in social and economic relations, as between city and country or supply and demand. **—mal′ad·just′ed** *adj.*
mal·ad·min·is·ter (măl′əd-mĭn′ĭ-stər) *tr.v.* **-tered, -ter·ing, -ters.** To administer or manage inefficiently or dishonestly. **—mal′ad·min′is·tra′tion** *n.*
mal·a·droit (măl′ə-droit′) *adj.* **1.** Characterized by a lack of dexterity; clumsy. **2.** Characterized by a lack of perception or judgment; tactless. [Fr. : *mal-*, mal- + *adroit,* adroit.] **—mal′a·droit′ly** *adv.*
mal·a·dy (măl′ə-dē) *n., pl.* **-dies. 1.** A disease, disorder, or ailment. **2.** An unwholesome condition: *the malady of national discontent.* [ME *maladie* < OFr. < *malade,* sick < Lat. *male habitus,* in poor condition.]
ma·la fi·de (mā′lə fī′dē) *adv. & adj.* In or with bad faith. [Lat.]
Mal·a·ga (măl′ə-gə) *n.* A sweet wine originally from Málaga, Spain.
Mal·a·gas·y (măl′ə-găs′ē) *n., pl.* **Malagasy** or **-gas·ies. 1.** A native of Madagascar. **2.** The Austronesian language of the Malagasy. **—Mal′a·gas′y** *adj.*
ma·la·gue·ña (mä′lə-gā′nyə) *n.* **1.** A dance native to Málaga, Spain, that is a variety of the fandango. **2.** A folk tune native to Málaga that is similar to the fandango. [Sp., fem. of *malagueño,* of Málaga, after *Málaga,* Spain.]
mal·aise (mă-lāz′, -lĕz′) *n.* A vague feeling of illness or depression. [Fr. < OFr. : *mal-*, mal- + *aise,* ease.]
mal·a·mute or **mal·e·mute** (măl′ə-myo͞ot′) *n.* Any of a powerful breed of dogs developed in Alaska as a sled dog, having a thick gray, black, or white coat. [*Malemute,* an Alaskan Eskimo people.]
mal·a·pert (măl′ə-pûrt′) *adj.* Saucy in speech or manner. *—n.* An impudent, saucy person. [ME < OFr. : *mal-*, mal- + *apert,* clever, alteration of Lat. *expertus.*] **—mal′a·pert′ly** *adv.* **—mal′a·pert′ness** *n.*
mal·ap·por·tioned (măl′ə-pôr′shənd, -pōr′-) *adj.* Characterized by an inappropriate or unfair proportional distribution of representatives to a legislative body. **—mal′ap·por′tion·ment** *n.*
mal·a·prop·ism (măl′ə-prŏp-ĭz′əm) *n.* A ludicrous misuse of a word. [After Mrs. *Malaprop,* a character in *The Rivals,* a play by Richard B. Sheridan (1751–1816).] **—mal′a·prop′i·an** (măl′ə-prŏp′ē-ən) *adj.*
mal·a·pro·pos (măl′ăp-rə-pō′) *adj.* Inappropriate; out of place. *—adv.* Inappropriately; inopportunely. [Fr. *mal à propos.*]
ma·lar (mā′lər, -lär′) *adj.* Of or pertaining to the cheekbone or the cheek. *—n.* The zygomatic bone in the cheek. [Lat. *malaris* < *mala,* cheekbone.]
ma·lar·i·a (mə-lâr′ē-ə) *n.* **1.** An infectious disease characterized by cycles of chills, fever, and sweating, transmitted by the bite of the infected female anopheles mosquito. **2.** *Archaic.* Bad or foul air; miasma. [Ital. *mal′aria* < *mala aria,* bad air.] **—ma·lar′i·al, ma·lar′i·an, ma·lar′i·ous** *adj.*
ma·lar·i·ol·o·gy (mə-lâr′ē-ŏl′ə-jē) *n.* The scientific study of malaria. **—ma·lar′i·ol′o·gist** *n.*
ma·lar·key also **ma·lar·ky** (mə-lär′kē) *n. Slang.* Exaggerated or foolish talk; nonsense. [Orig. unknown.]
mal·as·sim·i·la·tion (măl′ə-sĭm′ə-lā′shən) *n.* Incomplete assimilation of food.
mal·ate (măl′āt′, mā′lāt′) *n.* A salt or an ester of malic acid. [MAL(IC ACID) + -ATE[2]].
Mal·a·thi·on (măl′ə-thī′ŏn′). A trademark for the organic compound, $C_{10}H_{19}O_6PS_2$, used as an insecticide.
Ma·lay (mā′lā′, mə-lā′) *n.* **1.** One of a people inhabiting the Malay Peninsula, other parts of Malaysia, Indonesia, and some adjacent areas. **2.** The Austronesian language of the Malays. **3.** One of a breed of fowl with red and black plumage, domesticated in Asia. *—adj.* **1.** Of, pertaining to, or characteristic of the Malays or their language. **2.** Of or pertaining to Malaya or Malaysia. [Obs. Du. *Malayo* < Malay *Mĕlayu.*] **—Ma·lay′an** (mə-lā′ən) *adj. & n.*
Mal·a·ya·lam (măl′ə-yä′ləm) *n.* A Dravidian language of the Malabar coast in southwestern India.
Ma·lay·o-Pol·y·ne·sian (mə-lā′ō-pŏl′ə-nē′zhən, -shən) *n.* Austronesian. **—Ma·lay′o-Pol′y·ne′sian** *adj.*
mal·con·tent (măl′kən-tĕnt′) *adj.* Discontented with or in rebellion against existing conditions. *—n.* A discontented person. [OFr. : *mal-*, mal- + *content,* content.]
mal de mer (măl′də-mâr′) *n.* Seasickness. [Fr.]
mal·dis·tri·bu·tion (măl′dĭs-trə-byo͞o′shən) *n.* Faulty distribution or apportionment over an area or among a group.
male (māl) *adj.* **1.** Of, pertaining to, or designating the sex that has organs to produce spermatozoa for fertilizing ova. **2.** Of or characteristic of the male sex; masculine. **3.** Virile; manly. **4.** Composed of men or boys, or both: *a male choir.* **5.** *Bot.* **a.** Pertaining to or designating organs, such as stamens or anthers, that are capable of fertilizing female organs. **b.** Bearing stamens but not pistils; staminate: *male flowers.* **6.** Designating an object, such as an electric plug, designed for insertion into a fitted bore or socket. *—n.* **1.** An individual of the sex that begets young by fertilizing ova. **2.** A plant having only staminate flowers. [ME < OFr. < Lat. *masculus,* dim. of *mas,* male.] **—male′ness** *n.*
Synonyms: *male, masculine, manlike, manly, manful, virile, mannish.* The adjective *male* is confined to categorizing by sex, and applies to more than human beings. *Masculine,* when limited to human beings, pertains to qualities characteristic of males: *masculine charm. Manlike,* when applied to human beings, pertains to men as opposed to woman and children; said of other animals, it indicates resemblance to a human being. *Manly* pertains broadly to admirable qualities of men. *Manful* suggests braveness, resoluteness, or forcefulness. *Virile* stresses physical prowess or sexual potency. *Mannish* usually indicates affectation of masculine traits or style by women.
ma·le·ate (mā′lē-āt′, mə-lē′ət) *n.* A salt or ester of maleic acid. [MALE(IC ACID) + -ATE[2].]
Mal·e·cite (măl′ĭ-sīt′) also **Mal·i·seet** (-sēt′) *n., pl.* **Malecite** or **-cites** also **Maliseet** or **-seets. 1. a.** A tribe of Indians formerly inhabiting New Brunswick and northeastern Maine. **b.** A member of this tribe. **2.** The Algonquian language of the Malecites. [Prob. < Micmac *Maliisit.*]
mal·e·dict (măl′ĭ-dĭkt′) *adj.* Accursed. *—tr.v.* **-dict·ed, -dict·ing, -dicts.** To pronounce a curse against. [ME *maladicte* < Lat. *maledictus* < *maledicere,* to curse : *male,* ill (< *malus,* bad) + *dicere,* to speak.]
mal·e·dic·tion (măl′ĭ-dĭk′shən) *n.* **1.** A curse. **2.** Slander.
mal·e·fac·tor (măl′ə-făk′tər) *n.* **1.** One who has committed a crime; criminal. **2.** An evildoer. [ME *malefactour* < Lat. *malefactor* < *malefacere,* to do wrong : *male,* ill (< *malus,* bad) + *facere,* to do.] **—mal′e·fac′tion** (-făk′shən) *n.*
male fern *n.* A fern, *Dryopteris filix-mas,* that yields the drug used to treat tapeworm infestation.
ma·lef·ic (mə-lĕf′ĭk) *adj.* **1.** Having a malignant influence. **2.** Evil; malicious. [Lat. *maleficus* : *male,* ill (< *malus,* bad) + *facere,* to make.]
ma·lef·i·cence (mə-lĕf′ĭ-səns) *n.* **1.** Evil or harm; mischief. **2.** The quality or condition of being evil or malignant. [Lat. *maleficentia* < *maleficus,* malefic.] **—ma·lef′i·cent** *adj.*
ma·le·ic acid (mə-lē′ĭk) *n.* A colorless crystalline acid, $C_4H_4O_4$, used in the synthesis of resins and as an oil and fat preservative. [Fr. *acide maléique,* alteration of *acide malique,* malic acid.]
mal·e·mute (mă′lə-myo͞ot′) *n.* Variant of **malamute.**
mal·en·ten·du (măl′ŏn-tŏn-do͞o′) *n.* A misunderstanding. [Fr. < *mal entendu,* misunderstood.]
ma·lev·o·lence (mə-lĕv′ə-ləns) *n.* **1.** The quality or condition of being malevolent. **2.** Ill will; malice.
ma·lev·o·lent (mə-lĕv′ə-lənt) *adj.* **1.** Having or exhibiting ill will; malicious. **2.** Having an evil influence. [Lat. *malevolens, malevolent-,* malevolent : *male,* ill (< *malus,* bad) + *volens,* wishing (< *velle,* to wish).] **—ma·lev′o·lent·ly** *adv.*
mal·fea·sance (măl-fē′zəns) *n. Law.* Misconduct or wrongdoing, esp. by a public official. [MAL- + obs. *feasance,* doing < OFr. *faisance* < Med. Lat. *facientia* < Lat. *facere,* to do.] **—mal·fea′sant** *adj. & n.*
mal·for·ma·tion (măl′fôr-mā′shən) *n.* **1.** The condition of being malformed. **2.** An abnormal structure or form.
mal·formed (măl-fôrmd′) *adj.* Abnormally or imperfectly formed.
mal·func·tion (măl-fŭngk′shən) *intr.v.* **-tioned, -tion·ing, -tions. 1.** To fail to function. **2.** To function abnormally or imperfectly. *—n.* The act or an instance of malfunctioning.
mal·ic acid (măl′ĭk, mā′lĭk) *n.* A colorless, crystalline compound, $COOHCH_2CH(OH)COOH$, that occurs naturally in a wide variety of unripe fruit, including apples, cherries, and tomatoes, and is used as a flavoring and to aid in aging wine. [Fr. *acide malique* < Lat. *malum,* apple < Gk. *mēlon, malon.*]
mal·ice (măl′ĭs) *n.* **1.** A desire to harm others or to see others suffer. **2.** *Law.* The intent, without just cause or reason, to commit an unlawful act that will result in injury to another or others. [ME < OFr. < Lat. *malitia* < *malus,* bad.]
ma·li·cious (mə-lĭsh′əs) *adj.* Resulting from or having the nature of malice: *malicious gossip.* **—ma·li′cious·ly** *adv.* **—ma·li′cious·ness** *n.*
ma·lign (mə-līn′) *tr.v.* **-ligned, -lign·ing, -ligns.** To speak evil of. *—adj.* **1.** Evil in nature or intent. **2.** Evil in influence; baleful. [ME *malignen,* to attack < OFr. *malignier* < LLat. *malignari* < Lat. *malignus,* malign.] **—ma·lign′er** *n.* **—ma·lign′ly** *adv.*
Synonyms: *malign, defame, traduce, vilify, revile, vituperate, asperse, slander, calumniate, libel.* The verb *malign* applies in general to the expression of evil with malicious intent, and connotes falsehood or misrepresentation. *Defame* and *traduce* imply more open circulation of evil, maliciously motivated, and definite injury to character or reputation. *Vilify* pertains to open, deliberate, and forceful defaming or degrading. *Revile* and *vituperate* stress gross verbal abuse, which may be more spontaneous than calculated and may not involve falsehood. *Asperse* involves falsehood and calculated malicious intent, usually expressed orally but obliquely, as by innuendo. *Slander* and *calumniate* apply to malicious oral expression that is false and defamatory. *Libel* generally involves written or pictorial expression injurious to character or reputation.
ma·lig·nan·cy (mə-lĭg′nən-sē) also **ma·lig·nance** (-nəns) *n.,*

malamute

pl. **-nan·cies** also **-nanc·es. 1.** The state or quality of being malignant. **2.** A malignant tumor.
ma·lig·nant (mə-lĭg′nənt) *adj.* **1.** Showing great malevolence; evil. **2.** Highly injurious; pernicious. **3.** *Pathol.* **a.** Designating an abnormal growth that tends to metastasize. **b.** Threatening to life or health; virulent: *a malignant disease.* **—ma·lig′nant·ly** *adv.*
ma·lig·ni·ty (mə-lĭg′nĭ-tē) *n., pl.* **-ties. 1. a.** Intense ill will or hatred; great malice. **b.** An act or feeling of great malice. **2.** The condition or quality of being highly evil or injurious; deadliness.
ma·li·hi·ni (mä′lĭ-hē′nē) *n.* A newcomer, foreigner, or stranger among the people of Hawaii. [Hawaiian.]
ma·lines (mə-lēn′) *n.* **1.** Also **ma·line** (mə-lēn′). A thin, stiff veiling woven in a hexagonal pattern. **2.** Mechlin. [Fr. < *Malines,* Mechlin, Belgium.]
ma·lin·ger (mə-lĭng′gər) *intr.v.* **-gered, -ger·ing, -gers.** To pretend to be ill or injured in order to avoid duty or work. [< Fr. *malingre,* sickly.] **—ma·lin′ger·er** *n.*
Ma·lin·ke (mə-lĭng′kē) *n., pl.* **Malinke** or **-kes. 1. a.** A people of western Africa related to the Mandingos. **b.** A member of this people. **2.** The language of the Malinke.
Mal·i·seet (măl′ə-sēt′) *n.* Variant of **Malecite.**
mal·i·son (măl′ĭ-sən, -zən) *n.* A curse. [ME < OFr. *maleicon* < Lat. *maledictio* < *maledicere,* to speak ill. —see MALEDICT.]
mall[1] (môl, măl) *n.* **1.** A shady public walk or promenade. **2. a.** A street lined with shops and closed to vehicles. **b.** A shopping center. **c.** A large building or complex of buildings containing various shops, businesses, and restaurants usually accessible by common passageways. **3.** A median strip dividing a road or highway. [After *The Mall,* London, England, orig. a pall-mall alley.]

mallard

mall[2] (môl) *n. & v.* Variant of **maul.**
mal·lard (măl′ərd) *n., pl.* **mallard** or **-lards.** A wild duck, *Anas platyrhynchos,* of which the male has a green head and neck. [ME < OFr. *malarde,* poss. of Germanic orig.]
mal·le·a·ble (măl′ē-ə-bəl) *adj.* **1.** Capable of being shaped or formed, as by hammering or pressure: *a malleable metal.* **2.** Capable of being altered or influenced; tractable: *the malleable mind of the pragmatist.* [ME < OFr. < Med. Lat. *malleabilis* < *malleare,* to hammer < Lat. *malleus,* hammer.] **—mal′le·a·bil′i·ty, mal′le·a·ble·ness** *n.* **—mal′le·a·bly** *adv.*
mal·lee (măl′ē) *n.* **1.** Any of several low, scrubby, evergreen trees of the genus *Eucalyptus,* of western Australia. **2.** A thicket or growth of mallee. [Native word in Australia.]
mal·le·muck (măl′ə-mŭk′) *n.* Any of several sea birds, such as the fulmar, the albatross, or the shearwater. [Du. *mallemok,* fulmar : *mal,* silly + *mok,* gull.]
mal·let (măl′ĭt) *n.* **1. a.** A short-handled hammer, usually with a cylindrical head of wood, used chiefly to drive a chisel or wedge. **b.** A tool with a large head that is used to strike a surface without damaging it. **2.** *Sports.* A long-handled implement used to strike the ball, as in croquet and polo. **3.** A light hammer with a rounded head for striking a percussion instrument. [ME < OFr. *maillet,* dim. of *mail,* maul. —see MAUL.]
mal·le·us (măl′ē-əs) *n., pl.* **mal·le·i** (măl′ē-ī′). *Anat.* The largest of three small bones in the middle ear. [NLat. < Lat., hammer.]
mal·low (măl′ō) *n.* **1.** Any plant of the widely distributed genus *Malva,* characteristically having pink or white flowers. **2.** Any of various related plants, such as the rose mallow. [ME *malow* < OFr. *malve* < Lat. *malva.*]
malm (mäm) *n.* **1. a.** A soft, easily crumbled limestone. **b.** Loam formed by the disintegration of soft limestone. **2.** A mixture of clay and chalk used in making bricks. [ME, chalky soil < OE *mealm.*]

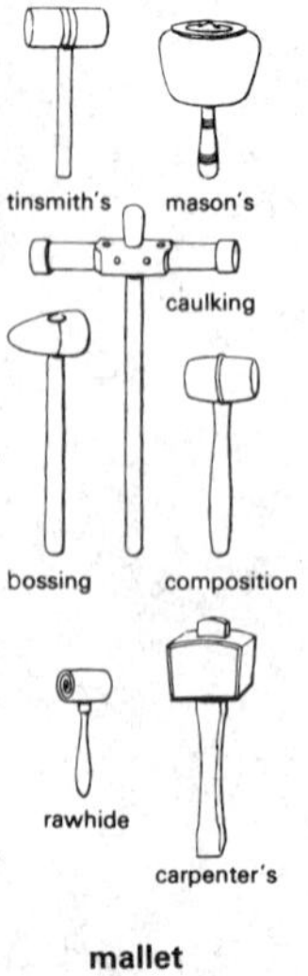

mallet

malm·sey (mäm′zē) *n., pl.* **-seys.** A sweet fortified white wine originally made in Greece. [ME < Med. Lat. *malmasia* < *Monembasia,* Monemvasia, Greece.]
mal·nour·ished (măl-nûr′ĭsht) *adj.* Suffering from improper nutrition or insufficient food.
mal·nu·tri·tion (măl′no͞o-trĭsh′ən, -nyo͞o-) *n.* Poor nutrition because of insufficient or poorly balanced diet or because of defective digestion or defective utilization of foods.
mal·oc·clu·sion (măl′ə-klo͞o′zhən) *n.* Faulty closure of teeth.
mal·o·dor·ous (măl-ō′dər-əs) *adj.* Having a bad odor; ill-smelling. **—mal·o′dor** *n.* **—mal·o′dor·ous·ly** *adv.* **—mal·o′dor·ous·ness** *n.*
ma·lo·nic acid (mə-lō′nĭk, -lŏn′ik) *n.* A colorless crystalline acid, $C_3H_4O_4$, derived from malic acid and used in making barbiturates. [Fr. *acide malonique,* alteration of *acide malique,* malic acid.]
Mal·pigh·i·an corpuscle (măl-pĭg′ē-ən) *n. Anat.* **1.** Also **Malpighian body.** A mass of arterial capillaries enveloped in a capsule and attached to a tubule in the kidney. **2.** A lymph nodule surrounding the smaller arteries in the spleen. [After Marcello *Malpighi* (1628–1694).]
Malpighian layer *n. Anat.* The deepest layer of the epidermis, from which the outer layers develop. [After Marcello *Malpighi* (1628–1694).]
Malpighian tube *n.* One of the excretory tubes leading from the digestive tract in insects. [After Marcello *Malpighi* (1628–1694).]
mal·po·si·tion (măl′pə-zĭsh′ən) *n.* An abnormal position, esp. of a fetus.
mal·prac·tice (măl-prăk′tĭs) *n.* **1.** Improper or negligent treatment of a patient by a physician, resulting in damage or injury. **2.** Improper or unethical conduct by the holder of an official or professional position. **3.** An act or instance of improper practice. **—mal′prac·ti′tion·er** (-tĭsh′ə-nər) *n.*
malt (môlt) *n.* **1.** Grain, usually barley, that has been allowed to sprout, used chiefly in brewing and distilling. **2.** An alcoholic beverage brewed from malt. **3.** Malted milk (sense 2). *—v.* **malt·ed, malt·ing, malts.** *—tr.* **1.** To process (grain) into malt. **2.** To treat or to mix with malt or a malt extract. *—intr.* To become malt. [ME < OE *mealt.*]
Mal·ta fever (môl′tə) *n.* Undulant fever.
mal·tase (môl′tās′, -tāz′) *n.* An enzyme that hydrolyzes maltose to glucose.
malt·ed milk (môl′tĭd) *n.* **1.** A soluble powder made of dried milk, malted barley, and wheat flour. **2.** Also **malt** or **malted.** A beverage made by mixing milk with malted milk powder and adding ice cream and flavoring.
Mal·tese (môl-tēz′, -tēs′) *adj.* **1.** Of or pertaining to Malta, its inhabitants, or the language spoken in Malta. **2.** Of or pertaining to the Knights of Malta. *—n., pl.* **Maltese. 1.** A native or inhabitant of Malta. **2.** The Semitic language of the Maltese. **3.** A small dog of an ancient breed, having long, silky white hair. **4.** A Maltese cat.
Maltese cat *n.* A domestic cat with short, silky, bluish-gray hair.
Maltese cross *n.* A cross having the form of four arrowheads placed with their points toward the center of a circle.
mal·tha (măl′thə) *n.* A black, viscous natural bitumen. [Lat. < Gk., a mixture of wax and pitch.]
Mal·thu·sian (măl-tho͞o′zhən, môl-) *adj.* Of or pertaining to the theory of Thomas Malthus that population tends to increase faster than food supply, with inevitably disastrous results unless the increase in population can be checked. **—Mal·thu′sian** *n.* **—Mal·thu′sian·ism** *n.*
malt liquor *n.* Fermented beer or ale made with malt.
mal·tose (môl′tōs′, -tōz′) *n.* A sugar, $C_{12}H_{22}O_{11}{\cdot}H_2O$. [Fr. < E. MALT.]
mal·treat (măl-trēt′) *tr.v.* **-treat·ed, -treat·ing, -treats.** To treat cruelly or roughly. [Fr. *maltraiter* : *mal-,* mal- + *traiter,* to treat.] **—mal·treat′ment** *n.*
malt sugar *n.* Maltose
mal·va·si·a (măl′və-zē′ə) *n.* **1.** A grape from which malmsey wine is made. **2.** Malmsey wine. [Ital., after *Monemvasia,* Greece.]
mal·ver·sa·tion (măl′vər-sā′shən) *n.* Misconduct in public office. [OFr. < *malverser,* to misbehave < Lat. *male versari.*]
mal·voi·sie (măl′vwə-zē′) *n.* Malmsey wine. [ME *malvesie* < OFr., after *Monemvasia,* Greece.]
ma·ma also **mam·ma** (mä′mə) *n.* **1.** (*also* mə-mä′). Mother. **2.** *Slang.* **a.** A woman. **b.** A wife. [Of baby-talk orig.]
mam·ba (mäm′bə) *n.* Any of several venomous snakes of the genus *Dendraspis,* found in tropical Africa, esp. *D. angusticeps,* a green or black tree snake. [Zulu *í-mâmbà.*]
mam·bo (mäm′bō) *n., pl.* **-bos. 1.** A dance of Latin-American origin, resembling the rumba. **2.** The syncopated music for the mambo, in 4/4 time. *—intr.v.* **-boed, -bo·ing, -bos.** To dance the mambo. [Sp. (Cuba) < *mamboo,* percussion instrument.]
Mam·e·luke (măm′ə-lo͝ok′) *n.* A member of a former military caste, originally composed of slaves from Turkey, that held the Egyptian throne from about 1250 until 1517 and remained powerful until 1811. [Ar. *mamlūk,* Mameluke, slave.]
mam·ma[1] (mä′mə) *n.* Variant of **mama.**
mam·ma[2] (măm′ə) *n., pl.* **mam·mae** (măm′ē). An organ of female mammals that contains milk-producing glands. [Lat.] **—mam′mate′** *adj.*
mam·mal (măm′əl) *n.* A member of the class Mammalia. [< LLat. *mammalis,* of the breast < Lat. *mamma,* breast.] **—mam·ma′li·an** (mă-mā′lē-ən) *adj. & n.*
Mam·ma·li·a (mə-mā′lē-ə) *pl.n.* A class of vertebrate animals of more than 15,000 species, including humans, distinguished by self-regulating body temperature, hair, and, in the females, milk-producing mammae. [NLat. < LLat. *mammalis,* of the breast < *mamma,* breast.]
mam·mal·o·gy (mə-măl′ə-jē, -mŏl′-) *n.* The branch of zoology dealing with the study of Mammalia. [MAMMA(L) + -LOGY.] **—mam′ma·log′i·cal** (măm′ə-lŏj′ĭ-kəl) *adj.* **—mam·mal′o·gist** *n.*
mam·ma·plas·ty (măm′ə-plăs′tē) *n., pl.* **-ties.** Plastic surgery of the breast.
mam·ma·ry (măm′ə-rē) *adj.* Of or pertaining to a breast or mamma.
mammary gland *n.* A milk-producing organ in female mammals, consisting of clusters of alveoli or small cavities with ducts terminating in a nipple or teat.
mam·mif·er·ous (mə-mĭf′ər-əs) *adj.* Having mammary glands. [Fr. *mammifère* : Lat. *mamma,* breast + *-fère,* -fer.]
mam·mil·la (mə-mĭl′ə) *n., pl.* **-mil·lae** (-mĭl′ē). **1.** A nipple; teat. **2.** A nipple-shaped protuberance. [Lat., dim of *mamma,* breast.] **—mam′mil·lar′y** (măm′ə-lĕr′ē) *adj.*
mam·mil·late (măm′ə-lāt′) also **mam·mil·lat·ed** (-lā′tĭd)

ă pat / ā pay / âr care / ä father / b bib / ch church / d deed / ĕ pet / ē be / f fife / g gag / h hat / hw which / ĭ pit / ī pie / îr pier / j judge / k kick / l lid, needle / m mum / n no, sudden / ng thing / ŏ pot / ō toe / ô paw, for / oi noise / ou out / o͝o took / o͞o boot /

adj. **1.** Having nipples or mammillae. **2.** Shaped like a nipple or mammilla. **—mam'mil·la'tion** *n.*

mam·mo·gram (măm'ə-grăm') *n.* An x-ray photograph or radiograph of the breast. [MAMM(A)² + -O- + -GRAM.]

mam·mog·ra·phy (mə-mŏg'rə-fē) *n.* Examination of the breast by x-rays in order to detect tumors before they can be felt by hand. [MAMM(A)² + -O- + -GRAPHY.]

Mam·mon (măm'ən) *n.* **1.** In the New Testament, riches, avarice, and worldly gain personified as a false god. **2.** Often **mammon.** Riches regarded as an object of worship or an evil influence. [ME < LLat. *mammon* < Gk. *mamōnas* < Aram. *māmōnā,* riches.]

mam·moth (măm'əth) *n.* **1.** An extinct elephant of the genus *Mammuthus,* once found throughout the Northern Hemisphere. **2.** Something of great size. *—adj.* Of enormous size; gigantic. [Obs. R. *mammot'.*]

mam·my (măm'ē) *n., pl.* **-mies. 1.** Mother. **2.** *Offensive.* A black nurse for white children, esp. formerly in the Southern United States. [Var. of MAMA.]

man (măn) *n., pl.* **men** (mĕn). **1.** An adult male human being. **2.** A human being, regardless of sex or age. **3.** The human race; mankind: *the accomplishments of man.* **4.** *Zool.* A member of the genus *Homo,* family Hominidae, order Primates, class Mammalia, characterized by erect posture and an opposable thumb, esp. a member of the only extant species, *Homo sapiens,* distinguished by the ability to communicate by means of organized speech and to record information in a variety of symbolic systems. **5.** A male human being endowed with qualities such as courage, strength, and fortitude, considered characteristic of manhood. **6.** *Theol.* In Christianity and Judaism, a being composed of a body and a soul or spirit. **7.** *Informal.* **a.** A husband. **b.** A lover or sweetheart. **8. men. a.** Workers as opposed to management. **b.** Enlisted servicemen of the armed forces: *officers and men.* **9.** A male servant or subordinate. **10.** *Informal.* Fellow. Used as a term of address. **11.** One who swore allegiance to a lord in the Middle Ages; vassal. **12.** *Games.* Any of the pieces used in a board game, such as chess or checkers. **13.** *Naut.* A ship: *merchantman; man-of-war.* **14. the Man.** *Slang.* A policeman. *—tr.v.* **manned, man·ning, mans. 1.** To supply or furnish with men for defense, support, or service: *manning a ship.* **2.** To be stationed at in order to defend, care for, or operate: *man the guns.* *—interj.* Used as an expletive to indicate intense feeling: *Man! It's hot in here.* **—idioms. one's own man.** Independent in judgment and action. **to a man.** With no exception: *They objected, to a man.* [ME < OE.]

Usage: The use of *man* to mean "a human being, regardless of sex" has a long history, but is now much less generally accepted. For many people, its general use in the primary sense of "adult male human being" has made it no longer broad enough to serve as the superordinate term: *The men who settled America's frontier were a sturdy race. Twentieth-century man has made great strides in improving health care. The man of the future will eat his meals in tablet form.* Many people feel that in such cases the sense of "male" is predominant over that of "person." Other means of expressing the idea while avoiding this possible confusion are: *men and women, humans, human beings. Man* in the sense of "mankind" is also sometimes felt to be too exclusive a term. Its use in phrases such as *the evolution of man* can be avoided with similar substitutions: *the evolution of humans.* Many occupational titles in which *man* occurs as an element are being replaced, sometimes officially, by terms which are considered neutral. For example, *firefighter* is used instead of *fireman,* or *Members of Congress* instead of *Congressmen.*

ma·na (mä'nə) *n.* **1.** An impersonal supernatural force believed to be inherent in a person, god, or sacred object. **2.** Power; authority. [Maori.]

man about town *n., pl.* **men about town.** A worldly and socially knowledgeable man who frequents fashionable places.

man·a·cle (măn'ə-kəl) *n.* **1.** A device for confining the hands, usually consisting of two metal rings that are fastened about the wrists and joined by a metal chain; handcuff. **2.** Something that confines or restrains. *—tr.v.* **-cled, -cling, -cles.** To confine or restrain with or as if with manacles; fetter. [ME < OFr. *manicle* < Lat. *manicula,* little hand, dim. of *manus,* hand.]

man·age (măn'ĭj) *v.* **-aged, -ag·ing, -ag·es.** *—tr.* **1.** To direct or control the use of. **2. a.** To exert control over. **b.** To make submissive to one's authority, discipline, or persuasion. **3.** To direct or administer (a business, for example). **4.** To contrive or arrange: *managed to wangle a promotion.* *—intr.* **1.** To direct, supervise, or carry on business or other affairs. **2.** To carry on; get along: *I don't know how they manage without him.* [Ital. *maneggiare* < VLat. **manidiare* < Lat. *manus,* hand.]

man·age·a·ble *adj.* Capable of being managed or controlled. **—man'age·a·bil'i·ty, man'age·a·ble·ness** *n.* **—man'age·a·bly** *adv.*

managed currency *n.* A monetary system in which the money supply and its buying power are regulated by a governmental agency or central bank, rather than automatically regulated by the gold standard.

man·age·ment (măn'ĭj-mənt) *n.* **1.** The act, manner, or practice of managing, supervising, or controlling. **2.** The person or persons who manage a business establishment, organization, or institution. **3.** Skill in managing; executive ability.

man·ag·er (măn'ĭ-jər) *n.* **1.** A person who manages a business or enterprise. **2.** A person who is in charge of the business affairs of an entertainer. **3. a.** A person in charge of the training and performance of an athlete or team. **b.** A student in charge of the equipment and records of a school or college team. **—man'ag·er·ship'** *n.*

man·a·ge·ri·al (măn'ĭ-jîr'ē-əl) *adj.* Of, pertaining to, or characteristic of a manager or management. **—man'a·ge'ri·al·ly** *adv.*

managing editor *n.* An executive who supervises editorial work.

man·a·kin (măn'ə-kĭn) *n.* **1.** Any of various small, colorful birds of the family Pipridae, found in forests of Central and South America. **2.** Variant of **manikin.** [Alteration of MANIKIN.]

ma·ña·na (mä-nyä'nə) *adv.* **1.** Tomorrow. **2.** At an unspecified future time. *—n.* An indefinite time in the future. [Sp. < *(cras) mañana,* early (tomorrow).]

Ma·nas·seh (mə-năs'ə) *n.* **1.** In the Old Testament, the elder son of Joseph. **2.** A tribe of Israel descended from Manasseh, son of Joseph. [Heb. *Mĕnashsheh.*]

man-at-arms (măn'ət-ärmz') *n., pl.* **men-at-arms.** A soldier, esp. a medieval cavalryman supplied with heavy arms.

man·a·tee (măn'ə-tē') *n.* An aquatic mammal of the genus *Trichechus,* found in Atlantic coastal waters of the tropical Americas and Africa. [Sp. *manatí* < Carib, breast.]

Man·ches·ter terrier (măn'chĕs'tər, -chĭ-stər) *n.* A short-haired, black-and-tan dog of a breed that originated in Manchester, England.

man·chi·neel (măn'chĭ-nēl') *n.* A tropical American tree, *Hippomane Mancinella,* having a poisonous fruit and a poisonous milky sap that causes skin blisters on contact. [Fr. *mancenille* < Sp. *manzanilla,* dim. of *manzana,* apple.]

Man·chu (măn'cho͞o, măn-cho͞o') *n., pl.* **Manchu** or **-chus. 1.** One of a nomadic Mongoloid people, native to Manchuria, who conquered China in 1644 and established a dynasty that was overthrown by revolution in 1911. **2.** The Tungusic language of the Manchu. [Manchu.] **—Man'chu** *adj.*

-mancy *suff.* Divination: *bibliomancy.* [ME < OFr. *-mancie* < LLat. *-mantia* < Gk. *manteia* < *manteuesthai,* to prophesy < *mantis,* prophet.]

Man·dae·an (măn-dē'ən) *n.* Variant of **Mandean.**

man·da·la (mŭn'də-lə) *n.* In Oriental art and religion, any of various designs symbolic of the universe. [Skt. *maṇḍalam,* circle, prob. < Tamil *muṭalai.*] **—man'dal·ic** *adj.*

mandala

man·da·mus (măn-dā'məs) *n. Law.* A writ issued by a superior court ordering a public official or body or a lower court to perform a specified duty. *—tr.v.* **-mused, -mus·ing, -mus·es.** To serve with a mandamus. [Lat., we order < *mandare,* to order.]

Man·dan (măn'dăn') *n., pl.* **Mandan** or **-dans. 1. a.** A tribe of Indians that inhabited the Missouri River Valley in North Dakota. **b.** A member of this tribe. **2.** The Siouan language of the Mandan.

man·da·rin (măn'də-rĭn) *n.* **1.** In imperial China, a member of any of the nine ranks of high public officials. **2. a.** A civil servant; bureaucrat. **b.** A person having influence or high status, esp. in intellectual or political circles. **3. Mandarin.** The standard vernacular language of China, which is based on the principal dialect spoken in and around Beijing. *—adj.* **1.** Of or like a mandarin. **2.** Marked by elaborate and refined language or literary style. [Port. < Malay *mĕntĕri* < Skt. *mantrī,* counselor < *mantraḥ* counsel.]

mandarin collar *n.* A narrow upright collar usually divided in front.

mandarin duck *n.* A waterfowl, *Aix galericulata,* of Asia, having brightly colored plumage and a crested head.

mandarin orange *n.* **1.** A small Chinese orange tree, *Citrus reticulata,* of the rue family. **2.** The small, loose-skinned fruit of the mandarin orange. [Fr. *mandarine* < Sp. *mandarina* < *mandarin,* mandarin < Port. (from the color of a mandarin's robe). —see MANDARIN.]

man·da·tar·y (măn'də-tĕr'ē) *n., pl.* **-ies.** One that receives a mandate.

man·date (măn'dāt') *n.* **1.** An authoritative command or instruction. **2.** The wishes of a political electorate, expressed by election results to its representatives in government. **3. a.** A commission from the League of Nations authorizing a nation to administer a territory. **b.** A region under such administration. **4.** *Law.* **a.** An order issued by a superior court of law to a lower court. **b.** A contract by which an individual agrees to perform services for another without payment. *—tr.v.* **-dat·ed, -dat·ing, -dates. 1.** To assign (a territory, for example) to a specified nation under a mandate. **2.** To make mandatory; require: *mandated desegregation in the schools.* [Lat. *mandatum* < *mandare,* to order.] **—man'da'tor** *n.*

man·da·to·ry (măn'də-tôr'ē, -tōr'ē) *adj.* **1.** Of, pertaining to, having the nature of, or containing a mandate. **2.** Required by or as if by mandate; obligatory. **3.** Holding a mandate over a region.

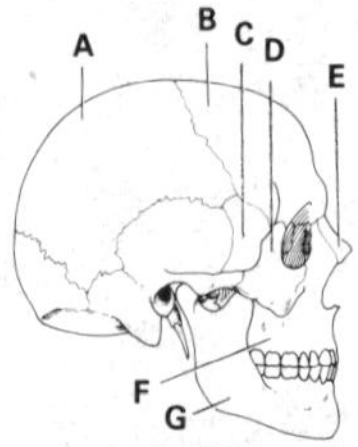

mandible
A. Parietal
B. Frontal
C. Sphenoid
D. Zygomatic
E. Nasal
F. Maxilla
G. Mandible

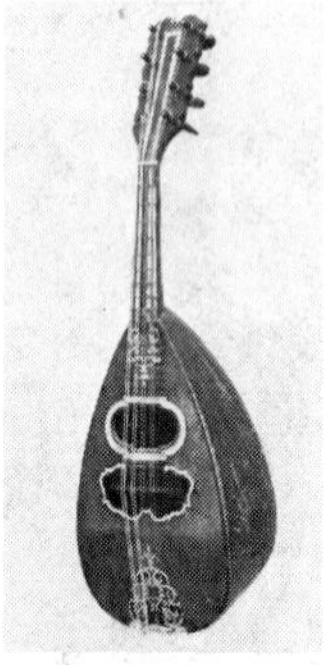

mandolin
18th-century Italian

mandrake

mane

man-day (măn′dā′) *n.* An industrial unit of production equal to the work a person can produce in one day.

Man·de (män′dā′) *n., pl.* **Mande** or **-des. 1.** A people of West Africa in the upper Niger valley. **2.** A branch of the Niger-Congo language family. [Mandingo.]

Man·de·an also **Man·dae·an** (măn-dē′ən) *n.* **1.** A member of an ancient Gnostic sect of Mesopotamia. **2.** A form of Aramaic used by the Mandeans. [Mandean *mandaya,* having knowledge < *manda,* knowledge.] **—Man·de′an** *adj.*

man·di·ble (măn′də-bəl) *n.* A jaw, esp.: **a.** The lower jaw in vertebrates. **b.** Either the upper or lower part of the beak in birds. **c.** Any of various mouth parts in insects. [OFr. < LLat. *mandibula* < *mandere,* to chew.] **—man·dib′u·lar** (măn-dĭb′yə-lər) *adj.*

man·dib·u·late (măn-dĭb′yə-lĭt, -lāt′) *n.* An animal having mandibles. **—man·dib′u·late′** *adj.*

Man·din·go (măn-dĭng′gō) *n., pl.* **-gos** or **-goes. 1.** A member of any of various Negroid peoples inhabiting the region of the upper Niger River valley of western Africa. **2.** Any of the languages of the Mandingos. [Mandingo.]

man·do·lin (măn′də-lĭn′, măn′də-lĭn′) *n.* A musical instrument with a usually pear-shaped body and a fretted neck over which several pairs of strings are stretched. [Fr. *mandoline* < Ital. *mandolino,* dim. of *mandola,* lute < Fr. *mandore* < LLat. *pandura,* three-string lute < Gk. *pandoura.*] **—man′do·lin′ist** *n.*

man·drag·o·ra (măn-drăg′ə-rə) *n.* The mandrake. [ME < Lat. *mandragoras* < Gk.]

man·drake (măn′drāk′) *n.* **1. a.** A Eurasian plant, *Mandragora officinarum,* having purplish flowers and a branched root thought to resemble the human body. **b.** The root of the mandrake, from which a narcotic was formerly prepared. **2.** The May apple (sense 1). [ME < MDu. *mandrage* and OE *mandragora,* both < Lat. *mandragoras* < Gk.]

man·drel or **man·dril** (măn′drəl) *n.* **1.** A spindle or axle used to secure or support material being machined or milled. **2.** A metal core around which wood and other materials may be cast and shaped. **3.** A shaft on which a working tool is mounted, as in dental drills. [Prob. alteration of Fr. *mandrin,* lathe.]

man·drill (măn′drəl) *n.* A large, fierce baboon, *Mandrillus sphinx,* of western Africa, having a beard, a crest, and a mane, tawny-greenish body hair with yellowish hair on the lower part, and brilliant blue, purple, and scarlet facial markings in the adult male. [MAN + DRILL[4].]

mane (mān) *n.* **1. a.** The long hair along the top and sides of the neck of such mammals as the horse and the male lion. **b.** The feathers on the back of the neck and head of some pigeons. **2.** A long, thick growth of human hair. [ME < OE *manu.*]

man-eat·er (măn′ē′tər) *n.* **1.** An animal that eats human flesh. **2.** A cannibal.

ma·nège also **ma·nege** (mă-nĕzh′) *n.* **1.** The art and practice of training a horse in the stylized and difficult exercises of classical riding. **2.** A riding academy. [Fr. < Ital. *maneggio* < *maneggiare,* to manage. —see MANAGE.]

ma·nes or **Ma·nes** (mā′nēz′, mä′nās′) *pl.n.* In ancient Rome: **a.** The spirits of the dead, esp. ancestors, deified as minor gods. **b.** A revered spirit of one who has died. [Lat. < *manus,* good.]

ma·neu·ver (mə-nōō′vər, -nyōō′-) *n.* **1. a.** A strategic or tactical military movement. **b.** Often **maneuvers.** A large-scale military training exercise simulating combat. **2. a.** A physical movement or way of doing something requiring skill and dexterity. **b.** A controlled change in flight path of an aircraft, rocket, or space vehicle. **3.** A calculated and skillful movement, act, or stratagem: *devious political maneuvers.* —*v.* **-vered, -ver·ing, -vers.** —*intr.* **1.** To perform or carry out a military maneuver. **2.** To make a change or a series of changes in position for some desired end. **3.** To shift ground or location; change tactics: *His opposition had no room in which to maneuver.* **4.** To attempt to bring about something by planning or scheming. —*tr.* **1.** To alter the tactical placement of (troops or warships). **2.** To manipulate into a desired position or toward a predetermined goal. [Fr. *manoeuvre* < OFr. *maneuvre,* manual work < Med. Lat. *manuopera* < Lat. *manu operari,* to work by hand.] **—ma·neu′ver·a·bil′i·ty** *n.* **—ma·neu′ver·a·ble** *adj.* **—ma·neu′ver·er** *n.*

man Friday *n.* A devoted male servant, aide, or employee. [After *Man Friday,* a character in *Robinson Crusoe,* a novel by Daniel Defoe (1660–1731).]

man·ful (măn′fəl) *adj.* **1.** Having or displaying qualities thought to befit a man; manly. **2.** Of, relating to, or suitable for men. **—man′ful·ly** *adv.* **—man′ful·ness** *n.*

man·ga·bey (măng′gə-bā′, -bē′) *n.* A monkey of the genus *Cercocebus,* of equatorial Africa, having a long tail and a relatively long muzzle. [After *Mangaby,* a region of Madagascar.]

mangan– *pref.* Variant of **mangano-.**

man·ga·nate (măng′gə-nāt′) *n.* A salt containing manganese in its anion, esp. a salt containing the MnO_4 radical.

man·ga·nese (măng′gə-nēz′, -nēs′) *n. Symbol* **Mn** A gray-white or silvery brittle metallic element, occurring in several allotropic forms, found worldwide, esp. in the ore pyrolusite, and alloyed with steel to increase strength, hardness, wear resistance, and other properties and with other metals to form highly ferromagnetic materials. Atomic number 25; atomic weight 54.9380; melting point 1,244°C; boiling point 2,097°C; specific gravity 7.21 to 7.44; valences 1, 2, 3, 4, 6, 7. [Fr. *manganèse* < Ital. *manganese* < Med. Lat. *magnesia.* —see MAGNESIA.] **—man′ga·ne′sian** *adj.*

manganese dioxide *n.* A black crystalline compound, MnO_2, used as a depolarizer of dry-cell batteries and in textile dyeing.

manganese spar *n.* **1.** Rhodonite. **2.** Rhodochrosite.

man·gan·ic (măn-găn′ĭk, măng-) *adj.* Pertaining to trivalent manganese or a compound containing trivalent manganese.

man·ga·nite (măng′gə-nīt′) *n.* A steel-gray to black mineral form of manganese oxide, $Mn_2O_3{\cdot}H_2O$, found in North America and Europe. It is an important ore of manganese.

mangano– or **mangan–** *pref.* Manganese: *manganite.* [< G. *Mangan* < Fr. *manganèse.*]

man·ga·nous (măng′gə-nəs) *adj.* Pertaining to bivalent manganese or to a compound containing bivalent manganese.

mange (mānj) *n.* A contagious skin disease of many mammals, occasionally including humans, caused by parasitic mites and characterized by itching and loss of hair. [ME *manjeue* < OFr. *manjue* < *mangier,* to eat. —see MANGER.]

man·gel-wur·zel (măng′gəl-wûr′zəl) *n.* A variety of the common beet having a large yellowish root, used chiefly as cattle feed. [G. *Mangoldwurzel* : *Mangold,* beet + *Wurzel,* root.]

man·ger (mān′jər) *n.* A trough in which feed for livestock is placed. [ME < OFr. *mangeoire* < *mangier,* to eat < Lat. *manducare* < *manduco,* glutton < *mandere,* to chew.]

man·gle¹ (măng′gəl) *tr.v.* **-gled, -gling, -gles. 1.** To mutilate or disfigure by battering, hacking, cutting, or tearing. **2.** To ruin or spoil through ineptitude or ignorance: *mangle a speech.* [ME *manglen* < AN *mangler.*] **—man′gler** *n.*

man·gle² (măng′gəl) *n.* **1.** A laundry machine for pressing fabrics. **2.** *Chiefly Brit.* A clothes wringer. —*tr.v.* **-gled, -gling, -gles.** To smooth or press with a mangle. [Du. < G. < MHG, dim. of *mange,* mangonel < LLat. *manganum,* catapult. —see MANGONEL.]

man·go (măng′gō) *n., pl.* **-goes** or **-gos. 1. a.** A tropical evergreen tree, *Mangifera indica,* native to Asia, cultivated for its edible fruit. **b.** The ovoid fruit of this tree, having a smooth rind and sweet, juicy, yellow-orange flesh. **2.** Any of various types of pickle, esp. a pickled stuffed sweet pepper. [Port. *manga,* fruit of the mango tree < Malay *mangā* < Tamil *mānkāy* : *mān,* mango tree + *kāy,* fruit.]

man·go·nel (măng′gə-nĕl′) *n.* A military machine used during the Middle Ages for hurling stones and other missiles. [ME < OFr. < Med. Lat. *mangonellus,* dim. of LLat. *manganum,* catapult < Gk. *manganon,* war machine.]

man·go·steen (măng′gə-stēn′) *n.* **1.** A tropical tree, *Garcinia Mangostana,* having thick, leathery leaves and edible fruit. **2.** The fruit of the mangosteen tree, having a hard rind and segmented, sweet, juicy pulp. [Malay *mangustan.*]

man·grove (măn′grōv′, măng′-) *n.* **1.** Any of various tropical evergreen trees or shrubs of the genus *Rhizophora,* having stiltlike roots and stems and forming dense thickets along tidal shores. **2.** Any of various shrubs or trees similar to the mangrove, esp. one of the genus *Avicennia.* [Prob. Port. *mangue,* mangrove (< Taino *mangle*) + GROVE.]

mang·y (mān′jē) *adj.* **-i·er, -i·est. 1.** Affected with or caused by mange. **2.** Having many bare spots; shabby: *a mangy old coat.* **—mang′i·ly** *adv.* **—mang′i·ness** *n.*

man·han·dle (măn′hăn′dəl) *tr.v.* **-dled, -dling, -dles. 1.** To handle roughly. **2.** To move by human strength, without machinery.

Man·hat·tan (măn-hăt′n, mən-) *n.* A cocktail made from vermouth and whiskey. [After *Manhattan,* a borough of New York City.]

man·hole (măn′hōl′) *n.* A hole through which a man may enter a sewer, boiler, pipe, conduit, or drain.

man·hood (măn′hŏŏd′) *n.* **1.** The state or condition of being an adult male: *Boys grow to manhood.* **2.** The composite of qualities, such as courage, determination, and vigor, often attributed to an adult male. **3.** Men collectively. **4.** The state or condition of being part of or endowed with humanity.

man-hour (măn′our′) *n.* An industrial unit of production equal to the work a person can produce in one hour.

man·hunt (măn′hŭnt′) *n.* An organized and extensive search for a person, usually a fugitive criminal.

ma·ni·a (mā′nē-ə, mān′yə) *n.* **1.** An inordinately intense desire or enthusiasm for something; craze. **2.** A manifestation of manic-depressive psychosis, characterized by profuse and rapidly changing ideas, exaggerated gaiety, and physical overactivity. **3.** Violent abnormal behavior. [ME, madness < LLat. < Gk.] **—man′ic** (măn′ĭk) *adj.*

–mania *suff.* An exaggerated or unreasonable desire or enthusiasm for: *balletomania.* [< MANIA.]

ma·ni·ac (mā′nē-ăk′) *n.* **1.** An insane person. **2.** A person who has an excessive enthusiasm or desire for something: *a bridge maniac.* —*adj.* Variant of **maniacal.** [< LLat. *maniacus,* maniacal < Gk. *maniakos* < *mania,* madness.]

ma·ni·a·cal (mə-nī′ə-kəl) also **ma·ni·ac** (mā′nē-ăk′) *adj.* **1.** Insane: *a maniacal killer.* **2.** Characterized by excessive enthusiasm: *a maniacal fondness for gambling.* **—ma·ni′a·cal·ly** *adv.*

man·ic-de·pres·sive (măn′ĭk-dĭ-prĕs′ĭv) *Psychiat.* —*adj.* Designating or afflicted with a psychosis in which periods of manic excitation alternate with melancholic depression. —*n.* A person afflicted with a manic-depressive psychosis.
Man·i·chae·an or **Man·i·che·an** (măn′ĭ-kē′ən) also **Man·i·chee** (măn′ĭ-kē′). —*n.* A believer in Manichaeism. —*adj.* Of or pertaining to Manichaeism. [ME *Maniche* < LLat. *Manichaeus* < LGk. *Manikhaios* < *Manikhaios,* Manes, the founder of the philosophy.]
Man·i·chae·ism (măn′ĭ-kē′ĭz′əm) also **Man·i·chae·an·ism** (măn′ĭ-kē′ə-nĭz′əm) *n.* **1.** The syncretic dualistic religious philosophy taught by the Persian prophet Manes about the third century A.D., combining elements of Zoroastrian, Christian, and Gnostic thought. **2.** A dualistic philosophy similar to Manichaeism, esp. one considered a heresy by the Roman Catholic Church.
Man·i·che·an (măn′ĭ-kē′ən) or **Man·i·chee** (-kē′) *n. & adj.* Variants of **Manichaean.**
man·i·cot·ti (măn′ĭ-kŏt′ē) *n.* An Italian dish consisting of pasta with a filling of chopped ham and ricotta cheese, usually served hot with a tomato sauce. [Ital., pl. of *manicotto,* muff < *manica,* sleeve < Lat. < *manus,* hand.]
man·i·cure (măn′ĭ-kyo͝or′) *n.* Treatment of the hands and fingernails, including shaping, cleaning, and polishing of the nails. —*tr.v.* **-cured, -cur·ing, -cures. 1.** To care for (the fingernails) by shaping, cleaning, and polishing. **2.** To clip or trim evenly and closely: *manicure a hedge.* [Fr. : Lat. *manus,* hand + Lat. *cura,* care.] **—man′i·cur′ist** *n.*
man·i·fest (măn′ə-fĕst′) *adj.* Clearly apparent to the sight or understanding; obvious. —*tr.v.* **-fest·ed, -fest·ing, -fests. 1.** To show or demonstrate plainly; reveal: *"Mercedes . . . manifested the chaotic abandonment of hysteria"* (Jack London). **2.** To be evidence of; prove. **3. a.** To record or list in a ship's manifest. **b.** To display or present a manifest of (cargo). —*n.* **1. a.** A list of cargo or passengers. **b.** A list of railroad cars according to owner and location. **2.** A fast freight train, usually one that carries perishable goods. [ME < Lat. *manifestus.*] **—man′i·fest′ly** *adv.*
man·i·fes·tant (măn′ə-fĕs′tənt) *n.* A participant in a manifestation or a public demonstration.
man·i·fes·ta·tion (măn′ə-fĕ-stā′shən) *n.* **1. a.** The act of manifesting. **b.** The state of being manifested. **c.** The demonstration of the existence, reality, or presence of a person, object, or quality: *a manifestation of ill will.* **d.** One of the forms in which someone or something, such as an individual, a divine being, or an idea, is revealed. **2.** A public demonstration, usually of a political nature.
Manifest Destiny *n.* **1.** A future event that is accepted as being inevitable. **2.** A policy of imperialistic expansion defended as necessary or benevolent.
man·i·fes·to (măn′ə-fĕs′tō) *n., pl.* **-toes** or **-tos.** A public declaration of principles or intentions, esp. of a political nature. —*intr.v.* **-toed, -to·ing, -toes.** To issue a manifesto. [Ital. < *manifesto,* clear < Lat. *manifestus.*]
man·i·fold (măn′ə-fōld′) *adj.* **1.** Of many kinds; multiple: *"the manifold exasperations of life"* (Thomas Mann). **2.** Having many features or forms: *manifold intelligence.* **3.** Consisting of or operating several of one kind. —*n.* **1.** A whole composed of diverse elements. **2.** One of many copies. **3.** A pipe so fitted that it has several apertures for making multiple connections. **4.** *Math.* A set of elements sharing a number of properties, usually of a topologic nature, such as orientability, differentiability, and dimensionality. —*tr.v.* **-fold·ed, -fold·ing, -folds. 1.** To make several copies of. **2.** To make manifold; multiply. [ME < OE *manigfeald* : *manig,* many + *-feald,* -fold.] **—man′i·fold′ly** *adv.* **—man′i·fold′ness** *n.*
man·i·kin or **man·ni·kin** (măn′ĭ-kĭn) *n.* **1.** A dwarf. **2.** A mannequin. [Du. *mannekijn* < MDu., dim. of *man,* man.]
ma·nil·a or **ma·nil·la** (mə-nĭl′ə) *n.* Often **Manila** or **Manilla. 1.** A cheroot made in Manila. **2.** Manila hemp. **3.** Manila paper. **4.** A light yellow brown.
Manila hemp *n.* The fiber of the abaca, used for making rope, cordage, and paper.
Manila paper *n.* Strong paper or thin cardboard with a smooth finish, usually buff in color, made from Manila hemp or wood fibers similar to it.
man in the street *n.* The ordinary citizen.
man·i·oc (măn′ē-ŏk′) also **man·i·o·ca** (măn′ē-ō′kə) *n.* Cassava (sense 1). [Fr., of Tupian orig.]
man·i·ple (măn′ə-pəl) *n.* **1.** An ornamental silk band hung as an ecclesiastical vestment on the left arm near the wrist. **2.** A subdivision of an ancient Roman legion, containing 60 or 120 men. [ME < OFr. < Lat. *manipulus,* handful.]
ma·nip·u·lar (mə-nĭp′yə-lər) *adj.* **1.** Of or pertaining to an ancient Roman maniple. **2.** Of or relating to manipulation. —*n.* A Roman soldier in a maniple.
ma·nip·u·late (mə-nĭp′yə-lāt′) *tr.v.* **-lat·ed, -lat·ing, -lates. 1.** To operate or control by skilled use of the hands; handle: *manipulated the lights to get just the effect she wanted.* **2.** To influence or manage shrewdly or deviously: *He manipulated public opinion in his favor.* **3.** To tamper with or falsify (financial records) for personal gain. [Back-formation < MANIPULATION.] **—ma·nip′u·la·bil′i·ty** *n.* **—ma·nip′u·la·ble** (-lə-bəl) *adj.* **—ma·nip′u·la′tive, ma·nip′u·la·to′ry** (-lə-tôr′ē, -tōr′ē) *adj.* **—ma·nip′u·la′tor** *n.*
ma·nip·u·la·tion (mə-nĭp′yə-lā′shən) *n.* **1.** The act of manipulating. **2.** Shrewd or devious management, esp. for one's own advantage. **3.** The state of being manipulated. [Fr. < *manipule,* handful < Lat. *manipulus* < *manus,* hand.]
man·i·tou or **man·i·tu** (măn′ĭ-to͞o′) also **man·i·to** (-tō′) *n.* **1.** A spirit or force of nature, either good or bad, deified in the religion of the Algonquian Indians. **2.** A representation or image of a manitou. [Fr. < Ojibwa *manitoo.*]
man·kind (măn′kīnd′) *n.* **1.** (*also* măn′kīnd′). The human race. **2.** Men as distinguished from women.
man·like (măn′līk′) *adj.* **1.** Resembling a man. **2.** Belonging to or befitting a man.
man·ly (măn′lē) *adj.* **-li·er, -li·est. 1.** Having qualities generally attributed to a man: *manly courage.* **2.** Belonging to or befitting a man; masculine: *manly clothes.* —*adv.* In a manly manner. **—man′li·ness** *n.*
man-made (măn′mād′) *adj.* Made by human beings; not of natural origin.
man·na (măn′ə) *n.* **1.** In the Old Testament, the food miraculously provided for the Israelites in the wilderness during their flight from Egypt. **2.** Spiritual nourishment of divine origin. **3.** Something of value that a person receives unexpectedly. **4.** The dried exudate of certain plants, esp. that of a Eurasian ash tree, *Fraxinus ornus,* formerly used as a laxative. [ME < OE < LLat. < Gk. < Aram. *mannā* < Heb. *mān.*]
man·nan (măn′ăn′, -ən) *n.* Any of a group of polysaccharides that are polymers of mannose. [MANN(OSE) + -AN.]
manned (mănd) *adj.* Transporting or operated by a human being: *a manned spacecraft.*
man·ne·quin (măn′ĭ-kĭn) *n.* **1.** A life-size full or partial representation of the human body, used for the fitting or displaying of clothes; dummy. **2.** A jointed model of the human body used by artists, esp. to demonstrate the arrangement of drapery. **3.** One who models clothes; model. [Fr. < MDu. *mannekijn,* manikin. —see MANIKIN.]
man·ner (măn′ər) *n.* **1.** A way of doing something or the way in which a thing is done or happens. **2.** A person's bearing or behavior: *a flirtatious manner.* **3. manners. a.** The socially correct way of acting; etiquette. **b.** The prevailing systems or modes of social conduct of a specific society, period, or group, esp. as the subject of a literary work. **4.** Practice, style, execution, or method in the arts: *This fresco is typical of the painter's early manner.* **5.** Kind; sort: *saw all manner of people at the mall.* [ME < OFr. *maniere* < VLat. **manuaria* < Lat. *manuarius,* of the hand < Lat. *manus,* hand.]
man·nered (măn′ərd) *adj.* **1.** Having manners of a specific kind: *ill-mannered.* **2.** Artificial or affected: *mannered speech.* **3.** Of, pertaining to, or exhibiting mannerisms.
man·ner·ism (măn′ə-rĭz′əm) *n.* **1.** A distinctive behavioral trait; idiosyncrasy. **2.** Exaggerated or affected style or habit, as in dress, speech, or art. **3. Mannerism.** An artistic style of the late 16th century characterized by distortion of such elements as scale and perspective. **—man′ner·ist** *n.*
man·ner·ly (măn′ər-lē) *adj.* Having good manners; polite. —*adv.* With good manners; politely. **—man′ner·li·ness** *n.*
man·ni·kin (măn′ĭ-kĭn) *n.* Variant of **manikin.**
man·nish (măn′ĭsh) *adj.* **1.** Of or befitting a man. **2.** Resembling a man. **—man′nish·ly** *adv.* **—man′nish·ness** *n.*
man·nite (măn′īt′) *n.* Mannitol. [Fr. < *manna,* manna < LLat.]
man·ni·tol (măn′ĭ-tôl′, -tōl′) *n.* An alcohol, $C_6H_8(OH)_6$, used as a nutrient, as a dietary supplement, and as the basis of dietetic sweets. [MANN(A) + -IT(E) + -OL.]
man·nose (măn′ōs′) *n.* A monosaccharide, $C_6H_{12}O_6$, obtained from the oxidation of mannitol. [MANN(A) + -OSE.]
ma·noeu·vre (mə-no͞o′vər, -nyo͞o′-) *n. & v. Chiefly Brit.* Variant of **maneuver.**
man of God *n.* A clergyman.
man of letters *n.* A man involved in literary or scholarly pursuits.
man of the cloth *n.* A clergyman.
man of the house *n.* The primary male in a household.
man of the world *n.* A sophisticated, worldly man.
man-of-war (măn′ə-wôr′) *n., pl.* **men-of-war** (mĕn′-). **1.** A warship. **2.** The Portuguese man-of-war.
ma·nom·e·ter (mă-nŏm′ĭ-tər) *n.* **1.** An instrument used for measuring the pressure of liquids and gases. **2.** A sphygmomanometer. [Fr. *manomètre* : Gk. *manos,* sparse + Fr. *-mètre,* -meter.] **—man′o·met′ric** (măn′ə-mĕt′rĭk), **man′o·met′ri·cal** *adj.* **—man′o·met′ri·cal·ly** *adv.* **—ma·nom′e·try** *n.*
man·or (măn′ər) *n.* **1. a.** The district over which a lord had domain in medieval western Europe. **b.** The lord's residence in such a district. **2.** A landed estate. **3.** The main house on an estate; mansion. **4.** In certain North American colonies, a tract of land with hereditary rights granted to the proprietor by royal charter. [ME < AN *maner* < OFr. *maneir,* to dwell < Lat. *manēre.*] **—ma·no′ri·al** (mə-nôr′ē-əl, -nōr′-) *adj.*
man-o'-war bird (măn′ə-wôr′) *n.* The frigate bird.
man·pow·er (măn′pou′ər) *n.* **1.** The power of human physical strength. **2.** Power in terms of the workers available to a particular group or required for a particular task.
man·qué (mäN-kā′) *adj.* Unfulfilled; frustrated: *an artist manqué.* [Fr. < *manquer,* to fail < VLat. **mancare* < Lat. *mancus,* maimed.]

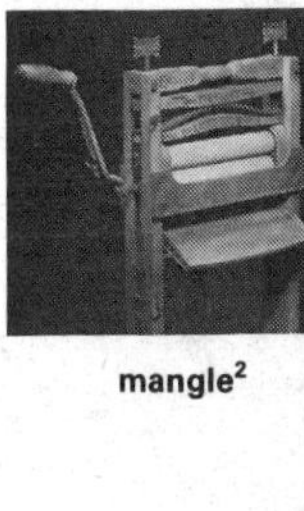
mangle[2]

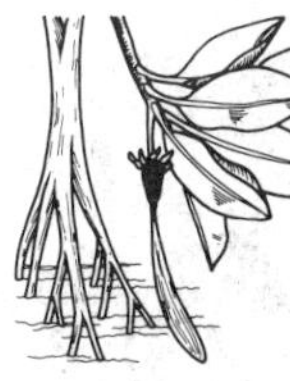
mangrove

manometer

mansard

mantel

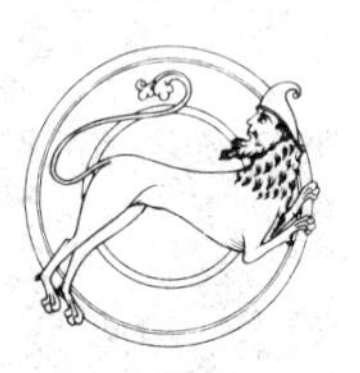

manticore
Drawing by T. H. White from a 12th-century bestiary

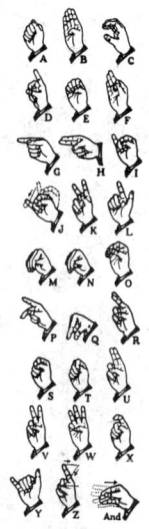

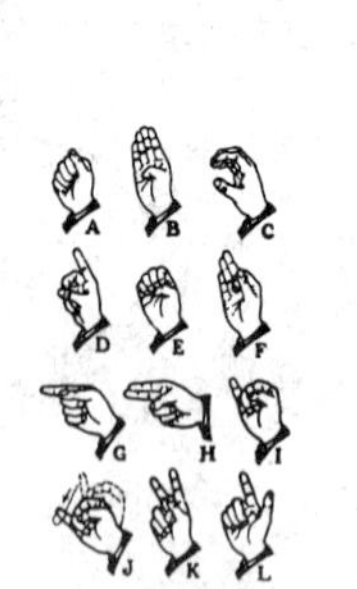

manual alphabet

man·rope (măn′rōp′) *n. Naut.* A rope rigged as a handrail on a gangplank or ladder.
man·sard (măn′särd′) *n.* **1.** A roof having two slopes on all four sides, with the lower slope almost vertical and the upper almost horizontal. **2.** The upper story formed by the lower slope of a mansard roof. [Fr. *mansarde,* after François *Mansart* (1598–1666).]
manse (măns) *n.* **1.** *Chiefly Scot.* A clergyman's house and land. **2.** *Archaic.* A mansion. [ME *manss,* a dwelling < Med. Lat. *mansa* < Lat. *manēre,* to dwell.]
man·ser·vant (măn′sûr′vənt) *n., pl.* **men·ser·vants.** A male servant, esp. a valet.
man·sion (măn′shən) *n.* **1.** A large, stately house. **2.** A manor house. **3.** *Archaic.* A dwelling; abode. **4. a.** A house (sense 8.b.). **b.** Any one of the 28 divisions of the moon's monthly path. [ME *mansioun,* a dwelling < OFr. *mansion* < Lat. *mansio* < *manēre,* to dwell.]
man-sized (măn′sīzd′) also **man-size** (-sīz′) *adj. Informal.* Very large: *a man-sized piece of pie; a man-sized job.*
man·slaugh·ter (măn′slô′tər) *n.* **1.** The taking of human life without premeditation. **2.** *Law.* The unlawful killing of one human being by another without express or implied intent to do injury.
man·slay·er (măn′slā′ər) *n.* A person or animal who kills a human being.
man·sue·tude (măn′swĭ-to͞od′, -tyo͞od′) *n.* Gentleness of manner; mildness. [ME < Lat. *mansuetudo* < *mansuescere,* to tame : *manus,* hand + *suescere,* to accustom.]
man·ta (măn′tə) *n.* **1.** A rough-textured cotton fabric or blanket made and used in Spanish America and the southwestern U.S. **2.** Also **manta ray.** Any of several fishes of the family Mobulidae, having large, extremely flattened bodies with winglike pectoral fins. [Sp., cape < Lat. *mantum.*]
manta ray *n.* A manta (sense 2).
man·teau (măn-tō′) *n., pl.* **-teaus** (-tōz′) or **-teaux** (-tō′). A loose cloak or mantle. [Fr. < OFr. *mantel.* —see MANTLE.]
man·tel also **man·tle** (măn′tl) *n.* **1.** An ornamental facing around a fireplace. **2.** The protruding shelf over a fireplace. [Var. of MANTLE.]
man·tel·et (măn′tl-ĭt, mănt′lĭt) *n.* **1.** A short cape. **2.** Also **mant·let** (mănt′lĭt). A mobile screen or shield formerly used to protect besieging soldiers. [ME < OFr., dim. of *mantel,* mantle. —see MANTLE.]
man·tel·let·ta (măn′tə-lĕt′ə) *n.* A knee-length, sleeveless vestment worn by Roman Catholic prelates. [Ital. < OFr. *mantelet,* mantelet.]
man·tel·piece also **man·tle·piece** (măn′tl-pēs′) *n.* A mantel (sense 2).
man·tel·tree (măn′tl-trē′) *n.* A beam, stone, or arch that functions as a lintel on a fireplace, supporting the masonry above. [ME.]
man·tes (măn′tēz) *n.* A plural of **mantis.**
man·tic (măn′tĭk) *adj.* Of, pertaining to, or having the power of divination; prophetic. [Gk. *mantikos* < *mantis,* prophet.]
man·ti·core (măn′tĭ-kôr′, -kōr′) *n.* A fabulous monster having the head of a man, the body of a lion, and the tail of a dragon or scorpion. [ME < Lat. *mantichōra* < Gk. *mantikhōras.*]
man·tid (măn′tĭd) *n.* Mantis. [< NLat. *Mantidae,* family name < *Mantis,* mantis genus < Gk. *mantis,* prophet.]
man·til·la (măn-tē′yə, -tĭl′ə) *n.* **1.** A scarf, usually of lace, worn over the head and shoulders, often over a high comb, by women in Spain and Latin America. **2.** A short cloak or cape. [Sp., dim. of *manta,* cape. —see MANTA.]
man·tis (măn′tĭs) *n., pl.* **-tis·es** or **-tes** (-tēz). Any of various insects of the family Mantidae, primarily tropical but including a few Temperate Zone species, usually pale-green and having two pairs of walking legs and powerful forelimbs that are often folded in a praying position. [NLat. *Mantis,* genus name < Gk. *mantis,* prophet.]
mantis crab *n.* The squilla.
man·tis·sa (măn-tĭs′ə) *n. Math.* The decimal part of a common logarithm when the logarithm is written as the sum of an integer and a decimal. [Lat., makeweight.]
mantis shrimp *n.* The squilla.
man·tle (măn′tl) *n.* **1.** A loose, sleeveless coat worn over outer garments; cloak. **2.** Something that covers, envelops, or conceals: *"On a summer night . . . a mantle of dust hangs over the gravel roads"* (John Dollard). **3.** Variant of **mantel. 4.** The outer covering of a wall. **5.** A zone of hot gases around a flame. **6.** A device in gas lamps consisting of a sheath of threads that gives off brilliant illumination when heated by the flame. **7.** *Anat.* The cerebral cortex. **8.** *Geol.* The layer of the earth between the crust and the core. **9.** The outer wall and casing of a blast furnace above the hearth. **10.** The wings, shoulder feathers, and back of a bird when differently colored from the rest of the body. **11.** *Zool.* In mollusks and brachiopods, a membrane between the body and the shell. —*v.* **-tled, -tling, -tles.** —*tr.* To cover with or as if with a mantle; conceal. —*intr.* **1.** To spread or become extended over a surface. **2.** To become covered with a coating, such as scum or froth on the surface of a liquid. **3.** To be or become covered or overspread by blushes or colors: *Her face mantled in joy.* [ME < OE *mentel* and OFr. *mantel,* both < Lat. *mantellum.*]
man·tle·piece (măn′tl-pēs′) *n.* Variant of **mantelpiece.**
mantle rock *n.* Regolith.
mant·let *n.* Variant of **mantelet** (sense 2).
man-to-man (măn′tə-măn′) *adj.* **1.** Marked by forthrightness and honesty: *a man-to-man discussion.* **2.** *Sports.* Of, pertaining to, or being a system of defense in which a defensive player guards a specific offensive player.
Man·toux test (măn′to͞o′, män-to͞o′) *n.* An intracutaneous test for tuberculin sensitivity that indicates past or present tuberculous infection. [After Charles *Mantoux* (1877–1947).]
man·tra (măn′trə, mŭn′-) *n. Hinduism.* A sacred formula believed to embody the divinity invoked and to possess magical power, used in prayer and incantation. [Skt. *mantraḥ.*]
man·tu·a (măn′cho͞o-ə, -to͞o-ə) *n.* A loose gown, open in front to reveal an underskirt, worn in the 17th and 18th centuries. [Alteration of MANTEAU.]
man·u·al (măn′yo͞o-əl) *adj.* **1. a.** Of, pertaining to, or done by the hands. **b.** Used by or operated with the hands: *manual controls.* **c.** Employing human rather than mechanical energy: *manual labor.* **2.** Of, pertaining to, or resembling a manual or guidebook. —*n.* **1.** A small reference book, esp. one giving instructions. **2.** A keyboard of an organ played with the hands. **3.** Prescribed movements in the handling of a weapon, esp. a rifle: *the military manual of arms.* [ME < OFr. *manuel* < Lat. *manualis* < *manus,* hand.] **—man′u·al·ly** *adv.*
manual alphabet *n.* An alphabet of hand signals used for communication by deaf-mutes.
manual training *n.* A course of training to develop manual dexterity in practical arts, as woodworking or handcrafts.
ma·nu·bri·um (mə-no͞o′brē-əm, -nyo͞o′-) *n., pl.* **-bri·a** (-brē-ə). **1.** The upper part of the breastbone or sternum. **2.** The handle-shaped projection of the malleus in the ear. [NLat. < Lat., handle < *manus,* hand.]
man·u·fac·to·ry (măn′yə-făk′tə-rē) *n., pl.* **-ries.** A factory. [MANUFACT(URE) + -ORY.]
man·u·fac·ture (măn′yə-făk′chər) *v.* **-tured, -tur·ing, -tures.** —*tr.* **1. a.** To make or process (a raw material) into a finished product, esp. by means of a large-scale industrial operation. **b.** To make or process (a product), esp. with the use of industrial machines. **2.** To create, produce, or turn out in a mechanical manner: *"His books seem to have been manufactured rather than composed"* (Dwight Macdonald). **3.** To concoct or invent; fabricate: *manufacture an excuse.* —*intr.* To make or process goods, esp. in large quantities and by means of industrial machines. —*n.* **1.** The act, craft, or process of manufacturing. **2.** A product that is manufactured. **3.** An industry. [< OFr., a making by hand < LLat. *manufactus* : Lat. *manus,* hand + Lat. *facere,* to make.] **—man′u·fac′tur·a·ble** *adj.*
manufactured gas *n.* A gaseous fuel made from various petroleum products or from soft coal.
man·u·fac·tur·er (măn′yə-făk′chər-ər) *n.* A person, enterprise, or entity that manufactures, esp. the owner or operator of a factory.
man·u·mit (măn′yə-mĭt′) *tr.v.* **-mit·ted, -mit·ting, -mits.** To free from slavery or bondage; emancipate. [ME *manumitten* < OFr. *manumitter* < Lat. *manumittere* : *manus,* hand + *mittere,* to send from.] **—man′u·mis′sion** (-mĭsh′ən) *n.*
ma·nure (mə-no͞or′, -nyo͞or′) *n.* Animal dung, compost, or other material used to fertilize soil. —*tr.v.* **-nured, -nur·ing, -nures.** To apply manure to. [< ME *manuren,* to cultivate land < AN *meinourer* < Med. Lat. *manuoperari* : Lat. *manus,* hand + Lat. *operari,* to work.] **—ma·nur′er** *n.*
ma·nus (mā′nəs, mä′-) *n., pl.* **manus.** The end of the forelimb in vertebrates, as the hand, claw, or hoof. [Lat., hand.]
man·u·script (măn′yə-skrĭpt′) *n.* **1.** A book, document, or other composition written by hand. **2.** A typewritten or handwritten version of a book, article, document, or other work, esp. the author's own copy, prepared and submitted for publication in print. **3.** Handwriting as opposed to printing. [< Med. Lat. *manuscriptus,* handwritten : Lat. *manus,* hand + Lat. *scriptus,* p.part. of *scribere,* to write.]
man·ward (măn′wərd) *adj. & adv.* Of, at, or toward man. **—man′wards** *adv.*
man·wise (măn′wīz′) *adv.* In a manner characteristic of man.
Manx (măngks) *adj.* Of or pertaining to the Isle of Man or the Manx language. —*n., pl.* **Manx. 1.** A native or resident of the Isle of Man. **2.** The nearly extinct Goidelic language of the Manx. **3.** A Manx cat.
Manx cat or **manx cat** *n.* A breed of domestic cat having short hair, usually solid color, and an internal vestigial tail.
man·y (mĕn′ē) *adj.* **more, most. 1.** Being one of a large, indefinite number; numerous: *many a man; many another day.* **2.** Amounting to or consisting of a large, indefinite number: *many friends.* —*n. (used with a pl. verb).* **1.** A large, indefinite number of persons or things: *Many of the children were ill.* **2.** Often **the many.** The great body of the people; the masses: *"The many fail; the one succeeds"* (Tennyson). —*pron. (used with a pl. verb).* A large number of persons or things: *"Many are called, but few are chosen"* (Matthew 22:14). [ME < OE *manig.*]
man·y·fold (mĕn′ē-fōld′) *adv.* By many times: *The state's population has increased manyfold.*
man·y·plies (mĕn′ĭ-plīz′) *n.* The omasum.

Man·za·ni·lla (măn'zə-nē'yə, -nĭl'ə) *n.* A pale dry sherry from Spain. [Sp., dim. of *manzana,* apple.]

man·za·ni·ta (măn'zə-nē'tə) *n.* Any of several evergreen shrubs of the genus *Arctostaphylos,* of the Pacific coast of North America, esp. *A. Manzanita,* bearing white or pink flowers in clusters. [Sp., dim. of *manzana,* apple.]

Mao·ism (mou'ĭz'əm) *n.* Marxism-Leninism developed in China chiefly by Mao Zedong. **—Mao'ist** *n.*

Mao·ri (mou'rē) *n., pl.* **Maori** or **-ris. 1.** A member of the aboriginal people of New Zealand, of Polynesian-Melanesian descent. **2.** The Austronesian language of the Maori. [Maori.] **—Mao'ri** *adj.*

map (măp) *n.* **1.** A representation, usually on a plane surface, of a region of the earth or heavens. **2.** Something that suggests a map in clarity of representation. **3.** *Slang.* The face. *—tr.v.* **mapped, map·ping, maps. 1.** To make a map of. **2.** To explore or make a survey of (a region) for the purpose of making a map. **3.** To plan or delineate, esp. in detail; arrange: *families mapping out their vacation plans.* **4.** *Math.* To establish a mapping of (a set or aggregate). ***—idioms.*** **put on the map.** To make famous or known. **wipe off the map.** To destroy completely; annihilate. [Med. Lat. *mappa* < Lat., napkin.] **—map'per** *n.*

ma·ple (mā'pəl) *n.* **1.** A tree or shrub of the genus *Acer,* found in the North Temperate Zone. Most are tall, deciduous trees having lobed leaves and winged seeds borne in pairs. **2.** The wood of a maple, esp. the hard, close-grained wood of the sugar maple, much used for furniture and flooring. **3.** The flavor of the concentrated sap of the sugar maple. [ME < OE *mapul.*]

maple sugar *n.* A sugar made by boiling down maple syrup.

maple syrup *n.* **1.** A sweet syrup made from the sap of the sugar maple. **2.** Syrup made from various sugars and flavored with maple syrup or artificial maple flavoring.

map·mak·er *n.* A person who makes maps; cartographer. **—map'mak·ing** *n.*

map·ping (măp'ĭng) *n. Math.* A rule of correspondence established between two mathematical sets that associates each member of the first set with a single member of the second.

ma·qui (mä'kē) *n.* **1.** An evergreen shrub, *Aristotelia Macqui,* of Chile, bearing purple berries. **2.** A Chilean wine made from maqui berries. [Sp., of Araucanian orig.]

ma·quil·lage (mä'kē-äzh') *n.* Makeup (sense 4). [Fr.]

ma·quis (mä-kē') *n., pl.* **maquis. 1.** In the Mediterranean area, a dense growth of small trees and shrubs. **2.** Often **Maquis. a.** The French underground organization that fought against German occupation forces during World War II; the resistance. **b.** A member of this organization. [Fr. < Ital. *macchie,* pl. of *macchia,* thicket < Lat. *macula,* spot.]

mar (mär) *tr.v.* **marred, mar·ring, mars. 1.** To damage or deface. **2.** To spoil the quality of. *—n.* A mark that disfigures; blemish. [ME *maren* < OE *mierran.*]

mar·a·bou also **mar·a·bout** (măr'ə-bo͞o') *n.* **1.** Any of several large Old World storks of the genus *Leptoptilus,* having a soft down used to trim women's garments. **2. a.** The down of the marabou or an imitation made from other bird feathers. **b.** A neckpiece, hat, dress, or coat trimmed with the down of the marabou or an imitation of it. **3. a.** A raw silk that can be dyed without being separated from the gum. **b.** A fabric or an article of apparel made from such silk. [Fr. *marabout,* Moslem hermit, marabout. —see MARABOUT[1].]

mar·a·bout[1] (măr'ə-bo͞o', -bo͞ot') *n.* **1.** A Moslem hermit or saint, esp. in northern Africa. **2.** The tomb of a marabout or a shrine to his memory. [Fr. *marabout* < Port. *marabuto* < Ar. *murābit.*]

mar·a·bout[2] (măr'ə-bo͞o') *n.* Variant of **marabou.**

ma·ra·ca (mə-rä'kə) *n.* A percussion instrument consisting of a hollow-gourd rattle containing pebbles or beans, and often played in pairs. [Port. *maracá* < Tupi.]

ma·ran·ta (mə-răn'tə) *n.* **1.** A plant of the tropical American genus *Maranta,* one species of which yields arrowroot. **2.** A starch made from arrowroot. [NLat. *Maranta,* genus name, after Bartolommeo *Maranta* (d. 1571).]

ma·ras·ca (mə-răs'kə) *n.* A European cherry tree, *Prunus Cerasus Marasca,* bearing bitter red fruit from which maraschino is made. [Ital.]

mar·a·schi·no (măr'ə-skē'nō, -shē'-) *n.* A cordial made from the fermented juice and crushed pits of the marasca cherry. [Ital. < *marasca,* marasca.]

maraschino cherry *n.* A maraschino-flavored preserved cherry.

ma·ras·mus (mə-răz'məs) *n.* A wasting away of the body, associated with inadequate or inadequately assimilated food. [LLat. < Gk. *marasmos* < *marainein,* to waste away.] **—ma·ras'mic** *adj.*

Ma·ra·tha also **Mah·rat·ta** (mə-rä'tə) *n., pl.* **Maratha** or **-thas** also **Mahratta** or **-tas. 1.** A Scytho-Dravidian people of southwestern India. **2.** A member of the Maratha people. [Marathi.]

Ma·ra·thi also **Mah·ra·ti** or **Mah·rat·ti** (mə-rä'tē) *n.* The principal Indic language of the state of Maharashtra, India. [Marathi < *Maratha,* Maratha.]

mar·a·thon (măr'ə-thŏn') *n.* **1.** A cross-country footrace of 26 miles, 385 yards. **2.** A long-distance race: *a swimming marathon.* **3.** A contest of endurance: *a dance marathon.* **4.** A task or action that requires prolonged effort or endurance: *a radio fund-raising marathon.* [After *Marathon,* Greece (so called because a messenger ran from there to Athens to announce a victory over the Persians in 490 B.C.).]

ma·raud (mə-rôd') *v.* **-raud·ed, -raud·ing, -rauds.** *—intr.* To rove in search of booty; raid for plunder. *—tr.* To invade for loot. [Fr. *marauder* < *maraud,* vagabond.] **—ma·raud'er** *n.*

mar·ble (mär'bəl) *n.* **1.** A metamorphic rock, chiefly calcium carbonate, $CaCO_3$, often irregularly colored by impurities, used for architectural and ornamental purposes. **2.** A piece of marble. **3.** A sculpture of marble: *the Elgin marbles.* **4.** A small hard ball, usually of glass, used in children's games. **5. marbles.** *(used with a sing. verb).* Any of various games played with marbles. **6. marbles.** *Slang.* Common sense; sanity: *must have lost his marbles.* **7.** Marbling. *—tr.v.* **-bled, -bling, -bles. 1.** To mottle and streak with colors and veins in imitation of marble. **2.** To intermix with flecks or thin strips of fat: *marble a steak.* *—adj.* Resembling marble in consistency, texture, venation, color, or coldness: *a marble heart.* [ME < OFr. *marbre* < Lat. *marmor* < Gk. *marmaros.*] **—mar'bly** *adj.*

marble cake *n.* A cake with a streaked or mottled appearance achieved by mixing light and dark batter.

mar·ble·ize (mär'bə-līz') *tr.v.* **-ized, -iz·ing, -iz·es.** To marble.

mar·ble·wood (mär'bəl-wo͝od') *n.* An Asian tree, *Diospyros kurzii,* having mottled gray wood used in cabinetwork.

mar·bling (mär'blĭng) *n.* **1.** A mottling or streaking that resembles marble. **2.** The process or operation of giving something the surface appearance of marble. **3.** The decorative imitation of marble patterns printed on page edges and endpapers of books. **4.** Flecks or thin strips of fat evenly distributed in a cut of meat.

marc (märk) *n.* **1.** The pulpy residue left after the juice has been pressed from grapes, apples, or other fruits. **2.** Brandy distilled from grape or apple residue. [Fr. < OFr. *marchier,* to trample.]

mar·ca·site (mär'kə-sīt', -zīt') *n.* **1.** A mineral of iron disulfide, FeS_2, having the same composition as pyrite but differing in crystalline structure. **2.** An ornament of pyrite, polished steel, or white metal. **3.** Any of several minerals resembling iron disulfide. [ME < Med. Lat. *marcasita* < Ar. *marqashīṭā* < Pers.] **—mar'ca·sit'i·cal** (-sĭt'ĭ-kəl) *adj.*

mar·cel (mär-sĕl') *n.* A former hair style characterized by deep, regular waves made by a heated curling iron. *—tr.v.* **-celled, -cell·ing, -cels.** To style (the hair) in a marcel. [After *Marcel* Grateau (1852–1936).]

mar·ces·cent (mär-sĕs'ənt) *adj.* Withering but not falling off, as a blossom that persists on a twig after flowering. [Lat. *marcescens, marcescent-,* becoming withered < *marcescere,* inchoative of *marcēre,* to wither.]

march[1] (märch) *v.* **marched, march·ing, march·es.** *—intr.* **1. a.** To walk in a formal military manner with measured steps at a steady rate. **b.** To begin to move in such a manner: *The troops will march at dawn.* **2.** To advance or proceed with steady movement. *—tr.* **1.** To cause to march: *march soldiers into battle.* **2.** To traverse by marching: *They marched the route in a day.* *—n.* **1.** The act of marching, esp.: **a.** The steady forward movement of a body of troops. **b.** A long tiring journey on foot. **2.** Forward movement; progression: *the march of time.* **3.** A regulated pace: *quick march.* **4.** The distance covered by marching: *a week's march away.* **5.** *Mus.* A musical composition in regularly accented usually duple meter to accompany marching. ***—idioms.*** **on the march.** Advancing; progressing: *Science is on the march.* **steal a march on.** To get ahead of, esp. by quiet enterprise. [ME *marchen* < OFr. *marchier,* prob. of Germanic orig.]

march[2] (märch) *n.* **1.** The border or boundary of a country or area of land; frontier. **2.** A tract of land bordering on two countries and claimed by both. *—intr.v.* **marched, march·ing, march·es.** To have a common boundary: *England marches with Scotland.* [ME < OFr. *marche,* of Germanic orig.]

March (märch) *n.* The third month of the Gregorian calendar. See table at **calendar.** [ME < AN < Lat. *martius* < *martius,* of Mars < *Mars,* Mars.]

Mär·chen (mĕr'KHən) *n., pl.* **Märchen.** A folk tale or fairy story. [G.]

march·er (mär'chər) *n.* One that marches, esp. for a specific cause: *a protest marcher.*

marching orders *pl.n.* Orders to move on or depart.

mar·chio·ness (mär'shə-nĭs, mär'shə-nĕs') *n., pl.* **-ness·es. 1.** The wife or widow of a marquis. **2.** A peeress of the rank of marquis in her own right. [Med. Lat. *marchionissa,* fem. of *marchio,* marquis < *marca,* boundary, of Germanic orig.]

march·land (märch'lănd') *n.* A borderland; march.

march·pane (märch'pān') *n.* Marzipan.

Mar·cion·ism (mär'shə-nĭz'əm) *n.* A Gnostic movement of the second and third centuries A.D. that rejected the Old Testament. [After *Marcion* (ca. 2nd cent. A.D.), its founder.]

Mar·co·ni rig (mär-kō'nē) *n.* A Bermuda rig. [After Guglielmo *Marconi* (1874–1937), from its resemblance to the early antennae used by him for his wireless telegraphy.]

Mar·di gras (mär'dē grä') *n.* Shrove Tuesday, the last day

Manx cat

maple
Above: Red maple in winter
Below: Detail showing leaves, flowers, and fruit

maraca

marathon
Boston Marathon

before Lent, celebrated by carnivals, masquerade balls, and parades of costumed merrymakers. [Fr.]

Mar·duk (mär'do͝ok) *n.* The chief god of ancient Babylonian myth. [Babylonian.]

mare¹ (mâr) *n.* A female horse or the female of other equine species. [ME < OE *mere.*]

ma·re² (mä'rā) *n., pl.* **-ri·a** (-rē-ə). *Astron.* Any of the large dark areas on the moon or Mars. [NLat. < Lat. *mare,* sea.]

ma·re clau·sum (mä'rā klou'səm, klô'-) *n.* A navigable body of water, as a sea, that is under the jurisdiction of one nation and closed to all others. [NLat : Lat. *mare,* sea + Lat. *clausum,* closed.]

ma·re li·be·rum (mä'rā lē'bə-ro͞om') *n.* A navigable body of water, as a sea, that is open to navigation by vessels of all nations. [NLat. : Lat. *mare,* sea + Lat. *liberum,* free.]

Ma·ren·go (mə-rĕng'gō) *adj.* Browned in oil and sautéed in a sauce of tomatoes, mushrooms, garlic or onion, and white wine: *chicken Marengo; veal Marengo.* [After *Marengo,* Italy, prob. from the chicken dish served to Napoleon following his victory here in 1800 over the Austrians.]

ma·re nos·trum (mä'rā nŏ'strəm) *n.* A navigable body of water, as a sea, that is under the jurisdiction of one nation or is shared by two or more nations. [Lat., our sea.]

mare's nest *n., pl.* **mare's nests** or **mares' nests. 1.** A hoax or fraud. **2.** An extraordinarily complicated situation.

mare's-tail (mârz'tāl') *n.* An aquatic plant, *Hippuris vulgaris,* of the North Temperate Zone, having minute flowers and whorls of tapering leaves.

marigold

mar·gar·ic (mär-găr'ĭk) *adj.* Resembling pearl; pearly. [< Gk. *margaron,* pearl.]

margaric acid *n.* A synthetic crystalline fatty acid, $C_{17}H_{34}O_2$. [Fr. *margarique* < Gk. *margaron,* pearl.]

mar·ga·rine also **mar·ga·rin** (mär'jər-ĭn) *n.* A fatty solid butter substitute consisting of a blend of hydrogenated vegetable oils mixed with emulsifiers, vitamins, coloring matter, and other ingredients. [Fr. < *margarique,* margaric acid.]

mar·ga·ri·ta (mär'gə-rē'tə) *n.* A cocktail made with tequila and lemon or lime juice, usually served with salt encrusted on the rim of the glass. [Sp., from the name *Margarita,* Margaret.]

mar·ga·rite¹ (mär'gə-rīt') *n.* A mineral, $CaAl_2(Si_2Al_2)O_{10}(OH)_2$, related to mica, with a pearly, translucent luster, formed in sheets of monoclinic crystals. [G. *Margarit* < Gk. *margaritēs,* pearl < *margaron.*]

mar·ga·rite² (mär'gə-rīt') *n.* **1.** *Archaic.* A pearl. **2.** A rock formation that resembles beads. [ME < OFr. < Lat. *margarita* < Gk. *margaritēs* < *margaron.*]

mar·gay (mär'gā', mär-gā') *n.* A spotted wildcat, *Felis weidii,* resembling a small, long-tailed ocelot, found from Texas to Brazil. [Sp. (South America) < Tupi *marakaya.*]

mar·gin (mär'jĭn) *n.* **1.** An edge and the area immediately adjacent to it; border. **2.** The blank space bordering the written or printed area on a page. **3.** A limit of a state or process: *the margin of reality.* **4.** An amount allowed beyond what is needed: *a margin of safety.* **5.** A measure, quantity, or degree of difference: *a margin of 500 votes.* **6.** *Econ.* **a.** The minimum return that an enterprise may earn and still pay for itself. **b.** The difference between the cost and the selling price of securities or commodities. **c.** The difference between the market value of collateral and the face value of a loan. **7.** An amount in money, or represented by securities, deposited by a customer with his broker as a provision against loss on transactions made on account. **8.** *Bot.* The border of a leaf. **9.** *Biol.* The boundary area of an insect's wing. —*tr.v.* **-gined, -gin·ing, -gins. 1.** To provide with a margin. **2.** To be a margin to; border. **3.** To inscribe or enter in the margin of a page. **4. a.** To add margin to: *margin up a brokerage account.* **b.** To deposit margin for: *margin a transaction.* **c.** To buy or hold (securities) by depositing or adding to a margin. [ME < Lat. *margo.*]

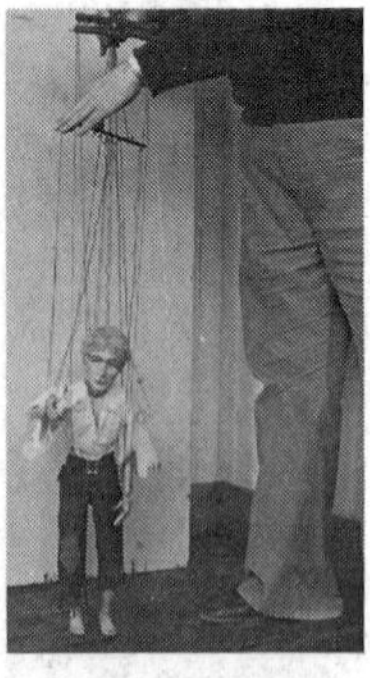

marionette

mar·gin·al (mär'jə-nəl) *adj.* **1.** Of, pertaining to, or constituting a margin: *the marginal strip of beach.* **2.** Geographically adjacent: *states marginal to Canada.* **3.** Written or printed in the margin of a book: *marginal notes.* **4.** Barely within a lower standard or limit of quality: *marginal writing ability.* **5.** *Econ.* **a.** Designating enterprises that produce goods or are capable of producing goods at a rate that barely covers production costs. **b.** Pertaining to commodities thus manufactured and sold. **6.** *Psychol.* Pertaining to or located at the fringe of consciousness. [Med. Lat. *marginalis* < Lat. *margo,* margin.] **—mar'gin·al'i·ty** *n.* **—mar'gin·al·ly** *adv.*

mar·gi·na·li·a (mär'jə-nā'lē-ə) *pl.n.* Notes in a book margin. [NLat. < Med. Lat. *marginalis,* marginal. —see MARGINAL.]

mar·gin·ate (mär'jə-nāt') *tr.v.* **-at·ed, -at·ing, -ates.** To provide with margins or a margin. —*adj.* (mär'jə-nĭt, -nāt). Also **mar·gin·at·ed** (-nā'tĭd). *Biol.* Having a border or edge of distinctive color or pattern. **—mar'gin·a'tion** *n.*

mar·gra·vate (mär'grə-vāt') *n.* Variant of **margraviate.**

mar·grave (mär'grāv') *n.* **1.** The lord or military governor of a medieval German border province. **2.** A hereditary title of certain princes in the Holy Roman Empire. [MDu. *markgrave* : *mark,* march, border, + *grave,* count.]

mar·gra·vi·ate (mär-grā'vē-ĭt, -āt') also **mar·gra·vate** (mär'grə-vāt') *n.* The territory governed by a margrave.

mar·gra·vine (mär'grə-vēn') *n.* The wife or widow of a margrave. [MDu. *markgravin* < *markgrave,* margrave. —see MARGRAVE.]

mar·gue·rite (mär'gə-rēt', -gyə-) *n.* **1.** A plant, *Chrysanthemum frutescens,* native to the Canary Islands, having white or pale-yellow flowers that resemble those of the common American daisy. **2.** Any of several plants similar or related to the marguerite, having daisylike flowers. [Fr. < OFr. *margarite,* daisy < Lat. *margarita,* pearl < Gk. *margaritēs* < *margaron.*]

ma·ri·a (mä'rē-ə) *n.* Plural of **mare².**

ma·ri·a·chi (mä'rē-ä'chē) *n.* **1.** A street band in Mexico. **2. a.** The music performed by a mariachi. **b.** A musician belonging to a mariachi. [Mex. Sp.]

Mar·i·an (mâr'ē-ən, măr'-) *n.* **1.** A devotee of the Virgin Mary. **2. a.** A supporter of Queen Mary I of England. **b.** A supporter of Mary, Queen of Scots. —*adj.* Of or pertaining to the Virgin Mary, Queen Mary I of England, or Mary, Queen of Scots.

mar·ic·o·lous (mə-rĭk'ə-ləs) *adj.* Inhabiting the sea. [Lat. *mare, mari-,* sea + -COLOUS.]

mar·i·cul·ture (măr'ĭ-kŭl'chər) *n.* The cultivation of marine organisms in their natural habitat. [Lat. *mare, mari-,* sea + CULTURE.]

mar·i·gold (măr'ĭ-gōld', mâr'-) *n.* **1.** Any of various plants of the genus *Tagetes,* native to tropical America and widely cultivated for their showy yellow or orange flowers. **2.** Any of several plants having flowers similar to those of the marigold, as the corn marigold and the marsh marigold. [ME : *Mary,* Mary + *gold,* gold.]

mar·i·jua·na or **mar·i·hua·na** (măr'ə-wä'nə) *n.* **1.** Hemp. **2.** The dried flower clusters and leaves of the hemp plant, esp. when taken to induce euphoria. [Mex. Sp. *marihuana.*]

ma·rim·ba (mə-rĭm'bə) *n.* A large xylophone with resonators. [Kimbundu.]

ma·ri·na (mə-rē'nə) *n.* A boat basin that has docks, moorings, supplies, and other facilities for small boats. [Ital., seashore < *marino,* belonging to the sea < Lat. *marinus.* —see MARINE.]

mar·i·nade (măr'ə-nād') *n.* A liquid mixture, usually of vinegar or wine and oil with various spices and herbs, in which meat, fowl, and fish are soaked before cooking. —*tr.v.* **-nad·ed, -nad·ing, -nades.** To marinate. [Fr. < Sp. *marinada* < *marinar,* to marinate < *marino,* belonging to the sea. —see MARINA.]

ma·ri·na·ra (măr'ə-năr'ə, mär'ə-när'ə) *adj.* Being or served with a sauce made of tomatoes, onions, garlic, and spices: *spaghetti marinara.* [Ital. *(alla) marinara,* in sailor style < *marinaro,* of sailors < *marino,* marine < Lat. *marinus.*]

mar·i·nate (măr'ə-nāt') *tr.v.* **-nat·ed, -nat·ing, -nates.** To soak (meat, for example) in a marinade. [Alteration of MARINADE.]

ma·rine (mə-rēn') *adj.* **1. a.** Of or pertaining to the sea: *marine exploration.* **b.** Native to or formed by the sea: *marine life.* **2.** Of or pertaining to shipping or maritime affairs. **3.** Of or pertaining to sea navigation; nautical: *a marine chart.* **4.** Designating or pertaining to troops that serve at sea as well as on land, specifically the U.S. Marine Corps. —*n.* **1.** The mercantile or naval ships or shipping fleet of a country. **2. a.** A soldier serving on a ship or at a naval installation. **b. Marine.** A member of the U.S. Marine Corps. **3.** In some nations, the governmental department in charge of naval affairs. **4.** A painting or photograph of the sea. [ME < OFr. < Lat. *marinus* < *mare,* sea.]

Marine Corps *n.* A branch of the U.S. Armed Forces composed chiefly of amphibious troops under the authority of the Secretary of the Navy.

mar·i·ner (măr'ə-nər) *n.* One who navigates a ship; sailor or seaman. [ME < AN < OFr. *marine,* marine.]

Mar·i·ol·a·try (mâr'ē-ŏl'ə-trē) *n.* Excessive or idolatrous worship of the Virgin Mary.

Mar·i·ol·o·gy also **Mar·y·ol·o·gy** (mâr'ē-ŏl'ə-jē) *n.* The body of belief relating to the Virgin Mary.

mar·i·o·nette (măr'ē-ə-nĕt') *n.* A jointed puppet manipulated by strings or wires attached to its limbs. [Fr., from the name *Marion.*]

mar·i·po·sa lily also **mar·i·po·sa tulip** (măr'ə-pō'zə, -sə) *n.* Any of several bulbous plants of the genus *Calochortus,* of the southwestern United States and Mexico, having variously colored, tuliplike flowers. [Sp. *mariposa,* butterfly : *Maria,* Mary + *posar,* to perch < LLat. *pausare,* to pause < Lat. *pausa,* pause.]

Mar·ist (mâr'ĭst, măr'-) *n.* **1.** A member of the Society of Mary, a congregation of Roman Catholic missionary priests founded in 1824. **2.** A member of the Little Brothers of Mary, a Roman Catholic teaching order founded in 1817.

mar·i·tal (măr'ĭ-təl) *adj.* **1.** Of or pertaining to marriage. **2.** Of or pertaining to a husband. [Lat. *maritalis* < *maritus,* married.] **—mar'i·tal·ly** *adv.*

mar·i·time (măr'ĭ-tīm') *adj.* **1.** Located on or near the sea. **2.** Of or concerned with shipping or navigation. **3.** Of or like a mariner. [Lat. *maritimus* < *mare,* sea.]

mar·jo·ram (mär'jər-əm) *n.* **1.** An aromatic plant, *Majorana hortensis,* having small purplish-white flowers and leaves used as seasoning. **2.** A plant, *Origanum vulgare,* similar to the marjoram, having spikes of pinkish flowers and leaves used in cooking. [ME *majorane* < OFr. < Med. Lat. *majorana.*]

mark¹ (märk) *n.* **1.** A visible trace or impression on something, as a spot, dent, or line. **2.** A cross or other sign made in lieu of a signature. **3.** A written or printed symbol used for punctuation; punctuation mark. **4. a.** A number, letter, or symbol used to indicate various grades of scholastic achievement: *A mark of 95 is excellent.* **b.** Often **marks.** An appraisal; rating: *got high marks from her superiors.* **5. a.** An inscription, name, stamp, label, or seal placed on an article to signify ownership, quality, manufacture, or origin. **b.** A notch in an animal's ear or hide indicating ownership. **6.** *Naut.* **a.** A knot or piece of material placed at various measured lengths on a lead line to indicate the depth of the water. **b.** A Plimsoll mark. **7. a.** A visible indication of a quality, property, or feature: *"The old Fort Prince George now bears no marks of a fortress, but is used as a trading house"* (William Bartram). **b.** A visible sign or symbol, as a badge or brand adopted by or imposed on a person. **c. Mark.** A particular mode, brand, size, or quality of a product: *This automobile is the Mark X model.* **8.** A recognized standard of quality: *schoolwork that is not up to the mark.* **9.** Quality; note; importance: *"A fellow of no mark nor likelihood"* (Shakespeare). **10.** Notice; attention; heed: *a matter unworthy of mark.* **11.** A target: *"A mounted officer would be a conspicuous mark"* (Ambrose Bierce). **12.** Something that one wishes to achieve; goal. **13.** An object or point that serves as a guide. **14.** *Slang.* A person who is the intended victim of a swindler; dupe. **15.** The place from which racers begin and sometimes end their contest. **16.** A point reached or gained: *the halfway mark of the race.* **17.** A record: *set a new mark in the long jump.* **18.** A strike or spare in bowling. **19.** A stationary ball in bowls; jack. **20.** A boundary between countries. **21.** In medieval England and Germany, a tract of land held in common by a community. **22.** The numerical value given for computational convenience to a statistical observation falling within one of a number of intervals. —*v.* **marked, mark·ing, marks.** —*tr.* **1.** To make a visible impression on, as with a spot, line, or dent. **2.** To form, make, or depict by making a visible impression, as with a spot, line, or dent: *He marked a square on the board.* **3. a.** To distinguish or indicate by making a visible impression: *He marked the spot where the treasure is buried.* **b.** To distinguish, indicate, or characterize: *the exuberance that marks her writings.* **4.** To set off or separate by or as if by a mark. **5.** To attach price tags, maker's labels, or other identification to (articles for sale). **6.** To grade and correct (scholastic work) by evaluating it according to a scale of letters and numbers. **7. a.** To give attention to; notice: *Mark her expression of discontent.* **b.** To take note of in writing; write down. **8.** To consider; study: *Mark my word.* **9.** To keep (score) in various games. —*intr.* **1.** To make a visible impression: *This pen will mark under water.* **2.** To receive a visible impression: *The floor marks easily.* **3.** To notice; pay attention. **4.** To keep score. **5.** To determine scholastic grades: *His teacher marks strictly.* —**phrasal verbs. mark down.** To mark for sale at a lower price. **mark up.** To mark for sale at a higher price. —***idioms.* beside the mark.** Beside the point; irrelevant. **mark time. 1.** To move the feet alternately in the rhythm of a marching step without advancing. **2.** To suspend progress for the time being; wait in readiness. [ME < OE *mearc.*]

mark² (märk) *n.* **1.** A former English and Scottish monetary unit equal to 13 shillings and 4 pence. **2.** Any of several former European units of weight equal to about eight ounces, used esp. for weighing gold and silver. **3.** See table at **currency.** [ME, unit of weight < OE *marc.*]

Mark (märk) *n.* **1.** One of the Apostles of Christ and traditionally accepted as the author of the second Gospel of the New Testament. **2.** See table at **Bible. 3.** In Arthurian legend, a king of Cornwall who was the husband of Iseult and the uncle of Tristan.

mark·down (märk′doun′) *n.* **1.** A reduction in price. **2.** The amount by which a price is reduced.

marked (märkt) *adj.* **1.** Having a mark or marks. **2.** Having a noticeable character; clearly defined: *noted marked variations in the color of the birds.* **3.** Singled out, esp. for a dire fate: *a marked man.* —**mark′ed·ly** (mär′kĭd-lē) *adv.*

mark·er (mär′kər) *n.* **1.** One that marks or distinguishes, as a bookmark, tombstone, or milestone. **2.** An implement used for marking or writing. **3.** A person who marks objects, esp. for industrial purposes. **4.** A person who grades scholastic papers. **5.** *Sports.* A device, as a line, stake, or flag, on a playing field that shows the playing or scoring position. **6. a.** One that keeps score in various games. **b.** A score in a game. **7.** *Slang.* A written, signed promissory note; IOU.

mar·ket (mär′kĭt) *n.* **1.** A public gathering held for buying and selling merchandise. **2.** A place where goods are offered for sale. **3.** A store or shop that sells a particular type of merchandise: *a meat market.* **4. a.** The business of buying and selling a specified commodity. **b.** A market price. **c.** A geographic region considered as a place for sales: *grain for the foreign market.* **d.** A subdivision of a population considered as buyers: *cosmetics for the teen-age market.* **5.** The opportunity to buy or sell; demand for merchandise. **6. a.** An exchange for buying and selling stocks or commodities: *securities sold on the New York market.* **b. the market.** The entire enterprise of buying and selling commodities and securities. —***modifier:*** *a market town.* —*v.* **-ket·ed, -ket·ing, -kets.** —*tr.* **1.** To offer for sale. **2.** To sell. —*intr.* **1.** To deal in a market. **2.** To buy household supplies: *He marketed for a special Sunday dinner.* —***idioms.* in the market.** Interested in buying. **on the market.** Up for sale. [ME < OE < ONFr. < Lat. *mercatus* < *mercari,* to buy < *merx,* merchandise.] —**mar′ket·er** *n.*

mar·ket·a·ble (mär′kĭ-tə-bəl) *adj.* **1.** Fit to be offered for sale. **2.** Salable: *a marketable product; a marketable idea.* **3.** Relating to selling or buying. —**mar′ket·a·bil′i·ty** *n.*

market basket *n.* **1.** A grocery cart. **2.** A selection of foods needed for a statistical household of 3.2 persons or for a family of four, considered in terms of its fluctuating cost.

mar·ket·ing (mär′kĭ-tĭng) *n.* **1.** The act or process of buying and selling in a market. **2.** The commercial functions involved in transferring goods from producer to consumer.

market order *n.* An order to buy or sell stocks or commodities at the prevailing market price.

mar·ket·place also **market place** (mär′kĭt-plās′) *n.* **1.** A place in which a market is set up. **2.** The world of business and commerce. **3.** The figurative place of assembly where works, opinions, and ideas are debated and exchanged: *the marketplace of ideas.*

market price *n.* The prevailing price at which merchandise, securities, or commodities are sold.

market value *n.* The amount that a seller may expect to obtain for merchandise, services, or securities in the open market.

mark·ing (mär′kĭng) *n.* **1.** A mark or marks. **2.** The characteristic pattern of coloration of a plant or animal.

mark·ka (mär′kä′) *n., pl.* **-kaa** (-kä′). See table at **currency.** [Finn. < Swed. *mark,* unit of value.]

marks·man (märks′mən) *n.* **1.** A person skilled at shooting a gun or other weapon. **2.** A classification in the U.S. Army and Marine Corps for the lowest of three ratings of rifle proficiency. **3.** A soldier in the U.S. Army who rates as a marksman. —**marks′man·ship′** *n.*

marks·wo·man (märks′wo͝om′ən) *n.* A woman skilled at shooting a gun or other weapon.

mark·up (märk′ŭp′) *n.* **1.** A raise in price. **2.** An amount added to a cost price in calculating a selling price, esp. an amount that takes into account overhead and profit.

marl (märl) *n.* A mixture of clays, carbonates of calcium and magnesium, and remnants of shells, forming a loam used as fertilizer. —*tr.v.* **marled, marl·ing, marls.** To fertilize with marl. [ME < OFr. < LLat. *margila,* dim. of Lat. *marga,* marl.]

mar·lin (mär′lĭn) *n.* Any of several large game fish of the genus *Makaira,* of the Atlantic and Pacific oceans. [Short for MARLINESPIKE (from the pointed shape of its snout).]

mar·line (mär′lĭn) also **mar·ling** (-lĭng) *n.* *Naut.* A light rope made of two loosely twisted strands. [MDu. *marlijn* : *marren,* to tie + *lijn,* line < Lat. *linea.*]

mar·line·spike (mär′lĭn-spīk′) also **mar·ling·spike** (-lĭng-spīk′) *n.* *Naut.* A pointed metal spike, used to separate strands of rope in splicing.

mar·lite (mär′līt′) *n.* A marl containing 25 to 75 per cent clay, the remainder being calcium carbonate, that is resistant to decomposition in air. —**mar·lit′ic** (-lĭt′ĭk) *adj.*

marl·stone (märl′stōn′) *n.* Marlite.

mar·ma·lade (mär′mə-lād′) *n.* A preserve made from the pulp and rind of fruits, esp. citrus fruits. [Fr. *marmelade* < Port. *mamelada* < *marmelo,* quince < Lat. *melimelum,* a kind of sweet apple < Gk. *melimēlon* : *meli,* honey + *mēlon,* apple.]

marmalade plum *n.* A tree, *Calocarpum zapota,* of the American tropics, having edible fruit.

mar·mo·re·al (mär-môr′ē-əl, -mōr′-) also **mar·mo·re·an** (-ē-ən) *adj.* Like marble, as in smoothness, whiteness, or hardness: *a complexion of marmoreal lustre.* [Lat. *marmoreus* < *marmor,* marble.]

mar·mo·set (mär′mə-sĕt′, -zĕt′) *n.* Any of various small monkeys of the genera *Callithrix, Cebuella, Saguinus,* and *Leontideus,* found in tropical forests of the Americas, having soft, dense fur, tufted ears, and long tails. [ME < OFr. < *marmouser,* to murmur.]

marmoset
Genus *Saguinus*

mar·mot (mär′mət) *n.* Any of various stocky, coarse-furred rodents of the genus *Marmota,* having short legs and ears and bushy tails, found throughout the Northern Hemisphere. [Fr. *marmotte.*]

Mar·o·nite (măr′ə-nīt′) *n.* A member of a Christian Uniat Church, chiefly of Lebanon, whose liturgy is conducted in Syriac. [Med. Lat. *maronita* < *Maro,* Syrian monk of the 5th cent. A.D.] —**Mar′o·nite′** *adj.*

ma·roon¹ (mə-ro͞on′) *tr.v.* **-rooned, -roon·ing, -roons. 1.** To put (a person) ashore on a deserted island or coast. **2.** To abandon or isolate (a person) with little hope of rescue or escape. —*n.* **1. a.** A fugitive Negro slave in the West Indies in the 17th and 18th centuries. **b.** A descendant of such a slave. **2.** A person who is marooned. [Fr., *marron,* fugitive slave < Am. Sp. *cimarrón,* poss. < *cima,* of a mountain.]

ma·roon² (mə-ro͞on′) *n.* A dark reddish brown to dark purplish red. [Fr. *marron* < Ital. *marrone.*]

mar·plot (mär′plŏt′) *n.* A stupid and officious meddler

marquetry

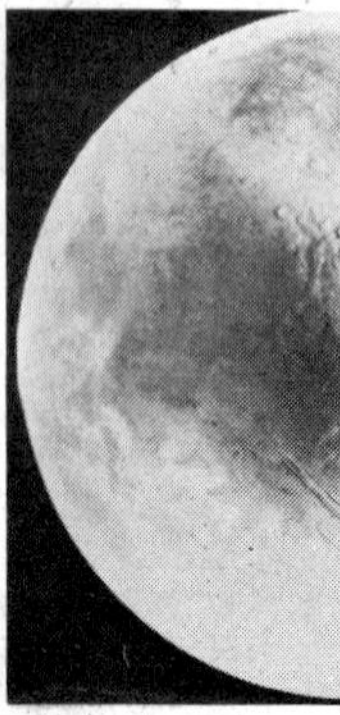

Mars
Above: View of the planet from the *Viking I* satellite
Below: 18th-century English statuette of the god

whose interference compromises the success of an undertaking. [After *Marplot,* a character in *The Busy Body,* a play by Susanna Centlivre (1667?–1723).]

mar·quee (mär-kē′) *n.* **1.** A large tent with open sides, used chiefly for outdoor entertainment. **2.** A rooflike structure, often bearing a signboard, projecting over an entrance to a theater or other building. [Fr. *marquise,* marquee, marquise.]

Mar·que·san (mär-kā′zən, -sən) *n.* **1.** An inhabitant of the Marquesas Islands. **2.** The Austronesian language of the Marquesans. —*adj.* Of or pertaining to the Marquesas Islands, their inhabitants, or their language.

mar·quess (mär′kwĭs) *n. Chiefly Brit.* Variant of **marquis.**

mar·que·try also **mar·que·terie** (mär′kĭ-trē) *n., pl.* **-tries.** An inlay, as of wood or ivory, used chiefly for decorating furniture. [OFr. *marqueterie* < *marqueter,* to checker < *marque,* mark, of Germanic orig.]

mar·quis (mär′kwĭs, mär-kē′) *n., pl.* **mar·quis·es** (mär′-kwĭ-sĭz) or **mar·quis** (mär-kēz′). The title of a nobleman ranking below a duke and above an earl or count. [ME < OFr. < *marche,* boundary, of Germanic orig.]

mar·quis·ate (mär′kwĭ-zĭt, -sĭt) *n.* The rank or territory of a marquis.

mar·quise (mär-kēz′) *n.* **1.** A marchioness. **2.** A marquee. **3. a.** A finger ring set with a pointed oval stone or cluster of pointed oval stones. **b.** A pointed oval shape of a gem. [Fr., fem. of *marquis,* marquis.]

mar·qui·sette (mär′kĭ-zĕt′, -kwĭ-) *n.* A sheer fabric of cotton, rayon, silk, or nylon, used for clothing, curtains, and mosquito nets. [MARQUISE + -ETTE.]

mar·ram (măr′əm) *n.* A beach grass, *Ammophila arenaria,* much planted to stabilize shifting dunes. [Of Scand. orig.]

mar·riage (măr′ĭj) *n.* **1. a.** The state of being married; wedlock. **b.** The legal union of a man and woman as husband and wife. **2.** The act of marrying or the ceremony of being married; wedding. **3.** A close union: *a true marriage of minds.* **4.** The combination of the king and queen of the same suit, as in pinochle. [ME *mariage* < OFr. < *marier,* to marry. —see MARRY.]

mar·riage·a·ble (măr′ĭ-jə-bəl) *adj.* Suitable for marriage: *of marriageable age.* —**mar′riage·a·bil′i·ty, mar′riage·a·ble·ness** *n.*

marriage of convenience *n.* A marriage or joint undertaking arranged for political, economic, or social benefit rather than from personal attachment.

mar·ried (măr′ēd) *adj.* **1. a.** Having a spouse: *a married man.* **b.** United in matrimony: *a married couple.* **2.** Of or pertaining to the state of marriage: *married bliss.* —*n.* A married person: *young marrieds.*

mar·ron (mă-rôɴ′) *n.* The Spanish chestnut (sense 2). [Fr. — see MAROON[2].]

mar·rons gla·cés (mă-rôɴ′ glă-sā′) *pl.n.* Chestnuts glazed with sugar or syrup. [Fr.]

mar·row (măr′ō) *n.* **1.** The soft material that fills bone cavities, consisting, in varying proportions, of fat cells and maturing blood cells together with supporting connective tissue and numerous blood vessels. **2.** Spinal marrow; the spinal cord. **3. a.** The inmost, choicest, or essential part; pith. **b.** Strength or vigor; vitality. **4.** *Chiefly Brit.* The vegetable marrow. [ME *marow* < OE *mearg.*]

mar·row·bone (măr′ō-bōn′) *n.* A bone for flavoring soup.

mar·row·fat (măr′ō-făt′) *n.* One of several varieties of pea that produces large seeds.

marrow pea *n.* The marrowfat.

marrow squash *n.* The vegetable marrow.

mar·ry[1] (măr′ē) *v.* **-ried, -ry·ing, -ries.** —*tr.* **1. a.** To become united with in matrimony: *They married each other in June.* **b.** To take as a husband or wife: *He married his sweetheart.* **c.** To give in marriage. **2.** To perform a marriage ceremony for. **3.** To obtain by marriage: *marry wealth.* **4.** *Naut.* To join (two ropes) end to end by interweaving their strands. **5.** To unite in a close, usually permanent way. —*intr.* **1.** To take a husband or wife; wed: *They married in their twenties.* **2.** To enter into a close relationship; unite. [ME *marien* < OFr. *marier* < Lat. *maritare* < *maritus,* married.]

mar·ry[2] (măr′ē) *interj. Archaic.* Used as an exclamation of surprise or emphasis. [ME *Marie,* Mary, the mother of Jesus.]

Mars (märz) *n.* **1.** *Rom. Myth.* The god of war. **2.** The fourth planet from the sun, having a sidereal period of revolution about the sun of 687 days at a mean distance of 227.8 million kilometers, or 141.6 million miles, a mean radius of approximately 3,363 kilometers, or 2,090 miles, and a mass approximately 0.15 that of Earth. [ME < Lat.]

mar·seille (mär-sāl′) also **mar·seilles** (-sālz′) *n.* A heavy cotton fabric with a raised pattern of stripes or figures. [After *Marseilles,* France.]

marsh (märsh) *n.* An area of low-lying wet land; fen, swamp, or bog. [ME < OE *mersc.*]

mar·shal (mär′shəl) *n.* **1.** In some countries, a military officer of the highest rank. **2.** In the United States: **a.** A Federal officer who carries out court orders. **b.** A city officer who carries out court orders. **c.** The head of a police or fire department. **3.** A person in charge of a parade or ceremony. **4.** A high official in a royal court, esp. one aiding the sovereign in military affairs. —*v.* **-shaled, -shal·ing, -shals** also **-shalled, -shal·ling, -shals.** —*tr.* **1.** To arrange or place (soldiers, for example) in line for a parade, maneuver, or review. **2.** To arrange, place, or set in methodical order: *marshal facts in preparation for an exam.* **3.** To enlist and organize: "*our interests in marshalling the French colonies against Germany*" (Winston Churchill). **4.** To guide (a person) ceremoniously; conduct or usher. —*intr.* To take up positions in or as if in a military formation. [ME < OFr. *mareschal,* of Germanic orig.] —**mar′shal·cy, mar′shal·ship′** *n.*

marsh elder *n.* Any of several shrubs of the genus *Iva,* of eastern and central North America, often growing in salt marshes.

marsh gas *n.* Methane.

marsh hawk *n.* A hawk, *Circus cyaneus,* found in marshy areas of North America and Eurasia.

marsh hen *n.* Any of various marsh birds of the family Rallidae, which includes the gallinules, coots, and rails.

marsh·land (märsh′lănd′) *n.* A marshy tract of land.

marsh·mal·low (märsh′mĕl′ō, -măl′ō) *n.* **1.** A confection of sweetened paste, formerly made from the root of the marsh mallow. **2.** A confection made of corn syrup, gelatin, sugar, and starch, and dusted with powdered sugar. **3.** *Slang.* A timid or cowardly person.

marsh mallow *n.* A plant, *Althaea officinalis,* native to Europe and naturalized in marshes of eastern North America, having showy pink flowers and a mucilaginous root used as a demulcent and in confectionery. [ME *mershmalwe* < OE *merscmealwe* : *mersc,* marsh + *mealwe,* mallow.]

marsh marigold *n.* A plant of the genus *Caltha,* esp. *C. palustris,* growing in swampy places and having bright yellow flowers.

marsh·y (mär′shē) *adj.* **-i·er, -i·est.** Of, like, or characterized by a marsh or marshes; boggy. —**marsh′i·ness** *n.*

mar·su·pi·a (mär-sōō′-pē-ə) *n.* Plural of **marsupium.**

mar·su·pi·al (mär-sōō′pē-əl) *n.* A mammal of the order Marsupialia, including kangaroos, opossums, bandicoots, and wombats, found principally in Australia and South and Central America. [NLat. *marsupialis* < *marsupium,* marsupium. —see MARSUPIUM.] —**mar·su′pi·al** *adj.*

mar·su·pi·um (mär-sōō′pē-əm) *n., pl.* **-pi·a** (-pē-ə). **1.** An external abdominal pouch in female marsupials that contains mammary glands and that shelters the young until fully developed. **2.** A temporary egg pouch in various animals. [NLat., pouch < Gk. *marsupion, marsipion,* dim. of *marsipos,* purse.]

mart (märt) *n.* **1.** A market; trading center. **2.** *Archaic.* A fair. [ME < MDu. < ONFr. *market,* market. —see MARKET.]

mar·ta·gon (mär′tə-gən) *n.* A lily, *Lilium martagon,* having pinkish-purple, spotted flowers. [ME < OFr. < OSp. < Turk. *martagān,* a kind of turban.]

Mar·tel·lo tower (mär-tĕl′ō) *n.* A small circular fort, formerly used in Europe for coastal defense. [After Cape *Mortella,* Corsica.]

mar·ten (mär′tn) *n., pl.* **marten** or **-tens.** **1.** Any of various carnivores of the genus *Martes,* found in northern wooded areas. **2.** The fur of the marten. [ME < OFr. *martrine* < Med. Lat. *martrina,* of Germanic orig.]

mar·ten·site (mär′tn-zīt′) *n.* A solid solution of iron and up to one per cent of carbon, the chief constituent of hardened carbon tool steels. [After Adolf *Martens* (1850–1914).] —**mar′ten·sit′ic** (-zĭt′ĭk) *adj.*

Mar·tha (mär′thə) *n.* In the New Testament, a sister of Lazarus and Mary, and friend of Jesus.

mar·tial (mär′shəl) *adj.* **1.** Of, pertaining to, or suggesting war. **2.** Pertaining to or connected with the armed forces or the military profession. **3.** Characteristic of or befitting a warrior: "*a bull-necked, martial-looking man*" (Dickens). [ME < Lat. *martialis* < *Mars,* Mars.] —**mar′tial·ism** *n.* —**mar′tial·ist** *n.* —**mar′tial·ly** *adv.*

martial art *n.* Any of several Oriental arts of combat or self-defense, as karate, judo, or tae kwon do, usually practiced as sport.

martial law *n.* Temporary rule by military authorities imposed upon a civilian population esp. in time of war or when civil authority is unable to maintain public safety.

Mar·tian (mär′shən) *adj.* Of or pertaining to the planet Mars. —*n.* A hypothetical inhabitant of the planet Mars, esp. as a stock fictional character. [ME < Lat. *martius* < *Mars,* Mars.]

mar·tin (mär′tn) *n.* Any of several birds resembling and closely related to the swallows, as the house martin and the purple martin. [OFr., prob. < the name *Martin,* Martin.]

mar·ti·net (mär′tn-ĕt′) *n.* **1.** A rigid military disciplinarian. **2.** A person who demands absolute adherence to rules: *a martinet about his children's schooling.* [After Jean *Martinet* (d. 1672), a French army officer.]

mar·tin·gale (mär′tn-gāl′) also **mar·tin·gal** (-găl′) *n.* **1.** The strap of a horse's harness that connects the girth to the nose band and is designed to prevent a horse from throwing back its head. **2.** *Naut.* Any of several parts of standing rigging strengthening the bowsprit and jib boom against the force of the head stays. **3.** A method of gambling in which one doubles the stakes after each loss. **4.** A loose half belt or strap placed on the back of a garment, as a coat or jacket. [OFr.]

mar·ti·ni (mär-tē′nē) *n., pl.* **-nis.** A cocktail made of gin or vodka and dry vermouth. [Orig. unknown.]

Martin Luther King Day *n.* January 15, Martin Luther

King's birthday, observed as a legal holiday by some U.S. states.

Mar·tin·mas (mär'tn-məs) *n.* A Christian festival celebrated annually on Saint Martin's Day, November 11. [ME *martinmesse* : *Martin,* Martin + *messe,* Mass.]

mart·let (märt'lĭt) *n.* **1.** The martin. **2.** In heraldry, a representation of a bird without feet, used as a crest or bearing to indicate a fourth son. [OFr. *martelet,* prob. alteration of *martinet,* dim. of *martin,* martin.]

mar·tyr (mär'tər) *n.* **1.** One who chooses to suffer death rather than renounce religious principles. **2.** A person who makes great sacrifices or suffers much in order to further a belief, cause, or principle. **3.** A person who endures great suffering: *a martyr to arthritis.* **4.** A person who makes a great show of suffering in order to arouse sympathy. —*tr.v.* **-tyred, -tyr·ing, -tyrs. 1.** To make a martyr of (a person). **2.** To inflict great pain upon; torment. [ME < OE < LLat. < Gk. *martus,* witness.]

mar·tyr·dom (mär'tər-dəm) *n.* **1.** The state of being a martyr; the suffering of death by a martyr. **2.** Extreme suffering.

mar·tyr·ize (mär'tə-rīz') *tr.v.* **-ized, -iz·ing, -iz·es.** To martyr.

mar·tyr·ol·o·gy (mär'tə-rŏl'ə-jē) *n., pl.* **-gies. 1.** A list or catalogue of religious martyrs. **2. a.** The history of religious martyrs, esp. Christian martyrs. **b.** A particular history or account of such martyrs. **—mar'tyr·ol'o·gist** *n.*

mar·vel (mär'vəl) *n.* **1.** Something that evokes surprise, admiration, or wonder. **2.** Strong surprise; astonishment. —*v.* **-veled, -vel·ing, -vels** also **-velled, -vel·ling, -vels.** —*intr.* To become filled with wonder or astonishment: *marveled at the child's genius.* —*tr.* To wonder at or about: *I marvel the fact that he came through safely.* [ME *marvail* < OFr. *merveille* < Lat. *marabilis,* wonderful < *mirari,* to wonder.]

mar·vel·ous also **mar·vel·lous** (mär'və-ləs) *adj.* **1.** Causing wonder or astonishment: *a marvelous cure.* **2.** Miraculous; supernatural: *"the Lord's doing; it is marvelous in our eyes"* (Psalm 118:23). **3.** Of the highest or best kind or quality; first-rate: *a marvelous recipe.* **—mar'vel·ous·ly** *adv.* **—mar'vel·ous·ness** *n.*

Marx·i·an (märk'sē-ən) *n.* One who studies, advocates, or makes use of Karl Marx's philosophical or socio-economic concepts as a method of analysis and interpretation, as in political economy or historical or literary criticism. **—Marx'i·an** *adj.* **—Marx'i·an·ism** *n.*

Marx·ism (märk'sĭz'əm) *n.* The political and economic ideas of Karl Marx and Friedrich Engels as developed into a system of thought that gives class struggle a primary role in leading society from bourgeois democracy under capitalism to a socialist society and thence to Communism.

Marx·ism-Len·in·ism (märk'sĭz'əm-lĕn'ĭ-nĭz'əm) *n.* The expansion of Marxism to include Lenin's concept of imperialism as the final form of capitalism, and a shift in the focus of struggle from the developed to the underdeveloped countries.

Marx·ist (märk'sĭst) *n.* One who believes in or follows the ideas of Marx and Engels, esp. a militant Communist.

Mar·y (mâr'ē) *n.* In the New Testament: **1.** The mother of Jesus. **2.** A sister of Lazarus and Martha, and a friend of Jesus.

Mary Jane (mâr'ē jān') *n. Slang.* Marijuana. [By folk ety. < MARIJUANA.]

Mary Mag·da·lene (măg'də-lēn', -lən, măg'də-lē'nē) also **Mary Mag·da·len** (măg'də-lən) *n.* In the New Testament, a woman whom Jesus cured of evil spirits and who saw Jesus near his tomb after he had risen from the dead.

Mar·y·ol·o·gy (mâr'ē-ol'ə-jē) *n.* Variant of **Mariology.**

mar·zi·pan (mär'zə-păn', märt'sə-păn') *n.* A confection made of ground almonds, egg whites, and sugar, molded into decorative forms. [G. < Ital. *marzapane,* marzipan, a medieval coin < Ar. *mawthabān,* a medieval coin.]

Ma·sai (mä-sī') *n., pl.* **Masai** or **-sais. 1.** A member of a people of Kenya and parts of Tanzania. **2.** The Nilotic language of the Masai. **—Ma·sai'** *adj.*

mas·ca·longe (măs'kə-lŏnj') *n.* Variant of **muskellunge.**

mas·car·a (mă-skăr'ə) *n.* A cosmetic applied to darken the eyelashes. [Sp. *máscara* < Ital. *maschera,* mask. —see MASK.]

mas·cot (măs'kŏt', -kət) *n.* A person, animal, or object believed to bring good luck, esp. one kept as the symbol of an athletic team or other organization. [Fr. *mascotte* < Prov. *mascoto* < *masca,* witch < LLat.]

mas·cu·line (măs'kyə-lĭn) *adj.* **1.** Of or pertaining to men or boys; male. **2.** Suggestive or characteristic of a man; mannish. **3.** Of, designating, or constituting the gender of words or grammatical forms denoting or referring normally to males: *a masculine suffix.* **4.** Of or having a stressed terminal syllable or syllables: *the masculine rhyme of "annoy, enjoy."* **5.** *Mus.* Ending on an accented beat: *a masculine cadence.* —*n.* **1.** The masculine gender. **2.** A word or word form of the masculine gender. **3.** A male. [ME < OFr. *masculin* < Lat. *masculinus* < *masculus,* male.] **—mas'cu·line·ly** *adv.* **—mas'cu·lin'i·ty, mas'cu·line·ness** *n.*

mas·cu·lin·ize (măs'kyə-lə-nīz') *tr.v.* **-ized, -iz·ing, -iz·es. 1.** To give a masculine appearance or character to. **2.** To cause to assume masculine characteristics.

ma·ser (mā'zər) *n.* Any of several devices that convert incident electromagnetic radiation from a wide range of frequencies to one or more discrete frequencies of highly amplified and coherent microwave radiation. [Acronym for *microwave amplification by stimulated emission of radiation.*]

mash (măsh) *n.* **1.** A fermentable starchy mixture from which alcohol or spirits can be distilled. **2.** A mixture of ground grain and nutrients fed to livestock and fowl. **3.** A soft, pulpy mixture or mass. **4.** A crushing or grinding. —*tr.v.* **mashed, mash·ing, mash·es. 1.** To convert (malt or grain) into mash. **2.** To convert into a soft, pulpy mixture: *mash potatoes.* **3.** To crush or grind. **4.** *Slang.* To flirt with or approach aggressively. [ME < OE *māsc.*]

mash·er (măsh'ər) *n.* **1.** A kitchen utensil for mashing vegetables or fruit. **2.** *Slang.* A man who attempts to force his amorous attentions upon a woman.

mash·ie also **mash·y** (măsh'ē) *n., pl.* **-ies.** A golf club of medium loft. [Orig. unknown.]

mas·jid (mŭs'jĭd) *n.* A mosque. [Ar.]

mask (măsk) *n.* **1.** A covering worn on the face to conceal one's identity, as: **a.** A cloth covering that has openings for the eyes, entirely or partly conceals the face, and is worn esp. at a masquerade ball. **b.** A representation of a grotesque face. **c.** A facial covering worn for ritual. **d.** A figure of a head worn by actors in Greek and Roman drama to identify a trait. **2.** A protective covering for the face or head. **3.** A gas mask. **4.** A representation of a face or head: **a.** A mold of a person's face, often made after death. **b.** An often grotesque representation of a head and face, used for ornamentation. **5.** The face or facial markings of certain animals, as a fox or dog. **6.** A face having a blank, fixed, or enigmatic expression. **7.** Something, often a trait, that disguises or conceals: *"If ever I saw misery under a mask, it was on her face"* (Erskine Childers). **8.** A natural or artificial feature of terrain that conceals and protects military forces or installations. **9. a.** An opaque border or pattern placed between a source of light and a photosensitive surface to prevent exposure of specified portions of the surface. **b.** The translucent border framing a television picture tube and screen. **10.** A cosmetic preparation applied as a covering and removed. **11.** Variant of **masque. 12.** A person wearing a mask. —*v.* **masked, mask·ing, masks.** —*tr.* **1.** To cover with a decorative or protective mask. **2.** To disguise by making indistinct or blurred to the senses: *The spice masks the meat's strong flavor.* **3.** To cover up for concealment or protection: *guns that were masked under heavy overcoats.* **4.** To block the view of: *Undergrowth masked the entrance.* **5.** To cover (a part of a photographic film) by the application of an opaque border. **6.** *Chem.* To inhibit (a compound or radical) with a reagent more active in a specific reaction. —*intr.* **1.** To put on a mask, esp. for a masquerade ball; disguise oneself. **2.** To conceal one's real personality, character, or intentions. [Fr. *masque* < Ital. *maschera,* poss. < Ar. *maskharah,* buffoon.]

mas·ka·longe (măs'kə-lŏnj') *n.* A muskellunge.

masked (măskt) *adj.* **1.** Wearing a mask. **2.** Disguised; concealed. **3.** Latent or hidden, as a symptom or disease. **4.** *Bot.* Personate. **5.** *Zool.* Having masklike markings on the head or face.

masked ball *n.* A ball at which the use of masks, often richly decorated, is required.

mas·keg (măs'kĕg') *n.* Variant of **muskeg.**

mask·er also **mas·quer** (măs'kər) *n.* A participant in a masquerade or masque.

mask·ing (măs'kĭng) *n.* **1.** *Psychol.* The concealment or screening of one sensory process by another. **2.** A piece of theatrical scenery used to conceal a part of the stage from the audience.

masking paper *n.* Paper used to cover and protect a surface that is not to be painted.

masking tape *n.* An adhesive tape used to cover and protect a surface that is not to be painted.

mas·ki·nonge (măs'kə-nŏng') *n.* A muskellunge.

mas·o·chism (măs'ə-kĭz'əm) *n.* **1.** *Psychiat.* An abnormal condition in which sexual excitement and satisfaction depend largely on being subjected to abuse or physical pain, whether by oneself or by another. **2. a.** The act or an instance of deriving pleasure from being offended, dominated, or mistreated in some way. **b.** The tendency to seek such mistreatment. **3.** The turning of any sort of destructive tendencies inward or upon oneself. [After Leopold von Sacher-*Masoch* (1836–1895), Austrian novelist.] **—mas'o·chist** *n.* **—mas'o·chis'tic** *adj.* **—mas'o·chis'ti·cal·ly** *adv.*

ma·son (mā'sən) *n.* **1.** A person who builds or works with stone or brick. **2.** A stonecutter. **3. Mason.** A Freemason (sense 2). —*tr.v.* **-soned, -son·ing, -sons.** To build of or strengthen with masonry. [ME < OFr., of Germanic orig.]

mason bee *n.* Any of various solitary bees of the genus *Anthidium,* found worldwide, that build clay nests.

Ma·son·ic (mə-sŏn'ĭk) *adj.* Of or pertaining to Freemasons or Freemasonry.

Ma·son·ite (mā'sə-nīt'). A trademark for a type of fiberboard used for insulation, paneling, or partitions.

Ma·son jar (mā'sən) *n.* A wide-mouthed glass jar with a screw top, used widely for home canning and preserving. [After John L. *Mason* (1832–1902), its inventor.]

ma·son·ry (mā'sən-rē) *n., pl.* **-ries. 1.** The trade of a mason.

martlet

mascot
Ornament from the hood of a truck

mask

2. Work done by a mason. 3. Stonework or brickwork. 4. **Masonry.** Freemasonry (sense 2).
masonry cement *n.* A kind of cement esp. prepared to be used in the mortar of block and brick masonry.
Ma·so·ra also **Ma·so·rah** (mə-sôr′ə, -sōr′ə) *n.* 1. The body of tradition relating to correct textual reading of the Old Testament. 2. The critical notes in which the Masora is embodied, made by Jewish scholars before the tenth century A.D. [Heb. *māsōrāh* < Heb. *māsar,* to hand over.] **—Mas′o·ret′ic** (măs′ə-rĕt′ĭk) *adj.*
masque also **mask** (măsk) *n.* 1. A dramatic entertainment, usually based on a mythological or allegorical theme, popular in England in the 16th and early 17th centuries. 2. A dramatic verse composition written for a masque production. 3. A masquerade (sense 1). [Fr. < Ital. *maschera,* mask.]
mas·quer (măs′kər) *n.* Variant of **masker.**
mas·quer·ade (măs′kə-rād′) *n.* 1. a. A costume party at which masks are worn; masked ball. b. A costume for such a party or ball. 2. a. A disguise or false outward show; pretense: *a masquerade of humility.* b. An involved scheme; charade. *—intr.v.* **-ad·ed, -ad·ing, -ades.** 1. To wear a mask or disguise, as at a masquerade: *She masqueraded as a shepherdess.* 2. To go about as if in disguise; have or put on a deceptive appearance: *The stowaway masqueraded as a crewman.* [OFr. *mascarade* < OSp. *mascarada,* poss. < Ar. *maskharah,* buffoon.] **—mas′quer·ad′er**
mass (măs) *n.* 1. A unified body of matter with no specific shape. 2. A grouping of individual parts or elements that compose a unified body of unspecified size or quantity: *"the heterogeneous, indistinguishable mass of college boys"* (F. Scott Fitzgerald). 3. A large but nonspecific amount or number: *a mass of bruises.* 4. The major part; majority: *the mass of the continent.* 5. The physical volume or bulk of a solid body. 6. *Physics.* The measure of a body's resistance to acceleration. The mass of a body is different from but proportional to its weight, is independent of the body's position but dependent on its motion with respect to other bodies, and may be expressed in mass units, as kilograms or slugs, or corresponding energy units, by means of the mass-energy relationship of the special theory of relativity. 7. An area of unified light, shade, or color in a painting. 8. A thick, pasty mixture of drugs used to form pills. 9. A mineral deposit with no specific shape. 10. **the masses.** The body of common people; the many. *—tr. & intr.v.* **massed, mass·ing, mass·es.** To gather or form into a mass. *—adj.* 1. Of, pertaining to, characteristic of, or attended by a large number of people: *mass education.* 2. Directed at or reaching a large number of people: *mass communication; mass marketing.* 3. Done on a large scale; involving great numbers or large amounts: *a mass evacuation.* 4. Total; complete: *The mass result is impressive.* [ME *masse* < OFr. < Lat. *massa* < Gk. *maza.*]
Mass also **mass** (măs) *n.* 1. a. In Roman Catholic and some Protestant churches, the celebration of the Eucharist. b. A service including this celebration. 2. A musical setting of certain parts of the Mass, esp. the Kyrie, Gloria, Credo, Sanctus, Benedictus, and Agnus Dei. [ME *masse* < OE *mæsse* < LLat. *missa* < Lat. *mittere,* to send.]
Mas·sa·chu·set also **Mas·sa·chu·sett** (măs′ə-cho͞o′sĭt, -zĭt) *n.* 1. a. A large tribe of Algonquian-speaking Indians who lived on or near Massachusetts Bay. b. A member of this tribe. 2. The Algonquian language of the Massachuset. [Massachuset.]
mas·sa·cre (măs′ə-kər) *n.* 1. The act or an instance of killing a number of human beings indiscriminately and cruelly. 2. The slaughter of a large number of animals. 3. *Informal.* A severe defeat, as in sports. *—tr.v.* **-cred** (-kərd), **-cring** (-krĭng, -kər-ĭng), **-cres.** 1. To kill indiscriminately and wantonly; slaughter. 2. *Informal.* To defeat decisively. [OFr.] **—mas′sa·crer** (-kər-ər, -krər) *n.*
mas·sage (mə-säzh′, -säj′) *n.* The rubbing or kneading of parts of the body to aid circulation or to relax the muscles. *—tr.v.* **-saged, -sag·ing, -sag·es.** 1. To give a massage to. 2. To treat by means of a massage. [Fr. < *masser,* to massage < Ar. *massa,* he touched.]
mas·sa·sau·ga (măs′ə-sô′gə) *n.* A brown and white venomous rattlesnake, *Sistrurus catenatus,* of North America. [After the *Missisauga* River, Ontario, Canada.]
mass·cult (măs′kŭlt′) *n.* Culture at the level of the masses: *American films, in the main, are masscult.* [MASS + CULT(URE).]
mass defect *n.* The amount by which the mass of an atomic nucleus is less than the sum of the masses of its constituent particles.
mass deficiency *n.* The mass defect.
mas·sé (mă-sā′) *n.* A stroke in billiards made by hitting the cue ball on its side with the cue held nearly perpendicular, so the cue ball will curve around one of the object balls. [Fr. < *masser,* to cue < *masse,* cue.]
mass-en·er·gy equivalence (măs′ĕn′ər-jē) *n.* The physical principle that a measured quantity of energy is equivalent to a measured quantity of mass. The equivalence is expressed by Einstein's equation, $E = mc^2$, where E represents energy, m the equivalent mass, and c the speed of light.
mas·se·ter (mə-sē′tər, mă-) *n.* A large muscle used in mastication that raises the lower jaw. [NLat. < Gk. *masētēr* < *masasthai,* to chew.]
mas·seur (mă-sûr′, mə-) *n.* A man who gives massages professionally. [Fr. < *masser,* to massage.]
mas·seuse (mă-soez′) *n.* A woman who gives massages professionally. [Fr., fem. of *masseur.*]
mas·si·cot (măs′ĭ-kŏt′, -kō′) *n.* The yellow crystalline mineral form of lead monoxide, PbO. [ME *masticot.*]
mas·sif (mă-sēf′) *n.* A large mountain mass or compact group of connected mountains forming an independent portion of a range. [Fr. < *massif,* massive < OFr. —see MASSIVE.]
mas·sive (măs′ĭv) *adj.* 1. Consisting of or making up a large mass; bulky: *a massive piece of furniture.* 2. Unusually large or impressive: *a massive head.* 3. Large or imposing in quantity, scope, degree, intensity, or scale: *a massive undertaking.* 4. *Med.* Large in comparison with the usual amount: *a massive dose.* 5. *Pathol.* Affecting a large area of bodily tissue; widespread and severe: *massive gangrene.* 6. Lacking crystalline structure; amorphous. [ME *massif* < OFr. < *masse,* mass. —see MASS[1].] **—mas′sive·ly** *adv.* **—mas′sive·ness** *n.*
mass·less (măs′lĭs) *adj.* Having no mass.
mass medium *n., pl.* **mass media.** A means of public communication reaching a large audience.
mass noun *n.* A noun, as *sugar, oil,* or *honesty,* typically denoting a concept or substance that in English is preceded in the singular by modifiers such as *some* or *much* rather than *a* or *an.*
mass number *n.* The total number of neutrons and protons in an atomic nucleus.
mass-pro·duce (măs′prə-do͞os′, -dyo͞os′) *tr.v.* **-duced, -duc·ing, -duc·es.** To manufacture in large quantities often by or as if by assembly-line techniques.
mass production *n.* The manufacture of goods in large quantities, using standardized designs and often assembly-line techniques.
mass spectrograph *n.* An instrument used to separate charged particles from a prepared beam by means of an electromagnetic field and to photograph the resulting distribution or spectrum of masses.
mass·y (măs′ē) *adj.* **-i·er, -i·est.** Having great mass or bulk; massive.
mast[1] (măst) *n.* 1. A tall vertical spar, sometimes sectioned, that rises from the keel of a sailing vessel to support the sails and running rigging. 2. A vertical pole. [ME < OE *mæst.*]
mast[2] (măst) *n.* The nuts of forest trees accumulated on the ground, used esp. as food for swine. [ME < OE *mæst.*]
mast– *pref.* Variant of **masto-.**
mas·ta·ba also **mas·ta·bah** (măs′tə-bə) *n.* An ancient Egyptian tomb with a rectangular base, sloping sides, and a flat roof. [Ar. *maṣṭabah,* stone bench.]
mast cell *n.* A cell found mainly in connective tissue that contains numerous basophilic granules of heparin. [Partial transl. of G. *Mast Zelle* : *Mast,* food + *Zelle,* cell.]
mas·tec·to·my (măs-tĕk′tə-mē) *n., pl.* **-mies.** Surgical removal of a breast.
mas·ter (măs′tər) *n.* 1. A person having control over the action of another or others. 2. The captain of a merchant ship. 3. a. A person who employs an apprentice. b. An employer. 4. The owner of a slave or an animal. 5. The man who serves as the head of a household. 6. One who has control over something; possessor: *the master of a large tea plantation.* 7. One who defeats another; victor. 8. A teacher, schoolmaster, or tutor. 9. a. A person whose teachings or doctrines are accepted by followers. b. **Master.** Christ. 10. A person of great learning; scholar. 11. a. A college or university degree signifying completion of at least one year of prescribed study beyond the bachelor's degree. b. A person holding such a degree. 12. An artist or performer of great and exemplary skill. 13. A workman qualified to teach apprentices and to carry on his craft independently. 14. An old master. 15. An expert: *a master of deceit.* 16. A former title for a man holding a naval office ranking next below a lieutenant on a warship. 17. The title of the head or presiding officer of certain societies, clubs, orders, or institutions. 18. *Chiefly Brit.* The title of any of various law court officers. 19. **Master.** The title of any of various officers having specified duties concerning the management of the British royal household. 20. **Master.** A man who owns a pack of hounds or is a chief officer of a hunt. 21. *Archaic.* A form of address for a man; mister. 22. **Master.** A prefix to the name of a boy or youth not considered old enough to be addressed as Mister. 23. An original from which copies can be made. *—adj.* 1. Of, pertaining to, or characteristic of a master. 2. Being the principal or leading force. 3. Being something specified in a superlative degree: *a master thief.* 4. Highly skilled; expert. 5. Controlling all other parts of a mechanism: *a master switch.* 6. Being an original from which copies are made. *—tr.v.* **-tered, -ter·ing, -ters.** 1. To act as or be the master of. 2. To make oneself a master of: *mastered the language in a year's study.* 3. To overcome or defeat: *finally mastered his addiction to drugs.* 4. To reduce to subjugation; break or tame (a person or animal). 5. To season or age (dyed goods). [ME < OE *magister* and OFr. *maistre,* both < Lat. *magister.*] **—mas′ter·dom** *n.*

mas·ter-at-arms (măs′tər-ət-ärmz′) *n., pl.* **mas·ters-at-arms.** A naval petty officer assigned to maintain order.
master bedroom *n.* A main bedroom, esp. one used by the head of the household.
mas·ter·ful (măs′tər-fəl) *adj.* **1.** Given to playing the master; imperious. **2.** Fit to command. **3.** Revealing mastery: *a masterful technique.* **4.** Expert; skillful: *masterful moviemaking.* —**mas′ter·ful·ly** *adv.* —**mas′ter·ful·ness** *n.*
Usage: *Masterful* has the undisputed meaning of "strong-willed, imperious, domineering." It is widely used also as a substitute for *masterly* in the sense of "having the skill of a master." A majority of the Usage Panel feels that the distinction between the two words should be respected, as in *a masterly* (not *masterful*) *performance of a Beethoven sonata.*
master key *n.* A key that opens several different locks whose keys are not the same.
mas·ter·ly (măs′tər-lē) *adj.* Having or showing the knowledge or skill of a master. —*adv.* With the skill of a master. —See Usage note at **masterful.** —**mas′ter·li·ness** *n.*
master mariner *n.* A master (sense 2).
master mason *n.* **1.** An expert mason. **2. Master Mason.** The third degree of Freemasonry.
mas·ter·mind (măs′tər-mīnd′) *n.* A highly intelligent person, esp. one who plans and directs a complex or difficult project. —*tr.v.* **-mind·ed, -mind·ing, -minds.** To direct, plan, or supervise (a project or activity).
master of ceremonies *n.* **1.** A person who acts as host at a formal event, making the welcoming speech and introducing other speakers. **2.** A performer who conducts a program of varied entertainment by introducing other performers to the audience.
mas·ter·piece (măs′tər-pēs′) *n.* **1.** An outstanding work of art or craft. **2.** The greatest work of an artist or craftsman. **3.** Something superlative: *a masterpiece of hypocrisy.* [Prob. transl. of Du. *meesterstuk* or G. *Meisterstück.*]
master plan *n.* A plan giving comprehensive guidance or instruction.
master race *n.* A people who hold themselves to be superior to other races and therefore suited to rule over them.
master sergeant *n.* A noncommissioned officer of the next to highest rating in the U.S. Army, Air Force, and Marine Corps.
mas·ter·ship (măs′tər-shĭp′) *n.* **1.** The office, function, or authority of a master. **2.** The skill or dexterity of a master.
mas·ter·sing·er (măs′tər-sĭng′ər) *n.* A Meistersinger.
mas·ter·stroke (măs′tər-strōk′) *n.* A masterly achievement or action: *a masterstroke of statesmanship.*
mas·ter·work (măs′tər-wûrk′) *n.* A masterpiece.
mas·ter·y (măs′tə-rē) *n., pl.* **-ies. 1.** Possession of consummate skill. **2.** The status of master or ruler; control: *mastery of the seas.* **3.** Full command of a subject of study: *a poet's mastery of the language.*
mast·head (măst′hĕd′) *n.* **1.** The top of a ship's mast. **2.** The listing in a newspaper, magazine, or other publication of information about its staff and operation.
mas·tic (măs′tĭk) *n.* **1.** The mastic tree. **2.** The aromatic resin of the mastic tree, used in varnishes and lacquers and as an astringent. **3.** A Near Eastern liquor, flavored with mastic resin and aniseed. **4.** A pastelike cement, esp. one made with powdered lime or brick and tar. [ME < OFr. < Lat. *mastiche* < Gk. *mastikhē.*]
mas·ti·cate (măs′tĭ-kāt′) *tr.v.* **-cat·ed, -cat·ing, -cates. 1.** To chew. **2.** To grind and knead. [LLat. *masticare, masticat-,* to masticate < Gk. *mastikhan,* to grind the teeth.] —**mas′ti·ca′tion** *n.* —**mas′ti·ca′tor** *n.*
mas·ti·ca·to·ry (măs′tĭ-kə-tôr′ē, -tōr′ē) *adj.* **1.** Of, pertaining to, or used in mastication. **2.** Adapted for chewing. —*n., pl.* **-ries.** A substance chewed to increase salivation.
mastic tree *n.* **1.** A small evergreen tree, *Pistacia lentiscus,* of the Mediterranean region. **2.** The pepper tree.
mas·tiff (măs′tĭf) *n.* A large dog of an ancient breed, probably originating in Asia, having a short fawn-colored coat. [ME *mastif* < OFr. *mastin* < Lat. *mansuetus,* tamed : *manus,* hand + *suescere,* to accustom.]
mastiff bat *n.* Any of various bats of the family Molossidae, found in the tropics, having narrow wings and brown, gray, or black fur.
mas·ti·goph·o·ran (măs′tĭ-gŏf′ə-rən) also **mas·tig·o·phore** (mă-stĭg′ə-fôr′, -fōr′) *n.* A member of the class Mastigophora, which includes protozoans with one or more flagella. [NLat. *Mastigophora,* class name : Gk. *mastix,* whip + Gk. *pherein,* to bear.] —**mas′ti·goph′o·ran** *adj.*
mas·ti·tis (mă-stī′tĭs) *n.* Inflammation of the breast or udder. —**mas·tit′ic** (-tĭt′ĭk) *adj.*
masto- or **mast-** *pref.* Breast; mammary gland; nipple: *mastectomy.* [NLat. < Gk. *mastos,* breast.]
mas·to·don (măs′tə-dŏn′) *n.* Any of several extinct mammals of the genus *Mammut* (sometimes called *Mastodon*), resembling the elephant. [NLat. *Mastodon,* genus name : Gk. *mastos,* nipple + Gk. *odous,* tooth.]
mas·to·dont (măs′tə-dŏnt′) *adj.* **1.** Having teeth like those of a mastodon. **2.** Of, pertaining to, or characteristic of mastodons.
mas·toid (măs′toid′) *n.* **1.** The mastoid process. **2.** Mastoiditis. —*adj.* **1.** Pertaining to the mastoid process. **2.** Shaped like a breast or nipple.
mastoid bone *n.* The mastoid process.
mastoid cell *n.* One of the small air-filled spaces in the mastoid process.
mas·toid·ec·to·my (măs′toid-ĕk′tə-mē) *n., pl.* **-mies.** Surgical removal of part or all of the mastoid process.
mas·toid·i·tis (măs′toid-ī′tĭs) *n.* Inflammation of part or all of the mastoid process.
mastoid process *n.* The rear portion of the temporal bone on each side of the head behind the ear in man and many other vertebrates.
mas·tur·bate (măs′tər-bāt′) *v.* **-bat·ed, -bat·ing, -bates.** —*intr.* To perform an act of masturbation. —*tr.* To perform an act of masturbation on. [Lat. *masturbari, masturbat-,* to masturbate.]
mas·tur·ba·tion (măs′tər-bā′shən) *n.* Excitation of the genital organs, usually to orgasm, by manual contact or means other than sexual intercourse. —**mas′tur·ba′tion·al, mas′tur·ba·to′ry** (-bə-tôr′ē, -tōr′ē) *adj.* —**mas′tur·ba′tor** *n.*
mat[1] (măt) *n.* **1.** A flat piece of fabric or other material used for wiping one's shoes or feet, or in various other forms as a floor covering. **2.** A small, flat piece of decorated material placed under a lamp, dish of food, or other object. **3.** A floor pad to protect athletes, as in wrestling or gymnastics. **4.** A densely woven or thickly tangled mass: *a mat of hair.* **5.** The solid part of a lace design. **6.** A heavy, woven net of rope or wire cable placed over a blasting site to keep debris from scattering. —*v.* **mat·ted, mat·ting, mats.** —*tr.* **1.** To cover, protect, or decorate with a mat or mats. **2.** To interweave into or cover with a thick mass: *A heavy growth of vines matted the tree.* —*intr.* To be interwoven into a thick mass; become entangled. [ME < OE *matta* < LLat.]
mat[2] (măt) *n.* **1.** A decorative border of cardboard or similar material placed around a picture to serve as a frame or act as a contrast between the picture and the frame. **2.** Also **matte. a.** A dull, often rough, finish, as on glass, metal, or paper. **b.** A special tool for producing such a surface or finish. **3.** *Printing.* A matrix (sense 10.b.). —*tr.v.* **mat·ted, mat·ting, mats. 1.** To put a mat around (a picture). **2.** To produce a dull finish on. —*adj.* Also **matte.** Having a dull finish. [< Fr., dull < OFr., helpless. —see MATE[2].]
Mat·a·be·le (măt′ə-bē′lē) *n., pl.* **Matabele** or **-les. 1. a.** A Zulu tribe driven out of the Transvaal by the Boers in 1837. **b.** A member of this tribe. **2.** The Bantu language of the Matabele.
mat·a·dor (măt′ə-dôr′) *n.* **1.** A bullfighter who performs the final passes and kills the bull. **2.** One of the highest trumps in certain card games. [Sp. < Lat. *mactare,* to sacrifice < *mactus,* sacred.]
match[1] (măch) *n.* **1. a.** A person or thing that is exactly like another; counterpart. **b.** A person or thing that is like another in one or more specified qualities: *He is John's match for bravery.* **2. a.** A person or thing that closely resembles or harmonizes with another: *The napkins were a nice match for the tablecloth.* **b.** A pair made up of two things or persons that resemble or harmonize with each other: *The colors were a close match.* **3.** A person or thing equal in qualities or able to compete with another of the same class or type: *The boxer had met his match.* **4.** *Sports.* **a.** An athletic contest or game in which two or more persons, animals, or teams oppose and compete with each other: *a soccer match.* **b.** A race between horses belonging to two different owners who have set the terms and conditions of the race. **c.** A tennis contest decided on the basis of victory in a specified number of sets, usually two out of three or three out of five. **5.** A marriage or an arrangement of marriage: *a royal match.* **6.** A person viewed as a prospective marriage partner. —*v.* **matched, match·ing, match·es.** —*tr.* **1. a.** To be exactly like; correspond exactly. **b.** To be like with respect to specified qualities: *The markings on the stamps matched each other.* **2.** To resemble or harmonize with: *The coat matches the dress.* **3.** To adapt or suit so that a balanced or harmonious result is achieved; cause to correspond: *"Let poets match their subject to their strength"* (Earl Roscommon). **4.** To fit together or cause to fit together, esp. to cut (boards) with a tongue and groove. **5.** To join or give in marriage. **6.** To place in opposition or competition; pit: *matched his skill against all comers.* **7.** To provide with an adversary or competitor. **8.** To do as well as or better than in competition; equal. **9.** To set in comparison; compare: *beauty that could never be matched.* **10.** To provide funds so as to equal or complement: *The government will match all private donations to the museum.* **11.** To flip or toss (coins) and compare the sides that land face up. **12.** To couple (electric circuits) by means of a transformer. —*intr.* To be a close counterpart; correspond. [ME *macch* < OE *gemæcca,* companion.] —**match′er** *n.*
match[2] (măch) *n.* **1.** A narrow strip of wood, cardboard, or wax coated on one end with a compound that ignites easily by friction. **2.** An easily ignited cord or wick, formerly used to detonate powder charges or to fire cannons and muzzle-loading firearms. [ME *matche,* lamp wick < OFr. *meche* < Med. Lat. *myxa* < Lat., a lamp's nozzle < Gk. *muxa,* lamp wick.]

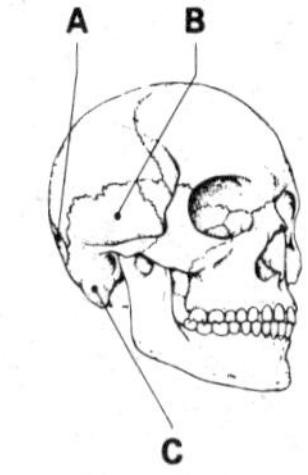

mastoid process
A. Occipital
B. Temporal
C. Mastoid process

matador

match·a·ble (măch′ə-bəl) *adj.* Capable of being matched. **—match′a·bil′i·ty** *n.*
match·board (măch′bôrd′, -bōrd′) *n.* A board cut with a tongue on one side and a matching groove on the other to fit with other boards of identical cut.
match·book (măch′bo͝ok′) *n.* A small folder containing matches.
match·box (măch′bŏks′) *n.* A box for keeping matches.
match·less (măch′lĭs) *adj.* Having no match or equal; unsurpassed: *matchless virtuosity at the keyboard.* **—match′less·ly** *adv.* **—match′less·ness** *n.*
match·lock (măch′lŏk′) *n.* **1.** A gunlock in which powder is ignited by a match. **2.** A musket having a matchlock.
match·mak·er (măch′mā′kər) *n.* **1.** One who habitually tries to arrange marriages. **2.** One who arranges athletic competitions.
match play *n. Sports.* A method of scoring golf games by counting only the number of holes won by each side rather than the number of strokes taken.
match point *n.* The final point needed to win a sports match, esp. in tennis.
match·wood (măch′wo͝od′) *n.* **1.** Wood in small pieces or splinters suitable esp. for making matches. **2.** Splinters: *The vessel was beaten to matchwood on the rocks.*

matzo

mate[1] (māt) *n.* **1.** One of a matched pair: *the mate to this glove.* **2.** A spouse. **3. a.** One of a conjugal pair of animals or birds. **b.** One of a pair of animals brought together for breeding. **4. a.** A person with whom one is in close association. **b.** A good friend or companion. **5.** A deck officer on a merchant ship ranking below the master. **6.** A U.S. Navy petty officer who is an assistant to the warrant officer. *—v.* **mat·ed, mat·ing, mates.** *—tr.* **1.** To join closely; pair. **2.** To unite in marriage. **3.** To pair (animals) for breeding. *—intr.* **1.** To become joined in marriage. **2.** To become mated; breed. [ME < MLG.]
mate[2] (māt) *n.* A checkmate. *—v.* **mat·ed, mat·ing, mates.** *—tr.* To checkmate. *—intr.* To achieve a checkmate. [ME < OFr. *mat,* checkmated < Pers. *māt,* helpless.]
ma·té (mä′tā′) *n.* **1.** An evergreen tree, *Ilex paraguayensis,* of South America, where it is widely cultivated. **2.** A mildly stimulant beverage, popular in South America, made from the dried leaves of the maté. [Am. Sp. < Quechua *mate,* beverage.]
mat·e·lote (măt′ə-lōt′) also **mat·e·lotte** (-lŏt′) *n.* **1.** A wine sauce for fish. **2.** Fish stewed in a wine sauce. [Fr. < *matelot,* sailor < OFr. *matenot,* prob. < MDu. *mattenoot* : *matte,* bed + *noot,* fellow.]
ma·ter (mā′tər) *n. Chiefly Brit.* Mother. [Lat.]
ma·ter·fa·mil·i·as (mā′tər-fə-mĭl′ē-əs) *n.* The mother of a family. [Lat. : *mater,* mother + *familia,* family.]
ma·te·ri·al (mə-tîr′ē-əl) *n.* **1.** The substance or substances out of which a thing is or can be constructed. **2.** Something, as an idea or sketch, to be refined and made or incorporated into a finished effort: *material for a comedy.* **3. materials.** Tools or apparatus for the performance of a given task: *writing materials.* **4.** Yard goods or cloth. *—adj.* **1.** Composed of or pertaining to physical substances; relating to matter. **2.** Of, pertaining to, or affecting physical well-being: *material comfort.* **3.** Of or concerned with the physical as distinct from the intellectual or spiritual. **4.** Substantial; noticeable: *a material improvement.* **5.** Of importance to a case; relevant: *discussed only the most material matters.* **6.** *Philos.* Of or pertaining to the matter of reasoning, rather than the form. [ME < *material,* consisting of matter < LLat. *materialis* < Lat. *materia,* matter.] **—ma·te′ri·al·ness** *n.*
ma·te·ri·al·ism (mə-tîr′ē-ə-lĭz′əm) *n.* **1.** The philosophical theory that physical matter in its movements and modifications is the only reality and that everything in the universe, including thought, feeling, mind, and will, can be explained in terms of physical laws. **2.** The theory or doctrine that physical well-being and worldly possessions constitute the greatest good and highest value in life. **3.** A great or excessive regard for worldly concerns. **—ma·te′ri·al·ist** *n.* **—ma·te′ri·al·is′tic** *adj.* **—ma·te′ri·al·is′ti·cal·ly** *adv.*
ma·te·ri·al·i·ty (mə-tîr′ē-ăl′ĭ-tē) *n., pl.* **-ties. 1.** The state or quality of being material. **2.** Physical substance; matter.
ma·te·ri·al·ize (mə-tîr′ē-ə-līz′) *v.* **-ized, -iz·ing, -iz·es.** *—tr.* To cause to become real or actual: *By building the house, he materialized his dream.* *—intr.* **1.** To assume material or effective form: *Their support on the eastern flank did not materialize.* **2.** To take physical form or shape. **3.** To appear, esp. suddenly. **—ma·te′ri·al·i·za′tion** *n.* **—ma·te′ri·al·iz′er** *n.*
Usage: *Materialize* as an intransitive verb has the primary sense of "to assume material form" or, more generally, "to take effective shape": *If our plans materialize, we will be independent for life* (acceptable to a majority of the Usage Panel). Though it is well established in the sense of "appear" or "happen," as in *Three more witnesses testified, but no new evidence materialized,* such a usage is not acceptable to a majority of the Usage Panel.
ma·te·ri·al·ly (mə-tîr′ē-ə-lē) *adv.* **1.** With regard to matter as distinguished from form. **2.** To a significant extent or degree; importantly. **3.** With regard to the physical world.
ma·te·ri·a med·i·ca (mə-tîr′ē-ə mĕd′ĭ-kə) *n. Med.* **1.** The study of remedies and their sources, preparation, and use. **2. a.** Substances used as or in preparing remedies; medicines. **b.** A particular medicine. [NLat. : Lat. *materia,* material + Lat. *medica,* medical.]
ma·te·ri·el or **ma·té·ri·el** (mə-tîr′ē-ĕl′) *n.* **1.** The equipment, apparatus, and supplies, as guns and ammunition, of a military force. **2.** The equipment, apparatus, and supplies of an organization. [Fr. < *matériel,* consisting of matter < OFr. *materiel* < LLat. *materialis.* —see MATERIAL.]
ma·ter·nal (mə-tûr′nəl) *adj.* **1.** Relating to or characteristic of a mother or motherhood; motherly: *maternal instinct.* **2.** Inherited from one's mother: *a maternal trait.* **3.** Related through one's mother: *my maternal uncle.* **4.** Of one's mother. [ME < OFr. *maternel* < Lat. *maternus* < *mater,* mother.] **—ma·ter′nal·ly** *adv.*
ma·ter·ni·ty (mə-tûr′nĭ-tē) *n.* **1.** The state of being a mother; motherhood. **2.** The feelings or characteristics associated with being a mother; motherliness. ***—modifier:*** *a maternity dress; maternity leave.* [Fr. *maternité* < Med. Lat. *maternitas* < Lat. *maternus,* maternal < *mater,* mother.]
mat·ey (mā′tē) *adj. Chiefly Brit. Informal.* Sociable; friendly.
math (măth) *n.* Mathematics.
math·e·mat·i·cal (măth′ə-măt′ĭ-kəl) also **math·e·mat·ic** (-ĭk) *adj.* **1.** Of or pertaining to mathematics. **2.** Precise; exact. **3.** Absolute; certain. [ME < Med. Lat. *mathematicus* < Lat. < Gk. *mathēmatikos* < *mathēma,* science < *manthanein,* to learn.] **—math′e·mat′i·cal·ly** *adv.*
mathematical induction *n.* Induction (sense 3.b.).
mathematical logic *n.* Symbolic logic.
math·e·ma·ti·cian (măth′ə-mə-tĭsh′ən) *n.* A person skilled or learned in mathematics.
math·e·mat·ics (măth′ə-măt′ĭks) *n. (used with a sing. verb).* The study of numbers, their form, arrangement, and associated relationships, using rigorously defined literal, numerical, and operational symbols. [ME *mathematik* < OFr. *matimatique* < Lat. *mathematica* < Gk. *mathēmatika* < *mathēmatikos,* mathematical. —see MATHEMATICAL.]
maths (măths) *n. Chiefly Brit.* Mathematics.
ma·til·i·ja poppy (mə-tĭl′ē-hä′) *n.* A shrubby plant, *Romneya Coulteri,* of California and Mexico, having very large, solitary white flowers. [After *Matilija* Canyon, California.]
mat·in (măt′n) also **mat·in·al** (-əl) *adj.* Of or pertaining to matins or to the early part of the day. [< MATINS.]
mat·i·nee or **mat·i·née** (măt′n-ā′) *n.* A dramatic or musical performance given in the daytime, usually in the afternoon. [Fr. *matinée* < *matin,* morning < Lat. *matutinus,* of the morning. —see MATINS.]
mat·ins (măt′nz) *n. (used with a sing. or pl. verb).* **1.** *Rom. Cath. Ch.* The office, together with lauds, that constitutes the first of the seven canonical hours. **2.** Often **Matins.** Morning Prayer. [ME *matines* < OFr. < Med. Lat. *(vigiliae) matutinae,* morning (vigils) < Lat. *matutinus,* of the morning < *Matuta,* goddess of dawn.]
matri– or **matro–** or **matr–** *pref.* Mother: *matrilineal.* [Lat. < *mater,* mother.]
ma·tri·arch (mā′trē-ärk′) *n.* **1.** A woman who rules a family, clan, or tribe. **2.** A woman who dominates a group or activity. **—ma′tri·ar′chal** (-är′kəl), **ma′tri·ar′chic** (-är′kĭk) *adj.* **—ma′tri·ar′chal·ism** *n.*
ma·tri·ar·chate (mā′trē-är′kĭt, -kāt′) *n.* **1. a.** A society, tribe, or state in which the dominant authority is held by women. **b.** The authority held by matriarchs in such a society. **2.** A hypothetical stage in the evolution of primitive society in which authority is held by matriarchs.
ma·tri·ar·chy (mā′trē-är′kē) *n., pl.* **-chies. 1.** A social system in which descent is traced through the mother's side of the family. **2.** A matriarchate.
ma·tri·ces (mā′trĭ-sēz′, măt′rĭ-) *n.* A plural of **matrix.**
mat·ri·cide (măt′rə-sīd′) *n.* **1.** The act of killing one's mother. **2.** One who kills his mother. [Lat. *matricidium* : *mater,* mother + *caedere,* to kill.] **—mat′ri·ci′dal** (-sīd′l) *adj.*
mat·ri·cli·nous (măt′rĭ-klī′nəs) also **mat·ro·cli·nous** (măt′rə-) *adj.* Having predominantly maternal hereditary traits. [MATRI- + Gk. *klinein,* to lean.]
ma·tric·u·lant (mə-trĭk′yə-lənt) *n.* A person who matriculates or is a candidate for matriculation.
ma·tric·u·late (mə-trĭk′yə-lāt′) *tr. & intr.v.* **-lat·ed, -lat·ing, -lates.** To admit or be admitted into a group, esp. a college or university; enroll. *—n.* A matriculant. [Med. Lat. *matriculare, matriculat-,* to matriculate < LLat. *matricula,* list < *matrix,* list. —see MATRIX.] **—ma·tric′u·la′tion** *n.*
mat·ri·lin·e·al (măt′rə-lĭn′ē-əl) *adj.* Relating to, based upon, or tracing ancestral descent through the maternal line. **—mat′ri·lin′e·al·ly** *adv.*
mat·ri·lo·cal (măt′rə-lō′kəl) *adj. Anthropol.* Pertaining to the home territory of a wife's kin group or clan in primitive societies. **—mat′ri·lo′cal·ly** *adv.*
mat·ri·mo·ny (măt′rə-mō′nē) *n., pl.* **-nies.** The act or state of being married; marriage. [ME < OFr. *matrimonie* < Lat. *matrimonium* < *mater,* mother.] **—mat′ri·mo′ni·al** *adj.* **—mat′ri·mo′ni·al·ly** *adv.*
matrimony vine *n.* Any of various often thorny shrubs of the genus *Lycium,* some species of which are cultivated for their purplish flowers and brightly colored berries.
ma·trix (mā′trĭks) *n., pl.* **ma·tri·ces** (mā′trĭ-sēz′, măt′rĭ-) or **ma·trix·es. 1.** A situation or surrounding substance within which something originates, develops, or is contained: *"Folklore must be maintained in the matrix of the culture for*

some time before it can be accepted as genuine" (Horace Beck). **2.** The womb. **3.** *Anat.* The formative cells of a fingernail or tooth. **4.** *Geol.* **a.** The solid matter in which a fossil or crystal is embedded. **b.** The impression left in a rock when an object, as a gemstone, has been removed. **5.** A mold or die. **6.** The principal metal in an alloy, as the iron in steel. **7.** A binding substance, as cement in concrete. **8.** *Math.* A rectangular array of numerical or algebraic quantities treated as an algebraic entity. **9.** *Computer Sci.* The network of intersections between input and output leads in a computer, functioning as an encoder or decoder. **10.** *Printing.* **a.** A metal plate used for casting typefaces. **b.** A mold used in stereotyping and designed to receive positive impressions of type or illustrations from which metal plates can be cast. [LLat. < Lat., breeding-animal < *mater,* mother.]

matro– *pref.* Variant of **matri-.**

mat·ro·cli·nous (măt′rə-klī′nəs) *adj.* Variant of **matriclinous.**

ma·tron (mā′trən) *n.* **1.** A married woman, esp. a mother of mature age with established dignity and social position. **2.** A woman who acts as a supervisor or monitor in a public institution, as a school, hospital, or prison. [ME *matrone* < OFr. < Lat. *matrona* < *mater,* mother.] **—ma′tron·al** *adj.* **—ma′tron·li·ness** *n.* **—ma′tron·ly** *adj. & adv.*

matron of honor *n., pl.* **matrons of honor.** A married woman serving as chief attendant of the bride at a wedding.

mat·ro·nym·ic (măt′rə-nĭm′ĭk) *adj. & n.* Variant of **metronymic.**

matte[1] (măt) *n.* Variant of **mat**[2] (sense 2). *—adj.* Variant of **mat**[2].

matte[2] (măt) *n.* A mixture of a metal with its oxides and sulfides, produced by smelting certain sulfide ores. [Fr.]

mat·ted (măt′ĭd) *adj.* **1.** Covered with or made from mats. **2.** Tangled in a dense mass: *matted undergrowth.*

mat·ter (măt′ər) *n.* **1. a.** Something that occupies space and can be perceived by one or more senses; a physical body or the universe as a whole. **b.** *Physics.* An entity displaying gravitation and inertia when at rest as well as when in motion. **2.** A specific type of substance: *inorganic matter.* **3.** Discharge or waste from a living organism, as pus or feces. **4.** The actual substance of thought or expression as distinguished from the manner in which it is stated or conveyed. **5.** *Philos.* In Aristotelian and Scholastic use, that which is in itself undifferentiated and formless and which, as the subject of change and development, receives form and becomes substance and experience. **6.** *Christian Science.* That which is postulated by the mortal mind, regarded as illusion and as the opposite of substance or God. **7.** Something that is the subject of concern, feeling, or action: *foreign-policy matters; a personal matter.* **8.** Trouble or difficulty: *What's the matter with you?* **9.** An approximated quantity, amount, or extent: *a matter of a few cents.* **10.** Something printed or otherwise set down in writing: *reading matter.* **11.** Something sent by mail. **12.** *Printing.* **a.** Composed type. **b.** Material to be set in type. *—intr.v.* **-tered, -ter·ing, -ters.** To be of importance: *It matters very much.* ***—idioms.*** **as a matter of fact.** In fact; actually. **for that matter.** So far as that is concerned; as for that. **no matter.** Regardless of: *would walk home no matter how late it was.* [ME < OFr. *matere* < Lat. *materia* < *mater,* mother.]

matter of course *n.* A natural or logical outcome.

mat·ter-of-fact (măt′ər-əv-făkt′) *adj.* Pertaining to or adhering to facts; literal: *a matter-of-fact description of a fanciful affair.* **—mat′ter-of-fact′ly** *adv.* **—mat′ter-of-fact′ness** *n.*

Mat·thew (măth′yo͞o) *n.* **1.** One of the Apostles of Christ and generally accepted as the author of the first Gospel of the New Testament. **2.** See table at **Bible.**

mat·ting[1] (măt′ĭng) *n.* **1.** A coarsely woven fabric used for covering floors and similar purposes. **2.** Mat-making.

mat·ting[2] (măt′ĭng) *n.* **1.** A dull surface or finish. **2.** The process of dulling a surface, as of metal. **3.** A border or mat used for framing a picture.

mat·tins (măt′nz) *n. Chiefly Brit.* Variant of **matins.**

mat·tock (măt′ək) *n.* A digging tool with a blade set at right angles to the handle and used with a downward motion. [ME < OE *mattuc.*]

mat·tress (măt′rĭs) *n.* **1. a.** A rectangular pad of heavy cloth filled with soft material, used as or on a bed. **b.** An airtight, inflatable pad used as or on a bed or as a cushion. **2.** A closely woven mat of brush and poles used to protect an embankment, dike, or dam from erosion. [ME *mattresse* < OFr. *materas* < OItal. *materasso* < Ar. *maṭraḥ,* place where something is thrown < *ṭaraḥ,* he threw.]

mat·u·rate (măch′ə-rāt′) *intr. & tr.v.* **-rat·ed, -rat·ing, -rates.** **1.** To mature or ripen. **2.** To suppurate or cause to suppurate. [Lat. *maturare, maturat-,* to maturate < *maturus,* mature.] **—mat′u·ra′tive** *adj.*

mat·u·ra·tion (măch′ə-rā′shən) *n.* **1.** The process of becoming mature. **2.** Suppuration (sense 1). **3.** *Biol.* **a.** Gametogenesis. **b.** The final differentiation processes in biological systems, as the final ripening of a seed.

maturation division *n.* Meiosis (sense 1).

ma·ture (mə-tyo͝or′, -to͝or′, -cho͝or′) *adj.* **-tur·er, -tur·est.** **1. a.** Having reached full natural growth or development: *a mature cell.* **b.** Fully developed; ripe: *a mature cheese.* **2.** Of, pertaining to, or characteristic of full development, either mental or physical: *mature for her age.* **3.** Worked out fully by the mind; considered: *a mature plan of action.* **4.** Having reached the limit of its time; due: *a mature bond.* **5.** *Geol.* Being a landscape in which hills and valleys predominate over flat areas as a result of erosion. *—v.* **-tured, -tur·ing, -tures.** *—tr.* **1.** To bring to full development; ripen. **2.** To work out fully in the mind: *"to be able to digest and mature my thoughts for my own mind only"* (J.S. Mill). *—intr.* **1.** To evolve toward full development: *The child's judgment matures as she grows older.* **2.** To become due. Used of notes and bonds. [ME < Lat. *maturus.*] **—ma·ture′ly** *adv.* **—ma·ture′ness** *n.*

ma·tur·i·ty (mə-tyo͝or′ĭ-tē, -to͝or′-, -cho͝or′-) *n., pl.* **-ties.** **1. a.** The state or quality of being mature; ripeness. **b.** The state or quality of being fully grown. **2. a.** The time at which a note or bond is due. **b.** The state of a note or bond being due. **3.** *Geol.* The state of being mature: *the maturity of an eroded landscape.* [ME *maturite* < OFr. < Lat. *maturitas* < *maturus,* mature.]

ma·tu·ti·nal (mə-to͞ot′n-əl, -tyo͞ot′-, măch′o͞o-tī′nəl) *adj.* Of, pertaining to, or occurring in the morning; early. [LLat. *matutinalis* < Lat. *matutinus.* —see MATINS.] **—ma·tu′ti·nal·ly** *adv.*

mat·zo (mät′sə, -sō) *n., pl.* **-zoth** (-sōth′, -sōt′, -sōs′) or **-zos** (-səz, -səs, -sōz′) or **-zot** (-sōt′). A brittle, flat piece of unleavened bread, eaten esp. during the Passover. [Yiddish *matse* < Heb. *maṣṣāh.*]

matzo ball *n.* A small dumpling made from matzo meal.

maud·lin (môd′lĭn) *adj.* Effusively or tearfully sentimental: *"Goering and Hitler displayed an almost maudlin concern for the welfare of animals"* (Aldous Huxley). [Alteration of Mary *Magdalen,* who was frequently depicted as a tearful penitent.] **—maud′lin·ly** *adv.* **—maud′lin·ness** *n.*

maul also **mall** (môl) *n.* A heavy, long-handled hammer used to drive stakes, piles, or wedges. *—tr.v.* **mauled, maul·ing, mauls** also **malled, mall·ing, malls.** **1.** To split (wood) with a maul and wedge. **2.** To handle roughly; bruise or tear: *a hunter mauled by a bear.* **3.** To injure by or as if by beating. [ME < OFr. *mail* < Lat. *malleus.*] **—maul′er** *n.*

maul·stick also **mahl·stick** (môl′stĭk′) *n.* A long wooden stick used by painters to support the hand that holds the brush. [Partial transl. of Du. *maalstok* : obs. Du. *malen,* to point + *stok,* stick.]

maund (mônd) *n.* A unit of weight varying in different countries of Asia from 11.2 to 37.358 kilograms or 24.7 to 82.286 pounds avoirdupois, the latter being the official maund in India. [Hindi *mān.*]

maun·der (môn′dər, män′-) *intr.v.* **-dered, -der·ing, -ders.** **1.** To talk incoherently or aimlessly. **2.** To move or act aimlessly or vaguely; wander. [Prob. imit.]

Maun·dy Thursday (môn′dē, män′-) *n.* The Thursday before Easter, commemorating Jesus' Last Supper. [ME *maunde,* ceremony of washing the feet of the poor on Maundy Thursday < OFr. *mande* < Lat. *mandatum,* mandate. —see MANDATE.]

Mau·ser (mou′zər). A trademark for a repeating rifle or pistol.

mau·so·le·um (mô′sə-lē′əm, mô′zə-) *n., pl.* **-le·ums** or **-le·a** (-lē′ə). A large and stately tomb or a building housing such a tomb or tombs. [ME < Lat. < Gk. *mausoleion,* < *Mausōlus,* Mausolus (d. 353 B.C.), satrap of Caria.] **—mau′so·le′an** *adj.*

mausoleum
Built about 350 B.C. for King Mausolos of Caria

mauve (mōv) *n.* A brilliant violet to strong or brilliant purple to moderate reddish purple. [Fr. < Lat. *malva,* mallow.] **—mauve** *adj.*

ma·ven also **ma·vin** (mā′vən) *n.* A person who has special knowledge or experience; expert. [Yiddish *meyvn* < Heb. *mēbhin.*]

mav·er·ick (măv′ər-ĭk, măv′rĭk) *n.* **1.** An unbranded or orphaned range calf or colt, traditionally considered the property of the first person who brands it. **2.** A horse or steer that has escaped from a herd. **3.** An independent-minded person who refuses to abide by the dictates of or resists adherence to a group; dissenter. ***—modifier:*** *maverick politicians.* [After Samuel A. *Maverick* (1803–1870).]

ma·vie (mā′vē) *n.* Variant of **mavis.**

ma·vin (mā′vən) *n.* Variant of **maven.**

ma·vis (mā′vĭs) also **ma·vie** (-vē) *n.* The song thrush. [ME < OFr. *mauvis.*]

ma·vour·neen also **ma·vour·nin** (mə-vo͝or′nēn′) *n. Ir.* My darling. [Ir. Gael. *mo mhuirnin.*]

maw (mô) *n.* **1.** The stomach, mouth, or gullet of a voracious animal. **2.** An opening that gapes as if with voracious appetite: *"Rome and Greece swept Art into their maw and destroyed it"* (Blake). [ME < OE *maga.*]

mawk·ish (mô′kĭsh) *adj.* **1.** Excessively and objectionably sentimental. **2.** Sickening or insipid in taste. [< ME *mawke,* maggot, var. of *magot.*] **—mawk′ish·ly** *adv.* **—mawk′ish·ness** *n.*

max·i (măk′sē) *n.* An ankle- or floor-length skirt or coat. [< MAXIMUM.]

max·il·la (măk-sĭl′ə) *n., pl.* **max·il·lae** (măk-sĭl′ē) or **max·il·las.** **1.** *Anat.* One of a pair of bones forming the upper jaw. **2.** *Zool.* Either of two laterally moving appendages behind the mandibles in insects and most other arthropods. [Lat., jaw bone.]

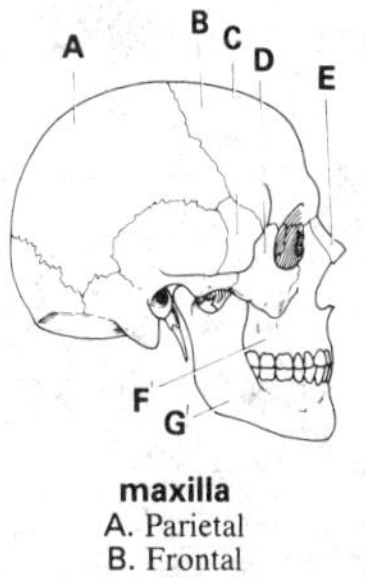

maxilla
A. Parietal
B. Frontal
C. Sphenoid
D. Zygomatic
E. Nasal
F. Maxilla
G. Mandible

May apple

Maypole

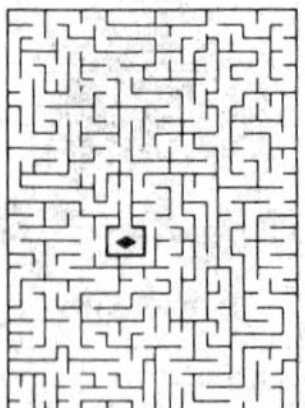
maze

max·il·lar·y (măk′sə-lĕr′ē) *n., pl.* **-ies.** A jaw or jawbone. —**max′il·lar′y** *adj.*
max·il·li·ped (măk-sĭl′ə-pĕd′) *n. Zool.* One of the three pairs of crustacean head appendages located just posterior to the maxillae. [MAXILL(A) + -PED.]
max·il·lo·fa·cial (măk-sĭl′ō-fā′shəl) *adj.* Pertaining to or involving the maxilla and the face. [MAXILL(A) + FACIAL.]
max·im (măk′sĭm) *n.* A concise formulation of a fundamental principle or rule of conduct; saying. [ME *maxime* < OFr. < Med. Lat. *maxima* < Lat. *maximus,* greatest < *magnus,* great.]
max·i·ma (măk′sə-mə) *n.* A plural of **maximum.**
max·i·mal (măk′sə-məl) *adj.* **1.** Of, pertaining to, or consisting of a maximum. **2.** Being the greatest or highest possible. **3.** *Math.* Designating the maximal of an ordered set. —*n. Math.* An element in an ordered set that is followed by no other. —**max′i·mal·ly** *adv.*
max·i·mal·ist (măk′sə-mə-lĭst) *n.* One who advocates direct revolutionary action to secure social and political gains. [Fr. *maximaliste,* prob. < E. *maximal.*]
max·i·mize (măk′sə-mīz′) *tr.v.* **-mized, -miz·ing, -miz·es.** **1.** To increase or make as great as possible: *"the ideal of maximizing opportunity through the equalizing of educational opportunity"* (Robert J. Havighurst). **2.** To assign the highest possible importance to. **3.** *Math.* To find a maximum value of (a function). —**max′i·mi·za′tion** *n.* —**max′i·miz′er** *n.*
max·i·mum (măk′sə-məm) *n., pl.* **-mums** or **-ma** (-mə). **1. a.** The greatest possible quantity, degree, or number. **b.** The time or period during which the highest point or degree is attained. **2.** An upper limit stipulated by law or other authority. **3.** *Astron.* **a.** The moment when a variable star is most brilliant. **b.** The magnitude of the star at such a moment. **4.** *Math.* **a.** The value of a function that is not exceeded by neighboring values. **b.** The greatest value assumed by a function within some subset of its domain of definition. **c.** The largest number in a set. —*adj.* **1.** Having or being the greatest quantity or the highest degree that has been or can be attained: *maximum temperature.* **2.** Of, pertaining to, or making up a maximum: *a maximum number in a series.* [< Lat., neuter of *maximus,* greatest. —see MAXIM.]
ma·xixe (mə-shēsh′, -shē′shə) *n.* A Brazilian dance similar to the two-step. [Port. (Brazil).]
max·well (măks′wĕl′, -wəl) *n.* A unit of magnetic flux in the centimeter-gram-second electromagnetic system, equal to the flux perpendicularly intersecting an area of one square centimeter in a region where the magnetic induction is one gauss. [After James *Maxwell* (1831–1879).]
may (mā) *aux.v.* Past **might** (mīt), present **may** for singular and plural. **1.** To be allowed or permitted to: *May I take a swim? You may.* **2.** Used to indicate a certain measure of likelihood or possibility: *It may rain this afternoon.* **3.** To be obliged; must. Used in statutes, deeds, and other legal documents. **4.** Used to express a desire or fervent wish: *Long may he live!* **5.** Used to express contingency, purpose, or result, in clauses introduced by *that* or *so that: expressing ideas so that the average man may understand.* —See Usage note at **can.** [ME, to be able < OE *mæg,* 1st and 3rd person singular indicative of *magan,* to be strong, be able.]
May (mā) *n.* **1.** The fifth month of the year according to the Gregorian calendar. See table at **calendar. 2.** The springtime of life; youth. **3.** The celebration of May Day. **4. may.** *Chiefly Brit.* The blossoms of the hawthorn. [ME < OFr. *Mai* < Lat. *Maius* < *Maia,* an Italic goddess.]
ma·ya (mä′yə) *n. Hinduism.* **1.** The origin of the world. **2.** The illusory appearance of the world. [Skt. *māyā.*]
Ma·ya (mä′yə) *n., pl.* **Maya** or **-yas. 1.** A member of a race of Indians in southern Mexico and Central America whose civilization reached its height around A.D. 1000. **2.** The Mayan language of the Maya. [Sp.] —**Ma′ya** *adj.*
Ma·yan (mä′yən) *adj.* Of or pertaining to the Mayas, their culture, their language or the language group to which it belongs. —*n.* **1.** A Maya. **2.** A linguistic stock of Central America that includes Maya and Yucatec.
May apple *n.* **1.** A plant, *Podophyllum peltatum,* of eastern North America, having a single, nodding white flower and oval yellow fruit. Although the pulp of the ripe fruit is edible, the roots, leaves, and seeds of this plant are poisonous. **2.** The fruit of the May apple.
may·be (mā′bē) *adv.* Perhaps; possibly.
May beetle *n.* The June beetle.
may·day (mā′dā′) *n.* An international radio-telephone signal word used by aircraft and ships in distress. [Alteration of Fr. *m'aidez,* help me!]
May Day *n.* **1.** The first day of May, marked by the celebration of spring. **2.** May 1, regarded in a number of places as an international holiday to celebrate labor organizations.
may·est (mā′ĭst) or **mayst** (māst) *aux.v. Archaic.* Second person singular present tense of **may**[1].
may·flow·er (mā′flou′ər) *n.* **1.** Any of a wide variety of plants that bloom in May. **2.** The trailing arbutus.
may·fly (mā′flī′) *n.* Any of various fragile, winged insects of the order Ephemeroptera that develop from aquatic nymphs and live in the adult stage for only a few hours.
may·hap (mā′hăp′, mā-hăp′) *adv.* Perhaps; perchance. [< the phrase *it may hap.*]
may·hem (mā′hĕm′, mā′əm) *n.* **1.** *Law.* The offense of willfully maiming or crippling a person. **2.** The infliction of violent injury upon a person or thing; wanton destruction: *children committing mayhem in the flower beds.* **3.** A state of violent disorder or riotous confusion; havoc. [ME < AN *mahem* < OFr. *mahaignier,* to maim.]
may·ing (mā′ĭng) *n.* Often **Maying.** The gathering of spring flowers, esp. during a May festival.
may·n't (mā′ənt, mānt). May not.
may·o (mā′ō) *n.* Mayonnaise.
may·on·naise (mā′ə-nāz′, mā′ə-nāz′) *n.* A dressing made of beaten raw egg yolk, butter or olive oil, lemon juice or vinegar, and seasonings. [Fr.]
may·or (mā′ər, mâr) *n.* The chief magistrate of a city, town, borough, or municipal corporation. [ME *maire* < OFr. < Med. Lat. *major* < Lat., greater. —see MAJOR.] —**may′or·al** *adj.* —**may′or·ship′** *n.*
may·or·al·ty (mā′ər-əl-tē, mâr′əl-) *n., pl.* **-ties. 1.** The office of a mayor. **2.** The term of office of a mayor. [ME *mairalte* < AN < OFr. *maire,* mayor. —see MAYOR.]
may·or·ess (mā′ər-ĭs, mâr′ĭs) *n.* **1.** A woman serving as the chief magistrate of a city, town, borough, or municipal corporation. **2.** The wife of a mayor.
May·pole also **may·pole** (mā′pōl′) *n.* A pole decorated with streamers that May Day celebrants hold while dancing.
may·pop (mā′pŏp′) *n.* **1.** A vine, *Passiflora incarnata,* of the southeastern United States, having purple and white flowers and edible yellow fruit. **2.** The fruit of the maypop. [Alteration of *maycock* < Powhatan *mahcawq.*]
mayst (māst) *aux.v.* Variant of **mayest.**
may tree *n. Chiefly Brit.* The hawthorn.
may·weed (mā′wēd′) *n.* A widespread weed, *Anthemis cotula,* having rank-smelling leaves and white flowers.
May wine *n.* **1.** A still white wine with woodruff flavoring, often containing orange or pineapple slices. **2.** A punch of champagne, claret, and Moselle or Rhine wine, flavored with woodruff. [Transl. of G. *Maiwein.*]
ma·zae·di·um (mə-zē′dē-əm) *n., pl.* **-di·a** (-dē-ə). A fruiting body of some lichens in which the spores lie freely in a powdery mass that is enclosed in a peridium. [NLat. : Gk. *maza,* lump + Lat. *aedes,* house.]
ma·zal tov (mä′zəl tôf′) *interj.* Variant of **mazel tov.**
Maz·da·ism also **Maz·de·ism** (măz′də-ĭz′əm) *n.* Zoroastrianism. [< Avestan *mazda,* the good principle.]
maze (māz) *n.* **1. a.** An intricate, usually confusing, network of walled or hedged pathways; labyrinth. **b.** A physical situation in which it is easy to get lost. **c.** Any of various networks of pathways, some blind and some leading to a goal, used experimentally to investigate learning in animals. **2.** A graphic puzzle, the solution of which is an uninterrupted path through an intricate pattern of line segments from a starting point to a goal. **3.** Something made up of many confused or conflicting elements; tangle. —*tr.v.* **mazed, maz·ing, maz·es. 1.** *Chiefly Regional.* To stupefy; daze. **2.** To bewilder. [ME *mase,* maze, confusion < *masen,* to confuse < OE *āmasian,* to confound.] —**maz′y** *adj.*
ma·zel tov also **ma·zal tov** (mä′zəl tôf′) *interj. Hebrew.* Congratulations. [Heb. *mazālṭob* : *mazāl,* luck + *ṭob,* good.]
ma·zer (mā′zər) *n.* A large drinking bowl or goblet made of hard wood or metal. [ME < OFr. *mazre,* of Germanic orig.]
ma·zour·ka (mə-zûr′kə, -zo͝or′-) *n.* Variant of **mazurka.**
ma·zu·ma (mə-zo͞o′mə) *n. Slang.* Money; cash. [Yiddish *mazumen* < Heb. *mzumān,* fixed.]
ma·zur·ka also **ma·zour·ka** (mə-zûr′kə, -zo͝or′-) *n.* **1.** A lively Polish dance resembling the polka, frequently adopted as a ballet form. **2.** A piece of music for a mazurka, written in 3/4 or 3/8 time with the second beat heavily accented. [Pol., accusative of *mazurek,* dim. of *mazur,* someone from Mazovia, a province of Poland.]
maz·zard (măz′ərd) *n.* A wild sweet cherry, *Prunus avium,* often used as grafting stock. [Orig. unknown.]
mbi·ra (ĕm-bîr′ə, əm-) *n.* A thumb piano. [Of Bantu orig.]
MC (ĕm′sē′) *n.* A master of ceremonies.
Mc·Car·thy·ism (mə-kär′thē-ĭz′əm) *n.* **1.** The political practice of publicizing accusations of disloyalty or subversion with insufficient regard to evidence. **2.** The use of methods of investigation and accusation regarded as unfair, in order to suppress opposition. [After Joseph R. *McCarthy,* (1908–1957).] —**Mc·Car′thy·ist** *n.*
Mc·Coy (mə-koi′) *n. Slang.* The authentic thing or quality; something that is not an imitation or substitute: *the real McCoy.* [After Kid *McCoy* (Norman Selby, 1873–1940), American boxer.]
Mc·In·tosh (măk′ĭn-tŏsh′) *n.* A variety of red eating apple, grown commercially in the northern United States. [After John *McIntosh* (fl. 1796), its first cultivator.]
Md The symbol for the element mendelevium.
M-day (ĕm′dā′) *n.* Mobilization day; the day on which national mobilization for war is ordered.
me (mē) *pron.* The objective case of the first person pronoun. Used: **1.** As the direct object of a verb: *He assisted me.* **2.** As the indirect object of a verb: *They offered me a ride.* **3.** As the object of a preposition: *This letter is addressed to me.* —See Usage notes at **be** and **I.** [ME < OE *mē.*]
me·a cul·pa (mā′ə ko͝ol′pə) *n.* An acknowledgment of a personal error or fault. [Lat., through my fault.]

mead[1] (mēd) *n.* An alcoholic beverage made from fermented honey and water. [ME < OE *medu.*]
mead[2] (mēd) *n. Archaic.* A meadow. [ME *meade* < OE *mǣd.*]
mead·ow (mĕd′ō) *n.* A tract of grassland, either in its natural state or used as pasture or for growing hay. [ME *medoue* < OE *mǣdwe* < *mǣd,* meadow.] **—mead′ow·y** *adj.*
meadow beauty *n.* A plant of the genus *Rhexia,* of eastern North America, growing in wet ground and having showy purple flowers.
meadow fescue *n.* A grass, *Festuca eliator,* used for hay.
meadow hen *n.* Any of various birds of the family Rallidae, esp. a rail or coot.
mead·ow·land (mĕd′ō-lănd′) *n.* A tract of land having the characteristics of or used for a meadow.
mead·ow·lark (mĕd′ō-lärk′) *n.* A bird of the genus *Sturnella,* with two species, *S. magna,* the eastern meadowlark, and *S. neglecta,* the western meadowlark, found in North America and noted for their song.
meadow mouse *n.* The field mouse.
meadow mushroom *n.* An edible mushroom, *Agaricus campestris,* that thrives in moist soil and is cultivated for human consumption.
meadow nematode *n.* Any of various nematodes of the genus *Pratylenchus* that are parasitic on the roots of plants.
meadow rue *n.* Any of various plants of the genus *Thalictrum,* having clusters of small white, yellowish, or purplish flowers.
meadow saffron *n.* The autumn crocus.
mead·ow·sweet (mĕd′ō-swēt′) *n.* Any of several plants of the genus *Spiraea,* esp. *S. alba* or *S. latifolia,* of eastern North America, having pyramidal clusters of flowers.
mea·ger also **mea·gre** (mē′gər) *adj.* **1.** Having little flesh; lean. **2.** Deficient in quantity, fullness, or extent; scanty. **3.** Deficient in richness, fertility, or vigor; feeble: *the meager soil of an eroded plain.* [ME *megre* < OFr. < Lat. *macer.*] **—mea′ger·ly** *adv.* **—mea′ger·ness** *n.*

Synonyms: *meager, spare, sparse, skimpy, scanty, scant. Meager* indicates deficient supply, often of general or intangible requisites: *meager resources; meager education. Spare* implies bare sufficiency, free of all excess. It is often applied to physical characteristics of persons (*spare of build*) and to manner of speech or writing (*spare style*). *Sparse* indicates lack of density and a spatial separation of units: *sparse vegetation; sparse hair. Skimpy* emphasizes conspicuous smallness or brevity: *a skimpy dress; a skimpy allowance. Scanty* conveys the same sense, most often of physical extent: *scanty living quarters. Scant* applies to what is barely enough or just short of a minimal amount: *a scant hour; a scant measure.*

meal[1] (mēl) *n.* **1.** The edible seed or other edible part of a grain, coarsely ground. **2.** A granular substance produced by grinding. [ME *meale* < OE *melu.*]
meal[2] (mēl) *n.* **1.** The food served and eaten in one sitting. **2.** A customary time or occasion of eating food. [ME < OE *mǣl.*]
meal·ie (mē′lē) *n. So. Afr.* **1.** An ear of corn. **2. mealies.** Corn; maize. [Afr. *milie* < Port. *milho,* millet < Lat. *milium.*]
meal ticket *n.* **1.** A card or ticket entitling the holder to a meal or meals. **2.** *Slang.* A person or thing depended on as a source of financial support.
meal·time (mēl′tīm′) *n.* The usual time for eating a meal.
meal·worm (mēl′wûrm′) *n.* The larva of any of several beetles of the genus *Tenebrio* that infest flour and other grain products and are raised for bird feed.
meal·y (mē′lē) *adj.* **-i·er, -i·est. 1.** Resembling meal in texture or consistency; granular: *mealy potatoes.* **2. a.** Made of or containing meal. **b.** Sprinkled or covered with meal or a similar granular substance. **3.** Flecked with spots; mottled. **4.** Lacking healthy coloring; pale. **5.** Mealy-mouthed. **—meal′i·ness** *n.*
meal·y·bug (mē′lē-bŭg′) *n.* Any of various insects of the genus *Pseudococcus,* some of which are destructive to plants, esp. citrus trees. [So called because it is covered with a white powdery substance.]
meal·y-mouthed (mē′lē-mouthd′, -moutht′) *adj.* Unwilling to state facts or opinions simply and directly.
mean[1] (mēn) *v.* **meant** (mĕnt), **mean·ing, means.** *—tr.* **1. a.** To be defined or described as; denote: *The word "dog" means a certain species of mammal.* **b.** To convey the same sense as; refer to the same thing as: *The French word "chien" means "dog."* **c.** To act as a symbol of; signify: *In this poem, the budding flower means youth.* **2.** To intend to convey or indicate: *What do you mean by that look?* **3.** To have as a purpose or intention; intend: *"Most of the girls who were not betrothed meant to be teachers"* (Sinclair Lewis). **4.** To design or intend for a certain purpose or end: *a building meant for storage.* **5.** To have as a consequence; bring about: *Friction means heat.* **6.** To be attended by or associated with: *Red sky at night means fair weather.* *—intr.* **1.** To be of a specified importance or significance; matter: *The opinions of critics meant little to him.* **2.** To have intentions of a specified kind; be disposed: *She means well, despite her blunders.* ***—idiom.*** **mean business.** *Informal.* To be in earnest. [ME *menen* < OE *mǣnan,* to tell of.]

Synonyms: *mean, signify, import, denote, represent, purport. Mean* is the least specific of the verbs considered here; it is used in the sense of conveying something meaningful. *Signify* is properly used after terms that are themselves objectively representative or symbolic of the ideas conveyed: *The Statue of Liberty signifies a haven for the oppressed. Import* makes this implication more strongly; it is often employed when what is conveyed is not merely an idea but associated ideas or implications. *Denote* is used when the idea transmitted is capable of precise statement, as a definition apart from connotations; it is also used after terms that are themselves clear indications (but not objective symbols) of the ideas conveyed: *Serenity denotes a clear conscience,* but *His crown signifies royal power. Represent* is employed when symbols convey the idea: *The shaded part of the map represents free soil,* or when a specific case serves as an example of the idea: *Crossing our borders represents aggression. Purport* may imply doubtful authenticity or pretense.

mean[2] (mēn) *adj.* **-er, -est. 1.** Low in quality or grade; inferior. **2.** Low in social status. **3.** Common or poor in appearance; shabby: *a mean hut.* **4.** Ignoble; base: *a mean motive.* **5.** Low in value or amount; paltry. **6.** Miserly; stingy. **7. a.** Lacking elevating human qualities, as kindness and good will. **b.** Reluctant to oblige or accommodate. **c.** Displaying bad temper; malicious. **8.** *Informal.* Ill-tempered: *a mean old dog.* **9.** *Slang.* **a.** Hard to cope with; difficult; troublesome: *a mean street to cross.* **b.** Hard to defeat: *He plays a mean game of bridge.* [ME < OE *gemǣne,* common.] **—mean′ly** *adv.*

Synonyms: *mean, low, base, abject, infamous, ignoble. Mean,* originally applied to persons of lowly birth, now emphasizes lack of those qualities that make man a superior form of life; it specifically pertains to pettiness, spite, and niggardliness. *Low* may indicate lack of refinement or apply to that which is deliberately pitched beneath a decent level, with evil intent: *a low trick. Base* emphasizes lack of honor or moral fiber. *Abject* stresses low condition without emotional connotation; it often indicates starkness or hopelessness: *abject squalor. Infamous* emphasizes bad reputation and its causes. *Ignoble* pertains to lack of qualities that give human beings distinction of mind and soul.

mean[3] (mēn) *n.* **1.** The middle point between two extremes. **2.** The avoidance of extremes of behavior; moderation: *"Every virtue, as we were taught in youth, is a mean between two extremes"* (Max Beerbohm). **3.** *Math.* **a.** A number that represents a set of numbers in any of several ways determined by a rule involving all members of the set; average. **b.** The arithmetic mean. **4.** *Logic.* The middle term in a syllogism. **5. means.** A method, course of action, or instrument by which an act can be accomplished or some end achieved: *thought that the end justified the means.* **6. means.** Money, property, or other wealth. *—adj.* **1.** Occupying a middle or intermediate position between two extremes. **2.** Intermediate in size, extent, quality, time, or degree; medium. ***—idioms.*** **by all means.** Without fail; certainly. **by any means.** In any way possible; in any case: *not by any means an easy opponent.* **by means of.** With the use of; owing to: *They succeeded by means of patience and sacrifice.* **by no means.** In no sense; certainly not. [ME, middle < OFr. < Lat. *medianus* < *medius.*]

Usage: In the sense of "financial resources," *means* takes a plural verb: *His means are more than adequate.* In the sense of "a way to an end," it may take a singular or plural verb; the choice of a modifier such as *any* or *all* generally determines the number of the verb: *Every means was tried. There are several means at our disposal.*

mean calorie *n.* A calorie (sense 2).
me·an·der (mē-ăn′dər) *intr.v.* **-dered, -der·ing, -ders. 1.** To follow a winding and turning course: *Streams tend to meander through level land.* **2.** To wander aimlessly and idly without fixed direction: *vagabonds meandering through life.* *—n.* **1. meanders.** Circuitous windings or sinuosities, as of a stream or path. **2.** Often **meanders.** A circuitous journey or excursion; ramble. **3.** The Greek fret or key pattern, used in art and architecture. [< Lat. *maeander,* circuitous windings < Gk. *maiandros,* after *Maeander,* a river in Turkey noted for its winding course.] **—me·an′der·er** *n.* **—me·an′der·ing·ly** *adv.* **—me·an′drous** (-drəs) *adj.*
mean deviation *n.* The arithmetic mean of the absolute values of deviations from the arithmetic mean, or from the median, in a statistical distribution.
mean·ing (mē′nĭng) *n.* **1.** Something that is signified; sense. **2.** Something that one wishes to convey, esp. by language. **3.** Something that is interpreted to be the goal, intent, or end. **4.** Something that is felt to be the inner significance of something: *"But who can comprehend the meaning of the voice of the city?"* (O. Henry). **5.** Functional value; efficacy: *customs now empty of all meaning.* *—adj.* **1.** Full of meaning; expressive. **2.** Intentioned or disposed in a specified manner: *a well-meaning fellow.*

Synonyms: *meaning, sense, significance, signification, acceptation, import, purport. Meaning,* being nonspecific, overlaps each of the following. *Sense,* in this context, may be used generally, as the equivalent of meaning (comprehensibility), or specifically, to denote a particular meaning (one of a group of meanings conveyed by a single word, symbol, or idea): *"Vision" has the distinct senses of sight and*

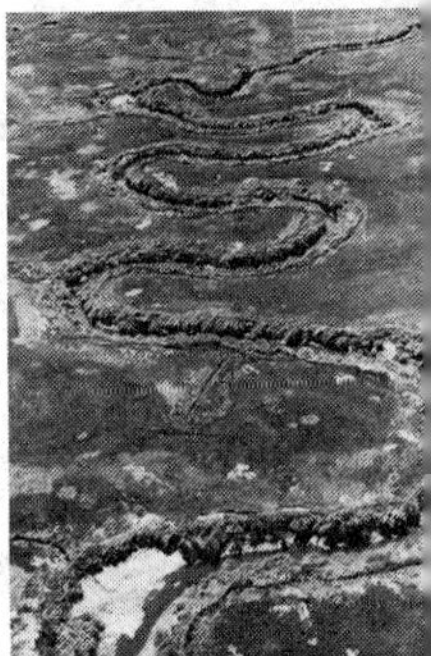
meander
A meandering river

foresight. Significance stresses meaning beyond immediate comprehension (underlying or long-range meaning); besides perception, it implies evaluation. In contrast, *signification* and *acceptation* apply to accepted or established meaning, directly conveyed. *Import* also pertains to ostensible meaning. *Purport* applies to broad understanding, often of an extensive subject.

mean·ing·ful (mē′nĭng-fəl) *adj.* Having meaning, function, or purpose; significant. **—mean′ing·ful·ly** *adv.* **—mean′ing·ful·ness** *n.*

mean·ing·less (mē′nĭng-lĭs) *adj.* Having no meaning or significance; senseless. **—mean′ing·less·ly** *adv.* **—mean′ing·less·ness** *n.*

mean·ly (mēn′lē) *adv.* In a poor, mean, or base manner.

mean·ness (mēn′nĭs) *n.* **1.** The state of being inferior in quality, character, or value; commonness. **2.** Selfishness; stinginess. **3.** A spiteful or malicious act.

mean solar day *n.* The period of time between two successive transits of the mean sun; the standard for the 24-hour day, measured from midnight to midnight.

mean square *n.* The arithmetic mean of the squares of a set of numbers.

mean sun *n.* A hypothetical sun defined as moving at a uniform rate along the celestial equator so that it completes its orbit in the same period as the apparent sun, used in computing the mean solar day.

meant (mĕnt) *v.* Past tense and past participle of **mean**[1].

mean·time (mēn′tīm′) *n.* The time between one occurrence and another; interval. *—adv.* During a period of intervening time; meanwhile: *"Meantime, let wonder seem familiar"* (Shakespeare).

Usage: *Meantime* serves principally as a noun: *In the meantime we waited.* In expressing the same sense as a single adverb, *meanwhile* is more common than *meantime: Meanwhile we waited.*

mean time *n.* Time measured with reference to the mean sun, giving equal 24-hour days throughout the year.

mean·while (mēn′hwīl′, -wīl′) *n.* The intervening time. *—adv.* **1.** During or in the intervening time: *Meanwhile, life goes on.* **2.** At the same time: *The court is deliberating; meanwhile, we must be patient.* —See Usage note at **meantime.**

mea·sles (mē′zəlz) *n. (used with a sing. verb).* **1. a.** An acute, contagious virus disease, usually occurring in childhood and characterized by the eruption of red spots. **b.** Any of several diseases displaying similar but milder symptoms, esp. German measles. **2.** A disease of cattle and swine, caused by tapeworm larvae. **3.** A plant disease, usually caused by fungi, and producing minute spots on leaves and stems. [ME *maseles,* pl. of *masel,* measles-spot, of MLG orig.]

mea·sly (mēz′lē) *adj.* **-sli·er, -sli·est. 1.** Infected or spotted with measles; measled. **2.** *Slang.* Contemptibly small; meager: *a measly tip.*

meas·ur·a·ble (mĕzh′ər-ə-bəl) *adj.* **1.** Able to be measured. **2.** Of distinguished importance; significant: *a measurable figure in literature.* **3.** Not so great as to escape all measure or comparison; moderate. **—meas′ur·a·bil′i·ty** *n.* **—meas′ur·a·bly** *adv.*

meas·ure (mĕzh′ər) *n.* **1.** The dimensions, quantity, or capacity of something as ascertained by measuring: *Length, area, volume, and mass are basic measures of material properties.* **2.** A reference standard or sample used for the quantitative comparison of properties: *The standard kilogram is maintained as a measure of mass.* **3.** A unit specified by a scale, as an inch, or by variable conditions, as a day's march. **4.** A system of measurement, as the metric system. **5.** A device, as a marked tape or a graduated container, used for measuring. **6.** An act of measurement. **7.** An evaluation or basis of comparison: *"the final measure of the worth of a society"* (Joseph Wood Krutch). **8.** The extent or degree of something. **9.** A fitting amount: *a measure of recognition.* **10.** A limited amount or degree: *"a measure of serenity"* (John Updike). **11.** Limit; bounds: *a generosity knowing no measure.* **12.** Appropriate restraint; moderation: *criticism in measure.* **13.** Often **measures.** An action taken as a means to an end; expedient: *desperate measures.* **14.** A legislative bill or enactment. **15.** Poetic meter. **16.** *Mus.* The metric unit between two bars on the staff; bar. *—v.* **-ured, -ur·ing, -ures.** *—tr.* **1.** To ascertain the dimensions, quantity, or capacity of. **2.** To mark, lay out, or establish dimensions for by measuring: *measure off an area.* **3.** To estimate by evaluation or comparison: *"I gave them an account . . . of the situation as far as I could measure it"* (Winston Churchill). **4.** To bring into opposition: *She measured her power with that of a dangerous adversary.* **5.** To mark off, usually with reference to a given unit of measurement; dole out: *measure out a pint of milk.* **6.** To serve as a measure of: *The inch measures length.* **7.** To allot or distribute as if by measuring; mete: *The revolutionary tribunal measured out harsh justice.* **8.** To consider or choose with care; weigh: *He measures his words with pedantic caution.* **9.** *Archaic.* To travel over: *"We must measure much ground today"* (Shakespeare). *—intr.* **1.** To have a measurement of: *The room measures 10 by 12 feet.* **2.** To allow of measurement: *White sugar measures more easily than brown.* ***—phrasal verb.*** **measure up. 1.** To be the equal of. **2.** To have the necessary qualifications: *a candidate who just didn't measure up.* ***—idioms.*** **beyond measure. 1.** In excess. **2.** Without limit. **for good measure.** In addition to the required amount. **in a** (or **some**) **measure.** To a degree: *The new law was in some measure harmful.* [ME < OFr. *mesure* < Lat. *mensura* < *metiri,* to measure.] **—meas′ur·er** *n.*

measure
First measure of "Frère Jacques"

meas·ured (mĕzh′ərd) *adj.* **1.** Determined by measurement: *The measured distance was less than a mile.* **2.** Regular in rhythm and number: *"A clock struck slowly in the house with a measured, solemn chime"* (Thomas Wolfe). **3.** Careful; restrained: *measured words.* **4.** Calculated; deliberate: *with measured irony.* **5.** Slow and stately. **6.** Written in meter. **7.** *Mus.* Mensural. **8.** Limited: *a measured capacity for action.* **—meas′ured·ly** *adv.* **—meas′ured·ness** *n.*

meas·ure·less (mĕzh′ər-lĭs) *adj.* Having no limits; infinite: *measureless happiness.* **—meas′ure·less·ly** *adv.*

meas·ure·ment (mĕzh′ər-mənt) *n.* **1.** The act of measuring or the process of being measured. **2.** A system of measuring: *measurement in miles.* **3.** The dimension, quantity, or capacity determined by measuring: *room measurements.*

measuring worm *n.* A geometrid caterpillar that moves in alternate contractions and expansions suggestive of measuring.

meat (mēt) *n.* **1.** The edible flesh of mammals, as distinguished from that of fish or poultry. **2.** An edible, fleshy, inner part: *crab meat.* **3.** The edible portions of eggs, fruits, or nuts. **4.** The essence or principal part of something: *the meat of the editorial.* **5.** *Slang.* Something one enjoys or excels in; forte: *Tennis is his meat.* **6.** Something eaten for nourishment; food: *meat and drink.* ***—modifier:*** *meat products.* [ME *mete* < OE, food.]

meat·ball (mēt′bôl′) *n.* **1.** A small ball of ground meat variously combined and cooked. **2.** *Slang.* A stupid, clumsy, or dull person.

meat·less (mēt′lĭs) *adj.* **1.** Lacking meat or food. **2.** Being or relating to a time when meat is not to be eaten: *meatless days.*

meat loaf *n.* A mounded or molded dish, usually baked, of ground beef or a combination of meats and other ingredients.

me·a·tus (mē-ā′təs) *n., pl.* **-tus·es** or **meatus.** A body canal or passage, as the opening of the ear or the urethral canal. [Lat., passage < *meare,* to pass.]

meat·y (mē′tē) *adj.* **-i·er, -i·est. 1. a.** Of or pertaining to meat. **b.** Having the flavor or smell of meat. **c.** Full of or containing meat. **2.** Heavily fleshed. **3.** Supplying ample food for thought: *a meaty theme for study and debate.* **—meat′i·ness** *n.*

mec·a·myl·a·mine (mĕk′ə-mĭl′ə-mēn′) *n.* A drug, $C_{11}H_{21}N \cdot HCl$, that is administered orally to bring down highly elevated blood pressure. [Orig. a trademark.]

mec·ca (mĕk′ə) *n.* **1. a.** A place that is regarded as the center of an activity or interest. **b.** A goal to which adherents of a religious faith or practice fervently aspire. **2.** A place visited by many people: *a mecca for tourists.* [After *Mecca,* Saudi Arabia, from its being a place of pilgrimage.]

mechan- *pref.* Variant of **mechano-**.

me·chan·ic (mĭ-kăn′ĭk) *n.* A worker skilled in making, using, or repairing machines and tools. [< ME, mechanical < OFr. *mecanique* < Lat. *mechanicus* < Gk. *mēkhanikos* < *mēkhanē,* machine < *mēkhos,* means.] **—me·chan′ic** *adj.*

me·chan·i·cal (mĭ-kăn′ĭ-kəl) *adj.* **1.** Of or pertaining to machines or tools. **2.** Operated or produced by a machine. **3.** Of, pertaining to, or governed by mechanics. **4.** Acting or performing like a machine; automatic: *The speaker's delivery was mechanical.* **5.** Pertaining to, produced by, or dominated by physical forces. **6.** Interpreting and explaining the phenomena of the universe by referring to causally determined material forces; mechanistic. **7.** Of or pertaining to manual labor, its tools, and its skills. *—n. Printing.* A layout consisting of type proofs, artwork, or both, exactly positioned and prepared for making an offset or other printing plate. [ME < *mechanic,* mechanical. —see MECHANIC.] **—me·chan′i·cal·ly** *adv.* **—me·chan′i·cal·ness** *n.*

mechanical advantage *n.* The ratio of the output force of a machine to the input force.

mechanical drawing *n.* **1.** Drafting. **2.** A drawing, such as an architect's plans, that enables measurements to be interpreted.

mechanical engineering *n.* The branch of engineering that encompasses the generation and application of heat and mechanical power and the design, production, and use of machines and tools. **—mechanical engineer** *n.*

mech·a·ni·cian (mĕk′ə-nĭsh′ən) *n.* A person who makes, uses, or repairs machines and tools.

me·chan·ics (mĭ-kăn′ĭks) *n. (used with a sing. or pl. verb).* **1.** The analysis of the action of forces on matter or material systems. **2.** The design, construction, operation, and application of machinery or mechanical structures. **3.** The functional and technical aspects of an activity: *The mechanics of football are learned with practice.*

mech·a·nism (mĕk′ə-nĭz′əm) *n.* **1. a.** A machine or mechanical appliance. **b.** The arrangement of connected parts in a machine. **2.** A system of parts that operate or interact like those of a machine: *the mechanism of the solar system.* **3.** An instrument or process, physical or mental, by which

MEASUREMENT

There are three major systems of measurement units in wide use: the U.S. Customary System, the British Imperial System, and the International (Metric) System.

The fundamental quantities of each system, together with their relationships to derived units within the same system and conversion to similar quantities in other systems, are shown in Table 1. This table is confined to units of "weights and measures," that is, measurements of length, mass (or weight), and capacity. Table II is a separate tabulation of some of the most common units of scientific measurement and other miscellaneous units.

Measurement of a quantity implies that a number is assigned to represent its magnitude. Usually the assignment can be made by a simple comparison. The magnitude of the quantity is compared to a "standard" quantity, the magnitude of which is arbitrarily chosen to have the measure 1.

Quantities having a scale of measurement chosen in this way, arbitrarily and independently of the scales of other quantities, are called "fundamental." All other quantities are measured in units defined in relation to, or "derived" from, fundamental quantities. The foot, defined as ⅓ of a yard, is an example of a derived unit. Another example is provided by the relationship between the weight and mass of a body. In the equation $W = mg$, W is the weight, m the mass, and g the acceleration of gravity at the place where the body is located. The units for g are derived units, given in terms of the fundamental quantities length and time. Thus, if mass is chosen as a fundamental quantity, the units for weight follow naturally from the above equation and are derived units. (It is, of course, possible to choose weight rather than mass as the fundamental quantity. This is in fact done when the resulting units are convenient for calculation.)

There is an important distinction between a "unit of measurement" and a "standard of measurement."

A *unit of measurement* is a precisely defined quantity in terms of which the magnitudes of all other quantities of the same kind can be stated.

A *standard of measurement* is an *object* which, under specified conditions, serves to define, represent, or record the magnitude of a unit.

In the U.S. Customary System, the fundamental units are the *yard* and the (avoirdupois) *pound*. There are no primary standards as such in the U.S. System. The fundamental units are defined in terms of standards used in the Metric System. The U.S. System has its origins in the British System, but they are not identical.

The fundamental units in the British Imperial System also are the yard and the pound. Until 1959, these were defined not by reference to a Metric standard, as in the United States, but by reference to primary standards created specifically for that purpose. In that year, by agreement between the United States and the British Commonwealth, the International Yard and the International Pound were defined in terms of the Metric standards (as given in Table 1) in the U.S. Customary System.

There are, however, significant differences between the U.S. and British systems. In the British System the units of dry measure (capacity) are the same as those of liquid measure. In the U.S. System they are not. In 1824 the British Imperial gallon was defined as the volume of 10 pounds of water at a temperature of 62°F (= 277.42 cubic inches, by calculation). The bushel was defined as 8 gallons. In 1879 the troy pound was abolished in England, only the troy ounce being retained. The troy pound, however, is still a legal, although infrequently used, unit.

The Metric System is the system used in most of the civilized world, and the one used almost exclusively for scientific work. With the addition of units of time (the second), electric current (the ampere), temperature (kelvin, or alternatively degree Kelvin), and luminous intensity (candela), the Metric System provides a complete, coherent system of units used for all physical measurements. It is called the International System of Units and its units are called SI units. The International System was adopted for scientific use by the U.S. National Bureau of Standards in February 1964.

The Metric System was first proposed in France by Gabriel Mouton, Vicar of Lyons, in 1670. However, it was not possible to introduce this entirely new system of weights and measures until the French Revolution provided the opportunity. The new system was presented to the National Assembly in 1790, and it was adopted in France by legislative action in April 1795.

In the United States the Metric System is the only system that has ever received specific legislative sanction by Congress (in 1866). Acceptance and use of the Metric System in the United States have grown steadily, until at present it is of nearly equal importance with the Customary System.

The fundamental units of the Metric System are the meter and the kilogram. The meter was defined in 1960 by the Eleventh General Conference on Weights and Measures to be equal to 1,650,763.73 wavelengths of the orange-red radiation in vacuum of krypton 86. The kilogram is defined as the mass of a platinum-iridium standard, the International Prototype Kilogram, kept at the International Bureau of Weights and Measures in Sèvres, France.

The International Kilogram is a standard of *mass*. Consequently, units such as the pound and gram derived from it should be regarded as units of mass. In common practice, however, the terms kilogram, pound, gram, etc., are used to designate the *weights* of these masses. This is permissible because equal masses have equal weights under identical conditions. Standards of mass (or "weights") are ordinarily calibrated (or "weighed") on an equal-arm analytical balance. On this instrument two identical masses balance each other independently of the local value of the acceleration of gravity (which determines weight). Thus standards of mass can also be used as standards of weight.

The Metric System is a decimal system, that is, one in which all derived units are multiples of ten. The prefixes listed below, in combination with the basic unit names, provide the multiples and submultiples in the International System. For example the unit *meter* with the prefix *kilo-* produces *kilometer*, meaning "1,000 meters."

Prefix	Symbol	Multiple*			
			deci-	d	10^{-1}
			centi-	c	10^{-2}
deca-	da	10	milli-	m	10^{-3}
hecto-	h	10^2	micro-	μ	10^{-6}
kilo-	k	10^3	nano-	n	10^{-9}
mega-	M	10^6	pico-	p	10^{-12}
giga-	G	10^9	femto-	f	10^{-15}
tera-	T	10^{12}	atto-	a	10^{-18}

* 10^{-1} means 0.1. Similarly, 10^{-6} = 0.000001, etc.: 10^3 = 1,000. 10^6 = 1,000,000, etc.

TABLE I. MEASUREMENT UNITS

LENGTH

U.S. Customary Unit	U.S. Equivalents	Metric Equivalents
inch	0.083 foot	2.540 centimeters
foot	⅓ yard, 12 inches	0.305 meter
yard	3 feet, 36 inches	0.914 meter
rod	5½ yards, 16½ feet	5.029 meters
mile (statute, land)	1,760 yards, 5,280 feet	1.609 kilometers
mile (nautical, international)	1.151 statute miles	1.852 kilometers

AREA

U.S. Customary Unit	U.S. Equivalents	Metric Equivalents
square inch	0.007 square foot	6.452 square centimeters
square foot	144 square inches	929.030 square centimeters
square yard	1,296 square inches, 9 square feet	0.836 square meters
acre	43,560 square feet, 4,840 square yards	4,047 square meters
square mile	640 acres	2.590 square kilometers

VOLUME OR CAPACITY

U.S. Customary Unit	U.S. Equivalents	Metric Equivalents
cubic inch	0.00058 cubic foot	16.387 cubic centimeters
cubic foot	1,728 cubic inches	0.028 cubic meter
cubic yard	27 cubic feet	0.765 cubic meter

U.S. Customary Liquid Measure	U.S. Equivalents	Metric Equivalents
fluid ounce	8 fluid drams, 1.804 cubic inches	29.573 milliliters
pint	16 fluid ounces, 28.875 cubic inches	0.473 liter
quart	2 pints, 57.75 cubic inches	0.946 liter
gallon	4 quarts, 231 cubic inches	3.785 liters
barrel	varies from 31 to 42 gallons, established by law or usage	

U.S. Customary Dry Measure	U.S. Equivalents	Metric Equivalents
pint	½ quart, 33.6 cubic inches	0.551 liter
quart	2 pints, 67.2 cubic inches	1.101 liters

VOLUME OR CAPACITY (continued)

U.S. Customary Dry Measure	U.S. Equivalents	Metric Equivalents
peck	8 quarts, 537.605 cubic inches	8.810 liters
bushel	4 pecks, 2,150.420 cubic inches	35.239 liters

British Imperial Liquid and Dry Measure	U.S. Customary Equivalents	Metric Equivalents
fluid ounce	0.961 U.S. fluid ounce, 1.734 cubic inches	28.413 milliliters
pint	1.032 U.S. dry pints, 1.201 U.S. liquid pints, 34.678 cubic inches	568.245 milliliters
quart	1.032 U.S. dry quarts, 1.201 U.S. liquid quarts, 69.354 cubic inches	1.136 liters
gallon	1.201 U.S. gallons, 277.420 cubic inches	4.546 liters
peck	554.84 cubic inches	0.009 cubic meter
bushel	1.032 U.S. bushels, 2,219.36 cubic inches	0.036 cubic meter

WEIGHT

U.S. Customary Unit (Avoirdupois)	U.S. Equivalents	Metric Equivalents
grain	0.036 dram, 0.002285 ounce	64.798 milligrams
dram	27.344 grains, 0.0625 ounce	1.772 grams
ounce	16 drams, 437.5 grains	28.350 grams
pound	16 ounces, 7,000 grains	453.592 grams
ton (short)	2,000 pounds	0.907 metric ton (1,000 kilograms)
ton (long)	1.12 short tons, 2,240 pounds	1.016 metric tons

Apothecary Weight Unit	U.S. Customary Equivalents	Metric Equivalents
scruple	20 grains	1.296 grams
dram	60 grains	3.888 grams
ounce	480 grains, 1.097 avoirdupois ounces	31.103 grams
pound	5,760 grains, 0.823 avoirdupois pound	373.242 grams

GUIDE TO THE METRIC SYSTEM

The metric system was first constructed by the French Academy of Sciences in 1790. The system was designed to set standards for weights and measures that had varied a great deal ever since the Greeks and Egyptians first based their unit of length on the human foot. One of the problems from the very beginning was whose foot to use — a peasant's or a king's? Volume was measured by how much a basket or a goatskin could hold. This system of weights and measures was capricious at best — Henry I of England even declared that a yard would henceforth be the distance from the tip of his nose to the end of his thumb.

The Academy of Sciences solved these differences by creating a rational, simple, and above all consistent system centered on sound scientific principles. Length, weight, and volume were derived from a single unit of measurement based on a fraction of the distance between the earth's equator and either pole (this later proved to be impractical and was changed to an atomic standard). The system's basic unit was named **meter** after the Greek word, **metron,** meaning "measure." Thus, all three basic forms of measurement were related to each other. In the metric system each unit is used to measure only one quantity. For example, in the customary system an ounce is used to measure both volume and weight and a pound is used to measure both weight and force; the metric system has separate units to measure length, weight, and volume. The system is also simple to use because it is a decimal system. It is based on the number ten so it is easy to add, subtract, multiply, and divide. The prefixes used with the basic metric unit names indicate the multiplication factor to be used with the basic unit.

LENGTH

Unit	Number of Meters	Approximate U.S. Equivalent
myriameter	10,000	6.214 miles
kilometer	1,000	0.621 mile
hectometer	100	109.361 yards
decameter	10	32.808 feet
meter	1	39.370 inches
decimeter	0.1	3.937 inches
centimeter	0.01	0.394 inch
millimeter	0.001	0.039 inch

AREA

Unit	Number of Square Meters	Approximate U.S. Equivalent
square kilometer	1,000,000	0.386 square mile
hectare	10,000	2.477 acres
are	100	119.599 square yards
deciare	10	11.960 square yards
centare	1	10.764 square feet
square centimeter	0.0001	0.155 square inch

VOLUME

Unit	Number of Cubic Meters	Approximate U.S. Equivalent
decastere	10	13.079 cubic yards
stere	1	1.308 cubic yards
decistere	0.10	3.532 cubic feet
cubic centimeter	0.000001	0.061 cubic inch

CAPACITY

Unit	Number of Liters	Cubic	Approximate U.S. Equivalents Dry	Liquid
kiloliter	1,000	1.308 cubic yards		
hectoliter	100	3.532 cubic feet	2.838 bushels	
decaliter	10	0.353 cubic foot	1.135 pecks	2.642 gallons
liter	1	61.024 cubic inches	0.908 quart	1.057 quarts
deciliter	0.10	6.102 cubic inches	0.182 pint	0.211 pint
centiliter	0.01	0.610 cubic inch		0.338 fluid ounce
milliliter	0.001	0.061 cubic inch		0.271 fluid dram

MASS AND WEIGHT

Unit	Number of Grams	Approximate U.S. Equivalent
metric ton	1,000,000	1.102 tons
quintal	100,000	220.462 pounds
kilogram	1,000	2.205 pounds
hectogram	100	3.527 ounces
decagram	10	0.353 ounce
gram	1	0.035 ounce
decigram	0.10	1.543 grains
centigram	0.01	0.154 grain
milligram	0.001	0.015 grain

METRIC CONVERSION CHART— APPROXIMATIONS

WHEN YOU KNOW	MULTIPLY BY	TO FIND
	Length	
millimeters	0.04	inches
centimeters	0.39	inches
meters	3.28	feet
meters	1.09	yards
kilometers	0.62	miles
inches	25.40	millimeters
inches	2.54	centimeters
feet	30.48	centimeters
yards	0.91	meters
miles	1.61	kilometers
	Area	
square centimeters	0.16	square inches
square meters	1.20	square yards
square kilometers	0.39	square miles
hectares (10,000m^2)	2.47	acres
square inches	6.45	square centimeters
square feet	0.09	square meters
square yards	0.84	square meters
square miles	2.60	square kilometers
acres	0.40	hectares
	Mass and Weight	
grams	0.035	ounce
kilograms	2.21	pounds
tons (100kg)	1.10	short tons
ounces	28.35	grams
pounds	0.45	kilograms
short tons (2000 lb)	0.91	tons
	Volume	
milliliters	0.20	teaspoons
milliliters	0.06	tablespoons
milliliters	0.03	fluid ounces
liters	4.23	cups
liters	2.12	pints

WHEN YOU KNOW	MULTIPLY BY	TO FIND
	Volume	
liters	1.06	quarts
liters	0.26	gallons
cubic meters	35.32	cubic feet
cubic meters	1.35	cubic yards
teaspoons	4.93	milliliters
tablespoons	14.78	milliliters
fluid ounces	29.57	milliliters
cups	0.24	liters
pints	0.47	liters
quarts	0.95	liters
gallons	3.79	liters
	Volume	
cubic feet	0.03	cubic meters
cubic yards	0.76	cubic meters
	Speed	
miles per hour	1.61	kilometers per hour
kilometers per hour	0.62	miles per hour
	Temperature (exact)	
Celsius temp.	9/5, +32	Fahrenheit temp.
Fahrenheit temp.	−32, 5/9 × remainder	Celsius temp.

Temperatures in degrees Celsius, as in the familiar Fahrenheit system, can only be learned through experience. The following temperatures are ones that are frequently encountered:

0°C	Freezing point of water (32°F)
10°C	A warm winter day (50°F)
20°C	A mild spring day (68°F)
30°C	A hot summer day (86°F)
37°C	Normal body temperature (98.6°F)
40°C	Heat wave conditions (104°F)
100°C	Boiling point of water (212°F)

MEASUREMENT *(continued)*

SCIENTIFIC MEASUREMENT

The units tabulated in Table II are commonly used in science and engineering. They are primarily chosen from the fields of mechanics and electricity and magnetism and are a representative, not an exhaustive, selection.

SI units are given for all physical quantities listed. For those units having a special name in the International System, the name appears, along with the derivation of the unit from the fundamental SI quantities, which are defined as: meter (m), kilogram (kg), second (s), ampere (A), kelvin (K) or alternatively degree Kelvin (°K), and candela (cd). Two supplementary units, the radian (rad), for measuring plane angles, and the steradian (sr), for measuring solid angles, are used. These are "geometrical" rather than "physical" units, in the sense that their definitions are based on abstract geometrical concepts rather than on physical standards.

In some instances, it is customary practice to measure a quantity in units other than SI units; in such cases the appropriate unit is given in the right-hand column, along with a conversion to SI units.

Additional information on individual scientific units, including those not tabulated, should be sought at the unit names in the text.

TABLE II. SCIENTIFIC UNITS

Quantity	SI Unit	Symbol	Derivation	Other Units
acceleration	meter per second squared	m/s^2		
angular acceleration	radian per second squared	rad/s^2		
angular velocity	radian per second	rad/s		
density	kilogram per cubic meter	kg/m^3		
electric capacitance	farad	F	(A·s/V)	
electric charge	coulomb	C	(A·s)	electrostatic unit (esu) = ⅓ $\times 10^{-9}$C
electric current	ampere	A		
electric field strength	volt per meter	V/m		
electric resistance	ohm		(V/A)	
energy, work, quantity of heat	joule	J	(N·m)	electronvolt (eV) = 1.60219 $\times 10^{-19}$J calorie (cal) = 4.184 J British thermal unit (Btu) = 1055.87 J erg = 10^{-7}J foot-pound (ft-lb) = 1.35582 J
flux of light	lumen	lm	(cd·sr)	
force	newton	N	($kg{\cdot}m/s^2$)	dyne (dyn) = 10^{-5} N
frequency	hertz	Hz	(s^{-1})	formerly cycle per second (cps, c/sec)
illumination	lux	lx	(lm/m^2)	
inductance	henry	H	(V·s/A)	
length	meter	m		angstrom (Å) = 10^{-10}m
luminance	candela per square meter	cd/m^2		
magnetic field strength	ampere per meter	A/m		oersted (Oe) = (1/4) $\times$ 10^3 A/m
magnetic flux	weber	Wb	(V/s)	maxwell (Mx) = 10^{-8} Wb
magnetic flux density	tesla	T	(Wb/m^2)	gauss (G) = 10^{-4} T
magnetomotive force	ampere	A		
mass	kilogram	kg		
power	watt	W	(J/s)	horsepower (hp) = 745.7 W
pressure	newton per square meter	N/m^2		atmosphere (atm) = 1.01325 $\times 10^5$ N/m^2 bar = 10^5 N/m^2
velocity	meter per second	m/s		
voltage, potential difference, electromotive force	volt	V	(W/A)	

something is done or comes into being: *"The mechanism of oral learning is largely that of continuous repetition"* (T.G.E. Powell). **4.** *Psychol.* **a.** The automatic and consistent response of an organism to various stimuli. **b.** A habitual manner of acting to achieve some end. **5.** *Psychoanal.* A usually unconscious mental and emotional pattern that dominates behavior: *a defense mechanism.* **6.** *Chem.* The sequence of steps in a chemical reaction. **7.** *Philos.* The doctrine that all natural phenomena are explicable by material causes and mechanical principles. [LLat. *mechanisma* < Gk. *mēkhanē,* machine. —see MECHANIC.]

mech·a·nist (mĕk'ə-nĭst) *n.* **1.** A person who believes in or employs in his work or thinking the philosophical doctrine of mechanism. **2.** A mechanician.

mech·a·nis·tic (mĕk'ə-nĭs'tĭk) *adj.* **1.** Mechanically determined. **2.** Of or pertaining to the philosophy of mechanism, esp. tending to explain phenomena only by reference to physical or biological causes. **3.** Mechanical. **—mech'a·nis'ti·cal·ly** *adv.*

mech·a·nize (mĕk'ə-nīz') *tr.v.* **-nized, -niz·ing, -niz·es. 1.** To equip with machinery: *mechanize a factory.* **2.** To equip (a military unit) with motor vehicles, as tanks and trucks. **3.** To make automatic or unspontaneous; render routine or monotonous. **4.** To produce by or as if by machines. **—mech'a·ni·za'tion** *n.* **—mech'a·niz'er** *n.*

mechano– or **mechan–** *pref.* **1.** Machine; machinery: *mechanize.* **2.** Mechanical: *mechanotherapy.* [ME *mechan-* < Lat. < Gk. *mēkhan-* < *mēkhanē,* machine.]

mech·a·no·chem·i·cal coupling (mĕk'ə-nō-kĕm'ĭ-kəl) *n.* The reversible conversion of chemical energy into mechanical work.

mech·a·no·re·cep·tor (mĕk'ə-nō-rĭ-sĕp'tər) *n.* A receptor

that responds to mechanical stimuli such as tension and pressure. **—mech′a·no·re·cep′tion** *n.* **—mech′a·no·re·cep′·tive** *adj.*
mech·a·no·ther·a·py (mĕk′ə-nō-thĕr′ə-pē) *n.* Medical treatment by mechanical methods, as massage. **—mech′an·o·ther′a·pist** *n.*
Mech·lin (mĕk′lĭn) *n.* A lace in which the pattern details are defined by a flat thread. [After *Mechlin,* Belgium.]
me·co·ni·um (mĭ-kō′nē-əm) *n.* Excrement in the fetal intestinal tract that is discharged at birth. [Lat. < Gk. *mēkōneion* < *mēkōn,* poppy.]
me·cop·ter·an (mĭ-kŏp′tər-ən) *n.* Any of various carnivorous insects of the order Mecoptera, distinguished by an elongated head that resembles a beak and has chewing mouthparts at the tip. [< NLat. *Mecoptera,* order name : Gk. *mēkos,* length + Gk. *pteron,* wing.]
me·da·ka (mĭ-dä′kə) *n.* **1.** The Japanese rice fish, *Oryzias latipes,* much used in biological research. **2.** A fish of the Asiatic and Indo-Malayan genus *Oryzias.* [J., killifish.]
med·al (mĕd′l) *n.* **1.** A flat piece of metal stamped with a design or inscription commemorating an event or person, often given as an award. **2.** A piece of metal stamped with a religious device, used as an object of veneration or commemoration. [Fr. *médaille* < OItal. *medaglia,* coin worth half a denarius, medal < VLat. **medalis* < LLat. *medialis,* middle < Lat. *medius.*]
Medal for Merit *n.* A decoration awarded by the United States to civilians for outstanding services in peace or war.
med·al·ist (mĕd′l-ĭst) *n.* **1.** One who designs, makes, or collects medals. **2.** One who has received a medal. **3.** *Sports.* The winner at medal play in a golf tournament.
me·dal·lion (mĭ-dăl′yən) *n.* **1.** A large medal. **2.** Any of various large ancient Greek coins. **3.** Something resembling a large medal, as an oval or circular design used as decoration. [Fr. *médaillon* < Ital. *medaglione,* aug. of *medaglia,* medal < OItal. —see MEDAL.]
med·al·list (mĕd′l-ĭst) *n. Chiefly Brit.* Variant of **medalist.**
Medal of Freedom *n.* A decoration awarded by the United States to civilians for outstanding achievement in various fields of endeavor.
Medal of Honor *n.* The highest U.S. military decoration, awarded in the name of Congress to members of the armed forces for gallantry and bravery beyond the call of duty in action against the enemy.
medal play *n.* Golf competition in which the total number of strokes taken is the basis of the score.
med·dle (mĕd′l) *intr.v.* **-dled, -dling, -dles. 1.** To intrude in other people's affairs or business; interfere. **2.** To handle something idly or ignorantly; tamper. [ME *medlen* < OFr. *medler,* var. of *mesler* < VLat. **misculare,* freq. of Lat. *miscēre,* to mix.] **—med′dler** (mĕd′lər, mĕd′l-ər) *n.*
med·dle·some (mĕd′l-səm) *adj.* Inclined to meddle or interfere. **—med′dle·some·ly** *adv.* **—med′dle·some·ness** *n.*
Me·de·a (mĭ-dē′ə) *n. Gk. Myth.* A princess and sorceress of Colchis who helped Jason obtain the Golden Fleece. [Lat. < Gk. *Mēdeia.*]
Med·fly also **med·fly** (mĕd′flī′) *n.* The Mediterranean fruit fly.
me·di·a¹ (mē′dē-ə) *n.* A plural of **medium.**
me·di·a² (mē′dē-ə) *n.* A medial (sense 1).
me·di·a·cy (mē′dē-ə-sē) *n.* **1.** The state or quality of being mediate. **2.** Mediation.
me·di·ae·val (mē′dē-ē′vəl, mĕd-ē′-) *adj.* Variant of **medieval.**
me·di·ae·val·ism (mē′dē-ē′və-lĭz′əm, mĕd-ē′-) *n.* Variant of **medievalism.**
me·di·ae·val·ist (mē′dē-ē′və-lĭst, mĕd-ē′-) *n.* Variant of **medievalist.**
me·di·al (mē′dē-əl) *adj.* **1.** Pertaining to, situated in, or extending toward the middle; median. **2.** Being a sound, syllable, or letter occurring between the initial and final positions in a word or morpheme. **3.** Being or pertaining to a mathematical average or mean. **4.** Average; ordinary. —*n.* **1.** A voiced stop, as *b, d,* or *g.* **2.** An element, such as a sound, letter, or form of a letter, that is used in the middle of a word. [LLat. *medialis* < Lat. *medius,* middle.] **—me′di·al·ly** *adv.*
me·di·an (mē′dē-ən) *adj.* **1.** Pertaining to, located in, or directed toward the middle; medial. **2.** *Anat. & Zool.* Of, pertaining to, or lying in the plane that divides a bilaterally symmetrical animal into right and left halves; mesial. **3.** *Statistics.* Relating to or constituting the middle value in a distribution. —*n.* **1.** A median point, plane, line, or part. **2.** *Statistics.* The middle value in a distribution, above and below which lie an equal number of values. **3.** *Math.* **a.** A line that joins a vertex of a triangle to the midpoint of the opposite side. **b.** The line that joins the midpoints of the nonparallel sides of a trapezoid. [Lat. *medianus* < *medius,* middle.] **—me′di·an·ly** *adv.*
median plane *n.* A plane dividing a bilaterally symmetrical animal into right and left halves.
median point *n.* The intersection of the medians of a triangle.
median strip *n.* The dividing area, either paved or landscaped, between opposing traffic on some highways.
me·di·ant (mē′dē-ənt) *n. Mus.* The third tone in a diatonic musical scale between the tonic and the dominant and traditionally related harmonically to them.
me·di·as·ti·na (mē′dē-ə-stī′nə) *n.* Plural of **mediastinum.**
me·di·as·ti·ni·tis (mē′dē-ăs′tə-nī′tĭs) *n.* Inflammation of the mediastinum.
me·di·as·ti·num (mē′dē-ə-stī′nəm) *n., pl.* **-na** (-nə). The septum that divides the pleural sacs in mammals, containing all the thoracic viscera except the lungs. [NLat. < Med. Lat. *mediastinus,* medial < Lat., drudge < *medius,* middle.] **—me′di·as·ti′nal** *adj.*
me·di·ate (mē′dē-āt′) *v.* **-at·ed, -at·ing, -ates.** —*tr.* **1.** To resolve or settle (differences) by acting as an intermediary agent between two or more conflicting parties. **2.** To bring about (a settlement, for example) by action as an intermediary. **3.** To convey or transmit as an intermediary agent or mechanism. —*intr.* **1.** To intervene between two or more disputing parties in order to effect an agreement, settlement, or compromise. **2.** To settle or reconcile differences. —*adj.* (mē′dē-ĭt). Acting through, involving, or dependent upon some intervening agency. [LLat. *mediare, mediat-,* to be in the middle < Lat. *medius,* middle.] **—me′di·ate·ly** (-ĭt-lē) *adv.*
me·di·a·tion (mē′dē-ā′shən) *n.* **1.** The act of mediating; intervention. **2.** The state of being mediated. **3.** *Law.* The attempt to bring about a peaceful settlement or compromise between disputing nations through the benevolent intervention of a neutral power. **—me′di·a′tive, me′di·a·tor′y** *adj.*

Synonyms: *mediation, conciliation, arbitration. Mediation* denotes only intervention in a dispute with intent to settle it equitably, but generally implies a favorable result. *Conciliation* stresses the settlement of difference and the assuaging of ill feeling. *Arbitration,* often the last resort among these processes, emphasizes finality and decision, usually achieved through legal apparatus and procedure agreed upon in advance.

me·di·a·tize (mē′dē-ə-tīz′) *tr.v.* **-tized, -tiz·ing, -tiz·es.** To annex (a lesser state) to a greater state as a means of permitting the ruler of the lesser power to retain his title and part of his former authority. [G. *mediatisieren* < *mediat,* mediate < LLat. *mediare,* to be in the middle. —see MEDIATE.] **—me′di·a·ti·za′tion** *n.*
me·di·a·tor (mē′dē-ā′tər) *n.* One that mediates, esp. a person who serves as an intermediary to reconcile differences.
med·ic¹ or **med·ick** (mĕd′ĭk) *n.* Any of several plants of the genus *Medicago,* native to the Old World and having clusters of small, usually yellow flowers and compound leaves with three leaflets. [ME *medike* < Lat. *Medica* < Gk. *Mēdikē* < *Mēdikos,* of Media, an ancient country of southwestern Asia < *Mēdos,* an inhabitant of Media < OPers. *mada.*]
med·ic² (mĕd′ĭk) *n. Informal.* **1.** A physician or surgeon. **2.** A medical student or intern. **3.** A military medical corpsman. [Lat. *medicus.* —see MEDICAL.]
med·i·ca·ble (mĕd′ĭ-kə-bəl) *adj.* Potentially responsive to treatment with medicine; curable.
Med·i·caid also **med·i·caid** (mĕd′ĭ-kād′) *n.* A program, jointly funded by the states and the federal government, that provides medical aid for people who are unable to finance their own medical expenses. [MEDIC(AL) + AID.]
med·i·cal (mĕd′ĭ-kəl) *adj.* **1.** Of or pertaining to the study or practice of medicine. **2.** Requiring medical as distinct from surgical treatment. —*n. Informal.* A thorough physical examination. [Fr. *médical* < LLat. *medicalis* < Lat. *medicus,* physician < *medēri,* to heal.]
medical examiner *n.* **1.** A physician officially authorized by a governmental unit (as a city or county) to ascertain causes of deaths, esp. those not occurring under natural circumstances. **2.** A physician who examines applicants for life insurance.
medical law *n.* A branch of law concerned with the legal regulation of medicine and medical practice.
me·dic·a·ment (mĭ-dĭk′ə-mənt, mĕd′ĭ-kə-) *n.* An agent that promotes recovery from injury or ailment; medicine. [Lat. *medicamentum* < *medicari,* to medicate.]
Med·i·care also **med·i·care** (mĕd′ĭ-kâr′) *n.* A program under the Social Security Administration that provides medical care for the aged. [MEDI(CAL) + CARE.]
med·i·cate (mĕd′ĭ-kāt′) *tr.v.* **-cat·ed, -cat·ing, -cates. 1.** To treat medicinally. **2.** To tincture or permeate with a medicinal substance. [Lat. *medicari, medicat-* < *medicus,* doctor < *medēri,* to heal.] **—med′i·ca′tive** *adj.*
med·i·ca·tion (mĕd′ə-kā′shən) *n.* **1.** A medicine; medicament. **2.** The act or process of being medicated. **3.** The administration of medicine.
me·dic·i·nal (mə-dĭs′ə-nəl) *adj.* Pertaining to or having the properties of medicine. **—me·dic′i·nal·ly** *adv.*
med·i·cine (mĕd′ĭ-sĭn) *n.* **1. a.** The science of diagnosing, treating, or preventing disease and other damage to the body or mind. **b.** The branch of this science encompassing treatment by drugs, diet, exercise, and other nonsurgical means. **2.** The practice of medicine. **3.** A drug or other agent used to treat disease or injury. **4.** Among North American Indians, something believed to control natural or supernatural powers and to serve as a preventive or remedy. [ME < Lat. *medicina* < *medicus,* physician. —see MEDICAL.]
medicine ball *n.* A large, heavy ball used for conditioning exercise.
medicine dance *n.* A ritual dance performed by some

medal

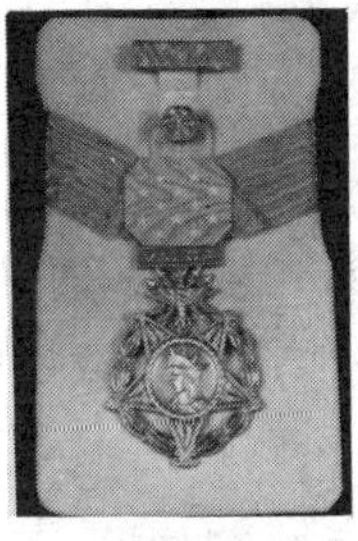

Medal of Honor
Congressional Medal of Honor

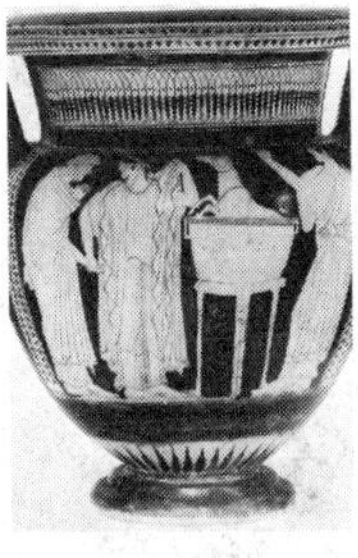

Medea
5th-century B.C. Greek vase painting

medicine man
American Blackfoot Indian

medlar

Medusa
Perseus holding the head of the slain Medusa

meerschaum
Meerschaum pipe

Plains Indians of North America to obtain supernatural assistance.

medicine lodge *n.* A large wooden structure used by some North American Indian tribes for ritualistic ceremonies.

medicine man *n.* **1.** A person believed among preliterate peoples to possess supernatural powers for healing, invoking spirits, and other purposes; shaman. **2.** A hawker of brews and potions among the audience in a medicine show.

medicine show *n.* A traveling show, popular esp. in 19th-century America, that offered varied entertainment, between the acts of which medicines were peddled.

med·ick (mĕd′ĭk) *n.* Variant of **medic**[1].

med·i·co (mĕd′ĭ-kō′) *n., pl.* **-cos.** *Informal.* **1.** A doctor. **2.** A medical student. [Ital. and Sp., both < Lat. *medicus.* —see MEDICAL.]

med·i·co·le·gal (mĕd′ĭ-kō-lē′gəl) *adj.* Of or pertaining to both medicine and law. [MEDIC(AL) + LEGAL.]

me·di·e·val also **me·di·ae·val** (mē′dē-ē′vəl, mĕd′ē-) *adj.* Pertaining or belonging to the Middle Ages. [Lat. *medius,* middle + Lat. *aevum,* age + -AL.] **—me′di·e′val·ly** *adv.*

Medieval Greek *n.* The Greek language as used from about 800 to 1500.

me·di·e·val·ism also **me·di·ae·val·ism** (mē′dē-ē′və-lĭz′əm, mĕd′ē-) *n.* **1.** The spirit or the body of beliefs, customs, or practices of the Middle Ages. **2.** Devotion to or acceptance of the ideas of the Middle Ages. **3.** Scholarly study of the Middle Ages.

me·di·e·val·ist also **me·di·ae·val·ist** (mē′dē-ē′və-lĭst, mĕd-ē′-) *n.* **1.** A specialist in medieval studies. **2.** A connoisseur of medieval culture.

Medieval Latin *n.* The Latin language as used from about 700 to 1500.

me·di·o·cre (mē′dē-ō′kər) *adj.* Of moderate to low quality; average. [Lat. *mediocris* < *medius,* middle.]

me·di·oc·ri·ty (mē′dē-ŏk′rĭ-tē) *n., pl.* **-ties.** **1.** The state or quality of being mediocre. **2.** Mediocre ability, achievement, or performance. **3.** A person who displays mediocre qualities.

med·i·tate (mĕd′ə-tāt′) *v.* **-tat·ed, -tat·ing, -tates.** *—tr.* **1.** To reflect upon; ponder. **2.** To plan or intend in the mind: *He meditated a just revenge.* *—intr.* To engage in contemplation. [Lat. *meditari, meditat-,* to meditate.] **—med′i·ta′tor** *n.*

med·i·ta·tion (mĕd′ĭ-tā′shən) *n.* **1. a.** The act or process of meditating. **b.** A devotional exercise of contemplation. **2.** A contemplative discourse, usually on a religious or philosophical subject.

med·i·ta·tive (mĕd′ĭ-tā′tĭv) *adj.* Devoted to, characterized by, or expressing meditation. **—med′i·ta′tive·ly** *adv.* **—med′i·ta′tive·ness** *n.*

med·i·ter·ra·ne·an (mĕd′ĭ-tə-rā′nē-ən, -rān′yən) *adj.* **1.** Surrounded nearly or completely by dry land. Used of large bodies of water, as lakes or seas. **2. Mediterranean.** Of, pertaining to, or characteristic of the Mediterranean Sea or the countries that border the Mediterranean Sea. [Lat. *mediterraneus* : *medius,* middle + *terra,* land.]

Mediterranean fever *n.* Undulant fever.

Mediterranean flour moth *n.* A small, pale-gray moth, *Ephestia kuehniella,* now found worldwide, the larvae of which destroy flour, whole grains, and beehive pollen.

Mediterranean fruit fly *n.* A black and white, two-winged fly, *Ceratitis capitata,* that attacks citrus and other fruits and is found in most subtropical countries.

me·di·um (mē′dē-əm) *n., pl.* **-di·a** (-dē-ə) or **-di·ums.** **1.** Something occupying a position or having a condition midway between extremes, as an intermediate course of action. **2.** An intervening substance through which something is transmitted or carried on, as an agency for transmitting energy. **3.** An agency by which something is accomplished, conveyed, or transferred: *"The principal use of money is as a medium of exchange"* (Melville Ullmer). **4.** *pl.* **media.** A means of mass communication, as newspapers, magazines, or television. **5.** *pl.* **mediums.** A person thought to have the power to communicate with the spirits of the dead. **6.** *pl.* **media. a.** A surrounding environment in which something functions and thrives. **b.** The substance in which a specific organism lives and thrives. **c.** A substance in which bacteria are cultivated for scientific purposes. **7. a.** A specific type of artistic technique or means of expression as determined by the materials used or the creative methods involved: *the medium of lithography.* **b.** The materials used in a specific artistic technique. **8.** A solvent with which paint is thinned to the proper consistency. **9.** *Chem.* A filtering substance, as filter paper. **10.** A size of paper, usually 18 × 23 inches or 17½ × 22 inches. *—adj.* **1.** Occurring or being between two degrees, amounts, or quantities; intermediate: *broil a medium steak.* **2.** Average; mean: *a medium-grade ore.* [Lat. < *medius,* middle.]

medium of exchange *n.* Something that is commonly used in a specific area or among a certain group of people as money.

med·lar (mĕd′lər) *n.* **1.** A tree, *Mespilus germanica,* cultivated for its fruit. **2.** The fruit of the medlar. [ME *medler* < OFr. < **medle,* var. of *mesle,* fruit of the medlar < Lat. *mespila* < Gk. *mespilē.*]

med·ley (mĕd′lē) *n., pl.* **-leys.** **1.** A jumbled assortment; mixture. **2.** A musical arrangement made from a series of melodies from various sources. [ME *medlee* < OFr., var. of *meslee* < VLat. **misculare.* —see MEDDLE.]

Mé·doc (mā-dôk′, -dŏk′) *n.* A red Bordeaux wine. [After *Médoc,* a region of France.]

me·dul·la (mə-dŭl′ə) *n., pl.* **-las** or **-lae** (-ē). **1.** *Anat.* The inner core of certain vertebrate body structures, as the marrow of bone. **2.** The medulla oblongata. **3.** *Bot.* The pith or central tissue in stems of certain plants. [Lat.] **—me·dul′lar, med′ul·lar′y** (mĕd′ə-lĕr′ē, mə-dŭl′ə-rē) *adj.*

medulla ob·lon·ga·ta (ŏb′lông-gä′tə) *n., pl.* **medulla ob·lon·ga·tas** or **medullae ob·lon·ga·tae** (-gä′tē). The nervous tissue at the bottom of the brain that controls respiration, circulation, and certain other bodily functions. [NLat., oblong medulla.]

medullary sheath *n.* **1.** *Anat.* Myelin. **2.** *Bot.* A layer of thick-walled cells surrounding the pith in the stems of various plants.

med·ul·lat·ed (mĕd′ə-lā′tĭd) *adj.* Myelinated. [LLat. *medullatus,* having marrow < Lat. *medulla,* medulla.]

med·ul·li·za·tion (mĕd′ə-lĭ-zā′shən) *n.* Replacement of bone tissue by marrow, as in inflammatory bone disease.

Me·du·sa (mə-do͞o′sə, -zə, -dyo͞o′-) *n., pl.* **-sas** or **-sae** (-sē, -zē). **1.** *Gk. Myth.* One of the three Gorgons. **2. medusa.** The tentacled, usually bell-shaped, free-swimming sexual stage in the life cycle of a coelenterate of the class Scyphozoa or Hydrozoa. [Lat. < Gk. *Medousa.*]

me·du·soid (mə-do͞o′soid′, -zoid′, dyo͞o′-) *n.* **1.** A shape resembling a jellyfish. **2.** A jellyfish. **—me·du′soid′** *adj.*

meed (mēd) *n.* **1.** *Archaic.* A merited gift or wage. **2.** A fitting recompense. [ME *mede* < OE *mēd.*]

meek (mēk) *adj.* **-er, -est.** **1.** Showing patience and humility; gentle. **2.** Easily imposed upon; submissive. [ME *meke* < ON *mjūkr,* soft.] **—meek′ly** *adv.*

meer·schaum (mîr′shəm, -shôm′) *n.* **1.** A tough, compact, usually white mineral of hydrous magnesium silicate, $H_4Mg_2Si_3O_{10}$, found in the Mediterranean area and used in fashioning tobacco pipes and as a building stone. **2.** A tobacco pipe with a bowl of meerschaum. [G. : *Meer,* sea + *Schaum,* foam.]

meet[1] (mēt) *v.* **met** (mĕt), **meet·ing, meets.** *—tr.* **1.** To come upon by chance or arrangement. **2.** To be present at the arrival of: *met the train.* **3.** To be introduced to. **4.** To come into conjunction with; join: *where the sea meets the sky.* **5.** To come into the company or presence of, as for a conference. **6.** To come to the notice of (the senses): *more here than meets the eye.* **7.** To experience; undergo: *met his fate with courage.* **8.** To deal with; oppose: *"We have met the enemy and they are ours"* (Oliver Hazard Perry). **9.** To cope or contend effectively with: *meet each problem as it arises.* **10.** To come into conformity with the views, wishes, or opinions of: *The firm has done its best to meet us on that point.* **11.** To satisfy (a need, for example); fulfill: *meet all the conditions in the contract.* **12.** To pay; settle: *enough money to meet the expenses.* *—intr.* **1.** To come together: *Let's meet tonight.* **2.** To come into conjunction; be joined: *"East is East, and West is West, and never the twain shall meet"* (Kipling). **3.** To come together as opponents; contend. **4.** To become introduced. **5.** To assemble. **6.** To experience or undergo: *The housing bill met with approval.* **7.** To occur together, esp. in one person or entity: *"The hopes and fears of all the years / Are met in thee tonight"* (Phillips Brooks). *—n.* A meeting or contest, esp. an athletic competition. ***—idiom.* meet (one) halfway.** To compromise. [ME *meten* < OE *mētan.*]

meet[2] (mēt) *adj.* Fitting; proper: *"It is not meet, nor wholesome to my place"* (Shakespeare). [ME *mete* < OE *gemǣte.*] **—meet′ly** *adv.*

meet·ing (mē′tĭng) *n.* **1.** The act or process of coming together; encounter. **2.** An assembly or gathering of people, as for a business, social, or religious purpose. ***—idiom.* meeting of the minds.** Agreement; concord.

meet·ing·house (mē′tĭng-hous′) *n.* A building used for public meetings and esp. for Quaker religious services.

mef·e·nam·ic acid (mĕf′ə-năm′ĭk) *n.* A crystalline compound, $C_{15}H_{15}NO_2$, used as an anti-inflammatory drug and as an analgesic. [(DI)ME(THYL) + *fen* (alteration of PHENYL) + AM(NIOBENZO)IC ACID.]

mega– *pref.* **1.** Large: *megadose.* **2.** One million (10^6): *megahertz.* [Gk. < *megas,* great.]

meg·a·buck (mĕg′ə-bŭk′) *n. Slang.* One million dollars.

meg·a·ceph·a·ly (mĕg′ə-sĕf′ə-lē) *n.* Macrocephaly. **—meg′a·ce·phal′ic** (-sə-făl′ĭk), **meg′a·ceph′a·lous** (-sĕf′ə-ləs) *adj.*

meg·a·cy·cle (mĕg′ə-sī′kəl) *n. Physics.* **1.** One million cycles. **2.** Megahertz.

me·ga·death (mĕg′ə-dĕth′) *n.* One million deaths. Used as a unit in reference to nuclear warfare.

Me·gae·ra (mə-jîr′ə) *n. Gk. Myth.* One of the Furies. [Lat. < Gk. *Megaira.*]

meg·a·gam·ete (mĕg′ə-găm′ēt′, -gə-mēt′) *n.* Macrogamete.

meg·a·ga·me·to·phyte (mĕg′ə-gə-mē′tə-fīt′) *n.* The female gametophyte that arises from a megaspore of a heterosporous plant.

meg·a·hertz (mĕg′ə-hûrts′) *n., pl.* **megahertz.** *Physics.* One million cycles per second, used esp. as a radio-frequency unit.

meg·a·kar·y·o·cyte (mĕg′ə-kăr′ē-ō-sīt′, -ə-sīt′) *n.* A large bone marrow cell with a lobulate nucleus that is the precursor to blood platelets.

megal– *pref.* Variant of **megalo-.**

meg·a·lith (mĕg′ə-lĭth′) *n.* A very large stone used in various prehistoric architectures or monumental styles, notably in western Europe during the second millennium B.C. **—meg′a·lith′ic** *adj.*

megalo– or **megal–** *pref.* Large; of exaggerated size or greatness: *megalocephaly.* [Gk. < *megas,* great.]

meg·a·lo·blast (mĕg′ə-lō-blăst′) *n.* A large nucleated erythroblast that is found in the blood in pernicious anemia. **—meg′a·lo·blas′tic** *adj.*

meg·a·lo·car·di·a (mĕg′ə-lō-kär′dē-ə) *n.* Enlargement of the heart. [MEGALO- + Gk. *kardia,* heart.]

meg·a·lo·ceph·a·ly (mĕg′ə-lō-sĕf′ə-lē) *n.* Macrocephaly. **—meg′a·lo·ce·phal′ic** (-sə-făl′ĭk), **meg′a·lo·ceph′a·lous** (-sĕf′ə-ləs) *adj.*

meg·a·lo·ma·ni·a (mĕg′ə-lō-mā′nē-ə, -mān′yə) *n.* A psychopathological condition in which fantasies of wealth, power, or omnipotence predominate. **—meg′a·lo·ma′ni·ac′** *n.* **—meg′a·lo·ma·ni′a·cal** (-mə-nī′ə-kəl), **—meg′a·lo·man′ic** (-măn′ĭk) *adj.*

meg·a·lop·o·lis (mĕg′ə-lŏp′ə-lĭs) also **me·gap·o·lis** (mə-găp′ə-lis, mĕ-) *n.* A region made up of several large cities and their surrounding areas in sufficiently close proximity to be considered a single urban complex. [MEGALO- + Gk. *polis,* city.] **—meg′a·lop·o·lis′tic** *adj.* **—meg′a·lo·pol′i·tan** (-lō-pŏl′ĭ-tən) *adj.*

meg·a·lo·saur (mĕg′ə-lə-sôr′) *n.* An extinct gigantic carnivorous dinosaur, genus *Megalosaurus,* of the Jurassic period. [NLat. *Megalosaurus,* genus name : MEGALO- + Gk. *sauros,* lizard.] **—meg′a·lo·sau′ri·an** *n. & adj.*

meg·a·phone (mĕg′ə-fōn′) *n.* A funnel-shaped device used to direct and amplify the voice. *—tr. & intr.v.* **-phoned, -phon·ing, -phones.** To transmit or speak through or as if through a megaphone. **—meg′a·phon′ic** (-fŏn′ĭk) *adj.* **—meg′a·phon′i·cal·ly** *adv.*

meg·a·pode (mĕg′ə-pōd′) *n.* Any of various birds of the family Megapodiidae, found in Australia and many South Pacific islands. [< NLat. *Megapodiidae,* family name : MEGA- + Gk. *pous,* foot.]

me·gap·o·lis (mə-găp′ə-lĭs, mĕ-) *n.* Variant of **megalopolis.**

meg·a·scop·ic (mĕg′ə-skŏp′ĭk) *adj.* Macroscopic (sense 2). **—meg′a·scop′i·cal·ly** *adv.*

meg·a·spo·ran·gi·um (mĕg′ə-spə-răn′jē-əm) *n., pl.* **-gi·a** (-jē-ə). A structure that encloses a megaspore.

meg·a·spore (mĕg′ə-spôr′, -spōr′) *n.* **1.** The larger of two types of spores formed by heterosporous plants, as ferns, giving rise to the female gametophyte. **2.** A spore that forms the embryo sac in seed plants. **—meg′a·spor′ic** *adj.*

meg·a·spo·ro·gen·e·sis (mĕg′ə-spôr′ə-jĕn′ĭ-sĭs, -spōr′-) *n.* The production or formation of megaspores.

meg·a·spo·ro·phyll (mĕg′ə-spôr′ə-fĭl′, -spōr′-) *n.* A leaflike structure that produces megasporangia.

meg·a·struc·ture (mĕg′ə-strŭk′chər) *n.* An extremely large, tall building.

meg·a·there (mĕg′ə-thîr′) *n.* A member of the extinct family Megatheriidae, composed of large ground sloths of the Miocene and Pleistocene epochs. [< NLat. *Megatheriidae,* family name : MEGA- + Gk. *thēr,* beast.] **—meg′a·the′ri·an** (-ē-ən) *adj.*

meg·a·ton (mĕg′ə-tŭn′) *n.* A unit of explosive force equal to one million tons of TNT. **—meg′a·ton′nage** *n.*

Me·gil·lah (mə-gĭl′ə) *n.* **1.** The Judaic scroll containing the Biblical narrative of the Book of Esther, traditionally read in synagogues to celebrate the festival of Purim. **2. megillah.** *Slang.* A tediously detailed or embroidered account. [Heb. *mĕgillāh* < *gālal,* to roll.]

Me·grez (mē′grĕz′) *n.* A star in the Big Dipper. [Short for Ar. *maghriz adh-Dhanab ad-Dubb al-Akbar,* the root of the tail of the greater bear.]

me·grim (mē′grĭm) *n.* **1.** A migraine. **2.** Often **megrims.** A caprice or fancy. **3. megrims.** Depression or unhappiness: *"If these megrims are the effect of Love, thank Heaven, I never knew what it was"* (Samuel Richardson). [ME *migrem* < OFr. *migraine,* migraine. —see MIGRAINE.]

mei·o·sis (mī-ō′sĭs) *n., pl.* **-ses** (-sēz′). **1.** *Biol.* The cell division in sexually reproducing organisms that reduces the number of chromosomes in reproductive cells, leading to the production of gametes in animals and spores in plants. **2.** Rhetorical understatement. [NLat. < Gk. *meiōsis,* diminution < *meioun,* to diminish < *meiōn,* less.] **—mei·ot′ic** (-ŏt′ĭk) *adj.* **—mei·ot′i·cal·ly** *adv.*

Meis·sen (mī′sən) *n.* A delicate porcelain ware made in Meissen, Germany.

Meis·ter·sing·er (mīs′tər-sĭng′ər) *n., pl.* **Meistersinger** or **-ers.** A member of one of the guilds organized in the principal cities of Germany in the 14th, 15th, and 16th centuries for the purpose of establishing competitive standards for the composition and performance of music and poetry. [G. < MHG : *meister,* master (< OHG *meistar* < Lat. *magister*) + *singer,* singer (< *singen,* to sing < OHG *singan*).]

mel·a·mine (mĕl′ə-mēn′) *n.* A white crystalline compound, $C_3H_6N_6$, used in making melamine resins. [G. *Melamin.*]

mel·a·mine resin (mĕl′ə-mēn′) *n.* A thermosetting resin used for molded products, adhesives, and surface coatings.

melan– *pref.* Variant of **melano-.**

mel·an·cho·li·a (mĕl′ən-kō′lē-ə) *n.* A mental disorder characterized by feelings of dejection and usually by withdrawal. It is often a phase of manic-depressive psychosis. [NLat. < LLat., melancholy.] **—mel′an·cho′li·ac** (-lē-ăk′) *adj. & n.*

mel·an·chol·ic (mĕl′ən-kŏl′ĭk) *adj.* **1.** Afflicted with or subject to melancholy. **2.** Of, pertaining to, or afflicted with melancholia. **—mel′an·chol′ic** *n.* **—mel′an·chol′i·cal·ly** *adv.*

mel·an·chol·y (mĕl′ən-kŏl′ē) *n.* **1.** Sadness or depression of the spirits; gloom. **2.** Pensive reflection or contemplation. **3. a.** Black bile. **b.** An emotional state characterized by sullenness and outbreaks of violent anger, believed to arise from black bile. *—adj.* **1.** Sad; depressed: *a melancholy mood.* **2.** Tending to promote sadness or gloom. **3.** Pensive; thoughtful. [ME *melancolie* < OFr. < Med. Lat. *melencholia* < LLat. *melancholia* < Gk. *melankholia* : *melas,* black + *kholē,* bile.] **—mel′an·chol′i·ly** *adv.* **—mel′an·chol′i·ness** *n.*

Mel·a·ne·sian (mĕl′ə-nē′zhən, -shən) *adj.* Of or pertaining to Melanesia, its people, or their languages. *—n.* **1.** An indigenous inhabitant of Melanesia. **2.** A subfamily of the Austronesian languages that includes the languages of Melanesia.

mé·lange also **me·lange** (mā-läNZH′) *n.* A mixture. [Fr. < OFr. < *mesler,* to mix. —see MEDDLE.]

me·la·ni·an (mə-lā′nē-ən) *adj.* Pertaining to dark or black pigmentation.

me·lan·ic (mə-lăn′ĭk) *adj.* **1.** Of, pertaining to, or exhibiting melanism. **2.** Afflicted with melanosis.

mel·a·nin (mĕl′ə-nĭn) *n.* A dark pigment found in the skin, retina, and hair.

mel·a·nism (mĕl′ə-nĭz′əm) *n.* **1.** Melanosis. **2.** Darkness of the skin, hair, or eyes resulting from high pigmentation. **—mel′a·nis′tic** *adj.*

mel·a·nite (mĕl′ə-nīt′) *n.* A black variety of garnet. [G. *Melanit* < Gk. *melas,* black.] **—mel′a·nit′ic** (-nĭt′ĭk) *adj.*

megaphone

melano– or **melan–** *pref.* Black; dark: *melanin.* [NLat. < Gk. < *melas,* black.]

mel·a·no·blast (mĕl′ə-nō-blăst′, mə-lăn′ə-) *n.* A precursor cell of a melanocyte or melanophore. **—mel′a·no·blas′tic** *adj.*

mel·a·no·blas·to·ma (mĕl′ə-nō-blă-stō′mə, mə-lăn′ə-) *n.* A malignant tumor composed mainly of melanoblasts.

mel·a·noch·ro·i (mĕl′ə-nŏk′rō-ī′, -nŏk′roi′) *pl.n.* Caucasian peoples having dark hair and light complexions. [NLat. : Gk. *melas,* dark + Gk. *ōkhros,* pale.] **—mel′a·no·chro·ic** (-nō-krō′ĭk), **mel′a·noch′roid′** (-nŏk′roid′) *adj.*

mel·a·no·cyte (mĕl′ə-nō-sīt′) *n.* An epidermal cell capable of synthesizing the black pigment melanin and responsible for color variations in the skin of humans and many animals.

mel·a·no·cyte-stim·u·lat·ing hormone (mĕl′ə-nō-sīt′stĭm′yə-lā′tĭng, mə-lăn′ə-) *n.* A hormone secreted by the pituitary gland that stimulates melanocytes or melanophores to disperse melanin.

mel·a·noid (mĕl′ə-noid′) *adj.* **1.** Black-pigmented. **2.** Afflicted with melanosis. **—mel′a·noid′** *n.*

mel·a·no·ma (mĕl′ə-nō′mə) *n., pl.* **-mas** or **-ma·ta** (-mə-tə). A dark-pigmented malignant tumor.

mel·a·no·phore (mĕl′ə-nə-fôr′, -fōr′, mə-lăn′ə-) *n.* A chromatophore that contains melanin.

mel·a·no·sis (mĕl′ə-nō′sĭs) *n.* Abnormally dark pigmentation of the skin or other tissues, resulting from sunburn and various dermatoses. **—mel′a·not′ic** (-nŏt′ĭk) *adj.*

mel·a·nous (mĕl′ə-nəs) *adj.* Having a swarthy or black complexion and black hair. **—mel′a·nos′i·ty** (-nŏs′ĭ-tē) *n.*

mel·a·phyre (mĕl′ə-fīr′) *n.* A dark, igneous porphyry embedded with feldspar crystals. [Fr. *mélaphyre* : Gk. *melas,* black + F. *porphyre,* porphyry < Med. Lat. *porphyrium.* —see PORPHYRY.]

Mel·ba toast (mĕl′bə) *n.* Very thinly sliced crisp toast. [After Nellie *Melba* (1861–1931).]

Mel·chiz·e·dek (mĕl-kĭz′ə-dĕk′). **1.** In the Old Testament, the king of Salem and high priest who blessed Abraham. **2.** The higher order of priesthood of the Mormon Church. [Gk. *Melkhisedek* < Heb. *Malkī-ṣedheq.*]

meld¹ (mĕld) *v.* **meld·ed, meld·ing, melds.** *—tr.* To declare or display (a card or combination of cards in a hand) for inclusion in one's score in various card games, as pinochle. *—intr.* To present a meld. *—n.* A combination of cards to be declared for a score. [G. *melden,* to announce < OHG *meldōn.*]

meld² (mĕld) *v.* **meld·ed, meld·ing, melds.** *—tr.* To cause to merge. *—intr.* To become merged. [Blend of MELT and WELD.]

me·lee (mā′lā′, mā-lā′) also **mê·lée** (mĕ-lā′) *n.* **1. a.** Confused, hand-to-hand fighting in a pitched battle. **b.** A violent free-for-all. **2.** A confused and tumultuous mingling, as of a crowd: *the rush-hour melee.* [Fr. *mêlée* < OFr. *meslee,* medley. —see MEDLEY.]

mel·i·lot (mĕl′ə-lŏt′) *n.* Any of several plants of the genus *Melilotus,* native to the Old World, having compound leaves and narrow clusters of small, fragrant, white or yellow flowers. [ME *melilote* < OFr. < Lat. *melilotos* < Gk. *melilōtos* : *meli,* honey + *lōtos,* lotus.]

mel·i·nite (mĕl′ə-nīt′) *n.* A high explosive made with picric acid. [Fr. *mélinite* < Gk. *mēlinos,* quince-yellow < *mēlon,* quince.]

mel·io·rate (mēl′yə-rāt′, mē′lē-ə-) *v.* **-rat·ed, -rat·ing, -rates.** *—tr.* To make better; improve. *—intr.* To grow better. [LLat. *meliorare, meliorat-* < *melior,* better.] **—mel′io·ra·ble** (-rə-bəl) *adj.* **—mel′io·ra′tive** *adj. & n.* **—mel′io·ra′tor** *n.*

mel·io·ra·tion (mēl′yə-rā′shən, mē′lē-ə-) *n.* **1. a.** The act or process of improving something or the state of being improved. **b.** An improvement. **2.** The linguistic process by which a word, over a period of time, grows more elevated in meaning or more positive in connotation.

mel·io·rism (mēl′yə-rĭz′əm, mē′lē-ə-) *n.* The belief that society has an innate tendency toward improvement and that this tendency may be furthered through conscious human effort. [Lat. *melior,* better + -ISM.] **—mel′io·rist** *n.* **—mel′io·ris′tic** *adj.*

me·lis·ma (mə-lĭz′mə) *n., pl.* **-ma·ta** (-mə-tə) or **-mas.** *Mus.* A passage sung to one syllable of text, as in Gregorian chant. [NLat. < Gk., song < *melizein,* to sing < *melos,* song.] **—mel′is·mat′ic** (mĕl′ĭz-măt′ĭk) *adj.*

mel·lif·er·ous (mə-lĭf′ər-əs) also **mel·lif·ic** (mə-lĭf′ĭk) *adj.* Forming or bearing honey. [< Lat. *mellifer* : *mel,* honey + *ferre,* to bear.]

mel·lif·lu·ent (mə-lĭf′lo͞o-ənt) *adj.* Mellifluous. **—mel·lif′lu·ent·ly** *adv.*

mel·lif·lu·ous (mə-lĭf′lo͞o-əs) *adj.* **1.** Flowing with honey or sweetness. **2.** Smooth and sweet; honeyed: *a mellifluous voice.* [Lat. *mellifluus* : *mel,* honey + *fluere,* to flow.] **—mel·lif′lu·ous·ly** *adv.* **—mel·lif′lu·ous·ness** *n.*

mel·lo·phone (mĕl′ō-fōn′) *n.* A brass musical wind instrument sometimes used as a substitute for the French horn, which it resembles in tone. [MELLO(W) + -PHONE.]

mel·low (mĕl′ō) *adj.* **-er, -est. 1. a.** Soft, sweet, juicy, and full-flavored because of ripeness: *a mellow fruit.* **b.** Suggesting softness, sweetness, juiciness, or full flavor: *"The mellow air brought in the feel of imminent autumn"* (Thomas Hardy). **2.** Rich and soft in quality: *a mellow sound; a mellow wine.* **3.** Having the gentleness, wisdom, or dignity often characteristic of maturity. **4.** Relaxed and at ease; genial. **5. a.** Slightly and pleasantly intoxicated. **b.** Pleasantly high from a drug, esp. from smoking marijuana. **6.** Moist, rich, soft, and loamy. Used of soil. *—v.* **-lowed, -low·ing, -lows.** *—tr. & intr.* To make or become mellow. [ME *melowe.*] **—mel′low·ly** *adv.* **—mel′low·ness** *n.*

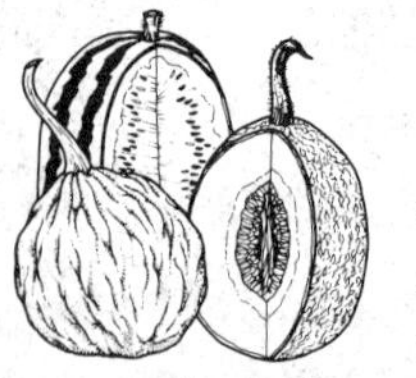

melon
Left to right: Crenshaw, watermelon, cantaloupe

me·lo·de·on (mə-lō′dē-ən) *n.* A small reed organ. [G. *Melodion* < *Melodie,* melody < OFr. —see MELODY.]

me·lod·ic (mə-lŏd′ĭk) *adj.* Of, pertaining to, or containing melody. **—me·lod′i·cal·ly** *adv.*

me·lo·di·ous (mə-lō′dē-əs) *adj.* **1.** Of, pertaining to, or containing a pleasing succession of sounds; tuneful. **2.** Agreeable to hear. **—me·lo′di·ous·ly** *adv.* **—me·lo′di·ous·ness** *n.*

mel·o·dize (mĕl′ə-dīz′) *v.* **-dized, -diz·ing, -diz·es.** *—tr.* **1.** To write a melody for (a song lyric). **2.** To make melodious. *—intr.* To compose a melody. **—mel′o·diz′er, mel′o·dist** *n.*

mel·o·dra·ma (mĕl′ə-drä′mə, -drăm′ə) *n.* **1. a.** A dramatic presentation characterized by heavy use of suspense, sensational episodes, romantic sentiment, and a conventionally happy ending. **b.** The dramatic genre characterized by this treatment. **2.** Behavior or occurrences having melodramatic characteristics. [Fr. *mélodrame* : Gk. *melos,* song + Fr. *drame,* drama < LLat. *drama.* —see DRAMA.]

mel·o·dra·mat·ic (mĕl′ə-drə-măt′ĭk) *adj.* **1.** Having the excitement and emotional appeal of melodrama: *"a melodramatic account of two perilous days spent among the planters"* (Frank O. Gatell). **2.** Exaggeratedly emotional or sentimental; histrionic: *"Accuse me, if you will, of melodramatic embroidery"* (Erskine Childers). **3.** Characterized by false pathos and sentiment. **—mel′o·dra·mat′i·cal·ly** *adv.*

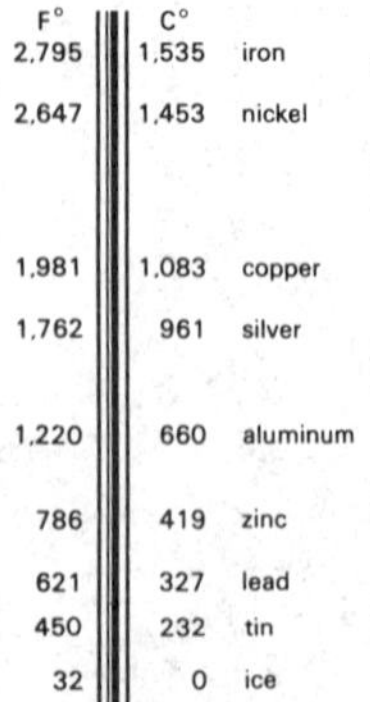

melting point

mel·o·dra·mat·ics (mĕl′ə-drə-măt′ĭks) *n. (used with a sing. or pl. verb).* **1.** Melodramatic theatrical performance. **2.** Melodramatic actions.

mel·o·dy (mĕl′ə-dē) *n., pl.* **-dies. 1.** A pleasing succession or arrangement of sounds. **2.** Musical quality: *the melody of verse.* **3.** *Mus.* **a.** A rhythmically organized sequence of single tones so related to one another as to make up a particular musical phrase or idea. **b.** The structure of music with respect to the arrangement of single notes in succession. **c.** The leading part or the air in a harmonic composition. **4.** A poem suitable for setting to music or singing. [ME *melodie* < OFr. < LLat. *melodia* < Gk. *melōidia,* choral song : *melos,* tune + *aoidein,* to sing.]

mel·oid (mĕl′oid′, mĕl′ō-ĭd) *n.* A blister beetle. *—adj.* Of or pertaining to blister beetles. [< NLat. *Meloidae,* family name < *Meloe,* beetle genus.]

mel·on (mĕl′ən) *n.* **1.** Any of several varieties of two related vines, *Cucumis melo* or *Citrullus vulgaris,* widely cultivated for their edible fruit. **2.** The fruit of a melon vine, characteristically having a hard rind and juicy flesh. [ME < LLat. *melo,* short for Lat. *melopepon* < Gk. *mēlopepōn* : *melon,* apple + *pepōn,* gourd.]

Mel·pom·e·ne (mĕl-pŏm′ə-nē′) *n. Gk. Myth.* The Muse of tragedy. [Lat. < Gk. *Melpomenē* < *melpesthai,* to sing.]

melt (mĕlt) *v.* **melt·ed, melt·ing, melts.** *—intr.* **1.** To be changed from a solid to a liquid state by the application of heat, pressure, or both. **2.** To dissolve: *Sugar melts in water.* **3.** To disappear or vanish gradually as if by dissolving. **4.** To pass or merge imperceptibly into something else: *Objects at a distance grew indistinct and seemed to melt into each other.* **5.** To become softened in feeling: *Her heart melted at the child's tears.* **6.** *Obs.* To be overcome or crushed, as by grief, dismay or fear. *—tr.* **1.** To reduce from a solid to a liquid state by the application of heat, pressure, or both. **2.** To dissolve: *melting honey in hot milk.* **3.** To cause to disappear gradually; disperse. **4.** To cause (units) to blend: *"Here individuals of all races are melted into a new race of men"* (H.J.S. Crevecoeur). **5.** To soften (someone's feelings); make gentle or tender. *—n.* **1.** A melted solid; fused mass. **2.** The state of being melted. **3. a.** The act or operation of melting. **b.** The quantity melted at a single operation or in one period. [ME *melten* < OE *meltan.*] **—melt′a·bil′i·ty** *n.* **—melt′a·ble** *adj.* **—melt′er** *n.*

Synonyms: *melt, fuse, liquefy, thaw, dissolve, deliquesce. Melt* is applied to physical liquefaction caused usually by heat and figuratively to gradual disappearance or transformation. *Fuse* is largely restricted to the process whereby metals are joined by melting and to figurative unions produced under stress: *courage and resolve fused by threat of conquest. Liquefy* is restricted to physical processes, but is said of both gases and solids, whereas the other terms apply only to solids. *Thaw* is applicable to that which is frozen and subjected to heat, but does not necessarily indicate complete liquefaction; figuratively it may refer to the softening of a harsh emotion or attitude. *Dissolve* specifies liquefaction by means of a solvent, a liquid that mingles its components with those of the original solid in a resultant liquid; figuratively it applies to melting, as by emotion. In both senses the term stresses complete transformation. *Deliquesce* refers to physical melting, usually gradual, through absorption of moisture from the air.

melt·age (mĕl′tĭj) *n.* **1.** The quantity or substance produced by a melting process. **2.** The process or act of melting.

melt·down (mĕlt′doun′) *n.* The melting of a nuclear reactor core.

melting point *n.* **1.** The temperature at which a solid becomes a liquid at standard atmospheric pressure. **2.** The temperature at which a solid and its liquid are in equilibrium, at any fixed pressure.

melting pot *n.* **1.** A container in which a substance is melted or fused. **2.** A place where immigrants of different cultures or races form an integrated society.

mel·ton (mĕl′tən) *n.* A heavy woolen cloth used chiefly for making overcoats and hunting jackets. [After *Melton* Mowbray, England.]

mem (mĕm) *n.* The 13th letter of the Hebrew alphabet. See table at **alphabet.** [Heb.]

mem·ber (mĕm′bər) *n.* **1.** A distinct part of a whole, esp.: **a.** A syntactic unit of a sentence; clause. **b.** A proposition of a syllogism. **c.** An element in a mathematical set. **2.** A part or organ of a human or animal body, as: **a.** A limb, such as an arm or leg. **b.** The penis. **3.** A part of a plant. **4.** A person who belongs to a group or organization. **5.** *Math.* The expression on either side of an equality sign. [ME < OFr. *membre* < Lat. *membrum.*]

mem·ber·ship (mĕm′bər-shĭp′) *n.* **1.** The state of being a member. **2.** The total number of members in a group.

mem·brane (mĕm′brān′) *n.* **1.** *Biol.* A thin, pliable layer of tissue covering surfaces or separating or connecting regions, structures, or organs of an animal or plant. **2.** A piece of parchment. **3.** *Chem.* A thin sheet of natural or synthetic material that is permeable to substances in solution. [Lat. *membrana,* skin < *membrum,* member.] **—mem′bra·nal** (-brə-nəl) *adj.*

membrane bone *n.* A bone formed directly in the connective tissue, as some cranial bones.

mem·bra·nous (mĕm′brə-nəs) *adj.* **1.** Made of or similar to a membrane. **2.** *Pathol.* Characterized by membrane formation.

membranous labyrinth *n.* The soft-tissue sensory structures of the inner ear.

me·men·to (mə-mĕn′tō) *n., pl.* **-tos** or **-toes.** A reminder of the past; keepsake. [ME < Lat. *memento,* imper. of *meminisse,* to remember.]

me·men·to mo·ri (mə-mĕn′tō môr′ē) *n.* **1.** A reminder of death or mortality, esp. a death's-head. **2.** A reminder of human failures or errors. [Lat., remember that you must die.]

Mem·non (mĕm′nŏn′) *n. Gk. Myth.* An Ethiopian king killed by Achilles and made immortal by Zeus. [Gk. *Memnōn.*]

mem·o (mĕm′ō) *n., pl.* **-os.** A memorandum.

mem·oir (mĕm′wär′, -wôr′) *n.* **1.** An account of the personal experiences of an author **2.** Often **memoirs.** An autobiography. **3.** A biography or biographical sketch. **4.** A report, esp. on a scientific or scholarly topic. **5. memoirs.** The report of the proceedings of a learned society. [Fr. *mémoire* < OFr. *memoire,* memory.]

mem·o·ra·bil·i·a (mĕm′ər-ə-bĭl′ē-ə, -bĭl′yə) *pl.n.* Remarkable things worthy of remembrance. [Lat. < *memorabilis,* memorable.]

mem·o·ra·ble (mĕm′ər-ə-bəl) *adj.* Worth being remembered or noted; remarkable: *a memorable event.* [ME < Lat. *memorabilis* < *memorare,* to remember < *memor,* mindful.]

—**mem'o·ra·bil'i·ty, mem'o·ra·ble·ness** *n.* —**mem'o·ra·bly** *adv.*

mem·o·ran·dum (mĕm'ə-răn'dəm) *n., pl.* **-dums** or **-da** (-də). **1.** A short note written as a reminder. **2.** A written record or communication, as in a business office. **3.** *Law.* A short, written statement outlining the terms of an agreement, transaction, or contract. **4.** A business statement made by a consignor about a shipment of goods that may be returned. **5.** A brief, unsigned diplomatic communication. [ME < Lat. *memorandus,* to be remembered < *memorare,* to remember. —see MEMORABLE.]

me·mo·ri·al (mə-môr'ē-əl, -mōr'-) *n.* **1.** Something, such as a monument or a holiday, designed or established to serve as a remembrance of a person or an event. **2.** A written statement of facts or a petition presented to a legislative body or an executive. —*adj.* **1.** Serving as a remembrance of a person or event; commemorative. **2.** Of, pertaining to, or in memory. [ME < LLat. *memoriale* < *memorialis,* belonging to memory < *memoria,* memory. —see MEMORY.] —**me·mo'ri·al·ly** *adv.*

Memorial Day *n.* May 30, a U.S. holiday officially celebrated on the last Monday in May in honor of members of the armed forces killed in war.

me·mo·ri·al·ist (mə-môr'ē-ə-lĭst, -mōr'-) *n.* **1.** A person who writes memoirs. **2.** A person who writes or signs a memorial.

me·mo·ri·al·ize (mə-môr'ē-ə-līz', mə-mōr'-) *tr.v.* **-ized, -iz·ing, -iz·es. 1.** To commemorate. **2.** To present a memorial to; petition. —**me·mo'ri·al·i·za'tion** *n.* —**me·mo'ri·al·iz'er** *n.*

mem·o·rize (mĕm'ə-rīz') *tr.v.* **-rized, -riz·ing, -riz·es.** To commit to memory; learn by heart. —**mem'o·riz'a·ble** *adj.* —**mem'o·ri·za'tion** *n.* —**mem'o·riz'er** *n.*

mem·o·ry (mĕm'ə-rē) *n., pl.* **-ries. 1.** The mental faculty of retaining and recalling past experience. **2.** An act or instance of remembrance; recollection. **3.** All that a person can remember. **4.** Something remembered: *pleasant childhood memories.* **5.** The fact of being remembered; remembrance. **6.** The period of time covered by the remembrance or recollection of a person or group of persons: *within the memory of man.* **7.** *Biol.* Persistent modification of behavior resulting from the organism's experience. **8.** *Computer Sci.* **a.** A unit of a computer that preserves data for retrieval. **b.** Capacity for storing information. **9.** *Statistics.* The set of past events affecting a given event in a stochastic process. [ME *memorie* < OFr. *memoire* < Lat. *memoria* < *memor,* mindful.]

Synonyms: *memory, remembrance, recollection, reminiscence, retrospect. Memory* overlaps each of these terms without having all of their specific senses; the plural *memories* sometimes implies a personal, cherished quality. *Remembrance* generally applies to a specific act of recall; in all senses, including the physical one of memento or keepsake, it usually connotes intimate associations. *Recollection* also is limited to a specific instance, which is deliberate and practical rather than sentimental. *Reminiscence* stresses pleasurable, casual recall of intimate matters; generally it involves the sharing of what is recalled. *Retrospect (retrospection)* emphasizes purposeful recall, often accompanied by evaluation.

memory engram *n.* Engram.

mem·sa·hib (mĕm'sä'ĭb) *n.* A title of respect applied to a white European woman in colonial India. [MA'AM + SAHIB.]

men (mĕn) *n.* Plural of **man.**

men– *pref.* Variant of **meno-.**

men·ace (mĕn'ĭs) *n.* **1. a.** A threat: *the menace of nuclear war.* **b.** The act of threatening. **2.** A troublesome or annoying person. —*v.* **-aced, -ac·ing, -ac·es.** —*tr.* **1.** To threaten. **2.** To constitute a threat to. —*intr.* To make threats. [ME < OFr. < Lat. *minacia* < *minax,* threatening < *minari,* to threaten.] —**men'ac·er** *n.* —**men'ac·ing·ly** *adv.*

men·a·di·one (mĕn'ə-dī'ōn') *n.* A yellow crystalline powder, $C_{10}H_5CH_3O_2$, having physiological effects similar to vitamin K. It is used as a medicine and as a fungicide. [ME(THYL) + NA(PHTHA) + DI-[1] + -ONE.]

mé·nage (mā-näzh') *n.* **1.** Persons living together as a unit; household. **2.** The management of a household. [Fr. < OFr. *mesnage,* dwelling < Lat. *mansio.* —see MANSION.]

ménage à trois (ä trwä) *n.* A relationship wherein three people, as a married couple and a lover, live together. [Fr., household for three.]

me·nag·er·ie (mə-năj'ə-rē, mə-năzh'-) *n.* **1.** A collection of live wild animals on exhibition. **2.** The enclosure in which wild animals are kept. [Fr. *ménagerie* < *ménage,* ménage.]

me·nar·che (mə-när'kē) *n.* The first occurrence of menstruation. [NLat. : MEN(O)- + Gk. *arkhē,* beginning.] —**me·nar'che·al** *adj.*

men·a·zon (mĕn'ə-zŏn') *n.* A colorless crystalline compound, $C_6H_{12}N_5O_2PS_2$, used as an insecticide. [(DI)ME(THYL) + (DIAMI)N(E) + (TRI)AZ(INE) + (THI)ON(ATE).]

mend (mĕnd) *v.* **mend·ed, mend·ing, mends.** —*tr.* **1.** To make right or correct; repair. **2.** To reform or improve: *mend one's ways.* —*intr.* **1. a.** To improve in health: *He is mending well.* **b.** To heal: *The bone mended in a month.* **2.** To correct errors; set right: *Least said, soonest mended.* —*n.* **1.** The act of mending. **2.** A mended place. —***idiom.* on the mend.** Improving, esp. in health. [ME *menden* < *amenden,* to amend. —see AMEND.] —**mend'a·ble** *adj.* —**mend'er** *n.*

men·da·cious (mĕn-dā'shəs) *adj.* **1.** Lying; untruthful: *a mendacious child.* **2.** False; untrue: *a mendacious statement.* [Lat. *mendax, mendac-,* mendacious.] —**men·da'cious·ly** *adv.*

men·dac·i·ty (mĕn-dăs'ĭ-tē) *n.* **1.** The condition of being mendacious; untruthfulness. **2.** A lie; falsehood.

men·de·le·vi·um (mĕn'də-lē'vē-əm) *n. Symbol* **Md** A radioactive transuranium element of the actinide series. Atomic number 101; mass numbers 255 and 256; half-lives approximately 30 minutes (Md^{255}) and 1.5 hours (Md^{256}). [After Dmitri *Mendeleev* (1834–1907).]

Men·de·li·an (mĕn-dē'lē-ən, -dēl'yən) *adj.* Of or pertaining to Gregor Mendel or his theories of genetics.

Men·del·ism (mĕn'dl-ĭz'əm) also **Men·de·li·an·ism** (mĕn-dē'lē-ə-nĭz'əm) *n.* The theoretical principles of heredity formulated by Gregor Mendel.

Men·del's law (mĕn'dlz) *n.* The principles of heredity of sexually reproducing organisms formulated by Gregor Mendel, now usually summarized in three laws: **a.** *Law of Segregation:* Certain paired characteristics, one from each parent, do not blend with or alter each other in the offspring, thus accounting for contrasting traits in successive generations. **b.** *Law of Independent Combination:* The genes determining such pairs of traits combine in the offspring according to the statistics of chance. **c.** *Law of Dominance:* If one of a pair of genes is dominant and the other recessive, the recessive trait may appear in an offspring only if both genes of its pair are recessive.

men·di·cant (mĕn'dĭ-kənt) *adj.* Depending upon alms for a living; practicing begging. —*n.* **1.** A beggar. **2.** A member of a mendicant order of friars. [Lat. *mendicans, mendicant-,* pr. part. of *mendicare,* to beg < *mendicus,* beggar < *mendum,* fault.] —**men'di·can·cy, men·dic'i·ty** (-dĭs'ĭ-tē) *n.*

Men·e·la·us (mĕn'ə-lā'əs) *n. Gk. Myth.* The king of Sparta, husband of Helen and brother of Agamemnon. [Lat. < Gk. *Menelaos.*]

men·folk (mĕn'fōk') or **men·folks** (-fōks') *pl.n.* **1.** Men collectively. **2.** The male members of a community or family.

men·ha·den (mĕn-hād'n) *n., pl.* **menhaden** or **-dens.** An abundant inedible fish, *Brevoortia tyrannus,* of American Atlantic and Gulf waters, used as a source of fish oil, fish meal, fertilizer, and bait. [Narraganset *munnawhatteaug.*]

men·hir (mĕn'hîr') *n.* A prehistoric monument of a class found chiefly in the British Isles and northern France, consisting of a single tall, upright megalith. [Fr. < Breton : *men,* stone + *hir,* long.]

me·ni·al (mē'nē-əl, mēn'yəl) *adj.* **1.** Of, pertaining to, or appropriate for a servant. **2.** Of or pertaining to work or a job regarded as servile. —*n.* **1.** A servant, esp. a domestic servant. **2.** A person who has a servile or low nature. [ME, belonging to a household < *meine,* household servants < AN < VLat. **mansionata* < Lat. *mansio,* house. —see MANSION.] —**me'ni·al·ly** *adv.*

mening– *pref.* Variant of **meningo-.**

me·nin·ge·al (mə-nĭn'jē-əl) *adj.* Of, relating to, or concerned with a meninx or meninges.

me·nin·ges (mə-nĭn'jēz) *n.* Plural of **meninx.**

meningi– *pref.* Variant of **meningo-.**

men·in·gi·tis (mĕn'ĭn-jī'tĭs) *n.* Inflammation of any or all of the meninges of the brain and the spinal cord, usually caused by a bacterial infection. —**men'in·git'ic** (-jĭt'ĭk) *adj.*

meningo– or **meningi–** or **mening–** *pref.* Meninges: *meningococcus.* [NLat. < *meninx,* meninx.]

me·nin·go·coc·cus (mə-nĭng'gə-kŏk'əs, -nĭn'jə-) *n., pl.* **-coc·ci** (-kŏk'sī). A bacterium, *Neisseria meningitidis,* that causes epidemic cerebrospinal meningitis. —**me·nin'go·coc'cal, me·nin'go·coc'cic** (-kŏk'sĭk) *adj.*

me·nin·go·en·ceph·a·li·tis (mə-nĭng'gō-ĕn-sĕf'ə-lī'tĭs) *n.* Inflammation of the brain and meninges. —**me·nin'go·en·ceph'a·lit'ic** (-lĭt'ĭk) *adj.*

me·ninx (mē'nĭngks) *n., pl.* **me·nin·ges** (mə-nĭn'jēz). Any of the membranes enclosing the brain and spinal cord in vertebrates. [NLat. < Gk. *mēninx,* membrane.]

me·nis·cus (mə-nĭs'kəs) *n., pl.* **-nis·ci** (-nĭs'ī') or **-nis·cus·es. 1.** A crescent-shaped body. **2.** A concavo-convex lens. **3.** The curved upper surface of a nonturbulent liquid in a container that is concave if the liquid wets the container walls and convex if it does not. **4.** *Anat.* A cartilage disk that acts as a cushion between the ends of bones that meet in a joint. [NLat. < Gk. *mēniskos,* dim. of *mēnē,* moon.] —**me·nis'cal** (-kəl), **me·nis'cate'** (-kāt'), **me·nis'coid'** (-koid'), **men'is·coi'dal** (mĕn'ĭs-koid'l) *adj.*

Men·non·ite (mĕn'ə-nīt') *n.* A member of an Evangelical Protestant Christian sect opposed to taking oaths, holding public office, or performing military service. [G. *Mennonit,* after *Menno* Simons (1492–1559).]

meno– or **men–** *pref.* **1.** Menstruation: *menarche.* **2.** Menses: *menorrhagia.* [NLat. < Gk. *meis, mēn-,* month.]

men·o·pause (mĕn'ə-pôz') *n.* The period of cessation of menstruation, occurring usually between the ages of 45 and 50. [Fr. : Gk. *meis, mēn-,* moon + Fr. *pause,* pause < Lat. *pausa.* —see PAUSE.] —**men'o·paus'al** *adj.*

Me·no·rah (mə-nôr'ə, -nōr'ə) *n.* **1.** A ceremonial seven-branched candelabrum of the Jewish Temple symbolizing

memorial
The Lincoln Memorial in Washington, D.C.

Menelaus
With Helen and Eros on a Greek vase

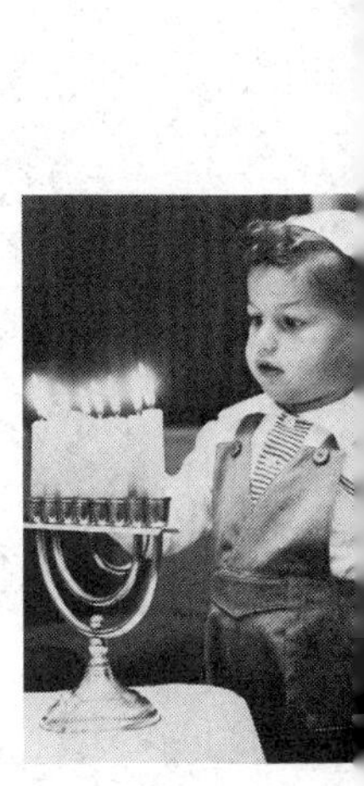

Menorah

the seven days of the Creation. **2.** A nine-branched candelabrum used in the celebration of Chanukah. [Heb. *mənorāh.*]

men·or·rha·gi·a (mĕn'ə-rā'jē-ə) *n. Pathol.* Abnormally heavy menstrual flow. **—men'or·rha'gic** (-jĭk) *adj.*

Men·sa (mĕn'sə) *n.* A southern constellation between Hydrus and Volans. [Lat. *mensa,* table.]

men·sal (mĕn'səl) *adj.* Belonging to or used at the table. [LLat. *mensalis* < Lat. *mensa,* table.]

mensch (mĕnsh) *n. Informal.* A person having admirable characteristics, as fortitude and firmness of purpose. [Yiddish < MHG, man < OHG *mennisco.*]

men·ses (mĕn'sēz) *pl.n. (used with a sing. or pl. verb). Physiol.* Blood and dead cell debris that is discharged from the uterus through the vagina by adult women at approximately monthly intervals between puberty and menopause. [Lat., pl. of *mensis,* month.]

Men·she·vik (mĕn'shə-vĭk) *n., pl.* **-viks** or **-vi·ki** (-vē'kē). A member of the liberal minority faction of the Russian Social Democratic Party that struggled against the Bolsheviks before and during the Russian Revolution. [R. *men'shevik* < *men'she,* less.] **—Men'she·vism** *n.* **—Men'she·vist** *n.*

men's room *n.* A restroom for men.

men·stru·a (mĕn'strōō-ə) *n.* A plural of **menstruum.**

men·stru·al (mĕn'strōō-əl) also **men·stru·ous** (mĕn'strōō-əs) *adj.* **1.** *Physiol.* Of or relating to menstruation. **2. a.** Taking place monthly. **b.** Having a monthly duration. [ME < Lat. *menstrualis* < *menstruus,* menstrual < *mensis,* month.]

men·stru·ate (mĕn'strōō-āt') *intr.v.* **-at·ed, -at·ing, -ates.** *Physiol.* To undergo menstruation. [Lat. *menstruare, menstruat-* < *menstruus,* menstrual.]

men·stru·a·tion (mĕn'strōō-ā'shən) *n.* The process or an instance of discharging the menses.

men·stru·ous (mĕn'strōō-əs) *adj.* Variant of **menstrual.**

men·stru·um (mĕn'strōō-əm) *n., pl.* **-stru·ums** or **-stru·a** (-strōō-ə). A solvent, esp. one used in extracting and preparing drugs. [ME, menstruation < Med. Lat. < Lat. *menstruus,* menstrual.]

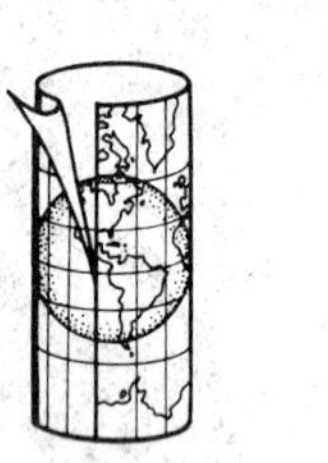

Mercator projection
Cylindrical projection showing meridians and North and South American continents

men·su·ra·ble (mĕn'sər-ə-bəl, -shər-) *adj.* **1.** Capable of being measured. **2.** Having fixed rhythm and measure, as in music; mensural. **—men'su·ra·bil'i·ty, men'su·ra·ble·ness** *n.*

men·su·ral (mĕn'sər-əl, -shər-) *adj.* **1.** Of or pertaining to measure. **2.** *Mus.* Having notes of fixed rhythmic value. [Lat. *mensuralis* < *mensura,* measure. —see MEASURE.]

men·su·ra·tion (mĕn'sə-rā'shən, -shə-) *n.* **1.** The process, act, or art of measuring. **2.** The measurement of geometric quantities. **—men'su·ra'tive** *adj.*

mens·wear (mĕnz'wâr') *n.* Clothing for men.

-ment *suff.* **1.** Action; process: *appeasement.* **2.** Result of an action or process: *advancement.* **3.** Means, instrument, or agent of an action or process: *adornment.* [ME < OFr. < Lat. *-mentum,* n. suffix.]

men·tal (mĕn'tl) *adj.* **1.** Of or relating to the mind; intellectual. **2.** Executed or performed by the mind; existing in the mind. **3.** Of, relating to, or affected by mental disorder. **4.** Intended for treatment of people affected with mental disorder: *a mental institution.* **5.** Of or relating to telepathy or mind reading. [ME < Lat. *mentalis* < *mens,* mind.] **—men'tal·ly** *adv.*

mental age *n.* A measure of mental development as determined by intelligence tests, generally restricted to children and expressed as the age at which that level is average.

mental deficiency *n.* Subnormal intellectual development, either congenital or induced by brain injury or disease, characterized broadly by deficiencies ranging in severity from impaired learning ability through social and vocational inadequacy to inability to learn connected speech or guard against common dangers.

men·tal·i·ty (mĕn-tăl'ĭ-tē) *n., pl.* **-ties. 1.** The sum of a person's intellectual capabilities or endowment. **2.** Cast or turn of mind.

mental retardation *n.* Mental deficiency.

mental telepathy *n.* Telepathy.

men·thol (mĕn'thôl') *n.* A white, crystalline, organic compound, $CH_3C_6H_9(C_3H_7)OH$, obtained from peppermint oil or synthesized. It is used in perfumes, as a mild anesthetic, and as a flavoring. [G. : Lat. *mentha,* mint + *-ol,* -ol.] **—men'tho·lat'ed** *adj.*

men·tion (mĕn'shən) *tr.v.* **-tioned, -tion·ing, -tions.** To cite or refer to incidentally. *—n.* **1. a.** The act of briefly or casually referring to something. **b.** An incidental reference or allusion. **2.** Honorable mention. [< ME, mention < OFr. < Lat. *mentio* < *mens,* mind.] **—men'tion·a·ble** *adj.*

Men·tor (mĕn'tôr', -tər) *n.* **1.** *Gk. Myth.* Odysseus' trusted counselor, under whose disguise Athena became the guardian and teacher of Telemachus. **2. mentor.** A wise and trusted counselor or teacher. [Lat. < Gk. *Mentōr.*]

men·u (mĕn'yōō, mā'nyōō) *n.* **1.** A list of the dishes to be served or available for a meal. **2.** The dishes served or available at a meal. [Fr. < *menu,* small < Lat. *minūtus.* —see MINUTE[2].]

me·ow (mē-ou') *n.* **1.** The cry of a cat. **2.** A malicious, spiteful comment. *—intr.v.* **-owed, -ow·ing, -ows.** To make the crying sound of a cat. [Imit.]

me·per·i·dine hydrochloride (mə-pĕr'ĭ-dēn') *n.* An organic compound, $C_{15}H_{21}NO_2 \cdot HCl$, used as an analgesic and sedative. [ME(THYL) + (PI)PERIDINE.]

Meph·i·stoph·e·les (mĕf'ĭ-stŏf'ə-lēz') *n.* The devil in the Faust legend to whom Faust sold his soul. [G.] **—Me·phis'to·phe'le·an, Me·phis'to·phe'li·an** (mə-fĭs'tō-fē'lē-ən, -fēl'yən, mĕf'ĭ-stō-) *adj.*

me·phi·tis (mə-fī'tĭs) *n.* **1.** An offensive smell; stench. **2.** A poisonous or foul-smelling gas emitted from the earth. [Lat.] **—me·phit'ic** (-fĭt'ĭk), **me·phit'i·cal** *adj.* **—me·phit'i·cal·ly** *adv.*

mep·ro·bam·ate (mĕp'rō-băm'āt', mĕ-prō'bə-māt') *n.* A white, bitter powder, $CH_3(C_3H_7)C(CH_2OOCNH_2)_2$, used as a tranquilizer. [ME(THYL) + PRO(PYL) + (DICAR)BAMATE.]

-mer *suff.* Variant of **-mere.**

mer·bro·min (mər-brō'mĭn) *n.* A green, crystalline, organic compound, $C_{20}H_8Br_2HgNa_2O_6$, that forms a red aqueous solution, used as a germicide and antiseptic. [MER(CURIC) + (DI)BROM(OFLORESCE)IN.]

mer·can·tile (mûr'kən-tēl', -tīl', -tĭl) *adj.* **1.** Of or pertaining to merchants or trade. **2.** Of or pertaining to mercantilism. [Fr. < Ital. < *mercante,* merchant < Lat. *mercans* < *mercari,* to trade.]

mer·can·til·ism (mûr'kən-tē-lĭz'əm, -tĭ-) *n.* **1.** The theory and system of political economy prevailing in Europe after the decline of feudalism based on national policies of accumulating bullion, establishing colonies and a merchant marine, and developing industry and mining to attain a favorable balance of trade. **2.** Commercialism. [MERCANTIL(E) + -ISM.] **—mer'can·til'ist** *n.* **—mer'can·til·is'tic** *adj.*

mer·cap·tan (mər-kăp'tăn') *n.* A sulfur-containing organic compound with the general formula RSH, R being any radical, for example, ethyl mercaptan, C_2H_5SH. [G. < Dan. < Med. Lat. *mercurium captans,* (one) seizing mercury.]

Mer·ca·tor projection (mər-kā'tər) *n.* A map projection in which the meridians and parallels of latitude appear as lines crossing at right angles and in which areas appear greater farther from the equator. [After Gerhardus *Mercator* (1512–1594).]

mer·ce·nar·y (mûr'sə-nĕr'ē) *adj.* **1.** Motivated solely by a desire for monetary or material gain. **2.** Hired for service in a foreign army. *—n., pl.* **-ies. 1.** A person who serves or works merely for monetary gain; hireling. **2.** A professional soldier who is hired by a foreign country. [ME, a mercenary < Lat. *mercenarius* < *merces,* wages.] **—mer'ce·nar'i·ly** *adv.* **—mer'ce·nar'i·ness** *n.*

mer·cer (mûr'sər) *n. Chiefly Brit.* A dealer in textiles, esp. silks. [ME < OFr. *mercier* < Lat. *merx,* merchandise.]

mer·cer·ize (mûr'sə-rīz') *tr.v.* **-ized, -iz·ing, -iz·es.** To treat (cotton thread) with sodium hydroxide so as to shrink the fiber and increase its color absorption and luster. [After John *Mercer* (1791–1866), its inventor.]

mer·chan·dise (mûr'chən-dīz', -dīs') *n.* Commodities or goods that may be bought or sold. *—v.* (mûr'chən-dīz') **-dised, -dis·ing, -dis·es.** *—tr.* **1.** To buy and sell (commodities). **2.** To promote the sale of, as by advertising or display. *—intr.* To trade commercially. [ME *merchaundise* < OFr. *marcheandise* < *marcheant,* merchant.] **—mer'chan·dis'er** *n.*

mer·chant (mûr'chənt) *n.* **1.** A person whose occupation is the wholesale purchase and retail sale of goods for profit. **2.** A person who runs a retail business; shopkeeper. *—adj.* **1.** Of or pertaining to a merchant, merchandise, or commercial trade: *a merchant guild.* **2.** Of or pertaining to the merchant marine: *merchant ships.* [ME < OFr. *marcheant* < VLat. **mercatans* < Lat. *mercari,* to trade.]

mer·chant·a·ble (mûr'chənt-ə-bəl) *adj.* Suitable for buying and selling; marketable.

mer·chant·man (mûr'chənt-mən) *n.* **1.** A ship used in commerce. **2.** *Archaic.* A merchant.

merchant marine *n.* **1.** A nation's ships that are engaged in commerce. **2.** The personnel of merchant ships.

merchant ship *n.* A merchantman (sense 1).

Mer·ci·an (mûr'shē-ən, -shən) *n.* **1.** A native or inhabitant of Mercia. **2.** The Old English dialect of Mercia. **—Mer'ci·an** *adj.*

mer·ci·ful (mûr'sĭ-fəl) *adj.* Full of mercy; compassionate. **—mer'ci·ful·ly** *adv.* **—mer'ci·ful·ness** *n.*

mer·ci·less (mûr'sĭ-lĭs) *adj.* Having no mercy; cruel. **—mer'ci·less·ly** *adv.* **—mer'ci·less·ness** *n.*

mercur- *pref.* Variant of **mercuro-.**

mer·cu·rate (mûr'kyə-rāt') *tr.v.* **-rat·ed, -rat·ing, -rates.** To treat or combine with mercury or a mercury compound. **—mer'cu·ra'tion** *n.*

mer·cu·ri·al (mər-kyŏŏr'ē-əl) *n.* A medical or chemical preparation containing mercury. *—adj.* **1.** Often **Mercurial.** Of or pertaining to the Roman god Mercury or the planet Mercury. **2.** Having the characteristics of eloquence, shrewdness, swiftness, and thievishness attributed to the god Mercury. **3.** Containing or caused by the action of the element mercury. **4.** Being quick and changeable in character: *a mercurial temperament.* [Lat. *mercurialis* < *Mercurius,* Mercury.] **—mer·cu'ri·al·ly** *adv.*

mer·cu·ri·al·ism (mər-kyŏŏr'ē-ə-lĭz'əm) *n.* Poisoning caused by mercury or its compounds.

mer·cu·ric (mər-kyŏŏr'ĭk) *adj. Chem.* Pertaining to or containing bivalent mercury.

mercuric chloride *n.* A poisonous white crystalline compound, $HgCl_2$, used as an antiseptic and disinfectant and in insecticides, preservatives, and batteries, and in metallurgy and photography.

mercuric sulfide *n.* A poisonous compound, HgS, having two forms: **a.** *Black mercuric sulfide,* a black powder obtained from mercury salts or by the reaction of mercury with sulfur, used as a pigment. **b.** *Red mercuric sulfide,* a bright scarlet powder derived from heating mercury with sulfur, used as a pigment.

mercuro– or **mercur–** *pref.* Mercury: *mercurous.* [< MERCURY.]

Mer·cu·ro·chrome (mər-kyo͝or′ə-krōm′) A trademark for a solution of merbromin, used as an antiseptic.

mer·cu·rous (mər-kyo͝or′əs, mûr′kyər-əs) *adj. Chem.* Pertaining to or containing monovalent mercury.

mercurous chloride *n.* Calomel.

Mer·cu·ry (mûr′kyə-rē) *n.* **1.** *Rom. Myth.* A god that served as messenger to the other gods and was himself the god of commerce, travel, and thievery. **2. mercury.** *Symbol* **Hg** A silvery-white poisonous metallic element, liquid at room temperature. It is used in thermometers, barometers, vapor lamps, and batteries, and in the preparation of chemical pesticides. Atomic number 80; atomic weight 200.59; melting point –38.87°C; boiling point 356.58°C; specific gravity 13.546; valences 1, 2. **3. mercury.** Temperature: *The mercury is falling quickly.* **4. mercury.** Any of several weedy plants of the genera *Mercurialis* or *Acalypha.* **5.** The smallest of the planets and the one nearest the Sun, having a sidereal period of revolution about the Sun of 88.0 days at a mean distance of 58.3 million kilometers, or 36.2 million miles, a mean radius of approximately 2,414 kilometers, or 1,500 miles, and a mass approximately 0.05 that of Earth. [ME *Mercurie* < OFr. < Lat. *Mercurius.*]

mer·cu·ry-va·por lamp (mûr′kyə-rē-vā′pər) *n.* A lamp in which ultraviolet and yellowish-green to blue visible light is produced by an electric discharge through mercury vapor.

mer·cy (mûr′sē) *n., pl.* **-cies. 1.** Kind and compassionate treatment of a person under one's power; clemency. **2.** A disposition to be kind and forgiving. **3.** Something for which to be thankful: *a mercy he survived.* **4.** Alleviation of distress; relief: *Her death was a mercy.* [ME < OFr. *merci* < Med. Lat. *merces* < Lat., reward.]

Synonyms: *mercy, leniency, clemency, forbearance, charity. Mercy* emphasizes compassion in a general way; it suggests reprieve from a fate of considerable severity, without further implication. *Leniency* applies to a specific act of indulgence. *Clemency* is usually applied to a specific act of a person or agency charged with administering justice; the recipient therefore is considered an offender. *Forbearance,* especially in its legal sense, is allied to *clemency* in denoting the act of foregoing the execution of a right. *Charity,* in this context, is a nonspecific term denoting benevolence.

mercy killing *n.* Euthanasia.

mercy seat *n.* **1.** The golden covering of the ark of the covenant, regarded as the resting place of God. **2.** The throne of God.

mere[1] (mîr) *adj.* Superlative **mer·est. 1.** Being nothing more than what is specified: *a mere trifle.* **2.** Pure; unadulterated. [ME, absolute < OFr. *mer* < Lat. *merus,* pure.] **—mere′ly** *adv.*

mere[2] (mîr) *n.* A small lake, pond, or marsh. [ME < OE.]

mere[3] (mîr) *n. Archaic.* A boundary. [ME < OE *mǣre.*]

–mere or **–mer** *suff.* Part; segment: *blastomere.* [Fr. *-mere* < Gk. *meros,* part.]

mer·e·tri·cious (mĕr′ĭ-trĭsh′əs) *adj.* **1.** Pertaining to or resembling a prostitute. **2. a.** Attracting attention in a vulgar manner: *meretricious ornamentation.* **b.** Lacking sincerity: *a meretricious argument.* [Lat. *meritricius* < *meretrix,* prostitute < *merēre,* to earn money.] **—mer′e·tri′cious·ly** *adv.* **—mer′e·tri′cious·ness** *n.*

mer·gan·ser (mər-găn′sər) *n.* A fish-eating duck of the genus *Mergus,* having a slim, hooked bill. [NLat. : Lat. *mergus,* diver (< *mergere,* to plunge) + Lat. *anser,* goose.]

merge (mûrj) *v.* **merged, merg·ing, merg·es.** *—tr.* **1.** To cause to be absorbed in gradual stages. **2.** To combine or unite, as sets of data. *—intr.* To blend together gradually. [Lat. *mergere,* to plunge.] **—mer′gence** *n.*

merg·er (mûr′jər) *n.* **1.** The union of two or more commercial interests or corporations. **2.** *Law.* The absorption of a lesser estate, liability, right, action, or offense into a greater one.

me·rid·i·an (mə-rĭd′ē-ən) *n.* **1. a.** A great circle on the earth's surface passing through both geophysical poles. **b.** Either half of such a great circle lying between the poles. **2.** *Astron.* A great circle passing through the two poles of the celestial sphere and the observer's zenith; the celestial meridian. **3.** *Math.* **a.** A curve on a surface of revolution, formed by the intersection of a plane containing the axis of revolution with the surface. **b.** A plane section of a surface of revolution containing the axis of revolution. **4.** The highest point or stage of development of something; zenith. **5.** *Archaic.* Noon. [ME < OFr. *meridiane,* midday < Lat. *meridianus,* of midday < *meridies,* midday : *medius,* middle + *dies,* day.] **—me·rid′i·an** *adj.*

me·rid·i·o·nal (mə-rĭd′ē-ə-nəl) *adj.* **1.** Of or pertaining to a meridian. **2.** Characteristic of southern areas or people. **3.** Located in the south; southerly. *—n.* An inhabitant of a southern region, esp. of France. [ME, pertaining to the sun's position at noon < OFr. *meridionel* < LLat. *meridionalis* < Lat. *meridianus,* of midday. —see MERIDIAN.]

me·ringue (mə-răng′) *n.* **1.** A topping for pastry or pies made of beaten and baked egg whites. **2.** A small pastry shell or cake made of meringue, often containing fruit or nutmeats. [Fr. *méringue.*]

me·ri·no (mə-rē′nō) *n., pl.* **-nos. 1. a.** A sheep of a breed originally from Spain. **b.** The fine wool of this sheep. **2.** A soft, lightweight fabric made originally of merino wool but now of any fine wool. **3. a.** A type of fine wool and cotton yarn used for knitting underwear, hosiery, and other articles of apparel. **b.** A knitted fabric made from merino yarn. [Sp.]

mer·i·stem (mĕr′ĭ-stĕm′) *n.* The growing point or area of rapidly dividing cells at the tip of a stem, root, or branch. [< Gk. *meristos,* divided < *merizein,* to divide < *meris,* division.] **—mer′i·ste·mat′ic** *adj.* **—mer′is·te·mat′i·cal·ly** *adv.*

me·ris·tic (mə-rĭs′tĭk) *adj.* **1.** Made up of segments, as some worms. **2.** Modified by changes in the number or placement of entire body parts, as contrasted with modification by gradual change of the entire organism. [Gk. *meristos,* divided. —see MERISTEM.] **—me·ris′ti·cal·ly** *adv.*

mer·it (mĕr′ĭt) *n.* **1.** Value, excellence, or superior quality. **2.** An aspect of a person's character or behavior deserving approval or disapproval: *to each according to his merits.* **3.** *Theol.* Spiritual credit granted for good works. **4. merits.** *Law.* **a.** A party's strict legal rights, excluding jurisdictional or technical aspects. **b.** The factual substance of a case as distinguished from its form and procedural aspects. **5.** The intrinsic right or wrong of any matter; the actual facts of a matter. *—v.* **-it·ed, -it·ing, -its.** *—tr.* **1.** To earn; deserve. **2.** *Theol.* To have the right to claim (a divine reward). *—intr. Theol.* To gain merit. [ME < OFr. *merite,* reward or punishment < Lat. *meritum* < *merēre,* to deserve.] **—mer′it·ed·ly** *adv.*

mer·i·toc·ra·cy (mĕr′ĭ-tŏk′rə-sē) *n., pl.* **-cies. 1.** A system in which advancement is based on ability or achievement. **2. a.** An elite composed of talented achievers. **b.** Leadership by such an elite. **—mer′it·o·crat′** (-tə-krăt′) *n.* **—mer′it·o·crat′ic** *adj.*

mer·i·to·ri·ous (mĕr′ĭ-tôr′ē-əs, -tōr′-) *adj.* Deserving reward or praise; having merit. [Lat. *meritorius,* earning money < *merēre,* to earn.] **—mer′i·to′ri·ous·ly** *adv.*

merit system *n.* A system of appointing and promoting civil service personnel on the basis of merit, determined by competitive examinations.

merle also **merl** (mûrl) *n.* A blackbird (sense 2). [ME < OFr. < Lat. *merulus.*]

mer·lin (mûr′lĭn) *n.* The pigeon hawk. [ME < AN *merilun,* of Germanic orig.]

Mer·lin (mûr′lĭn) *n.* In Arthurian legend, a magician and prophet serving as counselor to King Arthur.

mer·lon (mûr′lən) *n.* The solid portion of a crenelated wall between two open spaces. [Fr. < Ital. *merlone,* aug. of *merlo,* battlement < Med. Lat. *merulus* < Lat., merle.]

mer·maid (mûr′mād′) *n.* A fabled creature of the sea with the head and upper body of a woman and the tail of a fish. [ME : *mere,* sea + *maid,* maid.]

mer·man (mûr′măn′, -mən) *n.* A fabled creature of the sea with the head and upper body of a man and the tail of a fish. [MER(MAID) + MAN.]

mero– *pref.* **1.** Part; segment: *merozoite.* **2.** Partial; partially: *meropia.* [NLat. < Gk. *meros,* part.]

mer·o·blas·tic (mĕr′ə-blăs′tĭk) *adj.* Undergoing partial cleavage. Used of an egg with a large yolk. **—mer′o·blas′ti·cal·ly** *adv.*

mer·o·crine (mĕr′ə-krĭn, -krīn′, -krēn′) *adj.* Of or pertaining to a gland the cells of which remain intact during secretion. [MERO- + Gk. *krinein,* to separate.]

mer·o·my·o·sin (mĕr′ə-mī′ə-sĭn) *n.* Either of two protein subunits of a myosin molecule.

Mer·o·pe (mĕr′ə-pē′) *n.* **1.** *Gk. Myth.* One of the Pleiades, who hid her face in shame after marrying a mortal. **2.** The seventh star in the Pleiades cluster and the only one not visible to the naked eye. [Gk. *Meropē.*]

me·ro·pi·a (mə-rō′pē-ə) *n.* Partial blindness. **—me·ro′pic** (-rō′pĭk, -rŏp′ĭk) *adj.*

–merous *suff.* Having a specified kind or number of parts: *anisomerous.* [NLat. *-merus* < Gk. *meros,* part.]

Mer·o·vin·gi·an (mĕr′ə-vĭn′jē-ən, -jən) *adj.* Of or pertaining to the first dynasty of Frankish kings that ruled over Gaul from about A.D. 500 until A.D. 751. *—n.* A member of the first dynasty of Frankish kings. [Fr. *mérovingien* < Med. Lat. *Merovingi,* Merovingians < *Merovaeus,* Mérovée (d. 458), 2nd Frankish king.]

mer·o·zo·ite (mĕr′ə-zō′īt′) *n.* A cell produced by fission of a sporozoan.

mer·ri·ment (mĕr′ĭ-mənt) *n.* Gay conviviality; gaiety.

mer·ry (mĕr′ē) *adj.* **-ri·er, -ri·est. 1.** Full of high-spirited gaiety; jolly. **2.** Marked by or offering fun and gaiety; festive. **3.** Delightful; entertaining. **4.** Brisk: *a merry pace.* [ME *merri,* < OE *myrige.*] **—mer′ri·ly** *adv.* **—mer′ri·ness** *n.*

mer·ry-an·drew (mĕr′ē-ăn′dro͞o) *n.* A clown; buffoon. [MERRY + the name *Andrew.*]

Mercury

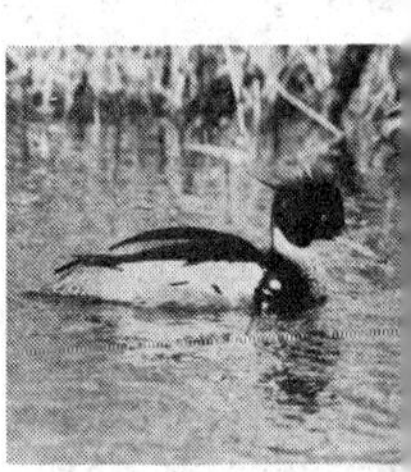

merganser

meridian
Earth encircled by meridians

mermaid
17th-century woodcut of a mermaid and a merman

mer·ry-bells (mĕr′ē-bĕlz′) *n.* *(used with a sing. or pl. verb).* The bellwort.

mer·ry-go-round (mĕr′ē-gō-round′) *n.* **1.** A revolving circular platform fitted with seats, often in the form of animals, ridden for amusement. **2.** A piece of playground equipment consisting of a small circular platform that revolves when pushed or pedaled. **3.** A whirl or swift round: *a merry-go-round of parties.*

mer·ry·mak·ing (mĕr′ē-mā′kĭng) *n.* **1.** Participation in a revel. **2.** A festivity; revelry. **—mer′ry·mak′er** *n.*

mer·ry·thought (mĕr′ē-thôt′) *n. Chiefly Brit.* A wishbone.

Mer·thi·o·late (mər-thī′ə-lāt′). A trademark for thimerosal.

mes– *pref.* Variant of **meso-**.

me·sa (mā′sə) *n.* A flat-topped elevation with one or more clifflike sides, common in the southwestern United States. [Sp. < OSp. < Lat. *mensa,* table.]

mé·sal·li·ance (mā′ză-lyäNs′, mā-zăl′ē-əns) *n.* A marriage with a person of inferior social position. [Fr. *més-,* mis- + *alliance,* alliance.]

mes·cal (mĕs-kăl′) *n.* **1.** A spineless, globe-shaped cactus, *Lophophora williamsii,* of Mexico and the southwestern United States, having buttonlike tubercles that are dried and chewed as a drug by certain Indian tribes. **2.** A Mexican liquor distilled from the fermented juice of certain species of agave. **3.** Maguey (sense 1). [Sp. < Nahuatl *mexcalli,* mescal liquor.]

mes·ca·line (mĕs′kə-lēn′, -lən) *n.* An alkaloid drug, $(CH_3O)_3C_6H_2(CH_2CH_2NH_2)$, that produces hallucinations and other psychedelic effects.

Mes·dames (mā-dăm′) *n.* Plural of **Madame** or **Madam.**

Mes·de·moi·selles (mād′mwä-zĕl′) *n.* Plural of **Mademoiselle.**

mes·en·ceph·a·lon (mĕz′ĕn-sĕf′ə-lŏn′, mĕs′-) also **mes·o·ceph·a·lon** (mĕz′ō-, mĕs′ō-) *n.* The middle section of the embryonic brain. **—mes′en·ce·phal′ic** (-sə-făl′ĭk) *adj.*

mes·en·chyme (mĕz′ən-kīm′, mĕs′-) also **mes·en·chy·ma** (mĕz-ĕng′kĭ-mə, mĕs-) *n.* The part of the embryonic mesoderm from which develop connective tissue, skeletal tissue, and the circulatory and lymphatic systems. [G. *Mesenchym* : *mes-,* meso- + *-enchym,* -enchyma.] **—mes·en′chy·mal, mes′en·chym′a·tous** (-kĭm′ə-təs, -kī′mē-) *adj.*

mes·en·ter·i·tis (mĕz-ĕn′tə-rī′tĭs, mĕs-) *n.* Inflammation of the mesentery.

mes·en·ter·i·um (mĕz′ən-tîr′ē-əm, mĕs′-) *n., pl.* **-i·a** (-ē-ə). Mesentery. [NLat. —see MESENTERY.]

mes·en·ter·on (mĕz-ĕn′tə-rŏn′, mĕs-) *n.* **1.** The midgut. **2.** The middle section of the gastrovascular cavity in anthozoans. **—mes·en′ter·on′ic** *adj.*

mes·en·ter·y (mĕz′ən-tĕr′ē, mĕs′-) *n., pl.* **-ies.** Any of several peritoneal folds that connect the intestines to the dorsal abdominal wall. [NLat. *mesenterium* < Gk. *mesenterion* : *mesos,* middle + *enteron,* enteron.] **—mes′en·ter′ic** *adj.*

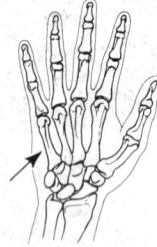

metacarpus

mesh (mĕsh) *n.* **1. a.** Any of the open spaces in a cord, thread, or wire network. **b.** Often **meshes.** The cords, threads, or wires surrounding these spaces. **2.** A net or network. **3.** A fabric with an open network of interlacing threads. **4.** Something that snares or entraps: *"Arabia had become entangled in the meshes of . . . politics"* (W. Montgomery Watt). **5. a.** The engagement of gear teeth. **b.** The state of being so engaged. *—v.* **meshed, mesh·ing, mesh·es.** *—tr.* **1.** To entangle or ensnare. **2.** To cause (gear teeth) to become engaged. **3.** To cause to work closely together. *—intr.* **1.** To be or become entangled. **2.** To be or become engaged or interlocked, as gear teeth. **3. a.** To coordinate or fit harmoniously and effectively. **b.** To accord with another; harmonize. [Prob. < MDu. *maesche.*] **—mesh′y** *adj.*

mesh·work (mĕsh′wûrk′) *n.* Meshes; network.

me·si·al (mē′zē-əl, -zhəl) *adj.* Of, in, near, or toward the middle. **—me′si·al·ly** *adv.*

me·sit·y·lene (mə-sĭt′l-ēn′) *n.* A hydrocarbon, $(CH_3)_3C_6H_3$, occurring in petroleum and coal tar and synthesized from acetone. [MESITYL(OXIDE) + -ENE.]

mes·i·tyl oxide (mĕs′ĭ-tĭl) *n.* An oily liquid, $(CH_3)_2C{:}CHCOCH_3$, obtained from acetones and used as a solvent and insect repellent. [< Gk. *mesitēs,* mediator < *mesos,* middle.]

mes·mer·ism (mĕz′mə-rĭz′əm, mĕs′-) *n.* **1.** Hypnotic induction believed to involve animal magnetism. **2.** Hypnotism. **3.** Hypnotic appeal. [After Franz *Mesmer* (1734–1815).] **—mes·mer′ic** (-mĕr′ĭk) *adj.* **—mes·mer′i·cal·ly** *adv.* **—mes′mer·ist** *n.*

mes·mer·ize (mĕz′mə-rīz′, mĕs′-) *tr.v.* **-ized, -iz·ing, -iz·es.** **1.** To hypnotize. **2.** To enthrall: *"He could mesmerize an audience by the sheer force of his presence"* (Justin Kaplan). **—mes′mer·iz′er** *n.*

mesne (mēn) *adj.* Intermediate; intervening. [OFr. < AN *meen* < OFr. *meien,* middle < Lat. *medianus* < *medius.*]

mesne lord *n.* A feudal lord intermediate between a superior lord and his own vassals or tenants.

meso– or **mes–** *pref.* **1.** Middle; in the middle: *mesoderm.* **2.** Intermediate: *mesomorph.* [Gk. < *mesos,* middle.]

mes·o·blast (mĕz′ə-blăst′, mĕs′-) *n.* The middle germinal layer of the embryo; the mesoderm in its early stage of development. **—mes′o·blas′tic** *adj.*

mes·o·carp (mĕz′ə-kärp′, mĕs′-) *n. Bot.* The middle, usually fleshy layer of a pericarp.

mes·o·ceph·a·lon (mĕz′ō-sĕf′ə-lŏn′, mĕs′ō-) *n.* Variant of **mesencephalon.**

mes·o·derm (mĕz′ə-dûrm′, mĕs′-) *n.* The embryonic germ layer, lying between the ectoderm and the endoderm, from which develop connective tissue, muscles, and the urogenital and vascular systems. **—mes′o·der′mal, mes′o·der′mic** *adj.*

mes·o·gle·a also **mes·o·gloe·a** (mĕz′ə-glē′ə, mĕs′-, mē′zə-, -sə-) *n.* A gelatinous substance between the ectoderm and endoderm in some coelenterates and ctenophores. [MESO- + Gk. *gloia,* glue.] **—mes′o·gle′al** *adj.*

Mes·o·lith·ic (mĕz′ə-lĭth′ĭk, mĕs′-) *adj.* Designating the cultural period between the Paleolithic and Neolithic ages, marked by the appearance of the bow and of cutting tools. *—n. Archaeol.* The Mesolithic age.

mes·o·morph (mĕz′ə-môrf′, mĕs′-) *n.* A human body characterized by powerful musculature and a predominantly bony framework.

mes·o·mor·phic (mĕz′ə-môr′fĭk, mĕs′-) *adj.* **1.** Also **mes·o·mor·phous** (-môr′fəs). Of, pertaining to, or existing in a state of matter intermediate between liquid and crystal. **2.** Of or pertaining to a mesomorph. **—mes′o·mor′phism, mes′o·mor′phy** *n.*

mes·on (mĕz′ŏn′, mē′zŏn′, mĕs′ŏn′, mē′sŏn′) *n.* Any of several subatomic particles having integral spins and masses generally intermediate between leptons and baryons. **—me·son′ic** (mē-zŏn′ĭk, -sŏn′ĭk, mĕ-) *adj.*

mes·o·neph·ros (mĕz′ə-nĕf′rəs, -rŏs′, mĕs′-) *n.* The midpart of the embryonic excretory system in vertebrates that becomes the functioning kidney in fish and amphibians. [MESO- + Gk. *nephros,* kidney.] **—mes′o·neph′ric** *adj.*

mes·o·pause (mĕz′ə-pôz′, mĕs′-) *n.* The atmospheric zone about 80 kilometers, or 50 miles, above the earth, forming the upper limit of the mesosphere.

mes·o·phyll (mĕz′ə-fĭl′, mĕs′-) *n.* The soft tissue of a leaf, between the top and bottom epidermis. **—mes′o·phyl′lic, mes′o·phyl′lous** *adj.*

mes·o·phyte (mĕz′ə-fīt′, mĕs′-) *n.* A land plant that grows in an environment having a moderate amount of moisture. **—mes′o·phyt′ic** (-fĭt′ĭk) *adj.*

mes·o·some (mĕz′ə-sōm′, mĕs′-, mē′zə-, -sə-) *n.* A convoluted invagination of the cytoplasmic membrane in some bacterial cells.

mes·o·sphere (mĕz′ə-sfîr′, mĕs′-) *n.* The portion of the atmosphere from about 30 to 80 kilometers, or 20 to 50 miles, above the earth, characterized by a temperature range that decreases from 50°F to −130°F with increasing altitude. **—mes′o·spher′ic** (-sfîr′ĭk, -sfĕr′-) *adj.*

mes·o·the·li·o·ma (mĕz′ə-thē′lē-ō′mə, mĕs′-, mē′zə-, -sə-) *n., pl.* **-ma·ta** (-mə-tə) or **-mas.** A tumor derived from mesothelium.

mes·o·the·li·um (mĕz′ə-thē′lē-əm, mĕs′-) *n., pl.* **-li·a** (-lē-ə). **1.** The layer of flat cells lining the embryonic body cavity. **2.** A layer of squamous cells of the epithelium lining the peritoneum, pericardium, and pleura. [MESO- + (EPI)THELIUM.] **—mes′o·the′li·al** *adj.*

mes·o·tho·rax (mĕz′ə-thôr′ăks′, -thōr′-, mĕs′-) *n., pl.* **-rax·es** or **-ra·ces** (-ə-sēz′). The midsection of an insect's thoracic region, bearing the middle legs and the rear wings. **—mes′o·tho·rac′ic** *adj.*

mes·o·tho·ri·um (mĕz′ə-thôr′ē-əm, -thōr′-, mĕs′-) *n.* Either of two decay products of thorium: **a.** Mesothorium I, an isotope of radium. **b.** Mesothorium II, an isotope of actinium.

mes·o·tron (mĕz′ə-trŏn′, mĕs′-) *n. Physics.* An obsolete term for meson. [MESO- + (ELEC)TRON.]

Mes·o·zo·ic (mĕz′ə-zō′ĭk, mĕs′-) *adj.* Of, belonging to, or designating the third era of geologic time, including the Cretaceous, Jurassic, and Triassic periods and characterized by the predominance of reptilian life forms. *—n.* The Mesozoic era.

mes·quite (mĕ-skēt′, mə-) *n.* Any of several shrubs or small trees of the genus *Prosopis,* esp. *P. juliflora,* of the southwestern United States and Mexico. Its pods are used as forage. [Sp. < Nahuatl *mizquitl.*]

mess (mĕs) *n.* **1.** A disorderly accumulation of items. **2.** A cluttered, untidy, usually dirty condition. **3. a.** A disturbing, confusing, and troublesome state of affairs; muddle. **b.** Senseless confusion and discontinuity; chaos. **4.** A person who looks dirty or untidy. **5. a.** *Archaic.* An amount of food for a meal, course, or dish. **b.** A serving of soft, semiliquid food. **c.** An amount or number acquired, usually of something edible: *a mess of fish.* **6. a.** A group of persons, usually in the military, who regularly eat meals together. **b.** A mess hall. **c.** A meal eaten in a mess hall. *—v.* **messed, mess·ing, mess·es.** *—tr.* **1.** To make disorderly and soiled; clutter: *messed up the kitchen with pots and pans.* **2.** To mismanage or botch: *He messed up the test.* **3.** *Slang.* To be rough with; manhandle: *a mugger messing up his victim.* *—intr.* **1.** To cause or make a mess. **2.** To interfere; meddle. **3.** To take a meal in a military mess. ***—phrasal verb.*** **mess around.** *Informal* **1.** To occupy time by puttering or tinkering. **2.** To associate with. **3. a.** To have a sexual affair with, esp. an adulterous one. **b.** To have sex with. [ME *mes,* course of a meal < OFr. < Lat. *missus* < *mittere,* to place.]

mes·sage (mĕs′ĭj) *n.* **1.** A communication transmitted by spoken or written words, signals, or other means from one person or group to another. **2.** A statement made or read before a gathering: *a farewell message.* **3.** The basic theme or significance of something. [ME < OFr. < VLat. **missaticum* < Lat. *mittere,* to send.]

mes·sa·line (mĕs′ə-lēn′) *n.* A lightweight, soft, shiny silk cloth with a twilled or satin weave. [Fr.]

Mes·sei·gneurs (mā-sĕ-nyœr′) *n.* Plural of **Monseigneur.**

mes·sen·ger (mĕs′ən-jər) *n.* **1.** One who is charged with transmitting messages or performing errands, as: **a.** A person employed to carry telegrams, letters, or parcels. **b.** A military or official courier. **c.** An envoy. **d.** A prophet: *a messenger of Allah.* **2.** A bearer of news. **3.** *Archaic.* A forerunner; harbinger. **4.** *Naut.* A chain or rope used for hauling in a cable. [ME *messanger* < OFr. < *message,* message.]

messenger ribonucleic acid *n.* Messenger RNA.

messenger RNA *n.* A ribonucleic acid that carries the genetic information required for protein synthesis in cells.

mess hall *n.* **1.** A hall in which mess is served. **2.** A building that is used for serving and eating meals.

Mes·si·ah (mə-sī′ə) *n.* **1. a.** Also **Mes·si·as** (mə-sī′əs) *Judaism.* The anticipated deliverer and king of the Jews. **b.** Jesus Christ. **2. messiah.** A deliverer or liberator. [Aram. *mĕshīḥa* or Heb. *māshiaḥ.*]

mes·si·an·ic also **Mes·si·an·ic** (mĕs′ē-ăn′ĭk) *adj.* **1.** Of or pertaining to a messiah. **2.** Invoking the aura of a messiah. [NLat. **messianicus* < LLat. *messias,* messiah < Gk. < Aram. *mĕshiḥa.*]

mes·si·a·nism (mĕs′ē-ə-nĭz′əm, mə-sī′-) *n.* **1.** Belief in a messiah. **2.** Belief that a cause is absolutely right.

Mes·si·as (mə-sī′əs) *n.* Variant of **Messiah** (sense 1).

Mes·sieurs (mĕs′ərz, mā-syœ′) *n.* Plural of **Monsieur.**

mess jacket *n.* A man's fitted, waist-length jacket, worn chiefly on semiformal occasions.

mess kit *n.* A compactly arranged set of cooking and eating utensils in a kit, used by soldiers and campers.

mess·mate (mĕs′māt′) *n.* A person with whom one eats regularly, as in a military mess.

mes·suage (mĕs′wĭj) *n. Law.* A dwelling house with its outbuildings and adjoining lands. [ME < AN, prob. alteration of OFr. *mesnage.* —see MÉNAGE.]

mess·y (mĕs′ē) *adj.* **-i·er, -i·est. 1.** Characterized by dirt and disorder. **2.** Devoid of neatness and precision: *a messy term paper.* **3.** Unpleasantly difficult to settle or resolve: *a messy divorce.* **—mess′i·ly** *adv.* **—mess′i·ness** *n.*

mes·ti·za (mĕs-tē′zə) *n.* A woman of mixed European and American Indian ancestry. [Sp., fem. of *mestizo.* —see MESTIZO.]

mes·ti·zo (mĕs-tē′zō) *n., pl.* **-zos** or **-zoes.** A man of mixed European and American Indian ancestry. [Sp. < *mestizo,* mixed < OSp. < Lat. *miscēre,* to mix.]

met (mĕt) *v.* Past tense and past participle of **meet.**

met– *pref.* Variant of **meta-.**

met·a (mĕt′ə) *adj. Chem.* **1.** Of, pertaining to, or designating positions in a benzene ring separated by one carbon atom. **2.** Designating closely related, esp. isomeric, compounds. [< META-.]

meta– or **met–** *pref.* **1. a.** Later in time: *metestrus.* **b.** At a later stage of development: *metanephros.* **2.** Situated behind: *metacarpus.* **3. a.** Change; transformation: *metachromatism.* **b.** Alternation: *metagenesis.* **4. a.** Beyond; transcending; more comprehensive: *metalinguistics.* **b.** At a higher state of development: *metazoan.* **5.** Having undergone metamorphosis: *metasomatic.* **6.** Derivative or related chemical substance: *metaprotein.* [Gk. < *meta,* beside, after.]

met·a·bol·ic (mĕt′ə-bŏl′ĭk) *adj.* **1.** *Biol.* Of, pertaining to, or exhibiting metabolism. **2.** *Zool.* Of, pertaining to, or undergoing metamorphosis. [Gk. *metabolikos,* changeable < *metabolē,* change. —see METABOLISM.] **—met′a·bol′i·cal·ly** *adv.*

me·tab·o·lism (mə-tăb′ə-lĭz′əm) *n. Biol.* **1.** The complex of physical and chemical processes involved in the maintenance of life. **2.** The functioning of a specific substance within the living body: *water metabolism; iodine metabolism.* [Gk. *metabolē,* change < *metaballein,* to change : *meta,* change + *ballein,* to throw.]

me·tab·o·lite (mə-tăb′ə-līt′) *n.* Any of various organic compounds produced by metabolism. [METABOL(ISM) + -ITE.]

me·tab·o·lize (mə-tăb′ə-līz′) *v.* **-lized, -liz·ing, -liz·es.** —*tr.* To subject (a substance) to metabolism. —*intr.* To undergo change by metabolism.

met·a·car·pal (mĕt′ə-kär′pəl) *adj.* Pertaining to the metacarpus. —*n.* Any of the bones of the metacarpus.

met·a·car·pus (mĕt′ə-kär′pəs) *n.* The part of the hand or forefoot that includes the five bones between the phalanges and the carpus.

met·a·cen·ter (mĕt′ə-sĕn′tər) *n.* The intersection of the verticals through the center of buoyancy of a floating body when in equilibrium and when tilted. **—met′a·cen′tric** (-sĕn′trĭk) *adj.*

met·a·chro·ma·tism (mĕt′ə-krō′mə-tĭz′əm) *n.* A change in color caused by variation of the physical conditions to which a body is subjected, as in heating. **—met′a·chro·mat′ic** (-măt′ĭk) *adj.*

met·a·eth·ics (mĕt′ə-ĕth′ĭks) *n. (used with a sing. verb).* The study of ethical terms, judgments, and arguments. **—met′a·eth′i·cal** *adj.*

met·a·gal·ax·y (mĕt′ə-găl′ək-sē) *n., pl.* **-ies.** The total physical universe including all galaxies.

met·age (mē′tĭj) *n.* **1.** The official measurement of weight or contents, as of trucks using state roads. **2.** The fee charged for metage.

met·a·gen·e·sis (mĕt′ə-jĕn′ĭ-sĭs) *n. Biol.* The occurrence in certain organisms of alternating sexual (gametophyte) and asexual (sporophyte) reproductive cycles. **—met′a·ge·net′ic** (-jə-nĕt′ĭk) *adj.*

me·tag·na·thous (mə-tăg′nə-thəs) *adj.* Having a beak in which the tips of the mandibles cross. Used of birds.

met·al (mĕt′l) *n.* **1.** Any of a category of electropositive elements that are usually whitish, lustrous, and, in the transition metals, typically ductile and malleable with high tensile strength. Typical metals form salts with nonmetals, basic oxides with oxygen, and alloys with one another. **2.** An alloy of two or more metallic elements. **3.** An object made of metal. **4.** Basic character; mettle. **5.** Broken stones used for road surfaces or railroad beds. **6.** Molten glass, esp. when used in glassmaking. **7.** Molten cast iron. **8.** *Printing.* Type made of metal. —*tr.v.* **-aled, -al·ing, -als.** To make (a road) with broken stones. [ME < OFr. < Lat. *metallum* < Gk. *metallon.*]

met·a·lin·guis·tics (mĕt′ə-lĭng-gwĭs′tĭks) *n. (used with a sing. verb).* The study of the interrelationship between language and other cultural behavioral phenomena.

metall– or **metalli–** *pref.* Variants of **metallo-.**

me·tal·lic (mə-tăl′ĭk) *adj.* **1.** Of, pertaining to, or having the characteristics of a metal. **2.** Containing a metal: *a metallic compound.* **3.** Having a quality resembling metal, as: **a.** Having iridescence: *metallic cloth.* **b.** Acrid: *a metallic taste to the tomato juice.* **4.** Harshly resonant: *heard a metallic voice on the phone.* **—me·tal′li·cal·ly** *adv.*

metallic bond *n.* The chemical bond characteristic of metals, produced by the sharing of valence electrons between atoms in a usually stable crystalline structure.

metallic soap *n.* A soft, waxlike organic compound composed of a metal oxide and a fatty acid, used as a drier or lubricant.

met·al·lif·er·ous (mĕt′l-ĭf′ər-əs) *adj.* Containing metal. [Lat. *metallifer* : *metallum,* metal + *ferre,* to bear.]

met·al·line (mĕt′l-īn, -ĭn′) *adj.* **1.** Of, resembling, or having the properties of a metal. **2.** Containing metal ions.

metallo– or **metalli–** or **metall–** *pref.* Metal: *metallotherapy.* [< Lat. *metallum,* metal.]

met·al·log·ra·phy (mĕt′l-ŏg′rə-fē) *n.* The study of the structure of metals and their compounds, esp. with a microscope. **—met′al·log′ra·pher** *n.* **—me·tal′lo·graph′ic** (mə-tăl′ə-grăf′ĭk) *adj.* **—me·tal′lo·graph′i·cal·ly** *adv.*

met·al·loid (mĕt′l-oid′) *n.* A nonmetallic element, such as arsenic, that has some of the chemical properties of a metal, or one, such as carbon, that can form an alloy with metals. —*adj.* also **met·al·loi·dal** (mĕt′l-oid′l). **1.** Relating to or having the properties of a metalloid. **2.** Having the appearance of a metal.

me·tal·lo·ther·a·py (mə-tăl′ō-thĕr′ə-pē) *n. Med.* The use of metals or metal compounds in the treatment of disease.

met·al·lur·gy (mĕt′l-ûr′jē) *n.* **1.** The science or procedures of extracting metals from their ores, of purifying metals, and of creating useful objects from metals. **2.** The knowledge and study of metals and their properties in bulk and at the atomic level. [NLat. *metallurgia* < Gk. *metallourgos,* miner : *metallon,* a mine + *ergon,* work.] **—met′al·lur′gic, met′al·lur′gi·cal** *adj.* **—met′al·lur′gi·cal·ly** *adv.* **—met′al·lur′gist** *n.*

met·al·work (mĕt′l-wûrk′) *n.* Work done in metal.

met·al·work·ing (mĕt′l-wûr′kĭng) *n.* The act or process of shaping things out of metal. **—met′al·work′er** *n.*

met·a·math·e·mat·ics (mĕt′ə-măth′ə-măt′ĭks) *n. (used with a sing. verb).* The study of the principles, conceptual elements, consistency, and other aspects of logical systems, esp. of mathematical systems. **—met′a·math′e·mat′i·cal** *adj.* **—met′a·math′e·ma·ti′cian** *n.*

met·a·mere (mĕt′ə-mîr′) *n. Zool.* One of a series of homologous body segments, as in worms and lobsters. **—met′a·mer′ic** (-mĕr′ĭk, -mîr′-) *adj.* **—met′a·mer′i·cal·ly** *adv.*

me·tam·er·ism (mə-tăm′ə-rĭz′əm) *n.* The condition of having the body divided into metameres.

met·a·mor·phic (mĕt′ə-môr′fĭk) also **met·a·mor·phous** (-fəs) *adj.* **1.** Of or relating to metamorphosis. **2.** *Geol.* Characteristic of, pertaining to, or changed by metamorphism. [METAMORPH(OSIS) + -IC.]

met·a·mor·phism (mĕt′ə-môr′fĭz′əm) *n. Geol.* An alteration in composition, texture, or structure of rock masses caused by great heat or pressure. [METAMORPH(OSIS) + -ISM.]

met·a·mor·phose (mĕt′ə-môr′fōz′, -fōs′) *v.* **-phosed, -phos·ing, -phos·es.** —*tr.* **1.** To transform, as by sorcery: "*His eyes turned bloodshot, and he was metamorphosed into a raging fiend*" (Jack London). **2.** To subject to metamorphosis or metamorphism. —*intr.* To be changed or transformed by or as if by metamorphosis or metamorphism. [OFr. *metamorphoser* < *metamorphose,* metamorphosis < Lat. *metamorphosis.* —see METAMORPHOSIS.]

met·a·mor·pho·sis (mĕt′ə-môr′fə-sĭs) *n., pl.* **-ses** (-sēz′). **1.** A transformation, as by magic or sorcery. **2.** A marked change in appearance, character, condition, or function. **3.** *Biol.* Change in the structure and habits of an animal

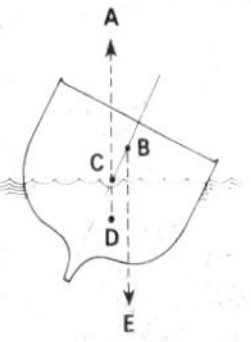

metacenter
A. Buoyant force
B. Center of gravity
C. Metacenter
D. Center of buoyancy
E. Weight

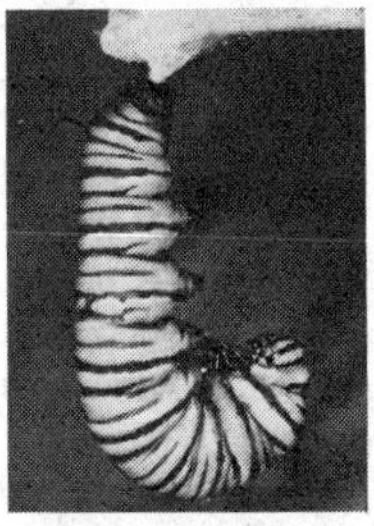

larva

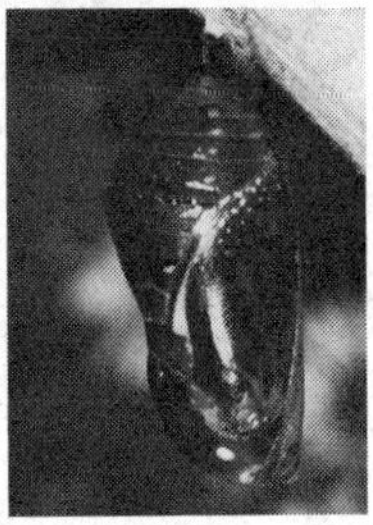

pupa

emerging adult

metamorphosis
Metamorphosis of the monarch butterfly

during normal growth, usually in the postembryonic stage. Metamorphosis includes, in insects, the emerging of an adult fly from a maggot or of a butterfly from a caterpillar, and, in amphibians, the changing of a tadpole into a frog. **4.** *Pathol.* Transformation of one kind of tissue into another, esp. degeneration. [Lat. < Gk. *metamorphōsis* < *metamorphoun,* to transform : *meta,* change + *morphē,* form.]

met·a·mor·phous (mĕt′ə-môr′fəs) *adj.* Variant of **metamorphic.**

met·a·neph·ros (mĕt′ə-nĕf′rŏs′) *n.* The embryonic vertebrate kidney, in its third stage, which becomes the adult kidney. [META- + Gk. *nephros,* kidney.]

met·a·phase (mĕt′ə-fāz′) *n.* The stage of mitosis during which the chromosomes are aligned along the equator of the mitotic spindle.

met·a·phor (mĕt′ə-fôr′, -fər) *n.* A figure of speech in which a term is transferred from the object it ordinarily designates to an object it may designate only by implicit comparison or analogy, as in the phrase *evening of life.* [OFr. *metaphore* < Lat. *metaphora* < Gk. < *metapherein,* to transfer : *meta,* change + *pherein,* to bear.] **—met′a·phor′ic, met′a·phor′i·cal** *adj.* **—met′a·phor′i·cal·ly** *adv.*

met·a·phos·phate (mĕt′ə-fŏs′fāt′) *n.* The inorganic anion PO_3^-, or a compound containing it.

met·a·phos·phor·ic acid (mĕt′ə-fŏs-fôr′ĭk, -fŏr′-) *n.* An inorganic compound, HPO_3, used as a dehydrating agent and in dental cements.

met·a·phrase (mĕt′ə-frāz′) *n.* A word-for-word translation. *—tr.v.* **-phrased, -phras·ing, -phras·es.** To manipulate the wording of (a text), esp. as a means of subtly altering the sense: *Reformists were accused of metaphrasing certain Marxian texts in order to justify their views.* [NLat. *metaphrasis* < Gk. < *metaphrazein,* to translate : *meta,* change + *phrazein,* tell.] **—met′a·phras′tic** (-frăs′tĭk) *adj.*

met·a·phrast (mĕt′ə-frăst′) *n.* One who renders a text into a different form, as by recasting prose in verse. [Med. Gk. *metaphrastēs* < Gk. *metaphrazein,* to translate. —see METAPHRASE.]

met·a·phys·i·cal (mĕt′ə-fĭz′ĭ-kəl) *adj.* **1.** Of or pertaining to metaphysics. **2.** Based on speculative or abstract reasoning. **3.** Too abstract; excessively subtle. **4. a.** Immaterial; incorporeal. **b.** Supernatural. **5.** Often **Metaphysical.** Of or designating a group of 17th-century poets whose verse is characterized by complex imagery and an abundance of conceits. [ME *metaphisicalle* < Med. Lat. *metaphysicalis* < *metaphysica,* metaphysics.] **—met′a·phys′i·cal·ly** *adv.*

met·a·phy·si·cian (mĕt′ə-fə-zĭsh′ən) *n.* One who is specialized or skilled in metaphysics.

met·a·phys·ics (mĕt′ə-fĭz′ĭks) *n. (used with a sing. verb).* **1.** The branch of philosophy that systematically investigates the nature of first principles and problems of ultimate reality, including the study of being (ontology) and, often, the study of the structure of the universe (cosmology). **2.** Speculative or critical philosophy in general. [Med. Lat. *metaphysica* < Gk. *Ta meta ta phusika,* the things after the physics, the title of Aristotle's treatise on first principles (so called because it followed his work on physics).]

met·a·pla·sia (mĕt′ə-plā′zhə, -zhē-ə) *n.* **1.** The metamorphosis of tissue from one type to another, as in ossification. **2.** The change of cells from a normal to an abnormal state. **—met′a·plas′tic** (-plăs′tĭk) *adj.*

met·a·plasm (mĕt′ə-plăz′əm) *n.* **1.** *Gram.* The changing of a word by adding, subtracting, or transposing letters or syllables. **2.** *Biol.* Inert material in the protoplasm of a cell, such as the yolk of an egg. [Lat. *metaplasmus,* transformation < Gk. *metaplasmos* < *metaplassein,* to remold : *meta,* change + *plassein,* to mold.] **—met′a·plas′mic** (-plăz′mĭk) *adj.*

met·a·pro·tein (mĕt′ə-prō′tēn′, -prō′tē-ĭn) *n.* Any of various organic compounds resulting from a reaction between an acid or alkali and a protein that are soluble in weak acids or alkalis and insoluble in neutral solutions.

met·a·psy·chol·o·gy (mĕt′ə-sī-kŏl′ə-jē) *n.* Philosophical speculation on the origin, structure, and function of the mind and on the relationship between the mind and objective reality.

met·a·so·ma·tism (mĕt′ə-sō′mə-tĭz′əm) also **met·a·so·ma·to·sis** (-tō′sĭs) *n. Geol.* Metamorphism in which chemical as well as physical changes occur as a result of reaction with external material. **—met′a·so·mat′ic** (-măt′ĭk) *adj.* **—met′a·so·mat′i·cal·ly** *adv.*

met·a·sta·ble (mĕt′ə-stā′bəl) *adj.* Designating a relatively unstable, transient, but significant state of a chemical or physical system, as of a supersaturated solution or an energetically excited atom. **—met′a·sta·bil′i·ty** (-stə-bĭl′ĭ-tē) *n.*

me·tas·ta·sis (mə-tăs′tə-sĭs) *n., pl.* **-ses** (-sēz′). **1.** *Pathol.* Transmission of disease from an original site to one or more sites elsewhere in the body, as in tuberculosis or cancer. **2.** In rhetoric, a sudden transition from one point to another. **3.** Paramorphism. [NLat. < LLat., transition < Gk. < *methistanai,* to change : *meta,* change + *histanai,* to cause to stand.] **—met′a·stat′ic** (mĕt′ə-stăt′ĭk) *adj.*

me·tas·ta·size (mə-tăs′tə-sīz′) *intr.v.* **-sized, -siz·ing, -siz·es.** To be transmitted, transferred, or transformed by or as if by metastasis.

met·a·tar·sal (mĕt′ə-tär′səl) *adj.* Of or pertaining to the metatarsus. *—n.* Any of the bones of the metatarsus. **—met′a·tar′sal·ly** *adv.*

met·a·tar·sus (mĕt′ə-tär′səs) *n., pl.* **-si** (-sī′). **1.** The middle part of the foot in man that forms the instep, composed of the five bones between the toes and the tarsus. **2.** A part of the hind foot in four-legged animals or of the foot in birds corresponding to the metatarsus.

me·tath·e·sis (mə-tăth′ĭ-sĭs) *n., pl.* **-ses** (-sēz′). **1.** Transposition within a word of letters, sounds, or syllables, as in the change from Old English *brid* to modern English *bird,* or in the confusion of *revelant* for *relevant.* **2.** *Chem.* Double decomposition. [Gk. < *metatithenai,* to transpose : *meta,* change + *tithenai,* to place.] **—met′a·thet′ic** (mĕt′ə-thĕt′ĭk), **met′a·thet′i·cal** *adj.* **—met′a·thet′i·cal·ly** *adv.*

me·tath·e·size (mə-tăth′ĭ-sīz′) *tr. & intr.v.* **-sized, -siz·ing, -siz·es.** To subject to or undergo metathesis.

met·a·tho·rax (mĕt′ə-thôr′ăks′, -thōr′-) *n., pl.* **-rax·es** or **-ra·ces** (-ə-sēz′). The hindmost of the three thoracic segments of an insect. **—me′ta·tho·rac′ic** *adj.*

met·a·zo·al (mĕt′ə-zō′əl) *adj.* Of or pertaining to metazoans.

met·a·zo·an (mĕt′ə-zō′ən) *n.* A member of one of two divisions of the animal kingdom, the Metazoa, which includes all animals more complex than the one-celled protozoan. [NLat. *Metazoa,* a subdivision of the animal kingdom : META- + Gk. *zōia,* pl. of *zōion,* animal.] **—met′a·zo′al, met′a·zo′an, met′a·zo′ic** *adj.*

mete¹ (mēt) *tr.v.* **met·ed, met·ing, metes. 1.** To distribute by or as if by measure; deal out: *mete out punishment.* **2.** *Archaic.* To measure. [ME *meten* < OE *metan.*]

mete² (mēt) *n.* A boundary line or limit: *metes and bounds.* [AN < Lat. *meta.*]

me·tem·psy·cho·sis (mə-tĕm′sĭ-kō′sĭs, mĕt′əm-sī-) *n., pl.* **-ses** (-sēz′). The transmigration of souls. [Gk. *metempsukhōsis* : *meta,* change + *empsukhos,* animate (*en,* in + *psukhē,* soul).]

met·en·ceph·a·lon (mĕt′ĕn-sĕf′ə-lŏn′) *n., pl.* **-la** (-lə). The part of the embryonic hindbrain from which the cerebellum and the pons develop. **—met′en·ce·phal′ic** (-sə-făl′ĭk) *adj.*

me·te·or (mē′tē-ər, -ôr′) *n.* **1.** The luminous trail or streak that appears in the sky when a meteoroid is made incandescent by friction with the earth's atmosphere. **2.** A meteoroid. **3.** An atmospheric phenomenon, such as a rainbow, lightning, or snow. [ME < OFr. *meteore* < Med. Lat. *meteorum* < Gk. *meteōron,* astronomical phenomenon < *meteōros,* high in the air.]

me·te·or·ic (mē′tē-ôr′ĭk, -ŏr′-) *adj.* **1.** Of, pertaining to, or formed by a meteor. **2.** Resembling a meteor in speed and brilliance: *a meteoric rise to fame.* **3.** Of or pertaining to the earth's atmosphere. **—me′te·or′i·cal·ly** *adv.*

me·te·or·ite (mē′tē-ə-rīt′) *n.* The stony or metallic material of a meteoroid that survives passage through the atmosphere and reaches the earth's surface. **—me′te·or·it′ic, me′te·or·it′i·cal** *adj.*

me·te·or·o·graph (mē′tē-ôr′ə-grăf′, -ŏr′-) *n.* An instrument that records simultaneously several meteorological conditions, such as temperature, barometric pressure, and moisture.

me·te·or·oid (mē′tē-ə-roid′) *n.* Any of numerous celestial bodies, ranging in size from specks of dust to asteroids weighing thousands of tons, which appear as meteors when entering the earth's atmosphere.

me·te·or·ol·o·gy (mē′tē-ə-rŏl′ə-jē) *n.* The science dealing with the phenomena of the atmosphere, esp. weather and weather conditions. [Gk. *meteōrologia,* discussion of astronomical phenomena : *meteōron,* astronomical phenomenon + *logos,* speech.] **—me′te·or·o·log′i·cal** (-ər-ə-lŏj′ĭ-kəl), **me′te·or·o·log′ic** *adj.* **—me′te·or·o·log′i·cal·ly** *adv.* **—me′te·or·ol′o·gist** *n.*

meteor shower *n.* A group of meteors that appear together and have an apparent common origin.

me·ter¹ (mē′tər) *n.* **1. a.** The measured rhythm characteristic of verse. **b.** A specified rhythmic pattern of verse, usually determined by the number and kinds of metrical units in a typical line: *trochaic meter.* **2. a.** The division of music into measures or bars. **b.** A specific musical rhythm determined by the number of beats and the time value assigned to each note in a measure. [ME < OFr. *metre* < Lat. *metrum* < Gk. *metron.*]

me·ter² (mē′tər) *n.* The fundamental unit of length, equivalent to 39.37 inches, in the metric system. It was defined in 1790 as one ten-millionth (10^{-7}) of the earth's quadrant passing through Paris but was redefined in 1960 as the length equal to 1,650,763.73 wavelengths in a vacuum of the orange-red radiation of krypton 86. [Fr. *mètre* < Gk. *metron,* measure.]

me·ter³ (mē′tər) *n.* **1.** Any of various devices designed to measure time, distance, speed, or intensity or to indicate and record or regulate the amount or volume of something, such as a flow of gas or an electric current. **2.** A postage meter. **3.** A parking meter. *—tr.v.* **-tered, -ter·ing, -ters. 1. a.** To measure with a metering device. **b.** To supply or regulate by means of a metering device. **2.** To imprint with postage or other revenue stamps by means of a postage meter or similar device. [< -METER.]

-meter *suff.* Measuring device: *anemometer.* [Fr. *-mètre* < Gk. *metron,* measure.]

me·ter-kil·o·gram-sec·ond system (mē′tər-kĭl′ə-grăm-sĕk′ənd) *n.* A coherent system of units for mechanics, using the meter, the kilogram, and the second as basic units of length, mass, and time.

meter maid *n.* A woman who is a member of a police traffic department and who is assigned the duty of writing parking tickets.

me·tes·trus (mĕ-tĕs′trəs) *n.* The period of sexual inactivity that follows estrus. **—me·tes′trous** (-trəs) *adj.*

meth– *pref.* Methyl: *methane.* [< METHYL.]

meth·ac·ry·late (mĕth-ăk′rə-lāt′) *n.* **1.** An ester of methacrylic acid, CH_2:C(CH_3)COOR, R being an organic radical. It is used in the manufacture of plastics. **2.** A resin derived from methacrylic acid. [METH- + ACRYL(IC) + -ATE.]

meth·a·cryl·ic acid (mĕth′ə-krĭl′ĭk) *n.* A colorless liquid, CH_2:C(CH_3)COOH, used in the manufacture of resins and plastics.

meth·a·done hydrochloride (mĕth′ə-dōn′) *n.* An organic compound, $C_{21}H_{27}NO{\cdot}HCl$, used as an analgesic and in treating heroin addiction. [(DI)METH(YL) + A(MINO) + D(IPHENYL) + *(heptan)one,* a ketone.]

meth·am·phet·a·mine (mĕth′ăm-fĕt′ə-mēn′, -mĭn) *n.* An amine derivative, $C_{10}H_{15}N$, of amphetamine that is used in the form of its crystalline hydrochloride as a stimulant.

meth·ane (mĕth′ān′) *n.* An odorless, colorless, flammable gas, CH_4, the major constituent of natural gas, that is used as a fuel and is an important source of hydrogen and a wide variety of organic compounds.

methane series *n.* The paraffin series.

meth·a·nol (mĕth′ə-nôl′, -nōl′) *n.* A colorless flammable liquid, $CH_2(OCH_3)_2$, used as an antifreeze, general solvent, fuel, and denaturant for ethyl alcohol.

meth·a·qua·lone (mĕth′ə-kwā′lōn′) *n.* A drug, $C_{16}H_{14}N_2O$, that is a habit-forming sedative and hypnotic. [Blend of METH- and *quinazoline,* a derivative of quinoline.]

Meth·e·drine (mĕth′ĭ-drēn′, -drĭn). A trademark for methamphetamine.

me·theg·lin (mə-thĕg′lĭn) *n.* A beverage typically made of fermented honey and water; mead. [Welsh *meddyglyn* : *meddyg,* medicinal (< Lat. *medicus* < *mederi,* to heal) + *llyn,* a liquid.]

met·he·mo·glo·bin (mĕt-hē′mə-glō′bĭn) *n.* A brownish-red, crystalline organic compound formed by oxidation of hemoglobin and found in the blood after poisoning by chlorates, nitrates, ferricyanides, or various other substances. [MET(A)- + HEMOGLOBIN.]

me·the·na·mine (mə-thē′nə-mēn′, -mĭn) *n.* An organic compound, $(CH_2)_6N_4$, used as a urinary tract antiseptic and in rubber vulcanizing. [METH- + -EN(E) + AMINE.]

meth·i·cil·lin (mĕth′ĭ-sĭl′ĭn) *n.* A synthetic penicillin that is resistant to penicillinase. [METH- + (PEN)ICILLIN.]

me·thinks (mĭ-thĭngks′) *v.* Past tense **me·thought** (-thôt′). *Archaic.* It seems to me. [ME *me thinketh* < OE *mē ðyncð* : *mē,* to me + *ðyncð,* it seems.]

me·thi·o·nine (mə-thī′ə-nēn′) *n.* An organic compound, $C_5H_{11}NO_2S$, derived from protein and used as a dietary supplement and in pharmaceuticals. [ME(TH)- + THION- + -INE.]

meth·od (mĕth′əd) *n.* **1.** A means or manner of procedure, esp. a regular and systematic way of accomplishing something. **2.** Orderly and systematic arrangement. **3.** The procedures and techniques characteristic of a particular discipline or field of knowledge: *the scientific method.* **4. Method.** A system of acting in which the actor recalls emotions and reactions from his past experience and utilizes them in the role he is playing. [Fr. *méthode* < Lat. *methodus* < Gk. *methodos* : *meta,* after + *hodos,* journey.]

Synonyms: *method, system, routine, manner, mode, fashion, way. Method* emphasizes procedures according to a detailed, logically ordered plan. *System,* broader in scope, stresses order and regularity affecting all parts of a relatively complex procedure. *Routine* stresses procedure from the standpoint of detail and rather rigid sequence; it involves only the mechanical skills necessary for unvarying practice. *Manner* emphasizes personal behavior and distinctive procedure characteristic of a group and influenced by local tradition and customs. *Mode* often applies to distinctive procedure characteristic of a group and influenced by local tradition and customs. *Fashion* usually applies to individual, highly personal behavior; *after a fashion* and *in one's fashion* suggest (unfavorably) idiosyncrasies or mannerisms. *Way* is most often an inclusive synonym for these terms, but it can indicate highly individual procedure, as in *It's just his way.*

me·thod·i·cal (mə-thŏd′ĭ-kəl) also **me·thod·ic** (-ĭk) *adj.* **1.** Arranged or proceeding in regular, systematic order. **2.** Characterized by ordered and systematic habits or behavior. **—me·thod′i·cal·ly** *adv.* **—me·thod′i·cal·ness** *n.*

Meth·od·ism (mĕth′ə-dĭz′əm) *n.* **1.** The beliefs, worship, and system of organization of the Methodists. **2. methodism.** Emphasis on systematic procedure.

Meth·od·ist (mĕth′ə-dĭst) *n.* **1.** A member of a Protestant Christian denomination (in the United States, the United Methodist Church) with a theology developed from the teachings of John and Charles Wesley and others in England in the early 18th century and characterized by an emphasis on the doctrines of free grace and individual responsibility. **2. methodist.** One who emphasizes or insists on systematic methods. **—Meth′od·is′tic** *adj.*

meth·od·ize (mĕth′ə-dīz′) *tr.v.* **-ized, -iz·ing, -iz·es.** To reduce to or organize according to a method; systematize. **—meth′od·i·za′tion** *n.* **—meth′od·iz′er** *n.*

meth·od·ol·o·gist (mĕth′ə-dŏl′ə-jĭst) *n.* One who studies methodology.

meth·od·ol·o·gy (mĕth′ə-dŏl′ə-jē) *n., pl.* **-gies. 1.** The system of principles, practices, and procedures applied to a specific branch of knowledge. **2.** The branch of logic dealing with the general principles of the formation of knowledge. **—meth′od·o·log′i·cal** (mĕth′ə-də-lŏj′ĭ-kəl) *adj.* **—meth′od·o·log′i·cal·ly** *adv.*

meth·o·trex·ate (mĕth′ə-trĕk′sāt′) *n.* A toxic antimetabolite, $C_{20}H_{22}N_8O_5$, used in the treatment of cancer. [METH- + *trex-* (of unknown orig.) + -ATE.]

me·thought (mĭ-thôt′) *v.* Past tense of **methinks.**

me·thox·y·chlor (mə-thŏk′sĭ-klôr′, -klōr′) *n.* A white crystalline compound, $C_{16}Cl_3H_{15}O_2$, used as an insecticide. [METH- + OXY- + (TRI)CHLOR(ETHANE).]

Me·thu·se·lah (mə-thōō′zə-lə) *n.* **1.** A Biblical patriarch said to have lived 969 years. **2. methuselah.** An extremely old man. [Heb. *Methūshelāh.*]

meth·yl (mĕth′əl) *n.* The univalent organic radical CH_3, derived from methane and occurring in many important organic compounds. [Fr. *méthyle,* back-formation < *méthylène,* methylene.] **—me·thyl′ic** (mə-thĭl′ĭk) *adj.*

methyl acetate *n.* An organic compound, $C_3H_6O_2$, used as a paint remover and general solvent and in the manufacture of perfumes.

meth·yl·al (mĕth′ə-lăl′) *n.* A colorless flammable liquid, $CH_2(OCH_3)_2$, used in the manufacture of perfumes, adhesives, and protective coatings.

methyl alcohol *n.* Methanol.

meth·yl·a·mine (mĕth′ə-lə-mēn′, -lăm′ēn′, mə-thĭl′ə-mēn′) *n.* A flammable gas, CH_3NH_2, produced by the decomposition of organic matter and synthesized for use as a solvent and in the manufacture of many products, such as dyes and insecticides.

meth·yl·ase (mĕth′ə-lās′, -lāz′) *n.* An enzyme that catalyzes a methylation reaction.

meth·yl·ate (mĕth′ə-lāt′) *n.* An organic compound in which the hydrogen of the hydroxyl group (OH) of methyl alcohol is replaced by a metal. *—tr.v.* **-at·ed, -at·ing, -ates. 1.** To mix or combine with methyl alcohol. **2.** To combine with the methyl radical. **—meth′yl·a′tion** *n.* **—meth′yl·a′tor** *n.*

methylated spirit *n.* Often **methylated spirits.** A denatured alcohol consisting of a mixture of ethyl alcohol and methyl alcohol.

methyl bromide *n.* A toxic gas, CH_3Br, used as a fumigant.

methyl chloride *n.* An explosive gas, CH_3Cl, used in organic synthesis and polymerization, as a refrigerant, and as an anesthetic.

meth·yl·ene (mĕth′ə-lēn′) *n.* A bivalent organic radical, CH_2, a component of unsaturated hydrocarbons. [Fr. *méthylène* : Gk. *methu,* wine + Gk. *hulē,* wood + *-ène,* -ene.]

methylene blue *n.* An organic compound, $C_{16}H_{18}N_3SCl{\cdot}3H_2O$, whose dark-green crystals or powder forms a deep-blue solution when dissolved in water and that is used as an antidote for cyanide poisoning and as a bacteriological stain.

methyl ethyl ketone *n. Chem.* Butanone.

methyl methacrylate *n.* A colorless liquid, CH_2:C(CH_3)$COOCH_3$, that is used as a monomer in plastics.

meth·yl·naph·tha·lene (mĕth′əl-năf′thə-lēn′, -năp′thə-) *n.* An organic compound, $C_{10}H_7CH_3$, obtained from coal tar in two isomeric forms, one a liquid, the other a solid.

me·tic·u·lous (mə-tĭk′yə-ləs) *adj.* **1.** Extremely careful and precise. **2.** Excessively concerned with details; overscrupulous. [Lat. *meticulosus,* timid < *metus,* fear.] **—me·tic′u·los′i·ty** (-lŏs′ĭ-tē), **me·tic′u·lous·ness** *n.* **—me·tic′u·lous·ly** *adv.*

Synonyms: *meticulous, conscientious, scrupulous, fastidious, punctilious. Meticulous* stresses extreme care, and sometimes exaggerated care for small details. *Conscientious* combines diligence with the dictates of conscience, thus involving duty and a sense of right and wrong. *Scrupulous* likewise implies strong concern for moral rectitude. *Fastidious,* said of personal tastes and appearance, stresses concern, often excessive, for niceties. *Punctilious* specifically applies to care in matters of etiquette.

mé·tier (mā-tyā′) *n.* **1.** An occupation, trade, or profession. **2.** Work or activity for which a person is particularly suited; specialty. [Fr. < OFr. *mestier* < Lat. *ministerium,* occupation.]

mé·tis (mā-tēs′) *n., pl.* **mé·tis. 1.** A person of mixed Indian and French-Canadian ancestry. **2.** A crossbred animal. [Canadian Fr. < OFr. *metis,* of mixed race < Lat. *miscēre,* to mix.]

Me·ton·ic cycle (mə-tŏn′ĭk) *n.* A period of 235 lunar months, or about 19 Julian years, at the end of which the phases of the moon recur in the same order and on the same days as in the preceding cycle. [After *Meton,* Athenian astronomer of the 5th cent. B.C., its discoverer.]

met·o·nym (mĕt′ə-nĭm′) *n.* A word used in metonymy.

me·ton·y·my (mə-tŏn′ə-mē) *n., pl.* **-mies.** A figure of speech in which an attribute or commonly associated feature is used to name or designate something, as in *The pen is mightier than the sword.* [LLat. *metonymia* < Gk. *metōnumia* : *meta-*, changing + *onoma,* name.] **—met'o·nym'ic** (mĕt'ə-nĭm'ĭk), **met'o·nym'i·cal** (-ĭ-kəl) *adj.* **—met'o·nym'i·cal·ly** *adv.*

me-too (mē'to͞o') *adj. Informal.* Advocating principles or practices copied from and closely similar to those of a rival. **—me'-too'er** *n.* **—me'-too'ism** *n.*

metope

met·o·pe (mĕt'ə-pē) *n.* The space between two triglyphs on a Doric frieze. [Lat. *metopa* < Gk. *metopē* : *meta,* between + *opē,* opening.]

me·top·ic (mə-tŏp'ĭk) *adj.* Of or pertaining to the forehead. [Gk. *metōpikos* < *metōpon,* forehead : *meta,* between + *ōps,* eye.]

met·o·pon hydrochloride (mĕt'ə-pŏn') *n.* A narcotic drug, $C_{18}H_{21}NO_3 \cdot HCl$, derived from morphine. [E. *metopon,* a morphine derivative + HYDROCHLORIDE.]

metr– *pref.* Variant of **metro-**.

Met·ra·zol (mĕt'rə-zôl', -zōl'). A trademark for pentylenetetrazol.

me·tre (mē'tər) *n. Chiefly Brit.* Variant of **meter**[1] and **meter**[2].

met·ric[1] (mĕt'rĭk) *adj.* Designating, pertaining to, or using the metric system. [Fr. *métrique* < *mètre,* meter < Gk. *metron,* measure.]

met·ric[2] (mĕt'rĭk) *n.* **1.** A standard of measurement. **2.** *Math.* A geometric function defined for a coordinate system such that the distance between any two points in that system may be determined from their coordinates.

met·ric[3] (mĕt'rĭk) *n.* Metrics. [Gk. *metrikē (tekhnē),* (the art) of meter.]

met·ri·cal (mĕt'rĭ-kəl) *adj.* **1.** Of, pertaining to, or composed in rhythmic meter. **2.** Of or pertaining to measurement. [Lat. *metricus* < Gk. *metrikos* < *metron,* meter.] **—met'ri·cal·ly** *adv.*

met·ri·ca·tion (mĕt'rĭ-kā'shən) *n.* Conversion to the metric system of weights and measures; metrification.

metric centner *n.* A unit of mass equal to 100 kilograms.

metric hundredweight *n.* A unit of mass equal to 50 kilograms.

met·rics (mĕt'rĭks) *n. (used with a sing. verb)*: The branch of prosody dealing with measure and metrical structures.

–metrics *suff.* The application of statistics and mathematical analysis to a specified field of study: *econometrics.* [< METRIC[2].]

metric system *n.* A decimal system of weights and measures based on the meter as a unit length and the kilogram as a unit mass. Derived units include the liter for liquid volume, the stere for solid volume, and the are for area.

metric ton *n.* A unit of mass equal to 1,000 kilograms.

met·ri·fy (mĕt'rə-fī') *tr. & intr.v.* **-fied, -fy·ing, -fies. 1.** To put into or compose in rhythmic meters. **2.** To convert to or adopt the metric system. [OFr. *metrifier* < Med. Lat. *metrificare* : Lat. *metrum,* measure (< Gk. *metron*) + Lat. *facere,* to make.] **—met'ri·fi·ca'tion** *n.*

me·tri·tis (mə-trī'tĭs) *n.* Inflammation of the uterus.

met·ro (mĕt'rō) *n., pl.* **-ros.** A subway system. [Fr., short for *(chemin de fer) métropolitain,* metropolitan (railway).]

metro– or **metr–** *pref.* Uterus: *metritis.* [NLat. < Gk. *mētro-* < *mētra,* uterus < *mētēr,* mother.]

me·trol·o·gy (mĕ-trŏl'ə-jē) *n., pl.* **-gies. 1.** The science that deals with measurement. **2.** A system of measurement. [Fr. *métrologie* < Gk. *metrologia,* theory of ratios : *metron,* measure + *logos,* reckoning.] **—met'ro·log'i·cal** (mĕt'rə-lŏj'ĭ-kəl) *adj.* **—met'ro·log'i·cal·ly** *adv.* **—me·trol'o·gist** *n.*

met·ro·nome (mĕt'rə-nōm') *n.* A device to mark time at a steady beat in adjustable intervals. [Gk. *metron,* measure + *nomos,* rule.] **—met'ro·nom'ic** (-nŏm'ĭk) *adj.* **—met'ro·nom'i·cal·ly** *adv.*

metronome

me·tro·nym·ic (mē'trə-nĭm'ĭk, mĕt'rə-) also **mat·ro·nym·ic** (măt'-) *adj.* Of, pertaining to, or derived from the name of one's mother or female ancestor. *—n.* A metronymic name. [Gk. *mētēr,* mother + Gk. *onuma,* name + -IC.]

me·trop·o·lis (mə-trŏp'ə-lĭs) *n.* **1.** A major city. **2.** A city or urban area regarded as the center of a specific activity: *a great cultural metropolis.* **3.** The chief see of a metropolitan bishop, esp. the main diocese of a specific ecclesiastical province. **4.** The mother city of a state or colony in ancient Greece. **5.** *Zool.* A region or area where a particular kind of organism lives and thrives. [LLat. < Gk. *mētropolis,* mother city : *mētēr,* mother + *polis,* city.]

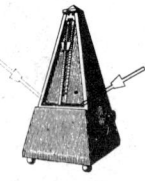

met·ro·pol·i·tan (mĕt'rə-pŏl'ĭ-tən) *adj.* **1. a.** Of, pertaining to, or characteristic of a metropolis. **b.** Making up a metropolis. **2.** Pertaining to or comprising the home territory of a sovereign state as distinguished from its dependencies, protectorates, or overseas territories and provinces. **3.** Of or pertaining to a metropolitan. *—n.* **1. a.** In the Roman Catholic and other episcopal churches, an archbishop who has authority over bishops. **b.** In the Eastern Orthodox Church, a bishop ranking next below the patriarch who serves as the head of an ecclesiastical province. **2.** One who resides in a metropolis, esp. one who displays big-city characteristics, attitudes, and values. [ME < LLat. *metropolitanus* < Gk. *mētropolitēs,* citizen of a metropolis < *mētropolis,* mother city. —see METROPOLIS.]

me·tror·rha·gi·a (mē'trə-rā'jē-ə, -jə) *n.* An abnormal hemorrhage of the uterus, esp. between menstrual flows. **—me'tror·rha'gic** (-rā'jĭk) *adj.*

–metry *suff.* Process or science of measuring: *isometry.* [ME *-metrie* < OFr. < Lat. *-metria* < Gk. < *metron,* measure.]

met·tle (mĕt'l) *n.* **1.** Inherent quality of character and temperament. **2.** Courage and fortitude; spirit: *show one's mettle in combat.* **—idiom. on (one's) mettle.** Prepared to put one's spirit, courage, or energy to the test. [Alteration of METAL.]

met·tle·some (mĕt'l-səm) *adj.* Full of courage; high-spirited.

mew[1] (myo͞o) *n.* **1.** A cage for hawks, esp. when molting. **2.** A secret place; hideaway. **3.** A small street behind a residential street, containing private stables, now mostly converted into small apartments. *—v.* **mewed, mew·ing, mews.** *—tr.* To confine in or as if in a cage. *—intr.* To molt. Used of a hawk. [ME < OFr. *mue* < *muer,* to molt < Lat. *mutare,* to change.]

mew[2] (myo͞o) *intr.v.* **mewed, mew·ing, mews.** To make the high-pitched, crying sound of a cat; meow. *—n.* The crying sound of a cat; meow. [ME *mewen.*]

mew[3] (myo͞o) *n.* A sea bird, *Larus canus,* one of the gulls found in northern Eurasia and western North America. [ME < OE *mæw.*]

mewl (myo͞ol) *intr.v.* **mewled, mewl·ing, mewls.** To cry weakly; whimper. [Imit.]

Mex·i·can (mĕk'sĭ-kən) *n.* A native or inhabitant of Mexico. *—adj.* Of or pertaining to Mexico or to its inhabitants, their language, or their culture.

Mexican hairless *n.* A small dog of a breed of unknown origin, found in Mexico, having a smooth hairless body except for tufts on the head and tail.

Mexican Spanish *n.* The Spanish language as used in Mexico.

me·ze·re·on (mə-zîr'ē-ən) *n.* **1.** A shrub, *Daphne mezereum,* native to Eurasia, having fragrant lilac-purple flowers and small scarlet fruit. **2.** Mezereum (sense 2). [ME *mizerion* < Med. Lat. *mezereon* < Ar. *māzaryūn.*]

me·ze·re·um (mə-zîr'ē-əm) *n.* **1.** The mezereon (sense 1). **2.** The dried bark of certain shrubs of the genus *Daphne,* once used externally as a vesicant and internally for arthritis. [Alteration of MEZEREON.]

me·zu·zah also **me·zu·za** (mə-zo͞oz'ə) *n.* A small piece of parchment inscribed with the biblical passages Deuteronomy 6:4–9 and 11:13–21 and marked with the word "Shaddai," a name of the Almighty, that is rolled up in a container and affixed to a door frame as a sign that a Jewish family lives within. [Heb. *mzūzāh,* doorpost.]

mez·za·nine (mĕz'ə-nēn', mĕz'ə-nēn') *n.* **1.** A partial story between two main stories of a building. **2.** The lowest balcony in a theater or the first few rows of that balcony. [Fr. < Ital. *mezzanino* < *mezzano,* middle < Lat. *medianus,* in the middle < *medius,* middle.]

mez·zo (mĕt'sō, mĕd'zō, mĕz'ō) *n., pl.* **-zos.** A mezzo-soprano.

mezzo for·te (fôr'tā') *adj. & adv. Mus.* Moderately loud. [Ital.]

mezzo pi·a·no (pē-ä'nō) *adj. & adv. Mus.* Moderately soft. [Ital.]

mez·zo-re·lie·vo (mĕt'sō-rĭ-lē'vō, -rĕl-yä'vō, mĕd'-, mĕz'-) *n., pl.* **-vos.** Sculptural relief composed of modeled forms that project approximately halfway from the background. [Ital. *mezzorilievo* : *mezzo,* half (< Lat. *medius)* + *rilievo,* relief < *rilevare,* to raise < Lat. *relevare,* to raise, relieve. —see RELIEVE.]

mez·zo-so·pran·o (mĕt'sō-sə-prăn'ō, -prä'nō, mĕd'-, mĕz'-) *n., pl.* **-os. 1. a.** A voice having a range between soprano and contralto. **b.** A vocal part calling for a voice having such a range. **2.** A woman having a mezzo-soprano voice. [Ital. : *mezzo,* half (< Lat. *medius)* + *soprano,* soprano. —see SOPRANO.]

mez·zo·tint (mĕt'sō-tĭnt', mĕd'-) *n.* **1.** A method of engraving a copper or steel plate by scraping and burnishing areas to produce effects of light and shadow. **2.** A print made from a plate engraved by mezzotint. [Ital. *mezzotinto* : *mezzo,* half (< Lat. *medius)* + *tinto,* tint < Lat. *tingere,* to dye.]

Mg The symbol for the element magnesium.

mho (mō) *n., pl.* **mhos.** A unit of conductance reciprocal to the ohm. [Backward spelling of OHM.]

mi (mē) *n. Mus.* The third tone of the diatonic scale in solfeggio. [Med. Lat. —see GAMUT.]

MIA (ĕm'ī-ā') *n.* A serviceman who is reported missing following a combat mission and whose death can be neither confirmed nor denied. [M(ISSING) I(N) A(CTION).]

Mi·am·i (mī-ăm'ē, -ăm'ə) *n., pl.* **Miami** or **-is.** A member of an Algonquian tribe of Indians who lived in what is now Ohio, Indiana, Illinois, and Wisconsin.

mi·as·ma (mī-ăz'mə, mē-) *n., pl.* **-mas** or **-ma·ta** (-mə-tə). **1. a.** A poisonous atmosphere formerly thought to rise from swamps and putrid matter and cause disease. **b.** A thick, vaporous atmosphere or emanation: *wreathed in a miasma of cigarette smoke.* **2.** A noxious atmosphere or influence: *a miasma of evil.* [Gk. < *miainein,* to pollute.] **—mi·as'mal** (-məl), **mi'as·mat'ic** (mī'əz-măt'ĭk), **mi·as'mic** (-mĭk) *adj.*

mi·ca (mī'kə) *n.* Any of a group of chemically and physically related mineral silicates, common in igneous and metamorphic rocks, each containing hydroxyl, alkali, and aluminum silicate groups, characteristically splitting into flexible sheets used in insulation. [NLat. < Lat., grain.] —**mi·ca′ceous** (-kā′shəs) *adj.*

Mi·cah (mī′kə) also **Mi·che·as** (mī-kē′əs) *n.* **1.** A Hebrew prophet of the eighth century B.C. **2.** See table at **Bible.** [Heb. *Mīkhāh.*]

mice (mīs) *n.* Plural of **mouse.**

mi·celle (mī-sĕl′) *n.* **1.** A submicroscopic aggregation of molecules, such as a droplet in a colloidal system. **2.** An organic particle of colloidal size found in coal. **3.** A coherent strand or structure in natural or synthetic fibers. **4.** A submicroscopic structural unit of protoplasm. [NLat. *micella* < Lat. *mica,* grain.] —**mi·cel′lar** (mī-sĕl′ər) *adj.*

Mi·chael (mī′kəl) *n.* The guardian archangel of the Jews in the Old Testament. [Heb. *Mīkā′ēl.*]

Mich·ael·mas (mĭk′əl-məs) *n.* A church festival celebrated on September 29 in honor of the archangel Michael. [ME *mychelmesse* < OE *Michaeles mæsse,* Michael's mass.]

Michaelmas daisy *n.* Any of several hybrid asters derived primarily from North American species such as the New England aster and the New York aster.

Mi·che·as (mī-kē′əs) *n.* Variant of **Micah.**

mick *n. Offensive Slang.* An Irishman. [Prob. < *Mick,* nickname for *Michael.*]

Mick·ey Finn (mĭk′ē fĭn′) *n. Slang.* An alcoholic beverage that is surreptitiously doctored to induce diarrhea or to stupefy, render unconscious, or otherwise incapacitate its imbiber. [Orig. unknown.]

mick·le (mĭk′əl) *Scot.* —*adj.* Great. —*adv.* Greatly. [ME *mikell* < OE *micel* and ON *mikill.*]

Mic·mac (mĭk′măk′) *n., pl.* **Micmac** or **-macs. 1. a.** A tribe of North American Indians formerly inhabiting the areas that are now Nova Scotia and New Brunswick. **b.** A member of the Micmac. **2.** The Algonquian language of the Micmac. [Micmac *miigemuaĝ.*]

micr– *pref.* Variant of **micro-.**

mi·cra (mī′krə) *n.* A plural of **micron.**

micro– or **micr–** *pref.* **1. a.** Small: *microcircuit.* **b.** Abnormally small: *microcephaly.* **c.** Requiring or involving microscopy: *microsurgery.* **2.** One-millionth (10^{-6}): *microcalorie.* [ME < Lat. < Gk. *mikro-* < *mikros,* small.]

mi·cro·a·nal·y·sis (mī′krō-ə-năl′ĭ-sĭs) *n.* The chemical analysis of quantities weighing one milligram or less. —**mi′cro·an′a·lyst** (-ăn′ə-lĭst) *n.* —**mi′cro·an′a·lyt′ic** (-ăn′ə-lĭt′ĭk), **mi′cro·an′a·lyt′i·cal** *adj.*

mi·cro·a·nat·o·my (mī′krō-ə-năt′ə-mē) *n.* Histology. —**mi′cro·an′a·tom′i·cal** (-ăn′ə-tŏm′ĭ-kəl) *adj.*

mi·crobe (mī′krōb′) *n.* A minute life form; microorganism, esp. one that causes disease. Not in technical use. [MICRO- + Gk. *bios,* life.] —**mi·cro′bi·al** (mī-krō′bē-əl), **mi·cro′bic** (-krō′bĭk) *adj.*

mi·cro·bi·cide (mī-krō′bĭ-sīd′) *n.* An agent that kills microbes. —**mi·cro′bi·cid′al** (-sīd′l) *adj.*

mi·cro·bi·ol·o·gy (mī′krō-bī-ŏl′ə-jē) *n.* The science that deals with microorganisms and esp. with their effects on other forms of life. —**mi′cro·bi′o·log′i·cal** (-bī′ə-lŏj′ĭ-kəl), **mi′cro·bi′o·log′ic** *adj.* —**mi′cro·bi′o·log′i·cal·ly** *adv.* —**mi′cro·bi·ol′o·gist** *n.*

mi·cro·bus (mī′krō-bŭs′) *n.* A station wagon in the shape of a small motorbus.

mi·cro·ceph·a·ly (mī′krō-sĕf′ə-lē) *n.* Abnormal smallness of the head, often associated with pathological mental conditions. —**mi′cro·ce·phal′ic** (-sə-făl′ĭk) *n.* & *adj.* —**mi′cro·ceph′a·lous** (-sĕf′ə-ləs) *adj.*

mi·cro·chem·is·try (mī′krō-kĕm′ĭ-strē) *n.* Chemistry that deals with minute quantities of materials weighing one milligram or less. —**mi′cro·chem′i·cal** (-ĭ-kəl) *adj.* —**mi′cro·chem′ist** *n.*

mi·cro·cir·cuit (mī′krō-sûr′kĭt) *n.* An electric circuit consisting of miniaturized components. —**mi′cro·cir′cuit·ry** (-kĭ-trē) *n.*

mi·cro·cli·mate (mī′krō-klī′mĭt) *n.* The climate of a specific place within an area contrasted with the climate of the area as a whole. —**mi′cro·cli·mat′ic** (-măt′ĭk) *adj.* —**mi′cro·cli′ma·to·log′ic** (-mə-tə-lŏj′ĭk), **mi′cro·cli′ma·to·log′i·cal** *adj.* —**mi′cro·cli′ma·tol′o·gy** (-mə-tŏl′ə-jē) *n.*

mi·cro·cline (mī′krō-klīn′) *n.* A mineral of the feldspar group, chiefly $KAlSi_3O_8$, used in making pottery. [G. *Mikroklin* : Gk. *mikros,* small + Gk. *klinein,* to lean.]

mi·cro·coc·cus (mī′krō-kŏk′əs) *n., pl.* **-coc·ci** (-kŏk′sī′, -kŏk′ī′). A spherical bacterium of several species of the genus *Micrococcus,* found in irregular clusters. [NLat. *Micrococcus,* genus name : MICRO- + *coccus,* coccus.] —**mi′cro·coc′cal** (-kŏk′əl) *adj.*

mi·cro·com·put·er (mī′krō-kəm-pyōō′tər) *n.* A very small computer built around a microprocessor.

mi·cro·cop·y (mī′krō-kŏp′ē) *n.* A greatly reduced photographic copy, usually reproduced by projection.

mi·cro·cosm (mī′krə-kŏz′əm) *n.* A diminutive, representative system more or less analogous to a larger system in constitution, configuration, or development: *The town meeting is a microcosm of American democracy.* [ME *microcosme* < Med. Lat. *microscosmus* < Gk. *mikros kosmos,* small world.] —**mi′cro·cos′mic** (-kŏz′mĭk), **mi′cro·cos′mi·cal** (-mĭ-kəl) *adj.* —**mi′cro·cos′mi·cal·ly** *adv.*

mi·cro·crys·tal·line (mī′krō-krĭs′tə-lĭn) *adj.* Having a crystalline structure that is visible only under the microscope. —**mi′cro·crys′tal** *n.*

mi·cro·cyte (mī′krə-sīt′) *n.* An abnormally small red blood cell, less than five microns in diameter. [MICRO- + (ERYTHRO)CYTE.] —**mi′cro·cyt′ic** (-sĭt′ĭk) *adj.*

mi·cro·e·lec·trode (mī′krō-ĭ-lĕk′trōd′) *n.* A very small electrode that is often used in the study of the electrical characteristics of living cells and tissues.

mi·cro·e·lec·tron·ics (mī′krō-ĭ-lĕk-trŏn′ĭks) *n.* (*used with a sing. verb*). The branch of electronics that deals with components of miniature size. —**mi′cro·e·lec·tron′ic** *adj.*

mi·cro·en·vi·ron·ment (mī′krō-ĕn-vī′rən-mənt) *n.* Microhabitat.

mi·cro·fiche (mī′krō-fēsh′) *n., pl.* **microfiche** or **-fich·es.** A sheet of microfilm capable of accommodating and preserving a considerable number of pages, as of printed text, in reduced form. [Fr. : *micro-,* small (< Gk. *mikros*) + *fiche,* card < OFr., peg < *fichier,* to drive in < Lat. *figere.*]

mi·cro·fi·lar·i·a (mī′krə-fə-lâr′ē-ə) *n.* A slender larval filaria. —**mi′cro·fi·lar′i·al** (-ē-əl) *adj.*

mi·cro·film (mī′krə-fĭlm′) *n.* **1.** A film upon which printed materials are photographed greatly reduced in size. **2.** A reproduction on microfilm. —*tr.v.* **-filmed, -film·ing, -films.** To reproduce (documents, for example) on microfilm.

mi·cro·form (mī′krə-fôrm′) *n.* An arrangement of images reduced in size, as on microfilm.

mi·cro·ga·mete (mī′krō-gə-mēt′, -găm′ēt′) *n.* The smaller of a pair of conjugating gametes, the male gamete.

mi·cro·ga·me·to·cyte (mī′krō-gə-mē′tə-sīt′) *n.* A gametocyte that gives rise to microgametes.

mi·crog·ra·phy (mī-krŏg′rə-fē) *n.* The representation, study, or description of microscopic objects. —**mi′cro·graph′ic** (mī′krə-grăf′ĭk) *adj.*

mi·cro·groove (mī′krō-grōōv′) *n.* A long-playing phonograph record. [Orig. a trademark.]

mi·cro·hab·i·tat (mī′krō-hăb′ĭ-tăt′) *n.* The smallest unit of a habitat, as a clump of grass or a space between rocks.

mi·cro·ma·nip·u·la·tor (mī′krō-mə-nĭp′yə-lā′tər) *n.* A device for manipulating minute instruments and needles under a microscope in order to perform microsurgery. —**mi′cro·ma·nip′u·la′tion** *n.*

mi·cro·mere (mī′krō-mîr′) *n.* A very small blastomere. [MICRO- + (BLASTO)MERE.]

mi·cro·me·te·or·ite (mī′krō-mē′tē-ə-rīt′) *n.* A micrometeoroid, esp. one found on the earth or the moon.

mi·cro·me·te·or·oid (mī′krō-mē′tē-ə-roid′) *n.* Any of numerous relatively small meteoroids distinguished by increasing occurrence as meteors with decreasing meteoric mass.

mi·cro·me·te·or·ol·o·gy (mī′krō-mē′tē-ə-rŏl′ə-jē) *n.* The study of meteorologic conditions in a small region, usually a shallow layer up to a few hundred feet above ground in which temperature and humidity extremes are found. —**mi′cro·me′te·or′o·log′i·cal** (-ôr′ə-lŏj′ĭ-kəl, -ər-ə-) *adj.* —**mi′cro·me′te·or·ol′o·gist** *n.*

mi·crom·e·ter (mī-krŏm′ĭ-tər) *n.* A device for measuring minute distances, esp. one based on the rotation of a finely threaded screw, as in relation to a microscope. [Fr. *micromètre* : *micro-,* small (< Gk. *mikros*) + *mètre,* meter < Gk. *metron,* measure.]

mi·crom·e·try (mī-krŏm′ĭ-trē) *n.* Measurement with a micrometer. —**mi′cro·met′ric** (mī′krō-mĕt′rĭk), **mi′cro·met′ri·cal** *adj.* —**mi′cro·met′ri·cal·ly** *adv.*

mi·cron also **mi·kron** (mī′krŏn′) *n., pl.* **-crons** or **-cra** (-krə) also **-krons** or **-kra.** A unit of length equal to one-millionth (10^{-6}) of a meter. [Gk., neuter of *mikros,* small.]

Mi·cro·ne·sian (mī′krə-nē′zhən, -shən) *adj.* Of or pertaining to Micronesia, its inhabitants, their languages, or their culture. —*n.* **1.** A native or inhabitant of Micronesia. **2.** A subfamily of the Austronesian language family that includes the languages of Micronesia.

mi·cron·ize (mī′krə-nīz′) *tr.v.* **-ized, -iz·ing, -iz·es.** To reduce to particles that are only a few microns in diameter.

mi·cro·nu·cle·us (mī′krō-nōō′klē-əs, -nyōō′-) *n., pl.* **-cle·i** (-klē-ī′) or **-cle·us·es.** The smaller nuclear mass in ciliated and suctorial protozoans as distinguished from the macronucleus in such animals.

mi·cro·nu·tri·ent (mī′krō-nōō′trē-ənt, -nyōō′-) *n.* A substance that in minute amounts is essential to life.

mi·cro·or·gan·ism (mī′krō-ôr′gə-nĭz′əm) *n.* An animal or plant of microscopic size, esp. a bacterium or a protozoan.

mi·cro·pa·le·on·tol·o·gy (mī′krō-pā′lē-ŏn-tŏl′ə-jē, -ən-) *n.* The scientific study of microscopic fossils. —**mi′cro·pa′le·on′to·log′ic** (-tə-lŏj′ĭk), **mi′cro·pa′le·on′to·log′i·cal** *adj.* —**mi′cro·pa′le·on·tol′o·gist** *n.*

mi·cro·phage (mī′krə-fāj′) *n.* A small phagocyte.

mi·cro·phone (mī′krə-fōn′) *n.* An instrument that converts acoustical waves into an electric current, usually fed into an amplifier, recorder, or broadcast transmitter. —**mi′cro·phon′ic** (-fŏn′ĭk) *adj.*

mi·cro·pho·to·graph (mī′krō-fō′tə-grăf′) *n.* **1.** A photograph requiring magnification for viewing. **2.** A photograph on microfilm. **3.** A photomicrograph. —**mi′cro·pho′to·graph′ic** (-grăf′ĭk) *adj.* —**mi′cro·pho·tog′ra·pher** (-fə-tŏg′rə-fər) *n.* —**mi′cro·pho·tog′ra·phy** (-rə-fē) *n.*

mi·cro·phys·ics (mī′krō-fĭz′ĭks) *n.* (*used with a sing. verb*).

micrometer

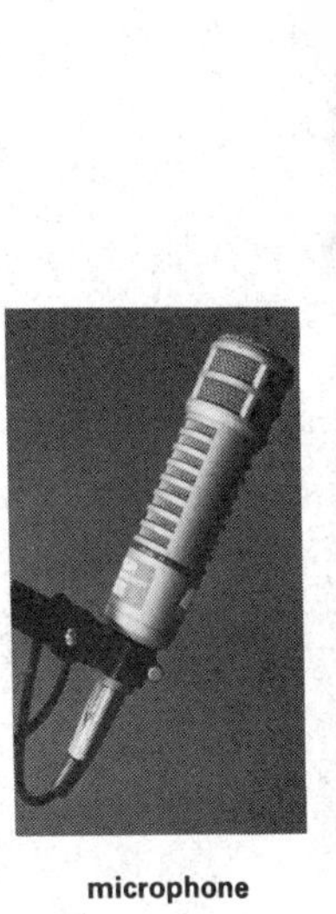

microphone

The physics of molecular, atomic, nuclear, and subnuclear systems. **—mi′cro·phys′i·cal** (-fĭz′ĭ-kəl) *adj.* **—mi′cro·phys′i·cal·ly** *adv.* **—mi′cro·phys′i·cist** (-fĭz′ĭ-sĭst) *n.*

mi·cro·phyte (mī′krə-fīt′) *n.* A plant of microscopic size. **—mi′cro·phyt′ic** (-fĭt′ĭk) *adj.*

mi·cro·print (mī′krə-prĭnt′) *n.* The printed or positive reproduction of a microphotograph.

mi·cro·proc·es·sor (mī′krō-prŏs′ĕs-ər) *n. Computer Sci.* A semiconductor central processing unit usually contained on a single integrated circuit chip.

mi·cro·pyle (mī′krə-pīl′) *n.* **1.** *Bot.* A minute opening in the ovule of a plant through which the pollen tube usually enters. **2.** *Zool.* A pore in the membrane of the ova of some animals through which the spermatozoon enters. [MICRO- + Gk. *pulē,* gate.]

mi·cro·scope (mī′krə-skōp′) *n.* An optical instrument that uses a combination of lenses to produce magnified images of small objects, esp. of objects too small to be seen by the unaided eye. [NLat. *microscopium* : MICRO- + *-scopium,* -scope.]

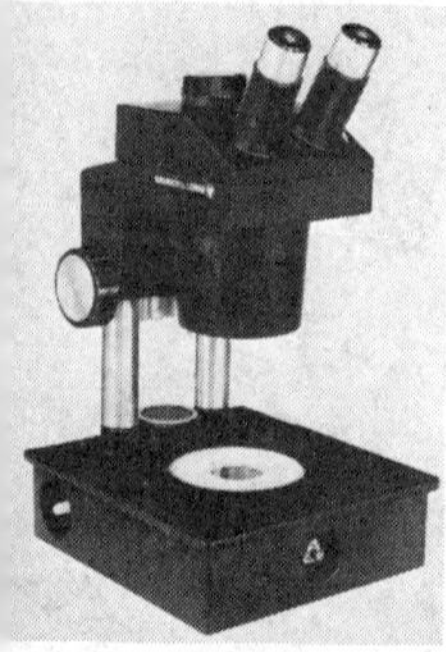

microscope

mi·cro·scop·ic (mī′krə-skŏp′ĭk) also **mi·cro·scop·i·cal** (-ĭ-kəl) *adj.* **1.** Too small to be seen by the unaided eye but large enough to be studied under a microscope. **2.** Exceedingly small; minute: *"The activities of men . . . were reduced to a microscopic scale"* (John Hersey). **3.** Characterized by or done with extreme attention to detail: *a microscopic investigation.* **4.** Of, pertaining to, or concerned with a microscope. **5.** Like or resembling a microscope in having the ability to observe very small objects. **—mi′cro·scop′i·cal·ly** *adv.*

Mi·cro·sco·pi·um (mī′krə-skō′pē-əm) *n.* A constellation in the Southern Hemisphere. [NLat., microscope.]

mi·cros·co·py (mī-krŏs′kə-pē) *n.* **1. a.** The study of microscopes. **b.** The use of microscopes. **2.** Investigation employing a microscope. **—mi·cros′co·pist** *n.*

mi·cro·seism (mī′krə-sī′zəm) *n.* A faint, recurrent tremor of the earth's crust. **—mi′cro·seis′mic** (-sīz′mĭk, -sīs′-) *adj.*

mi·cro·some (mī′krə-sōm′) *n.* A ribosome. [G. *Mikrosom* : Gk. *mikros,* small + Gk. *sōma,* body.] **—mi′cro·so′mi·al** (-sō′mē-əl), **mi′cro·so′mic** (-sō′mĭk) *adj.*

mi·cro·spo·ran·gi·um (mī′krō-spə-răn′jē-əm) *n., pl.* **-gi·a** (-jē-ə). A structure or receptacle in which microspores are formed. **—mi′cro·spo·ran′gi·ate** (-jē-ĭt) *adj.*

mi·cro·spore (mī′krə-spôr′, -spōr′) *n.* **1.** *Bot.* The smaller of two types of spores produced by heterosporous plants, such as ferns, giving rise to the male gametophyte. **2.** The smaller of two spores formed by Radiolaria and certain other protozoans. **—mi′cro·spo′ric, mi′cro·spo′rous** (mī′krə-spôr′əs, -spōr′-, mī-krŏs′pər-əs) *adj.*

mi·cro·spo·ro·cyte (mī′krə-spôr′ə-sīt′, -spōr′-) *n.* A cell that gives rise to microspores.

mi·cro·spo·ro·gen·e·sis (mī′krə-spôr′ə-jĕn′ĭ-sĭs, -spōr′-) *n.* The production or formation of microspores.

mi·cro·spo·ro·phyll (mī′krə-spôr′ə-fĭl′, -spōr′-) *n.* A structure that produces microsporangia.

mi·cro·state (mī′krō-stāt′) *n.* An independent country that is very small in area and population.

mi·cro·sur·ger·y (mī′krō-sûr′jə-rē) *n.* Surgery on minute living structures or cells by means of a micromanipulator. **—mi′cro·sur′gi·cal** (-jĭ-kəl) *adj.*

mi·cro·teach·ing (mī′krə-tē′chĭng) *n.* A method of practice teaching in which a videotape of a small segment of a student's classroom teaching is made and later evaluated.

mi·cro·tome (mī′krə-tōm′) *n.* An instrument used to cut tissue into thin sections for microscopic examination.

mi·crot·o·my (mī-krŏt′ə-mē) *n.* The preparation of specimens with a microtome. **—mi′cro·tom′ic** (mī′krə-tŏm′ĭk) *adj.*

mi·cro·tone (mī′krə-tōn′) *n. Mus.* An interval smaller than a half tone. **—mi′cro·ton′al** (-tō′nəl) *adj.* **—mi′cro·to·nal′i·ty** (-tō-năl′ĭ-tē) *n.* **—mi′cro·ton′al·ly** *adv.*

mi·cro·vil·lus (mī′krō-vĭl′əs) *n., pl.* **-vil·li** (-vĭl′ī′). Microscopic projections from the surface of a cell. **—mi′cro·vil′lar** *adj.*

mi·cro·wave (mī′krə-wāv′, -krō-) *n.* An electromagnetic wave having a wavelength in the approximate range from one millimeter to one meter, the region between infrared and short-wave radio wavelengths.

microwave oven *n.* An oven in which microwaves heat and cook the food.

mic·tu·rate (mĭk′chə-rāt′, mĭk′tə-) *intr.v.* **-rat·ed, -rat·ing, -rates.** To urinate. [< Lat. *micturire,* to want to urinate < *mingere,* to urinate.] **—mic′tu·ri′tion** (-rĭsh′ən) *n.*

mid[1] (mĭd) *adj.* **1.** Middle; central. **2.** Being the part in the middle or center: *in the mid Pacific.* **3.** Produced with the tongue in a position approximately intermediate between high and low. Used of vowel sounds. [ME < OE *midd.*]

mid[2] (mĭd) *prep.* Amid: *mid smoke and flame.*

mid– *pref.* Middle: *midsummer.* [< MID.]

Usage: Many compounds other than those entered here may be formed with *mid-*. In forming compounds, *mid-* is normally joined to the following word or element without a space or hyphen: *midpoint.* However, if the second element begins with a capital letter, it is always separated with a hyphen: *mid-May.* It is always acceptable to separate the elements with a hyphen to prevent possible confusion with another form, as for example, to distinguish *mid-den* (the middle of a den) from the word *midden.* Note that the adjective *mid*[1] above is a separate word, though, as with any adjective, it may be joined to another word with a hyphen when used as a unit modifier: *in the mid Pacific,* but *a mid-Pacific island.*

mid·air (mĭd′âr′) *n.* A point or region in the middle of the air; space: *floating in midair.*

Mi·das (mī′dəs) *n.* The fabled king of Phrygia to whom Dionysus gave the power of turning to gold all that he touched. [Lat. < Gk.]

mid·brain (mĭd′brān′) *n.* **1.** The mesencephalon. **2.** The parts of the brain that develop from the midbrain region.

mid·course (mĭd′kôrs′, -kōrs′) *n. Aerospace.* The part of a missile's flight between burnout and re-entry, during which corrective maneuvers are made.

mid·cult (mĭd′kŭlt′) *n.* A form of intellectual and artistic culture that has qualities of both high culture and mass culture without being either. [MID(DLEBROW) + CULT(URE).]

mid·day (mĭd′dā′) *n.* The middle of the day; noon. **—*modifier:*** *a midday snack.* [ME < OE *middæg* : *midd,* mid + *dæg,* day.]

mid·den (mĭd′n) *n.* **1.** A dunghill or refuse heap, esp. of a primitive habitation. **2.** A kitchen midden. [ME *myddung,* prob. of ON orig.]

mid·dle (mĭd′l) *adj.* **1.** Equally distant from extremes or limits; central: *the middle point on a line.* **2.** Being at neither one extreme nor the other; intermediate. **3. a.** Intervening between an earlier and a later period of time; part of a sequence or series: *the middle years.* **b. Middle.** *Geol.* Designating a division between an earlier and a later division: *the Middle Paleozoic.* **4. Middle.** Designating a stage in the development of a language or literature between earlier and later stages: *Middle English.* **5.** *Logic.* Designating a term that appears in both premises of a syllogism but not in the conclusion. **6.** *Gram.* Of a verb form or voice in which the subject both performs and is affected by the action specified. *—n.* **1.** An area or point equidistant between extremes; center: *the middle of a circle.* **2.** Something intermediate between extremes; mean. **3.** The interior portion: *the middle of the chain.* **4.** The middle part of the human body; waist. **5.** *Logic.* A middle term. *—tr.v.* **-dled, -dling, -dles. 1.** To place in the middle. **2.** *Naut.* To fold in the middle: *middle the sail.* [ME *middel* < OE.]

middle age *n.* The time of human life between youth and old age, usually reckoned as the years between 40 and 60.

mid·dle-aged (mĭd′l-ājd′) *adj.* Of or pertaining to middle age.

Middle Ages *pl.n.* The period in European history between antiquity and the Renaissance, often dated from A.D. 476 to A.D. 1453.

Middle America *n.* **1.** That part of the U.S. middle class thought of as being average in income and education and conservative in values and attitudes. **2.** The American heartland thought of as being made up of small towns, small cities, and suburbs. **—Middle American** *n.*

mid·dle·brow (mĭd′l-brou′) *n. Informal.* One who is somewhat cultured. **—mid′dle·brow′** *adj.*

middle C *n. Mus.* The musical tone represented by the first ledger line below the treble clef or the first ledger line above the bass clef.

middle class *n.* The members of society occupying a socioeconomic position intermediate between the laboring classes and the wealthy.

mid·dle-class (mĭd′l-klăs′) *adj.* Of, pertaining to, or characteristic of the middle class.

middle distance *n.* **1.** The area between the foreground and background in a painting, drawing, or photograph. **2.** *Sports.* A division of competition in racing with events usually ranging from 400 meters to 1,500 meters, or 440 yards to 1 mile.

Middle Dutch *n.* The Dutch language from the middle of the 12th through the 15th century.

middle ear *n.* The space between the tympanic membrane and the internal ear, containing the auditory ossicles that convey vibrations to the auditory tube.

Middle English *n.* The English language from about 1100 to 1500.

middle ground *n.* **1.** Middle distance (sense 1). **2.** A point of view midway between extremes.

Middle High German *n.* High German from the 11th through the 15th century.

Middle Irish *n.* Irish from the 10th through the 13th century.

Middle Low German *n.* Low German from the middle of the 13th through the 15th century.

mid·dle·man (mĭd′l-măn′) *n.* **1.** A trader who buys from producers and sells to retailers or consumers. **2.** An intermediary; go-between.

middle management *n.* A group of persons occupying an intermediate managerial position below the level of upper executives. **—middle manager** *n.*

mid·dle·most (mĭd′l-mōst′) *adj.* Midmost. [ME *middelmast* : *middel,* middle + *-mast,* -most.]

mid·dle-of-the-road (mĭd′l-əv-thə-rōd′) *adj.* **1.** Pursuing a course of action midway between extremes, esp. following a course in politics that is neither liberal nor conservative.

2. Of, relating to, or being a type of popular music that appeals to a wide audience.
middle school *n.* A school that usually includes grades five through eight.
middle term *n.* The term in a syllogism presented in both premises but not appearing in the conclusion.
Mid·dle·town (mĭd'l-toun') *n.* A hypothetical community regarded as representative of Middle America.
mid·dle·weight (mĭd'l-wāt') *n.* A boxer or wrestler weighing between 147 and 160 pounds.
Middle Welsh *n.* Welsh from the 12th through the 15th century.
mid·dling (mĭd'lĭng, -lĭn) *adj.* **1.** Of medium size, position, or quality. **2.** Mediocre. —*n.* **1.** Often **middlings.** *Chiefly Southeastern U.S.* Pork or bacon cut from between the ham and shoulder of a pig. **2.** Any of various products that are intermediate in quality, size, price, or grade. **3. middlings** *(used with a sing. or pl. verb).* Coarsely ground wheat mixed with bran. —*adv. Informal.* Fairly; moderately. [ME *mydlyn* : *mid,* mid + *-ling,* small.] **—mid'dling·ly** *adv.*
mid·dy (mĭd'ē) *n., pl.* **-dies. 1.** *Informal.* A midshipman. **2.** A middy blouse.
middy blouse *n.* A woman's or child's loose blouse with a sailor collar.
mid·field (mĭd'fēld') *n.* **1.** The section of a playing field midway between goals. **2.** Players on a team whose usual position is in the midfield. **—mid'field'er** *n.*
Mid·gard (mĭd'gärd') *n. Myth.* The part of the world inhabited by men, imagined as a fortress encircled by a huge serpent, built by the Norse gods around the middle region of the universe. [ON *Miðgarðr.*]
midge (mĭj) *n.* **1.** Any of various gnatlike flies of the family Chironomidae, found worldwide. **2.** A small person. [ME *migge* < OE *mycg.*]
midg·et (mĭj'ĭt) *n.* **1.** An extremely small person who is otherwise normally proportioned. **2.** A small or miniature version of something. **3.** A class of small objects, such as a class of very small sailboats or racing automobiles. —*adj.* **1.** Miniature; diminutive. **2.** Belonging to a type or class much smaller than what is considered standard: *a midget automobile.* [Dim. of MIDGE.]
mid·gut (mĭd'gŭt') *n.* The middle section of the digestive tract in the vertebrate embryo from which the ileum and the jejunum develop.
mid·i (mĭd'ē) *n.* A skirt or coat of mid-calf length. [< MIDDLE.]
Mid·i·an·ite (mĭd'ē-ə-nīt') *n.* One of the ancient Arabian tribe of Midian. **—Mid'i·an·ite'** *adj.*
mid·i·ron (mĭd'ī'ərn) *n.* An iron golf club that has more loft than a driver and less than a mashie, used for medium fairway shots and long approach shots.
mid·land (mĭd'lənd) *n.* The middle or interior part of a specific country or region. —*adj.* Of or in a midland.
mid·line (mĭd'līn') *n.* A medial line, esp. the medial line or plane of the body.
mid·most (mĭd'mōst') *adj.* **1.** Situated in the exact middle; middlemost. **2.** Situated nearest the middle. —*adv.* In the middle. [ME *midmest* < OE : *midd,* mid + *-mest,* -most.]
mid·night (mĭd'nīt') *n.* **1.** The middle of the night; specifically, 12 o'clock at night. **2. a.** Intense darkness or gloom. **b.** A period of darkness and gloom. **—*modifier:*** *a midnight swim; a midnight meeting; fell into a midnight mood from which nobody could rouse her.* **—*idiom.* burn the midnight oil.** To work or study very late at night. [ME < OE *midniht* : *midd,* mid + *niht,* night.]
midnight sun *n.* The sun as seen at midnight during the summer within the Arctic or Antarctic Circle.
mid·point (mĭd'point') *n.* **1.** The point of a line segment or curvilinear arc that divides it into two parts of the same length. **2.** A position midway between two extremes.
Mid·rash (mĭd'răsh') *n., pl.* **Mid·rash·im** (mĭd-rä'shĭm). Any of a group of Jewish commentaries on the Hebrew Scriptures written between A.D. 400 and 1200. [Heb. *midhrāsh,* commentary.]
mid·rib (mĭd'rĭb') *n.* The central or principal vein of a leaf.
mid·riff (mĭd'rĭf') *n.* **1.** The diaphragm (sense 1). **2.** The middle outer portion of the front of the human body extending roughly from just below the breast to the waistline. [ME *midrif* < OE *midhrif* : *midd,* mid + *hrif,* belly.] **—mid'riff'** *adj.*
mid·sec·tion (mĭd'sĕk'shən) *n.* A middle section, esp. the midriff of the human body.
mid·ship (mĭd'shĭp') *adj.* Of, pertaining to, or located in the middle of a ship.
mid·ship·man (mĭd'shĭp'mən, mĭd-shĭp'mən) *n.* **1.** A student training to be a commissioned naval officer, esp. a student at a naval academy. **2.** Any of various fishes of the genus *Porichthys,* having several rows of light-producing organs along their bodies.
mid·ships (mĭd'shĭps') *adv.* **1.** Amidships. **2.** In the center position. Used of the helm. [Short for AMIDSHIPS.]
midst (mĭdst, mĭtst) *n.* **1.** The middle position or part; center: *in the midst of the desert.* **2.** A position of proximity to other individuals or members: *a stranger in our midst.* **3.** The condition of being surrounded by or beset by something: *in the midst of all of our problems.* **4.** A time period about the middle of a continuing condition or act: *in the midst of the war.* —*prep.* Among. [ME *middest,* alteration of *middes* < *midde,* in the middle < OE, middle.]
mid·stream (mĭd'strēm') *n.* **1.** The middle part of a stream. **2.** The middle part of a course that is neither at the beginning nor at the end: *the midstream of life.*
mid·sum·mer (mĭd'sŭm'ər) *n.* **1.** The middle of the summer. **2.** The summer solstice, about June 21. **—*modifier:*** *a midsummer night.*
Midsummer Day *n.* The feast of the birth of John the Baptist, celebrated June 24.
mid·term (mĭd'tûrm') *n.* **1.** The middle of an academic term or a political term of office. **2. a.** An examination given at the middle of a school term. **b. midterms.** A series of such examinations.
mid·town (mĭd'toun') *n.* A central portion of a city, located between uptown and downtown.
mid-Vic·to·ri·an (mĭd'vĭk-tôr'ē-ən, -tōr'-) *adj.* Pertaining to, occurring in, or characteristic of the middle period of the reign of Queen Victoria in Great Britain (1837–1901), a period known for rigid social standards. —*n.* **1.** A person living in the mid-Victorian period. **2.** A person having mid-Victorian ideas.
mid·way (mĭd'wā') *n.* **1.** The area of a fair, carnival, circus, or exposition where side shows and other amusements are located. **2.** *Obs.* **a.** The middle of a way or distance. **b.** A middle way or course of action or thought. —*adv.* In the middle of a way or distance; halfway. **—mid'way'** *adj.*
mid·week (mĭd'wēk') *n.* The middle of the week. **—*modifier:*** *a midweek appointment with the dentist.* **—mid'week'ly** *adj. & adv.*
mid·wife (mĭd'wīf') *n.* **1.** A woman who assists women in childbirth. **2.** One who assists in bringing something about. —*tr.v.* **-wifed** or **-wived** (-wīvd'), **-wif·ing** or **-wiv·ing** (-wī'vĭng), **-wifes** or **-wives** (-wīvz'). To assist in bringing forth or about. [ME *midwif* : *mid,* with (< OE) + *wif,* woman < OE *wīf.*]
mid·wife·ry (mĭd'wīf'rē, -wĭ'fə-rē, mĭd-wĭf'ə-rē) *n.* The techniques and practice of a midwife.
mid·win·ter (mĭd'wĭn'tər) *n.* **1.** The middle of the winter. **2.** The period of the winter solstice, about December 22. **—*modifier:*** *a midwinter day.*
mid·year (mĭd'yîr') *n.* **1.** The middle of the calendar or academic year. **2. a.** An examination given in the middle of the school year. **b. midyears.** A series of such examinations.
mien (mēn) *n.* **1.** Bearing or manner; expression: *a person of noble mien.* **2.** An appearance or aspect. [< DEMEAN.]
miff (mĭf) *n.* **1.** A petulant, bad-tempered mood; huff. **2.** A petty quarrel or argument; tiff. —*tr.v.* **miffed, miff·ing, miffs.** To cause to become offended or annoyed. [Orig. unknown.]
mif·fy (mĭf'ē) *adj.* **-fi·er, -fi·est. 1.** *Informal.* Easily offended; oversensitive. **2.** *Bot.* Difficult to raise except under perfect conditions. Used of certain plants. **—mif'fi·ness** *n.*
might¹ (mīt) *n.* **1.** Tremendous power, force, or influence: *the might of the allied armies.* **2.** Physical or bodily strength. **3.** Strength or ability to do something: *tried with all her might.* [ME < OE *miht.*]
might² (mīt) *aux.v.* **1. a.** Used to indicate a condition or state contrary to fact: *She might help if she knew the truth.* **b.** Used to indicate a possibility or probability that is weaker than *may*: *We might discover a pot of gold at the end of the rainbow.* **2.** Used to express possibility or probability or permission in the past. **3.** Used to express a higher degree of deference or politeness than *may*: *Might I express my opinion?* [ME < OE *meahte,* 1st and 3rd person p. indicative of *magan,* to be able.]

Usage: In many Southern varieties of English, *might* is used in the "double modal" construction with *could,* as in *We might could park over there.* Less frequently, one hears *may can* and *might should.* These constructions are not familiar to the majority of American speakers and are best avoided in formal writing.

might·i·ly (mīt'l-ē) *adv.* **1.** In a mighty manner; powerfully. **2.** To a great degree; greatly.
might·y (mī'tē) *adj.* **-i·er, -i·est. 1.** Having or showing great power, skill, strength, or force: *a mighty orator; a mighty blow.* **2.** Imposing or awesome in size, degree, or extent: *a mighty stone fortress.* —*adv. Informal.* To a great degree; extremely. **—might'i·ness** *n.*
mi·gnon·ette (mĭn'yə-nĕt') *n.* A plant, *Reseda odorata,* native to the Mediterranean region and widely cultivated for its clusters of fragrant but inconspicuous greenish flowers. [Fr., fem. of obs. *mignonnet,* dim. of *mignon,* dainty.]
mi·graine (mī'grān') *n.* Severe, recurrent headache, usually affecting only one side of the head, characterized by sharp pain and often accompanied by nausea. [ME < OFr. < LLat. *hemicrania,* pain in one side of the head < Gk. *hēmikrania* : *hemi-,* half + *kranion,* head.] **—mi'grain·ous** *adj.*
mi·grant (mī'grənt) *n.* **1.** One that moves from one region to another by chance, instinct, or plan. **2.** An itinerant worker who travels from one area to another in search of work. —*adj.* Migratory. [Lat. *migrans, migrant-,* pr.part. of *migrare,* to migrate.]
mi·grate (mī'grāt') *intr.v.* **-grat·ed, -grat·ing, -grates. 1.** To move from one country or region and settle in another. **2.** To change location periodically, esp. to move seasonally

midget

migrant

from one region to another. [Lat. *migrare, migrat-.*] **—mi'gra'tor** *n.*

Usage: *Migrate* is used with reference to both the place of departure and the destination and can be followed by *from* or *to.* It is said of persons, animals, and birds and sometimes implies a lack of permanent settlement, especially as a result of seasonal or periodic movement. *Emigrate* pertains to a single move by persons, and implies permanence. It has specific reference to the place of departure and emphasizes movement from that place. If the place is mentioned, the preposition is *from: Since many people have emigrated from France, the population is declining. Immigrate* also pertains to a single move by persons and likewise implies permanence. But it refers to destination, emphasizes movement there, and is followed by *to: Since many people have immigrated to the United States, its population is increasing.*

mi·gra·tion (mī-grā′shən) *n.* **1.** The action or an act of migrating. **2.** A group migrating together. **3.** *Chem.* **a.** The movement of one or more atoms from one position in a molecule to another. **b.** The movement of ions toward one electrode or the other during electrolysis. **—mi·gra′tion·al** *adj.*

mi·gra·to·ry (mī′grə-tôr′ē, -tōr′ē) *adj.* **1.** Characterized by migration; migrating periodically: *migratory birds.* **2.** Of or relating to a migration. **3.** Roving; nomadic.

mi·ka·do (mĭ-kä′dō) *n., pl.* **-dos.** An emperor of Japan. [J. : *mi,* honorific prefix + *kado,* gate.]

mike (mīk) *n. Informal.* A microphone.

mi·kron (mī′krŏn′) *n.* Variant of **micron.**

mil[1] (mĭl) *n.* **1.** A unit of length equal to one-thousandth (10^{-3}) of an inch, or .0254 millimeter, used chiefly to specify the diameter of wire. **2.** A milliliter, or one cubic centimeter. **3.** A unit of angular measurement used in artillery and equal to $^1/_{6400}$ of a complete revolution. [< Lat. *mille,* thousand.]

mil[2] (mĭl) *n.* See table at **currency.** [< Lat. *mille,* thousand.]

mi·la·dy (mĭ-lā′dē) *n.* **1.** An English noblewoman or gentlewoman. Used as a title of respect. **2.** A chic or fashionable woman. [Fr. < E. *my lady.*]

mil·age (mī′lĭj) *n.* Variant of **mileage.**

milch (mĭlch) *adj.* Giving milk: *a milch cow.* [ME *milche* < OE *-milce.*]

mil·chig (mĭl′KHĭk) *adj.* Derived from or made of milk or dairy products. [Yiddish < *milch,* milk < MHG < OHG *miluh.*]

mild (mīld) *adj.* **-er, -est. 1.** Gentle or kind in disposition, manners, or behavior: *a strong but mild man.* **2. a.** Moderate in type, degree, effect, or force: *a mild pipe tobacco; a mild sedative.* **b.** Not extreme: *a mild winter storm.* **3.** Not very severe: *a mild fever.* **4.** Rather easily molded, shaped, or worked; malleable: *mild steel.* [ME < OE *milde.*] **—mild′ly** *adv.* **—mild′ness** *n.*

mil·dew (mĭl′do͞o′, -dyo͞o′) *n.* **1.** A plant disease in which a fungus forms a superficial growth on the plant. **2.** A superficial coating or discoloring of organic materials, such as paint, paper, cloth, or leather, caused by fungi, esp. under damp conditions. *—tr. & intr.v.* **-dewed, -dew·ing, -dews.** To affect or become affected with mildew. [ME < OE *mildēaw.*] **—mil′dew′y** *adj.*

mile (mīl) *n.* **1.** A unit of length equal to 5,280 feet, 1,760 yards, or 1,609.34 meters, used in the United States and other English-speaking countries. **2.** A nautical mile. **3.** An air mile. **4.** A race of a mile. **5.** A relatively great distance. [ME < OE *mīl* < Lat. *milia,* miles, pl. of *mille (passuum),* thousand (paces).]

mile·age also **mil·age** (mī′lĭj) *n.* **1.** Total length, extent, or distance measured or expressed in miles. **2.** Total miles covered or traveled in a given time. **3.** The amount of service, use, or wear estimated by miles used or traveled: *This tire will give very good mileage.* **4.** The number of miles traveled by a motor vehicle on a certain quantity of fuel. **5.** An allowance for travel expenses established at a specified rate per mile. **6.** Expense per mile, as for the use of a car. **7.** *Informal.* The amount of service something has yielded or may yield in the future; usefulness.

mile·post (mīl′pōst′) *n.* A post set up to indicate distance in miles, as along a highway.

mil·er (mī′lər) *n.* One trained to race a mile.

mi·les glo·ri·o·sus (mē′lās glôr′ē-ō′səs, glōr′-) *n., pl.* **mi·li·tes glo·ri·o·si** (mē′lĭ-tās glôr′ē-ō′sē, glōr′-). A bragging, swaggering soldier, esp. as a stock character in comedy. [Lat., after *Miles Gloriosus,* a comedy by Plautus.]

milestone

Mi·le·sian[1] (mī-lē′zhən, -shən) *adj.* Of or pertaining to Miletus or its inhabitants. *—n.* A native or inhabitant of Miletus.

Mi·le·sian[2] (mī-lē′zhən, -shən) *n.* A native of Ireland; Irishman. *—adj.* Of or pertaining to Ireland or its people; Irish. [After *Milesius,* legendary ancestor of the Irish people.]

mile·stone (mīl′stōn′) *n.* **1.** A stone marker set up on a roadside to indicate the distance in miles from a given point. **2.** An important event in one's history or career; turning point.

mil·foil (mĭl′foil′) *n.* **1.** The yarrow. **2.** Water milfoil. [ME < OFr. < Lat. *millefolium* : *mille,* thousand + *folium,* leaf.]

mil·i·a (mĭl′ē-ə) *n.* Plural of **milium.**

mil·i·ar·i·a (mĭl′ē-âr′ē-ə) *n.* A skin disease caused by an inflammation of the sweat glands and characterized by blebs, redness, and a prickling or burning sensation. [NLat. *(febris) miliaria,* miliary (fever).] **—mil′i·ar′i·al** *adj.*

mil·i·ar·y (mĭl′ē-ĕr′ē) *adj.* **1.** Designating a lesion or growth about one-eighth inch in diameter. **2.** Designating a disease marked by small skin lesions that look like millet seeds. [Lat. *miliarius,* of millet < *milium,* millet.]

miliary tuberculosis *n.* An acute form of tuberculosis characterized by very small tubercles in various body organs, caused by the spread of tubercle bacilli through the blood stream.

mi·lieu (mēl-yœ′) *n.* Environment; surroundings. [Fr. < OFr., center : *mi,* middle (< Lat. *medius*) + *lieu,* place < Lat. *locus.*]

mil·i·tant (mĭl′ĭ-tənt) *adj.* **1.** Fighting or warring. **2.** Having a combative character; aggressive, esp. in the service of a cause: *a militant political activist.* *—n.* A militant person. [ME < OFr. < Lat. *militans,* pr.part. of *militare,* to serve as a soldier < *miles,* soldier.] **—mil′i·tan·cy** *n.* **—mil′i·tant·ly** *adv.*

mil·i·ta·rism (mĭl′ĭ-tə-rĭz′əm) *n.* **1.** The glorification of the ideals of a professional military class. **2.** Predominance of the military in the administration or policy of the state. **3.** A policy in which military preparedness is of primary importance to the state. **—mil′i·ta·rist** *n.* **—mil′i·ta·ris′tic** (-rĭs′tĭk) *adj.* **—mil′i·ta·ris′ti·cal·ly** *adv.*

mil·i·ta·rize (mĭl′ĭ-tə-rīz′) *tr.v.* **-rized, -riz·ing, -riz·es. 1.** To equip or train for war. **2.** To imbue with militarism. **3.** To adopt for use by or in the military. **—mil′i·ta·ri·za′tion** *n.*

mil·i·tar·y (mĭl′ĭ-tĕr′ē) *adj.* **1.** Of, pertaining to, or characteristic of soldiers or the armed forces: *a military bearing; military attire.* **2.** Performed or supported by the armed forces. **3.** Of or pertaining to war: *military operations.* *—n.* Armed forces: *ruled by the military.* [Fr. *militaire* < Lat. *militaris* < *miles,* soldier.] **—mil′i·tar′i·ly** (-târ′ə-lē) *adv.*

military attaché *n.* An officer of the armed forces who is assigned to the official staff of an ambassador, consul general, or minister to a foreign country.

military intelligence *n.* **1.** Information important for its military value. **2.** The branch of the military that procures, analyzes, and uses information of tactical and strategic value.

military law *n.* Regulations and rules pertaining to the discipline and administration of the armed forces.

military police *n.* A branch of an army assigned to perform police duties. **—military policeman** *n.*

military science *n.* The tactical principles of warfare.

mil·i·tate (mĭl′ĭ-tāt′) *intr.v.* **-tat·ed, -tat·ing, -tates.** To have force or influence: *The facts available to us militate against this interpretation.* [Lat. *militare, militat-,* to serve as a soldier < *miles,* soldier.]

mi·li·tia (mə-lĭsh′ə) *n.* **1. a.** A citizen army as distinct from a body of professional soldiers. **b.** The armed citizenry as distinct from the regular army. **2.** A military force that is not part of a regular army and is subject to call for service in an emergency. **3.** The whole body of physically fit male civilians eligible by law for military service. [Lat., warfare < *miles,* soldier.]

mi·li·tia·man (mə-lĭsh′ə-mən) *n.* A member of a militia.

mil·i·um (mĭl′ē-əm) *n., pl.* **-i·a** (-ē-ə). A small, hard, white or yellowish mass just below the surface of the skin, caused by retention of the secretion of a sebaceous gland. [ME < Lat., millet.]

milk (mĭlk) *n.* **1. a.** A whitish liquid that is produced by the mammary glands of all mature female mammals after they have given birth and is used for feeding their young. **b.** The milk of cows, goats, or other animals, used as food by humans. **2.** A liquid similar to milk in appearance, as coconut milk, milkweed sap, or plant latex. **3.** Any of various medicinal emulsions. *—v.* **milked, milk·ing, milks.** *—tr.* **1.** To draw milk from the teat or udder of (a female mammal). **2.** To press out, drain off, or remove by or as if by milking: *milk a snake of its venom.* **3.** To draw out or extract something from as if by milking: *milk information from a person.* **4.** To use for one's own benefit; exploit: *corrupt officers milking the company's treasury.* *—intr.* **1.** To yield or supply milk. **2.** To draw milk from a female mammal. [ME < OE *milc.*] **—milk′er** *n.*

milk adder *n.* The milk snake.

milk-and-wa·ter (mĭlk′ən-wô′tər, -wŏt′ər) *adj.* Lacking forcefulness; insipid.

milk chocolate *n.* Sweetened chocolate made with milk and other ingredients.

milk fever *n.* **1.** A mild fever, usually occurring at the beginning of lactation, associated with infection following childbirth. **2.** A disease affecting dairy cows and occasionally sheep or goats, esp. soon after giving birth.

milk·fish (mĭlk′fĭsh′) *n., pl.* **milkfish** or **-fish·es.** A large fish, *Chanos chanos,* of the South Pacific and Indian oceans, widely used for food. [From its color.]

milk glass *n.* An opaque or translucent whitish glass.

milk leg *n.* A painful swelling of the leg occurring in women after childbirth as a result of clotting and inflammation of the femoral veins.

milk-liv·ered (mĭlk′lĭv′ərd) *adj.* Lacking courage; cowardly.

milk·maid (mĭlk′mād′) *n.* A girl or woman who milks cows.

milk·man (mĭlk′măn′) *n.* A man who sells or delivers milk to customers.

milk of magnesia *n.* A liquid suspension of magnesium hydroxide, $Mg(OH)_2$, used as an antacid and laxative.

milk punch *n.* A drink made of liquor, sugar, and milk.

milk run *n. Slang.* A military aerial mission that is either of short duration or lacking in danger. [From its being as uneventful and routine as the daily delivery of milk.]

milk shake *n.* A beverage made of milk, flavoring, and usually ice cream, shaken or whipped until foamy.

milk sickness *n.* **1.** An acute disease characterized by trembling, vomiting, and severe intestinal pain that is caused by eating the dairy products or flesh of cattle poisoned by eating white snakeroot. **2.** The trembles (sense 3.b.).

milk snake *n.* A nonvenomous grayish or tan snake, *Lampropeltis doliata* or *L. triangulum,* of the northeastern United States.

milk·sop (mĭlk′sŏp′) *n.* A male lacking in courage and manliness; weakling. **—milk′sop′py** *adj.*

milk sugar *n.* Lactose.

milk tooth *n.* Any of the temporary first teeth of a young mammal.

milk vetch *n.* Any of various plants of the genus *Astragalus,* having compound leaves and clusters of purple, white, or yellowish flowers. [From the belief that it increases the milk yield of goats.]

milk·weed (mĭlk′wēd′) *n.* **1.** A plant of the genus *Asclepias,* most of which have milky juice, esp. *A. syriaca,* the common milkweed of eastern North America, which has clusters of fragrant, dull-purple flowers and pointed pods that split open to release seeds with downy tufts. **2.** Any of various plants having milklike juice.

milkweed butterfly *n.* The monarch (sense 5).

milk·wort (mĭlk′wûrt′, -wôrt′) *n.* A plant of the genus *Polygala,* having variously colored, usually small flowers. [From the belief that it increases human lactation.]

milk·y (mĭl′kē) *adj.* **-i·er, -i·est. 1.** Like milk in color or consistency; opaque-white: *milky glass.* **2.** Filled with, consisting of, or yielding milk or a fluid resembling milk: *a milky kernel of corn.* **3.** Subdued. **—milk′i·ness** *n.*

milky disease *n.* A bacterial disease of Japanese beetle larvae and other scarabaeid grubs that eventually turns the blood of the grub a milky white color.

Milky Way *n.* The galaxy in which the solar system is located, visible as a luminous band in the night sky. [ME, transl. of Lat. *via lactea.*]

mill[1] (mĭl) *n.* **1.** A building equipped with machinery for grinding grain into flour or meal. **2.** A device or mechanism, such as rotating millstones, that grinds grain. **3.** A machine or device that reduces a solid or coarse substance into a pulp or minute grains by crushing, grinding, or pressing: *a pepper mill.* **4.** A machine that releases the juice of fruits and vegetables by pressing or grinding: *a cider mill.* **5. a.** A machine, as one for stamping coins, that produces something by the repetition of a simple process. **b.** Any of various machines for shaping, cutting, polishing, or dressing metal surfaces. **6. a.** A building or group of buildings equipped with machinery for processing raw materials into finished or industrial products: *a textile mill; a steel mill.* **b.** A building or collection of buildings that has machinery for manufacture; factory. **7.** A process, agency, or institution that operates in a routine way or turns out products in the manner of a factory: *The college was only a diploma mill.* **8.** A slow or laborious process: *took three years for the bill to get through the legislative mill.* **9.** A steel roller bearing a raised design, used for making a die or a printing plate by pressure. *—v.* **milled, mill·ing, mills.** *—tr.* **1.** To grind, pulverize, or break down into smaller particles in a mill. **2.** To transform or process mechanically in a mill. **3.** To shape, polish, dress, or finish in a mill or with a milling tool. **4. a.** To produce a ridge around the edge of (a coin). **b.** To groove or flute the rim of (a coin). **5.** To agitate or stir until foamy. *—intr.* **1.** To move around in churning confusion: *a crowd milling in the street.* **2.** *Slang.* To fight with the fists; box. **3.** To undergo milling. ***—idiom.* run of the mill.** Ordinary; commonplace. [ME *mille* < OE *mylen* < LLat. *molina* < *molinus,* of a mill < Lat. *mola,* millstone.]

mill[2] (mĭl) *n.* A monetary unit equal to 1/1000 of a U.S. dollar or 1/10 of a cent. [< Lat. *mille,* thousand.]

mill·board (mĭl′bôrd′, -bōrd′) *n.* A stiff, heavy paperboard used primarily for book covers. [Alteration of *milled board.*]

mill·dam (mĭl′dăm′) *n.* A dam constructed across a stream to raise the water level so the overflow will have sufficient power to turn a mill wheel.

mil·le·nar·i·an (mĭl′ə-nâr′ē-ən) *adj.* **1.** Of or pertaining to a thousand, esp. to a thousand years. **2.** Of, pertaining to, or believing in the doctrine of the millennium. *—n.* One who believes the millennium will occur. [LLat. *millenarius,* millenary.] **—mil′le·nar′i·an·ism** *n.*

mil·le·nar·y (mĭl′ə-nĕr′ē, mə-lĕn′ə-rē) *adj.* **1.** Of or pertaining to a thousand; millenarian. **2. a.** Of or relating to the doctrine of the millennium. **b.** Of or relating to the millenarians. *—n., pl.* **-ies. 1.** A sum or total of one thousand, esp. a thousand years. **2.** A millenarian. [LLat. *millenarius* < *milleni,* a thousand each < *mille,* thousand.]

mil·len·ni·um (mə-lĕn′ē-əm) *n., pl.* **-len·ni·ums** or **-len·ni·a** (-lĕn′ē-ə). **1.** A span of one thousand years. **2.** A thousand-year period of holiness during which Christ is to rule on earth. **3.** A hoped-for period of joy, serenity, prosperity, and justice. [NLat. : Lat. *mille,* thousand + Lat. *annus,* year.] **—mil·len′ni·al** *adj.* **—mil·len′ni·al·ism** *n.* **—mil·len′ni·al·ist** *n.* **—mil·len′ni·al·ly** *adv.*

mil·le·pede (mĭl′ə-pēd′) *n.* Variant of **millipede.**

mil·le·pore (mĭl′ə-pôr′, -pōr′) *n.* Any of various reef-building hydrocorals of the genus *Millepora,* of tropical marine waters, forming white or yellowish calcareous formations and resembling the true corals of the class Anthozoa. [NLat. *Millepora,* genus name : Lat. *mille,* thousand + *porus,* pore < Gk. *poros.*]

mill·er (mĭl′ər) *n.* **1.** One who works in, operates, or owns a mill, esp. a grain mill. **2.** A milling machine. **3.** Any of various moths having wings and bodies covered with a powdery substance.

mil·ler·ite (mĭl′ə-rīt′) *n.* A mineral of nickel sulfide, NiS, usually occurring in long slender crystals and used as a nickel ore. [G. *Millerit,* after William Hallowes *Miller* (1801–1880).]

miller's thumb *n.* Any of several freshwater fishes of the genus *Cottus,* found in Europe and North America and having spiny heads and fins. [ME *millarys thowmbe.*]

mil·les·i·mal (mə-lĕs′ə-məl) *adj.* **1.** Thousandth. **2.** Consisting of a thousandth. **3.** Pertaining to thousandths. *—n.* A thousandth. [Lat. *millesimus* < *mille,* thousand.] **—mil·les′i·mal·ly** *adv.*

mil·let (mĭl′ĭt) *n.* **1. a.** A grass, *Panicum miliaceum,* cultivated in Eurasia for its seed and in North America for hay. **b.** The white seeds of the millet used as a food grain in the Old World. **2.** Any of several grasses related or similar to the millet. [ME *milet* < OFr. < *mil,* millet < Lat. *milium.*]

mill finish *n.* A smooth surface made by machine on various papers.

milli– *pref.* One-thousandth (10^{-3}): *millisecond.* [Fr. < Lat. *milli-* < *mille,* thousand.]

mil·liard (mĭl′yərd, -yärd′, mĭl′ē-ärd′) *n. Chiefly Brit.* Billion (sense 1). [Fr. < OFr. *milliart* < *milion,* million.]

mil·li·ar·y (mĭl′ē-ĕr′ē) *adj.* Pertaining to or marking the distance of an ancient Roman mile, which equaled 1,000 paces. [Lat. *milliarius,* consisting of a thousand < *mille (passuum),* thousand (paces), mile.]

mil·lieme (mēl-yĕm′, mē-yĕm′) *n.* See table at **currency.** [Prob. < Fr. *millième,* thousandth < *mille,* thousand < OFr. < Lat.]

mil·li·li·ter (mĭl′ə-lē′tər) *n.* A unit of volume equal to one-thousandth of a liter, or 0.001 liquid quart or 0.0009 dry quart.

mil·li·me·ter (mĭl′ə-mē′tər) *n.* A unit of length equal to one-thousandth (10^{-3}) of a meter, or 0.0394 inch.

mil·li·me·tre (mĭl′ə-mē′tər) *n. Chiefly Brit.* Variant of **millimeter.**

mil·line (mĭl′līn′) *n.* **1.** A unit of advertising copy equal to one agate line one column wide printed in one million copies of a publication. **2.** The cost of a unit of advertising copy. [MIL(LION) + LINE.]

mil·li·ner (mĭl′ə-nər) *n.* A person who makes, trims, designs, or sells women's hats. [Alteration of obs. *Milaner,* native of Milan, Italy, from the importation of fashion accessories from Milan.]

mil·li·ner·y (mĭl′ə-nĕr′ē) *n.* **1.** Articles, esp. women's hats, sold by a milliner. **2.** The profession or business of a milliner.

mill·ing (mĭl′ĭng) *n.* **1.** The act or process of grinding, esp. grain into flour or meal. **2.** The operation of cutting, shaping, finishing, or working products manufactured in a mill. **3.** The ridges cut on the edges of coins. **4.** *Western U.S.* The process of halting a cattle stampede by turning the lead animals in a wide arc so that they form the center of a gradually tightening spiral.

mil·lion (mĭl′yən) *n., pl.* **million** or **-lions. 1.** The cardinal number equal to 1,000 × 1,000, or 10^6. **2.** A million monetary units, as dollars: *made a million in the stock market.* **3.** Often **millions.** An indefinitely large number: *millions of bicycles on the road.* **4.** The masses; the common people. [ME < OFr. *milion* < OItal. *milione,* aug. of *mille,* thousand < Lat.] **—mil′lion** *adj.*

mil·lion·aire (mĭl′yə-nâr′) *n.* A person whose wealth amounts to a million or more dollars or its equivalent in another currency. [Fr. *millionnaire* < *million,* million < OFr. *milion.* —see MILLION.]

mil·lionth (mĭl′yənth) *n.* **1.** The ordinal number that matches the number one million in a series. **2.** One of a million equal parts. **—mil′lionth** *adj. & adv.*

mil·li·pede or **mil·le·pede** (mĭl′ə-pēd′) *n.* A crawling, herbivorous arthropod of the class Diplopoda, found worldwide and having wormlike bodies with legs attached in double pairs to most body segments. [Lat. *millepeda,* a kind of insect : *mille,* thousand + *pes,* foot.]

mil·li·sec·ond (mĭl′ĭ-sĕk′ənd) *n.* One thousandth of a second.

mill·pond (mĭl′pŏnd′) *n.* A pond formed by a milldam.

mill·race (mĭl′rās′) *n.* **1.** The fast-moving stream of water that drives a mill wheel. **2.** The channel for the water that drives a mill wheel.

milkweed

mill[1]
Steel mill

millepore

mill·run (mĭl′rŭn′) *n.* **1.** A millrace. **2.** The output of a sawmill. **3. a.** A test of the mineral quality or content of a rock or an ore by the process of milling. **b.** The mineral yielded by this test.

mill-run (mĭl′rŭn′) *adj.* Being in the state in which a product leaves a mill; unsorted and uninspected: *mill-run fabric.*

mill·stone (mĭl′stōn′) *n.* **1.** One of a pair of cylindrical stones used in a mill for grinding grain. **2.** A heavy weight; burden.

mill·stream (mĭl′strēm′) *n.* The rapid stream of water flowing in a millrace.

mill·wright (mĭl′rīt′) *n.* A person who designs, builds, or repairs mills or mill machinery.

mil·neb (mĭl′nĕb′) *n.* A white crystalline compound, $C_{12}H_{22}N_4S_4$, used as an agricultural fungicide. [Orig. unknown.]

mi·lo (mī′lō) *n., pl.* **-los.** An early-growing, usually drought-resistant grain sorghum resembling millet. [Poss. < Afr. *mealie,* corn, prob. < Port. *milho* < Lat. *milium,* grain.]

mi·lord (mĭ-lôrd′) *n.* An English nobleman or gentleman. Used as a title of respect. [Fr. < E. *my lord.*]

milque·toast (mĭlk′tōst′) *n.* One who has a meek, timid, and retiring nature. [After Caspar *Milquetoast,* a comic-strip character created by H.T. Webster (d. 1952).]

milt (mĭlt) *n.* **1. a.** Fish sperm, including the seminal fluid. **b.** The reproductive glands of male fishes when filled with this fluid. **2.** *Zool.* The spleen (sense 2). *—tr.v.* **milt·ed, milt·ing, milts.** To fertilize (fish roe) with milt. [Prob. < MDu. *milte.*]

milt·er (mĭl′tər) *n.* A male fish that is ready to breed.

mime (mīm) *n.* **1. a.** A form of ancient Greek and Roman drama in which realistic characters and situations were farcically portrayed and actual persons mimicked on the stage. **b.** A performance of or dialogue for such a drama. **c.** An actor in such a drama. **2.** A modern actor or comedian who specializes in comic mimicry. **3. a.** Pantomime (sense 4). **b.** A performance of pantomime. **c.** An actor skilled in pantomime. *—v.* **mimed, mim·ing, mimes.** *—tr.* **1.** To ridicule by imitation; mimic. **2.** To act out with gestures and body movements. *—intr.* **1.** To act as a mimic. **2.** To portray characters and situations by wordless gesture and body movement. [Lat. *mimus* < Gk. *mimos.*] **—mim′er** *n.*

mim·e·o (mĭm′ē-ō′) *n., pl.* **-os.** A mimeographed publication.

mim·e·o·graph (mĭm′ē-ə-grăf′) *n.* **1.** A duplicator that makes copies of written, drawn, or typed material from a stencil that is fitted around an inked drum. **2.** A copy made by a mimeograph. *—v.* **-graphed, -graph·ing, -graphs.** *—tr.* To make (copies) on a mimeograph. *—intr.* To use a mimeograph. [Orig. a trademark.]

mi·me·sis (mĭ-mē′sĭs, mī-) *n.* **1.** The imitation or representation of nature, esp. in art and literature. **2.** *Biol.* Mimicry (sense 2). **3.** *Med.* The appearance, often due to hysteria, of symptoms of a disease not actually present. [Gk. *mimēsis* < *mimeisthai,* to imitate < *mimos,* imitator.]

mi·met·ic (mĭ-mĕt′ĭk, mī-) *adj.* **1.** Pertaining to, characteristic of, or showing mimicry. **2. a.** Of or pertaining to an imitation; imitative. **b.** Using imitative means of representation: *a mimetic dance.* [Gk. *mimētikos* < *mimeisthai,* to imitate < *mimos,* imitator.] **—mi·met′i·cal·ly** *adv.*

mim·ic (mĭm′ĭk) *tr.v.* **-icked, -ick·ing, -ics. 1.** To copy or imitate closely, esp. in speech, expression, and gesture; ape. **2.** To copy or imitate so as to ridicule; mock: *always mimicking his boss.* **3.** To resemble closely; simulate: *an insect mimicking a twig.* **4.** To take on the appearance of. *—n.* **1.** One who imitates, esp.: **a.** A mime. **b.** A person who copies or mimics others, as for amusement. **2.** A copy or imitation. *—adj.* **1.** Pertaining to, acting as, resembling, or characteristic of a mimic or mimicry. **2.** Make-believe; mock: *a mimic battle.* [Lat. *mimicus* < Gk. *mimikos* < *mimos,* imitator.] **—mim′ick·er** *n.*

mim·ic·ry (mĭm′ĭ-krē) *n., pl.* **-ries. 1. a.** The act, practice, or art of mimicking. **b.** An instance of mimicking. **2.** *Biol.* The resemblance, through natural selection, of one organism to another or to a natural object, as an aid in concealment.

Mi·mir (mē′mîr′) *n. Norse Myth.* A giant who dwelt by the roots of Yggdrasil, where he guarded the well of wisdom. [ON.]

mimosa

mi·mo·sa (mĭ-mō′sə, -zə) *n.* **1.** Any of various mostly tropical plants, shrubs, and trees of the genus *Mimosa,* having ball-like clusters of small flowers and compound leaves that are often sensitive to touch or light. **2.** The silk tree. [NLat. *Mimosa,* genus name < Lat. *mimus,* mime < Gk. *mimos.*]

mi·na¹ (mī′nə) *n., pl.* **-nas** or **-nae** (-nē). A varying unit of weight or money used in ancient Greece and Asia. [Lat. < Gk. *mna* < Akkadian *manru,* a unit of weight.]

mi·na² (mī′nə) *n.* Variant of **myna.**

mi·na·cious (mĭ-nā′shəs) *adj.* Of a menacing or threatening nature; minatory. [Lat. *minax, minac-* < *minari,* to threaten < *minae,* threats.] **—mi·na′cious·ly** *adv.* **—mi·na′cious·ness, mi·nac′i·ty** (mĭ-năs′ĭ-tē) *n.*

min·a·ret (mĭn′ə-rĕt′) *n.* A tall, slender tower on a mosque with one or more projecting balconies from which a muezzin summons the people to prayer. [Fr. < Turk. *minārat* < Ar. *manārat.*]

min·a·to·ry (mĭn′ə-tôr′ē, -tōr′ē) also **min·a·to·ri·al** (mĭn′ə-tôr′ē-əl, -tōr′-) *adj.* Menacing; threatening. [Fr. *minatoire* < LLat. *minatorius* < Lat. *minari,* to threaten < *minae,* threats.] **—min′a·to′ri·ly** *adv.*

mince (mĭns) *v.* **minced, minc·ing, minc·es.** *—tr.* **1.** To cut or chop into very small pieces. **2.** To pronounce in an affected way, as with forced elegance and refinement. **3.** To moderate or restrain for the sake of politeness and decorum; euphemize: *Let's not mince words: the man's a liar.* *—intr.* **1.** To walk with very short steps or with excessive primness. **2.** To speak in an affected way, as with forced elegance and refinement. *—n.* Food that is finely chopped; mincemeat. [ME *mincen* < OFr. *mincier* < VLat. **minutiare* < LLat. *minutia,* smallness. —see MINUTIA.] **—minc′er** *n.*

mince·meat (mĭns′mēt′) *n.* **1.** Finely chopped meat. **2.** A mixture of finely chopped apples, spices, suet, and sometimes meat, used esp. as a pie filling. ***—idiom.*** **make mincemeat of.** *Slang.* To destroy utterly as if by cutting into little pieces.

mince pie *n.* A pie filled with mincemeat.

minc·ing (mĭn′sĭng) *adj.* Affectedly refined or dainty. **—minc′ing·ly** *adv.*

mind (mīnd) *n.* **1.** The human consciousness that originates in the brain and is manifested esp. in thought, perception, feeling, will, memory, or imagination. **2.** The totality of conscious and unconscious processes of the brain and central nervous system that directs the mental and physical behavior of a sentient organism. **3.** The principle of intelligence; the spirit of consciousness regarded as an aspect of reality: *mind over matter.* **4.** The faculty of thinking, reasoning, and applying knowledge: *Follow your mind, not your heart.* **5.** A person of great mental ability; brain: *the greatest mind of the century.* **6. a.** Individual consciousness, memory, or recollection: *I'll bear the problem in mind.* **b.** An individual or a group that embodies certain mental qualities: *the public mind.* **c.** The thought processes characteristic of an individual or a group; psychology: *the criminal mind.* **7.** Opinion or sentiment: *I may change my mind when I hear the facts.* **8.** A desire for a particular thing or activity: *I have a mind to spend my vacation in the mountains.* **9.** Focus of thought; attention. **10.** A healthy mental state; sanity: *losing one's mind.* **11. Mind.** *Christian Science.* The Deity regarded as the perfect intelligence ruling over all of divine creation. *—v.* **mind·ed, mind·ing, minds.** *—tr.* **1.** *Chiefly Regional.* **a.** To put (a person) in mind of something; remind. **b.** To bring (an object or idea) to mind; remember. **2. a.** To become aware of; notice. **b.** *Chiefly Regional.* To have in mind as a goal or purpose; intend. **3.** To heed in order to obey: *The children minded their mother.* **4.** To attend to: *Mind closely what I tell you.* **5.** To be careful about: *Mind the icy sidewalk.* **6.** To object to; dislike. **7.** To take care or charge of; look after. **8.** To care about; be concerned about. *—intr.* **1.** To take notice; give heed. **2.** To behave obediently. **3.** To be concerned or troubled; care: *"Not minding about bad food has become a national obsession"* (Times Literary Supplement). **4.** To be cautious or careful. ***—idioms.*** **make up (one's) mind.** To decide between alternatives; come to a definite decision or opinion. **piece of (one's) mind.** *Informal.* One's bluntly expressed opinion, esp. a strongly worded rebuke or condemnation. **put (one) in mind.** *Informal.* To fill one with memories; remind one: *The novel put her in mind of her youth.* [ME *minde* < OE *gemynd.*]

Synonyms: *mind, intellect, intelligence, mentality, brains, wits, sense, reason. Mind,* which overlaps all of these terms, pertains broadly to capacities not distinctly physical and not associated with the heart, soul, or spirit. *Intellect* denotes capacity for knowing and thinking, as contrasted with feeling and willing, and emotion generally; it is closely allied to judgment and reason. *Intelligence* applies to adaptive behavior, as in solving problems, learning from experience, and reasoning abstractly. *Mentality* is now used most often in the sense of *intellect* (and *mental* and *cerebral* in the sense of *intellectual*). *Brains* is said of intellect, often with intent of emphasis. *Wits* pertains to intelligence, and stresses quickness or facility of comprehension. *Sense* involves natural power of understanding, reasonableness, and capacity for sound perception and judgment. *Reason,* the capacity for logical and analytic thought, embraces comprehending, evaluating, and drawing conclusions.

mind-blow·ing (mīnd′blō′ĭng) *adj. Slang.* **1.** Producing hallucinatory effects: *mind-blowing drugs.* **2.** Intensely affecting the mind or emotions: *a mind-blowing horror story.* **—mind′-blow′er** *n.*

mind-bog·gling (mīnd′bŏg′lĭng) *adj. Informal.* Overwhelming, as with wonder or perplexity.

mind·ed (mīn′dĭd) *adj.* **1.** Disposed; inclined: *I am not minded to answer any of your questions.* **2.** Having a specified kind of mind: *evil-minded.*

mind-ex·pand·ing (mīnd′ĭk-spăn′dĭng) *adj.* Psychedelic: *mind-expanding drugs.*

mind·ful (mīnd′fəl) *adj.* Attentive; heedful: *always mindful of her responsibilities.* **—mind′ful·ly** *adv.* **—mind′ful·ness** *n.*

mind·less (mīnd′lĭs) *adj.* **1. a.** Lacking intelligence or good sense; foolish. **b.** Without intelligent purpose, meaning, or direction: *mindless violence.* **2.** Giving or showing little attention or care; heedless: *mindless of the dangers.* **—mind′less·ly** *adv.* **—mind′less·ness** *n.*

mind reading *n.* **1.** The act of guessing what someone is thinking by observing facial expressions and other signs. **2.** The supposed faculty of discerning another's thoughts through extrasensory means of communication; telepathy. **—mind reader** *n.*

mind·set (mīnd′sĕt′) *n.* A mental attitude or disposition that predetermines a person's responses to and interpretations of situations.

mind's eye *n.* The inherent mental ability to imagine or remember scenes.

mine[1] (mīn) *n.* **1. a.** An excavation in the earth from which ore or minerals can be extracted. **b.** The site of such an excavation, with its surface buildings, elevator shafts, and equipment. **2.** A deposit of ore or minerals in the earth or on its surface. **3.** An abundant supply or source of something valuable: *Her guidebook is a mine of information.* **4. a.** A tunnel dug under an enemy emplacement to gain an avenue of attack or to lay explosives. **b.** An explosive device used to destroy enemy personnel, fortifications, or equipment, often placed in a concealed position and designed to be detonated by contact or by a time fuse. **5.** A burrow, tunnel, or gallery made by an insect. *—v.* **mined, min·ing, mines.** *—tr.* **1. a.** To extract (ore or minerals) from the earth. **b.** To dig a mine in (the earth) to obtain ore or minerals. **2. a.** To tunnel under (the earth or a surface feature). **b.** To make (a tunnel) by digging. **3.** To lay explosive mines in or under. **4.** To attack, damage, or destroy by underhanded means; subvert. **5.** To delve into and make use of; exploit: *mine the archives for detailed information.* *—intr.* **1. a.** To excavate the earth for the purpose of extracting ore or minerals. **b.** To work in a mine. **2.** To dig a tunnel under the earth, esp. under an enemy emplacement or fortification. **3.** To lay explosive mines. [ME < OFr.]

mine[2] (mīn) *pron. (used with a sing. or pl. verb).* That or those belonging to me: *The green books are mine. If you can't find your hat, take mine.* [ME *min* < OE *mīn.*]

mine detector *n.* Any of various electromagnetic devices used to locate explosive mines. **—mine detection** *n.*

mine·field (mīn′fēld′) *n.* An area in which explosive mines have been placed.

mine·lay·er (mīn′lā′ər) *n.* A ship equipped for laying explosive underwater mines.

min·er (mī′nər) *n.* **1.** One whose trade or business it is to extract ore or minerals from the earth. **2.** A machine for the automatic extraction of minerals, esp. of coal. **3.** A member of a military unit engaged in laying explosive mines. **4.** A leaf miner.

min·er·al (mĭn′ər-əl) *n.* **1.** A naturally occurring, homogeneous inorganic substance having a definite chemical composition and characteristic crystalline structure, color, and hardness. **2.** Any of various natural substances, as: **a.** An element, such as gold or silver. **b.** A mixture of inorganic compounds, such as hornblende or granite. **c.** An organic derivative, such as coal or petroleum. **3.** A substance that is neither animal nor vegetable; inorganic matter. **4.** An ore. **5. minerals.** *Chiefly Brit.* Mineral water. *—adj.* **1.** Of or pertaining to minerals: *a mineral deposit.* **2.** Impregnated with minerals: *mineral water.* [ME < Med. Lat. *minerale* < neuter of *mineralis,* of minerals < OFr. *miniere,* mine < *mine.*]

min·er·al·ize (mĭn′ər-ə-līz′) *v.* **-ized, -iz·ing, -iz·es.** *—tr.* **1.** To convert to a mineral substance; petrify. **2.** To transform a metal into a mineral by oxidation. **3.** To impregnate with minerals. *—intr.* To develop or hasten mineral formation. **—min′er·al·i·za′tion** *n.* **—min′er·al·iz′er** *n.*

mineral kingdom *n.* The group of objects and substances that are composed only of inorganic matter.

min·er·al·o·cor·ti·coid (mĭn′ər-ə-lō-kôr′tĭ-koid′) *n.* Any of a group of steroid hormones secreted by the adrenal cortex that regulate the concentrations of electrolytes, such as sodium and potassium, in the extracellular fluids.

min·er·al·o·gy (mĭn′ə-rŏl′ə-jē, -răl′-) *n.* The study of minerals, including their distribution, identification, and properties. [MINERA(L) + -LOGY.] **—min′er·a·log′i·cal** (-ər-ə-lŏj′ĭ-kəl) *adj.* **—min′er·a·log′i·cal·ly** *adv.* **—min′er·al′o·gist** *n.*

mineral oil *n.* **1.** Any of various light hydrocarbon oils, esp. a distillate of petroleum. **2.** A refined distillate of petroleum, used medicinally as a laxative.

mineral tar *n.* Maltha.

mineral water *n.* Naturally occurring or prepared water that contains dissolved minerals or gases, often used therapeutically.

mineral wax *n.* Ozocerite.

mineral wool *n.* An inorganic fibrous material that is produced by steam blasting and cooling molten silicate or a similar substance and is used as an insulator and filtering medium.

miner's lettuce *n.* Winter purslane.

Mi·ner·va (mĭ-nûr′və) *n. Rom. Myth.* The goddess of wisdom, invention, the arts, and martial prowess. [Lat.]

min·e·stro·ne (mĭn′ĭ-strō′nē) *n.* A soup of Italian origin containing assorted vegetables, vermicelli, and herbs in a meat or vegetable broth. [Ital., aug. of *minestra,* soup < *minestrare,* to serve < Lat. *ministrare* < *minister,* servant.]

mine sweeper *n.* A ship equipped for destroying, removing, or neutralizing explosive marine mines.

min·gle (mĭng′gəl) *v.* **-gled, -gling, -gles.** *—tr.* **1.** To mix or bring together in close association; combine. **2.** To mix so that the components become united; merge. *—intr.* **1.** To be or become mixed or united. **2.** To join or take part with others: *mingled with the crowd.* [ME *menglen,* freq. of *mengen,* to mix < OE *mengan.*] **—min′gler** *n.*

min·gy (mĭn′jē) *adj.* **-gi·er, -gi·est.** *Informal.* **1.** Small in quantity: *a mingy portion.* **2.** Mean and stingy: *a mingy old man.* [Perh. a blend of MEAN and STINGY.]

min·i (mĭn′ē) *n.* **1.** Something distinctively smaller or shorter than other members of its class. **2.** A miniskirt.

mini– *pref.* Small; miniature: *minicar.* [< MINIATURE.]

min·i·a·ture (mĭn′ē-ə-cho͝or′, mĭn′ə-, -chər) *n.* **1. a.** A copy or model that represents or reproduces something in a greatly reduced size. **b.** Something small of its class. **2. a.** A small painting executed with great detail, often on a surface such as ivory or vellum. **b.** A small portrait, picture, or decorative letter on an illuminated manuscript. **c.** The art of painting miniatures. *—adj.* On a small or greatly reduced scale: *miniature furniture.* [Ital. *miniatura,* illumination of manuscripts < *miniare,* to illuminate < Lat., to color red < *minium,* red lead.]

Usage: *Miniature* (adjective) describes a reduced model or version of something that normally has a larger size. It is not properly applied to something, such as a rug, that is simply small and for which there is no standard size.

miner

miniature golf *n.* A simplified version of golf played on a miniature course.

min·i·a·tur·ize (mĭn′ē-ə-chə-rīz′, mĭn′ə-) *tr.v.* **-ized, -iz·ing, -iz·es.** To plan or make on a greatly reduced scale. **—min′i·a·tur′i·za′tion** *n.*

min·i·bike (mĭn′ē-bīk′) *n.* A small motorbike having a low frame, small wheels, and elevated handlebars. [Orig. a trademark.]

min·i·bus (mĭn′ē-bŭs′) *n.* A small bus.

min·i·cab (mĭn′ē-kăb′) *n.* A minicar used as a taxicab, esp. in England.

min·i·car (mĭn′ē-kär′) *n.* A subcompact automobile, esp. one made in England.

min·i·com·put·er (mĭn′ē-kəm-pyo͞o′tər) *n.* A small computer having more memory and higher execution speed than a microcomputer.

min·ié ball (mĭn′ē, mĭn′ē-ā′) *n.* A conical rifle bullet with a hollow base that expanded when fired and was used in the 19th century. [After Claude Etienne *Minié* (1814–1879), its inventor.]

miniature
Page in Jeanne d'Evreux's book of hours, illuminated by Jean Pucelle. Actual size 3½ by 2 7/10 inches.

min·i·fy (mĭn′ə-fī′) *tr.v.* **-fied, -fy·ing, -fies.** To make smaller or less significant; reduce. [MIN(IMUM) + (MAGN)IFY.]

min·i·kin (mĭn′ĭ-kĭn) *n. Archaic.* A very small or delicate creature. [MDu. *minneken,* darling, dim. of *minne,* love.]

min·im (mĭn′əm) *n.* **1.** A unit of fluid measure: **a.** In the United States, 1/60 of a fluid dram, or 0.00376 cubic inches. **b.** In Great Britain, 1/20 of a scruple, or 0.00361 cubic inches. **2.** *Mus.* A half note. **3.** An insignificantly small portion or thing; jot. **4.** A downward vertical stroke in handwriting. [< Med. Lat. *minimus,* least < Lat.]

min·i·ma (mĭn′ə-mə) *n.* A plural of **minimum.**

min·i·mal (mĭn′ə-məl) *adj.* **1.** Smallest in amount or degree. **2.** Of, relating to, or being minimal art. *—n. Math.* In an ordered set, a member that precedes all others. **—min′i·mal′i·ty** (-măl′ĭ-tē) *n.* **—min′i·mal·ly** *adv.*

minimal art *n.* Nonrepresentational art that consists chiefly of basic geometric shapes and forms. **—minimal artist** *n.*

min·i·mal·ism (mĭn′ə-mə-lĭz′əm) *n.* Minimal art. **—min′i·mal·ist** *n.*

min·i·max (mĭn′ə-măks′) *adj. Math.* Of or pertaining to the strategic principle in game theory by which a player selects the strategy to minimize an opponent's greatest possible gain and maximize his own. [MINI(MUM) + MAX(IMUM).]

min·i·mize (mĭn′ə-mīz′) *tr.v.* **-mized, -miz·ing, -miz·es. 1.** To reduce to the smallest possible amount, extent, size, or degree. **2.** To represent as having the least degree of importance, value, or size: *minimized the magnitude of the crisis.* [< MINIMUM.] **—min′i·mi·za′tion** *n.* **—min′i·miz′er** *n.*

Usage: According to traditional grammar, *minimize* can mean only "to make as small as possible" and is therefore an absolute term, which cannot be modified by *greatly* or *somewhat,* which are appropriately used only with verbs like *reduce* and *lessen.* The newer use of *minimize* to mean "to make smaller than before," which can be so modified, is best avoided in formal writing.

min·i·mum (mĭn′ə-məm) *n., pl.* **-mums** or **-ma** (-mə). **1.** The least possible quantity or degree. **2.** The lowest degree or amount reached or recorded; the lower limit of variation. **3.** *Math.* **a.** A number not greater than any other in a finite set of numbers. **b.** A value of a function that is exceeded for any sufficiently small increase or decrease in the function's variables. *—adj.* Of, consisting of, or representing the lowest possible amount or degree permissible or attainable. [Lat., neuter of *minimus,* least.]

minimum wage *n.* **1.** The lowest wage, determined by law or contract, that an employer may pay an employee for a specified job. **2.** A living wage.

min·ing (mī′nĭng) *n.* **1.** The process or business of extracting ore or minerals from a mine. **2.** The process of laying explosive mines.

min·ion (mĭn′yən) *n.* **1.** One who is esteemed or favored.

2. a. An obsequious follower or dependent; sycophant. b. A subordinate official. [Fr. *mignon,* darling < OFr. *mignot.*]

min·i·se·ries (mĭn'ē-sîr'ēz) *n.* 1. A sequence of episodes that make up a televised dramatic production. 2. A short series of performances or athletic contests.

min·i·ski (mĭn'ē-skē') *n.* A short ski used by beginners or skibobbers.

min·i·skirt (mĭn'ē-skûrt') *n.* An extremely short skirt. **—min'i·skirt'ed** *adj.*

min·i·state (mĭn'ē-stāt') *n.* A microstate.

min·is·ter (mĭn'ĭ-stər) *n.* 1. A person serving as an agent for another by carrying out specified orders or functions. 2. a. A person authorized to perform religious functions in a church, esp. a Protestant church. b. *Rom. Cath. Ch.* The superior in certain orders. 3. A high officer of state appointed to head an executive or administrative department of government. 4. A person authorized to represent his government in diplomatic dealings with other governments, usually ranking next below an ambassador. *—v.* **-tered, -ter·ing, -ters.** *—intr.* 1. To attend to the wants and needs of others: *Volunteers ministered to the homeless after the flood.* 2. To perform the functions of a clergyman. *—tr.* To administer; dispense. [ME *ministre* < OFr. < Lat. *minister.*]

min·is·te·ri·al (mĭn'ĭ-stîr'ē-əl) *adj.* 1. Of, pertaining to, or characteristic of a minister of religion or of the ministry. 2. Of or pertaining to administrative and executive duties and functions of government. 3. *Law.* Of or designating a mandatory act or duty admitting of no personal discretion or judgment in its performance. 4. Acting or serving as an agent; instrumental. **—min'is·te'ri·al·ly** *adv.*

minister plenipotentiary *n.* A diplomatic representative with full authority to speak and act for his government; plenipotentiary.

minister resident *n.* A diplomatic agent ranking below a minister plenipotentiary.

Minotaur
Detail from a 6th-century B.C. Greek amphora showing Theseus slaying the Minotaur

min·is·trant (mĭn'ĭ-strənt) *n.* One who ministers. *—adj. Archaic.* Serving attendance on someone. [< Lat. *ministrans, ministrant-,* pr.part. of *ministrare,* to serve < *minister,* servant.]

min·is·tra·tion (mĭn'ĭ-strā'shən) *n.* 1. The act or process of serving or aiding. 2. The act of performing the duties of a clergyman. [Lat. *ministratio* < *ministrare,* to serve < *minister,* servant.] **—min'is·tra'tive** *adj.*

min·is·try (mĭn'ĭ-strē) *n., pl.* **-tries.** 1. a. The act of serving; ministration. b. One that serves as a means; instrumentality. 2. a. The profession, duties, and services of a minister of religion. b. The clergy. c. The period of service of a minister of religion. 3. a. A governmental department presided over by a minister. b. The building in which such a department is housed. c. The duties, functions, or term of a governmental minister and his staff. d. Often **Ministry.** Governmental ministers as a group. [ME *ministerie* < Lat. *ministerium* < *minister,* minister.]

min·i·track (mĭn'ē-trăk') *n.* An electronic measuring system designed to follow the course of satellites and rockets and to correlate radio signals received by a network of ground stations.

min·i·um (mĭn'ē-əm) *n.* Red lead. [Lat.]

min·i·ver (mĭn'ə-vər) *n.* A white or light-gray fur used as a rich trim on medieval robes and on ceremonial robes of state. [ME *meniver* < OFr. *menu vair,* small vair.]

mink (mĭngk) *n., pl.* **mink** or **minks.** 1. Any of various semiaquatic carnivores of the genus *Mustela,* esp. *M. vison* of North America, resembling the weasel and having short ears, a pointed snout, short legs, and partly webbed toes. 2. a. The soft, thick, lustrous fur of the mink. b. A coat or stole made of mink. [ME *mynk.*]

Min·nan (mĭ-năn') *n.* The dialect of Chinese spoken in Taiwan. [Chin. (Mandarin) *min^3 nan^2* : *min^3,* Fujian Province + *nan^2,* south.]

min·ne·sing·er (mĭn'ĭ-sĭng'ər, mĭn'ə-zĭng'ər) *n.* One of the German lyric poets and singers in the troubadour tradition who flourished from the 12th to the 14th centuries. [G. < MHG : *minne,* love (< OHG *minna*) + *singer,* singer < *singen,* to sing < OHG *singan.*]

min·now (mĭn'ō) *n., pl.* **minnow** or **-nows.** 1. Any of a large number of small, freshwater fishes of the family Cyprinidae, widely used as live bait. 2. A small, silver-colored fish. [ME *meneu.*]

Mi·no·an (mĭ-nō'ən) *adj.* Of or pertaining to the advanced Bronze Age culture that flourished in Crete from about 3000 to 1100 B.C. [Lat. *Minous,* of Minos < Gk. *Minōios* < *Minōs,* Minos.]

mi·nor (mī'nər) *adj.* 1. Lesser or smaller in amount, extent, or size. 2. Lesser in importance, rank, or stature: *a minor essayist.* 3. Lesser in seriousness or danger: *a minor injury.* 4. *Law.* Under legal age; not yet a legal adult. 5. *Chiefly Brit.* Designating the junior or younger of two pupils with the same surname. 6. Designating or relating to a secondary area of academic specialization. 7. *Logic.* Dealing with a more restricted category. 8. *Mus.* a. Designating a minor scale. b. Less in distance by a half step than the corresponding major interval. c. Based on a minor scale: *a minor key.* *—n.* 1. One that is lesser in comparison to others of the same class. 2. *Law.* One who has not reached full legal age. 3. a. A secondary area of specialized academic study. b. One studying a minor: *a chemistry minor.* 4. a. A minor premise. b. A minor term. 5. *Mus.* A minor key, scale, or interval. 6. **minors.** The minor leagues of a sport. *—intr.v.* **-nored, -nor·ing, -nors.** To pursue academic studies in a minor field: *minored in microbiology.* [ME < Lat.]

Mi·nor·ca (mĭ-nôr'kə) *n.* A domestic fowl of a breed originating in the Mediterranean region, having white or black plumage. [After *Minorca,* an island in the Mediterranean.]

Mi·nor·ite (mī'nə-rīt') *n.* A Franciscan friar. [< Med. Lat. *(Fratres) Minores,* minor (friars).]

mi·nor·i·ty (mə-nôr'ĭ-tē, -nŏr'-, mī-) *n., pl.* **-ties.** 1. The smaller in number of two groups forming a whole. 2. a. A racial, religious, political, national, or other group regarded as different from the larger group of which it is part. b. A member of a minority group. 3. The state or period of being under legal age: *an heir still in his minority.* [Fr. *minorité* < Med. Lat. *minoritas* < Lat. *minor,* smaller.]

minority leader *n.* The head of the minority party in a legislative body.

minor league *n.* A league of professional sports clubs, esp. baseball, not belonging to the major leagues.

mi·nor-league (mī'nər-lēg') *adj.* 1. Pertaining or belonging to a minor sports league. 2. Being of subordinate position or importance: *a minor-league politician.* **—mi'nor-leagu'er** *n.*

minor orders *pl.n. Rom. Cath. Ch.* The orders of acolyte, exorcist, reader or lector, and doorkeeper.

minor premise *n.* The premise in a syllogism containing the minor term, which will form the subject of the conclusion.

Minor Prophets *pl.n.* The Hebrew prophets Hosea, Joel, Amos, Obadiah, Jonah, Micah, Nahum, Habakkuk, Zephaniah, Haggai, Zechariah, and Malachi.

minor scale *n. Mus.* A diatonic scale having a minor third between the first and third tones and having several forms with different intervals above the fifth.

minor suit *n.* In bridge, the suit of clubs or of diamonds.

minor term *n.* The term in a syllogism that is stated in the minor premise and forms the subject of the conclusion.

Mi·nos (mī'nəs, -nŏs') *n. Gk. Myth.* A king of Crete, the son of Zeus and Europa. [Lat. < Gk. *Minōs.*]

Min·o·taur (mĭn'ə-tôr', mī'nə-) *n. Gk. Myth.* The son of Pasiphaë by a sacred bull, in body half man, half bull, slain by Theseus. [Lat. *Minotaurus* < Gk. *Minōtauros* : *Minōs,* Minos + *tauros,* bull.]

min·ster (mĭn'stər) *n. Chiefly Brit.* 1. A monastery church. 2. The title of certain large cathedrals. [ME < OE *mynster* < LLat. *monasterium,* monastery. —see MONASTERY.]

min·strel (mĭn'strəl) *n.* 1. A medieval musician who traveled from place to place singing and reciting poetry. 2. a. A lyric poet. b. A musician. 3. a. A performer in a minstrel show. b. A performance of a minstrel show. [ME *ministral* < OFr. *menestral* < LLat. *ministerialis,* official in the imperial household < Lat. *ministerium,* ministry < *minister,* minister.]

minstrel show *n.* A variety show in which performers sing, dance, tell jokes, and perform comic skits.

min·strel·sy (mĭn'strəl-sē) *n., pl.* **-sies.** 1. The art or profession of a minstrel. 2. A troupe of minstrels. 3. Ballads and lyrics sung by minstrels.

mint[1] (mĭnt) *n.* 1. A place where the coins of a country are manufactured by authority of the government. 2. An abundant amount, esp. of money. 3. Something that can be used as a source: *a mint of useful ideas.* *—tr.v.* **mint·ed, mint·ing, mints.** 1. To produce (money) by stamping metal; coin. 2. To invent or fabricate: *a phrase minted for one occasion.* *—adj.* Undamaged as if freshly minted. [ME *mynt* < OE *mynet,* money < Lat. *moneta.* —see MONEY.]

mint[2] (mĭnt) *n.* 1. Any of various plants of the genus *Mentha,* characteristically having aromatic foliage and two-lipped flowers that are often cultivated for their aromatic oil and used for flavoring. 2. Any of various plants, such as the mountain mint and the stone mint, that are related or similar to the mint. 3. A candy flavored with mint. [ME *minte* < OE < Lat. *menta* < Gk. *minthē.*] **—mint'y** *adj.*

mint·age (mĭn'tĭj) *n.* 1. The act or process of minting coins. 2. Coins manufactured in a mint. 3. The fee paid to a mint by a government. 4. The impression stamped on a coin.

mint julep *n.* A tall, frosted drink made of bourbon whiskey, sugar, crushed mint leaves, and shaved ice.

min·u·end (mĭn'yo͞o-ĕnd') *n. Math.* The quantity from which another quantity, the subtrahend, is to be subtracted. [Lat. *minuendum,* thing to be diminished, neuter gerund. of *minuere,* to lessen.]

min·u·et (mĭn'yo͞o-ĕt') *n.* 1. A slow, stately pattern dance in 3/4 time for groups of couples, originated in 17th-century France. 2. The music for or in the rhythm of the minuet. [Fr. *menuet* < OFr. *menu,* small < Lat. *minutus* < *minuere,* to lessen.]

mi·nus (mī'nəs) *prep.* 1. *Math.* Reduced by the subtraction of; less. 2. *Informal.* Lacking; without: *arrived at the door minus her gloves.* *—adj.* 1. *Math.* Negative or on the negative part of a scale: *a minus value; minus five degrees.* 2. Designating one subdivision of a grade less than: *a grade of B minus.* *—n.* 1. The minus sign (-). 2. A negative quantity. 3. A deficiency or defect. [ME < Lat. *minus,* less.]

min·us·cule (mĭn'ə-skyo͞ol', mĭ-nŭs'kyo͞ol') *n.* 1. A small, cursive script developed from uncial between the 7th and 9th centuries A.D. and used in medieval manuscripts. 2. A letter written in minuscule. **3.** A lower-case letter. *—adj.* **1.** Of, pertaining to, or written in minuscule. **2.** Very small; tiny. [Fr. < Lat. *minusculus,* very small, dim. of *minor,* smaller.] **—mi·nus'cu·lar** (mĭ-nŭs'kyə-lər) *adj.*

minus sign *n. Math.* The symbol (–), as in 4–2=2, that is used to indicate subtraction or a negative quantity.

min·ute¹ (mĭn'ĭt) *n.* **1. a.** A unit of time equal to one-sixtieth of an hour, or 60 seconds. **b.** A unit of angular measurement equal to one-sixtieth of a degree, or 60 seconds. **2.** A short interval of time: *wait a minute.* **3.** A specific point in time. **4.** A note or summary covering points to be remembered; memorandum. **5. minutes.** An official record of proceedings at the meeting of an organization. *—tr.v.* **-ut·ed, -ut·ing, -utes.** **1.** To record in a memorandum or other notation. **2.** To record in the minutes of a meeting. [ME < OFr. < LLat. *minuta* < Lat. *minutus,* small < *minuere,* to lessen.]

mi·nute² (mī-nōōt', -nyōōt', mĭ-) *adj.* **1.** Exceptionally small; tiny. **2.** Beneath notice; insignificant. **3.** Characterized by careful scrutiny and close examination. [Lat. *minutus* < *minuere,* to lessen.] **—mi·nute'ness** *n.*

minute hand *n.* The long hand on a clock or watch that indicates the minutes.

min·ute·ly¹ (mĭn'ĭt-lē) *adj. Archaic.* On a minute-by-minute basis.

mi·nute·ly² (mī-nōōt'lē, -nyōōt'-, mĭ-) *adv.* **1.** With attention to minutiae. **2.** On a very small scale.

min·ute·man (mĭn'ĭt-măn') *n.* An armed civilian pledged to be ready to fight on a minute's notice just before and during the Revolutionary War.

minute of arc *n.* A minute¹ (sense 1.b.).

minute steak *n.* A small, thin steak, often scored or cubed, that can be cooked quickly.

mi·nu·ti·a (mĭ-nōō'shē-ə, -shə, -nyōō'-) *n., pl.* **-ti·ae** (-shē-ē'). Often **minutiae.** A small or trivial detail: *the minutiae of daily life.* [Lat., smallness < *minutus,* small < *minuere,* to lessen.]

minx (mĭngks) *n.* **1.** A pert, impudent, or flirtatious young girl. **2.** *Obs.* A promiscuous woman. [Orig. unknown.]

Mi·o·cene (mī'ə-sēn') *adj.* Of, belonging to, or characteristic of the geologic time, rock series, and sedimentary deposits of the fourth epoch of the Tertiary period, characterized by the appearance of primitive apes, whales, and grazing animals. *—n.* **1.** The Miocene epoch. **2.** The deposits of the Miocene epoch. [Gk. *meiōn,* less + -CENE.]

mi·o·sis also **my·o·sis** (mī-ō'sĭs) *n., pl.* **-ses** (-sēz'). Excessive contraction of the pupil of the eye. [Gk. *muein,* to close the eyes + -OSIS.]

mi·ot·ic (mī-ŏt'ĭk) *n.* An agent that causes contraction of the pupil of the eye. *—adj.* Pertaining to or causing miosis. [< MIOSIS.]

mir (mîr) *n.* A prerevolutionary Russian peasant commune. [R.]

mi·ra·bi·le dic·tu (mĭ-rä'bĭ-lē dĭk'tōō) *adv.* Wonderful to relate. [Lat.]

mir·a·cle (mĭr'ə-kəl) *n.* **1.** An event that appears unexplainable by the laws of nature and so is held to be supernatural in origin or an act of God. **2.** One that excites admiring awe. **3.** A miracle play. [ME < OFr. < Lat. *miraculum* < *mirari,* to wonder at.]

miracle play *n.* A form of religious drama of the Middle Ages in which scenes and events in the lives of miracle-working saints and martyrs were represented.

mi·rac·u·lous (mĭ-răk'yə-ləs) *adj.* **1.** Of the nature of a miracle. **2.** Caused by or as if by a miracle: *a miraculous cure.* **3.** Having the power to work miracles. [OFr. *miraculeux* < Med. Lat. *miraculosus* < Lat. *miraculum,* miracle.] **—mi·rac'u·lous·ly** *adv.* **—mi·rac'u·lous·ness** *n.*

mi·rage (mĭ-räzh') *n.* **1.** An optical phenomenon that creates the illusion of water, often with inverted reflections of distant objects, and results from distortion of light by alternate layers of hot and cool air. **2.** Something that is illusory or insubstantial. [Fr. < *mirer,* to look at < Lat. *mirari,* to wonder at.]

mire (mīr) *n.* **1.** An area of wet, soggy, and muddy ground; bog. **2.** Deep, slimy soil or mud. *—v.* **mired, mir·ing, mires.** *—tr.* **1.** To cause to sink or become stuck in mire. **2.** To soil with mud. **3.** To trap or entangle as if in mire. *—intr.* To sink or become stuck in mire. [ME < ON *mýrr.*]

mi·rex (mī'rĕks') *n.* An insecticide, $C_{10}Cl_{12}$, used against ants. [Perh. (PIS)MIR(E) + EX(TERMINATE).]

mirk (mûrk) *n. & adj.* Variant of **murk.**

mirk·y (mûr'kē) *adj.* Variant of **murky.**

mir·ror (mĭr'ər) *n.* **1.** A surface capable of reflecting sufficient undiffused light to form a virtual image of an object placed in front of it. **2.** Something that faithfully reflects or gives a true picture of something else. **3.** Something worthy of imitation. *—tr.v.* **-rored, -ror·ing, -rors.** To reflect in or as if in a mirror. [ME *mirour* < OFr. < *mirer,* to look at < Lat. *mirari,* to wonder at.]

mirth (mûrth) *n.* Gladness and gaiety, esp. when expressed by laughter. [ME < OE *myrgð.*]

Synonyms: *mirth, merriment, hilarity, glee. Mirth* stresses lightheartedness and suggests easy laughter. *Merriment* strongly implies sociability and conviviality. *Hilarity* suggests also group activity; in modern usage it implies lack of restraint in expression of gaiety. *Glee* applies especially to reaction to particular circumstances, such as a sudden victory or an adversary's bad fortune; it emphasizes intensity of spirits, sometimes unworthily motivated, as by spite.

mirth·ful (mûrth'fəl) *adj.* **1.** Full of mirth. **2.** Characterized by or expressing mirth: *a warm, tender, and mirthful movie.* **—mirth'ful·ly** *adv.* **—mirth'ful·ness** *n.*

mirth·less (mûrth'lĭs) *adj.* Devoid of mirth. **—mirth'less·ly** *adv.* **—mirth'less·ness** *n.*

MIRV (mûrv) *n.* **1.** An offensive ballistic-missile system in which a number of warheads aimed at independent targets can be launched by a single booster rocket. **2.** Any of the warheads of a MIRV. [M(ULTIPLE) I(NDEPENDENTLY TARGETED) R(E-ENTRY) V(EHICLES).]

mir·y (mīr'ē) *adj.* **-i·er, -i·est.** **1.** Full of or resembling mire; swampy. **2.** Smeared with mire; muddy. **—mir'i·ness** *n.*

mis–¹ *pref.* **1.** Bad; badly; wrong; wrongly: *misconduct.* **2.** Failure; lack: *misfire.* **3.** Used as an intensive: *misdoubt.* [Partly < ME *mis-* (< OE), and partly < ME *mes-* < OFr. < Lat. *minus,* less.]

mis–² *pref.* Variant of **miso-.**

mis·ad·ven·ture (mĭs'əd-vĕn'chər) also **mis·ven·ture** (mĭs-vĕn'-) *n.* An instance of great misfortune; disaster. [ME *misaventure* < OFr. *mesaventure* < *mesavenir,* to result in misfortune : *mes-,* badly (< Lat. *minus,* less) + *avenir,* to turn out < Lat. *advenire,* to come to (*ad-,* to + *venire,* to come).]

mis·ad·vise (mĭs'əd-vīz') *tr.v.* **-vised, -vis·ing, -vis·es.** To advise wrongly.

mis·a·ligned (mĭs'ə-līnd') *adj.* Not correctly aligned. **—mis'a·lign'ment** *n.*

mis·al·li·ance (mĭs'ə-lī'əns) *n.* **1.** An unsuitable alliance, esp. an unsuitable marriage. **2.** A mésalliance. [Fr. *mésalliance* : *més-,* bad (< Lat. *minus,* less) + *alliance,* alliance < OFr. *aliance.* —see ALLIANCE.]

mis·al·lo·ca·tion (mĭs-ăl'ə-kā'shən) *n.* Faulty or inappropriate allocation.

mis·al·ly (mĭs'ə-lī') *tr.v.* **-lied, -ly·ing, -lies.** To ally badly.

mis·an·thrope (mĭs'ən-thrōp', mĭz'-) also **mis·an·thro·pist** (mĭs-ăn'thrə-pĭst) *n.* A person who hates or scorns mankind. [Fr. < Gk. *misanthrōpos,* hating mankind : *misein,* to hate + *anthrōpos,* man.]

mis·an·throp·ic (mĭs'ən-thrŏp'ĭk, mĭz'-) *adj.* **1.** Of or characteristic of a misanthrope. **2.** Characterized by a hatred or scorn for mankind. **—mis'an·throp'i·cal·ly** *adv.*

mis·an·thro·py (mĭs-ăn'thrə-pē, mĭz-) *n.* Hatred of mankind.

mis·ap·ply (mĭs'ə-plī') *tr.v.* **-plied, -ply·ing, -plies.** To use or apply wrongly. **—mis·ap'pli·ca'tion** (-ăp'lĭ-kā'shən) *n.*

mis·ap·pre·hend (mĭs-ăp'rĭ-hĕnd') *tr.v.* **-hend·ed, -hend·ing, -hends.** To fail to interpret correctly; misunderstand. **—mis·ap'pre·hen'sion** (-hĕn'shən) *n.*

mis·ap·pro·pri·ate (mĭs'ə-prō'prē-āt') *tr.v.* **-at·ed, -at·ing, -ates.** **1. a.** To appropriate wrongly: *misappropriating the theories of social science.* **b.** To appropriate dishonestly for one's own use; embezzle. **2.** To use illegally. **—mis'ap·pro'pri·a'tion** *n.*

mis·be·come (mĭs'bĭ-kŭm') *tr.v.* **-came** (-kām'), **-come, -com·ing, -comes.** To be unsuitable or inappropriate for.

mis·be·got·ten (mĭs'bĭ-gŏt'n) *adj.* **1.** Illegally or abnormally begotten, esp. illegitimate. **2.** Having an improper basis or origin; ill-conceived: *misbegotten ideas about education.*

mis·be·have (mĭs'bĭ-hāv') *v.* **-haved, -hav·ing, -haves.** *—intr.* To behave badly. *—tr.* To conduct oneself badly. **—mis'be·hav'er** *n.* **—mis'be·hav'ior** (-hāv'yər) *n.*

mis·be·lief (mĭs'bĭ-lēf') *n.* **1.** A wrong or faulty belief. **2.** A heretical or unorthodox religious belief.

mis·be·lieve (mĭs'bĭ-lēv') *intr.v.* **-lieved, -liev·ing, -lieves.** *Obs.* To hold a false or erroneous opinion, esp. in religious matters. **—mis'be·liev'er** *n.*

mis·cal·cu·late (mĭs-kăl'kyə-lāt') *tr. & intr. v.* **-lat·ed, -lat·ing, -lates.** To calculate wrongly. **—mis·cal'cu·la'tion** *n.*

mis·call (mĭs-kôl') *tr.v.* **-called, -call·ing, -calls.** To call by a wrong name.

mis·car·riage (mĭs-kăr'ĭj) *n.* **1. a.** Bad administration; mismanagement: *a miscarriage of justice.* **b.** Failure to attain the right or desired end: *the miscarriage of a cherished plan.* **2.** Premature expulsion of a nonviable fetus from the uterus.

mis·car·ry (mĭs-kăr'ē) *intr.v.* **-ried, -ry·ing, -ries.** **1.** To go astray; be lost in transit. **2.** To fail to reach the proper conclusion; go wrong. **3.** To bring forth a fetus prematurely; abort.

mis·cast (mĭs-kăst') *tr.v.* **-cast, -cast·ing, -casts.** **1.** To cast in an unsuitable role. **2.** To cast (a role or a theatrical production) inappropriately.

mis·ceg·e·na·tion (mĭ-sĕj'ə-nā'shən, mĭs'ĭ-jə-) *n.* The interbreeding of what are presumed to be distinct human races, esp. marriage or cohabitation between white and nonwhite persons. [Lat. *miscēre,* to mix + *genus,* race.] **—mis·ceg'e·na'tion·al** *adj.*

mis·cel·la·ne·a (mĭs'ə-lā'nē-ə) *pl.n.* A conglomeration of miscellaneous items. [Lat. < neuter pl. of *miscellaneus,* miscellaneous.]

mis·cel·la·ne·ous (mĭs'ə-lā'nē-əs) *adj.* **1.** Made up of a variety of parts or ingredients. **2.** Having a variety of characteristics, abilities, or appearances. **3.** Concerned with diverse

minuteman
Drawing of the minuteman statue in Concord, Massachusetts

mirror
18th-century American

subjects or aspects. [Lat. *miscellaneus* < *miscēre,* to mix.] **—mis′cel·la′ne·ous·ly** *adv.* **—mis′cel·la′ne·ous·ness** *n.*

Synonyms: *miscellaneous, heterogeneous, motley, mixed, varied, assorted. Miscellaneous* things are similar in kind but sufficiently unlike on secondary levels to defy orderly classification. *Heterogeneous* applies to large collections of persons or things that differ in basic kind. *Motley,* said of persons or things, emphasizes differences to the point of contradiction and discordance; it often expresses contempt. *Mixed* may indicate differences between persons or things in a general way, or specify the presence of both sexes, two or more races, or the like: *mixed doubles. Varied* emphasizes differences between things, emphatically but not specifically. *Assorted* is used when the differences are calculated and purposeful: *assorted nails for the job.*

mis·cel·la·nist (mĭs′ə-lā′nĭst, mĭ-sĕl′ə-) *n. Chiefly Brit.* One who compiles, writes, or edits miscellanies.

mis·cel·la·ny (mĭs′ə-lā′nē) *n., pl.* **-nies. 1.** A collection of various items, parts, or ingredients, esp. one composed of diverse literary works. **2. miscellanies.** A book or other publication containing a variety of literary works. [Lat. *miscellanea,* miscellanea.]

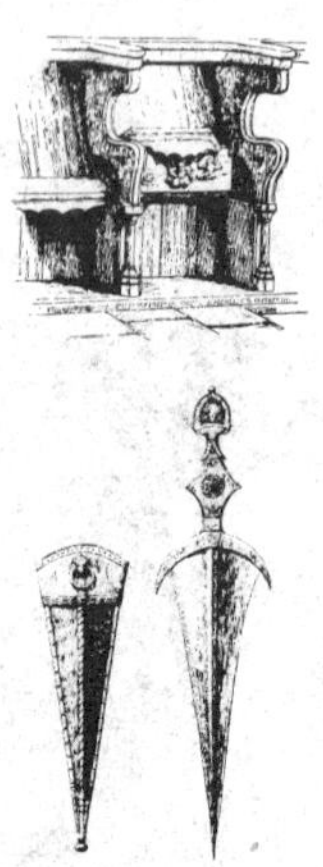
misericord
Above: Raised seat at right shows carving underneath
Below: 15th-century scabbard and dagger

mis·chance (mĭs-chăns′) *n.* **1.** An unfortunate occurrence; unlucky incident. **2.** Bad luck. [ME *mischaunce* < OFr. *meschance* : *mes-,* bad (< Lat. *minus,* less) + *chance,* chance. —see CHANCE.]

mis·chief (mĭs′chĭf) *n.* **1.** Behavior that causes discomfiture or annoyance in another. **2.** An inclination or tendency to play pranks or cause embarrassment: *full of mischief.* **3.** One that causes minor trouble or disturbance: *The child was a mischief in school.* **4.** Damage, destruction, or injury caused by a specific person or thing: *The broken window was the mischief of vandals.* **5.** The state or quality of being mischievous: *a little girl with mischief in her eyes.* [ME *mischef* < OFr. *meschef,* misfortune : *mes-,* badly (< Lat. *minus,* less) + *chef,* head, end < Lat. *caput.*]

mis·chie·vous (mĭs′chə-vəs) *adj.* **1.** Causing mischief. **2.** Playful; teasing. **3.** Troublesome; irritating: *a mischievous prank.* **4.** Causing harm, injury, or damage: *mischievous falsehoods.* [ME *meschevous* < AN < OFr. *meschef,* misfortune. —see MISCHIEF.] **—mis′chie·vous·ly** *adv.* **—mis′chie·vous·ness** *n.*

mis·ci·ble (mĭs′ə-bəl) *adj. Chem.* Capable of being mixed in all proportions. [Med. Lat. *miscibilis* < Lat. *miscēre,* to mix.] **—mis′ci·bil′i·ty** *n.*

mis·clas·si·fy (mĭs-klăs′ə-fī′) *tr.v.* **-fied, -fy·ing, -fies.** To classify incorrectly. **—mis·clas′si·fi·ca′tion** *n.*

mis·con·ceive (mĭs′kən-sēv′) *tr.v.* **-ceived, -ceiv·ing, -ceives.** To interpret incorrectly; misunderstand. **—mis′con·ceiv′er** *n.*

mis·con·cep·tion (mĭs′kən-sĕp′shən) *n.* An incorrect interpretation or understanding.

mis·con·duct (mĭs-kŏn′dŭkt) *n.* **1. a.** Behavior not conforming to prevailing standards or laws; impropriety. **b.** Adultery. **2.** Dishonest or bad management, esp. by persons entrusted or engaged to act on another's behalf. **3.** Malfeasance, esp. by governmental or military officials. **—mis′con·duct′** (mĭs′kən-dŭkt′) *v.* **(-duct·ed, -duct·ing, -ducts).**

mis·con·struc·tion (mĭs′kən-strŭk′shən) *n.* **1.** An inaccurate explanation, interpretation, or report; misunderstanding. **2.** A faulty construction, esp. of a sentence or clause.

mis·con·strue (mĭs′kən-stroo͞′) *tr.v.* **-strued, -stru·ing, -strues.** To mistake the meaning of; misinterpret.

mis·count (mĭs-kount′) *tr. & intr. v.* **-count·ed, -count·ing, -counts.** To count incorrectly; miscalculate. *—n.* (mĭs′kount′). An inaccurate count.

mis·cre·ant (mĭs′krē-ənt) *n.* **1.** An evildoer; villain. **2.** An infidel; heretic. [ME *miscreaunt,* heretic < OFr. *mescreant,* pr.part. of *mescroire,* to disbelieve : *mes-* (reversal < Lat. *minus,* less) + *croire,* to believe < Lat. *credere.*] **—mis′cre·ant** *adj.*

mis·cre·ate (mĭs′krē-āt′) *tr.v.* **-at·ed, -at·ing, -ates.** To make or shape badly. *—adj.* (mĭs′krē-ĭt, -āt′). Formed unnaturally; deformed. **—mis′cre·a′tion** *n.*

mis·cue (mĭs-kyoo͞′) *n.* **1.** A stroke in billiards that misses or just brushes the ball due to a slip of the cue. **2.** A blunder or mistake. *—intr.v.* **-cued, -cu·ing, -cues. 1.** To make a miscue. **2.** To miss a stage cue.

mis·deal (mĭs-dēl′) *v.* **-dealt** (-dĕlt′), **-deal·ing, -deals.** *—tr.* To deal (playing cards) improperly. *—intr.* To deal playing cards improperly. **—mis′deal′** *n.* **—mis·deal′er** *n.*

mis·deed (mĭs-dēd′) *n.* A wicked or illegal deed.

mis·de·mean·ant (mĭs′dĭ-mē′nənt) *n. Law.* One who is guilty of or has been convicted and sentenced for a misdemeanor.

mis·de·mean·or (mĭs′dĭ-mē′nər) *n.* **1.** A misdeed. **2.** *Law.* An offense of lesser gravity than a felony.

mis·de·mean·our (mĭs′dĭ-mē′nər) *n. Chiefly Brit.* Variant of **misdemeanor.**

mis·di·ag·nose (mĭs-dī′əg-nōs′, -nōz′) *tr.v.* **-nosed, -nos·ing, -nos·es.** To diagnose incorrectly.

mis·di·ag·no·sis (mĭs-dī′əg-nō′sĭs) *n.* An incorrect diagnosis.

mis·di·rect (mĭs′dĭ-rĕkt′, -dī-) *tr.v.* **-rect·ed, -rect·ing, -rects. 1.** To instruct incorrectly. **2.** To put a wrong address on.

mis·di·rec·tion (mĭs′dĭ-rĕk′shən, -dī-) *n.* **1.** Inaccurate or wrong instructions or guidance. **2.** *Law.* An error made by a judge in charging a jury.

mis·do (mĭs-doo͞′) *tr.v.* **-did** (-dĭd′), **-done** (-dŭn′), **-do·ing, -does** (-dŭz′). To do wrongly or awkwardly; botch. **—mis·do′er** *n.* **—mis·do′ing** *n.*

mis·doubt (mĭs-dout′) *tr.v.* **-doubt·ed, -doubt·ing, -doubts.** To feel wary of; suspect.

mise en scène (mēz′ äɴ sĕn′) *n.* **1.** The arrangement of performers and properties on a stage for a theatrical production. **2. a.** A stage setting. **b.** A physical environment. [Fr., putting on stage.]

mi·ser (mī′zər) *n.* **1.** One who deprives himself of all but the barest essentials in order to hoard money. **2.** A greedy or avaricious person. [< Lat., wretched.]

mis·er·a·ble (mĭz′ər-ə-bəl, mĭz′rə-bəl) *adj.* **1.** Very uncomfortable or unhappy; wretched. **2.** Causing or accompanied by wretchedness: *a miserable climate.* **3.** Mean; shameful: *a miserable trick.* **4.** Wretchedly inadequate: *miserable rations.* **5.** Of poor quality; inferior. [ME < OFr. < Lat. *miserabilis,* pitiable < *miserari,* to pity < *miser,* wretched.] **—mis′er·a·ble·ness** *n.* **—mis′er·a·bly** *adv.*

mis·e·re·re (mĭz′ə-râr′ē, -rîr′ē) *n.* **1. Miserere.** The 51st Psalm. **2.** A vocal lament or complaint. **3.** A misericord (sense 2). [Lat., have mercy, the first word of the psalm.]

mis·er·i·cord or **mis·er·i·corde** (mĭz′ər-ĭ-kôrd′, mĭ-zĕr′-ĭ-kôrd′) *n.* **1. a.** The relaxation of monastic rules, such as a dispensation from fasting. **b.** The room in a monastery used by monks granted such a dispensation. **2.** A bracket attached to the underside of a hinged seat in a church stall against which a standing person may lean. **3.** A narrow dagger used in medieval times to deliver the death stroke to a seriously wounded knight. [ME, pity < OFr. < Lat. *misericordia* < *misericors,* merciful : *miserēre,* to feel pity + *cors,* heart.]

mi·ser·ly (mī′zər-lē) *adj.* Characteristic of a miser, esp. tending to hoard money or possessions. **—mi′ser·li·ness** *n.*

mis·er·y (mĭz′ə-rē) *n., pl.* **-ies. 1. a.** A condition of suffering and want as a result of physical conditions or extreme poverty. **b.** A condition of mental or emotional unhappiness or distress. **2.** A cause or source of suffering. **3.** *Informal.* A physical ache or ailment. [ME *miserie* < OFr. < Lat. *miseria* < *miser,* wretched.]

mis·es·teem (mĭs′ə-stēm′) *tr.v.* **-teemed, -teem·ing, -teems.** To fail to regard with deserved esteem; disrespect.

mis·es·ti·mate (mĭs-ĕs′tə-māt′) *tr.v.* **-mat·ed, -mat·ing, -mates.** To estimate wrongly. **—mis·es′ti·ma′tion** *n.*

mis·fea·sance (mĭs-fē′zəns) *n. Law.* The improper and unlawful execution of an act that in itself is lawful and proper. [OFr. *mesfaisance* < *mesfaire,* to do wrong : *mes-,* wrongly (< Lat. *minus,* less) + *faire,* to do < Lat. *facere.*]

mis·fea·sor (mĭs-fē′zər) *n. Law.* One guilty of misfeasance. [OFr. *mesfesour* < *mesfaire,* to do wrong. —see MISFEASANCE.]

mis·file (mĭs-fīl′) *tr.v.* **-filed, -fil·ing, -files.** To file incorrectly.

mis·fire (mĭs-fīr′) *intr.v.* **-fired, -fir·ing, -fires. 1. a.** To fail to ignite when expected: *The engine misfired.* **b.** To fail to detonate or explode when expected: *The gun misfired.* **2.** To fail to achieve the anticipated result: *a scheme that misfired.* **—mis·fire′** (mĭs-fīr′, mĭs′fīr′) *n.*

mis·fit (mĭs′fĭt′, mĭs-fĭt′) *n.* **1.** Something of the wrong size or shape for its purpose. **2.** A person who is maladjusted or disturbingly different from those with whom he wishes to associate.

mis·for·tune (mĭs-fôr′chən) *n.* **1. a.** Bad fortune or ill luck. **b.** The condition resulting from bad fortune or ill luck: *wanted to help those in misfortune.* **2.** A distressing occurrence.

Synonyms: *misfortune, adversity, mishap, mischance, misadventure. Misfortune* applies broadly to bad fortune, usually over a long period and involving circumstances beyond the victim's control. *Adversity* differs principally in being more intense. (The related *calamity, catastrophe, cataclysm, debacle,* and *disaster* are much stronger still.) *Mishap* and *mischance* denote single instances of bad fortune having light consequences; *mischance* especially suggests that the victim was not at fault. *Misadventure* applies to a single instance; it is nonspecific as to severity, but implies some measure of fault or responsibility.

mis·give (mĭs-gĭv′) *v.* **-gave** (-gāv′), **-giv·en** (-gĭv′ən), **-giv·ing, -gives.** *—tr.* To arouse suspicion or apprehension in. *—intr.* To be suspicious, apprehensive, or doubtful. [MIS- + GIVE, to suggest (obs.).]

mis·giv·ing (mĭs-gĭv′ĭng) *n.* A feeling of uncertainty or apprehension: *viewed the proposal with misgiving; had misgivings about going to the dance.*

mis·gov·ern (mĭs-gŭv′ərn) *tr.v.* **-erned, -ern·ing, -erns.** To govern inefficiently or badly. **—mis·gov′ern·ment** *n.* **—mis·gov′er·nor** *n.*

mis·guide (mĭs-gīd′) *tr.v.* **-guid·ed, -guid·ing, -guides.** To give wrong or misleading directions to; lead astray. **—mis·guid′ance** *n.* **—mis·guid′ed·ly** (-gī′dĭd-lē) *adv.* **—mis·guid′er** *n.*

mis·han·dle (mĭs-hăn′dl) *tr.v.* **-dled, -dling, -dles. 1.** To deal with clumsily or inefficiently. **2.** To treat roughly; maltreat.

mis·hap (mĭs′hăp′, mĭs-hăp′) *n.* **1.** Bad luck or misfortune. **2.** An unfortunate accident.

mis·hear (mĭs-hîr′) *tr.v.* **-heard** (-hûrd′), **-hear·ing, -hears.** To hear wrongly or badly; misunderstand.

mish·mash (mĭsh′măsh′, -mäsh′) *n.* A collection or mixture of unrelated things; hodgepodge. [Redup. of MASH.]

Mish·nah also **Mish·na** (mĭsh′nə) *n.* **1.** The first section of the Talmud, comprising a collection of early oral interpretations of the scriptures as compiled about A.D. 200. **2.** A paragraph from the Mishnah. **3.** The teaching of a rabbi or other noted authority on Jewish laws. [Heb. *mishnāh,* instruction < *shānāh,* he repeated.] **—Mish·na′ic** (mĭsh-nā′ĭk) *adj.*

mis·i·den·ti·fy (mĭs′ī-dĕn′tə-fī′) *tr.v.* **-fied, -fy·ing, -fies.** To identify incorrectly. **—mis′i·den′ti·fi·ca′tion** *n.*

mis·im·pres·sion (mĭs′ĭm-prĕsh′ən) *n.* A faulty or mistaken impression.

mis·in·form (mĭs′ĭn-fôrm′) *tr.v.* **-formed, -form·ing, -forms.** To give wrong or inaccurate information to. **—mis′in·form′ant** (-fôr′mənt), **mis′in·form′er** *n.* **—mis·in′for·ma′tion** *n.*

mis·in·ter·pret (mĭs′ĭn-tûr′prĭt) *tr.v.* **-pret·ed, -pret·ing, -prets. 1.** To explain inaccurately. **2.** To err in understanding. **—mis′in·ter′pre·ta′tion** *n.* **—mis′in·ter′pret·er** *n.*

mis·join·der (mĭs-join′dər) *n. Law.* Improper joining of different causes of action or different parties to a lawsuit.

mis·judge (mĭs-jŭj′) *tr. & intr. v.* **-judged, -judg·ing, -judg·es.** To be wrong in judging. **—mis·judg′ment** *n.*

mis·la·bel (mĭs-lā′bəl) *tr.v.* **-beled, -bel·ing, -bels** also **-belled, -bel·ling, -bels.** To label inaccurately.

mis·lay (mĭs-lā′) *tr.v.* **-laid** (-lād′), **-lay·ing, -lays. 1.** To put in a place that is afterward forgotten: *She mislaid her hat.* **2.** To place or put down incorrectly: *mislaid the linoleum.* **—mis·lay′er** *n.*

mis·lead (mĭs-lēd′) *tr.v.* **-led** (-lĕd′), **-lead·ing, -leads. 1.** To lead in the wrong direction. **2.** To lead into error or wrongdoing in action or thought; deceive.

mis·lead·ing (mĭs-lē′dĭng) *adj.* Tending to mislead; deceptive. **—mis·lead′ing·ly** *adv.*

Synonyms: *misleading, deceptive, delusive. Misleading* is the most nonspecific of these terms; it makes no clear implication regarding intent. *Deceptive* applies almost exclusively to surface appearance, and may imply deliberate misrepresentation. *Delusive* stresses calculated misrepresentation or sham.

mis·like (mĭs-līk′) *tr.v.* **-liked, -lik·ing, -likes. 1.** *Archaic.* To be displeasing to. **2.** To disapprove of; dislike. *—n.* Disapproval; dislike. [ME *misliken* < OE *mislīcian* : *mis-,* ill + *līcian,* to please.]

mis·man·age (mĭs-măn′ĭj) *tr.v.* **-aged, -ag·ing, -ag·es.** To manage badly or carelessly. **—mis·man′age·ment** *n.*

mis·mar·riage (mĭs-măr′ĭj) *n.* A marriage that is not suitable.

mis·match (mĭs-măch′) *tr.v.* **-matched, -match·ing, -match·es.** To match unsuitably or inaccurately. **—mis·match′** (mĭs-măch′, mĭs′măch′) *n.*

mis·mate (mĭs-māt′) *tr.v.* **-mat·ed, -mat·ing, -mates.** To mate or match unsuitably.

mis·name (mĭs-nām′) *tr.v.* **-named, -nam·ing, -names.** To call by a wrong name.

mis·no·mer (mĭs-nō′mər) *n.* **1.** An error in naming a person or place. **2.** A name wrongly or unsuitably applied to a person or object. [ME < OFr. *mesnommer,* to misname : *mes-,* wrongly (< Lat. *minus,* less) + *nommer,* to name < Lat. *nominare* < *nomen,* name.]

mi·so (mē′sō) *n.* A thick fermented paste made by grinding together cooked soybeans, rice, and salt, used esp. in making soups. [J.]

miso- or **mis-** *pref.* Hatred: *misogamy.* [Gk. < *misein,* to hate.]

mi·sog·a·my (mĭ-sŏg′ə-mē) *n.* Hatred of marriage. **—mi·sog′a·mist** *n.*

mi·sog·y·ny (mĭ-sŏj′ə-nē) *n.* Hatred of women. [Gk. *misogunia* : *misein,* to hate + *gunē,* women.] **—mis′o·gyn′ic** (mĭs′ə-jĭn′ĭk, -gī′nĭk) *adj.* **—mi·sog′y·nist** *n.* **—mi·sog′y·nis′tic** (-sŏj′ə-nĭs′tĭk), **mi·sog′y·nous** (-sŏj′ə-nəs) *adj.*

mi·sol·o·gy (mĭ-sŏl′ə-jē) *n.* Hatred of reason, argument, or enlightenment. **—mi·sol′o·gist** *n.*

mis·o·ne·ism (mĭs′ə-nē′ĭz′əm) *n.* Hatred of change or innovation. [Ital. *misoneismo* : Gk. *misein,* to hate + Gk. *neos,* new.] **—mis′o·ne′ist** *n.*

mis·o·ri·ent (mĭs-ôr′ē-ənt, -ĕnt′, -ōr′-) *tr.v.* **-ent·ed, -ent·ing, -ents.** To orient incorrectly or inappropriately. **—mis·o′ri·en·ta′tion** *n.*

mis·per·ceive (mĭs′pər-sēv′) *tr.v.* **-ceived, -ceiv·ing, -ceives.** To misunderstand.

mis·place (mĭs-plās′) *tr.v.* **-placed, -plac·ing, -plac·es. 1. a.** To put in a wrong place. **b.** To lose; mislay. **2.** To bestow (confidence, for example) on an improper, unsuitable, or unworthy person or idea. **—mis·place′ment** *n.*

mis·play (mĭs-plā′, mĭs′plā′) *n.* A mistaken action in a game. *—tr.v.* (mĭs-plā′) **-played, -play·ing, -plays.** To make a misplay of.

mis·print (mĭs-prĭnt′) *tr.v.* **-print·ed, -print·ing, -prints.** To print incorrectly. *—n.* (mĭs′prĭnt′, mĭs-prĭnt′). An error in printing.

mis·pri·sion (mĭs-prĭzh′ən) *n. Law.* **1.** Maladministration of public office. **2.** Neglect in preventing or reporting a crime. [ME < OFr. *mesprison* < *mesprendre,* to make a mistake : *mes-,* wrongly (< Lat. *minus,* less) + *prendre,* to take < Lat. *prehendere.*]

mis·prize (mĭs-prīz′) *tr.v.* **-prized, -priz·ing, -priz·es.** To undervalue; disparage.

mis·pro·nounce (mĭs′prə-nouns′) *v.* **-nounced, -nounc·ing, -nounc·es.** *—tr.* To pronounce badly or incorrectly. *—intr.* To make a poor pronunciation. **—mis′pro·nun′ci·a′tion** (-nŭn′sē-ā′shən) *n.*

mis·quote (mĭs-kwōt′) *tr.v.* **-quot·ed, -quot·ing, -quotes.** To quote incorrectly. **—mis′quo·ta′tion** (-kwō-tā′shən) *n.*

mis·read (mĭs-rēd′) *tr.v.* **-read** (-rĕd′), **-read·ing, -reads. 1.** To read inaccurately. **2.** To misinterpret.

mis·reck·on (mĭs-rĕk′ən) *tr. & intr. v.* **-oned, -on·ing, -ons.** To miscalculate.

mis·re·mem·ber (mĭs′rĭ-mĕm′bər) *tr. v.* **-bered, -ber·ing, -bers.** To recollect incorrectly.

mis·re·port (mĭs′rĭ-pôrt′, -pōrt′) *tr.v.* **-port·ed, -port·ing, -ports.** To report mistakenly or falsely. *—n.* An inaccurate or wrong report. **—mis′re·port′er** *n.*

mis·rep·re·sent (mĭs-rĕp′rĭ-zĕnt′) *tr.v.* **-sent·ed, -sent·ing, -sents. 1.** To give an incorrect or misleading representation of. **2.** To serve incorrectly or dishonestly as an official representative of. **—mis·rep′re·sen·ta′tion** *n.* **—mis·rep′re·sen′ta·tive** (-zĕn′tə-tĭv) *adj.* **—mis·rep′re·sent′er** *n.*

mis·rule (mĭs-ro͞ol′) *tr.v.* **-ruled, -rul·ing, -rules.** To rule wrongly, unjustly, or unwisely; misgovern. *—n.* **1.** Misgovernment. **2.** Disorder or lawless confusion.

miss[1] (mĭs) *v.* **missed, miss·ing, miss·es.** *—tr.* **1.** To fail to hit, reach, attain, catch, meet, or otherwise make contact with (a specific object). **2.** To fail to perceive, understand, or otherwise experience: *missed the implications of what he said.* **3.** To fail to accomplish, achieve, or attain (a goal). **4.** To fail to attend or perform: *missed a day of work.* **5. a.** To leave out or omit. **b.** To let go by; let slip: *miss a chance.* **6.** To escape or avoid. **7.** To discover the absence or loss of. **8.** To feel the lack or loss of: *missed his wife.* *—intr.* **1.** To fail to hit or otherwise make contact with something: *He fired his final shot and missed again.* **2. a.** To be unsuccessful; fail. **b.** To lose a benefit or opportunity: *missed out on the promotion.* *—n.* A failure to hit, succeed, or find. [ME *missen* < OE *missan.*]

missel thrush

miss[2] (mĭs) *n.* **1. Miss.** A title of courtesy used before the name of an unmarried woman. **2.** A form of address used without a name in speaking to a usually young woman: *I beg your pardon, miss.* **3.** A young unmarried woman. [Short for MISTRESS.]

mis·sa cantata (mĭs′ə) *n.* A High Mass. [NLat., sung mass.]

mis·sal (mĭs′əl) *n.* **1.** *Rom. Cath. Ch.* A book containing all the prayers and responses necessary for celebrating the Mass throughout the year. **2.** A prayer book. [ME *messel* < Med. Lat. *missale* < neuter of *missalis,* of the Mass < LLat. *missa,* Mass < Lat. *mittere,* to send.]

mis·sel thrush also **mis·tle thrush** (mĭs′əl) *n.* A European thrush, *Turdus viscivorus,* that eats berries, mainly of the mistletoe. [< obs. *missel,* mistletoe < ME *mistel* < OE.]

mis·shape (mĭs-shāp′) *tr.v.* **-shaped** or **-shap·en** (-shā′pən), **-shap·ing, -shapes.** To shape badly; deform. **—mis·shap′en·ly** *adv.* **—mis·shap′er** *n.*

mis·sile (mĭs′əl, -īl′) *n.* **1.** An object or weapon that is fired, thrown, dropped, or otherwise projected at a target; projectile. **2.** A guided missile. **3.** A ballistic missile. [Lat. < neuter of *missilis,* able to be thrown < *mittere,* to let go.]

mis·sile·man (mĭs′əl-mən) *n.* A person skilled in the design, building, or launching of guided missiles.

mis·sile·ry also **mis·sil·ry** (mĭs′əl-rē) *n.* **1.** The art and science of making and using guided or ballistic missiles. **2.** Missiles collectively.

miss·ing (mĭs′ĭng) *adj.* **1.** Not present; lost. **2.** Lacking: *a book with 12 pages missing.*

missing link *n.* **1.** A theoretical primate postulated to bridge the evolutionary gap between the anthropoid apes and man. **2.** Something lacking but needed to complete a series.

mis·sion (mĭsh′ən) *n.* **1. a.** A body of persons sent to conduct negotiations or establish relations with a foreign country. **b.** The business with which such a body of persons is charged. **2. a.** A body of persons sent to do religious work in a foreign land. **b.** An establishment of missionaries abroad. **c.** The district assigned to a missionary. **d. missions.** Missionary duty or work. **e.** A missionary building or compound. **f.** An organization for carrying on missionary work in a territory. **3.** A permanent diplomatic office in a foreign country. **4.** A combat operation assigned to an individual or unit. **5.** A welfare or educational organization set up for the poor. **6.** A church or congregation with no priest of its own. **7.** A series of special religious services for purposes of proselytizing. **8.** A self-imposed duty. *—tr.v.* **-sioned, -sion·ing, -sions. 1.** To send on a mission. **2.** To organize or establish a mission among or in. [Fr. < Lat. *missio* < *mittere,* to send.] **—mis′sion·er** *n.*

mission
Carmel Mission,
Carmel, California

mis·sion·ar·y (mĭsh′ə-nĕr′ē) *n., pl.* **-ies. 1.** One who is sent on a mission, esp. one sent to do religious or charitable work in a territory or foreign country. **2.** A propagandist. *—adj.* **1.** Of or pertaining to missions or missionaries. **2.** Engaged in the activities of a mission or missionary.

3. Tending to propagandize or use insistent persuasion: *missionary fervor.*

mis·sis or **mis·sus** (mĭs′ĭz, -ĭs) *n. Informal.* **1.** The mistress of a household. **2.** One's wife. [Alteration of MISTRESS.]

Mis·sis·sip·pi·an (mĭs′ĭ-sĭp′ē-ən) *adj.* **1.** Of, belonging to, or designating the geologic time, system of rocks, and sedimentary deposits of the fifth period of the Paleozoic era, characterized by the submergence of extensive land areas under shallow seas. **2.** Of or concerned with the state of Mississippi. —*n.* **1.** *Geol.* The Mississippian period. **2.** A native or inhabitant of Mississippi.

mis·sive (mĭs′ĭv) *n.* A letter or message. [< ME *(letter) missive,* (letter) sent (by superior authority) < Med. Lat. *(littere) missive* < neuter of *missivus,* sent < Lat. *mittere,* to send.]

Mis·sou·ri (mĭ-zo͝or′ē) *n., pl.* **Missouri** or **-ris. 1. a.** A tribe of North American Indians formerly inhabiting what is now northern Missouri. **b.** A member of this tribe. **2.** The Siouan language of the Missouri.

mis·spell (mĭs-spĕl′) *tr.v.* **-spelled** or **-spelt** (-spĕlt′), **-spell·ing, -spells.** To spell incorrectly. **—mis·spell′ing** *n.*

mis·spend (mĭs-spĕnd′) *tr.v.* **-spent** (-spĕnt′), **-spend·ing, -spends.** To spend improperly or extravagantly; squander.

mis·state (mĭs-stāt′) *tr.v.* **-stat·ed, -stat·ing, -states.** To state wrongly or falsely. **—mis·state′ment** *n.*

mis·step (mĭs-stĕp′) *n.* **1.** A misplaced or awkward step. **2.** An instance of wrong or improper conduct; blunder.

mis·sus (mĭs′ĭz, -ĭs) *n.* Variant of **missis.**

miss·y (mĭs′ē) *n., pl.* **-ies.** *Informal.* A young girl; miss.

mist (mĭst) *n.* **1.** A mass of fine droplets of water in the atmosphere near or in contact with the earth. **2.** Water vapor condensed on and clouding the appearance of a surface. **3.** Fine drops of a liquid, as perfume, sprayed into the air. **4.** A colloidal suspension of a liquid in a gas. **5.** Something that dims or conceals. **6.** Something that produces or gives the impression of dimness or obscurity: *the mists of the past.* —*v.* **mist·ed, mist·ing, mists.** —*intr.* **1.** To be or become obscured or blurred by or as if by mist. **2.** To rain in a fine shower. —*tr.* To conceal or veil as if with mist. [ME < OE.]

mistletoe

mis·tak·a·ble (mĭ-stā′kə-bəl) *adj.* Capable of being mistaken or misunderstood. **—mis·tak′a·bly** *adv.*

mis·take (mĭ-stāk′) *n.* **1.** An error or fault. **2.** A misconception or misunderstanding. —*v.* **-took, -tak·en, -tak·ing, -takes.** —*tr.* **1.** To understand wrongly; misinterpret: *mistook her politeness for friendship.* **2.** To recognize or identify incorrectly: *He mistook her for her sister.* —*intr.* To make a mistake; err. [< ME *mistaken,* to misunderstand < ON *mistaka,* to take in error : *mis-,* wrongly + *taka,* to take.] **—mis·tak′er** *n.*

mis·tak·en (mĭ-stā′kən) *adj.* **1.** Wrong or incorrect in opinion, understanding, or perception. **2.** Based on error; wrong: *a mistaken view of the situation.* **—mis·tak′en·ly** *adv.*

Mis·ter (mĭs′tər) *n.* **1.** A title of courtesy used when speaking to or of a man, usually written in its abbreviated form and placed before a man's surname or title of office: *Mr. Jones; Mr. Secretary.* **2.** The official term of address for certain U.S. military personnel. **3. mister.** *Informal.* A form of address used without a name: *Watch your step, mister.* [Alteration of MASTER.]

Mister Char·lie (chär′lē) *n. Slang.* Mr. Charlie.

mist·flow·er (mĭst′flou′ər) *n.* A plant, *Eupatorium coelestinum,* of southeastern North America, having clusters of small, blue flowers.

mis·tle thrush (mĭs′əl) *n.* Variant of **missel thrush.**

mis·tle·toe (mĭs′əl-tō′) *n.* **1.** A Eurasian parasitic shrub, *Viscum album,* having leathery evergreen leaves and waxy white berries. **2.** Any of several American parasitic shrubs, such as *Phoradendron flavescens,* of eastern North America. **3.** A mistletoe sprig, often used as a Christmas decoration. [ME *mistelto* < OE *misteltān* : *mistel,* mistletoe + *tān,* twig.]

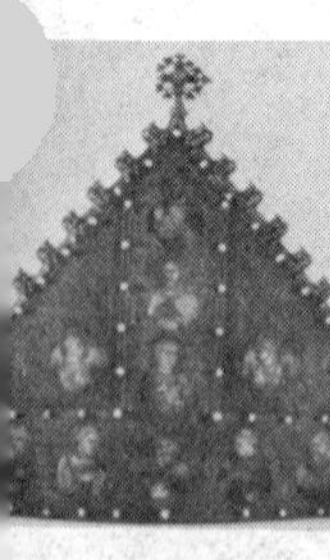

miter
14th-century Italian

mistletoe cactus *n.* A leafless, epiphytic tropical American cactus, *Rhipsalis cassytha.*

mis·took (mĭ-sto͝ok′) *v.* Past tense of **mistake.**

mis·tral (mĭs′trəl, mĭ-sträl′) *n.* A dry, cold northerly wind that blows in squalls through the Rhone Valley and nearby areas toward the Mediterranean coast of southern France. [Fr. < Prov. < Lat. *magistralis,* of a master < *magister,* master.]

mis·treat (mĭs-trēt′) *tr.v.* **-treat·ed, -treat·ing, -treats.** To handle or treat roughly or wrongly; abuse. **—mis·treat′ment** *n.*

mis·tress (mĭs′trĭs) *n.* **1.** A woman in a position of authority, control, or ownership, as the head of a household. **2.** A woman owning an animal or formerly a slave. **3.** A woman who has ultimate control over something: *the mistress of his heart.* **4. a.** A nation or country that has supremacy over others. **b.** Something that directs or reigns personified as female. **5.** A woman who has mastered a skill: *a mistress of cooking.* **6.** A woman who has a continuing sexual relationship with a man to whom she is not married, esp. one who receives financial support from the man. **7. Mistress.** A title of courtesy formerly used when speaking to or of a woman. **8.** *Chiefly Brit.* A female schoolteacher. [ME *mistres* < OFr. *maistresse* < *maistre,* master < Lat. *magister.*]

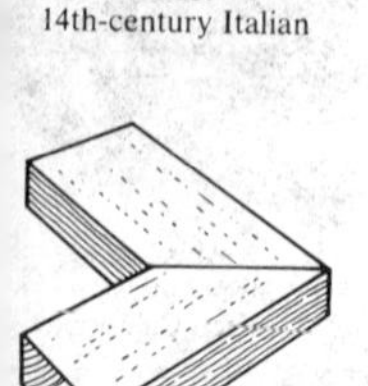

miter joint

mis·tri·al (mĭs-trī′əl, -trīl′) *n. Law.* **1.** A trial that becomes invalid because of basic error in procedure. **2.** An inconclusive trial, such as one in which the jurors fail to agree on a verdict.

mis·trust (mĭs-trŭst′) *n.* Lack of trust. —*v.* **-trust·ed, -trust·ing, -trusts.** —*tr.* To regard without confidence. —*intr.* To be wary or doubtful. **—mis·trust′ful** *adj.* **—mis·trust′ful·ly** *adv.* **—mis·trust′ful·ness** *n.*

mist·y (mĭs′tē) *adj.* **-i·er, -i·est. 1.** Consisting of or resembling mist: *a misty rain.* **2.** Obscured or clouded by or as if by mist. **3.** Lacking in clarity; vague. **—mist′i·ly** *adv.* **—mist′i·ness** *n.*

mist·y-eyed (mĭs′tē-īd′) *adj.* **1.** Having eyes blurred as if by mist. **2.** Having a sentimental or dreamy quality.

mis·un·der·stand (mĭs-ŭn′dər-stănd′) *tr.v.* **-stood** (-sto͝od′), **-stand·ing, -stands.** To understand incorrectly; misinterpret.

mis·un·der·stand·ing (mĭs-ŭn′dər-stăn′dĭng) *n.* **1.** A failure to understand correctly. **2.** A disagreement or quarrel.

mis·us·age (mĭs-yo͞o′sĭj, -zĭj) *n.* **1.** Abusive treatment. **2.** Improper application, as of words.

mis·use (mĭs-yo͞os′) *n.* Improper or incorrect use; misapplication. —*tr.v.* (mĭs-yo͞oz′) **-used, -us·ing, -us·es. 1.** To use wrongly or incorrectly. **2.** To mistreat or abuse.

mis·val·ue (mĭs-văl′yo͞o) *tr.v.* **-ued, -u·ing, -ues.** To value or estimate incorrectly.

mis·ven·ture (mĭs-vĕn′chər) *n.* Variant of **misadventure.**

mis·word (mĭs-wûrd′) *tr.v.* **-word·ed, -word·ing, -words.** To express incorrectly; word improperly.

mite[1] (mīt) *n.* Any of various small arachnids that are often parasitic. [ME < OE *mīte.*]

mite[2] (mīt) *n.* **1. a.** A very small amount of money or contribution. **b.** A widow's mite. **2.** A coin of very small value, esp. an obsolete British coin worth half a farthing. **3.** A very small object, creature, or particle. [ME < MDu., a small Flemish coin.]

mi·ter (mī′tər) *n.* **1.** A tall, pointed hat with peaks in front and back, worn by bishops and certain other ecclesiastics. **2. a.** A thong for binding the hair, worn by women in ancient Greece. **b.** The ceremonial headdress worn by ancient Jewish high priests. **3.** A covering or top of a chimney that permits the release of smoke while keeping out rain and debris. **4. a.** A miter joint. **b.** The edge of a piece of material that has been beveled preparatory to making a miter joint. **c.** A miter square. —*v.* **-tered, -ter·ing, -ters.** —*tr.* **1.** To bestow a miter upon. **2.** To make join with a miter joint. —*intr.* To meet in a miter joint. [ME *mitre* < OFr. < Lat. *mitra,* headband < Gk.]

miter box *n.* **1.** A box open at the ends, with sides slotted to guide a saw in cutting miter joints. **2.** A device for handsaws that may be set to guide cuts in lumber at various degrees.

miter joint *n.* A joint made by beveling each of two surfaces to be joined, usually at a 45° angle, to form a 90° corner.

miter square *n.* A carpenter's square with a blade that is set at a 45° angle or is adjustable.

mi·ter·wort (mī′tər-wûrt′, -wôrt′) *n.* Any of several North American plants of the genus *Mitella,* having heart-shaped leaves and clusters of small white flowers.

Mith·ra·ism (mĭth′rə-ĭz′əm, -rā-) *n.* A Persian religious cult that flourished in the late Roman Empire, rivaling Christianity. **—Mith·ra′ic** (mĭ-thrā′ĭk) *adj.* **—Mith·ra′ist** (mĭ-thrā′ĭst) *n.*

Mith·ras (mĭth′rəs) *n. Myth.* The Persian god of light and guardian against evil, often identified with the sun. [Lat. < Gk. < OPers. *mithra.*]

mith·ri·date (mĭth′rĭ-dāt′) *n.* A substance that is held to be an antidote against poison. [After *Mithridates* (132?–63 B.C.), who is said to have acquired tolerance for poison.]

mith·ri·da·tism (mĭth′rĭ-dā′tĭz′əm) *n.* Tolerance for a poison acquired by taking gradually larger doses of it. **—mith′ri·dat′ic** (-dăt′ĭk) *adj.*

mi·ti·cide (mī′tĭ-sīd′) *n.* An agent that kills mites. **—mi′ti·cid′al** (-sīd′l) *adj.*

mit·i·gate (mĭt′ĭgāt′) *tr. & intr.v.* **-gat·ed, -gat·ing, -gates.** To make or become less severe or intense; moderate. [ME *mitigaten* < Lat. *mitigare* < *mitis,* soft.] **—mit′i·ga·ble** (-gə-bəl) *adj.* **—mit′i·ga′tion** *n.* **—mit′i·ga′tive, mit′i·ga·to′ry** (-gə-tôr′ē, -tōr′ē) *adj.* **—mit′i·ga′tor** *n.*

mi·to·chon·dri·on (mī′tə-kŏn′drē-ən) *n., pl.* **-dri·a** (-drē-ə). *Biol.* A microscopic body found in the cells of almost all living organisms and containing enzymes responsible for the conversion of food to usable energy. [NLat. : Gk. *mitos,* thread + Gk. *khondrion,* dim. of *khondros,* grain.] **—mi′to·chon′dri·al** (-drē-əl) *adj.*

mi·to·gen (mī′tə-jən) *n.* An agent that induces mitosis. [MITO(SIS) + -GEN.] **—mi′to·gen′ic** (mī′tə-jĕn′ĭk, mĭt′ə-) *adj.* **—mi′to·ge·nic′i·ty** (-jə-nĭs′ĭ-tē) *n.*

mi·to·my·cin (mī′tə-mī′sĭn) *n.* A complex of antibiotics produced by the bacterium *Streptomyces caespitosus* that is sometimes used in the chemotherapeutic treatment of cancer. [MITO(SIS) + -MYCIN.]

mi·to·sis (mī-tō′sĭs) *n., pl.* **-ses** (-sēz′). *Biol.* **1.** The sequential differentiation and segregation of replicated chromosomes in a cell nucleus that precedes complete cell division. **2.** The entire sequence of processes in cell division in which the diploid number of chromosomes is retained in both daughter cells. [Gk. *mitos,* thread + -OSIS.] **—mi·tot′ic** (mī-tŏt′ĭk) *adj.* **—mi·tot′i·cal·ly** *adv.*

mi·tral (mī′trəl) *adj.* **1.** Pertaining to or resembling a miter. **2.** Pertaining to a mitral valve. [Fr. < Lat. *mitra,* miter.]

mitral valve *n.* The heart valve between the left auricle and the left ventricle that regulates blood flow from the auricle to the ventricle.

mi·tre (mī′tər) *n. & v. Chiefly Brit.* Variant of **miter.**

mitt (mĭt) *n.* **1.** A woman's glove that extends over the hand but only partially covers the fingers. **2.** A mitten. **3.** A baseball glove, esp. a large leather padded glove used by catchers and first basemen. **4.** *Slang.* A hand or fist. [Short for MITTEN.]

mit·ten (mĭt′n) *n.* A covering for the hand that encases the thumb separately and the four fingers together. [ME *mytan* < OFr. *mitaine,* prob. < Lat. *medietas,* half < *medius,* middle.]

mit·ti·mus (mĭt′ə-məs) *n., pl.* **-mus·es.** *Law.* A writ instructing a jailer to hold a prisoner. [Lat., we send (the first word of the writ).]

mitz·vah (mĭts′və) *n., pl.* **-voth** (-vōth′, -vōt′) or **-vahs. 1. a.** A commandment of the Jewish law. **b.** The fulfillment of such a commandment. **2.** A worthy deed. [Heb. *miṣwāh.*]

mix (mĭks) *v.* **mixed, mix·ing, mix·es.** *—tr.* **1. a.** To combine or blend into one mass or mixture so that the constituent parts are indistinguishable. **b.** To create or form by adding ingredients together. **c.** To add (an ingredient or element) to another. **2.** To combine or join: *mix joy with sorrow.* **3.** To bring into social contact: *mix boys and girls in a coeducational school.* **4.** To crossbreed. *—intr.* **1. a.** To become mixed or blended together. **b.** To be capable of being blended together: *Oil does not mix with water.* **2.** To associate socially or get along with others: *He does not mix well at parties.* **3.** To be crossbred. ***—phrasal verb.* mix up. 1.** To confuse; confound. **2.** To involve: *Don't let him mix you up in a power struggle.* *—n.* **1.** An act of mixing. **2.** A mixture, esp. of ingredients packaged and sold commercially: *a cake mix.* **3.** A tape recording or a phonograph record that is produced by combining and adjusting sounds. ***—idiom.* mix it up.** *Slang.* To fight. [Back-formation < obs. *mixte,* mixed < ME < OFr. < Lat. *mixtus,* p.part. of *miscēre,* to mix.] **—mix′a·ble** *adj.*

Synonyms: *mix, blend, mingle, coalesce, merge, amalgamate, combine, compound, fuse.* The verb *mix* is nonspecific, implying only components capable of existing together. *Blend* (transitive) denotes purposeful mixing; intransitively, it suggests that the components shade into each other. In either case the result is harmonious, and the components lose some or all of their original definition. *Mingle* implies no such loss of individual characteristics. *Coalesce* involves a union slowly achieved, with a distinct new identity. *Merge* also stresses new identity. *Amalgamate* implies a looser union, akin to a federation. *Combine* is usually applied to the union of a small number of elements, and implies resultant homogeneity. *Compound* stresses studious care in mixing distinct elements, which when united assume a new and independent character. *Fuse* emphasizes enduring union, as of molten metals, achieved under stress and strongly marked by loss of identity of parts.

mixed (mĭkst) *adj.* **1.** Blended together into one unit or mass; intermingled. **2.** Composed of a variety of differing, sometimes conflicting entities: *mixed emotions.* **3.** Made up of people of different sex, race, or social class.

mixed bag *n.* A collection of dissimilar things; assortment.

mixed drink *n.* A drink made of one or more kinds of liquor combined with other ingredients, usually shaken or stirred before serving.

mixed grill *n.* A dish consisting of a variety of broiled meats and vegetables, typically including a lamb chop.

mixed marriage *n.* Marriage between persons of different races or religions.

mixed-me·di·a (mĭkst′mē′dē-ə) *adj.* Multimedia.

mixed metaphor *n.* A succession of metaphors that produce an incongruous and ludicrous effect, as *His mounting ambition was soon bridled by a wave of opposition.*

mixed nerve *n.* A nerve that contains both sensory and motor fibers.

mixed number *n.* A number, such as 7¼, equal to the sum of an integer and a fraction.

mixed-up (mĭkst′ŭp′) *adj. Informal.* Being in a state of confusion; muddled: *just a mixed-up kid.*

mix·er (mĭk′sər) *n.* **1.** One that mixes. **2.** A sociable person. **3.** An informal dance or party arranged to give members of a group an opportunity to get acquainted. **4.** A device that blends or mixes substances or ingredients, esp. by mechanical agitation. **5.** A beverage, such as soda water or ginger ale, used in diluting alcoholic drinks.

mix·ol·o·gy (mĭk-sŏl′ə-jē) *n.* The study or skill of preparing mixed drinks. **—mix·ol′o·gist** *n.*

mixt (mĭkst) *v. Archaic.* A past tense and past participle of **mix.**

mix·ture (mĭks′chər) *n.* **1.** Something produced by mixing. **2.** Something consisting of diverse elements: *a mixture of joy and sorrow.* **3.** A fabric made of different kinds of thread or yarn. **4. a.** The act or process of mixing. **b.** The condition of being mixed. **5.** *Chem.* A composition of two or more substances that are not chemically bound to each other. [Fr. < Lat. *mixtura* < *miscēre,* to mix.]

Synonyms: *mixture, blend, admixture, combination, compound, composite, amalgam. Mixture,* being nonspecific, overlaps, in nontechnical use, all of these terms. *Blend* denotes a harmonious mixture in which the original components are modified substantially. *Admixture* applies when one ingredient is not in harmony with the fundamental quality of the new union. *Combination* applies broadly to any union of rather few components. *Compound* stresses careful, purposeful mixing; the new product has an independent identity not necessarily deducible from its components. *Composite* implies more components and less deliberation in mixing; the new product lacks the unity of a compound, since the components do not wholly lose their identities. *Amalgam* implies a union more homogeneous than a composite but less sharply defined than a compound.

mix-up (mĭks′ŭp′) *n.* **1.** A state of confusion; muddle. **2.** *Informal.* A fight or melee.

Mi·zar (mī′zär′) *n.* The star at the crook of the handle of the Big Dipper. [Ar. *mi'zar,* Mizar, veil.]

miz·zen or **miz·en** (mĭz′ən) *n.* **1.** A fore-and-aft sail set on the mizzenmast. **2.** A mizzenmast. [ME *meson* < OFr. *misaine,* prob. < OItal. *mezzana* < *mezzano,* middle < Lat. *medianus* < *medius,* half.] **—miz′zen** *adj.*

miz·zen·mast or **miz·en·mast** (mĭz′ən-məst, -măst′) *n.* **1.** The third mast aft on sailing ships carrying three or more masts. **2.** A jigger mast (sense 1).

miz·zle[1] (mĭz′əl) *intr.v.* **-zled, -zling, -zles.** To rain in fine, mistlike droplets. *—n.* A mistlike rain. [ME *misellen.*] **—miz′zly** *adv.*

miz·zle[2] (mĭz′əl) *intr.v.* **-zled, -zling, -zles.** *Chiefly Brit.* To make a sudden departure. [Orig. unknown.]

Mn The symbol for the element **manganese.**

mne·mon·ic (nĭ-mŏn′ĭk) *adj.* Relating to, assisting, or designed to assist the memory. *—n.* A device, such as a formula or rhyme, used as an aid in remembering. [Gk. *mnēmonikos,* of memory < *mnēmōn,* mindful < *mnasthai,* to remember.] **—mne·mon′i·cal·ly** *adv.*

mne·mon·ics (nĭ-mŏn′ĭks) *n. (used with a sing. verb).* A system to improve or develop the memory.

Mne·mos·y·ne (nĭ-mŏs′ə-nē, -mŏz′-) *n. Gk. Myth.* The goddess of memory, mother of the Muses. [Lat. < Gk. *Mnēmosunē* < *mnasthai,* to remember.]

-mo *suff.* Used after numerals to indicate the number of leaves that results from folding a sheet of paper: *twelvemo.* [< DUODECIMO.]

Mo The symbol for the element molybdenum.

mo·a (mō′ə) *n.* Any of various large, long-necked, flightless birds of the order Dinorthiformes, native to New Zealand and extinct for over a century. [Maori.]

Mo·ab·ite (mō′ə-bīt′) *n.* **1.** In the Old Testament, a descendant of Moab, the son of Lot. **2.** An inhabitant or native of Moab. **—Mo′a·bite′** *adj.*

moan (mōn) *n.* **1. a.** A low, sustained, mournful sound, usually indicative of sorrow or pain. **b.** A similar sound: *the moan of the wind.* **2.** Lamentation. *—v.* **moaned, moan·ing, moans.** *—intr.* **1. a.** To utter a moan. **b.** To make a sound resembling a moan. **2.** To complain, lament, or grieve. *—tr.* **1.** To bewail: *He moaned his misfortunes to anyone who would listen.* **2.** To utter with a moan. [ME *mone,* complaint.]

moat (mōt) *n.* A wide, deep ditch, usually filled with water, surrounding a medieval town, fortress, or castle as a protection against assault. *—tr.v.* **moat·ed, moat·ing, moats.** To surround with or as if with a moat. [ME *mote* < OFr., mound.]

mob (mŏb) *n.* **1.** A large, disorderly crowd or throng. **2.** The masses; the common people. **3.** *Informal.* An organized gang of criminals; crime syndicate. *—tr.v.* **mobbed, mob·bing, mobs. 1.** To crowd around and jostle or annoy, esp. in anger or excessive enthusiasm: *The audience mobbed the singer.* **2.** To crowd into: *Crowds mobbed the fairgrounds.* **3.** To attack violently, usually in a crowd or mob. [Short for obs. *mobile* < Lat. *mobile* (*vulgus*), fickle (crowd).]

mob·cap (mŏb′kăp′) *n.* A large, high cap trimmed with frills and ribbons, worn by women in the 18th and early 19th centuries. [Obs. *mob,* mobcap (poss. < obs. Du. *mop*) + CAP.]

mo·bile (mō′bəl, -bēl′, -bīl′) *adj.* **1.** Capable of moving or of being moved from place to place. **2.** Moving quickly from one state to another: *a mobile, expressive face.* **3. a.** Marked by the easy intermixing of different social groups: *a mobile society.* **b.** Having the possibility of relatively easy movement from one social class or level to another: *an upwardly mobile generation.* **4.** Flowing freely: *a mobile liquid.* *—n.* (mō′bēl′). A type of sculpture consisting of parts that move, esp. in response to air currents. —See Usage note at **movable.** [OFr. < Lat. *mobilis* < *movēre,* to move.] **—mo·bil′i·ty** (-bĭl′ĭ-tē) *n.*

mobile home *n.* A house trailer that is used as a permanent home and is usually hooked up to utilities.

mo·bi·lize (mō′bə-līz′) *v.* **-lized, -liz·ing, -liz·es.** *—tr.* **1.** To make mobile. **2. a.** To assemble, prepare, or put into operation for war or a similar emergency: *mobilize troops.* **b.** To assemble or coordinate for a particular purpose: *mobilized the country's economic resources.* *—intr.* To become prepared for war or a similar emergency. [Fr. *mobiliser* < *mobile,* mobile < OFr.] **—mo′bi·li·za′tion** *n.*

Mö·bi·us strip (mœ′bē-əs) *n.* A one-sided surface that can

mitt

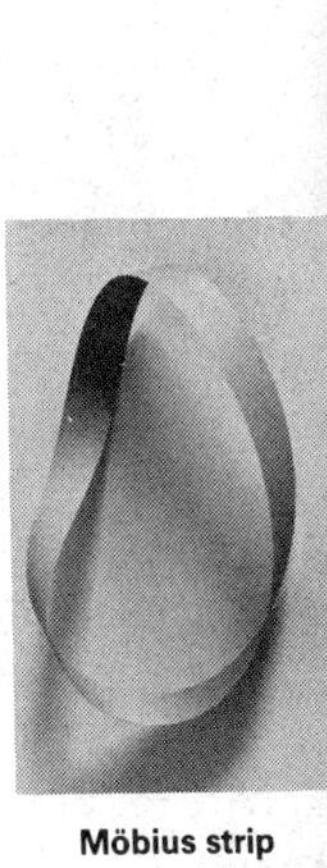

Möbius strip

be formed from a rectangular strip by rotating one end 180° and attaching it to the other end. [After August *Möbius* (1790–1868).]

moccasin

mob·oc·ra·cy (mŏb-ŏk′rə-sē) *n., pl.* **-cies. 1.** Political control by a mob. **2.** The mob as the source of political control. **—mob′o·crat** (mŏb′ə-krăt) *n.* **—mob′o·crat′ic** (-krăt′ĭk), **mob′o·crat′i·cal** *adj.*

mob·ster (mŏb′stər) *n. Slang.* A member of a criminal gang.

moc·ca·sin (mŏk′ə-sĭn) *n.* **1.** A soft leather slipper worn by American Indians. **2.** A shoe or slipper resembling an Indian moccasin. **3.** The water moccasin. [Natick *mohkussin.*]

moccasin flower *n.* Any of several North American orchids of the genus *Cypripedium,* esp. *C. acaule,* of eastern North America, having a solitary flower with a pouchlike pink lip.

mo·cha (mō′kə) *n.* **1.** A rich, pungent Arabian coffee. **2.** Coffee of high quality. **3.** A flavoring made of coffee often mixed with chocolate. **4.** A soft, thin glove leather usually made from goatskin. **5.** A dark olive brown. [After *Mocha,* a port of Yemen, from which it was orig. exported.]

mock (mŏk) *v.* **mocked, mock·ing, mocks.** *—tr.* **1.** To treat with ridicule or contempt; deride. **2. a.** To mimic, as in sport or derision. **b.** To imitate; counterfeit. **3.** To frustrate the hopes of. *—intr.* To express scorn or ridicule: *They mocked at the idea.* *—n.* **1. a.** An act of mocking. **b.** Mockery; derision. **2.** Something deserving of derision. **3.** An imitation or counterfeit. *—adv.* In an insincere or pretending manner: *mock-sorrowful.* *—adj.* Simulated; false; sham: *a mock battle.* [ME *mokken* < OFr. *mocquer.*] **—mock′er** *n.* **—mock′ing·ly** *adv.*

mock·er·y (mŏk′ə-rē) *n., pl.* **-ies. 1.** Scornful ridicule or derision. **2.** A specific action of ridicule or derision. **3.** An object of scorn or ridicule. **4.** A false, derisive, or impudent imitation. **5.** Something that is ludicrously futile or unsuitable.

mock-he·ro·ic (mŏk′hĭ-rō′ĭk) *n., pl.* **mock-he·ro·ics.** A satirical imitation or burlesque of the heroic manner or style. **—mock′-he·ro′ic** *adj.* **—mock′-he·ro′i·cal·ly** *adv.*

mock·ing·bird (mŏk′ĭng-bûrd′) *n.* Any of several species of New World birds of the family Mimidae, esp. *Mimus polyglottos,* a gray and white bird of the southern United States.

mock moon *n.* A paraselene.

mock orange *n.* **1.** Any of several deciduous shrubs of the genus *Philadelphus,* having white, usually fragrant flowers. **2.** Any of various shrubs or trees having flowers or fruit resembling those of the orange.

mock turtle soup *n.* Soup made from calf's head or veal and spiced to taste like green turtle soup.

mock·up also **mock-up** (mŏk′ŭp′) *n.* A scale model, usually full-sized, of a structure, used for demonstration, study, or testing.

mod (mŏd) *n.* A modern and unconventional style of fashionable dress originating in England. *—adj.* **1.** In or characteristic of the mod style. **2.** Stylishly up-to-date, esp. in dress. [After *the Mods,* name of several gangs of English youths, short for MODERN.]

mo·dal (mōd′l) *adj.* **1.** Of, pertaining to, or characteristic of a mode. **2.** *Gram.* Of, pertaining to, or expressing the mood of a verb. **3.** *Mus.* Of, pertaining to, characteristic of, or composed in any of the modes typical of medieval church music. **4.** *Philos.* Of or pertaining to mode as opposed to substance. **5.** *Logic.* Expressing or characterized by modality. **6.** *Statistics.* Of or pertaining to a statistical mode. [Med. Lat. *modalis* < Lat. *modus,* measure.] **—mo′dal·ly** *adv.*

modal auxiliary *n.* One of a set of English verbs, including *can, may, must, ought, shall, should, will,* and *would,* that are characteristically used with other verbs to express mood or tense.

mo·dal·i·ty (mō-dăl′ĭ-tē) *n., pl.* **-ties. 1.** The fact, state, or quality of being modal. **2.** A tendency to conform to a general pattern or type. **3.** *Logic.* The classification of propositions on the basis of whether they assert or deny the possibility, impossibility, contingency, or necessity of their content. **4.** *Med.* **a.** A method of therapy, usually physical, such as massage. **b.** An apparatus for such a therapy.

mode (mōd) *n.* **1. a.** Manner, way, or method of doing or acting: *modern modes of travel.* **b.** A particular form, variety, or manner: *a mode of expression.* **c.** A given condition of functioning; status: *The spacecraft was in its recovery mode.* **2.** The current or customary fashion or style. **3.** *Mus.* **a.** Any of certain arrangements of the diatonic tones of an octave. **b.** One of several patterned arrangements characteristic of classical Greek and medieval church music. **4.** *Philos.* The particular form or manner in which an underlying substance, or some permanent aspect or attribute of it, is manifested. **5.** *Logic.* **a.** The arrangement or order of the propositions in a syllogism according to both quality and quantity. **b.** The modality of a proposition. **6.** *Statistics.* The value or item occurring most frequently in a series of observations or statistical data. **7.** *Geol.* The mineral composition of a specific sample of igneous rock. **8.** *Physics.* Any of numerous patterns of wave motion, as of acoustic waves. [ME, tune < Lat. *modus,* tune, manner.]

mod·el (mŏd′l) *n.* **1.** A small object, usually built to scale, that represents another, often larger object. **2.** A preliminary pattern serving as the plan from which an item not yet constructed will be produced. **3.** A tentative description of a system or theory that accounts for all of its known properties. **4.** A style or design of an item. **5.** An example to be imitated or compared: *a model of decorum.* **6.** One that serves as the subject for an artist or photographer. **7.** A person employed to display merchandise. *—v.* **-eled, -el·ing, -els** also **-elled, -el·ling, -els.** *—tr.* **1.** To make or construct a model of. **2.** To plan or fashion according to a model. **3.** To make by shaping a plastic substance. **4.** To make conform to a chosen standard: *He modeled his manners on his father's.* **5.** To display by wearing or posing. **6.** In painting and drawing, to give a three-dimensional appearance to, as by shading. *—intr.* **1.** To make a model. **2.** To serve as a model. *—adj.* **1.** Serving as or used as a model. **2.** Worthy of imitation: *a model child.* [OFr. *modelle* < OItal. *modello* < Lat. *modulus,* dim. of *modus,* measure.] **—mod′el·er** *n.*

mo·dem (mō′dĕm′) *n.* A device that converts data from one form into another, as from one usable in data processing to one usable in telephonic transmission. [MO(DULATOR) + DEM(ODULATOR).]

mod·er·ate (mŏd′ər-ĭt) *adj.* **1.** Within reasonable limits; not excessive or extreme: *a moderate price.* **2.** Not violent; mild: *a moderate climate.* **3.** Of medium or average quantity, quality, or extent. **4.** Opposed to radical or extreme views or measures, esp. in politics and religion. *—n.* One who holds moderate views or opinions. *—v.* (mŏd′ə-rāt′) **-at·ed, -at·ing, -ates.** *—tr.* **1.** To make less violent, severe, or extreme. **2.** To preside over: *chosen to moderate the convention.* *—intr.* **1.** To become less violent, severe, or extreme; abate. **2.** To act as a moderator. [Lat. *moderatus,* p.part. of *moderare,* to reduce.] **—mod′er·ate·ly** *adv.* **—mod′er·a′tion** *n.*

mod·e·ra·to (mŏd′ə-rä′tō) *adv. Mus.* In moderate tempo; slower than allegretto but faster than andante. Used as a direction. **—mod′e·ra′to** *adj. & n.* [Ital. < Lat. *moderatus,* moderate.]

mod·er·a·tor (mŏd′ə-rā′tər) *n.* **1.** One that moderates. **2.** The officer who presides over a synod or general assembly of the Presbyterian Church. **3.** A substance, such as water or graphite, that is used in a nuclear reactor to decrease the speed of fast neutrons and increase the likelihood of fission.

mod·ern (mŏd′ərn) *adj.* **1.** Of, pertaining to, or characteristic of recent times or the present. **2.** Of or relating to advanced style, technique, or technology. *—n.* **1.** One who lives in modern times. **2.** One who has modern ideas, standards, or beliefs. **3.** *Printing.* Any of a variety of type faces characterized by strongly contrasted heavy and thin parts. [OFr. *moderne* < LLat. *modernus* < Lat. *modo,* just now < *modus,* measure.] **—mo·dern′i·ty** (mŏ-dûr′nĭ-tē), **mod′ern·ness** *n.* **—mod′ern·ly** *adv.*

Modern English *n.* English since about 1500.

Modern Greek *n.* Greek since the early 16th century.

Modern Hebrew *n.* New Hebrew.

mod·ern·ism (mŏd′ər-nĭz′əm) *n.* **1.** Modern thought, character, or practice. **2.** Something, as a peculiarity of usage or style, that is characteristic of modern times. **3.** Often **Modernism.** In Christian Churches, the name given to movements that attempt to define church teachings in the light of modern revolutions in science and philosophy. **4.** The theory and practice of modern art. **—mod′ern·ist** *n.* **—mod′ern·is′tic** *adj.*

mod·ern·ize (mŏd′ər-nīz′) *v.* **-ized, -iz·ing, -iz·es.** *—tr.* To make modern in appearance, style, or character. *—intr.* To accept or adopt modern ways, ideas, or style. **—mod′ern·i·za′tion** *n.*

modern pentathlon *n.* A pentathlon.

mod·est (mŏd′ĭst) *adj.* **1.** Having or showing a moderate estimation of one's own talents, abilities, and value. **2.** Having a shy and retiring nature; reserved. **3.** Observing conventional proprieties in speech, behavior, or dress. **4.** Quiet and humble in appearance; unpretentious: *a modest house.* **5.** Moderate; not extreme: *a modest charge.* [OFr. *modeste* < Lat. *modestus.*] **—mod′est·ly** *adv.*

mod·es·ty (mŏd′ĭ-stē) *n., pl.* **-ties. 1.** The state or quality of being modest. **2.** Reserve or propriety in speech, dress, or behavior. **3.** Lack of pretentiousness.

mod·i·cum (mŏd′ĭ-kəm) *n., pl.* **-cums** or **-ca** (-kə). A small amount or quantity. [ME < Lat., neuter of *modicus,* moderate < *modus,* measure.]

mod·i·fi·ca·tion (mŏd′ə-fĭ-kā′shən) *n.* **1.** The act of modifying or the condition of being modified. **2.** The result of modifying. **3.** A small alteration, adjustment, or limitation. **4.** *Biol.* A physical change in an organism due to environment or activity. **5.** *Ling.* **a.** A change undergone by a word as it passes from language to language. **b.** The linguistic change of a morpheme from one construction to another. **—mod′i·fi·ca′tor** *n.* **—mod′i·fi·ca·to·ry** (-kā′tə-rē), **mod′i·fi·ca′tive** (-kā′tĭv) *adj.*

modified American plan *n.* A system of hotel management in which guests pay a fixed daily or weekly rate for room, breakfast, and lunch or dinner.

mod·i·fi·er (mŏd′ə-fī′ər) *n.* **1.** One that modifies. **2.** *Gram.* A word, phrase, or clause that limits or qualifies the sense of another word or word group.

mod·i·fy (mŏd′ə-fī′) *v.* **-fied, -fy·ing, -fies.** *—tr.* **1.** To change in form or character; alter. **2.** To make less extreme, severe, or strong. **3.** *Gram.* To qualify or limit the meaning of. For example, *"summer"* modifies *"day"* in the phrase *a summer day.* **4.** *Ling.* To change (a vowel) by umlaut. *—intr.* To be or become modified. [ME *modifien,* to limit < OFr. *modifier* < Lat. *modificare* : *modus,* measure + *facere,* to make.] **—mod'i·fi'a·ble** *adj.*

mo·dil·lion (mō-dĭl'yən) *n. Archit.* An ornamental bracket used in series under the cornice of the Corinthian, Composite, or Ionic orders. [Ital. *modiglione* < VLat. **mutillio* < Lat. *mutulus.*]

mo·di·o·lus (mō-dī'ə-ləs) *n., pl.* **-li** (-lī'). The central, conical, bony shaft of the cochlea. [NLat. < Lat., dim. of *modius,* a measure for grain.]

mod·ish (mō'dĭsh) *adj.* Being in or conforming to the prevailing or current fashion; stylish. [< MODE.] **—mod'ish·ly** *adv.* **—mod'ish·ness** *n.*

mo·diste (mō-dēst') *n.* One who produces, designs, or deals in ladies' fashions. [Fr. < *mode,* fashion < Lat. *modus.*]

mod·u·lar (mŏj'ə-lər) *adj.* **1.** Of, relating to, or based on a module. **2.** Designed with standardized units or dimensions for flexible use: *modular furniture.* **—mod'u·lar'i·ty** (-lăr'ĭ-tē) *n.* **—mod'u·lar·ly** *adv.*

mod·u·lar·ized (mŏj'ə-lə-rīzd', mŏd'yə-) *adj.* Having or comprised of modules.

mod·u·late (mŏj'ə-lāt') *v.* **-lat·ed, -lat·ing, -lates.** *—tr.* **1.** To adjust or adapt to a certain proportion; temper. **2.** To change or vary the pitch, intensity, or tone of: *modulated his voice.* **3.** *Electronics.* To vary the frequency, amplitude, phase, or other characteristic of (a carrier wave). *—intr.* **1.** *Mus.* **a.** To pass from one key or tonality to another by means of a regular melodic chord or progression. **b.** To sing or play with modulation. **2.** *Electronics.* To vary the frequency, amplitude, phase, or other characteristic of any carrier wave. [Lat. *modulari, modulat-* < *modulus,* dim. of *modus,* measure.] **—mod'u·la·bil'i·ty** *n.* **—mod'u·la'tive, mod'u·la·to'ry** (-lə-tôr'ē, -tōr'ē) *adj.*

mod·u·la·tion (mŏj'ə-lā'shən) *n.* **1.** The act or process of modulating. **2.** The state of being modulated. **3.** *Mus.* A passing from one tonality to another by means of a regular melodic or chord progression. **4.** A change in pitch or loudness of the voice, esp. the use of a particular intonation or inflection of the voice to convey meaning. **5.** *Electronics.* The variation of a property of an electromagnetic wave or signal, such as its amplitude, frequency, or phase, in a manner determined by another wave or signal.

mod·u·la·tor (mŏj'ə-lā'tər) *n.* **1.** One that modulates. **2.** *Electronics.* A device or electric circuit used to modulate a carrier wave. **3.** *Anat.* A nerve fiber in the retina of the eye, related to color discrimination.

mod·ule (mŏj'o͞ol) *n.* **1.** A standard or unit of measurement. **2.** *Archit.* **a.** The part of a construction used as a standard to which the rest is proportioned. **b.** A uniform structural component used repeatedly in a building. **c.** A standardized unit designed for use with others of its kind. **3.** *Electronics.* A self-contained assembly of electronic components and circuitry, such as a stage in a computer. **4.** A self-contained unit of a spacecraft that performs a specific task or class of tasks in support of the major function of the craft. **5.** A unit of instruction that covers a single topic or a small section of a broad topic. [Lat. *modulus,* dim. of *modus,* measure.]

mod·u·lus (mŏj'ə-ləs) *n., pl.* **-li** (-lī'). **1.** *Physics.* A constant or coefficient that expresses the degree to which a substance possesses some property. **2.** *Math.* **a.** The absolute value of a complex number. **b.** A number or quantity that produces the same remainder when divided into each of two quantities. **c.** The number by which a logarithm in one system must be multiplied to obtain the corresponding logarithm in another system. **3.** A standard; norm. [NLat. < Lat., dim. of *modus,* measure.] **—mod'u·lar** (-lər) *adj.*

mo·dus op·er·an·di (mō'dəs ŏp'ə-răn'dē, -dī') *n.* A method of operating. [Lat.]

modus vi·ven·di (vĭ-vĕn'dē, -dī') *n.* **1.** A way of living. **2.** A temporary agreement between contending parties pending a final settlement. [Lat.]

mo·fette also **mof·fette** (mō-fĕt') *n.* **1.** An opening in the earth from which carbon dioxide and other gases escape, usually marking the last stage of volcanic activity. **2.** The gases escaping from a mofette. [Fr., gaseous exhalation < Ital. *moffetta,* prob. of Germanic orig.]

Mo·gen Da·vid (mô'gən dô'vĭd) *n.* Variant of **Magen David.**

Mo·ghul (mo͞o-gŭl') *n.* Variant of **Mogul** (sense 1).

mo·gul (mō'gəl) *n.* A small mound on a ski slope. [Prob. of Scand. orig.]

Mo·gul (mō'gəl, mō-gŭl') *n.* **1.** Also **Mo·ghul** (mo͞o-gŭl'). **a.** One of the followers of Baber who conquered India in 1526 and founded a Moslem empire that formally lasted until 1857. **b.** A descendant of a follower of Baber. **2.** A Mongol or Mongolian. **3. mogul.** A very rich or powerful person; magnate. [Pers. *Mughul* < Mongolian *Mongul.*] **—Mo'gul** *adj.*

mo·hair (mō'hâr') *n.* **1. a.** The hair of the Angora goat. **b.** A shiny, heavy, woolly fabric made of this hair, often with a mixture of cotton. **2.** An upholstery fabric with mohair pile. [Alteration of obs. *mocayare* < Ital. *moccaiaro* < Ar. *mukhayyar.*]

Mo·ham·med·an (mō-hăm'ĭ-dən) also **Mu·ham·mad·an** or **Mu·ham·med·an** (mo͞o-) *adj.* Of or pertaining to Mohammed or Islam; Moslem. *—n.* A follower of Mohammed or Islam; Moslem.

Mo·ham·med·an·ism (mō-hăm'ĭ-də-nĭz'əm) also **Mu·ham·mad·an·ism** (mo͞o-) *n.* Islam.

Mo·har·ram (mō-hăr'əm) *n.* Variant of **Muharram.**

Mo·ha·ve also **Mo·ja·ve** (mō-hä'vē) *n., pl.* **Mohave** or **-ves** also **Mojave** or **-ves. 1.** A tribe of Yuman-speaking Indians, formerly living along the Gila and Colorado rivers. **2.** A member of the Mohave. [Mohave *hamokhava,* three peaks.] **—Mo·ha've** *adj.*

Mo·hawk (mō'hôk') *n., pl.* **Mohawk** or **-hawks. 1. a.** A tribe of Iroquoian-speaking Indians who occupied the territory from the Mohawk River to the St. Lawrence. **b.** A member of this tribe. **2.** The Iroquoian language of the Mohawk. [Narraganset *mohowaugsuck.*] **—Mo'hawk'** *adj.*

Mo·he·gan (mō-hē'gən) *n., pl.* **Mohegan** or **-gans. 1.** A tribe of Algonquian-speaking Indians, formerly living in the area around the Thames River, Connecticut. **2.** A member of the Mohegan. [Prob. of Algonquian orig.] **—Mo·he'gan** *adj.*

Mo·hi·can (mō-hē'kən) *n.* Variant of **Mahican.**

Mo·hock (mō'hŏk') *n.* One of a band of young aristocrats who vandalized London in the early 18th century. [Alteration of MOHAWK.] **—Mo'hock·ism** *n.*

Mo·ho·ro·vi·čić discontinuity (mō'hə-rō'və-chĭch) *n.* The boundary between the earth's crust and the subjacent mantle rock, ranging in depth from 6 to 8 miles, or 9.65 to 12.87 kilometers, under ocean basins to 20 to 25 miles, or 32.18 to 40.23 kilometers, under continents. [After Andrija *Mohorovičić* (1857–1936).]

Mohs scale (mōz) *n.* A scale for determining the relative hardness of a mineral according to its resistance to scratching by one of the following minerals, arranged in order of increasing hardness: 1. talc; 2. gypsum; 3. calcite; 4. fluorite; 5. apatite; 6. feldspar; 7. vitreous silica; 8. quartz; 9. topaz; 10. garnet; 11. fused zirconia; 12. fused alumina; 13. silicon carbide; 14. boron carbide; 15. diamond. [After Friedrich *Mohs* (1773–1839).]

mo·hur (mō'ər, mə-ho͝or') *n.* A gold coin formerly used in India. [Hindi *muhar* < Pers. *muhr,* seal.]

moi·dore (moi'dôr', -dōr', moi-dôr', -dōr') *n.* A former Portuguese or Brazilian gold coin. [Alteration of Port. *moeda de ouro,* coin of gold.]

moi·e·ty (moi'ĭ-tē) *n., pl.* **-ties. 1.** A half. **2.** A part, portion, or share. **3.** Either of two basic units that make up a tribe on the basis of unilateral descent. [ME *moite* < OFr. < LLat. *medietas,* half < Lat. *medius,* middle.]

moil (moil) *intr.v.* **moiled, moil·ing, moils. 1.** To toil; slave. **2.** To churn about. *—n.* **1.** Toil; drudgery. **2.** Confusion; turmoil. [ME *moillen,* to wet < OFr. *moillier* < Lat. *mollis,* soft.] **—moil'er** *n.*

moi·ré (mwä-rā') also **moire** (mwär, mwä-rā') *n.* **1.** Cloth, esp. silk, that has a watered or wavy pattern. **2.** A watered pattern produced on cloth by engraved rollers. [Fr. < *moirer,* to water.] **—moi·ré'** *adj.*

moiré effect *n.* The effect of superimposing a repetitive design to produce a pattern distinct from its components.

moist (moist) *adj.* **-er, -est. 1.** Slightly wet or damp. **2.** Filled with moisture. **3.** Tearful. [ME *moiste* < OFr. < Lat. *mucidus,* moldy < *mucus,* mucus.] **—moist'ly** *adv.* **—moist'ness** *n.*

mois·ten (moi'sən) *tr. & intr.v.* **-tened, -ten·ing, -tens.** To make or become moist. **—mois'ten·er** *n.*

mois·ture (mois'chər) *n.* Diffuse wetness that can be felt as vapor in the atmosphere or as condensed liquid on the surfaces of objects; dampness. [ME < OFr. *moistour* < *moiste,* moist.]

mois·tur·ize (mois'chə-rīz') *—tr.v.* **-ized, -iz·ing, -iz·es.** To add moisture to: *lotion that moisturizes the face.* **—mois'tur·iz'er** *n.*

mo·jar·ra (mō-hăr'ə) *n., pl.* **mojarra** or **-ras. 1.** Any of several species of small American marine fishes of the family Gerridae, having extremely protrusile mouths. **2.** Any of several tropical American freshwater fishes of the family Cichlidae. [Am. Sp. < Sp., a kind of fish found off the coast of Spain < Ar. *muḥarrab,* pointed < *ḥarrab,* to sharpen.]

Mo·ja·ve (mō-hä'vē) *n.* Variant of **Mohave.**

moke (mōk) *n. Slang.* **1.** *Chiefly Brit.* A donkey. **2.** A dull or boring person. **3.** *Austral.* An old, broken-down horse. [Orig. unknown.]

mol (mōl) *n.* Variant of **mole[5].**

mo·lal (mō'ləl) *adj.* Of or designating a solution containing one mole of solute in 1,000 grams of solvent, usually water. [< MOLE (gram molecule).]

mo·lal·i·ty (mō-lăl'ĭ-tē) *n., pl.* **-ties.** The molal concentration of a solute, usually expressed as the number of moles of solute per 1,000 grams of solvent.

mo·lar[1] (mō'lər) *adj.* **1.** *Physics.* Of or pertaining to a body of matter as a whole, perceived apart from molecular or atomic properties. **2.** *Chem.* **a.** Containing one mole of a substance. **b.** Pertaining to or designating a solution that contains one mole of solute per liter of solution. [< MOLE[5].]

mo·lar[2] (mō'lər) *n.* A tooth with a broad crown for grinding food, located behind the bicuspids. *—adj.* **1.** Of or pertaining to the molar teeth. **2.** Capable of grinding. [Lat. *molaris* < *mola,* millstone.]

mo·lar·i·ty (mō-lăr'ĭ-tē) *n., pl.* **-ties.** The molar concentration

modular
Modular housing units

moiré effect

of a solute, usually expressed as the number of moles of solute per liter of solution.

mo·las·ses (mə-lăs′ĭz) *n.* Any of various thick syrups produced in refining sugar. [Port. *melaço* < LLat. *mellaceum,* must < Lat. *mel,* honey.]

mold[1] (mōld) *n.* **1.** A hollow form or matrix for shaping a fluid or plastic substance. **2.** A frame or model around or on which something is formed or shaped. **3.** Something that is made in or shaped on a mold. **4.** The pattern of a mold. **5.** General shape or form: *the oval mold of her face.* **6.** Distinctive character or type: *in the mold of his ancestors.* **7.** *Archit.* Molding (sense 2). —*tr.v.* **mold·ed, mold·ing, molds. 1.** To shape in or on a mold. **2. a.** To form into a particular shape. **b.** To guide or determine the growth or development of; influence. **3.** To fit closely. Used of clothes. **4.** To make a mold of or from, prior to casting. [ME *molde* < OFr. *modle* < Lat. *modulus,* dim. of *modus,* measure.] —**mold′a·ble** *adj.* —**mold′er** *n.*

mold[2] (mōld) *n.* **1.** Any of various fungous growths often causing disintegration of organic matter. **2.** A fungus that causes mold. —*intr.v.* **mold·ed, mold·ing, molds.** To become moldy. [ME *molde.*]

mold[3] (mōld) *n.* **1.** Loose, friable soil, rich in humus and fit for planting. **2.** *Brit. Regional.* **a.** The earth; the ground. **b.** The earth of the grave. **3.** *Obs.* Earth as the substance of the human body. [ME < OE *molde.*]

mold·board (mōld′bôrd′, -bōrd′) *n.* The curved plate of a plow that turns over the furrow slice. [MOLD (earth) + BOARD.]

mold·er (mōl′dər) *v.* **-ered, -er·ing, -ers.** —*intr.* To become dust gradually, by natural decay; crumble. —*tr.* To cause to decay or crumble. [Prob. of Scand. orig.]

mold·ing (mōl′dĭng) *n.* **1.** Something that is molded. **2.** *Archit.* An embellishment in strip form used to decorate a surface.

mold·y (mōl′dē) *adj.* **-i·er, -i·est. 1.** Covered with or containing mold: *moldy bread.* **2.** Musty or stale, as from age or decay. —**mold′i·ness** *n.*

mole[1] (mōl) *n.* A small congenital growth on the human skin, usually slightly raised and dark, and sometimes hairy, esp. a pigmented nevus. [ME < OE *māl.*]

mole[2] (mōl) *n.* **1.** Any of various small, insectivorous, burrowing mammals having thickset bodies with silky light-brown to dark-gray fur, rudimentary eyes, tough muzzles, and strong forefeet for digging and usually living underground. **2.** Moleskin (sense 1). **3.** A dark gray. [ME *molle,* poss. < MLG *mol.*]

mole[3] (mōl) *n.* **1.** A massive stone wall used esp. as a breakwater or to enclose an anchorage or harbor. **2.** The anchorage or harbor enclosed by a mole. [Fr. *môle* < LGk. *mōlos* < Lat. *moles,* mass.]

mole[4] (mōl) *n.* A mass or tumor in the uterus, caused by the degeneration or abortive development of an ovum. [Fr. *môle* < Lat. *mola,* millstone.]

mole[5] also **mol** (mōl) *n.* The amount of a substance that has a weight in grams numerically equal to the molecular weight of the substance. [G. *Mol,* short for *Molekulargewicht,* molecular weight.]

mole cricket *n.* Any of various burrowing crickets, with short wings and front legs well adapted for digging and shearing.

mo·lec·u·lar (mə-lĕk′yə-lər) *adj.* Pertaining to, consisting of, caused by, or existing between molecules. —**mo·lec′u·lar′i·ty** (-yə-lăr′ĭ-tē) *n.* —**mo·lec′u·lar·ly** *adv.*

molecular beam *n. Physics.* A highly collimated, internally collisionless stream of molecules that is used to study electromagnetic phenomena as the stream traverses an evacuated chamber.

molecular biology *n.* The field of biology in which the structure and development of biological systems are analyzed in terms of the physics and chemistry of their molecular constituents. —**molecular biologist** *n.*

molecular film *n.* A surface film of thickness comparable to that of a single molecule.

molecular formula *n.* A chemical formula that shows the number of atoms of each element in a molecule of a compound.

molecular weight *n.* The sum of the atomic weights of a molecule's constituent atoms.

mol·e·cule (mŏl′ĭ-kyōōl′) *n.* **1.** A stable configuration of atomic nuclei and electrons bound together by electrostatic and electromagnetic forces. It is the simplest structural unit that displays the characteristic physical and chemical properties of a compound. **2.** A small particle; bit. [Fr. *molécule* < NLat. *molecula,* dim. of Lat. *moles,* mass.]

mole·hill (mōl′hĭl′) *n.* A small mound of loose earth thrown up by a burrowing mole.

mole·skin (mōl′skĭn′) *n.* **1.** The short, soft, silky fur of the mole. **2. a.** A heavy-napped cotton twill fabric. **b. moleskins.** Clothing, esp. trousers, of this fabric.

mo·lest (mə lĕst′) *tr.v.* **-lest·ed, -lest·ing, -lests. 1.** To disturb, interfere with, or annoy. **2.** To accost and harass sexually. [ME *molesten* < OFr. *molester* < Lat. *molestare* < *molestus,* troublesome.] —**mo′les·ta′tion** (mō′lĕs-tā′shən) *n.* —**mo·lest′er** *n.*

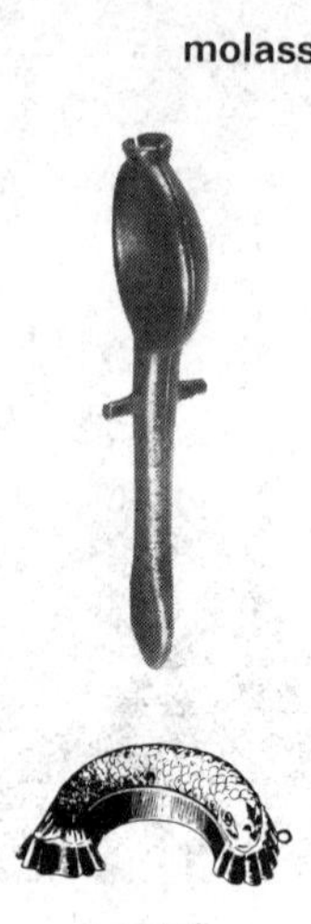

mold[1]
Above: 17th-century American mold for pewter spoons
Below: Copper fish for molding food

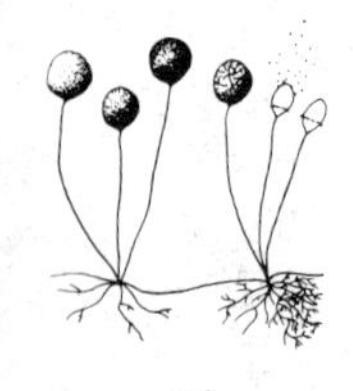

mold[2]
Bread mold

Moloch
Sacrifice of a child to the idol

moll (mŏl) *n. Slang.* **1.** A female companion of a gangster. **2.** A prostitute. [< *Moll,* nickname for *Mary.*]

mol·lie (mŏl′ē) *n.* Variant of **molly.**

mol·li·fy (mŏl′ə-fī′) *tr.v.* **-fied, -fy·ing, -fies. 1.** To allay the anger of; placate. **2.** To lessen in intensity; temper. **3.** To reduce the rigidity of; soften. [ME *mollifien* < OFr. *mollifier* < Lat. *mollificare* : *mollis,* soft + *facere,* to make.] —**mol′li·fi′a·ble** *adj.* —**mol′li·fi·ca′tion** *n.* —**mol′li·fi′er** *n.* —**mol′li·fy′ing·ly** *adv.*

mol·lusc (mŏl′əsk) *n.* Variant of **mollusk.**

mol·lus·can also **mol·lus·kan** (mə-lŭs′kən) *adj.* Of or relating to the mollusks. —*n.* A mollusk.

mol·lus·ci·cide (mə-lŭs′kĭ-sīd′) *n.* An agent that kills mollusks. [Lat. *molluscus,* soft (< *mollis*) + -CIDE.] —**mol·lus′ci·cid′al** *adj.*

mol·lusk also **mol·lusc** (mŏl′əsk) *n.* Any of various members of the phylum Mollusca, of largely marine invertebrates, including the edible shellfish and some 100,000 other species. [Fr. *mollusque* < NLat. *Mollusca,* phylum name < Lat. *molluscus,* soft < *mollis.*] —**mol·lus′cous** (mə-lŭs′kəs) *adj.*

mol·ly also **mol·lie** (mŏl′ē) *n., pl.* **-lies.** Any of several tropical and subtropical fishes of the genus *Mollienesia.* The males of some species have saillike dorsal fins and are raised in aquariums. [< NLat. *Mollienisia,* genus name, after Comte François N. *Mollien* (1758–1850).]

mol·ly·cod·dle (mŏl′ē-kŏd′l) *n.* A person, esp. a man or boy, who is pampered and protected. —*tr.v.* **-dled, -dling, -dles.** To be overprotective and indulgent toward. [Brit. slang *molly,* milksop (< the name *Molly*) + CODDLE.] —**mol′ly·cod′dler** *n.*

Mo·loch (mō′lŏk′, mŏl′ək) *n.* In the Old Testament, god of the Ammonites and Phoenicians to whom children were sacrificed. [LLat. *Moloch* < Gk. *Molokh* < Heb. *Molekh.*]

Mo·lo·tov cocktail (mŏl′ə-tôf′, môl′-, mō′lə-) *n.* A makeshift incendiary bomb made of a breakable container filled with flammable liquid and provided with a rag wick. [After Vyacheslav M. *Molotov* (1890–1981).]

molt (mōlt) *v.* **molt·ed, molt·ing, molts.** —*intr.* To shed an outer covering, such as feathers, cuticle, or skin, which is replaced periodically by a new growth. —*tr.* To shed or cast off by the process of molting. —*n.* **1.** The act or process of molting. **2.** The material cast off during molting. [ME *mouten* < OE *mūtian* < Lat. *mutare,* to change.]

mol·ten (mōl′tən) *v. Archaic.* A past participle of **melt.** —*adj.* **1.** Made liquid by heat; melted. **2.** Made by melting and casting: *a molten image.* **3.** Brilliantly glowing.

mol·to (mōl′tō) *adv. Mus.* Very; much. Used with directions to the performer. [Ital. < Lat. *multum.*]

mo·ly (mō′lē) *n., pl.* **-lies.** A mythical magic herb with black roots and white flowers. [Lat. < Gk. *mōlu.*]

mo·lyb·de·nite (mə-lĭb′də-nīt′) *n.* A mineral form of molybdenum sulfide, MoS_2, that is the principal ore of molybdenum. [MOLYBDEN(UM) + -ITE.]

mo·lyb·de·num (mə-lĭb′də-nəm) *n. Symbol* **Mo** A hard, gray, metallic element used to toughen alloy steels and soften tungsten alloy. It is also used in fertilizers, dyes, enamels, and reagents. Atomic number 42; atomic weight 95.94; melting point 2,620°C; boiling point 4,800°C; specific gravity 10.2; valences 2, 3, 4, 5. [NLat. < Lat. *molybdaena,* galena < Gk. *molubdaina* < *molubdos,* lead.]

mo·lyb·dic (mə-lĭb′dĭk) *adj.* Designating molybdenum or a compound containing molybdenum in its higher valences.

mo·lyb·dous (mə-lĭb′dəs) *adj.* Designating molybdenum or a compound containing molybdenum in its lower valences.

mom (mŏm) *n. Informal.* Mother. [Shortening and alteration of MAMMA.]

mom-and-pop (mŏm′ən-pŏp′) *adj.* Of or designating a small business that is run by the owners: *a mom-and-pop grocery store.*

mo·ment (mō′mənt) *n.* **1.** A brief, indefinite interval of time. **2.** A specific point in time, esp. the present time: *He is reading at the moment.* **3.** A particular period of importance, significance, or excellence. **4.** Outstanding significance or value; importance: *a discovery of great moment.* **5.** *Philos.* **a.** An essential or constituent element. **b.** A phase or aspect of a thing. **6.** *Physics.* **a.** The product of a quantity and its perpendicular distance from a reference point. **b.** The rotation produced in a body when a force is applied; torque. **7.** *Statistics.* The expected value of a positive integral power of a random variable. The first moment is the mean of the density function. [ME < OFr. < Lat. *momentum* < *movēre,* to move.]

mo·men·ta (mō-mĕn′tə) *n.* A plural of **momentum.**

mo·men·tar·i·ly (mō′mən-târ′ə-lē) *adv.* **1.** For only a moment. **2.** Very soon. **3.** From moment to moment.

mo·men·tar·y (mō′mən-tĕr′ē) *adj.* **1.** Lasting only a brief time. **2.** Occurring or present at every moment: *in momentary fear of being exposed.* **3.** Short-lived; ephemeral. Used of a living creature. [Lat. *momentarius* < *momentum,* moment < *movēre,* to move.] —**mo′men·tar′i·ness** *n.*

mo·ment·ly (mō′mənt-lē) *adv.* **1.** From moment to moment. **2.** At any moment. **3.** For a moment.

moment of inertia *n.* **1.** A measure of a body's resistance to angular acceleration, equal to: **a.** The product of the mass of a particle and the square of its distance from a reference.

b. The sum of the products of each mass element of a body multiplied by the square of its distance from an axis. **2.** The sum of the products of each element of an area multiplied by the square of its distance from a coplanar axis.

moment of momentum *n.* Angular momentum.

moment of truth *n.* **1.** The final kill in a bullfight. **2.** A crucial or decisive time on which much depends.

mo·men·tous (mō-mĕn′təs) *adj.* Of utmost importance or outstanding significance: *a momentous occasion.* **—mo·men′tous·ly** *adv.* **—mo·men′tous·ness** *n.*

mo·men·tum (mō-mĕn′təm) *n., pl.* **-ta** (-tə) or **-tums.** **1.** *Physics.* The product of a body's mass and linear velocity. **2. a.** Impetus. **b.** Impetus in human affairs. **3.** *Philos.* A constituent or essential element; moment. [Lat., movement < *movēre,* to move.]

Mo·mus (mō′məs) *n. Gk. Myth.* The god of blame and ridicule. [Gk. *Mōmos* < *mōmos,* blame.]

mon (mŏn) *n. Scot.* Man.

Mon (mōn) *n.* **1. a.** The principal native people of the Pegu region in Burma. **b.** A member of the Mon. **2.** The Mon-Khmer language of the Mon.

mon– *pref.* Variant of **mono-.**

mon·a·chism (mŏn′ə-kĭz′əm) *n.* Monasticism. [ME < Med. Lat. *monachismus* < LGk. *monakhismos* < *monakhos,* monk. —see MONK.]

mo·nad (mō′năd′) *n.* **1.** In the philosophy of Leibnitz, an indivisible and impenetrable unit of substance viewed as the basic constituent element of physical reality. **2.** *Biol.* A single-celled microscopic organism, esp. a flagellate protozoan. **3.** *Chem.* An atom or radical with a valence of 1. [LLat. *monas, monad-,* unit < Gk. < *monos,* single.] **—mo·nad′ic, mo·nad′i·cal** *adj.* **—mo·nad′i·cal·ly** *adv.*

mon·a·del·phous (mŏn′ə-dĕl′fəs, mō′nə-) *adj. Bot.* **1.** United by the filaments into a single tubelike group. Used of stamens. **2.** Having monadelphous stamens.

mon·a·des (mŏn′ə-dēz′) *n.* Plural of **monas.**

mo·nad·nock (mə-năd′nŏk′) *n.* A mountain or rocky mass that has resisted erosion and stands isolated in a plain or peneplain. [After Mt. *Monadnock* in New Hampshire.]

mo·nan·drous (mə-năn′drəs) *adj.* **1.** Having a single stamen. **2.** Having flowers bearing a single stamen. **3.** Of or relating to the custom of monandry.

mo·nan·dry (mə-năn′drē) *n.* **1.** The practice of having onc husband at a time. **2.** *Bot.* The condition of being monandrous.

mo·nan·thous (mə-năn′thəs) *adj. Bot.* Bearing a single flower.

mon·arch (mŏn′ərk, -ärk′) *n.* **1.** A sole and absolute ruler of a state. **2.** A sovereign, such as a king or emperor. **3.** One that presides over or rules. **4.** One that surpasses others in power or pre-eminence. **5.** A large orange and black butterfly, *Danaus plexippus,* having a wingspread of up to 10 centimeters or about 4 inches. [LLat. *monarcha* < Gk. *monarkhēs* : *monos,* single + *arkhein,* to rule.] **—mo·nar′chal** (mə-när′kəl), **mo·nar′chi·al, mo·nar′chic, mo·nar′chi·cal** *adj.* **—mo·nar′chal·ly, mo·nar′chi·cal·ly** *adv.*

monarch
Monarch butterfly

mo·nar·chi·an·ism (mə-när′kē-ə-nĭz′əm) *n.* A Christian heresy of the 2nd and 3rd centuries that denied the doctrine of the Trinity. [< LLat. *monarchiani,* the monarchians < *monarchia,* monarchy.] **—mo·nar′chi·an** (mə-när′kē-ən) *n.*

mon·ar·chism (mŏn′ər-kĭz′əm, -är′-) *n.* **1.** The principles of monarchy. **2.** Belief in or advocacy of monarchy. **—mon′ar·chist** (-kĭst) *n.* **—mon′ar·chis′tic** *adj.*

mon·ar·chy (mŏn′ər-kē, -är′-) *n., pl.* **-chies.** **1.** Government by a monarch. **2.** A state ruled by a monarch. [ME *monarchie* < OFr. < LLat. *monarchia* < Gk. *monarkhia* < *monarkhēs,* monarch.]

mo·nar·da (mə-när′də) *n.* An aromatic plant of the genus *Monarda,* such as the Oswego tea. [NLat. *Monarda,* genus name, after Nicolas *Monardes* (d. 1588).]

mo·nas (mō′năs′) *n., pl.* **mon·a·des** (mŏn′ə-dēz′). *Biol.* A monad (sense 2). [LLat. < Gk. < *monos,* single.]

mon·as·ter·y (mŏn′ə-stĕr′ē) *n., pl.* **-ies.** **1.** The dwelling place of a community of persons under religious vows, esp. monks. **2.** The community of monks living in a monastery. [ME *monasterie* < LLat. *monasterium* < LGk. *monastērion* < Gk. *monazein,* to live alone < *monos,* alone.] **—mon′as·te′ri·al** (mŏn′ə-stîr′ē-əl, -stĕr′-) *adj.*

mo·nas·tic (mə-năs′tĭk) also **mo·nas·ti·cal** (-tĭ-kəl) *adj.* Of, pertaining to, characteristic of, or resembling monasteries or persons living in religious or contemplative seclusion. *—n.* A monk. [LLat. *monasticus* < LGk. *monastikos* < Gk. *monazein,* to live alone < *monos,* alone.] **—mo·nas′ti·cal·ly** *adv.*

mo·nas·ti·cism (mə-năs′tĭ-sĭz′əm) *n.* The monastic life or system, esp. as practiced in a monastery.

mon·a·tom·ic (mŏn′ə-tŏm′ĭk) *adj.* **1.** Occurring as single atoms, as helium. **2.** Having one replaceable atom or radical. **3.** Univalent. **—mon′a·tom′ic·al·ly** *adv.*

mon·au·ral (mŏn-ôr′əl) *adj.* **1.** Designating sound reception by one ear. **2.** Relating to a system of transmitting, recording, or reproducing sound whereby one or more sources are channeled into a single carrier.

mon·ax·i·al (mŏn-ăk′sē-əl) *adj.* Uniaxial.

mon·ax·on (mŏn-ăk′sŏn′) *n. Zool.* A straight spicule in sponges. [MON(O)- + Gk. *axōn,* axis.]

mon·a·zite (mŏn′ə-zīt′) *n.* A reddish-brown mineral phosphate of rare-earth metals, chiefly cerium and lanthanum, usually together with thorium. [G. *Monazit* < Gk. *monazein,* to live alone < *monos,* alone.]

Mon·day (mŭn′dē, -dā′) *n.* The second day of the week, occurring after Sunday and before Tuesday. [ME < OE *Mōnandæg,* transl. of Lat. *dies lunae,* day of the moon.]

mo·ne·cious (mə-nē′shəs) *adj.* Variant of **monoecious.**

Mo·né·gasque (mô-nā-găsk′) *n.* A citizen of Monaco. [Fr. < Prov. *mounegasc* < *Mounegue,* Monaco.] **—Mo·né·gasque′** *adj.*

Mo·nel (mō-nĕl′). A trademark for an alloy of nickel, copper, iron, and manganese.

mon·es·trous (mŏn-ĕs′trəs) *adj.* Having one estrous cycle per year.

mon·e·tar·y (mŏn′ĭ-tĕr′ē, mŭn′-) *adj.* Of or pertaining to money or its means of circulation. [LLat. *monetarius* < Lat. *moneta,* money.] **—mon′e·tar′i·ly** *adv.*

mon·e·tize (mŏn′ĭ-tīz′, mŭn′-) *tr.v.* **-tized, -tiz·ing, -tiz·es.** **1.** To establish as legal tender. **2.** To coin (money). [< Lat. *moneta,* money.] **—mon′e·ti·za′tion** *n.*

mon·ey (mŭn′ē) *n., pl.* **mon·eys** or **mon·ies.** **1.** A commodity, such as gold or silver, that is legally established as an exchangeable equivalent of all other commodities and is used as a measure of their comparative values on the market. **2.** The official currency, coins, and negotiable paper notes issued by a government. **3.** Assets and property considered in terms of monetary value; wealth. **4.** Pecuniary profit or loss: *He made money on the sale of his properties.* **5.** An unspecified amount of currency: *money for groceries.* **6.** Often **moneys** or **monies.** Sums of money collected: *state tax money.* **—*idioms.* in the money.** Taking first, second, or third place in a dog or horse race. **on the money.** Exact; precise. [ME < OFr. *moneie* < Lat. *moneta* < *Moneta,* epithet of Juno, from the fact that her temple in Rome housed the mint.]

mon·ey·bag (mŭn′ē-băg′) *n.* **1.** A bag for holding money. **2. moneybags.** *(used with a sing. or pl. verb).* Wealth. **3. moneybags.** *(used with a sing. verb).* A rich and greedy person.

mon·ey·chang·er (mŭn′ē-chān′jər) *n.* **1.** A person who exchanges money, as from one currency to another. **2.** A machine that holds and dispenses coins.

mon·eyed also **mon·ied** (mŭn′ēd) *adj.* **1.** Having a great deal of money: *the moneyed classes.* **2.** Representing or arising from the possession of money: *the triumph of moneyed interests over landed interests.*

mon·ey·er (mŭn′ē-ər) *n.* A person authorized to coin or mint money. [ME *monyer* < OFr. *monier* < LLat. *monetarius* < *moneta,* money.]

mon·ey·lend·er (mŭn′ē-lĕn′dər) *n.* One whose business is lending money at an interest rate.

mon·ey·mak·ing (mŭn′ē-mā′kĭng) *n.* The acquisition of money or other wealth. *—adj.* **1.** Engaged in acquiring wealth. **2.** Actually or potentially profitable. **—mon′ey·mak′er** *n.*

money of account *n.* Any of the various monetary units in which accounts are kept, which may or may not correspond to actual current denominations.

money order *n.* An order for the payment of a specified amount of money, usually issued and payable at a bank or post office.

mon·ey·wort (mŭn′ē-wûrt′, -wôrt′) *n.* A creeping plant, *Lysimachia nummularia,* of Europe and eastern North America, having rounded, opposite leaves and yellow flowers. [From the round shape of its leaves.]

mon·ger (mŭng′gər, mŏng′-) *n.* **1.** A dealer in a specific commodity: *ironmonger.* **2.** A person promoting something undesirable: *scandalmonger, warmonger.* *—tr.v.* **-gered, -ger·ing, -gers.** To peddle. [ME *mongere* < OE *mangere* < Lat. *mango,* of Gk. orig.]

mon·go (mŏng′gō) *n., pl.* **mongo.** See table at **currency.** [Mongolian.]

Mon·gol (mŏng′gəl, -gōl′) *n.* **1.** A member of one of the nomadic tribes of Mongolia. **2.** A native of Mongolia. **3.** Mongolian (sense 3). **4.** A member of the Mongoloid ethnic group. [Mongol.] **—Mon′gol** *adj.*

Mon·go·li·an (mŏng-gō′lē-ən, -gōl′yən, mŏn-) *adj.* **1.** Of, pertaining to, or constituting the Mongolian People's Republic, the Mongols, or Mongolian. **2. mongolian.** Mongoloid (sense 3). *—n.* **1.** A native or inhabitant of Mongolia. **2.** A member of the Mongoloid race. **3.** Any of the Mongolic languages of Mongolia.

Mon·gol·ic (mŏng-gŏl′ĭk, mŏn-) *n.* A subfamily of the Altaic language family that includes Mongolian. *—adj.* **1.** Of or pertaining to the Mongoloid ethnic division. **2.** Of or pertaining to the subfamily of Altaic languages spoken in Mongolia.

mon·gol·ism also **Mon·gol·ism** (mŏng′gə-lĭz′əm, mŏn′-) *n.* Down's syndrome. [From the resemblance of the features of an affected person to those of Mongolians.]

Mon·gol·oid (mŏng′gə-loid′, mŏn′-) *adj.* **1.** *Anthropol.* **a.** Of, pertaining to, or designating a major ethnic division of the human species whose members are characterized by yellowish-brown to white pigmentation, coarse straight black hair, dark eyes with pronounced epicanthic folds, and prominent cheekbones. **b.** Characteristic of or like a Mon-

gol. **2. mongoloid.** Characterized by, affected with, or relating to Down's syndrome. —*n.* **1.** *Anthropol.* A member of the Mongoloid ethnic division of the human species. **2. mongoloid.** A person affected with Down's syndrome.
mon·goose (mŏng′go͞os′, mŏn′-) *n., pl.* **-goos·es.** Any of various Old World carnivorous mammals of the genus *Herpestes* and related genera, having a slender body and a long tail and notable for being able to kill venomous snakes. [Marathi *mangūs,* of Dravidian orig.]
mon·grel (mŭng′grəl, mŏng′-) *n.* **1.** An animal or plant, esp. a dog, resulting from various interbreedings. **2.** A cross between two different breeds. —*adj.* Of mixed origin or character. [Prob. < ME *mong,* mixture < OE *(ge)mang.*] **—mon·grel′ism** *n.* **—mon′grel·ly** *adv.*
mon·grel·ize (mŭng′grə-līz′, mŏng′-) *tr.v.* **-ized, -iz·ing, -iz·es.** To make mongrel in race, nature, or character. **—mon′-grel·i·za′tion** *n.*
mon·ick·er (mŏn′ĭ-kər) *n.* Variant of **moniker.**
mon·ied (mŭn′ēd) *adj.* Variant of **moneyed.**
mon·ies (mŭn′ēz′) *n.* A plural of **money.**
mon·i·ker or **mon·ick·er** (mŏn′ĭ-kər) *n. Slang.* A personal name or nickname. [Orig. unknown.]
mo·ni·li·a·sis (mō′nə-lī′ə-sĭs, mŏn′ə-) *n.* Candidiasis. [NLat. *Monilia,* fungus genus + -IASIS.]
mo·nil·i·form (mō-nĭl′ə-fôrm′) *adj.* Resembling a string of beads, as various plant roots, the antennae of certain insects, and the nuclei of some members of the Ciliata. [Lat. *monile,* necklace + -FORM.] **—mo·nil′i·form′ly** *adv.*
mon·ish (mŏn′ĭsh) *tr.v.* **-ished, -ish·ing, -ish·es.** To admonish; warn. [ME *monesen* < OFr. *monester* < VLat. **monestare* < Lat. *monēre,* to warn.]
mo·nism (mō′nĭz′əm, mŏn′ĭz′əm) *n. Philos.* A metaphysical system in which reality is conceived as a unified whole. **—mo′nist** *n.* **—mo·nis′tic** (mō-nĭs′tĭk, mŏ-) *adj.* **—mo·nis′ti·cal·ly** *adv.*
mo·ni·tion (mō-nĭsh′ən, mə-) *n.* **1.** A warning or intimation of impending danger. **2. a.** An admonition. **b.** A piece of advice; counsel. **3.** A formal order from a bishop or ecclesiastical court to refrain from a specified offense. [ME *monicion* < OFr. *monition* < Lat. *monitio* < *monēre,* to warn.]
mon·i·tor (mŏn′ĭ-tər) *n.* **1.** One that admonishes, cautions, or reminds. **2.** A pupil who assists a teacher in routine duties. **3. a.** A device used to record or control a process or activity. **b.** A screen used to view or check the picture being picked up by a television camera. **4.** An articulated device holding a rotating nozzle, used in mining and fire-fighting. **5. a.** A heavily ironclad warship of the 19th century with a low, flat deck and one or more gun turrets. **b.** A modern warship designed for coastal bombardment. **6.** Any of various tropical carnivorous lizards of the genus *Varanus,* ranging in length from several inches to ten feet. —*v.* **-tored, -tor·ing, -tors.** —*tr.* **1.** To check (the transmission quality of a signal) by means of a receiver. **2.** To test for radiation intensity. **3.** To keep track of by or as if by an electronic device. **4.** To check by means of a receiver for significant content. **5.** To scrutinize or check systematically with a view to collecting certain specified categories of data. **6.** To keep watch over; supervise: *monitor an examination.* **7.** To direct as a monitor. —*intr.* To act as a monitor. [Lat. < *monēre,* to warn.]
mon·i·to·ri·al (mŏn′ĭ-tôr′ē-əl, -tōr′-) *adj.* Of, pertaining to, or performed by monitors. **—mon′i·to′ri·al·ly** *adv.*
mon·i·to·ry (mŏn′ĭ-tôr′ē, -tōr′ē) *adj.* Conveying an admonition or warning: *a monitory glance.* —*n., pl.* **-ries.** A letter of admonition. [Lat. *monitorius* < *monitor,* monitor.]
monk (mŭngk) *n.* A member of a religious brotherhood living in a monastery and devoted to a discipline prescribed by his order. [ME *munk* < OE *munuc* < LLat. *monachus* < LGk. *monakhos* < Gk., single < *monos.*]
monk·er·y (mŭng′kə-rē) *n., pl.* **-ies. 1.** Monastic life or practices. **2.** Monks collectively. **3.** A monastery.
mon·key (mŭng′kē) *n., pl.* **-keys. 1.** A member of the order Primates, excluding man; specifically, most long-tailed primates, including the Old and New World monkeys and the marmosets, and usually excluding the anthropoid apes and the lemurs, lorises, tree shrews, and tarsiers. **2.** A mischievous, playful child or young person. **3.** The iron block of a pile driver. **4.** *Slang.* A person who is mocked, duped, or made to appear a fool. **5.** *Slang.* Drug addiction, regarded as a burdensome affliction: *have a monkey on one's back.* —*v.* **-keyed, -key·ing, -keys.** —*intr. Informal.* **1.** To play, fiddle, or tamper with something idly. **2.** To behave in a mischievous or apish manner. —*tr.* To imitate or mimic; ape. [Prob. of LG orig.]
monkey bread *n.* The fruit of the baobab.
monkey business *n. Slang.* Silly, mischievous, or deceitful acts.
mon·key-flow·er (mŭng′kē-flou′ər) *n.* Any of various plants of the genus *Mimulus,* having variously colored, two-lipped flowers.
monkey jacket *n.* **1.** A short, tight-fitting jacket, formerly worn by sailors. **2.** A mess jacket.
monkey pot *n.* **1. a.** The large, urn-shaped lidded pod of tropical trees of the genus *Lecythis.* **b.** A tree bearing this type of pod. **2.** A cylindrical or barrel-shaped melting pot used in making flint glass.

monkey
Callimico goeldi

monkey wrench

monocle

monkey puzzle *n.* An evergreen tree, *Araucaria araucana,* native to Chile, having intricately ramifying branches covered with stiff, prickle-tipped leaves.
mon·key·shine (mŭng′kē-shīn′) *n.* Often **monkeyshines.** *Slang.* A playful trick; prank.
monkey wrench *n.* **1.** A hand tool with adjustable jaws for turning nuts of varying sizes. **2.** *Informal.* Something that disrupts: *threw a monkey wrench into our plans.* [Orig. unknown.]
monk·fish (mŭngk′fĭsh′) *n., pl.* **monkfish** or **-fish·es.** The goosefish. [From the cowled appearance of its head.]
Mon-Khmer (mōn′kmĕr′) *n.* A subfamily of the Austro-Asiatic language family that includes Mon, Khmer and other languages of Southeast Asia.
monk·hood (mŭngk′ho͝od′) *n.* **1.** The state or profession of a monk; monasticism. **2.** Monks collectively.
monk·ish (mŭng′kĭsh) *adj.* **1.** Of, relating to, or characteristic of monks or monasticism. **2.** Of or inclined to self-denial.
monk's cloth *n.* A heavy cotton cloth in a coarse basket weave.
monks·hood (mŭngks′ho͝od′) *n.* Any of various usually poisonous plants of the genus *Aconitum,* having hooded flowers of various colors.
mon·o[1] (mŏn′ō) *n.* Mononucleosis (sense 2).
mon·o[2] (mŏn′ō) *adj.* Monaural (sense 2).
mono– or **mon–** *pref.* **1.** One; single; alone: *monomorphic.* **2.** Containing a single atom, radical, or group: *monobasic.* **3.** Monomolecular; monatomic: *monolayer.* [ME < OFr. < Lat. < Gk. < *monos,* single, alone.]
mon·o·ac·id (mŏn′ō-ăs′ĭd) also **mon·o·a·cid·ic** (mŏn′-ō-ə-sĭd′ĭk) *adj.* Having only one hydroxyl group to react with acids. —*n.* **monoacid.** An acid having one replaceable hydrogen atom.
mon·o·am·ine (mŏn′ō-ăm′ēn, -ə-mēn′) *n.* An amine compound having one amino group.
monoamine oxidase *n.* An enzyme that acts as a catalyst in the oxidative deamination of monoamines.
mon·o·ba·sic (mŏn′ə-bā′sĭk) *adj.* **1.** Monoprotic. **2.** Having only one metal ion or positive radical.
mon·o·carp (mŏn′ə-kärp′) *n.* A monocarpic plant.
mon·o·car·pel·lar·y (mŏn′ə-kär′pə-lĕr′ē) *adj.* Consisting of only one carpel.
mon·o·car·pic (mŏn′ə-kär′pĭk) also **mon·o·car·pous** (-kär′pəs) *adj.* Flowering and bearing fruit only once.
Mo·noc·er·os (mə-nŏs′ər-əs) *n.* **1.** A constellation near Canis Major and Canis Minor. **2. monoceros.** *Obs.* **a.** A one-horned fish, such as the swordfish. **b.** A unicorn. [ME, unicorn < OFr. < Lat. < Gk. *monokerōs,* having one horn : *monos,* one + *keras,* horn.]
mon·o·cha·si·um (mŏn′ə-kā′zē-əm, -zhē-əm) *n., pl.* **-si·a** (-zē-ə, -zhē-ə). A cyme having a single main stem. **—mon′o·cha′si·al** *adj.* [MONO- + (DI)CHASIUM.]
mon·o·chord (mŏn′ə-kôrd′) *n. Mus.* An acoustical instrument consisting of a sounding box with one string and a movable bridge, used to study musical tones. [ME *monocorde* < OFr. < Med. Lat. *monochordum* < Gk. *monokhordon* : *monos,* one + *khordē,* string.]
mon·o·chro·mat·ic (mŏn′ə-krō-măt′ĭk) also **mon·o·chro·ic** (-krō′ĭk) *adj.* **1.** Having only one color. **2.** Having or producing light of only one wavelength. [Lat. *monochromatos* < Gk. *monokhrōmatos* : *monos,* one + *khrōma,* color.] **—mon′o·chro·mat′i·cal·ly** *adv.* **—mon′o·chro′ma·tic′i·ty** (-mə-tĭs′ĭ-tē) *n.*
mon·o·chrome (mŏn′ə-krōm′) *n.* **1.** A painting done in different shades of one color. **2.** The technique of executing monochrome paintings. [Med. Lat. *monochroma* < Gk. *monokhrōmos,* of one color : *monos,* one + *khrōma,* color.] **—mon′o·chro′mic** (-krō′mĭk) *adj.*
mon·o·cle (mŏn′ə-kəl) *n.* An eyeglass for one eye. [Fr. < LLat. *monoculus,* having one eye : Gk. *monos,* one + Lat. *oculus,* eye.] **—mon′o·cled** (-kəld) *adj.*
mon·o·cline (mŏn′ə-klīn′) *n.* A geologic formation in which all strata are inclined in the same direction. **—mon′o·cli′nal** *adj.*
mon·o·clin·ic (mŏn′ə-klĭn′ĭk) *adj.* Of or pertaining to three unequal crystal axes, two of which intersect obliquely and are perpendicular to the third.
mon·o·cli·nous (mŏn′ə-klī′nəs) *adj.* Having pistils and stamens in the same flower. [NLat. *monoclinus* : Gk. *monos,* one + Gk. *klinē,* couch.]
mon·o·coque (mŏn′ə-kōk′, -kŏk′) *n.* A metal structure, as of an aircraft, in which the covering absorbs a large part of the stresses to which the body is subjected. [Fr. : Gk. *monos,* one + *coque,* shell < Lat. *coccum,* berry < Gk. *kokkos.*]
mon·o·cot·y·le·don (mŏn′ə-kŏt′l-ēd′n) also **mon·o·cot** (mŏn′ə-kŏt′) *n.* Any of various plants of the Monocotyledonae, one of the two major divisions of angiosperms, characterized by a single embryonic seed leaf that appears at germination. Included among the monocotyledons are such plants as grasses, orchids, and lilies. [NLat. *Monocotyledones,* class name : MONO- + Lat. *cotyledon,* navelwort. — see COTYLEDON.] **—mon′o·cot′y·le′don·ous** *adj.*
mo·noc·ra·cy (mō-nŏk′rə-sē, mə-) *n.* Government or rule by a single person; autocracy. **—mon′o·crat′** (mŏn′ə-krăt′) *n.* **—mon′o·crat′ic** *adj.*
mo·noc·u·lar (mŏ-nŏk′yə-lər, mə-) *adj.* **1.** Having or per-

taining to one eye. **2.** Adapted for the use of only one eye. [LLat. *monoculus,* having one eye. —see MONOCLE.] **—mo·noc'u·lar·ly** *adv.*

mon·o·cy·cle (mŏn'ə-sī'kəl) *n.* A unicycle.

mon·o·cyte (mŏn'ə-sīt') *n.* A large white blood corpuscle, having a pale, oval nucleus and more protoplasm than a lymphocyte. **—mon'o·cyt'ic** (-sĭt'ĭk), **mon'o·cy'toid'** (-sī'toid') *adj.*

mon·o·dac·tyl (mŏn'ə-dăk'tl) *n.* An animal having only one claw on each extremity. [< Gk. *monodaktulos,* having one toe : *monos,* one + *daktulos,* toe.] **—mon'o·dac'ty·lous** *adj.*

mon·o·dra·ma (mŏn'ə-drä'mə, -drăm'ə) *n.* A dramatic composition written for one performer. **—mon'o·dra·mat'ic** (-drə-măt'ĭk) *adj.*

mon·o·dy (mŏn'ə-dē) *n., pl.* **-dies. 1.** An ode for one voice or actor, as in Greek drama. **2.** An elegiac verse expressing personal lament. **3.** *Mus.* **a.** A style of composition in which one vocal part or melodic line predominates. **b.** A composition in this style. [LLat. *monodia* < Gk. *monōidia* : *monos,* one + *oidē,* song.] **—mo·nod'ic** (mə-nŏd'ĭk), **mo·nod'i·cal** *adj.* **—mo·nod'i·cal·ly** *adv.* **—mon'o·dist** (mŏn'ə-dĭst) *n.*

mo·noe·cious also **mo·ne·cious** (mə-nē'shəs) *adj.* **1.** *Bot.* Having male and female reproductive organs in separate flowers on a single plant. **2.** *Zool.* Hermaphroditic. [< NLat. *Monoecia,* class name : Gk. *monos,* one + Gk. *oikia,* house.] **—mo·noe'cious·ly** *adv.*

mon·o·es·ter (mŏn'ō-ĕs'tər) *n.* An ester having one ester group.

mo·nog·a·my (mə-nŏg'ə-mē) *n.* **1.** The custom or condition of being married to only one person at a time. **2.** The condition of having one mate for life. **—mo·nog'a·mist** *n.* **—mo·nog'a·mous** *adj.* **—mo·nog'a·mous·ly** *adv.*

mon·o·gen·e·sis (mŏn'ə-jĕn'ĭ-sĭs) *n.* **1.** The theory that all living organisms are descended from a single cell. **2.** Asexual reproduction, as by sporulation. **3.** The development of an ovum into an organism resembling the parent, without metamorphosis. **—mo·nog'e·nous** (mə-nŏj'ə-nəs) *adj.*

mon·o·ge·net·ic (mŏn'ə-jə-nĕt'ĭk) *adj.* **1.** Pertaining to or showing monogenesis. **2.** Asexual. **3.** Arising from a single formation process, as a mountain range.

mon·o·gen·ic (mŏn'ə-jĕn'ĭk) *adj.* **1.** Having a common or single origin, as igneous rocks composed of a single mineral. **2. a.** Of or pertaining to monogenesis; monogenetic. **b.** Relating to monogenism. **3.** Of or regulated by one gene or one of a pair of allelic genes. **4.** Producing offspring mostly of one sex. **—mon'o·gen'i·cal·ly** *adv.*

mo·nog·e·nism (mə-nŏj'ə-nĭz'əm) *n.* The theory that mankind has descended from a single pair of ancestors. **—mo·nog'e·nist** *n.* **—mo·nog'e·nis'tic** *adj.*

mon·o·gram (mŏn'ə-grăm') *n.* A design composed of one or more letters, usually the initials of a name. *—tr.v.* **-grammed, -gram·ming, -grams** also **-gramed, gram·ing, grams.** To mark with a monogram. [LLat. *monogramma* < Gk. *monogrammon* : *monos,* single + *gramma,* letter < *graphein,* to write.] **—mon'o·gram·mat'ic** (-grə-măt'ĭk) *adj.*

mon·o·graph (mŏn'ə-grăf') *n.* A scholarly book, article, or pamphlet on a specific and usually limited subject. **—mon'o·graph'** *v.* **(-graphed, -graph·ing, -graphs). —mo·nog'ra·pher** (mə-nŏg'rə-fər) *n.* **—mon'o·graph'ic** *adj.* **—mon'o·graph'i·cal·ly** *adv.*

mo·nog·y·ny (mə-nŏj'ə-nē) *n.* The practice or condition of having only one wife at a time. **—mo·nog'y·nist** *n.* **—mo·nog'y·nous** *adj.*

mon·o·hy·brid (mŏn'ō-hī'brĭd) *n.* Hybrid offspring of parents differing in a single characteristic or genetic factor.

mon·o·hy·drate (mŏn'ō-hī'drāt') *n.* A compound of singly hydrated molecules. **—mon'o·hy'drat'ed** *adj.*

mon·o·hy·dric (mŏn'ō-hī'drĭk) *adj.* Containing one replaceable hydroxyl radical.

mo·noi·cous (mə-noi'kəs) *adj.* Having archegonia and antheridia on the same plant; bisexual. [Alteration of MONOECIOUS.]

mon·o·lay·er (mŏn'ō-lā'ər) *n.* A film or stratum of a compound one molecule thick; monomolecular layer.

mon·o·lin·gual (mŏn'ə-lĭng'gwəl) *adj.* Using or knowing only one language. **—mon'o·lin'gual** *n.*

mon·o·lith (mŏn'ə-lĭth') *n.* **1.** A large block of stone, esp. one used in architecture or sculpture. **2.** A large organization, such as a corporation, that acts as a powerful unit. [Fr. *monolithe* < Gk. *monolithos,* consisting of a single stone : *monos,* one + *lithos,* stone.]

mon·o·lith·ic (mŏn'ə-lĭth'ĭk) *adj.* **1.** Consisting of a monolith. **2.** Massive, solid, and uniform: *monolithic proportions.* **—mon'o·lith'i·cal·ly** *adv.*

mon·o·logue also **mon·o·log** (mŏn'ə-lôg', -lŏg') *n.* **1.** A long speech made by one person, often monopolizing conversation. **2. a.** A dramatic soliloquy. **b.** A literary composition in the form of a soliloquy. **3.** A continuous series of jokes or comic stories delivered by a single comedian. [Fr. : Gk. *monos,* one + Gk. *logos,* speech.] **—mon'o·log'ic** (mŏn'ə-lŏj'ĭk), **mon'o·log'i·cal** *adj.* **—mo·nol'o·gist** (mə-nŏl'ə-jĭst, mŏn'ə-lôg'ĭst, -lŏg'-) *n.*

mon·o·ma·ni·a (mŏn'ə-mā'nē-ə, -mān'yə) *n.* **1.** Pathological obsession with one idea. **2.** Intent concentration on or exaggerated enthusiasm for a subject or an idea. **—mon'o·ma'ni·ac'** (-mā'nē-ăk') *n.* **—mon'o·ma·ni'a·cal** (-mə-nī'ə-kəl) *adj.*

mon·o·mer (mŏn'ə-mər) *n.* A molecule that can be chemically bound as a unit of a polymer. **—mon'o·mer'ic** (-mĕr'ĭk) *adj.*

mon·o·me·tal·lic (mŏn'ō-mə-tăl'ĭk) *adj.* **1.** Consisting of or containing one metal. **2.** Pertaining to monometallism.

mon·o·met·al·lism also **mon·o·met·al·ism** (mŏn'ō-mĕt'l-ĭz'əm) *n.* The economic theory or practice of using only one metal as a standard of money. **—mon'o·met'al·list** *n.*

mo·no·mi·al (mō-nō'mē-əl, mə-) *n.* **1.** *Math.* An algebraic expression consisting of only one term. **2.** *Biol.* A taxonomic name consisting of a single word. [MON(O)- + (BIN)OMIAL.] **—mo·no'mi·al** *adj.*

mon·o·mo·lec·u·lar (mŏn'ō-mə-lĕk'yə-lər) *adj.* **1.** Of or pertaining to a single molecule. **2.** Of or consisting of a layer one molecule thick. **—mon'o·mo·lec'u·lar·ly** *adv.*

mon·o·mor·phic (mŏn'ō-môr'fĭk) also **mon·o·mor·phous** (-fəs) *adj.* **1.** *Chem.* Having but one form, as one crystal form. **2.** *Zool.* Having a basic structure remaining unchanged through a series of developmental changes. **—mon'o·mor'phism** *n.*

mon·o·nu·cle·ar (mŏn'ō-no͞o'klē-ər, -nyo͞o'-) *adj.* Having one nucleus.

mon·o·nu·cle·o·sis (mŏn'ō-no͞o'klē-ō'sĭs, -nyo͞o-) *n.* **1.** The presence of an abnormally large number of leucocytes with single nuclei in the bloodstream. **2.** An acute, infectious disease producing mononucleosis. [MONO- + NUCLE(US) + -OSIS.]

mon·o·nu·cle·o·tide (mŏn'ō-no͞o'klē-ə-tīd', -nyo͞o'-) *n.* A nucleotide that contains one molecule each of a phosphoric acid, a pentose, and either a purine or pyrimidine base.

mon·o·pet·al·ous (mŏn'ə-pĕt'l-əs) *adj.* Having petals united to form one corolla; gamopetalous.

mo·noph·a·gous (mə-nŏf'ə-gəs) *adj.* Eating only one kind of food. **—mo·noph'a·gy** (-ə-jē) *n.*

mon·o·pho·bi·a (mŏn'ō-fō'bē-ə) *n.* Excessive fear of solitude. **—mon'o·pho'bic** (-fō'bĭk) *adj.*

mon·o·phon·ic (mŏn'ə-fŏn'ĭk) *adj.* **1.** *Mus.* Having a single melodic line; monodic. **2.** *Electronics.* Monaural (sense 2). **—mon'o·phon'i·cal·ly** *adv.*

mo·noph·o·ny (mə-nŏf'ə-nē) *n.* Music consisting of a single melodic line.

mon·oph·thong (mŏn'əf-thông', -thŏng') *n.* **1.** A single vowel sound made while the supraglottal speech organs are in a fixed position. **2.** Two written vowels representing a single sound. For example, *oa* in *boat* is a monophthong. [LGk. *monophthongos* : *monos,* single + *phthongos,* sound.] **—mon'oph·thon'gal** (-thông'gəl, -thŏng'-) *adj.*

mon·o·phy·let·ic (mŏn'ō-fī-lĕt'ĭk) *adj.* **1.** Of or concerning a single phylum of plants or animals. **2.** Descended or derived from one stock or source. **—mon'o·phy·let'ic·al·ly** *adv.*

Mo·noph·y·site (mə-nŏf'ə-sīt') *n. Theol.* An adherent of the doctrine that in the person of Christ there was but a single, divine nature. [Med. Lat. *monophysita* < Med. Gk. *monophusitēs* : *monos,* single + *phusis,* nature.] **—Mo·noph'y·sit'ic** (-sĭt'ĭk) *adj.* **—Mo·noph'y·sit'ism** *n.*

mon·o·plane (mŏn'ə-plān') *n.* An airplane with only one pair of wings.

mon·o·ple·gi·a (mŏn'ə-plē'jē-ə, -plē'jə) *n.* Paralysis of a single limb or part of the body, such as one side of the face. **—mon'o·ple'gic** (-plē'jĭk) *adj.*

mon·o·ploid (mŏn'ə-ploid') *adj.* Having a haploid set of chromosomes. *—n.* A monoploid individual.

mon·o·pode (mŏn'ə-pōd') *n.* **1.** A creature having only one foot, specifically a member of a fabled people in Africa. **2.** *Bot.* Monopodium. [LLat. *monopodius,* one-footed. —see MONOPODIUM.]

mon·o·po·di·um (mŏn'ə-pō'dē-əm) *n., pl.* **-dia** (-dē-ə). A main axis of a plant, such as the trunk of certain conifers, that maintains a single line of growth, giving off lateral branches. [NLat. < LLat. *monopodius,* one-footed < Gk. *monopous* : *monos,* one + *pous,* foot.] **—mon'o·po'di·al** *adj.*

mo·nop·o·lize (mə-nŏp'ə-līz') *tr.v.* **-lized, -liz·ing, -liz·es. 1.** To acquire or maintain a monopoly of. **2.** To dominate by excluding others: *monopolized the conversation.* **—mo·nop'o·li·za'tion** *n.* **—mo·nop'o·liz'er** *n.*

mo·nop·o·ly (mə-nŏp'ə-lē) *n., pl.* **-lies. 1.** *Econ.* Exclusive control by one group of the means of producing or selling a commodity or service. **2.** *Law.* A right granted by a government giving exclusive control over a specified commercial activity to a single party. **3. a.** A company or group having exclusive control over a commercial activity. **b.** A commodity or service so controlled. **4.** Exclusive possession or control. [Lat. *monopolium* < Gk. *monopōlion* : *monos,* one + *pōlein,* to sell.] **—mo·nop'o·lism** *n.* **—mo·nop'o·list** *n.* **—mo·nop'o·lis'tic** *adj.* **—mo·nop'o·lis'ti·cal·ly** *adv.*

mon·o·pro·pel·lant (mŏn'ō-prə-pĕl'ənt) *n.* A rocket propellant in which fuel and oxidizer are combined, such as a mixture of hydrogen peroxide and alcohol.

mon·o·pro·tic (mŏn'ə-prō'tĭk) *adj.* Having only one hydrogen ion to donate to a base in an acid-base reaction. [MONO- + PROT(ON) + -IC.]

mo·nop·so·ny (mə-nŏp'sə-nē) *n., pl.* **-nies.** A market situation in which the product or service of several sellers is sought by only one buyer. [MON(O)- + Gk. *opsōnia,* purchase of food < *opsōnein,* to buy food.]

mon·o·rail (mŏn'ə-rāl') *n.* **1.** A single rail on which a vehicle

Queen Anne of Great Britain and Ireland

Albrecht Dürer

monogram

monster
16th-century encyclopedia illustration

monstrance

montage
Montage of photographs

or train of cars travels. **2.** A railway system using a monorail.

mon·o·sac·cha·ride (mŏn′ə-săk′ə-rīd′, -rĭd) *n.* A simple sugar that cannot be decomposed by hydrolysis, esp. one of the hexoses, having the general formula $C_6H_{12}O_6$.

mon·o·sep·al·ous (mŏn′ə-sĕp′ə-ləs) *adj.* Having sepals united to form a single calyx; gamosepalous.

mon·o·sex·u·al (mŏn′ə-sĕk′sho͞o-əl) *adj.* Made up of or intended for individuals of one sex: *monosexual classrooms.*

mon·o·so·di·um glu·ta·mate (mŏn′ə-sō′dē-əm glo͞o′tə-māt′) *n.* Sodium glutamate.

mon·o·some (mŏn′ə-sōm′) *n.* **1.** A cell lacking one or more chromosomes. **2.** An unpaired X chromosome. **—mon′o·so′mic** (-sō′mĭk-) *adj.*

mon·o·sper·mous (mŏn′ə-spûr′məs) also **mon·o·sper·mal** (-məl) *adj.* Having a single seed.

mon·o·stome (mŏn′ə-stōm′) also **mo·nos·to·mous** (mə-nŏs′tə-məs) *adj.* Having one oral sucker only, as certain flatworms. *—n.* **monostome.** A trematode worm.

mon·o·sty·lous (mŏn′ə-stī′ləs) *adj. Bot.* Having one style.

mon·o·syl·lab·ic (mŏn′ə-sĭ-lăb′ĭk) *adj.* **1.** Having only one syllable. **2.** Characterized by or consisting of monosyllables. **—mon′o·syl·lab′ic·al·ly** *adv.*

mon·o·syl·la·ble (mŏn′ə-sĭl′ə-bəl) *n.* A word or utterance of one syllable. [LLat. *monosyllabum* < Gk. *monosullabon* : *monos,* one + *sullabē,* syllable. —see SYLLABLE.]

mon·o·syn·ap·tic (mŏn′ō-sə-năp′tĭk) *adj.* Having one neural synapse. **—mon′o·syn·ap′ti·cal·ly** *adv.*

mon·o·the·ism (mŏn′ə-thē-ĭz′əm) *n.* The doctrine or belief that there is only one God. **—mon′o·the′ist** *n.* **—mon′o·the·is′tic** *adj.* **—mon′o·the·is′ti·cal·ly** *adv.*

mon·o·the·mat·ic (mŏn′ō-thē-măt′ĭk) *adj. Mus.* Having but one theme.

mon·o·tint (mŏn′ə-tĭnt′) *n.* A monochrome (sense 1).

mon·o·tone (mŏn′ə-tōn′) *n.* **1.** A succession of sounds or words uttered in a single tone of voice. **2.** *Mus.* **a.** A single tone repeated with different words or time values, as in plainsong. **b.** A chant in a single tone. **3.** Sameness or dull repetition in sound, style, manner, or color. *—adj.* **1.** Of, pertaining to, or characteristic of sounds emitted at a single pitch. **2.** Of or having a single color. **3.** Also **mon·o·ton·ic** (mŏn′ə-tŏn′ĭk). *Math.* Designating sequences the successive members of which either consistently increase or decrease but do not oscillate in relative value. Each member of a *monotone increasing* sequence is greater than or equal to the preceding member; each member of a *monotone decreasing* sequence is less than or equal to the preceding member. [< Gk. *monotonos,* monotonous.] **—mon′o·ton′ic** (-tŏn′ĭk) *adj.* **—mon′o·ton′i·cal·ly** *adv.*

mo·not·o·nous (mə-nŏt′n-əs) *adj.* **1.** Sounded or spoken in an unvarying tone. **2.** Repetitiously dull or lacking in variety. [Gk. *monotonos* : *monos,* one + *tonos,* tone.] **—mo·not′o·nous·ly** *adv.* **—mo·not′o·nous·ness** *n.*

mo·not·o·ny (mə-nŏt′n-ē) *n.* **1.** Uniformity or lack of variation in pitch, intonation, or inflection. **2.** Wearisome sameness. [Gk. *monotonia* < *monotonos,* monotonous.]

mon·o·treme (mŏn′ə-trēm′) *n.* A member of the Monotremata, an order of egg-laying mammals restricted to Australia and New Guinea, and including the platypus and the echidna. [< NLat. *Monotremata,* order name : Gk. *monos,* one + Gk. *trēma,* hole < *tetrainein,* to perforate.] **—mon′o·trem′a·tous** (-trĕm′ə-təs) *adj.*

mo·not·ri·chous (mə-nŏt′rĭ-kəs) also **mon·o·trich·ic** (mŏn′ə-trĭk′ĭk) *adj.* Having one flagellum at only one pole or end, as certain bacteria.

mon·o·tro·phic (mŏn′ə-trŏ′fĭk) *adj.* Requiring only one kind of food; monophagous.

mon·o·type (mŏn′ə-tīp′) *n. Biol.* The sole member of its group, such as a species that also constitutes a genus. **—mon′o·typ′ic** (-tĭp′ĭk) *adj.*

Mon·o·type (mŏn′ə-tīp′). A trademark for a typesetting machine operated from a keyboard that activates a unit that casts individual letters from matrices and assembles them.

mon·o·va·lent (mŏn′ə-vā′lənt) *adj.* **1.** *Chem.* Possessing a valence of 1; univalent. **2.** *Pathol.* Able to resist a specific pathogen because the proper antibodies or antigens are present. **—mon′o·va′lence, mon′o·va′len·cy** *n.*

mon·ox·ide (mə-nŏk′sīd′) *n.* An oxide with each molecule containing one oxygen atom.

mon·o·zy·got·ic (mŏn′ō-zī-gŏt′ĭk) *adj.* Derived from a single fertilized ovum. Usually used of identical twins.

Monroe Doctrine *n.* The U.S. policy of opposition to outside interference in the Americas. [After James *Monroe* (1758–1831).]

mons (mŏnz) *n., pl.* **mon·tes** (mŏn′tēz). A protuberance of the human body, esp. that formed by the pubic bones. [Lat., mountain.]

Mon·sei·gneur (môN-sĕ-nyœr′) *n., pl.* **Mes·sei·gneurs** (mā-sĕ-nyœr′). A French title of honor or respect given to princes and prelates. [Fr. < OFr. : *mon,* my (< Lat. *meum*) + *seigneur,* sir, prob. < Lat. *senior,* older, comp. of *senex,* old.]

Mon·sieur (mə-syœ′) *n., pl.* **Mes·sieurs** (mĕs′ərz, mā-syœ′). A title of courtesy prefixed to the name or nobiliary or professional title of a Frenchman. [Fr. < OFr. : *mon,* my (< Lat. *meum*) + *sieur,* sir < *seigneur,* prob. < Lat. *senior,* older, comp. of *senex,* old.]

Mon·si·gnor also **mon·si·gnor** (mŏn-sēn′yər) *n., pl.* **-gnors.** *Rom. Cath. Ch.* A prelate having a rank or title, as of chamberlain, that is usually conferred by the Pope. Used as a title with a surname or with a first name and a surname. [Ital. < Fr. *Monseigneur.* —see MONSEIGNEUR.] **—Mon′si·gnor′i·al** *adj.*

mon·soon (mŏn-so͞on′) *n.* A wind system that influences large climatic regions and reverses direction seasonally, esp. the Asiatic monsoon that produces dry and wet seasons in India and southern Asia. [Obs. Du. *monssoen* < Port. *monção* < Ar. *mausim,* season.] **—mon·soon′al** *adj.*

mons pubis *n.* The male mons.

mon·ster (mŏn′stər) *n.* **1.** A creature having a bizarre or frightening shape or appearance. **2.** An animal or plant having structural defects or deformities. **3.** *Pathol.* A fetus or infant that is grotesquely abnormal. **4.** A very large animal, plant, or object. **5.** One who inspires horror or disgust. [ME < OFr. *monstre* < Lat. *monstrum,* portent, monster < *monēre,* to warn.]

mon·strance (mŏn′strəns) *n. Rom. Cath. Ch.* A receptacle in which the host is held. [ME < OFr. < Med. Lat. *monstrantia* < Lat. *monstrare,* to show < *monstrum,* portent, monster.]

mon·stros·i·ty (mŏn-strŏs′ĭ-tē) *n., pl.* **-ties.** **1.** One that is monstrous. **2.** The quality or character of being monstrous.

mon·strous (mŏn′strəs) *adj.* **1.** Deviating greatly from the norm in appearance or structure; abnormal. **2.** Exceptionally large; enormous. **3.** Hideous; frightful; shocking: *"a monstrous tyranny, never surpassed"* (Winston Churchill). [ME *monstrows* < OFr. *monstreux* < Lat. *monstruosus* < *monstrum,* monster.] **—mon′strous·ly** *adv.* **—mon′strous·ness** *n.*

mons ve·ne·ris (vĕn′ər-ĭs) *n.* The female mons.

mon·tage (mŏn-täzh′, môN-) *n.* **1. a.** The art, style, or process of making one pictorial composition by closely arranging or superimposing many pictures or designs. **b.** A picture so made. **2. a.** A rapid sequence of related short scenes or images used as a motion-picture technique to underscore a theme. **b.** A sequence using this effect. **3.** A mixture of miscellaneous elements; jumble. [Fr. < *monter,* to mount < OFr. —see MOUNT[1].] **—mon·tage′** *v.* **(-taged, -tag·ing, -tag·es).**

Mon·ta·gnard (mŏn′tən-yärd′) *n.* A member of a people inhabiting a mountainous region of southern Vietnam near the Cambodian border. [Fr., mountaineer < *montagne,* mountain. —see MOUNTAIN.]

mon·tane (mŏn-tān′, mŏn′tān′) *adj.* Of, growing in, or inhabiting mountain areas. [Lat. *montanus* < *mons,* mountain.]

mon·tan wax (mŏn′tən, -tăn′) *n.* A hard, white wax obtained from lignite and used in the manufacture of polishes, candles, and insulators. [< Lat. *montanus,* montane.]

mon·te (mŏn′tē) *n.* A card game in which two cards are chosen from four laid out and a player bets on one of the two to be matched by the dealer before the other one. [Sp., monte, mountain < Lat. *mons,* mountain.]

mon·te·ro (mŏn-târ′ō) *n., pl.* **-ros.** A huntsman's cap with side flaps. [Sp., hunter < *monte,* mountain < Lat. *mons.*]

mon·tes (mŏn′tēz) *n.* Plural of **mons.**

Mon·tes·so·ri·an (mŏn′tĭ-sôr′ē-ən, -sōr′-) *adj.* Of or relating to the Montessori method.

Mon·tes·so·ri method (mŏn′tə-sôr′ē, -sōr′ē) *n.* A method of instructing young children that stresses development of a child's own initiative. [After Maria *Montessori* (1870–1952).]

month (mŭnth) *n.* **1.** One of the 12 divisions of a year as determined by the Gregorian calendar. **2.** A period extending from a date in one calendar month to the corresponding date in the following month. **3. a.** A period of four weeks. **b.** A period of 30 days. **4.** The average period of revolution of the moon around the earth determined by using a fixed star as a reference point and equal to 27 days 7 hours 43 minutes. **5.** The average time between successive new, or full, moons; equal to 29 days 12 hours 44 minutes. **6.** One twelfth of a tropical year, totaling 30 days 10 hours 29 minutes 3.8 seconds. ***—idiom.* month of Sundays.** *Informal.* An indefinitely long period of time. [ME *moneth* < OE *mōnað.*]

month·ly (mŭnth′lē) *adj.* **1.** Occurring, appearing, or coming due every month. **2.** Continuing or lasting for a month. *—adv.* Once a month; every month. *—n., pl.* **-lies.** **1.** A periodical publication appearing once each month. **2. monthlies.** *Informal.* The menses.

mon·ti·cule (mŏn′tĭ-kyo͞ol′) *n.* A secondary volcanic cone of a volcano. [Fr. < LLat. *monticulus,* dim. of Lat. *mons,* mountain.]

mon·u·ment (mŏn′yə-mənt) *n.* **1.** A structure, such as a building or sculpture, erected as a memorial. **2.** An inscribed stone or other marker placed at a grave; tombstone. **3.** Something venerated for its historic or aesthetic significance. **4.** A national monument. **5. a.** An outstanding and enduring achievement. **b.** An exceptional example: *a monument of stupidity.* **6.** A boundary marker, as a stone or post. **7.** A written document, esp. a legal one. [ME < Lat. *monumentum,* memorial < *monēre,* to remind.]

mon·u·men·tal (mŏn′yə-mĕn′tl) *adj.* **1.** Of, resembling, or serving as a monument. **2.** Impressively large, sturdy, and enduring. **3.** Of outstanding significance: *Einstein's monu-*

mental contributions to physics. **4.** Astounding: *monumental cowardice; monumental talent.* **—mon'u·men·tal'i·ty** *n.* **—mon'u·men'tal·ly** *adv.*

mon·u·men·tal·ize (mŏn'yə-mĕn'tl-īz') *tr.v.* **-ized, -iz·ing, -iz·es.** To memorialize with a monument.

mon·u·ron (mŏn'yə-rŏn') *n.* A crystalline compound, $C_9H_{11}ClN_2O$, used as a herbicide for grasses and broadleaf weeds. [MON(O)- + UR(EA) + -ON.]

mon·zo·nite (mŏn-zō'nīt', mŏn'zə-nīt') *n.* An igneous rock composed chiefly of plagioclase and orthoclase, with small amounts of other minerals. [Fr., after Mt. *Monzoni* in northeastern Italy, where it was discovered.] **—mon'zo·nit'ic** *adj.*

moo (mōō) *intr.v.* **mooed, moo·ing, moos.** To emit the deep, bellowing sound made by a cow. *—n., pl.* **moos.** The lowing of a cow, or a similar sound. [Imit.]

mooch (mōōch) *v.* **mooched, mooch·ing, mooch·es.** *Slang.* *—tr.* **1.** To obtain (something) free of charge, as by cajolery. **2.** To steal or filch. *—intr.* **1.** To obtain free of charge; sponge. **2.** To wander around aimlessly. **3.** To skulk about. [ME *mowchen* < OFr. *muchier.*] **—mooch'er** *n.*

mood[1] (mōōd) *n.* **1.** A temporary state of mind or feeling, as evidenced by the tendency of one's thoughts: *a gloomy mood.* **2.** A pervading impression on the feelings of an observer: *the somber mood of the painting.* **3.** Sulking or angry behavior. **4.** Inclination; disposition. [ME *mod* < OE *mōd.*]

Synonyms: *mood, humor, temper. Mood* suggests greater duration than the other terms here. It pertains to persons and nonliving things (such as art and the times), and can indicate any segment of the emotional range, although when applied without qualification to a person, it generally implies antisocial behavior. *Humor,* said only of persons, emphasizes transitoriness; it sometimes implies variability of emotion. *Temper,* restricted to persons, stresses brief intensity of anger.

mood[2] (mōōd) *n.* **1.** *Gram.* A verb form or a set of verb forms inflected to indicate the manner in which the action or state expressed by a verb is viewed with respect to such functions as factuality, possibility, or command. **2.** *Logic.* The arrangement or form of a proposition. [Alteration of MODE.]

mood·y (mōō'dē) *adj.* **-i·er, -i·est.** **1.** Given to changeable emotional states, esp. of gloom. **2.** Gloomy; uneasy: *a moody silence.* **—mood'i·ly** *adv.* **—mood'i·ness** *n.*

moo goo gai pan (mōō' gōō' gī' păn') *n.* A Cantonese dish of chicken, mushrooms, vegetables, and spices, steamed together. [Cantonese, corresponding to Mandarin *mu[2] gu[2] ji[1] pian[1]* : *mu[2] gu[2],* mushroom + *ji[1],* chicken + *pian[1],* slice.]

moo·la or **moo·lah** (mōō'lə) *n.* *Slang.* Money. [Orig. unknown.]

moon (mōōn) *n.* **1.** The natural satellite of the earth, visible by reflection of sunlight, having a slightly elliptical orbit, approximately 356,00 kilometers, or 221,600 miles, distant at perigee and 406,997 kilometers, or 252,950 miles, at apogee. Its mean diameter is 3,475 kilometers, or 2,160 miles, its mass approximately one-eightieth that of the earth, and its average period of revolution around the earth 29 days 12 hours 44 minutes calculated with respect to the sun. **2.** A natural satellite revolving around a planet. **3.** The moon as it appears at a particular time in its cycle of phases: *the full moon; a half moon.* **4.** A month, esp. a lunar month. **5.** A disk, globe, or crescent resembling the moon. **6.** Moonlight. *—intr.v.* **mooned, moon·ing, moons.** **1.** To wander about or pass time languidly and aimlessly. **2.** To exhibit infatuation. [ME *moone* < OE *mōna.*] **—moon'like'** *adj.*

moon·beam (mōōn'bēm') *n.* A ray of moonlight.

moon·blind (mōōn'blīnd') *adj.* Suffering from moon blindness.

moon blindness *n.* **1.** Recurrent inflammation of a horse's eyes, often resulting in eventual blindness. **2.** Night blindness.

moon·calf (mōōn'kăf', -käf') *n.* **1.** A fool from birth. **2.** A freak.

moon dog *n.* A paraselene.

moon·eye (mōōn'ī') *n.* **1.** A silvery freshwater fish, *Hiodon tergisus,* of northern North America. **2.** Moon blindness (sense 1).

moon-faced (mōōn'fāst') *adj.* Having a round face.

moon·fish (mōōn'fĭsh') *n., pl.* **moonfish** or **-fish·es.** **1.** Either of two marine fishes of the family Carangidae, found in the warm coastal waters of the Americas. They have short, compressed bodies and are silver to yellowish in color. **2.** The opah.

moon·flow·er (mōōn'flou'ər) *n.* Any of several night-blooming vines related to the morning-glories.

moon·light (mōōn'līt') *n.* The light reflected from the surface of the moon, principally that originating at the sun. *—intr.v.* **-light·ed, -light·ing, -lights.** *Informal.* To work at another job, often at night, in addition to one's full-time job. **—moon'light'er** *n.*

moon·scape (mōōn'skāp') *n.* **1.** A view or picture of the surface of the moon. **2.** A desolate landscape.

moon·seed (mōōn'sēd') *n.* Any of several climbing vines of the genus *Menispermum* or related genera, having red or blackish fruit with crescent-shaped or ring-shaped seeds.

moon shell *n.* Any of various marine gastropod mollusks of the family Naticidae, having smooth spherical shells.

moon·shine (mōōn'shīn') *n.* **1.** Moonlight. **2.** *Informal.* Foolish or nonsensical talk, thought, or action. **3.** *Slang.* Illegally distilled whiskey. *—v.* **-shined, -shin·ing, -shines.** *—tr.* To distill (liquor) illegally. *—intr.* To operate an illegal still. **—moon'shine'** *adj.* **—moon'shin'er** *n.*

moon·stone (mōōn'stōn') *n.* A feldspar valued as a gem for its pearly translucence.

moon·struck (mōōn'strŭk') also **moon·strick·en** (-strĭk'ən) *adj.* **1.** Afflicted with insanity. **2.** Dazed or distracted with romantic sentiment. [From the belief that the moon caused insanity.]

moon·ward (mōōn'wərd) *adv.* Toward the moon.

moon·wort (mōōn'wûrt', -wôrt') *n.* A grape fern.

moon·y (mōō'nē) *adj.* **-i·er, -i·est.** **1. a.** Resembling the moon. **b.** Resembling moonlight. **2.** Moonlit. **3.** Dreamy in mood or nature; absent-minded.

moor[1] (mŏŏr) *v.* **moored, moor·ing, moors.** *—tr.* **1.** To secure or make fast (a vessel, for example) by means of cables, anchors, or lines. **2.** To fix in place; secure. *—intr.* **1.** To secure a vessel or aircraft. **2.** To be secured, as a vessel. [ME *moren* < MLG *mōren.*]

moor[2] (mŏŏr) *n.* A broad tract of open land, often high but poorly drained, with patches of heath and peat bogs. [ME *mor* < OE *mōr.*]

Moor (mŏŏr) *n.* **1.** One of a Moslem people of mixed Berber and Arab descent, now living chiefly in northern Africa. **2.** One of the Saracens who invaded Spain in the 8th century A.D. [ME *More* < OFr. < Lat. *Maurus.*]

moor·age (mŏŏr'ĭj) *n.* **1.** A place where a ship may be moored. **2.** The act of mooring or state of being moored. **3.** A charge for the use of mooring facilities.

moor·hen (mŏŏr'hĕn') *n.* *Chiefly Brit.* A common, widely distributed gallinule, *Gallinula chloropus.*

moor·ing (mŏŏr'ĭng) *n.* **1.** Equipment, such as anchors or chains, for holding fast a vessel or aircraft. **2.** The act of securing a vessel or aircraft. **3.** A place at which a vessel or aircraft can be moored. **4.** Often **moorings.** Elements providing stability or security: *lost his emotional moorings at the trial.*

Moor·ish (mŏŏr'ĭsh) *adj.* Of or characteristic of the Moors or their culture: *Moorish architecture.*

moor·land (mŏŏr'lănd') *n.* *Chiefly Brit.* A tract of moors.

moor·wort (mŏŏr'wûrt', -wôrt') *n.* The bog rosemary.

moose (mōōs) *n., pl.* **moose.** A hoofed mammal, *Alces alces* (also known as *A. americana*), of the deer family, found in forests of northern North America and in Eurasia. It has a broad, pendulous muzzle, and the male has large, flat antlers. [Natick *moos.*]

moose·bird (mōōs'bûrd') *n.* The Canada jay.

moose·wood (mōōs'wŏŏd') *n.* A slender maple, *Acer pennsylvanicum,* of eastern North America, having smooth bark with vertical whitish or greenish stripes.

moot (mōōt) *n.* **1.** An ancient English meeting, esp. a representative meeting of the freemen of a shire. **2.** A hypothetical case argued by law students as an exercise. *—tr.v.* **moot·ed, moot·ing, moots.** **1. a.** To bring up as a subject for discussion or debate. **b.** To discuss or debate. **2.** To plead or argue (a case) in a moot court. *—adj.* **1.** Subject to debate; arguable: *a moot question.* **2. a.** *Law.* Without legal significance, through having been previously decided or settled. **b.** Of no practical importance. [ME < OE *mōt.*]

moot court *n.* A mock court where hypothetical cases are tried for the training of law students.

mop (mŏp) *n.* **1.** A household implement made of absorbent material attached to a handle and used for dusting, washing, and drying floors. **2.** A loosely tangled bunch or mass: *a mop of hair.* *—tr.v.* **mopped, mop·ping, mops.** To wash or wipe with or as if with a mop. ***—phrasal verb.*** **mop up.** **1.** To clear (an area) of remaining enemy troops after a victory. **2.** *Informal.* To complete a task or action. [ME *mappe.*] **—mop'per** *n.*

mop·board (mŏp'bôrd', -bōrd') *n.* Baseboard.

mope (mōp) *intr.v.* **moped, mop·ing, mopes.** **1. a.** To be gloomy or dejected. **b.** To brood or sulk. **2.** To move in a leisurely or aimless manner; dawdle. *—n.* **1.** A person given to gloomy or dejected moods. **2. mopes.** Low spirits; the blues. [Orig. unknown.] **—mop'er** *n.* **—mop'ing·ly** *adv.* **—mop'ish** *adj.* **—mop'ish·ly** *adv.*

mop·pet (mŏp'ĭt) *n.* A young child. [< obs. *mop,* fool, child < ME.]

mop-up (mŏp'ŭp') *n.* A finishing action.

mo·quette (mō-kĕt') *n.* **1.** A heavy fabric with a thick nap, used for upholstery. **2.** A type of carpet with a deep, tufted pile. [Fr., alteration of *moucade.*]

mo·ra (môr'ə, mōr'ə) *n., pl.* **mo·rae** (môr'ē, mōr'ē) or **mo·ras.** In quantitative verse, the unit of metrical time equal to the short syllable. [< Lat., pause.]

mo·raine (mə-rān') *n.* An accumulation of boulders, stones, or other debris carried and deposited by a glacier. [Fr.] **—mo·rain'al, mo·rain'ic** *adj.*

mor·al (môr'əl, mŏr'-) *adj.* **1.** Of or concerned with the judgment principles of right and wrong in relation to human action and character. **2.** Teaching or exhibiting goodness or correctness of character and behavior: *a moral lesson.* **3.** Conforming to standards of what is right or just in behavior; virtuous. **4.** Arising from conscience or the sense of

monument

moray

Morgan

morion[1]
Made in 16th-century Italy

morning-glory

A	·–	V	···–
B	–···	W	·––
C	–·–·	X	–··–
D	–··	Y	–·––
E	·	Z	––··
F	··–·	Á	·––·–
G	––·	Ä	·–·–
H	····	É	··–··
I	··	Ñ	––·––
J	·–––	Ö	–––·
K	–·–	Ü	··––
L	·–··	1	·––––
M	––	2	··–––
N	–·	3	···––
O	–––	4	····–
P	·––·	5	·····
Q	––·–	6	–····
R	·–·	7	––···
S	···	8	–––··
T	–	9	––––·
U	··–	0	–––––
, (comma)	––··––		
. (period)	·–·–·–		
?	··––··		
;	–·–·–·		
:	–––···		
/	–··–·		
- (hyphen)	–····–		
apostrophe	·––––·		
parenthesis	–·––·–		
underline	··––·–		

Morse code

right and wrong: *a moral obligation.* **5.** Having psychological rather than physical or tangible effects: *a moral victory.* **6.** Based upon strong likelihood or firm conviction, rather than upon the actual evidence: *a moral certainty.* —*n.* **1.** The lesson or principle contained in or taught by a fable, story, or event. **2.** A concisely expressed precept or general truth; maxim. **3. morals.** Rules or habits of conduct, esp. sexual conduct, with reference to standards of right and wrong. [ME < OFr. < Lat. *moralis* < *mos,* custom.] **—mor′al·ly** *adv.*

Synonyms: *moral, ethical, virtuous, righteous. Moral* pertains to personal behavior (especially sexual) measured by prevailing standards of rectitude. *Ethical* approaches behavior from a philosophical standpoint; it stresses more objectively defined, but essentially idealistic, standards of right and wrong, such as those applicable to the practices of lawyers, doctors, and businessmen. *Virtuous* pertains to sexual continence, especially of women, or to loftiness of character in general. *Righteous* emphasizes one's credentials for salvation, especially the absence of guilt or sin, and implies zealousness and uprightness.

mo·rale (mə-răl′) *n.* The state of the spirits of an individual or group as shown by confidence, cheerfulness, discipline, and willingness to perform assigned tasks. [Fr. < fem. of *moral,* moral < OFr. —see MORAL.]

moral hazard *n.* A risk to an insurance company resulting from uncertainty about the honesty of the insured.

mor·al·ism (môr′ə-lĭz′əm, mŏr′-) *n.* **1.** A conventional moral maxim or attitude. **2.** The act or practice of moralizing. **3.** An often undue concern for morality.

mor·al·ist (môr′ə-lĭst, mŏr′-) *n.* **1.** A teacher or student of morals and moral problems. **2.** A person who follows a system of moral principles. **3.** One who is unduly concerned with the morals of others.

mor·al·is·tic (môr′ə-lĭs′tĭk, mŏr′-) *adj.* **1.** Characterized by or displaying an interest in or concern with morality. **2.** Marked by a narrow-minded morality. **—mor′al·is′ti·cal·ly** *adv.*

mo·ral·i·ty (mə-răl′ĭ-tē, mô-) *n., pl.* **-ties. 1.** The quality of being in accord with standards of right or good conduct. **2.** A system of ideas of right and wrong conduct. **3.** Virtuous conduct. **4.** A rule or lesson in moral conduct.

morality play *n.* An allegorical play of the 15th and 16th centuries in which moral instruction is given and in which the characters personify virtues and vices.

mor·al·ize (môr′ə-līz′, mŏr′-) *v.* **-ized, -iz·ing, -iz·es.** —*tr.* **1.** To interpret or explain the moral meaning of. **2.** To improve the morals of; reform. —*intr.* To think about or discuss moral or ethical issues. **—mor′al·i·za′tion** *n.* **—mor′al·iz′er** *n.*

moral philosophy *n.* Ethics.

mo·rass (mə-răs′, mô-) *n.* **1.** An area of low-lying, soggy ground; bog. **2.** Something that hinders, engulfs, or overwhelms. [Du. *moeras* < OFr. *maresc,* prob. of Germanic orig.]

mor·a·to·ri·um (môr′ə-tôr′ē-əm, -tōr′-, mŏr′-) *n., pl.* **-to·ri·ums** or **-to·ri·a** (-tôr′ē-ə, -tōr′-). **1.** *Law.* An authorization to a debtor, such as a bank or nation, permitting temporary suspension of payments. **2.** A suspension of action. [< LLat., neuter of *moratorius,* delaying. —see MORATORY.]

mor·a·to·ry (môr′ə-tôr′ē, -tōr′ē, mŏr′-) *adj.* Authorizing delay in payment. [Fr. *moratoire* < LLat. *moratorius,* delaying < Lat. *morari,* to delay < *mora,* delay.]

Mo·ra·vi·an (mə-rā′vē-ən) *n.* **1.** A native or inhabitant of Moravia. **2.** The Czech dialects of Moravia. **3.** A member of a Protestant denomination founded in Saxony in 1722 by Hussite emigrants from Moravia. **—Mo·ra′vi·an** *adj.*

mo·ray (môr′ā, mə-rā′) *n.* Any of various often voracious marine eels of the family Muraenidae, of chiefly tropical coastal waters. [Port. *moreia* < Lat. *murena* < Gk. *muraina.*]

mor·bid (môr′bĭd) *adj.* **1. a.** Of, relating to, or caused by disease. **b.** Psychologically unhealthy: *"She had a morbid fear of dance floors"* (Eric Berne). **2.** Susceptible to or overly preoccupied with unwholesome matters. **3.** Gruesome; grisly. [Lat. *morbidus,* diseased < *morbus,* disease.] **—mor·bid′i·ty, mor′bid·ness** *n.* **—mor′bid·ly** *adv.*

mor·da·cious (môr-dā′shəs) *adj.* **1.** Given to biting; biting. **2.** Caustic; sarcastic. [Lat. *mordax, mordac-* < *mordēre,* to bite.] **—mor·da′cious·ly** *adv.* **—mor·dac′i·ty** (-dăs′ĭ-tē) *n.*

mor·dant (môr′dnt) *adj.* **1. a.** Bitingly sarcastic. **b.** Incisive and trenchant. **2.** Bitingly painful. **3.** Serving to fix colors in dyeing. —*n.* **1.** A reagent, such as tannic acid, used to fix coloring matter in textiles, leather, or other materials. **2.** A corrosive substance, such as an acid, used in etching. —*tr.v.* **-dant·ed, -dant·ing, -dants.** To treat with a mordant. [Fr. < OFr. < pr.part. of *mordre,* to bite < Lat. *mordēre,* to bite.] **—mor′dan·cy** *n.* **—mor′dant·ly** *adv.*

mor·dent (môr′dnt, môr-dĕnt′) *n. Mus.* A melodic ornament in which a principal note is rapidly alternated with a note a half or full step below. [G. < Ital. *mordente* < *mordere,* to bite < Lat. *mordēre.*]

more (môr, mōr) *adj.* **1. a.** Greater in number. **b.** Greater in size, amount, extent, or degree. **2.** Additional; extra: *They need more food.* —*n.* A greater or additional quantity, number, degree, or amount: *More of them are coming.* —*pron.* **1.** Something greater or better: *More was expected of him because he was the oldest.* **2.** *(used with a pl. verb).* A greater number of persons or things: *opened only two bottles but there were more in the refrigerator.* —*adv.* **1.** To or in a greater extent or degree. Used to form the comparative of many adjectives and adverbs: *more difficult; more intelligently.* **2.** In addition. ***—idioms.*** **more and more.** To an increasing extent or degree: *She sees him more and more.* **more or less. 1.** About; approximately. **2.** To an undetermined degree. [ME < OE *māra.*]

mo·reen (mə-rēn′, mô-) *n.* A sturdy ribbed fabric of wool, cotton, or wool and cotton often with an embossed finish, used for clothing and upholstery. [Poss. < MOIRE.]

mo·rel (mə-rĕl′, mô-) *n.* Any of various edible mushrooms of the genus *Morchella* and related genera, characterized by a brownish, spongelike cap. [Fr. *morille* < OFr., prob. of Germanic orig.]

mo·rel·lo (mə-rĕl′ō) *n., pl.* **-los.** A variety of the sour cherry, *Prunus cerasus austera,* having fruit with dark-red skin. [Prob. < Ital. *amarello* < Med. Lat. *amarellum,* dim. of Lat. *amarus,* bitter.]

more·o·ver (môr-ō′vər, mōr-, môr′ō′vər, mōr′-) *adv.* Beyond what has been stated; further; besides.

mo·res (môr′āz′, -ēz, mōr′-) *pl.n.* **1.** The accepted traditional customs and usages of a particular social group. **2.** Moral attitudes. **3.** Manners; ways. [Lat., pl. of *mos,* custom.]

Mo·resque (mô-rĕsk′, mə-) *adj.* Characteristic of Moorish art and architecture. —*n.* An ornament or decoration in Moorish style. [Fr. < Sp. *Morisco,* Morisco.]

Mor·gan (môr′gən) *n.* One of a breed of American saddle and trotting horses. [After Justin *Morgan* (1747–1798).]

mor·ga·nat·ic (môr′gə-năt′ĭk) *adj.* Of or pertaining to a legal marriage between a person of royal or noble birth and a partner of lower rank, in which no titles or estates of the royal or noble partner are to be shared by the partner of inferior rank nor by any of the offspring of the marriage. [NLat. *morganaticus* < Med. Lat. *matrimonium ad morganaticam,* marriage for the morning-gift.] **—mor′ga·nat′i·cal·ly** *adv.*

mor·gan·ite (môr′gə-nīt′) *n.* A rosy-pink silicate of beryllium and aluminum valued as a semiprecious gem. [After John Pierpont *Morgan* (1837–1913).]

Mor·gan le Fay (môr′gən lə fā′) *n.* The sorceress sister and enemy of King Arthur according to Arthurian legend. [OFr. *Morgain la fee,* Morgan the fairy.]

mor·gen (môr′gən) *n., pl.* **morgen** or **-gens.** A Dutch and South African unit of land area equal to 2.116 acres. [Du. < MDu. *morghen,* morning.]

morgue (môrg) *n.* **1.** A place in which the bodies of persons found dead are kept until identified and claimed or until arrangements for burial have been made. **2.** A reference file in a newspaper or magazine office. [Fr.]

mor·i·bund (môr′ə-bŭnd′, mŏr′-) *adj.* Approaching the point of death; about to die. [Lat. *moribundus* < *mori,* to die.] **—mor′i·bun′di·ty** *n.* **—mor′i·bund′ly** *adv.*

mo·ri·on[1] (môr′ē-ŏn′, mōr′-) *n.* A crested metal helmet with a curved peak in front and back, worn by soldiers in the 16th and 17th centuries. [Fr. < Sp. *morrion* < *morro,* round object.]

mo·ri·on[2] (môr′ē-ŏn′, mōr′-) *n.* A variety of smoky quartz, often nearly black. [Alteration of Lat. *mormorion.*]

Mo·ris·co (mə-rĭs′kō) *n., pl.* **-cos** or **-coes.** A Spanish Moor. [Sp. < *Moro,* Moor < Lat. *Maurus.*] **—Mo·ris′co** *adj.*

Mor·mon (môr′mən) *n.* **1.** *Mormon Ch.* A prophet, warrior, and historian revealed to Joseph Smith as the author of a sacred history of the Americas which Smith translated as the Book of Mormon. **2.** A member of the Church of Jesus Christ of Latter-day Saints, founded by Joseph Smith in 1830 at Fayette, New York. **—Mor′mon·ism** *n.*

morn (môrn) *n.* **1.** The morning. **2.** The dawn. [ME < OE *morgen.*]

morn·ing (môr′nĭng) *n.* **1.** The first or early part of the day, lasting from midnight to noon or from sunrise to noon. **2.** The dawn. **3.** The first or early part of anything. [ME < *morn,* morn < OE *morgen.*]

morn·ing-glo·ry (môr′nĭng-glôr′ē, -glōr′ē) *n.* Any of various, usually twining vines of the genus *Ipomoea,* having funnel-shaped, variously colored flowers that close late in the day.

Morning Prayer *n.* The liturgical service of morning worship in the Anglican Church.

morn·ings (môr′nĭngz) *adv.* Regularly or habitually in the morning.

morning sickness *n.* Nausea and vomiting upon rising in the morning, esp. during the early stages of pregnancy.

morning star *n.* A planet, esp. Venus, visible in the east just before or at sunrise.

Mo·ro (môr′ō, mōr′ō) *n., pl.* **-ros. 1.** A member of any of the Moslem Malay tribes of the southern Philippines. **2.** Any of the Austronesian languages of the Moro. [Sp. < Lat. *Maurus,* Moor.] **—Mo′ro** *adj.*

mo·roc·co (mə-rŏk′ō) *n., pl.* **-cos.** A soft, fine leather of goatskin tanned with sumac. [After *Morocco,* where it was orig. made.]

mo·ron (môr′ŏn′, mōr′-) *n.* **1.** A mentally retarded person having a mental age between 7 and 12 years or an intelligence quotient between 50 and 75. **2.** A remarkably stupid person. [< Gk. *mōron,* neuter of *mōros,* stupid.] **—mo·ron′ic**

(mə-rŏn′ĭk, mô-) *adj.* —**mo·ron′i·cal·ly** *adv.* —**mo′ron′ism, mo·ron′i·ty** (mə-rŏn′ĭ-tē, mô-) *n.*

mo·rose (mə-rōs′, mô-) *adj.* **1.** Sullenly melancholy in nature or disposition. **2.** Characterized by or displaying gloom. [Lat. *morosus,* peevish < *mos,* manner.] —**mo·rose′ly** *adv.* —**mo·rose′ness** *n.*

morph (môrf) *n.* **1.** An allomorph. **2.** A phoneme or sequence of phonemes that is assumed to be an allomorph although its assignment to a particular morpheme has not been established.

morph– *pref.* Variant of **morpho-**.

–morph *suff.* **1.** Form; shape; structure: *endomorph.* **2.** Morpheme: *allomorph.* [Gk. *-morphos* < *morphē,* shape.]

mor·phal·lax·is (môr′fə-lăk′sĭs) *n. Biol.* The regeneration of a part or the transformation of one part into another by means of structural reorganization with only limited production of new cells, a process observed primarily in invertebrate organisms, such as certain lobsters. [NLat. : MORPH(O)- + Gk. *allaxis,* exchange < *allassein,* to exchange < *allos,* other.]

mor·pheme (môr′fēm′) *n.* A meaningful linguistic unit consisting of a word, such as *man,* or a word element, such as *-ed* of *walked,* that cannot be divided into smaller meaningful parts. [Fr. *morphème* < Gk. *morphē,* form.] —**mor·phem′ic** *adj.* —**mor·phem′i·cal·ly** *adv.*

mor·phem·ics (môr-fē′mĭks) *n.* *(used with a sing. verb).* **1.** The study of morphemes as a branch of linguistic analysis. **2.** The morphemic structure of a language.

Mor·phe·us (môr′fē-əs, -fyo͞os′) *n.* In Ovid's *Metamorphoses,* the god of dreams. [Lat.] —**Mor′phe·an** (-fē-ən) *adj.*

mor·phi·a (môr′fē-ə) *n.* Morphine. [NLat. < Lat. *Morpheus,* Morpheus.]

mor·phic (môr′fĭk) *adj.* Pertaining to form; morphological. —**mor′phi·cal·ly** *adv.*

–morphic *suff.* Having a specified form: *geomorphic.*

mor·phine (môr′fēn′) *n.* An organic compound, $C_{17}H_{19}NO_3$, extracted from opium, the soluble salts of which are used in human and veterinary medicine as a light anesthetic or as a sedative. [Fr. < *Morphée,* Morpheus < Lat. *Morpheus.*]

mor·phin·ism (môr′fē-nĭz′əm, môr′fə-) *n.* **1.** Morphine addiction. **2.** Poisoning caused by sustained or immoderate dosage of morphine, a chronic condition.

–morphism *suff.* The condition or quality of having a specified form: *homomorphism.*

morpho– or **morph–** *pref.* **1.** Form; shape; structure: *morphogenesis.* **2.** Morpheme: *morphophonemics.* [G. < Gk. < *morphē,* shape.]

mor·pho·gen·e·sis (môr′fō-jĕn′ĭ-sĭs) *n.* **1.** Evolutionary development of the structure of an organism or part. **2.** Embryological development of the structure of an organism or part. —**mor′pho·ge·net′ic** (-jə-nĕt′ĭk), **mor′pho·gen′ic** *adj.* —**mor′pho·ge·net′i·cal·ly** *adv.*

mor·phol·o·gy (môr-fŏl′ə-jē) *n.* **1.** The biological study of the form and structure of living organisms. **2.** The structure and form of an organism, excluding its functions. **3.** *Geol.* Geomorphology. **4.** *Ling.* The study of word formation in a language, including inflection, derivation, and the formation of compounds. [G. *Morphologie* : Gk. *morphē,* shape + Gk. *logos,* word, discussion.] —**mor′pho·log′i·cal** (-fə-lŏj′ĭ-kəl), **mor′pho·log′ic** *adj.* —**mor′pho·log′i·cal·ly** *adv.* —**mor·phol′o·gist** *n.*

mor·pho·pho·ne·mics (môr′fō-fə-nē′mĭks) *n.* *(used with a sing. verb).* **1.** Linguistic structure in terms of the phonological patterning of morphemes, as through variations, such as the addition, loss, or substitution of phonemes, including stress shifts, which determine the different shapes of morphemically related words. **2.** The study of the morphophonemics of a language. —**mor′pho·pho·ne′mic** *adj.*

mor·pho·sis (môr-fō′sĭs) *n., pl.* **-ses** (-sēz′). The manner in which an organism or one of its parts changes form or the manner or order of its development. [Gk. *morphōsis,* process of forming < *morphoun,* to form < *morphē,* form.]

–morphous *suff.* Having a specified form: *heteromorphous.*

mor·ris (môr′ĭs, mŏr′-) *n.* An English folk dance in which a story is acted by costumed dancers. [ME *moreys* *(dance),* morris (dance) < *moreys,* Moorish < *More,* Moor. —see MOOR.]

Mor·ris chair (môr′ĭs, mŏr′-) *n.* A large easy chair with arms, an adjustable back, and removable cushions. [After William *Morris* (1834–1896).]

mor·row (môr′ō, mŏr′ō) *n.* **1.** The day following some specified day. **2.** The time immediately subsequent to some particular event. **3.** *Archaic.* The morning. [ME *morow* < OE *morgen.*]

Morse code (môrs) *n.* One of the codes in which letters of the alphabet and numbers are represented by short and long elements esp. in the form of sounds or flashes of light. [After Samuel F. B. *Morse* (1791–1872).]

mor·sel (môr′səl) *n.* **1.** A small piece or bite of food. **2.** A small piece or amount. **3.** A tasty delicacy. **4.** One that is delightful and extremely pleasing. [ME < OFr., dim. of *mors,* bite < Lat. *morsus* < *mordēre,* to bite.]

mort[1] (môrt) *n.* The note sounded on a hunting horn to announce the death of a deer. [ME, death < OFr. < Lat. *mors.*]

mort[2] (môrt) *n.* A great number or quantity. [Poss. < MORTAL.]

mor·tal (môr′tl) *adj.* **1.** Liable or subject to death. **2.** Of or pertaining to human beings. **3.** Of, pertaining to, or accompanying death: *mortal throes.* **4.** Causing death; fatal: *a mortal wound.* **5.** Unrelenting; implacable: *a mortal enemy.* **6.** Of great intensity or severity; dire: *in mortal terror.* **7.** Conceivable: *no mortal reason for us to go.* **8.** Used as an intensifier: *spoke for six mortal hours.* —*n.* A human being. —*adv. Regional.* Extremely; very. [ME < OFr. < Lat. *mortalis* < *mors,* death.] —**mor′tal·ly** *adv.*

mor·tal·i·ty (môr-tăl′ĭ-tē) *n., pl.* **-ties. 1.** The quality or condition of being mortal. **2.** Frequency of number of deaths in proportion to a population; death rate. **3.** *Archaic.* Death. **4.** *Archaic.* Deadliness.

mortal sin *n. Theol.* A serious and deliberate sin, such as murder or suicide, that robs the soul of sanctifying grace.

mor·tar (môr′tər) *n.* **1.** A vessel in which substances are crushed or ground with a pestle. **2.** A machine in which materials are ground and blended or crushed. **3. a.** Also **trench mortar.** A muzzle-loading cannon used to fire shells at low velocities, short ranges, and great angular elevation. **b.** Any of several devices similar to a mortar used for various purposes, such as shooting life lines across a stretch of water. **4.** A mixture of cement or lime with sand and water used in building. —*tr.v.* **-tared, -tar·ing, -tars.** To plaster or join with mortar. [ME *morter* < OE *mortere* and OFr. *mortier,* both < Lat. *mortarium.*]

mor·tar·board (môr′tər-bôrd′, -bōrd′) *n.* **1.** A square board with a handle used for holding and carrying mortar. **2.** An academic cap topped by a flat square.

mort·gage (môr′gĭj) *n.* **1.** A temporary and conditional pledge of property to a creditor as security for the performance of an obligation or the repayment of a debt. **2.** A contract or deed specifying the terms of a mortgage. **3.** The claim that the mortgagee has upon mortgaged property. —*tr.v.* **-gaged, -gag·ing, -gag·es. 1.** To pledge or convey by means of a mortgage. **2.** To make subject to a pledge or claim. [ME *morgage* < OFr. : *mort,* dead (< Lat. *mortuus* < *mors,* death) + *gage,* pledge, of Germanic orig.]

mort·ga·gee (môr′gĭ-jē′) *n.* The holder of a mortgage.

mort·ga·gor (môr′gĭ-jôr′, môr′gĭ-jər) also **mort·gag·er** (môr′gĭ-jər) *n.* A person who mortgages his property.

mor·tice (môr′tĭs) *n.* & *v.* Variant of **mortise.**

mor·ti·cian (môr-tĭsh′ən) *n.* A funeral director; undertaker. [MORT(UARY) + -ICIAN.]

mor·ti·fi·ca·tion (môr′tə-fĭ-kā′shən) *n.* **1.** A feeling of shame, humiliation, or wounded pride. **2.** The mortifying of the body and appetites. **3.** The death or decay of one part of a living body; gangrene.

mor·ti·fy (môr′tə-fī′) *v.* **-fied, -fy·ing, -fies.** —*tr.* **1.** To cause to experience shame, humiliation, or wounded pride; humiliate. **2.** To discipline (one's body and physical appetites) by self-denial and austerity. —*intr.* **1.** To practice ascetic discipline or self-denial of the body and its appetites. **2.** To become gangrenous or necrosed. [ME *mortifien* < OFr. *mortifier* < LLat. *mortificare,* to kill : *mors,* death + *facere,* to make.] —**mor′ti·fy′ing** *adj.*

mor·tise also **mor·tice** (môr′tĭs) —*n.* **1.** A usually rectangular cavity in a piece of wood, stone, or other material, prepared to receive a tenon. **2.** *Printing.* A hole cut in a plate for the insertion of type. —*tr.v.* **-tised, -tis·ing, -tis·es** also **-ticed, -tic·ing, -tic·es. 1.** To join or fasten securely, as with a mortise and tenon. **2.** To cut or make a mortise in. **3.** *Printing.* **a.** To cut a hole in (a plate) for the insertion of type. **b.** To cut such a hole and insert (type). [ME *mortays* < OFr. *mortoise.*]

mort·main (môrt′mān′) *n.* **1.** *Law.* Perpetual ownership of real estate by institutions such as churches that cannot transfer or sell them. **2.** The often oppressive influence of the past upon the present. [ME *mortemayne* < OFr. *mortemain* : *morte,* fem. of *mort,* dead (< Lat. *mortuus* < *mors,* death) + *main,* hand < Lat. *manus.*]

mor·tu·ar·y (môr′cho͞o-ĕr′ē) *n., pl.* **-ies.** A place, esp. a funeral home, where dead bodies are kept prior to burial or cremation. [ME *mortuarie* < LLat. *mortuarium* < *mortuarius,* of burial < Lat. *mortuus,* dead < *mors,* death.]

mor·u·la (môr′yə-lə- môr′ə-) *n., pl.* **-lae** (-lē′). **1.** The spherical embryonic mass of blastomeres formed before complete blastulation. **2.** A spherical mass of developing male gametes occurring esp. in certain annelid worms. [NLat. < Lat. *morum,* mulberry.] —**mor′u·lar** (-lər) *adj.*

mo·sa·ic (mō-zā′ĭk) *n.* **1.** A picture or decorative design made by setting small colored pieces, such as tile, in mortar. **2.** Something that resembles a mosaic: *a mosaic of impressions.* **3.** A virus disease of plants, resulting in light and dark areas in the leaves, which often become shriveled and dwarfed. **4.** Overlapping photographs, usually aerial, assembled into a composite picture. **5.** A photosensitive surface in the iconoscope of a television camera. —*tr.v.* **-icked, -ick·ing, -ics. 1.** To make a mosaic. **2.** To adorn with or as if with mosaic. [ME *musycke* < OFr. *musaique* < OItal. *mosaico* < Med. Lat. *musaicus* < Gk. *mouseios,* of the Muses < *Mousa,* Muse.] —**mo·sa′i·cist** (mō-zā′ĭ-sĭst) *n.*

Mo·sa·ic (mō-zā′ĭk) *adj.* Of or pertaining to Moses or the laws and writings attributed to him.

mo·sa·i·cism (mō-zā′ĭ-sĭz′əm) *n.* The condition in which tis-

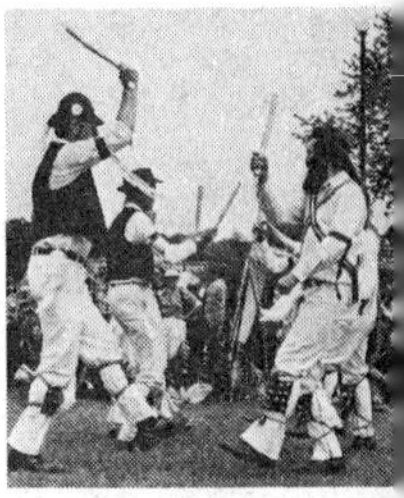

morris
Morris dancers

mortar
Above: Mortar and pestle
Below: Trench mortar

mortarboard

mortise

mosaic
4th-century mosaic from Asia Minor

sues of genetically different types occur in the same organism.

Mosaic Law *n.* The Pentateuch.

mos·cha·tel (mŏs′kə-tĕl′, mŏs′kə-tĕl′) *n.* A plant, *Adoxa moschatellina,* of northern regions, having greenish-white, musk-scented flowers. [Fr. *moscatelle* < Ital. *moscatella* < *moscato,* musk < LLat. *muscus.* —see MUSK.]

Mo·selle (mō-zĕl′) *n.* A light, dry white wine produced in the valley of the Moselle River.

Mo·ses (mō′zĭz, -zĭs) *n.* In the Old Testament, the Hebrew prophet and lawgiver who led the Israelites out of Egypt. [Lat. < Gk. *Mōsēs* < Heb. *Mosheh.*]

mo·sey (mō′zē) *intr.v.* **-seyed, -sey·ing, -seys.** *Informal.* **1.** To move in an idle, leisurely fashion. **2.** To get going; move along. [Orig. unknown.]

mo·shav (mō-shăv′) *n., pl.* **mo·sha·vim** (mō′shə-vēm′). An Israeli cooperative settlement consisting of small farms. [Mod. Heb. *mōshābh* < Heb., dwelling.]

Mos·lem (mŏz′ləm, mŏs′-) *n.* A believer in or adherent of Islam. [Ar. *muslim.*] **—Mos′lem** *adj.*

mosque (mŏsk) *n.* A Moslem house of worship. [Fr. *mosquée* < OItal. *moschea* < Ar. *masjid* < *sajada,* to worship.]

mos·qui·to (mə-skē′tō) *n., pl.* **-toes** or **-tos.** Any of various winged insects of the family Culicidae, in which the female of most species is distinguished by a long proboscis for sucking blood. Some species are vectors of diseases such as malaria and yellow fever. [Sp. < dim. of *mosca,* fly < Lat. *musca.*]

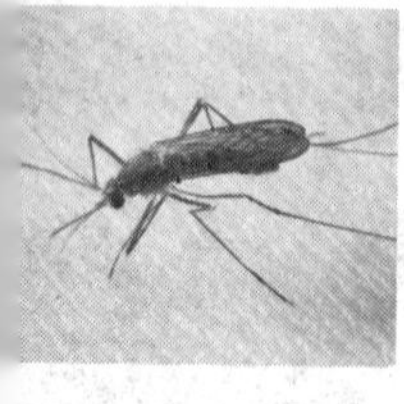

mosquito
Genus *Culex*

Mosquito *n., pl.* **-to** or **-tos. 1.** A South American people living in Nicaragua and Honduras. **2.** The language of the Mosquito.

mosquito net *n.* A fine net or screen used to keep out mosquitoes.

moss (mŏs, mŏs) *n.* **1. a.** Any of various green, usually small plants of the class Musci within the division Bryophyta. **b.** A patch or covering of such plants. **2.** Any of various other plants that are similar to moss in appearance or manner of growth, such as club moss, Irish moss, and Spanish moss. **3.** *Chiefly Scot.* A peat bog or moor. [ME < OE *mos.*]

moss·back (mŏs′băk′, mŏs′-) *n.* **1.** An old shellfish or turtle with a growth of algae on its back. **2.** *Slang.* An extremely conservative or old-fashioned person. **—moss′backed′** *adj.*

Möss·bau·er effect (mŏs′bou′ər) *n.* The recoilless fluorescence of gamma rays having an extremely narrow frequency range from atomic nuclei bound in solids. [After Rudolf *Mössbauer* (b. 1929).]

moss·bunk·er (mŏs′bŭng′kər, mŏs′-) *n.* The menhaden. [Du. *marsbanker.*]

moss campion *n.* A low-growing plant, *Silene acaulis,* of cool regions, having purplish-red flowers and forming dense, cushionlike mats.

moss green *n.* A moderate yellow green to grayish or moderate olive or dark yellowish green. **—moss′-green′** *adj.*

moss·grown (mŏs′grōn′, mŏs′-) *adj.* **1.** Overgrown with moss. **2.** Old-fashioned; antiquated.

mos·so (mŏs′sō) *adv. Mus.* With motion or animation. Used as a direction. [Ital. < *muovere,* to move < Lat. *movēre.*]

moss pink *n.* A low-growing plant, *Phlox subulata,* forming dense, mosslike mats and widely cultivated for its profuse pink or white flowers.

moss rose *n.* A variety of rose, *Rosa centifolia muscosa,* having fragrant pink flowers with a mossy flower stalk and calyx.

moss-troop·er (mŏs′trōō′pər, mŏs′-) *n.* **1.** One of a band of raiders operating in the bogs on the borders of England and Scotland during the 17th century. **2.** A plunderer; marauder.

moss·y (mŏ′sē, mŏs′ē) *adj.* **-i·er, -i·est. 1.** Covered with moss or something like moss. **2.** Resembling moss. **3.** Old-fashioned; antiquated. **—moss′i·ness** *n.*

most (mōst) *adj.* **1.** Greatest in number, quantity, size or degree. **2.** The greatest part of: *most people.* —*n.* The greatest amount: *had the most to say but did the least.* —*pron. (used with a sing. or pl. verb).* The greatest part: *Most of the children were absent. Most of the house was cold.* —*adv.* **1.** In the highest degree, quantity, or extent. Used with many adjectives and adverbs to form the superlative degree: *most honest; most impatiently.* **2.** Very: *a most impressive piece of writing.* **3.** *Informal.* Almost: *Most everyone agrees.* **—idioms. at (the) most.** At the maximum: *saw him for a quarter of an hour at the most.* **for the most part.** In most cases; usually. [ME < OE *mǣst.*]

Usage: The adverb *most* is sometimes used in the sense of "almost": *Most all the students took the oath.* However, a large majority of the Usage Panel terms this usage unacceptable in writing, and a small majority finds it unacceptable in speech. • In the sense of "very," as an intensive where no explicit comparison is involved, *most* is acceptable in both writing and speech: *a most ingenious solution.*

-most *suff.* **1.** Most: *innermost.* **2.** Nearest to: *aftmost.* [ME, alteration of *-mest,* as in *formest,* foremost.]

mos·tac·cio·li (mô-stä′chə-lē′) *n.* Pasta shaped like a short tube with slanted ends. [Ital. < *mostaccio,* mustache.]

most·ly (mōst′lē) *adv.* For the greatest part; almost entirely.

Usage: *Mostly* is used at all levels of style to refer to the largest number of a group: *The trees are mostly evergreens. They arrested mostly adolescents.* In speech and informal writing, it is also used to mean "in the greatest degree" or "for the most part," but this usage is best avoided in formal writing: *Those most* (not *mostly*) *affected are farmers. For the most part* (not *mostly*), *we eat out.*

mot (mō) *n.* A witty or incisive remark. [Fr. < OFr., word, prob. < Lat. *muttum,* grunt < *muttire,* to mutter.]

mote[1] (mōt) *n.* A very small particle; speck. [ME *mot* < OE.]

mote[2] (mōt) *aux.v. Archaic.* May; might. [ME *moten* < OE *mōtan.*]

mo·tel (mō-tĕl′) *n.* A hotel for motorists, usually with rooms opening directly on a parking area. [Blend of MOTOR and HOTEL.]

mo·tet (mō-tĕt′) *n.* A polyphonic musical composition based on a text of a sacred nature and usually sung without accompaniment. [ME < OFr. < *mot,* word. —see MOT.]

moth (môth, mŏth) *n., pl.* **moths** (môthz, mŏthz, môths, mŏths). **1.** Any of numerous insects of the order Lepidoptera, generally distinguished from butterflies by their nocturnal activity, hairlike or feathery antennae, and stout bodies. **2.** The clothes moth. [ME *motthe* < OE *moððe.*]

moth·ball (môth′bôl′, mŏth′-) *n.* **1.** A marble-sized ball, originally of camphor but now of naphthalene, stored with clothes to repel moths. **2. mothballs.** A condition of long storage: *battleships put into mothballs.*

moth-ball (môth′bôl′, mŏth′-) *tr.v.* **-balled, -ball·ing, -balls.** To remove (a ship, for example) from active service or use and put into storage.

moth-eat·en (môth′ēt′n, mŏth′-) *adj.* **1.** Eaten away by moths. **2.** Old and timeworn: *a moth-eaten phrase.* **3.** In shabby condition.

moth·er[1] (mŭth′ər) *n.* **1.** A female parent. **2.** A female who holds a position of authority or responsibility similar to that of a mother: *a house mother.* **3.** A creative source; origin: *Philosophy is the mother of the sciences.* **4.** An old or elderly woman. **5.** Qualities attributed to a mother, such as capacity to love. **—*modifier:*** *mother love.* —*tr.v.* **-ered, -er·ing, -ers. 1.** To give birth to; be the mother of. **2.** To create; produce. **3.** To watch over, nourish, and protect. [ME *moder* < OE *mōdor.*] **—moth′er·less** *adj.* **—moth′er·less·ness** *n.*

moth·er[2] (mŭth′ər) *n.* A stringy slime composed of yeast cells and bacteria that forms on the surface of fermenting liquids and is added to wine or cider to start production of vinegar. [Poss. < MOTHER[1].]

Mother Car·ey's chicken (kâr′ēz) *n.* Any of numerous petrels, esp. the storm petrel. [Orig. unknown.]

mother cell *n.* A cell that gives rise to other cells.

Mother Goose *n.* The supposed author of *"Mother Goose's Tales,"* a collection of English nursery rhymes first published in the 18th century.

moth·er·hood (mŭth′ər-hŏŏd′) *n.* The state or condition of being a mother.

moth·er·house (mŭth′ər-hous′) *n.* **1.** The convent in which the mother superior of a religious community lives. **2.** The original convent of a religious community.

Mother Hub·bard (hŭb′ərd) *n.* A woman's loose, unbelted dress.

moth·er-in-law (mŭth′ər-ĭn-lô′) *n., pl.* **moth·ers-in-law.** The mother of one's wife or husband.

moth·er·land (mŭth′ər-lănd′) *n.* **1.** The land or country of one's birth. **2.** The native land of one's ancestors. **3.** A country considered to be the place of origin, as of a movement.

moth·er·ly (mŭth′ər-lē) *adj.* Of, befitting, resembling, or characteristic of a mother; maternal. **—moth′er·li·ness** *n.*

moth·er-na·ked (mŭth′ər-nā′kĭd) *adj.* Completely naked.

moth·er-of-pearl (mŭth′ər-əv-pûrl′) *n.* The pearly internal layer of certain mollusk shells, used to make decorative objects. **—moth′er-of-pearl′** *adj.*

Mother's Day *n.* An annual day for honoring mothers and motherhood observed on the second Sunday in May.

mother superior *n.* A woman in charge of a religious community of women.

mother tongue *n.* **1.** One's native language. **2.** A language from which another is derived.

mother wit *n.* Innate intelligence or common sense.

moth·er·wort (mŭth′ər-wûrt′, -wôrt′) *n.* Any of several plants of the genus *Leonurus,* esp. *L. cardiaca,* a weed having clusters of small purple or pink flowers. [ME *moderwort* : *moder,* mother + *wort,* wort < OE *wyrt,* plant.]

moth·proof (môth′prōōf′, mŏth′-) *adj.* Resistant to damage by moths. —*tr.v.* **-proofed, -proof·ing, -proofs.** To make resistant to damage by moths. **—moth′proof′er** *n.*

moth·y (mô′thē, mŏth′ē) *adj.* **-i·er, -i·est.** Infested by moths.

mo·tif (mō-tēf′) also **mo·tive** (mō′tĭv, mō-tēv′) *n.* **1. a.** A recurrent thematic element used in an artistic or literary work. **b.** A dominant theme. **2.** A short significant phrase in a musical composition. **3.** A repeated figure or design in architecture or decoration. [Fr. < OFr., motive. —see MOTIVE.]

mo·tile (mōt′l, mō′tīl′) *adj.* Moving or having the power to move spontaneously, as certain spores and microorganisms. —*n. Psychol.* A person whose mental imagery chiefly consists of his own bodily motion. [MOT(ION) + -ILE[1].] **—mo·til′i·ty** (mō-tĭl′ĭ-tē) *n.*

mo·tion (mō′shən) *n.* **1.** The action or process of changing position. **2.** A meaningful or expressive change in the posi-

ă pat / ā pay / âr care / ä father / b bib / ch church / d deed / ĕ pet / ē be / f fife / g gag / h hat / hw which / ĭ pit / ī pie / îr pier / j judge / k kick / l lid, needle / m mum / n no, sudden / ng thing / ŏ pot / ō toe / ô paw, for / oi noise / ou out / ŏŏ took / ōō boot /

tion of the body or a part of the body; gesture. **3.** A state of active functioning. **4.** The ability or power to move. **5.** An inner impulse or inclination. **6.** *Mus.* Melodic ascent and descent of pitch. **7.** *Law.* An application to a court for a ruling. **8.** A formal proposal put to the vote under parliamentary procedures. *—v.* **-tioned, -tion·ing, -tions.** *—tr.* To direct by making a gesture. *—intr.* To signal by making a gesture. [ME *mocioun* < OFr. *motion* < Lat. *motio* < *movēre,* to move.]

mo·tion·less (mō′shən-lĭs) *adj.* Not moving. **—mo′tion·less·ly** *adv.* **—mo′tion·less·ness** *n.*

motion picture *n.* **1.** A series of filmed images viewed in sufficiently rapid succession to create the illusion of motion and continuity. **2.** A connected narrative represented through motion pictures.

motion sickness *n.* Sickness induced by motion, as in travel by airplane, car, ship, or other vehicle and characterized by nausea, vomiting, and often dizziness.

motion study *n.* A time study.

mo·ti·vate (mō′tə-vāt′) *tr.v.* **-vat·ed, -vat·ing, -vates.** To provide with an incentive or motive; impel.

mo·ti·va·tion (mō′tə-vā′shən) *n.* **1.** The act or process of motivating. **2.** Something that motivates. **—mo′ti·va′tion·al** *adj.* **—mo′ti·va′tion·al·ly** *adv.*

motivational research *n.* The use of certain techniques borrowed from psychology and sociology, esp. by advertisers and marketers, to assess consumer attitudes toward products and services.

mo·tive (mō′tĭv) *n.* **1.** An emotion, desire, physiological need, or similar impulse acting as an incitement to action. **2.** (mō′tĭv, mō-tēv′). Variant of **motif.** *—adj.* **1.** Causing or able to cause motion: *motive pleas.* **2.** Of, pertaining to, or constituting a motive. *—tr.v.* **-tived, -tiv·ing, -tives.** To motivate. [ME < OFr. *motif* < *motive,* causing motion < LLat. *motivus* < Lat. *movēre,* to move.] **—mo·tiv′i·ty** *n.*

mot juste (mō zhüst′) *n., pl.* **mots justes** (mō zhüst′). The most exact and suitable word or expression. [Fr. : *mot,* word + *juste,* right.]

mot·ley (mŏt′lē) *adj.* **1.** Having diverse components of great variety; heterogeneous: *"I did not realize how motley are the qualities that go to make up a human being"* (Maugham). **2.** Exhibiting or having many colors; multicolored. *—n.* **1.** The professional attire of a court jester. **2.** A heterogeneous mixture of elements. [ME, poss. < *mot,* speck < OE.]

mot·mot (mŏt′mŏt′) *n.* Any of several tropical American birds of the family Momotidae, usually having green and blue plumage. [Am. Sp. *mot-mot.*]

mo·to·cross (mō′tō-krôs′, -krŏs′) *n.* A cross-country motorcycle race over a course of rough terrain, such as steep hills and hairpin curves. [MOTO(R) + CROSS(-COUNTRY).]

mo·to·neu·ron (mō′tə-no͝or′ŏn′, -nyo͝or′-) *n.* A neuron that stimulates motion; motor nerve cell. [MOTO(R) + NEURON.]

mo·tor (mō′tər) *n.* **1.** Something that imparts or produces motion, such as a machine or engine. **2.** A device that converts any form of energy into mechanical energy, esp. an internal-combustion engine or an arrangement of coils and magnets that converts electric current into mechanical power. **3.** A motorized conveyance, esp. an automobile. *—adj.* **1.** Causing or producing motion: *motor power.* **2.** Of, pertaining to, or designating nerves carrying impulses from the nerve centers to the muscles. **3.** Of or relating to movements of the muscles: *motor coordination.* *—v.* **-tored, -tor·ing, -tors.** *—intr.* To drive or travel in a motor vehicle. *—tr.* To carry by motor vehicle. [Lat. < *movēre,* to move.]

mo·tor·bike (mō′tər-bīk′) *n.* **1.** A lightweight motorcycle. **2.** A pedal bicycle that has an attached motor.

mo·tor·boat (mō′tər-bōt′) *n.* A boat propelled by an internal-combustion engine.

mo·tor·bus (mō′tər-bŭs′) *n., pl.* **-bus·es** or **-bus·ses.** A passenger bus that is powered by a motor.

mo·tor·cade (mō′tər-kād′) *n.* A procession consisting of motor vehicles.

mo·tor·car (mō′tər-kär′) *n.* An automobile.

motor court *n.* A motel.

mo·tor·cy·cle (mō′tər-sī′kəl) *n.* A vehicle with two wheels in tandem, propelled by an internal-combustion engine and sometimes having a sidecar with a third wheel. *—intr.v.* **-cled, -cling, -cles.** To ride on or drive a motorcycle. **—mo′tor·cy′clist** *n.*

motor drive *n.* A system consisting of an electric motor and accessory parts, used to power machinery.

motor home *n.* A motor vehicle built on a truck or bus chassis and designed to serve as self-contained living quarters for recreational travel.

motor inn or **motor hotel** *n.* An urban motel usually having several stories and facilities for guest parking.

mo·tor·ist (mō′tər-ĭst) *n.* One who drives or travels in an automobile.

mo·tor·ize (mō′tə-rīz′) *tr.v.* **-ized, -iz·ing, -iz·es.** **1.** To equip with a motor. **2.** To supply with motor-driven vehicles. **3.** To provide with automobiles. **—mo′tor·i·za′tion** *n.*

motor lodge *n.* A motel.

mo·tor·man (mō′tər-mən) *n.* One who drives an electrically powered streetcar, locomotive, or subway train.

motor neuron *n.* Motoneuron.

motor pool *n.* A centrally managed group of motor vehicles intended for the use of personnel, as of a governmental agency or military installation.

motor scooter *n.* A two-wheeled vehicle with small wheels and a low-powered gasoline engine geared to the rear wheel.

mo·tor·ship (mō′tər-shĭp′) *n.* A ship powered by an internal-combustion engine.

motor vehicle *n.* A self-propelled, wheeled conveyance that does not run on rails.

mo·tor·way (mō′tər-wā′) *n.* *Chiefly Brit.* A superhighway.

motte also **mott** (mŏt) *n.* *Western U.S.* A copse or small stand of trees on a prairie. [Mex. Sp. *mata* < Sp., shrub, prob. < LLat. *matta,* mat.]

mot·tle (mŏt′l) *tr.v.* **-tled, -tling, -tles.** To cover (a surface) with spots or streaks of different shades or colors. *—n.* **1.** A spot or blotch of color. **2.** A variegated pattern, as on marble. [Prob. back-formation < MOTLEY.] **—mot′tler** *n.*

mottled enamel *n.* Discolored tooth enamel usually caused by excessive amounts of fluorides in drinking water.

mot·to (mŏt′ō) *n., pl.* **-toes** or **-tos.** **1.** A brief statement used to express a principle, goal, or ideal. **2.** A sentence, phrase, or word of appropriate character inscribed on or attached to an object. [Ital., motto, word < Lat. *muttum,* grunt < *muttire,* to mutter.]

mouch (mo͞och) *v.* *Chiefly Brit.* Variant of **mooch.**

moue (mo͞o) *n.* A grimace; pout. [Fr. < OFr., of Germanic orig.]

mou·flon also **mouf·flon** (mo͞of′lŏn′) *n., pl.* **mouflon** or **-flons** also **moufflon** or **-flons.** A wild sheep, *Ovis musimon,* of Sardinia and Corsica. [Fr. < dial. Ital. *muvrone* < LLat. *mufro.*]

mouil·lé (mo͞o-yā′) *adj.* Pronounced palatally, as the *ll* in the French word *mouillé.* [Fr. < *mouiller,* to moisten, palatalize < OFr. *moullier,* to soften by soaking < VLat. **molliare* < Lat. *mollis,* soft.]

mou·jik (mo͞o-zhēk′, -zhĭk′) *n.* Variant of **muzhik.**

mou·lage (mo͞o-läzh′) *n.* **1.** The making of a mold of a mark, such as a footprint, for identification in a criminal investigation. **2.** A mold used in a criminal investigation. [Fr. < OFr. < *mouler,* to mold < *modle,* mold. —see MOLD[1].]

mould (mōld) *n. & v.* *Chiefly Brit.* Variant of **mold.**

moul·der (mōl′dər) *v.* *Chiefly Brit.* Variant of **molder.**

mould·ing (mōl′dĭng) *n.* *Chiefly Brit.* Variant of **molding.**

mould·y (mōl′dē) *adj.* *Chiefly Brit.* Variant of **moldy.**

mou·lin (mo͞o-lăN′) *n.* A vertical shaft in a glacier, kept open by falling water and rock debris. [Fr., moulin, mill < OFr., mill < LLat. *molina.* —see MILL[1].]

moult (mōlt) *v. & n.* *Chiefly Brit.* Variant of **molt.**

mound (mound) *n.* **1.** A pile of earth, gravel, sand, rocks, or debris heaped for protection or concealment. **2.** A natural elevation, such as a small hill. **3.** A raised mass, as of hay. **4.** *Baseball.* The slightly elevated pitcher's area in the center of the diamond. *—tr.v.* **mound·ed, mound·ing, mounds.** **1.** To fortify or conceal with a mound. **2.** To heap in a mound. [Orig. unknown.]

Mound Builder *n.* A member of one of the prehistoric North American Indian tribes who built burial and effigy mounds, mainly in the Mississippi valley.

mount[1] (mount) *v.* **mount·ed, mount·ing, mounts.** *—tr.* **1.** To climb or ascend. **2.** To place oneself upon: *mount a horse.* **3.** To get up on in order to copulate. Used of male animals. **4.** To provide with a riding horse. **5. a.** To fix securely to a support. **b.** To place or fix on or in a secure place for display, study, or use. **6.** To provide with scenery, costumes, and other accessories: *mount a theatrical performance.* **7. a.** To set (guns) in position. **b.** To plan and start to carry out: *mount an attack.* **c.** To be equipped with: *The warship mounted ten guns.* **d.** To post (a guard): *mount sentries.* *—intr.v.* **1.** To go or move upward. **2.** To get or climb up on a horse or vehicle. **3.** To increase, as in amount, degree, extent, intensity, or number. *—n.* **1. a.** A horse, other animal, or vehicle on which to ride. **b.** The opportunity to ride a horse in a race. **2.** An object to which another is affixed or on which another is placed for accessibility, display, or use, esp.: **a.** A glass slide for use with a microscope. **b.** A setting for a jewel. **c.** An undercarriage or stand on which a device rests while in use. [ME *mounten* < OFr. *monter* < VLat. **montare* < Lat. *mons,* mountain.] **—mount′a·ble** *adj.* **—mount′er** *n.*

mount[2] (mount) *n.* **1.** A mountain or hill. Used esp. as part of a proper name. **2.** In palmistry, any of the seven fleshy cushions around the edges of the palm of the hand. [ME *mont* < OE *munt* < Lat. *mons.*]

moun·tain (moun′tən) *n.* **1.** A natural elevation of the earth's surface having considerable mass, generally steep sides, and a height greater than that of a hill. **2. a.** A large heap: *a mountain of ironing.* **b.** A huge quantity: *a mountain of trouble.* [ME < OFr. *montaigne* < VLat. **montanea* < Lat. *montanus,* of a mountain < *mons,* mountain.] **—moun′tain·y** *adj.*

mountain ash *n.* Any of various deciduous trees of the genus *Sorbus,* such as the rowan, having clusters of small white flowers and bright orange-red berries.

mountain cat *n.* The mountain lion.

mountain cranberry *n.* The cowberry.

mountain dew *n.* Illegally distilled corn liquor.

moun·tain·eer (moun′tə-nîr′) *n.* **1.** A native or inhabitant of

George Miksch Sutton

motmot

mountain ash
Foliage and berries

mountain laurel

a mountainous area. **2.** One who climbs mountains for sport. *—intr.v.* **-eered, -eer·ing, -eers.** To climb mountains for sport.
mountain goat *n.* A hoofed mammal, *Oreamnos americanus,* of the northwestern North American mountains, having short, curved black horns and yellowish-white hair and beard.
mountain laurel *n.* An evergreen shrub, *Kalmia latifolia,* of eastern North America, having leathery, poisonous leaves and clusters of pink or white flowers.
mountain lion *n.* A large, powerful, wild cat, *Felis concolor,* of mountainous regions of the Western Hemisphere, having an unmarked tawny body.
moun·tain·ous (moun'tə-nəs) *adj.* **1.** Of or pertaining to a region having many mountains. **2.** Of impressive size or height.
mountain range *n.* A series of mountain ridges alike in form, direction, and origin.
mountain sheep *n.* **1.** The bighorn. **2.** A wild sheep native to a mountainous area.
mountain sickness *n.* Shortness of breath, nausea, and other symptoms caused by insufficient oxygen at high altitudes.
moun·tain·side (moun'tən-sīd') *n.* Any of the sloping sides of a mountain.
Mountain Standard Time *n.* Time at the 105th meridian west of Greenwich, England, and in the seventh time zone based on it in North America.
moun·tain·top (moun'tən-tŏp') *n.* The summit of a mountain.
moun·te·bank (moun'tə-băngk') *n.* **1.** A roving hawker of quack medicines who attracts customers with stories, jokes, or tricks. **2.** A charlatan or trickster. *—v.* **-banked, -bank·ing, -banks.** *—intr.* To act as a mountebank. *—tr. Archaic.* To ensnare or prevail over with trickery. [Ital. *montambanco* < the phrase *monta im banco,* he gets up onto the bench.]
Mount·ie (moun'tē) also **Mount·y** *n., pl.* **-ies.** *Informal.* A Royal Canadian Mounted Policeman.
mount·ing (moun'tĭng) *n.* Something that provides a backing or appropriate setting for something else: *a mounting for a gem.*
Mount·y (moun'tē) *n.* Variant of **Mountie.**
mourn (môrn, mōrn) *v.* **mourned, mourn·ing, mourns.** *—intr.* **1.** To express or feel grief or sorrow. **2.** To express public grief for a death by conventional signs. *—tr.* To feel or express sorrow for. [ME *mournen* < OE *murnan.*] **—mourn'er** *n.*
mourn·ful (môrn'fəl, mōrn'-) *adj.* **1.** Feeling or expressing grief. **2.** Arousing or suggesting grief. **—mourn'ful·ly** *adv.* **—mourn'ful·ness** *n.*
mourn·ing (môr'nĭng, mōr'-) *n.* **1.** The actions or expressions of one who has suffered a bereavement. **2.** The symbols or conventional outward signs of grief for the dead, such as a black tie or armband or entirely black clothes. **3.** The period during which a death is mourned. **—mourn'ing·ly** *adv.*
mourning cloak *n.* A butterfly, *Nymphalis antiopa,* of Europe and North America, having purplish-brown wings with a broad yellow border.
mourning dove *n.* A wild dove, *Zenaidura macroura,* of North America, noted for its plaintive call.
mourning warbler *n.* A warbler, *Oporornis philadelphia,* of eastern North America, noted for its plaintive song.
mouse (mous) *n., pl.* **mice** (mīs). **1. a.** Any of numerous small rodents of the families Muridae and Cricetidae, such as the common house mouse, *Mus musculus,* characteristically having a long, naked or almost hairless tail. **b.** Any of various animals similar or related to the mouse, such as the jumping mouse or the pocket mouse. **2.** *Informal.* A cowardly or timid person. **3.** *Slang.* A black eye. *—intr.v.* (mouz) **moused, mous·ing, mous·es. 1.** To hunt, stalk, or catch mice. **2.** To search furtively for something; prowl. [ME < OE *mūs.*]
mouse deer *n.* A chevrotain.
mous·er (mou'zər) *n.* An animal that catches mice.
mouse-tail (mous'tāl') *n.* Any plant of the genus *Myosurus,* esp. *M. minimus,* having a taillike flower spike.
mouse·trap (mous'trăp') *n.* A trap for catching mice.
mous·ey (mou'sē, -zē) *adj.* Variant of **mousy.**
mous·ing (mou'zĭng) *n. Naut.* A binding or metal shackle around the point and shank of a hook to prevent it from slipping from an eye.
mous·sa·ka (mo͞o-sä'kə, mo͞o'sä-kä') *n.* A Greek dish consisting of layers of ground lamb or beef and sliced eggplant topped with a cheese sauce. [Mod. Gk. *moussakas.*]
mousse (mo͞os) *n.* **1.** Any of various chilled desserts made with whipped or flavored cream and gelatin. **2.** A molded dish made from a purée of meat, fish, or shellfish with whipped cream. [Fr., mousse, foam < Lat. *mulsa,* honey-water < *mulsus,* p.part. of *mulcēre,* to delight.]
mousse·line (mo͞os-lēn') *n.* A fine cotton fabric originally made in Mosul, Iraq. [Fr., muslin. —see MUSLIN.]
mous·tache (mŭs'tăsh', mə-stăsh') *n.* Variant of **mustache.**
Mous·te·ri·an (mo͞o-stîr'ē-ən) *adj.* Designating or belonging to a Middle Paleolithic culture following the Acheulian. [Fr. *moustérien* < *Le Moustier,* a cave in southwestern France where archaeological finds were made.]

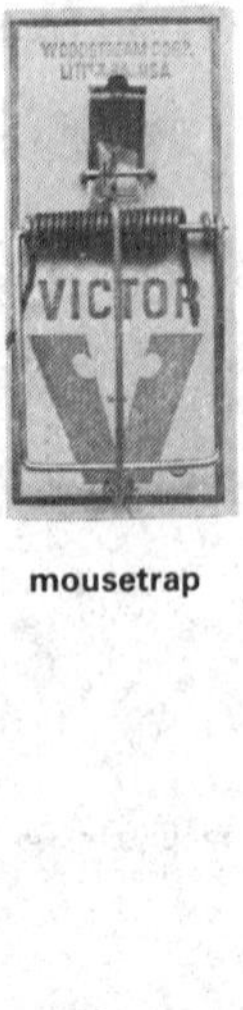

mousetrap

mous·y also **mous·ey** (mou'sē, -zē) *adj.* **-i·er, -i·est.** Mouselike in color, features, or shyness.
mouth (mouth) *n., pl.* **mouths** (mouthz). **1.** *Anat.* **a.** The body opening through which an animal takes in food. **b.** The system of related organs including the lips, teeth, tongue, and associated parts, with which food is chewed and swallowed and sounds and speech are articulated. **2.** The part of the lips visible on the human face. **3.** A person viewed as a consumer of food: *"Mouths without hands, maintained at vast expense"* (Dryden). **4.** A pout, grimace, or similar expression. **5. a.** Capacity of speech: *"A fool's mouth is his destruction"* (Proverbs 18:7). **b.** A tendency to talk excessively or injudiciously: *a big mouth.* **c.** Disrespectful or foul language: *watch your mouth.* **6.** A spokesman; mouthpiece. **7.** A natural opening, such as the part of a stream or river that empties into a larger body of water, or the entrance to a harbor, canyon, valley, or cave. **8.** An opening in a container. **9.** An opening in tools and devices whose function is to hold or grip. **10. a.** An opening in the pipe of an organ. **b.** The opening in the mouthpiece of a flute across which the player blows. *—v.* (mouth) **mouthed, mouth·ing, mouths.** *—tr.* **1.** To speak; pronounce. **2. a.** To utter in a declamatory manner: *constantly mouthing gems of homespun wisdom.* **b.** To utter mechanically, without conviction or understanding: *mouthing phrases.* **3.** To form or articulate words soundlessly: *mouthed Hamlet's soliloquy in time with the actor.* **4.** To put, take, or move around in the mouth. *—intr.* **1.** To orate affectedly; declaim. **2.** To grimace. ***—phrasal verb.* mouth off.** *Slang.* To complain, criticize, or brag loudly and indiscreetly. ***—idiom.* down in the mouth.** Crestfallen; depressed. [ME < OE *mūð.*]
mouth·breed·er (mouth'brē'dər) *n.* Any of various unrelated fishes that carry their eggs and young in their mouths.
mouth·ful (mouth'fo͝ol') *n.* **1.** The amount of food or other material that can be placed or held in the mouth at one time. **2.** A small amount to be tasted or eaten. **3.** An utterance that is complicated or difficult to pronounce. **4.** An important or perceptive remark.
mouth organ *n.* **1.** A harmonica (sense 1). **2.** A panpipe.
mouth·piece (mouth'pēs') *n.* **1.** A part, as of a musical instrument or a telephone, that functions in or near the mouth. **2.** A protective rubber device worn over the teeth by boxers. **3.** *Informal.* A spokesman. **4.** *Slang.* A defense lawyer.
mouth-to-mouth (mouth'tə-mouth') *adj.* Of, relating to, or being a method of artificial resuscitation in which the rescuer places his mouth directly over the victim's and forces air into the victim's lungs every few seconds.
mouth·wash (mouth'wŏsh', -wôsh') *n.* An antiseptic, usually flavored liquid for cleaning the mouth and freshening breath.
mouth·y (mou'thē, -thē) *adj.* **-i·er, -i·est.** Given to ranting; bombastic. **—mouth'i·ness** *n.*
mou·ton (mo͞o'tŏn') *n.* Sheepskin sheared and processed to resemble beaver or seal and used for garments. [Fr., sheep < OFr., of Celt. orig.]
mou·ton·née (mo͞o'tə-nā') also **mou·ton·néed** (-nād') *adj. Geol.* Rounded by glacial action to a shape likened to a sheep's back, as a rock formation. [Short for Fr. *roche moutonnée* : *roche,* rock + *moutonnée,* fleecy.]
mov·a·ble also **move·a·ble** (mo͞o'və-bəl) *—adj.* **1.** Capable of being moved. **2.** Varying in date from year to year: *a movable feast.* **3.** *Law.* Of or pertaining to personal property that can be moved, as opposed to real property such as land. *—n.* **1.** Often **movables.** Something that can be moved, esp. furniture, as opposed to permanent fixtures. **2.** *Law.* Personal property, as distinguished from real property such as land. **—mov'a·bil'i·ty, mov'a·ble·ness** *n.* **—mov'a·bly** *adv.*
Usage: Something is *movable* if it can be moved at all (*movable furniture, a movable wall*); it is *mobile* if it is designed for easy transportation (*a mobile home*) or if it moves frequently (*a mobile staff headquarters*). • The expression *movable feast* is used of a religious holiday, like Easter, that falls on different calendar days in different years.
move (mo͞ov) *v.* **moved, mov·ing, moves.** *—intr.* **1.** To change in position from one point to another: *moved away from the window.* **2.** To progress in sequence; go forward: *a novel that moves slowly.* **3.** To follow some specified course: *The earth moves in orbit around the sun.* **4.** To progress toward a certain state: *moving up in the company.* **5.** To settle in a new place of residence or business; relocate. **6.** To change hands commercially: *Furs move slowly in summer.* **7.** To change posture or position; stir: *he moved in his sleep.* **8.** To be stirred: *leaves moving in the breeze.* **9.** To be put into motion or to turn according to a prescribed motion. Used of machinery. **10.** To hum with activity; be busy. **11.** To initiate some action. **12.** To live or be active in a particular environment: *move in diplomatic circles.* **13.** To make a formal motion in parliamentary procedure: *move for an adjournment.* *—tr.* **1. a.** To change the place or position of: *move my office; move my toes.* **b.** To change from one position to another in a board game: *move a pawn.* **2.** To dislodge from a fixed point of view. **3.** To cause to take

action; rouse: *Disgust moved him to speak up.* **4. a.** To set or maintain in motion. **b.** To cause to function. **c.** To cause to progress or advance. **5.** To set astir; shake: *The wind moved the blossoms.* **6. a.** To arouse or stir the emotions of: *Her pitiable story moved him deeply.* **b.** To excite or provoke to the expression of some feeling: *"far too freely moved to tears"* (Hilaire Belloc). **7.** To propose or request in formal parliamentary procedure: *moved adjournment.* **8.** To cause to change hands commercially: *had trouble moving the big cars.* **9.** To cause (the bowels) to evacuate. ***—phrasal verbs.*** **move in.** To occupy a residence or place of business. **move in on. 1.** To make advances toward. **2.** To attempt to seize control of. *—n.* **1.** An act of moving. **2.** A change of residence or place of business. **3. a.** An act of transferring a piece from one position to another in board games. **b.** The prescribed manner in which a piece may be maneuvered. **c.** A player's turn to maneuver one of his pieces. **4.** One of a series of calculated actions undertaken to achieve some end. ***—idioms.*** **get a move on.** *Informal.* To get started; get going. **on the move. 1.** In the process of moving about. **2.** Making progress; advancing. [ME *moven* < AN *mover* < Lat. *movēre.*]

move·a·ble (mo͞o′və-bəl) *adj. & n.* Variant of **movable.**

move·ment (mo͞ov′mənt) *n.* **1. a.** An act of moving; change in position. **b.** A tactical or strategic change in the location of military troops, ships, or aircraft; maneuver. **2. a.** The activities of a group of people to achieve a specific goal: *the labor movement.* **b.** A tendency or trend. **3.** Activity, esp. in business or commerce. **4. a.** An evacuation of the bowels. **b.** The matter so evacuated. **5.** In the fine arts, the quality that manifests the effect or illusion of motion. **6.** In literature, the progression of events in the development of the plot. **7.** In poetry, the rhythmical or metrical structure of a poetic composition. **8.** *Mus.* A self-contained component section of a composition. **9.** A mechanism that produces or transmits motion, as the works of a watch. [ME < OFr. < Med. Lat. *movimentum* < Lat. *movēre,* to move.]

mov·er (mo͞o′vər) *n.* **1.** One that moves. **2.** One whose occupation is transporting furnishings.

mov·ie (mo͞o′vē) *n. Informal.* **1.** A motion picture. **2.** A theater that shows motion pictures. **3. movies. a.** A showing of a motion picture. **b.** The motion picture industry. [Short for MOVING PICTURE.]

mov·ie·dom (mo͞o′vē-dəm) *n.* Filmdom.

mov·ie·go·er (mo͞o′vē-gō′ər) *n.* A filmgoer.

mov·ie·mak·er (mo͞o′ve-mā′kər) *n.* One who makes movies, esp. professionally.

mov·ing (mo͞o′vĭng) *adj.* **1.** Changing or capable of changing position. **2.** Of or pertaining to a change of residence: *a moving van.* **3.** Causing or producing motion. **4.** Affecting the emotions: *a moving tale.* **—mov′ing·ly** *adv.*

Synonyms: *moving, stirring, poignant, touching, pathetic, affecting.* These words all refer to emotional reaction. *Moving* applies to that which calls forth any deeply felt emotion. *Stirring* stresses strong emotion, and is related to stimulation and inspiration. *Poignant* describes that which pierces or penetrates; it has wide-ranging application, from grief to sarcasm and (less often) to delight. *Touching* emphasizes sympathy and compassion. *Pathetic* stresses pity, and sometimes mild scorn (for that which is hopelessly inept or inadequate). *Affecting* applies to anything capable of moving the feelings, but usually pertains to that which inspires pity and tenderness.

moving picture *n.* A motion picture.

mow[1] (mou) *n.* **1.** A place for storing hay or grain. **2.** Feed stored, esp. in a barn. [ME, stack of hay < OE *mūga.*]

mow[2] (mō) *v.* **mowed, mowed** or **mown** (mōn), **mow·ing, mows.** *—tr.* **1.** To cut down with a scythe or a mechanical device. **2.** To cut (growth) from: *mow the lawn.* ***—phrasal verb.*** **mow down.** To destroy in great numbers, as in battle. [ME *mowen* < OE *māwan.*] **—mow′er** (mō′ər) *n.*

mox·ie (mŏk′sē) *n.* **1.** The ability to face difficulty with spirit; pluck. **2.** Energy or pep. [< MOXIE.]

Mox·ie (mŏk′sē). A trademark for a soft drink.

Moz·ar·ab (mō-zăr′əb) *n.* One of a group of Spanish Christians who practiced a modified form of their religion under the Moslems. [Sp. *Mozárabe* < Ar. *musta'rib,* would-be Arab < *'arab,* Arab.] **—Moz·ar′a·bic** *adj.*

mo·zet·ta (mō-zĕt′ə, mōt-sĕt′ə) *n. Rom. Cath. Ch.* A short, hooded cape worn by bishops. [Ital. < *almozetta* < Med. Lat. *almutia.*]

mo·zo (mō′zō) *n., pl.* **-zos.** *Western U.S.* A man who helps with a pack train or acts as a porter. [Sp., boy < OSp. *moço.*]

moz·za·rel·la (mŏt′sə-rĕl′ə, mōt′-) *n.* A soft, white Italian curd cheese, often melted in cookery. [Ital., dim. of *mozza,* a kind of cheese < *mozzare,* to cut off.]

Mpon·gwe (əm-pŏng′wā) *n.* A Bantu language spoken in the area around the estuary of the Gabon river.

Mr. (mĭs′tər) *n., pl.* **Messrs.** The abbreviated form of the title *Mister* when used with a name.

Mr. Charlie *n. Offensive Slang.* A white individual or white people collectively. [< *Charlie,* nickname for *Charles.*]

Mrs. (mĭs′ĭz) *n., pl.* **Mmes.** A title of courtesy used in speaking to or of a married woman, preceding the woman's surname. [Abbr. of MISTRESS.]

Mrs. Grun·dy (grŭn′dē) *n.* An extremely conventional or priggish individual. [After *Mrs. Grundy,* character alluded to in the play *Speed the Plough* by Thomas Morton (1764–1838).]

Ms. or **Ms** (mĭz) *n., pl.* **Mses.** or **Mss.** A title of courtesy used before a woman's surname or before her given name and surname without regard to her marital status. [Blend of MISS and MRS.]

Usage: As the title of respect for a woman used without regard for her marital status, *Ms.* is the equivalent of *Mr.,* the courtesy title for a man: *Ms. Smith, Ms. Judith Smith. Ms.* should not be used when a woman is addressed by her husband's given name and surname: *Ms. Green,* but not *Ms. Paul Green.* But *Ms.* is the appropriate courtesy title to use when a woman keeps her own name after marriage. If Kathleen Brown marries Roger Smith but does not change her name to Smith, she can be addressed as *Ms. Brown,* but *Mrs. Brown* is incorrect. Some women who keep their maiden name for professional purposes use the title *Miss* in that context, while others use *Ms.* Though *Ms.* was controversial when first introduced, it has come to be widely used in business and professional situations, on forms, and in many social contexts. While many women consider it both important and convenient to use this title in social as well as business contexts, others prefer *Miss* or *Mrs.*

mu (myo͞o, mo͞o) *n.* The 12th letter in the Greek alphabet. See table at **alphabet.** [Gk., of Phoenician orig; akin to Hebrew *mēm.*]

muc– *pref.* Variant of **muco-.**

much (mŭch) *adj.* **more, most.** Great in quantity, degree, or extent: *much rain.* *—n.* **1.** A large quantity or amount. **2.** Something remarkable or important: *As a leader, he is not much.* *—adv.* **more, most. 1.** To a great degree or extent: *much impressed.* **2.** Just about; almost: *much the same.* [ME *muche* < *muchel* < OE *mycel.*]

much as *conj.* However much.

much·ness (mŭch′nĭs) *n.* The quality or condition of being great in quantity, degree, or extent.

muci– *pref.* Variant of **muco-.**

mu·cic acid (myo͞o′sĭk) *n.* An organic acid, $HOOC(CHOH)_4COOH$, often derived from milk sugar. [< MUCUS.]

mu·cif·er·ous (myo͞o-sĭf′ər-əs) *adj.* Secreting or producing mucus.

mu·ci·lage (myo͞o′sə-lĭj) *n.* **1.** A sticky substance used as an adhesive. **2.** A gummy substance obtained from certain plants. [ME *muscilage* < OFr. *mucilage* < LLat. *mucilago,* musty juice < Lat. *mucus,* mucus.] **—mu′ci·lag′i·nous** (-lăj′ə-nəs) *adj.*

mu·cin (myo͞o′sĭn) *n.* Any of a group of organic compounds produced by mucous membranes. **—mu′cin·ous** *adj.*

muck (mŭk) *n.* **1.** A moist, sticky mixture, esp. of mud and filth. **2.** Moist animal dung mixed with decayed vegetable matter and used as a fertilizer; manure. **3.** Dark, fertile soil containing putrid vegetable matter. **4.** Something regarded as filthy or disgusting. **5.** Earth, rocks, or clay excavated in mining. *—tr.v.* **mucked, muck·ing, mucks. 1.** To fertilize with manure or compost. **2.** *Informal.* To soil or make dirty with or as if with muck. **3.** To remove muck or dirt from (a mine, for example). ***—phrasal verbs.*** **muck about.** *Chiefly Brit. Informal.* To spend time idly; putter. **muck up.** *Informal.* To bungle; botch. [ME *muk.*] **—muck′y** *adj.* **—muck′i·ly** *adv.*

muck·a·muck (mŭk′ə-mŭk′) *n. Slang.* A person of importance. [Short for HIGH MUCKAMUCK.]

muck·rake (mŭk′rāk′) *intr.v.* **-raked, -rak·ing, -rakes.** To search for and expose political or commercial corruption. **—muck′rak′er** *n.*

muco– or **muci–** or **muc–** *pref.* **1.** Mucus: *mucoprotein.* **2.** Mucous membrane: *mucin.* **3.** Mucin: *mucoid.* [< Lat. *mucus,* mucus.]

mu·co·cu·ta·ne·ous (myo͞o′kō-kyo͞o-tā′nē-əs) *adj.* Pertaining to the skin and a mucous membrane.

mu·coid (myo͞o′koid′) *n.* Any of a group of organic compounds similar to the mucins and found in connective tissue. **—mu′coid, mu·coi′dal** (myo͞o-koid′l) *adj.*

mu·co·lyt·ic (myo͞o′kə-lĭt′ĭk) *adj.* Breaking down or hydrolyzing mucin or mucopolysaccharides.

mu·co·pol·y·sac·cha·ride (myo͞o′kō-pŏl′ē-săk′ə-rīd′) *n.* Any of the polysaccharides that form chemical bonds with water to produce mucilaginous and lubricating fluids.

mu·co·pro·tein (myo͞o′kō-prō′tēn′, -prō′tē-ĭn) *n.* Any of a group of organic compounds, such as the mucins, that contain proteins and mucopolysaccharides.

mu·co·pu·ru·lent (myo͞o′kō-pyo͝or′ə-lənt, -yə-lənt) *adj.* Containing mucus and pus.

mu·co·sa (myo͞o-kō′sə) *n., pl.* **-sae** (-sē) or **-sas.** A mucous membrane. [NLat. < Lat., fem. of *mucosus,* mucous.] **—mu·co′sal** *adj.*

mu·cous (myo͞o′kəs) also **mu·cose** (-kōs′) *adj.* **1.** Producing or secreting mucus. **2.** Pertaining to, consisting of, or resembling mucus. [Lat. *mucosus* < *mucus,* mucus.]

mucous membrane *n.* The membrane lining all bodily channels that communicate with the air, such as the respiratory and alimentary tracts, the glands of which secrete mucus.

mu·cro (myo͞o′krō) *n., pl.* **mu·cro·nes** (myo͞o-krō′nēz). A

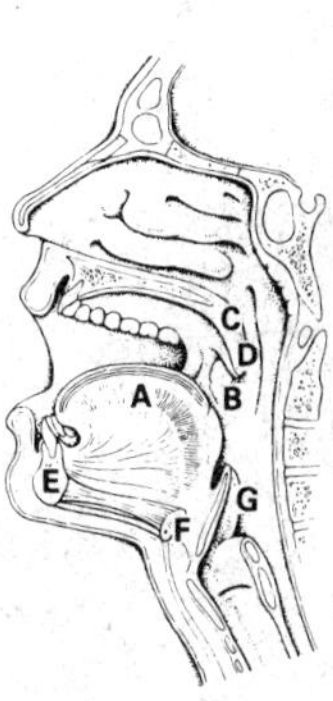

mouth
A. Tongue
B. Palatine tonsil
C. Soft palate
D. Uvula
E. Mandible
F. Hyoid bone
G. Epiglottis

sharp tip of some plant and animal organs. [NLat. < Lat., sword point.]

mu·cro·nate (myōō'krə-nāt') *adj. Biol.* Of or having a mucro. [Lat. *mucronatus* < *mucro,* sword point.] **—mu'cro·na'tion** *n.*

mu·cus (myōō'kəs) *n.* The viscous suspension of mucin, water, cells, and inorganic salts secreted as a protective, lubricant coating by glands in the mucous membrane. [Lat.]

mud (mŭd) *n.* **1.** Wet, sticky, soft earth. **2.** Slanderous or defamatory charges or comments. *—tr.v.* **mud·ded, mud·ding, muds.** To soil or bury with or as if with mud. [ME *mudde.*]

mud cat *n.* Any of several large American catfish of the Mississippi valley and southeastern U.S. streams.

mud dauber *n.* Any of several wasps having long hind legs and a slender abdomen terminating in a bulb. The female lays eggs in paralyzed insect larvae, which are placed in a nest of mud.

mud·der (mŭd'ər) *n.* In racing, a horse that runs well on a wet or muddy track.

mud·dle (mŭd'l) *v.* **-dled, -dling, -dles.** *—tr.* **1.** To make turbid; muddy. **2.** To mix confusedly; jumble. **3.** To confuse or befuddle, as with alcohol. **4.** To mismanage or bungle. **5.** To stir or mix (a beverage) gently. *—intr.* To act or think in a confused manner. ***—phrasal verb.* muddle through.** To push on to a successful conclusion in a disorganized way. *—n.* A confusion, jumble, or mess. [Poss. < obs. Du. *moddelen* < MDu. < *modde,* mud.] **—mud'dler** *n.*

mud·dle-head·ed (mŭd'l-hĕd'ĭd) *adj.* **1.** Mentally confused. **2.** Stupid; inept. **—mud'dle-head'ed·ness** *n.*

mud·dy (mŭd'ē) *adj.* **-di·er, -di·est.** **1.** Covered, full of, or spattered with mud. **2.** Not clear or pure, as a color or liquid. **3.** Dull: *a muddy complexion.* **4.** Confused, vague, or obscure, as in expression or meaning: *a muddy style of writing.* *—tr.v.* **-died, -dy·ing, -dies.** **1.** To make muddy or dirty. **2.** To make dull or cloudy. **3.** To make obscure or confused. **—mud'di·ly** *adv.* **—mud'di·ness** *n.*

mud eel *n.* An amphibian, *Siren lacertina,* found in swamps of the southeastern United States, that is eellike in appearance and has only front legs, which are inconspicuous.

mud·fish (mŭd'fĭsh') *n., pl.* **mudfish** or **-fish·es.** Any of various fishes found in mud or muddy water, such as the bowfin.

mud flat *n.* Land covered at high tide and exposed at low tide.

mud·guard (mŭd'gärd') *n.* A shield over a vehicle's wheel.

mud hen *n.* Any of various birds inhabiting marshy or coastal regions, such as a coot or rail.

mud minnow *n.* A fish of the genus *Umbra,* brown in color and found in the muddy areas of North American and European lakes and ponds.

mud puppy *n.* Any of various aquatic salamanders of the genus *Necturus,* esp. *N. maculosus,* of North America, having conspicuous clusters of external gills.

mu·dra (mə-drä') *n.* In East Indian classical dancing, a code of body postures and hand movements with which a dancer enacts a narrative.

mud·sill (mŭd'sĭl') *n.* The lowest sill, block, or timber supporting a building, located at or below ground level.

mud·skip·per (mŭd'skĭp'ər) *n.* Any of several species of fishes of the family Gobiidae that are found along the western coast of tropical Africa and in the Indo-Pacific region and are noted for their ability to maneuver on land.

mud·sling·er (mŭd'slĭng'ər) *n.* One who makes malicious charges against an opponent. **—mud'sling'ing** *n.*

mud snake *n.* A burrowing snake, *Farancia abacura,* of the southeastern United States, having black scales with reddish markings.

mud·stone (mŭd'stōn') *n.* A dark-gray, fine-grained shale that decomposes into mud when exposed to the atmosphere.

mud turtle *n.* Any of various turtles of the genus *Kinosternon,* found in sluggish fresh waters throughout the Western Hemisphere.

mud wasp *n.* The potter wasp.

Muen·ster or **Mun·ster** (mŭn'stər, mōōn'-) *n.* A semisoft, creamy, yellow fermented Alsatian cheese of mild flavor. [After *Munster,* city in northeastern France where it was originally made.]

mule[1]

mu·ez·zin (myōō-ĕz'ĭn, mōō-) *n. Islam.* The crier who calls the faithful to prayer five times a day. [Ar. *mu'adhdhin.*]

muff[1] (mŭf) *v.* **muffed, muff·ing, muffs.** *—tr.* **1.** To perform clumsily; bungle. **2.** *Sports.* To fail to catch (the ball). *—intr.* **1.** To perform some act clumsily; bungle. **2.** *Sports.* To fail to catch a ball. *—n.* A clumsy or bungled act. [Orig. unknown.]

muff[2] (mŭf) *n.* A small cylindrical fur or cloth cover, open at both ends, in which the hands are placed to keep them warm. [Du. *mof* < MDu. *moffel* < Med. Lat. *muffla.*]

muf·fin (mŭf'ĭn) *n.* A small, cup-shaped bread, often sweetened and usually served hot. [Poss. < LG *muffen,* pl. of *muffe,* cake.]

muf·fle[1] (mŭf'əl) *tr.v.* **-fled, -fling, -fles.** **1.** To wrap up in for warmth, protection, or secrecy. **2. a.** To wrap or pad in order to deaden a sound. **b.** To deaden (a sound). **3.** To make vague or obscure: *"his message was so muffled by learning and 'artiness'"* (Walter Blair). *—n.* **1.** Something that muffles. **2.** A kiln or part of a kiln in which pottery can be fired without being exposed to direct flame. [ME *muflen,* poss. < OFr. *moufle,* glove < Med. Lat. *muffla.*]

muf·fle[2] (mŭf'əl) *n.* The hairless snout of certain mammals. [Fr. *mufle.*]

muf·fler (mŭf'lər) *n.* **1.** A heavy scarf worn around the neck for warmth. **2.** A device that absorbs noise, esp. one used with an internal-combustion engine.

muf·ti[1] (mŭf'tē, mōōf'-) *n., pl.* **-tis.** A judge who interprets Moslem religious law. [Ar. *muftī* < *aftā,* give a decision.]

muf·ti[2] (mŭf'tē) *n.* Civilian dress, esp. such clothing when worn by one whose regular garb is a uniform. [Prob. < MUFTI[1].]

mug[1] (mŭg) *n.* **1.** A cylindrical drinking vessel often with a handle. **2.** The liquid contained in such a vessel. [Orig. unknown.]

mug[2] (mŭg) *n.* **1.** The face of a person. **2.** The area of the mouth, chin, and jaw. **3.** A photograph of the face, esp. one used by police for identification. **4.** A grimace. **5.** A thug; hoodlum. **6.** *Chiefly Brit.* A victim or dupe. *—v.* **mugged, mug·ging, mugs.** *—tr.* **1.** To photograph (a person's face) for police files. **2.** To waylay and beat severely, usually with intent to rob. *—intr.* To grimace, esp. to make exaggerated facial expressions. [Prob. < MUG[1].] **—mug'ger** *n.*

mug·ger (mŭg'ər) *n.* A large crocodile, *Crocodilus palustris,* of southwestern Asia, having an exceptionally broad, wrinkled snout. [Hindi *magar* < Skt. *makaraḥ,* crocodile, of Dravidian orig.]

mug·ging (mŭg'ĭng) *n.* An aggravated assault usually sprung by surprise and with intent to rob.

mug·gy (mŭg'ē) *adj.* **-gi·er, -gi·est.** Warm and extremely humid. [< dial. *mug,* mist < ME *muggen,* to drizzle.] **—mug'gi·ness** *n.*

mug·wump (mŭg'wŭmp') *n.* **1.** A Republican who bolted his party in 1884, refusing to support James G. Blaine as candidate for the U.S. presidency. **2.** A person who acts independently, esp. in politics. [Natick *mugwomp,* captain.] **—mug'wump'er·y** *n.*

Mu·ham·mad·an or **Mu·ham·med·an** (mōō-hăm'ə-dən) *adj. & n.* Variants of **Mohammedan.**

Mu·ham·mad·an·ism (mōō-hăm'ə-də-nĭz'əm) *n.* Variant of **Mohammedanism.**

Mu·har·ram (mōō-hăr'əm) also **Mo·har·ram** (mō-hăr'əm) or **Mu·har·rum** (mōō-hăr'əm) *n.* **1.** The first month of the Moslem calendar. See table at **calendar.** **2.** A festival held during the first ten days of Muharram. [Ar. *muḥarram,* p.part. of *ḥarrama,* he forbade.]

mu·jik (mōō-zhēk', -zhĭk') *n.* Variant of **muzhik.**

muk·luk (mŭk'lŭk') *n.* **1.** A soft Eskimo boot made of reindeer skin or sealskin. **2.** A slipper resembling the mukluk. [Eskimo *muklok,* large seal.]

mu·lat·to (mōō-lăt'ō, -lä'tō, myōō-) *n., pl.* **-tos** or **-toes.** **1.** A person having one white and one black parent. **2.** A person of mixed Caucasian and Negro ancestry. [Sp. *mulato,* mulatto, young mule < *mulo,* mule < Lat. *mulus.*]

mul·ber·ry (mŭl'bĕr'ē, -bə-rē) *n.* **1.** Any of several trees of the genus *Morus,* having edible fruit. **2.** The sweet, berrylike fruit of the mulberry. **3.** Any of several trees related or similar to the mulberry. **4.** A grayish to dark purple. [ME *mulberrie* : OFr. *moure,* mulberry (< Lat. *morum*) + OE *berie,* berry.] **—mul'ber'ry** *adj.*

mulch (mŭlch) *n.* A protective covering of various substances, esp. organic, placed around plants to prevent evaporation of moisture and freezing of roots and to control weeds. *—tr.v.* **mulched, mulch·ing, mulch·es.** To cover with a mulch. [Poss. < dial. *melch,* soft < ME *melsch.*]

mulct (mŭlkt) *n.* A fine or similar penalty. *—tr.v.* **mulct·ed, mulct·ing, mulcts.** **1.** To penalize by fining or demanding forfeiture. **2.** To acquire or take away from by trickery or deception. [Lat. *mulcta.*]

mule[1] (myōōl) *n.* **1.** A sterile hybrid of a male ass and a female horse. **2.** A sterile hybrid, as between a canary and other birds or between certain plants. **3.** *Informal.* A stubborn person. **4.** A type of spinning machine that makes thread or yarn from fibers. **5.** A small, usually electric tractor or locomotive used for hauling short distances. [ME < OFr. *mul* < Lat. *mulus.*]

mule[2] (myōōl) *n.* A slipper that has no counter or strap to fit around the heel of the foot. [OFr., slipper < Lat. *mulleus (calceus),* red (shoe).]

mule deer *n.* A hoofed mammal, *Odocoileus hemionus,* of western North America, having long ears and two-pronged antlers.

mule·skin·ner (myōōl'skĭn'ər) *n. Informal.* A driver of mules.

mu·le·ta (mōō-lā'tə, -lĕt'ə) *n.* A short red cape, suspended from a hollow staff, that is used by the matador to maneuver the bull during the final passes before the kill. [Sp., crutch < *mula,* she-mule < Lat., fem. of *mulus,* mule.]

mu·le·teer (myōō'lə-tîr') *n.* A mule driver. [OFr. *muletier* < *mulet,* dim. of *mul,* mule.]

mu·ley (myōō'lē, mōōl'ē, mōō'lē) *adj.* Hornless. Used of cattle. *—n., pl.* **-leys.** A hornless animal. [Of Celt. orig.]

mu·li·eb·ri·ty (myōō'lē-ĕb'rĭ-tē) *n.* **1.** The state of being a woman. **2.** The qualities characteristic of women. [LLat. *muliebritas* < Lat. *muliebris,* womanly < *mulier,* woman.]

mul·ish (myōō′lĭsh) *adj.* Characteristic of a mule; stubborn. —**mul′ish·ly** *adv.* —**mul′ish·ness** *n.*

mull[1] (mŭl) *tr.v.* **mulled, mull·ing, mulls.** To heat and spice (wine, for example). [Orig. unknown.]

mull[2] (mŭl) *v.* **mulled, mull·ing, mulls.** —*tr.* To go over mentally; deliberate. —*intr.* To ponder over something: *mull over a plan.* [ME *mullen,* to grind < *mul,* dust, prob. < MDu.]

mull[3] (mŭl) *n.* A soft, thin kind of muslin used in dresses and for trimmings. [Short for obs. *mulmull* < Hindi *malmal* < Pers.]

mul·lah also **mul·la** (mŭl′ə, mōōl′ə) *n.* A Moslem religious teacher or leader. Used as a title. [Turk., Pers. and Urdu *mullā,* all < Ar. *mawlā,* master.] —**mul′lah·ism** *n.*

mul·lein (mŭl′ən) *n.* **1.** Any of various plants of the genus *Verbascum,* esp. *V. thapsus,* native to Eurasia, a tall plant having leaves covered with dense, woolly down, and closely clustered yellow flowers. **2.** The Cretan mullein. [ME *moleyne* < OFr. *moleine.*]

mullein pink *n.* The rose campion.

mul·ler (mŭl′ər) *n.* A device with a stone or other hard base, used to grind paints or drugs. [ME *molour,* prob. < *mullen,* to grind. —see MULL[2].]

mul·let (mŭl′ĭt) *n., pl.* **mullet** or **-lets.** Any of various edible fishes of the family Mugilidae, found worldwide in tropical and temperate coastal waters and some freshwater streams. [ME *molet* < OFr. *mulet* < Lat. *mullus,* red mullet < Gk. *mullos.*]

mul·li·gan stew (mŭl′ĭ-gən) *n.* A stew of various meats and vegetables. [Prob. from the name *Mulligan.*]

mul·li·ga·taw·ny (mŭl′ĭ-gə-tô′nē) *n.* An East Indian meat soup strongly flavored with curry. [Tamil *miḷagutaṇṇī.*]

mul·lion (mŭl′yən) *n.* A vertical strip dividing the panes of a window. [Alteration of obs. *monial* < ME *moniel* < OFr. *moynel* < *moyen,* middle < Lat. *medianus* < *medius.*] —**mul′lioned** *adj.*

multi– *pref.* **1.** Many; much; multiple: *multicolored.* **2. a.** More than one: *multiparous.* **b.** More than two: *multilateral.* [ME < Lat. < *multus,* much.]

mul·ti·ad·dress (mŭl′tē-ăd′rĕs′) *adj. Computer Sci.* Designating a storage system of data-processing computers in which it is possible to store instructions or quantities in more than one position.

mul·ti·cel·lu·lar (mŭl′tĭ-sĕl′yə-lər) *adj.* Consisting of many cells. —**mul′ti·cel′lu·lar′i·ty** (-lăr′ĭ-tē) *n.*

mul·ti·col·ored (mŭl′tĭ-kŭl′ərd) *adj.* Having many colors.

mul·ti·cul·tur·al (mŭl′tĭ-kŭl′chər-əl) *adj.* Of, relating to, or intended for several individual cultures.

mul·ti·di·men·sion·al (mŭl′tĭ-dĭ-mĕn′shə-nəl) *adj.* Of, relating to, or having several dimensions. —**mul′ti·di·men′sion·al′i·ty** *n.*

mul·ti·di·rec·tion·al (mŭl′tĭ-dĭ-rĕk′shə-nəl) *adj.* Reaching in many directions: *a multidirectional campaign.*

mul·ti·dis·ci·pli·nar·y (mŭl′tĭ-dĭs′ə-plə-nĕr′ē) *adj.* Of, relating to, or making use of several disciplines at once: *a multidisciplinary approach to teaching.*

mul·ti·eth·nic (mŭl′tē-ĕth′nĭk) *adj.* Of, pertaining to, or including a variety of ethnic groups: *a multiethnic city.*

mul·ti·fac·et·ed (mŭl′tə-făs′ĭ-tĭd, -tē-) *adj.* Having several individual facets: *a multifaceted problem.*

mul·ti·fam·i·ly (mŭl′tĭ-făm′ə-lē) *adj.* Of, relating to, or intended for use by several individual families: *a multifamily house.*

mul·ti·far·i·ous (mŭl′tə-fâr′ē-əs) *adj.* Having great variety; diverse. [LLat. *multifarius* < *multus,* many.] —**mul′ti·far′i·ous·ly** *adv.* —**mul′ti·far′i·ous·ness** *n.*

mul·ti·fid (mŭl′tə-fĭd′) *adj. Biol.* Having many clefts forming lobes: *multifid leaves.* [Lat. *multifidus,* divided into many parts : *multus,* many + *findere,* to cleave.]

mul·ti·flo·ra rose (mŭl′tə-flôr′ə, -flōr′ə) *n.* A climbing or sprawling shrub, *Rosa multiflora,* native to Asia, having clusters of small, fragrant flowers. It is the origin of many horticultural varieties. [NLat. *Rosa multiflora,* species name : Lat. *rosa,* rose + Lat. *multiflora,* fem. of *multiflorus,* multiflorous.]

mul·ti·flo·rous (mŭl′tə-flôr′əs, -flōr′əs) *adj. Bot.* Bearing many flowers. [Lat. *multiflorus* : *multus,* many + *flos,* flower.]

mul·ti·foil (mŭl′tə-foil′) *n.* A flat object or opening with scalloped edges or ornaments.

mul·ti·fold (mŭl′tə-fōld′) *adj.* Many times doubled; manifold.

mul·ti·form (mŭl′tə-fôrm′) *adj.* Occurring in or having many forms, shapes, or appearances. [Lat. *multiformis* : *multus,* many + *forma,* shape.] —**mul′ti·for′mi·ty** *n.*

Mul·ti·graph (mŭl′tĭ-grăf′). A trademark for an office machine for typesetting and rotary printing.

mul·ti·lane (mŭl′tə-lān′, -tē-) *adj.* Having several lanes: *a multilane highway.*

mul·ti·lat·er·al (mŭl′tĭ-lăt′ər-əl) *adj.* **1.** Having many sides. **2.** Involving more than two nations: *multilateral trade agreements.* —**mul′ti·lat′er·al·ly** *adv.*

mul·ti·lay·ered (mŭl′tə-lā′ərd) *adj.* Consisting of or involving several individual layers or levels.

mul·ti·lev·el (mŭl′tə-lĕv′əl) also **mul·ti·lev·eled** (-lĕv′əld) *adj.* Having several levels: *a multilevel parking garage.*

mul·ti·lin·gual (mŭl′tə-lĭng′gwəl) *adj.* **1.** Of, including, or depicted in several languages: *multilingual signs.* **2.** Using or having the ability to use several languages: *a multilingual translator.* —**mul′ti·lin′gual·ism** *n.*

Mul·ti·lith (mŭl′tĭ-lĭth′). A trademark for a small rotary offset press.

mul·ti·me·di·a (mŭl′tĭ-mē′dē-ə) *adj.* Including or involving the use of several media: *a multimedia display.* —**mul′ti·me′di·a** *n.*

mul·ti·mil·lion·aire (mŭl′tĭ-mĭl′yə-nâr′) *n.* A person whose financial assets equal many millions of dollars.

mul·ti·na·tion·al (mŭl′tĭ-năsh′ə-nəl, -năsh′nəl) *adj.* **1.** Having operations, subsidiaries, or investments in more than one country: *a multinational corporation.* **2.** Of, in, or involving several or many countries: *a multinational research project.* —*n.* A multinational company or corporation. —**mul′ti·na′tion·al·ism** *n.*

mul·ti·no·mi·al (mŭl′tĭ-nō′mē-əl) *n.* A polynomial (sense 2.b.). [MULTI- + (BI)NOMIAL.] —**mul′ti·no′mi·al** *adj.*

multinomial theorem *n. Math.* The theorem that establishes the rule for forming the terms of a polynomial expansion.

mul·ti·nu·cle·ar (mŭl′tē-nōō′klē-ər, -nyōō′-) *adj.* Multinucleate.

mul·ti·nu·cle·ate (mŭl′tē-nōō′klē-ət, -nyōō′-) also **mul·ti·nu·cle·at·ed** (-ā′tĭd) *adj.* Having more than two nuclei.

mul·tip·a·rous (mŭl-tĭp′ər-əs) *adj.* **1.** Having borne more than one child. **2.** Giving birth to more than one offspring at one time.

mul·ti·par·tite (mŭl′tĭ-pär′tīt′) *adj.* **1.** Having many parts. **2.** Multilateral. [Lat. *multipartitus* : *multus,* many + *partitus,* p.part. of *partire,* to divide < *pars,* part.]

mul·ti·par·ty (mŭl′tə-pär′tē) *adj.* Of, relating to, or involving more than two political parties.

mul·ti·ped (mŭl′tə-pĕd′) also **mul·ti·pede** (-pēd′) *adj.* Having many feet. [Lat. *multipedes* : *multus,* many + *pes,* foot.]

mul·ti·ple (mŭl′tə-pəl) *adj.* Having, pertaining to, or consisting of more than one individual, element, part, or other component; manifold. —*n. Math.* A quantity into which another quantity may be divided with zero remainder: *4, 6, and 12 are multiples of 2.* A *common multiple* is a quantity into which each of two or more other quantities may be divided with zero remainder: *6, 12, and 24 are common multiples of 2 and 3.* A *least common multiple* is the least quantity into which two or more other quantities may be divided with zero remainder: *6 is the least common multiple of all common multiples of 2 and 3.* [Fr. < Lat. *multiplex,* multiplex.]

multiple allele *n. Genetics.* A set of three or more alleles, or alternative states of a gene, only two of which can be present in a somatic cell at the same time.

mul·ti·ple-choice (mŭl′tə-pəl-chois′) *adj.* Offering a number of solutions from which the correct one is to be chosen.

multiple factor *n. Genetics.* A combination of two or more genes acting as a unit to produce a quantitative inheritance trait, such as leaf shape or eye color.

multiple fruit *n.* A fruit, such as a pineapple, in which the fruits of several flowers are combined into a single structure.

multiple myeloma *n.* A malignant disease of bone marrow characterized by the presence of myelomas in many bones of the body.

multiple neuritis *n.* Inflammation of more than one nerve at a time.

multiple root *n.* A root (sense 9.c.).

multiple sclerosis *n.* A degenerative disease of the central nervous system in which hardening of tissue occurs throughout the brain or spinal cord or both.

multiple star *n.* Three or more stars, usually with a common gravitational center, that appear as one to the naked eye.

multiple store *n. Chiefly Brit.* A chain store.

mul·ti·plet (mŭl′tə-plĕt′, -plĭt) *n.* **1.** A spectral line having more than one component representing slight variations in energy states characteristic of an atom. **2.** Any of several classes or groupings of subatomic particles, such as the nucleon, each member of which has the same set of quantum numbers except for electric charge. [< MULTIPLE.]

mul·ti·plex (mŭl′tə-plĕks′) *adj.* **1.** Multiple; manifold: *"the whole complex and multiplex detail of the noble science of dinner"* (Peacock). **2.** Designating or being a simultaneous communication of two or more messages on the same wire or radio channel. —*v.* **-plexed, -plex·ing, -plex·es.** —*intr.* To send messages or signals in a multiplex system. —*tr.* To send simultaneously (more than one signal) using one radio frequency. [Lat. < *multus,* many.]

mul·ti·pli·a·ble (mŭl′tə-plī′ə-bəl) also **mul·ti·plic·a·ble** (-plĭk′ə-bəl) *adj.* Capable of being multiplied.

mul·ti·pli·cand (mŭl′tə-plĭ-kănd′) *n.* The number that is or is to be multiplied by another. [Lat. *multiplicandum,* neuter of *multiplicandus,* gerund. of *multiplicare,* to multiply. —see MULTIPLY.]

mul·tip·li·cate (mŭl-tĭp′lĭ-kĭt) *adj.* **1.** Having more than one layer or fold, as some shells or leaves. **2.** Multiple. [ME < Lat. *multiplicatus,* p. part. of *multiplicare,* to multiply. —see MULTIPLY.]

mul·ti·pli·ca·tion (mŭl′tə-plĭ-kā′shən) *n.* **1.** The act or process of multiplying or the condition of being multiplied.

multifoil

2. The propagation of plants and animals. **3.** *Math.* **a.** The conjunction of two real numbers in which the number of times either is taken in summation is determined by the value of the other. **b.** Any of certain analogous operations conjoining expressions other than real numbers. **4.** An increase or buildup achieved by adding. **—mul'ti·pli·ca'tion·al** *adj.*

multiplication sign *n.* The sign ×, placed between multiplicand and multiplier or operand and operator, as *a* × *b.*

multiplication table *n.* A table listing the products of certain numbers multiplied together, esp. the numbers 1 to 12.

mul·ti·pli·ca·tive (mŭl'tə-plĭk'ə-tĭv, mŭl'tə-plĭ-kā'tĭv) *adj.* **1.** Tending to multiply or capable of multiplying or increasing. **2.** Having to do with multiplication. **—mul'ti·pli'ca·tive·ly** *adv.*

multiplicative inverse *n.* Inverse (sense 2.a.).

mul·ti·plic·i·ty (mŭl'tə-plĭs'ĭ-tē) *n., pl.* **-ties. 1.** The state of being various or manifold. **2.** A large number: *a multiplicity of ideas.* **3.** *Physics.* The number of subatomic particles in a multiplet. [Fr. *multiplicité* < LLat. *multiplicitas* < *multiplex,* multiplex. —see MULTIPLEX.]

mul·ti·pli·er (mŭl'tə-plī'ər) *n.* **1.** One that multiplies. **2.** *Math.* The number by which the multiplicand is multiplied. **3.** *Physics.* A device, such as a phototube, used to enhance or increase an effect.

mul·ti·ply (mŭl'tə-plī') *v.* **-plied, -ply·ing, -plies.** *—tr.* **1.** To increase the amount, number, or degree of. **2.** *Math.* To perform multiplication on. *—intr.v.* **1.** To become more in number, amount, or degree. **2.** To breed; propagate. **3.** *Math.* To perform multiplication. [ME *multiplien* < OFr. *multiplier* < Lat. *multiplicare* < *multiplex,* multiplex.]

mul·ti·pur·pose (mŭl'tə-pûr'pəs) *adj.* Designed or used for several purposes.

mul·ti·ra·cial (mŭl'tē-rā'shəl) *adj.* Made up of, involving, or acting on behalf of various races: *a multiracial committee.*

mul·ti·sense (mŭl'tĭ-sĕns') *adj.* Having multiple meanings: *Make is a multisense word.*

mul·ti·sen·so·ry (mŭl'tĭ-sĕn'sə-rē) *adj.* Relating to or making use of several bodily senses: *multisensory methods of teaching reading.*

mul·ti·stage (mŭl'tĭ-stāj') *adj.* Functioning by stages.

multistage rocket *n.* A rocket composed of two or more stages, each stage firing in succession.

mul·ti·state (mŭl'tĭ-stāt') *adj.* Of, relating to, or involving several states: *a multistate antilitter campaign.*

mul·ti·sto·ry (mŭl'tĭ-stôr'ē, -stōr'ē) also **mul·ti·sto·ried** (-stôr'ēd, -stōr'-) *adj.* Having several stories: *a multistory motel.*

mul·ti·tude (mŭl'tĭ-to͞od', -tyo͞od') *n.* **1.** The condition or quality of being numerous. **2.** A great, indefinite number. **3.** The masses; the populace. [ME < OFr. < Lat. *multitudo* < *multus,* many.]

Synonyms: *multitude, host, legion, army, array. Multitude* denotes only great numbers; it applies to persons and things, but *in the multitude* indicates the people. The remaining terms suggest, besides numbers, some measure of orderliness and purposeful association. *Host,* applied to persons and things, and *legion,* largely confined to persons, stress impressiveness. *Army,* said chiefly of persons, emphasizes order and common purpose. *Array* primarily denotes imposing arrangement, but also applies to the persons and things thus arranged, with lesser emphasis on sheer numbers.

mul·ti·tu·di·nous (mŭl'tĭ-to͞od'n-əs, -tyo͞od'-) *adj.* **1.** Very numerous; existing in great numbers. **2.** Consisting of many parts. **3.** Crowded. **—mul'ti·tu'di·nous·ly** *adv.*

mul·ti·va·lent (mŭl'tĭ-vā'lənt, mŭl-tĭv'ə-lənt) *adj.* **1.** *Chem.* Polyvalent (sense 2.b.). **2.** *Biol.* Of or pertaining to homologous chromosomes in synapsis. **3.** Having various meanings or values. **—mul'ti·va'lence** *n.*

mul·ti·ver·si·ty (mŭl'tĭ-vûr'sĭ-tē) *n., pl.* **-ties.** A university that has numerous constituent and affiliated institutions such as separate colleges, campuses, and research centers. [MULTI- + (UNI)VERSITY.]

mul·ti·vi·ta·min (mŭl'tə-vī'tə-mĭn) *adj.* Containing many vitamins. *—n.* A multivitamin preparation.

mul·ture (mŭl'chər) *n.* A fee paid for grinding grain at a mill. [ME *multyr* < OFr. *molture,* grinding < Lat. *molere,* to grind.]

mum¹ (mŭm) *adj.* Silent. [ME.]

mum² (mŭm) *intr.v.* **mummed, mum·ming, mums. 1.** To act or play in a pantomime. **2.** To go merrymaking in a mask or disguise esp. during a festival. [ME *mummen* < OFr. *momer.*]

mum³ (mŭm) *n. Informal. Chiefly Brit.* Mother.

mum⁴ (mŭm) *n. Informal.* A chrysanthemum.

mural
By Diego Rivera

mum·ble (mŭm'bəl) *v.* **-bled, -bling, -bles.** *—tr.* **1.** To utter indistinctly by lowering the voice or partially closing the mouth. **2.** To chew slowly or painfully without or as if without teeth. *—intr.* **1.** To speak words indistinctly, as by lowering the voice or partially closing the mouth. **2.** To chew food slowly or painfully, as if without teeth. *—n.* A low, indistinct sound or speech. [ME *momelen.*] **—mum'bler** *n.*

mum·ble·ty·peg (mŭm'bəl-tē-pĕg', mŭm'blē-pĕg') also **mum·ble-the-peg** (mŭm'bəl-*thə*-pĕg') *n.* A game in which the players throw a knife from various positions with the object of having the blade stick firmly in the ground. [< the phrase *mumble the peg,* from the fact that orig. the loser had to pull up with his teeth a peg driven into the ground.]

mum·bo jum·bo (mŭm'bō jŭm'bō) *n.* **1.** An object believed to have supernatural powers; fetish. **2.** A complicated or obscure ritual. **3.** Language or ritualistic acitvity that is intended to confuse. **4.** Unintelligible or incomprehensible language; gibberish. [Prob. of Mandingo orig.]

mu meson *n. Physics.* The muon.

mum·mer (mŭm'ər) *n.* **1. a.** One who acts or plays in a pantomime. **b.** An actor. **2.** A masked merrymaker esp. at a festival. [ME *mummar* < OFr. *momeur* < *momer,* to pantomime.]

mum·mer·y (mŭm'ə-rē) *n., pl.* **-ies. 1.** A performance by mummers. **2.** A pretentious or hypocritical show or ceremony.

mum·mi·fy (mŭm'ə-fī') *v.* **-fied, -fy·ing, -fies.** *—tr.* **1.** To make into a mummy by embalming and drying. **2.** To cause to shrivel and dry up. *—intr.* To shrivel or dry up like a mummy. **—mum'mi·fi·ca'tion** *n.*

mum·my¹ (mŭm'ē) *n., pl.* **-mies. 1.** The body of a human being or animal embalmed after death according to the practice of the ancient Egyptians. **2.** A withered or shrunken body that resembles a mummy. [ME *mummie,* embalming ointment < OFr. *momie* < Med. Lat. *mumia* < Ar. *mūmiyā* < *mūm,* wax.]

mum·my² (mŭm'ē) *n., pl.* **-mies.** *Informal.* Mother. [Alteration of MAMMY.]

mumps (mŭmps) *pl.n. (used with a sing. or pl. verb).* An acute, inflammatory, contagious disease of the salivary glands, esp. the parotids and sometimes of the pancreas, ovaries, or testes, caused by a virus, *Rubula inflans.* [< pl. of dial. *mump,* grimace.]

munch (mŭnch) *tr.v.* **munched, munch·ing, munch·es.** To chew with a crunching sound. [ME *monchen.*] **—munch'er** *n.*

munch·ies (mŭn'chēz) *pl.n. Slang.* **1.** Food for snacking. **2.** A craving for snack foods: *have the munchies.*

mun·dane (mŭn'dān', mŭn'dān') *adj.* **1.** Of, relating to, or typical of this world. **2.** Typical of or concerned with the ordinary. [ME *mondeyne* < OFr. *mondain* < LLat. *mundanus* < Lat. *mundus,* world.] **—mun·dane'ly** *adv.*

mung bean (mŭng) *n.* A bean, *Phaseolus aureus,* cultivated esp. as the source of bean sprouts. [Hindi *mū̃g* < Skt. *mudgaḥ.*]

mun·go (mŭng'gō) *n.* Reclaimed wool of low quality. [Orig. unknown.]

mu·nic·i·pal (myo͞o-nĭs'ə-pəl) *adj.* **1. a.** Of, pertaining to, or typical of a municipality. **b.** Having local self-government. **2.** Of or pertaining to the internal affairs of a nation, as distinguished from its international affairs. [Lat. *municipalis* < *municipium,* town < *municeps,* citizen : *munus,* public office + *capere,* to take.] **—mu·nic'i·pal·ly** *adv.*

mu·nic·i·pal·i·ty (myo͞o-nĭs'ə-păl'ĭ-tē) *n., pl.* **-ties. 1.** A political unit, such as a city or town, incorporated for local self-government. **2.** A body of officials appointed to manage the affairs of a municipality.

mu·nic·i·pal·ize (myo͞o-nĭs'ə-pə-līz') *tr.v.* **-ized, -iz·ing, -iz·es. 1.** To place under municipal ownership. **2.** To make a municipality of. **—mu·nic'i·pal·i·za'tion** *n.*

mu·nif·i·cent (myo͞o-nĭf'ĭ-sənt) *adj.* **1.** Extremely liberal in giving; very generous. **2.** Showing great generosity: *a munificent gift.* [Lat. *munificens* < *munificus* : *munus,* gift + *facere,* to make.] **—mu·nif'i·cence** *n.* **—mu·nif'i·cent·ly** *adv.*

mu·ni·ment (myo͞o'nə-mənt) *n.* **1. muniments.** *Law.* Documentary evidence by which a person can defend a title to property or a claim to rights. **2.** *Archaic.* A means of defense or protection. [ME < OFr. < Med. Lat. *munimentum* < Lat., defense < *munire,* to fortify.]

mu·ni·tion (myo͞o-nĭsh'ən) *n.* Often **munitions.** War materiel, esp. weapons and ammunition. *—tr.v.* **-tioned, -tion·ing, -tions.** To supply with munitions. [OFr., fortification < Lat. *munitio* < *munire,* to defend.]

Mun·ster (mŭn'stər, mo͞on'-) *n.* Variant of **Muenster.**

munt·jac also **munt·jak** (mŭnt'jăk') *n.* Any of several small deer of the genus *Muntiacus,* of southeastern Asia and the East Indies. [Malay *menjangan,* deer.]

mu·on (myo͞o'ŏn') *n. Physics.* A subatomic particle in the lepton family, having a mass 207 times that of the electron, a negative electric charge, and a mean lifetime of 2.2 × 10^{-6} second.

mu·ral (myo͝or'əl) *n.* A work of art, such as a painting, applied directly to a wall or ceiling. *—adj.* **1.** Of, pertaining to, or like a wall. **2.** Painted on or applied to a wall. [OFr. < Lat. *muralis* < *murus,* wall.] **—mu'ral·ist** *n.*

mu·ram·ic acid (myo͞o-răm'ĭk) *n.* An amino sugar, $C_9H_{17}NO_7$, found in the murein in the cell walls of bacteria and blue-green algae. [Lat. *murus,* wall + AM(IDE) + -IC.]

mur·der (mûr'dər) *n.* **1.** The unlawful killing of one human being by another, esp. with premeditated malice. **2.** *Slang.* Something that is very uncomfortable, difficult, or hazardous. *—v.* **-dered, -der·ing, -ders.** *—tr.* **1.** To kill (a human being) unlawfully. **2.** To kill brutally or inhumanly. **3.** To destroy; put an end to. **4.** To spoil by ineptness; mutilate: *murdered the English language.* **5.** *Slang.* To defeat decisively; trounce. *—intr.* To commit murder. ***—idiom.* get away with murder.** *Informal.* To escape punishment for or

detection of a blameworthy act. [ME *murther* < OE *morðor.*] **—mur'der·er** *n.* **—mur'der·ess** *n.*
mur·der·ous (mûr'dər-əs) *adj.* **1.** Capable of, guilty of, or intending murder: *a murderous group of thugs.* **2.** Characteristic of or giving rise to murder or bloodshed. **3.** *Informal.* Capable of devastating or overwhelming: *a murderous exam.* **—mur'der·ous·ly** *adv.* **—mur'der·ous·ness** *n.*
mure (myo͝or) *tr.v.* **mured, mur·ing, mures.** To immure. [ME *muren* < OFr. *murer* < LLat. *murare,* to wall in < Lat. *murus,* wall.]
mu·re·in (myo͝or'ē-ĭn, myo͝or'ēn') *n.* A peptidoglycan that contains muramic acid and is found in procaryotic cell walls. [MUR(AMIC ACID) + -EIN.]
mu·rex (myo͝or'ĕks') *n., pl.* **mu·ri·ces** (myo͝or'ĭ-sēz') or **mu·rex·es.** Any of various marine gastropods of the genus *Murex,* that have rough, spiny shells, are common in warm seas, and yield a purple dye. [NLat. *Murex,* genus name < Lat. *murex,* purple-fish.]
mu·ri·cate (myo͝or'ĭ-kāt') also **mu·ri·cat·ed** (-kā'tĭd) *adj.* Having a roughened surface because of many short spines. [Lat. *muricatus,* shaped like a murex < *murex,* murex.]
mu·ri·ces (myo͝or'ĭ-sēz') *n.* A plural of **murex.**
mu·rine (myo͝or'īn') *adj.* **1.** Of or pertaining to a member of the rodent family Muridae, including rats and mice. **2.** Caused, transmitted, or affected by rodents of the family Muridae: *a murine plague.* [Lat. *murinus,* of mice < *mus,* mouse.] **—mu'rine** *n.*
murk also **mirk** (mûrk) *—n.* Darkness; gloom. *—adj. Archaic.* Dark; gloomy. [ME *mirke,* poss. < OE *mirce.*]
murk·y also **mirk·y** (mûr'kē) *adj.* **-i·er, -i·est. 1.** Dark or gloomy. **2. a.** Heavy and thick with smoke, mist, or fog; hazy. **b.** Turbid with sediment: *murky waters.* **3. a.** Cloudy in color; having no brightness. **b.** Cloudy in mind; muddled. **4.** Hard to understand; obscure. **—murk'i·ly** *adv.* **—murk'i·ness** *n.*
mur·mur (mûr'mər) *n.* **1.** A low, indistinct, and continuous sound: *the murmur of the waves.* **2.** An indistinct complaint; mutter. **3.** A whispered utterance: *a murmur of approval.* **4.** *Med.* An abnormal sound, usually in the thoracic cavity, derived from the heart or lungs and detected by the ear or a device such as a stethoscope. *—v.* **-mured, -mur·ing, -murs.** *—intr.* **1.** To make a low, continuous, and indistinct sound or succession of sounds. **2.** To complain in low mumbling tones; grumble. *—tr.* To say in a low indistinct voice; utter indistinctly. [ME *murmure* < OFr. < Lat. *murmur.*] **—mur'mur·er** *n.* **—mur'mur·ing·ly** *adv.* **—mur'mur·ous** *adj.* **—mur'mur·ous·ly** *adv.*
mur·phy (mûr'fē) *n., pl.* **-phies.** *Slang.* A potato. [< *Murphy,* a common Irish name, from the fact that the potato was a staple Irish food.]
Mur·phy bed (mûr'fē) *n.* A bed that folds or swings into a closet for concealment. [After William *Murphy* (1876–1959).]
mur·rain (mûr'ĭn) *n.* **1.** Any of various highly infectious and malignant diseases of domestic plants or animals, such as potato blight or anthrax. **2.** A pestilence or dire disease. [ME *moreyne* < OFr. *morine* < *morir,* to die < Lat. *mori.*]
murre (mûr) *n., pl.* **murre** or **murres.** Any of various sea birds of the genus *Uria,* found in north temperate and arctic regions. [Orig. unknown.]
mur·rey (mûr'ē) *n.* Mulberry (sense 4). [ME < OFr. *more* < Med. Lat. *moratus* < Lat. *morum,* mulberry.] **—mur'rey** *adj.*
mur·ther (mûr'*th*ər) *n. & v. Obs.* Variant of **murder.**
Mus·ca (mŭs'kə) *n.* A constellation in the polar region of the Southern Hemisphere near Apus and Carina. [< Lat. *musca,* fly.]
Mus·ca·det (mŭs'kə-dā') *n.* A dry white wine of French origin. [Fr. < Prov., muscadet grape < *musc,* musk odor.]
mus·ca·dine (mŭs'kə-dīn', -dĭn) *n.* A woody vine, *Vitis rotundifolia,* of the southeastern United States, bearing a musky grape used to make wine. [Alteration of MUSCATEL.]
mus·cae vo·li·tan·tes (mŭs'ē vŏl'ĭ-tăn'tēz) *pl.n.* Small motes and threads that seem to move about the field of vision, due to cell fragments or other defects in the vitreous humor and the lens of the eye. [Lat., flying flies.]
mus·ca·rine (mŭs'kə-rēn') *n.* A highly toxic organic compound, $C_9H_{21}O_3N$, related to the cholines, derived from the red form of the mushroom *Amanita muscaria* and occurring in dead animal tissue. [< NLat. *muscaria,* specific epithet of *Amanita muscaria,* fly agaric < Lat. *muscarius,* of flies < *musca,* fly.] **—mus'ca·rin'ic** *adj.*
mus·cat (mŭs'kăt', -kət) *n.* **1.** Any of various sweet white grapes used for making wine or raisins. **2.** Muscatel (sense 1). [OFr. < OProv. < *musc,* musk < LLat. *muscus.*]
mus·ca·tel (mŭs'kə-tĕl') *n.* **1.** A rich, sweet wine made from muscat grapes. **2.** A muscat grape or raisin. [ME *muscadelle* < OFr. *muscadel* < OProv. *muscadel,* dim. of *muscat,* muscat.]
mus·cle (mŭs'əl) *n.* **1.** A tissue composed of fibers capable of contracting and relaxing to effect bodily movement. **2.** A contractile organ consisting of muscle tissue. **3.** Muscular strength: *enough muscle to be a high jumper.* **4.** Power or authority: *put some muscle into law enforcement.* *—intr.v.* **-cled, -cling, -cles.** To make one's way by or as if by force: *muscled into the conversation.* [OFr. < Lat. *musculus,* dim. of *mus,* mouse.]
mus·cle-bound (mŭs'əl-bound') *adj.* **1.** Having stiff, overdeveloped muscles, usually as the result of excessive exercise. **2.** Characterized by inflexibility; rigid.
muscle fiber *n.* An elongated, contractile cell having highly striated cytoplasm.
muscle sugar *n.* Inositol.
mus·co·vite (mŭs'kə-vīt') *n.* A mineral, the most common form of mica, consisting essentially of hydrous potassium aluminum silicate, $KAl_2(AlSi_3O_{10})(OH)_2$, that ranges from colorless or pale yellow to gray and brown, has a pearly luster, and is used as an insulator. [< *Muscovy glass,* its former name.]
Mus·co·vite (mŭs'kə-vīt') *n.* A native or resident of Moscow or of Muscovy. **—Mus'co·vite'** *adj.*
Mus·co·vy duck (mŭs'kə-vē, -kō'-) *n.* A waterfowl, *Cairina moschata,* found wild from Mexico to Brazil but domesticated around the world for its succulent flesh. [After *Muscovy,* the principality of Moscow.]
mus·cu·lar (mŭs'kyə-lər) *adj.* **1.** Pertaining to or consisting of muscle. **2.** Accomplished with the use of the muscles. **3.** Having well-developed muscles. **4.** Of great strength; mighty. [< Lat. *musculus,* muscle.] **—mus'cu·lar'i·ty** (-lăr'ĭ-tē) *n.* **—mus'cu·lar·ly** *adv.*
muscular dystrophy *n.* A chronic, noncontagious disease of unknown cause in which complete incapacitation follows gradual but irreversible muscular deterioration.
mus·cu·la·ture (mŭs'kyə-lə-cho͝or') *n.* The system of muscles of an animal or a body part. [Fr. < Lat. *musculus,* muscle.]
mus·cu·lo·skel·e·tal (mŭs'kyə-lō-skĕl'ĭ-tl) *adj.* Pertaining to or involving the muscles and the skeleton. [Lat. *musculus,* muscle + SKELETAL.]
muse (myo͞oz) *v.* **mused, mus·ing, mus·es.** *—intr.* To consider or meditate upon something at length: *muse on the vanity of human wishes.* *—tr.* To consider reflectively: *muse the problem.* *—n.* A state of musing or deep meditation. [ME *musen* < OFr. *muser* < *mus,* snout < Med. Lat. *musum.*]
Muse (myo͞oz) *n.* **1.** *Gk. Myth.* Any of the nine daughters of Mnemosyne and Zeus, each of whom presided over a different art or science. **2. muse. a.** A guiding spirit. **b.** A source of inspiration. **3. muse.** A poet. [ME < OFr. < Lat. *Musa* < Gk. *Mousa.*]
mu·sette (myo͞o-zĕt') *n.* **1.** A small French bagpipe with a soft sound. **2.** A small canvas or leather bag with a shoulder strap. [ME < OFr. < *muser,* to play the musette, muse.]
mu·se·um (myo͞o-zē'əm) *n.* An institution for the acquisition, preservation, study, and exhibition of works of artistic, historical, or scientific value. [Lat. < Gk. *mouseion* < *mouseios,* of the Muses < *Mousa,* Muse.]
mush[1] (mŭsh) *n.* **1.** A thick mixture consisting of cornmeal boiled in liquid. **2.** Something thick, soft, and pulpy in texture. **3.** *Informal.* **a.** Maudlin sentimentality. **b.** Puerile and foolish amorousness. [Prob. alteration of MASH.]
mush[2] (mŭsh) *intr.v.* **mushed, mush·ing, mush·es.** To travel with a dog sled. Used often as a command to a team of dogs. *—n.* A journey by dog sled. [Canadian Fr. *mouche,* imper. of *moucher,* to hasten < Fr. *mouche,* fly < Lat. *musca.*] **—mush'er** *n.*
mush·room (mŭsh'ro͞om', -ro͝om') *n.* **1.** Any of various fleshy fungi of the class Basidiomycetes, characteristically having an umbrella-shaped cap borne on a stalk, esp. any of the edible varieties. **2.** Something resembling a mushroom in shape. *—intr.v.* **-roomed, -room·ing, -rooms. 1.** To multiply, grow, or expand rapidly: *The population mushroomed in the postwar decades.* **2.** To spread out, flatten, or swell into a mushroomlike shape. [ME *muscheron* < OFr. *mousseron.*]
mush·y (mŭsh'ē) *adj.* **-i·er, -i·est. 1.** Like mush in consistency; soft. **2.** *Informal.* **a.** Excessively sentimental. **b.** Foolishly amorous. **—mush'i·ly** *adv.* **—mush'i·ness** *n.*
mu·sic (myo͞o'zĭk) *n.* **1.** The art of organizing tones in a coherent sequence so as to produce a unified and continuous composition. **2.** Vocal or instrumental sounds possessing rhythm, melody, and harmony. **3. a.** A musical composition. **b.** The written or printed score for a musical composition. **4.** A musical accompaniment. **5.** A particular category or kind of music: *program music; country music.* **6.** An aesthetically pleasing or harmonious sound or combination of sounds: *the music of her voice.* [ME < OFr. *musique* < Lat. *musica* < Gk. *mousikē (tekhnē),* (art) of the Muses < *mousikos,* of the Muses < *Mousa,* Muse.]
mu·si·cal (myo͞o'zĭ-kəl) *adj.* **1.** Of, pertaining to, or capable of producing music: *a musical instrument.* **2.** Characteristic of or resembling music; melodious: *a musical speaking voice.* **3.** Set to or accompanied by music: *a musical revue.* **4.** Devoted to or skilled in music. *—n.* **1.** A musical comedy. **2.** *Archaic.* A musicale. **—mu'si·cal·ly** *adv.*
musical chairs *pl.n. (used with a sing verb).* **1.** A game in which the players walk to music around a row of chairs containing one chair fewer than the number of players and rush to sit down when the music stops. **2.** *Informal.* A rearrangement, as of the elements of a situation, having little practical influence or significance.
musical comedy *n.* A play or motion picture in which dialogue is interspersed with songs and dances.
Synonyms: *musical comedy, revue, operetta, light opera, vaudeville.* A *musical comedy* differs from a *revue* principally

Murphy bed
Landlady demonstrating the advantages of a Murphy bed to prospective tenant

Muse
Sarcophagus fragments with the nine Muses in relief

mushroom

in having a plot. A *revue* is a plotless series of comic sketches and songs, often topical and satiric. *Operetta,* used interchangeably with *light opera,* is a form having a plot with spoken dialogue; the libretto and the music are generally more serious and substantial than those of *musical comedy.* In modern usage, *vaudeville* denotes a plotless program of unrelated specialty acts; the approximate British equivalents are *music hall* and *variety.*

mu·si·cale (myōō′zĭ-kăl′) *n.* A program of music performed at a party or social gathering. [Fr. < *(soirée) musicale,* musical (evening).]

mu·si·cal·i·ty (myōō′zĭ-kăl′ĭ-tē) *n.* **1.** The condition or quality of being musical. **2.** Musical sensitivity or talent.

musical saw *n.* A handsaw on which musical notes are produced by flexing the blade and stroking it with a violin bow or a hammer.

music box *n.* A box containing a mechanical device that produces music when activated by a clockwork.

music drama *n.* An opera in which the continuity is not interrupted by arias, recitatives, or ensembles, and in which the music reflects or embodies the action of the drama.

music hall *n.* **1.** An auditorium for musical performances. **2.** *Chiefly Brit.* **a.** A vaudeville theater. **b.** Vaudeville.

mu·si·cian (myōō-zĭsh′ən) *n.* **1.** A person who composes or performs music. **2.** A performer esp. of instrumental music. [ME *musicien* < OFr. < Lat. *musica,* music.] **—mu·si′cian·ly** *adj.*

mu·si·cian·ship (myōō-zĭsh′ən-shĭp′) *n.* Skill, insight, and artistry in the performance of music.

music of the spheres *n.* An inaudible harmony thought by Pythagoras to be produced by the movements of celestial bodies.

mu·si·col·o·gy (myōō′zĭ-kŏl′ə-jē) *n.* The historical and scientific study of music. **—mu′si·col′o·gist** *n.*

mus·ing (myōō′zĭng) *adj.* Absorbed in thought; abstracted. *—n.* Contemplation; meditation. **—mus′ing·ly** *adv.*

mu·sique con·crète (mōō-sēk′ kŏn-krĕt′) *n.* A musical composite of heterogeneous recorded sounds randomly modified and arranged. [Fr. : *musique,* music + *concrète,* concrete.]

musk (mŭsk) *n.* **1. a.** A greasy secretion with a powerful odor, produced in a glandular sac beneath the skin of the abdomen of the male musk deer and used in perfumery. **b.** A similar secretion of certain other vertebrates, such as the otter or civet. **c.** A synthetic chemical resembling natural musk in odor or use. **2. a.** The odor of musk. **b.** An odor similar to musk **3.** The musk deer. [ME *muske* < OFr. *musc* < LLat. *muscus* < Gk. *moskhos* < Pers. *muskh,* prob. < Skt. *muṣkah,* testicle.] **—musk′i·ness** *n.* **—musk′y** *adj.*

musk ox

musk beaver *n.* The muskrat.

musk deer *n.* A small, hornless deer, *Moschus moschiferus,* of central and northeastern Asia, the male of which secretes musk.

musk duck *n.* **1.** The Muscovy duck. **2.** A waterfowl, *Biziura lobata,* of Australia, the male of which has a leathery chin lobe and emits a musky odor during the breeding season.

mus·keg (mŭs′kĕg′) also **mas·keg** (măs′-) *n.* A swamp or bog formed by an accumulation of sphagnum moss, leaves, and decayed matter resembling peat. [Cree *maskeek.*]

mus·kel·lunge (mŭs′kə-lŭnj′) *n., pl.* **muskellunge** or **-lunges.** A large game fish, *Esox masquinongy,* similar to the pike, found in the cooler fresh waters of North America. [Of Algonquian orig.]

mus·ket (mŭs′kĭt) *n.* A smoothbore shoulder gun used from the late 16th through the 18th centuries. [Fr. *mousquet* < Ital. *moschetto,* bolt for a crossbow, musket, dim. of *mosca,* fly < Lat. *musca.*]

mus·ket·eer (mŭs′kĭ-tîr′) *n.* **1.** A soldier armed with a musket. **2.** A member of the French royal household bodyguard in the 17th and 18th centuries. [Fr. *mousquetaire* < *mousquet,* musket.]

muskrat

mus·ket·ry (mŭs′kĭ-trē) *n.* **1.** Muskets collectively. **2.** The fire of muskets. **3.** The technique of using small arms.

Mus·kho·ge·an (mŭs-kō′gē-ən) *n.* A family of North American Indian languages that includes Chickasaw, Choctaw, Creek, and Seminole.

mus·kie or **mus·ky** (mŭs′kē) *n., pl.* **-kies.** The muskellunge.

musk·mel·on (mŭsk′mĕl′ən) *n.* **1.** Any of several varieties of the melon *Cucumis melo,* such as the cantaloupe, having fruit characterized by a netted rind and flesh with a musky aroma. **2.** The fruit of the muskmelon.

musk ox *n.* A large, hoofed mammal, *Ovibos moschatus,* of northern Canada and Greenland, that emits a musky odor and has horns and a long, shaggy, brown-to-black coat.

musk·rat (mŭs′krăt′) *n., pl.* **muskrat** or **-rats. 1.** An aquatic rodent, *Ondatra zibethica,* of North America, having a brown coat that is widely used as a fur. **2.** The fur of the muskrat.

musk rose *n.* A prickly shrub, *Rosa moschata,* native to the Mediterranean region, cultivated for its clustered, musk-scented white flowers.

musk turtle *n.* A small freshwater turtle of the genus *Sternotherus,* of the eastern United States and Canada, having a musky odor.

mustard

mus·ky (mŭs′kē) *n.* Variant of **muskie.**

Mus·lim (mŭz′ləm, mōōz′-, mŭs′-, mōōs′-) *n.* **1.** A Moslem. **2.** A Black Muslim. [Ar. *muslim,* active part. of *aslama,* he surrendered.] **—Mus′lim** *adj.*

mus·lin (mŭz′lĭn) *n.* **1.** Any of various sturdy, plain-weave cotton fabrics, used esp. for sheets. **2.** A model, as of a garment, to be used as a pattern. [Fr. *mousseline* < Ital. *mussolina* < *Mussolo,* Mosul, Iraq < Ar. *Al-Mawṣil.*]

mus·quash (mŭs′kwŏsh′, -kwôsh′) *n.* The muskrat. [Of Algonquian orig.]

muss (mŭs) *tr.v.* **mussed, muss·ing, muss·es.** To make messy or untidy; rumple. *—n.* **1.** A state of disorder; mess. **2.** *Regional.* A squabble; row. [Prob. alteration of MESS.] **—muss′i·ly** *adv.* **—muss′i·ness** *n.* **—muss′y** *adj.*

mus·sel (mŭs′əl) *n.* **1.** Any of several marine bivalve mollusks, esp. the edible *Mytilus edulis,* having a blue-black shell. **2.** Any of several freshwater bivalve mollusks of the genera *Anodonta* and *Unio,* found in the central United States, whose shells provide mother-of-pearl. [ME *muscle* < OE *muscelle.*]

Mus·sul·man (mŭs′əl-mən) *n., pl.* **-men** or **-mans.** A Moslem. [Turk. *musulmān,* prob. alteration of Ar. *muslim,* Muslim.]

must[1] (mŭst) *aux.v.* **1.** To be obliged or required by morality, law, or custom: *Citizens must register in order to vote.* **2.** To be compelled, as by a physical necessity or requirement: *Plants must have oxygen in order to live.* **3.** Used to express a command or admonition: *He must not go there alone. You simply must see the new play.* **4.** To be determined to; have as a fixed resolve: *If you must leave, do it quietly. I must have a proposal in writing before I can proceed.* **5.** Used to indicate: **a.** Inevitability or certainty: *Each of us must die.* **b.** Logical probability or presumptive certainty: *If the lights were on, they must have been at home.* *—intr.v. Archaic.* To be required or obliged to go: *"I must from hence"* (Shakespeare). *—n.* **1.** An absolute requirement: *Promptness on the job is a must.* **2.** Something that is indispensable. [ME *moste* < OE *mōste,* p.t. of *mōtan,* to be allowed.]

must[2] (mŭst) *n.* **1.** Staleness; mustiness. **2.** Musk. [Prob. back-formation < MUSTY.]

must[3] (mŭst) *n.* The unfermented or fermenting juice expressed esp. from grapes. [ME < OE < Lat. *mustum,* neuter of *mustus,* new.]

mus·tache (mŭs′tăsh′, mə-stăsh′) *n.* **1.** The hair growing on the human upper lip, esp. when it is cultivated and groomed. **2.** Something similar to a mustache in appearance and position, esp.: **a.** A group of bristles or hair about the mouth of an animal. **b.** Distinctive coloring or feathers near the beak of a bird. [OFr. *moustache* < Ital. *mustaccio* < Med. Gk. *moustakion* < Gk. *mustax,* mustache, upper lip.]

mus·ta·chio (mə-stăsh′ō, -stăsh′ē-ō′, -stä′shō, -shē-ō′) *n., pl.* **-chios.** A mustache, esp. a luxuriant one. [Ult. < Ital. *mustaccio,* mustache.]

mus·tang (mŭs′tăng′) *n.* A wild horse of the North American plains, descended from Spanish horses. [Sp. *mesteño,* stray animal < OSp. *mesta,* association of cattle owners < Lat. *miscere,* to mix.]

mus·tard (mŭs′tərd) *n.* **1.** Any of various plants of the genus *Brassica,* native to Eurasia, having four-petaled yellow flowers and slender pods, esp. *B. nigra* and *B. alba,* which are cultivated for their pungent seeds. **2. a.** Powdered mustard seeds used medicinally. **b.** A condiment made from powdered mustard seeds. **3.** A dark yellow to light olive brown. [ME < OFr. *moustarde* < Lat. *mustum,* must.]

mustard gas *n.* An oily, volatile liquid, $(ClCH_2CH_2)_2S$, used in warfare as a gaseous blistering agent.

mustard oil *n.* An oil obtained from mustard seeds.

mustard plaster *n.* A medicinal plaster made with a paste-like mixture of powdered mustard, flour, and water.

mus·te·line (mŭs′tə-lĭn′, -lĭn) *adj.* Of or pertaining to fur-bearing mammals of the family Mustelidae, which includes the badger, mink, otter, and weasel. [Lat. *mustelinus,* of a weasel < *mustela,* weasel, prob. < *mus,* mouse.]

mus·ter (mŭs′tər) *v.* **-tered, -ter·ing, -ters.** *—tr.* **1. a.** To summon or assemble (troops). **b.** To convene or collect together. **2.** To collect or gather: *Muster up your courage.* *—intr.* To assemble or gather: *mustering for inspection.* ***—phrasal verbs.*** **muster in** or **out.** To enlist (someone) in or discharge (someone) from military service: *mustered in at the age of eighteen.* *—n.* **1. a.** A gathering, esp. of troops, for service, inspection, review, or roll call. **b.** The persons assembled for such a gathering. **2.** A muster roll. **3.** A gathering or collection: *a muster of business leaders at a luncheon.* [ME *mustren* < OFr. *moustrer* < Lat. *monstrare,* to show < *monstrum,* portent < *monēre,* to warn.]

muster roll *n.* **1.** The official roll of persons in a military or naval unit. **2.** An inventory; roster.

must·n't (mŭs′ənt). Must not.

must·y (mŭs′tē) *adj.* **-i·er, -i·est. 1.** Having a stale or moldy odor or taste. **2. a.** Hackneyed; trite; dull. **b.** Antiquated. [Alteration of obs. *moisty* < MOIST.] **—must′i·ly** *adv.* **—must′i·ness** *n.*

mu·ta·ble (myōō′tə-bəl) *adj.* **1.** Capable of or subject to change or alteration. **2.** Prone to frequent change; inconstant. [Lat. *mutabilis* < *mutare,* to change.] **—mu′ta·bil′i·ty, mu′ta·ble·ness** *n.* **—mu′ta·bly** *adv.*

mu·ta·gen (myōō′tə-jən, -jĕn′) *n.* An agent, such as radioactive elements or ultraviolet light, that causes biological mutation. [MUTA(TION) + -GEN.] **—mu'ta·gen'i·cal·ly** *adv.*

mu·tant (myōōt'nt) *n.* An individual or organism differing from the parental strain or strains as a result of mutation. [Lat. *mutans, mutant-,* changing, pr.part. of *mutare,* to change.] **—mu'tant** *adj.*

mu·tate (myōō'tāt', myōō-tāt') *tr. & intr.v.* **-tat·ed, -tat·ing, -tates.** To cause to undergo or to undergo change by mutation. [Lat. *mutare, mutat-.*] **—mu'ta'tive** (-tā'tĭv, -tə-tĭv) *adj.*

mu·ta·tion (myōō-tā'shən) *n.* **1.** The act or process of being altered or changed. **2.** An alteration or change, as in nature, form, or quality. **3.** *Biol.* **a.** An heritable alteration of the genes or chromosomes of an organism. **b.** A mutant. **4.** The change that is caused in the sound of one vowel by its assimilation to another vowel, esp. an umlaut. [ME *mutacioun* < OFr. *mutation* < Lat. *mutatio* < *mutare,* to change.] **—mu·ta'tion·al** *adj.* **—mu·ta'tion·al·ly** *adv.*

mu·ta·tis mu·tan·dis (mōō-tä'tĭs mōō-tän'dĭs) *adv.* The necessary changes having been made; substituting new terms. [Lat.]

mutch·kin (mŭch'kĭn) *n. Scot.* A unit of liquid measure equal to 0.9 U.S. pint. [ME *muchekyn* < MDu. *mudseken.*]

mute (myōōt) *adj.* **mut·er, mut·est. 1.** Refraining from producing speech or vocal sound. **2. a.** Unable to speak. **b.** Unable to vocalize, as certain animals. **3.** Expressed without speech; unspoken: *a mute appeal.* **4.** *Law.* Refusing to plead when under arraignment: *stand mute.* **5. a.** Not pronounced; silent, as the *e* in *house.* **b.** Pronounced with a temporary stoppage of breath, as the sounds of *p* and *b;* plosive; stopped. *—n.* **1.** A person incapable of speech. **2.** *Law.* A defendant who refuses to plead when under arraignment. **3.** Any of various devices used to muffle or soften the tone of a musical instrument. **4. a.** A silent or unpronounced letter. **b.** A plosive; stop. *—tr.v.* **mut·ed, mut·ing, mutes. 1.** To muffle or soften the sound of. **2.** To soften the tone, color, shade, or hue of. [ME *muet* < OFr. < *mu* < Lat. *mutus.*] **—mute'ly** *adv.* **—mute'ness** *n.*

mut·ed (myōō'tĭd) *adj.* **1.** Produced by or provided with a mute. **2. a.** Subdued; softened. **b.** Muffled; indistinct. **—mut'ed·ly** *adv.*

mu·ti·late (myōōt'l-āt') *tr.v.* **-lat·ed, -lat·ing, -lates. 1.** To cut off or destroy a limb or other essential part. **2.** To render imperfect by excising or radically altering a part. [Lat. *mutilare, mutilat-* < *mutilus,* maimed.] **—mu'ti·la'tion** *n.* **—mu'ti·la'tive** *adj.* **—mu'ti·la'tor** *n.*

mu·ti·neer (myōōt'n-îr') *n.* One who takes part in a mutiny. [Obs. Fr. *mutinier* < OFr. *mutin,* rebellious. —see MUTINY.]

mu·ti·nous (myōōt'n-əs) *adj.* **1.** Pertaining to, engaged in, or disposed toward mutiny; rebellious. **2.** Unruly; disaffected: *a mutinous child.* **3.** Turbulent and uncontrollable: *"Mutinous passions, and conflicting fears"* (Shelley). [< obs. *mutine,* mutiny.] **—mu'ti·nous·ly** *adv.* **—mu'ti·nous·ness** *n.*

mu·ti·ny (myōōt'n-ē) *n., pl.* **-nies.** Open rebellion against constituted authority, esp. rebellion of sailors or soldiers against superior officers. *—intr.v.* **-nied, -ny·ing, -nies.** To commit mutiny. [Obs. *mutine* < OFr. *mutin,* rebellious < *muete,* revolt < VLat. **movita* < Lat. *movēre,* to move.]

mut·ism (myōō'tĭz'əm) *n.* The condition of being mute; inability to speak.

mutt (mŭt) *n. Slang.* **1.** A mongrel dog. **2.** A fool. [Short for MUTTONHEAD.]

mut·ter (mŭt'ər) *v.* **-tered, -ter·ing, -ters.** *—intr.* **1.** To speak indistinctly in low tones. **2.** To complain or grumble morosely. *—tr.* To utter or say in low, indistinct tones. *—n.* A low grumble or indistinct utterance. [ME *muttren.*] **—mut'ter·er** *n.*

mut·ton (mŭt'n) *n.* The flesh of fully grown sheep. [ME *motoun* < OFr. *moton,* of Celt. orig.]

mut·ton·chops (mŭt'n-chŏps) *pl.n.* Side whiskers shaped like chops of meat.

mut·ton·fish (mŭt'n-fĭsh') *n., pl.* **muttonfish** or **-fish·es.** The eelpout.

mut·ton·head (mŭt'n-hĕd') *n. Slang.* A stupid person. [From the stupidity of sheep.] **—mut'ton·head'ed** *adj.*

mu·tu·al (myōō'chōō-əl) *adj.* **1.** Having the same relationship each to the other: *mutual friends.* **2.** Directed and received in equal amount: *mutual respect.* **3.** Possessed in common: *mutual interests.* [ME *mutuall* < OFr. *mutuel* < Lat. *mutuus* < *mutare,* to change.] **—mu'tu·al'i·ty** (-ăl'ĭ-tē) *n.* **—mu'tu·al·ly** *adv.*

Usage: *Mutual* is usually used to describe a relation between two or more things, and in this use it can be paraphrased with expressions involving *between* or *each other.* Thus, *their mutual relations* means "their relations with each other" or "the relations between them." *Common* describes a relationship shared by the members of a group to something else, as in *their common interest in philately* or in the expression *common knowledge,* "the knowledge shared by all." The phrase *mutual friend,* however, has been used since Dickens to refer to a friend of each of the several members of a group: *We were introduced by a mutual friend. Reciprocal,* like *mutual,* applies to relations between the members of a group, with an added suggestion that an exchange of goods or favors is involved, as in *reciprocal trade. Joint* is usually used to describe an undertaking in which several partners are involved, as in *The joint efforts of federal and local officials will be required to stop the fire ant.*

mutual fund *n.* A company without fixed capitalization, freely buying and selling its own shares and using its capital to invest in other companies.

mutual inductance *n.* **1.** The ratio expressed by the flux linking one circuit with a neighboring circuit divided by the current in the neighboring circuit. **2.** The ratio expressed by the electromotive force induced in a circuit by a neighboring circuit divided by the corresponding change of current in the neighboring circuit.

mutual insurance *n.* An insurance system in which the insured persons become company members, each paying specified amounts into a common fund from which members are entitled to indemnification in case of loss.

mu·tu·al·ism (myōō'chōō-ə-lĭz'əm) *n.* An association, such as symbiosis, between two organisms.

mu·tu·al·ize (myōō'chōō-ə-līz') *tr.v.* **-ized, -iz·ing, -iz·es. 1.** To make mutual. **2.** To set up or reorganize (a corporation) so that the majority of common stock is owned by customers or employees. **—mu'tu·al·i·za'tion** *n.*

muu·muu (mōō'mōō') *n.* A long, loose dress that hangs free from the shoulders. [Hawaiian *mu'u mu'u.*]

Mu·zak (myōō'zăk'). A trademark for recorded background music transmitted by wire, as to places of business, on a subscription basis.

mu·zhik also **mou·jik** or **mu·jik** or **mu·zjik** (mōō-zhēk', -zhĭk') *n.* A peasant in czarist Russia. [R. < *muzh,* man.]

muz·zle (mŭz'əl) *n.* **1.** The forward, projecting part of the head of certain animals, including the jaws and nose. **2.** A leather or wire device that, when fitted over an animal's snout, prevents biting and eating. **3.** Something that restrains free movement or expression. **4.** The forward, discharging end of the barrel of a firearm. *—tr.v.* **-zled, -zling, -zles. 1.** To put a muzzle on (an animal). **2.** To restrain from expression. [ME *musell* < OFr. *musel* < LLat. *musum,* snout.] **—muz'zler** *n.*

muz·zy (mŭz'ē) *adj.* **-zi·er, -zi·est.** *Informal.* **1.** Mentally confused; muddled. **2.** Blurred; indistinct. [Orig. unknown.] **—muz'zi·ly** *adv.* **—muz'zi·ness** *n.*

my (mī) *pron.* The possessive form of I. **1.** Used attributively to indicate possession, agency, or reception of an action by the speaker: *my wallet; pursuing my tasks; suffered my first rebuff.* **2.** Used preceding various forms of polite, affectionate, or familiar address: *my lord; my dear Dr. Dressner; my good man.* **3.** Used in various interjectional phrases: *My word! My goodness!* *—interj.* Used as an exclamation of surprise, pleasure, or dismay: *Oh, my!* [ME < OE *mīn.*]

my– *pref.* Variant of **myo-.**

my·al·gi·a (mī-ăl'jē-ə, -jə) *n.* **1.** Muscular rheumatism. **2.** Muscular pain. [MY(O)- + -ALGIA.]

my·as·the·ni·a (mī'əs-thē'nē-ə) *n.* Abnormal muscular weakness or fatigue. [MY(O)- + ASTHENIA.] **—my'as·then'ic** (-thĕn'ĭk) *adj.*

myc– *pref.* Variant of **myco-.**

my·ce·li·um (mī-sē'lē-əm) *n., pl.* **-li·a** (-lē-ə). The vegetative part of a fungus, consisting of a mass of branching, threadlike filaments called hyphae. [NLat. : MYC(O)- + Gk. *hēlos,* wart.] **—my·ce'li·al** *adj.*

My·ce·nae·an (mī'sə-nē'ən) *adj.* Of, pertaining to, or designating the Aegean civilization that spread its influence from Mycenae to many parts of the Mediterranean region from about 1400 B.C. to 1150 B.C. **—My'ce·nae'an** *n.*

–mycete *suff.* Fungus: *actinomycete.* [NLat. *-mycetes* < Gk. *mukētes,* pl. of *mukēs,* fungus.]

my·ce·to·ma (mī'sĭ-tō'mə) *n., pl.* **-mas** or **-ma·ta** (-mə-tə). **1.** A chronic fungous infection usually affecting the foot, characterized by nodules that discharge oily pus. **2.** A mycetoma nodule. [Gk. *mukēs, mukēt-,* fungus + -OMA.] **—my'ce·to'ma·tous** (-tō'mə-təs, -tŏm'ə-təs) *adj.*

my·ce·to·zo·an (mī-sē'tə-zō'ən) *n.* A slime mold. [< NLat. *Mycetozoa,* order name : Gk. *mukēs,* fungus + Gk. *zōia,* pl. of *zōion,* animal.] **—my·ce'to·zo'an** *adj.*

–mycin *suff.* A substance derived from a fungus: *neomycin.* [MYC(O)- + IN.]

myco– or **myc–** *pref.* Fungus: *mycology.* [NLat. < Gk. *mukēs,* fungus.]

my·co·bac·te·ri·um (mī'kō-băk-tîr'ē-əm) *n., pl.* **-te·ri·a** (-tîr'ē-ə). Any of various slender, rod-shaped bacteria of the genus *Mycobacterium,* which includes the bacterium that causes tuberculosis.

my·col·o·gy (mī-kŏl'ə-jē) *n.* **1.** The branch of botany that deals with fungi. **2.** The fungi native to a region. **—my'co·log'i·cal** (-kə-lŏj'ĭ-kəl), **my'co·log'ic** *adj.* **—my·col'o·gist** *n.*

my·cor·rhi·za or **my·co·rhi·za** (mī'kə-rī'zə) *n., pl.* **-zae** (-zē) or **-zas.** *Bot.* The symbiotic association of the mycelium of a fungus with the roots of certain plants, such as conifers, beeches, or orchids. [MYCO- + Gk. *rhiza,* root.] **—my'cor·rhi'zal** *adj.*

my·co·sis (mī-kō'sĭs) *n., pl.* **-ses** (-sēz'). **1.** A fungous growth in the body. **2.** A disease caused by a fungous growth.

my·dri·a·sis (mĭ-drī'ə-sĭs) *n.* Prolonged and abnormal dilatation of the pupil of the eye as a result of disease or a drug. [Lat. < Gk. *mudriasis.*]

mute

muzzle

myd·ri·at·ic (mĭd′rē-ăt′ĭk) *n.* A drug that produces dilatation of the pupils. [< MYDRIASIS.] —**myd′ri·at′ic** *adj.*
myel– *pref.* Variant of **myelo-**.
my·e·len·ceph·a·lon (mī′ə-lĕn-sĕf′ə-lŏn′) *n.* The rear part of the embryonic hindbrain from which the medulla oblongata develops. —**my′e·len·ce·phal′ic** (-sə-făl′ĭk) *adj.*
my·e·lin (mī′ə-lĭn) also **my·e·line** (-lĭn, -lēn′) *n.* **1.** A white, fatty material encasing some nerve fibers. **2.** One of several fatlike substances found in body tissues. —**my′e·lin′ic** *adj.*
my·e·li·nat·ed (mī′ə-lə-nā′tĭd) *adj.* Having a myelin sheath: *myelinated nerve fibers.*
my·e·li·ni·za·tion (mī′ə-lə-nĭ-zā′shən) also **my·e·li·na·tion** (-nā′shən) *n.* **1.** The process of growing a myelin sheath. **2.** The condition of having a myelin sheath.
my·e·li·tis (mī′ə-lī′tĭs) *n.* Inflammation of the spinal column or bone marrow.
myelo– or **myel–** *pref.* Spinal cord; marrow: *myelitis.* [NLat. < Gk. *muelos,* marrow < *mus,* muscle.]
my·e·loid (mī′ə-loid′) *adj.* **1.** Of, related to, or derived from bone marrow. **2.** Of or pertaining to the spinal cord.
my·e·lo·ma (mī′ə-lō′mə) *n., pl.* **-mas** or **-ma·ta** (-mə-tə). A malignant tumor of the bone marrow. —**my′e·lo′ma·toid′** *adj.*
my·ia·sis (mī′ə-sĭs, mī-ī′ə-sĭs) *n., pl.* **my·ia·ses** (mī′ə-sēz). Infestation of human tissue by fly maggots or flies or a disease resulting from it. [Gk. *mua,* fly + -IASIS.]
My·lar (mī′lär′). A trademark for a thin strong polyester film.
my·lo·nite (mī′lə-nīt′) *n.* A fine-grained laminated rock formed by the shifting of rock layers. [Gk. *mulōn,* mill < *mulos* + -ITE.]
my·na or **my·nah** also **mi·na** (mī′nə) *n.* Any of various birds of the family Sturnidae, of southeastern Asia, related to the starlings and having blue-black to dark-brown coloration and yellow bills. Certain species are known for mimicry of human speech. [Hindi *mainā* < Skt. *madanah,* passion, lust.]

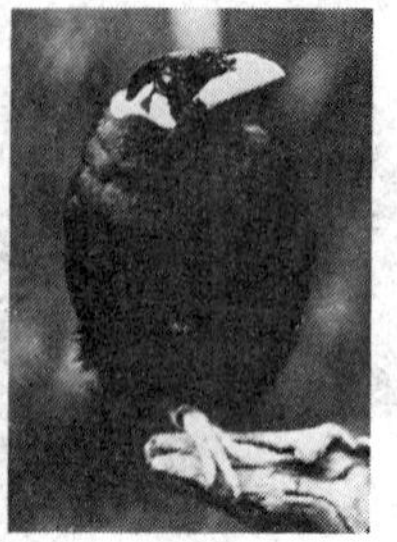
myna

myn·heer (mīn-hâr′, -hîr′) *n.* **1.** Often **Mynheer.** The Dutch title of courtesy and respect equivalent to the English *sir* or *Mr.* **2.** *Informal.* A Dutchman. [Du. *mijnheer* : *mijn,* my (< MDu. *mijni*) + *heer,* lord < MDu.]
myo– or **my–** *pref.* Muscle: *myograph.* [NLat. < Gk. *mus,* muscle.]
my·o·car·di·o·graph (mī′ō-kär′dē-ə-grăf′) *n.* An instrument for graphing the action of the heart muscle.
my·o·car·di·tis (mī′ō-kär-dī′tĭs) *n.* Inflammation of the myocardium. [MYOCARD(IUM) + -ITIS.]
my·o·car·di·um (mī′ō-kär′dē-əm) *n.* The muscle tissue of the heart. [NLat. : MYO- + Gk. *kardia,* heart.] —**my′o·car′di·al** *adj.*

myrtle

my·o·gen·ic (mī′ə-jĕn′ĭk) also **my·o·ge·net·ic** (mī′ō-jə-nĕt′ĭk) *adj.* **1.** Giving rise to or forming muscle tissue. **2.** Of muscular origin.
my·o·glo·bin (mī′ə-glō′bĭn) *n.* The form of hemoglobin found in muscle fibers.
my·o·graph (mī′ə-grăf′) *n.* An instrument for graphing muscular contractions.
my·ol·o·gy (mī-ŏl′ə-jē) *n.* The scientific study of muscles. —**my′o·log′ic** (mī′ə-lŏj′ĭk) *adj.* —**my·ol′o·gist** *n.*
my·o·ma (mī-ō′mə) *n., pl.* **-mas** or **-ma·ta** (-mə-tə). A tumor composed of muscle tissue. —**my·o′ma·tous** (-ō′mə-təs, -ŏm′ə-) *adj.*
my·ope (mī′ōp′) *n.* One who has myopia. [Fr. < LLat. *myops,* myopic < Gk. *muōps.* —see MYOPIA.]
my·o·pi·a (mī-ō′pē-ə) *n.* **1.** *Pathol.* A visual defect in which distant objects appear blurred because their images are focused in front of the retina rather than on it; nearsightedness. **2.** Shortsightedness or lack of discernment in thinking or planning: *"For Lorca, New York is a symbol of spiritual myopia"* (Edwin Honig). [Gk. *muōpia* < *muōps,* myopic : *muein,* to close the eyes + *ōps,* eye.] —**my·op′ic** (-ŏp′ĭk, -ō′pĭk) *adj.* —**my·op′i·cal·ly** *adv.*
my·o·sin (mī′ə-sĭn) *n.* The commonest protein in muscle; with actin it forms actomyosin.
my·o·sis (mī-ō′sĭs) *n.* Variant of **miosis.**
my·o·so·tis (mī′ə-sō′tĭs) *n.* A plant of the genus *Myosotis,* such as the forget-me-not. [NLat. *Myosotis,* genus name < Lat. *myosotis,* a kind of plant < Gk. *muosotis* : *mus,* mouse + *ous* ear.]
my·o·to·ni·a (mī′ə-tō′nē-ə) *n.* Tonic spasm or temporary muscular rigidity. —**my′o·ton′ic** (-tŏn′ĭk) *adj.*
myr·i·ad (mĭr′ē-əd) *adj.* **1.** Constituting a very large, indefinite number; innumerable. **2.** Comprised of numerous diverse elements or facets: *the myriad responsibilities of a chief executive.* —*n.* **1.** *Archaic.* Ten thousand. **2.** A vast number. [Gk. *murias,* ten thousand < *murios,* countless.]
myr·i·a·pod (mĭr′ē-ə-pŏd′) *n.* Any of several arthropods, such as the centipede, having segmented bodies and many legs. —**myr′i·ap′o·dan** (-ăp′ə-dən) *adj. & n.* —**myr′i·ap′o·dous** (-ăp′ə-dəs) *adj.*
my·ris·tic acid (mə-rĭs′tĭk, mī-) *n.* An organic compound, $CH_3(CH_2)_{12}COOH$, occurring in animal and vegetable fats and used in cosmetics and flavors. [Gk. *muristikos,* fragrant < *muron,* perfume.]
myrmeco– *pref.* Ant: *myrmecophagous.* [Gk. *murmeco-* < *murmēx,* ant.]
myr·me·col·o·gy (mûr′mĭ-kŏl′ə-jē) *n.* The scientific study of ants. —**myr′me·co·log′i·cal** (-kə-lŏj′ĭ-kəl) *adj.* —**myr′me·col′o·gist** *n.*
myr·me·coph·a·gous (mûr′mĭ-kŏf′ə-gəs) *adj.* Feeding on ants.
myr·me·co·phile (mûr′mĭ-kə-fīl′) *n.* An organism that habitually shares the nest of an ant colony. —**myr′me·coph′i·lous** (-kŏf′ə-ləs) *adj.* —**myr′me·coph′i·ly** (-kŏf′ə-lē) *n.*
Myr·mi·don (mûr′mə-dŏn′, -dən) *n.* **1.** One of a legendary Greek warrior people of ancient Thessaly who followed their king Achilles on the expedition against Troy. **2. myrmidon.** A faithful follower who carries out orders without question. [< Lat. *Myrmidones,* Myrmidons < Gk. *Murmidones.*]
my·rob·a·lan (mī-rŏb′ə-lən, mə-) *n.* **1.** A tree, *Prunus cerasifera,* native to Asia, bearing edible red or yellow fruit. **2.** The Indian almond. **3.** The fruit of a myrobalan. [OFr. *mirobalan* < Lat. *myrobalanum,* fruit of a myrobalan < Gk. *murobalanos* : *muron,* perfume + *balanos,* fruit shaped like an acorn.]
myrrh (mûr) *n.* **1.** An aromatic gum resin obtained from several trees and shrubs of the genus *Commiphora,* of India, Arabia, and eastern Africa, used in perfume and incense. **2.** Sweet cicely (sense 2). [ME *myrr* < OE *myrrha* < Lat. < Gk. *murrha,* prob. of Semitic orig.]
myr·tle (mûr′tl) *n.* **1.** Any of several evergreen shrubs or trees of the genus *Myrtus,* esp. *M. communis,* an aromatic shrub native to the Mediterranean region and western Asia, having pink or white flowers and blue-black berries. **2.** Periwinkle[2]. [ME *mirtille* < OFr. < Med. Lat. *myrtillus,* dim. of Lat. *myrtus* < Gk. *murtos.*]
my·self (mī-sĕlf′) *pron.* **1.** That one identical with me. Used: **a.** Reflexively as the direct or indirect object of a verb or the object of a preposition: *hurt myself; give myself time; talk to myself.* **b.** For emphasis: *I myself am involved.* **c.** In an absolute construction: *Myself in debt, I could offer no assistance.* **2.** My normal or healthy condition or state: *I have not been myself.* [ME < OE *mē self.*]
Usage: In informal speech, reflexive pronouns like *myself* and *yourself* are often used for emphasis in compound subjects and objects: *Mr. Jones and myself are undecided. I would assign the new department to John or yourself.* According to the Usage Panel, both constructions are to be avoided in writing.
my·so·phil·i·a (mī′sō-fĭl′ē-ə) *n.* A pathological interest in and attraction to excreta. [Gk. *musos,* filth + -PHILIA.]
my·so·pho·bi·a (mī′sō-fō′bē-ə) *n.* A pathological fear of dirt or contamination. [Gk. *musos,* filth + -PHOBIA.]
mys·ta·gogue (mĭs′tə-gôg′, -gŏg′) *n.* **1.** One who prepared candidates for initiation into a mystery cult. **2.** One who holds or spreads mystical doctrines. [OFr. < Lat. *mystagogus* < Gk. *mustagōgos* : *mustēs,* an initiate + *agōgos,* leader < *agein,* to lead.] —**mys′ta·gog′ic** (-gŏj′ĭk) *adj.* —**mys′ta·go′gy** (-gō′jē) *n.*
mys·te·ri·ous (mĭ-stîr′ē-əs) *adj.* **1.** Of, pertaining to, or being a mystery: *mysterious and infinite truths.* **2.** Simultaneously arousing and eluding the desire to know, comprehend, or explain: *a mysterious visitor; mysterious conduct.* [OFr. *mysterieux* < *mystere,* mystery < Lat. *mysterium,* mystery.] —**mys·te′ri·ous·ly** *adv.* —**mys·te′ri·ous·ness** *n.*
mys·ter·y[1] (mĭs′tə-rē) *n., pl.* **-ies. 1. a.** Something that is not fully understood or that baffles or eludes the understanding. **b.** A mysterious character or quality: *a landscape of mystery and charm.* **c.** A fictional work dealing with a puzzling crime. **2.** A specialized skill or practice of a particular profession or group. **3.** *Theol.* A religious truth incomprehensible to the reason and knowable only through divine revelation. **4.** One of 15 incidents, such as the Annuciation or the Ascension, serving as a subject for meditation during the recitation of the rosary. **5.** One of the Christian sacraments, esp. the Eucharist. **6. a.** A religious cult practicing secret rites to which only initiates were admitted. **b.** A secret rite of such a cult. [ME < Lat. *mysterium* < Gk. *mustērion,* secret rite < *muein,* to be closed.]
mys·ter·y[2] (mĭs′tə-rē) *n., pl.* **-ies. 1.** *Archaic.* A trade or occupation. **2.** *Archaic.* A guild. **3.** A mystery play. [ME < LLat. *misterium,* alteration of Lat. *ministerium,* occupation < *minister,* servant.]
mystery play *n.* A medieval drama based on scriptural events esp. in the life of Christ. [< MYSTERY[2].]
mys·tic (mĭs′tĭk) *adj.* **1.** Of or pertaining to religious mysteries or occult rites and practices. **2.** Of or pertaining to mysticism or mystics. **3.** Inspiring a sense of mystery and wonder. **4.** Mystical (sense 1). **5. a.** Mysterious; strange. **b.** Enigmatic; obscure. —*n.* One who practices or believes in mysticism or a specified form of mysticism. [ME < Lat. *mysticus* < Gk. *mustikos* < *mustērion,* secret rite. —see MYSTERY[1].]
mys·ti·cal (mĭs′tĭ-kəl) *adj.* **1.** Of or having a spiritual reality or import that is not apparent to the intelligence or senses. **2.** Of, pertaining to, or stemming from direct communion with ultimate reality or God. **3.** Of or founded on subjective experience: *a mystical religion.* **4.** Mystic (sense 1). **5.** Unintelligible; cryptic. —**mys′ti·cal·ly** *adv.* —**mys′ti·cal·ness** *n.*
mys·ti·cete (mĭs′tĭ-sēt′) *n.* Any of several whales having symmetrical skulls, paired blowholes, and plates of whalebone instead of teeth. [NLat. *mysticetus* < Gk. *mustikētos,* a

kind of whale, prob. alteration of *ho mus to kētos,* the whale (called) the mouse.] **—mys'ti·ce'tous** (-sē'təs) *adj.*

mys·ti·cism (mĭs'tĭ-sĭz'əm) *n.* **1. a.** A spiritual discipline aiming at direct union or communion with ultimate reality or God through deep meditation or trancelike contemplation. **b.** The experience of such communion as described by mystics. **2.** A belief in the existence of realities beyond perceptual or intellectual apprehension that are central to being and directly accessible by subjective experience, such as by intuition. **3.** Vague and groundless speculation.

mys·ti·fi·ca·tion (mĭs'tə-fĭ-kā'shən) *n.* **1.** The act or an instance of mystifying. **2.** The fact or condition of being mystified. **3.** Something intended to mystify.

mys·ti·fy (mĭs'tə-fī') *tr.v.* **-fied, -fy·ing, -fies. 1.** To perplex; bewilder. **2.** To make obscure or mysterious. [Fr. *mystifier* < *mystère,* mystery < Lat. *mysterium.* —see MYSTERY[1].] **—mys'ti·fi'er** *n.* **—mys'ti·fy'ing·ly** *adv.*

mys·tique (mĭ-stēk') *n.* **1.** A body of mystical attitudes and beliefs associated with a particular person, thing, or idea: *the mystique of power.* **2.** The specialized qualities or skills necessary for an occupation or activity. [Fr. < *mystique,* mystic < Lat. *mysticus.* —see MYSTIC.]

myth (mĭth) *n.* **1. a.** A traditional story originating in a preliterate society, dealing with supernatural beings, ancestors, or heroes that serve as primordial types in a primitive view of the world. **b.** A body of such stories told among a given people; mythology. **c.** All such stories collectively. **2.** A real or fictional story, recurring theme, or character type that appeals to the consciousness of a people by embodying its cultural ideals or by giving expression to deep, commonly felt emotions. **3.** A fiction or half-truth, esp. one that forms part of the ideology of a society: *the myth of racial superiority.* **4.** A fictitious story, person, or thing: *"German artillery superiority on the Western Front was a myth"* (Leon Wolff). [Lat. *mythos* < Gk. *muthos.*]

myth·i·cal (mĭth'ĭ-kəl) also **myth·ic** (-ĭk) *adj.* **1.** Having the nature of a myth. **2.** Of or existing in myth: *the mythical unicorn.* **3.** Imaginary; fictitious. **—myth'i·cal·ly** *adv.*

myth·i·cize (mĭth'ĭ-sīz') *tr.v.* **-cized, -ciz·ing, -ciz·es. 1.** To turn (a person or event) into myth. **2.** To interpret as a myth or in terms of mythology.

myth·mak·er (mĭth'mā'kər) *n.* One who creates myths or mythical situations. **—myth'mak·ing** *n.*

my·thog·ra·pher (mĭ-thŏg'rə-fər) *n.* A recorder or narrator of myths. [Gk. *mythographos* : *muthos,* myth + *-graphos,* writer < *graphein,* to write.]

my·thog·ra·phy (mĭ-thŏg'rə-fē) *n.* **1.** The artistic representation of mythical subjects. **2.** A collection of myths with critical commentary.

my·thoi (mī'thoi', mĭth'oi') *n.* Plural of **mythos.**

myth·o·log·i·cal (mĭth'ə-lŏj'ĭ-kəl) also **myth·o·log·ic** (-ĭk) *adj.* **1.** Of, pertaining to, or celebrated in mythology. **2.** Fabulous; imaginary. **3.** Mythmaking: *the mythological proclivities of children.* **—myth'o·log'i·cal·ly** *adv.*

my·thol·o·gist (mĭ-thŏl'ə-jĭst) *n.* A student of mythology.

my·thol·o·gize (mĭ-thŏl'ə-jīz') *v.* **-gized, -giz·ing, -giz·es.** *—tr.* To convert into myth; mythicize. *—intr.* **1.** To construct or relate a myth. **2.** To interpret or write about myths or mythology. **—my·thol'o·giz'er** *n.*

my·thol·o·gy (mĭ-thŏl'ə-jē) *n., pl.* **-gies. 1. a.** A collection of myths about the origin and history of a people and their deities, ancestors, and heroes. **b.** A body of myths concerning some individual, event, or institution: *"A new mythology, essential to the . . . American funeral rite, has grown up"* (Jessica Mitford). **2.** The field of scholarship dealing with the systematic collection and study of myths. [Fr. *mythologie* < LLat. *mythologia* < Gk. *muthologia,* story-telling : *muthos,* story + *logos,* speech.]

myth·o·ma·ni·a (mĭth'ə-mā'nē-ə, -mān'yə) *n.* A compulsion to embroider the truth, exaggerate, or tell lies. [Gk. *muthos,* story + -MANIA.] **—myth'o·ma'ni·ac'** (-ăk') *n.*

myth·o·poe·ic also **myth·o·pe·ic** (mĭth'ə-pē'ĭk) *adj.* Productive of myths; mythmaking. [< Gk. *muthopoios,* composer of fiction < *mythopoiein,* to relate a story : *muthos,* story + *poiein,* to make.] **—myth'o·poe'ia** (-pē'ə), **myth'o·po·e'sis** (-pō-ē'sĭs) *n.*

my·thos (mī'thŏs', mĭth'ŏs') *n., pl.* **my·thoi** (mī'thoi', mĭth'oi'). **1.** Myth. **2.** Mythology. **3.** The pattern of basic values and attitudes of a people, characteristically transmitted through the arts. **4.** A deliberately fostered cult or aura. [Gk. *muthos.*]

myx– *pref.* Variant of **myxo-.**

myx·e·de·ma or **myx·oe·de·ma** (mĭk'sĭ-dē'mə) *n.* A disease caused by decreased activity of the thyroid gland in adults, and characterized by dry skin, swellings around the lips and nose, mental deterioration, and a subnormal basal metabolic rate. **—myx'e·dem'a·tous** (-dĕm'ə-təs, -dē'mə-), **myx'e·dem'ic** (-dĕm'ĭk) *adj.*

myxo– or **myx–** *pref.* Mucus: *myxocyte.* [NLat. < Gk. *muxa,* mucus, slime.]

myx·o·cyte (mĭk'sə-sīt') *n.* A large cell found in mucous tissue.

myx·oid (mĭk'soid') *adj.* Containing mucus; mucoid.

myx·o·ma (mĭk-sō'mə) *n., pl.* **-mas** or **-ma·ta** (-mə-tə). A benign tumor composed of connective tissue and mucous elements. **—myx·o'ma·tous** (-sō'mə-təs, -sŏm'ə-) *adj.*

myx·o·ma·to·sis (mĭk-sō'mə-tō'sĭs) *n., pl.* **-ses** (-sēz). **1.** *Pathol.* A condition characterized by the growth of many myxomas. **2.** A highly infectious, usually fatal, viral disease of rabbits characterized by many skin tumors similar to myxomas.

myx·o·my·cete (mĭk'sō-mī-sēt', -mī'sēt') *n.* A slime mold. [NLat. *Myxomycetes,* class name : MYXO- + Gk *mukētes,* pl. of *mukēs,* fungus.] **—myx'o·my·ce'tous** (-mī-sē'təs) *adj.*

N

Around 1000 B.C. the Phoenicians and other Semitic peoples began to use graphic signs to represent individual speech sounds instead of syllables or words. They used a symbol in the forms (1,2) to represent the sound of the consonant "n" and called it *nūn,* their word for "fish." The Greeks, adapting the Phoenician alphabet, retained the phonetic value of *nūn* but changed its shape and orientation (3,4,5) and altered its name to *nū.* The Romans borrowed the alphabet from the Greeks via the Etruscans and adapted it for monumental inscriptions. Monumental script (8) is the prototype of modern capital letters (11,12). Medieval scribes adapted the Roman capitals to being quickly written on paper, parchment, and vellum. These uncial and cursive minuscules (9,10) are the prototypes of modern lower-case letters, both written and printed (14,13).

n

n or **N** (ĕn) *n., pl.* **n's** or **N's.** **1.** The 14th letter of the modern English alphabet. **2.** Any of the speech sounds represented by the letter *n.* **3.** The 14th in a series.
N The symbol for the element nitrogen.
Na The symbol for the element sodium. [< NLat. *natrium* < NATRON.]
nab (năb) *tr.v.* **nabbed, nab·bing, nabs.** *Slang.* **1.** To seize (a fugitive or wrongdoer); arrest. **2.** To grab; snatch. [Perh. var. of dial. *nap,* to seize.] **—nab'ber** *n.*
na·bob (nā'bŏb') *n.* **1.** A governor in India under the Mogul Empire. **2.** A man of wealth and prominence. [Port. *nababo* < Hindi *nawwāb.* —see NAWAB.]
na·celle (nə-sĕl') *n.* A separate streamlined enclosure on an aircraft for sheltering the crew or cargo or housing an engine. [Fr., nacelle, small boat < LLat. *navicella,* dim. of Lat. *navis,* ship.]
na·cho (nä'chō') *n.* A small, often triangular piece of tortilla topped with cheese or chili-pepper sauce and broiled. [Poss. < Sp., flat-nosed.]
na·cre (nā'kər) *n.* Mother-of-pearl. [Fr. < OItal. *nacarra,* nacre, drum < Ar. *naqqārah,* drum.] **—na'cred** (-kərd), **na'cre·ous** (-krē-əs) *adj.*
Na-Den·e also **Na-Dé·né** (nä-dĕn'ē) *n.* A phylum of North American Indian languages spoken in western North America from Alaska to Mexico. [Of Athapascan orig.]
na·dir (nā'dər, -dîr') *n.* **1.** A point on the celestial sphere diametrically opposite the zenith. **2.** The lowest point: *the nadir of her fortunes.* [ME < Med. Lat. < Ar. *nadīr assamt,* opposite the zenith.]
nae (nā) *adv. Scot.* **1.** No. **2.** Not.
nag[1] (năg) *v.* **nagged, nag·ging, nags.** *—tr.* **1.** To annoy by constant scolding, complaining, or urging. **2.** To torment persistently, as with anxiety. *—intr.* **1.** To scold, complain, or find fault constantly: *nagging at his children.* **2.** To be a continuing source of anxiety or annoyance: *The half-remembered quotation nagged at his mind.* *—n.* A person who nags. [Prob. of Scand. orig.] **—nag'ger** *n.* **—nag'ging·ly** *adv.*
Usage: In some dialects of American English, *nag* is used with *on,* as in *He is always nagging on me.* In formal writing, however, the direct object construction should be used: *He is always nagging me.*
nag[2] (năg) *n.* **1.** A horse, esp.: **a.** An old or worn-out horse. **b.** *Slang.* A racehorse. **2.** *Archaic.* A small saddle horse or pony. [ME.]
na·ga·na also **n'ga·na** (nə-gä'nə) *n.* An often fatal disease of African livestock transmitted by the bite of the tsetse or other flies. [Zulu *u-nakane.*]
Na·hua·tl (nä'wät'l) *n., pl.* **Nahuatl** or **-tls.** **1. a.** A group of Mexican and Central American Indian tribes, including the Aztecs. **b.** A member of any of these tribes. **2.** The Uto-Aztecan language of the Nahuatl. [Sp. < Nahuatl *Nahuatl,* sing. of *Nahua,* the Nahuatl people.]
Na·hum (nā'həm, nā'əm) *n.* **1.** A Hebrew prophet of the 7th century B.C. who predicted the fall of Nineveh. **2.** See table at **Bible.** [Heb. *Naḥūm.*]
nai·ad (nā'əd, -ăd', nī'-) *n., pl.* **-a·des** (-ə-dēz') or **-ads.** **1.** *Gk. Myth.* One of the nymphs living in and presiding over brooks, springs, and fountains. **2.** The aquatic nymph of certain insects, such as the mayfly. **3.** A freshwater mussel of the family Unionidae. **4.** An aquatic plant of the genus *Naias.* [Gk. *naias, naiad-.*]
na·if or **na·ïf** (nä-ēf') *adj. & n.* Variants of **naive.**
nail (nāl) *n.* **1.** A slim, pointed piece of metal hammered into wood or other materials as a fastener. **2. a.** A fingernail or toenail. **b.** A claw or talon. **3.** Something resembling a nail in shape, sharpness, or use. **4.** A former measure of length for cloth, equal to 1/16 yard. *—tr.v.* **nailed, nail·ing, nails.** **1.** To fasten, join, or attach with or as if with a nail. **2.** To cover, enclose, or shut by fastening with nails: *nail up a window.* **3.** To keep fixed, motionless, or intent: *Fear nailed him to his seat.* **4.** *Informal.* To stop and seize; catch. **5.** *Informal.* To detect and expose: *nail a lie.* **6.** *Informal.* To strike or bring down, esp. with something shot or hurled: *nail a bird in flight.* **7.** *Baseball.* To put out (a base runner). ***—phrasal verb.*** **nail down.** **1.** To discover or establish conclusively: *nailed down the story.* **2.** To win. [ME < OE *nægl.*] **—nail'er** *n.*
nail·brush (nāl'brŭsh') *n.* A small brush with firm bristles used for washing the hands and cleaning the fingernails.
nail file *n.* A small, flat file used for shaping the fingernails.
nail fold *n.* A keratinous material overlapping the base of a fingernail or toenail as a circular fold; cuticle.
nail polish *n.* A clear or colored cosmetic lacquer applied to the fingernails or toenails.
nail scissors *pl.n. (used with a sing. or pl. verb).* Small scissors with short, curved blades for trimming and shaping fingernails or toenails.
nain·sook (nān'sŏŏk') *n.* A soft, light cotton material, often with a woven stripe. [Hindi *nainsukh,* pleasant : *nain,* eye (< Skt. *nayanam* < *nayati,* he leads) + *sukh,* pleasure (< Skt. *sukha-,* pleasant).]
nai·ra (nī'rə) *n.* See table at **currency.** [Alteration of *Nigeria.*]
na·ive or **na·ïve** (nä-ēv') also **na·if** or **na·ïf** (nä-ēf') *—adj.* **1. a.** Lacking worldliness and sophistication; artless. **b.** Simple and credulous as a child; ingenuous. **2.** Lacking critical ability or analytical insight; not subtle or learned. **3.** Not previously subjected to experiments: *testing naive mice.* *—n.* A naive person. [Fr. *naïve,* fem. of *naïf* < OFr. < Lat. *nativus,* natural < *nasci,* to be born.] **—na·ive'ly** *adv.* **—na·ive'ness** *n.*
Synonyms: *naive, simple, innocent, ingenuous, unsophisticated, natural, unaffected, guileless, artless.* These words signify lack of artifice and affectation. *Naive* generally implies lack of perception, or intuitive judgment, that is the basis of sound behavior in a practical world. *Simple* stresses utter lack of deviousness or deceit as well; it may imply a favorable quality or an unfavorable one, such as lack of good sense. *Innocent* primarily signifies freedom from guilt or sin; applied to an adult, it too may imply lack of practical wisdom. *Ingenuous* denotes childlike simplicity and directness; it connotes lack of ability to mask one's feelings, without implying a desire to dissemble. *Unsophisticated* specifically indicates absence of worldly wisdom; it is not as strong as the foregoing words in its implication of innate simplicity or innocence. *Natural* stresses spontaneity, the result of freedom from self-consciousness or other inhibitions—the state of "being oneself." *Unaffected* likewise signifies merely lack of pretense, without implying simplicity, naiveté, or even sophistication. *Guileless* signifies absence of deceit. *Artless* also stresses absence of deceit, but implies a detached quality of a person either actually or seemingly unconcerned about, or unaware of, the reaction of others.
na·ive·té or **na·ïve·té** (nä'ēv-tā', nä-ē'vĭ-tā') *n.* **1.** The state or quality of being naive. **2.** A naive statement or action. [Fr. < *naïf,* artless. —see NAIVE.]
na·ive·ty or **na·ïve·ty** (nä-ēv'tē, -ē'vĭ-tē) *n., pl.* **-ties.** Naiveté.
na·ked (nā'kĭd) *adj.* **1.** Without clothing on the body; nude. **2.** Without covering, esp. the usual covering: *a naked sword.* **3.** Devoid of vegetation, trees, or foliage; stripped or bare. **4.** Without addition, concealment, disguise, or embellishment: *the naked facts.* **5.** Devoid of something specified: *naked of all pretense.* **6.** Defenseless; vulnerable. **7.** *Bot.* **a.** Not encased in ovaries: *naked seeds.* **b.** Unprotected by scales: *naked buds.* **c.** Lacking a perianth: *naked flowers.* **d.** Without leaves or pubescence: *naked stalks.* **8.** Lacking protective covering such as scales, fur, feathers, or a shell. **9.** *Law.* Unsupported or uncorroborated by authority, evidence, or proof. [ME < OE *nacod.*] **—na'ked·ly** *adv.* **—na'ked·ness** *n.*
naked eye *n.* The eye unassisted by an optical instrument.
naked option *n.* A securities option sold by a trader who does not own the optioned stock.
na·led (nā'lĕd') *n.* A nonpersistent chemical, $C_4H_7O_4PBr_2Cl_2$, used as an insecticide against crop pests and mosquitoes. [Orig. unknown.]
nal·ox·one (năl'ək-sōn') *n.* A drug, $C_{19}H_{21}NO_4$, used in the form of its hydrochloride as an antagonist to narcotic drugs, such as morphine. [NAL(LYL) + (HYDR)OX(Y) + -ONE.]
nam·by-pam·by (năm'bē-păm'bē) *adj.* **1.** Insipid and sentimental. **2.** Lacking vigor or decisiveness; weak. *—n., pl.* **-bies.** Something or someone that is namby-pamby. [After *Namby-Pamby,* a satire on the poetry of Ambrose Philips by Henry Carey (d. 1743).]
name (nām) *n.* **1.** A word or words by which an entity is designated and distinguished from others. **2.** A word or words used to describe or evaluate, often disparagingly: *called his opponent names.* **3.** Representation or repute as opposed to reality: *a democracy in name, a police state in fact.* **4. a.** General reputation: *a bad name.* **b.** A distinguished reputation; renown. **5.** *Informal.* A famous or outstanding person: *a big name in state politics.* *—tr.v.* **named, nam·ing, names.** **1.** To give a name to. **2.** To identify by name. **3.** To mention, specify, or cite by name. **4.** To call by an epithet: *named them all cowards.* **5.** To nominate or appoint to a specific duty, office, or honor. **6.** To specify or fix: *name the time of our meeting.* *—adj. Informal.* Well-known by a name: *name brands.* ***—idioms.*** **in the name of.** By the authority of. **to (one's) name.** Belonging to one: *not a book to his name.* [ME < OE *nama.*] **—nam'a·ble, name'a·ble** *adj.* **—nam'er** *n.*
Synonyms: *name, designation, denomination, title, appellation, nickname, sobriquet, cognomen, moniker. Name* is the general term among these related words. A *designation* is a name given expressly to classify according to distinguishing characteristics. A *denomination* is also a categorizing name and is applied to persons or things, often religious groups or monetary units, having close relationship. A *title,* applied to persons, indicates specific rank or position, and generally connotes distinction and respect; applied to things, such as literary or musical works, it is a form of proper name. An *appellation* is a name, other than a proper one, that describes or characterizes, generally in pictorial terms, and that gains currency more through use than through a formal act of designation; "Great Emancipator" is thus an appellation for Lincoln. A *nickname* is an appellation with informal, sometimes humorous, overtones, such as "Honest Abe." A *sobriquet* is an especially humorous or picturesque nickname. *Cognomen* (in its informal sense) and *moniker* (a slang word) are rather loosely employed as the equivalent of proper name or, more often, of nickname.
name day *n.* **1.** The feast day of the saint after whom one is named. **2.** The day on which one is baptized.

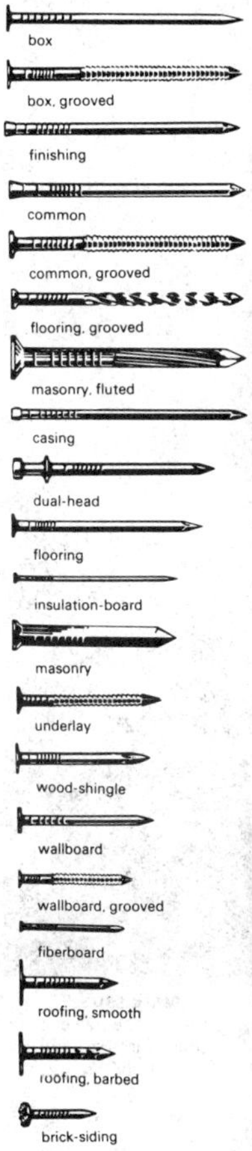

nail

name·less (nām′lĭs) *adj.* **1.** Having or bearing no name: *nameless stars.* **2.** Unknown by name; obscure: *the nameless dead.* **3.** Not designated by name; anonymous: *a nameless benefactor.* **4.** Incapable of being described; inexpressible: *nameless horror.* **—name′less·ly** *adv.* **—name′less·ness** *n.*
name·ly (nām′lē) *adv.* That is to say; specifically.
name·plate (nām′plāt′) *n.* **1.** A plate or plaque, as on an office door, inscribed with a name. **2.** A brand of merchandise.
name·sake (nām′sāk′) *n.* A person or thing named after another.
nan·a (năn′ə, nä′nə) *n.* **1.** A nurse or nursemaid. **2.** A grandmother. [Of baby-talk orig.]
nance (năns) *n. Slang.* An effeminate male, esp. a homosexual. [Short for the name *Nancy.*]
NAND (nănd) *n.* A machine logic circuit that produces an output inverse to that of an AND circuit. [N(OT) + AND.]
nan·din (năn′dĭn) *n.* An evergreen Asiatic shrub, *Nandina domestica,* having compound leaves and small white flowers that grow in a branching cluster and are followed by bright-red berries. [NLat. *Nandina,* genus name < J. *nanten,* southern sky < Chin. (Mandarin) *nan*[2] *tian*[1] : *nan*[2], south + *tian*[1], sky.]
nan·keen (năn-kēn′) *n.* **1. a.** A sturdy yellow or buff cotton cloth. **b. nankeens.** Trousers made of this cloth. **2. Nankeen.** A kind of Chinese porcelain with a blue-and-white pattern. [After *Nanjing* (Nanking), China.]
nan·ny also **nan·nie** (năn′ē) *n., pl.* **-nies.** *Chiefly Brit.* A children's nurse. [Alteration of NANA.]
nan·ny·ber·ry (năn′ē-bĕr′ē) *n.* The sheepberry.
nanny goat *n.* A female goat. [< *Nanny,* nickname for *Ann.*]
nano– *pref.* **1.** Extremely small: *nanoplankton.* **2.** One-billionth (10^{-9}): *nanosecond.* [Lat. *nanus,* dwarf < Gk. *nanos.*]
nan·o·gram (năn′ə-grăm′) *n.* One-billionth (10^{-9}) of a gram.
nan·o·me·ter (năn′ə-mē′tər) *n.* One-billionth (10^{-9}) of a meter.
na·no·plank·ton (nā′nə-plăngk′tən, năn′ə-) also **nan·no·plank·ton** (năn′ə-plăngk′tən) *n.* Aquatic animal and plant organisms of microscopic size comprising the smallest of the plankton.
nan·o·sec·ond (năn′ə-sĕk′ənd) *n.* One-billionth (10^{-9}) of a second.
Nan·sen bottle (năn′sən, nän′-) *n.* An ocean-water sampling bottle with spring-loaded valves at both ends that are closed at an appropriate depth by a messenger device sent down the wire connecting the bottle to the surface. [After Fridtjof *Nansen* (1861–1930).]
Nan·sen passport (năn′sən) *n.* A passport issued after World War I by the League of Nations to stateless persons. [After Fridtjof *Nansen* (1861–1930).]
nap[1] (năp) *n.* A brief sleep, often during the day. *—intr.v.* **napped, nap·ping, naps. 1.** To sleep for a brief period, often during the day; doze. **2.** To be unaware of imminent danger or trouble. [< ME *nappen,* to doze < OE *hnappian.*]
nap[2] (năp) *n.* A soft or fuzzy surface on fabric or leather. *—tr.v.* **napped, nap·ping, naps.** To form or raise a nap on (fabric or leather). [ME *noppe* < MDu.]
na·palm (nā′päm′) *n.* **1. a.** An aluminum soap of various fatty acids that when mixed with gasoline makes a firm jelly used in flame throwers and incendiary bombs. **b.** This jelly used in flame throwers and bombs. **2.** An incendiary mixture similar to napalm and made of polystyrene, benzene, and gasoline. *—tr.v.* **-palmed, -palm·ing, -palms.** To attack with napalm. [E. *naphthenate,* salt of naphthenic acid (< NAPHTHENE) + PALM(ITATE).]
nape (nāp, năp) *n.* The back of the neck. [ME.]
na·per·y (nā′pə-rē) *n.* Household linen, esp. table linen. [ME *naperie* < OFr. < *nape,* tablecloth < Lat. *mappa,* napkin.]
Naph·ta·li (năf′tə-lī′) *n.* A son of Jacob and legendary ancestor of one of the tribes of Israel. [Heb. *Naphtālī* < *niphtal,* he wrestled.]
naph·tha (năf′thə, năp′-) *n.* **1.** A colorless flammable liquid obtained from crude petroleum and used as a solvent and cleaning fluid and as a raw material for gasoline. **2.** Any of several volatile hydrocarbon liquids derived from coal tar and other materials and used as solvents. **3.** *Obs.* Petroleum. [Gk., liquid bitumen.]
naph·tha·lene (năf′thə-lēn′, năp′-) also **naph·tha·line** or **naph·tha·lin** (-lĭn) *n.* A white crystalline compound, $C_{10}H_8$, derived from coal tar or petroleum and used to manufacture dyes, moth repellents, explosives, and solvents. [NAPHTH(A) + AL(COHOL) + -ENE.] **—naph′tha·len′ic** (-lĕn′ĭk) *adj.*
naph·thene (năf′thēn′, năp′-) *n.* Any of several cycloparaffin hydrocarbons having the general formula C_nH_{2n}, found in various petroleums. [NAPHTH(A) + -ENE.] **—naph·then′ic** (-thĕn′ĭk) *adj.*
naph·thol (năf′thôl′, -thōl′, năp′-) also **naph·tol** (-tôl′, -tōl′) *n.* An organic compound, $C_{10}H_7OH$, occurring in two isomeric forms: **a.** *alpha-naphthol,* colorless or yellow prisms or powder used in dyes, organic synthesis, and perfumes. **b.** *beta-naphthol,* white lustrous leaflets or powder used in dyes, insecticides, and in the manufacture of rubber. [NAPHTH(ALENE) + -OL[2].]
Na·pier·i·an logarithm (nə-pîr′ē-ən, nā-) *n. Math.* A logarithm to the base *e* (=2.71828...). For example, $\ln 10 = \log_e 10 = 2.30258$. [After John *Napier* (1550–1617).]

Narcissus
Above: The flower
Below: Narcissus and Echo

Na·pi·er's bones (nā′pē-ərz) *n.* A data or logarithm table used to perform multiplication quickly. [After John *Napier* (1550–1617).]
na·pi·form (nā′pə-fôrm′) *adj.* Shaped like a turnip: *napiform roots.* [Lat. *napus,* turnip + -FORM.]
nap·kin (năp′kĭn) *n.* **1.** A piece of cloth or absorbent paper used at table to protect the clothes or wipe the lips and fingers. **2.** A cloth or towel. **3.** *Chiefly Brit.* A diaper. **4.** A sanitary napkin. [ME, dim. of *nape,* tablecloth < OFr. < Lat. *mappa,* napkin.]
na·po·le·on (nə-pō′lē-ən, -pōl′yən) *n.* **1.** A rectangular piece of pastry made with crisp, flaky layers filled with custard cream. **2.** A former 20-franc gold coin of France. [After *Napoleon* I (1769–1821).]
nappe (năp) *n.* **1.** A sheet of water flowing over a dam or similar structure. **2.** *Geol.* **a.** A recumbent anticline or fold of strata. **b.** A mass of rock moved from its original position by an anticline. **3.** *Math.* Either of the two parts into which a cone is divided by the vertex. [Fr., sheet < OFr., tablecloth < Lat. *mappa,* napkin.]
nap·py[1] (năp′ē) *adj.* **-pi·er, -pi·est. 1.** Having a nap; fuzzy. **2.** Kinky (sense 1).
nap·py[2] (năp′ē) *n., pl.* **-pies.** A round, shallow cooking or serving dish with a flat bottom and sloping sides. [Prob. < dial. *nap,* bowl < ME < OE *hnæp.*]
nap·py[3] (năp′ē) *n., pl.* **-pies.** *Chiefly Brit.* An infant's diaper. [Shortening and alteration of NAPKIN.]
narc or **nark** (närk) *n. Slang.* A law-enforcement officer who deals with narcotics violations. [Short for *narcotics agent.*]
nar·cism (När′sĭz′əm) *n.* Variant of **narcissism.**
nar·cis·si (när-sĭs′ī′, -sĭs′ē) *n.* A plural of **narcissus** (sense 2).
nar·cis·sism (när′sĭ-sĭz′əm) also **nar·cism** (när′sĭz′əm) *n.* **1.** Excessive love or admiration of oneself. **2.** *Psychoanal.* An arresting of development at or a regression to the infantile stage of development in which one's own body is the object of erotic interest. [After NARCISSUS.] **—nar′cis·sist** *n.* **—nar′cis·sis′tic** *adj.*
Nar·cis·sus (när-sĭs′əs) *n.* **1.** *Gk. Myth.* A youth who pined away in love for his own image in a pool of water and was transformed into the flower that bears his name. **2. narcissus,** *pl.* **-cis·sus·es** or **-cis·si** (-sĭs′ī′, -sĭs′ē). Any of several widely cultivated plants of the genus *Narcissus,* having narrow, grasslike leaves and usually white or yellow flowers characterized by a cup-shaped or trumpet-shaped central crown. [Lat. < Gk. *Narkissos.*]
narco– *pref.* **1.** Numbness; stupor; lethargy: *narcolepsy.* **2.** Narcotic drug: *narcoanalysis.* [Gk. *narko-* < *narkoun,* to numb < *narkē,* numbness.]
nar·co (när′kō) *n., pl.* **-cos.** *Slang.* A narc.
nar·co·a·nal·y·sis (när′kō-ə-năl′ĭ-sĭs) *n.* Psychoanalysis conducted while the patient is in a drug-induced drowsy state. **—nar′co·an′a·lyt′ic** (-ăn′ə-lĭt′ĭk) *adj.*
nar·co·lep·sy (när′kə-lĕp′sē) *n.* A condition characterized by sudden and uncontrollable attacks of deep sleep. **—nar′co·lep′tic** (-lĕp′tĭk) *adj. & n.*
nar·co·sis (när-kō′sĭs) *n.* **1.** Deep unconsciousness produced by a drug. **2.** *Biol.* Immobility in an organism caused by chemicals such as carbon dioxide. [Gk. *narkōsis,* a numbing < *narkoun,* to numb < *narkē,* numbness.]
nar·co·syn·the·sis (när′kō-sĭn′thĭ-sĭs) *n.* Narcoanalysis directed toward making the patient recall suppressed memories and emotional traumas for later interpretation.
nar·cot·ic (när-kŏt′ĭk) *n.* **1.** A drug that dulls the senses, induces sleep, and becomes addictive with prolonged use. **2.** Something that numbs, soothes, or induces a dreamlike state. *—adj.* **1.** Inducing sleep or stupor. **2.** Of or pertaining to narcotics, their effects, or their use. **3.** Of or pertaining to one addicted to a narcotic drug. [ME *narkotik* < Med. Lat. *narcoticum* < Gk. *narkōtikos,* numbing < *narkoun,* to numb < *narkē,* numbness.] **—nar·cot′i·cal·ly** *adv.*
nar·co·tism (när′kə-tĭz′əm) *n.* **1.** Addiction to narcotics such as opium, heroin, or morphine. **2.** Narcosis (sense 1). [NARCOT(IC) + -ISM.]
nar·co·tize (när′kə-tīz′) *tr.v.* **-tized, -tiz·ing, -tiz·es. 1.** To place under the influence of a narcotic. **2.** To put to sleep; lull. **3.** To dull; deaden. **—nar′co·ti·za′tion** *n.*
nard (närd) *n.* **1.** The spikenard (sense 1). **2.** A balm made from spikenard. **3.** Any of several plants of the genus *Valeriana* or related plants whose aromatic roots have been used in medicine. [ME *narde* < OFr. < Lat. *nardus* < Gk. *nardos.*]
nar·es (nâr′ēz) *n.* Plural of **naris.**
nar·ghi·le also **nar·gi·leh** (när′gə-lē′) *n.* An Oriental tobacco pipe in which smoke is drawn through a container of water by a flexible tube. [Fr. *narguilé* < Pers. *nārgīleh* < *nārgīl,* coconut.]
nar·is (nâr′ĭs) *n., pl.* **-es** (-ēz) An opening in the nasal cavity of a vertebrate; nostril. [Lat.] **—nar′i·al** (-ē-əl) *adj.*
nark[1] (närk) *n. Slang.* Variant of **narc.**
nark[2] (närk) *Chiefly Brit. Slang. —n.* An informer, esp. to the police. *—intr.v.* **narked, nark·ing, narks.** To be a nark. [Perh. < Romany *nāk,* nose.]
Nar·ra·gan·set also **Nar·ra·gan·sett** (năr′ə-găn′sĭt) *n., pl.* **Narraganset** or **-sets** also **Narragansett** or **-setts. 1. a.** A tribe of Indians that formerly inhabited the area of Rhode Island. **b.** A member of this tribe. **c.** The Algonquian lan-

guage of the Narraganset. **2.** A small, sturdy saddle horse of a breed developed in Rhode Island. [Alteration of Narraganset *Nanhigganeuck.*] **—Nar′ra·gan′set** *adj.*

nar·rate (năr′āt′, nă-rāt′) *v.* **-rat·ed, -rat·ing, -rates.** —*tr.* To give an account of; relate. —*intr.* **1.** To give an account or description. **2.** To supply a running commentary for a motion picture or other performance. [Lat. *narrare, narrat-* < *gnarus,* knowing.] **—nar′ra′tor, nar′rat′er** *n.*

nar·ra·tion (nă-rā′shən, nə-) *n.* **1. a.** The act or process of narrating. **b.** An instance of narrating. **2.** Something narrated. **—nar·ra′tion·al** *adj.*

nar·ra·tive (năr′ə-tĭv) *n.* **1.** A narrated account; story. **2.** The act, technique, or process of narrating. **3.** *Computer Sci.* Information included in a computer program that does not function in the program itself but that is used by the programmer to identify and correct individual machine instructions. —*adj.* **1.** Consisting of or characterized by the telling of a story: *narrative poetry.* **2.** Of or pertaining to narration: *narrative skill.* **—nar′ra·tive·ly** *adv.*

nar·row (năr′ō) *adj.* **-er, -est. 1.** Of small or slender width, esp. in comparison with length. **2.** Limited in area or scope; cramped. **3.** Lacking flexibility; rigid: *narrow opinions.* **4.** Barely sufficient; close: *a narrow margin of victory.* **5.** Painstakingly thorough or attentive; meticulous: *a narrow scrutiny.* **6.** *Regional.* Miserly; stingy. **7.** *Ling.* Tense[1] (sense 4). —*v.* **-rowed, -row·ing, -rows.** —*tr.* **1.** To make narrower; contract. **2.** To limit or restrict: *narrowed down the possibilities.* —*intr.* To become narrower; contract. —*n.* **1.** A narrow part, such as a narrow pass through mountains. **2. a. narrows** *(used with a sing. or pl. verb).* A narrow body of water connecting two larger ones. **b.** A narrow part of a river or ocean current. [ME *narwe* < OE *nearu.*] **—nar′row·ly** *adv.* **—nar′row·ness** *n.*

narrow gauge *n.* **1.** A distance between the rails of a railroad track that is less than the standard width of 56½ inches. **2.** A locomotive, car, or railway of a narrow gauge. **—nar′row-gauge′, nar′row-gauged′** *adj.*

nar·row-mind·ed (năr′ō-mīn′dĭd) *adj.* Lacking tolerance, breadth of view, or sympathy; petty. **—nar′row-mind′ed·ly** *adv.* **—nar′row-mind′ed·ness** *n.*

nar·thex (när′thĕks′) *n. Archit.* **1.** A portico or lobby of an early Christian or Byzantine church or basilica. **2.** An entrance hall leading to the nave of a church. [LGk. *narthēx* < Gk., box, giant fennel.]

nar·whal also **nar·wal** (när′wəl) or **nar·whale** (-hwāl′, -wāl′) *n.* An arctic aquatic mammal, *Monodon monoceros,* that has a spotted pelt and is characterized in the male by a long spirally twisted tusk that furnishes ivory. [Norw. or Dan. *narhval* < ON *nāhvalr* : *nār,* corpse + *hvalr,* whale (so called from its whitish color).]

nar·y (nâr′ē) *adj. Regional.* Not one; no. [Alteration of *ne'er a.*]

na·sal (nā′zəl) *adj.* **1.** Of or pertaining to the nose. **2.** Uttered by lowering the soft palate and occluding the mouth so that most of the air passes through the nose, as in sounding *m, n,* and *ng.* **3.** Characterized by or resembling a resonant sound produced through the nose: *a nasal whine.* —*n.* **1.** A nasal consonant. **2.** A nasal part or bone. **3.** The nosepiece of a helmet. [Med. Lat. *nasalis* < Lat. *nasus,* nose.] **—na·sal′i·ty** (nā-zăl′ĭ-tē) *n.* **—na′sal·ly** *adv.*

na·sal·ize (nā′zə-līz′) *tr. & intr.v.* **-ized, -iz·ing, -iz·es.** To make nasal or produce nasal sounds. **—na′sal·i·za′tion** *n.*

nas·cent (năs′ənt, nā′sənt) *adj.* Coming into existence; emerging. [Lat. *nascens, nascent-,* pr.part. of *nasci,* to be born.] **—nas′cence, nas′cen·cy** *n.*

nase·ber·ry (nāz′bĕr′ē) *n.* The sapodilla (sense 2). [Sp. *néspera* < Lat. *mespila,* medlar < Gk. *mespilē.*]

Nash·ville (năsh′vĭl′) *n.* **1.** Country music. **2.** The country music industry. [After *Nashville,* Tennessee.]

naso– *pref.* Nose: *nasopharynx.* [NLat. < Lat. *nasus,* nose.]

na·so·fron·tal (nā′zō-frŭn′təl) *adj.* Of or pertaining to the nasal and frontal bones.

na·so·phar·ynx (nā′zō-făr′ĭngks) *n.* The portion of the pharynx directly behind the nasal cavity and above the soft palate. **—na′so·pha·ryn′ge·al** (-fə-rĭn′jē-əl, -jəl, -făr′ən-jē′əl) *adj.*

nas·tic (năs′tĭk) *adj.* Of, pertaining to, or characterized by a tendency in plants to grow or change according to internal cell pressures as distinguished from environmental influences. [< Gk. *nastos,* pressed close < *nassein,* to press.]

nas·tur·tium (nə-stûr′shəm, nă-) *n.* **1.** Any of various plants of the genus *Tropaeolum,* having flowers with five broad petals that are usually yellow, orange, or red. **2.** A brilliant orange yellow. [Lat., a kind of cress : *nasus,* nose + **tortare,* freq. of *torquēre,* to twist (from its pungent smell).]

nas·ty (năs′tē) *adj.* **-ti·er, -ti·est. 1. a.** Disgustingly dirty; filthy. **b.** Physically repellent; foul. **2.** Morally offensive; indecent. **3.** Malicious; mean. **4.** Causing discomfort or trouble; unpleasant: *nasty weather.* **5.** Painful or dangerous; grave: *a nasty accident.* **6.** Difficult to solve or handle; exasperating. [ME *nasti,* of Scand. orig.] **—nas′ti·ly** *adv.* **—nas′ti·ness** *n.*

-nasty *suff.* Nastic response or change: *epinasty.* [G. *nastie* < Gk. *nastos,* pressed down < *nassein,* to press.]

na·tal (nāt′l) *adj.* **1.** Of, relating to, or accompanying birth: *natal injuries.* **2.** Of or pertaining to the time or place of one's birth. [Lat. *natalis* < *nasci,* to be born.]

na·tal·i·ty (nā-tăl′ĭ-tē, nə-) *n., pl.* **-ties.** Birth rate.

Na·tal plum (nə-tăl′, -täl′) *n.* A South African shrub, *Carissa grandiflora,* having forked spines, white flowers, and an edible scarlet berry. [After *Natal,* South Africa.]

na·tant (nāt′nt) *adj.* Floating or swimming in the water. [Lat. *natans, natant-,* pr.part. of *natare,* to swim.]

na·ta·tion (nā-tā′shən, nă-) *n.* The action or skill of swimming. [Lat. *natatio* < *natare,* to swim.]

na·ta·to·ri·a (nā′tə-tôr′ē-ə, -tōr′-, năt′ə-) *n.* A plural of **natatorium.**

na·ta·to·ri·al (nā′tə-tôr′ē-əl, -tōr′-, năt′ə-) also **na·ta·to·ry** (nā′tə-tôr′ē, -tōr′ē, năt′ə-) *adj.* Of, pertaining to, or adapted for swimming. [LLat. *natatorius* < Lat. *natare,* to swim.]

na·ta·to·ri·um (nā′tə-tôr′ē-əm, -tōr′-, năt′ə-) *n., pl.* **-to·ri·ums** or **-to·ri·a** (-tôr′ē-ə, -tōr′-). An indoor swimming pool. [LLat. < Lat. *natare,* to swim.]

na·ta·to·ry (nā′tə-tôr′ē, -tōr′ē, năt′ə-) *adj.* Variant of **natatorial.**

natch (năch) *adv. Slang.* Of course; naturally. [Shortening and alteration of NATURALLY.]

Natch·ez (năch′ĭz) *n., pl.* **Natchez. 1. a.** A tribe of Indians, formerly living in the area of Mississippi. **b.** A member of this tribe. **2.** The Muskhogean language of the Natchez. [Fr.] **—Natch′ez** *adj.*

na·tes (nā′tēz′) *pl.n.* The buttocks. [Lat., pl. of *natis,* buttock.]

nathe·less (nāth′lĭs) also **nath·less** (năth′-) *adv. Archaic.* Nevertheless; notwithstanding. [ME *nathles* < OE *nā ðē lǣs,* not less by that.]

Na·tick (nā′tĭk) *n.* A dialect of Massachuset. [Orig. unknown.]

na·tion (nā′shən) *n.* **1.** A people who share common customs, origins, history, and frequently language; nationality. **2.** A relatively large group of people organized under a single, usually independent government; country. **3.** The government of a sovereign state. **4. a.** A federation or tribe, esp. one composed of North American Indians. **b.** The territory occupied by such a federation or tribe. [ME *nacioun* < OFr. *nacion* < Lat. *natio* < *nascī,* to be born.]

Synonyms: *nation, state, commonwealth, country, land, people, race, folk. Nation* primarily signifies a political body rather than a physical territory—the citizens united under one independent government, without close regard for their origins; secondarily it denotes institutional ties, a community of economic and cultural interests. *State* even more specifically indicates political (governmental) organization, generally on a sovereign basis and pertaining to a well-defined area. *Commonwealth* is also used in a variety of political senses; to a much lesser degree it retains an earlier sense of union based on mutual interests. *Country,* in strict usage, is a geographic term signifying the territory of one nation, but it is often used in the extended sense of *nation. Land,* specifically, is a somewhat less precise geographic term for an area inhabited by one people, but not necessarily a single political unit. *People,* in this context, signifies a group united over a long period by common cultural and social ties, although not necessarily by racial and national bonds. *Race* refers to those recognizable physical traits, stemming from common ancestry, that succeeding generations have in common. *Folk,* somewhat narrower than *people,* has specific reference to distinctive cultural characteristics of long standing.

na·tion·al (năsh′ə-nəl, năsh′nəl) *adj.* **1.** Of, pertaining to, or belonging to a nation as an organized whole. **2.** Of or relating to nationality. **3.** Characteristic of or peculiar to the people of a nation. **4.** Of or maintained by the government of a nation. **5.** In the interest of one's own nation. **6.** Devoted to one's own nation or its interests; nationalistic. —*n.* **1.** A citizen of a particular nation. **2.** Often **nationals.** A contest or tournament involving participants from all parts of a nation. **—na′tion·al·ly** *adv.*

national bank *n.* **1.** A bank in a system of federally chartered privately owned banks in the United States, each required by law to be an investing member of its district Federal Reserve Bank and to be insured by the Federal Deposit Insurance Corporation. **2.** A bank associated with national finances and usually owned or controlled by a government.

national debt *n.* The total financial obligations of a national government.

national forest *n.* A large expanse of forest that is protected by a government and that may be harvested only under controlled conditions.

National Guard *n.* The military reserve units controlled by each state of the United States, equipped by the federal government and subject to the call of either the federal or the state government.

national income *n.* The total net value of all goods and services produced within a nation over a specified period of time, representing the sum of wages, profits, rents, interest, and pension payments to residents of the nation.

na·tion·al·ism (năsh′ə-nə-lĭz′əm, năsh′nə-) *n.* **1.** Devotion to the interests or culture of a particular nation. **2.** The belief that nations would benefit from acting independently rather

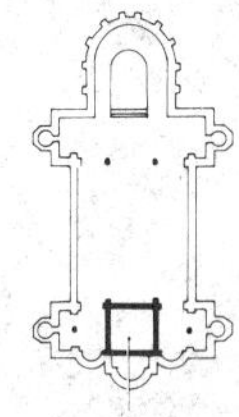

narthex
Plan of Troyes Cathedral, France

narwhal
Female (*left*), and male (*right*)

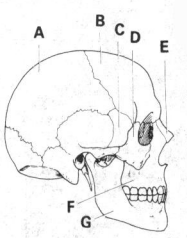

nasal
A. Parietal
B. Frontal
C. Sphenoid
D. Zygomatic
E. Nasal
F. Maxilla
G. Mandible

nasturtium

than collectively, emphasizing national rather than international goals. **3.** Aspirations for national independence in a country under foreign domination. **—na'tion·al·ist** *n.* **—na'tion·al·is'tic** *adj.* **—na'tion·al·is'ti·cal·ly** *adv.*

na·tion·al·i·ty (năsh'ə-năl'ĭ-tē, năsh-năl'-) *n., pl.* **-ties. 1.** The status of belonging to a particular nation by origin, birth, or naturalization. **2.** A people having common origins or traditions and often constituting a nation. **3.** Existence as a politically autonomous entity; national independence. **4.** National character. **5.** Nationalism.

na·tion·al·ize (năsh'ə-nə-līz', năsh'nə-) *tr.v.* **-ized, -iz·ing, -iz·es. 1.** To convert from private to governmental ownership and control: *nationalize an industry.* **2.** To make national in character. **—na'tion·al·i·za'tion** *n.* **—na'tion·al·iz'er** *n.*

national monument *n.* A natural landmark or a structure or site of historic interest set aside by a national government and maintained for enjoyment or study by the public.

national park *n.* A tract of land declared public property by a national government with a view to its preservation and development for purposes of recreation and culture.

national seashore *n.* A seacoast recreational area that is protected and maintained by the federal government.

National Socialism *n.* Nazism.

na·tion·hood (nā'shən-ho͝od') *n.* The state of being a nation.

nation-state (nā'shən-stāt') *n.* A type of political organization consisting of an autonomous state inhabited esp. by a predominantly homogeneous people.

na·tion·wide (nā'shən-wīd') *adj.* Throughout a whole nation.

na·tive (nā'tĭv) *adj.* **1.** Existing in or belonging to one by nature; innate: *native ability.* **2.** Being such by birth or origin: *a native Englishman.* **3.** Being one's own because of the place or circumstances of one's birth: *our native land.* **4.** Originally living, growing, or produced in a certain place; indigenous: *a plant native to Asia.* **5.** Of, belonging to, or characteristic of the original inhabitants of a particular place, esp. those of primitive culture. **6.** Occurring in nature pure or uncombined with other substances: *native copper.* **7.** Natural; unaffected: *native beauty.* **8.** *Archaic.* Closely related, as by birth or race. *—n.* **1.** One born in or connected with a place by birth. **2.** One of the original inhabitants or lifelong residents of a place as distinguished from immigrants or visitors. **3.** One belonging to a people of primitive culture originally occupying a country as distinguished from visitors or invaders. **4.** Something, esp. an animal or a plant, that originated in a particular place. [ME *natif* < OFr. < Lat. *nativus* < *nasci,* to be born.] **—na'tive·ly** *adv.* **—na'tive·ness** *n.*

Synonyms: *native, indigenous, endemic, aboriginal. Native,* said of people and cultural products, indicates birth or immediate origin in a specified place without eliminating the possibility of foreign origin through an earlier generation or historical period: *a native American. Indigenous* goes further in eliminating introduction from outside. *Indigenous* is used in this strict sense in the life sciences, but *native* is also commonly applied by biologists in the same sense. *Endemic,* said of plant life and diseases, emphasizes restriction to a limited area in which an organism especially thrives. *Aboriginal,* applied principally to people, describes the earliest-known inhabitants of a place.

Native American *n.* An American Indian.

Usage: The term *Indian* has always been a misnomer for the first inhabitants of the Western Hemisphere. Many now prefer the designation *Native American,* but usage varies according to tribe and region. In Canada and Alaska, in particular, *American Indian* is still preferred as suggesting a useful distinction from Eskimos. *Native American* has also been used to refer to Hawaiians of Polynesian descent.

na·tive-born (nā'tĭv-bôrn') *adj.* Belonging to a place by birth.

na·tiv·ism (nā'tĭ-vĭz'əm) *n.* **1.** A sociopolitical policy, esp. in the United States in the 19th century, favoring the interests of native inhabitants over those of immigrants. **2.** *Philos.* The doctrine that the mind produces ideas that are not derived from external sources. **3.** The re-establishment or perpetuation of native cultural traits, esp. in opposition to acculturation. **—na'tiv·ist** *n.* **—na'tiv·is'tic** *adj.*

nativity
Woodcut of the Nativity made in 1511 by Albrecht Dürer

na·tiv·i·ty (nə-tĭv'ĭ-tē, nā-) *n., pl.* **-ties. 1.** Birth, esp. the place, conditions, or circumstances of being born. **2. Nativity. a.** The birth of Jesus. **b.** A representation, such as a painting, of this. **c.** Christmas. **3.** A horoscope for the time of one's birth. [ME *nativite* < Lat. *nativitas* < *nativus,* born < *nasci,* to be born.]

na·tro·lite (nā'trə-līt') *n.* A colorless to white zeolite with composition $Na_2(Al_2Si_3O_{10})\cdot 2H_2O$. [G. *Natrolith* : *natron,* natron (< Fr.) + *-lith,* -lite.]

na·tron (nā'trŏn', -trən) *n.* A mineral of hydrous sodium carbonate, $Na_2CO_3\cdot 10H_2O$, often found crystallized with other salts. [Fr. < Sp. *natrón* < Ar. *naṭrūn,* niter < Gk. *nitron,* of Semitic orig.]

nat·ter (năt'ər) *intr.v.* **-tered, -ter·ing, -ters.** *Chiefly Brit.* To talk idly; chatter. [Imit.]

nat·ty (năt'ē) *adj.* **-ti·er, -ti·est.** *Informal.* Neat, trim, and smart; dapper. [Perh. var. of obs. *netty* < *net,* elegant < Fr. < OFr. —see NEAT.] **—nat'ti·ly** *adv.* **—nat'ti·ness** *n.*

nat·u·ral (năch'ər-əl, năch'rəl) *adj.* **1.** Present in or produced by nature. **2.** Of, pertaining to, or concerning nature: *natural science.* **3.** Conforming to the usual or ordinary course of nature: *a natural death.* **4. a.** Not acquired; inherent: *Love of power is natural to man.* **b.** Having a particular character by nature: *a natural leader.* **5.** Free from affectation or artificiality; spontaneous. **6.** Not altered, treated, or disguised: *natural coloring.* **7.** Faithfully representing nature or life. **8.** Expected and accepted: *Marriage seemed the natural and logical sequence to love.* **9.** Established by moral certainty or conviction: *natural rights.* **10.** In a primitive, uncivilized, or unregenerate state. **11. a.** Related by blood rather than adoption. **b.** Born of unwed parents; illegitimate: *a natural child.* **12.** *Math.* Of or pertaining to positive integers. **13.** *Mus.* **a.** Not sharped or flatted. **b.** Having no sharps or flats. **14.** Afro. *—n.* **1. a.** One having all the qualifications necessary for success: *a natural for the job.* **b.** One suited by nature for a certain purpose or function. **2.** An idiot; moron. **3.** *Mus.* **a.** The sign (♮) placed before a note to cancel a preceding sharp or flat. **b.** A note so affected. **4.** A yellowish gray to pale orange yellow. **5.** In certain card and dice games, a combination that wins immediately. **6.** An Afro hairstyle. [ME < Lat. *naturalis* < *natura,* nature < *nasci,* to be born.] **—nat'u·ral·ness** *n.*

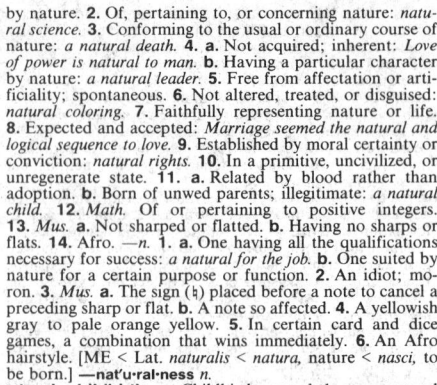

natural childbirth *n.* Childbirth regarded as a natural process involving little pain or stress and requiring preparatory training and medical supervision but no anesthesia or surgical aid.

natural food *n.* Food that contains no additives, as preservatives or artificial coloring or flavoring.

natural gas *n.* A mixture of hydrocarbon gases that occurs with petroleum deposits, principally methane together with varying quantities of ethane, propane, butane, and other gases, and that is used as a fuel and in the manufacture of organic compounds.

natural history *n.* The study of natural objects and organisms and their origins, evolution, interrelationships, and description.

nat·u·ral·ism (năch'ər-ə-lĭz'əm, năch'rə-) *n.* **1.** Conformity to nature; factual or realistic representation, esp. in art and literature. **2.** *Philos.* The system of thought holding that all phenomena can be explained in terms of natural causes and laws without attributing moral, spiritual, or supernatural significance to them. **3.** *Theol.* The doctrine that all religious truths are derived from nature and natural causes and not from revelation. **4.** Conduct or thought prompted by natural desires or instincts.

nat·u·ral·ist (năch'ər-ə-lĭst, năch'rə-) *n.* **1.** One versed in natural history, esp. in zoology or botany. **2.** One who believes in and follows the tenets of naturalism.

nat·u·ral·is·tic (năch'ər-ə-lĭs'tĭk, năch'rə-) *adj.* **1.** Imitating or producing the effect or appearance of nature. **2.** Of, pertaining to, or in accordance with the doctrines of naturalism. **—nat'u·ral·is'ti·cal·ly** *adv.*

nat·u·ral·ize (năch'ər-ə-līz', năch'rə-) *v.* **-ized, -iz·ing, -iz·es.** *—tr.* **1.** To grant full citizenship to (one of foreign birth). **2.** To adopt (something foreign) into general use. **3.** To adapt or acclimate (a plant, for example) to life in a new environment. **4.** To cause to conform to nature. *—intr.* To become naturalized or acclimated; adapt. **—nat'u·ral·i·za'tion** *n.*

natural language *n.* A human written or spoken language as opposed to machine language.

natural law *n.* A law or body of laws that derives from nature and is believed to be binding upon human actions apart from or in conjunction with laws established by human authority.

natural logarithm *n.* A Napierian logarithm.

nat·u·ral·ly (năch'ər-ə-lē, năch'rə-) *adv.* **1.** In a natural manner. **2.** By nature; inherently. **3.** Without a doubt; surely.

natural number *n.* *Math.* One of the set of positive whole numbers; positive integer.

natural philosophy *n.* The study of nature and the physical universe. **—natural philosopher** *n.*

natural resource *n.* A material source of wealth, such as timber, fresh water, or a mineral deposit, that occurs in a natural state.

natural science *n.* A science, such as biology, chemistry, or physics, based chiefly on objective quantitative hypotheses.

natural selection *n.* The principle that individuals possessing characteristics advantageous for survival in a specific environment constitute an increasing proportion of their species in that environment with each succeeding generation.

natural theology *n.* A theology holding that knowledge of God may be acquired without recourse to revelation.

na·ture (nā'chər) *n.* **1.** The material world and its phenomena. **2.** The forces and processes that produce and control all the phenomena of the material world: *the laws of nature.* **3.** The world of living things and the outdoors: *the beauties of nature.* **4.** A primitive state of existence, untouched and uninfluenced by civilization or artificiality. **5.** *Theol.* Man's natural state as distinguished from the state of grace. **6.** Kind; type: *something of that nature.* **7.** The essential characteristics and qualities of a person or a thing: *the nature of the problem.* **8.** The fundamental character or disposition of an individual; temperament: *had a sweet nature.*

9. The natural or real aspect of a person, place, or thing. **10.** The processes and functions of the body: *the call of nature.* [ME, essential properties of a thing < Lat. *natura* < *nasci,* to be born.]
nature trail *n.* A trail, as through woods or by a seashore, usually with natural features labeled esp. for study.
na·tur·op·a·thy (nā'chə-rŏp'ə-thē) *n.* A system of therapy that relies exclusively on natural remedies, such as sunlight supplemented with diet and massage, to treat the sick. [NATUR(E) + -PATHY.] **—na'tur·o·path'** (nā'chər-ə-păth', nə-cho͝or'-) *n.* **—na·tur'o·path'ic** (nə-cho͝or'ə-păth'ĭk) *adj.*
Nau·ga·hyde (nô'gə-hīd'). A trademark for fabrics coated with vinyl.
naught also **nought** (nôt) *—n.* **1.** Nothing: *All her work was for naught.* **2.** The figure 0; cipher; zero. *—adj.* Of no value; worthless. *—adv.* Not in the least. [ME *nauht* < OE *nāwiht* : *nā,* no + *wiht,* thing.]
naugh·ty (nô'tē) *adj.* **-ti·er, -ti·est. 1.** Behaving disobediently or mischievously. **2.** Indecent; improper: *a naughty wink.* **3.** *Archaic.* Wicked; immoral. [< ME *noughti,* wicked < *nought,* evil < OE *nāwiht,* nothing, evil. —see NAUGHT.] **—naugh'ti·ly** *adv.* **—naugh'ti·ness** *n.*
nau·pli·us (nô'plē-əs) *n., pl.* **-pli·i** (-plē-ī'). The microscopic free-swimming first stage of the larva of certain crustaceans. [Lat., a kind of shellfish < Gk. *nauplios.*]
nau·se·a (nô'zē-ə, -zhə, -sē-ə, -shə) *n.* **1.** A stomach disturbance characterized by a feeling of the need to vomit. **2.** Strong aversion; disgust. [Lat. < Gk. *nausia,* seasickness < *naus,* ship.]
nau·se·ate (nô'zē-āt', -zhē-, -sē-, -shē-) *intr. & tr.v.* **-at·ed, -at·ing, -ates. 1.** To feel or cause to feel nausea. **2.** To feel or cause to feel loathing or disgust. —See Usage note at **nauseous.** [Lat. *nauseare, nauseat-* < *nausea,* nausea.] **—nau'se·a'tion** *n.*
nau·seous (nô'shəs, -zē-əs) *adj.* **1.** Causing nausea; sickening. **2.** Affected with nausea. **—nau'seous·ly** *adv.*
Usage: Traditionally, *nauseous* means "causing nausea"; *nauseated* means "suffering from nausea." The use of *nauseous* in the sense of *nauseated* is unacceptable to a great majority of the Usage Panel and should be avoided in writing.
nautch (nôch) *n.* A dance form of northern India for a single girl dancer accompanied by several musicians and sometimes by a singer. [Hindi *nāc* < Prakrit *nacca,* dance < Skt. *nṛtyam* < *nṛyati,* he dances.]
nau·ti·cal (nô'tĭ-kəl) *adj.* Of, pertaining to, or characteristic of ships, shipping, seamen, or navigation on a body of water. [Lat. *nauticus* < Gk. *nautikos* < *nautēs,* sailor < *naus,* ship.] **—nau'ti·cal·ly** *adv.*
Synonyms: *nautical, naval. Nautical* is a general term pertaining to sailors, ships, and navigation. *Naval,* once synonymous with *nautical,* now pertains specifically to the personnel and ships of a navy or military sea force.
nautical mile *n.* A unit of length used in sea and air navigation, based on the length of one minute of arc of a great circle, esp. an international and U.S. unit equal to 1,852 meters, or about 6,076 feet.
nau·ti·li (nôt'l-ī') *n.* A plural of **nautilus.**
nau·ti·loid (nôt'l-oid') *n.* A mollusk of the subclass Nautiloidea, which includes the nautiluses and numerous extinct species known only as fossils. [< NLat. *Nautiloidea,* subclass name < Lat. *nautilus,* nautilus.]
nau·ti·lus (nôt'l-əs) *n., pl.* **-ti·lus·es** or **-ti·li** (-l-ī'). **1.** A mollusk of the genus *Nautilus,* found in the Indian and Pacific oceans and having a spiral shell with a series of air-filled chambers. **2.** The chambered nautilus. [Lat. < Gk. *nautilos,* nautilus, sailor < *nautēs,* sailor < *naus,* ship.]
Nav·a·jo also **Nav·a·ho** (năv'ə-hō', nä'və-) *n., pl.* **Navajo, -jos,** or **-joes** also **Navaho, -hos,** or **-hoes. 1.** A group of Indians occupying an extensive reservation in parts of New Mexico, Arizona, and Utah. **2.** A member of the Navajo. **3.** The Athapascan language of the Navajo. [Mex. Sp. *(Apache de) Navajo,* (Apache of) Navajo < Tewa *Navahu,* the name of a Tewa pueblo.] **—Nav'a·jo** *adj.*
na·val (nā'vəl) *adj.* **1.** Of or pertaining to ships or shipping. **2.** Of or pertaining to a navy. **3.** Having a navy: *a great naval power.* [Lat. *navalis* < *navis,* ship.]
naval architect *n.* An architect who designs ships.
naval stores *pl.n.* Products such as turpentine or pitch, originally used to caulk the seams of wooden ships.
nav·ar (năv'är') *n.* A method of air navigation in which traffic in a pilot's vicinity is observed by ground radar and relayed to the pilot's radarscope. [NAV(IGATIONAL) + (RADAR).]
nave[1] (nāv) *n.* The central part of a church, extending from the narthex to the chancel and flanked by aisles. [Med. Lat. *navis* < Lat., ship.]
nave[2] (nāv) *n.* The hub of a wheel. [ME < OE *nafa.*]
na·vel (nā'vəl) *n.* **1.** The mark on the abdomen of mammals where the umbilical cord was attached during gestation. **2.** A central point; middle. [ME < OE *nafela.*]
navel orange *n.* A sweet, usually seedless orange having at its apex a navellike formation enclosing an underdeveloped fruit.
na·vel·wort (nā'vəl-wûrt', -wôrt') *n.* **1.** The pennywort (sense 2). **2.** A plant of the genus *Omphalodes,* having one-sided clusters of usually blue flowers. [From the navellike depression on its leaves.]
na·vic·u·lar (nə-vĭk'yə-lər) *n.* **1.** A bone of the wrist shaped like a comma. **2.** The concave bone in front of the anklebone on the instep of the foot. *—adj.* Shaped like a boat. [LLat. *navicularis* < Lat. *navicula,* dim. of *navis,* ship.]
nav·i·ga·ble (năv'ĭ-gə-bəl) *adj.* **1.** Sufficiently deep or wide to provide passage for vessels. **2.** Capable of being steered. Used of vessels or aircraft. **—nav'i·ga·bil'i·ty, nav'i·ga·ble·ness** *n.* **—nav'i·ga·bly** *adv.*
nav·i·gate (năv'ĭ-gāt') *v.* **-gat·ed, -gat·ing, -gates.** *—tr.* **1.** To plan, record, and control the course and position of (a ship or aircraft). **2.** To follow a planned course on, across, or through: *navigate a stream.* *—intr.* **1.** To control the course of a ship or aircraft. **2.** To voyage over water in a boat or ship; sail. **3.** *Informal.* **a.** To make one's way. **b.** To walk: *too unsteady on his legs to navigate.* [Lat. *navigare, navigat-* : *navis,* ship + *agere,* to direct.]
nav·i·ga·tion (năv'ĭ-gā'shən) *n.* **1.** The theory and practice of navigating, esp. the charting of a course for a ship or aircraft. **2.** Travel or traffic by vessels, esp. commercial shipping. **—nav'i·ga'tion·al** *adj.*
nav·i·ga·tor (năv'ĭ-gā'tər) *n.* **1.** One who navigates. **2.** A device that directs the course of an aircraft or missile.
nav·vy (năv'ē) *n., pl.* **-vies.** *Chiefly Brit.* A laborer, esp. one employed in construction or excavation projects. [Alteration of NAVIGATOR, canal laborer (obs.).]
na·vy (nā'vē) *n., pl.* **-vies. 1.** All of a nation's warships. **2.** Often **Navy.** A nation's entire military organization for sea warfare and defense, including vessels, personnel, and shore establishments. **3.** A group of ships; fleet. **4.** Navy blue. [ME *navie* < OFr. < VLat. **navia* < Lat. *navis,* ship.]
navy bean *n.* Any of several varieties of the kidney bean, cultivated for their nutritious white seeds. [From its former use as a standard provision of the U.S. Navy.]
navy blue *n.* A dark grayish blue. [From the color of the British naval uniform.]
Navy Cross *n.* A decoration awarded by the U.S. Navy for exceptional heroism in action.
navy yard *n.* A dockyard for the construction, repair, equipping, or docking of naval ships.
na·wab (nə-wŏb') *n.* A governor or ruler in India under the Mogul empire. [Hindi *nawwāb* < Ar. *nuwwāb,* pl. of *na'ib,* deputy.]
nay (nā) *adv.* **1.** No: *All but four Democrats voted nay.* **2.** And moreover: *He was ill-favored, nay, hideous.* *—n.* **1.** A denial or refusal. **2.** A negative vote or voter. [ME < ON *nei* : *ne,* not + *ei,* ever.]
Naz·a·rene (năz'ə-rēn', năz'ə-rēn') *n.* **1. a.** A native or inhabitant of Nazareth. **b.** Jesus. **2.** A member of a sect of early Christians of Jewish origin who retained many of the prescribed Jewish observances. **3.** A member of an American Protestant denomination, the Church of the Nazarene, that follows many of the doctrines of early Methodism. [ME < LLat. *Nazarenus* < Gk. *Nazarēnos* < *Nazaret,* Nazareth.]
Na·zi (nät'sē, năt'-) *n., pl.* **-zis. 1.** A member of the National Socialist German Workers' Party, founded in Germany in 1919 and brought to power in 1933 under Adolf Hitler. **2.** Often **nazi.** An adherent or advocate of policies characteristic of Nazism; fascist. *—adj.* Of, relating to, controlled by, or typical of Nazis. [G., contraction of *Nationalsozialist,* National Socialist.] **—Na'zi·fi·ca'tion** (-sə-fĭ-kā'shən) *n.* **—Na'zi·fy'** (-sə-fī') *v.* **(-fied, -fy·ing, -fies).**
Na·zism (nät'sĭz'əm, năt'-) also **Na·zi·ism** (-sē-ĭz'əm) *n.* The ideology and practice of the Nazis, esp. the policy of state control of the economy, racist nationalism, and national expansion.
Nb The symbol for the element niobium.
Nd The symbol for the element neodymium.
Ne The symbol for the element neon.
Ne·an·der·thal (nē-ăn'dər-thôl', -tôl', nā-än'dər-täl') *n.* **1.** Neanderthal man. **2.** *Slang.* A crude or boorish person. *—adj.* **1.** Of, pertaining to, or resembling Neanderthal man. **2.** *Slang.* Crude or boorish. **—Ne·an'der·thal'oid'** (-thô'loid', -tô'-, -tä'-) *adj.*
Neanderthal man *n.* An extinct species or race of man, *Homo neanderthalensis,* living during the late Pleistocene age in the Old World and associated with Middle Paleolithic tools. [After *Neanderthal,* a valley near Düsseldorf, West Germany.]
ne·an·throp·ic (nē'ən-thrŏp'ĭk) *adj.* Of or pertaining to members of the extant species *Homo sapiens* as compared with other, now extinct species of *Homo.* [NE(O)- + ANTHROP(O)- + -IC.]
Ne·a·pol·i·tan (nē'ə-pŏl'ĭ-tən) *adj.* Of, belonging to, or characteristic of Naples, Italy. *—n.* A native or resident of Naples, Italy.
Neapolitan ice cream *n.* Ice cream in brick form, with layers of different colors and flavors.
neap tide (nēp) *n.* A tide of lowest range, occurring when the sun and moon are in quadrature. [ME **neep* < OE *nēp(flōd),* neap (tide).]
near (nîr) *adv.* **-er, -est. 1.** To, at, or within a short distance or interval in space or time. **2.** Almost; nearly: *near exhausted.* **3.** With or in a close relationship. *—adj.* **-er, -est. 1.** Close in time, space, position, or degree: *near equals.*

nautch

nautilus

nave[1]

2. Closely related by kinship or association; intimate. **3.** Failing or succeeding by a very small margin: *a near miss.* **4.** Closely corresponding to or resembling an original: *a near likeness.* **5. a.** Closer of two or more. **b.** On the left side of a vehicle or draft team. **6.** Short and direct: *the nearest route to town.* **7.** Stingy; parsimonious. *—prep.* Close to: *an inn near London.* *—v.* **neared, near·ing, nears.** *—tr.* To come close or closer to. *—intr.* To draw near or nearer; approach. [ME *ner* < OE *nēar,* comp. adv. of *nēah,* near.] **—near'ness** *n.*

near beer *n.* A malt liquor that does not contain enough alcohol to be considered an alcoholic beverage.

near·by (nîr'bī') *adj.* Located a short distance away; close at hand. *—adv.* Not far away.

Ne·arc·tic (nē-ärk'tĭk, -är'tĭk) *adj.* Of or designating the zoogeographic region that includes the Arctic and Temperate areas of North America and Greenland. [NE(O)- + ARCTIC.]

near·ly (nîr'lē) *adv.* **1.** Almost but not quite. **2.** Closely; intimately: *a matter nearly affecting our interests.*

near·sight·ed (nîr'sī'tĭd) *adj.* Unable to see distant objects clearly; myopic. **—near'sight'ed·ly** *adv.* **—near'sight'ed·ness** *n.*

neat¹ (nēt) *adj.* **-er, -est. 1.** Orderly and clean; tidy. **2.** Orderly and precise in procedure; systematic. **3.** Marked by ingenuity and skill; adroit: *a neat turn of phrase.* **4.** Not diluted or mixed with other substances: *neat whiskey.* **5.** Left after all deductions; net: *neat profit.* **6.** *Slang.* Wonderful; terrific: *That was a neat party.* *—adv.* Without dilution; straight: *takes his Scotch neat.* [OFr. *net* < Lat. *nitidus,* elegant < *nitēre,* to shine.] **—neat'ly** *adv.* **—neat'ness** *n.*

Synonyms: *neat, tidy, trim. Neat* primarily denotes simplicity, close attention to detail, and cleanliness. *Tidy* emphasizes precise arrangement and consequent good order. *Trim* stresses especially pleasing or smart appearance, resulting from neatness, tidiness, sense of proportion, and deftness of design.

neckerchief

neat² (nēt) *n., pl.* **neat.** *Archaic.* A domestic bovine animal. [ME *net* < OE *nēat.*]

neat·en (nēt'n) *tr.v.* **-ened, -en·ing, -ens.** To put in order; make neat.

neath or **'neath** (nēth) *prep.* Beneath.

neat·herd (nēt'hûrd') *n. Archaic.* A cowherd.

neat's-foot oil (nēts'fo͝ot') *n.* A light yellow oil obtained from the feet and shinbones of cattle, used chiefly to dress leather.

neb (nĕb) *n.* **1. a.** A beak of a bird. **b.** A nose; snout. **2.** A projecting part, esp. a nib. [ME < OE.]

neb·bish (nĕb'ĭsh, -ĭKH) *n.* A weak-willed and timid person. [Yiddish *nebech.*]

neb·u·la (nĕb'yə-lə) *n., pl.* **-lae** (-lē') or **-las. 1.** *Astron.* **a.** A diffuse mass of interstellar dust or gas or both, visible as luminous patches or areas of darkness depending on the way the mass absorbs or reflects incident radiation. **b.** Such a mass that absorbs ultraviolet radiation from stars and reemits it as visible light. **c.** Such a mass that absorbs all incident radiation without re-emission. **d.** Such a mass that reflects visible radiation. **e.** A galactic nebula. **2.** *Pathol.* **a.** A cloudy spot on the cornea. **b.** Cloudiness in the urine. **3.** A liquid medication applied by spraying. [Lat., cloud.] **—neb'u·lar** *adj.*

nebular hypothesis *n.* A theory of the origin of the solar system according to which a rotating nebula cooled and contracted, throwing off rings of matter that contracted into the planets and their moons, while the great mass of the condensing nebula became the sun.

neb·u·lize (nĕb'yə-līz') *tr.v.* **-lized, -liz·ing, -liz·es. 1.** To convert (a liquid) to a fine spray; atomize. **2.** To treat with a medicated spray. [< NEBULA.] **—neb'u·li·za'tion** *n.* **—neb'u·liz'er** *n.*

neb·u·los·i·ty (nĕb'yə-lŏs'ĭ-tē) *n., pl.* **-ties. 1.** The quality or condition of being nebulous. **2. a.** A nebula. **b.** A mass of material constituting a nebula.

neb·u·lous (nĕb'yə-ləs) *adj.* **1.** Cloudy, misty, or hazy. **2.** Lacking definite form or limits; vague. **3.** Of, pertaining to, or characteristic of a nebula. [Lat. *nebulosus* < *nebula,* cloud.] **—neb'u·lous·ly** *adv.* **—neb'u·lous·ness** *n.*

nec·es·sar·i·ly (nĕs'ĭ-sâr'ə-lē) *adv.* Of necessity; inevitably.

nec·es·sar·y (nĕs'ĭ-sĕr'ē) *adj.* **1.** Absolutely essential; indispensable. **2.** Needed to achieve a certain result or effect; requisite: *the necessary tools.* **3. a.** Unavoidably determined by prior conditions or circumstances; inevitable: *the necessary results of overindulgence.* **b.** Logically inevitable. **4.** Required by obligation, compulsion, or convention: *made the necessary apologies.* *—n., pl.* **-ies.** Something that is indispensable or necessary. [ME *necessarie* < Lat. *necessarius* < *necesse.*]

Synonyms: *necessary, essential, vital, indispensable, requisite, required, prerequisite, necessitous, needy, needful. Necessary* denotes that which fills an urgent need, but not invariably an all-compelling need. The stronger *essential* and *vital* are applied to that without which something, by its nature, cannot exist, or without which it cannot exist or continue in normal condition or form. *Indispensable* even more specifically denotes that which cannot be sacrificed; frequently it is applied to part of a whole. *Requisite* and *required* are more specific and less powerful terms; they usually signify a need that complements other needs and is imposed externally rather than by the nature of the subject itself. *Prerequisite* adds the dimension of need that must be met beforehand; it specifies a prior condition that determines whether something desired is to follow. *Necessitous* and *needy* signify want in the subjective sense of privation, and are applied to persons in a condition of great want. *Needful* expresses want much less urgently than any of the foregoing.

necessary condition *n.* **1.** *Logic.* A proposition whose falsity assures the falsity of another proposition derived from it. **2.** A condition that is an essential antecedent of another.

ne·ces·si·tar·i·an·ism (nə-sĕs'ĭ-târ'ē-ə-nĭz'əm) *n.* The doctrine that events are inevitably determined by preceding causes. **—ne·ces'si·tar'i·an** *adj. & n.*

ne·ces·si·tate (nə-sĕs'ĭ-tāt') *tr.v.* **-tat·ed, -tat·ing, -tates. 1.** To make necessary or unavoidable. **2.** To require or compel. [Med. Lat. *necessitare, necessitat-* < Lat. *necessitas,* necessity < *necesse,* necessary.] **—ne·ces'si·ta'tion** *n.* **—ne·ces'si·ta'tive** *adj.*

ne·ces·si·tous (nə-sĕs'ĭ-təs) *adj.* **1.** Needy; indigent. **2.** Compelling; urgent. [Fr. *nécessiteux* < OFr. *necessite,* necessity.] **—ne·ces'si·tous·ly** *adv.*

ne·ces·si·ty (nə-sĕs'ĭ-tē) *n., pl.* **-ties. 1. a.** The condition or quality of being necessary. **b.** Something that is necessary. **2. a.** Something that is dictated by invariable physical laws. **b.** The force exerted by circumstance. **3.** The state or fact of being in need. **4.** Pressing or urgent need, esp. that arising from poverty. **—*idiom.* of necessity.** As an inevitable consequence; necessarily. [ME *necessite* < OFr. < Lat. *necessitas* < *necesse,* necessary.]

neck (nĕk) *n.* **1.** The part of the body joining the head to the trunk. **2.** The part of a garment around or near the neck. **3.** *Anat.* A relatively narrow portion of a structure, as of a bone or organ, that joins its parts. **4.** A relatively narrow elongation, projection, or connecting part: *a neck of land; the neck of a flask.* **5.** The narrow part along which the strings of a stringed instrument extend to the pegs. **6.** *Geol.* Solidified lava filling the vent of an extinct volcano. **7.** The siphon of a bivalve mollusk, such as a clam. **8.** A narrow margin: *won by a neck.* *—v.* **necked, neck·ing, necks.** *—intr. Slang.* To kiss and caress. *—tr.* To strangle or decapitate (a fowl). **—*idioms.* neck and neck.** Even in a race or contest. **stick (one's) neck out.** To risk criticism, trouble, or danger unnecessarily. [ME *nekke* < OE *hnecca.*]

neck·er·chief (nĕk'ər-chĭf, -chēf') *n.* A kerchief worn around the neck.

neck·ing (nĕk'ĭng) *n.* **1.** A molding between the upper part of a column and the projecting part of the capital. **2.** The act or practice of amorously kissing and petting.

neck·lace (nĕk'lĭs) *n.* An ornament worn around the neck.

neck·line (nĕk'līn') *n.* The line formed by the edge of a garment at or near the neck.

neck·tie (nĕk'tī') *n.* A long, narrow band of fabric worn around the neck and tied in a knot or bow close to the throat.

neck·wear (nĕk'wâr') *n.* Articles, such as neckties or scarfs, worn around the neck.

necro– or **necr–** *pref.* **1.** Dead body; corpse: *necrophilia.* **2.** Death: *necrobiosis.* [NLat. < Gk. *nekros,* corpse.]

nec·ro·bi·o·sis (nĕk'rō-bī-ō'sĭs) *n.* The natural degeneration and death of cells and tissues as opposed to death from injury or disease and distinguished from death of the entire organism. **—nec'ro·bi·ot'ic** (-ŏt'ĭk) *adj.*

ne·crol·o·gy (nə-krŏl'ə-jē, nĕ-) *n., pl.* **-gies. 1.** A list of people who have died, esp. in the recent past. **2.** An obituary. **—nec'ro·log'ic** (nĕk'rə-lŏj'ĭk), **nec'ro·log'i·cal** *adj.* **—ne·crol'o·gist** *n.*

nec·ro·man·cy (nĕk'rə-măn'sē) *n.* **1.** The practice of communicating with the spirits of the dead in order to predict the future. **2.** Black magic; sorcery. **3.** Magical qualities. [Alteration of ME *nigromancie* < OFr. *nigremancie* < Med. Lat. *nigromantia,* alteration of *necromantia* < Gk. *nekromanteia* : *nekros,* corpse + *manteia,* divination. —see -MANCY.] **—nec'ro·man'cer** *n.* **—nec'ro·man'tic** (-măn'tĭk) *adj.*

nec·ro·pha·gia (nĕk'rə-fā'jə) also **ne·croph·a·gy** (nə-krŏf'ə-jē) *n.* The act or practice of eating the flesh of corpses or carrion.

ne·croph·a·gous (nə-krŏf'ə-gəs, nĕ-) *adj.* Feeding on carrion or corpses.

ne·croph·a·gy (nə-krŏf'ə-jē) *n.* Variant of **necrophagia.**

nec·ro·phil·i·a (nĕk'rə-fĭl'ē-ə) *n.* **1.** An obsessive fascination with death and corpses. **2.** The practice or an instance of engaging in sexual intercourse with a corpse. **—nec'ro·phil'ic** (-fĭl'ĭk) *adj.*

nec·ro·pho·bi·a (nĕk'rə-fō'bē-ə) *n.* A morbid fear of death or corpses. **—nec'ro·pho'bic** *adj.*

ne·crop·o·lis (nə-krŏp'ə-lĭs, nĕ-) *n., pl.* **-lis·es** or **-leis** (-lās'). A cemetery, esp. a large and elaborate one belonging to an ancient city.

nec·rop·sy (nĕk'rŏp'sē) *n., pl.* **-sies.** An autopsy. **—nec'rop'sy** *v.* **(-sied, -sy·ing, -sies).**

ne·crose (nĕ-krōs', -krōz', nĕk'rōs', -rōz') *tr. & intr.v.* **-crosed, -cros·ing, -cros·es.** To affect or be affected with necrosis. [Back-formation < NECROSIS.]

ne·cro·sis (nə-krō'sĭs, nĕ-) *n., pl.* **-ses** (-sēz'). The pathologic death of living tissue in a plant or animal. [LLat. < Gk. *nekrōsis,* death < *nekroun,* to make dead < *nekros,* corpse.] **—ne·crot'ic** (-krŏt'ĭk) *adj.*

nec·ro·tize (nĕk'rə-tīz') *tr. & intr.v.* **-tized, -tiz·ing, -tiz·es.** To necrose.

nec·tar (nĕk'tər) *n.* **1.** *Gk. & Rom. Myth.* The drink of the gods. **2.** A delicious or invigorating drink. **3.** A sweet liquid secreted by flowers of various plants and gathered by bees for making honey. [Lat. < Gk. *nektar.*] **—nec'tar·ous** *adj.*

nec·tar·ine (nĕk'tə-rēn') *n.* A variety of peach of ancient origin, having a smooth, waxy skin. [< obs. *nectarine,* sweet as nectar < NECTAR.]

nec·ta·ry (nĕk'tə-rē) *n., pl.* **-ries. 1.** A glandlike organ, usually at the base of a flower, that secretes nectar. **2.** The part of a flower in which a nectary is contained. [NLat. *nectarium* < NECTAR.] **—nec·tar'i·al** (-târ'ē-əl) *adj.*

née also **nee** (nā) *adj.* Born. Used to indicate the maiden name of a married woman: *Mary Smith, née Jones.* [Fr., fem. p.part. of *naître,* to be born < Lat. *nasci.*]

need (nēd) *n.* **1.** A lack of something required or desirable: *crops in need of water; a need for affection.* **2.** Something required or wanted; requisite: *Our needs are modest.* **3.** Necessity; obligation: *There is no need for you to go.* **4.** A condition of poverty or misfortune: *He is in dire need.* *—v.* **need·ed, need·ing, needs.** *—aux.* To be under the necessity of or the obligation to: *He need not come.* *—tr.* To have need of; require. *—intr.* **1.** To be in need or want. **2.** *Archaic.* To be necessary. [ME *nede* < OE *nēod.*]

Synonyms: *need, necessity, exigency, requisite. Need,* as a noun, is the most general of the words compared here and the least strong in signifying urgency. *Necessity* greatly intensifies urgency to the point of denying that the particular need can be ignored. *Exigency* (usually plural in this sense) stresses great urgency brought about by particular conditions or circumstances, often those of an emergency. *Requisite* specifies need closely associated with attainment of a given goal; like *exigency,* but unlike the other terms, it connotes need imposed by external requirements rather than by inner compulsion.

Usage: When combined with another verb, *need* has two forms, one regular and one irregular. The regular form is marked for person and is followed by the infinitive with *to: She needs to go. Does she need to go?* The irregular form occurs only in questions, negations, and *if* clauses. Like the modal verbs (*must, can,* etc.), it is not marked for person and is followed by a bare verb with no *to*; moreover, its negated and questioned forms are not formed with *do.* Thus, we say *he need not go,* not *he doesn't need go, he need not to go,* or *he needs not go.* Similarly, the questioned form with the irregular *need* would be *Need it be done in a hurry?* rather than *Does it need be done?* or *Need it to be done?* • The two forms of *need* are subtly different in meaning. The irregular form is roughly equivalent to "to be obliged to" and is generally reserved for situations in which there is some question as to whether its subject is under an externally imposed obligation to perform the action named by the accompanying verb. Thus, *you needn't come* means "you are under no obligation to come." Where the subject is under no external compulsion to perform the action of the accompanying verb, the regular form of *need* is used. Thus, we would say: *Since I was there at the game, I don't need to read the newspaper accounts* (not *needn't read,* since the decision not to read the newspaper is entirely the subject's own). But a teacher might say, *If you have already done all the homework assignments, you needn't take the final* (not *don't need to take,* since it is the students' obligations and not their interests that are at issue).

need·ful (nēd'fəl) *adj.* Necessary; required. **—need'ful·ly** *adv.* **—need'ful·ness** *n.*

nee·dle (nēd'l) *n.* **1.** A small, slender sewing implement, usually of polished steel, with an eye at one end through which a length of thread is passed and held. **2.** Any of various implements similar to a needle in appearance and use, as one used in knitting or crocheting. **3.** A small, pointed stylus used to transmit vibrations from the grooves of a phonograph record. **4. a.** A slender pointer or indicator on a dial, scale, or similar part of a mechanical device. **b.** A magnetic needle. **5.** A hypodermic needle. **6.** A stiff, narrow leaf, such as those of conifers. **7.** A fine, sharp projection, such as a spine of a sea urchin or a crystal. **8.** A sharp, pointed instrument used in engraving. *—v.* **-dled, -dling, -dles.** *—tr.* **1.** To prick, pierce, or stitch with or as if with a needle. **2.** *Informal.* To goad, provoke, or tease. **3.** *Slang.* To increase the alcoholic content of (a beverage). *—intr.* To sew or do similar work with a needle. [ME *nedle* < OE *nædl.*] **—nee'dler** *n.*

nee·dle·fish (nēd'l-fĭsh') *n., pl.* **needlefish** or **-fish·es. 1.** Any of several marine fishes of the family Belonidae, having slender bodies and narrow jaws. **2.** Any of various fishes with projecting jaws, as the pipefish.

nee·dle·point (nēd'l-point') *n.* **1.** Decorative needlework on canvas, usually in a diagonal stitch covering the entire surface of the material. **2.** A type of lace worked on paper patterns with a needle. **—modifier:** *a needlepoint pillow.*

need·less (nēd'lĭs) *adj.* Not needed or wished for; unnecessary. **—need'less·ly** *adv.* **—need'less·ness** *n.*

needle valve *n.* A valve having a slender point fitting into a conical seat, for accurately regulating the flow of a liquid or gas.

nee·dle·wom·an (nēd'l-wo͝om'ən) *n.* A woman who does needlework, esp. a seamstress.

nee·dle·work (nēd'l-wûrk') *n.* Work done with a needle, such as sewing or embroidery. **—nee'dle·work'er** *n.*

need·n't (nēd'nt). Need not.

needs (nēdz) *adv.* Of necessity; necessarily: *He must needs go.* [ME *nedes* < *nede,* necessarily < OE *nēde.*]

need·y (nē'dē) *adj.* **-i·er, -i·est.** Being in need; impoverished. **—need'i·ness** *n.*

ne'er (nâr) *adv.* Never.

ne'er-do-well (nâr'do͞o-wĕl') *n.* An idle, irresponsible person. **—ne'er'-do-well'** *adj.*

ne·far·i·ous (nə-fâr'ē-əs) *adj.* Extremely wicked or infamous; evil. [Lat. *nefarius* < *nefas,* crime : *ne-,* not + *fas,* law.] **—ne·far'i·ous·ly** *adv.* **—ne·far'i·ous·ness** *n.*

ne·gate (nĭ-gāt') *tr.v.* **-gat·ed, -gat·ing, -gates. 1.** To make ineffective or invalid; nullify. **2.** To rule out; deny. **3.** *Computer Sci.* To perform the machine logic operation NOT. [Lat. *negare, negat-,* to deny.] **—ne·ga'tor, ne·gat'er** *n.*

ne·ga·tion (nĭ-gā'shən) *n.* **1.** The act or process of negating. **2.** A denial, contradiction, or negative statement. **3.** The opposite or absence of something regarded as actual, positive, or affirmative. **—ne·ga'tion·al** *adj.*

neg·a·tive (nĕg'ə-tĭv) *adj.* **1.** Expressing, containing, or consisting of a negation, refusal, or denial: *a negative answer.* **2. a.** Lacking the quality of being positive or affirmative: *negative ideas.* **b.** Indicating opposition or resistance: *a negative reaction to an advertising campaign.* **3.** Not positive or constructive: *negative criticism.* **4.** Not indicative of the presence of microorganisms, disease, or a specific condition. **5.** *Logic.* Denying agreement between a subject and its predicate. Used of a proposition. **6.** *Math.* Pertaining to or denoting: **a.** A quantity less than zero. **b.** The sign (–). **c.** A quantity to be subtracted from another. **d.** A quantity, number, angle, velocity, or direction, in a sense opposite to another of the same magnitude indicated or understood to be positive. **7.** *Physics.* Pertaining to or denoting: **a.** Electric charge of the same sign as that of an electron, designated by the symbol (–). **b.** A body having an excess of electrons. **8.** *Chem.* Pertaining to or denoting an ion, the anion, that is attracted to a positive electrode. **9.** *Biol.* Indicating resistance to, opposition to, or motion away from a stimulus: *a negative tropism.* *—n.* **1.** A statement or act indicating or expressing a contradiction, denial, or refusal. **2.** Something that is the counterpart of something positive. **3.** *Gram.* A word or part of a word, such as *no, not,* or *non-,* that indicates negation. **4.** The side in a debate that contradicts or opposes the question being debated. **5. a.** An image in which the light areas of the object rendered appear dark and the dark areas appear light. **b.** A film, plate, or other photographic material containing such an image. **6.** *Math.* A negative quantity. *—tr.v.* **-tived, -tiv·ing, -tives. 1.** To refuse to approve; veto. **2.** To deny; contradict. **3.** To demonstrate to be false; disprove. **4.** To counteract or neutralize. —See Usage note at **affirmative.** [LLat. *negatitivus* < *negare,* to deny.] **—neg'a·tive·ly** *adv.* **—neg'a·tive·ness, neg'a·tiv'i·ty** (-tĭv'ĭ-tē) *n.*

negative feedback *n.* Feedback that reduces the output of a system, as the action of heat on a thermostat to limit the output of a furnace.

negative income tax *n.* A system of government payments to those whose income is below a specified level, proposed as an alternative to welfare.

negative transfer *n.* Interference with current learning or performance as a result of the transfer of previously learned responses.

neg·a·tiv·ism (nĕg'ə-tĭ-vĭz'əm) *n.* **1.** A habitual attitude of skepticism or resistance to the suggestions, orders, or instructions of others. **2.** Behavior characterized by the stubborn refusal to carry out the suggestions, orders, or instructions of others. **—neg'a·tiv·ist** *n.* **—neg'a·tiv·is'tic** *adj.*

neg·a·tron (nĕg'ə-trŏn') *n.* An electron. [NEGA(TIVE) + (ELEC)TRON.]

ne·glect (nĭ-glĕkt') *tr.v.* **-glect·ed, -glect·ing, -glects. 1.** To ignore or pay no attention to; disregard. **2.** To fail to care for or give proper attention to. **3.** To fail to do or carry out, as through carelessness or oversight. *—n.* **1.** The act or an instance of neglecting something. **2.** The state of being neglected. **3.** Habitual lack of care. [Lat. *neglegere, neglect-* : *neg-,* not + *legere,* to choose.] **—ne·glect'er** *n.*

ne·glect·ful (nĭ-glĕkt'fəl) *adj.* Characterized by neglect; heedless: *neglectful of responsibilities.* **—ne·glect'ful·ly** *adv.* **—ne·glect'ful·ness** *n.*

neg·li·gee also **neg·li·gée** or **neg·li·gé** (nĕg'lĭ-zhā', nĕg'lĭ-zhā') *n.* **1.** A woman's loose dressing gown, often of soft, delicate fabric. **2.** Informal or incomplete attire. [Fr. < *négliger,* to neglect < Lat. *neglegere.*]

neg·li·gence (nĕg'lĭ-jəns) *n.* **1.** The state or quality of being negligent. **2.** A negligent act or failure to act. **3.** *Law.* The omission or neglect of reasonable precaution, care, or action.

neg·li·gent (nĕg'lĭ-jənt) *adj.* **1.** Characterized by or inclined to neglect, esp. habitually. **2.** Extremely careless or casual.

needlepoint

[ME < OFr. < Lat. *negligens,* pr.part. of *negligere,* to neglect.] —**neg'li·gent·ly** *adv.*

neg·li·gi·ble (nĕg'lĭ-jə-bəl) *adj.* Not significant or important enough to be worth considering; trifling. [< Lat. *neglegere,* to neglect.] —**neg'li·gi·bil'i·ty, neg'li·gi·ble·ness** *n.* —**neg'li·gi·bly** *adv.*

ne·go·tia·ble (nĭ-gō'shə-bəl, -shē-ə-) *adj.* **1.** Capable of being negotiated. **2.** Capable of being legally transferred from one person to another, either by delivery or by delivery and endorsement. —**ne·go'tia·bil'i·ty** *n.* —**ne·go'tia·bly** *adv.*

ne·go·ti·ant (nĭ-gō'shē-ənt, -shənt) *n.* One who negotiates.

ne·go·ti·ate (nĭ-gō'shē-āt') *v.* **-at·ed, -at·ing, -ates.** —*intr.* To confer with another in order to come to terms or reach an agreement. —*tr.* **1.** To arrange or settle by conferring or discussing: *negotiate a union contract.* **2. a.** To transfer title to or ownership of (notes, for example) to another person or party in return for value received. **b.** To sell or discount. **3.** To succeed in going over, accomplishing, or coping with: *negotiate a sharp curve.* [Lat. *negotiari, negotiat-,* to transact business < *negotium,* business : *neg-,* not + *otium,* leisure.] —**ne·go'ti·a'tor** *n.* —**ne·go'tia·to'ry** (-shə-tôr'ē, -tōr'ē, -shē-ə-) *adj.*

ne·go·ti·a·tion (nĭ-gō'shē-ā'shən) *n.* Often **negotiations.** The act or process of negotiating.

Ne·gress (nē'grĭs) *n.* A female Negro.

Ne·gril·lo (nĭ-grĭl'ō, -grē'yō) *n., pl.* **-los** or **-loes.** One of a group of Negroid peoples of Africa, including the Bushmen and the Pygmies, who are short in stature. [Sp., dim. of *negro,* black person. —see NEGRO.]

Ne·gri·to (nĭ-grē'tō) *n., pl.* **-tos** or **-toes. 1.** A Negrillo. **2.** One of various groups of Negroid people of short stature inhabiting parts of Malaysia, the Philippines, and southeastern Asia. [Sp., dim. of *negro,* black person. —see NEGRO.]

ne·gri·tude (nē'grĭ-tōōd', -tyōōd', nĕg'rĭ-) *n.* An aesthetic and ideological concept affirming the independent validity of Negro culture. [Fr. *négritude* < *nègre,* Negro < Sp. *negro.*]

Ne·gro (nē'grō) *n., pl.* **-groes. 1.** A member of the Negroid ethnic division of the human species, esp. one of various peoples of central and southern Africa. **2.** A person of Negro descent. [Sp. and Port. < *negro,* black < Lat. *niger.*] —**Ne'gro** *adj.*

Ne·groid (nē'groid') *adj.* **1.** Of, pertaining to, or designating a major ethnic division of the human species whose members are characterized by brown to black pigmentation and often by tightly curled hair. **2.** Of or characteristic of Negroes. —*n.* A member of the Negroid ethnic division of the human species. [NEGR(O)- + -OID.]

ne·gro·phile (nē'grə-fīl') *n.* Often **Negrophile.** One who is friendly to Negroes and their interests. —**ne'gro·phil'ism** *n.*

ne·gro·phobe (nē'grə-fōb') *n.* Often **Negrophobe.** One who feels intense aversion to or fear of Negroes. —**ne'gro·pho'bi·a** (-fō'bē-ə) *n.*

ne·gus (nē'gəs) *n.* A beverage made of wine, hot water, lemon juice, sugar, and nutmeg. [After Colonel Francis *Negus* (d. 1732).]

Ne·gus (nē'gəs, nĭ-gōōs') *n.* The title of the emperor of Ethiopia. [Amharic *negūs* < Ethiopic *nĕgūśă.*]

Ne·he·mi·ah (nē'hə-mī'ə, nē'ə-) *n.* **1.** A Jewish leader and governor of Judea in the fifth century B.C. during the Babylonian Captivity. **2.** See table at **Bible.** [Heb. *Nĕḥemyāh.*]

neigh (nā) *n.* The long, high-pitched sound made by a horse. —*intr.v.* **neighed, neigh·ing, neighs.** To utter a neigh. [< ME *neighen,* to neigh < OE *hnægan.*]

neigh·bor (nā'bər) *n.* **1.** One who lives or is located near or next to another. **2.** A fellow human being. —*v.* **-bored, -bor·ing, -bors.** —*tr.* To lie close to or border directly upon. —*intr.* To live or be situated close by. [ME *neighebor* < OE *nēahgebūr* : *nēah,* near + *gebūr,* dweller.]

neigh·bor·hood (nā'bər-hōōd') *n.* **1.** A district or area with distinctive characteristics. **2.** The people who live in a particular district or area. **3.** *Informal.* Approximate amount or range: *in the neighborhood of ten million dollars.* **4.** *Math.* The set of points surrounding a specified point, each of which is at a distance from the specified point less than an arbitrary bound.

neigh·bor·ly (nā'bər-lē) *adj.* Appropriate to, characteristic of, or showing the feelings of a friendly neighbor. —**neigh'bor·li·ness** *n.*

neigh·bour (nā'bər) *n. & v. Chiefly Brit.* Variant of **neighbor.**

nei·ther (nē'*th*ər, nī'-) *adj.* Not either; not one or the other: *Neither shoe fits comfortably.* —*pron.* Not either one; not the one nor the other: *Neither of them fits.* —*conj.* **1.** Not either; not in either case. Used with the correlative conjunction *nor: Neither we nor they want it.* **2.** Also not: *If I can't have it, neither can she.* —*adv.* Similarly not: *Just as you would not, so neither would they.* [ME < OE *nāwðer* : *nā,* not + *hwæðer,* which of two.]

Usage: According to the traditional rule, *neither* should be construed as singular when it occurs as the subject of a sentence: *Neither of the houses is* (not *are*) *finished.* Accordingly, a pronoun with *neither* as an antecedent must also be singular: *Neither of the doctors is likely to reveal her* (not *their*) *identity.* • As a conjunction, *neither* is supposed to be followed by *nor,* not *or: Neither prayer nor curses brought relief* (not *or curses*). When *neither. . . nor* connects two singular elements, the following verb is singular, as in *Neither Kim nor Pat is coming.* When both elements are plural, the verb is plural: *Neither the students nor the teachers have read the report.* When one element is singular and the other is plural, many have suggested that the verb should agree with the element closest to it. Thus, we would write *neither the students nor the teacher has read the report,* but *neither the teacher nor the students have read the report.* Other grammarians, however, have insisted that these sentences must be avoided entirely and that one must instead seek a paraphrase in which the problem does not arise, such as *The students have not read the report, and neither has the teacher.* • When *neither. . . nor* is used as an adverb, it should be placed in such a way that each of its elements is followed by a construction of the same type. Instead of *the report neither specified time nor place,* one should write *the report specified neither time nor place.* Instead of *he was neither told that the meeting was canceled nor that the bank was closed,* one should write *he was told neither that the meeting was canceled nor that the bank was closed.* See also Usage note at **everyone.**

nek·ton (nĕk'tən, -tŏn') *n.* The total population of marine animal organisms that swim independently of currents, ranging in size from microscopic organisms to whales. [G. < Gk. *nēkton,* neuter of *nēktos,* swimming < *nēkhein,* to swim.] —**nek·ton'ic** (-tŏn'ĭk) *adj.*

nel·ly or **nel·lie** (nĕl'ē) *n., pl.* **-lies.** *Slang.* An effeminate male homosexual. [Poss. < *Nelly,* nickname for *Helen.*]

nel·son (nĕl'sən) *n.* A wrestling hold in which the user places an arm under the opponent's arm and applies pressure with the palm of the hand against the opponent's neck. [Perh. < the name *Nelson.*]

nemato– or **nemat–** *pref.* **1.** Thread; threadlike: *nematocyst.* **2.** Nematode: *nematocide.* [NLat. < Gk. *nēma,* thread.]

nem·a·to·cyst (nĕm'ə-tə-sĭst', nĭ-măt'ə-) *n. Zool.* A stinging organ in various coelenterates, such as jellyfish, that when stimulated ejects a coiled tube that chemically paralyzes its victim. —**nem'a·to·cys'tic** *adj.*

nem·a·tode (nĕm'ə-tōd') *n.* A worm of the phylum Nematoda, having unsegmented, threadlike bodies, many of which, as the hookworm, are parasitic. [NLat. *Nematoda,* phylum name < Gk. *nemā,* thread.]

Nem·bu·tal (nĕm'byə-tôl'). A trademark for the drug pentobarbital sodium.

ne·mer·te·an (nĭ-mûr'tē-ən) also **nem·er·tine** (nĕm'ər-tīn') or **nem·er·tin·e·an** (nĕm'ər-tĭn'ē-ən) *adj.* Of, pertaining to, or belonging to the phylum Nemertea, consisting chiefly of marine worms having soft cylindrical or flattened bodies, usually brightly colored. [< NLat. *Nemertea,* phylum name < *Nemertes,* genus name < Gk. *Nēmertēs,* name of a Nereid.] —**ne·mer'te·an** *n.*

nem·e·sis (nĕm'ĭ-sĭs) *n., pl.* **-ses** (-sēz'). **1. Nemesis.** *Gk. Myth.* The goddess of retributive justice or vengeance. **2.** One that inflicts retribution or vengeance. **3.** An unbeatable rival. **4.** Retributive justice in its execution or outcome: *invite nemesis.* **5.** A source of injury or destruction: *Unthinking trust was her nemesis.* [Gk. < *nemesis,* retribution < *nemein,* to deal out.]

ne·ne (nā'nā) *n.* A goose, *Branta sandvicensis,* of the Hawaiian Islands, now very rare. [Hawaiian *nēnē.*]

neo– *pref.* **1.** New; recent: *Neolithic.* **2. a.** New and different: *neoimpressionism.* **b.** New and abnormal: *neoplasm.* **3.** New World: *Neotropical.* [Gk. < *neos,* new.]

Usage: Many compounds other than those entered here may be formed with *neo-.* In forming compounds, *neo-* is normally joined to the following word without space or hyphen: *neocolonialism.* However, if the second element begins with a capital letter, it is separated with a hyphen and the *N* of *Neo-* is also capitalized: *Neo-Platonism.* (The *N* may be capitalized in other words, too: *Neolithic*). If the second element begins with *o,* it is separated by a hyphen: *neo-orthodoxy.*

ne·o·ars·phen·a·mine (nē'ō-ärs-fĕn'ə-mēn') *n.* A yellow powder, $C_{13}H_{13}As_2N_2NaO_4S$, containing arsenic, used chiefly in the treatment of syphilis and yaws.

Ne·o·cene (nē'ə-sēn') *n.* A division of the Tertiary period comprising the Miocene and Pliocene. —**Ne'o·cene'** *adj.*

ne·o·clas·si·cism (nē'ō-klăs'ĭ-sĭz'əm) *n.* A revival of classical aesthetics and forms, esp. in art, music, and literature. —**ne'o·clas'sic, ne'o·clas'si·cal** *adj.*

ne·o·col·on·i·al·ism (nē'ō-kə-lō'nē-ə-lĭz'əm) *n.* **1.** Control of former colonies by colonial powers, esp. by economic means. **2.** The indirect economic or political influencing of other nations or peoples by a very powerful nation. —**ne'o·co·lo'ni·al** *adj.* —**ne'o·co·lo'ni·al·ist** *n.*

ne·o·cor·tex (nē'ō-kôr'tĕks') *n.* The dorsal region of the cerebral cortex. —**ne'o·cor'ti·cal** (-tĭ-kəl) *adj.*

Ne·o-Dar·win·ism (nē'ō-där'wə-nĭz'əm) *n.* The theory that the evolutionary development of plants and animals is principally determined by natural selection and that acquired characteristics cannot be inherited. —**Ne'o-Dar·win'i·an** (-där-wĭn'ē-ən) *adj.* —**Ne'o-Dar'win·ist** *n.*

ne·o·dym·i·um (nē'ō-dĭm'ē-əm) *n. Symbol* **Nd** A bright, silvery rare-earth metal element, found in the minerals monazite and bastnaesite and used for coloring glass and for doping some glass lasers. Atomic number 60; atomic weight

144.24; melting point 1,024°C; boiling point 3,027°C; specific gravity 6.80 or 7.004 (depending on allotropic form); valence 3. [NEO- + (DI)DYMIUM.]

Ne·o-Freud·i·an (nē′ō-froi′dē-ən) *adj. Psychoanal.* Of or relating to a theory based on Freudian philosophy but emphasizing the significance of social and cultural influences on personality development. **—Ne′o-Freud′i·an** *n.*

Ne·o·gae·a also **Ne·o·ge·a** (nē′ə-jē′ə) *n.* A region that is coextensive with the Neotropical region and is considered one of the primary zoogeographic realms. [NEO- + Gk. *gaia,* earth.] **—Ne′o·gae′an** *adj.*

ne·o·gen·e·sis (nē′ō-jĕn′ĭ-sĭs) *n.* The regeneration of tissue. **—ne′o·ge·net′ic** (-jə-nĕt′ĭk) *adj.*

ne·o·im·pres·sion·ism also **ne·o-im·pres·sion·ism** (nē′ō-ĭm-prĕsh′ə-nĭz′əm) *n.* A movement in 19th-century painting that sought to make impressionism more formal and meticulous, characterized by the juxtaposition of dots of primary colors to achieve brighter secondary colors, the mixture of pure tones being left for the eye itself to complete. **—ne′o·im·pres′sion·ist** *n. & adj.*

Ne·o-La·marck·ism (nē′ō-lə-mär′kĭz′əm) *n.* The theory that acquired characteristics can be inherited but that natural selection is also a valid evolutionary principle. **—Ne′o-La·marck′i·an** (-kē-ən) *adj. & n.*

ne·o·lith (nē′ə-lĭth′) *n.* A stone implement of the Neolithic period. [Back-formation < NEOLITHIC.]

Ne·o·lith·ic (nē′ə-lĭth′ĭk) *adj.* Of or denoting the cultural period beginning around 10,000 B.C. in the Middle East and later elsewhere and characterized by the invention of farming and the making of technically advanced stone implements.

ne·ol·o·gism (nē-ŏl′ə-jĭz′əm) *n.* **1.** A newly coined word, phrase, or expression. **2.** A meaningless word or phrase coined or used by a psychotic. **—ne·ol′o·gist** *n.* **—ne·ol′o·gis′tic, ne·ol′o·gis′ti·cal** *adj.*

ne·ol·o·gy (nē-ŏl′ə-jē) *n., pl.* **-gies. 1.** A neologism. **2.** The use of a newly coined word, phrase, or expression or of a new meaning for an established word. **—ne′o·log′i·cal** (nē′ə-lŏj′ĭ-kəl) *adj.* **—ne′o·log′i·cal·ly** *adv.*

ne·o·morph (nē′ə-môrf′) *n.* A biological structure that has not evolved from a similar structure in an ancestor. **—ne′o·morph′ic** (-môr′fĭk) *adj.*

ne·o·my·cin (nē′ə-mī′sĭn) *n.* An antibiotic drug consisting of a group of organic complexes produced by the metabolism of bacteria.

ne·on (nē′ŏn′) *n. Symbol* **Ne** A rare, inert gaseous element occurring in the atmosphere to the extent of 18 parts per million and obtained by fractional distillation of liquid air. It is colorless but glows reddish-orange in an electric discharge and is used in display and television tubes. Atomic number 10; atomic weight 20.183; melting point -248.67°C; boiling point -245.95°C; valence 0. [< Gk., neuter of *neos,* new.]

ne·o·nate (nē′ə-nāt′) *n.* A newborn child. [NEO- + Lat. *natus,* p.part. of *nasci,* to be born.] **—ne′o·na′tal** (nē′ō-nāt′l) *adj.*

neon tetra *n.* A small tropical American freshwater fish, *Hyphessobrycon innesi,* having blue and red markings.

ne·o-or·tho·dox·y (nē′ō-ôr′thə-dŏk′sē) *n.* A Protestant movement of the 20th century that opposes liberalism and aims to revive adherence to certain theological doctrines of the Reformation. **—ne′o-or′tho·dox′** *adj.*

ne·o·phyte (nē′ə-fīt′) *n.* **1.** A recent convert. **2. a.** A newly ordained Roman Catholic priest. **b.** A novice of a religious order. **3.** A beginner; novice. [LLat. *neophytus* < Gk. *neophutos* : *neous,* new + *phuton,* plant < *phuein,* to bring forth.]

ne·o·plasm (nē′ə-plăz′əm) *n.* An abnormal new growth of tissue in animals or plants; tumor.

ne·o·plas·tic (nē′ə-plăs′tĭk) *n.* Of, pertaining to, or being a neoplasm.

Ne·o-Pla·to·nism also **Ne·o·pla·to·nism** (nē′ō-plāt′n-ĭz′əm) *n.* **1.** A philosophical system developed at Alexandria in the third century A.D., based on a modified form of Platonism combined with elements of Oriental mysticism and some Judaic and Christian concepts and positing a single source from which all existence emanates and with which an individual soul can be mystically united. **2.** A revival of Neo-Platonism or a system derived from it, as in the Middle Ages. **—Ne′o-Pla·ton′ic** (-plə-tŏn′ĭk) *adj.* **—Ne′o-Pla′to·nist** *n.*

ne·o·prene (nē′ə-prēn′) *n.* A synthetic rubber produced by polymerization of chloroprene and used in weather-resistant products, adhesives, shoe soles, paints, and rocket fuels. [NEO- + PR(OPYL) + -ENE.]

Ne·op·tol·e·mus (nē′ŏp-tŏl′ə-məs) *n. Gk. Myth.* A son of Achilles who slew Priam during the taking of Troy.

Ne·o-Scho·las·ti·cism (nē′ō-skə-lăs′tĭ-sĭz′əm) *n.* A movement that seeks to revive medieval Scholasticism by infusing it with modern concepts. **—Ne′o-Scho·las′tic** (-lăs′tĭk) *adj.*

ne·o·ter·ic (nē′ə-tĕr′ĭk) *adj.* Of recent origin; modern. [LLat. *neotericus* < Gk. *neōterikos,* modern < *neōteros,* younger, comp. of *neos,* new.]

Ne·o·trop·i·cal (nē′ō-trŏp′ĭ-kəl) *adj.* Of or designating the zoogeographic region stretching southward from the tropic of Cancer and including southern Mexico, Central and South America, and the West Indies.

Ne·o·zo·ic (nē′ə-zō′ĭk) *adj.* Of, pertaining to, or designating the geologic period from the end of the Mesozoic era to the present.

Nep·al·ese (nĕp′ə-lēz′, -lēs′) *n., pl.* **Nepalese. 1.** A native or resident of Nepal. **2.** The Indic language of Nepal. *—adj.* Of, pertaining to, or designating Nepal, its inhabitants, its language, or its culture.

ne·pen·the (nĭ-pĕn′thē) *n.* **1.** A legendary drug of ancient times, used as a remedy for grief. **2.** Something that induces forgetfulness of sorrow or eases pain. [Gk. *nēpenthes (pharmakon),* grief-banishing (drug) : *ne-,* not + *penthos,* grief.] **—ne·pen′the·an** (-thē-ən) *adj.*

neph·e·line (nĕf′ə-lēn′, -lĭn) also **neph·e·lite** (-līt′) *n.* A mineral of sodium- or potassium-aluminum silicate, occurring worldwide in igneous rocks and used in the manufacture of ceramics and enamels. [Fr. *néphéline* < Gk. *nephelē,* cloud (because it becomes cloudy when placed in nitric acid).] **—neph′e·lin′ic** (-lĭn′ĭk) *adj.*

neph·e·lin·ite (nĕf′ə-lĭ-nīt′) *n.* An igneous rock consisting chiefly of pyroxene and nepheline.

neph·e·lite (nĕf′ə-līt′) *n.* Variant of **nepheline.**

neph·e·lom·e·ter (nĕf′ə-lŏm′ĭ-tər) *n.* An apparatus used to measure the size and concentration of particles in a liquid by analysis of light transmitted through or reflected by the liquid. [Gk. *nephelē,* cloud + -METER.] **—neph′e·lo·met′ric** (-lō-mĕt′rĭk) *adj.* **—neph′e·lom′e·try** *n.*

neph·ew (nĕf′yo͞o) *n.* **1.** The son of one's brother or sister or of one's brother-in-law or sister-in-law. **2.** A son of a celibate ecclesiastic. [ME *neveu* < OFr. < Lat. *nepos.*]

ne·phol·o·gy (nĕ-fŏl′ə-jē) *n.* The science of clouds. [Gk. *nephos,* cloud + -LOGY.] **—neph′o·log′i·cal** (nĕf′ə-lŏj′ĭ-kəl) *adj.*

nephr- *pref.* Variant of **nephro-.**

ne·phrec·to·my (nə-frĕk′tə-mē) *n., pl.* **-mies.** The surgical removal of a kidney.

Neptune

ne·phrid·i·um (nə-frĭd′ē-əm) *n., pl.* **-i·a** (-ē-ə). **1.** An excretory organ in many invertebrates. **2.** The excretory organ of a vertebrate embryo from which the kidney develops. **—ne·phrid′i·al** *adj.*

neph·rite (nĕf′rīt′) *n.* A white to dark green variety of jade, chiefly a metasilicate of iron, calcium, and magnesium. [G. *Nephrit* < Gk. *nephros,* kidney, from the belief that it cured kidney diseases.]

ne·phrit·ic (nə-frĭt′ĭk) *adj.* **1.** Of or pertaining to the kidneys. **2.** Of, pertaining to, or affected with nephritis.

ne·phri·tis (nə-frī′tĭs) *n.* Any of various acute or chronic inflammations of the kidneys. [LLat. < Gk. < *nephros,* kidney.]

nephro- or **nephr-** *pref.* Kidney; kidneylike structure: *nephrotomy.* [< Gk. *nephros,* kidney.]

neph·ro·gen·ic (nĕf′rə-jĕn′ĭk) *adj.* Nephrogenous.

ne·phrog·e·nous (nə-frŏj′ə-nəs) *adj.* **1.** Originating in the kidney. **2.** Having the capacity to generate new kidney tissue.

neph·rol·o·gy (nə-frŏl′ə-jē) *n.* The science that deals with the kidneys, esp. their functions or diseases. **—ne·phrol′o·gist** *n.*

ne·phro·sis (nə-frō′sĭs) *n.* A disease of the kidneys, esp. when marked by degenerative lesions of the renal tubules as opposed to the inflammation characteristic of nephritis. **—ne·phrot′ic** (-frŏt′ĭk) *adj.*

ne·phrot·o·my (nə-frŏt′ə-mē) *n., pl.* **-mies.** Surgical incision into the kidney.

ne plus ul·tra (nē′ plŭs ŭl′trə, nā′ plo͝os o͝ol′trä) *n.* The extreme or utmost point, esp. of excellence or achievement. [Lat., (go) no more beyond (this point).]

nep·o·tism (nĕp′ə-tĭz′əm) *n.* Favoritism shown or patronage granted by persons in high office to relatives or close friends. [Fr. *népotisme* < Ital. *nepotismo* < *nepote,* nephew < Lat. *nepos.*] **—nep′o·tist** *n.* **—nep′o·tis′tic, nep′o·tis′ti·cal** *adj.*

Nep·tune (nĕp′to͞on′, -tyo͞on′) *n.* **1. a.** *Rom. Myth.* The god of the sea, corresponding to the Greek Poseidon. **b.** The ocean or sea. **2.** The eighth planet from the sun, having a sidereal period of revolution around the sun of 164.8 years at a mean distance of 4.5 billion kilometers, or 2.8 billion miles, a mean radius of 22,500 kilometers, or 14,000 miles, and a density 17.2 times that of earth. [Lat. *Neptunus.*] **—Nep·tu′ni·an** (-to͞o′nē-ən, -tyo͞o′-) *adj.*

nep·tu·ni·um (nĕp-to͞o′nē-əm, -tyo͞o′-) *n. Symbol* **Np** A silvery, metallic, naturally radioactive element, atomic number 93, the first of the transuranium elements, having thirteen isotopes with mass numbers from 231 to 241 and half-lives ranging from 7.3 minutes to 2.2 million years. It is found in trace quantities in uranium ores and is produced synthetically by nuclear reactions. [After the planet *Neptune,* so called because Neptune is the next planet after Uranus and neptunium follows uranium in the periodic table.]

nerd also **nurd** (nûrd) *n. Slang.* A socially inept, foolish, or ineffectual person. [Prob. alteration of NUT.]

Ne·re·id (nîr′ē-ĭd) *n.* **1.** *Gk. Myth.* Any of the sea nymphs, daughters of Nereus. **2.** The smaller of the two satellites of the planet Neptune. [Gk. *Nēreis, Nēreid-* < *Nēreus,* Nereus.]

ne·re·is (nîr′ē-ĭs) *n., pl.* **ne·re·i·des** (nə-rē′ĭ-dēz′). Any of sev-

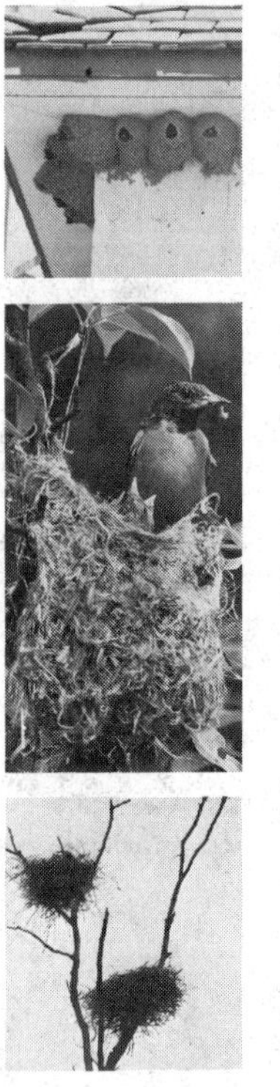

nest
Above: Cliff swallow nests
Center: Baltimore oriole nest
Below: Heron nests

netsuke
Above: Lacquer case suspended from netsuke
Below: Ivory netsuke

eral marine worms of the genus *Nereis,* having a long, flat, segmented body and a pair of paddles on each segment. [NLat. *Nereis,* genus name < Lat., Nereid < Gk. —see NEREID.]

Ne·re·us (nîr′ē-əs, nîr′o͞os′) *n. Gk. Myth.* A sea god, father of the Nereids. [Gk. *Nēreus.*]

ne·rit·ic (nə-rĭt′ĭk) *adj.* Of or pertaining to the waters and deposits of a shoreline. [Perh. < Lat. *nerita,* sea snail < Gk. *nēritēs* < *Nēreus,* Nereus.]

ner·o·li oil (nĕr′ə-lē) *n.* An essential oil distilled from orange flowers and used in perfumery. [Fr., after Anna Maria de la Trémoille, 17th-cent. princess of *Neroli.*]

nerts (nûrts) *interj. Slang.* Used to express disgust, contempt, or refusal. [Alteration of NUTS.]

ner·vate (nûr′vāt′) *adj. Bot.* Having veins. Used of leaves.

ner·va·tion (nûr-vā′shən) *n.* Venation.

nerve (nûrv) *n.* **1.** Any of the bundles of fibers interconnecting the central nervous system and the organs or parts of the body, capable of transmitting both sensory stimuli and motor impulses from one part of the body to another. **2.** A tendon or muscle: *strain every nerve.* **3.** A sensitive point or subject. **4.** A source from which energy or dynamic action emanates. **5. a.** Patience; endurance. **b.** Forcefulness; stamina. **c.** Courage. **d.** *Informal.* Audacity; effrontery. **6.** Nervous agitation caused by fear, anxiety, or stress; hysteria: *an attack of nerves.* **7.** A vein in an insect's wing. **8.** The midrib and larger veins in a leaf. —*tr.v.* **nerved, nerv·ing, nerves.** To give strength or courage to. [Lat. *nervus.*]

nerve cell *n.* A neuron.

nerve center *n.* **1.** A group of nerve cells that perform a specific function. **2.** A source or focus of power or control.

nerve fiber *n.* A threadlike process that is part of a nerve; axon or dendrite.

nerve impulse *n.* The wavelike progression of chemical and electrical disturbance along a stimulated nerve fiber.

nerve·less (nûrv′lĭs) *adj.* **1. a.** Lacking strength or energy. **b.** Lacking courage. **2.** Undisturbed by danger or upsetting circumstances; cool. **—nerve′less·ly** *adv.* **—nerve′less·ness** *n.*

nerve-rack·ing also **nerve-wrack·ing** (nûrv′răk′ĭng) *adj.* Intensely distressing or irritating to the nerves.

nerv·ous (nûr′vəs) *adj.* **1. a.** Of or pertaining to the nerves or nervous system. **b.** Stemming from or affecting the nerves or nervous system: *a nervous disorder.* **2.** Easily excited or distraught; high-strung. **3.** Marked by uneasiness or fearfulness; apprehensive. **4.** *Archaic.* Strong; vigorous. [ME, containing nerves < Lat. *nervosus* < *nervus,* nerve.] **—nerv′ous·ly** *adv.* **—nerv′ous·ness** *n.*

nervous breakdown *n.* **1.** Neurasthenia. **2.** A severe or incapacitating emotional disorder.

nervous Nel·lie or **nervous Nel·ly** (nĕl′ē) *n., pl.* **-lies.** *Informal.* A person who is unduly timid or given to excessive worrying.

nervous system *n. Anat.* A coordinating mechanism in all multicellular animals, except sponges, that regulates internal body functions and responses to external stimuli. In vertebrates it consists of the brain, spinal cord, nerves, ganglia, and parts of receptor and effector organs.

ner·vure (nûr′vyər) *n.* **1.** One of the vascular ridges that form the framework of a leaf. **2.** One of the thickened ribs of tissue that form the framework of an insect's wing. [Fr. < Lat. *nervus,* sinew.]

nerv·y (nûr′vē) *adj.* **-i·er, -i·est. 1.** Impudently confident; brazen. **2.** Showing or requiring fortitude, energy, or endurance. **3.** *Chiefly Brit.* Jumpy; nervous. **4.** *Archaic.* Full of muscular force; sinewy. **—nerv′i·ness** *n.*

nes·cience (nĕsh′əns, nĕsh′ē-əns, nēsh′-, nĕs′ē-əns, nē′sē-) *n.* Absence of knowledge or awareness; ignorance. [LLat. *nescientia* < *nesciens,* ignorant, pr.part. of *nescire,* to be ignorant : *ne-,* not + *scire,* to know.] **—nes′cient** *adj. & n.*

ness (nĕs) *n.* A cape or headland. [ME *nasse* < OE *naessa.*]

-ness *suff.* State; quality; condition; degree: *brightness.* [ME *-nes* < OE.]

Nes·sel·rode (nĕs′əl-rōd′) *n.* A mixture of chestnuts, cherries, candied fruits, and liqueur, used in puddings, ice cream, or pies. [After Count Karl von *Nesselrode* (1780–1862).]

nest (nĕst) *n.* **1. a.** A container or shelter made by a bird for holding its eggs and young. **b.** A similar shelter or structure in which fishes or insects deposit eggs or keep their young. **c.** A place where young are reared; lair. **d.** A number of insects, birds, or other animals occupying such a place. **2.** A place affording snug seclusion or lodging. **3. a.** A place or environment fostering rapid growth or development; hotbed. **b.** The persons occupying or frequenting such a place or environment. **4.** A set of objects of graduated size that can be stacked together, each fitting within the immediately larger one. **5.** *Computer Sci.* A subroutine or set of data contained sequentially within another. —*v.* **nest·ed, nest·ing, nests.** —*intr.* **1.** To build or occupy a nest. **2.** To hunt for birds' nests, esp. in order to collect the eggs. —*tr.* **1.** To place in or as if in a nest. **2.** To put snugly together or inside one another. [ME < OE.]

nest egg *n.* **1.** An artificial or natural egg placed in a nest to induce a bird to lay. **2.** A sum of money put by as a reserve.

nest·er (nĕs′tər) *n.* **1.** One that nests. **2.** *Western U.S.* A squatter, farmer, or homesteader who settles in cattle-grazing territory.

nes·tle (nĕs′əl) *v.* **-tled, -tling, -tles.** —*intr.* **1. a.** To settle snugly and comfortably. **b.** To lie in a sheltered location: *a cottage that nestled in the wood.* **2.** To draw or press close, esp. in an affectionate manner: *The child nestled up to her mother.* **3.** *Archaic.* To nest. —*tr.* To rest, snuggle, or press contentedly. [ME *nestlen* < OE *nestlian,* to make a nest < *nest,* nest.] **—nes′tler** *n.*

nest·ling (nĕst′lĭng) *n.* **1.** A bird too young to leave its nest. **2.** A young child.

Nes·tor (nĕs′tər, -tôr′) *n.* **1.** In the Homeric poems, a hero celebrated for his age and for the wisdom of his counsel. **2.** Often **nestor.** A venerable and wise old man. [Gk. *Nestōr.*]

Nes·to·ri·an (nĕ-stôr′ē-ən, -stōr′-) *adj.* Designating a church of the East that adheres to the doctrines of Nestorius, which assert that Christ had two distinct natures, divine and human. —*n.* A member of the Nestorian church. **—Nes·to′ri·an·ism** *n.*

net[1] (nĕt) *n.* **1.** An openwork fabric made of threads, cords, or ropes that are woven or knotted together at regular intervals. **2.** Something made of net, esp.: **a.** A device for capturing birds, fish, butterflies, or other animals. **b.** A mesh for holding the hair in place. **3.** *Sports.* **a.** A barrier of meshwork cord or rope strung between two posts to divide a tennis, badminton, or volleyball court in half. **b.** A ball that is hit into a net. **c.** The goal in ice hockey. **4.** A meshed network of lines, figures, or fibers. **5.** Something that entraps. —*tr.v.* **net·ted, net·ting, nets. 1.** To catch in or as if in a net. **2.** To cover, protect, or surround with or as if with a net. **3.** To hit (a ball) into a net. **4.** To make into a net. [ME < OE *nett.*] **—net′ter** *n.*

net[2] (nĕt) *adj.* **1.** Remaining after all deductions and adjustments have been made: *net profit; net weight.* **2.** Ultimate; final: *the net result.* —*n.* A net amount, as of profit or weight. —*tr.v.* **net·ted, net·ting, nets. 1.** To bring in or yield as profit. **2.** To clear as profit. [ME < OFr., elegant. —see NEAT.]

neth·er (nĕ*th*′ər) *adj.* Located beneath or below; lower or under: *the nether regions of the earth.* [ME < OE *niðera* < *niðer,* down.]

neth·er·most (nĕ*th*′ər-mōst′) *adj.* Farthest down; lowest.

neth·er·world (nĕ*th*′ər-wûrld′) *n.* **1.** The world of the dead; Hades. **2.** The underworld; hell.

net·keep·er (nĕt′kē′pər) *n.* A goalkeeper.

net·su·ke (nĕt′sə-kē) *n.* A small Japanese toggle, usually decorated with inlays or carving, used to fasten a purse or other article to a kimono sash. [J.]

net·ting (nĕt′ĭng) *n.* **1.** An openwork fabric; net. **2.** The act or process of making a net. **3.** The act or process of fishing with a net.

net·tle (nĕt′l) *n.* **1.** A plant of the genus *Urtica,* having toothed leaves covered with hairs that secrete a stinging fluid that affects the skin on contact. **2.** Any of various stinging or prickly plants. —*tr.v.* **-tled, -tling, -tles. 1.** To sting with or as if with a nettle. **2.** To irritate; vex. [ME < OE *netele.*]

nettle rash *n.* Urticaria.

net·tle·some (nĕt′l-səm) *adj.* Causing annoyance; vexatious.

net ton *n.* A ton (sense 1.b.).

net·work (nĕt′wûrk′) *n.* **1.** An openwork fabric or structure in which rope, thread, or wires cross at regular intervals. **2.** Something resembling a net in consisting of a number of parts, passages, lines, or routes that cross, branch out, or interconnect: *an espionage network; a network of railways.* **3.** A chain of interconnected radio or television broadcasting stations, usually sharing a large proportion of their programs. **4.** A group or system of electric components and connecting circuitry designed to function in a specific manner. —*tr.v.* **-worked, -work·ing, -works. 1.** To overlay with or as if with a network. **2.** To broadcast over a radio or television network.

Neuf·châ·tel (no͞o′shə-tĕl′, nœ′shä-) *n.* A soft, white cheese made from skimmed or whole milk or cream. [After *Neufchâtel,* France.]

neume or **neum** (no͞om, nyo͞om) *n.* A sign used in the notation of plainsong during the Middle Ages, surviving today in transcriptions of Gregorian chant. [ME, series of notes sung on one syllable < Med. Lat. *pneuma* < Gk., breath.] **—neu·mat′ic** (no͞o-măt′ĭk, nyo͞o-) *adj.*

neur- *pref.* Variant of **neuro-.**

neu·ral (no͝or′əl, nyo͝or′-) *adj.* **1.** Of or pertaining to a nerve or the nervous system. **2.** Of, pertaining to, or located on the same side of the body as the spinal cord; dorsal. **—neu′ral·ly** *adv.*

neu·ral·gia (no͞o-răl′jə, nyo͞o-) *n.* Paroxysmal pain along a nerve. **—neu·ral′gic** *adj.*

neu·ras·the·ni·a (no͝or′əs-thē′nē-ə, nyo͝or′-) *n.* A condition marked by fatigue, loss of energy and memory, and feelings of inadequacy, once thought to result from exhaustion of the nervous system. **—neu′ras·then′ic** (-thĕn′ĭk) *adj.* **—neu′ras·then′i·cal·ly** *adv.*

neu·rec·to·my (no͞o-rĕk′tə-mē, nyo͞o-) *n., pl.* **-mies.** Surgical removal of a nerve or part of a nerve.

neu·ri·lem·ma (no͝or′ə-lĕm′ə, nyo͝or′-) *n.* The outer covering of a nerve fiber. [NEUR- + Gk. *eilēma,* veil < *eilein,* to wind.] **—neu'ri·lem'mal** *adj.*

neu·ris·tor (no͞o-rĭs'tər, nyo͞o-) *n.* An electronic device that is capable of relaying a signal without attenuation in velocity. [NEUR(ON) + (TRANS)ISTOR.]

neu·ri·tis (no͞o-rī'tĭs, nyo͞o-) *n.* Inflammation of a nerve, causing pain, loss of reflexes, and muscular atrophy. **—neu·rit'ic** (-rĭt'ĭk) *adj.*

neuro- or **neur-** *pref.* **1.** Nerve: *neuroblast.* **2.** Neural: *neuropathology.* [NLat. < Gk. *neuron,* tendon, nerve.]

neu·ro·blast (no͝or'ə-blăst', nyo͝or'-) *n.* An embryonic cell from which a nerve cell develops.

neu·ro·cyte (no͝or'ə-sīt', nyo͝or'-) *n.* A nerve cell and its processes.

neu·rog·li·a (no͞o-rŏg'lē-ə, nyo͞o-, no͞o'rə-glē'ə, nyo͞o'-, -glī'-) *n.* The network of branched cells and fibers that supports the tissue of the central nervous system. [NEURO- + Med. Gk. *glia,* glue.] **—neu·rog'li·al** *adj.*

neu·rol·o·gy (no͞o-rŏl'ə-jē, nyo͞o-) *n.* The medical science of the nervous system and its disorders. **—neu'ro·log'i·cal** (no͝or'ə-lŏj'ĭ-kəl, nyo͝or'-) *adj.* **—neu·rol'o·gist** *n.*

neu·ro·ma (no͞o-rō'mə, nyo͞o-) *n., pl.* **-mas** or **-ma·ta** (-mə-tə). A tumor made of nerve tissue.

neu·ron (no͝or'ŏn', nyo͝or'-) also **neu·rone** (-ōn') *n.* Any of the cells of nerve tissue consisting of a nucleated portion and cytoplasmic extensions, the cell body, and the dendrites and axons. [Gk. nerve.] **—neu·ron'ic** *adj.* **—neu·ron'i·cal·ly** *adv.*

neu·ro·path (no͝or'ə-păth', nyo͝or'-) *n.* One suffering from or having a hereditary tendency toward nervous disorders or neurosis. **—neu'ro·path'ic, neu'ro·path'i·cal** *adj.* **—neu'ro·path'i·cal·ly** *adv.*

neu·ro·pa·thol·o·gy (no͝or'ō-pə-thŏl'ə-jē, nyo͝or'-) *n.* The medical study of diseases of the nervous system. **—neu'ro·path'o·log'ic** (-păth'ə-lŏj'ĭk), **neu'ro·path'o·log'i·cal** *adj.* **—neu'ro·pa·thol'o·gist** *n.*

neu·rop·a·thy (no͞o-rŏp'ə-thē, nyo͞o-) *n.* Disease or abnormality of the nervous system.

neu·ro·psy·chi·a·try (no͝or'ō-sĭ-kī'ə-trē, -sī-, nyo͝or'-) *n.* The integrated medical study of both neurological and psychiatric disorders. **—neu'ro·psy'chi·at'ric** (-sī'kē-ăt'rĭk) *adj.* **—neu'ro·psy·chi'a·trist** *n.*

neu·rop·ter·an (no͞o-rŏp'tər-ən, nyo͞o-) *n.* An insect of the order Neuroptera, as the ant lion, dobson fly, or lacewing, having four net-veined wings. *—adj.* Of or belonging to the Neuroptera. [< NLat. *Neuroptera,* order name : NEURO- + Gk. *pteron,* wing.] **—neu·rop'ter·ous** *adj.*

neu·ro·sis (no͞o-rō'sĭs, nyo͞o-) *n., pl.* **-ses** (-sēz'). Any of various functional disorders of the mind or emotions without obvious organic lesion or change and involving anxiety, phobia, or other abnormal behavior symptoms.

neu·ro·sur·ger·y (no͝or'ō-sûr'jə-rē, nyo͝or'-) *n.* Surgery of any part of the nervous system. **—neu'ro·sur'geon** *n.* **—neu'ro·sur'gi·cal** *adj.*

neu·rot·ic (no͞o-rŏt'ĭk, nyo͞o-) *adj.* **1.** Of, pertaining to, or derived from a neurosis. **2.** Of, pertaining to, or afflicted with neurosis. *—n.* A person suffering from a neurosis. **—neu·rot'i·cal·ly** *adv.*

neu·rot·o·my (no͞o-rŏt'ə-mē, nyo͞o-) *n., pl.* **-mies**. The surgical cutting or stretching of a nerve, usually to relieve pain.

neu·ter (no͞o'tər, nyo͞o'-) *adj.* **1.** *Gram.* **a.** Neither masculine nor feminine in gender. **b.** Neither active nor passive. Used of verbs. **2. a.** *Biol.* Having no sexual organs. **b.** *Bot.* Having no pistils or stamens; asexual. **c.** *Zool.* Sexually undeveloped. **3.** Taking no side; neutral. *—n.* **1.** *Gram.* **a.** The neuter gender. **b.** A neuter word. **2. a.** A castrated animal. **b.** A sexually undeveloped or imperfectly developed female insect; worker. **c.** A plant without stamens or pistils. **3.** A neutral person. *—tr.v.* **-tered, -ter·ing, -ters.** To castrate or spay. [ME *neutre* < OFr. < Lat. *neuter,* neither : *ne-,* not + *uter,* either.]

neu·tral (no͞o'trəl, nyo͞o'-) *adj.* **1.** Not allied with, supporting, or favoring either side in a war, dispute, or contest. **2.** Belonging to neither side nor party: *on neutral ground.* **3.** Not one thing or the other; indifferent. **4.** Of no sex; neuter. **5.** *Chem.* **a.** Of or pertaining to a compound that is neither acidic nor alkaline. **b.** Of or pertaining to a solution in which the concentrations of positive and negative ions are equal. **6.** *Physics.* **a.** Of or pertaining to a particle, object, or system that has neither positive nor negative electric charge. **b.** Of or pertaining to a particle, object, or system that has a net electric charge of zero. **7.** Of or indicating a color, such as gray, black, or white, that lacks hue; achromatic. **8.** Pronounced with the tongue in a relaxed middle position, as the *a* in *around.* *—n.* **1.** One that is neutral. **2.** A neutral color: *decorated in neutrals.* **3.** A position in which a set of gears is disengaged so that power cannot be transmitted. [Lat. *neutralis,* grammatically neuter < *neuter.* —see NEUTER.] **—neu'tral·ly** *adv.*

neu·tral·ism (no͞o'trə-lĭz'əm, nyo͞o'-) *n.* **1.** Neutrality. **2.** A political attitude of nonalignment or noninvolvement with conflicting alliances. **—neu'tral·ist** *n.* **—neu'tral·is'tic** *adj.*

neu·tral·i·ty (no͞o-trăl'ĭ-tē, nyo͞o-) *n.* The state or policy of being neutral, esp. nonparticipation in war.

neu·tral·i·za·tion (no͞o'trə-lĭ-zā'shən, nyo͞o'-) *n.* **1.** The act or process of neutralizing. **2.** *Chem.* A reaction between an acid and a base that yields a salt and water.

neu·tral·ize (no͞o'trə-līz', nyo͞o'-) *tr.v.* **-ized, -iz·ing, -iz·es. 1.** To make neutral. **2.** To counterbalance the effect of; make ineffective. **3.** To make neutral and immune from invasion, use, or control by a warring nation. **4.** *Chem.* **a.** To make (a solution) chemically neutral. **b.** To cause (an acid or base) to undergo neutralization. **5.** *Med.* To counteract the effect of (a drug or toxin). **—neu'tral·iz'er** *n.*

Synonyms: *neutralize, negate, nullify, counteract. Neutralize,* in nonscientific usage, is employed to indicate a state of ineffectiveness, inaction, or inoperativeness. *Negate* and *nullify* imply finality rather than a stalemate; often they also imply loss incurred through the rendering of something useless or valueless. *Counteract* is frequently used when the contending forces are thought of as desirable and undesirable; it suggests positive action to correct or set right.

neutral spirits *n. (used with a sing. or pl. verb).* Ethyl alcohol distilled at or above 190 proof and used frequently in alcoholic beverage blends.

neu·tri·no (no͞o-trē'nō, nyo͞o-) *n., pl.* **-nos.** *Physics.* Either of two massless, electrically neutral, stable subatomic particles in the lepton family. [Ital., dim. of *neutrone,* neutron < E. NEUTRON.]

neu·tron (no͞o'trŏn', nyo͞o'-) *n.* An electrically neutral subatomic particle in the baryon family, having a mass 1,839 times that of the electron, stable when bound in an atomic nucleus, and having a mean lifetime of approximately 16.6 minutes as a free particle. It and the proton combine to form nearly the entire mass of atomic nuclei and in numbers characteristic of each nuclear species. [NEUTR(AL) + -ON[1].]

neutron star *n.* A celestial body hypothesized to occur in a terminal stage of stellar evolution, consisting of a superdense mass essentially of neutrons, and having a powerful gravitational attraction from which only neutrinos and high-energy photons could escape, thus rendering the body invisible except to x-ray detection.

neu·tro·phil (no͞o'trə-fĭl', nyo͞o'-) also **neu·tro·phile** (-fīl') or **neu·tro·phil·ic** (no͞o'trə-fĭl'ĭk, nyo͞o'-) *adj.* Easily stained by neutral dyes. Used of such cells as leucocytes. [NEUTR(AL) + -PHIL(E).] **—neu'tro·phil', neu'tro·phile'** *n.*

né·vé (nā-vā') *n.* **1.** The upper part of a glacier where the snow turns into ice. **2. a.** A field of snow at the head of a glacier. **b.** The granular snow typically found in such a field. [Fr., ult. < Lat. *nix,* snow.]

nev·er (nĕv'ər) *adv.* **1.** Not ever; on no occasion: *I have never been here before.* **2.** Not at all; in no way: *Never fear. Never mind.* [ME < OE *nǣfre* : *ne,* not + *ǣfre,* ever.]

nev·er·more (nĕv'ər-môr', -mōr') *adv.* Never again.

nev·er-nev·er land (nĕv'ər-nĕv'ər) *n.* An imaginary place where all is idyllic or ideal.

nev·er·the·less (nĕv'ər-*th*ə-lĕs') *adv.* None the less; however: *The plan may fail, but we must try it nevertheless.*

ne·vus (nē'vəs) *n., pl.* **-vi** (-vī'). A congenital growth or mark on the skin, such as a birthmark. [Lat. *naevus.*] **—ne'void'** (-void') *adj.*

new (no͞o, nyo͞o) *adj.* **-er, -est. 1.** Having existed or been made for only a short time; recent: *a new movie.* **2. a.** Not yet old; fresh: *a new coat of paint.* **b.** Never used or worn; not old or secondhand: *a new car.* **3.** Just found, discovered, or learned: *new information.* **4.** Unfamiliar; novel: *ideas that are new to me.* **5.** Starting over again in a cycle: *the new moon.* **6.** Recently obtained or acquired: *new political power.* **7.** Additional: *needed new sources of energy.* **8.** Recently arrived or established in a place, position, or relationship: *new neighbors; a new secretary.* **9.** Changed for the better; rejuvenated: *A nap made a new man of him.* **10.** Coming after or taking the place of a previous one or ones: *a new edition.* **11. a.** Modern; current: *a new dance.* **b. New.** In the most recent form, period, or development: *New Latin.* **12.** Inexperienced or untrained: *new at the job.* *—adv.* Freshly; recently: *the smell of new-mown hay.* [ME *newe* < OE *nīwe.*] **—new'ness** *n.*

Synonyms: *new, novel, original. New* is a broad, general term having reference to both time and condition. *Novel,* which emphasizes condition, is applied to that which is both new and strikingly unusual: *His symphony is not only new* (chronologically), *but novel in its treatment of folk songs. Original* also emphasizes state rather than time, and is said of that which is the first of its kind.

new·born (no͞o'bôrn', nyo͞o'-) *adj.* **1.** Very recently born. **2.** Born anew. *—n.* A neonate.

New·burg also **New·burgh** (no͞o'bûrg', nyo͞o'-) *adj.* Served in a rich sauce made of cream, egg yolks, butter, wine, and usually nutmeg: *lobster Newburg.* [Orig. unknown.]

new·com·er (no͞o'kŭm'ər, nyo͞o'-) *n.* One who has only recently arrived.

New Criticism *n.* A method of literary analysis developed in the mid-20th century that stresses a close examination of the language, structure, imagery, and thematic tensions of the text and posits that the facts of an author's life or his intentions for the work are irrelevant. **—New Critic** *n.*

New Deal *n.* **1.** The programs and policies for economic recovery and reform, relief, and social security introduced during the 1930's by President Franklin D. Roosevelt and his administration. **2.** The period during which the pro-

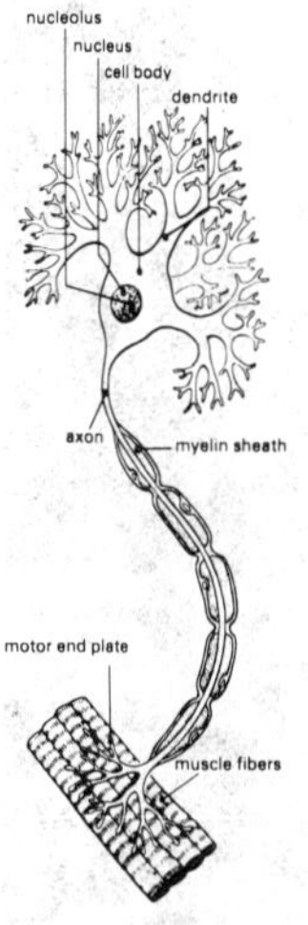

neuron

newel

Newfoundland

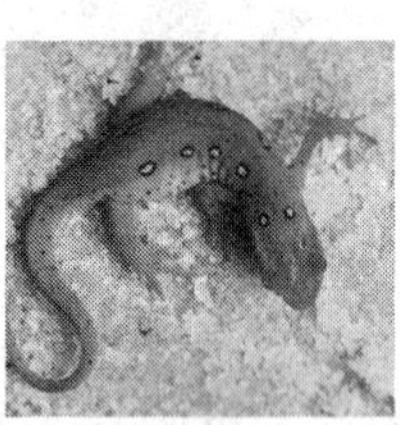
newt

grams and policies of the New Deal were developed. —**New Dealer** *n.*
new·el (no͞o'əl, nyo͞o'-) *n.* **1.** The vertical support at the center of a circular staircase. **2.** A post that supports a handrail at the bottom or at the landing of a staircase. [ME *novel* < OFr. < VLat. **nucale* < Lat. *nux,* nut.]
New English Bible *n.* A British interdenominational translation of the Bible first published in complete form in 1970.
new·fan·gled (no͞o'făng'gəld, nyo͞o'-) *adj.* **1.** New; novel. **2.** Fond of novelty. [< ME *neuefangel,* fond of novelty.] —**new'fan'gled·ness** *n.*
new-fash·ioned (no͞o'făsh'ənd, nyo͞o'-) *adj.* **1.** Up-to-date. **2.** Created in a new form or fashion.
new·found (no͞o'found', nyo͞o'-) *adj.* Recently discovered: *a newfound pastime.*
New·found·land (no͞o'fən-lənd, nyo͞o'-) *n.* A large breed of dog with a broad head and square muzzle, a powerful body, and a dense, usually black coat. [After *Newfoundland,* Canada.]
New·gate (no͞o'gāt', -gĭt, nyo͞o'-) *n.* A famous prison in London, England, that was demolished in 1902.
New Greek *n.* Modern Greek.
New Hebrew *n.* The Hebrew language used in Israel at the present time.
New Jerusalem *n.* **1.** The final resting place of souls having experienced redemption by Christ. **2.** An ideal community on earth.
New Journalism *n.* Journalism that is characterized by the reporter's subjective interpretations and personal involvement and that often features fictional dramatized elements to emphasize that involvement. —**New Journalist** *n.*
New Latin *n.* Latin as used since about 1500.
New Left *n.* A U.S. radical political movement originating in the 1960's and marked by active advocacy of revolutionary changes, as in government, politics, education, and society. —**New Leftist** *n.*
new·ly (no͞o'lē, nyo͞o'-) *adv.* **1.** Lately; recently: *newly baked bread.* **2.** Once more; anew: *a newly painted room.* **3.** In a new or different way; freshly: *an old idea newly phrased.*
new·ly·wed also **new·ly-wed** (no͞o'lē-wĕd', nyo͞o'-) *n.* A person recently married.
new math *n.* Mathematics taught in elementary and secondary schools that constructs mathematical relationships from set theory.
new mathematics *n.* New math.
new moon *n.* **1.** The phase of the moon occurring when it passes between the earth and the sun and is invisible or visible only as a narrow crescent at sunset. **2.** The crescent moon.
news (no͞oz, nyo͞oz) *pl.n. (used with a sing. verb).* **1.** Recent events and happenings, esp. those that are unusual or notable. **2. a.** Information about recent events of general interest, esp. as reported by newspapers, periodicals, radio, or television. **b.** A presentation or broadcast of such information; newscast. **3.** Newsworthy material.
news agency *n.* An organization that provides news coverage to subscribers, as newspapers or periodicals.
news·boy (no͞oz'boi', nyo͞oz'-) *n.* A boy who sells or delivers newspapers.
news·break (no͞oz'brāk', nyo͞oz'-) *n.* An event worthy of reporting, as on television or in the newspaper.
news·cast (no͞oz'kăst', nyo͞oz'-) *n.* A radio or television broadcast of events in the news. [NEWS + (BROAD)CAST.] —**news'cast'er** *n.*
news conference *n.* A press conference.
news·let·ter (no͞oz'lĕt'ər, nyo͞oz'-) *n.* A printed report giving news or information of interest to a special group.
news·man (no͞oz'măn', -mən, nyo͞oz'-) *n.* One who gathers, reports, or edits news.
news·mon·ger (no͞oz'mŭng'gər, -mŏng'-, nyo͞oz'-) *n.* A person who gathers and repeats news, esp. a gossip.
news·pa·per (no͞oz'pā'pər, nyo͞oz'-) *n.* **1.** A typically daily or weekly publication containing current news, editorials, feature articles, and usually advertising. **2.** Newsprint.
news·pa·per·man (no͞oz'pā'pər-măn', nyo͞oz'-) *n.* One who owns or is employed on a newspaper.
new·speak (no͞o'spēk', nyo͞o'-) *n.* Ambiguous and contradictory language used for propagandistic purposes. [< *Newspeak,* a language invented by George Orwell (1903–1950) in the novel *Nineteen Eighty-Four.*]
news·person (no͞oz'pûr'sən, nyo͞oz'-) *n.* A reporter or newscaster.
news·print (no͞oz'prĭnt', nyo͞oz'-) *n.* Inexpensive paper made from wood pulp, used chiefly for printing newspapers.
news·reel (no͞oz'rēl', nyo͞oz'-) *n.* A short motion picture dealing with recent news events.
news release *n.* A handout (sense 3).
news·room (no͞oz'ro͞om', -ro͝om', nyo͞oz'-) *n.* A room, as in a newspaper office or a radio or television station, in which news is prepared for release.
news·stand (no͞oz'stănd', nyo͞oz'-) *n.* A shop or open booth at which newspapers and periodicals are sold.
New Style *n.* The method of reckoning the months and days of the year according to the Gregorian calendar.
news·wom·an (no͞oz'wo͝om'ən, nyo͞oz'-) *n.* A woman who gathers, reports, or edits news.
news·wor·thy (no͞oz'wûr'thē, nyo͞oz'-) *adj.* Worthy of reporting to the general public: *a newsworthy event.*
news·y (no͞o'zē, nyo͞o'-) *adj.* **-i·er, -i·est.** *Informal.* Full of news; informative. —**news'i·ness** *n.*
newt (no͞ot, nyo͞ot) *n.* Any of several small, semiaquatic salamanders of the genus *Triturus* and related genera. [ME *a neute,* alteration of *an eute,* var. of *evete* < OE *efete.*]
New Testament *n.* The Gospels, Acts, Pauline and other Epistles, and the Book of Revelation, together viewed by Christians as forming the record of the new dispensation belonging to the Church. See table at **Bible.**
New Thought *n.* A modern religious movement that emphasizes spiritual healing and the creative power of positive thought.
new·ton (no͞ot'n, nyo͞ot'n) *n. Physics.* In the meter-kilogram-second system, the unit of force required to accelerate a mass of one kilogram one meter per second per second that is equal to 100,000 dynes. [After Sir Isaac *Newton* (1642–1727).]
New·to·ni·an (no͞o-tō'nē-ən, nyo͞o-) *adj.* Of, pertaining to, or in accordance with the work of Sir Isaac Newton, esp. that in mechanics and gravitation: *Newtonian physics.*
new town *n.* A planned urban community designed for self-sufficiency and comprising housing, industrial, commercial, and recreational facilities.
New Wave *n.* **1.** A film-making movement that is characterized by unconventional techniques, as abstraction and subjective symbolism, and often by experimental photography. **2.** A new movement in a particular area, as popular music or gourmet cooking. **3.** Rock music marked by ensemble playing rather than lengthy solo passages and by lyrics that express anger or social alienation.
New Year *n.* **1.** The first day or days of the calendar year. **2.** Rosh Hashanah.
New Year's Day *n.* The first day of the year, January 1, celebrated as a holiday in many countries.
New York aster (yôrk) *n.* A wild aster, *Aster novi-belgi,* of eastern North America, with pointed leaves and bluish-violet flowers.
next (nĕkst) *adj.* **1.** Closest or nearest in space or position; adjacent: *the next room.* **2.** Immediately preceding or following in time, order, or sequence: *next Monday; the next President.* —*adv.* **1.** In the time, position, or order nearest or immediately following: *What comes next?* **2.** On the first subsequent occasion: *when next I write.* —*prep.* Close to; nearest. [ME *nexte* < OE *nēahst,* superl. of *nēah,* near.]
next door *adv.* To or in the adjacent house, building, room, or apartment. —**next'-door'** (nĕkst'dôr', -dōr') *adj.*
next friend *n. Law.* One who is appointed by or admitted to a court to sue as the representative of a minor or other person under legal disability.
next of kin *n.* **1.** The person or persons most nearly related to another person. **2.** *Law.* **a.** The closest relative of a deceased person. **b.** Those relatives entitled to the estate of a deceased person in accordance with the statutes of distribution.
nex·us (nĕk'səs) *n., pl.* **nexus** or **-us·es. 1.** A means of connection; link or tie. **2.** A connected series or group. [Lat. < *nectere,* to bind.]
Nez Perce (nĕz' pûrs', nĕs') *n., pl.* **Nez Perce** or **Nez Perc·es** (pûr'sĭz). **1.** A tribe of Indians formerly occupying much of the Pacific Northwest. **2.** A member of the Nez Perce. **3.** The Sahaptin language of the Nez Perce. [Canadian Fr.]
n'ga·na (nə-gä'nə) *n.* Variant of **nagana.**
ngul·trum (ĕn-gŭl'trəm, ĕng-) *n.* See table at **currency.** [Native word in Bhutan.]
ngwee (ĕn-gwē') *n., pl.* **ngwee.** See table at **currency.** [Of Bantu orig.]
Ni The symbol for the element nickel.
ni·a·cin (nī'ə-sĭn) *n.* Nicotinic acid. [NI(COTINIC) AC(ID) + -IN.]
nib (nĭb) *n.* **1. a.** The point of a quill pen, esp. when sharpened. **b.** The point of a pen. **2.** A sharp point or tip. **3.** A bird's beak or bill. [Perh. alteration of NEB.]
nib·ble (nĭb'əl) *v.* **-bled, -bling, -bles.** —*tr.* **1.** To bite at gently and repeatedly. **2.** To eat with small, quick bites or in small morsels. —*intr.* To take small or hesitant bites: *fish nibbling at the bait.* —*n.* **1.** A small quantity, esp. of food; morsel. **2.** An act of nibbling. [Orig. unknown.]
Ni·be·lung (nē'bə-lo͝ong') *n. Germanic Myth.* **1.** Any of a race of subterranean dwarfs whose hoard of riches and magic ring were taken from them by Siegfried. **2.** A follower of Siegfried. **3.** One of the Burgundian kings in the *Nibelungenlied.* [G. < MHG *Nibelungen.*]
Ni·be·lung·en·lied (nē'bə-lo͝ong'ən-lēd') *n.* A Middle High German epic poem written in the early 13th century and based on the legends of Siegfried and of the Burgundian kings.
nib·lick (nĭb'lĭk) *n.* A nine iron. [Orig. unknown.]
nic·co·lite (nĭk'ə-līt') *n.* A nickel ore, essentially nickel arsenide, NiAs, found in America and Europe. [NLat. *niccolum,* nickel (perh. < Swed. *nickel*) + -ITE.]
nice (nīs) *adj.* **nic·er, nic·est. 1.** Pleasing and agreeable in nature; enjoyable: *a nice time.* **2.** Having a pleasant or attractive appearance: *a nice dress; a nice face.* **3.** Courteous and polite; considerate: *a nice gesture.* **4.** Of good character

and reputation; respectable: *a nice family.* **5.** Characterized by sometimes excessive delicacy or fastidiousness; fussy. **6.** Showing or marked by great precision and sensitive discernment; subtle: *a nice distinction.* **7.** Executed with delicacy, accuracy, and skill: *a nice bit of craftsmanship.* **8.** Used as an intensive with *and*: *nice and warm.* **9.** *Obs.* **a.** Wanton; profligate. **b.** Affectedly modest; coy. [ME, foolish < OFr. < Lat. *nescius,* ignorant < *nescire,* to be ignorant. —see NESCIENCE.] **—nice'ly** *adv.* **—nice'ness** *n.*

Ni·cene Creed (nī'sēn', nī-sēn') *n.* A formal statement of doctrine of the Christian faith adopted at the Council of Nicaea in A.D. 325 and expanded in later councils.

nice-nel·ly (nīs'nĕl'ē) *adj.* **1.** Priggish. **2.** Marked by the use of euphemism: *nice-nelly language.* [< the name *Nelly.*]

ni·ce·ty (nī'sĭ-tē) *n., pl.* **-ties. 1.** The quality of showing or requiring careful and precise treatment. **2.** Delicacy of feeling or taste; fastidiousness. **3.** A fine point, small detail, or subtle distinction. **4.** An elegant or refined feature; amenity: *the niceties of civilized life.* [ME *nicete,* exactitude, silliness < OFr., silliness < *nice,* silly. —see NICE.]

niche (nĭch, nēsh) *n.* **1.** A recess in a wall, as for holding a statue. **2.** A cranny, hollow, or crevice, as in rock. **3.** A situation or activity specially suited to a person's abilities or character. **4.** *Ecol.* **a.** The set of functional relationships of an organism or population to the environment it occupies. **b.** The area within a habitat occupied by an organism. *—tr.v.* **niched, nich·ing, nich·es.** To place in a niche. [Fr. < OFr. < *nichier,* to nest < VLat. **nidicare* < Lat. *nidus,* nest.]

nick (nĭk) *n.* A shallow notch, cut, or indentation on a surface. *—tr.v.* **nicked, nick·ing, nicks. 1. a.** To cut a nick or notch in. **b.** To graze and wound slightly: *a sliver of glass that nicked his hand.* **2.** To cut short; check. **3.** *Slang.* To cheat or defraud, esp. to overcharge. **—*idiom.* in the nick of time.** Just at the critical moment. [ME *nik.*]

nick·el (nĭk'əl) *n.* **1.** *Symbol* **Ni** A silvery, hard, ductile, ferromagnetic metallic element used in alloys, in corrosion-resistant surfaces and batteries, and for electroplating. Atomic number 28; atomic weight 58.71; melting point 1,453°C; boiling point 2,732°C; specific gravity 8.902; principal valence 2. **2.** A U.S. coin worth five cents, made of a nickel and copper alloy. *—tr.v.* **-eled, -el·ing, -els** or **-elled, -el·ling, -els.** To coat with a thin layer of nickel. [Swed., short for G. *kupfernickel,* niccolite : *kupfer,* copper (< OHG *kupfar* < LLat. *cuprum*) + *Nickel,* demon, from the deceptive copper color of the ore.]

nick·el-and-dime (nĭk'əl-ən-dīm') *Informal. —adj.* **1.** Consisting of, involving, or paying only a small amount of money: *a nickel-and-dime job.* **2.** Minor; small-time: *nickel-and-dime speculators.* *—v.* **-dimed, -dim·ing, -dimes.** *—intr.* To spend money carefully, esp. out of necessity. *—tr.* To change for the worse, esp. to diminish or destroy gradually through persistent attention to petty financial details: *nickel-and-dimed the research project out of existence.*

nick·el·ic (nĭ-kĕl'ĭk) *adj.* **1.** Of or containing nickel. **2.** Of or containing trivalent nickel, Ni^{3+}.

nick·el·if·er·ous (nĭk'ə-lĭf'ər-əs) *adj.* Bearing or containing nickel. Used of ores.

nick·el·o·de·on (nĭk'ə-lō'dē-ən) *n.* **1.** An early movie house charging an admission price of five cents. **2. a.** A player piano. **b.** A juke box. [NICKEL + (MEL)ODEON.]

nick·el·ous (nĭk'ə-ləs) *adj.* **1.** Of or containing nickel. **2.** Of or containing bivalent nickel, Ni^{2+}.

nickel silver *n.* A silvery, hard, corrosion-resistant, malleable alloy of copper, zinc, and nickel.

nick·er (nĭk'ər) *intr.v.* **-ered, -er·ing, -ers.** To neigh softly. [Perh. alteration of NEIGH.] **—nick'er** *n.*

nick·nack (nĭk'năk') *n.* Variant of **knickknack.**

nick·name (nĭk'nām') *n.* **1.** A descriptive name added to or replacing the actual name of a person, place, or thing. **2.** A familiar or shortened form of a proper name. *—tr.v.* **-named, -nam·ing, -names. 1.** To give a nickname to. **2.** To call by an incorrect name; misname. [ME *a nekename,* alteration of *an ekename* : *eke,* addition (< OE *ēaca*) + *name,* name < OE *nama.*] **—nick'nam'er** *n.*

ni·co·ti·an·a (nĭ-kō'shē-ăn'ə, -ä'nə, -ā'nə) *n.* Any of various flowering tobacco plants of the genus *Nicotiana,* native to the Americas. [NLat. *(herba) nicotiana,* (herb of) Nicot, after Jean *Nicot* (1530?–1600).]

nicotin– *pref.* **1.** Nicotine: *nicotinic.* **2.** Nicotinic acid: *nicotinamide.* [< NICOTINE.]

nic·o·tin·a·mide-ad·e·nine di·nu·cle·o·tide (nĭk'ə-tē'nə-mĭd-ăd'n-ēn' dī-nōō'klē-ə-tīd', -nyōō'-, -tĭn'ə-) *n.* An enzyme, $C_{21}H_{27}N_7O_{14}P_2$, occurring in most living cells and utilized alternately as an oxidizing or reducing agent in various metabolic processes.

nicotinamide-adenine dinucleotide phosphate *n.* An enzyme, $C_{21}H_{28}N_7O_{17}P_3$, occurring in most living cells and utilized similarly to nicotinamide-adenine dinucleotide but interacting with different metabolites.

nic·o·tine (nĭk'ə-tēn') *n.* A poisonous alkaloid, $C_5H_4NC_4H_7NCH_3$, derived from the tobacco plant and used in medicine and as an insecticide. [Fr. < NLat. *nicotiana.* —see NICOTIANA.]

nic·o·tin·ic (nĭk'ə-tĭn'ĭk, -tē'nĭk) *adj.* **1.** Of or pertaining to nicotine. **2.** Of or pertaining to nicotinic acid.

nicotinic acid *n.* A member of the vitamin B complex, C_5H_4NCOOH, occurring in living cells as an essential substance for growth and synthesized for use in treating pellagra. [So called because it is often obtained by oxidizing nicotine.]

nic·o·tin·ism (nĭk'ə-tē-nĭz'əm) *n.* Nicotine poisoning.

nic·ti·tate (nĭk'tĭ-tāt') also **nic·tate** (nĭk'tāt') *intr.v.* **-tat·ed, -tat·ing, -tates.** To wink. [Med. Lat. *nictitare, nictitat-,* freq. of Lat. *nictare,* to wink.] **—nic'ti·ta'tion** *n.*

nictitating membrane also **nictating membrane** *n.* An inner eyelid in birds, reptiles, and some mammals that helps to keep the eye clean.

nid·der·ing (nĭd'ər-ĭng) *n. Archaic.* A cowardly person; wretch. [Alteration of ME *nithing* < OE *nīðing* < ON *nīðingr.*]

nide (nīd) *n.* A nest or brood of pheasants. [Lat. *nidus,* nest.]

ni·di (nī'dī') *n.* A plural of **nidus.**

nid·i·fy (nĭd'ə-fī') *intr.v.* **-fied, -fy·ing, -fies.** To build a nest. [Lat. *nidificare* : *nidus,* nest + *facere,* to make.] **—nid'i·fi·ca'tion** *n.*

ni·dus (nī'dəs) *n., pl.* **-dus·es** or **-di** (-dī'). **1.** A nest, esp. one for the eggs of insects or spiders. **2.** A cavity where spores develop. **3.** *Pathol.* The seat of bacterial growth in a living organism. [Lat.]

niece (nēs) *n.* **1.** A daughter of one's brother, brother-in-law, sister, or sister-in-law. **2.** The daughter of a celibate ecclesiastic. [ME *nece* < OFr. < VLat. **neptia* < Lat. *neptis.*]

ni·el·lo (nē-ĕl'ō) *n., pl.* **-el·li** (-ĕl'ē) or **-el·los. 1.** Any of several black metallic alloys of sulfur with copper, silver, or lead, used to fill an incised design on the surface of another metal. **2.** A surface or object decorated with niello. **3.** The art or process of ornamenting metal surfaces with niello. *—tr.v.* **-loed, -lo·ing, -los.** To decorate or inlay with niello. [Ital. < Med. Lat. *nigellum* < Lat. *nigellus,* dim. of *niger,* black.] **—ni·el'list** *n.*

niche

Nif·l·heim (nĭv'əl-hām') *n.* The realm of the dead in Norse mythology. [ON *niflheimr* : *nifl,* mist + *heimr,* home.]

nif·ty (nĭf'tē) *Slang. —adj.* **-ti·er, -ti·est.** Very good; first-rate. *—n., pl.* **-ties.** Something regarded as being nifty. [Orig. unknown.] **—nif'ti·ly** *adv.* **—nif'ti·ness** *n.*

Ni·ger-Con·go (nī'jər-kŏng'gō) *n.* A large language family of south, central, and west Africa that includes the Mande, Kwa, and Bantu groups.

nig·gard (nĭg'ərd) *n.* A stingy, grasping person; miser. *—adj.* Stingy; niggardly. [ME *nigard,* of Scandinavian orig.]

nig·gard·ly (nĭg'ərd-lē) *adj.* **1.** Unwilling to give, spend, or share; stingy. **2.** Scanty; meager. **—nig'gard·li·ness** *n.* **—nig'gard·ly** *adv.*

nig·ger (nĭg'ər) *n. Offensive Slang.* A black or member of any dark-skinned people. [Alteration of dial. *neger,* black person < Fr. *nègre* < Sp. *negro.* —see NEGRO.]

nig·gle (nĭg'əl) *intr.v.* **-gled, -gling, -gles. 1.** To be preoccupied with trifles or petty details. **2.** To find fault constantly and trivially; carp. [Orig. unknown.] **—nig'gler** *n.*

nig·gling (nĭg'lĭng) *adj.* **1.** Excessively concerned with details; fussy. **2.** Persistently nagging; petty. **3.** Showing or requiring close attention to details; exacting: *niggling paperwork.* **—nig'gling** *n.* **—nig'gling·ly** *adv.*

nigh (nī) *adv.* **-er, -est. 1.** Near in time, place, or relationship: *I'd perch by her window as evening drew nigh.* **2.** Nearly; almost: *nigh onto two hours.* *—adj.* **-er, -est. 1.** Being near in time, place, or relationship; close. **2.** *Regional.* Short; direct. *—prep.* Not far from; near. *—tr. & intr.v.* **nighed, nigh·ing, nighs.** To come near to or draw near. [ME *neigh* < OE *nēah.*]

night (nīt) *n.* **1.** The period between sunset and sunrise, esp. the hours of darkness. **2.** Nightfall: *worked from morning to night.* **3.** Darkness: *vanished into the night.* **4.** A time or condition of gloom, obscurity, ignorance, or sorrow: *"In a real dark night of the soul it is always three o'clock in the morning"* (F. Scott Fitzgerald). **—*modifier:*** *a night game; a night light.* [ME < OE *niht.*]

night-blind (nīt'blīnd') *adj.* Suffering from night blindness.

night blindness *n.* Vision that is normal in daylight but abnormally weak when the light is dim.

night-bloom·ing cereus (nīt'blōō'mĭng) *n.* Any of several flowering cacti having large, fragrant flowers that open at night.

night·cap (nīt'kăp') *n.* **1.** A cloth cap worn esp. in bed. **2.** *Informal.* A drink, usually alcoholic, taken just before bedtime. **3.** *Slang.* The last event in a day's competition, esp. the final game in a baseball double-header.

night·clothes (nīt'klōz', -klōthz') *pl.n.* Clothes worn in bed.

night·club (nīt'klŭb') *n.* An establishment that stays open late at night and provides food, drink, and entertainment.

night crawler *n.* Any of various earthworms that crawl out from the ground at night.

night·dress (nīt'drĕs') *n.* **1.** A nightgown. **2.** Nightclothes.

night·fall (nīt'fôl') *n.* The approach of darkness; dusk.

night·glow (nīt'glō') *n.* Airglow occurring at night.

night·gown (nīt'goun') *n.* A loose garment worn to bed.

night·hawk (nīt'hôk') *n.* **1. a.** Any of several mainly nocturnal birds of the genus *Chordeiles,* having buff to black mottled feathers, esp. *C. minor,* of North America. **b.** A related European bird, the nightjar. **2.** *Informal.* A night owl.

night heron *n.* Any of several nocturnal herons of the genus *Nycticorax,* esp. the black-crowned heron, *N. nycticorax.*

nightingale

George Miksch Sutton
nightjar

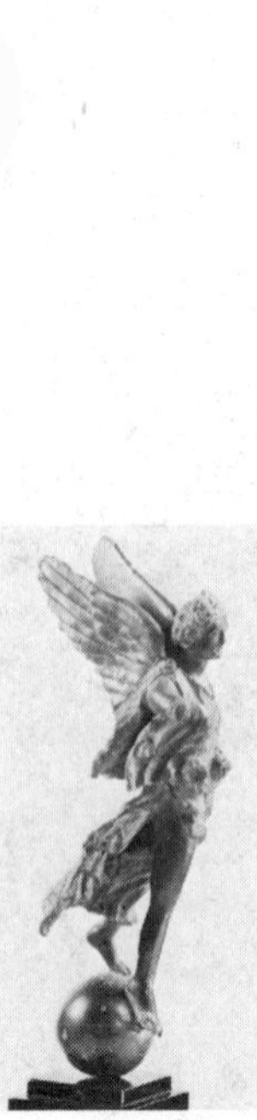
Nike

night·ie or **night·y** (nī′tē) *n., pl.* **-ies.** *Informal.* A woman's nightgown. [Shortening and alteration of NIGHTGOWN.]
night·in·gale (nīt′n-gāl′, nī′tĭng-) *n.* **1.** A European songbird, *Luscinia megarhynchos,* with brownish plumage, noted for its nocturnal song. **2.** Any of various nocturnal songbirds. [ME *nightegale* < OE *nihtegale* : *niht,* night + *galan,* to sing.]
night·jar (nīt′jär′) *n.* Any of various nocturnal birds of the family Caprimulgidae, esp. the common European nightjar, *Caprimulgus europaeus.*
night jasmine *n.* **1.** A shrub, *Nyctanthes arbortristis,* cultivated for its small, white, fragrant flowers. **2.** A West Indian shrub, *Cestrum nocturnum,* having small, greenish-white flowers that are very fragrant at night.
night latch *n.* A spring lock that can be opened from the inside by turning a knob but from the outside only with a key.
night letter *n.* A telegram sent at night at a reduced rate for delivery the next morning.
night·life (nīt′līf′) *n.* Social activities or entertainment available or pursued in the evening.
night-light (nīt′līt′) *n.* A usually small light left on all night.
night·long (nīt′lông′, -lŏng′) *adj.* Lasting through the whole night. —*adv.* Through the night; all night.
night·ly (nīt′lē) *adj.* **1.** Of or occurring during the night; nocturnal: *nightly prowling.* **2.** Happening or done every night: *nightly rounds.* **—night′ly** *adv.*
night·mare (nīt′mâr′) *n.* **1.** A dream arousing feelings of intense, inescapable fear, horror, and distress. **2.** Something, as an event or experience, that is as intensely distressing as a nightmare. **3.** A demon or spirit once thought to plague sleeping people. [ME, a female demon that afflicts sleeping people : *night,* night + *mare,* goblin < OE.] **—night′mar′ish** *adj.* **—night′mar′ish·ly** *adv.* **—night′mar′ish·ness** *n.*
night owl *n.* A person who habitually stays up late at night.
night·rid·er (nīt′rī′dər) *n.* One of a band of mounted and usually masked men who engaged in nocturnal terrorism for revenge or intimidation in the southern United States.
nights (nīts) *adv.* Regularly or habitually in the nighttime: *works nights and Saturdays.*
night-scent·ed stock (nīt′sĕn′tĭd) *n.* Evening stock.
night school *n.* A school that holds classes in the evening.
night·shade (nīt′shād′) *n.* Any of several plants of the genus *Solanum,* many of them having a poisonous juice, esp. the deadly nightshade and the bittersweet. [ME < OE *nihtscada.*]
night·shirt (nīt′shûrt′) *n.* A long shirt worn in bed.
night soil *n.* Human excrement collected for use as fertilizer.
night·stand (nīt′stănd′) *n.* A night table.
night·stick (nīt′stĭk′) *n.* A club carried by a policeman.
night table *n.* A small table or stand placed at a bedside.
night·tide (nīt′tīd′) *n.* Nighttime.
night·time (nīt′tīm′) *n.* The time between sunset and sunrise.
night·walk·er (nīt′wô′kər) *n.* **1.** One who walks around in the streets at night. **2.** A night crawler.
night·y (nī′tē) *n.* Variant of **nightie.**
ni·gres·cence (nī-grĕs′əns) *n.* **1.** The process of becoming black or dark. **2.** Blackness or darkness, as of complexion. [< Lat. *nigrescens, nigrescent-,* pr.part. of *nigrescere,* to become black < *niger,* black.] **—ni·gres′cent** *adj.*
ni·gri·tude (nī′grĭ-to͞od′, -tyo͞od′, nĭg′rĭ-) *n.* Blackness. [Lat. *nigritudo* < *niger,* black.]
ni·gro·sine (nī′grə-sēn′, -sĭn) *n.* Any of a class of dyes, varying from blue to black, used in the manufacture of inks and for dyeing wood and textiles. [Lat. *niger, nigr-,* black + -OS(E) + -INE.]
ni·hil·ism (nī′ə-lĭz′əm, nī′hə-, nē′-) *n.* **1.** A doctrine that all values are baseless and that nothing is knowable or can be communicated. **2.** Rejection of all distinctions in moral value, constituting a willingness to refute all previous theories of morality. **3.** The belief that destruction of existing political or social institutions is necessary for future improvement. **4.** Also **Nihilism.** The doctrine of a 19th-century Russian movement that advocated assassination and terrorism. [< Lat. *nihil,* nothing.] **—ni′hil·ist** (-lĭst) *n.* **—ni′hil·is′tic** *adj.*
ni·hil·i·ty (nī-hĭl′ĭ-tē, nē-) *n.* Nonexistence; nothingness.
ni·hil ob·stat (nī′hĭl ŏb′stăt′, -stät′, nē′-) *n.* **1.** An attestation by a Roman Catholic censor that a book contains nothing damaging to faith or morals. **2.** Official approval, esp. of an artistic work. [Lat., nothing hinders.]
-nik *suff.* One associated with or characterized by: *peacenik.* [Yiddish, of Slavic orig.]
Ni·ke (nī′kē) *n. Gk. Myth.* The goddess of victory. [Gk. *Nikē.*]
nil (nĭl) *n.* Nothing; zero. [Lat., short for *nihil.*] **—nil** *adj.*
Nile blue (nīl) *n.* A light bluish green.
Nile green *n.* A moderate yellow green to vivid pale green.
nill (nĭl) *v.* **nilled, nill·ing, nills.** *Obs.* —*tr.* Not to will; not to wish. —*intr.* To be unwilling. [ME *nilen* < OE *nyllan* : *ne,* not + *wyllan,* to wish.]
Ni·lot·ic (nī-lŏt′ĭk) *adj.* **1.** Of or pertaining to the Nile or the Nile Valley. **2.** Of or pertaining to a Negroid group of peoples in eastern Africa. —*n.* A large group of related African languages spoken in southern Sudan, Uganda, Kenya, and northern Tanzania. [Lat. *Niloticus* < Gk. *Neilotikos* < *Neilos,* Nile.]
nil·po·tent (nĭl-pōt′nt, nĭl′pōt′nt) *n.* An algebraic quantity that when raised to some power equals zero. **—nil·po′ten·cy** *n.*
nim (nĭm) *tr. & intr.v.* **nimmed, nim·ming, nims.** *Archaic.* To steal; pilfer. [ME *nimen,* to take < OE *niman.*]
nim·bi (nĭm′bī′) *n.* A plural of **nimbus.**
nim·ble (nĭm′bəl) *adj.* **-bler, -blest. 1.** Quick, light, or agile in movement or action; deft: *nimble fingers.* **2.** Quick and clever in thinking, understanding, or responding: *a nimble wit.* [ME *nemel,* prob. of OE orig.] **—nim′ble·ness** *n.* **—nim′bly** *adv.*
Synonyms: *nimble, agile, quick, brisk, facile, spry, sprightly, chipper. Nimble* is applied to both mental capacity (*nimble wit*) and physical ability; in each case it indicates lightness, speed, and adroitness. *Agile* primarily applies to physical dexterity. *Quick,* in this context applicable to both physical and mental capacity, connotes readiness born more of alertness than of innate ability. *Brisk* may indicate either animated physical movement or, applied to nouns that do not themselves have the sense of movement, that which is conducive to such activity: *a brisk climate. Facile,* used in describing physical and mental activity and speech, befits ease bordering on effortlessness; sometimes it has the disparaging implications of superficiality, cursoriness, or glibness. *Spry* usually pertains to physical alacrity in elderly persons. *Sprightly* and *chipper* are said of one showing animation of spirit.
nim·bo·stra·tus (nĭm′bō-strā′təs, -străt′əs) *n.* A low, gray cloud, often dark, that precipitates rain, snow, or sleet. [NIMB(US) + STRATUS.]
nim·bus (nĭm′bəs) *n., pl.* **-bi** (bī′) or **-bus·es. 1.** A cloudy radiance said to surround a deity when on earth. **2.** A radiant light that appears usually in the form of a circle about the head in the representation of a deity or saint. **3.** An atmosphere or aura, as of glamour, that surrounds someone or something. **4.** A uniformly gray rain cloud that extends over the sky. [Lat., cloud.]
ni·mi·e·ty (nĭ-mī′ĭ-tē) *n.* Excess; redundancy. [LLat. *nimietas* < Lat. *nimius,* excessive < *nimis,* excessively.]
nim·i·ny-pim·i·ny (nĭm′ə-nē-pĭm′ə-nē) *adj.* Affectedly delicate or refined. [Perh. alteration of NAMBY-PAMBY.] **—nim′i·ny-pim′i·ny** *n.*
Nim·rod (nĭm′rŏd′) *n.* **1.** A mighty hunter and king and Noah's great-grandson in the Old Testament. **2.** Also **nimrod.** A hunter. [Heb. *Nimrōdh.*]
nin·com·poop (nĭn′kəm-po͞op′, nĭng′-) *n.* A silly or stupid person; fool. [Orig. unknown.] **—nin′com·poop′er·y** *n.*
nine (nīn) *n.* **1.** The cardinal number that is next after the number 8 and equal to the sum of 8 + 1. **2.** The ninth in a set or sequence. **3.** Something having nine parts, units, or members. **4.** A set of nine persons or things, esp.: **a.** A baseball team. **b. Nine.** The nine Muses. ***—idiom.* to the nines.** To the highest degree: *dressed to the nines.* [ME < OE *nigon;* akin to G. *neun,* Lat. *novem,* Gk. *ennea,* Skt. *nava.*] **—nine** *adj. & pron.*
nine·bark (nīn′bärk′) *n.* A shrub, *Physocarpus opulifolius,* of eastern North America, having peeling or shredding bark and clusters of small, white flowers. [From the many layers in its bark.]
nine days' wonder *n.* Something that creates a brief sensation.
nine·fold (nīn′fōld′) *adj.* **1.** Having nine parts. **2.** Nine times as many or as much. **—nine′fold′** *adv.*
nine iron *n.* An iron-headed golf club with a face slanted at a greater angle than any other iron.
nine·pin (nīn′pĭn′) *n.* **1.** A wooden pin used in the game of ninepins. **2. ninepins.** *(used with a sing. verb).* A bowling game in which nine wooden pins are the target.
nine·teen (nīn-tēn′) *n.* **1.** The cardinal number that is next after the number 18 and equal to the sum of 18 + 1. **2.** The nineteenth in a set or sequence. [ME *nintene* < OE *nigontȳne* < *nigon,* nine.] **—nine·teen′** *adj. & pron.*
nine·teenth (nīn-tēnth′) *n.* **1.** The ordinal number that matches the number nineteen in a series. **2.** One of nineteen equal parts. **—nine·teenth′** *adj. & adv.*
nine·ti·eth (nīn′tē-ĭth) *n.* **1.** The ordinal number that matches the number ninety in a series. **2.** One of ninety equal parts. **—nine′ti·eth** *adj. & adv.*
nine-to-fiv·er (nīn′tə-fī′vər) *n.* A person who works regular daytime hours, as in an office.
nine·ty (nīn′tē) *n., pl.* **-ties.** The cardinal number equal to 9 × 10. [ME *ninti* < OE *nigontig* : *nigon,* nine + *-tig,* -ty.] **—nine′ty** *adj. & pron.*
nin·ny (nĭn′ē) *n., pl.* **-nies.** A fool; simpleton. [Perh. alteration of INNOCENT.]
ni·non (nē′nŏn′) *n.* A sheer fabric of silk, rayon, or nylon made in a variety of tight smooth weaves or open lacy patterns. [Prob. < Fr. *Ninon,* nickname for *Anne.*]
ninth (nīnth) *n.* **1.** The ordinal number that matches the number nine in a series. **2.** One of nine equal parts. **3.** *Mus.* **a.** A harmonic or melodic interval of an octave and a second. **b.** The tone at the upper limit of such an interval. **c.** A chord consisting of a root with its third, seventh, and ninth. [ME *ninthe* < *nine,* nine < OE *nigon.*] **—ninth** *adj. & adv.*
Ni·nus (nī′nəs) *n.* The legendary founder of Nineveh and husband of Semiramis. [Lat. < Gk. *Ninos.*]

Ni·o·be (nī'ə-bē) *n. Gk. Myth.* The daughter of Tantalus who turned to stone while bewailing the loss of her children. [Gk. *Niobē.*]

ni·o·bi·um (nī-ō'bē-əm) *n. Symbol* **Nb** A silvery, soft, ductile metallic element that occurs chiefly in columbite-tantalite and is used in steel alloys, arc welding, and superconductivity research. Atomic number 41; atomic weight 92.906; melting point 2,468°C; boiling point 4,927°C; specific gravity 8.57; valences 2, 3, 5. [After *Niobe,* so called because it is obtained from tantalite. —see TANTALITE.]

nip¹ (nĭp) *v.* **nipped, nip·ping, nips.** *—tr.* **1.** To seize and pinch or bite: *The lobster nipped the wader's toe.* **2.** To remove or sever by or as if by nipping: *nipped off the plant leaf.* **3.** To sting with the cold; chill. **4.** To stop the further growth or development of: *nipped the scandal in the bud.* **5.** *Slang.* **a.** To snatch up hastily. **b.** To steal. *—intr. Chiefly Brit. Slang.* To move quickly; dart. *—n.* **1.** The act of nipping; a small, sharp bite or pinch. **2.** A small bit or portion. **3. a.** A sharp, stinging quality, as of frosty air. **b.** Severely sharp cold. **4.** A cutting or stinging remark. **5.** A sharp, biting flavor; tang. ***—idiom.*** **nip and tuck.** Very close; neck and neck. [ME *nippen* < MDu. *nipen.*]

nip² (nĭp) *n.* A small amount of liquor. *—v.* **nipped, nip·ping, nips.** *—tr.* To drink (alcoholic liquor) in small amounts: *had been nipping brandy. —intr.* To take a nip or nips of alcoholic liquor: *nips all day.* [< *nip,* a small amount of spirits, prob. short for *nipperkin,* of Germanic orig.] **—nip'per** *n.*

ni·pa (nē'pə) *n.* **1.** A large palm, *Nipa frutescens,* of the Philippines and Australia, having long leaves much used for thatching. **2.** An alcoholic beverage made from the sap of the nipa. [New Latin < Malay *nipah.*]

nip·per (nĭp'ər) *n.* **1.** Often **nippers.** A tool, such as pliers or pincers, used for grasping or nipping. **2.** A pincerlike part, such as the large claw of a crustacean. **3.** *Chiefly Brit.* A small boy.

nip·ping (nĭp'ĭng) *adj.* Sharp and biting, as the cold. **—nip'ping·ly** *adv.*

nip·ple (nĭp'əl) *n.* **1.** The small conical protuberance near the center of the mammary gland containing the outlets of the milk ducts. **2. a.** The rubber cap on a bottle from which a baby nurses. **b.** A pacifier for an infant. **3.** Any of various devices resembling or functioning like a nipple, esp.: **a.** A regulated opening for discharging a liquid, as in a small stopcock. **b.** A pipe coupling threaded on both ends. **c.** A short extension of pipe to which a nozzle can be attached. **4.** A natural projection resembling a nipple, as a mountain crest. [< obs. *neble,* dim of NEB.]

nip·ple·wort (nĭp'əl-wûrt', -wôrt') *n.* A plant, *Lapsana communis,* having a milky juice and small, yellow flower heads. [From its former use in folk medicine to cure breast tumors.]

Nip·pon·ese (nĭp'ə-nēz', -nēs') *adj. & n.* Japanese. [< *Nippon* (Japan).]

nip·py (nĭp'ē) *adj.* **-pi·er, -pi·est. 1.** Sharp or biting: *nippy cheese.* **2.** Bitingly cold: *a nippy fall day.* **—nip'pi·ly** *adv.* **—nip'pi·ness** *n.*

nip-up (nĭp'ŭp') *n.* An acrobatic spring from a supine to an upright position.

nir·va·na (nîr-vä'nə, nər-) *n.* **1. Nirvana.** *Buddhism.* **a.** The state of absolute blessedness, characterized by release from the cycle of reincarnations and attained through the extinction of the self. **b.** A similar state in which reunion with Brahma is attained through the suppression of individual existence. **2.** An ideal condition of rest, harmony, stability, or joy. [Skt. *nirvāṇam* : *nir-,* out, away + *vāti,* he blows.]

Ni·san (nĭs'ən, nē-sän') *n.* In the Hebrew calendar, the seventh month of the civil year and the first of the religious year. See table at **calendar.** [Heb. *Nīsān* < Akkadian *Nissanu.*]

Ni·sei (nē-sā', nē'sā') *n., pl.* **Nisei** or **-seis.** A person born in America of parents who emigrated from Japan. [J. : *ni,* second + *sei,* generation.]

ni·si (nī'sī') *adj. Law.* Taking effect at a specified date unless cause is shown for modification or nullification: *a decree nisi.* [Lat. : *ne-,* not + *si,* if.]

Nis·sen hut (nĭs'ən) *n.* A prefabricated building of corrugated steel in the shape of a half cylinder, used esp. as a military shelter. [After Lieut. Col. Peter N. *Nissen* (1871–1930).]

ni·sus (nī'səs) *n., pl.* **nisus.** An effort or endeavor to realize an aim. [Lat. < *niti,* to strive.]

nit (nĭt) *n.* **1.** The egg or young of a parasitic insect, such as a louse. **2.** A unit of illuminative brightness equal to one candle per square meter, measured perpendicular to the rays of the source. [ME *nite* < OE *hnitu.*] **—nit'ty** *adj.*

ni·ter (nī'tər) *n.* A white, gray, or colorless mineral of potassium nitrate, KNO_3, used in making gunpowder. [ME *nitre* < OFr. < Lat. *nitrum,* natron < Gk. *nitron,* of Semitic orig.]

nit-pick (nĭt'pĭk') *intr.v.* **-picked, -pick·ing, -picks.** *Informal.* To be concerned with or find fault with insignificant details. **—nit'-pick'er** *n.*

nitr- *pref.* Variant of **nitro-.**

ni·trate (nī'trāt', -trĭt) *n.* **1.** The radical NO_3^- or a compound containing it, as a salt or ester of nitric acid. **2.** Fertilizer consisting of sodium nitrate or potassium nitrate. *—tr.v.* **-trat·ed, -trat·ing, -trates.** To treat with nitric acid or with a nitrate, usually to change an organic compound into a nitrate. **—ni·tra'tion** *n.* **—ni'tra'tor** *n.*

ni·tre (nī'tər) *n. Chiefly Brit.* Variant of **niter.**

ni·tric (nī'trĭk) *adj.* Of, derived from, or containing nitrogen, esp. in a valence state higher than that in a comparable nitrous compound.

nitric acid *n.* A transparent, colorless to yellowish, fuming corrosive liquid, HNO_3, a highly reactive oxidizing agent, used in the production of fertilizers, explosives, and rocket fuels and in a wide variety of industrial metallurgical processes.

nitric oxide *n.* A colorless, poisonous gas, NO, produced as an intermediate during the manufacture of nitric acid from ammonia or atmospheric nitrogen.

ni·tride (nī'trīd') *n.* A compound containing nitrogen with another more electropositive element.

ni·tri·fy (nī'trə-fī') *tr.v.* **-fied, -fy·ing, -fies. 1.** To oxidize into nitric acid, nitrous acid, or any nitrate or nitrite, as by the action of nitrobacteria. **2.** To treat or combine with nitrogen or compounds containing nitrogen. **—ni'tri·fi·ca'tion** *n.* **—ni'tri·fi'er** *n.*

ni·trile also **ni·tril** (nī'trəl) *n.* A compound containing trivalent nitrogen, N^{-3}, in a cyanogen group.

ni·trite (nī'trīt') *n.* A salt or ester of nitrous acid. [NITR(O)- + -ITE.]

nitro- or **nitr-** *pref.* **1.** Nitrate; niter: *nitrobacterium.* **2. a.** Nitrogen: *nitrile.* **b.** Containing the univalent group NO_2: *nitromethane.* [NLat. < Lat. *nitrum,* natron < Gk. *nitron,* of Semitic orig.]

ni·tro·bac·te·ri·um (nī'trō-băk-tîr'ē-əm) *n.* A soil bacterium that produces nitrification.

ni·tro·ben·zene (nī'trō-bĕn'zēn', -bĕn-zēn') *n.* A poisonous organic compound, $C_6H_5NO_2$, either bright-yellow crystals or an oily liquid, having the odor of almonds and used in the manufacture of aniline, insulating compounds, and polishes.

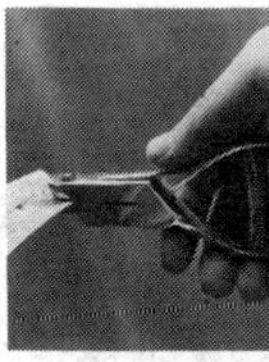

nipper

ni·tro·cel·lu·lose (nī'trō-sĕl'yə-lōs', -lōz') *n.* A pulpy or cottonlike polymer derived from cellulose treated with sulfuric and nitric acids and used in the manufacture of explosives, collodion, plastics, and solid monopropellants. **—ni'tro·cel'lu·los'ic** (-lŏ'sĭk, -zĭk) *adj.*

ni·tro·chlo·ro·form (nī'trō-klôr'ə-fôrm', -klōr'-) *n.* Chloropicrin.

ni·tro·gen (nī'trə-jən) *n. Symbol* **N** A nonmetallic element that constitutes nearly four-fifths of the air by volume, occurring as a colorless, odorless, almost inert diatomic gas, N_2, in various minerals and in all proteins, and that is used in a wide variety of important manufactures, including ammonia, nitric acid, TNT, and fertilizers. Atomic number 7; atomic weight 14.0067; melting point −209.86°C; boiling point −195°C; valence 3, 5. **—ni·trog'e·nous** (nī-trŏj'ə-nəs) *adj.*

ni·trog·e·nase (nī-trŏj'ə-nās', nī'trə-jə-) *n.* An enzyme utilized in nitrogen fixation to convert molecular nitrogen to ammonia.

nitrogen balance *n.* The difference between the amounts of nitrogen taken into and lost by the body or the soil.

nitrogen cycle *n.* **1.** The continuous cyclic progression of chemical reactions in which atmospheric nitrogen is compounded, dissolved in rain, deposited in the soil, assimilated and metabolized by bacteria and plants, and returned to the atmosphere by organic decomposition. **2.** Carbon-nitrogen cycle.

nitrogen dioxide *n.* A mildly poisonous brown gas, NO_2, often found in smog and automobile exhaust fumes and synthesized for use as a nitrating agent, catalyst, and oxidizing agent.

nitrogen fixation *n.* **1.** The conversion of atmospheric nitrogen into nitrogenous compounds by natural agencies or by various industrial processes. **2.** The conversion by certain algae and soil bacteria of inorganic nitrogen compounds into organic compounds assimilable by plants. **—ni'tro·gen-fix'ing** (nī'trə-jən-fĭk'sĭng) *adj.*

ni·trog·en·ize (nī-trŏj'ə-nīz', nī'trə-jə-nīz') *tr.v.* **-ized, -iz·ing, -iz·es.** To combine or treat with nitrogen.

ni·tro·glyc·er·in also **ni·tro·glyc·er·ine** (nī'trō-glĭs'ər-ĭn) *n.* A thick, pale-yellow liquid, $CH_2NO_3CHNO_3CH_2NO_3$, that is explosive on concussion or exposure to sudden heat and is used in the production of dynamite and blasting gelatin and as a vasodilator in medicine.

ni·tro·hy·dro·chlo·ric acid (nī'trō-hī'drə-klôr'ĭk, -klōr'-) *n.* Aqua regia.

ni·tro·meth·ane (nī'trō-mĕth'ān') *n.* An oily, colorless liquid, CH_3NO_2, used in making dyes and resins, in organic synthesis, and as a rocket propellant.

ni·tro·par·af·fin (nī'trō-păr'ə-fĭn) *n.* Any of a group of organic compounds formed by replacing one or more of the hydrogen atoms of a paraffin hydrocarbon with the nitro group, NO_2^-, as in nitromethane, CH_3NO_2.

ni·tro·starch (nī'trō-stärch') *n.* A highly explosive orange-colored powder, $C_{12}H_{12}(NO_2)_8O_{10}$, derived from starch and used for demolition.

ni·trous (nī'trəs) *adj.* Of, derived from, or containing nitrogen, esp. in a valence state lower than that in a comparable nitric compound.

nitrous acid *n.* An unstable inorganic acid, HNO_2, existing in solution only.
nitrous oxide *n.* A colorless, sweet inorganic gas, N_2O, used as a mild anesthetic.
nits-and-lice (nĭts'ənd-līs') *n.* *(used with a sing. or pl. verb).* A plant, *Hypericum drummondii,* of the central United States, having narrow leaves and yellow flowers.
nit·ty-grit·ty (nĭt'ē-grĭt'ē, nĭt'ē-grĭt'ē) *n. Slang.* The specific or practical details; core. [Orig. unknown.]
nit·wit (nĭt'wĭt') *n. Informal.* A stupid or silly person.
ni·val (nī'vəl) *adj.* Of or growing in or under snow. [Lat. *nivalis* < *nix,* snow.]
niv·e·ous (nĭv'ē-əs) *adj.* Like snow; snowy. [Lat. *niveus* < *nix,* snow.]
nix[1] (nĭks) *n.* A water sprite of German mythology, usually in human form or half-human and half-fish. [G. < MHG *nickes* < OHG *nihhus.*]
nix[2] (nĭks) *Slang.* —*n.* Nothing. —*adv.* No. —*tr.v.* **nixed, nix·ing, nix·es.** To forbid; veto. [< G. *nichts,* nothing < MHG *nihtes* < *niht* < OHG *niwiht* : *ni-,* no + *wiht,* thing.]
nix·ie also **nix·y** (nĭk'sē) *n., pl.* **-ies.** *Slang.* A misaddressed piece of mail. [< NIX[2].]
Ni·zam (nĭ-zäm', -zăm', nī-) *n.* The title of the former rulers of Hyderabad, India. [Hindi *nizām (-almulk),* governor (of the empire) < *niẓām,* government < Ar. *niẓām* < *naẓama,* he arranged.]
no[1] (nō) *adv.* **1.** Not so. Used to express refusal, denial, or disagreement: *No, I'm not going.* **2.** Not at all. Used with the comparative: *no better; no more.* **3.** Not: *whether or no.* —*n., pl.* **noes. 1.** A negative response; denial or refusal: *The proposal produced only noes.* **2.** A negative vote or voter. [ME < OE *nā* : *ne,* not + *ā,* ever.]
no[2] (nō) *adj.* **1.** Not any; not one: *No cookies are left.* **2.** Not at all; not close to being: *He is no child.* [ME < OE *nā* < *nān,* none.]

Usage: When *no* introduces a compound phrase, its elements should be connected with *or* rather than with *nor.* Thus we write: *He has no experience or interest in chemistry* (not *nor interest*). *No modification or change will be acceptable to them* (not *nor change*).

No[1]
Print of a No actor

No[1] also **Noh** (nō) *n., pl.* **No** also **Noh.** The classical drama of Japan, with music and dance performed in a highly stylized manner by elaborately dressed actors on an almost bare stage. [J. *nō,* talent, ability < Chin. *neng*[2].]
No[2] The symbol for the element nobelium.
no-ac·count (nō'ə-kount') *adj.* Worthless; good-for-nothing: *a no-account fellow.*
No·a·chi·an (nō-ā'kē-ən) *adj.* **1.** Of or relating to Noah or his time. **2.** Antiquated; ancient.
No·ah (nō'ə) *n.* The Old Testament patriarch chosen by God to build the ark in which Noah, his family, and many animals were saved from the Flood. [Heb. *Nōah.*]
nob[1] (nŏb) *n. Slang.* The head. [Perh. var. of KNOB.]
nob[2] (nŏb) *n. Slang.* A person of wealth or social standing. [Orig. unknown.]
nob·ble (nŏb'əl) *tr.v.* **-bled, -bling, -bles.** *Chiefly Brit. Slang.* **1.** To disable (a racehorse), esp. by drugging. **2. a.** To win (a person) over. **b.** To outdo or get the better of by devious means. **c.** To filch or steal. [Orig. unknown.] —**nob'bler** *n.*
nob·by (nŏb'ē) *adj.* **-bi·er, -bi·est.** Fashionable; stylish. [< NOB[2].]
No·bel·ist (nō-bĕl'ĭst) *n.* A recipient of a Nobel prize.
no·bel·i·um (nō-bĕl'ē-əm) *n.* *Symbol* **No** A radioactive transuranic element in the actinide series, artificially produced in trace amounts. Atomic number 102; isotopic masses 252, 253, 254, 255, 256; half-lives 4.5, 95, 75, 180, 8 seconds. [After the *Nobel* Institute at Stockholm.]
No·bel Prize (nō-bĕl') *n.* Any of the international prizes awarded annually by the Nobel Foundation for outstanding achievements in the fields of physics, chemistry, physiology or medicine, literature, and economics and for the promotion of world peace.

node
Left to Right: Rye grass, horsetail, buckwheat

no·bil·i·ar·y (nō-bĭl'ē-ĕr'ē, -bĭl'yə-rē) *adj.* Of or pertaining to the nobility. [Fr. *nobiliaire* < Lat. *nobilis,* noble.]
no·bil·i·ty (nō-bĭl'ĭ-tē) *n., pl.* **-ties. 1.** A class of persons distinguished by high birth or rank; aristocracy. **2.** Noble rank or status: *Congress may not grant titles of nobility.* **3.** The state or quality of being noble. [ME *nobilite,* the quality of being noble < OFr. < Lat. *nobilitas* < *nobilis,* noble.]
no·ble (nō'bəl) *adj.* **-bler, -blest. 1.** Of, in, or belonging to the nobility. **2.** Having or showing qualities of high moral character, as courage, generosity, or honor: *a noble spirit.* **3. a.** Superior in nature or character; exalted: *a noble ideal.* **b.** Grand and stately in appearance; majestic: *noble mountain peaks.* **4.** Designating an esp. corrosion-resistant metal, such as gold. **5.** *Chem.* Inactive or inert. —*n.* **1.** A member of the nobility. **2.** A former English gold coin worth six shillings and eight pence. [ME < OFr. < Lat. *nobilis.*] —**no'ble·ness** *n.* —**no'bly** *adv.*
no·ble·man (nō'bəl-mən) *n.* A man of noble rank.
no·blesse (nō-blĕs') *n.* **1.** Noble birth or condition. **2.** The members of the nobility; aristocracy. [ME < OFr. < *noble,* noble < Lat. *nobilis.*]
noblesse o·blige (ō-blēzh') *n.* Benevolent and honorable behavior considered to be the responsibility of persons of high birth or rank. [Fr. : *noblesse,* nobility + *oblige,* obligates.]
no·ble·wom·an (nō'bəl-wo͝om'ən) *n.* A woman of noble rank.
no·bod·y (nō'bŏd'ē, -bə-dē) *pron.* No person; no one. —*n., pl.* **-ies.** A person of no importance or influence. —See Usage note at **everyone.**
no·cent (nō'sənt) *adj.* Causing injury; harmful. [ME *nocent,* guilty < Lat. *nocens,* pr.part. of *nocēre,* to harm.]
nock (nŏk) *n.* **1.** The groove at either end of a bow for holding the bowstring. **2.** The notch in the end of an arrow that fits on the bowstring. —*tr.v.* **nocked, nock·ing, nocks. 1.** To put a nock in (a bow or arrow). **2.** To fit (an arrow) to a bowstring. [ME *nokke.*]
noct- *pref.* Variant of **nocti-.**
noc·tam·bu·lism (nŏk-tăm'byə-lĭz'əm) also **noc·tam·bu·la·tion** (-tăm'byə-lā'shən) *n.* Somnambulism. [NOCTI- + Lat. *ambulare,* to walk + -ISM.] —**noc·tam'bu·list** *n.*
nocti- or **noct-** *pref.* Night: *noctilucent.* [NLat. < Lat. *nox,* night.]
noc·ti·lu·ca (nŏk'tə-lo͞o'kə) *n.* Any of various plantlike, bioluminescent marine organisms of the genus *Noctiluca* that when grouped in large numbers make the sea phosphorescent. [NLat. *Noctiluca,* genus name < Lat. *noctiluca,* lantern : *nox,* night + *lucēre,* to shine.]
noc·ti·lu·cent (nŏk'tə-lo͞o'sənt) *adj.* Luminous at night. Used esp. of certain high clouds.
noc·tu·id (nŏk'cho͞o-ĭd) *n.* Any of the night-flying moths of the family Noctuidae, the larvae of which are destructive pests. [< NLat. *Noctuidae,* family name < Lat. *noctua,* night owl.]
noc·tule (nŏk'cho͞ol') *n.* A large, reddish-brown, insectivorous bat of the genus *Nyctalus,* found in Eurasia, Indonesia, and the Philippines. [Fr. < Ital. *nottola* < LLat. *noctula,* dim. of Lat. *noctua,* night owl < *nox,* night.]
noc·turn (nŏk'tûrn') *n.* Any of the three canonical divisions of the office of matins. [ME *nocturne* < Med. Lat. *nocturna* < Lat. *nocturnus,* of the night < *nox,* night.]
noc·tur·nal (nŏk-tûr'nəl) *adj.* **1.** Of, pertaining to, or occurring in the night: *nocturnal stillness.* **2.** *Bot.* Having flowers that open during the night. **3.** *Zool.* Active at night, as certain animals. [LLat. *nocturnalis* < Lat. *nocturnus* < *nox,* night.] —**noc·tur'nal·ly** *adv.*
noc·turne (nŏk'tûrn') *n.* **1.** A painting of a night scene. **2.** A romantic musical composition intended to suggest or evoke thoughts and feelings of night. [Fr. < *nocturne,* nocturnal < Lat. *nocturnus* < *nox,* night.]
noc·u·ous (nŏk'yo͞o-əs) *adj.* Harmful; noxious. [Lat. *nocuus* < *nocēre,* to harm.] —**noc'u·ous·ly** *adv.*
nod (nŏd) *v.* **nod·ded, nod·ding, nods.** —*intr.* **1.** To lower the head quickly, as in agreement. **2.** To doze momentarily. **3.** To be careless or momentarily inattentive. **4.** To sway, droop, or bend downward, as flowers in the wind. —*tr.* **1.** To lower and raise (the head) quickly in agreement or acknowledgment. **2.** To express by lowering and raising the head: *He nodded his acceptance.* **3.** To summon, guide, or send by nodding the head: *nodded her into the room.* —*n.* **1.** An act or instance of nodding: *gave a nod of affirmation.* **2.** An indication of approval or assent: *The contestant got the nod from the judges.* [ME *nodden.*] —**nod'der** *n.*
nod·al (nōd'l) *adj.* Of, pertaining to, being, or situated near or at a node. —**nod'al·ly** *adv.*
nodding pogonia *n.* A North American orchid, *Triphora trianthophora,* having pink or white flowers.
nod·dle (nŏd'l) *n.* The head. [ME *nodel,* back of the head.]
nod·dy (nŏd'ē) *n., pl.* **-dies. 1.** A dunce or fool; simpleton. **2.** A tern of the genus *Anous* that is found in tropical waters and is dark brown with a white head. [Prob. < obs. *noddy,* foolish.]
node (nōd) *n.* **1.** A protuberance or swelling. **2.** *Bot.* The often enlarged point on a stem where a leaf, bud, or other organ diverges from the stem to which it is attached; joint. **3.** *Physics.* A point or region of minimum or zero amplitude in a periodic system. **4.** *Math.* The point at which a continuous curve crosses itself. **5.** The intersection or terminating point of two or more lines or curves; vertex. **6.** *Astron.* **a.** Either of two diametrically opposite points at which the orbit of a planet intersects the ecliptic. **b.** Either of two points at which the orbit of a satellite intersects the orbital plane of a planet. [Lat. *nodus,* knot.]
no·di (nō'dī') *n.* Plural of **nodus.**
nod·ule (nŏj'o͞ol) *n.* **1.** A small node, as of body tissue. **2.** *Anat.* A localized swelling. **3.** *Bot.* A small, knoblike outgrowth, such as those found on the roots of most leguminous plants. **4.** A small lump of a mineral or mixture of minerals. [Lat. *nodulus,* dim. of *nodus,* knot.] —**nod'u·lar** (nŏj'ə-lər), **nod'u·lose'** (-lōs'), **nod'u·lous** (-ləs) *adj.*
no·dus (nō'dəs) *n., pl.* **-di** (-dī'). A difficult situation or problem; complication. [Lat., knot.]
No·ël also **No·el** (nō-ĕl') *n.* **1.** Christmas. **2. noël** also **noel.** A Christmas carol. [Fr. < OFr. *novel* < Lat. *natalis (dies),* (day) of birth < *nasci,* to be born.]
no·e·sis (nō-ē'sĭs) *n. Psychol.* The cognitive process; cognition. [Gk. *noēsis,* understanding < *noein,* to perceive < *nous,* mind.]
no·et·ic (nō-ĕt'ĭk) *adj.* Of, pertaining to, originating in, or

apprehended by the intellect. [Gk. *noētikos* < *noēsis,* understanding. —see NOESIS.]
no-fault (nō′fôlt′) *adj.* **1.** Of or indicating a system of automobile insurance in which accident victims are compensated by their insurance companies without assignment of blame. **2.** Of or indicating a type of divorce in which no blame is assigned to either party.
no-frills (nō′frĭlz′) *adj.* Marked by the absence of extra or special features; basic: *bought the no-frills model of the car.*
nog¹ (nŏg) *n.* A wooden block built into a masonry wall to hold nails that support joinery structures. [Orig. unknown.]
nog² (nŏg) *n.* Eggnog. [Orig. unknown.]
nog·gin (nŏg′ĭn) *n.* **1.** A small mug or cup. **2.** A unit of liquid measure equal to one-quarter of a pint. **3.** *Slang.* The head. [Orig. unknown.]
no-go (nō′gō′) *adj. Slang.* Not in a suitable condition for proceeding or functioning properly: *The space launch was no-go.*
no-good (no′go͝od′) *adj.* **1.** Having no value, use, or merit. **2.** Despicable; vile. —*n.* One that is no-good.
Noh (nō) *n.* Variant of **No**¹.
no-hit (nō′hĭt′) *adj. Baseball.* Of, pertaining to or being a game in which one pitcher allows his opponents no hits and no runs.
no-hit·ter (nō′hĭt′ər) *n. Baseball.* A no-hit game.
no·how (nō′hou′) *adv. Nonstandard.* In no way; not at all.
noil (noil) *n.* A short fiber combed from long fibers during the preparation of textile yarns. [OFr. *noel* < Med. Lat. *nodellus,* dim. of Lat. *nodus,* knot.]
noise (noiz) *n.* **1. a.** Sound or a sound that is loud, unpleasant, unexpected or undesired. **b.** Sound or a sound of any kind: *The only noise was the wind in the pines.* **2.** A loud outcry or commotion. **3.** *Physics.* A disturbance, esp. a random and persistent disturbance, that obscures or reduces the clarity or quality of a signal. **4.** *Computer Sci.* Irrelevant or meaningless date generated by a computer along with desired data. **5.** *Informal.* **a.** A complaint or protest. **b.** Rumor; talk. —*v.* **noised, nois·ing, nois·es.** —*tr.* To spread the rumor or report of. —*intr.* **1.** To talk much or volubly. **2.** To be noisy; make noise. [ME < OFr. < Lat. *nausea,* seasickness. —see NAUSEA.]
  Synonyms: *noise, din, racket, uproar, pandemonium, hullabaloo, hubbub, clamor, babel. Noise* is the most general and least forceful of these words. Both *din,* associated with prolonged, ear-splitting sound, and *racket,* which is more general and somewhat less emphatic, are subjective terms that indicate strong discomfort on the part of the user. *Uproar, pandemonium,* and the somewhat weaker *hullabaloo* all strongly imply uncontrolled commotion together with loud, confused sound. *Hubbub* also emphasizes physical movement and resultant confusing sound, but not necessarily disorder; the term is often applied to commercial activity conducted with great intensity. *Clamor* stresses intense and prolonged sound designed to express a purpose, such as protest, and only secondarily implies movement. *Babel* is concerned expressly with vocal sound, not primarily with volume but with the confusion resulting from diversity of language and from simultaneous utterance.
noise·less (noiz′lĭs) *adj.* Creating no noise; quiet. **—noise′less·ly** *adv.* **—noise′less·ness** *n.*
noise·mak·er (noiz′mā′kər) *n.* One that makes noise, esp. a device such as a horn or rattle used to make noise at a party. **—noise′mak′ing** *n.*
noise pollution *n.* Noise occurring in the environment that is annoying, distracting, or harmful.
noi·some (noi′səm) *adj.* **1.** Offensive to the point of arousing disgust; foul: *a noisome odor.* **2.** Harmful or dangerous: *noisome fumes.* [ME *noisom* : *noi,* harm (< *anoi,* annoyance < OFr. < Lat. *in odio,* hateful) + *-some,* -some.] **—noi′some·ly** *adv.* **—noi′some·ness** *n.*
nois·y (noi′zē) *adj.* **-i·er, -i·est. 1.** Making noise. **2.** Full of, characterized by, or accompanied by noise. **—nois′i·ly** *adv.* **—nois′i·ness** *n.*
no·li-me-tan·ge·re (nō′lē-mē-tăn′jə-rē) *n.* A warning or prohibition against meddling, touching, or interfering. [Lat., don't touch me.]
nol·le pros·e·qui (nŏl′ē prŏs′ĭ-kwī′) *n. Law.* A declaration that the plaintiff in a civil case or the prosecutor in a criminal case will drop prosecution of all or part of a suit or indictment. [Lat., to be unwilling to pursue.]
no·lo (nō′lō) *n.* Nolo contendere.
no-load (nō′lōd′) *adj.* Sold at net asset value without a sales commission: *a no-load mutual fund.*
no·lo con·ten·de·re (nō′lō kən-tĕn′də-rē) *n. Law.* A plea made by the defendant in a criminal action that is equivalent to an admission of guilt and subjects him to punishment but leaves open the possibility for him to deny the alleged facts in other proceedings. [Lat., I do not wish to contend.]
nol-pros (nŏl′prŏs′) *tr.v.* **-prossed, -pros·sing, -pros·ses.** *Law.* To drop prosecution of by entering a nolle prosequi on the court records.
no·ma (nō′mə) *n.* A severe, often gangrenous inflammation of the mouth, occurring esp. in a young child after a debilitating disease. [Lat. < Gk. *nomē* < *nemein,* to spread.]
no·mad (nō′măd′) *n.* **1.** A member of a group of people who have no fixed home and move from place to place in search of food, water, and grazing land. **2.** A person who roams about; wanderer. [Lat. *nomas, nomad-* < Gk. *nomas,* wandering around for pasture < *nemein,* to pasture.] **—no′mad′ism** (nō′măd′ĭz′əm) *n.*
no·mad·ic (nō-măd′ĭk) *adj.* Leading the life of a nomad; wandering: *nomadic herdsmen.* **—no·mad′i·cal·ly** *adv.*
no man's land *n.* **1.** An unclaimed or unowned piece of land. **2.** Land under dispute by two opposing parties, esp. the field of battle between two opposing entrenched armies. **3.** An area of uncertainty or ambiguity.
nom·bril (nŏm′brəl) *n. Heraldry.* The point on an escutcheon between the fess point and the base point. [OFr., nombril, navel, alteration of *ombril,* navel < Lat. *umbilicus.*]
nom de guerre (nŏm′ də gâr′) *n.* A fictitious name; pseudonym. [Fr., war name.]
nom de plume (nŏm′ də plo͞om′) *n.* A pseudonym adopted by a writer. [Fr., pen name.]
nome (nōm) *n.* **1.** A province of ancient Egypt. **2.** A province of modern Greece. [Gk. *nomos,* district, habitation.]
no·men·cla·tor (nō′mən-klā′tər) *n.* One who assigns names, as in scientific classification. [Lat., a slave who accompanied his master to tell him the names of people he met : *nomen,* name + *calare,* to call.]
no·men·cla·to·ri·al (nō′mən-klə-tôr′ē-əl, -tōr′-) *adj.* Of or pertaining to nomenclature.
no·men·cla·ture (nō′mən-klā′chər, nō-mĕn′klə-) *n.* A system of names used in an art or science. [Lat. *nomenclatura* < *nomenclator,* nomenclator.]
nom·i·nal (nŏm′ə-nəl) *adj.* **1. a.** Of, like, pertaining to, or consisting of a name or names. **b.** Bearing a person's name: *nominal shares.* **2.** Existing in name only and not in actuality. **3.** Insignificantly small; trifling: *a nominal sum.* **4.** *Gram.* Of or pertaining to a noun or a word group that functions as a noun. **5.** According to plan: *a nominal flight check.* —*n. Gram.* A word or group of words that functions as a noun. [Lat. *nominalis* < *nomen,* name.] **—nom′i·nal·ly** *adv.*
  Usage: *Nominal* in one of its senses means "in name only." Hence a *nominal payment* is a token payment, bearing no relation to the real value of what is being paid for. The word is often extended in use, especially by sellers, to describe a low or bargain price.
nom·i·nal·ism (nŏm′ə-nə-lĭz′əm) *n. Philos.* The doctrine that abstract concepts, general terms, or universals have no objective reference but exist only as names. **—nom′i·nal·ist** *n.* **—nom′i·nal·is′tic** *adj.*
nominal value *n.* The stated, par, or book value of a share of stock as opposed to the actual or market value.
nom·i·nate (nŏm′ə-nāt′) *tr.v.* **-nat·ed, -nat·ing, -nates. 1.** To propose as a candidate, as for election. **2.** To designate or appoint to an office, responsibility, or honor. [Lat. *nominare, nominat-* < *nomen,* name.] **—nom′i·na′tor** *n.*
nom·i·na·tion (nŏm′ə-nā′shən) *n.* **1.** The act or process of nominating. **2.** The state of being nominated.
nom·i·na·tive (nŏm′ə-nā′tĭv) *adj.* **1. a.** Appointed to office. **b.** Nominated as a candidate for office. **2.** Having or bearing a person's name: *nominative shares.* **3.** (-nə-tĭv). *Gram.* Of, pertaining to, or belonging to a case that usually indicates the subject of a verb. —*n.* (-nə-tĭv). *Gram.* The nominative case.
nom·i·nee (nŏm′ə-nē′) *n.* Someone who has been nominated. [NOMIN(ATE) + -EE.]
nom·o·gram (nŏm′ə-grăm′, nō′mə-) *n.* A nomograph. [Gk. *nomos,* law + -GRAM.]
nom·o·graph (nŏm′ə-grăf′, nō′mə-) *n.* **1.** A graph consisting of three coplanar curves, usually parallel straight lines, each graduated for a different variable so that a straight line cutting all three curves intersects the related values of each variable. **2.** A chart representing numerical relationships. [Gk. *nomos,* law + -GRAPH.] **—nom′o·graph′ic** (-grăf′ĭk) *adj.* **—no·mog′ra·phy** (nō-mŏg′rə-fē) *n.*
-nomy *suff.* A system of laws governing or a body of knowledge about a specified field: *aeronomy.* [Lat. *-nomia* < Gk. < *nomos,* law < *nemnein,* to arrange.]
non- *pref.* Not: *noncombatant.* [ME < OFr. < Lat. *non,* not.]
  Usage: Many compounds other than those entered here may be formed with *non-*. In forming compounds, *non-* is normally joined with the following element without space or hyphen: *nonnutritive.* However, if the second element begins with a capital letter, it is separated with a hyphen: *non-French.*
nona- *pref.* Ninth; nine: *nonagon.* [< Lat. *nonus,* ninth.]
non·ad·di·tive (nŏn-ăd′ĭ-tĭv) *adj.* **1.** Having a numerical value different from the sum of the component parts. **2.** Of, pertaining to, or being a genic effect that is nonadditive. **—non′ad·di·tiv′i·ty** *n.*
non·age (nŏn′ĭj, nō′nĭj) *n.* **1.** The period during which one is legally underage. **2.** A period of immaturity. [ME *nounage* < AN < OFr. *nonage* : *non-,* non- + *age,* age.]
non·a·ge·nar·i·an (nŏn′ə-jə-nâr′ē-ən, nō′nə-) *adj.* Being ninety years old or between ninety and one hundred years old. [< Lat. *nonagenarius* < *nonageni,* ninety each < *nonagintia,* : *novem,* nine + *-ginta,* ten times.] **—non′a·ge·nar′i·an** *n.*
non·a·gon (nŏn′ə-gŏn′, nō′nə-) *n.* A polygon with nine sides.

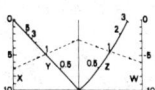

nomograph
Combination straight-line and curved-scale nomograph for equation $xy + wz = z^2$. Dashed line graphically determines that $w = -6$ when $x = 7$, $y = 1$, and $z = 1$

non·a·ligned (nŏn′ə-līnd′) *adj.* Not in alliance with any other nation or bloc; neutral. **—non′a·lign′ment** *n.*
non·a·no·ic acid (nŏn′ə-nō′ĭk) *n.* Pelargonic acid. [< *nonane,* a paraffin : NONA- + -ANE (so called because it is ninth in the methane series).]
non·ca·lor·ic (nŏn′kə-lôr′ĭk, -lŏr′-) *adj.* Having few or no calories: *a noncaloric beverage.*
non·can·di·date (nŏn-kăn′dĭ-dāt′, -dĭt) *n. Slang.* One who has announced that he is not a candidate, esp. for political office.
nonce (nŏns) *n.* The present or particular occasion: *for the nonce.* [< ME *for the nones,* for the occasion.]
nonce word *n.* A word occurring, invented, or used just for a particular occasion.
non·cha·lance (nŏn′shə-läns′) *n.* The state or quality of being nonchalant.
non·cha·lant (nŏn′shə-länt′) *adj.* Cool, carefree, and casually unconcerned. [Fr. < OFr. < *nonchaloir,* to be unconcerned : *non-,* non- + *chaloir,* to be concerned < Lat. *calere,* to be warm.] **—non′cha·lant′ly** *adv.*
non·chro·mo·som·al (nŏn′krō-mə-sō′məl) *adj.* Not situated on or involving a chromosome.
non·com (nŏn′kŏm′) *n. Informal.* A noncommissioned officer.
non·com·bat·ant (nŏn′kəm-băt′nt, -kŏm′bə-tənt) *n.* **1.** A member of the armed forces, as a chaplain, whose duties lie outside combat. **2.** A civilian in wartime, esp. one in a war zone.
non·com·mis·sioned officer (nŏn′kə-mĭsh′ənd) *n.* An enlisted member of the armed forces, as a sergeant, appointed to a rank conferring leadership over others.
non·com·mit·tal (nŏn′kə-mĭt′l) *adj.* Not revealing what one feels or thinks: *a noncommittal reply.* **—non′com·mit′tal·ly** *adv.*
non·com·pli·ance (nŏn′kəm-plī′əns) *n.* Failure or refusal to comply. **—non′com·pli′ant** *adj. & n.*
non com·pos men·tis (nŏn kŏm′pəs mĕn′tĭs) *adj. Law.* Not of sound mind and hence not legally responsible. [Lat., not in control of the mind.]
non·con·duc·tor (nŏn′kən-dŭk′tər) *n.* A substance that conducts little or no electricity or heat.
non·con·form·ist (nŏn′kən-fôr′mĭst) *n.* **1.** One who does not conform to accepted beliefs, customs, or practices. **2.** Often **Nonconformist.** A person who does not belong to a national or established church, esp. to the Church of England.
non·con·form·i·ty (nŏn′kən-fôr′mĭ-tē) *n.* **1.** Refusal or failure to conform to accepted customs, beliefs, or practices. **2.** Often **Nonconformity.** Refusal to accept or conform to the doctrines of the Church of England.
non·co·op·er·a·tion (nŏn′kō-ŏp′ə-rā′shən) *n.* Failure or refusal to cooperate, esp. with the government of a country. **—non′co·op′er·a′tion·ist** *n.* **—non′co·op′er·a·tive** (-ŏp′ər-ə-tĭv, -ŏp′ə-rā′-) *adj.* **—non′co·op′er·a′tor** *n.*
non·cred·it (nŏn-krĕd′ĭt) *adj.* Of, pertaining to, or comprising an educational course that does not offer credit toward an academic degree.
non·dair·y (nŏn-dâr′ē) *adj.* Containing no milk or dairy products.
non·de·duct·i·ble (nŏn′dĭ-dŭk′tə-bəl) *adj.* Not deductible, esp. for income-tax purposes.
non·de·nom·i·na·tion·al (nŏn′dĭ-nŏm′ə-nā′shə-nəl) *adj.* Not restricted to or associated with a religious denomination.
non·de·script (nŏn′dĭ-skrĭpt′) *adj.* Lacking in distinctive qualities; without individual character or form. [NON- + Lat. *descriptus,* p.part. of *describere,* to describe. —see DESCRIBE.] **—non′de·script′** *n.*
non·de·struc·tive (nŏn′dĭ-strŭk′tĭv) *adj.* Of, pertaining to, or being a process that does not result in the destruction of the material under investigation. **—non′de·struc′tive·ly** *adv.*
non·di·rec·tive (nŏn′dĭ-rĕk′tĭv, -dī-) *adj.* Of, pertaining to, or being a psychotherapeutic technique in which the therapist takes an unobtrusive role in order to encourage free expression by the client.
non·dis·crim·i·na·tion (nŏn′dĭ-skrĭm′ə-nā′shən) *n.* **1.** Absence of discrimination. **2.** The practice or policy of refraining from discrimination. **—non′dis·crim′i·na·to′ry** (-nə-tôr′ē, -tōr′ē) *adj.*
non·dis·junc·tion (nŏn′dĭs-jŭngk′shən) *n. Biol.* The failure of paired chromosomes to separate during mitosis. **—non′dis·junc′tion·al** *adj.*
non·dis·tinc·tive (nŏn′dĭs-tĭngk′tĭv) *adj. Ling.* Not phonemically distinctive; not serving to distinguish meaning.
non·drink·er (nŏn-drĭng′kər) *n.* One who does not drink alcoholic beverages.
none (nŭn) *pron.* **1.** No one; not one; nobody: *None dared to do it.* **2.** Not any: *None of my classmates survived the war.* **3.** No part; not any: *none of his business.* —*adv.* In no way; not at all: *He is none too happy.* —See Usage note at **every·one.** [ME < OE *nān* : *ne,* no + *ān,* one.]
non·e·go (nŏn-ē′gō) *n.* All that is not part of the ego or the conscious self. [Transl. of G. *Nichtich* : *nicht,* not + *Ich,* I.]
non·en·ti·ty (nŏn-ĕn′tĭ-tē) *n., pl.* **-ties.** **1.** Nonexistence. **2.** Something that does not exist or that exists only in the imagination. **3.** A person of no importance or significance.
nones (nōnz) *pl.n.* **1.** In the ancient Roman calendar, the seventh day of March, May, July or October and the fifth day of the other months. **2.** *Eccles.* **a.** The fifth of the seven canonical hours. **b.** The time of day set aside for this prayer, usually the ninth hour after sunrise. [ME < Lat. *nonae,* fem. pl. of *nonus,* ninth.]
none·such also **non·such** (nŭn′sŭch′) *n.* **1.** A person or thing without equal. **2.** The black medic. **—none′such′** *adj.*
none·the·less (nŭn′*th*ə-lĕs′) *adv.* Nevertheless; however.
non-Eu·clid·e·an (nŏn′yo͞o-klĭd′ē-ən) *adj.* Designating any of several modern geometries that are not based on the postulates of Euclid.
non·e·vent (nŏn′ĭ-vĕnt′) *n. Slang.* An anticipated event that does not occur or that proves anticlimactic.
non·ex·ist·ence (nŏn′ĭg-zĭs′təns) *n.* **1.** The condition of not existing. **2.** Something that does not exist. **—non′ex·ist′ent** *adj.*
non·fat (nŏn′făt′) *adj.* Lacking fat solids or having the fat content removed: *nonfat milk.*
non·fea·sance (nŏn-fē′zəns) *n. Law.* Failure to perform an act that is either an official duty or a legal requirement. [NON- + obs. *feasance,* a doing < OFr. *faisance.* —see MALFEASANCE.]
non·fer·rous (nŏn-fĕr′əs) *adj.* **1.** Not composed of or containing iron. **2.** Of or pertaining to metals other than iron.
non·fic·tion (nŏn-fĭk′shən) *n.* Literary works other than fiction. **—non·fic′tion·al** *adj.*
non·flam·ma·ble (nŏn-flăm′ə-bəl) *adj.* Not flammable, esp. not readily ignited.
non·food (nŏn′fo͞od′) *adj. Slang.* Of, relating to, or being something that is not food, as articles sold in a supermarket.
non·grad·ed (nŏn-grā′dĭd) *adj.* Being without grade levels: *a nongraded elementary school.*
non·he·ro (nŏn-hîr′ō) *n.* An antihero.
non·i·den·ti·cal (nŏn′ī-dĕn′tĭ-kəl) *adj.* **1.** Not the same; different. **2.** Fraternal (sense 3).
no·nil·lion (nō-nĭl′yən) *n.* **1.** The cardinal number that is equal to 10^{30}. **2.** *Chiefly Brit.* The cardinal number that is equal to 10^{54}. [Fr. < OFr. : Lat. *nonus,* nine + Fr. *million,* million < OFr. *milion.* —see MILLION.] **—no·nil′lion** *adj.*
no·nil·lionth (nō-nĭl′yənth) *n.* The ordinal number nonillion in a series. **—no·nil′lionth** *adj. & adv.*
non·in·duc·tive (nŏn′ĭn-dŭk′tĭv) *adj.* Having low inductance.
non·in·ter·ven·tion (nŏn′ĭn-tər-vĕn′shən) *n.* Failure or refusal to intervene, esp. in the affairs of another nation. **—non′in·ter·ven′tion·ist** *n.*
non·in·volve·ment (nŏn′ĭn-vŏlv′mənt) *n.* **1.** Lack of emotional involvement. **2.** Nonintervention.
non·join·der (nŏn-join′dər) *n. Law.* The omission of a party, plaintiff, defendant, or cause of action that should have been included as a part of an action or suit.
non·judg·men·tal (nŏn′jŭj-mĕn′tl) *adj.* Refraining from judgment, esp. one based on personal standards.
non·ju·ror (nŏn-jo͝or′ər, -ôr′) *n.* **1.** One who refuses to take an oath, as of allegiance. **2.** **Nonjuror.** An Anglican clergyman who refused to swear allegiance to William and Mary in 1689. [NON- + JUROR, one who takes an oath (obs.).]
non·lin·e·ar (nŏn-lĭn′ē-ər) *adj.* **1.** Not in a straight line. **2.** Occurring as a result of a nonadditive operation.
non·lit·er·ate (nŏn-lĭt′ər-ĭt) *adj.* Having no written language. **—non·lit′er·ate** *n.*
non·met·al (nŏn-mĕt′l) *n. Chem.* Any of a number of elements, such as oxygen or sulfur, that generally occur as negatively charged ions or radicals, form oxides that produce acids, and are poor conductors of heat and of electricity when solid.
non·me·tal·lic (nŏn′mə-tăl′ĭk) *adj.* **1.** Not metallic. **2.** *Chem.* Of, pertaining to, or being a nonmetal.
non·mor·al (nŏn-môr′əl, -mŏr′-) *adj.* Unrelated to moral or ethical considerations.
non·neg·a·tive (nŏn-nĕg′ə-tĭv) *adj.* Of, pertaining to, or being a quantity that is either positive or zero.
non·nu·cle·ar (nŏn-no͞o′klē-ər, -nyo͞o′-) *adj.* **1.** Not causing, involving, or operated by nuclear energy. **2.** Not possessing nuclear weapons.
no-no (nō′nō′) *n. Informal.* **1.** Something that is unacceptable or impermissible. **2.** A faux pas.
non·ob·jec·tive (nŏn′əb-jĕk′tĭv) *adj.* Designating or being a style of graphic art in which natural objects are not represented realistically.
non ob·stan·te (nŏn′ əb-stăn′tē, nōn′-) *prep.* Notwithstanding. [Lat.]
no-non·sense (nō-nŏn′sĕns′, -səns) *adj.* Practical; businesslike.
non·pa·reil (nŏn′pə-rĕl′) *adj.* Having no equal; peerless. —*n.* **1.** A person or thing that has no equal; paragon. **2.** The painted bunting. **3.** A small, flat chocolate drop covered with white pellets of sugar. [ME *nonparail* < OFr. *nonpareil* : *non-,* non- + *pareil,* equal < VLat. **pariculus,* dim. of Lat. *par,* equal.]
non·par·ti·san (nŏn-pär′tĭ-zən, -sən) *adj.* **1.** Not partisan. **2.** Not based on, influenced by, affiliated with, or supporting the interests or policies of a political party. **—non·par′ti·san** *n.* **—non·par′ti·san·ship′** *n.*
non·per·sis·tent (nŏn′pər-sĭs′tənt) *adj.* Of or pertaining to a

chemical or biological agent that has a short life or existence under natural conditions.

non·per·son (nŏn-pûr′sən) *n.* A person whose expunction from the attention and memory of the public is sought, esp. by governmental action and usually for reasons of ideological or political deviation.

non·plus (nŏn-plŭs′) *n.* A state of perplexity, confusion, or bewilderment. —*tr.v.* **-plused, -plus·ing, -plus·es** also **-plussed, -plus·sing, -plus·ses.** To put at a loss as to what to think, say, or do; bewilder. [< Lat. *non plus,* no more.]

non·pol·lut·ing (nŏn′pə-lo͞o′tĭng) *adj.* Not causing pollution.

non pos·su·mus (nŏn pŏs′ə-məs, nōn) *n.* A statement indicating inability to do a particular thing. [Lat., we cannot.]

non·pro·duc·tive (nŏn′prə-dŭk′tĭv) *adj.* **1.** Not yielding or producing. **2.** Not engaged in the direct production of goods, as clerical personnel. **—non′pro·duc′tive·ly** *adv.*

non·pro·fes·sion·al (nŏn′prə-fĕsh′ə-nəl) *n.* One who is not a professional. —*adj.* Not professional. **—non′pro·fes′sion·al·ly** *adv.*

non·prof·it (nŏn-prŏf′ĭt) *adj.* Not seeking profit.

non·pro·lif·er·a·tion (nŏn′prə-lĭf′ə-rā′shən) *adj.* Of, pertaining to, involving, or calling for cessation of the proliferation of nuclear weapons: *a nonproliferation treaty.*

non·pros (nŏn′prŏs′) *tr.v.* **-prossed, -pros·sing, -pros·ses.** *Law.* To enter a judgment of non prosequitur against (a plaintiff). [Short for NON PROSEQUITUR.]

non pro·se·qui·tur (nŏn′ prə-sĕk′wĭ-tər, nōn′) *n. Law.* The judgment entered against a plaintiff who fails to appear in court to prosecute his suit. [Lat., he does not prosecute.]

non·read·er (nŏn-rē′dər) *n.* One who does not or is unable to read, esp. a child who takes a long time learning to read.

non·rep·re·sen·ta·tion·al (nŏn-rĕp′rĭ-zĕn-tā′shə-nəl) *adj.* Nonobjective.

non·re·pro·duc·tive (nŏn′rē-prə-dŭk′tĭv) *adj.* Not reproducing or not capable of reproducing.

non·res·i·dent (nŏn-rĕz′ĭ-dənt, -dĕnt′) *adj.* Not living in a particular place. **—non·res′i·dent** *n.* **—non·res′i·dence, non·res′i·den·cy** *n.*

non·re·sis·tance (nŏn′rĭ-zĭs′təns) *n.* **1.** The practice or principle of complete obedience to authority even if unjust or arbitrary. **2.** The practice or principle of refusing to resort to force even in defense against violence.

non·re·sis·tant (nŏn′rĭ-zĭs′tənt) *adj.* Not resistant, esp. unable to resist illness or infection. **—non′re·sis′tant** *n.*

non·re·stric·tive (nŏn′rĭ-strĭk′tĭv) *adj.* **1.** Not restrictive. **2.** *Gram.* Of or designating a word, clause, or phrase that is descriptive of but not essential to the basic meaning of the sentence element it modifies.

non·re·turn·a·ble (nŏn′rĭ-tûr′nə-bəl) *adj.* **1.** Not capable of being returned. **2.** Not exchangeable for a deposit: *nonreturnable bottles.*

non·rig·id (nŏn-rĭj′ĭd) *adj.* **1.** Not rigid. **2.** Designating a lighter-than-air aircraft that holds its shape by gas pressure.

non·sched·uled (nŏn-skĕj′o͞old) *adj.* Operating without a regular schedule of passenger or cargo flights: *a nonscheduled airline.*

non·sec·tar·i·an (nŏn′sĕk-târ′ē-ən) *adj.* Not limited to or associated with a particular religious denomination. **—non′sec·tar′i·an·ism** *n.*

non·sense (nŏn′sĕns′, -səns) *n.* **1.** Behavior or language that is foolish or absurd. **2.** Extravagant foolishness or frivolity. **3.** Something of little or no importance or usefulness; trifle. **4.** Insolent or pretentious behavior: *wouldn't take any nonsense from anyone.*

nonsense verse *n.* Verse characterized by humor or whimsy and often featuring nonce words.

non·sen·si·cal (nŏn-sĕn′sĭ-kəl) *adj.* Foolish; absurd. **—non·sen′si·cal′i·ty** (-kăl′ĭ-tē), **non·sen′si·cal·ness** *n.* **—non·sen′si·cal·ly** *adv.*

non se·qui·tur (nŏn sĕk′wĭ-tər, -to͝or′) *n.* **1.** An inference or conclusion that does not follow from the premises or evidence. **2.** A statement that does not follow logically from what preceded it. [Lat., it does not follow.]

non·sex·ist (nŏn-sĕk′sĭst) *adj.* Not discriminating against individuals, esp. women, on the basis of gender.

non·sig·nif·i·cant (nŏn′sĭg-nĭf′ĭ-kənt) *adj.* Having, producing, or being a value obtained from a statistical test that lies within the limits for being of random occurrence. **—non′sig·nif′i·cant·ly** *adv.*

non·sked (nŏn′skĕd′) *n. Informal.* A nonscheduled airline or cargo plane. [Short for NONSCHEDULED.]

non·skid (nŏn′skĭd′) *adj.* Designed to prevent or inhibit skidding.

non·stan·dard (nŏn-stăn′dərd) *adj.* **1.** Varying from or not adhering to the standard. **2.** Of, pertaining to, or indicating a level of language usage that is usually avoided by educated speakers and writers.

non·stick (nŏn′stĭk′) *adj.* Facilitating removal of adhered food particles: *a frying pan with a nonstick surface.*

non·stop (nŏn′stŏp′) *adv.* Performed or accomplished without a stop. —*adj.* **1.** Making or having made no stops: *a nonstop flight.* **2.** Unceasing; unremitting.

non·such (nŭn′sŭch′) *n.* Variant of **nonesuch.**

non·suit (nŏn-so͞ot′) *n. Law.* A judgment against a plaintiff for failure to prosecute his case or to introduce sufficient evidence. —*tr.v.* **-suit·ed, -suit·ing, -suits.** To dismiss the lawsuit of. [ME, failure of a plaintiff to prosecute < AN *nounsute* : *non-,* no (< Lat. *non*) + *suite,* suit.]

non·sup·port (nŏn′sə-pôrt′, -pōrt′) *n. Law.* Failure to provide for the maintenance of one's legal dependents.

non·tar·get (nŏn-tär′gĭt) *adj.* Of, relating to, or being an object not intended to be acted upon by an agent.

non·ten·ured (nŏn-tĕn′yərd, -yo͝ord′) *adj.* Not having or leading to tenure.

non·triv·i·al (nŏn-trĭv′ē-əl) *adj. Math.* Of, relating to, or being an expression in which at least one variable is not equal to zero.

non trop·po (nŏn trô′pō, nōn) *adv. & adj. Mus.* In moderation. Used to modify a direction: *adagio non troppo.* [Ital., not too much.]

non-U (nŏn-yo͞o′) *adj. Chiefly Brit. Informal.* Not belonging or appropriate to upper-class custom.

non·un·ion (nŏn-yo͞on′yən) *adj.* **1.** Not belonging to a labor union: *nonunion workers.* **2.** Not recognizing or dealing with a labor union or employing union members: *a nonunion shop.*

non·u·ple (nŏn′yə-pəl) *adj.* **1.** Consisting of nine members, parts, or elements; ninefold. **2.** Multiplied by nine. —*n.* A number or total that is nine times as great as another. [OFr. < Lat. *nonus,* nine.]

non·us·er (nŏn-yo͞o′zər) *n.* One who refrains from the use of something, as of narcotic drugs or alcohol.

non·ver·bal (nŏn-vûr′bəl) *adj.* **1.** Being other than verbal: *nonverbal gestures.* **2. a.** Involving little use of language: *a nonverbal intelligence test.* **b.** Measuring low on a scale of verbal ability.

non·vi·a·ble (nŏn-vī′ə-bəl) *adj.* **1.** Not capable of living or developing: *a nonviable fetus.* **2.** Not workable or practicable.

non·vi·o·lence (nŏn-vī′ə-ləns) *n.* **1.** Lack of violence. **2.** The doctrine, policy, or practice of rejecting violence in favor of peaceful tactics as a means of gaining esp. political objectives. **—non·vi′o·lent** *adj.* **—non·vi′o·lent·ly** *adv.*

non·vot·er (nŏn-vō′tər) *n.* A person who does not vote or who has no right to vote.

noo·dle[1] (no͞od′l) *n.* **1.** *Slang.* The head. **2.** A stupid person; fool. [Poss. alteration of NODDLE.]

noo·dle[2] (no͞od′l) *n.* A narrow, ribbonlike strip of dried dough, usually made of flour, eggs, and water. [G. *Nudel.*]

noo·dle[3] (no͞od′l) *intr.v.* **-dled, -dling, -dles.** To improvise music on an instrument in an idle and haphazard fashion. [Orig. unknown.]

nook (no͝ok) *n.* **1.** A small corner, alcove, or recess, esp. one that is part of a larger room. **2.** A hidden or secluded spot. [ME *nok,* prob. of Scand. orig.]

noon (no͞on) *n.* **1. a.** Twelve o'clock in the daytime; midday. **b.** The time or the point in the sun's path when it is on the local meridian. **2.** The highest point; zenith. **3.** *Archaic.* Midnight: *the noon of night.* ***—modifier:*** *a noon meal.* [ME *non* < OE, ninth hour after sunrise < LLat. *nona (hora)* < Lat. *nonus,* ninth.]

noon·day (no͞on′dā′) *n.* Noon.

no one also **no-one** (nō′wŭn′) *pron.* No person; nobody. —See Usage note at **everyone.**

noon·tide (no͞on′tīd′) *n.* Noon; noontime. [ME *nontide* < OE *nōntīd* : *nōn,* noon + *tīd,* time.]

noon·time (no͞on′tīm′) *n.* Noon.

noose (no͞os) *n.* **1.** A loop formed in a rope by means of a slipknot so that it binds tighter as the rope is pulled. **2.** A snare or trap. —*tr.v.* **noosed, noos·ing, noos·es. 1.** To capture or hold by or as if by a noose. **2.** To make a noose of or in. [ME *nose.*]

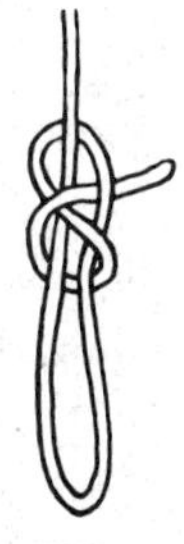
noose
Figure-eight noose

Noot·ka (no͞ot′kə, no͝ot′-) *n.* **1. a.** A tribe of North American Indians living on Vancouver Island, British Columbia, and Cape Flattery, northwestern Washington. **b.** A member of this tribe. **2.** The Wakashan language of the Nootka. **—Noot′ka** *adj.*

Nootka cypress *n.* A tall evergreen tree, *Chamaecyparis nootkatensis,* of the northwestern coast of North America. [After *Nootka* Sound, Canada.]

no·pal (nō′pəl, nō-päl′, -păl′) *n.* **1.** A cactus of the genus *Nopalea,* esp. *N. coccinellifera,* found chiefly in Mexico. **2.** A species of prickly pear, *Opuntia lindheimeri,* having yellow or red flowers and purple fruit. [Sp. < Nahuatl *nopalli.*]

no-par (nō′pär′) *adj.* Without face value; having no par value: *a no-par stock certificate.*

no-par-val·ue (nō′pär-văl′yo͞o) *adj.* No-par.

nope (nōp) *adv. Slang.* No. [Alteration of NO.]

nor[1] (nôr; nər *when unstressed*) *conj.* And not; or not; not either: *He has no experience nor does he want any. He is neither willing nor able to do anything.* —See Usage notes at **neither** and **no.** [ME : *ne,* no + *or,* or.]

nor[2] (nôr; nər *when unstressed*) *conj. Regional.* Than. [ME.]

NOR (nôr) *n.* A machine logic circuit that produces an output inverse to that of an OR circuit. [N(OT) + OR.]

nor– *pref.* An unaltered parent compound: *norepinephrine.* [< NORMAL.]

nor·a·dren·a·lin (nôr′ə-drĕn′ə-lĭn) *n.* Norepinephrine.

Nor·dic (nôr′dĭk) *adj.* **1.** Of, pertaining to, or belonging to the subdivision of the Caucasoid ethnic group that is most predominant in Scandinavia. **2.** Of or pertaining to a class consisting of people who are typically tall, long-headed, blond, and blue-eyed. **3.** *Sports.* Of or pertaining to ski competition featuring ski jumping and cross-country racing. [Fr. *nordique* < OFr. *nord,* north < OE *norð.*] **—Nor'dic** *n.*

Nord·mann fir (nôrd'mən) *n.* A widely planted evergreen tree, *Abies nordmanniana,* having reddish-brown, erect cones. [After A. von *Nordmann* (d. 1866).]

nor·ep·i·neph·rine (nôr'ĕp-ə-nĕf'rĭn, -rēn') *n.* A hormone, $(OH)_2C_6H_3 \cdot CHOH \cdot CH_2 \cdot NH_2$, that is formed naturally in the body's sympathetic nerve endings and is a vasoconstrictor.

Nor·folk Island pine (nôr'fək) *n.* An evergreen tree, *Araucaria excelsa,* native to Norfolk Island in the South Pacific.

Norfolk jacket *n.* A belted jacket with two box pleats in front and back. [After *Norfolk,* England.]

no·ri·a (nôr'ē-ə, nōr'-) *n.* A water wheel with buckets attached to its rim that are used to raise water from a stream, esp. for transferal to an irrigation trough. [Sp. < Ar. *nā'ūrah* < *na'ara,* to creak.]

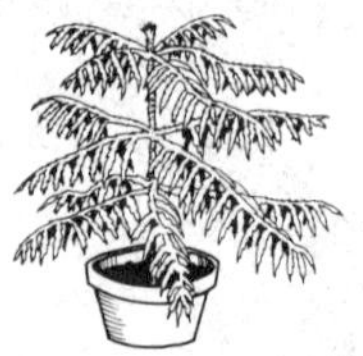

Norfolk Island pine

nor·ite (nôr'īt') *n.* Gabbro. [Norw. *norit* < *Norge,* Norway.] **—nor·it'ic** (nô-rĭt'ĭk) *adj.*

norm (nôrm) *n.* **1.** A standard, model, or pattern regarded as typical for a specific group. **2.** *Math.* **a.** A mode. **b.** An average. **c.** The length of a vector. [Lat. *norma,* carpenter's square.]

Nor·ma (nôr'mə) *n.* A constellation in the Southern Hemisphere within the Milky Way near Lupus and Ara. [NLat. < Lat. *norma,* carpenter's square.]

nor·mal (nôr'məl) *adj.* **1.** Conforming, adhering to, or constituting a usual or typical standard, pattern, level, or type: *normal room temperature; his normal weight.* **2.** *Biol.* **a.** Not affected, immunized, or changed by experimentation. **b.** Functioning or occurring in a natural way. **3.** *Chem.* **a.** Describing a solution having one gram equivalent weight of solute per liter of solution. **b.** Describing an aliphatic hydrocarbon having a straight and unbranched chain of carbon atoms. **4.** *Math.* Being perpendicular; at right angles. **5. a.** Relating to or marked by average intelligence or development. **b.** Free from physical or emotional disorder. *—n.* **1.** Something that is normal; the standard. **2.** The usual or expected state, form, amount, or degree. **3. a.** Correspondence to a norm. **b.** An average. **4.** *Math.* A perpendicular, esp. a perpendicular to a line tangent to a plane curve or to a plane tangent to a space curve. [Lat. *normalis,* made according to the square < *norma,* carpenter's square.] **—nor'mal·ly** *adv.*

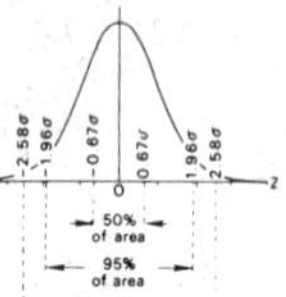

normal distribution
Frequency curve of the normal distribution; σ is the standard deviation

Synonyms: *normal, regular, standard, natural, typical.* Nontechnically, all these words suggest group characteristics. *Normal* stresses adherence to an established level or pattern that is associated with well-being, although based on group tendencies rather than on an arbitrary ideal. *Regular* and *standard* indicate unvarying conformity to a pattern in a narrower, impersonal sense. *Natural* emphasizes harmony between something (such as an act or an emotion) and the essence of the individual or object considered as a representative of a group. *Typical* stresses adherence to those qualities considered collectively and impersonally that identify a group.

nor·mal·cy (nôr'məl-sē) *n.* Normality.

normal distribution *n.* A theoretical frequency distribution for a set of variable data, usually represented by a bell-shaped curve symmetrical about the mean.

nor·mal·i·ty (nôr-măl'ĭ-tē) *n.* The state or fact of being normal.

nor·mal·ize (nôr'mə-līz') *tr.v.* **-ized, -iz·ing, -iz·es. 1.** To cause to conform to a standard or norm. **2.** *Metallurgy.* To remove strains and reduce coarse crystalline structures by applying heat. **—nor'mal·i·za'tion** *n.* **—nor'mal·iz'er** *n.*

normal pentane *n.* A pentane.

normal school *n.* A school that trains teachers, chiefly for the elementary grades. [Transl. of Fr. *école normale* (so called because the first school so named was intended as a model) < Lat. *normalis,* according to the square < *norma,* carpenter's square.]

Nor·man (nôr'mən) *n.* **1.** A member of a Scandinavian people who conquered Normandy in the 10th century. **2.** A member of a people of Norman and French blood who conquered England in 1066. **3.** A native or inhabitant of Normandy. *—adj.* **1.** Of or pertaining to Normandy, the Normans, their culture, or their language. **2.** *Archit.* Of or designating a style of Romanesque architecture that was introduced from Normandy into England before 1066 and flourished until about 1200. [ME < OFr. *Normant* (< ON *Northmaðr* : *norðr,* north + *maðr,* man) and OE, var. of *Norðman* (*norð,* north + *man,* man).]

Norman Conquest *n.* The conquest of England by the Normans under William the Conqueror beginning in 1066.

Norman French *n.* The dialect of Old French used in Normandy.

nor·ma·tive (nôr'mə-tĭv) *adj.* Of, relating to, or prescribing a norm or standard. [Fr. *normatif* < *norme,* norm < Lat. *norma,* carpenter's square.] **—nor'ma·tive·ly** *adv.* **—nor'ma·tive·ness** *n.*

nor·mo·blast (nôr'mə-blăst') *n.* An immature red blood cell characterized by abundant hemoglobin and a small nucleus.

Norn (nôrn) *n.* One of the three Fates in Norse mythology. [ON.]

nor·nic·o·tine (nôr-nĭk'ə-tēn') *n.* A colorless liquid alkaloid, $C_9H_{12}N_2$, extracted from tobacco and used as a plant insecticide.

Norse (nôrs) *adj.* **1.** Of or pertaining to ancient Scandinavia, its people, or their language. **2. a.** Of or pertaining to West Scandinavia or the languages of its inhabitants. **b.** Of or pertaining to Norway, its people, or their language. *—n., pl.* **Norse. 1. a.** The people of Scandinavia; the Scandinavians. **b.** The people of West Scandinavia; the West Scandinavians, esp. the Norwegians. **c.** The ancient Norwegians. **2. a.** North Germanic. **b.** Any of the western Scandinavian languages, esp. Norwegian. [Du. *noorsch,* a Norwegian, alteration of *noordsch* < *noord,* north < MDu. *nort.*]

Norse·man (nôrs'mən) *n.* A member of one of the peoples of ancient Scandinavia.

north (nôrth) *n.* **1. a.** The direction along a meridian 90 degrees counterclockwise from east; the direction to the left of sunrise. **b.** The cardinal point on the mariner's compass located at 0 degrees. **2.** Often **North.** The northern part of a country or region. *—adj.* **1.** To, toward, of, facing, or in the north. **2.** Coming from or originating in the north. *—adv.* In, from, or toward the north. [ME < OE *norð.*]

north·bound (nôrth'bound') *adj.* Going toward the north.

north by east *n.* The direction or point on the mariner's compass halfway between due north and north-northeast. It is 11 degrees 15 minutes east of due north. *—adv. & adj.* To or from north by east.

north by west *n.* The direction or point on the mariner's compass halfway between due north and north-northwest. It is 11 degrees 15 minutes west of due north. *—adv. & adj.* To or from north by west.

north·east (nôrth-ēst', nôr-ēst') *n.* **1.** The direction or point on the mariner's compass halfway between north and east. It is 45 degrees east of due north. **2.** An area or region lying in the northeast. *—adj.* **1.** Situated toward, facing, or in the northeast. **2.** Coming from or originating in the northeast, as a wind. *—adv.* In, from, or toward the northeast. **—north·east'ern** *adj.*

northeast by east *n.* The direction or point on the mariner's compass halfway between northeast and east-northeast. It is 56 degrees 15 minutes east of due north.

northeast by north *n.* The direction or point on the mariner's compass halfway between northeast and north-northeast. It is 33 degrees 45 minutes east of due north.

north·east·er (nôrth-ē'stər, nôr-ē'-) *n.* A storm or gale from the northeast.

north·east·er·ly (nôrth-ē'stər-lē, nôr-ē'-) *adj.* **1.** Situated toward or in the northeast. **2.** From the northeast. **—north·east'er·ly** *adv.*

north·east·ward (nôrth-ēst'wərd, nôr-ēst'-) *adv.* Toward the northeast. *—adj.* Situated toward or facing the northeast. *—n.* A direction or region to the northeast. **—north·east'ward·ly** *adj. & adv.* **—north·east'wards** (-wərdz) *adv.*

north·er (nôr'*th*ər) *n.* A sudden, cold gale from the north.

north·er·ly (nôr'*th*ər-lē) *adj.* **1.** Situated toward the north. **2.** From the north, as a wind. *—n., pl.* **-lies.** A storm or wind from the north. **—north'er·ly** *adv.*

north·ern (nôr'*th*ərn) *adj.* **1.** Situated toward, in, or facing the north. **2.** Coming from the north, as a wind. **3.** Growing in the north. **4.** Often **Northern.** Of, pertaining to, or characteristic of northern regions or the North. **5.** *Astron.* North of the celestial equator. [ME *northerne* < OE *norðerne.*]

Northern Cross *n.* Cygnus.

Northern Crown *n.* Corona Borealis.

north·ern·er (nôr'*th*ər-nər) *n.* A native or inhabitant of the north, esp. of the northeastern United States.

Northern Hemisphere *n.* The half of the earth north of the equator.

northern lights *pl.n.* The aurora borealis.

north·ern·most (nôr'*th*ərn-mōst') *adj.* Farthest north.

Northern Spy *n.* A large, yellowish-red, late-ripening apple.

North Germanic *n.* A subdivision of the Germanic languages that includes Norwegian, Icelandic, Swedish, Danish, and Faroese.

north·ing (nôr'thĭng, -*th*ĭng) *n.* **1.** The difference in latitude between two positions as a result of a movement to the north. **2.** Progress toward the north.

north·land (nôrth'lănd', -lənd) *n.* Often **Northland.** A region in the north, as of a country or territory. **—north'land'er** *n.*

North·man (nôrth'mən) *n.* A Norseman.

north-north·east (nôrth'nôrth-ēst', nôr'nôr-ēst') *n.* The direction or point on the mariner's compass halfway between due north and northeast. It is 22 degrees 30 minutes east of due north. *—adj. & adv.* In, from, or toward the north-northeast.

north-north·west (nôrth'nôrth-wĕst', nôr'nôr-wĕst') *n.* The direction or point on the mariner's compass halfway between due north and northwest. It is 22 degrees 30 minutes west of due north. *—adj. & adv.* In, from, or toward the north-northwest.

North Pole *n.* **1. a.** The northern end of the earth's axis of rotation. **b.** The celestial zenith of this terrestrial point, slightly more than 1 degree from Polaris. **2. north pole.** The north-seeking magnetic pole of a magnet.

North Star *n.* Polaris (sense 1).

North·um·bri·an (nôr-thŭm'brē-ən) *adj.* **1.** Of or pertaining to Northumbria or its Old English dialect. **2.** Of or pertaining to Northumberland. —*n.* **1.** A native or inhabitant of Northumbria. **2.** A native or inhabitant of Northumberland. **3.** The Old English dialect of Northumbria.

north·ward (nôrth′wərd) *adj. & adv.* Toward, to, or in the north. —*n.* A northern direction, point, or region. —**north′ward·ly** *adj. & adv.* —**north′wards** (-wərdz) *adv.*

north·west (nôrth-wĕst′, nôr-wĕst′) *n.* **1.** The direction or point on the mariner's compass halfway between north and west. It is 45 degrees west of due north. **2.** An area or region lying in the northwest. —*adj.* **1.** To, toward, of, facing, or in the northwest. **2.** Coming from the northwest. —*adv.* In, from, or toward the northwest. —**north·west′ern** *adj.*

northwest by north *n.* The direction or point on the mariner's compass halfway between northwest and north-northwest. It is 33 degrees 45 minutes west of due north.

northwest by west *n.* The direction or point on the mariner's compass halfway between northwest and west-northwest. It is 56 degrees 15 minutes west of due north.

north·west·er (nôrth-wĕs′tər) *n.* A storm or gale from the northwest.

north·west·er·ly (nôrth-wĕs′tər-lē, nôr-wĕs′-) *adj.* **1.** Toward or in the northwest. **2.** From the northwest. —**north·west′er·ly** *adv.*

north·west·ward (nôrth-wĕst′wərd) *adv.* Toward the northwest. —*adj.* Situated toward, facing, or in the northwest. —*n.* A direction or region toward the northwest. —**north·west′ward·ly** *adj. & adv.* —**north·west′wards** (-wərdz) *adv.*

Nor·way maple (nôr′wā′) *n.* A tall Eurasian tree, *Acer platanoides,* widely used in North America as a shade tree.

Norway pine *n.* The red pine. [After *Norway,* Maine.]

Norway rat *n.* The common brown rat, *Rattus norvegicus,* which is highly destructive and is found worldwide, esp. in populated areas.

Norway spruce *n.* A tall evergreen tree, *Picea abies,* of northern regions, having long, dark-green needles.

Nor·we·gian (nôr-wē′jən) *n.* **1.** A native or inhabitant of Norway. **2.** The North Germanic language of the Norwegians. [< Med. Lat. *Norwegia,* Norway < ON *Norvegr* : *norðr,* north + *vegr,* region.] —**Nor·we′gian** *adj.*

Norwegian elkhound *n.* The elkhound.

nose (nōz) *n.* **1. a.** In man and other primates, the structure on the face or the forward part of the head that contains the nostrils and organs of smell and forms the beginning of the respiratory tract. **b.** A similar feature or organ in the face, muzzle, snout, or front end of many other animals. **2.** The sense of smell: *a dog with a good nose.* **3.** The ability to detect, sense, or discover as if by smell: *a nose for gossip.* **4.** *Informal.* The nose considered as a symbol of prying: *Keep your nose out of my business.* **5.** Something that resembles a nose in shape or position, as the forward end of an aircraft, rocket, or submarine. —*v.* **nosed, nos·ing, nos·es.** —*tr.* **1.** To find out by or as if by smell. **2.** To touch or examine with the nose; nuzzle. **3.** To cause to move or advance cautiously: *nosed the car into the flow of traffic.* —*intr.* **1.** To smell or sniff. **2.** *Informal.* To pry curiously or in a meddlesome way: *nosing around in someone else's business.* **3.** To push forward with caution: *The ship nosed into its berth.* —***phrasal verb.* nose out.** To defeat by a very narrow margin. —***idioms.* follow (one's) nose. 1.** To move straight ahead. **2.** To be guided by instinct. **look down (one's) nose at.** *Informal.* To regard or treat with disapproval, contempt, or arrogance. **on the nose.** Exactly; precisely: *predicted the amount on the nose.* [ME < OE *nosu.*]

nose·band (nōz′bănd′) *n.* The part of a bridle or halter that passes over an animal's nose.

nose·bleed (nōz′blēd′) *n.* A nasal hemorrhage; bleeding from the nose.

nose cone *n.* The forwardmost and usually separable section of a rocket or guided missile, shaped to offer minimum aerodynamic resistance and often bearing a protective cladding against heat.

nose dive *n.* **1.** A very steep dive of an aircraft, nose toward the earth. **2.** A sudden, swift drop or plunge.

nose-dive (nōz′dīv′) *intr.v.* **-dived** or **-dove** (-dōv′), **-div·ing, -dives.** To perform a nose dive.

no-see-um (nō-sē′əm) *n.* The punkie. [Alteration of *no see them.*]

nose·gay (nōz′gā′) *n.* A small bunch of flowers. [ME : *nose,* nose + *gay,* ornament < *gay,* joyous < OFr. *gai.*]

nose job *n. Slang.* Plastic surgery performed on the nose, esp. to improve appearance.

nose·piece (nōz′pēs′) *n.* **1.** A piece of armor that forms part of a helmet and protects the nose. **2.** The part of a pair of eyeglasses that fits across the nose. **3.** A noseband. **4.** The part of a microscope, often rotatable, to which one or more objective lenses are attached.

nos·ey (nō′zē) *adj.* Variant of **nosy.**

nosh (nŏsh) *Informal.* —*n.* A tidbit; snack. —*intr.v.* **noshed, nosh·ing, nosh·es.** To eat snacks between meals. [Short for Yiddish *nosherai,* tidbits < OHG *hnascōn,* to nibble.] —**nosh′er** *n.*

no-show (nō-shō′) *n. Slang.* **1. a.** A traveler who reserves a place, esp. on an airplane, but neither claims nor cancels the reservation before the time of departure. **b. no-shows.** Those who purchase tickets for an event but do not attend esp. out of protest or disapproval. **2.** A person who unexplainedly fails to keep an engagement or appointment.

nos·ing (nō′zĭng) *n.* **1. a.** The horizontally projecting edge of a stair tread. **b.** A shield covering this edge. **2.** A projecting edge of a molding.

noso– *pref.* Disease: *nosography.* [Gk. < *nosos,* a disease.]

no·sog·ra·phy (nō-sŏg′rə-fē, -zŏg′-) *n.* The systematization and description of diseases. —**no·sog′ra·pher** *n.* —**no′so·graph′ic** (nō′sə-grăf′ĭk), **no′so·graph′i·cal** *adj.*

no·sol·o·gy (nō-sŏl′ə-jē, -zŏl′-) *n.* **1.** The branch of medicine that deals with the classification of diseases. **2.** A classification of diseases. —**no′so·log′i·cal** (-sə-lŏj′ĭ-kəl), **no′so·log′ic** *adj.* —**no′so·log′i·cal·ly** *adv.* —**no·sol′o·gist** *n.*

nos·tal·gi·a (nŏ-stăl′jə, nə-) *n.* **1.** A bittersweet longing for things, persons, or situations of the past. **2.** The condition of being homesick; homesickness. [Gk. *nostos,* home + -ALGIA.] —**nos·tal′gic** (-jĭk) *adj.* —**nos·tal′gi·cal·ly** *adv.*

nos·toc (nŏs′tŏk′) *n.* A freshwater alga of the genus *Nostoc,* forming colonies of blue-green cells embedded in a jelly. [Coined by Paracelsus (1493–1541).]

nos·tril (nŏs′trəl) *n.* Either of the external openings of the nose. [ME *nostrille* < OE *nosðyrl* : *nosu,* nose + *thyrl,* hole.]

nos·trum (nŏs′trəm) *n.* **1.** A medicine, esp. a quack remedy, whose ingredients are usually secret. **2.** A favorite but untested remedy for problems or evils. [Lat., our own, neuter of *noster,* ours.]

nos·y or **nos·ey** (nō′zē) *adj.* **-i·er, -i·est.** *Informal.* Prying; inquisitive. [< NOSE.] —**nos′i·ly** *adv.* —**nos′i·ness** *n.*

not (nŏt) *adv.* In no way; to no degree. Used to express negation, denial, refusal, or prohibition: *I will not go. You may not have any.* [ME, alteration of *nought* < OE *nōwiht* : *nā,* no + *wiht,* thing.]

Usage: Care should be taken with the placement of *not* and other negatives in a sentence in order to avoid ambiguity. *All elephants are not friendly* could be taken to mean either "all elephants are unfriendly" or "not all elephants are friendly." Similarly, the sentence *Kim didn't sleep until noon* could mean either "Kim went to sleep at noon" or "Kim got up before noon." • In formal writing, the *not only. . .but also* construction should be used in such a way that each of its elements is followed by a construction of the same type. Instead of *she not only bought a new car but a new lawnmower,* write *she bought not only a new car but a new lawnmower;* in the second version, both *not only* and *but also* are followed by noun phrases. • In the *not only* construction, *also* is often omitted when the second part of the sentence merely intensifies the first: *She is not only smart but brilliant. He not only wanted the diamond but wanted it desperately.*

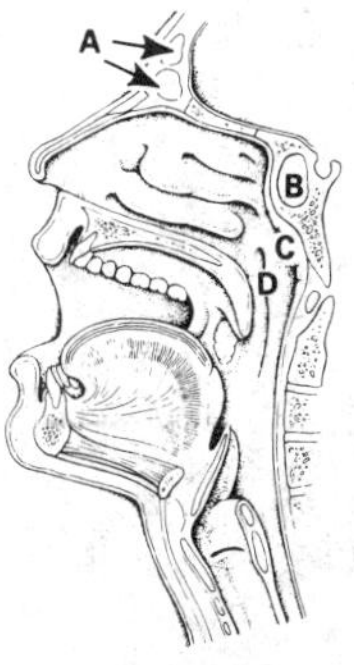

nose
A. Frontal sinuses
B. Sphenoid sinus
C. Pharyngeal tonsil
D. Eustachian tube

NOT (nŏt) *n.* A machine logic circuit that produces an output inverse to the input. [< NOT.]

no·ta be·ne (nō′tə bē′nē, bĕn′ē). Used to direct attention to something particularly important. [Lat., note well.]

no·ta·bil·i·ty (nō′tə-bĭl′ĭ-tē) *n., pl.* **-ties. 1.** The state or quality of being notable. **2.** A notable or prominent person.

no·ta·ble (nō′tə-bəl) *adj.* **1. a.** Worthy of notice; striking: *notable beauty; a notable accomplishment.* **b.** Prominent or distinguished: *many notable politicians were in attendance.* **2.** (*also* nŏt′ə-bəl). *Archaic & Regional.* Diligent and efficient, esp. in household duties. —*n.* **1.** A person of distinction or great reputation. **2.** Often **Notable.** One of a council of prominent persons before the French revolution called into assembly to deliberate at times of emergency. [ME < OFr. < Lat. *notabilis* < *notare,* to note < *nota,* note.] —**no′ta·ble·ness** *n.* —**no′ta·bly** *adv.*

no·tar·i·al (nō-târ′ē-əl) *adj.* **1.** Of or pertaining to a notary public. **2.** Executed or drawn up by a notary public. —**no·tar′i·al·ly** *adv.*

no·ta·rize (nō′tə-rīz′) *tr.v.* **-rized, -riz·ing, -riz·es.** To authenticate or attest to as a notary public. [< NOTARY.] —**no′ta·ri·za′tion** *n.*

no·ta·ry (nō′tə-rē) *n., pl.* **-ries. 1.** *Obs.* A stenographer. **2.** A notary public. [ME *notarie* < OFr. *notaire* < Lat. *notarius* < *notarius,* shorthand < *nota,* mark.]

notary public *n., pl.* **notaries public.** A person legally empowered to witness and certify documents and to take affidavits and depositions.

no·tate (nō′tāt′) *tr.v.* **-tat·ed, -tat·ing, -tates.** To put into notation.

no·ta·tion (nō-tā′shən) *n.* **1. a.** A system of figures or symbols used in specialized fields to represent numbers, quantities, tones, or values: *musical notation.* **b.** The act or process of using such a system. **2.** A brief note; annotation. [Lat. *notatio* < *notare,* to note < *nota,* note.] —**no·ta′tion·al** *adj.*

notch (nŏch) *n.* **1. a.** A V-shaped cut. **b.** Such a cut used for keeping a record. **2.** A narrow pass between mountains. **3.** *Informal.* A level or degree: *He is a notch better than his brother.* —*tr.v.* **notched, notch·ing, notch·es. 1.** To cut a notch in. **2.** To record by or as if by making notches. [*a notch,* alteration of *an otch* < OFr. *oche* < *ochier,* to notch < Lat. *absecare,* to cut off : *ab-,* off + *secare,* to cut.] —**notched** *adj.*

notch·back (nŏch′băk′) *n.* An automobile with a sloping roof and a pronounced rear compartment.

note
Musical notes

note (nōt) *n.* **1.** A brief record, esp. one written down to aid the memory. **2.** A brief, informal letter or message. **3.** A formal written diplomatic or official communication. **4.** A comment or explanation, as on a passage in a text. **5. a.** A piece of paper currency. **b.** A certificate issued by a government or a bank and sometimes negotiable as money. **c.** A promissory note. **6.** *Mus.* **a.** A tone of definite pitch. **b.** A symbol for such a tone, indicating pitch by its position on the staff and duration by its shape. **c.** A key of a piano or similar instrument. **7.** A characteristic animal call or cry: *the clear note of a cardinal.* **8.** A sign of a certain quality: *ended his plea on a note of despair.* **9.** Importance; consequence: *Nothing of note happened.* **10.** Notice; observation: *He took note of what had happened.* **11.** *Archaic.* A song, melody, or tune. *—tr.v.* **not·ed, not·ing, notes. 1.** To observe carefully; notice. **2.** To write down; make a note of. **3.** To show; indicate. **4.** To make mention of; remark. ***—idiom.* compare notes.** To exchange ideas, views, or opinions. [Lat. *nota,* mark.] **—not'er** *n.*

note·book (nōt'bo͝ok') *n.* A book of blank pages for notes.

not·ed (nō'tĭd) *adj.* Distinguished by reputation; famous: *a noted author.* **—not'ed·ly** *adv.* **—not'ed·ness** *n.*

Synonyms: *noted, notable, noteworthy, notorious.* Applied to persons, *noted* emphasizes actual celebrity without stressing worthiness. *Notable* and *noteworthy* stress worthiness more strongly than celebrity. *Notorious* is usually unfavorable, implying disreputable celebrity.

note of hand *n.* A promissory note.

note·wor·thy (nōt'wûr'*thē*) *adj.* Deserving notice or attention; remarkable: *a noteworthy advance in cancer research.* **—note'wor'thi·ly** *adv.* **—note'wor'thi·ness** *n.*

noth·ing (nŭth'ĭng) *pron.* **1.** No thing; not anything: *I've heard nothing about it.* **2.** No significant or notable thing: *There is nothing on television tonight.* **3.** No part; no portion: *Nothing remains of its former glory.* **4.** Insignificance; obscurity: *rising from nothing.* **5.** Something or someone of no consequence, significance, or interest: *It's nothing to me.* **6.** Absence of anything perceptible; nonexistence: *The sound faded into nothing.* *—n.* **1.** Something that has no existence. **2.** Something that has no quantitative value; zero. **3. a.** Something that is trivial; trifle: *a novel that is a real nothing.* **b.** A trivial or inane word or remark. **c.** An exceedingly inconsequential, insignificant, or uninteresting person; nonentity: *Her mother-in-law is a big nothing.* *—adj. Slang.* Insignificant or worthless; trifling: *a nothing part in a play.* *—adv.* In no way or degree; not at all: *She looks nothing like me.* ***—idiom.* nothing doing.** *Informal.* Certainly not. [ME < OE *nāthing* : *nān,* none + *thing,* thing.]

Usage: *Nothing* takes a singular verb, even when it is followed by a phrase containing a plural noun or pronoun: *Nothing except your fears stands* (not *stand*) *in your path. Nothing but roses meets* (not *meet*) *the eye.* See also Usage note at **double negative.**

noth·ing·ness (nŭth'ĭng-nĭs) *n.* **1.** The condition or quality of being nothing; nonexistence. **2.** Empty space; void. **3.** Lack of consequence; insignificance. **4.** Something inconsequential or insignificant.

no·tice (nō'tĭs) *n.* **1.** Attention; observation: *That detail escaped my notice.* **2.** Respectful attention or consideration. **3.** A written or printed announcement. **4. a.** A formal announcement of purpose, esp. of intention to withdraw from an agreement or leave a job. **b.** The condition of being notified of such purpose. **5.** A critical review, as of a play or book. **6.** An indication or warning of something. *—tr.v.* **-ticed, -tic·ing, -tic·es. 1.** To take note of; observe. **2.** To consider; mark. **3.** To comment on; mention. **4.** To treat with courteous attention. [ME, knowledge < OFr. *notere* < Lat. *notitia* < *notus,* known, p.part. of *noscere,* to come to know.]

no·tice·a·ble (nō'tĭ-sə-bəl) *adj.* **1.** Readily observed; evident. **2.** Worthy of notice; significant. **—no'tice·a·bly** *adv.*

no·ti·fi·ca·tion (nō'tə-fĭ-kā'shən) *n.* **1.** The act or an instance of notifying. **2.** Something, as a letter, by which notice is given.

no·ti·fy (nō'tə-fī') *tr.v.* **-fied, -fy·ing, -fies. 1.** To give notice to; inform: *notified his client of the hearing.* **2.** *Chiefly Brit.* To give notice of; make known. [ME *notifien* < OFr. *notifier* < Lat. *notificare,* to make known : *notus,* known (p.part. of *noscere,* to come to know) + *facere,* to make.] **—no'ti·fi'er** *n.*

no·tion (nō'shən) *n.* **1.** A belief; opinion. **2.** A mental image or representation; idea. **3.** A fanciful impulse; whim. **4. notions.** Small useful items, such as needles, buttons, or thread. [Lat. *notio* < *noscere,* to come to know.]

no·tion·al (nō'shə-nəl) *adj.* **1.** Of, pertaining to, or being a notion. **2.** Speculative or theoretical rather than actual. **3.** Existing in the mind; imaginary rather than factual. **4.** Conveying an idea of a thing or action; having full lexical meaning as distinguished from relational meaning: *The word* did *is notional in "we did the work" and relational in "we did not agree."* **—no'tion·al·ly** *adv.*

no·to·chord (nō'tə-kôrd') *n.* **1.** A flexible rodlike structure in some lower vertebrates that provides dorsal support; the primitive backbone. **2.** A structure similar to the notochord in embryos of higher vertebrates from which the spine develops. [Gk. *nōtos,* back + CHORD[3].] **—no'to·chord'al** *adj.*

no·to·ri·e·ty (nō'tə-rī'ĭ-tē) *n.* The quality or condition of being notorious.

no·to·ri·ous (nō-tôr'ē-əs, -tōr'-) *adj.* Known widely and usually unfavorably. [Med. Lat. *notorius* < Lat. *notus,* known, p.part. of *noscere,* to come to know.] **—no·to'ri·ous·ly** *adv.* **—no·to'ri·ous·ness** *n.*

no·tor·nis (nō-tôr'nĭs) *n., pl.* **notornis.** A flightless bird, now rare, of the genus *Notornis,* found in New Zealand. [NLat. *Notornis,* genus name : Gk. *notos,* south + Gk. *ornis,* bird.]

no-trump (nō'trŭmp') *n.* **1.** In bridge and other card games, a declaration to play a hand without a trump suit. **2.** A hand played without a trump suit. **—no'-trump'** *adj.*

not·with·stand·ing (nŏt'wĭth-stăn'dĭng, -wĭ*th*-) *prep.* In spite of. *—adv.* All the same; nevertheless. *—conj.* In spite of the fact that; although. [ME *notwithstanding* : *not,* not + *withstanding,* pr.part. of *withstanden,* to resist. —see WITHSTAND.]

Synonyms: *notwithstanding, despite, in spite of. Notwithstanding* is the weakest of three terms used to indicate opposition of varying intensity to contrary forces or circumstances. *Despite* is used when the opposition is relatively stronger and *in spite of* when the forces are resisted most actively and vigorously.

nou·gat (no͞o'gət) *n.* A confection made from a sugar or honey paste into which nuts are mixed. [Fr. < Prov. < Lat. *nux,* nut.]

nought (nôt) *n., adj., & adv.* Variant of **naught.**

nou·me·non (no͞o'mə-nŏn') *n., pl.* **-na** (-nə). *Philos.* **1.** An object of purely intellectual intuition as opposed to an object of sensuous perception. **2.** A thing-in-itself that is independent of the sensuous or intellectual perception of it. [Gk., concept < *nouein,* to conceive < *nous,* mind.] **—nou'me·nal** *adj.*

noun (noun) *n. Gram.* A word that is used to name a person, place, thing, quality, or action and can function as the subject or object of a verb, the object of a preposition, or an appositive. [ME < AN < OFr. *non* < Lat. *nomen,* name.]

nour·ish (nûr'ĭsh, nŭr'-) *tr.v.* **-ished, -ish·ing, -ish·es. 1.** To provide with food or other substances necessary for life and growth; feed. **2.** To foster the development of; promote. **3.** To keep alive; maintain. [ME *norishen* < OFr. *norrir* < Lat. *nutrire.*] **—nour'ish·er** *n.*

nour·ish·ment (nûr'ĭsh-mənt, nŭr'-) *n.* **1. a.** The act of nourishing. **b.** The state of being nourished. **2.** Something that nourishes.

nous (no͞os) *n. Philos.* Mind; reason, esp. the principle of divine reason. [Gk.]

nou·veau riche (no͞o'vō rēsh') *n., pl.* **nou·veaux riches** (no͞o'vō rēsh'). A person who has recently become rich, esp. one who flaunts his wealth; parvenu. [Fr., new rich.]

nou·velle cuisine (no͞o-vĕl') *n.* A contemporary school of French cooking that seeks to bring out the natural flavors of foods and substitutes light, low-caloric sauces and stocks for the traditional heavy butter- and cream-based preparations. [Fr., new cuisine.]

nouvelle vague (väg') *n.* New wave (sense 1). [Fr.]

no·va (nō'və) *n., pl.* **-vae** (-vē) or **-vas.** *Astron.* A variable star that suddenly increases in brightness to several times its normal magnitude and returns to its original appearance in a few weeks to several months or years. [NLat. *(stella) nova,* new star < Lat. *novus,* new.]

no·vac·u·lite (nō-văk'yə-līt') *n.* A very hard, dense, even-textured silica-bearing rock used in whetstones. [Lat. *novacula,* razor + -ITE.]

no·vae (nō'vē) *n.* A plural of **nova.**

no·va·tion (nō-vā'shən) *n. Law.* The substitution of a new obligation for an old one. [LLat. *novatio* < Lat. *novare,* to make new < *novus,* new.]

nov·el[1] (nŏv'əl) *n.* **1.** A fictional prose narrative of considerable length, typically having a plot that is unfolded by the actions, speech, and thoughts of the characters. **2.** The literary genre represented by novels. [Ital. *(storia) novella,* new story < *novello,* new < Lat. *novellus,* dim. of *novus.*]

nov·el[2] (nŏv'əl) *adj.* Strikingly new, unusual, or different. [ME < OFr. < Lat. *novellus,* dim. of *novus.*] **—nov'el·ly** *adv.*

nov·el·ette (nŏv'ə-lĕt') *n.* A short novel.

nov·el·ist (nŏv'ə-lĭst) *n.* A writer of novels.

nov·el·is·tic (nŏv'ə-lĭs'tĭk) *adj.* Of, relating to, or characteristic of novels. **—nov'el·is'ti·cal·ly** *adv.*

no·vel·la (nō-vĕl'ə) *n., pl.* **-vel·las** or **-vel·le** (-vĕl'ē). **1.** A short prose tale characterized by wit, terseness, or satire. **2.** A short novel. [Ital. —see NOVEL[1].]

nov·el·ty (nŏv'əl-tē) *n., pl.* **-ties. 1.** The quality of being novel; newness. **2.** Something new and unusual; innovation. **3. novelties.** Small mass-produced articles, as toys or trinkets. [ME *novelte* < OFr. < *novel,* new. —see NOVEL[2].]

No·vem·ber (nō-vĕm'bər) *n.* The 11th month of the Gregorian calendar. See table at **calendar.** [ME *Novembre* < OFr. < Lat. *November,* ninth month < *novem,* nine.]

no·ve·na (nō-vē'nə) *n., pl.* **-nas** or **-nae** (-nē). *Rom. Cath. Ch.* Prayers and devotions for a special purpose, repeated for nine consecutive days. [Med. Lat. < Lat. *novenus,* nine each < *novem,* nine.]

no·ver·cal (nō-vûr'kəl) *adj.* Of, pertaining to, or characteristic of a stepmother. [Lat. *novercalis* < *noverca,* stepmother.]

nov·ice (nŏv'ĭs) *n.* **1.** A person new to a field or activity; beginner. **2.** A person who has entered a religious order but has not yet taken final vows. [ME, probationary member of a religious order < OFr. < Med. Lat. *novicius* < Lat. *novus,* new.]

no·vi·ti·ate also **no·vi·ci·ate** (nō-vĭsh′ē-ĭt, -āt′) *n.* **1.** The period of being a novice. **2.** A place where novices live. **3.** A novice (sense 2). [Fr. *noviciat* < Med. Lat. *noviciatus* < *novicius,* novice < Lat. *novus,* new.]
No·vo·cain (nō′və-kān′). A trademark for the anesthetic procaine hydrochloride.
now (nou) *adv.* **1.** At the present time: *can't leave now.* **2.** At once; immediately: *Stop now.* **3.** In the immediate past; very recently: *He left just now.* **4.** In the immediate future; very soon: *They are going just now.* **5.** At this point in the series of events; then: *The ship was now listing to port.* **6.** Nowadays. **7.** In these circumstances; as things are: *Now we won't be able to stay.* **8.** —Used esp. to introduce a command, reproof, or request: *Now pay attention.* —*conj.* Since; seeing that: *Now that we have eaten, let's go out and party.* —*n.* The present time or moment: *wouldn't work up to now.* —*adj.* **1.** *Informal.* Of the present time; current: *the now generation.* **2.** *Slang.* In tune with the latest trends: *wore now clothing.* **—idiom. now and again** (or **then**). Occasionally. [ME < OE *nū.*]
NOW account (nou) *n.* A savings account against which drafts can be written and which usually bears interest. [N(EGOTIATED) O(RDER OF) W(ITHDRAWAL).]
now·a·days (nou′ə-dāz′) *adv.* During the present time. [ME *nou a daies,* on this day, at the present time.]
no·way (nō′wā′) also **no·ways** (-wāz′) *adv.* Nowise.
no way *interj. Informal.* Used to indicate definite negation.
no·where (nō′hwâr′, -wâr′) *adv.* **1.** Not anywhere. **2.** To no place or result: *You'll get nowhere doing it that way.* —*n.* A remote or unknown place: *a cabin in the middle of nowhere.*
no·wheres (nō′hwârz′, -wârz′) *adv. Nonstandard.* Nowhere.
no·whith·er (nō′hwĭ*th*′ər, -wĭ*th*′-) *adv.* In no definite direction.
no-win (nō′wĭn′) *adj.* Incapable of affording victory or success: *found herself trapped in a no-win predicament.*
no·wise (nō′wīz′) *adv.* In no way, manner, or degree; not at all. [ME : *no,* no + *wise,* way < OE *wīse.*]
nox·ious (nŏk′shəs) *adj.* **1.** Injurious or harmful to health: *noxious chemical wastes.* **2.** Injurious or harmful to the mind or morals; corrupting: *noxious ideas.* [Lat. *noxius* < *noxa,* damage.] **—nox·ious·ly** *adv.* **—nox′ious·ness** *n.*
noz·zle (nŏz′əl) *n.* **1.** A projecting part with an opening, as at the end of a hose, through which something is discharged. **2.** *Slang.* The nose. [Dim. of NOSE.]
Np The symbol for the element Neptunium.
nth (ĕnth) *adj.* **1.** Pertaining to an indefinitely large ordinal number: *ten to the nth power.* **2.** Highest; utmost: *delighted to the nth degree.*
nth root *n.* Root (sense 9.a.).
nu (no͞o, nyo͞o) *n.* The 13th letter of the Greek alphabet. See table at **alphabet.** [Gk., of Semitic orig.; akin to Heb. *nūn,* nun.]
nu·ance (no͞o-äns′, nyo͞o-, no͞o′äns′, nyo͞o′-) *n.* A subtle or slight degree of difference, as in meaning, color, or tone; gradation. [Fr., shade < OFr. < *nuer,* to show different shades < *nue,* cloud < Lat. *nubes.*]
nub (nŭb) *n.* **1.** A protuberance or knob. **2.** A small lump. **3.** The essence; core: *the nub of a story.* [Var. of *knub* < MLG *knubbe,* knot of a tree.] **—nub′by** *adj.*
Nu·ba (no͞o′bə, nyo͞o′-) *n., pl.* **Nuba. 1.** A Nubian. **2.** A member of any of several Negroid tribes of southern Sudan. **3.** The language of the Nuba.
nub·bin (nŭb′ĭn) *n.* **1.** Something, as an ear of corn, that is stunted or imperfectly developed. **2.** A small chunk or piece: *a nubbin of chalk.* [Dim. of NUB.]
nub·ble (nŭb′əl) *n.* A small protuberance or lump. [Dim. of NUB.] **—nub′bly** *adj.*
Nu·bi·an (no͞o′bē-ən, nyo͞o′-) *n.* **1.** A native or inhabitant of Nubia. **2.** Any of the languages of Nubia. **—Nu′bi·an** *adj.*
nu·bile (no͞o′bĭl, -bīl′, nyo͞o′-) *adj.* Ready for marriage; of a marriageable age or condition. Used of young women. [Fr. < Lat. *nubilis* < *nubere,* to take a husband.] **—nu·bil′i·ty** (no͞o-bĭl′ĭ-tē, nyo͞o-) *n.*
nu·cel·lus (no͞o-sĕl′əs, nyo͞o-) *n., pl.* **-cel·li** (-sĕl′ī′). *Bot.* The center of the rudimentary seed of a plant, containing the embryo sac. [NLat., alteration of Lat. *nucella,* dim. of *nux,* nut.] **—nu·cel′lar** *adj.*
nu·cha (no͞o′kə, nyo͞o′-) *n.* The nape of the neck. [ME < Med. Lat. < Ar. *nukhā′.*] **—nu′chal** *adj.*
nucle– *pref.* Variant of **nucleo-.**
nu·cle·ar (no͞o′klē-ər, nyo͞o′-) *adj.* **1.** *Biol.* Of, pertaining to, or forming a nucleus: *a nuclear membrane.* **2.** *Physics.* Of or concerning atomic nuclei: *nuclear physics.* **3.** Using or derived from the energy of atomic nuclei; atomic: *nuclear power plants.* **4.** Of, using, or possessing atomic or hydrogen bombs: *nuclear war; nuclear nations.* [< NUCLEUS.]
nuclear emulsion *n. Physics.* Any of several photographic emulsions used to detect and visually display the paths of charged subatomic particles, esp. of charged cosmic-ray particles.
nuclear energy *n.* The energy released by a nuclear reaction, esp. by fission, fusion, or radioactive decay.
nuclear family *n.* A self-contained family unit consisting of a mother and father and their children.
nuclear fission *n. Physics.* Fission (sense 2).
nuclear force *n.* Strong interaction.
nuclear fusion *n. Physics.* Fusion (sense 5).
nuclear magnetic resonance *n.* The magnetic resonance of an atomic nucleus.
nuclear magneton *n. Physics.* A unit of the magnetic moment of the nucleon.
nuclear physics *n.* The scientific study of the forces, reactions, and internal structures of atomic nuclei.
nuclear reaction *n.* A reaction that alters the energy, composition, or structure of an atomic nucleus.
nuclear reactor *n.* Any of several devices in which a chain reaction is initiated and controlled with the consequent production of heat typically used for power generation and the neutrons and fission products used for a variety of experimental and medical purposes.
nuclear resonance *n.* The resonance absorption of a gamma ray by an atomic nucleus identical to the nucleus that emitted the ray.
nu·cle·ase (no͞o′klē-ās′, -āz′, nyo͞o′-) *n.* Any of several enzymes that hydrolize nucleic acids.
nu·cle·ate (no͞o′klē-ĭt, nyo͞o′-) *adj.* Having a nucleus or nuclei. —*v.* (-āt′) **-at·ed, -at·ing, -ates.** —*tr.* **1.** To bring together into a nucleus. **2.** To act as a nucleus for. —*intr.* To form a nucleus. **—nu′cle·a′tion** *n.* **—nu′cle·a′tor** *n.*
nu·cle·i (no͞o′klē-ī′, nyo͞o′-) *n.* A plural of **nucleus.**
nu·cle·ic acid (no͞o-klē′ĭk, nyo͞o-) *n.* A member of either of two groups of complex compounds found in all living cells and composed of purines, pyrimidines, carbohydrates, and phosphoric acid.
nucleo– or **nucle–** *pref.* **1.** Nucleus: *nucleon, nucleoplasm.* **2.** Nucleic acid: *nucleoprotein.* [< NUCLEUS.]
nu·cle·o·late (no͞o′klē-ə-lāt′, nyo͞o′-) also **nu·cle·o·lat·ed** (-lā′tĭd) *adj.* Having a nucleolus or nucleoli. [NUCLEOL(US) + -ATE.]
nu·cle·o·lus (no͞o-klē′ə-ləs, nyo͞o-) *n., pl.* **-li** (-lī′). *Biol.* **1.** A small, usually round body composed of protein and ribonucleic acid in the nucleus of a cell. **2.** A discrete, cellular particle that resembles a nucleolus, other than a chromosome. [Lat., dim. of *nucleus,* kernel < *nux,* nut.] **—nu·cle′o·lar** (-lər) *adj.*
nu·cle·on (no͞o′klē-ŏn′, nyo͞o′-) *n.* A proton or a neutron, esp. as part of an atomic nucleus. **—nu′cle·on′ic** *adj.*
nu·cle·on·ics (no͞o′klē-ŏn′ĭks, nyo͞o′-) *n. (used with a sing. verb).* The technology of nuclear energy. [< NUCLEON.]
nucleon number *n. Physics.* Mass number.
nu·cle·o·phile (no͞o′klē-ə-fīl′, nyo͞o′-) *n.* A substance that donates electrons.
nu·cle·o·plasm (no͞o′klē-ə-plăz′əm, nyo͞o′-) *n.* The protoplasm of a cell nucleus. **—nu′cle·o·plas′mic, nu′cle·o·plas·mat′ic** (-ō-plăz-măt′ĭk) *adj.*
nu·cle·o·pro·tein (no͞o′klē-ō-prō′tēn′, -prō′tē-ĭn, nyo͞o′-) *n.* Any of a group of substances found in all living cells and viruses and composed of a protein and a nucleic acid.
nu·cle·o·side (no͞o′klē-ə-sīd′, nyo͞o′-) *n.* A compound made of a sugar and a purine or pyrimidine base, esp. one obtained by hydrolysis of a nucleic acid, such as adenosine.
nu·cle·o·some (no͞o′klē-ə-sōm′) *n.* Any of the basic globular subunits of chromatin consisting of DNA and histone. **—nu′cle·o·som′al** (-sō′məl) *adj.*
nu·cle·o·syn·the·sis (no͞o′klē-ō-sĭn′thĭ-sĭs, nyo͞o′-) *n.* The process by which heavier chemical elements are synthesized from hydrogen nuclei in the interiors of stars. **—nu′cle·o·syn·thet′ic** (-sĭn-thĕt′ĭk) *adj.*
nu·cle·o·tide (no͞o′klē-ə-tīd′, nyo͞o′-) *n.* Any of various organic compounds consisting of a nucleoside combined with phosphoric acid.
nu·cle·us (no͞o′klē-əs, nyo͞o′-) *n., pl.* **-cle·i** (-klē-ī′) or **-cle·us·es. 1.** A central or essential part around which other parts are grouped or collected; core: *the nucleus of a city.* **2.** Something regarded as a basis for future development and growth; kernel. **3.** *Biol.* A complex, usually spherical protoplasmic body within a living cell that contains the cell's hereditary material and controls its metabolism, growth, and reproduction. **4.** *Bot.* **a.** The nucellus. **b.** The central kernel of a nut or seed. **c.** The central point of a starch granule. **5.** *Anat.* A group of nerve cells or localized mass of gray matter in the brain, where nerve fibers interconnect. **6.** *Physics.* The positively charged central region of an atom, composed of protons and neutrons and containing almost all of the mass of the atom. **7.** *Chem.* A group of atoms chemically bound in a structure resistant to alteration in chemical reactions. **8.** *Astron.* **a.** The central portion of the head of a comet. **b.** The central or brightest part of a nebula or of a galaxy. **9.** *Meteorol.* A particle on which water vapor molecules accumulate in free air to form a droplet or ice crystal. [Lat., kernel < *nux,* nut.]
nu·clide (no͞o′klīd′, nyo͞o′-) *n. Physics.* An atomic nucleus specified by its atomic number, atomic mass, and energy state. **—nu·clid′ic** (no͞o-klĭd′ĭk, nyo͞o-) *adj.*
nude (no͞od, nyo͞od) *adj.* **nud·er, nud·est. 1.** Without clothing; naked. **2.** Lacking any of various legal requisites, such as evidence. —*n.* **1.** The nude human figure, esp. in artistic representation. **2.** The condition of being unclothed: *in the nude.* [Lat. *nudus.*] **—nude′ly** *adv.* **—nude′ness, nu′di·ty** (no͞o′dĭ-tē, nyo͞o′-) *n.*
nudge¹ (nŭj) *tr.v.* **nudged, nudg·ing, nudg·es. 1.** To push against gently, esp. in order to gain attention or give a sig-

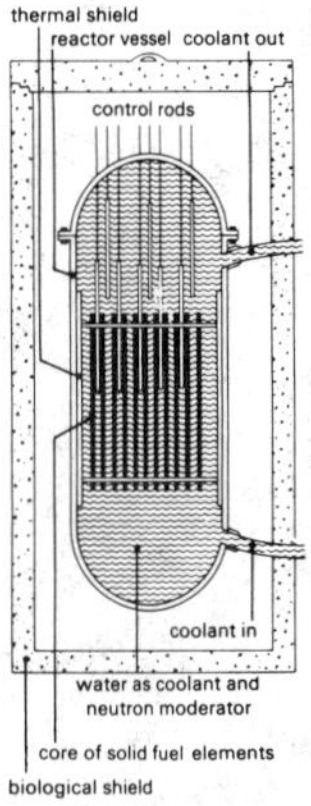

nuclear reactor

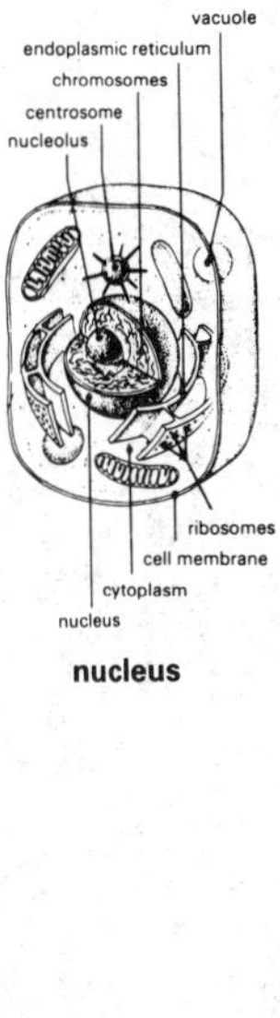

nucleus

nal. **2.** To come close to; near: *She's nudging 60 years of age.* —*n.* A gentle push. [Prob. of Scandinavian orig.]

nudge² also **nudzh** (no͝oj) *Slang.* —*n.* One who persistently pesters, annoys, or complains. —*v.* **nudged, nudg·ing, nudg·es** also **nudzhed, nudzh·ing, nudzh·es.** —*tr.* To annoy or pester (someone) persistently. —*intr.* To complain or carp persistently. [< Yiddish *nudyen,* to pester, bore < R. *nudnyi,* tedious, boring < *nudnost',* tedium.]

nudi– *pref.* Naked; bare: *nudibranch.* [< Lat. *nudus,* nude.]

nu·di·branch (no͞o'də-brăngk', nyo͞o'-) *n.* A mollusk of the order Nudibranchia; sea slug. [< NLat. *Nudibranchia,* order name : NUDI- + Gk. *brankhia,* gills.] —**nu'di·bran'chi·ate** (-brăng'kē-ĭt), **nu'di·bran'chi·an** (-kē-ən) *adj. & n.*

nud·ism (no͞o'dĭz'əm, nyo͞o'-) *n.* The belief in or practice of going nude. —**nud'ist** *n.*

nud·nik also **nud·nick** (no͝od'nĭk) *n. Slang.* A dense, boring, or bothersome person; pest. [Yiddish < Pol. *nudny,* tiresome < *nuda,* boredom.]

nudzh (no͝oj) *n. & v. Slang.* Variant of **nudge².**

nu·ga·to·ry (no͞o'gə-tôr'ē, -tōr'ē, nyo͞o'-) *adj.* **1.** Of little or no importance; trifling. **2.** Without force; invalid. [Lat. *nugatorius* < *nugari,* to trifle < *nugae,* jokes.]

nug·get (nŭg'ĭt) *n.* **1.** A small, solid lump, esp. of gold. **2.** Something resembling a nugget, as in value: *nuggets of information.* [Dial. E., dim. of *nug,* lump.]

nui·sance (no͞o'səns, nyo͞o'-) *n.* **1.** Something that is inconvenient, annoying, or vexatious; bother. **2.** *Law.* A use of property or course of conduct that interferes with the legal rights of others by causing damage, annoyance, or inconvenience. [ME *noisaunce* < OFr. *nuisance* < *nuire,* to harm < Lat. *nocēre.*]

nuisance tax *n.* A tax levied on separate purchases and collected directly from the purchaser.

nuke (no͞ok, nyo͞ok) *Slang.* —*n.* **1.** A nuclear weapon. **2.** A nuclear-powered electric generating plant. —*tr.v.* **nuked, nuk·ing, nukes.** To attack with nuclear weapons. [Shortening and alteration of NUCLEAR.]

null (nŭl) *adj.* **1.** Having no legal force; invalid. **2.** Of no consequence, effect, or value; insignificant. **3.** Amounting to nothing; absent; nonexistent. **4.** *Math.* Of or pertaining to a set having no members or to zero magnitude. —*tr.v.* **nulled, null·ing, nulls.** To make null. —*n.* **1.** Zero; nothing. **2.** An instrumental reading of zero. [OFr. *nul* < Lat. *nullus* : *ne,* not + *ullus,* any.]

nul·lah (nŭl'ə) *n.* A ravine or gully. [Hindi *nāla,* rivulet, prob. of Dravidian orig.]

null character *n.* A data control character that fills computer time by adding nonsignificant zeros to a data sequence.

nul·li·fi·ca·tion (nŭl'ə-fĭ-kā'shən) *n.* **1. a.** The act of nullifying. **b.** The state of being nullified. **2.** The refusal or failure of a state to recognize or enforce a U.S. law within its boundaries. —**nul'li·fi·ca'tion·ist** *n.*

nul·li·fi·er (nŭl'ə-fī'ər) *n.* **1.** One that nullifies. **2.** One who believes in nullification, esp. on the part of a U.S. state.

nul·li·fy (nŭl'ə-fī') *tr.v.* **-fied, -fy·ing, -fies. 1.** To make null; invalidate. **2.** To counteract the force or effectiveness of. [LLat. *nullificare,* to despise : Lat. *nullus,* none + *facere,* to make.]

Synonyms: *nullify, negate, abolish, annul, void, invalidate, abrogate, cancel, repeal, revoke, rescind. Nullify* and *negate,* as compared here, both indicate reduction to ineffectiveness. *Abolish* goes further and stresses complete removal. *Annul* and *void* are general terms indicating deprivation of effectiveness or validity. *Invalidate* is also applied to action that destroys effectiveness or validity, but it is narrower in that it implies a specific cause; a contract may be invalidated by faulty execution or by lack of fulfillment of a single term. *Abrogate,* applied to treaties or other formal agreements, stresses executive action that terminates. *Cancel* has the same force as the preceding term, but is applied to more commonplace agreements, such as contracts, leases, and deeds. *Repeal* is usually confined to a legislative act that terminates existing legislation. *Revoke* and *rescind* involve the taking back by executive action of a previous grant of privilege or power.

nul·lip·a·ra (nə-lĭp'ə-rə) *n.* A female who has not borne offspring. [Lat. *nullus,* none + -PARA.] —**nul·lip'a·rous** *adj.*

nul·li·ty (nŭl'ĭ-tē) *n., pl.* **-ties. 1.** The state or quality of being null. **2.** Something that is null, esp. an act having no legal validity.

numb (nŭm) *adj.* **-er, -est. 1.** Deprived of the power to feel or move normally; benumbed: *toes numb with cold.* **2.** Stunned or paralyzed, as from shock or strong emotion: *too numb with fear to cry out.* —*tr. & intr.v.* **numbed, numb·ing, numbs.** To make or become numb. [ME *nomen,* p. part. of *nimen,* to seize < OE *niman.*] —**numb'ly** *adv.* —**numb'ness** *n.*

num·ber (nŭm'bər) *n.* **1.** *Math.* **a.** A member of the set of positive integers; one of a series of symbols of unique meaning in a fixed order that can be derived by counting. **b.** A member of any of the further sets of mathematical objects, such as negative integers and real numbers, that can be derived from the positive integers by mathematical induction. **2. numbers.** Arithmetic. **3. a.** A symbol used to represent a number. **b.** A numeral or series of numerals for reference or identification: *a telephone number.* **4.** A total; sum: *the number of feet in a mile.* **5.** Quantity of units or individuals: *The crowd was small in number.* **6. numbers. a.** A large quantity or collection; multitude: *Numbers of people visited the fair.* **b.** Numerical superiority: *The South had leaders, the North numbers.* **7.** One item in a group or series considered esp. in numerical order. **8.** One of the separate offerings in a program of music. **9.** *Informal.* A person or thing singled out from a group for some characteristic. **10.** *Gram.* The indication, as by inflection, of the singularity or plurality of a linguistic form. **11. a. numbers.** Metrical periods or feet; verses. **b.** Measured rhythm in verse; meter. **12. numbers.** *Archaic.* Musical periods or measures. **13. numbers.** The numbers game. **14. Numbers.** See table at **Bible.** —*v.* **-bered, -ber·ing, -bers.** —*tr.* **1.** To total in number or amount; add up to. **2.** To count or determine the number or amount of. **3.** To include in a group or category: *He was numbered among the lost.* **4.** To mention one by one; enumerate. **5.** To assign a number to. **6.** To limit or restrict in number: *numbered the visits each prisoner was allowed a month.* —*intr.* **1.** To count or call off numbers: *numbering to ten.* **2.** To constitute a group or number: *The applicants numbered in the thousands.* —*idioms.* **do a number on.** *Slang.* **1.** To harm or abuse, esp. by trickery. **2.** To make fun of; ridicule. **get** (or **have**) **(someone's) number.** To determine or know someone's real character or motives. **without** (or **beyond**) **number.** Too many to be counted; countless. [ME *nombre* < OFr. < Lat. *numerus.*] —**num'ber·er** *n.*

Usage: As a collective noun, *number* may take either a singular or a plural verb. It takes a singular verb when it is preceded by the definite article *the: The number of skilled workers is small.* It takes a plural verb when preceded by the indefinite article *a: A number of the workers are unskilled.*

number cruncher *n. Slang.* A computer able to perform complex and lengthy calculations. —**number crunching** *n.*

num·ber·less (nŭm'bər-lĭs) *adj.* Innumerable; countless.

number line *n.* A line that graphically expresses the real numbers as a series of points distributed about a point arbitrarily designated as zero and in which the magnitude of each number is represented by the distance of the corresponding point from zero.

numbers game *n.* A kind of lottery in which bets are made on an unpredictable number, such as a daily stock-exchange figure.

numb·fish (nŭm'fĭsh') *n.* The electric ray.

numb·skull (nŭm'skŭl') *n.* Variant of **numskull.**

nu·men (no͞o'mən, nyo͞o'-) *n., pl.* **-mi·na** (-mə-nə). **1.** A presiding divinity or spirit of a place. **2.** A spirit believed by animists to inhabit certain natural phenomena or objects. **3.** Creative energy; genius. [Lat.]

nu·mer·a·ble (no͞o'mər-ə-bəl, nyo͞o'-) *adj.* Capable of being counted; countable. [Lat. *numerabilis* < *numerare,* to count < *numerus,* number.]

nu·mer·al (no͞o'mər-əl, nyo͞o'-) *n.* **1.** A symbol or mark used to represent a number. **2. numerals.** The numbers, usually the last two digits, indicating by year a graduating class in a school or college. —*adj.* Of, pertaining to, or expressing numbers. [LLat. *numeralis* < Lat. *numerus,* number.] —**nu'mer·al·ly** *adv.*

nu·mer·ar·y (no͞o'mə-rĕr'ē, nyo͞o'-) *adj.* Of or pertaining to a number or numbers. [Med. Lat. *numerarius* < Lat. *numerus,* number.]

nu·mer·ate (no͞o'mə-rāt', nyo͞o'-) *tr.v.* **-at·ed, -at·ing, -ates.** To enumerate; count. [Lat. *numerare, numerat-,* to count < *numerus,* number.]

nu·mer·a·tion (no͞o'mə-rā'shən, nyo͞o'-) *n.* **1.** The act or process of counting or numbering; enumeration. **2.** A system of enumeration.

nu·mer·a·tor (no͞o'mə-rā'tər, nyo͞o'-) *n.* **1.** *Math.* **a.** The expression written above the line in a common fraction. **b.** An expression to be divided by another; dividend. **2.** One that numbers; enumerator.

nu·mer·ic (no͞o-mĕr'ĭk, nyo͞o-) *n.* A number or numeral. —*adj.* Variant of **numerical.**

nu·mer·i·cal (no͞o-mĕr'ĭ-kəl, nyo͞o-) also **nu·mer·ic** (-mĕr'ĭk) *adj.* **1.** Of or pertaining to a number or series of numbers: *numerical order.* **2.** Denoting number or a number: *a numerical symbol.* **3.** Expressed in or counted by numbers: *numerical strength.* [< Lat. *numerus,* number.] —**nu·mer'i·cal·ly** *adv.*

numerical analysis *n.* The study of approximate solutions to mathematical problems, taking into account the extent of possible errors.

numerical control *n.* Control of a process or machine by a digital computer.

numerical taxonomy *n.* A branch of taxonomy that deals with the quantitative relationships between the elements classified.

numerical value *n. Math.* The absolute value of a number regardless of sign.

nu·mer·ol·o·gy (no͞o'mə-rŏl'ə-jē, nyo͞o'-) *n.* The study of the occult meanings of numbers and of their supposed influence on human life. [Lat. *numerus,* number + -LOGY.] —**nu'mer·o·log'i·cal** (-mər-ə-lŏj'ĭ-kəl) *adj.* —**nu'mer·ol'o·gist** *n.*

nu·mer·ous (no͞o'mər-əs, nyo͞o'-) *adj.* Consisting of many persons or items. [Lat. *numerosus* < *numerus,* number.] —**nu'mer·ous·ly** *adv.* —**nu'mer·ous·ness** *n.*

Usage: *Numerous* is not used as a pronoun in standard English. In writing, expressions like *numerous of the firemen* should be avoided.

nu·mi·na (no͞o'mə-nə, nyo͞o'-) *n.* Plural of **numen.**

nu·mi·nous (no͞o'mə-nəs, nyo͞o'-) *adj.* **1.** Of or pertaining to a numen; supernatural. **2.** Spiritually elevated; supernatural. **3.** Incapable of being described or understood; mysterious. [< Lat. *numen,* numen.]

nu·mis·mat·ic (no͞o'mĭz-măt'ĭk, -mĭs-, nyo͞o'-) *adj.* **1.** Of or pertaining to coins or currency. **2.** Of or pertaining to numismatics. —**nu'mis·mat'i·cal·ly** *adv.*

nu·mis·mat·ics (no͞o'mĭz-măt'ĭks, -mĭs-, nyo͞o'-) *n. (used with a sing. verb).* The study or collection of money, coins, and often medals. [< *numismatic,* pertaining to coins < Fr. *numismatique* < Lat. *numisma,* coin < Gk. *nomisma,* current coin < *nomizein,* to have in use < *nomos,* custom.] —**nu·mis'ma·tist** (no͞o-mĭz'mə-tĭst, -mĭs'-, nyo͞o-) *n.*

nu·mis·ma·tol·o·gy (no͞o-mĭz'mə-tŏl'ə-jē, -mĭs'-, nyo͞o-) *n.* Numismatics.

num·mu·lar (nŭm'yə-lər) *adj.* Shaped like a coin; oval or circular. [Fr. *nummulaire* < Lat. *nummulus,* dim. of *nummus,* coin.]

num·mu·lite (nŭm'yə-līt') *n.* A protozoan of the family Nummulitidae, chiefly marine, tiny, mostly extinct, and characterized by a coin-shaped shell. [NLat. *Nummulites,* genus name < Lat. *nummulus,* dim. of *nummus,* coin.] —**num'mu·lit'ic** (-lĭt'ĭk) *adj.*

num·skull also **numb·skull** (nŭm'skŭl') *n.* A stupid person; blockhead.

nun[1] (nŭn) *n.* A woman who belongs to a religious order devoted to religious service or meditation, usually under vows of poverty, chastity, and obedience. [ME *nonne* < OE *nunne* and OFr. *nonne,* both < LLat. *nonna.*]

nun[2] (no͞on) *n.* The 14th letter of the Hebrew alphabet. See table at **alphabet.** [Heb. *nūn.*]

Nunc Di·mit·tis (nŭngk' dĭ-mĭt'ĭs, no͝ongk') *n.* The canticle of Simeon, beginning *"Nunc dimittis servum tuum"* ("Now lettest thou thy servant depart").

nun·ci·a·ture (nŭn'sē-ə-cho͝or', -chər, no͝on'-) *n.* The office or term of office of a nuncio. [Ital. *nunciatura* < *nuncio,* nuncio < Lat. *nuntius,* messenger.]

nun·ci·o (nŭn'sē-ō', no͝on'-) *n., pl.* **-os.** A papal ambassador or representative. [Ital. < Lat. *nuntius,* messenger.]

nun·cle (nŭng'kəl) *n. Archaic.* An uncle. [Alteration of UNCLE.]

nun·cu·pa·tive (nŭn'kyə-pā'tĭv, nŭng'-, nŭn-kyo͞o'pə-tĭv) *adj. Law.* Designating a will delivered orally to witnesses rather than written. [Med. Lat. *nuncupativus* < Lat. *nuncupare,* to name : *nomen,* name + *capere,* to take.]

nun·ner·y (nŭn'ə-rē) *n., pl.* **-ies.** A convent of nuns.

nup·tial (nŭp'shəl, -chəl) *adj.* **1.** Of or pertaining to marriage or the wedding ceremony. **2.** Of, pertaining to, or occurring in the mating season. —*n.* Often **nuptials.** A wedding ceremony. [Lat. *nuptialis* < *nuptiae,* wedding < *nubere,* to take a husband.] —**nup'tial·ly** *adv.*

nurd (nûrd) *n.* Variant of **nerd.**

nurse (nûrs) *n.* **1.** A person trained to care for the sick or disabled esp. under the supervision of a physician. **2. a.** A person employed to take care of a child; nursemaid. **b.** A woman employed to suckle children other than her own; wet nurse. **3.** One that serves as a nurturing or fostering influence or means. **4.** A worker ant or bee that cares for the young in an insect colony. —*v.* **nursed, nurs·ing, nurs·es.** —*tr.* **1.** To feed at the breast; suckle. **2.** To serve as a nurse for. **3.** To try to cure or treat: *nurse a cough.* **4.** To take special care of; foster: *nursed his business through the depression.* **5.** To bear in the mind: *nursing a grudge.* **6.** To treat carefully, esp. in order to prevent pain: *nursed his bruised knee.* **7.** To consume slowly, esp. in order to conserve. —*intr.* **1.** To take nourishment from the breast; suckle. **2.** To serve as a nurse. [ME *norice,* nursemaid < OFr. *norrice* < LLat. *nutricia* < *nutrire,* to nourish.] —**nurs'er** *n.*

nurse·maid (nûrs'mād') *n.* A woman employed to take care of children.

nurs·er·y (nûr'sə-rē, nûrs'rē) *n., pl.* **-ies. 1.** A room or area set apart for the use of children. **2. a.** A nursery school. **b.** A place for the temporary care of children. **3.** A place where plants are grown for sale, transplanting, or experimentation. **4.** A place in which something is produced, fostered, or developed. [ME *noricere* < OFr. *norricerie* < *norrice,* nursemaid. —see NURSE.]

nurs·er·y·maid (nûr'sə-rē-mād', nûrs'rē-) *n.* A nursemaid.

nurs·er·y·man (nûr'sə-rē-mən, nûrs'rē-) *n.* One who owns or works in a nursery for plants.

nursery rhyme *n.* A short, rhymed poem or tale for children.

nursery school *n.* A school for children who are not old enough to attend kindergarten.

nurs·ing (nûr'sĭng) *n.* **1.** The occupation of a nurse. **2.** The tasks of a nurse.

nursing home *n.* A private hospital for the care of the aged or chronically ill.

nurs·ling (nûrs'lĭng) *n.* **1.** A nursing infant or young animal. **2.** A carefully nurtured person or thing.

nur·tur·ance (nûr'chər-əns) *n.* The providing of loving care and attention. —**nur'tur·ant** *adj.*

nur·ture (nûr'chər) *n.* **1.** Something that nourishes; sustenance. **2.** The act of bringing up; rearing. **3.** *Biol.* The sum of environmental influences and conditions acting on an organism. —*tr.v.* **-tured, -tur·ing, -tures. 1.** To nourish; feed. **2.** To educate; train. **3.** To help grow or develop; cultivate. [ME *norture* < OFr. < LLat. *nutritia,* a suckling < Lat. *nutrire,* to suckle.] —**nur'tur·er** *n.*

nut (nŭt) *n.* **1. a.** A hard-shelled, solid-textured, one-celled fruit, such as an acorn or a hazelnut, that does not split open. **b.** A seed borne in a fruit having a hard shell, as the peanut or almond. **c.** The kernel of any of these. **2.** *Slang.* **a.** A crazy or eccentric person. **b.** An enthusiast; buff: *a movie nut.* **3.** *Informal.* A difficult endeavor or problem. **4.** *Slang.* A person's head. **5. a.** A ridge of wood at the top of the fingerboard or neck of a stringed instrument over which the strings pass. **b.** A device at the lower end of the bow, as of a violin used for adjusting the hairs. **6.** A small block of metal or wood with a central, threaded hole that is designed to fit around and secure a bolt or screw. **7.** Often **nuts.** *Slang.* The testicles. —*intr.v.* **nut·ted, nut·ting, nuts.** To gather or hunt for nuts. [ME *note* < OE *hnutu.*] —**nut'ter** *n.*

nu·ta·tion (no͞o-tā'shən, nyo͞o-) *n.* **1.** The act of nodding the head. **2.** *Astron.* A small periodic motion of the celestial pole of the earth with respect to the pole of the ecliptic. **3.** *Bot.* A slight curving or circular movement in the stem of a plant caused by irregular growth rates of different parts. [Lat. *nutatio* < *nutare,* to nod.] —**nu·ta'tion·al** *adj.*

nut·crack·er (nŭt'krăk'ər) *n.* **1.** An implement used to crack nuts, typically consisting of two hinged metal levers between which the nut is squeezed. **2. a.** A bird, *Nucifraga caryocatactes,* of northern Eurasia. **b.** A bird, *N. columbianus,* of western North America. **c.** The nuthatch.

nut·gall (nŭt'gôl') *n.* A nutlike swelling produced on an oak or other tree by certain parasitic wasps.

nut·hatch (nŭt'hăch') *n.* Any of several small birds of the family Sittidae, having long, sharp bills and noted for their insectlike ability to maneuver on tree trunks and branches. [ME *notehatch* : *note,* nut + *hache,* hatchet, of Germanic orig.]

nut house *n. Slang.* A mental institution.

nut·let (nŭt'lĭt) *n.* **1.** A small nut. **2.** The stone or pit of certain fruits such as the peach or cherry.

nut·meat (nŭt'mēt') *n.* The edible kernel of a nut.

nut·meg (nŭt'mĕg') *n.* **1.** An evergreen tree, *Myristica fragrans,* native to the East Indies. **2.** The hard, aromatic seed of the nutmeg, used as a spice when grated or ground. **3.** A grayish to moderate brown. [ME *notemugge,* prob. ult. < OFr. *nois mugede* < VLat. **nuce muscata* : Lat. *nux,* nut + Lat. *muscus,* musk.]

nut pick also **nut·pick** (nŭt'pĭk') *n.* A small, sharp-pointed tool used for digging the meat from nuts.

nut pine *n.* The piñon.

nu·tri·a (no͞o'trē-ə, nyo͞o'-) *n.* **1.** The coypu. **2.** The light-brown fur of the coypu. [Sp., var. of *lutra,* otter < Lat.]

nu·tri·ent (no͞o'trē-ənt, nyo͞o'-) *n.* Something that nourishes, esp. a nourishing ingredient in a food. —*adj.* Providing nourishment. [< Lat. *nutriens, nutrient-,* pr.part. of *nutrire,* to feed.]

nu·tri·ment (no͞o'trə-mənt, nyo͞o'-) *n.* **1.** Something that nourishes; food. **2.** Something that promotes growth or development. [Lat. *nutrimentum* < *nutrire,* to feed.] —**nu'tri·men'tal** (-mĕn'tl) *adj.*

nu·tri·tion (no͞o-trĭsh'ən, nyo͞o-) *n.* The process of nourishing or being nourished, esp. the process by which a living organism assimilates food and uses it for growth and for replacement of tissues. [OFr. < LLat. *nutritio* < Lat. *nutrire,* to feed.] —**nu·tri'tion·al** *adj.* —**nu·tri'tion·al·ly** *adv.*

nu·tri·tion·ist (no͞o-trĭsh'ə-nĭst, nyo͞o-) *n.* A person who specializes in the study of nutrition.

nu·tri·tious (no͞o-trĭsh'əs, nyo͞o-) *adj.* Providing nourishment; nourishing. [Lat. *nutritius* < *nutrix,* nurse.] —**nu·tri'tious·ly** *adv.* —**nu·tri'tious·ness** *n.*

nu·tri·tive (no͞o'trĭ-tĭv, nyo͞o'-) *adj.* **1.** Nourishing. **2.** Of or pertaining to nutrition. [ME *nutritif* < OFr. < LLat. *nutritivus* < Lat. *nutrire,* to feed.] —**nu'tri·tive·ly** *adv.*

nuts (nŭts) *Slang.* —*adj.* **1.** Crazy; insane. **2.** Extremely enthusiastic: *nuts about opera.* —*interj.* Used to express contempt, disappointment, or refusal. [< NUT.]

nuts and bolts *pl.n.* The basic working components or practical aspects of something.

nut·shell (nŭt'shĕl') *n.* The shell enclosing the meat of a nut. —***idiom.* in a nutshell.** In a few words; concisely.

nut·ty (nŭt'ē) *adj.* **-ti·er, -ti·est. 1.** Containing or producing nuts. **2.** Having a flavor like that of nuts. **3.** *Informal.* Crazy. —**nut'ti·ly** *adv.* —**nut'ti·ness** *n.*

nux vom·i·ca (nŭks vŏm'ĭ-kə) *n.* A tree, *Strychnos nux-vomica,* native to southeastern Asia, having poisonous seeds that are the source of strychnine and brucine. [Med. Lat., emetic nut : Lat. *nux,* nut + Lat. *vomere,* to vomit.]

nuz·zle (nŭz'əl) *v.* **-zled, -zling, -zles.** —*tr.* **1.** To rub or push against gently with or as if with the nose or snout. **2.** To

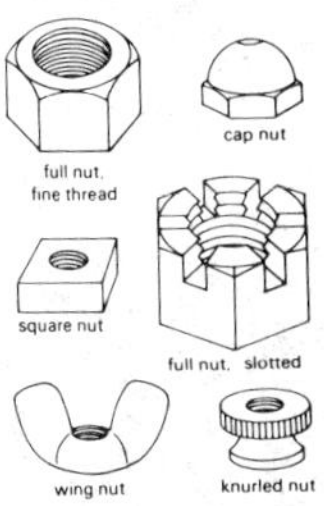

nut

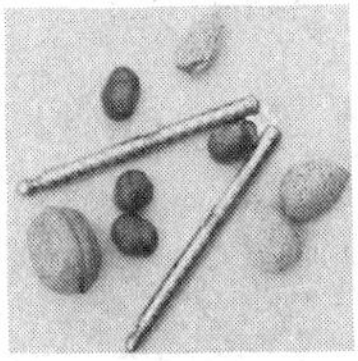

nutcracker

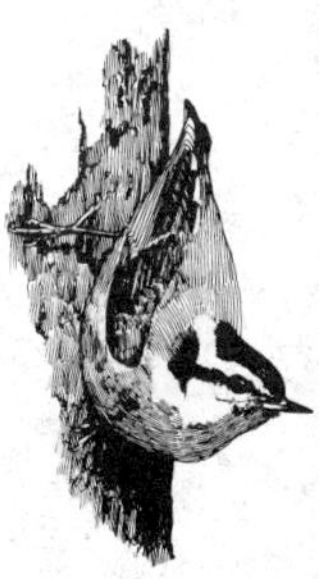

George Miksch Sutton

nuthatch

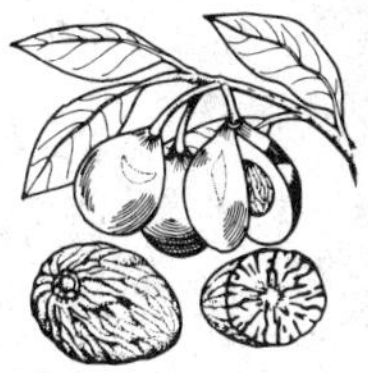

nutmeg

nux vomica

root or move with the snout. —*intr.* **1.** To make rubbing or pressing motions with or as if with the nose or snout. **2.** To nestle together. [ME *noselen,* to bring the nose close to the ground < *nose,* nose.] —**nuz'zler** *n.*
Ny·an·ja (nē-ăn'jə) *n.* A Bantu language of Malawi.
nyc·ta·lo·pi·a (nĭk'tə-lō'pē-ə) *n.* Night blindness. [LLat. < Gk. *nuktalōps,* night-blind : *nux,* night + *alaos,* blind + *ops,* eye.] —**nyc'ta·lo'pic** (-lō'pĭk, -lŏp'ĭk) *adj.*
nyc·tit·ro·pism (nĭk-tĭt'rə-pĭz'əm) *n. Bot.* The tendency of the leaves of some plants to change their position at nightfall. [Gk. *nux, nukt-,* night + -TROPISM.] —**nyc'ti·tro'pic** (-tĭ-trō'pĭk, -trŏp'ĭk) *adj.*
ny·lon (nī'lŏn') *n.* **1.** Any of a family of high-strength, resilient synthetic materials the long-chain molecule of which contains the recurring amide group CONH. **2.** Cloth or yarn made from nylon. **3. nylons.** Stockings made of nylon. [Coined by its inventors, E.I. duPont de Nemours & Co., Inc.]
nymph (nĭmf) *n.* **1.** *Gk. & Rom. Myth.* One of numerous female spirits inhabiting and animistically representing features of nature, as woodlands and waters. **2.** A girl, esp. a beautiful one. **3.** One of the young of any insect that undergoes incomplete metamorphosis. [ME *nimphe* < Lat. *nympha* < Gk. *numphē.*] —**nymph'al** (nĭm'fəl) *adj.*
nym·pha (nĭm'fə) *n., pl.* **-phae** (-fē). **1.** A nymph (sense 3). **2. nymphae.** *Anat.* The labia minora. [Lat., nymph < Gk. *numphē.*]
nym·pha·lid (nĭm'fə-lĭd) *n.* Any of various medium to large butterflies of the family Nymphalidae, found worldwide and often brilliantly colored. [< NLat. *Nymphalidae,* family name < *Nymphalis,* genus name < Lat. *nympha,* nymph < Gk. *numphē.*]
nym·phet (nĭm-fĕt', nĭm'fĭt) *n.* **1.** A young nymph. **2.** A pubescent girl regarded as sexually desirable.
nym·pho·lep·sy (nĭm'fə-lĕp'sē) *n., pl.* **-sies. 1.** A frenzy supposed by ancient peoples to have been induced by nymphs. **2.** An emotional frenzy. [< NYMPHOLEPT.] —**nym'pho·lep'tic** (-lĕp'tĭk) *adj.*
nym·pho·lept (nĭm'fə-lĕpt') *n.* One who is in a state of nympholepsy. [Gk. *numpholēptos,* raptured : *numphē,* nymph + *lambanein,* to seize.]
nym·pho·ma·ni·a (nĭm'fə-mā'nē-ə, -măn'yə) *n.* Inordinate sexual desire in a woman. —**nym'pho·ma'ni·ac'** (-nē-ăk') *adj. & n.* —**nym'pho·ma·ni'a·cal** (-mə-nī'ə-kəl) *adj.* [NYMPH(A) + -MANIA.]
Ny·norsk (nōō-nôrsk') *n.* Landsmål. [Norw., new Norwegian.]
nys·tag·mus (nĭ-stăg'məs) *n. Pathol.* A spasmodic, involuntary motion of the eyeball. [Gk. *nustagmos,* drowsiness < *nustazein,* to be sleepy.] —**nys·tag'mic** *adj.*

O

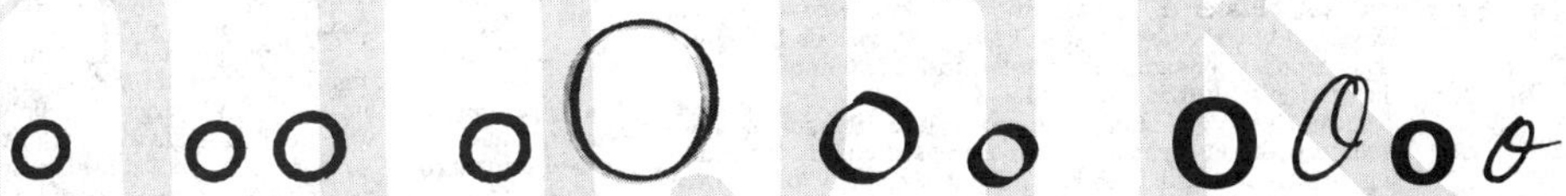

Around 1000 B.C. the Phoenicians and other Semitic peoples began to use graphic signs to represent individual speech sounds instead of syllables or words. They used a circular symbol (1) to represent a laryngeal consonant that is not found in English or any other Indo-European language and called it *ʿayin,* their word for "eye." The Greeks, adapting the Phoenician alphabet, used *ʿayin* to represent the sound of the short vowel "o" and called it *omikron,* or "small o" to distinguish it from *ōmega,* or "long o." The Romans borrowed the alphabet from the Greeks via the Etruscans. They used *omikron* to represent both long and short "o" and adapted it for monumental inscriptions. Monumental script (5) is the prototype of modern capital letters (8,9). Medieval scribes adapted the Roman capitals to being quickly written on paper, parchment, and vellum. These uncial and cursive minuscules (6,7) are the prototypes of modern lower-case letters, both written and printed (11,10).

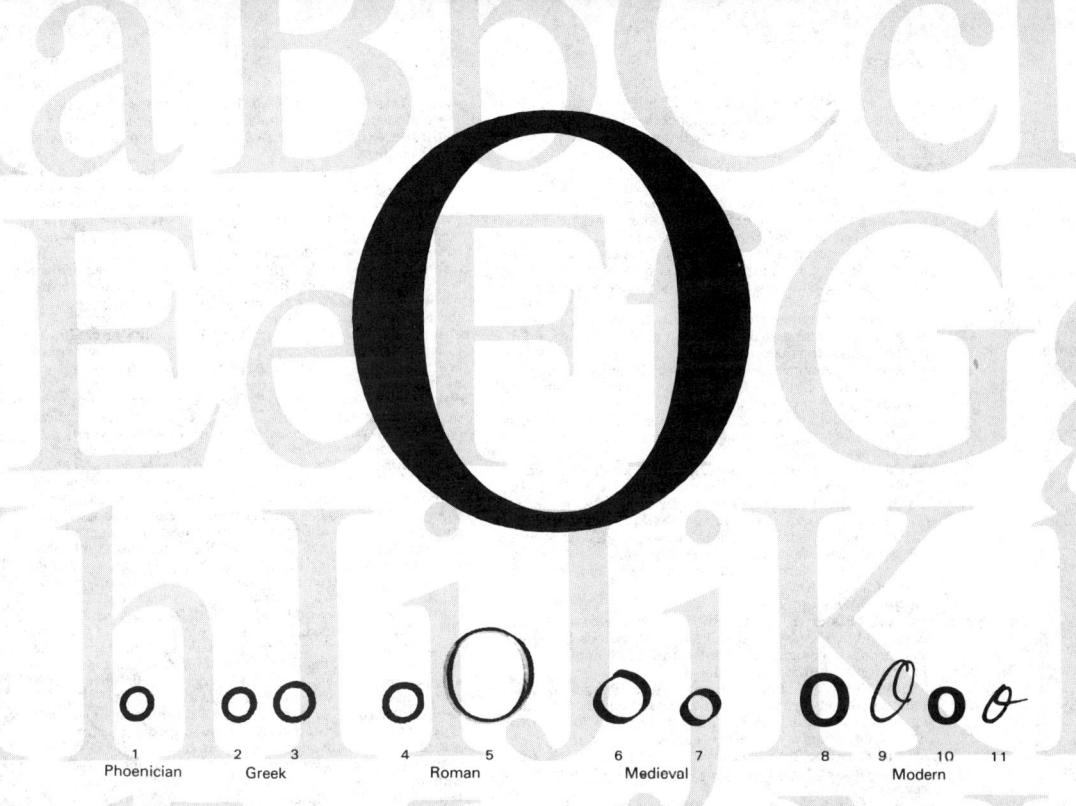

o

oarfish

obelisk

obi

o or **O** (ō) *n., pl.* **o's** or **O's. 1.** The 15th letter of the modern English alphabet. **2.** Any of the speech sounds represented by the letter *o.* **3.** A zero. **4.** Something shaped like the letter O. **5.** The 15th in a series.

O¹ (ō) *interj.* **1.** Used before the name of a person or thing being formally addressed: *Hear us, O Lord.* **2.** Used to express surprise or strong emotion: *O my goodness!*

Usage: *O* is used chiefly in religious or poetic invocations: *O God on High! O mighty ocean!* It is always capitalized and is never followed directly by punctuation. The interjection *oh* can stand alone or as part of a sentence to express strong emotions or merely a reflective pause: *Oh! What a horse! Oh, I see.* It is only capitalized when it is the first word of a sentence and is usually followed by a comma or, when the emphasis is strong, by an exclamation point.

O² The symbol for the element oxygen.

-o- Used as a connective to join word elements: *acidophilic.* [ME < OFr. < Lat. < Gk., thematic vowel of nouns and adjectives used in combination.]

oaf *n.* **1.** A stupid person. **2.** A big, clumsy, thickheaded person. [Obs. *aufe,* elf < ON *alfr.*] **—oaf'ish** *adj.* **—oaf'ish·ly** *adv.* **—oaf'ish·ness** *n.*

oak (ōk) *n.* **1.** Any of various deciduous or evergreen trees or shrubs of the genus *Quercus,* bearing acorns as fruit. **2.** The durable wood of the oak. **3.** Any of various trees or shrubs resembling the oak, as the poison oak. **4.** Something made of oak wood. **5.** Any of various brown shades resembling oak wood. [ME *ok* < OE *āc.*] **—oak'en** *adj.*

oak apple *n.* A harmless gall on oak trees, caused by the larva of a type of wasp.

oak gall *n.* Oak apple.

oak leaf cluster *n.* A decoration of bronze or silver oak leaves and acorns awarded to holders of various U.S. military medals in recognition of acts entitling them to a second decoration with the same medal.

oa·kum (ō'kəm) *n.* Loose hemp or jute fiber, sometimes treated with tar, creosote, or asphalt, used chiefly for caulking seams in wooden ships and packing pipe joints. [ME *okum* < OE *ācumba* : *ā-,* off + *cemban,* to comb.]

oak wilt *n.* A disease of oak trees caused by a fungus, *Chalara quercina,* and often resulting in wilting and dropping of leaves.

oar (ôr, ōr) *n.* **1.** A long, thin, usually wooden pole with a blade at one end, used to row and, occasionally, to steer a boat. **2.** An oarsman. *—v.* **oared, oar·ing, oars.** *—tr.* **1.** To propel with or as if with oars. **2.** To traverse with or as if with oars: *an hour to oar the strait.* *—intr.* To move forward by or as if by rowing. [ME *or* < OE *ār.*] **—oared** *adj.*

oar·fish (ôr'fĭsh', ōr'-) *n., pl.* **oarfish** or **-fish·es.** A marine fish, *Regalecus glesne,* having a slender body up to 10 meters, or approximately 30 feet, in length, a dorsal fin extending the entire body length, and red-tipped rays above the head.

oar·lock (ôr'lŏk', ōr'-) *n.* A device used as a fulcrum to hold an oar in place while rowing, usually a U-shaped metal hoop on a swivel in the gunwale.

oars·man (ôrz'mən, ōrz'-) *n.* A person who rows; rower. [*oar's,* possessive of OAR + MAN.]

o·a·sis (ō-ā'sĭs) *n., pl.* **-ses** (-sēz'). **1.** A fertile or green spot in a desert or waste, made so by the presence of water. **2.** A small place preserved from surrounding unpleasantness: *an oasis of serenity amidst the chaos.* [LLat. < Gk., of Egypt. orig.]

oast (ōst) *n.* A kiln for drying hops or malt or for drying and curing tobacco. [ME *ost* < OE *āst.*]

oat (ōt) *n.* **1.** Often **oats** *(used with a sing. or pl. verb).* **a.** A grass of the genus *Avena,* esp. *A. sativa,* widely cultivated for its edible seeds. **b.** The seeds of the oat, used as food and fodder. **2.** *Archaic.* A musical pipe made of an oat straw. [ME *ote* < OE *āte.*]

oat·cake (ōt'kāk') *n.* A flattened cake of baked oatmeal.

oat·en (ōt'n) *adj.* Of, made of, or containing oats, oatmeal, or oat straw: *oaten fodder.*

oat grass *n.* **1.** Any of various grasses of the genus *Arrhenatherum,* common in meadows. **2.** Any of several oatlike grasses.

oath (ōth) *n., pl.* **oaths** (ōthz, ōths). **1. a.** A solemn, formal declaration or promise to fulfill a pledge, often calling upon God or a god as witness. **b.** The words or formula of such a declaration or promise. **c.** Something that that is promised or declared. **2.** An irreverent or blasphemous use of the name of God or something held sacred. **3.** An imprecation. [ME *ooth* < OE *āð.*]

oat·meal (ōt'mēl') *n.* **1.** Meal made from oats; rolled or ground oats. **2.** A porridge made from rolled or ground oats.

ob- *pref.* Inverse; inversely: *obcordate.* [NLat. < Lat., toward, against < *ob,* toward.]

O·ba·di·ah (ō'bə-dī'ə) *n.* **1.** A Hebrew prophet of the 6th century B.C. **2.** See table at **Bible.** [Heb. *Ōbhadyāh.*]

ob·bli·ga·to (ŏb'lĭ-gä'tō) *Mus.* *—adj.* Not to be left out; indispensable. Used of an accompaniment that is an integral part of a piece. *—n., pl.* **-tos** or **-ti** (-tē). An obbligato musical accompaniment. [Ital., p.part. of *obbligare,* to obligate < Lat. *obligare,* to oblige.]

ob·cor·date (ŏb-kôr'dāt') *adj.* Heart-shaped, with the tapering end at the point of attachment: *an obcordate leaf.*

ob·du·ra·cy (ŏb'dōō-rə-sē, -dyōō-) *n.* The state or quality of being obdurate.

ob·du·rate (ŏb'dōō-rĭt, -dyōō-) *adj.* **1. a.** Hardened in wrongdoing or wickedness. **b.** Hardened against feeling; hardhearted. **2.** Not giving in to persuasion; intractable. [ME *obdurat* < Lat. *obduratus,* p.part. of *obdurare,* to harden : *ob-* (intensive) + *durare,* to harden < *durus,* hard.] **—ob'du·rate·ly** *adv.* **—ob'du·rate·ness** *n.*

o·be·ah (ō'bē-ə) *n.* A form of religious belief, practiced in some parts of the West Indies and nearby tropical America, involving witchcraft or sorcery. [Efik *ubio,* something put in the ground to cause sickness or death.]

o·be·di·ence (ō-bē'dē-əns) *n.* **1. a.** The quality or condition of being obedient. **b.** The act of obeying. **2. a.** A sphere of ecclesiastical authority. **b.** A group of persons under such authority.

o·be·di·ent (ō-bē'dē-ənt) *adj.* Obeying or carrying out a request or command; dutiful. [ME < OFr. < Lat. *oboediens, oboedient-,* p.part. of *oboedire,* to obey.] **—o·be'di·ent·ly** *adv.*

Synonyms: *obedient, compliant, acquiescent, submissive, docile, amenable, obsequious, servile, tractable, dutiful. Obedient,* said of persons and animals, refers to acceptance of authority in general; its implications, if any, are favorable. *Compliant* and *acquiescent* suggest innate disposition of persons to yield to authority without protest. This sense is intensified in *submissive* and *docile;* the latter, also applicable to animals, specifies capacity for being taught. *Amenable* pertains to congenial acceptance of authority in a more positive sense; besides agreeableness, it sometimes also indicates accountability and responsibility. *Obsequious* and *servile* refer to slavish, truckling obedience in persons. *Tractable* applies to persons, animals, and things with the capacity for being handled or led; *dutiful* signifies a scrupulous sense of responsibility, an interest or reliability in carrying out what is specifically assigned or required.

o·bei·sance (ō-bā'səns, ō-bē'-) *n.* **1.** A gesture or movement of the body, such as a curtsy, expressing deference or homage. **2.** An attitude of deference or homage. [ME < OFr. *obeissance* < *obeissant,* p.part. of *obeir,* to obey.] **—o·bei'sant** *adj.*

ob·e·li (ŏb'ə-lī') *n.* Plural of **obelus.**

o·be·lia (ō-bēl'yə) *n.* Any of various colonial marine hydroids of the genus *Obelia.* [NLat. *Obelia,* genus name, prob. < Gk. *obelias,* a loaf baked on a spit < *obelos,* a spit.]

ob·e·lisk (ŏb'ə-lĭsk) *n.* **1.** A tall, four-sided shaft of stone, usually tapering and monolithic, that rises to a pyramidal point. **2.** *Printing.* The dagger sign (†), used esp. as a reference mark. [OFr. *obelisque* < Lat. *obeliscus* < Gk. *obeliskos,* dim. of *obelos,* a spit.] **—ob'e·lis'cal** (-lĭs'kəl) *adj.* **—ob'e·lis'koid'** (-koid') *adj.*

ob·e·lize (ŏb'ə-līz') *tr.v.* **-lized, -liz·ing, -liz·es.** To mark or annotate with an obelus. [Gk. *obelizein* < *obelos,* a spit.]

ob·e·lus (ŏb'ə-ləs) *n., pl.* **-li** (-lī'). **1.** A mark (— or ÷) used in ancient manuscripts to indicate a doubtful or spurious passage. **2.** *Printing.* An obelisk (sense 2). [LLat. *obelus* < Gk. *obelos,* a spit.]

O·ber·on (ō'bə-rŏn', -rən) *n.* The king of the fairies and husband of Titania in medieval folklore. [Fr. < OFr. *Auberon,* of Frankish orig.]

o·bese (ō-bēs') *adj.* Extremely fat; corpulent. [Lat. *obesus,* grown fat from eating < p.part. of *obedere,* to eat away : *ob,* away + *edere,* to eat.] **—o·be'si·ty** (ō-bē'sĭ-tē) *n.*

o·bey (ō-bā') *v.* **o·beyed, o·bey·ing, o·beys.** *—tr.* **1.** To carry out or fulfill the command, order, or instruction of. **2.** To carry out or comply with (a command, for example). *—intr.* To behave obediently. [ME *obeien* < OFr. *obeir* < Lat. *oboediere,* to listen to : *ob,* to + *audire,* to hear.] **—o·bey'er** *n.*

ob·fus·cate (ŏb'fə-skāt', ŏb-fŭs'kāt') *tr.v.* **-cat·ed, -cat·ing, -cates. 1. a.** To render obscure. **b.** To darken. **2.** To confuse: *His emotions obfuscated his judgment.* [LLat. *obfuscare,* to darken : *ob* (intensive) + Lat. *fuscare,* to darken < *fuscus,* dark.] **—ob'fus·ca'tion** *n.* **—ob·fus'ca·to'r'y** (ŏb-fŭs'kə-tôr'ē, -tōr'ē, əb-) *adj.*

o·bi (ō'bē) *n.* A wide sash fastened in the back with a large flat bow, worn by women in Japan as a part of the traditional dress. [J., belt.]

O·bie (ō'bē) *n.* An award given annually for exceptional achievement in off-Broadway theater. [< O.B., abbr. for OFF-BROADWAY.]

o·bit (ō'bĭt, ō-bĭt') *n. Informal.* An obituary.

o·bi·ter dic·tum (ō'bĭ-tər dĭk'təm) *n., pl.* **obiter dic·ta** (dĭk'tə). **1.** *Law.* An opinion voiced by a judge that has only incidental bearing on the case in question and is therefore not binding. **2.** An incidental remark or observation. [Lat., something said in passing.]

o·bit·u·ar·y (ō-bĭch'ōō-ĕr'ē) *n., pl.* **-ies.** A published notice of a death, usually with a brief biography of the deceased. [Med. Lat. *obituarius,* (report) of death < Lat. *obitus,* death < *obire,* to die : *ob,* down + *ire,* to go.] **—o·bit'u·ar'y** *adj.*

ob·ject¹ (əb-jĕkt') *v.* **-ject·ed, -ject·ing, -jects.** *—intr.* **1.** To present a dissenting or opposing argument; raise an objection. **2.** To feel adverse to or express disapproval of something: *object to modern materialism.* *—tr.* To put forward in or as a reason for opposition: *They objected that discipline* *was lacking.* [ME *objecten* < Lat. *obicere,* to oppose : *ob,* toward + *jacere,* to throw.] **—ob·jec'tor** *n.*

Synonyms: *object, protest, kick, complain, dissent, demur, remonstrate, expostulate, boggle. Object* is a general term for denoting expression of opposition; the following terms have this basic sense, together with specific implications. *Protest* suggests strong opposition forthrightly expressed; *kick,* used informally, stresses the same implications even more forcefully. *Complain* applies to opposition usually stemming from a sense of personal injury or wrong. *Dissent* often implies formal expression of opposition, along with finality of judgment not inherent in the other terms. *Demur* is applicable to more tentative opposition or expression of doubt that may delay ultimate decision or action pending reconsideration. *Remonstrate* specifies objection in the form of argument or pleading; *expostulate,* objection in the form of earnest reasoning. *Boggle* pertains to opposition in the sense of hesitancy or shying away caused by fear or scruples.

ob·ject² (ŏb'jĭkt, -jĕkt') *n.* **1.** Something perceptible esp. to the sense of vision or touch. **2.** *Philos.* Something intelligible or perceptible by the mind. **3.** A focus of attention, feeling, thought, or action: *an object of contempt.* **4.** The purpose, aim, or goal of a specific action or effort: *the object of the game.* **5.** *Gram.* **a.** A noun or substantive that receives or is affected by the action of a verb within a sentence. **b.** A noun or substantive following and governed by a preposition. [ME < Lat. *objectus,* p.part. of *obicere,* to throw before —see OBJECT¹.]

object glass *n.* An objective (sense 4).

ob·jec·ti·fy (əb-jĕk'tə-fī') *tr.v.* **-fied, -fy·ing, -fies. 1. a.** To present (something) as an object; externalize. **b.** To make objective. **2.** To rationalize (sense 3). [< OBJECT².] **—ob·jec'ti·fi·ca'tion** *n.*

ob·jec·tion (əb-jĕk'shən) *n.* **1.** An act of objecting. **2.** A statement presented in opposition. **3.** A ground, reason, or cause for expressing opposition.

ob·jec·tion·a·ble (əb-jĕk'shə-nə-bəl) *adj.* Arousing disapproval; offensive. **—ob·jec'tion·a·bil'i·ty** *n.* **—ob·jec'tion·a·bly** *adv.*

ob·jec·tive (əb-jĕk'tĭv) *adj.* **1.** Of or having to do with a material object as distinguished from a mental concept. **2.** Having actual existence or reality. **3. a.** Uninfluenced by emotion, surmise, or personal prejudice. **b.** Based on observable phenomena; presented factually: *an objective appraisal.* **4.** *Med.* Indicating a symptom or condition perceived as a sign of disease by someone other than the person afflicted. **5.** *Gram.* **a.** Denoting the case of a noun or pronoun serving as the object of the verb. **b.** Pertaining to a noun or pronoun used in such a case. *—n.* **1.** Something that actually exists as distinguished from something thought or felt to exist. **2.** Something worked toward or striven for; goal. **3.** *Gram.* **a.** The objective case. **b.** A noun or pronoun in the objective case. **4. a.** The lens or lens system in a microscope or telescope that is closest to the object. **b.** A lens or lens system in a camera or projector that forms the image of the object. [Med. Lat. *objectivus* < Lat. *objectus,* object. —see OBJECT².] **—ob·jec'tive·ly** *adv.* **—ob·jec'tive·ness** *n.*

objective complement *n. Gram.* A noun, adjective, or pronoun serving as a complement to a verb and qualifying its direct object, as *governor* in *They elected him governor.*

objective correlative *n.* A situation that objectifies an emotion, often used as a literary device to elicit a particular emotional response in the reader.

ob·jec·tiv·ism (ŏb-jĕk'tĭ-vĭz'əm) *n.* **1.** *Philos.* One of several doctrines holding that all reality is objective and external to the mind and that knowledge is reliably based on observed objects and events. **2.** An emphasis on objective themes or subjects in art and literature. **—ob·jec'tiv·ist** *n.* **—ob·jec'tiv·is'tic** *adj.*

ob·jec·tiv·i·ty (ŏb'jĕk-tĭv'ĭ-tē) *n.* **1.** The state or quality of being objective. **2.** External or material reality.

object language *n.* A target language.

object lens *n.* An objective (sense 4).

object lesson *n.* **1.** A lesson taught by using a material object. **2.** A concrete illustration of a moral or principle.

ob·jet d'art (ôb'zhĕ där') *n., pl.* **ob·jets d'art** (ôb'zhĕ där'). An object of artistic merit. [Fr., object of art.]

ob·jet trou·vé (ôb-zhā' trōō-vā') *n.* A found object. [Fr.]

ob·jur·gate (ŏb'jər-gāt', ŏb-jûr'gāt') *tr.v.* **-gat·ed, -gat·ing, -gates.** To scold or rebuke sharply; berate. [Lat. *objurgare, objurgat-* : *ob,* against + *jurgare,* to scold (*jus,* law + *agere,* to carry on).] **—ob'jur·ga'tion** *n.* **—ob·jur'ga·to'ri·ly** (ŏb-jûr'gə-tôr'ə-lē, -tōr'-) *adv.* **—ob·jur'ga·to'ry** (-tôr'ē, -tōr'ē) *adj.*

ob·lan·ce·o·late (ŏb-lăn'sē-ə-lāt') *adj.* Broader and rounded at the apex and tapering at the base: *an oblanceolate leaf.*

o·blast (ô'bləst, ô'blăst') *n.* In the Soviet Union, a territorial administrative division within a republic. [R. *oblast'.*]

ob·late¹ (ŏb'lāt', ŏ-blāt') *adj.* **1.** Having the shape of a spheroid; spheroidal. **2.** Having an equatorial diameter greater than the distance between poles; compressed along or flattened at the poles: *The earth is an oblate solid.* [Prob. Med. Lat. *oblatus* : Lat. *ob* (intensive) + Lat. *latus,* p.part. of *ferre,* to carry.] **—ob'late'ly** *adv.* **—ob'late'ness** *n.*

ob·late² (ŏb'lāt') *n.* **1.** A lay person dedicated to a religious life. **2. Oblate.** *Rom. Cath. Ch.* A member of one of various religious communities for men or women. [Med. Lat. *oblatus* < Lat., p.part. of *offerre,* to offer : *ob,* toward + *ferre,* to carry.]

ob·la·tion (ə-blā'shən, ō-blā'-) *n.* **1.** The act of offering something, such as worship or thanks, to a deity. **2. Oblation. a.** The act of offering the bread and wine of the Eucharist. **b.** Something that is offered, esp. the bread and wine of the Eucharist. **3.** A charitable offering or gift. [ME *oblacioun* < OFr. *oblacion* < Lat. *oblatio* < *offerre,* to offer : *ob,* toward + *ferre,* to carry.] **—ob·la'tion·al, ob'la·to'ry** (ŏb'lə-tôr'ē, -tōr'ē) *adj.*

ob·li·gate (ŏb'lĭ-gāt') *tr.v.* **-gat·ed, -gat·ing, -gates. 1. a.** To bind, compel, or constrain by a legal or moral tie. **b.** To oblige (sense 2). **2.** To commit (money, for example) in order to fulfill an obligation. *—adj.* (-gĭt, -gāt'). **1.** *Biol.* Able to survive in only one environment. Used of certain parasites. **2.** Absolutely indispensable; essential. [Lat. *obligare, obligat-.* —see OBLIGE.] **—ob'li·ga·ble** (-gə-bəl) *adj.* **—ob'li·gate·ly** *adv.* **—ob'li·ga'tor** *n.*

Usage: *Obligate* has fewer meanings than *oblige. Obligate* is used chiefly to mean "to bind, compel, or constrain." In that sense it is often but not always interchangeable with *oblige.* When the constraint is from the outside, either is appropriate: *I am obliged* (or *obligated*) *to pay the bill.* When the constraint is in one's mind, *oblige* is the choice: *I feel obliged to accept the invitation.* • *Obligate* used to be interchangeable with *oblige* in the sense of "to put under debt of gratitude." Although this meaning is not wholly obsolete, *oblige* is preferred in that sense: *I am obliged* (better than *obligated*) *to you for all you have done.*

ob·li·ga·tion (ŏb'lĭ-gā'shən) *n.* **1.** The act of binding oneself by a social, legal, or moral tie. **2. a.** A duty, contract, promise, or other social, moral, or legal requirement that compels one to follow or avoid a given course of action. **b.** A course of action imposed by law, society, or conscience by which one is bound or restricted. **3.** The constraining power of a law, promise, contract, or sense of duty. **4.** *Law.* **a.** A legal agreement stipulating a specified payment or action, esp. if the agreement also specifies the penalty for failure to comply. **b.** The document containing the terms of such an agreement. **5. a.** Something owed as payment or in return for a special service or favor. **b.** The service or favor for which one is indebted to another. **6.** The state, fact, or feeling of being indebted to another for a special service or favor received.

Synonyms: *obligation, responsibility, duty.* Each of these terms involves a constraint in conduct or choice of course. *Obligation* applies to a specific instance of constraint in which the constraining factors are immediate and objectively defined (as by terms of a contract or treaty). *Responsibility* lacks the implication of a single instance and immediate constraint; in a more general way, it stresses that for which one is accountable. *Duty* involves continuing constraint deriving from moral or ethical considerations.

o·blig·a·to·ry (ə-blĭg'ə-tôr'ē, -tōr'ē, ŏb'lĭ-gə-) *adj.* **1.** Legally or morally constraining; binding. **2.** Imposing or recording an obligation: *a bill obligatory.* **3.** Of the nature of an obligation; compulsory: *Attendance is obligatory.* **4.** *Biol.* Obligate (sense 1). **—o·blig'a·to'ri·ly** *adv.*

o·blige (ə-blīj') *v.* **o·bliged, o·blig·ing, o·blig·es.** *—tr.* **1.** To constrain by physical, legal, social, or moral means. **2.** To make indebted or grateful: *They were obliged to him for his hospitality.* **3.** To do a service or favor for: *He obliged us by arriving early.* *—intr.* To do a service or favor: *The pianist will oblige with an encore.* —See Usage note at **obligate.** [ME *obligen* < OFr. *obligier* < Lat. *obligare* : *ob,* to + *ligare,* to bind.] **—o·blig'er** *n.*

ob·li·gee (ŏb'lə-jē') *n.* **1.** A person who is under obligation to another. **2.** *Law.* A person to whom another is bound by contract or legal agreement.

o·blig·ing (ə-blī'jĭng) *adj.* Ready to do favors for others; accommodating. **—o·blig'ing·ly** *adv.* **—o·blig'ing·ness** *n.*

ob·li·gor (ŏb'lĭ-gôr', -jôr') *n. Law.* A person who binds himself to another by contract or legal agreement.

o·blique (ō-blēk', ə-blēk') *adj.* **1. a.** Having a slanting or sloping direction, course, or position; inclined. **b.** Designating geometric lines or planes that are neither parallel nor perpendicular. **2. a.** Indirect or evasive: *oblique maneuvers.* **b.** Devious, misleading, or dishonest: *oblique answers.* **3.** Not direct in descent; collateral. **4.** *Bot.* Having sides of unequal length or form: *an oblique leaf.* **5.** *Gram.* Designating any noun case except the nominative or the vocative. *—n.* **1.** An oblique thing, such as a line, direction, or muscle. **2.** *Naut.* The act of changing course by less than 90 degrees. *—adv.* (ō-blīk', ə-blīk). At an angle of 45 degrees: *Right oblique, march!* [ME < OFr. < Lat. *obliquus.*] **—o·blique'ly** *adv.* **—o·blique'ness** *n.*

oblique angle *n.* An acute or obtuse angle.

oblique triangle *n.* A triangle having no right angle.

o·bliq·ui·ty (ō-blĭk'wĭ-tē, ə-blĭk'-) *n., pl.* **-ties. 1.** The quality or condition of being oblique. **2. a.** A deviation from a vertical or horizontal line, plane, position, or direction. **b.** The angle or extent of such a deviation. **3. a.** A mental deviation or aberration. **b.** Immoral conduct. **4. a.** Obscurity or indirectness in conduct or verbal expression. **b.** An obscure, cloudy statement. [ME *obliquite* < Lat. *obliquitas* < *obliquus,* oblique.] **—o·bliq'ui·tous** *adj.*

o·blit·er·ate (ə-blĭt'ə-rāt', ō-blĭt'-) *tr.v.* **-at·ed, -at·ing, -ates. 1.** To do away with completely so as to leave no trace. **2.** To wipe out, rub off, or erase (writing or other markings). [Lat. *oblitterare, oblitterat-,* to erase : *ob,* against + *littera,* letter.] **—o·blit'er·a'tion** *n.* **—o·blit'er·a'tive** (-ə-rā'tĭv, -ər-ə-tĭv) *adj.* **—o·blit'er·a'tor** *n.*

o·bliv·i·on (ə-blĭv'ē-ən) *n.* **1.** The quality or condition of being completely forgotten. **2.** An act or an instance of forgetting. **3.** Official overlooking of offenses. [ME *oblivioun* < OFr. *oblivion* < Lat. *oblivio* < *oblivisci,* to forget.]

o·bliv·i·ous (ə-blĭv'ē-əs) *adj.* **1.** Lacking all memory; forgetful. **2.** Lacking conscious awareness; unmindful. **—o·bliv'i·ous·ly** *adv.* **—o·bliv'i·ous·ness** *n.*

ob·long (ŏb'lông', -lŏng') *adj.* **1.** Having a long dimension, esp. having one of two perpendicular dimensions, as length or width, greater than the other; elongated. **2.** Having the shape of or resembling a rectangle or an ellipse. **3.** *Bot.* Having a somewhat elongated form with approximately parallel sides: *an oblong leaf.* —*n.* An object or figure, such as a rectangle, with an elongated shape. [ME < Lat. *oblongus* : *ob* (intensive) + *longus,* long.]

ob·lo·quy (ŏb'lə-kwē) *n., pl.* **-quies. 1.** Abusively detractive language or utterance; calumny. **2.** Loss of or damage to one's reputation. [ME *obloqui* < Med. Lat. *obloquium* < Lat. *obloqui,* to speak against : *ob,* against + *loqui,* to speak.]

ob·nox·ious (ŏb-nŏk'shəs, əb-) *adj.* **1.** Highly disagreeable or offensive; odious. **2.** Exposed to harm, injury, or evil: *"The town . . . now lies obnoxious to its foes"* (Bunyan). **3.** *Archaic.* Deserving of or liable to censure. [Lat. *obnoxiosus,* hurtful < *obnoxius,* punishable : *ob,* to + *noxa,* injury.] **—ob·nox'ious·ly** *adv.* **—ob·nox'ious·ness** *n.*

oboe

o·boe (ō'bō) *n.* **1.** A slender woodwind musical instrument with a conical bore and a double-reed mouthpiece, having a range of three octaves and a penetrating, poignant sound. **2.** A reed stop in an organ that produces a sound similar to that of the oboe. [Ital. < Fr. *hautbois.* —see HAUTBOY.] **—o'bo·ist** *n.*

ob·o·vate (ŏb-ō'vāt') *adj.* Egg-shaped in outline, with the narrow end attached to the stalk: *an obovate leaf.*

ob·o·void (ŏb-ō'void') *adj.* Egg-shaped, with the narrow end attached to the stem: *an obovoid fruit.*

ob·scene (ŏb-sēn', əb-) *adj.* **1.** Offensive to accepted standards of decency or modesty. **2.** Inciting lustful feelings; lewd. **3.** Offensive or repulsive to the senses; loathsome: *an obscene lie.* [Lat. *obscenus.*] **—ob·scene'ly** *adv.*

ob·scen·i·ty (ŏb-sĕn'ĭ-tē, əb-) *n., pl.* **-ties. 1.** The state or quality of being obscene. **2.** Indecency, lewdness, or offensiveness in behavior, expression, or appearance. **3.** Something, such as a word, act, or expression, that is obscene.

ob·scur·ant (ŏb-skyo͝or'ənt, əb-) *n.* One who opposes intellectual advancement and political reform. —*adj.* **1.** Characteristic of an obscurant. **2.** Tending to make obscure. [Lat. *obscurans, obscurant-,* pr.part. of *obscurare,* to darken < *obscurus,* dark.]

ob·scur·ant·ism (ŏb-skyo͝or'ən-tĭz'əm, əb-, ŏb'skyo͝o-răn'-) *n.* **1.** The principles or practice of obscurants. **2.** A policy of withholding information from the public. **3. a.** A style in art and literature characterized by deliberate vagueness or obliqueness. **b.** An act or example of this style. **—ob·scur'ant·ist** *n.*

ob·scure (ŏb-skyo͝or', əb-) *adj.* **-scur·er, -scur·est. 1.** Deficient in light; dark. **2. a.** So faintly perceptible as to lack clear delineation; indistinct. **b.** Indistinctly heard; faint. **c.** *Ling.* Having the mid-central unstressed sound represented by the schwa (ə). **3.** Far from centers of human population: *an obscure village.* **4.** Not readily noticed or seen; inconspicuous: *an obscure flaw.* **5.** Of undistinguished or humble station or reputation: *an obscure poet.* **6.** Not easily understood or not clearly expressed; ambiguous. —*tr.v.* **-scured, -scur·ing, -scures. 1.** To make dim or indistinct: *Smog obscured our view.* **2.** To conceal in obscurity: *details obscured in a maze of legal jargon.* **3.** *Ling.* To reduce (a vowel) to the mid-central unstressed sound represented by the schwa (ə). —*n.* Obscurity. [ME < Lat. *obscurus.*] **—ob·scure'ly** *adv.* **—ob·scure'ness** *n.*

observatory

ob·scu·ri·ty (ŏb-skyo͝or'ĭ-tē, əb-) *n., pl.* **-ties. 1.** Deficiency or absence of light; darkness. **2. a.** The quality or condition of being unknown: *from obscurity to fame.* **b.** One that is obscure. [ME *obscurite* < OFr. < Lat. *obscuritas* < *obscurus,* dark.]

ob·se·qui·ous (ŏb-sē'kwē-əs, əb-) *adj.* Full of or exhibiting servile compliance; fawning: *obsequious gestures and grimaces.* [ME < Lat. *obsequiosus* < *obsequium,* compliance < *obsequi,* to comply : *ob,* to + *sequi,* to follow.] **—ob·se'qui·ous·ly** *adv.* **—ob·se'qui·ous·ness** *n.*

ob·se·quy (ŏb'sĭ-kwē) *n., pl.* **-quies.** Often **obsequies.** A funeral rite or ceremony. [ME *obsequi* < OFr. *obseque* < Med. Lat. *obsequiae* < Lat. *obsequium,* compliance. —see OBSEQUIOUS.]

ob·serv·a·ble (əb-zûr'və-bəl) *adj.* **1.** Capable of being observed; discernible. **2.** Deserving or worthy of note; noteworthy. —*n. Physics.* A physical property, such as weight or temperature, that can be observed or measured directly as distinguished from a quantity, such as work or entropy, that must be derived from observed quantities. **—ob·serv'a·bly** *adv.*

ob·ser·vance (əb-zûr'vəns) *n.* **1.** The act or practice of observing or complying with a law, custom, command, or rule. **2.** The act or custom of keeping or celebrating a holiday or other ritual occasion. **3.** A customary rite or ceremony. **4.** The action of watching; observation. **5.** *Rom. Cath. Ch.* The rule governing a religious order.

ob·ser·vant (əb-zûr'vənt) *adj.* **1.** Quick to perceive or apprehend; alert: *an observant traveler.* **2.** Diligent in observing a law, custom, duty, or principle: *observant of the speed limit.* [Fr. < Lat. *observans,* pr.part. of *observare,* to watch. —see OBSERVE.] **—ob·ser'vant·ly** *adv.*

ob·ser·va·tion (ŏb'zər-vā'shən) *n.* **1. a.** The act or faculty of observing. **b.** The fact of being observed. **2. a.** The act of noting and recording something, as a phenomenon, with instruments. **b.** The result or record of such notation: *a meteorological observation.* **3.** A comment or remark. **4.** An inference or judgment that is acquired from or based on observing. [Lat. *observatio* < *observare,* to watch. —see OBSERVE.] **—ob'ser·va'tion·al** *adj.* **—ob'ser·va'tion·al·ly** *adv.*

ob·ser·va·to·ry (əb-zûr'və-tôr'ē, -tōr'ē) *n., pl.* **-ries. 1.** A building designed and equipped for making observations of astronomical, meteorological, or other natural phenomena. **2.** A structure overlooking an extensive view. [Prob. Fr. *observatorie* < OFr. *observatorie,* to observe. —see OBSERVE.]

ob·serve (əb-zûrv') *v.* **-served, -serv·ing, -serves.** —*tr.* **1.** To perceive; notice. **2.** To watch attentively: *observe a child's behavior.* **3.** To make a systematic or scientific observation of: *observe the moon's orbit.* **4.** To say casually; remark. **5.** To adhere to or abide by: *observe the terms of a contract.* **6.** To keep or celebrate (a holiday, for example): *observe an anniversary.* —*intr.* **1.** To take notice. **2.** To make a comment or remark. **3.** To watch or be present without participating actively. [ME *observen* < OFr. *observer* < Lat. *observare* : *ob,* to + *servare,* to watch.] **—ob·serv'ing·ly** *adv.*

Synonyms: *observe, keep, celebrate, solemnize, commemorate.* These are compared in the sense of heeding, marking, or complying with rules, customs, ceremonials, holidays, and the like. *Observe* stresses respectful adherence (to law or tradition, for example), often in the form of compliance with prescribed rites. *Keep* may be used broadly, in opposition to breaking or violating (a promise or the Sabbath, for example), or it may imply rigid adherence. *Celebrate* stresses observance in the form of demonstrations or other group activity; it generally suggests festivity, but can also be applied to religious rites. *Solemnize* is restricted to functions, especially religious ones, characterized by dignity and gravity. *Commemorate* refers to the marking, in the present, of a past event; almost always it implies reverential activity.

ob·serv·er (əb-zûr'vər) *n.* One that observes, as: **a.** A delegate sent to observe and report on the proceedings of an assembly or meeting but not to vote or otherwise participate. **b.** A military aircraft crew member who makes observations. **c.** A soldier watching and reporting from an observation post.

ob·sess (əb-sĕs', ŏb-) *tr.v.* **-sessed, -sess·ing, -sess·es.** To preoccupy the mind of excessively. [Lat. *obsidēre, obsess-,* to beset, possess : *ob,* on + *sedēre,* to sit.]

ob·ses·sion (əb-sĕsh'ən, ŏb-) *n.* **1.** Compulsive preoccupation with a fixed idea or unwanted feeling or emotion, often accompanied by symptoms of anxiety. **2.** A compulsive, often unreasonable idea or emotion. **—ob·ses'sion·al** *adj.*

ob·ses·sive (əb-sĕs'ĭv, ŏb-) *adj.* **1.** Of, relating to, or characteristic of an obsession. **2.** Tending to cause an obsession. **3.** Excessive in degree or nature: *an obsessive need to win.* **—ob·ses'sive** *n.* **—ob·ses'sive·ly** *adv.* **—ob·ses'sive·ness** *n.*

ob·sid·i·an (ŏb-sĭd'ē-ən) *n.* An acid-resistant, lustrous volcanic glass, usually black or banded and displaying curved, shiny surfaces when fractured. [Lat. *obsidianus,* alteration of *obsianus* (*lapis*), (stone) of Obsius, who reportedly discovered it.]

ob·so·lesce (ŏb'sə-lĕs') *intr.v.* **-lesced, -lesc·ing, -lesc·es.** To become obsolescent.

ob·so·les·cent (ŏb'sə-lĕs'ənt) *adj.* In the process of passing out of use; becoming obsolete. [Lat. *obsolescens, obsolescent-,* pr.part. of *obsolescere,* to wear out : *ob* (intensive) + *solēre,* to use.] **—ob'so·les'cence** *n.* **—ob'so·les'cent·ly** *adv.*

ob·so·lete (ŏb'sə-lēt', ŏb'sə-lēt') *adj.* **1.** No longer in use: *an obsolete word.* **2.** Outmoded in design, style, or construction: *an obsolete locomotive.* **3.** *Biol.* Increasingly vestigial or disappearing in each succeeding generation. Used of plant or animal characteristics or organs. —*tr.v.* **-let·ed, -let·ing, -letes.** To cause to become obsolete. [Lat. *obsoletus,* p.part. of *obsolescere,* to wear out. —see OBSOLESCENT.] **—ob'so·lete'ly** *adv.* **—ob'so·lete'ness** *n.* **—ob'so·let'ism** *n.*

ob·sta·cle (ŏb'stə-kəl) *n.* One that opposes, stands in the way of, or holds up progress. [ME < OFr. < Lat. *obstaculum* < *obstare,* to hinder : *ob,* against + *stare,* to stand.]

obstacle course *n.* **1.** A military training course filled with obstacles, as ditches and walls, that must be negotiated. **2.** A situation full of obstacles that must be negotiated.

ob·stet·ric (ŏb-stĕt'rĭk, əb-) also **ob·stet·ri·cal** (-rĭ-kəl) *adj.* Of or pertaining to the profession of obstetrics or to the care of women during and after pregnancy. [Lat. *obstetricus* <

obstetrix, midwife < *obstare,* to stand before : *ob,* before + *stare,* to stand.] **—ob·stet'ri·cal·ly** *adv.*
ob·ste·tri·cian (ŏb'stĭ-trĭsh'ən) *n.* A physician specializing in obstetrics.
ob·stet·rics (ŏb-stĕt'rĭks, əb-) *n. (used with a sing. or pl. verb).* The branch of medicine concerned with the care of women during pregnancy, childbirth, and the recuperative period following delivery.
ob·sti·na·cy (ŏb'stə-nə-sē) *n., pl.* **-cies. 1.** The state or quality of being obstinate. **2.** An act or instance of stubbornness.
ob·sti·nate (ŏb'stə-nĭt) *adj.* **1.** Stubbornly adhering to an attitude, opinion, or course of action; obdurate. **2.** Difficult to manage, control, or subdue; refractory. **3.** Difficult to alleviate or cure: *an obstinate headache.* [ME < Lat. *obstinatus,* p.part. of *obstinare,* to persist.] **—ob'sti·nate·ly** *adv.* **—ob'sti·nate·ness** *n.*

Synonyms: *obstinate, stubborn, headstrong, stiff-necked, bullheaded, pigheaded, mulish, dogged, pertinacious. Obstinate* applies specifically to unreasonable rigidity in the face of external stimulus, such as persuasion or attack. *Stubborn* pertains to innate unyieldingness of persons, animals, and things; it does not imply a specific instance of provocation. *Headstrong,* said of persons, pertains to inflexibility combined with reckless willfulness; more than the other terms, it implies action along with resistance. *Stiff-necked* applies to extreme inflexibility in persons, combined with arrogance. *Bullheaded* is said of obstinacy viewed as foolish or irrational; *pigheaded,* of obstinacy as blindly stupid; and *mulish,* of human stubbornness on the level of a beast. *Dogged,* applied to persons and their attributes, emphasizes perseverance in the face of odds, but not necessarily in the sense of contrariness. *Pertinacious,* said of persons, stresses tenacity of purpose viewed as perverse.

ob·strep·er·ous (ŏb-strĕp'ər-əs, əb-) *adj.* **1.** Noisily and stubbornly defiant. **2.** Aggressively boisterous. [Lat. *obstreperus,* noisy < *obstrepere,* to clamor against : *ob,* against + *strepere,* to make a noise.] **—ob·strep'er·ous·ly** *adv.* **—ob·strep'er·ous·ness** *n.*
ob·struct (əb-strŭkt', ŏb-) *tr.v.* **-struct·ed, -struct·ing, -structs. 1.** To block or fill (a passage) with obstacles. **2.** To impede, retard, or interfere with; hinder. **3.** To cut off from sight. [Lat. *obstruere, obstruct-* : *ob,* against + *struere,* to pile up.] **—ob·struct'er, ob·struc'tor** *n.* **—ob·struc'tive** *adj.* **—ob·struc'tive·ly** *adv.* **—ob·struc'tive·ness** *n.*
ob·struc·tion (əb-strŭk'shən, ŏb-) *n.* **1.** One that obstructs; obstacle. **2.** An act or instance of obstructing. **3.** The act of causing delay or an attempt to cause a delay in the conduct of business, esp. in a legislative body.
ob·struc·tion·ist (əb-strŭk'shə-nĭst, ŏb-) *n.* One who systematically interrupts progress, esp. one who impedes the passage of legislation, as by filibuster. **—ob·struc'tion·ism** *n.* **—ob·struc'tion·is'tic** *adj.*
ob·tain (əb-tān', ŏb-) *v.* **-tained, -tain·ing, -tains.** *—tr.* To succeed in gaining possession of as the result of planning or endeavor; procure or acquire. *—intr.* **1.** To be established, accepted, or customary: *Certain formal customs still obtain today.* **2.** *Archaic.* To succeed. [ME *obteinen* < OFr. *obtenir* < Lat. *obtinēre* : *ob* (intensive) + *tenēre,* to hold.] **—ob·tain'a·ble** *adj.* **—ob·tain'er** *n.*
ob·tect (ŏb-tĕkt') also **ob·tect·ed** (-tĕk'tĭd) *adj.* Enclosed or covered by a hardened secretion. Used esp. of pupae having wings, antennae, and legs enclosed and sealed against the body surface by such a covering. [Lat. *obtectus,* p.part. of *obtegere,* to cover over : *ob,* over + *tegere,* to cover.]
ob·test (ŏb-tĕst') *tr.v.* **-test·ed, -test·ing, -tests.** To supplicate; entreat. [Lat. *obtestari* : *ob,* to + *testari,* to call as a witness < *testis,* witness.] **—ob'tes·ta'tion** *n.*
ob·trude (ŏb-tro͞od', əb-) *v.* **-trud·ed, -trud·ing, -trudes.** *—tr.* **1.** To force (oneself or one's ideas) upon others with undue insistence or without invitation. **2.** To thrust out; push forward. *—intr.* To force oneself upon others or upon their attention. [Lat. *obtrudere* : *ob-,* against + *trudere,* to thrust.] **—ob·trud'er** *n.* **—ob·tru'sion** (-tro͞o'zhən) *n.*
ob·tru·sive (ŏb-tro͞o'sĭv, -zĭv, əb-) *adj.* **1.** Projecting; protruding: *an obtrusive rock formation.* **2.** Tending to push self-assertively forward; brash: *the obtrusive behavior of a spoiled child.* **3.** Undesirably noticeable: *an obtrusive scar.* [< Lat. *obtrudere, obtrus-,* to obtrude.] **—ob·tru'sive·ly** *adv.* **—ob·tru'sive·ness** *n.*
ob·tund (ŏb-tŭnd') *tr.v.* **-tund·ed, -tund·ing, -tunds.** To make less intense; dull or deaden. [ME *obtunden* < Lat. *obtundere* : *ob-,* against + *tundere,* to beat.] **—ob·tund'ent** *adj. & n.*
ob·tu·rate (ŏb'tə-rāt', -tyə-) *tr.v.* **-rat·ed, -rat·ing, -rates.** To close or obstruct. [Lat. *obturare, obturat-.*] **—ob'tu·ra'tion** *n.*
ob·tu·ra·tor (ŏb'tə-rā'tər, -tyə-) *n.* One that closes or obstructs, as: **a.** An organic structure, such as the soft palate, that closes an opening in the body. **b.** A prosthetic device serving the same purpose.
ob·tuse (ŏb-to͞os', -tyo͞os', əb-) *adj.* **1.** Not sharp, pointed, or acute in form; blunt. **2.** *Bot.* Having a blunt or rounded tip: *an obtuse leaf.* **3.** Lacking keenness or quickness in comprehending or discerning. [Lat. *obtusus,* p.part. of *obtundere,* to blunt. —see OBTUND.] **—ob·tuse'ly** *adv.* **—ob·tuse'ness** *n.*
obtuse angle *n.* An angle greater than 90 degrees and less than 180 degrees.
ob·verse (ŏb-vûrs', əb-, ŏb'vûrs') *adj.* **1.** Facing or turned toward the observer: *the obverse side of a statue.* **2.** *Bot.* Having a narrower base than top, as certain leaves; inverse. **3.** Serving as a counterpart or complement. *—n.* (ŏb'vûrs', ŏb-vûrs', əb-). **1.** The side of a coin, medal, or badge that bears the principal stamp or design. **2.** The more conspicuous of two possible alternatives, cases, or sides: *the obverse of this issue.* **3.** *Logic.* The counterpart of a proposition obtained by exchanging the affirmative for the negative quality of the whole proposition and then negating the predicate: *The obverse of "every act is predictable" is "no act is unpredictable."* [Lat. *obversus,* p.part. of *obvertere,* to turn toward. —see OBVERT.] **—ob·verse'ly** *adv.*
ob·vert (ŏb-vûrt', əb-) *tr.v.* **-vert·ed, -vert·ing, -verts. 1.** To turn so as to present another side or aspect to view. **2.** To alter the appearance of. [Lat. *obvertere,* to turn toward : *ob,* toward + *vertere,* to turn.]
ob·vi·ate (ŏb'vē-āt') *tr.v.* **-at·ed, -at·ing, -ates.** To prevent by anticipating; make unnecessary. [LLat. *obviare, obviat-,* to hinder : *ob-,* against + *via,* way.] **—ob'vi·a'tion** *n.* **—ob'vi·a'tor** *n.*
ob·vi·ous (ŏb'vē-əs) *adj.* **1.** Easily perceived or understood; quite apparent. **2.** Easily seen through due to a lack of subtlety; transparent: *an obvious political ploy.* **3.** *Archaic.* Standing in the way or in front. [Lat. *obvius* : *ob-,* against + *via,* way.] **—ob'vi·ous·ly** *adv.* **—ob'vi·ous·ness** *n.*
ob·vo·lute (ŏb'və-lo͞ot', ŏb'və-lo͞ot') *adj.* Folded together with overlapping edges. Used of leaves and petals in a bud. [Lat. *obvolutus,* p.part. of *obvolvere,* to wrap around : *ob,* over + *volvere,* to wrap.] **—ob'vo·lu'tion** *n.* **—ob'vo·lu'tive** *adj.*
oc·a·ri·na (ŏk'ə-rē'nə) *n.* A small terra-cotta or plastic wind instrument with a mouthpiece, finger holes, and an elongated ovoid shape. [Ital., dim. of *oca,* goose < Lat. *avicula,* dim. of *avis,* bird.]
Oc·cam's razor (ŏk'əmz) *n.* Variant of **Ockham's razor.**
oc·ca·sion (ə-kā'zhən) *n.* **1. a.** An event or happening; incident. **b.** The time at which an event occurs. **2.** A significant event. **3.** A favorable time; opportunity. **4.** Something that brings on or precipitates an action or event; immediate cause. **5.** Something that provides a reason or justification. **6.** A need created by a particular circumstance. **7. occasions.** *Archaic.* Personal requirements or necessities. **8. occasions.** Personal affairs or business matters. **9.** A large or important social gathering. *—tr.v.* **-sioned, -sion·ing, -sions.** To provide occasion for; cause. ***—idiom.* on occasion.** From time to time; now and then. [ME *occasioun* < OFr. *occasion* < Lat. *occasio* < *occidere,* to fall : *ob,* down + *cadere,* to fall.]
oc·ca·sion·al (ə-kā'zhə-nəl) *adj.* **1. a.** Occurring from time to time. **b.** Occurring on a particular occasion. **2.** Created for a special occasion: *occasional verse.* **3.** Designed for use as the occasion requires: *an occasional chair.* **4.** Acting as the cause of something. **5.** Acting in a specified capacity from time to time: *an occasional hunter.*
oc·ca·sion·al·ly (ə-kā'zhə-nə-lē) *adv.* Now and then; from time to time.
oc·ci·dent (ŏk'sĭ-dənt, -dĕnt') *n.* **1.** The west; western lands or regions. **2. Occident.** The countries of Europe and the Western Hemisphere. [ME < OFr. *ocident* < Lat. *occidens* < pr.part. of *occidere,* to set (used of the sun).]
oc·ci·den·tal or **Oc·ci·den·tal** (ŏk'sĭ-dĕnt'l). *—adj.* Of or pertaining to the countries of the Occident, their peoples, or their culture; western. *—n.* A native or inhabitant of a western country.
Oc·ci·den·tal·ism (ŏk'sĭ-dĕn'tl-ĭz'əm) *n.* The characteristic traits or customs of Occidental peoples.
oc·ci·den·tal·ize or **Oc·ci·den·tal·ize** (ŏk'sĭ-dĕnt'l-īz'). *tr.v.* **-ized, -iz·ing, -iz·es.** To make occidental in character, outlook, or way of life. **—oc'ci·den'tal·i·za'tion** *n.*
oc·cip·i·ta (ŏk-sĭp'ĭ-tə) *n.* A plural of **occiput.**
oc·cip·i·tal (ŏk-sĭp'ĭ-tl) *adj.* Of or pertaining to the occiput or to the occipital bone: *an occipital fracture.* *—n.* The occipital bone. [OFr. < Med. Lat. *occipitalis* < Lat. *occiput,* occiput.] **—oc·cip'i·tal·ly** *adv.*
occipital bone *n.* A curved, trapezoidal, compound bone that forms the lower posterior part of the skull.
occipital lobe *n.* The posterior lobe of the cerebral hemisphere that has the shape of a three-sided pyramid.
oc·ci·put (ŏk'sə-pŭt', -pət) *n., pl.* **oc·cip·i·ta** (ŏk-sĭp'ĭ-tə) or **oc·ci·puts.** The back of the skull, esp. the occipital area. [Lat. : *ob-,* against + *caput,* head.]
oc·clude (ə-klo͞od') *v.* **-clud·ed, -clud·ing, -cludes.** *—tr.* **1.** To cause to become closed; obstruct: *occlude an artery.* **2.** To prevent the passage of: *occlude light.* **3.** *Chem.* To absorb or adsorb (a substance) in great quantity. **4.** *Meteorol.* To force (air) upward from the earth's surface, as when a cold front overtakes and undercuts a warm front. **5.** To bring together (the upper and lower teeth) in proper alignment for chewing. *—intr.* To close so that the cusps fit together. Used of the teeth of the upper and lower jaws. [Lat. *occludere* : *ob* (intensive) + *claudere,* to close.] **—oc·clud'ent** *adj.*
occluded front *n.* The air front established when a cold front occludes a warm front.

obtuse angle

ocelot

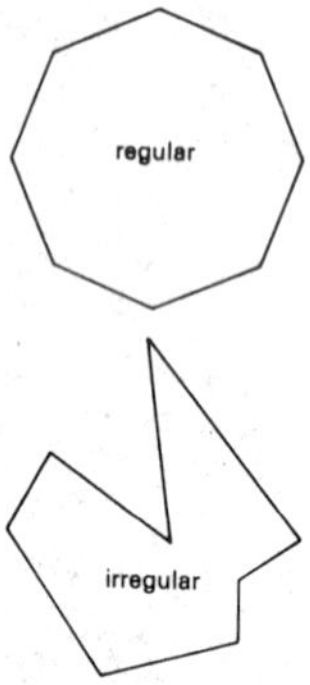

octagon

octahedron

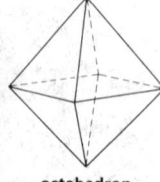

oc·clu·sal (ə-klo͞o′zəl, -səl) *adj.* Of or pertaining to occlusions of the teeth.

oc·clu·sion (ə-klo͞o′zhən) *n.* **1. a.** The process of occluding. **b.** Something that occludes or blocks. **2.** *Meteorol.* **a.** The process of occluding air masses. **b.** An occluded front. **3.** The fit of the teeth when brought together. **4.** *Ling.* **a.** The closing of the breath passage in a stop. **b.** The blocking of the mouth passage in a nasal consonant.

oc·clu·sive (ə-klo͞o′sĭv, -zĭv) *adj.* Occluding or tending to occlude. —*n. Ling.* **1.** A closing of the breath passage; stop. **2.** A nasal consonant.

oc·cult (ə-kŭlt′, ŏ-kŭlt′, ŏk′ŭlt′) *adj.* **1.** Of, pertaining to, or dealing with supernatural influences, agencies, or phenomena. **2.** Beyond the realm of human comprehension; inscrutable. **3.** Available only to the initiate; secret: *occult lore.* **4.** Hidden from view; concealed. —*n.* Occult practices or techniques: *a student of the occult.* —*v.* (ə-kŭlt′, ŏ-kŭlt′) **-cult·ed, -cult·ing, -cults.** —*tr.* **1.** To conceal or cause to disappear from view. **2.** *Astron.* To conceal by occultation: *The moon occulted Mars.* —*intr.* To become concealed or extinguished at regular intervals: *a lighthouse beacon that occults every 45 seconds.* [Lat. *occultus,* secret, p.part. of *occulere,* to conceal.] **—oc·cult′ly** *adv.* **—oc·cult′ness** *n.*

oc·cul·ta·tion (ŏk′ŭl-tā′shən) *n.* **1.** *Astron.* **a.** The passage of a celestial body across a line between an observer and another celestial object, as when the moon moves between earth and sun in a solar eclipse. **b.** The progressive blocking of light, radio waves, or other radiation from a celestial source during such a passage. **c.** An observational technique for determining the position or radiant structure of a celestial source so occulted: *a lunar occultation of a quasar.* **2.** The act of occulting or the state of being occulted. [Lat. *occultatio* < *occultare,* freq. of *occulere,* to conceal.]

oc·cult·ism (ə-kŭl′tĭz′əm, ŏ-kŭl′-, ŏk′ŭl-) *n.* **1.** The study of the supernatural. **2.** A belief in the occult **—oc·cult′ist** *n.*

oc·cu·pan·cy (ŏk′yə-pən-sē) *n., pl.* **-cies. 1. a.** The act of taking or holding possession. **b.** The condition of being occupied. **2. a.** The period during which one owns, rents, or uses certain premises or land. **b.** The use to which something occupied is put: *commercial occupancy.* **3.** The state of being an occupant or tenant. **4.** *Law.* The act of taking possession of previously unowned property with the intent of obtaining the right to own it.

oc·cu·pant (ŏk′yə-pənt) *n.* **1.** One who occupies a position or place, esp. a resident. **2.** One who has certain legal rights to or control over the premises he occupies; tenant or owner. **3.** *Law.* One who is the first to take possession of something previously unowned.

oc·cu·pa·tion (ŏk′yə-pā′shən) *n.* **1. a.** An activity that serves as one's regular source of livelihood; vocation. **b.** An activity engaged in esp. as a means of passing time. **2. a.** The act or process of holding or possessing a place. **b.** The state of being held or possessed. **3. a.** The invasion, conquest, and control of a nation or territory by a foreign military force. **b.** The military government exercising such control. [ME *occupacioun* < OFr. *ocupacion* < Lat. *occupatio* < *occupare,* to employ. —see OCCUPY.]

oc·cu·pa·tion·al (ŏk′yə-pā′shə-nəl) *adj.* Of, pertaining to, or caused by engagement in a particular occupation: *occupational disease.* **—oc′cu·pa′tion·al·ly** *adv.*

occupational therapy *n.* Therapy in which the principal element is some form of productive or creative activity. **—occupational therapist** *n.*

oc·cu·py (ŏk′yə-pī′) *tr.v.* **-pied, -py·ing, -pies. 1.** To seize possession of and maintain control over by military conquest. **2.** To fill up (time or space): *a lecture that occupied three hours.* **3.** To dwell or reside in. **4.** To hold or fill (an office or position). **5.** To engage, employ, or busy (oneself): *occupied himself with cleaning.* [ME *occupien* < OFr. *ocuper* < Lat. *occupare,* to seize : *ob-* (intensive) + *capere,* to take.] **—oc′cu·pi′er** *n.*

oc·cur (ə-kûr′) *intr.v.* **-curred, -cur·ring, -curs. 1.** To take place; come about. **2.** To be found to exist or appear: *Heavy rains occur during a summer monsoon.* **3.** To come to mind: *The idea never occurred to me.* [Lat. *occurrere* : *ob,* toward + *currere,* to run.]

oc·cur·rence (ə-kûr′əns) *n.* **1.** An act or instance of occurring. **2.** Something that takes place; incident. **—oc·cur′rent** *adj.*

Synonyms: *occurrence, happening, event, incident, episode, circumstance. Occurrence* and *happening* pertain, without implication, to anything that takes place. *Event* denotes a notable occurrence, usually considered as the result of antecedent happenings. *Incident* may apply to any minor occurrence or, in a special sense, to that part of an event that takes on sharp identity and momentary significance: *a border incident* (considered as part of a diplomatic event). *Episode* denotes a progression of occurrences that has independent character and significance within a larger sequence. *Circumstance,* in this context, denotes a detail of an event that, in combination with others of its kind, explains or interprets the nature of the event.

o·cean (ō′shən) *n.* **1. a.** The entire body of salt water that covers about 72 per cent of the earth's surface. **b.** Often **Ocean.** Any of the principal divisions of the ocean, including the Atlantic, Pacific, and Indian oceans, their southern extensions in Antarctica, and the Arctic Ocean. **2.** A great expanse or amount: *oceans of money.* [ME *occean* < OFr. < Lat. *oceanus* < Gk. *ōkeanos,* a great river encircling the earth.]

o·cean·ar·i·um (ō′shə-nâr′ē-əm) *n., pl.* **-i·ums** or **-i·a** (-ē-ə). A large aquarium for the study or display of marine life.

o·ce·an·ic (ō′shē-ăn′ĭk) *adj.* **1.** Of or pertaining to the ocean. **2.** Produced by or living in an ocean, esp. in the open sea rather than in shallow coastal waters. **3.** Resembling an ocean in expanse; vast.

O·ce·a·nid (ō-sē′ə-nĭd) *n., pl.* **O·ce·an·i·des** (ō′sē-ăn′ĭ-dēz′). *Gk. Myth.* Any of the ocean nymphs held to be the daughters of Oceanus and Tethys. [Gk. *ōkeanis, ōkeanid-* < *Ōkeanos,* Oceanus.]

o·cean·og·ra·phy (ō′shə-nŏg′rə-fē) *n.* The exploration and scientific study of the ocean and its phenomena. **—o′cean·og′ra·pher** *n.* **—o′cean·o·graph′ic** (-nə-grăf′ĭk), **o′cean·o·graph′i·cal** *adj.* **—o′cean·o·graph′i·cal·ly** *adv.*

o·cean·ol·o·gy (ō′shə-nŏl′ə-jē) *n.* Oceanography. **—o′cean·o·log′ic** (-nə-lŏj′ĭk), **o′cean·o·log′i·cal** *adj.* **—o′cean·o·log′i·cal·ly** *adv.* **—o′cean·ol′o·gist** (-nŏl′ə-jĭst) *n.*

ocean sunfish *n.* A marine fish, *Mola mola,* with a large globular body, found in warm seas.

O·ce·a·nus (ō-sē′ə-nəs) *n. Gk. Myth.* A Titan, the god of the outer sea encircling the earth and the father of the Oceanides and of the river gods. [Gk. *Ōkeanos.*]

oc·el·lat·ed (ŏs′ə-lā′tĭd, ō′sə-, ō-sĕl′ā′-) also **oc·el·late** (-lāt′) *adj.* **1.** Having an ocellus or ocelli. **2.** Resembling an ocellus. **3.** Having spots. [Lat. *ocellatus,* having little eyes < *ocellus,* dim. of *oculus,* eye.] **—oc′el·la′tion** *n.*

o·cel·lus (ō-sĕl′əs) *n., pl.* **o·cel·li** (ō-sĕl′ī′). **1.** A small simple eye, found in many invertebrates. **2.** A marking that resembles an eye. [Lat., dim. of *oculus,* eye.] **—o·cel′lar** (ō-sĕl′ər) *adj.*

oc·e·lot (ŏs′ə-lŏt′, ō′sə-) *n.* A brush- and forest-dwelling cat, *Felis pardalis,* of the southwestern United States and Central and South America, having a tawny-grayish or yellow coat with black spots. [Fr. < Nahuatl *ocelotl.*]

o·cher or **o·chre** (ō′kər) *n.* **1.** Any of several earthy mineral oxides of iron mingled with varying amounts of clay and sand, occurring in yellow, brown, or red, and used either untreated or processed for color intensification as pigments. **2.** A moderate orange yellow, from moderate or deep orange to moderate or strong yellow. [ME *oker* < OFr. *ocre* < Med. Lat. *ochra* < Gk. *ōkhra* < *ōkhros,* pale yellow.] **—o′cher·ous** (ō′kər-əs), **o′cher·y** (ō′krē) *adj.*

och·loc·ra·cy (ŏk-lŏk′rə-sē) *n., pl.* **-cies.** Government by the masses; mob rule. [OFr. *ochlocratie* < Gk. *okhlokratia* : *okhlos,* mob + *kratos,* power.] **—och′lo·crat′** (ŏk′lə-krăt′) *n.* **—och′lo·crat′ic, och′lo·crat′i·cal** *adj.* **—och′lo·crat′i·cal·ly** *adv.*

och·lo·pho·bi·a (ŏk′lə-fō′bē-ə) *n.* Abnormal dread of crowds. [Gk. *okhlos,* crowd + -PHOBIA.] **—och′lo·pho′bic** *adj. & n.*

Ock·ham's razor also **Oc·cam's razor** (ŏk′əmz) *n.* A rule in science and philosophy stating that entities should not be multiplied needlessly, which is interpreted to mean that the simplest of two or more competing theories is preferable and that an explanation for unknown phenomena should first be attempted in terms of what is already known. [After William of *Ockham* (1285?–1349).]

o'clock (ə-klŏk′) *adv.* **1.** Of or according to the clock: *three o'clock.* **2.** According to an imaginary clock dial with the observer at the center and 12 o'clock considered as straight ahead in horizontal position or straight up in vertical position: *enemy planes at 10 o'clock.* [Short for *of the clock.*]

o·co·ti·llo (ō′kə-tē′yō) *n., pl.* **-llos.** A cactuslike tree, *Fouquieria splendens,* of Mexico and the southwestern United States, having clusters of scarlet tubular flowers. [Mex. Sp., dim. of *ocote,* a Mexican pine < Nahuatl *ocotl,* pitch pine.]

oc·re·a (ŏk′rē-ə) *n., pl.* **-re·ae** (-rē-ē′). *Bot.* A sheath composed of one or more stipules, enclosing the leafstalks of certain plants. [Lat., greave.]

oct– or **octa–** *pref.* Variants of **octo-.**

oc·tad (ŏk′tăd′) *n.* A group or sequence of eight. [Gk. *oktas, oktad-* < *okto,* eight.] **—oc·tad′ic** *adj.*

oc·ta·gon (ŏk′tə-gŏn′) *n.* A polygon with eight sides and eight angles.

oc·tag·o·nal (ŏk-tăg′ə-nəl) *adj.* Having eight sides and eight angles. **—oc·tag′o·nal·ly** *adv.*

oc·ta·he·dra (ŏk′tə-hē′drə) *n.* A plural of **octahedron.**

oc·ta·he·dral (ŏk′tə-hē′drəl) *adj.* Having eight plane surfaces. **—oc′ta·he′dral·ly** *adv.*

oc·ta·he·dron (ŏk′tə-hē′drən) *n., pl.* **-drons** or **-dra** (-drə). A polyhedron with eight plane surfaces.

oc·tal (ŏk′təl) *adj.* Of, relating to, or being a number expressed in a numbering system of base eight.

oc·tam·e·ter (ŏk-tăm′ĭ-tər) *adj.* Having eight measures or metrical feet to a line of verse. —*n.* A verse having eight measures or metrical feet to each line.

oc·tan·dri·ous (ŏk-tăn′drē-əs) *adj. Bot.* Having eight stamens. [OCT(O) + -ANDRY + -OUS.]

oc·tane (ŏk′tān′) *n.* **1.** Any of various isomeric paraffin hydrocarbons with the formula C_8H_{18}. **2.** A colorless inflammable hydrocarbon, $CH_3(CH_2)_6CH_3$, found in petroleum and used as a solvent. **3.** Octane number.

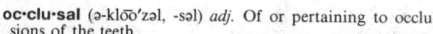

ă pat / ā pay / âr care / ä father / b bib / ch church / d deed / ĕ pet / ē be / f fife / g gag / h hat / hw which / ĭ pit / ī pie / îr pier / j judge / k kick / l lid, needle / m mum / n no, sudden / ng thing / ŏ pot / ō toe / ô paw, for / oi noise / ou out / o͝o took / o͞o boot /

octane number *n.* A numerical measure of the antiknock properties of motor fuel, based on the percentage by volume of isooctane in a standard reference fuel.

octane rating *n.* Octane number.

Oc·tans (ŏk'tănz') *n.* The constellation that includes the south celestial pole. [Lat., half-quadrant < *octo,* eight.]

oc·tant (ŏk'tənt) *n.* **1.** One-eighth of a circle: **a.** A 45° arc. **b.** The area enclosed by two radii at a 45° angle and the intersected arc. **2.** An instrument based on the principle of the sextant but employing only a 45° angle, used as an aid in navigation. **3.** *Astron.* The position of a celestial body when it is separated from another by a 45° angle. **4.** One of eight parts into which three-dimensional space is divided by three usually perpendicular coordinate planes. [Lat. *octans, octant-,* half-quadrant < *octo,* eight.] **—oc·tan'tal** (ŏk-tăn'təl) *adj.*

oc·tave (ŏk'tĭv, -tāv') *n.* **1.** *Mus.* **a.** The interval of eight diatonic degrees between two tones, one of which has twice as many vibrations per second as the other. **b.** A tone that is eight full tones above or below another given tone. **c.** Two tones eight diatonic degrees apart that are sounded together. **d.** The consonance that results when two tones eight diatonic degrees apart are sounded. **e.** A series of tones included within this interval or the keys of an instrument that produce such a series. **f.** An organ stop that produces tones an octave above those usually produced by the keys played. **2.** *Eccles.* **a.** The eighth day after a feast day, counting the feast day as one. **b.** The entire period between a feast day and the eighth day following it. **3.** A group or series of eight. **4. a.** A stanza of eight lines in poetry. **b.** An octet (sense 4). **5.** A rotating parry in fencing. [OFr. < Lat. *octavus,* eighth < *octo,* eight.] **—oc·ta'val** (ŏk-tā'vəl, ŏk'tə-vəl) *adj.*

oc·ta·vo (ŏk-tā'vō, -tä') *n., pl.* **-vos.** **1.** The page size, from 5 × 8 inches to 6 × 9½ inches, of a book composed of printer's sheets folded into eight leaves, originally printed on one side of each sheet. **2.** A book composed of octavo pages. [< Lat. *octavus,* eighth < *octo,* eight.]

oc·ten·ni·al (ŏk-tĕn'ē-əl) *adj.* **1.** Happening or recurring every eight years. **2.** Lasting eight years. [< LLat. *octennium,* period of eight years : Lat. *octo,* eight + Lat. *annus,* year.] **—oc·ten'ni·al·ly** *adv.*

oc·tet (ŏk-tĕt') *n.* **1.** A musical composition written for eight voices or eight instruments. **2.** A group of eight singers or eight instrumentalists. **3.** A group of eight. **4.** The first eight lines of an Italian sonnet. [Ital. *ottetto* < *otto,* eight < Lat. *octo.*]

oc·til·lion (ŏk-tĭl'yən) *n.* **1.** The cardinal number equal to 10^{27}. **2.** *Chiefly Brit.* The cardinal number equal to 10^{48}. [OCT- + (M)ILLION.]

oc·til·lionth (ŏk-tĭl'yənth) *n.* The ordinal number that matches the number octillion in a series. **—oc·til'lionth** *adj. & adv.*

octo– or **octa–** or **oct–** *pref.* Eight: *octane.* [Gk. *okta-, oktō-* (< *oktō*) and Lat. *octo-* (< *octo*).]

Oc·to·ber (ŏk-tō'bər) *n.* **1.** The tenth month of the Gregorian calendar. See table at **calendar.** **2.** *Chiefly Brit.* Ale brewed in October. [ME < Lat., eighth month < *octo,* eight.]

oc·to·dec·i·mo (ŏk'tə-dĕs'ə-mō') *n., pl.* **-mos.** **1.** The page size, 4 × 6½ inches, of a book composed of printer's sheets folded into 18 leaves or 36 pages. **2.** A book composed of octodecimo pages. [< Lat. *octodecimus,* eighteenth < *octodecim,* eighteen : *octo,* eight + *decem,* ten.]

oc·to·ge·nar·i·an (ŏk'tə-jə-nâr'ē-ən) *adj.* Being between 80 and 90 years of age. *—n.* A person between 80 and 90 years of age. [< Lat. *octogenarius,* containing eighty < *octogeni,* eighty each < *octoginta,* eighty : *octo,* eight + *-ginta,* times ten.]

oc·to·nar·y (ŏk'tə-nĕr'ē) *adj.* **1.** Of or pertaining to the number eight. **2.** Consisting of eight members or of groups containing eight. *—n., pl.* **-ies.** **1.** An octet (sense 4). **2.** A group or set of eight. [Lat. *octonarius,* containing eight < *octo,* eight.]

oc·to·pi (ŏk'tə-pī') *n.* A plural of **octopus.**

oc·to·ploid (ŏk'tə-ploid') *adj.* Having eight haploid sets of chromosomes in a body cell. **—oc'to·ploid'** *n.*

oc·to·pod (ŏk'tə-pŏd') *n.* Any of various mollusks of the order Octopoda, such as an octopus, having eight arms. [NLat. *Octopoda,* order name < Gk. *oktopous,* octopus.] **—oc'to·pod', oc'to·pod'ous** *adj.*

oc·to·pus (ŏk'tə-pəs) *n., pl.* **-pus·es** or **-pi** (-pī'). **1.** Any of numerous carnivorous nocturnal marine mollusks of the genus *Octopus* or related genera, found worldwide. It has a rounded, saclike body, eight tentacles, each bearing two rows of suckers, a large distinct head, and a strong beaklike mouth. **2.** Something, such as a multinational corporation, that resembles an octopus in its many powerful centrally controlled branches. [NLat. *Octopus,* genus name < Gk. *oktōpous,* eight-footed : *okto,* eight + *pous,* foot.]

oc·to·roon (ŏk'tə-ro͞on') *n.* A person whose ancestry is one-eighth Negro. [OCTO- + (QUAD)ROON.]

oc·to·syl·la·ble (ŏk'tə-sĭl'ə-bəl) *n.* **1.** Also **oc·to·syl·lab·ic** (ŏk'tō-sĭ-lăb'ĭk). **a.** A line of verse containing eight syllables. **b.** A verse with eight syllables in each line. **2.** A word of eight syllables. **—oc'to·syl·lab'ic** *adj.*

oc·troi (ŏk'troi', -trwä') *n., pl.* **-trois** (-troiz'; ôk-trwȧ'). A local tax levied on certain items brought into some European cities. [Fr. < OFr. < *octroyer,* to grant, perh. < Med. Lat. *auctorizare.* —see AUTHORIZE.]

oc·tu·ple (ŏk'tə-pəl, -to͞o'pəl, ŏk-tyo͞o'-) *adj.* **1.** Having eight parts, members, or copies. **2.** Multiplied by eight; eightfold. *—n.* A quantity eight times as great as another. *—tr.v.* **-pled, -pling, -ples.** To multiply by eight.

oc·u·lar (ŏk'yə-lər) *adj.* **1. a.** Of or pertaining to the eye: *ocular exercises.* **b.** Resembling the eye in form or function. **2.** Of or pertaining to the sense of sight: *an ocular aberration.* **3.** Seen by the eye; visual: *ocular proof.* *—n.* The eyepiece of an optical instrument. [LLat. *ocularis* < Lat. *oculus,* eye.]

oc·u·list (ŏk'yə-lĭst) *n.* **1.** A physician who treats diseases of the eyes; ophthalmologist. **2.** An optometrist. [Fr. *oculiste* < Lat. *oculus,* eye.]

oc·u·lom·e·ter (ŏk'yə-lŏm'ĭ-tər) *n.* A device designed for measuring the direction, speed, and extent of eye movement. [Lat. *oculus,* eye + -METER.]

oc·u·lo·mo·tor (ŏk'yə-lō-mō'tər) *adj.* **1.** Pertaining to movements of the eyeball. **2.** Pertaining to the oculomotor nerve. [Lat. *oculus,* eye + MOTOR.]

oculomotor nerve *n.* Either of the two cranial nerves that control the muscles of the eyeballs.

Od or **Odd** (ŏd) *interj. Archaic.* God. Used as a mild oath.

OD (ō'dē') *Slang.* *—n.* **1.** An overdose of a narcotic drug. **2.** One who has taken an overdose. *—intr. v.* **OD'd, OD'ing, OD's.** To overdose. [O(VER)D(OSE).]

o·da·lisque also **o·da·lisk** (ō'də-lĭsk') *n.* A female slave or concubine in a harem. [Fr. < Turk. *ōdalik,* chambermaid : *ōdah,* room + *-lik,* suffix expressing function.]

odd (ŏd) *adj.* **-er, -est.** **1.** Deviating from what is customary or accepted: *an odd name; odd behavior.* **2. a.** In excess of the indicated or approximate number, extent, or degree: *thirty-odd guests.* **b.** Being a remainder: *had some odd dollars left over.* **c.** Small in amount: *only odd change in my pocket.* **3. a.** Being one of an incomplete pair or set: *an odd shoe.* **b.** Remaining after others are paired or grouped: *odd man at the dinner party.* **4.** *Math.* Designating an integer not divisible by two, as: 1, 3, and 5. **5.** Not expected, regular, or planned: *called at odd intervals.* **6.** Remote; out-of-the-way. *—n.* **1.** Something odd. **2. a.** In the United States, a golf score one stroke higher than the score of one's opponent. **b.** In Great Britain, a golfing handicap of one stroke given to a player as odds or an advantage of one stroke taken away from a player's score as odds. **—*idiom.* odd man out.** One who, by the strangeness of his behavior or belief, stands alone in a group. [ME *odde* < ON *oddi,* odd number.] **—odd'ly** *adv.* **—odd'ness** *n.*

Usage: *Odd,* when used to indicate a few more than a given number, should be preceded by a hyphen in order to avoid ambiguity: *thirty-odd guests. Odd* in that sense is used only with round numbers.

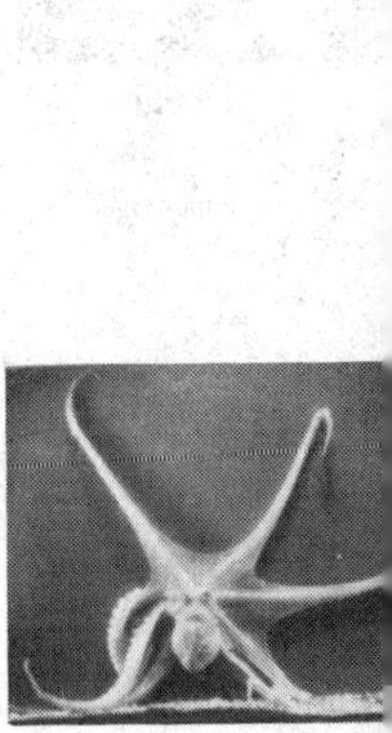

octopus

odd·ball (ŏd'bôl') *n. Informal.* A person marked by eccentric behavior or thinking.

Odd Fellow *n.* A member of the Independent Order of Odd Fellows, a fraternal and benevolent secret society.

odd·ish (ŏd'ĭsh) *adj.* Somewhat odd.

odd·i·ty (ŏd'ĭ-tē) **1.** One that is odd. **2.** The state or quality of being odd; strangeness.

odd lot *n.* A quantity that differs from a standard trading unit, esp. an amount of stock of fewer than 100 shares.

odd·ment (ŏd'mənt) *n.* **1. a.** Something left over. **b. oddments.** Odds and ends. **2.** An oddity.

odd-pin·nate (ŏd'pĭn'āt') *adj.* Pinnate with a single, unpaired leaflet at the end of the leafstalk. **—odd'-pin'nate'ly** *adv.*

odds (ŏdz) *pl.n.* **1.** A certain number of points given beforehand to a weaker side in a contest to equalize the chances of all participants. **2.** A ratio expressing the probability of an event or outcome: *The odds on the champion winning are three to two.* **3.** A ratio expressing the amount by which the stake of one bettor differs from that of his opposing bettor. **4.** The likelihood of one thing occurring rather than another in a contest or issue of indefinite outcome: *The odds are that he will get the nomination on the first ballot.* **5.** An amount or degree by which one thing exceeds or falls short of another: *won the contest by considerable odds.* **—*idioms.* at odds.** In disagreement; in conflict. **by all odds.** In every possible way; unquestionably: *by all odds the best film of the year.* [Pl. of ODD.]

odds and ends *pl.n.* Miscellaneous items, remnants, or pieces.

ode (ōd) *n.* **1.** In classical literature, a poem intended to be sung by a chorus at a public festival or as part of a drama. **2.** A lengthy lyrical poem, usually rhymed, often addressed to a praised object, person, or quality and characterized by exalted style. [Fr. < OFr. < LLat. *oda* < Gk. *aoidē,* song.] **—od'ic** (ō'dĭk) *adj.*

odalisque
Detail from "Odalisque" by Jean Auguste Ingres

–ode *suff.* **1.** Way; path: *electrode.* **2.** Electrode: *dynode.* [Gk. *-odos* < *hodos,* way.]

o·de·um (ō-dē'əm, ō'dē-) *n., pl.* **o·de·a** (ō-dē'ə, ō'dē-ə). **1.** A small building of ancient Greece and Rome used for public performances of music and poetry. **2.** A contemporary theater or concert hall. [Lat. < Gk. *ōideion* < *aoidē,* song.]

O·din (ō'dĭn) *n.* In Norse mythology, the supreme deity and creator of the cosmos and man; the god of wisdom, war, art, culture, and the dead. [ON *Ōdhinn.*]

o·di·ous (ō'dē-əs) *adj.* Exciting hatred or repugnance; abhorrent. [ME < OFr. *odios* < Lat. *odiosus* < *odium,* hatred < *odisse,* to hate.] **—o'di·ous·ly** *adv.* **—o'di·ous·ness** *n.*

o·di·um (ō'dē-əm) *n.* **1.** The state or quality of being odious. **2.** Strong dislike; contempt or aversion. **3.** Disgrace resulting from hateful conduct. [Lat., hatred < *odisse,* to hate.]

o·do·graph (ō'də-grăf') *n.* **1.** A device for recording speed and distance traveled on foot. **2.** An instrument for recording the distance and course traveled by a vehicle. [Gk. *hodos,* journey + -GRAPH.]

o·dom·e·ter (ō-dŏm'ĭ-tər) *n.* An instrument that indicates distance traveled by a vehicle. [Fr. *odomètre* : Gk. *hodos,* journey + Fr. *-mètre,* -meter.] **—o·dom'e·try** *n.*

–odon *suff.* An animal having a specified kind of teeth: *sphenodon.* [NLat. < Gk. *odous,* tooth.]

o·do·nate (ŏd'n-āt', ō-dŏn'-) *n.* Any of various predacious winged insects of the order Odonata, which includes the dragonflies and damselflies, characterized by two pairs of membranous wings and large compound eyes. [NLat. *Odonata,* order name < Gk. *odous, odor,* tooth.]

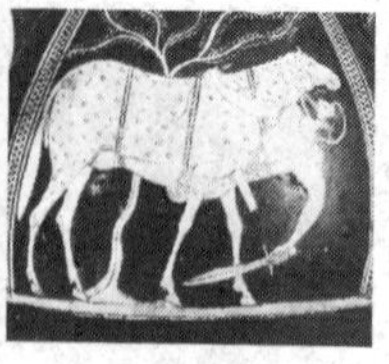

Odysseus
Detail from a 5th-century B.C. Attic vase painting

odont– *pref.* Variant of **odonto-**.

–odont *suff.* Having teeth of a specified kind: *pleurodont.* [< Gk. *odous, odont-,* tooth.]

–odontia *suff.* The form of, condition of, or manner of treating the teeth: *orthodontia.* [NLat. < Gk. *odous,* tooth.]

odonto– or **odont–** *pref.* Tooth: *odontophore.* [Gk. < *odous,* tooth.]

o·don·to·blast (ō-dŏn'tə-blăst') *n.* A tooth cell in the outer surface of dental pulp that produces dentine. **—o·don'to·blas'tic** *adj.*

o·don·toid (ō-dŏn'toid') *adj.* **1.** Resembling a tooth. **2.** Of or pertaining to the odontoid process.

odontoid process *n. Anat.* A small, toothlike projection from the second vertebra of the neck around which the first vertebra rotates.

o·don·tol·o·gy (ō'dŏn-tŏl'ə-jē) *n.* The study of the anatomy, growth, and diseases of the teeth. **—o·don'to·log'i·cal** (-tə-lŏj'ĭ-kəl) *adj.* **—o·don'to·log'i·cal·ly** *adv.* **—o'don·tol'o·gist** *n.*

o·don·to·phore (ō-dŏn'tə-fôr', -fōr') *n.* A protrusile structure at the base of the mouth of most mollusks, supporting the radula. **—o'don·toph'o·ral** (ō'dŏn-tŏf'ər-əl), **o'don·toph'o·rine'** (-ə-rīn', -rĭn), **o'don·toph'o·rous** (-ər-əs) *adj.*

o·dor (ō'dər) *n.* **1.** The property or quality of a thing that affects, stimulates, or is perceived by the sense of smell. **2.** A sensation, stimulation, or perception of the sense of smell. **3.** A strong, pervasive quality: *an odor of sadness.* **4.** Esteem; repute: *a doctrine that is not currently in good odor.* [ME *odour* < OFr. < Lat. *odor.*] **—o'dored** *adj.*

o·dor·if·er·ous (ō'də-rĭf'ər-əs) *adj.* Having or giving off an odor. **—o'dor·if'er·ous·ly** *adv.* **—o'dor·if'er·ous·ness** *n.*

o·dor·less (ō'dər-lĭs) *adj.* Having no odor: *an odorless gas.* **—o'dor·less·ly** *adv.* **—o'dor·less·ness** *n.*

o·dor·ous (ō'dər-əs) *adj.* Having a distinctive odor, as: **a.** Fragrant. **b.** Malodorous. **—o'dor·ous·ly** *adv.* **—o'dor·ous·ness** *n.*

o·dour (ō'dər) *n. Chiefly Brit.* Variant of **odor**.

O·dys·seus (ō-dĭs'yo͞os', ō-dĭs'ē-əs) *n. Gk. Myth.* The king of Ithaca, a leader of the Greeks in the Trojan War, who reached home after ten years of wandering. [Gk. *Odusseus.*]

od·ys·sey (ŏd'ĭ-sē) *n., pl.* **-seys. 1.** An extended adventurous wandering. **2.** An intellectual or spiritual quest. [After the *Odyssey,* a Homeric epic recounting the wanderings of Odysseus after the fall of Troy < Fr. *Odyssée* < Lat. *Odyssea* < Gk. *Odusseia* < *Odusseus,* Odysseus.]

Oedipus

oe·de·ma (ĭ-dē'mə-) *n.* Variant of **edema**.

oed·i·pal (ĕd'ə-pəl, ē'də-) *adj.* Often **Oedipal.** Of, relating to, or characteristic of the Oedipus complex. **—oed'i·pal·ly** *adv.*

Oed·i·pus (ĕd'ə-pəs, ē'də-) *n. Gk. Myth.* A son of Laius and Jocasta, who was abandoned at birth and who unwittingly killed his father and married his mother. [Gk. *Oidipeus* : *oidan,* to swell + *pous,* foot.]

Oedipus complex *n.* Libidinal feelings in a child, esp. a male child, for the parent of the opposite sex, usually accompanied by hostility to the parent of the same sex and generally manifesting itself first between ages three and five.

oe·nol·o·gy (ē-nŏl'ə-jē) *n.* The study of wines. [Gk. *oinos,* wine + -LOGY.] **—oe'no·log'i·cal** (ē'nə-lŏj'ĭ-kəl) *adj.* **—oe·nol'o·gist** *n.*

oe·no·mel (ē'nə-mĕl') *n.* A beverage of ancient Greece, consisting of wine and honey. [Gk. *oinomeli* : *oinos,* wine + *meli,* honey.]

o'er (ôr, ōr) *prep. & adv.* Over.

oer·sted (ûr'stĕd') *n.* The centimeter-gram-second electromagnetic unit of magnetic intensity, equal to the magnetic intensity one centimeter from a unit magnetic pole. [After Hans Christian *Oersted* (1777–1851).]

oe·soph·a·gus (ĭ-sŏf'ə-gəs) *n.* Variant of **esophagus**.

oes·tro·gen (ĕs'trə-jən) *n.* Variant of **estrogen**.

oes·trus (ĕs'trəs) *n.* Variant of **estrus**.

oeu·vre (œ'vrə) *n., pl.* **oeu·vres** (œ'vrə). **1.** A work of art. **2.** The sum of an artist's lifework. [Fr. < Lat. *opus,* work.]

of (ŭv, ŏv; *unstressed* əv) *prep.* **1.** Derived or coming from; originating at or from: *men of the north.* **2.** Caused by; resulting from: *his death of tuberculosis.* **3.** Away from; at a distance from: *a mile east of here.* **4.** So as to be separated or relieved from: *robbed of his dignity; cured of distemper.* **5.** From the total or group comprising: *give of one's time; two of his friends; most of the cases.* **6.** Composed or made from: *a dress of silk.* **7.** Associated with or adhering to: *a man of your religion.* **8.** Belonging or connected to: *the rungs of a ladder.* **9. a.** Possessing; having: *a man of honor.* **b.** On the part of: *very nice of you.* **10.** Containing or carrying: *a basket of groceries.* **11.** Specified as; named or called: *a depth of ten feet; the Garden of Eden.* **12.** Centering upon; directed toward: *a love of horses.* **13.** Produced by; issuing from: *products of the vine.* **14.** Characterized or identified by: *a year of famine.* **15. a.** With reference to; about: *think highly of his proposals; speak of it later.* **b.** In respect to: *slow of speech.* **16.** Set aside for; taken up by: *a day of rest.* **17.** Before; until: *five minutes of two.* **18.** During or on a specified time: *of recent years.* **19.** By: *beloved of his family.* **20.** Used to indicate an appositive: *that idiot of a driver.* **21.** *Archaic.* On: *"A plague of all cowards, I say."* (Shakespeare). [ME < OE.]

Usage: Grammarians have sometimes condemned categorically the "double genitive" construction, as in *a friend of my father's, a book of mine.* The usage is well supported by literary precedent, however, and should be regarded as entirely acceptable at all levels. There is a subtle difference between the forms *a friend of my father's* and *a friend of my father:* With the double genitive like *a friend of my father's,* it is assumed that the father has more than one friend. For this reason, the double genitive is not used in constructions like *a mother of his* or *a president of the school board,* where it is assumed that the object of *of* possesses only one of the entities in question.

o·fay (ō'fā') *n. Offensive Slang.* A white person. [Orig. unknown.]

off (ôf, ŏf) *adv.* **1.** From a place or position: *drive off.* **2. a.** At a certain distance in space or time: *a mile off; a week off.* **b.** From a given course or route; aside: *swerved off into a ditch.* **c.** Into a state of unconsciousness: *I must have dozed off.* **3. a.** So as to be no longer on, attached, or connected: *shaved off his mustache.* **b.** So as to be divided: *marked off the playing fields by yards.* **4.** So as to be no longer continuing, operating, or functioning: *turn off the radio.* **5.** So as to be completely removed, finished, or eliminated: *write off a report; kill off the mice.* **6.** So as to be smaller, fewer, or less: *Sales dropped off.* **7.** So as to be away from work or duty: *They took a day off.* **8.** Offstage. *—adj.* **1. a.** Distant or removed; farther: *the off side of the barn.* **b.** Remote; slim: *on the off chance that he's home.* **2.** Not on, attached, or connected: *with his shoes off.* **3.** Not operating or operational: *The oven is off.* **4.** No longer taking place; canceled: *The wedding is off.* **5.** Slack: *Production was off this year.* **6. a.** Not up to standard; below a normal or satisfactory level: *Your pitching is off today.* **b.** Not accurate; incorrect: *Your statistical results are off.* **c.** Somewhat crazy; eccentric: *He's a little off.* **7.** Started on the way; going: *I'm off to see the president.* **8. a.** Absent or away from work or duty: *He's off every Tuesday.* **b.** Spent away from work or duty: *My off day is Saturday.* **9.** On the right side of a vehicle or draft team: *The off horse is lame.* **10.** *Naut.* Farthest from the shore; seaward. **11.** Designating or toward the side of the field facing the batsman in cricket. **12.** Off-color. *—prep.* **1.** So as to be removed or distant from: *The bird hopped off the branch.* **2.** Away or relieved from: *off duty.* **3. a.** By consuming: *living off locusts and honey.* **b.** With the means provided by: *living off his pension.* **c.** *Nonstandard.* From: *got a loan off him.* **4.** Extending or branching out from: *an artery off the heart.* **5.** Not up to the usual standard of: *off his game.* **6.** So as to abstain from: *He went off narcotics.* **7.** To seaward of: *a mile off Sandy Hook.* *—v.* **offed, off·ing, offs.** *—intr.* To go away; leave. *—tr. Slang.* To murder. ***—idiom.*** **off and on.** Intermittently: *slept off and on.* [ME *of* < OE.]

Usage: Particularly in written usage, *off* should not be followed by *of* or *from: He stepped off* (not *off of* or *off from*) *the platform.* Nor should *off* be used for *from* to indicate a source in such a sentence as: *I got a loan from* (not *off*) *him.*

of·fal (ô'fəl, ŏf'əl) *n.* **1.** Waste parts, esp. of a butchered animal. **2.** Refuse; rubbish. [ME : *of-,* off + *fal,* fall.]

off·beat (ôf'bēt', ŏf'-) *n.* An unaccented beat in a musical measure. *—adj.* (ôf'bēt', ŏf'-). *Slang.* Not conforming to an ordinary type or pattern; unconventional.

off-Broad·way (ôf'brôd'wā', ŏf'-) *adj.* **1.** Designating or pertaining to theatrical activity, often experimental and low-cost, presented in theaters outside the Broadway entertainment district of New York City. **2.** Located outside of the Broadway entertainment district.

off·cast (ôf'kăst', ŏf'-) *adj.* Rejected; discarded.

off-col·or (ôf'kŭl'ər, ŏf'-) *adj.* **1.** Varying from the usual, expected, or required color. **2.** In bad taste; improper: *an off-color joke.* **3.** *Chiefly Brit.* Not in good health or spirits.

of·fence (ə-fĕns') *n. Chiefly Brit.* Variant of **offense**.

of·fend (ə-fĕnd') *v.* **-fend·ed, -fend·ing, -fends.** *—tr.* **1.** To create or excite anger, resentment, or annoyance in. **2.** To be displeasing or disagreeable to: *Onions offend his sense of smell.* **3. a.** To transgress; violate. **b.** To cause to sin. *—intr.* **1.** To cause displeasure: *Bad manners may offend.* **2. a.** To violate a moral or divine law; sin. **b.** To violate a rule or law: *offend against the law.* [ME *offenden* < OFr. *ofendre* < Lat. *offendere.*] **—of·fend'er** *n.*

Synonyms: *offend, insult, affront, outrage. Offend* is the least specific of these verbs denoting the act of giving displeasure; it often makes no implication regarding intent. *Insult* applies to a deliberate act calculated to cause humiliation; *affront* adds to this a stress on openness of attack, a sense of an insult to one's face. *Outrage,* stronger still, emphasizes that which causes extreme resentment by flagrantly violating one's standards of right and decency.

of·fense (ə-fĕns') *n.* **1. a.** The act of offending or causing anger, resentment, displeasure, or affront. **b.** The state of being offended: *took offense at the comment.* **2. a.** A violation or infraction of a moral or social code; transgression or sin. **b.** A transgression of law; crime. **3.** Something that outrages moral sensibilities: *Genocide is an offense to all civilized human beings.* **4.** (ŏf'ĕns'). The act of attacking or assaulting. **5.** (ŏf'ĕns'). *Sports.* **a.** An athletic team in possession of the ball or puck. **b.** Scoring ability or potential. **c.** The means or tactics used in an attempt to score points. [ME < OFr. *ofense* < Lat. *offensa* < p.part. of *offendere,* to offend.]

Synonyms: *offense, crime, sin, error.* These terms are related in denoting infraction of a code. *Offense* is broadly applicable to any such infraction. *Crime* applies to transgression of law, generally to a serious violation, which, like its punishment, is defined by law. *Sin* pertains less specifically to serious violation of moral law. *Error,* like *offense,* is nonspecific as to magnitude and code; it differs from all of the others by stressing lack of knowledge or bad judgment rather than willfull violation.

of·fen·sive (ə-fĕn'sĭv) *adj.* **1.** Disagreeable to the senses: *an offensive odor.* **2.** Causing anger, displeasure, resentment, or affront: *an offensive gesture.* **3. a.** Making an attack. **b.** Of, pertaining to, or designed for attack: *offensive infantry weapons.* **c.** Of or pertaining to a team having possession of a ball or puck: *the offensive line.* —*n.* **1.** An attitude of attack: *on the offensive.* **2.** An attack; assault: *led a massive military offensive.* **—of·fen'sive·ly** *adv.* **—of·fen'sive·ness** *n.*

Synonyms: *offensive, insulting, forward, obnoxious.* These adjectives describe unpleasant effects to the senses or feelings. *Offensive* generally applies to sight, smell, or sound or to the intellect or feelings. While *insulting* can apply to an action, particularly a gesture, it most commonly refers to a verbal offense. *Forward* implies a breach in propriety or etiquette and is applied to persons as the approximate equivalent of the informal "pushy." *Obnoxious* emphasizes an extremely unpleasant quality.

of·fer (ô'fər, ŏf'ər) *v.* **-fered, -fer·ing, -fers.** —*tr.* **1.** To present for acceptance or rejection; proffer: *offered him a drink.* **2. a.** To put forward for consideration; propose: *offer an opinion.* **b.** To present in order to meet a need or satisfy a requirement: *offered new statistics to aid in decision-making.* **3.** To present for sale. **4.** To propose as payment; bid. **5.** To present as an act of worship: *offer up prayers.* **6.** To exhibit readiness or desire to do; volunteer: *The gentleman offered to escort her.* **7.** To put up; mount: *partisans who offered strong resistance to the invaders.* **8.** To threaten: *offered to strike him with his stick.* **9.** To provide; furnish: *a hotel that offers conference facilities.* **10.** To produce or introduce on the stage: *The repertory group is offering two new plays this season.* —*intr.* **1.** To present an offering in worship or devotion. **2.** To make an offer or proposal, esp. to make an offer of marriage. **3.** To present itself: *"This plan was dropped, because of its risk, and because a better offered"* (T.E. Lawrence). —*n.* **1.** The act of offering: *an offer of assistance.* **2.** Something offered, such as a suggestion, proposal, bid, or recommendation. **3.** *Law.* A proposal that if accepted constitutes a legally binding contract. **4.** The condition of being offered, esp. for sale: *thousands of bushels of wheat on offer.* **5. a.** An attempt; try. **b.** A show of intention. [ME *offren,* ult. < Lat. *offerre* : *ob,* to + *ferre,* to bring.] **—of'fer·er, of'fer·or** *n.*

Synonyms: *offer, proffer, tender, present. Offer* is the basic general term among this group. *Proffer,* used in polite discourse, is somewhat more emphatic through its implication of voluntary action motivated by courtesy or generosity. *Tender,* in business or legal usage, may stress formality (*tender one's resignation*), or it may apply specifically to discharge of an obligation (*tender payment*); in more general usage it emphasizes formality and observance of amenities (*tender one's respects*). *Present* stresses both formality and overt show.

of·fer·ing (ô'fər-ĭng, ŏf'ər-) *n.* **1.** The act of making an offer. **2.** Something that is offered. **3.** A presentation made to a deity as an act of religious worship or sacrifice; oblation. **4.** A contribution or gift, esp. one made at a religious service. [ME *offring* < OE *offrung* < *offrian,* to offer a sacrifice or gift < Lat. *offerre,* to offer.]

of·fer·to·ry (ô'fər-tôr'ē, -tōr'ē, ŏf'ər-) *n., pl.* **-ries. 1.** Often **Offertory. a.** One of the principal parts of the Eucharistic liturgy at which bread and wine are offered to God by the celebrant. **b.** A musical setting of the Offertory. **2.** A collection of offerings at a religious service. [Med. Lat. *offertorium* < Lat. *offerre,* to offer.]

off·hand (ôf'hănd', ŏf'-) *adv.* Without preparation or forethought; extemporaneously. —*adj.* Also **off·hand·ed** (-hăn'dĭd). Performed or expressed offhand. **—off'hand'ed·ly** *adv.* **—off'hand'ed·ness** *n.*

off-hour (ôf'our', ŏf'-) *n.* A period of time that is not a rush hour.

of·fice (ô'fĭs, ŏf'ĭs) *n.* **1. a.** A place in which business, clerical, or professional activities are conducted. **b.** The administrative personnel, executives, or staff working in such a place. **2.** A duty or function assigned to or assumed by someone. **3.** A position of authority, duty, or trust given to a person, as in a government or corporation: *the office of vice president.* **4. a.** A subdivision of a governmental department: *the U.S. Patent Office.* **b.** A major executive division of a government: *the British Home Office.* **5.** A public position: *seek office.* **6. offices.** *Chiefly Brit.* The parts of a house, such as the laundry and kitchen, in which servants carry out household work. **7.** Often **offices.** A usually beneficial act performed for another. **8.** *Eccles.* A ceremony, rite, or service, usually prescribed by liturgy, esp.: **a.** *Rom. Cath. Ch.* The canonical hours. **b.** A prayer service in the Anglican Church, as Morning or Evening Prayer. **c.** A ceremony, rite, or service for a special purpose, esp. a rite for the dead. ***—modifier:*** *office buildings; office work.* [ME < OFr., position of responsibility < Lat. *officium.*]

office boy *n.* A boy or young man employed in a business office to do odd jobs.

of·fice·hold·er (ô'fĭs-hōl'dər, ŏf'ĭs-) *n.* One who holds a public office.

of·fi·cer (ô'fĭ-sər, ŏf'ĭ-) *n.* **1.** One who holds an office of authority or trust in an organization, such as a corporation or a government. **2.** One holding a commission in the armed forces. **3.** A person licensed in the merchant marine as master, mate, chief engineer, or assistant engineer. **4.** One performing police duties. [ME < OFr. *officier* < Med. Lat. *officarius* < Lat. *officium,* office.]

officer of the day *n.* A military officer who for a given day assumes responsibility for security, order, and the performance of the guard.

officer of the deck *n.* A naval officer assigned to represent the commanding officer of a vessel or installation for a specified period during which he is superior to all officers below the executive officer.

of·fi·cial (ə-fĭsh'əl) *adj.* **1.** Of or pertaining to an office or post of authority: *official duties.* **2.** Authorized by a proper authority; authoritative: *official permission.* **3.** Holding office or serving in a public capacity: *an official representative.* **4.** Characteristic of or befitting a person of authority; formal: *an official banquet.* **5.** Designating drugs that are authorized by or contained in the U.S. Pharmacopoeia or National Formulary. —*n.* **1.** One who holds an office or position, esp. one who acts in a subordinate capacity for an institution such as a corporation or governmental agency. **2.** A referee or an umpire in various sports. [< ME, ecclesiastical officer < OFr. < LLat. *officialis* < Lat., of an office < *officium,* office.] **—of·fi'cial·dom** *n.* **—of·fi'cial·ly** *adv.*

of·fi·cial·ese (ə-fĭsh'ə-lēz', -lēs') *n.* Language characteristic of official documents or statements, often considered obscure, pretentiously wordy, or formal in style.

of·fi·cial·ism (ə-fĭsh'ə-lĭz'əm) *n.* Rigid adherence to official regulations, forms, and procedures.

of·fi·ci·ant (ə-fĭsh'ē-ənt) *n.* One who officiates at a religious service or ceremony; celebrant.

of·fi·ci·ar·y (ə-fĭsh'ē-ĕr'ē) *n., pl.* **-ies. 1.** A body of officials or officers. **2.** An official or officer. —*adj.* **1.** Attached to or resulting from an office held. Used of a title. **2.** Having a title resulting from the holding of an office. Used of a dignitary.

of·fi·ci·ate (ə-fĭsh'ē-āt') *intr.v.* **-at·ed, -at·ing, -ates. 1.** To perform the duties and functions of an office or position of authority. **2.** To serve as a priest or minister at a religious service. **3.** To serve as referee or umpire in any of various sports. [Med. Lat. *officiare, officiat-,* to conduct a religious service < Lat. *officium,* office.] **—of·fi'ci·a'tion** *n.* **—of·fi'ci·a'tor** *n.*

of·fic·i·nal (ə-fĭs'ə-nəl, ô'fĭ-sī'nəl, ŏf'ĭ-) *adj.* **1.** Designating a drug available without prescription. **2.** Designating a plant used in medicine. —*n.* An officinal drug. [Med. Lat. *officinalis,* kept in stock < Lat. *officina,* workshop < *opifex,* workman : *opus,* work + *facere,* to do.] **—of·fic'i·nal·ly** *adv.*

of·fi·cious (ə-fĭsh'əs) *adj.* **1.** Excessively forward in offering one's services or advice to others, esp. where these services are unnecessary and unwanted. **2.** *Archaic.* Eager to render services or help others. **3.** Of an informal nature; unofficial. [Lat. *officiosus,* obliging < *officium,* duty.] **—of·fi'cious·ly** *adv.* **—of·fi'cious·ness** *n.*

off·ing (ô'fĭng, ŏf'ĭng) *n.* **1.** The part of the sea that is distant yet visible from the shore. **2.** The near or immediate future: *Success is in the offing.*

off·ish (ô'fĭsh, ŏf'ĭsh) *adj.* Inclined to be distant and reserved; aloof. **—off'ish·ly** *adv.* **—off'ish·ness** *n.*

off-key (ôf'-kē', ŏf'-) *adj.* **1.** Pitched higher or lower than the correct notes of a melody. **2.** Being out of accord with what is considered normal or appropriate; irregular. **—off'key'** *adv.*

ogee
Gothic ogee in the framework of a classical doorway

oilcan
Left: Bench oilcan
Right: Direct-pump oilcan

off-lim·its (ôf-lĭm′ĭts, ŏf-) *adj.* Forbidden to a designated group: *a bar off-limits to military personnel.*
off-line (ôf′līn′, ŏf′-) *adj.* Not under the control of a central computer, as in a manufacturing process or an experiment.
off-load (ôf′lōd′, ŏf′-) *tr.v.* **-load·ed, -load·ing, -loads. 1.** To launch (a guided missile or rocket) with propellant tanks less than fully loaded in order to alter the center of gravity of the vehicle. **2.** To unload (a vehicle, esp. an airplane).
off of *prep.* Off.
off-off-Broadway (ôf′ôf-brôd′wā′, ŏf′ŏf-) *n.* A theatrical movement in New York City that is involved in avant-garde, experimental techniques and productions.
off·print (ôf′prĭnt′, ŏf′-) *n.* A reproduction of or excerpt from a printed article that was originally contained in a larger publication. *—tr.v.* **-print·ed, -print·ing, -prints.** To reproduce or reprint (an excerpt).
off-put·ting (ôf′po͝ot′ĭng, ŏf′-) *adj.* Tending to disconcert or repel: *has an off-putting habit of scowling.*
off·scour·ing (ôf′skour′ĭng, ŏf′-) *n.* **1.** Something that is scoured off; refuse. **2.** A social outcast or misfit.
off-screen (ôf′-skrēn′, ŏf′-) *adj & adv.* **1.** Out of sight of the viewer of a motion-picture or television screen. **2.** Out of public view; in private.
off-sea·son (ôf′-sē′zən, ŏf′-) *n.* A period of time marked by the cessation or lessening of activity. ***—modifier:*** *off-season motel rates.*
off·set (ôf′sĕt′, ŏf′-) *n.* **1.** Something that balances, counteracts, or compensates. **2.** Something deriving or originating from but set off from something else. **3.** *Archit.* A ledge or recess in a wall formed by a reduction in thickness above; setoff. **4.** *Bot.* A shoot that develops laterally at the base of a plant, often rooting to form a new plant. **5.** *Geol.* A spur of a range of mountains or hills. **6.** A bend in a pipe or bar to allow it to pass around an obstruction. **7.** A crosscut or drift from a main level of a mine. **8.** In surveying, a short distance measured perpendicularly from the main line, used to help in calculating the area of an irregular plot. **9.** A descendant of a race or family; offshoot. **10.** *Printing.* **a.** Offset printing. **b.** The unintentional or faulty transfer of ink not yet dry from a printed sheet to a surface, such as the next sheet, that is laid over it. *—v.* (ôf′sĕt′, ŏf′-, ôf-sĕt′, ŏf-) **-set, -set·ting, -sets.** *—tr.* **1.** To counterbalance, counteract, or compensate for. **2.** *Printing.* **a.** To print by offset. **b.** To smear with an offset. **3.** To make or form an offset in (a wall, bar, or pipe). *—intr.* To develop as an offset. **—off′set′** *adj.*
offset printing *n.* Planographic printing by indirect image transfer, as: **a.** Printing from photomechanical plates. **b.** Printing from paper mats.
off·shoot (ôf′sho͞ot′, ŏf′-) *n.* **1.** Something that branches out or derives its existence or origin from a particular source. **2.** A branch, descendant, or member of a family or social group. **3.** A lateral shoot from the main stem of a plant.
off·shore (ôf′shôr′, -shōr′, ŏf′-) *adj.* **1.** Moving or directed away from the shore: *an offshore wind.* **2. a.** Located or occurring at a distance from the shore: *an offshore mooring.* **b.** Located or based outside the United States and not subject to United States tax laws: *offshore bank accounts; offshore investments.* *—adv.* **1.** Away from the shore: *The storm moved offshore.* **2.** At a distance from the shore: *a boat moored offshore.*
off·side also **off side** (ôf′sīd′, ŏf′-) *adj. Sports.* Illegally ahead of the ball or puck.
off·spring (ôf′sprĭng′, ŏf′-) *n., pl.* **offspring. 1.** The progeny of a person, animal, or plant. **2.** A result; product. [ME *ofspring* < OE : *of,* off + *springan,* to rise.]
off-stage (ôf′stāj′, ŏf′-) *adj.* Located or occurring in the area of a stage not visible to the audience. *—adv.* **1.** Away from the area of a stage visible to the audience. **2. a.** In private life: *an actor known off-stage by another name.* **b.** Behind the scenes; not visible to the public: *The meetings between the leaders took place off-stage.*
off-the-rack (ôf′*thə*-răk′, ŏf′-) *adj.* Ready-made (sense 1).
off-the-rec·ord (ôf′*thə*-rĕk′ərd, ŏf′-) *adj.* Not for publication or attribution. **—off′-the-rec′ord** *adv.*
off-the-shelf (ôf′*thə*-shĕlf′, ŏf′-) *adj.* Of or pertaining to merchandise carried in stock that is deliverable without alteration. **—off′-the-shelf′** *adv.*
off-the-wall (ôf′*thə*-wôl′, ŏf′-) *adj. Informal.* Very unconventional, unusual, or bizarre: *off-the-wall humor.*
off-track (ôf′trăk′, ŏf′-) *adj.* Of or pertaining to gambling on horse races that is conducted away from a racetrack.
off-track betting *n.* A system of placing bets away from a racetrack.
off-white (ôf′hwīt′, -wīt′, ŏf′-) *n.* A grayish or yellowish white. **—off′-white′** *adj.*
off year *n.* **1.** A year in which no major political elections occur. **2.** A year of reduced activity or production: *an off year for soybean crops.*
oft (ôft, ŏft) *adv.* Often. [ME < OE.]
of·ten (ô′fən, ŏf′ən) *adv.* Many times; frequently. [ME < *oft* < OE.]
of·ten·times (ô′fən-tīmz′, ŏf′ən-) also **oft·times** (ôf′tīmz′, ŏf′-) *adv.* Frequently; repeatedly.
O·ga·la·la (ō′gə-lä′lə) *n.* Variant of **Oglala.**
og·am (ŏg′əm, ō′əm) *n.* Variant of **ogham.**
o·gee (ō′jē′) *n. Archit.* **1.** A double curve with the shape of an elongated S. **2.** A molding having in profile an S-shaped curve. **3.** An arch of two curves meeting at a point. [Alteration of OGIVE.]
og·ham or **og·am** (ŏg′əm, ō′əm) *n.* **1. a.** An alphabet used for writing Irish from the 4th or 5th century A.D. to the early 7th century. **b.** A character in this alphabet. **2. a.** An inscription in the ogham alphabet. **b.** A stone inscribed in the ogham alphabet. [Ir. Gael. < OIr. *ogom.*]
o·give (ō′jīv′) *n.* **1.** *Statistics.* **a.** The graphic representation of a frequency distribution in which every ordinate represents the sum of frequencies in preceding intervals. **b.** A frequency distribution. **2.** *Archit.* **a.** A diagonal rib of a Gothic vault. **b.** A pointed arch. [< Fr., diagonal rib of a vault < OFr. *augive.*] **—o·gi′val** *adj.*
O·gla·la (ō-glä′lə) also **O·ga·la·la** (ō′gə-lä′lə) *n., pl.* **Oglala** or **-las** also **Ogalala** or **-las. 1. a.** A tribe of North American Indians of the Teton Dakota group, inhabiting the area west of the Missouri River in South Dakota. **b.** A member of the Oglala. **2.** The Siouan language of the Oglala.
o·gle (ō′gəl, ŏ′gəl) *v.* **o·gled, o·gling, o·gles.** *—tr.* **1.** To stare at. **2.** To stare at impertinently, flirtatiously, or amorously. *—intr.* To stare impertinently, flirtatiously, or amorously. *—n.* An impertinent, flirtatious, or amorous stare. [Perh. < LG *oegeln,* freq. of *oegen,* to eye < *oog,* eye.] **—o′gler** *n.*
o·gre (ō′gər) *n.* **1.** A fabled man-eating giant or monster. **2.** One who is particularly cruel, brutish, or hideous. [Fr.] **—o′gre·ish** (ō′gər-ĭsh, ō′grĭsh) *adj.*
o·gress (ō′grĭs) *n.* A woman who behaves like an ogre.
oh (ō) *interj.* **1.** Used to express strong emotion, such as surprise, fear, anger, or pain. **2.** Used in direct address: *Oh, sir! You forgot your keys.* **3.** Used to indicate understanding or acknowledgment of a statement. —See Usage note at **O.**
O·hi·o buckeye (ō-hī′ō) *n.* A tree, *Aesculus glabra,* of the central United States, having compound leaves and yellowish-green flowers.
ohm (ōm) *n.* A unit of electrical resistance equal to that of a conductor in which a current of one ampere is produced by a potential of one volt across its terminals. [After Georg S. *Ohm* (1787–1854).] **—ohm′ic** (ō′mĭk) *adj.* **—ohm′i·cal·ly** *adv.*
ohm·age (ō′mĭj) *n.* Resistance expressed in ohms.
ohm·me·ter (ōm′mē′tər) *n.* An instrument for direct measurement of the resistance of a conductor in ohms.
o·ho (ō-hō′) *interj.* Used esp. to express surprise or mock astonishment.
-oic *suff.* Containing a carboxyl group or one of its derivatives: *decanoic acid.* [-O- + -IC.]
-oid *suff.* **1.** Resembling; having the appearance of: *acanthoid.* **2.** One that resembles something specified or has a specified quality: *humanoid.* [Gk. *-oeidēs* < *eidos,* shape, form.]
o·id·i·um (ō-ĭd′ē-əm) *n., pl.* **-i·a** (-ē-ə). A thin-walled spore produced by fragmentation in some filamentous fungi. [NLat. *Oidium,* fungus genus < Gk. *oiōn,* egg.]
oil (oil) *n.* **1.** Any of numerous mineral, vegetable, and synthetic substances and animal and vegetable fats that are generally slippery, combustible, viscous, liquid or liquefiable at room temperatures, soluble in various organic solvents, such as ether, but not in water, and used in a great variety of products, esp. lubricants and fuels. **2. a.** Petroleum. **b.** A petroleum derivative, such as a machine oil or lubricant. **3.** A substance with an oily consistency. **4.** An oil color. **5.** An oil painting (sense 1). **6.** *Informal.* Insincere flattery. ***—modifier:*** *an oil lamp; oil companies.* *—v.* **oiled, oil·ing, oils.** *—tr.* To lubricate, supply, cover, or polish with oil. *—intr.* To load up with or take on fuel oil. ***—idiom.*** **oil (someone's) hand** (or **palm**). *Informal.* **1.** To bribe. **2.** To give a tip to: *oiled the headwaiter's hand.* [ME < OFr. *oile* < Lat. *oleum,* olive oil < Gk. *elaion* < *elaia,* olive.]
oil beetle *n.* Any of various insects of the subfamily Meloinae that exude an oily yellow substance when disturbed.
oil·bird (oil′bûrd′) *n.* The guacharo.
oil burner *n.* **1.** A heating unit, furnace, or boiler that burns fuel oil. **2.** A device for spraying fine droplets of oil into an oil-burning heating unit prior to ignition.
oil cake *n.* The solid residue that is left after certain oily seeds, such as cottonseed and linseed, have been pressed free of their oil and that is used after grinding as cattle feed or fertilizer.
oil·can (oil′kăn′) *n.* A can for oil, esp. a can with a spout constructed to release oil drop by drop, as for lubricating machinery.
oil·cloth (oil′klôth′, -klŏth′) *n.* A fabric that is treated with clay, oil, and pigments to make it waterproof.
oil color *n.* A color consisting of pigment ground in oil.
oiled (oild) *adj.* **1.** Treated with oil. **2.** *Slang.* Drunk.
oil·er (oi′lər) *n.* **1.** One that oils machinery and engines. **2.** An oil tanker. **3.** An oilcan. **4.** A well that produces oil. **5.** A ship that burns oil. **6.** *Informal.* An oilskin garment.
oil field *n.* An area with reserves of recoverable petroleum, esp. one with several oil-producing wells.
oil gland *n.* **1.** A gland that secretes oil. **2.** The uropygial gland.
oil of turpentine *n.* Refined turpentine.
oil of vitriol *n.* Sulfuric acid.
oil paint *n.* A paint in which the vehicle is a drying oil.

oil painting *n.* **1.** A painting done in oil colors. **2.** The art or practice of painting with oil colors.

oil palm *n.* **1.** A tall palm tree, *Elaeis guineensis,* native to tropical Africa, having nutlike fruits that yield a commercially valuable oil. **2.** Any of several palms yielding oil.

oil pan *n.* The bottom of the crankcase in an internal-combustion engine, serving as an oil reservoir.

oil·pa·per (oil′pā′pər) *n.* Paper that is soaked in oil to make it transparent and water-resistant.

oil sand *n.* **1.** A stratum or rock formation containing oil. **2.** A stratum of porous sandstone from which petroleum can be extracted through drilled wells.

oil shale *n.* A black or dark-brown shale containing hydrocarbons that yield petroleum by distillation.

oil·skin (oil′skĭn′) *n.* **1.** Cloth treated with oil so that it is waterproof. **2.** A garment made of oilskin. **—*modifier:*** *an oilskin poncho.*

oil slick *n.* A thin film of oil on water.

oil·stone (oil′stōn′) *n.* A smooth whetstone lubricated with oil, used for fine sharpening.

oil well *n.* A hole dug or drilled in the earth from which petroleum flows or is pumped.

oil·y (oi′lē) *adj.* **-i·er, -i·est. 1.** Of or pertaining to oil. **2.** Impregnated or smeared with oil; greasy. **3.** Excessively suave in action or behavior; unctuous. **—oil′i·ly** *adv.* **—oil′i·ness** *n.*

oink (oingk) *n.* The natural grunting noise of a hog. [Imit.] **—oink** *v.* **(oinked, oink·ing oinks).**

oint·ment (oint′mənt) *n.* A highly viscous or semisolid substance used on the skin as a cosmetic, an emollient, or a medicament; salve. [ME *oinement* < OFr. *oignement* < Lat. *unguentum* < *unguere,* to anoint.]

O·jib·wa (ō-jĭb′wā′, -wə) also **O·jib·way** (-wā′) *n., pl.* **Ojibwa** or **-was** also **Ojibway** or **-ways. 1. a.** A tribe of North American Indians inhabiting regions of the United States and Canada around Lake Superior. **b.** A member of the Ojibwa. **2.** The Algonquian language of the Ojibwa. [Ojibwa *Očipwee.*]

O.K. or **OK** or **o·kay** (ō-kā′) *Informal.* —*n., pl.* **O.K.'s** or **OK's** or **okays.** Approval; agreement: *got her supervisor's O.K. before taking a day off.* —*tr.v.* **O.K.'d, O.K.'ing, O.K.'s** or **OK'd, OK'ing, OK's** or **o·kayed, o·kay·ing, o·kays.** To approve of or agree to; authorize. —*interj.* Used to express approval or agreement. [Prob. abbreviation of *oll korrect,* slang respelling of *all correct.*] **—O.K.** *adj. & adv.*

o·ka·pi (ō-kä′pē) *n., pl.* **okapi** or **-pis.** A ruminant forest mammal, *Okapia johnstoni,* related to the giraffe but smaller and having a short neck, found in the Congo region in Africa. [Perh. of Mbuba orig.]

o·kay (ō-kā′) *n., v., & interj.* Variant of **O.K.**

O·kie (ō′kē) *n. Slang.* A migrant farm worker, esp. one from Oklahoma in the 1930's. [Shortening and alteration of *Oklahoma.*]

o·kra (ō′krə) *n.* **1.** A tall tropical and semitropical plant, *Hibiscus esculentus,* having edible, mucilaginous green pods. **2.** The edible pods of the okra plant, used in soups and as a vegetable. **3.** Gumbo (sense 2). [Twi *nkruma.*]

Ok·to·ber·fest (ŏk-tō′bər-fĕst′) *n.* A festival held in autumn that usually features the consumption of beer. [G. : *Oktober,* October + *Fest,* festival.]

-ol[1] *suff.* An alcohol or a phenol: *glycerol.* [< ALCOHOL.]

-ol[2] *suff.* Variant of **-ole.**

old (ōld) *adj.* **-er, -est. 1. a.** Having lived or existed for a relatively long time; far advanced in years or life. **b.** Relatively advanced in age. **2.** Made long ago; in existence for many years: *an old book.* **3.** Of or pertaining to a long life or to persons who have had a long life: *a ripe old age.* **4.** Having or exhibiting the physical characteristics of age: *a prematurely old face.* **5.** Having or exhibiting the wisdom of age; mature: *a child that is old for her years.* **6.** Having lived for a specified amount of time: *She was twelve years old.* **7. a.** Belonging to a remote or former period in history; ancient: *old fossils.* **b.** Belonging to or being of an earlier time: *his old classmates.* **8.** Often **Old.** Being the earlier or earliest of two or more related objects, stages, versions, or periods: *the Old Testament; Old High German.* **9.** *Geol.* **a.** Having become slower in flow and less vigorous in action. Used of rivers. **b.** Having become simpler in form and of lower relief. Used of land forms. **10.** Exhibiting the effects of time or long use; worn: *an old coat.* **11.** Known through long acquaintance; long familiar: *an old friend.* **12.** Skilled or able through long experience; practiced. **13.** *Informal.* Used as an intensive: *a high old time; any old time.* —*n.* **1.** Former times; yore: *in days of old.* **2.** An individual of a specified age: *a five-year-old.* —See Usage note at **elder.** [ME < OE *eald.*] **—old′ness** *n.*

Synonyms: *old, elderly, aged, venerable, superannuated.* These terms are compared in their application to persons. *Old,* though ostensibly general, often stresses advanced years strongly. *Elderly* specifies the period past late middle age without necessarily implying marked decline. *Aged* emphasizes advanced years and often suggests infirmity. *Venerable* suggests dignity and qualities associated with age that are worthy of great respect. *Superannuated,* in contrast, applies narrowly to the state of being pensioned or retired or, more generally, to one figuratively discarded or outmoded. *Olden, ancient, archaic, obsolete, obsolescent, antique, antiquated,* and *old-fashioned* are terms that are applied principally to inanimate objects and historical associations. *Old* is the general term. *Olden* connotes a bygone age, often with some nostalgia. *Ancient* pertains to the distant past and usually to what no longer exists. *Archaic* similarly specifies a very early, often primitive period but does not always imply the fact of being discarded; archaic language, though not in general use, is preserved for historical value and limited application. *Obsolete* indicates merely the fact of having passed from use, and *obsolescent* the state of becoming obsolete. *Antique* may indicate association with the ancient past; more often it characterizes that which is valued for its membership in a class of things from the more recent past. *Antiquated,* in contrast, indicates that which is discarded as now out-of-date or discredited. *Old-fashioned* pertains more generally to something from the recent past that is no longer in vogue or general use; it does not invariably imply low regard or the fact of having been discarded.

old boy *n. Chiefly Brit.* A graduate of a boys' public school.

Old Bulgarian *n.* Old Church Slavonic.

Old Catholic *n.* A member of an independent religious organization formed by a group of German Roman Catholics who refused to accept the doctrine of papal infallibility proclaimed by the Vatican Council in 1870.

Old Church Slavonic *n.* The literary language of the oldest Slavic manuscripts and the liturgical language of several Eastern churches.

old country *n.* The native country of an immigrant.

Old Danish *n.* The Danish language from the beginning of the 12th to the end of the 14th century.

Old Dutch *n.* The Dutch language from the beginning of the 12th to the middle of the 13th century.

old·en (ōl′dən) *adj.* Old; ancient: *in olden times.* [ME < *old,* old < OE *eald.*]

Old English *n.* **1.** The English language from the middle of the 5th to the beginning of the 12th century. **2.** *Printing.* Black letter.

Old English sheepdog *n.* A sturdy dog of a breed derived from Scottish and Russian ancestors, having a thick, shaggy, bluish-gray and white coat that hangs over the eyes.

old fashioned *n.* A cocktail made of whiskey, bitters, sugar, and fruit.

old-fash·ioned (ōld′făsh′ənd) *adj.* **1.** Of a style or method formerly in vogue; outdated. **2.** Attached to or favoring methods, ideas, or customs of an earlier time: *an old-fashioned girl.*

old fogy also **old fogey** *n.* One who is tiresomely conservative or old-fashioned. [Sc. < obs. *fogey,* invalid soldier.] **—old′fo′gy·ish, old′fo′gey·ish** (ōld′fō′gē-ĭsh) *adj.*

Old French *n.* The French language from the 9th to the early 16th century.

Old Glory *n.* The United States flag.

old gold *n.* A dark yellow, from light olive or olive brown to deep or strong yellow. **—old′-gold′** *adj.*

old guard *n.* Often **Old Guard.** A conservative, often reactionary element of a given class, society, or political group.

old hand *n.* One who is experienced; veteran: *an old hand at politics.*

old hat *adj. Informal.* **1.** Behind the times; old-fashioned. **2.** Trite.

Old High German *n.* High German from the middle of the 9th to the end of the 11th century.

Old Icelandic *n.* Icelandic from the middle of the 12th to the middle of the 16th century.

old·ie (ōl′dē) *n.* Something that is old, esp. a song that was popular in the past.

Old Iranian *n.* Any of the Iranian languages in use before the beginning of the Christian era.

Old Irish *n.* The Irish language from 725 to about 950.

Old Italian *n.* The Italian language until the middle of the 16th century.

old lady *n. Slang.* **1.** One's mother. **2. a.** One's wife **b.** One's girlfriend.

old-line (ōld′līn′) *adj.* **1.** Adhering to conservative or reactionary principles. **2.** Long established; traditional.

old maid *n.* **1.** *Informal.* A woman, esp. an older woman, who is not married; spinster. **2.** *Informal.* A primly fastidious person. **3.** A card game in which the player who holds a designated card at the end is an "old maid." **—old′-maid′ish** *adj.*

old man *n.* **1.** *Slang.* **a.** One's father. **b.** One's husband. **c.** One's boyfriend. **d.** A man in authority. **2.** The southernwood.

old-man-and-wom·an (ōld′măn′ənd-wo͝om′ən) *n.* The houseleek.

old-man cactus (ōld′măn′) *n.* A treelike cactus, *Cephalocereus senilis,* having tufts of long, white hair on the tips of its branches.

old-man's-beard (ōld′mănz-bîrd′) *n.* Any of various plants having parts suggestive of a beard, as virgin's bower and Spanish moss.

old master *n.* **1.** A distinguished European artist of the period from around 1500 to the early 1700's, esp. one of the great painters of this period. **2.** A work created by an old master.

oil well
The first oil well in the United States. Drilled near Titusville, Pennsylvania, in 1859

okapi

okra

Old English sheepdog

old moon *n.* A phase of the waning moon; the last quarter.
Old Nick *n.* The devil; Satan.
Old Norse *n.* **1.** The North Germanic languages until the middle of the 14th century. **2. a.** Old Icelandic. **b.** Old Norwegian.
Old North French *n.* The dialects of Old French spoken in northern France, esp. in Normandy and Picardy.
Old Norwegian *n.* The Norwegian language from the middle of the 12th to the end of the 14th century.
Old Persian *n.* An Old Iranian language attested in cuneiform inscriptions dating from the 6th to the 5th centuries B.C.
Old Portuguese *n.* The Portuguese language until the middle of the 16th century.
Old Provençal *n.* Provencal before the middle of the 16th century.
Old Prussian *n.* The Baltic language of Eastern Prussia that became extinct in the 18th century.
old rose *n.* A dark pink to grayish or moderate red.
Old Russian *n.* The Russian language as used in documents from the middle of the 11th to the end of the 16th century.
Old Saxon *n.* The Low German language of the continental Saxons until the 12th century.
old school *n.* A group committed to traditional ideas or practices.
old-school tie (ōld′sko͞ol′) *n.* **1.** A necktie that has the colors of an English public school. **2.** The upper-middle-class solidarity and system of mutual assistance attributed to graduates of the English public schools. **3.** A narrow, clannish attitude among members of a clique.
Old Spanish *n.* Spanish before the middle of the 16th century.
old squaw *n.* A marine duck, *Clangula hyemalis,* that is black with a white breast and is found in Arctic and North Temperate regions.
old·ster (ōld′stər) *n. Informal.* An old person.
Old Stone Age *n.* The Paleolithic age.
old style *n.* **1.** A style of printing type originating in the 18th century and characterized by slight contrast between light and heavy strokes and by slanting serifs. **2. Old Style.** The method of reckoning dates according to the Julian calendar.
Old Swedish *n.* Swedish from the early 13th to the late 14th century.
Old Testament *n.* **1.** The first of the two main divisions of the Christian Bible, containing the Hebrew Scriptures. **2.** The covenant of God with Israel as distinguished in Christianity from the dispensation of Christ constituting the New Testament. [ME, transl. of LLat. *Vetus Testamentum,* transl. of Gk. *Palaia Diathēkē.*]
old-time (ōld′tīm′) *adj.* Of, pertaining to, or characteristic of a time in the past.
old-tim·er (ōld′tī′mər) *n. Informal.* **1. a.** A veteran. **b.** An oldster. **2.** Something that is very old or antiquated.
Old Welsh *n.* The Welsh language before the 12th century.
old·wife (ōld′wīf′) *n.* **1.** The old squaw. **2.** Any of several fishes such as the alewife and the menhaden.
old wives' tale *n.* A bit of superstitious folklore.
Old World *n.* The Eastern Hemisphere, esp. Europe.
old-world (ōld′wûrld′) *adj.* **1.** Antique and quaint. **2.** Often **Old-World.** Of, native to, or pertaining to the Old World.
o·lé (ō-lā′) *interj.* Used to express excited approval. —*n.* A cry of olé. [Sp. < Ar. *wa-llāh,* by God!, used as an expression of admiration.]
ole– *pref.* Variant of **oleo-.**
–ole or **–ol** *suff.* **1.** A usually heterocyclic chemical compound containing a five-membered ring: *pyrrole.* **2.** A chemical compound, esp. an ether, that does not contain hydroxyl: *eucalyptol.* [< Lat. *oleum,* oil. —see OLEO-.]
o·le·a (ō′lē-ə) *n.* A plural of **oleum.**
o·le·ag·i·nous (ō′lē-ăj′ə-nəs) *adj.* **1.** Of or pertaining to oil. **2.** Oily; unctuous. [Fr. *oléagineux* < Lat. *oleaginus,* of the olive tree < *olea,* olive tree < Gk. *elaia.*] **—o′le·ag′i·nous·ly** *adv.* **—o′le·ag′i·nous·ness** *n.*

oleander

o·le·an·der (ō′lē-ăn′dər, ō′lē-ăn′dər) *n.* A poisonous evergreen shrub of the genus *Nerium,* found in warm climates, esp. *N. oleander,* having fragrant white, rose, or purple flowers. [Med. Lat.]
o·le·an·do·my·cin (ō′lē-ăn′də-mī′sĭn) *n.* An antibiotic, $C_{35}H_{61}NO_{12}$, produced by *Streptomyces antibioticus,* that is mainly effective against Gram-positive microorganisms. [OLEAND(ER) + -MYCIN.]
o·le·as·ter (ō′lē-ăs′tər) *n.* A small Eurasian tree, *Elaeagnus angustifolia,* having oblong silvery leaves, fragrant greenish flowers, and olivelike fruit. [Lat. < *olea,* olive tree < Gk. *elaia.*]
o·le·ate (ō′lē-āt′) *n.* An ester or salt of oleic acid.
o·lec·ra·non (ō-lĕk′rə-nŏn′) *n.* The large point on the upper end of the ulna that projects behind the elbow joint and forms the point of the elbow. [Gk. *ōlekranon* : *ōlenē,* elbow + *kranion,* head.] **—o·lec′ra·nal** (-nəl), **o′le·cra′ni·al** (ō′-lĭ-krā′nē-əl), **o′le·cra′ni·an** (-nē-ən) *adj.*
o·le·fin (ō′lə-fĭn) *n.* Any of a class of unsaturated hydrocarbons, such as ethylene, having the general formula C_nH_{2n} and characterized by relatively great chemical activity. [Fr. *(gaz) oléfiant,* oil-forming (gas) < Lat. *oleum,* oil < Gk. *elaion,* olive oil < *elaia,* olive.] **—o′le·fin′ic** (-fĭn′ĭk) *adj.*
o·le·ic (ō-lē′ĭk) *adj. Chem.* Of, pertaining to, or derived from oil.
oleic acid *n.* An oily liquid, $CH_3(CH_2)_7CH$:-$CH(CH_2)_7COOH$, occurring in animal and vegetable oils.
o·le·in (ō′lē-ĭn) also **o·le·ine** (-ĭn, -ēn′) *n.* A yellow oily liquid, $(C_{17}H_{33}COO)_3C_3H_5$, occurring naturally in most fats and oils, including olive oil, of which it is the major constituent, and used as a textile lubricant.
o·le·o (ō′lē-ō′) *n.* Margarine.
oleo– or **ole–** *pref.* Oil: *oleoresin.* [Fr. *oléo-* < Lat. *oleo-* < *oleum,* oil < Gk. *elaion* < *elaia,* olive.]
o·le·o·graph (ō′lē-ə-grăf′) *n.* **1.** A chromolithograph printed in imitation of an oil painting. **2.** The lacelike pattern that is formed by a drop of oil on the surface of water. **—o′le·og′ra·pher** (-ŏg′rə-fər) *n.* **—o′le·o·graph′ic** *adj.* **—o′le·og′ra·phy** *n.*
o·le·o·mar·ga·rine (ō′lē-ō-mär′jə-rĭn, -rēn′) *n.* Margarine.
o·le·o·res·in (ō′lē-ō-rĕz′ĭn) *n.* **1.** A naturally occurring mixture of an oil and resin, such as the exudate from pine trees. **2.** An oil-resin mixture extracted from plants, such as capsicum. **—o′le·o·res′in·ous** *adj.*
o·le·um (ō′lē-əm) *n., pl.* **-le·a** (-lē-ə) or **-le·ums.** A corrosive solution of sulfur trioxide in sulfuric acid. [Lat., olive oil. —see OIL.]
ol·fac·tion (ŏl-făk′shən, ōl-) *n.* **1.** The sense of smell. **2.** The act of smelling. [< Lat. *olfacere,* to smell. —see OLFACTORY.]
ol·fac·tom·e·ter (ŏl′făk-tŏm′ĭ-tər, ōl′-) *n.* An instrument for measuring the acuity of the sense of smell. [OLFACT(ION) + -METER.] **—ol·fac′to·met′ric** (-tə-mĕt′rĭk) *adj.* **—ol′fac·tom′e·try** *n.*
ol·fac·to·ry (ŏl-făk′tə-rē, -trē, ōl-) *adj.* Of, pertaining to, or contributing to the sense of smell. [< Lat. *olfacere,* to smell : *olēre,* to smell + *facere,* to do.]
olfactory lobe *n.* A projection of the lower anterior portion of each cerebral hemisphere.
olfactory nerve *n.* Either of two bundles of nerve fibers, one on each side of the nasal cavity, that conduct chemical indications of smell.
ol·fac·tron·ics (ŏl′făk-trŏn′ĭks, ōl′-) *n. (used with a sing. verb).* The scientific study of the detection and identification of odors. [Blend of OLFACTION and ELECTRONICS.]
olig– *pref.* Variant of **oligo-.**
ol·i·garch (ŏl′ĭ-gärk′, ō′lĭ-) *n.* A member of an oligarchy. [Gk. *oligarkhēs* : *oligos,* few + *arkhein,* to rule.]
ol·i·gar·chy (ŏl′ĭ-gär′kē, ō′lĭ-) *n., pl.* **-chies. 1. a.** Government by a few, esp. by a small faction of persons or families. **b.** Those making up such a faction. **2.** A state governed by oligarchy. **—ol′i·gar′chic, ol′i·gar′chi·cal** *adj.*
oligo– or **olig–** *pref.* Few: *oligosaccharide.* [Gk. < *oligos,* few, little.]
Ol·i·go·cene (ŏl′ĭ-gō-sēn′, ō′lĭ-) *Geol.* —*adj.* Of or designating the geologic time and deposits of the epoch in the Tertiary period of the Cenozoic era that extended from the Eocene to the Miocene. —*n.* **1.** The Oligocene epoch. **2.** The deposits of the Oligocene epoch.
ol·i·go·chaete (ŏl′ĭ-gō-kēt′, ō′lĭ-) *n.* Any of various worms of the class Oligochaeta, including the earthworms. [NLat. *Oligochaeta,* class name : OLIGO- + Gk. *khaitē,* long hair.] **—ol′i·go·chae′tous** (-kē′təs) *adj.*
ol·i·go·clase (ŏl′ĭ-gō-klās′, -klāz′, ō′lĭ-) *n.* Plagioclase.
ol·i·go·cy·the·mi·a also **ol·i·go·cy·thae·mi·a** (ŏl′-ĭ-gō-sī-thē′mē-ə, ō′lĭ-) *n.* Deficiency of the cellular elements of the blood, causing a form of anemia. [OLIGO- + CYT(O)- + -(H)EMIA.]
ol·i·go·gene (ŏl′ĭ-gō-jēn′, ō′lĭ-) *n.* A gene that determines major qualitative hereditary characteristics. **—ol′i·go·gen′ic** (-jĕn′ĭk) *adj.*
o·lig·o·mer (ə-lĭg′ə-mər) *n.* A polymer that consists of two, three, or four monomers. **—o·lig′o·mer′ic** (-mĕr′ĭk) *adj.* **—o·lig′o·mer′i·za′tion** *n.*
ol·i·goph·a·gous (ŏl′ĭ-gŏf′ə-gəs, ō′lĭ-) *adj.* Feeding on a limited variety of food substances. **—ol′i·goph′a·gy** (-jē) *n.*
ol·i·go·phre·ni·a (ŏl′ĭ-gō-frē′nē-ə, ō′lĭ-) *n.* Mental deficiency. **—ol′i·go·phren′ic** (-frĕn′ĭk) *adj.*
ol·i·gop·o·ly (ŏl′ĭ-gŏp′ə-lē, ō′lĭ-) *n., pl.* **-lies.** *Econ.* A market condition in which sellers are so few that the actions of any one of them will materially affect price and hence have a measurable impact upon competitors. [OLIGO- + (MONO)POLY.] **—ol′i·gop′o·lis′tic** (-lĭs′tĭk) *adj.*
ol·i·gop·so·ny (ŏl′ĭ-gŏp′sə-nē, ō′lĭ-) *n., pl.* **-nies.** A market condition in which purchasers are so few that the actions of any one of them can materially affect price and hence the costs that competitors must pay. [OLIG(O)- + (MON)OPSONY.] **—ol′i·gop′so·nis′tic** (-nĭs′tĭk) *adj.*
ol·i·go·sac·cha·ride (ŏl′ĭ-gō-săk′ə-rīd′, ō′lĭ-) *n.* A sugar consisting of a small number of monosaccharide units.
ol·i·go·tro·phic (ŏl′ĭ-gō-trō′fĭk, -trŏf′ĭk, ō′lĭ-) *adj.* Lacking in plant nutrients and having an abundance of dissolved oxygen throughout. Used of a pond or lake.
o·li·o (ō′lē-ō′) *n., pl.* **-os. 1.** A heavily spiced stew of meat, vegetables, and chickpeas. **2. a.** A mixture or medley; hodgepodge. **b.** A collection of various artistic or literary works or musical pieces; miscellany. **3.** Vaudeville or musical entertainment presented between the acts of a burlesque or minstrel show. [Alteration of Sp. *olla,* pot. —see OLLA.]
ol·i·va·ceous (ŏl′ə-vā′shəs) *adj.* Olive-green.

ol·i·var·y (ŏl′ə-vĕr′ē) *adj.* **1.** Shaped like an olive. **2.** *Anat.* Of, pertaining to, or designating one of the two oval bodies of nervous tissue found on either side of the medulla oblongata. [Lat. *olivarius,* of olives < *oliva,* olive < Gk. *elaia.*]

ol·ive (ŏl′ĭv) *n.* **1.** An Old World semitropical evergreen tree, *Olea europaea,* having an edible fruit, yellow flowers, and leathery leaves. **2.** The small ovoid fruit of the olive tree, an important food and a source of oil. **3.** A yellow green of low to medium lightness and low to moderate saturation. [ME < Lat. *oliva* < Gk. *elaia.*] **—ol′ive** *adj.*

olive branch *n.* **1.** A branch of an olive tree regarded as an emblem of peace. **2.** An offer of peace.

olive drab *n.* **1.** A grayish olive to dark olive brown or olive gray. **2. a.** Cloth of an olive-drab color, often used in military uniforms. **b.** Also **olive drabs.** A uniform made from olive-drab cloth. **—ol′ive-drab′** *adj.*

olive green *n.* A green yellow hue of low to medium lightness and low to moderate saturation. **—ol′ive-green′** *adj.*

o·liv·e·nite (ō-lĭv′ə-nīt′) *n.* A basic arsenate of copper, $Cu_2(AsO_4)(OH)$, brown, olive green, or gray in color, found in copper deposits. [G. *Olivenite* : *olive,* olive + *-it,* -ite.]

olive oil *n.* Oil pressed from olives, used in salad dressings, for cooking, as an ingredient of soaps, and as an emollient.

ol·i·vine (ŏl′ə-vēn′) *n.* A mineral silicate of iron and magnesium, principally Fe_2SiO_4 and Mg_2SiO_4, found in igneous and metamorphic rocks and used as a structural material in refractories and in cements. [G. *Olivin* < *olive,* olive, so called because of its color.] **—ol′i·vin′ic** (-vĭn′ĭk), **ol′i·vi·nit′ic** (-və-nĭt′ĭk) *adj.*

o·lla (ŏl′ə, oi′ə) *n.* **1.** An earthenware pot or jar with a wide mouth. **2.** An olla podrida. [Sp. < OSp. < Lat., var. of *aulla,* jar.]

olla po·dri·da (pə-drē′də) *n.* **1.** A stew of highly seasoned meat and vegetables. **2.** An assorted mixture; miscellany. [Sp.: *olla,* olla + *podrida,* rotten < Lat. *putridus* < *putrere,* to rot < *puter,* decaying.]

ol·o·gy (ŏl′ə-jē) *n., pl.* **-gies.** *Informal.* A branch of learning: "*amphibology, parisology, and other ologies*" (Evan Esar). [< -LOGY.]

O·lym·pi·ad (ō-lĭm′pē-ăd′) *n.* **1.** The interval of four years between celebrations of the Olympic games, by which the ancient Greeks reckoned dates. **2.** A celebration of the modern Olympic games. [ME *olimpias* < Lat. *Olympics* < Gk. *Olumpias* < *Olumpios,* Olympian < *Olumpas,* Olympus, a mountain in Greece and fabled abode of the gods.]

O·lym·pi·an (ō-lĭm′pē-ən) *adj.* **1.** Of or pertaining to the greater gods of the ancient Greek pantheon, whose abode was Olympus. **2. a.** Majestic in manner. **b.** Superior to mundane affairs. **3.** Of or pertaining to the Olympic games. *—n.* **1.** One of the 12 major gods inhabiting Olympus. **2.** A contestant in the ancient Olympic games.

Olympian games *pl.n.* Olympic games (sense 1).

O·lym·pic (ō-lĭm′pĭk) *adj.* Of or pertaining to the Olympic games.

Olympic games *pl.n.* **1.** In ancient Greece, a Pan-Hellenic festival of athletic games and contests of choral poetry and dance, first celebrated in 776 B.C. and held every four years until A.D. 393 on the plain of Olympia in honor of the Olympian Zeus. **2.** A modern international revival of athletic contests patterned after the Olympic games and held every four years.

O·lym·pics (ō-lĭm′pĭks) *pl.n.* Olympic games (sense 2).

-oma *suff.* Tumor: *lipoma.* [NLat. < Gk. *-ōma,* n. suffix.]

O·ma·ha (ō′mə-hô′, -hä′) *n., pl.* **Omaha** or **-has. 1.** A tribe of Siouan-speaking Indians of northeastern Nebraska. **2.** A member of the Omaha. [Dhegia *umăhă.*] **—O′ma·ha′** *adj.*

o·ma·sum (ō-mā′səm) *n., pl.* **-sa** (-sə). The third stomach of a ruminant animal, located between the abomasum and the reticulum. [Lat., bullock's tripe, prob. of Celtic orig.]

om·bre also **om·ber** (ŏm′bər) *n.* A card game, played by three players with 40 cards, that was popular in Europe during the 17th and 18th centuries. [Sp. *hombre,* man < Lat. *homo.*]

om·buds·man (ŏm′bŭdz′mən, -bədz-, -bo͝odz′-) *n.* **1.** A government official, esp. in Scandinavian countries, who investigates citizens' complaints against the government or its functionaries. **2.** One that investigates complaints, as from consumers, reports findings, and assists in achieving fair settlements. [Norw. < ON *umboðsmaðr,* steward, manager: *um,* about + *boð,* command + *maðr,* man.] **—om′buds′-man·ship′** *n.*

-ome *suff.* Mass: *biome.* [NLat. *-oma* < Gk. *-ōma,* n. suffix.]

o·me·ga (ō-mĕg′ə, ō-mē′gə, ō-mā′-) *n.* **1.** The 24th and final letter of the Greek alphabet. See table at **alphabet. 2.** The end; last. **3.** *Physics.* A subatomic particle in the baryon family having a mass 3,276 times that of the electron, a negative electric charge, and a mean lifetime of 1.5×10^{-10} second. **4.** An omega meson. [Gk. *ō mega,* large *o.*]

omega meson *n.* An unstable meson having a mass 1,532 times that of the electron.

om·e·let also **om·e·lette** (ŏm′ə-lĭt, ŏm′lĭt) *n.* A dish consisting of beaten eggs cooked and folded, often around a filling. [Fr. *omelette* < OFr. *amlette,* alteration of *alumette,* var. of *alumelle* < *lemelle,* knife blade < Lat. *lamella,* dim. of *lamina,* thin plate.]

o·men (ō′mən) *n.* **1.** A phenomenon supposed to portend good or evil; prophetic sign. **2.** Prognostication; portent: *birds of ill omen.* *—tr.v.* **o·mened, o·men·ing, o·mens.** To be an omen of; portend. [Lat.]

o·men·tum (ō-mĕn′təm) *n., pl.* **-ta** (-tə) or **-tums.** *Anat.* One of two pairs of peritoneal folds: **a.** The greater omentum, consisting of a double fold of peritoneum, passes from the stomach to the transverse colon. **b.** The lesser omentum is doubled to join the lesser curve of the stomach and duodenum to the liver. [Lat.] **—o·men′tal** *adj.*

o·mer (ō′mər) *n.* An ancient Hebrew dry measure roughly equal to 3.7 quarts. [Heb. *'ōmer.*]

om·i·cron (ŏm′ĭ-krŏn′, ō′mĭ-) *n.* The 15th letter of the Greek alphabet. See table at **alphabet.** [Gk. *o mikron,* small o.]

om·i·nous (ŏm′ə-nəs) *adj.* **1.** Of or being an omen, esp. an evil one. **2.** Menacing; threatening: *ominous black clouds.* [Lat. *ominosus* < *omen,* omen.] **—om′i·nous·ly** *adv.* **—om′i·nous·ness** *n.*

o·mis·si·ble (ō-mĭs′ə-bəl) *adj.* **1.** Capable of being omitted. **2.** Suitable for omission. [< Lat. *omittere, omiss-,* to disregard. —see OMIT.]

o·mis·sion (ō-mĭsh′ən) *n.* **1.** The act or an instance of omitting. **2.** The state of being omitted. **3.** Something that is omitted or neglected. [ME *omissioun* < OFr. < LLat. *omissio* < Lat. *omittere,* to disregard.]

o·mis·sive (ō-mĭs′ĭv) *adj.* Characterized by omission.

o·mit (ō-mĭt′) *tr.v.* **o·mit·ted, o·mit·ting, o·mits. 1.** To fail to include; leave out. **2. a.** To pass over; neglect. **b.** To fail to do; forbear. [ME *omitten* < Lat. *omittere* : *ob,* away + *mittere,* to send.]

om·ma·tid·i·um (ŏm′ə-tĭd′ē-əm) *n., pl.* **-i·a** (-ē-ə). One of the elements, resembling a single simplified eye, that make up the compound eye of arthropods. [NLat., dim. of Gk. *omma,* eye.] **—om′ma·tid′i·al** *adj.*

om·mat·o·phore (ō-măt′ə-fôr′, -fōr′) *n.* A movable stalk ending with an eye, as found in snails. [Gk. *omma, ommat-* + -PHORE.] **—om′ma·toph′o·rous** (ŏm′ə-tŏf′ər-əs) *adj.*

omni- *pref.* All: *omnidirectional.* [Lat. < *omnis,* all.]

om·ni·bus (ŏm′nĭ-bŭs′) *n.* **1.** A bus (sense 1). **2.** A printed anthology of the works of one author or of writings on related subjects. *—adj.* Including or covering many things or classes: *an omnibus law.* [Fr. < Lat., for all < *omnis,* all.]

om·ni·di·rec·tion·al (ŏm′nē-dĭ-rĕk′shə-nəl, -dī-) *adj.* Capable of transmitting or receiving signals in all directions.

omnidirectional radio range *n.* Omnirange.

om·ni·far·i·ous (ŏm′nĭ-fâr′ē-əs) *adj.* Of all kinds: *omnifarious knowledge.* [LLat. *omnifarius* < *omnis,* all.] **—om′ni·far′i·ous·ness** *n.*

om·nip·o·tent (ŏm-nĭp′ə-tənt) *adj.* Having unlimited or universal power, authority, or force; all-powerful. *—n.* **Omnipotent.** God. [ME < OFr. < Lat. *omnipotens* : *omnis,* all + *potens,* pr.part. of *posse,* to be able.] **—om·nip′o·tence, om·nip′o·ten·cy** *n.* **—om·nip′o·tent·ly** *adv.*

om·ni·pres·ence (ŏm′nĭ-prĕz′əns) *n.* The fact of being present everywhere. [Med. Lat. *omnipraesentia* < *omnipraesens,* omnipresent : Lat. *omnis,* all + Lat. *praesens,* pr.part. of *praeese,* to be present. —see PRESENT[1].] **—om′ni·pres′ent** *adj.*

om·ni·range (ŏm′nĭ-rānj′, -nē-) *n.* A radio network that provides complete bearing information for aircraft.

om·nis·cient (ŏm-nĭsh′ənt) *adj.* Having total knowledge; knowing everything. *—n.* **Omniscient.** God. [NLat. *omnisciens, omniscient-* < Med. Lat. *omniscientia* : Lat. *omnis,* all + Lat. *scientia,* knowledge < *scire,* to know.] **—om·nis′cience, om·nis′cien·cy** *n.* **—om·nis′cient·ly** *adv.*

om·ni·um-gath·er·um (ŏm′nē-əm-găth′ər-əm) *n.* A miscellaneous collection; hodgepodge. [Lat. *omnis,* all + GATHER.]

om·ni·vore (ŏm′nə-vôr′, -vōr′) *n.* An omnivorous animal. [< Lat. *omnivorus,* omnivorous.]

om·niv·o·rous (ŏm-nĭv′ər-əs) *adj.* **1.** *Zool.* Eating both animal and vegetable substances. **2.** Taking in everything available, as with the mind: *an omnivorous reader.* [Lat. *omnivorus* : *omnis,* all + *vorare,* to swallow up.] **—om·niv′o·rous·ly** *adv.* **—om·niv′o·rous·ness** *n.*

om·pha·los (ŏm′fə-lŏs′, -ləs) *n., pl.* **-li** (-lī′). **1.** *Anat.* The navel. **2.** A central part; focal point. [Gk.]

on (ŏn, ôn) *prep.* **1.** Used to indicate: **a.** Position above and in contact with: *The vase is on the table.* **b.** Contact with any surface, regardless of position: *a picture on the wall.* **c.** Location at or along: *a house on the beach.* **d.** Proximity: *a town on the border.* **e.** Attachment to or suspension from: *beads on a string.* **2.** Used to indicate: **a.** Motion or direction toward a position: *He threw the books on the floor.* **b.** Motion toward, against, or onto: *jump on the table; the march on Washington.* **3.** Used to indicate: **a.** Occurrence at a given time: *on July third.* **b.** The particular occasion or circumstance: *On entering the room, she saw him.* **c.** The exact moment or point of: *on the hour.* **4.** Used to indicate: **a.** The object affected by actual, perceptible action: *The spotlight fell on the actress.* **b.** The agent or agency of a specified action: *cut his foot on the broken glass; talked on the telephone.* **c.** The object affected by a figurative action: *Have pity on them.* **d.** The object of an action directed, tending, or moving against it: *an attack on the fortress.* **5.** Used to indicate a source or basis; *live on bread and water; make a profit on gambling.* **6.** Used to indicate: **a.** The state or process of: *on leave; on fire.* **b.** The purpose of: *travel on business.* **c.** A

olive

Olympic games
The opening of the 1980 Olympic games in Lake Placid, New York

means of conveyance: *ride on a train.* **d.** Availability by means of: *beer on tap; a nurse on call.* **e.** Association with: *a doctor on the hospital staff.* **f.** Addition or repetition: *error on error.* **7. a.** Concerning; about: *a book on astronomy.* **b.** To the disadvantage of: *We have some evidence on him.* **8.** In one's possession; with: *I haven't a cent on me.* **9.** At the expense of: *drinks on the house.* —*adv.* **1.** In or into a position of being attached to or covering something: *Put your clothes on.* **2.** In or into a position or condition of being supported by or in contact with something: *Put the coffee on.* **3.** In the direction of: *He looked on while the ship docked.* **4. a.** Toward or at a point lying ahead in space or time; forward: *The army moved on to the next town.* **b.** At or to a more distant point in time or space: *I'll do it later on.* **5.** In a continuous course: *He worked on quietly.* **6. a.** In or into performance or operation: *Turn on the radio.* **b.** In progress or action; in a state of activity: *The show goes on.* **7.** In or at the present position: *stay on; hang on.* **8.** In a condition of being scheduled for or decided upon: *There is a party on tonight.* —*adj.* **1.** In operation: *The television is on.* **2.** Engaged in a given function or activity, such as a vocal or dramatic role. **3. a.** Planned; intended: *has nothing on for this weekend.* **b.** Happening; taking place: *The parade is on.* —*idioms.* **and so on.** And like the preceding; and so forth. **be on to.** *Informal.* To be aware of or have information about. **on and off.** Intermittently. **on and on.** Without stopping; continuously. [ME < OE.]

Usage: To indicate motion toward a position, both *on* and *onto* can be used: *The cat jumped on the table. The cat jumped onto the table. Onto* is more specific, however, in indicating that the motion was initiated from an outside point. *He wandered onto the battlefield* means that he began his wandering at some point off the battlefield. *He wandered on the battlefield* may mean that his wandering began on the battlefield. • In constructions where *on* is an adverb attached to a verb, it should not be joined with *to* to form a single word *onto: move on to* (not *onto*) *new subjects; hold on to* (not *onto*) *our gains.* • In their uses to indicate spatial relations, *on* and *upon* are often interchangeable: *It was resting on* (or *upon*) *two supports. She took it on* (or *upon*) *herself to finish the project. We saw a finch light on* (or *upon*) *a bough.* To indicate a relation between two things, however, instead of between an action and an end point, *upon* cannot always be used: *Hand me the book on* (not *upon*) *the table. It was the only town on* (not *upon*) *the main line.* Similarly, *upon* cannot always be used in place of *on* when the relation is not spatial: *He wrote a book on* (not *upon*) *alchemy. She will be here on* (not *upon*) *Tuesday.*

–on¹ *suff.* **1. a.** Subatomic particle: *baryon.* **b.** Unit; quantum: *photon.* **2.** Basic hereditary unit: *codon.* [< ION.]

–on² *suff.* Inert gas: *radon.* [NLat. < ARGON.]

–on³ *suff.* A chemical compound that is not a ketone or a compound that contains oxygen in a carbonyl group: *parathion.* [Alteration of -ONE.]

on·a·ger (ŏn'ə-jər) *n.* **1.** A wild ass, *Equus hemionus onager,* of central Asia. **2.** An ancient and medieval stone-propelling siege engine. [ME < Lat. < Gk. *onagros* : *onos,* ass + *agros,* field.]

o·nan·ism (ō'nə-nĭz'əm) *n.* **1.** Masturbation. **2.** Coitus interruptus. **3.** Self-gratification. [After *Onan,* son of Judah.] —**o'nan·ist** *n.* —**o'nan·is'tic** *adj.*

on·board (ŏn-bôrd', -bōrd', ôn-) *adj.* Carried aboard a vehicle.

once (wŭns) *adv.* **1.** One time only: *once a day.* **2.** At one time in the past; formerly. **3.** At any time; ever: *Once known, never forgotten.* **4.** By one degree of relationship: *my first cousin once removed.* —*n.* A single occurrence; one time: *You can go this once.* —*conj.* As soon as; if ever; when: *Once he goes, we can clean up.* —*adj.* Having been formerly; former: *the once capital of the nation.* [ME *ones* < *on,* one < OE *ān.*]

once-o·ver (wŭns'ō'vər) *n. Informal.* A quick but comprehensive survey or performance: *Let's give this memorandum a quick once-over.*

on·co·gen·e·sis (ŏn'kō-jĕn'ĭ-sĭs, ŏng'-) *n.* The process of tumor formation and development. [Gk. *onkos,* mass, tumor + -GENESIS.]

on·co·gen·ic (ŏn'kō-jĕn'ĭk, ŏng'-) *adj.* Tending to cause the formation of tumors. —**on'co·ge·nic'i·ty** (-jə-nĭs'ĭ-tē) *n.*

on·col·o·gy (ŏn-kŏl'ə-jē) *n.* The scientific study of tumors. [Gk. *onkos,* mass + -LOGY.] —**on'co·log'i·cal** (-kə-lŏj'ĭ-kəl), **on'co·log'ic** *adj.* —**on·col'o·gist** *n.*

on·com·ing (ŏn'kŭm'ĭng, ôn'-) *adj.* Coming nearer; approaching: *the oncoming storm.* —*n.* An approach; advance.

one (wŭn) *adj.* **1.** Being a single entity, unit, object, or being: *one dog.* **2.** Characterized by unity; undivided: *They spoke with one voice.* **3.** Occurring or existing as something indefinite, as in time or position: *He will come one day.* **4. a.** Of the same kind or quality: *two animals of one species.* **b.** Forming a single entity of two or more components: *three chemicals combined into one solution.* **5. a.** Being one in particular: *late one evening.* **b.** Used as an intensifier of the quality specified: *That is one fine dog.* **6.** Being the only person of a specified or implied kind: *the one man I could marry.* —*n.* **1. a.** A single person or thing; unit. **b.** The cardinal number, represented by the symbol 1, designating the first such unit in a series. **2.** A one-dollar bill. —*pron.* **1.** An indefinitely specified individual. **2.** An unspecified individual member of a group or class: *one of the Elizabethans.* —*idioms.* **at one.** In accord or unity. **one and all.** Everyone. **one by one.** Individually and in succession. [ME *on* < OE *ān*; akin to G. *ein,* Lat. *unus,* Gk. *oinē* (ace on dice), Skt. *eka.*]

Usage: Constructions employing *one* often raise questions whether verbs should be singular or plural. One such construction is exemplified by this sentence: *One in every ten men was found deficient.* Although the plural *are* is sometimes used in such a sentence, a large majority of the Usage Panel feels that in formal writing a singular verb should be used, in agreement with the subject *one.* • A more controversial construction involves *one of those who* or a variant: *He is one of those men who always complain about their wives. The defeat was one of the most costly blows that have been inflicted on our forces.* A majority of the Panel feels that only the plural verbs (as used above) are possible, since the antecedents of *who* and *that* are plural nouns (*men* and *blows*). In other examples, however, *one* may be construed as the subject of the verb in the relative clause: *He is the only one of those men who has* (not *have*) *taken the test.* • The construction *more than one* is always singular, despite the fact that logic would seem to require a plural verb: *More than one of the boys has failed the exam.* Conversely, *fewer than two* is always plural: *Fewer than two have failed.*

–one *suff.* **1.** A ketone or a related oxygen-containing compound: *acetone.* **2.** A chemical compound containing oxygen, esp. in a carbonyl group: *lactone.* [Alteration of -ENE.]

one-base hit (wŭn'bās') *n. Baseball.* A base hit by which a batter can reach first base safely.

one-di·men·sion·al (wŭn'dĭ-mĕn'shə-nəl) *adj.* Lacking depth; superficial.

one-hand·ed (wŭn'hăn'dĭd) *adj.* **1.** Having or making use of only one hand. **2.** Calling for or brought about by the use of only one hand.

one-horse (wŭn'hôrs') *adj.* **1.** Drawn by or using only one horse: *a one-horse carriage.* **2.** Very small or insignificant: *a one-horse town.*

O·nei·da (ō-nī'də) *n., pl.* **Oneida** or **-das. 1. a.** One of the five tribes belonging to the league of the Iroquois. **b.** A member of this tribe. **2.** The Iroquoian language of the Oneida. [Iroquois *onẽyóte'.*]

o·nei·ric (ō-nī'rĭk) *adj.* Of or pertaining to dreams. [< Gk. *oneiros,* dream.]

o·nei·ro·man·cy (ō-nī'rə-măn'sē) *n.* Divination by dreams. [Gk. *oneiros,* dream + -MANCY.] —**o·nei'ro·man'cer** *n.*

one-man (wŭn'măn') *adj.* **1.** Consisting of one individual: *a one-man team.* **2.** Featuring the work of one individual: *a one-man show.* **3.** Designed for or restricted to one individual: *a one-man sled.*

one·ness (wŭn'nĭs) *n.* **1.** The quality or state of being one; singleness: *the infinite oneness of God.* **2.** Singularity; uniqueness. **3.** The condition of being undivided; wholeness. **4.** Identity of character (of several things): *the disagreeable oneness of roadside landscapes.* **5.** Unison; agreement: *oneness of mind and purpose.*

one-night stand (wŭn'nīt') *n.* **1. a.** A performance by a traveling musical or dramatic performer or group in one place on one night only. **b.** The place at which such a performance is given. **2.** *Informal.* A sexual encounter that is limited to only one occasion.

one-on-one (wŭn'ŏn-wŭn') *adj. Sports.* **1.** Man-to-man (sense 2). **2.** Directly encountering or confronting another person.

one-piece (wŭn'pēs') *adj.* Consisting of or fashioned in a single whole piece: *a one-piece swimsuit.*

on·er·ous (ŏn'ər-əs, ō'nər-) *adj.* **1.** Troublesome or oppressive; burdensome. **2.** *Law.* Entailing obligations that exceed any advantage. [ME < OFr. *oneros* < Lat. *onerosus* < *onus,* burden.] —**on'er·ous·ly** *adv.* —**on'er·ous·ness** *n.*

one·self (wŭn-sĕlf') also **one's self** (wŭn sĕlf', wŭnz sĕlf') *pron.* **1.** One's own self: *have faith in oneself.* **2.** One's normal or healthy condition or state: *come to oneself.*

one-shot (wŭn'shŏt') *adj.* **1.** Being effective after only one attempt: *looked for a one-shot solution to the problem.* **2.** Being the only one and unlikely to be repeated: *the funding was a one-shot deal.*

one-sid·ed (wŭn'-sī'dĭd) *adj.* **1.** Favoring one side or group; partial; biased: *a one-sided view.* **2.** Larger or more developed on one side: *a one-sided pattern.* **3.** Existing or occurring on one side only. —**one'sid'ed·ly** *adv.* —**one'-sid'ed·ness** *n.*

one-step (wŭn'stĕp') *n.* A ballroom dance consisting of a series of unbroken rapid steps in 2/4 time. —*intr.v.* **-stepped, -step·ping, -steps.** To dance the one-step.

one·time (wŭn'tīm') *adj.* Former: *a onetime boxing champion.*

Usage: *Onetime* (single word) means "former." *One-time* (hyphenated) means "only once." Thus, *a onetime champion* is a former champion; *a one-time champion* was champion only once.

one-time (wŭn'tīm') *adj.* Only once: *a one-time winner in 1970.*

one-to-one (wŭn'tə-wŭn') *adj.* **1. a.** Allowing the pairing of each member of a class uniquely with a member of another class. **b.** *Math.* Pertaining to a correspondence that assigns to each member of one set a unique member of another set. **2.** Characterized by proportional amounts on both sides.

one-track (wŭn′trăk′) *adj.* Obsessively limited to a single idea or purpose: *a one-track mind.*

one-up (wŭn′ŭp′) *tr.v.* **-upped, -up·ping, -ups.** *Informal.* To practice one-upmanship on.

one-up·man·ship (wŭn-ŭp′mən-shĭp′) *n. Informal.* The practice and technique of keeping one step ahead of a competitor.

one-way (wŭn′wā′) *adj.* **1.** Moving, or permitting movement, in one direction only: *a one-way street.* **2.** Providing for travel in one direction only: *a one-way ticket.*

on·go·ing (ŏn′gō-ĭng, ôn′-) *adj.* **1.** Currently taking place: *ongoing festival.* **2.** Progressing or evolving.

on·ion (ŭn′yən) *n.* **1.** A bulbous plant, *Allium cepa,* cultivated worldwide as a vegetable. **2.** The rounded, edible bulb of the onion plant, composed of tight, concentric layers, and having a pungent odor and taste. [ME *oinyon* < OFr. *oignon* < Lat. *unio.*]

on·ion·skin (ŭn′yən-skĭn′) *n.* A thin, strong, translucent paper.

on-line (ŏn′līn′, ôn′-) *adj.* **1.** *Computer Sci.* Under the control of a central computer, as in a manufacturing process or experiment. **2.** In progress; ongoing: *on-line editorial projects.*

on·look·er (ŏn′lo͝ok′ər, ôn′-) *n.* One that looks on; spectator.

on·ly (ōn′lē) *adj.* **1.** Alone in kind or class; sole. **2.** Standing alone by reason of superiority or excellence. —*adv.* **1.** Without anyone or anything else; alone: *Only three survived.* **2. a.** At the very least: *If you would only come home. The story was only too true.* **b.** Merely: *I only work here.* **3.** Exclusively; solely: *facts known only to us.* **4. a.** In the last analysis or final outcome: *actions that will only make things worse.* **b.** With the final result; nevertheless: *received a raise only to be laid off.* **5. a.** As recently as: *called me only last month.* **b.** In the immediate past: *only just saw her.* —*conj.* **1.** Were it not that; except. **2. a.** With the restriction that; but: *You may go, only be careful.* **b.** However; and yet: *The merchandise is well made, only we can't use it.* [ME < OE *ānlīc* : *ān,* one + *-līc,* -ly.]

Usage: When used as an adverb, *only* should be placed with care to avoid ambiguity. Generally this means having *only* adjoin the word or words that it limits. Variation in the placement of *only* can change the meaning of the sentence, as the following examples show: *Dictators respect only force, they are not moved by words. Dictators only respect force, they do not worship it. She picked up the receiver only when he entered, not before. She only picked up the receiver when he entered, she didn't dial the number.* Though strict grammarians insist that the rule for placement of *only* should always be followed, there are occasions when placement of *only* earlier in the sentence seems much more natural. In the following example, *only* is placed according to the rule: *The committee can make its decision by Friday of next week only if it receives a copy of the latest report.* Placement of *only* earlier in the sentence, immediately after *can,* would serve the rhetorical function of warning the reader that a condition on the statement follows. *Only* is often used as a conjunction equivalent to *but* in the sense of "were it not that": *They would have come, only the automobile broke down.* This example is considered unacceptable in writing by a large majority of the Usage Panel. See also Usage note at **not**.

on·o·mas·tic (ŏn′ə-măs′tĭk) *adj.* Of or pertaining to a name or names. [Gk. *onomastikos* < *onomazein,* to name < *onoma,* name.]

on·o·mas·tics (ŏn′ə-măs′tĭks) *n.* (*used with a sing. or pl. verb*). **1. a.** The study of the origins and forms of words, esp. those used in specialized fields. **b.** The study of the origins and forms of proper names. **2.** The system that underlies the formation and use of words, esp. specialized vocabulary and proper names.

on·o·mat·o·poe·ia (ŏn′ə-măt′ə-pē′ə) *n.* The formation or use of words, such as *buzz* or *cuckoo,* that imitate what they denote. [LLat. < Gk. *onomotopoiia* < *onomatopoiein,* to coin names: *onoma,* name + *poiein,* to make.] —**on′o·mat′o·poe′ic, on′o·mat′o·po·et′ic** (-pō-ĕt′ĭk) *adj.* —**on′o·mat′o·po·et′i·cal·ly** *adv.*

On·on·da·ga (ŏn′ən-dô′gə, -dä′gə) *n., pl.* **Onondaga** or **-gas. 1.** A tribe of Indians, formerly inhabiting upper New York state and Ontario. **2.** A member of the Onondaga. **3.** The Iroquoian language of the Onondaga. [Iroquois *onōtáge′,* the name of their chief village.] —**On′on·da′gan** *adj.*

on·rush (ŏn′rŭsh′, ôn′-) *n.* **1.** A forward rush or flow. **2.** An assault (sense 1). —**on′rush′ing** *adj.*

on·set (ŏn′sĕt′, ôn′-) *n.* **1.** An onslaught; assault. **2.** A beginning; start: *the onset of a cold.*

on·shore (ŏn′shôr′, -shōr′, ôn′-) *adj.* **1.** Moving or directed toward the shore: *an onshore gale.* **2.** Located or operating on the shore: *an onshore patrol.* **3.** Domestic; *onshore oil drilling.* —*adv.* Toward the shore: *The wind shifted onshore.*

on·slaught (ŏn′slôt′, ôn′-) *n.* A violent attack. [Obs. *anslaight* < MDu. *aenslag,* a striking at : *aan,* on + *slag,* a striking.]

on-stage (ŏn-stāj′, ôn-) *adj.* Located or occurring in the area of a stage visible to the audience. —*adv.* In the area of a stage visible to the audience.

ont– *pref.* Variant of **onto-**.

-ont *suff.* Cell; organism: *biont.* [< Gk. *ōn, ont-,* pr.part. of *einai,* to be.]

on-the-job (ŏn′thə-jŏb′, ôn′-) *adj.* Of or relating to something learned, experienced, or done, often under supervision, while employed at a job: *on-the-job training.*

on-the-scene (ŏn′thə-sēn′, ôn′-) *adj.* Being at the site of an action or event: *an on-the-scene reporter.*

on·to (ŏn′to͞o′, -tə, ôn′-) *prep.* **1.** On top of; to a position on; upon: *The dog jumped onto the chair.* **2.** *Informal.* Aware or cognizant of; informed about: *I'm onto your schemes.* —*adj. Math.* Of, relating to, or being a mapping such that every element of the set referred to is the image of an element in another. —See Usage note at **on**.

onion

onto– or **ont–** *pref.* **1.** Existence; being: *ontology.* **2.** Organism: *ontogeny.* [LGk. < Gk. *ōn,* pr.part. of *einai,* to be.]

on·tog·e·ny (ŏn-tŏj′ə-nē) *n., pl.* **-nies.** The course of development of an individual organism. —**on′to·ge·net′ic** (ŏn′tō-jə-nĕt′ĭk) *adj.* —**on′to·ge·net′i·cal·ly** *adv.*

on·tol·o·gy (ŏn-tŏl′ə-jē) *n.* The branch of philosophy that deals with being. —**on′to·log′i·cal** (ŏn′tə-lŏj′ĭ-kəl) *adj.* —**on′to·log′i·cal·ly** *adv.* —**on·tol′o·gist** *n.*

o·nus (ō′nəs) *n.* **1.** Something that is burdensome, esp. a disagreeable responsibility or necessity. **2. a.** A stigma. **b.** Blame. [Lat., burden.]

on·ward (ŏn′wərd, ôn′-) *adj.* Moving or tending forward. —*adv.* Also **on·wards** (-wərdz). In a direction or toward a position that is ahead in space or time; forward.

-onym *suff.* Word; name: *acronym.* [Lat. *-onymum* < Gk. *-ōnumon* < *onuma,* name.]

-onymy *suff.* A set of names; the study of a kind of names: *toponymy.* [Gk. *-ōnumia* < *-ōnumos,* having a specified kind of name < *onuma,* name.]

on·yx (ŏn′ĭks) *n.* A kind of chalcedony that occurs in bands of different colors and that is used as a gemstone, esp. in cameos and intaglios. [ME *oniche* < OFr. < Lat. *onyx* < Gk.]

oo– *pref.* Egg; ovum: *oophyte.* [Gk. *ōio-* < *ōion,* egg.]

o·o·cyst (ō′ə-sĭst′) *n.* The encysted form of some sporozoan zygotes.

o·o·cyte (ō′ə-sīt′) *n.* **1.** A cell, derived from an oogonium, that undergoes meiosis and produces an ovum. **2.** A female gamete in certain protozoa.

oo·dles (o͞od′lz) *pl.n. Informal.* A great amount; a lot. [Orig. unknown.]

o·o·ga·mete (ō′ə-găm′ēt′, -gə-mēt′) *n.* A female gamete of sporozoans.

o·og·a·mous (ō-ŏg′ə-məs) *adj.* **1.** Characterized by small male gametes and large, less mobile female gametes. **2.** Pertaining to reproduction by oogamy.

o·og·a·my (ō-ŏg′ə-mē) *n., pl.* **-mies.** The fertilization of oogamous gametes.

o·o·gen·e·sis (ō′ə-jĕn′ə-sĭs) *n.* The enlargement and meiotic division of an oogonium that produces an ovum. —**o′o·ge·net′ic** (-jə-nĕt′ĭk) *adj.*

o·o·go·ni·um (ō′ə-gō′nē-əm) *n., pl.* **-ni·a** (-nē-ə) or **-ni·ums. 1.** *Biol.* One of the cells that form the bulk of ovarian tissue. **2.** *Bot.* A female reproductive structure in certain fungi, containing oospores. [OO- + NLat. *gonium,* cell < Gk. *gonos,* seed.]

o·o·lite (ō′ə-līt′) also **o·o·lith** (-lĭth′) *n.* **1.** A small, round, calcareous grain found, for example, in limestones and dolomites. **2.** Rock, usually limestone, composed of oolites. —**o′o·lit′ic** (ō′ə-lĭt′ĭk) *adj.*

o·ol·o·gy (ō-ŏl′ə-jē) *n.* The branch of ornithology that deals with birds' eggs. —**o′o·log′ic** (ō′ə-lŏj′ĭk), **o′o·log′i·cal** *adj.* —**o′o·log′i·cal·ly** *adv.* —**o·ol′o·gist** *n.*

oo·long (o͞o′lông′, -lŏng′) *n.* A dark Chinese tea that is partly fermented before drying. [Chin. (Mandarin) *wu[1] long[2]* : *wu[1],* black + *long[2],* dragon.]

oo·mi·ak (o͞o′mē-ăk′) *n.* Variant of **umiak**.

oomph (o͞omf) *n. Slang.* **1.** Irrepressible enthusiasm; spirited vigor. **2.** Sex appeal. [Orig. unknown.]

o·o·pho·rec·to·my (ō′ə-fə-rĕk′tə-mē) *n., pl.* **-mies.** The surgical removal of one or both ovaries.

o·o·pho·ri·tis (ō′ə-fə-rī′tĭs) *n.* Ovarian inflammation.

o·o·phyte (ō′ə-fīt′) *n.* The stage in plants undergoing metagenesis during which the sexual organs are developed. —**o′o·phyt′ic** (-fĭt′ĭk) *adj.*

o·o·sperm (ō′ə-spûrm′) *n.* A fertilized ovum.

o·o·sphere (ō′ə-sfîr′) *n.* A nonmotile female gamete or egg, formed in an oogonium and ready for fertilization.

o·o·spore (ō′ə-spôr′, -spōr′) *n.* A thick-walled spore, developed from a fertilized oosphere or by parthenogenesis. —**o′o·spor′ic** (-spôr′ĭk, -spōr′-), **o·os′po·rous** (ō-ŏs′pər-əs, ō′ə-spôr′əs, -spōr′-) *adj.*

o·o·the·ca (ō′ə-thē′kə) *n., pl.* **-cae** (-sē). The capsule or egg case of certain insects and mollusks. —**o′o·the′cal** *adj.*

o·o·tid (ō′ə-tĭd′) *n.* One of the four sections into which a mature ovum divides. [OO- + (SPERMA)TID.]

ooze[1] (o͞oz) *v.* **oozed, ooz·ing, ooz·es.** —*intr.* **1.** To flow or leak out slowly, as through small openings. **2.** To disappear or ebb slowly: *His courage oozed away.* **3.** To progress slowly but steadily. **4.** To emit or exude moisture. —*tr.* **1.** To give off; exude. **2.** To emit or radiate in pervasive abundance: *She oozes confidence.* —*n.* **1.** The act of oozing. **2.** Something that oozes. **3.** An infusion of vegetable matter, as from oak bark, used in tanning. [ME *wosen* < *wose,* juice < OE *wōs.*]

ooze² (o͞oz) *n.* **1.** Soft, thin mud. **2.** The layer of mudlike sediment covering the floor of oceans and lakes, composed chiefly of remains of microscopic sea animals. **3.** Muddy ground; bog. [ME *wose* < OE *wāse.*]

ooz·y¹ (o͞o′zē) *adj.* **-i·er, -i·est.** Slowly leaking; dripping. **—ooz′i·ness** *n.*

ooz·y² (o͞o′zē) *adj.* **-i·er, -i·est.** Of, resembling, or containing ooze: *an oozy riverbed.* **—ooz′i·ly** *adv.* **—ooz′i·ness** *n.*

o·pac·i·fi·er (ō-păs′ə-fī′ər) *n.* A chemical agent added to a material to make it opaque.

o·pac·i·ty (ō-păs′ĭ-tē) *n., pl.* **-ties. 1.** The quality or state of being opaque. **2.** Something that is opaque. **3.** Obscurity; impenetrability. [Fr. *opacité* < Lat. *opacitas* < Lat. *opacus,* dark.]

opah

o·pah (ō′pə) *n.* A large, vividly colored marine fish, *Lampris regius,* found in all oceans and having edible red flesh. [Of West African orig.]

o·pal (ō′pəl) *n.* A translucent mineral of hydrated silicon dioxide, often used as a gem. [Lat. *opalus* < Gk. *opallios* < Skt. *upalaḥ* < *upara-,* lower < *upa,* below.] **—o′pal·ine′** (ō′pə-līn′, -lēn′) *adj.*

o·pal·esce (ō′pə-lĕs′) *intr.v.* **-esced, -esc·ing, -esc·es.** To emit or show an iridescent shimmer of colors. [Back-formation < OPALESCENCE.]

o·pal·es·cence (ō′pə-lĕs′əns) *n.* The quality or state of exhibiting a milky iridescence like that of an opal. **—o′pal·es′cent** *adj.*

o·paque (ō-pāk′) *adj.* **1. a.** Impervious to the passage of light. **b.** Not reflecting light; without luster: *an opaque finish.* **2.** Impenetrable by a form of radiant energy other than visible light: *a chemical solution opaque to x rays.* **3. a.** Obtuse; dense. **b.** So obscure as to be unintelligible. —*n.* Something that is opaque, esp. an opaque pigment used to darken parts of a photographic print or negative. [Partly < ME *opake,* and partly < OFr. *opaque,* both < Lat. *opacus,* dark.] **—o·paque′ly** *adv.* **—o·paque′ness** *n.*

op art (ŏp) *n.* Optical art.

op-ed page (ŏp-ĕd′) *n.* A newspaper section, usually located opposite the editorial page, that features articles expressing personal viewpoints. [OP(POSITE) + ED(ITORIAL).]

o·pen (ō′pən) *adj.* **1. a.** Affording unobstructed entrance and exit; not shut or closed. **b.** Affording unobstructed passage or view. **2.** Having no protecting or concealing cover: *an open fire; an open car.* **3.** Not sealed, tied, or folded: *an open package.* **4. a.** Having interspersed gaps, spaces, or intervals: *open columns; an open weave.* **b.** Distributed sparsely: *open population.* **5. a.** Accessible to all; unrestricted: *an open meeting.* **b.** Free from limitations, boundaries, or restrictions: *open housing laws.* **c.** Enterable by registered voters regardless of political affiliation: *an open primary.* **d.** Lacking effective commercial regulation: *an open town.* **e.** Not legally controlled: *open drug trafficking.* **6.** Susceptible; vulnerable: *open to attack; open to question.* **7. a.** Available; obtainable: *The job is still open.* **b.** Available for use: *an open account; the only course open to us.* **8.** Ready to transact business: *The store is open.* **9. a.** Unengaged; unoccupied: *an hour open for emergency cases.* **b.** Not yet decided; subject to further thought: *an open question.* **10. a.** Characterized by lack of pretense; candid: *an open nature.* **b.** Free of prejudice; receptive to new ideas and arguments: *an open mind.* **11. a.** Widely spaced or leaded. Used of printed matter. **b.** Having constituent elements separated by space in printing or writing: *"French window" is an open compound.* **12.** *Mus.* **a.** Not stopped by a finger. Used of a string or hole of an instrument. **b.** Produced by an unstopped string or hole, or without the use of slides, valves, or keys: *an open note on a trumpet.* **c.** Played without a mute: *an open wind instrument.* **13. a.** Articulated with the tongue in a low position: *The vowel sound in the word "far" is open.* **b.** Ending in a vowel or diphthong: *an open syllable.* **14.** Having the lips parted: *stood with her mouth wide open.* **15.** Designating a method of punctuation in which commas and other pause marks are used sparingly. **16.** *Elect.* Containing a gap across which electricity cannot pass. **17.** *Math.* **a.** Of, relating to, or being an interval containing neither of its end points. **b.** Of, relating to, or being a set such that every point or at least one neighborhood of every point in the set is within the set. —*v.* **o·pened, o·pen·ing, o·pens.** —*tr.* **1.** To cause to become open; release from a closed or fastened position. **2.** To remove obstructions from; clear. **3.** To make or force an opening in: *open an old wound.* **4.** To form spaces or gaps between: *soldiers opening ranks.* **5. a.** To remove the cover or lid from; expose. **b.** To remove the wrapping from; undo. **6.** To unfold so that the inner parts are displayed; spread out: *open a newspaper.* **7. a.** To begin; commence: *open a meeting.* **b.** To commence the operation of: *open a new business.* **c.** To begin (the action in a game of cards) by making the first bid, by placing a first bet, or by playing the first lead. **8.** To permit the use of; make available. **9.** To make more responsive or understanding: *opened her heart to their pleas.* **10.** To reveal the secrets of; bare. **11.** *Law.* To recall (an order or judgment) for a re-examination of its merits. —*intr.* **1.** To become open or unfastened. **2.** To draw apart; separate: *The wound opened under pressure.* **3.** To spread apart; unfold. **4.** To come into view; become revealed: *The plain opened before us.* **5.** To become receptive or understanding. **6. a.** To begin; commence: *We opened with a list of complaints.* **b.** To begin business or operation. **c.** To give the first public performance. **d.** To make a bid, bet, or lead in starting a game of cards. **7.** To give access or view: *The windows open onto a lawn.* **—phrasal verb. open up. 1.** To spread out and come into view: *The road opens up five miles ahead.* **2.** To begin firing: *artillery opening up.* **3.** *Informal.* To speak or act freely and unrestrainedly. **4.** To make an opening in by cutting: *The surgeon opened up the patient.* **5.** To make available: *open up new markets.* —*n.* **1. a.** An unobstructed area of land or water. **b.** The outdoors: *lived in the open.* **2.** An undisguised or unconcealed state: *bring a matter out into the open.* **3.** A tournament or contest in which both professional and amateur players may participate. [ME < OE.] **—o′pen·ly** *adv.* **—o′pen·ness** *n.*

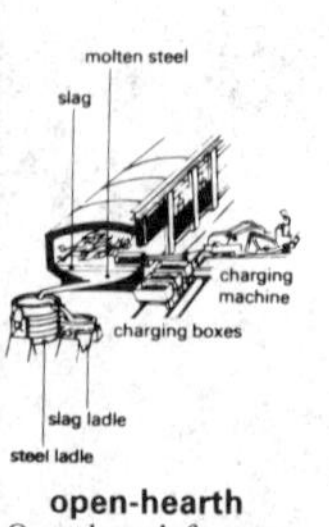

open-hearth
Open-hearth furnace

open admission *n.* Open enrollment.

o·pen-air (ō′pən-âr′) *adj.* Outdoor: *an open-air concert.*

o·pen-and-shut (ō′pən-ən-shŭt′) *adj.* Presenting no difficulties; easily settled: *an open-and-shut case.*

open chain *n. Chem.* A linear arrangement of atoms that is the basic form of various carbon and silicon compounds.

open-circuit (ō′pən-sûr′kĭt) *adj.* Of, relating to, or being an open transmission circuit.

open city *n.* A city that is declared demilitarized during a war, thus, under international law, gaining immunity from attack.

open classroom *n.* A system of elementary education in which open-ended discussion is encouraged and instruction and activities are informal, flexible, and individualized.

open door *n.* **1.** An unhindered opportunity for progress; free access. **2.** Admission to all on equal terms. **3.** A policy whereby a nation opens its foreign and internal trade to nationals of all other nations on equal terms. **—o′pen-door′** (ō′pən-dôr′, -dōr) *adj.*

o·pen-end (ō′pən-ĕnd′) *adj.* **1.** Having no definite limit of duration or amount: *an open-end contract.* **2.** Permitting the borrowing of additional funds under existing terms: *an open-end mortgage.*

o·pen-end·ed (ō′pən-ĕn′dĭd) *adj.* **1.** Not restrained by definite limits, restrictions, or structure. **2.** Open or adaptable to change. **3.** Inconclusive or indefinite. **4.** Allowing for a spontaneous, unstructured response: *an open-ended question.*

open-end investment company *n.* A mutual fund.

open enrollment *n.* A policy that permits enrollment of a student in a college or university without regard to academic qualifications.

o·pen·er (ō′pə-nər) *n.* **1.** One that opens, esp. a device used to cut open cans or pry up bottle caps. **2. a.** The player who starts the betting in a card game. **b. openers.** Cards of sufficient value for the holder to open the betting legally in a card game. **3. a.** The first act in a theatrical variety show. **b.** The first game in a series. **4. openers.** A beginning; start: *For openers, let's try the soup.*

o·pen-eyed (ō′pən-īd′) *adj.* **1.** Having the eyes wide open as in surprise. **2.** Watchful and alert.

o·pen-faced (ō′pən-fāst′) *adj.* **1.** Having an undisguised or sincere face or expression. **2.** Having one side uncovered: *an open-faced sandwich.*

o·pen·hand·ed (ō′pən-hăn′dĭd) *adj.* Giving freely; generous. **—o′pen·hand′ed·ly** *adv.* **—o′pen·hand′ed·ness** *n.*

o·pen-heart (ō′pən-härt′) *adj.* Of, pertaining to, or designating surgery in which the heart is open while its normal functions in the circulatory system are assumed by external apparatus.

o·pen·heart·ed (ō′pən-här′tĭd) *adj.* **1.** Frank. **2.** Kindly. **—o′pen·heart′ed·ly** *adv.* **—o′pen·heart′ed·ness** *n.*

o·pen-hearth (ō′pən-härth′) *adj.* **1.** Designating a reverberatory furnace used in the production of high-quality steel. **2.** Describing steel produced in an open-hearth furnace.

open house *n.* An event in which hospitality is extended to all.

o·pen·ing (ō′pə-nĭng) *n.* **1.** An open space serving as a passage or gap. **2.** A breach or aperture. **3.** The first period or stage. **4.** The first occasion: *the opening of a new play.* **5.** A specific pattern or series of beginning moves in certain games, esp. chess. **6.** A favorable opportunity or chance. **7.** An unfilled job or position; vacancy. **8.** The act of becoming open or being made to open.

open letter *n.* A letter on a subject of general interest, addressed to an individual but intended for general readership.

open loop *n. Computer Sci.* A computer control system that is not self-correcting.

open marriage *n.* A marriage in which the spouses agree to permit sexual activity outside the marriage.

o·pen-mind·ed (ō′pən-mīn′dĭd) *adj.* Receptive to new ideas or to reason; free from prejudice or bias. **—o′pen-mind′ed·ly** *adv.* **—o′pen-mind′ed·ness** *n.*

o·pen-mouthed (ō′pən-mouthd′, -moutht′) *adj.* **1.** Having an open mouth. **2.** Affected with great amazement or wonder. **3.** Vociferous; clamorous. **—o'pen-mouth'ed·ly** *adv.* **—o'pen-mouth'ed·ness** *n.*

open season *n.* **1.** A period when hunting is permitted for a specified game animal. **2.** *Informal.* A situation in which criticism is unconstrained: *After the exposé, it was open season on government officials.*

open secret *n.* Something ostensibly secret but in fact generally known.

open sentence *n.* A mathematical expression that contains at least one unknown quantity and that becomes true or false when a test value is substituted for the unknown.

open ses·a·me (sĕs'ə-mē) *n.* A seemingly unfailing means of gaining admittance or attaining success. [From the magical formula used by Ali Baba in the *Arabian Nights* to open the door of the robbers' cave.]

open shop *n.* A business establishment or factory in which workers are employed without regard to union membership.

open stock *n.* **1.** A form of merchandising in which replacements for articles sold in sets are carried at all times. **2.** Open stock collectively.

o·pen·work (ō'pən-wûrk') *n.* Ornamental or structural work containing numerous openings, usually in set patterns.

op·er·a¹ (ŏp'ər-ə, ŏp'rə) *n.* **1.** A form of theatrical presentation in which a dramatic performance is set to music. **2.** A work of opera. **3.** A theater designed primarily for operas. [Ital. < Lat., work produced < *opus,* work.]

o·pe·ra² (ō'pər-ə, ŏp'ər-ə) *n.* A plural of **opus.**

op·er·a·ble (ŏp'ər-ə-bəl, ŏp'rə-) *adj.* **1.** Capable of being used or operated: *an operable machine.* **2.** Capable of being put into practice; practicable: *an operable plan.* **3.** Capable of being treated by surgical operation: *an operable stage of cancer.* **—op'er·a·bil'i·ty** *n.* **—op'er·a·bly** *adv.*

opera bouffe (bo͞of) *n.* A comic often satirical opera. [Fr. < Ital. *opera buffa.*]

o·pe·ra buf·fa (ŏp'ər-ə bo͞o'fə, ŏp'rə) also **o·pé·ra bouffe** (ô-pā-rä bo͞of') *n.* A comic opera, esp. one of the 18th century. [Ital., comic opera.]

o·pé·ra co·mique (ŏp'ər-ə kŏ-mēk', ŏp'rə, ô-pā-rä kô-mēk') *n.* Opera that, in addition to musical solos and ensembles, has dialogue that is spoken rather than sung. [Fr., comic opera.]

opera glasses *pl.n.* Small, low-powered binoculars for use esp. at a theatrical performance.

op·er·a·go·er (ŏp'ər-ə-gō'ər, ŏp'rə-) *n.* A person who attends operas, esp. frequently.

opera hat *n.* A collapsible top hat.

opera house *n.* A theater designed chiefly for operas.

op·er·and (ŏp'ər-ənd) *n.* A quantity on which a mathematical operation is performed. [< Lat. *operandum,* neuter gerund. of *operari,* to operate < *opus,* work.]

op·er·ant (ŏp'ər-ənt) *adj.* **1.** Operating to produce effects; effective. **2.** *Psychol.* Characterizing a response or behavior elicited by an environment rather than by a specific stimulus and identified by its consequences in the environment. —*n.* **1.** One that operates. **2.** *Psychol.* An element of operant behavior. [Lat. *operans, operant-,* pr.part. of *operari,* to work < *opus,* work.] **—op'er·ant·ly** *adv.*

op·er·ate (ŏp'ə-rāt') *v.* **-at·ed, -at·ing, -ates.** —*intr.* **1.** To function effectively; work. **2.** To bring about a desired or proper effect. **3.** To perform surgery. **4.** To carry on a military or naval action or campaign. —*tr.* **1.** To run or control the functioning of: *operate a machine.* **2.** To conduct the affairs of; manage: *operate a business.* **3.** To perform surgery upon. **4.** To bring about or effect. [Lat. *operari, operat-* < *opus,* work.]

op·er·at·ic (ŏp'ə-răt'ĭk) *adj.* **1.** Of, related to, or typical of the opera: *an operatic aria.* **2.** Histrionic or implausible in a way considered characteristic of grand opera. [< OPERA.] **—op'er·at'i·cal·ly** *adv.*

op·er·at·ics (ŏp'ə-răt'ĭks) *n.* *(used with a sing. or pl. verb).* Histrionics.

operating system *n.* Computer software designed to complement the hardware of a specific data processing system.

op·er·a·tion (ŏp'ə-rā'shən) *n.* **1.** An act, process, or way of operating. **2.** The condition of being operative or functioning: *in operation.* **3.** A process or series of acts performed to effect a certain purpose or result: *the operation of preparing a meal for 20.* **4.** A process or method of productive activity. **5.** *Med.* A procedure for remedying an injury, ailment, or dysfunction in a living body, esp. one performed with instruments. **6.** *Math.* A process or action, such as addition, substitution, transposition, or differentiation, performed in a specified sequence and in accordance with specific rules of procedure. **7.** *Computer Sci.* An action resulting from a single computer instruction. **8. a.** A military or naval action, campaign, or project. **b. operations.** The office at an airport or air base where pilots file flight plans and where flying from the field is controlled. **c. operations.** The agency of a business organization that carries out planning and operating functions on an executive level: *a vice president of operations.* [ME *operacioun* < OFr. *operacion* < Lat. *operatio* < *operari,* to work < *opus,* work.]

op·er·a·tion·al (ŏp'ə-rā'shə-nəl) *adj.* **1.** Of or pertaining to an operation or a series of operations. **2.** Of, for, or engaged in military operations. **3. a.** Serviced and declared fit for proper functioning: *an operational aircraft.* **b.** Observed to be properly functioning: *an operational computer.* **—op'er·a'tion·al·ly** *adv.*

op·er·a·tion·al·ism (ŏp'ə-rā'shə-nə-lĭz'əm) *n.* *Philos.* The doctrine that the meanings of concepts are derived from or given by specific operations. **—op'er·a'tion·al·ist** *n.*

operations research *n.* Mathematical or scientific analysis of the systematic efficiency and performance of manpower, machinery, equipment, and policies used in a governmental, military, or commercial operation.

op·er·a·tive (ŏp'ər-ə-tĭv, ŏp'rə-, -ə-rā'tĭv) *adj.* **1.** Exerting influence or force. **2.** Functioning effectively; efficient. **3.** Being in force, in effect, or in operation: *operative regulations.* **4.** Engaged in, concerned with, or related to physical or mechanical activity. **5.** Of, pertaining to, or resulting from a surgical operation. —*n.* **1.** A skilled worker, esp. in industry. **2. a.** A secret or trusted agent. **b.** A private detective. **—op'er·a·tive·ly** *adv.*

op·er·a·tor (ŏp'ə-rā'tər) *n.* **1.** One that operates a mechanical device: *a telephone operator.* **2.** The owner or director of a business or industrial concern. **3.** A dealer in stocks or commodities. **4.** A symbol, such as a plus sign, that represents a mathematical operation. **5.** *Informal.* A shrewd and sometimes unscrupulous person who gets what he wants by devious means. **6.** A chromosomal sequence that is the region of an operon responsible for regulation of structural genes.

o·per·cu·la (ō-pûr'kyə-lə) *n.* A plural of **operculum.**

o·per·cu·late (ō-pûr'kyə-lĭt) also **o·per·cu·lat·ed** (-lā'tĭd) *adj.* Having an operculum.

o·per·cu·lum (ō-pûr'kyə-ləm) *n., pl.* **-la** (-lə) or **-lums. 1.** *Biol.* A lid or flap covering an aperture, such as the gill cover in some fishes or the horny shell cover in snails or other mollusks. **2.** *Anat.* A flap or lid, such as the layer of tissue over an erupting tooth. [Lat., lid < *operire,* to cover.] **—o·per'cu·lar** *adj.* **—o·per'cu·lar·ly** *adv.*

op·e·ret·ta (ŏp'ə-rĕt'ə) *n.* A theatrical production that has many of the musical elements of opera, but is lighter and more popular in subject and style and contains spoken dialogue. [Ital., dim. of *opera,* opera.]

op·er·on (ŏp'ə-rŏn') *n.* A cluster of genes in physical proximity to one another, together with a distant gene that regulates the cluster's production of a set of different but functionally related enzymes. [< OPERATE.]

op·er·ose (ŏp'ə-rōs') *adj.* **1.** Involving great labor; laborious. **2.** Industrious; diligent. [Lat. *operosus* < *opus,* work.] **—op'er·ose'ly** *adv.* **—op'er·ose'ness** *n.*

o·phid·i·an (ō-fĭd'ē-ən) *adj.* Of or pertaining to limbless reptiles or snakes; snakelike. —*n.* A member of the suborder Ophidia or Serpentes; snake. [< NLat. *Ophidia,* suborder name < Gk. *ophis,* snake.]

oph·i·ol·o·gy (ŏf'ē-ŏl'ə-jē, ō'fē-) *n.* A branch of herpetology dealing with snakes. [Gk. *ophis,* snake + -LOGY.] **—oph'i·o·log'i·cal** (-ə-lŏj'ĭ-kəl) *adj.* **—oph'i·ol'o·gist** *n.*

o·phi·oph·a·gous (ō'fē-ŏf'ə-gəs) *adj.* Feeding on snakes.

oph·ite (ŏf'īt', ō'fīt') *n.* **1.** A mottled-green rock composed of diabase. **2.** Any of various green rocks, such as serpentine. [Lat. *ophites* < Gk. *ophitēs (lithos),* serpentlike (stone) < *ophis,* serpent.]

o·phit·ic (ō-fĭt'ĭk, ō-fĭt'-) *adj.* **1.** Of or pertaining to ophite. **2.** Having a texture composed of plagioclase crystals in a matrix of pyroxene crystals.

Oph·i·u·chus (ŏf'ē-yo͞o'kəs, ō'fē-) *n.* A constellation in the equatorial region near Hercules and Scorpius. [Lat. < Gk. *ophioukhos* : *ophis,* serpent + *ekhein,* to hold.]

ophthalm– *pref.* Variant of **ophthalmo-.**

oph·thal·mia (ŏf-thăl'mē-ə, ŏp-) also **oph·thal·mi·tis** (ŏf'thəl-mī'tĭs, -thăl-) *n.* Inflammation of the eye, esp. of the conjunctiva. [ME *obtalmia* < LLat. *ophthalmia* < Gk. < *ophthalmos,* eye.]

oph·thal·mic (ŏf-thăl'mĭk, ŏp-) *adj.* **1.** Of or pertaining to the eye; ocular. **2.** Having ophthalmia. [Gk. *ophthalmikos* < *ophthalmos,* eye.]

oph·thal·mi·tis (ŏf'thəl-mī'tĭs, -thăl-) *n.* Variant of **ophthalmia.**

ophthalmo– or **ophthalm–** *pref.* Eye; eyeball: *ophthalmoscope.* [Gk. < *ophthalmos,* eye.]

oph·thal·mol·o·gist (ŏf'thăl-mŏl'ə-jĭst, ŏf'thəl-, ŏp'-) *n.* A physician specializing in the treatment of diseases of the eye.

oph·thal·mol·o·gy (ŏf'thăl-mŏl'ə-jē, ŏf'thəl-, ŏp'-) *n.* The medical specialty encompassing the anatomy, functions, pathology, and treatment of the eye. **—oph·thal'mo·log'ic** (-thăl'mə-lŏj'ĭk), **oph·thal'mo·log'i·cal** *adj.* **—oph·thal'mo·log'i·cal·ly** *adv.*

oph·thal·mom·e·ter (ŏf'thăl-mŏm'ĭ-tər, ŏf'thəl-, ŏp'-) *n.* An optical instrument for measuring astigmatism. **—oph·thal'mo·met'ric** (ŏf-thăl'mə-mĕt'rĭk, ŏp-), **oph·thal'mo·met'ri·cal** *adj.*

oph·thal·mo·scope (ŏf-thăl'mə-skōp', ŏp-) *n.* An instrument consisting essentially of a mirror with a central hole through which the eye is examined. **—oph·thal'mo·scop'ic** (-skŏp'ĭk), **oph·thal'mo·scop'i·cal** *adj.* **—oph'thal·mos'co·py** (ŏf'thăl-mŏs'kə-pē, ŏp'-) *n.*

-opia *suff.* A visual condition or defect of a specified kind: *anisometropia.* [NLat. < Gk. *-ōpia* < *ōps,* eye.]

o·pi·ate (ō'pē-ĭt, -āt') *n.* **1.** Any of various sedative narcotics

opera glasses
"At the Opera" by Mary Cassatt

opera hat
Above: Hat as worn
Below: Hat collapsed

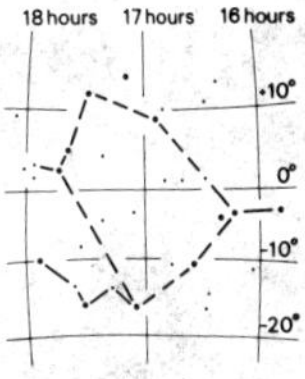

Ophiuchus

containing opium or one or more of its derivatives. **2.** A sedative or narcotic drug. **3.** Something that relaxes or that induces sleep or torpor. —*adj.* **1.** Consisting of or containing opium. **2.** Causing or producing sleep or sedation. **3.** Dulling the senses or mental processes; deadening. —*tr.v.* (ō'pē-āt') **-at·ed, -at·ing, -ates. 1.** To subject to the action of an opiate. **2.** To dull or deaden as if with a narcotic drug. [Med. Lat. *opiatum* < *opiatus,* treated with opium < Lat. *opium,* opium.]

o·pine (ō-pīn') *tr.v.* **o·pined, o·pin·ing, o·pines.** To hold or state as an opinion; think: *"They were, he opined, mere imitations of Arthur Symons"* (Stanislaus Joyce). [OFr. *opiner* < Lat. *opinari,* to suppose.]

o·pin·ion (ə-pĭn'yən) *n.* **1.** A belief or conclusion held with confidence, but not substantiated by positive knowledge or proof. **2.** An evaluation or judgment based on special knowledge and given by an expert: *a medical opinion.* **3.** A judgment or estimation of the worth or value of a person or thing: *had a low opinion of gamblers.* **4.** The common, usual, or prevailing feeling or sentiment: *public opinion.* **5.** *Law.* A formal statement by a judge or jury of the legal reasons and principles for the conclusions of the court. [ME *opinioun* < Lat. *opinio* < *opinari,* to suppose.]

Synonyms: *opinion, view, sentiment, feeling, impression, inclination, belief, conviction, persuasion, judgment. Opinion* is applicable to any conclusion to which one adheres without ruling out the possibility of debate. *View* differs principally in that it stresses individuality of outlook as a determinant of the conclusion. *Sentiment* and especially *feeling* stress the role of emotion as a determinant. *Impression* and *inclination,* in this context, denote tentative conclusions. *Belief* pertains to a conclusion, not necessarily derived firsthand, to which one subscribes strongly. *Conviction* denotes belief that excludes doubt and that proceeds usually from weight of evidence. *Persuasion* applies to strong belief, but does not necessarily suggest an intellectual basis. *Judgment,* strictly, is opinion based on reasoning and evaluation rather than emotion or will.

o·pin·ion·at·ed (ə-pĭn'yə-nā'tĭd) *adj.* Holding stubbornly and often unreasonably to one's own opinions. **—o·pin'ion·at'ed·ly** *adv.* **—o·pin'ion·at'ed·ness** *n.*

o·pin·ion·a·tive (ə-pĭn'yə-nā'tĭv) *adj.* **1.** Pertaining to, based on, or of the nature of an opinion. **2.** Opinionated. **—o·pin'ion·a'tive·ly** *adv.*

o·pis·tho·branch (ə-pĭs'thə-brăngk') *n., pl.* **-branchs.** Any of various marine gastropods of the order Opisthobranchia characterized by gills, a shell that is reduced or absent, and two pairs of tentacles. [NLat. *Opisthobranchia,* order name : Gk. *opisthen,* behind + Gk. *brankhion,* gill.]

op·is·thog·na·thous (ŏp'ĭs-thŏg'nə-thəs) *adj.* Having receding jaws. [Gk. *opisthen,* behind + -GNATHOUS.] **—op'is·thog'na·thism** *n.*

o·pi·um (ō'pē-əm) *n.* **1.** A bitter, yellowish-brown, strongly addictive drug prepared from the dried juice of unripe pods of the opium poppy, containing alkaloids such as morphine, narcotine, codeine, and papaverine, and used as an anesthetic. **2.** Something that numbs or stupefies. [ME < Lat. < Gk. *opion,* dim. of *opos,* juice.]

opium poppy *n.* A plant, *Papaver somniferum,* originally of Asia Minor, having grayish-green leaves and variously colored flowers. The juice of its unripe pods is the original source of opium.

o·pos·sum (ə-pŏs'əm, pŏs'əm) *n., pl.* **opossum** or **-sums. 1.** Any of various nocturnal, arboreal marsupials of the family Didelphidae, esp. *Didelphis marsupialis,* of the Western Hemisphere. **2.** Any of several Australian marsupials of the family Phalangeridae, some of which have valuable fur. [Powhatan *aposoum.*]

opossum

op·po·nent (ə-pō'nənt) *n.* One that opposes another or others in a battle, contest, controversy, or debate. —*adj.* **1.** Acting against an antagonist or an opposing force: *opponent armies.* **2.** Located in front. [Lat. *opponens, opponent-,* pr.part. of *opponere,* oppose.] **—op·po'nen·cy** *n.*

Synonyms: *opponent, adversary, antagonist, competitor, rival.* These nouns all describe persons engaged in contests or struggles. *Opponent,* somewhat impersonal, means one who takes a contrary position. *Adversary* suggests a more formidable opponent and can imply animosity, while an *antagonist* is an actively hostile opponent. *Competitor,* a milder word, suggests a person trying to outdo one or more opponents, as in sports or business. *Rival* most frequently implies a single, more personal opponent. Rivals are opponents competing for an objective.

op·por·tune (ŏp'ər-to͞on', -tyo͞on') *adj.* **1.** Suited or right for a particular purpose: *chose an opportune moment to put in her request.* **2.** Occurring at a time that is fitting or advantageous: *an opportune meeting.* [ME < OFr. *oportune* < Lat. *opportunus* : *ob,* to + *portus,* harbor.] **—op'por·tune'ly** *adv.* **—op'por·tune'ness** *n.*

op·por·tun·ist (ŏp'ər-to͞o'nĭst, -tyo͞o'-) *n.* A person who takes advantage of opportunities for achieving an end or for self-advancement, usually with no regard for principles or consequences. **—op'por·tun'ism** *n.* **—op'por·tun·is'tic** *adj.*

op·por·tu·ni·ty (ŏp'ər-to͞o'nĭ-tē, -tyo͞o'-) *n., pl.* **-ties. 1.** A favorable or advantageous combination of circumstances; suitable occasion or time. **2.** A chance for progress or advancement: *seized the opportunity to improve her lifestyle.* [ME *opportunite* < OFr. < Lat. *opportunitas* < *opportunus,* opportune.]

op·pos·a·ble (ə-pō'zə-bəl) *adj.* **1.** Capable of being opposed. **2.** Capable of being placed opposite or in opposition to something: *The thumb is an opposable digit.* **—op·pos'a·bil'i·ty** *n.*

op·pose (ə-pōz') *v.* **-posed, -pos·ing, -pos·es.** —*tr.* **1.** To be in contention or conflict with: *oppose the enemy force.* **2.** To be resistant to: *oppose new ideas.* **3.** To place in opposition or be in opposition to; contrast or counterbalance by antithesis. **4.** To move so as to be opposite something else; place in contraposition. —*intr.* To act or be in opposition. [Fr. *opposer* < OFr. < Lat. *opponere* : *ob-,* against + *ponere,* to put.] **—op·pos'er** *n.*

op·po·site (ŏp'ə-zĭt) *adj.* **1.** Placed or located directly across from something else or from each other: *opposite sides of a building.* **2.** Facing the other way; moving or tending away from each other: *opposite directions.* **3.** Contrary or antithetical in nature or tendency; altogether different. **4.** *Bot.* Growing in pairs on either side of a stem: *opposite leaves.* —*n.* **1.** One that is opposite or contrary to another. **2.** An opponent or antagonist. **3.** An antonym. —*adv.* In an opposite position or positions: *They sat opposite at the table.* —*prep.* **1.** Across from or facing: *Park your car opposite the bank.* **2.** In a complementary dramatic role to: *She played opposite him.* [ME < OFr. *oposite* < Lat. *oppositus,* p.part. of *opponere,* oppose.] **—op'po·site·ly** *adv.* **—op'po·site·ness** *n.*

Synonyms: *opposite, contrary, antithetical, contradictory.* These adjectives have the common meaning of being irreconcilably set apart. When two things have a definite relationship and yet differ to the extent of revealing marked contrast, they are *opposite: opposite sides of the street; opposite points of view. Contrary* stresses extreme divergence and may imply stubbornness. *Antithetical* emphasizes sharp, diametrical opposition, usually intellectual. *Contradictory* implies denial of one view by another.

opposite number *n.* A person who holds a position in an organization which corresponds to that of a person in another organization.

op·po·si·tion (ŏp'ə-zĭsh'ən) *n.* **1.** The act or condition of opposing or of being in conflict. **2. a.** A position or location opposite to or facing another. **b.** Placement in such a position or location. **3.** Something that is or serves as an obstacle. **4.** Often **Opposition.** A political party or organized group opposed to the group, party, or government in power. **5.** *Astron.* **a.** A geometric configuration in which the earth lies on a straight line between the sun and a planet. **b.** The position of the exterior planet in this configuration. **6.** *Logic.* The relation existing between two propositions having an identical subject and predicate but differing in quantity, quality, or both. **7.** *Ling.* Contrast between two phonemes or other elements of a language that have a relationship such that the contrast is significant. ***—modifier:*** *opposition parties.* [ME *opposicioun,* a placement opposite, a contradiction < Lat. *oppositio,* an opposing < *opponere,* to oppose.] **—op'po·si'tion·al** *adj.* **—op'po·si'tion·ist** *n.*

op·press (ə-prĕs') *tr.v.* **-pressed, -press·ing, -press·es. 1.** To subjugate or persecute by unjust or tyrannical use of force or authority. **2.** To weigh heavily upon, esp. so as to depress the mind or spirits. **3.** *Obs.* To overwhelm or crush. [ME *oppressen,* to crush < OFr. *opresser* < Med. Lat. *oppressare,* freq. of Lat. *opprimere* : *ob-,* against + *premere,* to press.] **—op·pres'sor** *n.*

op·pres·sion (ə-prĕsh'ən) *n.* **1.** The act of oppressing or the state of being oppressed. **2.** Something that oppresses or burdens. **3.** A feeling of being heavily weighed down, either mentally or physically.

op·pres·sive (ə-prĕs'ĭv) *adj.* **1. a.** Difficult to bear; harsh: *oppressive tax laws.* **b.** Tyrannical. **2.** Weighing heavily on the spirit or senses: *oppressive heat.* [Med. Lat. *oppressivus* < Lat. *opprimere,* to press down. —see OPPRESS.] **—op·pres'sive·ly** *adv.* **—op·pres'sive·ness** *n.*

op·pro·bri·ous (ə-prō'brē-əs) *adj.* **1.** Expressing or carrying a sense of disgrace or contemptuous scorn: *opprobrious epithets.* **2.** Shameful; infamous. [ME < LLat. *opprobriosus* < Lat. *opprobrium,* opprobrium.] **—op·pro'bri·ous·ly** *adv.*

op·pro·bri·um (ə-prō'brē-əm) *n.* **1.** Disgrace inherent in or arising from shameful conduct; ignominy. **2.** Scornful reproach or contempt: *a term of opprobrium.* **3.** A cause of shame or disgrace. [Lat. : *ob-,* against + *probrum,* reproach.]

op·pugn (ə-pyo͞on') *tr.v.* **-pugned, -pugn·ing, -pugns.** To oppose, contradict, or call into question. [ME *oppugnen* < Lat. *oppugnare,* to attack : *ob-,* against + *pugnare,* to fight.] **—op·pugn'er** *n.*

op·sin (ŏp'sĭn) *n.* The protein constituent of rhodopsin. [Gk. *opsis,* sight + -IN.]

-opsis *suff.* Something resembling a specified thing: *caryopsis.* [NLat. < Gk. < *opsis,* sight, appearance.]

op·son·ic (ŏp-sŏn'ĭk) *adj.* Of, pertaining to, or having the effect of opsonin. [OPSON(IN) + -IC.]

op·son·i·fy (ŏp-sŏn'ə-fī') *tr.v.* **-fied, -fy·ing, -fies.** To make (bacteria) susceptible to phagocytosis by opsonic action; opsonize. [OPSON(IN) + -FY.] **—op·son'i·fi·ca'tion** *n.*

op·so·nin (ŏp'sə-nĭn) *n.* A substance naturally present in the blood that renders bacteria susceptible to phagocytosis. [< Lat. *opsonium,* relish < Gk. *opsōnion* < *opson.*]

op·so·nize (ŏp′sə-nīz′) *tr.v.* **-nized, -niz·ing, -niz·es. 1.** To form opsonins in. **2.** To opsonify. [< OPSONIN.] **—op′so·ni·za′tion** *n.*

-opsy *suff.* Examination: *biopsy.* [NLat. *-opsia* < Gk. < *opsis,* sight.]

opt (ŏpt) *intr.v.* **opt·ed, opt·ing, opts.** To make a choice or decision. ***—phrasal verb.* opt out.** To choose not to engage in something: *opted out of big business.* [Fr. *opter* < Lat. *optare.*]

op·ta·tive (ŏp′tə-tĭv) *adj.* **1.** Expressing a wish or choice. **2.** *Gram.* **a.** Denoting a mood of verbs in some languages, such as Greek, used to express a wish. **b.** Designating a statement using a verb in the subjunctive mood to indicate a wish or desire; for example, *Had I the means, I would do it.* *—n. Gram.* **1.** The optative mood. **2.** A verb or expression in the optative mood. [ME *optatif* < OFr. < LLat. *optativus* < Lat. *optare,* to wish.] **—op′ta·tive·ly** *adv.*

op·tic (ŏp′tĭk) *adj.* **1.** Of or pertaining to the eye or to vision. **2.** Of or pertaining to the science of optics. *—n.* **1.** An eye. **2.** Any of the components of an optical instrument. [OFr. *optique* < Med. Lat. *opticus* < Gk. *optikos* < *optos,* visible.]

op·ti·cal (ŏp′tĭ-kəl) *adj.* **1.** Of or pertaining to sight: *an optical illusion.* **2.** Designed to assist sight: *optical instruments.* **3.** Of or pertaining to optics. **4.** Pertaining to or using light: *optical astronomy.* **5.** Using light-sensitive devices: *optical character recognition.* **—op′ti·cal·ly** *adv.*

optical activity *n. Chem.* A property of a substance that enables it to rotate the plane of incident polarized light.

optical art *n.* Abstract art that features the use of geometric shapes or patterns, esp. to create optical illusions.

optical fiber *n.* A flexible optically transparent fiber, as of glass or plastic, through which light can be transmitted by successive internal reflections.

optical illusion *n.* A visually perceived image that is deceptive or misleading.

optical maser *n.* A laser, esp. one that produces visible radiation.

optic axis *n.* An optical path through a crystal along which a ray of light can pass without undergoing double refraction.

optic chiasm *n.* Optic chiasma.

optic chiasma *n.* The partial decussation of the optic nerve fibers on the undersurface of the hypothalamus in the brain.

optic disk *n. Anat.* Blind spot (sense 1).

op·ti·cian (ŏp-tĭsh′ən) *n.* **1.** One who makes lenses and eyeglasses. **2.** One who sells lenses, eyeglasses, and other optical instruments. [Fr. *opticien* < Med. Lat. *optica,* optics.]

optic nerve *n.* Either of two sensory nerves that connect the retinas of the eyes with the brain.

op·tics (ŏp′tĭks) *n.* *(used with a sing. verb). Physics.* The scientific study of light and vision, chiefly of the generation, propagation, and detection of electromagnetic radiation having wavelengths greater than x rays and shorter than microwaves. [Med. Lat. *optica* < Gk. *optikos,* of sight < *optos,* visible.]

op·ti·ma (ŏp′tə-mə) *n.* A plural of **optimum.**

op·ti·mal (ŏp′tə-məl) *adj.* Most favorable or desirable; optimum. **—op′ti·mal·ly** *adv.*

op·ti·mism (ŏp′tə-mĭz′əm) *n.* **1.** A tendency or disposition to expect the best possible outcome or to dwell upon the most hopeful aspects of a situation. **2.** *Philos.* **a.** The doctrine, asserted by Leibnitz, that our world is the best of all possible worlds. **b.** The belief that the universe is improving and that good will ultimately triumph over evil. [Fr. *optimisme* < Lat. *optimus,* best.]

op·ti·mist (ŏp′tə-mĭst) *n.* **1.** One who habitually or in a particular case expects a favorable outcome. **2.** A believer in philosophical optimism. **—op′ti·mis′tic** *adj.* **—op′ti·mis′ti·cal·ly** *adv.*

op·ti·mize (ŏp′tə-mīz′) *tr.v.* **-mized, -miz·ing, -miz·es. 1.** To make as good or as effective as possible. **2.** To make the most effective use of.

op·ti·mum (ŏp′tə-məm) *n., pl.* **-ma** (-mə) or **-mums. 1.** The best or most favorable condition, degree, or amount. **2.** The most favorable conditions for growth and reproduction. *—adj.* Most favorable or advantageous; best. [Lat. < *optimus,* best.]

op·tion (ŏp′shən) *n.* **1.** An act of choosing; choice. **2.** The power or right of choosing; freedom to choose. **3. a.** The exclusive right, usually obtained for a fee, to buy or sell property within a specified time and at a specified price. **b.** The privilege of demanding fulfillment of a contract during a specified future time. **c.** A right to buy or sell specific securities at a specified price within a specified time. **d.** A clause in an insurance policy permitting the policyholder to specify the manner in which payments are to be made or credited to him. **4.** Something chosen or available as a choice. *—tr.v.* **-tioned, -tion·ing, -tions. 1. a.** To acquire an option on: *optioned the neighboring lot.* **b.** To grant an option on. **2.** *Baseball.* To transfer (a player) to a minor-league club with the option of recalling him within a specified period of time. [Fr. < Lat. *optio.*]

op·tion·al (ŏp′shə-nəl) *adj.* Left to choice; not compulsory or automatic. **—op′tion·al·ly** *adv.*

option play *n. Football.* An offensive play in which a back has the choice of running with the ball or throwing a forward pass.

op·tom·e·trist (ŏp-tŏm′ĭ-trĭst) *n.* One who specializes in optometry.

op·tom·e·try (ŏp-tŏm′ĭ-trē) *n.* The profession of examining, measuring, and treating certain visual defects by means of corrective lenses or other methods that do not require license as a physician. [Gk. *optos,* visible + -METRY.] **—op′to·met′ric** (ŏp′tə-mĕt′rĭk), **op′to·met′ri·cal** *adj.*

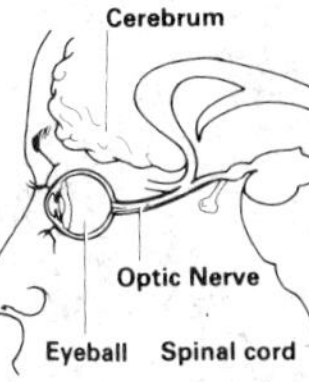

optic nerve

op·u·lent (ŏp′yə-lənt) *adj.* **1.** Having or characterized by great wealth; affluent. **2. a.** Abundant; plentiful. **b.** Characterized by fullness and vitality. [Lat. *opulentus* < *ops,* wealth.] **—op′u·lence, op′u·len·cy** *n.* **—op′u·lent·ly** *adv.*

o·pun·ti·a (ō-pŭn′shē-ə, -shə) *n.* **1.** Any of various cacti of the genus *Opuntia.* **2.** A prickly pear. [NLat. *Opuntio,* genus name < Lat. *(herba) Opuntia,* (herb) of Opus, an ancient city in Greece.]

o·pus (ō′pəs) *n., pl.* **o·pe·ra** (ō′pər-ə, ŏp′ər-ə) or **o·pus·es.** A creative work, esp. a musical composition numbered to designate the order of a composer's works. [Lat.]

o·pus·cule (ō-pŭs′kyo͞ol) *n.* A small and minor work. [Fr. < Lat. *opusculum,* dim. of *opus,* work.]

o·quas·sa (ō-kwăs′ə, ō-kwä′sə) *n., pl.* **oquassa** or **-sas.** A freshwater fish, *Salvelinus oquassa,* found in the Rangeley Lakes in Maine. [After Lake *Oquassa,* Maine.]

or[1] (ôr; *unstressed* ər) *conj.* Used to indicate: **1. a.** An alternative, usually only before the last term of a series: *hot or cold; this, that, or the other.* **b.** The second of two alternatives, the first being preceded by *either* or *whether: Your answer is either ingenious or wrong. She didn't know whether to laugh or cry.* **c.** *Archaic.* Either. **2.** A synonymous or equivalent expression: *acrophobia, or fear of great heights.* **3.** Uncertainty or indefiniteness: *two or three.* [ME, contraction of *other,* perh. < OE *oððe.*]

Usage: When all the elements in a series connected by *or* are singular, the verb they govern is singular: *Tom or Jack is coming. Beer, ale, or wine is included in the charge.* When all the elements are plural, the verb is plural. When the elements do not agree in number, some have suggested that the verb be governed by the element to which it is nearer: *Tom or his sisters are coming. The girls or their brother is coming. Cold symptoms or headache is the usual first sign.* Other grammarians, however, have argued that such constructions must be avoided and that substitutes be found in which the problem of agreement does not arise: *Either Tom is coming or his sisters are. The usual first sign may be either cold symptoms or a headache.* See also Usage notes at **and/or** and **no**[2].

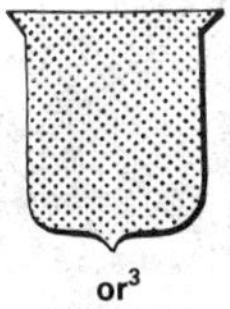
or[3]

or[2] (ôr) *Archaic. —conj.* Before. Followed by *ever* or *ere: "I doubt he will be dead or ere I come"* (Shakespeare). *—prep.* Before. [ME < OE *ǣr* and ON *ār.*]

or[3] (ôr) *n.* Gold, represented in heraldic engraving by a white field sprinkled with small dots. [OFr. < Lat. *aurum.*]

-or[1] *suff.* One that performs a specified action: *accelerator.* [ME *-our* < OFr. *-eor, -eur,* partly < Lat. *-or,* and partly < Lat. *-ator.*]

-or[2] *suff.* State; quality; activity: *behavior.* [ME *-our* < OFr. *-eur* < Lat. *-or.*]

o·ra (ôr′ə, ōr′ə) *n.* Plural of **os**[1].

or·ach also **or·ache** (ôr′ĭch, ŏr′-) *n.* Any of various plants of the genus *Atriplex,* esp. *A. hortensis,* whose edible leaves resemble spinach. [ME *arage* < OFr. *arrache* < Lat. *atriplex* < Gk. *atraphaxus.*]

or·a·cle (ôr′ə-kəl, ŏr′-) *n.* **1. a.** A shrine consecrated to the worship and consultation of a prophetic god. **b.** A person who transmits prophecies from a deity at such a shrine. **c.** A prophecy made known at such a shrine, often in the form of an enigmatic statement or allegory. **2. a.** A person or agency considered to be a source of wise counsel or prophetic opinions. **b.** An authoritative statement or prediction from such an agency. **3.** *Theol.* A command or revelation from God. **4.** In the Old Testament, the sanctuary of the Temple. [ME < Lat. *oraculum* < *orare,* to speak.]

o·rac·u·lar (ô-răk′yə-lər, ō-răk′-) *adj.* **1.** Of, pertaining to, or being an oracle. **2.** Resembling or characteristic of an oracle: **a.** Solemnly prophetic: *an oracular warning.* **b.** Brief and enigmatic; cryptic. [< Lat. *oraculum,* oracle < *orare,* to speak.] **—o·rac′u·lar·ly** *adv.*

o·ral (ôr′əl, ōr′-) *adj.* **1.** Spoken rather than written. **2.** Of or pertaining to the mouth: *oral hygiene.* **3.** Used in or taken through the mouth: *an oral vaccine.* **4.** Consisting of or using speech: *oral instruction.* **5.** Designating a speech sound emitted through the mouth only, with the nasal passages closed. **6.** *Psychol.* Of, pertaining to, or denoting the first stage of psychosexual development of the infant when sexual gratification is derived chiefly from stimulation of the mouth parts. *—n.* Often **orals.** A school or college examination in which questions and answers are spoken rather than written. —See Usage note at **verbal.** [< Lat. *ōs, ōr-,* mouth.] **—o′ral·ly** *adv.*

oral contraceptive *n.* Any of various hormone compounds in pill form, used in specific sequence to prevent ovulation and conception.

oral history *n.* **1.** Historical information obtained in tape-

orange

orangutan
Bornean orangutans

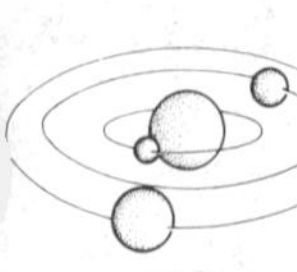

orbit

orchid

recorded interviews with persons having firsthand knowledge. **2.** A written account based on oral history.

or·ange (ôr′ĭnj, ŏr′-) *n.* **1. a.** Any of several evergreen trees of the genus *Citrus,* cultivated in tropical and subtropical regions, and having fragrant white flowers and round fruit with a yellowish-red rind and a sectioned, pulpy interior, esp. *C. sinensis,* the sweet orange, and *C. aurantium,* the Seville or sour orange. **b.** The fruit of these trees, having a sweetish, acid juice. **2.** Any of several plants or trees resembling the orange in some respect, such as the Osage orange and the mock orange. **3.** Any of a group of colors between red and yellow in hue, of medium lightness and moderate saturation. [ME < OFr. < Ar. *nāranj* < Pers. *nārang* < Skt. *nārangaḥ.*] **—or′ange** *adj.*

or·ange·ade (ôr′ĭn-jād′, ŏr′-) *n.* A beverage of orange juice, sugar, and water.

orange hawkweed *n.* A plant, *Hieracium aurantiacum,* native to Europe, having hairy leaves and clusters of orange-red flowers.

Or·ange·man (ôr′ĭnj-mən, ŏr′-) *n.* **1.** A member of a Protestant secret society founded in Northern Ireland in 1795. **2.** A Protestant Irishman. [After William, Prince of *Orange,* later King William III of England (1650–1702).]

orange milkweed *n.* Butterfly weed.

orange pekoe *n.* **1.** A grade of black tea consisting of the end buds and their surrounding leaves. **2.** A grade of black tea consisting of small leaves obtained by screening. **3.** A grade of black tea consisting of the first two full leaves of the shoot.

or·ange·ry (ôr′ĭnj-rē, ŏr′-) *n., pl.* **-ries.** A place where orange trees are cultivated, usually an enclosure or greenhouse. [Fr. *orangerie* < *orange,* orange < OFr. —see ORANGE.]

orange stick *n.* A stick of orangewood, used in manicuring.

or·ange·wood (ôr′ĭnj-wo͝od′, ŏr′-) *n.* The fine-grained wood of the orange tree, used in fine woodwork.

o·rang·u·tan (ō-răng′ə-tăn′, ə-răng′-) also **o·rang·ou·tan** (-tăng′) *n.* An arboreal anthropoid ape, *Pongo pygmaeus,* of Borneo and Sumatra, having a shaggy reddish-brown coat, very long arms, and no tail. [Malay *ōrang hūtan* : *ōrang,* man + *hūtan,* forest.]

o·rate (ô-rāt′, ō-rāt′, ôr′āt′, ŏr′-) *intr.v.* **o·rat·ed, o·rat·ing, o·rates.** To speak in a pompous, oratorical manner. [Back-formation < *oration.*]

o·ra·tion (ô-rā′shən, ō-rā′-) *n.* **1.** A formal address or speech, esp. one given on a special occasion such as a civic holiday, academic celebration, or funeral. **2.** A high-flown speech. [Lat. *oratio, oration-* < *orare,* to speak.]

or·a·tor (ôr′ə-tər, ŏr′-) *n.* **1.** A person who delivers an oration. **2.** A person skilled in the art of public speaking. [ME *oratour* < Lat. *orator* < *orare,* to speak.] **—or′a·tor·ship′** *n.*

or·a·tor·i·cal (ôr′ə-tôr′ĭ-kəl, -tŏr′-) *adj.* Of or pertaining to an orator or to oratory. **—or′a·tor′i·cal·ly** *adv.*

or·a·to·ri·o (ôr′ə-tôr′ē-ō′, -tōr′-, ŏr′-) *n., pl.* **-os.** A musical composition for voices and orchestra, telling a sacred story without costumes, scenery, or dramatic action. [Ital. < *Oratorio,* the Oratory of St. Philip Neri at Rome, where famous musical services were held in the 16th century < LLat. *oratorium,* oratory, chapel.]

or·a·to·ry¹ (ôr′ə-tôr′ē, -tōr′ē, ŏr′-) *n.* **1.** The art of public speaking; rhetoric. **2.** Rhetorical style or skill. **3.** Public speaking, esp. when conventional or bombastic. [Lat. *(ars) oratoria,* (art) of speaking < *oratorius,* oratorical < *orator,* speaker < *orare,* to speak.]

or·a·to·ry² (ôr′ə-tôr′ē, -tōr′ē, ŏr′-) *n., pl.* **-ries.** A place for prayer, such as a small private chapel. [ME *oratorie* < OFr. *oratori* < Lat. *(templum) oratorium,* (place) of prayer < *oratorius,* of prayer. —see ORATORY¹.]

orb (ôrb) *n.* **1. a.** A sphere, esp. a celestial sphere. **b.** A range of endeavor, influence, or activity; province. **2.** A heavenly body. **3.** One of a series of concentric transparent spheres thought by ancient and medieval astronomers to revolve about the earth and support the celestial bodies. **4.** A jeweled globe surmounted by a cross that is part of a sovereign's regalia and that symbolizes monarchial power and justice. **5.** An eye. **6.** *Archaic.* A circle or an object of circular form. *—v.* **orbed, orb·ing, orbs.** *—tr.* **1.** To shape into a circle or sphere. **2.** *Archaic.* To encircle; enclose. *—intr. Archaic.* To move in an orbit. [OFr. *orbe* < Lat. *orbis.*]

or·bic·u·lar (ôr-bĭk′yə-lər) *adj.* **1.** Circular or spherical. **2.** *Bot.* Circular and flat, as a leaf. [ME *orbiculer* < LLat. *orbicularis* < Lat. *orbiculus,* dim. of *orbis,* orb.] **—or·bic′u·lar′i·ty** (-lăr′ĭ-tē) *n.* **—or·bic′u·lar·ly** *adv.*

or·bic·u·late (ôr-bĭk′yə-lĭt, -lāt′) also **or·bic·u·lat·ed** (-lā′tĭd) *adj.* Orbicular. [Lat. *orbiculatus* < *orbiculus,* dim. of *orbis,* orb.] **—or·bic′u·late·ly** *adv.*

or·bit (ôr′bĭt) *n.* **1. a.** The path of a celestial body or manmade satellite as it revolves around another body. **b.** One complete revolution of such a body. **2.** The path of a body in a field of force surrounding another body; for example, the movement of an atomic electron in relation to a nucleus. **3. a.** A range of activity, experience, or knowledge: *one's social orbit.* **b.** A range of control or influence: *"What magnetism drew these quaking ruined creatures into his orbit?"* (Malcolm Lowry). **4.** Either of two bony cavities in the skull containing an eye and its external structures; eye socket. *—v.* **-bit·ed, -bit·ing, -bits.** *—tr.* **1.** To put into or cause to move in an orbit: *The first manmade satellite was orbited in 1957.* **2.** To revolve around (a center of attraction): *The moon orbits the earth.* *—intr.* To move in an orbit. [Lat. *orbita* < *orbitus,* circular < *orbis,* circle.] **—or′bit·al** *adj.* **—or′bit·al·ly** *adv.*

orbital velocity *n.* The minimum velocity required to place a satellite in orbit about a celestial body.

orc (ôrk) *n.* The killer whale. [Fr. *orque* < Lat. *orca,* whale.]

or·chard (ôr′chərd) *n.* **1.** An area of land devoted to the cultivation of fruit or nut trees. **2.** The trees cultivated in an orchard. [ME < OE *ortgeard* : Lat. *hortus,* garden + OE *geard,* yard.]

orchard grass *n.* An Old World grass, *Dactylis glomerata,* widely planted in pastures.

or·ches·tra (ôr′kĭ-strə, ôr′kĕs′trə) *n.* **1. a.** A large group of musicians who play together on various musical instruments, usually including strings, woodwinds, brass instruments, and percussion instruments. **b.** The instruments played by such a group of musicians. **2.** In theaters and concert halls, the area where the musicians sit, immediately in front of and below the stage. **3. a.** The front section of seats nearest the stage in a theater. **b.** The entire main floor of a theater. **4.** In ancient Greek theaters, a semicircular space in front of the stage on which the chorus danced. [Lat., the semicircular space in front of the stage < Gk. *orkhēstra* < *orkheisthai,* to dance.] **—or·ches′tral** (ôr-kĕs′trəl) *adj.* **—or·ches′tral·ly** *adv.*

or·ches·trate (ôr′kĭ-strāt′) *tr.v.* **-trat·ed, -trat·ing, -trates. 1.** To compose or arrange (music) for performance by an orchestra. **2.** To arrange, put together, or organize so as to achieve a desired or effective combination: *orchestrate a multimedia advertising campaign.*

or·ches·tra·tion (ôr′kĭ-strā′shən) *n.* **1.** A musical composition that has been orchestrated. **2.** Arrangement of music for performance by an orchestra.

or·ches·tri·on (ôr-kĕs′trē-ən) also **or·ches·tri·na** (ôr′kĭ-strē′nə) *n.* A large mechanical musical instrument resembling a barrel organ and producing sound in imitation of an orchestra. [ORCHESTR(A) + (MELOD)ION.]

or·chid (ôr′kĭd) *n.* **1. a.** Any of numerous epiphytic or terrestrial plants of the family Orchidaceae, found worldwide, but chiefly in the tropics, and often having brightly colored flowers of irregular and unusual shapes. **b.** The flower of one of these plants, esp. one cultivated for ornament or personal adornment. **2.** A pale to light purple, from grayish to purplish pink to strong reddish purple. [Lat. *orchis* < Gk. *orkhis,* orchid, testicle.] **—or′chid** *adj.*

or·chi·da·ceous (ôr′kĭ-dā′shəs) *adj.* **1.** Of, relating to, or characteristic of the orchid family of plants. **2.** Suggesting ostentatious luxury; showy. [< NLat. *Orchidaceae,* family name < Lat. *orchis,* orchid.]

orchid tree *n.* **1.** A small tree, *Bauhinia variegata,* native to southeastern Asia, and having showy lavender or purple flowers. **2.** A tree, *Amherstia nobilis,* of India, having compound leaves and a great profusion of large, yellow-spotted, scarlet flowers.

or·chil (ôr′kĭl, -chĭl) *n.* **1.** Any of several lichens, chiefly of the genera *Roccella* and *Lecanora,* from which a dye is obtained. **2.** The reddish dyestuff obtained from the orchil. [OFr. *orchel.*]

or·chis (ôr′kĭs) *n.* Any of various orchids of the genus *Orchis,* having magenta, white, or magenta-spotted flowers. [NLat. *Orchis,* genus name < Lat., orchid.]

Or·cus (ôr′kəs) *n. Rom. Myth.* **1.** The world of the dead; Hades. **2.** The underworld god Pluto. [Lat.]

or·dain (ôr-dān′) *tr.v.* **-dained, -dain·ing, -dains. 1. a.** To invest with ministerial or priestly authority; confer holy orders upon. **b.** To authorize as a rabbi. **2.** To order by virtue of superior authority; decree or enact. **3.** To prearrange unalterably; predestine: *by fate ordained.* [ME *ordeinen* < OFr. *ordener* < Lat. *ordinare,* to organize < *ordo,* order.] **—or·dain′er** *n.* **—or·dain′ment** *n.*

or·deal (ôr-dēl′) *n.* **1.** A difficult or painful experience, esp. one that severely tests character or endurance. **2.** A former method of determining guilt or innocence in which the accused was subjected to physically painful or dangerous tests, the result being regarded as a divine judgment. [ME *ordal,* trial by ordeal < OE *ordāl.*]

ordeal bark *n.* The poisonous bark of an African tree, *Erythrophloeum guineense.* [From its use in trials by ordeal.]

ordeal tree *n.* The upas (sense 1).

or·der (ôr′dər) *n.* **1.** A condition of logical or comprehensible arrangement among the separate elements of a group. **2. a.** A condition of methodical or prescribed arrangement among component parts, such that proper functioning or appearance is achieved; a state of sound readiness. **b.** Systematic arrangement and design. **3. a.** The existing structure or method of social organization: *"Every revolution exaggerates the evils of the old order"* (C. Wright Mills). **b.** The rule of law and custom or the observance of prescribed procedure: *Order was restored after the riot.* **4.** A sequence or arrangement of successive things. **5.** An established sequence; customary procedure: *the order of worship.* **6.** An authoritative indication to be obeyed; command. **7. a.** A command given by a superior military officer requiring execution of a task or other obedience. **b. orders.**

Formal written instructions to report for military duty at a specified time and place. **8. a.** A commission or instruction to buy, sell, or supply something. **b.** That which is supplied, bought, or sold. **9.** *Informal.* An assigned task; undertaking. **10.** A portion of food requested by a customer at a restaurant. **11.** *Law.* A direction or command delivered by a court and entered into the court record, but not included in the final judgment or verdict. **12.** *Eccles.* **a.** Any of several grades of the Christian ministry: *the order of priesthood.* **b. orders.** The office and rank of an ordained minister or priest. **c. orders.** Holy orders. **13.** Any of the nine grades or choirs of angels. **14.** A group of persons living under a religious rule: *Order of St. Benedict.* **15.** An organization of people united by some common fraternal bond or social aim. **16. a.** A group of persons upon whom a government or sovereign has formally conferred honor for unusual service or merit, entitling such persons to wear a special insignia: *the Order of the Garter.* **b.** The insignia worn by such persons. **17.** Often **orders.** A social class. **18.** Degree of quality or importance; rank: *poetry of a high order.* **19.** *Archit.* **a.** Any of several styles of classical architecture characterized by the type of column employed. **b.** A style of architecture: *a cathedral of the Gothic order.* **20.** *Biol.* A taxonomic category of plants and animals ranking above the family and below the class. **21.** *Math.* **a.** An indicated number of successive differentiations to be performed. **b.** The number of elements in a finite group. **c.** The number of rows or columns in a determinant or matrix. **22.** A class that is defined by the common attribute or attributes possessed by all its members; kind. *—v.* **-dered, -der·ing, -ders.** *—tr.* **1.** To issue a command or instruction to. **2.** To give a command or instruction for: *The judge ordered a recount of the ballots.* **3.** To give an order for; request to be supplied with. **4.** To put into a methodical and systematic arrangement. **5.** To ordain: *He was ordered priest.* *—intr.* To give an order or orders; request that something be done or supplied: *Order now, before prices go up.* **—*phrasal verb.* order up.** To summon (personnel) for active military duty: *ordered up the reservists.* **—*idioms.* in order.** Called for; appropriate: *A reappraisal is in order.* **in order that.** So that. **in order to.** For the purpose of; so that. **in short order.** With no delay; quickly. **on order.** Requested but not yet delivered. **on the order of. 1.** In a fashion similar to; like: *a plane on the order of the U-2.* **2.** Approximately; about: *equipment costing on the order of a million dollars.* **to order.** According to the buyer's specifications. [ME *ordre* < OFr. < Lat. *ordo.*] **—or′der·er** *n.*

order arms *n.* **1.** A position in the military manual of arms in which the rifle is held vertically next to the right leg, with the butt resting on the ground. **2.** A command to assume order arms.

or·der·ly (ôr′dər-lē) *adj.* **1.** Having a methodical and systematic arrangement; tidy: *an orderly room.* **2.** Devoid of violence or disruption; peaceful: *an orderly transition of governments.* *—n., pl.* **-lies. 1.** An attendant who does unskilled work in a hospital. **2.** A soldier assigned to attend a superior officer and carry orders or messages. *—adv.* Systematically; regularly. **—or′der·li·ness** *n.*

Synonyms: *orderly, methodical, systematic.* These mean procedural in manner or nature and imply neatness or efficiency. *Orderly* means correctly conducted, properly arranged, or peaceable, and is used particularly where disorder is considered possible: *orderly evacuation of the school. Methodical* means scrupulous in execution and planned or paced in a logical way, often slowly. Its emphasis on a set procedure may suggest plodding rigidity: *methodical study habits; a performance too methodical for romantic music. Systematic* is more impersonal and suggests efficiency, thoroughness, and precision. Often it also implies activity of rather broad scope: *systematic check of each candidate's campaign expenditures.*

order of business *n.* Something, such as a task, that must be addressed.

order of magnitude *n.* **1.** An estimate of size or magnitude expressed as a power of ten: *The earth's mass is of the order of magnitude of 10^{22} tons; that of the sun is 10^{27} tons.* **2.** A range of values between a designated lower value and an upper value ten times as large: *The masses of the earth and the sun differ by five orders of magnitude.*

order of the day *n.* **1.** The business or jobs that must be addressed by a group for a particular day. **2.** The characteristic or most significant aspect or event: *devising a new ad campaign is the order of the day.*

or·di·nal (ôr′dn-əl) *adj.* **1.** Being of a specified position in a numbered series: *an ordinal rank of seventh.* **2.** Pertaining to a biological order. *—n.* **1.** An ordinal number. **2.** *Eccles.* **a.** A book of instructions for daily services. **b.** A book of forms for ordination. [LLat. *ordinalis* < Lat. *ordo,* order.]

ordinal number *n.* A number indicating position in a series or order. The ordinal numbers are first (1st), second (2nd), third (3rd), etc.

or·di·nance (ôr′dn-əns) *n.* **1.** An authoritative command or order. **2.** A custom or practice established by long usage. **3.** A religious rite, esp. Holy Communion. **4.** A statute or regulation, esp. one enacted by a city government. [ME *ordinaunce* < OFr. *ordenance* < Med. Lat. *ordinantia* < Lat. *ordinare,* to ordain < *ordo,* order.]

or·di·nar·i·ly (ôr′dn-âr′ə-lē, ôr′dn-ĕr′-) *adv.* **1.** As a general rule; usually. **2.** In the regular or usual manner: *ordinarily dressed.* **3.** To the usual extent or degree: *ordinarily large profits.*

or·di·nar·y (ôr′dn-ĕr′ē) *adj.* **1.** Commonly encountered; usual. **2.** *Math.* Designating a differential equation containing no more than two variables and derivatives of one with respect to the other. **3.** Of no exceptional degree or quality; average. **4.** Having immediate rather than delegated jurisdiction, as a judge. *—n., pl.* **-ies. 1.** The usual or normal condition or course of events: *Nothing out of the ordinary occurred.* **2.** *Law.* A judge or other official with immediate rather than delegated jurisdiction. **3.** In some states of the United States, the judge of a probate court. **4.** Often **Ordinary.** *Eccles.* **a.** The part of the Mass that remains unchanged from day to day. **b.** A division of the Roman Breviary containing the unchangeable parts of the office other than the Psalms. **c.** A cleric, such as the residential bishop of a diocese, with ordinary jurisdiction in the external forum over a specified territory. **5.** One of the simplest and commonest charges in heraldry, such as the bend and the cross. [ME *ordinarie* < Lat. *ordinarius* < *ordo,* order.] **—or′di·nar′i·ness** *n.*

ordinary seaman *n.* A seaman of the lowest grade in the merchant marine.

or·di·nate (ôr′dn-ĭt, -āt′) *adj.* Arranged in regular rows, as spots on an insect's wings. *—n. Math.* The plane Cartesian coordinate representing the distance from a specified point to the *x*-axis, measured parallel to the *y*-axis. [Lat. *ordinatus,* p.part. of *ordinare,* to set in order < *ordo,* order.]

or·di·na·tion (ôr′dn-ā′shən) *n.* **1.** The act of ordaining or the condition of being ordained. **2.** *Eccles.* **a.** The ceremony during which a person is admitted to the ministry of a church. **b.** The admission itself. **3.** A proper arrangement.

or·di·nes (ôr′də-nēz′) *n.* A plural of **ordo.**

ord·nance (ôrd′nəns) *n.* **1. a.** Military weapons collectively, along with ammunition and the equipment to keep them in good repair. **b.** The branch of a military force that designs, develops, procures, stores, maintains, and issues weapons. **2.** Heavy guns; artillery. [ME *ordinaunce.* —see ORDINANCE.]

or·do (ôr′dō) *n., pl.* **-di·nes** (-də-nēz′) or **-dos.** *Rom. Cath. Ch.* An annual calendar containing instructions for the Mass and office to be celebrated on each day of the year. [Med. Lat. < Lat., order.]

or·don·nance (ôr′də-näNs′) *n.* The arrangement of elements in a literary or artistic composition or architectural plan. [Fr., var. of OFr. *ordenance,* an arranging. —see ORDINANCE.]

Or·do·vi·cian (ôr′də-vĭsh′ən) *adj.* Of, pertaining to, or designating the geologic time, system of rocks, and sedimentary deposits of the second period of the Paleozoic era, characterized by the appearance of primitive fishes. *—n.* The Ordovician period. [After the *Ordovices,* an ancient Celtic tribe of North Wales.]

or·dure (ôr′jər) *n.* **1.** Excrement; dung. **2.** Something morally offensive; filth. [ME < OFr. < *ord,* filthy < Lat. *horridus,* frightful < *horrēre,* to shudder.]

ore (ôr, ōr) *n.* A mineral or aggregate of minerals from which a valuable constituent, esp. a metal, can be profitably mined or extracted. [ME < OE *ōra.*]

ö·re (œ′rə) *n., pl.* **öre.** See table at **currency.** [Dan. and Norw. *øre* and Swed. *öre,* all < Lat. *aureus,* gold coin < *aurum,* gold.]

o·re·ad (ôr′ē-ăd′, ōr′-) *n. Gk. Myth.* A mountain nymph. [Gk. *Oreias, Oreiad-* < *oreios,* of a mountain < *oros,* mountain.]

o·reg·a·no (ə-rĕg′ə-nō′, ô-rĕg′-) *n.* An herb seasoning made from the dried leaves of a species of marjoram, *Origanum vulgare.* [Sp. *orégano,* marjoram < Lat. *origanum* < Gk. *origanon,* prob. of North African orig.]

Or·e·gon fir (ôr′ə-gən, -gŏn′, ŏr′-) *n.* The Douglas fir.

Oregon grape *n.* An evergreen shrub, *Mahonia aquifolium,* of northwestern North America, having fragrant yellow flowers and small, edible, bluish berries.

Oregon maple *n.* A tree, *Acer macrophyllum,* of the Pacific coast of North America, having very large, lobed leaves.

Oregon myrtle *n.* The California laurel.

Oregon pine *n.* The wood of the Douglas fir.

o·re·ide (ôr′ē-īd′, ōr′-) *n.* Variant of **oroide.**

O·res·tes (ô-rĕs′tēz) *n. Gk. Myth.* The son of Agamemnon and Clytemnestra, who, with his sister Electra, avenged his father by slaying his mother and Aegisthus. [Gk. *Orestēs* < *orestēs,* mountaineer < *oros,* mountain.]

or·fray (ôr′frā′) *n.* Variant of **orphrey.**

or·gan (ôr′gən) *n.* **1.** A musical instrument consisting of a number of pipes that sound tones when supplied with air and a keyboard that operates a mechanism controlling the flow of air to the pipes. **2.** Any of various instruments, such as the electronic organ, that resemble the organ either in mechanism or sound. **3.** *Biol.* A differentiated part of an organism, adapted for a specific function. **4.** An organization that performs certain specified functions: *The FBI is an organ of the Justice Department.* **5.** An instrument or vehicle of communication, esp. a periodical publication issued by a

Orestes
Orestes slaying Aegisthus

organ grinder

organ-pipe cactus

oriel
Sketch showing oriel on late 19th-century house designed by Richard Morris Hunt

Oriental rug

political party, business firm, or other group. ***—modifier:*** *organ music.* [ME < OFr. *organe* < LLat. *organum* < Lat., instrument < Gk. *organon.*]

organ– *pref.* Variant of **organo-**.

or·ga·na[1] (ôr′gə-nə) *n.* A plural of **organon.**

or·ga·na[2] (ôr′gə-nə) *n.* A plural of **organum**[1].

or·gan·dy also **or·gan·die** (ôr′gən-dē) *n., pl.* **-dies.** A transparent crisp fabric of cotton or silk, used for trim, curtains, and light apparel. [Fr. *organdi.*]

or·gan·elle (ôr′gə-nĕl′) *n.* A specialized part of a cell that resembles and functions as an organ. [NLat. *organella* < Lat., dim. of *organum,* implement < Gk. *organon.*]

organ grinder *n.* A street musician who plays a hurdy-gurdy.

or·gan·ic (ôr-găn′ĭk) *adj.* **1.** Of, pertaining to, or affecting an organ of the body. **2.** Of, pertaining to, or derived from living organisms. **3. a.** Using or grown with fertilizers and mulches consisting only of animal or vegetable matter, with no use of chemical fertilizers or pesticides: *organic gardening.* **b.** Free from chemical injections or additives: *organic foods.* **c.** Simple, basic, and close to nature: *an organic lifestyle.* **4.** Having properties associated with living organisms. **5.** Likened to an organism in organization or development: *He saw society as an organic whole.* **6. a.** Constituting an integral part; constitutional. **b.** *Law.* Designating or pertaining to the fundamental laws and precepts of a government or organization. **7.** *Chem.* Of or designating carbon compounds. [OFr. *organique* < Lat. *organicus,* of an implement < Gk. *organikos* < *organon,* implement.] **—or·gan′i·cal·ly** *adv.*

organic chemistry *n.* The chemistry of carbon compounds.

or·gan·i·cism (ôr-găn′ĭ-sĭz′əm) *n.* **1.** The theory that all disease is associated with structural alterations of organs. **2.** The theory that the total organization of an organism, rather than the functioning of individual organs, is the principal or exclusive determinant of every life process. **3.** The concept that society is analogous to a biological organism. **—or·gan′i·cist** *n.*

or·gan·ism (ôr′gə-nĭz′əm) *n.* **1.** A living individual; a plant or animal. **2.** A system regarded as analogous to a living body: *the social organism.* **—or′gan·is′mal** (-nĭz′məl), **or′gan·is′mic** *adj.* **—or′gan·is′mi·cal·ly** *adv.*

or·gan·ist (ôr′gə-nĭst) *n.* One who plays the organ.

or·gan·i·za·tion (ôr′gə-nĭ-zā′shən) *n.* **1. a.** An act of organizing. **b.** The process of being organized. **2.** The state or manner of being organized: *a high degree of organization.* **3.** Something that has been organized or made into an ordered whole. **4.** Something comprising elements with varied functions that contribute to the whole and to collective functions; organism. **5.** A number of persons or groups having specific responsibilities and united for a particular purpose. **—or′gan·i·za′tion·al** *adj.* **—or′gan·i·za′tion·al·ly** *adv.*

or·gan·ize (ôr′gə-nīz′) *v.* **-ized, -iz·ing, -iz·es.** *—tr.* **1.** To put together into an orderly, functional, structured whole. **2. a.** To arrange in a coherent form; systematize: *organize one's thoughts before speaking.* **b.** To arrange in a desired pattern or structure: *"The painting is organized about a young reaper enjoying his noonday rest"* (William Carlos Williams). **3.** To arrange systematically for harmonious or united action: *organize a strike.* **4. a.** To establish as an organization: *organize a club.* **b.** To cause (employees) to form or join a labor union. **c.** To induce the employees of (a business or industry) to form or join a union: *organize a department store.* *—intr.* **1.** To develop into or assume an organic structure. **2. a.** To form a group (as a labor union). **b.** To join such a group. [ME *organisen* < Med. Lat. *organizare* < Lat. *organum,* instrument < Gk. *organon.*] **—or′gan·iz′er** *n.*

organo– or **organ–** *pref.* **1.** Organ: *organotherapy.* **2.** Organic: *organomercurial.* [ME < Med. Lat. *organum,* organ of the body < Lat., implement. —see ORGAN.]

or·gan·o·chlo·rine (ôr-găn′ə-klôr′ēn′, -ĭn, -klōr′-) *n.* Any of various hydrocarbon pesticides, such as DDT, that contain chlorine.

organ of Cor·ti (kôr′tē) *n.* A specialized structure located on the inner surface of the basilar membrane of the cochlea that contains a series of sensory receptors that respond to sound vibrations. [After Alfonso *Corti* (1822–1888).]

or·gan·o·gen·e·sis (ôr′gə-nō-jĕn′ĭ-sĭs, ôr-găn′ə-) *n., pl.* **-ses** (-sēz′). The origin and development of biological organs. **—or′gan·o·ge·net′ic** (-jə-nĕt′ĭk) *adj.* **—or′gan·o·ge·net′i·cal·ly** *adv.*

or·ga·nog·ra·phy (ôr′gə-nŏg′rə-fē) *n.* The scientific description of the organs of animals and plants. **—or′gan·o·graph′ic** *adj.* **—or′ga·no·graph′i·cal·ly** *adv.*

or·gan·o·lep·tic (ôr′gə-nō-lĕp′tĭk, ôr-găn′ə-) *adj.* Pertaining to or perceived by a sensory organ. [Fr. *organoleptique* : *organe,* organ (< Lat. *organum,* implement < Gk. *organon*) + Gk. *lēptikos,* receptive < *lambanein,* to take.] **—or′gan·o·lep′ti·cal·ly** *adv.*

or·gan·ol·o·gy (ôr′gə-nŏl′ə-jē) *n.* The study of plant and animal organs and their functions. **—or′gan·o·log′ic** (ôr′gə-nə-lŏj′ĭk, ôr-găn′ə-), **or′gan·o·log′i·cal** *adj.*

or·gan·o·mer·cu·ri·al (ôr-găn′ō-mər-kyŏŏr′ē-əl) *n.* An organic substance that contains mercury.

or·ga·non (ôr′gə-nŏn′) also **or·ga·num** (-nəm) *n., pl.* **-na** (-nə) or **-nons.** A set of principles or methods used in scientific investigation. [Gk., tool.]

or·gan·o·ther·a·py (ôr′gə-nō-thĕr′ə-pē, ôr-găn′ō-) *n.* The treatment of disease with animal organs or extracts such as insulin and thyroxin. **—or′gan·o·ther′a·peu′tic** (-thĕr′-ə-pyōō′tĭk) *adj.*

or·gan·ot·ro·pism (ôr′gə-nŏt′rə-pĭz′əm) also **or·gan·ot·ro·py** (-pē) *n. Med.* The attraction of certain chemical compounds or microorganisms to specific tissues or organs of the body. **—or′gan·o·trop′ic** (ôr′gə-nō-trŏp′ĭk, ôr-găn′ō-) *adj.* **—or′gan·o·trop′i·cal·ly** *adv.*

or·gan-pipe cactus (ôr′gən-pīp′) *n.* A tall cactus, *Pachycereus marginatus,* of Mexico and the southwestern United States.

organ point *n.* A pedal point.

or·ga·num[1] (ôr′gə-nəm) *n., pl.* **-na** (-nə) or **-nums.** Any of several types of vocal polyphonic music, in two, three, or four parts, of the 9th to the early 13th century. [Med. Lat. < LLat., organ. —see ORGAN.]

or·ga·num[2] (ôr′gə-nəm) *n.* Variant of **organon.**

or·gan·za (ôr-găn′zə) *n.* A sheer, stiff fabric of silk or synthetic material used for trimming, neckwear, or evening dresses. [Orig. unknown.]

or·gan·zine (ôr′gən-zēn′) *n.* A raw-silk thread, usually used as a warp thread. [Fr. *organsin* < Ital. *organzino.*]

or·gasm (ôr′găz′əm) *n.* The climax of sexual excitement, marked normally by ejaculation of semen by the male and by the release of tumescence in erectile organs of both sexes. [Fr. *orgasme* < Gk. *orgasmos* < *organ,* to swell up, to be excited.] **—or·gas′mic** (ôr-găz′mĭk), **or·gas′tic** *adj.*

or·geat (ôr′zhä′) *n.* A sweet flavoring of orange and almond used in cocktails and food. [Fr. < OFr. < OProv. *orjat* < *ordī,* barley < Lat. *hordeum.*]

or·gi·as·tic (ôr′jē-ăs′tĭk) *adj.* Of, pertaining to, or characteristic of an orgy. [Gk. *orgiastikos* < *orgia,* secret rites.]

or·gy (ôr′jē) *n., pl.* **-gies. 1.** A secret rite in the cults of ancient Greek or Roman deities, typically involving frenzied singing, dancing, drinking, and sexual activity. **2.** A revel involving unrestrained indulgence, esp. sexual activity. **3.** Excessive indulgence in an activity: *an orgy of reading.* [< *orgies,* secret rites < OFr. < Lat. *orgia* < Gk.]

o·ri·bi (ôr′ə-bē, ŏr′-) *n., pl.* **oribi** or **or·i·bis.** A small, brownish African antelope, *Ourebia ourebia.* [Afr. < Hottentot *arab* : *ara,* to provide with strips + *-b,* masc. noun-forming suffix.]

o·ri·el (ôr′ē-əl, ōr′-) *n.* A projecting bay window, supported from below with a corbel or bracket. [ME < Med. Lat. *oriolum,* porch.]

o·ri·ent (ôr′ē-ənt, -ĕnt′, ōr′-) *n.* **1.** The east; eastern regions. **2. Orient. a.** The countries of Asia, esp. of eastern Asia. **b.** In ancient times, the lands and regions east of the Mediterranean. **3. a.** The luster characteristic of a pearl of high quality. **b.** A pearl having exceptional luster. *—adj.* **1.** *Archaic.* Eastern; oriental. **2.** Having exceptional luster: *orient gemstones.* **3.** *Archaic.* Rising in the sky; ascending. *—v.* (ôr′ē-ĕnt′, ōr′-) **-ent·ed, -ent·ing, -ents.** *—tr.* **1.** To locate or place in a particular relation to the points of the compass: *orient the swimming pool north and south.* **2. a.** To locate or place so as to face the east. **b.** To build (a church) with the nave laid out west to east and the altar at the eastern end. **3.** To align or position with respect to a reference system. **4.** To determine the bearings of: *He oriented himself by finding a familiar landmark.* **5.** To cause to become familiar with or adjusted to facts, principles, or a situation. *—intr.* **1.** To turn toward the east. **2.** To become adjusted or aligned. [ME < OFr. < Lat. *oriens,* rising sun, east, pr.part. of *oriri,* to rise.]

o·ri·en·tal (ôr′ē-ĕn′tl, ōr′-) *adj.* **1.** Eastern. **2.** Often **Oriental.** Pertaining to the countries or regions of the Orient or to their peoples, languages, or culture. **3. Oriental.** *Ecol.* Of or designating the zoographic region that includes tropical Asia and the adjacent islands of the Malay Archipelago. **4.** Lustrous and valuable: *oriental pearls.* **5.** Pertaining to or designating precious varieties of corundum: *an oriental ruby.* *—n.* Often **Oriental.** An inhabitant of the Orient, esp. a native of an Oriental country or tribe. **—o′ri·en′tal·ly** *adv.*

O·ri·en·tal·ism also **o·ri·en·tal·ism** (ôr′ē-ĕn′tl-ĭz′əm, ōr′-) *n.* **1.** A quality, mannerism, or custom peculiar to or characteristic of the Orient. **2.** Scholarly knowledge of eastern cultures, languages, and peoples. **—O′ri·en′tal·ist** *n.*

O·ri·en·tal·ize also **o·ri·en·tal·ize** (ôr′ē-ĕn′tl-īz′, ōr′-) *v.* **-ized, -iz·ing, -iz·es.** *—tr.* To give an Oriental character or appearance to. *—intr.* To become Oriental.

Oriental poppy *n.* A plant, *Papaver orientale,* native to the Mediterranean region, and widely cultivated for its brilliant scarlet and black flowers.

Oriental rug *n.* Any of numerous kinds of rugs made by hand in the Orient.

or·i·en·tate (ôr′ē-ĕn-tāt′, -ən-, ōr′-) *tr. & intr.v.* **-tat·ed, -tat·ing, -tates.** To orient.

o·ri·en·ta·tion (ôr′ē-ĕn-tā′shən, -ən-, ōr′-) *n.* **1.** The act of orienting or the state of being oriented. **2.** Location or position relative to the points of the compass. **3.** *Archit.* The construction of a church so that its longitudinal axis is from west to east and its main altar at the eastern end. **4.** The line or direction followed in the course of a trend, movement, or development. **5.** A tendency of thought; general inclination:

a Marxist orientation. **6.** An adjustment or adaptation to a new environment, situation, custom, or set of ideas. **7.** *Psychol.* Individual awareness of the objective world in its relation to the self. **8.** Introductory instruction concerning a new situation.

or·i·en·teer·ing (ôr′ē-ĕn-tîr′ĭng, -ən-, ōr′-) *n.* A cross-country race in which competitors use a map and compass to find their way through unfamiliar territory. [Orig. a trademark.]

or·i·fice (ôr′ə-fĭs, ŏr′-) *n.* A mouth or vent; opening. [OFr. < LLat. *orificium* : Lat. *ōs,* mouth + Lat. *facere,* to make.] —**or′i·fi′cial** *adj.*

or·i·flamme (ôr′ə-flăm′, ŏr′-) *n.* **1.** The red or orange-red flag of the Abbey of St. Denis, France, used as a standard by the early kings of France. **2.** An inspiring standard or symbol. [ME *oriflamble* < OFr. *oriflambe* < Med. Lat. *auriflamma* : Lat. *aurum,* gold + Lat. *flamma,* flame.]

o·ri·ga·mi (ôr′ĭ-gä′mē) *n.* **1.** The art or process, originating in Japan, of folding paper into flower, bird, or other shapes. **2.** A decorative object made by folding paper. [J. : *ori,* a folding + *kami,* paper.]

origami
Folded paper bird

or·i·gin (ôr′ə-jĭn, ŏr′-) *n.* **1.** A point of origination; source. **2.** Ancestry; derivation: *"We cannot escape our origins, however hard we try"* (James Baldwin). **3.** A coming into being. **4.** *Anat.* The point of attachment of a muscle. **5.** *Math.* The point of intersection of coordinate axes, as in the Cartesian coordinate system. [ME *origine,* ancestry < Lat. *origo* < *oriri,* to rise.]

Synonyms: *origin, inception, source, root.* These nouns relate to beginnings. *Origin,* applicable to persons as well as things, indicates the often remote place and time when something began. *Inception,* more specific, marks the actual start of an action or process. *Source,* also more specific, stresses the place from which something is derived or comes into being. It may also denote a person or printed work considered as a giver of information. *Root* usually refers to beginnings in the sense of fundamental cause or basic reason for something of consequence.

o·rig·i·nal (ə-rĭj′ə-nəl) *adj.* **1.** Preceding all others in time; first. **2. a.** Not derived from something else; fresh and unusual: *an original play, not an adaptation.* **b.** Showing a marked departure from previous practice; new: *a truly original approach.* **3.** Productive of new things or new ideas; inventive. **4.** Being the source from which a copy, reproduction, or translation is made. —*n.* **1.** A first form from which varieties arise or imitations are made: *Later models retained many features of the original.* **2.** An authentic work of art, as distinguished from a copy or reproduction. **3.** One that is the model for an artistic or literary work. **4.** A person who is appealingly odd or curious; character. [ME < OFr. < Lat. *originalis* < *origo,* source < *oriri,* to rise.]

o·rig·i·nal·i·ty (ə-rĭj′ə-năl′ĭ-tē) *n., pl.* **-ties. 1.** The quality of being original. **2.** The capacity to act or think independently. **3.** Something original.

o·rig·i·nal·ly (ə-rĭj′ə-nə-lē) *adv.* **1.** With reference to origin. **2.** At first. **3.** In a highly distinctive manner.

original sin *n.* According to Christian theology, the condition of sin that marks all human beings as a result of Adam's first act of disobedience.

o·rig·i·nate (ə-rĭj′ə-nāt′) *v.* **-nat·ed, -nat·ing, -nates.** —*tr.* To bring into being; create. —*intr.* To come into being; start. —**o·rig′i·na′tion** *n.* —**o·rig′i·na′tive** *adj.* —**o·rig′i·na′tive·ly** *adv.* —**o·rig′i·na′tor** *n.*

o·ri·na·sal (ôr′ə-nā′zəl, ōr′-) *adj.* Pronounced with both nasal and oral passages open. —*n.* An orinasal speech sound, such as a French nasal vowel. [Lat. *ōs, ōr-,* mouth + NASAL.]

o·ri·ole (ôr′ē-ōl′, ōr′-) *n.* **1.** Any of various Old World birds of the family Oriolidae, of which the males are characteristically bright yellow and black. **2.** Any of various New World birds of the family Icteridae, of which the males are black and orange or yellow. [Fr. *oriol* < OFr. < Med. Lat. *oriolus* < Lat. *aureolus,* golden < *aureus* < *aurum,* gold.]

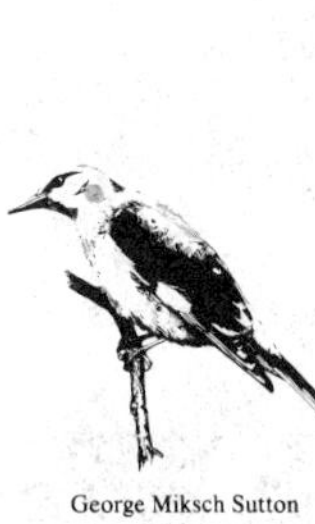

George Miksch Sutton
oriole

O·ri·on (ō-rī′ən) *n.* **1.** *Gk. Myth.* A giant hunter, pursuer of the Pleiades and lover of Eos, killed by Artemis. **2.** A constellation in the celestial equator near Gemini and Taurus, containing the stars Betelgeuse and Rigel. [Gk. *Ōriōn.*]

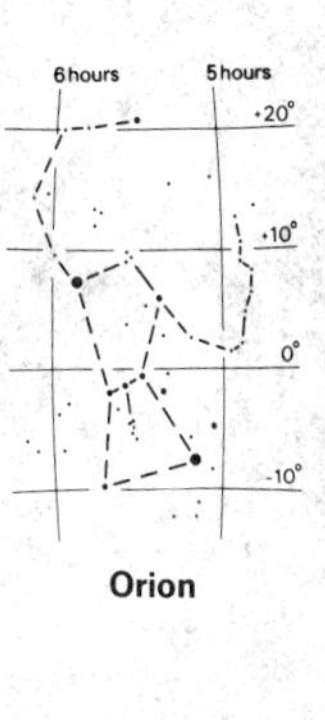

Orion

or·i·son (ôr′ĭ-sən, -zən, ŏr′-) *n.* A prayer. [ME *orisoun* < OFr. *oraison* < Lat. *oratio,* speech < *orare,* to speak.]

O·ri·ya (ō-rē′yə) *n.* The Indic language of Orissa, a state in eastern India.

Or·le·an·ist (ôr′lē-ə-nĭst) *n.* A supporter of the Orléans branch of the French royal family, descended from a younger brother of Louis XIV.

Or·lon (ôr′lŏn′). A trademark for a synthetic acrylic fiber.

or·lop (ôr′lŏp′) *n. Naut.* The lowest deck of a ship, esp. a warship. [ME *overloper,* floor covering a ship's hold < MDu. *overloop* : *over,* over + *loopen,* to leap.]

Or·mazd also **Or·muzd** (ôr′məzd) *n.* The chief deity of Zoroastrianism, the creator of the world, the source of light, and the embodiment of good. [Pers. *Ormazd* < Avestan *Ahura-Mazda* : *ahura,* spirit + *mazdā,* wise.]

or·mer (ôr′mər) *n. Chiefly Brit.* An abalone shell, esp. the shell of an edible species, *Haliotis tuberculata,* found chiefly in the Channel Islands. [Dial. Fr. < Fr. *ormier,* short for *oreille-de-mer,* ear of the sea < Lat. *auris maris.*]

or·mo·lu (ôr′mə-lo͞o′) *n.* **1.** Any of several copper and tin or zinc alloys resembling gold in appearance and used to decorate furniture, moldings, architectural ornamentations, and jewelry. **2.** An imitation of gold. [Fr. *or moulu,* ground gold.]

Or·muzd (ôr′məzd) *n.* Variant of **Ormazd.**

or·na·ment (ôr′nə-mənt) *n.* **1.** Something that decorates or adorns; embellishment. **2.** A person considered as a source of pride, honor, or credit: *He is an ornament to his profession.* **3.** *Mus.* A note or group of notes that embellishes a melody. —*tr.v.* (-mĕnt′) **-ment·ed, -ment·ing, -ments. 1.** To furnish with ornaments. **2.** To be an ornament to. [ME *ournement* < OFr. *ornement* < Lat. *ornamentum* < *ornare,* to embellish.] —**or′na·ment′er** *n.*

or·na·men·tal (ôr′nə-mĕn′tl) *adj.* Of, pertaining to, or serving as an ornament. —*n.* Something that is ornamental, esp. a plant grown for its beauty. —**or′na·men′tal·ly** *adv.*

or·na·men·ta·tion (ôr′nə-mĕn-tā′shən) *n.* **1. a.** The act or process of ornamenting. **b.** The state of being ornamented. **2.** That which ornaments; embellishment.

or·nate (ôr-nāt′) *adj.* **1.** Elaborately and heavily ornamented; excessively decorated. **2.** Flashy, showy, or florid in style or manner; flowery. [ME < Lat. *ornatus,* p.part. of *ornare,* to embellish.] —**or·nate′ly** *adv.* —**or·nate′ness** *n.*

Synonyms: *ornate, florid, flamboyant, lavish, gaudy, showy, ostentatious.* These adjectives indicate colorful and often excessive display in words, actions, or aspects. *Ornate* pertains to what is lavishly decorated, and can apply in that sense to use of words: *an ornate style. Florid* stresses excesses of adornment in design, writing, or speech. *Flamboyant* strongly implies vivid color, boldness of design, or personal behavior marked by boldness and dash: *flamboyant gestures; a flamboyant speech. Lavish* emphasizes opulent display or very generous action: *a lavish dinner party; a lavish donor. Gaudy* implies vulgarity or poor taste in color or style in general. *Showy,* a weaker word, describes a flashy display which is usually in poor taste. *Ostentatious* always implies a deliberate effort to attract attention or to outdo another by means of display.

or·ner·y (ôr′nə-rē) *adj.* **-i·er, -i·est.** Of a stubborn and mean-spirited nature. [Alteration of ORDINARY.]

ornith– *pref.* Variant of **ornitho-.**

or·nith·ic (ôr-nĭth′ĭk) *adj.* Of, relating to, or characteristic of birds. [Gk. *ornithikos* < *ornis,* bird.]

or·ni·thine (ôr′nə-thēn′) *n.* An amino acid, $C_5H_{12}N_2O_{12}$, that functions in urea formation. [E. *ornith(uric acid),* an acid found in birds' urine + -INE[2].]

ornitho– or **ornith–** *pref.* Bird: *ornithosis.* [NLat. < Gk. < *ornis,* bird.]

or·ni·thol·o·gy (ôr′nə-thŏl′ə-jē) *n.* The scientific study of birds as a branch of zoology. —**or′ni·tho·log′ic** (-thə-lŏj′ĭk), **or′ni·tho·log′i·cal** (-lŏj′ĭ-kəl) *adj.* —**or′ni·tho·log′i·cal·ly** *adv.* —**or′ni·thol′o·gist** *n.*

or·ni·thop·ter (ôr′nə-thŏp′tər) *n.* A hypothetical aircraft held aloft and propelled by wing movements. [ORNITHO- + (HELICO)PTER.]

or·ni·tho·sis (ôr′nə-thō′sĭs) *n.* A contagious virus disease, resembling psittacosis, that infects domestic fowl and other birds and is transmissible to man. —**or′ni·thot′ic** (-thŏt′ĭk) *adj.*

oro– *pref.* Mountain: *orogeny.* [< Gk. *oros,* mountain.]

o·rog·e·ny (ô-rŏj′ə-nē) also **or·o·gen·e·sis** (ôr′ə-jĕn′ĭ-sĭs, ōr′-) *n.* The process of mountain formation, esp. by a folding and faulting of the earth's crust. —**or′o·gen′ic** (ôr′ə-jĕn′ĭk, ōr′-) *adj.* —**or′o·gen′i·cal·ly** *adv.*

o·rog·ra·phy (ô-rŏg′rə-fē) *n.* The study of the physical geography of mountains and mountain ranges. —**or′o·graph′ic** (ôr′ə-grăf′ĭk, ōr′-), **or′o·graph′i·cal** *adj.* —**or′o·graph′i·cal·ly** *adv.*

o·ro·ide (ôr′ō-īd′, ōr′-) also **o·re·ide** (ôr′ē-īd′, ōr′-) *n.* An inexpensive alloy of copper, zinc, and tin, used in imitation gold jewelry. [Fr. *oréide* : *or,* gold (< Lat. *aurum*) + *-éide,* -oid.]

o·rol·o·gy (ô-rŏl′ə-jē) *n.* The study of mountains. —**o′ro·log′i·cal** (ôr′ə-lŏj′ĭ-kəl, ōr′-) *adj.* —**o′ro·log′i·cal·ly** *adv.* —**o·rol′o·gist** *n.*

o·ro·tund (ôr′ə-tŭnd′, ōr′-) *adj.* **1.** Full in sound; sonorous: *orotund tones.* **2.** Pompous and bombastic: *orotund talk.* [Lat. *ōre rotundo,* with a round mouth.] —**o′ro·tun′di·ty** (ôr′ə-tŭn′dĭ-tē, ōr′-) *n.*

or·phan (ôr′fən) *n.* A child whose parents are dead. —*adj.* **1.** Being an orphan. **2.** Intended for orphans: *an orphan home.* —*tr.v.* **-phaned, -phan·ing, -phans.** To deprive (a child) of one or both parents. [LLat. *orphanus* < Gk. *orphanos,* without parents.] —**or′phan·hood′** *n.*

or·phan·age (ôr′fə-nĭj) *n.* **1.** A public institution for the care and protection of orphans and abandoned children. **2.** The condition of being an orphan.

Or·phe·us (ôr′fē-əs, -fyo͞os′) *n. Gk. Myth.* A legendary Thracian poet and musician whose music had the power to move even inanimate objects and who almost succeeded in rescuing his wife Euridice from Hades. [Gk.] —**Or·phe′an** (ôr-fē′ən, ôr′fē-ən) *adj.*

Or·phic (ôr′fĭk) *adj.* **1.** Of or ascribed to Orpheus: *the Orphic poems; Orphic mysteries.* **2.** Of, pertaining to, or characteristic of the dogmas, mysteries, and philosophical principles set forth in the poems ascribed to Orpheus. **3.** Capable of casting a charm or spell as Orpheus did by his singing.

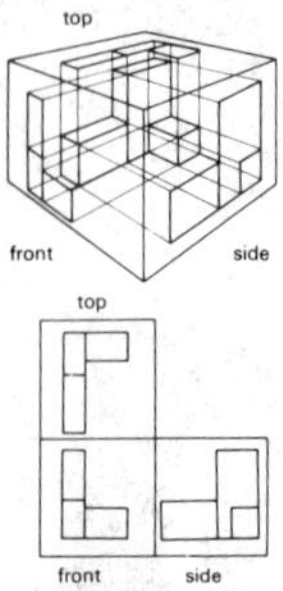

orthogonal projection

oryx

4. Often **orphic.** Mystic or occult in nature. [Gk. *Orphikos* < *Orpheus,* Orpheus.] **—Or'phi·cal·ly** *adv.*

Or·phism (ôr'fĭz'əm) *n.* An ancient Greek mystery religion arising in the 6th century B.C. from a synthesis of pre-Hellenic beliefs with the Thracian cult of Zagreus and soon becoming mingled with the Eleusinian mysteries and the doctrines of Pythagoras. [Fr. *orphisme* < *Orphée,* Orpheus < Gk. *Orpheus.*] **—Or'phist** *n.*

or·phrey (ôr'frē) also **or·fray** (ôr'frā') *n., pl.* **-phreys** also **-frays. 1.** A band of elaborate embroidery decorating the front of certain ecclesiastical vestments. **2.** Elaborate embroidery, esp. when made of gold. [ME *orfrey* < OFr. *orfrois* < Med. Lat. *aurifrigium* : Lat. *aurum,* gold + Lat. *Phrygius,* Phrygian.]

or·pi·ment (ôr'pə-mənt) *n.* Arsenic trisulfide, As_2S_3, a lemon-yellow pigment, used in tanning and in linoleum manufacture. [ME < OFr. < Lat. *auripigmentum* : *aurum,* gold + *pigmentum,* pigment < *pingere,* to paint.]

or·pine (ôr'pĭn) *n.* Any of several plants of the genus *Sedum,* esp. *S. telephium,* native to Eurasia, having clusters of reddish-purple flowers. [ME *orpin* < OFr. < *orpiment,* orpiment.]

Or·ping·ton (ôr'pĭng-tən) *n.* A breed of domestic fowls having a large body, a single comb, and unfeathered legs. [After *Orpington,* England.]

or·re·ry (ôr'ə-rē, ŏr'-) *n., pl.* **-ries.** A mechanical model of the solar system. [After Charles Boyle (1676–1731), fourth Earl of *Orrery.*]

or·ris (ôr'ĭs, ŏr'-) *n.* **1.** Any of several species of iris having a fragrant rootstock, esp. *Iris florentina.* **2.** Orrisroot. [Var. of IRIS.]

or·ris·root (ôr'ĭs-ro͞ot', -ro͝ot', ŏr'-) *n.* The fragrant rootstock of the orris, used in perfumes and cosmetics.

ort (ôrt) *n.* **1.** A small scrap or leaving of food after a meal is completed. **2.** A scrap; bit. [ME *orte,* food left by animals < MDu. : *oor,* out + *eten,* to eat.]

orth– *pref.* Variant of **ortho-.**

or·thi·con (ôr'thĭ-kŏn') *n.* A television camera pickup tube that uses a low-velocity electron beam to scan a photoactive mosaic. [ORTH(O)- + ICON(OSCOPE).]

or·tho (ôr'thō) *adj.* **1.** *Chem.* **a.** Designating the most fully hydrated form of an acid or of its salts. **b.** Of, pertaining to, or designating adjacent carbon positions in a benzene ring. **2.** *Physics.* Designating diatomic molecules in which the nuclei have the same spin directions. **3.** Orthochromatic. [< ORTHO-.]

ortho– or **orth–** *pref.* **1.** Straight; upright; vertical: *orthotropous.* **2.** Perpendicular: *orthorhombic.* **3.** Correct; correction: *orthopsychiatry.* [ME < OFr. < Lat. < Gk. < *orthos,* straight, correct, right.]

or·tho·cen·ter (ôr'thō-sĕn'tər) *n.* The point of intersection of the three altitudes of a triangle.

or·tho·ce·phal·ic (ôr'thō-sə-făl'ĭk) also **or·tho·ceph·a·lous** (-sĕf'ə-ləs) *adj.* Having a ratio of skull height to skull length between 0.70 and 0.75. **—or'tho·ceph'a·ly** (-sĕf'ə-lē) *n.*

or·tho·chro·mat·ic (ôr'thō-krō-măt'ĭk) *adj.* **1.** Of, having, or accurately reproducing the colors of nature. **2.** Of or pertaining to a film, plate, or emulsion that renders all colors, except red, in tones of gray approximating the relative brilliance of these colors. **—or'tho·chro'ma·tism** (-krō'mə-tĭz'-əm) *n.*

or·tho·clase (ôr'thə-klās', -klāz') *n.* A feldspar, essentially potassium aluminum silicate, $KAlSi_3O_8$, characterized by a monoclinic crystalline structure and found in igneous or granitic rock. [ORTHO- + Gk. *klasis,* a breaking < *klan,* to break.]

or·tho·clas·tic (ôr'thə-klăs'tĭk) *adj. Geol.* Having right-angled cleavage.

or·tho·don·tia (ôr'thə-dŏn'shə) *n.* The dental specialty and practice of correcting abnormally aligned or positioned teeth. **—or'tho·don'tic** (-tĭk) *adj.* **—or'tho·don'tist** *n.*

or·tho·don·tics (ôr'thə-dŏn'tĭks) *n.* *(used with a sing. verb).* Orthodontia.

or·tho·dox (ôr'thə-dŏks') *adj.* **1.** Adhering to the accepted or traditional and established faith, esp. in religion. **2.** Adhering to the Christian faith as expressed in the early Christian ecumenical creeds. **3.** Adhering to what is commonly accepted, customary, or traditional. **4. Orthodox. a.** Of, pertaining to, or designating any of the churches of the Eastern Orthodox Church. **b.** Of, pertaining to, or denoting Orthodox Judaism. *—n.* **1.** One that is orthodox. **2. Orthodox.** A member of an Eastern Orthodox Church. [OFr. *orthodoxe* < LLat. *orthodoxus* < Gk. *orthodoxos* : *orthos,* correct + *doxa,* opinion < *dokein,* to think.] **—or'tho·dox'ly** *adv.*

Orthodox Church *n.* The Eastern Orthodox Church.

Orthodox Judaism *n.* The branch of the Jewish faith that adheres to the Mosaic Law as interpreted in the Talmud, and considers it binding in modern as well as ancient times.

or·tho·dox·y (ôr'thə-dŏk'sē) *n., pl.* **-ies. 1.** The quality or state of being orthodox. **2.** Orthodox practice, custom, or belief.

or·tho·e·py (ôr-thō'ə-pē, ôr'thō-ĕp'ē) *n.* **1.** The study of the pronunciation of words. **2.** The customary pronunciation of words. [Gk. *orthoepeia,* correctness of diction : *orthos,* correct + *epos,* word.] **—or'tho·ep'ic** (-ĕp'ĭk), **or'tho·ep'i·cal** (-ĕp'ĭ-kəl) *adj.* **—or·tho'e·pist** *n.*

or·tho·gen·e·sis (ôr'thō-jĕn'ĭ-sĭs) *n.* **1.** *Biol.* The theory that evolutionary change is predetermined by the constitution of germ plasm and independent of external factors. **2.** The theory that all cultures pass through sequential periods in the same order. **—or'tho·ge·net'ic** (-jə-nĕt'ĭk) *adj.* **—or'tho·ge·net'i·cal·ly** *adv.*

or·tho·gen·ic (ôr'thō-jĕn'ĭk) *adj.* Pertaining to the correction or treatment of mental and emotional abnormalities in children.

or·thog·na·thous (ôr-thŏg'nə-thəs) also **or·thog·nath·ic** (ôr'thŏg-năth'ĭk) *adj.* Having the lower jaw aligned with the upper so that it does not protrude or recede. **—or·thog'na·thism, or·thog'na·thy** *n.*

or·thog·o·nal (ôr-thŏg'ə-nəl) *adj. Math.* Pertaining to or composed of right angles. [Gk. *orthogōnios* : *orthos,* right + *gōnia,* angle.] **—or·thog'o·nal·ly** *adv.*

orthogonal projection *n.* The two-dimensional graphic representation of an object formed by the perpendicular intersections of lines drawn from points on the object to a plane of projection.

or·tho·graph·ic (ôr'thə-grăf'ĭk) also **or·tho·graph·i·cal** (-kəl) *adj.* **1.** Of or pertaining to orthography. **2.** Spelled correctly. **3.** *Math.* Having perpendicular lines. **—or'tho·graph'i·cal·ly** *adv.*

orthographic projection *n.* Orthogonal projection.

or·thog·ra·phy (ôr-thŏg'rə-fē) *n., pl.* **-phies. 1.** The art or study of correct spelling according to established usage. **2.** The aspect of language study concerned with letters and their sequences in words. **3.** A method of representing the sounds of language by literal symbols. **—or·thog'ra·pher, or·thog'ra·phist** *n.*

or·tho·mo·lec·u·lar (ôr'thō-mə-lĕk'yə-lər) *adj.* Of, pertaining to, or being a theory that holds that mental illness results from various chemical imbalances or deficiencies and can be cured by the restoration of proper levels of chemical substances in the body.

or·tho·pe·dics also **or·tho·pae·dics** (ôr'thə-pē'dĭks) *n.* *(used with a sing. verb).* The surgical or manipulative treatment of disorders of the skeletal system and associated motor organs. [< Fr. *orthopedique,* orthopedic : Gk. *orthos,* correct + Gk. *pais,* child.] **—or'tho·pe'dic** *adj.* **—or'tho·pe'di·cal·ly** *adv.* **—or'tho·pe'dist** *n.*

or·tho·psy·chi·a·try (ôr'thō-sĭ-kī'ə-trē, -sī-) *n.* The psychiatric study and treatment of incipient and borderline mental disorders, esp. their development in the young. **—or'tho·psy'chi·at'ric** (-sī'kē-ăt'rĭk), **or'tho·psy'chi·at'ri·cal** *adj.* **—or'tho·psy·chi'a·trist** *n.*

or·thop·ter·an (ôr-thŏp'tər-ən) also **or·thop·ter·on** (-tə-rŏn', -tər-ən) *n.* An insect of the order Orthoptera, characterized by membranous, folded hind wings covered by leathery, narrow forewings, and including the locusts, cockroaches, crickets, and grasshoppers. [NLat. *Orthoptera,* order name : Gk. *orthos,* straight + Gk. *pteron,* wing.] **—or·thop'ter·an, or·thop'ter·ous, or·thop'ter·al** *adj.*

or·tho·rhom·bic (ôr'thō-rŏm'bĭk) *adj.* Of or pertaining to a crystalline structure of three mutually perpendicular axes of different length.

or·tho·scope (ôr'thə-skōp') *n.* An instrument for examining the eye through a layer of water that compensates for the curvature of the cornea.

or·tho·scop·ic (ôr'thə-skŏp'ĭk) *adj.* **1.** Having normal vision. **2.** Pertaining to the use of the orthoscope. **3.** Giving an undistorted image.

or·thos·ti·chous (ôr-thŏs'tĭ-kəs) *adj. Biol.* Characterized by parallel arrangement in a vertical row. [ORTHO- + Gk. *stikhos,* row.] **—or·thos'ti·chy** *n.*

or·thot·ics (ôr-thŏt'ĭks) *n.* *(used with a sing. verb).* A branch of medicine that deals with the use of specialized mechanical devices to support or supplement weakened joints or limbs. [< Gk. *orthōsis,* a straightening < *orthoun,* to straighten < *orthos,* straight.] **—or·thot'ic** *adj.* **—or·thot'ist** (ôr-thŏt'ĭst, ôr'thə-tĭst) *n.*

or·tho·trop·ic (ôr'thə-trŏp'ĭk) *adj.* Tending to grow or form along a vertical axis. **—or'tho·trop'i·cal·ly** *adv.* **—or·thot'ro·pism** (ôr-thŏt'rə-pĭz'əm) *n.*

or·thot·ro·pous (ôr-thŏt'rə-pəs) *adj.* Growing straight, so that the micropyle is at the side opposite the stalk: *an orthotropous ovule.*

or·to·lan (ôr'tə-lən) *n.* **1.** A small, brownish bird, *Emberiza hortulana,* of the Old World, eaten as a delicacy. **2.** Any of several New World birds, such as the bobolink and the sora. [Fr. < Prov., gardener < Lat. *hortulanus* < *hortus,* garden.]

–ory *suff.* **1.** Of, pertaining to, or characterized by: *advisory.* **2.** A place or thing used for or connected with: *crematory.* [ME *-orie* < OFr. < Lat. *-orium,* n. suffix and *-orius,* adj. suffix.]

o·ryx (ôr'ĭks, ŏr'-, ōr'-) *n., pl.* **o·ryx·es** or **oryx.** Any of several antelopes of the genus *Oryx,* of Africa and southwestern Asia, having long, straight or arching horns. [Lat. < Gk. *orux.*]

os[1] (ŏs) *n., pl.* **o·ra** (ôr'ə, ōr'ə). A mouth or opening. [Lat. *ōs,* mouth.]

os[2] (ŏs) *n., pl.* **os·sa** (ŏs'ə). A bone. [Lat., bone.]

os[3] (ōs) *n., pl.* **os·ar** (ō'sär'). An esker. [Swed. *ås,* ridge < ON *āss.*]

Os The symbol for the element osmium.

O·sage (ō′sāj′, ō-sāj′) *n., pl.* **O·sage** or **O·sag·es. 1. a.** A tribe of North American Indians formerly inhabiting the region between the Missouri and Arkansas rivers. **b.** A member of this tribe. **2.** The Siouan language of the Osage. [Fr. < Osage *Wazházhe,* tribal name.] **—O′sage′** *adj.*

Osage orange *n.* A tree, *Maclura pomifera,* native to midwestern North America, bearing inedible, orangelike fruit.

os·ar (ō′sär′) *n.* Plural of **os**[3].

Os·can (ŏs′kən) *n.* **1.** One of an ancient people of Campania. **2.** The Italic language of the Oscans. **—Os′can** *adj.*

Os·car (ŏs′kər). A trademark for any of the golden statuettes awarded annually by the Academy of Motion Picture Arts and Sciences for achievement in motion pictures.

os·cil·late (ŏs′ə-lāt′) *intr.v.* **-lat·ed, -lat·ing, -lates. 1.** To swing back and forth with a steady uninterrupted rhythm. **2.** To waver between two or more thoughts or courses of action; vacillate. **3.** *Physics.* To vary between alternate extremes, usually with a definable period. [Lat. *oscillare, oscillat-* < *oscillum,* swing.] **—os′cil·la′tor** *n.* **—os′cil·la·to′ry** (-lə-tôr′ē, -tōr′ē) *adj.*

os·cil·la·tion (ŏs′ə-lā′shən) *n.* **1.** The state or act of oscillating. **2.** A single oscillatory cycle. **—os′cil·la′tion·al** *adj.*

os·cil·lo·gram (ō-sĭl′ə-grăm′, ə-sĭl′-) *n.* **1.** The graph traced by an oscillograph. **2.** An instantaneous oscilloscope trace or photograph. [OSCILLO(GRAPH) + -GRAM.]

os·cil·lo·graph (ō-sĭl′ə-grăf′) *n.* A device that records oscillations as a continuous graph of corresponding variation in an electric current. [OSCILL(ATION) + -GRAPH.] **—os·cil′lo·graph′ic** *adj.* **—os·cil′lo·graph′i·cal·ly** *adv.* **—os′cil·log′ra·phy** (ŏs′ə-lŏg′rə-fē) *n.*

os·cil·lo·scope (ō-sĭl′ə-skōp′, ə-sĭl′-) *n.* An electronic instrument that produces an instantaneous visual display or trace of electron motion on the screen of a cathode-ray tube corresponding to some external oscillatory motion. [OSCILL(ATION) + -SCOPE.] **—os·cil′lo·scop′ic** (-skŏp′ĭk) *adj.*

os·cine (ŏs′īn′) *adj.* Of or pertaining to the Oscines, a large suborder of the passerine birds that includes most songbirds. [NLat. *Oscines,* suborder name < Lat. *oscines,* pl. of *oscen,* bird used in augury : *ob-,* before + *canere,* to sing.] **—os′cine′** *n.*

os·ci·tance (ŏs′ĭ-təns) *n.* Oscitancy.

os·ci·tan·cy (ŏs′ĭ-tən-sē) *n., pl.* **-cies. 1.** The act of yawning. **2.** The state of being drowsy or inattentive; dullness. [< Lat. *oscitans,* pr.part. of *oscitare,* to yawn : *ōs,* mouth + *citare,* to move.] **—os′ci·tant** *adj.*

Os·co-Um·bri·an (ŏs′kō-ŭm′brē-ən) *n.* A subdivision of the Italic languages that consists of Oscan and Umbrian.

os·cu·la (ŏs′kyə-lə) *n.* Plural of **osculum.**

os·cu·lant (ŏs′kyə-lənt) *adj.* **1.** *Biol.* Intermediate in characteristics between two similar or related taxonomic groups. **2.** Closely adhering or joined; embracing. [Lat. *osculans, osculant-,* pr.part. of *osculari,* to kiss. —see OSCULATE.]

os·cu·late (ŏs′kyə-lāt′) *v.* **-lat·ed, -lat·ing, -lates.** *—tr.* To kiss. *—intr. Biol.* To have characteristics that are intermediate between those of two similar or related taxonomic groups. [Lat. *osculari, osculat-* < *osculum,* kiss, dim. of *ōs,* mouth.]

os·cu·la·tion (ŏs′kyə-lā′shən) *n.* **1. a.** The act of kissing. **b.** A kiss. **2.** *Math.* A point where two branches of a curve have a common tangent and extend in both directions of the tangent. **—os′cu·la·to′ry** (ŏs′kyə-lə-tôr′ē, -tōr′ē) *adj.*

os·cu·lum (ŏs′kyə-ləm) also **os·cule** (ŏs′kyo͞ol′) *n., pl.* **-cu·la** (-kyə-lə) also **-cules.** An opening in a sponge for expelling water. [Lat., dim. of *ōs,* mouth.] **—os′cu·lar** *adj.*

-ose[1] *suff.* Possessing; having the characteristics of; full of: *cymose.* [ME < Lat. *-osus.*]

-ose[2] *suff.* **1.** Carbohydrate: *fructose.* **2.** Product of protein hydrolysis: *proteose.* [< GLUCOSE.]

o·sier (ō′zhər) *n.* **1. a.** Any of several willows having long, rodlike twigs used in basketry, esp. *Salix viminalis* and *S. purpurea,* both native to Eurasia. **b.** A twig of an osier. **2.** Any of various trees similar to the osier. [ME < OE *oser* and OFr. *osier,* both < Med. Lat. *osaria,* willow bed.]

O·si·ris (ō-sī′rĭs) *n.* The ancient Egyptian god whose annual death and resurrection personified the self-renewing vitality and fertility of nature. [Lat. < Gk., of Egypt. orig.]

-osis *suff.* **1.** Condition; process: *osmosis.* **2.** Diseased or abnormal condition: *neurosis.* **3.** Increase; formation: *leukocytosis.* [ME < Lat. < Gk. *-ōsis,* n. suffix.]

Os·man·li (ŏz-măn′lē, ŏs-) *n., pl.* **-lis. 1.** An Ottoman Turk. **2.** Turkish. *—adj.* Ottoman. [Turk. : *Osman,* Osman I (1259–1326) + *-li,* adj. suffix.]

os·mat·ic (ŏz-măt′ĭk) also **os·mic** (ŏz′mĭk) *adj.* Having or characterized by a sense of smell. [Gk. *osmē,* odor + -ATE[1] + -IC.]

os·mic[1] (ŏz′mĭk) *adj.* Of, pertaining to, or containing osmium in a compound with a valence higher than that in a comparable osmous compound. [OSM(IUM) + -IC.]

os·mic[2] (ŏz′mĭk) *adj.* Variant of **osmatic.**

os·mi·ous (ŏz′mē-əs) *adj.* Variant of **osmous.**

os·mi·rid·i·um (ŏz′mə-rĭd′ē-əm) *n.* A natural alloy of osmium and iridium with small inclusions of platinum, rhodium, and other metals, used in needles and wearing points. [OSM(IUM) + IRIDIUM.]

os·mi·um (ŏz′mē-əm) *n. Symbol* **Os** A bluish-white, hard, metallic element, found in small amounts in osmiridium, nickel, and platinum ores. It is used as a platinum hardener, in making pen points, phonograph needles, and instrument pivots and also as a catalyst in cortisone synthesis. Atomic number 76; atomic weight 190.2; melting point 3,000°C; boiling point 5,000°C; specific gravity 22.57; valences 2, 3, 4, 8. [NLat. < Gk. *osmē,* odor (from the odor of osmium tetroxide).]

os·mom·e·ter (ŏz-mŏm′ĭ-tər, ŏs-) *n.* A device for measuring osmotic pressure. [OSMO(SIS) + -METER.] **—os′mo·met′ric** (ŏz′mə-mĕt′rĭk, ŏs′-) *adj.* **—os·mom′e·try** *n.*

os·mo·reg·u·la·tion (ŏz′mə-rĕg′yə-lā′shən, ŏs′-) *n.* The maintenance of an optimal and constant osmotic pressure in the body of a living organism. [OSMO(SIS) + REGULATION.] **—os′mo·reg′u·la·to′ry** (-lə-tôr′ē, -tōr′ē) *adj.*

os·mose (ŏz′mōs′, ŏs′-) *intr. & tr.v.* **-mosed, -mos·ing, -mos·es.** To diffuse or cause to diffuse by the process of osmosis. [Back-formation < OSMOSIS.]

os·mo·sis (ŏz-mō′sĭs, ŏs-) *n.* **1. a.** The diffusion of fluid through a semipermeable membrane until there is an equal concentration of fluid on both sides of the membrane. **b.** The tendency of fluids to diffuse in such a manner. **2.** A gradual, often unconscious process of assimilation or absorption that resembles fluid osmosis: *learn a language by osmosis.* [< obs. *osmose,* ult. < Gk. *ōsmos,* thrust < *ōthein,* to push.] **—os·mot′ic** (-mŏt′ĭk) *adj.* **—os·mot′i·cal·ly** *adv.*

os·mous (ŏz′məs) also **os·mi·ous** (ŏz′mē-əs) *adj.* Of, pertaining to, or containing osmium in a compound with a valence lower than that in a comparable osmic compound. [OSM(IUM) + -OUS.]

os·mun·da (ŏz-mŭn′də) also **os·mund** (ŏz′mənd) *n.* Any fern of the genus *Osmunda,* having erect, compound fronds and, in some species, fibrous roots used as a potting medium for cultivated plants. [NLat. *Osmunda,* genus name < ME *osmunde,* a kind of fern < OFr. *osmonde.*]

os·na·burg (ŏz′nə-bûrg′) *n.* A heavy, coarse cotton fabric, used for grain sacks, upholstery, and draperies. [After *Osnaburg,* Osnabrück, West Germany.]

os·prey (ŏs′prē, -prā′) *n., pl.* **-preys. 1.** A fish-eating hawk, *Pandion haliaetus,* having plumage that is dark on the back and white below. **2.** A plume formerly used to trim women's hats. [ME *osprai* < AN < Lat. *avis praedae,* bird of prey.]

os·sa (ŏs′ə) *n.* Plural of **os**[2].

os·se·in (ŏs′ē-ĭn) *n.* The residue of bone after acid dissolution, used in gelatin and glue. [OSSE(OUS) + -IN.]

os·se·ous (ŏs′ē-əs) *adj.* Composed of, containing, or resembling bone; bony. [Lat. *osseus* < *os,* bone.] **—os′se·ous·ly** *adv.*

Os·set (ŏs′ĭt, ŏ-sĕt′) also **Os·sete** (ŏs′ēt′, ŏ-sēt′) *n.* One of a people of Iranian origin living in Ossetia. **—Os·set′ic** *adj.*

os·si·a (ō-sē′ə) *conj. Mus.* Or else. Used as a direction to the performer to designate an alternative section or passage. [Ital. < *o sia,* or whether.]

Os·sian (ŏsh′ən, ŏs′ē-ən) *n.* A legendary Gaelic hero and bard of the 3rd century A.D. [Gael. *Oisin.*]

os·si·cle (ŏs′ĭ-kəl) *n. Anat.* A small bone, esp. one of the three bones of the inner ear. [Lat. *ossiculum,* dim. of *os,* bone.] **—os·sic′u·lar** (ŏ-sĭk′yə-lər), **os·sic′u·late** (-lĭt) *adj.*

os·si·fi·ca·tion (ŏs′ə-fĭ-kā′shən) *n.* **1.** The natural process of bone formation. **2. a.** The abnormal hardening or calcification of soft tissue into a bonelike material. **b.** A mass or deposit of such material. **3.** The process of becoming or state of being set in a rigidly conventional pattern, as of behavior, habits, or beliefs. **—os·sif′i·ca·to′ry** (ŏ-sĭf′ĭ-kə-tôr′ē, -tōr′ē) *adj.*

os·si·frage (ŏs′ə-frĭj, -frāj′) *n.* **1.** Osprey. **2.** Lammergeier. [Lat. *ossifraga* < *ossifragus,* bone-breaking : *os,* bone + *frangere,* to break.]

os·si·fy (ŏs′ə-fī′) *v.* **-fied, -fy·ing, -fies.** *—intr.* **1.** To change into bone; become bony. **2.** To become set in a rigidly conventional pattern. *—tr.* **1.** To convert (a membrane or cartilage, for example) into bone. **2.** To mold into a rigidly conventional pattern. [Lat. *os, oss-,* bone + -FY.] **—os·sif′ic** (ŏ-sĭf′ĭk) *adj.*

os·so bu·co (ō′sō bo͞o′kō) *n.* An Italian dish consisting of braised veal shanks in white wine. [Ital. *ossobuco,* marrowbone.]

os·su·ar·y (ŏsh′o͞o-ĕr′ē, ŏs′yo͞o-) *n., pl.* **-ies.** A container or receptacle, such as an urn or vault, for holding the bones of the dead. [LLat. *ossuarium,* neut. of Lat. *ossuarius,* of bones < *os,* bone.]

oste– *pref.* Variant of **osteo-.**

os·te·al (ŏs′tē-əl) *adj.* **1.** Bony; osseous. **2.** Pertaining to bone or to the skeleton.

os·te·i·tis (ŏs′tē-ī′tĭs) *n.* Inflammation of bone or bony tissue.

os·ten·si·ble (ŏ-stĕn′sə-bəl) *adj.* Represented or appearing as such; seeming; professed: *His ostensible purpose was charity, his real goal popularity.* [Fr. < Med. Lat. *ostensibilis* < Lat. *ostendere,* to show : *ob-,* before + *tendere,* to stretch.] **—os·ten′si·bly** *adv.*

os·ten·sive (ŏ-stĕn′sĭv) *adj.* **1.** Ostensible. **2.** Obviously or manifestly demonstrative. [LLat. *ostensivus* < Lat. *ostendere,* to show. —see OSTENSIBLE.] **—os·ten′sive·ly** *adv.*

os·ten·so·ri·um (ŏs′tən-sôr′ē-əm, -sōr′ē-) also **os·ten·so·ry** (ŏ-stĕn′sə-rē) *n., pl.* **-so·ri·a** (-sôr′ē-ə, -sōr′-) also **-so·ries.**

Osiris
Papyrus showing a man making an offering to Osiris

osprey

osculation

Rom. Cath. Ch. A monstrance. [Med. Lat. < Lat. *ostendere,* to show. —see OSTENSIBLE.]

os·ten·ta·tion (ŏs′tĕn-tā′shən, -tən-) *n.* **1.** Pretentious display meant to impress others; boastful showiness. **2.** *Archaic.* An act of showing; exhibition. [ME *ostentacioun* < Lat. *ostentatio* < *ostentare,* freq. of *ostendere,* to show. —see OSTENSIBLE.]

os·ten·ta·tious (ŏs′tĕn-tā′shəs, -tən-) *adj.* Characterized by or given to ostentation; showy; pretentious. **—os′ten·ta′tious·ly** *adv.*

osteo– or **oste–** *pref.* Bone: *osteocranium.* [Gk. < *osteon,* bone.]

os·te·o·ar·thri·tis (ŏs′tē-ō-är-thrī′tĭs) *n.* Degenerative joint disease. **—os′te·o·ar·thrit′ic** *adj.*

os·te·o·blast (ŏs′tē-ə-blăst′) *n.* A cell from which bone develops. **—os′te·o·blas′tic** *adj.*

os·te·oc·la·sis (ŏs′tē-ŏk′lə-sĭs) *n.* **1.** Surgical fracture of a bone, performed to correct a deformity. **2.** The process of dissolution and resorption of bony tissue in the regeneration of bone. [OSTEO- + Gk. *klasis,* breakage < *klan,* to break.]

os·te·o·clast (ŏs′tē-ə-klăst′) *n.* **1.** An instrument used in surgical osteoclasis. **2.** A large multinuclear cell that resorbs bony tissue in osteoclasis. [OSTEO- + Med. Lat. *-clastes,* breaker < Med. Gk. *-klastēs* < Gk. *klan,* to break.] **—os′te·o·clas′tic** *adj.*

os·te·o·cra·ni·um (ŏs′tē-ō-krā′nē-əm) *n.* The ossified embryonic cranium as distinguished from the chondrocranium. **—os′te·o·cra′ni·al** *adj.*

os·te·o·cyte (ŏs′tē-ə-sīt′) *n.* A bone cell.

os·te·o·gen·ic sarcoma (ŏs′tē-ə-jĕn′ĭk) *n.* Osteosarcoma.

os·te·oid (ŏs′tē-oid′) *adj.* Resembling bone. —*n.* The bone matrix, esp. before calcification.

os·te·ol·o·gy (ŏs′tē-ŏl′ə-jē) *n.* **1.** The anatomical study of bones. **2.** The bone structure or system of an animal. **—os′te·o·log′i·cal** (-ə-lŏj′ĭ-kəl) *adj.* **—os′te·ol′o·gist** *n.*

os·te·o·ma (ŏs′tē-ō′mə) *n., pl.* **-mas** or **-ma·ta** (-mə-tə). A benign bony tumor, esp. one in the skull.

os·te·o·ma·la·cia (ŏs′tē-ō-mə-lā′shə, -shē-ə) *n.* Softening of the bones because of a deficiency of vitamin D or of calcium and phosphorus. [OSTEO- + Gk. *malakia,* softness < *malakos,* soft.]

os·te·o·my·e·li·tis (ŏs′tē-ō-mī′ə-lī′tĭs) *n.* Inflammation of the bone marrow.

os·te·o·path (ŏs′tē-ə-păth′) also **os·te·op·a·thist** (ŏs′tē-ŏp′ə-thĭst) *n.* One who practices osteopathy.

os·te·op·a·thy (ŏs′tē-ŏp′ə-thē) *n.* A medical therapy that emphasizes manipulative techniques for correcting somatic abnormalities thought to cause disease and inhibit recovery. **—os′te·o·path′ic** (-ə-păth′ĭk) *adj.* **—os′te·o·path′i·cal·ly** *adv.*

os·te·o·phyte (ŏs′tē-ə-fīt′) *n.* A small abnormal bony outgrowth. **—os′te·o·phyt′ic** (-fĭt′ĭk) *adj.*

os·te·o·plas·tic (ŏs′tē-ə-plăs′tĭk) *adj.* **1.** *Med.* Of or pertaining to osteoplasty. **2.** *Physiol.* Pertaining to or functioning in bone formation.

os·te·o·plas·ty (ŏs′tē-ə-plăs′tē) *n., pl.* **-ties.** The surgical repair or alteration of bone.

os·te·o·sar·co·ma (ŏs′tē-ō-sär-kō′mə) *n.* A malignant sarcoma of the bone.

os·te·ot·o·my (ŏs′tē-ŏt′ə-mē) *n., pl.* **-mies.** The surgical division or sectioning of bone. **—os′te·ot′o·mist** *n.*

os·ti·a (ŏs′tē-ə) *n.* Plural of **ostium.**

Os·ti·ak (ŏs′tē-ăk′) *n.* Variant of **Ostyak.**

os·ti·ar·y (ŏs′tē-ĕr′ē) *n., pl.* **-ies. 1.** *Rom. Cath. Ch.* One who is ordained in the lowest of the minor orders. **2.** A doorkeeper at a church. [Lat. *ostiarius,* doorkeeper < *ostium,* door < *ōs,* mouth.]

os·ti·na·to (ŏs′tĭ-nä′tō) *n., pl.* **-tos.** *Mus.* A short melody or phrase that is constantly repeated in the same pitch. [Ital. < Lat. *obstinatus,* stubborn, p.part. of *obstinare,* to persist.]

os·ti·ole (ŏs′tē-ōl′) *n.* A small opening or pore. [Lat. *ostiolum,* dim. of *ostium,* opening < *ōs,* mouth.] **—os′ti·o′lar** *adj.*

os·ti·um (ŏs′tē-əm) *n., pl.* **-ti·a** (-tē-ə). A small opening; ostiole. [Lat. < *ōs,* mouth.]

os·tler (ŏs′lər) *n.* Variant of **hostler.**

ost·mark (ôst′märk′, ŏst′-) *n.* See table at **currency.** [G. : *Ost,* east (< OHG *ōstan*) + *Mark,* Deutsche mark.]

ostrich

os·to·my (ŏs′tə-mē) *n., pl.* **-mies.** The surgical construction of an artificial excretory opening, such as a colostomy. [< COLOSTOMY.]

os·tra·cism (ŏs′trə-sĭz′əm) *n.* **1.** Banishment or exclusion from a group; disgrace. **2. a.** The act of ostracizing. **b.** The state or condition of being ostracized. **3.** In Athens and other cities of ancient Greece, the temporary banishment by popular vote of a citizen considered dangerous to the state. [Fr. *ostracisme* < Gk. *ostrakismos* < *ostrakizein,* to ostracize. —see OSTRACIZE.]

os·tra·cize (ŏs′trə-sīz′) *tr.v.* **-cized, -ciz·ing, -ciz·es. 1.** To banish or exclude from a group; shun. **2.** To banish by ostracism, as in ancient Greece. [Gk. *ostrakizein* < *ostrakon,* potsherd, from the potsherds used as ballots in voting for ostracism.]

os·tra·cod (ŏs′trə-kŏd′) *n.* Any of various minute, chiefly freshwater crustaceans of the order Ostracoda, having a bivalve carapace. [NLat. *Ostracoda,* order name < Gk. *ostrakōdēs,* testaceous < *ostrakon,* shell.]

os·trich (ŏs′trĭch, ôs′-) *n., pl.* **-trich·es** or **ostrich. 1. a.** Any of several large, flightless African birds of the genus *Struthio,* characterized by long, bare necks and legs, two-toed feet, and plumage used for decoration and brushes. **b.** The rhea. **2.** One who tries to avoid disagreeable situations by refusing to face them. [ME < OFr. *ostruce* and Med. Lat. *ostrica,* both < VLat. **avis struthio* : Lat. *avis,* bird + LLat. *struthio,* ostrich. —see STRUTHIOUS.]

ostrich fern *n.* A fern, *Matteuccia Struthiopteris,* of northern temperate regions, having long, plumelike fronds.

Os·tro·goth (ŏs′trə-gŏth′) *n.* One of a tribe of eastern Goths that conquered and ruled Italy from A.D. 493 to 555. [LLat. *Ostrogothi,* Ostrogoths : *ostro-,* eastward (of Germanic orig.) + *Gothi,* Goths, of Germanic orig.] **—Os′tro·goth′ic** *adj.*

Os·ty·ak also **Os·ti·ak** (ŏs′tē-ăk′) *n.* **1.** One of a Finno-Ugric people inhabiting western Siberia. **2.** The Ugric language of the Ostyaks. [R. < Ostyak *āsyakh,* dwellers on the Ob River < *Ās,* the Ob River.]

Os·we·go tea (ŏs-wē′gō) *n.* An aromatic plant, *Monarda didyma,* of North America, having clusters of fragrant scarlet flowers. [After the *Oswego* River, New York.]

ot– *pref.* Variant of **oto-.**

O·ta·hei·te orange (ō′tə-hē′tē) *n.* A widely cultivated house plant, *Citrus taitensis,* resembling a miniature orange tree, and having lemon-shaped, insipid fruit. [After *Otaheite,* var. of *Tahiti.*]

oth·er (ŭth′ər) *adj.* **1. a.** Being or designating the remaining one of two or more: *the other ear.* **b.** Being or designating the remaining ones of several: *His other books are still in storage.* **2.** Different from that or those implied or specified: *Any other man would tell the truth.* **3.** Of a different character or quality: *He has no friends other than classmates.* **4.** Of a different time or era either future or past: *other centuries; other generations.* **5.** Additional; extra: *I have no other shoes.* **6.** Opposite or contrary; reverse: *the other side.* **7.** Alternate; second: *every other day.* **8.** Of the recent past: *just the other day.* —*n.* **1. a.** The remaining one of two or more: *One took a taxi, and the other walked home.* **b. others.** The remaining ones of several: *After his departure the others resumed the discussion.* **2. a.** A different person or thing: *one hurricane after the other.* **b.** An additional person or thing: *How many others will come later?* —*pron.* **1.** A different or another person or thing: *something or other.* **2. others.** People aside from oneself: *"Others may indeed talk"* (Anthony Berkeley). —*adv.* In another way; otherwise; differently: *She performed other than perfectly.* [ME < OE *ōðer.*]

oth·er-di·rect·ed (ŭth′ər-dĭ-rĕk′tĭd, -dī-) *adj.* Directed or guided chiefly by external standards as opposed to one's own standards or values. **—oth′er-di·rect′ed·ness** *n.*

oth·er·wise (ŭth′ər-wīz′) *adv.* **1.** In another way; differently: *She thought otherwise.* **2.** Under other circumstances: *Otherwise I might have helped.* **3.** In other respects: *an otherwise logical mind.* —*adj.* Other than supposed; different: *The evidence is otherwise.* [ME < OE *(on) ōðre wīsan,* (in) another manner.]

oth·er·world (ŭth′ər-wûrld′) *n.* A world or existence beyond earthly reality.

oth·er·world·ly (ŭth′ər-wûrld′lē) *adj.* **1.** Of, pertaining to, or characteristic of another world, esp. a mystical or transcendental world. **2.** Devoted to the world of the mind; concerned with intellectual or imaginative things. **—oth′er·world′li·ness** *n.*

o·tic (ō′tĭk) *adj.* Of, pertaining to, or located near the ear; auricular. [Gk. *ōtikos* < *ous,* ear.]

–otic *suff.* **1.** Of, pertaining to, or characterized by a specified condition or process: *anabiotic.* **2.** Having a specified disease or abnormal condition: *epizootic.* **3.** Characterized by an increase or formation of a specified kind: *leukocytotic.* [Fr. *-otique* < Lat. *-oticus* < Gk. *-ōtikos,* adj. suffix.]

o·ti·ose (ō′shē-ōs′, ō′tē-) *adj.* **1.** Having a lazy nature; indolent. **2.** Of no use. **3.** Ineffective; futile. [Lat. *otiosus,* idle < *otium,* leisure.] **—o′ti·ose′ly** *adv.* **—o′ti·os′i·ty** (-ŏs′ĭ-tē) *n.*

o·ti·tis (ō-tī′tĭs) *n.* Inflammation of the ear. **—o·tit′ic** (ō-tĭt′ĭk) *adj.*

oto– or **ot–** *pref.* Ear: *otology.* [NLat. < Gk. *ous,* ear.]

o·to·cyst (ō′tə-sĭst′) *n.* **1.** The auditory capsule in a vertebrate embryo. **2.** A statocyst. **—o′to·cys′tic** *adj.*

o·to·lar·yn·gol·o·gy (ō′tō-lăr′ĭng-gŏl′ə-jē) *n.* The branch of medicine that combines treatment of the ear and throat. **—o′to·lar′yn·go·log′i·cal** (-lə-rĭng′gə-lŏj′ĭ-kəl) *adj.* **—o′to·lar′yn·gol′o·gist** *n.*

o·to·lith (ō′tə-lĭth′) *n.* One of many minute calcareous particles found in the inner ear of certain vertebrates and in the statocysts of many invertebrates. **—o′to·lith′ic** *adj.*

o·tol·o·gy (ō-tŏl′ə-jē) *n.* The anatomy, physiology, and pathology of the ear. **—o′to·log′i·cal** (ō′tə-lŏj′ĭ-kəl) *adj.* **—o·tol′o·gist** *n.*

o·to·rhi·no·lar·yn·gol·o·gy (ō′tō-rī′nō-lăr′ĭng-gŏl′ə-jē) *n.* The branch of medicine that combines treatment of the ear, nose, and throat. **—o′to·rhi′no·la·ryn′go·log′i·cal** (-lə-rĭng′gə-lŏj′ĭ-kəl) *adj.* **—o′to·rhi′no·lar′yn·gol′o·gist** *n.*

ot·tar (ŏt′ər) *n.* Variant of **attar.**

ot·ta·va (ō-tä′və) *adv. Mus.* At an octave higher or lower than indicated. Used as a direction. [Ital.]

ottava ri·ma (rē′mə) *n.* A stanza of verse consisting of eight lines of eleven syllables each in iambic pentameter and having a rhyme pattern *abababcc.* [Ital., eighth rhyme.]

Ot·ta·wa (ŏt′ə-wə, -wä′, -wô′) *n.* **1. a.** A group of Indians inhabiting Michigan and southern Ontario. **b.** A member of this group. **2.** The dialect of Ojibwa spoken by the Ottawas. [After the *Ottawa* River.]

ot·ter (ŏt′ər) *n., pl.* **otter** or **-ters. 1.** Any of various aquatic, carnivorous mammals of the genus *Lutra* and allied genera, having webbed feet and dense, dark-brown fur. **2.** The fur of the otter. [ME *oter* < OE *otor.*]

ot·to (ŏt′ō) *n.* Variant of **attar.**

ot·to·man (ŏt′ə-mən) *n., pl.* **-mans. 1. a.** An upholstered sofa or divan without arms or a back. **b.** An upholstered low seat or cushioned footstool. **2.** A heavy silk or rayon fabric with a corded texture, usually used for coats and trimmings. [Fr. *ottomane,* fem. of *ottoman,* Ottoman.]

Ot·to·man (ŏt′ə-mən) *n., pl.* **-mans.** A Turk. *—adj.* Of or pertaining to the Turks; Turkish. [Fr. < Med. Lat. *Ottomanus* < Ar. *Othmānī,* Turkish < Turk. *Osman,* Osman I (1259-1326).]

oua·ba·in (wä-bā′ĭn) *n.* A white poisonous glucoside, $C_{29}H_{44}O_{12}{\cdot}8H_2O$, extracted from the seeds of the African trees *Strophanthus gratus* and *Acokanthera ouabaio,* and used as a heart stimulant, and by some African tribes as a dart poison. [< Fr. *ouabaio* < Somali *wabayo.*]

ou·bli·ette (o͞o′blē-ĕt′) *n.* A dungeon with a trap door in the ceiling as its only means of entrance or exit. [Fr. < *oublier,* to forget < OFr. *oblider* < Lat. *oblivisci.*]

ouch[1] (ouch) *interj.* Used to express sudden pain or displeasure.

ouch[2] (ouch) *n.* **1.** A setting for a precious stone. **2.** A brooch or a buckle set with jewels. **3.** *Obs.* A clasp; brooch. [ME *an ouche,* an ouch, alteration of *a nouche* < AN *nouch,* brooch, of Germanic orig.]

oud (o͞od) *n.* A musical instrument of northern Africa and southwest Asia resembling a lute. [Ar. *'ūd.*]

ought[1] (ôt) *aux.* Indicates: **1.** Obligation or duty: *You ought to work harder than that.* **2.** Advisability or prudence: *You ought to wear a raincoat.* **3.** Desirability: *You ought to have been there; it was great fun.* **4.** Probability or likelihood: *She ought to finish by next week.* [ME *oughten,* to be obliged to < *oughte,* owned < OE *āhte,* p.t. of *āgan,* to possess.]

Usage: *Ought to* is sometimes used without a following verb if the meaning is clear: *Should we begin soon? Yes, we ought to.* The omission of *to,* however (as in *no, we ought not*), is not standard. • Usages like *he hadn't ought to come* and *she shouldn't ought to say that* are common in many varieties of American English. They should be avoided in written English, however, in favor of the more standard variant *ought not to.*

ought[2] (ôt) *pron. & adv.* Variant of **aught**[1].

ought[3] (ôt) *n.* Variant of **aught**[2].

ought[4] (ôt) *v. Obs.* A past participle of **owe.**

ou·gui·ya (o͞o-gē′yə) *n.* See table at **currency.** [Native word in Mauritania.]

Oui·ja (wē′jə, -jē). A trademark for a board with the alphabet and other symbols on it, and a planchette that is thought, when touched with the fingers, to move in such a way as to spell out spiritualistic and telepathic messages on the board.

ounce[1] (ouns) *n.* **1. a.** A unit of weight in the U.S. Customary System, an avoirdupois unit equal to 437.5 grains or 28.350 grams. **b.** A unit of apothecary weight, equal to 480 grains or 31.103 grams. **2. a.** A unit of volume or capacity in the U.S. Customary System, used in liquid measure, equal to 8 fluid drams or 29.573 milliliters. **b.** A unit of volume or capacity in the British Imperial System, used in dry and liquid measure, equal to 1.734 cubic inches or 28.412 milliliters. **3.** A tiny bit. [ME *unce* < OFr. < Lat. *uncia* < *unus,* unit.]

ounce[2] (ouns) *n.* The snow leopard. [ME *once* < OFr., alteration of *lonce* < Lat. *lynx,* lynx < Gk. *lunx.*]

our (our) *pron.* The possessive form of **we.** Used to indicate possession or the agent or recipient of an action: *our children; our questioning of the witness; our first setback.* [ME *oure* < OE *ūre.*]

Our Father *n.* The Lord's Prayer.

Our Lady *n.* The Virgin Mary.

ours (ourz) *pron. (used with a sing. or pl. verb).* That or those belonging to us: *That house is ours. Ours were the only suggestions adopted.* [ME *oures* < *oure,* our < OE *ūre.*]

our·self (our-sĕlf′, är-) *pron.* Myself. Used as a reflexive when *we* is used instead of *I* by a singular speaker or author, as in an editorial or royal proclamation.

our·selves (our-sĕlvz′, är-) *pron.* **1.** Those identical with us. Used: **a.** Reflexively as the direct or indirect object of a verb or the object of a preposition: *We injured ourselves.* **b.** For emphasis: *We ourselves are excluded from the contract.* **c.** In an absolute construction: *In difficulty ourselves, we were unable to help others.* **2.** Our normal or healthy condition or state: *We have not been ourselves since he left.* — See Usage note at **myself.**

-ous *suff.* **1.** Possessing; full of; characterized by: *joyous.* **2.** Having a valence lower than that of a specified element in compounds or ions named with adjectives ending in *-ic*: *ferrous.* [ME < OFr. *-ous, -eus, -eux* < Lat. *-osus* and *-us,* adj. suffixes.]

ou·sel (o͞o′zəl) *n.* Variant of **ouzel.**

oust (oust) *tr.v.* **oust·ed, oust·ing, ousts. 1.** To eject from a position or place; force out: *"the American Revolution, which ousted the English"* (Virginia S. Eifert). **2.** To take the place of, esp. by force; supplant. [Norman Fr. *ouster* < Lat. *obstare,* to hinder. —see OBSTACLE.]

oust·er (ous′tər) *n.* **1. a.** The act of ousting. **b.** The state of being ousted. **2.** One that ousts. **3.** *Law.* The act of forcing one out of possession or occupancy of material property to which he is entitled; illegal or wrongful dispossession. [Norman Fr. < *ouster,* to oust.]

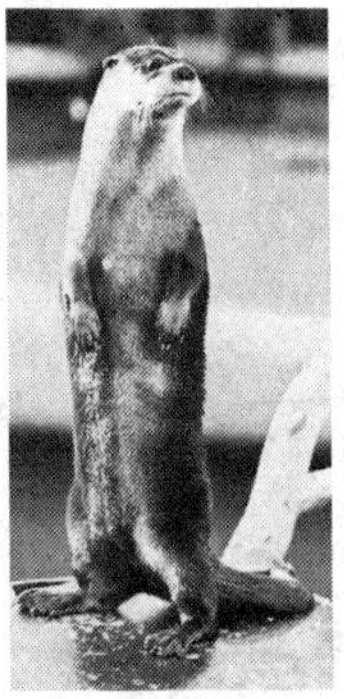

otter

out (out) *adv.* **1.** In a direction away from the inside: *go out of the office.* **2.** Away from the center or middle: *The troops fanned out.* **3. a.** Away from a usual place: *stepped out for a minute.* **b.** Out of normal position: *threw his back out.* **4.** From inside a building or shelter into the open air; outside: *The boy went out to play.* **5. a.** From within a container or source: *drain the water out.* **b.** From among others. **6. a.** To exhaustion or depletion: *The supplies have run out.* **b.** Into extinction or imperceptibility: *The fire has gone out.* **c.** To a finish or conclusion: *Play the game out.* **d.** To the fullest extent or degree: *all decked out for the dance.* **e.** In or into competition: *went out for the basketball team.* **7. a.** Into being or evident existence: *The new car models have come out.* **b.** Into public circulation: *The paper came out early today.* **8.** Into view: *The moon came out.* **9.** Without inhibition; boldly: *Speak out.* **10.** Into possession of another or others; into distribution: *giving out free passes.* **11. a.** Into disuse or an unfashionable status: *Knee-length hems have gone out.* **b.** Into a state of deprivation or loss: *voted the incompetent governor out.* **12.** *Baseball.* So as to be retired, or counted as an out: *He grounded out to the shortstop.* **13.** Used in two-way radio transmission to indicate that a message is terminated. *—adj.* **1.** Exterior; external: *the out surface of a ship's hull.* **2.** Located outside of a building or shelter. **3.** Located away from home or business; absent: *She was out when I called.* **4.** Directed away from a place or center; outgoing. **5.** In evidence or view: *The sun may be out later.* **6.** Exhausted or depleted: *The oil supply is out.* **7.** Extinguished. **8.** Not operating, functioning, or flowing: *The power is out.* **9.** Not available for consideration; impossible: *A taxi is out, because we haven't the money.* **10.** Not in power: *After the election, the liberals were out.* **11.** No longer fashionable. **12.** *Informal.* Without an amount possessed previously: *I'm out ten dollars.* **13.** Bare or threadbare: *a jacket out at the elbow.* **14.** *Baseball.* Not allowed to continue to bat or run; retired. **15.** Intent; determined: *She's out for the chairmanship. He is out to win.* *—prep.* **1.** Through; forth from: *He fell out the window.* **2.** Beyond or outside of: *Out this door is the garage.* *—n.* **1.** A person or thing that is out, esp. one who is out of power. **2.** A means of escape: *The window was my only out.* **3.** *Baseball.* **a.** A play in which a batter or base runner is retired. **b.** The player retired in such a play. **4.** *Sports.* A serve or return that falls out of bounds in a court game. **5.** *Printing.* A word or other part of a manuscript omitted from the printed copy. *—v.* **out·ed, out·ing, outs.** *—intr.* To be disclosed or revealed; come out: *Truth will out.* *—tr.* **1.** To put (a person or thing) out. **2.** *Chiefly Brit. Slang.* To knock unconscious. ***—idiom.* on the outs.** *Informal.* Not on friendly terms; disagreeing. [ME < OE *ūt.*]

out– *pref.* In a way that surpasses, exceeds, or goes beyond: *outdistance.* [< OUT.]

out·age (ou′tĭj) *n.* **1.** A quantity or portion of something lacking after delivery or storage. **2.** A temporary suspension of operation, esp. of electric power.

out-and-out (out′n-out′) *adj.* Complete; thoroughgoing.

out-and-outer (out′ən-ou′tər) *n.* A person who goes to extremes.

out·back (out′băk′) *adv.* Out to or in remote, rural country, esp. in Australia or New Zealand. *—n.* (out′băk′). The remote, rural part of a country, esp. of Australia or New Zealand. ***—modifier:*** *outback life.* **—out′back′er** *n.*

out·bid (out-bĭd′) *tr.v.* **-bid, -bid·den** (-bĭd′n) or **-bid, -bid·ding, -bids.** To bid higher than: *He outbid his rivals at the auction.*

out·board (out′bôrd′, -bōrd′) *adj.* **1.** *Naut.* **a.** Situated outside the hull of a vessel. **b.** Being away from the center line of the hull of a ship. **2.** Situated toward or nearer the end of a wing of an aircraft. **—out′board′** *adv.*

outboard motor *n.* A detachable engine mounted on the stern of a boat or on outboard brackets.

out·bound (out′bound′) *adj.* Outward bound; headed away.

out·break (out′brāk′) *n.* **1.** A sudden increase in something: *an outbreak of influenza.* **2.** A sudden eruption; outburst: *"an outbreak of strikes, violent agitation, and arrests"* (Samuel Chew).

out·breed (out′brēd′) *tr.v.* **-bred** (-brĕd′), **-breed·ing, -breeds.** To subject to outbreeding.

out·breed·ing (out′brē′dĭng) *n.* **1.** The breeding of distantly related or unrelated stocks of animals. **2.** *Anthropol.* The mating of persons from different groups, often as a consequence of taboos against marriage within the group.

out·build·ing (out′bĭl′dĭng) *n.* A building separate from but associated with a main building.

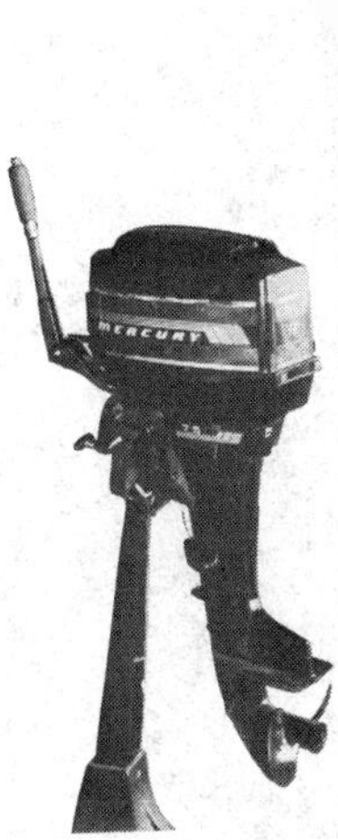

outboard motor

out·burst (out′bûrst′) *n.* A sudden, violent display, as of activity or emotion; flare-up: *an outburst of hatred.*
out·cast (out′kăst′) *n.* One that has been excluded from a society or system. **—out′cast′** *adj.*
out·caste (out′kăst′) *n.* A native of India who has been expelled from or has abandoned his caste.
out·class (out-klăs′) *tr.v.* **-classed, -class·ing, -class·es.** To surpass decisively, so as to appear of a higher class.
out·come (out′kŭm′) *n.* A natural result; consequence.
out·crop (out′krŏp′) *n.* A portion of bedrock or other stratum protruding through the soil level. *—intr.v.* (out-krŏp′) **-cropped, -crop·ping, -crops.** *Geol.* To protrude above the soil, as rock formations.
out·cross (out′krôs′, -krŏs′) *tr.v.* **-crossed, -cross·ing, -cross·es.** To breed (animals) that belong to different strains of the same breed. *—n.* **1.** The process of outcrossing. **2.** An offspring produced by outcrossing.
out·cry (out′krī′) *n.* **1.** A loud cry or clamor. **2.** A strong protest or objection: *public outcry over the price rise.* **3.** An auction.
out·curve (out′kûrv′) *n. Baseball.* A pitched ball that curves away from the batter.
out·date (out-dāt′) *tr.v.* **-dat·ed, -dat·ing, -dates.** To replace or make obsolete, antiquated, or old-fashioned.
out·dat·ed (out-dā′tĭd) *adj.* Out-of-date; antiquated.
out·dis·tance (out-dĭs′təns) *tr.v.* **-tanced, -tanc·ing, -tanc·es.** **1.** To outrun, esp. in a long-distance race. **2.** To surpass by a wide margin, esp. through superior skill or endurance: *completely outdistanced by younger salesmen.*
out·do (out-do͞o′) *tr.v.* **-did** (-dĭd′), **-done** (-dŭn′), **-do·ing, -does** (-dŭz′). To exceed in performance.
out·door (out′dôr′, -dōr′) also **out-of-door** (out′əv-dôr′, -dōr′) *adj.* Located in, done in, or suited to the open air.
out·doors (out-dôrz′, -dōrz′) also **out-of-doors** (out′-əv-dôrz′, -dōrz′) *—adv.* In or into the open; outside of a house or shelter: *walking outdoors for fresh air.* *—n.* The open air; the area away from human habitation.
out·doors·man (out-dôrz′mən, -dōrz′-) *n.* One who spends considerable leisure time in outdoor activities, as hunting or fishing.
out·er (ou′tər) *adj.* **1.** Located on the outside; external. **2.** Farther from the center or middle. **3.** Relating to the body or its appearance rather than the mind or spirit.
outer ear *n.* The external ear.
out·er·most (ou′tər-mōst′) *adj.* Most distant from the center or inside; farthest out; outmost.
outer space *n.* Any region of space beyond limits determined with reference to the boundaries of a celestial body or system.
out·face (out-fās′) *tr.v.* **-faced, -fac·ing, -fac·es.** **1.** To overcome with a bold or self-assured look; stare down. **2.** To defy or resist.
out·fall (out′fôl′) *n.* The place where a sewer, drain, or stream discharges.
out·field (out′fēld′) *n.* **1.** The grass-covered playing area extending outward from a baseball diamond, divided into right, center, and left field. **2.** The members of a baseball team playing in the outfield. **—out′field′er** *n.*
out·fit (out′fĭt′) *n.* **1.** A set of tools or equipment for a specialized purpose: *a mountain-climber's outfit; a welder's outfit.* **2.** A set of clothing with accessories. **3.** *Informal.* An association of persons, esp. a military unit or a business organization. **4.** The act of equipping. *—tr.v.* **-fit·ted, -fit·ting, -fits.** To provide with necessary equipment: *This store outfits skiers.* **—out′fit′ter** *n.*
out·flank (out-flăngk′) *tr.v.* **-flanked, -flank·ing, -flanks.** **1.** To maneuver around and behind the flank of (an opposing force). **2.** To gain a tactical advantage over.
out·flow (out′flō′) *n.* **1.** The act of flowing out. **2.** Something that flows out. **3.** The amount flowing out.
out·fox (out-fŏks′) *tr.v.* **-foxed, -fox·ing, -fox·es.** To outsmart.
out·gas (out′găs′) *tr.v.* **-gassed, -gas·sing, -gas·ses.** To remove embedded gas from (a solid) by heating.
out·go (out-gō′) *tr.v.* **-went** (-wĕnt′), **-gone** (-gôn′, -gŏn′), **-go·ing, -goes** (-gōz′). To exceed; surpass. *—n.* (out′gō′), *pl.* **-goes.** **1.** Something that goes out, esp. expenditure or cost. **2.** The act of going out.
out·go·ing (out′gō′ĭng) *adj.* **1. a.** Departing; going out; *an outgoing steamship.* **b.** Retiring from or relinquishing a place, position, or office: *the outgoing chairman.* **2.** Friendly; sociable.
out-group (out′gro͞op′) *n.* A group of people excluded from or not belonging to an in-group.
out·grow (out-grō′) *tr.v.* **-grew** (-gro͞o′), **-grown** (-grōn′), **-grow·ing, -grows.** **1.** To grow too large for: *He outgrew his new suit.* **2.** To lose or discard in the course of maturation: *outgrew his former idealism.* **3.** To surpass in growth.
out·growth (out′grōth′) *n.* **1.** Something that grows out of something else; offshoot: *an outgrowth of new shoots on a branch.* **2.** A result or consequence: *Inflation is an outgrowth of war.*
out·guess (out-gĕs′) *tr.v.* **-guessed, -guess·ing, -guess·es.** **1.** To anticipate correctly the actions of. **2.** To gain the advantage over by cleverness or forethought; outwit.
out·haul (out′hôl′) *n. Naut.* A rope used to extend a sail along a spar or boom.
out·house (out′hous′) *n.* An outdoor toilet housed in a small structure.
out·ing (ou′tĭng) *n.* **1.** An excursion or pleasure trip. **2.** A walk outdoors; airing.
outing flannel *n.* A soft, lightweight cotton fabric, usually with a short nap on both sides.
out·land (out′lănd′, -lənd) *n.* **1.** A foreign land. **2. outlands.** The outlying areas of a country; provinces. [ME < OE *ūtland* : *ūt,* out + *land,* land.] **—out′land′** *adj.* **—out′land′er** *n.*
out·land·ish (out-lăn′dĭsh) *adj.* **1.** Strikingly foreign; unfamiliar. **2.** *Archaic.* Of foreign origin; not native. **3.** Geographically remote from the familiar world. **4.** Conspicuously unconventional; bizarre; absurd. [ME < OE *ūtlandisc* : *ūtland,* outland + *-isc,* -ish.] **—out·land′ish·ly** *adv.* **—out·land′ish·ness** *n.*
out·last (out-lăst′) *tr.v.* **-last·ed, -last·ing, -lasts.** To endure or live longer than.
out·law (out′lô′) *n.* **1.** A habitual criminal. **2.** A fugitive from the law. **3.** A person excluded from normal legal protection and rights. **4.** A wild or vicious animal. *—tr.v.* **-lawed, -law·ing, -laws.** **1.** To declare illegal. **2.** To ban. **3.** To deprive of the protection of the law. [ME *outlaue* < OE *ūtlaga* < ON *ūtlagi* : *ūt,* out + *lög,* law.]
out·law·ry (out′lô′rē) *n., pl.* **-ries.** **1.** The act or process of outlawing. **2.** The state of being outlawed. **3.** Defiance of the law. [ME *outlauerie* < AN *utlagerie* < OE *ūtlaga,* outlaw.]
out·lay (out′lā′) *n.* **1.** The spending or disbursing of money: *"A few pennies had survived his weekly outlay on comics"* (Alan Sillitoe). **2.** An amount spent; expenditure. *—tr.v.* (out-lā′), **-laid** (-lād′), **-lay·ing, -lays.** To expend (money).
out·let (out′lĕt′, -lĭt) *n.* **1.** A passage for escape or exit; vent. **2. a.** A means of release, as for energies, drives, or desires: *exercised as an outlet for frustration.* **b.** A means of achieving self-expression. **3. a.** A commercial market for goods or services. **b.** A store that sells the goods of a particular manufacturer or wholesaler. **4.** *Elect.* A receptacle, esp. one mounted in a wall, that is connected to a power supply and equipped with a socket for a plug.
out·li·er (out′lī′ər) *n.* **1.** One whose domicile lies at some appreciable remove from his place of business. **2.** *Geol.* A portion of stratified rock separated from a main formation by erosion.
out·line (out′līn′) *n.* **1. a.** A line marking the outer contours or boundaries of an object or figure. **b.** The shape of an object or figure. **2.** A style of drawing in which objects are delineated in contours without shading. **3. a.** A general description covering the main points of a subject. **b.** An abstract. **c.** A summary of a written work or speech, usually analyzed in headings and subheadings. **d.** A preliminary draft or plan. *—tr.v.* **-lined, -lin·ing, -lines.** **1.** To draw an outline of. **2.** To display or accentuate the outline of. **3.** To give the main points of; summarize.
out·live (out-lĭv′) *tr.v.* **-lived, -liv·ing, -lives.** **1.** To live longer than; outlast. **2.** To live through; survive.
Synonyms: *outlive, outlast, survive.* These verbs all mean to exist longer than another person or thing. *Outlive* often implies the capacity for endurance in competition: *outlive one's enemies.* Sometimes it refers to going beyond a certain time: *He outlived his usefulness. Outlast* can often be used interchangeably with *outlive,* but it more commonly applies to things, stressing duration, rather than to persons. When applied to persons, *outlast* suggests endurance. *Survive* may be used with reference merely to living longer than another: *He is survived by his wife.* However, *survive* has the more common meaning of remaining alive after a dangerous event: *He survived the auto accident.*
out·look (out′lo͝ok′) *n.* **1.** The act of looking out. **2. a.** A place where something can be viewed. **b.** The view seen from such a place. **3.** A point of view; attitude. **4.** Prospect; expectation.
out loud *adv.* Aloud.
out·ly·ing (out′lī′ĭng) *adj.* Comparatively distant or remote from a center or middle.
out·ma·neu·ver (out′mə-no͞o′vər, -nyo͞o′-) *tr.v.* **-vered, -ver·ing, -vers.** **1.** To overcome by more artful maneuvering. **2.** To excel in maneuverability: *The car outmaneuvers all others of its class.*
out·mod·ed (out-mō′dĭd) *adj.* **1.** Not in fashion. **2.** No longer usable or practical; obsolete: *outmoded machinery.*
out·most (out′mōst′) *adj.* Farthest out; outermost.
out·num·ber (out-nŭm′bər) *tr.v.* **-bered, -ber·ing, -bers.** To exceed the number of; be more numerous than.
out of *prep.* **1. a.** From within to the outside of: *ran out of the room.* **b.** From a given condition: *came out of her trance.* **c.** From an origin, source, or cause: *made out of wood.* **2. a.** In a position or situation beyond the range, boundaries, limits, or sphere of: *She went out of sight.* **b.** In a state or position away from the expected or usual: *out of practice.* **3.** Because of; owing to: *did it out of malice.* **4.** With headquarters in: *works out of the main office.* **5.** From among: *five out of six votes.*
out-of-bounds (out′əv-boundz′) *adv. & adj.* Beyond the designated boundaries or limits.

out-of-date (out′əv-dāt′) *adj.* Outmoded; old-fashioned.
out-of-door (out′əv-dôr′, -dōr′) *adj.* Variant of **outdoor.**
out-of-doors (out′əv-dôrz′, -dōrz′) *adv.* Variant of **outdoors.**
out-of-pock•et (out′əv-pŏk′ĭt) *adj.* Calling for the spending of cash: *out-of-pocket expenses.*
out-of-stat•er (out′əv-stā′tər) *n.* **1.** A visitor, as a tourist, from another state. **2.** A legal resident of one state who lives for a period of time in another state, as to attend school.
out-of-the-way (out′əv-*th*ə-wā′) *adj.* **1.** Remote; secluded. **2.** Out of the ordinary; unusual.
out-of-town•er (out′əv-tou′nər) *n.* A visitor from another town or city.
out•pa•tient (out′pā′shənt) *n.* A patient who receives treatment at a hospital or clinic without being hospitalized. **—modifier:** *an outpatient clinic.*
out•per•form (out′pər-fôrm′) *tr.v.* **-formed, -form•ing, -forms.** To surpass in performance.
out•play (out-plā′) *tr.v.* **-played, -play•ing, -plays.** To surpass (one's opponent) in playing a game.
out•post (out′pōst′) *n.* **1. a.** A detachment of troops stationed at a distance from a main unit of forces. **b.** The station occupied by such troops. **2.** An outlying settlement.
out•pour (out-pôr′, -pōr′) *tr.v.* **-poured, -pour•ing, -pours.** To flow out rapidly; pour out. *—n.* (out′pôr′, -pōr′). A rapid outflow; an outpouring. **—out•pour′er** *n.*
out•pour•ing (out′pôr′ĭng, -pōr′-) *n.* **1.** The act of pouring out. **2.** Something that pours out or is poured out; outflow: *an outpouring of lava.*
out•put (out′po͝ot′) *n.* **1.** The act of producing; production. **2.** The amount of something produced or manufactured, esp. during a given time. **3. a.** The energy, power, or work produced by a system. **b.** The information produced by a computer from a specific input. *—tr.v.* **-put•ted** or **-put, -put•ting, -puts.** To produce or manufacture as output.
out•rage (out′rāj′) *n.* **1.** An act of extreme violence or viciousness. **2.** Any act grossly offensive to decency, morality, or good taste. **3.** A severe insult or offense. **4.** Resentful anger aroused by a violent or offensive act. *—tr.v.* **-raged, -rag•ing, -rag•es. 1.** To commit an outrage upon. **2.** To rape. **3.** To produce anger or resentment in: *Incompetence outraged him.* [ME, excess < OFr. < *outre,* beyond < Lat. *ultra.*]
out•ra•geous (out-rā′jəs) *adj.* **1. a.** Being an outrage; grossly offensive; heinous. **b.** Disgraceful; shameful. **2.** Having no regard for morality. **3.** Violent or unrestrained in temperament or behavior. **4.** Extravagant; immoderate; extreme: *She spends an outrageous amount on clothes.* **—out•ra′geous•ly** *adv.* **—out•ra′geous•ness** *n.*
Synonyms: *outrageous, flagrant, infamous, monstrous.* These adjectives describe behavior grossly offensive or revolting to society, and are often used interchangeably. *Outrageous* applies to any action, or result of an action, so distasteful or appalling as to be shocking or intolerable: *an outrageous remark; an outrageous price. Flagrant* adds to outrageous the idea of defiance of recognized authority: *a flagrant violation of the law. Infamous* has a personal sense, suggesting scandalous, odious, or treasonable actions. *Monstrous* describes actions so outrageous as to be inhuman: *Kidnaping is a monstrous act.*
out•rank (out-răngk′) *tr.v.* **-ranked, -rank•ing, -ranks.** To rank higher than.
ou•tré (o͞o-trā′) *adj.* Highly unconventional; eccentric. [Fr., p.part. of *outrer,* to go beyond < *outre,* beyond < Lat. *ultra.*]
out•reach (out-rēch′) *v.* **-reached, -reach•ing, -reach•es.** *—tr.* **1.** To reach or go beyond; surpass. **2.** To extend (something) outward. *—intr.* To reach out. *—n.* (out′rēch′). **1.** An act of reaching out. **2.** The extent of reach. **3.** A systematic attempt to provide services beyond conventional limits, as to particular segments of a community: *an educational outreach to adult illiterates.*
out•ride¹ (out-rīd′) *tr.v.* **-rode** (-rōd′), **-rid•den** (-rĭd′n), **-rid•ing, -rides.** To ride faster, farther, or better than; outstrip.
out•ride² (out′rīd′) *n.* An unstressed syllable or cluster of syllables within a given metrical unit that is omitted from the scansion pattern in sprung rhythm. [Coined by Gerard Manley Hopkins (1844–1889).]
out•rid•er (out′rī′dər) *n.* **1.** A mounted attendant who rides in front of or beside a carriage. **2.** A guide; escort.
out•rig•ger (out′rĭg′ər) *n.* **1. a.** A long, thin float attached parallel to a seagoing canoe by projecting spars as a means of preventing it from capsizing. **b.** A vessel fitted with such a float. **2.** A projecting frame extending laterally beyond the main structure of a vessel, vehicle, aircraft, or machine to stabilize the structure or to support an extending part.
out•right (out′rīt′, -rīt′) *adv.* **1.** Without reservation or qualification; openly. **2.** Entirely; utterly. **3.** Without delay; straightway: *kill outright. —adj.* (out′rīt′). **1.** Without reservation; unqualified: *an outright gift.* **2. a.** Complete; total: *the outright cost.* **b.** Thoroughgoing; out-and-out: *outright viciousness.* **3.** *Archaic.* Directed straight on; moving straight onward.
out•run (out-rŭn′) *tr.v.* **-ran** (-răn′), **-run, -run•ning, -runs. 1.** To run faster than. **2.** To escape from: *outrun one's creditors.* **3.** To go beyond; exceed: *"Man's ingenuity has outrun his intelligence"* (Joseph Wood Krutch).
out•sell (out-sĕl′) *tr.v.* **-sold** (-sōld′), **-sell•ing, -sells. 1.** To surpass in amount sold. **2.** To outdo in selling.
out•set (out′sĕt′) *n.* **1.** Beginning; start. **2.** An initial stage, as of an activity.
out•shine (out-shīn′) *v.* **-shone** (-shōn′), **-shin•ing, -shines.** *—tr.* **1.** To shine brighter than. **2.** To surpass in beauty or obvious excellence. *—intr.* To shine forth.
out•shoot (out-sho͞ot′) *v.* **-shot** (-shŏt′), **-shoot•ing, -shoots.** *—tr.* **1.** To shoot better than. **2.** To extend beyond. *—intr.* To protrude or project. *—n.* (out′sho͞ot′). **1.** A protuberance, projection, or outgrowth. **2.** A flowing or gushing forth.
out•shout (out-shout′) *tr.v.* **-shout•ed, -shout•ing, -shouts.** To shout more forcefully than.
out•side (out-sīd′, out′sīd′) *n.* **1.** The part or parts that face out; outer surface; exterior. **2. a.** The part or side of an object that is presented to the viewer; external aspect. **b.** A superficial or obvious aspect. **3.** The space beyond a boundary or limit. **4.** An utmost limit; maximum: *We'll be leaving in ten days at the outside. —adj.* **1.** Acting, occurring, originating, or existing at a place beyond certain limits; outer; foreign: *outside assistance.* **2.** Of, restricted to, or situated on the outside of an enclosure or boundary; external: *an outside door lock.* **3.** Extreme; uttermost: *The cost exceeded even my outside estimate.* **4.** Slight; slim: *an outside possibility. —adv.* **1.** On or into the outside. **2.** Outdoors. *—prep.* **1.** On or to the outer side of. **2.** Beyond the limits of. **3.** With the exception of; except: *no information outside the figures given.*
outside of *prep.* Outside.
out•sid•er (out-sī′dər) *n.* **1. a.** A person who is excluded from a particular party, association, or set. **b.** One who is isolated or detached from the activities or concerns of the community in which he lives. **2.** A contestant given little chance of winning; long shot.
out•size (out′sīz′) *n.* **1.** An unusual size, esp. a very large size. **2.** An outsize garment. *—adj.* Also **out•sized** (out′sīzd′). Unusually large.
out•skirts (out′skûrts′) *pl.n.* The parts or regions remote from a central district; peripheral areas.
out•smart (out-smärt′) *tr.v.* **-smart•ed, -smart•ing, -smarts.** To gain the advantage over by cunning; outwit.
out•speak (out-spēk′) *v.* **-spoke** (-spōk′), **-spok•en** (-spō′kən), **-speak•ing, -speaks.** *—tr.* **1.** To outdo in speech; speak better or more cogently than. **2.** To say candidly and frankly. *—intr.* To speak out.
out•spend (out-spĕnd′) *tr.v.* **-spent** (-spĕnt), **-spend•ing, -spends. 1.** To spend beyond the limits of: *outspends his earnings.* **2.** To outdo in spending: *outspends all the relatives at Christmas.*
out•spo•ken (out-spō′kən) *adj.* **1.** Spoken without reserve; candid. **2.** Frank and unsparing in speech. **—out•spo′ken•ly** *adv.* **—out•spo′ken•ness** *n.*
out•spread (out-sprĕd′) *intr. & tr.v.* **-spread, -spread•ing, -spreads.** To spread out or cause to spread out. *—n.* (out′sprĕd′). The act of spreading out. *—adj.* Spread out; extended.
out•stand (out-stănd′) *intr.v.* **-stood** (-sto͝od′), **-stand•ing, -stands. 1.** To stand out plainly; be outstanding. **2.** *Naut.* To set sail; put out to sea.
out•stand•ing (out-stăn′dĭng, out′stăn′-) *adj.* **1.** Standing out; projecting upward or outward. **2.** Standing out among others of its kind; prominent. **3.** Superior to others of its kind; distinguished; excellent. **4.** Still in existence; not settled or resolved: *outstanding debts; a long outstanding problem.*
out•stare (out-stâr′) *tr.v.* **-stared, -star•ing, -stares.** To stare out of countenance; face down; outface.
out•sta•tion (out′stā′shən) *n.* A remote station or post.
out•stay (out-stā′) *tr.v.* **-stayed, -stay•ing, -stays. 1.** To stay longer than; overstay. **2.** To show greater endurance than.
out•stood (out-sto͝od′) *v.* Past tense of **outstand.**
out•stretch (out-strĕch′) *tr.v.* **-stretched, -stretch•ing, -stretch•es. 1.** To stretch out; extend. **2.** To stretch beyond.
out•strip (out-strĭp′) *tr.v.* **-stripped, -strip•ping, -strips. 1.** To leave behind; outrun. **2.** To exceed; surpass: *"Material development outstripped human development"* (Edith Hamilton).
out•stroke (out′strōk′) *n.* An outward stroke, esp. the stroke of an engine piston moving toward the crankshaft.
out•take (out′tāk′) *n.* **1. a.** A section or scene, as of a motion picture, that is filmed but not used in the final version. **b.** A complete version of something, as a recording of a song, that is dropped in favor of another version. **2.** An opening for outward discharge; vent.
out•talk (out-tôk′) *tr.v.* **-talked, -talk•ing, talks. 1.** To outdo in talking. **2.** To outwit by talking.
out•think (out-thĭngk′) *tr.v.* **-thought** (-thôt), **-think•ing, -thinks. 1.** To outdo in thinking. **2.** To outwit by thinking.
out•turn (out′tûrn′) *n.* A total amount produced during a given period; output.
out•ward (out′wərd) *adj.* **1.** Of, located on, or moving toward the outside or exterior; outer. **2.** Pertaining to the physical self, as distinguished from the mind or spirit. **3.** Purely external; superficial. *—adv.* Also **out•wards** (-wərdz). **1.** Toward the outside; away from a central point. **2.** On the outside; externally. **3.** Obviously; apparently. *—n.* **1.** The outside; exterior. **2.** Outward appearance.

3. The material or external world. [ME < OE *ūtweard* : *ūt,* out + *-weard,* -ward.] **—out′ward·ly** *adv.* **—out′ward·ness** *n.*
out·wear (out-wâr′) *tr.v.* **-wore** (-wôr′, -wōr′), **-worn** (-wôrn′, -wōrn′), **-wear·ing, -wears. 1.** To wear out; exhaust by using. **2.** To last longer than; outlast. **3.** To outgrow or outlive: *ethics outworn by a changing people.*
out·weigh (out-wā′) *tr.v.* **-weighed, -weigh·ing, -weighs. 1.** To weigh more than. **2.** To be more significant than.
out·wit (out-wĭt′) *tr.v.* **-wit·ted, -wit·ting, -wits. 1.** To surpass in cleverness or cunning. **2.** *Archaic.* To surpass in intelligence.
out·work[1] (out-wûrk′) *tr.v.* **-worked** or **-wrought** (-rôt′), **-work·ing, -works. 1.** To work better or faster than. **2.** To work out to a finish; complete.
out·work[2] (out′wûrk′) *n.* A fortification constructed beyond a main defensive position or fortification.
out·wrought (out-rôt′) *v.* A past tense and past participle of **outwork**[1].
ou·zel also **ou·sel** (o͞o′zəl) *n.* **1.** Any of various European birds of the genus *Turdus.* **2.** The water ouzel. [ME *osel* < OE *ōsle.*]
ou·zo (o͞o′zō) *n., pl.* **-zos.** An aniseed-flavored Greek liqueur. [Mod. Gk.]
ov– *pref.* Variant of **ovi-.**
o·va (ō′və) *n.* Plural of **ovum.**
o·val (ō′vəl) *adj.* **1.** Resembling an egg in shape. **2.** Resembling an ellipse in shape; ellipsoidal or elliptical. *—n.* **1.** An oval form or figure. **2.** An oval track, as for horse racing or athletic events. [Med. Lat. *ovalis* < Lat. *ovum,* egg.] **—o′val·ly** *adv.* **—o′val·ness** *n.*

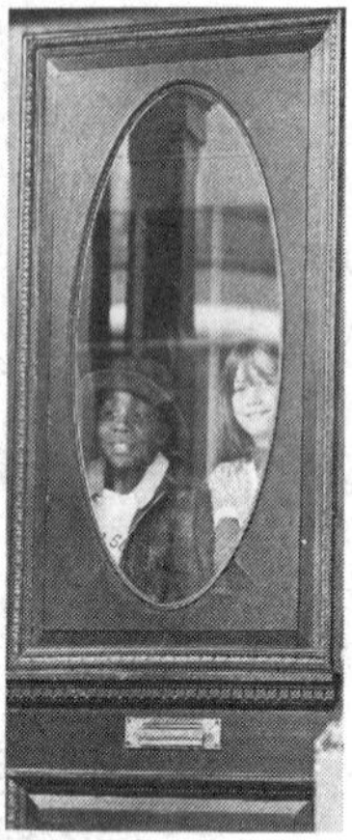

oval

oval window *n.* The oval-shaped opening in the middle ear to which the ossicles of the ear are connected.
o·var·i·ec·to·my (ō-vâr′ē-ĕk′tə-mē) *n., pl.* **-mies.** Surgical excision of an ovary. [OVAR(Y) + -ECTOMY.]
o·var·i·ot·o·my (ō-vâr′ē-ŏt′ə-mē) *n., pl.* **-mies. 1.** Ovariectomy. **2.** Surgical incision into an ovary. [OVAR(Y) + -TOMY.]
o·va·ri·tis (ō′və-rī′tĭs) *n.* Oophoritis. [OVAR(Y) + -ITIS.]
o·va·ry (ō′və-rē) *n., pl.* **-ries. 1.** One of a pair of female reproductive glands that produce ova. **2.** *Bot.* The part of a pistil containing the ovules. [NLat. *ovarium* < Lat. *ovum,* egg.] **—o·var′i·an** (ō-vâr′ē-ən), **o·var′i·al** *adj.*
o·vate (ō′vāt′) *adj.* **1.** Shaped like an egg; oval. **2.** *Bot.* Broad and rounded at the base and tapering toward the end: *an ovate leaf.* [Lat. *ovatus* < *ovum,* egg.] **—o′vate′ly** *adv.*
o·va·tion (ō-vā′shən) *n.* **1.** Enthusiastic and prolonged applause. **2.** A show of public homage or welcome. **3.** An ancient Roman victory ceremony of somewhat less importance than a triumph. [Lat. *ovatio,* a Roman victory ceremony < *ovare,* to rejoice.]
ov·en (ŭv′ən) *n.* A chamber or enclosed compartment, as in a stove, equipped to heat objects placed within. [ME < OE *ofen.*]
ov·en·bird (ŭv′ən-bûrd′) *n.* **1.** A thrushlike North American warbler, *Seiurus aurocapillus,* having a shrill call, and characteristically building a domed nest on the ground. **2.** Any of various, often nest-building South American birds of the family Furnariidae. [From its oven-shaped nest.]
ov·en·proof (ŭv′ən-pro͞of′) *adj.* Capable of resisting the heat produced in an oven: *an ovenproof casserole.*
o·ver (ō′vər) *prep.* **1.** In or at a position above or higher than: *a sign over the door.* **2.** Above and across from one end or side to the other: *a jump over the fence.* **3.** On the other side of: *a village over the border.* **4.** Upon the surface of: *a coat of varnish over the woodwork.* **5.** All through; through the extent of: *a tour over the nation.* **6.** So as to cover or close: *put rocks over a cave entrance.* **7.** Up to or higher than the level or height of: *water over the dike.* **8. a.** Through the period or duration of: *records maintained over two years.* **b.** Until or beyond the end of: *stay over the holidays.* **9.** More than in degree, quantity, or extent: *over ten miles.* **10.** In preference to: *respected over all others.* **11.** In a position to rule or control: *preside over the meeting.* **12.** Upon; directed toward: *his influence over children.* **13.** While occupied with or engaged in: *a chat over coffee.* **14.** With reference to; concerning: *an argument over methods.* *—adv.* **1.** Above the top or surface. **2. a.** Across to another or opposite side. **b.** Across the edge or brim: *The coffee spilled over.* **3. a.** Across a distance in a particular direction or at a location: *over in Europe.* **b.** To another specified place or position: *Move your chair over toward the fire.* **4.** Throughout an entire area or region: *wander all over.* **5.** To a different opinion or allegiance: *win someone over.* **6.** To a different person, condition, or title: *sign over land.* **7.** So as to be completely enclosed or covered: *The river froze over.* **8.** Completely through; from beginning to end: *Think the problem over.* **9. a.** From an upright position: *The lamp fell over.* **b.** From an upward position to an inverted or reversed position: *turn the book over.* **10.** Another time; again: *Count your cards over.* **11.** In repetition: *ten times over.* **12.** In addition or excess; in surplus: *three pennies left over.* **13.** Beyond or until a specified time: *stay a day over.* **14. a.** At an end. **b.** Used in two-way radio transmissions to indicate that a message is complete and a reply is awaited. *—adj.* **1. a.** Upper; higher. **b.** External; outer. **2. a.** In excess; excessive. **b.** Not yet used up; remaining. *—n.* A series of six balls bowled from one end of a cricket pitch. *—tr.v.* **o·vered, o·ver·ing, o·vers.** To jump over. **—*idioms.* over a barrel.** At the mercy of others. **over (one's) head.** Beyond one's comprehension or abilities. [ME < OE *ofer.*]

ovary
Longitudinal section of a chickweed-flower ovary showing the ovules

ovate
An ovate leaf

over– *pref.* Excessive; excessively: *overextend.* [< OVER.]
o·ver·a·bun·dance (ō′vər-ə-bŭn′dəns) *n.* Lavish abundance; excess. **—o′ver·a·bun′dant** *adj.*
o·ver·a·chieve (ō′vər-ə-chēv′) *intr.v.* **-chieved, -chiev·ing, -chieves.** To perform better than expected. **—o′ver·a·chiev′er** *n.* **—o′ver·a·chieve′ment** *n.*
o·ver·act (ō′vər-ăkt′) *v.* **-act·ed, -act·ing, -acts.** *—tr.* To act (a part) with unnecessary exaggeration. *—intr.* To exaggerate a part; overplay.
o·ver·ac·tive (ō′vər-ăk′tĭv) *adj.* Active to an excessive or abnormal degree.
o·ver·age[1] (ō′vər-ĭj) *n.* **1.** An amount, as of money or goods, actually on hand that exceeds the listed amount in records or books of account. **2.** A surplus or excess.
o·ver·age[2] (ō′vər-āj′) *adj.* Beyond the proper or required age.
o·ver·ag·gres·sive (ō′vər-ə-grĕs′ĭv) *adj.* Aggressive to an excessive degree.
o·ver·all also **o·ver-all** (ō′vər-ôl′) *adj.* **1.** From one end to the other. **2.** Including everything; comprehensive. *—adv.* On the whole; generally. *—n.* A loose-fitting protective outer garment; smock.
o·ver·alls (ō′vər-ôlz′) *pl.n.* Loose-fitting, coarse trousers with a bib front and shoulder straps, often worn over regular clothing as protection from dirt and wear.
o·ver·arch (ō′vər-ärch′) *tr.v.* **-arched, -arch·ing, -arch·es. 1.** To form an arch over. **2.** To extend over or throughout.
o·ver·arm (ō′vər-ärm′) *adj.* *Sports.* Executed with the arm raised above the shoulder: *an overarm throw.*
o·ver·awe (ō′vər-ô′) *tr.v.* **-awed, -aw·ing, -awes.** To subdue by inspiring awe; overcome with awe.
o·ver·bal·ance (ō′vər-băl′əns) *v.* **-anced, -anc·ing, -anc·es.** *—tr.* **1.** To have greater weight or importance than. **2.** To throw off balance. *—intr.* To lose one's balance. *—n.* (ō′vər-băl′əns). Something that overbalances; an excess of weight or quantity.
o·ver·bear (ō′vər-bâr′) *v.* **-bore** (-bôr′), **-borne** (bôrn′), **-bear·ing, -bears.** *—tr.* **1.** To crush or press down upon with physical force. **2.** To prevail over, as if by superior weight or force; dominate. **3.** To be more important than; outweigh. *—intr.* To bear too much fruit or offspring.
o·ver·bear·ing (ō′vər-bâr′ĭng) *adj.* **1.** Overwhelming in power or significance; predominant. **2.** Domineering in manner; arrogant: *an overbearing person.* **—o′ver·bear′ing·ly** *adv.*
o·ver·bid (ō′vər-bĭd′) *v.* **-bid, -bid·den** (-bĭd′n) or **-bid, -bid·ding, -bids.** *—tr.* To outbid (a person) for something. *—intr.* To bid higher than the actual value of something. *—n.* (ō′vər-bĭd′). A bid that is higher than another bid.
o·ver·bite (ō′vər-bīt′) *n.* Dental malocclusion in which the front upper incisor and canine teeth project over the lower.
o·ver·blow (ō′vər-blō′) *tr.v.* **-blew** (-blo͞o′), **-blown** (-blōn′), **-blow·ing, -blows.** To blow (a wind instrument) so as to produce an overtone instead of a fundamental tone.
o·ver·blown (ō′vər-blōn′) *adj.* **1.** Blown down or over. **2.** Blown up with conceit; inflated. **3.** Past the stage of full bloom. **4.** Very fat; obese.
o·ver·board (ō′vər-bôrd′, -bōrd′) *adv.* Over the side of a boat or ship. **—*idiom.* go overboard.** *Informal.* To show excessive enthusiasm.
o·ver·book (ō′vər-bo͝ok′) *v.* **-booked, -book·ing, -books.** *—tr.* To book passengers for (an airline flight, for example) beyond the seating capacity. *—intr.* To book passengers beyond the seating capacity.
o·ver·build (ō′vər-bĭld′) *v.* **-built** (-bĭlt′), **-build·ing, -builds.** *—tr.* **1.** To build over or on top of. **2.** To build more buildings in (an area) than necessary. **3.** To build with excessive size or elaboration. *—intr.* To build more buildings than needed.
o·ver·bur·den (ō′vər-bûr′dn) *tr.v.* **-dened, -den·ing, -dens. 1.** To burden with too much weight. **2.** To burden with too much work, care, or responsibility. *—n.* (ō′vər-bûr′dn). **1.** *Geol.* **a.** Material overlying a useful mineral deposit. **b.** Sedimentary rock covering older crystalline layers. **2.** *Archaeol.* A sterile stratum overlying a stratum bearing traces of the culture being studied.
o·ver·buy (ō′vər-bī′) *v.* **-bought** (-bôt′), **-buy·ing, -buys.** *—tr.* **1.** To buy in excessive amounts. **2.** To buy (stock) on margin in excess of one's ability to provide further security if prices drop. *—intr.* To buy goods beyond one's means or needs.
o·ver·call (ō′vər-kôl′) *tr.v.* **-called, -call·ing, -calls. 1.** To overbid. **2.** To bid higher than (one's opponent) when one's partner has not bid in a bridge game. *—n.* (ō′vər-kôl′). **1.** An overbid. **2.** An instance of overcalling in bridge.
o·ver·cap·i·tal·ize (ō′vər-kăp′ĭ-tl-īz′) *tr.v.* **-ized, -iz·ing, -iz·es. 1.** To provide an excess amount of capital for (a business enterprise). **2.** To estimate the value of (property) too highly. **3.** To place an unlawfully or unreasonably high value on the nominal capital of (a corporation). **—o′ver·cap′i·tal·i·za′tion** *n.*
o·ver·cast (ō′vər-kăst′, ō′vər-kăst′) *adj.* **1. a.** Covered or ob-

scured, as with clouds or mist. **b.** Clouded over. **2.** Gloomy; melancholy. **3.** Sewn with long, overlying stitches in order to prevent raveling, as the edges of fabric. —*n.* (ō′vər-kăst′). **1.** A covering, as of mist or clouds. **2.** An arch or support for a passage over another passage in a mine. **3.** A fishing cast falling beyond the point intended. **4.** An overcast stitch or seam. —*tr.v.* (ō′vər-kăst′, ō′vər-kăst′) **-cast·ed, -cast·ing, -casts. 1.** To make cloudy or gloomy. **2.** To cast beyond (the intended point) with a fishing rod. **3.** To sew with an overcast stitch.

o·ver·cast·ing (ō′vər-kăst′ĭng) *n.* An overcast stitch or seam.

o·ver·cau·tious (ō′vər-kô′shəs) *adj.* Excessively cautious.

o·ver·charge (ō′vər-chärj′) *tr.v.* **-charged, -charg·ing, -charg·es. 1.** To charge (a person) too high a price for something. **2.** To fill too full; overload. **3.** To exaggerate. —*n.* (ō′vər-chärj′). **1.** An excessive charge or price. **2.** A load or burden that is too full or heavy.

o·ver·cloud (ō′vər-kloud′) *v.* **-cloud·ed, -cloud·ing, -clouds.** —*tr.* **1.** To cover with clouds. **2.** To make dark and gloomy. —*intr.* To become cloudy.

o·ver·coat (ō′vər-kōt′) *n.* A heavy coat worn over ordinary clothing in cold weather.

o·ver·come (ō′vər-kŭm′) *v.* **-came** (-kām′), **-come, -com·ing, -comes.** —*tr.* **1.** To defeat in competition or conflict; conquer. **2.** To surmount; prevail over: *overcome the obstacles of poverty.* **3.** To overpower, as with emotion; affect deeply. —*intr.* To surmount opposition; be victorious. [ME *overcomen* < OE *ofercuman.*]

o·ver·com·pen·sate (ō′vər-kŏm′pən-sāt′) *v.* **-sat·ed, -sat·ing, -sates.** —*intr.* **1.** To make a greater effort than required to achieve compensation. **2.** To engage in overcompensation. —*tr.* To compensate excessively. **—o′ver·com·pen′sa·to′ry** (-kəm-pĕn′sə-tôr′ē, -tōr′ē) *adj.*

o·ver·com·pen·sa·tion (ō′vər-kŏm′pən-sā′shən) *n.* The exertion of effort in excess of that needed to compensate for a physical or psychological characteristic or defect.

o·ver·con·fi·dent (ō′vər-kŏn′fĭ-dənt) *adj.* Excessively confident. **—o′ver·con′fi·dence** *n.* **—o′ver·con′fi·dent·ly** *adv.*

o·ver·crop (ō′vər-krŏp′) *tr.v.* **-cropped, -crop·ping, -crops.** To exhaust the fertility of (land) by overcultivation.

o·ver·crowd (ō′vər-kroud′) *tr.v.* **-crowd·ed, -crowd·ing, -crowds.** To cause to be excessively crowded.

o·ver·de·vel·op (ō′vər-dĭ-vĕl′əp) *tr.v.* **-oped, -op·ing, -ops. 1.** To develop to excess: *muscles overdeveloped by weightlifting.* **2.** To process (a photographic plate or film) too long or in too concentrated a solution. **—o′ver·de·vel′op·ment** *n.*

o·ver·do (ō′vər-do͞o′) *v.* **-did** (-dĭd′), **-done** (-dŭn′), **-do·ing, -does** (-dŭz′). —*tr.* **1.** To do, use, or stress to excess; carry too far: *overdid his diet and became malnourished.* **2.** To wear out the strength of; overtax. **3.** To cook too much or too long. —*intr.* To do something to excess.

o·ver·dom·i·nance (ō′vər-dŏm′ə-nəns) *n.* The condition of a heterozygote having a phenotype that is more pronounced or better adapted than that of either homozygote. **—o′ver·dom′i·nant** *adj.*

o·ver·dose (ō′vər-dōs′) *n.* An excessive dose esp. of a narcotic. —*intr. & tr.v.* (ō′vər-dōs′) **-dosed, -dos·ing, -dos·es.** To take or administer an overdose.

o·ver·draft (ō′vər-drăft′, -drăft′) *n.* **1. a.** The act of overdrawing an account. **b.** The amount overdrawn. **2.** Also **o·ver·draught. a.** A current of air made to pass over the ignited fuel in a furnace. **b.** A series of flues in a brick kiln designed to force air down from the top. **c.** The air so forced.

o·ver·draw (ō′vər-drô′) *tr.v.* **-drew** (-dro͞o′), **-drawn** (-drôn′), **-draw·ing, -draws. 1.** To draw against (an account) in excess of credit. **2.** To pull back too far: *overdraw a bow.* **3.** To spoil the effect of by exaggeration in telling or describing.

over·drawn (ō′vər-drôn′) *adj.* Having an account that has been drawn against in excess of credit.

o·ver·dress (ō′vər-drĕs′) *intr.v.* **-dressed, -dress·ing, -dress·es.** To dress in a more formal or elaborate manner than is desirable. —*n.* A skirted garment, such as a pinafore, worn over other outer clothing.

o·ver·drive (ō′vər-drīv′) *n.* A gearing mechanism of an automotive engine that reduces the power output required to maintain driving speed in a specific range by increasing the ratio of drive shaft to engine speed. —*tr.v.* (ō′vər-drīv′) **-drove** (-drōv′), **-driv·en** (-drĭv′ən), **-driv·ing, -drives. 1.** To drive (a vehicle) too far or too long. **2.** To push (oneself) too far; overwork.

o·ver·dub (ō′vər-dŭb′) *tr.v.* **-dubbed, -dub·bing, -dubs.** To blend, as recorded sound, with previously recorded sound to produce a multiple effect. **—o′ver·dub′** *n.*

o·ver·due (ō′vər-do͞o′, -dyo͞o′) *adj.* **1.** Being unpaid after becoming due. **2.** Past due; expected or required but not come: *"Such an invention has been overdue for about fifty years"* (Arthur C. Clarke).

o·ver·eat (ō′vər-ēt′) *intr.v.* **-ate** (-āt), **-eat·ing, -eats.** To eat too much, esp. habitually. **—o′ver·eat′er** *n.*

o·ver·em·pha·size (ō′vər-ĕm′fə-sīz′) *v.* **-sized, -siz·ing, -siz·es.** —*tr.* To place too much emphasis on. —*intr.* To employ too much emphasis. **—o′ver·em′pha·sis** (-sĭs) *n.*

o·ver·es·ti·mate (ō′vər-ĕs′tə-māt′) *tr.v.* **-mat·ed, -mat·ing, -mates. 1.** To estimate too highly. **2.** To esteem too greatly. **—o′ver·es′ti·mate** (-mĭt) *n.* **—o′ver·es′ti·ma′tion** *n.*

o·ver·ex·ert (ō′vər-ĭg-zûrt′) *tr.v.* **-ert·ed, -ert·ing, -erts.** To exert too much; overtax. **—o′ver·ex·er′tion** *n.*

o·ver·ex·pose (ō′vər-ĭk-spōz′) *tr.v.* **-posed, -pos·ing, -pos·es. 1.** To expose too long or too much. **2.** To expose (a photographic film or plate) too long or with too much light. **—o′ver·ex·po′sure** *n.*

o·ver·ex·tend (ō′vər-ĭk-stĕnd′) *tr.v.* **-tend·ed, -tend·ing, -tends.** To expand or disperse beyond a safe or reasonable limit: *overextended their defenses.* **—o′ver·ex·ten′sion** *n.*

o·ver·fa·tigue (ō′vər-fə-tēg′) *n.* Fatigue often to a degree beyond an individual's power to recover.

o·ver·fish (ō′vər-fĭsh′) *tr.v.* **-fished, -fish·ing, -fish·es.** To fish (a body of water) to such a degree as to upset ecological balance or cause depletion of living creatures.

o·ver·flow (ō′vər-flō′) *v.* **-flowed, -flow·ing, -flows.** —*intr.* **1.** To flow or run over the top, brim, or banks. **2.** To be filled beyond capacity, as a container or waterway. **3.** To have a boundless supply; be superabundant: *overflowing with gratitude.* —*tr.* **1.** To flow over the top, brim, or banks of. **2.** To spread or cover over; flood. **3.** To cause to fill beyond capacity. —*n.* (ō′vər-flō′). **1.** The act of overflowing. **2.** Something that flows over; excess. **3.** An outlet or vent through which excess liquid may escape.

o·ver·gar·ment (ō′vər-gär′mənt) *n.* An outer garment.

o·ver·glaze (ō′vər-glāz′) *n.* An outer coat of glaze on a piece of pottery. —*tr.v.* (ō′vər-glāz′, ō′vər-glāz′) **-glazed, -glaz·ing, -glaz·es.** To apply an overglaze to.

o·ver·graze (ō′vər-grāz′) *tr.v.* **-grazed, -graz·ing, -graz·es.** To graze to excess.

o·ver·grow (ō′vər-grō′, ō′vər-grō′) *v.* **-grew** (-gro͞o′), **-grown** (-grōn′), **-grow·ing, -grows.** —*tr.* **1.** To spread over with growth. **2.** To grow too large for. —*intr.* To grow beyond normal size.

o·ver·growth (ō′vər-grōth′) *n.* **1.** A growth over or upon something. **2.** Excessively abundant or luxuriant growth.

o·ver·hand (ō′vər-hănd′) also **o·ver·hand·ed** (ō′vər-hăn′dĭd) *adj.* **1.** Thrown, struck, or executed with the hand above the level of the shoulder: *an overhand pitch.* **2.** Sewn with stitches drawing two edges together, with each stitch passing over the seam formed by the edges. —*adv.* In an overhand manner. —*n.* **1.** An overhand throw, stroke, or delivery. **2.** An overhand stitch or seam. —*tr.v.* **-hand·ed, -hand·ing, -hands.** To sew with an overhand seam or stitches.

overhand knot *n.* A knot formed by making a loop in a piece of cord and pulling the end through it.

o·ver·hang (ō′vər-hăng′) *v.* **-hung** (-hŭng′), **-hang·ing, -hangs.** —*tr.* **1.** To project or extend beyond. **2.** To threaten or menace; loom over. **3.** To ornament with hangings. —*intr.* To hang or project over something. —*n.* (ō′vər-hăng′). **1.** A projecting part of something, such as an architectural structure or rock formation. **2.** Amount of projection: *an overhang of six inches.* **3.** The part of a ship's bow or stern that projects over the water.

o·ver·haul (ō′vər-hôl′, ō′vər-hôl′) *tr.v.* **-hauled, -haul·ing, -hauls. 1. a.** To examine or go over carefully for needed repairs. **b.** To dismantle in order to make repairs. **c.** *Naut.* To slacken (a line) or to release and separate the blocks of (a tackle). **2.** To make all needed repairs on; renovate. **3.** To catch up with; overtake. —*n.* (ō′vər-hôl′). **1.** An act of overhauling. **2.** A repair job.

o·ver·head (ō′vər-hĕd′) *adj.* **1.** Located or functioning above the level of the head: *an overhead light.* **2.** Of or pertaining to the operating expenses of a business concern. —*n.* (ō′vər-hĕd′). **1.** The operating expenses of a business, including the costs of rent, utilities, interior decoration, and taxes, and excluding labor and materials. **2.** The top surface in an enclosed space of a ship. **3.** Something, such as a light fixture, that is located above head height. —*adv.* (ō′vər-hĕd′). Over or above the level of the head: *look overhead.*

o·ver·hear (ō′vər-hîr′) *tr.v.* **-heard** (-hûrd′), **-hear·ing, -hears.** To hear (something spoken or someone speaking) without being addressed by the speaker. **—o′ver·hear′er** *n.*

o·ver·heat (ō′vər-hēt′) *v.* **-heat·ed, -heat·ing, -heats.** —*tr.* **1.** To heat too hot. **2.** To cause to become hot or excited: *overheated by a sharp exchange of insults.* **3.** To overstimulate. —*intr.* To become overheated.

o·ver·in·dulge (ō′vər-ĭn-dŭlj′) *v.* **-dulged, -dulg·ing, -dulg·es.** —*tr.* To indulge excessively. —*intr.* To indulge in something to excess. **—o′ver·in·dul′gence** *n.* **—o′ver·in·dul′gent** *adj.* **—o′ver·in·dul′gent·ly** *adv.*

o·ver·joyed (ō′vər-joid′) *adj.* Filled with joy; delighted.

o·ver·kill (ō′vər-kĭl′) *n.* **1.** Nuclear destructive capacity exceeding the amount needed to destroy an enemy. **2.** Excessive killing. **3.** A greatly excessive action or response: *government overkill in dealing with dissent.* —*tr.v.* (ō′vər-kĭl′) **-killed, -kill·ing, -kills.** To destroy (an enemy target) with more nuclear force than is needed.

o·ver·lad·en (ō′vər-lād′n) *adj.* Overloaded; overburdened.

o·ver·land (ō′vər-lănd′, -lənd) *adj.* Passing over or traversing land: *an overland journey.* —*adv.* By way of land.

o·ver·lap (ō′vər-lăp′) *v.* **-lapped, -lap·ping, -laps.** —*tr.* **1.** To lie or extend over and cover part of. **2.** To have an area or range in common with; coincide partly with. —*intr.* **1.** To lie over and partly cover something. **2.** To coincide partly: *Their duties overlap.* —*n.* (ō′vər-lăp′). **1.** A part or portion that overlaps or is overlapped. **2.** An instance of overlapping.

o·ver·lay (ō′vər-lā′) *tr.v.* **-laid, -lay·ing, -lays. 1.** To lay or spread over or upon. **2. a.** To cover the surface of with a decorative layer or design: *overlay wood with silver.* **b.** To embellish superficially: *a simple tune overlaid with ornate harmonies.* **3.** *Printing.* To put an overlay upon. —*n.* (ō′vər-lā′). **1.** Something that is laid over or covers something else. **2.** A layer of decoration, such as gold leaf or wood veneer, applied to a surface. **3.** *Printing.* A piece of paper used on a pressure tympan to vary the pressure that produces light and dark tones. **4.** A transparent sheet containing graphic matter, such as labels or colored areas, placed on illustrative matter to be incorporated into it.

o·ver·leap (ō′vər-lēp′) *tr.v.* **-leaped** or **-leapt** (-lĕpt′), **-leap·ing, -leaps. 1.** To leap across or over. **2.** To defeat (oneself or one's purpose) by going too far.

o·ver·learn (ō′vər-lûrn′) *tr.v.* **-learned** or **-learnt** (-lûrnt′), **-learn·ing, -learns.** To continue working at (a skill, for example) after becoming proficient.

o·ver·lie (ō′vər-lī′) *tr.v.* **-lay** (-lā′), **-lain** (-lān′), **-ly·ing, -lies. 1.** To lie over or upon. **2.** To kill by lying upon.

o·ver·load (ō′vər-lōd′) *tr.v.* **-load·ed, -load·ing, -loads.** To load too heavily. —*n.* (ō′vər-lōd′). An excessive load.

o·ver·long (ō′vər-lông′, -lŏng′) *adj.* Excessively long. —*adv.* For too long.

o·ver·look (ō′vər-lo͝ok′) *tr.v.* **-looked, -look·ing, -looks. 1.** To look over or at from a higher place. **2.** To rise above, esp. so as to afford a view over: *The tower overlooks the sea.* **3.** To fail to notice or consider; miss. **4.** To ignore deliberately or indulgently; disregard. **5.** To look over; examine. **6.** To watch over; oversee. **7.** To cast a spell over with an evil eye. —*n.* (ō′vər-lo͝ok′). **1.** An elevated place that affords an extensive view. **2.** An act of overlooking something.

o·ver·lord (ō′vər-lôrd′) *n.* **1.** A lord having power or supremacy over other lords. **2.** One who is in a position of supremacy or domination over others. **—o′ver·lord′ship** *n.*

o·ver·ly (ō′vər-lē) *adv.* To an excessive degree; too.

o·ver·man *n.* **1.** (ō′vər-mən, -măn′). A person having authority over others, esp. an overseer or foreman. **2.** (ō′vər-măn′). Superman (sense 2). —*tr.v.* (ō′vər-măn′) **-manned, -man·ning, -mans.** To provide with more personnel than are needed.

o·ver·mas·ter (ō′vər-măs′tər) *tr.v.* **-tered, -ter·ing, -ters.** To overpower; overcome.

o·ver·match (ō′vər-măch′) *tr.v.* **-matched, -match·ing, -match·es. 1.** To be more than the match of; exceed. **2.** To match with a superior opponent. —*n.* (ō′vər-măch′). A contest in which one opponent is distinctly superior.

o·ver·much (ō′vər-mŭch′) *adj.* Too much; excessive. —*adv.* In excess. —*n.* (ō′vər-mŭch′, ō′vər-mŭch′). An excessive amount.

o·ver·night (ō′vər-nīt′) *adj.* **1.** Lasting for, extending over, or remaining during a night: *an overnight journey.* **2.** For use over a single night or for a short journey: *overnight supplies.* **3.** Happening as if in a single night; sudden: *an overnight success.* —*adv.* (ō′vər-nīt′). **1.** During or for the length of the night. **2.** On the preceding night or evening. **3.** In or as if in the course of one night; suddenly: *The situation changed overnight.*

overnight bag *n.* A small piece of luggage used to carry items needed for an overnight stay.

o·ver·nu·tri·tion (ō′vər-no͞o-trĭsh′ən, -nyo͞o-) *n.* Excessive intake of food.

o·ver·op·ti·mis·tic (ō′vər-ŏp′tə-mĭs′tĭk) *adj.* Excessively optimistic. **—o′ver·op′ti·mism** *n.* **—o′ver·op′ti·mis′ti·cal·ly** *adv.*

o·ver·pass (ō′vər-păs′) *n.* A passage, roadway, or bridge that crosses above another roadway or thoroughfare. —*tr.v.* (ō′vər-păs′, -päs′), **-passed** or **-past, -pass·ing, -pass·es. 1.** To pass over or across; traverse. **2.** To go beyond; surpass. **3.** To overlook; disregard.

o·ver·pay (ō′vər-pā′) *v.* **-paid** (-pād′), **-pay·ing, -pays.** —*tr.* **1.** To pay (someone) too much. **2.** To pay an amount in excess of (a sum due). —*intr.* To pay too much. **—o′ver·pay′ment** *n.*

overpass

o·ver·per·suade (ō′vər-pər-swād′) *tr.v.* **-suad·ed, -suad·ing, -suades.** To persuade (someone) to act contrary to inclination. **—o′ver·per·sua′sion** *n.*

o·ver·play (ō′vər-plā′) *tr.v.* **-played, -play·ing, -plays. 1.** To play (a dramatic role) in an exaggerated manner; overact. **2.** To overestimate the strength of (one's holding or position) and thus contribute to one's own defeat: *overplay one's hand.* **3.** To hit (a golf ball) beyond the green.

o·ver·plus (ō′vər-plŭs′) *n.* An amount in excess of need.

o·ver·pop·u·la·tion (ō′vər-pŏp′yə-lā′shən) *n.* Excessive population of an area to the point of overcrowding, depletion of natural resources, or environmental deterioration. **—o′ver·pop′u·lat′ed** (-lā′tĭd) *adj.*

o·ver·pow·er (ō′vər-pou′ər) *tr.v.* **-ered, -er·ing, -ers. 1.** To overcome or vanquish by superior force; subdue. **2.** To affect so strongly as to make helpless or ineffective; overwhelm. **3.** To furnish with excessive mechanical power.

o·ver·pow·er·ing (ō′vər-pou′ər-ĭng) *adj.* So strong as to overpower; overwhelming. **—o′ver·pow′er·ing·ly** *adv.*

o·ver·praise (ō′vər-prāz′) *tr.v.* **-praised, -prais·ing, -prais·es.** To give too much praise to.

o·ver·price (ō′vər-prīs′) *tr.v.* **-priced, -pric·ing, -pric·es.** To put too high a price or value on.

o·ver·print (ō′vər-prĭnt′) *tr.v.* **-print·ed, -print·ing, -prints.** To imprint over something already printed, esp. to print over (printed images) with another color. —*n.* (ō′vər-prĭnt′). **1.** A mark or impression made by overprinting. **2. a.** A mark or words printed over a postage stamp to note a change in use or a special occasion. **b.** A stamp so marked.

o·ver·prize (ō′vər-prīz′) *tr.v.* **-prized, -priz·ing, -priz·es.** To prize too much.

o·ver·pro·duce (ō′vər-prə-do͞os′, -dyo͞os′) *tr.v.* **-duced, -duc·ing, -duc·es.** To produce too much of. **—o′ver·pro·duc′tion** (-dŭk′shən) *n.*

o·ver·proof (ō′vər-pro͞of′) *adj.* Containing a greater proportion of alcohol than proof spirit, esp. containing more than 50 per cent alcohol by volume.

o·ver·pro·tect (ō′vər-prə-tĕkt′) *tr.v.* **-tect·ed, -tect·ing, -tects.** To protect too much. **—o′ver·pro·tec′tive** *adj.*

o·ver·qual·i·fied (ō′vər-kwŏl′ə-fīd′) *adj.* Having qualifications beyond what is necessary or desired.

o·ver·rate (ō′vər-rāt′) *tr.v.* **-rat·ed, -rat·ing, -rates.** To rate too highly; overestimate the merits of.

o·ver·reach (ō′vər-rēch′) *v.* **-reached, -reach·ing, -reach·es.** —*tr.* **1.** To reach or extend over or beyond. **2.** To miss by reaching too far or attempting too much: *overreach a goal.* **3.** To defeat (oneself) by going too far or by doing or trying to gain too much. **4.** To get the better of. —*intr.* **1.** To reach or go too far. **2.** To outwit or cheat others. **3.** To strike the front part of a hind foot against the rear or side part of a forefoot or foreleg on the same side of the body. **—o′ver·reach′er** *n.*

o·ver·re·act (ō′vər-rē-ăkt′) *intr.v.* **-act·ed, -act·ing, -acts.** To react unduly. **—o′ver·re·ac′tion** *n.*

o·ver·re·fine·ment (ō′vər-rĭ-fīn′mənt) *n.* Undue refinement. **—o′ver·re·fined′** *adj.*

o·ver·ride (ō′vər-rīd′) *tr.v.* **-rode** (-rōd′), **-rid·den** (-rĭd′n), **-rid·ing, -rides. 1.** To ride across. **2.** To trample upon. **3.** To ride (a horse) too hard. **4.** To prevail over; conquer: *Budgetary concerns overrode all other considerations.* **5.** To declare null and void; set aside. —*n.* (ō′vər-rīd′). A sales commission collected by an executive in addition to the commission received by the subordinate salesman.

o·ver·ripe (ō′vər-rīp′) *adj.* **1.** More than ripe; too ripe. **2.** Jaded; decadent. **—o′ver·ripe′ness** *n.*

o·ver·rule (ō′vər-ro͞ol′) *tr.v.* **-ruled, -rul·ing, -rules. 1. a.** To disallow the action or arguments of (a person), esp. by virtue of higher authority. **b.** To decide or rule against: *overrule a policy decision.* **c.** To declare null and void; reverse. **2.** To dominate by strong influence.

o·ver·run (ō′vər-rŭn′) *v.* **-ran** (-răn′), **-run, -run·ning, -runs.** —*tr.* **1.** To defeat conclusively and seize the positions of: *"A large party of screeching warriors had overrun our company"* (James D. Horan). **2.** To spread or swarm over destructively: *Locusts overran the prairie.* **3.** To spread swiftly throughout: *The new fashion overran the country.* **4.** To overflow: *The river overran its banks.* **5.** To run or extend beyond: *His speech has overrun the time limit.* **6.** *Printing.* **a.** To rearrange or move (set type or pictures) from one column, line, or page to another. **b.** To print (a job order) in a quantity larger than that ordered. —*intr.* **1.** To run over; overflow. **2.** To go beyond the normal or desired limit. —*n.* (ō′vər-rŭn′). **1.** An act of overrunning. **2.** The amount by which something overruns. **3. a.** The act of exceeding estimated costs for work covered by contract. **b.** The amount by which actual costs exceed estimates.

o·ver·score (ō′vər-skôr′, -skōr′) *tr.v.* **-scored, -scor·ing, -scores.** To cross out by drawing a line or lines over or through.

o·ver·seas (ō′vər-sēz′, ō′vər-sēz′) also **o·ver·sea** (ō′vər-sē′, ō′vər-sē′) *adv.* Beyond the sea; abroad. —*adj.* Of, pertaining to, originating in, or situated in areas across the sea.

overseas cap *n.* A garrison cap.

o·ver·see (ō′vər-sē′) *tr.v.* **-saw** (-sô′), **-seen, -see·ing, -sees. 1.** To watch over and direct; supervise. **2.** To scrutinize; inspect.

o·ver·se·er (ō′vər-sē′ər) *n.* **1.** One who keeps watch over and directs the work of others, esp. laborers. **2.** A supervisor or superintendent.

o·ver·sell (ō′vər-sĕl′) *tr.v.* **-sold** (-sōld′), **-sell·ing, -sells. 1.** To contract to sell more of (a stock or commodity) than can be delivered within the terms of a contract. **2.** To be too eager or insistent in attempting to sell something to (someone). **3.** To present with excessive or unwarranted enthusiasm.

o·ver·sen·si·tive (ō′vər-sĕn′sĭ-tĭv) *adj.* Unduly sensitive. **—o′ver·sen′si·tive·ness, o′ver·sen′si·tiv′i·ty** *n.*

o·ver·set (ō′vər-sĕt′) *v.* **-set, -set·ting, -sets.** —*tr.* **1.** To tip or push over; overturn. **2.** To throw into a confused or disturbed state; upset. **3.** *Printing.* **a.** To set too much (type). **b.** To set too much type for (a given space). —*intr.* **1.** To fall over; overturn. **2.** *Printing.* To set too much printed matter for a given space. —*n.* (ō′vər-sĕt′). **1.** An upset. **2.** *Printing.* An excess of set type.

o·ver·sew (ō′vər-sō′, ō′vər-sō′) *tr.v.* **-sewed, -sewn** (-sōn′) or **-sewed, -sew·ing, -sews.** To sew with overhand stitches.

o·ver·sexed (ō′vər-sĕkst′) *adj.* Exhibiting an unusually large sexual appetite.

o·ver·shad·ow (ō′vər-shăd′ō) *tr.v.* **-owed, -ow·ing, -ows. 1.** To cast a shadow over. **2.** To make insignificant by comparison; dominate.

o·ver·shoe (ō′vər-sho͞o′) *n.* An article of footwear worn over shoes as protection from water, snow, or cold.

o·ver·shoot (ō′vər-sho͞ot′) *v.* **-shot** (-shŏt′), **-shoot·ing, -shoots.** —*tr.* **1.** To shoot or pass over or beyond. **2.** To miss by or as if by shooting, hitting, or propelling something too far. **3.** To fly beyond or past: *The plane overshot the runway.* **4.** To go beyond; exceed. —*intr.* To shoot or go too far.

o·ver·shot (ō′vər-shŏt′) *adj.* **1.** Having an upper part projecting beyond the lower: *an overshot jaw.* **2.** Moved or put into motion by the weight of water passing over and flowing from the top: *an overshot mill wheel.*

o·ver·sight (ō′vər-sīt′) *n.* **1.** An unintentional omission or mistake. **2.** Watchful care or management; supervision.

o·ver·sim·ple (ō′vər-sĭm′pəl) *adj.* Too simple; not thorough: *an oversimple explanation of a complex phenomenon.*

o·ver·sim·pli·fy (ō′vər-sĭm′plə-fī′) *v.* **-fied, -fy·ing, -fies.** —*tr.* To distort by presenting in too simple a form. —*intr.* To cause distortions by presenting a subject too simply. **—o′ver·sim′pli·fi·ca′tion** *n.*

o·ver·size (ō′vər-sīz′) also **o·ver·sized** (-sīzd′) *adj.* Larger in size than usual or necessary. —*n.* (ō′vər-sīz′). **1.** An unusually large size. **2.** An article made in an unusually large size.

o·ver·skirt (ō′vər-skûrt′) *n.* An outer skirt, esp. a shorter one worn draped over another skirt.

o·ver·sleep (ō′vər-slēp′) *v.* **-slept** (-slĕpt′), **-sleep·ing, -sleeps.** —*intr.* To sleep beyond one's usual or intended time for waking. —*tr.* To sleep beyond the time for: *overslept my appointment.*

o·ver·soul (ō′vər-soul′) *n.* In New England transcendentalism, a spiritual essence or vital force in the universe in which all souls participate and which therefore transcends individual consciousness.

o·ver·spend (ō′vər-spĕnd′) *v.* **-spent** (-spĕnt′), **-spend·ing, -spends.** —*intr.* To spend more than is prudent or necessary. —*tr.* **1.** To spend in excess of: *overspend one's income.* **2.** To exhaust: *overspent with toil.*

o·ver·spread (ō′vər-sprĕd′) *tr.v.* **-spread, -spread·ing, -spreads.** To spread over or overhead. **—o′ver·spread′** *n.*

o·ver·state (ō′vər-stāt′) *tr.v.* **-stat·ed, -stat·ing, -states.** To state in exaggerated terms. **—o′ver·state′ment** *n.*

o·ver·stay (ō′vər-stā′) *tr.v.* **-stayed, -stay·ing, -stays.** To stay beyond the set limits or expected duration of: *He overstayed his welcome.*

o·ver·step (ō′vər-stĕp′) *tr.v.* **-stepped, -step·ping, -steps.** To go beyond (a limit): *overstep the bounds of taste.*

o·ver·stock (ō′vər-stŏk′) *tr.v.* **-stocked, -stock·ing, -stocks.** To stock with too much of (a commodity). —*n.* (ō′vər-stŏk′). An excessive supply.

o·ver·stuff (ō′vər-stŭf′) *tr.v.* **-stuffed, -stuff·ing, -stuffs. 1.** To stuff too much into. **2.** To upholster overall and thickly.

o·ver·sub·scribe (ō′vər-səb-skrīb′) *tr.v.* **-scribed, -scrib·ing, -scribes.** To subscribe for (something) in excess of available supply or accommodation: *The opera season was oversubscribed.* **—o′ver·sub·scrip′tion** (-skrĭp′shən) *n.*

o·ver·sub·tle (ō′vər-sŭt′l) *adj.* Subtle to the point of failing to accomplish one's objective.

o·ver·sup·ply (ō′vər-sə-plī′) *n., pl.* **-plies.** A supply in excess of what is required. —*tr.v.* (ō′vər-sə-plī′) **-plied, -ply·ing, -plies.** To supply in excess.

o·vert (ō-vûrt′, ō′vûrt′) *adj.* Open and observable; not concealed or hidden: *overt hostility.* [ME < OFr., p.part. of *ovrir,* to open < Lat. *aperire.*] **—o·vert′ly** *adv.*

o·ver·take (ō′vər-tāk′) *tr.v.* **-took** (-to͝ok′), **-tak·en, -tak·ing, -takes. 1.** To catch up with; draw even or level with. **2.** To pass after catching up with. **3.** To come upon unexpectedly; take by surprise.

o·ver·tax (ō′vər-tăks′) *tr.v.* **-taxed, -tax·ing, -tax·es. 1.** To impose an excessive tax or taxes on. **2.** To subject to an excessive burden or strain. **—o′ver·tax·a′tion** *n.*

o·ver-the-count·er (ō′vər-*th*ə-koun′tər) *adj.* **1.** Not listed or available on an officially recognized stock exchange but traded in direct negotiation between buyers and sellers: *over-the-counter stocks.* **2.** Capable of being sold legally without a prescription: *over-the-counter drugs.* **3.** *Informal.* Legitimate; aboveboard.

o·ver·throw (ō′vər-thrō′) *tr.v.* **-threw** (-thro͞o′), **-thrown** (-thrōn), **-throw·ing, -throws. 1.** To throw over; overturn. **2.** To bring about the downfall or destruction of, esp. by force or concerted action: *a plot to overthrow the government.* **3.** To throw something over and beyond (an intended mark): *The infielder overthrew first base.* —*n.* (ō′vər-thrō′). **1.** An instance of overthrowing. **2.** Downfall; destruction. **3.** The throwing of a ball over and beyond a target, esp. in baseball.

o·ver·time (ō′vər-tīm′) *n.* **1.** Time beyond an established limit, such as: **a.** Working hours in addition to those of the regular schedule. **b.** *Sports.* A period of playing time added after the expiration of the set time limit of an athletic contest. **2.** Payment for additional work done outside of regular working hours. —*adv.* Beyond the established time limit, esp. that of the normal working day: *The staff worked overtime.* —*tr.v.* (ō′vər-tīm′) **-timed, -tim·ing, -times.** To exceed the desired timing for: *overtime a photographic exposure.*

o·ver·tone (ō′vər-tōn′) *n.* **1.** *Mus.* A harmonic (sense 1). **2.** Often **overtones.** An implication; hint: *praise with overtones of envy.*

o·ver·top (ō′vər-tŏp′) *tr.v.* **-topped, -top·ping, -tops. 1.** To extend or rise over or beyond the top of; tower above. **2.** To be superior to; override: *"Religion overtopped the common affairs of life"* (Albert C. Baugh).

o·ver·train (ō′vər-trān′) *v.* **-trained; -train·ing; -trains.** —*tr.* To train too much. —*intr.* To practice something excessively.

o·ver·trick (ō′vər-trĭk′) *n.* A trick won in excess of contract or game, as in bridge.

o·ver·trump (ō′vər-trŭmp′, ō′vər-trŭmp′) *v.* **-trumped, -trump·ing, -trumps.** —*intr.* To play a trump higher than one previously played on a trick. —*tr.* To trump with a higher trump.

o·ver·ture (ō′vər-cho͝or′) *n.* **1.** *Mus.* **a.** An instrumental composition intended esp. as an introduction to an extended musical work, such as an opera or an oratorio. **b.** A similar orchestral work, such as one written as introductory music to a play or as a concert piece. **2.** An introductory section or part, as of a poem. **3.** An act, offer, or proposal that indicates readiness to undertake a course of action or to open a relationship: *"I wanted revenge for her snub of my flirting overture"* (John Updike). —*tr.v.* **-tured, -tur·ing, -tures. 1.** To present as an overture or proposal. **2.** To present or offer an overture to. **3.** To introduce with an overture or prelude. [ME < OFr. < Lat. *apertura,* opening < *aperire,* to open.]

o·ver·turn (ō′vər-tûrn′) *v.* **-turned, -turn·ing, -turns.** —*tr.* **1.** To cause to turn over or capsize; upset. **2.** To overthrow; defeat. —*intr.* To turn over or capsize; become upset. —*n.* (ō′vər-tûrn′). **1.** The act or process of overturning. **2.** The state of being overturned. **3.** Turnover (sense 5).

o·ver·use (ō′vər-yo͞oz′) *tr.v.* **-used, -us·ing, -us·es.** To use to excess. —*n.* (ō′vər-yo͞os′). Excessive use.

o·ver·val·ue (ō′vər-văl′yo͞o) *tr.v.* **-ued, -u·ing, -ues.** To set too high a value on. **—o′ver·val′u·a′tion** *n.*

o·ver·view (ō′vər-vyo͞o′) *n.* **1.** A broad, comprehensive view; survey. **2.** A summary or review.

o·ver·wear (ō′vər-wâr′) *tr.v.* **-wore** (-wôr′, -wōr′), **-worn** (-wôrn′, -wōrn′), **-wear·ing, -wears.** To wear out.

o·ver·wea·ry (ō′vər-wîr′ē) *adj.* Weary to the point of exhaustion —*tr. v.* **-ried, -ry·ing, -ries.** To tire out; exhaust.

o·ver·ween·ing (ō′vər-wē′nĭng) *adj.* **1.** Presumptuously arrogant; overbearing: *overweening vanity.* **2.** Excessive; immoderate: *overweening ambition.*

o·ver·weigh (ō′vər-wā′) *tr.v.* **-weighed, -weigh·ing, -weighs. 1.** To have more weight than. **2.** To weigh down excessively; overburden.

o·ver·weight (ō′vər-wāt′) *adj.* Weighing more than is normal, necessary, or allowed. —*n.* (ō′vər-wāt′). **1.** More weight than is normal, necessary, or allowed. **2.** Greater weight or importance; preponderance. —*tr.v.* (ō′vər-wāt′) **-weight·ed, -weight·ing, -weights. 1.** To weigh down too heavily; overload. **2.** To give too much emphasis, importance, or consideration to.

o·ver·whelm (ō′vər-hwĕlm′, -wĕlm′) *tr.v.* **-whelmed, -whelm·ing, -whelms. 1.** To surge over and submerge; engulf: *waves overwhelming the rocky shoreline.* **2.** To overcome completely, either physically or emotionally; overpower: *overwhelmed by the enthusiastic reception.* **3.** To turn over; upset.

o·ver·whelm·ing (ō′vər-hwĕl′mĭng, -wĕl′-) *adj.* Overpowering in effect or strength: *overwhelming news; an overwhelming majority.* **—o′ver·whelm′ing·ly** *adv.*

o·ver·wind (ō′vər-wīnd′) *tr.v.* **-wound** (-wound), **-wind·ing, -winds.** To wind too tightly.

o·ver·win·ter (ō′vər-wĭn′tər) *intr.v.* **-tered, -ter·ing, -ters.** To remain alive, as small game, through the winter. —*adj.* Occurring during the period of winter.

o·ver·work (ō′vər-wûrk′) *v.* **-worked, -work·ing, -works.** —*tr.* **1.** To force to work too hard or too long. **2.** To use or rework too often or to excess: *overwork a metaphor.* —*intr.* To work too long or too hard. —*n.* (ō′vər-wûrk′). Excess work, esp. work done on overtime.

o·ver·write (ō′vər-rīt′) *v.* **-wrote** (-rōt′), **-writ·ten** (rĭt′n), **-writ·ing, -writes.** —*tr.* **1.** To write (something) over other writing. **2.** To write about in an excessively flowery, mannered, or prolix style. —*intr.* To write at unnecessarily great length.

o·ver·wrought (ō′vər-rôt′) *adj.* **1.** Excessively nervous or excited; agitated: *"The Queen was so overwrought that she became physically ill"* (Philip Magnus). **2.** Extremely elaborate or ornate; overdone: *an overwrought prose style.*

ovi– or **ovo–** or **ov–** *pref.* Egg; ovum: *oviferous.* [Lat. < *ovum,* egg.]

o·vi·bos (ō′və-bŏs′) *n.* The musk ox. [Lat. *ovis,* sheep + Lat. *bos,* ox.]

o·vi·ci·dal (ō′vĭ-sīd′l) *adj.* Capable of killing eggs. **—o′vi·cide′** *n.*

o·vi·duct (ō′və-dŭkt′) *n.* A tube through which ova travel from an ovary. **—o′vi·duc′tal** *adj.*

o·vif·er·ous (ō-vĭf′ər-əs) *adj.* Bearing or producing ova.

o·vi·form (ō′və-fôrm′) *adj.* Egg-shaped.

o·vine (ō′vīn′) *adj.* Of or characteristic of sheep; sheeplike. *—n.* An ovine animal. [LLat. *ovinus* < Lat. *ovis,* sheep.]
o·vip·a·rous (ō-vĭp′ər-əs) *adj.* Producing eggs that hatch outside the body. **—o′vi·par′i·ty** (ō′və-păr′ĭ-tē) *n.* **—o·vip′a·rous·ly** *adv.*
o·vi·pos·it (ō′və-pŏz′ĭt) *intr.v.* **-it·ed, -it·ing, -its.** To lay eggs, esp. with an ovipositor. **—o′vi·po·si′tion** (-pə-zĭsh′ən) *n.* **—o′vi·po·si′tion·al** *adj.*
o·vi·pos·i·tor (ō′və-pŏz′ə-tər) *n.* A tubular structure, sometimes extending outside the abdomen, with which many insects lay eggs.
o·vi·sac (ō′və-săk′) *n.* An egg-containing capsule, such as an ootheca or a Graafian follicle.
ovo– *pref.* Variant of **ovi-.**
o·void (ō′void′) also **o·voi·dal** (ō-void′l) *adj.* Egg-shaped. *—n.* **ovoid.** Something egg-shaped.

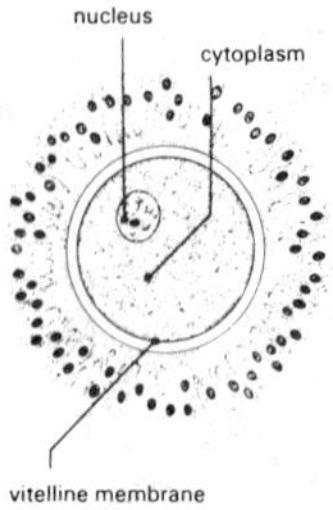

ovum
Human ovum

o·vo·lo (ō′və-lō′) *n., pl.* **-li** (-lī′). *Archit.* A rounded convex molding, often a quarter section of a circle or ellipse. [Ital., dim. of *ovo,* egg < Lat. *ovum.*]
o·von·ic (ō-vŏn′ĭk) *n.* A device whose operation is based on the Ovshinsky effect. [OV(SHINSKY EFFECT) + (ELECTR)ONIC.]
o·vo·tes·tis (ō′vō-tĕs′tĭs) *n., pl.* **-tes** (-tēz′). The hermaphroditic reproductive gland of some gastropods.
o·vo·vi·vip·a·rous (ō′vō-vī-vĭp′ər-əs) *adj.* Producing eggs that hatch within the female's body, as do some fishes and reptiles. **—o′vo·vi·vip′a·rous·ly** *adv.* **—o′vo·vi′vi·par′i·ty** (-vī′və-păr′ĭ-tē), **o′vo·vi·vip′a·rous·ness** *n.*
Ov·shin·sky effect (ŏv-shĭn′skē, ôv-) *n.* The effect by which a specific glassy thin film switches from a nonconductor to a semiconductor upon application of a minimum voltage. [After Stanford R. *Ovshinsky* (b. 1922).]
o·vu·late (ō′vyə-lāt′, ŏv′yə-) *intr.v.* **-lat·ed, -lat·ing, -lates. 1.** To produce ova. **2.** To discharge ova. [< OVULE.] **—o′vu·la′tion** *n.*
o·vule (ō′vyo͞ol, ŏv′yo͞ol) *n.* **1.** *Zool.* An immature ovum. **2.** *Bot.* A minute structure which after fertilization becomes a plant seed. [Fr. < NLat. *ovulum,* dim. of Lat. *ovum,* egg.] **—o′vu·lar** (ō′vyə-lər, ŏv′yə-), **o′vu·lar′y** (-lĕr′ē) *adj.*
o·vum (ō′vəm) *n., pl.* **o·va** (ō′və). The female reproductive cell of animals; egg. [Lat., egg.]

George Miksch Sutton
owl

owe (ō) *v.* **owed, ow·ing, owes.** *—tr.* **1.** To be indebted to the amount of: *He owes me five dollars.* **2.** To have a moral obligation to render or offer: *I owe him an apology.* **3.** To be in debt to: *owes the porter for his services.* **4. a.** To be indebted or obliged for. **b.** To be indebted for the existence or origin of: *She owes her success to talent and luck.* **5.** To bear (a certain feeling) toward a person: *He owes them a grudge.* **6.** *Obs.* To own; have. *—intr.* To be in debt: *He owes for everything he has.* [ME *owen* < OE *āgan,* to possess.]
ow·ing (ō′ĭng) *adj.* Still to be paid; due.
owing to *prep.* Because of; on account of.
owl (oul) *n.* **1.** Any of various often nocturnal birds of prey of the order Strigiformes, having hooked and feathered talons, large heads with short hooked beaks, and eyes set in a frontal facial plane. **2.** Any of a breed of domestic pigeons resembling owls. [ME *owle* < OE *ūle.*]
owl·et (ou′lĭt) *n.* A young owl.
owl·ish (ou′lĭsh) *adj.* Resembling an owl. **—owl′ish·ly** *adv.* **—owl′ish·ness** *n.*
owl's claws (oulz) *n.* *(used with a sing. or pl. verb).* A plant, *Helenium hoopesii,* of western North America, having large yellow flower heads.
owl's-clo·ver (oulz′klō′vər) *n.* Any of various New World plants of the genus *Orthocarpus,* having spikes of red or purple flowers. [From the resemblance of the flowers of some species to owl's faces.]
own (ōn) *adj.* Of or belonging to oneself or itself: *He made his own bed.* *—n.* That which belongs to one: *It is my own.* *—v.* **owned, own·ing, owns.** *—tr.* **1.** To have or possess: *He owns the store.* **2.** To acknowledge or admit: *He owned his mistake.* *—intr.* To confess: *He owned to being annoyed.* ***—phrasal verb.*** **own up.** To confess fully and openly. ***—idioms.*** **come into (one's) own. 1.** To obtain possession of what belongs to one. **2.** To obtain rightful recognition and prosperity. **hold (one's) own.** To maintain one's place in spite of attack or criticism. **of one's own.** Belonging completely to oneself. **on (one's) own.** Completely independent; responsible for oneself. [ME *owen* < OE *āgen.*] **—own′er** *n.*
own·er·ship (ō′nər-shĭp′) *n.* **1.** The state or fact of being an owner. **2.** Legal right to the possession of a thing.

ox
Yoked oxen

ox (ŏks) *n., pl.* **ox·en** (ŏk′sən). **1.** An adult castrated bull of the genus *Bos.* **2.** A bovine mammal. [ME < OE *oxa.*]
ox– *pref.* Variant of **oxo-.**
ox·a·cil·lin (ŏk′sə-sĭl′ĭn) *n.* A semisynthetic penicillin effective against penicillinase-producing staphylococci. [OX(O) + A(ZOLE) + (PENI)CILLIN.]
ox·a·late (ŏk′sə-lāt′) *n.* A salt or ester of oxalic acid. *—tr.v.* **-lat·ed, -lat·ing, -lates.** To treat (a specimen) with an oxalate or oxalic acid. [Fr. : *oxalique,* oxalic acid + *-ate,* -ate.]
ox·al·ic acid (ŏk-săl′ĭk) *n.* A poisonous, crystalline organic acid, $HOOCCOOH \cdot 2H_2O$, used as a cleansing agent for automobile radiators and for metals in general, as a laundry bleach, and in textile finishing and cleaning. [Fr. *oxalique* < Lat. *oxalis,* wood sorrel. —see OXALIS.]
ox·a·lis (ŏk′sə-lĭs, ŏk-săl′ĭs) *n.* Any of various plants of the genus *Oxalis,* having pink, yellow, or white flowers. [NLat. *Oxalis,* genus name < Lat. *oxalis,* wood sorrel < Gk. < *oxus,* sour.]
ox·blood red (ŏks′blŭd′) *n.* A dark or deep red to medium reddish brown.
ox·bow (ŏks′bō′) *n.* **1.** A U-shaped piece of wood that fits under and around the neck of an ox, with its upper ends attached to the bar of the yoke. **2. a.** A U-shaped bend in a river. **b.** The land within such a bend of a river.
oxen (ŏk′sən) *n.* Plural of **ox.**
ox·eye (ŏk′sī′) *n.* **1.** Any of various Eurasian plants of the genus *Buphthalmum,* having daisylike flowers with yellow rays and dark centers. **2.** Any of various North American plants of the genus *Heliopsis,* having flowers similar to those of the oxeye. **3.** A round or oval dormer window. [ME.]
oxeye daisy *n.* The daisy (sense 1).
ox·ford (ŏks′fərd) *n.* **1.** A stout, low shoe that laces over the instep. **2.** A cotton cloth of a tight basket weave, used primarily for shirts. [After *Oxford,* England.]
oxford gray *n.* A dark gray.
Oxford movement *n.* A movement within the Church of England, originating at Oxford University in 1833, that sought to link the Anglican Church more closely to the Roman Catholic Church.
ox·heart (ŏks′härt′) *n.* A variety of cultivated cherry having sweet, juicy fruit.
ox·i·dant (ŏk′sĭ-dənt) *n.* A chemical reagent that oxidizes.
ox·i·dase (ŏk′sə-dās′) *n.* Any of various plant or animal enzymes that act as oxidants. [OXID(ATION) + -ASE.] **—ox′i·da′sic** *adj.*
ox·i·da·tion (ŏk′sĭ-dā′shən) *n.* **1.** The combination of a substance with oxygen. **2.** A reaction in which the atoms in an element lose electrons and the element's valence is correspondingly increased. [Fr. < *oxider,* to oxidize < *oxide,* oxide. —see OXIDE.] **—ox·i·da·tive** *adj.* **—ox′i·da′tive·ly** *adv.*
ox·i·da·tion-re·duc·tion (ŏk′sĭ-dā′shən-rĭ-dŭk′shən) *n.* A chemical reaction in which an atom or molecule loses electrons to another atom or molecule.
ox·i·da·tive phos·pho·ryl·a·tion (ok′sĭ-dā′tĭv fŏs′fə-rə-lā′shən) *n.* A vital process of intracellular respiration occurring within the mitochondria of the cell, responsible for most adenosine triphosphate formation.
ox·ide (ŏk′sīd′) *n.* A binary compound of an element or radical with oxygen. [Fr. < *oxygène,* oxygen. —see OXYGEN.] **—ox·id′ic** (ŏk-sĭd′ĭk) *adj.*
ox·i·dize (ŏk′sĭ-dīz′) *v.* **-dized, -diz·ing, -diz·es.** *Chem.* *—tr.* **1.** To combine with oxygen; make into an oxide. **2.** To increase the positive charge or valence of (an element) by removing electrons. **3.** To coat with oxide. *—intr.* To become oxidized. [< OXIDE.] **—ox′i·diz′a·ble** *adj.* **—ox′i·di·za′tion** *n.*
ox·i·diz·er (ŏk′sĭ-dī′zər) *n.* A substance that oxidizes or induces another substance to oxidize; an oxidizing agent.
ox·i·do·re·duc·tase (ŏk′sĭ-dō-rĭ-dŭk′tās) *n.* An enzyme that catalyzes an oxidation-reduction reaction. [OXID(ATION) + REDUC(TION) + -ASE.]
ox·lip (ŏks′lĭp′) *n.* A Eurasian primrose, *Primula elatior,* having clusters of yellow flowers. [OE *oxanslyppe* : *oxa,* ox + *slipa,* slimy substance.]
oxo– or **ox–** *pref.* Oxygen: *oxophenarsine.* [Fr. < *oxygène,* oxygen.]
Ox·o·ni·an (ŏk-sō′nē-ən) *adj.* Of, pertaining to, or characteristic of Oxford or Oxford University. *—n.* **1.** A native or inhabitant of Oxford. **2.** A student or graduate of Oxford University. [< Med. Lat. *Oxonia,* Oxford < OE *Oxnaford.*]
ox·o·phen·ar·sine hydrochloride (ŏk′sō-fĕ-när′sēn′) *n.* A drug, $C_6H_3AsO(OH)NH_2HCl$, formerly used in treating syphilis.
ox·peck·er (ŏks′pĕk′ər) *n.* Either of two African birds, *Buphagus africanus* or *B. erythrorhyncus,* that feed upon ticks on the hides of large wild or domestic animals.
ox·tail (ŏks′tāl′) *n.* The tail of an ox, esp. when used in soup.
oxy– *pref.* Oxygen, esp. additional oxygen: *oxyacetylene.* [< OXYGEN.]
ox·y·a·cet·y·lene (ŏk′sē-ə-sĕt′l-ĭn, -ēn′) *adj.* Containing a mixture of acetylene and oxygen, as commonly used in metal welding and cutting torches.
ox·y·ac·id (ŏk′sē-ăs′ĭd) *n.* An oxygen-containing acid.
ox·y·ceph·a·ly (ŏk′sē-sĕf′ə-lē) *n.* A congenital cephalic abnormality in which the skull assumes a conical shape. [Gk. *oxus,* sharp + -CEPHALY.] **—ox′y·ce·phal′ic** (-sə-făl′ĭk), **ox′y·ceph′a·lous** *adj.*
ox·y·gen (ŏk′sĭ-jən) *n.* *Symbol* **O** A colorless, odorless, tasteless gaseous element constituting 21 per cent of the atmosphere by volume from which the pure liquid form is obtained by fractional distillation. It combines with most elements, is essential for plant and animal respiration, and is required for nearly all combustion and combustive processes. Atomic number 8; atomic weight 15.9994; melting point −218.4°C; boiling point −183.0°C; gas density at 0°C 1.429 grams per liter; valence 2. [Fr. *oxygène* : Gk. *oxus,* sharp, acid + *-gène,* -gen.] **—ox′y·gen′ic** (ŏk′sĭ-jĕn′ĭk) *adj.* **—ox′y·gen′i·cal·ly** *adv.* **—ox·yg′e·nous** (ŏk-sĭj′ə-nəs) *adj.*
ox·y·gen·ase (ok′sĭ-jə-nās′) *n.* An oxidoreductase that catalyzes the transfer of free oxygen to its substrate.

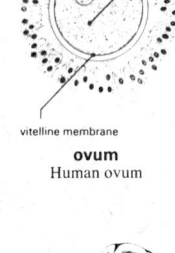

ă pat / ā pay / âr care / ä father / b **bib** / ch **church** / d **deed** / ĕ pet / ē be / f **fife** / g **gag** / h **hat** / hw **which** / ĭ pit / ī pie / îr **pier** / j **judge** / k **kick** / l lid, needle / m **mum** / n no, sudden / ng **thing** / ŏ pot / ō toe / ô paw, for / oi **noise** / ou **out** / o͝o **took** / o͞o **boot** /

ox·y·gen·ate (ŏk′sĭ-jə-nāt′) also **ox·y·gen·ize** (-nīz′) *tr.v.* **-at·ed, -at·ing, -ates** also **-ized, -iz·ing, -iz·es.** To treat, combine, or infuse with oxygen. **—ox′y·gen·a′tion** *n.*

oxygen mask *n.* A masklike device covering the mouth and nose and through which oxygen is supplied from a tank or other source.

oxygen tent *n.* A canopy placed over the head and shoulders of a patient to provide oxygen therapy.

ox·y·he·mo·glo·bin (ŏk′sē-hē′mə-glō′bĭn, -hĕm′ə-) *n.* A bright-red chemical complex of hemoglobin and oxygen that transports oxygen from the lungs to the tissues via the blood.

ox·y·hy·dro·gen blowpipe (ŏk′sē-hī′drə-jən) *n.* A torch that burns a mixture of hydrogen and oxygen for welding.

ox·y·mo·ron (ŏk′sē-môr′ŏn′, -mōr′-) *n., pl.* **-mo·ra** (-môr′ə, -mōr′ə). A rhetorical figure in which incongruous or contradictory terms are combined, as in "a deafening silence" and "a mournful optimist." [Gk. *oxumōron,* neuter of *oxumōros,* pointedly foolish : *oxus,* sharp + *mōros,* foolish.]

ox·y·sul·fide (ŏk′sē-sŭl′fīd′) *n.* A compound consisting of sulfur and oxygen combined with a metal or positive radical in which part of the sulfur has been replaced by oxygen.

ox·y·tet·ra·cy·cline (ŏk′sē-tĕt′rə-sī′klīn, -klēn′) *n.* An antibiotic, $C_{22}H_{24}N_2O_9 \cdot 2H_2O$, derived from the mold *Streptomyces rimosus,* and used to treat bacterial infection in people and animals.

ox·y·to·cic (ŏk′sĭ-tō′sĭk) *n.* A drug that hastens the process of childbirth, esp. by inducing contraction of the uterine muscle. [Gk. *oxus,* sharp + *tokos,* childbirth < *tiktein,* to give birth.] **—ox′y·to′cic** *adj.*

ox·y·to·cin (ŏk′sĭ-tō′sĭn) *n.* An oxytocic pituitary hormone.

ox·y·tone (ŏk′sĭ-tōn′) *adj.* **1.** Designating a Greek word that has an acute accent on its last syllable. **2.** Designating a word that has a heavy stress accent on its last syllable. *—n.* A word having the stress or the acute accent on the last syllable. [Gk. *oxutonos* : *oxus,* sharp + *tonos,* tone.]

ox·y·u·ri·a·sis (ŏk′sē-yŏŏ-rī′ə-sĭs) *n.* Infestation with pinworms (family Oxyuridae). [NLat. *Oxyuris,* worm genus (Gk. *oxus,* sharp + Gk. *oura,* tail) + -IASIS.]

oy·er and ter·mi·ner (oi′ər; tûr′mə-nər) *n. Law.* **1.** A hearing or trial. **2.** A high criminal court in some states of the United States. **3.** In Great Britain: **a.** A commission to a judge by which he is empowered to hear and rule on a criminal case at the assizes. **b.** The court in which such a hearing is held. [ME < Norman Fr. *oyer et terminer,* to hear and determine.]

o·yez (ō′yĕs′, ō′yĕz′, ō′yā′) also **o·yes** (ō′yĕs′) *interj.* Used three times in succession to introduce the opening of a court of law. *—n., pl.* **o·yes·ses** (ō′yĕs′ĭz). The cry "oyez." [ME < Norman Fr., hear ye, imper. pl. of *oyer,* to hear < OFr. *oïr* < Lat. *audire.*]

oys·ter (oi′stər) *n.* **1. a.** Any of several edible bivalve mollusks of the genus *Ostrea,* chiefly of shallow marine waters, having an irregularly shaped shell. **b.** Any of various similar or related bivalve mollusks, such as the pearl oyster. **2.** A bit of muscle, regarded as a delicacy, found in the hollow of the pelvic bone of a fowl. **3. a.** A special delicacy. **b.** Something from which benefits may be extracted. **4.** *Slang.* A close-mouthed person. *—intr.v.* **-tered, -ter·ing, -ters.** To gather, dredge for, or raise oysters. [ME *oistre* < OFr. < Lat. *ostrea* < Gk. *ostreon.*]

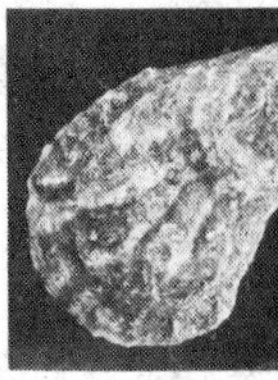
oyster

oyster bed *n.* A place where oysters breed or are raised.

oys·ter·catch·er (oi′stər-kăch′ər) *n.* Any of several shore birds of the genus *Haematopus,* having black and white plumage and a long orange-red bill.

oyster crab *n.* A small crab, *Pinnotheres ostreum,* that lives inside the shells of living oysters.

oyster cracker *n.* A small, dry soda cracker.

oys·ter·man (oi′stər-mən) *n.* **1.** One who cultivates or sells oysters. **2.** An oyster-dredging vessel.

oyster plant *n.* The salsify.

oysters Rock·e·fel·ler (rŏk′ə-fĕl′ər) *pl.n.* Oysters cooked with spinach and a seasoned cream sauce. [After John D. *Rockefeller* (1839–1937).]

oyster white *n.* A pale yellowish green to light gray.

oystercatcher
American oystercatcher

o·zo·ce·rite (ō′zō-sîr′īt′) also **o·zo·ke·rite** (-kîr′-) *n.* A yellow-brown to black or green mineral hydrocarbon wax, used in making electrical insulation, lubricants, and inks. [G. *Ozokerit* : Gk. *ozein,* to smell + Gk. *kēros,* wax + G. *-it,* ite.]

o·zone (ō′zōn′) *n.* **1.** A blue gaseous allotrope of oxygen, O_3, derived or formed naturally from diatomic oxygen by electric discharge or exposure to ultraviolet radiation. It is an unstable, powerfully bleaching, poisonous, oxidizing agent with a pungent, irritating odor, used to purify and deodorize air, to sterilize water, and as a bleach. **2.** *Informal.* Fresh, pure air. [G. *Ozon* < Gk. *ozōn,* pr.part. of *ozein,* to smell.] **—o·zo′nic** (ō-zō′nĭk, ō-zŏn′ĭk), **o′zon′ous** (ō′zō′nəs) *adj.*

ozone layer *n.* Ozonosphere.

o·zo·nide (ō′zō-nīd′) *n.* Any of various, often explosive chemicals formed by attachment of ozone to the double bond of an unsaturated compound and used in analytical chemistry to locate such bonds.

o·zo·nize (ō′zō-nīz′) *tr.v.* **-nized, -niz·ing, -niz·es. 1.** To treat or impregnate with ozone. **2.** To convert (oxygen) to ozone. **—o′zon·iz′er** *n.*

o·zo·no·sphere (ō-zō′nə-sfîr′) *n.* A region of the upper atmosphere, between ten and twenty miles in altitude, containing a relatively high concentration of ozone that absorbs solar ultraviolet radiation in a wavelength range not screened by other atmospheric components. **—o·zo′no·spher′ic** (-sfîr′ĭk, -sfĕr′-), **o·zo′no·spher′i·cal** *adj.*

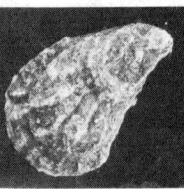

P

Around 1000 B.C. the Phoenicians and other Semitic peoples began to use graphic signs to represent individual speech sounds instead of syllables or words. They used a symbol in the forms (1,2) to represent the sound of the consonant "p" and called it *pē*, their word for "mouth." The Greeks, adapting the Phoenician alphabet, kept the phonetic value of *pē* but reversed its orientation (3,4,5,6), gave it a symmetrical angular shape (7), and altered its name to *pi*. The Romans borrowed the alphabet from the Greeks via the Etruscans who had adopted the earlier, rounded shape of P. The Romans closed the curve into a loop and adapted P for monumental inscriptions. Monumental script (10) is the prototype of modern capital letters (13,14). Medieval scribes adapted the Roman capitals to being quickly written on paper, parchment, and vellum. These uncial and cursive minuscules (11,12) are the prototypes of modern lower-case letters, both written and printed (16,15).

p

p or **P** (pē) *n., pl.* **p's** or **P's. 1.** The 16th letter of the modern English alphabet. **2.** Any of the speech sounds represented by the letter *p.* **3.** The 16th in a series.
P The symbol for the element phosphorus.
pa (pä) *n. Informal.* Papa; father. [Short for PAPA.]
Pa The symbol for the element protactinium.
pa'an·ga (päng'gə) *n.* See table at **currency.** [Tongan.]
PABA (pä'bə) *n.* Para-aminobenzoic acid.
pab·u·lum (păb'yə-ləm) *n.* **1.** A substance that gives nourishment; food. **2.** Insipid intellectual nourishment. [Lat.]
pac also **pack** (păk) *n.* A type of moccasin or soft shoe designed to be worn inside a boot. [Delaware *paku.*]
pa·ca (pä'kə, păk'ə) *n.* A nocturnal tropical American rodent of the genus *Cuniculus,* having a short tail and blackish or brown fur. [Port. (Brazil) and Am. Sp., both < Tupi *páca.*]
pace¹ (pās) *n.* **1.** A step made in walking; stride. **2.** The distance spanned by a step or stride, esp.: **a.** A unit of length equal to 30 inches. **b.** Thirty inches at quick marching time or 36 inches at double time. **c.** Five Roman feet or 58.1 English inches, measured from the point at which the heel of one foot is raised to the point at which it is set down again after an intervening step by the other foot. **d.** The modern version of the Roman pace, measuring five English feet. **3. a.** The rate of speed at which a person, animal, or group walks or runs. **b.** The rate of speed at which an activity or movement proceeds. **4.** A manner of walking or running: *a jaunty pace.* **5.** A gait of a horse in which both feet on one side leave and return to the ground together. —*v.* **paced, pac·ing, pac·es.** —*tr.* **1.** To walk or stride back and forth across. **2.** To measure by counting the number of steps needed to cover a distance. **3.** To set or regulate the rate of speed for. **4.** To train (a horse) in a particular gait, esp. the pace. —*intr.* **1.** To walk with long, deliberate steps. **2.** To go at the pace. Used of a horse or rider. —***idioms.*** **put one through (one's) paces.** To test or demonstrate one's abilities. **set the pace. 1.** To go at a speed that other competitors attempt to match or surpass. **2.** To behave or perform in a way that others try to emulate. [ME < OFr. *pas* < Lat. *passus* < *pandere,* to stretch.]
pa·ce² (pā'sē) *prep.* With the permission of; with deference to: *I have not, pace my detractors, entered into any "deals."* [Lat. < ablative of *pax,* peace.] —**pa'ce** *adv.*
pace car *n.* A usually high-performance automobile that leads a group of competing race cars through the pace lap of a race but that does not participate in the race.
pace lap *n.* The initial lap of a motor vehicle race in which the racers warm up their engines and get set for a fast start.
pace·mak·er (pās'mā'kər) *n.* **1.** One who sets the pace in a race; pacer. **2.** A leader in any field: *This fashion house is the pacemaker.* **3. a.** *Physiol.* A mass of specialized muscle fibers of the heart that regulate the heartbeat. **b.** *Med.* Any of several usually miniaturized and surgically implanted electronic devices used to regulate, or to aid in the regulation of, the heartbeat. **4.** *Biochem.* A substance that regulates a series of related reactions.
pac·er (pā'sər) *n.* **1.** A horse trained to pace. **2.** A pacemaker (sense 1).
pace·set·ter (pās'sĕt'ər) *n.* A pacemaker (senses 1 and 2).
pa·cha (pä'shə, păsh'ə, pə-shä') *n.* Variant of **pasha.**
pa·chi·si (pə-chē'zē) *n.* **1.** An ancient game of India similar to backgammon but using cowry shells instead of dice. **2.** Parcheesi. [Hindi *pacīsī* < *pacīs,* twenty-five : Skt. *pañcan,* five + *viṃsatiḥ,* twenty.]
pach·ou·li (păch'ə-lē, pə-cho͞o'lē) *n.* Variant of **patchouli.**
pach·y·derm (păk'ĭ-dûrm') *n.* Any of various large, thick-skinned, hoofed mammals, such as the elephant, rhinoceros, or hippopotamus. [Fr. *pachyderme* < Gk. *pakhudermos,* thick-skinned : *pakhus,* thick + *derma,* skin.] —**pach'y·der'ma·tous** (-dûr'mə-təs), **pach'y·der'mous** (-dûr'məs) *adj.*
pach·y·san·dra (păk'ĭ-săn'drə) *n.* Any of several plants of the genus *Pachysandra,* esp. *P. terminalis,* native to Japan, having evergreen leaves and inconspicuous white flowers. [NLat. *Pachysandra,* genus name : Gk. *pakhus,* thick + NLat. *-andrus,* -androus.]
pa·cif·ic (pə-sĭf'ĭk) also **pa·cif·i·cal** (-ĭ-kəl) *adj.* **1.** Tending to diminish or put an end to conflict; appeasing. **2.** Of a peaceful nature; serene. [OFr. *pacifique* < Lat. *pacificus* : *pax,* peace + *facere,* to make.] —**pa·cif'i·cal·ly** *adv.*
pac·i·fi·ca·tion (păs'ə-fĭ-kā'shən) *n.* **1.** The act of pacifying or the condition of being pacified; appeasement. **2. a.** Reduction, as of a rebellious district, to peaceful submission: *"Real pacification is hard to get in the Vietnamese countryside"* (McGeorge Bundy). **b.** Policy or practical measures aiming to effect this. **3.** Often **Pacification.** A peace treaty: *the Pacification of Ghent.* [OFr. < Lat. *pacificatio* < *pacificare,* to pacify. —see PACIFY.] —**pa·cif'i·ca'tor** (pə-sĭf'ĭ-kā'tər) *n.* —**pa·cif'i·ca·to'ry** (pə-sĭf'ĭ-kə-tôr'ē, -tōr'ē) *adj.*
Pacific Standard Time *n.* One of the four standard time zones of North America, operative from longitude 120 degrees to 140 degrees, with wide local variations in boundary.
pac·i·fi·er (păs'ə-fī'ər) *n.* **1.** One that pacifies. **2.** A rubber or plastic nipple or teething ring for a baby to suck or chew on.
pac·i·fism (păs'ə-fĭz'əm) *n.* **1.** The belief that disputes between nations should and can be settled peacefully. **2. a.** Opposition to war or violence as a means of resolving disputes. **b.** Such opposition demonstrated by refusal to participate in military action. [Fr. *pacifisme* < *pacifique,* pacific < OFr. —see PACIFIC.] —**pac'i·fist** *n.* —**pac'i·fis'tic** *adj.* —**pac'i·fis'ti·cal·ly** *adv.*
pac·i·fy (păs'ə-fī') *tr.v.* **-fied, -fy·ing, -fies. 1.** To ease the anger or agitation of. **2.** To establish peace in; end war, fighting, or violence in. [ME *pacifien* < Lat. *pacificare* : *pax,* peace + *facere,* to make.] —**pac'i·fi'a·ble** *adj.*
Synonyms: *pacify, placate, mollify, conciliate, appease, quiet.* These words all suggest leading someone hostile or demanding to moderation, accord, or satisfaction. *Pacify* applies broadly to any alleviation of hostility by diplomatic means. *Placate* more strongly suggests gratification of demands, and usually implies that the person so gratified is difficult to please. *Mollify* stresses mitigation of hostile feeling by soothing. *Conciliate* usually pertains to winning over by reasoning, and may imply a more lasting solution than the other terms. *Appease* (more strongly than *placate*) stresses overt gratification of a claim, often to the point of surrender of principle, and often implies that the claim is unworthy. *Quiet* is general, in this context, but often is used to indicate response to urgent demands.

paca

Pa·cin·i·an corpuscle (pə-sĭn'ē-ən) *n.* An encapsulated sensory nerve ending found in deep layers of the skin that functions as a receptor for heavy pressure and touch. [After Filippo *Pacini* (1812–1888).]
pack¹ (păk) *n.* **1. a.** A collection of items tied up or wrapped; bundle. **b.** A container made to be carried on the back of a person or an animal. **2.** The amount of something, such as food, that is processed and packaged at one time or in one season. **3.** A small package containing a standard number of identical or similar items: *a pack of matches.* **4. a.** A complete set of related items: *a pack of cards.* **b.** A large amount; heap. **5. a.** A group of animals, such as dogs or wolves, that run and hunt together. **b.** A gang of people: *a pack of hoodlums.* **c.** An organized troop having common interests: *a Cub Scout pack.* **6.** A mass of large pieces of floating ice driven together. **7.** *Med.* **a.** The swathing of a patient in hot, cold, wet, or dry sheets or blankets. **b.** The sheets or blankets so used. **c.** A material, such as gauze, therapeutically inserted into a body cavity or wound. **8.** An ice pack (sense 2). **9.** A cosmetic paste applied to the skin and allowed to dry. —*v.* **packed, pack·ing, packs.** —*tr.* **1.** To fold, roll, or combine into a bundle; wrap up. **2. a.** To put into a receptacle for transporting or storing: *pack one's belongings.* **b.** To fill up with items: *pack one's trunk.* **3.** To process and put into containers in order to preserve, transport, or sell. **4. a.** To bring together (persons or things) closely; crowd together. **b.** To fill up tight; cram. **5.** *Med.* To wrap (a patient) in a pack. **6.** To wrap tightly for protection or to prevent leakage: *pack a valve stem.* **7.** To press together; compact firmly: *packing clay and straw into bricks.* **8.** *Informal.* To have available for action: *pack a pistol; pack a hard punch.* **9.** To send peremptorily: *They packed him off to camp.* **10.** To rig (a voting panel) to be fraudulently favorable: *pack the jury.* —*intr.* **1.** To place one's belongings in boxes or luggage for transporting or storing. **2.** To be susceptible of compact storage: *Dishes pack more easily than glasses.* **3.** To become compacted; form lumps or masses. **4.** To depart abruptly. —***idioms.*** **pack it in.** To call it quits: *Let's pack it in for the day.* **send packing.** To dismiss (someone) abruptly. [ME, of LG orig.] —**pack'a·bil'i·ty** *n.* —**pack'a·ble** *adj.*
pack² (păk) *n.* Variant of **pac.**
pack·age (păk'ĭj) *n.* **1.** A wrapped or boxed object; parcel. **2.** A container in which something is packed for storage or transporting. **3. a.** A preassembled unit. **b.** A commodity, such as food, uniformly processed and containerized. **4.** A proposition or offer made up of several items each of which must be accepted: *a package deal.* —*tr.v.* **-aged, -ag·ing, -ag·es.** To place in a package or make a package of.
package store *n.* A store that sells sealed bottles of alcoholic beverages for consumption away from its premises.
pack·ag·ing (păk'ə-jĭng) *n.* The act, process, industry, art, or style of packing.
pack animal *n.* An animal, such as a mule, used to carry loads.
packed (păkt) *adj.* **1.** Crowded to capacity: *a packed auditorium.* **2.** Being compressed: *ground covered with wet, packed leaves.* **3.** *Informal.* Filled with: *a thrill-packed television series.*
pack·er (păk'ər) *n.* One that packs, esp. one whose occupation is the processing and packing of wholesale goods, usually meat products.
pack·et (păk'ĭt) *n.* **1.** A small package or bundle. **2.** *Slang.* A sizable sum of money. **3.** A boat, usually a coastal or river steamer, that plies a regular route carrying passengers, freight, and mail. [OFr. *pacquet,* of Germanic orig.]
pack·horse (păk'hôrs) *n.* A horse used as a pack animal.
pack ice *n.* Floating ice driven together into a single mass.
pack·ing (păk'ĭng) *n.* **1.** The act or process of one that packs, esp. the processing and packaging of food products. **2.** A material used to prevent leakage or seepage, as around a pipe joint. **3.** The application of a medical pack.
packing fraction *n. Physics.* The quotient of the algebraic difference between the isotopic mass and the mass number

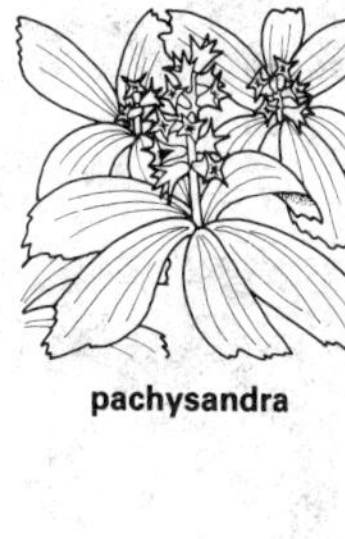
pachysandra

of a nuclide, divided by its mass number, often interpreted as a measure of stability.

packing house *n.* **1.** A firm that slaughters, processes, and packs livestock into meat and meat products. **2.** A firm that processes and packs food products other than meats.

pack·man (păk′măn′, -mən) *n.* A peddler.

pack rat *n.* **1.** Any of various small North American rodents of the genus *Neotoma,* that collect in their nests a great variety of small objects. **2.** *Western U.S. Slang.* A petty thief. **3.** *Slang.* A collector of miscellaneous objects.

pack·sack (păk′săk′) *n.* A canvas or leather traveling bag designed to be carried strapped to the shoulders.

pack·sad·dle (păk′săd′l) *n.* A saddle for a pack animal on which loads can be secured.

pack·thread (păk′thrĕd′) *n.* A strong two-ply or three-ply twine for sewing or tying packages or bundles.

pack train *n.* A line of animals, such as horses or mules, loaded with supplies for an expedition.

pact (păkt) *n.* **1.** A formal agreement, as between nations; treaty. **2.** A compact; bargain. [ME < OFr. < Lat. *pactum* < *pascisci,* to agree.]

pad[1]

pad[1] (păd) *n.* **1.** A thin, cushionlike mass of soft material used as filling or for protection against jarring, scraping, or other injury. **2.** A flexible saddle made without a frame. **3.** An ink-soaked cushion used to ink a rubber stamp. **4.** A number of sheets of paper of the same size stacked one on top of the other and glued together at one end; tablet. **5.** The broad, floating leaf of an aquatic plant, such as the water lily. **6. a.** The cushionlike flesh on the underpart of the toes and feet of many animals. **b.** The foot of such an animal. **7.** The fleshy underside of the end of a finger or toe: *the pad of one's thumb.* **8.** A launch pad. **9.** *Slang.* One's apartment or room. —*tr.v.* **pad·ded, pad·ding, pads. 1.** To line or stuff with soft material. **2.** To lengthen (something written or spoken) with extraneous material. —***idiom.* on the pad.** *Slang.* Taking bribes; on the take. [Orig. unknown.]

pad[2] (păd) *v.* **pad·ded, pad·ding, pads.** —*intr.* **1.** To go about on foot. **2.** To move or walk about almost inaudibly. —*tr.* To go along (a route) on foot: *padding the long road into town.* —*n.* **1.** A muffled sound resembling that of soft footsteps. **2.** A horse with a plodding gait. [Prob. < MDu. *paden,* to walk along a path < *pad,* path.] **—pad′der** *n.*

pa·dauk (pə-dôk′) also **pa·douk** (-do͝ok′) *n.* **1.** Any of various tropical trees of the genus *Pterocarpus,* having reddish wood with a mottled or striped grain. **2.** The wood of the padauk tree, used for decorative cabinetwork. [Native word in Burma.]

pad·ding (păd′ĭng) *n.* **1.** The act of stuffing, filling, or lining something. **2.** A soft material used to make a pad. **3.** Matter added to a speech or written work to make it longer.

pad·dle[1] (păd′l) *n.* **1.** A wooden implement having a blade at one end, or sometimes at both ends, used without an oarlock to propel a canoe or small boat. **2.** Any of various implements resembling a paddle, as: **a.** An iron tool for stirring molten ore in a furnace. **b.** A tool with a shovellike blade used to mix materials in glassmaking. **c.** A pallet with which to mix and shape clay. **d.** A narrow board used to beat clothes in hand-laundering. **e.** A flattened board used to administer physical punishment. **f.** A light wooden racket used in playing table tennis. **3.** A board of a paddle wheel. **4.** A flipper or flattened appendage of certain animals. **5.** The act of paddling. —*v.* **-dled, -dling, -dles.** —*intr.* **1.** To propel a watercraft with a paddle. **2.** To row slowly and gently. **3.** To move through water by means of repeated short strokes of the limbs. —*tr.* **1.** To propel (a watercraft) with a paddle or paddles. **2.** To convey in a watercraft propelled by paddles. **3.** To beat with a paddle, esp. to punish by spanking with a paddle. **4.** To stir or shape (material) with a paddle. [ME *padell,* implement used for cleaning a plowshare.] **—pad′dler** *n.*

pad·dle[2] (păd′l) *intr.v.* **-dled, -dling, -dles. 1.** To dabble about in shallow water; splash gently with the hands or feet. **2.** To move with a waddling motion; toddle. [Orig. unknown.]

pad·dle·ball (păd′l-bôl′) *n.* **1.** A game for two to four players played with a wooden or plastic paddle and a ball similar to a tennis ball on a one-, three-, or four-walled court. **2.** The ball used in paddleball.

pad·dle·board (păd′l-bôrd′) *n.* A long, narrow floatable board that is used in riding the surf or in rescuing swimmers.

paddy wagon

paddle boat *n.* A steamship propelled through the water by paddle wheels on each side or by one paddle wheel astern.

pad·dle·fish (păd′l-fĭsh′) *n., pl.* **paddlefish** or **-fish·es.** A large fish, *Polyodon spathula,* of the Mississippi River basin, having a long, paddle-shaped snout.

paddle wheel *n.* A steam-driven wheel with boards or paddles affixed around its circumference, used to propel a ship.

padlock

pad·dling (păd′lĭng, păd′l-ĭng) *n.* **1.** The act of moving a boat by means of a paddle. **2.** A spanking with a paddle.

pad·dock (păd′ək) *n.* **1.** A fenced area, usually near a stable, used chiefly for grazing horses. **2.** An enclosure at a racetrack where the horses are assembled, saddled, and paraded before each race. **3.** An area at an automobile racetrack where cars are prepared before a race. **4.** *Austral.* A piece of fenced-in land. —*tr.v.* **-docked, -dock·ing, -docks.** To confine in a paddock. [Alteration of ME *parrok* < OE *pearroc.*]

pad·dy (păd′ē) *n., pl.* **-dies. 1.** Rice, esp. in the husk, whether gathered or still in the field. **2.** A specially irrigated or flooded field where rice is grown. [Malay *padi.*]

Pad·dy (păd′ē) *n. Offensive Slang.* An Irishman. [A nickname for *Patrick.*]

paddy wagon *n. Slang.* A police van for taking suspects into custody. [< PADDY.]

Pa·di·shah (pä′dĭ-shä′) *n.* **1.** A title of the former monarch of Iran. **2.** A title of the former sultan of Turkey. [Pers. *pādshāh* : OPers. *pati,* master + *shāh,* king.]

pad·lock (păd′lŏk′) *n.* A detachable lock with a U-shaped bar hinged at one end, designed to be passed through the staple of a hasp or a link in a chain and then snapped shut. —*tr.v.* **-locked, -lock·ing, -locks.** To lock up with or as if with a padlock. [ME *padlok* : *pad-* (of unknown orig.) + *lok,* lock.]

pa·douk (pə-do͝ok′) *n.* Variant of **padauk.**

pa·dre (pä′drā, -drē) *n.* **1.** Father. Used as a title of address for a priest in Italy, Spain, Portugal, and Latin America. **2.** *Informal.* A military chaplain. **3.** *Chiefly Brit. Informal.* A parson. [Sp., Ital., or Port., all < Lat. *pater,* father.]

pa·dro·ne (pə-drō′nē, -nā) *n., pl.* **-nes** (-nēz, -nāz) or **-ni** (-nē). **1.** An owner or manager, esp. of an inn; proprietor. **2.** A man who exploitatively employs or finds work for Italian immigrants in America. [Ital. < Lat. *patronus,* patron. —see PATRON.] **—pa·dro′nism** (pə-drō′nĭz′əm) *n.*

pad·u·a·soy (păj′o͞o-ə-soi′) *n.* **1.** A rich, heavy silk fabric with a corded effect. **2.** A hanging or garment made of paduasoy. [Alteration of Fr. *pou-de-soie.*]

pae·an also **pe·an** (pē′ən) *n.* **1.** A song of joyful praise or exultation. **2.** A fervent expression of joy or praise: *"The art . . . was a paean to paganism"* (Will Durant). **3.** An ancient Greek hymn of thanksgiving to a god, esp. to Apollo. [Lat. *paean,* hymn of thanksgiving, often addresed to Apollo < Gk. *paian, paiōn* < *Paiōn,* a title of Apollo.]

paed– or **paedo–** *pref.* Variants of **pedo-[2].**

pae·do·gen·e·sis (pē′dō-jĕn′ĭ-sĭs) *n.* Reproduction of young during the larval or preadult stage, occurring chiefly in insects. **—pae′do·ge·net′ic** (-jə-nĕt′ĭk) *adj.*

pae·do·mor·phism (pē′də-môr′fĭz′əm) *n.* The retention of juvenile characteristics in the adult. **—pae′do·mor′phic** (-fĭk) *adj.*

pae·do·mor·pho·sis (pē′də-môr′fə-sĭs) *n.* Phylogenetic change in which juvenile characteristics are retained by the adults.

pa·e·lla (pä-ĕl′ə, pä-ā′lyä, -ā′yä) *n.* A saffron-flavored Spanish dish made with varying combinations of rice, vegetables, meat, chicken, and seafood. [Catalan < OFr. *paelle,* pan < Lat. *patella,* dim. of *patina,* pan.]

pae·on (pē′ən, -ŏn′) *n.* A metrical foot of poetry having one long syllable and three short syllables occurring in random order. [Lat. < Gk. *paiōn.* —see PAEAN.]

pa·gan (pā′gən) *n.* **1.** A person who is not a Christian, Moslem, or Jew; heathen. **2.** One who has no religion. **3.** A non-Christian. **4.** A hedonist. —*adj.* **1.** Not Christian, Moslem, or Jewish. **2.** Not religious; heathen. [ME < LLat. *paganus* < Lat., country-dweller < *pagus,* country.] **—pa′gan·dom** (-dəm) *n.* **—pa′gan·ish** *adj.* **—pa′gan·ism** *n.*

pa·gan·ize (pā′gə-nīz′) *tr. & intr.v.* **-ized, -iz·ing, -iz·es.** To make or become pagan. **—pa′gan·i·za′tion** *n.*

page[1] (pāj) *n.* **1.** In chivalry, a boy attending a knight as the first stage of training for knighthood. **2.** A youth in ceremonial employment or attendance at court. **3. a.** A person employed to run errands, carry messages, or act as a guide, as in a hotel, theater, or club. **b.** A person similarly employed in Congress or another legislature. **4.** A boy who bears the bride's train at a wedding. —*tr.v.* **paged, pag·ing, pag·es. 1.** To summon or call (a person) by name. **2.** To attend as a page. [ME < OFr. < Ital. *paggio.*]

page[2] (pāj) *n.* **1.** One side of a leaf, as of a book, letter, newspaper, or manuscript, esp. the entire leaf: *tearing out a page.* **2.** The writing or printing on one side of a leaf. **3.** *Printing.* The type set for printing a page. **4.** A noteworthy or memorable event: *a new page in history.* **5.** *Computer Sci.* **a.** A quantity of computer memory storage equal to between 512 and 4,096 bytes. **b.** A quantity of source program coding equal to between 8 and 64 lines. **6. pages.** A source or record of knowledge: *in the pages of science.* —*v.* **paged, pag·ing, pag·es.** —*tr.* To number the pages of; paginate. —*intr.* To turn pages: *page through a magazine.* [OFr. < Lat. *pagina.*]

pag·eant (păj′ənt) *n.* **1.** An elaborate public dramatic presentation, usually depicting some historical or traditional event. **2.** A spectacular procession or celebration. **3.** Colorful display; pageantry. **4.** Showy display; pomp. [ME *padgin,* scene of a play < Med. Lat. *pagina* < Lat., page.]

pag·eant·ry (păj′ən-trē) *n., pl.* **-ries. 1.** Pageants and their presentation. **2.** Grand display; pomp. **3.** Empty pomp or show; flashy display.

pag·i·nal (păj′ə-nəl) *adj.* **1.** Of, pertaining to, or consisting of pages. **2.** Page for page: *paginal facsimile.* [LLat. *paginalis* < Lat. *pagina,* page.]

pag·i·nate (păj′ə-nāt′) *tr.v.* **-nat·ed, -nat·ing, -nates.** To number the pages of; page. [< Lat. *pagina,* page.]

pag·i·na·tion (păj′ə-nā′shən) *n.* **1.** The system with which

pages are numbered. **2.** The arrangement and number of pages in a book, as noted in a catalogue or bibliography.
pag·ing (pā′jĭng) *n. Computer Sci.* The transfer of pages of data from a computer's main memory to an auxiliary memory.
pa·go·da (pə-gō′də) *n.* **1.** A religious building of the Far East, esp. a many-storied Buddhist tower, erected as a memorial or shrine. **2.** A structure, such as a garden pavilion, built in imitation of a pagoda. [Port. *pagode,* poss. of Dravidian orig.]
pah (pä) *interj.* Used to express disgust or irritation.
pah·la·vi (pä′lə-vē′) *n., pl.* **-vis.** A gold coin formerly in use in Iran. [Pers. *pahlawī,* after Mohammed Riza *Pahlavi* (1919–1980), Shah of Iran.]
Pah·la·vi (pä′lə-vē′) also **Peh·le·vi** (pā′lə-vē′) *n.* An Iranian language used in Persia during the reign of the Sassanids. [Pers. *pahlawī* < *Pahlav,* Parthia.]
paid[1] (pād) *v.* Past tense and past participle of **pay**[1].
paid[2] (pād) *v.* A past tense and a past participle of **pay**[2].
pail (pāl) *n.* **1.** A watertight cylindrical vessel, open at the top and fitted with a handle; bucket. **2.** The amount contained in a pail. [ME *payle* < OE *pægel.*] **—pail′ful′** *adj.*
pail·lasse also **pal·liasse** (păl-yăs′, păl′yăs′) *n.* A thin mattress filled with straw or sawdust. [Fr. < *paille,* straw < Lat. *palea.*]
pail·lette (pä-yĕt′, pā-, pă-lĕt′) *n.* **1.** A small piece of metal or foil, used in enamel painting. **2.** A spangle used to ornament a dress or costume. [Fr., dim. of *paille,* straw. —see PAILLASSE.]
pain (pān) *n.* **1.** An unpleasant sensation, occurring in varying degrees of severity as a consequence of injury, disease, or emotional disorder. **2.** Suffering or distress. **3. pains.** The pangs of childbirth. **4. pains.** Great care or effort: *take pains with one's work.* **5.** *Informal.* A nuisance. *—v.* **pained, pain·ing, pains.** *—tr.* To hurt or injure; cause pain to. *—intr.* To be the cause of pain. ***—idioms.*** **on** (or **upon** or **under**) **pain of.** Subject to the penalty of some specified punishment, as death. **pain in the neck.** A source of annoyance; nuisance. [ME < OFr. *peine* < Lat. *poena* < Gk. *poinē,* penalty.]
pain·ful (pān′fəl) *adj.* **1.** Causing pain; hurtful. **2.** Full of pain; distressing. **3.** Requiring care and labor; irksome: *a painful task.* **4.** *Archaic.* Diligent; careful. **—pain′ful·ly** *adv.* **—pain′ful·ness** *n.*
pain·kill·er (pān′kĭl′ər) *n.* Something, such as a drug, that relieves pain. **—pain′kill′ing** *adj.*
pain·less (pān′lĭs) *adj.* Free from complication or pain: *a painless operation.* **—pain′less·ly** *adv.* **—pain′less·ness** *n.*
pain principle *n. Psychoanal.* The unconscious tendency to seek death or forgetfulness; the desire for pain or destruction.
pains·tak·ing (pānz′tā′kĭng) *adj.* Taking great pains; careful. *—n.* The act of taking pains; extremely careful and diligent work or effort. **—pains′tak′ing·ly** *adv.*
paint (pānt) *n.* **1. a.** A liquid mixture, usually of a solid pigment in a liquid vehicle, used as a decorative or protective coating. **b.** The thin dry film formed by such a mixture applied to a surface. **c.** The solid pigment before it is mixed with a vehicle. **2.** A cosmetic, esp. one that colors, as rouge. **3.** A pinto. *—v.* **paint·ed, paint·ing, paints.** *—tr.* **1.** To make (a picture) with paints. **2. a.** To represent in a picture with paints. **b.** To depict vividly in words. **3.** To coat or decorate with paint: *paint a house.* **4.** To apply cosmetics to. **5.** To apply medicine to; swab: *paint a wound.* *—intr.* **1.** To practice the art of painting pictures. **2.** To cover something with paint. **3.** To apply cosmetics to oneself: *"Let her paint an inch thick, to this favor she must come"* (Shakespeare). **4.** To serve as a surface to be coated with paint: *These nonporous surfaces paint badly with a brush.* ***—idiom.*** **paint the town red.** *Slang.* To go on an elaborate or wild spree. [< ME *painten,* to paint < OFr. *peindre* < Lat. *pingere.*]
paint·brush (pānt′brŭsh′) *n.* A brush for applying paint.
paint·ed (pān′tĭd) *adj.* **1.** Represented in paint. **2. a.** Covered or adorned with paint. **b.** Brightly colored; gaudy. **3.** Excessively or improperly made up with cosmetics. **4.** Having no reality; artificial: *painted expressions.*
painted bunting *n.* A small bird, *Passerina ciris,* of the southern United States, having brilliant multicolored plumage.
painted cup *n.* The Indian paintbrush.
painted lady *n.* A widely distributed butterfly, *Vanessa cardui,* having brown, black, and orange markings.
paint·er[1] (pān′tər) *n.* One who paints, either as an artist or as a worker.
pain·ter[2] (pān′tər) *n. Naut.* A rope attached to the bow of a boat, used for tying up. [ME *paynter,* poss. < OFr. *pentoir,* strong rope < *pendre,* to hand < Lat. *pendēre.*]
pain·ter[3] (pān′tər) *n. Regional.* A mountain lion or lynx. [Alteration of PANTHER.]
paint·er·ly (pān′tər-lē) *adj.* **1.** Of, pertaining to, or characteristic of a painter; artistic. **2. a.** Having qualities unique to the art of painting as distinguished from other visual arts. **b.** Designating a style of painting marked by openness of form, with shapes distinguished by variations of color, rather than by outline or contour. **—paint′er·li·ness** *n.*
painter's colic *n.* Chronic intestinal pains and constipation caused by lead poisoning. [So called because the disease is often caused by exposure to lead-base paint.]
paint·ing (pān′tĭng). **1.** The process, art, or occupation of coating surfaces with paint, for either a utilitarian or an artistic effect. **2.** A picture or design in paint.
pair (pâr) *n., pl.* **pair** also **pairs. 1.** Two corresponding persons or items, similar in form or function and matched or associated: *a pair of shoes.* **2.** One object composed of two joined, similar parts that are dependent upon each other: *a pair of pliers.* **3. a.** Two persons joined together in marriage or engagement. **b.** Two persons having something in common and considered together: *a pair of hunters.* **c.** Two mated animals. **d.** Two animals joined together in work. **4.** Two playing cards of the same denomination. **5.** Two members of a deliberative body with opposing opinions on a given issue who agree to abstain from voting on the issue, thereby offsetting each other. **6.** *Chem.* An electron pair. *—v.* **paired, pair·ing, pairs.** *—tr.* **1.** To arrange in sets of two; couple. **2.** To join in a pair; mate. **3.** To provide a partner for. *—intr.* **1.** To form a pair or pairs. **2.** To join in marriage; mate. [ME < OFr. *paire* < Lat. *paria* < *par,* equal.]
Usage: *Pair* as a noun can be followed by a singular or plural verb. The singular is always used when *pair* denotes the set taken as a single entity: *This pair of shoes is on sale.* A plural verb is used when the members are considered as individuals: *The pair are working more harmoniously now.* After a numeral other than one, *pair* itself can be either singular or plural, but the plural is now more common: *She bought six pairs* (or *pair*) *of stockings.*
pair of compasses *n.* Compass (sense 1.c.).
pair of virginals *n.* A virginal.
pair production *n.* The simultaneous creation of a positron and electron from a high-energy gamma ray in a very strong electric field, esp. in that of an atomic nucleus.
pai·sa (pī-sä′) *n., pl.* **pai·se** (pī-sā′) or **pai·sas.** See table at **currency.** [Hindi *paisā.*]
pai·sa·no (pī-zä′nō) also **pai·san** (pī-zän′) *n., pl.* **-sa·nos** also **-sans. 1.** Countryman; compatriot. **2.** *Slang.* Friend; pal. [Sp. < Fr. *paysan* < OFr. *paisant,* peasant. —see PEASANT.]
pais·ley (pāz′lē) *adj.* **1.** Made of a soft wool fabric with a woven or printed colorful, swirled pattern of abstract, curved shapes, ultimately derived from the palmette motif of Persian rugs. **2.** Marked with a paisley pattern. *—n., pl.* **-leys.** A shawl or other article of clothing made of paisley fabric. [After *Paisley,* Scotland.]
Pai·ute also **Pi·ute** (pī′yo͞ot′) *n., pl.* **Paiute** or **-utes** also **Pi·ute** or **-utes. 1.** Either of two distinct North American Indian peoples, the Northern Paiute and the Southern Paiute, belonging to the Shoshonean subfamily of the Uto-Aztecan language family, who formerly lived in the southwestern United States. **2.** A member of either of the Paiute peoples. **3.** The Shoshonean language of the Paiute. **—Pai′ute′** *adj.*
pa·ja·mas (pə-jä′məz, -jăm′əz) *pl.n.* **1.** A loose-fitting garment consisting of trousers and a jacket, worn for sleeping or lounging. **2.** Loose-fitting trousers worn in the Orient by both sexes. [Hindi *pāejāma,* loose-fitting trousers : Pers. *pāī,* leg + Pers. *jāmah,* garment.]
pak choi (bäk′ choi′) *n.* A Chinese plant, *Brassica chinensis,* that is similar to the common cabbage and is used as a vegetable. [Chin. *bai*[2] *car*[4] : *bai*[2], white + *cai*[4], vegetable.]
pal (păl) *Informal.* *—n.* A friend; chum. *—intr.v.* **palled, pal·ling, pals.** To associate as pals: *palling around together.* [Romany *phal, phrall* < Skt. *bhrātṛ,* brother.]
pal·ace (păl′ĭs) *n.* **1.** The official residence of a royal person. **2.** *Chiefly Brit.* The official residence of a high dignitary, as a bishop or archbishop. **3. a.** A large or splendid residence. **b.** A large, often gaudy and ornate building used for entertainment, exhibitions, and the like. [ME < OFr. *palais* < Lat. *palatium* < *Palatium,* Palatine Hill, Rome, Italy (from its being the site where emperors built their homes).]
pal·a·din (păl′ə-dĭn) *n.* **1.** Any of the 12 peers of Charlemagne's court. **2.** A paragon of chivalry; heroic champion. [Fr. < Ital. *paladino* < Lat. *palatinus,* palatine.]
palae– or **palaeo–** *pref.* Variants of **paleo-.**
pa·laes·tra (pə-lĕs′trə) *n.* Variant of **palestra.**
pal·an·quin also **pal·an·keen** (păl′ən-kēn′) *n.* An east Asian covered litter, carried on poles on the shoulders of two or four men. [Port. *palanquin* < Javanese *pĕlangki* < Skt. *palyankaḥ, paryankaḥ,* bed : *pari,* around + *añcati,* he bends.]
pal·at·a·ble (păl′ə-tə-bəl) *adj.* **1.** Acceptable to the taste; sufficiently agreeable in flavor to be eaten. **2.** Acceptable to the mind or sensibilities; agreeable: *a palatable solution to the problem.* [< PALATE.] **—pal′at·a·bil′i·ty, pal′at·a·ble·ness** *n.* **—pal′at·a·bly** *adv.*
pal·a·tal (păl′ə-təl) *adj.* **1.** Of or pertaining to the palate. **2. a.** Produced with the front of the tongue near or against the hard palate, as the (y) in English *young.* **b.** Produced with the blade of the tongue near the hard palate, as the (ch) in English *chin.* **c.** Produced with the front of the tongue in a forward position. Used of a vowel. *—n.* A palatal sound. **—pal′a·tal·ly** *adv.*
pal·a·tal·ize (păl′ə-tə-līz′) *tr.v.* **-ized, -iz·ing, -iz·es.** To pronounce as or alter to a palatal sound. **—pal′a·tal·i·za′tion** *n.*

pagoda
Indonesian pagoda

painter[1]

painter[2]

paisley
A paisley design

palanquin

pal·ate (păl′ĭt) *n.* **1.** The roof of the mouth in vertebrates having a complete or partial separation of the mouth cavity and nasal passage, consisting of a bony front, the hard palate, backed by the fleshy soft palate. **2.** A part, as in a lipped flower, similar to a palate. **3.** The sense of taste: *delicacies pleasing to the most refined palate.* [ME < Lat. *palatum.*]
pa·la·tial (pə-lā′shəl) *adj.* **1.** Of or suitable for a palace: *palatial gardens.* **2.** Of the nature of a palace; spacious and ornate. [< Lat. *palatium,* palace.] **—pa·la′tial·ly** *adv.* **—pa·la′tial·ness** *n.*
pa·lat·i·nate (pə-lăt′n-āt′, -ĭt) *n.* The office, powers, or territory of a palatine. [Med. Lat. *palatinatus* < Lat. *palatinus,* a palatine < *palatinus,* palatine.]
pal·a·tine[1] (păl′ə-tīn′) *n.* **1. a.** A soldier of the palace guard of the Roman emperors formed in the time of Diocletian. **b.** A soldier of a major division of the Roman army formed in the time of Constantine. **2.** A title of various administrative officials of the late Roman and Byzantine empires. **3.** A feudal lord exercising sovereign power over his lands. *—adj.* **1.** Belonging to or fit for a palace. **2.** Pertaining to or designating a palatine or palatinate. [Lat. *palatinus* < *palatinus,* of a palace < *palatium,* palace. —see PALACE.]

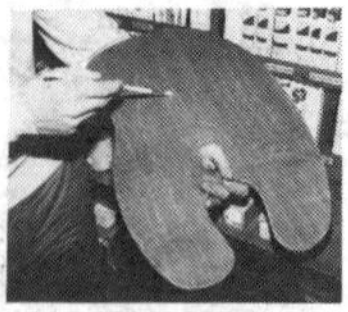
palette

pal·a·tine[2] (păl′ə-tēn′) *n.* A fur cape and hood worn by women. [Fr., after Princess *Palatine,* Charlotte Elizabeth of Bavaria (1652–1722).]
pal·a·tine[3] (păl′ə-tīn′) *adj.* Of or pertaining to the palate. *—n.* Either of the two bones that make up the hard palate.
pa·lav·er (pə-lăv′ər, -lä′vər) *n.* **1. a.** Idle chatter. **b.** Talk intended to charm or beguile. **2.** *Obs.* A parley between European explorers and representatives of local populations, esp. in Africa. *—v.* **-ered, -er·ing, -ers.** *—tr.* To flatter or cajole. *—intr.* To chatter idly. [Port. *palavra,* speech < LLat. *parabola.* —see PARABLE.]
pale[1] (pāl) *n.* **1.** A stake or pointed stick; picket. **2.** A fence enclosing an area. **3.** The area enclosed by a fence or boundary. **4.** *Heraldry.* A wide vertical band in the center of an escutcheon. **5. the Pale.** The medieval dominions of the English in Ireland. *—tr.v.* **paled, pal·ing, pales.** To enclose with pales; fence in. ***—idiom.* beyond the pale.** Irrevocably unacceptable or unreasonable. [ME < OFr. *pal* < Lat. *palus.*]
pale[2] (pāl) *adj.* **pal·er, pal·est. 1.** Whitish in complexion; pallid. **2.** Of a low intensity of color; light. **3.** Of a color having high lightness and low saturation. **4.** Of a low intensity of light; dim; faint. **5.** Feeble; weak. *—v.* **paled, pal·ing, pales.** *—tr.* To cause to turn pale. *—intr.* **1.** To become pale; blanch. **2.** To decrease in relative importance. [ME < OFr. < Lat. *pallidus* < *pallēre,* to be pale.] **—pale′ly** *adv.* **—pale′ness** *n.*
pale– *pref.* Variant of **paleo-.**
pa·le·a (pā′lē-ə) *n., pl.* **-le·ae** (-lē-ē′). A small, chafflike bract enclosing the flower of a grass spikelet. [NLat. < Lat., chaff.]
Pa·le·arc·tic (pā′lē-ärk′tĭk, -är′tĭk) *adj.* Of or designating the zoogeographic region that includes Europe, the northwestern coast of Africa, and Asia north of the Himalayas.
pale-dry (pāl′drī′) *adj.* Light colored and dry in flavor: *pale-dry ginger ale.*
pa·le·eth·nol·o·gy also **pa·le·ëth·nol·o·gy** (pā′lē-ĕth-nŏl′ə-jē) *n.* The ethnology of early man. **—pa′le·eth′no·log′ic** (-ĕth′nə-lŏj′ĭk), **pa′le·eth′no·log′i·cal** *adj.*
paleo– or **pale–** or **palaeo–** or **palae–** *pref.* **1.** Ancient; prehistoric: *paleobotany.* **2.** Early; primitive: *paleoanthropology.* [Gk. *palaio-* < *palaios,* ancient < *palai,* long ago.]
pa·le·o·an·throp·ic (pā′lē-ō-ăn-thrŏp′ĭk) *adj.* Of or pertaining to extinct members of the genus *Homo* that preceded *H. sapiens.*
pa·le·o·an·thro·pol·o·gy (pā′lē-ō-ăn′thrə-pŏl′ə-jē) *n.* The study of manlike creatures more primitive than *Homo sapiens.* **—pa′le·o·an′thro·po·log′ic** (-pə-lŏj′ĭk), **pa′le·o·an′thro·po·log′i·cal** *adj.* **—pa′le·o·an′thro·pol′o·gist** *n.*
pa·le·o·bot·a·ny (pā′lē-ō-bŏt′n-ē) *n.* The study of plant fossils and ancient vegetation. **—pa′le·o·bo·tan′ic** (-bə-tăn′ĭk), **pa′le·o·bo·tan′i·cal** *adj.* **—pa′le·o·bo·tan′i·cal·ly** *adv.* **—pa′le·o·bot′a·nist** *n.*
Pa·le·o·cene (pā′lē-ə-sēn′) *adj.* Of, belonging to, or designating the geologic time, rock series, and sedimentary deposits of the first epoch of the Tertiary period, preceding the Eocene and characterized by the appearance of placental mammals. *—n.* **1.** The Paleocene epoch. **2.** The deposits of the Paleocene epoch.
pa·le·o·e·col·o·gy (pā′lē-ō-ĭ-kŏl′ə-jē) *n.* A branch of ecology that deals with the interaction between ancient organisms and their environment. **—pa′le·o·ec′o·log′i·cal** (-ĕk′ə-lŏj′ĭ-kəl, -ē′kə-), **pa′le·o·ec′o·log′ic** *adj.* **—pa′le·o·e·col′o·gist** *n.*
pa·le·og·ra·phy (pā′lē-ŏg′rə-fē) *n.* **1.** The study and scholarly interpretation of ancient written documents. **2.** The documents studied in paleography. **—pa′le·og′ra·pher** *n.* **—pa′le·o·graph′ic** (-ə-grăf′ĭk), **pa′le·o·graph′i·cal** *adj.*
pa·le·o·lith (pā′lē-ə-lĭth′) *n.* A stone implement of the Paleolithic period.
Pa·le·o·lith·ic (pā′lē-ə-lĭth′ĭk) *adj.* Of, belonging to, or designating the cultural period beginning with the earliest chipped stone tools, about 750,000 years ago, until the beginning of the Mesolithic, about 15,000 years ago. *—n.* The Paleolithic Age.
pa·le·on·tol·o·gy (pā′lē-ŏn-tŏl′ə-jē) *n.* **1.** The study of fossils. **2.** Paleozoology. **—pa′le·on′to·log′ic** (-ŏn′tə-lŏj′ĭk), **pa′le·on′to·log′i·cal** *adj.* **—pa′le·on·tol′o·gist** *n.*
Pa·le·o·zo·ic (pā′lē-ə-zō′ĭk) *adj.* Of, belonging to, or designating the era of geologic time that includes the Cambrian, Ordovician, Silurian, Devonian, Mississippian, Pennsylvanian, and Permian periods, and is characterized by the appearance of marine invertebrates, primitive fishes, land plants, and primitive reptiles. *—n.* The Paleozoic era.
pa·le·o·zo·ol·o·gy (pā′lē-ō-zō-ŏl′ə-jē) *n.* The study of animal fossils and ancient animal life. **—pa′le·o·zo′o·log′i·cal** (-zō′ə-lŏj′ĭ-kəl) *adj.* **—pa′le·o·zo·ol′o·gist** *n.*
pa·les·tra also **pa·laes·tra** (pə-lĕs′trə) *n., pl.* **-trae** (-trē) or **-tras.** In ancient Greece, a public place for training and practice in wrestling and other athletics. [Lat. *palaestra* < Gk. *palaistra* < *palaiein,* to wrestle.] **—pa·les′tral, pa·les′tri·an** *adj.*
pal·ette (păl′ĭt) *n.* **1.** A board, typically with a hole for the thumb, upon which an artist mixes colors. **2. a.** The range of colors used in a particular painting or by a particular artist: *a limited palette.* **b.** The range of qualities inherent in other art forms, such as music. [Fr. < OFr., small potter's shovel, dim. of *pale,* shovel < Lat. *pala.*]
palette knife *n.* A knife with a thin, flexible blade, used by artists for mixing, scraping, or applying paint.
pal·frey (pôl′frē) *n., pl.* **-freys.** *Archaic.* A woman's saddle horse. [ME < OFr. *palefrei* < Med. Lat. *palefredus* < LLat. *paraveredus,* extra post horse : Gk. *para,* extra + Lat. *veredus,* post horse.]
Pa·li (pä′lē) *n.* An ancient Indic language that is a scriptural and liturgical language of Hinayana Buddhism. [Skt. *pāliḥ,* row, of Dravidian orig.]
pal·i·mo·ny (păl′ə-mō′nē) *n. Informal.* An allowance for support made under court order and given usually by a man to his former mistress or live-in companion after they have separated. [Blend of PAL and ALIMONY.]
pal·imp·sest (păl′ĭmp-sĕst′) *n.* A written document, typically on vellum or parchment, that has been written upon several times, often with remnants of earlier, imperfectly erased writing still visible. Remnants of this kind are a major source for the recovery of lost literary works of classical antiquity. [Lat. *palimpsestus* < Gk. *palimpsēstos,* scraped again : *palin,* again + *psēn,* to scrape.]
pal·in·drome (păl′ĭn-drōm′) *n.* A word, phrase, verse, or sentence which reads the same backward or forward, as *A man, a plan, a canal, Panama!* [Gk. *palindromos,* running back again : *palin,* again + *dromos,* a running.] **—pal′in·dro′mic** (-drō′mĭk, -drŏm′ĭk) *adj.*
pal·ing (pā′lĭng) *n.* **1.** One of a row of upright, pointed sticks forming a fence. **2.** Pointed sticks used in making fences; pales. **3.** A fence made of pales or pickets.
pal·in·gen·e·sis (păl′ĭn-jĕn′ĭ-sĭs) *n., pl.* **-ses** (-sēz′). **1.** The doctrine of transmigration of souls; metempsychosis. **2.** *Biol.* The repetition by a single organism of various stages in the evolution of its species during embryonic development. [Gk. *palin,* again + -GENESIS.] **—pal′in·ge·net′ic** (-jə-nĕt′ĭk) *adj.* **—pal′in·ge·net′i·cal·ly** *adv.*
pal·i·node (păl′ə-nōd′) *n.* **1.** A poem in which the poet retracts something said in a previous poem. **2.** A formal statement of retraction. [LLat. *palinodia* < Gk. *palinōidia* : *palin,* again + *ōidē,* song.]
pal·i·sade (păl′ĭ-sād′) *n.* **1. a.** A fence of pales forming a defense barrier or fortification. **b.** One of the pales of such a fence. **2. palisades.** A line of lofty, steep cliffs, usually along a river. *—tr.v.* **-sad·ed, -sad·ing, -sades.** To equip or fortify with a palisade. [Fr. *palissade* < OProv. *palissada* < *palissa,* stake < Lat. *palus.*]
palisade cell *n. Bot.* One of the columnar cells of palisade parenchyma.
palisade parenchyma *n. Bot.* A leaf tissue composed of columnar cells that contain numerous chloroplasts.
pal·ish (pā′lĭsh) *adj.* Slightly pale.
pall[1] (pôl) *n.* **1.** A cover for a coffin, bier, or tomb, often made of black, purple, or white velvet. **2.** A coffin, esp. one being borne to a grave or tomb. **3. a.** A covering that darkens or obscures: *a pall of smoke over the city.* **b.** A gloomy effect or atmosphere: *Defeat cast a pall over the troops.* **4.** *Eccles.* **a.** A linen cloth, or a square of cardboard faced with cloth, used to cover the chalice. **b.** The pallium (sense 2). *—tr.v.* **palled, pall·ing, palls.** To cover with or as with a pall. [ME *palle* < OE *pæll,* purple robe < Lat. *pallium,* cloak.]
pall[2] (pôl) *v.* **palled, pall·ing, palls.** *—intr.* **1.** To become insipid, boring, or wearisome. **2.** To have a dulling, wearisome, or unpleasant effect. **3.** To become cloyed or satiated. *—tr.* **1.** To cloy; satiate. **2.** To make vapid or wearisome. [ME *pallen,* short for *appallen,* to grow faint. —see APPALL.]
pal·la·di·a (pə-lā′dē-ə) *n.* A plural of **palladium[2].**
Pal·la·di·an[1] (pə-lā′dē-ən) *adj.* **1.** Of, pertaining to, or characteristic of Athena. **2.** Of, pertaining to, or characterized by wisdom or study. [< Lat. *palladius* < Gk. *palladios* < *Pallas,* Pallas Athena.]
Pal·la·di·an[2] (pə-lā′dē-ən) *adj.* **1.** Of or designating the Renaissance architectural style of Andrea Palladio. **2.** Of or designating a mid-18th-century architectural style derived from that of Palladio, esp. in Britain.

pal·la·dic (pə-lā′dĭk, -lăd′ĭk) *adj.* Of or designating compounds containing trivalent or tetravalent palladium.

pal·la·di·um[1] (pə-lā′dē-əm) *n. Symbol* **Pd** A soft, ductile, steel-white, tarnish-resistant, metallic element occurring naturally with platinum, esp. in gold, nickel, and copper ores. It is used as a catalyst in hydrogenation process, as a purification filter for hydrogen, and is alloyed for use in electric contacts, jewelry, nonmagnetic watch parts, and surgical instruments. Atomic number 46; atomic weight 106.4; melting point 1552°C; boiling point 2927°C; specific gravity 12.02 (20°C); valence 2, 3, 4. [< PALLAS.]

pal·la·di·um[2] (pə-lā′dē-əm) *n., pl.* **-di·a** (-dē-ə) or **-di·ums. 1.** A sacred object having the power to preserve a city or state possessing it. **2.** A safeguard, esp. one viewed as a guarantee of the integrity of social institutions: *the Bill of Rights, palladium of American civil liberties.* [Lat. *Palladium,* a statue of Pallas Athena believed to protect Troy < Gk. *Palladion* < *Pallas,* Pallas Athena.]

pal·la·dous (pə-lā′dəs, păl′ə-dəs) *adj.* Of, pertaining to, or containing palladium, esp. bivalent palladium.

Pal·las (păl′əs) *n.* The second-largest asteroid of the solar system, approximately 483 kilometers, or 300 miles, in diameter. [Peter S. *Pallas* (1741–1811), its discoverer.]

Pallas Athena or **Pallas Athene** *n.* Athena.

pall·bear·er (pôl′bâr′ər) *n.* One of the persons who carry or attend a coffin at a funeral.

pal·let[1] (păl′ĭt) *n.* **1.** A machine part that converts reciprocating motion to rotary motion or vice versa, such as a click or pawl for controlling the motion of a ratchet wheel in a watch escapement. **2.** The lip or projection of a pawl for engaging the teeth on a ratchet wheel. **3.** A wooden, paddle-like potter's tool for mixing and shaping clay. **4.** A tool used for printing or gilding letters on book bindings or taking up and applying gold leaf. **5.** A portable platform for storing or moving cargo or freight. **6.** A painter's palette. [OFr. *palette,* small potter's shovel. —see PALETTE.]

pal·let[2] (păl′ĭt) *n.* A narrow, hard bed or straw-filled mattress. [ME *pailet* < AN *paillete,* bundle of straw < *paille,* straw < Lat. *palea,* chaff.]

pal·lette (pă-lĕt′) *n.* A plate that protects the armpit on a suit of armor. [Alteration of PALETTE.]

pal·li·a (păl′ē-ə) *n.* A plural of **pallium.**

pal·li·al (păl′ē-əl) *adj.* **1.** Of or pertaining to the cerebral cortex. **2.** Of or pertaining to the mantle of a mollusk or brachiopod. [< NLat. *pallium,* cerebral cortex < Lat., cloak.]

pal·liasse (păl-yăs′, păl′yăs′) *n.* Variant of **paillasse.**

pal·li·ate (păl′ē-āt′) *tr.v.* **-at·ed, -at·ing, -ates. 1.** To make (an offense or crime) seem less serious; extenuate. **2.** To make less severe or intense; mitigate: *tried to palliate the widespread discontent.* [LLat. *palliare, palliat-,* to cloak < Lat. *pallium,* cloak.] **—pal′li·a′tion** *n.* **—pal·li·a′tor** *n.*

pal·li·a·tive (păl′ē-ā′tĭv, -ē-ə-tĭv) *adj.* Tending or serving to palliate. *—n.* Something that palliates. **—pal′li·a′tive·ly** *adv.*

pal·lid (păl′ĭd) *adj.* **1.** Having an abnormally pale or wan complexion: *the pallid face of an invalid.* **2.** Lacking intensity of hue or luminousness. **3.** Lacking in radiance or vitality; dull. [Lat. *pallidus* < *pallēre,* to be pale.] **—pal′lid·ly** *adv.* **—pal′lid·ness** *n.*

pal·li·um (păl′ē-əm) *n., pl.* **-li·ums** or **-li·a** (-ē-ə). **1.** A cloak worn by the Romans. **2.** A vestment worn by the pope, and conferred by him on archbishops and sometimes on bishops. **3. a.** *Biol.* The cerebral cortex. **b.** The mantle of a mollusk or brachiopod. [Lat.]

pall-mall (pĕl′mĕl′, păl′măl′, pôl′môl′) *n.* **1.** A 17th-century game in which a boxwood ball was struck with a mallet to drive it through an iron ring suspended at the end of an alley. **2.** The alley in which pall-mall was played. [Obs. Fr. *pallemaille* < Ital. *pallamaglio* : *palla,* ball (of Germanic orig.) + *maglio,* mallet (< Lat. *malleus*).]

pal·lor (păl′ər) *n.* Extreme or unnatural paleness. [Lat. < *pallēre,* to be pale.]

pal·ly (păl′ē) *adj.* **-li·er, -li·est.** *Informal.* Having the relationship of pals.

palm[1] (päm) *n.* **1. a.** The inner surface of the hand, extending from the wrist to the base of the fingers. **b.** The similar part of the forefoot of a quadruped. **2.** A unit of length equal to either the width or the length of the hand. **3.** The part of a glove or mitten that covers the palm of the hand. **4.** A metal shield worn by sailmakers over the palm of the hand and used to force a needle through heavy canvas. **5.** The blade of an oar or paddle. **6.** The flattened part of the antlers of certain animals, such as the moose. *—tr.v.* **palmed, palm·ing, palms. 1.** To conceal (something) in the palm of the hand, as in cheating at dice or cards or in a sleight-of-hand trick. **2.** To pick up furtively. **3.** *Basketball.* To commit a violation by letting (the ball) rest momentarily in the palm of the hand while dribbling. **—phrasal verb. palm off.** To dispose of or pass off by deception. **—*idioms.* cross one's palm.** To pay, tip, or bribe. **grease the palm of.** To bribe. **have an itching palm.** To have a craving for money. [ME *paume* < OFr. < Lat. *palma,* palm of the hand, palm tree.]

palm[2] (päm) *n.* **1.** Any of various chiefly tropical evergreen trees or shrubs of the family Palmaceae, characteristically having unbranched trunks with a crown of large pinnate or palmate leaves. **2.** A leaf or frond of a palm tree, carried as an emblem of victory, success, or joy. **3.** Triumph; victory. **4.** A small metallic representation of a palm leaf added to a military decoration that has been awarded a second time. **—*idiom.* bear** (or **carry off**) **the palm.** To win the prize in a given contest. [ME *palme* < OE *palm* < Lat. *palma,* palm tree, palm of the hand.] **—palm′like′** *adj.*

pal·mar (păl′mər, päl′-, pä′mər) *adj.* Of, pertaining to, or corresponding to the palm of the hand or an animal's paw: *palmar folds.* [NLat. *palmaris* < Lat. *palma,* palm.]

pal·ma·ry (păl′mə-rē, päl′-, pä′mə-) *adj.* Worthy of the palm; outstanding. [Lat. *palmarius,* deserving the palm < *palma,* palm tree.]

pal·mate (păl′māt′, päl′-, pä′māt′) also **pal·mat·ed** (-mā′tĭd) *adj.* **1.** Resembling a hand with the fingers extended: *palmate antlers; palmate coral.* **2.** *Bot.* Having leaflets or lobes radiating from one point: *a palmate leaf.* **3.** *Zool.* Having webbed toes, as the feet of many water birds. [Lat. *palmatus* < *palma,* palm.] **—pal′mate′ly** *adv.* **—pal·ma′tion** *n.*

pal·ma·tion (păl-mā′shən, päl-, pä-mā′-) *n.* **1.** The state of being palmate. **2. a.** A palmate structure or form. **b.** A division or part of a palmate structure.

palm·er (pä′mər) *n.* A medieval European pilgrim who carried a palm branch as a token of having visited the Holy Land. [ME < AN < Med. Lat. *palmarius* < Lat. *palma,* palm.]

pallet[1]

palm·er·worm (pä′mər-wûrm′) *n.* Any of several caterpillars that injure fruit trees by feeding upon their leaves, esp. the small green caterpillar of a North American moth, *Dichomeris ligulella.*

pal·mette (păl-mĕt′) *n.* A stylized palm leaf used as a decorative element, notably in Persian rugs and in classical moldings, reliefs, frescoes, and vase paintings. [Fr., dim. of *palme,* palm < Lat. *palma.*]

pal·met·to (păl-mĕt′ō) *n., pl.* **-tos** or **-toes.** Any of several small, mostly tropical palms having fan-shaped leaves, esp. *Sabal palmetto,* of the southeastern United States. [Sp. *palmito,* dim. of *palma,* palm < Lat.]

palm·ist (pä′mĭst) also **palm·is·ter** (-mĭ-stər) *n.* One who practices palmistry. [Prob. back-formation < PALMISTRY.]

palm·is·try (pä′mĭ-strē) *n.* The practice or art of telling fortunes from the lines, marks, and patterns on the palms of the hands; chiromancy. [ME *pawmestrie* < *paume,* palm. —see PALM[1].]

pal·mi·tate (păl′mĭ-tāt′, päl′-, pä′mĭ-) *n.* An ester or salt of palmitic acid. [PALMIT(IN) + -ATE[2].]

pal·mit·ic acid (păl-mĭt′ĭk, päl-, pä-mĭt′-) *n.* A common fatty acid, $CH_3(CH_2)_{14}COOH$, occurring in many natural oils and fats, used in making soaps. [< PALMITIN.]

pal·mi·tin (păl′mĭ-tĭn, päl′-, pä′mĭ-) *n.* The glyceryl ester, $C_3H_5(OC_{16}H_{31}O)_3$, of palmitic acid, found in palm oil and animal fats, and used to manufacture soap. [Fr. *palmitine,* perh. < *palmite,* pith of the palm tree < *palme,* palm < Lat. *palma.*]

palm oil *n.* A yellowish fatty oil obtained esp. from the crushed nuts of the West African palm, *Elaeis guineensis,* and used to manufacture soaps, chocolates, cosmetics, and candles.

palm sugar *n.* Sugar made from the sap of various palm trees.

Palm Sunday *n.* The Sunday before Easter, commemorating Christ's entry into Jerusalem when palm branches were strewn before him.

palm·y (pä′mē) *adj.* **-i·er, -i·est. 1.** Of or pertaining to palm trees. **2.** Covered with palm trees. **3.** Prosperous; flourishing.

pal·my·ra (păl-mī′rə) *n.* A tall palm, *Borassus flabellifera,* of tropical Asia, having large, fanlike leaves. [Port. *palmeira* < *palma,* palm < Lat.]

palmyra palm *n.* The palmyra.

pal·o·mi·no (păl′ə-mē′nō) *n., pl.* **-nos.** A type of horse having a golden or tan coat and a white or cream-colored mane and tail. [Am. Sp. < Sp., dove-colored < Lat. *palumbinus,* pertaining to ringdoves < *palumbes,* ringdove.]

pa·loo·ka (pə-lo͞o′kə) *n. Slang.* An incompetent or easily defeated person, esp. a prizefighter. [Orig. unknown.]

pa·lo·ver·de (păl′ō-vûr′dē, -vûrd′) *n.* **1.** A spiny, nearly leafless shrub, *Cercidium Torreyanum,* of southwestern North America, having showy yellow flowers. **2.** Any of several shrubs similar or related to the paloverde. [Mex. Sp. : Sp. *palo,* tree (< Lat. *pallus,* stake) + Sp. *verde,* green (< Lat. *virdis*).]

palp (pălp) *n. Zool.* An elongated sensory organ, usually near the mouth, in invertebrate organisms such as mollusks, crustaceans, and insects. [Fr. *palpe* < Lat. *palpus,* a touching.]

pal·pa·ble (păl′pə-bəl) *adj.* **1.** Capable of being handled, touched, or felt; tangible. **2.** Easily perceived; obvious. **3.** *Med.* Perceptible by palpation: *a palpable tumor.* [ME < LLat. *palpabilis* < Lat. *palpare,* to touch.] **—pal′pa·bil′i·ty** *n.* **—pal′pa·bly** *adv.*

pal·pate[1] (păl′pāt′) *tr.v.* **-pat·ed, -pat·ing, -pates.** To examine or explore by touching (an organ or area of the body) as a diagnostic aid. [Lat. *palpare, palpat-,* to touch.] **—pal·pa′tion** *n.* **—pal′pa′tor** *n.*

pal·pate[2] (păl′pāt′) *adj.* Having a palp or palps.

pal·pe·bral (păl′pə-brəl, păl-pē′brəl, -pĕb′rəl) *adj.* Of or re-

Pan
Fragment from a
4th-century Roman bowl

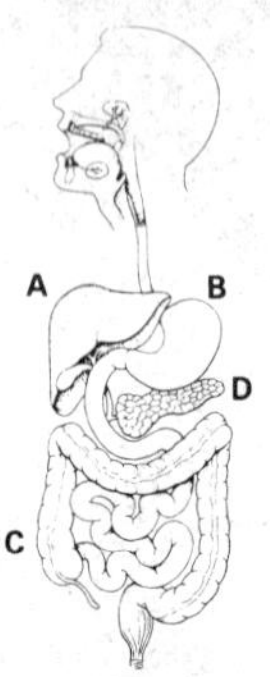

pancreas
A. Liver
B. Stomach
C. Large intestine
D. Pancreas

lating to the eyelids. [LLat. *palpebralis* < Lat. *palpebra,* eyelid.]

pal·pi (păl′pī) *n.* Plural of **palpus.**

pal·pi·tant (păl′pĭ-tənt) *adj.* Palpitating; trembling; quivering. [Lat. *palpitans, palpitant-,* pr.part. of *palpitare,* to palpitate.]

pal·pi·tate (păl′pĭ-tāt′) *intr.v.* **-tat·ed, -tat·ing, -tates. 1.** To shake; quiver; flutter. **2.** To beat more quickly than normal; throb. Used of the heart. [Lat. *palpitare, palpitat-,* freq. of *palpare,* to touch.] **—pal′pi·tat′ing·ly** *adv.*

pal·pi·ta·tion (păl′pĭ-tā′shən) *n.* **1.** A trembling or shaking. **2.** Irregular, rapid beating or pulsation of the heart.

pal·pus (păl′pəs) *n., pl.* **-pi** (-pī′). *Zool.* A palp. [NLat. < Lat., a feeling.]

pals·grave (pôlz′grāv′) *n.* A palatine[1] (sense 3). [MDu. *paltsgrave* : *palts,* palatine + *grave,* count.]

pal·sied (pôl′zēd) *adj.* **1.** Afflicted with palsy. **2.** Trembling; shaking.

pal·sy (pôl′zē) *n., pl.* **-sies. 1.** Paralysis. **2.** A condition marked by loss of power to feel or to control movement in any part of the body. **3. a.** A weakening or debilitating influence. **b.** An enfeebled condition or debilitated state thought to result from such an influence. **4.** A fit of strong emotion marked by an inability to act. *—tr.v.* **-sied, -sy·ing, -sies. 1. a.** To paralyze. **b.** To deprive of strength. **2.** To make helpless, as with fear. [ME < OFr. *paralisie* < Lat. *paralysis.* —see PARALYSIS.]

pal·sy-wal·sy (păl′zē-wăl′zē) *adj. Slang.* Appearing to have the close relationship of pals. [Redup. of *palsy,* alteration of PALLY.]

pal·ter (pôl′tər) *intr.v.* **-tered, -ter·ing, -ters. 1.** To talk or act insincerely; equivocate. **2.** To be capricious; trifle. **3.** To quibble, esp. in bargaining. [Orig. unknown.] **—pal′ter·er** *n.*

pal·try (pôl′trē) *adj.* **-tri·er, -tri·est. 1.** Petty; trifling; insignificant. **2.** Worthless; contemptible. [< obs. *paltry,* trash.] **—pal′tri·ly** *adv.* **—pal′tri·ness** *n.*

pa·lu·dal (pə-lo͞od′l, păl′yə-dəl) *adj.* Of or pertaining to a swamp; marshy. [< Lat. *palus, palud-,* marsh.]

pal·u·dism (păl′yə-dĭz′əm) *n.* Malaria (sense 1). [< Lat. *palus, palud-,* marsh.]

pal·y (pā′lē) *adj.* Pale.

pal·y·nol·o·gy (păl′ə-nŏl′ə-jē) *n.* The scientific study of spores and pollen. [Gk. *palunein,* to sprinkle (< *palē,* dust) + -LOGY.] **—pal′y·no·log′i·cal** (-nə-lŏj′ĭ-kəl), **pal′y·no·log′ic** *adj.* **—pal′y·no·log′i·cal·ly** *adv.* **—pal′y·nol′o·gist** *n.*

pam (păm) *n.* The jack of clubs and highest trump in certain variations of loo. [Prob. short for Gk. *pamphilos,* loved by all : *pan,* all + *philos,* beloved.]

pam·pa (păm′pə) *n., pl.* **-pas** (-pəz, -pəs). A nearly treeless grassland area of South America, chiefly in central Argentina and Uruguay between the Andes and the Atlantic. [Am. Sp. < Quechua, flat field.]

pam·pas grass (păm′pəs) *n.* A tall grass, *Cortaderia argentea,* of southern South America, having silvery plumes.

pam·pe·an (păm′pē-ən, păm-pē′ən) *adj.* Of or pertaining to the pampas or the Indian people who inhabit them. *—n.* **Pampean.** An Indian of the pampas.

pam·per (păm′pər) *tr.v.* **-pered, -per·ing, -pers. 1.** To treat with excessive indulgence; coddle. **2.** *Archaic.* To indulge with rich food; glut. [ME *pamperem,* of Du. orig.] **—pam′per·er** *n.*

Synonyms: *pamper, indulge, humor, spoil, coddle, baby.* These all mean to cater excessively to another's (or one's own) desires or feelings, typically those of a child and more pejoratively those of an adult. To *pamper* is to be overattentive to somebody's physical comforts. *Indulge* is applied principally to instincts or appetites, sometimes without very strong condemnation. *Humor* usually implies short-term submission to another's mood or idiosyncrasies as a means to an end. *Spoil* usually implies a long-term oversolicitude that badly affects a person's character. *Coddle* points to overprotecting, serving, or favoring somebody. *Baby* suggests bestowing on someone the indulgence and attention appropriate to an infant, and is always unfavorable.

pam·pe·ro (păm-pâr′ō, päm-) *n., pl.* **-ros.** A strong, cold southwest wind that blows across the pampas. [Am. Sp. < *pampa,* pampas.]

pam·phlet (păm′flĭt) *n.* **1.** An unbound printed work, usually with a paper cover. **2.** A short essay or treatise, usually on a current topic, published without a binding. [ME *pamflet* < Med. Lat. *Pamphilus,* a short amatory Latin poem of the 12th cent.] **—pam′phlet·ar′y** (păm′flĭ-tĕr′ē) *adj.*

pam·phlet·eer (păm′flĭ-tîr′) *n.* A writer of pamphlets or other short works taking a partisan stand on an issue. *—intr.v.* **-eered, -eer·ing, -eers.** To write and publish pamphlets.

pan[1] (păn) *n.* **1.** A shallow, wide, open container, usually of metal and without a lid, used for holding liquids, cooking, and other domestic purposes. **2.** A vessel similar in form to a pan, esp.: **a.** An open, metal dish used to separate gold or other metal from gravel or waste by washing. **b.** Either of the receptacles on a balance or pair of scales. **c.** A vessel used for boiling and evaporating liquids. **3. a.** A basin or depression in the earth, often containing mud or water. **b.** A natural or artificial basin used to obtain salt by evaporating brine. **4.** A piece of drift ice that has broken off a larger floe. **5.** In flintlocks, the small cavity in the lock used to hold powder. **6.** *Slang.* The face. **7.** *Informal.* Severe criticism, esp. a negative review: *gave the film a devastating pan.* *—v.* **panned, pan·ning, pans.** *—tr.* **1.** To wash (gravel, for example) in a pan for precious metal. **2.** To cook (food) in a pan. **3.** *Informal.* To criticize or review harshly. *—intr.* **1.** To wash gravel, sand, or other sediments in a pan. **2.** To yield gold as a result of washing in a pan. ***—phrasal verb.* pan out.** *Informal.* To turn out well; be successful: *"If I don't pan out as an actor I can still go back to school"* (Saul Bellow). [ME < OE *panne,* poss. < Lat. *patina* < Gk. *patanē.*]

pan[2] (pän) *n.* **1.** The leaf of the betel tree. **2.** A preparation of pan with betel nuts and lime, used for chewing in the Orient. [Hindi *pān* < Skt. *parṇam,* feathery leaf.]

pan[3] (păn) *v.* **panned, pan·ning, pans.** *—intr.* To move a motion-picture or television camera to follow a moving object or create a panoramic effect. *—tr.* To move (a camera) so as to follow a moving object or create a panoramic effect. [Short for PANORAMA.]

Pan (păn) *n. Gk. Myth.* The god of woods, fields, and flocks, having a human torso with goat's legs, horns, and ears. [Lat. < Gk.]

pan– *pref.* **1.** All: *panorama.* **2.** Involving all of or the union of a specified group: *Pan-Hellenic.* **3.** General; whole: *panleucopenia.* [Gk. < *pas,* all.]

pan·a·ce·a (păn′ə-sē′ə) *n.* **1.** A remedy for all diseases, evils, or difficulties; cure-all. **2.** Elixir (sense 2). [Lat. < Gk. *panakeia* < *panakēs,* all-healing : *pan-,* all + *akos,* cure.] **—pan′a·ce′an** *adj.*

pa·nache (pə-năsh′, -näsh′) *n.* **1.** A bunch of feathers or a plume, esp. on a helmet. **2.** Dash; swagger; verve. [Fr. < Ital. *pennachio* < LLat. *pinnaculum,* dim. of Lat. *pinna,* feather.]

pa·na·da (pə-nä′də) *n.* A paste or gruel of bread crumbs, toast, or flour combined with milk, stock, or water, used for soups, for binding forcemeats, or for thickening sauces. [Sp. < *pan,* bread < Lat. *panis.*]

pan·ag·glu·ti·nin (păn′ə-glo͞ot′n-ĭn) *n.* An agglutinin that is capable of agglutinating red blood cells of every blood group.

Pan·a·ma hat (păn′ə-mä′) *n.* A natural-colored, hand-plaited hat made from leaves of the jipijapa plant of South and Central America.

Panama Red *n.* Marijuana of Panamanian origin that is slightly red and very potent.

Pan-A·mer·i·can (păn′ə-mĕr′ĭ-kən) *adj.* Of or pertaining to North, South, and Central America collectively.

pan·a·tel·a also **pan·e·tel·a** or **pan·e·tel·la** (păn′ə-tĕl′ə) *n.* A long, slender cigar. [Sp., cigar, biscuit < Ital. *panatella,* biscuit < *panata,* panada < *pane,* bread < Lat. *panis.*]

pan-broil (păn′broil′) *tr.v.* **-broiled, -broil·ing, -broils.** To cook (steak, for example) over direct heat in an uncovered, usually ungreased skillet.

pan·cake (păn′kāk′) *n.* A thin cake made of batter, poured on a hot, greased skillet and cooked on both sides until brown. *—v.* **-caked, -cak·ing, -cakes.** *—intr.* To make a pancake landing in an aircraft. *—tr.* To cause (an airplane) to make a pancake landing.

pancake landing *n.* An irregular or emergency landing in which an aircraft drops flat to the ground from a low altitude.

Pan-Cake Make-Up (păn′kāk′). A trademark for a semi-solid face-powder cosmetic pressed into a flat cake.

pan·chax (păn′chăks′) *n.* Any of various small, brightly colored Old World tropical fishes of the genus *Aplocheilus* and related genera, often kept in home aquariums. [NLat.]

Pan·chen La·ma (pän′chən lä′mə) *n.* One of Tibet's two grand lamas, the other being the Dalai Lama. [Tibetan : *paṇchen,* great scholar (Skt. *paṇḍitaḥ,* scholar + Tibetan *chen-po,* great) + *bla-ma,* monk.]

pan·chro·mat·ic (păn′krō-măt′ĭk) *adj.* Sensitive to all colors: *panchromatic film for a camera.* **—pan·chro′ma·tism** (-krō′mə-tĭz′əm) *n.*

pan·cra·ti·um (păn-krā′shē-əm) *n.* An athletic contest in ancient Greece that involved boxing and wrestling. [Lat. < Gk. *pankration* : *pan-,* all + *kratos,* strength.]

pan·cre·as (păng′krē-əs, păn′-) *n. Anat.* A long, soft, irregularly shaped gland lying behind the stomach that secretes pancreatic juice into the duodenum and, in the islands of Langerhans, produces insulin that is taken up by the blood stream. [Gk. *pankreas* : *pan-,* all + *kreas,* flesh.] **—pan′cre·at′ic** (păng′krē-ăt′ĭk, păn′-) *adj.*

pancreat– *pref.* Variant of **pancreato-.**

pan·cre·a·tec·to·my (păng′krē-ə-tĕk′tə-mē, păn′-) *n., pl.* **-mies.** The surgical excision of the pancreas.

pancreatic juice *n.* A clear, alkaline secretion of the pancreas containing enzymes that aid in the digestion of proteins, carbohydrates, and fats.

pan·cre·a·tin (păng′krē-ə-tĭn, păn′-, păn-krē′ə-tĭn) *n.* A mixture of enzymes extracted from the pancreases of cattle or hogs and used as a digestive aid.

pan·cre·a·ti·tis (păng′krē-ə-tī′tĭs, păn′-) *n.* Inflammation of the pancreas.

pancreato– or **pancreat–** *pref.* Pancreas: *pancreatin.* [Gk. *pankreas, pankreat-,* pancreas.]

pan·cre·o·zy·min (păng′krē-ō-zī′mĭn, păn′-) *n.* A hormone produced by the intestinal mucosa that stimulates the secretion of pancreatic juice. [PANCRE(AS) + -O- + ZYM(O)- + -IN.]

pan·da (păn′də) *n.* **1.** A bearlike mammal, *Ailuropoda melanoleuca,* of the mountains of China and Tibet, having woolly fur with distinctive black and white markings. **2.** A small, raccoonlike mammal, *Ailurus fulgens,* of northeastern Asia, having reddish fur and a long, ringed tail. [Fr., perh. < a native word in Nepal.]

panda car *n. Chiefly Brit.* A police cruiser. [From a similarity of color tone distribution.]

pan·dae·mo·ni·um (păn′də-mō′nē-əm) *n.* Variant of **pandemonium.**

pan·da·nus (păn-dā′nəs, -dăn′əs) *n.* Any of various palmlike trees and shrubs of the genus *Pandanus,* of southeastern Asia, having large prop roots and a crown of narrow leaves that yield a fiber used in weaving mats and similar articles. [NLat. *Pandanus,* genus name < Malay *pandan,* screw pine.] **—pan′da·na′ceous** (păn′də-nā′shəs) *adj.*

Pan·da·rus (păn′də-rəs) also **Pan·dar** (păn′dər) *n.* **1.** In the *Iliad,* the leader of the Lycians, slain by Diomedes. **2.** In medieval romance, the procurer of Cressida for Troilus. [Lat. < Gk. *Pandaros.*]

Pandean pipes (păn-dē′ən) *pl.n.* A panpipe. [< PAN.]

pan·dect (păn′dĕkt′) *n.* **1.** A comprehensive digest or complete treatise. **2. pandects.** A complete body of laws; a legal code. **3. Pandects.** A digest of Roman civil law, compiled for the emperor Justinian in the 6th century A.D. and part of the Corpus Juris Civilis. [LLat. *Pandectae,* the Pandects, a digest of Roman civil law < *pandecta,* encyclopedia < Gk. *pandektēs,* all-receiving : *pan-,* all + *dektēs,* receiver < *dekheisthai,* to receive.]

pan·dem·ic (păn-dĕm′ĭk) *adj.* **1.** Widespread; general. **2.** *Med.* Epidemic over an esp. wide geographic area. *—n.* A pandemic disease. [LLat. *pandemus* < Gk. *pandēmos,* of all the people : *pan-,* all + *dēmos,* people.]

pan·de·mo·ni·um also **pan·dae·mo·ni·um** (păn′də-mō′nē-əm) *n.* **1.** A place characterized by uproar and noise: *"The whole lobby was a perfect pandemonium, and the din was terrific"* (Jerome K. Jerome). **2.** Wild uproar or noise: *pandemonium in the audience.* [After *Pandæmonium,* capital of Hell in *Paradise Lost,* an epic poem by John Milton (1608–1674).] **—pan′de·mo′ni·ac** (-mō′nē-ăk′) *adj.*

pan·der (păn′dər) also **pan·der·er** (păn′dər-ər) *n.* **1.** A go-between or liaison in sexual intrigues; procurer. **2.** One who caters to the lower tastes and desires of others or exploits their weaknesses. *—v.* **-dered, -der·ing, -ders.** *—tr.* To act as a pander for. *—intr.* To act as a pander. [ME *Pandare,* Pandarus < OItal. *Pandaro* < Lat. *Pandarus* < Gk. *Pandaros.*] **—pan′der·ism** *n.*

Pan·do·ra's box (păn-dôr′əz, -dōr′-) *n.* A source of many unforeseen troubles. [Gk. *Pandōra* : *pan,* all + *-dōra,* giving (from the myth that the first woman, *Pandora,* came to man with a box which was not to be opened, but which she opened out of curiosity and thereby released all that is evil to mankind).]

pan·dore (păn′dôr′, -dōr′) *n.* A bandore. [Gk. *pandoura.*]

pan·dow·dy (păn-dou′dē) *n., pl.* **-dies.** Sliced fruit baked with sugar and spices in a deep dish, with a thick top crust. [Orig. unknown.]

pan·du·rate (păn-dŏŏr′ĭt, -dyŏŏr′-) also **pan·du·ri·form** (-ə-fôrm′) *adj.* Resembling a violin in shape. Used of leaves. [NLat. *panduratus* < LLat. *pandura,* three-string lute < Gk. *pandoura.*]

pane (pān) *n.* **1. a.** One of the glass-filled divisions of a window or door. **b.** The glass used in such a division. **2.** A panel, as of a door or wall. **3.** One of the flat surfaces or facets of an object, such as a bolt, having many sides. [ME, section < OFr. *pan,* piece of cloth < Lat. *pannus,* cloth.]

pan·e·gyr·ic (păn′ə-jĭr′ĭk, -jī′rĭk) *n.* **1.** A formal eulogistic composition intended as a public compliment. **2.** Elaborate praise or laudation; encomium. [Fr. *panégyrique* < Lat. *panegyricus* < Gk. *panēgurikos* < *panēgurikos,* of a public assembly < *panēguris,* public assembly : *pan-,* all + *aguris,* assembly.] **—pan′e·gyr′i·cal** *adj.* **—pan′e·gyr′i·cal·ly** *adv.*

pan·e·gyr·ist (păn′ə-jĭr′ĭst, -jī′rĭst) *n.* One who writes or delivers panegyrics; eulogist.

pan·e·gy·rize (păn′ə-jə-rīz′) *v.* **-rized, -riz·ing, -riz·es.** *—tr.* To eulogize. *—intr.* To compose, deliver, or indulge in panegyrics.

pan·el (păn′əl) *n.* **1.** A flat, usually rectangular piece forming a part of a surface in which it is set, and being raised, recessed, or framed. **2.** The space or section in a fence or railing between two posts. **3.** A vertical section of fabric; gore. **4. a.** A thin wooden board, used as a surface for oil painting. **b.** A painting on such a board. **5. a.** A board having switches to control parts of an electric device. **b.** An instrument panel. **6.** A section of a telephone switchboard. **7. a.** The complete list of persons summoned for jury duty. **b.** Those persons selected from the list to compose a jury. **c.** A jury. **8. a.** A group of people gathered to plan or discuss an issue, judge a contest, or act as a team on a radio or television quiz program. **b.** A discussion by such a group. *—tr.v.* **-eled, -el·ing, -els** also **-elled, -el·ling, -els. 1.** To cover or furnish with panels. **2.** To decorate with panels. **3.** To separate into panels. **4.** To select or impanel (a jury). [ME, piece of cloth < OFr. < Lat. *pannus,* cloth.]

panel discussion *n.* A usually formal discussion of a subject of public interest by a group of persons forming a panel.

pan·el·ing (păn′ə-lĭng) *n.* A section of panels or paneled wall.

pan·el·ist (păn′ə-lĭst) *n.* A member of a panel.

panel truck *n.* A small delivery truck with a fully enclosed body.

pan·e·tel·a or **pan·e·tel·la** (păn′ə-tĕl′ə) *n.* Variants of **panatela.**

pan·et·to·ne (păn′ə-tō′nē) *n., pl.* **-nes** or **-ni** (-nē). A festive Italian yeast cake made with candied fruit peels and raisins. [Ital. < *panetto,* a small loaf, dim. of *pane,* bread < Lat. *panis.*]

pan fish *n.* A fish small enough to be fried whole in a pan.

pan-fry (păn′frī′) *tr.v.* **-fried, -fry·ing, -fries.** To fry in a frying pan or skillet with a small amount of shortening.

pan·ful (păn′fŏŏl′) *n.* The amount that a pan will hold.

pang (păng) *n.* **1.** A sudden, sharp spasm of pain. **2.** A sudden, sharp feeling of emotional distress. *—tr.v.* **panged, pang·ing, pangs.** To cause anguish. [Orig. unknown.]

pan·gen·e·sis (păn-jĕn′ĭ-sĭs) *n.* The discredited hypothesis that every somatic cell generates self-representative hereditary materials that enter the blood stream and eventually coalesce in reproductive cells, making possible the inheritance of acquired characteristics. **—pan′ge·net′ic** (-jə-nĕt′ĭk) *adj.* **—pan′ge·net′i·cal·ly** *adv.*

Pan·gloss·i·an (păn-glŏs′ē-ən, -glôs′-, păng-) *adj.* Blindly expecting a favorable outcome or naively dwelling on hopeful aspects. [After *Pangloss,* an optimist in *Candide,* a satire by Voltaire (1694–1778).]

pan·go·lin (păng′gə-lĭn, păn′-) *n.* Any of several long-tailed, scale-covered mammals of the genus *Manis,* of tropical Africa and Asia, having a long snout and a sticky tongue with which it catches and eats ants. [Malay *pĕngguling* < *guling,* to roll.]

pan·han·dle¹ (păn′hăn′dl) *v.* **-dled, -dling, -dles.** *Informal. —intr.* To beg, esp. on the streets. *—tr.* To obtain by panhandling; beg from. [Back-formation < *panhandler,* beggar, from the resemblance of a beggar's outstretched arm to the handle of a pan.] **—pan′han′dler** *n.*

pan·han·dle² (păn′hăn′dl) *n.* **1.** The handle of a pan. **2.** Often **Panhandle.** A narrow strip of territory projecting from a larger, broader area to which it belongs in such a way that its borders as drawn on a map appear to outline the handle of a pan.

Pan-Hel·len·ic also **Pan·hel·len·ic** (păn′hə-lĕn′ĭk) *adj.* **1.** Of or pertaining to Greek peoples or a movement to unify them. **2.** Of or pertaining to Greek-letter fraternities and sororities.

pan·hu·man (păn-hyōō′mən) *adj.* Of or relating to all of humanity.

pan·ic (păn′ĭk) *n.* **1.** A sudden, overpowering terror, often affecting many people at once. **2.** Mass alarm concerning finances, often resulting in a depression. **3.** *Slang.* One that is uproariously funny. *—adj.* **1.** Of, pertaining to, or resulting from sudden, overwhelming terror. **2.** Often **Panic.** Of or pertaining to Pan. *—tr. & intr.v.* **-icked, -ick·ing, -ics.** To affect or be affected with panic. [< Fr. *panique,* terrified < Gk. *panikos* < *Pan,* Pan.] **—pan′ick·y** *adj.*

panic button *n.* **1.** A device for setting off an alarm in an emergency. **2.** *Slang.* A hasty, emotional response.

panic grass *n.* Any of numerous grasses of the genus *Panicum,* many of which are grown for grain and fodder. [ME *panik* < Lat. *panicum.*]

pan·i·cle (păn′ĭ-kəl) *n. Bot.* A flower cluster that is loosely and irregularly branched. [Lat. *panicula,* dim. of *panus,* a swelling.] **—pan′i·cled** *adj.*

pan·ic-strick·en (păn′ĭk-strĭk′ən) also **pan·ic-struck** (-strŭk′) *adj.* Overcome by panic; terrified.

pa·nic·u·late (pə-nĭk′yə-lĭt, -lāt′) also **pa·nic·u·lat·ed** (-lā′tĭd) *adj. Bot.* Growing or arranged in a panicle. [NLat. *paniculatus* < Lat. *panicula,* panicle. —see PANICLE.] **—pa·nic′u·late·ly** *adv.*

Pan·ja·bi (pŭn-jä′bē, -jăb′ē) *n.* Variant of **Punjabi.**

pan·jan·drum (păn-jăn′drəm) *n.* A muckamuck: *"Once an editor of ladies' magazines and now a panjandrum of the publishing business"* (Nat Hentoff). [After the Grand *Panjandrum,* a character in a nonsense farrago written by Samuel Foote (1720–1777).]

pan·mic·tic (păn-mĭk′tĭk) *adj.* Of or pertaining to panmixis. [PAN- + Gk. *miktos,* mixed < *mignunai,* to mix.]

pan·mix·is (păn-mĭk′sĭs) *n.* Random mating within a breeding population. [PAN- + Gk. *mixis,* act of mingling < *mignunai,* to mix.]

panne (păn) *n.* A special finish for velvet and satin that produces a high luster. [Fr. < OFr., fur lining < Lat. *penna,* feather.]

pan·nier (păn′yər, păn′ē-ər) *n.* **1.** A large wicker basket, esp.: **a.** One of a pair of baskets carried on either side of a pack animal. **b.** A basket carried on a person's back. **2. a.** A framework of wire, bone, or other material formerly used to expand a woman's skirt at the hips. **b.** A skirt or overskirt

panda
Ailuropoda melanoleuca

panicle

pannier

pansy

pantile

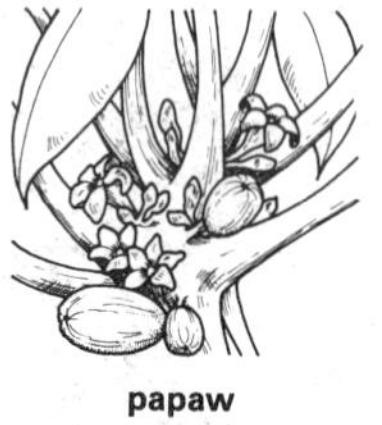
papaw

papaya
Above: Tree and fruit
Below: Fruit with cross section

puffed out at the hips. [ME *panier* < OFr. < Lat. *panarium,* breadbasket < *panis,* bread.] **—pan′niered** *adj.*
pan·ni·kin (păn′ĭ-kĭn) *n. Chiefly Brit.* A small saucepan or metal cup. [Dim. of PAN[1].]
pa·no·cha (pə-nō′chə) also **pa·no·che** (-chē) *n.* **1.** A coarse grade of Mexican sugar. **2.** Penuche. [Mex. Sp., pressed cakes of brown sugar, dim. of Sp. *pan,* bread < Lat. *panis.*]
pan·o·pho·bi·a (păn′ə-fō′bē-ə) *n.* Fear of everything. [PAN- + -PHOBIA.]
pan·o·ply (păn′ə-plē) *n., pl.* **-plies. 1.** The complete arms and armor of a warrior. **2.** A magnificent, shining array that covers or protects. [Gk. *panoplia* : *pan-,* all + *hoplon,* weapon.]
pan·op·tic (păn-ŏp′tĭk) also **pan·op·ti·cal** (-tĭ-kəl) *adj.* Including everything visible in one view. [< Gk. *panoptēs,* all-seeing : *pan-,* all + *optos,* visible.]
pan·o·ram·a (păn′ə-răm′ə, -rä′mə) *n.* **1.** An unlimited view of all visible objects over a wide area. **2.** A comprehensive picture of a chain of events or a specific subject: *a panorama of ancient history.* **3.** A picture or series of pictures representing a continuous scene, exhibited a part at a time by being unrolled and passed before the spectator. [PAN- + Gk. *horama,* sight < *horan,* to see.] **—pan′o·ram′ic** (-răm′ĭk) *adj.* **—pan′o·ram′i·cal·ly** *adv.*
pan·pipe (păn′pīp′) *n.* Often **panpipes.** A primitive wind instrument consisting of a series of pipes or reeds of graduated length bound together, played by blowing across the top open ends. [PAN + PIPE.]
pan·sy (păn′zē) *n., pl.* **-sies. 1.** A garden plant hybridized from *Viola tricolor hortensis,* having rounded, velvety petals of various colors. **2.** A deep to strong violet. **3.** *Slang.* An effeminate man, esp. a homosexual. [OFr. *pensée* < *pensée,* thought < *penser,* to think. —see PENSIVE.]
pant (pănt) *v.* **pant·ed, pant·ing, pants.** *—intr.* **1.** To breathe rapidly in short gasps, as after exertion. **2.** To give off or emit in loud puffs. **3.** To pulsate rapidly; throb. **4.** To yearn with frantic exhaustion. *—tr.* To utter hurriedly or breathlessly. *—n.* **1.** The act of panting. **2.** A short, labored breath; gasp. **3.** A short, loud puff, as of steam from an engine. **4.** A throb; pulsation. [ME *panten* < OFr. *pantaisier* < VLat. **phantasiare* < Gk. *phantasioun,* to cause to imagine < *phantasia,* appearance. —see FANTASY.] **—pant′ing·ly** *adv.*
pan·ta·lets also **pan·ta·lettes** (păn′tə-lĕts′) *pl.n.* **1.** Long underpants trimmed with ruffles extending below the skirt, worn by women in the mid-19th century. **2.** Frills attached to the legs of underpants. [< PANTALOON.]
pan·ta·loon (păn′tə-lo͞on′) *n.* **1. pantaloons. a.** Men's wide breeches extending from waist to ankle, and worn in England during the reign of Charles II. **b.** Tight trousers extending from waist to ankle with straps passing under the instep, worn esp. in the 19th century. **2. Pantaloon.** A character in the commedia dell'arte, portrayed as a foolish old man with slippers and tight trousers. **3.** A stock character, the butt of a clown's jokes in modern pantomime. [OFr. *pantalon,* a kind of trouser, after *Pantalon,* Pantaloon < OItal. *Pantalone.*]
pant·dress (pănt′drĕs′) *n.* **1.** Culottes. **2.** A dress worn over a matching set of shorts.
pan·tech·ni·con (păn-tĕk′nĭ-kŏn′, -kən) *n. Chiefly Brit.* **1.** A storage warehouse, esp. for furniture. **2.** A large truck, esp. a furniture van. [After *Pantechnicon,* London, England, a 19th-cent. bazaar that became a furniture warehouse.]
pan·the·ism (păn′thē-ĭz′əm) *n.* **1.** The doctrine identifying the Deity with the various forces and workings of nature. **2.** Belief in and worship of all gods. **—pan′the·ist** *n.* **—pan′the·is′tic, pan′the·is′ti·cal** *adj.* **—pan′the·is′ti·cal·ly** *adv.*
pan·the·on (păn′thē-ŏn′, -ən) *n.* **1. Pantheon.** A circular temple in Rome, completed in 27 B.C., and dedicated to all the gods. **2.** A temple dedicated to all gods. **3.** All the gods of a people. **4.** A public building commemorating and dedicated to the great persons of a nation. **5.** A group of famous persons. [ME *Panteon,* Pantheon < Lat. *Pantheon* < Gk. *pantheion,* pantheon : *pan-,* all + *theos,* god.]
pan·ther (păn′thər) *n.* **1.** The leopard, *Panthera pardus,* esp. in its black, unspotted form. **2.** The mountain lion. [ME *pantere* < OFr. < Lat. *panthera* < Gk. *panthēr.*]
pant·ies (păn′tēz) *pl.n.* Short underpants for women or children. [< PANTS.]
pan·tile (păn′tīl′) *n.* An S-curved roofing tile, laid so the down curve of one tile overlaps the up curve of the next one. [PAN[1] + TILE.] **—pan′tiled′** *adj.*
pan·tof·fle also **pan·to·fle** (păn-tŏf′əl, -tō′fəl, -to͞o′fəl, păn′tə-fəl) *n.* A slipper. [ME *pantufle* < OFr. *pantoufle.*]
pan·to·graph (păn′tə-grăf′) *n.* **1.** An instrument for copying a plane figure to any desired scale, consisting of styluses for tracing and copying mounted on four jointed rods in the form of a parallelogram with extended sides. **2.** A linked framework, such as a power-collecting trolley on an electric locomotive or an extensible telephone arm. [Fr. *pantographe* : Gk. *panto-,* all + Gk. *graphein,* to write.] **—pan′to·graph′ic** *adj.*
pan·to·mime (păn′tə-mīm′) *n.* **1. a.** A genre of theatrical performance, invented in Rome in the reign of Augustus, in which one actor played all the parts in dumb show, with music and singing in the background. **b.** The actor in this genre. **c.** Any of various revivals or derivatives of this genre. **2.** A British genre of musical plays for children, usually based on fairy stories, having specific conventions derived from the commedia dell'arte. **3.** Acting that consists mostly of gesture. **4.** Dumb show used for expressive communication. *—v.* **-mimed, -mim·ing, -mimes.** *—tr.* To represent by pantomime. *—intr.* To express oneself in pantomime. [Lat. *pantominus* < Gk. *pantomimos,* pantomimic actor : *pas,* all + *mimos,* mime.] **—pan′to·mim′ic** (-mĭm′ĭk), **pan′to·mim′i·cal** *adj.* **—pan′to·mim′ist** (-mī′mĭst) *n.*
pan·to·then·ate (păn′tə-thĕn′āt′, păn-tŏth′ə-nāt′) *n.* A salt or ester of pantothenic acid. [PANTOTHEN(IC ACID) + -ATE.]
pan·to·then·ic acid (păn′tə-thĕn′ĭk) *n.* A component of the vitamin B complex, $C_9H_{17}NO_5$, common in liver but found in all living tissue. [< Gk. *pantothen,* from all sides < *pas,* all.]
pan·toum (păn-to͞om′) *n.* A verse form that is comprised of quatrains in which the second and fourth lines are repeated as the first and third lines of the following quatrain, and in which the final line of the poem repeats the opening line. [Fr. < Malay *pantun.*]
pan·try (păn′trē) *n., pl.* **-tries. 1.** A small room or closet, usually off a kitchen, where food, china, silver, linens, and similar items are stored. **2.** A small room used for the preparation of cold foods. [ME *pantrie* < AN *panetrie,* bread-closet < OFr. *panetier,* pantry servant < *pan,* bread < Lat. *panis.*]
pan·try·man (păn′trē-măn′, -mən) *n.* A person who works in or is in charge of a pantry, as at a hotel.
pants (pănts) *pl.n.* **1.** Trousers. **2.** Underpants. ***—idiom.* with one's pants down.** In an embarrassing position. [Short for *pantaloons,* plural of PANTALOON.]
pant·suit also **pants suit** (pănt′so͞ot′) *n.* A woman's suit having trousers instead of a skirt.
pant·y·hose (păn′tē-hōz′) *n., pl.* **pantyhose.** A garment consisting of stretchable stockings and underpants in one piece.
pant·y raid (păn′tē) *n.* A raid on a girls' dormitory usually by college boys ostensibly to obtain undergarments as trophies.
pant·y·waist (păn′tē-wāst′) *n.* **1.** A child's undergarment consisting of a shirt and pants buttoned together at the waist. **2.** *Slang.* A weak, effeminate man. **—pant′y·waist′** *adj.*
pan·zer (păn′zər, pănt′sər) *adj.* **1.** Protected by armor; armored. **2.** Using or equipped with armored or mechanized units: *a panzer division.* *—n.* An armored tank. [G. < *Panzer,* armor < MHG *panzier* < OFr. *pancier* < *pance,* body. —see PAUNCH.]
panzer division *n.* A German division of armored vehicles, esp. tanks.
pap[1] (păp) *n.* **1.** *Chiefly Regional.* A teat or nipple. **2.** Something resembling a nipple. [ME.]
pap[2] (păp) *n.* **1.** Soft or semiliquid food, as for infants. **2.** Something lacking real value or substance and considered to be unsuitable for the minds of adults. **3.** *Slang.* Money and favors obtained as political patronage: *"uncouth, self-seeking politicians primarily interested in patronage, privilege, and pap"* (Fiorello LaGuardia). [ME.]
pa·pa (pä′pə, pə-pä′) also **pop·pa** (pä′pə) *n.* Father. [Fr.]
pa·pa·cy (pā′pə-sē) *n., pl.* **-cies. 1.** The office and jurisdiction of a pope. **2.** The period of time during which a pope is in office. **3. Papacy.** *Rom. Cath. Ch.* The system of church government headed by the pope. [ME *papacie* < Med. Lat. *papatia* < LLat. *papa,* pope. —see POPE.]
pa·pa·in (pə-pā′ĭn, -pī′ĭn) *n.* An enzyme capable of digesting protein, obtained from the unripe fruit of the papaya and used as a meat tenderizer and in medicine as a protein digestant. [< PAPAYA.]
pa·pal (pā′pəl) *adj.* **1.** Of, pertaining to, or issued by the pope: *a papal bull.* **2.** Of or pertaining to the papacy: *papal succession.* **3.** Of or pertaining to the Roman Catholic Church. [ME < OFr. < Med. Lat. *papalis* < LLat. *papa,* pope. —see POPE.] **—pa′pal·ly** *adv.*
Pa·pa·ni·co·laou's test (pä′pə-nē′kə-louz′) *n.* A Pap test.
pa·pa·raz·zo (pä′pə-rät′sō) *n., pl.* **-zi** (-sē). A reporter or photographer, esp. a free-lance one, who doggedly searches for sensational stories about or takes candid pictures of celebrities for magazines and newspapers. [After Signor *Paparazzo,* a character in *La Dolce Vita,* a movie, by Federico Fellini (b. 1920) < dial. Ital. *paparazzo,* a kind of buzzing insect.]
pa·pav·er·ine (pə-păv′ə-rēn′, -ər-ĭn) *n.* A nonaddictive opium derivative, $C_{20}H_{21}NO_4$, used medicinally as an antispasmodic. [Lat. *papaver,* poppy + -INE.]
pa·paw also **paw·paw** (pô′pô′) *n.* **1.** A tree, *Asimina triloba,* of central North America, having small, fleshy, edible fruit. **2.** The fruit of the papaw tree. [Prob. < Sp. *papaya,* papaya. —see PAPAYA.]
pa·pa·ya (pə-pä′yə) *n.* **1.** An evergreen tropical American tree, *Carica Papaya,* bearing large, yellow, edible fruit. **2.** The fruit of the papaya tree. [Sp., of Cariban orig.]
pa·per (pā′pər) *n.* **1.** A thin sheet material made of cellulose pulp, derived mainly from wood, rags, and certain grasses, processed into flexible leaves or rolls by deposit from an aqueous suspension, and used chiefly for writing, printing, drawing, wrapping, and covering walls. **2.** A single sheet of this material. **3.** One or more sheets of paper, bearing writ-

ing or printing, as: **a.** An official document. **b.** An essay, treatise, or scholarly dissertation. **c.** An examination, report, theme, or other written academic assignment. **d.** A newspaper. **4. papers.** A collection of letters, diaries, and other writings, esp. those produced by one person: *the Kennedy papers.* **5. papers.** Documents establishing the identity of the bearer. **6. papers.** Ship's papers. **7.** A negotiable note, such as a bill, check, or letter of credit; commercial paper. **8.** *Slang.* **a.** A free pass to a theater. **b.** The audience admitted with free passes. *—tr.v.* **-pered, -per·ing, -pers. 1.** To wrap or cover in paper. **2.** To supply with paper. **3.** To cover with wallpaper. **4.** *Slang.* To issue free passes for (a theater, for example). ***—phrasal verb.*** **paper over. 1.** To put or keep out of sight; conceal. **2.** To play down the significance of (a dispute, for example) by treating lightly or glossing over. *—adj.* **1.** Made of paper. **2.** Resembling paper in thinness or flimsiness. **3.** Existing only in printed or written form; planned but not realized; theoretical: *paper profits.* ***—idiom.*** **on paper. 1.** In writing or print. **2.** In theory, as distinguished from actual performance or fact: *a good team on paper, but the members really don't play well together.* [ME *papir* < OFr. *papier* < Lat. *papyrus,* papyrus paper < Gk. *papuros,* papyrus.] **—pa'per·er** *n.* **—pa'per·y** *adj.*

pa·per·back (pā'pər-băk') *n.* A book having a flexible paper binding. **—pa'per·backed'** *adj.*

paper birch *n.* A North American birch tree, *Betula papyrifera,* having paperlike white bark used to make baskets, toy canoes, and other articles.

pa·per·board (pā'pər-bôrd', -bōrd') *n.* Cardboard; pasteboard.

pa·per·bound (pā'pər-bound') *adj.* Bound in paper.

paper boy *n.* A person who sells or delivers newspapers.

paper cutter *n.* A usually square, often calibrated board with a long pivoting cutting knife attached to one side, used to trim paper to specific dimensions.

pa·per·hang·er (pā'pər-hăng'ər) *n.* **1.** A person whose occupation is covering or decorating walls with wallpaper; paperer. **2.** *Slang.* A person who passes bad checks. **—pa'per·hang'ing** *n.*

pa·per·knife (pā'pər-nīf') *n.* A thin, dull knife used for opening sealed envelopes, slitting uncut pages of books, and creasing paper.

paper money *n.* Currency in the form of government notes and bank notes.

paper mulberry *n.* A shade tree, *Broussonetia papyrifera,* native to Asia, having bark that can be processed into a paperlike fabric.

paper nautilus *n.* A marine mollusk, *Argonauta argo,* having a paper-thin spiral shell.

pa·per-thin (pā'pər-thĭn') *adj.* Very thin or shallow: *made of paper-thin material.*

paper tiger *n.* One that is seemingly dangerous and powerful but is in fact impotent and weak.

pa·per-train (pā'pər-trān') *tr.v.* **-trained, -train·ing, -trains.** To train (a dog, for example) to urinate and defecate indoors on paper.

paper wasp *n.* A wasp, such as a hornet, that builds paperlike nests.

pa·per·weight (pā'pər-wāt') *n.* A small heavy object, often decorative, placed on top of loose papers to keep them in place.

pa·per·work also **paper work** (pā'pər-wûrk') *n.* Work involving the handling of reports, letters, and forms.

pap·e·terie (păp'ĭ-trē, păp-trē') *n.* A box used to hold paper and other writing materials. [Fr. < *papier,* paper < OFr. — see PAPER.]

pa·pier-mâ·ché (pā'pər-mə-shā', pă-pyā'-) *n.* A material made from paper pulp or shreds of paper mixed with glue or paste, that can be molded into various shapes when wet and that becomes hard and suitable for painting and varnishing when dry. ***—modifier:*** *papier-mâché decorations.* [Fr. : *papier,* paper + *mâché,* p.part of *mâcher,* to chew.]

pa·pil·la (pə-pĭl'ə) *n., pl.* **-pil·lae** (-pĭl'ē). A small, nipplelike projection, such as a protuberance on the top of the tongue, at the root of a hair, or at the base of a developing tooth. [Lat., nipple.] **—pap'il·lar'y** (păp'ə-lĕr'ē, pə-pĭl'ə-rē) *adj.* **—pap'il·late'** (păp'ə-lāt', pə-pĭl'ĭt) *adj.* **—pap·il·lose** (păp'ə-lōs', pə-pĭl'ōs') *adj.*

pap·il·lo·ma (păp'ə-lō'mə) *n., pl.* **-ma·ta** (-mə-tə) or **-mas.** A small, benign epithelial tumor in the breast, intestine, mucous membrane, or skin, seen as an overgrowth of cells on a core of smooth connective tissue. [PAPILL(A) + -OMA.] **—pap'il·lom'a·tous** *adj.*

pap·il·lote (pä'pē-yōt', păp'ē-) *n.* **1.** A frilled paper cover used to decorate the bone end of a cooked chop or cutlet. **2.** Oiled parchment in which certain foods are baked. [Fr. < *papillon,* butterfly < Lat. *papilio.*]

pa·pist (pā'pĭst) *n. Offensive.* A Roman Catholic. [Fr. *papiste* < *pape,* pope < LLat. *papa.* —see POPE.] **—pa·pis'tic** (pə-pĭs'tĭk) *adj.* **—pa'pist·ry** *n.*

pa·poose (pă-pōōs', pə-) *n.* A North American Indian infant or young child. [Algonquian *papoos.*]

pa·po·va·vi·rus (pə-pō'və-vī'rəs) *n.* Any of a group of animal viruses that are associated with various tumors, such as warts or papillomas. [PA(PILLOMA) + PO(LYOMA) + VA(CUOLATION) + VIRUS.]

pap·pus (păp'əs) *n., pl.* **pap·pi** (păp'ī'). A tuft of bristles, or a similar structure, surmounting the achene of certain plants, such as dandelions and thistles. [Lat. < Gk. *pappos.*] **—pap'pose** (-ōs), **pap'pous** (-əs) *adj.*

pap·py¹ (păp'ē) *adj.* **-pi·er, -pi·est.** Of or like pap; mushy.

pap·py² (păp'ē) *n., pl.* **-pies.** Father. [Dim. of PAPA.]

pa·pri·ka (pă-prē'kə, pə-, păp'rĭ-kə) *n.* **1.** A mild, powdered seasoning made from sweet red peppers. **2.** A dark to deep or vivid reddish orange. [Hung. < Serbian < *papar,* pepper < Gk. *peperi.*]

Pap smear (păp) *n.* A Pap test.

Pap test *n. Med.* A test in which a smear of a bodily secretion, esp. from the cervix or vagina, is immediately fixed and examined for exfoliated cells to detect cancer in an early stage or to evaluate hormonal condition. [After George *Papanicolaou* (1883–1962), its inventor.]

Pap·u·an (păp'yōō-ən) *n.* **1.** A native or inhabitant of New Guinea. **2.** A member of a subgroup of an Oceanic Negroid people of Melanesia. **3.** Any of the indigenous languages of New Guinea, New Britain, and the Solomon Islands.

pap·ule (păp'yōōl) also **pap·u·la** (-yə-lə) *n., pl.* **-ules** also **-u·lae** (-yə-lē'). A small, inflammatory, congested spot on the skin; pimple. [Lat. *papula.*] **—pap'u·lar** (-yə-lər), **pap'u·lif'er·ous** (-yə-lĭf'ər-əs) *adj.*

pa·py·ri (pə-pī'rī') *n.* A plural of **papyrus.**

pap·y·rol·o·gy (păp'ə-rŏl'ə-jē) *n.* The study of papyrus manuscripts.

pa·py·rus (pə-pī'rəs) *n., pl.* **-rus·es** or **-ri** (-rī'). **1.** A tall aquatic sedge, *Cyperus papyrus,* of southern Europe and northern Africa. **2. a.** A paper made from the pith or the stems of the papyrus, used in antiquity as a writing material. **b.** A document written on this paper: *the Oxyrhynchus papyri.* [ME < Lat. < Gk. *papuros.*]

par (pär) *n.* **1.** An accepted average; normal standard: *up to par.* **2.** An equality of status, level, or value; equal footing: *on a par.* **3. a.** The established face value of a monetary unit expressed in terms of a monetary unit of another country using the same metal standard. **b.** A condition of equality between the face value of a stock, bond, or other negotiable instrument and its current market value: *sell at par.* **4.** The number of golf strokes considered necessary to complete a hole or course in expert play. *—tr.v.* **parred, par·ring, pars.** To score par on (a hole or course) in golf. *—adj.* **1.** Equal to the standard; normal. **2.** Of or pertaining to monetary face value. [< Lat., equal.]

par– *pref.* Variant of **para-¹.**

par·a¹ (păr'ə) *adj.* **1.** Of, pertaining to, or designating positions in a benzene ring separated by two carbon atoms. **2.** Designating a diatomic molecule in which the nuclei have opposite spin directions. [< PARA-¹.]

pa·ra² (pä-rä', pä'rä) *n.* See table at **currency.** [Turk. < Pers. *parāh.*]

para–¹ or **par–** *pref.* **1.** Beside; near; alongside: *parathyroid.* **2.** Beyond: *paranormal.* **3.** Incorrect; abnormal: *paresthesia.* **4.** Resembling; similar to: *paratyphoid.* **5.** Subsidiary; assistant: *paraprofessional.* **6.** Isomeric; polymeric: *paraldehyde.* **7.** Substitution of radicals at two opposite ends of the benzene ring: *paradichlorobenzene.* [ME < OFr. < Lat. < Gk. < *para,* beside.]

para–² *pref.* Parachute; parachutist: *paratroops.* [< PARACHUTE.]

–para *suff.* A woman who has given birth to a specified number of children: *multipara.* [Lat. < *parere,* to give birth.]

par·a-a·mi·no·ben·zo·ic acid (păr'ə-ə-mē'nō-bĕn-zō'ĭk, -ăm'ə-) *n.* A crystalline para form of aminobenzoic acid that is part of the vitamin B complex.

par·a·bi·o·sis (păr'ə-bī-ō'sĭs) *n.* The natural or artificial fusion of two organisms, as in the development of Siamese twins or the experimental joining of animals for research. **—par'a·bi·ot'ic** *adj.* **—par'a·bi·ot'i·cal·ly** *adv.*

par·a·blast (păr'ə-blăst') *n.* The food yolk of a meroblastic egg. **—par'a·blas'tic** *adj.*

par·a·ble (păr'ə-bəl) *n.* A simple story illustrating a moral or religious lesson. [ME < OFr. *parabole* < LLat. *parabola* < Gk. *parabolē* < *paraballein,* to compare : *para,* beside + *ballein,* to throw.]

pa·rab·o·la (pə-răb'ə-lə) *n.* A plane curve formed by: **a.** A conic section taken parallel to an element of the intersected cone. **b.** The locus of points equidistant from a fixed line and a fixed point not on the line. [NLat. < Gk. *parabolē* < *paraballein,* to compare. —see PARABLE.]

par·a·bol·ic (păr'ə-bŏl'ĭk) also **par·a·bol·i·cal** (-ĭ-kəl) *adj.* **1.** Of or like a parable. **2.** Of or having the form of a parabola. **—par'a·bol'i·cal·ly** *adv.*

pa·rab·o·loid (pə-răb'ə-loid') *n.* A surface having parabolic sections parallel to a single coordinate axis, such as a paraboloid of revolution. [PARABOL(A) + -OID.] **—pa·rab'o·loi'dal** (-loid'l) *adj.*

par·a·chute (păr'ə-shōōt') *n.* **1.** An apparatus used to retard free fall from an aircraft, consisting of a hemispherical canopy attached by conically arrayed cords to a harness and worn or stored folded until deployed in descent. **2.** Any of various unpowered devices similar to a parachute that are used for retarding free-speeding or free-falling motion. **3.** A membranous, winglike extension between the limbs of flying squirrels and certain lizards; patagium. *—v.* **-chut·ed,**

papoose

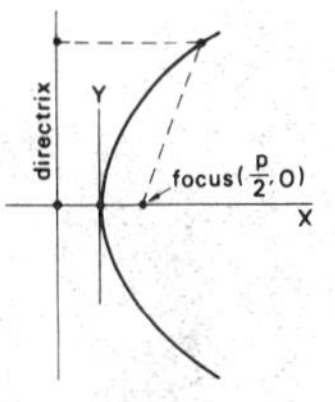

parabola
Dashed lines, from focus and directrix to any point on parabola, are equal. Equation of parabola is $y^2 = 2px$

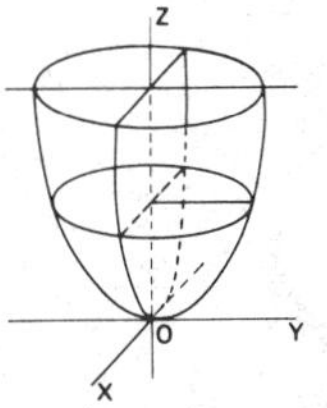

paraboloid
Equation of paraboloid shown is

$$\frac{x^2}{a^2} + \frac{y^2}{b^2} = 2cz,$$

where *a*, *b*, and *c* are constants

parachute

p **pop** / r **roar** / s **sauce** / sh **ship, dish** / t **tight** / th **thin, path** / *th* **this, bathe** / ŭ **cut** / ûr **urge** / v **valve** / w **with** / y **yes** / z **zebra, size** / zh **vision** / ə **about, item, edible, gallop, circus** / œ *Fr.* **feu,** *Ger.* **schön** / ü *Fr.* **tu,** *Ger.* **über** / KH *Ger.* **ich,** *Scot.* **loch** / N *Fr.* **bon.**

-chut·ing, -chutes. —*tr.* To drop (supplies, for example) by means of a parachute. —*intr.* To descend by means of a parachute. [Fr., blend of *parasol,* parasol + *chute,* fall.] **—par'a·chut'ic** *adj.* **—par'a·chut'ist** *n.*

parachute spinnaker *n. Naut.* An oversized spinnaker used on racing yachts.

Par·a·clete (păr'ə-klēt') *n.* The Holy Ghost. [ME *Paraclit* < OFr. *Paraclet* < LLat. *Paracletus* < Gk. *Paraklētos* < *parakalein,* to invoke : *para,* to the side of + *kalein,* to call.]

pa·rade (pə-rād') *n.* **1. a.** A public procession on a festive or ceremonial occasion. **b.** The occasion or action of making such a procession. **c.** The event itself or the persons involved. **d.** An assembly or congregation, as of strollers. **2. a.** A ceremonial review of troops. **b.** The troops taking part in a review. **c.** The place of assembly for a review of troops. **3.** A succession: *the parade of fads and styles.* **4.** A movement deriving momentum and strength from the increasing popularity of its approach to a political issue; bandwagon. **5.** An ostentatious show; a pompous display: *make a parade of humanitarian zeal.* **6.** A public square or promenade. —*v.* **-rad·ed, -rad·ing, -rades.** —*tr.* **1.** To assemble (troops) for a formal display or review. **2.** To march or walk through or around. **3.** To exhibit ostentatiously; flaunt. —*intr.* **1.** To assemble for a formal military review. **2.** To take part in a parade. **3.** To promenade in a public place. [Fr. < Ital. *parata* < Lat. *parare,* to prepare.] **—pa·rad'er** *n.*

par·a·di·chlo·ro·ben·zene (păr'ə-dī-klôr'ə-bĕn'zēn', -bĕn-zēn', -klōr'-) *n.* A white crystalline compound, $C_6H_4Cl_2$, used as a germicide and insecticide.

parallel bars

par·a·digm (păr'ə-dīm', -dĭm') *n.* **1.** A list of all the inflectional forms of a word taken as an illustrative example of the conjugation or declension to which it belongs. **2.** An example or model. [ME, example < LLat. *paradigma* < Gk. *paradeigma* < *paradeiknunai,* to exhibit : *para,* alongside + *deiknunai,* to show.] **—par'a·dig·mat'ic** (-dĭg-măt'ĭk) *adj.*

par·a·dise (păr'ə-dīs', -dīz') *n.* **1.** Often **Paradise.** The Garden of Eden. **2.** *Theol.* **a.** The abode of righteous souls after death; heaven. **b.** An intermediate resting place for righteous souls awaiting the Resurrection. **3.** A place of ideal beauty or loveliness. **4.** A state of delight. [ME *paradis* < OFr. < LLat. *paradisus* < Gk. *paradeisos,* garden < Avestan *pairi-daēza-* : *pairi,* around + *daēza-,* wall.] **—par'a·di·si'a·cal** (păr'ə-dĭ-sī'ə-kəl, -zī'ə-kəl), **par'a·di·sa'i·cal** (-dĭ-sā'ĭ-kəl, -zā'ĭ-kəl) *adj.* **—par'a·di·si'a·cal·ly, par'a·di·sa'i·cal·ly** *adv.*

par·a·dox (păr'ə-dŏks') *n., pl.* **-dox·es. 1.** A seemingly contradictory statement that may nonetheless be true. **2.** One exhibiting inexplicable or contradictory aspects. **3.** An assertion that is essentially self-contradictory, although based on a valid deduction from acceptable premises. **4.** A statement contrary to received opinion. [Lat. *paradoxum* < Gk. *paradoxon* < *paradoxos,* conflicting with expectation : *para,* beyond + *doxa,* opinion < *dokein,* to think.] **—par'a·dox'i·cal** *adj.* **—par'a·dox'i·cal·ly** *adv.* **—par'a·dox'i·cal·ness** *n.*

par·a·drop (păr'ə-drŏp') *n.* The delivery of supplies to a place by parachute. —*tr.v.* **-dropped, -drop·ping, -drops.** To deliver by parachute.

par·aes·the·sia (păr'ĭs-thē'zhə) *n.* Variant of **paresthesia.**

par·af·fin (păr'ə-fĭn) *n.* **1.** *Chem.* A waxy, white or colorless, solid hydrocarbon mixture used to make candles, wax paper, lubricants, and sealing materials. **2.** *Chem.* A member of the paraffin series. **3.** *Chiefly Brit.* Kerosene. —*tr.v.* **-fined, -fin·ing, -fins.** To saturate, impregnate, or coat with paraffin. [G. : Lat. *parum,* too little + Lat. *affinis,* associated with (from its lack of affinity with other material).] **—par'af·fin'ic** *adj.*

paraffin series *n. Chem.* A homologous group of saturated aliphatic hydrocarbons having the general formula C_nH_{2n+2}, the simplest and most abundant of which is methane.

paraffin wax *n.* Paraffin (sense 1).

parallelogram

par·a·for·mal·de·hyde (păr'ə-fôr-măl'də-hīd') *n.* A white solid polymer of formaldehyde, $(HCHO)_n$, where *n* is at least 6, used as a disinfectant, a fumigant, and a fungicide.

par·a·gen·e·sis (păr'ə-jĕn'ĭ-sĭs) also **par·a·ge·ne·sia** (-jə-nē'zhə, -zhē-ə) *n.* The successive order in which a formation of associated minerals is generated. **—par'a·ge·net'ic** (-jə-nĕt'ĭk) *adj.*

par·a·gon (păr'ə-gŏn', -gən) *n.* **1.** A model or pattern of excellence or perfection of a kind; peerless example: *a paragon of virtue.* **2. a.** An unflawed diamond weighing at least 100 carats. **b.** A very large spherical pearl. **3.** *Printing.* A type size of 20 points. —*tr.v.* **-goned, -gon·ing, -gons.** To parallel or match. [OFr. < OItal. *paragone* < *paragonare,* to test on a touchstone < Gk. *parakonan,* to sharpen : *para,* alongside + *akonē,* whetstone.]

par·a·graph (păr'ə-grăf') *n.* **1.** A distinct division of a written work or composition that expresses a thought or point relevant to the whole but is complete in itself, and may consist of a single sentence or several sentences. **2.** A mark (¶) used to indicate where a new paragraph should begin or to serve as a reference mark. **3.** A brief article, notice, or announcement, as in a newspaper. —*tr.v.* **-graphed, -graph·ing, -graphs.** To divide or arrange in paragraphs. [OFr. *paragraphe* < Med. Lat. *paragraphus,* sign marking a new paragraph < Gk. *paragraphos,* line in a dialogue showing a change of speakers < *paragraphein,* to write beside : *para,* beside + *graphein,* to write.] **—par'a·graph'ic, par'a·graph'i·cal** *adj.*

Par·a·guay tea (păr'ə-gwī', -gwā') *n.* Maté (sense 2).

par·a·jour·nal·ism (păr'ə-jûr'nə-lĭz'əm) *n.* Very subjective journalism. **—par'a·jour'nal·ist** *n.* **—par'a·jour'nal·is'tic** *adj.*

par·a·keet (păr'ə-kēt') *n.* Any of various small parrots, usually having long, tapering tails. [OFr. *paroquet.*]

par·a·kite (păr'ə-kīt') *n.* A specialized parachute that is towed by an automobile or motorboat and that lifts a person in its harness up and through the air.

par·al·de·hyde (pă-răl'də-hīd') *n.* A colorless aromatic liquid polymer, $C_6H_{12}O_3$, of acetaldehyde, used as a solvent and as a sedative. [PAR(A)-[1] + (ACET)ALDEHYDE.]

par·a·le·gal (păr'ə-lē'gəl) *adj.* Of, relating to, or being a person with specialized training who assists a lawyer. **—par'a·le'gal** *n.*

par·al·lax (păr'ə-lăks') *n.* An apparent change in the direction of an object, caused by a change in observational position that provides a new line of sight. [Fr. *parallaxe* < Gk. *parallaxis* < *parallassein,* to change : *para,* among + *allassein,* to exchange < *allos,* other.] **—par'al·lac'tic** (-lăk'tĭk) *adj.*

par·al·lel (păr'ə-lĕl') *adj.* **1.** Being an equal distance apart at every point. **2. a.** Designating two or more straight coplanar lines that do not intersect. **b.** Designating two or more planes that do not intersect. **c.** Designating a line and a plane that do not intersect. **d.** Designating curves or surfaces everywhere equidistant. **3. a.** Having comparable parts, analogous aspects, or readily recognized similarities. **b.** Having the same tendency or direction. **4.** *Gram.* Containing or characterized by corresponding syntactical forms or constructions. **5.** *Mus.* Moving consistently by the same intervals. Used of two or more melodies. **6.** *Elect.* Designating a circuit or part of a circuit connected in parallel. —*adv.* In a parallel relationship or manner. —*n.* **1.** A surface or line that is equidistant from another. **2.** One of a set of parallel geometric figures, usually lines. **3. a.** Something that closely resembles or is analogous to something else. **b.** A comparison indicating likeness or analogy. **4.** The condition of being parallel; near similarity or exact agreement in particulars. **5.** Any of the imaginary lines representing degrees of latitude that encircle the earth parallel to the plane of the equator. **6.** *Printing.* A sign indicating material referred to in a note or reference. **7.** *Elect.* A configuration of two or more two-terminal components connected between two points in a circuit with one terminal of each connected to each of the two points. Used chiefly in the phrase *in parallel.* —*tr.v.* **-leled, -lel·ing, -lels. 1.** To make or place parallel to. **2.** To be or extend parallel to. **3.** To be similar or analogous to. **4.** To be or provide an equal or match for. **5.** To show to be analogous; compare or liken. [Lat. *parallelus* < Gk. *parallēlos* : *para,* beside + *allēlōn,* of one another < *allos,* other.]

parallel bars *pl.n.* Two horizontal poles set parallel to each other in adjustable upright supports and used in gymnastic exercises.

par·al·lel·e·pi·ped (păr'ə-lĕl'ə-pī'pĭd, -pĭp'ĭd) *n.* A solid with six faces, each a parallelogram. [Gk. *parallēlepipedon* : *parallēlos,* parallel + *epipedon,* plane surface < *epipedos,* level (*epi,* on + *pedon,* ground).]

par·al·lel·ism (păr'ə-lĕ-lĭz'əm) *n.* **1.** The state or position of being parallel; a parallel relationship. **2.** Likeness, correspondence, or similarity in aspect, course, or tendency. **3.** *Gram.* **a.** The use of corresponding syntactical forms. **b.** An instance of this. **4.** *Philos.* The doctrine that to every mental change there corresponds a concomitant, but causally unconnected, physical alteration.

par·al·lel·o·gram (păr'ə-lĕl'ə-grăm') *n.* A four-sided plane figure with opposite sides parallel. [LLat. *parallelogrammum,* Gk. *parallēlogrammon* < *parallēlogrammos,* bound by parallel lines : *parallēlos,* parallel + *grammē,* line.]

pa·ral·o·gism (pə-răl'ə-jĭz'əm) *n. Logic.* Fallacious or illogical reasoning, esp. a faulty argument of whose fallacy the reasoner is not aware. [Fr. *paralogisme* < LLat. *paralogismus* < Gk. *paralogismos* < *paralogos,* unreasonable : *para,* beyond + *logos,* reason.] **—pa·ral'o·gist** *n.* **—pa·ral'o·gis'tic** *adj.*

par·a·lyse (păr'ə-līz') *v. Chiefly Brit.* Variant of **paralyze.**

pa·ral·y·sis (pə-răl'ĭ-sĭs) *n., pl.* **-ses** (-sēz'). **1.** Loss or impairment of the ability to move or have sensation in a bodily part as a result of injury to or disease of its nerve supply. **2.** Partial or complete inability to move or function; stoppage or impairment of activity. [Lat. < Gk. *paralusis* < *paraluein,* to disable : *para-,* in an injurious way + *luein,* to release.] **—par'a·lyt'ic** (păr'ə-lĭt'ĭk) *adj. & n.*

paralysis ag·i·tans (ăj'ĭ-tănz') *n.* Parkinson's disease. [NLat. : Lat. *paralysis,* palsy + Lat. *agitans,* pr.part. of *agitare,* to shake.]

par·a·lyze (păr'ə-līz') *tr.v.* **-lyzed, -lyz·ing, -lyz·es. 1.** To affect with paralysis; cause to be paralytic. **2.** To make helpless or unable to move: *paralyzed by fear.* **3.** To impair the progress or functioning of; make inoperative or powerless. [Fr. *paralyser* < *paralysie,* paralysis < Lat. *paralysis.*] **—par'a·ly·za'tion** *n.* **—par'a·lyz'er** *n.*

par·a·mag·net (păr'ə-măg'nĭt) *n.* A paramagnetic substance.

par·a·mag·net·ic (păr'ə-măg-nĕt'ĭk) *adj.* Pertaining to or denoting a substance in which an induced magnetic field is in the same direction as and greater in strength than the magnetizing field, but much weaker than in ferromagnetic materials. **—par′a·mag·net′i·cal·ly** *adv.* **—par′a·mag′net·ism** (-măg′nĭ-tĭz′əm) *n.*

par·a·mat·ta or **par·ra·mat·ta** (păr′ə-măt′ə) *n.* A fine, lightweight, silk-and-wool or cotton-and-wool dress fabric. [After *Parramatta,* Australia.]

par·a·me·ci·um (păr′ə-mē′shē-əm, -sē-əm) *n., pl.* **-ci·a** (-shē-ə, -sē-ə) or **-ci·ums.** Any of various ciliate protozoans of the genus *Paramecium,* usually oval and having an oral groove for feeding. [NLat. *Paramecium,* genus name < Gk. *paramēkes,* oblong : *para,* alongside + *mēkos,* length.]

par·a·med·ic (păr′ə-mĕd′ĭk) *n.* A person who is trained to supply emergency medical treatment or to assist medical professionals.

par·a·med·i·cal (păr′ə-mĕd′ĭ-kəl) *adj.* Of or designating the work of paramedics; relating to auxiliary medical personnel.

par·a·ment (păr′ə-mənt) *n., pl.* **-ments** or **-men·ta** (-mĕn′tə). Often **paraments** or **paramenta.** Ecclesiastical vestments or hangings. [ME < Med. Lat. *paramentum* < *parare,* to decorate < Lat., to prepare.]

pa·ram·e·ter (pə-răm′ĭ-tər) *n.* **1.** A variable or an arbitrary constant appearing in a mathematical expression, each value of which restricts or determines the specific form of the expression. **2.** *Informal.* **a.** A fixed limit or boundary; constant. **b.** A characteristic element: *terrorism as a parameter of this generation.* **—par′a·met′ric** (păr′ə-mĕt′rĭk), **par′a·met′ri·cal** *adj.* **—par′a·met′ri·cal·ly** *adv.*

Usage: This scientific term has been adapted to general usage. It is sometimes used in the sense of "a constant, a given, or a precondition" and sometimes in the sense of "a limit or boundary" (perhaps influenced by *perimeter*): *We must stay within the parameters of the present budget. They want to narrow the parameters of public debate. Violence and rebellion are parameters of modern life.* None of these examples is acceptable to a majority of the Usage Panel.

par·a·mil·i·tar·y (păr′ə-mĭl′ĭ-tĕr′ē) *adj.* Of, relating to, or designating forces organized after a military pattern, esp. as an auxiliary military force.

par·am·ne·sia (păr′ăm-nē′zhə) *n.* A distortion of memory in which fantasy and experience are confused.

pa·ra·mo (pä′rə-mō′, păr′ə-) *n., pl.* **-mos.** A high, treeless plain of tropical South America. [Sp. *páramo,* open desolate land.]

par·a·morph (păr′ə-môrf′) *n.* A mineral crystal formed or affected by paramorphism.

par·a·mor·phine (păr′ə-môr′fēn′) *n.* Thebaine.

par·a·mor·phism (păr′ə-môr′fĭz′əm) *n.* Structural alteration of a mineral without change of chemical composition. **—par′a·mor′phic, par′a·mor′phous** *adj.*

par·a·mount (păr′ə-mount′) *adj.* **1.** Of chief concern or importance; foremost. **2.** Supreme in rank, power, or authority. *—n.* A person of the highest power or authority; supreme ruler. [AN *paramont* : OFr. *par,* by (< Lat. *per*) + OFr. *amont,* above.] **—par′a·mount′cy** *n.* **—par′a·mount′ly** *adv.*

par·a·mour (păr′ə-mo͝or′) *n.* A lover of either sex, esp. one in an adulterous relationship. [ME < *par amour,* by way of love < OFr. : *par,* by (< Lat. *per*) + *amour,* love (< Lat. *amor* < *amare,* to love).]

par·am·y·lum (pă-răm′ə-ləm) *n.* A reserve carbohydrate resembling starch that is found in various protozoans and algae.

pa·rang (pä′răng′) *n.* A short, heavy, straight-edged knife used in Malaysia and Indonesia as a tool and weapon. [Malay.]

par·a·noi·a (păr′ə-noi′ə) *n.* A nondegenerative, limited, usually chronic psychosis characterized by delusions of persecution or of grandeur, strenuously defended by the afflicted with apparent logic and reason. [NLat. < Gk., *madness* < *paranoos,* demented : *para,* beyond + *nous,* mind.]

par·a·noi·ac (păr′ə-noi′ăk′, -noi′ĭk) *n.* One who is afflicted with paranoia. *—adj.* Of, pertaining to, or resembling paranoia.

par·a·noid (păr′ə-noid′) *adj.* **1.** Pertaining to, characteristic of, or afflicted with paranoia. **2.** Suggestive of paranoia; showing unreasonable distrust, suspicion, or an exaggerated sense of one's own importance. *—n.* One afflicted with paranoia.

par·a·nor·mal (păr′ə-nôr′məl) *adj.* Not within the range of normal experience or scientifically explainable phenomena. **—par′a·nor·ma′li·ty** *n.* **—par′a·nor′mal·ly** *adv.*

par·an·thro·pus (păr′ən-thrō′pəs, pă-răn′thrə-pəs) *n., pl.* **-pus·es.** One of a genus, *Paranthropus,* of extinct anthropoid apes, known from remains found in Olduvai Gorge, Tanzania. [NLat. *Paranthropus,* genus name : PARA-[1] + Gk. *anthropos,* man.]

par·a·pet (păr′ə-pĭt, -pĕt′) *n.* **1.** A low, protective wall or railing along the edge of a roof, balcony, or similar structure. **2.** An earthen or stone embankment protecting soldiers from enemy fire. [Fr. < Ital. *parapetto* : *parare,* to shield + *petto,* chest < Lat. *pectus.*] **—par′a·pet′ed** (-pĕt′ĭd) *adj.*

par·aph (păr′əf, pə-răf′) *n.* A flourish made after or below a signature, originally to prevent forgery. [OFr. *parraphe* < Med. Lat. *paragraphus,* paragraph sign. —see PARAGRAPH.]

par·a·pher·na·lia (păr′ə-fər-nāl′yə, -fə-nāl′yə) *pl.n. (used with a sing. or pl. verb).* **1.** Personal belongings. **2.** The articles used in a given activity; equipment: *drug paraphernalia.* **3.** A married woman's personal property exclusive of her dowry, according to common law. [Med. Lat., a married woman's property exclusive of her dowry < Gk. *parapherna* : *para,* beyond + *phernē,* dowry.]

par·a·phrase (păr′ə-frāz′) *n.* **1.** A restatement of a text or passage in another form or other words, often to clarify meaning. **2.** The making of paraphrases, often used as a teaching device. *—v.* **-phrased, -phras·ing, -phras·es.** *—tr.* To express in a paraphrase. *—intr.* To compose a paraphrase. [OFr. < Lat. *paraphrasis* < Gk. < *paraphrazein,* to paraphrase : *para,* alongside + *phrazein,* to show.] **—par′a·phras′a·ble** *adj.* **—par′a·phras′er** *n.*

par·a·phras·tic (păr′ə-frăs′tĭk) or **par·a·phras·ti·cal** (-tĭ-kəl) *adj.* **1.** Of the nature of a paraphrase. **2.** Explaining or translating more amply or clearly. [Fr. *paraphrastique* < Gk. *paraphrastikos* < *paraphrazein,* to paraphrase.] **—par′a·phras′ti·cal·ly** *adv.*

parapet

pa·raph·y·sis (pə-răf′ĭ-sĭs) *n., pl.* **-ses** (-sēz′). One of the sterile filaments accompanying the spore-carrying or sexual organs of certain fungi or other cryptogamic plants. [PARA-[1] + Gk. *phusis,* nature.]

par·a·ple·gi·a (păr′ə-plē′jē-ə, -jə) *n.* Complete paralysis of the lower half of the body including both legs that is caused by injury to or disease of the spinal cord. [NLat. < Gk. *paraplēgia,* hemiplegia < *paraplēssein,* to strike on one side : *para,* beside + *plēssein,* to strike.] **—par′a·ple′gic** (-plē′jĭk) *adj. & n.*

par·a·po·di·um (păr′ə-pō′dē-əm) *n., pl.* **-di·a** (dē-ə). One of the fleshy paired appendages of each body segment in some annelids that function in locomotion and breathing.

par·a·pro·fes·sion·al (păr′ə-prə-fĕsh′ə-nəl) *n.* A worker who is not a member of a given profession but who assists a professional.

par·a·psy·chol·o·gy (păr′ə-sī-kŏl′ə-jē) *n.* The study of phenomena, such as telepathy, clairvoyance, and psychokinesis, that are not explainable by known natural laws. **—par′a·psy′cho·log′i·cal** *adj.* **—par′a·psy·chol′o·gist** *n.*

par·a·quat (păr′ə-kwŏt′) *n.* A yellow compound, $C_{12}H_{14}N_2Cl_2$, used as a herbicide. [PARA- + QUAT(ERNARY).]

Pa·rá rubber (pə-rä′, păr′ə) *n.* Rubber obtained from various tropical South American trees of the genus *Hevea,* esp. *H. brasiliensis.* [After *Pará,* a state in Brazil.]

par·a·sang (păr′ə-săng′) *n.* An ancient Persian unit of distance, usually estimated at $3^1/_2$ miles. [Lat. *parasanga* < Gk. *parasangas,* of Iranian orig.]

par·a·se·le·ne (păr′ə-sĭ-lē′nē) *n., pl.* **-nae** (-nē). A luminous spot on a lunar halo. [PARA-[1] + Gk. *selēnē,* moon.] **—par′a·se·le′nic** (-lē′nĭk, -lĕn′ĭk) *adj.*

par·a·site (păr′ə-sīt′) *n.* **1.** *Biol.* An organism that grows, feeds, and is sheltered on or in a different organism while contributing nothing to the survival of its host. **2.** A person who habitually takes advantage of the generosity of others without making any useful return. **3.** A professional dinner guest, esp. in ancient Greece. **4.** A sycophant. [OFr., a person who continually eats at the expense of another < Lat. *parasitus* < Gk. *parasitos* : *para,* beside + *sitos,* grain.]

par·a·sit·ic (păr′ə-sĭt′ĭk) also **par·a·sit·i·cal** (-ĭ-kəl) *adj.* **1.** Of, pertaining to, or characteristic of a parasite. **2.** Caused by a parasite, as certain diseases. **—par′a·sit′i·cal·ly** *adv.*

par·a·sit·i·cide (păr′ə-sĭt′ĭ-sīd′) *n.* An agent or preparation used to destroy parasites. *—adj.* Destructive to parasites. **—par′a·sit′i·ci′dal** (-sīd′l) *adj.*

par·a·sit·ism (păr′ə-sĭ-tĭz′əm, -sī-) *n.* **1.** The characteristic behavior or mode of existence of a parasite. **2.** A diseased condition resulting from parasitic infestation.

par·a·sit·ize (păr′ə-sĭ-tīz′, -sī-) *tr.v.* **-ized, -iz·ing, -iz·es.** To live on (a host) as a parasite.

par·a·si·tol·o·gy (păr′ə-sĭ-tŏl′ə-jē, -sī-) *n.* The scientific study of parasitism. **—par′a·si′to·log′ic** (-sĭ′tə-lŏj′ĭk), **par′a·si′to·log′i·cal** *adj.* **—par′a·si·tol′o·gist** *n.*

par·a·sit·o·sis (păr′ə-sĭ-tō′sĭs, -sī-) *n.* A disease that results from parasitism.

parasol

par·a·sol (păr′ə-sôl′, -sŏl′) *n.* A light, usually small umbrella carried esp. by women as protection from the sun. [Fr. < OItal. *parasole* : *parare,* to shield + *sole,* sun < Lat. *sol.*]

par·a·sym·pa·thet·ic nervous system (păr′ə-sĭm′pə-thĕt′ĭk) *n. Anat.* The part of the autonomic nervous system originating in the central and back parts of the brain and in the lower part of the spinal cord that, in general, inhibits or opposes the physiological effects of the sympathetic nervous system, as in tending to stimulate digestive secretions, slowing the heart, and dilating blood vessels.

par·a·syn·the·sis (păr′ə-sĭn′thĭ-sĭs) *n. Gram.* The formation of words by a combination of compounding and adding an affix, as in *downhearted,* formed from *down* plus *heart* plus *-ed,* not *down* plus *hearted.* **—par′a·syn·thet′ic** (-thĕt′ĭk) *adj.*

par·a·tax·is (păr′ə-tăk′sĭs) *n.* The coordination of grammatical elements such as phrases or clauses without the use of coordinating elements such as conjunctions, as *It was cold; the snows came.* [Gk., a placing side by side < *paratassein,* to arrange side by side : *para,* beside + *tassein,* to arrange.]

—**par′a·tac′tic** (-tăk′tĭk), **par′a·tac′ti·cal** *adj.* —**par′a·tac′ti·cal·ly** *adv.*

par·a·thi·on (păr′ə-thī′ŏn′) *n.* A highly poisonous yellowish liquid agricultural insecticide, $(C_2H_5O)_2P(S)OC_6H_4NO_2$. [PARA-¹ + thio(phosphate) + -ON.]

par·a·thy·roid·ec·to·my (păr′ə-thī′roi-dĕk′tə-mē) *n., pl.* **-mies.** The surgical excision of the parathyroid glands.

par·a·thy·roid gland (păr′ə-thī′roid′) *n.* Any of four small kidney-shaped glands that lie in pairs near the lateral lobes of the thyroid gland and secrete a hormone necessary for calcium and phosphorus metabolism.

par·a·troop (păr′ə-tro͞op′) *adj.* Of or pertaining to paratroops: *a paratroop landing.*

par·a·troop·er (păr′ə-tro͞o′pər) *n.* A member of the paratroops.

par·a·troops (păr′ə-tro͞ops′) *pl.n.* Infantry trained and equipped to parachute.

par·a·ty·phoid fever (păr′ə-tī′foid′) *n.* An acute intestinal disease, similar to typhoid fever but less severe and caused by any of three bacteria of the genus *Salmonella.*

par·a·vane (păr′ə-vān′) *n.* A device equipped with sharp teeth and towed alongside a ship to cut the mooring cables of submerged mines.

par·boil (pär′boil′) *tr.v.* **-boiled, -boil·ing, -boils. 1.** To cook partially by boiling for a brief period. **2.** To subject to intense, often uncomfortable heat. [ME *parboilen* < *parboilen,* to boil thoroughly < OFr. *parboillir* < LLat. *perbullire* : Lat. *per,* thoroughly + *bullire,* to boil.]

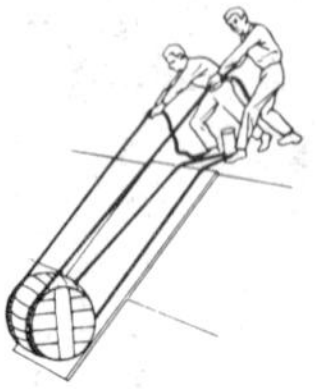

parbuckle

par·buck·le (pär′bŭk′əl) *n.* **1.** A rope sling for rolling cylindrical objects up or down an inclined plane. **2.** A sling for raising or lowering an object vertically. —*tr.v.* **-led, -ling, -les.** To raise or lower with a parbuckle. [Orig. unknown.]

Par·cae (pär′sē) *pl.n. Rom. Myth.* The Three Fates. [Lat.]

par·cel (pär′səl) *n.* **1.** Something wrapped up or packaged; package. **2.** A portion or plot of land, usually a division of a larger area. **3.** A quantity of merchandise offered for sale. **4.** A group or company; pack: *a parcel of idiots.* —*tr.v.* **-celed, -cel·ing, -cels. 1.** To divide into allotments and distribute. **2.** To make into a parcel; package. **3.** *Naut.* To wind protective strips of canvas around (rope). [ME, portion < OFr. *parcelle* < Lat. *particula,* dim. of *pars,* part.]

parcel post *n.* The branch of the postal service that handles and delivers parcels sent through the mail.

par·ce·nar·y (pär′sə-nĕr′ē) *n., pl.* **-ies.** *Law.* Coparcenary (sense 1). [AN *parcenarie* < OFr. *parçonerie* < *parçonier,* partner. —see PARCENER.]

par·ce·ner (pär′sə-nər) *n. Law.* A coparcener. [ME < AN < OFr. *parçonier* < *parçon,* partition < Lat. *partitio.* —see PARTITION.]

parch (pärch) *v.* **parched, parch·ing, parch·es.** —*tr.* **1.** To make very dry, esp. by the action of heat. **2.** To make thirsty. **3.** To dry or roast (corn, for example) by exposing to heat. —*intr.* **1.** To become very dry. **2.** To become thirsty. [ME *parchen.*]

Par·chee·si (pär-chē′zē). A trademark for a board game based on the ancient game of pachisi.

parch·ment (pärch′mənt) *n.* **1.** The skin of a sheep or goat prepared for writing or painting on. **2.** A written text or drawing on a sheet of parchment. **3.** Paper made in imitation of parchment. [ME *perchement* < OFr. *parchemin,* alteration of Lat. *pergamina* < Gk. *pergamēnē* < *Pergamēnos,* of Pergamum, after *Pergamon* (Pergamum), an ancient Greek city in Asia Minor.]

pard (pärd) *n.* A leopard or other large cat. [ME *parde* < OFr. < Lat. *pardus* < Gk. *pardos.*]

par·don (pär′dn) *tr.v.* **-doned, -don·ing, -dons. 1.** To release (a person) from punishment; forgive. **2.** To pass over (an offense) without punishment. **3.** To make courteous allowance for; excuse. —*n.* **1.** The act of forgiving. **2.** *Law.* **a.** The exemption of a convicted person from the penalties of an offense or crime by the power of the executor of the laws. **b.** The official document or warrant declaring such an exemption. **3.** *Rom. Cath. Ch.* An indulgence. [ME *pardonen* < OFr. *pardoner* < LLat. *perdonare,* to give wholeheartedly : Lat. *per* (intensive) + Lat. *donare,* to give.] —**par′don·a·ble** *adj.* —**par′don·a·ble·ness** *n.* —**par′don·a·bly** *adv.*

par·don·er (pär′dn-ər) *n.* **1.** One who pardons. **2.** A medieval ecclesiastic authorized to raise money for religious works by granting papal indulgences to contributors.

pare (pâr) *tr.v.* **pared, par·ing, pares. 1.** To remove the outer covering or skin of by peeling with a knife or similar instrument. **2.** To remove by or as if by cutting, clipping, or shaving. **3.** To whittle away. [ME *paren* < OFr. *parer,* to prepare < Lat. *parare.*] —**par′er** *n.*

par·e·gor·ic (păr′ə-gôr′ĭk, -gŏr′-) *n.* Camphorated tincture of opium, taken internally for the relief of diarrhea and intestinal pain. [LLat. *paregoricus,* soothing < Gk. *parēgorikos* < *parēgoros,* consoling.]

pa·ren·chy·ma (pə-rĕng′kə-mə) *n.* **1.** *Anat.* The tissue characteristic of an organ, as distinguished from connective tissue. **2.** *Bot.* Tissue composed of soft, unspecialized, thin-walled cells. [NLat. < Gk. *parenkhuma,* visceral flesh < *parenkhein,* to pour in beside : *para,* beside + *en,* in + *khein,* to pour.] —**pa·ren′chy·mal, par′en·chym′a·tous** (păr′ĕn-kĭm′ə-təs) *adj.* —**par′en·chym′a·tous·ly** *adv.*

par·ent (pâr′ənt) *n.* **1.** A father or mother. **2.** A forefather; ancestor; progenitor. **3.** An organism that produces or generates another. **4.** A guardian; protector. **5.** The source or cause of something; origin. —*v.* **-ent·ed, -ent·ing, -ents. 1.** To act or serve as a parent to. **2.** To cause to come into existence; originate. [ME < OFr. < Lat. *parens* < pr.part. of *parere,* to give birth.] —**par′ent·hood′** *n.*

Usage: The use of *parent* as a verb is unacceptable to a large majority of the Usage Panel. There is no acceptable one-word substitute, so paraphrases like "perform the duties of parenthood" are recommended.

par·ent·age (pâr′ən-tĭj) *n.* **1.** Descent or derivation from parents or ancestors; lineage. **2.** Derivation from a source; origin or cause. **3.** The state or relationship of being a parent.

pa·ren·tal (pə-rĕn′tl) *adj.* **1.** Of, pertaining to, or characteristic of a parent. **2.** *Genetics.* Designating the generation from which a genetic experiment begins. —**pa·ren′tal·ly** *adv.*

par·en·ter·al (pă-rĕn′tər-əl) *adj.* **1.** *Physiol.* Located outside the alimentary canal. **2.** *Med.* Taken into the body or administered in a manner other than through the digestive tract, as by intravenous or intramuscular injection.

pa·ren·the·sis (pə-rĕn′thə-sĭs) *n., pl.* **-ses** (-sēz′). **1.** Either or both of the upright curved lines, ( ), used to mark off explanatory or qualifying remarks in writing or printing. **2.** *Math.* A parenthesis used as one of a pair to enclose a sum, product, or other expression considered or treated as a collective entity in a mathematical operation. **3. a.** A qualifying or amplifying phrase occurring within a sentence in such a way as to form an interpolation independent of the surrounding syntactical structure. **b.** A comment departing from the theme of discourse; digression. **4.** An interruption of continuity. [LLat. < Gk. < *parentithenai,* to insert : *para,* beside + *en,* in + *tithenai,* to put.]

par·en·thet·i·cal (păr′ən-thĕt′ĭ-kəl) also **par·en·thet·ic** (-ĭk) *adj.* **1.** Contained in or as if contained in parentheses; qualifying or explanatory: *a parenthetical remark.* **2.** Using or containing parentheses. —**par′en·thet′i·cal·ly** *adv.*

par·ent·ing (pâr′ən-tĭng, păr′-) *n.* The rearing of a child or children, esp. the care, love, and guidance given by parents.

pa·re·sis (pə-rē′sĭs, păr′ĭ-sĭs) *n. Pathol.* **1.** Slight or partial paralysis. **2.** General paresis. [NLat. < Gk. < *parienai,* to let fall : *para,* beside + *hienai,* to throw.] —**pa·ret′ic** (pə-rĕt′ĭk) *n. & adj.* —**pa·ret′i·cal·ly** *adv.*

par·es·the·sia also **par·aes·the·sia** (păr′ĭs-thē′zhə) *n. Pathol.* Abnormal or impaired skin sensation, such as burning, prickling, itching, or tingling. —**par′es·thet′ic** (-thĕt′ĭk) *adj.*

pa·re·u (pä′rā-o͞o′) *n.* A rectangular piece of cloth worn in Polynesia as a wraparound skirt or loincloth. [Tahitian.]

pa·re·ve (pä′rə-və) also **par·ve** (pär′və) *adj. Judaism.* Designating or pertaining to foods that are prepared without meat, milk, or their derivatives, and that therefore may be eaten with meat or dairy dishes. [Yiddish *parev*†.]

par ex·cel·lence (pär ĕk-sə-läɴs′) *adv.* Pre-eminently. —*adj.* Being the highest degree; pre-eminent: *a conductor par excellence.* [Fr. : *par,* by + *excellence,* excellence.]

par·fait (pär-fā′) *n.* **1.** A dessert made of cream, eggs, sugar, and flavoring frozen together and served in a tall glass. **2.** A dessert made of several layers of different flavors of ice cream or ices, variously garnished and served in a tall glass. [Fr. < *parfait,* perfect < Lat. *perfectus.* —see PERFECT.]

parfait glass *n.* A slender glass of medium height with a short stem, used in serving a parfait.

par·fleche (pär′flĕsh′) *n.* **1.** Rawhide soaked in lye and water to remove the hair and then dried on a stretcher. **2.** An article, such as a shield, made of parfleche. [Canadian Fr.]

par·get (pär′jĭt) *n.* **1.** Plaster, roughcast, or a similar mixture used to coat walls or line chimneys. **2.** Ornamental plasterwork. **3.** A cement mixture used to waterproof outer walls. —*tr.v.* **-get·ed, -get·ing, -gets.** To cover or adorn with parget. [ME < *pargetten,* to parget < OFr. *parjeter,* to throw onto a surface : *par,* onto (< Lat. *per*) + *jeter,* to throw (< Lat. *jacere*).] —**par′get·ing** *n.*

par·he·li·a (pär-hē′lē-ə, -hēl′yə) *n.* Plural of **parhelion.**

par·he·lic circle also **par·he·lic ring** (pär-hē′lĭk) *n.* A luminous halo visible at the height of the sun and parallel to the horizon, caused by the sun's rays reflecting off atmospheric ice crystals.

par·he·li·on (pär-hē′lē-ən, -hēl′yən) *n., pl.* **-he·li·a** (-hē′lē-ə, -hēl′yə). A bright spot sometimes appearing to either side of the sun, often on a luminous ring or halo. [Lat. *parelion* < Gk. *parēlion* : *para,* beside + *hēlios,* sun.] —**par·he′lic** (-hē′lĭk) *adj.*

pa·ri·ah (pə-rī′ə) *n.* **1.** A member of a low caste of agricultural and domestic workers in southern India and Burma. **2.** A social outcast. [Tamil *paṛaiyan* < *paṛai,* drum.]

pa·ri·es (pâr′ē-ēz′) *n., pl.* **pa·ri·e·tes** (pə-rī′ə-tēz′). *Biol.* Often **parietes.** The wall of an organ. [NLat. < Lat., wall.]

pa·ri·e·tal (pə-rī′ĭ-təl) *adj.* **1.** *Biol.* Pertaining to or forming the wall of a hollow structure. **2.** *Anat.* Of or relating to either of the parietal bones. **3.** *Bot.* Attached to the ovary wall. Used of the ovules or placenta in certain plants. **4.** Dwelling within or having authority within the walls or buildings of a college. —*n.* **1.** A parietal part, as a wall, bone, or plate. **2. parietals.** The rules governing the visiting privileges of members of the opposite sex in college or university dormitories. [Fr. *pariétal* < LLat. *parietalis* < Lat. *paries,* wall.]

parietal bone *n. Anat.* Either of two large, irregularly quadrilateral bones between the frontal and occipital bones that together form the sides and top of the skull.

parietal cell *n.* One of the large peripheral cells of the gastric mucosa that secrete hydrochloric acid.

parietal lobe *n. Anat.* The division of each hemisphere of the brain that lies beneath each parietal bone.

pa·ri·e·tes (pə-rī′ə-tēz′) *n.* Plural of **paries.**

par·i-mu·tu·el (păr′ĭ-myōō′chōō-əl) *n.* **1.** A system of betting on races whereby the winners divide the total amount bet, after deducting management expenses, in proportion to the sums they have wagered individually. **2.** The machine that records pari-mutuel bets. [Fr. *pari mutuel* : *pari,* wager + *mutuel,* mutual.]

par·ing (pâr′ĭng) *n.* **1.** Something, such as a skin or peeling, that has been pared off. **2.** The act of cutting back or shaving off: *a drastic paring of the budget.*

paring knife *n.* A small knife with a short blade and a firm handle used esp. in paring fruit or vegetables.

pa·ri pas·su (păr′ē păs′ōō) *adv.* With equal pace, speed, or progress; side by side: *proceed pari passu.* [Lat.]

Par·is (păr′ĭs) *n. Gk. Myth.* The prince of Troy whose abduction of Helen provoked the Trojan War. [Lat. < Gk.]

Paris daisy *n.* The marguerite (sense 1).

Paris green *n.* A poisonous emerald-green powder, $(CuO)_3As_2O_3 \cdot Cu(C_2H_3O_2)_2$, used as a pigment, insecticide, and wood preservative. [After *Paris,* France.]

par·ish (păr′ĭsh) *n.* **1.** In the Anglican, Roman Catholic, and some other churches, an administrative part of a diocese that has its own church. **2.** *Chiefly Brit.* A political division of a county for local civil government, usually corresponding to the ecclesiastical parish. **3.** An administrative subdivision in Louisiana that corresponds to a county in other states of the United States. **4.** Members of a parish; a community of parishioners. [ME *parisshe* < OFr. *paroche* < LLat. *parochia* < LGk. *paroikia* < *paroikos,* Christian < Gk., neighbor : *para,* beside + *oikos,* house.]

pa·rish·ion·er (pə-rĭsh′ə-nər) *n.* A member of a parish. [ME *parisshoner* < *paroschien,* parishioner < OFr. *paroissien* < *paroisse,* parish, var. of *paroche.* —see PARISH.]

par·i·ty¹ (păr′ĭ-tē) *n., pl.* **-ties. 1.** Equality, as in amount, status, or value. **2.** Functional equivalence, as in the development of strategic arms. **3.** The equivalent in value of a sum of money expressed in terms of a different currency at a fixed, official rate of exchange. **4.** Equality of prices of goods or securities in two different markets. **5.** A level for farm-product prices maintained by governmental support and intended to give farmers the same purchasing power they had during a chosen base period. **6.** *Math.* The comparative odd-even relationship between two integers. If both are odd, or even, they are said to have the same parity; if one is odd and one even, they have different parity. **7. a.** An intrinsic symmetry property of subatomic particles that is characterized by the behavior of the wave function of such particles under reflection through the origin of spatial coordinates. **b.** A quantum number, either +1 (even) or -1 (odd), that mathematically describes this property. **8. a.** The state of a binary-coded computer character under a system in which a character having an even number of digits is assigned the code 0 and one having an odd number is assigned the code 1. **b.** Parity bit. [LLat. *paritas* < *par,* equal.]

par·i·ty² (păr′ĭ-tē) *n. Med.* **1.** The condition of having borne offspring. **2.** The number of children borne by one woman. [Lat. *parere,* to give birth, bring forth + -ITY.]

parity bit *n.* A bit added to a group of bits that indicates parity and is used to check the accuracy of computer data.

park (pärk) *n.* **1.** A tract of land set aside for public use, as: **a.** An expanse of enclosed grounds for recreational use within or adjoining a town. **b.** A landscaped city square. **c.** A tract of land kept in its natural state. **2.** A stadium or enclosed playing field: *a ball park.* **3.** A country estate, esp. when including extensive gardens, woods, pastures, and game preserves. **4. a.** An area where military vehicles and artillery are stored and serviced. **b.** The materiel kept in such an area. —*v.* **parked, park·ing, parks.** —*tr.* **1.** To put or leave (a vehicle) for a time in a certain location. **2.** *Informal.* To place, put, set, or leave (something) somewhere. **3.** To assemble (artillery or other equipment) in order. —*intr.* To station an automobile or other vehicle in a parking space. [ME, royal land set aside for hunting < OFr. *parc.*] —**park′er** *n.*

par·ka (pär′kə) *n.* **1.** A hooded fur jacket worn as an outer garment by Eskimos. **2.** An outer garment of warm cloth. [Aleut. < R., pelt < Samoyed.]

Par·ker House roll (pär′kər) *n.* A yeast-leavened roll, shaped by folding a flat round of dough in half. [After the *Parker House,* a hotel in Boston, Massachusetts.]

parking lot *n.* An area for parking motor vehicles.

parking meter *n.* A coin-operated device which registers the amount of time purchased for the parking of a motor vehicle, at the expiration of which the driver is liable for a fine.

parking orbit *n. Aerospace.* A temporary orbit for spacecraft.

Par·kin·son·ism (pär′kĭn-sə-nĭz′əm) *n.* **1.** A chronic neurological condition marked by muscular rigidity, tremor, and impaired motor control. **2.** Parkinson's disease. [< PARKINSON'S DISEASE.]

Par·kin·son's disease (pär′kĭn-sənz) *n.* A progressive nervous disease of the later years, characterized by muscular tremor, slowing of movement, partial facial paralysis, peculiarity of gait and posture, and weakness. [After James *Parkinson* (1755–1824).]

Par·kin·son's Law (pär′kĭn-sənz) *n.* Any of several satirical observations propounded as economic laws, as "work expands to fill the time available for its completion." [After C. Northcote *Parkinson* (b. 1909).]

park·way (pärk′wā′) *n.* A broad landscaped highway, often divided by planted median strips.

par·lance (pär′ləns) *n.* **1.** A particular manner of speaking; idiom: *legal parlance.* **2.** Conversation, esp. a parley or debate. [OFr. < *parler,* to speak. —see PARLEY.]

par·lan·do (pär-län′dō) also **par·lan·te** (-tā) *adj. Mus.* That is to be sung in a style suggestive of speech. Used as a direction. [Ital. < *parlare,* to speak < Med. Lat. *parabolare.* —see PARLEY.] —**par·lan′do** *adv.*

par·lay (pär′lā′, -lē) *tr.v.* **-layed, -lay·ing, -lays. 1.** To bet (an original wager and its winnings) on a subsequent event. **2.** To maneuver (an asset) to great advantage: *parlayed her small investments into a large fortune.* —*n.* A bet comprising the sum of an original wager plus its winnings, or a series of bets made in such a manner. [Fr. *paroli* < dial. Ital., pl. of *parolo,* a set of dice < *paro,* pair < Lat. *par,* equal.]

parle (pärl) *n. & v. Archaic.* Variant of **parley.**

par·ley (pär′lē) *n., pl.* **-leys.** A discussion or conference, esp. one between enemies over terms of truce or other matters. —*intr.v.* **-leyed, -ley·ing, -leys.** To discuss, confer, or debate with another, esp. with an enemy. [Fr. *parlée* < *parler,* to talk < OFr. < Med. Lat. *parabolare* < LLat. *parabola,* discourse. —see PARABLE.]

par·lia·ment (pär′lə-mənt) *n.* **1.** A national representative body having supreme legislative powers within the state. **2. Parliament.** The legislative body of various countries, esp. that of the United Kingdom, made up of the House of Lords and the House of Commons. [ME, a meeting about national concerns < OFr. *parlement* < *parler,* to talk. —see PARLEY.]

par·lia·men·tar·i·an (pär′lə-mĕn-târ′ē-ən) *n.* **1.** One who is expert in parliamentary procedures, rules, or debate. **2. Parliamentarian.** A supporter of the Long Parliament during the English Civil War and the Commonwealth; Roundhead. —*adj.* Of or pertaining to the Long Parliament or to the Roundheads.

par·lia·men·ta·ry (pär′lə-mĕn′tə-rē, -mĕn′trē) *adj.* **1.** Of, pertaining to, or like a parliament. **2.** Proceeding from, passed, or decreed by a parliament. **3.** In accordance with the rules and customs of a parliament. **4.** Having a parliament.

parliamentary law *n.* A body of rules governing procedure in legislative and deliberative assemblies.

par·lor (pär′lər) *n.* **1.** A room in a private home set apart for the entertainment of visitors. **2.** A small lounge or sitting room affording limited privacy, such as at an inn or tavern. **3.** A room equipped and furnished for a special function or business: *a beauty parlor.* [ME *parlur* < AN < OFr. *parler,* to talk. —see PARLEY.]

parlor car *n.* A railroad car for day travel fitted with individual reserved seats.

parlor game *n.* A game that can be played indoors.

parlor grand *n.* A grand piano shorter in length than a concert grand yet longer than a baby grand.

par·lour (pär′lər) *n. Chiefly Brit.* Variant of **parlor.**

par·lous (pär′ləs) *adj.* **1.** Perilous; dangerous. **2.** *Obs.* Dangerously cunning. [ME, alteration of *perilous,* perilous < *peril,* peril. —see PERIL.] —**par′lous·ly** *adv.*

Par·ma violet (pär′mə) *n.* A variety of violet, *Viola odorata sempervirens,* cultivated for its fragrant lavender flowers. [After *Parma,* Italy.]

Par·me·san (pär′mə-zän′, -zăn′, -zən) *n.* A hard, sharp, dry Italian cheese made from skim milk and usually served grated as a garnish. —*adj.* Of or from Parma. [Orig. a trademark.]

par·mi·gia·na (pär′mĭ-zhä′nə, -jä′-) *adj.* Made or covered with Parmesan cheese: *eggplant parmigiana.* [Ital., fem. of *parmigiano,* of *Parma,* after *Parma,* Italy.]

Par·nas·si·an¹ (pär-năs′ē-ən) *adj.* Of or pertaining to poetry. [Lat. *parnassius,* of Parnassus < *parnasios,* after *Parnasos* (Parnassus), a mountain in Greece sacred to Apollo and the Muses.]

Par·nas·si·an² (pär-năs′ē-ən) *n.* A member of a school of late 19th-century French poets whose work is characterized by detachment and emphasis on metrical form. [Fr. *parnassien,* after *Le Parnasse contemporain,* The Contemporary Parnassian, the group's first anthology of poetry (1866).] —**Par·nas′si·an** *adj.*

pa·ro·chi·al (pə-rō′kē-əl) *adj.* **1.** Of, pertaining to, supported by, or located in a parish. **2.** Narrowly restricted; provincial: *parochial attitudes.* [ME *parochiell* < OFr. *parochial* < LLat. *parochialis* < *parochia,* parish. —see PARISH.] —**pa·ro′chi·al·ism** *n.* —**pa·ro′chi·al·ist** *n.* —**pa·ro′chi·al·ly** *adv.*

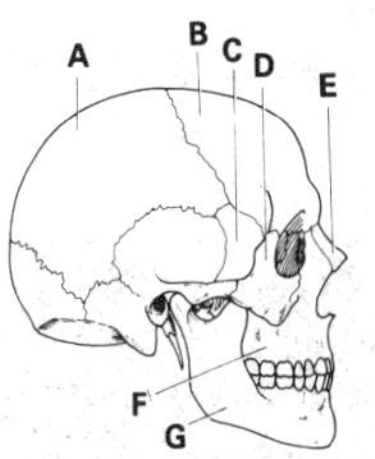

parietal bone
A. Parietal
B. Frontal
C. Sphenoid
D. Zygomatic
E. Nasal
F. Maxilla
G. Mandible

Paris
Detail from a Greek bowl, 460 B.C.

parquetry

parrot

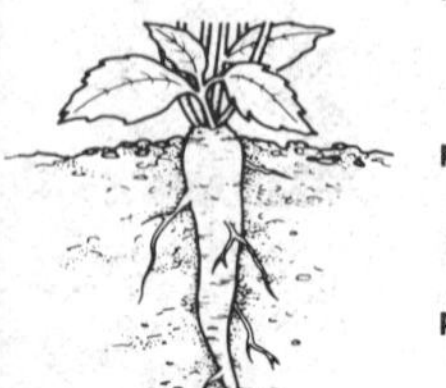

parsnip

parochial school *n.* A school supported by a church parish.

par·o·dy (păr'ə-dē) *n., pl.* **-dies. 1.** A literary or artistic work that broadly mimics an author's characteristic style and holds it up to ridicule. **2.** A performance so bad as to be equivalent to intentional mockery; travesty: *The trial was a parody of justice.* —*tr.v.* **-died, -dy·ing, -dies.** To make a parody of. [Lat. *parodia* < Gk. *parōidia* : *para-*, subsidiary to + *ōidē*, song.] —**pa·rod'ic** (pə-rŏd'ĭk), **pa·rod'i·cal** *adj.* —**par'o·dist** *n.*

pa·rol (pə-rōl', păr'əl) *n. Law.* An oral utterance; word of mouth: *by parol.* —*adj. Law.* Given by word of mouth. [OFr. *parole* < LLat. *parabola,* discourse. —see PARABLE.]

pa·role (pə-rōl') *n.* **1.** *Law.* **a.** The release of a prisoner before his term has expired on condition of continued good behavior. **b.** The duration of such conditional release. **2.** A password used by a military officer of the day or an officer on guard. **3.** Word of honor; promise. —***modifier:*** *parole violations.* —*tr.v.* **-roled, -rol·ing, -roles.** To release (a prisoner) on parole. [Fr., promise < OFr. —see PAROL.]

pa·rol·ee (pə-rō'lē') *n.* One who is released on parole.

par·o·no·ma·sia (păr'ə-nō-mā'zhə, -zhē-ə) *n.* Word play, esp. a pun. [Lat. < Gk. < *paronomazein,* to call by a different name : *para,* besides + *onomazein,* to name < *onoma,* name.] —**par'o·no·mas'tic** (-măs'tĭk), **par'o·no·ma'sial** *adj.* —**par'o·no·mas'ti·cal·ly** *adv.*

par·o·nych·i·a (păr'ə-nĭk'ē-ə) *n. Med.* Inflammation of the tissue surrounding a nail. [Lat. < Gk. *parōnukhia* : *para-*, around + *onux,* nail.]

par·o·nym (păr'ə-nĭm') *n.* A paronymous word. [Gk. *parōnumon* < *parōnumos,* derivative. —see PARONYMOUS.] —**par'o·nym'ic** *adj.*

pa·ron·y·mous (pə-rŏn'ə-məs) *adj.* Allied by derivation from the same root; having the same stem; for example, *beautiful* and *beauteous.* [Gk. *parōnumos,* derivative : *para,* besides + *onuma,* name.]

pa·rot·id (pə-rŏt'ĭd) *n.* A parotid gland. —*adj.* Of or pertaining to the parotid gland.

pa·rot·i·dec·to·my (pə-rŏt'ĭ-dĕk'tə-mē) *n., pl.* **-mies.** The surgical excision of the parotid gland.

pa·rot·id gland (pə-rŏt'ĭd) *n.* Either of the largest of the paired salivary glands, located below and in front of each ear. [< Gk. *parōtis, parōtid-,* tumor near the ear : *para,* beside + *ous,* ear.]

par·o·ti·tis (păr'ə-tī'tĭs) also **pa·rot·i·di·tis** (pə-rŏt'ĭ-dī'tĭs) *n.* Inflammation of the parotid glands, as in mumps. —**par'o·tit'ic** (-tĭt'ĭk) *adj.*

-parous *suff.* Giving birth to; producing: *multiparous.* [Lat. *-parous* < *parere,* to give birth.]

Par·ou·si·a (pär'o͞o-sē'ə, pə-ro͞o'zē-ə) *n.* The Second Coming. [Gk., presence, arrival < *pareinai,* to be present.]

par·ox·ysm (păr'ək-sĭz'əm) *n.* **1.** A sudden outburst of emotion or action: *a paroxysm of laughter.* **2.** *Pathol.* **a.** A crisis in or recurrent intensification of a disease. **b.** A spasm or fit; convulsion. [Fr. *paroxysme* < Med. Lat. *paroxysmus* < Gk. *paroxusmos* < *paroxunein,* to stimulate : *para* (intensive) + *oxunein,* to goad < *oxus,* sharp.] —**par'ox·ys'mal** (-sĭz'məl) *adj.* —**par'ox·ys'mal·ly** *adv.*

par·ox·y·tone (pă-rŏk'sĭ-tōn') *adj.* Having an acute accent on the penultimate syllable. Used of certain words in Greek and certain Romance languages, such as French and Portuguese. —*n.* A paroxytone word. [Gk. *paroxutonos* : *para,* beside + *oxutonos,* oxytone.]

par·quet (pär-kā') *n.* **1. a.** The part of the main floor of a theater between the orchestra pit and the parquet circle. **b.** Orchestra (sense 3.b.). **2.** A floor of parquetry. —*tr.v.* **-quet·ed** (-kăd'), **-quet·ing** (-kā'ĭng), **-quets** (-kāz'). **1.** To furnish (a room) with a floor of parquetry. **2.** To make (a floor) of parquetry. [Fr., parquetry < OFr., dim. of *parc,* enclosure.]

parquet circle *n.* The section of a parquet in a theater that lies under a rear balcony.

par·quet·ry (pär'kĭ-trē) *n., pl.* **-ries.** Wood, often of contrasting colors, worked into an inlaid mosaic, used esp. for floors. [Fr. *parqueterie* < *parquet,* parquetry. —see PARQUET.]

parr (pär) *n., pl.* **parr** or **parrs. 1.** A young salmon during the first two years of its life when it lives in fresh water. **2.** The young of various fishes. [Orig. unknown.]

par·ral (păr'əl) *n.* Variant of **parrel.**

par·ra·mat·ta (păr'ə-măt'ə) *n.* Variant of **paramatta.**

par·rel also **par·ral** (păr'əl) *n. Naut.* A sliding loop of rope or chain to which a running yard or gaff is fastened, permitting movement of the yard up and down the mast. [ME *perell,* alteration of *parail,* equipment, short for *appareil,* apparel. —see APPAREL.]

par·ri·cide (păr'ĭ-sīd') *n.* **1. a.** One who murders his father or mother or other near relative. **b.** The act of committing such a murder. **2.** One who murders someone to whom he owes reverence. [Lat. *parricida.*] —**par'ri·cid'al** (-sīd'l) *adj.* —**par'ri·cid'al·ly** *adv.*

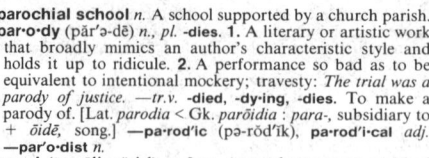

par·rot (păr'ət) *n.* **1.** Any of numerous tropical and semitropical birds of the order Psittaciformes, characterized by short, hooked bills, brightly colored plumage, and, in some species, the ability to mimic human speech or other sounds. **2.** One who mindlessly imitates the words or actions of another. —*tr.v.* **-rot·ed, -rot·ing, -rots.** To repeat or imitate without meaning or understanding. [Prob. from *Perrot,* dim. of *Pierre,* Peter.] —**par'rot·er** *n.*

parrot fever *n.* Psittacosis.

par·rot·fish (păr'ət-fĭsh') *n., pl.* **parrotfish** or **-fish·es.** Any of various brightly colored tropical marine fishes of the family Scaridae, having jaws resembling a parrot's beak.

par·ry (păr'ē) *v.* **-ried, -ry·ing, -ries.** —*tr.* **1.** To deflect or ward off (a fencing thrust, for example). **2.** To avoid, evade, or turn aside: *He skillfully parried her questions.* —*intr.* To deflect or ward off a blow. —*n., pl.* **-ries. 1.** The act of deflecting or warding off a blow, esp. in fencing. **2.** An evasive answer or action; evasion. [Prob. < Fr. *parez,* imper. of *parer,* to defend < Ital. *parare* < Lat., to prepare.]

parse (pärs) *v.* **parsed, pars·ing, pars·es.** —*tr.* **1.** To break (a sentence) down into its component parts of speech with an explanation of the form, function, and syntactical relationship of each part. **2.** To describe (a word) by stating its part of speech, form, and syntactical relationships in a sentence. —*intr.* To admit of being parsed: *His sentences do not parse easily.* [< Lat. *pars orationis,* part of speech.] —**pars'er** *n.*

par·sec (pär'sĕk') *n.* A unit of astronomical length based on the distance from earth at which stellar parallax is one second of arc and equal to 3.258 light years, 3.086×10^{13} kilometers, or 1.918×10^{13} miles. [PAR(ALLAX) + SEC(OND).]

Par·see also **Par·si** (pär'sē, pär-sē') *n.* **1.** A member of a Zoroastrian religious sect in India, descended from Persians. **2.** The Iranian dialect used in the religious literature of the Parsees. [Pers. *Pārsī* < *Pārs,* Persia.] —**Par'see'ism** *n.*

par·si·mo·ni·ous (pär'sə-mō'nē-əs) *adj.* Marked by parsimony; stingy. —**par'si·mo'ni·ous·ly** *adv.* —**par'si·mo'ni·ous·ness** *n.*

par·si·mo·ny (pär'sə-mō'nē) *n.* **1.** Unusual or excessive frugality; stinginess. **2.** Economy or simplicity of assumptions in logical formulation. [ME *parcimony* < Lat. *parsimonia* < *parcere,* to spare.]

pars·ley (pär'slē) *n.* A cultivated herb, *Petroselinum crispum,* having much-divided, curled leaves that are used as a garnish and for seasoning. [ME *persely* < OE *petersilie* < LLat. *petrosilium* < Lat. *petroselinum* < Gk. *petroselinon* : *petra,* rock + *celinon,* celery.]

pars·nip (pär'snĭp') *n.* **1.** A strong-scented plant, *Pastinaca sativa,* cultivated for its long, white, edible root. **2.** The root of the parsnip. [ME *pasnepe,* alteration of OFr. *pasnaie* < Lat. *pastinaca* < *pastinum,* a kind of two-pronged dibble.]

par·son (pär'sən) *n.* **1.** An Anglican clergyman with full legal control of a parish under ecclesiastical law. **2.** A clergyman in the Reformed tradition. [ME, rector < OFr. *persone* < Med. Lat. *persona* < Lat., character.]

par·son·age (pär'sə-nĭj) *n.* The official residence of a parson.

parson's nose *n.* A pope's nose.

Par·sons table (pär'sənz) *n.* A table, usually rectangular, having straight legs that form its four corners. [Prob. < the name *Parsons.*]

part (pärt) *n.* **1.** A portion, division, or segment of a whole; piece. **2.** Any of several equal portions or fractions into which a whole may be divided. **3.** *Math.* An aliquot part. **4. a.** An organ, member, or other division of an animal or plant. **b. parts.** The external genitals. **5.** A component that can be separated from a system: *a machine part.* **6.** A role. **7.** One's proper or expected share in responsibility or obligation; duty. **8.** Often **parts.** Individual endowment or ability. **9.** Often **parts.** A region, land, or territory: *foreign parts.* **10.** The line where the hair on the head is parted. **11.** *Mus.* **a.** One of the melodic lines in concerted music or in harmony. **b.** The individual score for it. —*v.* **part·ed, part·ing, parts.** —*tr.* **1.** To divide or break (something) into separate pieces. **2.** To break up or end (a relationship) by separating: *part company.* **3.** To separate by or as if by coming between; put or keep apart. **4.** To comb (the hair) away from a dividing line on the scalp. **5.** *Archaic.* To divide into shares or portions. —*intr.* **1.** To divide or break; come apart: *The curtain parted in the middle.* **2.** To go away from one another; separate: *They parted as friends.* **3.** To separate into ways going in different directions: *The road parts in the forest.* **4.** To leave; depart. **5.** To die. —***phrasal verb.*** **part with.** To give up; relinquish. —*adv.* Partially; in part: *part yellow, part green.* —*adj.* Not full or complete; partial: *a part owner.* —***idioms.*** **for one's part.** So far as one is concerned. **for the most part.** To the greater extent; generally. **in good part.** With good grace; without taking offense: *take a joke in good part.* **in part.** To some extent; partly. **part and parcel.** A basic part or essential function. **on the part of.** Regarding the one specified. **take part.** To join in; participate: *He took part in the celebration.* **take (someone's) part.** To side with someone in a disagreement; support. [ME < OFr. and OE, both < Lat. *pars.*]

par·take (pär-tāk') *v.* **-took** (-to͝ok'), **-tak·en, -tak·ing, -takes.** —*intr.* **1.** To take part or have a share; participate: *partake in the festivities.* **2.** To take or be given part or portion: *partook of the delicious dinner.* **3.** To have a given quality or characteristic; show evidence: *a nature that partook of the ferocity of the lion.* —*tr.* To take or have part of; share. [Back-formation < *partaker,* one who partakes : PART + TAKER.] —**par·tak'er** *n.*

part·ed (pär'tĭd) *adj.* **1.** Separated or divided into parts;

cleft. **2.** Kept apart; separated. **3.** *Bot.* Cleft almost to the base, so as to have distinct divisions or lobes. **4.** *Archaic.* Deceased.

par·terre (pär-târ′) *n.* **1.** A parquet circle. **2.** A flower garden having the beds and paths arranged to form a pattern. [Fr. < OFr., ornamental garden < *par terre,* on the ground.]

par·the·no·car·py (pär′thə-nō-kär′pē) *n.* The production of fruit without fertilization. [Gk. *parthenos,* virgin + *karpos,* fruit.] **—par′the·no·car′pic** *adj.* **—par′the·no·car′pi·cal·ly** *adv.*

par·the·no·gen·e·sis (pär′thə-nō-jĕn′ĭ-sĭs) *n.* Reproduction of organisms without conjunction of gametes of opposite sexes. [Gk. *parthenos,* virgin + GENESIS.] **—par′the·no·ge·net′ic** (-jə-nĕt′ĭk) *adj.* **—par′the·no·ge·net′i·cal·ly** *adv.*

Par·thi·an (pär′thē-ən) *adj.* Of or pertaining to a shot fired by one who is in actual or feigned retreat. [After *Parthia,* an ancient country in Western Asia (from the tactics of Parthian archers, who shot at the enemy while feigning flight).]

par·tial (pär′shəl) *adj.* **1.** Of, pertaining to, or affecting only part; not total. **2.** Favoring one person or side over another or others; biased: *a decision that was partial to the plaintiff.* **3.** Having a particular liking for someone or something: *partial to detective novels.* **4.** *Math.* Of, designating, or pertaining to operations or sequences of operations, such as differentiation and integration, when applied to only one of several variables at a time. *—n.* **1.** *Mus.* A harmonic (sense 1). **2.** A partial derivative. [ME *parcial,* biased < OFr. *partial* < LLat. *partialis* < Lat. *pars,* part.] **—par′tial·ness** *n.*

partial derivative *n.* The derivative with respect to a single variable of a function of two or more variables, regarding other variables as constants.

partial differential equation *n.* A differential equation containing at least one partial derivative.

partial differentiation *n.* Differentiation with respect to a single variable in a function of several variables, regarding other variables as constants.

partial fraction *n.* One of a set of fractions having an algebraic sum equal to a specified fraction.

par·ti·al·i·ty (pär′shē-ăl′ĭ-tē, pär-shăl′-) *n., pl.* **-ties. 1.** The state of being partial. **2.** Favorable prejudice or bias. **3.** A special fondness; predilection: *"an almost feminine partiality for old china"* (Lamb).

par·tial·ly (pär′shə-lē) *adv.* To a degree; not totally. —See Usage note at **partly.**

partial pressure *n.* The pressure that one component of a mixture of gases would exert if it were alone in a container.

partial tone *n. Mus.* A harmonic (sense 1).

par·ti·ble (pär′tə-bəl) *adj.* Capable of being parted, divided, or separated; divisible. [LLat. *partibilis* < Lat. *partiri,* to divide < *pars,* part.]

par·tic·i·pant (pär-tĭs′ə-pənt) *n.* One that participates or takes part in something. *—adj.* Participating; taking part.

par·tic·i·pate (pär-tĭs′ə-pāt′) *v.* **-pat·ed, -pat·ing, -pates.** *—intr.* To take part; join or share with others: *participate in a discussion.* *—tr.* To share in; partake of. [Lat. *participare, participat-* < *particeps,* partaker : *pars,* part + *capere,* to take.] **—par·tic′i·pance** *n.* **—par·tic′i·pa′tive** *adj.* **—par·tic′i·pa′tor** *n.*

par·tic·i·pa·tion (pär-tĭs′ə-pā′shən) *n.* **1.** The act of participating: *participation in a game.* **2.** A taking part or sharing: *each investor's participation in the profits.*

par·tic·i·pa·to·ry (pär-tĭs′ə-pə-tôr′ē, -tōr′ē) *adj.* Marked by or involving participation, esp. affording the opportunity for individual participation: *participatory democracy.*

par·ti·cip·i·al (pär′tĭ-sĭp′ē-əl) *adj.* Of, pertaining to, consisting of, or formed with a participle. [Lat. *participialis* < *participium,* participle.] **—par′ti·cip′i·al·ly** *adv.*

par·ti·ci·ple (pär′tĭ-sĭp′əl) *n. Gram.* A nominal form of a verb that is used with an auxiliary verb to indicate certain tenses and that can also function independently as an adjective. [ME < OFr. < Lat. *participium.*]

Usage: When a *participle* is used as a modifier, there should be no ambiguity or illogicality about the element it modifies. Special care should be taken to avoid the dangling participle, one that is wrongly attached to (and seemingly modifies) a noun, pronoun, or other substantive and thus produces an absurdity: *Turning the corner, the view was much changed.* (Since it was not the view that turned the corner, a better phrasing would be: *Turning the corner, he discovered that the view was much changed.*) Similarly: *Lacking a better candidate, it was decided to postpone the election.* This is better rewritten: *In the absence of a better candidate, it was decided . . . .* Many participlelike constructions are well established as prepositions, however, and may be used freely. These include *speaking of, owing to, concerning, failing, considering, granting,* and *judging by.* Thus, we may write: *Speaking of politics, the election has been postponed. Considering the hour, it is surprising that he arrived at all.*

par·ti·cle (pär′tĭ-kəl) *n.* **1.** A very small piece or part; speck. **2.** A very small amount, trace, or degree: *not a particle of doubt.* **3.** *Physics.* **a.** A body whose spatial extent and internal motion and structure, if any, are irrelevant in a specific problem. **b.** An elementary particle. **4.** *Gram.* **a.** One of a class of forms, such as prepositions or conjunctions, consisting of a single word that has no inflection. **b.** A suffix or prefix, such as *-ness* or *in-.* **5.** A small division or section of something written, such as a clause of a document. **6.** *Rom. Cath. Ch.* **a.** A small piece of a consecrated Host. **b.** One of the smaller, individual Hosts. [ME < Lat. *particula,* dim. of *pars,* part.]

SUBATOMIC PARTICLES

Family Name	Particle Name	Particle Symbol*	Anti-particle Symbol	Mass**	Particle's Electric Charge†	Average Lifetime‡ (sec)
	photon	γ	(γ)	0	0	stable
lepton	electron's neutrino	ν_e	$\bar{\nu}_e$	0	0	stable
	muon's neutrino	ν_μ	$\bar{\nu}_\mu$	0	0	stable
	electron	e^-	e^+	1	−1	stable
	muon	μ^-	μ^+	207	−1	2.2×10^{-6}
meson	pion	π^0	π^0	264	0	0.8×10^{-16}
		π^+	π^-	273	+1	2.6×10^{-8}
	kaon	K^+	K^-	966	+1	1.2×10^{-8}
		K^0	$\bar{K}^0$	975	0	0.9×10^{-10} or 5.2×10^{-8}
baryon	***nucleon***					
	proton	p	$\bar{p}$	1,836	+1	stable
	neutron	n	$\bar{n}$	1,839	0	$1.0 \times 10^{+3}$
	hyperon					
	lambda	Λ	$\bar{\Lambda}$	2,183	0	2.6×10^{-10}
	sigma	Σ^+	$\bar{\Sigma}^-$	2,328	+1	0.8×10^{-10}
		Σ^0	$\bar{\Sigma}^0$	2,333	0	$< 1.0 \times 10^{-14}$
		Σ^-	$\bar{\Sigma}^+$	2,343	−1	1.7×10^{-10}
	xi	Ξ^0	$\bar{\Xi}^0$	2,572	0	3.0×10^{-10}
		Ξ^-	$\bar{\Xi}^-$	2,585	−1	1.7×10^{-10}
	omega	Ω^-	Ω^+	3,276	−1	1.5×10^{-10}

*Particle symbols are frequently written without superscripts indicating charge; antiparticles are commonly identified by a bar over the particle symbol, but variations using parentheses, or no distinguishing marks at all, are also widely used.

**Approximate masses expressed in terms of the electron's mass.

†Given in terms of the electron's charge, and for particles only; antiparticles have the opposite charge or are neutral if the particle is neutral.

‡Stable means the particle lasts an indefinitely long time and has no known decay mode; the neutral kaon is a composite of two particles, the average lifetime of each of which is given; when bound in a nucleus, the neutron is stable.

par·ti-col·ored (pär′tē-kŭl′ərd) *adj.* Having different parts or sections colored differently; pied. [Obs. *party,* parti-colored + COLORED.]

par·tic·u·lar (pər-tĭk′yə-lər) *adj.* **1.** Of, belonging to, or associated with a single person, group, thing, or category; not general or universal. **2.** Separate and distinct from others; specific. **3.** Worthy of note; exceptional. **4.** Especially or excessively attentive to or concerned with details or niceties; fussy. **5.** *Logic.* Encompassing some, but not all, of a class or group; restricted. Used of a proposition. **6.** *Math.* Designating a solution of a differential equation, as distinguished from the general representation of the set of all solutions. *—n.* **1.** An individual item, fact, or detail: *correct in every particular.* **2.** Often **particulars.** Items or details of information or news. **3.** Often **particulars.** A separate case or individual instance. **4.** *Logic.* A particular proposition. ***—idiom.*** **in particular.** Particularly; especially. [ME < *particuler* < OFr. < LLat. *particularis* < Lat. *particula,* dim. of *pars,* part.]

par·tic·u·lar·ism (pər-tĭk′yə-lə-rĭz′əm) *n.* **1.** Exclusive adherence to or interest in one's own group, party, sect, or nation. **2.** A policy of allowing each state in a nation or federation to act independently. **3.** *Theol.* The belief that a particular individual is elected to salvation and grace by God's free choice rather than by God's foreseeing the individual's response. **—par·tic′u·lar·ist** *n.* **—par·tic′u·lar·is′tic** *adj.*

par·tic·u·lar·i·ty (pər-tĭk′yə-lăr′ĭ-tē) *n., pl.* **-ties. 1.** The quality or state of being particular rather than general. **2.** Exactitude of detail, esp. in description. **3.** Attention to or concern with details; fastidiousness. **4.** A specific point or detail; particular. **5.** An individual characteristic; peculiarity.

par·tic·u·lar·ize (pər-tĭk′yə-lə-rīz′) *v.* **-ized, -iz·ing, -iz·es.** *—tr.* **1.** To state or enumerate in detail; itemize. **2.** To mention or treat individually; specify. *—intr.* To give details or particulars. **—par·tic′u·lar·i·za′tion** *n.* **—par·tic′u·lar·iz′er** *n.*

par·tic·u·lar·ly (pər-tĭk′yə-lər-lē) *adv.* **1.** To a great degree; especially. **2.** With particular reference or emphasis; specifically. **3.** In a particular manner; individually: *"Everyone has a moment in history which belongs particularly to him"* (John Knowles). **4.** With regard to particulars; in detail.

par·tic·u·late (pər-tĭk′yə-lĭt, -lāt′) *adj.* Of, pertaining to, or formed of separate particles. *—n.* A particulate substance.

part·ing (pär′tĭng) *n.* **1.** The act or process of separating or dividing. **2.** A division or separation: *the parting of the ways.* **3.** A departure or leave-taking. *—adj.* Pertaining to, done, given, or said on departing or separating: *a parting gift.* ***—idiom.*** **parting of the ways.** A point of divergence.

par·ti pris (pär'tē prē') *n.* An inclination for or against something or someone that inhibits impartial judgment; bias. [Fr. : *parti,* decision + *pris,* p.part. of *prendre,* to take.]
par·ti·san[1] (pär'tĭ-zən) *n.* **1.** A militant supporter of a party, cause, faction, person, or idea: *"I avow myself the partisan of truth alone"* (William Harvey). **2.** A member of a detached, often unofficially organized body of fighters who attack or harass an enemy within occupied territory; guerrilla. *—adj.* **1.** Of, pertaining to, or characteristic of a partisan or partisans. **2.** Devoted to or biased in support of a single party or cause: *partisan politics.* [Fr. < OItal. *partigiano* < *parte,* part < Lat. *pars.*] **—par'ti·san·ship'** *n.*
par·ti·san[2] also **par·ti·zan** (pär'tĭ-zən) *n.* A weapon having a long shaft surmounted by a blade with broad, horizontally projecting cutting edges, used chiefly in the 16th and 17th centuries. [OFr. *partizane* < OItal. *partesana,* var. of *partigiano,* supporter. —see PARTISAN[1].]
par·ti·ta (pär-tē'tə) *n. Mus.* A set of related instrumental pieces, such as a series of variations or a suite. [Ital. < *partire,* divide < Lat. —see PARTITE.]
par·tite (pär'tīt') *adj.* Divided into parts; parted. [Lat. *partitus* < *partire,* to divide < *pars,* part.]
par·ti·tion (pär-tĭsh'ən) *n.* **1. a.** The act or process of dividing something into parts. **b.** The state of being so divided. **2.** Something that separates, such as a partial wall dividing a larger area. **3.** A part or section into which something has been divided. **4.** *Math.* **a.** An expression of a positive integer as a sum of positive integers. **b.** The decomposition of a set into a family of mutually exclusive sets. **5.** *Logic.* The analysis of a class into its component parts. *—tr.v.* **-tioned, -tion·ing, -tions. 1.** To divide into parts, pieces, or sections. **2.** To divide or separate by means of a partition: *partition off an alcove.* [ME *particioun* < OFr. *partition* < Lat. *partitio* < *partire,* to divide < *pars,* part.] **—par·ti'tion·ist** *n.* **—par·ti'tion·ment** *n.*
par·ti·tive (pär'tĭ-tĭv) *adj.* **1.** Serving to divide something into parts. **2.** *Gram.* Indicating a part as distinct from a whole; for example, in the sentence *She drank some of the coffee, some of the coffee* is a partitive construction. *—n. Gram.* **1.** A partitive word, such as *many* or *less.* **2.** A partitive construction or case. [Lat. *partitivus* < *partire,* to divide. —see PARTITE.] **—par'ti·tive·ly** *adv.*
par·ti·zan (pär'tĭ-zən) *n.* Variant of **partisan[2]**.
part·let (pärt'lĭt) *n.* A woman's garment worn esp. in the 16th century, consisting of a covering for the neck and shoulders, and having a band or ruffle at the neck. [ME *patelet* < OFr. *patelete,* band of cloth, dim. of *patte,* paw.]
part·ly (pärt'lē) *adv.* In part; in some degree.
Usage: *Partly* and *partially* are not always interchangeable. *Partly* is the better choice when reference is made to a part as opposed to the whole, especially when speaking of physical objects: *The flag is partly red and partly green. Partially* is used to mean "to a degree" when referring to conditions or states: *We are only partially covered by the insurance. They are partially dependent on welfare.*
part·ner (pärt'nər) *n.* A person associated with another or others in some activity of common interest, esp.: **a.** A member of a business partnership. **b.** A spouse. **c.** Either of two persons dancing together. **d.** One of a pair or a team in a game or sport, such as bridge or tennis. *—tr.v.* **-nered, -ner·ing, -ners. 1.** To make a partner of. **2.** To bring together as partners. **3.** To be the partner of. [ME *partener,* alteration of *parcener,* parcener. —see PARCENER.]
Synonyms: *partner, colleague, ally, confederate, accomplice, associate.* These all denote one who cooperates in a venture, occupation, or challenge. *Partner* implies a relationship, frequently between two people, in which each has equal status and a certain independence but also implicit or formal obligations to the other or others. A *colleague* is any coworker in a given occupation, usually a profession. An *ally* is one who, out of a common cause, has taken one's side and can ostensibly be relied upon, at least temporarily. *Confederate* and *accomplice* are both derogatory, usually applied to alleged criminals and suggesting guilt by willful association. *Confederate* is the more general, signifying any collaborator in a suspicious relationship or venture. An *accomplice* is more specifically somebody who assists another in a single crime. An *associate* is broadly anybody who works in the same place (as distinct from the same field) as another, usually in direct contact with him.
part·ner·ship (pärt'nər-shĭp') *n.* **1.** The state of being a partner; an association of partners. **2.** A contract entered into by two or more persons in which each agrees to furnish a part of the capital and labor for a business enterprise, and by which each shares in some fixed proportion in profits and losses.
part of speech *n.* **1.** One of a group of traditional classifications of words according to their functions in context, including the noun, pronoun, verb, adjective, adverb, preposition, conjunction, and interjection, and sometimes the article. **2.** A word considered as a part of speech.
par·ton (pär'tŏn') *n.* A hypothetical elementary particle that is believed to be a constituent of hadrons.
par·tridge (pär'trĭj) *n., pl.* **partridge** or **-tridg·es. 1.** Any of several plump-bodied Old World game birds, esp. of the genera *Perdix* and *Alectoris.* **2.** Any of several birds, such as the ruffed grouse or the bobwhite, similar or related to the partridge. [ME *partrich* < OFr. *perdriz* < Lat. *perdix* < Gk.]

partridge

par·tridge·ber·ry (pär'trĭj-bĕr'ē) *n., pl.* **-ries.** A creeping, woody, evergreen plant, *Mitchella repens,* of eastern North America, having small white flowers and scarlet berries.
partridge pea *n.* A plant, *Cassia fasciculata,* of eastern and central North America, having yellow flowers.
part song *n.* A song with two or more voice parts.
part-time (pärt'tīm') *adj.* For or during less than the customary time: *a part-time job.* **—part'-time'** *adv.* **—part'-tim'er** *n.*
par·tu·ri·ent (pär-tyo͝or'ē-ənt, -to͝or'-) *adj.* **1.** About to bring forth young; being in labor. **2.** Of or pertaining to giving birth. **3.** About to produce or come forth with something, such as an idea or discovery. [Lat. *parturiens, parturient-,* pr.part. of *parturire,* to be in labor < *parere,* to bear.]
par·tu·ri·fa·cient (pär-tyo͝or'ə-fā'shənt, pär-to͝or'-) *adj.* Inducing or facilitating labor during childbirth. *—n.* A drug facilitating childbirth. [PARTURI(TION) + FACIENT.]
par·tu·ri·tion (pär'tyo͞o-rĭsh'ən, -to͞o-, pär'chə-) *n.* The act of giving birth; childbirth. [LLat. *parturitio* < Lat. *parturire,* to be in labor. —see PARTURIENT.]
part·way (pärt'wā') *adv. Informal.* In part; to a certain degree.
par·ty (pär'tē) *n., pl.* **-ties. 1. a.** A social gathering esp. for pleasure or amusement: *a cocktail party.* **b.** A group of persons gathered together to participate in an activity: *a sailing party.* **2.** A permanent political group organized to promote and support its principles and candidates for public office. **3.** *Law.* A person or group involved in a legal proceeding. **4.** A participant or accessory. **5.** *Informal.* A person: *He's an amusing old party.* **6.** A selected group of soldiers: *a raiding party.* **7.** *Slang.* **a.** An act of sexual intercourse. **b.** An orgy. *—intr.v.* **-tied, -ty·ing, -ties.** *Informal.* **1.** To have or attend a party. **2.** To carouse. [ME, a company of persons < OFr. *partie* < *partir,* to divide < Lat. *partire.* —see PARTITE.]
Usage: A person may be called a *party* in the sense of "participant" *(a party to the conspiracy)* or in a humorous sense *(a wise old party).* But except in legal usage, *party* should not be used as a general synonym for *person,* as in this example: *The party who made the disturbance was taken into custody.*
party line *n.* **1.** A telephone circuit connecting two or more subscribers with the exchange. **2.** The official policies and principles of a political party to which loyal members are expected to adhere. **—party liner** *n.*
par·ty-poop·er (pär'tē-po͞o'pər) *n. Slang.* One who declines to participate enthusiastically in the recreation of a group.
party wall *n. Law.* A wall built on the boundary line of adjoining properties and shared by two owners or tenants.
pa·rure (pə-ro͝or') *n.* A set of matched jewelry or other ornaments. [Fr. < OFr., adornment < *parer,* to adorn. —see PARE.]
par value *n.* The value imprinted on a stock certificate or bond which provides the basis for bond interest, preferred stock dividend, or share of equity capital; face value.
par·ve (pär'və) *adj. Judaism.* Variant of **pareve**.
par·ve·nu (pär'və-no͞o', -nyo͞o') *n.* A person who has suddenly risen above his social and economic class without the background or qualifications for his new status. [Fr. < p.part of *parvenir,* to arrive < Lat. *pervenire* : *per,* through + *venire,* to come.] **—par've·nu'** *adj.*
par·vis (pär'vĭs) *n.* **1.** An enclosed courtyard or space in front of a palace or church. **2.** A portico or colonnade in front of a church. [ME < OFr. < LLat. *paradisus,* garden, paradise. —see PARADISE.]
par·vo·vi·rus (pär'vō-vī'rəs) *n.* Any of a group of DNA-containing animal viruses. [Lat. *parvus,* small + VIRUS.]
pas (pä) *n., pl.* **pas** (pä). **1. a.** In ballet, a step or series of steps. **b.** A ballet dance. **2.** The right to go before; precedence. [Fr. < Lat. *passus,* step. —see PACE[1].]
pas·cal (päs-käl', pä-skäl') *n.* A unit of pressure equal to one newton per square meter. [After Blaise *Pascal* (1623–1662).]
pas·cal celery also **Pas·chal celery** (păs'kəl) *n.* Any of several types of commercially grown celery having green, unblanched stalks. [Orig. unknown.]
pas·chal (păs'kəl) *adj.* Of or pertaining to Passover or to Easter. [ME *paskal* < OFr. *pascal* < LLat. *paschalis* < *pascha,* Passover, Easter < LGk. *paskha* < Heb. *pesaḥ,* Pesach.]
paschal lamb *n.* **1.** A lamb eaten at the feast of the Passover. **2. Paschal Lamb.** Christ.
pas de deux (pä də dœ') *n., pl.* **pas de deux.** A ballet figure or dance for two persons. [Fr. *pas,* step + *de,* of + *deux,* two.]
pa·se (pä'sā) *n.* A presentation and movement of the cape by the matador to attract, receive, and direct the charge of the bull. [Sp. < *pasar,* to pass < VLat. **passare.* —see PASS.]
pa·sha also **pa·cha** (pä'shə, păsh'ə, pə-shä') *n.* A former title of honor placed after the name of Turkish military and civil officials. [Turk. *paşa.*]
Pash·to (pŭsh'tō) also **Push·tu** (pŭsh'to͞o) *n.* An Iranian language that is the principal vernacular language of Afghanistan and parts of western Pakistan. [Pers. *pashtu* < Pashto.]
Pa·siph·a·ë (pə-sĭf'ə-ē') *n. Gk. Myth.* The wife of Minos and mother, by a white bull, of the Minotaur. [Lat. < Gk. *Pasiphaē.*]

pasque·flow·er (păsk′flou′ər) *n.* Any of several plants of the genus *Anemone,* having large blue, purple, or white flowers and conspicuously plumed fruit. [Blend of OFr. *pasque,* Easter and E. *passeflower,* pasqueflower < OFr. *passefleur* : *passer,* to pass + *fleur,* flower.]

pas·qui·nade (păs′kwə-nād′) *n.* **1.** A lampoon posted in a public place. **2.** Satire. —*tr.v.* **-nad·ed, -nad·ing, -nades.** To ridicule with a pasquinade. [Fr. < Ital. *pasquinata,* after *Pasquino,* the nickname given to a statue in Rome, Italy on which lampoons were posted.] —**pas′qui·nad′er** *n.*

pass (păs) *v.* **passed, pass·ing, pass·es.** —*intr.* **1.** To move on or ahead; proceed. **2.** To run; extend: *The river passes through our land.* **3.** To gain passage despite obstacles: *pass through difficult years.* **4.** To catch up with and move past another vehicle: *The sports car passed on the right.* **5.** To move past in time; elapse: *The days passed quickly.* **6.** To be transferred from one to another; circulate: *The wine passed around the table.* **7.** To be communicated or exchanged between persons: *Loud words passed.* **8.** To be transferred or conveyed to another by will, deed, or the like: *The title passed to the older son.* **9.** To undergo transition from one condition, form, quality, or characteristic to another: *Daylight passed into darkness.* **10.** To come to an end; be terminated: *His anger passed suddenly.* **11.** To cease to exist; die: *passed on in his sleep.* **12.** To happen; take place: *What passed during the morning?* **13.** To be allowed to happen without notice or challenge: *Let their rude remarks pass.* **14.** To undergo an examination or trial with favorable results. **15.** To be approved or adopted: *The motion to adjourn passed.* **16.** *Law.* **a.** To sit in judicial or legal investigation. **b.** To pronounce an opinion, judgment, or sentence. **c.** To sit in adjudication. **17.** *Sports.* To transfer a ball or puck to a teammate. **18.** To thrust or lunge in fencing. **19.** *Games.* To let one's turn to play or bid go by. —*tr.* **1.** To go by without stopping; leave behind. **2. a.** To go by without paying attention to; let go unmentioned. **b.** To fail to pay (a dividend). **3.** To go beyond; exceed: *The returns passed all expectations.* **4.** To go across; go through: *pass enemy lines.* **5. a.** To undergo (a trial or examination) with favorable results: *He passed every test.* **b.** To cause or allow to go through a trial, test, or examination successfully: *The instructor passed all the candidates.* **6. a.** To cause to move: *He passed his hand over the fabric.* **b.** To cause to move into a certain position: *pass a cable around a cylinder.* **c.** To cause to move as part of a process: *pass liquid through a filter.* **7.** To cause to go by: *pass foot soldiers in review.* **8.** To allow to go by or elapse; spend: *He passed his winter in Vermont.* **9. a.** To cause to be transferred from one to another; circulate: *They passed the news quickly.* **b.** To hand over to someone else: *pass the bread.* **c.** To circulate fraudulently: *pass counterfeit money.* **d.** *Law.* To transfer title or ownership of. **10.** *Sports.* **a.** To throw (a ball) to a teammate. **b.** *Baseball.* To walk (a batter). **11.** To cross over; issue from: *No secrets pass her lips.* **12.** To discharge (bodily waste); void. **13. a.** To approve; adopt: *The legislature passed the bill.* **b.** To be sanctioned, ratified, or approved by: *The bill passed the House of Representatives.* **14.** To pronounce; utter: *pass judgment.* **15.** To go past without noticing: *He passed them by without even a nod.* —***phrasal verbs.*** **pass away. 1.** To go away in time; end. **2.** To die. **3.** To spend or while away (time). **pass for.** To be accepted as being something one is not: *pass for a doctor.* **pass off.** To offer, sell, or put into circulation (an imitation of something) as genuine. **pass out. 1.** To lose consciousness. **2.** To die. **pass over.** To leave out; disregard. **pass up.** *Informal.* To reject; let go by: *pass up an opportunity.* —*n.* **1.** The act of passing; passage. **2.** A way through or on which one can move or travel, esp. a narrow gap between mountain peaks. **3. a.** A permit, ticket, or authorization to come and go at will. **b.** A free ticket entitling one to transportation or admission. **c.** Written leave of absence from military duty. **4.** A sweep or run by an aircraft over an area or target. **5.** A condition or situation, often critical in nature; predicament. **6.** A sexual invitation or overture. **7.** A motion of the hand or the waving of a wand for magic. **8. a.** *Sports.* A transfer of a ball or puck between teammates. **b.** *Sports.* A lunge or thrust in fencing. **c.** *Baseball.* A walk. **9.** *Games.* A refusal to bid, draw, bet, or play. **10.** A winning throw of the dice in the game of craps. **11.** A pase. —***idioms.*** **bring to pass.** To cause to happen. **come to pass.** To happen. **in passing.** By the way; parenthetically. **pass muster.** To pass an examination or an inspection; measure up to a given standard. **pass the buck.** To shift responsibility or blame to another. **pass the hat.** To take up a collection. **pretty pass.** A bad or difficult situation. [ME *passen* < OFr. *passer* < VLat. **passare* < Lat. *passus,* step. —see PACE[1].] —**pass′er** *n.*

Usage: The past tense and past participle of *pass* is *passed: They passed* (or *have passed*) *our home. Time had passed slowly. Past* is the corresponding adjective (*in centuries past*), adverb (*drove past*), and preposition (*past midnight; past the crisis*).

pass·a·ble (păs′ə-bəl) *adj.* **1.** Able to be passed, traversed, or crossed, as a road or stream. **2.** Acceptable for general circulation: *passable currency.* **3.** Satisfactory but not outstanding. —**pass′a·ble·ness** *n.* —**pass′a·bly** *adv.*

pas·sa·ca·glia (pä′sə-käl′yə, păs′ə-käl′yə) *n. Mus.* A 17th- and 18th-century musical form consisting of continuous variations on a ground bass in slow triple meter. [Ital. < Sp. *passacalle* : *pasar,* to pass + *calle,* street < Lat. *callis,* path.]

pas·sage (păs′ĭj) *n.* **1.** The act or process of passing, esp.: **a.** A movement from one place to another; transit. **b.** The process of elapsing. **c.** The process of passing from one condition or stage to another; transition. **d.** *Obs.* Death. **e.** The enactment into law of a legislative measure. **2.** A journey, esp. one by air or water. **3. a.** The right to travel on something, esp. a ship: *book a passage.* **b.** The price paid for this. **4.** The right, permission, or power to come and go freely. **5. a.** A path, channel, or duct through, over, or along which something may pass: *the nasal passages.* **b.** A corridor. **6.** An occurrence between two persons, esp.: **a.** An exchange of words, arguments, or vows. **b.** An exchange of blows: *passage at arms.* **7.** A segment of a literary work: *a celebrated passage from Shakespeare.* **8.** *Mus.* A segment of a composition. **9.** *Med.* An emptying of the bowels. [ME < OFr. < *passer,* to pass.]

pas·sage·way (păs′ĭj-wā′) *n.* A corridor.

Pas·sa·ma·quod·dy (păs′ə-mə-kwŏd′ē) *n., pl.* **Passamaquoddy** or **-dies. 1.** A tribe of Algonquian-speaking North American Indians, formerly inhabiting Maine and New Brunswick, Canada. **2.** A member of the Passamaquoddy. **3.** The Algonquian language of the Passamaquoddy.

pas·sant (păs′ənt) *adj. Heraldry.* Designating a beast facing and walking toward the viewer's right with one front leg raised. [ME < OFr. < pr.part. of *passer,* to pass.]

pass·book (păs′bo͝ok′) *n.* **1.** A bankbook. **2.** A book in which a merchant records credit sales.

pas·sé (pă-sā′) *adj.* **1.** Out-of-date; no longer current or in fashion. **2.** Past the prime; aged. [Fr. p.part. of *passer,* to pass < OFr.]

passed ball *n. Baseball.* A pitch missed by the catcher that he should have been able to field and that allows a base runner to advance a base.

pas·sel (păs′əl) *n. Informal.* A large quantity or number: *They had a whole passel of children.* [Alteration of PARCEL.]

passe·men·terie (păs-mĕn′trē) *n.* Ornamental trimming for a garment, such as braid, lace, or metallic beads. [Fr. < *passement,* ornamental braid < *passer,* to pass < OFr.]

pas·sen·ger (păs′ən-jər) *n.* **1.** A person who travels in a train, airplane, ship, bus, or other conveyance without participating in its operation. **2.** A wayfarer or traveler. [ME *passager* < OFr. < *passager,* passing < *passage,* passage < *passer,* to pass.]

passenger pigeon *n.* An extinct migratory bird, *Ectopistes migratorius,* abundant in North America until the latter part of the 19th century.

passe par·tout (păs pär-to͞o′) *n.* **1.** Something enabling one to pass or go everywhere, esp. a master key. **2. a.** A mounting for a picture in which colored tape forms the frame. **b.** The tape so used. **3.** A mat used in mounting a picture. [Fr. : *passe,* imper. of *passer,* to pass + *partout,* everywhere.]

pas·ser-by also **pas·ser·by** (păs′ər-bī′) *n., pl.* **pas·sers-by** also **pas·sers·by** A person who passes by, often by chance.

pas·ser·ine (păs′ə-rīn′) *adj.* Pertaining to or designating birds of the order Passeriformes, which includes perching birds and songbirds such as the jays, blackbirds, finches, warblers, and sparrows. —*n.* A bird of the order Passeriformes. [Lat. *passerinus,* of sparrows < *passer,* sparrow.]

pas seul (pä sœl′) *n.* A dance or ballet figure performed by one person. [Fr.]

pass-fail (păs′fāl′) *n.* A system of grading in which traditional letter grades are not used and the student either passes or fails. —***modifier:*** *a pass-fail course.*

pas·si·ble (păs′ə-bəl) *adj.* Capable of suffering; sensitive. [ME < OFr. < Med. Lat. *passibilis* < LLat. < Lat. *pati,* to suffer.] —**pas′si·bil′i·ty** *n.*

pas·sim (păs′ĭm) *adv.* Throughout; frequently. Used in textual annotation to indicate that the word or passage occurs frequently in the work cited. [Lat. < *passus,* scattered < *pandere,* to scatter.]

pass·ing (păs′ĭng) *adj.* **1.** Of brief duration; transitory: *a passing fancy.* **2.** Cursory; superficial; casual: *a passing glance.* **3.** Allowing one to pass a test, course of study, or other examination; satisfactory: *a passing grade.* **4.** *Obs.* Very; great; surpassing: " *'Tis a passing shame*" (Shakespeare). —*adv.* Very; surpassingly: *a girl who was passing fair.* —*n.* **1.** The act of one that passes or the fact of having passed. **2.** A place where or a means by which one can pass. **3.** Death.

passing note *n. Mus.* A note that is not part of a particular chord but is placed between two chords to provide a smooth transition from one to the other.

pas·sion (păsh′ən) *n.* **1.** A powerful emotion or appetite, such as love, joy, hatred, anger, or greed. **2. a.** Ardent, adoring love. **b.** Strong sexual desire; lust. **c.** The object of such love or desire. **3. a.** Boundless enthusiasm: *has a passion for literature.* **b.** The object of such enthusiasm: *literature is his passion.* **4.** An abandoned display of emotion, esp. of anger. **5. Passion. a.** The sufferings of Christ in the period following the Last Supper and including the Crucifixion. **b.** A narrative of this, as in one of the Gospels, or a musical setting or serial pictorial representation of it. [ME < OFr. < LLat.

passio, suffering < Lat. *passus,* p.part. of *pati,* to suffer.] **—pas'sion·less** *adj.*

Synonyms: *passion, fervor, enthusiasm, zeal, ardor.* These all denote strong feeling, either sustained or passing, for or about something or somebody. *Passion* is a deep, overwhelming feeling or emotion. When directed toward a person, it usually connotes love as well as sexual desire, although it can also refer to hostile emotions such as anger and hatred. Used lightly, it suggests an avid interest, as in a hobby: *a passion for gardening. Fervor* is a highly intense, sustained emotional state, frequently (like *passion*) with a potential loss of control implied: *he fought with fervor.* Quite different is *enthusiasm,* which reflects excitement and responsiveness to more specific or concrete things. *Zeal,* sometimes reflecting strong, forceful devotion to a specific cause, expresses a driving attraction to something that grows out of motivation or attitude: *zeal for the project. Ardor* can be for a cause but commonly connotes a warm, rapturous feeling directed toward persons.

pas·sion·al (păsh'ə-nəl) *adj.* Of or pertaining to passion. *—n.* A book of the sufferings of saints and martyrs.

pas·sion·ate (păsh'ə-nĭt) *adj.* **1.** Capable of or having intense feelings. **2.** Wrathful by temperament; choleric. **3.** Amorous; lustful. **4.** Showing or expressing strong emotion; ardent: *a passionate speech against injustice.* **5.** Arising from or marked by passion: *a passionate rage.* **—pas'sion·ate·ly** *adv.* **—pas'sion·ate·ness** *n.*

passionflower

pas·sion·flow·er (păsh'ən-flou'ər) *n.* Any of various chiefly tropical American vines of the genus *Passiflora,* usually having large, showy flowers. [So called from the resemblance of its parts to the instruments of the Passion.]

passion fruit *n.* The edible fruit of the passionflower.

Passion play *n.* A play representing the Passion of Christ.

Passion Sunday *n.* The second Sunday before Easter.

Pas·sion·tide (păsh'ən-tīd') *n.* The fortnight between Passion Sunday and Easter.

Passion Week *n.* The week between Passion Sunday and Palm Sunday.

pas·sive (păs'ĭv) *adj.* **1.** Receiving or subjected to an action without responding or initiating an action in return. **2.** Accepting without objection or resistance; compliant. **3.** Not participating, acting, or operating; inert. **4.** Designating certain bonds or shares that do not bear financial interest. **5.** *Gram.* Denoting a verb form or voice used to indicate that the grammatical subject is the object of the action or the effect of the verb. For example, in the sentence *They were impressed by his manner, were impressed* is in the passive voice. **6.** Inert (sense 3). **7.** *Electronics.* Exhibiting no gain or contributing no energy: *a passive circuit element. —n. Gram.* **1.** The passive voice. **2.** A verb or construction in the passive voice. [ME < Lat. *passivus,* capable of suffering < *passus,* p.part. of *pati,* to suffer.] **—pas'sive·ly** *adv.* **—pas'sive·ness** *n.*

passive immunity *n.* Immunity acquired by an individual after the transfer of antibodies through injection or by natural means, as by placental transfer to a fetus. **—passive immunization** *n.*

passive resistance *n.* Resistance to authority or law by nonviolent methods, such as refusal to comply, peaceful demonstrations, or fasting. **—passive resister** *n.*

passive restraint *n.* An automatic safety device, such as an air bag, on a vehicle that acts to protect a person during a crash.

pas·siv·ism (păs'ĭv-ĭz'əm) *n.* Passive character, quality, or behavior. **—pas'siv·ist** *n.*

pas·siv·i·ty (pă-sĭv'ĭ-tē) *n.* The condition or quality of being passive; inactivity; quiescence.

pass·key (păs'kē') *n.* A master key.

Pass·o·ver (păs'ō'vər) *n.* A Jewish festival beginning on the 14th of Nisan and traditionally celebrated for eight days. It commemorates the escape of the Jews from Egypt. [Transl. of Heb. *pesaḥ,* Pesach.]

pass·port (păs'pôrt', -pōrt') *n.* **1.** An official governmental document that certifies the identity and citizenship of an individual and grants him permission to travel abroad. **2.** A permit issued by a foreign country allowing one to transport goods or to travel through that country. **3.** An official document issued to a ship, esp. a neutral merchant ship in time of war, authorizing it to leave port or to enter certain waters freely. **4.** Something that enables one to be admitted or accepted: *intelligence as a passport to success.* [Fr. *passeport* : *passer,* to pass + *port,* port.]

pass·word (păs'wûrd') *n.* A secret word or phrase which indicates that the speaker is to be admitted.

past (păst) *adj.* **1.** No longer current; gone by; over: *His youth is past.* **2.** Having existed or occurred in an earlier time; bygone: *past events; past centuries.* **3. a.** Earlier than the present time; ago: *forty years past.* **b.** Just gone by or elapsed: *in the past month.* **4.** Having served formerly in a given official capacity: *a past vice president.* **5.** *Gram.* Of, pertaining to, or denoting a verb tense or form used to express an action or condition prior to the time it is expressed. *—n.* **1.** The time before the present. **2. a.** Former background, career, experiences, and activities: *a man with a distinguished past.* **b.** A former period of someone's life kept secret. **3.** *Gram.* **a.** The past tense. **b.** A verb form in the past tense. *—adv.* So as to pass by or go beyond: *He waved as he walked past. —prep.* **1.** Beyond in time; later than; after: *It is past midnight.* **2.** Beyond in position: *the lake past the meadow.* **3.** Beyond the power, scope, extent, or influence of: *The problem is past understanding.* **4.** Beyond the number or amount of: *The child couldn't count past 20.* — See Usage note at **pass.** [ME < p.part. of *passen,* to pass. — see PASS.]

pas·ta (päs'tə) *n.* **1.** Paste or dough made of flour and water, used dried, as in macaroni, or fresh, as in ravioli. **2.** A prepared dish of pasta. [Ital. < LLat.]

paste[1] (pāst) *n.* **1.** A smooth viscous adhesive, such as flour and water or starch and water, used to join light materials, such as paper and cloth. **2.** A soft, smooth, thick mixture similar to paste. **3.** A smooth dough of water, flour, and butter or other shortening, used in making pastry. **4.** A food that has been pounded until it is reduced to a smooth, creamy mass: *anchovy paste.* **5.** A sweet, doughy candy or confection. **6.** Moistened clay used in making porcelain or pottery. **7. a.** A hard, brilliant glass used in making artificial gems. **b.** A gem made of this glass. *—tr.v.* **past·ed, past·ing, pastes. 1.** To cause to adhere by applying paste. **2.** To cover with something to which paste has been applied: *He pasted the wall with burlap.* **—*phrasal verb.* paste up.** *Printing.* To prepare a mechanical of. [ME < OFr. < LLat. *pasta.*]

paste[2] (pāst) *Slang. —tr.v.* **past·ed, past·ing, pastes.** To punch. *—n.* A hard blow. [Alteration of BASTE[3].]

paste·board (pāst'bôrd', -bōrd') *n.* **1.** A thin, firm board made of sheets of paper pasted together or of pressed paper pulp, used esp. to make book covers. **2. a.** A ticket. **b.** A playing card. **c.** A visiting card.

pas·tel (pă-stĕl') *n.* **1. a.** A dried paste made of ground and mixed pigment, chalk, water, and gum, used to make crayons. **b.** A crayon of this material. **2.** A picture or sketch drawn with this type of crayon. **3.** The art or process of drawing with pastels. **4.** A soft, delicate hue; a light tint. **5.** A sketchy or brief prose work. [Fr. < Ital. < LLat. *pastellus,* woad, dim. of *pasta,* paste.] **—pas·tel'ist** *n.*

pas·tern (păs'tərn) *n.* **1.** The part of a horse's foot between the fetlock and hoof. **2.** A part of the leg of a dog or other quadruped that is comparable to the pastern. [ME *pastron,* hobble < OFr. *pasturon* < *pasture,* pasture.]

paste-up (pāst'ŭp') *n.* **1.** A composition of light, flat objects pasted on a sheet of paper or other backing; collage. **2.** *Printing.* A mechanical.

pas·teur·i·za·tion (păs'chər-ĭ-zā'shən, păs'tər-) *n.* The act or process of destroying most disease-producing microorganisms and limiting fermentation in milk, beer, and other liquids by partial or complete sterilization. [After Louis *Pasteur* (1822–1895).]

pas·teur·ize (păs'chə-rīz', păs'tə-) *tr.v.* **-ized, -iz·ing, -iz·es.** To subject (a liquid) to pasteurization. **—pas'teur·iz'er** *n.*

Pas·teur treatment (pă-stûr') *n.* A rabies treatment in which the growth of antibodies is stimulated during the incubation of the disease by increasingly strong inoculations of the attenuated rabies virus. [After Louis *Pasteur* (1822–1895).]

pas·tic·cio (pă-stē'chō, -chē-ō, päs-) *n., pl.* **-ci** (-chē). A work, esp. a musical work, produced by borrowing fragments or motifs from various sources; potpourri. [Ital. < Med. Lat. *pasticius,* pasty < Lat. *pasta,* paste.]

pas·tiche (pă-stēsh', pä-) *n.* **1.** A dramatic, literary, or musical piece openly imitating the previous work of another artist, often with satirical intent. **2.** A hodgepodge; pasticcio. [Fr. < Ital. *pasticcio,* pasticcio.]

pas·tille (pă-stēl') also **pas·til** (păs'tĭl) *n.* **1.** A small medicated or flavored tablet; troche. **2.** A tablet containing aromatic substances that is burned to fumigate or deodorize the air. **3.** Pastel (sense 1). [Fr. < Lat. *pastillus.*]

pas·time (păs'tīm') *n.* An activity that occupies one's spare time pleasantly.

pas·ti·na (pă-stē'nə) *n.* Tiny pieces of macaroni, usually cooked in soups or used as baby food. [Ital., dim. of *pasta,* pasta.]

past master *n.* **1.** One who has formerly held the position of master in an organization such as a lodge or club. **2.** A person thoroughly experienced and skilled in a particular craft.

pas·tor (păs'tər) *n.* **1.** A Christian minister in his capacity of having spiritual charge over a congregation or other group. **2.** A shepherd. [ME *pastour* < AN < Lat. *pastor,* shepherd < *pascere,* to pasture.] **—pas'tor·ship'** *n.*

pas·tor·al (păs'tər-əl) *adj.* **1.** Of or pertaining to shepherds, herdsmen, and others directly involved in animal husbandry. **2. a.** Of or pertaining to the country or country life; rural. **b.** Having the qualities of idealized country life, such as charming simplicity and a leisurely, carefree pace. **3.** Of or designating an artistic work that portrays country life in an idealized way. **4.** Of or pertaining to a pastor or his duties. *—n.* **1.** A literary or other artistic work that portrays rural life, usually in an idealized manner. **2.** *Mus.* A pastorale. [ME < Lat. *pastoralis* < *pastor,* shepherd. —see PASTOR.] **—pas'tor·al·ism** *n.* **—pas'tor·al·ist** *n.* **—pas'tor·al·ly** *adv.*

pas·to·rale (păs'tə-räl', -răl', -rä'lē, päs'-) *n., pl.* **-ra·li** (-rä'lē) or **-rales.** *Mus.* **1.** An opera or other vocal composition based on a rural theme or subject. **2.** An instrumental composition with a tender melody in a moderately slow rhythm,

ă **pat** / ā **pay** / âr **care** / ä **father** / b **bib** / ch **church** / d **deed** / ĕ **pet** / ē **be** / f **fife** / g **gag** / h **hat** / hw **which** / ĭ **pit** / ī **pie** / îr **pier** / j **judge** / k **kick** / l **lid, needle** / m **mum** / n **no, sudden** / ng **thing** / ŏ **pot** / ō **toe** / ô **paw, for** / oi **noise** / ou **out** / o͝o **took** / o͞o **boot** /

suggestive of idyllic rural life. [Ital. < *pastorale,* pastoral < Lat. *pastoralis* < *pastor,* shepherd. —see PASTOR.]
pas·tor·ate (păs′tər-ĭt) *n.* **1.** The office, rank, or jurisdiction of a pastor. **2.** A pastor's term of office with one congregation. **3.** A body of pastors.
pas·to·ri·um (pă-stôr′ē-əm, -stōr′-) *n. Chiefly Southern U.S.* The residence of a pastor; parsonage.
past participle *n.* A verb form indicating past or completed action or time that is used as a verbal adjective in phrases such as *finished work, baked beans,* and with auxiliaries to form the passive voice or perfect and pluperfect tenses in constructions such as *The work was finished* and *She had baked the beans.*
past perfect *n.* The pluperfect.
pas·tra·mi (pə-strä′mē) *n.* A highly seasoned smoked cut of beef, usually from the breast or shoulder. [Yiddish < Rum. *pastramă* < *păstra,* to preserve.]
pas·try (pās′trē) *n., pl.* **-tries. 1.** A baked paste of flour, water, and shortening, used for the crusts of such foods as pies and tarts. **2.** Baked foods made with pastry. [< PASTE[1].]
past tense *n.* A verb tense used to express an action or condition that occurred in or during the past; for example, in *While she was sewing, he read aloud, was sewing* and *read* are in the past tense.
pas·tur·age (păs′chər-ĭj) *n.* **1.** The grass or other vegetation eaten by grazing animals. **2. a.** Land covered with grass or vegetation suitable for grazing animals. **b.** The right to graze animals on such land. **3.** The business of grazing cattle.
pas·ture (păs′chər) *n.* **1. a.** Grass or other vegetation eaten as food by grazing animals. **b.** Ground on which such vegetation grows. **2.** The feeding or grazing of animals. *—v.* **-tured, -tur·ing, -tures.** *—tr.* **1.** To herd (animals) into a pasture to graze. **2.** To provide (animals) with pasturage. Used of land. *—intr.* To graze in a pasture. [ME < OFr. < LLat. *pastura* < Lat. *pascere,* to pasture.] **—pas′tur·a·ble** *adj.* **—pas′tur·er** *n.*
pas·ture·land (păs′chər-lănd′) *n.* Land suitable for grazing.
past·y[1] (pā′stē) *adj.* **-i·er, -i·est. 1.** Resembling paste in color or consistency. **2.** Having a pale and lifeless appearance. *—n., pl.* **-ies.** A patch used by striptease performers to conceal the nipple. **—past′i·ness** *n.*
pas·ty[2] (păs′tē) *n., pl.* **-ties.** A pie with a filling of seasoned meat or fish. [ME < OFr. *pastee* < *paste,* paste.]
PA system (pē′ā′) *n.* A public-address system.
pat (păt) *v.* **pat·ted, pat·ting, pats.** *—tr.* **1. a.** To tap gently with the open hand or with something flat. **b.** To stroke lightly as a gesture of affection. **2.** To mold by tapping gently with the hands or a flat implement. *—intr.* **1.** To run or walk with a tapping sound. **2.** To hit something or against something gently or lightly. *—n.* **1.** A light stroke or tap. **2.** The sound made by a light stroke or tap, or by light footsteps. **3.** A small mass of something shaped by or as if by patting: *a pat of butter.* *—adj.* **1.** Timely; opportune; fitting. **2.** Needing no change; exactly right. **3.** Contrived: *a pat answer.* *—adv. Informal.* **1.** Without changing position; steadfastly: *stand pat on that issue.* **2.** Perfectly; precisely; aptly. **—*idiom.* down pat.** *Informal.* Known and understood completely. [< ME *patte,* a light blow.] **—pat′ly** *adv.* **—pat′ness** *n.*
pa·ta·ca (pə-tä′kə) *n.* See table at **currency.** [Port.]
pa·ta·gi·um (pə-tā′jē-əm) *n., pl.* **-gi·a** (-jē-ə) *Zool.* **1.** A thin membrane extending between the fore and hind limb to form a wing or winglike extension, as in bats and flying squirrels. **2.** An expandable, membranous fold of skin between the wing and body of a bird. [NLat. < Lat., gold edging on a woman's tunic < Gk. **patageion* < *patagos,* clatter.]
patch (păch) *n.* **1.** A small piece of material affixed to another, larger piece to conceal or reinforce a weakened or worn area. **2. a.** A small piece of cloth used for patchwork. **b.** A small cloth badge affixed to a sleeve to indicate the military unit to which one belongs. **3.** A dressing or covering applied to protect a wound or sore. **4.** A small pad or shield of cloth worn over an injured eye. **5.** A beauty spot. **6. a.** A small piece of land. **b.** The produce grown on such a piece of land: *a patch of beans.* **7.** A small part or section of a surface that differs from or contrasts with the whole: *The flowers made white patches against the grass.* **8.** A small piece or part of something. *—tr.v.* **patched, patch·ing, patch·es. 1.** To put a patch or patches on. **2. a.** To make by sewing scraps of material together: *patch a quilt.* **b.** To make by piecing various elements together, esp. hastily: *They patched together a treaty.* **3.** To mend, repair, or put together, esp. hastily, clumsily, or poorly: *patching old costumes for the tour.* **—*phrasal verb.* patch up.** To settle; make up: *They patched up their quarrel.* [ME *pacche.*] **—patch′a·ble** *adj.* **—patch′er** *n.*
patch·ou·li also **patch·ou·ly** or **pach·ou·li** (păch′ə-lē, pə-cho͞o′lē) *n., pl.* **-lis** also **-lies** or **-lis. 1.** Any of several Asiatic trees of the genus *Pogostemon,* esp. *P. patchouly* and *P. cablin,* having leaves that yield a fragrant oil used in the manufacture of perfumes. **2.** A perfume made from the oil of the patchouli. [Tamil *paccilai.*]
patch pocket *n.* An unfitted flat pocket on the outside of a garment.
patch test *n.* A test for allergic sensitivity made by applying a suspected allergen to the skin in a small surgical pad.
patch·work (păch′wûrk′) *n.* **1.** Needlework consisting of varicolored patches of material sewed together, as in a quilt. **2.** A collection of miscellaneous or incongruous parts; jumble.
patch·y (păch′ē) *adj.* **-i·er, -i·est. 1.** Made up of or marked by patches: *patchy trousers.* **2.** Uneven in quality or performance: *patchy work.* **—patch′i·ly** *adv.* **—patch′i·ness** *n.*
pate (pāt) *n.* **1.** The head, esp. the top of the head: *a bald pate.* **2.** The brains; intellect. [ME.] **—pat′ed** *adj*
pâte (pät) *n.* Paste used in making porcelain and pottery. [Fr. < OFr. *paste,* paste.]
pâ·té (pä-tā′) *n.* **1.** A meat paste, esp. pâté de foie gras. **2.** A small pastry filled with meat or fish. [Fr. < OFr. *pastee,* pasty (pie) < *paste,* paste.]
pâ·té de foie gras (pä-tā′ də fwä grä′) *n.* A paste made from goose liver, usually with truffles. [Fr. : *pâté,* pâté + *de,* of + *foie,* liver + *gras,* fat]
pa·tel·la (pə-tĕl′ə) *n., pl.* **-lae** (-ē). **1. a.** A flat, triangular bone located at the front of the knee joint. **b.** A dish-shaped anatomical formation. **2.** An ancient Roman pan or dish. [Lat. < dim. of *patina,* plate. —see PATEN.] **—pa·tel′lar, pa·tel′late** (-ĭt, -āt′) *adj.*
pa·tel·li·form (pə-tĕl′ə-fôrm′) *adj.* Shaped like a pan, dish, or cup: *the patelliform shell of the limpet.* [PATELL(A) + -FORM.]
pat·en also **pat·in** (păt′n) or **pa·tine** (pă-tēn′) *n.* **1.** A plate used to hold the Eucharistic bread. **2.** A plate. **3.** A thin disk of metal. [ME < OFr. *patene* < Lat. *patina,* plate < Gk. *patanē.*]
pa·ten·cy (pāt′n-sē) *n.* The state or quality of being obvious.
pat·ent (păt′nt) *n.* **1. a.** A grant made by a government to an inventor, assuring him the sole right to make, use, and sell his invention for a certain period of time. **b.** Letters patent. **c.** Something that is protected by such a grant. **2. a.** A grant made by a government to an individual, conveying to him fee-simple title to public lands. **b.** The official document of such a grant. **c.** The land so granted. **3.** An exclusive right or title. *—adj.* **1.** Obvious; plain. **2.** Protected by a patent. **3.** Of, pertaining to, or dealing in patents: *patent law.* **4.** (pāt′nt) *Biol.* Spreading open; expanded. **5.** Of high quality. Used of flour. *—tr.v.* **-ent·ed, -ent·ing, -ents. 1.** To obtain a patent on. **2.** To grant a patent to. [ME, unsealed < OFr. < Lat. *patens* < pr.part. of *patēre,* to be opened.] **—pat′ent·a·bil′i·ty** *n.* **—pat′ent·a·ble** *adj.* **—pat′ent·ly** (pāt′nt-lē) *adv.*
pat·ent·ee (păt′n-tē′) *n.* One who has been granted a patent.
pat·ent leather (păt′nt) *n.* **1.** Black leather finished to a hard, glossy surface. **2.** Any of several synthetic materials resembling patent leather. [So called because it is made by a once-patented process.]
patent log *n. Naut.* A screw log.
patent medicine *n.* A drug or other medical preparation that is protected by a patent and can be bought without a prescription.
patent office *n.* A government bureau that studies claims for and grants patents.
pat·en·tor (păt′n-tər, păt′n-tôr′) *n.* One that grants a patent.
patent right *n.* The right granted by a patent, esp. the right to have exclusive manufacture and sale of an invention.
pa·ter (pā′tər) *n. Chiefly Brit.* Father. [Lat.]
pa·ter·fa·mil·i·as (pā′tər-fə-mĭl′ē-əs, pä′tər-) *n., pl.* **pa·tres·fa·mil·i·as** (pā′trēz-fə-mĭl′ē-əs, pä′-). **1.** The male head of a household. **2.** The father of a family. [Lat. : *pater,* father + *familia,* family.]
pa·ter·nal (pə-tûr′nəl) *adj.* **1.** Of, pertaining to, or characteristic of a father; fatherly. **2.** Received or inherited from a father. **3.** Of or pertaining to the father's side of a family. [Med. Lat. *paternalis* < Lat. *paternus* < *pater,* father.] **—pa·ter′nal·ly** *adv.*
pa·ter·nal·ism (pə-tûr′nə-lĭz′əm) *n.* A policy or practice of treating or governing people in a fatherly manner, esp. by providing for their needs without giving them responsibility. **—pa·ter′nal·is′tic** *adj.* **—pa·ter′nal·is′ti·cal·ly** *adv.*
pa·ter·ni·ty (pə-tûr′nĭ-tē) *n.* **1.** The fact or condition of being a father; fatherhood. **2.** Descent on a father's side; paternal descent. **3.** Authorship; origin. [OFr. *paternite* < LLat. *paternitas* < Lat. *paternus,* paternal < *pater,* father.]
paternity test *n.* A test using blood group identification of a mother, child, and suspected father that establishes the probability of paternity.
pa·ter·nos·ter (pā′tər-nŏs′tər, pä′tər-, păt′ər-) *n.* **1.** Often **Paternoster.** The Lord's Prayer. **2.** One of the large beads on a rosary on which the Lord's Prayer is said. **3.** A sequence of words spoken as a prayer or as a magic formula. **4.** A weighted fishing line having several jointed attachments for hooks connected by beadlike swivels. [ME < Med. Lat. < Lat. *pater noster,* our father.]
path (păth, päth) *n., pl.* **paths** (pă*th*z, pä*th*z, păths, päths). **1.** A track or way made by footsteps. **2.** A road or track made for a particular purpose: *a bicycle path.* **3.** The route or course along which something moves: *the path of a hurricane.* **4.** A course of action or conduct: *the path of righteousness.* [ME < OE *pæð.*]
path- *pref.* Variant of **patho-.**
-path *suff.* **1.** A practitioner of a specified kind of medical treatment: *naturopath.* **2.** One suffering from a specified kind of disorder: *sociopath.* [Back-formation < -PATHY.]

patchwork

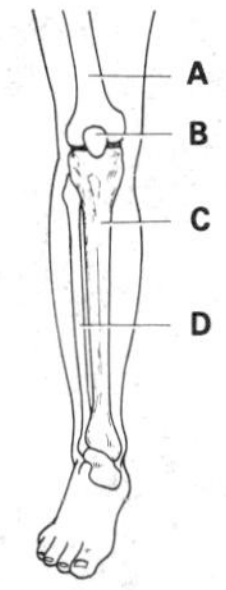

patella
A. Femur
B. Patella
C. Tibia
D. Fibula

Pa·than (pə-tän′) *n.* An Afghan, esp. one of Indo-Iranian stock and Moslem religion. [Hindi *Paṭhan* < Pashto *Pĕṣtana,* pl. of *Pĕṣtūn,* an Afghan < *pashtu,* Pashto.]

pa·thet·ic (pə-thĕt′ĭk) also **pa·thet·i·cal** (-ĭ-kəl) *adj.* **1.** Of, pertaining to, expressing, or arousing pity, sympathy, or tenderness; full of pathos: *a pathetic tale of hardship.* **2.** Distressing and inadequate: *a pathetic attempt to appear worldly.* [Fr. *pathétique* < LLat. *patheticus* < Gk. *pathētikos* sensitive < *pathētos,* liable to suffer < *pathos,* suffering.] **—pa·thet′i·cal·ly** *adv.*

Synonyms: *pathetic, pitiful, regrettable, lamentable.* These describe a person or an unfortunate condition that inspires profound concern and, often, either sympathy or rather mild scorn. *Pathetic* and *pitiful* apply expressly to what is rendered helpless through misfortune, to what is abject or cast down, and in some contexts to what is hopelessly inadequate. Often they express genuine compassion; where ineptitude or inadequacy is stressed, the terms usually suggest contempt. *Regrettable* applies to whatever offers ground for regret or apprehension, without necessarily implying sympathy or scorn. Similarly, *lamentable,* a much stronger term, suggests only extreme concern for what is gravely unfortunate.

pathetic fallacy *n.* The attribution of human emotions or characteristics to things; for example, *angry clouds, a cruel wind.*

path·find·er (păth′fīn′dər, päth′-) *n.* One who discovers a way through or into unexplored regions.

path·less (păth′lĭs) *adj.* Unmarked by trails or paths.

patho– or **path–** *pref.* Disease; suffering: *pathogen.* [NLat. < Gk. < *pathos,* suffering.]

path·o·gen (păth′ə-jən) *n.* An agent that causes disease, esp. a microorganism such as a bacterium or fungus.

path·o·gen·e·sis (păth′ə-jĕn′ĭ-sĭs) also **pa·thog·e·ny** (pă-thŏj′ə-nē) *n.* The development of a diseased or morbid condition.

path·o·gen·ic (păth′ə-jĕn′ĭk) also **path·o·ge·net·ic** (păth′-ō-jə-nĕt′ĭk) *adj.* Capable of causing disease. **—path′o·gen′i·cal·ly** *adv.* **—path′o·ge·nic′i·ty** (-jə-nĭs′ĭ-tē) *n.*

pa·thog·no·mon·ic (pə-thŏg′nə-mŏn′ĭk, păth′əg-nō-) *adj.* Characteristic of a particular disease or condition. [Gk. *pathognōmonikos* : *pathos,* suffering + *gnōmonikos,* able to judge < *gnōmon,* interpreter.]

path·o·log·i·cal (păth′ə-lŏj′ĭ-kəl) also **path·o·log·ic** (-ĭk) *adj.* **1.** Of or pertaining to pathology. **2.** Pertaining to or caused by disease. **3.** Disordered in behavior: *a pathological liar.* **—path′o·log′i·cal·ly** *adv.*

pa·thol·o·gy (pă-thŏl′ə-jē) *n., pl.* **-gies. 1.** The scientific study of the nature of disease, its causes, processes, development, and consequences. **2.** The anatomic or functional manifestations of disease. **—pa·thol′o·gist** *n.*

pa·thos (pā′thŏs′, -thôs′) *n.* **1.** A quality that arouses feelings of pity, sympathy, tenderness, or sorrow. **2.** A feeling of sympathy or pity. **3.** In aesthetics, the transient, emotional, or subjective elements in a work of art, as distinguished from the ideal or objective. [Gk., suffering.]

path·way (păth′wā′, päth′-) *n.* A path.

-pathy *suff.* **1.** Feeling; suffering; perception: *telepathy.* **2. a.** Disease: *neuropathy.* **b.** A system of treating disease: *homeopathy.* [Lat. *-pathia* < Gk. *-patheia* < *pathos,* suffering.]

pa·tience (pā′shəns) *n.* **1.** The quality of being patient; capacity of calm endurance. **2.** *Chiefly Brit.* A game of solitaire.

Synonyms: *patience, resignation, forbearance.* These all denote tolerance of something or somebody over a period of time, generally without complaint though not necessarily without annoyance. *Patience* is any admirable endurance of a trying situation or person, usually through a passiveness which comes out of understanding. *Resignation,* on the other hand, implies a feeling of failure with an attitude of seeing something through out of despair or necessity: *his resignation to defeat. Forbearance* denotes restraint, usually in the face of considerable provocation: *forbearance to one's enemies.*

pa·tient (pā′shənt) *adj.* **1.** Capable of bearing affliction with calmness. **2.** Tolerant; understanding. **3.** Persevering; constant: *a patient worker.* **4.** Capable of bearing delay; not hasty. *—n.* **1.** One under medical treatment. **2.** *Archaic.* One who suffers. [ME *pacient* < OFr. < Lat. *patiens* < *pati,* to endure.] **—pa′tient·ly** *adv.*

pat·in (păt′n) *n.* Variant of **paten.**

pat·i·na[1] (păt′ə-nə) *n., pl.* **-nae** (-nē). A paten (sense 3). [Med. Lat. < Lat., plate. —see PATEN.]

pat·i·na[2] (păt′ə-nə, pə-tē′nə) also **pa·tine** (pă-tēn′) *n.* **1.** A thin layer of corrosion, usually brown or green, that appears on copper or copper alloys, such as bronze, as a result of natural or artificial oxidation. **2.** The sheen produced by age and use on any antique surface. [Ital. < Lat., plate. —see PATEN.]

pa·tine (pă-tēn′) *tr.v.* **-tined, -tin·ing, -tines.** To coat with a patina. *—n.* **1.** Variant of **paten. 2.** Variant of **patina**[2]. [< PATINA[2].]

pat·i·o (păt′ē-ō′, pä′tē-ō′) *n., pl.* **-os. 1.** An inner, roofless courtyard. **2.** A space for dining or recreation, usually paved, that adjoins a residence. [Sp. < OSp. < Lat. *patēre,* to be open.]

pa·tis·se·rie (pä-tēs-rē′) *n.* A bakery specializing in French pastry. [Fr. *pâtisserie* < OFr. *pâtissier,* pastry cook, ult. < LLat. *pasta,* dough.]

pat·ois (păt′wä′, pă-twä′) *n., pl.* **pat·ois** (păt′wäz′, pă-twä′). **1. a.** A regional dialect. **b.** Illiterate or substandard speech. **2.** The special jargon of a group; cant. [Fr. < OFr.]

patr– *pref.* Variant of **patri-.**

pa·tres·fa·mil·i·as (pā′trēz-fə-mĭl′ē-əs, pä′trēz-) *n.* Plural of **paterfamilias.**

patri– or **patr–** *pref.* Father: *patrilineal.* [Lat. < *pater,* father.]

pa·tri·arch (pā′trē-ärk′) *n.* **1.** The male leader of a family or tribe. **2. a.** Any of the Old Testament fathers of the human race. **b.** Abraham, Isaac, Jacob, or any of the founders of the 12 tribes of Israel. **3.** A former title for the bishops of Rome, Constantinople, Jerusalem, Antioch, and Alexandria. **4.** *Rom. Cath. Ch.* A bishop who holds the highest episcopal rank after the pope. **5.** The bishop of various Eastern Orthodox and Greek Orthodox churches. **6.** *Mormon Ch.* A high dignitary of the priesthood empowered to invoke blessings. **7.** Someone regarded as the founder or original head of an enterprise, organization, or tradition. **8.** A very old and venerable man; elder. **9.** The most venerable specimen in a group: *patriarch of the herd.* [ME *patriarche* < OFr. < LLat. *patriarcha* < Gk. *patriarkhēs* : *patria,* family (< *patēr,* father) + *arkhos,* ruler (< *arkhein,* to rule).]

pa·tri·ar·chal (pā′trē-är′kəl) also **pa·tri·ar·chic** (-är′kĭk) *adj.* **1.** Pertaining to or characteristic of a patriarch; venerable; dignified. **2.** Of or pertaining to a patriarchy: *a patriarchal social system.* **3.** Ruled by a patriarch: *a patriarchal see.* **—pa′tri·ar′chal·ism** *n.* **—pa′tri·ar′chal·ly** *adv.*

patriarchal cross *n.* A Latin cross having two horizontal bars, of which the upper is the shorter.

pa·tri·ar·chate (pā′trē-är′kĭt, -kāt′) *n.* **1.** The territory, rule, or rank of a patriarch. **2.** A patriarchy.

pa·tri·ar·chy (pā′trē-är′kē) *n., pl.* **-chies. 1.** A system of social organization in which descent and succession are traced through the male line. **2.** The rule of a tribe or family by men.

pa·tri·cian (pə-trĭsh′ən) *n.* **1.** A member of one of the noble families of the ancient Roman Republic. **2.** An aristocrat. **3.** A person of refined manners and tastes. [ME *patricion* < OFr. *patricien* < Lat. *patricius* < *patres,* senators < pl. of *pater,* father.] **—pa·tri′cian** *adj.* **—pa·tri′cian·ly** *adv.*

pa·tri·ci·ate (pə-trĭsh′ē-ĭt, -āt′) *n.* **1.** The rank of patrician. **2.** Patricians as a class; nobility; aristocracy. [Lat. *patriciatus* < *patricius,* patrician.]

pat·ri·cide (păt′rĭ-sīd′) *n.* **1.** The act of murdering one's father. **2.** One who murders one's father. [LLat. *patricidium* : Lat. *pater,* father + Lat. *caedere,* to kill.] **—pat′ri·cid′al** (păt′rə-sīd′l) *adj.*

pat·ri·cli·nous also **pat·ro·cli·nous** (păt′rĭ-klī′nəs) *adj.* Derived from the male line. [PATRI- + Gk. *klinein,* to lean.]

pat·ri·lin·e·al (păt′rə-lĭn′ē-əl) *adj.* Relating to, based on, or tracing descent through the male line.

pat·ri·lo·cal (păt′rə-lō′kəl) *adj.* Pertaining to the home territory of a husband's family or tribe in primitive societies.

pat·ri·mo·ny (păt′rə-mō′nē) *n., pl.* **-nies. 1.** An inheritance from a father or other ancestor. **2.** Legacy; heritage. **3.** An endowment or estate belonging to a church. [ME < OFr. *patrimoine* < Lat. *patrimonium* < *pater,* father.] **—pat′ri·mo′ni·al** *adj.* **—pat′ri·mo′ni·al·ly** *adv.*

pa·tri·ot (pā′trē-ət, -ŏt′) *n.* A person who loves, supports, and defends his country. [OFr. *patriote,* compatriot < LLat. *patriota* < Gk. *patriōtēs* < *patrios,* of one's fathers < *patris,* fatherland < *patēr,* father.]

pa·tri·ot·ic (pā′trē-ŏt′ĭk) *adj.* Feeling, expressing, or inspired by love for one's country. **—pa′tri·ot′i·cal·ly** *adv.*

pa·tri·ot·ism (pā′trē-ə-tĭz′əm) *n.* Love of and devotion to one's country.

Patriots' Day *n.* April 19, the anniversary of the battles of Lexington and Concord in 1775, celebrated as a legal holiday in Maine and Massachusetts.

pa·tris·tic (pə-trĭs′tĭk) also **pa·tris·ti·cal** (-tĭ-kəl) *adj.* Of or relating to the fathers of the early Christian church or to their writings. **—pa·tris′ti·cal·ly** *adv.*

pat·ro·cli·nous (păt′rə-klī′nəs) *adj.* Variant of **patriclinous.**

Pa·tro·clus (pə-trō′kləs) *n. Gk. Myth.* A Greek warrior, the friend of Achilles. [Lat. < Gk. *Patroklos.*]

pa·trol (pə-trōl′) *n.* **1.** The action of moving about an area for purposes of observation or security. **2.** A person or group of persons who carry out such an action. **3. a.** A military unit sent out on a reconnaissance mission. **b.** One or more vehicles, boats, ships, or aircraft assigned to guard or reconnoiter a given area. **4.** A group of eight Boy Scouts, a division of a troop. *—v.* **-trolled, -trol·ling, -trols.** *—tr.* To engage in a patrol of. *—intr.* To engage in a patrol. [Fr. *patrouille* < *patrouiller,* to patrol < *patouiller,* to paddle about in mud < *patte,* paw.] **—pa·trol′ler** *n.*

patrol car *n.* A squad car.

pa·trol·man (pə-trōl′mən) *n.* A policeman or guard who patrols an assigned area.

patrol torpedo boat *n.* A PT boat.

patrol wagon *n.* A police truck used to convey prisoners.

pa·tron (pā′trən) *n.* **1.** One that supports, protects, or champions; benefactor: *a patron of the arts.* **2.** A regular customer. [ME < OFr. < Med. Lat. *patronus* < Lat. < *pater,* father.] **—pa′tron·al** (pā′trə-nəl) *adj.*

pa·tron·age (pā′trə-nĭj, păt′rə-) *n.* **1.** Support, encouragement, or championship from a patron. **2.** A patronizing manner. **3.** The trade given to a commercial establishment by its customers. **4.** Customers or patrons collectively; clientele: *an old shop with a large, loyal patronage.* **5. a.** The power of appointing people to governmental or political positions. **b.** The positions so made.

pa·tron·ize (pā′trə-nīz′, păt′rə-) *tr.v.* **-ized, -iz·ing, -iz·es. 1.** To act as a patron to; support. **2.** To go to regularly as a customer. **3.** To treat in an offensively condescending manner. **—pa′tron·iz′er** *n.* **—pa′tron·iz′ing·ly** *adv.*

patron saint *n.* The guardian saint of a nation, place, craft, activity, class, or person.

pat·ro·nym·ic (păt′rə-nĭm′ĭk) *n.* A name received from a paternal ancestor, esp. one formed by an affix, as in *Johnson,* the son of John. [LLat. *patronymicum* < *patronymicus,* of a patronymic < Gk. *patrōnumikos* < *patrōnumia* : *pater,* father + *onuma,* name.] **—pat′ro·nym′ic** *adj.* **—pat′ro·nym′i·cal·ly** *adv.*

pa·troon (pə-tro͞on′) *n.* A landholder in New York and New Jersey who was granted certain proprietary and manorial powers under Dutch colonial rule. [Du. < Fr. *patron,* patron < OFr.]

pat·sy (păt′sē) *n., pl.* **-sies.** *Slang.* A person who is cheated, victimized, or made the butt of a joke. [Orig. unknown.]

pat·ten (păt′n) *n.* A wooden sandal, shoe, or clog. [ME *patin* < OFr. < *patte,* paw.]

pat·ter[1] (păt′ər) *v.* **-tered, -ter·ing, -ters.** *—intr.* **1.** To make a quick succession of light, soft taps: *Rain pattered on the roof.* **2.** To move with quick, light, softly audible steps. *—tr.* To cause to patter. *—n.* A succession of quick, light, tapping sounds. [Freq. of PAT.]

pat·ter[2] (păt′ər) *v.* **-tered, -ter·ing, -ters.** *—intr.* **1.** To chatter glibly and rapidly. **2.** To mumble prayers in a mechanical manner. *—tr.* To utter in a glib, rapid, or mechanical manner. *—n.* **1.** The jargon of a particular group; cant. **2.** Glib, rapid-fire speech, as of an auctioneer, salesman, or comedian. **3.** Meaningless talk; chatter. [ME *patren* < *paternoster,* paternoster (from the mechanical and rapid recitation of the prayer).] **—pat′ter·er** *n.*

pat·tern (păt′ərn) *n.* **1. a.** An archetype. **b.** An ideal worthy of imitation: *a pattern of womanly virtues.* **2.** A plan, diagram, or model to be followed in making things: *dress patterns.* **3.** A representative sample; specimen. **4. a.** An artistic or decorative design: *a paisley pattern.* **b.** A design of natural or accidental origin: *snowflake patterns.* **5.** A composite of traits or features characteristic of an individual: *behavioral patterns.* **6.** Form and style in an artistic work or body of artistic works. **7. a.** The configuration of identically aimed rifle shots upon a target. **b.** The distribution and spread of shot from a shotgun. **8.** Enough material to make a complete garment. **9.** A standardized diagram transmitted to test television picture quality. **10.** The ordered flight path of an aircraft about to land. *—tr.v.* **-terned, -tern·ing, -terns. 1.** To make, mold, or design by following a pattern. **2.** To cover or ornament with a design or pattern. [ME *patron* < OFr. —see PATRON.]

pat·ty (păt′ē) *n., pl.* **-ties. 1. a.** A small, oval, flattened cake of chopped or minced food. **b.** A similarly shaped candy: *a peppermint patty.* **2.** A patty shell. [Fr. *pâté* < OFr. *paste,* paste. —see PASTE[1].]

pat·ty·pan squash (păt′ē-păn′) *n.* The cymling.

patty shell *n.* A shell of baked puff pastry made to be filled with creamed meat, seafood, vegetables, or fruit.

pat·u·lous (păch′ə-ləs) also **pat·u·lent** (-lənt) *adj. Bot.* Spreading or expanded: *patulous branches.* [Lat. *patulus* < *patēre,* to be open.] **—pat′u·lous·ly** *adv.* **—pat′u·lous·ness** *n.*

pau·ci·ty (pô′sə-tē) *n.* **1.** Smallness of number; fewness: *a paucity of soldiers.* **2.** Smallness of quantity; scarcity; dearth: *a paucity of natural resources.* [ME *paucite* < OFr. < Lat. *paucitas* < *paucus,* few.]

Paul Bunyan (pôl′bŭn′yən) *n.* A giant lumberjack in American folklore.

Pau·li exclusion principle (pô′lē, pou′-) *n.* Exclusion principle. [After Wolfgang *Pauli* (1900–1958).]

Paul·ist (pô′lĭst) *n.* A priest belonging to the Roman Catholic Missionary Society of Saint Paul the Apostle.

pau·low·ni·a (pô-lō′nē-ə) *n.* Any of several trees of the genus *Paulownia,* native to the Orient, having large, heart-shaped leaves and clusters of purplish or white flowers. [After Princess Anna *Paulovna* (1795–1865), queen of William II of the Netherlands.]

paunch (pônch) *n.* **1.** The belly, esp. a potbelly. **2.** The rumen. [ME *paunche* < AN, var. of OFr. *pance* < Lat. *pantex.*]

paunch·y (pôn′chē, pän′-) *adj.* **-i·er, -i·est.** Having a potbelly. **—paunch′i·ness** *n.*

pau·per (pô′pər) *n.* **1.** One who is extremely poor. **2.** One living on public charity. *—tr.v.* **-pered, -per·ing, -pers.** To pauperize. [< Lat., poor.]

pau·per·ism (pô′pə-rĭz′əm) *n.* **1.** The quality or state of being a pauper. **2.** Paupers collectively.

pau·per·ize (pô′pə-rīz′) *tr.v.* **-ized, -iz·ing, -iz·es.** To make a pauper of; impoverish. **—pau′per·i·za′tion** *n.*

pause (pôz) *intr.v.* **paused, paus·ing, paus·es. 1.** To cease or suspend an action for a time. **2.** To linger; tarry: *pausing for a while at the café.* **3.** To hesitate: *He paused before replying.* *—n.* **1.** A temporary stop. **2.** A delay or suspended reaction, as from uncertainty; hesitation: *After a pause the audience burst into cheers.* **3.** A break, stop, or rest for a calculated purpose or effect: *a pause to let the words sink in.* **4.** *Mus.* **a.** A sign indicating that a note or rest is to be held. **b.** A measured break or rest; caesura. **5.** A reason for hesitation: *The size of the task gives one pause.* [ME, pause < Lat. *pausa* < Gk. *pausis* < *pauein,* to stop.]

pa·vane also **pa·van** (pə-vän′, -văn′) *n.* **1.** A slow, stately court dance of the 16th century. **2.** Music for the pavane. [OFr. *pavane* < OSp. *pavana* < OItal.]

pave (pāv) *tr.v.* **paved, pav·ing, paves. 1.** To cover with a hard, smooth surface that will bear travel. **2.** To cover uniformly, as if with pavement. **3.** To be or compose the pavement of. **—*idiom.* pave the way.** To make progress or development easier: *experiments that paved the way for future research.* [ME *paven* < OFr. *paver* < Lat. *pavire,* to stamp.] **—pav′er** *n.*

pa·vé (pă-vā′) *n.* A setting of precious stones placed together so closely that no metal shows: *diamonds in pavé.* [Fr. < p.part. of *paver,* to pave.] **—pa·vé** *adj.*

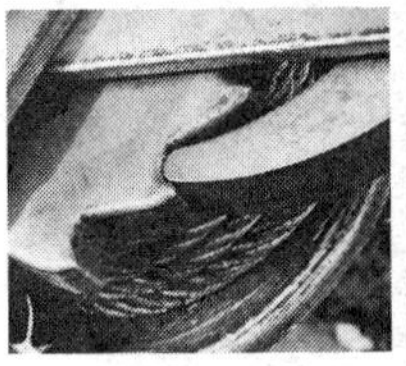

pave·ment (pāv′mənt) *n.* **1. a.** A hard, paved surface, esp. of a public area or thoroughfare. **b.** The material of which such a surface is made. **2.** *Chiefly Brit.* A sidewalk.

pav·id (păv′ĭd) *adj.* Timid. [Lat. *pavidus* < *pavēre,* to fear.]

pa·vil·ion (pə-vĭl′yən) *n.* **1.** An ornate tent. **2. a.** A light, sometimes ornamental, roofed structure, used at parks or fairs for amusement or shelter. **b.** A usually temporary structure erected at a fair or show for use by an exhibitor. **3.** A building or other structure connected to a larger building; annex. **4.** One of a group of related buildings forming a complex, as of a hospital. **5.** The surface of a brilliant-cut gem that slants outward from girdle to culet. *—tr.v.* **-ioned, -ion·ing, -ions.** To shelter in or as if in a pavilion. [ME *pavilon* < OFr. *pavillon* < Lat. *papilio.*]

pawl
Ratchet wheel with pawl (*above*) and diagram (*below*)

pav·ing (pā′vĭng) *n.* **1.** The laying of pavement. **2.** A pavement. **3.** Material used for pavement.

pav·ior (pāv′yər) *n.* **1.** One that paves. **2.** Material or tools used for paving. [ME *pavier* < *paven,* to pave.]

pav·iour (pāv′yər) *n.* *Chiefly Brit.* Variant of **pavior.**

pav·is also **pav·isse** (păv′ĭs) *n.* A medieval shield large enough to cover the whole body. [ME < OFr. *pavais* < OItal. *pavese,* after *Pavia,* Italy.]

Pa·vo (pā′vō) *n.* A constellation in the Southern Hemisphere near Apus and Indus. [Lat. *pavo,* peacock.]

pav·o·nine (păv′ə-nīn′) *adj.* **1.** Of or like a peacock. **2.** Resembling a peacock's tail in color, design, or iridescence. [Lat. *pavoninus* < *pavo,* peacock.]

paw (pô) *n.* **1.** The nailed or clawed foot of an animal. **2.** *Informal.* A human hand, esp. a large, clumsy one: *"Lennie dabbled his big paw in the water"* (Steinbeck). *—v.* **pawed, paw·ing, paws.** *—tr.* **1.** To strike with the paw or paws. **2.** To strike or scrape with a beating motion. **3.** To handle clumsily, rudely, or with too much familiarity. *—intr.* **1.** To scrape the ground with the forefeet: *The horse pawed restlessly.* **2.** To make clumsy, grasping motions with the hands: *always pawing at everything he sees.* [ME *pawe* < OFr. *powe,* of Germanic orig.] **—paw′er** *n.*

pawl (pôl) *n.* A hinged or pivoted device adapted to fit into a notch of a ratchet wheel to impart forward motion or prevent backward motion. [Poss. < Du. *pal.*]

pawn[1] (pôn) *n.* **1.** Something given as security for a loan; pledge; guaranty. **2.** The condition of being held as a pledge against the payment of a loan: *jewels at pawn.* **3.** A person serving as security; hostage. **4.** The act of pawning. *—tr.v.* **pawned, pawn·ing, pawns. 1.** To give or deposit as security for the payment of money borrowed. **2.** To risk; hazard: *pawn one's honor.* [ME *paun* < OFr. *pan.*] **—pawn′a·ble** *adj.* **—pawn′age** *n.* **—pawn′er** (pô′nər), **paw′nor** (-nôr′) *n.*

pawn[2] (pôn) *n.* **1.** A chessman of lowest value, enabled to move forward one square at a time, or two squares for the first move, and capture on a one-space diagonal forward move. **2.** A person or entity composed of persons used to further the purposes of another: *an underdeveloped nation that was a pawn in the struggle between Russia and the United States.* [ME < OFr. *paon* < Med. Lat. *pedo,* foot soldier < LLat., one who has wide feet < Lat. *pes,* foot.]

pawn·bro·ker (pôn′brō′kər) *n.* One who lends money at interest in exchange for personal property left with him as security. **—pawn′bro′king** *n.*

Paw·nee (pô-nē′) *n., pl.* **Pawnee** or **-nees. 1. a.** A confederation of four North American Plains Indian tribes of Caddoan linguistic stock in the region of Kansas and Nebraska, now living on a reservation in Oklahoma. **b.** A member of this confederation. **2.** The language of the Pawnee.

pawnshop

pawn·shop (pôn′shŏp′) *n.* The shop of a pawnbroker.

pawn ticket *n.* A receipt for goods pawned.

paw·paw (pô′pô) *n.* Variant of **papaw.**

pay[1] (pā) *v.* **paid, pay·ing, pays.** *—tr.* **1.** To give money to in return for goods or services rendered: *pay the cashier.* **2.** To give (money) in exchange for goods or services: *paid three dollars for a hamburger.* **3.** To give the indicated amount of: *pay taxes.* **4.** To gain revenge for or upon; requite; punish: *paid him back for his insults.* **5.** To yield as a return: *banks* *paying 12 per cent.* **6.** To bear the cost of: *He paid my way through school.* **7.** To afford an advantage to; profit: *It paid him to be generous.* **8.** To give or bestow: *pay compliments.* **9.** To make (a visit or call). **10.** *past tense* **payed.** *Naut.* To let out (a line or cable) by slackening. —*intr.* **1.** To make payment. **2.** To discharge a debt or obligation. **3.** To be profitable or worthwhile. —***phrasal verbs.*** **pay off. 1. a.** To pay the full amount on (a debt). **b.** To get revenge for or on; requite. **2.** To pay the wages due to (an employee) and discharge. **3.** *Informal.* To bribe. **4.** To allow (a rope, for example) to run off a reel or spool. **5.** *Naut.* To turn or cause to turn (a vessel) to leeward. **pay up.** To pay the full amount demanded. —*adj.* **1.** Of, pertaining to, giving, or receiving payments. **2.** Requiring payment to operate: *a pay telephone.* **3.** Yielding valuable metal in mining: *a pay streak.* —*n.* **1.** The act of paying or state of being paid. **2.** Money given in return for work done; salary; wages; hire. **3. a.** Recompense or reward: *His thanks were pay enough.* **b.** Retribution or punishment. **4.** Paid employment: *the men in our pay.* **5.** A person considered with regard to his credit or willingness to pay. —***idioms.*** **pay (one's) dues.** To earn a given right or position through hard work, long-term experience, or suffering. **pay (one's) way.** To contribute one's own share; pay for oneself. **pay the piper.** To bear the consequences of something. **pay through the nose.** To pay excessively. [ME *payen* < OFr. *paier* < Med. Lat. *pacare* < Lat., to pacify < *pax,* peace.]

pay² (pā) *tr.v.* **payed** or **paid, pay·ing, pays.** *Naut.* To coat or cover (seams of a ship, for example) with waterproof materials such as tar or asphalt. [Obs. Fr. *peier* < Lat. *picare* < *pix,* pitch.]

pea

pay·a·ble (pā'ə-bəl) *adj.* **1.** Requiring payment on a certain date; due. **2.** Specifying payment to a particular person. **3.** Capable of producing profit: *a payable business venture.* —**pay'a·bly** *adv.*

pay cable *n.* Pay-TV that is received over a cable.

pay·check (pā'chĕk') *n.* **1.** A check issued to an employee in payment of salary or wages. **2.** Salary or wages: *a larger paycheck.*

pay·day (pā'dā') *n.* The day on which wages are paid.

pay dirt *n.* **1.** Earth, ore, or gravel with a rich enough metal content to make mining profitable. **2.** *Slang.* A useful or profitable discovery.

payed (pād) *v.* **1.** Past tense and past participle of **pay¹** (sense 10). **2.** A past tense and past participle of **pay².**

pay·ee (pā-ē') *n.* A person to whom money is paid.

pay·er (pā'ər) *n.* **1.** One that pays. **2.** A person named responsible for paying a bill or note.

peach¹

pay·load (pā'lōd') *n.* **1.** The revenue-producing part of a cargo, as distinguished from the weight of the vehicle. **2.** The explosive charge carried in the warhead of a missile. **3. a.** The total weight of passengers and cargo that an aircraft carries or can carry. **b.** *Aerospace.* The total weight of the instruments, crew, and life-support systems that a spacecraft can carry. **c.** The passengers, crew, instruments, or equipment carried by an aircraft, spacecraft, or rocket.

pay·mas·ter (pā'măs'tər) *n.* A person in charge of paying wages and salaries.

pay·ment (pā'mənt) *n.* **1.** The act of paying or state of being paid. **2.** The amount that is paid: *received a large payment.* **3.** One's due, reward, or punishment; requital.

pay·nim (pā'nĭm) *n. Archaic.* **1. a.** A non-Christian, esp. a Moslem. **b.** A pagan or heathen. **2.** The pagan world. [ME *painim* < OFr. *paienisme,* heathendom < LLat. *paganismus* < *paganus,* pagan. —see PAGAN.]

pay·off (pā'ôf', -ŏf') *n.* **1. a.** Full payment of a salary or wages. **b.** The time of such payment. **2.** *Informal.* **a.** Final settlement or reckoning. **b.** The climax of a narrative or of a sequence of events. **3.** Final retribution or revenge. **4.** *Informal.* A bribe. **5.** *Math.* In game theory, the amount gained or lost by a player.

pay·o·la (pā-ō'lə) *n. Slang.* **1.** Bribery, esp. the bribing of disc jockeys to promote records. **2.** A bribe, esp. one given to a disc jockey. [PAY + *(Victr)ola,* a trademark for a phonograph.]

pay·out (pā'out') *n.* A percentage of corporate earnings that is paid to shareholders as dividends.

peacock

pay·roll also **pay roll** (pā'rōl') *n.* **1.** A list of employees receiving wages, with the amounts due to each. **2.** The total sum of money to be paid out to employees at a given time.

pay station *n.* A coin-operated telephone for public use.

pay television *n.* Pay-TV.

pay toilet *n.* A public toilet in a booth that is equipped with a coin-operated door.

pay-TV (pā'tē-vē') *n.* A system for receiving television broadcasts that requires a monthly subscription payment.

Pb The symbol for the element lead. [Lat. *plumbum,* lead.]

Pd The symbol for the element palladium.

pe (pā) *n.* The 17th letter of the Hebrew alphabet. See table at **alphabet.** [Heb. *peh.*]

pea (pē) *n.* **1.** A climbing annual vine, *Pisum sativum,* cultivated in all temperate zones, and having compound leaves, small white flowers, and edible seeds in a green, elongated pod. **2.** One of the rounded green seeds of the pea, used as a vegetable. **3. peas.** The unopened pods of the pea plant. **4.** Any of several plants of the genus *Lathyrus,* such as the sweet pea or the beach pea. [Back-formation < ME *pease* (taken as pl.) < OE *pise* < LLat. *pisa,* ult. < Gk. *pison.*]

pea bean *n.* The navy bean.

pea·bod·y bird (pē'bŏd'ē, -bə-dē) *n.* The white-throated sparrow. [Prob. imit. of its song.]

peace (pēs) *n.* **1.** The absence of war or other hostilities. **2.** An agreement or treaty to end hostilities. **3.** Freedom from quarrels and disagreement; harmonious relations: *They made peace with each other.* **4.** Public security and order: *disturbing the peace.* **5.** Inner contentment; serenity: *peace of mind.* —*interj.* Used as a greeting or farewell, and as a request for silence. —***idioms.*** **at peace. 1.** In a state of tranquillity; serene. **2.** Free from strife. **hold (or keep) one's peace.** To be silent. **keep the peace.** To maintain or observe law and order. [ME *pees* < OFr. *pais* < Lat. *pax.*]

peace·a·ble (pē'sə-bəl) *adj.* **1.** Inclined or disposed to peace; promoting calm: *They met in a peaceable spirit.* **2.** Peaceful; undisturbed. —**peace'a·ble·ness** *n.* —**peace'a·bly** *adv.*

Peace Corps *n.* A Federal government organization, set up in 1961, that trains and sends American volunteers abroad to work with people of developing countries on projects for technological, agricultural, and educational improvement.

peace·ful (pēs'fəl) *adj.* **1.** Undisturbed by strife, turmoil, or disagreement; tranquil. **2.** Opposed to strife; peaceable. **3.** Of or characteristic of a condition of peace. —**peace'ful·ly** *adv.* —**peace'ful·ness** *n.*

peaceful coexistence *n.* An existing together peacefully rather than in a state of hostility or war: *peaceful coexistence between the U.S. and the U.S.S.R.*

peace keeping also **peace-keeping** (pēs'kē'pĭng) *adj.* Of or relating to the preservation of peace, esp. the international supervision of a truce between hostile nations.

peace·mak·er (pēs'mā'kər) *n.* One who makes peace, esp. by settling the disputes of others. —**peace'mak'ing** *n. & adj.*

peace offering *n.* An offering made to an adversary in the interests of peace or reconciliation.

peace officer *n.* A law officer, such as a sheriff, responsible for maintaining civil peace.

peace pipe *n.* The calumet.

peace sign *n.* A hand sign made with the palm forward and with the middle and index fingers forming a V used to express a desire for peace.

peace·time (pēs'tīm') *n.* A time of peace.

peach¹ (pēch) *n.* **1. a.** A small tree, *Prunus persica,* native to China but widely cultivated throughout the temperate zones, having pink flowers and edible fruit. **b.** The soft, juicy, single-seeded fruit of this tree, having yellow flesh and downy, red-tinted, yellow skin. **2.** A light moderate to strong yellowish pink to light orange. **3.** *Slang.* A particularly admirable or pleasing person or thing. [ME *peche* < OFr., a peach < LLat. *persica* < Lat. *Persicus,* Persian.]

peach² (pēch) *v.* **peached, peach·ing, peach·es.** *Slang.* —*intr.* To inform on someone; turn informer. —*tr.* To inform against: *He peached me to the cops.* [ME *pechen* < *apechen,* to accuse, prob. < AN **anpecher* < LLat. *impedicare,* to entangle. —see IMPEACH.]

peach·y (pē'chē) *adj.* **-i·er, -i·est. 1.** Like a peach, esp. in color or texture. **2.** *Slang.* Splendid; fine. —**peach'i·ness** *n.*

pea coat *n.* A pea jacket.

pea·cock (pē'kŏk') *n.* **1.** The male peafowl, distinguished by its crested head, brilliant blue or green feathers, and long tail feathers that are marked with eyelike, iridescent spots, and that can be spread in a fanlike form. **2.** A vain person given to self-display; dandy. —*intr.v.* **-cocked, -cock·ing, -cocks.** To strut about like a peacock; exhibit oneself vainly. [ME *pecok* : OE *pēa,* peafowl (< Lat. *pavo,* peacock) + *cok,* cock < OE *coc.*] —**pea'cock'ish, pea'cock'y** *adj.*

peacock blue *n.* A moderate to dark or strong greenish blue. —**pea'cock'-blue'** (pē'kŏk'blo͞o) *adj.*

pea·fowl (pē'foul') *n., pl.* **peafowl** or **-fowls.** Either of two large pheasants, *Pavo cristatus,* of India and Ceylon, or *P. muticus,* of southeastern Asia. [PEA(COCK) + FOWL.]

peag also **peage** (pēg) *n.* Wampum. [Narraganset *wampompeag.*]

pea green *n.* A moderate, strong, or brilliant yellow green to moderate yellowish green. —**pea'-green'** (pē'grēn') *adj.*

pea·hen (pē'hĕn') *n.* The female peafowl.

pea jacket *n.* A short, warm, double-breasted coat of heavy wool, worn esp. by sailors. [By folk etymology < Du. *pijjekker* : *pij,* a kind of coarse cloth + *jekker,* jacket.]

peak¹ (pēk) *n.* **1.** A tapering, projecting point; pointed extremity: *peak of a cap; peak of a roof.* **2. a.** The pointed summit of a mountain. **b.** The mountain itself: *Pikes Peak.* **3. a.** The point of a beard. **b.** A widow's peak. **4.** The point of greatest development, value, height, or intensity: *a novel written at the peak of his career.* **5.** *Physics.* The highest value attained by a varying quantity: *a current peak.* **6.** *Naut.* **a.** The narrow portion of a ship's hull at the bow or stern. **b.** The upper after corner of a fore-and-aft sail. **c.** The outermost end of a gaff. —*v.* **peaked, peak·ing, peaks.** —*tr.* **1.** *Naut.* To raise (a gaff) above the horizontal. **2.** To bring to a maximum of development, growth, value, or intensity. —*intr.* **1.** To be formed into a peak or peaks: *Beat the egg whites until they peak.* **2.** To achieve a maximum of development, growth, value, or intensity. —*adj.* Approaching or constituting the maximum: *peak efficiency.* [Prob. alteration of PIKE[4].]

peak[2] (pēk) *intr.v.* **peaked, peak·ing, peaks.** To become sickly, emaciated, or pale. [Orig. unknown.]

peaked[1] (pēkt, pē′kĭd) *adj.* Ending in a peak; pointed.

peak·ed[2] (pē′kĭd) *adj.* Having a sickly appearance.

peal (pēl) *n.* **1.** A ringing of a set of bells, esp. a change or set of changes rung on bells. **2.** A set of bells tuned to each other; chime. **3.** A loud burst of noise: *peals of laughter.* —*v.* **pealed, peal·ing, peals.** —*intr.* To sound in a peal; ring. —*tr.* To utter loudly and sonorously. [ME *pele,* summons to church by bell, short for *apel,* appeal. —see APPEAL.]

pe·an (pē′ən) *n.* Variant of **paean.**

pea·nut (pē′nŭt′) *n.* **1.** A vine, *Arachis hypogaea,* native to tropical America and widely cultivated in semitropical regions, having yellow flowers on stalks that bend over so that the seed pods ripen underground. **2.** The edible, nutlike, oily seed of the peanut, used for food and as a source of oil. **3.** *Slang.* A small or insignificant person. **4. peanuts.** *Slang.* A very small amount of money; trifling sum. —*adj. Slang.* Having little or no importance; insignificant: *peanut politicians.*

peanut brittle *n.* A hard candy containing peanuts.

peanut butter *n.* A paste made from roasted ground peanuts.

peanut oil *n.* The oil pressed from peanuts, used for cooking, in soaps, and as a pharmaceutical vehicle.

pear (pâr) *n.* **1.** A widely cultivated tree, *Pyrus communis,* having glossy leaves, white flowers, and edible fruit. **2.** The fruit of the pear, spherical at the base and tapering toward the top. [ME *pere* < OE *peru,* a pear < Lat. *pirum.*]

pear haw *n.* A shrub or small tree, *Crataegus uniflora,* of southeastern North America, having white flowers and small, orange-red, pear-shaped fruit.

pearl[1] (pûrl) *n.* **1.** A smooth, lustrous, variously colored deposit, chiefly calcium carbonate, formed around a grain of sand or other foreign matter in the shells of certain mollusks and valued as a gem. **2.** Mother-of-pearl; nacre. **3.** One that is likened to a pearl in beauty or value. **4.** *Printing.* A type size measuring 5 points. **5.** A yellowish white. —*v.* **pearled, pearl·ing, pearls.** —*tr.* **1.** To decorate or cover with or as with pearls. **2.** To make into the shape or color of pearls. —*intr.* **1.** To dive or fish for pearls or pearl-bearing mollusks. **2.** To form beads resembling pearls. —**modifier:** *a pair of pearl earrings.* —*adj.* Having the shape or color of pearls. [ME *perle* < OFr. < VLat. **pernula,* dim. of Lat. *perna,* sea-mussel.]

pearl[2] (pûrl) *v. & n.* Variant of **purl.**

pearl ash *n.* Potassium carbonate.

pearl danio *n.* A slender freshwater tropical fish, *Brachydanio albolineatus,* having silvery scales and popular as an aquarium fish. [NLat. *Danio,* genus name.]

pearl diver *n.* A person who dives in search of mollusks containing pearls.

pearl·er (pûr′lər) *n.* **1.** A pearl diver. **2.** A boat engaged in seeking or trading pearls.

pearl·es·cent (pûr-lĕs′ənt) *adj.* Having a pearly shine or gloss.

pearl gray *n.* A light gray, from yellowish to light bluish gray. —**pearl′-gray′** (pûrl′grā′) *adj.*

Pearl Harbor *n.* A swift, surprise attack that usually causes great destruction. [After *Pearl Harbor,* Oahu, Hawaii, from the surprise attack there by the Japanese in 1941.]

pearl·ite (pûr′līt′) *n.* **1.** A mixture of ferrite and cementite forming distinct layers or bands in slowly cooled carbon steels. **2.** Variant of **perlite.** [Fr. *perlite* < *perle,* pearl.]

pearl millet *n.* A tropical grass, *Pennisetum glaucum,* having long, dense flowering spikes and whitish seeds that are used as food.

pearl oyster *n.* Any of several bivalve marine mollusks of the genus *Pinctada* and related genera, of tropical waters, esp. *P. margaritifera,* a major commercial source of pearls.

pearl·y (pûr′lē) *adj.* **-i·er, -i·est. 1.** Resembling pearls. **2.** Covered or decorated with pearls or mother-of-pearl.

pearly everlasting *n.* A plant, *Anaphalis margaritaceae,* having woolly, gray-green foliage and whitish, long-lasting flowers.

pearly nautilus *n.* The chambered nautilus.

pear·main (pâr′mān′) *n.* An old variety of red-skinned apple. [ME *parmain,* a kind of pear < OFr.]

peas·ant (pĕz′ənt) *n.* **1.** A member of the class comprising small farmers and tenants, sharecroppers, and laborers on the land where these constitute the main labor force in agriculture. **2.** A countryman; rustic. **3.** An uncouth, crude, or ill-bred person; boor. [ME *paissaunt* < OFr. *paisant* < *païs,* country < LLat. *pagensis,* inhabitant of a district < Lat. *pagus,* district.]

peas·ant·ry (pĕz′ən-trē) *n.* **1.** The social class constituted by peasants. **2.** The condition, rank, or conduct of a peasant.

pease (pēz) *n., pl.* **pease** or **peas·en** (pē′zən). *Obs.* A pea.

pease·cod also **peas·cod** (pēz′kŏd′) *n. Obs.* The pod of the pea. [ME *pesecod* : *pese,* pea + *cod,* cod. —see COD[2].]

pea·shoot·er (pē′sho͞o′tər) *n.* A toy consisting of a small tube through which dried peas or other pellets are blown.

pea soup *n.* **1.** A purée or soup made of dried peas. **2.** *Slang.* Dense fog.

peat (pēt) *n.* Partially carbonized vegetable matter, usually mosses, found in bogs, and used as fertilizer and fuel. [ME *pete* < Med. Lat. *peta.*] —**peat′y** *adj.*

peat bog *n.* A bog or swamp where peat has accumulated.

peat moss *n.* **1.** Any of various mosses of the genus *Sphagnum,* growing in very wet places. **2.** The partly carbonized remains of peat moss, used as a mulch and plant food.

pea·vey also **pea·vy** (pē′vē) *n., pl.* **-veys** also **-vies.** A wooden lever with a metal point and a hinged hook near the end, used by lumbermen to handle logs. [After Joseph *Peavey* (fl. 1875), American inventor.]

peb·ble (pĕb′əl) *n.* **1.** A small stone worn smooth by erosion. **2. a.** Clear, colorless quartz; rock crystal. **b.** A lens made of such quartz. **3.** A crinkled surface, as on leather or paper. —*tr.v.* **-bled, -bling, -bles. 1.** To pave or pelt with pebbles. **2.** To impart an irregularly rough, grainy surface to (leather or paper). [ME *pobble* < OE *papolstān.*] —**peb′bly** *adj.*

pe·can (pĭ-kän′, -kăn′) *n.* **1.** A tree, *Carya illinoensis,* of the southern United States, having deeply furrowed bark and edible nuts. **2.** The smooth, thin-shelled, oval nut of the pecan. [Algonquian *paccan.*]

pec·ca·ble (pĕk′ə-bəl) *adj.* Liable to sin. [OFr. < Lat. *peccare,* to sin.] —**pec′ca·bil′i·ty** *n.*

pec·ca·dil·lo (pĕk′ə-dĭl′ō) *n., pl.* **-loes** or **-los.** A small sin or fault. [Sp. *pecadillo,* dim. of *pecado,* sin < Lat. *peccatum* < *peccare,* to sin.]

pec·cant (pĕk′ənt) *adj.* **1.** Sinful; guilty. **2.** Violating a rule or accepted practice; erring. [Lat. *peccans, peccant-,* pr.part. of *peccare,* to sin.] —**pec′can·cy** *n.* —**pec′cant·ly** *adv.*

pec·ca·ry (pĕk′ə-rē) *n., pl.* **-ries.** Either of two piglike, hoofed mammals, *Tayassu tajacu* or *T. pecari,* of southern North America, Central America, and South America, having dense, long, dark bristles. [Sp. *pécari* < Cariban *pakira.*]

pec·ca·vi (pĕ-kä′wē, -vē, -kā′vī′) *n., pl.* **-vis.** A confession of sin. [Lat., I have sinned < *peccare,* to sin.]

peck[1] (pĕk) *v.* **pecked, peck·ing, pecks.** —*tr.* **1.** To strike with a beak or some sharp-pointed instrument. **2.** To make (a hole, for example) by striking repeatedly with the beak or a pointed instrument. **3.** To grasp and pick up with the beak: *The bird pecked insects from the log.* **4.** *Informal.* To kiss briefly and casually. —*intr.* **1.** To make strokes with the beak or something pointed like a beak. **2.** To eat in small, sparing bits; nibble: *pecked at her dinner.* **3.** To criticize repeatedly; carp. —*n.* **1. a.** A stroke or light blow with the beak. **b.** A mark or hole made by such a stroke. **2.** *Informal.* A light, quick kiss. [ME *pecken,* prob. < MLG *pekken.*]

peck[2] (pĕk) *n.* **1. a.** A unit of volume or capacity in the U.S. system, used in dry measure, equal to 8 quarts or 537.605 cubic inches. **b.** A unit of volume or capacity in the British Imperial System, used in dry and liquid measure, equal to 554.84 cubic inches. **2.** A container holding or measuring a peck. **3.** *Informal.* A large quantity; lot: *a peck of troubles.* [ME < OFr. *pek.*]

peck·er (pĕk′ər) *n.* **1.** One that pecks. **2.** *Chiefly Brit. Slang.* Courage; pluck. **3.** *Vulgar Slang.* Penis (sense 1).

pecking order *n.* **1.** A hierarchy within flocks of poultry, according to which each member submits to pecking and domination by the stronger or more aggressive members, and has the privilege of pecking and dominating the weaker members. **2.** A hierarchy in a human group.

Peck's bad boy (pĕks) *n.* A person whose bad behavior embarrasses and annoys others. [After *Peck's Bad Boy and His Pa,* a book by George Wilbur Peck (1840–1916).]

Peck·sniff·i·an (pĕk-snĭf′ē-ən) *adj.* Hypocritically benevolent; sanctimonious. [After Seth *Pecksniff,* a character in *Martin Chuzzlewit,* a novel by Charles Dickens (1812–1870).]

pec·tase (pĕk′tās′, -tāz′) *n.* An enzyme found in certain fruits that catalyzes the conversion of pectins to pectic acids. [PECT(IN) + -ASE.]

pec·tate (pĕk′tāt′) *n.* A salt or ester of pectic acid. [PECT(IC ACID) + -ATE.]

pec·ten (pĕk′tən) *n., pl.* **-ti·nes** (-tə-nēz′). *Zool.* **1.** A body structure or organ resembling a comb, such as the ridged part of the eyelid of reptiles and birds. **2.** A scallop of the genus *Pecten.* [NLat. < Lat., comb.]

pec·tic acid (pĕk′tĭk) *n.* Any of several colloidal substances, essentially complex organic acids, derived from pectin. [Fr. *pectique,* related to pectin. —see PECTIN.]

pec·tin (pĕk′tĭn) *n.* Any of a group of complex colloidal substances of high molecular weight found in ripe fruits, such as apples, and used to jell various foods, drugs, and cosmetics. [Fr. *pectine* < *pectique,* related to pectin < Gk. *pēktikos,* coagulating < *pēktos,* coagulated, *pēgnunai,* to coagulate.] —**pec′tic, pec′tin·ous** *adj.*

pec·tin·ase (pĕk′tə-nās′, -nāz′) *n.* A plant enzyme that catalyzes the hydrolysis of pectin.

pec·ti·nate (pĕk′tə-nāt′) also **pec·ti·nat·ed** (-nā′tĭd) *adj.* Having teeth like a comb; comblike. [Lat. *pecten, pectin-,* comb + -ATE.] —**pec′ti·na′tion** *n.*

pec·tin·es·ter·ase (pĕk′tə-nĕs′tə-rās′, -rāz′) *n.* An enzyme that catalyzes the hydrolysis of pectins into pectic acids.

pec·to·ral (pĕk′tər-əl) *adj.* **1.** *Anat.* Pertaining to the breast or chest: *a pectoral muscle.* **2.** *Med.* Useful in diseases of the chest. **3.** Worn on the chest or breast: *a pectoral cross.* —*n.* **1.** A chest muscle or organ. **2.** A pectoral fin. **3.** A medicine

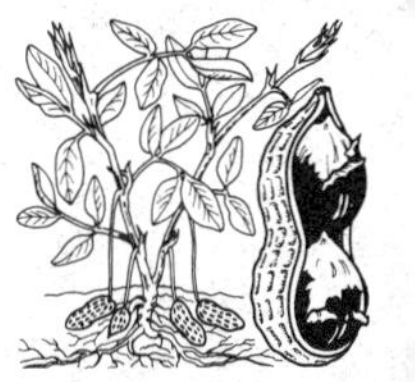

peanut

pear

peavey

pecan

peccary

for chest diseases. **4.** An ornament or decoration worn on the chest. [ME, something worn on the chest < OFr. < Lat. *pectorale,* breastplate < *pectoralis,* pectoral < *pectus,* breast.]

pectoral arch *n.* The pectoral girdle.

pectoral fin *n.* Either of the anterior pair of fins attached to the pectoral girdle of fishes.

pectoral girdle *n.* A skeletal structure in vertebrates, attached to and supporting the forelimbs or fins.

pectoral muscle *n.* One of the four muscles of the upper anterior chest.

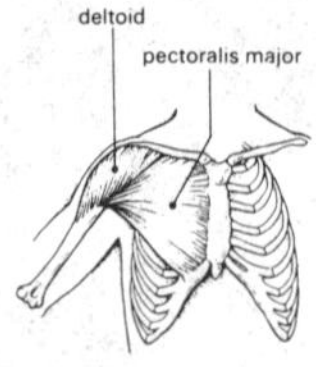

pectoral muscle

pectoral sandpiper *n.* A New World sandpiper, *Erolia melanotos,* having brownish streaks on the upper part of the breast.

pec·u·late (pĕk'yə-lāt') *v.* **-lat·ed, -lat·ing, -lates.** —*tr.* To embezzle or take for one's own use. —*intr.* To steal money or goods entrusted to one. [Lat. *peculari, peculat-* < *peculium,* private property < *pecu,* cattle.] —**pec'u·la'tion** *n.* —**pec'u·la'tor** *n.*

pe·cu·liar (pĭ-kyo͞ol'yər) *adj.* **1.** Unusual or eccentric; odd: *peculiar behavior.* **2.** Standing apart from others; distinct and particular: *a problem of peculiar complexity.* **3. a.** Exclusive; unique. **b.** Belonging distinctively or primarily to one person, group, or kind. —*n.* **1.** Some privilege or property that is exclusively one's own. **2.** *Chiefly Brit.* A church or parish under the jurisdiction of a diocese different from that in which it lies. [ME *peculier,* of private property < Lat. *peculiaris* < *peculium,* private property < *pecu,* cattle.] —**pe·cu'liar·ly** *adv.*

pe·cu·li·ar·i·ty (pĭ-kyo͞o'lē-ăr'ĭ-tē, -kyo͞ol-yăr'-) *n., pl.* **-ties.** **1.** The quality or state of being peculiar. **2.** A notable or distinctive feature or characteristic. **3.** An eccentricity; idiosyncrasy.

pe·cu·ni·ar·y (pĭ-kyo͞o'nē-ĕr'ē) *adj.* **1.** Consisting of or pertaining to money: *a pecuniary loss; pecuniary motives.* **2.** Requiring the payment of money: *a pecuniary offense.* [Lat. *pecuniarius* < *pecunia,* money.]

ped–[1] *pref.* Variant of **pedo-**[1].

ped–[2] *pref.* Variant of **pedo-**[2].

–ped or **–pede** *suff.* Foot: *maxilliped.* [< Lat. *pes, ped-,* foot.]

pedestal

ped·a·gog·ic (pĕd'ə-gŏj'ĭk, -gō'jĭk) also **ped·a·gog·i·cal** (-gŏj'ĭ-kəl, -gō'jĭ-kəl) *adj.* **1.** Of, pertaining to, or characteristic of teaching. **2.** Characterized by pedantic formality: *a haughty, pedagogic manner.* —**ped'a·gog'i·cal·ly** *adv.*

ped·a·gog·ics (pĕd'ə-gŏj'ĭks, -gō'jĭks) *n.* *(used with a sing. verb).* The art of teaching; pedagogy.

ped·a·gogue (pĕd'ə-gŏg', -gôg') *n.* **1.** A schoolteacher; educator. **2.** One who instructs in a pedantic or dogmatic manner. [ME *pedagoge* < OFr. < Lat. *paedagogus* < Gk. *paidagōgos* : *pais,* boy + *agōgos,* leader < *agein,* to lead.] —**ped'a·gogu'ish** *adj.*

ped·a·go·gy (pĕd'ə-gō'jē, -gŏj'ē) *n.* **1.** The art or profession of teaching. **2.** Preparatory training or instruction.

ped·al (pĕd'l) *n.* **1.** A lever operated by the foot on various musical instruments, such as the piano or harp. **2.** A pedal point. **3.** A lever worked by the foot in a machine, such as a bicycle or sewing machine; treadle. —*adj.* **1.** Of or pertaining to a foot or footlike part: *the pedal extremities.* **2.** *Mus.* Of or pertaining to a pedal. —*v.* **-aled, -al·ing, -als** or **-alled, -al·ling, -als.** —*intr.* **1.** To use or operate a pedal or pedals. **2.** To ride a bicycle. —*tr.* To operate the pedals of. [Fr. *pedale* < Ital. < Lat. *pedalis,* of the foot < *pes,* foot.]

pe·dal·fer (pĭ-dăl'fər) *n.* Soil rich in alumina and iron and deficient in carbonates, characteristic of humid, high-temperature regions with forest cover. [PED(O)-[1] + AL(UM) + Lat. *ferrum,* iron.]

pedal keyboard *n.* A keyboard of pedals in a musical instrument such as a pipe organ.

pedal piano *n.* A piano with a pedal keyboard.

pedal point *n.* *Mus.* A note, usually in the bass and on the tonic or the dominant, sustained through harmonic changes in the other parts.

pedal pushers *pl.n.* Women's and girls' calf-length slacks.

ped·ant (pĕd'nt) *n.* **1.** One who pays undue attention to book learning and formal rules without having an understanding or experience of practical affairs. **2.** One who exhibits his learning or scholarship ostentatiously. **3.** *Obs.* A schoolmaster. [OFr. < OItal. *pedante,* poss. < Lat. *paedagogans,* pr.part. of *paedagogare,* to instruct < *paedagogus,* pedagogue.]

pe·dan·tic (pə-dăn'tĭk) *adj.* Characterized by a narrow, often ostentatious concern for book learning and formal rules: *a pedantic attention to details.* —**pe·dan'ti·cal·ly** *adv.*

ped·ant·ry (pĕd'n-trē) *n., pl.* **-ries.** **1.** Pedantic attention to detail or rules. **2. a.** The habit of mind or manner characteristic of a pedant. **b.** An instance of pedantic behavior.

ped·ate (pĕd'āt') *adj.* **1.** *Zool.* Having feet. **2.** Resembling or functioning as a foot: *pedate appendages.* **3.** *Bot.* Having radiating lobes or divisions, with the lateral lobes cleft or divided: *a pedate leaf.* [Lat. *pedatus,* p.part. of *pedare,* to furnish with feet < *pes,* foot.]

ped·dle (pĕd'l) *v.* **-dled, -dling, -dles.** —*tr.* **1.** To travel about selling (wares): *peddling goods from door to door.* **2.** To give out; seek to disseminate: *peddling lies.* **3.** To engage in the illicit sale of (narcotics). —*intr.* **1.** To travel about selling wares. **2.** To occupy oneself with trifles. [Back-formation < PEDDLER.]

ped·dler (pĕd'lər) *n.* One who peddles for a living; hawker. [ME *pedlere,* prob. alteration of *peddere* < *pedde,* covered basket.]

–pede *suff.* Variant of **-ped.**

ped·er·ast (pĕd'ə-răst') *n.* One who engages in anal intercourse, esp. with a boy. [Gk. *paiderastēs,* lover of boys : *pais,* boy + *erasthēs,* lover < *erasthai,* to love.] —**ped'er·as'ty** *n.*

pe·des (pĕd'ās') *n.* Plural of **pes.**

ped·es·tal (pĕd'ĭ-stəl) *n.* **1.** An architectural support or base, as for a column or statue. **2.** A support or foundation. **3.** A position of high regard or adoration. —*tr.v.* **-taled, -tal·ing, -tals.** To place on or provide with a pedestal. [OFr. *piedestal* < OItal. *piedestallo* < *pie di stallo,* foot of a stall.]

pe·des·tri·an (pə-dĕs'trē-ən) *n.* A person traveling on foot; walker. —*adj.* **1.** Of, relating to, or made for pedestrians. **2.** Going or performed on foot: *a pedestrian journey.* **3.** Undistinguished; ordinary: *pedestrian prose.* [Lat. *pedester,* going on foot < *pedes,* a pedestrian < *pes,* foot.] —**pe·des'tri·an·ism** *n.*

pe·des·tri·an·ize (pĭ-dĕs'trē-ə-nīz') *tr.v.* **-ized, -iz·ing, -iz·es.** To convert (a street) into a mall or a pedestrian walkway. —**pe·des'tri·an·i·za'tion** *n.*

pedi– *pref.* Foot: *pediform.* [< Lat. *pes, ped-,* foot.]

pe·di·a·tri·cian (pē'dē-ə-trĭsh'ən) also **pe·di·at·rist** (pē'dē-ăt'rĭst) *n.* A physician who specializes in pediatrics.

pe·di·at·rics (pē'dē-ăt'rĭks) *n.* *(used with a sing. verb).* The branch of medicine that deals with the care of infants and children and the treatment of their diseases. —**pe'di·at'ric** *adj.*

ped·i·cab (pĕd'ĭ-kăb') *n.* A small, hooded, three-wheeled passenger vehicle that is pedaled.

ped·i·cel (pĕd'ĭ-səl, -sĕl') also **ped·i·cle** (-kəl) *n.* **1.** A small stalk, part, or organ, esp. one serving as a support. **2.** *Bot.* **a.** Any of several small stalks bearing a single flower in an inflorescence. **b.** A support for a fern sporangium or moss capsule. [NLat. *pedicellus* < Lat. *pediculus,* dim. of *pes,* foot.] —**ped'i·cel'lar** (pĕd'ĭ-sĕl'ər) *adj.*

ped·i·cel·late (pĕd'ĭ-sĕl'ĭt, -āt') *adj.* Having or supported by a pedicel.

ped·i·cle (pĕd'ĭ-kəl) *n.* Variant of **pedicel.**

pe·dic·u·lar (pə-dĭk'yə-lər) *adj.* Of, pertaining to, or caused by lice. [Lat. *pedicularis* < *pediculus,* dim. of *pedis,* louse.]

pe·dic·u·late (pə-dĭk'yə-lĭt, -lāt') *adj.* Of or pertaining to marine fishes of the order Pediculati or Lophiiformes, which includes the anglerfishes. —*n.* A pediculate fish. [< NLat. *Pediculati,* order name < Lat. *pediculus,* dim. of *pes,* foot.]

pe·dic·u·lo·sis (pə-dĭk'yə-lō'sĭs) *n.* Infestation with lice; lousiness. [Lat. *pediculus,* dim of *pedis,* louse + -OSIS.] —**pe·dic'u·lous** (-ləs) *adj.*

ped·i·cure (pĕd'ĭ-kyo͝or') *n.* **1. a.** Podiatry. **b.** A podiatrist. **2. a.** Cosmetic care of the feet and toenails. **b.** A single cosmetic treatment of the feet and toenails. —*tr.v.* **-cured, -cur·ing, -cures.** To give a pedicure to. [Fr. *pédicure* : Lat. *pes,* foot + Lat. *curare,* to take care of < *cura,* care.] —**ped'i·cur'ist** *n.*

ped·i·form (pĕd'ə-fôrm') *adj.* Shaped like a foot.

ped·i·gree (pĕd'ĭ-grē') *n.* **1.** A line of ancestors; lineage. **2.** A list of ancestors; family tree. **3.** A list of the ancestors of a purebred animal. [ME *pedegru* < OFr. *pie de grue,* crane's foot (from the resemblance of a crane's foot to the lines of succession on a genealogical chart).] —**ped'i·greed'** *adj.*

ped·i·ment (pĕd'ə-mənt) *n.* **1.** A wide, low-pitched gable surmounting the facade of a building in the Grecian style. **2.** An element, similar to or derivative of a pediment, used widely in architecture and decoration. [Obs. *perement,* prob. alteration of PYRAMID.] —**ped'i·men'tal** (-mĕn'tl) *adj.* —**ped'i·ment'ed** (-mĕn'tĭd) *adj.*

ped·i·palp (pĕd'ə-pălp') *n.* *Zool.* One of the second pair of appendages of an arachnid that are modified for various sensory functions.

ped·lar (pĕd'lər) *n.* *Chiefly Brit.* Variant of **peddler.**

pedo–[1] or **ped–** *pref.* Soil: *pedocal.* [< Gk. *pedon,* soil, earth.]

pedo–[2] or **ped–** or **paedo–** or **paed–** *pref.* Child: *pedodontia.* [Gk. *paido-* < *pais,* child, boy.]

ped·o·cal (pĕd'ə-kăl') *n.* A lime-rich soil of cool, semiarid, and arid regions. [PEDO-[1] + Lat. *calx,* lime < Gk. *khalix,* pebble.] —**ped'o·cal'ic** *adj.*

pe·do·don·tia (pē'də-dŏn'shə) *n.* The dentistry of children's teeth. —**pe'do·don'tist** (-dŏn'tĭst) *n.*

ped·o·gen·e·sis (pĕd'ə-jĕn'ĭ-sĭs) *n.* The process of soil formation.

pe·dol·o·gy[1] (pē-dŏl'ə-jē) *n.* The study of the behavior and development of children. —**pe'do·log'ic** (-də-lŏj'ĭk), **pe'do·log'i·cal** *adj.* —**pe'do·log'i·cal·ly** *adv.* —**pe·dol'o·gist** *n.*

pe·dol·o·gy[2] (pĭ-dŏl'ə-jē, pĕ-) *n.* The scientific study of soils, their origins, characteristics, and uses. —**ped'o·log'ic** (pĕd'ə-lŏj'ĭk), **ped'o·log'i·cal** *adj.* —**ped'o·log'i·cal·ly** *adv.* —**pe·dol'o·gist** *n.*

pe·dom·e·ter (pĭ-dŏm'ĭ-tər) *n.* An instrument that gauges the approximate distance traveled on foot by registering the number of steps taken. [Fr. *pédomètre* : Lat. *pes,* foot + Gk. *metron,* measure.]

pe·dun·cle (pĭ-dŭng'kəl, pē'dŭng'kəl) *n.* **1.** *Bot.* The main stalk of an inflorescence, or a stalk or stem bearing a solitary flower. **2.** *Zool.* A stalklike structure in invertebrate animals. **3.** *Anat.* A stalklike bundle of fibers, esp. of nerve fibers, connecting different parts of the central nervous system. [NLat. *pedunculus,* dim. of Lat. *pes,* foot.] **—pe·dun'cu·lar** (pĭ-dŭng'kyə-lər) *adj.*

pe·dun·cu·late (pĭ-dŭng'kyə-lĭt, -lāt') also **pe·dun·cu·lat·ed** (-lā'tĭd) *adj.* Having or supported on a peduncle.

pee¹ (pē) *n.* The letter *p.*

pee² (pē) *Vulgar Slang.* *—intr.v.* **peed, pee·ing, pees.** To urinate. *—n.* Urine. [From the first letter of PISS.]

peek (pēk) *intr.v.* **peeked, peek·ing, peeks. 1.** To glance quickly. **2.** To look or peer furtively, as from a place of concealment. **3.** To become gradually visible, as if emerging from hiding: *tiny crocuses peeking through the snow.* *—n.* A furtive or brief look. [ME *piken.*]

peek·a·boo (pēk'ə-bo͞o') *n.* A game for amusing a child, in which one repeatedly covers and exposes one's face, exclaiming "peekaboo!" *—adj.* Made of a sheer or transparent fabric: *a peekaboo blouse.* [Orig. unknown.]

peel¹ (pēl) *n.* The skin or rind of certain fruits, such as the orange or banana. *—v.* **peeled, peel·ing, peels.** *—tr.* **1.** To strip or cut away the skin, rind, or bark from; pare. **2.** To strip away; pull off: *peel the label from the jar.* *—intr.* **1.** To lose or shed skin, bark, or other covering. **2.** To come off in thin strips or pieces, as bark, skin, or paint: *Her sunburn began to peel.* **3.** *Slang.* To remove one's clothes; undress. ***—phrasal verb.* peel off. 1.** To leave flight formation in order to land or make a dive. **2.** To leave or depart. —See Usage note at **unloose.** [< ME *pelen,* to peel < OFr. *peler* < Lat. *pilare,* to deprive of hair < *pilus,* hair.]

peel² (pēl) *n.* **1.** A long-handled, shovellike tool used by bakers to move bread or pastries into and out of an oven. **2.** A T-shaped pole used by printers for hanging freshly printed sheets of paper to dry. [ME < OFr. *pele* < Lat. *pala.*]

peel³ (pēl) *n.* One of a class of fortified houses or towers constructed in the borderland of Scotland and England in the 16th century. [ME *pel,* small castle < AN < Lat. *palus,* stake.]

peel·er¹ (pē'lər) *n.* **1.** One that peels, esp. a kitchen implement for peeling the rind or skin from a fruit or vegetable. **2.** *Slang.* A stripteaser.

peel·er² (pē'lər) *n.* *Chiefly Brit. Slang.* A policeman. [After Sir Robert *Peel* (1788–1850).]

peel·ing (pē'lĭng) *n.* A piece or strip, as of skin or bark, that has been peeled off.

peen (pēn) *n.* The end of a hammerhead opposite the flat striking surface, often wedge-shaped or ball-shaped and used for chipping, indenting, and metalworking. *—tr.v.* **peened, peen·ing, peens.** To hammer, bend, or shape with a peen. [Prob. of Scand. orig.]

peep¹ (pēp) *intr.v.* **peeped, peep·ing, peeps. 1.** To utter short, soft, high-pitched sounds, like those of a baby bird; cheep. **2.** To speak in a hesitant, thin, high-pitched voice. *—n.* **1.** A weak, shrill sound or utterance, like that of a young bird. **2.** A slight sound or utterance: *I don't want to hear a peep out of you.* **3.** Any of various small North American sandpipers. [ME *pepen.*]

peep² (pēp) *v.* **peeped, peep·ing, peeps.** *—intr.* **1.** To peek furtively; steal a quick glance. **2.** To peer through a small aperture or from behind something. **3.** To become visible gradually, as though emerging from a hiding place: *At dawn the sun peeped over the horizon.* *—tr.* To cause to emerge or become partly visible. *—n.* **1.** A quick or furtive look; glance. **2.** A first glimpse or first appearance: *the peep of dawn.* [ME *pepen,* prob. alteration of *piken,* to peek.]

peep·er¹ (pē'pər) *n.* A creature that peeps, esp. a frog.

peep·er² (pē'pər) *n.* **1.** One who looks furtively. **2.** *Slang.* An eye.

peep·hole (pēp'hōl') *n.* A small hole or crevice through which one may peep.

peeping Tom *n.* A person who gets pleasure, esp. sexual pleasure, from secretly watching others; voyeur. [After the legendary *Peeping Tom* of Coventry who was the only person to see the naked Lady Godiva.]

peep·show also **peep show** (pēp'shō') *n.* **1.** An exhibition of pictures or objects viewed through a small hole or magnifying glass. **2.** A short, sexually explicit film presentation seen usually in a small coin-operated projection booth.

peep sight *n.* A rear sight of a firearm consisting of an adjustable eyepiece with a small opening through which the front sight and the target are aligned.

pee·pul also **pi·pal** (pē'pəl) *n.* A fig tree, *Ficus religiosa,* of India, regarded as sacred by Buddhists. [Hindi *pīpal* < Skt. *pippalam.*]

peer¹ (pîr) *intr.v.* **peered, peer·ing, peers. 1.** To look intently, searchingly, or with difficulty. **2.** To be partially visible; show: *The moon peered from behind a cloud.* [Perh. alteration of APPEAR.]

peer² (pîr) *n.* **1.** A person who has equal standing with another, as in rank, class, or age. **2.** *Archaic.* A companion; fellow. **3. a.** A nobleman. **b.** A member of the British peerage; a duke, marquis, earl, viscount, or baron. ***—modifier:*** *peer group.* [ME < OFr. *per* < *per,* equal < Lat. *par.*]

Usage: *Peer* is sometimes misused in the sense of "a superior": *She is the equal, if not the peer, of any player in the tournament. Peer* refers to an equal, not a superior. Its misuse may stem from the fact that English noblemen are called *peers;* but they are so called because they are equals of each other, not because they are the superiors of English commoners. *Peer* is properly used in the expressions *peer group* and *jury of one's peers.*

peer·age (pîr'ĭj) *n.* **1.** The rank or title of a peer. **2.** Peers collectively. **3.** A book listing peers and their families.

peer·ess (pîr'ĭs) *n.* **1.** The wife or widow of a peer. **2.** A woman who holds a peerage by descent or appointment.

peer·less (pîr'lĭs) *adj.* Without peer; unmatched. **—peer'less·ly** *adv.* **—peer'less·ness** *n.*

peet·weet (pēt'wēt') *n.* The spotted sandpiper. [Imit. of its song.]

peeve (pēv) *tr.v.* **peeved, peev·ing, peeves.** To annoy or make resentful; vex. *—n.* **1.** A vexation; grievance: *a pet peeve.* **2.** A resentful mood: *be in a peeve.* [Back-formation < PEEVISH.]

pee·vish (pē'vĭsh) *adj.* **1.** Querulous; discontented; fretful. **2.** Ill-tempered. **3.** Contrary; fractious. [ME *pevish,* spiteful.] **—pee'vish·ly** *adv.* **—pee'vish·ness** *n.*

pee·wee (pē'wē) *n.* **1.** *Informal.* One that is relatively or unusually small. **2.** Variant of **pewee.** [Prob. redup. of WEE.] **—pee'wee** *adj.*

peg (pĕg) *n.* **1. a.** A small cylindrical or tapered pin, as of wood, used to fasten things or to plug a hole. **b.** A similar pin forming a projection that may be used as a support or as a boundary marker. **2.** One of the pins of a stringed musical instrument that are turned to tighten or slacken the strings so as to regulate their pitch. **3.** An implement fitted with a pointed prong or claw for tearing or catching. **4.** A degree or notch, esp. in estimation. **5.** *Chiefly Brit.* A shot of liquor. **6.** A pretext or occasion for: *a peg to hang one's grievances on.* **7.** *Baseball.* A low and fast throw made to put a baserunner out. **8.** *Informal.* A wooden leg. *—v.* **pegged, peg·ging, pegs.** *—tr.* **1.** To fasten or plug with a peg. **2.** To designate or mark by means of pegs. **3.** To fix (a price) at a certain level or within a certain range. **4.** *Informal.* To classify; categorize. **5.** *Informal.* To throw. *—intr.* To work steadily; persist: *pegging steadily away until his luck turned.* ***—idiom.* take one down a peg.** To reduce the pride of; humble. [ME *pegge.*]

Peg·a·sus (pĕg'ə-səs) *n.* **1.** *Gk. Myth.* A winged horse that with a stroke of his hoof caused the fountain Hippocrene to spring forth from Mount Helicon. **2.** A constellation in the Northern Hemisphere near Aquarius and Andromeda. [Gk. *Pēgasos.*]

peg leg *n.* *Informal.* An artificial leg.

peg·ma·tite (pĕg'mə-tīt') *n.* A coarse-grained igneous rock, largely granite, sometimes rich in rare elements such as uranium, tungsten, and tantalum. [Fr. < Gk. *pēgma,* framework < *pēgnunai,* to fasten.] **—peg'ma·tit'ic** (-tĭt'ĭk) *adj.*

Peh·le·vi (pā'lə-vē') *n.* Variant of **Pahlavi.**

pei·gnoir (pān-wär', pĕn-) *n.* A woman's loose-fitting dressing gown. [Fr. < OFr. *peigner,* to comb the hair < Lat. *pectinare* < *pecten,* comb.]

pej·o·ra·tion (pĕj'ə-rā'shən, pē'jə-) *n.* **1.** The process or condition of worsening or degenerating. **2.** *Ling.* The process by which the semantic status of a word changes for the worse, over a period of time. For example, *egregious,* which formerly meant "distinguished or remarkable," has come to mean "conspicuously bad or flagrant." [Med. Lat. *pejoratio* < LLat. *pejorare,* to make worse < Lat. *pejor,* worse.]

pe·jor·a·tive (pĭ-jôr'ə-tĭv, -jŏr'-, pĕj'ə-rā'tĭv, pē'jə-) *adj.* Tending to make or become worse; disparaging; downgrading. *—n.* A pejorative word. **—pe·jor'a·tive·ly** *adv.*

pek·an (pĕk'ən) *n.* The fisher (sense 2.a.). [Canadian Fr. *pékan,* of Algonquian orig.]

pe·kin (pē'kĭn') *n.* **1.** A striped or figured silk fabric. **2. Pekin.** A large white duck of an Oriental breed, widely raised in the United States for food. [Fr. *pékin,* after *Pékin* (Beijing), China.]

Pe·king·ese (pē'kĭng-ēz', -ēs') also **Pe·kin·ese** (pē'kə-nēz', -nēs') *n., pl.* **Pekingese** also **Pekinese. 1.** A resident or native of Peking (now Beijing), China. **2.** The Chinese dialect of Peking. **3.** (pē'kə-nēz', -nēs'). A toy dog of a breed developed in China, having a flat nose, a long-haired coat, and short, bowed forelegs. **—Pe'king·ese'** *adj.*

Pe·king man (pē'kĭng) *n.* An extinct hominid primate of the genus *Sinanthropus,* known from fossil remains of the Pleistocene epoch. [After *Peking* (Beijing), China.]

pe·koe (pē'kō) *n.* A grade of black tea consisting of the leaves around the buds. [Chin. (Amoy) *peh ho* : *peh,* white + *ho,* down, fine feathers.]

pel·age (pĕl'ĭj) *n.* The coat of a mammal, consisting of hair, fur, wool, or other soft covering, as distinct from bare skin. [Fr. < OFr. *poil,* hair < Lat. *pilus.*]

Pe·la·gi·an·ism (pə-lā'jē-ə-nĭz'əm) *n.* The theological doctrine propounded by Pelagius, a British or Irish monk, and condemned as heresy by the Roman Catholic Church in A.D. 416. Included in its tenets were denial of original sin and affirmation of man's ability to be righteous by the exercise of free will. **—Pe·la'gi·an** *adj. & n.*

pe·lag·ic (pə-lăj'ĭk) *adj.* Of, pertaining to, or living in open oceans or seas rather than waters adjacent to land or inland waters. [Lat. *pelagicus* < Gk. *pelagikos* < *pelagos,* sea.]

pel·ar·gon·ic acid (pĕl'är-gŏn'ĭk, -gō'nĭk) *n.* A colorless or

peel²
18th-century engraving of a baker's peel

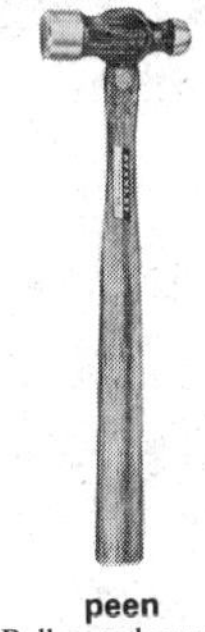

peen
Ball peen hammer

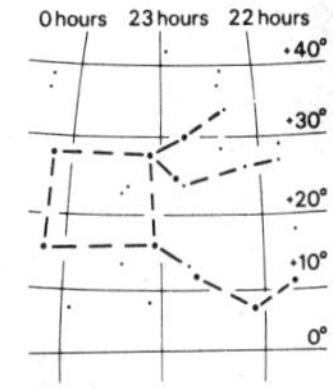

Pegasus
Above: Detail from a Greek vase
Below: The constellation

Pekingese

pelican

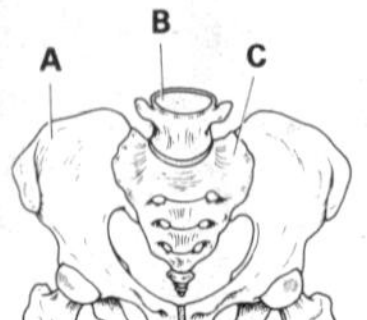

pelvis
A. Ilium
B. Vertebra
C. Sacrum

yellow oil, $CH_3(CH_2)_7COOH$, used as a gasoline additive and in the manufacture of lacquers, plastics, and pharmaceuticals. [PELARGON(IUM) + -IC.]

pel·ar·go·ni·um (pĕl′är-gō′nē-əm) *n.* Any of various plants and shrubs of the genus *Pelargonium,* which includes the geraniums. [NLat. *Pelargonium,* genus name < Gk. *pelargos,* stork.]

Pe·las·gi·an (pə-lăz′jē-ən) *n.* One of a people living in the region of the Aegean Sea before the coming of the Greeks. [< Gk. *Pelasgoi.*] **—Pe·las′gi·an, Pe·las′gic** (pə-lăz′jĭk) *adj.*

pe·lec·y·pod (pə-lĕs′ə-pŏd′) *n.* A lamellibranch. [< NLat. *Pelecypoda,* class name : Gk. *pelekus,* ax + Gk. *pous,* foot.]

pel·er·ine (pĕl′ə-rēn′, pĕl′ər-ĭn) *n.* A woman's cape, usually short, with points in front. [Fr. *pèlerine* < fem. of *pèlerin,* pilgrim < LLat. *pelegrinus.* —see PILGRIM.]

Pe·le·us (pē′lē-əs, pēl′yo͞os′) *n. Gk. Myth.* A son of Aeacus and father of Achilles. [Lat. < Gk. *Pēleus.*]

pelf (pĕlf) *n.* Wealth or riches, esp. when dishonestly acquired. [ME < OFr. *pelfre.*]

pel·i·can (pĕl′ĭ-kən) *n.* Any of various large, web-footed birds of the genus *Pelecanus,* of tropical and warm regions, having under the lower bill a large pouch used for catching and holding fish. [ME < OE *pellican* < LLat. *pelicanus* < Gk. *pelekan, pelekinos* < *pelekus,* ax.]

pe·lisse (pə-lēs′) *n.* **1.** A long cloak or outer robe, usually of fur or with a fur lining. **2.** A woman's loose, light cloak, often with openings for the arms. [Fr. < Med. Lat. *pellicia* < Lat. *pellicius,* made of skin < *pellis,* skin.]

pe·lite (pē′līt′) *n.* Rock composed of fine fragments, as of clay, quartz particles, or rock flour. [Gk. *pēlos,* clay + -ITE.] **—pe·lit′ic** (pĭ-lĭt′ĭk) *adj.*

pel·lag·ra (pə-lăg′rə, -lā′grə, -lä′grə) *n.* A chronic disease caused by niacin deficiency, and characterized by skin eruptions, digestive and nervous disturbances, and eventual mental deterioration. [Ital. : *pelle,* skin (< Lat. *pellis*) + Gk. *agra,* seizure.] **—pel·lag′rous** *adj.*

pel·lag·rin (pə-lăg′rĭn, -lā′grĭn, -lä′grĭn) *n.* A person afflicted with pellagra. [< PELLAGRA.]

pel·let (pĕl′ĭt) *n.* **1.** A small, solid or densely packed ball or mass, as of bread, wax, or medicine. **2.** A bullet or piece of small shot. **3.** A stone ball, used as a catapult missile or as a primitive cannonball. *—tr.v.* **-let·ed, -let·ing, -lets. 1.** To make or form into pellets. **2.** To strike with pellets. [ME *pelet* < OFr. *pelote* < VLat. **pilotta,* dim. of Lat. *pila,* ball.]

pel·li·cle (pĕl′ĭ-kəl) *n.* A thin skin or film, such as an organic membrane or a liquid film. [OFr. < Med. Lat. *pellicula* < Lat., dim. of *pellis,* skin.] **—pel·lic′u·lar** (pə-lĭk′yə-lər) *adj.*

pel·li·to·ry[1] (pĕl′ĭ-tôr′ē, -tōr′ē) *n., pl.* **-ries.** A small plant, *Anacyclus pyrethrum,* of the Mediterranean region, containing a volatile oil once used for the relief of toothache and facial neuralgia. [ME *peletre* < OFr. *piretre* < Lat. *pyrethrum.*]

pel·li·to·ry[2] (pĕl′ĭ-tôr′ē, -tōr′ē) *n., pl.* **-ries.** Any of various plants of the genus *Parietaria,* having long, narrow leaves with hairy tufts at the base. [ME *peritorie* < OFr. *paritaire* < LLat. *parietaria* < *parietarius,* belonging to walls < Lat. *paries,* wall.]

pell-mell also **pell·mell** (pĕl′mĕl′) *adv.* **1.** In a jumbled, confused manner; helter-skelter. **2.** In frantic, disorderly haste; headlong. [Fr. *pêle-mêle* < OFr. *pesle mesle,* prob. redup. of *mesle,* imper. of *mesler,* to mix. —see MEDDLE.] **—pell′-mell′** *adj. & n.*

pel·lu·cid (pə-lo͞o′sĭd) *adj.* **1.** Admitting the maximum passage of light; transparent; translucent. **2.** Transparently clear in style or meaning: *pellucid prose.* [Lat. *pellucidus* < *pellucēre,* to shine through : *per,* through + *lucēre,* to shine.] **—pel·lu·cid′i·ty** (-sĭd′ĭ-tē), **pel·lu′cid·ness** *n.* **—pel·lu′cid·ly** *adv.*

Pe·lops (pē′lŏps′) *n. Gk. Myth.* The son of Tantalus and father of Atreus. [Lat. < Gk. : *pelios,* dark + *ops,* face.]

pe·lo·ri·a (pə-lôr′ē-ə, -lōr′-) *n.* Unusual regularity in the form of a flower that is normally irregular. [NLat. < Gk. *pelōros,* monstrous < *pelōr,* monster.] **—pe·lor′ic** (pə-lôr′ĭk, -lōr′-) *adj.*

pe·lo·rus (pə-lôr′əs, -lōr′-) *n., pl.* **-rus·es.** A fixed compass card on which bearings relative to a ship's heading are taken. [Orig. unknown.]

pe·lo·ta (pə-lō′tə) *n.* **1.** Jai alai. **2.** The ball used in jai alai. [Sp. < OFr. *pelote,* pellet.]

pelt[1] (pĕlt) *n.* **1.** The skin of an animal with the fur or hair still on it. **2.** A stripped animal skin ready for tanning. [ME.]

pelt[2] (pĕlt) *v.* **pelt·ed, pelt·ing, pelts.** *—tr.* **1.** To strike or assail repeatedly with or as if with blows or missiles; bombard: *pelted each other with snowballs.* **2.** To cast, hurl, or throw (missiles): *pelting stones at windows.* **3.** To strike repeatedly: *Hailstones pelted the tent.* *—intr.* **1.** To beat or strike heavily and repeatedly. **2.** To move at a vigorous gait. *—n.* **1.** A sharp blow; whack. **2.** A rapid pace; speed: *galloped away at full pelt.* [ME *pelten.*] **—pelt′er** *n.*

pel·tate (pĕl′tāt′) *adj.* Having the leaf stalk attached near the center of the surface, rather than at or near the margin: *the peltate leaf of the nasturtium.* [NLat. *peltatus* < Lat. *pelta,* small shield < Gk. *peltē.*] **—pel′tate′ly** *adv.*

pelt·ing (pĕl′tĭng) *adj. Archaic.* Paltry; petty; contemptible. [Orig. unknown.]

pel·try (pĕl′trē) *n.* Undressed pelts collectively. [ME < AN *pelterie* < OFr. *peletier,* furrier, prob. < *pel,* skin < Lat. *pellis.*]

pel·vic (pĕl′vĭk) *adj.* Of, in, near, or pertaining to the pelvis: *a pelvic artery.*

pelvic arch *n.* Pelvic girdle.

pelvic fin *n.* Either of a pair of lateral hind fins of fishes, attached to the pelvic girdle.

pelvic girdle *n.* The skeletal structure of bone or cartilage by which the hind limbs or analogous parts are supported and joined to the vertebral column.

pel·vis (pĕl′vĭs) *n., pl.* **-vis·es** or **-ves** (-vēz). *Anat.* **1.** A basin-shaped skeletal structure, composed of the innominate bones on the sides, the pubis in front, and the sacrum and coccyx behind, that rests on the lower limbs and supports the spinal column. **2.** The hollow funnel in the outlet of the kidney, into which urine is discharged before entering the ureter. [NLat. < Lat., basin.]

pem·mi·can also **pem·i·can** (pĕm′ĭ-kən) *n.* **1.** A food prepared by North American Indians from lean, dried strips of meat pounded into paste, mixed with fat and berries, and pressed into small cakes. **2.** A food made chiefly from beef, dried fruit, and suet, used as emergency rations. [Cree *pimikân* < *pimii,* fat.]

pem·phi·gus (pĕm′fĭ-gəs, pĕm-fī′gəs) *n.* Any of several acute or chronic skin diseases characterized by groups of itching blisters. [NLat. < Gk. *pemphix,* pustule.]

pen[1] (pĕn) *n.* **1.** An instrument for writing or drawing with ink or similar fluid, esp.: **a.** A quill. **b.** A pen point. **c.** A penholder and its pen point. **d.** A ball-point pen. **e.** A fountain pen. **2.** An instrument for writing that is a means of expression. **3.** A writer or author: *a hired pen.* **4.** A style of writing: *a witty pen.* **5. pens.** Pinions. **6.** *Zool.* The chitinous internal shell of a squid. *—tr.v.* **penned, pen·ning, pens.** To write or compose with a pen. [ME *penne* < OFr. < Lat. *penna,* feather.] **—pen′ner** *n.*

pen[2] (pĕn) *n.* **1. a.** A fenced enclosure for animals. **b.** The animals kept in such an enclosure. **c.** Any of various other enclosures, such as a bullpen or playpen. **2.** A repair dock for submarines. *—tr.v.* **penned** or **pent** (pĕnt), **pen·ning, pens.** To confine in or as if in a pen. [ME < OE *penn.*]

pen[3] (pĕn) *n.* A female swan. [Orig. unknown.]

pen[4] (pĕn) *n. Slang.* A penitentiary (sense 1). [Short for PENITENTIARY.]

pe·nal (pē′nəl) *adj.* **1.** Of, relating to, or prescribing punishment, as for breaking the law. **2.** Subject to punishment; legally punishable: *a penal offense.* **3.** Serving as or constituting a means or place of punishment: *penal servitude.* [ME < OFr. < Lat. *poenalis* < *poena,* penalty.] **—pe′nal·ly** *adv.*

penal code *n.* The body of laws relating to crimes and offenses and the penalties for their commission.

pe·nal·ize (pē′nə-līz′, pĕn′ə-) *tr.v.* **-ized, -iz·ing, -iz·es. 1.** To subject to a penalty, esp. for infringement of a law or official regulation. **2.** To impose a handicap on; place at a disadvantage. **—pe′nal·i·za′tion** *n.*

pen·al·ty (pĕn′əl-tē) *n., pl.* **-ties. 1.** A punishment established by law or authority for a crime or offense. **2.** Something, esp. a sum of money, required as a forfeit for an offense. **3.** The disadvantage or painful consequences resulting from an action or condition: *neglected his health and paid the penalty.* **4.** *Sports.* A punishment, handicap, or loss of advantage imposed on a team or competitor for infraction of a rule. **5.** Often **penalties.** *Games.* In contract bridge, points scored by the opponents when the declarer fails to make his bid. [Med. Lat. *poenalitas* < Lat. *peonalis,* penal.]

penalty box *n. Sports.* An area to the side of an ice-hockey rink in which penalized players wait out the time of their penalties.

pen·ance (pĕn′əns) *n.* **1.** An act of self-mortification or devotion performed voluntarily to show sorrow for a sin or other wrongdoing. **2.** In some Christian churches, a sacrament that includes contrition, confession to a priest, acceptance of punishment, and absolution. *—tr.v.* **-anced, -anc·ing, -ances.** To impose penance upon. [ME < OFr. < Lat. *paenitentia,* penitence < *paenitens,* penitent.]

Pe·na·tes (pə-nā′tēz, -nä′-) *pl.n.* The Roman gods of the household, tutelary deities of the home and of the state, whose cult was closely connected and often identified with that of the Lares. [Lat.]

pence (pĕns) *n. Chiefly Brit.* A plural of **penny** (sense 1).

pen·cel also **pen·sil** (pĕn′səl) *n.* A narrow flag, streamer, or pennon, esp. one carried at the top of a lance or spear. [ME < OFr. *penoncel,* dim. of *penon,* pennon.]

pen·chant (pĕn′chənt) *n.* A strong inclination; a definite and continued liking. [Fr. < pr.part. of *pencher,* to incline < Lat. *pendēre,* to hang.]

pen·cil (pĕn′səl) *n.* **1.** A narrow, generally cylindrical implement for writing, drawing, or marking, consisting of a thin rod of graphite, crayon, or similar substance encased in wood or held in a plastic or metal mechanical device. **2.** Something shaped or used like a pencil, esp. a narrow medicated or cosmetic stick. **3. a.** *Archaic.* An artist's brush, esp. a fine one. **b.** An artist's style or technique in drawing or delineating. **c.** Descriptive skill. **4.** A cluster of rays, esp. light rays, radiating from or converging on a single point. **5.** *Math.* A one-parameter family of three-dimensional or plane figures, such as all straight lines in a plane that pass through a fixed point. *—tr.v.* **-ciled, -cil·ing, -cils** also **-cilled, -cil·ling, -cils. 1.** To write or produce by using a pencil. **2.** To mark or color with or as if with a pencil. [ME *pencel,* artist's brush < OFr. *pincel* < Lat. *pennicillus* < *peniculus,* brush, dim. of *penis,* tail.] **—pen'cil·er** *n.*

pencil pusher *n. Informal.* One whose job involves writing.

pen·dant also **pen·dent** (pĕn'dənt) *n.* **1.** Something suspended from something else, esp. an ornament or piece of jewelry attached to a necklace or bracelet. **2.** A hanging lamp or chandelier. **3.** A sculptured ornament suspended from a vaulted Gothic roof or ceiling. **4. a.** One of a matched pair; a parallel or companion piece. **b.** An additional thing or part that supplements or complements another; complement. *—adj.* Variant of **pendent.** [ME *pendaunt* < OFr. *pendant* < pr.part. of *pendre,* to hang < Lat. *pendēre.*]

pen·dent also **pen·dant** (pĕn'dənt) *adj.* **1.** Hanging down; dangling; suspended. **2.** Projecting; jutting; overhanging. **3.** Awaiting settlement; pending. *—n.* Variant of **pendant.** [ME *pendant* < OFr. —see PENDANT.] **—pen'dent·ly** *adv.*

pen·den·tive (pĕn-dĕn'tĭv) *n. Archit.* An overhanging, triangular section of vaulting between the rim of a dome and each adjacent pair of the arches that support it. [Fr. *pendentif* < Lat. *pendens,* hanging < *pendēre,* to hang.]

pend·ing (pĕn'dĭng) *adj.* **1.** Not yet decided or settled; awaiting conclusion or confirmation. **2.** Impending; imminent. *—prep.* **1.** While in the process of; during. **2.** While awaiting; until. [Fr. *pendant,* pendant, pending (< OFr.) + -ING[1].]

pen·drag·on (pĕn-drăg'ən) *n.* The title of the supreme war leader of the post-Roman Celts of southern Britain. [ME < Welsh : *pen,* chief + *dragon,* leader.] **—pen·drag'on·ship'** *n.*

pen·du·lar (pĕn'jə-lər, pĕn'dyə-) *adj.* Of or resembling the motion of a pendulum; swinging back and forth.

pen·du·lous (pĕn'jə-ləs, pĕn'dyə-) *adj.* **1.** Hanging loosely; suspended so as to swing or sway. **2.** Wavering; undecided. [Lat. *pendulus* < *pendēre,* to hang.] **—pen'du·lous·ly** *adv.* **—pen'du·lous·ness** *n.*

pen·du·lum (pĕn'jə-ləm, pĕn'dyə-, pĕn'də-) *n.* **1.** An object suspended from a fixed support so that it swings freely back and forth under the influence of gravity, and commonly used to regulate various devices, esp. clocks. **2.** Something that swings back and forth from one course, opinion, or condition to another: *the pendulum of public opinion.* [NLat. < Lat. *pendulus,* hanging < *pendēre,* to hang.]

Pe·nel·o·pe (pə-nĕl'ə-pē) *n. Gk. Myth.* The wife of Odysseus and mother of Telemachus, celebrated for her faithfulness. [Lat. < Gk. *Pēnelopeia.*]

pe·ne·plain also **pe·ne·plane** (pē'nə-plān') *n. Geol.* A nearly flat land surface representing an advanced stage of erosion. [Lat. *paene, pene,* almost + PLAIN.]

pe·nes (pē'nēz) *n.* A plural of **penis.**

pen·e·tra·ble (pĕn'ĭ-trə-bəl) *adj.* Capable of being penetrated. [Lat. *penetrabilis* < *penetrare,* to penetrate.] **—pen'e·tra·bil'i·ty** *n.* **—pen'e·tra·bly** *adv.*

pen·e·tra·li·a (pĕn'ĭ-trā'lē-ə) *pl.n.* The innermost or most secret parts. [Lat. < *penetralis,* inner < *penetrare,* to penetrate.]

pen·e·tram·e·ter (pĕn'ĭ-trăm'ĭ-tər) *n.* Variant of **penetrometer.**

pen·e·trance (pĕn'ĭ-trəns) *n.* The degree or frequency with which a gene manifests its effect. [< PENETRANT.]

pen·e·trant (pĕn'ĭ-trənt) *adj.* Penetrating; piercing. *—n.* Something that penetrates or is capable of penetrating. [Lat. *penetrans, penetrant-,* pr.part. of *penetrare,* to enter.]

pen·e·trate (pĕn'ĭ-trāt') *v.* **-trat·ed, -trat·ing, -trates.** *—tr.* **1.** To enter or force a way into; pierce. **2. a.** To enter into and permeate. **b.** To cause to be permeated or diffused; steep. **3.** To grasp the inner significance of; understand. **4.** To see through. **5.** To affect deeply, as by piercing the consciousness or emotions. *—intr.* **1.** To pierce or enter into something; make a way in or through something; get in or through. **2.** To gain admittance or access. **3.** To gain insight. [Lat. *penetrare, penetrat-.*]

pen·e·trat·ing (pĕn'ĭ-trā'tĭng) *adj.* **1.** Able or seeming to penetrate: *a penetrating wind.* **2.** Keenly perceptive or understanding: *penetrating insight.* **—pen'e·trat'ing·ly** *adv.*

pen·e·tra·tion (pĕn'ĭ-trā'shən) *n.* **1.** The act or process of piercing or penetrating something: **a.** The act of entering a country so as to establish influence: *penetration of spies.* **b.** An attack that penetrates enemy territory or a military front. **2.** The power or ability to penetrate. **3.** The depth reached by a projectile after hitting its target. **4.** The capacity or action of understanding; insight.

pen·e·tra·tive (pĕn'ĭ-trā'tĭv) *adj.* Capable of penetrating; tending to penetrate; piercing.

pen·e·trom·e·ter (pĕn'ĭ-trŏm'ĭ-tər) also **pen·e·tram·e·ter** (-trăm'ĭ-tər) *n.* **1.** A device for measuring the penetrating power of x-rays. **2.** A device for measuring the penetrability of semisolids.

pen·guin (pĕn'gwĭn, pĕng'gwĭn) *n.* **1.** Any of various flightless marine birds of the family Spheniscidae, of cool regions of the Southern Hemisphere, having scalelike, barbless feathers, flipperlike wings, and webbed feet. **2.** *Obs.* The great auk. [Poss. < Welsh *pen gwyn,* white head.]

pen·hold·er (pĕn'hōl'dər) *n.* A holder for a pen point.

-penia *suff.* Lack; deficiency: *leukopenia.* [NLat. < Gk. *penia,* poverty, lack.]

pen·i·cil·la·mine (pĕn'ĭ-sĭl'ə-mēn') *n.* A degradation product of penicillin, $C_5H_{11}NO_2S$, that is used as a chelating agent and in the medical treatment of rheumatoid arthritis. [PENICILL(IN) + AMINE.]

pen·i·cil·late (pĕn'ĭ-sĭl'ĭt, -āt') *adj.* Having or resembling a tuft or brush of fine hairs, such as those on caterpillars and certain grasses. [Lat. *penicillus,* brush + -ATE.] **—pen'i·cil'late·ly** *adv.* **—pen'i·cil·la'tion** (-sə-lā'shən) *n.*

pen·i·cil·lin (pĕn'ĭ-sĭl'ĭn) *n.* Any of several isomeric antibiotic compounds obtained from penicillium molds, esp. *Penicillium notatum* and *P. chrysogenum,* or produced biosynthetically, and used to prevent or treat a wide variety of diseases and infections. [PENICILL(IUM) + -IN.]

pen·i·cil·lin·ase (pĕn'ĭ-sĭl'ĭ-nās') *n.* A bacterial enzyme that inactivates penicillin by hydrolysis.

pen·i·cil·li·um (pĕn'ĭ-sĭl'ē-əm) *n., pl.* **-cil·li·ums** or **-cil·li·a** (-sĭl'ē-ə). Any of various molds of the genus *Penicillium,* having a characteristic blue-green color, and producing tufts of fine filaments that grow on decaying fruits and ripening cheese, and are used in the production of penicillin and in making cheese. [NLat. *Penicillium,* genus name < Lat. *penicillus,* brush. —see PENCIL.]

pen·in·su·la (pə-nĭn'syə-lə, -sə-lə) *n.* A long projection of land into water, connected with the mainland by an isthmus. [Lat. : *paene,* almost + *insula,* island.] **—pen·in'su·lar** *adj.*

pe·nis (pē'nĭs) *n., pl.* **-nis·es** or **-nes** (-nēz). *Anat.* **1.** The male organ of copulation in higher vertebrates, and usually of urinary excretion in mammals. **2.** Any of various copulatory organs in males of lower animals. [Lat.]

pen·i·tent (pĕn'ĭ-tənt) *adj.* Feeling or expressing remorse for one's misdeeds or sins. *—n.* **1.** One who is penitent. **2.** A person performing penance under the direction of a confessor. [ME < OFr. < Lat. *paenitens* < *paenitēre,* to repent.] **—pen'i·tence** *n.* **—pen'i·tent·ly** *adv.*

pen·i·ten·tial (pĕn'ĭ-tĕn'shəl) *adj.* **1.** Of, pertaining to, or expressing penitence. **2.** Pertaining to or of the nature of penance. *—n.* **1.** A book or set of church rules concerning the sacrament of penance. **2.** A penitent. **—pen'i·ten'tial·ly** *adv.*

pen·i·ten·tia·ry (pĕn'ĭ-tĕn'shə-rē) *n., pl.* **-ries. 1.** A prison for those convicted of major crimes. **2.** *Rom. Cath. Ch.* **a.** A tribunal of the Roman Curia, presided over by a cardinal designated in this office as the Grand Penitentiary, having jurisdiction in matters relating to penance, dispensations, and papal absolutions. **b.** In cathedrals or churches having a chapter of canons, a canon whose special function is the administration of the sacrament of penance. *—adj.* **1.** Of or for the purpose of penance; penitential. **2.** Pertaining to or used for punishment or reform of criminals or wrongdoers. **3.** Resulting in or punishable by imprisonment in a penitentiary: *a penitentiary offense.* [ME *penitenciary,* penance officer < Med. Lat. *penitentiarius* < Lat. *paenitentia,* penitence < *paenitens,* penitent.]

pen·knife (pĕn'nīf') *n.* A small pocketknife.

pen·light (pĕn'līt') *n.* A small flashlight having the size and shape of a fountain pen.

pen·man (pĕn'mən) *n.* **1.** A copyist; scribe. **2.** An expert in penmanship. **3.** An author; writer.

pen·man·ship (pĕn'mən-shĭp') *n.* The art, skill, style, or manner of handwriting; calligraphy.

pen·na (pĕn'ə) *n., pl.* **pen·nae** (pĕn'ē). Any of the larger feathers forming the visible plumage of a bird, as distinguished from the down feathers. [Lat., feather.] **—pen·na'ceous** (pĕ-nā'shəs) *adj.*

pen name also **pen·name** (pĕn'nām') *n.* A literary pseudonym.

pen·nant (pĕn'ənt) *n.* **1.** *Naut.* A long, tapering flag, often triangular, used on ships for signaling or for identification. **2.** A flag or emblem similar in shape to a ship's pennant. **3.** *Sports.* **a.** A flag that serves as the emblem of the championship in a professional baseball league. **b.** The yearly championship in such a league. [Blend of PENDANT and PENNON.]

pen·nate (pĕn'āt') also **pen·nat·ed** (pĕn'ā'tĭd) *adj.* Feathered or winged; pinnate. [Lat. *penatus* < *penna,* wing.]

pen·ni (pĕn'ē) *n., pl.* **pen·nis** or **pen·ni·a** (pĕn'ē-ə). See table at **currency.** [Finn.]

pen·ni·less (pĕn'ē-lĭs, pĕn'ə-lĭs) *adj.* **1.** Entirely without money. **2.** Very poor. **—pen'ni·less·ly** *adv.* **—pen'ni·less·ness** *n.*

pen·non (pĕn'ən) *n.* **1.** A long, narrow banner or streamer borne upon a lance. **2.** A banner, flag, or pennant. **3.** A pinion; wing. [ME < OFr. *penon,* aug. of *penne,* wing < Lat. *penna.*] **—pen'noned** *adj.*

pen·non·cel also **pen·on·cel** or **pen·non·celle** (pĕn'ən-sĕl') *n.* A small pennon, flag, or streamer borne upon a lance. [ME *penoncelle* < OFr. *penoncel,* dim. of *penon,* pennon.]

Penn·syl·va·nia Dutch (pĕn'səl-vān'yə, -vā'nē-ə) *n.* **1.** The descendants of German and Swiss immigrants who settled in Pennsylvania in the 17th and 18th centuries. **2.** The dialect of High German spoken by the Pennsylvania Dutch.

Pennsylvania German *n.* Pennsylvania Dutch (sense 2).

Penn·syl·va·nian (pĕn'səl-vān'yən, -vā'nē-ən) *Geol. —adj.*

pendant

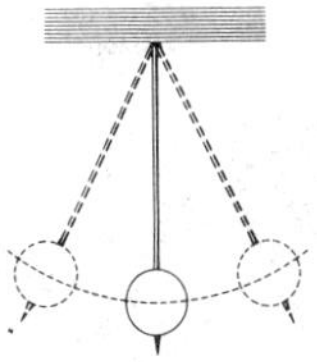

pendulum

George Miksch Sutton

penguin

pennant

pennon
Pennon of Sir Philip Sidney carried at his funeral procession

Of, belonging to, or designating the geologic time, system of rocks, and sedimentary deposits of the sixth period of the Paleozoic era, characterized by the development of coal-bearing rock formations. —*n.* The Pennsylvanian period. [After *Pennsylvania.*]

penny
U.S. currency

pen·ny (pĕn′ē) *n., pl.* **-nies. 1.** See table at **currency. 2.** Any of various coins of small denomination. **3.** A sum of money. —***idiom.*** **pretty penny.** *Informal.* A relatively large sum of money. [ME, an English coin < OE *penig.*]
penny ante *n.* **1.** A poker game in which the highest bet is limited to a penny or some other small sum. **2.** *Informal.* A business transaction on a small scale. **—pen′ny-an′te** *adj.*
penny arcade *n.* A hall or building, esp. in an amusement park, where various coin-operated devices are played for entertainment.
pen·ny·cress (pĕn′ē-krĕs′) *n.* Any of several plants of the genus *Thlaspi,* native to Europe, and characteristically having small, winged seed pods, esp. *T. arvense,* which grows as a weed throughout North America.
pen·ny-pinch (pĕn′ē-pĭnch′) *intr. v.* **-pinched, -pinch·ing, -pinch·es.** *Informal.* To be stingy or ungenerous.
penny pincher *n. Informal.* A person who is very stingy with money. **—pen′ny-pinch′ing** *adj. & n.*
pen·ny·roy·al (pĕn′ē-roi′əl) *n.* **1.** A Eurasian plant, *Mentha pulegium,* having hairy leaves and small lilac-blue flowers, that yields a useful aromatic oil. **2.** An aromatic plant, *Hedeoma pulegioides,* of eastern North America, similar to the pennyroyal in appearance and use. [Prob. by folk etymology < AN *puliol real* : OFr. *poliol,* thyme (< Lat. *pulegium*) + AN *real,* royal (< OFr. *roial* < Lat. *regalis* < *rex,* king).]
pen·ny·weight (pĕn′ē-wāt′) *n.* A unit of troy weight equal to 24 grains, 1/20 of a troy ounce or approximately 1.555 grams.
pen·ny-wise (pĕn′ē-wīz′) *adj.* Careful in dealing only with small sums of money or small matters.
pen·ny·wort (pĕn′ē-wûrt′, -wôrt′) *n.* Any of several plants having rounded leaves suggestive of pennies, such as: **a.** A North American plant, *Obolaria virginica,* having fleshy leaves and small white or purplish flowers. **b.** A Eurasian plant, *Cotyledon umbilicus,* having thick, rounded leaves and yellowish-green flowers.
pen·ny·worth (pĕn′ē-wûrth′) *n.* **1.** As much as a penny will buy. **2.** A small amount; modicum. **3.** A bargain.
Pe·nob·scot (pə-nŏb′skət, -skŏt′) *n., pl.* **Penobscot** or **-scots. 1. a.** A tribe of North American Indians who were part of the Algonquin federation and formerly inhabited central Maine. **b.** A member of this Indian tribe. **2.** The Algonquian language of the Penobscot. **—Pe·nob′scot** *adj.*
pe·nol·o·gy also **poe·nol·o·gy** (pē-nŏl′ə-jē) *n.* The theory and practice of prison management and criminal rehabilitation. [Gk. *poinē,* penalty + -LOGY.] **—pe′no·log′i·cal** (pē′nə-lŏj′ĭ-kəl) *adj.* **—pe′no·log′i·cal·ly** *adv.* **—pe·nol′o·gist** *n.*
pen·on·cel (pĕn′ən-sĕl′) *n.* Variant of **pennoncel.**
pen pal *n.* A friend with whom one is acquainted only by correspondence.
pen point *n.* A tapering metal device with a split point that fits into a holder and is used for writing.
pen·sil (pĕn′səl) *n.* Variant of **pencel.**
pen·sile (pĕn′sīl′) *adj.* **1.** Hanging down loosely; suspended: *the pensile nest of the Baltimore oriole.* **2.** Building a hanging nest. Used of birds. [Lat. *pensilis* < *pendēre,* to hang.] **—pen′sile′ness, pen·sil′i·ty** (pĕn-sĭl′ĭ-tē) *n.*
pen·sion[1] (pĕn′shən) *n.* A sum of money paid regularly as a retirement benefit or by way of patronage. —*tr.v.* **-sioned, -sion·ing, -sions. 1.** To grant a pension to. **2.** To retire or dismiss with a pension. [ME, payment < OFr. < Lat. *pensio* < *pendere,* to pay.]
pen·sion[2] (päN-syôN′) *n.* A boarding house or small hotel in Europe. [Fr. < OFr., payment. —see PENSION[1].]
pen·sion·ar·y (pĕn′shə-nĕr′ē) *adj.* **1.** Constituting a pension. **2.** Mercenary; venal. —*n., pl.* **-ies. 1.** A pensioner. **2.** A hireling.
pen·sion·er (pĕn′shə-nər) *n.* **1.** One who receives a pension. **2.** One who is dependent on the bounty of another. **3.** *Obs.* A pensionary.
pen·sive (pĕn′sĭv) *adj.* **1.** Engaged in deep thoughtfulness. **2.** Suggesting or expressing deep, often melancholy thoughtfulness. [ME *pensif* < OFr. < *penser,* to think < Lat. *pensare,* freq. of *pendere,* to weigh.] **—pen′sive·ly** *adv.* **—pen′sive·ness** *n.*

Synonyms: *pensive, contemplative, reflective, meditative.* These describe the quality or nature of being mentally or spiritually preoccupied, usually in a quiet way but one which is or would be apparent to other people. One is *pensive* when one is silently thinking in a serious way about some matter or problem, frequently despite oneself. It can be in a rational (if troubled) way, but it more often has a wistful, dreamy, or sad sense. *Contemplative* implies a slow, directed consideration of a lofty object of thought, or physical object, with conscious intent of better understanding or of spiritual or aesthetic enrichment: *a contemplative attitude toward nature. Reflective* expresses a more analytical deliberation about past experience or about something which has just happened, often as a process of second thought or reappraisal of a particular occurrence. *Meditative* means to be consciously intent or reflective in a spiritual sense. It differs from *contemplative* in that the object of one's thought is usually inward, as a self-examination, rather than outward.

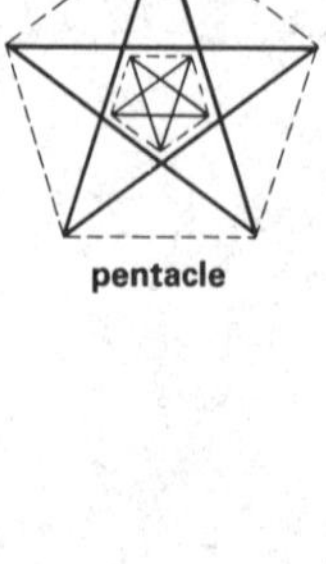

pentacle

pen·ste·mon (pĕn-stē′mən, pĕn′stə-mən) *n.* A plant of the genus *Penstemon,* which includes the beard-tongues. [NLat. *Penstemon,* genus name : Gk. *pente,* five + Gk. *stēmōn,* thread.]
pen·stock (pĕn′stŏk′) *n.* **1.** A sluice or gate used to control a flow of water. **2.** A pipe or conduit used to carry water to a water wheel or turbine.
pent (pĕnt) *v.* A past tense and past participle of **pen**[2]. —*adj.* Penned or shut up; closely confined.
penta– or **pent–** *pref.* Five: *pentamerous.* [Gk. < *pente,* five.]
pen·ta·chlo·ro·phe·nol (pĕn′tə-klôr′ə-fē′nōl′, -nôl′, -klōr′-) *n.* A compound, C_6Cl_5OH, used in solution as a fungicide and wood preservative.
pen·ta·cle (pĕn′tə-kəl) *n.* A five-pointed star formed by five straight lines connecting the vertices of a pentagon and enclosing another pentagon in the completed figure. [Med. Lat. **pentaculum* : Gk. *penta-,* five + Lat. *-culum,* dim. suffix.]
pen·tad (pĕn′tăd′) *n.* A group of five. [Gk. *pentas, pentad-,* the number five < *pente,* five.]
pen·ta·dac·tyl (pĕn′tə-dăk′təl) also **pen·ta·dac·ty·late** (-dak′tə-lĭt, -lāt′) *adj.* Having five fingers or toes on each hand or foot. [Lat. *pentadactylus* < Gk. *pentadaktulos* : *penta-,* five + *daktulos,* finger.] **—pen′ta·dac′tyl·ism** *n.*
pen·ta·gon (pĕn′tə-gŏn′) *n.* **1.** A polygon having five sides and five interior angles. **2. Pentagon.** The United States military establishment. [Lat. *pentagonum* < Gk. *pentagōnon* : *penta-,* five + *gōnia,* angle.] **—pen·tag′o·nal** (pĕn-tăg′ə-nəl) *adj.* **—pen·tag′o·nal·ly** *adv.*
Pen·ta·gon·ese (pĕn′tə-gŏn-ēz′, -ēs′) *n.* Military jargon.
pen·ta·gram (pĕn′tə-grăm′) *n.* A pentacle.
pen·ta·he·dron (pĕn′tə-hē′drən) *n., pl.* **-drons** or **-dra** (-drə). A solid having five plane faces. **—pen′ta·he′dral** *adj.*
pen·tam·er·ous (pĕn-tăm′ər-əs) *adj.* **1.** Having five similar parts. **2.** *Bot.* Having flower parts, such as petals, sepals, and stamens, in sets of five. **—pen·tam′er·ism** *n.*
pen·tam·e·ter (pĕn-tăm′ĭ-tər) *n.* **1.** A line of verse composed of five metrical feet. **2.** English verse composed in iambic pentameter; heroic verse. [Lat. < Gk. *pentametros* : *penta-,* five + *metron,* measure.]
pen·tane (pĕn′tān′) *n.* Any of three isomeric hydrocarbons, C_5H_{12}, of the methane series: **a.** *Normal pentane,* a colorless flammable liquid used as an anesthetic, a general solvent, and in the manufacture of artificial ice. **b.** *Isopentane,* a colorless flammable liquid used as a solvent and in the manufacture of polystyrene foam. **c.** *Neopentane,* a colorless gas used in the manufacture of synthetic rubber.
pen·tan·gu·lar (pĕn-tăng′gyə-lər) *adj.* Having five angles.
pen·ta·ploid (pĕn′tə-ploid′) *adj.* Having five haploid sets of chromosomes in each nucleus. —*n.* An organism having pentaploid chromosomes.
pen·ta·quine (pĕn′tə-kwēn′, -kwĭn) also **pen·ta·quin** (-kwĭn) *n.* A drug used with quinine in the treatment of malaria. [PENTA- + QUIN(OLIN)E.]
pen·tar·chy (pĕn′tär′kē) *n., pl.* **-chies. 1.** Government by five rulers. **2.** A body of five rulers governing jointly. **3.** An association or federation of five governments, each ruled by a different leader. [Gk. *pentarkhia* : *penta-,* five + *arkhein,* to rule.] **—pen·tar′chi·cal** (pĕn-tär′kĭ-kəl) *adj.*
pen·ta·stich (pĕn′tə-stĭk′) *n.* A poem or stanza containing five lines. [< LGk. *pentastikhos,* of five lines : *penta-,* five + *stikhos,* line.]
Pen·ta·teuch (pĕn′tə-to͝ok′, -tyo͝ok′) *n.* **1.** The first five books of the Old Testament. **2.** See table at **Bible.** [LLat. *Pentateuchus* < Gk. *Pentateukos* : *penta-,* five + *teukhos,* scroll.] **—Pen′ta·teuch′al** *adj.*
pen·tath·lon (pĕn-tăth′lən, -lŏn′) *n.* An athletic contest consisting of five events for each participant, usually running, horseback riding, swimming, fencing, and pistol shooting. [Gk. : *pente,* five + *athlon,* contest.]
pen·ta·ton·ic scale (pĕn′tə-tŏn′ĭk) *n.* Any of various five-tone musical scales, esp. one composed of the first, second, third, fifth, and sixth tones of a diatonic scale.
pen·ta·va·lent (pĕn′tə-vā′lənt) *adj.* Having a valence of 5.
pen·taz·o·cine (pĕn-tăz′ə-sēn′) *n.* A synthetic drug, $C_{19}H_{27}NO$, used as an analgesic. [Orig. unknown.]
Pen·te·cost (pĕn′tĭ-kôst′, -kŏst′) *n.* **1.** A festival of the Christian Church occurring on the seventh Sunday after Easter, to celebrate the descent of the Holy Ghost upon the disciples. **2.** A Jewish festival, Shavuot. [ME < OE *Pentecosten* < LLat. *Pentecoste* < Gk. *pentēkostē (hēmera),* fiftieth (day) < *pentēkostos,* fiftieth < *pentēkonta,* fifty : *pente,* five + *-konta,* times ten.]
Pen·te·cos·tal (pĕn′tĭ-kŏs′təl, -kôs′-) *adj.* **1.** Of, pertaining to, or occurring at Pentecost. **2.** Of, pertaining to, or designating any of various Christian religious congregations that seek to be filled with the Holy Ghost, in emulation of the disciples at Pentecost. **—Pen′te·cos′tal** *n.* **—Pen′te·cos′tal·ism** *n.*
pent·house (pĕnt′hous′) *n.* **1. a.** An apartment or dwelling situated on the roof of a building. **b.** A residence, often with a terrace, comprising the top floor of an apartment house. **c.** A structure housing machinery on the roof of a building. **2.** A shed or sloping roof attached to the side of a building or wall. [ME *pentis,* a shed attached to a wall of a building

< OFr. *appentis* < Med. Lat. *appenticium,* appendage < Lat. *appendix.* —see APPENDIX.]

pent·land·ite (pĕnt′lən-dīt′) *n.* The principal ore of nickel, a light-brown nickel iron sulfide. [Fr., after Joseph B. *Pentland* (1797–1873).]

pen·to·bar·bi·tal sodium (pĕn′tə-bär′bĭ-tôl′) *n.* A white crystalline or powdery barbiturate, $C_{11}H_{17}N_2O_3Na$, used as a sedative.

pen·tode (pĕn′tōd′) *n.* A vacuum tube with five electrodes that can be used as a logic element in a computer.

pen·to·san (pĕn′tə-săn′) *n.* Any of a group of complex carbohydrates found with cellulose in many woody plants and yielding pentoses on hydrolysis.

pen·tose (pĕn′tōs′, -tōz′) *n.* A sugar having five carbon atoms per molecule.

pen·to·side (pĕn′tə-sīd′) *n.* A glycoside that produces a pentose on hydrolysis.

Pen·to·thal (pĕn′tə-thôl′). A trademark for a thiopental sodium.

pent·ox·ide (pĕnt-ŏk′sīd′) *n.* An oxide having five atoms of oxygen in the molecule.

pent-up (pĕnt′ŭp′) *adj.* Not given expression; repressed: *pent-up emotions.*

pen·tyl (pĕn′təl) *n.* Amyl.

pen·tyl·ene·tet·ra·zol (pĕn′tə-lēn′tĕt′rə-zōl′, -zŏl′) *n.* A drug, $C_6H_{10}N_4$, used as a stimulant of the central nervous system. [PENT(A)- + (METH)YLENE + TETR(A)- + AZ(O)- + -OL.]

pe·nu·che also **pe·nu·chi** (pə-no͞o′chē) *n.* A fudgelike confection of brown sugar, water or milk, and chopped nuts. [Var. of PANOCHA.]

pe·nuch·le or **pe·nuck·le** (pē′nŭk′əl) *n.* Variants of **pinochle.**

pe·nult (pē′nŭlt′, pĭ-nŭlt′) also **pe·nul·ti·ma** (pĭ-nŭl′tə-mə) *n.* **1.** The next to the last syllable in a word. **2.** The next to the last item in a series. [Lat. *paenultima* < *paenultimus,* next to last : *paene,* almost + *ultimus,* last.]

pe·nul·ti·mate (pĭ-nŭl′tə-mĭt) *adj.* **1.** Next to last. **2.** Of or pertaining to the penult of a word: *penultimate stress.* —*n.* The next to the last. [Lat. *paenultimus.* —see PENULT.]

pe·num·bra (pĭ-nŭm′brə) *n., pl.* **-brae** (-brē) or **-bras. 1.** A partial shadow, as in an eclipse, between regions of complete shadow and complete illumination. **2.** The partly darkened fringe around a sunspot. **3.** An outlying, surrounding region; periphery; fringe. [Lat. *paene,* almost + Lat. *umbra,* shadow.] **—pe·num′bral, pe·num′brous** *adj.*

pe·nu·ri·ous (pə-no͝or′ē-əs, -nyo͝or′-) *adj.* **1.** Miserly; stingy. **2.** Yielding little; barren: *a penurious land.* **3.** Poverty-stricken; needy. [Med. Lat. *penuriosus* < Lat. *penuria,* want.] **—pe·nu′ri·ous·ly** *adv.* **—pe·nu′ri·ous·ness** *n.*

pen·u·ry (pĕn′yə-rē) *n.* **1.** Extreme want or poverty; destitution. **2.** Extreme dearth; barrenness; insufficiency. [ME < Lat. *penuria,* want.]

Pe·nu·ti·an (pə-no͞o′tē-ən, -shən) *n.* A stock of North American Indian languages spoken in Pacific coastal areas from California into British Columbia.

pe·on (pē′ŏn′, pē′ən) *n.* **1. a.** An unskilled laborer or farm worker of Latin America or the southwestern United States. **b.** Such a worker bound in servitude to a landlord creditor. **2.** (pyo͞on). A native Indian or Ceylonese messenger, servant, or foot soldier. **3.** A menial worker; drudge. [Am. Sp. *peón* < Med. Lat. *pedo,* foot soldier. —see PAWN[2].]

pe·on·age (pē′ə-nĭj) also **pe·on·ism** (-nĭz′əm) *n.* **1.** The condition of being a peon. **2.** A system by which debtors are bound in servitude to their creditors until their debts are paid.

pe·o·ny (pē′ə-nē) *n., pl.* **-nies.** Any of various garden plants of the genus *Paeonia,* having large pink, red, white, or creamy flowers. [ME *pione* < OE *peonie* < Lat. *peonia* < Gk. *paiōnia,* after *Paiōn,* Apollo's title as physician.]

peo·ple (pē′pəl) *n., pl.* **people. 1.** A body of persons living in the same country under one national government; nationality. **2.** *pl.* **peo·ples.** A body of persons sharing a common religion, culture, language, or inherited condition of life. **3.** Persons with regard to their residence, class, profession, or group: *sales people.* **4. the people.** The mass of ordinary persons; the populace. **5.** The citizens of a nation, state, or other political unit; electorate. **6.** Persons subordinate to or loyal to a ruler, superior, or employer. **7.** Family, relatives, or ancestors. **8.** Members of the community; persons in general. **9.** Human beings considered as distinct from lower animals or inanimate things. **10.** A class or kind of beings distinct from human beings: *rabbits and squirrels: the furry little people of the woods.* —*tr.v.* **-pled, -pling, -ples.** To furnish with a population; populate. [ME < OFr. *pueple* < Lat. *populus.*] **—peo′pler** *n.*

Usage: *People* and *persons* are distinguished in usage. *People* is the proper term when referring to a large group of individuals, collectively and indefinitely: *People can be pushed only so far. Persons* is applicable to a specific and relatively small number: *Ten persons were killed.* In modern usage, however, *people* is also acceptable with any plural number: *I counted twenty people.* • The possessive form is *people's (the people's rights)* except when *people* is used in the plural to refer to two or more groups considered to be political or cultural entities: *the Slavic peoples' history.* • *The people* and *the public* are sometimes interchangeable, but only *people* has the political sense of an electorate. See also Usage note at **collective noun.**

People's Party *n.* The Populist Party.

People's Republic *n.* A political unit controlled and organized by a national Communist party.

pep (pĕp) *Informal.* —*n.* Energy; high spirits; vim. —*tr.v.* **pepped, pep·ping, peps.** To bring energy or liveliness to; invigorate: *Good news pepped her up.* [Short for PEPPER.] **—pep′pi·ness** *n.* **—pep′py** *adj.*

pep·los (pĕp′ləs, -lōs′) also **pep·lus** (-ləs) *n., pl.* **-los·es** also **-lus·es.** A loose outer robe worn by women in ancient Greece. [Gk.]

peony

pep·lum (pĕp′ləm) *n., pl.* **-lums. 1.** A short overskirt or ruffle attached at the waistline of a jacket, blouse, or dress. **2.** A peplos. [Lat., robe of state < Gk. *peplos,* peplos.]

pep·lus (pĕp′ləs) *n.* Variant of **peplos.**

pe·po (pē′pō) *n., pl.* **-pos.** The fruit of any of various related plants, such as the cucumber, squash, pumpkin, and melon, having a hard rind, fleshy pulp, and numerous seeds. [Lat., a kind of melon < Gk. *pepōn.*]

pep·per (pĕp′ər) *n.* **1. a.** A woody vine, *Piper nigrum,* of the East Indies, having small, berrylike fruit. **b.** The dried, blackish fruit of this plant, used as a pungent condiment. **2.** Any of several other plants of the genus *Piper,* such as cubeb, betel, and kava. **3. a.** Any of several varieties of a woody plant, *Capsicum frutescens* or *C. annuum,* of tropical origin. **b.** The podlike fruit of any of these plants, varying in size, shape, and degree of pungency, with the milder types including the bell pepper and pimiento, and the more pungent types including the cherry pepper. **4.** Any of various condiments made from the more pungent varieties of *C. frutescens,* such as cayenne pepper and chili. —*tr.v.* **-pered, -per·ing, -pers. 1.** To season or sprinkle with pepper. **2.** To sprinkle liberally; dot. **3.** To pelt or shower with small missiles. **4.** To make lively and vivid with wit or invective, as a speech or article. [ME *peper* < OE *pipor* < Lat. *piper* < Gk. *peperi,* < Skt. *pippalī,* berry.]

pep·per-and-salt (pĕp′ər-ən-sôlt′) *adj.* Having a close mixture of black and white: *a pepper-and-salt beard.*

pep·per·box (pĕp′ər-bŏks′) *n.* A container with small holes in the top for sprinkling ground pepper.

pep·per·bush (pĕp′ər-bo͝osh′) *n.* Sweet pepperbush.

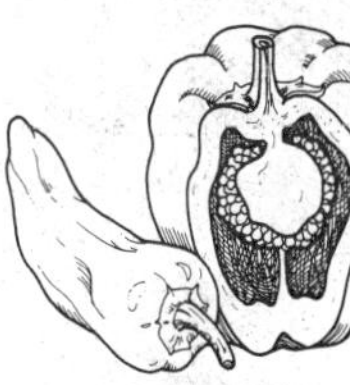

pepper
Genus *Capsicum*

pep·per·corn (pĕp′ər-kôrn′) *n.* **1.** A dried berry of the pepper vine *Piper nigrum.* **2.** A small or insignificant thing.

pep·per·grass (pĕp′ər-grăs′) *n.* Any of several plants of the genus *Lepidium,* esp. *L. virginicum,* having small white flowers and pungent seeds.

pep·per·idge (pĕp′ər-ĭj) *n.* The sour gum. [Orig. unknown.]

pepper mill *n.* A utensil for grinding peppercorns.

pep·per·mint (pĕp′ər-mĭnt′) *n.* **1.** A plant, *Mentha piperita,* having small purple or white flowers and downy leaves that yield a pungent oil. **2.** The oil from the peppermint, or a preparation made from it, used as flavoring. **3.** A candy or lozenge with peppermint flavoring.

pep·per·o·ni (pĕp′ə-rō′nē) *n.* A highly spiced pork and beef sausage. [Ital. *peperoni,* pl. of *peperone,* chili, aug. of *pepe,* pepper < Lat. *piper.* —see PEPPER.]

pepper pot *n.* **1.** A soup made with vegetables and tripe or other meat, seasoned with pepper, and often containing dumplings. **2.** A thick West Indian stew of meat or fish, vegetables, and regional condiments. **3.** A pepperbox.

pepper tree *n.* Any of several trees of the genus *Schinus,* esp. *S. molle,* native to South America, having compound leaves and yellowish-white flowers.

pep·per·wort (pĕp′ər-wûrt′, -wôrt′) *n.* **1.** Any of various aquatic or marsh plants of the genus *Marsilea,* having floating leaves rising from long runners. **2.** Peppergrass.

pep·per·y (pĕp′ə-rē) *adj.* **1.** Of, like, or containing pepper; sharp or pungent in flavor. **2.** Vigorously sharp-tempered in disposition and manner. **3.** Sharp and stinging in style or content; vivid; fiery. **—pep′per·i·ness** *n.*

pep pill *n. Slang.* A tablet or capsule containing an ingredient that stimulates the central nervous system, esp. one of the amphetamines.

pep·sin also **pep·sine** (pĕp′sĭn) *n.* **1.** A digestive enzyme found in gastric juice that catalyzes the breakdown of protein to peptides. **2.** A substance containing pepsin, obtained from the stomachs of hogs and used as a digestive aid. [G. < Gk. *pepsis,* digestion < *peptein,* to digest.]

pep·sin·o·gen (pĕp-sĭn′ə-jən) *n.* An inert substance found in the cells of the gastric mucosa that is converted to pepsin during digestion by the action of hydrochloric acid.

pep talk *n.* A speech of exhortation delivered by a leader, as to his team or staff.

pep·tic (pĕp′tĭk) *adj.* **1. a.** Of, pertaining to, or assisting digestion: *peptic secretion.* **b.** Induced by or associated with the action of digestive secretions: *a peptic ulcer.* **2.** Of, pertaining to, or involving pepsin. **3.** Capable of digesting. —*n.* A digestive agent. [Lat. *pepticus* < Gk. *peptikos* < *peptein,* to digest.]

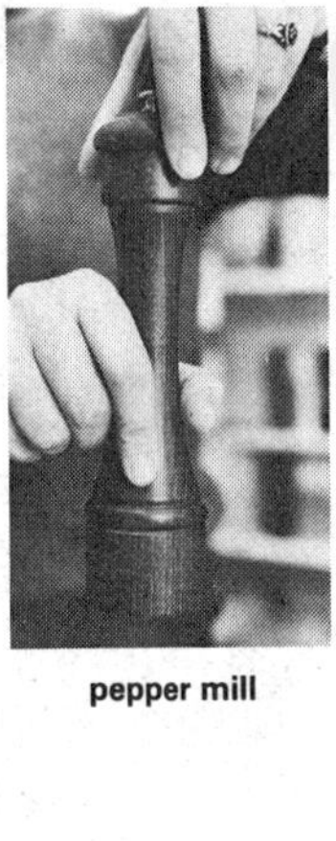

pepper mill

pep·ti·dase (pĕp′tĭ-dās′, -dāz′) *n.* An enzyme that hydrolyzes peptides, releasing amino acids.

pep·tide (pĕp′tīd′) also **pep·tid** (pĕp′tĭd) *n.* Any of various natural or synthetic compounds containing two or more amino acids linked by the carboxyl group of one amino acid and the amino group of another. [PEPT(ONE) + -IDE.] **—pep·tid'ic** (-tĭd'ĭk) *adj.* **—pep·tid'i·cal·ly** *adv.*

peptide bond *n.* The chemical bond between the organic acid groups and amine groups of neighboring amino acids, constituting the primary linkage of all protein structures.

pep·ti·do·gly·can (pĕp'tĭ-dō-glī'kən, -kăn') *n.* A polymer found in the cell walls of procaryotes that consists of polysaccharide and peptide chains in a strong molecular network. [PEPTIDE + *glycan,* a polysaccharide.]

pep·tize (pĕp'tīz') *tr.v.* **-tized, -tiz·ing, -tiz·es. 1.** To increase the dispersion of (a colloidal solution). **2.** To liquefy (a colloidal gel) to form a sol. [Gk. *peptein,* to digest + -IZE.] **—pep'ti·za'tion** *n.* **—pep'tiz'er** *n.*

pep·tone (pĕp'tōn') *n.* Any of various protein compounds obtained by acid or enzyme hydrolysis of natural protein and used as nutrients and culture media. [G. *Pepton* < Gk. *peptos,* digested.] **—pep·ton'ic** (-tŏn'ĭk) *adj.*

pep·to·nize (pĕp'tə-nīz') *tr.v.* **-nized, -niz·ing, -niz·es. 1.** To convert (protein) into a peptone. **2.** To dissolve (food) by means of a proteolytic enzyme. **3.** To combine with peptone. **—pep'to·ni·za'tion** *n.*

Pe·quot (pē'kwŏt') *n., pl.* **Pequot** or **-quots. 1. a.** A tribe of Indians formerly living in southern New England. **b.** A member of this Indian tribe. **2.** The Algonquian language of the Pequot. [Prob. alteration of Narraganset *paquatanog,* destroyers.] **—Pe'quot** *adj.*

per (pûr) *prep.* **1.** Through; by means of: *per bearer.* **2.** To, for, or by each; for every: *40 cents per gallon.* **3.** According to; by: *per instructions.* [Lat.]

Usage: *Per* is used with reference to statistics and units of measurement: *per mile; per day; per person.* Its more general use (as in *per the terms of the contract*) is best left to business correspondence.

per– *pref.* **1.** Thoroughly; completely; intensely: *perfervid.* **2.** Containing an element in its highest oxidation state: *perchloric acid.* **3.** Containing a large or the largest possible proportion of an element: *peroxide.* **4.** Containing the peroxy group: *peracid.* [< Lat. *per,* through.]

per·ac·id (pûr'ăs'ĭd) *n.* **1.** Any of various acids containing the peroxy group. **2.** An inorganic acid, such as perchloric acid, containing the largest proportion of oxygen in a series of related acids.

perambulator

per·ad·ven·ture (pûr'əd-vĕn'chər, pĕr'-) *adv. Archaic.* Perhaps; perchance. *—n.* Chance or uncertainty; doubt; question. [ME *per aventure* < OFr., by chance.]

per·am·bu·late (pə-răm'byə-lāt') *v.* **-lat·ed, -lat·ing, -lates.** *—tr.* To walk through, esp. so as to inspect. *—intr.* To walk about; roam; stroll. [Lat. *perambulare, perambulat-* : *per-,* through + *ambulare,* to walk.] **—per·am'bu·la'tion** *n.* **—per·am'bu·la·to'ry** (pə-răm'byə-lə-tôr'ē, -tōr'ē) *adj.*

per·am·bu·la·tor (pə-răm'byə-lā'tər) *n. Chiefly Brit.* A baby carriage.

George Miksch Sutton

perch[1]
Bird on a perch

per an·num (pər ăn'əm) *adv.* By the year; annually. [Lat.]

per·bo·rate (pər-bôr'āt', -bōr'-) *n.* A salt containing the radical BO_3, formed from a borate and hydrogen peroxide.

per·cale (pər-kāl') *n.* An opaque cotton fabric used to make sheets and clothing. [Fr. < Pers. *pargālah.*]

per·ca·line (pûr'kə-lēn') *n.* A glazed fine cotton fabric used for dress goods, shirting, and linings. [Fr., dim. of *percale,* percale.]

per cap·i·ta (pər kăp'ĭ-tə) *adv. & adj.* **1.** Per unit of population; per person: *income per capita.* **2.** Equally to each individual. [Med. Lat., by heads.]

per·ceive (pər-sēv') *tr.v.* **-ceived, -ceiv·ing, -ceives. 1.** To become aware of directly through any of the senses, esp. to see or hear. **2.** To take notice of; observe. **3.** To become aware of in one's mind; achieve understanding of. [ME *perceiven* < OFr. *perceivre* < Lat. *percipere* : *per-* (intensive) + *capere,* to seize.] **—per·ceiv'a·ble** *adj.* **—per·ceiv'a·bly** *adv.*

per cent also **per·cent** (pər-sĕnt') *—adv.* Out of each hundred; per hundred. *—n., pl.* **per cent** also **percent. 1.** One part in a hundred. **2.** A percentage: *a large per cent of her salary.* *—adj.* Paying interest at a specified percentage. [Lat. *per centum,* by the hundred.]

Usage: *Per cent,* which also may be written as one word (*percent*), is generally used with a specific figure. The number of a noun that follows it or is understood to follow it governs the number of the verb: *Twenty per cent of the stock is owned by a conglomerate. Twenty per cent of the students are slow learners.*

per·cent·age (pər-sĕn'tĭj) *n.* **1.** A fraction or ratio with 100 fixed and understood as the denominator, formed by multiplying a decimal equivalent of a fraction by 100; for example, 0.98 equals a percentage of 98. **2.** A proportion or share in relation to a whole; part. **3.** An amount, such as an allowance, duty, or commission, that varies in proportion to a larger sum, such as total sales: *work for a percentage.* **4.** *Informal.* Advantage; gain: *There is no percentage in work without pay.*

Usage: *Percentage,* when preceded by *the,* takes a singular verb: *The percentage of unskilled workers is small.* When preceded by *a,* it takes either a singular or plural verb, depending on the number of the noun in the prepositional phrase that follows: *A small percentage of the workers are unskilled. A large percentage of the crop has spoiled.*

per·cen·tile (pər-sĕn'tīl') *n.* A number that corresponds to one of 100 equal divisions of the range of a statistic in a given sample and characterizes a contained value of the statistic as not exceeded by a specified percentage of all the values in the sample. For example, a score higher than 97 per cent of those attained on an examination is said to be in the ninety-seventh percentile.

per cen·tum (pər sĕn'təm) *n.* Per cent. [Lat.]

per·cept (pûr'sĕpt') *n.* **1.** The object of perception. **2.** An impression in the mind of something perceived by the senses, viewed as the basic component in the formation of concepts. [Back-formation < PERCEPTION.]

per·cep·ti·ble (pər-sĕp'tə-bəl) *adj.* Capable of being perceived; discernible by the senses or mind. **—per·cep'ti·bil'i·ty** *n.* **—per·cep'ti·bly** *adv.*

Synonyms: *perceptible, palpable, appreciable, noticeable, discernible.* These are used to convey the sense of being real, apprehensible, or discriminable. *Perceptible* basically means perceivable, but differs in more often being used of comparisons themselves: *a perceptible difference. Palpable* means tangible or readily ascertainable. It is sometimes used for emphasis: *a palpable case of indigestion. Appreciable* means considerable in a quantitative sense and suggests the admitted possibility of apprehending what is in question: *an appreciable quantity. Noticeable* has the broad sense of visible or remarkable (in its weaker literal meaning), describing something which is adequately revealed or observable to anybody: *a noticeable tremor in his voice. Discernible,* like *perceptible* and *noticeable,* need not be visual in connotation. It means only apparent through scrutiny: *a discernible symptom.*

per·cep·tion (pər-sĕp'shən) *n.* **1.** The process, act, or faculty of perceiving. **2.** The effect or product of perceiving. **3. a.** Insight, intuition, or knowledge gained by perceiving. **b.** The capacity for such insight. [Lat. *perceptio* < *percipere,* to perceive.] **—per·cep'tion·al** *adj.*

per·cep·tive (pər-sĕp'tĭv) *adj.* **1.** Of or pertaining to perception: *perceptive faculties.* **2. a.** Having the ability to perceive; keen in discernment. **b.** Marked by discernment and understanding; sensitive. **—per·cep'tive·ly** *adv.* **—per'cep·tiv'i·ty** (pûr'sĕp-tĭv'ĭ-tē) *n.*

per·cep·tu·al (pər-sĕp'chōō-əl) *adj.* Of, based on, or involving perception. **—per·cep'tu·al·ly** *adv.*

perch[1] (pûrch) *n.* **1.** A rod or branch serving as a roost for a bird. **2.** A place for resting or sitting. **3.** A pole used in acrobatics. **4.** *Chiefly Brit.* **a.** The rod (sense 12.a.). **b.** One square rod of land. **5.** A unit of cubic measure used in stonework, usually 16.5 feet (one rod) by one foot by 1.5 feet, or .70 cubic meter. **6.** A frame on which cloth is laid for examination of quality. *—v.* **perched, perch·ing, perch·es.** *—intr.* **1.** To alight or rest on a perch; roost. **2.** To stand, sit, or rest on an elevated place or position. *—tr.* **1.** To place on or as if on a perch. **2.** To lay (cloth) on a perch in order to examine it. [ME *perche* < OFr. < Lat. *pertica.*]

perch[2] (pûrch) *n., pl.* **perch** or **perch·es. 1.** Any of various freshwater fishes of the genus *Perca,* esp. either of two edible species, *P. flavescens,* of North America, and *P. fluviatilis,* of Europe. **2.** Any of various fishes, such as the pike perch, similar to or related to the perch. [ME *perche* < OFr. < Lat. *perca* < Gk. *perkē.*]

per·chance (pər-chăns') *adv.* Perhaps; possibly. [ME < AN *par chance* : *par,* by + *chance,* chance.]

per·chlo·rate (pər-klôr'āt', -klōr'-) *n.* An ester or a salt of perchloric acid.

per·chlo·ric acid (pər-klôr'ĭk, -klōr'-) *n.* A clear, colorless liquid, $HClO_4$, explosively unstable under some conditions, that is a powerful oxidant used as a catalyst and in explosives.

per·chlo·ride (pər-klôr'īd', -klōr'-) also **per·chlo·rid** (-klôr'ĭd, -klōr'-) *n.* A chloride having more chlorine than other chlorides of the same element.

per·chlor·o·eth·yl·ene (pər-klôr'ō-ĕth'ə-lēn', -klōr'-) *n.* A colorless, nonflammable organic solvent, $Cl_2C{:}CCl_2$, used in dry-cleaning solutions and to dissolve a variety of waxes, tars, rubbers, and gums.

per·cip·i·ent (pər-sĭp'ē-ənt) *adj.* Having the power of perceiving, esp. perceiving keenly and readily. *—n.* One that perceives. [Lat. *percipiens, percipient-,* pr.part. of *percipere,* to perceive.] **—per·cip'i·ence, per·cip'i·en·cy** *n.*

per·coid (pûr'koid') also **per·coi·de·an** (pər-koi'dē-ən) *adj.* Of or pertaining to the Percoidea, a large suborder of fishes that includes the perches, sunfishes, groupers, and grunts. *—n.* Any fish of the percoid group. [NLat. *Percoidea,* suborder name < Lat. *perca,* perch. —see PERCH[2].]

per·co·late (pûr'kə-lāt') *v.* **-lat·ed, -lat·ing, -lates.** *—tr.* **1.** To cause (liquid, powder, or small particles) to pass through a porous substance or small holes; filter. **2.** To pass or ooze through: *Water percolated the sand.* **3.** To make (coffee) in a percolator. *—intr.* **1.** To drain or seep through a porous substance or filter. **2.** *Informal.* To become lively or active. *—n.* (pûr'kə-lĭt, -lāt'). A liquid that has been percolated. [Lat. *percolare, percolat-* : *per,* through + *colare,* to filter < *colum,* sieve.] **—per'co·la'tion** *n.*

per·co·la·tor (pûr'kə-lā'tər) *n.* A type of coffeepot in which boiling water is forced repeatedly up through a center tube to filter back down through a basket of ground coffee.

per con·tra (pər kŏn′trə) *adv.* **1. a.** On the contrary. **b.** By way of contrast. **2.** As an offset. [Lat.]
per·cur·rent (pər-kûr′ənt) *adj.* Designating a midrib of a leaf that extends from base to apex. [Lat. *percurrens, percurrent-,* pr.part. of *percurrere,* to run through : *per,* through + *currere,* to run.]
per·cuss (pər-kŭs′) *tr.v.* **-cussed, -cuss·ing, -cuss·es.** To strike or tap firmly, as in medical percussion: *percuss a patient's chest.* [Lat. *percutere, percuss-,* to strike hard : *per-* (intensive) + *quatere,* to strike.]
per·cus·sion (pər-kŭsh′ən) *n.* **1.** The striking together of two bodies, esp. when noise is produced. **2.** The sound, vibration, or shock caused by the striking together of two bodies. **3.** The act of detonating a percussion cap in a firearm. **4.** A method of medical diagnosis in which various areas of the body, esp. the chest, back, and abdomen, are tapped to determine by resonance the condition of internal organs. **5.** Musical percussion instruments collectively. [Lat. *percussio* < *percutere,* to percuss.]
percussion cap *n.* A thin metal cap containing gunpowder or another detonator that explodes on being struck.
percussion instrument *n.* A musical instrument in which sound is produced by striking, such as a drum, xylophone, or piano.
per·cus·sion·ist (pər-kŭsh′ə-nĭst) *n.* One who plays percussion instruments.
per·cus·sive (pər-kŭs′ĭv) *adj.* Of, pertaining to, or characterized by percussion. **—per·cus′sive·ly** *adv.* **—per·cus′sive·ness** *n.*
per·cu·ta·ne·ous (pûr′kyo͞o-tā′nē-əs) *adj. Med.* Passed, done, or effected through or by means of the skin. **—per′cu·ta′ne·ous·ly** *adv.*
per di·em (pər dē′əm, dī′əm) *adv.* By the day; per day. *—n., pl.* **per diems.** An allowance for daily expenses. *—adj.* **1.** Reckoned on a daily basis. **2.** Paid by the day. [Lat.]
per·di·tion (pər-dĭsh′ən) *n.* **1. a.** The loss of the soul; eternal damnation. **b.** Hell. **2.** *Archaic.* Utter ruin. [ME *perdicion* < LLat. *perditio* < Lat. *perdere,* to lose : *per,* away + *dare,* to give.]
per·du or **per·due** (pər-do͞o′, -dyo͞o′) *n. Obs.* A soldier sent on a dangerous mission. [Fr. *sentinelle perdue* : *sentinelle,* sentinel + *perdre,* to lose.]
per·du·ra·ble (pər-do͝or′ə-bəl, -dyo͝or′-) *adj.* Extremely durable; permanent. [ME < OFr. < LLat. *perdurabilis* < Lat. *perdurare,* to endure : *per-,* throughout + *durare,* to last.] **—per·du′ra·bil′i·ty** *n.* **—per·du′ra·bly** *adv.*
per·e·gri·nate (pĕr′ĭ-grə-nāt′) *v.* **-nat·ed, -nat·ing, -nates.** *—intr.* To journey or travel from place to place. *—tr.* To travel through or over. [Lat. *peregrinari, peregrinat-* < *peregrinus,* foreigner. —see PEREGRINE.] **—per′e·gri·na′tion** *n.* **—per′e·gri·na′tor** *n.*
per·e·grine (pĕr′ə-grĭn, -grēn′) *adj.* **1.** Foreign; alien. **2.** Roving or wandering; migratory. *—n.* The peregrine falcon. [Med. Lat. *peregrinus* < Lat., foreigner < *pereger,* being abroad : *per,* through + *ager,* land.]
peregrine falcon *n.* A widely distributed bird of prey, *Falco peregrinus,* having gray and white plumage, formerly much used in falconry. [ME, transl. of Med. Lat. *falco peregrinus* (so called because the falcons were caught in passage rather than taken from the nest as were eyas falcons).]
pe·rei·ra bark (pə-râr′ə) *n.* The bark of a South American tree, *Geissospermum vellosii,* the source of a substance formerly used in the treatment of malaria. [After Jonathan *Pereira* (1804–1853).]
per·emp·to·ry (pə-rĕmp′tə-rē) *adj.* **1.** Putting an end to all debate or action: *a peremptory decree.* **2.** Not allowing contradiction or refusal; imperative: *peremptory commands.* **3.** Having the nature of or expressing a command; urgent: *spoke in a peremptory tone.* **4.** Offensively self-assured; dictatorial: *a swaggering, peremptory manner.* [LLat. *peremptorius* < *perimere,* to take away : *per-* (intensive) + *emere,* to obtain.] **—per·emp′to·ri·ly** *adv.* **—per·emp′to·ri·ness** *n.*
per·en·ni·al (pə-rĕn′ē-əl) *adj.* **1.** Lasting or active through the year or through many years. **2. a.** Lasting an indefinitely long time; everlasting; perpetual: *perennial happiness.* **b.** Appearing again and again; continually recurring. **3.** *Bot.* Having a life span of more than two years. *—n. Bot.* A perennial plant. [Lat. *perennis* : *per-,* throughout + *annus,* year.] **—per·en′ni·al·ly** *adv.*
per·fect (pûr′fĭkt) *adj.* **1.** Lacking nothing essential to the whole; complete of its nature or kind. **2.** In a state of undiminished or highest excellence; without defect; flawless: *a perfect specimen.* **3.** Completely skilled or talented in a certain field or area: *a perfect artist.* **4.** Completely reproducing or corresponding to a type or original; accurate; exact: *a perfect reproduction of a painting.* **5.** Complete; thorough; utter: *a perfect fool.* **6.** Pure; undiluted; unmixed: *perfect red.* **7.** Excellent and delightful in all respects: *a perfect day.* **8.** *Bot.* Having both stamens and pistils in the same flower; monoclinous. **9.** *Gram.* Of, pertaining to, or constituting a verb form expressing action completed prior to a fixed point of reference in time. **10.** *Mus.* **a.** Designating the three basic intervals of the octave, fourth, and fifth. **b.** Designating a cadence in which the final chord has its root in both bass and soprano. *—n. Gram.* **1.** The perfect tense. **2.** A verb or verb form in the perfect tense. *—tr.v.* (pər-fĕkt′) **-fect·ed, -fect·ing, -fects.** To bring to perfection or completion. [ME *perfit* < OFr. *parfit* < Lat. *perfectus* < p.part. of *perficere,* to finish : *per-* (intensive) + *facere,* to do.] **—per·fect′er** *n.* **—per′fect·ness** *n.*
Usage: *Perfect* has traditionally been considered an absolute term, like *chief* and *prime,* and not subject to comparison with *more, less, almost,* and other modifiers of degree. The comparative form nonetheless has the sanction of the U.S. Constitution, in the phrase *a more perfect union,* and must be regarded as entirely correct, especially when *perfect* is used to mean "ideal for the purposes," as in *A more perfect spot for a picnic could not be found.*
per·fec·ta (pər-fĕk′tə) *n.* An exacta. [Short for Am. Sp. *quiniela perfecta,* perfect quinella.]
per·fect·i·ble (pər-fĕk′tə-bəl) *adj.* Capable of becoming or being made perfect. **—per·fect′i·bil′i·ty** *n.*
per·fec·tion (pər-fĕk′shən) *n.* **1.** The state, quality, or condition of being perfect. **2.** The process or act of perfecting: *The perfection of the invention took years.* **3.** A person or thing considered to be perfect. **4.** An instance or quality of excellence.
per·fec·tion·ism (pər-fĕk′shə-nĭz′əm) *n.* **1.** A propensity for setting extremely high standards and being displeased with anything less. **2.** A belief that moral or spiritual perfection can be achieved by people in this life. **—per·fec′tion·ist** *n.*
per·fec·tive (pər-fĕk′tĭv) *adj.* **1.** Tending toward perfection. **2.** *Gram.* Of or designating a verb in the perfective aspect. *—n. Gram.* **1.** The perfective aspect. **2.** A verb in the perfective aspect. **—per·fec′tive·ly** *adv.* **—per·fec′tive·ness, per′fec·tiv′i·ty** (pûr′fĕk-tĭv′ĭ-tē) *n.*
perfective aspect *n.* An aspect of verbs that expresses a completed action as distinct from a continuing or not necessarily completed action.
per·fect·ly (pûr′fĭkt-lē) *adv.* **1.** In a perfect manner or to a perfect degree. **2.** Completely; fully; wholly: *perfectly content.*
Usage: In writing, *perfectly* is sometimes objected to when it is used as a mere intensive denoting "quite," "altogether," or "just," as in *perfectly good* and *perfectly dreadful.* But it is widely used by educated speakers in this sense.
perfect number *n.* A positive integer that is equal to the sum of its integral factors, including 1 but excluding itself.
per·fec·to (pər-fĕk′tō) *n., pl.* **-tos.** A cigar of standard length, thick in the center and tapering at each end. [< Sp., perfect < Lat. *perfectus.*]
perfect participle *n.* The past participle.
perfect pitch *n.* Absolute pitch (sense 2).
perfect rhyme *n.* **1.** The commonest English rhyme, having identity in sound for the last accented vowel and any final consonants or syllables but with variation in the preceding consonant, for example, *great, late; rider, beside her; dutiful, unbeautiful.* **2.** A rhyme of two words pronounced identically but differing in meaning, for example, *right, rite.*
perfect square *n.* An integer that is the square of an integer.
perfect year *n.* In the Hebrew calendar, a year having 355 days or a leap year having 385 days.
per·fer·vid (pər-fûr′vĭd) *adj.* Impassioned; zealous; extremely or extravagantly eager. **—per·fer′vid·ly** *adv.* **—per·fer′vid·ness** *n.*
per·fi·dy (pûr′fĭ-dē) *n., pl.* **-dies.** Deliberate breach of faith; calculated violation of trust; treachery. [Lat. *perfidia* < *perfidus,* treacherous : *per,* through + *fides,* faith.] **—per·fid′i·ous** (pər-fĭd′ē-əs) *adj.* **—per·fid′i·ous·ly** *adv.*
per·fo·li·ate (pər-fō′lē-ĭt) *adj.* Designating a leaf that completely clasps the stem and is apparently pierced by it. [NLat. *perfoliatus* : Lat. *per,* through + Lat. *foliatus,* bearing leaves < *folium,* leaf.] **—per·fo′li·a′tion** *n.*
per·fo·rate (pûr′fə-rāt′) *tr.v.* **-rat·ed, -rat·ing, -rates. 1.** To pierce, punch, or bore a hole or holes in; penetrate. **2.** To pierce or stamp with rows of holes, such as those between postage stamps, to allow easy separation. *—adj.* (pûr′fər-ĭt, -fə-rāt′). Perforated. [Lat. *perforare, perforat-* : *per* (intensive) + *forare,* to bore.] **—per′fo·ra·ble** (-fər-ə-bəl) *adj.* **—per′fo·ra′tive, per′fo·ra·to′ry** (-fər-ə-tôr′ē, -tōr′ē) *adj.* **—per′fo·ra′tor** *n.*
per·fo·rat·ed (pûr′fə-rā′tĭd) *adj.* Having a perforation or perforations.
per·fo·ra·tion (pûr′fə-rā′shən) *n.* **1. a.** The act of perforating. **b.** The state of being perforated. **2.** A hole or series of holes punched or bored through something, esp. a hole in a series, separating sections in a sheet or roll.
per·force (pər-fôrs′, -fōrs′) *adv.* By necessity; willy-nilly. [ME *par force* < OFr. : *par,* by + *force,* force.]
per·form (pər-fôrm′) *v.* **-formed, -form·ing, -forms.** *—tr.* **1.** To begin and carry through to completion; do: *perform surgery.* **2.** To take action in accordance with the requirements of; fulfill: *perform contractual obligations.* **3. a.** To enact (a feat or role) before an audience. **b.** To give a public presentation of. *—intr.* **1.** To carry on; function: *a car that performs well on curves.* **2.** To fulfill an obligation or requirement; accomplish something as promised or expected. **3.** To portray a role or demonstrate a skill before an audience. **4.** To present a dramatic or musical work or other entertainment before an audience. [ME *performen* < AN *parformer* < OFr. *parfornir* : *par-* (intensive < Lat. *per-*) + *fornir,* to

percussion instrument

peregrine falcon

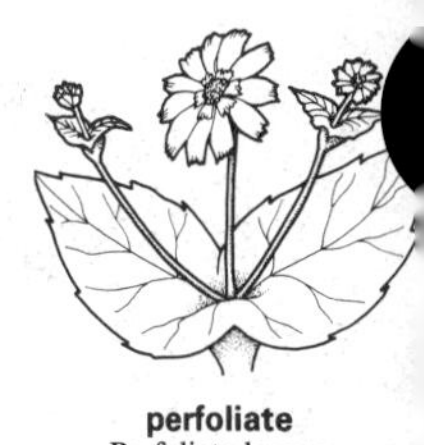

perfoliate
Perfoliate leaves

furnish, of Germanic orig.] **—per·form'a·ble** *adj.* **—per·form'er** *n.*

Synonyms: *perform, execute, accomplish, achieve, effect, fulfill, discharge, render.* These synonyms for *do* stress the action, effort, or completion of a prescribed or significant deed or task. *Perform* stresses the skill or care involved in carrying something out by established procedures. It can also mean, as with machines, to function routinely. *Execute* implies doing a planned task with efficiency, precision, or finality: *execute the maneuver. Accomplish* connotes completion of a job or feat which reflects a person's impressive talents. *Achieve* places more weight on the effort, significance, or difficulty involved. *Effect* suggests practical carrying out of something, often collectively or impersonally: *A new policy was effected.* To *fulfill* means to live up to the expectations or demands of somebody or some challenge: *fulfill one's obligation.* To *discharge* a duty is to complete it from a purely mechanical standpoint: *Your duties must be correctly discharged. Render* refers less to doing a task than to the effect of one's action: *render a service.*

per·form·ance (pər-fôr'məns) *n.* **1.** The act of performing, or the state of being performed. **2.** The act or style of performing a work or role before an audience. **3.** The way in which someone or something functions: *rated the machine's performance.* **4.** A presentation, esp. a theatrical one, before an audience. **5.** Something performed; an accomplishment.

per·fume (pûr'fyo͞om', pər-fyo͞om') *n.* **1.** A volatile liquid, distilled from flowers or prepared synthetically, that emits and diffuses a fragrant odor. **2.** A pleasing, agreeable scent or odor. *—tr.v.* (pər-fyo͞om') **-fumed, -fum·ing, -fumes.** To impregnate with fragrance; impart a pleasant odor to. [OFr. *parfum* < OItal. *parfumo* < *parfumare,* to fill with smoke : *par-* (intensive < Lat. *per-*) + *fumare,* to smoke < Lat. < *fumus,*. smoke.]

per·fum·er (pər-fyo͞o'mər) *n.* A maker or seller of perfumes.

per·fum·er·y (pər-fyo͞o'mə-rē) *n., pl.* **-ies. 1.** Perfumes in general. **2.** An establishment that specializes in making or selling perfume. **3.** The art of making perfume.

per·func·to·ry (pər-fŭngk'tə-rē) *adj.* Done or acting routinely and with little interest or care. [LLat. *perfunctorius* < Lat. *perfungi,* to get through with : *per-* (intensive) + *fungi,* to perform.] **—per·func'to·ri·ly** *adv.* **—per·func'to·ri·ness** *n.*

per·fuse (pər-fyo͞oz') *tr.v.* **-fused, -fus·ing, -fus·es. 1.** To coat, suffuse, or permeate with liquid, color, or light. **2.** To pour or diffuse (a liquid) over or through something. [Lat. *perfundere, perfus-,* to pour over : *per-* (intensive) + *fundere,* to pour.] **—per·fu'sive** (pər-fyo͞o'sĭv, -zĭv) *adj.*

per·fu·sion (pər-fyo͞o'zhən) *n.* The injection of fluid into an artery in order to reach tissues.

per·go·la (pûr'gə-lə) *n.* An arbor or passageway with a roof of trelliswork on which climbing plants are trained to grow. [Ital. < Lat. *pergula.*]

pergola

per·haps (pər-hăps') *adv.* Maybe; possibly.

peri– *pref.* **1.** Around; about; enclosing: *perimysium.* **2.** Near: *perinatal.* [Lat. < Gk. < *peri,* around, near.]

per·i·anth (pĕr'ē-ănth') *n. Bot.* The outer envelope of a flower, consisting of the calyx and corolla, or of one of these if the other is absent. [NLat. *perianthus* : Gk. *peri,* around + Gk. *anthos,* flower.]

per·i·apt (pĕr'ē-ăpt') *n.* An amulet or charm worn as protection against mischief and disease. [OFr. *periapte* < Gk. *periapton* : *peri,* around + *haptos,* fastened < *haptein,* to fasten.]

per·i·car·di·tis (pĕr'ĭ-kär-dī'tĭs) *n.* Inflammation of the pericardium.

per·i·car·di·um (pĕr'ĭ-kär'dē-əm) *n., pl.* **-di·a** (-dē-ə). The membranous sac enclosing the heart. [NLat. < Gk. *perikardion* < *perikardios,* around the heart : *peri,* around + *kardia,* heart.] **—per'i·car'di·al, per'i·car'di·ac'** *adj.*

per·i·carp (pĕr'ĭ-kärp') *n.* The wall of a ripened ovary or fruit. [NLat. *pericarpium* < Gk. *perikarpion,* pod : *peri,* around + *karpos,* fruit.] **—per'i·car'pi·al** *adj.*

per·i·chon·dri·um (pĕr'ĭ-kŏn'drē-əm) *n., pl.* **-dri·a** (-drē-ə). *Anat.* The fibrous membrane covering the surface of cartilage except at joint endings. [NLat. : PERIC + Gk. *khondros,* cartilage.] **—per'i·chon'dri·al** *adj.*

per·i·clase (pĕr'ĭ-klās', -klāz') *n.* A mineral form of magnesium oxide, MgO, usually occurring in isomeric crystals or grains. [G. *Periklas* : Gk. *peri-* (intensive) + *klasis,* breaking (so called in reference to its perfect cleavage).]

per·i·cline (pĕr'ĭ-klīn') *n.* A variety of albite occurring as elongated white crystals. [< Gk. *periklinēs,* sloping on all sides : *peri,* around + *klinein,* to slope.]

per·i·cra·ni·um (pĕr'ĭ-krā'nē-əm) *n., pl.* **-ni·a** (-nē-ə). The external periosteum that covers the outer surface of the skull. [NLat. < Gk. *perikranion* < *perikranios,* around the skull : *peri,* around + *kranion,* cranium.] **—per'i·cra'ni·al** *adj.*

per·i·cy·cle (pĕr'ĭ-sī'kəl) *n.* The growing layer of parenchyma cells and fibers between the endodermis and the conducting tissue in plant roots and stems. [Fr. *péricycle* < Gk. *perikuklos,* spherical : *peri,* around + *kuklos,* circle.] **—per'i·cy'clic** (-sī'klĭk, -sĭk'lĭk) *adj.*

per·i·derm (pĕr'ĭ-dûrm') *n.* An outer layer of tissue of plant roots and stems, consisting of the bark and the layer of growing tissue beneath the bark. **—per'i·der'mal** (-dûr'məl), **per'i·der'mic** *adj.*

pe·rid·i·um (pə-rĭd'ē-əm) *n., pl.* **-i·a** (-ē-ə). The covering of the spore-bearing organ in many fungi. [NLat. < Gk. *pēridion,* dim. of *pēra,* leather pouch.] **—pe·rid'i·al** *adj.*

per·i·dot (pĕr'ĭ-dŏt', -dō') *n.* A green variety of olivine used as a gem. [Fr. *péridot* < OFr. *peritot.*] **—per'i·dot'ic** (-dŏt'ĭk, -dō'tĭk) *adj.*

per·i·do·tite (pĕr'ĭ-dō-tīt', pə-rĭd'ə-tīt') *n.* Any of a group of igneous rocks having a granitelike texture and composed mainly of olivine and various pyroxenes and amphiboles.

per·i·gee (pĕr'ə-jē) *n.* The point nearest the earth in the orbit of the moon or a satellite. [OFr. < Med. Lat. *perigeum* < LGk. *perigeion* : Gk. *peri,* near + Gk. *gē,* earth.] **—per'i·ge'al** (pĕr'ə-jē'əl), **per'i·ge'an** *adj.*

pe·rig·y·nous (pə-rĭj'ə-nəs) *adj. Bot.* **1.** Having sepals, petals, and stamens around the edge of a cuplike receptacle containing the ovary. **2.** Designating perigynous flower parts: *perigynous stamens.* **—pe·rig'y·ny** (pə-rĭj'ə-nē) *n.*

per·i·he·li·on (pĕr'ə-hē'lē-ən, -hēl'yən) *n., pl.* **-he·li·a** (-hē'lē-ə, -hēl'yə). The point nearest the sun in the orbit of a planet or other celestial body. [PERI- + Gk. *hēlios,* sun.] **—per'i·he'li·al** *adj.*

per·i·kar·y·on (pĕr'ĭ-kăr'ē-ŏn', -ən) *n., pl.* **-kar·y·a** (kăr'ē-ə). The cell body of a neuron containing the nucleus. **—per'i·kar'y·al** *adj.*

per·il (pĕr'əl) *n.* **1.** A condition of imminent danger; exposure to the risk of harm or loss. **2.** Something that endangers; serious risk. *—tr.v.* **-iled, -il·ing, -ils** also **-illed, -il·ling, -ils.** To expose to danger or the chance of injury; imperil. [ME < OFr. < Lat. *periculum.*] **—per'il·ous** *adj.* **—per'il·ous·ly** *adv.*

per·i·lymph (pĕr'ə-lĭmf') *n.* The fluid in the space between the membranous and bony labyrinths of the internal ear.

pe·rim·e·ter (pə-rĭm'ĭ-tər) *n.* **1. a.** *Math.* A closed curve bounding a plane area. **b.** The length of such a boundary. **2.** A fortified strip or boundary usually protecting a military position. **3.** The outer limits of an area. [Fr. *périmètre* < Lat. *perimetros* < Gk. : *peri,* around + *metron,* measure.] **—per'i·met'ric** (pĕr'ə-mĕt'rĭk), **per'i·met'ri·cal** *adj.* **—per'i·met'ri·cal·ly** *adv.*

per·i·morph (pĕr'ə-môrf') *n.* A mineral that encloses a different mineral. **—per'i·mor'phic, per'i·mor'phous** *adj.* **—per'i·mor'phism** *n.*

per·i·my·si·um (pĕr'ə-mĭzh'ē-əm, -mĭz'ē-əm) *n., pl.* **-my·si·a** (-mĭzh'ē-ə, -mĭz'ē-ə). A sheath of connective tissue enveloping bundles of muscle fibers. [NLat. : PERI- + Gk. *mus,* muscle.]

per·i·na·tal (pĕr'ə-nāt'l) *adj.* Occurring near the time of birth.

per·i·neph·ri·um (pĕr'ə-nĕf'rē-əm) *n., pl.* **-ri·a** (-rē-ə). The connective and fatty tissue surrounding the kidney. [NLat. < Gk. *perinephros,* fat around the kidneys : *peri,* around + *nephros,* kidney.] **—per'i·neph'ral, per'i·neph'ri·al, per'i·neph'ric** *adj.*

per·i·ne·um (pĕr'ə-nē'əm) *n., pl.* **-ne·a** (-nē'ə). **1.** The portion of the body in the pelvis occupied by urogenital passages and the rectum, bounded in front by the pubic arch, in the back by the coccyx, and laterally by part of the hipbone. **2.** The region between the scrotum and the anus in males, and between the posterior vulva junction and the anus in females. [NLat. < LLat. *perinaion* < Gk. : *peri,* around + *inan,* to excrete.] **—per'i·ne'al** *adj.*

per·i·neu·ri·um (pĕr'ə-no͝or'ē-əm, -nyo͝or'-) *n., pl.* **-neu·ri·a** (-no͝or'ē-ə, -nyo͝or'-). A sheath of connective tissue enclosing a primary bundle of nerve fibers. **—per'i·neu'ri·al** *adj.*

pe·ri·od (pîr'ē-əd) *n.* **1.** An interval of time characterized by the occurrence of certain conditions or events: *a period of 12 months.* **2.** An interval of time characterized by the prevalence of a specified culture, ideology, or technology: *artifacts of the pre-Columbian period.* **3.** A unit of geologic time, longer than an epoch and shorter than an era. **4.** An interval regarded as a distinct evolutionary or developmental phase; stage: *Picasso's blue period.* **5.** Any of various arbitrary temporal units, esp.: **a.** Any of the divisions of the academic day. **b.** A division of the playing time of a game. **6.** *Physics & Astron.* The time interval between two successive occurrences of a recurrent event; cycle. **7.** An instance or occurrence of menstruation. **8.** A point or portion of time at which something is ended; completion; conclusion. **9.** The full pause at the end of a spoken sentence. **10.** A punctuation mark (.) indicating a full stop, placed at the end of declarative sentences and other statements thought to be complete, and after many abbreviations. **11.** In formal writing, a sentence of several carefully balanced clauses. **12.** A metrical unit of Greek verse consisting of two or more cola. **13.** *Mus.* A group of two or more phrases within a composition, made up of 8 or 16 measures and terminating with a cadence. **14.** *Math.* **a.** The least interval in the range of the independent variable of a periodic function of a real variable in which all possible values of the dependent variable are assumed. **b.** A group of digits separated by commas in a written number. **c.** The number of digits that repeat in a repeating decimal. For example, $1/7$ = 0.142857142857 . . . has a six-digit period. *—adj.* Of, belonging to, or representing a certain historical age or time: *a period piece; period furniture.* [ME *paryode* < OFr. *periode* < Med. Lat. *periodus* < Lat., cycle < Gk. *periodos,* circuit : *peri,* around + *hodos,* way.]

Synonyms: *period, time, epoch, era, age, term.* These are general words for an imprecise portion of time, usually of actual or seemingly long duration. A *period* can be a roughly specified interval or it can objectively denote a time historically: *an endless waiting period; the Romantic period. Time,* used here in its concrete rather than conceptual sense, often implies a period with certain diversities or possibilities as seen from a more personal vantage: *those times were the best. Time* can also be used loosely for a period of not precisely defined limits: *it was a time of sorrow. Epoch* is a formal word for more precise historical emphasis, implying usually that the given period is one of change and is seen as but one among many. More colorful is *era,* which conjures up associations of a notable flavor or way of life over a long and important span of time. *Age* accents the great duration of a period with a salient characteristic, seen from a distant or at least hypothetical perspective. Used of geologic and historical periods, an *age* can cover centuries but it is often used hyperbolically: *ages ago.* A *term* is a formally delimited period, usually relating to particular institutions: *his term of imprisonment; her term of office.*

pe•ri•od•ic (pĭr′ē-ŏd′ĭk) *adj.* **1.** Having periods or repeated cycles. **2.** Happening or appearing at regular intervals. **3.** Taking place now and then; intermittent. [Lat. *periodicus* < Gk. *periodikos* < *periodos,* circuit. —see PERIOD.] **—pe′ri•od′i•cal•ly** *adv.*

Synonyms: *periodic, sporadic, intermittent, occasional, fitful.* These specify recurrence over a period of time. Something is *periodic* which occurs at intervals that are, if not regular, at least generally predictable. *Sporadic* emphasizes the irregularity of what recurs, as well as its unpredictability. *Intermittent* describes anything which comes and goes, usually infrequently but somewhat expectedly, and stresses the pauses or interruptions rather than the occurrences. It usually implies recurrence within understood limits, and may hint at a significant pattern: *intermittent periods of rationality.* What is *occasional* happens at random, usually infrequently, and is generally not considered very important or disruptive. Something is *fitful* which comes abruptly, at odd times, and does not last long.

per•i•od•ic acid (pûr′ī-ŏd′ĭk) *n.* A white, crystalline inorganic acid, $H_5IO_4 \cdot 2H_2O$, used as an oxidizer.

pe•ri•od•i•cal (pĭr′ē-ŏd′ĭ-kəl) *adj.* **1.** Periodic. **2. a.** Published at regular intervals of more than one day. **b.** Of or pertaining to a publication issued at such intervals. —*n.* A publication issued at regular intervals of more than one day.

periodical cicada *n.* Seventeen-year locust.

pe•ri•o•dic•i•ty (pĭr′ē-ə-dĭs′ĭ-tē) *n.* The quality of being periodic; recurrence at regular intervals.

periodic law *n. Chem.* The principle that the properties of the elements recur periodically with increasing atomic number.

periodic table *n. Chem.* A tabular arrangement of the elements according to their atomic number.

per•i•o•don•tal (pĕr′ē-ō-dŏn′tl) *adj.* Of or designating tissue and structures surrounding and supporting the teeth. **—per′i•o•don′tal•ly** *adv.*

per•i•o•don•tics (pĕr′ē-ō-dŏn′tĭks) *n. (used with a sing. verb).* The dental specialty of periodontal disease. **—per′i•o•don′tic, per′i•o•don′ti•cal** *adj.* **—per′i•o•don′tist** *n.*

per•i•o•nych•i•um (pĕr′ē-ō-nĭk′ē-əm) *n., pl.* **-i•a** (-ē-ə). *Anat.* The border tissue surrounding the nail. [NLat. : PERI- + Gk. *onux,* nail.]

per•i•os•te•um (pĕr′ē-ŏs′tē-əm) *n., pl.* **-te•a** (-tē-ə). A fibrous membrane covering all bones, except at points of articulation. [NLat. < LLat. *periosteon* < Gk. < *periosteos,* around the bone : *peri,* around + *osteon,* bone.] **—per′i•os′te•al, per′i•os′te•ous** *adj.*

per•i•os•ti•tis (pĕr′ē-ŏs-tī′tĭs) *n.* Inflammation of the periosteum. **—per′i•os•tit′ic** (-tĭt′ĭk) *adj.*

per•i•o•tic (pĕr′ē-ō′tĭk) *adj.* **1.** Situated around the ear. **2.** Of or designating the bones immediately around the inner ear.

per•i•pa•tet•ic (pĕr′ə-pə-tĕt′ĭk) *adj.* **1.** Of or relating to walking. **2. Peripatetic.** Of or pertaining to the philosophy or methods of teaching of Aristotle. —*n.* **1.** A person who walks from place to place; itinerant. **2. Peripatetic.** A follower of the philosophy of Aristotle; Aristotelian. [OFr. *peripatetique* < Lat. *peripateticus* < Gk. *peripatētikos* < *peripatein,* to walk about : *peri,* around + *patein,* to walk.]

per•i•pe•te•ia (pĕr′ə-pə-tē′ə, -tī′ə) *n.* An abrupt or unexpected change in a course of events or situation, esp. in a literary work. [Gk. < *peripiptein,* to change suddenly : *peri,* around + *piptein,* to fall.]

pe•rip•e•ty (pə-rĭp′ĭ-tē) *n.* Peripeteia.

pe•riph•er•al (pə-rĭf′ər-əl) *adj.* **1.** Pertaining to, located on, or comprising the periphery. **2.** Auxiliary. —*n.* An auxiliary device, such as a printer or plotter, that works in conjunction with a computer. **—pe•riph′er•al•ly** *adv.*

peripheral nervous system *n.* The part of the nervous system comprising the cranial nerves, the spinal nerves, and the sympathetic nervous system.

pe•riph•er•y (pə-rĭf′ə-rē) *n., pl.* **-ies. 1. a.** The outermost part or region within a precise boundary. **b.** The region or area immediately beyond a precise boundary. **c.** A zone constituting an imprecise boundary. **2.** *Math.* **a.** A perimeter (sense 1.a.). **b.** The surface of a solid. **3.** *Anat.* A region in which nerves end. [ME *peripherie* < LLat. *peripheria* < Gk. *periphereia* < *peripherēs,* carrying around : *peri,* around + *pherein,* to carry.]

pe•riph•ra•sis (pə-rĭf′rə-sĭs) *n., pl.* **-ses** (-sēz′). **1.** The use of circumlocution. **2.** A circumlocution. [Lat. < Gk. < *periphrazein,* to express periphrastically : *peri,* around + *phrazein,* to say.]

per•i•phras•tic (pĕr′ə-frăs′tĭk) *adj.* **1.** Having the nature of or characterized by periphrasis. **2.** *Gram.* Constructed by using an auxiliary word rather than an inflected form; for example, the phrases *the word of his father* and *his father did say* are periphrastic, while *his father's word* and *his father said* are inflected. **—per′i•phras′ti•cal•ly** *adv.*

pe•riph•y•ton (pə-rĭf′ĭ-tŏn′) *n.* Sessile organisms that live attached to surfaces projecting from the bottom in a freshwater aquatic environment. [NLat. < Gk. *periphutos,* planted all over : *peri,* around + *phuein,* to grow.]

pe•rip•ter•al (pə-rĭp′tər-əl) *adj. Archit.* Built with a row of columns on all sides. —*n.* A structure with rows of columns on all sides. [Lat. *peripteros* < Gk. : *peri,* around + *pteron,* wing.]

pe•rique (pə-rēk′) *n.* A strongly flavored, black tobacco grown in Louisiana and used in various blends. [Louisiana Fr.]

per•i•sarc (pĕr′ĭ-särk′) *n.* A horny external covering that encloses the polyp colonies of certain hydrozoans. [PERI- + Gk. *sarx,* flesh.] **—per′i•sar′cal, per′i•sar′cous** *adj.*

per•i•scope (pĕr′ĭ-skōp′) *n.* Any of various tubular optical instruments that contain reflecting elements, such as mirrors and prisms, to permit observation from a position displaced from a direct line of sight. **—per′i•scop′ic** (-skŏp′ĭk), **per′i•scop′i•cal** *adj.*

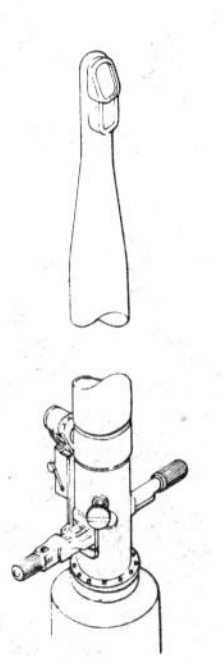

periscope
Periscope of a submarine
Above: Optical head that projects above the water
Below: Directional control and eyepiece inside the ship

per•ish (pĕr′ĭsh) *intr.v.* **-ished, -ish•ing, -ish•es. 1.** To die, esp. in a violent or untimely manner. **2.** To pass from existence; disappear gradually. **3.** *Regional.* To spoil or deteriorate. [ME *perisshen* < OFr. *perir, periss-,* to perish < Lat. *perire* : *per-,* away + *ire,* to go.]

per•ish•a•ble (pĕr′ĭ-shə-bəl) *adj.* Liable to perish, decay, or spoil; easily injured or destroyed. —*n.* Often **perishables.** Something, esp. foodstuff, apt to decay or spoil. **—per′ish•a•bil′i•ty, per′ish•a•ble•ness** *n.* **—per′ish•a•bly** *adv.*

pe•ris•so•dac•tyl (pə-rĭs′ō-dăk′təl) *Zool.* —*adj.* **1.** Having an odd number of toes. **2.** Of or pertaining to certain hoofed mammals, such as horses and rhinoceroses, of the order Perissodactyla, that have an odd number of toes. —*n.* A hoofed mammal of the order Perissodactyla. [Gk. *perissodaktulos* : *perissos,* uneven (< *peri,* beyond) + *daktulos,* finger.] **—pe•ris′so•dac′ty•lous** (-dăk′tə-ləs) *adj.*

per•i•stal•sis (pĕr′ĭ-stôl′sĭs, -stăl′-) *n., pl.* **-ses** (-sēz). Wavelike muscular contractions that propel contained matter along tubular organs, as in the alimentary canal. [NLat. < Gk. *peristaltikos,* peristaltic < *peristellein,* to wrap around : *peri,* around + *stellein,* to place.] **—per′i•stal′tic** (-stôl′tĭk, -stăl′-) *adj.* **—per′i•stal′ti•cal•ly** *adv.*

per•i•stome (pĕr′ĭ-stōm′) *n.* **1.** *Bot.* A circular row of toothlike appendages surrounding the mouth of a moss capsule. **2.** *Zool.* The area around the mouth in certain invertebrates. [PERI- + Gk. *stoma,* mouth.] **—per′i•sto′mal** (-stō′məl), **per′i•sto′mi•al** (-stō′mē-əl) *adj.*

per•i•style (pĕr′ĭ-stīl′) *n. Archit.* **1.** A series of columns surrounding a temple or other structure, or enclosing a court. **2.** A court enclosed by columns. [Fr. *péristyle* < Lat. *peristylum* < Gk. *peristulon* < *peristulos,* surrounded by columns : *peri,* around + *stulos,* pillar.] **—per′i•sty′lar** (-stī′lər) *adj.*

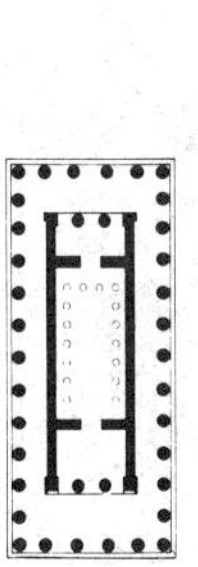

peristyle

per•i•the•ci•um (pĕr′ə-thē′shē-əm, -sē-əm) *n., pl.* **-ci•a** (-shē-ə, -sē-ə). A small fruiting body in certain fungi, containing ascospores. [NLat. : PERI- + Gk. *thēkion,* dim. of *thēkē,* case.]

per•i•to•ne•um also **per•i•to•nae•um** (pĕr′ĭ-tə-nē′əm) *n., pl.* **-ne•a** also **-nae•a** (-nē′ə). The membrane lining the walls of the abdominal cavity and enclosing the viscera. [LLat. < Gk. *peritonaion* < *peritonaios,* stretched across < *peritonos,* stretched around : *peri,* around + *teinein,* to stretch.] **—per′i•to•ne′al** *adj.* **—per′i•to•ne′al•ly** *adv.*

per•i•to•ni•tis (pĕr′ĭ-tə-nī′tĭs) *n.* Inflammation of the peritoneum.

per•i•trich (pĕr′ĭ-trĭk′) *n., pl.* **pe•rit•ri•cha** (pə-rĭt′rĭ-kə). A bell-shaped or tubular microorganism of the order Peritrichida, characterized by a wide oral opening surrounded by cilia. [NLat. *Peritrichida,* order name : PERI- + Gk. *thrix,* hair.] **—pe•rit′ri•chous** (pə-rĭt′rĭ-kəs) *adj.*

per•i•wig (pĕr′ĭ-wĭg′) *n.* A wig or peruke. [Alteration of OFr. *perruque.* —see PERUKE.]

per•i•win•kle[1] (pĕr′ĭ-wĭng′kəl) *n.* **1.** Any of several small, edible marine snails, esp. of the genus *Littorina,* having thick, cone-shaped, whorled shells. **2.** The shell of any of the periwinkles. [ME **periwinkle,* prob. alteration of OE *pīnewincle* : Lat. *pīna,* mussel (< Gk. *pinē*) + OE *-wincel,* snail shell.]

per•i•win•kle[2] (pĕr′ĭ-wĭng′kəl) *n.* Any of several trailing, evergreen plants of the genus *Vinca,* esp. *V. minor,* having glossy, dark-green leaves and blue flowers. [ME *pervenke* < OFr. *pervenche* < Lat. *pervinca.*]

periwinkle[2]

per•jure (pûr′jər) *tr.v.* **-jured, -jur•ing, -jures.** To render (oneself) guilty of perjury by deliberately testifying falsely under oath. [ME *perjuren* < OFr. *perjurer* < Lat. *perjurare* : *per,* through + *jurare,* to swear.] **—per′jur•er** *n.*

per·ju·ry (pûr′jə-rē) *n., pl.* **-ries.** The deliberate, willful giving of false, misleading, or incomplete testimony under oath. [ME *perjurie* < AN < Lat. *perjurium* < *perjurare,* to perjure.] **—per·ju′ri·ous** (pər-jo͝or′ē-əs) *adj.* **—per·ju′ri·ous·ly** *adv.*

perk¹ (pûrk) *v.* **perked, perk·ing, perks.** *—intr.* **1.** To stick up or jut out: *dogs' ears that perk.* **2.** To carry oneself in a lively and jaunty manner; rise up spiritedly. *—tr.* To cause to stick up or jut out: *The dog perked its ears at the noise.* ***—phrasal verb.* perk up. 1.** To regain or cause to regain one's good spirits or liveliness. **2.** To add to the appearance of; spruce up. *—adj.* Perky. [ME *perken,* to be lively < ONFr. *perquer,* to perch < *perque,* perch < Lat. *pertica.*]

perk² (pûrk) *n.* Often **perks.** A perquisite: *"The high-flying corporate perks—office refrigerators stocked with Perrier water, first-class trips for employees"* (Newsweek).

perk·y (pûr′kē) *adj.* **-i·er, -i·est.** Cheerful and brisk; animated; jaunty. **—perk′i·ly** *adv.* **—perk′i·ness** *n.*

per·lite also **pearl·ite** (pûr′līt′) *n.* A natural volcanic glass similar to obsidian but having distinctive concentric cracks and a relatively high water content that in a fluffy heat-expanded form is used as a lightweight aggregate in plaster and concrete and in thermal and acoustic insulation. [Fr. < *perle,* pearl < OFr. —see PEARL¹.] **—per·lit′ic** (pər-lĭt′ĭk) *adj.*

perm (pûrm) *n.* A permanent wave. *—tr. & intr.v.* **permed, perm·ing, perms.** To wave hair by applying chemicals, winding it on curlers, and drying it with heat.

per·ma·frost (pûr′mə-frôst′, -frŏst′) *n.* Permanently frozen subsoil continuous in underlying polar regions and occurring locally in perennially frigid areas. [PERMA(NENT) + FROST.]

perm·al·loy (pûr′mə-loi′, pûrm-ăl′oi′) *n.* Any of several alloys of nickel and iron having high magnetic permeability. [PERM(EABLE) + ALLOY.]

per·ma·nence (pûr′mə-nəns) *n.* The condition or quality of being permanent.

per·ma·nen·cy (pûr′mə-nən-sē) *n., pl.* **-cies. 1.** Permanence. **2.** One that is permanent.

per·ma·nent (pûr′mə-nənt) *adj.* **1.** Fixed and changeless; lasting or meant to last indefinitely. **2.** Not expected to change in status, condition, or place: *a permanent address; permanent secretary to the president.* *—n.* **1.** A permanent wave. **2.** A long-lasting hair setting. [ME < OFr. < Lat. *permanens,* pr.part. of *permanēre,* to endure : *per,* throughout + *manēre,* to remain.] **—per′ma·nent·ly** *adv.* **—per′ma·nent·ness** *n.*

permanent magnet *n.* A material that retains induced magnetic properties after it is removed from a magnetic field.

permanent press *n.* Durable press.

permanent tooth *n.* One of the 32 teeth of the second set of teeth in mammals that grow as the milk teeth are shed.

permanent wave *n.* **1.** Artificial waves in the hair produced by applying chemicals to it while wet, winding it on curlers, and drying with heat. **2.** The process used in making permanent waves. **3.** A preparation used in the process of making permanent waves.

per·man·ga·nate (pər-măn′gə-nāt′) *n.* Any of the salts of permanganic acid, all of which are strong oxidizing agents. [PERMANGAN(IC ACID) + -ATE².]

per·man·gan·ic acid (pûr′măn-găn′ĭk) *n.* An unstable inorganic acid, $HMnO_4$, existing as a strongly oxidizing, purple aqueous solution.

per·me·a·bil·i·ty (pûr′mē-ə-bĭl′ĭ-tē) *n.* **1.** The property or condition of being permeable. **2.** *Physics.* Magnetic permeability. **3.** The rate of diffusion of a pressurized gas through a porous material.

per·me·a·ble (pûr′mē-ə-bəl) *adj.* Capable of being permeated. [LLat. *permeabilis* < Lat. *permeare,* to penetrate. —see PERMEATE.] **—per′me·a·bly** *adv.*

per·me·ance (pûr′mē-əns) *n.* A measure of the ability of a magnetic circuit to conduct magnetic flux; the reciprocal of reluctance. [< Lat. *permeans,* pr.part. of *permeare,* to penetrate. —see PERMEATE.]

per·me·ase (pûr′mē-ās′) *n.* Any of a group of enzymes that regulate the transport of substances across a cell membrane. [PERME(ATE) + -ASE.]

per·me·ate (pûr′mē-āt′) *v.* **-at·ed, -at·ing, -ates.** *—tr.* **1.** To spread or flow throughout; pervade. **2.** To pass through the openings or interstices of: *liquid permeating a membrane.* *—intr.* To spread; penetrate; diffuse. [Lat. *permeare, permeat-,* to penetrate : *per,* through + *meare,* to pass.] **—per′me·ant** (-ənt), **per′me·a′tive** *adj.* **—per′me·a′tion** *n.*

Per·mi·an (pûr′mē-ən, pĕr′-) *Geol. —adj.* Of, belonging to, or designating the geologic time, system of rocks, and sedimentary deposits of the seventh and last period of the Paleozoic era. *—n.* The Permian period. [After *Perm,* an oblast of the USSR.]

per·mis·si·ble (pər-mĭs′ə-bəl) *adj.* That can be permitted; allowable. **—per·mis′si·bil′i·ty, per·mis′si·ble·ness** *n.* **—per·mis′si·bly** *adv.*

per·mis·sion (pər-mĭsh′ən) *n.* **1.** The act of permitting. **2.** Consent, esp. formal consent; leave; authorization. [ME < OFr. < Lat. *permissio* < *permittere,* to permit.]

per·mis·sive (pər-mĭs′ĭv) *adj.* **1.** Granting permission; allowing. **2.** Not forbidden; permitted; allowed. **3.** Lenient; tolerant. **4.** Permitting discretion; optional. **—per·mis′sive·ly** *adv.* **—per·mis′sive·ness** *n.*

per·mit (pər-mĭt′) *v.* **-mit·ted, -mit·ting, -mits.** *—tr.* **1.** To allow (something); consent to; tolerate. **2.** To give consent; authorize. **3.** To afford opportunity to. *—intr.* To afford opportunity; allow: *if circumstances permit.* *—n.* (pûr′mĭt, pər-mĭt′). **1.** Permission, esp. in written form. **2.** A document or certificate giving permission to do something; license; warrant. [Lat. *permittere* : *per,* through + *mittere,* to let go.] **—per·mit′ter** *n.*

Usage: *Permit of* is sometimes used for the transitive verb *permit* ("to allow," "to admit") as in *permits of two interpretations.*

per·mit·tiv·i·ty (pûr′mĭ-tĭv′ĭ-tē) *n., pl.* **-ties.** *Physics.* The ratio of electric flux density produced by an electric field in a medium to that produced in a vacuum by the same field.

per·mu·ta·tion (pûr′myo͞o-tā′shən) *n.* **1.** A complete change; transformation. **2.** The act of altering a given set of objects in a group. **3.** *Math.* An ordered arrangement of all or some of the elements of a set. **—per′mu·ta′tion·al** *adj.*

per·mute (pər-myo͞ot′) *tr.v.* **-mut·ed, -mut·ing, -mutes. 1.** To change the order of. **2.** *Math.* To subject to permutation. [ME *permuten* < OFr. *permuter* < Lat. *permutare* : *per-* (intensive) + *mutare,* to change.] **—per·mut′a·ble** *adj.*

per·ni·cious (pər-nĭsh′əs) *adj.* **1. a.** Tending to cause death or serious injury; deadly: *a pernicious virus.* **b.** Causing great harm; destructive; ruinous: *pernicious gossip.* **2.** *Archaic.* Evil; wicked. [Lat. *perniciosus* < *pernicies,* destruction : *per-* (intensive) + *nex,* violent death.] **—per·ni′cious·ly** *adv.* **—per·ni′cious·ness** *n.*

pernicious anemia *n.* A severe anemia associated with failure to absorb vitamin B_{12} and characterized by the presence of abnormally large red blood cells, gastrointestinal disturbances, and lesions of the spinal cord.

per·nick·e·ty (pər-nĭk′ĭ-tē) *adj.* Variant of **persnickety.**

per·o·ne·al (pĕr′ə-nē′əl) *adj.* Of or pertaining to the fibula or to the outer portion of the leg. [NLat. *peroneus* < *perone,* fibula < Gk. *peronē.*]

per·o·ral (pər-ôr′əl, -ōr′) *adj.* Administered by way of the mouth. [Lat. *per,* through + Lat. *ōs, ōr-,* mouth.] **—per·o′ral·ly** *adv.*

per·o·rate (pĕr′ə-rāt′) *intr.v.* **-rat·ed, -rat·ing, -rates. 1.** To conclude a speech with a formal recapitulation. **2.** To speak at great length, often in a grandiloquent manner; declaim. [Lat. *perorare, perorat-,* to harangue at length : *per-* (intensive) + *orare,* to speak.] **—per′o·ra′tion** *n.* **—per′o·ra′tion·al** *adj.*

per·ox·i·dase (pə-rŏk′sĭ-dās′, -dāz′) *n.* An enzyme found in most plant cells and some animal cells that catalyzes peroxide oxidation reactions.

per·ox·ide (pə-rŏk′sīd′) also **per·ox·id** (-sĭd) *n.* **1.** Hydrogen peroxide. **2.** A compound containing oxygen that yields hydrogen peroxide with an acid, such as sodium peroxide, Na_2O_2. *—tr.v.* **-id·ed, -id·ing, -ides. 1.** To treat with peroxide. **2.** To bleach (hair) with hydrogen peroxide. **—per·ox′ide′** *adj.*

per·ox·i·some (pə-rŏk′sĭ-sōm′) *n.* A cell organelle containing enzymes that catalyze the production and breakdown of hydrogen peroxide. [PEROXI(DE) + -SOME³.] **—per·ox′i·som′al** (-sō′məl) *adj.*

per·ox·y (pə-rŏk′sē) *adj.* Containing the bivalent group O_2. [PER- + OXY-.]

per·pend (pər-pĕnd′) *v.* **-pend·ed, -pend·ing, -pends.** *—tr.* To wonder about; ponder. *—intr.* To be attentive; reflect. [Lat. *perpendere,* to consider carefully : *per-* (intensive) + *pendere,* to consider.]

per·pen·dic·u·lar (pûr′pən-dĭk′yə-lər) *adj.* **1.** *Math.* Intersecting at or forming right angles. **2.** At right angles to the horizontal; vertical. **3.** Often **Perpendicular.** Designating a style of English Gothic architecture of the 14th and 15th centuries, characterized by emphasis of the vertical element. *—n.* **1.** A line or plane perpendicular to a given line or plane. **2.** A perpendicular position. **3.** A device, such as a plumb line, used in marking the vertical from a given point. **4.** A vertical or nearly vertical line or plane. [ME *perpendiculer* < OFr. < Lat. *perpendicularius* < *perpendiculum,* plumb line : *per-* (intensive) + *pendēre,* to hang.] **—per′pen·dic′u·lar′i·ty** (-lăr′ĭ-tē) *n.* **—per′pen·dic′u·lar·ly** *adv.*

per·pe·trate (pûr′pĭ-trāt′) *tr.v.* **-trat·ed, -trat·ing, -trates.** To be guilty of; commit: *perpetrate a crime; perpetrate a practical joke.* [Lat. *perpetrare, perpetrat-,* to accomplish : *per-* (intensive) + *patrare,* to bring about.] **—per′pe·tra′tion** *n.* **—per′pe·tra′tor** *n.*

per·pet·u·al (pər-pĕch′o͞o-əl) *adj.* **1.** Lasting for eternity: *the perpetual fires of hell.* **2.** Lasting for an indefinitely long duration. **3.** Instituted to be in effect or have tenure for an unlimited duration: *a treaty of perpetual friendship.* **4.** Ceaselessly repeated or continuing without interruption: *perpetual nagging.* **5.** Flowering throughout the growing season. [ME *perpetuel* < OFr. < Lat. *perpetualis* < *perpetuus,* continuous < *perpes,* uninterrupted : *per-* (intensive) + *petere,* to go toward.] **—per·pet′u·al·ly** *adv.*

perpetual calendar *n.* A chart or mechanical device that indicates the day of the week corresponding to any given date over a period of many years.

perpetual motion *n.* The hypothetical continuous operation of an isolated mechanical device or other closed system without a sustaining energy source.

per·pet·u·ate (pər-pĕch′o͞o-āt′) *tr.v.* **-at·ed, -at·ing, -ates. 1.** To make perpetual. **2.** To prolong the existence of; cause to be remembered for a long time: *The new library will perpetuate its founder's great love of learning.* [Lat. *perpetuare, perpetuat-* < *perpetuus,* continuous. —see PERPETUAL.] **—per·pet′u·ance, per·pet′u·a′tion** *n.* **—per·pet′u·a′tor** *n.*

per·pe·tu·i·ty (pûr′pĭ-to͞o′ĭ-tē, -tyo͞o′-) *n., pl.* **-ties. 1.** The quality, state, or condition of being perpetual: *"The perpetuity of the Church was an article of faith"* (Morris L. West). **2.** Time without end; eternity. **3.** *Law.* **a.** The condition of an estate that is limited so as to be inalienable either perpetually or longer than the period determined by law. **b.** An estate so limited. **4.** An annuity payable indefinitely.

per·plex (pər-plĕks′) *tr.v.* **-plexed, -plex·ing, -plex·es. 1.** To confuse or puzzle; bewilder. **2.** To make confusedly intricate. [< obs. *perplex,* perplexed < Lat. *perplexus* : *per-* (intensive) + *plectere,* to entwine.]

per·plexed (pər-plĕkst′) *adj.* **1.** Puzzled; bewildered; confused. **2.** Complicated; involved. **—per·plex′ed·ly** (pər-plĕk′sĭd-lē) *adv.*

per·plex·i·ty (pər-plĕk′sĭ-tē) *n., pl.* **-ties. 1.** The state or condition of being perplexed or puzzled. **2.** The state or condition of being intricate or complicated: *"the perplexity of life in twentieth-century America"* (Daniel J. Boorstin). **3.** Something that perplexes.

per·qui·site (pûr′kwĭ-zĭt) *n.* **1.** A payment or profit received in addition to a regular wage or salary, esp. a benefit expected as one's due. **2.** A tip; gratuity. **3.** Something claimed as an exclusive right: *"Politics was the perquisite of the upper class"* (Richard B. Sewall). [ME, property acquired otherwise than by inheritance < Med. Lat. *perquisitum,* acquisition < p.part. of Lat. *perquirere,* to search diligently for : *per-* (intensive) + *quaerere,* to seek.]

per·ry (pĕr′ē) *n., pl.* **-ries.** A fermented beverage, similar to cider, made from pears. [ME *perrye* < OFr. *pere* < VLat. **piratum* < Lat. *pirum,* pear.]

per se (pər sā′, sē′) *adv.* In or by itself; intrinsically. [Lat.]

per·se·cute (pûr′sĭ-kyo͞ot′) *tr.v.* **-cut·ed, -cut·ing, -cutes. 1.** To oppress or harass with ill-treatment. **2.** To annoy persistently; bother. [OFr. *persecuter* < LLat. *persequi* < Lat., to pursue : *per-* (intensive) + *sequi,* to follow.] **—per′se·cu′tive, per′se·cu·to′ry** (-kyo͞o-tôr′ē, -tōr′ē, -kyo͞o′tə-rē) *adj.* **—per′se·cu′tor** *n.*

per·se·cu·tion (pûr′sĭ-kyo͞o′shən) *n.* **1.** The act or practice of persecuting. **2.** The state or condition of being persecuted. **—per′se·cu′tion·al** *adj.*

Per·se·id (pûr′sē-ĭd) *n., pl.* **-ids** or **Per·se·i·des** (pər-sē′ĭ-dēz′). One of a shower of meteors that appears to originate in the vicinity of the constellation Perseus during the second week of August. [< Lat. *Perseus,* the constellation Perseus.]

Per·seph·o·ne (pər-sĕf′ə-nē) *n. Gk. Myth.* The wife of Hades and queen of the underworld. [Lat. < Gk. *Persephonē.*]

Per·se·us (pûr′sē-əs, -so͞os′) *n.* **1.** *Gk. Myth.* The son of Zeus and Danae who slew Medusa and rescued Andromeda. **2.** A constellation in the Northern Hemisphere near Andromeda and Auriga. [Lat. < Gk.]

per·se·ver·ance (pûr′sə-vîr′əns) *n.* **1.** Adherence to a course of action, belief, or purpose without giving way; steadfastness. **2.** *Theol.* The Calvinistic doctrine that those who have been chosen by God will continue in a state of grace to the end and will finally be saved.

Synonyms: *perseverance, persistence, tenacity, steadfastness.* Each of these conveys a sense of endurance in the pursuit of a desired end. *Perseverance,* which is favorable, suggests continuing strength or patience in dealing with something arduous. It particularly implies withstanding difficulty or resistance. *Persistence* is usually but not always unfavorable. It implies dogged resolve in dealing with others and hence often a willful insistency which is unreasonable or annoying: *her suitor's persistence. Tenacity* means tough, aggressive persistence, and accents will power. Whereas *perseverance* and *persistence* largely apply to striving for a goal, *tenacity* basically denotes holding on to something: *his tenacity in defending his position. Steadfastness* is moral in connotation and implies unswerving adherence to principles, usually in the face of opposition.

per·sev·er·a·tion (pər-sĕv′ə-rā′shən) *n. Psychol.* Continued or repetitive activity or actions: **a.** The uncontrollable repetition of a word, phrase, or gesture. **b.** The spontaneous recurrence of a thought, image, phrase, or tune in the mind.

per·se·vere (pûr′sə-vîr′) *intr.v.* **-vered, -ver·ing, -veres.** To persist in or remain constant to a purpose, idea, or task in the face of obstacles or discouragement. [ME *perseveren* < OFr. *perseverer* < Lat. *perseverare* < *perseverus,* very serious : *per-* (intensive) + *severus,* severe.] **—per′se·ver′ing·ly** *adv.*

Per·sian (pûr′zhən) *adj.* Of or pertaining to Persia or Iran, its people, language, or culture. *—n.* **1.** A native or inhabitant of ancient Persia or modern Iran. **2. a.** Any of the Iranian languages of the Persians in use during various historical periods. **b.** The modern Iranian language of Iran and western Afghanistan.

Persian cat *n.* A stocky domestic cat having long silky fur.

Persian lamb *n.* **1.** The lamb of the karakul sheep of Asia. **2.** The glossy, tightly curled fur obtained from the Persian lamb, usually when it is three or four days old.

Persian melon *n.* A melon, *Cucumis melo inodorus,* having a light-colored, unridged rind and orange-colored flesh.

per·si·flage (pûr′sə-fläzh′) *n.* **1.** Light, bantering style in writing or speaking. **2.** Idle, good-natured banter. [Fr. < *persifler,* to banter : *per-* (intensive < Lat.) + *siffler,* to whistle (< Lat. *sibilare*).]

per·sim·mon (pər-sĭm′ən) *n.* **1.** Any of various chiefly tropical trees of the genus *Diospyros,* having hard wood and orange-red fruit that is edible only when completely ripe. **2.** The fruit of any of the persimmon trees. [Of Algonquian orig.]

per·sist (pər-sĭst′, -zĭst′) *intr.v.* **-sist·ed, -sist·ing, -sists. 1.** To be obstinately repetitious, insistent, or tenacious. **2.** To hold firmly and steadfastly to a purpose, state, or undertaking, despite obstacles, warnings, or setbacks. **3.** To continue in existence; last: *hostilities that have persisted for years.* [Lat. *persistere* : *per-* (intensive) + *sistere,* to stand.] **—per·sis′ter** *n.*

per·sist·ence (pər-sĭs′təns, -zĭs′-) also **per·sist·en·cy** (-tən-sē) *n.* **1.** The act of persisting. **2.** The quality of being persistent; perseverance; tenacity. **3.** The continuance of an effect after the cause is removed: *persistence of vision.*

per·sist·ent (pər-sĭs′tənt, -zĭs′-) *adj.* **1.** Refusing to give up or let go; persevering obstinately. **2.** Insistently repetitive or continuous: *a persistent ringing of the phone.* **3.** Enduring. **4.** *Bot.* Lasting past maturity without falling off, as certain leaves or flowers. **5.** *Zool.* Retained permanently, rather than disappearing in an early stage of development: *the persistent gills of fishes.* **—per·sist′ent·ly** *adv.*

per·snick·e·ty (pər-snĭk′ĭ-tē) also **per·nick·e·ty** (-nĭk′ĭ-tē) *adj. Informal.* **1.** Fastidious; exacting. **2.** Requiring strict attention to detail. [Orig. unknown.] **—per·snick′e·ti·ness** *n.*

per·son (pûr′sən) *n.* **1.** A living human being, esp. as distinguished from an animal or thing. **2.** The composite of characteristics that make up an individual personality. **3.** An individual of specified character: *a person of importance.* **4.** The living body of a human being: *searched the prisoner's person for drugs.* **5.** Guise; character: *"Well, in her person, I say I will not have you"* (Shakespeare). **6.** Physique and general appearance. **7.** *Law.* A human being or organization with legal rights and duties. **8.** *Theol.* The separate individualities of the Father, Son, and Holy Spirit, as distinguished from the essence of the Godhead that unites them. **9.** *Gram.* **a.** Any of three groups of pronoun forms with corresponding verb inflections that distinguish between the speaker (first person), the individual addressed (second person), and the individual or thing spoken of (third person). **b.** Any of the different forms or inflections expressing these distinctions. ***—idiom.* in person.** Physically present. [ME < OFr. *persone* < Lat. *persona,* prob. < Etruscan *phersu,* mask.]

Usage: *Person* is used increasingly to create compounds which may refer to either a man or woman: *chairperson; spokesperson; anchorperson; salesperson.* These forms can be used when reference is to the position itself, regardless of who might hold it: *The committee should elect a chairperson at its first meeting.* They are also appropriate when speaking of the specific individual holding the position: *She was the best anchorperson the local station had ever had. The group asked him to act as their spokesperson.* In such cases, the alternatives *anchorwoman* and *spokesman,* would also be appropriate, and are sometimes preferred by the one holding the position. See also Usage note at **people.**

per·so·na (pər-sō′nə, -nä′) *n.* **1.** *pl.* **-nae** (-nē). A character in a dramatic or literary work. **2.** *pl.* **-nas** *Psychol.* The role that a person assumes in order to display his conscious intentions to himself and to others. [Lat. —see PERSON.]

per·son·a·ble (pûr′sə-nə-bəl) *adj.* Pleasing in appearance or personality; attractive; comely. **—per′son·a·ble·ness** *n.*

per·son·age (pûr′sə-nĭj) *n.* **1.** A character in a literary work. **2. a.** A person. **b.** A person of distinction. [ME < OFr. < *persone,* person. —see PERSON.]

per·so·na gra·ta (pər-sō′nə grä′tə, grăt′ə) *adj.* Fully acceptable or welcome, esp. to a foreign government: *diplomats who were persona grata.* [Lat., an acceptable person.]

per·son·al (pûr′sə-nəl) *adj.* **1.** Of or pertaining to a particular person; private; one's own: *personal affairs.* **2. a.** Done, made, or performed in person: *a personal appearance.* **b.** Done to or for or directed toward a particular person: *a personal favor.* **3.** Concerning a particular individual and his intimate affairs, interests, or activities; intimate: *I have something personal to tell you.* **4. a.** Aimed pointedly at the most intimate aspects of a person, esp. in a critical or hostile manner: *an uncalled-for, highly personal remark.* **b.** Tending to make remarks, or be unduly questioning, about another's affairs: *He always becomes personal in an argument.* **5.** Of or pertaining to the body or physical being: *personal cleanliness.* **6.** Pertaining to or having the nature of a person or self-conscious being: *a personal God.* **7.** *Law.* Pertaining to a person's movable property: *personal possessions.* **8.** *Gram.* Indicating grammatical person. *—n.* A personal item or notice in a newspaper.

personal effects *pl.n.* Privately owned items, as keys, an identification card, or a wallet or watch that are regularly worn or carried on one's person.

personal equation *n.* The characteristics of a person as

Persephone
5th-century B.C.
Greek vase

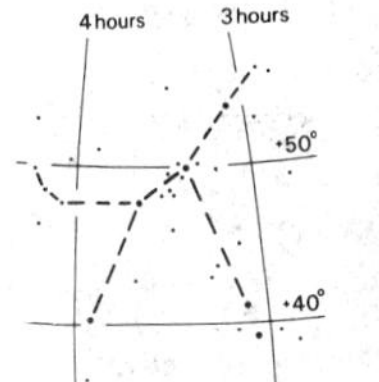

Perseus

Persian cat

persimmon

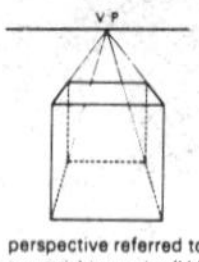

perspective referred to one vanishing point (V.P.)

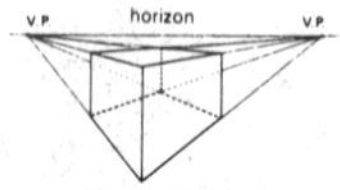

perspective referred to two vanishing points (V.P.)

perspective
Above: "The Annunciation" by Antoniazzo Romano showing linear perspective
Below: Two representations of the same cube

they tend to cause variation in observation, judgment, and reasoning.

per·son·al·ism (pûr′sə-nə-lĭz′əm) *n.* **1.** The quality of being characterized by purely personal modes of expression or behavior; idiosyncrasy. **2.** *Philos.* Any of various trends of subjective idealism regarding personality as the key to the interpretation of reality. **—per′son·al·ist** *n. & adj.* **—per′son·al·is′tic** *adj.*

per·son·al·i·ty (pûr′sə-năl′ĭ-tē) *n., pl.* **-ties. 1.** The state or quality of being a person. **2. a.** The totality of qualities and traits, as of character or behavior, that are peculiar to an individual person. **b.** A person as the embodiment of distinctive traits of mind and behavior: *a dynamic political personality.* **3.** The pattern of collective character, behavioral, temperamental, emotional, and mental traits of an individual. **4.** Distinctive qualities of an individual, esp. those distinguishing personal characteristics that make one socially appealing: *won the election more on personality than on capability.* **5.** *Informal.* A person of prominence or notoriety: *television personalities.* **6.** Often **personalities.** An offensively personal remark: *Let's not engage in personalities.* **7.** The characteristics of a place or situation that give it a distinctive character: *colors that give a room personality.* [ME *personalite* < LLat. *personalitas* < *personalis,* personal < Lat. *persona,* person. —see PERSON.]

Usage: *Personality,* meaning "celebrity" or "notable," is widely used in speech and journalism. In more formal writing, however, it is considered unacceptable by a majority of the Usage Panel.

per·son·al·ize (pûr′sə-nə-līz′) *tr.v.* **-ized, -iz·ing, -iz·es. 1.** To take (a remark or characterization) personally. **2.** To personify. **3.** To have printed, engraved, or monogrammed with one's name or initials: *personalized stationery.* **—per′son·al·i·za′tion** *n.*

per·son·al·ly (pûr′sə-nə-lē) *adv.* **1.** In person; without the intervention of another: *I thanked them personally.* **2.** As far as oneself is concerned: *Personally, I don't mind.* **3.** As a person: *I admire his skill but dislike him personally.* **4.** In a personal manner: *Don't take her disparaging remarks personally.*

personal pronoun *n. Gram.* A pronoun denoting the person speaking (*I, me, we, us*), the person spoken to (*you*), or the person or thing spoken about (*he, she, it, they, him, her, them*).

personal property *n. Law.* Temporary or movable property as distinguished from real property.

per·son·al·ty (pûr′sə-nəl-tē) *n., pl.* **-ties.** *Law.* Personal property; chattels. [AN *personalte* < LLat. *personalitas,* personality. —see PERSONALITY.]

per·so·na non gra·ta (pər-sō′nə nŏn grä′tə, grăt′ə) *adj.* Fully unacceptable or unwelcome, esp. to a foreign government: *diplomats who were persona non grata.* [Lat., an unacceptable person.]

per·son·ate¹ (pûr′sə-nāt′) *tr.v.* **-at·ed, -at·ing, -ates. 1.** To impersonate (a character); play the role or portray the part of. **2.** To endow with personal qualities; personify. **3.** *Law.* To assume the identity of, with intent to deceive. [< PERSON.] **—per′son·a′tion** *n.* **—per′son·a′tive** *adj.* **—per′son·a′tor** *n.*

per·son·ate² (pûr′sə-nĭt) *adj. Bot.* Two-lipped, with the base closed by a prominent palate. Used of a corolla. [Lat. *personatus,* masked < *persona,* mask. —see PERSON.]

per·son·hood (pûr′sən-hŏŏd′) *n.* The state or condition of being a person, esp. those qualities that confer distinct individuality.

per·son·i·fi·ca·tion (pər-sŏn′ə-fĭ-kā′shən) *n.* **1.** The act of personifying. **2.** A person or thing typifying a certain quality or idea that is outstanding; an embodiment; exemplification: *"He's invisible, a walking personification of the Negative"* (Ralph Ellison). **3.** A rhetorical figure of speech in which inanimate objects or abstractions are endowed with human qualities or are represented as possessing human form, as in *Hunger sat shivering on the road* or *Flowers danced about the lawn.* **4.** The artistic representation of an abstract quality or idea as a person.

per·son·i·fy (pər-sŏn′ə-fī′) *tr.v.* **-fied, -fy·ing, -fies. 1.** To think of or represent (an inanimate object or abstraction) as having personality or the qualities, thoughts, or movements of a living being. **2.** To represent (an object or abstraction) by a human figure. **3.** To represent (an abstract quality or idea): *This character personifies evil.* **4.** To be the embodiment or perfect example of: *"Stalin now personified bolshevism in the eyes of the world"* (A.J.P. Taylor). [Fr. *personnifier* < *personne,* person < OFr. *persone.* —see PERSON.] **—per·son′i·fi′er** *n.*

per·son·nel (pûr′sən-ĕl′) *n.* **1.** The body of persons employed by or active in an organization, business, or service. **2.** An administrative division of an organization concerned with the body of persons employed by or active in it. **—modifier:** *a personnel manager.* [Fr. < *personnel,* personal < OFr. *personal* < LLat. *personalis.* —see PERSONALITY.]

Usage: *Personnel* is a collective noun and never refers to an individual; therefore it is unacceptable when used with a numeral. It is acceptable, however, to use another qualifying word: *A number of armed forces personnel* (not *six armed forces personnel*) *testified.* See also Usage note at **collective noun.**

per·spec·tive (pər-spĕk′tĭv) *n.* **1.** The technique of representing three-dimensional objects and depth relationships on a two-dimensional surface. **2.** A view or vista. **3.** The appearance of objects in depth as perceived by normal binocular vision. **4.** The relationship of aspects of a subject to each other and to a whole: *a perspective of history.* **5.** Subjective evaluation of relative significance; point of view. *—adj.* Of, seen, or represented in perspective. [OItal. *perspectiva* < LLat., of a view < Lat. *perspicere,* to inspect : *per-* (intensive) + *specere,* to look.] **—per·spec′tive·ly** *adv.*

per·spi·ca·cious (pûr′spĭ-kā′shəs) *adj.* Able to perceive or understand keenly; mentally perceptive. [< Lat. *perspicax, perspicac-* < *perspicere,* to look through. —see PERSPECTIVE.] **—per′spi·ca′cious·ly** *adv.* **—per′spi·ca′cious·ness** *n.*

per·spi·cac·i·ty (pûr′spĭ-kăs′ĭ-tē) *n.* Acuteness of perception, discernment, or understanding.

per·spi·cu·i·ty (pûr′spĭ-kyōō′ĭ-tē) *n.* **1.** The quality of being perspicuous: *"He was at pains to insist on the perspicuity of what he wrote"* (Lionel Trilling). **2.** Perspicacity.

per·spic·u·ous (pər-spĭk′yōō-əs) *adj.* Clearly expressed or presented; easy to understand; lucid. [Lat. *perspicuus* < *perspicere,* to see through. —see PERSPECTIVE.] **—per·spic′u·ous·ly** *adv.* **—per·spic′u·ous·ness** *n.*

per·spi·ra·tion (pûr′spə-rā′shən) *n.* **1.** The saline moisture excreted through the pores of the skin by the sweat glands; sweat. **2.** The act or process of perspiring. **—per·spir′a·to′ry** (pər-spīr′ə-tôr′ē, -tōr′ē, pûr′spər-ə-) *adj.*

per·spire (pər-spīr′) *v.* **-spired, -spir·ing, -spires.** *—intr.* To excrete perspiration through the pores of the skin. *—tr.* To expel through external pores; exude. [Fr. *perspirer* < OFr. < Lat. *perspirare,* to breathe through : *per,* through + *spirare,* to breathe.]

per·suade (pər-swād′) *tr.v.* **-suad·ed, -suad·ing, -suades. 1. a.** To cause (someone) to do something by means of argument, reasoning, or entreaty. **b.** To win over (someone) to a course of action by reasoning or inducement. **2.** To make (someone) believe something; convince: *"to make children fit to live in a society by persuading them to learn and accept its codes"* (Alan W. Watts). —See Usage note at **convince.** [Lat. *persuadēre* : *per-* (intensive) + *suadēre,* to urge.] **—per·suad′a·ble** *adj.* **—per·suad′er** *n.*

Synonyms: *persuade, induce, prevail on, convince.* Frequently interchangeable, these are compared as they relate to influencing successfully another's thinking toward a decision or in a direction in accord with one's own will. *Persuade* means to resolve, change, or form another's feelings or opinion, in any effective but reputable manner. One can be persuaded by reasoning, by personal forcefulness, or even impersonally by circumstances or an event. *Induce* implies a more significant but subtle—if not deceptive—form of persuasion, often by promise of reward, where the focus is on the success of the effort: *If I could only induce you to stay.* To *prevail on* (or *upon*) suggests persuasion which is an imposition. One *prevails on* somebody who resists or who is indifferent, so that a reluctant submission rather than genuine agreement is often implied. *Convince* means to persuade one decisively of a truth or necessity.

per·sua·si·ble (pər-swā′zə-bəl, -sə-bəl) *adj.* That can be persuaded; persuadable. **—per·sua′si·bil′i·ty, per·sua′si·ble·ness** *n.*

per·sua·sion (pər-swā′zhən) *n.* **1.** The act of persuading or the state of being persuaded: *"The persuasion of a democracy to big changes is at best a slow process."* (Harold J. Laski). **2.** The ability or power to persuade. **3.** A strong conviction or belief. **4.** A body of religious beliefs; religion: *worshipers of various persuasions.* **5.** A faction; party. [Lat. *persuasio* < *persuadēre,* to persuade. —see PERSUADE.]

per·sua·sive (pər-swā′sĭv, -zĭv) *adj.* Tending or having the power to persuade: *a persuasive argument.* **—per·sua′sive·ly** *adv.* **—per·sua′sive·ness** *n.*

pert (pûrt) *adj.* **-er, -est. 1.** Impudently bold; saucy. **2.** High-spirited; vivacious: *a pert old lady.* **3.** Jaunty: *a pert little hat.* [ME < OFr. *apert* < Lat. *apertus,* open, p.part. of *aperire,* to open.] **—pert′ly** *adv.* **—pert′ness** *n.*

per·tain (pər-tān′) *intr.v.* **-tained, -tain·ing, -tains. 1.** To have reference; relate: *evidence pertaining to the accident.* **2.** To belong as an adjunct or accessory: *the farm and all the lands which pertain to it.* **3.** To be fitting or suitable. [ME *pertenen* < OFr. *partenir* < Lat. *pertinēre* : *per-* (intensive) + *tenēre,* to hold.]

per·ti·na·cious (pûr′tn-ā′shəs) *adj.* **1.** Holding firmly or tenaciously to a purpose, belief, or opinion. **2.** Stubbornly or perversely persistent. [< Lat. *pertinax, pertinac-* : *per-* (intensive) + *tenax,* tenacious < *tenēre,* to hold.] **—per′ti·na′cious·ly** *adv.* **—per′ti·na′cious·ness** *n.*

per·ti·nac·i·ty (pûr′tn-ăs′ĭ-tē) *n.* The quality or state of being pertinacious.

per·ti·nent (pûr′tn-ənt) *adj.* Of, relating to, or connected with a specific matter; apposite: *a pertinent fact.* [ME < OFr. < Lat. *pertinens,* pr.part. of *pertinēre,* to pertain. —see PERTAIN.] **—per′ti·nence, per′ti·nen·cy** *n.* **—per′ti·nent·ly** *adv.*

per·turb (pər-tûrb′) *tr.v.* **-turbed, -turb·ing, -turbs. 1.** To disturb greatly; make uneasy or anxious. **2.** To throw into great confusion. **3.** *Physics.* To cause perturbation, as of an electronic or celestial orbit. [ME *perturben* < OFr. *perturber* < Lat. *perturbare* : *per-* (intensive) + *turbare,* to throw into disorder.] **—per·turb'a·ble** *adj.*

per·tur·ba·tion (pûr'tər-bā'shən) *n.* **1. a.** The act of perturbing. **b.** The state or condition of being perturbed; agitation. **2.** Variation in a designated orbit, as of an electron or planet, resulting from the influence of one or more external bodies. **—per'tur·ba'tion·al** *adj.*

per·tus·sis (pər-tŭs'ĭs) *n.* Whooping cough. [NLat. : Lat. *per-* (intensive) + Lat. *tussis,* cough.] **—per·tus'sal** *adj.*

Pe·ru balsam (pə-rōō') *n.* Balsam of Peru.

pe·ruke (pə-rŏŏk') *n.* A wig, esp. one worn by men in the 17th and 18th centuries; periwig. [Fr. *perruque* < OFr., wig < OItal. *perrucca.*]

pe·ruse (pə-rōōz') *tr.v.* **-rused, -rus·ing, -rus·es.** To read or examine, esp. with great care. [ME *perusen,* to use up : Lat. *per-* (intensive) + ME *usen,* to use.] **—pe·rus'a·ble** *adj.* **—pe·rus'al** *n.* **—pe·rus'er** *n.*

Pe·ru·vi·an bark (pə-rōō'vē-ən) *n.* Cinchona (sense 2).

per·vade (pər-vād') *tr.v.* **-vad·ed, -vad·ing, -vades.** To be present throughout; permeate. [Lat. *pervadere* : *per,* through + *vadere,* to go.] **—per·vad'er** *n.* **—per·va'sion** (-vā'zhən) *n.*

per·va·sive (pər-vā'sĭv, -zĭv) *adj.* Having the quality or tendency to pervade or permeate. [< Lat. *pervadere, pervas-,* to pervade.] **—per·va'sive·ly** *adv.* **—per·va'sive·ness** *n.*

per·verse (pər-vûrs', pûr'vûrs') *adj.* **1.** Directed away from what is right or good; perverted. **2.** Obstinately persisting in an error or fault; wrongly self-willed or stubborn. **3. a.** Marked by a disposition to oppose and contradict. **b.** Characterized by or arising from such a disposition. **4.** Cranky; peevish. [ME *pervers* < OFr. < Lat. *pervertere,* to pervert. —see PERVERT.] **—per·verse'ly** *adv.* **—per·verse'ness** *n.*

per·ver·sion (pər-vûr'zhən, -shən) *n.* **1.** The act of perverting or the state of being perverted. **2.** A sexual practice or act considered deviant. **—per·ver'sive** (-sĭv, -zĭv) *adj.*

per·ver·si·ty (pər-vûr'sĭ-tē) *n., pl.* **-ties. 1.** The quality or state of being perverse. **2.** An instance of being perverse.

per·vert (pər-vûrt') *tr.v.* **-vert·ed, -vert·ing, -verts. 1.** To cause to turn from what is considered morally right; corrupt: *"We forbid bad men to pervert society."* (John Stuart Mill). **2.** To bring to a worse condition; debase; vitiate: *He will not allow bribery to pervert his sense of honor.* **3.** To employ wrongly or incorrectly; misuse: *He perverted the law to suit his own needs.* **4.** To interpret incorrectly; misconstrue: *an analysis that perverts the meaning of the poem.* —*n.* (pûr'vûrt'). One who practices sexual perversion. [ME *perverten* < OFr. *pervertir* < Lat. *pervertere* : *per-* (intensive) + *vertere,* to turn.] **—per·vert'er** *n.* **—per·vert'i·ble** *adj.*

per·vert·ed (pər-vûr'tĭd) *adj.* **1.** Deviating greatly from what is considered right and correct: *a perverted idea of justice.* **2.** Of, pertaining to, or practicing sexual perversion. **3.** Misinterpreted; misconstrued: *a perverted translation of an epic poem.* **—per·vert'ed·ly** *adv.* **—per·vert'ed·ness** *n.*

per·vi·ous (pûr'vē-əs) *adj.* **1.** Open to passage or entrance; permeable. **2.** Open to arguments, ideas, or change. [Lat. *pervius* : *per,* through + *via,* way.] **—per'vi·ous·ly** *adv.* **—per'vi·ous·ness** *n.*

pes (pās) *n., pl.* **pe·des** (pĕd'ās'). A foot or footlike part, esp. the foot of a four-footed vertebrate. [Lat.]

Pe·sach (pā'säkh') *n.* Passover. [Heb. *pesaḥ* < *pāsaḥ,* he passed over.]

pe·sade (pə-säd', -zäd') *n.* The act or position of a horse when rearing on its hind legs with its forelegs in the air. [Fr., var. of obs. *posade* < OFr. < OItal. *posata* < *posare,* to pause < LLat. *pausare* < Lat. *pausa,* pause. —see PAUSE.]

pe·se·ta (pə-sā'tə) *n.* See table at **currency.** [Sp., dim. of *peso,* peso.]

pe·se·wa (pā-sā'wä) *n., pl.* **pesewa** or **-was.** See table at **currency.** [Native word in Ghana.]

pes·ky (pĕs'kē) *adj.* **-ki·er, -ki·est.** *Informal.* Troublesome; annoying: *a pesky mosquito.* [Prob. alteration of PEST.] **—pes'ki·ly** *adv.* **—pes'ki·ness** *n.*

pe·so (pā'sō) *n., pl.* **-sos.** See table at **currency.** [Sp. < Lat. *pensum,* something weighed < *pendere,* to weigh.]

pes·sa·ry (pĕs'ə-rē) *n., pl.* **-ries. 1.** Any of various contraceptive or supportive devices placed and worn in the vagina. **2.** A medicated vaginal suppository. [ME *pessarie* < Med. Lat. *pessarium* < LLat. *pessum* < Gk. *pessos.*]

pes·si·mism (pĕs'ə-mĭz'əm) *n.* **1.** A tendency to take the gloomiest possible view of a situation. **2.** The doctrine or belief that this is the worst of all possible worlds and that all things ultimately tend toward evil. **3.** The doctrine or belief that the evil in the world outweighs the good. [Fr. *pessimisme* < Lat. *pessimus,* worst.] **—pes'si·mist** *n.* **—pes'si·mis'tic** *adj.* **—pes'si·mis'ti·cal·ly** *adv.*

pest (pĕst) *n.* **1.** An annoying person or thing; nuisance. **2.** An injurious plant or animal, esp. one harmful to humans. **3.** A pestilence. [OFr. *peste,* pestilence < Lat. *pestis.*]

pes·ter (pĕs'tər) *tr.v.* **-tered, -ter·ing, -ters.** To harass with petty annoyances; bother. [Prob. < OFr. *empestrer,* to hobble < VLat. **impastoriare* : Lat. *in-,* in + LLat. *pastura,* pasture < Lat. *pascere,* to pasture.] **—pes'ter·er** *n.*

pest house *n.* A hospital for patients suffering from plague or other infectious disease.

pes·ti·cide (pĕs'tĭ-sīd') *n.* A chemical used to kill pests, esp. insects and rodents.

pes·tif·er·ous (pĕs-tĭf'ər-əs) *adj.* **1.** Producing or breeding infectious disease. **2.** Infected with or contaminated by an epidemic disease. **3.** Morally evil or deadly; pernicious. **4.** *Informal.* Bothersome; annoying. [ME < Lat. *pestiferus* : *pestis,* pestilence + *ferre,* to carry.] **—pes·tif'er·ous·ly** *adv.* **—pes·tif'er·ous·ness** *n.*

pes·ti·lence (pĕs'tə-ləns) *n.* **1. a.** A usually fatal epidemic disease, esp. bubonic plague. **b.** An epidemic of such a disease. **2.** A pernicious, evil influence or agent.

pes·ti·lent (pĕs'tə-lənt) also **pes·ti·len·tial** (pĕs'tə-lĕn'shəl) *adj.* **1.** Tending to cause death; deadly; fatal. **2.** Likely to cause an epidemic disease. **3.** Infected or contaminated with a contagious disease. **4.** Morally, socially, or politically harmful; pernicious. **5.** Causing annoyance or disfavor. [ME < Lat. *pestilens* < *pestis,* pestilence.]

pes·tle (pĕs'əl, pĕs'təl) *n.* **1.** A club-shaped hand tool for grinding or mashing substances in a mortar. **2.** A large bar moved vertically to stamp or pound, as in a press or mill. —*v.* **-tled, -tling, -tles.** —*tr.* To pound, grind, or mash with a pestle. —*intr.* To use a pestle. [ME *pestel* < OFr. < Lat. *pistillum.*]

pet[1] (pĕt) *n.* **1.** An animal kept for amusement or companionship. **2.** An object of the affections. **3.** A person esp. loved or indulged; favorite: *teacher's pet.* —*adj.* **1.** Kept as a pet: *a pet cat.* **2.** Particularly cherished or indulged; favorite: *a pet daughter; a pet aversion.* —*v.* **pet·ted, pet·ting, pets.** —*tr.* To stroke or caress gently; pat. —*intr.* *Informal.* To make love by fondling and caressing. [Orig. unknown.] **—pet'ter** *n.*

pet[2] (pĕt) *n.* A fit of bad temper or pique. —*intr.v.* **pet·ted, pet·ting, pets.** To be sulky and peevish. [Orig. unknown.]

pet·al (pĕt'l) *n.* A separate, often brightly colored segment of a corolla. [NLat. *petalum* < Gk. *petalon,* leaf.] **—pet'aled, pet'alled** *adj.*

-petal *suff.* Moving toward: *basipetal.* [< NLat. *-petus* < Lat. *petere,* to seek.]

pet·al·if·er·ous (pĕt'l-ĭf'ər-əs) *adj.* Bearing petals.

pet·al·ine (pĕt'l-ĭn, -īn') *adj.* Of or resembling a petal.

pet·al·oid (pĕt'l-oid') *adj.* Resembling a petal; petallike.

pet·al·ous (pĕt'l-əs) *adj.* Having petals.

pe·tard (pĭ-tärd') *n.* **1.** A small bell-shaped bomb used to breach a gate or wall. **2.** A firecracker. [Fr. *pétard* < OFr. *peter,* to break wind < *pet,* a breaking of wind < Lat. *peditum* < *pedere,* to break wind.]

pet·cock also **pet cock** (pĕt'kŏk') *n.* A small valve or faucet used to drain or reduce pressure from pipes, radiators, and boilers. [Perh. PET(TY) + COCK[1].]

pe·te·chi·a (pə-tē'kē-ə) *n., pl.* **-chi·ae** (-kē-ī'). A small spot on a body surface, such as the skin or mucous membrane, caused by a minute hemorrhage and often seen in typhus. [NLat. < Ital. *petecchia,* skin spot.] **—pe·te'chi·al** *adj.* **—pe·te'chi·ate** (-ĭt) *adj.*

pe·ter[1] (pē'tər) *intr.v.* **-tered, -ter·ing, -ters. 1.** To come to an end slowly; diminish, dwindle. **2.** To become exhausted. [Orig. unknown.]

pe·ter[2] (pē'tər) *n.* *Vulgar Slang.* Penis (sense 1). [< the name *Peter.*]

Pe·ter (pē'tər) *n.* **1.** Chief of the Apostles and traditional author of two books of the New Testament. **2.** See table at **Bible.**

Peter Principle *n.* The notion that an employee within an organization will advance to his highest level of incompetence and remain there. [After Laurence Johnston *Peter* (b. 1919), its formulator.]

Peter's pence also **Peter pence** *n.* **1.** A tax of one penny per household paid in medieval England to the Papal See. **2.** An annual voluntary contribution made by Roman Catholics toward the expenses of the Holy See. [After St. *Peter,* from the tradition that he founded the papacy.]

pet·i·o·lar (pĕt'ē-ō'lər) *adj.* Of, pertaining to, or growing on a petiole.

pet·i·o·late (pĕt'ē-ə-lāt', pĕt'ē-ō'lĭt) *adj.* Having a petiole.

pet·i·ole (pĕt'ē-ōl') *n.* **1.** *Bot.* The stalk by which a leaf is attached to a stem; a leafstalk. **2.** *Zool.* The slender, stalklike connection between the thorax and abdomen in certain insects. [NLat. *petiolus* < LLat., fruit stalk, dim. of Lat. *pes,* foot.]

pet·i·o·lule (pĕt'ē-ō-lōōl', pĕt'ē-ŏl'yōōl) *n.* The stalk of a leaflet in a compound leaf. [NLat. *petiolulus,* dim. of *petiolus,* petiole. —see PETIOLE.]

pet·it also **pet·ty** (pĕt'ē) *adj.* *Law.* Lesser; minor. [ME, insignificant < OFr., small.]

pet·it bour·geois also **pet·ty bour·geois** (pĕt'ē bŏŏr-zhwä') *n.* A member of the petty bourgeoisie. [Fr. *petit-bourgeois* : *petit,* small + *bourgeois,* bourgeois.]

pe·tite (pə-tēt') *adj.* Small, slender, and trim. Used of a girl or woman. —*n.* A clothing size for short women. [Fr., fem. of *petit* < OFr.]

pe·tite bour·geoi·sie (pə-tēt' bŏŏr'zhwä-zē') *n.* The petty bourgeoisie. [Fr. *petite-bourgeoise* : *petite,* small + *bourgeoisie,* bourgeoisie.]

pe·tite mar·mite (pə-tēt' mär-mēt') *n.* Broth made and served in a small, covered earthenware casserole. [Fr. : *petite,* little + *marmite,* kettle.]

peruke
Two of the perukes shown in "The Five Orders of Periwigs," a 1761 engraving by Hogarth

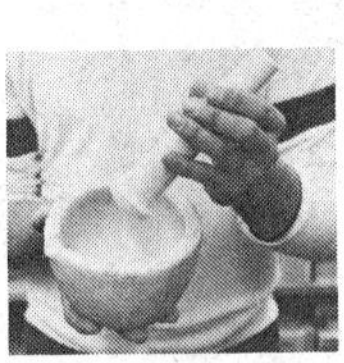

pestle

petard

pe·tit four (pĕt′ē fôr′, fōr′) *n., pl.* **pe·tits fours** or **pe·tit fours** (pĕt′ē fôrz′, fōrz′). A small, rich tea cake, frosted and decorated. [Fr. : *petit,* little + *four,* oven.]

pe·ti·tion (pə-tĭsh′ən) *n.* **1.** A solemn supplication or request to a superior authority; an entreaty. **2.** A formal written document requesting a right or a benefit from a person or group in authority. **3.** *Law.* **a.** A formal written application requesting a court for a specific judicial action: *a petition for appeal.* **b.** The judicial action that is asked for in any such request. —*v.* **-tioned, -tion·ing, -tions.** —*tr.* **1.** To address a petition to. **2.** To ask for by petition; request formally. —*intr.* To make an entreaty: *petition for retrial.* [ME *peticion* < OFr. *petition* < Lat. *petitio* < *petere,* to request.] **—pe·ti′tion·ar′y** (pə-tĭsh′ə-nĕr′ē) *adj.* **—pe·ti′tion·er** *n.*

pe·ti·ti·o prin·ci·pi·i (pə-tĭsh′ē-ō′ prĭn-sĭp′ē-ē′) *n. Logic.* The fallacy of assuming in the premise of an argument that which one wishes to prove in the conclusion; begging the question. [Med. Lat. : Lat. *petitio,* request + Lat. *principii,* of the beginning.]

pet·it juror also **pet·ty juror** (pĕt′ē) *n.* A member of a petit jury.

pet·it jury also **pet·ty jury** (pĕt′ē) *n.* A jury of 12 persons that sits at civil and criminal trials.

pet·it larceny also **pet·ty larceny** (pĕt′ē) *n.* The theft of objects whose value is below a certain arbitrary standard.

pe·tit mal (pĕt′ē mäl′, măl′) *n.* A form of epilepsy characterized by frequent but transient lapses of consciousness and only rare spasms or falling. [Fr. : *petit,* small + *mal,* illness.]

pet·it point (pĕt′ē point′) *n.* **1.** A small stitch used in needlepoint. **2.** Needlepoint done with a small stitch. [Fr.]

pet·nap (pĕt′năp′) *tr.v.* **-napped, -nap·ping, -naps.** To steal (a pet), usually for profit. **—pet′nap′per** *n.* **—pet′nap′ping** *n.* [PET + (KID)NAP.]

petr– *pref.* Variant of **petro-.**

Pe·trar·chan sonnet (pĭ-trär′kən) *n.* A sonnet form of Italian origin comprising an octave with the rhyme pattern *abbaabba,* and a sestet of various rhyme patterns such as *cdecde* or *cdecde.* [After *Petrarch* (1304–1374).]

George Miksch Sutton

petrel

pet·rel (pĕt′rəl) *n.* Any of various sea birds of the order Procellariiformes, esp. the storm petrel. [Orig. unknown.]

petri– *pref.* Variant of **petro-.**

Pe·tri dish (pē′trē) *n.* A shallow dish with a loose-fitting cover, used esp. to culture microorganisms for research. [After Julius R. *Petri* (1852–1921).]

pet·ri·fac·tion (pĕt′rə-făk′shən) also **pet·ri·fi·ca·tion** (-fĭ-kā′shən) *n.* **1.** The process of petrifying, esp. the conversion of organic matter into stone or a stony substance. **2.** The state of being petrified, as by fear.

pet·ri·fy (pĕt′rə-fī′) *v.* **-fied, -fy·ing, -fies.** —*tr.* **1.** To convert (wood or other organic matter) into a stony replica by structural impregnation with dissolved minerals. **2.** To cause to become stiff or stonelike; deaden. **3.** To stun or paralyze with terror; daze. —*intr.* To become stony, esp. by mineral replacement of organic matter. [OFr. *petrifier* : Lat. *petra,* rock (< Gk.) + Lat. *facere,* to make.]

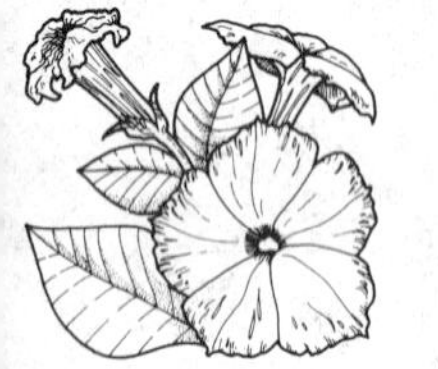

petunia

Pe·trine (pē′trīn′) *adj.* Of or pertaining to Saint Peter. [LLat. *Petrus,* Peter + -INE[1].]

petro– or **petri–** or **petr–** *pref.* **1.** Rock; stone: *petroglyph.* **2.** Petroleum: *petrochemistry.* [< Gk. *petros,* stone and *petra,* rock.]

pet·ro·chem·i·cal (pĕt′rō-kĕm′ĭ-kəl) *n.* A chemical derived from petroleum or natural gas. **—pet′ro·chem′i·cal** *adj.*

pet·ro·chem·is·try (pĕt′rō-kĕm′ĭ-strē) *n.* The chemistry of petroleum and its derivatives.

pet·ro·dol·lar (pĕt′rō-dŏl′ər) *n.* A unit of hard currency, as a dollar, held by oil-exporting countries as a result of the sharp increases in oil prices that generated a transfer of purchasing power to oil-exporting nations and a balance-of-payments deficit for oil-importing nations.

pet·ro·gen·e·sis (pĕt′rō-jĕn′ĭ-sĭs) *n.* A branch of petrology that deals with the origin of rocks. **—pet′ro·ge·net′ic** (-jə-nĕt′ĭk) *adj.*

pet·ro·glyph (pĕt′rə-glĭf′) *n. Archaeol.* A carving or line drawing on rock. **—pet′ro·glyph′ic** *adj.*

pe·trog·ra·phy (pə-trŏg′rə-fē) *n.* The description and classification of rocks. **—pe·trog′ra·pher** *n.* **—pet′ro·graph′ic** (pĕt′rə-grăf′ĭk), **pet′ro·graph′i·cal** *adj.* **—pet′ro·graph′i·cal·ly** *adv.*

pewter

pet·rol (pĕt′rəl) *n. Chiefly Brit.* Gasoline. [Fr. *(essence de) petrole,* (essence of) petroleum < OFr. *petrole,* petroleum < Med. Lat. *petroleum.*]

pet·ro·la·tum (pĕt′rə-lā′təm, -lä′təm) *n.* A colorless-to-amber gelatinous semisolid, obtained from petroleum, consisting of various methane and olefin hydrocarbons, and used in lubricants and medicinal ointments. [NLat. < Med. Lat. *petroleum,* petroleum.]

pe·tro·le·um (pə-trō′lē-əm) *n.* A natural, yellow-to-black, thick, flammable liquid hydrocarbon mixture found principally beneath the earth's surface and processed for fractions including natural gas, gasoline, naphtha, kerosene, fuel and lubricating oils, paraffin wax, asphalt, and a wide variety of derivative products. [Med. Lat. : Lat. *petra,* rock (< Gk.) + Lat. *oleum,* oil.]

petroleum jelly *n.* Petrolatum.

pe·trol·ic (pə-trŏl′ĭk) *adj.* Derived from petroleum. [PETRO-L(EUM) + -IC.]

pe·trol·o·gy (pə-trŏl′ə-jē) *n.* The study of the origin, composition, structure, and alteration of rocks. **—pet′ro·log′ic** (pĕt′rə-lŏj′ĭk), **pet′ro·log′i·cal** *adj.* **—pet′ro·log′i·cal·ly** *adv.* **—pe·trol′o·gist** *n.*

pet·ro·pol·i·tics (pĕt′rō-pŏl′ĭ-tĭks) *n. (used with a sing. or pl. verb).* The strategic practice of controlling petroleum sales so as to achieve international political and economic ends and goals.

pe·tro·sal (pə-trō′səl) also **pet·rous** (pĕt′rəs) *adj. Anat.* Pertaining to or located near the portion of the temporal bone that surrounds the inner ear. [< Lat. *petrosus,* rocky. —see PETROUS.]

pet·rous (pĕt′rəs) *adj.* **1.** Of, pertaining to, or resembling rock; stony; hard. **2.** Variant of **petrosal.** [Lat. *petrosus,* rocky < *petra,* rock < Gk.]

pet·ti·coat (pĕt′ē-kōt′) *n.* **1.** A skirt, esp. a woman's slip or underskirt. **2.** Something, such as a decorative hanging, that resembles a woman's slip. **3.** *Slang.* A woman or girl. —*adj.* **1.** Female; feminine. **2.** Of or by women: *a petticoat government.* [ME *petycote* : *pety,* small + *cote,* coat.] **—pet′ti·coat′ed** *adj.*

petticoat narcissus *n.* A small daffodil, *Narcissus bulbocodium,* native to the Mediterranean region, having yellow or white flowers.

pet·ti·fog (pĕt′ē-fŏg′, -fôg′) *intr.v.* **-fogged, -fog·ging, -fogs.** To act like a pettifogger. [Back-formation < PETTIFOGGER.]

pet·ti·fog·ger (pĕt′ē-fŏg′ər, -fô′gər) *n.* **1.** A petty, quibbling, unscrupulous lawyer. **2.** A person who quibbles over trivia. [Orig. unknown.]

pet·ting (pĕt′ĭng) *n. Informal.* Caressing and kissing.

pet·ting zoo (pĕt′ĭng) *n.* A collection of farm animals, as goats, ducks, and sheep, and sometimes docile wild animals such as turtles or deer, for children to feed and pet.

pet·tish (pĕt′ĭsh) *adj.* Ill-tempered; peevish; petulant. [Prob. < PET[2].] **—pet′tish·ly** *adv.* **—pet′tish·ness** *n.*

pet·ty (pĕt′ē) *adj.* **-ti·er, -ti·est. 1.** Small, trivial, or insignificant in quantity or quality: *petty grievances.* **2.** Of contemptibly narrow mind or views: *a petty outlook.* **3.** *Informal.* Spiteful; mean. **4.** Of subordinate or inferior rank. **5.** *Law.* Variant of **petit.** [ME *pety,* alteration of *petit.* —see PETIT.] **—pet′ti·ly** *adv.* **—pet′ti·ness** *n.*

petty bourgeois *n.* Variant of **petit bourgeois.**

petty bour·geoi·sie (bo͝or′zhwä-zē′) *n.* The class of small businessmen, tradesmen, and professional people.

petty cash *n.* A small fund of money for incidental expenses, as in an office.

petty juror *n.* Variant of **petit juror.**

petty jury *n.* Variant of **petit jury.**

petty larceny *n.* Variant of **petit larceny.**

petty officer *n.* A naval noncommissioned officer.

pet·u·lant (pĕch′ə-lənt) *adj.* **1.** Unreasonably irritable or ill-tempered; peevish. **2.** Contemptuous in speech or behavior. [OFr. < Lat. *petulans* < **petulare,* dim. of *petere,* to assail.] **—pet′u·lance, pet′u·lan·cy** *n.* **—pet′u·lant·ly** *adv.*

pe·tu·nia (pĭ-to͞on′yə, -tyo͞on′-) *n.* **1.** Any of various widely cultivated plants of the genus *Petunia,* native to South America, having funnel-shaped flowers in colors from white to purple. **2.** A moderate to dark purple. [NLat. *Petunia,* genus name < obs. Fr. *petun,* tobacco < Tupi *petyn.*]

pe·tun·tze or **pe·tun·tse** (pə-to͞on′tsē) *n.* A variety of feldspar sometimes mixed with kaolin in Chinese porcelain. [Chin. (Mandarin) *bai*[1] *dun*[1]*zi*[5] : *bai*[1], white + *dun*[1]*zi*[5], block of stone.]

pew (pyo͞o) *n.* **1.** A bench for the congregation in a church. **2.** A compartment that provides seating for a number of people in a church. [ME *pewe* < OFr. *puie,* raised seat < Lat. *podia,* pl. of *podium,* balcony < Gk. *podion,* base, dim. of *pous,* foot.]

pe·wee also **pee·wee** (pē′wē) *n.* Any of various small, olive-brown North American woodland birds of the genus *Contopus.* [Imit. of its cry.]

pe·wit (pē′wĭt′, pyo͞o′ĭt) *n.* The lapwing. [Imit. of its cry.]

pew·ter (pyo͞o′tər) *n.* **1.** Any of numerous silver-gray alloys of tin with various amounts of antimony, copper, and lead, formerly used widely for fine kitchen utensils and tableware. **2.** Pewter articles collectively. —*adj.* Made of pewter. [ME *pewtre* < OFr. *peutre.*]

pew·ter·er (pyo͞o′tər-ər) *n.* One who makes pewter objects, as dishes or candlesticks.

pe·yo·te (pā-ō′tē) also **pe·yo·tl** (pā-ōt′l) *n.* **1.** Mescal (sense 1). **2.** A hallucinatory drug derived from the tubercles of peyote. [Mex. Sp. < Nahuatl *peyotl.*]

pfen·nig (fĕn′ĭg) *n., pl.* **pfen·nigs** or **pfen·ni·ge** (fĕn′ĭ-gə). See table at **currency.** [G. < OHG *pfenning.*]

PG (pē′jē′) *adj.* Indicating a motion-picture rating that allows admission of persons of all ages but suggests parental guidance in the case of children. [Short for P(ARENTAL) G(UIDANCE).]

pH (pē′āch′) *n. Chem.* A measure of the acidity or alkalinity of a solution, numerically equal to 7 for neutral solutions, increasing with increasing alkalinity and decreasing with increasing acidity. [P(OTENTIAL OF) H(YDROGEN).]

Phae·dra (fē′drə, fĕ′-) *n. Gk. Myth.* The wife of Theseus who fell in love with her stepson, Hippolytus. [Lat. < Gk. *Phaidra* < fem. of *phaidros,* shining.]

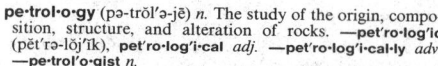

Pha·ë·thon (fā′ə-thŏn′) *n. Gk. Myth.* A son of the sun god

Helios who was killed when he drove his father's chariot across the sky. [Lat. < Gk. *Phaethōn* < *phaethōn,* shining.]

pha·e·ton (fā'ĭ-tən) *n.* **1.** A light, open, four-wheeled carriage, usually drawn by a pair of horses. **2.** A touring car. [After PHAETHON.]

phage (fāj) *n.* A bacteriophage.

-phage *suff.* One that eats: *macrophage.* [Gk. *-phagos* < *phagein,* to eat.]

-phagia *suff.* The eating of a specified substance or eating in a specified manner: *dysphagia.* [Gk. < *phagein,* to eat.]

phago– *pref.* Eating; consuming: *phagocyte.* [Gk. < *phagein,* to eat.]

phag·o·cyte (făg'ə-sīt') *n.* A cell such as a leukocyte that engulfs and digests cells, microorganisms, or other foreign bodies in the bloodstream and tissues. **—phag'o·cyt'ic** (-sĭt'ĭk) *adj.*

phag·o·cy·tin (făg'ə-sī'tĭn) *n.* A bactericidal substance liberated by the disintegration of phagocytes.

phag·o·cy·tize (făg'ə-sĭ-tīz', -sī'-) *tr.v.* **-tized, -tiz·ing, -tiz·es.** To ingest by phagocytosis.

phag·o·cy·to·sis (făg'ə-sī-tō'sĭs) *n.* The envelopment and digestion of bacteria or other foreign bodies by phagocytes. [PHAGOCYT(E) + -OSIS.] **—phag'o·cy·tot'ic** (-tŏt'ĭk) *adj.*

phag·o·some (făg'ə-sōm) *n.* An intracellular membrane-bound vesicle that contains material taken into the cell by phagocytosis.

-phagous *suff.* Eating; feeding on: *ichthyophagous.* [Lat. *-phagus* < Gk. *-phagos* < *phagein,* to eat.]

-phagy *suff.* -phagia.

pha·lange (fă'lănj', fə-lănj') *n. Anat.* A phalanx (sense 3). [Fr. < Gk. *phalanx.*]

pha·lan·ge·al (fə-lăn'jē-əl, fā-) also **pha·lan·gal** (fə-lăng'gəl, fā-) or **pha·lan·ge·an** (fə-lăn'jē-ən, fā-) *adj. Anat.* Of or pertaining to a phalanx.

pha·lan·ger (fə-lăn'jər) *n.* Any of various small, arboreal marsupials of the family Phalangeridae, of Australia and adjacent islands, having a long tail and dense, woolly fur. [Prob. < Fr. < Gk. *phalanx,* toe bone.]

pha·lanx (fā'lăngks') *n., pl.* **pha·lanx·es** or **pha·lan·ges** (fə-lăn'jēz, fā-). **1.** A formation of infantry carrying overlapping shields and long spears, developed by Philip II of Macedonia and used by Alexander the Great. **2.** A close-knit or compact body of people: *"formed a solid phalanx in defence of the Constitution and Protestant religion"* (G.M. Trevelyan). **3.** *pl.* **phalanges.** *Anat.* A bone of a finger or toe. [Lat. < Gk.]

phal·a·rope (făl'ə-rōp') *n.* Any of several wading birds of the family Phalaropodidae, having lobed toes that enable them to swim. [Fr. < NLat. *phalaropus* : Gk. *phalaris,* coot + Gk. *pous,* foot.]

phal·lic (făl'ĭk) *adj.* **1.** Of, pertaining to, or resembling a phallus. **2.** Of or pertaining to the cult of the phallus as an embodiment of generative power: *phallic worship.* [Gk. *phallikos* < *phallos,* phallus.] **—phal'li·cal·ly** *adj.*

phal·lus (făl'əs) *n., pl.* **phal·li** (făl'ī') or **phal·lus·es. 1.** *Anat.* **a.** The penis. **b.** The sexually undifferentiated tissue in the embryo that becomes the penis or clitoris. **2.** A representation of the penis and testes as an embodiment of generative power. **3.** *Psychoanal.* The immature penis considered as the libidinal object of infantile sexuality. [LLat. < Gk. *phallos.*]

-phane or **-phan** *suff.* A substance resembling something specified: *tryptophan.* [< Gk. *-phanēs,* appearing < *phainesthai.* to appear.]

phan·er·o·gam (făn'ər-ə-găm', fə-năr'ə-) *n.* A plant that produces flowers and true seeds. [NLat. *phanerogramus* : Gk. *phaneros,* visible + Gk. *gamos,* marriage.] **—phan'er·o·gam'ic** (făn'ər-ə-găm'ĭk, fə-năr'ə-), **phan'er·og'a·mous** (făn'ə-rŏg'ə-məs) *adj.*

phan·tasm (făn'tăz'əm) *n.* **1.** Something apparently seen but having no physical reality; a phantom. **2.** An illusory mental image. **3.** In Platonic philosophy, objective reality as perceived and distorted by the five senses. [ME *fantasme* < OFr. < Lat. *phantasma* < Gk. < *phantazein,* to make visible < *phainein,* to show.] **—phan·tas'mal** (-tăz'məl), **phan·tas'mic** (-tăz'mĭk) *adj.*

phan·tas·ma (făn-tăz'mə) *n., pl.* **-ma·ta** (-mə-tə). A phantasm.

phan·tas·ma·go·ri·a (făn-tăz'mə-gôr'ē-ə, -gōr'-) also **phan·tas·ma·go·ry** (făn-tăz'mə-gôr'ē, -gōr'ē) *n.* **1.** A fantastic sequence of haphazardly associative imagery, as seen in dreams or fever. **2.** Fantastic imagery as represented in art. [Poss. < Gk. *phantasma,* phantasm + *agora,* assembly.] **—phan·tas'ma·gor'ic** (-gôr'ĭk, -gŏr'-), **phan·tas'ma·gor'i·cal** *adj.*

phan·tom (făn'təm) *n.* **1.** Something apparently seen, heard, or sensed, but having no physical reality; ghost; specter. **2.** An image that appears only in the mind. *—adj.* Unreal; ghostlike. [ME *fantom* < OFr. *fantosme* < Lat. *phantasma.* —see PHANTASM.]

Phar·aoh also **phar·aoh** (fâr'ō, fā'rō) *n.* **1.** A king of ancient Egypt. **2.** A tyrant. [LLat. *Pharao* < Gk. *Pharaō* < Heb. *Par'ōh,* of Egyptian orig.] **—Phar'a·on'ic** (fâr'ā-ŏn'ĭk) *adj.*

pharaoh ant *n.* A very small, reddish ant, *Monomorium pharaonis,* that infests human dwellings.

phar·i·sa·ic (făr'ĭ-sā'ĭk) also **phar·i·sa·i·cal** (-sā'ĭ-kəl) *adj.* **1. Pharisaic** also **Pharisaical.** Of, relating to, or characteristic of the Pharisees. **2.** Hypocritically self-righteous and condemnatory. **—phar'i·sa'i·cal·ly** *adv.*

phar·i·sa·ism (făr'ĭ-sā-ĭz'əm) also **phar·i·see·ism** (-sē-ĭz'əm) *n.* **1. Pharisaism** also **Phariseeism.** The doctrines and practices of the Pharisees. **2.** Hypocritical observance of the letter of religious or moral law without regard for the spirit; sanctimoniousness.

phar·i·see (făr'ĭ-sē) *n.* **1. Pharisee.** A member of an ancient Jewish sect that emphasized strict interpretation and observance of the Mosaic law in both its oral and written form. **2.** A hypocritically self-righteous person. [ME *pharise* < OE *farise* < LLat. *pharisaeus* < Gk. *pharisaios* < Aram. *perīshayyā.*]

phar·i·see·ism (făr'ĭ-sē-ĭz'əm) *n.* Variant of **pharisaism.**

phar·ma·ceu·ti·cal (fär'mə-sōō'tĭ-kəl) also **phar·ma·ceu·tic** (-tĭk) *—adj.* Of or pertaining to pharmacy or pharmacists. *—n.* A pharmaceutical product or preparation. [< LLat. *pharmaceuticus* < Gk. *pharmakeutikos* < *pharmakeuein,* to administer drugs < *pharmakon,* drug.] **—phar'ma·ceu'ti·cal·ly** *adv.*

phar·ma·ceu·tics (fär'mə-sōō'tĭks) *n. (used with a sing. verb).* The science of preparing and dispensing drugs.

phar·ma·cist (fär'mə-sĭst) *n.* A person trained in pharmacy; druggist.

pharmaco– *pref.* Drug; medicine: *pharmacognosy.* [< Gk. *pharmakon,* drug, poison.]

phar·ma·co·dy·nam·ics (fär'mə-kō'dī-năm'ĭks) *n. (used with a sing. verb).* The study of drug action on living organisms. **—phar'ma·co'dy·nam'ic** *adj.* **—phar'ma·co'dy·nam'i·cal·ly** *adv.*

phar·ma·co·ge·net·ics (fär'mə-kō-jə-nĕt'ĭks) *n. (used with a sing. verb).* The study of hereditary influences to drug response. **—phar'ma·co·ge·net'ic** *adj.*

phar·ma·cog·no·sy (fär'mə-kŏg'nə-sē) *n.* The branch of pharmacology dealing with crude natural drugs. [PHARMACO- + Gk. *gnōsis,* knowledge.] **—phar'ma·cog'no·sist** *n.* **—phar'ma·cog·nos'tic** (-kŏg-nŏs'tĭk) *adj.*

phar·ma·co·ki·net·ics (fär'mə-kō-kĭ-nĕt'ĭks) *n. (used with a sing. verb).* The study of the absorption, metabolism, and action of drugs. **—phar'ma·co·ki·net'ic** *adj.*

phar·ma·col·o·gy (fär'mə-kŏl'ə-jē) *n.* The science of drugs, including their composition, uses, and effects. **—phar'ma·co·log'ic** (-kə-lŏj'ĭk), **phar'ma·co·log'i·cal** *adj.* **—phar'ma·co·log'i·cal·ly** *adv.* **—phar'ma·col'o·gist** *n.*

phar·ma·co·poe·ia (fär'mə-kə-pē'ə) *n., pl.* **-ias. 1.** A book containing an official list of medicinal drugs together with articles on their preparation and use. **2.** A collection or stock of drugs. [Gk. *pharmakopoiia,* preparation of drugs < *pharmakopoios,* preparing drugs : *pharmakon,* drug + *poiein,* to make.] **—phar'ma·co·poe'ial** (-pē'əl) *adj.* **—phar'ma·co·poe'ist** (-pē'ĭst) *n.*

phar·ma·cy (fär'mə-sē) *n., pl.* **-cies. 1.** The art of preparing and dispensing drugs. **2.** A place where drugs are sold; drugstore. [ME *farmacie* < OFr. < LLat. *pharmacia* < Gk. *pharmakeia* < *pharmakon,* drug.]

pha·ros (fâr'ŏs') *n.* A lighthouse. [Lat. < Gk., after *Pharos,* an island in the bay of Alexandria, Egypt, and the site of a famous ancient lighthouse.]

pharyng– *pref.* Variant of **pharyngo-.**

pha·ryn·ge·al (fə-rĭn'jē-əl, -jəl, făr'ĭn-jē'əl) also **pha·ryn·gal** (fə-rĭng'gəl) *—adj.* Of, pertaining to, located in, or coming from the pharynx: *pharyngeal speech sounds.* *—n.* A speech sound produced in the pharynx. [< NLat. *pharyngeus* < *pharynx,* pharynx.]

pha·ryn·ges (fə-rĭn'jēz) *n.* A plural of **pharynx.**

phar·yn·gi·tis (făr'ĭn-jī'tĭs) *n.* Inflammation of the pharynx.

pharyngo– or **pharyng–** *pref.* Pharynx: *pharyngoscope.* [NLat. < Gk. *pharungo-* < *pharunx,* throat.]

phar·yn·gol·o·gy (făr'ĭn-gŏl'ə-jē) *n.* The medical study of the pharynx and its diseases.

pha·ryn·go·scope (fə-rĭng'gə-skōp') *n.* An instrument used in examining the pharynx. **—phar'yn·gos'co·py** (făr'ĭn-gŏs'kə-pē) *n.*

phar·yn·got·o·my (făr'ĭn-gŏt'ə-mē) *n., pl.* **-mies.** A surgical incision of the pharynx.

phar·ynx (făr'ĭngks) *n., pl.* **pha·ryn·ges** (fə-rĭn'jēz) or **phar·ynx·es.** The section of the digestive tract that extends from the nasal cavities to the larynx, there becoming continuous with the esophagus. [NLat. *pharynx, pharyng-* < Gk. *pharunx,* throat.]

phase (fāz) *n.* **1.** A distinct stage of development: *"The American occupation of Japan fell into three successive phases"* (Edwin Reischauer). **2.** A temporary manner, attitude, or pattern of behavior: *a passing phase.* **3.** An aspect; part: *every phase of the operation.* **4.** *Astron.* One of the cyclically recurring apparent forms of the moon or a planet. **5.** *Physics.* **a.** A particular stage in a periodic process or phenomenon. **b.** The fraction of a complete cycle elapsed as measured from a specified reference point and often expressed as an angle. **6.** *Chem.* A discrete homogeneous part of a material system that is mechanically separable from the rest, as is ice from water. **7.** *Biol.* A characteristic form or appearance that occurs in a cycle or that distinguishes some individuals of a group. *—tr.v.* **phased, phas·ing, phas·es.** To plan or carry out systematically by phases. *—phrasal verbs.* **phase in.** To introduce, one stage at a time. **phase**

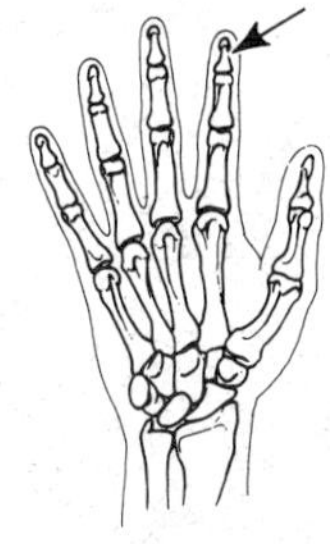

phalanx
Phalanges of the hand

George Miksch Sutton
phalarope

Pharaoh
3rd-millennium B.C.
Egyptian sculpture

out. To eliminate, one stage at a time. —*idioms.* **in phase.** In a correlated or synchronized way. **out of phase.** In an unsynchronized or uncorrelated way. [NLat. *phasis,* phase of the moon < Gk. < *phainein,* to show.] —**pha'sic** (fā'zĭk) *adj.*

Synonyms: *phase, aspect, facet, angle, side, stage.* These terms refer to various particular or possible views or levels of a process, consideration, or object. The visual astronomical meaning of *phase* has more and more given way to a sequential one, though the word still connotes change in an object itself rather than in viewpoint. A *phase,* in scientific or organizational usage, is often a stage or period of development. In everyday life, it refers to a temporary attitude or manner: *going through a new phase.* An *aspect* is a single area of interest from a chosen vantage point, usually as a matter for study, judgment, or emotional reaction: *a neglected aspect of medicine.* A *facet* is in this context usually one of several theoretical or practical aspects of a situation or problem: *the unexpected facets of a new concept; many facets of the welfare state. Angle* more informally expresses a deliberate limitation of perspective, with emphasis on the observer's own view of the object under consideration: *a loser from any angle. Side* is used in discussion and argumentation of an issue over which opinion has been divided into two contradictory points of view: *You've got to look at this side of it. Stage* is similar to *phase* and always denotes a point or interval of time, change, or achievement.

phase contrast microscope also **phase microscope** *n.* A microscope that renders differences in the phase of light transmitted or reflected by a specimen as variations in contrast.

phase modulation *n.* Variation of the phase of a carrier wave by an amount proportional to the amplitude of a modulating signal.

phase·out (fāz'out') *n.* A cessation of operations or production by gradually slowing down through phases.

phase rule *n.* A rule stating that the number of degrees of freedom in a material system at equilibrium is equal to the number of components minus the number of phases plus the constant 2. For example, the system of water vapor, water, and ice has zero degrees of freedom, since three phases of one component coexist.

-phasia *suff.* A speech disorder of a specified kind: *aphasia.* [NLat. < Gk., speech < *phasis,* utterance < *phanai,* to say, speak.]

pheasant

pheas·ant (fĕz'ənt) *n., pl.* **pheas·ants** or **pheasant. 1.** Any of various birds of the family Phasianidae, native to the Old World, characteristically having long tails and, in the males of many species, brilliantly colored plumage. **2.** A ruffed grouse. [ME *fesant* < OFr. *fesan* < Lat. *phasianus* < Gk. *phasianos (ornis),* (bird) of the Phasis River < *Phasis,* the Phasis River in the Caucasus.]

phel·lem (fĕl'əm, -ĕm') *n.* Cork (sense 4). [< Gk. *phellos,* cork.]

phel·lo·derm (fĕl'ə-dûrm') *n.* The soft, green cortex tissue that forms on the inner side of the phellogen of some trees. [Gk. *phellos,* cork + -DERM.] —**phel'lo·der'mal** *adj.*

phel·lo·gen (fĕl'ə-jən) *n.* A tissue in woody plants, from which cork and phelloderm develop. [Gk. *phellos,* cork + -GEN.] —**phel'lo·ge·net'ic** (-jə-nĕt'ĭk), **phel'lo·gen'ic** *adj.*

phen- *pref.* Variant of **pheno-**.

phe·na·caine (fē'nə-kān', fĕn'ə-) *n.* A white crystalline compound, $C_{18}H_{22}N_2O_2$, used in the form of its hydrochloride as a local anesthetic. [Alteration of PHENO- + -CAINE.]

phe·nac·e·tin (fə-năs'ĭ-tĭn) also **phe·nac·e·tine** (-tēn') *n.* Acetophenetidin.

phen·a·cite (fĕn'ə-sīt') *n.* A natural beryllium silicate, Be_2SiO_4, occurring as vitreous crystals sometimes used as gems. [< Gk. *phenax, phenak-,* imposter.]

phe·nan·threne (fə-năn'thrēn') *n.* A colorless crystalline compound, $C_{14}H_{10}$, obtained by fractional distillation of coal-tar oils and used in dyes, drugs, and explosives. [PHEN(O)- + ANTHR(AC)ENE.]

phen·ar·sa·zine chloride (fə-när'sə-zēn') *n.* A highly poisonous yellow crystalline compound, $C_{12}H_9AsClN$, used as a poison gas and sometimes with tear gas. [PHEN(O)- + AR-S(ENIC) + AZINE.]

phen·a·zine (fĕn'ə-zēn') also **phen·a·zin** (-zĭn) *n.* A yellow crystalline compound, $C_6H_4N_2C_6H_4$, used in the manufacture of dyes.

phen·cy·cli·dine (fĕn-sī'klĭ-dēn', -dĭn, -sĭk'lĭ-) *n.* A drug, $C_{17}H_{25}N$, used in veterinary medicine as an anesthetic and illegally as a hallucinogen. [PHEN(O)- + CYCL(O)- + -ID(E) + -INE.]

phe·nix (fē'nĭks) *n.* Variant of **phoenix.**

pheno- or **phen-** *pref.* **1.** Showing; displaying: *phenocryst.* **2. a.** Related to or derived from benzene: *phenol.* **b.** Containing phenyl: *phenothiazine.* [< Gk. *phainein,* to show.]

Phe·no·bar·bi·tal (fē'nō-bär'bĭ-tôl'). A trademark for a crystalline compound, $C_{12}H_{12}N_2O_3$, used in medicine as a sedative and hypnotic.

phe·no·cop·y (fē'nə-kŏp'ē) *n., pl.* **-ies.** An environmentally induced phenotypic variation that closely resembles a genetically determined character. [PHENO(TYPE) + COPY.]

phe·no·cryst (fē'nə-krĭst') *n.* A conspicuous, usually large, crystal embedded in porphyritic igneous rock. [PHENO- + CRYST(AL).] —**phe'no·crys'tic** *adj.*

phe·nol (fē'nōl', -nôl') *n.* **1.** A caustic, poisonous, white, crystalline compound, C_6H_5OH, derived from benzene and used in various resins, plastics, disinfectants, and pharmaceuticals. **2.** Any of a class of aromatic organic compounds having at least one hydroxyl group attached directly to the benzene ring.

phe·no·lic (fĭ-nō'lĭk, -nŏl'ĭk) *adj.* Of, pertaining to, containing, or derived from phenol.

phenolic resin *n.* Any of various synthetic thermosetting resins, obtained by the reaction of phenols with simple aldehydes and used to make molded products and as coatings and adhesives.

phe·nol·o·gy (fĭ-nŏl'ə-jē) *n.* The study of periodic biological phenomena, such as flowering, breeding, and migration, esp. as related to climate. [PHENO(MENON) + -LOGY.] —**phe'no·log'i·cal** (fē'nə-lŏj'ĭ-kəl) *adj.* —**phe·nol'o·gist** *n.*

phe·nol·phthal·ein (fē'nōl-thăl'ēn', -thăl'ē-ĭn, -thā'lēn', -thā'lē-ĭn) *n.* A pale-yellow crystalline powder, $(C_6H_4OH)_2C_2O_2C_6H_4$, used as an acid-base indicator, in making dyes, and as a cathartic.

phe·nom·e·nal (fĭ-nŏm'ə-nəl) *adj.* **1.** Of, pertaining to, or constituting a phenomenon or phenomena. **2.** Extraordinary; outstanding; remarkable: *a phenomenal feat of memory.* **3.** *Philos.* Known or derived through the senses, rather than through the mind. —**phe·nom'e·nal·ly** *adv.*

phe·nom·e·nal·ism (fĭ-nŏm'ə-nə-lĭz'əm) *n. Philos.* The doctrine, set forth by Hume and his successors, that percepts and concepts actually present in the mind constitute the sole object of knowledge, the objects of perception themselves, their origin outside the mind, or the nature of the mind itself remaining forever beyond inquiry. —**phe·nom'e·nal·ist** *n.* —**phe·nom'e·nal·is'tic** *adj.* —**phe·nom'e·nal·is'ti·cal·ly** *adv.*

phe·nom·e·nol·o·gy (fĭ-nŏm'ə-nŏl'ə-jē) *n.* **1.** The study of all possible appearances in human experience, during which considerations of objective reality and of purely subjective response are temporarily left out of account. **2.** A philosophical movement based on phenomenology, originated about 1905 by Edmund Husserl (1859–1938, German philosopher). —**phe·nom'e·no·log'i·cal** (-nə-lŏj'ĭ-kəl) *adj.* —**phe·nom'e·no·log'i·cal·ly** *adv.* —**phe·nom'e·nol'o·gist** *n.*

phe·nom·e·non (fĭ-nŏm'ə-nŏn', -nən) *n., pl.* **-na** (-nə) or **-nons. 1.** *pl.* **phenomena.** An occurrence or fact that is directly perceptible by the senses. **2.** *pl.* **phenomenons. a.** An unusual, significant, or unaccountable fact or occurrence; marvel. **b.** A person outstanding for an extreme quality or achievement; paragon: *a man who was a phenomenon of respectability.* **3.** *pl.* **phenomena.** *Philos.* That which appears real to the senses, regardless of whether its underlying existence is proved or its nature understood. **4.** *pl.* **phenomena.** *Physics.* An observable event. [LLat. *phaenomenon* < Gk. *phainomenon* < *phainomenos,* pr.part. of *phainesthai,* to appear < *phainein,* to show.]

Usage: *Phenomenon* is the only singular form of this noun; *phenomena* is the usual plural. *Phenomenons* may also be used as the plural in nonscientific writing when the meaning is "extraordinary things or occurrences" or "prodigies": *They were phenomenons in the history of music.*

phe·no·thi·a·zine (fē'nō-thī'ə-zēn') *n.* A greenish organic compound, $C_{12}H_9NS$, used in insecticides, livestock anthelmintics, and dyes.

phe·no·type (fē'nə-tīp') *n.* **1.** The environmentally and genetically determined observable appearance of an organism, esp. as considered with respect to all possible genetically influenced expressions of one specific character. **2.** An individual or group of organisms exhibiting a particular phenotype. [G. *Phänotypus* : Gk. *phainein,* to show + Gk. *typos,* type.] —**phe'no·typ'ic** (-tĭp'ĭk), **phe'no·typ'i·cal** *adj.* —**phe'no·typ'i·cal·ly** *adv.*

phe·nox·ide (fĭ-nŏk'sīd') *n.* A salt of carbolic acid.

phen·yl (fĕn'əl, fē'nəl) *n.* The organic radical C_6H_5, derived from benzene by the removal of one hydrogen atom. —**phe·nyl'ic** (fĭ-nĭl'ĭk) *adj.*

phen·yl·al·a·nine (fĕn'əl-ăl'ə-nēn', fē'nəl-) *n.* A natural amino acid, $C_6H_5CH_2CH(NH_2)COOH$, that occurs as a constituent of many proteins and is extracted for use as a dietary supplement.

phen·yl·bu·ta·zone (fĕn'əl-byōō'tə-zōn') *n.* A white compound, $C_{19}H_{20}N_2O_2$, used medically as an anti-inflammatory and analgesic drug in the treatment of arthritis.

phen·yl·ene (fĕn'ə-lēn', fē'nə-) *n.* An organic radical, C_6H_4, derived from benzene by removal of two hydrogen atoms.

phen·yl·ke·to·nur·i·a (fĕn'əl-kĕt'n-ŏŏr'ē-ə, -yŏŏr'-, fē'nəl-) *n.* A hereditary disorder of phenylalanine metabolism characterized by brain damage and mental retardation due to accumulation of toxic metabolic products.

pher·o·mone (fĕr'ə-mōn') *n.* Any of various chemical substances secreted by an animal that influence specific patterns of behavior by other members of the same species. [Gk. *pherein,* to carry + (HOR)MONE.]

phew (fyōō) *interj.* Used to express relief, fatigue, surprise, or disgust.

phi (fī) *n.* The 21st letter of the Greek alphabet. See table at **alphabet.** [Med. Gk. < Gk. *phei.*]

phi·al (fī′əl) *n.* A vial. [ME *fiol* < OFr. *fiole* < Lat. *phiala,* shallow vessel < Gk. *phialē.*]

Phi Be·ta Kap·pa (fī′ bā′tə kăp′ə) *n.* **1.** An honorary fraternity (founded in 1776) of college students and graduates whose members are chosen on the basis of high academic standing. **2.** A member of Phi Beta Kappa. [< the initials of the society's Gk. motto *philosophia biou kubernētēs,* philosophy the guide of life.]

phil– *pref.* Variant of **philo-**.

–phil *suff.* Variant of **-phile**.

Phil·a·del·phi·a lawyer (fĭl′ə-dĕl′fē-ə) *n.* A shrewd lawyer adept at the discovery and manipulation of legal technicalities. [After *Philadelphia,* Pennsylvania.]

Philadelphia pepper pot *n.* Pepper pot (sense 1).

phi·lan·der (fĭ-lăn′dər) *intr.v.* **-dered, -der·ing, -ders.** To engage in love affairs frivolously or casually. [< obs. *philander,* lover < Gk. *philandros,* loving men : *philos,* loving + *anēr,* man.] **—phi·lan′der·er** *n.*

phi·lan·thro·py (fĭ-lăn′thrə-pē) *n., pl.* **-pies. 1.** The effort or inclination to increase the well-being of mankind, as by charitable aid or donations. **2.** Love of mankind in general. **3.** An action or institution designed to promote human welfare. [LLat. *philanthropia* < Gk. *philanthrōpia* < *philanthrōpos,* loving mankind : *philos,* loving + *anthrōpos,* mankind.] **—phil′an·throp′ic** (fĭl′ən-thrŏp′ĭk), **phil′an·throp′i·cal** *adj.* **—phi·lan′thro·pist** *n.*

phi·lat·e·ly (fĭ-lăt′l-ē) *n.* The collection and study of postage stamps, postmarks, and related materials; stamp collecting. [Fr. *philatélie* : Gk. *philos,* loving + Gk. *ateleia,* exemption from payment (*a-,* without + *telos,* charge).] **—phil′a·tel′ic** (fĭl′ə-tĕl′ĭk), **phil′a·tel′i·cal** *adj.* **—phil′a·tel′i·cal·ly** *adv.* **—phi·lat′e·list** *n.*

–phile or **–phil** *suff.* **1.** One that loves or has a strong affinity or preference for: *audiophile.* **2.** Loving; having a strong affinity or preference for: *Francophile.* [Partly < Fr. *-phile,* and partly < NLat. *-philus* (< Lat.), both < Gk. *-philos* < *philos,* beloved, dear.]

Phi·le·mon (fĭ-lē′mən, fī-) *n.* See table at **Bible**.

phil·har·mon·ic (fĭl′här-mŏn′ĭk, fĭl′ər-) *adj.* **1.** Devoted to or appreciative of music. **2.** Pertaining to a symphony orchestra. *—n.* Also **Philharmonic**. A symphony orchestra or the group that supports it. [Fr. *philharmonique* < Ital. *filarmonico* : Gk. *philos,* loving + *armonico,* harmonic < Lat. *harmonicus.* —see HARMONIC.]

phil·hel·lene (fĭl-hĕl′ēn′) also **phil·hel·len·ist** (fĭl-hĕl′ə-nĭst) *n.* One who admires Greece or the Greeks. [Gk. *philellēn* : *philos,* loving + *Hellēn,* a Greek.] **—phil′hel·len′ic** (fĭl′hĕ-lĕn′ĭk) *adj.* **—phil·hel′len·ism** *n.*

–philia *suff.* **1.** Tendency towards: *hemophilia.* **2.** Abnormal attraction to: *necrophilia.* [NLat. < Gk. *philia,* friendship < *philos,* loving.]

–philiac *suff.* **1.** One that has a tendency toward: *hemophiliac.* **2.** One that has an abnormal attraction to: *coprophiliac.* [NLat. *-philia,* -philia + Gk. *-akos,* adj. suffix.]

–philic *suff.* -philous.

Phi·lip·pi·ans (fĭ-lĭp′ē-ənz) *n.* See table at **Bible**.

Phi·lip·pic (fĭ-lĭp′ĭk) *n.* **1.** Any of the orations of Demosthenes against Philip of Macedonia in the 4th century B.C. **2.** Any of the orations of Cicero against Antony in 44 B.C. **3. philippic.** A verbal denunciation characterized by invective.

Phil·ip·pine mahogany (fĭl′ə-pēn′) *n.* Any of various Philippine hardwood trees of the genus *Shorea* and related genera.

Phil·is·tine (fĭl′ĭ-stēn′, fĭ-lĭs′tĭn, -tēn′) *n.* **1.** One of the people of ancient Philistia. **2. a.** A smug, ignorant, esp. middle-class person who is held to be indifferent or antagonistic to artistic and cultural values. **b.** One who lacks knowledge in a specific area. *—adj.* Often **philistine**. Boorish; barbarous. [ME < LLat. *Philistini,* Philistines < LGk. *Philistinoi* < Heb. *pelishtīm* < *pelesheth,* Philistia.]

Phil·is·tin·ism also **phi·lis·tin·ism** (fĭl′ĭ-stē-nĭz′əm, fĭ-lĭs′tə-nĭz′əm, -tē-nĭz′əm) *n.* Smug conventionalism: *"the contrast between intellect and philistinism"* (Richard Hofstadter).

phil·lu·men·ist (fə-lo͞o′mə-nĭst) *n.* One who collects matchbooks or matchboxes. [PHIL(O)- + Lat. *lumen,* light + -IST.]

philo– or **phil–** *pref.* Having a strong affinity or preference for; loving: *philoprogenitive.* [NLat. < Gk. < *philos,* beloved, dear.]

phil·o·den·dron (fĭl′ə-dĕn′drən) *n., pl.* **-drons** or **-dra** (-drə). Any of various climbing tropical American plants of the genus *Philodendron,* many of which are cultivated as house plants. [NLat. *Philodendron,* genus name < Gk., neuter of *philodendros,* loving trees : *philos,* loving + *dendron,* tree.]

phi·lol·o·gy (fĭ-lŏl′ə-jē) *n.* **1.** Historical linguistics. **2.** Literary study or classical scholarship. [Fr. *philologie* < Lat. *philologia,* love of learning < Gk. < *philologos,* loving learning : *philos,* loving + *logos,* reason, speech.] **—phi·lol′o·ger, phi·lol′o·gist** *n.* **—phil′o·log′ic** (fĭl′ə-lŏj′ĭk), **phil′o·log′i·cal** *adj.* **—phil′o·log′i·cal·ly** *adv.*

phil·o·mel (fĭl′ə-mĕl′) *n.* A nightingale. [After PHILOMELA.]

Phil·o·me·la (fĭl′ə-mē′lə) *n. Gk. Myth.* A princess of Athens who, after being raped and having her tongue cut out by Tereus, was turned into either a swallow or a nightingale. [Lat. < Gk. *Philomelē.*]

phil·o·pro·gen·i·tive (fĭl′ō-prō-jĕn′ĭ-tĭv) *adj.* **1.** Producing many offspring; prolific. **2.** Loving one's own offspring or children in general. **3.** Of or pertaining to love of children. **—phil′o·pro·gen′i·tive·ly** *adv.* **—phil′o·pro·gen′i·tive·ness** *n.*

phi·lo·sophe (fē′lə-zôf′) *n.* Any of the leading philosophical, political, and social writers of the 18th-century French Enlightenment. [Fr. < OFr., philosopher.]

phi·los·o·pher (fĭ-lŏs′ə-fər) *n.* **1.** A student of or specialist in philosophy. **2.** A person who lives and thinks according to a particular philosophy. **3.** A person who is calm and rational under any circumstances. [ME < OFr. *philosophe* < Lat. *philosophus* < Gk. *philosophos,* loving wisdom, philosopher : *philos,* loving + *sophia,* wisdom.]

philosophers' stone also **philosopher's stone** *n.* A substance that was held to have the power of transmuting base metal into gold.

phil·o·soph·i·cal (fĭl′ə-sŏf′ĭ-kəl) also **phil·o·soph·ic** (-ĭk) *adj.* **1.** Of, pertaining to, or based on a system of philosophy. **2.** Characteristic of a philosopher, as in enlightenment and wisdom. **—phil′o·soph′i·cal·ly** *adv.*

phi·los·o·phize (fĭ-lŏs′ə-fīz′) *v.* **-phized, -phiz·ing, -phiz·es.** *—intr.* **1.** To speculate in a philosophical manner. **2.** To set forth or express a moralistic, often superficial philosophy. *—tr.* To consider (a matter) from a philosophical standpoint. **—phi·los′o·phiz′er** *n.*

phi·los·o·phy (fĭ-lŏs′ə-fē) *n., pl.* **-phies. 1. a.** Love and pursuit of wisdom by intellectual means and moral self-discipline. **b.** The investigation of causes and laws underlying reality. **c.** A system of philosophical inquiry or demonstration. **2.** Inquiry into the nature of things based on logical reasoning rather than empirical methods. **3.** The critique and analysis of fundamental beliefs as they come to be conceptualized and formulated. **4.** The synthesis of all learning. **5.** The investigation of natural phenomena and its systematization in theory and experiment, as in alchemy, astrology, or astronomy: *hermetic philosophy; natural philosophy.* **6.** All learning except technical precepts and practical arts. **7.** All the disciplines presented in university curriculums of science and the liberal arts, except medicine, law, and theology: *Doctor of Philosophy.* **8.** The science comprising logic, ethics, aesthetics, metaphysics, and epistemology. **9.** A system of motivating concepts or principles: *the philosophy of a culture.* **10.** A basic theory; viewpoint: *an original philosophy of advertising.* **11.** The system of values by which one lives: *his philosophy of life.* **12.** The calmness, equanimity, and detachment thought to befit a philosopher. [ME *philosophie* < OFr. < Lat. *philosophia* < Gk. < *philosophos,* loving wisdom, philosopher.]

–philous *suff.* Having a strong affinity or preference for; loving: *anemophilous.* [< Gk. *philos,* beloved, dear.]

phil·ter also **phil·tre** (fĭl′tər) *—n.* **1.** A love potion. **2.** A magic potion or charm. *—tr.v.* **-tered, -ter·ing, -ters** also **-tred, -tring, -tres.** To enchant with or as if with a philter. [Fr. *philtre* < OFr. < Lat. *philtrum* < Gk. *philtron* < *philein,* to love.]

phleb– *pref.* Variant of **phlebo-**.

phle·bi·tis (flĭ-bī′tĭs) *n.* Inflammation of a vein. **—phle·bit′ic** (-bĭt′ĭk) *adj.*

phlebo– or **phleb–** *pref.* Vein: *phlebology.* [Gk. < *phleps,* blood vessel.]

phle·bog·ra·phy (flĭ-bŏg′rə-fē) *n.* Roentgenography of a vein following injection of a radiopaque substance. **—phle′bo·gram′** (flē′bə-grăm′) *n.* **—phle′bo·graph′ic** *adj.*

phle·bol·o·gy (flĭ-bŏl′ə-jē) *n.* The medical study of the diseases and functioning of veins.

phle·bot·o·mize (flĭ-bŏt′ə-mīz′) *tr.v.* **-mized, -miz·ing, -miz·es.** To perform a phlebotomy on.

phle·bot·o·my (flĭ-bŏt′ə-mē) *n., pl.* **-mies.** The therapeutic practice of opening a vein to draw blood. [ME *flebotomie* < OFr. < LLat. *phlebotomia* < Gk. *phlebotomia* < *phlebotomos,* opening a vein : *phleps,* vein + *-tomos,* cutting < *temnein,* to cut.] **—phleb′o·tom′ic** (flĕb′ə-tŏm′ĭk), **phleb′o·tom′i·cal** *adj.* **—phle·bot′o·mist** *n.*

Phleg·e·thon (flĕg′ə-thŏn′) *n. Gk. Myth.* A river of fire, one of the six rivers of Hades. [Lat. < Gk. *Phlegethōn* < *phlegethein,* to blaze < *phlegein,* to burn.]

phlegm (flĕm) *n.* **1.** *Physiol.* Stringy, thick mucus secreted by the respiratory mucosa. **2.** One of the four humors of ancient physiology. **3.** Sluggishness of temperament. **4.** Calm self-possession; equanimity. [ME *fleume* < OFr. < LLat. *phlegma,* clammy humor of the body < Gk. *phlegma,* clammy humor of the body, heat < *phlegein,* to burn.] **—phlegm′y** (flĕm′ē) *adj.*

phleg·mat·ic (flĕg-măt′ĭk) also **phleg·mat·i·cal** (-ĭ-kəl) *adj.* **1.** Of or pertaining to phlegm; phlegmy. **2.** Having or suggesting a calm, sluggish temperament; unemotional. [ME *fleumatike* < OFr. *flaumatique* < LLat. *phlegmaticus,* full of phlegm < Gk. *phlegmatikos* < *phlegma,* clammy humor of the body, heat < *phlegein,* to burn.]

phlo·em (flō′ĕm′) *n.* The food-conducting tissue of vascular plants, consisting of sieve tubes and other cellular material. [G. < Gk. *phloios,* bark.]

phlo·gis·tic (flō-jĭs′tĭk) *adj.* **1.** Of or pertaining to phlogiston. **2.** *Med.* Of or pertaining to inflammation or fever.

phlo·gis·ton (flō-jĭs′tŏn′, -tən) *n.* A hypothetical substance formerly thought to be a volatile constituent of all combus-

philodendron

phlox

tible substances released as flame in combustion. [NLat. < Gk., neuter of *phlogistos,* inflammable < *phlogizein,* to set on fire < *phlox,* flame.]

phlog·o·pite (flŏg′ə-pīt′) *n.* A yellow to dark-brown mica, $KMg_3AlSi_3O_{10}(OH)_2$, used in insulation. [G. *Phlogopit* < Gk. *phlogōpos,* fiery-looking : *phlox,* flame + *ōps,* face.]

phlox (flŏks) *n., pl.* **phlox** or **phlox·es.** A plant of the genus *Phlox,* chiefly of North America, having lance-shaped leaves and clusters of white, red, or purple flowers. [NLat. *Phlox,* genus name < Lat. *phlox,* a kind of flower < Gk. wallflower, flame.]

phlyc·te·na also **phlyc·tae·na** (flĭk-tē′nə) *n., pl.* **-nae** (-nē). A small blister; vesicle. [Gk. *phluktaina* < *phluzein,* to boil over.]

-phobe *suff.* One that fears or is averse to a specified thing: *ailurophobe.* [< Gk. *-phobos,* fearing < *phobos,* fear.]

pho·bi·a (fō′bē-ə) *n.* **1.** A persistent, abnormal, or illogical fear of a specific thing or situation. **2.** A strong fear, dislike, or aversion. [NLat. < LLat. *-phobia,* -phobia.] **—pho′bic** (fō′bĭk) *adj.*

-phobia *suff.* An intense, abnormal, or illogical fear of a specified thing: *xenophobia.* [NLat. < LLat. < Gk. < *phobos,* fear.]

-phobic *suff.* **1.** Having a fear of or an aversion for: *xenophobic.* **2.** Lacking an affinity for: *lyophobic.* [Fr. *-phobique* < LLat. *-phobicus* < Gk. *-phobikos* < *-phobia,* -phobia.]

Pho·bos (fō′bŏs′, fŏb′ŏs′) *n.* The larger and inner of the two satellites of the planet Mars. [Gk. *phobos,* fear.]

-phobous *suff.* -phobic.

phoe·be (fē′bē) *n.* Any of several small dull-colored North American birds of the genus *Sayornis.* [Poss. alteration of PEWIT.]

Phoe·be (fē′bē) *n.* **1.** *Gk. Myth.* The goddess Artemis. **2.** The moon. **3.** *Astron.* The ninth satellite of Saturn. [Lat. < Gk. *Phoibē* < *phoibos,* shining.]

Phoe·bus (fē′bəs) *n.* **1.** *Gk. Myth.* Apollo, the god of the sun. **2.** The sun. [Lat. < Gk. *Phoibos* < *phoibos,* shining.]

Phoe·ni·cian (fĭ-nĭsh′ən, -nē′shən) *n.* **1.** A native, inhabitant, or subject of ancient Phoenicia. **2.** The Semitic language of ancient Phoenicia. [ME *Phenecien* < OFr. < Lat. *Phoenicius* < Gk. *phoinix,* Phoenician, phoenix.] **—Phoe·ni′cian** *adj.*

phoe·nix also **phe·nix** (fē′nĭks) *n.* **1.** A bird in Egyptian mythology that consumed itself by fire after 500 years, and rose renewed from its ashes. **2.** A person or thing of unsurpassed excellence or beauty; paragon. **3. Phoenix.** A constellation in the Southern Hemisphere near Tucana and Sculptor. [ME *fenix* < OFr. < Lat. *phoenix* < Gk. *phoinix.*] **—phoe′nix·like′** *adj.*

phon- *pref.* Variant of **phono-.**

pho·nate (fō′nāt′) *v.* **-nat·ed, -nat·ing, -nates.** *—intr.* To utter speech sounds; vocalize. *—tr.* To utter (a sound). **—pho·na′tion** *n.*

phone[1] (fōn) *n. Ling.* An individual speech sound. [Gk. *phōnē,* sound.]

phone[2] (fōn) *Informal. —n.* **1.** A telephone. **2.** An earphone. *—v.* **phoned, phon·ing, phones.** *—intr.* To telephone. *—tr.* **1.** To telephone (someone). **2.** To impart (information or news, for example) by telephone. [Short for TELEPHONE.]

-phone *suff.* **1.** Sound: *allophone.* **2.** Device that receives or emits sound: *geophone.* [< Gk. *phōnē,* sound, voice.]

pho·ne·mat·ic (fō′nĭ-măt′ĭk) *adj.* Phonemic.

pho·neme (fō′nēm′) *n. Ling.* One of the set of the smallest units of speech, as the *m* of *mat* and the *b* of *bat* in English, that distinguish one utterance or word from another in a given language. [Fr. *phonème* < Gk. *phōnēma,* utterance < *phōnein,* to speak.]

pho·ne·mic (fə-nē′mĭk, fō-) *adj.* **1.** Of or pertaining to phonemes. **2.** Of or pertaining to phonemics. **3.** Serving to distinguish phonemes or distinctive features. **—pho·ne′mi·cal·ly** *adv.*

pho·ne·mics (fə-nē′mĭks, fō-) *n. (used with a sing. verb). Ling.* The study and establishment of the phonemes of a language. **—pho·ne′mi·cist** (-mĭ-sĭst) *n.*

pho·net·ic (fə-nĕt′ĭk) *adj.* **1.** Of or pertaining to phonetics. **2.** Representing the sounds of speech with a set of distinct symbols, each denoting a single sound: *phonetic spelling.* [Gk. *phōnētikos* < *phōnein,* to speak.] **—pho·net′i·cal·ly** *adv.*

phonetic alphabet *n.* **1.** A standardized set of symbols used in phonetic transcription. **2.** Any of various systems of code words for identifying letters in voice communication.

pho·ne·ti·cian (fō′nĭ-tĭsh′ən) also **pho·net·i·cist** (fə-nĕt′ĭ-sĭst) *n.* An expert in phonetics.

pho·net·ics (fə-nĕt′ĭks) *n. (used with a sing. verb).* **1.** The branch of linguistics dealing with the study of the sounds of speech, their production, combination, description, and representation by written symbols. **2.** The system of sounds of a particular language.

pho·ney (fō′nē) *adj. & n.* Variant of **phony.**

-phonia *suff.* Speech disorder of a specified kind: *dysphonia.* [Gk. *-phōnia,* sound < *phōnē.*]

phon·ic (fŏn′ĭk) *adj.* Of, pertaining to, or having the nature of sound, esp. speech sounds. **—phon′i·cal·ly** *adv.*

phon·ics (fŏn′ĭks) *n. (used with a sing. verb).* **1.** The study or science of sound; acoustics. **2.** The use of elementary phonetics in the teaching of reading.

phono- or **phon-** *pref.* Sound; voice; speech: *phonology.* [< Gk. *phōnē,* sound, voice.]

pho·no·car·di·o·gram (fō′nə-kär′dē-ə-grăm′) *n.* A graphic record of heart sounds.

pho·no·car·di·o·graph (fō′nə-kär′dē-ə-grăf′) *n.* An instrument used in making phonocardiograms. **—pho′no·car′di·o·graph′ic** *adj.* **—pho′no·car′di·og′ra·phy** (-ŏg′rə-fē) *n.*

pho·no·gram (fō′nə-grăm′) *n.* A character or symbol, as in a phonetic alphabet, representing a word or phoneme in speech. **—pho′no·gram′ic, pho′no·gram′mic** *adj.* **—pho′no·gram′i·cal·ly, pho′no·gram′mi·cal·ly** *adv.*

pho·no·graph (fō′nə-grăf′) *n.* A machine that reproduces sound from a disc. **—pho′no·graph′ic** *adj.* **—pho′no·graph′i·cal·ly** *adv.*

pho·nog·ra·phy (fə-nŏg′rə-fē, fō-) *n.* **1.** The science or practice of transcribing speech by means of symbols representing elements of sound; phonetic transcription. **2.** A system of shorthand based on phonetic transcription. **—pho·nog′ra·pher, pho·nog′ra·phist** *n.*

pho·no·lite (fō′nə-līt′) *n. Mineral.* A volcanic rock composed principally of orthoclase and nepheline. [Fr. < G. *Phonolith* : Gk. *phōnē,* sound + Gk. *lithos,* stone.] **—pho′no·lit′ic** (fō′nə-lĭt′ĭk) *adj.*

pho·nol·o·gy (fə-nŏl′ə-jē, fō-) *n.* The science of speech sounds, including phonetics and phonemics. **—pho·no·log′ic** (fō′nə-lŏj′ĭk), **pho′no·log′i·cal** *adj.* **—pho′no·log′i·cal·ly** *adv.* **—pho·nol′o·gist** *n.*

pho·non (fō′nŏn′) *n. Physics.* The quantum of acoustic or vibrational energy, considered a discrete particle and used esp. in mathematical models to calculate thermal and vibrational properties of solids.

pho·no·re·cep·tion (fō′nō-rĭ-sĕp′shən) *n.* Perception of or response to sound waves. **—pho′no·re·cep′tor** (-tər) *n.*

pho·no·scope (fō′nə-skōp′) *n.* A device that produces a visible display of the mechanical properties of a sounding body, esp. of musical instruments.

pho·no·type (fō′nə-tīp′) *n.* **1.** A phonetic symbol used in printing. **2.** Text printed in phonetic symbols. **—pho′no·typ′ic** (fō′nə-tĭp′ĭk), **pho′no·typ′i·cal** *adj.* **—pho′no·typ′i·cal·ly** *adv.*

pho·no·typ·y (fō′nə-tī′pē) *n.* The practice of transcribing speech sounds by means of phonetic symbols. **—pho′no·typ′ist** *n.*

pho·ny also **pho·ney** (fō′nē) *Informal. —adj.* **-ni·er, -ni·est.** Not genuine or real; spurious; fake. *—n., pl.* **-nies** also **-neys. 1.** Something not genuine; a fake. **2.** A person who is an impostor; hypocrite. [Orig. unknown.] **—pho′ni·ly** *adv.* **—pho′ni·ness** *n.*

-phony *suff.* Sound: *telephony.* [Gk. *-phōnia* < *phōnē,* sound.]

phoo·ey (fo͞o′ē) *interj.* Used as an exclamation of disgust or contempt.

pho·rate (fôr′āt′, fōr′-) *n.* A toxic liquid, $C_7H_{17}O_2PS_3$, used as an insecticide. [(PHOS)PHOR(OUS) + (THION)ATE.]

-phore *suff.* Bearer; carrier: *chromatophore.* [< Gk. *-phoros,* bearing < *pherein,* to bear.]

-phoresis *suff.* Transmission: *electrophoresis.* [Gk. *phorēsis,* act of bearing < *phorein,* to carry, freq. of *pherein,* to bear.]

-phorous *suff.* Bearing: *gonophorous.* [Gk. *-phoros* < *pherein,* to bear.]

phos- *pref.* Light: *phosgene.* [< Gk. *phōs,* light.]

phos·gene (fŏs′jēn′, fŏz′-) *n.* A colorless volatile liquid or gas, $COCl_2$, used as a poison gas and in making glass, dyes, resins, and plastics.

phosph- *pref.* Variant of **phospho-.**

phos·pha·tase (fŏs′fə-tās′, -tāz′) *n.* Any of numerous enzymes that catalyze the hydrolysis of esters to phosphoric acid and are distinguished by activity in carbohydrate and nucleotide metabolism and in bone formation. [PHOSPHAT(E) + -ASE.]

phos·phate (fŏs′fāt′) *n.* **1.** *Chem.* A salt or ester of phosphoric acid containing mainly pentavalent phosphorus and oxygen. **2.** A fertilizer containing phosphorus compounds. **3.** A carbonated beverage of water, flavoring, and a small amount of phosphoric acid. [Fr. < *acide phosphorique,* phosphoric acid.] **—phos·phat′ic** (fŏs-făt′ĭk) *adj.*

phosphate rock *n.* Any of various sedimentary rocks composed largely of apatite, used as fertilizer and as a source of phosphorous compounds.

phos·pha·tide (fŏs′fə-tīd′) *n.* Any of a group of lipid compounds, such as lecithin and cephalin, composed mainly of glycerol and phosphoric acid, and found in great abundance in plant and animal tissues with stored fats. [PHOSPHAT(E) + -IDE.]

phos·pha·tize (fŏs′fə-tīz′) *tr.v.* **-tized, -tiz·ing, -tiz·es. 1.** To change into a phosphate or phosphates. **2.** To treat with phosphate or phosphoric acid. **—phos′pha·ti·za′tion** *n.*

phos·pha·tu·ri·a (fŏs′fə-to͝or′ē-ə, -tyo͝or′-) *n.* A condition in which excessive phosphates are discharged in the urine. [PHOSPHAT(E) + -URIA.] **—phos′pha·tu′ric** *adj.*

phos·phene (fŏs′fēn′) *n.* A luminous visual sensation experienced when the eyeball is pressed. [PHOS- + Gk. *phainein,* to show.]

phos·phide (fŏs′fīd′) also **phos·phid** (-fĭd) *n.* A compound of phosphorus and a more electropositive element.

phos·phine (fŏs′fēn′) also **phos·phin** (-fĭn) *n.* **1.** A colorless, spontaneously flammable poisonous gas, PH_3, having a garliclike odor and used as a doping agent for solid-state components. **2.** A synthetic yellow dye.

phos·phite (fŏs′fīt′) *n.* A salt of phosphorous acid.

phospho– or **phosph–** *pref.* **1.** Phosphorus: *phosphine.* **2.** Phosphate: *phospholipid.* [Fr. < *phosphore,* phosphorus < NLat. *phosphorus.*]

phos·pho·cre·a·tine (fŏs′fō-krē′ə-tēn′) also **phos·pho·cre·a·tin** (-tĭn) *n.* An organic compound, $C_4H_{10}N_3O_5$, capable of providing physiologic energy, as in muscular contraction.

phos·pho·lip·id (fŏs′fō-lĭp′ĭd) *n.* A phosphatide.

phos·pho·ni·um (fŏs-fō′nē-əm) *n.* A univalent radical, PH_4, derived from phosphine. [PHOSPH(O)- + (AMM)ONIUM.]

phos·pho·pro·tein (fŏs′fō-prō′tēn′, -prō′tē-ĭn) *n.* Any of a group of proteins, such as casein, containing chemically bound phosphoric acid.

phos·phor (fŏs′fər, -fôr′) *n.* **1.** A substance that can be stimulated to emit light by incident radiation. **2.** Something exhibiting phosphorescence. [Fr. *phosphore* < NLat. *phosphorus,* phosphorus. —see PHOSPHORUS.]

phosphor bronze *n.* A hard, strong, corrosion-resistant bronze containing up to 0.5 per cent phosphorus and used in electric switches, springs, and chains.

phos·pho·resce (fŏs′fə-rĕs′) *intr.v.* **-resced, -resc·ing, -resc·es.** To persist in emitting light, unaccompanied by sensible heat or combustion, after exposure to and removal of a source of radiation. [Prob. back-formation < PHOSPHORESCENCE.]

phos·pho·res·cence (fŏs′fə-rĕs′əns) *n.* **1.** Persistent emission of light following exposure to and removal of incident radiation. **2.** Organically generated light emission; bioluminescence: *"He saw the phosphorescence of the Gulf weed in the water"* (Hemingway). [< PHOSPHOR.] **—phos′pho·res′cent** *adj.* **—phos′pho·res′cent·ly** *adv.*

phos·phor·ic (fŏs-fôr′ĭk, -fŏr′-) *adj.* Of, pertaining to, or containing phosphorus, esp. in a valence state higher than that of a comparable phosphorous compound.

phosphoric acid *n.* A clear colorless liquid, H_3PO_4, used in fertilizers, soaps and detergents, food flavoring, pharmaceuticals, and animal feed.

phos·pho·rism (fŏs′fə-rĭz′əm) *n.* Chronic phosphorus poisoning from ingestion or inhalation. [PHOSPHOR(US) + -ISM.]

phos·pho·rite (fŏs′fə-rīt′) *n.* **1.** A fibrous variety of apatite. **2.** A concretionary mass of rock consisting predominantly of calcium phosphate. [PHOSPHOR(US) + -ITE.]

phos·pho·rous (fŏs′fər-əs, fŏs-fôr′əs, -fōr′-) *adj.* Of, pertaining to, or containing phosphorus, esp. with valence 3.

phosphorous acid *n.* A white or yellowish hygroscopic crystalline solid, H_3PO_3, used as a reducing agent and to produce phosphite salts.

phos·pho·rus (fŏs′fər-əs) *n.* **1.** *Symbol* **P** A highly reactive, poisonous, nonmetallic element occurring naturally in phosphates, esp. apatite, and existing in three allotropic forms, white (sometimes yellow), red, and black. It is an essential constituent of protoplasm and, depending on the allotropic form, is used in safety matches, pyrotechnics, incendiary shells, fertilizers, glass, and steel. Atomic number 15; atomic weight 30.9738; melting point (white) 44.1°C; boiling point 280°C; specific gravity (white) 1.82; valences 3, 5. **2.** A phosphorescent substance. [NLat. < Gk. *phōsphoros,* bringing light : *phōs,* light + *-phoros,* bearing < *pherein,* to bear.]

phos·pho·ryl·ase (fŏs′fər-ə-lās′, -lāz′) *n.* An enzyme that catalyzes the production of phosphates from glycogen. [PHOSPHOR(US) + -YL + -ASE.]

phos·pho·ryl·ate (fŏs′fər-ə-lāt′) *tr.v.* **-at·ed, -at·ing, -ates.** To change (an organic substance) into an organic phosphate. [PHOSPHOR(US) + -YL + -ATE.] **—phos′pho·ry·la′tion** *n.*

phot (fōt) *n. Physics.* A unit of illumination equal to one lumen per square centimeter. [Gk. *phōs, phōt-,* light.]

phot– *pref.* Variant of **photo-.**

pho·tic (fō′tĭk) *adj.* **1.** Of or pertaining to light. **2.** *Biol.* Pertaining to the production of light by organisms. **3.** Pertaining to or designating the upper zone or region of a body of water, into which sunlight penetrates.

pho·to (fō′tō) *Informal.* —*n., pl.* **-tos.** A photograph. —*tr. & intr.v.* **-toed, -to·ing, -tos.** To photograph.

photo– or **phot–** *pref.* **1.** Light; radiant energy: *photosynthesis.* **2.** Photographic: *photomontage.* **3.** Photoelectric: *photoemission.* [< Gk. *phōs, phōt-,* light.]

pho·to·ac·tive (fō′tō-ăk′tĭv) *adj.* **1.** Capable of responding to light photoelectrically. **2.** Capable of responding to light by chemical reaction. **—pho′to·ac·tiv′i·ty** *n.*

pho·to·au·to·tro·phic (fō′tō-ô′tə-trō′fĭk, -trŏf′ĭk) *adj.* Capable of using light as a source of energy in the synthesis of food from inorganic materials. **—pho′to·au′to·troph′** *n.*

pho·to·bi·ot·ic (fō′tō-bī-ŏt′ĭk) *adj. Biol.* Depending on light for the continuance of life and growth.

pho·to·cell (fō′tō-sĕl′) *n.* A photoelectric cell.

pho·to·chem·is·try (fō′tō-kĕm′ĭ-strē) *n.* The chemistry of the interactions of radiant energy and chemical systems. **—pho′to·chem′i·cal** *adj.* **—pho′to·chem′i·cal·ly** *adv.*

pho·to·co·ag·u·la·tion (fō′tō-kō-ăg′yə-lā′shən) *n.* The surgical coagulation of tissue by means of intense light energy, as a laser beam.

pho·to·com·pose (fō′tō-kəm-pōz′) *tr.v.* **-posed, -pos·ing, -pos·es.** To prepare (written matter) for printing by photocomposition. **—pho′to·com·pos′er** *n.*

pho·to·com·po·si·tion (fō′tō-kŏm′pə-zĭsh′ən) *n.* The preparation of manuscript for printing by the projection of images of type characters on photographic film, which is then used to make printing plates.

pho·to·con·duc·tiv·i·ty (fō′tō-kŏn′dŭk-tĭv′ĭ-tē) *n.* Electrical conductivity affected by illumination. **—pho′to·con·duc′tion** *n.* **—pho′to·con·duc′tive** *adj.*

pho·to·cop·i·er (fō′tə-kŏp′ē-ər) *n.* A device for photographically reproducing written, printed, or graphic material.

pho·to·cop·y (fō′tə-kŏp′ē) *tr.v.* **-cop·ied, -cop·y·ing, -cop·ies.** To make a photographic reproduction of (printed material). —*n., pl.* **-cop·ies.** A photographic reproduction.

pho·to·cur·rent (fō′tō-kûr′ənt) *n. Physics.* An electric current produced by illumination of a photoelectric material.

pho·to·de·com·po·si·tion (fō′tō-dē-kŏm′pə-zĭsh′ən) *n.* Chemical breakdown caused by radiant energy.

pho·to·dis·in·te·gra·tion (fō′tō-dĭs-ĭn′tĭ-grā′shən) *n.* Nuclear disintegration or transformation caused by absorption of high-energy radiation, as of gamma rays.

pho·to·dra·ma (fō′tə-drä′mə, -drăm′ə) *n.* A photoplay.

pho·to·du·pli·cate (fō′tō-dōō′plĭ-kāt′, -dyōō′-) *tr.v.* **-cat·ed, -cat·ing, -cates.** To photocopy. **—pho′to·du′pli·cate** (-kĭt) *n.* **—pho′to·du′pli·ca′tion** *n.*

pho·to·dy·nam·ic (fō′tō-dī-năm′ĭk) *adj.* Producing or increasing in organisms a toxic reaction to light.

pho·to·e·lec·tric (fō′tō-ĭ-lĕk′trĭk) also **pho·to·e·lec·tri·cal** (-trĭ-kəl) *adj.* Of or pertaining to electric effects, esp. increased electrical conduction, caused by illumination. **—pho′to·e·lec′tri·cal·ly** *adv.*

photoelectric cell *n.* An electronic device having an electrical output that varies in response to incident radiation, esp. to visible light.

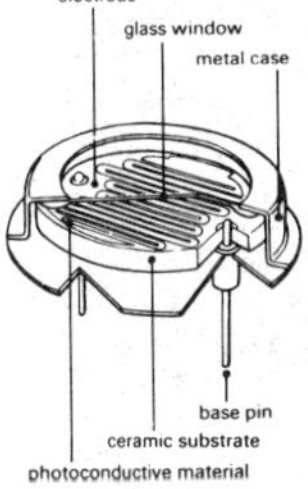

photoelectric cell

photoelectric effect *n. Physics.* The ejection of electrons from a substance by incident electromagnetic radiation, esp. by visible light.

pho·to·e·lec·tron (fō′tō-ĭ-lĕk′trŏn′) *n.* An electron released or ejected from a substance by the photoelectric effect.

pho·to·e·mis·sion (fō′tō-ĭ-mĭsh′ən) *n.* The emission of photoelectrons, esp. from metallic surfaces.

pho·to·en·grave (fō′tō-ĕn-grāv′) *tr.v.* **-graved, -grav·ing, -graves.** To reproduce by photoengraving. **—pho′to·en·grav′er** *n.*

pho·to·en·grav·ing (fō′tō-ĕn-grā′vĭng) *n.* **1.** The process of reproducing graphic material by transferring the image photomechanically to a plate or other surface in etched relief for printing. **2.** A plate prepared by photoengraving. **3.** A reproduction made by photoengraving.

pho·to-es·say (fō′tō-ĕs′ā′) *n.* A commentary dealing with a subject chiefly through photographs. **—pho′to-es′say·ist** *n.*

photo finish *n.* **1.** A race in which the leading contestants cross the finish line so close together that the winner must be determined by a photograph taken at the moment of crossing. **2.** *Informal.* An extremely close competition.

pho·to·flash (fō′tō-flăsh′) *n.* A flash bulb.

pho·to·flood (fō′tō-flŭd′) *n.* A reusable electric lamp that produces a bright continuous light for photographic illumination.

pho·to·fluor·o·gram (fō′tə-flŏŏr′ə-grăm′) *n.* A photograph made by photofluorography.

pho·to·fluor·og·ra·phy (fō′tō-flŏŏ-rŏg′rə-fē) *n. Med.* The photography of fluoroscopic images. **—pho′to·fluor·o·graph′ic** (-flŏŏr′ə-grăf′ĭk) *adj.*

pho·to·gel·a·tin process (fō′tō-jĕl′ə-tĭn) *n.* Collotype.

pho·to·gene (fō′tə-jēn′) *n. Physiol.* An afterimage.

pho·to·gen·ic (fō′tə-jĕn′ĭk) *adj.* **1.** Attractive as a subject for photography. **2.** *Biol.* Producing or emitting light; phosphorescent. **3.** Caused or produced by light. **—pho′to·gen′i·cal·ly** *adv.*

pho·to·gram (fō′tə-grăm′) *n.* **1.** A shadowy image produced without a camera by placing an object in contact with film or photosensitive paper and exposing it to light. **2.** A photograph.

pho·to·gram·me·try (fō′tə-grăm′ĭ-trē) *n.* **1.** The process of making maps or scale drawings by aerial or other photography. **2.** The process of making precise measurements by the use of photography. **—pho′to·gram·met′ric** (-grə-mĕt′rĭk) *adj.* **—pho′to·gram′me·trist** *n.*

pho·to·graph (fō′tə-grăf′) *n.* An image, esp. a positive print, recorded by a camera and reproduced on a photosensitive surface. —*v.* **-graphed, -graph·ing, -graphs.** —*tr.* To take a photograph of. —*intr.* **1.** To practice photography. **2.** To be the subject for photographs: *She photographs well.* **—pho·tog′ra·pher** *n.*

pho·to·graph·ic (fō′tə-grăf′ĭk) also **pho·to·graph·i·cal** (-ĭ-kəl) *adj.* **1.** Of, pertaining to, or consisting of photography or a photograph. **2.** Used in photography: *a photographic lens.* **3.** Resembling a photograph, esp. representing or simulating something with great accuracy and fidelity of detail. **4.** Capable of forming accurate and lasting impressions: *a photographic memory.* **—pho′to·graph′i·cal·ly** *adv.*

pho·tog·ra·phy (fə-tŏg′rə-fē) *n.* **1.** The process of rendering optical images on photosensitive surfaces. **2.** The art, practice, or occupation of taking and printing photographs. **3.** A body of photographs.

pho·to·gra·vure (fō'tə-grə-vyŏŏr') *n.* The process of printing from an intaglio plate, etched according to a photographic image.
pho·to·he·li·o·graph (fō'tō-hē'lē-ə-grăf') *n.* A telescope equipped to photograph the sun.
pho·to·jour·nal·ism (fō'tō-jûr'nə-lĭz'əm) *n.* Journalism making primary use of photographs. **—pho'to·jour'nal·ist** *n.* **—pho'to·jour'nal·is'tic** *adj.*
pho·to·ki·ne·sis (fō'tō-kĭ-nē'sĭs, -kī-) *n. Biol.* Movement as a response to light. **—pho'to·ki·net'ic** (-nĕt'ĭk) *adj.*
pho·to·lith·o·graph (fō'tō-lĭth'ə-grăf') *tr.v.* **-graphed, -graph·ing, -graphs.** To reproduce by means of photolithography. *—n.* A picture made by photolithography. **—pho'to·li·thog'ra·pher** (fō'tō-lĭ-thŏg'rə-fər) *n.*
pho·to·li·thog·ra·phy (fō'tō-lĭ-thŏg'rə-fē) *n.* A planographic printing process using plates made according to a photographic image. **—pho'to·lith'o·graph'ic** (-lĭth'ə-grăf'ĭk) *adj.*
pho·tol·y·sis (fō-tŏl'ĭ-sĭs) *n.* Chemical decomposition induced by light or other radiant energy. **—pho'to·lyt'ic** (fō'tə-lĭt'ĭk) *adj.* **—pho'to·lyt'i·cal·ly** *adv.*
pho·to·map (fō'tə-măp') *n.* A map made by superimposing orienting data on an aerial photograph. *—v.* **-mapped, -map·ping, -maps.** *—tr.* To make a photomap of. *—intr.* To make a photomap.
pho·to·me·chan·i·cal (fō'tō-mĭ-kăn'ĭ-kəl) *adj.* Of, pertaining to, or designating any of various methods by which plates are prepared for printing by means of photography. **—pho'to·me·chan'i·cal·ly** *adv.*
pho·tom·e·ter (fō-tŏm'ĭ-tər) *n.* An instrument for measuring a property of light, esp. luminous intensity or flux.
pho·tom·e·try (fō-tŏm'ĭ-trē) *n. Physics.* The measurement of the properties of light, esp. of luminous intensity. **—pho'to·met'ric** (fō'tə-mĕt'rĭk), **pho'to·met'ri·cal** *adj.* **—pho·tom'e·trist** *n.*
pho·to·mi·cro·graph (fō'tō-mī'krə-grăf') *n.* A photograph made through a microscope. *—tr.v.* **-graphed, -graph·ing, -graphs.** To make (a photograph) through a microscope. **—pho'to·mi·crog'ra·pher** (-mī-krŏg'rə-fər) *n.* **—pho'to·mi'cro·graph'ic** *adj.* **—pho'to·mi·crog'ra·phy** *n.*
pho·to·mi·cro·scope (fō'tō-mī'krə-skōp') *n.* An instrument used for making photomicrographs. **—pho'to·mi'cro·scop'ic** (-skŏp'ĭk) *adj.*
pho·to·mon·tage (fō'tō-mŏn-täzh', -môn-) *n.* **1.** The technique of making a picture by assembling pieces of photographs, often in combination with other types of graphic material. **2.** The composite picture produced by photomontage.
pho·ton (fō'tŏn') *n.* The quantum of electromagnetic energy, generally regarded as a discrete particle having zero mass, no electric charge, and an indefinitely long lifetime. **—pho·ton'ic** *adj.*
pho·to·nu·cle·ar (fō'tō-nōō'klē-ər, -nyōō'-) *adj. Physics.* Designating a nuclear reaction induced by photons.
pho·to-off·set (fō'tō-ôf'sĕt', -ŏf'-) *n.* Offset printing.
pho·to·pe·ri·od (fō'tō-pĭr'ē-əd) *n.* The relative exposure of an organism to daylight as a proportion of the total day, considered esp. with regard to the effect on growth and functioning. **—pho'to·pe'ri·od'ic** (-ŏd'ĭk), **pho'to·pe'ri·od'i·cal** *adj.* **—pho'to·pe'ri·od·ism** *n.*
pho·toph·i·lous (fō-tŏf'ə-ləs) also **pho·to·phil·ic** (fō'tə-fĭl'ĭk) *adj. Biol.* Growing or functioning best in strong light. **—pho·toph'i·ly** *n.*
pho·to·pho·bi·a (fō'tə-fō'bē-ə) *n.* Abnormal intolerance of light. **—pho'to·pho'bic** (-fō'bĭk) *adj.*
pho·to·phos·phor·y·la·tion (fō'tō-fŏs'fôr-ə-lā'shən, -fər-) *n.* Phosphorylation induced by radiant energy in photosynthesis.
pho·to·pi·a (fō-tō'pē-ə) *n.* Adaptation of the eyes to light; daylight vision. **—pho·to'pic** (-tō'pĭk, -tŏp'ĭk) *adj.*
pho·to·play (fō'tə-plā') *n.* A play filmed or arranged for filming as a motion picture.
pho·to·re·al·ism (fō'tō-rē'ə-lĭz'əm) *n.* A style of painting that resembles photography in its meticulous attention to detail. **—pho'to·re'al·ist** *n.*
pho·to·re·cep·tion (fō'tō-rĭ-sĕp'shən) *n.* The detection or perception of visible light; vision; sight. **—pho'to·re·cep'tive** *adj.*
pho·to·re·cep·tor (fō'tō-rĭ-sĕp'tər) *n.* A photoreceptive nerve.
pho·to·re·con·nais·sance (fō'tō-rĭ-kŏn'ə-səns, -zəns) *n.* Photographic aerial reconnaissance of military targets.
pho·to·res·pi·ra·tion (fō'tō-rĕs'pə-rā'shən) *n.* Oxidation of carbohydrates in plants with the release of carbon dioxide during photosynthesis.
pho·to·sen·si·tive (fō'tō-sĕn'sĭ-tĭv) *adj.* Sensitive to light. **—pho'to·sen'si·tiv'i·ty** *n.*
pho·to·sen·si·ti·za·tion (fō'tō-sĕn'sĭ-tĭ-zā'shən) *n.* **1.** The act or process of photosensitizing something. **2.** *Med.* Hypersensitivity of the skin to sunlight or ultraviolet radiation, caused by ingestion of endocrine products, fluorescent dyes, or small amounts of heavy metals, and resulting in skin eruptions.
pho·to·sen·si·tize (fō'tō-sĕn'sĭ-tīz') *tr.v.* **-tized, -tiz·ing, -tiz·es.** To make (an organism or substance) sensitive to light.
pho·to·set (fō'tō-sĕt') *tr.v.* **-set, -set·ting, -sets.** *Printing.* To photocompose. **—pho'to·set'ter** *n.*
pho·to·sphere (fō'tə-sfîr') *n.* The surface of a star, esp. of the sun. **—pho'to·spher'ic** (-sfîr'ĭk, -sfĕr'ĭk) *adj.*
Pho·to·stat (fō'tə-stăt'). A trademark for a device used to make quick, direct-reading negative or positive copies.
pho·to·syn·the·sis (fō'tō-sĭn'thĭ-sĭs) *n.* The process by which chlorophyll-containing cells in green plants convert incident light to chemical energy and synthesize organic compounds from inorganic compounds, esp. carbohydrates from carbon dioxide and water, with the simultaneous release of oxygen. **—pho'to·syn·thet'ic** (-sĭn-thĕt'ĭk) *adj.* **—pho'to·syn·thet'i·cal·ly** *adv.*
pho·to·syn·the·size (fō'tō-sĭn'thĭ-sīz') *v.* **-sized, -siz·ing, -siz·es.** *—tr.* To synthesize by the process of photosynthesis. *—intr.* To perform the process of photosynthesis.
pho·to·tax·is (fō'tō-tăk'sĭs) also **pho·to·tax·y** (fō'tō-tăk'sē) *n. Biol.* The movement of an organism in response to a source of light. **—pho'to·tac'tic** (-tăk'tĭk) *adj.*
pho·to·tel·e·graph (fō'tō-tĕl'ə-grăf') *tr.v.* **-graphed, -graph·ing, -graphs.** To transmit (printed or other graphic material) by facsimile. **—pho'to·tel'e·graph'ic, pho'to·tel'e·graph'i·cal** *adj.* **—pho'to·tel'e·graph'i·cal·ly** *adv.* **—pho'to·te·leg'ra·phy** (-tə-lĕg'rə-fē) *n.*
pho·to·ther·a·peu·tics (fō'tō-thĕr'ə-pyōō'tĭks) *n. (used with a sing. or pl. verb).* Phototherapy.
pho·to·ther·a·py (fō'tō-thĕr'ə-pē) *n.* The treatment of disease, esp. certain skin conditions, with light, including infrared and ultraviolet radiation.
pho·tot·o·nus (fō-tŏt'ə-nəs) *n. Biol.* Sensitivity to light. **—pho'to·ton'ic** (fō'tə-tŏn'ĭk) *adj.*
pho·to·tran·sis·tor (fō'tō-trăn-zĭs'tər, -sĭs'-) *n.* A transistor having highly photosensitive electrical characteristics.
pho·to·troph (fō'tə-trŏf') *n.* An organism that obtains metabolic energy through photosynthesis. [PHOTO- + Gk. *trophē,* food.]
pho·tot·ro·pism (fō-tŏt'rə-pĭz'əm) also **pho·tot·ro·py** (-pē) *n.* Growth or movement in response to a source of light. **—pho'to·tro'pic** (fō'tə-trō'pĭk, -trŏp'ĭk) *adj.* **—pho'to·tro'pi·cal·ly** *adv.*
pho·to·tube (fō'tō-tōōb', -tyōōb') *n.* An electron tube with a photosensitive cathode.
pho·to·type·set·ter (fō'tō-tīp'sĕt'ər) *n. Printing.* Any of various machines used in photocomposition.
pho·to·type·set·ting (fō'tō-tīp'sĕt'ĭng) *n. Printing.* Photocomposition.
pho·to·ty·pog·ra·phy (fō'tō-tī-pŏg'rə-fē) *n.* Photomechanical printing that resembles metal typography. **—pho'to·ty'po·graph'ic** (-tī'pə-grăf'ĭk), **pho'to·ty'po·graph'i·cal** *adj.* **—pho'to·ty'po·graph'i·cal·ly** *adv.*
pho·to·vol·ta·ic (fō'tō-vŏl-tā'ĭk, -vōl-) *adj.* Capable of producing a voltage when exposed to radiant energy, esp. light.
pho·to·zin·co·graph (fō'tō-zĭng'kə-grăf') *tr.v.* **-graphed, -graph·ing, -graphs.** To make (prints) by photozincography. *—n.* A print produced by photozincography.
pho·to·zin·cog·ra·phy (fō'tō-zĭng-kŏg'rə-fē) *n.* A photoengraving process in which sensitized zinc plates are used.
phrase (frāz) *n.* **1.** A sequence of words intended to have meaning. **2.** A brief, apt, and cogent expression, such as *behind the Iron Curtain.* **3.** A word or group of words read or spoken as a unit and separated by pauses or other junctures. **4.** *Gram.* Two or more words in sequence that form a syntactic unit or group of syntactic units, less completely predicated than a sentence. **5.** A series of dance movements forming a unit in a choreographic pattern. **6.** *Mus.* A segment of a composition, usually consisting of four or eight measures. *—v.* **phrased, phras·ing, phras·es.** *—tr.* **1.** To express orally or in writing: *He phrased several opinions.* **2.** To pace or mark off (something read aloud or spoken) by pauses. **3.** *Mus.* **a.** To divide (a passage) into phrases. **b.** To combine (notes) in a phrase. *—intr.* To make or render phrases. [Lat. *phrasis,* style of speech < Gk. < *phrazein,* to explain.] **—phras'al** *adj.* **—phras'al·ly** *adv.*
phrase book *n.* A book of idiomatic foreign language expressions and their translations.
phrase·maker (frāz'mā'kər) *n.* **1.** One who coins cogent phrases. **2.** One who makes superficially attractive but often inane and meaningless phrases.
phra·se·o·gram (frā'zē-ə-grăm') *n.* A symbol, such as one used in shorthand, that denotes a particular phrase.
phra·se·o·graph (frā'zē-ə-grăf') *n.* A phrase having a phraseogram. **—phra'se·o·graph'ic** *adj.*
phra·se·ol·o·gy (frā'zē-ŏl'ə-jē) *n., pl.* **-gies. 1.** The way in which words and phrases are used in speech or writing; style. **2.** A set of expressions used by a particular person or group: *nautical phraseology.* **—phra'se·o·log'i·cal** (frā'zē-ə-lŏj'ĭ-kəl) *adj.* **—phra'se·ol'o·gist** *n.*
phras·ing (frā'zĭng) *n.* **1.** The act of making phrases. **2.** The manner in which an expression is phrased; wording. **3.** *Mus.* The manner in which a phrase is rendered or interpreted.
phra·try (frā'trē) *n., pl.* **-tries. 1.** A kinship group constituting an intermediate division in the primitive structure of the Hellenic tribe or phyle, consisting of several patrilinear clans, and surviving in classical times as a territorial subdivision in the political and military organization of the Athenian state. **2.** *Anthropol.* An exogamous subdivision of the tribe, comprising two or more related clans. [Gk. *phratria* < *phratēr,* member of a phratry.] **—phra'tric** *adj.*

phre·at·ic (frē-ăt′ĭk) *adj.* Of or pertaining to ground water. [< Gk. *phrear,* well.]
phren– *pref.* Variant of **phreno-.**
phre·net·ic (frə-nĕt′ĭk) or **phre·net·i·cal** (-ĭ-kəl) *adj.* Variants of **frenetic.**
-phrenia *suff.* Mental disorder: *schizophrenia.* [< Gk. *phrēn,* mind.]
phren·ic (frĕn′ĭk, frē′nĭk) *adj.* **1.** Of or pertaining to the mind. **2.** *Anat.* Of or pertaining to the diaphragm: *the phrenic nerve.* [PHREN(O) + -IC.]
phre·ni·tis (frĭ-nī′tĭs) *n. Pathol.* **1.** Inflammation of the diaphragm. **2.** Frenzy; delirium. **—phre·nit′ic** (-nĭt′ĭk) *adj.*
phreno– or **phren–** *pref.* **1.** Mind: *phrenology.* **2.** Diaphragm: *phrenitis.* [< Gk. *phrēn,* diaphragm, mind.]
phre·nol·o·gy (frĭ-nŏl′ə-jē) *n.* The study of the conformation of the skull based on a belief that it is indicative of character and mental capacity. **—phren′o·log′ic** (frĕn′ə-lŏj′ĭk, frē′nə-), **phren′o·log′i·cal** *adj.* **—phre·nol′o·gist** *n.*
phren·sy (frĕn′zē) *n. & v.* Variant of **frenzy.**
Phryg·i·an (frĭj′ē-ən) *adj.* Of or pertaining to Phrygia or its people, language, and culture. *—n.* **1.** A native or inhabitant of Phrygia. **2.** The Indo-European language of the Phrygians.
Phrygian cap *n.* A soft cap with a forward-curving peak, represented in ancient Greek art as part of the attire worn by Phrygians.
phthal·ein also **phthal·eine** (thăl′ēn′, thăl′ē-ĭn, thā′lēn′, thā′lē-ĭn) *n.* Any of a group of chemical compounds formed by a combination of phthalic anhydride with a phenol, from which certain synthetic dyes are derived. [PHTHAL(IC) + -EIN.]
phthal·ic (thăl′ĭk, thā′lĭk) *adj.* **1.** Of, pertaining to, or derived from naphthalene. **2.** Pertaining to phthalic acid. [Short for *naphthalic* : NAPHTH(A) + AL(COHOL) + -IC.]
phthalic acid *n.* A colorless, crystalline organic acid, $C_6H_4(COOH)_2$, prepared from naphthalene and used in the synthesis of dyes, perfumes, and other organic compounds.
phthalic anhydride *n.* A white, crystalline compound, $C_6H_4(CO)_2O$, prepared by oxidizing naphthalene and used in the manufacture of phthaleins and other dyes, resins, plasticizers, and insecticides.
phthal·in (thăl′ĭn, thā′lĭn) *n.* Any of various colorless compounds derived from the reduction of phthaleins.
phthal·o·cy·a·nine (thăl′ō-sī′ə-nēn′, thā′lō-) *n.* Any of several stable, light-fast, blue or green organic pigments derived from the basic compound $(C_6H_4C_2N)_4N_4$, and used in enamels, printing inks, linoleum, and plastics. [PHTHAL(IC) + CYANINE.]
phthi·ri·a·sis (thĭ-rī′ə-sĭs, thī-) *n.* Infestation with lice; pediculosis. [Lat. < Gk. *phtheiriasis* : *phtheir,* louse + *-iasis,* -iasis.]
phthis·ic (tĭz′ĭk) *n.* **1.** Variant of **phthisis. 2.** *Archaic.* Asthma. [ME *ptisike* < OFr. *tisique* < Lat. *phthisicus,* consumptive < Gk. *phthisikos* < *phthisis,* phthisis.] **—phthis′ic, phthis′i·cal** *adj.*
phthi·sis (thī′sĭs) also **phthis·ic** (tĭz′ĭk) *n.* **1.** Tuberculosis of the lungs; pulmonary tuberculosis. **2.** A wasting away or emaciation and atrophy of the body or part of the body. [Lat. < Gk. < *phthinein,* to waste away.]
phyco– *pref.* Seaweed: *phycology.* [< Gk. *phukos,* seaweed.]
phy·co·bi·lin (fī′kō-bī′lĭn) *n.* Any of a group of water-soluble pigments that occur in some algae. [PHYCO- + Lat. *bilis,* bile + -IN.]
phy·co·cy·a·nin (fī′kō-sī′ə-nĭn) *n.* A blue phycobilin that occurs in the cells of blue-green algae.
phy·co·er·y·thrin (fī′kō-ĕr′ĭ-thrĭn) *n.* A red phycobilin that occurs in the cells of red algae.
phy·col·o·gy (fī-kŏl′ə-jē) *n.* The branch of botany concerned with the study of seaweeds and algae. **—phy′co·log′i·cal** (fī′kə-lŏj′ĭ-kəl) *adj.* **—phy·col′o·gist** *n.*
phy·co·my·cete (fī′kō-mī′sēt′, -mī-sēt′) *n.* Any of various fungi that resemble algae, including certain molds and mildews. [NLat. *Phycomycetes,* class name : PHYCO- + -MYCETE.] **—phy′co·my·ce′tous** *adj.*
phy·la (fī′lə) *n.* Plural of **phylum.**
phy·lac·ter·y (fĭ-lăk′tə-rē) *n., pl.* **-ies. 1.** *Judaism.* Either of two small leather boxes, each containing strips of parchment inscribed with quotations from the Hebrew Scriptures, one of which is strapped to the forehead and the other to the left arm by observant Jewish men during morning worship, except on Sabbath and holidays. **2. a.** An amulet. **b.** A reminder. [ME *filakterie* < LLat. *phylacterium* < Gk. *phulaktērion,* phylactery, safeguard < *phulaktēr,* guard < *phulassein,* to guard.]
phy·lax·is (fĭ-lăk′sĭs) *n.* Inhibiting of infection by the body. [Gk. *phulaxis,* act of guarding < *phulassein,* to guard.] **—phy·lac′tic** (-lăk′tĭk) *adj.*
phy·le (fī′lē) *n., pl.* **-lae** (-lē). A large citizens' organization, based on kinship, constituting the largest political subdivision of an ancient Greek city-state. [Gk. *phulē,* tribe.] **—phy′lic** *adj.*
phy·let·ic (fī-lĕt′ĭk) *adj.* Of or pertaining to phylogeny or phylogenetic development. [< NLat. *phylesis,* course of evolutionary development < Gk. *phulon,* race.] **—phy·let′i·cal·ly** *adv.*
phyll– *pref.* Variant of **phyllo-.**
-phyll *suff.* Leaf: *sporophyll.* [< Gk. *phullon,* leaf.]
phyl·lite (fĭl′īt′) *n.* A green, gray, or red metamorphic rock, similar to slate but often having a wavy surface and a distinctive micaceous luster.
phyllo– or **phyll–** *pref.* Leaf: *phylloid.* [< Gk. *phullon,* leaf.]
phyl·lo·clade (fĭl′ə-klăd′) also **phyl·lo·clad** (-klăd′) *n.* A flattened branch or stem that performs the functions of a leaf, as in some cacti. [NLat. *phyllocladium* : PHYLLO- + Gk. *klados,* branch.]
phyl·lode (fĭl′ōd′) also **phyl·lo·di·um** (fĭ-lō′dē-əm) *n., pl.* **-lodes** also **-lo·di·a** (-lō′dē-ə). A flattened leafstalk that serves as a leaf. [< Gk. *phullōdes,* like leaves : *phullon,* leaf + *eidos,* shape.] **—phyl·lo′di·al** *adj.*
phyl·loid (fĭl′oid′) *adj.* Resembling a leaf; leaflike.
phyl·lome (fĭl′ōm′) *n.* A leaf or a plant structure that functions as a leaf. **—phyl·lo′mic** (fĭ-lō′mĭk, -lŏm′ĭk) *adj.*
phyl·loph·a·gous (fĭ-lŏf′ə-gəs) *adj.* Feeding on leaves.
phyl·lo·pod (fĭl′ə-pŏd′) *n.* Any of various crustaceans of the order Phyllopoda, having swimming and respiratory appendages that resemble leaves. *—adj.* Also **phyl·lop·o·dous** (fĭ-lŏp′ə-dəs). **1.** Possessing leaflike feet. **2.** Of or relating to the phyllopods. [NLat. *Phyllopoda,* order name : PHYLLO- + -POD.] **—phyl·lop′o·dan** (fĭ-lŏp′ə-dən) *adj. & n.*
phyl·lo·tax·y (fĭl′ə-tăk′sē) also **phyl·lo·tax·is** (fĭl′ə-tăk′sĭs) *n.* **1.** The arrangement of leaves on a stem. **2.** The principles governing leaf arrangement. [NLat. *phyllotaxis* : PHYLLO- + -TAXIS.] **—phyl′lo·tac′tic** (-tăk′tĭk), **phyl′lo·tac′ti·cal** *adj.*
-phyllous *suff.* Having a specified kind or number of leaves: *gamophyllous.* [NLat. *-phyllus* < Gk. *phullon,* leaf.]
phyl·lox·e·ra (fĭl′ŏk-sîr′ə, fĭ-lŏk′sər-ə) *n., pl.* **-rae** (-rē). Any of several small insects of the genus *Phylloxera,* esp. *P. vitifoliae,* a widely distributed species very destructive to grape crops. [NLat. *Phylloxera,* genus name : PHYLLO- + Gk. *xēros,* dry.] **—phyl′lox·e′ran** *adj. & n.*
phy·log·e·ny (fī-lŏj′ə-nē) *n., pl.* **-nies. 1.** The evolutionary development of a species of plant or animal. **2.** The historical development of a tribe or racial group. [Gk. *phulon,* race, class + -GENY.] **—phy′lo·ge·net′ic** (fī′lō-jə-nĕt′ĭk), **phy′lo·gen′ic** *adj.* **—phy′lo·ge·net′i·cal·ly** *adv.*
phy·lum (fī′ləm) *n., pl.* **-la** (-lə). **1.** *Biol.* A taxonomic division of the animal kingdom or, less commonly, the plant kingdom, next above a class in size. **2.** *Ling.* A large division of genetically related families of languages or linguistic stocks. [NLat. < Gk. *phulon,* class.]
physi– *pref.* Variant of **physio-.**
phys·i·at·rics (fĭz′ē-ăt′rĭks) *n. (used with a sing. verb). Med.* Physical therapy.
phys·i·at·rist (fĭz′ē-ăt′rĭst) *n. Med.* A physician who specializes in physical medicine or physical therapy.
phys·i·at·ry (fĭz′ē-ăt′rē) *n. Med.* Physical therapy.
phys·ic (fĭz′ĭk) *n.* **1.** A medicine or drug. **2.** A cathartic. **3.** *Archaic.* The profession of medicine. *—tr.v.* **-icked, -icking, -ics. 1.** *Archaic.* To treat with or as if with medicine. **2.** To act upon as a cathartic. **3.** To cure or heal. [ME *phisik* < OFr. *fisique,* medical science, natural science < Lat. *physica* < Gk. *phusikē,* fem. of *phusikos,* of nature < *phusis,* nature.]
phys·i·cal (fĭz′ĭ-kəl) *adj.* **1.** Of or pertaining to the body, as distinguished from the mind or spirit; bodily; corporeal: *physical strength.* **2.** Of or pertaining to material things: *physical environment.* **3.** Of or pertaining to matter and energy or the sciences dealing with them, esp. physics. *—n.* A physical examination. [ME *phisycal,* medical < Med. Lat. *physicalis* < Lat. *physica,* physics. —see PHYSICS.] **—phys′i·cal·ly** *adv.*
physical anthropology *n.* The science of human evolutionary biology, racial variation, and classification. **—physical anthropologist** *n.*
physical chemistry *n.* The scientific analysis of the properties and behavior of chemical systems primarily by physical theory and technique as, for example, the thermodynamic analysis of macroscopic chemical phenomena.
physical education *n.* Education in the care and development of the human body, stressing athletics and including hygiene.
physical examination *n.* A medical examination to detect illness or dysfunction and esp. to determine physical fitness for a specified activity or service.
physical geography *n.* The study of the structure and phenomena of the earth's surface, esp. in its current aspects, including land formation, climate, currents, and distribution of flora and fauna.
phys·i·cal·ism (fĭz′ĭ-kə-lĭz′əm) *n. Philos.* The doctrine that all phenomena can be described in spatiotemporal terms and consequently that any descriptive scientific statement can in principle be reduced to an empirically verifiable physical statement. **—phys′i·cal·ist** *n.* **—phys′i·cal·is′tic** *adj.*
physical medicine *n.* The branch of medicine that diagnoses and treats disease by essentially physical means, including manipulation, massage, and exercise, often with mechanical devices, and the application of heat, cold, electricity, radiation, and water.
physical science *n.* Any of the sciences, such as physics, chemistry, astronomy, and geology, that analyze the nature and properties of energy and nonliving matter.
physical therapy *n.* The treatment of disease and injury by

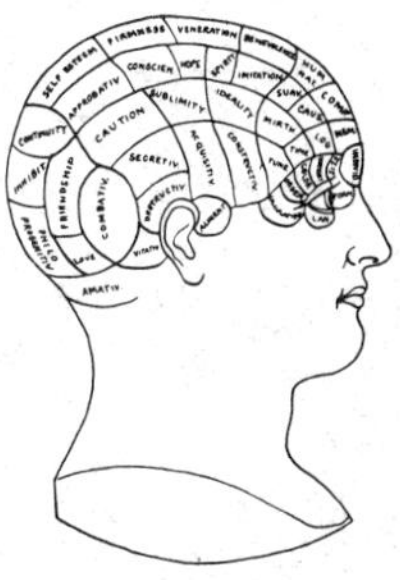

phrenology
Diagram showing location on the human head of brain segments believed to control various characteristics

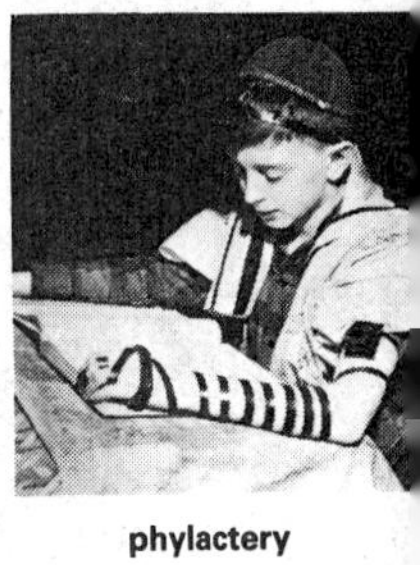

phylactery

mechanical means such as exercise, heat, light, and massage.

phy·si·cian (fĭ-zĭsh′ən) *n.* **1.** A person licensed to practice medicine; medical doctor. **2.** A person who heals or exerts a healing influence. [ME *fisicien* < OFr. < *fisique,* medical science. —see PHYSIC.]

phy·si·cian·ly (fĭ-zĭsh′ən-lē) *adj.* Suitable to or characteristic of a physician.

phys·i·cist (fĭz′ĭ-sĭst) *n.* A scientist who specializes in physics.

phys·i·co·chem·i·cal (fĭz′ĭ-kō-kĕm′ĭ-kəl) *adj.* **1.** Pertaining to properties that are both physical and chemical. **2.** Pertaining to physical chemistry.

phys·ics (fĭz′ĭks) *n. (used with a sing. verb).* **1.** The science of matter and energy and of interactions between the two, grouped in traditional fields such as acoustics, optics, mechanics, thermodynamics, and electromagnetism, as well as in modern extensions including atomic and nuclear physics, cryogenics, solid-state physics, particle physics, and plasma physics. **2.** Physical properties, interactions, processes, or laws: *the physics of supersonic flight.* **3.** *Archaic.* The study of the natural or material world and phenomena; natural philosophy. [Lat. *physica* < Gk. *phusika,* neuter pl. of *phusikos,* of nature < *phusis,* nature.]

physio– or **physi–** *pref.* **1.** Nature; natural: *physiography.* **2.** Physical: *physiatry.* [Gk. *phusio-* < *phusis,* nature < *phuein,* to grow.]

phys·i·og·no·my (fĭz′ē-ŏg′nə-mē, -ŏn′ə-mē) *n., pl.* **-mies.** **1. a.** The art of judging human character from facial features. **b.** Divination based on facial features. **2. a.** Facial features, esp. when regarded as revealing character. **b.** Aspect and character of an inanimate or abstract entity: *the physiognomy of New England.* [ME *phisonomie* < OFr. < LLat. *physiognomia* < Gk. *phusiognomonia* : *phusis,* appearance + *gnōmōn,* interpreter < *gignōskein,* to know.] **—phys′i·og·nom′ic** (fĭz′ē-ŏg-nŏm′ĭk, fĭz′ē-ə-nŏm′ĭk), **phys′i·og·nom′i·cal** *adj.* **—phys′i·og·nom′i·cal·ly** *adv.* **—phys′i·og′no·mist** *n.*

phys·i·og·ra·phy (fĭz′ē-ŏg′rə-fē) *n.* Physical geography. **—phys′i·og′ra·pher** *n.* **—phys′i·o·graph′ic** (fĭz′ē-ə-grăf′ĭk), **phys′i·o·graph′i·cal** *adj.* **—phys′i·o·graph′i·cal·ly** *adv.*

phys·i·o·log·i·cal (fĭz′ē-ə-lŏj′ĭ-kəl) also **phys·i·o·log·ic** (-ĭk) *adj.* **1.** Of or pertaining to physiology. **2.** In accord with or characteristic of the normal functioning of a living organism. **—phys′i·o·log′i·cal·ly** *adv.*

physiological saline *n.* A sterile salt solution that is isotonic to body fluids.

phys·i·ol·o·gy (fĭz′ē-ŏl′ə-jē) *n.* **1.** The biological science of essential and characteristic life processes, activities, and functions. **2.** All the vital processes of an organism. [Lat. *physiologia* < Gk. *phusiologia* : *phusis,* nature + *logos,* account.] **—phys′i·ol′o·gist** *n.*

piano[1]

phys·i·o·ther·a·py (fĭz′ē-ō-thĕr′ə-pē) *n.* Physical therapy. **—phys′i·o·ther′a·peu′tic** (-thĕr′ə-pyōō′tĭk) *adj.*

phy·sique (fĭ-zēk′) *n.* The body considered with reference to its proportions, muscular development, and appearance: *"a short man with . . . the physique of a swimmer"* (John LeCarré). [Fr. < *physique,* physical < Lat. *physicus,* of nature < Gk. *phusikos* < *phusis,* nature.] **—phy·siqued′** *adj.*

phy·so·stig·mine (fī′sō-stĭg′mēn′) also **phy·so·stig·min** (-mĭn) *n.* A colorless or pink poisonous crystalline compound, $C_{15}H_{21}N_3O_2$, extracted from the Calabar bean, and used in a variety of medicines. [< NLat. *Physostigma,* genus name of the Calabar bean : Gk. *phusa,* bellows + Gk. *stigma,* tattoo.]

phy·sos·to·mous (fī-sŏs′tə-məs) *adj.* Having a connecting tube between the air bladder and a part of the alimentary canal, as in certain fishes. [Gk. *phusa,* bladder + -STOM(E) + -OUS.]

phyt– *pref.* Variant of **phyto–**.

–phyte *suff.* **1.** A plant with a specified character or habitat: *halophyte.* **2.** A pathological growth: *osteophyte.* [Gk. *phuton,* plant < *phuein,* to grow.]

phyto– or **phyt–** *pref.* Plant: *phytogenesis.* [NLat. < Gk. *phuto-* < *phuton,* plant < *phuein,* to grow.]

phy·to·chem·is·try (fī′tō-kĕm′ĭ-strē) *n.* The chemistry of plants. **—phy′to·chem′i·cal** (-ĭ-kəl) *adj.* **—phy′to·chem′i·cal·ly** *adv.* **—phy′to·chem′ist** *n.*

phy·to·gen·e·sis (fī′tō-jĕn′ĭ-sĭs) also **phy·tog·e·ny** (fī-tŏj′ə-nē) *n.* The origin and evolutionary development of plants. **—phy′to·ge·net′ic** (-jə-nĕt′ĭk), **phy′to·ge·net′i·cal** *adj.* **—phy′to·ge·net′i·cal·ly** *adv.*

phy·to·gen·ic (fī′tō-jĕn′ĭk) also **phy·tog·e·nous** (fī-tŏj′ə-nəs) *adj.* Having a plant origin, as coal.

phy·to·ge·og·ra·phy (fī′tō-jē-ŏg′rə-fē) *n.* The study of the distribution of plants. **—phy′to·ge·og′ra·pher** *n.* **—phy′to·ge′o·graph′i·cal** (-jē′ə-grăf′ĭ-kəl), **phy′to·ge′o·graph′ic** *adj.*

phy·tog·ra·phy (fī-tŏg′rə-fē) *n.* The science of plant description; descriptive botany.

phy·to·hor·mone (fī′tō-hôr′mōn′) *n.* A hormone produced by a plant, esp. one that affects plant growth.

phy·tol (fī′tôl′) *n.* A liquid alcohol, $C_{20}H_{40}O$, used in the synthesis of vitamins E and K.

phy·to·lite (fī′tə-līt′) also **phy·to·lith** (-lĭth′) *n.* A fossil plant.

phy·tol·o·gy (fī-tŏl′ə-jē) *n.* The study of plants; botany. **—phy′to·log′ic** (fī′tə-lŏj′ĭk), **phy′to·log′i·cal** *adj.*

phy·ton (fī′tŏn′) *n.* A unit of plant structure, esp. the smallest part of a plant that, when cut off, is able to grow. [NLat. < Gk. *phuton,* plant < *phuein,* to grow.] **—phy·ton′ic** *adj.*

phy·to·path·o·gen (fī′tō-păth′ə-jən) *n.* An organism that is pathogenic to a plant. **—phy′to·path′o·gen′ic** (-jĕn′ĭk) *adj.*

phy·to·pa·thol·o·gy (fī′tō-pə-thŏl′ə-jē) *n.* The science of plant diseases. **—phy′to·path′o·log′ic** (-păth′ə-lŏj′ĭk), **phy′to·path′o·log′i·cal** *adj.* **—phy′to·pa·thol′o·gist** *n.*

phy·toph·a·gous (fī-tŏf′ə-gəs) *adj.* Feeding on plants, including shrubs and trees. Used esp. of certain insects.

phy·to·plank·ton (fī′tō-plăngk′tən) *n.* Minute, floating aquatic plants. **—phy′to·plank·ton′ic** (-plăngk-tŏn′ĭk) *adj.*

phy·to·so·ci·ol·o·gy (fī′tō-sō′sē-ŏl′ə-jē, -shē-) *n.* The branch of ecology that deals with the characteristics, relationships, and distribution of associated plants. **—phy′to·so′ci·o·log′i·cal** (-sō′sē-ə-lŏj′ĭ-kəl, -shē-) *adj.* **—phy′to·so′ci·o·log′i·cal·ly** *adv.* **—phy′to·so′ci·ol′o·gist** *n.*

phy·to·tox·ic (fī′tō-tŏk′sĭk) *adj.* Poisonous to plants. **—phy′to·tox·ic′i·ty** (-tŏk-sĭs′ĭ-tē) *n.*

pi[1] (pī) *n., pl.* **pis.** **1.** The 16th letter of the Greek alphabet. See table at **alphabet.** **2.** *Symbol* π *Math.* A transcendental number, approximately 3.14159, representing the ratio of the circumference to the diameter of a circle and appearing as a constant in a wide range of mathematical problems. [Med. Gk. < Gk. *pei,* of Phoenician orig.; akin to Heb. *pē.*]

pi[2] also **pie** (pī) *Printing.* —*n., pl.* **pis** also **pies.** An amount of type that has been jumbled or thrown together at random. —*v.* **pied, pi·ing, pies** also **pied, pie·ing, pies.** —*tr.* To jumble or mix up (type). —*intr.* To become jumbled. [Orig. unknown.]

pia (pī′ə, pē′ə) *n.* The pia mater. **—pi′al** *adj.*

pi·ac·u·lar (pī-ăk′yə-lər) *adj.* **1.** Making expiation or atonement for a sacrilege: *piacular sacrifice.* **2.** Requiring expiation; wicked; blameworthy. [Lat. *piacularis* < *piaculum,* propitiatory sacrifice < *piare,* to appease < *pius,* dutiful.]

piaffe (pyăf) *intr.v.* **piaffed, piaf·fing, piaffes.** To perform the piaffer. [Fr. *piaffer.*]

piaf·fer (pyăf′ər) *n.* A movement in which a horse trots in place with high action of the legs. [Fr. < *piaffer,* to piaffe.]

pia ma·ter (mā′tər, mä′tər) *n.* The fine vascular membrane that envelops the brain and spinal cord under the arachnoid membrane and the dura mater. [ME < Med. Lat., tender mother.]

pi·an·ism (pē-ăn′ĭz′əm, pē′ə-nĭz′əm) *n.* The technique or execution of piano playing.

pi·a·nis·si·mo (pē′ə-nĭs′ə-mō′) *Mus.* —*adv.* Very softly or quietly. Used as a direction. —*n., pl.* **-mos.** A very quietly played part of a composition. [Ital., superl. of *piano,* soft < Lat. *planus,* level.] **—pi′a·nis′si·mo′** *adj.*

pi·an·ist (pē-ăn′ĭst, pē′ə-nĭst) *n.* One who plays the piano.

pi·a·nis·tic (pē′ə-nĭs′tĭk) *adj.* **1.** Of or pertaining to the piano. **2.** Well-adapted to the piano. **—pi′a·nis′ti·cal·ly** *adv.*

pi·a·nis·tics (pē′ə-nĭs′tĭks) *n. (used with a sing. or pl. verb).* **1.** The art or principles of piano playing. **2.** A show of virtuosity in playing the piano.

pi·an·o[1] (pē-ăn′ō) *n., pl.* **-os.** A musical instrument with a manual keyboard actuating hammers that strike wire strings, producing sounds that may be softened or sustained by means of pedals. [Ital., short for *pianoforte.* —see PIANOFORTE.]

pi·a·no[2] (pē-ä′nō) *Mus.* —*adv.* Softly; quietly. Used as a direction. —*n., pl.* **-nos.** A passage to be played softly. [Ital. < Lat. *planus,* flat.] **—pi·a′no** *adj.*

piano bar *n.* A cocktail lounge featuring entertainment by a pianist.

pi·an·o·for·te (pē-ăn′ō-fôr′tā, -fôr′tē, -fôrt′) *n.* A piano. [Ital. < *piano e forte,* soft and loud.]

piano hinge *n.* A long narrow hinge with a pin running the entire length of its joint.

pi·as·sa·va (pē′ə-sä′və) also **pi·as·sa·ba** (-sä′bə) *n.* **1.** Either of two South American palm trees, *Attalea funifera* or *Leopoldina piassaba,* from which a strong, coarse fiber is obtained. **2.** The fiber of the piassava, used for making ropes, brushes, and brooms. [Port. *piassaba* < Tupi *piaçaba.*]

pi·as·ter also **pi·as·tre** (pē-ăs′tər, -ä′stər) *n.* **1.** See table at **currency.** **2.** A piece of eight. [Fr. *piastre* < Ital. *piastra,* thin metal plate < Lat. *emplastrum,* medical dressing. —see PLASTER.]

pi·az·za (pē-ăz′ə, -ä′zə) *n., pl.* **-zas.** **1.** (*also* -ät′sə) *pl.* **pi·az·ze** (-ät′sā). A public square in an Italian town. **2.** A roofed and arcaded passageway; colonnade. **3.** A verandah. [Ital. < Lat. *platea,* street < Gk. *plateia (hodos),* broad (way).]

pi·broch (pē′brŏkh′) *n.* A series of variations on a traditional dirge or martial theme for the highland bagpipe. [Sc. Gael. *piobaireachd,* pipe music.]

pic (pĭk) *n., pl.* **pics** or **pix.** *Slang.* **1.** A photograph. **2.** A movie. [Short for PICTURE.]

pi·ca[1] (pī′kə) *n.* **1. a.** A printer's unit of type size, equal to 12 points or about 1/6 inch. **b.** An equivalent unit of composition measurement used in determining the dimensions of lines, illustrations, or printed pages. **2.** A type size for typewriters, providing 10 characters to the inch. [Prob. < Med. Lat., list of church services.]

pi·ca[2] (pī′kə) *n.* A craving for unnatural food, as seen in hysteria and pregnancy. [NLat. < Lat. *pica,* magpie.]

pic·a·dor (pĭk′ə-dôr′) *n., pl.* **pic·a·dors** or **pic·a·do·res** (pĭk′-ə-dôr′ās). A horseman in a bullfight who lances the bull's neck muscles so that it will tend to keep its head low for the subsequent stages of the fight. [Sp. < *picar,* to prick.]
pi·ca·ra (pē′kä-rä′) *n., pl.* **-ras** (-räz′, -räs′). A woman who behaves like a picaro; an adventuress.
pic·a·resque (pĭk′ə-rĕsk′, pē′kə-) *adj.* **1.** Of or involving clever rogues or adventurers. **2.** Of, belonging to, or characteristic of a literary genre in which the rogue-hero and his escapades are depicted with broad realism and satire. *—n.* One that is picaresque. [Fr. < Sp. *picaresco* < *pícaro,* picaro.]
pi·ca·ro (pē′kä-rō) *n., pl.* **-ros** (-rōz′, -rōs′). A bohemian adventurer; rogue. [Sp. *pícaro* < *picar,* to prick < VLat. **piccare* < Lat. *picus,* woodpecker.]
pic·a·roon (pĭk′ə-ro͞on′) *n.* **1. a.** A pirate. **b.** A picaro. **2.** A pirate ship. *—intr.v.* **-rooned, -roon·ing, -roons.** To act as a pirate. [Sp. *picarón,* aug. of *pícaro,* picaro.]
pic·a·yune (pĭk′ə-yo͞on′) *adj.* **1.** Of little value or importance; paltry. **2.** Petty; mean. *—n.* **1.** A Spanish-American half-real piece formerly used in parts of the southern United States. **2.** A five-cent piece. **3.** Something of very small value; trifle: *not worth a picayune.* [Fr. *picaillon,* small coin < Prov. *picaioun.*] **—pic′a·yun′ish** *adj.*
pic·ca·lil·li (pĭk′ə-lĭl′ē) *n., pl.* **-lis.** A pickled relish made of various chopped vegetables. [Prob. alteration of PICKLE.]
pic·co·lo[1] (pĭk′ə-lō′) *n., pl.* **-los.** A small flute pitched an octave above a regular flute. [Ital., short for *piccolo flauto,* small flute.] **—pic′co·lo′ist** *n.*
pic·co·lo[2] (pĭk′ə-lō′) *adj.* Designating a musical instrument considerably smaller than the usual size: *a piccolo trumpet; a piccolo concertina.* [Ital., small.]
pice (pīs) *n., pl.* **pice.** See table at **currency.** [Hindi *paisā.*]
pi·ce·ous (pī′sē-əs) *adj.* **1.** Of or pertaining to pitch. **2.** Glossy black in color. [Lat. *piceus* < *pix,* pitch.]
pich·i·ci·e·go (pĭch′ĭ-sē-ā′gō) also **pich·i·ci·a·go** (-ā′gō, -ä′-gō) *n., pl.* **-gos.** **1.** A small armadillo, *Chlamyphorus truncatus,* of Argentina, having pale-pink armor and soft, silky white hair. **2.** A South American armadillo, *Burmeisteria retusa,* similar to the pichiciego, having yellow-brown armor and whitish hair. [Poss. < Allentiac.]
pick[1] (pĭk) *v.* **picked, pick·ing, picks.** *—tr.* **1.** To select from a group: *The best swimmer was picked.* **2. a.** To select or cull. **b.** To gather in; harvest: *They were picking cotton.* **c.** To gather the harvest from: *We picked the whole field in one day.* **3. a.** To remove the outer covering of; pluck: *pick a chicken clean of feathers.* **b.** To tear off bit by bit: *pick meat from the bones.* **4.** To remove extraneous matter from (the teeth). **5.** To poke and pull at with the fingers. **6.** To break up, separate, or detach by means of a sharp, pointed instrument. **7.** To pierce or make (a hole) with a sharp instrument. **8.** To seek and discover (a flaw): *He picked holes in their argument.* **9.** To take up (food) with the beak; peck: *The parrot picked its seed.* **10.** To steal the contents of: *My pocket has been picked.* **11.** To open (a lock) without the use of the key. **12.** To make (one's way) carefully: *She picked her way through the underbrush.* **13.** To provoke: *pick a fight.* **14. a.** To pluck (the strings) of a musical instrument. **b.** To play (a tune) by plucking strings. *—intr.* **1.** To decide with care or forethought. **2.** To work with a pick. **3.** To find fault or make petty criticisms; carp: *He's always picking about something.* **4.** To be harvested or gathered: *The ripe apples picked easily.* ***—phrasal verbs.*** **pick apart. 1.** To separate into pieces by picking: *He picked apart an old quilt.* **2.** To refute or find flaws in by close examination: *The lawyer picked apart his testimony.* **pick at. 1.** To pluck or pull at with the fingers. **2.** To eat sparingly or without appetite: *He picked at his meal.* **3.** *Informal.* To nag: *She picks at him day and night.* **pick off. 1.** To shoot after singling out: *I picked the ducks off one by one.* **2.** *Baseball.* To put (a base runner) out with a quick throw, as from the pitcher or catcher. **3.** *Sports.* To intercept, as a football pass. **pick on.** To tease or bully. **pick out. 1.** To choose or select. **2.** To discern from the surroundings; distinguish. **3.** To play (music) slowly by ear: *He managed to pick out the tune.* **pick over.** To sort out or examine item by item. **pick up. 1. a.** To take up (something) by hand: *pick up a book.* **b.** To collect or gather: *picked up the broken pieces of glass.* **c.** To tidy up: *picked up the living room.* **2.** To take on (passengers or freight, for example). **3.** *Informal.* **a.** To acquire casually or by accident: *picked up a mink coat on sale.* **b.** To acquire (knowledge) by learning or experience: *picked up French very quickly.* **c.** To claim: *picked up her shoes at the repair shop.* **d.** To buy: *picked up some beverages on the way home.* **e.** To accept (a bill) in order to pay it: *Let me pick up the tab.* **f.** To come down with (a disease): *picked up a virus.* **g.** To gain: *picked up five yards on that play.* **4.** *Slang.* To take into custody: *The coast guard picked up five smugglers.* **5.** *Slang.* To make casual acquaintance with, usually in anticipation of sexual relations. **6.** To come upon and follow: *The dog picked up the deer's scent.* **7.** To continue after a break: *Let's pick up the discussion after lunch.* **8.** *Informal.* To improve in condition or activity: *Sales picked up last fall.* **9.** *Informal.* To pack one's belongings: *She just picked up and left.* *—n.* **1. a.** The act of picking, esp. with a pointed instrument. **b.** A long-toothed comb used in grooming Afros and some perms. **2.** The act of selecting or choosing; choice. **3.** Something that is selected as the most desirable; the best or choicest part: *the pick of the crop.* **4.** The amount or quantity of a crop that is picked by hand. ***—idiom.*** **pick and choose.** To select with great care. [ME *piken,* to prick, prob. < OFr. *piquer* < VLat. **piccare* < Lat. *picus,* woodpecker.] **—pick′er** *n.*
pick[2] (pĭk) *n.* **1.** A tool for breaking hard surfaces, consisting of a curved bar sharpened at both ends and fitted to a long handle. **2.** Something used for picking, as an ice pick, a toothpick, or a picklock. **3.** *Mus.* A plectrum. [ME *pik.*]
pick[3] (pĭk) *n.* **1.** A weft thread in weaving. **2.** A passage or throw of the shuttle in a loom. *—tr.v.* **picked, pick·ing, picks. 1.** To throw (a shuttle) across the loom. **2.** *Archaic.* To cast; pitch. [< ME *pykken,* to stick in the ground.]
pick·a·back (pĭk′ə-băk′) *adv. & n.* Variant of **piggyback.** [Orig. unknown.]
pick·a·nin·ny (pĭk′ə-nĭn′ē) *n., pl.* **-nies.** *Offensive.* A small black child. [Prob. Sp. *pequeño,* little + *niño,* child.]
pick·ax or **pick·axe** (pĭk′ăks′) *n.* A pick, esp. with one end of the head pointed and the other end with a chisel edge for cutting through roots. *—v.* **-axed, -ax·ing, -ax·es.** *—intr.* To use a pickax. *—tr.* To use a pickax on. [Alteration of ME *pikois* < OFr. *picois* < *pic,* pick, prob. < Lat. *picus,* woodpecker.]

pickax

picked[1] (pĭkt) *adj.* **1.** Chosen by careful selection. **2.** Cleaned by picking out damaged or undesirable parts. **3.** Gathered; plucked; harvested. **4.** Worked upon with a pick. **5.** In tailoring, ornamented with a hand-worked line of short running stitches along the edges.
picked[2] (pĭkt) *adj. Regional.* Pointed: *a picked cap.* [< PICK[2].]
pick·er·el (pĭk′ər-əl, pĭk′rəl) *n., pl.* **pickerel** or **-els. 1.** Any of several North American freshwater game and food fishes of the genus *Esox,* esp. *E. niger* and *E. vermiculatus.* **2.** Any of various fishes, such as the walleye, similar to or related to the pickerel. **3.** *Chiefly Brit.* A young pike. [ME *pikerel,* dim. of *pike,* pike.]
pick·er·el·weed (pĭk′ər-əl-wēd′, pĭk′rəl-) *n.* A plant, *Pontederia cordata,* growing in freshwater shallows of North America, and having heart-shaped leaves and spikes of violet-blue flowers.
pick·et (pĭk′ĭt) *n.* **1.** A pointed stake driven into the ground to support a fence, secure a tent, tether animals, mark points in surveying, or, when pointed at the top, serve as a defense. **2.** A detachment of one or more soldiers advanced or held in readiness to warn of an enemy's approach. **3. a.** A person or persons stationed outside a place of employment, usually during a strike, to express grievance or protest and discourage entry by nonstriking employees or customers. **b.** A person or persons present outside a building to protest. *—v.* **-et·ed, -et·ing, -ets.** *—tr.* **1.** To enclose, secure, tether, mark out, or fortify with pickets. **2. a.** To post as a picket. **b.** To guard with a picket. **3.** To post a picket or pickets during a strike or demonstration. *—intr.* To act or serve as a picket. [Fr. *piquet* < OFr. < *piquer,* to prick. —see PICK[1].] **—pick′et·er** *n.*

picket fence

picket fence *n.* A fence of pointed, upright pickets.
picket line *n.* A line or procession of people picketing a place of business or otherwise staging a public protest.
pick·ing (pĭk′ĭng) *n.* **1.** The act of someone or something that picks. **2. pickings.** Something that is or may be picked. **3.** Often **pickings. a.** Leftovers. **b.** A share of spoils.
pick·le (pĭk′əl) *n.* **1.** An edible product, such as a cucumber, that has been preserved and flavored in a solution of brine or vinegar. **2.** A solution of brine or vinegar, often spiced, for preserving and flavoring food. **3.** An acid or other chemical solution used as a bath to remove scale and oxides from the surface of metals before plating or finishing. **4.** *Informal.* A troublesome, embarrassing, or difficult situation. *—tr.v.* **-led, -ling, -les. 1.** To preserve or flavor in a solution of brine or vinegar. **2.** To treat (metal) in a chemical bath. [ME *pekille,* prob. < MDu. *pekel.*]
pick·led (pĭk′əld) *adj.* **1.** Preserved in or treated with pickle. **2.** *Slang.* Drunk.
pick·lock (pĭk′lŏk′) *n.* **1.** A person who picks locks, esp. a thief. **2.** An instrument for picking a lock.
pick-me-up (pĭk′mē-ŭp′) *n. Informal.* A drink, often an alcoholic beverage, taken as a stimulant or hangover cure.
pick·pock·et (pĭk′pŏk′ĭt) *n.* One who steals from pockets.
pick·proof (pĭk′pro͞of′) *adj.* Designed to prevent picking: *a pickproof lock.*
pick·up (pĭk′ŭp′) *n.* **1. a.** The action or process of picking up: *the pickup and delivery of farm produce.* **b.** *Sports.* The act of striking or fielding a ball after it has touched the ground: *a good pickup and throw from third base.* **c.** Capacity for acceleration: *a sports car with good pickup.* **d.** *Informal.* An improvement in condition or activity: *a pickup in sales.* **e.** *Slang.* An arrest. **2.** One that is picked up, esp.: **a.** Passengers or freight: *Taxi drivers expect good tips from airport pickups.* **b.** A balance brought forward in accounting. **c.** Previous journalistic copy to which succeeding copy is added. **d.** *Mus.* The unstressed note or notes introductory to a phrase or composition. **e.** *Informal.* A hitchhiker. **f.** *Slang.* A stranger with whom casual acquaintance is made, usually in anticipation of sexual relations. **3.** One that picks up, esp.: **a.** A pickup truck. **b.** The rotary rake on machinery such as a harvester that picks up windrowed hay

or straw. **4.** *Electronics.* **a.** A device that converts the oscillations of a phonograph needle into electrical impulses for subsequent conversion into sound. **b.** The tone arm of a record player. **5. a.** The reception of light or sound waves for conversion to electrical impulses. **b.** The apparatus used for such reception. **c.** A telecast originating outside of a studio. **d.** The apparatus for transmitting a broadcast from an outside place to the broadcasting station.

pickup truck *n.* A light truck with an open body and low sides.

pick·y (pĭk′ē) *adj.* **-i·er, -i·est.** *Informal.* Excessively meticulous; fussy.

pic·lo·ram (pĭk′lə-răm′, pī′klə-) *n.* A colorless compound, $C_6H_3Cl_3N_2O_2$, used as a herbicide. [PIC(OLINE) + (CH)LOR(O)- + AM(INE).]

pic·nic (pĭk′nĭk) *n.* **1.** A meal eaten outdoors on an excursion. **2.** *Slang.* An easy task or pleasant experience. **3.** A shoulder of pork from which most of the butt has been removed. —*intr.v.* **-nicked, -nick·ing, -nics.** To go on or participate in a picnic. [Fr. *piquenique,* prob. redup. of *piquer,* to pick.] —**pic′nick·er** *n.* —**pic′nick·y** *adj.*

pico– *pref.* **1.** One-trillionth (10^{-12}): *picosecond.* **2.** Very small: *picornavirus.* [Sp. *pico,* small quantity < *picar,* to prick. —see PICARO.]

pi·co·gram (pē′kə-grăm′, pī′-) *n.* One trillionth (10^{-12}) of a gram.

pic·o·line (pĭk′ə-lēn′, pī′kə-) *n.* Any of three isomeric liquid methylpyridine bases, C_6H_7N, derived from coal tar, horse urine, and bone oil and used as an industrial solvent. [Lat. *pix,* pitch + -OL + -INE.]

pi·cor·na·vi·rus (pē-kôr′nə-vī′rəs, pī-) *n.* Any of a group of very small RNA-containing viruses that includes the Coxsackie virus. [PICO- + RNA + VIRUS.]

pi·co·sec·ond (pē′kə-sĕk′ənd, pī′-) *n.* One trillionth (10^{-12}) of a second.

pi·cot (pē′kō, pē-kō′) *n.* A small embroidered loop forming an ornamental edging on some ribbon and lace. —*tr.v.* **-coted** (-kōd), **-cot·ing** (-kō-ĭng), **-cots** (-kōz). To trim with edging. [Fr. < OFr. < *pic,* point < *piquer,* to prick. —see PICK[1].]

pic·o·tee (pĭk′ə-tē′) *n.* A type of carnation having pale petals bordered by a darker color. [Fr. *picoté,* marked with points < *picoter,* to mark with points < *picot,* point, picot.]

pic·quet (pĭ-kā′) *n.* Variant of **piquet.**

picr– *pref.* Variant of **picro-.**

pic·rate (pĭk′rāt′) *n.* A salt or ester of picric acid.

pic·ric acid (pĭk′rĭk). A poisonous, explosive yellow crystalline solid, $C_6H_2(NO_2)_3OH$, used in explosives, dyes, and antiseptics.

picro– or **picr–** *pref.* **1.** Bitter: *picrotoxin.* **2.** Picric acid: *picrate.* [Gk. *pikro-* < *pikros,* bitter.]

pic·ro·tox·in (pĭk′rə-tŏk′sĭn) *n.* A bitter powder, $C_{30}H_{34}O_{13}$, used as a stimulant and antidote for barbiturate poisoning.

Pict (pĭkt) *n.* One of the ancient people of North Britain, who were absorbed by the invading Scots between the 6th and 9th centuries A.D. [ME < LLat. *Picti,* Picts.]

pic·to·gram (pĭk′tə-grăm′) *n.* A pictorial representation of numerical data or relationships. [PICTO(GRAPH) + -GRAM.]

pic·to·graph (pĭk′tə-grăf′) *n.* **1.** A picture representing a word or idea; hieroglyph. **2.** A record in hieroglyphic symbols. [Lat. *pictus,* p.part. of *pingere,* to paint + -GRAPH.] —**pic′to·graph′ic** *adj.* —**pic′to·graph′i·cal·ly** *adv.* —**pic·tog′ra·phy** (pĭk-tŏg′rə-fē) *n.*

Pic·tor (pĭk′tər) *n.* A constellation in the Southern Hemisphere near Columba and Dorado. [Lat. *pictor,* painter < *pingere,* to paint.]

pic·to·ri·al (pĭk-tôr′ē-əl, -tōr′-) *adj.* **1.** Pertaining to, characterized by, or composed of pictures. **2.** Represented as if in a picture: *pictorial prose.* **3.** Illustrated by pictures. —*n.* An illustrated periodical. [< LLat. *pictorius* < Lat. *pictor,* painter < *pingere,* to paint.] —**pic·to′ri·al·ly** *adv.* —**pic·to′ri·al·ness** *n.*

pic·ture (pĭk′chər) *n.* **1.** A visual representation or image painted, drawn, photographed, or otherwise rendered on a flat surface. **2.** A visible image, esp. one on a flat surface: *the picture reflected in the lake.* **3.** A vivid or realistic verbal description: *a Shakespearean picture of guilt.* **4.** A person or object that bears a striking resemblance to another: *She's the picture of her mother.* **5.** A person, object, or scene that typifies or embodies an emotion, state of mind, or mood: *Her face was a picture of horror.* **6.** The chief circumstances of an event or time; situation. **7.** A motion picture. **8.** A tableau vivant. —*tr.v.* **-tured, -tur·ing, -tures. 1.** To make a visible representation or picture of. **2.** To form a mental image of; visualize. **3.** To describe vividly in words; make a verbal picture of: *He pictured her heroism in glowing language.* [ME < Lat. *pictura* < *pingere,* to paint.]

Pic·ture·phone (pĭk′chər-fōn′). A trademark for a device that combines telephone and television communications.

picture puzzle *n.* A jigsaw puzzle.

pic·tur·esque (pĭk′chə-rĕsk′) *adj.* **1.** Of or suggesting a picture; suitable for a picture: *picturesque rocky shores.* **2.** Striking or interesting in an unusual way; irregularly or quaintly attractive; charming: *a picturesque French café.* **3.** Strikingly expressive or vivid: *picturesque language.* [Fr. *pittoresque* < Ital. *pittoresco* < *pittore,* painter < Lat. *pictor* < *pingere,* to paint.] —**pic′tur·esque′ly** *adv.* —**pic′tur·esque′ness** *n.*

pier

picture window *n.* A large, usually single-paned window that provides a broad outside view.

pic·ul (pĭk′əl) *n.* Any of various units of weight used in the Far East, esp. a Chinese unit equal to 214.53 pounds, or 133.33 kilograms. [Malay *pīkul.*]

pid·dle (pĭd′l) *v.* **-dled, -dling, -dles.** —*tr.* To use triflingly; squander: *piddle away one's time.* —*intr.* **1.** To spend time aimlessly; diddle. **2.** *Informal.* To urinate. [Orig. unknown.]

pid·dling (pĭd′lĭng) *adj.* Beneath consideration; trifling; trivial.

pid·dock (pĭd′ək) *n.* Any of various marine bivalve mollusks of the family Pholadidae, capable of boring into wood, rock, and clay. [Orig. unknown.]

pidg·in (pĭj′ən) *n.* A simplified form of speech, usually a mixture of two or more languages, that has a rudimentary grammar and vocabulary and is used for communication between groups speaking different languages. [< PIDGIN ENGLISH.] —**pidg′in·i·za′tion** *n.* —**pidg′in·ize′** *v.* **(-ized, -iz·ing, -iz·es).**

Pidgin English also **pidgin English** *n.* A pidgin based on English that is used as a trade language in parts of Eastern Asia and Melanesia. [Alteration of *business English.*]

pie[1] (pī) *n.* **1.** A baked food composed of a shell of pastry that is filled with fruit, meat, cheese, or other ingredients, and usually covered with a pastry crust. **2.** A layer cake having cream, custard, or jelly filling. —*idiom.* **pie in the sky.** An empty promise. [ME.]

pie[2] (pī) *n.* The magpie (sense 1). [ME < OFr. < Lat. *pica.*]

pie[3] (pī) *n.* A former monetary unit of India and Pakistan. [Hindi *pā′ī* < Skt. *pādika-,* quarter < *pādah,* foot, leg.]

pie[4] (pī) *n.* An almanac of services used in the English church before the Reformation. [Med. Lat. *pica.*]

pie[5] (pī) *n. & v. Printing.* Variant of **pi**[2].

pie·bald (pī′bôld′) *adj.* Spotted or patched, esp. in black and white: *a piebald horse.* —*n.* A piebald animal, esp. a horse. [PIE[2] + BALD.]

piece (pēs) *n.* **1.** A thing considered as a unit or element of a larger quantity or class; portion: *a piece of string.* **2.** A portion or part that has been separated from a whole: *a piece of cake.* **3.** An object that is one member of a group or class: *a piece of furniture.* **4.** An artistic, musical, or literary work or composition: *"They are lively and well-plotted pieces, both in prose"* (Tucker Brooke). **5.** An instance; specimen: *a piece of folly.* **6.** One's fully expressed opinion; one's mind: *speak one's piece.* **7.** A coin: *a ten-cent piece.* **8.** In various board games, one of the counters or men used in playing. **9.** Any of the chess figures other than a pawn. **10.** A firearm, esp. a rifle. **11.** A given distance: *"There was farm country down the road on the right a piece"* (James Agee). **12.** *Vulgar Slang.* A sexually attractive person. —*tr.v.* **pieced, piec·ing, piec·es. 1.** To mend by adding a piece to. **2.** To join or unite the pieces of: *He pieced together the vase.* —*idioms.* **a piece of (one's) mind.** *Informal.* Frank and severe criticism; censure. **go to pieces. 1.** To shatter into small pieces; fall apart. **2.** *Informal.* To lose mental and emotional self-control; break down. **of a piece.** Belonging to the same class or kind. **piece of the action.** *Informal.* A share of an activity or of profits. [ME *pece* < OFr. < Med. Lat. *pecia,* prob. of Gaulish orig.]

pièce de ré·sis·tance (pyĕs də rā-zē-stäNs′) *n.* **1.** The principal dish of a meal. **2.** An outstanding accomplishment. [Fr.]

piece goods *pl.n.* Fabrics made and sold in standard lengths.

piece·meal (pēs′mēl′) *adv.* **1.** Piece by piece; gradually: *articles acquired piecemeal.* **2.** In pieces; apart. —*adj.* Accomplished or made piece by piece. [ME *pecemele* : *pece,* piece + *-mele,* by a fixed measure < OE *mæl,* appointed time.]

piece of eight *n.* An old Spanish silver coin.

piece·work (pēs′wûrk′) *n.* Work paid for according to the number of products turned out. —**piece′work′er** *n.*

pie chart *n.* A circular chart having radii dividing the circle into sectors proportional in angle and area to the relative size of the quantities represented.

pied[1] (pīd) *adj.* Patchy in color; splotched; piebald. [ME < *pie,* magpie. —see PIE[2].]

pied[2] (pīd) *v. Printing.* A past tense and a past participle of **pi**[2].

pied-à-terre (pyā-dä-târ′) *n., pl.* **pieds-à-terre** (pyā-dä-târ′). A secondary or temporary lodging: *They live in the country but have a small pied-à-terre in the city.* [Fr. : *pied,* foot + *à,* to + *terre,* ground.]

pied·mont (pēd′mŏnt′) *adj.* Formed or lying at the foot of a mountain or mountain range: *a piedmont plain.* —*n.* A piedmont area or region. [After *Piedmont,* a region in Italy.]

pied piper *n.* **1.** A person who offers others strong yet delusive enticement. **2.** A leader who makes promises irresponsibly. [After *The Pied Piper of Hamelin,* title and hero of a poem by Robert Browning (1812–1889).]

pie·plant (pī′plănt′) *n.* Rhubarb (sense 1).

pier (pîr) *n.* **1. a.** A platform extending from a shore over water and supported by piles or pillars, used to secure, protect, and provide access to ships or boats. **b.** Such a structure used predominantly for entertainment. **2.** A supporting structure at the junction of connecting spans of a bridge. **3.** *Archit.* Any of various vertical supporting structures, esp.: **a.** A pillar, rectangular in cross section, supporting an arch or roof. **b.** The portion of a wall between windows. **c.** A reinforcing structure that projects from a wall; buttress. [ME *per* < OE < Med. Lat. *pera.*]

pierce (pîrs) *v.* **pierced, pierc·ing, pierc·es.** —*tr.* **1.** To cut or pass through with or as if with a sharp instrument; stab; penetrate. **2.** To make a hole or opening in; perforate. **3.** To make a way through: *The path pierced the wilderness.* **4.** To sound sharply through: *His shout pierced the din.* **5.** To succeed in discerning or understanding: *He pierced the heart of the mystery.* **6.** To affect penetratingly; move deeply; transfix: *She was pierced by anguish.* —*intr.* To penetrate into or through something: *The rocket pierced through space.* [ME *percen* < OFr. *percer* < VLat. **pertusiare* < Lat. *pertundere,* to bore through : *per-,* through + *tundere,* to beat.] **—pierc'er** *n.* **—pierc'ing** *adj.* **—pierc'ing·ly** *adv.*

Pi·e·ri·an Spring (pī-îr'ē-ən) *n.* **1.** *Gk. Myth.* A spring in Macedonia, sacred to the Muses. **2.** A source of inspiration. [< Lat. *Pierius,* sacred to the Muses < Gk. *Pieria,* a region of Macedonia.]

Pier·rot (pē'ə-rō', pyĕ-rō') *n.* A character in French pantomime, dressed in a floppy white outfit. [Fr., dim. of the name *Pierre,* Peter < Lat. *Petrus.*]

pie·tà also **Pie·tà** (pyā-tä') *n.* A painting or sculpture of the Virgin Mary holding and mourning over the dead body of Jesus. [Ital., pity < Lat. *pietas.* —see PIETY.]

pi·e·tism (pī'ĭ-tĭz'əm) *n.* **1.** Piety. **2.** Affected or exaggerated piety. **3. Pietism.** A reform movement in the German Lutheran Church during the 17th and 18th centuries, which strove to renew the devotional ideal in the Protestant religion. [G. *Pietismus* < Lat. *pietas,* piety.] **—pi'e·tist** *n.* **—pi'e·tis'tic, pi'e·tis'ti·cal** *adj.* **—pi'e·tis'ti·cal·ly** *adv.*

pi·e·ty (pī'ĭ-tē) *n., pl.* **-ties. 1.** Religious devotion and reverence to God. **2.** Devotion and reverence to parents and family. **3.** A pious act or thought. **4.** The state or quality of being pious. [Fr. *pieté* < Lat. *pietas,* dutiful conduct < *pius,* dutiful.]

piezo– *pref.* Pressure: *piezoelectricity.* [< Gk. *piezein,* to squeeze.]

pi·e·zo·e·lec·tric·i·ty (pī-ē'zō-ə-lĕk-trĭs'ĭ-tē, pē-ā'zō-) *n.* *Physics.* The generation of electricity or of electric polarity in dielectric crystals subjected to mechanical stress, and, conversely, the generation of stress in such crystals subjected to an applied voltage. **—pi·e'zo·e·lec'tric, pi·e'zo·e·lec'tri·cal** *adj.* **—pi·e'zo·e·lec'tri·cal·ly** *adv.*

pi·e·zom·e·ter (pī'ĭ-zŏm'ĭ-tər, pē'ĭ-) *n.* An instrument for measuring pressure, esp. high pressure. **—pi·e'zo·met'ric** (pī-ē'zə-mĕt'rĭk, pē-ā'zə-), **pi'e'zo·met'ri·cal** *adj.* **—pi·e'zom'e·try** *n.*

pif·fle (pĭf'əl) *intr.v.* **-fled, -fling, -fles.** To talk or act in a feeble or futile way. —*n.* Foolish or futile talk or ideas; nonsense. [Orig. unknown.]

pig (pĭg) *n.* **1.** Any of several mammals of the family Suidae, having short legs, cloven hoofs, bristly hair, and a cartilaginous snout used for digging, esp. the domesticated hog, *Sus scrofa,* when young or of comparatively small size. **2.** The edible parts of a pig. **3.** *Informal.* A person regarded as being piglike, greedy, or gross. **4.** The guinea pig (sense 1). **5. a.** An oblong block of metal, chiefly iron or lead, poured from a smelting furnace. **b.** A mold in which such metal is cast. **c.** Pig iron. **6.** *Offensive Slang.* A police officer. —*intr.v.* **pigged, pig·ging, pigs.** To give birth to pigs; farrow. **—*idioms.* pig in a poke.** Something that is offered in a manner that conceals its true nature or value. **pig it.** To live in a piglike fashion. [ME *pigge.*]

pig bed *n.* A bed of sand in which pigs of iron are cast.

pig·boat (pĭg'bōt') *n. Slang.* A submarine.

pi·geon (pĭj'ən) *n.* **1.** Any of various birds of the widely distributed family Columbidae, characteristically having deep-chested bodies, small heads, and short legs, esp. *Columba livia* or any of its domesticated varieties. **2.** *Slang.* One who is easily swindled; dupe. [ME < OFr. *pijon* < Lat. *pipio,* young chirping bird < *pipire,* to chirp.]

pigeon breast *n.* Chicken breast. **—pi'geon-breast'ed** *adj.*

pigeon hawk *n.* A small falcon, *Falco columbarius.*

pi·geon·hole (pĭj'ən-hōl') *n.* **1.** The small hole or holes for nesting in a pigeon loft. **2.** A small compartment or recess, as in a desk, for holding papers; cubbyhole. **3.** A specific, often oversimplified category. —*tr.v.* **-holed, -hol·ing, -holes. 1.** To place or file in a pigeonhole. **2.** To classify mentally; categorize. **3.** To put aside and ignore; shelve.

pigeon pea *n.* **1.** A tropical shrub, *Cajanus indicus,* having showy orange-yellow flowers. **2.** The edible brown seed of the pigeon pea.

pi·geon-toed (pĭj'ən-tōd') *adj.* Having the toes turned inward.

pi·geon·wing (pĭj'ən-wĭng') *n.* A dance step performed by jumping and clapping the feet together.

pig·fish (pĭg'fĭsh') *n., pl.* **pigfish** or **-fish·es.** A marine fish, *Orthopristis chrysopterus,* of Atlantic waters along the U.S. coast.

pig·ger·y (pĭg'ə-rē) *n., pl.* **-ies.** A place where pigs are kept.

pig·gin (pĭg'ĭn) *n.* A small wooden bucket with one stave projecting above the rim for use as a handle. [Orig. unknown.]

pig·gish (pĭg'ĭsh) *adj.* **1.** Greedy: *a piggish appetite.* **2.** Stubborn; pigheaded. **—pig'gish·ly** *adv.* **—pig'gish·ness** *n.*

pig·gy (pĭg'ē) *n., pl.* **-gies.** A little pig.

pig·gy·back (pĭg'ē-băk') also **pick·a·back** (pĭk'ə-băk') *adv.* **1.** On the shoulders or back: *ride piggyback.* **2.** By a method of transportation in which truck trailers are carried on trains, or cars on specially designed trucks. —*n.* The act of transporting piggyback —*v.* **-backed, -back·ing, -backs.** —*tr.* To cause to be aligned with something, such as an issue, that is larger or more important. —*intr.* To function as if carried on the back of another. [Alteration of PICKABACK.] **—pig'gy·back'** *adj.*

piggy bank *n.* A child's coin bank shaped like a pig.

pig·head·ed (pĭg'hĕd'ĭd) *adj.* Stubborn. **—pig'head'ed·ly** *adv.* **—pig'head'ed·ness** *n.*

pig iron *n.* Crude iron cast in blocks.

pig Latin *n.* A jargon systematically formed by the transposition of the initial consonant to the end of the word and the suffixation of an additional syllable, as *igpay atinlay* for *pig Latin.*

pig lead *n.* Crude lead cast in blocks.

pig·let (pĭg'lĭt) *n.* A young pig.

pig·ment (pĭg'mənt) *n.* **1.** A substance used as coloring. **2.** Dry coloring matter, usually an insoluble powder to be mixed with water, oil, or another base to produce paint and similar products. **3.** *Biol.* A substance, such as chlorophyll or hemoglobin, that produces a characteristic color in plant or animal tissue. —*tr.v.* **-ment·ed, -ment·ing, -ments.** To color with pigment. [Lat. *pigmentum* < *pingere,* to paint.] **—pig'men·tar'y** (pĭg'mən-tĕr'ē) *adj.*

pig·men·ta·tion (pĭg'mən-tā'shən) *n. Biol.* **1.** Coloration of tissues by pigment. **2.** Deposition of pigment by cells.

Pig·my (pĭg'mē) *n. & adj.* Variant of **Pygmy.**

pig·nut (pĭg'nŭt') *n.* **1.** Either of two trees, *Carya glabra* or *C. ovalis,* of the eastern United States, bearing nuts with somewhat bitter kernels. **2.** The nut of either of the pignut trees. **3.** The earthnut.

pig·pen (pĭg'pĕn') *n.* **1.** A pen for pigs. **2.** A dirty place.

pig·skin (pĭg'skĭn') *n.* **1.** The skin of a pig. **2.** Leather made from pigskin. **3.** *Informal.* **a.** A football. **b.** A saddle.

pigs·ney (pĭgz'nē) *n. Obs.* **1.** A darling. **2.** An eye. [ME *piggesnye* : *pigge,* pig + *nye,* alteration of *eye,* eye.]

pig·sty (pĭg'stī') *n., pl.* **-sties.** A shelter where pigs are kept.

pig·tail (pĭg'tāl') *n.* **1.** A plait of braided hair that hangs down the back. **2.** A twisted roll of tobacco. **—pig'tailed'** *adj.*

pig·weed (pĭg'wēd') *n.* **1.** A common wild plant, *Chenopodium album,* having leaves with a mealy surface and small green flowers. **2.** A coarse weed, *Amaranthus retroflexus,* having hairy leaves and spikes of green flowers.

pi·ka (pē'kə) *n.* Any of several small, tailless, harelike mammals of the genus *Ochotona,* of the mountains of North America and Eurasia. [Tungus *piika.*]

pike[1] (pīk) *n.* A long spear formerly used by infantry. —*tr.v.* **piked, pik·ing, pikes.** To pierce with a pike. [OFr. *pique* < *piquer,* to prick. —see PICK[1].] **—piked** *adj.*

pike[2] (pīk) *n., pl.* **pike** or **pikes. 1.** A freshwater game and food fish, *Esox lucius,* of the Northern Hemisphere, having a long snout and attaining a length of over four feet. **2.** Any of various fishes similar or related to the pike. [ME.]

pike[3] (pīk) *n.* **1.** A turnpike. **2. a.** A tollgate on a turnpike. **b.** The toll paid. —*intr.v.* **piked, pik·ing, pikes.** To move quickly. [Short for TURNPIKE.]

pike[4] (pīk) *n. Chiefly Brit.* A hill with a pointed summit. [ME, poss. of Scand. orig.]

pike[5] (pīk) *n.* A spike or sharp point, such as the tip of a spear. [ME < OE *pīc.*]

pike perch *n.* Any of various fishes related to the perches and resembling the pike, such as the walleye.

pik·er (pī'kər) *n. Slang.* A stingy, petty person, esp. one who gambles cautiously. [Orig. unknown.]

pike·staff (pīk'stăf') *n.* **1.** The shaft of a pike. **2.** A walking stick tipped with a metal spike.

pi·laf or **pi·laff** (pĭ-läf', pē-) also **pi·lau** (pĭ-lō', pē-) *n.* A steamed rice dish with meat, shellfish, or vegetables in a seasoned broth. [Turk. *pilāw.*]

pi·lar (pī'lər) *adj.* Of, pertaining to, or covered with hair. [NLat. *pilaris* < Lat. *pilus,* hair.]

pi·las·ter (pĭ-lăs'tər) *n. Archit.* A pillar or column with a capital and base, set into a wall as an ornamental motif. [OFr. *pilastre* < Ital. *pilastro* < Med. Lat. *pilastrum* < Lat. *pila,* pillar.]

pi·lau (pĭ-lō', pē-) *n.* Variant of **pilaf.**

pil·chard (pĭl'chərd) *n.* Any of various small marine fishes related to the herrings, esp. a commercially important edible species, *Sardina pilchardus,* of European waters. [Orig. unknown.]

pile[1] (pīl) *n.* **1.** A quantity of objects stacked or thrown together in a heap. **2.** *Informal.* A large accumulation or quantity: *a pile of trouble.* **3.** *Slang.* A large sum of money; fortune. **4.** A funeral pyre. **5.** A very large building or complex of buildings. **6.** *Physics.* A nuclear reactor. **7.** *Elect.* Voltaic pile. —*v.* **piled, pil·ing, piles.** —*tr.* **1.** To set or stack in a pile or heap. **2.** To load with a pile: *He piled the table*

pietà
Sculpture by
Giuseppe Bernardi

George Miksch Sutton

pigeon

pilaster

p **pop** / r **roar** / s **sauce** / sh **ship, dish** / t **tight** / th **thin, path** / *th* **this, bathe** / ŭ **cut** / ûr **urge** / v **valve** / w **with** / y **yes** / z **zebra, size** / zh **vision** / ə **about, item, edible, gallop, circus** / œ *Fr.* **feu**, *Ger.* **schön** / ü *Fr.* **tu**, *Ger.* **über** / KH *Ger.* **ich**, *Scot.* **loch** / N *Fr.* **bon.**

pilgrim
Detail from "Pilgrims Going to Church" by George Henry Boughton

piling

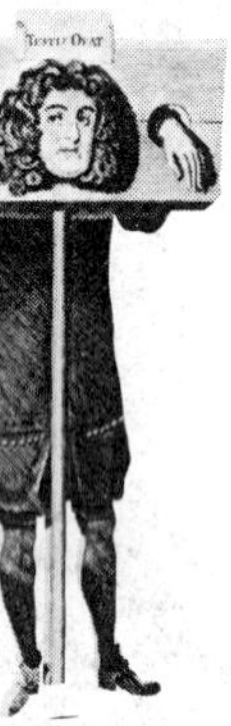

pillory
Titus Oates in the pillory

pimpernel

with books. —*intr.* **1.** To form a heap or pile. **2.** To move in a disorderly mass or group: *pile out of a car; pile into a bus.* —***phrasal verb.* pile up. 1.** To accumulate. **2.** To undergo a serious vehicular collision. [ME < OFr. < Lat. *pila,* pillar.]

pile[2] (pīl) *n.* **1.** A heavy beam of timber, concrete, or steel, driven into the earth as a foundation or support for a structure. **2.** *Heraldry.* A wedge-shaped charge pointing downward. **3.** A Roman javelin. —*tr.v.* **piled, pil·ing, piles. 1.** To drive piles into. **2.** To support with piles. [ME < OE *pīl* < Lat. *pilum,* spear.]

pile[3] (pīl) *n.* **1. a.** Cut or uncut loops of yarn forming the surface of certain fabrics, such as velvet, plush, and carpeting. **b.** The surface so formed. **2.** Soft, fine hair, fur, or wool. [ME < Lat. *pilus,* hair.] —**piled** *adj.*

pi·le·a (pī′lē-ə) *n.* Plural of **pileum.**

pi·le·at·ed (pī′lē-ā′tĭd) also **pi·le·ate** (-ĭt) *adj.* **1.** *Bot.* Having a pileus. **2.** Having a crest covering the pileum. [< Lat. *pileatus,* wearing a pileus < *pileus,* felt cap.]

pileated woodpecker *n.* A large North American woodpecker, *Dryocopus pileatus,* having black and white plumage and a bright red crest.

pile driver *n.* **1.** A machine that drives piles by raising a weight between guideposts and dropping it on the head of the pile. **2.** An operator of a pile driver.

piles (pīlz) *pl.n.* Hemorrhoids (sense 2). [< Lat. *pila,* ball.]

pi·le·um (pī′lē-əm) *n., pl.* **-le·a** (-lē-ə). The top of a bird's head, extending from the base of the bill to the nape. [NLat. < Lat. *pileus,* felt cap.]

pile·up (pīl′ŭp′) *n.* A serious collision usually involving several motor vehicles.

pi·le·us (pī′lē-əs) *n., pl.* **-le·i** (-lē-ī′). **1.** *Bot.* The umbrellalike cap of a stalked, fleshy fungus, such as a mushroom. **2.** A round, brimless skullcap worn by ancient Romans. [NLat. < Lat., cap.]

pile·wort (pīl′wûrt′, -wôrt′) *n.* Any of several plants reputed to be effective in treating piles, such as the lesser celandine and the fireweed.

pil·fer (pĭl′fər) *v.* **-fered, -fer·ing, -fers.** —*tr.* To steal (a small amount or item); filch. —*intr.* To steal or filch. [OFr. *pelfrer,* to rob < *pelfre,* booty.] —**pil′fer·age** (-ĭj) *n.* —**pil′fer·er** *n.*

pil·grim (pĭl′grəm) *n.* **1.** A religious devotee who journeys to a shrine or sacred place. **2.** One who embarks on a quest for some end conceived as sacred. **3.** A traveler. **4. Pilgrim.** One of the English Puritans who founded the colony of Plymouth in New England in 1620. [ME < OFr. *peligrin* < LLat. *pelegrinus,* alteration of Lat. *peregrinus,* foreigner.]

pil·grim·age (pĭl′grə-mĭj) *n.* **1.** A journey to a sacred place or shrine. **2.** A long journey or search, esp. one of exalted purpose or moral significance. —*intr.v.* **-aged, -ag·ing, -ag·es.** To go on a pilgrimage.

pi·li (pī′lī′) *n.* Plural of **pilus.**

pil·ing (pī′lĭng) *n.* **1.** The act of driving piles. **2.** Piles collectively. **3.** A structure composed of piles.

Pil·i·pi·no (pĭl′ə-pē′nō) *n.* A language based on Tagalog that is the official language of the Republic of the Philippines. [Tagalog < *pilipino,* Filipino < Sp.]

pill[1] (pĭl) *n.* **1.** A small pellet or tablet of medicine, often coated, taken by swallowing whole or chewing. **2. the pill.** *Informal.* An oral contraceptive. **3.** *Slang.* Something, such as a baseball, that resembles a pill. **4.** Something that is distasteful or unpleasant but necessary. **5.** *Slang.* An insipid or ill-natured person. —*v.* **pilled, pil·ling, pills.** —*tr.* **1.** To dose with pills. **2.** To make into pills. **3.** *Slang.* To blackball. —*intr.* To form small balls resembling pills: *a sweater that pills.* [Lat. *pilula,* dim. of *pila,* ball.]

pill[2] (pĭl) *v.* **pilled, pil·ling, pills.** —*tr. Archaic.* To subject to extortion. —*intr. Chiefly Brit.* To come off, as in flakes or scales. [ME *pillen* < OFr. *piller.*]

pil·lage (pĭl′ĭj) *v.* **-laged, -lag·ing, -lag·es.** —*tr.* **1.** To rob of goods by force, esp. in time of war; plunder. **2.** To take as spoils. —*intr.* To take spoils by force. —*n.* **1.** The act of pillaging. **2.** Something pillaged; spoils. [ME < OFr. < *piller,* to plunder < *peille,* rag < Lat. *pilleus, pileus,* felt cap.] —**pil′lag·er** *n.*

pil·lar (pĭl′ər) *n.* **1.** A slender, freestanding, vertical support; column. **2.** A pillar or similar structure used for decoration. **3.** One who occupies a central or responsible position: *a pillar of the state.* —*tr.v.* **-lared, -lar·ing, -lars.** To support or decorate with a pillar or pillars. —***idiom.* from pillar to post.** From one resource to another; hither and thither. [ME *piller* < OFr. *pilier* < Med. Lat. *pilare* < Lat. *pila.*]

pill·box (pĭl′bŏks′) *n.* **1.** A small box for pills. **2.** A woman's small, round hat. **3.** A low-roofed concrete emplacement for a machine gun or antitank gun.

pill bug *n.* Any of various small, terrestrial crustaceans of the genus *Armadillidium* or related genera, having convex, segmented bodies capable of being curled into a ball.

pil·lion (pĭl′yən) *n.* **1.** A pad or cushion for an extra rider behind the saddle on a horse or motorcycle. **2.** A bicycle or motorcycle saddle. [Prob. < Sc. Gael. *pillean,* dim. of *peall,* covering < Lat. *pellis,* skin.]

pil·lo·ry (pĭl′ə-rē) *n., pl.* **-ries.** A wooden framework on a post, with holes for the head and hands, in which offenders were formerly locked to be exposed to public scorn as punishment. —*tr.v.* **-ried, -ry·ing, -ries. 1.** To put in a pillory as punishment. **2.** To expose to ridicule and abuse. [ME < OFr. *pilori.*]

pil·low (pĭl′ō) *n.* **1.** A cloth case, stuffed with something soft, such as down, feathers, or foam rubber, and used to cushion the head esp. during sleep. **2.** A decorative cushion. **3.** The pad on which bobbin lace is made. —*v.* **-lowed, -low·ing, -lows.** —*tr.* **1.** To rest (one's head) on or as if on a pillow. **2.** To act as a pillow for: *Grass pillows my head.* —*intr.* To rest on or as if on a pillow. [ME *pilwe* < OE *pyle* < Lat. *pulvinus.*] —**pil′low·y** *adj.*

pillow block *n.* A block that encloses and supports a journal or shaft; bearing.

pil·low·case (pĭl′ō-kās′) *n.* A removable covering for a pillow.

pillow lace *n.* Bobbin lace.

pil·low·slip (pĭl′ō-slĭp′) *n.* A pillowcase.

pi·lo·car·pine (pī′lō-kär′pēn′) *n.* A poisonous, colorless or yellow compound, $C_{11}H_{16}N_2O_2$, obtained from the leaves of the jaborandi tree and used to induce sweating. [< NLat. *Pilocarpus,* jaborandi genus : Gk. *pilos,* wool + Gk. *karpos,* fruit.]

pi·lose (pī′lōs′) *adj.* Covered with fine, soft hair. [Lat. *pilosus* < *pilus,* hair.] —**pi·los′i·ty** (-lŏs′ĭ-tē) *n.*

pi·lot (pī′lət) *n.* **1.** One who operates or is licensed to operate an aircraft in flight. **2. a.** One who, though not belonging to a ship's company, is licensed to conduct a ship into and out of port or through dangerous waters. **b.** The helmsman of a ship. **3.** One who guides or directs a course of action for others. **4.** The part of a tool, device, or machine that leads or guides the whole: *a pilot parachute.* **5.** A pilot light (sense 1). **6.** A television program produced as a prototype of a series being considered for adoption by a network. —*tr.v.* **-lot·ed, -lot·ing, -lots. 1.** To serve as the pilot of. **2.** To steer or control the course of. —*adj.* **1.** Serving as a tentative model for future experiment or development: *a pilot project.* **2.** Serving or leading as guide. [OFr. *pilote* < OItal. *pilota,* alteration of *pedota,* prob. < Med. Gk. ***pēdōtēs** < Gk. *pēdon,* rudder.] —**pi′lot·less** *adj.*

pi·lot·age (pī′lə-tĭj) *n.* **1.** *Naut.* **a.** The technique or act of piloting. **b.** The fee paid to a pilot. **2.** Aerial navigation by visual identification of landmarks.

pilot balloon *n.* A small balloon used to determine wind velocity.

pilot bread *n.* Hardtack.

pilot burner *n.* **1.** A small service burner, as in a boiler system, kept lighted to ignite main fires. **2.** A pilot light (sense 1).

pilot cell *n.* A storage battery cell tested to determine the condition of the entire battery.

pilot engine *n.* A locomotive sent ahead of a train to check the track for safety and clearance.

pilot fish *n.* A marine fish, *Naucrates ductor,* that often swims in company with larger fishes, esp. sharks.

pi·lot·house (pī′lət-hous′) *n.* An enclosed area on the deck or bridge of a vessel from which the vessel is controlled when under way.

pi·lot·ing (pī′lə-tĭng) *n.* **1.** The occupation or service of a pilot. **2.** *Naut.* Coastal navigation by reference to landmarks, such as buoys and soundings.

pilot lamp *n.* A small electric lamp wired to light in response to specified conditions in an electric circuit.

pilot light *n.* **1.** A small jet of gas that is kept burning in order to ignite a gas burner, as in a stove. **2.** A pilot lamp.

pilot whale *n.* Any of several small, dark-colored whales of the genus *Globicephala.*

Pilt·down man (pĭlt′doun′) *n.* A supposedly early genus and species of man, *Eoanthropus dawsoni,* postulated from bones allegedly found in an early Pleistocene gravel bed between 1909 and 1915 and proved in 1953 to have been a forgery based on the artificial modification and juxtaposition of the cranium of a man and the mandible of an ape. [After *Piltdown* Common, East Sussex, England.]

pil·ule (pĭl′yo͞ol) *n.* A small pill. [OFr. < Lat. *pilula,* dim. of *pila,* ball.] —**pil′u·lar** (pĭl′yə-lər) *adj.*

pi·lus (pī′ləs) *n., pl.* **-li** (-lī′). A hair or hairlike structure. [Lat.]

Pi·ma (pē′mə) *n., pl.* **Pima** or **-mas. 1.** A tribe of North American Indians living in southern Arizona and northern Mexico. **2.** A member of the Pima. **3.** The Uto-Aztecan language of the Pima. —**Pi′man** *adj.*

pi·ma cotton (pē′mə) *n.* A very strong high-grade cotton of medium staple developed from selected Egyptian cottons in the southwestern United States. [After *Pima* County, Arizona, where it was developed.]

pi·men·to (pĭ-mĕn′tō) *n., pl.* **-tos. 1.** Allspice (sense 2). **2.** The pimiento. [Sp. *pimienta,* pepper < Med. Lat. *pigmentum* < Lat., pigment < *pingere,* to paint.]

pi meson *n. Physics.* The pion.

pi·mien·to (pĭ-mĕn′tō, -myĕn′tō) *n., pl.* **-tos.** A garden pepper, *Capsicum anuum,* or its mild, ripe, red fruit, used in salads, cookery, and as stuffing for green olives. [Sp. < *pimienta,* pepper. —see PIMENTO.]

pimp (pĭmp) *n.* A procurer; pander. —*intr.v.* **pimped, pimp·ing, pimps.** To serve as a pimp. [Orig. unknown.]

pim·per·nel (pĭm′pər-nĕl′, -nəl) *n.* Any of various plants of the genus *Anagallis,* esp. the scarlet pimpernel, *A. arvensis,*

ă pat / ā pay / âr care / ä father / b bib / ch church / d deed / ĕ pet / ē be / f fife / g gag / h hat / hw which / ĭ pit / ī pie / îr pier / j judge / k kick / l lid, needle / m mum / n no, sudden / ng thing / ŏ pot / ō toe / ô paw, for / oi noise / ou out / o͝o took / o͞o boot /

whose red, purple, or white flowers close in bad weather. [ME *pympernel* < OFr. *pimpernelle* < LLat. *pimpinella* < Lat. *piper,* pepper.]

pim·ple (pĭm′pəl) *n.* A small swelling of the skin, sometimes containing pus; papule or pustule. [ME *pinple.*] **—pim′pled, pim′ply** *adj.*

pin (pĭn) *n.* **1.** A short, straight, stiff piece of wire with a blunt head and a sharp point, used esp. for fastening. **2.** Something, such as a hairpin or a safety pin, that resembles a pin in shape or use. **3.** An ornament fastened to the clothing by means of a clasp. **4.** Something of little or no value: *didn't care a pin about the matter.* **5.** A slender, cylindrical piece of wood or metal for holding or fastening parts together, or serving as a support for suspending one thing from another, as: **a.** A thin rod for securing the ends of fractured bones. **b.** A peg for fixing the crown to the root of a tooth. **c.** A cotter pin. **6.** *Naut.* **a.** A belaying pin. **b.** A thole pin. **7.** *Mus.* One of the pegs securing the strings and regulating their tension on a stringed instrument. **8.** The part of a key stem entering a lock. **9.** A rolling pin. **10.** One of the wooden clubs at which the ball is aimed in bowling. **11.** *Sports.* The pole bearing a pennant to mark a hole in golf. **12. pins.** *Informal.* The legs: *spry for his age, and steady on his pins.* *—tr.v.* **pinned, pin·ning, pins. 1.** To fasten or secure with or as if with a pin or pins. **2. a.** To transfix. **b.** To place in a position of trusting dependence: *He pinned his faith on an absurdity.* **3. a.** To win a fall from in wrestling. **b.** To hold fast; immobilize: *He was pinned under the wreckage.* **4.** To give (a girl) a fraternity pin in token of attachment. ***—phrasal verbs.* pin down.** To fix or establish clearly: *finally able to pin down the cause of the disease.* **pin on.** To attribute (a wrongdoing or crime): *The murder was pinned on the wrong man.* *—adj.* Having a grain suggestive of the heads of pins. [ME < OE *pinn,* prob. < Lat. *pinna,* feather.]

pi·ña cloth (pēn′yə) *n.* A soft, sheer fabric made from the fibers of pineapple leaves. [Sp. *piña,* pineapple < Lat. *pinea,* pine cone < *pinus,* pine.]

pi·ña co·la·da (pēn′yə kō-lä′də, kə-, pĭn′-) *n.* A mixed drink made of rum, coconut cream, and unsweetened pineapple juice. [Sp., strained pineapple.]

pin·a·fore (pĭn′ə-fôr′, -fōr′) *n.* A sleeveless garment like an apron, worn esp. by small girls as a dress or overdress. [PIN + AFORE.]

pi·nas·ter (pī-năs′tər) *n.* A pine tree, *Pinus pinaster,* native to the Mediterranean region, having a characteristic pyramidal form. [Lat., wild pine < *pinus,* pine.]

pi·ña·ta (pēn-yä′tə) *n.* A decorated container filled with candy and toys and suspended from the ceiling to be broken by a blindfolded child with a stick, used as part of the Christmas celebration in certain Latin American countries.

pin·ball (pĭn′bôl′) *n.* A game played on a device in which the player operates a plunger to shoot a ball down a slanted surface having obstacles and targets.

pince-nez (păns′nā′, pĭns′-) *n., pl.* **pince-nez** (-nāz′, -nā′). Eyeglasses that are clipped to the bridge of the nose. [Fr. : *pincer,* to pinch (< OFr. *pincier*) + *nez,* nose < Lat. *nasus.*]

pin·cer (pĭn′sər) *n.* Something resembling one of the grasping parts of pincers.

pin·cers (pĭn′sərz) also **pinch·ers** (pĭn′chərz) *pl.n. (used with a sing. or pl. verb).* **1.** A grasping tool having a pair of jaws and handles pivoted together to work in opposition. **2.** The articulated, prehensile claws of certain arthropods, such as the lobster. **3.** A military maneuver in which the enemy is attacked from two flanks and the front. [ME *pynsour,* pincer < OFr. *pincier,* to pinch.]

pinch (pĭnch) *v.* **pinched, pinch·ing, pinch·es.** *—tr.* **1.** To squeeze between the thumb and a finger, the jaws of a tool, or other edges. **2.** To squeeze or bind (a part of the body) in such a way as to cause discomfort or pain: *The shoes pinch my toes.* **3.** To nip, wither, or shrivel: *buds pinched by the frost; her face all pinched with grief.* **4.** To straiten: *"A year and a half of the blockade has pinched Germany"* (William L. Shirer). **5.** *Slang.* To steal. **6.** *Slang.* To arrest. **7.** To move by means of a pinch bar. **8.** *Naut.* To head (a boat) very close into the wind. *—intr.* **1.** To press, squeeze, or bind painfully: *This collar pinches.* **2.** To be miserly. **3.** To drag an oar at the end of a stroke. *—n.* **1.** The act of pinching. **2.** An amount of something that can be held between thumb and forefinger: *a pinch of rosemary.* **3.** A painful, difficult, or straitened circumstance: *feel the pinch of recession.* **4.** An emergency situation. **5.** *Informal.* A theft or robbery. **6.** *Slang.* An arrest. ***—idiom.* pinch pennies.** To be thrifty or miserly. [ME *pinchen* < OFr. *pincier.*]

pinch bar *n.* A crowbar with a pointed projection at one end.

pinch·beck (pĭnch′bĕk′) *n.* **1.** An alloy of zinc and copper used as imitation gold. **2.** A cheap imitation. *—adj.* **1.** Made of pinchbeck. **2.** Imitation; spurious. [After Christopher *Pinchbeck* (1670? –1732), its inventor.]

pinch·cock (pĭnch′kŏk′) *n.* A clamp used to regulate or close a flexible tube, esp. in laboratory apparatus.

pinch effect *n. Physics.* The radial constriction of a plasma, caused by the interaction of its internal electric currents and its self-generated magnetic field.

pinch·ers (pĭn′chərz) *n.* Variant of **pincers.**

pinch-hit (pĭnch′hĭt′) *intr.v.* **-hit, -hit·ting, -hits. 1.** *Baseball.* To bat in place of a player scheduled to bat, esp. when a hit is badly needed. **2.** *Informal.* To substitute for another in an emergency. **—pinch hitter** *n.*

pin curl *n.* A coiled strand of hair, usually damp, secured with a bobby pin or clip and combed into a wave or curl when dry.

pin·cush·ion (pĭn′ko͝osh′ən) *n.* A small, firm cushion in which pins are stuck when not in use.

Pin·dar·ic (pĭn-dăr′ĭk) *adj.* **1.** Pertaining to or characteristic of the poetic style of Pindar. **2.** Of or characteristic of a Pindaric ode. *—n.* A Pindaric ode.

Pindaric ode *n.* **1.** An ode in the form developed by Pindar, consisting of a series of triads formed by the strophe, antistrophe, and epode. **2.** An adaptation of the ode developed by Pindar, with irregular stanzas and rhyme schemes, esp. as practiced by English poets of the 17th and 18th centuries.

pine¹ (pīn) *n.* **1.** Any of various evergreen trees of the genus *Pinus,* having needle-shaped leaves in clusters and bearing cones, and valued for shade and ornament and for their wood and resinous sap, which yields turpentine and pine tar. **2. a.** A coniferous tree, esp. of the family Pinaceae, such as the cedar, spruce, or fir. **b.** The wood of any of these trees. [ME < OE *pīn* < Lat. *pinus.*]

pine² (pīn) *v.* **pined, pin·ing, pines.** *—intr.* **1.** To suffer intense longing or yearning: *pined for her family.* **2.** To wither or waste away from longing or grief: *pined away and died.* *—tr. Archaic.* To grieve or mourn for. *—n. Archaic.* Intense longing or grief. [ME *pinen* < OE *pīnian,* prob. < Lat. *poena,* punishment < Gk. *poinē.*]

pin·e·al (pĭn′ē-əl, pī′nē-) *adj.* **1.** Having the form of a pine cone. **2.** Pertaining to the pineal body. [Fr. *pinéal* < OFr. *pineal* < Lat. *pinea,* pine cone < *pineus,* of pine < *pinus,* pine.]

pineal body *n.* A small, rudimentary glandular body of uncertain function, in the brain at the roof of the third ventricle.

pineal eye *n.* Pineal body.

pineal gland *n.* Pineal body.

pineal organ *n.* Pineal body.

pine·ap·ple (pīn′ăp′əl) *n.* **1. a.** A tropical American plant, *Ananas comosus,* having large, swordlike leaves and a large, fleshy, edible fruit consisting of the flowers fused into a compound whole with a terminal tuft of leaves. **b.** The fruit of this plant. **2.** *Slang.* A small hand grenade. [ME, pine cone : *pine,* pine + *apple,* apple.]

pineapple weed *n.* A North American plant, *Matricaria matricarioides,* having greenish-yellow, rayless flower heads and an odor of pineapple when crushed.

pine·drops (pīn′drŏps′) *pl.n. (used with a sing. or pl. verb).* A purplish-brown, leafless, parasitic plant, *Pterospora andromedea,* having reddish or white flowers.

pine finch *n.* The pine siskin.

pine mouse *n.* Any of various voles of the genus *Pitymys,* esp. *P. pinetorum,* a tiny forest animal of eastern North America.

pi·nene (pī′nēn′) *n.* Either of two isomeric terpene liquids, $C_{10}H_{16}$, that are the main constituents of oil or spirits of turpentine.

pine needle *n.* The needle-shaped leaf of a pine tree.

pine nut *n.* The edible seed of certain pines, such as the piñon.

pin·er·y (pī′nə-rē) *n., pl.* **-ies. 1.** A hothouse or plantation for growing pineapples. **2.** A forest of pine trees.

pine·sap (pīn′săp′) *n.* A fleshy white or reddish plant, *Monotropa hypopithys,* growing as a saprophyte or parasite on tree roots.

pine siskin *n.* A North American finch, *Spinus pinus,* having streaked, brownish plumage.

pine tar *n.* A viscous or semisolid brown to black substance produced by the destructive distillation of pine wood and used in roofing compositions, paints and varnishes, expectorants, and as an antiseptic.

pi·ne·tum (pī-nē′təm) *n., pl.* **-ta** (-tə). An area planted with pine trees or related conifers, esp. for botanical study. [Lat., pine grove < *pinus,* pine.]

pine vole *n.* The pine mouse.

pine warbler *n.* A small, yellow-breasted songbird, *Dendroica pinus,* of eastern North America.

pin·y (pī′nē) *adj.* Variant of **piny.**

pin·feath·er (pĭn′fĕth′ər) *n.* A growing feather still enclosed in its horny sheath, esp. one just emerging through the skin.

pin·fish (pĭn′fĭsh′) *n., pl.* **pinfish** or **-fish·es.** A small, spiny-finned fish, *Lagodon rhomboides,* of the waters off the southeastern coast of the United States.

pin·fold (pĭn′fōld′) *n.* A pound for stray animals. *—tr.v.* **-fold·ed, -fold·ing, -folds.** To confine in or as if in a pinfold. [ME *pynfold* < OE *pundfald* : *pund-,* enclosure + *fald,* fold.]

ping (pĭng) *n.* A brief, high-pitched sound, such as that made by a bullet striking metal. *—intr.v.* **pinged, ping·ing, pings.** To produce a ping. [Imit.]

Ping-Pong (pĭng′pông′, -pŏng′). A trademark for table tennis.

pin·head (pĭn′hĕd′) *n.* **1.** The head of a pin. **2.** Something small, trifling, or insignificant. **3.** *Slang.* A stupid person. **—pin′head′ed** *adj.* **—pin′head′ed·ness** *n.*

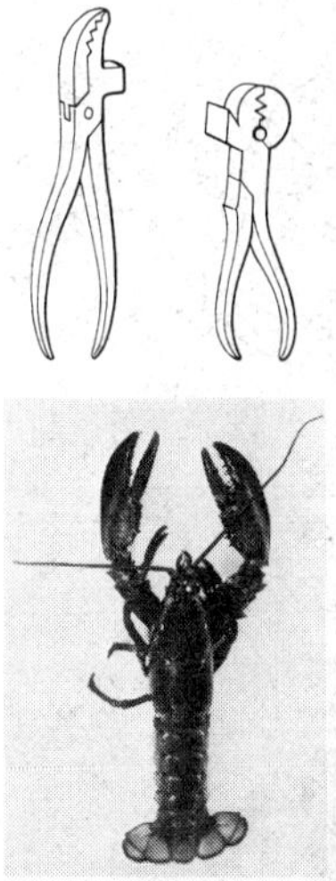

pincers
Above: Saddler's pincers (*left*) and shoe pincers (*right*)
Below: Pincers on a lobster

pineapple

pin·hole (pĭn′hōl′) *n.* A tiny puncture made by or as if by a pin.

pin·ion[1] (pĭn′yən) *n.* **1.** A bird's wing. **2.** The outer rear edge of a bird's wing, containing the primary feathers. **3.** A primary feather of a bird. —*tr.v.* **-ioned, -ion·ing, -ions. 1. a.** To remove or bind the wing feathers of (a bird) to prevent flight. **b.** To cut or bind (the wings of a bird). **2.** To restrain or immobilize (a person) by binding the arms. **3.** To fix in one place; make fast. [ME *pynyon* < OFr. *pignon* < VLat. **pinnio* < Lat. *penna,* feather.]

pin·ion[2] (pĭn′yən) *n.* A small cogwheel that engages or is engaged by a larger cogwheel or a rack. [Fr. *pignon* < OFr. < *peigne,* comb < Lat. *pecten* < *pectere,* to comb.]

pin·ite (pĭn′īt′, pē′nīt′) *n.* A hydrous, usually amorphous mineral silicate of aluminum and potassium. [G. *Pinit,* after *Pini,* a mine in Saxony where it was found.]

pink[1]

pink[1] (pĭngk) *n.* **1. a.** Any of various plants of the genus *Dianthus,* often cultivated for their fragrant flowers. **b.** Any of various plants such as the wild pink and the moss pink. **c.** A flower of any of these plants. **2.** The highest degree of excellence or perfection: *He is in the pink of health.* **3.** Any of a group of colors reddish in hue, of medium to high lightness, and low to moderate saturation. **4. pinks.** Light-brown trousers formerly worn as part of the winter semi-dress uniform by U.S. Army officers. **5.** *Slang.* A person regarded as sympathetic with or influenced by Communist doctrine. —*adj.* **-er, -est. 1.** Pink in color. **2.** Designating the scarlet coat worn by fox hunters. **3.** *Slang.* Sympathetic with or influenced by Communist doctrine. [Orig. unknown.] **—pink′ness** *n.*

pink[2] (pĭngk) *tr.v.* **pinked, pink·ing, pinks. 1.** To stab lightly with a pointed weapon; prick: *"it was as if Nixon were wielding a club while Kennedy pinked him with a rapier"* (Theodore H. White). **2.** To decorate with a perforated pattern. **3.** To cut with pinking shears. [ME *pinken,* prob. of LG orig.]

pink[3] (pĭngk) also **pink·ie** (pĭng′kē) or **pink·y** *n., pl.* **pinks** also **pink·ies.** *Naut.* A sailing vessel with a narrow stern. [ME < MDu. *pinke.*]

pink·eye also **pink eye** (pĭngk′ī′) *n.* Acute contagious conjunctivitis, characterized by inflamed eyelids and eyeballs. [Partial trans. of obs. Du. *pinck oogen,* small eyes.]

pink·ie[1] also **pink·y** (pĭng′kē) *n., pl.* **-ies.** *Informal.* The fifth or little finger. [Prob. < Du. *pinkje,* dim. of *pink,* little finger.]

pink·ie[2] (pĭng′kē) *n. Naut.* Variant of **pink**[3].

pinking shears

pinking shears *pl.n.* Sewing scissors with notched or serrated blades, used to finish edges of cloth with a scalloped or zigzag pattern for decoration or to prevent raveling.

pink·ish (pĭng′kĭsh) *adj.* Somewhat pink. **—pink′ish·ness** *n.*

pink lady *n.* A cocktail of gin, brandy, lemon or lime juice, egg white, and grenadine, shaken with cracked ice and strained.

pink·o (pĭng′kō) *n., pl.* **-os.** *Slang.* Pink[1] (sense 5).

pink·root (pĭngk′ro͞ot′, -ro͝ot′) *n.* A plant, *Spigelia marilandica,* of eastern North America, having red and yellow flowers, whose root was once used as a vermifuge.

pink root *n.* A disease of onions and related plants caused by a fungus, *Pyrenochaeta terrestris,* resulting in small plants with shriveled pink roots.

Pink·ster also **Pinx·ter** (pĭngk′stər) *n. Regional.* Whitsunday or Whitsuntide. [Du. < MDu. *pinxter* < Goth. *paintekuste* < Gk. *pentēkostē,* fiftieth. —see PENTECOST.]

pinkster flower also **pinxter flower** *n.* A North American shrub, *Rhododendron nudiflorum,* having fragrant pink flowers that bloom before the leaves appear.

pink·y[1] (pĭng′kē) *n.* Variant of **pinkie**[1].

pink·y[2] (pĭng′kē) *n.* Variant of **pink**[3].

pin money *n.* Money for incidental expenses.

pin·na (pĭn′ə) *n., pl.* **pin·nae** (pĭn′ē) or **pin·nas. 1.** *Bot.* Any of the leaflets of a pinnate leaf. **2.** *Zool.* A feather, wing, fin, or similar appendage. **3.** *Anat.* The external part of the ear; auricle. [NLat. < Lat., feather.] **—pin′nal** *adj.*

pin·nace (pĭn′ĭs) *n. Naut.* **1.** A small sailing boat formerly used as a tender for merchant and war vessels. **2.** A small ship or ship's boat. [OFr. *pinace,* prob. < OSp. *pinaza* < *pino,* pine < Lat. *pinus.*]

pin·na·cle (pĭn′ə-kəl) *n.* **1.** *Archit.* A small turret or spire on a roof or buttress. **2.** A tall, pointed formation, such as a mountain peak. **3.** The highest point; summit; acme: *the pinnacle of achievement.* —*tr.v.* **-cled, -cling, -cles. 1.** To furnish with a pinnacle. **2.** To place on or as if on a pinnacle. [ME < OFr. *pinacle* < LLat. *pinnaculum* < Lat. *pinna,* pinnacle, feather.]

pin·nae (pĭn′ē) *n.* A plural of **pinna.**

pin·nate (pĭn′āt′) also **pin·nat·ed** (pĭn′ā′tĭd) *adj.* **1.** Resembling a feather; pennate. **2.** *Bot.* Having leaflets, lobes, or divisions in a featherlike arrangement on each side of a common axis, as many compound leaves do. [Lat. *pinnatus,* feathered < *pinna,* feather.] **—pin′nate′ly** *adv.*

pintail

pinnati– *pref.* Resembling a feather: *pinnatifid.* [< Lat. *pinnatus,* feathered < *pinna,* feather.]

pin·nat·i·fid (pĭ-năt′ə-fĭd) *adj.* Having pinnately cleft lobes or divisions. Used of certain leaves. **—pin·nat′i·fid·ly** *adv.*

pin·nat·i·sect (pĭ-năt′ĭ-sĕkt′) *adj.* Divided nearly to the midrib. Used of certain leaves.

pin·ni·ped (pĭn′ə-pĕd′) *adj.* Of or belonging to the Pinnipedia, an order of aquatic mammals that includes the seals, walruses, and similar animals having finlike flippers as organs of locomotion. —*n.* A mammal belonging to the Pinnipedia. [NLat. *Pinnipedia,* order name : Lat. *pinna,* feather + Lat. *pes,* foot.]

pin·nule (pĭn′yo͞ol) also **pin·nu·la** (pĭn′yə-lə) *n., pl.* **pin·nules** also **pin·nu·lae** (pĭn′yə-lē′). **1.** *Bot.* Any of the leaflets of a pinnately compound leaf. **2.** *Zool.* A featherlike or plumelike organ or part, such as a small fin, or one of the appendages of a crinoid. [NLat. *pinnula* < Lat., little feather, dim. of *pinna,* feather.] **—pin′nu·lar** (pĭn′yə-lər) *adj.*

pin oak *n.* A tree, *Quercus palustris,* of eastern North America, having horizontal or drooping branches and sharply lobed leaves.

pi·noch·le or **pi·noc·le** (pē′nŭk′əl, -nŏk′əl) also **pe·nuch·le** or **pe·nuck·le** (pē′nŭk′əl) *n.* **1.** A game of cards for 2 to 4 persons, played with a special deck of 48 cards, with points being scored by taking tricks and forming certain combinations. **2.** The combination of the queen of spades and jack of diamonds in the game of pinochle. [Orig. unknown.]

pin·o·cy·to·sis (pĭn′ə-sī-tō′sĭs, -sī-, pī′nə-) *n.* The introduction of fluids into a cell by invagination of the cell membrane, followed by the formation of vesicles within the cells. [Gk. *pinein,* to drink + CYT(O)- + -OSIS.] **—pin′o·cy·tot′ic** (-tŏt′ĭk) *adj.* **—pin′o·cy·tot′i·cal·ly** *adv.*

pi·no·le (pĭ-nō′lē) *n.* Meal of ground corn or wheat and mesquite beans. [Mex. Sp. < Nahuatl *pinolli.*]

pi·ñon also **pin·yon** (pĭn′yōn′, -yən) *n., pl.* **pi·ñons** or **pi·ño·nes** (pĭn-yō′nēz) also **pin·yons.** Any of several pine trees bearing edible, nutlike seeds, esp. *Pinus cembroides edulis,* of the western United States and Mexico. [Sp., pine cone < *piña* < Lat. *pinea,* fem. of *pineus,* of pine < *pinus,* pine.]

piñon jay also **pinyon jay** *n.* A small, dull-blue, uncrested jay, *Gymnorhinus cyanocephala,* of western North America.

pin·point (pĭn′point′) *n.* **1.** An extremely small thing or spot; particle; bit: *a pinpoint of light.* **2. a.** A point on a map designating a strictly defined military target. **b.** A precisely identified and limited target. —*tr.v.* **-point·ed, -point·ing, -points. 1.** To pierce with or as if with a pin; punctuate: *The ship's running lights pinpointed the darkness.* **2.** To locate and identify precisely: *Our radar pinpointed the attacking planes.* **3.** To take precise aim at: *pinpoint a target.* —*adj.* **1.** Characterized by meticulous precision: *pinpoint accuracy.* **2.** Minuscule: *Pinpoint creatures swarmed on the leaf.*

pin·prick (pĭn′prĭk′) *n.* **1.** A slight puncture made by a pin. **2.** An insignificant wound. **3.** A minor annoyance. —*v.* **-pricked, -prick·ing, -pricks.** —*tr.* To puncture with a pin. —*intr.* To make a slight puncture with a pin.

pins and needles *pl.n.* Tingling felt in a part of the body that has been numbed from lack of circulation. ***—idiom.*** **on pins and needles.** In a state of anxiety or tense anticipation.

pin·scher (pĭn′shər) *n.* A Doberman pinscher.

pin·set·ter (pĭn′sĕt′ər) *n.* One that is employed to set up pins in a bowling alley.

pin·stripe (pĭn′strīp′) *n.* **1.** A thin stripe on a fabric. **2.** A kind of fabric with thin stripes, often used for suits. **—pin′-striped′** *adj.*

pint (pīnt) *n.* **1. a.** A unit of volume or capacity in the U.S. Customary System, used in liquid measure, equal to 16 fluid ounces or .473 liter. **b.** A unit of volume or capacity in the U.S. Customary System, used in dry measure, equal to 1/2 quart or .551 liter. **c.** A unit of volume or capacity in the British Imperial System, used in dry and liquid measure, equal to .568 liter. **2. a.** A container with a pint capacity. **b.** The amount of a substance that can be contained in such a container. [ME *pinte,* a unit of volume < OFr.]

pin·ta (pĭn′tə, pĕn′tä) *n.* A contagious skin disease prevalent in tropical America, caused by spirochete microorganisms, and characterized by extreme thickening and spotty discoloration of the skin. [Am. Sp. < Sp., painted mark < Lat. *pingere,* to paint.]

pin·tail (pĭn′tāl′) *n., pl.* **pintail** or **-tails.** A duck, *Anas acuta,* of the Northern Hemisphere, having gray, brown, and white plumage and a sharply pointed tail.

pin·ta·no (pĭn-tä′nō) *n., pl.* **pintano** or **-nos.** A dark-banded fish, *Abudefduf marginatus,* of southern Atlantic waters. [Am. Sp.]

pin·tle (pĭn′tl) *n.* An upright pin or bolt used as a pivot, esp.: **a.** *Naut.* The pin on which a rudder turns. **b.** The pin on a gun carriage. [ME *pintel* < OE, penis.]

pin·to (pĭn′tō) *n., pl.* **-tos** or **-toes.** A horse with irregular spots or markings. —*adj.* Irregularly marked; piebald. [Sp., piebald < VLat. **pinctus* < Lat. *pictus,* p.part. of *pingere,* to paint.]

pinto bean *n.* A form of the common string bean that has mottled seeds and is grown chiefly in the southwestern United States.

pint·size (pīnt′sīz′) also **pint·sized** (-sīzd′) *adj. Informal.* Of small dimensions; diminutive.

pin·up (pĭn′ŭp′) *n.* **1.** A picture to be pinned up on a wall, esp. a photograph of a sexually attractive woman or movie star. **2.** A woman considered a suitable model for a pinup. —*adj.* **1.** Pertaining to or suitable for a pinup. **2.** Designed to be attached to a wall: *a pinup lamp.*

pin·wale (pĭn′wāl′) *n.* A corduroy made with narrow ribs or wales. —*adj.* Of, pertaining to, or designating pinwale.
pin·weed (pĭn′wēd′) *n.* Any of various plants of the genus *Lechea,* having narrow leaves and numerous small flowers.
pin·wheel (pĭn′hwēl′, -wēl′) *n.* **1.** A toy consisting of vanes of colored paper or plastic pinned to the end of a stick in such a way that they turn when blown upon. **2.** A firework that forms a rotating wheel of colored flames. **3.** A wheel with a circle of pins at right angles to its face, used as a tripping device.
pin·work (pĭn′wûrk′) *n.* The fine stitches raised in needlepoint lace from the surface of a motif.
pin·worm (pĭn′wûrm′) *n.* A small nematode worm, *Enterobius vermicularis,* that infects the human intestines and rectum, esp. in children.
pin·wrench (pĭn′rĕnch′) *n.* A wrench having a projection designed to fit a hole in the object to be turned.
Pinx·ter (pĭngk′stər) *n.* Variant of **Pinkster.**
pinxter flower *n.* Variant of **pinkster flower.**
pin·y also **pine·y** (pī′nē) *adj.* **-i·er, -i·est.** Resembling, characteristic of, consisting of, or covered with pines.
Pin·yin or **pin·yin** (pĭn′yĭn′, -yĭn) *n.* A system for transliterating Chinese ideograms into the roman alphabet. [Chin. (Mandarin) *pin*[1] *yin*[1], to combine sounds into syllables : *pin*[1], to combine + *yin*[1], sound.]
pin·yon (pĭn′yōn′, -yən) *n.* Variant of **piñon.**
pinyon jay *n.* Variant of **piñon jay.**
pi·o·let (pē′ə-lā′) *n.* A kind of ice ax used in mountain climbing. [Fr. < dial. Fr. *piola,* ax < OProv. *apcha,* of Germanic orig.]
pi·on (pī′ŏn′) *n.* Either of two subatomic particles in the meson family: **a.** *pi zero,* having a mass 264 times that of the electron, zero electric charge, and a mean lifetime of 0.9×10^{-16} second. **b.** *pi plus,* having a mass 273 times that of the electron, a positive electric charge, and a mean lifetime of 2.6×10^{-8} second. [Contraction of PI MESON.]
pi·o·neer (pī′ə-nîr′) *n.* **1.** One who ventures into unknown or unclaimed territory to settle. **2.** An innovator: *a pioneer in aviation.* **3.** A military engineer employed in the construction and fortification of positions and the maintenance of communication lines. **4.** *Ecol.* An animal or plant species that establishes itself in a previously barren environment. —*adj.* **1.** Of the nature of a pioneer; trailblazing; innovating: *a pioneer chemist.* **2.** Of or relating to early settlers or their time: *the pioneer spirit.* —*v.* **-neered, -neer·ing, -neers.** —*tr.* **1. a.** To explore or open up (a region): *Our rockets pioneered outer space.* **b.** To settle: *The taiga is still being pioneered.* **2.** To innovate or participate in the development of: *men who pioneered rocketry.* —*intr.* To act as a pioneer. [OFr. *pionier,* foot soldier < *pion* < Med. Lat. *pedo* < Lat. *pes,* foot.]
pi·os·i·ty (pī-ŏs′ĭ-tē) *n., pl.* **-ties.** Ostentatious piousness; exaggerated devoutness. [< PIOUS.]
pi·ous (pī′əs) *adj.* **1.** Having or exhibiting reverence and earnest compliance in the observance of religion; devout. **2. a.** Marked by conspicuous devoutness: *a pious and holy observation.* **b.** Marked by false devoutness; solemnly hypocritical: *a pious fraud.* **3.** Devotional: *pious readings.* **4.** Professing or exhibiting a strict, traditional sense of virtue and morality; high-minded. **5.** Commendable; worthy: *pious giving.* [Lat. *pius,* dutiful.] —**pi′ous·ly** *adv.* —**pi′ous·ness** *n.*
pip[1] (pĭp) *n.* **1.** The small seed of a fruit, such as an apple or orange. **2.** *Informal.* Something remarkable of its kind: *a pip of a plan.* [Short for PIPPIN.]
pip[2] (pĭp) *tr.v.* **pipped, pip·ping, pips.** *Chiefly Brit. Slang.* **1.** To strike with a gunshot; hit. **2.** To blackball. [Poss. < PIP[3].]
pip[3] (pĭp) *n.* **1. a.** A dot indicating a unit of numerical value on dice or dominoes. **b.** A spot or speck. **2.** A rootstock of certain flowering plants, esp. the lily of the valley. **3.** *Informal.* A shoulder insignia of certain officers in the British Army. **4.** A radar signal. [Orig. unknown.]
pip[4] (pĭp) *v.* **pipped, pip·ping, pips.** —*tr.* To break through (an eggshell) in hatching. —*intr.* To peep or chirp, as a chick or young bird does. —*n.* A short, high-pitched radio signal. [Orig. unknown.]
pip[5] (pĭp) *n.* **1. a.** A disease of birds, characterized by a thick mucous discharge that forms a crust in the mouth and throat. **b.** The crust symptomatic of this disease. **2.** *Slang.* A minor or imaginary human ailment. [ME *pippe* < MDu. < Lat. *pituita.*]
pip·age also **pipe·age** (pī′pĭj) *n.* **1. a.** The transmission of liquids through pipes. **b.** The charge for such transmission. **2.** Pipes; piping.
pi·pal (pē′pəl) *n.* Variant of **peepul.**
pipe (pīp) *n.* **1. a.** A hollow cylinder or tubular conveyance for a fluid or gas. **b.** A section or piece of such a tube. **2. a.** An instrument for smoking, consisting of a tube of wood or clay with a mouthpiece at one end and a small bowl at the other. **b.** Sufficient tobacco or other smoking material to fill the bowl of a pipe; pipeful. **3. a.** *Biol.* A tubular part or organ. **b. pipes.** *Informal.* The human respiratory system. **4. a.** A wine cask having a capacity of 126 gallons. **b.** This volume as a unit of liquid measure. **5.** *Mus.* **a.** A tubular wind instrument, such as a flute. **b.** Any of the tubes in an organ. **c. pipes.** A small wind instrument, consisting of tubes of different lengths bound together: *pipes of Pan.* **d. pipes.** A bagpipe. **6.** The sound of the voice, esp. as used in singing or acting. **7.** A birdcall. **8.** *Naut.* A kind of whistle used for signaling crewmen: *a boatswain's pipe.* **9.** *Mining.* **a.** A vertical, cylindrical vein of ore. **b.** One of the vertical veins of eruptive origin in which diamonds are found in South Africa. **10.** *Geol.* An eruptive passageway opening into the crater of a volcano. **11.** *Metallurgy.* A cone-shaped cavity in a steel ingot, formed during cooling by escaping gases. **12.** *Slang.* An easy task, esp. an easy course in school. —*v.* **piped, pip·ing, pipes.** —*tr.* **1.** To convey (liquid or gas) by means of pipes. **2.** To provide or connect with pipes. **3. a.** To play (a tune) on a pipe or pipes. **b.** To lead by playing on pipes. **4.** *Naut.* **a.** To call (the crew) by sounding a boatswain's pipe. **b.** To receive aboard or mark the departure of by playing a boatswain's pipe: *piped the admiral aboard the battleship.* **5.** To utter in a shrill, reedy tone. **6.** To furnish (a garment or fabric) with piping. —*intr.* **1.** To play on a pipe. **2.** To speak shrilly; make a shrill sound. **3.** To chirp or whistle, as a bird does. **4.** *Naut.* To signal the crew with a boatswain's pipe. **5.** *Metallurgy.* To develop conical cavities. —***phrasal verbs.*** **pipe down.** *Slang.* To stop talking; be quiet. **pipe up.** To speak up in a small, shrill voice. [ME < OE *pīpe* < VLat. **pipa* < Lat. *pipare,* to chirp.]
pipe·age (pī′pĭj) *n.* Variant of **pipage.**
pipe clay *n.* A fine white clay used in making tobacco pipes and pottery, in calico printing, and in whitening leather.
pipe cleaner *n.* A pliant, tufted rod used for cleaning the stem of a tobacco pipe.
pipe dream *n.* A wishful, fantastic notion or hope. [From the fantasies induced by smoking a pipe of opium.]
pipe·fish (pīp′fĭsh′) *n., pl.* **pipefish** or **-fish·es.** Any of various slim, elongated marine or freshwater fishes of the family Syngnathidae, characterized by a tubelike snout and an external covering of bony plates.
pipe fitter *n.* One who installs and repairs piping systems.
pipe·fit·ting (pīp′fĭt′ĭng) *n.* **1. a.** The act or work of joining pipes together. **b.** A branch of the plumbing trade that deals specifically with the installation and repair of piping systems. **2.** A section of pipe used to join two or more pipes together.
pipe·ful (pīp′fo͝ol′) *n.* Sufficient tobacco to fill a pipe.
pipe·line (pīp′līn′) *n.* **1.** A conduit of pipe for the conveyance of water or petroleum products. **2.** A channel by which information of a generally secret or confidential nature is transmitted. **3.** A line of communication or route of supply: *a new pipeline for medical supplies.* —*tr.v.* **-lined, -lin·ing, -lines.** **1.** To convey by means of a pipeline. **2.** To lay a pipeline through.

pipeline

pipe organ *n.* An organ (sense 1).
pip·er (pī′pər) *n.* **1.** One who plays on a pipe. **2.** One who lays or installs piping. **3.** One who applies piping to a garment or fabric.
pi·per·a·zine (pī-pĕr′ə-zēn′, pĭ-) *n.* A colorless, crystalline compound, $C_4H_{10}N_2$, used to inhibit corrosion, in insecticides, and as an anthelmintic. [PIPER(INE) + AZ(O)- + -INE[2].]
pi·per·i·dine (pī-pĕr′ĭ-dēn′, pĭ-) *n.* A strongly basic, colorless liquid, $C_5H_{10}NH$, used in the manufacture of rubber and as a curing agent in epoxy resins. [PIPER(INE) + -IDE + -INE[2].]
pip·er·ine (pĭp′ə-rēn′) *n.* A crystalline solid, $C_{17}H_{19}NO_3$, extracted from black pepper, and used as flavoring and as an insecticide. [Lat. *piper,* pepper + -INE[2].]
pi·per·o·nal (pī-pĕr′ə-năl′, pĭ-) *n.* A white powder, $C_8H_6O_3$, having a floral odor, used as flavoring and in perfume. [PIPER(INE) + -ON(E) + -AL[3].]
pipe·stone (pīp′stōn′) *n.* A heat-hardened, compacted, red clay used by American Indians for making tobacco pipes.
pi·pette also **pi·pet** (pī-pĕt′) *n.* Any of variously shaped glass tubes, open at both ends, usually calibrated, and used esp. to transfer small volumes of liquid. [Fr., dim. of *pipe,* pipe < VLat. **pipa.* —see PIPE.]
pipe vine *n.* A woody vine, *Aristolochia durior,* of the eastern United States, having greenish, brown-mottled flowers shaped like a curved pipe.
pipe wrench *n.* A wrench with two serrated jaws, one adjustable, for gripping and turning pipe.
pip·ing (pī′pĭng) *n.* **1.** A system of pipes, such as one used in plumbing. **2.** *Mus.* **a.** The act of playing on a pipe. **b.** The music produced by a pipe. **3.** A shrill, high-pitched sound. **4.** A rounded strip of cloth used for trimming garments or decorative fabrics. **5.** A rounded ribbon of icing on a pastry. —*adj.* **1.** Playing on a pipe. **2.** Making a high-pitched sound with little resonance, as a pipe does. —*adv.* Extremely: *piping hot biscuits.*
pip·it (pĭp′ĭt) *n.* Any of various widely distributed songbirds of the genus *Anthus,* characteristically having brownish upper plumage and a streaked breast. [Imit. of its song.]
pip·kin (pĭp′kĭn) *n.* **1.** A small earthenware or metal cooking pot. **2.** A piggin. [Poss. PIPE + -KIN.]
pip·pin (pĭp′ĭn) *n.* **1.** Any of several varieties of apple. **2.** The seed of a fruit; pip. **3.** *Slang.* An admired person or thing. [ME *pipin* < OFr. *pepin.*]
pip·sis·se·wa (pĭp-sĭs′ə-wô′) *n.* Any of several North American evergreen plants of the genus *Chimaphila,* esp. *C. umbel-*

piranha

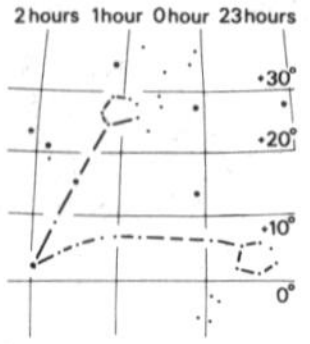

Pisces

pistachio

pitcher[2]
18th-century French

lata, having white or pinkish flowers. [Cree *pipisisikweu.*]

pip-squeak (pĭp'skwēk') *n.* A contemptibly small or insignificant person.

pi·quant (pē'kənt, -känt', pē-känt') *adj.* **1.** Pleasantly pungent in taste or odor; spicy. **2.** Pleasantly or appealingly provocative: *touched by the piquant faces of children.* **3.** *Archaic.* Causing hurt pride or feelings; stinging. [OFr. < pr.part. *piquer,* to prick. —see PICK[1].] **—pi'quan·cy, pi'quant·ness** *n.* **—pi'quant·ly** *adv.*

pique (pēk) *n.* A feeling of resentment or vexation arising from wounded pride or vanity. *—tr.v.* **piqued, piqu·ing, piques. 1.** To cause to feel resentment or vexation; injure the feelings of. **2.** To provoke; arouse: *The portrait piqued my curiosity.* **3.** To pride (oneself): *They piqued themselves on their modish attire.* [OFr., animosity < *piquer,* to prick. —see PICK[1].]

pi·qué (pĭ-kā', pē-) *n.* A tightly woven fabric with various patterns of wales, produced esp. by a double warp. [Fr. < *piquer,* to quilt < OFr., to backstitch, prick. —see PICK[1].]

pi·quet also **pic·quet** (pĭ-kā') *n.* A card game for two people, played with a deck from which all cards below the seven (aces being high) are omitted. [Fr.]

pi·ra·cy (pī'rə-sē) *n., pl.* **-cies.** The act or practice of pirating. [Med. Lat. *piratia* < LGk. *peirateia* < Gk. *peiratēs,* pirate.]

pi·ra·gua (pĭ-rä'gwə) *n.* **1.** A canoe made by hollowing out a tree trunk; dugout. **2.** A flat-bottomed sailing boat with two masts. [Sp. < Carib.]

pi·ra·nha also **pi·ra·ña** (pĭ-rän'yə, -răn'yə) *n.* Any of several tropical American freshwater fishes of the genus *Serrasalmus* that are voraciously carnivorous and often attack and destroy living animals. [Port. < Tupi : *pirá,* fish + *sainha,* tooth.]

pi·ra·ru·cu (pĭ-rär'ə-kōō') *n.* The arapaima. [Port. *pirarucú* < Tupi *pirá-rucú* : *pirá,* fish + *urucú,* red.]

pi·rate (pī'rĭt) *n.* **1. a.** One who robs at sea or plunders the land from the sea without commission from a sovereign nation. **b.** A ship used for this purpose. **2.** One who makes use of or reproduces the work, esp. the literary work, of another, illicitly or without permission. *—v.* **-rat·ed, -rat·ing, -rates.** *—tr.* **1.** To attack and rob (a ship at sea). **2.** To seize (goods) by piracy. **3.** To make use of or reproduce (another's work) illicitly. *—intr.* To act as a pirate; practice piracy. [ME < Lat. *pirata* < Gk. *peiratēs* < *peiran,* to attempt.] **—pi·rat'ic** (pī-răt'ĭk), **pi·rat'i·cal** *adj.* **—pi·rat'i·cal·ly** *adv.*

pirate perch *n.* A small North American freshwater fish, *Aphredoderus sayanus,* that is unusual because its anal opening is in the throat.

pi·rog (pĭ-rōg') *n., pl.* **-ro·ghi** (-rō'gē) or **-ro·gi.** A large Russian pastry made of dough stuffed with various combinations of meat, fish, eggs, or cabbage. [R., prob. < *pir,* feast.]

pi·rogue (pĭ-rōg') *n.* A canoe made from a hollowed tree trunk; piragua. [Fr. < Sp. *piragua* < Carib.]

pir·ou·ette (pĭr'ōō-ĕt') *n.* A full turn of the body on the tip of the toe or on the ball of the foot in ballet. *—intr.v.* **-et·ted, -et·ting, -ettes.** To execute a pirouette. [Fr. < OFr. *pirouet,* spinning top.]

pi·rozh·ki also **pi·rosh·ki** or **pi·roj·ki** (pĭ-rôzh'kē) *pl.n.* Small Russian pastries made esp. with meat or cabbage fillings. [Yiddish *pirozhke* < R. *pirozhki,* pl. of *pirozhok,* small pocket of pastry, dim. of *pirog,* pirog.]

pis al·ler (pē ză-lā') *n.* The final recourse or expedient; last resort. [Fr., to go worse.]

pis·ca·ry (pĭs'kə-rē) *n., pl.* **-ries. 1.** The right to fish in waters owned by another party. **2.** A fishery. [ME < Med. Lat. *piscaria* < Lat., neuter pl. of *piscarius,* of fish < *piscis,* fish.]

pis·ca·to·ri·al (pĭs'kə-tôr'ē-əl, -tōr'-) also **pis·ca·to·ry** (pĭs'kə-tôr'ē, -tōr'ē) *adj.* **1.** Of or pertaining to fish, fishermen, or fishing. **2.** Involved in fishing. [< Lat. *piscatorius* < *piscator,* fisherman < *piscari,* to fish < *piscis,* fish.] **—pis'ca·to'ri·al·ly** *adv.*

Pi·sces (pī'sēz) *n.* **1.** A constellation in the equatorial region of the Northern Hemisphere near Aries and Pegasus. **2.** The 12th sign of the zodiac. [ME < Lat. < pl. of *piscis,* fish.] **—Pi'sce·an** (pī'sē-ən) *adj.*

pisci– *pref.* Fish: *piscivorous.* [< Lat. *piscis,* fish.]

pi·sci·cul·ture (pī'sĭ-kŭl'chər, pĭs'ĭ-) *n.* The breeding, hatching, and rearing of fish under controlled conditions. **—pi'sci·cul'tur·al** *adj.* **—pi'sci·cul'tur·ist** *n.*

pi·sci·form (pī'sĭ-fôrm', pĭs'ĭ-) *adj.* Having the shape of a fish.

pi·sci·na (pĭ-sē'nə, -sī'nə, -shē'nə) *n., pl.* **-nae** (-nē). *Eccles.* A stone basin with a drain for carrying away the water used in ceremonial ablutions. [Med. Lat. < Lat., fish-pond < *piscis,* fish.] **—pis'ci·nal** (pĭs'ə-nəl) *adj.*

pi·scine (pī'sēn', pĭs'īn') *adj.* Of, pertaining to, or typical of a fish or fishes. [Med. Lat. *piscinus* < Lat. *piscis,* fish.]

Pi·scis Aus·tri·nus (pī'sĭs ôs-trī'nəs) *n.* A constellation in the Southern Hemisphere near Aquarius and Grus. [NLat., the Southern Fish.]

pi·sciv·o·rous (pĭ-sĭv'ər-əs, pī-) *adj.* Habitually feeding on fish; fish-eating.

pish (pĭsh) *interj.* Used to express disdain.

pi·shogue also **pi·shoge** (pĭ-shōg') *n. Ir.* **1.** Black magic; sorcery; witchcraft. **2.** An evil spell; incantation. [Ir. Gael. *pĭseog* < MIr. *pisōc.*]

pi·si·form (pī'sə-fôrm') *adj.* Suggestive of a pea in size or shape; pealike. *—n. Anat.* A small bone at the junction of the ulna and the wrist. [Lat. *pisum,* pea + -FORM.]

pis·mire (pĭs'mīr', pĭz'-) *n.* An ant. [ME *pissemyre* : *pisse,* urine + *mire,* ant, of Scand. orig.]

pis·mo clam (pĭz'mō) *n.* An edible marine clam, *Tivela stultorum,* of the southern Pacific coast of North America. [After *Pismo* Beach, California.]

pi·so·lite (pī'sə-līt') *n.* A small round accretionary limestone mass. [Gk. *pisos,* pea + -LITE.] **—pi'so·lit'ic** (-lĭt'ĭk) *adj.*

piss (pĭs) *Vulgar Slang.* *—v.* **pissed, piss·ing, piss·es** *—intr.* To urinate. *—tr.* To urinate on or in. *—n.* **1.** Urine. **2.** The act of urinating. [ME *pisser* < OFr. *pissier.*]

piss ant also **piss-ant** or **piss·ant** (pĭs'ănt') *Slang.* *—n.* A stickler for petty details. *—adj.* Showing concern for petty details; niggling.

piss·er (pĭs'ər) *n. Vulgar Slang.* A person or situation that is extremely difficult, disappointing, or repulsive.

pis·soir (pē-swär') *n.* A public urinal located on streets in some countries of Europe. [Fr. < *pisser,* to urinate < OFr. *pissier.*]

pis·ta·chi·o (pĭ-stăsh'ē-ō', -stä'shē-ō') *n., pl.* **-os. 1. a.** A tree, *Pistacia vera,* of the Mediterranean region and western Asia, bearing small hard-shelled nuts. **b.** The nut of this tree, having an edible, oily, green kernel. **2.** The flavor of pistachio nuts. [Ital. *pistacchio* < Lat. *pistacium,* pistachio nut < Gk. *pistakion* < *pistakē,* pistachio tree < Pers. *pistah.*]

pistachio green *n.* A moderate to light yellowish or yellow green.

pis·ta·reen (pĭs'tə-rēn') *n.* A small silver coin used in America and the West Indies during the 18th century. [Prob. alteration of Sp. *peseta,* peseta. —see PESETA.]

pis·til (pĭs'təl) *n.* The seed-bearing organ of a flower, including the stigma, style, and ovary. [Fr. < Lat. *pistillum,* pestle.]

pis·til·late (pĭs'tə-lāt', -lĭt) *adj.* **1.** Having a pistil or pistils. **2.** Bearing pistils but no stamens: *pistillate flowers.*

pis·tol (pĭs'təl) *n.* A firearm designed to be held and fired with one hand. *—tr.v.* **-toled, -tol·ing, -tols.** To shoot with a pistol. [Fr. *pistole* < G. *Pistole* < Czech *pištala,* pipe.]

pis·tole (pĭ-stōl') *n.* An old gold coin, used in various European countries until the late 19th century. [Fr.]

pis·to·leer (pĭs'tə-lîr') *n.* One armed with a pistol.

pistol grip *n.* **1. a.** The grip of a pistol, shaped to fit the hand. **b.** A similar grip sometimes used on a rifle or other firearm. **2.** A grip used on certain tools, such as a saw, shaped to fit the hand.

pis·tol-whip (pĭs'təl-hwĭp', -wĭp') *tr.v.* **-whipped, -whip·ping, -whips. 1.** To beat with a pistol barrel. **2.** To beat while threatening with a gun. **3.** To attack violently.

pis·ton (pĭs'tən) *n.* **1.** A solid cylinder or disk that fits snugly into a larger cylinder and moves back and forth under fluid pressure, as in a reciprocating engine, or displaces or compresses fluids, as in pumps and compressors. **2.** *Mus.* A valve mechanism in brass instruments for altering pitch. [Fr. < OFr. < OItal. *pistone,* large pestle < *pistare,* to pound < Lat. *pinsare.*]

piston ring *n.* An adjustable metal ring that fits around a piston and closes the gap between the piston and cylinder wall.

piston rod *n.* A connecting rod that transmits power to or is powered by a piston.

pit[1] (pĭt) *n.* **1.** A relatively deep hole in the ground, either natural, such as a pothole or sinkhole, or manmade, such as a mine shaft. **2.** A trap consisting of a concealed hole in the ground; pitfall. **3.** A hidden danger or unexpected trouble. **4. a.** Hell. **b.** A very dirty, unattractive place: *This house is a pit.* **c. the pits.** *Slang.* The worst imaginable: *"New York politics are the pits"* (Washington Star). **5.** An enclosed space, often one dug in the ground, in which animals, such as dogs or gamecocks, are placed for fighting. **6. a.** A natural depression in the surface of a body, organ, or part. **b.** A small indentation in the skin left by disease or injury; pockmark. **7. a.** The section directly in front of the stage of a theater, in which the musicians sit. **b.** The area behind the stalls of a theater. **8.** The section of an exchange where trading in a specific commodity is carried on. **9.** A refueling area at an auto racecourse. **10.** *Football.* The middle areas of the defensive and offensive lines. **11.** *Bot.* A thin-walled spot or depression in the wall of some plant cells. *—v.* **pit·ted, pit·ting, pits.** *—tr.* **1.** To make cavities, depressions, or scars in. **2.** To place in contest against another; set in direct opposition: *a civil war that pitted brother against brother.* *—intr.* **1.** To become marked with small pits. **2.** To stop at one's refueling area during an auto race. [ME < OE *pytt.*]

pit[2] (pĭt) *n.* The single, central kernel of certain fruits, such as a peach or cherry; stone. *—tr.v.* **pit·ted, pit·ting, pits.** To extract pits from (fruit). [Du. < MDu.]

pi·ta[1] (pē'tə) *n.* Round, flat bread with a pocket inside. [Mod. Gk., pie, cake.]

pi·ta[2] (pē'tə) *n.* **1.** Any of several plants of the genus *Agave* that yield a strong fiber. **2.** A species of pineapple, *Ananas magdalenae,* from whose leaves a fine, whitish fiber is obtained. **3.** The fiber of the pita plant, used in making cordage and paper. [Sp. < Quechua, to complicate.]

pita fiber *n.* Pita[2] (sense 3).

pit·a·pat (pĭt'ə-păt') *intr.v.* **-pat·ted, -pat·ting, -pats. 1.** To move with a series of quick, tapping steps. **2.** To make a repeated tapping sound. *—n.* A series of quick steps, taps, or beats. *—adv.* With a rapid tapping sound. [Imit.]

pitch¹ (pĭch) *n.* **1.** Any of various thick, dark, sticky substances obtained from the distillation residue of coal tar, wood tar, or petroleum, and used for waterproofing, roofing, caulking, and paving. **2.** Any of various natural bitumens, such as mineral pitch or asphalt. **3.** A resin derived from the sap of various coniferous trees, such as the pines. *—tr.v.* **pitched, pitch·ing, pitch·es.** To smear or cover with or as if with pitch. [ME *pich* < OE *pic* < Lat. *pix.*]

pitch² (pĭch) *v.* **pitched, pitch·ing, pitch·es.** *—tr.* **1.** To throw, usually in a specific, intended direction; hurl; toss. **2.** *Baseball.* **a.** To throw (the ball) from the mound to the batter. **b.** To play (a game or part of one) in the position of pitcher. **3.** To put up or in position; establish: *pitching a tent.* **4.** To set firmly; implant; embed: *pitch stakes.* **5. a.** To fix the level of: *pitch one's expectations high.* **b.** To set the character and course of: *He pitched his speech to the party line.* **6. a.** To set at a specified downward slant: *pitched the roof at a steep angle.* **b.** *Mus.* To set in a particular key. **7.** *Games.* To lead (a card), thus establishing the trump suit. **8.** To sell or present in a high-pressure fashion. *—intr.* **1.** To throw or toss something, such as a ball, horseshoe, or bale. **2.** *Baseball.* To play in the position of pitcher. **3.** To plunge; fall, esp. forward: *He pitched over the railing.* **4. a.** To stumble around; lurch. **b.** To buck, as a horse. **5. a.** *Naut.* To dip bow and stern alternately. **b.** To revolve about a lateral axis so that the nose lifts or descends in relation to the tail. Used of an airplane. **c.** To revolve about a lateral axis that is both perpendicular to the longitudinal axis and horizontal to the earth. Used of a space vehicle. **6.** To slope downward. **7.** To set up living quarters; encamp; settle. **8.** To make a casual, usually hurried decision: *They pitched on his solution as the best.* **—phrasal verbs. pitch in.** *Informal.* **1.** To set to work vigorously. **2.** To join forces with others; help; cooperate. **pitch into.** *Informal.* To attack verbally or physically; assault. *—n.* **1.** An act or instance of pitching. **2.** *Baseball.* **a.** A throw of the ball by the pitcher for action by the batter. **b.** A ball so thrown: *The pitch was fouled off.* **3.** The rectangular area between the wickets in cricket, 22 yards by 10 feet. **4.** *Naut.* The alternate dip and rise of a ship's bow and stern. **5. a.** A steep downward slant. **b.** The degree of such a slant. **6.** *Archit.* **a.** The angle of a roof. **b.** The highest point of a structure: *the pitch of an arch.* **7.** A point or stage of development or intensity: *worked at a feverish pitch.* **8.** *Acoustics.* The subjective quality of a complex sound, dependent on frequency, loudness, and intensity, and often measured as the frequency of a pure tone of specified intensity judged equivalent to the complex sound by a normal ear. **9.** *Mus.* **a.** The relative position of a tone in a scale, as determined by its frequency. **b.** Any of various standards that establish a frequency for each tone, used in the tuning of instruments. **10. a.** The distance traveled by a machine screw in a single revolution. **b.** The distance between two corresponding points on adjacent screw threads or gear teeth. **11.** The distance a propeller would travel in an ideal medium during one complete revolution, measured parallel to the shaft of the propeller. **12. a.** *Slang.* A set talk designed to persuade: *a sales pitch.* **b.** The stand of a vender or hawker. **13.** *Games.* Seven-up. [ME *pichen.*]

pitch accent *n. Ling.* Tonic accent.

pitch-black (pĭch′blăk′) *adj.* Extremely black; black as pitch.

pitch·blende (pĭch′blĕnd′) *n.* The principal ore of uranium, a brownish-black mineral of uraninite and uranium trioxide with small amounts of water and uranium decay products. [G. *Pechblend* : *Pech,* pitch (< Lat. *pix*) + *Blende,* blende. —see BLENDE.]

pitch-dark (pĭch′därk′) *adj.* Extremely dark.

pitched battle *n.* **1.** A fierce, intensive battle fought by opponents in close contact. **2.** A fierce dispute.

pitch·er¹ (pĭch′ər) *n.* **1.** One that pitches. **2.** *Baseball.* The player who throws the ball from the mound for action by the batter. **3.** A golf iron with a sharply inclined head.

pitch·er² (pĭch′ər) *n.* **1.** A vessel for liquids, with a handle and a lip or spout for pouring. **2.** *Bot.* A pitcherlike part such as the leaf of a pitcher plant. [ME *picher* < OFr. *pichier* < Med. Lat. *bicarium,* drinking cup < Gk. *bikos,* jar.]

pitcher plant *n.* Any of various insectivorous plants of the genera *Sarracenia, Nepenthes,* or *Darlingtonia,* having leaves modified to form pitcherlike organs that attract and trap insects.

pitch·fork (pĭch′fôrk′) *n.* A large fork with sharp, widely spaced prongs for pitching hay and breaking ground. *—tr.v.* **-forked, -fork·ing, -forks.** To lift or toss with a pitchfork. [ME *pikforke* : *pik,* pick + *forke,* fork.]

pitch·man (pĭch′mən) *n.* A peddler or vender of small wares, esp. one with a colorful sales talk.

pitch·out (pĭch′out′) *n.* **1.** *Baseball.* A pitch deliberately thrown high and away from the batter to make it easier for the catcher to throw out a base runner attempting to steal. **2.** *Football.* A lateral pass from the back receiving the snap from the center to another back behind the line of scrimmage.

pitch pine *n.* Any of various American pine trees yielding pitch or turpentine, such as *Pinus rigida* or *P. echinata,* of eastern North America.

pitch pipe *n. Mus.* A small pipe that, when sounded, gives the standard pitch for a piece of music or for tuning an instrument.

pitch·stone (pĭch′stōn′) *n.* Any of various volcanic glasses distinguished by their pitchlike luster and relatively high water content. [Transl. of G. *Pechstein.*]

pitch·y (pĭch′ē) *adj.* **-i·er, -i·est. 1.** Full of pitch; covered or smeared with pitch. **2.** Resembling pitch; having the texture of pitch. **3.** Extremely dark; black. **—pitch′i·ness** *n.*

pit·e·ous (pĭt′ē-əs) *adj.* **1.** Exciting pity; pathetic. **2.** Pitying; compassionate. [ME *piteus* < OFr. < *pite,* pity. —see PITY.] **—pit′e·ous·ly** *adv.* **—pit′e·ous·ness** *n.*

pit·fall (pĭt′fôl′) *n.* **1.** A trap made by digging a hole in the ground and concealing its opening. **2.** Danger or difficulty that is not easily anticipated or avoided.

pith (pĭth) *n.* **1.** *Bot.* The soft, spongelike substance in the center of stems and branches of most vascular plants. **2. a.** The most central and material part; heart. **b.** A basic trait or set of traits that define and establish the character of something. **3.** Force; strength; vigor. **4.** Significance or importance. *—tr.v.* **pithed, pith·ing, piths. 1.** To remove the pith from (a plant stem). **2.** To sever or destroy the spinal cord of (a laboratory animal), usually by means of a needle inserted into the vertebral canal. **3.** To kill (cattle) by cutting the spinal cord. [ME < OE *piða.*]

pith·e·can·thro·pus (pĭth′ĭ-kăn′thrə-pəs, -kăn-thrō′pəs) *n.* A member of a genus formerly designated *Pithecanthropus,* based on bone fragments found in Java and thought to indicate the existence of a primate between man and ape but now reclassified in the extinct species *Homo erectus.* [NLat. *Pithecanthropus,* genus name : Gk. *pithēkos,* ape + Gk. *anthrōpos,* man.]

pith helmet *n.* A light sun hat made from dried pith; topi.

pith·y (pĭth′ē) *adj.* **-i·er, -i·est. 1.** Consisting of or resembling pith. **2.** Precisely meaningful; cogent and terse. **—pith′i·ly** *adv.* **—pith′i·ness** *n.*

pit·i·a·ble (pĭt′ē-ə-bəl) *adj.* **1.** Arousing or deserving of pity or compassion; lamentable. **2.** Arousing disdainful pity; paltry; despicable. **—pit′i·a·ble·ness** *n.* **—pit′i·a·bly** *adv.*

pit·i·ful (pĭt′ĭ-fəl) *adj.* **1.** Arousing pity; pathetic. **2.** So inferior or insignificant as to be contemptible; mean; paltry. **3.** *Archaic.* Filled with pity or compassion. **—pit′i·ful·ly** *adv.* **—pit′i·ful·ness** *n.*

pit·i·less (pĭt′ĭ-lĭs) *adj.* **1.** Having no pity; without mercy. **2.** Totally uncompromising and unmitigating. **—pit′i·less·ly** *adv.* **—pit′i·less·ness** *n.*

pit·man (pĭt′mən) *n.* **1.** *pl.* **pit·men.** A worker employed inside a pit in various industrial operations, as in a coal mine. **2.** *pl.* **pit·mans.** A connecting rod.

pi·ton (pē′tŏn′) *n.* A metal spike fitted at one end with an eye or ring through which to pass a rope, used in mountain climbing as a hold. [Fr. < OFr., nail.]

Pi·tot-stat·ic tube (pē′tō-stăt′ĭk, pē-tō′-) *n.* A device consisting of a Pitot tube and a static tube combined to simultaneously measure total and static pressure in a fluid stream. It can be used in aircraft to determine relative wind speed.

Pi·tot tube (pē′tō, pē-tō′) *n.* A device used to measure the total pressure of a fluid stream. It is essentially a tube attached to a manometer at one end and pointed upstream at the other. [After Henri *Pitot* (1695–1771), its inventor.]

pit·saw also **pit saw** (pĭt′sô′) *n.* A large saw for cutting logs, hand-operated by two people, one of whom stands on the log and the other in a pit underneath.

pit stop *n.* **1.** A stop at a pit during a motor vehicle race, usually for fuel or a change of tires. **2. a.** *Informal.* A stop during a trip for rest, food, or fuel. **b.** A place where such a stop is made.

pit·tance (pĭt′ns) *n.* **1.** A meager monetary allowance. **2.** A very small salary or remuneration. **3.** A small amount or portion. [ME *pitaunce* < OFr. *pitance,* donation to a monastery < Med. Lat. *pietantia* < Lat. *pietas,* piety < *pius,* dutiful.]

pit·ted (pĭt′ĭd) *adj.* **1.** Marked by pits. **2.** Having the pit removed: *pitted dates.*

pit·ter-pat·ter (pĭt′ər-păt′ər) *n.* A rapid series of light, tapping sounds. **—pit′ter-pat′ter** *v.* **(-tered, -ter·ing, -ters).** [Imit.]

pi·tu·i·cyte (pĭ-to͞o′ĭ-sēt′, -tyo͞o′-) *n.* A modified neuroglia cell of the posterior lobe of the pituitary gland. [PITUI(TARY) + -CYTE.]

pi·tu·i·tar·y (pĭ-to͞o′ĭ-tĕr′ē, -tyo͞o′-) *n., pl.* **-ies. 1.** *Anat.* The pituitary gland. **2.** *Med.* An extract from the anterior or posterior lobes of the pituitary gland, prepared for therapeutic use. *—adj.* **1.** Of the pituitary gland. **2.** Of or designating a type of body structure characterized by obesity, enlarged bones, and soft parts of arms, legs, and face, believed to be due to excessive secretion from the pituitary gland. **3.** Of or secreting phlegm or mucus; mucous. [< Lat. *pituitarius,* of phlegm < *pituita,* phlegm.]

pituitary gland *n.* A small, oval endocrine gland attached to the base of the vertebrate brain, the secretions of which control the other endocrine glands and influence growth, metabolism, and maturation.

pi·tu·i·tous (pĭ-to͞o′ĭ-təs, -tyo͞o′-) *adj.* Containing, discharg-

pitcher plant

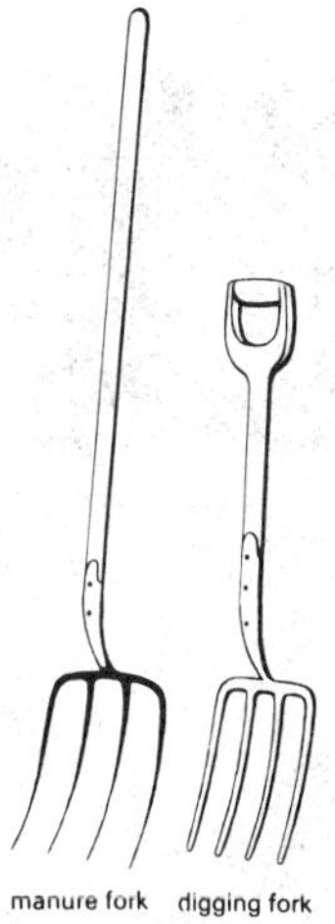

pitchfork

pitch pipe

pith helmet

p **pop** / r **roar** / s **sauce** / sh **ship, dish** / t **tight** / th **thin, path** / *th* **this, bathe** / ŭ **cut** / ûr **urge** / v **valve** / w **with** / y **yes** / z **zebra, size** / zh **vision** / ə **about, item, edible, gallop, circus** / œ *Fr.* **feu**, *Ger.* **schön** / ü *Fr.* **tu**, *Ger.* **über** / KH *Ger.* **ich**, *Scot.* **loch** / N *Fr.* **bon.**

ing, or resembling mucus. [Lat. *pituitosus* < *pituita,* phlegm.]

pit viper *n.* Any of various venomous snakes of the family Crotalidae, such as a copperhead or rattlesnake, characterized by a small pit on each side of the head.

pit·y (pĭt′ē) *n., pl.* **-ies. 1.** Sorrow or grief aroused by the misfortune of another; compassion for suffering. **2.** A regrettable or disagreeable fact or necessity. *—v.* **-ied, -y·ing, -ies.** *—tr.* To feel pity for. *—intr.* To feel pity. ***—idiom.*** **take pity on.** To attempt to alleviate the misfortune of. [ME *pite* < OFr. < Lat. *pietas* < *pius,* dutiful.] **—pit′y·ing·ly** *adv.*

Synonyms: *pity, compassion, commiseration, sympathy, condolence, empathy.* These are words for grief or concern felt for someone in misfortune. *Pity* implies a disposition to help but not necessarily empathetic involvement. *Compassion* always favorably connotes broad or profound feeling for the misfortunes of others and a desire to aid them. A more casual involvement is conveyed by *commiseration,* which signifies an expressed, sometimes superficial, solace. *Sympathy* is as broad as *pity* but connotes spontaneous emotion rather than considered attitude. *Condolence* expresses commiseration extended on specific occasions of loss common to all people, usually to relatives upon a death in their family. *Empathy,* with literary and psychological overtones, is a conscious involvement with a person's situation in the sense of vicarious identification.

pit·y·ri·a·sis (pĭt′ĭ-rī′ə-sĭs) *n.* Any of various skin diseases of humans and animals, characterized by epidermal shedding of flaky scales. [NLat. < Gk. *pituriasis* < *pituron,* grain husk.]

più (pyo͞o) *adv. Mus.* More. Used to qualify an adverb or adjective in directions. [Ital. < Lat. *plus.*]

Pi·ute (pī′yo͞ot′) *n.* Variant of **Paiute.**

piv·ot (pĭv′ət) *n.* **1.** A short rod or shaft about which a related part rotates or swings. **2.** One that determines the direction or effect of something; the essential component. **3.** The act of turning on or as if on a pivot. *—v.* **-ot·ed, -ot·ing, -ots.** *—tr.* **1.** To mount on, attach by, or furnish with a pivot or pivots. **2.** To cause to turn on a pivot, esp. to place under the control of a determining factor: *"In Egypt the whole cycle of agriculture is pivoted round the inundation"* (V. Gordon Childe). *—intr.* To turn on or as if on a pivot; wheel: *"The plot . . . lacks direction, pivoting on Hamlet's incertitude"* (G. Wilson Knight). [Fr. < OFr.] **—piv′ot·a·ble** *adj.* **—piv′ot·al** *adj.* **—piv′ot·al·ly** *adv.*

place kick

pix[1] (pĭks) *n. Slang.* A plural of **pic.**

pix[2] (pĭks) *n.* Variant of **pyx.**

pix·ie (pĭk′sē) *n.* Variant of **pixy.**

pix·i·lat·ed (pĭk′sə-lā′tĭd) *adj.* **1.** Behaving as if somewhat mentally unbalanced; bemused. **2.** Whimsical. **3.** *Slang.* Drunk. [< PIXY.] **—pix′i·la′tion** *n.*

pix·y or **pix·ie** (pĭk′sē) *n., pl.* **-ies.** A fairylike or elfin creature. *—adj.* Playfully mischievous. [Orig. unknown.] **—pix′y·ish, pix′ie·ish** *adj.*

piz·za (pēt′sə) *n.* An Italian baked dish consisting of a shallow pie crust covered usually with a spiced mixture of tomatoes, cheese, and other toppings. [Ital., prob. < VLat.* *picea* < Lat., fem. of *piceus,* of pitch < *pix,* pitch.]

piz·zazz (pĭ-zăz′) *n. Slang.* Flamboyance; zest; flair. [Orig. unknown.]

piz·ze·ri·a (pēt′sə-rē′ə) *n.* A place where pizzas are made and sold.

piz·zi·ca·to (pĭt′sĭ-kä′tō) *adj.* Played by plucking rather than bowing the strings of a musical instrument. [Ital., past participle of *pizzicare,* to pluck < *pizzare,* to prick.] **—piz′zi·ca′to** *adv. & n.*

piz·zle (pĭz′əl) *n.* **1.** The penis of an animal. **2.** A whip made from an animal's penis. [Poss. < LG *pēsel,* dim. of MLG *pese,* penis.]

PL/1 (pē′ĕl-wŭn′) *n.* A computer programming language designed for scientific and commercial uses at varying levels of complexity. [P(ROGRAMMING) L(ANGUAGE) 1.]

plac·a·ble (plăk′ə-bəl, plā′kə-) *adj.* Easily calmed or pacified; tolerant. [ME, agreeable < OFr. < Lat. *placabilis* < *placare,* to calm.] **—plac′a·bil′i·ty** *n.* **—plac′a·bly** *adv.*

plac·ard (plăk′ärd′, -ərd) *n.* **1.** A printed or written announcement for display in a public place; poster. **2.** A nameplate, as on the door of a house. *—tr.v.* **-ard·ed, -ard·ing, -ards. 1.** To announce or advertise (a message or product) on a placard. **2.** To post placards on or in. **3.** To display as or as if a placard. [ME *placquart,* official document < OFr. < *plaquier,* to plate < MDu. *placker,* to patch.] **—plac′ard′er** *n.*

pla·cate (plā′kāt′, plăk′āt′) *tr.v.* **-cat·ed, -cat·ing, -cates.** To allay the anger of, esp. by yielding concessions; appease. [Lat. *placare, placat-.*] **—pla′cat′er** *n.* **—pla·ca′tion** (plā-kā′shən) *n.* **—pla′ca·to′ry** (-tôr′ē, -tōr′ē), **pla′ca′tive** *adj.*

place (plās) *n.* **1.** A portion of space; an area with definite or indefinite boundaries. **2.** An area occupied by or set aside for a specific person or purpose. **3.** A definite location, esp.: **a.** An abode, such as a house or an apartment. **b.** A business establishment or office. **c.** A particular town or city. **4. Place.** A public square or thoroughfare in a town. **5. a.** A space for one person to sit or stand, as a passenger or spectator. **b.** A setting for one person at a table. **6.** A position regarded as possessed by someone or something else; stead: *I was chosen in his place.* **7.** A particular point up to which one has read in a book: *I lost my place.* **8.** A position figuratively occupied by a thing, group, or activity in a larger complex; function; role. **9.** Proper or customary location or order: *Everything is in place.* **10.** A social station entailing a certain mode of behavior: *He overstepped his place.* **11.** High rank or office. **12.** A relative position in a series; standing: *fourth place.* **13.** *Math.* The position of a number in relation to other numbers in a series. *—v.* **placed, plac·ing, plac·es.** *—tr.* **1. a.** To put in a particular position; set. **b.** To offer for consideration: *placed the matter before the board.* **2.** To put in a relation or order: *Place the words in alphabetical order.* **3.** To find living quarters for (someone): *placed the orphan in a foster home.* **4.** To arrange for the publication or production of (a literary or dramatic work): *place a novel.* **5.** To appoint to a post: *She was placed in a key position by the president.* **6.** To rank (someone or something) in an order or sequence: *I'd place him second best.* **7.** To date or identify in a particular context: *We placed the artifacts as Paleolithic.* **8.** To recollect clearly: *I remember that face, but I can't place her now.* **9.** To give order for: *place a bet.* **10.** To apply for; request formally: *place an order.* **11.** To invest (money): *place the interest with a broker.* **12.** To adjust (one's voice) for the best possible effects. *—intr. Sports.* **1.** To arrive among the first three finishers in a race. **2.** To finish second in a race. ***—idiom.*** **in place of.** Instead of. [ME < OFr., open space < Lat. *platea,* broad street < Gk. *plateia (hodos),* broad (street).] **—place′a·ble** *adj.*

pla·ce·bo (plə-sē′bō) *n., pl.* **-bos** or **-boes. 1.** (plä-chā′bō). *Rom. Cath. Ch.* The service or office of vespers for the dead. **2. a.** *Med.* A substance containing no medication and given merely to humor a patient. **b.** An inactive substance used as a control in an experiment. **3.** Something lacking intrinsic remedial value and that is done or given to humor another. [ME < Lat., I shall please, the first word of the first antiphon of the service.]

place kick *n. Football.* A kick, as for a field goal, for which the ball is held or propped up in a fixed position. **—place′-kick′** *v.* **(-kicked, -kick·ing, -kicks). —place′-kick′er** *n.*

place mat *n.* A decorative and protective mat for a single setting of dishes and silver at mealtime.

place·ment (plās′mənt) *n.* **1. a.** The act of placing or arranging. **b.** The state of being placed or arranged. **2.** The act or business of finding jobs, lodgings, or other positions for applicants. **3.** *Football.* **a.** The setting of the ball in position for a place kick. **b.** A place kick.

pla·cen·ta (plə-sĕn′tə) *n., pl.* **-tas** or **-tae** (-tē). **1. a.** *Anat.* A vascular, membranous organ that develops in female mammals during pregnancy, lining the uterine wall and partially enveloping the fetus, to which it is attached by the umbilical cord. Following birth, the placenta is expelled. **b.** An organ in certain other animals, including certain sharks and reptiles, with similar functions. **2.** *Bot.* **a.** The part of the ovary to which the ovules are attached. **b.** In nonflowering plants, the tissue that bears the spore cases. [NLat. < Lat., flat cake < Gk. *plakous* < *plax,* flat surface.] **—pla·cen′tal** *adj.*

plac·en·ta·tion (plăs′ən-tā′shən) *n.* **1.** *Zool.* **a.** The process of the formation of a placenta. **b.** The type or structure of a placenta. **2.** *Bot.* The way in which the placenta is arranged in or attached to the ovary.

plac·er (plăs′ər) *n.* **1.** A glacial or alluvial deposit of sand or gravel containing eroded particles of valuable minerals. **2.** A place where a placer deposit is washed to extract its mineral content. [Sp. < *plaza,* place < Lat. *platea,* broad street. —see PLACE.]

placer mining *n.* The obtaining of minerals from placers by washing or dredging. **—placer miner** *n.*

place setting *n.* A table service for one person.

plac·id (plăs′ĭd) *adj.* **1.** Having an undisturbed surface or aspect; outwardly calm or composed: *"Rosemary waited, placid but inwardly on fire"* (F. Scott Fitzgerald). **2.** Self-satisfied; complacent. [Lat. *placidus* < *placēre,* to please.] **—pla·cid′i·ty** (plə-sĭd′ĭ-tē), **plac′id·ness** *n.* **—plac′id·ly** *adv.*

plack·et (plăk′ĭt) *n.* **1.** A slit in a dress, blouse, or skirt to make the garment easy to put on or take off. **2.** A pocket, esp. in a woman's skirt. [Orig. unknown.]

plac·oid (plăk′oid) *adj.* Platelike, as the hard, toothlike scales of sharks, skates, and rays are. [Gk. *plax, plak-,* flat surface + -OID.]

pla·gal (plā′gəl) *adj. Mus.* **1.** Designating a medieval mode having a range from the fourth below to the fifth above its final tone. **2.** Designating a cadence with the subdominant chord immediately preceding the tonic chord. [Med. Lat. *plagalis* < Gk. *plagios,* oblique < *plagos,* side.]

pla·gia·rism (plā′jə-rĭz′əm) *n.* **1.** The act of plagiarizing. **2.** Something plagiarized. [< PLAGIARY.] **—pla′gia·rist** *n.* **—pla′gia·ris′tic** *adj.*

pla·gia·rize (plā′jə-rīz′) *v.* **-rized, -riz·ing, -riz·es.** *—tr.* **1.** To steal and use (the ideas or writings of another) as one's own. **2.** To appropriate passages or ideas from and use them as one's own. *—intr.* To take and use as one's own the writings or ideas of another. [< PLAGIARY.] **—pla′gia·riz′er** *n.*

pla·gia·ry (plā′jə-rē) *n., pl.* **-ries. 1.** Plagiarism. **2.** *Archaic.* One who plagiarizes. [Lat. *plagiarius,* plunderer < *plagium,* kidnapping < *plaga,* net.]

plagio– *pref.* Slanting; inclining: *plagiotropism.* [< Gk. *plagios,* oblique < *plagos,* side.]

pla·gi·o·clase (plā′jē-ə-klās′, -klāz′, plăj′ē-) *n.* Any of a common rock-forming series of triclinic feldspars, consisting of mixtures of sodium and calcium aluminum silicates. [G. *Plagioklas* : Gk. *plagios,* oblique (< *plagos,* side) + Gk. *klasis,* breaking < *klan,* to break.]

pla·gi·ot·ro·pism (plā′jē-ŏt′rə-pĭz′əm) *n. Biol.* The tendency to grow at an oblique or horizontal angle. Used chiefly of roots, stems, or branches. **—pla′gi·o·tro′pic** (-ə-trŏ′pĭk, -trŏp′ĭk) *adj.* **—pla′gi·o·tro′pi·cal·ly** *adv.*

plague (plāg) *n.* **1.** A pestilence, affliction, or calamity, originally one of divine retribution. **2.** A sudden influx, as of destructive or injurious insects: *a plague of locusts.* **3.** A cause for annoyance; nuisance: *"the plague of social jabbering"* (George Santayana). **4.** A highly infectious, usually fatal, epidemic disease, esp. the bubonic plague. *—tr.v.* **plagued, plagu·ing, plagues. 1.** To harass, pester, or annoy: *children who plagued the neighbors.* **2.** To afflict with or as if with plague or any other evil; to worry or distress: *"Runaway inflation further plagued the wage- or salary-earner"* (Edwin Reischauer). [ME *plage* < OFr., wound < Lat. *plaga* < Gk. *plēgē.*] **—plagu′er** *n.* **—plague′some** *adj.*

pla·guy also **pla·guey** (plā′gē) *adj. Informal.* Irritating; bothersome. **—pla′guy, pla′gui·ly** *adv.*

plaice (plās) *n., pl.* **plaice** or **plaic·es. 1.** An edible marine flatfish, *Pleuronectes platessa,* of western European waters. **2.** Any of various flatfishes, such as *Hippoglossoides platessoides* of North American Atlantic waters, related to the plaice. [ME < OFr. *plaïs* < LLat. *platessa,* ult. < Gk. *platus,* broad.]

plaid (plăd) *n.* **1.** A rectangular woolen scarf of a checked or tartan pattern worn over one shoulder by Scottish Highlanders. **2.** Cloth with a tartan or checked pattern. **3.** A tartan or checked pattern. [Sc. Gael. *plaide.*] **—plaid′ed** *adj.*

plain (plān) *adj.* **-er, -est. 1.** Free from obstructions; open to view; clear: *plain sight.* **2.** *Archaic.* Having no visible elevation or depression; flat; level. **3.** Easily understood; clearly evident: *make one's intent plain.* **4.** Uncomplicated; easily done; simple. **5.** Straightforward; frank; candid: *plain dealing.* **6.** Not mixed with other substances; pure: *plain water.* **7.** Common in rank or station; average; ordinary: *a plain man.* **8.** Unpretentious; unaffected; unsophisticated. **9.** Not rich; ordinary; simple: *plain food.* **10.** With little ornamentation or decoration: *a plain dress.* **11.** Not dyed, twilled, or patterned: *a plain fabric.* **12.** Not beautiful or handsome: *a plain face.* **13.** Sheer; utter; unqualified: *plain terror.* *—n.* **1.** An extensive, level, treeless land region, such as a valley floor or a plateau summit. **2.** Something devoid of ornamentation or extraneous matter. *—adv.* In a clear or intelligible manner. [ME < OFr. < Lat. *planus,* flat.] **—plain′ly** *adv.* **—plain′ness** *n.*

plain·chant (plān′chănt′) *n.* Plainsong (sense 2). [Fr., transl. of Med. Lat. *cantus planus,* plain song.]

plain·clothes man (plān′klōz′) also **plain·clothes·man** (plān′klōz′mən) *n.* A member of a police force, esp. a detective, who wears civilian clothes on duty.

plain-laid (plān′lād′) *adj.* Designating a rope made of three strands laid together with a right-hand twist.

Plain People *n.* Members of the Mennonite, Amish, or Dunker sects, noted for their custom of wearing plain dress.

plain sailing *n.* Easy progress over a direct course.

Plains Indian *n.* A member of any of the tribes of North American Indians that once inhabited the Great Plains of the United States and Canada.

plains·man (plānz′mən) *n.* An inhabitant or settler of the prairie regions of the United States.

plain·song (plān′sông′, -sŏng′) *n. Mus.* **1.** Gregorian chant. **2.** The general designation for the various bodies of medieval liturgical music without strict meter and sung without accompaniment. [Transl. of Med. Lat. *cantus planus.*]

plain·spo·ken (plān′spō′kən) *adj.* Frank; straightforward: *a plainspoken critic.* **—plain′spo′ken·ness** *n.*

plaint (plānt) *n.* **1.** A complaint. **2.** An utterance of grief or sorrow; lamentation. **3.** *Law.* A statement of grievance submitted to a court as a request for redress. [ME < OFr. *plainte* < Lat. *planctus,* lament < p.part. of *plangere,* to beat one's breast.]

plain·tiff (plān′tĭf) *n. Law.* The party that institutes a suit in a court. [ME *playntif* < OFr. *plaintif* < *plaintif,* plaintive.]

plain·tive (plān′tĭv) *adj.* Expressing sorrow; mournful; melancholy. [ME *playntif* < OFr. *plaintif* < *plainte,* plaint.] **—plain′tive·ly** *adv.* **—plain′tive·ness** *n.*

plain weave *n.* A weave in which the filling threads and the warp threads interlace alternately, forming a checkerboard pattern.

plait (plāt, plăt) *n.* **1.** A braid, esp. of hair. **2.** A pleat. *—tr.v.* **plait·ed, plait·ing, plaits. 1.** To braid. **2.** To pleat. **3.** To make by braiding or pleating. [ME, fold < OFr. *pleit* < Lat. *plicare,* to fold.] **—plait′er** *n.*

plan (plăn) *n.* **1.** A detailed scheme, program, or method worked out beforehand for the accomplishment of an object: *a plan of attack.* **2.** A proposed or tentative project or goal: *Do you have any plans for the evening?* **3.** A systematic arrangement of details; an outline or sketch: *the plan of a story.* **4.** A drawing or diagram made to scale showing the structure or arrangement of something. **5.** In perspective rendering, one of several imaginary planes perpendicular to the line of vision between the viewer and the object being depicted. *—v.* **planned, plan·ning, plans.** *—tr.* **1.** To formulate a scheme or program for the accomplishment or attainment of: *plan a campaign.* **2.** To have as a specific aim or purpose; intend: *They plan to go to the beach.* **3.** To draw or make a graphic representation of. *—intr.* To make plans. [Fr. < *planter,* to plant < Lat. *plantare* < *planta,* sole of the foot.] **—plan′ner** *n.*

plan– *pref.* Variant of **plano-.**

pla·nar (plā′nər, -när′) *adj.* **1.** Of, pertaining to, or situated in a plane. **2.** Flat: *a planar surface.* **3.** Having a two-dimensional characteristic. [LLat. *planaris,* flat < Lat. *planus.*] **—pla·nar′i·ty** (plā-năr′ĭ-tē) *n.*

pla·nar·i·a (plə-nâr′ē-ə) *n.* Planarian.

pla·nar·i·an (plə-nâr′ē-ən) *n.* Any of various flatworms of the order Tricladida, having broad, ciliated bodies and a three-branched digestive cavity. [< NLat. *Planaria,* genus name < LLat. *planarius,* on level ground < *planus,* flat.]

pla·na·tion (plā-nā′shən) *n.* Lateral mechanical erosion, as of a valley, by a running stream. [< PLANE[1].]

planch·et (plăn′chĭt) *n.* **1.** A flat disk of metal ready for stamping as a coin; a coin blank. **2.** A small disk of metal on which a radioactive substance is deposited for measurement of its activity. [Dim. of dial. *planch,* board < ME *plaunche* < OFr. *planche* < Lat. *planca.*]

plan·chette (plăn-shĕt′) *n.* A small triangular board with a pointer supported by two casters and a vertical pencil which is said to spell out messages from the spirit world when the operator's fingers are placed lightly upon it. [Fr., dim. of OFr. *planche,* board. —see PLANCHET.]

Planck's constant (plängks) *n. Physics.* The constant of proportionality relating the quantum of energy that can be possessed by radiation to the frequency of that radiation. Its value is approximately 6.625×10^{-27} erg-second. [After Max K.E.L. *Planck* (1858–1947).]

plane[1] (plān) *n.* **1.** *Math.* A surface containing all the straight lines connecting any two points on it. **2.** A flat or level surface. **3.** A level of development, existence, or achievement: *scholarship on a high plane.* **4.** An airplane or hydroplane. **5.** A supporting surface of an airplane; airfoil or wing. *—adj.* **1.** *Math.* Designating a figure lying in a plane: *a plane curve.* **2.** Flat. [Lat. *planum,* flat surface < *planus,* flat.] **—plane′ness** *n.*

plane[2] (plān) *n.* **1.** A carpenter's tool with an adjustable blade for smoothing and leveling wood. **2.** A trowel-shaped tool for smoothing the surface of clay, sand, or plaster in a mold. *—v.* **planed, plan·ing, planes.** *—tr.* **1.** To smooth or finish with or as with a plane. **2.** To remove with a plane. *—intr.* **1.** To undergo planing: *Poplar planes easily.* **2.** To act as a plane. [ME < OFr. < LLat. *plana* < *planare,* to plane < *planus,* flat.]

plane[3] (plān) *intr.v.* **planed, plan·ing, planes. 1.** To rise partly out of the water, as a hydroplane does at high speeds. **2.** To soar or glide. **3.** To travel by airplane. [Fr. *planer,* to glide < *plan,* level surface < Lat. *planum* < *planus,* flat.]

plane[4] (plān) *n.* The plane tree. [ME < OFr. < Lat. *platanus* < Gk. *platanos* < *platus,* broad.]

plane angle *n.* An angle formed by two straight lines.

plane geometry *n.* The geometry of planar figures.

plane·load (plān′lōd′) *n.* The load an airplane is able to carry.

plan·er (plā′nər) *n.* **1.** One that planes. **2.** A machine tool for smoothing and planing the surfaces of wood or metal. **3.** *Printing.* A smooth block of wood used to level a form of type.

pla·ner tree (plā′nər) *n.* A small swamp tree, *Planera aquatica,* of the southern United States, having small, rough, nutlike fruit. [After J.J. *Planer* (1743–1789).]

plane·side (plān′sīd′) *n.* The area adjacent to an airplane.

plan·et (plăn′ĭt) *n.* **1.** A nonluminous celestial body illuminated by light from a star, such as the sun, around which it revolves. In the solar system there are nine known major planets: Mercury, Venus, Earth, Mars, Jupiter, Saturn, Uranus, Neptune, and Pluto. **2.** In ancient astronomy, one of the seven celestial bodies (Mercury, Venus, the Moon, the Sun, Mars, Jupiter, and Saturn) visible to the naked eye and thought to revolve in the heavens about a fixed Earth and among fixed stars. **3.** In astrology, one of the seven revolving celestial bodies that in conjunction with the stars are supposed to influence human affairs and personalities. [ME < OFr. *planete* < LLat. *planeta* < Gk. *planēs,* wanderer < *planasthai,* to wander.]

plane table *n.* A portable surveying instrument consisting essentially of a drawing board and a ruler mounted on a tripod and used to sight and map topographical details.

plan·e·tar·i·um (plăn′ĭ-târ′ē-əm) *n., pl.* **-i·ums** or **-i·a** (-ē-ə). **1.** An apparatus or model representing the solar system. **2.** A device for projecting images of celestial bodies in their courses onto the inner surface of a hemispherical dome. **3.** A building or room containing a planetarium, with seats for an audience.

plan·e·tar·y (plăn′ĭ-tĕr′ē) *adj.* **1.** Of, pertaining to, or resembling the physical or orbital characteristics of a planet or the planets. **2.** Terrestrial; mundane; earthly. **3.** Wandering; er-

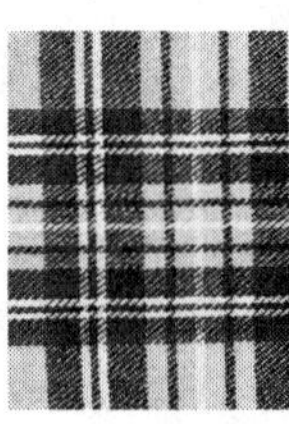

plaid

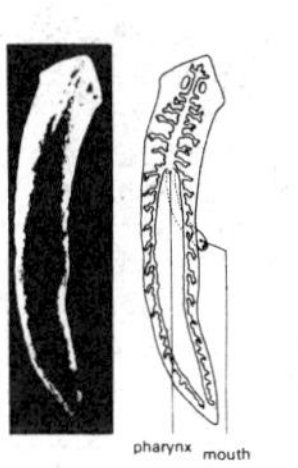

planarian
Diagram (*right*) showing branched digestive tract

plane[2]

ratic: *planetary life.* **4.** Denoting or pertaining to a gear train consisting of a central gear with an internal ring gear and one or more pinions.

planetary nebula *n.* Any of several objects in the Galaxy consisting of a hot, blue-white, central star surrounded by an envelope of expanding gas.

plan·e·tes·i·mal (plăn′ĭ-tĕs′ə-məl, -tĕz′-) *n.* Any of innumerable small bodies thought to have orbited the sun during the formation of the planets. [PLANET + (INFINIT)ESIMAL.] **—plan′e·tes′i·mal** *adj.*

planetesimal hypothesis *n.* The hypothesis that the planets and satellites of the solar system were formed by gravitational aggregation of planetesimals.

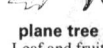

plane tree
Leaf and fruit

plan·e·toid (plăn′ĭ-toid′) *n. Astron.* An asteroid (sense 1). **—plan′e·toi′dal** *adj.*

plane tree *n.* Any of several trees of the genus *Platanus,* having ball-shaped fruit clusters and, usually, outer bark that flakes off in patches.

planet wheel *n.* One of the small gear wheels in an epicyclic train.

plan·gent (plăn′jənt) *adj.* **1.** Striking with a deep, reverberating sound, as waves against the shore. **2. a.** Loud and resounding, as the sound of bells. **b.** Expressing sadness; plaintive. [Lat. *plangens, plangent-,* pr.part. of *plangere,* to strike.] **—plan′gen·cy** *n.* **—plan′gent·ly** *adv.*

plani– *pref.* Variant of **plano-**.

pla·nim·e·ter (plə-nĭm′ĭ-tər, plā-) *n.* An instrument that measures the area of a plane figure as a mechanically coupled pointer traverses the figure's perimeter. [Fr. *planimètre* : Lat. *planum,* level surface (< *planus,* flat) + *mètre,* meter < Gk. *metron,* measure.] **—pla′ni·met′ric** (plā′nə-mĕt′rĭk), **pla′ni·met′ri·cal** *adj.* **—pla′ni·met′ri·cal·ly** *adv.* **—pla·nim′e·try** *n.*

plan·ish (plăn′ĭsh) *tr.v.* **-ished, -ish·ing, -ish·es.** To flatten, smooth, toughen, or polish (metal) by rolling or hammering. [OFr. *planir, planiss-,* to make smooth < *plan,* level < Lat. *planus.*] **—plan′ish·er** *n.*

pla·ni·sphere (plā′nĭ-sfîr′) *n.* **1.** A representation of a sphere or part of a sphere on a plane surface. **2.** *Astron.* A polar projection of the celestial sphere on a chart equipped with an adjustable overlay to show the stars visible at a particular time and place. [ME *planisperie* < Med. Lat. *planisphaerium* : Lat. *planus,* flat + Lat. *sphaera,* sphere < Gk. *sphaira.*] **—pla′ni·spher′ic** (-sfîr′ĭk, -sfĕr′-), **pla′ni·spher′i·cal** *adj.*

plantain[1]

plank (plăngk) *n.* **1. a.** A piece of lumber cut thicker than a board. **b.** Such pieces of lumber considered collectively; planking. **2.** A foundation; support. **3.** One of the articles of a political platform. *—tr.v.* **planked, plank·ing, planks. 1.** To furnish, lay, or cover with planks. **2.** To bake or broil and serve (fish or meat) on a plank. **3.** To put or set down emphatically or with force. **4.** *Informal.* To pay at once: *planked down $10 for the fare.* [ME < ONFr. *planke* < Lat. *planca.*]

plank·ing (plăng′kĭng) *n.* **1.** The act of laying planks. **2.** Planks collectively. **3.** Something made of planks.

plank-sheer (plăngk′shîr′) *n.* A horizontal timber forming the outer edge of the upper deck of a wooden ship. [Alteration of obs. *plancher,* planking < ME *plauncher* < OFr. *planchier* < *planche,* plank < Lat. *planca.*]

plantain[2]

plank·ter (plăngk′tər) *n.* One of the minute organisms that collectively constitute plankton. [< Gk. *planktēr,* wanderer < *planktos,* wandering. —see PLANKTON.]

plank·ton (plăngk′tən) *n.* Plant and animal organisms, generally microscopic, that float or drift in great numbers in fresh or salt water. [G. < Gk., neuter of *planktos,* wandering < *plazein,* to drive astray.] **—plank·ton′ic** (-tŏn′ĭk) *adj.*

Planned Parenthood (plănd). A service mark for an organization that provides family planning services.

plano– or **plani–** or **plan–** *pref.* Flat: *planoconvex.* [< Lat. *planus,* flat.]

pla·no·con·cave (plā′nō-kŏn-kāv′, -kŏn′kāv′) *adj.* Flat or plane on one side and concave on the other.

pla·no·con·vex (plā′nō-kŏn-vĕks′, -kŏn′vĕks′) *adj.* Flat or plane on one side and convex on the other.

pla·nog·ra·phy (plə-nŏg′rə-fē, plā-) *n.* A process for printing from a smooth surface, as lithography or offset. **—pla′no·graph′ic** (plā′nə-grăf′ĭk) *adj.* **—pla′no·graph′i·cal·ly** *adv.*

pla·nom·e·ter (plə-nŏm′ĭ-tər, plā-) *n.* A flat metal plate for gauging the accuracy of a plane surface in precision metalworking; surface plate. **—pla·nom′e·try** *n.*

plant (plănt) *n.* **1.** An organism of the vegetable kingdom, characteristically having cellulose cell walls, growing by synthesis of inorganic substances, and lacking the power of locomotion. **2.** A plant having no permanent woody stem; an herb, as distinguished from a tree or shrub. **3.** The equipment, including machinery, tools, instruments, and fixtures and the buildings containing them, necessary for an industrial or manufacturing operation; factory. **4.** The buildings, equipment, and fixtures of an institution. **5.** A seemingly trivial passage or line in a play or story that becomes important later. **6. a.** A person placed in an audience to encourage applause or contribute to the action of the play. **b.** *Slang.* A person placed or stationed in a given location in order to observe, spy, or inform. **7.** A misleading piece of evidence placed so as to be discovered. **8.** *Slang.* A scheming trick; swindle. *—tr.v.* **plant·ed, plant·ing, plants. 1.** To place or set (seeds, for example) in the ground to grow. **2. a.** To furnish or supply (a plot of land) with plants or seeds. **b.** To stock (water) with fish or spawn. **c.** To introduce (an animal) into an area. **3.** To fix or set firmly in position: *He planted both feet on the ground.* **4.** To establish or set up; found: *plant a colony.* **5.** To implant (an idea, for example) in the mind; introduce and establish firmly: *"The right of revolution is planted in the heart of man"* (Clarence Darrow). **6.** *Slang.* **a.** To place or station (a person) for the purposes of observation, spying, or informing: *Detectives were planted all over the store.* **b.** To place (something) for the purpose of deception: *plant false evidence.* **7.** *Informal.* To hide by burying. **8.** *Slang.* To deliver (a blow or punch). [ME < OE < Lat. *planta,* shoot.] **—plant′a·ble** *adj.* **—plant′like′** *adj.*

plan·tain[1] (plăn′tən) *n.* Any of various plants of the genus *Plantago,* esp. *P. major,* a weed with broad leaves and a spike of small, greenish flowers. [ME < OFr. < Lat. *plantago* < *planta,* sole of the foot.]

plan·tain[2] (plăn′tən) *n.* **1.** A large tropical plant, *Musa paradisiaca,* resembling the banana and bearing similar fruit. **2.** The fruit of the plantain, used as a staple food in tropical regions. [Sp. *plántano* < Med. Lat. *plantanus,* plane tree < Lat. *platanus.* —see PLANE[4].]

plantain lily *n.* Any of several plants of the genus *Hosta,* native to Asia, widely cultivated for their white, blue, or lilac flowers.

plan·tar (plăn′tər, -tär′) *adj.* Of, pertaining to, or occurring on the sole of the foot. [Lat. *plantaris* < *planta,* sole of the foot.]

plan·ta·tion (plăn-tā′shən) *n.* **1.** An area under cultivation. **2.** A group of cultivated trees or plants. **3.** A large estate or farm on which crops are raised, often by resident workers. **4.** A newly established colony or settlement.

plant·er (plăn′tər) *n.* **1. a.** One who plants. **b.** A machine or tool for planting or sowing seeds. **2.** The owner or manager of a plantation. **3.** An early settler or colonist. **4.** A decorative container for house plants.

planter's punch (plăn′tərz) *n.* A drink of rum with lemon or lime juice, sugar syrup, water or soda, bitters, and grenadine.

plant hormone *n.* Phytohormone.

plan·ti·grade (plăn′tĭ-grăd′) *adj.* Walking with the entire lower surface of the foot on the ground, as humans and bears do. *—n.* A plantigrade animal. [Fr. : Lat. *planta,* sole of the foot + Lat. *-gradus,* going < *gradi,* to step.]

plant louse *n.* An aphid.

plan·u·la (plăn′yə-lə) *n., pl.* **-lae** (-lē′). The free-swimming, ciliated larva of a coelenterate. [NLat. < Lat., little plane < *planus,* flat.] **—plan′u·lar** *adj.*

plaque (plăk) *n.* **1.** A flat plate, slab, or disk that is ornamented or engraved for mounting, as on a wall for decoration or on a monument for information. **2.** A small pin or brooch worn as an ornament or a badge of membership. **3.** *Pathol.* **a.** A small, disk-shaped formation or growth; patch. **b.** A thin film consisting of mucus and microorganisms on a tooth surface. [Fr. < OFr., metal plate < MDu. *placke* < *placken,* to patch.]

plash (plăsh) *n.* **1.** A light splash. **2.** The sound of a plash. *—v.* **plashed, plash·ing, plash·es.** *—tr.* To spatter (liquid) about; splash. *—intr.* To splash lightly. [Prob. imit.]

–plasia *suff.* Growth; development: *achondroplasia.* [NLat. < Gk. *plasis,* molding < *plassein,* to mold.]

plasm (plăz′əm) *n.* **1.** Germ plasm (sense 3). **2.** Variant of **plasma**.

plasm– *pref.* Variant of **plasmo-**.

–plasm *suff.* Material forming cells or tissue: *cytoplasm.* [< PLASMA.]

plas·ma (plăz′mə) also **plasm** (plăz′əm) *n.* **1. a.** *Physiol.* The clear, yellowish fluid portion of blood, lymph, or intramuscular fluid in which cells are suspended. **b.** *Med.* Cell-free, sterilized blood plasma, used in transfusions. **2.** Protoplasm or cytoplasm. **3.** The fluid portion of milk from which the curd has been separated by coagulation; whey. **4.** *Physics.* An electrically neutral, highly ionized gas composed of ions, electrons, and neutral particles. [NLat. < LLat., image < Gk. < *plassein,* to mold.] **—plas·mat′ic** (plăz-măt′ĭk), **plas′mic** *adj.*

plasma cell *n.* A large oval-shaped cell that contains deeply staining chromatin material and is associated with the production of immunoglobulins.

plas·ma·gel (plăz′mə-jĕl′) *n.* A jellylike state of cytoplasm, characteristically occurring in the periphery of the amoeba.

plas·ma·gene (plăz′mə-jēn′) *n. Genetics.* A self-reproducing hereditary structure thought to exist in cytoplasm and function in a manner analogous to, but independent of, chromosomal genes. **—plas′ma·gen′ic** (-jē′nĭk, -jĕn′ĭk) *adj.*

plasma membrane *n. Biol.* The semipermeable membrane that encloses the cytoplasm of a cell.

plas·ma·pher·e·sis (plăz′mə-fĕr′ĭ-sĭs) *n.* A process in which blood is withdrawn from a donor, the plasma and erythrocytes are separated from the blood, and the erythrocytes are returned to the circulatory system of the donor. [PLASMA + Gk. *aphairesis,* removal. —see APHAERESIS.]

plas·ma·sol (plăz′mə-sôl′, -sŏl′, -sōl′) *n. Biol.* A state of cytoplasm that is more liquid than plasmagel. [PLASMA + SOL4.]

plas·mid (plăz′mĭd) *n.* A genetic element occurring outside of the nucleus that is found in the cytoplasm of some bacterial cells. [PLASM(A) + -ID.]

plas·min (plăz′mĭn) *n.* A proteolytic enzyme in plasma that dissolves fibrin and other clotting factors in blood.

plas·min·o·gen (plăz-mĭn′ə-jən) *n.* The precursor to plasmin that is found in body fluids and blood plasma.

plasmo– or **plasm–** *pref.* Plasma: *plasmin.* [< PLASMA.]

plas·mo·des·ma (plăz′mə-dĕz′mə) also **plas·mo·desm** (plăz′mə-dĕz′əm) *n., pl.* **-ma·ta** (-mə-tə) or **-mas.** A strand of living cytoplasm connecting two cells that are otherwise functionally separate. [PLASMO- + Gk. *desma,* bond < *dein,* to bind.]

plas·mo·di·um (plăz-mō′dē-əm) *n., pl.* **-di·a** (-dē-ə). **1.** A protozoan of the genus *Plasmodium,* which includes the parasites that cause malaria. **2.** A naked, multinucleate mass of protoplasm such as that characteristic of the vegetative phase of the slime molds. [NLat. *Plasmodium,* genus name: PLASM(O)- + *-odium,* resembling < Gk. *-oeidēs,* -oid.]

plas·mol·y·sis (plăz-mŏl′ĭ-sĭs) *n.* Shrinkage or contraction of the protoplasm in a cell, esp. a plant cell, caused by loss of water through osmosis. **—plas′mo·lyt′ic** (plăz′mə-lĭt′ĭk) *adj.* **—plas′mo·lyt′i·cal·ly** *adv.*

plas·mo·lyze (plăz′mə-līz′) *v.* **-lyzed, -lyz·ing, -lyz·es.** *—tr.* To subject to plasmolysis. *—intr.* To undergo plasmolysis. [< PLASMOLYSIS.]

plas·mo·some (plăz′mə-sōm′) *n.* A nucleolus.

-plast *suff.* An organized unit of living matter; cell: *chloroplast.* [< Gk. *plastos,* molded < *plassein,* to mold.]

plas·ter (plăs′tər) *n.* **1.** A mixture of lime, sand, and water, sometimes with hair or other fiber added, that hardens to a smooth solid and is used for coating walls and ceilings. **2.** Plaster of Paris. **3.** A pastelike mixture applied to a part of the body for healing or cosmetic purposes. **4.** Mustard plaster. *—tr.v.* **-tered, -ter·ing, -ters. 1.** To cover, coat, or repair with plaster. **2.** To cover by or as if by pasting, esp. to cover conspicuously. **3.** To apply a plaster to. **4.** To cause to adhere to another surface. **5.** To make smooth by applying a sticky substance: *plastered his hair with pomade.* **6.** *Informal.* **a.** To inflict heavy damage or injury on. **b.** To defeat decisively. [ME < OE < Lat. *emplastrum,* medical dressing < Gk. *emplastron* < *emplassein,* to plaster on : *en-,* in + *plassein,* to mold.] **—plas′ter·er** *n.* **—plas′ter·y** *adj.*

plas·ter·board (plăs′tər-bôrd′, -bōrd′) *n.* A thin, rigid board or sheet of layers of fiberboard or paper, usually bonded to a plaster core and used to cover walls and ceilings.

plaster cast *n.* **1.** A sculptured mold or cast in plaster of Paris. **2.** A cast (sense 11).

plas·tered (plăs′tərd) *adj. Slang.* Drunk.

plas·ter·ing (plăs′tər-ĭng) *n.* **1.** The act of applying or working with plaster. **2.** A layer or coating of plaster. **3.** A resounding defeat; licking.

plaster of Paris *n.* Any of a group of gypsum cements, essentially hemihydrated calcium sulfate, $CaSo_4 \cdot {}^1/_2H_2O$, a white powder that forms a paste when mixed with water and hardens into a solid, used in making casts, molds, and sculpture. [After *Paris,* France, where it was originally made.]

plas·tic (plăs′tĭk) *adj.* **1.** Capable of being shaped or formed; pliable. **2.** Pertaining to or dealing with shaping or modeling: *the plastic arts.* **3.** Giving form or shape to a substance. **4.** Easily influenced; impressionable. **5.** Having the qualities of a piece of sculpture; well-formed. **6.** Made of a plastic or plastics: *a plastic garden hose.* **7.** *Physics.* Capable of undergoing continuous deformation without rupture or relaxation. **8.** *Biol.* Capable of building tissue; formative. **9.** Marked by artificiality, pretension, or lack of originality: *the plastic world of Madison Avenue hype.* *—n.* Any of various complex organic compounds produced by polymerization, capable of being molded, extruded, or cast into various shapes and films, or drawn into filaments used as textile fibers. [Lat. *plasticus* < Gk. *plastikos* < *plassein,* to mold.] **—plas′ti·cal·ly** *adv.* **—plas·tic′i·ty** (plăs-tĭs′ĭ-tē) *n.*

-plastic *suff.* Forming; growing; developing: *cytoplastic.* [Gk. *plastikos,* fit for molding. —see PLASTIC.]

plas·ti·cize (plăs′tĭ-sīz′) *tr. & intr. v.* **-cized, -ciz·ing, -ciz·es.** To make or become plastic. **—plas′ti·ci·za′tion** *n.*

plas·ti·ciz·er (plăs′tĭ-sī′zər) *n.* Any of various substances added to plastics or other materials to keep them soft or pliable.

plastic surgery *n.* Surgery to remodel, repair, or restore injured or defective body parts, esp. by the transfer of tissue. **—plastic surgeon** *n.*

plas·tid (plăs′tĭd) *n.* Any of several specialized cytoplasmic structures occurring in plant cells and in some plantlike organisms, and having various physiological functions. [G. < Gk. *plastos,* molded < *plassein,* to mold.] **—plas·tid′i·al** (plăs-tĭd′ē-əl) *adj.*

plas·to·mer (plăs′tə-mər) *n.* Any of various tough, hard polymers, such as acrylate resin. [Gk. *plastos,* molded + (POLY)MER.]

plas·tron (plăs′trən) *n.* **1.** A breastplate worn under a coat of mail. **2.** A protective breastplate worn by fencers. **3.** A trimming on the front of a bodice. **4.** The front of a man's dress shirt. **5.** *Zool.* The ventral surface of the shell of a turtle or tortoise. [OFr. < OItal. *piastrone,* aug. of *piastra,* thin metal plate. —see PIASTER.] **—plas′tral** (-trəl) *adj.*

-plasty *suff.* Plastic surgery: *dermatoplasty.* [Gk. *-plastia* < *plastos,* molded < *plassein,* to mold.]

-plasy *suff.* -plasia.

plat (plăt) *tr.v.* **plat·ted, plat·ting, plats.** To plait or braid. *—n.* A braid. [ME *platen,* alteration of *plaiten,* to fold < *plait,* fold. —see PLAIT.]

plate (plāt) *n.* **1.** A smooth, flat, relatively thin, rigid body of uniform thickness. **2. a.** A sheet of hammered, rolled, or cast metal. **b.** A very thin plated coat or layer of metal. **3. a.** A flat piece of metal forming part of a machine: *a boiler plate.* **b.** A flat piece of metal on which something is engraved. **4. a.** A thin piece of metal used for armor. **b.** Armor made of this. **5.** *Printing.* **a.** A sheet of metal, plastic, rubber, paperboard, or other material converted into a printing surface, such as an electrotype or stereotype. **b.** A print of a woodcut, lithograph, or other engraved material, esp. when reproduced in a book. **c.** A full-page book illustration, often in color and printed on paper different from that used on the text pages. **6.** A light-sensitive sheet of glass or metal upon which a photographic image can be recorded. **7.** A thin metallic or plastic support fitted to the gums to anchor artificial teeth. **8.** *Archit.* In wood-frame construction, a horizontal member, capping the exterior wall studs, upon which the roof rafters rest. **9.** *Baseball.* Home plate. **10. a.** A shallow dish in which food is served or from which it is eaten. **b.** The contents of such a dish. **c.** A whole course served on such a dish. **11.** Service and food for one person at a meal: *dinner at a set price per plate.* **12.** Household articles, such as hollowware, covered with a precious metal, such as gold or silver. **13.** A dish passed among a congregation for the collection of offerings. **14.** *Sports.* **a.** A dish, cup, or other article of silver or gold offered as a prize. **b.** A contest, esp. a horse race, offering such a prize. **15.** A thin cut of beef from the brisket. **16.** *Anat. & Zool.* **a.** A thin, flat layer or scale. **b.** A platelike part or organ. **17.** *Electronics.* **a.** An electrode, as in a storage battery or capacitor. **b.** The anode in an electron tube. **18.** *Geol.* A large rigid section of the earth's lithosphere that floats upon the earth's mantle according to the theory of plate tectonics. *—tr.v.* **plat·ed, plat·ing, plates. 1.** To coat or cover with a thin layer of metal. **2.** To armor. **3.** *Printing.* To make a stereotype or electrotype from. **4.** To give a glossy finish to (paper) by pressing between metal sheets or rollers. [ME < OFr. < fem. of *plat,* flat < VLat. **plattus* < Gk. *platus.*] **—plate′like′** *adj.*

pla·teau (plă-tō′) *n., pl.* **-teaus** or **-teaux** (-tōz′). **1.** An elevated and comparatively level expanse of land; tableland. **2.** A relatively stable or quiescent period or state. [Fr. < OFr., platter < *plat,* flat. —see PLATE.]

plat·ed (plā′tĭd) *adj.* **1.** Coated with a thin layer of metal: *gold-plated.* **2.** Covered or furnished with plates or sheets of metal, as armor. **3.** Knitted with two kinds of yarn, one on the face and one on the back.

plate·ful (plāt′fo͝ol′) *n., pl.* **-fuls. 1.** The amount that a plate will hold. **2.** A generous portion of food.

plate glass *n.* A strong rolled and polished glass containing few impurities and used for mirrors and large windows.

plate·let (plāt′lĭt) *n.* A protoplasmic disk, smaller than a red blood cell, found in the blood of vertebrates and thought to promote coagulation.

plat·en (plăt′n) *n.* **1.** One of the two flat members of the printing unit of a printing press that serves to position the paper and hold it against the inked type. **2.** The roller on a typewriter against which the keys strike. [ME *plateyne,* paten < OFr. *platine,* metal plate < *plate,* plate. —see PLATE.]

platen

plate proof *n.* A proof taken from a master printing plate.

plat·er (plā′tər) *n.* **1.** One that plates. **2.** *Slang.* An inferior racehorse.

plate tectonics *n. (used with a sing. verb).* **1.** A branch of geology concerned with seismic activity and continental movement, based on the theory that the earth's surface is comprised of a small number of large, semirigid sections that float across the mantle, with seismic activity and volcanism occurring primarily at the junction of these sections. **2.** The dynamics of plate movement.

plat·form (plăt′fôrm′) *n.* **1.** A floor or horizontal surface raised above the level of the adjacent area, such as a stage for public speaking or a landing alongside railroad tracks. **2.** A vestibule at the end of a railway car. **3.** A formal declaration of the principles on which a group, such as a political party, makes its appeal to the public. **4. a.** A layer of leather between the inner and outer soles of a shoe. **b.** A shoe having such a construction. [OFr. *plate-forme,* diagram : *plate,* flat + *forme,* form.]

platform
Subway platform

platform balance *n.* An equal-arm balance having two flat platforms above the beam and frequently using a sliding rider instead of weights.

platform car *n.* A railroad car having no sides or roof; flatcar.

platform scale *n.* An industrial weighing instrument consisting of a platform coupled to an automatic system of levers and adjustable weights, used to weigh large or heavy objects.

platin– *pref.* Variant of **platino-**.

pla·ti·na (plə-tē′nə) *n.* Platinum, esp. as found naturally. [Sp., dim. of *plata,* silver, flat < VLat. **plattus* < Gk. *platus,* flat.]

plat·ing (plā′tĭng) *n.* **1.** A thin layer or coating of metal, such as gold or silver. **2.** A covering or layer of metal sheets or plates.

platini– *pref.* Variant of **platino-**.

pla·tin·ic (plə-tĭn′ĭk) *adj. Chem.* Of, pertaining to, or containing platinum, esp. with valence 4.

plat·i·nize (plăt′n-īz′) *tr.v.* **-nized, -niz·ing, -niz·es.** To electroplate with platinum.

platino– or **platini–** or **platin–** *pref.* Platinum: *platinotype.* [< PLATINUM.]

plat·i·no·cy·a·nide (plăt′n-ō-sī′ə-nīd′) *n.* A complex salt of platinous cyanide and another cyanide.

plat·i·noid (plăt′n-oid′) *adj.* Like platinum. —*n.* **1.** An alloy of copper, nickel, tungsten, and zinc, formerly used in electric coils. **2.** A metal resembling platinum chemically, esp. osmium, iridium, or palladium.

plat·i·no·type (plăt′n-ō-tīp′) *n.* **1.** A process formerly used for making photographic prints, using a finely precipitated platinum salt and an iron salt in the sensitizing solution to produce photographic prints in platinum black. **2.** A photographic print produced by platinotype.

plat·i·nous (plăt′n-əs) *adj.* Of, pertaining to, or containing platinum, esp. with valence 2.

plat·i·num (plăt′n-əm) *n.* **1.** *Symbol* **Pt** A silver-white metallic element occurring worldwide, usually mixed with other metals such as iridium, osmium, or nickel. It is ductile and malleable, does not oxidize in air, and is used in electrical components, jewelry, dentistry, electroplating, and as a catalyst. Atomic number 78; atomic weight 195.09; melting point 1769°C; boiling point 3827°C; specific gravity 21.45; valences 1, 2, 3, 4. **2.** A medium to light gray. [NLat. < Sp. *platina,* platinum. —see PLATINA.]

platinum black *n.* A fine black powder of metallic platinum, used as a catalyst and as a gas absorbent.

platinum blond *n.* **1.** A very light silver-blond hair color, esp. when artificially produced. **2.** A person having platinum blond hair.

plat·i·tude (plăt′ĭ-to͞od′, -tyo͞od′) *n.* **1.** A trite or banal remark or statement. **2.** Lack of originality; triteness. [Fr. < *plat,* flat < OFr. —see PLATE.] **—plat′i·tu′di·nal, plat′i·tu′di·nous** *adj.* **—plat′i·tu′di·nous·ly** *adv.*

plat·i·tu·di·nar·i·an (plăt′ĭ-to͞od′n-âr′ē-ən, -tyo͞od′-) *n.* One who habitually uses platitudes. [PLATITUDIN(OUS) + -ARIAN.]

plat·i·tu·di·nize (plăt′ĭ-to͞od′n-īz′, -tyo͞od′-) *intr.v.* **-nized, -niz·ing, -niz·es.** To use platitudes in speaking or writing.

Pla·ton·ic (plə-tŏn′ĭk, plā-) *adj.* **1.** Also **Pla·ton·i·cal** (-ĭ-kəl). Of, pertaining to, or characteristic of Plato or his philosophy. **2.** Often **platonic.** Transcending physical desire and tending toward the purely spiritual or ideal: *platonic love.* **3.** Often **platonic.** Speculative or theoretical. [After *Plato* (427?–347 B.C.), Greek philosopher.] **—Pla·ton′i·cal·ly** *adv.*

Pla·to·nism (plāt′n-ĭz′əm) *n.* The philosophy of Plato, esp. insofar as it asserts ideal forms as an absolute and eternal reality of which the phenomena of the world are an imperfect and transitory reflection. **—Pla′to·nist** *n.* **—Pla′to·nis′tic** *adj.*

pla·toon (plə-to͞on′) *n.* **1.** A subdivision of a military company divided into squads or sections and usually commanded by a lieutenant. **2.** A body of persons working together. **3.** *Sports.* A group of players within a team, esp. a football team, used for offense or defense. —*v.* **-tooned, -toon·ing, -toons.** *Sports.* —*tr.* To play (a player) in alternation with another player in the same position. —*intr.* **1.** To use different players at the same position. **2.** To be platooned with another player. [Fr. *peloton* < OFr. *pelote,* little ball. —see PELLET.]

platoon sergeant *n.* The senior noncommissioned officer in an army platoon or comparable unit.

Platt·deutsch (plät′doich′) *n.* The Low German vernacular of northern Germany. [G. < Du. *platduits,* Low German : *plat,* low, flat (< MDu. < OFr.) + *Duitsch,* German < MDu. *duutsch.*]

plat·ter (plăt′ər) *n.* **1.** A large, shallow dish or plate, used esp. for serving food. **2.** A meal or course served on a platter. **3.** *Slang.* A phonograph record. **—*idiom.* on a platter.** Effortlessly. [ME *plater* < AN < OFr. *plate,* plate.]

plat·y[1] (plā′tē) *adj.* **-i·er, -i·est.** Designating soil or minerals occurring in flaky layers.

plat·y[2] (plăt′ē) *n., pl.* **-ys** or **-ies.** Any of several small freshwater fish of the genus *Xiphophorus,* of southern North America, esp. *X. maculatus,* a colorful aquarium fish. [< NLat. *Platypoecilus,* genus name of platys : PLATY- + Gk. *poikilos,* many-colored.]

platy– *pref.* Flat: *platyhelminth.* [< Gk. *platus,* broad, flat.]

plat·y·fish (plăt′ē-fĭsh′) *n.* Platy[2].

plat·y·hel·minth (plăt′ĭ-hĕl′mĭnth) *n.* Any of various parasitic and nonparasitic worms of the phylum Platyhelminthes, such as a tapeworm or a planarian, characteristically having a flattened body. [PLATY- + Gk. *helmis,* parasitic worm.] **—plat′y·hel·min′thic** *adj.*

platypus

plat·y·pus (plăt′ĭ-pəs) *n., pl.* **-pus·es.** A semiaquatic, egg-laying mammal, *Ornithorhynchus anatinus,* of Australia and Tasmania, having a broad, flat tail, webbed feet, and a snout resembling a duck's bill. [NLat. < Gk. *platupous,* flat-footed : *platus,* flat + *pous,* foot.]

plat·yr·rhine (plăt′ĭ-rīn′) also **plat·yr·rhin·i·an** (plăt′ĭ-rĭn′ē-ən) *adj.* **1.** *Anthropol.* Having a broad, flat nose. **2.** *Zool.* Of or designating the New World monkeys, many of which are characterized by widely separated nostrils. —*n.* A platyrrhine person or monkey. [NLat. *Platyrrhina,* group name < Gk. *platurrhis,* broad-nosed : *platus,* wide + *rhis,* nose.] **—plat′yr·rhi′ny** (-rī′nē) *n.*

plau·dit (plô′dĭt) *n.* Often **plaudits.** An enthusiastic expression of approbation or praise. [< Lat. *plaudite,* pl. imper. of *plaudere,* to applaud.]

plau·si·ble (plô′zə-bəl) *adj.* **1.** Seemingly or apparently valid, likely, or acceptable: *a plausible excuse.* **2.** Giving a deceptive impression of truth, acceptability, or reliability; specious. [Lat. *plausibilis,* deserving applause < *plaudere,* to applaud.] **—plau′si·bil′i·ty, plau′si·ble·ness** *n.* **—plau′si·bly** *adv.*

plau·sive (plô′zĭv, -sĭv) *adj.* **1.** Showing or expressing praise or approbation; applauding. **2.** *Obs.* Plausible. [< Lat. *plaudere, plaus-,* to applaud.]

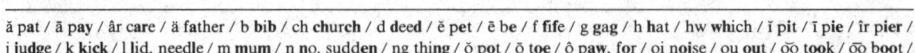

play (plā) *v.* **played, play·ing, plays.** —*intr.* **1.** To occupy oneself in amusement, sport, or other recreation. **2. a.** To take part in a game. **b.** To participate in a betting game; gamble. **3.** To act in jest or sport. **4.** To deal or behave carelessly or indifferently; toy; trifle. **5.** To make love in a sportive or playful way. **6.** To act or behave in a specified way: *play fair.* **7.** To act or perform, esp. in a dramatic production. **8.** To perform on a musical instrument. **9.** To emit sound or be sounded in performance: *The band is playing.* **10.** To be performed, as in a theater or on television: *A good movie is playing next week.* **11.** To move or seem to move quickly, lightly, or irregularly: *The breeze played on the water.* **12.** To function or operate uninterruptedly, esp. to discharge a steady stream: *The fountains played in the courtyard.* **13.** To move or operate freely within a bounded space, as machine parts do. —*tr.* **1. a.** To perform or act (a role or part) in a dramatic performance. **b.** To assume the role of; act as: *play the villain.* **2.** To put on or perform (a theatrical work) on or as if on the stage. **3.** To put on or produce a theatrical performance in (a given place): *They played Detroit last week.* **4.** To pretend to be; mimic the activities of: *The boys played cowboy.* **5.** To participate in (a game or sport). **6.** To compete against in a game or sport. **7. a.** To occupy or work at (a position) in a game: *She plays first base.* **b.** To employ (a player) in a game or position: *play her at first base.* **c.** To use or move (a card, piece, or ball) in a game or sport: *play the queen of hearts.* **8.** To perform or put into effect, esp. as a jest or deception: *play a joke on someone.* **9.** To use or manipulate, esp. for one's own interests: *He played his two opponents against each other.* **10. a.** To bet; wager. **b.** To make a wager on. **11. a.** To perform on (a musical instrument): *play the guitar.* **b.** To perform (music) on an instrument or instruments. **12.** To cause (a record or phonograph, for example) to emit recorded sounds. **13.** To discharge, set off, or cause to operate in or as if in a continuous stream: *play a hose on a fire.* **14.** To cause to move rapidly, lightly, or irregularly: *play lights over the dance floor.* **15.** To exhaust (a hooked fish) by allowing it to pull on the line. **—*phrasal verbs.* play along.** *Informal.* To agree to participate in or cooperate with an activity or plan. **play at. 1.** To participate in; engage in. **2.** To do or take part in half-heartedly. **play back.** To perform a playback of (a recently recorded tape or disc). **play down.** To minimize the importance of; make little of: *play down one's failings.* **play off. 1.** *Sports.* **a.** To establish the winner of (a tie) by playing in an additional game or series of games. **b.** To participate in a play-off. **2.** To set (one individual or party) in opposition to another, so as to advance one's own interests. **play on (or upon).** To take advantage of (another's attitudes or feelings) for one's own interests: *He played on her sympathies.* **play out. 1.** To do or play until completed; finish. **2.** To use up; exhaust. **play up.** *Informal.* To emphasize or publicize: *play up one's conquests.* —*n.* **1. a.** A literary work written for performance on the stage; drama. **b.** The performance of such a work. **2.** Activity engaged in for enjoyment or recreation. **3.** Fun or jesting: *It was done in play.* **4. a.** The act of carrying on or engaging in a game or sport. **b.** The manner or way of playing a game or sport. **5.** A manner or method of dealing with people generally: *fair play.* **6.** A move or action in a game: *It's your play.* **7.** Participation in betting; gambling. **8.** Action, motion, or use: *the play of the imagination.* **9.** Quick, often irregular movement or action, esp. of light or color: *the play of color on iridescent feathers.* **10.** Movement or space for movement, as of mechanical parts. **—*idioms.* in play.** *Sports.* In a position to be played. **make a play for.** *Informal.* To make an attempt to attract or obtain by using artifice, wiles, or skill. **out of play.** *Sports.* Not in play. **play ball.** *Informal.* To cooperate. **play both ends against the middle.** To set opposing parties or interests against one another so as to advance one's own goals. **play by ear.** To deal with extemporaneously: *played it by ear until the schedule was firm.* **play catch up.** *Informal.* To act speedily in order to move ahead from a lagging position. **play down to.** To simplify one's manner or the meaning of, esp. to win support or favor. **play games.** *Informal.* To conceal the truth from by use of deceptiveness. **play hardball.** To use rough, unscrupulous tactics in order to achieve a goal: *"This is a judicious way of accusing the Court of playing political hardball on the sly"* (Edwin M. Yoder, Jr.). **play in Peoria.** *Informal.* To be acceptable, esp. to middle-class standards. **play into the hands of.** To act or behave so as to give an advantage to (an opponent). **play (one's) cards.** *Informal.* To act with all the means at one's disposal. **play possum.** To pretend to be sleeping or dead. **play the field.** To date more than one person. **play the game.** To behave according to prevailing custom or standards. **play up to.** *Informal.* To curry favor with. [ME *playen* < OE *plegan.*] **—play'a·bil'i·ty** *n.* **—play'a·ble** *adj.*

pla·ya (plī'ə) *n.* **1.** The beach or bank of a river. **2.** A nearly level area at the bottom of a desert basin, sometimes temporarily covered with water. [Sp. < Med. Lat. *plagia,* prob. < Gk., sides.]

play-act (plā'ăkt') *intr.v.* **-act·ed, -act·ing, -acts. 1.** To play a role in a dramatic performance. **2.** To play a pretended role; make believe. **3.** To behave in an overdramatic or artificial manner.

play·back (plā'băk') *n.* **1.** The act or process of replaying a newly made record or tape. **2.** A method of or apparatus for reproducing sound recordings.

play·bill (plā'bĭl') *n.* A poster announcing a theatrical performance.

Play·bill (plā'bĭl'). A trademark for a program of a theatrical performance.

play·boy (plā'boi') *n.* A man who is devoted to the pursuit of pleasurable activities.

play-by-play (plā'bī-plā') *adj.* Consisting of a detailed running commentary or account, as of the action of a sports event.

play·date (plā'dāt') *n.* The scheduled showing of a production, as a movie, esp. on pay-TV.

play·er (plā'ər) *n.* **1.** One who participates in a game or sport. **2.** One who performs in theatrical roles; actor. **3.** One who plays a musical instrument. **4.** The mechanism actuating a player piano. **5.** A phonograph. **6.** A gambler. **7.** A trifler.

player piano *n.* A mechanically operated piano that uses a perforated paper roll to actuate the keys.

play·fel·low (plā'fĕl'ō) *n.* A companion in play; playmate.

play·ful (plā'fəl) *adj.* **1.** Full of fun and good spirits; frolicsome; sportive: *a playful kitten.* **2.** Humorous; jesting. **—play'ful·ly** *adv.* **—play'ful·ness** *n.*

play·girl (plā'gûrl') *n.* A woman devoted to the pursuit of pleasurable activities.

play·go·er (plā'gō'ər) *n.* One who attends the theater.

play·ground (plā'ground') *n.* **1.** An outdoor area set aside for recreation and play, esp. one containing equipment such as seesaws or swings. **2.** A field or sphere of unrestricted activity: *"Foreign affairs had been T.R.'s personal playground during his Presidency"* (John Dos Passos).

play·house (plā'hous') *n.* **1.** A theater. **2.** A small house for children to play in. **3.** A child's toy house; doll house.

playing card *n.* A card marked with its rank and suit belonging to any of several decks used in playing various games.

playing field *n.* A field for games such as cricket and soccer.

play·let (plā'lĭt) *n.* A short play.

play·mate (plā'māt') *n.* A companion in play or recreation.

play-off (plā'ôf', -ŏf') *n. Sports.* **1.** A final game or series of games played to break a tie. **2.** A series of games played to determine a championship.

play·pen (plā'pĕn') *n.* A portable enclosure in which a baby or young child can be left to play.

play·room (plā'ro͞om', -ro͝om') *n.* A room designed or set aside for recreation or playing.

play·thing (plā'thĭng') *n.* **1.** Something to play with; toy. **2.** One treated as a toy: *a plaything of fate.*

play·wear (plā'wâr') *n.* Garments suitable for recreational activities.

play·wright (plā'rīt') *n.* One who writes plays; dramatist.

pla·za (plä'zə, plăz'ə) *n.* **1.** A public square or similar open area in a town or city. **2.** A broad paved area for automobiles, esp.: **a.** The widened roadway forming the approach to tollbooths on a highway. **b.** A parking or servicing area next to a highway. [Sp. < Lat. *platea,* broad street. —see PLACE.]

plea (plē) *n.* **1.** An appeal or entreaty: *a plea for leniency.* **2.** An excuse; pretext. **3.** *Law.* **a.** An allegation offered in pleading a case. **b.** In common law, a defendant's establishment of an allegation of fact in answer to the declaration made by the plaintiff. **c.** In criminal law, the answer of the accused to a charge or indictment. **d.** In equity law, a special answer depending upon or demonstrating one or more reasons why a suit should be delayed, dismissed, or barred. **e.** An action or suit. [ME *plai,* lawsuit < OFr. *plaid* < Med. Lat. *placitum* < Lat., decision < *placēre,* to please.]

plea-bar·gain (plē'bär'gən) *intr.v.* **-gained, -gain·ing, -gains.** To make an agreement that will permit a defendant to plead guilty to a lesser charge instead of a more serious one. **—plea'-bar'gain·ing** *n.*

pleach (plēch, plăch) *tr.v.* **pleached, pleach·ing, pleach·es.** To plait or interlace (branches or twigs, for example), esp. in making a hedge or an arbor. [ME *plechen* < ONFr. *plechier* < Lat. *plectere.*]

pleached (plēcht, plăcht) *adj.* Bordered or shaded with interlaced branches or vines: *a pleached walk.*

plead (plēd) *v.* **plead·ed** or **pled** (plĕd), **plead·ing, pleads.** *—intr.* **1.** To appeal earnestly; beg. **2.** To argue or offer persuasive reasons for or against something. **3.** To furnish or provide an argument or appeal: *His misfortunes plead for him.* **4.** *Law.* **a.** To put forward a plea of a specific nature in a court of law: *plead guilty.* **b.** To file an answer or pleading on behalf of a defendant or as part of the prosecution in a law action. **c.** To address a court as a lawyer or advocate. *—tr.* **1.** To assert or urge as defense, vindication, or excuse; submit as a plea: *plead illness.* **2.** To present as an answer to a charge, indictment, or declaration made against one. **3.** To argue or present (a case) in a court or similar tribunal, or to an authorized person. [ME *pleden* < OFr. *plaidier* < Med. Lat. *placitare* < *placitum,* lawsuit. —see PLEA.] **—plead'a·ble** *adj.* **—plead'er** *n.* **—plead'ing·ly** *adv.*

Usage: In strict legal usage, one is said to *plead guilty* or *plead not guilty,* but not to *plead innocent.* In nonlegal contexts, however, *plead innocent* is well established.

plead·ing (plē'dĭng) *n.* **1. a.** The act of entreating or making a plea. **b.** A plea or entreaty thus made. **2.** *Law.* **a.** The act or procedure of one who acts as an advocate in a law court. **b.** The act or technique of drawing up or presenting pleas in legal cases. **c.** A formal statement, generally written, propounding the cause of action or the defense of a legal case. **d. pleadings.** The consecutive statements, allegations, and counter allegations made in turn by plaintiff and defendant, or prosecutor and accused, until a single issue is reached upon which the trial may be held.

pleas·ance (plĕz'əns) *n.* **1.** A secluded garden or landscaped area. **2.** Pleasure or a source of pleasure. [ME < OFr. *plaisance* < *plaisant,* pleasant.]

pleas·ant (plĕz'ənt) *adj.* **1.** Giving or affording pleasure or enjoyment; agreeable. **2.** Pleasing in manner, appearance, or other personal qualities. **3.** Fair and comfortable: *pleasant weather.* **4.** Merry; lively. [ME *plesant* < OFr. *plaisant,* pr.part. of *plaisir,* to please < Lat. *placēre.*] **—pleas'ant·ly** *adv.* **—pleas'ant·ness** *n.*

player piano

pleas·ant·ry (plĕz'ən-trē) *n., pl.* **-ries. 1.** A jesting, entertaining, or humorous remark or action. **2.** Pleasingly humorous style or manner in conversation or social situations. [Fr. *plaisanterie* < OFr. < *plaisant,* pleasant.]

please (plēz) *v.* **pleased, pleas·ing, pleas·es.** *—tr.* **1.** To give enjoyment, pleasure, or satisfaction to; make glad or contented. **2.** To be the will or desire of: *May it please the court to admit this gun as evidence.* **3.** To be willing to; be so obliging as to: *Please pick up your clothes.* *—intr.* **1.** To give satisfaction or pleasure; be agreeable. **2.** To have the will or desire; wish: *Do whatever you please.* **—idiom. if you please. 1.** If it is your will, desire, or pleasure. **2.** If you can believe or imagine it. Used as an ironical expression of indignation or surprise. [ME *plesen* < OFr. *plaisir* < Lat. *placēre.*]

pleas·ing (plē'zĭng) *adj.* Giving pleasure or enjoyment; agreeable. **—pleas'ing·ly** *adv.* **—pleas'ing·ness** *n.*

pleas·ur·a·ble (plĕzh'ər-ə-bəl) *adj.* Agreeable; gratifying. **—pleas'ur·a·bil'i·ty, pleas'ur·a·ble·ness** *n.* **—pleas'ur·a·bly** *adv.*

pleas·ure (plĕzh'ər) *n.* **1.** An enjoyable sensation or emotion; delight. **2.** A source of enjoyment, gratification, or delight. **3.** Amusement, diversion, or worldly enjoyment. **4.** Sensual gratification or indulgence. **5.** One's preference, wish, or choice: *What is your pleasure?* *—v.* **-ured, -ur·ing, -ures.** *—tr.* To give pleasure or enjoyment to; gratify. *—intr.* **1.** To take pleasure; delight: *She pleasures in the sounds of the forest.* **2.** *Informal.* To go in search of pleasure or enjoyment. [ME *plesure* < OFr. *plaisir* < *plaisir,* to please < Lat. *placēre.*] **—pleas'ure·less** *adj.*

Synonyms: *pleasure, enjoyment, delight, joy.* These nouns denote, with varying force, a state of happiness or personal satisfaction. *Pleasure* is the least forceful. Sometimes, though not invariably, it suggests superficial and transitory emotion resulting from the conscious pursuit of happiness, and sometimes it is merely a form in polite address: *the pleasure of announcing your appointment. Enjoyment* is relatively stronger in its implication of sustained happiness. *Delight* suggests keen, intense, often transitory emotion. *Joy,* also a strong term, implies a more sustained state, and is often associated with sharing, self-realization, and high-mindedness in general.

pleasure principle *n.* The tendency to seek immediate gratification of instinctual needs, and to reduce pain. [Transl. of G. *Lustprinzip.*]

pleat (plēt) *n.* A fold in cloth or other material, made by doubling the material upon itself and then pressing or stitching into place; plait. *—tr.v.* **pleat·ed, pleat·ing, pleats.** To press or arrange in pleats; plait. [ME *plete,* var. of *plait,* pleat, fold. —see PLAIT.]

pleat

pleat·er (plē′tər) *n.* A sewing-machine attachment that pleats.

pleb (plĕb) *n.* **1.** A commoner; plebeian. **2.** A freshman; plebe. [Short for PLEBEIAN.]

plebe (plēb) *n.* A freshman at the U.S. Military or Naval Academy. [Obs. *plebe,* common people < Fr. *plèbe* < Lat. *plebs.*]

ple·be·ian (plĭ-bē′ən) *adj.* **1.** Of or pertaining to the Roman plebs. **2.** Of, belonging to, or characteristic of commoners. **3.** Crude; low: *plebeian tastes.* —*n.* **1.** One of the Roman plebs. **2.** A member of the lower classes. **3.** Someone who is vulgar or coarse. [Lat. *plebeius* < *plebs,* common people.] **—ple·be′ian·ism** *n.* **—ple·be′ian·ly** *adv.*

ple·bes (plē′bēz) *n.* Plural of **plebs.**

pleb·i·scite (plĕb′ĭ-sīt′, -sĭt) *n.* **1.** A direct vote in which the entire people is invited to accept or refuse the measure, program, or government of the person or party initiating the consultation. **2.** A consultation whereby a population exercises the right of national self-determination. [Fr. *plebiscite* < Lat. *plebiscitum* : *plebs,* common people + *scitum,* decree < *sciscere,* to decree.] **—ple·bis′ci·tar′y** (plə-bĭs′ĭ-tĕr′ē, plĕb′-ĭ-sī′tə-rē) *adj.*

plebs (plĕbz) *n., pl.* **ple·bes** (plē′bēz). **1.** The common people of ancient Rome. **2.** The common people; populace. [Lat.]

ple·cop·ter·an (plĭ-kŏp′tər-ən) *n.* Stonefly. [< NLat. *Plecoptera,* order name : Gk. *plekein,* to braid + Gk. *pteron,* wing.] **—ple·cop′ter·an** *adj.*

plec·tog·nath (plĕk′tŏg-năth′) *n.* Any of various tropical marine fishes of the order Tetraodontiformes or Plectognathi, which includes the triggerfishes, puffers, and trunkfishes. [NLat. *Plectognathi,* order name : Gk. *plektos,* twisted + Gk. *gnathos,* jaw.] **—plec′tog·nath′** *adj.*

plec·trum (plĕk′trəm) *n., pl.* **-trums** or **-tra** (-trə). A small, thin, flexible piece of metal, plastic, bone, or other material, used to pluck the strings of certain musical instruments, such as the guitar or lute. [Lat. < Gk. *plēktron* < *plēssein,* to strike.]

pled (plĕd) *v.* A past tense and past participle of **plead.**

pledge (plĕj) *n.* **1.** A formal promise to do something, as the performance of an obligation or duty, or to refrain from doing something. **2. a.** Something given or held as security to guarantee payment of a debt or fulfillment of an obligation. **b.** The condition of something thus given or held: *put an article in pledge.* **3.** *Law.* **a.** A delivery of goods or personal property as security for a debt or obligation. **b.** The contract by which such delivery is made. **4.** A token or sign. **5.** A person who has been accepted for membership in a fraternity or similar organization, and has promised to join, but has not yet been initiated. **6.** The act of drinking to someone; toast. —*v.* **pledged, pledg·ing, pledg·es.** —*tr.* **1.** To offer or guarantee by a solemn promise. **2.** To bind or secure by or as if by a pledge. **3.** To deposit as security; pawn. **4.** To drink a toast to. **5. a.** To promise to join (a fraternity or similar organization). **b.** To accept as a prospective member of such an organization. —*intr.* **1.** To make a solemn promise. **2.** To drink a toast to someone. —***idiom.* take the pledge.** To make a solemn vow to abstain from drinking alcoholic liquor. [ME < OFr. *plege* < LLat. *plevium,* a security, of Germanic orig.]

pledg·ee (plĕj-ē′) *n.* **1.** A person to whom something is pledged. **2.** A person with whom something is deposited as a pledge.

pledg·er (plĕj′ər) *n.* One who makes or gives a pledge.

pledg·or also **pledge·or** (plĕj′ər, plĕj-ôr′) *n. Law.* A person who deposits property as a pledge.

-plegia *suff.* Paralysis: *monoplegia.* [NLat. < Gk. *plēgē,* stroke < *plēssein,* to strike.]

Ple·iad (plē′əd,-ăd′) *n., pl.* **Ple·ia·des** (plē′ə-dēz′). **1.** One of the Pleiades. **2.** Also **ple·iad.** A group of seven illustrious persons. [Back-formation < PLEIADES.]

Ple·ia·des (plē′ə-dēz′) *pl. n.* **1.** *Gk. Myth.* The seven daughters of Atlas (Maia, Electra, Celaeno, Taygeta, Merope, Alcyone, and Sterope), who were metamorphosed into stars. **2.** An open star cluster in the constellation Taurus, consisting of several hundred stars, of which six are visible to the naked eye. [Lat. < Gk.]

pleio– *pref.* Variant of **pleo-.**

plei·o·tax·y (plī′ə-tăk′sē) *n.* An increase in the number of whorls in an inflorescence. [Gk. *pleiōn,* more + -TAXY.]

plei·ot·ro·pism (plī-ŏt′rə-pĭz′əm) also **plei·ot·ro·py** (-pē) *n.* The control or determination of more than one characteristic or function by a single gene. [Gk. *pleiōn,* more + -TROPISM.] **—plei′o·tro′pic** (plī′ə-trō′pĭk, -trŏp′ĭk) *adj.* **—plei′o·tro′pi·cal·ly** *adv.*

Pleis·to·cene (plī′stə-sēn′) *Geol.* —*adj.* Of, belonging to, or designating the geologic time, rock series, and sedimentary deposits of the earlier of the two epochs of the Quaternary period, characterized by the alternate appearance and recession of northern glaciation and the appearance of the progenitors of man. —*n.* The Pleistocene epoch or system of deposits. [Gk. *pleistos,* most + -CENE.]

ple·na (plē′nə, plĕn′ə) *n.* A plural of **plenum.**

ple·na·ry (plē′nə-rē, plĕn′ə-) *adj.* **1.** Complete in all aspects or essentials; full: *a diplomat with plenary powers.* **2.** Fully attended by all qualified members: *a plenary session of the council.* [LLat. *plenarius* < Lat. *plenus,* full.] **—ple′na·ri·ly** *adv.* **—ple′na·ri·ness** *n.*

plenary indulgence *n. Rom. Cath. Ch.* An indulgence that remits the full temporal punishment incurred by a sinner.

plench (plĕnch) *n.* A hand tool used for gripping, pulling, and turning objects under zero gravity, operated by squeezing the handle. [PL(IERS) + (WR)ENCH.]

plen·i·po·ten·ti·ar·y (plĕn′ē-pə-tĕn′shē-ĕr′ē, -shə-rē) *adj.* Invested with or conferring full powers. —*n., pl.* **-ies.** A diplomatic agent, such as an ambassador, fully authorized to represent his government. [Med. Lat. *plenipotentarius* < LLat. *plenipotens,* invested with full power : Lat. *plenus,* full + Lat. *potens,* powerful.]

plen·i·tude (plĕn′ĭ-to͞od′, -tyo͞od′) *n.* **1.** Abundance; copiousness. **2.** The condition of being full, ample, or complete. [ME < OFr. < Lat. *plenitudo* < *plenus,* full.] **—plen′i·tu′di·nous** (-to͞od′n-əs, -tyo͞od′-) *adj.*

plen·te·ous (plĕn′tē-əs) *adj.* **1.** Abundant; copious. **2.** Producing or yielding in abundance. [ME *plentivous* < OFr. *plentiveus* < *plentif* < *plente,* plenty.] **—plen′te·ous·ly** *adv.* **—plen′te·ous·ness** *n.*

plen·ti·ful (plĕn′tĭ-fəl) *adj.* **1.** Existing in great quantity or ample supply. **2.** Providing or producing an abundance: *a plentiful harvest.* **—plen′ti·ful·ly** *adv.* **—plen′ti·ful·ness** *n.*

plen·ty (plĕn′tē) *n.* **1.** A full or completely adequate amount or supply; as much as one could want: *plenty of time.* **2.** A large quantity or amount; abundance: *goods in plenty.* **3.** A condition of general abundance or prosperity. —*adj.* Plentiful; abundant. —*adv. Informal.* Sufficiently; very: *It's plenty hot.* [ME *plentie* < OFr. *plente* < Lat. *plenitas* < *plenus,* full.]

ple·num (plē′nəm, plĕn′əm) *n., pl.* **ple·nums** or **ple·na** (plē′-nə, plĕn′ə). **1.** An enclosure in which air or other gas is at a pressure greater than that outside the enclosure. **2.** An assembly or meeting with all members present. **3.** Fullness. [Lat. < neuter of *plenus,* full.]

pleo– or **pleio–** or **plio–** *pref.* More: *pleopod.* [< Gk. *pleiōn, pleōn,* more.]

ple·och·ro·ism (plē-ŏk′rō-ĭz′əm) *n.* The property possessed by some crystals of exhibiting different colors, esp. three different colors, when viewed along different axes. [PLEO- + Gk. *khrōs,* color + -ISM.] **—ple′o·chro′ic** (plē′ə-krō′ĭk) *adj.*

ple·o·mor·phism (plē′ə-môr′fĭz′əm) *n.* **1.** *Chem.* Polymorphism (sense 2). **2.** *Biol.* The occurrence of two or more structural forms during a life cycle, esp. of certain plants. **—ple′o·mor′phic** *adj.*

ple·o·nasm (plē′ə-năz′əm) *n.* **1.** The use of more words than are required to express an idea; redundancy. **2.** An instance of redundancy. **3.** A superfluous word or phrase. [LLat. *pleonasmus* < Gk. *pleonasmos* < *pleonazein,* to be excessive < *pleōn,* more.] **—ple′o·nas′tic** *adj.* **—ple′o·nas′ti·cal·ly** *adv.*

ple·o·pod (plē′ə-pŏd′) *n.* A swimmeret.

ple·ro·cer·coid (plîr′ō-sûr′koid′) *n.* The infective larva of some tapeworms, characterized by its solid elongated body. [< Gk. *plērēs,* full + *kerkos,* tail.]

ple·si·o·sau·rus (plē′sē-ə-sôr′əs, plē′zē-) also **ple·si·o·saur** (plē′sē-ə-sôr′, plē′zē-) *n., pl.* **-sau·ri** (-sôr′ī′) also **-saurs.** *Paleontol.* A large marine reptile of the extinct suborder Plesiosauria, common in Europe and North America during the Mesozoic era. [Gk. *plēsios,* near + -SAURUS.]

ples·sim·e·ter (plĕ-sĭm′ĭ-tər) *n.* Variant of **pleximeter.**

ples·sor (plĕs′ər) *n.* Variant of **plexor.**

pleth·o·ra (plĕth′ər-ə) *n.* **1.** Superabundance; excess. **2.** An excess of blood in the circulatory system or in one organ or area. [Med. Lat. < Gk. *plēthōra* < *plēthein,* to be full.]

ple·thor·ic (plĕ-thôr′ĭk, -thŏr′-, plĕth′ər-ĭk) *adj.* **1. a.** Excessive in quantity; superabundant: *plethoric wealth.* **b.** Excessive in style; turgid: *plethoric prose.* **2.** Characterized by an overabundance of blood. **—ple·thor′i·cal·ly** *adv.*

ple·thys·mo·graph (plĕ-thĭz′mə-grăf′, plə-) *n.* An instrument that measures variations in the size of an organ or body part on the basis of the amount of blood passing through or present in the part. [Gk. *plēthusmos,* increase (< *plēthunein,* to increase < *plēthus,* quantity < *plēthein,* to be full) + -GRAPH.] **—ple·thys′mo·graph′ic** *adj.* **—ple·thys′mo·graph′i·cal·ly** *adv.* **—pleth′ys·mog′ra·phy** (plĕth′ĭz-mŏg′-rə-fē) *n.*

pleur– *pref.* Variant of **pleuro-.**

pleu·ra[1] (plo͝or′ə) *n., pl.* **pleu·rae** (plo͝or′ē). Either of two membranous sacs, each of which lines one side of the thoracic cavity and envelops the contiguous lung, reducing the friction of respiratory movements to a minimum. [Med. Lat. < Gk., side.] **—pleu′ral** *adj.*

pleu·ra[2] (plo͝or′ə) *n.* Plural of **pleuron.**

pleu·ri·sy (plo͝or′ĭ-sē) *n. Pathol.* Inflammation of the pleura, often characterized when acute by exudation into the pleural cavity and production of adhesions that may become permanent or, if infected, result in empyema. [ME *pluresy* < OFr. *pleuresie* < Med. Lat. *pleuresis* < LLat. *pleuritis* < Gk. < *pleura,* side.] **—pleu·rit′ic** (plo͝o-rĭt′ĭk) *adj.*

pleurisy root *n.* Butterfly weed.

pleuro– or **pleur–** *pref.* **1.** Side; lateral: *pleurodont.* **2.** Pleura; pleural: *pleurotomy.* [NLat. < Gk. *pleura,* side, rib.]

pleu·ro·dont (plo͝or′ə-dŏnt′) *adj.* Having the teeth attached by their sides to the inner side of the jaw, as in some lizards. —*n.* A lizard with pleurodont teeth.

pleu·ron (plo͝or′ŏn′) *n., pl.* **pleu·ra** (plo͝or′ə). An external, lateral part of the body segments of arthropods. [NLat. < Gk., side.]
pleu·ro·pneu·mo·nia (plo͝or′ō-no͞o-mōn′yə, -nyo͞o-) *n.* Pneumonia aggravated by pleurisy.
pleu·rot·o·my (plo͞o-rŏt′ə-mē) *n., pl.* **-mies.** Surgical incision of the pleura.
pleus·ton (plo͞o′stən, -stŏn′) *n.* Plants that float upon the surface of bodies of fresh water. [Gk. *pleusis,* sailing + (PLANK)TON.] **—pleus·ton′ic** (plo͞o-stŏn′ĭk) *adj.*
plex·i·form (plĕk′sə-fôrm′) *adj.* Similar to or having the form of a plexus; complicated in structure. [PLEX(US) + -FORM.]
Plex·i·glas (plĕk′sĭ-glăs′). A trademark for a light, permanently transparent, weather-resistant thermoplastic.
plex·im·e·ter (plĕk-sĭm′ĭ-tər) also **ples·sim·e·ter** (plĕ-sĭm′ĭ-tər) *n.* A small, thin plate held against the body and struck with a plexor. [PLEX(OR) + -METER.] **—plex′i·met′ric** (plĕk′sə-mĕt′rĭk) *adj.* **—plex·im′e·try** *n.*
plex·or (plĕk′sər) also **ples·sor** (plĕs′ər) *n.* A small, rubber-headed hammer used in diagnosis by percussion. [< Gk. *plexis,* stroke < *plēssein,* to strike.]
plex·us (plĕk′səs) *n., pl.* **plexus** or **-us·es. 1.** A structure in the form of a network, esp. of nerves, blood vessels, or lymphatics: *the solar plexus.* **2.** An interlacing of parts; network. [NLat. < Lat., braid < *plectere,* to plait.]
pli·a·ble (plī′ə-bəl) *adj.* **1.** Easily bent or shaped; flexible. **2. a.** Receptive to change; adaptable. **b.** Easily influenced, persuaded, or swayed; tractable. **—pli′a·bil′i·ty, pli′a·ble·ness** *n.* **—pli′a·bly** *adv.*
pli·ant (plī′ənt) *adj.* **1.** Easily bent or flexed; supple. **2.** Easily altered or modified to fit conditions; adaptable. **3.** Yielding readily to influence or domination; compliant. [ME *plyante* < OFr. *pliant,* pr.part. of *plier,* to fold < Lat. *plicare.*] **—pli′an·cy** *n.* **—pli′ant·ly** *adv.* **—pli′ant·ness** *n.*
pli·ca (plī′kə) *n., pl.* **pli·cae** (plī′sē). **1.** *Zool.* A fold or ridge as of skin, membrane, or shell. **2.** *Pathol.* A matted and encrusted state of the hair, resulting from uncleanliness and vermin. [Med. Lat., fold < Lat. *plicare,* to fold.] **—pli′cal** (plī′kəl) *adj.*
pli·cate (plī′kāt′) also **pli·cat·ed** (plī′kā′tĭd) *adj.* Arranged in folds like those of a fan; pleated. [Lat. *plicatus,* p.part. of *plicare,* to fold.] **—pli′cate′ly** *adv.* **—pli′cate′ness** *n.*
pli·ca·tion (plī-kā′shən) also **plic·a·ture** (plĭk′ə-cho͝or′) *n.* **1. a.** The act or process of folding. **b.** The state of being folded. **2.** A fold.
plied[1] (plīd) *v.* Past tense and past participle of **ply**[1].
plied[2] (plīd) *v.* Past tense and past participle of **ply**[2].
pli·er (plī′ər) *n.* One who plies a trade.
pli·ers (plī′ərz) *pl.n.* Any of variously shaped tools having a pair of pivoted jaws, used for holding, bending, or cutting.
plies[1] (plīz) *v.* Third person singular present tense of **ply**[1]. *—n.* Plural of **ply**[1].
plies[2] (plīz) *v.* Third person singular present tense of **ply**[2].
plight[1] (plīt) *n.* A condition or situation of difficulty or adversity. [ME *plit,* fold, condition < Norman Fr. < Lat. *plicitum,* p.part. of *plicare,* to fold.]
plight[2] (plīt) *tr.v.* **plight·ed, plight·ing, plights. 1.** To promise or bind by a solemn pledge, esp. to betroth. **2.** To give or pledge (one's word or oath, for example). *—n.* A solemn pledge, as of faith; engagement. ***—idiom.*** **plight one's troth. 1.** To become engaged to marry. **2.** To give one's solemn oath. [ME *plighten* < OE *plihtan,* to endanger < *pliht,* danger.] **—plight′er** *n.*
plim·soll (plĭm′səl, -sôl′) also **plim·sol** or **plim·sole** (plĭm′sōl′) *n. Chiefly Brit.* A rubber-soled cloth shoe; sneaker. [Prob. from the resemblance of its mudguard to a PLIMSOLL MARK.]
Plimsoll mark *n.* One of a set of lines on the hull of a merchant ship that indicate the depth to which it may be legally loaded under specified conditions. [After Samuel *Plimsoll* (1824–1898).]
plink (plĭngk) *v.* **plinked, plink·ing, plinks.** *—tr.* **1.** To cause to make a metallic clinking sound. **2.** To shoot at in a casual manner. *—intr.* **1.** To make a clinking sound. **2.** To shoot at randomly selected targets. [Imit.]
plinth (plĭnth) *n. Archit.* **1.** A block or slab upon which a pedestal, column, or statue is placed. **2.** The base block at the intersection of the horizontal baseboard and vertical trim around an opening. **3.** A continuous course of stones supporting a wall. **4.** A square base, as of a vase. [Fr. *plinthe* < Lat. *plinthus* < Gk. *plinthos,* tile.]
plio– *pref.* Variant of **pleo-.**
Pli·o·cene (plī′ə-sēn′) *Geol. —adj.* Of, belonging to, or designating the geologic time, rock series, and sedimentary deposits of the last of the five epochs of the Tertiary period, characterized by the appearance of distinctly modern plants and animals. *—n.* The Pliocene epoch or system of deposits. [Gk. *pleiōn,* more + -CENE.]
Pli·o·film (plī′ə-fĭlm′). A trademark for a pliant, transparent rubber compound used for waterproof items.
pli·o·tron (plī′ə-trŏn′) *n.* A vacuum tube running with a high-temperature cathode that has one or more grids. [Orig. a trademark.]
plis·sé also **plis·se** (plĭ-sā′) *n.* **1.** A puckered texture of cloth created by treating fabric with a caustic soda. **2.** Fabric having a plissé texture. [Fr. < p.part. of *plisser,* to pleat < OFr. < *pli,* fold < *plier,* to fold < Lat. *plicare.*]
plod (plŏd) *v.* **plod·ded, plod·ding, plods.** *—intr.* **1.** To move or walk heavily or laboriously; trudge. **2.** To work or act perseveringly or monotonously; drudge. *—tr.* To trudge heavily and slowly along or over. *—n.* **1.** The act of moving or walking heavily and slowly. **2.** The sound made by a heavy step. [Imit.] **—plod′der** *n.* **—plod′ding·ly** *adv.*
-ploid *suff.* Having a number of chromosomes that has a specified relationship to the basic number of chromosomes of a group: *heteroploid.* [Back-formation < DIPLOID and HAPLOID.]
ploi·dy (ploi′dē) *n.* A multiple of a set of chromosomes. [Back-formation < DIPLOIDY and HAPLOIDY.]
plonk (plŏngk, plŭngk) *v., n., & adv.* Variant of **plunk.**
plop (plŏp) *v.* **plopped, plop·ping, plops.** *—intr.* **1.** To fall with a sound like that of an object falling into water without splashing. **2.** To drop or sink heavily: *plop into a chair.* *—tr.* To drop or move so as to make a plopping sound. *—n.* A plopping sound or movement. [Imit.] **—plop** *adv.*
plo·sion (plō′zhən) *n.* **1.** The articulation of a plosive sound. **2.** The sudden release of occluded air characteristically occurring in the articulation of certain stop consonants. [< EXPLOSION.]
plo·sive (plō′sĭv, -zĭv) *adj.* Designating a speech sound whose articulation requires, at some stage, the complete closure of the oral passage, as in the sound of (p) in *top* or (d) in *adorn.* *—n.* A plosive speech sound. [Fr.]
plot (plŏt) *n.* **1. a.** A small piece of ground, generally used for a specific purpose: *a garden plot.* **b.** A measured area of land; lot. **2.** A ground plan, as for a building; diagram. **3.** The series of events consisting of an outline of the action of a narrative or drama. **4.** A secret plan to accomplish a hostile or illegal purpose; scheme. *—v.* **plot·ted, plot·ting, plots.** *—tr.* **1.** To represent graphically, as on a chart: *plot a ship's course.* **2.** To form a plot for; prearrange secretly or deviously: *plot an assassination.* **3.** To conceive and arrange the action and incidents of: *plotted her new novel.* **4.** *Math.* **a.** To locate (points or other figures) on a graph by means of coordinates. **b.** To draw (a curve) connecting points on a graph. *—intr.* **1.** To devise secretly; conspire. **2.** To be located by means of coordinates, as on a chart or with data. [ME < OE.] **—plot′less** *adj.* **—plot′less·ness** *n.* **—plot′ter** *n.*
plot line *n.* A story line.
plottage (plŏt′ĭj) *n.* The area of land in a plot.
plotting board *n.* A computer output device that plots the curves of functions of variables.
plotting table *n.* A plotting board.
plough (plou) *n. & v. Chiefly Brit.* Variant of **plow.**
plov·er (plŭv′ər, plō′vər) *n., pl.* **plover** or **-ers. 1.** Any of various widely distributed wading birds of the family Charadriidae, having rounded bodies, short tails, and short bills. **2.** Any of various birds similar or related to the plover. [ME < OFr. *plovier* < VLat. **plovarius* < *pluvia,* rain. —see PLUVIAL.]
plow (plou) *n.* **1. a.** A farm implement consisting of a heavy blade at the end of a beam, usually hitched to a draft team or motor vehicle, and used for breaking up soil and cutting furrows in preparation for sowing. **b.** An implement of similar function, as a snowplow. **2. Plow.** The Big Dipper. *—v.* **plowed, plow·ing, plows.** *—tr.* **1.** To break and turn over (earth) with a plow. **2. a.** To form (a furrow, for example) with a plow. **b.** To make or form with driving force: *plowed his way through the crowd.* **3.** To make furrows or indentations in. **4.** To cut through (water): *plow the high seas.* *—intr.* **1.** To break and turn up earth with a plow. **2.** To be capable of being plowed: *Rocky earth plows poorly.* **3.** To move or progress with driving force: *plowed through the crowd impatiently.* **4.** To proceed laboriously; plod. ***—phrasal verbs.*** **plow back.** To reinvest (earnings or profits) in one's business. **plow into.** *Informal.* **1.** To strike with force. **2.** To undertake (a task, for example) with eagerness and vigor. **plow under. 1.** To overwhelm. **2.** To cause to vanish. [ME < OE *plōg,* plowland.] **—plow′a·ble** *adj.* **—plow′er** *n.*
plow·boy (plou′boi′) *n.* **1.** A boy who leads or guides a team of animals in plowing. **2.** A country boy.
plow·head (plou′hĕd′) *n.* The metal shackle at the leading end of the beam of a plow, used to attach the plow to a tractor or draft animal; clevis.
plow·land (plou′lănd′) *n.* **1.** In medieval England, a unit of land area roughly equivalent to the area capable of being plowed by a team of eight oxen in a single year. **2.** Land under cultivation or suitable for cultivation.
plow·man (plou′mən) *n.* **1.** A person who plows. **2.** A farmer or rustic.
plow·share (plou′shâr′) *n.* The cutting blade of a plow; share.
plow steel *n.* A high-strength steel having a carbon content of 0.5 to 0.95% and used primarily to make wire rope.
ploy (ploi) *n.* A stratagem or artifice to obtain an advantage over one's opponent. [Orig. unknown.]
pluck (plŭk) *v.* **plucked, pluck·ing, plucks.** *—tr.* **1.** To detach by grasping and pulling abruptly with the fingers; pick: *pluck a flower; pluck feathers from a chicken.* **2.** To pull out the hair or feathers of: *pluck a chicken.* **3.** To give an

pliers

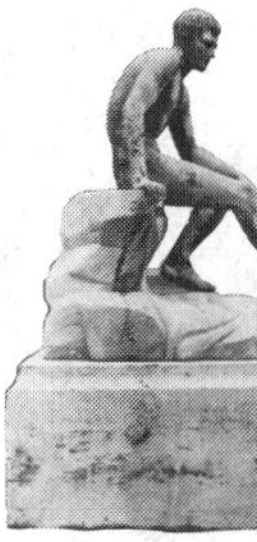

plinth

plow

plum[1]

George Miksch Sutton

plumage
Of a nightjar

plumb

plunger

abrupt pull to; tug at: *pluck a sleeve.* **4.** *Mus.* To sound (the strings of an instrument) by pulling and releasing them with the fingers or a plectrum. **5.** *Slang.* To rob or swindle. —*intr.* To give an abrupt pull; tug. —*n.* **1.** The act of plucking; tug. **2.** Resourceful courage and daring in the face of difficulties; spirit. **3.** The heart, liver, windpipe, and lungs of a slaughtered animal. [ME *plukken* < OE *pluccian,* prob. < VLat. **piluccare* < Lat. *pilus,* hair.] **—pluck'er** *n.*

pluck·y (plŭk'ē) *adj.* **-i·er, -i·est.** Having or showing courage or spirited resourcefulness in trying circumstances. **—pluck'i·ly** *adv.* **—pluck'i·ness** *n.*

plug (plŭg) *n.* **1.** An object, such as a cork or wad of cloth, used to stop a hole or gap. **2.** *Elect.* **a.** A fitting, commonly with two metal prongs for insertion in a fixed socket, used to connect an appliance to a power supply. **b.** A spark plug. **3.** A fireplug. **4. a.** A flat cake of pressed or twisted tobacco. **b.** A portion of chewing tobacco. **5.** *Geol.* A mass of igneous rock filling the opening, or vent, of a volcano. **6.** *Informal.* A favorable public mention of a commercial product, business, or performance, esp. when spoken over television or radio. **7.** *Slang.* Something inferior, useless, or defective, esp. an old, worn-out horse. **8.** *Slang.* A gunshot or bullet: *a plug in the back.* **9.** *Slang.* A plug hat. —*v.* **plugged, plug·ging, plugs.** —*tr.* **1.** To fill (a hole) tightly with or as with a plug or stopper; stop up. **2.** To use as a plug: *plugged a cork in a bottle.* **3.** To connect (an electrical appliance) to a socket: *He plugged in the toaster.* **4.** *Slang.* **a.** To hit with a bullet; shoot. **b.** To hit with the fist; punch. **5.** *Informal.* **a.** To make favorable public mention of (a product, for example). **b.** To publicize (a song, for example) by constant repetition. —*intr.* **1.** *Informal.* To work doggedly and persistently at some activity. **2.** *Informal.* To work for a particular cause or person: *plug for a promotion.* **3.** *Slang.* To fire bullets. ***—phrasal verb.* plug in. 1.** To function by being connected to an electrical outlet. **2.** *Slang.* To be attuned or responsive to. [Du. < MDu. *plugge.*] **—plug'ger** *n.*

plug board *n.* **1.** A control panel or wiring panel. **2.** A removable panel in a computing device that may be rewired at will to sort data by a prescribed pattern.

plug-com·pat·i·ble (plŭg'kəm-păt'ə-bəl) *adj.* Capable of being connected peripherally to a computer without modification.

plug hat *n. Slang.* A man's high silk hat.

plug-in (plŭg'ĭn') *adj.* Designed to be plugged in to an electric circuit: *a plug-in game.*

plug·ug·ly (plŭg'ŭg'lē) *n., pl.* **-lies.** *Slang.* A gangster or ruffian, esp. one hired to intimidate. [Orig. unknown.]

plum¹ (plŭm) *n.* **1. a.** Any of several shrubs or small trees of the genus *Prunus,* bearing smooth-skinned, fleshy, edible fruit with a single hard-shelled seed. **b.** The fruit of any of these trees. **2. a.** Any of several trees bearing plumlike fruit. **b.** The fruit of such a tree. **3.** A raisin, when added to a pudding or cake. **4.** A sugarplum. **5.** A dark purple to deep reddish purple. **6.** Something esp. desirable, as a good position. [ME < OE *plūme* < Lat. *prunum* < Gk. *proumnon.*] **—plum'like'** *adj.*

plum² (plŭm) *adj. & adv. Informal.* Variant of **plumb.**

plum·age (plo͞o'mĭj) *n.* **1.** The feathers of a bird. **2.** Feathers used ornamentally. **3.** Elaborate dress; finery. [ME < OFr. < *plume,* plume < Lat. *pluma.*] **—plum'aged** *adj.*

plu·mate (plo͞o'māt') *adj.* Resembling a plume or feather. [Lat. *plumatus,* feathered < *pluma,* feather.]

plumb (plŭm) *n.* **1.** A weight suspended from the end of a line, used to determine water depth. **2.** A plumb used to establish a true vertical. —*adj.* **1.** Exactly vertical. **2.** Also **plum.** *Informal.* Utter; absolute; sheer: *a plumb fool.* —*adv.* **1.** In a vertical or perpendicular line. **2.** Also **plum.** *Informal.* Utterly; completely: *plumb tired.* —*v.* **plumbed, plumb·ing, plumbs.** —*tr.* **1.** To test the alignment or angle of with a plumb. **2.** To straighten or make perpendicular: *plumb up the wall.* **3.** To determine the depth of; sound. **4.** To examine closely; probe into: *"Shallow ideas are plumbed and discarded"* (Gilbert Highet). **5.** To seal with lead. —*intr.* To work as a plumber. ***—idiom.* out of** (or **off**) **plumb.** Not vertical. [ME < OFr. *plomme* < Lat. *plumbum,* lead.] **—plumb'a·ble** *adj.*

plum·ba·go (plŭm-bā'gō) *n., pl.* **-gos. 1.** Graphite. **2.** Any of various plants of the genus *Plumbago*; leadwort. [Lat., lead ore < *plumbum,* lead.]

plumb bob *n.* A usually conical piece of metal attached to the end of a plumb line.

plumb·er (plŭm'ər) *n.* **1.** A worker who installs and repairs pipes and plumbing. **2.** *Slang.* A person who investigates and tries to plug leaks of sensitive information: *"The plumbers pushed the departments to investigate with interviews and polygraph tests"* (Richard M. Nixon). [ME *plummer* < OFr. *plommier* < LLat. *plumbarius,* lead worker < Lat. *plumbum,* lead.]

plumber's helper *n.* A device having a large suction cup at the end of a handle, used to clear drains.

plumber's snake *n.* Snake (sense 4).

plumb·er·y (plŭm'ə-rē) *n., pl.* **-ies. 1.** A plumber's workshop or place of business. **2.** A plumber's work; plumbing.

plum·bif·er·ous (plŭm-bĭf'ər-əs) *adj.* Containing lead. [Lat. *plumbum,* lead + -FEROUS.]

plumb·ing (plŭm'ĭng) *n.* **1.** The pipes, fixtures, and other apparatus of a water, gas, or sewage system. **2.** The work or trade of a plumber. **3.** The act of using a plumb line.

plum·bism (plŭm'bĭz'əm) *n.* Chronic lead poisoning. [< Lat. *plumbum,* lead.]

plumb line *n.* **1.** A line from which a weight is suspended to determine verticality or depth. **2.** A line regarded as directed exactly toward the earth's center of gravity.

plumb rule *n.* A narrow strip of wood with a plumb line and bob attached, used to test verticality.

plum duff *n.* A flour pudding with raisins or currants, boiled in a cloth bag.

plume (plo͞om) *n.* **1.** A feather, esp. one that is large and ornamental. **2.** A large feather or cluster of feathers worn as an ornament or symbol of rank, as on a helmet. **3.** A token of honor or achievement. **4.** A featherlike structure, form, or object: *a plume of smoke.* **5.** *Geol.* A column of molten rock hypothesized to rise from the earth's lower mantle and believed to be the driving force in plate tectonics. —*tr.v.* **plumed, plum·ing, plumes. 1.** To decorate, cover, or supply with or as with plumes. **2.** To smooth (feathers); preen. **3.** To pride or congratulate (oneself): *plumed himself on his victory.* [ME < OFr. < Lat. *pluma.*]

plume·let (plo͞om'lĭt) *n.* A small plume.

plum·met (plŭm'ĭt) *n.* **1.** A plumb bob. **2.** Something that weighs down or oppresses. —*intr.v.* **-met·ed, -met·ing, -mets.** To drop straight down; plunge. [ME *plomet* < OFr. *plombet,* ball of lead, dim. of *plomme,* lead < Lat. *plumbum.*]

plum·my (plŭm'ē) *adj.* **-mi·er, -mi·est. 1.** Filled with plums. **2.** Choice; desirable: *got a plummy job with the state.* **3.** Mellow and rich, often to the point of sounding affected: *a plummy voice.*

plu·mose (plo͞o'mōs') *adj.* **1.** Having plumes or feathers; feathered. **2.** Resembling a feather or plume; feathery. [Lat. *plumosus* < *pluma,* feather.] **—plu'mose'ly** *adv.* **—plu·mos'i·ty** (-mŏs'ĭ-tē) *n.*

plump¹ (plŭmp) *adj.* **-er, -est. 1.** Well-rounded and full in form; chubby. **2.** Abundant; ample: *a plump reward.* —*v.* **plumped, plump·ing, plumps.** —*tr.* To make chubby or well-rounded: *plump up a pillow.* —*intr.* To become rounded or chubby. [ME, dull, prob. < MLG *plomp.*] **—plump'ly** *adv.* **—plump'ness** *n.*

plump² (plŭmp) *v.* **plumped, plump·ing, plumps.** —*intr.* **1.** To drop abruptly or heavily: *plump into a chair.* **2.** To come or go abruptly or hurriedly. **3.** To give full support or praise: *plumped for her appointment as department head.* —*tr.* To drop or throw down heavily or abruptly: *plump an ice cube into a glass.* —*n.* **1.** A heavy or abrupt fall or collision. **2.** The sound of a heavy fall or collision. —*adj.* Blunt; direct. —*adv.* **1.** With a heavy or abrupt impact. **2.** Straight down. **3.** Without qualification; bluntly. [MLG *plumpen.*] **—plump'ly** *adv.* **—plump'ness** *n.*

plump·ish (plŭm'pĭsh) *adj.* Somewhat plump.

plum pudding *n.* A rich boiled or steamed pudding made with flour, suet, raisins, currants, citron, and spices.

plum tomato *n.* A form of the cherry tomato, having somewhat oblong fruit.

plu·mule (plo͞om'yo͞ol) *n.* **1.** A down feather. **2.** *Bot.* The rudimentary bud of a plant embryo. [Lat. *plumula,* dim. of *pluma,* feather.] **—plu'mu·lose'** *adj.*

plum·y (plo͞o'mē) *adj.* **1.** Consisting of or covered with feathers. **2.** Resembling a feather or plume.

plun·der (plŭn'dər) *v.* **-dered, -der·ing, -ders.** —*tr.* **1.** To rob of goods by force, esp. in time of war; pillage. **2.** To seize wrongfully or by force; steal. —*intr.* To take booty; rob. —*n.* **1.** Property stolen by fraud or force; booty. **2.** The act or practice of plundering. [G. *plündern* < MHG *plundern* < *plunder,* household goods.] **—plun'der·a·ble** *adj.* **—plun'der·er** *n.* **—plun'der·ous** *adj.*

plun·der·age (plŭn'dər-ĭj) *n.* **1.** Robbery. **2.** *Law.* **a.** The embezzling of goods on board a ship. **b.** The goods so acquired.

plunge (plŭnj) *v.* **plunged, plung·ing, plung·es.** —*tr.* **1.** To thrust or throw forcefully into a substance or place: *"Plunge the lobsters head first into a large pot of boiling salted water"* (Craig Claiborne). **2.** To cast suddenly or violently into a given state or situation. —*intr.* **1.** To throw oneself into a substance or place. **2.** To throw oneself earnestly or wholeheartedly into a given state or activity. **3.** To enter violently or speedily. **4.** To descend steeply; fall precipitously, as a road or cliff. **5.** To move forward and downward violently. **6.** *Informal.* To speculate or gamble extravagantly. —*n.* **1.** An act or instance of plunging. **2. a.** A place or area for diving or plunging, as a swimming pool. **b.** A swim; dip. [ME *plungen* < OFr. *plonger* < VLat. **plumbicare* < Lat. *plumbum,* lead.]

plung·er (plŭn'jər) *n.* **1.** One that plunges. **2.** A part that operates with a repeated thrusting or plunging movement, such as a piston. **3.** A device consisting of a rubber suction cup attached to the end of a stick, used to clean out clogged drains and pipes.

plunk (plŭngk) also **plonk** (plŏngk, plŭngk) *Informal.* —*v.* **plunked, plunk·ing, plunks** also **plonked, plonk·ing, plonks.** —*tr.* **1.** To strum or pluck (the strings of a musical instrument). **2.** To throw or place heavily or abruptly: *plunk one's money down.* —*intr.* **1.** To emit a hollow, twanging sound.

2. To drop or fall abruptly or heavily; plump. *—n.* **1.** A short, hollow, twanging sound. **2.** A heavy blow or stroke. *—adv.* **1.** With a short, hollow thud. **2.** Exactly; precisely: *The dart landed plunk in the center of the target.* [Imit.] **—plunk'er** *n.*

plu·per·fect (plo͞o-pûr'fĭkt) *Gram. —adj.* Of or designating a verb tense used to express action completed prior to a specified or implied past time. *—n.* **1.** The pluperfect tense, formed in English with the past participle of a verb and one or more auxiliaries, as *had been gone* in the sentence *He had been gone an hour when we arrived.* **2.** A verb or form in the pluperfect tense. [Alteration of LLat. *plus quam perfectum,* more than perfect.]

plu·ral (plo͝or'əl) *adj.* **1.** Relating to or composed of more than one member, set, or kind. **2.** *Gram.* Of or relating to a grammatical form that designates more than one of the things specified. *—n. Gram.* **1.** The plural number or form. **2.** A word or term in the plural form. [ME < OFr. *plurel* < Lat. *pluralis* < *plus,* more.] **—plu'ral·ly** *adv.*

plu·ral·ism (plo͝or'ə-lĭz'əm) *n.* **1.** The condition of being plural. **2.** A condition of society in which numerous distinct ethnic, religious, or cultural groups coexist within one nation. **3.** The holding by one person of more than one position or office, esp. two or more ecclesiastical benefices, at the same time. **4.** *Philos.* **a.** The doctrine that reality is composed of many ultimate substances. **b.** The belief that no single explanatory system or view of reality can account for all the phenomena of life.

plu·ral·ist (plo͝or'ə-lĭst) *n.* **1.** A person who holds more than one office, esp. two or more ecclesiastical benefices, at the same time. **2.** One who adheres to philosophical pluralism. **—plu'ral·is'tic** *adj.*

plu·ral·i·ty (plo͞o-răl'ĭ-tē) *n., pl.* **-ties. 1.** The state or fact of being plural. **2.** A large number or amount; multitude: *"Man burst forth with a plurality of tools and art"* (Edmund Carpenter). **3.** *Eccles.* **a.** Pluralism (sense 3). **b.** The offices or benefices held by a pluralist. **4. a.** In a contest of more than two alternatives, the number of votes cast for the winning alternative if this number is not more than one half of the total votes cast. **b.** The number by which the vote of a winning candidate exceeds that of his closest opponent. **5.** The larger or greater part of something.

plu·ral·ize (plo͝or'ə-līz') *v.* **-ized, -iz·ing, -iz·es.** *—tr.* **1.** To make plural. **2.** To express in the plural. *—intr.* **1.** To become plural. **2.** To hold more than one position or ecclesiastical benefice at one time. **—plu'ral·i·za'tion** *n.*

plus (plŭs) *prep.* **1.** Added to. **2.** Increased by; along with: *earnings plus dividends. —adj.* **1. a.** Involving or pertaining to addition. **b.** Positive, as on a scale. **2.** Added or extra: *a plus benefit.* **3.** *Informal.* Increased to a further degree: *personality plus.* **4.** Slightly more than: *a grade of C plus.* **5.** Positive (sense 12). *—n., pl.* **plus·es** or **plus·ses. 1.** The plus sign (+). **2.** A positive quantity. **3.** A favorable factor: *The clear weather was a plus for the golf tournament. —conj. Informal.* And. [Lat., more.]

Usage: Traditionally, *plus* as a preposition does not have the conjunctive force of *and.* Therefore, when *plus* is used after a singular subject, the verb remains singular: *Two* (the numeral considered as a singular noun) *plus two equals four. Her skill plus their connections makes them a formidable couple.* • *Plus* is sometimes used loosely as a conjunction to connect two independent clauses: *She has a great deal of talent, plus she is willing to work hard.* Such use is unacceptable in writing to a large majority of the Usage Panel.

plus fours *pl.n.* Loose knickerbockers bagging below the knees, worn for sports. [From the fact that they are four inches longer than ordinary knickerbockers.]

plush (plŭsh) *n.* A fabric of silk, rayon, cotton, or other material, having a thick, deep pile. *—adj.* **1.** Made of or covered with plush. **2.** *Informal.* Luxurious. [OFr. *pluche* < *peluchier,* to pluck, prob. < VLat. **piluccare* < Lat. *pilus,* hair.] **—plush'ly** *adv.* **—plush'ness** *n.*

plush·y (plŭsh'ē) *adj.* **-i·er, -i·est. 1.** Resembling plush in texture. **2.** *Informal.* Ostentatiously luxurious: *a plushy office.* **—plush'i·ly** *adv.* **—plush'i·ness** *n.*

plus sign *n.* The symbol (+), as in *2 + 2 = 4,* used to indicate addition or a positive quantity.

Plu·to (plo͞o'tō) *n.* **1.** *Rom. Myth.* The god of the dead and the ruler of the underworld. **2.** The ninth and farthest planet from the sun, having a sidereal period of revolution about the sun of 248.4 years, 4.5 billion kilometers or 2.8 billion miles distant at perihelion and 7.4 billion kilometers or 4.6 billion miles at aphelion, and a diameter approximately half that of the earth. [Lat. < Gk. *ploutōn* < *ploutos,* wealth.]

plu·toc·ra·cy (plo͞o-tŏk'rə-sē) *n., pl.* **-cies. 1.** Government by the wealthy. **2.** A wealthy class that controls a government. **3.** A government or state in which the wealthy rule. [Gk. *ploutokratia* : *ploutos,* wealth + *kratos,* strength.]

plu·to·crat (plo͞o'tə-krăt') *n.* **1.** A member of a governing wealthy class. **2.** Someone having political influence or control because of wealth. [< PLUTOCRACY.] **—plu'to·crat'ic** *adj.* **—plu'to·crat'i·cal·ly** *adv.*

plu·ton (plo͞o'tŏn') *n.* Igneous rock formed beneath the surface of the earth by consolidation of magma. [Prob. back-formation < PLUTONIC.]

Plu·to·ni·an (plo͞o-tō'nē-ən) also **Plu·ton·ic** (-tŏn'ĭk) *adj.* **1.** Of or pertaining to Pluto or the underworld. **2.** Of or pertaining to the planet Pluto.

plu·ton·ic (plo͞o-tŏn'ĭk) *adj.* Of deep igneous or magmatic origin: *plutonic water.* [< PLUTO.]

plu·to·ni·um (plo͞o-tō'nē-əm) *n. Symbol* **Pu** A naturally radioactive, silvery, metallic transuranic element, occurring in uranium ores and produced artificially by neutron bombardment of uranium, having 15 isotopes with masses ranging from 232 to 246 and half-lives from 20 minutes to 76 million years. It is a radiological poison, specifically absorbed by bone marrow, and is used, esp. the highly fissionable isotope Pu239, as a reactor fuel and in nuclear weapons. Atomic number 94; melting point 639.5°C; boiling point 3,235°C; specific gravity 19.8; valence 3, 4, 5, 6. [Lat. *Pluto, Pluton-,* Pluto + -IUM.]

plu·vi·al (plo͞o'vē-əl) also **plu·vi·an** (-ən) *adj.* **1.** Of or pertaining to rain; rainy. **2.** *Geol.* Caused by rain. [Lat. *pluvialis* < *pluvia,* rain < *pluvius,* rainy < *pluvere,* to rain.]

plu·vi·om·e·ter (plo͞o'vē-ŏm'ĭ-tər) *n.* A rain gauge. [Fr. *pluviomètre* : Lat. *pluvia,* rain < *pluvius,* rainy < *pluvere,* to rain + Gk. *metron,* measure.] **—plu'vi·o·met'ric** (-ə-mĕt'rĭk), **plu'vi·o·met'ri·cal** *adj.* **—plu'vi·o·met'ri·cal·ly** *adv.* **—plu'vi·om'e·try** *n.*

plu·vi·ous (plo͞o'vē-əs) also **plu·vi·ose** (-ōs') *adj.* Characterized by heavy rainfall; rainy. [ME *pluvyous* < Lat. *pluviosus* < *pluvia,* rain. —see PLUVIAL.] **—plu'vi·os'i·ty** (-ŏs'ĭ-tē) *n.*

ply[1] (plī) *tr.v.* **plied, ply·ing, plies. 1.** To join together, as by molding or twisting. **2.** To double over (cloth, for example). *—n., pl.* **plies. 1.** A layer, as of doubled-over cloth or of paperboard. **2.** One of the sheets of wood glued together to form plywood. **3.** One of the strands twisted together to make yarn, rope, or thread. **4.** A bias; inclination. [ME *plien* < OFr. *plier* < Lat. *plicare,* to fold.]

ply[2] (plī) *v.* **plied, ply·ing, plies.** *—tr.* **1.** To use diligently as a tool or weapon; wield: *He plies an ax with the assurance of a lumberjack.* **2.** To engage in (a trade, for example); practice diligently. **3.** To traverse or sail over regularly: *Trading ships plied the routes between coastal ports.* **4.** To continue supplying or offering to: *plying her guests with food.* **5.** To assail vigorously. *—intr.* **1.** To traverse a route or course regularly: *The boat plies between the islands on a weekly schedule.* **2.** To perform or work diligently or regularly: *He plied at the weaver's trade.* **3.** *Naut.* To work against the wind by a zigzag course; tack. [ME *plien* < *applien,* to apply. —see APPLY.]

Plym·outh Rock (plĭm'əth) *n.* An American breed of fowl raised for both meat and eggs. [After *Plymouth Rock,* legendary landing place of the Pilgrims in 1620.]

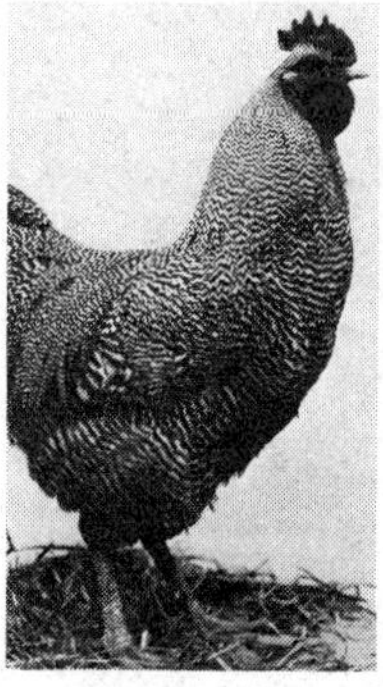

Plymouth Rock

ply·wood (plī'wo͝od') *n.* A structural material made of layers of wood glued tightly together, usually with the grains of adjoining layers at right angles to each other. [PLY[1] + WOOD.]

Pm The symbol for the element promethium.

pneum– *pref.* Variant of **pneumo-.**

pneu·ma (no͞o'mə, nyo͞o'-) *n.* The soul or vital spirit. [Gk.]

pneumat– *pref.* Variant of **pneumato-.**

pneu·mat·ic (no͞o-măt'ĭk, nyo͞o-) also **pneu·mat·i·cal** (-ĭ-kəl) *adj.* **1.** Of or pertaining to air or other gases. **2.** Of or pertaining to pneumatics. **3.** Run by or using compressed air: *a pneumatic drill.* **4.** Filled with air, esp. compressed air: *a pneumatic tire.* **5.** *Zool.* Having air cavities, as the bones of certain birds. **6.** Having or pertaining to a shapely, ample bust. **7.** Of or pertaining to the pneuma; spiritual. [Fr. *pneumatique* < Lat. *pneumaticus* < Gk. *pneumatikos* < *pneuma,* wind.] **—pneu·mat'i·cal·ly** *adv.* **—pneu'ma·tic'i·ty** (no͞o'mə-tĭs'ĭ-tē, nyo͞o'-) *n.*

pneu·mat·ics (no͞o-măt'ĭks, nyo͞o-) *n. (used with a sing. verb).* The study of the mechanical properties of air and other gases.

pneumato– or **pneumat–** *pref.* **1.** Air; gas: *pneumatolysis.* **2.** Breath; respiration: *pneumatometer.* [< Gk. *pneuma, pneumat-,* wind, breath.]

pneu·mat·o·graph (no͞o-măt'ə-grăf', nyo͞o-) *n.* Variant of **pneumograph.**

pneu·ma·tol·o·gy (no͞o'mə-tŏl'ə-jē, nyo͞o'-) *n.* **1.** The doctrine or study of spiritual beings and phenomena, esp. the belief in spirits intervening between man and God. **2.** The Christian doctrine of the Holy Ghost. **—pneu'ma·to·log'ic** (-tə-lŏj'ĭk), **pneu'ma·to·log'i·cal** *adj.* **—pneu'ma·tol'o·gist** *n.*

pneu·ma·tol·y·sis (no͞o'mə-tŏl'ĭ-sĭs, nyo͞o'-) *n.* A process of rock alteration or mineral formation brought about by the action of gases emitted from solidifying magma. **—pneu'ma·to·lyt'ic** (-tə-lĭt'ĭk) *adj.*

pneu·ma·tom·e·ter (no͞o'mə-tŏm'ĭ-tər, nyo͞o'-) *n.* A device for measuring the pressure of inspiration or expiration in the lungs. **—pneu'ma·tom'e·try** *n.*

pneu·mat·o·phore (no͞o-măt'ə-fôr', -fōr', nyo͞o-) *n.* **1.** *Zool.* A gas-filled sac serving as a float in some colonial organisms, such as the Portuguese man-of-war. **2.** *Bot.* A specialized respiratory root structure in certain aquatic plants. **—pneu·mat'o·phor'ic** *adj.*

pneu·mec·to·my (no͞o-mĕk'tə-mē, nyo͞o-) *n., pl.* **-mies.** The surgical excision of a lung or part of a lung.

pneumo– or **pneum–** *pref.* **1.** Air; gas: *pneumothorax.* **2.** Lung; pulmonary: *pneumoconiosis.* **3.** Respiration: *pneu-*

pocketknife

mograph. **4.** Pneumonia: *pneumococcus.* [< Gk. *pneuma,* wind, breath.]

pneu·mo·ba·cil·lus (no͞o′mō-bə-sĭl′əs, nyo͞o′-) *n., pl.* **-cil·li** (-sĭl′ī′). A bacterium, *Klebsiella pneumoniae,* associated with respiratory infections, esp. pneumonia.

pneu·mo·coc·cus (no͞o′mə-kŏk′əs, nyo͞o′-) *n., pl.* **-coc·ci** (-kŏk′sī′, -kŏk′ī′). A bacterium, *Diplococcus pneumoniae,* that causes pneumonia. **—pneu′mo·coc′cal** (-kŏk′əl) *adj.*

pneu·mo·co·ni·o·sis (no͞o′mō-kō′nē-ō′sĭs, nyo͞o′-) *n.* A lung disease caused by long-continued inhalation of mineral or metallic dusts. [PNEUMO- + Gk. *konis,* dust + -OSIS.]

pneu·mo·gas·tric (no͞o′mō-găs′trĭk, nyo͞o′-) *adj.* **1.** Of or involving the lungs and the stomach. **2.** Relating to the vagus nerve.

pneumogastric nerve *n. Anat.* The vagus.

pneu·mo·graph (no͞o′mə-grăf′, nyo͞o′-) also **pneu·mat·o·graph** (no͞o-măt′ə-grăf′, nyo͞o-) *n.* A device for recording chest movements during respiration. **—pneu′mo·graph′ic** *adj.*

pneu·mo·nec·to·my (no͞o′mə-nĕk′tə-mē, nyo͞o′-) *n., pl.* **-mies.** Surgical removal of lung tissue. [Gk. *pneumōn,* lung + -ECTOMY.]

pneu·mo·nia (no͞o-mōn′yə, nyo͞o-) *n.* An acute or chronic disease marked by inflammation of the lungs, and caused by viruses, bacteria, and physical and chemical agents. [NLat. < Gk., alteration of *pleumonia* < *pleumōn,* lung.]

pneu·mon·ic (no͞o-mŏn′ĭk, nyo͞o-) *adj.* **1.** Pertaining to, affected by, or similar to pneumonia. **2.** Of, affecting, or pertaining to the lungs; pulmonary. [NLat. *pneumonicus* < Gk. *pneumonikos,* of the lungs < *pneumōn,* lung.]

pneu·mo·tho·rax (no͞o′mō-thôr′ăks′, -thōr′-, nyo͞o′-) *n.* Accumulation of air or gas in the pleural cavity, occurring as a result of disease or injury, or sometimes induced to collapse the lung in the treatment of tuberculosis and other lung diseases.

Po The symbol for the element polonium.

poach[1] (pōch) *tr.v.* **poached, poach·ing, poach·es.** To cook in a boiling or simmering liquid: *fish poached in wine.* [ME *pochen* < OFr. *pochier,* to put in a bag < *poche,* bag, of Germanic orig.]

poach[2] (pōch) *v.* **poached, poach·ing, poach·es.** *—intr.* **1.** To trespass on another's property in order to take fish or game. **2.** To take fish or game in a forbidden area. **3.** To become muddy or broken up from being trampled. Used of land. **4.** To sink into soft earth when walking. *—tr.* **1.** To trespass on (another's property) for fishing or hunting. **2.** To take (fish or game) illegally. **3.** To make (land) muddy or broken up by trampling. [OFr. *pocher,* to trample, of Germanic orig.]

poach·er[1] (pō′chər) *n.* A vessel or dish designed for the poaching of food, as eggs or fish.

poach·er[2] (pō′chər) *n.* **1.** One who hunts or fishes illegally on the property of another. **2.** Any of various marine fishes of the family Agonidae, chiefly of northern Pacific waters, having an external covering of bony plates.

po·chard (pō′chərd) *n.* Any of various ducks of the genera *Aythya* and *Netta,* esp. *A. ferina,* of Europe, having gray and black plumage and a reddish head. [Orig. unknown.]

pock (pŏk) *n.* **1.** A pustule caused by smallpox or a similar eruptive disease. **2.** A mark or scar left in the skin by such a pustule; pockmark. *—tr.v.* **pocked, pock·ing, pocks.** To mark with pocks; pit. [ME *pokke* < OE *pocc.*]

pock·et (pŏk′ĭt) *n.* **1. a.** A small, flat pouch sewed into a garment and used to carry small articles. **b.** A piece of material sewed onto the outside of a garment with the top edge open. **2.** A small sack or bag. **3.** A receptacle, cavity, or opening. **4.** Supply of money; financial means. **5. a.** A small cavity in the earth containing ore. **b.** A small body or accumulation of ore. **6.** One of the pouchlike receptacles at the corners and sides of a billiard or pool table. **7.** A racing position in which a contestant has no room to pass a group of contestants immediately to his front or side. **8.** A small, isolated, or protected area or group. **9.** An air pocket. **10.** A bin for storing ore, grain, or other materials. *—adj.* **1.** Suitable for or capable of being carried in one's pocket: *pocket money; a pocket edition.* **2.** Tiny; miniature. *—tr.v.* **-et·ed, -et·ing, -ets. 1.** To place in or as if in one's pocket. **2.** To take possession of for oneself, esp. dishonestly. **3.** To accept or tolerate (an insult, for example). **4.** To suppress or conceal: *He pocketed his pride.* **5.** To prevent (a bill) from becoming law by delaying its signing until the adjournment of the legislature. **6.** To hem in (a competitor) in a race. **7.** To hit (a ball) into a pocket of a pool or billiard table. *—idioms.* **in one's pocket.** In one's power or possession. **in pocket. 1.** Having funds. **2.** Having made a profit. **out of pocket. 1.** Low on funds. **2.** Having experienced a loss. [ME *poket* < ONFr. *pokete,* dim. of *poke,* bag, of Germanic orig.] **—pock′et·a·ble** *adj.* **—pock′et·er** *n.*

pocket billiards *pl.n.* Pool[2] (sense 6).

pock·et·book (pŏk′ĭt-bo͝ok′) *n.* **1.** A pocket-sized folder or case used to hold money and papers; billfold. **2.** A bag used by women to carry money, papers, and other small articles; purse. **3.** Supply of money; financial resources. **4.** A pocket-sized, usually paperbound book.

pocket borough *n.* A borough in England, prior to the Parliamentary reform of 1832, whose representation was controlled by a single person or family.

pocket bread *n.* Pita[1].

pocket calculator *n.* A small calculator designed to be carried in a pocket.

pocket edition *n.* Pocketbook (sense 4).

pock·et·ful (pŏk′ĭt-fo͝ol′) *n., pl.* **pock·et·fuls** or **pock·ets·ful.** The amount that a pocket will hold.

pocket gopher *n.* Gopher (sense 1).

pock·et·knife (pŏk′ĭt-nīf′) *n.* A small knife with a blade or blades folding into the handle.

pocket money *n.* Money for incidental or minor expenses.

pocket mouse *n.* Any of various small, North American burrowing rodents of the genus *Perognathus,* having fur-lined external cheek pouches.

pock·et-sized (pŏk′ĭt-sīzd′) or **pock·et·size** (-sīz′) *adj.* **1.** Small. **2.** Of a size suitable to be carried in a pocket: *a pocket-sized radio.*

pocket veto *n.* **1.** The President's indirect veto of a bill presented to him within ten days of Congressional adjournment, by his retaining the bill unsigned until Congress adjourns. **2.** An action similar to the pocket veto exercised by a state governor or other chief executive. **—pocket veto** *v.* **(-toed, -to·ing, -toes).**

pock·mark (pŏk′märk′) *n.* A pitlike scar left on the skin by smallpox or another eruptive disease. *—tr.v.* To cover with pockmarks; pit. **—pock′marked′** *adj.*

pock·y (pŏk′ē) *adj.* **-i·er, -i·est. 1.** Pertaining to, resembling, or having pocks. **2.** Pertaining to, having, or resembling syphilis.

po·co (pō′kō) *adv. Mus.* Somewhat; a little. Used as a direction. [Ital. < Lat. *paucus.*]

po·co a po·co (pō′kō ä pō′kō) *adv. Mus.* Gradually; little by little. Used as a direction. [Ital.]

po·co·cu·ran·te (pō′kō-ko͞o-răn′tē, -rän′tē) *adj.* Indifferent; apathetic. *—n.* One who does not care. [Ital. : *poco,* little (< Lat. *paucus*) + *curante,* pr.part. of *curare,* to care for (< Lat. < *cura,* care).] **—po′co·cu·ran′tism** *n.*

po·co·sin (pə-kō′sĭn) *n. Chiefly Southeastern U.S.* A swamp in an upland coastal region. [Delaware *pâkwesen.*]

pod[1] (pŏd) *n.* **1.** *Bot.* **a.** A dehiscent seed vessel or fruit of a leguminous plant such as the pea. **b.** A fruit that contains several seeds, and that usually dries and splits open. **2.** A podlike protective covering. **3.** A streamlined housing that encloses aircraft engines, machine guns, or fuel, carried externally. **4.** *Aeronautics.* A compartment for personnel or instrumentation that may be detached from the spacecraft carrying it. *—v.* **pod·ded, pod·ding, pods.** *—intr.* **1.** To bear or produce pods. **2.** To expand or swell like a pod. *—tr.* To remove (seeds) from a pod. [Prob. alteration of obs. *cod* < ME < OE *codd.*]

pod[2] (pŏd) *n.* A school of seals or whales. [Orig. unknown.]

pod[3] (pŏd) *n.* **1.** The lengthwise groove in certain boring tools, such as augers. **2.** The socket for holding the bit in a boring tool. [Orig. unknown.]

-pod or **-pode** *suff.* Foot; footlike part: *pleopod.* [NLat. *-podius, -poda* < Gk. *pous,* foot.]

po·dag·ra (pə-dăg′rə) *n. Pathol.* Gout, esp. of the great toe. [ME < Lat. < Gk. : *pous,* foot + *agra,* trap, seizure.] **—po·dag′ral, po·dag′ric** *adj.*

-pode *suff.* Variant of **-pod.**

po·des·ta (pō-dĕs′tə, pō′dĕ-stä′) *n.* The chief magistrate in any of the republics of medieval Italy. [Ital. *podestà* < OItal. *podestate* < Lat. *potestas,* power.]

po·di·a (pō′dē-ə) *n.* A plural of **podium.**

po·di·a·try (pə-dī′ə-trē) *n.* The study and treatment of foot ailments. **—po′di·at′ric** (pō′dē-ăt′rĭk) *adj.* **—po·di′a·trist** *n.*

pod·ite (pŏd′īt′) *n.* A limb segment of an arthropod appendage. [Gk. *pous, pod-,* foot + -ITE[1].] **—po·dit′ic** (pə-dĭt′ĭk) *adj.*

po·di·um (pō′dē-əm) *n., pl.* **-di·a** (-dē-ə) or **-di·ums. 1.** An elevated platform, as for an orchestra conductor or lecturer. **2.** *Archit.* A low wall serving as foundation. **3.** A wall circling the arena of an ancient amphitheater. **4.** *Biol.* A structure resembling or functioning as a foot. [Lat. < Gk. *podion,* base, dim. of *pous,* foot.]

pod·o·phyl·lin (pŏd′ə-fĭl′ĭn) *n.* A bitter-tasting resin obtained from the dried root of the May apple, and used as a cathartic. [< NLat. *Podophyllum,* genus name : Gk. *pous,* foot + Gk. *phullon,* leaf.]

-podous *suff.* Having a specified kind or number of feet or footlike parts: *gastropodous.* [-POD + -OUS.]

Po·dunk (pō′dŭngk′) *n. Slang.* A small, isolated, and unimportant town. [After *Podunk,* name of two New England towns.]

pod·zol (pŏd′zôl′) *n.* A leached soil formed mainly in cool, humid climates. [R. : *pod,* ground + *zola,* ashes.] **—pod·zol′ic** (pŏd-zŏl′ĭk, -zô′lĭk) *adj.*

pod·zol·i·za·tion (pŏd′zô-lĭ-zā′shən) *n.* **1.** The process by which soils are depleted of bases and become acidic. **2.** The development of a podzol.

po·em (pō′əm, -ĭm) *n.* **1.** A composition designed to convey a vivid and imaginative sense of experience, characterized by the use of condensed language chosen for its sound and suggestive power as well as its meaning, and by the use of such literary techniques as structured meter, natural cadences, rhyme, or metaphor. **2.** A composition in verse rather than in prose. **3.** A literary composition written with an intensity or beauty of language more characteristic of poetry than of prose: *a prose poem.* **4.** A creation, object, or experience thought to embody the lyrical beauty or structural perfection characteristic of poetry. [OFr. *poeme* < Lat. *poema* < Gk. *poiēma* < *poiein,* to create.]

poe·nol·o·gy (pē-nŏl′ə-jē) *n.* Variant of **penology.**

po·e·sy (pō′ĭ-zē, -sē) *n., pl.* **-sies. 1.** Poetry. **2.** The art or practice of composing poems. **3.** The inspiration involved in composing poetry. [ME *poesie* < OFr. < Lat. *poesis* < Gk. *poiēsis* < *poiein,* to create.]

po·et (pō′ĭt) *n.* **1.** A writer of poems. **2.** One who is esp. gifted in the perception and expression of the beautiful or lyrical. [ME < OFr. *poete* < Lat. *poeta* < Gk. *poiētēs* < *poiein,* to create.]

Synonyms: *poet, bard, versifier, rhymer, rhymester, poetaster.* These nouns denote persons who write in verse. *Poet* is the most inclusive, but usually identifies one who composes verse of considerable merit; sometimes the term is applied to anyone gifted in artistic expression. *Bard,* in its original meaning, denoted a Celtic poet who composed and sang verses dealing with legendary events. Now the term can apply to any poet, but especially to a lyric poet. *Versifier, rhymer,* and *rhymester,* all lesser terms than *poet,* now refer principally to minor writers of verse. *Poetaster,* the lowest of these terms, applies to a verse writer of little or no merit.

po·et·as·ter (pō′ĭt-ăs′tər) *n.* An inferior poet. [NLat. : Lat. *poeta,* poet + Lat. *-aster,* partially resembling.]

po·et·ess (pō′ĭ-tĭs) *n.* A woman who writes poems.

po·et·ic (pō-ĕt′ĭk) *adj.* **1.** Of or pertaining to poetry: *poetic works.* **2.** Having a quality or style characteristic of poetry: *poetic diction.* **3.** Suitable as a subject for poetry: *a poetic love affair.* **4.** Of, pertaining to, or befitting a poet: *poetic insight.* **5.** Characterized by romantic imagery: *"Turner's vision of the rainbow . . . was poetic"* (Lawrence Gowing). [OFr. *poetique* < Lat. *poeticus* < Gk. *poiētikos,* inventive < *poiein,* to make.]

po·et·i·cal (pō-ĕt′ĭ-kəl) *adj.* **1.** Poetic. **2.** Fancifully depicted or embellished; idealized. **—po·et′i·cal·ly** *adv.* **—po·et′i·cal·ness** *n.*

po·et·i·cism (pō-ĕt′ĭ-sĭz′əm) *n.* A poetic term or expression that has become no longer vivid or evocative.

poetic justice *n.* An outcome whereby a person receives his just deserts in a manner peculiarly or ironically appropriate.

poetic license *n.* The liberty taken, esp. by an artist or writer, in deviating from conventional form or fact to achieve a desired effect.

po·et·ics (pō-ĕt′ĭks) *n. (used with a sing. verb).* **1.** Literary criticism that deals with the nature, forms, and laws of poetry. **2.** A treatise on or study of poetry or aesthetics. **3.** Poetic utterances or feelings.

po·et·ize (pō′ĭ-tīz′) *v.* **-ized, -iz·ing, -iz·es.** *—intr.* To write or express oneself in poetry. *—tr.* To give poetic expression to. **—po′et·iz′er** *n.*

poet laureate *n., pl.* **poets laureate** or **poet laureates. 1.** A poet appointed by the British sovereign to a lifetime position as chief poet of the kingdom. **2.** A poet acclaimed as the most excellent or most representative of a locality or group. **3.** A poet honored for excellence.

po·et·ry (pō′ĭ-trē) *n.* **1.** The art or work of a poet. **2. a.** Poems regarded as forming a division of literature. **b.** The poetic works of a given author, group, nation, or kind. **3.** A piece of literature written in meter; verse. **4.** Prose that resembles a poem in some respect, as form or sound. **5.** The essence of or characteristic quality possessed by a poem. **6.** The quality of a poem, as possessed by an object, act, or experience: *the poetry of her dance movements.* [ME *poetrie* < OFr. < Med. Lat. *poetria* < Lat. *poeta,* poet. —see POET.]

po·go·ni·a (pə-gō′nē-ə, -gōn′yə) *n.* Any of various small terrestrial orchids of the genus *Pogonia,* of the North Temperate Zone, having pink or whitish flowers. [NLat. *Pogonia,* genus name < Gk. *pogōn,* beard.]

pog·o·nip (pŏg′ə-nĭp′) *n.* A dense fog of suspended ice particles, occurring esp. in mountain valleys of the western United States. [Paiute.]

po·go stick (pō′gō) *n.* A strong stick with footrests and a heavy spring set into the bottom end, propelled along the ground by hopping. [< *Pogo,* a former trademark.]

po·grom (pə-grŏm′, pō′grəm) *n.* An organized and often officially encouraged massacre or persecution of a minority group, esp. one conducted against the Jews. *—tr.v.* To massacre in a pogrom. [R. : *po-,* like < *po,* next to + *grom,* thunder.]

po·gy (pō′gē) *n., pl.* **pogy** or **-gies.** The menhaden. [Of Algonquian orig.]

poi (poi) *n.* A Hawaiian food made from taro root cooked, pounded to a paste, and fermented. [Hawaiian.]

-poiesis *suff.* Production; creation; formation: *hematopoiesis.* [< Gk. *poiēsis,* creation < *poiein,* to make.]

-poietic *suff.* Productive; formative: *galactopoietic.* [< Gk. *poiētikos,* creative < *poiētēs,* maker < *poiein,* to make.]

poign·ant (poin′yənt) *adj.* **1. a.** Physically painful. **b.** Keenly distressing to the mind: *poignant anxiety.* **c.** Appealing to the emotions; touching: *poignant sentiment.* **2.** Piercing; incisive: *poignant criticism.* **3. a.** Neat, skillful, and to the point: *poignant illustrations supplementing the text.* **b.** Astute and pertinent; relevant: *poignant suggestions.* **4.** Agreeably intense or stimulating: *poignant delight.* **5. a.** *Archaic.* Sharp or sour to the taste; piquant. **b.** Sharp or pungent to the smell: *a poignant perfume.* [ME *poinaunt* < OFr. *poignant,* pr.part. of *poindre,* to sting < Lat. *pungere.*] **—poign′ance, poign′an·cy** *n.* **—poign′ant·ly** *adv.*

poi·kil·o·therm (poi-kĭl′ə-thûrm′) *n.* A poikilothermous organism, such as a fish or reptile. [Gk. *poikilos,* variegated + -THERM.]

poi·kil·o·ther·mous (poi′kĭl-ə-thûr′məs) also **poi·kil·o·ther·mal** (-məl) *adj.* Having a body temperature that varies with the external environment; cold-blooded. **—poi′kil·o·ther′mism** *n.*

poi·lu (pwä-lü′) *n. Slang.* A French front-line soldier in World War I. [Fr. < *poilu,* hairy < OFr. < *poil,* hair < Lat. *pilus,* hair.]

poin·ci·an·a (poin′sē-ăn′ə, -ä′nə) *n.* **1.** Any of various tropical trees of the genus *Poinciana,* having large orange or red flowers. **2.** The royal poinciana. [NLat. *Poinciana,* genus name, after M. de *Poinci,* 17th-cent. governor of French Antilles.]

poin·set·ti·a (poin-sĕt′ē-ə, -sĕt′ə) *n.* A tropical American shrub, *Euphorbia pulcherrima,* having showy, usually scarlet bracts beneath the small yellow flowers. [NLat., after Joel R. *Poinsett* (1799–1851), its discoverer.]

point (point) *n.* **1.** The sharp or tapered end of something. **2.** Something that has a sharp or tapered end, as a knife or needle. **3.** A tapering extension of land projecting into water; cape. **4.** A mark formed by or as if by the sharp end of something. **5.** A mark or dot used in printing or writing. **6.** A mark used in punctuation, esp. a period. **7.** A decimal point. **8.** The vowel point. **9.** One of the protruding marks used in certain methods of writing and printing for the blind. **10.** *Math.* A dimensionless geometric object having no property but location. **11.** A position, place, or locality; spot: *a good point to begin; connections to Chicago and points west.* **12.** A specified degree, condition, or limit, as in a scale or course. **13. a.** Any of the 32 equal divisions marked at the circumference of a mariner's compass card that indicate direction. **b.** The distance or interval of 11 degrees, 15 minutes between any two adjacent markings. **14.** A distinct condition or degree: *the point of no return.* **15.** A specific moment in time: *At this point, we are ready to proceed.* **16.** A crucial situation in a course of events. **17.** An important, essential, or primary factor. **18.** A purpose, goal, advantage, or reason: *What's the point of discussing it?* **19.** The major idea or essential part of a concept or narrative. **20.** A significant, outstanding, or effective idea, argument, or suggestion. **21.** A separate or individual item or element; detail. **22.** A quality or characteristic that is important or distinctive, esp. a standard characteristic used to judge an animal. **23.** A single unit, as in counting, rating, or measuring. **24. a.** A unit of academic credit usually equal to one hour of class work per week during one semester. **b.** A numerical unit equal to a letter grade in grading academic achievement. **25.** A unit of scoring or counting in a game or sport. **26.** The stiff and attentive stance taken by a hunting dog. **27.** *Elect.* **a.** An electrical contact, esp. one in the distributor of an automobile engine. **b.** *Chiefly Brit.* A socket or outlet. **28. a.** A unit equal to one dollar and used to quote or state the current prices of stocks or commodities. **b.** A unit equal to one percentage point, used in reference to ownership. **29.** *Mus.* A phrase, such as a fugue subject, in contrapuntal music. **30.** *Printing.* A unit of type size equal to 0.01384 inch, or approximately $1/_{72}$ of an inch. **31.** A jeweler's unit of mass equal to 2 milligrams or 0.01 carat. **32. a.** Needlepoint. **b.** Bobbin lace. **33. a.** A movable rail, tapered at the end, such as that used in a railroad switch. **b.** The vertex or tip of the angle created by the intersection of rails in a frog or switch. **34.** A ribbon or cord with a metal tag at the end, used to fasten clothing in the 16th and 17th centuries. *—v.* **point·ed, point·ing, points.** *—tr.* **1.** To direct or aim: *point a weapon.* **2.** To bring to notice: *pointed out the error in his reasoning.* **3.** To indicate the position or direction of. **4.** To sharpen (a pencil, for example); provide with a point. **5.** To separate with a decimal point. **6.** To mark with a point or period; punctuate. **7.** To mark (a consonant) with a vowel point. **8.** To give emphasis to (a remark, for example); stress. **9.** To indicate the presence and position of (game) by standing immobile and directing the muzzle toward it. **10.** To fill and finish the joints of (brickwork) with cement or mortar. *—intr.* **1.** To direct attention or indicate position with or as if with the finger. **2.** To turn the mind or thought in a particular direction. **3.** To be turned or faced in a given direction; aim. **4.** To show the location of animals hunted as game by standing still and facing in that direction, as a hunting dog does. **5.** *Naut.* To sail close to the wind. **—*idioms.* beside the point.** Irrelevant to the matter at hand. **in point of.** With reference to; in the matter of. **stretch (or strain) a point. 1.** To make an exception. **2.** To exaggerate. **to the point.** Relevant to the matter at hand. [ME < OFr. < VLat. *puncta < Lat. *punctus* < *pungere,* to prick.]

point·blank (point′blăngk′) *adj.* **1.** Aimed straight at the

pogo stick

poinsettia

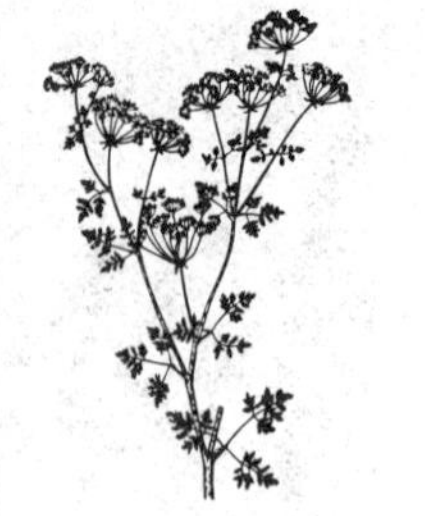

poison hemlock

poison ivy

poison oak

poker[1]

polar bear

mark or target, esp. aimed straight without allowing for the drop in a projectile's course. **2. a.** So close to a target that a weapon may be aimed directly at it: *pointblank range.* **b.** Close enough so that missing the target is unlikely or impossible: *a pointblank shot.* **3.** Straightforward; blunt: *a pointblank accusation.* —*adv.* **1.** With a straight aim; directly: *fired pointblank.* **2.** Without hesitation, deliberation, or equivocation: *answer pointblank.* [Orig. unknown.]

point defect *n.* A departure from symmetry in the alignment of atoms in a crystal that affects only one or two lattice sites.

point-de·vice (point′dĭ-vīs′) *adj. Archaic.* Scrupulously correct or neat; precise. [ME *at point devis,* prob. < OFr. **a point devis,* to the arranged point.] —**point′-de·vice′** *adv.*

point·ed (poin′tĭd) *adj.* **1.** Having an end coming to a point. **2.** Sharp; cutting: *a pointed question.* **3.** Obviously directed at or making reference to a particular person or thing: *a pointed comment.* **4.** Clearly evident or conspicuous; marked: *a pointed lack of interest.* **5.** Characterized by the use of a pointed crown, as in Gothic architecture: *a pointed arch.* —**point′ed·ly** *adv.* —**point′ed·ness** *n.*

point·er (poin′tər) *n.* **1.** One that sharpens, directs, indicates, or points. **2.** A scale indicator on a watch, balance, or other measuring instrument. **3.** A long, tapered stick for indicating objects, as on a chart or blackboard. **4.** One of a breed of hunting dogs having a short-haired coat that is usually white with black or brownish spots. **5.** A suggestion; piece of advice. **6.** *Computer Sci.* A computer word that directs the user to the address of a core storage location.

point estimate *n.* The single value assigned to a parameter in point estimation.

point estimation *n.* A method of making a mathematical estimate by assigning a single value to a parameter.

poin·til·lism (pwăn′tē-ĭz′əm, point′l-ĭz′əm) *n.* A postimpressionist school of painting exemplified by Seurat and his followers in late 19th-century France and characterized by the application of paint in small dots and brush strokes so as to create an effect of blending and luminosity. [Fr. *pointillisme* < *pointiller,* to paint small dots < *pointille,* small dot < Ital. *puntiglio,* dim. of *punto,* point < Lat. *punctum* < *pungere,* to prick.] —**poin′til·list** *n.* —**poin′til·lis′tic** *adj.*

point lace *n.* Needlepoint.

point·less (point′lĭs) *adj.* **1.** Meaningless; irrelevant. **2.** Ineffectual. —**point′less·ly** *adv.* —**point′less·ness** *n.*

point man *n.* **1.** A soldier who is assigned some distance ahead of a patrol as a lookout. **2.** One who speaks for or represents another, esp. in confrontational matters with opponents.

point of accumulation *n.* A limit point.

point of honor *n.* A matter that affects one's honor or reputation.

point of no return *n.* **1.** The point in the flight of an aircraft beyond which the aircraft must proceed, there being insufficient fuel for return to the starting point. **2.** The point in a course of action beyond which reversal is not possible.

point of order *n.* A question as to whether that which is being discussed is in order or allowed by the rules.

point-of-sale (point′əv-sāl′) *adj.* Of, pertaining to, or being the physical place where an item or service is purchased.

point of view *n.* **1.** The position from which something is observed or considered; standpoint. **2.** One's manner of viewing things; attitude.

points (points) *pl.n.* A percentage of the face value of a mortgage or loan charged as a placement or service fee.

point system *n.* **1.** *Printing.* A system of measurement by the point. **2.** A system of printing or writing for the blind that uses an alphabet of raised symbols or dots that correspond to letters, such as Braille. **3.** A system of evaluating and averaging a student's academic achievement by using numerical units or points that are equivalent to letter grades.

point·y (poin′tē) *adj.* **-i·er, -i·est.** Having an end tapering to a point.

poise[1] (poiz) *v.* **poised, pois·ing, pois·es.** —*tr.* To carry or hold in equilibrium; balance. —*intr.* To be balanced or held in suspension; hover: *poised on the brink of disaster.* —*n.* **1.** The state or condition of being balanced or held in equilibrium; stability. **2.** Freedom from affectation or embarrassment; composure. **3.** The bearing or deportment of the head or body; mien. **4.** A state or condition of hovering or being suspended. [ME *poisen,* to weigh < OFr. *poiser* < VLat. **pesare* < Lat. *pensare.*]

poise[2] (poiz) *n.* A centimeter-gram-second unit of dynamic viscosity equal to one dyne-second per square centimeter. [Fr., after Jean Louis Marie *Poiseuille* (1799–1869).]

poi·son (poi′zən) *n.* **1.** A substance that causes injury, illness, or death, esp. by chemical means. **2.** Something that is destructive or fatal. **3.** *Chem.* A substance that inhibits or retards a chemical reaction. —*tr.v.* **-soned, -son·ing, -sons.** **1.** To kill or harm with poison. **2.** To put poison on or into: *poison a drink.* **3. a.** To pollute: *Noxious fumes poison the air.* **b.** To have a harmful influence on; corrupt: *Jealousy poisoned their friendship.* **4.** *Chem.* To inhibit or retard (a chemical reaction). —*adj.* Poisonous. [ME < OFr. < Lat. *potio,* drink < *potare,* to drink.] —**poi′son·er** *n.*

poison elder *n.* Poison sumac.

poison gas *n.* A lethal or crippling vapor used in warfare.

poison hemlock *n.* A poisonous plant, *Conium maculatum,* native to Eurasia but naturalized in North America, having compound leaves and umbels of small, white flowers.

poison ivy *n.* A North American shrub or vine, *Rhus radicans,* having leaflets in groups of three, small green flowers, and whitish berries, and causing a rash on contact.

poison oak *n.* **1.** Either of two shrubs, *Rhus toxicodendron* of the southeastern United States, or *R. diversiloba* of western North America, related to poison ivy and causing a rash on contact. **2.** Poison ivy.

poi·son·ous (poi′zə-nəs) *adj.* **1.** Capable of harming or killing by or as if by poison; toxic or venomous. **2.** Containing a poison. **3.** Marked by apparent ill will: *a poisonous glance.* —**poi′son·ous·ly** *adv.* —**poi′son·ous·ness** *n.*

poison sumac *n.* A swamp shrub, *Rhus vernix,* of the southeastern United States, having compound leaves and greenish-white berries, and causing an itching rash on contact with the skin.

Pois·son distribution (pwä-sôN′) *n.* A probability distribution used to describe the occurrence of unlikely events in a large number of independent repeated trials. [After Siméon Denis *Poisson* (1781–1840).]

poke[1] (pōk) *v.* **poked, pok·ing, pokes.** —*tr.* **1.** To push or jab at, as with a finger or arm; prod. **2.** To make (a hole or pathway, for example) by or as if by prodding, thrusting, or poking: *He poked his way to the front of the crowd.* **3.** To push; thrust: *A seal poked its head out of the water.* **4.** To stir (a fire) by prodding the wood or coal with a poker or stick. **5.** To strike; punch. —*intr.* **1.** To make thrusts or jabs, as with a stick or poker. **2.** To pry or meddle; intrude: *poking into another's business.* **3.** To search or look curiously in a desultory manner. **4.** To live or proceed in a slow or lazy manner; putter. **5.** To thrust forward; appear: *His head poked from under the blankets.* —*n.* **1.** A push, thrust, or jab. **2.** A punch or blow with the fist. **3.** A person who moves slowly or aimlessly; dawdler. —***idiom.* poke fun at.** To ridicule in a mischievous manner; tease. [ME *poken,* prob. < MLG.]

poke[2] (pōk) *n.* **1.** A large bonnet having a projecting brim at the front. **2.** The brim of a poke. [< POKE[1].]

poke[3] (pōk) *n. Chiefly Regional.* A sack or bag. [ME < ONFr. *poke,* of Germanic orig.]

poke[4] (pōk) *n.* Pokeweed. [Algonquian (Virginia) *pakon,* any plant used for dyeing < *pak,* blood.]

poke·ber·ry (pōk′bĕr′ē) *n., pl.* **-ries.** **1.** The blackish-red berry of the pokeweed. **2.** Pokeweed.

pok·er[1] (pō′kər) *n.* One that pokes, esp. a metal rod used to stir a fire.

pok·er[2] (pō′kər) *n.* Any of various card games played by two or more players who bet on the value of their hands. [Orig. unknown.]

poker face *n.* A face lacking any interpretable expression, as that of an expert poker player. —**pok′er-faced′** (pō′kər-fāst′) *adj.*

poke·root (pōk′ro͞ot′, -ro͝ot′) *n.* Pokeweed.

poke·weed (pōk′wēd′) *n.* A tall North American plant, *Phytolacca americana,* having small white flowers, blackish-red berries, and a poisonous root. [POKE[4] + WEED.]

po·key (pō′kē) *n., pl.* **-keys.** *Slang.* Jail; prison. [Orig. unknown.]

pok·y also **poke·y** (pō′kē) *adj.* **pok·i·er, pok·i·est.** *Informal.* **1.** Dawdling; slow. **2.** Frumpish; shabby: *always wearing those poky old clothes.* **3.** Small and cramped: *a poky apartment.* [< POKE[1].] —**pok′i·ly** *adv.* —**pok′i·ness** *n.*

pol (pôl) *n.* A politician.

Po·lack (pō′lŏk′, -lăk′) *n.* **1.** *Obs.* A native of Poland; Pole. **2.** *Offensive Slang.* A person of Polish descent or birth. [Pol. *Polak.*]

Poland China *n.* A large black-and-white pig of a breed developed in North America.

po·lar (pō′lər) *adj.* **1. a.** Of, pertaining to, or designating a pole. **b.** Measured from or referred to a pole: *polar distance; polar diameter.* **2.** Pertaining to, connected with, or located near the North Pole or South Pole. **3. a.** Passing over a planet's north and south poles. **b.** Traveling in a polar orbit. **4.** Occupying or characterized by opposite extremes. **5.** Serving as a guide, such as a polestar or a pole of the earth. **6.** Central or pivotal.

polar angle *n.* The angle formed by the polar axis and the radius vector in a polar coordinate system.

polar axis *n.* The fixed reference axis from which the polar angle is measured in a polar coordinate system.

polar bear *n.* A large, white-furred bear, *Thalarctos maritimus,* of Arctic regions.

polar body *n.* A minute cell produced and ultimately discarded in the development of an oocyte, containing little or no cytoplasm but having one of the nuclei derived from the first or second meiotic division.

polar cap *n.* **1. a.** A high-altitude icecap. **b.** The polar regions of ice. **2.** *Astron.* A differentiated polar region of a planet.

polar circle *n.* Either the Arctic Circle or Antarctic Circle.

polar coordinate *n.* Either of two coordinates, the radius vector or the polar angle, that together specify the position of a point in a plane.

po·lar·im·e·ter (pō′lə-rĭm′ĭ-tər) *n.* An instrument used to measure the rotation of the plane of polarization of polarized light, or the degree of polarization of light passing through an optical structure or sample. **—po′lar·i·met′ric** (-lər-ə-mĕt′rĭk) *adj.* **—po′lar·im′e·try** *n.*

Po·lar·is (pə-lăr′ĭs, -lär′ĭs) *n.* **1.** A star of the second magnitude, at the end of the handle of the Little Dipper and almost at the north celestial pole. **2.** A U.S. Navy intermediate range surface-to-surface ballistic missile. [NLat. (*Stella*) *Polaris,* polar (star).]

po·lar·i·scope (pō-lăr′ĭ-skōp′) *n.* An instrument for ascertaining, measuring, or exhibiting the properties of polarized light, or for studying the interactions of polarized light with optically transparent media.

po·lar·i·ty (pō-lăr′ĭ-tē) *n., pl.* **-ties. 1.** Intrinsic polar separation, alignment, or orientation, esp. of a physical property: *magnetic polarity; ionic polarity.* **2.** The possession or manifestation of two opposing attributes, tendencies, or principles: *political polarity.* **3.** An indicated polar extreme: *an electric terminal with positive polarity.*

po·lar·i·za·tion (pō′lər-ĭ-zā′shən) *n.* **1.** The production or condition of polarity, as: **a.** The uniform and nonrandom elliptical, circular, or linear variation of a wave characteristic, esp. of vibrational orientation, in light or other radiation. **b.** *Physics & Chem.* The partial or complete polar separation of positive and negative electric charge in a nuclear, atomic, molecular, or chemical system. **2.** A concentration, as of groups, forces, or interests, about two conflicting or contrasting positions.

po·lar·ize (pō′lə-rīz′) *v.* **-ized, -iz·ing, -iz·es.** *—tr.* **1.** To induce polarization in; impart polarity to. **2.** To cause to concentrate about two conflicting or contrasting positions. *—intr.* To acquire polarity. **—po′lar·iz′a·ble** *adj.* **—po′lar·iz′er** *n.*

polarizing microscope *n.* A microscope in which the object viewed is illuminated by polarized light.

polar nucleus *n.* Either of two nuclei located centrally in a seed plant embryo sac that eventually fuse to form the endosperm nucleus.

po·lar·og·ra·phy (pō′lə-rŏg′rə-fē) *n.* An electrochemical method of quantitative or qualitative analysis based on the relationship between an increasing current passing through the solution being analyzed and the increasing voltage used to produce the current. [POLAR(IZATION) + -GRAPHY.] **—po·lar′o·graph′ic** (-lăr′ə-grăf′ĭk) *adj.* **—po·lar′o·graph′i·cal·ly** *adv.*

Po·lar·oid (pō′lə-roid′). A trademark for a specially treated, transparent plastic capable of polarizing light passing through it, used in glare-reducing optical devices.

Polar Regions *n.* The land and water areas surrounding the North and South Poles.

polar star *n.* Polaris (sense 1).

pol·der (pōl′dər) *n.* An area of low-lying land, esp. in the Netherlands, that has been reclaimed from a body of water and is protected by dikes. [Du. < MDu.]

pole[1] (pōl) *n.* **1.** Either axial extremity of an axis through a sphere. **2.** Either of the regions contiguous to the extremities of the earth's rotational axis, the North Pole or the South Pole. **3.** *Physics.* A magnetic pole. **4.** *Elect.* Either of two oppositely charged terminals, as in an electric cell or battery. **5.** *Astron.* A celestial pole. **6.** *Biol.* A structurally or physiologically distinct region at either axial extremity of a nucleus, cell, or organism. **7.** Either of two antithetical ideas, propensities, forces, or positions. **8.** A fixed point of reference. **9.** *Math.* The origin in a polar coordinate system; the polar angle vertex. [ME < Lat. *polus* < Gk. *polos.*]

pole[2] (pōl) *n.* **1.** A long, relatively slender, and generally rounded piece of wood or other material. **2.** The long, tapering, wooden shaft extending up from the front axle of a vehicle to the collars of the animals drawing it; tongue. **3. a.** A rod (sense 12. a.). **b.** A unit of area equal to a square rod. **4.** *Naut.* A small or light spar. *—v.* **poled, pol·ing, poles.** *—tr.* **1.** To propel with a pole. **2.** To support (plants) with a pole. **3.** To strike, poke, or stir with a pole. *—intr.* **1.** To propel a boat or raft with a pole. **2.** To use ski poles to gain speed. [ME < OE *pāl* < Lat. *palus,* stake.]

Pole (pōl) *n.* A native or inhabitant of Poland.

pole·ax or **pole·axe** (pōl′ăks′) *—n.* **1.** A battle-ax used in the Middle Ages and consisting of an ax, or an ax, hammer, and pick combination, with a long shaft. **2.** An ax having a hammer face opposite the blade, used to slaughter cattle. *—tr.v.* **-axed, -ax·ing, -ax·es.** To strike or fell with or as if with a poleax. [ME *pollax* : *poll,* head (< MLG *polle*) + *ax,* ax < OE *æxa.*]

pole bean *n.* Any of various cultivated climbing beans trained to grow on poles or supports.

pole·cat (pōl′kăt′) *n.* **1.** A carnivorous mammal, *Mustela putorius,* of Eurasia and northern Africa, having dark-brown or black fur. **2.** The skunk (sense 1). [ME *polcat.*]

pole horse *n.* A horse harnessed to the pole, or tongue, of a vehicle.

po·leis (pō′lās′) *n.* Plural of **polis.**

pole jump *n. Sports.* A pole vault.

pole lamp *n.* A usually spring-loaded pole that extends from the ceiling to the floor, having attached lamp fixtures.

po·lem·ic (pə-lĕm′ĭk) *n.* **1.** A controversy or argument, esp. one that is a refutation of or an attack upon a specified opinion or doctrine. **2. polemics.** *(used with a sing. verb).* **a.** The art or practice of argumentation or controversy. **b.** The practice of theological controversy to refute errors of doctrine. **3.** A person engaged in or inclined to controversy, argument, or refutation. *—adj.* Also **po·lem·i·cal** (-ĭ-kəl). Of or pertaining to a controversy, argument, or refutation. [Med. Lat. *polemicus,* controversialist < Gk. *polemikos,* hostile < *polemos,* war.] **—po·lem′i·cal·ly** *adv.*

po·lem·i·cist (pə-lĕm′ĭ-sĭst) also **po·lem·ist** (pə-lĕm′ĭst, pŏl′ə-mĭst) *n.* A person skilled or involved in polemics.

pol·er (pō′lər) *n.* **1.** One that propels, supports, conveys, or strikes with a pole. **2.** A pole horse.

pole·star (pōl′stär′) *n.* **1.** Polaris (sense 1). **2.** A guiding principle.

pole vault *n. Sports.* **1.** A field event in which the contestant jumps or vaults over a high crossbar with the aid of a long pole. **2.** A vault made with the aid of a long pole.

pole-vault (pōl′vôlt′) *intr.v.* **-vault·ed, -vault·ing, -vaults.** *Sports.* To perform or complete a pole vault. **—pole′-vault′er** *n.*

po·lice (pə-lēs′) *n., pl.* **police. 1.** The regulation and control of the affairs of a community, esp. with respect to the maintenance of order, law, health, morals, safety, and other matters affecting general welfare. **2. a.** The governmental department charged with the regulation and control of the affairs of a community, now chiefly the department established to maintain order, enforce the law, and prevent and detect crime. **b.** The official civil force, or body of persons, established and maintained for this purpose; police force. **c.** *(used with a pl. verb).* The members of such a force; police officers. **3. a.** A group of persons resembling the police force of a community in organization or function: *campus police.* **b.** The members of such a group. **4.** The cleaning of a military base or other military area: *Police of the barracks must be completed.* **5.** The soldiers assigned to a specified maintenance duty: *kitchen police.* *—tr.v.* **-liced, -lic·ing, -lic·es. 1.** To regulate, control, or keep in order with or as if with police. **2.** To make (a military area) neat in appearance. [OFr., government < LLat. *politia* < Gk. *politeia* < *polis,* city.]

police action *n.* A localized military action undertaken without a formal declaration of war.

police court *n.* An inferior court having the power to prosecute minor criminal offenses and to hold for trial persons charged with more serious offenses.

police dog *n.* A dog trained to aid the police, esp. the German shepherd.

police force *n.* A body of persons trained in methods of law enforcement and crime prevention and detection, and given authority to maintain the peace, safety, and order of the community.

po·lice·man (pə-lēs′mən) *n.* A member of a police force.

police officer *n.* A policeman or a policewoman.

police power *n.* The inherent authority of a government to impose restrictions on private rights for the sake of public welfare, order, and security.

police reporter *n.* A newspaper reporter whose assignment is to obtain and cover news in a local police department.

police state *n.* A political unit in which the government exercises rigid and repressive controls over the social, economic, and political life, esp. by means of a secret police force.

police station *n.* The headquarters of a unit of a police force where those under arrest are first charged.

po·lice·wom·an (pə-lēs′wo͝om′ən) *n.* A female member of a police force.

pol·i·clin·ic (pŏl′ē-klĭn′ĭk) *n.* The department of a hospital that treats outpatients. [G. *Poliklinik* : Gk. *polis,* city + Gk. *klinikos,* of a bed < *klinein,* to lie down.]

pol·i·cy[1] (pŏl′ĭ-sē) *n., pl.* **-cies. 1.** A plan or course of action, as of a government, political party, or business, designed to influence and determine decisions, actions, and other matters: *American foreign policy; the company's personnel policy.* **2. a.** A course of action, guiding principle, or procedure considered to be expedient, prudent, or advantageous: *Honesty is the best policy.* **b.** Prudence, shrewdness, or sagacity in practical matters. [ME *policie* < OFr., government < Lat. *politia.* —see POLICE.]

pol·i·cy[2] (pŏl′ĭ-sē) *n., pl.* **-cies. 1.** A written contract or certificate of insurance. **2.** The numbers game. [OFr. *police,* certificate < OItal. *polizza* < Med. Lat. *apodixa,* receipt < Med. Gk. *apodeixis* < Gk., proof < *apodeiknunai,* to demonstrate. —see APODICTIC.]

pol·i·cy·hol·der (pŏl′ĭ-sē-hōl′dər) *n.* One that holds an insurance contract or policy.

pol·i·cy·mak·ing or **pol·i·cy-mak·ing** (pŏl′ĭ-sē-mā′kĭng) *n.* The top-level development of policy, esp. official government policy. **—pol′i·cy·mak′er** *n.*

po·li·o (pō′lē-ō′) *n.* Poliomyelitis.

po·li·o·my·e·li·tis (pō′lē-ō-mī′ə-lī′tĭs) *n.* An infectious viral disease occurring mainly in children and in its acute forms attacking the central nervous system and producing paralysis, muscular atrophy, and often deformity. [Gk. *polios,* gray + MYELITIS.] **—po′li·o·my′e·lit′ic** (-lĭt′ĭk) *adj.*

po·li·o·vi·rus (pō′lē-ō-vī′rəs) *n.* A virus that can be sepa-

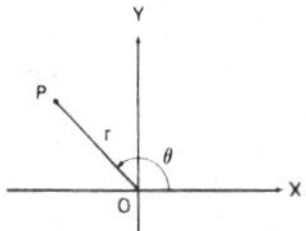

polar coordinate
r. Radius vector
θ. Polar angle
P. A point in the X-Y plane
O, Origin of pole

pole vault
A pole-vaulter

rated into three serotypes and is the causative agent of poliomyelitis.

po·lis (pō′lĭs) *n., pl.* **-leis** (-lās′). A city-state of ancient Greece. [Gk.]

pol·ish (pŏl′ĭsh) *v.* **-ished, -ish·ing, -ish·es.** —*tr.* **1.** To make smooth and shiny by rubbing or chemical action. **2.** To free from coarseness; refine. **3.** To remove flaws from; perfect or complete. —*intr.* **1.** To become smooth or shiny by or as if by rubbing. **2.** To become perfect or refined. —***phrasal verb.* polish off.** *Informal.* To finish or dispose of quickly and easily. —*n.* **1.** Smoothness or shininess of surface or finish. **2.** A substance containing chemical agents or abrasive particles and applied to smooth or shine a surface. **3.** The act or process of polishing. **4.** Elegance of style or manners; refinement. [ME *polisshen* < OFr. *polir, poliss-* < Lat. *polire.*] —**pol′ish·er** *n.*

Po·lish (pō′lĭsh) *adj.* Of or pertaining to Poland, its inhabitants, or their language or culture. —*n.* The Slavic language of the Poles.

pol·ished (pŏl′ĭsht) *adj.* **1. a.** Made shiny and smooth. **b.** Naturally shiny and smooth. **2.** Refined; cultured. **3.** Having no imperfections or errors; flawless.

pol·it·bu·ro (pŏl′ĭt-byŏŏr′ō, pə-lĭt′-) *n.* The chief political and executive committee of a Communist party. [R., contraction of *politisheskoe buro,* political bureau.]

po·lite (pə-līt′) *adj.* **-lit·er, -lit·est. 1.** Marked by consideration for others, correct manners, or tact. **2.** Refined; elegant: *polite society.* [ME *polyt,* polished < Lat. *polire,* to polish.] —**po·lite′ly** *adv.* —**po·lite′ness** *n.*

Synonyms: *polite, civil, courteous, genteel.* These all describe social behavior as being proper or commendatory. *Polite* means duly respectful or indulgent with other people according to social norms. *Civil,* suggesting only the barest agreeability or tact in manners, means friendly in a reserved, correct sense. *Courteous* is similar to *polite* but implies a more voluntary, generous consideration which is of a helpful nature. *Genteel* refers to the quality of good taste or propriety in a cultured person. It can suggest fine sensibilities and respectability but now usually suggests overrefinement to the point of artificiality.

polo

pol·i·tesse (pŏl′ĭ-tĕs′, pô′lĭ-) *n.* Courteous formality; politeness. [Fr. < OFr., cleanliness < OItal. *politezza* < *pulire,* to polish < Lat. *polire.*]

pol·i·tic (pŏl′ĭ-tĭk) *adj.* **1.** Artful; shrewd: *a politic senator.* **2.** Using, displaying, or proceeding from policy; judicious: *a politic decision.* **3.** Crafty; cunning. [ME *polytyk* < OFr. *politique* < Lat. *politicus,* political < Gk. *politikos* < *politēs,* citizen < *polis,* city.] —**pol′i·tic·ly** *adv.*

po·lit·i·cal (pə-lĭt′ĭ-kəl) *adj.* **1.** Of, pertaining to, or dealing with the study, structure, or affairs of government, politics, or the state. **2.** Having a definite or organized policy or structure of government. **3.** Characteristic of or resembling politics, political parties, or politicians. —**po·lit′i·cal·ly** *adv.*

political economy *n.* The science of economics.

political science *n.* The study of the processes, principles, and structure of government and of political institutions; politics.

pol·i·ti·cian (pŏl′ĭ-tĭsh′ən) *n.* **1. a.** One who is actively involved in politics, esp. party politics. **b.** One who holds or seeks a political office. **2.** One who seeks personal or partisan gain, often by cunning or dishonest means. **3.** One who is skilled or experienced in the science or administration of government.

po·lit·i·cize (pə-lĭt′ĭ-sīz′) *v.* **-cized, -ciz·ing, -ciz·es.** —*intr.* To engage in or discuss politics. —*tr.* To make political. —**po·lit′i·ci·za′tion** *n.*

pol·i·tick (pŏl′ĭ-tĭk) *intr.v.* **-ticked, -tick·ing, -ticks.** To engage in or talk politics.

po·lit·i·co (pə-lĭt′ĭ-kō′) *n., pl.* **-cos.** A politician. [Ital., political < Lat. *politicus.* —see POLITIC.]

pol·i·tics (pŏl′ĭ-tĭks) *n.* **1.** *(used with a sing. verb).* The art or science of government; political science. **2.** *(used with a sing. verb).* The activities or affairs of a government, politician, or political party. **3.** *(used with a sing. verb).* **a.** The conducting of or engaging in political affairs, often professionally. **b.** The business, activities, or profession of a person so involved. **4.** *(used with a sing. verb).* The methods or tactics involved in managing a state or government. **5.** *(used with a pl. verb).* Intrigue or maneuvering within a group: *office politics.* **6.** *(used with a pl. verb).* A person's general position or attitude on political subjects: *His politics are conservative.*

pol·i·ty (pŏl′ĭ-tē) *n., pl.* **-ties. 1.** The form of government of a nation, state, church, or organization. **2.** An organized society, such as a nation, having one specific form of government. [OFr. *politie* < Lat. *politia,* government. —see POLICE.]

pol·ka (pōl′kə, pō′kə) *n.* **1.** A lively round dance originating in Bohemia, performed by couples in duple meter. **2.** Music for the polka. —*intr.v.* **-kaed, -ka·ing, -kas.** To dance the polka. [Czech < Pol. < *Polka,* Polish woman, fem. of *Polak,* Pole.]

pol·ka dot (pō′kə) *n.* **1.** One of a number of dots or round spots forming a pattern on cloth. **2.** A pattern or fabric with dots.

poll (pōl) *n.* **1.** The casting and registering of votes in an election. **2.** The number of votes cast or recorded. **3.** Often **polls.** The place where votes are cast and registered. **4.** A survey of the public or of a sample of the public to acquire information or record opinion. **5.** The head, esp. the top of the head where hair grows. **6.** The blunt or broad end of a tool, such as a hammer or ax. —*v.* **polled, poll·ing, polls.** —*tr.* **1.** To receive (a given number of votes). **2.** To receive or record the votes of: *poll a jury.* **3.** To cast (a vote or ballot). **4.** To question in a survey; canvass. **5.** To cut off or trim (hair, horns, or wool, for example); clip. **6.** To trim or cut off the hair, wool, branches, or horns of; shear: *poll sheep.* —*intr.* To vote at the polls or in an election. [ME *pol,* head < MLG *polle.*] —**poll′er** *n.*

pol·lack (pŏl′ək) *n.* Variant of **pollock.**

pol·lard (pŏl′ərd) *n.* **1.** A tree whose top branches have been cut back to the trunk so that it may produce a dense growth of new shoots. **2.** An animal, such as an ox, goat, or sheep, that no longer has its horns. —*tr.v.* **-lard·ed, -lard·ing, -lards.** To convert or change into a pollard. [< POLL.]

polled (pōld) *adj.* Having no horns; hornless.

pol·len (pŏl′ən) *n.* The fine, powderlike material produced by the anthers of flowering plants, and functioning as the male element in fertilization. [NLat. < Lat., flour.]

pol·len·ate (pŏl′ə-nāt′) *v.* Variant of **pollinate.**

pollen count *n.* The average number of pollen grains, usually of ragweed, in a cubic yard or other standard volume of air over a 24-hour period at a specified time and place, used to estimate the possible severity of hay-fever attacks.

pol·len·if·er·ous (pŏl′ə-nĭf′ər-əs) *adj.* Variant of **polliniferous.**

pol·len·o·sis (pŏl′ə-nō′sĭs) *n.* Variant of **pollinosis.**

pollen tube *n. Bot.* The slender tube that is emitted by a grain of pollen and that penetrates an ovule and fertilizes it.

pol·lex (pŏl′ĕks′) *n., pl.* **pol·li·ces** (pŏl′ĭ-sēz′). The innermost forelimb digit; thumb. [Lat.]

pol·li·cal (pŏl′ĭ-kəl) *adj.* Of or pertaining to the thumb.

pollin– *pref.* Variant of **pollini-.**

pol·li·nate also **pol·len·ate** (pŏl′ə-nāt′) *tr.v.* **-nat·ed, -nat·ing, -nates** also **-at·ed, -at·ing, -ates.** *Bot.* To convey or transfer pollen from an anther to a stigma of (a plant or flower) in the process of fertilization. [< NLat. *pollen, pollin-,* pollen < Lat., flour.] —**pol′li·na′tion** *n.* —**pol′li·na′tor** *n.*

pollini– or **pollin–** *pref.* Pollen: *polliniferous.* [< NLat. *pollen, pollin-,* pollen.]

pol·lin·i·a (pŏ-lĭn′ē-ə) *n.* Plural of **pollinium.**

pol·lin·ic (pŏ-lĭn′ĭk) *adj.* Of or pertaining to pollen.

pol·li·nif·er·ous also **pol·len·if·er·ous** (pŏl′ə-nĭf′ər-əs) *adj.* **1.** Producing or yielding pollen. **2.** Adapted for carrying pollen.

pol·lin·i·um (pŏ-lĭn′ē-əm) *n., pl.* **-i·a** (-ē-ə). A mass of agglutinated pollen grains, found in the flowers of most orchids and milkweeds.

pol·li·nize (pŏl′ə-nīz′) *tr.v.* **-nized, -niz·ing, -niz·es.** To pollinate. —**pol′li·ni·za′tion** *n.* —**pol′li·niz′er** *n.*

pol·li·no·sis also **pol·len·o·sis** (pŏl′ə-nō′sĭs) *n.* Allergic reaction to pollen, as in disorders such as hay fever or asthma.

pol·li·wog also **pol·ly·wog** (pŏl′ē-wŏg′, -wôg′) *n.* A tadpole. [ME *polwygle* : *pol,* head (< MLG *polle*) + *wiglen,* to wiggle. —see WIGGLE.]

pol·lock also **pol·lack** (pŏl′ək) *n., pl.* **pollock** or **-locks** also **pollack** or **-lacks.** A marine food fish, *Pollachius virens,* of northern Atlantic waters. [Sc. *podlok.*]

poll·ster (pōl′stər) *n.* A person who takes public-opinion surveys.

poll tax *n.* A tax levied on persons rather than on property, often as a requirement for voting.

pol·lut·ant (pə-lōōt′nt) *n.* Something that pollutes, esp. a waste material that contaminates air, soil, or water.

pol·lute (pə-lōōt′) *tr.v.* **-lut·ed, -lut·ing, -lutes. 1.** To render morally impure; corrupt. **2.** To make unfit for or harmful to living things, esp. by the addition of waste matter. [ME *polluten* < Lat. *polluere.*] —**pol·lut′er** *n.*

pol·lu·tion (pə-lōō′shən) *n.* **1.** The act or process of polluting or the state of being polluted. **2.** The contamination of soil, water, or the atmosphere by the discharge of harmful substances.

Pol·lux (pŏl′əks) *n.* **1.** *Gk. Myth.* One of the Dioscuri. **2.** A bright star in the constellation Gemini. [Lat. < Gk. *Polludeukēs.*]

Pol·ly·an·na (pŏl′ē-ăn′ə) *n.* A foolishly or blindly optimistic person. [After *Pollyanna,* the heroine of *Pollyanna,* novel by Eleanor Porter (1868–1920).]

pol·ly·wog (pŏl′ē-wŏg′, -wôg′) *n.* Variant of **polliwog.**

po·lo (pō′lō) *n.* **1.** A game played by two teams of three or four players on horseback, equipped with long-handled mallets for driving a small wooden ball through the opponents' goal. **2.** Water polo. [Of Tibeto-Burman orig.] —**po′lo·ist** *n.*

polo coat *n.* A kind of loose-fitting, tailored overcoat made from camel's hair or a similar material.

pol·o·naise (pŏl′ə-nāz′, pō′lə-) *n.* **1.** A stately, marchlike Polish dance in triple time. **2.** Music for or in the style of the polonaise. **3.** A woman's dress of the 18th century, having a fitted bodice and draped cutaway skirt, worn over an elaborate underskirt. [Fr. < fem. of *polonais,* Polish < Med. Lat. *Polonia,* Poland.]

po·lo·ni·um (pə-lō′nē-əm) *n. Symbol* **Po** A naturally radioactive metallic element, occurring in minute quantities as a product of radium disintegration and produced by bombarding bismuth or lead with neutrons. It has 27 isotopes ranging in mass number from 192 to 218, of which Po 210, with a half-life of 138.39 days, is the most readily available. Atomic number 84; melting point 254°C; boiling point 962°C; specific gravity 9.32; valence 2, 4, 6. [< Med. Lat. *Polonia,* Poland.]

polo shirt *n.* A pullover sport shirt of knitted cotton.

pol·ter·geist (pōl′tər-gīst′) *n.* A ghost that manifests itself by noises and rappings. [G. : *poltern,* to make noises (< MHG *boldern*) + *Geist,* ghost < OHG.]

pol·troon (pŏl-tro͞on′) *n. Archaic.* A base coward. [OFr. *poltron* < OItal. *poltrone,* aug. of *poltro,* colt < Lat. *pullus,* young animal.] **—pol·troon′er·y** *n.*

poly– *pref.* **1.** More than one; many; much: *polyatomic.* **2.** More than usual; excessive; abnormal: *polydipsia.* **3.** Polymer; polymeric: *polyethylene.* [< Gk. *polus,* much, many.]

pol·y·a·cryl·a·mide (pŏl′ē-ə-krĭl′ə-mīd′) *n.* A white polyamide (–$CH_2CHCONH_2$–) of acrylic acid. [POLY- + ACRYL(IC ACID) + AMIDE.]

polyacrylamide gel *n.* A hydrated polyacrylamide of stiff consistency used as a medium for electrophoresis because of its white coloring and thickening action in water-based solutions.

pol·y·al·co·hol (pŏl′ē-ăl′kə-hôl′) *n.* An alcohol containing more than one hydroxy group.

pol·y·am·ide (pŏl′ē-ăm′īd′) *n.* A polymer containing repeated amide groups, as in various kinds of nylon.

pol·y·an·dric (pŏl′ē-ăn′drĭk) *adj.* Of or relating to polyandry.

pol·y·an·drous (pŏl′ē-ăn′drəs) *adj.* **1.** Pertaining to or practicing polyandry. **2.** *Bot.* Having an indefinite number of stamens.

pol·y·an·dry (pŏl′ē-ăn′drē) *n.* **1.** The state or practice of having more than one husband at a single time. **2.** *Bot.* The condition of being polyandrous.

pol·y·an·thus (pŏl′ē-ăn′thəs) *n., pl.* **-thus·es.** Any of a group of hybrid garden primroses having clusters of variously colored flowers. [NLat. < Gk. *poluanthos,* having many flowers : *polus,* many + *anthos,* flower.]

polyanthus narcissus *n.* A bulbous plant, *Narcissus tazetta,* native to Eurasia, having clusters of fragrant white or yellow flowers.

pol·y·a·tom·ic (pŏl′ē-ə-tŏm′ĭk) *adj.* Having three or more atoms as constituents. Used esp. of molecules.

pol·y·ba·sic (pŏl′ē-bā′sĭk) *adj.* Polyprotic.

pol·y·ba·site (pŏl′ē-bā′sīt′) *n.* A black mineral with a metallic luster, containing silver, copper, antimony, and sulfur, essentially $(Ag, Cu)_{16}Sb_2S_{11}$, often found in veins of silver. [G. *Polybasit* : Gk. *polus,* many + Gk. *basis,* base.]

pol·y·car·bon·ate (pŏl′ĭ-kär′bə-nāt′) *n.* Any of a family of thermoplastics characterized by a high softening temperature and high impact strength.

pol·y·car·pel·lar·y (pŏl′ē-kär′pə-lĕr′ē) *adj.* Having or consisting of many carpels. [POLY- + CARPEL + -ARY.]

pol·y·car·pous (pŏl′ē-kär′pəs) also **po·ly·car·pic** (-pĭk) *adj.* Having fruit with two or more carpels. **—pol′y·car′py** *n.*

pol·y·chaete also **pol·y·chete** (pŏl′ĭ-kēt′) *n.* Any of various marine worms of the class Polychaeta, having paired, flattened, bristle-tipped organs of locomotion. [NLat. *Polychaeta,* class name < Gk. *polukhaitēs,* with much hair : *polus,* much + *khaitē,* long hair.] **—pol′y·chaete, pol′y·chae′tous** *adj.*

pol·y·chlo·rin·at·ed biphenyl (pŏl′ĭ-klôr′ə-nā′tĭd, -klōr′-) *n.* Any of a family of industrial compounds produced by chlorination of biphenyl, noted primarily as an environmental pollutant that accumulates in animal tissue with resultant pathogenic and teratogenic effects.

pol·y·chro·mat·ic (pŏl′ē-krō-măt′ĭk) also **pol·y·chro·mic** (-krō′mĭk) or **pol·y·chro·mous** (-krō′məs) *adj.* **1.** Having many colors or manifesting changes of color. **2.** Referring to radiation of more than one wavelength.

pol·y·chro·mat·o·phil·i·a (pŏl′ē-krō-măt′ə-fĭl′ē-ə) also **pol·y·chro·mo·phil·i·a** (-krō′mə-fĭl′ē-ə) *n.* Susceptibility to staining with more than one type of dye, as seen in diseased red blood cells. **—pol′y·chro·mat′o·phil′ic** *adj.*

pol·y·chrome (pŏl′ē-krōm′) *adj.* **1.** Having many or various colors; polychromatic. **2.** Made or decorated in many or various colors. *—n.* An object having or decorated in many colors.

pol·y·chro·my (pŏl′ē-krō′mē) *n.* The art of employing many colors in decoration, esp. in architecture and statuary.

pol·y·clin·ic (pŏl′ē-klĭn′ĭk) *n.* A clinic or hospital that treats all types of diseases and injuries.

pol·y·con·ic projection (pŏl′ē-kŏn′ĭk) *n.* A conic map projection having distances between meridians along every parallel equal to those distances on a globe. The central geographic meridian is a straight line and the others are curved, while the parallels are arcs of circles.

pol·y·cot·y·le·don (pŏl′ē-kŏt′l-ēd′n) also **pol·y·cot** (pŏl′ē-kŏt′) *n.* A plant having several cotyledons. **—pol′y·cot′y·le′don·ous** *adj.*

pol·y·cy·clic (pŏl′ĭ-sī′klĭk, -sĭk′lĭk) *adj. Chem.* Having two or more atomic rings in a molecule.

pol·y·cy·the·mi·a (pŏl′ē-sī-thē′mē-ə) *n. Pathol.* A condition marked by an abnormally large number of red cells in the blood.

pol·y·dac·tyl (pŏl′ē-dăk′təl) also **pol·y·dac·ty·lous** (-tə-ləs) *—adj.* Having more than the normal number of fingers or toes. *—n.* A polydactyl person or animal. **—pol′y·dac′tyl·ism, pol′y·dac′ty·ly** *n.*

pol·y·dem·ic (pŏl′ē-dĕm′ĭk) *adj.* Occurring in or inhabiting two or more regions. [POLY- + (EN)DEMIC.]

pol·y·dip·si·a (pŏl′ē-dĭp′sē-ə) *n.* Excessive or abnormal thirst. [NLat. : POLY- + Gk. *dipsa,* thirst.] **—pol′y·dip′sic** *adj.*

pol·y·e·lec·tro·lyte (pŏl′ē-ĭ-lĕk′trə-līt′) *n.* An electrolyte having a high molecular weight, such as a protein or polysaccharide.

pol·y·em·bry·o·ny (pŏl′ē-ĕm′brē-ə-nē, -ĕm-brī′-) *n.* The development of more than one embryo from a single egg or ovule. **—pol′y·em′bry·on′ic** (-brē-ŏn′ĭk) *adj.*

pol·y·ene (pŏl′ē-ēn′) *n.* An organic compound containing many double bonds.

pol·y·es·ter (pŏl′ē-ĕs′tər) *n.* Any of numerous synthetic resins, produced chiefly by reaction of dibasic acids with dihydric alcohols. Reinforced polyester resins are light, strong, and weather-resistant, and are used in boat hulls, swimming pools, waterproof fibers, adhesives, and molded parts. **—pol′y·es′ter·i·fi·ca′tion** (-ə-fĭ-kā′shən) *n.*

pol·y·e·ther (pŏl′ē-ē′thər) *n.* A polymer containing a carbon-oxygen bond in the repeating unit, esp. when derived from an epoxide or an aldehyde.

pol·y·eth·yl·ene (pŏl′ē-ĕth′ə-lēn′) *n. Chem.* A polymerized ethylene resin, used esp. in the form of films and sheets for packaging or molded for a wide variety of containers, kitchenware, and tubing.

polyethylene glycol *n.* Any of a number of high molecular weight liquids that are colorless and soluble in water and in many organic solvents, used primarily as emulsifying agents and plasticizers and in detergents.

po·lyg·a·la (pə-lĭg′ə-lə) *n.* A plant of the genus *Polygala;* milkwort. [NLat. *Polygala,* genus name < Gk. *polugalon,* milkwort : *polus,* much + *gala,* milk.]

po·lyg·a·mist (pə-lĭg′ə-mĭst) *n.* One who practices polygamy.

po·lyg·a·mous (pə-lĭg′ə-məs) *adj.* **1.** Of, relating to, engaged in, or characterized by polygamy. **2.** *Bot.* **a.** Having both hermaphroditic and unisexual flowers on the same plant. **b.** Having either hermaphroditic or unisexual flowers on different plants of the same species. **—po·lyg′a·mous·ly** *adv.*

po·lyg·a·my (pə-lĭg′ə-mē) *n.* The state or practice of having more than one wife or husband at a time. [Fr. *polygamie* < LLat. *polygamia* < Gk. *polugamia* : *polus,* many + *gamos,* marriage.]

pol·y·gene (pŏl′ē-jēn′) *n.* One of a set of cooperating genes, each producing a small quantitative effect.

pol·y·gen·e·sis (pŏl′ē-jĕn′ĭ-sĭs) *n.* The derivation of a species or type from more than one ancestor. **—pol′y·gen′e·sist** *n.* **—pol′y·ge·net′ic** (-jə-nĕt′ĭk), **pol′y·gen′ic** (-jĕn′ĭk), **po·lyg′e·nous** (pə-lĭj′ə-nəs) *adj.*

pol·y·glot (pŏl′ē-glŏt′) *adj.* Speaking, writing, written in, or composed of several languages. *—n.* **1.** A person with a reading, writing, or speaking knowledge of several languages. **2.** A book, esp. a Bible, containing several versions of the same text in different languages. **3.** A mixture or confusion of languages. [Fr. *polyglotte* < Gk. *poluglōttos* : *polus,* many + *glōtta,* tongue.] **—pol′y·glot′ism, pol′y·glot′tism** *n.*

pol·y·gon (pŏl′ē-gŏn′) *n.* A closed plane figure bounded by three or more line segments. [LLat. *polygonum* < Gk. *polugōnon* < *polugōnos,* having many angles : *polus,* many + *gōnia,* angle.] **—po·lyg′o·nal** (pə-lĭg′ə-nəl) *adj.* **—po·lyg′o·nal·ly** *adv.*

po·lyg·o·num (pə-lĭg′ə-nəm) *n.* Any of numerous plants of the widely distributed genus *Polygonum,* characterized by stems with knotlike joints. [NLat. *Polygonum,* genus name < Gk. *polugonon,* knotgrass : *polus,* many + *gonu,* knee.]

pol·y·graph (pŏl′ē-grăf′) *n.* An instrument that simultaneously records changes in such physiological processes as heartbeat, blood pressure, and respiration, often used as a lie detector. **—pol′y·graph′ic** *adj.*

po·lyg·y·ny (pə-lĭj′ə-nē) *n.* The condition or practice of having more than one wife at a single time. [POLY- + Gk. *gunē,* woman.] **—po·lyg′y·nous** *adj.*

pol·y·he·dra (pŏl′ē-hē′drə) *n.* A plural of **polyhedron.**

pol·y·he·dral angle (pŏl′ē-hē′drəl) *n.* The configuration formed by three or more planes having intersections that form a common vertex.

pol·y·he·dron (pŏl′ē-hē′drən) *n., pl.* **-drons** or **-dra** (-drə). A solid bounded by polygons. **—pol′y·he′dral** *adj.*

pol·y·his·tor (pŏl′ē-hĭs′tər) *n.* A polymath. [< Gk. *poluistōr,* very learned : *polus,* much + *histōr,* learned.] **—pol′y·his·tor′ic** (-hĭ-stôr′ĭk, -stŏr′-) *adj.*

pol·y·hy·dric (pŏl′ē-hī′drĭk) *adj. Chem.* Containing at least two hydroxyl groups.

Pol·y·hym·ni·a (pŏl′ē-hĭm′nē-ə) also **Po·lym·ni·a** (pə-lĭm′nē-ə) *n. Gk. Myth.* The Muse of singing, rhetoric, and mime. [Lat. < Gk. *Polumnia* < *polumnos,* abounding in songs : *polus,* many + *humnos,* hymn.]

pol·y·im·ide (pŏl′ē-ĭm′īd′) *n.* A synthetic polymeric resin of

polyconic projection
Polyconic projection of North America

a class resistant to high temperatures, wear, and corrosion, used primarily as a coating or film on a substrate substance.

pol·y·mas·ti·gote (pŏl′ē-măs′tĭ-gōt′) *adj.* Having a tuftlike arrangement of flagella. [Alteration of E. *polymastigate* : POLY- + Gk. *mastix,* whip + -ATE[1].]

pol·y·math (pŏl′ē-măth′) *n.* A person of great or varied learning. [Gk. *polumathēs* : *polus,* much + *manthanein,* to learn.] **—pol′y·math′, pol′y·math′ic** *adj.*

pol·y·mer (pŏl′ə-mər) *n.* Any of numerous natural and synthetic compounds of usually high molecular weight consisting of up to millions of repeated linked units, each a relatively light and simple molecule. [Back-formation < POLYMERIC.]

pol·y·mer·ase (pŏl′ə-mə-rās′, -rāz′) *n.* Any of various enzymes that aid in the linkage of nucleotides in the formation of DNA or RNA with an existing strand of DNA or RNA acting as a template.

pol·y·mer·ic (pŏl′ə-mĕr′ĭk) *adj.* Of, pertaining to, or consisting of a polymer. [Gk. *polumerēs,* having many parts : *polus,* many + *meros,* part.] **—pol′y·mer′i·cal·ly** *adv.* **—po·lym′er·ism** (pə-lĭm′ə-rĭz′əm, pŏl′ə-mə-) *n.*

po·lym·er·i·za·tion (pə-lĭm′ər-ĭ-zā′shən, pŏl′ə-mər-) *n.* **1.** The uniting of two or more monomers to form a polymer. **2.** A chemical process that effects polymerization.

pol·y·mer·ize (pŏl′ə-mə-rīz′, pə-lĭm′ə-) *intr.* & *tr.v.* **-ized, -iz·ing, -iz·es.** To undergo or subject to polymerization.

po·lym·er·ous (pə-lĭm′ər-əs) *adj.* Consisting of numerous parts.

Po·lym·ni·a (pə-lĭm′nē-ə) *n.* Variant of **Polyhymnia.**

pol·y·morph (pŏl′ē-môrf′) *n.* **1.** *Biol.* An organism characterized by polymorphism. **2.** *Chem.* A specific crystalline form of a compound that can crystallize in different forms.

pol·y·mor·phism (pŏl′ē-môr′fĭz′əm) *n.* **1.** *Biol.* The occurrence of different forms, stages, or color types in individual organisms or in organisms of the same species. **2.** *Chem.* Crystallization of a compound in at least two distinct forms. **—pol′y·mor′phic, pol′y·mor′phous** *adj.*

pol·y·mor·pho·nu·cle·ar (pŏl′ĭ-môr′fə-no͞o′klē-ər, -nyo͞o′-) *adj.* Having a lobed nucleus. Used of leukocytes.

pol·y·myx·in (pŏl′ē-mĭk′sĭn) *n.* Any of various mainly toxic antibiotics derived from strains of the soil bacterium *Bacillus polymyxa.* [< NLat. *polymyxa,* specific epithet of *Bacillus polymyxa* : POLY- + Gk. *muxa,* slime.]

Pol·y·ne·sian (pŏl′ə-nē′zhən, -shən) *adj.* Of or pertaining to Polynesia, its inhabitants, culture, or languages. *—n.* **1.** A native of Polynesia. **2.** A subfamily of the Austronesian language family spoken in Polynesia.

Pol·y·ni·ces (pŏl′ə-nī′sēz) *n. Gk. Myth.* A son of Oedipus for whom an expedition against Thebes was raised. [Lat. < Gk. *Poluneikēs.*]

pol·y·no·mi·al (pŏl′ē-nō′mē-əl) *adj.* Of, pertaining to, or consisting of more than two names or terms. *—n.* **1.** *Biol.* A taxonomic designation consisting of more than two terms. **2.** *Math.* **a.** An algebraic function of two or more summed terms, each term consisting of a constant multiplier and one or more variables raised, in general, to integral powers. For example, the general form of a polynomial of degree *n* in a single real variable *x* is $a_0x^n + a_1x^{n-1} + \cdots + a_{n-1}x + a_n$ where $a_0, a_1, \cdots, a_n$ are real numbers with $a_0 \neq 0$ and *n* is a positive integer. **b.** A mathematical expression of two or more terms. [POLY- + (BI)NOMIAL.]

pol·y·nu·cle·o·tide (pŏl′ĭ-no͞o′klē-ə-tīd′, -nyo͞o′-) *n.* A polymeric chain of nucleotides.

po·lyn·ya (pŏl′ən-yä′) *n.* A large area of open water surrounded by sea ice. [R. *polyn′ya* < *polyĭ,* open.]

pol·yp (pŏl′ĭp) *n.* **1.** *Zool.* A coelenterate having a cylindrical body and an oral opening usually surrounded by tentacles, as a hydra or coral. **2.** *Pathol.* A growth protruding from the mucous lining of an organ such as the nose. [Fr. *polype,* octopus < Lat. *polypus* < Gk. *polupous* : *polus,* many + *pous,* foot.] **—pol′yp·oid′** *adj.*

pol·y·par·y (pŏl′ə-pĕr′ē) also **pol·y·par·i·um** (pŏl′ə-pâr′ē-əm) *n., pl.* **-ies** also **-i·a** (-ē-ə). *Zool.* The common framework and base of a polyp colony, esp. of coral.

pol·y·pep·tide (pŏl′ē-pĕp′tīd′) *n.* A peptide containing between 10 and 100 amino acids.

pol·y·pet·al·ous (pŏl′ē-pĕt′l-əs) *adj.* Having distinctly separate petals: *a polypetalous corolla.*

pol·y·pha·gi·a (pŏl′ē-fā′jē-ə, -jə) *n.* An excessive or pathological desire to eat. **—pol′y·pha′gi·an** *adj.*

po·lyph·a·gous (pə-lĭf′ə-gəs) *adj.* Feeding on or utilizing a variety of foods.

Pol·y·phe·mus (pŏl′ə-fē′məs) *n. Gk. Myth.* The Cyclops who confined Odysseus and his companions in a cave until Odysseus blinded him and escaped. [Lat. < Gk. *Poluphēmos.*]

pol·y·phe·mus moth (pŏl′ə-fē′məs) *n.* A large North American moth, *Antheraea polyphemus,* having an eyelike spot on each hind wing. [After POLYPHEMUS.]

pol·y·phone (pŏl′ē-fōn′) *n.* A written character or combination of characters having two or more phonetic values, such as the letter *a.*

pol·y·phon·ic (pŏl′ē-fŏn′ĭk) *adj. Mus.* Of, pertaining to, or characteristic of polyphony. **—pol′y·phon′i·cal·ly** *adv.*

po·lyph·o·ny (pə-lĭf′ə-nē) *n., pl.* **-nies.** *Mus.* Music with two or more independent melodic parts sounded together. **—po·lyph′o·nous** *adj.* **—po·lyph′o·nous·ly** *adv.*

pol·y·phy·let·ic (pŏl′ē-fī-lĕt′ĭk) *adj.* Pertaining to or characterized by development from more than one ancestral type. **—pol′y·phy·let′i·cal·ly** *adv.*

pol·y·pi (pŏl′ə-pī′) *n.* A plural of **polypus.**

pol·y·ploid (pŏl′ē-ploid′) *adj.* Having more than twice the normal haploid chromosome number. *—n.* An organism with more than two sets of chromosomes. **—pol′y·ploi′dy** *n.*

pol·yp·ne·a (pŏl′ĭp-nē′ə) *n.* Very rapid breathing; panting. [NLat. : POLY- + Gk. *pnoia,* breathing.] **—pol′yp·ne′ic** (-nē′ĭk) *adj.*

pol·y·pod (pŏl′ē-pŏd′) also **po·lyp·o·dous** (pə-lĭp′ə-dəs) *adj.* Having numerous feet.

pol·y·po·dy (pŏl′ē-pō′dē) *n., pl.* **-dies.** Any of various ferns of the widely distributed genus *Polypodium,* having simple or compound fronds and creeping rootstocks. [ME *polypodie* < Lat. *polypodium* < Gk. *polupodion* < dim. of *polupous,* octopus. —see POLYP.]

pol·y·pore (pŏl′ē-pôr′, -pōr′) *n.* A pore fungus.

pol·y·pro·pyl·ene (pŏl′ĭ-prō′pə-lēn′) *n.* Any of various thermoplastic resins that are polymers of propylene.

pol·y·pro·tic (pŏl′ē-prō′tĭk) *adj.* Designating an acid with two or more replaceable hydrogen atoms in each molecule. [POLY- + PROT(ON) + -IC.]

pol·yp·tych (pŏl′ĭp-tĭk′) *n.* A decorated altarpiece or panel having three or more hinged sections that can be folded together. [< Gk. *poluptukhos,* having many folds : *polus,* many + *ptukhē,* fold.]

pol·y·pus (pŏl′ə-pəs) *n., pl.* **-pi** (-pī′) or **-pus·es.** A polyp (sense 2). [Lat., polypus, octopus. —see POLYP.]

pol·y·ri·bo·some (pŏl′ĭ-rī′bə-sōm′) *n.* A cluster of ribosomes connected by a molecule of messenger RNA.

pol·y·sac·cha·ride (pŏl′ē-săk′ə-rīd′) also **pol·y·sac·cha·rid** (-rĭd) or **pol·y·sac·cha·rose** (-rōs′, -rōz′) *n.* A group of nine or more monosaccharides joined by glycosidic bonds, such as starch and cellulose.

pol·y·sep·al·ous (pŏl′ē-sĕp′ə-ləs) *adj.* Having distinctly separated sepals.

pol·y·some (pŏl′ĭ-sōm′) *n.* Polyribosome.

pol·y·so·mic (pŏl′ē-sō′mĭk) *adj.* Having an excess number of one or more chromosomes. [POLY- + (CHROMO)SOM(E) + -IC.]

pol·y·sor·bate (pŏl′ĭ-sôr′bāt′) *n.* Any of a class of emulsifiers used in food preparation and in some pharmaceuticals.

pol·y·sper·my (pŏl′ē-spûr′mē) *n.* The entry of several sperms into an ovum during fertilization. **—pol′y·sper′mic** *adj.*

po·lys·ti·chous (pə-lĭs′tĭ-kəs) *adj.* Arranged in two or more series or rows. [POLY- + LLat. *-stichus* < Gk. *-stikhos* < *stikhos,* row.]

pol·y·sty·rene (pŏl′ē-stī′rēn′) *n.* A hard, rigid, dimensionally stable, clear thermoplastic polymer that is easily colored and molded for a wide variety of applications as a structural material.

pol·y·sul·fide (pŏl′ē-sŭl′fīd′) *n.* A sulfide compound containing at least two sulfur atoms per molecule.

pol·y·syl·lab·ic (pŏl′ē-sĭ-lăb′ĭk) *adj.* **1.** Having more than three syllables. **2.** Characterized by words having more than three syllables. **—pol′y·syl·lab′i·cal·ly** *adv.*

pol·y·syl·la·ble (pŏl′ē-sĭl′ə-bəl) *n.* A word of more than three syllables.

pol·y·syn·de·ton (pŏl′ē-sĭn′dĭ-tŏn′) *n.* The repetition of connectives or conjunctions in close succession for rhetorical effect, as in the phrase *here and there and everywhere.* [LGk. *polusundeton,* neuter of *polusundetos,* using many connectives : *polus,* many + *sundetos,* bound together. —see SYNDETIC.]

pol·y·syn·thet·ic (pŏl′ē-sĭn-thĕt′ĭk) *adj. Ling.* Designating a language, such as Eskimo, in which many of the elements of a sentence or phrase are combined into one utterance and do not exist separately.

pol·y·tech·nic (pŏl′ē-tĕk′nĭk) *adj.* Pertaining to or dealing with many arts or sciences. *—n.* A school specializing in the teaching of industrial arts and applied sciences. [Fr. *polytechnique* < Gk. *polutekhnos,* skilled in many arts : *polus,* many + *tekhnē,* skill.]

pol·y·tene (pŏl′ĭ-tēn′) *adj.* Pertaining to or having chromosomes that are large, multistranded, and have corresponding chromomeres in contact. [POLY- + Lat. *taenia,* band < Gk. *tainia,* ribbon.]

pol·y·tet·ra·fluor·o·eth·yl·ene (pŏl′ē-tĕt′rə-flo͝or′ō-ĕth′ə-lēn′) *n.* A waxy, opaque-white, thermoplastic resin, $(C_2F_4)_n$, thermally stable, resistant to acids, alkalis, and oxidizing agents, and having an extremely low coefficient of friction. It is used as a low-friction coating, esp. for cooking vessels, and for chemical-resistant gaskets, seals, and hoses.

pol·y·the·ism (pŏl′ē-thē-ĭz′əm) *n.* The worship of or belief in more than one god. [Fr. *polythéisme* < Gk. *polutheos,* polytheistic : *polus,* many + *theos,* god.] **—pol′y·the′ist** *n.* **—pol′y·the·is′tic** *adj.*

pol·y·thene (pŏl′ə-thēn′) *n. Chiefly Brit.* Variant of **polyethylene.**

po·lyt·o·cous (pə-lĭt′ə-kəs) *adj. Biol.* Producing many offspring or ova at a single time. [Gk. *polutokos,* bearing many offspring : *polus,* many + *tokos,* offspring.]

pol·y·to·nal·i·ty (pŏl′ē-tō-năl′ĭ-tē) *n. Mus.* Simultaneity of two or more tonalities in a composition. **—pol′y·ton′al** *adj.* **—pol′y·ton′al·ly** *adv.*

pol·y·tro·phic (pŏl′ē-trō′fĭk, -trŏf′ĭk) *adj.* **1.** *Biol.* Subsisting on various types of organic material. **2.** *Pathol.* Characterized by or relating to excessive nutrition.

pol·y·typ·ic (pŏl′ē-tĭp′ĭk) also **pol·y·typ·i·cal** (-ĭ-kəl) *adj.* Existing in, having, or involving many different forms or types.

pol·y·un·sat·u·rat·ed (pŏl′ē-ŭn-săch′ə-rā′tĭd) *adj.* Pertaining to long-chain carbon compounds, esp. fats, having many unsaturated bonds.

pol·y·ur·e·thane (pŏl′ē-yo͝or′ə-thān′) *n.* Any of various thermoplastic or thermosetting resins, widely varying in flexibility, used in tough chemical-resistant coatings and in adhesives, foams, and electrical insulation.

pol·y·u·ri·a (pŏl′ē-yo͝or′ē-ə) *n.* Excessive passage of urine, as in diabetes. **—pol′y·u′ric** *adj.*

pol·y·va·lent (pŏl′ē-vā′lənt) *adj.* **1.** *Microbiol.* Containing, sensitive to, or interacting with more than one kind of antigen, antibody, toxin, or microorganism. **2.** *Chem.* **a.** Having more than one valence. **b.** Having a valence of 3 or higher. **—pol′y·va′lence, pol′y·va′len·cy** *n.*

pol·y·vi·nyl (pŏl′ē-vī′nəl) *adj.* Designating any of a group of polymerized thermoplastic vinyls, such as polyvinyl chloride.

polyvinyl chloride *n.* A common thermoplastic resin, used in a wide variety of manufactured products, including rainwear, garden hoses, phonograph records, and floor tiles.

pol·y·zo·an (pŏl′ē-zō′ən) *n.* A bryozoan. [< NLat. *Polyzoa,* phylum name : POLY- + Gk. *zōia,* pl. of *zōion,* animal.] **—pol′y·zo′an** *adj.*

pol·y·zo·ar·i·um (pŏl′ē-zō-âr′ē-əm) also **pol·y·zo·a·ry** (-zō′ə-rē) *n., pl.* **-ar·i·a** (-âr′ē-ə) also **-a·ries.** A bryozoan colony or its supporting skeletal structure. [NLat. < *Polyzoa,* phylum name. —see POLYZOAN.]

pol·y·zo·ic (pŏl′ē-zō′ĭk) *adj. Biol.* **1.** Forming or consisting of a colony of zooids. **2.** Containing numerous sporozoites.

pom·ace (pŭm′ĭs, pŏm′-) *n.* **1.** The pulpy refuse remaining after the juice has been pressed from apples or other fruit. **2.** Pulpy material remaining after the extraction of oil from nuts, seeds, or fish. [Med. Lat. *pomacium,* cider < Lat. *pomum,* fruit.]

pomace fly *n.* The fruit fly.

po·ma·ceous (pō-mā′shəs) *adj.* **1.** Of, pertaining to, or characteristic of apples. **2.** Of, pertaining to, or bearing pomes. [< Lat. *pomum,* fruit.]

po·made (pō-măd′, -mäd′) *n.* A perfumed ointment applied to the hair. *—tr.v.* **-mad·ed, -mad·ing, -mades.** To anoint with pomade. [Fr. *pommade* < Ital. *pomata* < *pomo,* apple < Lat. *pomum,* fruit.]

po·man·der (pō′măn′dər, pō-măn′-) *n.* **1.** A mixture of aromatic substances, formerly worn enclosed in a bag or box as a protection against odor and infection. **2.** A case, box, or bag for holding pomander. [ME, alteration of OFr. *pome d'embre,* apple of amber.]

pome (pōm) *n.* A fleshy fruit having seeds but no stone, such as the apple, pear, or quince. [ME < OFr., apple < Lat. *pomum,* fruit.]

pome·gran·ate (pŏm′grăn′ĭt, pŏm′ĭ-, pŭm′-, pŭm′ĭ-) *n.* **1.** A semitropical shrub or small tree, *Punica granatum,* native to Asia, and widely cultivated for its edible fruit. **2.** The fruit of the pomegranate tree, having a tough, reddish rind, and containing many seeds enclosed in a juicy red pulp with a mildly acid flavor. [ME *pomegranard* < OFr. *pome grenate* : *pome,* apple + *grenate,* having many seeds.]

pom·e·lo (pŏm′ə-lō′) *n., pl.* **-los.** The grapefruit. [Alteration of POMPELMOUS.]

Pom·er·a·ni·an (pŏm′ə-rā′nē-ən, -rān′yən) *adj.* Of or relating to Pomerania or its people. *—n.* **1.** A native of Pomerania. **2.** One of a breed of small dogs having long, silky hair.

po·mi·cul·ture (pō′mĭ-kŭl′chər) *n.* The cultivation of fruit. [Lat. *pomum,* fruit + CULTURE.]

po·mif·er·ous (pō-mĭf′ər-əs) *adj.* Bearing pomes. [Lat. *pomifer,* fruit-bearing : *pomum,* fruit + *ferre,* to bear.]

pom·mel (pŭm′əl, pŏm′-) *n.* **1.** A knob on the hilt of a sword or other weapon. **2.** The upper front part of a saddle; saddlebow. *—tr.v.* **-meled, -mel·ing, -mels** also **-melled, -mel·ling, -mels.** To beat; pummel. [ME *pomel* < OFr. < VLat. **pomellum* < Lat. *pomum,* fruit.]

po·mol·o·gy (pō-mŏl′ə-jē) *n.* The scientific study and cultivation of fruit. [Lat. *pomum,* fruit + -LOGY.] **—po′mo·log′i·cal** (pō′mə-lŏj′ĭ-kəl) *adj.* **—po′mo·log′i·cal·ly** *adv.* **—po·mol′o·gist** *n.*

pomp (pŏmp) *n.* **1.** Dignified or magnificent display; splendor. **2.** Vain or ostentatious display. [ME < OFr. *pompe* < Lat. *pompa* < Gk. *pompē,* procession < *pempein,* to send.]

pom·pa·dour (pŏm′pə-dôr′, -dōr′) *n.* **1.** A woman's hair style formed by sweeping the hair straight up from the forehead. **2.** A man's hair style with the hair brushed up from the forehead. [After Jeanne Antoinette Poisson (1721–1764), Marquise de *Pompadour,* its inventor.]

pom·pa·no (pŏm′pə-nō′, pŭm′-) *n., pl.* **pompano** or **-nos. 1.** Any of several marine food fishes of the genus *Trachinotus,* esp. *T. carolinus,* of tropical and temperate Atlantic waters. **2.** Any of several fishes, such as *Palometa simillima,* a butterfish of American Pacific coastal waters. [Sp. *pámpano salpa,* a kind of fish.]

pomander

Pom·pe·ian red (pŏm-pā′ən) *n.* A grayish to moderate red.

pom·pel·mous (pŏm′pəl-mo͞os′) *n.* The shaddock (sense 2). [Du. *pompelmoes.*]

pom·pom (pŏm′pŏm′) also **pom·pon** (-pŏn′) *n.* **1.** A tuft or ball of wool, feathers, or other material worn as decoration. **2.** A small, buttonlike flower of some chrysanthemums and dahlias. [Fr. *pompon.*]

pom-pom (pŏm′pŏm′) *n.* An automatic, rapid-fire antiaircraft cannon usually mounted on ships. [Imit.]

pom·pous (pŏm′pəs) *adj.* **1.** Characterized by an exaggerated show of dignity or self-importance. **2.** Bombastic or self-important. **3.** Characterized by pomp or stately display; ceremonious. [ME < OFr. *pompeux* < LLat. *pomposus* < Lat. *pompa,* pomp. —see POMP.] **—pom·pos′i·ty** (-pŏs′ĭ-tē), **pom′pous·ness** *n.* **—pom′pous·ly** *adv.*

pon·cho (pŏn′chō) *n., pl.* **-chos. 1.** A blanketlike cloak having a hole in the center for the head. **2.** A garment, similar to the poncho, used as a raincoat. [Am. Sp. < Araucanian *pontho,* woolen fabric.]

pond (pŏnd) *n.* A still body of water smaller than a lake, often of artificial construction. [ME *ponde* < OE *pund-,* enclosure.]

pon·der (pŏn′dər) *v.* **-dered, -der·ing, -ders.** *—tr.* To weigh mentally; consider carefully. *—intr.* To meditate; reflect. [ME *ponderen* < OFr. *ponderer* < Lat. *ponderare* < *pondus,* weight.] **—pon′der·er** *n.*

Synonyms: *ponder, consider, deliberate, ruminate.* These mean to think deeply about something, usually in terms of its outcome or significance. *Ponder* suggests painstaking care and thoroughness. *Consider* is less subjective and suggests orderly evaluation. *Deliberate* can apply to the thought of a single person, but more often is used with reference to several persons engaged in seeking a decision. *Ruminate* designates a slow but less orderly process.

pomegranate

pon·der·a·ble (pŏn′dər-ə-bəl) *adj.* Capable of being weighed or assessed; appreciable. **—pon′der·a·bil′i·ty** *n.*

pon·der·o·sa pine (pŏn′də-rō′sə) *n.* A tall timber tree, *Pinus ponderosa,* of western North America, having long, dark-green needles. [NLat. *Pinus ponderosa,* ponderous pine.]

pon·der·ous (pŏn′dər-əs) *adj.* **1.** Having great weight; massive. **2.** Graceless or unwieldy from weight. **3.** Lacking fluency; labored: *a ponderous speech.* [ME < OFr. *pondereux* < Lat. *ponderosus* < *pondus, weight.*] **—pon′der·os′i·ty** (-ŏs′ĭ-tē), **pon′der·ous·ness** *n.* **—pon′der·ous·ly** *adv.*

pond lily *n.* The water lily.

pond scum *n.* Any of various freshwater algae that form a usually greenish scum on the surface of stagnant water.

pond·weed (pŏnd′wēd′) *n.* Any of various submerged or floating aquatic plants of the genus *Potamogeton.*

pone (pōn) *n.* Corn pone. [Of Algonquian orig.]

pon·gee (pŏn-jē′, pŏn′jē) *n.* A soft, thin cloth of Chinese or Indian silk with a knotty weave. [Chin. (Mandarin) *ben^{3}zhi^1* : *ben^3,* one's own + *zhi^1,* to weave, spin.]

pommel

pon·iard (pŏn′yərd) *n.* A dagger. *—tr.v.* **-iard·ed, -iard·ing, -iards.** To stab with a poniard. [Fr. *poignard* < *poing,* fist < OFr. < Lat. *pugnus.*]

pons (pŏnz) *n., pl.* **pon·tes** (pŏn′tēz). *Anat.* **1.** A slender tissue joining two parts of an organ. **2.** The pons varolii. [NLat. < Lat., bridge.]

pons as·i·no·rum (pŏnz′ ăs′ə-nôr′əm, -nōr′əm) *n.* A problem that severely tests the ability of someone inexperienced. [Lat., asses' bridge.]

pons va·ro·li·i (pŏnz′ və-rō′lē-ī′) *n.* A band of nerve fibers in the brain connecting the medulla oblongata and the mesencephalon below the cerebellum. [NLat., bridge of Varoli, after Constanzo *Varoli* (1542–1575).]

pon·tes (pŏn′tēz) *n.* Plural of **pons.**

pon·ti·fex (pŏn′tə-fĕks′) *n., pl.* **pon·tif·i·ces** (pŏn-tĭf′ĭ-sēz′). In ancient Rome, a member of the Pontifical College, the highest college of priests, headed by the Pontifex Maximus. [Lat.]

pon·tiff (pŏn′tĭf) *n.* **1. a.** The pope. **b.** A bishop. **2.** A pontifex. [Fr. < Lat. *pontifex,* pontifex]

pon·tif·i·cal (pŏn-tĭf′ĭ-kəl) *adj.* **1.** Pertaining to, characteristic of, or suitable for a pope or bishop. **2.** Having the dignity, pomp, or authority of a pontiff. **3.** Pompously authoritative. *—n.* **1. pontificals.** The vestments and insignia of a pontiff. **2.** A book of ceremonies and rites for a bishop. [Lat. *pontificalis,* of a pontifex < *pontifex,* pontifex.] **—pon·tif′i·cal·ly** *adv.*

Pontifical Mass *n. Eccles.* A celebration of the Eucharist performed by a bishop in all Roman Catholic churches, many Anglican churches, and some Lutheran churches.

pon·tif·i·cate (pŏn-tĭf′ĭ-kĭt, -kāt′) *n.* The office or term of office of a pontiff. *—intr.v.* (pŏn-tĭf′ĭ-kāt′) **-cat·ed, -cat·ing, -cates. 1.** To administer the office of a pontiff. **2.** To speak or behave with pompous authority. [Lat. *pontificatus* < *pontifex,* pontifex.]

pon·tif·i·ces (pŏn-tĭf′ĭ-sēz′) *n.* Plural of **pontifex.**

pon·til (pŏn′tĭl) *n.* A punty. [Fr., poss. < Ital. *puntello,* dim. of *punto,* point < Lat. *punctum* < *pungere,* to prick.]

pon·tine (pŏn′tīn′) *adj.* **1.** Of or pertaining to bridges. **2.** *Anat.* Of or pertaining to the pons varolii. [< Lat. *pons, pont-,* bridge.]

poncho

Pont l'É·vêque (pôɴ' lā-vĕk') *n.* A French cheese that is mild and soft-centered, made of whole milk. [After *Pont L'Évêque,* France.]
pon·to·nier (pŏn'tə-nîr') *n.* One in charge of pontoons or engaged in the construction of pontoon bridges. [Fr. *pontonnier* < *ponton,* pontoon.]
pon·toon (pŏn-to͞on') *n.* **1. a.** A flat-bottomed boat or other structure used to support a floating bridge. **b.** A floating structure serving as a dock. **2.** A float on a seaplane. [Fr. *ponton* < OFr. < Lat. *ponto,* boat bridge < *pons,* bridge.]
pontoon bridge *n.* A temporary floating bridge using pontoons for support.
po·ny (pō'nē) *n., pl.* **-nies. 1.** Any of several types or breeds of horses that are small in size when full grown. **2.** *Informal.* A racehorse. **3.** Something small for its kind. **4.** *Informal.* A word-for-word translation of a foreign language text, esp. one used secretly by students. **5.** *Chiefly Brit. Slang.* The sum of 25 pounds. *—v.* **-nied, -ny·ing, -nies.** *Slang. —tr.* To prepare (lessons) with a pony. *—intr.* To prepare lessons with a pony. ***—phrasal verb.*** **pony up.** *Slang.* To pay money owed or due. [Prob. < obs. Fr. *poulenet,* dim. of *poulain,* colt < Lat. *pullus,* foal.]

pony express
19th-century lithograph

pony car *n.* One of a group of downsized sporty American automobiles that are similar in styling, price range, and performance. [So called because several brands of such cars are named after horse breeds.]
pony express *n.* A system of mail transportation by relays of ponies, esp. the system in operation from St. Joseph, Missouri to Sacramento, California (1860–1861).
po·ny·tail (pō'nē-tāl') *n.* A hair style in which the hair is clasped in the back so as to hang down like a pony's tail.
pooch (po͞och) *n. Slang.* A dog. [Orig. unknown.]
pood (po͞od) *n.* A Russian weight equivalent to slightly over 36 pounds avoirdupois. [R. *pud* < ON *pund,* pound < OE < Lat. *pondo.*]
poo·dle (po͞od'l) *n.* Any of a breed of dogs originally developed in Europe as hunting dogs, having thick, curly hair, and ranging widely in size. [G. *Pudel,* short for *Pudelhund* : LG *pudeln,* to splash + *hund,* dog.]

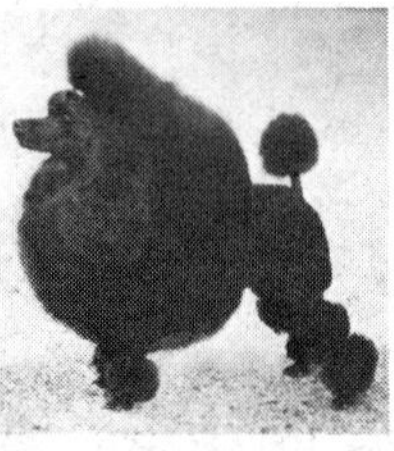

poodle

pooh (po͞o) *interj.* Used to express disdain.
Pooh-Bah (po͞o'bä') *n.* **1.** A pompous, ostentatious official, esp. one who, holding many offices, fulfills none of them. **2.** A person who holds high office. [After *Pooh-Bah,* Lord-High-Everything-Else, character in *The Mikado* by Sir William Schwenck Gilbert (1836–1911) and Sir Arthur Seymour Sullivan (1842–1900).]
pooh-pooh (po͞o'po͞o') *tr.v.* **-poohed, -pooh·ing, -poohs.** *Informal.* To express contempt or disdain for; make light of. [Redup. of POOH.]
pool[1] (po͞ol) *n.* **1.** A small body of still water; small pond. **2.** A puddle: *in a pool of blood.* **3.** A deep place in a river or stream. **4.** A swimming pool. [ME *pool* < OE *pōl.*]
pool[2] (po͞ol) *n.* **1. a.** A game of chance, resembling a lottery, in which the contestants put money into a common fund that is later paid to the winner. **b.** The fund containing the bets made in a game of chance or on a horse race. **2.** A grouping of resources for the common advantage of the participants: *a car pool.* **3. a.** A mutual fund established by a group of stockholders for speculating in or manipulating prices of securities. **b.** The persons or parties participating in such a combination. **4.** An agreement between competing business concerns to establish controls over production, market, and prices for common profit. **5.** *Sports.* A fencing match in which each member of a team fences successively with each member of an opposing team. **6.** Any of several games played on a six-pocket billiard table usually with 15 object balls and a cue ball. *—v.* **pooled, pool·ing, pools.** *—tr.* To put into a common fund for use by all: *pool our resources. —intr.* To join or form a pool. [Fr. *poule,* stakes < Lat. *pullus,* young of an animal.]
pool·room (po͞ol'ro͞om', -ro͝om') *n.* A commercial establishment or room for the playing of pool or billiards.
pool table *n.* A six-pocket billiard table on which pool is played.
poon (po͞on) *n.* Any of several trees of the genus *Calophyllum,* of southern Asia, having light, hard wood used for masts and spars. [Singhalese *pūna.*]
poop[1] (po͞op) *n. Naut.* **1.** The stern superstructure of a ship. **2.** The poop deck. [OFr. *poupe* < Lat. *puppis.*]
poop[2] (po͞op) *tr.v.* **pooped, poop·ing, poops.** *Slang.* To cause to become fatigued or exhausted; tire. ***—phrasal verb.*** **poop out. 1.** To quit because of exhaustion: *poop out of the race.* **2.** To decide not to participate, esp. at the last moment. [Orig. unknown.]
poop[3] (po͞op) *n. Slang.* Inside information. [Orig. unknown.]
poop deck *n. Naut.* The aftermost deck of a ship.
poor (po͝or) *adj.* **-er, -est. 1. a.** Having little or no wealth and few or no possessions. **b.** *Law.* Dependent on charity or public funds; destitute. **c.** Lacking in financial or other resources: *an area poor in timber and coal.* **2. a.** Lacking in mental or moral quality: *a poor spirit.* **b.** Inferior; inadequate: *a poor choice.* **3. a.** Lacking fertility: *poor soil.* **b.** Undernourished; lean. **4. a.** Lacking in value; trivial. **b.** Lacking in quantity: *poor attendance.* **5. a.** Humble: *in my poor opinion.* **b.** Pitiable: *the poor fellow.* [ME *poure* < OFr. *povre* < Lat. *pauper.*] **—poor'ness** *n.*

Synonyms: *poor, indigent, impoverished, destitute.* These adjectives describe a person without income. *Poor* is the most general and means, broadly, lacking money or means for an adequate existence. One who is *poor* is usually characteristically or continually so. *Indigent* more specifically refers to one suffering severe financial hardship. Like *poor,* it sometimes denotes a social class. *Impoverished* means abjectly poor, usually conspicuously so. The strongest of these words is *destitute,* which suggests poverty due to misfortune and particularly implies urgent need.

Usage: *Poor* is an adjective, not an adverb. In formal usage it should not be used to qualify a verb, as in *did poor* or *never played poorer. Poorly* and *more poorly* are required in such examples.

poor box *n.* A box, esp. in a church, for collecting alms.
poor boy *n.* A hero (sense 6).
poor farm *n.* A farm that houses, supports, and employs paupers at public expense.
poor·house (po͝or'hous') *n.* An establishment maintained at public expense as housing for the needy or poverty-stricken.
poo·ri also **pu·ri** (po͝or'ē) *n.* A light, flat wheat cake of Pakistan and northern India, usually fried in deep fat. [Hindi *puri* < Skt. *pūraḥ,* cake.]
poor·ish (po͝or'ĭsh) *adj.* Somewhat poor.
poor law *n.* A law or system of laws providing for public relief and support of the poor.
poor·ly (po͝or'lē) *adv.* In a poor manner. *—adj. Regional.* In poor health; ill: *feeling poorly.*
poor·mouth (po͝or'mouth', -mouth') *v.* **-mouthed, -mouth·ing, -mouths.** *—tr.* To speak ill of; badmouth. *—intr.* To claim poverty as an excuse for one's position or actions. *—n.* An exaggerated assertion of poverty.
poor white *n.* A member of an exploited, often expropriated and pauperized class of white farmers and laborers, esp. in the American South.
pop[1] (pŏp) *v.* **popped, pop·ping, pops.** *—intr.* **1.** To make a short, sharp, explosive sound. **2.** To burst open with a short, sharp, explosive sound. **3.** To move quickly or unexpectedly; appear abruptly: *popped into view.* **4.** To open wide suddenly: *Her eyes popped with disbelief.* **5.** *Baseball.* To hit a short high fly ball, esp. one that can be caught by an infielder. **6.** To shoot a pistol or other firearm. *—tr.* **1.** To cause to make a sharp bursting sound. **2.** To cause to explode with a sharp bursting sound: *popped the balloon.* **3.** To put or thrust suddenly or unexpectedly: *popped the grape into his mouth.* **4.** To fire (a pistol or other firearm). **5.** To fire at; shoot. **6.** To hit or strike: *popped him on the head.* **7.** *Baseball.* To hit (a ball) high in the air but not far. **8.** *Slang.* **a.** To take (drugs), esp. orally: *always popping pills.* **b.** To have (a drink): *popped a few beers after work.* ***—phrasal verb.*** **pop off.** *Informal* **1. a.** To leave abruptly or hurriedly. **b.** To die suddenly and unexpectedly. **2.** To speak in a burst of vehement anger. *—n.* **1.** A sudden sharp, explosive sound. **2.** A shot with a firearm. **3.** A nonalcoholic, flavored, carbonated beverage; soda pop. **4.** An alcoholic drink. **5.** *Baseball.* A pop fly. *—adv.* **1.** With a popping sound. **2.** Abruptly or unexpectedly. ***—idiom.*** **pop the question** *Informal.* To propose marriage. [ME *poppen.*]
pop[2] (pŏp) *n.* Father. [Short for *poppa,* var. of PAPA.]
pop[3] (pŏp) *adj. Informal.* **1.** Of, pertaining to, or specializing in popular music: *a pop singer.* **2.** Suggestive of pop art. [Short for POPULAR.]
pop art *n.* A form of art that depicts objects of everyday life and adapts techniques of commercial art, such as comic strips.
pop·corn (pŏp'kôrn') *n.* **1.** A variety of corn, *Zea mays everta,* having hard kernels that burst to form white, irregularly shaped puffs when heated. **2.** The edible, popped kernels of popcorn. [Contraction of *popped corn.*]
popcorn flower *n.* Any of several plants of the genus *Plagiobothrys,* of northwestern North America, having clusters of small white flowers.
pope (pōp) *n.* **1.** Often **Pope.** The bishop of Rome and head of the Roman Catholic Church, acting (by apostolic succession from Saint Peter) as vicar of Christ on earth. **2.** A priest in the Eastern Orthodox Church. **3.** A figure considered to have unquestioned authority: *the pope of surrealism.* [ME < OE *papa* < LLat., title of bishops < LGk. *pappas,* father.]
pope·dom (pōp'dəm) *n.* The office, jurisdiction, or tenure of a pope; papacy.
pop·er·y (pō'pə-rē) *n.* The doctrines, practices, and rituals of the Roman Catholic Church. Used disparagingly.
pope's nose *n.* The rump of a cooked fowl.
pop·eyed (pŏp'īd') *adj.* **1.** Having bulging eyes. **2.** Amazed; astonished: *popeyed with wonder.*
pop fly *n. Baseball.* A short high fly ball.
pop·gun (pŏp'gŭn') *n.* A toy gun that usually shoots corks and makes a popping noise.
pop·in·jay (pŏp'ĭn-jā') *n.* A vain, talkative, conceited person. [ME *papenjay,* parrot < OFr. *papegai* < Ar. *babaghā.*]
pop·ish (pō'pĭsh) *adj.* Of or pertaining to the popes or the Roman Catholic Church. Used disparagingly. **—pop'ish·ly** *adv.* **—pop'ish·ness** *n.*
pop·lar (pŏp'lər) *n.* **1. a.** Any of several fast-growing deciduous trees of the genus *Populus.* **b.** The wood of these trees.

ă pat / ā pay / âr care / ä father / b **bib** / ch **church** / d **deed** / ĕ pet / ē be / f **fife** / g **gag** / h **hat** / hw **which** / ĭ pit / ī pie / îr pier / j **judge** / k **kick** / l **lid,** needle / m **mum** / n **no,** sudden / ng thing / ŏ pot / ō toe / ô paw, for / oi noise / ou out / o͝o took / o͞o boot /

2. The tulip tree. [ME *poplere* < OFr. *poplier* < Lat. *populus.*]

pop·lin (pŏp′lĭn) *n.* A ribbed fabric of silk, rayon, wool, or cotton, used in making clothing and upholstery. [Fr. *papeline* < Ital. *papalina,* fem. of *papalino,* papal < Med. Lat. *papalis* < LLat. *papa,* pope. —see POPE.]

pop·lit·e·al (pŏp-lĭt′ē-əl, pŏp′lĭ-tē′əl) *adj.* Of or pertaining to the part of the leg behind the knee joint. [< NLat. *popliteus* < Lat. *poples,* ham of the knee.]

pop·o·ver (pŏp′ō′vər) *n.* A very light, puffy, hollow muffin made with eggs, milk, and flour.

pop·pa (pä′pə) *n.* Variant of **papa.**

pop·per (pŏp′ər) *n.* **1.** One that pops. **2.** A container or pan for making popcorn. **3.** *Slang.* An ampule of amyl nitrate used illicitly as a stimulant.

pop·pet (pŏp′ĭt) *n.* **1.** A poppet valve. **2.** *Naut.* **a.** A small wooden strip on the gunwale of a boat that forms or supports the oarlocks. **b.** One of the beams of a launching cradle supporting a ship's hull. **3.** *Chiefly Brit.* A darling. [ME *popet,* small child, ult. < Lat. *pupa,* doll.]

poppet valve *n.* An intake or exhaust valve, operated by springs and cams, that plugs and unplugs its opening by axial motion.

pop·ple[1] (pŏp′əl) *intr.v.* **-pled, -pling, -ples.** To move in a tossing, bubbling, or rippling manner, as choppy water. —*n.* **1.** Choppy water. **2.** The sound made by boiling liquid. [ME *poplen.*]

pop·ple[2] (pŏp′əl) *n. Informal.* A poplar. [ME *popul* < OE < Lat. *populus.*]

pop·py (pŏp′ē) *n., pl.* **-pies. 1.** Any of numerous plants of the genus *Papaver,* of temperate regions, having showy red, orange, or white flowers, and a milky white juice. **2.** Any of several plants similar or related to the poppy, such as the California poppy. **3.** The narcotic extracted from the opium poppy. **4.** A vivid red to reddish orange. [ME *popi* < OE *popig* < Lat. *papaver.*]

pop·py·cock (pŏp′ē-kŏk′) *n.* Senseless talk; humbug. [Du. dial. *pappekak* : *pap,* pap (< MDu. *pappe*) + *kak,* dung < *kakken,* to defecate < Lat. *cacare.*]

Pop·si·cle (pŏp′sĭ-kəl, -sĭk′əl). A trademark for colored, flavored ice molded into a rectangle with two flat sticks for handles.

pop-top (pŏp′tŏp′) *adj.* Designating or made with a tab that can be pulled up or off to make an opening: *pop-top beer cans.* **—pop′-top′** *n.*

pop·u·lace (pŏp′yə-lĭs) *n.* **1.** The common people; the masses. **2.** A population. [Fr. < Ital. *popolaccio,* rabble < *popolo,* the people < Lat. *populus.*]

pop·u·lar (pŏp′yə-lər) *adj.* **1.** Widely liked or appreciated: *a popular resort.* **2.** Liked by friends, associates, or acquaintances; sought after for company. **3.** Of, representing, or carried on by the people at large: *the popular vote.* **4.** Fit for or reflecting the taste and intelligence of the people at large: *popular entertainment.* **5.** Accepted by or prevalent among the people in general: *a popular misunderstanding.* **6.** Suited to or within the means of ordinary people: *popular prices.* **7.** Originating among the people: *popular legend.* [Lat. *popularis,* of the people < *populus,* the people.] **—pop′u·lar·ly** *adv.*

popular front *n.* A political coalition of a kind formed in European countries during the 1930's, as an alliance of democratic and revolutionary parties having common interests in the struggle against reaction and fascism.

pop·u·lar·i·ty (pŏp′yə-lăr′ĭ-tē) *n.* The quality or state of being popular, esp. the state of being widely admired, accepted, or sought after.

pop·u·lar·ize (pŏp′yə-lə-rīz′) *tr.v.* **-ized, -iz·ing, -iz·es.** To make popular, esp. to cause to become readily intelligible to the layman. **—pop′u·lar·i·za′tion** *n.* **—pop′u·lar·iz′er** *n.*

pop·u·late (pŏp′yə-lāt′) *tr.v.* **-lat·ed, -lat·ing, -lates. 1.** To supply with inhabitants, as by colonization; people. **2.** To inhabit or become inhabitants of. [Med. Lat. *populare, populat-* < Lat. *populus,* the people.]

pop·u·la·tion (pŏp′yə-lā′shən) *n.* **1. a.** All of the people inhabiting a specified area. **b.** The total number of such people. **2.** The total number of inhabitants of a particular race, class, or group in a specified area. **3.** The act or process of furnishing with inhabitants. **4.** *Ecol.* All the organisms that constitute a specific group or occur in a specified habitat. **5.** The set of individuals, items, or data from which a statistical sample is taken. [LLat. *populatio* < Lat. *populus,* the people.]

population explosion *n.* The geometrical expansion of a biological population, esp. the unchecked growth in human population resulting from a decrease in infant mortality and an increase in longevity.

Pop·u·lism (pŏp′yə-lĭz′əm) *n.* **1.** The philosophy of the Populist Party. **2. populism.** A political philosophy directed to the needs of the common people and advocating a more equitable distribution of wealth and power.

Pop·u·list (pŏp′yə-lĭst) *n.* **1.** A member or supporter of the Populist Party. **2. populist.** An advocate of populism. —*adj.* **1.** Of or pertaining to the Populist Party. **2. populist.** Of, pertaining to, or characteristic of populism or its advocates.

Populist Party *n.* An American political party that sought to represent the interests of farmers and laborers in the 1890's, advocating increased currency issue, free coinage of gold and silver, public ownership of railroads, and a graduated federal income tax.

pop·u·lous (pŏp′yə-ləs) *adj.* **1.** Containing many people or inhabitants; thickly settled. **2.** Numerous; manifold. [ME *populus* < Lat. *populosus* < *populus,* the people.] **—pop′u·lous·ly** *adv.* **—pop′u·lous·ness** *n.*

pop-up (pŏp′ŭp′) *n. Baseball.* A pop fly.

pop wine *n.* A sweet, often fruit-flavored, inexpensive wine.

por·bea·gle (pôr′bē′gəl) *n.* A shark, *Lamna nasus,* of temperate Atlantic waters. [Cornish *porghbugel.*]

por·ce·lain (pôr′sə-lĭn, pōr′-) *n.* **1.** A hard, white, translucent ceramic made by firing a pure clay and then glazing with variously colored fusible materials; china. **2.** An object made of porcelain. [OFr. *porcelaine,* cowry shell, porcelain < OItal. *porcellana* < *porcello,* little pig, vulva < Lat. *porcellus,* dim. of *porcus,* pig, vulva.] **—por′ce·la′ne·ous** (-lā′nē-əs) *adj.*

porcelain enamel *n.* A silicate glass fired on metal.

porch (pôrch, pōrch) *n.* **1.** A covered platform, usually having a separate roof, at an entrance to a house. **2.** An open or enclosed gallery or room attached to the outside of a building; verandah. **3.** *Obs.* A portico or covered walk. [ME *porche* < OFr. < Lat. *porticus,* portico < *porta,* gate.]

por·cine (pôr′sīn′) *adj.* Of or resembling swine or a pig. [Lat. *porcinus* < *porcus,* pig.]

por·cu·pine (pôr′kyə-pīn′) *n.* Any of various rodents, including members of the Old World genus *Hystrix,* the New World genus *Erethizon,* and related genera, characteristically covered with long, sharp quills or spines. [ME *porkepin* < OFr. *porc espin,* spiny pig.]

porcupine fish *n.* A spiny tropical marine fish, *Diodon hystrix,* capable of inflating itself when attacked.

pore[1] (pôr, pōr) *intr.v.* **pored, por·ing, pores. 1.** To gaze steadily or earnestly. **2.** To read or study carefully and attentively. **3.** To meditate deeply; ponder. [ME *pouren.*]

pore[2] (pôr, pōr) *n.* **1.** A minute orifice, such as one in the skin of an animal, serving as an outlet for perspiration, or in a plant leaf or stem, serving as a means of absorption and transpiration. **2.** A minute surface opening or passageway, as in a rock. [ME < OFr. < Lat. *porus* < Gk. *poros.*]

pore fungus *n.* A fungus having a crustlike fruiting body with a pitted or porous surface.

por·gy (pôr′gē) *n., pl.* **porgy** or **-gies. 1.** Any of various deep-bodied marine fishes of the family Sparidae. **2.** Any of several fishes similar or related to the porgy. [Sp. *pargo* < Lat. *pagrus,* a kind of fish < Gk. *phagros.*]

po·rif·er·an (pə-rĭf′ər-ən) *n.* Any of various animals of the phylum Porifera; sponge. [NLat. *Porifera,* phylum name : Lat. *porus,* pore (< Gk. *poros*) + Lat. *ferre,* to bear.] **—po·rif′er·al, po·rif′er·an** *adj.*

po·rif·er·ous (pə-rĭf′ər-əs) *adj.* **1.** Having pores. **2.** *Zool.* Of or relating to the phylum Porifera, which includes the sponges. [Lat. *porus,* pore (< Gk. *poros*) + -FEROUS.]

pork (pôrk, pōrk) *n.* **1.** The flesh of a pig or hog used as food. **2.** *Slang.* Government funds, appointments, or other favors acquired by a representative for his constituency as political patronage. [ME < OFr. *porc,* pig < Lat. *porcus.*]

pork barrel *n. Slang.* A government project or appropriation benefiting a specific locale and a legislator's constituents.

pork·er (pôr′kər, pōr′-) *n.* A fattened young pig.

pork·pie also **pork pie** (pôrk′pī′, pōrk′-) *n.* **1.** A thick-crusted pie filled with chopped pork. **2.** A man's hat having a low, flat crown and a snap brim.

por·ky (pôr′kē) *n., pl.* **-kies.** *Informal.* A porcupine. [Shortening and alteration of PORCUPINE.]

por·no (pôr′nō) also **porn** (pôrn) *Slang. n.* **1.** Pornography. **2.** Pornographic material, such as a picture, movie, or book.

por·nog·ra·phy (pôr-nŏg′rə-fē) *n.* The presentation of sexually explicit behavior, as in a photograph, intended to arouse sexual excitement. [< Gk. *pornographos,* writing about prostitutes : *pornē,* prostitute + *graphein,* to write.] **—por·nog′ra·pher** *n.* **—por′no·graph′ic** (pôr′nə-grăf′ĭk) *adj.*

po·ro·mer·ic (pôr′ə-mĕr′ĭk, pōr′-) *n.* Any of several tough, porous leather substitutes. [Gk. *poros,* pore + (POLY)-MERIC.]

po·ros·i·ty (pə-rŏs′ĭ-tē, pô-) *n., pl.* **-ties. 1.** The state or property of being porous. **2.** A structure or part that is porous. [Med. Lat. *porositas* < *porosus,* porous.]

po·rous (pôr′əs, pōr′-) *adj.* **1.** Having or full of pores. **2.** Admitting the passage of gas or liquid through pores or interstices. [ME < Med. Lat. *porosus* < Lat. *porus,* pore < Gk. *poros.*] **—po′rous·ly** *adv.* **—po′rous·ness** *n.*

por·phyr·i·a (pôr-fîr′ē-ə) *n.* A hereditary pathological disorder of porphyrin metabolism characterized by photosensitivity and the excretion of porphyrins in the urine. [NLat. < PORPHYRIN.]

por·phy·rin (pôr′fə-rĭn) *n.* Any of various nitrogen-containing organic compounds occurring universally in protoplasm and providing the foundation structure for hemoglobin, chlorophyll, and certain enzymes. [< Gk. *porphura,* purple.]

por·phy·rit·ic (pôr′fə-rĭt′ĭk) also **por·phy·rit·i·cal** (-ĭ-kəl) *adj.* **1.** Of or containing porphyry. **2.** Containing relatively large isolated crystals in a mass of fine texture.

por·phy·roid (pôr′fə-roid′) *n.* Metamorphic rock having porphyritic texture.

poppy

porcelain
18th-century English figurine

porcupine

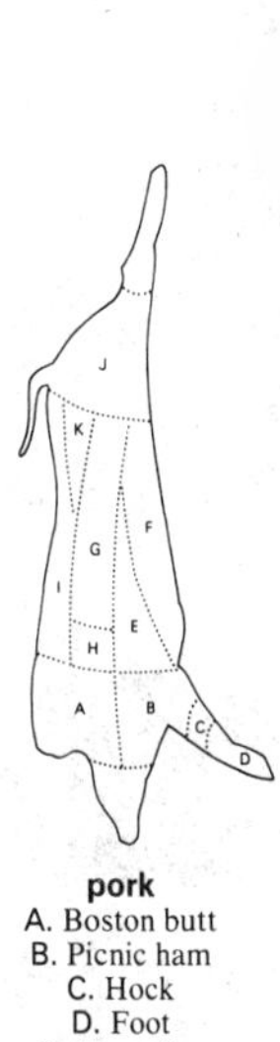

pork
A. Boston butt
B. Picnic ham
C. Hock
D. Foot
E. Spareribs
F. Bacon
G. Center loin
H. Rib chops
I. Fatback for salt pork
J. Ham
K. Tenderloin

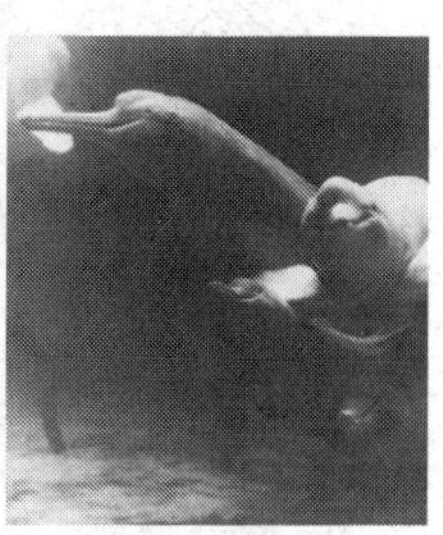
porpoise

porringer
18th-century American

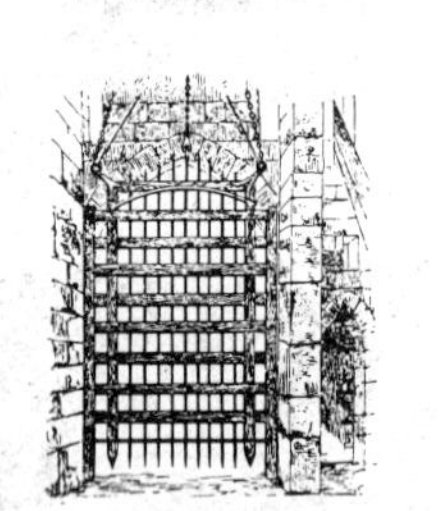
portcullis

porthole

por·phy·ry (pôr′fə-rē) *n., pl.* **-ries.** Rock containing relatively large conspicuous crystals, esp. feldspar, in a fine-grained igneous matrix. [ME *porfurie* < Med. Lat. *porphyrium* < Lat. *porphyrites* < Gk. *porphuritēs* < *porphura,* purple.]

por·poise (pôr′pəs) *n., pl.* **porpoise** or **-pois·es. 1.** Any of several gregarious aquatic mammals of the genus *Phocaena* and related genera, of oceanic waters, characteristically having a blunt snout and a triangular dorsal fin. **2.** Any of several aquatic mammals related to the porpoise, such as the dolphin. [ME *porpoys* < OFr. *porpois* < Med. Lat. *porcopiscis* : Lat. *porcus,* pig + Lat. *piscis,* fish.]

por·ridge (pôr′ĭj, pŏr′-) *n.* Boiled cereal, such as oatmeal, usually eaten with milk. [Alteration of POTTAGE.]

por·rin·ger (pôr′ĭn-jər, pŏr′-) *n.* A shallow cup or bowl with a handle. [Alteration of ME *potinger* < OFr. *potager* < *potage,* soup < *pot,* pot.]

port[1] (pôrt, pōrt) *n.* **1. a.** A town having a harbor for ships taking on or discharging cargo. **b.** A place on a waterway that provides a harbor for a nearby city. **c.** The harbor or waterfront district of a city. **2.** A place of anchorage or shelter; haven. **3.** A port of entry. **4.** *Computer Sci.* An entrance to or exit for a data network. [ME < OE < Lat. *portus.*]

port[2] (pôrt, pōrt) *n.* The left-hand side of a ship or aircraft facing forward. *—adj.* Of, pertaining to, or on the port. *—tr.v.* **port·ed, port·ing, ports.** To turn or shift (the helm of a vessel) to the left. [Orig. unknown.]

port[3] (pôrt, pōrt) *n.* **1.** *Naut.* **a.** A porthole. **b.** A covering for this. **2.** An opening, as in a cylinder or valve face, for the passage of steam or fluid. **3.** A hole in an armored vehicle or fortified structure through which weapons may be fired. **4.** *Scot.* A gateway or portal, as to a town. [ME < OFr. *porte,* gate < Lat. *porta.*]

port[4] (pôrt, pōrt) *n.* A rich sweet fortified wine. [After *Oporto,* Portugal.]

port[5] (pôrt, pōrt) *tr.v.* **port·ed, port·ing, ports.** To carry (a weapon) diagonally across the body, with the muzzle or blade near the left shoulder. *—n.* **1.** The position of a rifle or other weapon when ported. **2.** The manner in which a person carries himself; bearing. [OFr. *porter,* to carry < Lat. *portare.*]

port·a·ble (pôr′tə-bəl, pōr′-) *adj.* **1.** Capable of being carried. **2.** Easily carried or moved. **3.** *Archaic.* Endurable; supportable; bearable. *—n.* Something that is portable, such as a light typewriter. [ME < OFr. < LLat. *portabilis* < Lat. *portare,* to carry.] **—port′a·bil′i·ty, port′a·ble·ness** *n.* **—port′a·bly** *adv.*

port·age (pôr′tĭj, pōr′-, pôr-täzh′) *n.* **1.** The carrying of boats and supplies overland between two waterways. **2.** A track or route used for portage. *—v.* **-aged, -ag·ing, -ag·es.** *—tr.* To transport by portage; pack: *"They had illegally portaged back to Canada a small fortune in beaver skins"* (Irving Stone). *—intr.* To make a portage. [ME < OFr. < *porter,* to carry < Lat. *portare.*]

por·tal (pôr′tl, pōr′-) *n.* **1.** A doorway, entrance, or gate, esp. one that is large and imposing. **2.** An entrance or means of entrance: *a portal of knowledge.* **3.** The portal vein. *—adj.* Of or pertaining to the portal vein. [ME < OFr. < Med. Lat. *portale,* city gate < *portalis,* of a gate < Lat. *porta,* gate.]

por·tal-to-por·tal (pôr′tl-tə-pôr′tl, pōr′tl-tə-pōr′tl) *adj.* Of or based on the time spent by a worker on the employer's property, from the moment of arrival to that of departure: *portal-to-portal pay.*

portal vein *n. Anat.* A vein that conducts blood from the digestive organs, spleen, pancreas, and gall bladder to the liver.

por·ta·men·to (pôr′tə-mĕn′tō, pōr′-) *n., pl.* **-ti** (-tē). A smooth, uninterrupted glide in passing from one tone to another, esp. with the voice or a bowed stringed instrument. [Ital. < *portare,* to carry < Lat.]

por·ta·tive (pôr′tə-tĭv, pōr′-) *adj.* **1.** Portable. **2.** Capable of carrying. [ME *portatif* < OFr. < Lat. *portare,* to carry.]

port·cul·lis (pôrt-kŭl′ĭs, pōrt-) *n.* A sliding grille of iron or wood suspended in the gateway of a fortified place in such a way that it can be quickly lowered in case of attack. [ME *portculis* < OFr. *porte coleïce,* sliding door.]

Port du Sa·lut (pôr′ dü să-lo͞o′) *n.* Variant of **Port Salut.**

Porte (pôrt, pōrt) *n.* The government of the Ottoman Empire. [Fr., short for *la Sublime Porte,* the High Gate.]

porte-co·chère or **porte-co·chere** (pôrt′kō-shâr′, pōrt′-) *n.* **1.** A carriage entrance leading into the courtyard of a town house. **2.** A porch roof projecting over a driveway at the entrance to a building, providing shelter for those getting in and out of vehicles. [Fr. *porte cochère,* coach door.]

por·tend (pôr-tĕnd′, pōr-) *tr.v.* **-tend·ed, -tend·ing, -tends. 1.** To serve as an omen or warning of; presage. **2.** To indicate or suggest: *economic declines that portend trouble.* [ME *portenden* < Lat. *portendere.*]

por·tent (pôr′tĕnt′, pōr′-) *n.* **1.** An indication of something momentous or calamitous about to occur; omen. **2.** Prophetic or threatening significance. **3.** Something amazing or marvelous; prodigy. [Lat. *portentum* < *portendere,* to portend.]

por·ten·tous (pôr-tĕn′təs, pōr-) *adj.* **1.** Of the nature of or constituting a portent; foreboding. **2.** Full of unspecifiable significance; exciting wonder and awe. **3.** Marked by pompousness; pretentiously weighty. **—por·ten′tous·ly** *adv.* **—por·ten′tous·ness** *n.*

por·ter[1] (pôr′tər, pōr′-) *n.* **1.** A person employed to carry travelers' luggage. **2.** A railroad employee who waits on passengers in a sleeping car or parlor car. [ME *portour* < OFr. *porteur* < LLat. *portator* < Lat. *portare,* to carry.]

por·ter[2] (pôr′tər, pōr′-) *n. Chiefly Brit.* A gatekeeper; doorman. [ME < OFr. *portier* < LLat. *portarius* < Lat. *porta,* gate.]

por·ter[3] (pôr′tər, pōr′-) *n.* A dark beer resembling light stout, made from malt browned or charred by drying at a high temperature. [Short for *porter's beer.*]

por·ter·age (pôr′tər-ĭj, pōr′-) *n.* **1.** The carrying of parcels or goods as done by porters. **2.** The charge for porterage.

por·ter·ess (pôr′tər-ĭs, pōr′-) *n.* Variant of **portress.**

por·ter·house (pôr′tər-hous′, pōr′-) *n.* **1.** In 19th-century America, an alehouse or chophouse. **2.** A cut of beef taken from the thick end of the short loin, having a T-bone and a sizable piece of tenderloin.

porterhouse steak *n.* Porterhouse (sense 2).

port·fo·li·o (pôrt-fō′lē-ō′, pōrt-) *n., pl.* **-os. 1. a.** A portable case for holding loose papers, photographs, or drawings. **b.** The materials collected in such a case, esp. when representative of a person's work: *a photographer's portfolio.* **2.** The office or post of a cabinet member or minister of state. **3.** An itemized list of the investments, securities, and commercial paper owned by a bank, investment organization, or other investor. [Ital. *portafoglio* : *portare,* to carry (< Lat.) + *foglio,* sheet < Lat. *folium,* leaf.]

port·hole (pôrt′hōl′, pōrt′-) *n.* **1.** A small, usually circular window in a ship's side. **2.** An embrasure.

por·ti·co (pôr′tĭ-kō′, pōr′-) *n., pl.* **-coes** or **-cos.** A porch or walkway with a roof supported by columns, often leading to the entrance of a building. [Ital. < Lat. *porticus* < *porta,* gate.] **—por′ti·coed′** *adj.*

por·tière or **por·tiere** (pôr-tyâr′, pōr-) *n.* A heavy curtain hung across a doorway. [Fr. < OFr., fem. of *portier,* porter < LLat. *portarius* < Lat. *porta,* gate.]

por·tion (pôr′shən, pōr′-) *n.* **1.** A section or quantity within a larger thing; a part of a whole. **2.** A part separated from a whole. **3.** A part that is allotted to a person or group, as: **a.** A helping of food. **b.** The part of an estate received by an heir. **c.** A woman's dowry. **4.** A person's lot or fate. *—tr.v.* **-tioned, -tion·ing, -tions. 1.** To divide into parts or shares for distribution; parcel. **2.** To provide with a share, inheritance, or dowry. [ME < OFr. < Lat. *portio.*] **—por′tion·a·ble** *adj.* **—por′tion·er** *n.* **—por′tion·less** *adj.*

Port·land cement (pôrt′lənd, pōrt′-) *n.* A hydraulic cement made by heating a mixture of limestone and clay, containing oxides of calcium, aluminum, iron, and silicon, in a kiln and pulverizing the resultant clinker. [After *Portland,* England, from its resemblance to limestone quarried there.]

port·ly (pôrt′lē, pōrt′-) *adj.* **-li·er, -li·est. 1.** Comfortably stout; corpulent. **2.** *Archaic.* Stately; majestic; imposing. [< PORT[5].] **—port′li·ness** *n.*

port·man·teau (pôrt-măn′tō, pōrt-, pôrt′măn-tō′, pōrt′-) *n., pl.* **-teaus** or **-teaux** (-tōz). *Chiefly Brit.* A large leather suitcase that opens into two hinged compartments. [Fr. *portemanteau* < OFr. : *porter,* to carry (< Lat. *portare*) + *manteau,* cloak < Lat. *mantellum.*]

portmanteau word *n.* A word formed by merging the sounds and meanings of two different words; for example, *slithy,* from *lithe* and *slimy; chortle,* from *chuckle* and *snort.*

port of call *n.* A port where ships dock in the course of voyages to load or unload cargo, obtain supplies, or undergo repairs.

port of entry *n.* A place where travelers or goods may enter or leave a country under official supervision.

por·trait (pôr′trĭt, -trāt′, pōr′-) *n.* **1.** A painting, photograph, or other likeness of a person, esp. one showing the face. **2.** A verbal picture or description, esp. of a person. [Fr. < OFr. < *portraire,* to portray.]

por·trait·ist (pôr′trə-tĭst, pōr-) *n.* A person who makes portraits, esp. a painter or photographer.

por·trai·ture (pôr′trĭ-cho͝or′, pōr′-) *n.* **1.** The practice or art of making portraits. **2.** A portrait. **3.** Portraits collectively.

por·tray (pôr-trā′, pōr-) *tr.v.* **-trayed, -tray·ing, -trays. 1.** To depict or represent pictorially; make a picture of. **2.** To depict or describe in words. **3.** To represent dramatically, as on the stage. [ME *portraien* < OFr. *portraire* < Lat. *protrahere,* to reveal : *pro-,* forth + *trahere,* to draw.] **—por·tray′a·ble** *adj.* **—por·tray′er** *n.*

por·tray·al (pôr-trā′əl, pōr-) *n.* **1.** The act or process of depicting or portraying. **2.** A representation or description.

por·tress (pôr′trĭs, pōr′-) also **por·ter·ess** (pôr′tər-ĭs, pōr′-) *n.* A female doorkeeper or porter, esp. in a convent.

Port Sa·lut (pôr′ să-lo͞o′) also **Port du Sa·lut** (pôr′ dü să-lo͞o′) *n.* A semihard fermented cheese, made originally by Trappist monks in France. [After *Port du Salut,* Trappist abbey in France.]

Por·tu·guese (pôr′chə-gēz′, -gēs′, pōr′-) *adj.* Of or pertaining to Portugal, its people, or their language. *—n., pl.* **Portuguese. 1. a.** A native or inhabitant of Portugal. **b.** A person of Portuguese descent. **2.** The Romance language of Portugal and Brazil.

Portuguese man-of-war *n.* A complex colonial organism

of the genus *Physalia,* of warm seas, having a bluish, bladderlike float from which are suspended numerous long stinging tentacles capable of inflicting severe injury.

por·tu·lac·a (pôr'chə-lăk'ə, pōr'-) *n.* Any of various plants of the genus *Portulaca,* having fleshy stems and leaves, esp. *P. grandiflora,* cultivated for its showy flowers that open only in sunlight. [NLat. *Portulaca,* genus name < Lat. *portulaca,* purslane < *portula,* dim. of *porta,* gate.]

pose[1] (pōz) *v.* **posed, pos·ing, pos·es.** —*intr.* **1.** To assume or hold a particular position or posture, as in sitting for a portrait. **2.** To affect a particular mental attitude. **3.** To represent oneself falsely; pretend to be other than what one is. —*tr.* **1.** To place (a model, for example) in a specific position. **2.** To present or put forward: *pose a threat.* —*n.* **1.** A bodily attitude or position, esp. one assumed for an artist or photographer. **2.** An affected attitude of mind or body. [ME *posen* < OFr. *poser* < LLat. *pausare,* to rest < Lat. *pausa,* pause. —see PAUSE.]

pose[2] (pōz) *tr.v.* **posed, pos·ing, pos·es.** To puzzle or confuse with a difficult question or problem. [ME *apposen,* alteration of *opposen* < OFr. *opposer,* to oppose. —see OPPOSE.]

Po·sei·don (pō-sīd'n) *n. Gk. Myth.* The god of the waters, earthquakes, and horses, and brother of Zeus. [Lat. < Gk. *Poseidōn.*]

pos·er[1] (pō'zər) *n.* One who poses.

pos·er[2] (pō'zər) *n.* A baffling question or problem.

po·seur (pō-zœr') *n.* A person who affects a particular attitude, character, or manner to impress others. [Fr. < OFr. *poser,* to pose. —see POSE[1].]

posh (pŏsh) *adj.* Smart and fashionable. [Orig. unknown.]

pos·i·grade (pŏz'ĭ-grād') *adj.* Of, relating to, or being an auxiliary rocket on a spacecraft that provides additional thrust in the direction of the spacecraft's motion. [POSI(TIVE) + (RETRO)GRADE.]

pos·it (pŏz'ĭt) *tr.v.* **-it·ed, -it·ing, -its. 1.** To place in position. **2.** To put forward as a fact or truth; postulate. [< Lat. *positus,* p.part. of *ponere,* to place.]

po·si·tion (pə-zĭsh'ən) *n.* **1.** A place or location. **2.** The right or appropriate place: *The guns were in position.* **3. a.** The way in which something or someone is placed: *in a conspicuous position.* **b.** The arrangement of bodily parts; posture: *a standing position.* **4.** An advantageous place or location: *jockeys maneuvering for position.* **5.** A situation as it relates to the surrounding circumstances: *in a position to bargain.* **6.** A point of view or attitude on a certain question. **7.** Social standing or status; rank. **8.** A post of employment; job. **9.** *Sports.* The area for which a particular player is responsible. **10. a.** The act or process of positing. **b.** The principle or proposition posited. —*tr.v.* **-tioned, -tion·ing, -tions.** To place in proper position. [OFr. < Lat. *positio* < *ponere,* to place.] —**po·si'tion·al** *adj.* —**po·si'tion·er** *n.*

position paper *n.* **1.** A detailed policy report that usually explains, justifies, or recommends a particular course of action. **2.** An aide-mémoire.

pos·i·tive (pŏz'ĭ-tĭv) *adj.* **1.** Characterized by or displaying certainty, acceptance, or affirmation: *a positive answer.* **2.** Measured or moving in a direction of increase, progress, or forward motion. **3.** Explicitly or openly expressed or laid down: *a positive demand.* **4.** Admitting of no doubt; irrefutable. **5. a.** Determined or settled in opinion or assertion; confident: *a positive manner.* **b.** Overconfident; dogmatic. **6.** Formally or arbitrarily determined; prescribed. **7.** Concerned with practical rather than theoretical matters. **8.** Composed of or characterized by the presence of particular qualities or attributes; real. **9.** *Philos.* Of or pertaining to positivism. **10.** *Informal.* Utter; absolute: *a positive darling.* **11.** *Math.* Pertaining to or designating: **a.** A quantity greater than zero. **b.** The sign (+). **c.** A quantity, number, angle, or direction opposite to another designated as negative. **12.** *Physics.* Pertaining to or designating electric charge of a sign opposite to that of an electron. **13.** *Med.* Indicating the presence of a particular disease, condition, or organism: *a positive Wassermann test.* **14.** *Biol.* Indicating or characterized by response or motion toward the source of a stimulus: *positive tropism.* **15.** Having the areas of light and dark in their original and normal relationship, as in a photographic print made from a negative. **16.** *Gram.* Of, pertaining to, or denoting the simple uncompared degree of an adjective or adverb, as opposed to either the comparative or superlative. **17.** Driven by or generating power directly through intermediate machine parts having little or no play: *positive drive.* —*n.* **1.** Something positive. **2.** *Philos.* Something perceptible to the senses. **3.** *Math.* A quantity greater than zero. **4.** *Physics.* A positive electric charge. **5.** A photographic image in which the lights and darks appear as they do in nature. **6.** *Gram.* **a.** The uncompared degree of an adjective or adverb. **b.** A word in this degree. [ME < OFr. *positif* < Lat. *positivus,* formally laid down < *ponere,* to place.] —**pos'i·tive·ly** *adv.* —**pos'i·tive·ness** *n.*

positive prescription *n. Law.* Prescription (sense 4.a.).

pos·i·tiv·ism (pŏz'ĭ-tĭ-vĭz'əm) *n.* **1. a.** A philosophical doctrine contending that sense perceptions are the only admissible basis of human knowledge and precise thought. **b.** The application of this doctrine in logic, epistemology, and ethics. **2.** The system of Auguste Comte designed to supersede theology and metaphysics, and depending on a hierarchy of the sciences, beginning with mathematics and culminating in sociology. **3.** The state or quality of being positive. —**pos'i·tiv·ist** *n.* —**pos'i·tiv·is'tic** *adj.*

pos·i·tron (pŏz'ĭ-trŏn') *n.* The antiparticle of the electron. [POSI(TIVE) + (ELEC)TRON.]

pos·i·tro·ni·um (pŏz'ĭ-trō'nē-əm) *n.* A short-lived association of an electron and a positron bound together in a configuration resembling the hydrogen atom. [NLat. < POSITRON.]

pos·se (pŏs'ē) *n.* **1.** A group of people summoned by a sheriff to aid in law enforcement. **2.** A search party. [Short for Med. Lat. *posse comitatus,* power of the county.]

pos·sess (pə-zĕs') *tr.v.* **-sessed, -sess·ing, -sess·es. 1.** To have as property; own. **2.** To have as a quality, characteristic, or other attribute: *possessed great tact.* **3.** To acquire mastery of or have knowledge of: *possess valuable data.* **4.** To gain or exert influence or control over; dominate: *Fury possessed him.* **5.** To control or maintain (one's nature) in a particular condition: *He possessed his temper despite the insult.* **6.** To cause to own, hold, or master something, such as property or knowledge: *possessed herself of the unclaimed goods.* **7.** To cause to be influenced or controlled, as by an idea or emotion: *The thought of getting rich possessed her.* **8.** *Obs.* To gain or seize. [ME *possessen* < OFr. *possesser* < Lat. *possidere* : *potis,* capable + *sedere,* to sit.] —**pos·ses'sor** *n.*

pos·sessed (pə-zĕst') *adj.* **1.** Having as a possession. **2.** Controlled by or as if by a spirit or other force; obsessed. **3.** Calm; collected: *possessed in time of trial.*

pos·ses·sion (pə-zĕsh'ən) *n.* **1.** The act or fact of possessing. **2.** The state of being possessed. **3.** Something that is owned or possessed. **4. possessions.** Wealth or property. **5.** *Law.* Actual holding or occupancy with or without rightful ownership. **6.** A territory subject to foreign control. **7.** Self-control. **8.** The state of being dominated by or as if by evil spirits or by an obsession.

pos·ses·sive (pə-zĕs'ĭv) *adj.* **1.** Of or pertaining to ownership or possession. **2.** Having or manifesting a desire to control or dominate: *a possessive father.* **3.** *Gram.* Of, pertaining to, or designating a noun or pronoun case that indicates possession. —*n. Gram.* **1.** The possessive case. **2.** A possessive form or construction. —**pos·ses'sive·ly** *adv.* —**pos·ses'sive·ness** *n.*

possessive adjective *n. Gram.* A pronominal adjective expressing possession.

possessive pronoun *n. Gram.* One of several pronouns denoting possession and capable of substituting for noun phrases.

pos·ses·so·ry (pə-zĕs'ə-rē) *adj.* **1.** Of, pertaining to, or having possession. **2.** *Law.* Depending on or arising from possession: *possessory interest.*

pos·set (pŏs'ĭt) *n.* A spiced drink of hot sweetened milk curdled with wine or ale. [ME *poshet.*]

pos·si·bil·i·ty (pŏs'ə-bĭl'ĭ-tē) *n., pl.* **-ties. 1.** The fact or state of being possible. **2.** Something possible. **3. possibilities.** Potentially favorable results: *The idea has tremendous possibilities.*

pos·si·ble (pŏs'ə-bəl) *adj.* **1.** Capable of happening, existing, or being true without contradicting proven facts, laws, or circumstances. **2.** Capable of occurring or being done without offense to character, nature, or custom. **3.** Capable of favorable development; potential: *a possible site for the new capital.* **4.** Of uncertain likelihood. [ME < OFr. < Lat. *possibilis* < *posse,* to be able.] —**pos'si·bly** *adv.*

Synonyms: *possible, practical, workable,, practicable, feasible, viable.* These adjectives refer to the likelihood that, or ease with which, something can be done. *Possible* indicates that something is realizable as an end. It can imply either a moderate degree of probability or the barest chance within the limits of circumstances: *admittedly possible; not at all possible. Practical* emphasizes the prudence, efficiency, or economy of an act, solution, or agent: *a practical way to do it; a practical person. Workable* is used of proposed ideas or plans, the success of which is likely if properly managed: *a workable production schedule. Practicable,* meaning fitted for actual use or application, is often used to describe projects where an initial forecast is important: *hardly practicable at this time.* Something is *feasible* if it is clearly possible and applicable; the word often connotes closer scrutiny and more guarded approval than *workable* or *practicable. Viable,* in current usage, has come to denote likelihood of continued effectiveness or success; it tends to be used comparatively: *a more viable method of negotiating a settlement.*

pos·sum (pŏs'əm) *n.* Variant of **opossum.**

possum haw *n.* **1.** A holly, *Ilex decidua,* of the southeastern United States, having bright-red fruit. **2.** A shrub, *Viburnum nudum,* of the eastern United States, having white flowers and bluish-black fruit.

post[1] (pōst) *n.* **1.** A stake of wood or other material set upright into the ground to serve as a marker or support. **2.** A goal post. **3.** The starting gate at a racetrack. —*tr.v.* **post·ed, post·ing, posts. 1. a.** To fasten up (an announcement) in a place of public view. **b.** To cover (a wall, for example) with posters. **2.** To announce by or as if by posters: *post banns.* **3.** To put up signs on (property) warning against trespass-

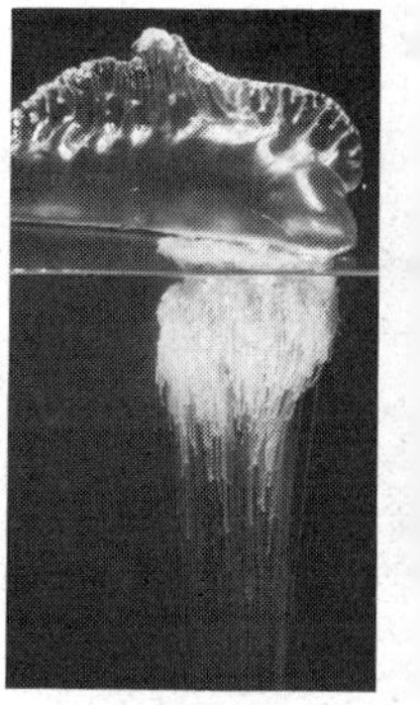

Portuguese man-of-war

portulaca

Poseidon
4th-century B.C. Greek vase painting

ing. **4.** To denounce publicly: *post a man as a thief.* **5.** To publish (a name) on a list. [ME < OE < Lat. *postis.*]

post[2] (pōst) *n.* **1. a.** A military base where troops are stationed. **b.** The grounds and buildings of a military base. **2.** A local organization of military veterans. **3.** Either of two bugle calls in the British Army, sounded in the evening as a signal to retire to quarters. **4.** An assigned position or station, as of a guard or sentry. **5.** A position of employment, esp. an appointed public office. **6.** A place to which someone is assigned for duty. **7.** A trading post. —*tr.v.* **post·ed, post·ing, posts. 1.** To assign to a specific position or station: *post a sentry.* **2.** To appoint to a naval or military command. **3.** To put forward; present: *post bail.* [Fr. *poste* < OItal. *posto* < VLat. **postum* < Lat. *positum,* p.part. of *ponere,* to place.]

postage stamp
U.S. two-cent stamp issued in 1928 to commemorate Washington's winter at Valley Forge

post[3] (pōst) *n.* **1. a.** A delivery of mail. **b.** The mail delivered. **2. a.** One of a series of relay stations along a fixed route, furnishing fresh riders and horses for the delivery of mail on horseback. **b.** A rider on such a mail route; courier. **3.** *Chiefly Brit.* **a.** A governmental system for transporting and delivering the mail. **b.** A post office. —*v.* **post·ed, post·ing, posts.** —*intr.* **1.** To travel in stages or relays. **2.** To travel quickly; speed or hasten. **3.** To bob up and down in the saddle in rhythm with a horse's trotting gait. —*tr.* **1.** To send by mail in a system of relays on horseback. **2.** To mail (a letter). **3.** To inform of the latest news. **4. a.** To transfer (an item) to a ledger in bookkeeping. **b.** To make the necessary entries in (a ledger). **5.** *Computer Sci.* To enter a unit of information on a record or into a section of computer storage. —*adv.* **1.** By post horse. **2.** By mail. **3.** With great speed; rapidly. [Fr. *poste* < Ital. *posta* < Lat. *posita,* p.part. of *ponere,* to place.]

poster[1]

post– *pref.* **1.** After; later: *postmillenial.* **2.** Behind; posterior to: *postaxial.* [Lat. < *post,* behind, after.]

post·age (pō′stĭj) *n.* The charge for mailing an item.

postage meter *n.* A machine used in bulk mailing to print the correct amount of postage on each piece of mail.

postage stamp *n.* A small engraved, usually adhesive label issued by a government and sold in various denominations to be affixed to items of mail as evidence of the payment of postage.

post·al (pō′stəl) *adj.* Of or pertaining to the post office or mail service. —*n.* A postal card. **—post′al·ly** *adv.*

postal card *n.* A card printed with a postage stamp, issued by a government and sold by a governmental agency, for sending messages at low rates.

postal order *n. Chiefly Brit.* A money order.

postal service *n.* Post office (sense 1).

post·ax·i·al (pōst-ăk′sē-əl) *adj.* Located behind an axis of the body, esp. posterior to the fibula of the leg or the ulna of the arm. **—post·ax′i·al·ly** *adv.*

post-bel·lum (pōst-bĕl′əm) *adj.* Happening after a war, esp. the American Civil War. [Lat. *post,* after + Lat. *bellum,* war.]

post·box also **post box** (pōst′bŏks′) *n.* A mailbox.

post card also **post·card** (pōst′kärd′) *n.* **1.** An unofficial card, usually bearing a picture on one side, with space for an address, postage stamp, and short message. **2.** A postal card.

post·ca·va (pōst-kā′və) *n.* The inferior vena cava. **—post·ca′val** *adj.*

post chaise *n.* A closed, four-wheeled, horse-drawn carriage, formerly used to transport mail and passengers.

post·clas·si·cal (pōst-klăs′ĭ-kəl) *adj.* Of, relating to, or being a time following a classical period, as in art or literature.

post·co·lo·ni·al (pōst′kə-lō′nē-əl) *adj.* Of, relating to, or being the time following the establishment of independence in a colony: *postcolonial economics.*

post·date (pōst-dāt′) *tr.v.* **-dat·ed, -dat·ing, -dates. 1.** To put a date on (a check, for example) that is later than the actual date. **2.** To occur later than; follow in time.

post·di·lu·vi·an (pōst′dĭ-lo͞o′vē-ən) also **post·di·lu·vi·al** (-əl) *adj.* Existing or occurring after the biblical Flood. —*n.* A person or thing living after the biblical Flood. [POST + Lat. *diluvium,* flood. —see DILUVIAL.]

post·doc·tor·al (pōst-dŏk′tər-əl) also **post·doc·tor·ate** (-ĭt) *adj.* Of, pertaining to, or engaged in academic study beyond the level of a doctor's degree.

postimpressionism
Detail from "The Pond" by Paul Cézanne

post·er[1] (pō′stər) *n.* **1.** A large printed placard, bill, or announcement, often illustrated, posted to advertise or publicize something. **2.** One who posts bills or notices.

post·er[2] (pō′stər) *n. Archaic.* One who traveled post.

poster color *n.* Tempera (sense 1).

poste res·tante (pōst′ rĕ-stänt′) *n.* A notation written on a letter indicating that the letter should be held at the post office until claimed by the addressee. [Fr. : *poste,* mail + *restante,* pr.part. of *rester,* to remain.]

pos·te·ri·or (pŏ-stîr′ē-ər, pō-) *adj.* **1.** Located behind a part or toward the rear of a structure. **2.** Pertaining to the caudal end of the body in an animal or the dorsal side in man. **3.** *Bot.* Next to or nearest the main stem or axis. **4.** Coming after in order; following. **5.** Following in time; subsequent. —*n.* Often **posteriors.** The buttocks. [Lat., comp. of *posterus,* coming after < *post,* after.] **—pos·te′ri·or·ly** *adv.*

pos·te·ri·or·i·ty (pŏ-stîr′ē-ôr′ĭ-tē, -ŏr′-, pō-) *n.* The condition of being posterior in location or time.

pos·ter·i·ty (pŏ-stĕr′ĭ-tē) *n.* **1.** Future generations. **2.** All of a person's descendants. [ME *posterite* < OFr. < Lat. *posteritas* < *posterus,* coming after < *post,* after.]

pos·tern (pō′stərn, pŏs′tərn) *n.* A small rear gate, esp. one in a fort or castle. —*adj.* Situated in back or at the side. [ME *posterne* < OFr., alteration of *posterle* < LLat. *posterula,* dim. of Lat. *posterus,* behind < *post,* after.]

poster paint *n.* Tempera (sense 1).

Post Exchange. A trademark for a store on a military base that sells goods to military personnel and their families or to authorized civilians.

post·ex·il·i·an (pōst′ĕg-zĭl′ē-ən, -zĭl′yən, -ĕk-sĭl′ē-ən, -sĭl′yən) also **post·ex·il·ic** (-ĕg-zĭl′ĭk, -ĕk-sĭl′ĭk) *adj.* Of or pertaining to the period of Jewish history following the Babylonian captivity (after 586 B.C.).

post·fix (pōst-fĭks′) *tr.v.* **-fixed, -fix·ing, -fix·es.** To suffix. —*n.* (pōst′fĭks′). A suffix. **—post·fix′al, post·fix′i·al** *adj.*

post-free (pōst′frē′) *adj. Chiefly Brit.* Postpaid.

post·gan·gli·on·ic (pōst′găng-glē-ŏn′ĭk) *adj.* Located posterior or distal to a ganglion.

post·gla·cial (pōst-glā′shəl) *adj.* Pertaining to or occurring during the time following a glacial period.

post·grad·u·ate (pōst-grăj′o͞o-ĭt, -āt′) *adj.* Of, pertaining to, or pursuing advanced study after graduation from high school or college. —*n.* A person engaged in postgraduate study.

post·haste (pōst′hāst′) *adv.* With great speed; rapidly. —*n. Archaic.* Great speed; rapidity. [From the phrase *post, haste,* a direction on letters.]

post·hole (pōst′hōl′) *n.* A hole dug in the ground to hold a fence post.

post·hu·mous (pŏs′chə-məs) *adj.* **1.** Occurring or continuing after one's death: *a posthumous award.* **2.** Published after the author's death: *a posthumous book.* **3.** Born after the death of the father; *a posthumous child.* [Lat. *posthumus,* alteration of *postumus,* superl. of *posterus,* coming after < *post,* after.] **—post′hu·mous·ly** *adv.* **—post′hu·mous·ness** *n.*

post·hyp·not·ic suggestion (pōst′hĭp-nŏt′ĭk) *n.* A suggestion made to a hypnotized person specifying an action to be performed in a subsequent waking state.

pos·tiche (pô-stēsh′, pŏ-) *n.* **1.** Something false; sham. **2.** A small hairpiece; toupee. [Fr., out of place < Ital. *posticcio,* counterfeit < *posto,* added < Lat. *positus,* p.part. of *ponere,* to place.]

pos·til·ion also **pos·til·lion** (pō-stĭl′yən, pŏ-) *n.* One who rides the near horse of the leaders to guide the horses drawing a coach. [Fr. *postillion* < Ital. *postiglione* < *posta,* mail coach. —see POST[3].]

post·im·pres·sion·ism (pōst′ĭm-prĕsh′ə-nĭz′əm) *n.* A school of painting in France in the late 19th century that rejected the objective naturalism of impressionism and used form and color in more personally expressive ways. **—post′im·pres′sion·ist** *n.* **—post′im·pres′sion·is′tic** *adj.*

post·ir·ra·di·a·tion (pōst′ĭ-rā′dē-ā′shən) *adj.* Occurring after irradiation.

post·lude (pōst′lo͞od′) *n.* **1. a.** An organ voluntary played at the end of a church service. **b.** A concluding piece of music. **2.** A final chapter or phase. [POST- + (PRE)LUDE.]

post·man (pōst′mən) *n.* A letter carrier.

post·mark (pōst′märk′) *n.* An official mark printed over the stamp on a piece of mail, esp. one that cancels the stamp and records the date and place of mailing. —*tr.v.* **-marked, -mark·ing, -marks.** To stamp with a postmark.

post·mas·ter (pōst′măs′tər) *n.* A government official in charge of the operations of a local post office. **—post′mas′ter·ship′** *n.*

postmaster general *n., pl.* **postmasters general.** The executive head of a national postal service.

post·me·rid·i·an (pōst′mə-rĭd′ē-ən) *adj.* Of, pertaining to, or taking place in the afternoon. —See Usage note at **ante meridian.** [Lat. *postmeridianus* : *post,* after + *meridianus,* of midday. —see MERIDIAN.]

post me·rid·i·em (pōst′ mə-rĭd′ē-əm) *adj.* After noon. Used chiefly in the abbreviated form to specify the hour: *10:30* P.M. —See Usage note at **ante meridiem.** [Lat., after midday.]

post·mil·le·nar·i·an (pōst′mĭl-ə-nâr′ē-ən) *adj.* Of or pertaining to postmillennialism. —*n.* A person who believes in postmillennialism.

post·mil·le·nar·i·an·ism (pōst′mĭl-ə-nâr′ē-ə-nĭz′əm) *n.* Postmillennialism.

post·mil·len·ni·al (pōst′mə-lĕn′ē-əl) also **post·mil·len·ni·an** (-ən) *adj.* Happening or existing after the millennium.

post·mil·len·ni·al·ism (pōst′mə-lĕn′ē-ə-lĭz′əm) *n.* The doctrine that Christ's second coming will follow the millennium. **—post′mil·len′ni·al·ist** *n.*

post·mis·tress (pōst′mĭs′trĭs) *n.* A female government official in charge of the operations of a local post office.

post·mor·tem (pōst-môr′təm) *adj.* **1.** Occurring or done after death. **2.** Of or pertaining to a postmortem examination. —*n.* **1.** An autopsy. **2.** *Informal.* An analysis or review of a completed event. [Lat. *post mortem,* after death.]

postmortem examination *n.* An autopsy.

post·na·sal (pōst-nā′zəl) *adj.* Posterior to the nose.

postnasal drip *n.* The chronic secretion of mucus from the posterior nasal cavities, resulting in congestion and soreness of the throat.

post·na·tal (pōst-nāt′l) *adj.* Of or occurring during the period immediately after birth. —**post·na′tal·ly** *adv.*

post·nup·tial (pōst-nŭp′shəl, -chəl) *adj.* Happening after marriage. —**post·nup′tial·ly** *adv.*

post-o·bit (pōst-ō′bĭt) *adj.* Happening or taking effect after a person's death. —*n.* A bond given by a borrower promising to repay the debt after the death of a specified person from whose estate he expects to inherit. [Lat. *post obitum,* after death.]

post-obit bond *n.* A post-obit.

post office *n.* **1.** The public department responsible for the transportation and delivery of the mails. **2.** A local office where mail is received, sorted, and delivered, and where stamps and other postal matter are sold.

post·op·er·a·tive (pōst-ŏp′ər-ə-tĭv, -ŏp′rə-tĭv, -ŏp′ə-rā′tĭv) *adj.* Happening or done after surgery. —**post·op′er·a·tive·ly** *adv.*

post·or·bi·tal (pōst-ôr′bĭt-l) *adj.* Located behind the eye socket: *a postorbital bone.*

post·paid (pōst′pād′) *adj.* With the postage paid in advance.

post·par·tum (pōst-pär′təm) *adj.* Of or occurring in the period shortly after childbirth. [Lat. *post partum,* after birth.]

post·pone (pōst-pōn′, pōs-pōn′) *tr.v.* **-poned, -pon·ing, -pones. 1.** To delay until a future time; put off. **2.** To place after in importance; subordinate. [Lat. *postponere* : *post,* after + *ponere,* to put.] —**post·pon′a·ble** *adj.* —**post·pone′ment** *n.* —**post·pon′er** *n.*

post·po·si·tion (pōst′pə-zĭsh′ən) *n. Gram.* **1.** The placing of a word or suffixed element after the word to which it is grammatically related. **2.** A word or element placed postpositionally, such as a preposition placed after its object. [Fr. < OFr. *postposer,* to put after < Lat. *postponere.* —see POSTPONE.] —**post′po·si′tion·al** *adj.* —**post′po·si′tion·al·ly** *adv.*

post·pos·i·tive (pōst-pŏz′ĭ-tĭv) *Gram.* —*adj.* Placed after or suffixed to another word. —*n.* An appended or suffixed word or word element; postposition. [LLat. *postpositivus* < Lat. *postponere,* to put after. —see POSTPONE.] —**post·pos′i·tive·ly** *adv.*

post·pran·di·al also **post-pran·di·al** (pōst-prăn′dē-əl) *adj.* Following a meal, esp. dinner.

post·script (pōst′skrĭpt′, pōs′skrĭpt′) *n.* **1.** A message appended at the end of a letter after the writer's signature. **2.** Additional information appended to a manuscript, such as to a book or article. [Lat. *postscriptum,* p.part. of *postscribere,* to write after : *post,* after + *scribere,* to write.]

post time *n.* The time set immediately before the official start of a race after which point no further betting is allowed.

post·trau·mat·ic (pōst′trou-măt′ĭk, -trô-) *adj.* Following injury or resulting from it: *posttraumatic amnesia.*

pos·tu·lant (pŏs′chə-lənt) *n.* **1.** A person submitting a request or application; petitioner. **2.** A candidate for admission into a religious order. [Fr. < OFr. < Lat. *postulans,* pr.part. of Lat. *postulare,* to request.] —**pos′tu·lan·cy, pos′tu·lant·ship′** *n.*

pos·tu·late (pŏs′chə-lāt′) *tr.v.* **-lat·ed, -lat·ing, -lates. 1.** To make claim for; demand. **2.** To assume the truth or reality of with no proof, esp. to do so as a basis of an argument. **3.** To assume as a premise or axiom; take for granted. —*n.* (pŏs′cho͞o-lĭt, -lāt′). **1.** Something assumed without proof as being self-evident or generally accepted, esp. when used as a basis for an argument. **2.** A fundamental element; basic principle. **3.** *Math.* An axiom. **4.** A requirement; prerequisite. [Lat. *postulare, postulat-,* to request.] —**pos′tu·la′tion** *n.*

pos·tu·la·tor (pŏs′chə-lā′tər) *n.* **1.** One who postulates. **2.** *Rom. Cath. Ch.* A church official who presents a plea for canonization or beatification.

pos·ture (pŏs′chər) *n.* **1.** A position or attitude of the body or of bodily parts: *a sitting posture.* **2.** A characteristic way of bearing one's body; carriage: *learning good posture.* **3.** A bodily position assumed by an artist's model. **4.** The present condition or tendency of something: *the military posture of a nation.* **5.** A frame of mind affecting one's thoughts or behavior; overall attitude. —*v.* **-tured, -tur·ing, -tures.** —*intr.* To assume an exaggerated or unnatural pose or mental attitude; attitudinize. —*tr.* To put in a posture; pose. [Fr. < Ital. *postura* < Lat. *positura,* position < *ponere,* to place.] —**pos′tur·al** *adj.* —**pos′tur·er, pos′tur·ist** *n.*

post·vo·cal·ic (pōst′vō-kăl′ĭk) *adj.* Designating a consonant or consonantal sound directly following a vowel.

post·war (pōst′wôr′) *adj.* Occurring after a war.

po·sy (pō′zē) *n., pl.* **-sies. 1.** A flower or bunch of flowers; nosegay. **2.** *Archaic.* A brief verse or sentimental phrase, esp. one inscribed on a trinket. [Alteration of POESY.]

pot (pŏt) *n.* **1. a.** A round, fairly deep cooking vessel with a handle. **b.** Such a vessel and its contents: *a pot of soup.* **c.** The amount that such a vessel will hold; potful. **2. a.** A large drinking cup; tankard. **b.** A drink of liquor contained in such a cup. **3.** An artistic or decorative ceramic vessel. **4.** A flowerpot. **5.** Something resembling a round cooking vessel in appearance or function, such as a chimney pot or chamber pot. **6.** A trap for fish, crustaceans, or eels, consisting of a wicker or wire basket. **7. a.** The total amount staked by all the players in one hand of a card game. **b.** The area on a card table where stakes are placed. **8.** *Informal.* A common fund to which members of a group contribute. **9.** *Computer Sci.* A section of computer storage reserved for storing accumulated data. **10.** *Informal.* A pot shot. **11.** *Informal.* A potbelly. **12.** *Slang.* Marijuana. —*v.* **pot·ted, pot·ting, pots.** —*tr.* **1.** To place or plant in a pot: *pot a plant.* **2.** To preserve (food) in a pot. **3.** To cook in a pot. **4.** To shoot (game) for food rather than for sport. **5.** *Informal.* To shoot with a pot shot. **6.** *Informal.* To win or capture; bag. —*intr. Informal.* To take a pot shot. —*idiom.* **go to pot.** *Informal.* To deteriorate. [ME < OE *pott.*]

po·ta·ble (pō′tə-bəl) *adj.* Fit to drink. —*n.* **potables.** Drinkables. [Fr. < LLat. *potabilis* < Lat. *potare,* to drink.] —**po′ta·bil′i·ty, po′ta·ble·ness** *n.*

pot·ash (pŏt′ăsh′) *n.* **1.** Potassium carbonate. **2.** Potassium hydroxide. **3.** Any of several compounds containing potassium, esp. soluble compounds, such as potassium oxide, potassium chloride, and various potassium sulfates, used chiefly in fertilizers. [Sing. of obs. *pot ashes.*]

potash feldspar *n.* Orthoclase.

potash muriate *n.* Potassium chloride.

po·tas·si·um (pə-tăs′ē-əm) *n. Symbol* **K** A soft, silver-white, light, highly or explosively reactive metallic element obtained by electrolysis of its common hydroxide and found in, or converted to, a wide variety of salts used esp. in fertilizers and soaps. Atomic number 19; atomic weight 39.102; melting point 63.65°C; boiling point 774°C; specific gravity 0.862; valence 1. [< POTASH.] —**po·tas′sic** *adj.*

po·tas·si·um-ar·gon (pə-tăs′ē-əm-är′gŏn′) *adj.* Of, relating to, or being a geological dating method relying on the percentage of potassium in a specimen that has radioactively decayed to argon.

potassium bitartrate *n.* A white crystalline solid or powder, $KHC_4H_4O_6$, used in baking powder, in the tinning of metals, and as a component of laxatives.

potassium bromide *n.* A white crystalline solid or powder, KBr, used as a sedative, in photographic emulsion, and in spectroscopy.

potassium carbonate *n.* A transparent, white, deliquescent, granular powder, K_2CO_3, used in making glass, pigments, ceramics, and soaps.

potassium chlorate *n.* A poisonous crystalline compound, $KClO_3$, used as an oxidizing agent, bleach, and disinfectant, and in making explosives, matches, and fireworks.

potassium chloride *n.* A colorless crystalline solid or powder, KCl, used widely in fertilizers and in the preparation of most potassium compounds.

potassium cyanide *n.* An extremely poisonous white compound, KCN, used in the extraction of gold and silver from ores, electroplating, photography, and as a fumigant and insecticide.

potassium dichromate *n.* A bright yellowish-red crystalline compound, $K_2Cr_2O_7$, used as an oxidizing agent, and in pyrotechnics, explosives, and safety matches.

potassium hydroxide *n.* A caustic deliquescent solid, KOH, used as a bleach and in the manufacture of liquid detergents and soaps, oxalic acid, matches, and many potassium compounds.

potassium iodide *n.* A white crystalline compound, KI, used in photography and as an analytical reagent.

potassium muriate *n.* Potassium chloride.

potassium nitrate *n.* A transparent white crystalline compound, KNO_3, used to pickle meat and in the manufacture of pyrotechnics, explosives, matches, rocket propellants, and fertilizers.

potassium permanganate *n.* A dark-purple crystalline compound, $KMnO_4$, used as an oxidizing agent, disinfectant, and in deodorizers and dyes.

potassium sulfate *n.* A colorless or white crystalline compound, K_2SO_4, used in medicine, glassmaking, fertilizers, and as a reagent in analytical chemistry.

po·ta·tion (pō-tā′shən) *n.* **1.** The act of drinking. **2.** A drink, esp. of an alcoholic beverage. [ME *potacion* < OFr. < Lat. *potatio* < *potare,* to drink.]

po·ta·to (pə-tā′tō) *n., pl.* **-toes. 1.** A plant, *Solanum tuberosum,* native to South America and widely cultivated for its starchy, edible tubers. **2.** A tuber of the potato plant. [Sp. *patata* < Taino *batata.*]

potato

potato beetle *n.* A small yellow-and-black striped beetle, *Leptinotarsa decemlineata,* that is a major agricultural pest.

potato blight *n.* Any of various highly destructive fungus diseases of the potato.

potato bug *n.* The potato beetle.

potato chip *n.* A thin slice of potato fried in deep fat until crisp and then salted.

po·ta·to·ry (pō′tə-tôr′ē, -tōr′ē) *adj.* Of, pertaining to, or given to drinking. [Lat. *potatorius* < *potare,* to drink.]

pot-au-feu (pô-tō-fœ′) *n.* A French dish of boiled meats and vegetables. [Fr. : *pot,* pot + *au,* on the + *feu,* fire.]

Pot·a·wat·o·mi (pŏt′ə-wŏt′ə-mē) *n., pl.* **Potawatomi** or **-mis. 1.** A tribe of North American Indians inhabiting Michigan. **2.** A member of the Potawatomi tribe. **3.** The Algonquian language of the Potawatomi.

pot·bel·lied stove (pŏt′bĕl′ēd) *n.* A potbelly stove.

pot·bel·ly (pŏt′bĕl′ē) *n., pl.* **-lies. 1.** A protruding abdominal region. **2.** A potbelly stove. —**pot′bel′lied** *adj.*

potbelly stove

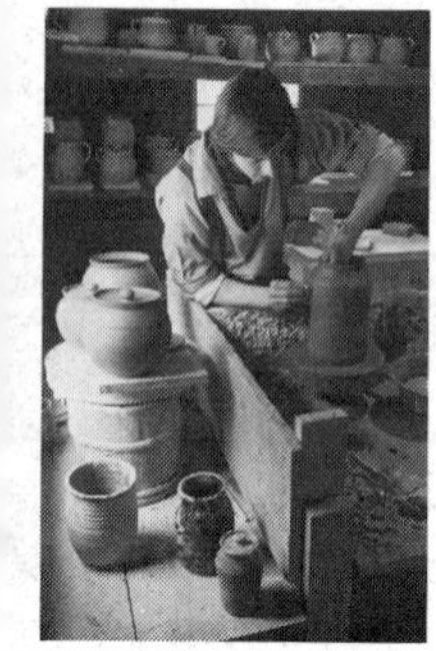

potter[1]

potter's wheel

potbelly stove *n.* A short rounded stove in which wood or coal is burned.

pot·boil·er (pŏt′boi′lər) *n.* A sensational literary or artistic work of poor quality, produced quickly for profit.

pot·boy (pŏt′boi′) *n. Chiefly Brit.* A boy or man who works in an inn or a public house serving customers and doing chores.

pot cheese *n.* Cottage cheese.

po·teen (pō-tēn′) *n.* Irish whiskey that is distilled unlawfully. [Ir. Gael. *poitīn* < *pota,* pot.]

po·tence (pōt′ns) *n.* Potency.

po·ten·cy (pōt′n-sē) *n., pl.* **-cies. 1.** The quality or state of being potent. **2.** Inherent capacity for growth and development; potentiality.

po·tent (pōt′nt) *adj.* **1.** Possessing inner or physical strength; powerful. **2.** Having a strong effect or influence; cogent: *potent arguments.* **3.** Having great control or authority: "*The police were potent only so long as they were feared*" (Thomas Burke). **4.** Capable of causing strong physiological or chemical effects, as medicines or alcoholic beverages do. **5.** Able to perform sexually. Used of a male. [ME < Lat. *potens,* pr.part. of *posse,* to be able.] **—po′tent·ly** *adv.* **—po′tent·ness** *n.*

po·ten·tate (pōt′n-tāt′) *n.* **1.** One who has the power and position to rule over others; monarch. **2.** One who dominates or leads a group or endeavor: *industrial potentates.* [ME *potentat* < OFr. < LLat. *potentatus* < Lat., power < *potens,* pr.part. of *posse,* to be able.]

po·ten·tial (pə-tĕn′shəl) *adj.* **1.** Capable of being but not yet in existence; latent: *a potential problem.* **2.** *Gram.* Denoting possibility, capability, or power; designating a verb form with auxiliaries such as *may* or *can*; for example, *It may snow.* —*n.* **1.** The inherent ability or capacity for growth, development, or coming into being. **2.** Something possessing the capacity for growth or development. **3.** *Gram.* A potential verb form. **4.** *Physics.* The work required to bring a unit electric charge, magnetic pole, or mass from an infinitely distant position to a designated point in a static electric, magnetic, or gravitational field, respectively. **5.** *Elect.* The potential energy of a unit charge at any point in an electric circuit measured with respect to a specified reference point in the circuit or to ground; voltage. [ME *potencial* < OFr. < LLat. *potentialis,* powerful < Lat. *potentia,* power < *potens,* pr.part. of *posse,* to be able.] **—po·ten′tial·ly** *adv.*

potential energy *n.* The energy of a particle or system of particles derived from position, rather than motion, with respect to a specified datum in a field of force.

po·ten·ti·al·i·ty (pə-tĕn′shē-ăl′ĭ-tē) *n., pl.* **-ties. 1.** Inherent capacity for growth, development, or coming into existence. **2.** Something possessing potentiality.

po·ten·til·la (pōt′n-tĭl′ə) *n.* Any of numerous plants or shrubs of the genus *Potentilla,* of the North Temperate Zone. [Med. Lat., garden valerian < Lat. *potens,* pr.part. of *posse,* to be able.]

po·ten·ti·om·e·ter (pə-tĕn′shē-ŏm′ĭ-tər) *n.* **1.** An instrument for measuring an unknown voltage or potential difference by comparison to a standard voltage. **2.** A three-terminal resistor with an adjustable center connection, widely used for volume control in radio and television receivers. [POTENTI(AL) + -METER.] **—po·ten′ti·o·met′ric** *adj.*

pot·ful (pŏt′fo͝ol′) *n.* **1.** The amount that a pot will hold. **2.** *Informal.* A large amount: *made a potful of money on the horses.*

pot·head (pŏt′hĕd′) *n. Slang.* One who habitually smokes marijuana.

poth·er (pŏ*th*′ər) *n.* **1.** A commotion; disturbance. **2.** A state of nervous activity; fuss. **3.** A cloud of smoke or dust that chokes or smothers. —*v.* **-ered, -er·ing, -ers.** —*tr.* To make confused; trouble; worry. —*intr.* To take too much concern with trifles; fuss. [Orig. unknown.]

pot·herb (pŏt′ûrb′, -hûrb′) *n.* A plant whose leaves, stems, or flowers are cooked and eaten or used as seasoning.

pot·hold·er (pŏt′hōl′dər) *n.* A small fabric pad used to handle hot cooking utensils.

pot·hole (pŏt′hōl′) *n.* **1.** A deep hole or pit, esp. one in a road surface. **2.** A deep, round hole worn in rock by loose stones whirling in strong rapids or waterfalls. **3.** *Western U.S.* A place filled with mud or quicksand that is a hazard to cattle.

pot·hook (pŏt′ho͝ok′) *n.* **1.** A bent or hooked piece of iron for hanging a pot or kettle over a fire. **2.** A curved iron rod with a hooked end used for lifting hot pots, irons, or stove lids. **3.** A curved, S-shaped mark made in writing. **4.** Often **pothooks. a.** Illegible handwriting or aimless scribbling. **b.** *Informal.* Stenographic writing.

pot·house (pŏt′hous′) *n. Chiefly Brit.* A tavern.

pot·hunt·er (pŏt′hŭn′tər) *n.* **1.** One who hunts game for food, ignoring the rules of sport. **2.** One who participates in contests simply to win prizes. **3.** A nonprofessional archaeologist. **—pot′hunt′ing** *n.*

po·tiche (pô-tēsh′) *n.* A vase or jar with a round or polygonal body tapering at the neck and having a removable cover. [Fr. < *pot,* pot < OFr.]

po·tion (pō′shən) *n.* A liquid dose, esp. one of medicinal, magic, or poisonous content: *a love potion.* [ME *pocion* < OFr. < Lat. *potio* < *potare,* to drink.]

pot·latch (pŏt′lăch′) *n.* A ceremonial feast among Indian tribes living on the northwest Pacific coast in which the host distributes gifts requiring reciprocation. [Chinook < Nootka *patshatl,* gift.]

pot·luck (pŏt′lŭk′) *n.* Whatever food happens to be available for a meal, esp. when offered to a guest.

pot marigold *n.* A plant, *Calendula officinalis,* often grown for its showy yellow or orange flowers, the dried florets of which were formerly used for seasoning.

pot marjoram *n.* Marjoram (sense 2).

pot·pie (pŏt′pī′) *n.* **1.** A mixture of meat or poultry and vegetables covered with a pastry crust and baked in a deep dish. **2.** A meat or poultry stew with dumplings.

pot·pour·ri (pō′po͞o-rē′) *n., pl.* **-ris. 1.** A combination of various incongruous elements. **2.** A miscellaneous anthology or collection. **3.** A mixture of dried flower petals and spices kept in a jar and used to scent the air. [Fr. *pot pourri,* transl. of Sp. *olla podrida.* —see OLLA PODRIDA.]

pot roast *n.* A cut of beef that is browned and then cooked until tender, often with vegetables, in a covered pot.

pot·sherd (pŏt′shûrd′) also **pot·shard** (-shärd′) *n.* A fragment of broken pottery, esp. one found in an archaeological excavation. [ME *potschoord* : *pot,* pot + *schoord,* var. of *shard,* shard < OE *sceard.*]

pot shot *n.* **1.** A shot fired without taking careful aim or fired at a target within easy range. **2.** A criticism made without careful thought and aimed at a handy target for attack: *reporters taking pot shots at the mayor.* [So called because such a shot is fired by a hunter whose main purpose is to get food for his pot.]

pot·stone (pŏt′stōn′) *n.* An impure variety of steatite once used to make cooking vessels.

pot·tage (pŏt′ĭj) *n.* **1.** A thick soup or stew of vegetables and sometimes meat. **2.** *Archaic.* Porridge. [ME *potage* < OFr. < *pot,* pot.]

pot·ted (pŏt′ĭd) *adj.* **1. a.** Placed in a pot. **b.** Grown in a pot, as a plant. **2.** Preserved in a pot, can, or jar. **3.** *Slang.* **a.** Intoxicated. **b.** Stoned (sense 2).

pot·ter[1] (pŏt′ər) *n.* One who makes earthenware pots, dishes, or other vessels. [ME *pottere* < OE < *pott,* pot.]

pot·ter[2] (pŏt′ər) *v. Chiefly Brit.* Variant of **putter.**

potter's clay *n.* A clay low in iron content that is suitable for making pottery or for modeling.

potter's earth *n.* Potter's clay.

potter's field *n.* A place for the burial of indigent or unknown persons. [From the potter's field mentioned in the Gospel according to St. Matthew.]

potter's wheel *n.* A device composed of a revolving, often treadle-operated horizontal disk upon which clay is shaped manually.

potter wasp *n.* Any of various wasps of the genus *Eumenes,* characteristically building pot-shaped nests of clay.

pot·ter·y (pŏt′ə-rē) *n., pl.* **-ies. 1.** Ware, such as vases, pots, bowls, or plates, shaped from moist clay and hardened by heat. **2.** The craft or occupation of a potter. **3.** The place where a potter works. [OFr. *poterie* < *potier,* potter, prob. < *pot,* pot.]

pot·tle (pŏt′l) *n.* **1.** A pot or drinking vessel with a two-quart capacity. **2.** The liquid contained in a pottle. **3.** An old liquid measure equal to about two quarts. [ME *potel* < OFr. < *pot,* pot.]

pot·to (pŏt′ō) *n., pl.* **-tos.** Any of several small African primates of the genera *Perodicticus* and *Arctocebus,* having woolly fur and hands and feet adapted for grasping. [Of Niger-Congo orig.]

Pott's disease (pŏts) *n.* Partial destruction of the bones of the vertebrae, usually caused by a tuberculous infection and often producing deformity and curvature of the spine. [After Percival *Pott* (1714–1788).]

pot·ty[1] (pŏt′ē) *adj.* **-ti·er, -ti·est.** *Chiefly Brit.* **1.** Of little importance; trivial. **2.** Slightly intoxicated. **3.** Somewhat silly or crazy; addlebrained. [Poss. < POT.]

pot·ty[2] (pŏt′ē) *n., pl.* **-ties.** A small pot for use as a toilet by an infant or young child.

pot·ty-chair (pŏt′ē-châr′) *n.* A small chair with an opening in the seat and a receptacle beneath, used for toilet-training young children.

pouch (pouch) *n.* **1.** A small bag closed with a drawstring and used esp. for carrying loose pipe tobacco in one's pocket. **2.** A small or medium-sized bag of flexible material used for holding or carrying various things, esp. one used to carry mail or diplomatic dispatches. **3.** *Archaic.* A purse for small coins. **4.** A leather bag for carrying powder or small-arms ammunition. **5.** Something resembling a bag in shape: *He had pouches under his eyes.* **6.** *Zool.* A saclike structure, such as the cheek pockets of the gopher or the external abdominal pocket in which marsupials carry their young. **7.** *Scot.* A pocket. —*v.* **pouched, pouch·ing, pouch·es.** —*tr.* **1.** To place in or as if in a pouch; pocket: *He pouched all the money.* **2.** To cause to resemble a pouch in shape. **3.** To swallow. Used of certain birds or fishes. —*intr.* To assume the form of a pouch or pouchlike cavity. [ME *pouche* < OFr., of Germanic orig.] **—pouch′y** *adj.*

pouf (po͞of) *n.* **1.** A woman's hair style popular in the 18th century, characterized by high rolled puffs. **2.** A part of a dress or other garment gathered into a puff. **3.** A rounded ottoman. [Fr.]

pouil·ly-fuis·sé (pōō-yē'fwē-sā') *n.* A dry white Burgundy. [After Solutré-*Pouilly* and *Fuissé,* villages in France.]

pou·lard also **pou·larde** (pōō-lärd') *n.* A young hen that has been spayed for fattening. [Fr. *poularde* < OFr. *pollarde* < *polle,* hen < Lat. *pullus,* chicken.]

poult (pōlt) *n.* A young fowl, esp. a turkey. [ME *pult,* short for *polet* < OFr. *poulet,* dim. of *poule, polle,* hen. —see POULARD.]

poul·ter·er (pōl'tər-ər) *n. Chiefly Brit.* A poultry dealer. [Alteration of ME *pulter* < OFr. *pouletier* < *poulet,* young fowl. —see POULT.]

poul·ter's measure (pōl'tərz) *n.* A metrical pattern originally consisting of a couplet whose first line had 12 syllables and the second 14. [< obs. *poulter,* poulterer, from the practice of giving a few extra eggs in the dozen.]

poul·tice (pōl'tĭs) *n.* A moist, soft mass of bread, meal, clay, or other adhesive substance, usually heated, spread on cloth, and applied to warm, moisten, or stimulate an aching or inflamed part of the body. —*tr.v.* **-ticed, -tic·ing, -tic·es.** To apply a poultice to. [Med. Lat. *pultes,* thick paste < Lat., pl. of *puls,* pap, poss. < Gk. *poltos,* porridge.]

poul·try (pōl'trē) *n.* Domestic fowls, such as chickens, turkeys, ducks, or geese, raised for flesh or eggs. [ME *pultrie* < OFr. *pouletrie* < *pouletier,* poulterer. —see POULTERER.]

pounce¹ (pouns) *v.* **pounced, pounc·ing, pounc·es.** —*intr.* **1.** To spring or swoop with intent to seize someone or something. **2.** To attack or seize suddenly and unexpectedly: *pounce on an opportunity.* —*tr.* To seize with or as if with talons. —*n.* **1.** The act of pouncing. **2.** The talon or claw of a bird of prey. [< ME, talon of a bird of prey, perh. var. of *ponson,* a pointed tool. —see PUNCHEON.] **—pounc'er** *n.*

pounce² (pouns) *n.* **1.** A fine powder formerly used to smooth and finish writing paper and to soak up ink. **2.** A fine powder, such as pulverized charcoal, dusted over a stencil to transfer a design to an underlying surface. —*tr.v.* **pounced, pounc·ing, pounc·es. 1.** To sprinkle, smooth, or treat with pounce. **2.** To transfer (a stenciled design) with pounce. [Fr. *ponce* < Lat. *pumex,* pumice.] **—pounc'er** *n.*

pounce³ (pouns) *tr.v.* **pounced, pounc·ing, pounc·es.** To ornament (metal, for example) by perforating from the back with a pointed implement. [ME *pounsen,* prob. < OFr. *poiçonner,* to prick < *poinon,* a pointed tool. —see PUNCHEON.]

pounce box *n.* A small box with a perforated top, formerly used to sprinkle sand or pounce on writing paper to dry the ink.

poun·cet box (poun'sĭt) *n.* A small perfume box with a perforated top. [Prob. alteration of *pounce box.*]

pound¹ (pound) *n., pl.* **pound** or **pounds. 1. a.** A unit of weight equal to 16 ounces, 7,000 grains, or 453.592 grams. **b.** A unit of apothecary weight equal to 5,760 grains or 373.242 grams. **2.** A unit of weight differing in various countries and times. **3.** A British unit of force equal to the weight of a standard one-pound mass where the local acceleration of gravity is 32.174 feet per second per second. **4.** See table at **currency. 5.** A monetary unit of Scotland before the Union, usually worth a small fraction of the pound sterling. [ME < OE *pund* < Lat. *pondo,* a unit of weight.]

pound² (pound) *v.* **pound·ed, pound·ing, pounds.** —*tr.* **1.** To strike or hammer with a heavy blow or blows. **2.** To drive (something) in or out with repeated blows; hammer. **3.** To beat to a powder or pulp; pulverize or crush. **4.** To instill by persistent and emphatic repetition: *pound knowledge into their heads.* —*intr.* **1.** To strike vigorous, repeated blows: *He pounded on the table.* **2.** To move along heavily and noisily: *pounded through the hallway.* **3.** To pulsate rapidly and heavily: *Her heart pounded.* **4.** To work or move laboriously: *a ship pounding through heavy seas.* —*n.* **1.** A heavy blow. **2.** The sound of a heavy blow; thump. **3.** The act of pounding. [ME *pounen* < OE *pūnian.*] **—pound'er** *n.*

pound³ (pound) *n.* **1.** A public enclosure for the confinement of stray dogs or livestock. **2.** A place in which impounded property is held until redeemed. **3.** An enclosure in which animals or fish are trapped or kept. **4.** A place of confinement for lawbreakers. —*tr.v.* **pound·ed, pound·ing, pounds.** To confine in or as if in a pound; impound. [ME.]

pound·age¹ (poun'dĭj) *n.* **1.** A tax or commission based on value per pound sterling. **2.** A rate or charge based on weight in pounds. **3.** Weight measured in pounds.

pound·age² (poun'dĭj) *n.* **1.** The confinement of animals in a pound. **2.** A fee charged for the redemption of impounded animals or other property.

pound·al (poun'dl) *n.* A unit of force in the foot-pound-second system of measurement, equal to the force required to accelerate a standard one-pound mass one foot per second per second. [POUND + (QUINT)AL.]

pound cake *n.* A rich cake containing a large proportion of eggs, flour, butter, and sugar.

pound-fool·ish (pound'fōō'lĭsh) *adj.* Unwise in dealing with large sums of money or large matters.

pound of flesh *n.* A debt harshly insisted upon. [From Antonio's debt to Shylock in *The Merchant of Venice* by William Shakespeare (1564–1616).]

pound scots *n.* Pound¹ (sense 5).

pound sterling *n.* Pound¹ (sense 4).

pour (pôr, pōr) *v.* **poured, pour·ing, pours.** —*tr.* **1.** To make (a liquid or granular solid) stream or flow. **2.** To send forth, produce, express, or utter copiously, as if in a stream or flood: *poured money into the project.* —*intr.* **1.** To stream or flow continuously or profusely. **2.** To rain hard or heavily. **3.** To go forth or stream in large numbers or quantity: *The army poured into enemy territory.* —*n.* A pouring or flowing forth, esp. a downpour of rain. [ME *pouren.*] **—pour'er** *n.*

pour·boire (pōōr-bwär') *n.* Money given as a gratuity; tip. [Fr. < *pour boire,* for drinking.]

pour·par·ler (pōōr'pär-lā') *n.* Conversation or discussion preliminary to negotiation. [Fr. < *pour parler,* for speaking.]

pour point *n.* The lowest temperature at which an oil or other liquid will pour when cooled under given conditions.

pousse-ca·fé (pōōs'kă-fā') *n.* **1.** A drink consisting of several liqueurs of different densities, poured to form differently colored layers. **2.** A brandy or liqueur served after dinner with coffee. [Fr. : *pousse,* a push + *café,* coffee.]

pous·sette (pōō-sĕt') *n.* A country-dance figure in which a couple or couples join hands and swing around the floor. [Fr. < *pousse,* a push < *pousser,* to push < OFr. < Lat. *pulsare,* freq. of *pellere,* to impel.]

pout¹ (pout) *v.* **pout·ed, pout·ing, pouts.** —*intr.* **1.** To protrude the lips in an expression of displeasure or sulkiness. **2.** To show displeasure or disappointment; sulk. **3.** To project or protrude. —*tr.* **1.** To push out or protrude (the lips). **2.** To utter or express with a pout. —*n.* **1.** A protrusion of the lips, esp. as an expression of sullen discontent. **2.** Often **pouts.** A fit of petulant sulkiness. [ME *pouten.*]

pout² (pout) *n., pl.* **pout** or **pouts.** Any of various freshwater or marine fishes, esp. an eelpout. [ME **poute* < OE *-pūte,* as in *aelepūte,* eelpout.]

pout·er (pou'tər) *n.* One of a breed of pigeons capable of distending the crop until the breast becomes puffed out.

pov·er·ty (pŏv'ər-tē) *n.* **1.** The state of being poor; lack of the means of providing material needs or comforts. **2.** Deficiency in amount; scantiness: *the poverty of his vocabulary.* **3.** Unproductiveness; infertility: *the poverty of the soil.* **4.** The renunciation made by a member of a religious order of the right to own property. [ME *poverte* < OFr. < Lat. *paupertas* < *pauper,* poor.]

poverty grass *n.* Any of several North American grasses that grow in poor or sandy soil.

poverty level *n.* A minimum income level below which a person is considered to lack adequate subsistence and to be living in poverty.

pov·er·ty-strick·en (pŏv'ər-tē-strĭk'ən) *adj.* Having little or no money or wealth; poor.

pow·der (pou'dər) *n.* **1.** A substance consisting of ground, pulverized, or otherwise finely dispersed solid particles. **2.** Any of various preparations in the form of powder, such as certain cosmetics and medicines. **3.** Gunpowder or a similar explosive mixture. **4.** Light, dry snow. —*v.* **-dered, -der·ing, -ders.** —*tr.* **1.** To reduce to powder; pulverize. **2.** To dust or cover with or as if with powder. **3.** *Slang.* To defeat handily or decisively. —*intr.* **1.** To become pulverized; turn to powder. **2.** To use powder as a cosmetic. —*idiom.* **take a powder.** *Slang.* To make a quick departure; run away. [ME *poudre* < OFr. < Lat. *pulvis.*] **—pow'der·er** *n.*

powder blue *n.* A moderate to pale blue or purplish blue. [From the color of powdered smalt.]

powder flask *n.* A small flask or similar receptacle used for carrying gunpowder.

powder horn *n.* A container consisting of an animal's horn capped at the open end used to carry gunpowder.

powder keg *n.* **1.** A small cask for holding gunpowder or other explosives. **2.** A potentially explosive thing or situation.

powder metallurgy *n.* The technology of powdered metals, esp. the production and utilization of metallic powders for massive materials and shaped objects.

powder puff *n.* A soft pad for applying powder to the skin.

pow·der-puff (pou'dər-pŭf') *adj.* Of, relating to, or being a usually competitive activity in which only women take part: *powder-puff baseball.*

powder room *n.* A lavatory for women.

pow·der·y (pou'də-rē) *adj.* **1.** Composed of or similar to powder. **2.** Dusted or covered with or as if with powder. **3.** Easily made into powder; friable.

powdery mildew *n.* **1.** Any of various fungi of the family Erysiphaceae or genus *Oidium* that produce powdery conidia on the host. **2.** A plant disease caused by a powdery mildew.

pow·er (pou'ər) *n.* **1.** The ability or capacity to act or perform effectively. **2.** Often **powers.** A specific capacity, faculty, or aptitude: *his powers of concentration.* **3.** Strength or force exerted or capable of being exerted; might. **4.** The ability or official capacity to exercise control; authority. **5.** A person, group, or nation having great influence or control over others: *the powers that be; the western powers.* **6.** The might of a nation, political organization, or similar group. **7.** Forcefulness; effectiveness: *a novel of unusual power.* **8.** *Regional.* A large number or amount. **9.** *Physics.* The rate at which work is done, mathematically expressed as the first derivative of work with respect to time and commonly measured in units such as the watt and horsepower. **10.** *Elect.* **a.** The product of applied potential difference and current in a direct-current circuit. **b.** The product of the effective values of the voltage and current with the cosine of the phase angle between current and voltage in an alternating-current circuit. **11.** *Math.* **a.** An exponent (sense 3). **b.** The number of elements in a finite set. **12.** *Statistics.* The probability of rejecting the null hypothesis where it is false. **13.** A measure of the magnification of an optical instrument, as a microscope or telescope. **14. powers.** *Theol.* The sixth group of angels in the hierarchical order of nine. **15.** *Archaic.* An armed force. —*tr.v.* **-ered, -er·ing, -ers.** To supply with power, esp. mechanical power. [ME *pouer* < OFr. *poeir* < *poeir,* to be able < Lat. **potēre* < *potis,* able.]

pow·er·boat (pou'ər-bōt') *n.* A motorboat.

power brake *n.* A motor vehicle brake that is assisted by a power mechanism operated by the engine that amplifies pressure applied to the brake pedal.

power broker *n.* A person, esp. a politician, who exerts strong influence by virtue of the individuals and votes he controls.

power dive *n.* A downward plunge of an aircraft accelerated by both gravity and engine power.

pow·er-dive (pou'ər-dīv') *v.* **-dived** or **-dove** (-dōv'), **-div·ing, -dives.** —*intr.* To execute a power dive. —*tr.* To cause to execute a power dive.

power drill *n.* **1.** A portable electric drill. **2.** A large drilling machine having a vertical, motorized drill set in a table stand.

pow·er·ful (pou'ər-fəl) *adj.* **1.** Having or capable of exerting power. **2.** Effective or potent: *a powerful drug.* **3.** *Regional.* Great: *It did a powerful lot of good.* —*adv. Regional.* Very: *It was powerful hot.* **—pow'er·ful·ly** *adv.* **—pow'er·ful·ness** *n.*

pow·er·house (pou'ər-hous') *n.* **1.** A station for the generating of electricity. **2.** One who possesses great force or energy.

pow·er·less (pou'ər-lĭs) *adj.* **1.** Lacking strength or power; helpless; ineffectual. **2.** Lacking legal or other authority. **—pow'er·less·ly** *adv.* **—pow'er·less·ness** *n.*

power mower *n.* A lawn mower that is powered by a gasoline or electric motor.

power of appointment *n. Law.* Authority granted to one person by another to succeed to property upon the death of the latter.

power of attorney *n. Law.* A legal instrument authorizing one to act as another's attorney or agent.

power pack *n.* A usually compact, portable device that converts supply current to direct or alternating current as required by specific equipment.

power plant

power plant *n.* **1.** All the equipment, including structural members, that constitutes a unit power source: *the power plant of a truck.* **2.** A complex of structures, machinery, and associated equipment for generating power, esp. electric power.

power play *n.* **1.** *Sports.* **a.** An offensive maneuver in a team game, esp. in football, in which a massive concentration of players is applied in a certain area. **b.** A situation in ice hockey in which one team has a temporary numerical advantage because the other team has one or more players in the penalty box. **2.** A strategic action or maneuver, as in politics, diplomacy, business, or warfare, based on the use or threatened use of power as a means of coercion.

power politics *n. (used with a sing. or pl. verb).* International diplomacy in which each nation uses or threatens to use military or economic power to further its own interests. [Transl. of G. *Machtpolitik.*]

power series *n.* A sum of successively higher integral powers of a variable or combination of variables, each multiplied by a constant coefficient.

power shovel *n.* A large, usually mobile machine having a boom, a dipper stick, and a bucket for excavating.

power station *n.* A power plant (sense 2).

power steering *n.* A power-assisted device on an automobile that facilitates the turning of the steering wheel by the driver.

power structure *n.* Establishment (sense 5).

power take-off *n.* A mechanism attached to a motor vehicle engine that supplies power to nonvehicular devices, as a pump or backhoe.

power train *n.* An assembly of gears and associated parts by which power is transmitted from an engine to a driving axle.

Pow·ha·tan (pou'ə-tăn') *n., pl.* **Powhatan** or **-tans. 1.** One of various tribes of North American Indians formerly inhabiting eastern Virginia. **2.** A member of one of the Powhatan tribes. **3.** The Algonquian language of the Powhatan tribes.

pow·wow (pou'wou') *n.* **1.** A North American Indian medicine man. **2.** A North American Indian ceremony in which incantations and dancing are used to invoke divine aid in hunting, in battle, or against disease. **3.** A conference or meeting with or of North American Indians. **4.** *Informal.* A conference or gathering. —*intr.v.* **-wowed, -wow·ing, -wows.** To hold a powwow. [Of Algonquian orig.]

pox (pŏks) *n.* **1.** A disease characterized by purulent skin eruptions, such as chicken pox or smallpox. **2.** Syphilis. **3.** *Archaic.* Misfortune and calamity. [Alteration of *pocks,* pl. of POCK.]

pox·vi·rus (pŏks'vī'rəs) *n.* Any of a group of DNA-containing animal viruses that includes the causative agents of smallpox and vaccinia.

poz·zuo·la·na (pŏt'swə-lä'nə) also **poz·zo·la·na** (pŏt'sə-) *n.* **1.** A siliceous volcanic ash used to produce hydraulic cement. **2.** Any of various artificially produced substances resembling pozzuolana ash. [Ital. *pozzolana* < *Pozzuoli,* Italy.] **—poz'zuo·la'nic** *adj.*

PPLO (pē'pē-ĕl-ō') *n., pl.* **PPLO.** Mycoplasma. [P(LEURO)-P(NEUMONIA)L(IKE) + O(RGANISM).]

Pr The symbol for the element praseodymium.

praam also **pram** (präm) *n.* **1.** A flat-bottomed boat used esp. in the Baltic as a barge. **2.** *Chiefly Brit.* A small dinghy having a flat, snub-nosed bow. [Du. < MDu. *praem* < Czech.]

prac·ti·ca·ble (prăk'tĭ-kə-bəl) *adj.* **1.** Capable of being effected, done, or executed; feasible. **2.** Capable of being used for a specified purpose: *a practicable way of entry.* [Fr. < *pratiquer,* to practice. —see PRACTICE.] **—prac'ti·ca·bil'i·ty** *n.* **—prac'ti·ca·bly** *adv.*

Usage: *Practicable* describes that which can be put into effect. *Practical* describes that which is also sensible and worthwhile. It might be *practicable* to transport children to school by balloon, but it would not be *practical.*

prac·ti·cal (prăk'tĭ-kəl) *adj.* **1.** Of, relating to, governed by, or acquired through practice or action, rather than theory, speculation, or ideals. **2.** Manifested in or involving practice. **3.** Actually engaged in some work or occupation. **4.** Capable of being used or put into effect; useful: *practical knowledge of German.* **5.** Designed to serve a purpose without elaboration: *practical low-heeled shoes.* **6.** Concerned with the production or operation of something useful: *Woodworking is a practical art.* **7.** Level-headed, efficient, and unspeculative. **8.** Being actually so in almost every respect; virtual: *a practical disaster.* —See Usage note at **practicable.** [< LLat. *practicus* < Gk. *praktikos* < *prattein,* to act.] **—prac'ti·cal'i·ty** (-kăl'ĭ-tē), **prac'ti·cal·ness** *n.*

practical joke *n.* A mischievous trick played on a person esp. to cause him to feel embarrassment or indignity.

prac·ti·cal·ly (prăk'tĭk-lē) *adv.* **1.** In a way that is practical. **2.** In every important respect; virtually. **3.** Almost: *practically everyone was there.*

Usage: *Practically* is used unexceptionally in its primary sense of "in a way that is practical." In other senses it has become almost interchangeable with *virtually.* Such use is acceptable when the meaning is "for all practical purposes." Thus, a man whose liabilities exceed his assets may be said to be *practically bankrupt,* even though he has not been legally declared insolvent. By a slight extension of this meaning, however, *practically* is often used to mean "nearly" or "all but": *He had practically finished his meal when I arrived.* In that sense it is unacceptable to a small majority of the Usage Panel and should be avoided in writing.

practical nurse *n.* A licensed practical nurse.

prac·tice (prăk'tĭs) *v.* **-ticed, -tic·ing, -tic·es.** —*tr.* **1.** To do or perform habitually or customarily; make a habit of: *practice restraint.* **2.** To exercise or perform repeatedly in order to acquire or polish a skill: *practice a dance step.* **3.** To give lessons or repeated instructions to; drill: *practice students in handwriting.* **4.** To work at, esp. as a profession: *practice law.* **5.** To carry out in action; observe: *practice one's religion.* **6.** *Obs.* To plot (something evil). —*intr.* **1.** To do or perform something habitually or repeatedly. **2.** To do something repeatedly in order to acquire or polish a skill. **3.** To work at a profession. **4.** *Obs.* To intrigue or plot. —*n.* **1.** A habitual or customary action or way of doing something: *make a practice of being punctual.* **2. a.** Repeated performance of an activity in order to learn or perfect a skill. **b.** *Archaic.* The skill so learned or perfected. **c.** The condition of being skilled through repeated exercise: *out of practice.* **3.** The act or process of doing something; performance. **4.** The exercise of an occupation or profession: *the practice of law.* **5.** The business of a professional person. **6.** Often **practices.** A habitual action or act: *questionable business practices; a standard accounting practice.* **7.** The methods of procedure used in a court of law. **8.** *Archaic.* **a.** The act of tricking. **b.** A stratagem; trick. [ME *practisen* < OFr. *practiser* < Med. Lat. *practicare* < LLat. *practicus,* practical.] **—prac'tic·er** *n.*

prac·ticed (prăk'tĭst) *adj.* **1.** Proficient; skilled: *a practiced marksman.* **2.** Acquired or brought to perfection by practice.

practice teaching *n.* Classroom teaching by a college student under the supervision of an experienced teacher that is done as an internship in teaching methodology prior to certification as a professional teacher.

prac·tic·ing (prăk'tĭ-sĭng) *adj.* Actively working in a particular profession or occupation: *a practicing attorney.*

prac·ti·cum (prăk'tĭ-kəm) *n.* Supervised practical application of a previously studied theory: *an advanced practicum for teaching reading to visually impaired pupils.* [G. *Praktikum* < LLat. *practicum,* neuter of *practicus,* practical.]

prac·tise (prăk'tĭs) *v. & n. Chiefly Brit.* Variant of **practice.**

prac·ti·tion·er (prăk-tĭsh′ə-nər) *n.* **1.** One who practices an occupation, profession, or technique. **2.** In Christian Science, a person engaged in the public ministry of spiritual healing. [OFr. *practicien* < *pratique,* practice < LLat. *practicus,* practical.]
prae·di·al also **pre·di·al** (prē′dē-əl) *adj.* **1.** Pertaining to land or its products. **2.** Attached to or arising from land or landed property: *praedial serfs.* [Med. Lat. *praedialis,* of an estate < Lat. *praedium,* estate < *praes,* surety.]
prae·fect (prē′fĕkt′) *n.* Variant of **prefect.**
prae·lect (prĭ-lĕkt′) *v.* Variant of **prelect.**
prae·mu·ni·re (prē′myo͞o-nī′rē) *n.* **1.** In English history, the offense of appealing to or obeying a foreign court or authority, thus challenging the supremacy of the Crown. **2. a.** The writ charging praemunire. **b.** The penalty for this offense. [ME *premunire facias* < Med. Lat. *praemunire facias,* that you cause to warn, words used in the writ.]
prae·no·men (prē-nō′mən) *n., pl.* **-nom·i·na** (-nŏm′ə-nə, -nō′mə-nə) or **-no·mens.** A first or given name. [Lat. : *prae-,* before + *nomen,* name.] **—prae·nom′i·nal** (-nŏm′ə-nəl) *adj.*
prae·tor (prē′tər) *n.* A high elected magistrate of the ancient Roman Republic, ranking below the consuls and serving as a judge. [Lat. < *praeire,* to go before : *prae-,* before + *ire,* to go.] **—prae′tor·ship′** *n.*
prae·to·ri·an (prē-tôr′ē-ən, -tōr′-) *adj.* **1.** Of or pertaining to a praetor. **2. Praetorian.** Of, comprising, or belonging to the elite bodyguard of Roman emperors. *—n.* **1.** A praetor. **2. Praetorian.** A member of the bodyguard of the Roman emperors.
prag·mat·ic (prăg-măt′ĭk) *adj.* **1.** Concerned with causes and effects or with needs and results rather than with ideas or theories; practical. **2.** Of or pertaining to pragmatism. *—n.* **1.** A pragmatic sanction. **2.** A meddler; busybody. [Lat. *pragmaticus,* skilled in business < Gk. *pragmatikos* < *pragma,* deed < *prattein,* to do.] **—prag·mat′i·cal** *adj.* **—prag·mat′i·cal·ly** *adv.*
prag·mat·ics (prăg-măt′ĭks) *n. (used with a sing. or pl. verb).* The branch of semiotics concerned with the relations between signs or expressions and their users.
pragmatic sanction *n.* An edict issued by a sovereign that becomes part of the fundamental law of the land.
prag·ma·tism (prăg′mə-tĭz′əm) *n.* **1.** *Philos.* The theory, developed by Charles S. Peirce and William James, that the meaning of a proposition or course of action lies in its observable consequences and that the sum of these consequences constitutes its meaning. **2.** A practical way of solving problems. **—prag′ma·tist** *n.* **—prag′ma·tis′tic** *adj.*
prai·rie (prâr′ē) *n.* An extensive area of flat or rolling grassland, esp. the plain of central North America. [Fr. < OFr. *praerie* < Lat. *pratum,* meadow.]
prairie breaker *n.* A plow that cuts a wide furrow and turns the earth completely over.
prairie chicken *n.* Either of two birds, *Tympanuchus cupido* or *T. pallidicinctus,* of western North America, having deep-chested bodies and mottled brownish plumage.
prairie dog *n.* Any of several burrowing rodents of the genus *Cynomys,* of west-central North America, having yellowish fur and a barklike call and living in large communities.
prairie oyster *n.* **1.** *Slang.* A raw egg immersed in liquid and swallowed whole, esp. as a palliative for a hangover. **2.** *Chiefly Regional.* The testis of a calf, cooked and served as food.
prairie schooner *n.* A canvas-covered wagon used by pioneers crossing the North American prairies.
praise (prāz) *n.* **1.** An expression of warm approval or admiration; strong commendation. **2.** The extolling of a deity, ruler, or hero. **3.** *Archaic.* A reason for praise; merit. *—tr.v.* **praised, prais·ing, prais·es. 1.** To express warm approval of or admiration for; commend. **2.** To extol or exalt; worship. [ME *preisen* < OFr. *presier* < LLat. *pretiare,* to prize < Lat. *pretium,* price.] **—prais′er** *n.*
Synonyms: *praise, acclaim, commend, extol, laud.* These are words for expressing the highest approval of somebody or something and often imply public accord for such favor. *Praise* means to express one's esteem of a person for his virtues or accomplishment, though one can also praise things or ideas. To *acclaim* somebody is collectively to praise or pronounce him or something he has done worthy of honor, but it is often used literally to mean actual applause or cheering. *Commend* suggests approval accorded by higher quarters in a judicious manner, often for a particular service rendered in the interests of society. *Extol* suggests resounding praise in a lofty style. It means to proclaim excellence, often repeatedly or excessively. *Laud* expresses respectful tribute given formally and decisively, usually for a particular deed.
praise·wor·thy (prāz′wûr′*th*ē) *adj.* Meriting praise; highly commendable. **—praise′wor′thi·ly** *adv.* **—praise′wor′thi·ness** *n.*
Pra·krit (prä′krĭt) *n.* Any of the ancient or modern vernacular Indic languages as opposed to the literary language, Sanskrit. [Skt. *prākŗtam* < *prākŗta-,* natural, vulgar, vernacular.] **—Pra·krit′ic** *adj.*
pra·line (prä′lēn, prā′-, prô′-) *n.* A crisp confection made of nut kernels stirred in boiling sugar syrup until brown. [Fr., after César de Choiseul, Count du Plessis-*Praslin* (1598–1675).]
prall·tril·ler (präl′trĭl′ər) *n. Mus.* A mordent using the auxiliary note above the principal note. [G. : *prallen,* to rebound + *Triller,* trill < Ital. *trillo* < *trillare,* to trill.]
pram[1] (prăm) *n. Chiefly Brit.* A perambulator.
pram[2] (präm) *n.* Variant of **praam.**

prairie dog

prance (prăns) *v.* **pranced, pranc·ing, pranc·es.** *—intr.* **1. a.** To spring forward on the hind legs. Used of a horse. **b.** To move with a succession of such springs or bounds. **2.** To ride a horse that prances. **3.** To walk or move about in a lively manner; strut. *—tr.* To cause (a horse) to prance. *—n.* An act of prancing; caper. [ME *prauncen.*] **—pranc′er** *n.* **—pranc′ing·ly** *adv.*
pran·di·al (prăn′dē-əl) *adj.* Of or relating to a meal. [< Lat. *prandium,* late breakfast.] **—pran′di·al·ly** *adv.*
prank[1] (prăngk) *n.* A mischievous trick; practical joke. [Orig. unknown.]
prank[2] (prăngk) *v.* **pranked, prank·ing, pranks.** *—tr.* To decorate or dress ostentatiously or gaudily. *—intr.* To make an ostentatious display. [Of Germanic orig.]
prank·ish (prăng′kĭsh) *adj.* Characterized by impish, mischievous behavior. **—prank′ish·ly** *adv.* **—prank′ish·ness** *n.*
prank·ster (prăngk′stər) *n.* One who plays tricks or pranks.
pra·se·o·dym·i·um (prā′zē-ō-dĭm′ē-əm, prā′sē-) *n. Symbol* **Pr** A soft, silvery, malleable, ductile rare-earth element that develops a characteristic green tarnish in air. It occurs naturally with other rare earths in monazite and is used to color glass yellow, as a core material for carbon arcs, and in metallic alloys. Atomic number 59; atomic weight 140.907; melting point 935°C; boiling point 3,127°C; specific gravity 6.8; valence 3, 4. [Gk. *prasios,* leek-green (< *prason,* leek) + (DI)DYMIUM.]
prat (prăt) *n. Slang.* The buttocks. [Orig. unknown.]
prate (prāt) *v.* **prat·ed, prat·ing, prates.** *—intr.* To talk idly and at great length; chatter. *—tr.* To utter idly or to little purpose. *—n.* Empty, foolish, or trivial talk. [ME *praten.*] **—prat′er** *n.* **—prat′ing·ly** *adv.*
prat·fall (prăt′fôl′) *n.* A fall on the buttocks.

George Miksch Sutton
pratincole

prat·in·cole (prăt′n-kōl′, prāt′-, prăt′ĭng-, prā′tĭng-) *n.* Any of several Old World birds of the genus *Glareola,* having brown and black plumage, long, pointed wings, and a forked tail. [NLat. *pratincola* : Lat. *pratum,* meadow + Lat. *incola,* inhabitant.]
pra·tique (pră-tēk′) *n. Naut.* Clearance granted to a ship to proceed into port after compliance with quarantine or health regulations. [Fr., ult. < Lat. *practicus,* practical. —see PRACTICAL.]
prat·tle (prăt′l) *v.* **-tled, -tling, -tles.** *—intr.* To talk idly or meaninglessly; babble. *—tr.* To utter in a childish or silly way. *—n.* Childish or meaningless sounds; babble. [Freq. of PRATE.] **—prat′tler** *n.*
prawn (prôn) *n.* Any of various edible crustaceans of the genus *Palaemonetes* and related genera, closely related to and resembling the shrimps. *—intr.v.* **prawned, prawn·ing, prawns.** To fish for prawns. [ME *prayne.*] **—prawn′er** *n.*
prax·es (prăk′sēz′) *n.* Plural of **praxis.**
prax·i·ol·o·gy or **prax·e·ol·o·gy** (prăk′sē-ŏl′ə-jē) *n.* The study of human conduct. [PRAXI(S) + -LOGY.]
prax·is (prăk′sĭs) *n., pl.* **-es** (-sēz′). **1.** Practical application or exercise of a branch of learning. **2.** Habitual or established practice; custom. [Med. Lat. < Gk., action < *prattein,* to do.]
pray (prā) *v.* **prayed, pray·ing, prays.** *—intr.* **1.** To utter or address a petition to God or another deity. **2.** To make a fervent request; plead. *—tr.* **1.** To say a prayer or prayers to. **2.** To implore; beseech: *Pray be careful.* **3.** To make a devout or earnest request for: *I pray your indulgence.* **4.** To move or bring by prayer or entreaty. [ME *preyen* < OFr. *preier* < Lat. *precari* < *prex,* prayer.]
pray·er[1] (prā′ər) *n.* One who prays.
prayer[2] (prâr) *n.* **1. a.** A reverent petition made to God or another deity. **b.** The act of making such a petition. **2.** An act of communion with God, such as a confession, praise, or thanksgiving. **3.** A specially worded form used in addressing God. **4. prayers.** A religious service in which praying predominates. **5. a.** A fervent request. **b.** The thing requested: *His safe arrival was their prayer.* **6.** The slightest chance or hope: *didn't have a prayer of winning.* **7.** *Law.* **a.** The request of a complainant, as stated in a bill in equity, that the court grant the aid or relief solicited. **b.** The section of the bill that contains this request. [ME *preiere* < OFr. < Med. Lat. *precaria* < Lat. *precarius,* obtained by entreaty < *precari,* to entreat < *prex,* prayer.]
prayer beads *pl.n.* A string of beads for keeping count of the prayers one is saying; rosary.
prayer book *n.* A book containing prayers and other forms of worship.
prayer·ful (prâr′fəl) *adj.* Inclined to pray frequently; devout. **—prayer′ful·ly** *adv.* **—prayer′ful·ness** *n.*
prayer meeting *n.* An evangelical service, esp. one held on a weekday evening, in which the laity participate by singing, praying, or testifying.
prayer shawl *n.* A tallith.
prayer wheel *n.* A cylinder inscribed with or containing written prayers and revolved on an axis, used esp. by the Buddhists of Tibet.
praying mantis *n.* A green or brownish predatory insect,

praying mantis

Mantis religiosa, that while at rest folds its front legs as if in prayer.

pre– *pref.* **1. a.** Earlier; before; prior to: *prehistoric* **b.** Preparatory; preliminary: *premedical.* **c.** In advance: *prepay.* **2.** Anterior; in front of: *preaxial.* [ME < OFr. < Lat. *prae-* < *prae,* before, in front.]

preach (prēch) *v.* **preached, preach·ing, preach·es.** *—tr.* **1.** To expound upon, esp. to urge acceptance of or compliance with: *preach tolerance.* **2.** To deliver or put forth (religious instruction, for example). *—intr.* **1.** To deliver a sermon. **2.** To give religious or moral instruction, esp. in a drawn-out, tiresome manner. [ME *prechen* < OFr. *prechier* < LLat. *praedicare* < Lat., to announce : *prae-,* before + *dicare,* to proclaim.]

preach·er (prē′chər) *n.* **1.** A Protestant clergyman; minister. **2.** One who preaches.

preach·i·fy (prē′chə-fī′) *intr.v.* **-fied, -fy·ing, -fies.** *Informal.* To preach tediously and didactically. **—preach′i·fi·ca′tion** *n.*

preach·ment (prēch′mənt) *n.* **1.** The act of preaching. **2.** A tiresome or unwelcome moral lecture; tedious sermonizing.

preach·y (prē′chē) *adj.* **-i·er, -i·est.** Inclined to preach.

pre·ad·o·les·cence (prē′ăd-l-ĕs′əns) *n.* The period between childhood and adolescence, often designated as between the ages of ten and twelve. **—pre′ad·o·les′cent** *n. & adj.*

pre·ag·ri·cul·tur·al (prē′ăg-rĭ-kŭl′chər-əl) *adj.* Occurring or existing before the advent of agriculture.

pre·am·ble (prē′ăm′bəl, prē-ăm′-) *n.* **1.** A preliminary statement, esp. the introduction to a formal document that explains its purpose. **2.** An introductory occurrence or fact; preliminary. [ME < OFr. *preambule* < Med. Lat. *praeambulum* < LLat. *praeambulus,* walking in front : *prae-,* in front + *ambulare,* to walk.] **—pre·am′bu·lar′y** (-byə-lĕr′ē) *adj.*

pre·am·pli·fi·er (prē-ăm′plə-fī′ər) *n.* An electronic circuit or device that detects and sufficiently amplifies weak signals, esp. from a radio receiver, for subsequent amplification stages.

pre·ar·range (prē′ə-rānj′) *tr.v.* **-ranged, -rang·ing, -rang·es.** To arrange in advance. **—pre′ar·range′ment** *n.*

pre·as·signed (prē′ə-sīnd′) *adj.* Assigned beforehand: *preassigned seating.*

pre·a·tom·ic (prē′ə-tŏm′ĭk) *adj.* Of or pertaining to the period preceding the use of atomic energy.

pre·ax·i·al (prē-ăk′sē-əl) *adj.* Anatomically positioned in front of a body axis. **—pre·ax′i·al·ly** *adv.*

preb·end (prĕb′ənd) *n.* **1.** A clergyman's stipend, drawn from a special endowment belonging to his cathedral or church. **2.** The property or tithe providing the endowment for a stipend. **3.** The clergyman who receives a stipend; prebendary. [ME *prebende* < OFr. < Med. Lat. *praebenda* < Lat., state allowance, neuter pl. gerund. of *praebere,* to grant : *prae-,* forward + *habēre,* to hold.] **—pre·ben′dal** (prĭ-bĕn′dl, prĕb′ən-dəl) *adj.*

preb·en·dar·y (prĕb′ən-dĕr′ē) *n., pl.* **-ies. 1.** A clergyman who receives a prebend. **2.** An Anglican clergyman holding the honorary title of prebend without a stipend.

Pre·cam·bri·an (prē-kăm′brē-ən) *adj.* Of, belonging to, or designating the oldest and largest division of geologic time, preceding the Cambrian, often subdivided into the Archeozoic and Proterozoic eras, and characterized by the appearance of primitive forms of life. *—n.* The Precambrian era.

pre·can·cel (prē-kăn′səl) *tr.v.* **-celed, -cel·ing, -cels** or **-celled, -cel·ling, -cels.** To cancel (a postage stamp) before mailing. *—n.* A precanceled stamp or envelope.

pre·can·cer·ous (prē-kăn′sər-əs) *adj.* Exhibiting a likelihood of becoming cancerous.

pre·car·i·ous (prĭ-kâr′ē-əs) *adj.* **1.** Dangerously lacking in security or stability. **2.** Subject to chance or unknown conditions. **3.** Based upon uncertain or unproved premises. **4.** *Archaic.* Dependent on the will or favor of another. [Lat. *precarius,* obtained by entreaty < *precari,* to entreat < *prex,* prayer.] **—pre·car′i·ous·ly** *adv.* **—pre·car′i·ous·ness** *n.*

prec·a·to·ry (prĕk′ə-tôr′ē, -tōr′ē) also **prec·a·tive** (-tĭv) *adj.* Relating to or expressing entreaty or supplication. [LLat. *precatorius* < *precari,* to entreat < *prex,* prayer.]

pre·cau·tion (prĭ-kô′shən) *n.* **1.** An action taken in advance to protect against possible failure or danger; safeguard. **2.** Caution practiced in advance; circumspection. [Fr. *précaution* < LLat. *praecautio* < Lat. *praecavēre,* to guard against : *prae-,* before + *cavēre,* to beware.]

pre·cau·tion·ar·y (prĭ-kô′shə-nĕr′ē) also **pre·cau·tion·al** (-nəl) *adj.* **1.** Of or constituting a precaution. **2.** Advising or exercising precaution.

pre·cau·tious (prĭ-kô′shəs) *adj.* Exercising precaution. **—pre·cau′tious·ly** *adv.* **—pre·cau′tious·ness** *n.*

pre·ca·va (prē-kā′və, -kä′-) *n., pl.* **-vae** (-vē). The superior vena cava. [PRE- + (VENA) CAVA.] **—pre·ca′val** *adj.*

pre·cede (prĭ-sēd′) *v.* **-ced·ed, -ced·ing, -cedes.** *—tr.* **1.** To come before in time. **2.** To come before in order or rank; outrank. **3.** To be in a position in front of; go in advance of. **4.** To preface; introduce: *precede a speech with an anecdote.* *—intr.* To exist or go before. [ME *preceden* < OFr. *preceder* < Lat. *praecedere* : *prae-,* before + *cedere,* to go.]

prec·e·dence (prĕs′ĭ-dəns, prĭ-sēd′ns) also **prec·e·den·cy** (prĕs′ĭ-dən-sē, prĭ-sēd′n-sē) *n.* **1.** The act, state, or right of preceding; priority. **2.** A ceremonial order of rank observed on formal occasions.

prec·e·dent (prĕs′ĭ-dənt) *n.* **1. a.** An act or instance that may be used as an example in dealing with subsequent similar cases. **b.** *Law.* A judicial decision that may be used as a standard in subsequent similar cases. **2.** Convention or custom. *—adj.* **pre·ced·ent** (prĭ-sēd′nt, prĕs′ĭ-dənt). Preceding; prior. [ME < OFr. < Lat. *praecedens,* pr.part. of *praecedere,* to go before. —see PRECEDE.]

prec·e·den·tial (prĕs′ĭ-dĕn′shəl) *adj.* **1.** Of or pertaining to a precedent. **2.** Having precedence.

pre·ced·ing (prĭ-sē′dĭng) *adj.* Existing or coming before in time, place, rank, or sequence; previous.

pre·cen·sor (prē-sĕn′sər) *tr.v.* **-sored, -sor·ing, -sors.** To censor (a publication, for example) prior to public release.

pre·cen·tor (prĭ-sĕn′tər) *n.* One who directs the singing of a church choir. [LLat. *praecentor* < Lat. *praecinere,* to sing before : *prae-,* before + *canere,* to sing.] **—pre′cen·to′ri·al** (prē′sĕn-tôr′ē-əl, -tōr′-) *adj.*

pre·cept (prē′sĕpt′) *n.* **1.** A rule or principle imposing a particular standard of action or conduct. **2.** *Law.* A writ. [ME < Lat. *praeceptum* < *praecipere,* to advise, teach : *prae-,* before + *capere,* to take.]

pre·cep·tive (prĭ-sĕp′tĭv) *adj.* **1.** Of or expressing a precept. **2.** Giving precepts; didactic. **—pre·cep′tive·ly** *adv.*

pre·cep·tor (prĭ-sĕp′tər, prē′sĕp′tər) *n.* A teacher; instructor. [ME *preceptur* < Lat. *praeceptor* < *praecipere,* to teach. —see PRECEPT.] **—pre′cep·to′ri·al** (prē′sĕp-tôr′ē-əl, -tōr′-) *adj.* **—pre′cep·to′ri·al·ly** *adv.*

pre·cess (prē-sĕs′, prē′sĕs′) *intr.v.* **-cessed, -cess·ing, -cess·es.** To move in or be subjected to precession. [Back-formation < PRECESSION.]

pre·ces·sion (prē-sĕsh′ən) *n.* **1.** The act or state of preceding; precedence. **2.** *Physics.* A complex motion executed by a rotating body subjected to a torque tending to change its axis of rotation, characterized for constant speed of rotation and constant magnitude of the applied torque by a conical locus of the axis. **3.** *Astron.* Precession of the equinoxes. [LLat. *praecessio* < Lat. *praecedere,* to go before. —see PRECEDE.] **—pre·ces′sion·al** *adj.*

precession of the equinoxes *n. Astron.* A slow westward shift of the equinoctial points along the plane of the ecliptic at a rate of 50.27 seconds of arc per year, resulting from precession of the earth's axis of rotation.

pre-Chris·tian (prē-krĭs′chən) *adj.* Of, pertaining to, or being the period of time before Christianity.

pre·cinct (prē′sĭngkt′) *n.* **1. a.** A subdivision or district of a city patrolled by a unit of its police force. **b.** The police station in such a district. **2.** An election district of a city or town. **3.** Often **precincts. a.** A place or enclosure marked off by definite limits. **b.** A boundary. **4. precincts.** Neighborhood; environs. **5. precincts.** An area of thought or action; province. [ME *precincte,* an enclosed space < Med. Lat. *praecinctum* < Lat. *praecingere,* to encircle : *prae-,* before + *cingere,* to gird.]

pre·ci·os·i·ty (prĕsh′ē-ŏs′ĭ-tē, prĕs′-) *n., pl.* **-ties.** Extreme meticulousness or overrefinement, as in language. [ME *preciousite* < OFr. *preciosite* < Lat. *pretiositas* < *pretiosus,* precious < *pretium,* price.]

pre·cious (prĕsh′əs) *adj.* **1.** Of high cost or worth; valuable. **2.** Highly esteemed; cherished. **3.** Dear; beloved. **4.** Affectedly dainty or overrefined. **5.** *Informal.* Arrant; thoroughgoing. *—adv.* Used as an intensifier: *"He had precious little right to complain"* (James Agee). [ME < OFr. *precios* < Lat. *pretiosus* < *pretium,* price.] **—pre′cious·ly** *adv.* **—pre′cious·ness** *n.*

precious stone *n.* Any of various minerals, such as diamond, emerald, ruby, or sapphire, valued for their rarity or appearance.

prec·i·pice (prĕs′ə-pĭs) *n.* **1.** An extremely steep or overhanging mass of rock, such as a crag or the face of a cliff. **2.** The brink of a dangerous situation. [OFr. < Lat. *praecipitium* < *praeceps,* headlong. —see PRECIPITATE.]

pre·cip·i·ta·ble (prĭ-sĭp′ĭ-tə-bəl) *adj.* Capable of being precipitated. [< PRECIPITATE.]

pre·cip·i·tance (prĭ-sĭp′ĭ-təns) also **pre·cip·i·tan·cy** (-tən-sē) *n.* The quality of being precipitant.

pre·cip·i·tant (prĭ-sĭp′ĭ-tənt) *adj.* **1.** Rushing or falling headlong. **2.** Impulsive in thought or action; rash. **3.** Abrupt or unexpected; sudden. *—n.* A substance that causes precipitation. —See Usage note at **precipitate.** [Lat. *praecipitans, praecipitant-,* pr.part. of *praecipitare,* to throw headlong. —see PRECIPITATE.] **—pre·cip′i·tant·ly** *adv.*

pre·cip·i·tate (prĭ-sĭp′ĭ-tāt′) *v.* **-tat·ed, -tat·ing, -tates.** *—tr.* **1.** To throw from or as if from a great height; hurl downward: *"The finest bridge in all Peru broke and precipitated five travelers into the gulf below"* (Thornton Wilder). **2.** To cause to happen before anticipated or required. **3.** To cause (water vapor) to condense and fall as rain or snow. **4.** *Chem.* To cause (a solid substance) to be separated from a solution. *—intr.* **1.** To condense and fall as rain or snow. **2.** *Chem.* To be separated from a solution as a precipitate. **3.** To fall headlong. *—adj.* (-tĭt). **1.** Speeding headlong; moving rapidly and heedlessly. **2.** Acting with excessive haste or impulse; lacking due deliberation. **3.** Occurring suddenly or unexpectedly. *—n.* (-tāt′, -tĭt). *Chem.* A solid or solid phase separated from a solution. [Lat. *praecipitare, praecipitat-,* to throw headlong < *praeceps,* headlong : *prae-,* in front + *caput,* head.] **—pre·cip′i·tate·ly** (-tĭt-lē) *adv.* **—pre·cip′i·tate·ness** *n.* **—pre·cip′i·ta′tive** *adj.* **—pre·cip′i·ta′tor** *n.*

Usage: *Precipitate* (adjective) and *precipitately* apply primarily to rash, overhasty human actions. *Precipitant* (adjective) and *precipitantly* are used also in the foregoing sense, with stress on rushing forward or falling headlong (literally or figuratively). *Precipitous* and *precipitously* are used primarily of physical steepness, as in *a precipitous slope,* or in the figurative extensions of such literal uses, as in *a precipitous drop in interest rates.*

pre·cip·i·ta·tion (prĭ-sĭp′ĭ-tā′shən) *n.* **1.** A headlong fall or rush. **2.** Abrupt or impulsive haste. **3. a.** Water droplets or ice particles condensed from atmospheric water vapor and sufficiently massive to fall to the earth's surface, such as rain or snow. **b.** The quantity of such precipitation falling in a specific area within a specific period. **4.** *Chem.* The production of a precipitate.

pre·cip·i·tin (prĭ-sĭp′ĭ-tĭn) *n.* An antibody that reacts with an antigen to cause a precipitate. [PRECIPIT(ATE) + -IN.]

pre·cip·i·tin·o·gen (prĭ-sĭp′ĭ-tĭn′ə-jən) *n.* An antigen that induces the formation of a specific precipitin.

pre·cip·i·tous (prĭ-sĭp′ĭ-təs) *adj.* **1.** Like a precipice; extremely steep. **2.** Having several precipices: *a precipitous bluff.* **3.** Abrupt and ill-considered; precipitate. —See Usage note at **precipitate**. [Fr. *précipiteux* < OFr. < Lat. *praecipitium,* precipice. —see PRECIPICE.] **—pre·cip′i·tous·ly** *adv.* **—pre·cip′i·tous·ness** *n.*

pré·cis (prā′sē, prā-sē′) *n., pl.* **pré·cis** (prā′sēz, prā-sēz′). A concise summary of the essential facts or statements of a book, article, or other text; abstract. *—tr.v.* **-cised, -cis·ing, -cis·es.** To make a précis of. [Fr. < *précis,* condensed < OFr. *precis.* —see PRECISE.]

pre·cise (prĭ-sīs′) *adj.* **1.** Clearly expressed or delineated; definite: *a precise description.* **2.** Capable of, resulting from, or designating an action, performance, or process executed or successively repeated within close specified limits: *a precise measurement.* **3.** Exactly corresponding to what is indicated; correct: *the precise amount of seasoning.* **4.** Strictly distinguished from others; very: *at that precise moment.* **5.** Distinct and correct in sound or statement: *precise articulation.* **6.** Conforming strictly to rule or proper form: *precise etiquette.* [OFr. *precis,* condensed < Lat. *praecisus,* p.part. of *praecidere,* to shorten : *prae-,* in front + *caedere,* to cut.] **—pre·cise′ly** *adv.* **—pre·cise′ness** *n.*

pre·ci·sian (prĭ-sĭzh′ən) *n.* **1.** A person who is strict and precise in adherence to established rules, forms, or standards. **2.** A person who is very strict about the forms of religious observance or moral behavior, esp. an English Puritan of the 16th or 17th century. [< PRECISE.] **—pre·ci′sian·ism** *n.* **—pre·ci′sian·ist** *n.*

pre·ci·sion (prĭ-sĭzh′ən) *n.* The state or quality of being precise. *—adj.* **1.** Used or intended for precise measurement: *a precision tool.* **2.** Made so as to vary minimally from a set standard: *precision components.* [Fr. *précision* < Lat. *praecisio,* a cutting off < *praecidere,* to cut off. —see PRECISE.] **—pre·ci′sion·ism** *n.*

pre·ci·sion·ist (prĭ-sĭzh′ə-nĭst) *n.* One who values precision.

pre·clin·i·cal (prē-klĭn′ĭ-kəl) *adj.* Occurring before the diagnosis of disease is possible.

pre·clude (prĭ-klo͞od′) *tr.v.* **-clud·ed, -clud·ing, -cludes.** To make impossible or impracticable by previous action; prevent. [Lat. *praecludere* : *prae-,* in front + *claudere,* to close.] **—pre·clu′sion** (-klo͞o′zhən) *n.* **—pre·clu′sive** (-klo͞o′sĭv, -zĭv) *adj.* **—pre·clu′sive·ly** *adv.*

pre·co·cial (prĭ-kō′shəl) *adj.* Of or characterizing birds that are covered with down and capable of moving about when first hatched. [< NLat. *praecoces,* precocial birds < Lat. *praecox,* premature. —see PRECOCIOUS.]

pre·co·cious (prĭ-kō′shəs) *adj.* **1.** Manifesting or characterized by unusually early development or maturity, esp. in mental aptitude. **2.** *Bot.* Blossoming before the leaves sprout. [Lat. *praecox,* premature < *praecoquere,* to boil before : *prae-,* before + *coquere,* to cook.] **—pre·co′cious·ly** *adv.* **—pre·co′cious·ness, pre·coc′i·ty** (-kŏs′ĭ-tē) *n.*

pre·cog·ni·tion (prē′kŏg-nĭsh′ən) *n.* Knowledge of something in advance of its occurrence. [LLat. *praecognitio* < Lat. *praecognoscere,* to foresee : *prae-,* before + *cognoscere,* to know. —see COGNITION.] **—pre·cog′ni·tive** *adj.*

pre-co·lo·ni·al (prē′kə-lō′nē-əl) *adj.* Of, pertaining to, or being the period of time before colonization.

pre-Co·lum·bi·an (prē′kə-lŭm′bē-ən) *adj.* Of, relating to, or originating in the Americas before the voyages of Columbus.

pre·con·ceive (prē′kən-sēv′) *tr.v.* **-ceived, -ceiv·ing, -ceives.** To form an opinion or conception of beforehand.

pre·con·cep·tion (prē′kən-sĕp′shən) *n.* **1.** An opinion or conception formed in advance of actual knowledge. **2.** A prejudice.

pre·con·cert (prē′kən-sûrt′) *tr.v.* **-cert·ed, -cert·ing, -certs.** To agree on or arrange in advance.

pre·con·di·tion (prē′kən-dĭsh′ən) *n.* A condition that must exist or be established before something can occur or be considered; prerequisite. *—tr.v.* **-tioned, -tion·ing, -tions.** To condition, train, or accustom in advance.

pre·con·scious (prē-kŏn′shəs) *adj. Psychoanal.* Capable of being recalled although not present in the conscious mind. **—pre·con′scious·ly** *adv.*

pre·cook (prē-ko͝ok′) *tr.v.* **-cooked, -cook·ing, -cooks.** To cook in advance or cook partially before final cooking.

pre·crit·i·cal (prē-krĭt′ĭ-kəl) *adj.* Prior to the occurrence of a critical condition.

pre·cur·sive (prĭ-kûr′sĭv) *adj.* Precursory.

pre·cur·sor (prĭ-kûr′sər, prē′kûr′sər) *n.* **1.** One that precedes and indicates or announces someone or something to come; forerunner. **2.** One that precedes another; predecessor. [Lat. *praecursor* < *praecurrere,* to run before : *prae-,* before + *currere,* to run.]

pre·cur·so·ry (prĭ-kûr′sə-rē) *adj.* **1.** Preceding in the manner of a precursor; preliminary. **2.** Suggesting or indicating something to follow; premonitory.

pre·da·cious or **pre·da·ceous** (prĭ-dā′shəs) *adj.* Living by seizing or taking prey; predatory. [< Lat. *praedari,* to plunder < *praeda,* booty.] **—pre·da′cious·ness, pre·dac′i·ty** (-dăs′ĭ-tē) *n.*

pre·date (prē-dāt′) *tr.v.* **-dat·ed, -dat·ing, -dates. 1.** To mark or designate with an earlier date than the actual one. **2.** To precede in time; antedate.

pre·da·tion (prĭ-dā′shən) *n.* **1.** The act or practice of plundering or marauding. **2.** The capturing of prey as a means of maintaining life. [Lat. *praedatio* < *praedari,* to plunder < *praeda,* booty.]

pred·a·tor (prĕd′ə-tər, -tôr′) *n.* **1.** An animal that lives by preying upon others. **2.** One who plunders or abuses other people for his own profit. [Lat. *praedator,* pillager < *praedari,* to plunder < *praeda,* booty.]

pred·a·to·ry (prĕd′ə-tôr′ē, -tōr′ē) *adj.* **1.** Of, relating to, or characterized by plundering, pillaging, or marauding. **2.** Preying on other animals; predacious. **3.** Addicted to or characterized by a tendency to victimize or destroy others for one's own gain. [Lat. *praedatoris* < *praedari,* to plunder < *praeda,* booty.] **—pred′a·to′ri·ly** *adv.* **—pred′a·to′ri·ness** *n.*

pre·dawn (prē′dôn′) *n.* The time just before dawn.

pre·de·cease (prē′dĭ-sēs′) *tr.v.* **-ceased, -ceas·ing, -ceas·es.** To die before (another person).

pred·e·ces·sor (prĕd′ĭ-sĕs′ər, prē′dĭ-) *n.* **1.** One who precedes another in time, esp. in an office or position. **2.** Something that has been succeeded by another. **3.** An ancestor or forefather. [ME *predecessour* < OFr. *predecesseur* < LLat. *praedecessor* : Lat. *prae-,* before + Lat. *decessor,* someone who leaves < *decedere,* to depart (*de-,* away + *cedere,* to go).]

pre·des·ti·nar·i·an (prē-dĕs′tə-nâr′ē-ən) *adj.* **1.** Of or pertaining to predestination. **2.** Believing in or based on the doctrine of predestination. *—n.* One who believes in the doctrine of predestination. **—pre·des′ti·nar′i·an·ism** *n.*

pre·des·ti·nate (prē-dĕs′tə-nāt′) *tr.v.* **-nat·ed, -nat·ing, -nates. 1.** To destine or determine in advance; foreordain. **2.** *Theol.* To predestine. *—adj.* (prē-dĕs′tə-nĭt, -nāt′). Foreordained; predestined. [ME *predestinaten* < Lat. *praedestinare.* —see PREDESTINE.]

pre·des·ti·na·tion (prē-dĕs′tə-nā′shən) *n.* **1.** The act of predestining or the condition of being predestined. **2.** *Theol.* **a.** The act whereby God is believed to have foreordained all things. **b.** The relegation of all souls to either salvation or damnation by this act. **c.** The doctrine that God has foreordained all things, esp. the salvation of individual souls. **3.** Destiny; fate.

pre·des·tine (prē-dĕs′tĭn) *tr.v.* **-tined, -tin·ing, -tines. 1.** To fix upon, decide, or decree in advance; foreordain. **2.** *Theol.* To foreordain by divine will or decree. [ME *predestinen* < OFr. *predestiner* < Lat. *praedestinare* : *prae-,* before + *destinare,* to determine.]

pre·de·ter·mine (prē′dĭ-tûr′mĭn) *tr.v.* **-mined, -min·ing, -mines. 1.** To determine, decide, or establish in advance: *factors that predetermine an outcome.* **2.** To influence or sway toward an action or opinion; predispose. [LLat. *praedeterminare* : Lat. *prae-,* before + Lat. *determinare,* to limit. —see DETERMINE.] **—pre′de·ter′mi·na′tion** *n.* **—pre′de·ter′mi·na′tive** (-mə-nā′tĭv, -nə-tĭv) *adj.* **—pre′de·ter′min·er** *n.*

pre·di·al (prē′dē-əl) *adj.* Variant of **praedial**.

pred·i·ca·ble (prĕd′ĭ-kə-bəl) *adj.* Able to be stated or predicated. *—n.* **1.** Something that can be predicated; quality; attribute. **2.** *Logic.* One of five general attributes of a class —genus, species, property, difference, and accident—designating the peculiar relation that a predicate bears to its subject regardless of the quantity or quality of a proposition. [Med. Lat. *praedicabilis* < LLat. *praedicare,* to proclaim. —see PREACH.] **—pred′i·ca·bil′i·ty, pred′i·ca·ble·ness** *n.*

pre·dic·a·ment (prĭ-dĭk′ə-mənt) *n.* **1.** A troublesome, embarrassing, or ludicrous situation. **2.** *Logic.* A category (sense 2). [ME, something predicated < LLat. *praedicamentum* < *praedicare,* to proclaim. —see PREACH.] **—pre·dic′a·men′tal** (-mĕn′tl) *adj.* **—pre·dic′a·men′tal·ly** *adv.*

Synonyms: *predicament, plight, dilemma, quandary.* A *predicament* is a problematic situation seen in terms of a difficult decision and implies that one does not know what to do and is considering it rationally. A *plight* is a more serious pass, which may have been imposed on an individual with a course of action being less clear. *Dilemma* more abstractly denotes a problem which poses two alternatives, each of which must be carefully weighed. The term is some-

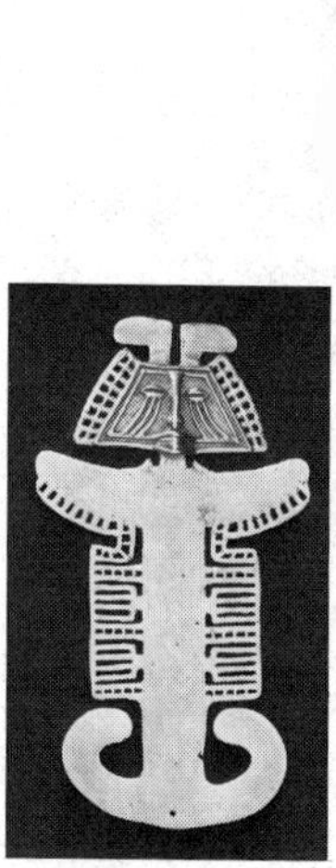

pre-Columbian
Pendant in the form of a stylized figure

times loosely used of any problem. *Quandary,* somewhat more formal, suggests a complicated stalemate with numerous possibilities.

pred·i·cate (prĕd′ĭ-kāt′) *v.* **-cat·ed, -cat·ing, -cates.** —*tr.* **1.** To base or establish (a statement, for example): *He predicates his argument on these facts.* **2.** To state or affirm as an attribute or quality of something: *predicate the perfectibility of mankind.* **3.** To carry the connotation of; imply. **4.** *Logic.* To make (a term or expression) the predicate of a proposition. **5.** To proclaim; assert. —*intr.* To make a statement or assertion. —*n.* (prĕd′ĭ-kĭt). **1.** *Gram.* The part of a sentence or clause that expresses something about the subject, consisting of a verb and often including objects, modifiers, or complements of the verb. **2.** *Logic.* Whatever is stated about the subject of a proposition. —*adj.* (prĕd′ĭ-kĭt). **1.** *Gram.* Of or belonging to the predicate of a sentence or clause. **2.** Predicated; stated. [Lat. *praedicare, praedicat-,* to proclaim. —see PREACH.] **—pred′i·ca′tive** *adj.* **—pred′i·ca′tive·ly** *adv.*

Usage: *Predicate* as a transitive verb is now employed widely in the sense of "to base upon" or "to found" as a means of indicating dependence: *Success is predicated on continuing effort.* This example is acceptable to a majority of the Usage Panel.

predicate nominative *n. Gram.* A noun or pronoun that follows a linking verb and refers to the same person or thing as the subject of the verb.

pred·i·ca·tion (prĕd′ĭ-kā′shən) *n.* **1.** The act or procedure of predicating, esp. a logical assertion or affirmation. **2.** Something predicated. **—pred′i·ca′tion·al** *adj.*

pred·i·ca·to·ry (prĕd′ĭ-kə-tôr′ē, -tōr′ē) *adj.* Of, pertaining to, or characteristic of preaching or a preacher. [LLat. *praedicatorius* < Lat. *praedicare,* to proclaim. —see PREACH.]

pre·dict (prĭ-dĭkt′) *v.* **-dict·ed, -dict·ing, -dicts.** —*tr.* To state, tell about, or make known in advance, esp. to do so on the basis of special knowledge; foretell: *predict the weather.* —*intr.* To foretell what will happen; prophesy. [Lat. *praedicere, praedict-* : *prae-,* before + *dicere,* to say.] **—pre·dict′a·bil′i·ty** *n.* **—pre·dict′a·ble** *adj.* **—pre·dict′a·bly** *adv.* **—pre·dic′tor** *n.*

pre·dic·tion (prĭ-dĭk′shən) *n.* **1.** The act of predicting. **2.** Something foretold or predicted; prophecy. **—pre·dic′tive** *adj.* **—pre·dic′tive·ly** *adv.* **—pre·dic′tive·ness** *n.*

pre·di·gest (prē′dĭ-jĕst′, -dī-jĕst′) *tr.v.* **-gest·ed, -gest·ing, -gests.** To subject to partial digestion. **—pre′di·ges′tion** *n.*

pred·i·lec·tion (prĕd′l-ĕk′shən, prē′d-) *n.* A partiality or disposition in favor of something; preference. [Fr. *prédilection* < Med. Lat. *praediligere,* to prefer : Lat. *prae-,* before + Lat. *diligere,* to love. —see DILIGENT.]

pre·dis·pose (prē′dĭ-spōz′) *tr.v.* **-posed, -pos·ing, -pos·es.** **1.** To make (someone) inclined to something in advance: *His good manners predispose people to like him.* **2.** To make susceptible or liable: *conditions that predispose miners to lung disease.* **3.** *Archaic.* To settle or dispose of in advance. **—pre′dis·pos′al** *n.*

pre·dis·po·si·tion (prē′dĭs-pə-zĭsh′ən) *n.* The state of being predisposed; tendency or inclination.

pred·ni·sone (prĕd′nĭ-sōn′,-zōn′) *n.* An analog of cortisone, $C_{21}H_{26}O_5$, that is used as an anti-inflammatory agent in the treatment of arthritis. [E. *pregnane,* a hydrocarbon + D(I)- + -(E)N(E) + (CORT)ISONE.]

pre·doc·tor·al (prē-dŏk′tər-əl) *adj.* Of, pertaining to, or engaged in advanced academic study in preparation for a doctorate.

pre·dom·i·nance (prĭ-dŏm′ə-nəns) also **pre·dom·i·nan·cy** (-nən-sē) *n.* The state or quality of being predominant; preponderance.

pre·dom·i·nant (prĭ-dŏm′ə-nənt) *adj.* **1.** Having greatest ascendancy, importance, influence, authority, or force. **2.** Most common or conspicuous; prevalent: *the predominant color in a design.* [OFr. < Med. Lat. *praedominans,* pr.part. of *praedominari,* to predominate.] **—pre·dom′i·nant·ly** *adv.*

pre·dom·i·nate (prĭ-dŏm′ə-nāt′) *v.* **-nat·ed, -nat·ing, -nates.** —*intr.* **1.** To be of greater power, importance, or quantity; be most important or outstanding. **2.** To have authority, power, or controlling influence; prevail. —*tr.* To dominate or prevail over. [Med. Lat. *praedominari, praedominat-* : Lat. *prae-,* before + Lat. *dominari,* to rule < *dominus,* master.] **—pre·dom′i·nate·ly** (-nĭt-lē) *adv.* **—pre·dom′i·nat′ing·ly** *adv.* **—pre·dom′i·na′tion** *n.* **—pre·dom′i·na′tor** *n.*

pree·mie also **pre·mie** (prē′mē) *n. Informal.* An infant born prematurely. [Shortening and alteration of PREMATURE.]

pre-em·i·nent or **pre·em·i·nent** (prē-ĕm′ə-nənt) *adj.* Superior to or notable above all others; outstanding. [LLat. *praeeminens,* pr.part of Lat. *praeeminēre,* to excel : *prae-,* before + *eminēre,* to stand out.] **—pre-em′i·nence** *n.* **—pre-em′i·nent·ly** *adv.*

pre·em·ploy·ment (prē′ĕm-ploi′mənt) *adj.* Of, pertaining to, or occurring at a time before employment: *preëmployment testing.*

pre-empt or **pre·empt** (prē-ĕmpt′) *v.* **-empt·ed, -empt·ing, -empts.** —*tr.* **1.** To gain possession of by prior right or opportunity, esp. to settle on (public land) so as to obtain the right to buy before others. **2.** To appropriate, seize, or act for oneself before others. **3.** To be presented in place of; displace: *The special news program pre-empted the scheduled shows.* **4.** To take precedence over: *The issue of energy has pre-empted discussion of all others.* **5.** To gain a pre-eminent place in: *a candidate who pre-empted all others in the race.* —*intr.* To make a pre-emptive bid in bridge. [Back-formation < PRE-EMPTION.] **—pre-emp′tor′** (-ĕmp′tôr′) *n.* **—pre·emp′to·ry** (-ĕmp′tə-rē) *adj.*

pre-emp·tion or **pre·emp·tion** (prē-ĕmp′shən) *n.* **1. a.** The right to purchase something, esp. government-owned land, before others. **b.** A purchase made when such a right is granted. **2.** Acquisition or appropriation of something beforehand. [< Med. Lat. *praeemere,* to buy before : Lat. *prae-,* before + Lat. *emere,* to buy.]

pre-emp·tive or **pre·emp·tive** (prē-ĕmp′tĭv) *adj.* **1.** Of, pertaining to, or characteristic of pre-emption. **2.** Having or granted by the right of pre-emption. **3.** Designating or characteristic of a bid in bridge that is unnecessarily high and is intended to prevent the opposing players from bidding. **4.** Constituting or relating to a military strike made so as to gain an advantage when an enemy strike is imminent: *a pre-emptive attack.* **—pre-emp′tive·ly** *adv.*

preen (prēn) *v.* **preened, preen·ing, preens.** —*tr.* **1.** To smooth or clean (feathers) with the beak or bill. **2.** To dress or groom (oneself) with elaborate care or vanity; primp. **3.** To take pride or satisfaction in (oneself); gloat. —*intr.* To dress up; primp. [ME *preinen,* poss. var. of *prouynen,* to prune. —see PRUNE².] **—preen′er** *n.*

pre-en·gi·neered (prē′ĕn-jə-nîrd′) *adj.* Prefabricated.

pre-es·tab·lish or **pre·es·tab·lish** (prē′ĭ-stăb′lĭsh) *tr.v.* **-lished, -lish·ing, -lish·es.** To establish beforehand.

pre-ex·il·i·an (prē′ĕg-zĭl′ē-ən, -zĭl′yən, -ĕk-sĭl′ē-ən, -sĭl′yən) also **pre-ex·il·ic** (-ĕg-zĭl′ĭk, -ĕk-sĭl′ĭk) *adj.* Pertaining to the history of the Jewish people prior to their exile in Babylonia at the end of the 6th century B.C.

pre-ex·ist or **pre·ex·ist** (prē′ĭg-zĭst′) *v.* **-ist·ed, -ist·ing, -ists.** —*intr.* To exist before. —*tr.* To exist before (something): *dinosaurs that pre-existed mammals.* **—pre′-ex·is′tence** *n.* **—pre′-ex·is′tent** *adj.*

pre·fab (prē′făb′) *n.* A prefabricated part or structure.

pre·fab·ri·cate (prē-făb′rĭ-kāt′) *tr.v.* **-cat·ed, -cat·ing, -cates.** **1.** To construct or manufacture in advance. **2.** To construct in standard sections that can be easily shipped and assembled. **—pre·fab′ri·ca′tion** *n.* **—pre·fab′ri·ca′tor** *n.*

pref·ace (prĕf′ĭs) *n.* **1. a.** A statement or essay, usually by the author, introducing a book and explaining its scope, intention, or background. **b.** The introductory section of a speech. **2.** An introductory approach; preliminary. **3.** Often **Preface.** A thanksgiving prayer ending with the Sanctus and introducing the canon of the Roman Catholic Mass. —*tr.v.* **-aced, -ac·ing, -ac·es.** **1.** To introduce by or provide with a preliminary statement or essay. **2.** To serve as an introduction to. [ME < OFr. < Med. Lat. *prefatia* < Lat. *praefatio,* something said before < *praefari,* to say before : *prae-,* before + *fari,* to say.] **—pref′ac·er** *n.*

pref·a·to·ry (prĕf′ə-tôr′ē, -tōr′ē) also **pref·a·to·ri·al** (prĕf′ə-tôr′ē-əl, -tōr′-) *adj.* Of the nature of or serving as an introductory statement or essay; preliminary. [< Lat. *praefatio,* preface.] **—pref′a·to′ri·ly** *adv.*

pre·fect also **prae·fect** (prē′fĕkt′) *n.* **1.** Any of several high military or civil officials, such as magistrates or administrators of ancient Rome. **2.** A high administrative official, esp. the chief of police of Paris, France. **3.** The dean in a Jesuit school. **4.** A student officer, esp. in a private school. [ME < OFr. < Lat. *praefectus* < p.part. of *praeficere,* to place at the head of : *prae-,* before + *facere,* to make.]

prefect apostolic *n., pl.* **prefects apostolic.** A Roman Catholic priest with broad jurisdiction in a missionary territory.

pre·fec·ture (prē′fĕk′chər) *n.* **1.** The district, office, or authority of a prefect. **2.** The domicile or housing of a prefect. **—pre·fec′tur·al** (prĭ-fĕk′chər-əl) *adj.*

pre·fer (prĭ-fûr′) *tr.v.* **-ferred, -fer·ring, -fers.** **1.** To choose as more desirable; like better: *prefers classical music to popular music.* **2.** *Law.* To give priority or precedence to (a creditor). **3.** *Law.* To file, prosecute, or offer for consideration or resolution before a magistrate, court, or other legal person or body: *prefer charges.* **4.** *Archaic.* To recommend for advancement or appointment. [ME *preferren* < OFr. *preferer* < Lat. *praeferre* : *prae-,* before + *ferre,* to bear.]

pref·er·a·ble (prĕf′ər-ə-bəl, prĕf′rə-) *adj.* More desirable or worthy; preferred. **—pref′er·a·bil′i·ty, pref′er·a·ble·ness** *n.* **—pref′er·a·bly** *adv.*

pref·er·ence (prĕf′ər-əns, prĕf′rəns) *n.* **1. a.** The act of preferring. **b.** The exercise of choice. **c.** One that is preferred. **d.** The state of being preferred. **2.** *Law.* **a.** The paying of one or more creditors by an insolvent debtor before or to the exclusion of other creditors. **b.** The right to be so paid. **3.** The granting of precedence or advantage to one over others. [Fr. *préférence* < Med. Lat. *praeferentia* < Lat. *praeferre,* to prefer.]

pref·er·en·tial (prĕf′ə-rĕn′shəl) *adj.* **1.** Of, having, providing, or obtaining advantage or preference: *preferential treatment.* **2.** Manifesting or originating from partiality or preference: *preferential tariff rates.* **—pref′er·en′tial·ism** *n.* **—pref′er·en′tial·ist** *n.* **—pref′er·en′tial·ly** *adv.*

preferential shop *n.* A union shop whose management

gives priority or advantage to union members in hiring, promoting, or laying off.

preferential voting *n.* A system of voting in which the voter indicates his choices in order of preference.

pre·fer·ment (prĭ-fûr′mənt) *n.* **1.** The act of advancing to a higher position or office; promotion. **2.** A position, appointment, or rank giving advancement.

preferred stock *n.* The portion of a corporation's stock having a priority or preference over the common stock in the distribution of dividends and assets.

pre·fig·u·ra·tion (prē-fĭg′yə-rā′shən) *n.* **1.** The act of representing, suggesting, or imagining in advance; foreshadowing. **2.** Something that prefigures. **—pre·fig′ur·a·tive** (-fĭg′yər-ə-tĭv) *adj.* **—pre·fig′ur·a·tive·ly** *adv.* **—pre·fig′ur·a·tive·ness** *n.*

pre·fig·ure (prē-fĭg′yər) *tr.v.* **-ured, -ur·ing, -ures. 1.** To suggest, indicate, or represent by an antecedent form or model; presage: *The art and theories of Cézanne prefigured the cubist school of art.* **2.** To imagine or picture to oneself in advance. [ME *prefiguren* < LLat. *praefigurare* : Lat. *prae-*, before + Lat. *figurare*, to shape < *figura*, shape.] **—pre·fig′ure·ment** *n.*

pre·fix (prē-fĭks′, prē′fĭks′) *tr.v.* **-fixed, -fix·ing, -fix·es. 1.** To put or fix before. **2.** (prē-fĭks′). To settle or arrange in advance. *—n.* (prē′fĭks′). **1.** *Gram.* An affix, such as *dis-* in *disbelieve*, put before a word to produce a derivative word or an inflected form. **2.** A title placed before a person's name. [OFr. *prefixer* : *pre-*, before (< Lat. *prae-*) + *fixer*, to place < *fixe*, fastened < Lat. *fixus*, p.part. of *figere*, to fasten.] **—pre′fix′al** *adj.* **—pre′fix′al·ly** *adv.*

pre·flight (prē′flīt′) *adj.* Preparing for or occurring prior to flight.

pre·form (prē′fôrm′) *tr.v.* **-formed, -form·ing, -forms.** To shape or form beforehand.

pre·for·ma·tion (prē′fôr-mā′shən) *n.* **1.** The act of shaping or forming in advance; prior formation. **2.** A now invalidated biological theory that all parts of a future organism exist completely formed in the germ cell and develop only by increasing in size. **—pre′for·ma′tion·ism** *n.*

pre·fron·tal (prē-frŭn′tl) *adj.* Located in the forward part of the frontal lobe of the brain.

prefrontal lobotomy *n.* An operation in which the white fibers connecting the prefrontal and frontal lobes of the brain to the thalamus are severed.

pre·gan·gli·on·ic (prē-găng′glē-ŏn′ĭk) *adj.* Located proximal or anterior to a ganglion.

preg·na·ble (prĕg′nə-bəl) *adj.* Vulnerable to seizure or capture, as a fort. [ME *prenable* < OFr. < *prendre*, to capture < Lat. *prehendere*.] **—preg′na·bil′i·ty** *n.*

preg·nan·cy (prĕg′nən-sē) *n., pl.* **-cies. 1. a.** The condition of being pregnant. **b.** An instance of being pregnant. **c.** The period during which a developing fetus is carried within the uterus. **2.** The quality of being pregnant, as with significance.

preg·nant[1] (prĕg′nənt) *adj.* **1.** Carrying a developing fetus within the uterus. **2.** Creative; inventive. **3.** Fraught with significance or implication: *The room was filled with a pregnant silence.* **4. a.** Abounding; profuse. **b.** Overflowing; replete. **c.** Filled; fraught: *pregnant with fate.* **5.** Producing results; fruitful: *a pregnant decision.* [ME < Lat. *praegnans.*] **—preg′nant·ly** *adv.*

preg·nant[2] (prĕg′nənt) *adj. Archaic.* Convincing; cogent. Used of an argument or proof. [ME *preignant* < OFr., pr.part. of *preindre*, to press < Lat. *premere.*]

preg·nen·o·lone (prĕg-nĕn′ə-lōn′) *n.* A steroid ketone, $C_{21}H_{32}O_2$, that results from the oxidation of cholesterol and other steroids. [E. *pregnene*, a hydrocarbon + -OL[1] + -ONE.]

pre·heat (prē-hēt′) *tr.v.* **-heat·ed, -heat·ing, -heats.** To heat beforehand. **—pre·heat′er** *n.*

pre·hen·sile (prē-hĕn′səl, -sīl′) *adj.* Adapted for seizing or holding, esp. by wrapping around an object: *a prehensile tail.* [Fr. *préhensile* < Lat. *prehendere*, to grasp.] **—pre′hen·sil′i·ty** (-sĭl′ĭ-tē) *n.*

pre·hen·sion (prē-hĕn′shən) *n.* **1.** The act of grasping or seizing. **2. a.** Apprehension by the senses. **b.** Understanding. [Lat. *prehensio* < *prehendere*, to seize.]

pre·his·tor·ic (prē′hĭ-stôr′ĭk, -stŏr′-) also **pre·his·tor·i·cal** (-ĭ-kəl) *adj.* Of, pertaining to, or belonging to the era before recorded history. **—pre′his·tor′i·cal·ly** *adv.*

pre·his·to·ry (prē-hĭs′tə-rē) *n.* The history of mankind in the period before written or recorded history. **—pre′his·tor′i·an** (-hĭ-stôr′ē-ən, -stŏr′-) *n.*

pre·ig·ni·tion (prē′ĭg-nĭsh′ən) *n.* The ignition of fuel in an internal-combustion engine before the spark passes through the fuel, resulting from a hot spot in the cylinder or from too great a compression ratio for the fuel.

pre·in·duc·tion (prē′ĭn-dŭk′shən) *adj.* Taking place prior to induction into the armed services.

pre·in·dus·tri·al (prē′ĭn-dŭs′trē-əl) *adj.* Of, pertaining to, or taking place prior to industrialization.

pre·judge (prē-jŭj′) *tr.v.* **-judged, -judg·ing, -judg·es.** To judge beforehand without adequate evidence. **—pre·judg′er** *n.* **—pre·judg′ment, pre·judge′ment** *n.*

prej·u·dice (prĕj′ə-dĭs) *n.* **1. a.** An adverse judgment or opinion formed beforehand or without knowledge or examination of the facts. **b.** A preconceived preference or idea; bias. **2.** The act or state of holding unreasonable preconceived judgments or convictions. **3.** Irrational suspicion or hatred of a particular group, race, or religion. **4.** Detriment or injury caused to a person by the preconceived and unfavorable conviction of another or others. *—tr.v.* **-diced, -dic·ing, -dic·es. 1.** To cause (someone) to judge prematurely and irrationally; bias. **2.** To affect injuriously or detrimentally by some judgment or act. [ME < OFr. < Lat. *praejudicium* : *prae-*, before + *judicium*, judgment < *judex*, judge.]

prej·u·di·cial (prĕj′ə-dĭsh′əl) *adj.* Causing or of the nature of prejudice; detrimental. **—prej′u·di′cial·ly** *adv.* **—prej′u·di′cial·ness** *n.*

prej·u·di·cious (prĕj′ə-dĭsh′əs) *adj.* Prejudicial. **—prej′u·di′cious·ly** *adv.*

prel·a·cy (prĕl′ə-sē) *n., pl.* **-cies. 1. a.** The office or station of a prelate. **b.** Prelates collectively. **2.** Church government administrated by prelates.

pre·lap·sar·i·an (prē′lăp-sâr′ē-ən) *adj.* Of or pertaining to the period before the fall of man. [PRE- + Lat. *lapsus*, fall + -ARIAN.]

prel·ate (prĕl′ĭt) *n.* A high-ranking clergyman, such as a bishop or an abbot. [ME *prelat* < OFr. < Med. Lat. *praelatus* < Lat., p.part. of *praeferre*, to carry before : *prae-*, before + *ferre*, to carry.] **—pre·lat′ic** (prĭ-lăt′ĭk) *adj.*

prelate nul·li·us (nōō-lē′əs) *n.* A Roman Catholic prelate, usually a titular bishop, who has jurisdiction over a territory not in a diocese but subject directly to the Holy See. [PRELATE + NLat. *nullius (dioecesis)*, of no (diocese).]

pre·launch (prē′lônch′, -lŏnch′) *adj.* Preparatory or preliminary to the launch of a spacecraft or missile.

pre·lect also **prae·lect** (prĭ-lĕkt′) *intr.v.* **-lect·ed, -lect·ing, -lects.** To lecture or discourse in public. [Lat. *praelegere*, *praelect-* : *prae-*, in front of + *legere*, to read.] **—pre·lec′tion** *n.* **—pre·lec′tor** *n.*

pre·li·ba·tion (prē′lī-bā′shən) *n.* A foretaste. [Lat. *praelibatio* < *praelibare*, to taste beforehand : *prae-*, before + *libare*, to taste.]

pre·lim (prē′lĭm′, prĭ-lĭm′) *n. Informal* A preliminary (sense 2.b.).

pre·lim·i·nar·y (prĭ-lĭm′ə-nĕr′ē) *adj.* Prior to or preparing for the main matter, action, or business; prefatory. *—n., pl.* **-ies. 1.** Something antecedent or preparatory, as a statement or action. **2. a.** An academic test or examination that is preparatory to one that is longer, more complex, or more important. **b.** *Sports.* An event that precedes the main event of a particular program, esp. in boxing or wrestling. **3. preliminaries.** *Printing.* Matter that precedes the actual text of a book, such as the title page, preface, or dedication. [Fr. *préliminaire* < Med. Lat. *praeliminaris* : Lat. *prae-* before + Lat. *limen*, threshold.] **—pre·lim′i·nar′i·ly** (-nâr′ə-lē) *adv.*

pre·lit·er·ate (prē-lĭt′ər-ĭt) *adj.* Of or pertaining to a culture not having a written language. **—pre·lit′er·ate** *n.*

prel·ude (prĕl′yōōd′, prā′lōōd′, prē′-) *n.* **1.** An introductory performance, event, or action preceding a more important one. **2.** *Mus.* A piece or movement serving as an introduction to a musical composition, esp.: **a.** An independent piece of moderate length that precedes a fugue. **b.** The first or opening section of a suite. **c.** The overture to an opera or oratorio, or a similar piece played before one of the acts of an opera. **d.** A piece played before a church service; an introductory voluntary. **e.** A relatively short composition in a free style, usually for piano or orchestra. *—v.* **-ud·ed, -ud·ing, -udes.** *—tr.* **1.** To serve as a prelude to. **2.** To introduce with or as if with a prelude. *—intr.* To serve as a prelude or introduction. [OFr. < Med. Lat. *praeludium* < Lat. *praeludere*, to play beforehand : *prae-*, before + *ludere*, to play < *ludus*, game.] **—prel′ud′er** *n.* **—pre·lu′di·al** (prĭ-lōō′dē-əl) *adj.*

pre·ma·lig·nant (prē′mə-lĭg′nənt) *adj.* Precancerous.

pre·mar·i·tal (prē-măr′ĭ-tl) *adj.* Taking place or existing prior to marriage. **—pre·mar′i·tal·ly** *adv.*

pre·ma·ture (prē′mə-tyōōr′, -tōōr′, -chōōr′) *adj.* **1.** Occurring, growing, or existing prior to the customary, correct, or assigned time; uncommonly or unexpectedly early: *a premature end.* **2.** Born after a gestation period of less than the normal time: *a premature baby.* [Lat. *praematurus* : *prae-*, before + *maturus*, ripe.] **—pre′ma·ture′ly** *adv.* **—pre′ma·ture′ness, pre′ma·tu′ri·ty** *n.*

pre·max·il·la (prē′măk-sĭl′ə) *n., pl.* **-il·lae** (-sĭl′ē). Either of two bones located in front of and between the maxillary bones in the upper jaw of vertebrates. **—pre·max′il·lar′y** (-măk′sə-lĕr′ē) *adj.*

pre·med (prē′mĕd′) *Informal. —adj.* Premedical. *—n.* A premedical student.

pre·med·i·cal (prē-mĕd′ĭ-kəl) *adj.* Preparing for or pertaining to the studies that prepare for the study of medicine.

pre·med·i·tate (prē-mĕd′ĭ-tāt′) *v.* **-tat·ed, -tat·ing, -tates.** *—tr.* To plan, arrange, or plot (a deed or events) in advance. *—intr.* To meditate or deliberate beforehand. [Lat. *praemeditari, praemeditat-* : *prae-*, before + *meditari*, to consider.] **—pre·med′i·ta′tive** *adj.* **—pre·med′i·ta′tor** *n.*

pre·med·i·tat·ed (prē-mĕd′ĭ-tā′tĭd) *adj.* Characterized by deliberate purpose, previous consideration, and some degree of planning. **—pre·med′i·tat′ed·ly** *adv.*

pre·med·i·ta·tion (prē-mĕd′ĭ-tā′shən) *n.* **1.** The act of speculating, arranging, or plotting in advance. **2.** *Law.* The con-

prehensile
Spider monkey hanging from branch by means of a prehensile tail

templation and plotting of a crime in advance, showing intent to commit the crime.
pre·men·stru·al (prē-mĕn′strōō-əl) *adj.* Of, pertaining to, or occurring in the period just before menstruation. **—pre·men′stru·al·ly** *adv.*
pre·mie (prē′mē) *n.* Variant of **preemie.**
pre·mi·er (prē′mē-ər, prĕm′ē-, prĭ-mîr′) *adj.* **1.** First in status or importance; chief. **2.** First to occur or exist; earliest. *—n.* (prĭ-mîr′). **1.** A prime minister. **2.** The chief executive of a Canadian province. [ME *primier* < OFr. *premier* < Lat. *primarius* < *primus,* first.] **—pre·mier′ship′** *n.*
pre·mière (prĭ-mîr′, -myâr′) *n.* **1.** The first public performance, as of a movie or play. **2.** The leading lady of a theatrical company. *—v.* **-mièred, -mièr·ing, -mières.** *—tr.* To present the first public performance of. *—intr.* To have the first public performance. *—adj.* Premier; paramount. [Fr. < fem. of *premier,* first < OFr. —see PREMIER.]
Usage: *Première* as a verb is unacceptable to a large majority of the Usage Panel, despite its wide usage in the world of entertainment.
pre·mil·le·nar·i·an (prē-mĭl′ə-nâr′ē-ən) *adj.* Of or pertaining to premillennialism. *—n.* A person who believes in premillennialism. **—pre·mil′le·nar′i·an·ism** *n.*
pre·mil·len·ni·al (prē′mĭ-lĕn′ē-əl) *adj.* Of or happening before the millennium. **—pre′mil·len′ni·al·ly** *adv.*
pre·mil·len·ni·al·ism (prē′mĭ-lĕn′ē-ə-lĭz′əm) *n.* The belief that Christ's second coming will immediately precede the millennium. **—pre′mil·len′ni·al·ist** *n.*
prem·ise (prĕm′ĭs) *n.* **1. a.** A proposition upon which an argument is based or from which a conclusion is drawn. **b.** *Logic.* One of the first two propositions (major or minor) of a syllogism, from which the conclusion is drawn. **2. premises.** *Law.* The preliminary or explanatory statements or facts of a document, as in an equity bill or deed. **3. premises. a.** Land and the buildings upon it. **b.** A building or part of a building. *—v.* **-ised, -is·ing, -is·es.** *—tr.* **1.** To state in advance as an introduction or explanation. **2.** To state or assume as a proposition in an argument. *—intr.* To make a premise. [ME *premisse* < OFr. < Med. Lat. *praemissa* < Lat., p.part. of *praemittere,* to set in front : *prae-,* before + *mittere,* to send.]
pre·mi·um (prē′mē-əm) *n.* **1.** A prize awarded for a particular act. **2.** Something offered free or at a reduced price as an inducement to buy. **3.** A sum of money or bonus paid in addition to a regular price, salary, or other amount. **4.** The amount paid, often in addition to the interest, to obtain a loan. **5.** The amount paid or payable, often in installments, for an insurance policy. **6.** The amount at which something is valued above its par or nominal value, as money or securities. **7.** Payment for training in a trade or profession. **8.** An unusual or high value: *put a premium on honesty and hard work.* [Lat. *praemium,* profit : *prae-,* before + *emere,* to take.]
pre·mix (prē′mĭks′) *n.* A mixture, as powdered ingredients for a cake, that is made beforehand and designed to be blended later with other ingredients, as eggs or water.
pre·mo·lar (prē-mō′lər) *n.* One of eight bicuspid teeth located in pairs on each side of the upper and lower jaws behind the canines and in front of the molars. **—pre·mo′lar** *adj.*
pre·mo·ni·tion (prē′mə-nĭsh′ən, prĕm′ə-) *n.* **1.** A warning in advance; forewarning. **2.** A presentiment of the future; foreboding. [OFr. *premonicion* < LLat. *praemonitio* < Lat. *praemonēre,* to forewarn : *prae-,* before + *monēre,* to warn.] **—pre·mon′i·to′ri·ly** (-mŏn′ĭ-tôr′ə-lē, -tōr′-) *adv.* **—pre·mon′i·to′ry** *adj.*
pre·morse (prĭ-môrs′) *adj. Biol.* Abruptly truncated, as though bitten or broken off. [Lat. *praemorsus,* p.part. of *praemordēre,* to bite off in front : *prae-,* in front + *mordēre,* to bite.]
pre·mu·ni·tion (prē′myōō-nĭsh′ən) *n.* Relative immunity to severe infection as a result of inducing an active low-grade infection. [Lat. *praemunitio,* fortification beforehand : *prae-,* before + *munire,* to fortify.] **—pre·mune′** (prē-myōōn′) *adj.*
pre·name (prē′nām′) *n.* A forename.
pre·na·tal (prē-nāt′l) *adj.* Existing or taking place prior to birth. **—pre·na′tal·ly** *adv.*
pre·oc·cu·pan·cy (prē-ŏk′yə-pən-sē) *n.* **1.** The act or right of taking possession before others; preoccupation. **2.** The state of being preoccupied or engrossed.
pre·oc·cu·pa·tion (prē-ŏk′yə-pā′shən) *n.* **1.** The state of being preoccupied; absorption of the attention or intellect. **2.** Something that preoccupies or engrosses the mind: *Increasing profits was his sole preoccupation.* **3.** Possession or occupation in advance; preoccupancy.
pre·oc·cu·pied (prē-ŏk′yə-pīd′) *adj.* **1. a.** Absorbed in thought; engrossed. **b.** Excessively concerned with something; distracted. **2.** Formerly or already occupied. **3.** Already used and therefore unavailable for further use. Used of taxonomic names.
pre·oc·cu·py (prē-ŏk′yə-pī′) *tr.v.* **-pied, -py·ing, -pies. 1.** To occupy completely the mind or attention of; engross. **2.** To occupy or take possession of in advance or before another.
pre·op·er·a·tive (prē-ŏp′ər-ə-tĭv, -ŏp′rə-, -ŏp′ə-rā′-) *adj.* Occurring prior to surgery. **—pre·op′er·a·tive·ly** *adv.*
pre·or·bit·al (prē-ôr′bĭ-tl) *adj.* Occurring prior to the establishing of an orbit, esp. the orbital flight of a spacecraft.
pre·or·dain (prē′ôr-dān′) *tr.v.* **-dained, -dain·ing, -dains.** To appoint, decree, or ordain in advance; foreordain. **—pre′or·dain′ment** *n.* **—pre·or′di·na′tion** (-ôr′dn-ā′shən) *n.*
prep (prĕp) *adj. Informal.* Preparatory: *a prep course.* *—n.* **1.** *Informal.* A preparatory school. **2.** *Chiefly Brit. Slang.* The preparing of lessons; homework. *—v.* **prepped, prep·ping, preps.** *Informal.* *—intr.* **1.** To be enrolled in and attend a preparatory school. **2.** To study or train in preparation for something. *—tr.* To prepare (someone) for medical examination or surgery.
pre·pack·age (prē-păk′ĭj) *tr.v.* **-aged, -ag·ing, -ag·es.** To wrap or package (products) before marketing them.
prep·a·ra·tion (prĕp′ə-rā′shən) *n.* **1.** The act or process of preparing. **2.** The state of being prepared; readiness. **3.** Often **preparations.** Preliminary measures that serve to make ready for something: *preparations for the wedding.* **4.** A substance, such as a medicine, prepared for a particular purpose. **5.** *Mus.* **a.** The anticipation of a dissonant tone by means of its introduction as a consonant tone in the preceding chord. **b.** The tone so used.
pre·par·a·tive (prĭ-păr′ə-tĭv, -pâr′-) *adj.* Serving or tending to prepare or make ready. *—n.* Something that prepares for something following. **—pre·par′a·tive·ly** *adv.*
pre·par·a·tor (prĭ-păr′ə-tər, -pâr′-) *n.* A person who prepares specimens for scientific investigation or for display.
pre·par·a·to·ry (prĭ-păr′ə-tôr′ē, -tōr′ē, -pâr′-) *adj.* **1.** Serving to make ready or prepare; introductory. **2.** Occupied in or pertaining to preparation, esp. for admission to college. *—**idiom.*** **preparatory to.** In preparation for. **—pre·par′a·to′ri·ly** *adv.*
preparatory school *n.* A secondary school, usually private, preparing students for college or, in Britain, for public school.
pre·pare (prĭ-pâr′) *v.* **-pared, -par·ing, -pares.** *—tr.* **1.** To make ready beforehand for a specific purpose, event, or occasion. **2.** To put together or make by combining various elements or ingredients; manufacture. **3.** To fit out; equip: *The troops were prepared for service in the Arctic.* **4.** *Mus.* To lead up to and soften (a dissonance or its impact) by means of preparation. *—intr.* To get ready. [ME *preparen* < OFr. *preparer* < Lat. *praeparare* : *prae-,* before + *parare,* to make ready.] **—pre·par′ed·ly** (-pâr′ĭd-lē) *adv.* **—pre·par′er** *n.*
pre·par·ed·ness (prĭ-pâr′ĭd-nĭs) *n.* The state of being prepared, esp. military readiness for war.
pre·pay (prē-pā′) *tr.v.* **-paid, -pay·ing, -pays.** To pay or pay for beforehand. **—pre·pay′ment** *n.*
pre·pense (prĭ-pĕns′) *adj.* Contemplated or arranged in advance; premeditated: *malice prepense.* [Alteration of obs. *purpensed* < ME, p.part. of *purpensen,* to premeditate < OFr. *pourpenser* : *pour,* before (< Lat. *pro-*) + *penser,* to think < Lat. *pensare,* freq. of *pendere,* to weigh.] **—pre·pense′ly** *adv.*
pre·plan (prē-plăn′) *intr. & tr.v.* **-planned, -plan·ning, -plans.** To make plans or plan in advance.
pre·pon·der·ance (prĭ-pŏn′dər-əns) also **pre·pon·der·an·cy** (-ən-sē) *n.* Superiority in weight, quantity, power, or importance.
pre·pon·der·ant (prĭ-pŏn′dər-ənt) *adj.* Having superior power, force, or importance; predominant. **—pre·pon′der·ant·ly** *adv.*
pre·pon·der·ate (prĭ-pŏn′də-rāt′) *intr.v.* **-at·ed, -at·ing, -ates. 1.** To exceed something else in weight. **2.** To be greater in power, force, quantity, or importance; predominate. **3.** *Archaic.* To be weighed down, as one end of a balance. *—adj.* (-dər-ĭt). Preponderant. [Lat. *praeponderare, praeponderat-* : *prae-,* in front of + *ponderare,* to weigh < *pondus,* weight.] **—pre·pon′der·ate·ly, pre·pon′der·at′ing·ly** *adv.*
prep·o·si·tion (prĕp′ə-zĭsh′ən) *n. Gram.* **1.** In some languages, a word that indicates the relation of a substantive to a verb, an adjective, or another substantive, as English *at, by, in, to, from,* and *with.* **2.** A word or construction similar in function to a preposition, such as *in regard to* or *concerning.* [ME *preposicioun* < Lat. *praepositio* < *praeponere,* to put in front : *prae-,* in front + *ponere,* to put.]
Usage: There is nothing inherently bad about ending a sentence with a preposition. Such placement may cause awkwardness by giving undue stress to the preposition (*the arrogant manner he always spoke with*) or it may provide a weak ending: *He welcomed the invitation, for Maine was the state he hoped to spend most of his time in.* But often the final position is the only natural one for the preposition: *We have much to be thankful for.* Where rearrangement would give an awkward or stilted effect, as in the example immediately preceding, the natural order should be kept.
prep·o·si·tion·al (prĕp′ə-zĭsh′ə-nəl) *adj.* Relating to, composed of, or used as a preposition. **—prep′o·si′tion·al·ly** *adv.*
prepositional phrase *n. Gram.* A phrase that consists of a preposition and the noun it governs and has adjectival or adverbial value.
pre·pos·i·tive (prĭ-pŏz′ĭ-tĭv) *Gram.* *—adj.* Put before; prefixed. *—n.* A word or particle put before another word. [LLat. *praepositivus* < Lat. *praeponere,* to put in front. —see PREPOSITION.] **—pre·pos′i·tive·ly** *adv.*
pre·pos·sess (prē′pə-zĕs′) *tr.v.* **-sessed, -sess·ing, -sess·es.**

1. To preoccupy the mind of to the exclusion of other thoughts or feelings. 2. To influence beforehand against or in favor of someone or something; prejudice. 3. To impress favorably in advance.
pre·pos·sess·ing (prē'pə-zĕs'ĭng) *adj.* 1. Impressing favorably; pleasing. 2. *Archaic.* Causing prejudice. **—pre'pos·sess'ing·ly** *adv.* **—pre'pos·sess'ing·ness** *n.*
pre·pos·ses·sion (prē'pə-zĕsh'ən) *n.* 1. A preconception or prejudice. 2. The state of being preoccupied with thoughts, opinions, or feelings.
pre·pos·ter·ous (prĭ-pŏs'tər-əs) *adj.* Contrary to nature, reason, or common sense; absurd. [Lat. *praeposterus* : *prae-*, before + *posterus,* coming after < *post,* after.] **—pre·pos'ter·ous·ly** *adv.* **—pre·pos'ter·ous·ness** *n.*
pre·po·ten·cy (prē-pōt'n-sē) *n.* The condition of being prepotent; predominance.
pre·po·tent (prē-pōt'nt) also **pre·po·ten·tial** (prē'pə-tĕn'shəl) *adj.* Greater in power, influence, or force; predominant. [ME < Lat. *praepotens,* pr.part. of *praeposse,* to be more powerful : *prae-*, before + *posse,* to be powerful.] **—pre·po'tent·ly** *adv.*
prep·pie or **prep·py** (prĕp'ē) *n., pl.* **-pies.** *Informal.* 1. A student in a preparatory school. 2. A student or young adult whose manner and dress are traditional and conservative. [Shortening and alteration of PREPARATORY SCHOOL.] **—prep'pie, prep'py** *adj.*
pre·proc·ess (prē-prŏs'ĕs', -prō'sĕs') *tr.v.* **-essed, -ess·ing, -ess·es.** To perform preliminary processing on.
pre·pro·duc·tion (prē'prə-dŭk'shən) *adj.* 1. Taking place or existing prior to production: *preproduction planning.* 2. Of, pertaining to, or being a prototype: *preproduction models of next year's automobiles.*
pre·pro·fes·sion·al (prē'prə-fĕsh'ə-nəl) *adj.* Preparatory to the practice of a profession or to its specialized field of study.
pre·pro·gram (prē-prō'grăm', -grəm) *tr.v.* **-grammed, -gram·ming, -grams** or **-gramed, -gram·ing, -grams.** To program in advance; preset.
prep school *n. Informal.* A preparatory school.
pre·pu·ber·ty (prē-pyōō'bər-tē) *n.* The period just before puberty.
pre·pu·bes·cence (prē'pyōō-bĕs'əns) *n.* Prepuberty.
pre·pu·bes·cent (prē'pyōō-bĕs'ənt) *adj.* Of or relating to prepuberty.
pre·pub·li·ca·tion (prē-pŭb'lĭ-kā'shən) *adj.* Of or pertaining to a time just prior to the publication date of a book: *prepublication orders.*
pre·puce (prē'pyōōs') *n.* 1. The loose fold of skin that covers the glans of the penis. 2. A loose fold of skin covering the glans of the clitoris. [ME < OFr. < Lat. *praeputium.*] **—pre·pu'tial** (-pyōō'shəl) *adj.*
pre·punch (prē-pŭnch') *tr.v.* **-punched, -punch·ing, -punch·es.** To punch data cards or tape before an anticipated use.
pre-Raph·a·el·ite (prē-răf'ē-ə-līt', -rā'fē-) *n.* A painter or writer belonging to or influenced by the pre-Raphaelite Brotherhood, a society founded in 1848 to advance the style and spirit of Italian painting before Raphael. *—adj.* Of, pertaining to, or characteristic of the pre-Raphaelites. **—pre-Raph'a·el·it'ism** *n.*
pre·re·cord (prē'rĭ-kôrd') *tr.v.* **-cord·ed, -cord·ing, -cords.** To record (a television program, for example) at an earlier time for later use.
pre·reg·is·tra·tion (prē-rĕj'ĭ-strā'shən) *n.* An early registration, as for returning college students, that takes place prior to general registration.
pre·req·ui·site (prē-rĕk'wĭ-zĭt) *adj.* Required as a prior condition to something: *Competence is prerequisite to promotion.* *—n.* Something that is prerequisite.
pre·rog·a·tive (prĭ-rŏg'ə-tĭv) *n.* 1. An exclusive right or privilege held by a person or group, esp. a hereditary or official right. 2. A characteristically exclusive right or privilege. 3. A natural gift or advantage making one superior. 4. Priority or pre-eminence; superiority. *—adj.* Of, arising from, or exercising a prerogative. [ME < OFr. < Lat. *praerogativa* < *praerogativus,* asked first : *prae-*, before + *rogare,* to ask.] **—pre·rog'a·tived** *adj.*
pres·age (prĕs'ĭj) *n.* 1. An indication or warning of a future occurrence; omen. 2. A feeling or intuition of what is going to occur; presentiment. 3. Prophetic significance or meaning. 4. A prediction. *—v.* **pre·sage** (prĭ-sāj', prĕs'ĭj) **-saged, -sag·ing, -sag·es.** *—tr.* 1. To indicate or warn of in advance; portend. 2. To have a presentiment of. 3. To foretell or predict. *—intr.* To make or utter a prediction. [ME < Lat. *praesagium* < *praesagire,* to perceive beforehand : *prae-*, before + *sagire,* to perceive acutely.] **—pre·sage'ful** (prĭ-sāj'fəl) *adj.* **—pre·sag'er** (prĭ-sā'jər) *n.*
pres·by·o·pi·a (prĕz'bē-ō'pē-ə, prĕs'-) *n.* The inability of the eye to focus sharply on nearby objects, resulting from hardening of the crystalline lens with advancing age. [Gk. *presbus,* old man + -OPIA.] **—pres'by·op'ic** (-ŏp'ĭk, -ō'pĭk) *adj.*
pres·by·ter (prĕz'bĭ-tər, prĕs'-) *n.* 1. In the early Christian church, an elder of the congregation. 2. In various hierarchical churches, a priest. 3. a. A teaching elder in the Presbyterian Church. b. A ruling elder in the Presbyterian Church. [LLat. < Gk. *presbuteros* < comp. of *presbus,* old man.]
pres·byt·er·ate (prĕz-bĭt'ər-ĭt, -ə-rāt', prĕs-) *n.* 1. The office of a presbyter. 2. The body or order of presbyters.
pres·by·te·ri·al (prĕz'bĭ-tîr'ē-əl, prĕs'-) *adj.* Of or pertaining to a presbyter or the presbytery. **—pres'by·te'ri·al·ly** *adv.*
pres·by·te·ri·an (prĕz'bĭ-tîr'ē-ən, prĕs'-) *adj.* 1. Of or pertaining to ecclesiastical government by presbyters. 2. **Presbyterian.** Of or pertaining to a Presbyterian Church. *—n.* **Presbyterian.** A member or adherent of a Presbyterian Church. **—pres'by·te'ri·an·ism** *n.*
Presbyterian Church *n.* Any of various Protestant churches governed by presbyters and traditionally Calvinist in doctrine.
pres·by·ter·y (prĕz'bĭ-tĕr'ē, prĕs'-) *n., pl.* **-ies.** 1. a. A court composed of Presbyterian Church ministers and representative elders of a particular locality. b. The district represented by this court. 2. Presbyters collectively. 3. Government of a church by presbyters. 4. The section of a church reserved for the clergy. 5. *Rom. Cath. Ch.* The residence of a priest. [LLat. *presbyterium,* council of elders < Gk. *presbuterion* < *presbuteros,* elder. —see PRESBYTER.]
pre·school (prē'skōōl') *adj.* Of, pertaining to, or designed for a child of nursery-school age. *—n.* A nursery school. **—pre'school'er** *n.*
pre·sci·ence (prē'shē-əns, -shəns, prĕsh'ē-əns, prĕsh'əns) *n.* Knowledge of actions or events before they occur; foreknowledge; foresight.
pre·sci·ent (prē'shē-ənt, -shənt, prĕsh'ē-ənt, prĕsh'ənt) *adj.* 1. Of or pertaining to prescience. 2. Possessing prescience. [Lat. *praesciens, praescient-*, pr.part. of *praescire,* to know beforehand : *prae-*, before + *scire,* to know.] **—pre'sci·ent·ly** *adv.*
pre·sci·en·tif·ic (prē-sī'ən-tĭf'ĭk) *adj.* Of, pertaining to, or occurring at a time before the advent of modern science and the application of its methods.
pre·scind (prĭ-sĭnd') *v.* **-scind·ed, -scind·ing, -scinds.** *—tr.* To separate or divide in thought; consider individually. *—intr.* To withdraw one's attention. [Lat. *praescindere,* to cut off in front : *prae-*, in front + *scindere,* to cut off.]
pre·screen (prē-skrēn') *tr.v.* **-screened, -screen·ing, -screens.** 1. To view a motion picture before it is released for public showing. 2. To screen beforehand: *prescreen applicants for interviews.*
pre·scribe (prĭ-skrīb') *v.* **-scribed, -scrib·ing, -scribes.** *—tr.* 1. To set down as a rule or guide; enjoin. 2. *Med.* To order or recommend the use of (a drug or treatment). *—intr.* 1. To establish rules, laws, or directions. 2. *Med.* To order or recommend a remedy or treatment. 3. *Law.* a. To assert a right or title to something on the grounds of prescription. b. To become invalidated or unenforceable by the process of prescription. [Lat. *praescribere* : *prae-*, before + *scribere,* to write.] **—pre·scrib'er** *n.*
pre·script (prē'skrĭpt') *n.* Something prescribed, esp. a rule or regulation of conduct. *—adj.* (prē'skrĭpt', prĭ-skrĭpt'). Established as a rule; prescribed. [Lat. *praescriptum* < *praescribere,* to order. —see PRESCRIBE.]
pre·scrip·ti·ble (prĭ-skrĭp'tə-bəl) *adj.* 1. Capable of being prescribed. 2. Requiring or derived from prescription. **—pre·scrip'ti·bil'i·ty** *n.*
pre·scrip·tion (prĭ-skrĭp'shən) *n.* 1. a. The act of prescribing. b. Something that is prescribed. 2. *Med.* a. A written instruction by a physician for the preparation and administration of a medicine. b. A prescribed medicine. c. An ophthalmologist's or optometrist's written instruction for the grinding of corrective lenses. 3. A formula directing the preparation of something. 4. *Law.* a. The process of acquiring title to property by reason of uninterrupted possession of specified duration. b. The limitation of time beyond which an action, debt, or crime is no longer valid or enforceable. [Lat. *praescriptio,* precept < *praescribere,* to order. —see PRESCRIBE.]
prescription drug *n.* A controlled drug available only by the order of a physician's prescription.
pre·scrip·tive (prĭ-skrĭp'tĭv) *adj.* 1. Sanctioned or authorized by long-standing custom or usage. 2. Making or giving injunctions, directions, laws, or rules. 3. *Law.* Acquired by or based upon uninterrupted possession. **—pre·scrip'tive·ly** *adv.* **—pre·scrip'tive·ness** *n.*
pre·sell (prē-sĕl') *tr.v.* **-sold** (-sōld'), **-sell·ing, -sells.** To promote (a product not yet on the market).
pres·ence (prĕz'əns) *n.* 1. The state or fact of being present. 2. Immediate proximity in time or space. 3. The area immediately surrounding a great personage, esp. a sovereign. 4. A person who is present. 5. a. A person's manner of carrying himself; bearing. b. The quality of self-assurance and confidence. 6. A supernatural influence felt to be nearby.
presence of mind *n.* The ability to think and act efficiently, esp. in an emergency.
pres·ent[1] (prĕz'ənt) *n.* 1. A moment or period in time perceptible as intermediate between past and future; now. 2. *Gram.* a. The present tense. b. A verb form in the present tense. 3. **presents.** *Law.* The document or instrument in question: *be it known by these presents.* *—adj.* 1. Being, pertaining to, or occurring at a moment or period in time considered as the present. 2. Being at hand. 3. *Obs.* Alert to circumstances; attentive. 4. *Archaic.* Readily available; immediate. 5. *Gram.* Denoting a verb tense or form that ex-

presses current time. —***idioms.*** **at present.** At the present time; right now. **for the present.** For the time being; temporarily. [ME < OFr. < Lat. *praesens,* pr.part. of *praeesse,* to be present : *prae-,* in front + *esse,* to be.] —**pres'ent·ness** *n.*

pre·sent² (prĭ-zĕnt') *v.* **-sent·ed, -sent·ing, -sents.** —*tr.* **1. a.** To introduce, esp. with formal ceremony. **b.** To introduce (a girl) to society with conventional ceremony. **2.** To bring before the public: *present a play.* **3. a.** To make a gift or award of. **b.** To make a gift to. **4.** To offer to view; display: *present one's credentials.* **5.** To offer for consideration. **6.** To salute with or aim (a weapon). **7.** *Eccles.* To recommend (a clergyman) for a benefice. **8.** *Law.* **a.** To offer to a legislature or court for consideration. **b.** To bring a charge or indictment against. —*n.* **pres·ent** (prĕz'ənt). Something presented; gift. [ME *presenten* < OFr. *presentare,* to show < *praesens,* pr.part. of *praeesse,* to be in front of. —see PRESENT¹.] —**pre·sent'er** *n.*

pre·sent·a·ble (prĭ-zĕn'tə-bəl) *adj.* **1.** Capable of being given, displayed, or offered. **2.** Fit for introduction to others. —**pre·sent'a·bil'i·ty, pre·sent'a·ble·ness** *n.* —**pre·sent'a·bly** *adv.*

pres·en·ta·tion (prĕz'ən-tā'shən, prē'zən-) *n.* **1. a.** The act of presenting. **b.** The state of being presented. **2.** A performance, as of a drama. **3.** Something, as an award, that is presented. **4. a.** A formal introduction. **b.** A social debut. **5.** *Eccles.* The act or right of naming a clergyman to a benefice. **6.** The process of offering for consideration. **7.** *Med.* The position of the fetus in the uterus at birth with respect to the mouth of the uterus. —**pres'en·ta'tion·al** *adj.*

pre·sent·a·tive (prĭ-zĕn'tə-tĭv) *adj.* **1.** Having the capacity or function of bringing an idea or image to mind. **2. a.** Perceived or capable of being perceived directly rather than through association. **b.** Having the ability to so perceive. **3.** *Eccles.* Capable of naming or of being named to a benefice. —**pre·sent'a·tive·ness** *n.*

pres·ent-day (prĕz'ənt-dā') *adj.* Current.

pres·ent·ee (prĕz'ən-tē', prĭ-zĕn'-) *n.* **1.** A person who is presented. **2.** A person to whom something is given.

pre·sen·tient (prē-sĕn'shənt, -shē-ənt, -zĕn'-, prĭ-) *adj.* Having a presentiment. [Lat. *praesentiens, praesentient-,* pr.part. of *praesentire,* to feel beforehand. —see PRESENTIMENT.]

pre·sen·ti·ment (prĭ-zĕn'tə-mənt) *n.* A sense of something about to occur; premonition. [Obs. Fr. < OFr. *presentir,* to feel beforehand < Lat. *praesentire* : *prae-,* before + *sentire,* to feel.] —**pre·sen'ti·men'tal** (-mĕn'tl) *adj.*

pres·ent·ly (prĕz'ənt-lē) *adv.* **1.** In a short time; soon: *She will arrive presently.* **2.** At this time or period; now: *He is presently staying with us.* **3.** *Archaic.* At once; immediately.

Usage: *Presently* is now used primarily in the sense of "soon." Confusingly, it is also used in the sense of "at the present time." The Usage Panel is about evenly divided on the acceptability of its use in the latter sense. Writers who use the word should take care that the meaning is clear from the context.

pre·sent·ment (prĭ-zĕnt'mənt) *n.* **1.** The act of presenting; presentation. **2.** Something presented, as a picture or exhibition. **3.** *Law.* **a.** The act of submitting or presenting a formal statement of a legal matter to a court or authorized person. **b.** The report concerning an offense written by a grand jury and based on the jury's own knowledge and observation. **4.** The act of presenting a bill or note for payment.

present participle *n. Gram.* A participle expressing present action, in English formed by the infinitive plus *-ing* and used to express present action in relation to the time indicated by the finite verb in its clause, to form progressive tenses with modal auxiliaries, and to function as a verbal adjective.

present perfect *n. Gram.* **1.** The verb tense expressing action completed at the present time, formed in English by combining the present tense of *have* with a past participle, as in *He has spoken.* **2.** A verb in the present perfect tense.

present tense *n. Gram.* The verb tense expressing action in the present time, as in *She sews.*

pres·er·va·tion·ist (prĕz'ər-vā'shə-nĭst) *n.* One who advocates preservation, as of a building having historical value.

pre·ser·va·tive (prĭ-zûr'və-tĭv) *adj.* Tending to preserve or capable of preserving. —*n.* Something used to preserve, esp. a chemical used in foods to inhibit spoilage.

pre·serve (prĭ-zûrv') *v.* **-served, -serv·ing, -serves.** —*tr.* **1.** To keep safe from injury, peril, or other adversity; protect. **2.** To keep in perfect or unaltered condition; maintain unchanged. **3.** To keep or maintain intact: *tried to preserve family harmony.* **4.** To prepare (food) for future use, as by canning or salting. **5.** To prevent (organic bodies) from decaying or spoiling. **6.** To keep or protect (game or fish) for one's private hunting or fishing. —*intr.* **1.** To treat fruit or other foods so as to prevent decay. **2.** To maintain a private area stocked with game or fish. —*n.* **1.** Something that acts to preserve; preservative. **2.** Often **preserves.** Fruit cooked with sugar to protect against decay or fermentation; jam or confiture. **3.** An area maintained for the protection of wildlife or natural resources. **4.** Something considered restricted to the use of certain persons: *Ancient Greek is the preserve of scholars.* [ME *preserven* < OFr. *preserver* < LLat. *praeservare* : Lat. *prae-,* before + Lat. *servare,* to guard.] —**pre·serv'a·bil'i·ty** *n.* —**pre·serv'a·ble** *adj.* —**pres'er·va'tion** (prĕz'ər-vā'shən) *n.* —**pre·serv'er** *n.*

pre·set (prē-sĕt') *tr.v.* **-set, -set·ting, -sets.** To set beforehand: *preset a microwave oven.*

pre·shrunk also **pre-shrunk** (prē'shrŭngk') *adj.* Shrunk during manufacture to minimize subsequent shrinkage.

pre·side (prĭ-zīd') *intr.v.* **-sid·ed, -sid·ing, -sides.** **1.** To hold the position of authority; act as chairperson or president. **2.** To possess or exercise authority or control. **3.** *Mus.* To be the featured instrumental performer. [Fr. *presider* < Lat. *praesidēre* : *prae-,* in front of + *sedēre,* to sit.] —**pre·sid'er** *n.*

pres·i·den·cy (prĕz'ĭ-dən-sē, -dĕn'-) *n., pl.* **-cies.** **1.** The office, function, or term of a president. **2.** Often **Presidency.** The office of president of a republic, esp. of the United States. **3.** *Mormon Ch.* **a.** A governing body on a local level consisting of three men. **b.** Often **Presidency.** The chief administrative body of the church.

pres·i·dent (prĕz'ĭ-dənt, -dĕnt') *n.* **1.** One appointed or elected to preside over an organized body of people, as an assembly or meeting. **2.** Often **President.** The chief executive of a republic, esp. of the United States. **3.** The chief officer of a branch of government, a corporation, a board of trustees, a university, or a similar body. [ME < OFr. < Lat. *praesidens,* pr.part. of *praesidēre,* to preside. —see PRESIDE.] —**pres'i·dent·ship'** *n.*

pres·i·dent-e·lect (prĕz'ĭ-dənt-ĭ-lĕkt') *n.* A person who has been elected president but has not yet begun his term of office.

pres·i·den·tial (prĕz'ĭ-dĕn'shəl) *adj.* **1.** Of or relating to a president or presidency. **2.** Providing for a president elected independently of the legislature. —**pres'i·den'tial·ly** *adv.*

president pro tem (prō tĕm') *n. Informal.* A president pro tempore.

president pro tem·po·re (prō tĕm'pə-rē) *n.* The senator who presides over the U.S. Senate in the absence of the Vice President.

pre·sid·i·a (prĭ-sĭd'ē-ə) *n.* A plural of **presidium.**

pre·sid·i·al (prĭ-sĭd'ē-əl) also **pre·sid·i·ar·y** (-ĕr'ē) *adj.* Of, pertaining to, or possessing a presidio.

pre·si·di·o (prĭ-sē'dē-ō', -sĭd'ē-ō') *n., pl.* **-os.** A garrison, esp. a fortress of the kind established in the U.S. Southwest by the Spanish to protect their holdings and missions. [Sp. < Lat. *praesidium* < *praesidēre,* to guard. —see PRESIDE.]

pre·sid·i·um (prĭ-sĭd'ē-əm) *n., pl.* **-i·a** (-ē-ə) or **-i·ums.** **1.** Any of various permanent executive committees in Communist countries having power to act for a larger governing body. **2. Presidium.** A committee of the Supreme Soviet headed by the premier and constituting the highest policy-making body of the Soviet Union. [R. *prezidium* < Lat. *praesidium,* garrison < *praesidēre,* to guard. —see PRESIDE.]

pre·sig·ni·fy (prē-sĭg'nə-fī') *tr.v.* **-fied, -fy·ing, -fies.** To betoken or signify beforehand; prefigure.

pre·soak (prē-sōk') *tr.v.* **-soaked, -soak·ing, -soaks.** To soak (clothes, for example) before washing. —*n.* (prē'sōk'). A cycle on an automatic washing machine for presoaking clothes.

pre·sort (prē-sôrt') *tr.v.* **-sort·ed, -sort·ing, -sorts.** To sort (mail) according to Zip Codes before delivering to a post office.

press¹ (prĕs) *v.* **pressed, press·ing, press·es.** —*tr.* **1.** To exert steady weight or force against; bear down on. **2. a.** To squeeze the juice or other contents from. **b.** To extract (juice, for example) by squeezing or compressing. **3. a.** To make compact or reshape by applying steady force. **b.** To iron (clothing, for example). **4.** To clasp or embrace closely. **5.** To seek to influence, as by insistent arguments; entreat insistently. **6.** To attempt to force to action; urge on. **7.** To place in trying or constraining circumstances; harass. **8.** To lay stress upon; emphasize. **9.** To advance or carry on vigorously: *"Far from backing down, he pressed the attack"* (Justin Kaplan). **10.** To put forward importunately or insistently. —*intr.* **1.** To exert force or pressure. **2.** To weigh heavily, as on the mind. **3.** To advance eagerly; push forward. **4.** To require haste; be urgent. **5.** To iron clothes or other material. **6.** To assemble closely and in large numbers; crowd. **7.** To employ urgent persuasion or entreaty; ask earnestly or persistently. —*n.* **1.** Any of various machines or devices that apply pressure. **2.** Any of various machines used for printing; printing press. **3.** A place or establishment where matter is printed. **4.** The method, art, or business of printing. **5. a.** Printed matter as a whole, esp. newspapers and periodicals. **b.** The people involved with such publications, as editors and reporters. **c.** The matter dealt with in such publications, as news and criticism. **6.** The act of gathering in large numbers or of pushing forward. **7.** A large gathering; throng. **8. a.** The act of applying pressure. **b.** The state of being pressed. **9.** The haste or urgency of business or affairs. **10.** The set of proper creases in a garment or fabric, formed by ironing. **11.** An upright closet or case used for storing clothing, books, or other articles. —***idioms.*** **be (hard) pressed for.** To be lacking in. **press (one's) luck.** To push for something in spite of odds against it. **press the flesh.** *Informal.* To glad-hand and mix with people, esp. while campaigning for political office. [ME *pressen* < OFr. *presser* < Lat. *pressare,* freq. of *premere,* to press.]

press[2] (prĕs) *tr.v.* **pressed, press·ing, press·es. 1.** To force into service in the army or navy; impress. **2.** To use in a manner different from the usual or intended. —*n.* **1.** Conscription or impressment into service, esp. into the navy. **2.** An official warrant for impressing men. [Alteration of obs. *prest,* to hire for military service < ME, enlistment money < OFr. < *prester,* to lend < Med. Lat. *prestare* < Lat., to furnish.]

press agency *n.* A news agency.

press agent *n.* A person employed to arrange advertising and publicity, as for an actor or a business. **—press′-a′gent·ry** (-ā′jən-trē) *n.*

press association *n.* A news agency.

press·board (prĕs′bôrd′, -bōrd′) *n.* **1.** A heavy glazed paper or pasteboard used esp. to cover the platen or cylinder of a printing press. **2.** A small ironing board.

press box *n.* A section for reporters, as in a stadium.

press conference *n.* An interview held for newsmen by a political figure or celebrity.

press·er (prĕs′ər) *n.* **1.** A person who presses clothes. **2.** Any of various devices that apply pressure to a product in manufacturing or canning.

press gang also **press·gang** (prĕs′găng′) *n.* A company of men under an officer detailed to press men into military or naval service.

press·ing (prĕs′ĭng) *adj.* **1.** Demanding immediate attention; urgent: *a pressing need.* **2.** Importunate; insistent: *a pressing invitation.* **—press′ing·ly** *adv.*

press·man (prĕs′mən, -măn′) *n.* **1.** A printing press operator. **2.** *Chiefly Brit.* A newspaperman.

press·mark (prĕs′märk′) *n.* **1.** A notation in or on a book indicating where it should be placed in a library. **2.** *Printing.* A notation or figure in the margin of a printed sheet indicating the press upon which it was printed.

press of sail *n. Naut.* The greatest amount of sail that a ship can carry safely.

pres·sor (prĕs′ôr′, -ər) *adj.* Causing an increase in blood pressure. [< Lat. *pressus,* p.part. of *premere,* to press.]

press release *n.* An announcement of an event, performance, or other news or publicity item issued to the press.

press·room (prĕs′ro͞om′, -ro͝om′) *n.* The room in a printing or newspaper publishing establishment that contains the presses.

press·run (prĕs′rŭn′) *n.* The specific number of copies printed during a continuous operation of a printing press.

press secretary *n.* A person who manages the public affairs and press conferences of a public figure.

pres·sure (prĕsh′ər) *n.* **1. a.** The act of pressing. **b.** The condition of being pressed. **2.** The application of continuous force by one body upon another that it is touching; compression. **3.** *Physics.* Force applied over a surface, measured as force per unit of area. **4.** A constraining influence upon the mind or will, as a moral force. **5.** Urgent claim or demand: *under the pressure of business.* **6.** A burdensome, distressing, or weighty condition. **7.** *Archaic.* A mark made by application of force or weight; impression. —*tr.v.* **-sured, -sur·ing, -sures.** To force, as by overpowering influence or persuasion. [Lat. *pressura* < *premere,* to press.]

pressure cabin *n.* A pressurized section of an aircraft.

pressure cooker *n.* **1.** An airtight metal pot that uses steam under pressure at high temperature to cook food quickly. **2.** A position of difficulty, stress, or anxiety; hot seat.

pressure gauge *n.* **1.** A device for measuring fluid pressure. **2.** A device for measuring the pressure of explosions.

pressure group *n.* A group that exerts pressure to advance or protect its interests.

pressure point *n.* Any of a number of areas on the body where an artery runs near a bone so that when pressure is applied to the artery by pressing it against the bone bleeding can be controlled.

pressure suit *n.* A garment that is worn in high-altitude aircraft or in spacecraft to compensate for low-pressure conditions.

pres·sur·ize (prĕsh′ə-rīz′) *tr.v.* **-ized, -iz·ing, -iz·es. 1.** To maintain normal air pressure in (an enclosure, as an aircraft or submarine). **2.** To put (gas or liquid) under a greater than normal pressure. **3.** To design to resist pressure. **—pres′sur·i·za′tion** *n.* **—pres′sur·iz′er** *n.*

press·work (prĕs′wûrk′) *n.* **1.** The management or operation of a printing press. **2.** The matter printed by a printing press.

Pres·ter John (prĕs′tər jŏn′) *n.* A legendary medieval Christian priest and king thought to have reigned over a Christian kingdom in the Far East or in Ethiopia. [ME *prestre,* priest < OFr. < LLat. *presbyter.* —see PRESBYTER.]

pres·ti·dig·i·ta·tion (prĕs′tĭ-dĭj′ĭ-tā′shən) *n.* Manual skill and dexterity in the execution of tricks; sleight of hand. [Fr. < *prestidigitateur,* conjurer : *preste,* nimble (< Ital. *presto* < LLat. *praestus* < Lat. *praesto,* at hand) + Lat. *digitus,* finger.] **—pres′ti·dig′i·ta′tor** *n.*

pres·tige (prĕ-stēzh′, -stēj′) *n.* **1.** Prominence or influential status achieved through success, renown, or wealth. **2.** The power to command admiration in a group: *His new position has much prestige.* **—modifier:** *the prestige schools of the Ivy League.* [Fr., illusion < Lat. *prestigiae,* tricks < *praestringere,* to dazzle : *prae-,* before + *stringere,* to bind.] **—pres·tige′ful** *adj.*

pres·ti·gious (prĕ-stē′jəs, -stĭj′əs) *adj.* Having prestige; esteemed. **—pres·ti′gious·ly** *adv.* **—pres·ti′gious·ness** *n.*

pres·tis·si·mo (prĕ-stĭs′ə-mō′) *Mus.* —*adv.* At as fast a tempo as possible. Used as a direction. —*n., pl.* **-mos.** A section or passage to be played prestissimo. [Ital., superl. of *presto,* presto.] **—pres·tis′si·mo′** *adj.*

pres·to (prĕs′tō) *adv.* **1.** *Mus.* In rapid tempo. Used as a direction. **2.** Suddenly; at once. —*n., pl.* **-tos.** *Mus.* A section or passage to be played presto. [Ital. < LLat. *praestus,* quick < Lat. *praesto,* at hand.] **—pres′to** *adj.*

pre·sum·a·ble (prĭ-zo͞o′mə-bəl) *adj.* Capable of being presumed or taken for granted; reasonable as a supposition. **—pre·sum′a·bly** *adv.*

pre·sume (prĭ-zo͞om′) *v.* **-sumed, -sum·ing, -sumes.** —*tr.* **1.** To take for granted; assume to be true in the absence of proof to the contrary. **2.** To give reasonable evidence for assuming; appear to prove. **3.** To engage oneself in without authority or permission; dare: *He presumed to invite himself to dinner.* —*intr.* **1.** To act overconfidently; take liberties. **2.** To take unwarranted advantage of something: *Don't presume on their hospitality.* [ME *presumen* < OFr. *presumer* < LLat. *praesumere* < Lat., to anticipate : *prae-,* before + *sumere,* to take.] **—pre·sum′ed·ly** (-zo͞o′mĭd-lē) *adv.* **—pre·sum′er** *n.*

Synonyms: *presume, presuppose, suppose, postulate, assume, posit.* These verbs signify the step of inferring certain things to be true as a probability, hypothesis, or convenience, sometimes without full justification. To *presume* something is to guess it as being reasonable or possible beforehand or without full knowledge, but it may imply an unwarranted conclusion and is often used in a questioning tone of voice: *I presume you're going?* It may indicate to take advantage of: *He presumed upon my good nature.* To *suppose* something is more hesitantly and objectively to subscribe to its likelihood, sometimes out of seeming disinterestedness. *Presuppose* implies a working or assumptive speculation about something based on some preceding evidence or condition. *Postulate* has a more exact philosophical usage and means to assert or construe a hypothetical proposal formally and without proof: *He postulated a complete lie.* To *assume* something is to take it for granted without proof but sometimes on safe, if incomplete, grounds: *You can only assume so much.* To *posit* something is to affirm or present it flatly for consideration. It is close to *postulate* in meaning but is more decisive in spirit: *posited a sound proof of the Devil's existence.*

pre·sum·ing (prĭ-zo͞o′mĭng) *adj.* Having or exhibiting excessive and arrogant self-confidence; presumptuous. **—pre·sum′ing·ly** *adv.*

pre·sump·tion (prĭ-zŭmp′shən) *n.* **1.** Behavior or language that is boldly arrogant or offensive; effrontery. **2.** The act of presuming or accepting as true. **3.** Acceptance or belief based on reasonable evidence; assumption or supposition. **4.** A condition or basis for accepting or presuming. **5.** *Law.* An inference as to the truth of an allegation or proposition, based on probable reasoning in the absence of or prior to actual proof or disproof. [ME *presumpcion* < OFr. < LLat. *praesumptio* < *praesumere,* to presume.]

pre·sump·tive (prĭ-zŭmp′tĭv) *adj.* **1.** Providing a reasonable basis for belief or acceptance. **2.** Founded on probability or presumption: *an heir presumptive.* **—pre·sump′tive·ly** *adv.*

pre·sump·tu·ous (prĭ-zŭmp′cho͞o-əs) *adj.* Excessively forward or confident; arrogant. [ME < OFr. *presumptueux* < LLat. *presumptuosus* < *praesumptio,* presumption.] **—pre·sump′tu·ous·ly** *adv.* **—pre·sump′tu·ous·ness** *n.*

pre·sup·pose (prē′sə-pōz′) *tr.v.* **-posed, -pos·ing, -pos·es. 1.** To assume or suppose in advance. **2.** To require or involve necessarily as an antecedent condition. **—pre·sup′po·si′tion** (-sŭp′ə-zĭsh′ən) *n.*

pre·tax (prē′tăks′) *adj.* Existing before tax deductions: *pretax income.*

pre·teen (prē′tēn′) *adj.* **1.** Pertaining to or designed for preadolescent children: *preteen clothing.* **2.** Being a preadolescent child. —*n.* A preadolescent child.

pre·tence (prē′tĕns′, prĭ-tĕns′) *n. Chiefly Brit.* Variant of **pretense.**

pre·tend (prĭ-tĕnd′) *v.* **-tend·ed, -tend·ing, -tends.** —*tr.* **1.** To affect; feign: *"All princes pretend a regard to the rights of other princes"* (Hume). **2.** To claim or allege insincerely or falsely; profess. **3.** To represent fictitiously in play; make believe. **4.** To take upon oneself; venture: *I cannot pretend to say that you are wrong.* —*intr.* **1.** To feign an action or character, as in play. **2.** To put forward a claim. [ME *pretenden* < Lat. *praetendere* : *prae-,* in front + *tendere,* to extend.]

Synonyms: *pretend, feign, dissemble, fake, simulate.* These all mean to assume falsely an identity, manner, or skill. *Pretend* is mild in force, implying no evil end, but it can suggest a vain or transparent attempt to fool others. *Feign* implies more strongly the false assumption of some condition so as to evade the responsibilities incurred by being sincere: *She feigned illness and left early. Dissemble* suggests artful deception in speech or manner to conceal one's

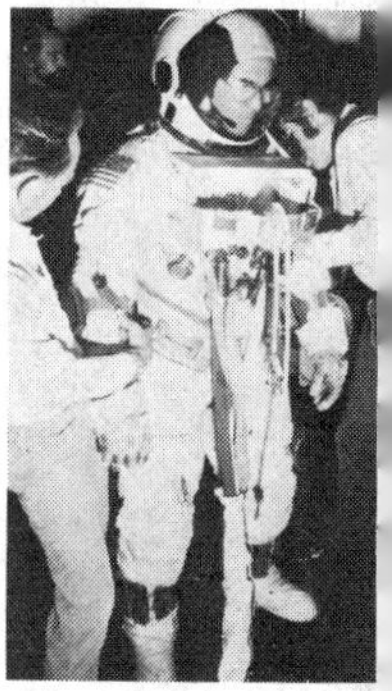

pressure suit

true purposes or feelings. *Fake,* an informal term, suggests counterfeiting, proceeding as often from ineptitude as from deceitfulness. *Simulate* emphasizes misleading appearance rather than deceptive action and implies the taking on of a false aspect that closely resembles reality.

pre·tend·ed (prĭ-tĕn′dĭd) *adj.* **1.** Reputed or asserted; alleged. **2.** False; feigned. **—pre·tend′ed·ly** *adv.*

pre·tend·er (prĭ-tĕn′dər) *n.* **1.** One who simulates, pretends, or alleges falsely; hypocrite or dissembler. **2. a.** One who sets forth a claim. **b.** A claimant to a throne.

pre·tense (prē′tĕns′, prĭ-tĕns′) *n.* **1.** The act of pretending; a false appearance or action intended to deceive. **2.** A false or studied show; affectation. **3.** A false reason or excuse; pretext. **4.** Something imagined or pretended; make-believe. **5.** A mere show without reality; outward appearance. **6.** A right asserted with or without foundation; claim. **7.** Ostentation; pretentiousness. [ME < AN, ult. < Lat. *praetendere,* to pretend.]

pre·ten·sion (prĭ-tĕn′shən) *n.* **1.** A specious allegation; pretext. **2.** A claim to something, such as a privilege or right. **3.** The advancing of a claim. **4.** Pretentiousness; ostentation.

pre·ten·tious (prĭ-tĕn′shəs) *adj.* **1.** Claiming or demanding a position of distinction or merit, esp. when unjustified. **2.** Making an extravagant outward show; ostentatious. **—pre·ten′tious·ly** *adv.* **—pre·ten′tious·ness** *n.*

pret·er·it or **pret·er·ite** (prĕt′ər-ĭt) *Gram.* *—adj.* Denoting the verb tense that expresses or describes a past or completed action or condition. *—n.* **1.** The verb form expressing or describing a past or completed action or condition; past tense. **2.** A verb in the preterit form. [ME < OFr. < Lat. *praeteritus,* p.part. of *praeterire,* to go by : *praeter,* beyond (comp. of *prae,* before) + *ire,* to go.]

pret·er·i·tion (prĕt′ə-rĭsh′ən) *n.* **1.** The act of passing by, disregarding, or omitting. **2.** *Law.* The neglect of a testator to mention a legal heir in his will. **3.** *Theol.* The Calvinist doctrine that God neglected to designate those who would be damned, positively determining only the elect. [LLat. *praeteritio* < Lat. *praeterire,* to go by. —see PRETERIT.]

pre·ter·mit (prē′tər-mĭt′) *tr.v.* **-mit·ted, -mit·ting, -mits. 1.** To disregard intentionally or allow to pass unnoticed or unmentioned. **2.** To fail to do or include; omit. **3.** To interrupt or terminate. [Lat. *praetermittere* : *praeter,* beyond (comp. of *prae,* before) + *mittere,* to let go.] **—pre′ter·mis′sion** (-mĭsh′ən) *n.* **—pre′ter·mit′ter** *n.*

pre·ter·nat·u·ral (prē′tər-năch′ər-əl, -năch′rəl) *adj.* **1.** Out of or beyond the normal course of nature; differing from the natural. **2.** Transcending the natural or material order; supernatural. [Med. Lat. *praeternaturalis* : Lat. *praeter,* beyond (comp. of *prae,* before) + Lat. *natura,* nature.] **—pre′ter·nat′u·ral·ism** *n.* **—pre′ter·nat′u·ral·ly** *adv.* **—pre′ter·nat′u·ral·ness** *n.*

pre·test (prē′tĕst′) *n.* **1. a.** A test given to determine whether a class is sufficiently prepared for a new course. **b.** The condition of a sample prior to experimental modification. **2.** The advance testing of something, such as a questionnaire, product, or idea. *—tr. & intr.v.* (prē-tĕst′) **-test·ed, -test·ing, -tests.** To subject to or conduct a pretest.

pre·text (prē′tĕkst′) *n.* An ostensible or professed purpose; excuse. *—tr.v.* **-text·ed, -text·ing, -texts.** To allege as an excuse. [Lat. *praetextum* < p.part. of *praetexere,* to disguise : *prae-,* before + *texere,* to weave.]

pre·treat (prē-trēt′) *tr.v.* **-treat·ed, -treat·ing, -treats.** To treat beforehand. **—pre·treat′ment** *n.*

pre·tri·al (prē-trī′əl, -trīl′) *adj.* Existing or occurring before a trial: *pretrial hearings.*

pret·ti·fy (prĭt′ĭ-fī′) *tr.v.* **-fied, -fy·ing, -fies.** To make pretty. **—pret′ti·fi·ca′tion** *n.* **—pret′ti·fi′er** *n.*

pret·ty (prĭt′ē) *adj.* **-ti·er, -ti·est. 1.** Pleasing or attractive in a graceful or delicate way. **2.** Excellent; good. **3.** *Archaic.* Elegant; fine. **4.** Effeminate; foppish. **5.** *Informal.* Considerable in size or extent: *a pretty fortune.* *—adv.* **1.** To a fair degree; moderately: *a pretty good student.* **2.** *Regional.* Prettily; pleasingly. *—n., pl.* **-ties.** One that is pretty. *—tr.v.* **-tied, -ty·ing, -ties.** *Informal.* To make pretty: *pretty up the house.* ***—idiom.*** **sitting pretty.** *Informal.* In favorable circumstances; in a good position. [ME *prety,* clever, fine < OE *prættig,* cunning < *prætt,* trick.] **—pret′ti·ly** *adv.* **—pret′ti·ness** *n.*

pre·tu·ber·cu·lous (prē′to͝o-bûr′kyə-ləs, -tyo͝o-) *adj.* Pertaining to lesions of tuberculosis occurring before the actual development of the disease.

pret·zel (prĕt′səl) *n.* A glazed biscuit that is salted on the outside and usually baked in the form of a loose knot or stick. [G. < OHG *brezitella* < Lat. *bracchium,* arm < Gk. *brakhiōn.*]

pre·vail (prĭ-vāl′) *intr.v.* **-vailed, -vail·ing, -vails. 1.** To be greater in strength or influence; triumph: *prevailed against great odds; will prevail over the enemy.* **2.** To be or become effective; win out. **3.** To be most common or frequent; be predominant. **4.** To be in force, use, or effect; be current. ***—phrasal verb.*** **prevail on** (or **upon).** To persuade successfully. [ME *prevayllen* < Lat. *praevalēre,* to be stronger : *prae-,* beyond + *valēre,* to be strong.] **—pre·vail′er** *n.*

pre·vail·ing (prĭ-vā′lĭng) *adj.* **1.** Most frequent or common; predominant. **2.** Generally current; widespread. **—pre·vail′ing·ly** *adv.* **—pre·vail′ing·ness** *n.*

Synonyms: *prevailing, prevalent, current, rife.* The widespread existence of some condition is implied by these adjectives. *Prevailing* implies predominance at a certain time: *prevailing opinion. Prevalent* suggests a condition that is merely widespread, with less emphasis on time. *Current* stresses the immediate present: *current trends.* It is often applied to things subject to frequent change. *Rife* emphasizes rapidity of multiplication.

prev·a·lent (prĕv′ə-lənt) *adj.* Widely or commonly occurring or existing; generally accepted or practiced. [Lat. *praevalens, praevalent-,* pr.part. of *praevalere,* to be stronger. —see PREVAIL.] **—prev′a·lence** *n.* **—prev′a·lent·ly** *adv.*

pre·var·i·cate (prĭ-văr′ĭ-kāt′) *intr.v.* **-cat·ed, -cat·ing, -cates.** To stray from or evade the truth; equivocate. [Lat. *praevaricari, praevaricat-* : *prae-,* before + *varicare,* to straddle < *varicus,* straddling < *varus,* bent.] **—pre·var′i·ca′tion** *n.* **—pre·var′i·ca′tor** *n.*

pre·ven·ience (prĭ-vēn′yəns) *n.* **1.** The act or state of being antecedent or prevenient. **2.** Attention to another's needs.

pre·ven·ient (prĭ-vēn′yənt) *adj.* **1.** Antecedent; preceding. **2.** Expectant; anticipatory. [Lat. *praeveniens, praevenient-,* pr.part. of *praevenire,* to precede : *prae-,* before + *venire,* to come.] **—pre·ven′ient·ly** *adv.*

pre·vent (prĭ-vĕnt′) *v.* **-vent·ed, -vent·ing, -vents.** *—tr.* **1.** To keep from happening; avert. **2.** To keep (someone) from doing something; impede: *prevented him from winning.* **3.** To anticipate or counter in advance. **4.** *Archaic.* To come before; precede. *—intr.* To present an obstacle: *There will be a picnic if nothing prevents.* [ME *preventen,* to anticipate < Lat. *praevenire* : *prae-,* before + *venire,* to come.] **—pre·vent′a·bil′i·ty, pre·vent′i·bil′i·ty** *n.* **—pre·vent′a·ble, pre·vent′i·ble** *adj.* **—pre·vent′er** *n.*

Synonyms: *prevent, preclude, obviate, forestall.* These verbs refer to stopping or hindering an action or eliminating a situation or condition that could produce an action. *Prevent* strongly implies decisive counteraction to stop something from happening. *Preclude* makes an event or action impossible or largely ineffectual by removing the conditions for it, while *obviate* makes an event or action unnecessary in the same way. *Forestall* less forcefully implies anticipatory action to prevent or hinder an imminent happening, but not by eliminating the conditions for it.

pre·ven·ta·tive (prĭ-vĕn′tə-tĭv) *adj. & n.* Variant of **preventive.**

pre·ven·tion (prĭ-vĕn′shən) *n.* **1.** The act of preventing. **2.** A hindrance; obstacle.

pre·ven·tive (prĭ-vĕn′tĭv) also **pre·ven·ta·tive** (-tə-tĭv) *—adj.* **1.** Designed or used to prevent or hinder; acting as an obstacle. **2.** *Med.* Thwarting or warding off illness or disease; prophylactic. *—n.* **1.** Something that prevents; obstacle. **2.** *Med.* Something used to ward off illness. **—pre·ven′tive·ly** *adv.* **—pre·ven′tive·ness** *n.*

preventive detention *n.* The pretrial imprisonment without the right to bail of a person accused of a felony and judged dangerous to society.

pre·view also **pre·vue** (prē′vyo͞o′) *—n.* **1.** An advance showing of a motion picture, an art exhibition, or another event to an invited audience prior to public presentation. **2.** An advance viewing or exhibition, esp. the presentation of several scenes advertising a forthcoming motion picture. **3.** An introductory or limited experience. *—tr.v.* **-viewed, -view·ing, -views** also **-vued, -vu·ing, -vues.** To view or exhibit in advance.

pre·vi·ous (prē′vē-əs) *adj.* **1.** Existing or occurring prior to something else in time or order; antecedent. **2.** *Informal.* Premature; hasty. [Lat. *praevius,* going before : *prae-,* before + *via,* way.] **—pre′vi·ous·ly** *adv.* **—pre′vi·ous·ness** *n.*

previous question *n.* In parliamentary procedure, the motion to take an immediate vote on the main question being considered or on any other questions so designated.

previous to *prep.* Prior to; before.

pre·vise (prĭ-vīz′) *tr.v.* **-vised, -vis·ing, -vis·es. 1.** To foresee. **2.** To notify in advance. [Lat. *praevidēre, praevis-* : *prae-,* before + *vidēre,* to see.] **—pre·vi′sion** (-vĭzh′ən) *n.* **—pre·vi′sion·al, pre·vi′sion·ar′y** (-ə-nĕr′ē) *adj.* **—pre·vi′sor** *n.*

pre·vo·cal·ic (prē′vō-kăl′ĭk) *adj.* Preceding a vowel.

pre·vo·ca·tion·al (prē′vō-kā′shə-nəl) *adj.* Of or pertaining to instruction given in preparation for vocational school.

pre·vue (prē′vyo͞o′) *n. & v.* Variant of **preview.**

pre·war (prē′wôr′) *adj.* Existing or occurring before a war.

prex·y (prĕk′sē) *n., pl.* **-ies.** *Slang.* A president, esp. of a college or university. [Shortening and alteration of PRESIDENT.]

prey (prā) *n.* **1.** A creature hunted or caught for food; quarry. **2.** A victim. **3.** The act of preying. *—intr.v.* **preyed, prey·ing, preys. 1.** To hunt, catch, or eat as prey: *Owls prey on mice.* **2.** To victimize or make a profit at someone's expense. **3.** To plunder or pillage. **4.** To exert a baneful or injurious effect: *Remorse preyed upon his mind.* [ME *preie* < OFr. < Lat. *praeda.*] **—prey′er** *n.*

Pri·am (prī′əm) *n.* *Gk. Myth.* King of Troy, the father of Paris and Hector, who was killed when his city fell to the Greeks. [Lat. *Priamus* < Gk. *Priamos.*]

pri·a·pic (prī-ăʹpĭk, -ăpʹĭk) also **pri·a·pe·an** (prīʹə-pēʹən) *adj.* Phallic. [< PRIAPUS.]
pri·a·pism (prīʹə-pĭzʹəm) *n.* Persistent, usually painful erection of the penis, esp. as a consequence of disease. [Fr. *priapisme* < LLat. *priapismus* < Gk. *priapismos* < *priapizein,* to have an erection < *Priapos,* Priapus.]
pri·a·pus (prī-āʹpəs) *n.* **1. Priapus.** The Greco-Roman god of procreation, guardian of gardens and vineyards, and personification of the erect phallus. **2.** An image of the god Priapus, often used as a scarecrow in ancient gardens. **3.** A representation of the phallus. [Lat. < Gk. *Priapos.*]
price (prīs) *n.* **1.** The sum of money or goods asked or given for something. **2.** The cost at which something is obtained. **3.** The cost of bribing someone: *Every man has his price.* **4.** A reward offered for the capture or killing of a person. **5.** Value or worth. *—tr.v.* **priced, pric·ing, pric·es. 1.** To fix or establish a price for: *shoes priced at nine dollars.* **2.** To find out the price of: *spent the day pricing dresses.* **—idiom. price out of the market.** To charge so much for goods or services that people no longer buy or use them. [ME *pris* < OFr. < Lat. *pretium.*]
Synonyms: *price, charge, cost, expense, expenditure, outlay, fee.* These nouns apply to money or other valuable consideration, such as labor and time, asked for or spent in payment for goods or services or for attainment of desired conditions. *Price* is the amount of money needed to purchase an object. *Charge* is the sum asked for the rendering of a service: *the charge for insuring the parcel. Cost,* a more inclusive term, generally applies to the total amount to be spent, including all *prices* and *charges. Expense* suggests cost in the aggregate or in relation to a larger allocation of funds: *traveling expenses. Expenditure* usually refers to the total of money, time, or effort actually involved, sometimes with the suggestion of detailed accounting. *Outlay* refers to the act of spending money or to the total spent. *Fee* is used specifically in connection with professional services.
price cutting *n.* The reduction of retail prices to a level low enough to eliminate competition.
price-earn·ings ratio (prīsʹûrʹnĭngz) *n.* The ratio of a common stock's market price to its earnings per share, used as an indicator of a company's profitability.
price index *n.* A number relating prices of a group of commodities to their prices during an arbitrarily chosen base period.
price·less (prīsʹlĭs) *adj.* **1.** Of inestimable worth; invaluable. **2.** Highly amusing, absurd, or odd.
price tag *n.* **1.** A label attached to a piece of merchandise indicating its price. **2.** The cost of something.
price war *n.* A period of intense competition among businesses in which each competitor tries to cut retail prices below those of the others.
pric·ey (prīʹsē) *adj.* **-i·er, -i·est.** Expensive: *a pricey restaurant.*
prick (prĭk) *n.* **1. a.** The act of piercing or pricking. **b.** The sensation of being pierced or pricked. **2.** A painful or stinging feeling of sorrow or remorse. **3.** A small mark or puncture made by a pointed object. **4.** A hare's track or footprint. **5.** A pointed object, as an ice pick, goad, thorn, or bee sting. **6.** *Vulgar Slang.* The penis. **7.** *Vulgar Slang.* A highly unpleasant man. *—v.* **pricked, prick·ing, pricks.** *—tr.* **1.** To puncture lightly. **2.** To sting with a mental or emotional pang. **3.** To incite; impel: *"My duty pricks me on"* (Shakespeare). **4.** To mark or delineate on a surface by means of small punctures: *prick a pattern on a board.* **5.** *Naut.* To measure with dividers on a chart. **6.** To pierce the quick of (a horse's hoof) while shoeing. **7.** To transplant (seedlings) preliminary to a final planting. *—intr.* **1.** To pierce or puncture something. **2.** To feel a stinging or pricking sensation. **3.** To ride at a gallop. **4.** To point upward. **—idiom. prick up (one's) ears.** To listen with attentive interest. [ME < OE *prica,* puncture.]
prick·er (prĭkʹər) *n.* **1.** One that pricks. **2.** A pricking tool. **3.** A prickle or thorn.
prick·et (prĭkʹĭt) *n.* **1. a.** A small point or spike for holding a candle upright. **b.** A candlestick having such a spike. **2.** A buck in his second year, before his horns branch. [ME *priket* < *prik,* prick < OE *prica,* puncture.]
prick·le (prĭkʹəl) *n.* **1.** A small sharp point, spine, or thorn. **2.** A tingling or pricking sensation. *—v.* **-led, -ling, -les.** *—tr.* **1.** To prick as if with a thorn. **2.** To cause a tingling or pricking sensation in. *—intr.* **1.** To feel a tingling or pricking sensation. **2.** To rise or stand up like prickles. [ME *prikel* < OE *pricel.*]
prick·ly (prĭkʹlē) *adj.* **-li·er, -li·est. 1.** Having prickles. **2.** Tingling; smarting. **3.** Bristling or irritable. **—prickʹli·ness** *n.*
prickly ash *n.* An aromatic shrub or small tree, *Zanthoxylum americanum,* of eastern North America, having prickly stems and feathery leaves.
prickly heat *n.* Miliaria.
prickly pear *n.* **1.** Any of various cacti of the genus *Opuntia,* having bristly flattened or cylindrical joints, showy, usually yellow flowers, and ovoid, sometimes edible fruit. **2.** The fruit of a prickly pear.
prickly poppy *n.* Any of various plants of the genus *Argemone,* chiefly of tropical America, having large yellow or white flowers and prickly leaves, stems, and pods.
prick·y (prĭkʹē) *adj.* **-i·er, -i·est.** Prickly.
pride (prīd) *n.* **1.** A sense of one's own proper dignity or value; self-respect: *One should not be robbed of his pride.* **2.** Pleasure or satisfaction taken in one's work, achievements, or possessions. **3. a.** A cause or source of pride: *These men were their country's pride.* **b.** The most successful or thriving condition; prime: *the flush and pride of youth.* **4. a.** An excessively high opinion of oneself; conceit. **b.** *Theol.* The consideration or personification of this condition as the first of the seven cardinal sins. **5.** Mettle or spirit in horses. **6.** A company of lions. *—v.* **prid·ed, prid·ing, prides.** *—tr.* To esteem (oneself) for: *I pride myself on this garden. —intr.* To indulge in self-esteem; glory. [ME < OE *prȳde* < *prūd,* proud < OFr.] **—prideʹful** *adj.* **—prideʹful·ly** *adv.* **—prideʹful·ness** *n.*
prie·dieu (prē-dyœʹ) *n., pl.* **-dieus** or **-dieux** (-dyœzʹ). A low desk with space for a book above and with a foot piece below for kneeling in prayer. [Fr. *prie Dieu,* pray God.]
pri·er also **pry·er** (prīʹər) *n.* One who pries.
priest (prēst) *n.* **1.** In the Roman Catholic, Eastern Orthodox, Anglican, Armenian, and separated Catholic hierarchies, a member of the second grade of clergy ranking below a bishop but above a deacon and having authority to pronounce absolution and administer all sacraments save that of ordination. **2.** A minister in a non-Christian religion. **3.** One whose role is considered comparable to that of a priest. *—tr.v.* **priest·ed, priest·ing, priests.** To ordain or admit to the priesthood. [ME *preost* < OE *prēost* < VLat. **prester* < LLat. *presbyter.* —see PRESBYTER.]
priest·ess (prēʹstĭs) *n.* A woman who functions as a priest.
priest·hood (prēstʹhŏodʹ) *n.* **1.** The character, office, or vocation of a priest. **2.** The clergy.
priest·ly (prēstʹlē) *adj.* **-li·er, -li·est.** Of, pertaining to, or befitting a priest or priests. **—priestʹli·ness** *n.*
prig (prĭg) *n.* **1.** A person regarded as overprecise, affectedly arrogant, smug, or narrow-minded. **2.** *Archaic.* A coxcomb. **3.** *Chiefly Brit. Slang.* A petty thief or pickpocket. *—tr.v.* **prigged, prig·ging, prigs.** *Chiefly Brit. Slang.* To steal or pilfer. [Orig. unknown.] **—prigʹger·y** *n.* **—prigʹgish** *adj.* **—prigʹgish·ly** *adv.* **—prigʹgish·ness** *n.*
prim¹ (prĭm) *adj.* **prim·mer, prim·mest. 1.** Precise or proper to the point of affectation. **2.** Formal; decorous. **3.** Neat; trim. *—v.* **primmed, prim·ming, prims.** *—tr.* To fix (the face or mouth) in a prim expression. *—intr.* To assume a prim expression. [Orig. unknown.] **—primʹly** *adv.* **—primʹness** *n.*
prim² (prĭm) *n.* The privet (sense 1). [Orig. unknown.]
pri·ma ballerina (prēʹmə) *n., pl.* **prima ballerinas.** The leading female dancer in a ballet company. [Ital., first ballerina.]
pri·ma·cy (prīʹmə-sē) *n., pl.* **-cies. 1.** The state or condition of being first or foremost. **2.** The office or province of an ecclesiastical primate.
pri·ma donna (prēʹmə, prĭmʹə) *n., pl.* **prima donnas. 1.** The leading female soloist in an opera company. **2.** A temperamental and conceited person. [Ital., first lady.]
pri·ma fa·cie (prīʹmə fāʹshē, fāʹshə) *adv.* At first sight; before closer inspection. [Lat.] **—priʹma-faʹcie** *adj.*
prima-facie evidence *n. Law.* Evidence that would if uncontested establish a fact or raise a presumption of a fact.
pri·mal (prīʹməl) *adj.* **1.** Being first in time; original. **2.** Of first importance; primary. [Med. Lat. *primalis* < Lat. *primus,* first.] **—pri·malʹi·ty** (-mălʹĭ-tē) *n.*
pri·mar·i·ly (prī-mârʹə-lē, -mĕrʹ-) *adv.* **1.** At first; originally. **2.** Chiefly; principally.
pri·mar·y (prīʹmĕrʹē, -mə-rē) *adj.* **1.** Occurring first in time or sequence; original: *a primary source.* **2.** Primitive; unsophisticated: *the primary instinct of motherhood.* **3.** Being or standing first in a list, series, or sequence. **4.** Being first or best in degree, quality, or importance. **5.** *Geol.* Of, pertaining to, or designating the earliest periods of geological development up to and including the Paleozoic era; Precambrian. **6.** Being a fundamental or basic part of an organized whole: *a primary element.* **7.** Immediate; direct: *a primary effect.* **8.** Of or pertaining to the basic colors from which all other colors may be derived. **9.** *Ling.* **a.** Having a word root or other linguistic element as a basis that cannot be further analyzed or broken down. Used of the derivation of a word or word element. **b.** Referring to present or future time. Used as a collective designation for various present and future verb tenses in Latin, Greek, and Sanskrit. **10.** *Elect.* Of, pertaining to, or designating an inducting current, circuit, or coil. **11.** Of, pertaining to, or designating the main flight feathers projecting along the outer edge of a bird's wing. **12.** *Chem.* **a.** Pertaining to the replacement of one of several atoms or radicals in a compound by another atom or radical. **b.** Having a carbon atom attached solely to one other carbon atom in a molecule. **13.** *Biochem.* Of, relating to, or being the sequence of amino acids in a protein. *—n., pl.* **-ies. 1. a.** One that is first in time, order, or sequence. **b.** One that is first or best in degree, quality, or importance. **c.** One that is fundamental, basic, or elemental. **2. a.** A meeting of the registered voters of a political party for the purpose of nominating candidates and for choosing delegates to their party convention. **b.** A preliminary election in which the registered voters of a political party nominate candidates for office. **3.** A primary color. **4.** One of the main flight feathers projecting along the outer edge of a

pricket
15th-century German candlestick

prickly pear

priedieu
18th-century French

bird's wing. **5.** *Elect.* An inducting current, circuit, or coil. **6.** *Astron.* A celestial body, esp. a star, to which the orbit of a satellite, or secondary, is referred. **7.** A cosmic ray. [Lat. *primarius,* chief < *primus,* first.]

primer[1]
Page from an early edition of the *New England Primer*

primary accent *n.* **1.** The strongest degree of stress placed on a syllable in the pronunciation of a word. **2.** The mark (′) used to indicate the strongest degree of stress.
primary atypical pneumonia *n.* A mild pneumonia, probably caused by a virus.
primary cell *n.* A cell in which an irreversible chemical reaction generates electricity.
primary coil *n.* An electrically conducting coil, as in a transformer, that carries an inducting current.
primary color *n.* A color belonging to any three groups each of which is regarded as generating all colors. These groups are: **a.** Additive, physiological, or light primaries—red, green, and blue. Lights of red, green, and blue wavelengths may be mixed to produce all colors. **b.** Subtractive or colorant primaries—magenta, yellow, and cyan. Substances that reflect light of one of these wavelengths and absorb (subtract) other wavelengths may be mixed to produce all colors. **c.** Psychological primaries—red, yellow, green, and blue, plus the achromatic pair black and white. All colors may be subjectively conceived as mixtures of these.
primary election *n.* A preliminary election in which voters nominate party candidates for office.
primary school *n.* A school usually comprising the first three or four grades of elementary school and sometimes kindergarten.
pri·mate (prī′mĭt, -māt′) *n.* **1.** A bishop of highest rank in a province or country. **2.** (prī′māt′). Any of the order Primates, which includes the monkeys, apes, and man. [ME *primat* < OFr. < Med. Lat. *primas* < Lat., principal < *primus,* first.] **—pri′mate·ship′** *n.* **—pri·ma′tial** (-mā′shəl) *adj.*

primitive
American primitive painting

pri·ma·ve·ra (prē′mə-vĕr′ə) *n.* **1.** A tree, *Cybistax donnell-smithii,* of Central America, having yellow flowers and close-grained, light-colored wood. **2.** The wood of the primavera, used in cabinetwork. [Am. Sp. < Sp., spring < Lat. *prima vera* : *primus,* first + *ver,* spring.]
prime (prīm) *adj.* **1.** First in excellence, quality, or value. **2.** First in degree or rank; chief. **3.** First or early in time, order, or sequence. **4.** Of the highest U.S. Government grade of meat. **5.** *Math.* Designating a prime number. *—n.* **1.** The earliest hours of the day; dawn. **2.** The first season of the year; spring. **3.** The age of ideal physical perfection and intellectual vigor. **4.** The period or phase of ideal or peak condition. **5.** The first position of thrust and parry in fencing. **6.** A mark (′) written above and to the right of a letter in order to distinguish it from the same letter already in use or to designate a related quantity or thing, as feet, minutes of angle, or minutes of time. **7.** *Eccles.* **a.** The second of the seven canonical hours. **b.** The time of day set aside for this prayer, usually about 6:00 A.M. **8.** *Math.* A prime number. *—v.* **primed, prim·ing, primes.** *—tr.* **1.** To make ready; prepare. **2.** To prepare (a gun or mine) for firing by inserting a charge of gunpowder or a primer. **3.** To prepare for operation, as by pouring water into a pump or gasoline into a carburetor. **4.** To prepare (a surface) for painting by covering with size, primer, or an undercoat. **5.** To prepare with information; coach. *—intr.* To prepare someone or something for future action or operation. ***—idiom.* prime the pump.** *Informal.* To encourage the growth of something. [ME, first in occurrence < OFr. < Lat. *primus.*] **—prime′ly** *adv.* **—prime′ness** *n.*
prime meridian *n.* The zero meridian (0°), used as a reference line from which longitude east and west is measured. It passes through Greenwich, England.
prime minister *n.* **1.** A chief minister appointed by a ruler. **2.** The head of the cabinet and often also the chief executive of a parliamentary democracy. **—prime ministership, prime ministry** *n.*
prime mover *n.* **1.** The initial force that engages or moves a machine, as electricity, wind, or gravity. **2.** Something regarded as the initial source of energy directed toward a goal: *Patriotism was the prime mover of the revolution.* **3.** A machine or mechanism that converts natural energy into work. **4.** Any of various heavy-duty trucks or tractors. **5.** In Aristotelian philosophy, the self-moved being that causes all motion.
prime number *n.* A number that has itself and unity as its only factors.
prim·er[1] (prĭm′ər) *n.* **1.** An elementary textbook. **2.** A book that covers the basic elements of a subject. [ME < Norman Fr. < Med. Lat. *primarius,* first < Lat. < *primus.*]
prim·er[2] (prī′mər) *n.* **1.** One that primes or causes to be primed. **2.** A cap or tube containing a small amount of explosive used to detonate the main explosive charge of a firearm or mine. **3.** An undercoat of paint or size applied to prepare a surface, as for painting.

primrose

prime rate *n.* The lowest rate of interest on bank loans at a given time and place, offered to preferred borrowers.
pri·me·ro (prĭ-mâr′ō) *n.* A gambling card game, popular in Elizabethan England. [Alteration of Sp. *primera,* fem. of *primero,* first < Lat. *primarius,* principal < *primus,* first.]
prime time *n.* The hours, usually during the evening, when the largest television audience is available.
pri·me·val (prī-mē′vəl) *adj.* Belonging to the first or earliest age or ages; original. [< Lat. *primaevus,* young : *primus,* first + *aevum,* age.] **—pri·me′val·ly** *adv.*
pri·mi (prē′mē) *n.* Plural of **primo.**
prim·ing (prī′mĭng) *n.* **1.** The explosive used to ignite a charge. **2.** A preliminary coat of paint or size applied to a surface.
pri·mip·a·ra (prī-mĭp′ər-ə) *n., pl.* **-a·ras** or **-a·rae** (-ə-rē′). *Med.* **1.** A woman who is pregnant for the first time. **2.** A woman who has borne only one child. [Lat. : *primus,* first + *parere,* to give birth.] **—pri′mi·par′i·ty** (-mĭ-păr′ĭ-tē) *n.* **—pri·mip′a·rous** *adj.*
prim·i·tive (prĭm′ĭ-tĭv) *adj.* **1. a.** Of or pertaining to an earliest or original stage or state. **b.** Archetypal. **2.** Characterized by simplicity or crudity; unsophisticated: *primitive weapons.* **3.** Of or pertaining to early stages in the evolution of human culture: *primitive societies.* **4.** *Ling.* **a.** Serving as the basis for derived or inflected forms: *"Pick" is the primitive word from which "picket" is derived.* **b.** Being a protolanguage: *primitive Germanic.* **5.** *Math.* A form in geometry or algebra from which another form is derived. **6. a.** Having a painting style of an early or unsophisticated culture. **b.** Self-taught. **c.** Of or pertaining to late medieval European painters. **7.** *Geol.* Of or pertaining to rocks formed by the first solidification of the earth's crust. **8.** *Biol.* Occurring in or characteristic of an early stage of development or evolution. *—n.* **1.** A person belonging to a primitive society. **2.** One that is at a low or early stage of development. **3. a.** One belonging to an early stage in the development of a culture or artistic trend. **b.** An artist having or affecting a primitive style. **c.** A self-taught artist. **4.** *Ling.* A word or word element from which another word or inflected form of the word is derived. **5.** *Computer Sci.* A basic or fundamental unit of machine instruction or translation. [ME *primitif* < OFr. < Lat. *primitivus* < *primus,* first.] **—prim′i·tive·ly** *adv.* **—prim′i·tive·ness, prim′i·tiv′i·ty** *n.*
prim·i·tiv·ism (prĭm′ĭ-tĭ-vĭz′əm) *n.* **1.** The state or quality of being primitive. **2.** A belief in primitive customs or ideas. **3.** The style of primitive painters. **4.** A belief that the acquisitions of civilization are evil or that the earliest period of human history was the best. **—prim′i·tiv·ist** *n.* **—prim′i·tiv·is′tic** *adj.*
pri·mo (prē′mō) *n., pl.* **-mi** (-mē). *Mus.* The principal part in a duet or ensemble composition. [Ital. < Lat. *primus,* first.] **—pri′mo** *adj.*
pri·mo·gen·i·tor (prī′mō-jĕn′ĭ-tər) *n.* The earliest ancestor or forefather. [Med. Lat. : Lat. *primus,* first + Lat. *genitor,* begetter < *gignere,* to beget.]
pri·mo·gen·i·ture (prī′mō-jĕn′ĭ-chŏŏr′) *n.* **1.** The state or condition of being the first-born or eldest child of the same parents. **2.** *Law.* The right of the eldest child, esp. the eldest son, to inherit the entire estate of one or both of his parents. [Med. Lat. *primogenitura* : Lat. *primus,* first + Lat. *genitura,* birth < *gignere,* to beget.] **—pri′mo·gen′i·tar′y** (-jĕn′ĭ-tĕr′ē), **pri′mo·gen′i·tal** *adj.*
pri·mor·di·al (prī-môr′dē-əl) *adj.* **1.** Being or happening first in sequence of time; original. **2.** Primary or fundamental: *play a primordial role.* **3.** *Biol.* Belonging to or characteristic of the earliest stage of development of an organism or part. *—n.* A basic principle. [ME < LLat. *primordialis* < Lat. *primordium,* origin : *primus,* first + *ordiri,* to begin.] **—pri·mor′di·al·ly** *adv.*
pri·mor·di·um (prī-môr′dē-əm) *n., pl.* **-di·a** (-dē-ə). An organ or part in its most rudimentary form or stage. [Lat. —see PRIMORDIAL.]
primp (prĭmp) *v.* **primped, primp·ing, primps.** *—tr.* To neaten (one's appearance) with considerable attention to detail. *—intr.* To preen. [Orig. unknown.]
prim·rose (prĭm′rōz′) *n.* **1.** Any of various plants of the genus *Primula,* having tubular, variously colored flowers with five lobes. **2.** The evening primrose. [ME *primerose* < OFr. < Med. Lat. *prima rosa,* first rose.]
primrose path *n.* A way of life of worldly ease or pleasure.
pri·mum mo·bi·le (prī′məm mō′bə-lē′, prē′məm mō′bĭ-lā′) *n.* **1.** In medieval astronomy, the tenth and outermost concentric sphere of the universe thought to revolve around the earth from east to west in 24 hours and believed to cause the other nine spheres to revolve with it. **2.** A prime mover (senses 2, 5). [Med Lat., first mover, transl. of Ar. *almuḥarrik alawwal.*]
pri·mus (prī′məs) *n., pl.* **-mus·es.** The first in rank of the bishops of Scotland. [Med. Lat. < Lat., first.]
pri·mus in·ter pa·res (prī′məs ĭn′tər pâr′ēz, prē′mŏŏs ĭn′tər pä′rās′) *n.* The first among equals. [Lat.]
prince (prĭns) *n.* **1.** A hereditary ruler; king. **2.** The ruler of a principality. **3.** A male member of a royal family other than the monarch. **4.** A nobleman of varying status or rank. **5.** An outstanding man in a group or class: *a merchant prince.* [ME < OFr. < Lat. *princeps* < *primus,* first.] **—prince′ship′** *n.*
Prince Al·bert (ăl′bərt) *n.* A man's long, double-breasted frock coat. [After *Prince Albert* Edward (1841–1910), later Edward VII.]
prince charming *n.* A man who fulfills all the romantic expectations of a woman. [After *Prince Charming,* hero of *Cinderella,* a fairy tale.]

prince consort *n.* The husband of a sovereign queen.
prince·dom (prĭns′dəm) *n.* **1.** The territory ruled by a prince; principality. **2.** The rank or status of a prince.
prince·ling (prĭns′lĭng) also **prince·let** (prĭns′lĭt) *n.* A prince of minor status or importance.
prince·ly (prĭns′lē) *adj.* **-li·er, -li·est. 1.** Of or pertaining to a prince; royal. **2.** Befitting a prince; munificent. **—prince′li·ness** *n.* **—prince′ly** *adv.*
Prince of Wales *n.* **1.** A title conferred by the sovereign on the male heir to the British throne. **2.** The male heir to the British throne, upon whom the title Prince of Wales has been conferred.
prince regent *n.* A prince who rules during the minority, absence, or incapacity of a sovereign.
prince's-feath·er (prĭn′sĭz-fĕth′ər) *n.* **1.** A tall plant, *Polygonum orientale,* having hairy stems and long spikes of pink or rose flowers. **2.** A plant, *Amaranthus hybridus hypochondriacus,* having reddish foliage and dense, brownish-red flower clusters.
prince's-pine (prĭn′sĭz-pīn′) *n.* The pipsissewa.
prin·cess (prĭn′sĭs, -sĕs′, prĭn-sĕs′) *n.* **1.** *Archaic.* A hereditary female ruler; queen. **2.** The female ruler of a principality. **3.** A female member of a royal family other than the monarch. **4.** A noblewoman of varying status or rank. **5.** The wife of a prince. **6.** A woman thought of as having the status or qualities of a princess. *—adj.* Also **prin·cesse** (prĭn-sĕs′). Designed to hang in smooth, close-fitting, unbroken lines from shoulder to flared hem: *a princess dress.* [ME *princesse* < OFr. < *prince,* prince.]
princess royal *n.* The eldest daughter of a sovereign.
prin·ci·pal (prĭn′sə-pəl) *adj.* First, highest, or foremost in importance, rank, worth, or degree; chief. *—n.* **1.** One who holds a position of presiding rank, esp. the head of an elementary school or high school. **2.** A main participant in a given situation. **3.** A person having a leading or starring role. **4. a.** The capital or main body of an estate or financial holding as distinguished from the interest or revenue from it. **b.** A sum of money owed as a debt, upon which interest is calculated. **5.** *Law.* **a.** A person who empowers another to act as his representative. **b.** The person having prime responsibility for an obligation as distinguished from one who acts as surety or as an endorser. **c.** One who commits or is an accomplice to a crime. **6.** The main truss or rafter that supports and gives form to a roof. [ME < OFr. < Lat. *principalis* < *princeps,* ruler < *primus,* first.] **—prin′ci·pal·ly** *adv.* **—prin′ci·pal·ship′** *n.*
Usage: *Principal* and *principle* are often confused but have no meanings in common. *Principle* is only a noun, and all its senses are abstract. *Principal* is both a noun and an adjective. As a noun (aside from its specialized meanings in law and finance) it generally denotes a person who holds a high position or plays an important role: *a meeting between all the principals in the transaction.* As an adjective it has the same sense of "chief" or "leading."
principal diagonal *n.* The diagonal in a square matrix that goes from the upper left corner to the lower right corner.
principal focus *n.* A focal point.
prin·ci·pal·i·ty (prĭn′sə-păl′ĭ-tē) *n., pl.* **-ties. 1.** A territory ruled by a prince or from which a prince derives his title. **2.** The position, authority, or jurisdiction of a prince; sovereignty. **3. principalities.** *Theol.* One of the nine orders of angels.
principal parts *pl.n. Gram.* In traditional grammars of inflected languages, the primary forms of a verb from which all other forms may be derived, including in English the present infinitive *(play, eat),* the past tense *(played, ate),* the past participle *(played, eaten),* and the present participle *(playing, eating).*
prin·cip·i·um (prĭn-sĭp′ē-əm) *n., pl.* **-i·a** (-ē-ə). A principle, esp. one that is basic. [Lat. —see PRINCIPLE.]
prin·ci·ple (prĭn′sə-pəl) *n.* **1.** A basic truth, law, or assumption: *the principles of democracy.* **2. a.** A rule or standard, esp. of good behavior: *a man of principle.* **b.** Moral or ethical standards or judgments collectively: *a decision based on principle rather than expediency.* **3.** A fixed or predetermined policy or mode of action: *acting on the principle of every man for himself.* **4.** A basic, or essential, quality or element determining intrinsic nature or characteristic behavior: *the principle of self-preservation natural to man.* **5.** A rule or law concerning the functioning of natural phenomena or mechanical processes: *the principle of jet propulsion.* **6.** A basic source. **7. Principle.** *Christian Science.* God. ***—idiom.* in principle.** With regard to basics: *an idea that is acceptable in principle.* —See Usage note at **principal.** [ME < OFr. *principe* < Lat. *principium* < *princeps,* first < *primus.*]
prin·ci·pled (prĭn′sə-pəld) *adj.* Motivated by or based on moral or ethical principles.
prink (prĭngk) *v.* **prinked, prink·ing, prinks.** *—tr.* To adorn (oneself) in a showy manner. *—intr.* To primp. [Prob. alteration of PRANK[2].] **—prink′er** *n.*
print (prĭnt) *n.* **1.** A mark or impression made in or upon a surface by pressure: *the print of footsteps in the sand.* **2. a.** A device or implement, such as a stamp, die, or seal, used to press markings on or into a surface. **b.** Something formed or marked by such a device: *a print of butter.* **3. a.** Lettering or other impressions produced in ink from type by a printing press or other means. **b.** Matter so produced. **c.** The state or form of matter so produced. **4.** A design or picture transferred from an engraved plate, wood block, lithographic stone, or other medium. **5.** A photographic image transferred to paper or a similar surface, usually from a negative. **6. a.** A fabric or garment with a dyed pattern that has been pressed onto it, usually by engraved rollers. **b.** The pattern itself. *—v.* **print·ed, print·ing, prints.** *—tr.* **1.** To press (a mark or design, for example) onto or into a surface. **2.** To make an impression on or in (a surface) with a stamp, seal, die, or similar device. **3.** To press (a stamp or similar device) onto or into a surface to leave a marking. **4.** To produce by means of pressed type on a paper surface, with or as if with a printing press. **5.** To offer in printed form; publish. **6.** To write (something) in characters similar to those commonly used in print. **7.** To impress firmly in the mind or memory. **8.** To produce (a positive photograph) by passing light through a negative onto sensitized paper. *—intr.* **1.** To work as a printer. **2.** To write characters similar to those commonly used in print. **3.** To produce or receive an impression, marking, or image. ***—phrasal verb.* print out.** To print as a computer function; produce print-out. ***—idioms.* in print. 1.** In printed or published form. **2.** Still offered for sale by the publisher: *books in print.* **out of print.** No longer offered for sale by the publisher. [ME *preinte* < OFr. < p.part. of *preindre,* to press < Lat. *premere.*]
print·a·ble (prĭn′tə-bəl) *adj.* **1.** Capable of being printed or of producing a print. **2.** Regarded as fit for publication. **—print′a·bil′i·ty** *n.*
print bar *n.* A mechanism in a printing device that carries the template of the final form of the alphanumeric characters to be printed.
printed circuit *n.* An electric circuit in which the conducting connections are formed by depositing a conducting metal, such as copper, in predetermined patterns on an insulating substrate, while other materials, esp. semiconductors, are deposited to form various electronic components.

printed circuit

printed matter *n.* Printed material, as a book or magazine, that is not considered first-class mail and qualifies for a special postal rate.
print·er (prĭn′tər) *n.* **1.** One that prints, esp. a person whose occupation is printing. **2.** The part of a computer that produces printed matter.
printer's devil *n.* An apprentice in a printing establishment.
print·er·y (prĭn′tə-rē) *n., pl.* **-ies. 1.** A place where typographic printing is done. **2.** A factory where fabrics are printed.
print·ing (prĭn′tĭng) *n.* **1.** The process, art, or business of producing printed matter by means of inked type and a printing press or by similar means. **2. a.** The act of one that prints. **b.** Matter that is printed. **3.** All the copies of a book or other publication that are printed at one time. **4.** Written characters not connected to one another and resembling those appearing in print.
printing ink *n.* Ink made esp. for use in printing.
printing office *n.* An establishment where printed material is produced, esp. an officially authorized one.
printing press *n.* A machine that transfers lettering or images by contact with various forms of inked surface onto paper or similar material fed into it in various ways.

printing press

print·mak·ing (prĭnt′mā′kĭng) *n.* The artistic design and manufacture of prints, as woodcuts or silkscreens. **—print′mak′er** *n.*
print-out (prĭnt′out′) *n.* The printed output of a computer.
print wheel *n.* A disk-shaped mechanism in a printing device that carries the template of the characters to be printed around its rim and prints one character at a time, revolving after each character to the proper position for the next.
pri·or[1] (prī′ər) *adj.* **1.** Preceding in time or order: *a prior commitment.* **2.** Preceding in importance or value: *a prior consideration.* ***—idiom.* prior to.** Before. [Lat.] **—pri′or·ly** *adv.*
pri·or[2] (prī′ər) *n.* **1.** A monastic officer in charge of a priory, or ranking next under the abbot of an abbey. **2.** One of the ruling magistrates of the medieval Italian republic of Florence. [ME *priour* < OE and OFr. *prior,* both < Med. Lat. < Lat., superior.] **—pri′or·ate** (-ĭt), **pri′or·ship′** *n.*
pri·or·ess (prī′ər-ĭs) *n.* A nun at the head of a priory or ranking next below an abbess in an abbey. [ME *prioresse* < OFr., fem. of *prior,* a prior.]
pri·or·i·tize (prī-ôr′ĭ-tīz′, -ŏr′-) *tr.v.* **-tized, -tiz·ing, -tiz·es.** To arrange or deal with in order of importance: *had to prioritize his debts.* [PRIORIT(Y) + -IZE.]
Usage: *Prioritize* is condemned by a large majority of the Usage Panel. See also Usage note at **-ize.**
pri·or·i·ty (prī-ôr′ĭ-tē, -ŏr′-) *n., pl.* **-ties. 1.** Precedence, esp. established by order of importance or urgency. **2. a.** An established right to precedence. **b.** An authoritative rating that establishes such precedence. **3.** A preceding or coming earlier in time. [ME *priorite* < OFr. < Med. Lat. *prioritas* < Lat. *prior,* first.]
pri·or·y (prī′ə-rē) *n., pl.* **-ies.** A monastery or convent governed by a prior or prioress. [ME *priorie* < Norman Fr. < Med. Lat. *prioria,* a prior < Lat., superior.]
prise (prīz) *v. & n.* Variant of **prize[3].**
pri·sere (prī′sîr′) *n.* The succession of vegetation that occurs

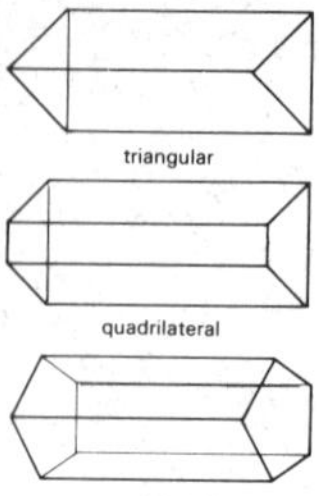

prism
Geometric prisms

in an area not previously occupied by a community as it passes from barren earth or water to a climax community. [PRI(MARY) + SERE².]

prism (prĭz′əm) *n.* **1.** A polyhedron having parallel, congruent polygons as bases and parallelograms as sides. **2.** A homogeneous transparent solid, usually with triangular bases and rectangular sides, used to produce or analyze a continuous spectrum. **3.** A cut-glass object, such as a pendant of a chandelier. **4.** A crystalline solid having three or more similar faces parallel to a single axis. [LLat. < Gk. < *prizein,* to saw.]

pris·mat·ic (prĭz-măt′ĭk) also **pris·mat·i·cal** (-ĭ-kəl) *adj.* **1.** Of, pertaining to, or resembling a prism. **2.** Refracting light, as a prism. **3.** Multicolored; iridescent. **—pris·mat′i·cal·ly** *adv.*

pris·ma·toid (prĭz′mə-toid′) *n.* A polyhedron having all vertices lying in one of two parallel planes. [Gk. *prisma, prismat-,* prism + -OID.] **—pris′ma·toi′dal** *adj.*

pris·moid (prĭz′moid′) *n.* A prismatoid having polygons with the same number of sides as bases, and faces that are parallelograms or trapezoids. **—pris·moi′dal** *adj.*

pris·on (prĭz′ən) *n.* **1.** A place where persons convicted or accused of crimes are confined; penitentiary or jail. **2.** A place or condition of confinement or forcible restraint. **3.** Imprisonment. *—tr.v.* **-oned, -on·ing, -ons.** To imprison. [ME < OFr. < Lat. *prensio,* a seizing, short for *prehensio* < *prehendere,* to seize.]

prison camp *n.* **1.** A camp for prisoners of war. **2.** A minimum security facility for the internment of trustworthy prisoners.

pris·on·er (prĭz′ə-nər, prĭz′nər) *n.* **1.** A person held in custody, captivity, or a condition of forcible restraint, esp. while on trial or serving a prison sentence. **2.** One deprived of freedom of action or expression: *a prisoner of fate.*

prisoner of war *n.* A person taken by or surrendering to enemy forces during wartime.

prisoner's base *n.* A children's game in which two teams try to capture opposing players by tagging them and bringing them to a base.

prison fever *n.* Typhus. [So called because it formerly prevailed in prisons.]

pris·sy (prĭs′ē) *adj.* **-si·er, -si·est.** Finicky, fussy, and prudish. [Blend of PRIM and SISSY.] **—pris′si·ly** *adv.* **—pris′si·ness** *n.*

pris·tine (prĭs′tēn′, prĭ-stēn′) *adj.* **1.** Of, pertaining to, or typical of the earliest time or condition; primitive or original. **2.** Remaining in a pure state; uncorrupted. [Lat. *pristinus.*] **—pris·tine′ly** *adv.*

prith·ee (prĭ*th*′ē, prĭth′ē) *interj. Archaic.* Please. [Alteration of *(I) pray thee.*]

pri·va·cy (prī′və-sē) *n., pl.* **-cies.** **1.** The condition of being secluded or isolated from the view of, or from contact with, others. **2.** Concealment; secrecy.

pri·vate (prī′vĭt) *adj.* **1.** Secluded from the sight, presence, or intrusion of others: *a private bathroom.* **2.** Of or confined to one person; personal: *private opinions.* **3.** Not available for public use, control, or participation: *a private club.* **4.** Belonging to a particular person or persons, as opposed to the public or the government: *private property.* **5.** Not holding an official or public position: *a former President, now a private citizen.* **6.** Not public; intimate: *a private tragedy.* *—n.* **1. a.** An enlisted man ranking below private first class in the Army or Marine Corps. **b.** One having a similar rank in other military organizations. **2. privates.** The genitals. **—*idiom.* in private.** Secretly or confidentially. [ME *privat* < Lat. *privatus,* not in public life, p.part. of *privare,* to release < *privus,* individual.] **—pri′vate·ly** *adv.* **—pri′vate·ness** *n.*

private detective *n.* A privately employed detective as distinguished from one belonging to a public police force.

private enterprise *n.* **1.** Business activities unregulated by state ownership or control; privately owned business in general. **2.** A privately owned business enterprise, esp. one operating under a system of free enterprise or laissez-faire capitalism.

pri·va·teer (prī′və-tîr′) *n.* **1.** A ship privately owned and manned but authorized by a government during wartime to attack and capture enemy vessels. **2.** The commander or one of the crew of a privateer. *—intr.v.* **-teered, -teer·ing, -teers.** To sail as a privateer.

private eye *n. Informal.* A private detective.

private first class *n.* An enlisted man ranking below corporal and above private in the Army or Marine Corps.

private investigator *n.* A private detective.

private law *n.* The branch of law which deals with or affects the rights of, and the relations between, private individuals.

private member *n. Chiefly Brit.* A member of Parliament who does not hold office in the government or in his party.

private parts *pl.n.* The genitals.

private school *n.* A secondary or elementary school run and supported by private individuals or a corporation rather than by a government or public agency.

pri·va·tion (prī-vā′shən) *n.* **1. a.** Lack of the basic necessities or comforts of life. **b.** The condition resulting from such lack. **2.** An act, condition, or result of deprivation or loss. [ME *privacion* < OFr. *privation* < Lat. *privatio* < *privare,* to deprive < *privus,* without.]

pri·vat·ism (prī′və-tĭz′əm) *n.* The social position of being noncommittal to or uninvolved with anything other than one's own immediate interests and lifestyle. **—pri′va·tis′tic** *adj.*

priv·a·tive (prĭv′ə-tĭv) *adj.* **1.** Causing deprivation, lack, or loss. **2.** *Gram.* Altering the meaning of a term from positive to negative. *—n. Gram.* A privative prefix or suffix, such as *a-, non-, un-,* or *-less.* [Lat. *privativus* < *privare,* to deprive < *privus,* without.] **—priv′a·tive·ly** *adv.*

priv·et (prĭv′ĭt) *n.* **1.** Either of two shrubs, *Ligustrum vulgare* or *L. ovalifolium,* having pointed leaves and clusters of white flowers, widely used for hedges. **2.** Any of several plants similar or related to the privet. [Orig. unknown.]

priv·i·lege (prĭv′ə-lĭj) *n.* **1. a.** A special advantage, immunity, permission, right, or benefit granted to or enjoyed by an individual, class, or caste. **b.** Such a right or advantage held as a prerogative of status or rank, and exercised to the exclusion or detriment of others. **2.** The principle of granting and maintaining privileges: *a society based on privilege.* **3.** An option to buy or sell a stock, including put, call, spread, and straddle. *—tr.v.* **-leged, -leg·ing, -leg·es.** **1.** To grant a privilege to. **2.** To free or exempt. [ME < OFr. < Lat. *privilegium,* a law affecting one person : *privus,* single + *lex,* law.]

priv·i·leged (prĭv′ə-lĭjd) *adj.* Enjoying a privilege or having privileges: *privileged students.*

privileged communication *n. Law.* **1.** A confidential communication that one cannot be made to divulge. **2.** A communication that is not subject to charges of slander or libel.

priv·i·ly (prĭv′ə-lē) *adv.* In a privy manner; privately.

priv·i·ty (prĭv′ĭ-tē) *n., pl.* **-ties.** **1.** Knowledge of something private or secret shared between individuals, esp. with the implication of approval or consent. **2.** *Law.* **a.** A relation between parties that is held to be sufficiently close and direct to support a legal claim on behalf of or against another person with whom this relation exists. **b.** A successive or mutual interest in or relationship to the same property. [ME *privete,* secret < OFr. < Med. Lat. *privitas* < Lat. *privus,* private.]

priv·y (prĭv′ē) *adj.* **1.** Made a participant in knowledge of something private or secret: *was privy to government secrets.* **2.** Belonging or proper to a person, such as the British sovereign, in a private rather than official capacity. **3.** *Archaic.* Concealed; secret. *—n., pl.* **-ies.** **1. a.** A latrine. **b.** An outhouse. **2.** *Law.* One of the parties having an interest in the same matter. [ME *prive* < OFr. < Lat. *privatus,* private < *privus.*]

Privy Council *n.* **1.** A council of the British sovereign that until the 17th century was the supreme legislative body, that now consists of cabinet ministers ex officio and others appointed as a high honor, membership being for life, and that has no important function except through its Judicial Committee, which in certain cases acts as a supreme appellate court in the Commonwealth. **2. privy council.** An advisory council to an executive. **—Privy Councillor** *n.*

prix fixe (prē′ fēks′) *n., pl.* **prix fixes** (prē′ fēks′). **1.** A table d'hôte (sense 2). **2.** The price at which a table d'hôte meal is offered. [Fr., fixed price.]

prize¹ (prīz) *n.* **1.** Something offered or won as an award for achieving superiority or excellence in competition with others. **2.** Something offered for winning in a game of chance. **3.** Something worth striving for or aspiring to. *—adj.* **1.** Offered or given as a prize: *a prize cup.* **2.** Given a prize, or likely to win a prize: *a prize cow.* **3.** Worthy of a prize; first-class. *—tr.v.* **prized, priz·ing, priz·es.** **1.** To value highly; esteem; treasure. **2.** To estimate the worth of; evaluate. [ME *pris.* —see PRICE.]

prize² (prīz) *n.* **1.** Something seized by force or taken as booty, esp. an enemy ship and cargo captured at sea during wartime. **2.** The act of seizing; capture. [ME *prise* < OFr. < VLat. **presa* < Lat. *prehendere,* to seize.]

prize³ also **prise** (prīz) *tr.v.* **prized, priz·ing, priz·es** also **prised, pris·ing, pris·es.** To move or force with or as if with a lever; pry. *—n.* **1.** Leverage. **2.** *Regional.* Something used as a lever or for prying. [< obs. *prize,* instrument for prizing < ME *prise* < OFr., grasp. —see PRIZE².]

prize·fight (prīz′fīt′) *n.* A match fought between professional boxers for money. **—prize′fight′er** *n.* **—prize′fight′ing** *n.*

prize ring *n.* **1.** The platform enclosed by ropes in which contending boxers meet. **2.** Professional boxing.

prize winner *n.* One that wins a prize.

prize-win·ning (prīz′wĭn′ĭng) *adj.* Having won a prize or being judged worthy of such: *a prize-winning recipe.*

pro¹ (prō) *n., pl.* **pros.** **1.** An argument in favor of something; affirmative consideration or vote. **2.** One who supports a proposal or takes the affirmative side in debate. *—adv.* In favor of; affirmatively. *—adj.* Favoring; supporting. [ME < Lat., for.]

pro² (prō) *Informal.* *—n., pl.* **pros.** **1.** A professional, esp. in sports. **2.** An expert in a field of endeavor. *—adj.* Professional: *pro football.* [Short for PROFESSIONAL.]

pro–¹ *pref.* **1.** Acting in the place of; substituting for: *progesterone.* **2.** Supporting; favoring: *prorevolutionary.* [ME < Lat. *pro,* for.]

pro–² *pref.* **1. a.** Earlier; prior to: *prothrombin.* **b.** Rudimentary: *pronucleus.* **2.** Anterior; in front of: *procambium.* [< Gk. *pro,* before, in front of.]

pro·a (prō′ə) *n.* A swift Malayan sailboat with a triangular sail and a single outrigger. [< Malay *pĕrāhū,* prob. Marathi *pạdāv.*]

pro-a·bor·tion (prō′ə-bôr′shən) *adj.* Favoring or supporting legalized clinical abortions. **—pro-a·bor′tion·ist** *n.*

prob·a·bi·lism (prŏb′ə-bə-lĭz′əm) *n.* **1.** *Philos.* The doctrine that probability is a sufficient basis for belief and action, since certainty in knowledge is unattainable. **2.** *Rom. Cath. Ch.* The doctrine that when there is doubt as to the moral rectitude of an action, the opinion that favors liberty may be followed, provided that it is solidly probable, even though the contrary may be equally, or even more, probable. **—prob′a·bi·list** *n.* **—prob′a·bi·lis′tic** *adj.*

prob·a·bil·i·ty (prŏb′ə-bĭl′ĭ-tē) *n., pl.* **-ties. 1.** The quality or condition of being probable; likelihood. **2.** A probable situation, condition, or event. **3.** *Math.* A number expressing the likelihood of occurrence of a specific event, such as the ratio of the number of experimental results that would produce the event to the total number of results considered possible. **—*idiom.* in all probability.** Most probably; very likely.

probability density *n.* **1.** A function of a continuous random variable, the integral of which, over a given interval, gives the probability that the value of the variable will fall within the interval. **2.** The calculated value of a probability density.

probability distribution *n.* **1.** Probability density. **2.** A function of a discrete random variable yielding the probability that the variable will have a given value.

probability theory *n.* A branch of mathematics that studies the likelihood of occurrence of random events in order to predict the behavior of defined systems.

prob·a·ble (prŏb′ə-bəl) *adj.* **1.** Likely to happen or to be true. **2.** Relatively likely but not certain; plausible. **3.** *Theol.* Of or pertaining to moral opinions and actions for the lawfulness of which intrinsic reasons or extrinsic authority may be adduced; possible; provable. [ME, provable < OFr. < Lat. *probabilis* < *probare,* to prove.]

probable cause *n. Law.* Reasonable grounds for belief that an accused person is guilty as charged.

prob·a·bly (prŏb′ə-blē) *adv.* Most likely; presumably.

pro·bang (prō′băng′) *n.* A long, slender, flexible rod having a tuft or sponge at the end, used to remove foreign bodies from the larynx or esophagus. [Alteration of obs. *provang.*]

pro·bate (prō′bāt′) *n.* **1. a.** Legal establishment of the validity of a will. **b.** The process of legally establishing the validity of a will. **2.** The right to validate wills. *—tr.v.* **-bat·ed, -bat·ing, -bates.** To establish the validity of (a will). [ME *probat* < Lat. *probatum,* something proved < *probare,* to prove < *probus,* good.]

probate court *n.* A court limited to the jurisdiction of probating wills and administering estates.

pro·ba·tion (prō-bā′shən) *n.* **1.** A trial period in which a person's fitness for membership in a working or social group is tested. **2.** *Law.* The action of suspending the sentence of one convicted of a minor offense and granting him provisional freedom on the promise of good behavior. **3.** A trial period in which a student is permitted to redeem failing grades or bad conduct. **4.** The status of a person on probation. [ME *probacion* < OFr. < Lat. *probatio,* trial < *probare,* to test < *probus,* good.] **—pro·ba′tion·al, pro·ba′tion·ar′y** *adj.* **—pro·ba′tion·al·ly** *adv.*

pro·ba·tion·er (prō-bā′shə-nər) *n.* A person on probation.

pro·ba·tive (prō′bə-tĭv) also **pro·ba·to·ry** (-tôr′ē, -tōr′ē) *adj.* **1.** Serving to test, try, or prove. **2.** Furnishing evidence or proof. [ME *probatiffe* < Lat. *probativus* < *probare,* to prove < *probus,* good.]

probe (prōb) *n.* **1.** An object or device used to investigate an unknown configuration, condition, or region. **2.** A slender, flexible instrument used to explore a wound or body cavity. **3.** The act of exploring or searching with the aid of a probe. **4.** An investigation into the nature of something, esp. an investigation of unlawful practices. *—v.* **probed, prob·ing, probes.** *—tr.* **1.** To explore with a probe. **2.** To examine or investigate; delve into. *—intr.* To conduct an exploratory investigation; search. [< Med. Lat. *proba,* examination < Lat. *probare,* to test < *probus,* good.] **—prob′er** *n.*

pro·ben·e·cid (prō-bĕn′ĭ-sĭd) *n.* A derivative of benzoic acid, $C_{13}H_{19}NO_4S$, that is used medically as a drug in the treatment of gout. [PRO(PYL) + BEN(ZOIC) + (A)CID.]

pro·bi·ty (prō′bĭ-tē) *n.* Complete and confirmed integrity; uprightness. [OFr. *probite* < Lat. *probitas* < *probus,* honest.]

prob·lem (prŏb′ləm) *n.* **1.** A question or situation that presents uncertainty, perplexity, or difficulty. **2.** A person who is difficult to deal with. **3.** A question put forward for consideration, discussion, or solution. **—*modifier:*** *a problem child; a problem play.* [ME *probleme* < OFr. < Lat. *problema* < Gk. *problēma* < *proballein,* to throw out : *pro-,* forward + *ballein,* to throw.]

prob·lem·at·i·cal (prŏb′lə-măt′ĭ-kəl) also **prob·lem·at·ic** (-ĭk) *adj.* **1.** Posing a problem; difficult to solve. **2.** Open to doubt; debatable. **—prob′lem·at′i·cal·ly** *adv.*

prob·lem-o·ri·ent·ed language (prŏb′ləm-ôr′ē-ĕn′tĭd, -ōr-) *n.* A computer programming language designed for use in solving a particular set of problems.

pro·bos·cid·i·an (prō′bŏs-ĭd′ē-ən) also **pro·bos·ci·de·an** (prō-bŏs′ĭ-dē′ən) *adj.* Of or belonging to the Proboscidea, an order of mammals that is characterized by a trunk or proboscis and includes the elephant. *—n.* An animal of the order Proboscidea. [< NLat. *Proboscidea,* order name < Lat. *proboscis,* proboscis.]

pro·bos·cis (prō-bŏs′ĭs) *n., pl.* **-cis·es** or **-ci·des** (-ĭ-dēz′). **1.** A long, flexible snout or trunk, as of an elephant. **2.** The slender, tubular feeding and sucking structure of some insects and worms. **3.** A human nose, esp. a prominent one. [Lat. < Gk. *proboskis* : *pro-,* in front + *boskein,* to feed.]

pro-bus·ing (prō-bŭs′ĭng) *adj.* Favoring or supporting the busing of children to schools outside their neighborhoods as a means of achieving racial integration.

pro·caine hydrochloride (prō′kān′) *n.* A white crystalline powder, $C_{13}H_{20}O_2N_2{\cdot}HCl$, used as a local anesthetic in medicine and dentistry. [PRO-[1] + (CO)CAIN.]

pro·cam·bi·um (prō-kăm′bē-əm) *n.* A layer of undifferentiated plant cells from which the vascular tissue is formed. **—pro·cam′bi·al** *adj.*

pro·carp (prō′kärp′) *n.* A specialized female sex organ in certain algae.

pro·car·y·ote also **pro·kar·y·ote** (prō-kăr′ē-ōt′) *n.* A cellular organism, such as a bacterium or blue-green alga, whose nucleus lacks a limiting membrane. [PRO-[2] + Gk. *karuōtos,* having nuts.] **—pro·car′y·ot′ic** (-ŏt′ĭk) *adj.*

pro·ce·dur·al (prə-sē′jər-əl) *adj.* Of or concerning procedure, esp. of a court of law or parliamentary body. **—pro·ce′dur·al·ly** *adv.*

pro·ce·dure (prə-sē′jər) *n.* **1.** A manner of proceeding; way of performing or effecting something. **2.** An act composed of steps; course of action. **3.** A set of established forms or methods for conducting the affairs of a business, legislative body, or court of law. [Fr. *procédure* < OFr. < *proceder,* to proceed.]

pro·ceed (prō-sēd′, prə-) *intr.v.* **-ceed·ed, -ceed·ing, -ceeds.** **1.** To go forward or onward, esp. after an interruption; continue. **2.** To undertake and carry on some action or process. **3.** To move on in an orderly manner. **4.** To issue forth; originate. **5.** To institute and conduct legal action: *proceeded against the defendant.* [ME *proceden* < OFr. *proceder* < Lat. *procedere* : *pro-,* forward + *cedere,* to go.] **—pro·ceed′er** *n.*

pro·ceed·ing (prō-sē′dĭng, prə-) *n.* **1.** A course of action; procedure. **2.** A continuing of an action. **3. proceedings.** A sequence of events occurring at a particular place or occasion. **4. proceedings.** A record of business carried on by a society or other organization; minutes. **5.** *Law.* **a. proceedings.** Legal action; litigation. **b.** The instituting or conducting of litigation.

pro·ceeds (prō′sēdz′) *pl.n.* The amount of money derived from a commercial or fund-raising venture; yield.

pro·ce·phal·ic (prō′sə-făl′ĭk) *adj.* Anatomically located on or near the front of the head.

proc·ess[1] (prŏs′ĕs′, prō′sĕs′) *n., pl.* **proc·ess·es** (prŏs′ĕs′ĭz, prō′sĕs′-, prŏs′ĭ-sēz′, prō′sĭ-). **1.** A system of operations in the production of something. **2.** A series of actions, changes, or functions that bring about an end or result. **3.** Course or passage of time. **4.** Ongoing movement; progression. **5.** *Law.* **a.** A summons or writ ordering a defendant to appear in court. **b.** The total quantity of summonses or writs issued in a particular proceeding. **c.** The entire course of a judicial proceeding. **6.** *Biol.* A part extending or projecting from an organ or organism; appendage. **7.** Any of various photomechanical or photoengraving methods. *—tr.v.* **-essed, -ess·ing, -ess·es. 1.** To put through the steps of a prescribed procedure. **2.** To prepare, treat, or convert by subjecting to some special process. **3.** *Law.* To serve with a summons or writ. **4.** To institute legal proceedings against; prosecute. **5.** *Computer Sci.* To perform operations on data. *—adj.* **1.** Prepared or converted by a special treatment: *process cheese.* **2.** Made by or used in photomechanical or photoengraving methods: *a process print.* [ME *proces* < OFr. < Lat. *processus,* advance < p.part. of *procedere,* to advance. —see PROCEED.]

pro·cess[2] (prə-sĕs′) *intr.v.* **-cessed, -cess·ing, -cess·es.** To move along in or as if in a procession. [Back-formation < PROCESSION.]

pro·ces·sion (prə-sĕsh′ən) *n.* **1.** The act of proceeding, moving along, or issuing forth. **2. a.** A group of persons, vehicles, or objects moving along in an orderly and formal manner, usually in a long line. **b.** The movement of such a group. **3.** A continuous and orderly course: *the procession of the seasons.* *—intr.v.* **-sioned, -sion·ing, -sions.** To form or go in a procession. [ME < OFr. < Lat. *processio,* advance < *procedere,* to advance. —see PROCEED.]

pro·ces·sion·al (prə-sĕsh′ə-nəl) *adj.* Of, pertaining to, or suitable for a procession. *—n.* **1.** A book containing the ritual observed during a religious procession. **2.** A hymn sung when the clergy enter a church at the beginning of the service. **3.** Music intended to be played or sung during a procession. **—pro·ces′sion·al·ly** *adv.*

pro·ces·sor (prŏs′ĕs′ər) *n.* **1.** One that processes. **2.** A computer. **3.** A central processing unit. **4.** A computer program

probe
Space probe orbiting Venus

that translates another program into a form acceptable to the computer being used.

process printing *n.* Printing from multiple, usually four, halftone images, each inked with a different color such that the composite impression will reproduce the colors of the original.

pro·cès-ver·bal (prō-sā′vĕr-băl′) *n., pl.* **-ver·baux** (-vĕr-bō′). **1.** An official record of diplomatic negotiations. **2.** A detailed official record of legal or other proceedings. [Fr. : *procès,* proceedings + *verbal,* oral.]

pro-choice (prō-chois′) *adj.* Pro-abortion.

pro·claim (prō-klām′, prə-) *tr.v.* **-claimed, -claim·ing, -claims. 1.** To announce officially and publicly; declare. **2.** To indicate unmistakably; make plain. **3.** To praise; extol. [ME *proclaymen* < OFr. *proclamer* < Lat. *proclamare* : *pro-,* forward + *clamare,* to cry out.] **—pro·claim′er** *n.*

proc·la·ma·tion (prŏk′lə-mā′shən) *n.* **1.** The act of proclaiming. **2.** Something proclaimed, esp. an official public announcement.

pro·clit·ic (prō-klĭt′ĭk) *adj. Ling.* Forming an accentual unit with the following word and thus having no independent accent. *—n.* A proclitic word. [NLat. *procliticus* < Gk. *proklinein,* to lean forward : *pro-,* forward + *klinein,* to lean.]

pro·cliv·i·ty (prō-klĭv′ĭ-tē) *n., pl.* **-ties.** A natural propensity or inclination; predisposition. [Lat. *proclivitas* < *proclivus,* inclined : *pro-,* forward + *clivus,* slope.]

Proc·ne (prŏk′nē) *n. Gk. Myth.* The sister of Philomela and betrayed wife of Tereus who was changed into a nightingale before Tereus was able to kill her. [Lat. < Gk. *Proknē.*]

pro·con·sul (prō-kŏn′səl) *n.* **1.** A Roman provincial governor of consular rank. **2.** A high administrator in one of the European colonial empires. [ME < Lat. < *pro consule,* for the consul.] **—pro·con′su·lar** (-sə-lər) *adj.* **—pro·con′su·late** (-sə-lĭt) *n.* **—pro·con′sul·ship′** *n.*

produce

pro·cras·ti·nate (prō-krăs′tə-nāt′, prə-) *v.* **-nat·ed, -nat·ing, -nates.** *—intr.* To put off doing something until a future time. *—tr.* To postpone or delay needlessly. [Lat. *procrastinare, procrastinat-* : *pro-,* forward + *cras,* tomorrow.] **—pro·cras′ti·na′tion** *n.* **—pro·cras′ti·na′tor** *n.*

pro·cre·ate (prō′krē-āt′) *v.* **-at·ed, -at·ing, -ates.** *—tr.* **1.** To beget (offspring). **2.** To produce or create; originate. *—intr.* To beget offspring; reproduce. [Lat. *procreare, procreat-* : *pro-,* forward + *creare,* to create.] **—pro′cre·ant** (-ənt) *adj.* **—pro′cre·a′tion** *n.* **—pro′cre·a′tor** *n.*

pro·cre·a·tive (prō′krē-ā′tĭv) *adj.* **1.** Capable of reproducing; generative. **2.** Of or directed to procreation: *procreative instinct.*

pro·crus·te·an also **Pro·crus·te·an** (prō-krŭs′tē-ən) *adj.* **1.** Producing or designed to produce conformity by ruthless or arbitrary means. **2.** Having merciless disregard for individual differences or special circumstances. [After *Procrustes,* a mythical Greek giant who stretched or shortened captives to make them fit his beds < *prokrouein,* to stretch out : *pro-,* forth + *krouein,* to beat.]

procrustean bed also **Procrustean bed** *n.* An arbitrary standard to which exact conformity is forced.

pro·cryp·tic (prō-krĭp′tĭk) *adj. Biol.* Having a pattern or coloration adapted for natural camouflage. [Prob. PRO(TECT) + CRYPTIC.]

proc·ti·tis (prŏk-tī′tĭs) *n.* Inflammation of the rectum or anus. [Gk. *prōktos,* anus + -ITIS.]

proc·tol·o·gy (prŏk-tŏl′ə-jē) *n.* The physiology and pathology of the rectum and anus. [Gk. *prōktos,* anus + -LOGY.] **—proc′to·log′ic** (-tə-lŏj′ĭk), **proc′to·log′i·cal** *adj.* **—proc′to·log′i·cal·ly** *adv.* **—proc·tol′o·gist** *n.*

proc·tor (prŏk′tər) *n.* A dormitory and examination supervisor in a school. *—tr.v.* **-tored, -tor·ing, -tors.** To supervise (an examination). [ME, university officer < *procuratour,* procurator.] **—proc·to′ri·al** (-tôr′ē-əl, -tōr′-) *adj.* **—proc′tor·ship′** *n.*

proc·to·scope (prŏk′tə-skōp′) *n.* An instrument for dilating and examining the rectum. [Gk. *prōktos,* anus + -SCOPE.] **—proc′to·scop′ic** (-skŏp′ĭk) *adj.* **—proc·tos′co·py** (-tŏs′kə-pē) *n.*

pro·cum·bent (prō-kŭm′bənt) *adj.* **1.** *Bot.* Trailing along the ground: *a procumbent vine.* **2.** Lying face down; prone. [Lat. *procumbens, procumbent-,* pr.part. of *procumbere,* to bend down : *pro-,* forward + *cumbere,* to lie down.]

proc·u·ra·tor (prŏk′yə-rā′tər) *n.* **1.** An agent having power of attorney. **2.** An official of the Roman Empire acting as a financial agent of the emperor or as the administrator of a minor province. [ME *procuratour* < OFr. < Lat. *procurator* < *procurare,* to take care of. —see PROCURE.] **—proc′u·ra·to′ri·al** (-yər-ə-tôr′ē-əl, -tōr′-) *adj.*

pro·cure (prō-kyŏŏr′, prə-) *v.* **-cured, -cur·ing, -cures.** *—tr.* **1.** To obtain; acquire. **2.** To bring about; effect: *procure a solution.* **3.** To obtain for another (a person) for sexual intercourse. *—intr.* To work as a procurer. [ME *procuren* < OFr. *procurer* < Lat. *procurare,* to manage : *pro-,* for + *curare,* to care for.] **—pro·cur′a·ble** *adj.* **—pro·cur′ance, pro·cure′ment** *n.*

pro·cur·er (prō-kyŏŏr′ər, prə-) *n.* **1.** One who procures. **2.** A pander.

pro·cur·ess (prō-kyŏŏr′ĭs, prə-) *n.* A woman who procures.

Pro·cy·on (prō′sē-ŏn′) *n.* A double star in the constellation Canis Minor. [Lat. < Gk. *Prokuon* : *pro-,* before + *kuōn,* dog.]

prod (prŏd) *tr.v.* **prod·ded, prod·ding, prods. 1.** To jab or poke, as with a pointed instrument. **2.** To rouse to action; goad. *—n.* **1.** Something that is used to prod; goad. **2.** An incitement or stimulus. [Orig. unknown.] **—prod′der** *n.*

prod·i·gal (prŏd′ĭ-gəl) *adj.* **1.** Recklessly wasteful; extravagant. **2.** Profuse in giving; exceedingly abundant. **3.** Profuse; lavish: *prodigal praise.* *—n.* A person given to luxury or extravagance. [Lat. *prodigus* < *prodigere,* to squander : *prod-,* before (var. of *pro-*) + *agere,* to drive.] **—prod′i·gal·ly** *adv.*

prod·i·gal·i·ty (prŏd′ĭ-găl′ĭ-tē) *n., pl.* **-ties. 1.** Extravagant wastefulness. **2.** Profuse generosity. **3.** Extreme abundance; lavishness.

pro·di·gious (prə-dĭj′əs) *adj.* **1.** Impressively great in size, force, or extent; enormous. **2.** Extraordinary; marvelous. **3.** Portentous; ominous. [Lat. *prodigiousus* < *prodigium,* omen.] **—pro·di′gious·ly** *adv.* **—pro·di′gious·ness** *n.*

prod·i·gy (prŏd′ə-jē) *n., pl.* **-gies. 1.** A person with exceptional talents or powers: *a child prodigy.* **2.** An act or event so extraordinary or rare as to inspire wonder. **3.** An omen or portent. [Lat. *prodigium,* omen.]

pro·drome (prō′drōm′) *n., pl.* **-dromes** or **-dro·ma·ta** (-drō′mə-tə). A symptom of the onset of a disease. [Fr. < Gk. *prodromos,* precursor : *pro-,* forward + *dromos,* running.] **—pro·dro′mal** (-drō′məl), **pro·drom′ic** (-drŏm′ĭk) *adj.*

pro·duce (prə-dōōs′, -dyōōs′, prō-) *v.* **-duced, -duc·ing, -duc·es.** *—tr.* **1.** To bring forth; yield. **2.** To create by mental or physical effort. **3.** To manufacture. **4.** To cause to occur or exist; give rise to. **5.** To bring forward; exhibit. **6.** To sponsor and present to the public: *produce a play.* **7.** To extend (an area or volume) or lengthen (a line). *—intr.* To make or yield the customary product or products. *—n.* (prŏd′ōōs, prō′dōōs). Something produced; a product, esp. farm products collectively. [Lat. *producere* : *pro-,* forward + *ducere,* to lead.] **—pro·duc′i·ble** *adj.*

pro·duc·er (prə-dōō′sər, -dyōō′-, prō-) *n.* **1.** One that produces, esp. a person or organization that grows or manufactures goods or services for sale. **2.** One who finances and supervises the production of a play or other public entertainment. **3.** A furnace that manufactures producer gas. **4.** *Ecol.* An autotrophic organism in an ecosystem.

producer gas *n.* A gas used as fuel, generated by passing air with steam over burning coke or coal to yield a combustible mixture of nitrogen, carbon monoxide, and hydrogen.

producer goods or **producers' goods** *pl.n. Econ.* Goods, such as raw materials or tools, used to make consumer goods.

prod·uct (prŏd′əkt) *n.* **1.** Something produced by human or mechanical effort or by a natural process. **2.** A direct result; consequence. **3.** *Chem.* A substance produced by a chemical change. **4.** *Math.* **a.** The result obtained by performing multiplication. **b.** A scalar product. **c.** A vector product. [Lat. *productum* < p.part. of *producere,* to bring forth. —see PRODUCE.]

pro·duc·tion (prə-dŭk′shən, prō-) *n.* **1.** The act or process of producing. **2.** The creation of value or wealth by producing goods and services. **3.** Something produced; product. **4.** The total number of products; output. **5.** A public performance or showing of a play or other form of entertainment. **—pro·duc′tion·al** *adj.*

pro·duc·tive (prə-dŭk′tĭv, prō-) *adj.* **1.** Producing or capable of producing. **2.** Producing abundantly; fertile. **3.** Yielding favorable or useful results; constructive. **4.** *Econ.* Of or involved in the creation of goods and services to produce wealth or value. **5.** Resulting in: *difficulties productive of dispute.* **—pro·duc′tive·ly** *adv.* **—pro′duc·tiv′i·ty** (prō′dŭk-tĭv′ĭ-tē, prŏd′ək-), **pro·duc′tive·ness** *n.*

pro·em (prō′ĕm′) *n.* A short introduction; preface. [ME *proheme* < OFr. < Lat. *prooemium* < Gk. *prooimion,* prelude : *pro-,* before + *oimē,* song.] **—pro·e′mi·al** (prō-ē′mē-əl, -ĕm′ē-) *adj.*

pro·en·zyme (prō-ĕn′zīm′) *n.* Zymogen.

pro·es·trus (prō-ĕs′trəs) *n.* The period of preparation for pregnancy that immediately precedes estrus in female mammals.

prof (prŏf) *n. Informal.* A professor.

prof·a·na·tion (prŏf′ə-nā′shən) *n.* The act or an instance of profaning; desecration.

pro·fane (prō-fān′, prə-) *adj.* **1.** Showing contempt or irreverence toward God or sacred things; blasphemous. **2.** Nonreligious in subject matter, form, or use; secular: *sacred and profane music.* **3.** Not initiated into the mysteries of ritual. **4.** Vulgar; coarse. *—tr.v.* **-faned, -fan·ing, -fanes. 1.** To treat with irreverence. **2.** To put to an improper, unworthy, or degrading use; abuse. [ME *prophane* < OFr. < Lat. *profanus* : *pro-,* before + *fanum,* temple.] **—pro·fan′a·to′ry** (prō-făn′ə-tôr′ē, -tōr′ē, prə-) *adj.* **—pro·fane′ly** *adv.* **—pro·fane′ness** *n.* **—pro·fan′er** *n.*

Synonyms: *profane, blasphemous, sacrilegious.* The most common meaning of these adjectives refers to irreverence toward God or things held sacred. *Profane,* the most general, describes abusive disrespect of a sacred name by word or deed. *Blasphemous,* in careful use, refers to profane utterances about God. *Sacrilegious* usually implies extremely profane actions or desecration of sacred objects.

pro·fan·i·ty (prō-făn′ĭ-tē, prə-) *n., pl.* **-ties. 1.** The condition or quality of being profane. **2. a.** Abusive, vulgar, or irreverent language. **b.** The use of such language.

pro·fess (prə-fĕs′, prō-) *v.* **-fessed, -fess·ing, -fess·es.** —*tr.* **1.** To affirm openly; declare or claim: *professed his innocence.* **2.** To make a pretense of: *"He professed to despise everything that had happened since 1850"* (Louis Auchincloss). **3.** To claim skill in or knowledge of: *profess medicine.* **4.** To affirm belief in: *profess Catholicism.* **5.** To receive into a religious order. —*intr.* **1.** To make an open affirmation. **2.** To take the vows of a religious order. [Lat. *profiteri, profess-* : *pro-,* forth + *fateri,* to acknowledge.] **—pro·fess′ed·ly** (-fĕs′ĭd-lē) *adv.*

pro·fes·sion (prə-fĕsh′ən) *n.* **1.** An occupation or vocation requiring training in the liberal arts or the sciences and advanced study in a specialized field. **2.** The body of qualified persons of one specific occupation or field. **3.** The act or an instance of professing; declaration. **4.** An avowal of faith in a religion. [ME, vow made on entering a religious order < OFr. < Lat. *professio,* declaration < *profiteri,* to declare. —see PROFESS.]

pro·fes·sion·al (prə-fĕsh′ə-nəl) *adj.* **1.** Of, relating to, engaged in, or suitable for a profession. **2.** Engaged in a specific activity as a source of livelihood: *a professional actor.* **3.** Performed by persons receiving pay: *professional football.* **4.** Having great skill or experience in a particular field or activity. —*n.* **1.** A person following a profession. **2.** One who earns his livelihood as an athlete. **3.** One who has an assured competence in a particular field or occupation. **—pro·fes′sion·al·ly** *adv.*

pro·fes·sion·al·ism (prə-fĕsh′ə-nə-lĭz′əm) *n.* **1.** Professional status, methods, character, or standards. **2.** The use of professional players in organized athletics.

pro·fes·sion·al·ize (prə-fĕsh′ə-nə-līz′) *tr.v.* **-ized, -iz·ing, -iz·es.** To make professional; put into professional form. **—pro·fes′sion·al·i·za′tion** *n.*

pro·fes·sor (prə-fĕs′ər) *n.* **1. a.** A teacher of the highest rank in an institution of higher learning. **b.** A teacher or instructor. **2.** One who professes. [ME *professour* < Lat. *professor* < *profiteri,* to profess.] **—pro′fes·so′ri·al** (prō′fĭ-sôr′ē-əl, -sōr′-, prŏf′ĭ-) *adj.* **—pro′fes·so′ri·al·ly** *adv.* **—pro·fes′sor·ship′** *n.*

pro·fes·so·ri·ate or **pro·fes·so·ri·at** (prō′fĭ-sôr′ē-ət, -āt′, -sōr′-, prŏf′ĭ-) *n.* **1.** The rank or office of a professor. **2.** College and university professors collectively.

prof·fer (prŏf′ər) *tr.v.* **-fered, -fer·ing, -fers.** To offer; tender. —*n.* The act of proffering; offer. [ME *profren* < OFr. *poroffrir* : *por-,* forth (< Lat. *pro-*) + *offrir,* to offer < Lat. *offerre.* —see OFFER.] **—prof′fer·er** *n.*

pro·fi·cien·cy (prə-fĭsh′ən-sē) *n., pl.* **-cies.** The state or quality of being proficient; competence.

pro·fi·cient (prə-fĭsh′ənt) *adj.* Performing in a given art, skill, or branch of learning with expert correctness and facility; adept. —*n.* An adept; expert. [Lat. *proficiens, proficient-,* pr.part. of *proficere,* to advance. —see PROFIT.] **—pro·fi′cient·ly** *adv.*

pro·file (prō′fīl′) *n.* **1. a.** A side view of an object or structure, esp. of a human head. **b.** A representation of an object or structure seen from the side. **2.** An outline of an object. **3.** A biographical essay presenting the subject's most noteworthy characteristics and achievements. **4.** A graph or table representing numerically the extent to which a person or thing shows various tested characteristics: *an organizational profile.* —*tr.v.* **-filed, -fil·ing, -files. 1.** To draw or shape a profile of. **2.** To write a profile of. [Obs. Ital. *profilo* < *profilare,* to draw in outline : *pro-,* forward (< Lat.) + *filare,* to draw a line < LLat., to spin < Lat. *filum,* thread.]

prof·it (prŏf′ĭt) *n.* **1.** An advantageous gain or return; benefit. **2.** The return received on a business undertaking after all operating expenses have been met. **3.** Often **profits. a.** The return received on an investment after all charges have been paid. **b.** The rate of increase in the net worth of a business enterprise in a given accounting period. **c.** Income received from investments or property. **d.** The amount received for a commodity or service in excess of the original cost. —*v.* **-it·ed, -it·ing, -its.** —*intr.* **1.** To make a gain or profit. **2.** To be advantageous; benefit. —*tr.* To be beneficial to. [ME < OFr. < Lat. *profectus* < p.part. of *proficere,* to gain : *pro-,* forward + *facere,* to make.] **—prof′it·a·bil′i·ty, prof′it·a·ble·ness** *n.* **—prof′it·a·ble** *adj.* **—prof′it·a·bly** *adv.* **—prof′it·less** *adj.*

profit and loss *n.* An account showing net profit and loss over a given period.

prof·i·teer (prŏf′ĭ-tîr′) *n.* One who makes excessive profits on commodities in short supply. —*intr.v.* **-teered, -teer·ing, -teers.** To act as a profiteer.

profit sharing *n.* A system by which employees receive a share of the profits of a business enterprise.

profit system *n.* Free enterprise.

prof·li·gate (prŏf′lĭ-gĭt, -gāt′) *adj.* **1.** Given over to dissipation; dissolute. **2.** Recklessly wasteful; wildly extravagant. —*n.* A wastrel. [Lat. *profligatus,* p.part. of *profligare,* to ruin : *pro-,* forward + *fligere,* to strike.] **—prof′li·ga·cy** (-gə-sē) *n.* **—prof′li·gate·ly** *adv.*

pro for·ma (prō fôr′mə) *adj.* **1.** Done or carried out in a perfunctory way. **2.** Provided in advance so as to prescribe form or to describe items. [Lat., according to form.]

pro·found (prə-found′, prō-) *adj.* **-er, -est. 1.** Situated at, extending to, or coming from a great depth; deep. **2.** Coming as if from the depths of one's being: *profound contempt.* **3.** Thoroughgoing; far-reaching. **4.** Penetrating beyond what is superficial or obvious. **5.** Unqualified; absolute: *a profound silence.* [ME *profounde* < OFr. *profund* < Lat. *profundus* : *pro-,* before + *fundus,* bottom.] **—pro·found′ly** *adv.* **—pro·found′ness** *n.*

pro·fun·di·ty (prə-fŭn′dĭ-tē, prō-) *n., pl.* **-ties. 1.** Great depth. **2.** Depth of intellect, feeling, or meaning. **3.** Something profound or abstruse. [ME *profundite* < OFr. < LLat. *profunditas* < Lat. *profundus,* deep. —see PROFOUND.]

pro·fuse (prə-fyo͞os′, prō-) *adj.* **1.** Plentiful; copious. **2.** Giving or given freely and abundantly; extravagant: *profuse in his compliments.* [ME < Lat. *profusus,* p.part. of *profundere,* to pour forth : *pro-,* forward + *fundere,* to pour.] **—pro·fuse′ly** *adv.* **—pro·fuse′ness** *n.*

pro·fu·sion (prə-fyo͞o′zhən, prō-) *n.* **1.** The state of being profuse; abundance. **2.** Lavish or unrestrained expense; extravagance. **3.** A profuse outpouring or display.

pro·gen·i·tor (prō-jĕn′ĭ-tər) *n.* **1.** A direct ancestor. **2.** An originator of a line of descent. [ME *progenitour* < OFr. *progeniteur* < Lat. *progenitor* < *progignere,* to beget : *pro-,* forward + *gignere,* to beget.]

prog·e·ny (prŏj′ə-nē) *n., pl.* **-nies. 1.** Children or descendants; offspring. **2.** A result of creative effort; product. [ME *progenie* < OFr. < Lat. *progenies* < *progignere,* to beget. —see PROGENITOR.]

pro·ges·ta·tion·al (prō′jĕs-tā′shə-nəl) *adj.* **1.** Preceding gestation. **2.** Preceding ovulation.

pro·ges·ter·one (prō-jĕs′tə-rōn′) *n.* A female hormone, $C_{21}H_{30}O_2$, secreted by the corpus luteum of the ovary prior to implantation of the fertilized ovum. [PRO-[1] + GES(TATION) + STER(OL) + -ONE.]

pro·ges·to·gen (prō-jĕs′tə-jən) *n.* Any of several natural or synthetic progestational hormones. [PROGEST(ATIONAL) + (ESTR)OGEN.]

pro·glot·tid (prō-glŏt′ĭd) also **pro·glot·tis** (-glŏt′ĭs) *n., pl.* **-glot·tids** also **-glot·ti·des** (-glŏt′ĭ-dēz′). One of the segments of a tapeworm, containing both male and female reproductive organs. [Gk. *proglōttis, proglōttid-,* tip of the tongue (from its shape) : *pro-,* before + *glotta,* tongue.] **—pro·glot′tic, pro′glot·ti·de′an** (-glŏt-ĭ-dē′ən, -glŏ-tĭd′ē-ən) *adj.*

prog·na·thous (prŏg′nə-thəs, prŏg-nā′-) also **prog·nath·ic** (prŏg-năth′ĭk, -nā′thĭk) *adj.* Having jaws that project forward to a considerable degree. **—prog′na·thism** (-nə-thĭz′əm) *n.*

prog·no·sis (prŏg-nō′sĭs) *n., pl.* **-ses** (-sēz′). **1. a.** A prediction of the probable course and outcome of a disease. **b.** The likelihood of recovery from a disease. **2.** A forecast or prediction. [LLat. < Gk. *prognōsis* < *progignōskein,* to foreknow : *pro-,* before + *gignōskein,* to know.]

prog·nos·tic (prŏg-nŏs′tĭk) *adj.* **1.** Of, relating to, or acting as a prognosis. **2.** Predicting; foretelling. —*n.* **1.** A sign or omen of some future happening. **2.** A symptom indicating the future course of a disease. [Med. Lat. *prognosticus* < Gk. *prognōstikos* < *progignōskein,* to foreknow. —see PROGNOSIS.]

prog·nos·ti·cate (prŏg-nŏs′tĭ-kāt′) *tr.v.* **-cat·ed, -cat·ing, -cates. 1.** To predict, using present indications as a guide. **2.** To foreshadow; portend. [Med. Lat. *prognosticare, prognosticat-* < Lat. *prognosticum,* sign of the future < Gk. *prognōstikon* < *prognōstikos,* foreknowing. —see PROGNOSTIC.] **—prog·nos′ti·ca′tion** *n.* **—prog·nos′ti·ca′tive** *adj.* **—prog·nos′ti·ca′tor** *n.*

pro·gram (prō′grăm′, -grəm) *n.* **1. a.** A listing of the order of events and other pertinent information for a public presentation. **b.** The presentation itself. **2.** A scheduled radio or television show. **3.** An organized list of procedures; schedule. **4. a.** A procedure for solving a problem, including collection of data, processing, and presentation of results. **b.** Such a procedure coded for a computer. **5.** An instruction sequence in programmed instruction. —*tr.v.* **-grammed, -gram·ming, -grams** also **-gramed, -gram·ing, -grams. 1.** To include or schedule in a program. **2.** To design or schedule programs. **3.** To train or regulate (the mind or the senses, for example) to perform in a certain way: *continually trying to program their behavior.* **4. a.** To prepare an instructional sequence in programmed instruction. **b.** To instruct by such a sequence. **5.** *Computer Sci.* To provide (a computer) with a set of instructions for solving a problem. [Fr. *programme* < LLat. *programma,* public notice < Gk. < *prographein,* to set forth as a public notice : *pro-,* forth + *graphein,* to write.] **—pro·gram′ma·bil′i·ty** *n.* **—pro′gram′ma·ble** *adj.* **—pro′gram·mat′ic** (prō′grə-măt′ĭk) *adj.* **—pro·gram·mat′i·cal·ly** *adv.*

program director *n.* A radio or television station director who is responsible for selecting, planning, and scheduling programs.

pro·gramme (prō′grăm′, -grəm) *n. & v. Chiefly Brit.* Variant of **program.**

pro·grammed or **pro·gramed** (prō′grămd′, -grəmd) *adj.* Of, pertaining to, or occurring by programmed instruction: *programmed learning.*

profile

prohibition
Federal agents smashing beer kegs during Prohibition

programmed instruction *n.* A method of teaching in which the information to be learned is presented in discrete units, with a correct response to each unit required from the learner before advancing to the next unit.

pro·gram·mer or **pro·gram·er** (prō′grăm′ər) *n.* **1.** One who prepares a computer program. **2.** One who prepares an instructional program.

pro·gram·ming or **pro·gram·ing** (prō′grăm′ĭng, -grə-mĭng) *n.* The designing, scheduling, or planning of a program.

program music *n.* Music embodying the episodes of a known story.

prog·ress (prŏg′rĕs′, -rəs, prō′grĕs′) *n.* **1.** Movement toward a goal. **2.** Development; unfolding. **3.** Steady improvement, as of a society or civilization: *a believer in progress.* **4.** A state journey made by a sovereign through his realm. *—intr.v.* **pro·gress** (prə-grĕs′) **-gressed, -gress·ing, -gress·es. 1.** To advance; proceed. **2.** To advance toward a more desirable form. **—*idiom.* in progress.** Going on or occurring. [ME *progresse* < Lat. *progressus,* p.part. of *progredi,* to advance : *pro-,* forward + *gradi,* to step.]

pro·gres·sion (prə-grĕsh′ən) *n.* **1.** Progress. **2.** Advance. **3.** A sequence, as of events. **4.** *Math.* A series of numbers or quantities each derived from the one preceding by a consistent operation. **5.** *Mus.* **a.** A succession of tones or chords. **b.** A series of repetitions of a phrase, each in a new position on the scale. **—pro·gres′sion·al** *adj.*

pro·gres·sive (prə-grĕs′ĭv) *adj.* **1.** Moving forward; advancing. **2.** Proceeding in steps; continuing steadily by increments. **3.** Promoting or favoring political or social reform; liberal. **4. Progressive.** Of or belonging to a Progressive Party. **5.** Of, relating to, or influenced by a theory of education characterized by emphasis on the individual needs and capacities of each child and informality of curriculum. **6.** Of or denoting a tax system in which the rate of taxation increases as the taxable amount increases. **7.** *Pathol.* Continuously spreading or increasing in severity. **8.** *Gram.* Designating a verb form that expresses an action or condition in progress. *—n.* **1.** A person who favors or strives for reform in politics, education, or other fields. **2. Progressive.** One who belongs to a Progressive Party. **3.** *Gram.* A progressive verb form. **—pro·gres′sive·ly** *adv.* **—pro·gres′sive·ness** *n.*

Pro·gres·sive-Con·ser·va·tive Party (prə-grĕs′ĭv-kən-sûr′və-tĭv) *n.* A leading Canadian political party advocating close ties with Britain and economic nationalism.

Progressive Party *n.* **1.** A primarily agrarian American political party organized under the leadership of Theodore Roosevelt in 1912. **2.** A political party organized in 1924 and led by Robert M. La Follette. **3.** A political party formed in 1948, originally led by Henry A. Wallace.

pro·gres·siv·ism (prə-grĕs′ĭ-vĭz′əm) *n.* The doctrines and practice of political or educational progressives. **—pro·gres′siv·ist** *n.* **—pro·gres′siv·is′tic** *adj.*

pro·hib·it (prō-hĭb′ĭt) *tr.v.* **-it·ed, -it·ing, -its. 1.** To forbid by authority. **2.** To prevent or debar. [ME *prohibiten* < Lat. *prohibēre,* to prevent : *pro-,* in front + *habēre,* to hold.]

pro·hi·bi·tion (prō′ə-bĭsh′ən) *n.* **1.** The act of prohibiting. **2.** A law, order, or decree that forbids something. **3. a.** The forbidding by law of the manufacture, transportation, sale, and possession of alcoholic beverages. **b. Prohibition.** The period (1920–33) during which a law forbidding the manufacture and sale of alcoholic beverages was in force in the United States.

pro·hi·bi·tion·ist (prō′ə-bĭsh′ə-nĭst) *n.* **1.** One in favor of outlawing the manufacture and sale of alcoholic beverages. **2.** Often **Prohibitionist.** A member of the Prohibition Party.

Prohibition Party *n.* An American political party that was organized in 1869 and advocated prohibition.

pro·hib·i·tive (prō-hĭb′ĭ-tĭv) also **pro·hib·i·to·ry** (-tôr′ē, -tōr′ē) *adj.* **1.** Prohibiting; forbidding. **2.** Preventing or discouraging purchase or use: *prohibitive prices.* **—pro·hib′i·tive·ly** *adv.* **—pro·hib′i·tive·ness** *n.*

proj·ect (prŏj′ĕkt′, -ĭkt) *n.* **1.** A plan or proposal; scheme. **2.** An undertaking requiring concerted effort. **3.** A research undertaking. *—v.* **pro·ject** (prə-jĕkt′) **-ject·ed, -ject·ing, -jects.** *—tr.* **1.** To thrust outward or forward. **2.** To throw forward; hurl. **3.** To transport in one's imagination. **4.** To externalize and attribute (an emotion, for example) to someone or something else. **5.** To direct (one's voice) so as to be heard clearly at a distance. **6.** To form a plan or intention for. **7.** To cause (an image) to appear upon a surface. **8.** *Math.* To produce a projection. *—intr.* **1.** To extend forward or out; protrude. **2.** To direct one's voice so as to be heard clearly at a distance. [ME *proiecte* < Lat. *projectus,* p.part. of *proicere,* to throw out : *pro-,* forth + *jacere,* to throw.] **—pro·ject′a·ble** *adj.*

pro·jec·tile (prə-jĕk′təl, -tīl′) *n.* **1.** A fired, thrown, or otherwise projected object, such as a bullet, having no capacity for self-propulsion. **2.** A self-propelling missile, such as a rocket. *—adj.* **1.** Capable of being impelled or hurled forward. **2.** Driving forward; impelling. **3.** *Zool.* Capable of being thrust outward; protrusile. [NLat. *projectilis* < Lat. *proicere,* to throw out. —see PROJECT.]

pro·jec·tion (prə-jĕk′shən) *n.* **1.** The act of projecting. **2.** Something that thrusts outward; protuberance. **3.** A plan for an anticipated course of action. **4. a.** The process of projecting a filmed image onto a screen or other viewing surface. **b.** The image so projected. **5.** The image of a geometric figure produced by a coordinate mapping. **6.** A system of intersecting lines, such as the grid of a map, on which part or all of the globe or the celestial sphere may be represented as a plane surface. **7.** *Psychol.* The naive or unconscious attribution of one's own feelings, attitudes, or desires to others.

projection booth *n.* A booth, as in a theater, from which a film projector is operated.

pro·jec·tion·ist (prə-jĕk′shə-nĭst) *n.* **1.** One who operates a motion-picture projector. **2.** A map-maker.

projection room *n.* **1.** A room equipped with facilities for the private viewing of a motion picture. **2.** A projection booth.

pro·jec·tive (prə-jĕk′tĭv) *adj.* **1.** Pertaining to or made by projection. **2.** Extending outward; projecting. **3.** Designating a property of a geometric figure that does not vary when the figure undergoes projection. **—pro·jec′tive·ly** *adv.*

projective geometry *n.* The study of geometric properties that are invariant under projection.

projective test *n.* A psychological test in which a subject's responses to relatively unstructured standard stimuli, such as a series of cartoons, abstract patterns, or incomplete sentences, are analyzed for determinants of personality or sometimes cognition.

pro·jec·tor (prə-jĕk′tər) *n.* **1.** A machine for projecting an image onto a screen. **2.** A device for projecting a beam of light. **3.** One who devises plans or projects.

pro·jec·tu·al (prə-jĕk′cho͞o-əl) *n.* A piece of instructional material designed to be projected onto a screen by a projector. [PROJECT + (VIS)UAL.]

pro·kar·y·ote (prō-kăr′ē-ōt′) *n.* Variant of **procaryote.**

pro·lac·tin (prō-lăk′tĭn) *n.* A pituitary hormone that stimulates the secretion of milk.

pro·la·mine also **pro·la·min** (prō′lə-mĭn, -mēn′) *n.* Any of a class of simple proteins found in wheat, rye, and other grains. [PROL(INE) + AM(MONIA) + -INE.]

pro·lan (prō′lăn′) *n.* The gonadotropic hormone in pregnant women's urine, used to indicate pregnancy. [G. < Lat. *proles,* offspring.]

pro·lapse (prō-lăps′) *Med.* *—intr.v.* **-lapsed, -laps·ing, -laps·es.** To fall or slip out of place. *—n.* (prō′lăps′, prō-lăps′) also **pro·lap·sus** (prō-lăp′səs). The falling down or slipping out of place of an organ or part, such as the uterus. [LLat. *prolapsus,* a falling < Lat., p.part. of *prolabi,* to fall down : *pro-,* forward + *labi,* to fall.]

pro·late (prō′lāt′) *adj.* Designating the shape of a solid, esp. of a spheroid, having its polar axis longer than its equatorial diameter; cigar-shaped. [Lat. *prolatus,* p.part. of *proferre,* to stretch out : *pro-,* forth + *ferre,* to carry.] **—pro′late′ly** *adv.* **—pro′late′ness** *n.*

prole (prōl) *n.* A proletarian. [Short for PROLETARIAN.]

pro·leg (prō′lĕg′) *n.* One of the stubby limbs on the abdominal segments of caterpillars and some other insect larvae.

pro·le·gom·e·non (prō′lĭ-gŏm′ə-nŏn′, -nən) *n., pl.* **-na** (-nə). A critical introduction. [Gk. < passive neuter pr.part. of *prolegein,* to say beforehand : *pro-,* before + *legein,* to say.] **—pro′le·gom′e·nous** *adj.*

pro·lep·sis (prō-lĕp′sĭs) *n., pl.* **-ses** (-sēz′). **1.** The anticipation and answering of an objection or argument before one's opponent has put it forward. **2.** The use of a descriptive word in anticipation of the act or circumstances that would make it applicable. [LLat. < Gk. *prolēpsis* < *prolambanein,* to anticipate : *pro-,* before + *lambanein,* to take.] **—pro·lep′tic** (-lĕp′tĭk), **pro·lep′ti·cal** *adj.*

pro·le·tar·i·an (prō′lĭ-târ′ē-ən) *adj.* Of, pertaining to, or characteristic of the proletariat. *—n.* A member of the proletariat. [< Lat. *proletarius* < a Roman citizen of the lowest class < *proles,* offspring (from the fact that propertyless citizens were deemed by a Roman constitution to be of service to the state only by having children).] **—pro′le·tar′i·an·ism** *n.*

pro·le·tar·i·at (prō′lĭ-târ′ē-ĭt) *n.* **1. a.** The class of industrial wage earners who, possessing neither capital nor production means, must earn their living by selling their labor. **b.** The poorest class of working people. **2.** The propertyless class of ancient Rome, constituting the lowest class of citizens. [Fr. *prolétariat* < Lat. *proletarius,* a Roman citizen of the lowest class. —see PROLETARIAN.]

pro-life (prō-līf′) *adj.* Opposed to legalized abortions. **—pro-lif′er** *n.*

pro·lif·er·ate (prə-lĭf′ə-rāt′) *v.* **-at·ed, -at·ing, -ates.** *—intr.* **1.** To reproduce or produce new growth or parts rapidly and repeatedly: *proliferating cells.* **2.** To increase or spread at a rapid rate. *—tr.* To cause to grow or increase rapidly. [Back-formation < E. *proliferation,* the act of proliferating < Fr. *prolifération* < *prolifère,* procreative < Med. Lat. *prolifer.* —see PROLIFEROUS.] **—pro·lif′er·a′tion** *n.* **—pro·lif′er·a′tive** *adj.*

pro·lif·er·ous (prə-lĭf′ər-əs) *adj.* **1.** *Biol.* Reproducing freely by means of buds and side branches. **2.** *Bot.* Freely producing buds or offshoots, sometimes from unusual places. [Med. Lat. *prolifer* < Lat. *proles,* offspring.] **—pro·lif′er·ous·ly** *adv.*

pro·lif·ic (prə-lĭf′ĭk) *adj.* **1.** Producing offspring or fruit in great abundance; fertile. **2.** Producing abundant works or results. [Fr. *prolifique* < Med. Lat. *prolificus* < Lat. *proles,* offspring.] **—pro·lif′i·ca·cy** (-ĭ-kə-sē), **pro·lif′ic·ness** *n.* **—pro·lif′i·cal·ly** *adv.*

pro·line (prō′lēn′) *n.* An amino acid, $C_5H_9O_2N$, found in many proteins. [G. *Prolin* < *Pyrol,* pyrole.]

pro·lix (prō-lĭks′, prō′lĭks′) *adj.* **1.** Wordy and tedious. **2.** Tending to speak or write at great length. [ME < OFr. *prolixe* < Lat. *prolixus,* extended.] **—pro·lix′i·ty** (-lĭk′sĭ-tē) *n.* **—pro·lix′ly** *adv.*

pro·loc·u·tor (prō-lŏk′yə-tər) *n.* A presiding officer or chairman, esp. of the lower house of a convocation in the Anglican Church. [ME < Lat., advocate < *proloqui,* to speak out : *pro-,* forth + *loqui,* to speak.]

pro·logue also **pro·log** (prō′lôg′, -lŏg′) *n.* **1.** The lines introducing a discourse or play. **2.** An introductory act or event. [ME *prolog* < OFr. *prologue* < Lat. *prologus* < Gk. *prologos* : *pro-,* before + *legein,* to speak.]

pro·long (prə-lông′, -lŏng′) *tr.v.* **-longed, -long·ing, -longs. 1.** To lengthen in duration; protract. **2.** To lengthen in extent. [ME *prolongen* < OFr. *prolonguer* < LLat. *prolongare* : Lat. *pro-,* out + Lat. *longus,* long.] **—pro·long′er** *n.*

pro·lon·gate (prə-lông′gāt′, -lŏng′-, prō-) *tr.v.* **-gat·ed, -gat·ing, -gates.** To prolong. **—pro′lon·ga′tion** (prō′lông-gā′shən, -lŏng-) *n.*

pro·lu·sion (prō-lo͞o′zhən) *n.* **1.** A preliminary exercise. **2.** An essay written as a preface to a more detailed work. [Lat. *prolusio* < *proludere,* to practice beforehand : *pro-,* before + *ludere,* to play.] **—pro·lu′so·ry** (-sə-rē, -zə-) *adj.*

prom (prŏm) *n.* A ball or formal dance held for a high-school or college class. [Short for PROMENADE.]

pro·me·carb (prō′mĭ-kärb′) *n.* A colorless crystalline compound used as an agricultural insecticide on potatoes and fruit. [PRO(PYL) + ME(THYL) + CARB(AMATE).]

prom·e·nade (prŏm′ə-nād′, -näd′) *n.* **1. a.** A leisurely walk, esp. one taken in a public place as a social activity. **b.** A public place for such walking. **2. a.** A formal ball. **b.** A formal march by the guests at the opening of a ball. **3.** A march executed between the figures of a square dance. *—v.* **-nad·ed, -nad·ing, -nades.** *—intr.* **1.** To go on a leisurely walk. **2.** To execute a promenade in square dancing. *—tr.* **1.** To take a promenade along or through. **2.** To take or display on or as if on a promenade. [Fr. < *(se) promener,* to take a walk < LLat. *prominare,* to drive forward : *pro-,* forward + *minare,* to drive < *minari,* to threaten < *minae,* threats.] **—prom′e·nad′er** *n.*

promenade deck *n.* The upper deck or a section of the upper deck on a passenger ship where the passengers can promenade.

Pro·me·the·an (prə-mē′thē-ən) *adj.* **1.** Pertaining to or suggestive of Prometheus. **2.** Boldly creative; original. *—n.* One who is Promethean in manner or actions.

Pro·me·the·us (prə-mē′thē-əs, -thyo͞os′) *n. Gk. Myth.* A Titan who stole fire from Olympus and gave it to man. [Lat. < Gk. *Promētheus.*]

pro·me·thi·um (prə-mē′thē-əm) *n. Symbol* **Pm** A radioactive rare-earth element prepared by fission of uranium or by neutron bombardment of neodymium, having 14 isotopes with mass numbers ranging from 141 to 154, and used as a source of beta rays. Atomic number 61; melting point 1,035°C; boiling point 2,730°C; valence 3. [< PROMETHEUS.]

prom·i·nence (prŏm′ə-nəns) also **prom·i·nen·cy** (-nən-sē) *n.* **1.** The condition or quality of being prominent. **2.** Something that is prominent. **3.** *Astron.* A tonguelike cloud of flaming gas rising from the sun's surface, visible as part of the corona during a total solar eclipse.

prom·i·nent (prŏm′ə-nənt) *adj.* **1.** Projecting outward from a line or surface; protuberant. **2.** Immediately noticeable; conspicuous. **3.** Widely known; eminent. [Lat. *prominens, prominent-,* pr.part. of *prominēre,* to jut out.] **—prom′i·nent·ly** *adv.*

prom·is·cu·i·ty (prŏm′ĭ-skyo͞o′ĭ-tē, prō′mĭ-) *n., pl.* **-ties. 1.** The state or character of being promiscuous. **2.** Promiscuous sexual intercourse. **3.** An indiscriminate mixture; hodgepodge.

pro·mis·cu·ous (prə-mĭs′kyo͞o-əs) *adj.* **1.** Consisting of diverse and unrelated parts or individuals; confused. **2.** Lacking standards of selection; indiscriminate. **3.** Indiscriminate in sexual relations. **4.** Casual; random. [Lat. *promiscuus* : *pro-* (intensive) + *miscēre,* to mix.] **—pro·mis′cu·ous·ly** *adv.* **—pro·mis′cu·ous·ness** *n.*

prom·ise (prŏm′ĭs) *n.* **1.** A declaration assuring that one will or will not do something; vow. **2.** Something promised. **3.** Indication of future excellence or success. *—v.* **-ised, -is·ing, -is·es.** *—tr.* **1.** To pledge or offer assurance: *We promise to return.* **2.** To make a promise of. **3.** To afford a basis for expecting. *—intr.* **1.** To make a promise. **2.** To afford a basis for expectation: *a future that promises well.* [ME *promys* < Lat. *promissum,* neuter p.part. of *promittere,* to promise : *pro-,* forth + *mittere,* to send.] **—prom′is·er** *n.*

Promised Land *n.* **1.** In the Old Testament, the land of Canaan, promised to Abraham and his descendants. **2. promised land.** A place of anticipated happiness.

prom·is·ee (prŏm′ĭ-sē′) *n. Law.* An individual to whom a promise is made.

prom·is·ing (prŏm′ĭ-sĭng) *adj.* Likely to develop in a desirable manner. **—prom′is·ing·ly** *adv.*

prom·i·sor (prŏm′ĭ-sôr′) *n. Law.* An individual who makes a promise.

prom·is·so·ry (prŏm′ĭ-sôr′ē, -sōr′ē) *adj.* **1.** Containing, involving, or having the nature of a promise. **2.** Indicating how the provisions of an insurance contract will be carried out after it is signed. [Med. Lat. *promissorius* < Lat. *promissor,* one who promises < *promittere,* to promise.]

promissory note *n.* A written promise to pay or repay a specified sum of money at a stated time or on demand.

pro·mo (prō′mō) *n., pl.* **-mos.** *Informal.* A promotional presentation, such as a television spot, radio announcement, or personal appearance. [Short for PROMOTION.]

prom·on·to·ry (prŏm′ən-tôr′ē, -tōr′ē) *n., pl.* **-ries. 1.** A high ridge of land or rock jutting out into a sea or other expanse of water. **2.** *Anat.* A projecting bodily part. [Med. Lat. *promontorium,* alteration of Lat. *promuntorium.*]

pro·mot·a·ble (prə-mō′tə-bəl) *adj.* **1.** Having the qualities necessary for advancement to a higher position or rank: *a promising, promotable young woman.* **2.** Suitable for consumer marketing and promotion: *a promotable item.* **—pro·mot′a·bil′i·ty** *n.*

pro·mote (prə-mōt′) *tr.v.* **-mot·ed, -mot·ing, -motes. 1. a.** To raise to a more important or responsible job or rank. **b.** To advance (a student) to the next higher grade. **2.** To contribute to the progress or growth of; further. **3.** To urge the adoption of; advocate. **4.** To attempt to sell or popularize by advertising or by securing financial support: *promote a new product; promote a Broadway show.* [ME *promoten* < Lat. *promovēre,* to advance : *pro-,* forward + *movēre,* to move.]

pro·mot·er (prə-mō′tər) *n.* **1.** An active supporter; advocate. **2.** A financial and publicity organizer, as of a boxing match.

pro·mo·tion (prə-mō′shən) *n.* **1.** The act of promoting. **2.** An advancement in rank or responsibility. **3.** Encouragement; furtherance. **4.** Advertising or other publicity. **—pro·mo′tion·al** *adj.* **—pro·mo′tion·al·ly** *adv.*

pro·mo·tive (prə-mō′tĭv) *adj.* Tending to promote. **—pro·mo′tive·ness** *n.*

prompt (prŏmpt) *adj.* **-er, -est. 1.** On time; punctual. **2.** Done without delay. *—tr.v.* **prompt·ed, prompt·ing, prompts. 1.** To press into action; incite. **2.** To give rise to; inspire. **3.** To assist with a reminder; remind. **4.** To give a cue to, as in a play. *—n.* **1. a.** The act of prompting or giving a cue. **b.** The information suggested; reminder or cue. **2. a.** A prompt note. **b.** The time limit stipulated in a prompt note. [ME < OFr. < Lat. *promptus,* p.part. of *promere,* to bring forth : *pro-,* forth + *emere,* to take.] **—promp′ti·tude′** (prŏmp′tĭ-to͞od′, -tyo͞od′), **prompt′ness** *n.* **—prompt′ly** *adv.*

prompt·book (prŏmpt′bo͝ok′) *n.* An annotated script used by a theater prompter.

prompt·er (prŏmp′tər) *n.* **1.** One who prompts. **2.** One who gives cues to actors.

prompt·ing (prŏmp′tĭng) *n.* A computer language function that alerts a user to the need for additional input in order to continue processing data.

prompt note *n.* A notice sent to the purchaser of goods as a reminder of the amount that is due the seller and the date that it is due.

prom·ul·gate (prŏm′əl-gāt′, prō-mŭl′gāt′) *tr.v.* **-gat·ed, -gat·ing, -gates. 1.** To make known (a decree, for example) by public declaration; announce officially. **2.** To put (a law) into effect by formal public announcement. [Lat. *promulgare, promulgat-.*] **—prom′ul·ga′tion** (prŏm′əl-gā′shən, prō′məl-) *n.* **—prom′ul·ga′tor** *n.*

pro·na·tal·ism (prō-nāt′l-ĭz′əm) *n.* An attitude or policy that encourages childbearing, as by exalting or rewarding parenthood. **—pro·na′tal·ist** *n.* **—pro·na′tal·is′tic** *adj.*

pro·nate (prō′nāt′) *tr.v.* **-nat·ed, -nat·ing, -nates.** To turn (the palm or inner surface of the hand or forelimb) downward or backward. [LLat. *pronare, pronat-,* to bend forward < *pronus,* turned forward.] **—pro·na′tion** *n.*

pro·na·tor (prō′nā′tər) *n., pl.* **pro·na·to·res** (prō′nə-tôr′ēz, -tōr′-). The forearm or forelimb muscle that effects pronation.

prone (prōn) *adj.* **1.** Lying with the front or face downward; prostrate. **2.** Tending: *prone to mischief.* *—adv.* In a prone manner: *lying prone on the bed.* [ME < Lat. *pronus,* inclined forward.] **—prone′ly** *adv.* **—prone′ness** *n.*

Synonyms: *prone, supine, prostrate, recumbent. Prone* always means lying face downward, the front of the body turned toward the surface it rests on. *Supine* also means lying down, but always on one's back. *Prostrate* can mean lying down in either position, and suggests a person's placing himself, being thrown, or collapsing into this position. *Recumbent* means lying down but emphasizes a position of comfort or rest.

pro·neph·ros (prō-nĕf′rəs, -rŏs′) *n.* A primitive kidney that disappears early in the embryonic development of higher vertebrates. [PRO-[2] + Gk. *nephros,* kidney.] **—pro·neph′ric** (-rĭk) *adj.*

prong (prông, prŏng) *n.* **1.** A sharply pointed part of a tool or instrument, such as a tine of a fork. **2.** A sharply pointed projection. *—tr.v.* **pronged, prong·ing, prongs.** To pierce

Prometheus
17th-century German sculpture

PROOFREADERS' MARKS

Instruction	Mark in Margin	Mark in Type	Corrected Type
Delete		the ~~good~~ word	the word
Insert indicated material	good	the ‸ word	the good word
Let it stand	stet	the ~~good~~ word	the good word
Make capital	cap	the word	the Word
Make lower case	lc	/The Word	the Word
Set in small capitals	SC	See word.	See WORD.
Set in italic type	ital	The word is word.	The word is *word.*
Set in roman type	rom	the *word*	the word
Set in boldface type	bf	the entry word	the entry **word**
Set in lightface type	lf	the entry **word**	the entry word
Transpose	tr	the word good	the good word
Close up space		the wo rd	the word
Delete and close up space		the woord	the word
Spell out	sp	2 words	two words
Insert: space	#	theword	the word
period	⊙	This is the word‸	This is the word.
comma	‸	words‸ words, words	words, words, words
hyphen	=/=	word‸for‸word test	word-for-word test
colon	(:)	The following words‸	The following words:
semicolon	;	Scan the words‸ skim the words.	Scan the words; skim the words.
apostrophe	’	Johns words	John's words
quotation marks	“/ ”/	the word word	the word “word”
parentheses	(/)/	The word‸ word‸ is in parentheses.	The word (word) is in parentheses.
brackets	[/]/	He read from the Word ‸the Bible‸.	He read from the Word [the Bible].
en dash	N	1964‸1972	1964–1972
em dash	M/ M/	The dictionary‸ how often it is needed‸ belongs in every home.	The dictionary—how often it is needed—belongs in every home.
superior type	2	2 = 4	$2^2 = 4$
inferior type	2	HO	H_2O
asterisk	*	word	word*
dagger	†	a word‸	a word†
double dagger	‡	words and words‸	words and words‡
section symbol	§	‸Book Reviews	§Book Reviews
virgule	/	either‸or	either/or
Start paragraph	¶	“Where is it?” ‸“It's on the shelf.”	“Where is it?” “It's on the shelf.”
Run in	run in	The entry word is printed in boldface. The pronunciation follows.	The entry word is printed in boldface. The pronunciation follows.
Turn right side up		the word	the word
Move left	⊏	⊏ the word	the word
Move right	⊐	the word	the word
Move up		the word	the word
Move down		the word	the word
Align	‖	the word / the word / the word	the word / the word / the word
Straighten line		the word	the word
Wrong font	wf	the word	the word
Broken type	×	the word	the word

with or as if with a prong. [ME *pronge,* forked instrument.]

prong·horn (prông′hôrn′, prŏng′-) *n., pl.* **pronghorn** or **-horns.** A small deer, *Antilocapra americana,* resembling an antelope and having small forked horns, found on western North American plains.

pro·nom·i·nal (prō-nŏm′ə-nəl) *adj. Gram.* **1.** Of, pertaining to, or functioning as a pronoun. **2.** Resembling a pronoun, as by specifying a person, place, or thing, while functioning primarily as another part of speech. *His* in *his choice* is a pronominal adjective. [LLat. *pronominalis* < Lat. *pronomen,* pronoun : *pro-,* in place of + *nomen,* name.] **—pro·nom′i·nal·ly** *adv.*

pro·noun (prō′noun′) *n. Gram.* One of a class of words that function as substitutes for nouns or noun phrases and denote persons or things asked for, previously specified, or understood from the context.

pro·nounce (prə-nouns′) *v.* **-nounced, -nounc·ing, -nounc·es.** *—tr.* **1.** To articulate (a word or speech sound). **2.** To transcribe (a word) in phonetic symbols. **3.** To state officially and formally; declare. **4.** To declare to be in a specified condition. *—intr.* **1.** To declare one's opinion or make a pronouncement. **2.** To articulate words. [ME *pronouncen* < OFr. *prononcier* < Lat. *pronuntiare,* to declare : *pro-,* forth + *nuntiare,* to announce < *nuntius,* message.] **—pro·nounce′a·ble** *adj.* **—pro·nounc′er** *n.*

pro·nounced (prə-nounst′) *adj.* **1.** Spoken; voiced. **2.** Distinct; strongly marked: *walks with a pronounced limp.* **—pro·nounc′ed·ly** (-noun′sĭd-lē) *adv.* **—pro·nounc′ed·ness** *n.*

pro·nounce·ment (prə-nouns′mənt) *n.* **1.** A formal declaration. **2.** An authoritative statement.

pro·nounc·ing (prə-noun′sĭng) *adj.* Pertaining to, designed for, or showing pronunciation: *a pronouncing dictionary.*

pron·to (prŏn′tō) *adv. Informal.* Without delay; quickly. [Sp. < Lat. *promptus.* —see PROMPT.]

pro·nu·cle·us (prō-no͞o′klē-əs, -nyo͞o′-) *n., pl.* **-cle·i** (-klē-ī′). The haploid nucleus of a sperm or egg prior to fusion of the nuclei in fertilization. **—pro·nu′cle·ar** *adj.*

pro·nun·ci·a·men·to (prō-nŭn′sē-ə-mĕn′tō) *n., pl.* **-tos** or **-toes. 1.** An edict announcing a coup d'état. **2.** An authoritarian pronouncement. [Sp. *pronunciamiento* < *pronunciar,* to pronounce < Lat. *pronuntiare.*]

pro·nun·ci·a·tion (prə-nŭn′sē-ā′shən) *n.* **1.** The act or manner of articulating speech. **2.** A phonetic transcription of a given word. **—pro·nun′ci·a′tion·al** *adj.*

proof (pro͞of) *n.* **1.** The evidence establishing the validity of a given assertion. **2.** Conclusive demonstration of something. **3.** The proving of something by experiment, test, or trial: *put one's beliefs to the proof.* **4.** *Archaic.* Proven impenetrability. **5.** *Law.* The whole body of evidence that determines the verdict or judgment in a case. **6.** The validation of a proposition by application of specified rules, as of induction or deduction, to assumptions, axioms, and sequentially derived conclusions. **7.** The strength of a liquor with reference to proof spirit. **8. a.** *Printing.* A trial sheet of printed material that is checked against the original manuscript and on which corrections are made. **b.** A trial impression of a plate, stone, or block taken at any of various stages in engraving. **c.** A trial photographic print. *—adj.* **1.** Fully or successfully resistant; impervious: *proof against fire.* **2.** Of standard alcoholic strength. **3.** Used in proving or making corrections. *—v.* **proofed, proof·ing, proofs.** *—tr.* **1.** To run off (a printed or engraved proof). **2.** To proofread (copy). **3.** To work (dough) into proper lightness. **4.** To make resistant. *—intr.* To proofread. [ME *prove* < LLat. *proba* < Lat. *probare,* to prove.]

-proof *suff.* Impervious to; able to withstand: *bulletproof.* [< PROOF.]

proof·like (pro͞of′līk′) *adj.* Having the appearance of a coin, esp. its mint luster, that is not for circulation.

proof·read (pro͞of′rēd′) *v.* **-read** (-rĕd′), **-read·ing, -reads.** *—tr.* To read (copy or a printer's proof) against the original manuscript for corrections. *—intr.* To correct a printer's proof while reading against the original manuscript. **—proof′read′er** *n.*

proof sheet *n.* A proof (sense 8.a.).

proof spirit *n.* An alcohol-water mixture or a beverage containing a standard amount of alcohol, the U.S. standard being 100 proof, or 50 per cent, of ethyl alcohol by volume at 60°F.

prop¹ (prŏp) *n.* **1.** A device used to shore something up. **2.** One that serves as a support or stay. *—tr.v.* **propped, prop·ping, props.** To keep from falling; support. [ME *proppe,* prob. of MDu. orig.]

prop² (prŏp) *n.* A property (sense 4).

prop³ (prŏp) *n. Informal.* A propeller.

prop- *pref.* Related to or derived from propionic acid: *propane.* [< PROPIONIC ACID.]

pro·pae·deu·tic (prō′pĭ-do͞o′tĭk, -dyo͞o′-) *adj.* Providing introductory instruction. *—n.* Preparatory instruction. [< Gk. *propaideuein,* to teach beforehand : *pro-,* before + *paideuein,* to teach < *pais,* child.]

prop·a·gan·da (prŏp′ə-găn′də) *n.* **1.** The systematic propagation of a given doctrine or of allegations reflecting its views and interests: *Marxist propaganda.* **2.** Material disseminated by the advocates of a doctrine. **3. Propaganda.** The Congregation of the Roman Curia that has authority in the matter of preaching the gospel and of establishing the Church in non-Christian countries and of administering Church missions in territories where there is no properly organized hierarchy. [Ital., short for NLat. *Sacra Congregatio de Propaganda Fide,* Sacred Congregation for Propagating the Faith.] **—prop'a·gan'dism** *n.* **—prop'a·gan'dist** *n.* **—prop'a·gan·dis'tic** *adj.* **—prop'a·gan·dis'ti·cal·ly** *adv.*

prop·a·gan·dize (prŏp'ə-găn'dīz') *v.* **-dized, -diz·ing, -diz·es.** *—tr.* **1.** To spread (a doctrine or opinion) by means of propaganda. **2.** To subject (a person or group of persons) to propaganda. *—intr.* To spread propaganda.

prop·a·gate (prŏp'ə-gāt') *v.* **-gat·ed, -gat·ing, -gates.** *—tr.* **1.** To cause (animals or plants) to multiply or breed. **2.** To breed (offspring). **3.** To transmit (characteristics) from one generation to another. **4.** To make known; publicize: *propagate a rumor.* **5.** *Physics.* To cause (a wave, for example) to move through a medium; transmit. *—intr.* **1.** *Physics.* To move through a medium. **2.** To breed or multiply. [Lat. *propagare, propagat-* < *propages,* offspring.] **—prop'a·ga·ble** (-gə-bəl) *adj.* **—prop'a·ga'tive** *adj.* **—prop'a·ga'tor** *n.*

prop·a·ga·tion (prŏp'ə-gā'shən) *n.* **1.** Increase or spread, as by natural reproduction. **2.** Dissemination, as of a belief. **—prop'a·ga'tion·al** *adj.*

pro·pane (prō'pān') *n.* A colorless gas, C_3H_8, found in natural gas and petroleum and widely used as a fuel.

pro·par·ox·y·tone (prō'păr-ŏk'sĭ-tōn') *adj.* Having an acute accent on the antepenult in Classical Greek. *—n.* A proparoxytone word. [Gk. *proparoxutonos* : *pro-,* before + *paroxutonos,* paroxytone. —see PAROXYTONE.] **—pro'par·ox'y·ton'ic** (-tŏn'ĭk) *adj.*

pro·pel (prə-pĕl') *tr.v.* **-pelled, -pel·ling, -pels.** To cause to move or sustain in motion. [ME *propellen* < Lat. *propellere* : *pro-,* forward + *pellere,* to drive.]

pro·pel·lant also **pro·pel·lent** (prə-pĕl'ənt) *n.* **1.** Something that propels or provides thrust, as an explosive charge or a rocket fuel. **2.** A gas, as a fluorocarbon, that acts as a vehicle for discharging the contents of an aerosol container. *—adj.* Serving to propel; propelling.

pro·pel·ler also **pro·pel·lor** (prə-pĕl'ər) *n.* Any of various related simple machines for propelling aircraft or boats, esp. one having radiating blades mounted on a revolving power-driven shaft.

pro·pend (prō-pĕnd') *intr.v.* **-pend·ed, -pend·ing, -pends.** To have a propensity toward. [Lat. *propendēre* : *pro-,* forward + *pendēre,* to hang.]

pro·pene (prō'pēn') *n.* Propylene.

pro·pen·si·ty (prə-pĕn'sĭ-tē) *n., pl.* **-ties.** An innate inclination; tendency. [< obs. *propense,* inclined < Lat. *propensus,* p.part. of *propendere,* to be inclined. —see PROPEND.]

prop·er (prŏp'ər) *adj.* **1.** Suitable; appropriate: *the proper moment.* **2.** Out-and-out; thorough: *a proper whipping.* **3.** Worthy of the name: *take one's medicine like a proper man.* **4.** Meeting a requisite standard of competence or validity. **5. a.** Within the strict limitation of the term: *France proper.* **b.** Rigorously correct; exact. **6.** Characteristically belonging to the being or thing in question: *an optical effect proper to fluids.* **7. a.** Seemly; decorous. **b.** Displaying exaggerated propriety or gentility. **8.** *Math.* Designating a subset of a given set when the latter has at least one element not in the subset. *—adv.* Thoroughly: *He got his ears pinned back good and proper.* *—n.* Also **Proper.** *Eccles.* **1.** The parts of the Mass that vary according to the particular day or feast. **2.** An office to be said on an appointed day or feast. [ME *propre* < OFr. < Lat. *proprius,* one's own.] **—prop'er·ly** *adv.* **—prop'er·ness** *n.*

proper adjective *n.* An adjective formed from a proper noun.

pro·per·din (prō-pûr'dn) *n.* A natural protein in human blood serum that helps provide immunity to infectious diseases. [Perh. PRO-[1] + Lat. *perdere,* to destroy + -IN.]

proper fraction *n.* **1.** A numerical fraction in which the numerator is less than the denominator. **2.** A polynomial fraction in which the numerator is of lower degree than the denominator.

proper noun *n.* A noun designating by name a being or thing without a limiting modifier.

prop·er·tied (prŏp'ər-tēd) *adj.* Owning land or securities as a principal source of revenue.

prop·er·ty (prŏp'ər-tē) *n., pl.* **-ties. 1.** Ownership. **2. a.** A possession. **b.** Possessions collectively. **3.** Something tangible or intangible to which its owner has legal title. **4.** An article, except costumes and scenery, used as part of a dramatic production. **5. a.** A characteristic trait or peculiarity. **b.** A special capability or power; virtue. **c.** A quality serving to define or describe an object or substance. **d.** A characteristic attribute possessed by all members of a class. **e.** *Logic.* A predicable that is common and peculiar to the whole of a species and is necessarily predicated of its essence without being part of that essence. [ME *proprete* < OFr. *propriete* < Lat. *proprietas,* ownership < *proprius,* one's own.] **—prop'er·ty·less** *adj.*

property damage insurance *n.* Liability insurance for claims brought against a person who causes damage to another's property, as by an automobile accident.

property tax *n.* A tax levied against the owner of real or personal property.

pro·phage (prō'fāj') *n.* A noninfectious association between a bacterial virus and a bacterium in which the viral chromosomes link with the bacterial chromosomes but do not cause disruption of the bacterial cell or promote replication of the virus itself.

pro·phase (prō'fāz') *n.* The first stage in cell division by mitosis, during which chromosomes form from the chromatin of the nucleus. **—pro·pha'sic** (-fā'zĭk) *adj.*

proph·e·cy (prŏf'ĭ-sē) *n., pl.* **-cies. 1.** A prediction. **2. a.** The inspired utterance of a prophet, viewed as a declaration of divine will. **b.** Such a revelation transmitted orally or in writing. [ME *prophecie* < OFr. < Lat. *prophetia* < Gk. *prophetēs,* prophet.]

proph·e·sy (prŏf'ĭ-sī') *v.* **-sied, -sy·ing, -sies.** *—tr.* **1.** To reveal by divine inspiration. **2.** To predict. **3.** To prefigure; foreshow. *—intr.* **1.** To reveal the will or message of God. **2.** To predict the future. **3.** To speak as a prophet. [ME *prophecien* < OFr. *prophecier* < *prophecie,* prophecy.] **—proph'e·si'er** *n.*

proph·et (prŏf'ĭt) *n.* **1.** A person who speaks by divine inspiration or as the interpreter through whom the will of a god is expressed. **2.** A predictor; soothsayer. **3.** The chief spokesman of a movement or cause. [ME < OFr. < Lat. *propheta* < Gk. *prophētēs* : *pro-,* before + *phanai,* to speak.]

proph·et·ess (prŏf'ĭ-tĭs) *n.* **1.** A woman who speaks by divine inspiration or as the interpreter through whom the will of a god is expressed. **2.** A predictor. **3.** The chief spokesperson of a movement or cause.

pro·phet·ic (prə-fĕt'ĭk) also **pro·phet·i·cal** (-ĭ-kəl) *adj.* **1.** Of or belonging to a prophet or prophecy. **2.** Of the nature of prophecy. **—pro·phet'i·cal·ly** *adv.* **—pro·phet'i·cal·ness** *n.*

pro·phy·lac·tic (prō'fə-lăk'tĭk, prŏf'ə-) *adj.* Acting to defend against or prevent something, esp. disease; protective. *—n.* A prophylactic medicine, device, or measure, esp. a condom. [Gk. *prophulaktikos* < *prophulassein,* to take precautions against : *pro-,* before + *phulassein,* to protect < *phulax,* guard.] **—pro'phy·lac'ti·cal·ly** *adv.*

pro·phy·lax·is (prō'fə-lăk'sĭs, prŏf'ə-) *n., pl.* **-lax·es** (-lăk'sēz'). The prevention of or protective treatment for disease. [NLat. < Gk. *prophulaktikos,* prophylactic.]

pro·pin·qui·ty (prə-pĭng'kwĭ-tē) *n.* **1.** Nearness; proximity. **2.** Kinship. **3.** Similarity in nature. [ME *propinquite* < Lat. *propinquitas* < *propinquus,* near.]

pro·pi·on·al·de·hyde (prō'pē-ŏn-ăl'də-hīd') *n.* A flammable liquid, C_3H_6O, used in the manufacture of plastics and rubber chemicals. [PROPION(IC ACID) + ALDEHYDE.]

pro·pi·o·nate (prō'pē-ə-nāt') *n.* A salt or ester of propionic acid. [PROPION(IC ACID) + -ATE.]

pro·pi·on·ic acid (prō'pē-ŏn'ĭk) *n.* A fatty acid, $CH_3CH_2CO_2H$, prepared synthetically and widely used in a salt form as a mold inhibitor in bread. [Fr. *propionique* : Gk. *pro-,* first + Gk. *piōn,* fat (so called because it is first in order among the fatty acids).]

pro·pi·ti·ate (prō-pĭsh'ē-āt') *tr.v.* **-at·ed, -at·ing, -ates.** To conciliate (an offended power); appease. [Lat. *propitiare, propitiat-* < *propitius,* favorable.] **—pro·pi'ti·a·ble** (-pĭsh'ē-ə-bəl, -pĭsh'ə-bəl) *adj.* **—pro·pi'ti·at'ing·ly** *adv.* **—pro·pi'ti·a'tive** *adj.* **—pro·pi'ti·a'tor** *n.*

pro·pi·ti·a·tion (prō-pĭsh'ē-ā'shən) *n.* **1.** The act of propitiating. **2.** Something that propitiates, esp. a conciliatory offering to a god.

pro·pi·ti·a·to·ry (prō-pĭsh'ē-ə-tôr'ē, -tōr'ē, -pĭsh'ə-) *adj.* Of or offered in propitiation; conciliatory. **—pro·pi'ti·a·to'ri·ly** *adv.*

pro·pi·tious (prə-pĭsh'əs) *adj.* **1.** Presenting favorable circumstances; auspicious. **2.** Kindly; gracious. [ME *propicius* < OFr. < Lat. *propitius.*] **—pro·pi'tious·ly** *adv.* **—pro·pi'tious·ness** *n.*

prop-jet (prŏp'jĕt') *n.* A turboprop.

pro·plas·tid (prō-plăs'tĭd) *n.* The precursor of a cell plastid.

prop·o·lis (prŏp'ə-lĭs) *n.* A resinous substance collected from various plants by bees, and used together with beeswax in the construction of their hives. [Lat. < Gk., suburb, bee glue : *pro-,* before + *polis,* city.]

pro·po·nent (prə-pō'nənt) *n.* One who argues in support of something; advocate. [Lat. *proponens, proponent-,* pr.part. of *proponere,* to set forth. —see PROPOSE.]

pro·por·tion (prə-pôr'shən, -pōr'-) *n.* **1.** A part considered in relation to the whole. **2.** A relationship between things or parts of things with respect to comparative magnitude, quantity, or degree. **3.** A relationship between quantities such that if one varies then another varies in a manner dependent on the first; ratio: *"We do not always find visible happiness in proportion to visible virtue"* (Samuel Johnson). **4.** Harmonious relation. **5.** Often **proportions.** Dimensions; size. **6.** *Math.* A relation of equality between two ratios. Four quantities, *a, b, c, d,* are said to be in proportion if $a/b = c/d$. *—tr.v.* **-tioned, -tion·ing, -tions. 1.** To adjust so that proper relations between parts are attained. **2.** To form with proportion. [ME *proporcioun* < OFr. *proportion* < Lat. *proportio* < *pro portione,* for its share.] **—pro·por'tion·a·ble** *adj.* **—pro·por'tion·a·bly** *adv.* **—pro·por'tion·er** *n.* **—pro·por'tion·ment** *n.*

Synonyms: *proportion, harmony, symmetry, balance.* All these nouns are compared as they apply to aesthetic pleasure derived from proper arrangement. *Proportion* is the desirable, correct, or perfect relationship of parts within a

pronghorn

whole. *Harmony* generally means the smooth and flowing joining of details. *Symmetry* and *balance* both imply an arrangement of parts and details on either side of a median line. They differ, however, in that *symmetry* emphasizes duplicate or mirror-image arrangement of parts, while *balance* emphasizes dissimilar or opposing parts that offset each other to make a harmonious whole.

pro·por·tion·al (prə-pôr′shə-nəl, -pōr′-) *adj.* **1.** Forming a relationship with other parts or quantities; being in proportion. **2.** Properly related in size or other measurable characteristics. **3.** *Math.* Having a constant ratio. —*n.* One of the quantities in a mathematical proportion. —**pro·por′tion·al′i·ty** (-năl′ĭ-tē) *n.* —**pro·por′tion·al·ly** *adv.*

proportional representation *n.* Representation of all parties in a legislature in proportion to their popular vote.

pro·por·tion·ate (prə-pôr′shə-nĭt, -pōr′-) *adj.* Being in due proportion; proportional. —*tr.v.* (-nāt′-) **-at·ed, -at·ing, -ates.** To make proportionate. —**pro·por′tion·ate·ly** *adv.* —**pro·por′tion·ate·ness** *n.*

pro·pos·al (prə-pō′zəl) *n.* **1.** The act of proposing. **2.** A plan or scheme that is proposed. **3.** An offer of marriage.

pro·pose (prə-pōz′) *v.* **-posed, -pos·ing, -pos·es.** —*tr.* **1.** To put forward for consideration, discussion, or adoption; suggest: *propose new methods.* **2.** To present or nominate (a person) for a position, office, or membership. **3.** To offer (a toast to be drunk). **4.** To purpose; intend. —*intr.* To form or make a proposal, esp. of marriage. [ME *proposen* < OFr. *proposer* < Lat. *proponere* : *pro-*, forth + *ponere,* to put.] —**pro·pos′er** *n.*

prop·o·si·tion (prŏp′ə-zĭsh′ən) *n.* **1.** A plan or scheme suggested for acceptance. **2.** *Informal.* A matter requiring special handling: *a difficult proposition.* **3.** *Informal.* A dubious or immoral proposal. **4.** A subject for discussion or analysis. **5.** *Logic.* **a.** A statement in which the subject is affirmed or denied by the predicate. **b.** Something that is expressed in a statement, as opposed to the way it is expressed. **c.** A statement containing only logical constants and having a fixed truth-value. —*tr.v.* **-tioned, -tion·ing, -tions.** *Informal.* To propose a private bargain to, esp. to make a sexual overture to. [ME *proposicioun* < OFr. *proposition* < Lat. *propositio* < *proponere,* to set forth. —see PROPOSE.] —**prop′o·si′tion·al** *adj.* —**prop′o·si′tion·al·ly** *adv.*

propositional function *n. Logic.* An expression having the form of a proposition but containing undefined symbols for the substantive elements, and becoming a proposition when appropriate values are assigned to the symbols.

pro·pos·i·tus (prō-pŏz′ĭ-təs) *n., pl.* **-ti** (-tī′). **1.** *Law.* One from whom a line of descent is traced. **2.** The person immediately affected by an action. [Lat., p.part. of *proponere,* to set forth. —see PROPOSE.]

pro·pound (prə-pound′) *tr.v.* **-pound·ed, -pound·ing, -pounds.** To put forward for consideration; set forth. [ME *proponen* < Lat. *proponere,* to set forth. —see PROPOSE.] —**pro·pound′er** *n.*

pro·prae·tor (prō-prē′tər) *n.* A Roman official appointed, usually immediately after holding the praetorship, to be the chief administrator of a province. [Lat. : *pro-*, for + *praetor,* praetor. —see PRAETOR.] —**pro′prae·to′ri·al** (prō′prĭ-tôr′ē-əl, -tōr′-), **pro′prae·to′ri·an** *adj.*

pro·pran·o·lol (prō-prăn′ə-lôl′, -lōl′) *n.* A drug, $C_{16}H_{21}NO_2$, used in the treatment of angina pectoris and cardiac arrhythmia. [Alteration of PROPANE + -OL + -OL.]

pro·pri·e·tar·y (prə-prī′ĭ-tĕr′ē) *adj.* **1.** Of or pertaining to a proprietor or to proprietors collectively. **2.** Exclusively owned; private. **3.** Befitting an owner: *a proprietary air.* **4.** Owned by a private individual or corporation under a trademark or patent: *a proprietary drug.* —*n., pl.* **-ies. 1.** A proprietor. **2.** A group of proprietors. **3.** Ownership; proprietorship. **4.** The governor of a proprietary colony. **5.** A proprietary medicine. [LLat. *proprietarius* < Lat. *proprietas,* property < *proprius,* one's own.] —**pro·pri′e·tar′i·ly** *adv.*

proprietary colony *n.* Any of certain early North American colonies, such as Carolina and Pennsylvania, organized in the 17th century in territories granted by the Crown to one or more Lords Proprietary who had full governing rights.

pro·pri·e·tor (prə-prī′ĭ-tər) *n.* **1.** A person who has legal title to something; owner. **2.** The owner or owner-manager of a business or other institution. —**pro·pri′e·to′ri·al** (-tôr′ē-əl, -tōr′-) *adj.* —**pro·pri′e·to′ri·al·ly** *adv.* —**pro·pri′e·tor·ship′** *n.*

pro·pri·e·tress (prə-prī′ĭ-trĭs) *n.* **1.** A woman who has legal title to something; owner. **2.** The owner or owner-manager of a business or other institution.

pro·pri·e·ty (prə-prī′ĭ-tē) *n., pl.* **-ties. 1.** The quality of being proper; appropriateness. **2.** Conformity to prevailing customs and usages. **3. proprieties.** The usages and customs of polite society. [ME *propriete,* particular character < OFr. — see PROPERTY.]

pro·pri·o·cep·tion (prō′prē-ō-sĕp′shən) *n.* The reception of stimuli arising within the organism. [Lat. *proprius,* one's own + (RE)CEPTION.]

pro·pri·o·cep·tor (prō′prē-ō-sĕp′tər) *n.* A sensory receptor, chiefly in muscles, tendons, and joints, that responds to stimuli arising within the organism. [Lat. *proprius,* one's own + (RE)CEPTOR.] —**pro′pri·o·cep′tive** *adj.*

prop root *n.* A root growing from above ground into the soil and helping to support the plant stem, as in corn.

prop root

prop·to·sis (prŏp-tō′sĭs) *n., pl.* **-ses** (-sēz′). Forward displacement of an organ, esp. the eyeball. [LLat. < Gk. *proptōsis,* prolapse : *pro-*, forward + *piptein,* to fall.]

pro·pul·sion (prə-pŭl′shən) *n.* **1.** The process of driving or propelling. **2.** A driving or propelling force. [Med. Lat. *propulsio* < Lat. *propellere,* to drive forward. —see PROPEL.] —**pro·pul′sive, pro·pul′so·ry** *adj.*

pro·pyl (prō′pĭl) *n.* A univalent organic radical with composition C_3H_7, derived from propane. —**pro·pyl′ic** *adj.*

prop·y·la (prŏp′ə-lə, prō′pə-) *n.* Plural of **propylon.**

prop·y·lae·um (prŏp′ə-lē′əm, prō′pə-) *n., pl.* **-lae·a** (-lē′ə). *Archit.* An entrance or vestibule to a temple or group of buildings. [Lat. < Gk. *propulaion* : *pro-*, before + *pulē,* gate.]

propyl alcohol *n.* A clear colorless liquid, $CH_3CH_2CH_2OH$, widely used as a solvent.

pro·pyl·ene (prō′pə-lēn′) *n.* A flammable gas, $CH_3CH{:}CH_2$, derived from petroleum hydrocarbon cracking and used in organic synthesis.

propylene glycol *n.* A colorless viscous hygroscopic liquid, $CH_3CHOHCH_2OH$, used in antifreeze solutions, in hydraulic fluids, and as a solvent.

prop·y·lon (prŏp′ə-lŏn′, prō′pə-) *n., pl.* **-la** (-lə). A propylaeum. [Gk. *propulon* : *pro-*, before + *pulē,* gate.]

pro ra·ta (prō rā′tə, răt′ə, rä′tə) *adv.* In proportion. [Lat. *pro rata (parte),* according to the calculated (share).]

pro·rate (prō-rāt′, prō′rāt′) *v.* **-rat·ed, -rat·ing, -rates.** —*tr.* To divide, distribute, or assess proportionately. —*intr.* To settle affairs on the basis of proportional distribution. [< PRO RATA.] —**pro·rat′a·ble** *adj.* —**pro·ra′tion** *n.*

pro·rogue (prō-rōg′) *tr.v.* **-rogued, -rogu·ing, -rogues. 1.** To discontinue a session of (a parliament or similar body). **2.** To postpone; defer. [ME *prorogen* < OFr. *proroger,* to postpone < Lat. *prorogare* : *pro-*, forward + *rogare,* to ask.] —**pro′ro·ga′tion** (prō′rō-gā′shən) *n.*

pros– *pref.* **1.** Near; toward: *prosenchyma.* **2.** In front of: *prosencephalon.* [Gk. < *pros,* near, at.]

pro·sa·ic (prō-zā′ĭk) *adj.* **1. a.** Of or like prose. **b.** Matter-of-fact; straightforward. **2.** Lacking in imagination and spirit; ordinary. [LLat. *prosaicus* < Lat. *prosa,* prose. —see PROSE.] —**pro·sa′i·cal·ly** *adv.* —**pro·sa′ic·ness** *n.*

pro·sa·ism (prō′zā-ĭz′əm) *n.* **1.** A quality or style that is prosaic. **2.** A prosaic expression, phrase, or word.

pro·sce·ni·um (prō-sē′nē-əm) *n.* **1.** *pl.* **-ni·ums.** The area of a modern theater that is located between the curtain and the orchestra. **2.** *pl.* **-ni·a** (-nē-ə). The stage of an ancient theater, located between the background and the orchestra. [Lat. < Gk. *proskēnion* : *pro-*, before + *skēnē,* buildings at the back of the stage.]

pro·sciut·to (prō-shōō′tō) *n.* An aged, dry-cured Italian ham that is ready to eat and usually sliced thin. [Ital.]

pro·scribe (prō-skrīb′) *tr.v.* **-scribed, -scrib·ing, -scribes. 1.** To denounce or condemn. **2.** To prohibit; forbid. **3.** To publish the name of (a person) as outlawed. [Lat. *proscribere,* to put up someone's name as outlawed : *pro-*, in front + *scribere,* to write.] —**pro·scrib′er** *n.*

pro·scrip·tion (prō-skrĭp′shən) *n.* **1.** The act of proscribing; prohibition. **2.** The condition of being proscribed; outlawry. —**pro·scrip′tive** *adj.* —**pro·scrip′tive·ly** *adv.*

prose (prōz) *n.* **1.** Ordinary speech or writing, as distinguished from verse. **2.** Commonplace expression or quality. **3.** *Rom. Cath. Ch.* A hymn of irregular meter sung after the gradual. —*v.* **prosed, pros·ing, pros·es.** —*tr.* To make into prose. —*intr.* **1.** To write prose. **2.** To speak or write in a dull, tiresome style. [ME < OFr. < Lat. *prosa (oratio),* straightforward (discourse) < *proversus,* p.part. of *provertere,* to turn forward : *pro-*, forward + *vertere,* to turn.]

pros·e·cute (prŏs′ĭ-kyōōt′) *v.* **-cut·ed, -cut·ing, -cutes.** —*tr.* **1.** To pursue or persist in so as to complete. **2.** To carry on; practice. **3. a.** To initiate legal or criminal court action against. **b.** To seek to obtain or enforce by legal action. —*intr.* **1.** To initiate and conduct legal proceedings. **2.** To act as prosecutor. [ME *prosecuten* < Lat. *prosequi* : *pro-*, forward + *sequi,* to follow.] —**pros′e·cut′a·ble** *adj.*

prosecuting attorney *n.* An attorney empowered to prosecute cases on behalf of a government and the people.

pros·e·cu·tion (prŏs′ĭ-kyōō′shən) *n.* **1.** The act of prosecuting. **2.** The institution and conduct of a legal proceeding. **3.** A prosecuting attorney.

pros·e·cu·tor (prŏs′ĭ-kyōō′tər) *n.* **1.** One who prosecutes. **2.** One who initiates and carries out a legal action, esp. criminal proceedings. **3.** A prosecuting attorney.

pros·e·cu·to·ri·al (prŏs′ĭ-kyōō-tôr′ē-əl, -tōr′-) *adj.* Of, pertaining to, or concerned with prosecution.

pros·e·lyte (prŏs′ə-līt′) *n.* A new convert to a religion or doctrine. —*tr. & intr.v.* **-lyt·ed, -lyt·ing, -lytes.** To proselytize. [ME *proselite* < LLat. *proselytus* < Gk. *proselutos.*] —**pros′e·lyt′er** *n.*

pros·e·ly·tism (prŏs′ə-lĭ-tĭz′əm, -lī-) *n.* **1.** The practice of proselytizing. **2.** The state of being a proselyte. —**pros′e·lyt′i·cal** (-lĭt′ĭ-kəl) *adj.*

pros·e·ly·tize (prŏs′ə-lĭ-tīz′) *v.* **-tized, -tiz·ing, -tiz·es.** —*intr.* To make proselytes. —*tr.* To convert from one belief or faith to another. —**pros′e·ly·ti·za′tion** *n.* —**pros′e·ly·tiz′er** *n.*

pros·en·ceph·a·lon (prŏs′ĕn-sĕf′ə-lŏn′) *n.* The forebrain. —**pros′en·ce·phal′ic** (-sə-făl′ĭk) *adj.*

pros·en·chy·ma (prō-sĕng′kĭ-mə) *n.* Tissue consisting of elongated, unspecialized cells, occurring in most flowering plants. [PROS- + (PAR)ENCHYMA.] **—pros'en·chym'a·tous** (-kĭm'ə-təs) *adj.*

prose poem *n.* A work that is predominately prose but has characteristics and qualities of poetry.

Pro·ser·pi·na (prō-sûr'pə-nə) also **Pros·er·pi·ne** (prŏs'-ər-pīn', prō-sûr'pə-nē) *n. Rom. Myth.* The wife of Pluto and daughter of Ceres and the goddess of the underworld. [Lat.]

pro·sim·i·an (prō-sĭm'ē-ən) *adj.* Of or belonging to the Prosimii, a suborder of primates that includes the lemurs, lorises, and tarsiers. *—n.* A primate of the suborder Prosimii. [< NLat. *Prosimii,* suborder name : Lat. *pro-,* before + Lat. *simia,* ape. —see SIMIAN.]

pro·sit (prō'sĭt, prō'zĭt) *interj.* Used as a drinking toast to someone's health. [G. < Lat., may it benefit.]

pros·o·dist (prŏs'ə-dĭst) *n.* A specialist in prosody.

pros·o·dy (prŏs'ə-dē) *n.* **1.** The study of the metrical structure of verse. **2.** A particular system of versification. [ME *prosodye* < Lat. *prosodia,* accent < Gk. *prosōidia,* singing in accord : *pros-,* corresponding to + *ōidē,* song.] **—pro·sod'ic** (prə-sŏd'ĭk) *adj.* **—pro·sod'i·cal·ly** *adv.*

pro·so·ma (prō-sō'mə) *n. Zool.* The anterior portion of the body of an invertebrate when primitive segmentation is not evident. [PRO-[2] + Gk. *sōma,* body.] **—pro·so'mal** *adj.*

pro·so·po·pe·ia also **pro·so·po·poe·ia** (prə-sō'pə-pē'ə) *n.* **1.** The impersonation of an absent or imaginary speaker. **2.** Personification (sense 3). [Lat. *prosopopoeia* < Gk. *prosōpopoiia* : *pros,* toward + *ōpon,* face + *poiein,* to make.] **—pro·so'po·pe'ial** *adj.*

pros·pect (prŏs'pĕkt') *n.* **1.** Something expected; possibility. **2. prospects.** Chances for success. **3. a.** A potential customer or purchaser. **b.** A candidate deemed likely to succeed. **4.** The direction in which an object, such as a building, faces; outlook. **5.** Something presented to the eye; scene: *a pleasant prospect.* **6.** The act of surveying or examining. **7. a.** The location or probable location of a mineral deposit. **b.** An actual or probable mineral deposit. **c.** The mineral yield obtained by working an ore. *—v.* **-pect·ed, -pect·ing, -pects.** *—tr.* To search for or explore (a region) for gold or other mineral deposits. *—intr.* To explore for mineral deposits. [ME *prospecte* < Lat. *prospectus,* distant view < p.part. of *prospicere,* to look out : *pro-,* forward + *specere,* to look.]

pro·spec·tive (prə-spĕk'tĭv) *adj.* **1.** Likely to happen; expected. **2.** Likely to become or be: *a prospective client.* **—pro·spec'tive·ly** *adv.*

pros·pec·tor (prŏs'pĕk'tər) *n.* One who explores an area for natural deposits, such as gold or oil.

pro·spec·tus (prə-spĕk'təs) *n.* A formal summary of a proposed commercial, literary, or other venture. [Lat., distant view. —see PROSPECT.]

pros·per (prŏs'pər) *v.* **-pered, -per·ing, -pers.** *—intr.* To be fortunate or successful; thrive. *—tr. Archaic.* To cause to thrive. [ME *prosperen* < OFr. *prosperer* < Lat. *prosperare,* to render fortunate < *prosperus,* fortunate.]

pros·per·i·ty (prŏ-spĕr'ĭ-tē) *n., pl.* **-ties.** The condition of being prosperous.

pros·per·ous (prŏs'pər-əs) *adj.* **1.** Having success; flourishing. **2.** Well-to-do; well-off. **3.** Propitious; favorable. **—pros'per·ous·ly** *adv.* **—pros'per·ous·ness** *n.*

pros·ta·glan·din (prŏs'tə-glăn'dĭn) *n.* Any of a group of physiologically active hormonelike substances derived from fatty acids and found in various human body tissues and that may affect blood pressure, metabolism, and smooth muscle activity. [PROSTA(TE) + GLAND + -IN.]

pros·tate (prŏs'tāt') *n.* A gland in male mammals composed of muscular and glandular tissue that surrounds the urethra at the bladder. [NLat. *prostata* < Gk. *prostatēs* < *proïstanai,* to set before : *pro-,* in front + *histanai,* to cause to stand.] **—pro·stat'ic** (prō-stăt'ĭk) *adj.*

pros·ta·tec·to·my (prŏs'tə-tĕk'tə-mē) *n., pl.* **-mies.** The surgical removal of all or part of the prostate.

pros·ta·ti·tis (prŏs'tə-tī'tĭs) *n.* Inflammation of the prostate.

pros·the·sis (prŏs-thē'sĭs) *n., pl.* **-ses** (-sēz'). **1.** The artificial replacement of a limb, tooth, or other part of the body. **2.** An artificial device used in prosthetic replacement. [Gk., addition < *prostithenai,* to add : *pros-,* in addition + *tithenai,* to put.]

pros·thet·ic (prŏs-thĕt'ĭk) *adj.* Of or pertaining to prosthetics or a prosthesis. **—pros·thet'i·cal·ly** *adv.*

prosthetic group *n.* A link other than an amino acid in a protein chain.

pros·thet·ics (prŏs-thĕt'ĭks) *n. (used with a sing. verb).* Prosthetic surgery. **—pros'the·tist** (prŏs'thĭ-tĭst) *n.*

pros·tho·don·tics (prŏs'thə-dŏn'tĭks) *n. (used with a sing. verb).* Prosthetic dentistry, esp. the replacement of missing teeth by bridges and dentures. [PROSTH(ESIS) + Gk. *odons, odont-,* tooth.] **—pros'tho·don'tist** *n.*

pros·ti·tute (prŏs'tĭ-to͞ot', -tyo͞ot') *n.* **1.** One who solicits and accepts payment for sexual intercourse. **2.** One who sells his abilities or name to an unworthy cause. *—tr.v.* **-tut·ed, -tut·ing, -tutes. 1.** To offer (oneself or another) for sexual hire. **2.** To sell (oneself or one's talents) to an unworthy cause. [Lat. *prostituta* < p.part. of *prostituere,* to prostitute : *pro-,* forward + *statuere,* to place.] **—pros'ti·tu'tor** *n.*

pros·ti·tu·tion (prŏs'tĭ-to͞o'shən, -tyo͞o'-) *n.* **1.** The act or practice of prostituting. **2.** The act of offering or devoting one's talents to an unworthy use or cause.

pro·sto·mi·um (prō-stō'mē-əm) *n., pl.* **-mi·a** (-mē-ə). The portion of the head in annelids and mollusks that is situated anterior to the mouth. [NLat. : PRO- + Gk. *stoma,* mouth.]

pros·trate (prŏs'trāt') *tr.v.* **-trat·ed, -trat·ing, -trates. 1.** To make (oneself) bow or kneel down in humility or adoration. **2.** To throw down flat. **3.** To lay low; overcome. *—adj.* **1.** Lying face down, as in submission or adoration. **2.** Lying down full-length. **3.** Physically or emotionally exhausted; incapacitated. **4.** *Bot.* Growing flat along the ground. [Lat. *prosternere, prostrat-* : *pro-,* forward + *sternere,* to cast down.] **—pros'tra'tor** *n.*

pros·tra·tion (prŏ-strā'shən) *n.* **1. a.** The act of prostrating oneself. **b.** The state of being prostrate. **2.** Total exhaustion.

pro·style (prō'stīl') *adj. Archit.* Having a row of columns across the front only, as in some Greek temples. [Lat. *prostylos* < Gk. *prostulos* : *pro-,* in front + *stulos,* pillar.]

pros·y (prō'zē) *adj.* **-i·er, -i·est. 1.** Matter-of-fact; dry. **2.** Dull; commonplace. [< PROSE.] **—pros'i·ly** *adv.* **—pros'i·ness** *n.*

prot– *pref.* Variant of **proto-.**

pro·tac·tin·i·um (prō'tăk-tĭn'ē-əm) *n. Symbol* **Pa** A rare radioactive element chemically similar to uranium, having 12 known isotopes, the most common of which is Pa 231 with a half-life of 32,480 years. Atomic number 91; melting point 1,230°C; specific gravity 15.37; valence 4 or 5.

pro·tag·o·nist (prō-tăg'ə-nĭst) *n.* **1.** The leading character in Greek drama or any other literary form. **2. a.** A leading or principal figure. **b.** *Informal.* The leader of a cause; champion. [Gk. *prōtagōnistēs* : *prōtos,* first + *agōnistēs,* actor < *agōnizesthai,* to contend < *agōn,* contest.]

Usage: *Protagonist* denotes the leading figure in a theatrical drama or, by extension, in any work or undertaking. Sometimes in modern usage the sense of singularity is lost: *There are three protagonists in this sluggish novel.* This watered-down meaning, though well established, is unacceptable to a majority of the Usage Panel. *Protagonist* is informally used to indicate a champion or advocate.

pro·ta·mine (prō'tə-mēn', -mĭn) also **pro·ta·min** (-mĭn) *n.* Any of the group of the simplest proteins that are highly basic, soluble in water, not coagulated by heat, and yield only amino acids, chiefly arginine, upon hydrolysis.

pro·ta·no·pi·a (prō'tə-nō'pē-ə) *n.* A form of colorblindness in which red and bluish-green stimuli are confused with neutral stimuli and with each other.

prot·a·sis (prŏt'ə-sĭs) *n., pl.* **-ses** (-sēz'). **1.** *Gram.* A subordinate clause, esp. in a conditional sentence. **2.** The introductory part of a classical drama. [LLat., proposition < Gk. < *proteinein,* to propose : *pro-,* forward + *teinein,* to stretch.] **—pro·tat'ic** (prō-tăt'ĭk, prō-) *adj.*

prospector

prote– *pref.* Variant of **proteo-.**

pro·te·an (prō'tē-ən, prō-tē'-) *adj.* Readily taking on different shapes or forms; variable. [< PROTEUS.]

pro·te·ase (prō'tē-ās', -āz') *n.* An enzyme that catalyzes the hydrolytic breakdown of proteins.

pro·tect (prə-tĕkt') *tr.v.* **-tect·ed, -tect·ing, -tects. 1.** To keep from harm, attack, or injury; guard. **2.** *Econ.* To help (domestic industry) with tariffs on imported goods. **3.** To assure payment of (drafts or notes, for example) by setting aside funds. [Lat. *protegere, protect-* : *pro-,* in front + *tegere,* to cover.] **—pro·tect'ing·ly** *adv.*

pro·tec·tant (prə-tĕk'tənt) *n.* One that protects: *applied a protectant to the raw wood.*

pro·tect·er (prə-tĕk'tər) *n.* Variant of **protector.**

pro·tec·tion (prə-tĕk'shən) *n.* **1.** The act of protecting. **2.** The condition of being protected. **3.** One that protects. **4.** A pass guaranteeing safe-conduct to travelers. **5.** *Econ.* A tariff system protecting domestic industries from foreign competition. **6.** Money extorted by racketeers in exchange for a promise of freedom from molestation. **—pro·tec'tion·al** *adj.*

pro·tec·tion·ism (prə-tĕk'shə-nĭz'əm) *n.* The economic theory and system of protection. **—pro·tec'tion·ist** *n.*

pro·tec·tive (prə-tĕk'tĭv) *adj.* Adapted or intended to afford protection. *—n.* Something that protects. **—pro·tec'tive·ly** *adv.* **—pro·tec'tive·ness** *n.*

pro·tec·tor also **pro·tect·er** (prə-tĕk'tər) *n.* **1.** A person who protects; guardian. **2.** A device that protects; guard. **3. Protector. a.** A person who rules a kingdom during the monarch's minority. **b.** The head of the Commonwealth of England, Scotland, and Ireland from 1653 to 1659. **—pro·tec'tor·al** *adj.* **—pro·tec'tor·ship'** *n.*

pro·tec·tor·ate (prə-tĕk'tər-ĭt) *n.* **1. a.** A relationship of protection and partial control assumed by a superior power over a dependent country or region. **b.** The protected country or region. **2. Protectorate. a.** The government, office, or term of a protector. **b.** The government of England under Oliver Cromwell (1653–58) and his son Richard (1658–59).

pro·tec·to·ry (prə-tĕk'tə-rē) *n., pl.* **-ries.** An institution providing for the welfare of destitute children.

pro·té·gé (prō'tə-zhā', prō'tə-zhā') *n.* A man or boy whose welfare, training, or career is promoted by an influential person. [Fr. < p.part. of *protéger,* to protect < Lat. *protegere.* —see PROTECT.]

pro·té·gée (prō'tə-zhā', prō'tə-zhā') *n.* A woman or girl whose welfare, training, or career is promoted by an influential person. [Fr., fem. of *protégé,* protégé.]

pro·te·i (prō′tē-ī′) *n.* Plural of **proteus.**

pro·te·id (prō′tē-ĭd) *n.* A protein.

pro·tein (prō′tēn′, -tē-ĭn) *n.* Any of a group of complex nitrogenous organic compounds of high molecular weight that contain amino acids as their basic structural units and that occur in all living matter and are essential for the growth and repair of animal tissue. [Fr. *protéine* < LGk. *proteios,* primary < Gk. *prōtos,* first.] **—pro′tein·a′ceous** (prōt′n-ā′shəs, prō′tē-nā′-), **pro′te·in′ic** (prō′tē-ĭn′ĭk) *adj.*

pro·tein·ase (prōt′n-ās′, -āz′, prō′tē-nās′, -nāz′) *n.* A protease that hydrolyzes proteins into polypeptides.

pro·tein·ate (prōt′n-āt′, prō′tē-nāt′) *n.* A protein compound.

pro·tein·oid (prōt′n-oid′, prō′tē-noid′) *n.* Any of several polypeptides prepared by polymerization of mixtures of amino acids, generally through electrical stimulation, that resembles organized naturally produced proteins and may represent an early form of protein evolution.

pro·tein·u·ri·a (prōt′n-o͝or′ē-ə, -yo͝or′-, prō′tē-no͝or′-, -nyo͝or′-) *n.* A condition of protein in the urine, commonly caused by kidney disease.

pro tem (prō tĕm′) *adv.* Pro tempore.

pro tem·po·re (prō tĕm′pə-rē) *adv.* For the time being; temporarily. [Lat.]

proteo– or **prote–** *pref.* Protein: *proteolysis.* [< PROTEIN.]

pro·te·o·clas·tic (prō′tē-ō-klăs′tĭk) *adj.* Of, pertaining to, or causing proteolysis; proteolytic. [PROTEO- + Gk. *klastos,* broken < *klan,* to break.]

pro·te·ol·y·sis (prō′tē-ŏl′ĭ-sĭs) *n.* The breaking down of proteins into simpler, soluble substances, as in digestion. **—pro′te·o·lyt′ic** (-ə-lĭt′ĭk) *adj.*

pro·te·ose (prō′tē-ōs′, -ōz′) *n.* Any of several water-soluble proteins produced during digestion.

Prot·er·o·zo·ic (prŏt′ər-ə-zō′ĭk, prō′tər-) *adj.* Of, belonging to, or designating the geologic time and deposits of the Precambrian era between the Archeozoic era and the Cambrian period of the Paleozoic era. *—n.* The Proterozoic era. [Gk. *proteros,* earlier + -ZOIC.]

pro·test (prə-tĕst′, prō-, prō′tĕst′) *v.* **-test·ed, -test·ing, -tests.** *—tr.* **1.** To object to, esp. in a formal statement. **2.** To promise or affirm with earnest solemnity. **3.** *Law.* To declare (a bill) dishonored or refused. **4.** *Archaic.* To proclaim or make known. *—intr.* **1.** To express strong objection. **2.** To make an earnest avowal or affirmation. *—n.* (prō′tĕst′). **1.** A formal declaration of disapproval or objection issued by a concerned party. **2.** An individual or collective gesture or display of disapproval. **3.** *Law.* **a.** A formal statement drawn up by a notary for a creditor declaring that the debtor has refused to accept or honor a bill. **b.** A formal declaration made by a taxpayer stating that the tax demanded is illegal or excessive and reserving the right to contest it. [ME *protesten* < OFr. *protester* < Lat. *protestari* : *pro-,* forth + *testari,* to testify < *testis,* witness.] **—pro·test′er** *n.* **—pro·test′ing·ly** *adv.*

Prot·es·tant (prŏt′ĭ-stənt) *n.* **1.** A Christian belonging to a sect descending from those that seceded from the Church of Rome at the time of the Reformation. **2.** One of those who adhered to the doctrine of Luther and in 1529 protested against the decree of the Diet of Spires commanding submission to the authority of Rome. **3. protestant** (*also* prə-tĕs′tənt). One who makes a declaration or avowal. *—adj.* Of or pertaining to Protestants or Protestantism. [< Lat. *protestans, protestant-,* pr. part. of *protestari,* to protest.]

Protestant Episcopal Church *n.* A church body in the United States originally associated with the Church of England, but since 1789 organized as a separate entity.

Prot·es·tant·ism (prŏt′ĭ-stən-tĭz′əm) *n.* **1.** Adherence to a Protestant church. **2.** The religion and religious tendencies fostered by the Protestant movement. **3.** Protestants collectively.

prot·es·ta·tion (prŏt′ĭ-stā′shən, prō′tĭ-) *n.* **1.** An emphatic declaration. **2.** A strong or formal expression of dissent.

pro·te·us (prō′tē-əs) *n., pl.* **-te·i** (-tē-ī′). Any of various gram-negative, rod-shaped bacteria of the genus *Proteus* that include some species associated with human enteritis. [NLat. *Proteus,* genus name < Lat., Proteus.]

Pro·te·us (prō′tē-əs, -tyo͞os′) *n. Gk. Myth.* A sea god who could change his shape at will. [Lat. < Gk. *Prōteus.*]

pro·tha·la·mi·on (prō-thə-lā′mē-ən, -ŏn′) *n., pl.* **-mi·a** (-mē-ə). A song in celebration of a wedding; epithalamium. [PRO-[2] + Gk. *epithalamion,* epithalamium. —see EPITHALAMIUM.]

pro·thal·lus (prō-thăl′əs) also **pro·thal·li·um** (prō-thăl′ē-əm) *n., pl.* **-thal·li** (-thăl′ī′) also **-thal·li·a** (-thăl′ē-ə). A small, flat mass of tissue produced by a germinating spore of ferns and some mosses and related plants. It bears sexual organs and eventually develops into a mature plant. [PRO-[2] + Gk. *thallos,* shoot.] **—pro·thal′li·al** *adj.*

proth·e·sis (prŏth′ĭ-sĭs) *n., pl.* **-ses** (-sēz′). **1.** *Ling.* The addition of a phoneme at the beginning of a word to ease pronunciation or to form a new word. **2.** The preparation of the Eucharistic elements for consecration in the Eastern Orthodox Church. [Gk., prefixing < *protithenai,* to put before : *pro-,* before + *tithenai,* to put.] **—pro·thet′ic** (prō-thĕt′ĭk) *adj.* **—pro·thet′i·cal·ly** *adv.*

Proteus
Menelaus wrestling Proteus in an illustration by Walter Crane

pro·thon·o·tar·y (prō-thŏn′ə-tĕr′ē, prō′thə-nō′tə-rē) also **pro·ton·o·tar·y** (prō-tŏn′ə-tĕr′ē, prō′tə-nō′tə-rē) *n., pl.* **-ies. 1.** The principal clerk in certain courts of law. **2.** *Rom. Cath. Ch.* One of a college of twelve ecclesiastics charged with the registry of important pontifical proceedings. **3.** A chief scribe. [ME < LLat. *protonotarius* : Gk. *prōtos,* first + Lat. *notarius,* secretary < *nota,* mark.] **—pro·thon′o·tar′i·al** (prō-thŏn′ə-târ′ē-əl, prō′thə-nō-târ′-) *adj.*

prothonotary warbler *n.* A small bird, *Protonotaria citrea,* of southeastern North America, having a deep-yellow head and breast and grayish wings. [Probably from the bright-yellow robes worn by ecclesiastics at important meetings.]

pro·tho·rax (prō-thôr′ăks′, -thōr′-) *n., pl.* **-tho·rax·es** or **-tho·ra·ces** (-thôr′ə-sēz′, -thōr′-). The anterior division of the thorax of an insect, bearing the first pair of legs. **—pro′tho·rac′ic** (prō′thə-răs′ĭk) *adj.*

pro·throm·bin (prō-thrŏm′bĭn) *n.* A plasma protein that is converted into thrombin during blood coagulation.

pro·tist (prō′tĭst) *n.* Any of the unicellular organisms of the kingdom Protista, which includes protozoans, bacteria, some algae, and other forms not readily classified as either plants or animals. [NLat. *Protista,* kingdom name < Gk. *prōtista,* neuter pl. of *prōtistos,* the very first < *prōtos,* first.] **—pro·tis′tan** (-tĭs′tən) *adj. & n.* **—pro′tis·tol′o·gy** (prō′tĭ-stŏl′ə-jē) *n.*

pro·ti·um (prō′tē-əm, prō′shē-) *n.* The most abundant isotope of hydrogen, H^1, with atomic mass 1.

proto– or **prot– 1.** Earliest; first in time: *protolithic.* **2.** First formed; primitive: *protohuman.* **3. Proto-.** Being a form of a language that is the ancestor of a language or group of related languages: *Proto-Germanic.* **4.** Having the least amount of a specified element or radical: *protoporphyrin.* [< Gk. *prōtos,* first.]

Pro·to-Al·gon·qui·an (prō′tō-ăl-gŏng′kwē-ən, -kē-ən) *n.* The earliest reconstructed ancestor of the Algonquian languages.

pro·to·col (prō′tə-kôl′, -kōl′, -kŏl′) *n.* **1.** The forms of ceremony and etiquette observed by diplomats and heads of state. **2.** The first copy of a treaty or other document prior to its ratification. **3.** A preliminary draft or record of a transaction. **4.** The plan for a medical or scientific experiment. *—intr.v.* **-coled, -col·ing, -cols** or **-colled, -col·ling, -cols.** To form or issue protocols. [OFr. *prothocole,* formula for drawing up state documents < Med. Lat. *protocollum* < LGk. *prōtokollon,* table of contents : Gk. *prōtos,* first + LGk. *kollema,* sheets of a papyrus glued together < *kollan,* to glue together < *kolla,* glue.] **—pro′to·col′ar** (-kŏl′ər), **pro′to·col′a·ry** (-kŏl′ə-rē) *adj.*

pro·to·derm (prō′tə-dûrm′) *n. Bot.* Dermatogen. **—pro′to·derm′al** *adj.*

Pro·to-Ger·man·ic (prō′tō-jûr-măn′ĭk) *n.* The reconstructed prehistoric ancestor of the Germanic languages.

pro·to·his·to·ry (prō′tō-hĭs′tə-rē, -hĭs′trē) *n.* The study of a culture just prior to its earliest recorded history. **—pro′to·his·tor′i·an** (-hĭ-stôr′ē-ən, -stōr′-) *n.* **—pro′to·his·tor′ic** (-hĭ-stôr′ĭk, -stōr′-) *adj.*

pro·to·hu·man (prō′tō-hyo͞o′mən) *adj.* Of or pertaining to several species of prehistoric primates resembling modern man but more primitive in development. *—n.* A protohuman primate.

Pro·to-In·do-Eur·o·pe·an (prō′tō-ĭn′dō-yo͝or′ə-pē′ən) *n.* The earliest reconstructed stage of Indo-European.

pro·to·lan·guage (prō′tō-lăng′gwĭj) *n.* A language that is the recorded or hypothetical ancestor of another language or group of languages.

pro·to·lith·ic (prō′tə-lĭth′ĭk) *adj.* Of, pertaining to, or characteristic of the very beginning of the Stone Age; eolithic.

pro·to·mar·tyr (prō′tō-mär′tər) *n.* The first martyr in a cause. Used esp. of the first Christian martyr, Saint Stephen.

pro·to·mor·phic (prō′tə-môr′fĭk) *adj.* Primitive in structure or form.

pro·ton (prō′tŏn′) *n.* A stable, positively charged subatomic particle in the baryon family having a mass 1,836 times that of the electron. [Gk. *prōton,* neuter of *prōtos,* first.] **—pro·ton′ic** *adj.*

pro·to·ne·ma (prō′tə-nē′mə) *n., pl.* **-ne·ma·ta** (-nē′mə-tə, -nĕm′ə-tə). *Bot.* A green, threadlike structure that arises on germination of a moss spore and that eventually develops into a mature plant. [PROTO- + Gk. *nēma,* thread.] **—pro′to·ne′mal** (-nē′məl), **pro′to·ne′ma·tal** (-nē′mə-təl, -nĕm′ə-təl) *adj.*

pro·ton·o·tar·y (prō-tŏn′ə-tĕr′ē, prō′tə-nō′tə-rē) *n.* Variant of **prothonotary.**

proton synchrotron *n. Physics.* A ring-shaped synchrotron that uses a frequency-modulated accelerating voltage to accelerate protons to energies of several billion electron volts.

pro·to·path·ic (prō′tə-păth′ĭk) *adj.* Of or designating the cutaneous sensory reception of gross pressure, pain, heat, or cold. [< LGk. *prōtopathēs,* affected first < Gk. *prōtopathein,* to feel first : *prōto-,* first + *paskhein,* to feel.] **—pro·top′a·thy** (prō-tŏp′ə-thē) *n.*

pro·to·plasm (prō′tə-plăz′əm) *n.* A complex, jellylike colloidal substance conceived of as constituting the living matter of plant and animal cells and performing the basic life functions. —**pro'to·plas'mic** (-plăz'mĭk), **pro'to·plas'mal, pro'to·plas·mat'ic** (-plăz-măt'ĭk) *adj.*

pro·to·plast (prō'tə-plăst') *n.* **1.** Something that is the first made or formed; prototype. **2.** *Biol.* The living material of a cell as distinguished from inert portions. [OFr. *protoplaste* < LLat. *protoplastus* < Gk. *prōtoplastos* : *prōtos,* first + *plassein,* to form.] —**pro'to·plas'tic** *adj.*

pro·to·por·phy·rin (prō'tō-pôr'fə-rĭn) *n.* A metal-free porphyrin, $C_{34}H_{34}N_4O_4$, derived from the hemin of blood.

pro·to·stele (prō'tə-stēl', prō'tə-stē'lē) *n.* A stele that lacks pith and has a solid core of xylem. —**pro'to·ste'lic** (-stē'lĭk) *adj.*

pro·to·tro·phic (prō'tə-trō'fĭk, -trŏf'ĭk) *adj.* Obtaining nourishment by the assimilation of inorganic materials: *prototrophic bacteria.* —**pro'to·troph'** *n.*

pro·to·type (prō'tə-tīp') *n.* **1.** An original type, form, or instance that serves as a model on which later stages are based or judged. **2.** An early and typical example. **3.** *Biol.* A primitive or ancestral form or species. [Fr. < Gk. *prōtotupon,* archetype : *prōtos,* first + *tupos,* model.] —**pro'to·typ'al** (-tī'pəl), **pro'to·typ'ic** (-tĭp'ĭk), **pro'to·typ'i·cal** *adj.*

pro·to·xy·lem (prō'tə-zī'ləm) *n.* *Bot.* The first formed xylem that differentiates from the procambium.

pro·to·zo·an (prō'tə-zō'ən) also **pro·to·zo·on** (-ŏn') *n., pl.* **-zo·ans** also **-zo·a** (-zō'ə). Any of the single-celled, usually microscopic organisms of the phylum or subkingdom Protozoa, which includes the most primitive forms of animal life. [< NLat. *Protozoa,* subkingdom name : PROTO- + Gk. *zōia,* pl. of *zōion,* animal.] —**pro'to·zo'an, pro'to·zo'ic** (-zō'ĭk) *adj.*

pro·to·zo·ol·o·gy (prō'tə-zō-ŏl'ə-jē) *n.* The biological study of protozoans. —**pro'to·zo'o·log'i·cal** (-zō'ə-lŏj'ĭ-kəl) *adj.* —**pro'to·zo·ol'o·gist** *n.*

pro·to·zo·on (prō'tə-zō'ŏn') *n.* Variant of **protozoan.**

pro·tract (prō-trăkt', prə-) *tr.v.* **-tract·ed, -tract·ing, -tracts. 1.** To draw out or lengthen in time; prolong. **2.** To draw to scale by means of a scale and protractor; plot. **3.** *Anat.* To extend or protrude. [Lat. *protrahere, protract-* : *pro-,* forth + *trahere,* to drag.] —**pro·tract'ed·ly** (-trăk'tĭd-lē) *adv.* —**pro·tract'ed·ness** *n.* —**pro·trac'tive** *adj.*

pro·trac·tile (prō-trăk'təl, -tīl', prə-) also **pro·tract·i·ble** (-tə-bəl) *adj.* Capable of being protracted; extensible. —**pro'trac·til'i·ty** (prō'trăk-tĭl'ĭ-tē) *n.*

pro·trac·tion (prō-trăk'shən, prə-) *n.* **1. a.** The act of protracting. **b.** The state of being protracted. **2.** The irregular lengthening of a normally short syllable.

pro·trac·tor (prō-trăk'tər, prə-) *n.* **1.** A semicircular instrument for measuring and constructing angles. **2.** An adjustable pattern used by tailors. **3.** *Anat.* An extensor.

pro·trude (prō-trōōd') *v.* **-trud·ed, -trud·ing, -trudes.** —*tr.* To push or thrust outward. —*intr.* To jut out; project. [Lat. *protrudere* : *pro-,* forward + *trudere,* to thrust.] —**pro·trud'ent** (-trōōd'nt) *adj.*

pro·tru·sile (prō-trōō'səl, -sīl') also **pro·tru·si·ble** (prō-trōō'sə-bəl) *adj.* Capable of being thrust outward, as the tongue. [PROTRUS(ION) + -ILE.] —**pro'tru·sil'i·ty** (prō'-trōō-sĭl'ĭ-tē) *n.*

pro·tru·sion (prō-trōō'zhən) *n.* **1. a.** The act of protruding. **b.** The state of being protruded. **2.** Something that protrudes. [< Lat. *protrusus,* p.part. of *protrudere,* to protrude.]

pro·tru·sive (prō-trōō'sĭv, -zĭv) *adj.* **1.** Tending to protrude; protruding. **2.** Unduly or disagreeably conspicuous; obtrusive. —**pro·tru'sive·ly** *adv.* —**pro·tru'sive·ness** *n.*

pro·tu·ber·ance (prō-tōō'bər-əns, -tyōō'-) *n.* **1.** Something that protrudes; a bulge or knob. **2.** The condition of being protuberant.

pro·tu·ber·an·cy (prō-tōō'bər-ən-sē, -tyōō'-) *n., pl.* **-cies.** Protuberance.

pro·tu·ber·ant (prō-tōō'bər-ənt, -tyōō'-) *adj.* Swelling outward; bulging. [LLat. *protuberans, protuberant-,* pr.part. of *protuberare,* to bulge out. —see PROTUBERATE.] —**pro·tu'ber·ant·ly** *adv.*

pro·tu·ber·ate (prō-tōō'bə-rāt', -tyōō'-) *intr.v.* **-at·ed, -at·ing, -ates.** To swell or bulge out. [LLat. *protuberare* : Lat. *pro-,* forth + Lat. *tuber,* a swelling.] —**pro·tu'ber·a'tion** *n.*

proud (proud) *adj.* **-er, -est. 1.** Feeling pleasurable satisfaction over an attribute or act by which one's stature or sense of self is measured: *proud of one's daughter; proud to serve one's country.* **2.** Occasioning pride; gratifying: *a proud moment.* **3.** Marked by exacting or constraining self-respect. **4.** Having excessive self-esteem; haughty. **5.** Of great dignity; honored: *a proud name.* **6.** Majestic; magnificent. **7.** Spirited. [ME < OE *prūd* < OFr. *prud, preu,* brave, virtuous < LLat. *prode,* advantageous < Lat. *prodesse,* to be good : *prod-,* for (var. of *pro-*) + *esse,* to be.] —**proud'ly** *adv.* —**proud'ness** *n.*

Synonyms: *proud, arrogant, haughty, disdainful, supercilious.* These adjectives imply self-esteem, most of them to the degree of belief in one's superiority over others. Although *proud* can suggest conceit or vanity, it more often implies justifiable satisfaction with oneself. *Arrogant* suggests one who demands more power or consideration than is rightly his. *Haughty* refers to a more consciously assumed manner, as of one who affects superiority by reason of birth or station. *Disdainful* emphasizes scorn or contempt. *Supercilious* combines the meanings of *haughty* and *disdainful* and adds the idea of aloofness.

proud flesh *n.* *Pathol.* The swollen flesh around a healing wound due to granulation tissue. [So called because of its swelling up.]

prove (prōōv) *v.* **proved, proved** or **prov·en** (prōō'vən), **prov·ing, proves.** —*tr.* **1.** To establish the truth or validity of by presentation of argument or evidence. **2.** *Law.* To establish the authenticity of (a will). **3.** To determine the quality of by testing; try out. **4.** *Math.* **a.** To validate (a hypothesis or proposition) by a proof. **b.** To verify (the result of a calculation). **5.** *Printing.* To make a sample impression of (type). **6.** *Archaic.* To experience; undergo. —*intr.* To be shown to be; turn out: *a theory that proved impractical in practice.* —***phrasal verb.*** **prove out.** *Informal.* To turn out well; succeed. [ME *proven* < OFr. *prover* < Lat. *probare,* to test < *probus,* good.] —**prov'a·bil'i·ty, prov'a·ble·ness** *n.* —**prov'a·ble** *adj.* —**prov'a·bly** *adv.* —**prov'er** *n.*

Usage: The regular form *proved* is the preferred form of the past participle: *He has proved his point. The theory has not been proved.* The alternative *proven* is unacceptable to a large majority of the Usage Panel in such examples. *Proven* is a Scots variant made familiar through its legal use: *The charges were not proven.* But *proven* is more widely employed as an adjective that is used directly before a noun: *a proven talent.*

prov·en (prōō'vən) *adj.* Proved; verified. —*v.* A past participle of **prove.** —See Usage note at **prove.** —**prov'en·ly** *adv.*

prov·e·nance (prŏv'ə-nəns, -näns') *n.* Place of origin; derivation. [Fr. < *provenir,* to originate < Lat. *provenire* : *pro-,* forth + *venire,* to come.]

Pro·ven·çal (prō'vən-säl', prŏv'ən-) *n.* The Romance language of Provence. —**Pro'ven·çal'** *adj.*

prov·en·der (prŏv'ən-dər) *n.* **1.** Dry food, such as hay, used as feed for livestock. **2.** Food or provisions. [ME *provendre* < OFr. < Med. Lat. *probenda,* var. of *praebenda.* —see PREBEND.]

pro·ve·nience (prə-vēn'yəns, -vē'nē-əns) *n.* A source or origin of something. [< Lat. *proveniens,* pr.part. of *provenire,* to originate. —see PROVENANCE.]

pro·ven·tric·u·lus (prō'vĕn-trĭk'yə-ləs) *n., pl.* **-li** (-lī'). **1.** A division of the stomach anterior to the gizzard in birds. **2.** A digestive division in insects and some worms similar to the proventriculus. [PRO-[2] + Lat. *ventriculus,* stomach, dim. of *venter,* belly.] —**pro'ven·tric'u·lar** (-lər) *adj.*

prov·erb (prŏv'ûrb') *n.* **1.** A short, pithy saying in frequent and widespread use that expresses a well-known truth or fact. **2.** One that is recognized as a typical example. [ME *proverbe* < OFr. < Lat. *proverbium* : *pro-,* forth + *verbum,* word.]

pro·ver·bi·al (prə-vûr'bē-əl) *adj.* **1.** Of the nature of a proverb. **2.** Expressed in a proverb. **3.** Widely referred to, as if the subject of a proverb; famous. —**pro·ver'bi·al·ly** *adv.*

Prov·erbs (prŏv'ûrbz') *n. (used with a sing. verb).* See table at **Bible.**

pro·vide (prə-vīd') *v.* **-vid·ed, -vid·ing, -vides.** —*tr.* **1.** To furnish; supply. **2.** To make ready; prepare. **3.** To make available; afford. **4.** To set down as a stipulation. —*intr.* **1.** To take measures in preparation. **2.** To supply means of subsistence. **3.** To make a stipulation or condition: *The Constitution provides for a bicameral legislature.* [ME *providen* < Lat. *providēre,* to prepare for : *pro-,* forward + *vidēre,* to see.] —**pro·vid'er** *n.*

pro·vid·ed (prə-vī'dĭd) *conj.* On the condition; if: *will pay the bonus provided the job is completed on time.*

Usage: As a conjunction meaning "on condition that" *provided* is often held to be preferable to *providing: You may go provided your work is done.* In this usage a majority of the Usage Panel finds *providing* unacceptable for writing.

prov·i·dence (prŏv'ĭ-dəns, -dĕns') *n.* **1.** Care or preparation in advance; foresight. **2.** Prudent management; economy. **3.** The care, guardianship, and control exercised by a deity; divine direction: *"Some sought the key to history in the working of divine providence"* (William Ebenstein). **4. Providence.** God.

prov·i·dent (prŏv'ĭ-dənt, -dĕnt') *adj.* **1.** Providing for future needs or events. **2.** Frugal; economical. [ME < Lat. *providens,* pr.part.of *providēre,* to provide for. —see PROVIDE.] —**prov'i·dent·ly** *adv.*

prov·i·den·tial (prŏv'ĭ-dĕn'shəl) *adj.* **1.** Of or resulting from divine providence. **2.** Happening as if through divine intervention; opportune. —**prov'i·den'tial·ly** *adv.*

pro·vid·ing (prə-vī'dĭng) *conj.* On the condition; provided. —See Usage note at **provided.**

prov·ince (prŏv'ĭns) *n.* **1.** A territory governed as an administrative or political unit of a country or empire. **2.** *Eccles.* A division of territory under the jurisdiction of an archbishop. **3. provinces.** Areas of a country situated away from the capital or population center. **4.** A comprehensive area of knowledge, activity, or interest: *a topic falling within the province of ancient history.* **5.** The range of one's proper duties and functions; scope; jurisdiction. **6.** *Ecol.* A subdivision of a region. **7.** Any of various lands outside Italy conquered by the Romans and administered by them as self-contained units. [ME *provynce* < OFr. *province* < Lat. *provincia.*]

pro·vin·cial (prə-vĭn'shəl) *adj.* **1.** Of or pertaining to a province. **2.** Of or characteristic of people from the provinces;

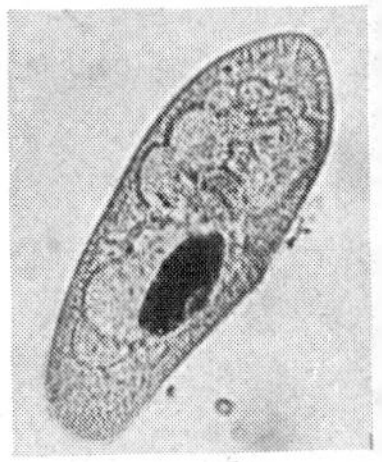

protozoan

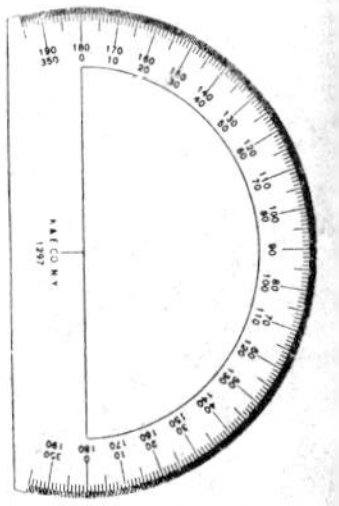

protractor

not fashionable or sophisticated: *"Well-educated professional women . . . made me feel uncomfortably provincial"* (J.R. Salamanca). **3.** Limited in perspective; narrow and self-centered. *—n.* **1.** A native or inhabitant of the provinces. **2.** A person who has provincial ideas or habits. **—pro·vin'cial·ism, pro·vin'ci·al'i·ty** (-shē-ăl'ĭ-tē) *n.* **—pro·vin'cial·ly** *adv.*

pro·vin·cial·ize (prə-vĭn'shə-līz') *tr.v.* **-ized, -iz·ing, -iz·es.** To make provincial. **—pro·vin'cial·i·za'tion** *n.*

proving ground *n.* A place for testing new devices or theories.

pro·vi·sion (prə-vĭzh'ən) *n.* **1.** The act of supplying or fitting out. **2.** Something that is provided. **3.** A preparatory action or measure. **4. provisions.** A stock of necessary supplies, esp. food. **5.** A stipulation or qualification, esp. a clause in a document or agreement. *—tr.v.* **-sioned, -sion·ing, -sions.** To supply with provisions. [ME < OFr., forethought < Lat. *provisio* < *providēre,* to foresee. —see PROVIDE.] **—pro·vi'sion·er** *n.*

pro·vi·sion·al (prə-vĭzh'ə-nəl) also **pro·vi·sion·ar·y** (-vĭzh'ə-nĕr'ē) *adj.* Provided for the time being, pending permanent arrangements: *a provisional capital.* **—pro·vi'sion·al·ly** *adv.*

pro·vi·so (prə-vī'zō) *n., pl.* **-sos** or **-soes.** A clause in a document making a qualification, condition, or restriction. [ME < Med. Lat. *proviso quod,* provided that.]

pro·vi·so·ry (prə-vī'zə-rē) *adj.* Depending on a proviso; conditional. **—pro·vi'so·ri·ly** *adv.*

pro·vi·ta·min (prō-vī'tə-mĭn) *n.* A substance converted to a vitamin within the body, as carotene into vitamin A.

Pro·vo (prō'vō) *n.* A member of the extremist faction of the Irish Republican Army. [Shortening and alteration of *provisional* (*wing*), name of the faction.]

pro·vo·ca·teur (prō-vŏk'ə-tûr') *n.* An agent provocateur. [Fr.]

prov·o·ca·tion (prŏv'ə-kā'shən) *n.* **1.** The act of provoking or inciting. **2.** Something that provokes. [ME *provocacioun* < OFr. *provocation* < Lat. *provocatio* < *provocare,* to challenge. —see PROVOKE.]

pro·voc·a·tive (prə-vŏk'ə-tĭv) *adj.* Tending to provoke; stimulating. *—n.* Something that provokes. **—pro·voc'a·tive·ly** *adv.* **—pro·voc'a·tive·ness** *n.*

pro·voke (prə-vōk') *tr.v.* **-voked, -vok·ing, -vokes. 1.** To cause anger, resentment, or deep feeling in. **2.** To cause to take action. **3.** To bring on by inciting: *provoke a fight.* [ME *provoken* < OFr. *provoker* < Lat. *provocare,* to challenge : *pro-,* forth + *vocare,* to call.] **—pro·vok'ing·ly** *adv.*

Synonyms: *provoke, incite, excite, stimulate, arouse, rouse, stir.* These verbs are compared in the sense of causing a person to take action or feel emotion. *Provoke,* the least explicit with respect to means, does little more than state the consequences produced: *He was provoked to anger. Incite* implies the urging on and directing of energies toward a certain course. *Excite* stresses a playing upon the emotions generally. The remaining terms suggest increasing degrees of emotional awakening. *Stimulate* and *arouse* connote immediate, often brief sensations, and *rouse* and *stir,* deeper, stronger responses.

pro·vok·ing (prə-vō'kĭng) *adj.* Troubling the nerves or peace of mind, as by repeated vexations. **—pro·vok'ing·ly** *adv.*

pro·vost (prō'vōst', -vəst, prŏv'əst) *n.* **1.** The chief magistrate of certain Scottish cities. **2.** The chief officer of some colleges. **3.** The highest official in certain cathedrals or collegiate churches. **4.** The keeper of a prison. [ME < OE *profost* and OFr. *provost,* both < Med. Lat. *propositus* < Lat. *praepositus,* superintendent < p.part. of *praeponere,* to place over : *prae-,* before + *ponere,* to put.]

pro·vost court (prō'vō) *n.* A military court for the trial of minor offenses committed in occupied hostile territories.

pro·vost guard (prō'vō) *n.* A detail of soldiers on police duty under a provost marshal.

pro·vost marshal (prō'vō) *n.* **1.** The head of military police. **2.** A naval officer responsible for the disposition of prisoners facing court-martial.

pro·vost sergeant (prō'vō) *n.* A noncommissioned officer who heads a detail of military police.

prow (prou) *n.* **1.** The forward part of a ship's hull; bow. **2.** A projecting part similar in configuration to the prow of a ship, as the forward end of a ski. [OFr. *proue* < Lat. *prora* < Gk. *prōira.*]

prow·ess (prou'ĭs) *n.* **1.** Superior skill or ability. **2.** Superior strength, courage, or daring, esp. in battle. [ME *prowesse* < OFr. *proesse* < *prou,* var. of *prud,* brave. —see PROUD.]

prowl (proul) *v.* **prowled, prowl·ing, prowls.** *—tr.* To roam through stealthily, as in search of prey or plunder. *—intr.* To rove furtively or with predatory intent. *—n.* An act of prowling. **—*idiom.* on the prowl.** Actively looking for something. [ME *prollen.*] **—prowl'er** *n.*

prowl car *n.* A squad car.

prox·i·mal (prŏk'sə-məl) *adj.* **1.** Nearest; proximate. **2.** *Biol.* Near the central part of the body or a point of attachment or origin: *the proximal end of a bone.* [< Lat. *proximus,* superl. of *propior,* near.] **—prox'i·mal·ly** *adv.*

prox·i·mate (prŏk'sə-mĭt) *adj.* **1.** Closely related in space, time, or order; very near. **2.** Approximate. [Lat. *proximatus,* p.part. of *proximare,* to come near < *proximus,* superl. of *propior,* near.] **—prox'i·mate·ly** *adv.* **—prox'i·mate·ness** *n.*

prox·im·i·ty (prŏk-sĭm'ĭ-tē) *n.* The state, quality, or fact of being near or next; closeness. —See Usage note at **close.** [OFr. *proximite* < Lat. *proximitas* < *proximus,* superl. of *propior,* near.]

proximity fuze *n.* An electronic device for detonating a projectile as it approaches a target, used in antiaircraft shells.

prox·i·mo (prŏk'sə-mō') *adv. Archaic.* Of or in the following month. [Lat. *proximo mense,* in the next month.]

prox·y (prŏk'sē) *n., pl.* **-ies. 1.** A person authorized to act for another; agent or substitute. **2.** The authority to act for another. **3.** The written authorization to act in place of another. **—*modifier:*** *a proxy vote.* [ME *proxcy* < Norman Fr. *procuracie* < Med. Lat. *procuratia* < Lat. *procurare,* to take care of. —see PROCURE.]

prude (prōōd) *n.* A person who is excessively concerned with being or seeming to be proper, modest, or righteous. [Fr., short for OFr. *preudefemme,* virtuous woman : *preu,* virtuous, proud + *de,* of (< Lat.) + *femme,* woman (< Lat. *femina*).]

pru·dence (prōōd'ns) *n.* **1.** The state, quality, or fact of being prudent. **2.** Careful management; economy.

Synonyms: *prudence, discretion, circumspection.* These nouns are compared as they express caution and wisdom in the conduct of affairs. *Prudence,* the most comprehensive, implies not only caution but the capacity for judging in advance the probable results of one's actions. *Discretion* suggests prudence coupled with self-restraint and sound judgment. *Circumspection* adds to discretion the implication of wariness in one's actions out of consideration for social and moral consequences.

pru·dent (prōōd'nt) *adj.* **1.** Wise in handling practical matters; exercising good judgment or common sense. **2.** Careful in regard to one's own interests; provident. **3.** Careful about one's conduct; circumspect. [ME < OFr. < Lat. *prudens,* short for *providens.* —see PROVIDENT.] **—pru'dent·ly** *adv.*

pru·den·tial (prōō-dĕn'shəl) *adj.* **1.** Arising from or characterized by prudence. **2.** Exercising prudence, good judgment, or common sense. **—pru·den'tial·ly** *adv.*

prud·er·y (prōō'də-rē) *n., pl.* **-ies. 1.** The state or quality of being prudish. **2.** An instance of prudish behavior or talk. [Fr. *pruderie* < *prude,* prude. —see PRUDE.]

prud·ish (prōō'dĭsh) *adj.* Marked by or exhibiting the characteristics of a prude; priggish. **—prud'ish·ly** *adv.* **—prud'ish·ness** *n.*

pru·i·nose (prōō'ə-nōs') *adj. Bot.* Having a white, powdery covering or bloom. [Lat. *pruinosus,* frosty < *pruina,* hoarfrost.]

prune[1] (prōōn) *n.* **1. a.** The partially dried fruit of any of several varieties of the common plum, *Prunus domestica.* **b.** Any kind of plum that can be dried without spoiling. **2.** *Slang.* An ill-tempered person. [ME < OFr. < Lat. *prunum,* plum.]

prune[2] (prōōn) *v.* **pruned, prun·ing, prunes.** *—tr.* **1.** To cut off or remove dead or living parts or branches of (a plant, for example) to improve shape or growth. **2.** To remove or cut out as superfluous. **3.** To reduce: *prune the budget.* *—intr.* To remove what is superfluous or undesirable. [ME *prouynen* < OFr. *proignier* < VLat. **prorotundiare* : Lat. *pro-,* in front + Lat. *rotundus,* round.] **—prun'er** *n.*

pru·nel·la (prōō-nĕl'ə) also **pru·nel·lo** (-nĕl'ō) *n., pl.* **-las** also **-los.** A strong, heavy fabric of worsted twill, used chiefly for shoe uppers, clerical robes, and academic gowns. [Fr. *prunelle,* sloe, dim. of *prune,* prune.]

pru·nelle (prōō-nĕl') *n.* A brownish, sloe-flavored French liqueur. [Fr., dim. of *prune,* prune.]

pru·nel·lo (prōō-nĕl'ō) *n.* Variant of **prunella.**

pruning hook *n.* A long pole with a curved saw blade and usually a clipping mechanism on one end, used esp. for pruning small trees.

pru·ri·ent (prŏŏr'ē-ənt) *adj.* **1.** Obsessively interested in matters of a sexual nature. **2. a.** Characterized by an obsessive interest in sex: *prurient thoughts.* **b.** Arousing or appealing to an obsessive interest in sex: *prurient literature.* [Lat. *pruriens, prurient-,* pr.part. of *prurire,* to feel desire, itch.] **—pru'ri·ence, pru'ri·en·cy** *n.* **—pru'ri·ent·ly** *adv.*

pru·ri·go (prōō-rī'gō) *n.* A chronic, inflammatory skin disease characterized by eruption and severe itching. [Lat., an itching < *prurire,* to itch.] **—pru·rig'i·nous** (-rĭj'ə-nəs) *adj.*

pru·ri·tus (prōō-rī'təs) *n.* Severe itching, usually of undamaged skin. [Lat. < *prurire,* to itch.] **—pru·rit'ic** (-rĭt'ĭk) *adj.*

Prus·sian (prŭsh'ən) *adj.* **1.** Of or pertaining to Prussia, its people, or their language and culture. **2.** Like or suggestive of the Junkers and the military class of Prussia. *—n.* **1.** One of the western Balts anciently inhabiting the region between the Vistula and Neman. **2.** A Baltic inhabitant of Prussia. **3.** A German inhabitant of Prussia.

Prussian blue *n.* **1.** An insoluble, dark-blue pigment and dye, ferric ferrocyanide or one of its modifications. **2.** Iron blue. **3.** A moderate to strong blue or deep greenish blue. [After *Prussia,* where the dye was discovered.]

prus·si·ate (prŭs'ē-āt') *n.* **1.** A ferrocyanide or ferricyanide. **2.** A salt of hydrocyanic acid; cyanide. [Fr. < *(acide) prussique,* prussic acid.]

prus·sic acid (prŭs'ĭk) *n.* Hydrocyanic acid. [So called because it is obtained from Prussian blue.]

pru·tah (proo-tä′) *n., pl.* **-toth** or **-tot** (-tōt′, -tōth′, -tōs′). See table at **currency**. [Mod. Heb. *perūṭāh*.]

pry¹ (prī) *intr.v.* **pried, pry·ing, pries.** To look or inquire closely, curiously, or inquisitively, often in a furtive manner; snoop: *always prying into the affairs of others.* —*n., pl.* **pries. 1.** An act of prying. **2.** An excessively inquisitive person; snoop. [ME *prien.*] —**pry′ing·ly** *adv.*

pry² (prī) *tr.v.* **pried, pry·ing, pries. 1.** To raise, move, or force open with a lever. **2.** To obtain with effort or difficulty: *pried a confession out of the suspect.* —*n., pl.* **pries. 1.** Something, as a crowbar, that is used to apply leverage. **2.** Leverage. [Alteration of PRIZE³.]

pry·er (prī′ər) *n.* Variant of **prier.**

psalm (säm) *n.* **1.** A sacred song; hymn. **2. Psalms** *(used with a sing. verb).* See table at **Bible.** —*tr.v.* **psalmed, psalm·ing, psalms.** To sing of or celebrate in psalms. [ME < OE *psealm* < LLat. *psalmus* < Gk. *psalmos* < *psallein,* to play the harp.]

psalm·ist (sä′mĭst) *n.* A writer or composer of psalms.

psalm·o·dy (sä′mə-dē, săl′mə-) *n., pl.* **-dies. 1.** The act or practice of singing psalms in divine worship. **2.** The composition or arranging of psalms for singing. **3.** A collection of psalms. [ME *psalmodie* < LLat. *psalmodia* < Gk. *psalmōdia,* singing to the harp : *psalmos,* psalm (< *psallein,* to play the harp) + *ōidē,* song.] —**psalm′o·dist** *n.*

Psal·ter also **psal·ter** (sôl′tər) *n.* A book containing the Book of Psalms or a particular version of, musical setting for, or selection from it. [ME < OE *psaltere* and OFr. *psautier,* both < LLat. *psalterium* < Gk. *psaltērion,* harp. —see PSALTERY.]

psal·te·ri·um (sôl-tîr′ē-əm) *n., pl.* **-ri·a** (-ē-ə). The omasum. [LLat., psalter, so called because when slit open its folds fall apart like the leaves of a book.] —**psal·te′ri·al** *adj.*

psal·ter·y (sôl′tə-rē) also **psal·try** (sôl′trē) *n., pl.* **-ter·ies** also **-tries.** An ancient stringed musical instrument played by plucking the strings with the fingers or a plectrum. [ME *psalterie* < OFr. < Lat. *psalterium* < Gk. *psaltērion* < *psallein,* to play the harp.]

p's and q's (pēz′ ən kyooz′) *pl. n.* **1.** Socially correct behavior; manners. **2.** The way one acts; conduct: *was told to watch his p's and q's or he would be fired.*

pse·phol·o·gy (sē-fŏl′ə-jē) *n.* The study of political elections. [Gk. *psēphos,* pebble, ballot (from the ancient Greeks' use of pebbles for voting) + -LOGY.] —**pse′pho·log′i·cal** (sē′fə-lŏj′ĭ-kəl) *adj.* —**pse·phol′o·gist** *n.*

pseud– *pref.* Variant of **pseudo-.**

pseud·ax·is (soo-dăk′sĭs) *n.* A sympodium.

pseud·e·pig·ra·pha (soo′dĭ-pĭg′rə-fə) *pl.n.* **1.** Spurious writings, esp. writings falsely attributed to Biblical characters or times. **2.** A body of Jewish religious texts written between 200 B.C. and A.D. 200 and spuriously ascribed to various prophets and kings of Hebrew Scriptures. [Gk. : *pseudēs,* false (< *pseudein,* to lie) + *epigraphein,* to ascribe (*epi-,* upon + *graphein,* to write).] —**pseud′e·pig′ra·phal, pseud′ep·i·graph′ic** (soo′dĕp′ĭ-grăf′ĭk), **pseud′ep·i·graph′i·cal, pseud′e·pig′ra·phous** *adj.*

pseudo– or **pseud–** *pref.* **1.** False; deceptive; sham: *pseudoscience.* **2.** Apparently similar: *pseudocarp.* [ME < LLat. < Gk. *pseudēs,* false < *pseudein,* to lie.]

pseu·do·carp (soo′də-kärp′) *n.* An accessory fruit. —**pseu′do·car′pous** *adj.*

pseu·do·coel (soo′də-sēl′) also **pseu·do·coe·lom** (soo′də-sē′ləm) *n.* A body cavity not formed by gastrulation and lacking a mesodermal lining.

pseu·do·coe·lo·mate (soo′dō-sē′lə-māt′) *adj.* Having a pseudocoel.

pseu·do·cy·e·sis (soo′dō-sī-ē′sĭs) *n.* A psychosomatic condition in which physical symptoms of pregnancy, such as weight gain and amenorrhea, are manifested without conception.

pseu·do-e·vent (soo′dō-ĭ-vĕnt′) *n. Informal.* A staged event that is designed to attract attention: *the pseudo-events of a political campaign.*

pseu·do·mo·nad (soo′də-mō′năd′) *n.* Any of various gram-negative, rod-shaped bacteria of the genus *Pseudomonas,* including some plant and animal pathogens. [NLat. *Pseudomonas, Pseudomonad-,* genus name : PSEUDO- + Gk. *monas,* unit < *monos,* one.]

pseu·do·morph (soo′də-môrf′) *n.* **1.** A false, deceptive, or irregular form. **2.** *Mineral.* A mineral having the crystalline form of another mineral rather than that normally characteristic of its composition. —**pseu′do·mor′phism** *n.* —**pseu′do·mor′phic, pseu′do·mor′phous** *adj.*

pseu·do·nym (sood′n-ĭm′) *n.* A fictitious name assumed by an author; pen name. [Fr. *pseudonyme* < Gk. *pseudonumon* : *pseudēs,* false + *onoma,* name.] —**pseu·don′y·mous** (soo-dŏn′ə-məs) *adj.* —**pseu·don′y·mous·ly** *adv.* —**pseu·don′y·mous·ness** *n.*

pseu·do·po·di·um (soo′də-pō′dē-əm) also **pseu·do·pod** (soo′də-pŏd′) *n., pl.* **-po·di·a** (-pō′dē-ə) also **-pods.** A temporary protrusion of the cytoplasm of a cell, serving as a means of locomotion and of surrounding and ingesting food in organisms such as the amoeba. [NLat. : PSEUDO- + Gk. *podion,* dim. of *pous,* foot.]

pseu·do·preg·nan·cy (soo′dō-prĕg′nən-sē) *n.* **1.** A condition resembling pregnancy that occurs in some mammals following infertile copulation. **2.** Pseudocyesis.

pseu·do·ran·dom (soo′dō-răn′dəm) *adj.* Of, relating to, or being random numbers generated by a definite, nonrandom computational process.

pseu·do·sci·ence (soo′dō-sī′əns) *n.* A theory, methodology, or activity that appears to be or is presented as being scientific. —**pseu′do·sci′en·tif′ic** (-ən-tĭf′ĭk) *adj.* —**pseu′do·sci′en·tist** *n.*

pshaw (shô) *interj.* Used to indicate impatience, irritation, disapproval, or disbelief.

psi (sī, psī) *n.* The 23rd letter of the Greek alphabet. See table at **alphabet.** [LGk. < Gk. *psei.*]

psil·o·cy·bin (sĭl′ə-sī′bĭn, sī′lə-) *n.* A compound, $C_{12}H_{17}N_2O_4P$, obtained from the mushroom *Psilocybe mexicana,* that is a strong hallucinogen. [NLat. *Psilocybe,* genus name + -IN.]

psi·lom·e·lane (sī-lŏm′ə-lān′) *n.* A hard, black hydrated oxide ore of manganese. [Gk. *psilos,* bare + Gk. *melas, melan-,* black.]

psit·ta·cine (sĭt′ə-sīn′) *adj.* Of, pertaining to, or characteristic of parrots. [Lat. *psittacinus* < *psittacus,* parrot < Gk. *psittakos.*]

psit·ta·co·sis (sĭt′ə-kō′sĭs) *n.* A virus disease of parrots and related birds that is communicable to human beings, in whom it produces high fever and complications similar to pneumonia. [Lat. *psittacus,* parrot (< Gk. *psittakos*) + -OSIS.] —**psit′ta·cot′ic** (-kŏt′ĭk, -kō′tĭk) *adj.*

pso·ri·a·sis (sə-rī′ə-sĭs) *n.* A chronic, noncontagious skin disease characterized by inflammation and white, scaly patches. [Gk. *psōriasis* < *psōrian,* to have the itch < *psōra,* itch.] —**pso′ri·at′ic** (sôr′ē-ăt′ĭk, sōr′-) *adj.*

psych (sīk) *Informal.* —*n.* Psychology. —*tr.v.* **psyched, psych·ing, psychs. 1.** To put into the right psychological frame of mind: *The coach psyched the team up before the game.* **2.** To undermine the confidence of by psychological means: *He psyched out his opponent.*

psych– *pref.* Variant of **psycho-.**

psy·che (sī′kē) *n.* **1. Psyche.** *Gk. Myth.* A maiden who was loved by Eros and united with him after Aphrodite's jealousy was overcome and who subsequently became the personification of the soul. **2.** The soul or spirit as distinguished from the body. **3.** *Psychiat.* The mind functioning as the center of thought, feeling, and behavior and consciously or unconsciously adjusting and relating the body to its social and physical environment. [Lat. < Gk. *psukhē,* soul.]

psy·che·de·li·a (sī′kĭ-dē′lē-ə, -dēl′yə) *n.* The subcultural realm of people associated with psychedelic drugs.

psy·che·del·ic (sī′kĭ-dĕl′ĭk) *adj.* Of, pertaining to, or generating hallucinations, distortions of perception, and, occasionally, states resembling psychosis. [PSYCHE + Gk. *dēlos,* visible.] —**psy′che·del′i·cal·ly** *adv.*

psy·chi·a·try (sĭ-kī′ə-trē, sī-) *n.* The medical study, diagnosis, treatment, and prevention of mental illness. —**psy′chi·at′ric** (sī′kē-ăt′rĭk), **psy′chi·at′ri·cal** *adj.* —**psy′chi·at′ri·cal·ly** *adv.* —**psy·chi′a·trist** *n.*

psy·chic (sī′kĭk) also **psy·chi·cal** (-kĭ-kəl) *adj.* **1.** Of or pertaining to the human mind or psyche. **2. a.** Of or pertaining to extraordinary, esp. extrasensory and nonphysical, mental processes, such as extrasensory perception and mental telepathy. **b.** Proceeding from, produced by, or responding to such processes. —*n.* **psychic. 1.** An individual apparently responsive to psychic forces. **2.** A medium. [Gk. *psukhikos* < *psukhē,* soul.] —**psy′chi·cal·ly** *adv.*

psy·cho (sī′kō) *Slang.* —*n., pl.* **-chos.** A psychopath. —*adj.* Crazy; insane.

psycho– or **psych–** *pref.* **1. a.** Mind; mental: *psychogenic.* **b.** Mental activities or processes: *psychomotor.* **2.** Psychology; psychological: *psychohistory.* [< Gk. *psukhē,* spirit, life.]

psy·cho·ac·tive (sī′kō-ăk′tĭv) *adj.* Affecting the mind or mental processes. Used of a drug or chemical.

psy·cho·a·nal·y·sis (sī′kō-ə-năl′ĭ-sĭs) *n.* **1.** The analytic technique originated by Sigmund Freud that uses free association, dream interpretation, and analysis of resistance and transference to investigate mental processes. **2.** The theory of human psychology founded by Freud on the concepts of the unconscious, resistance, repression, sexuality, and the Oedipus complex. **3.** A psychiatric therapy incorporating psychoanalysis. —**psy′cho·an′a·lyst** (-ăn′ə-lĭst) *n.* —**psy′cho·an′a·lyt′ic** (-ăn′ə-lĭt′ĭk), **psy′cho·an′a·lyt′i·cal** *adj.* —**psy′cho·an′a·lyt′i·cal·ly** *adv.*

psy·cho·an·a·lyze (sī′kō-ăn′ə-līz′) *tr.v.* **-lyzed, -lyz·ing, -lyz·es.** To analyze and treat by psychoanalysis.

psy·cho·bi·og·ra·phy (sī′kō-bī-ŏg′rə-fē, -bē-) *n.* **1.** A biography that analyzes the psychological make-up or characteristics of an individual. **2.** A character analysis. —**psy′cho·bi·og′ra·pher** *n.* —**psy′cho·bi′o·graph′i·cal** (-bī′ə-grăf′ĭ-kəl) *adj.*

psy·cho·bi·ol·o·gy (sī′kō-bī-ŏl′ə-jē) *n.* The study of interactions between mental and biological processes. —**psy′cho·bi′o·log′i·cal** (-bī′ə-lŏj′ĭ-kəl) *adj.* —**psy′cho·bi·ol′o·gist** *n.*

psy·cho·chem·i·cal (sī′kō-kĕm′ĭ-kəl) *n.* A psychoactive substance.

psy·cho·dra·ma (sī′kə-drä′mə, -drăm′ə) *n.* **1.** A psychotherapeutic and analytic technique in which individuals are

psaltery
12th-century manuscript illustration of King David

psyche
Psyche and Eros

assigned roles to be spontaneously played within a dramatic context devised by a therapist. **2.** A dramatization in which psychodrama is employed. **—psy′cho·dra·mat′ic** (-drə-măt′ĭk) *adj.*

psy·cho·dy·nam·ics (sī′kō-dī-năm′ĭks, -dĭ-) *n. (used with a sing. verb).* **1.** The interaction of various mental or emotional processes, esp. when they are considered as constituents of a system of interrelated forces. **2.** Behavioral analysis in terms of motives or drives. **—psy′cho·dy·nam′ic** *adj.* **—psy′cho·dy·nam′i·cal·ly** *adv.*

psy·cho·gen·e·sis (sī′kə-jĕn′ĭ-sĭs) *n.* **1.** The generation and development of psychological processes, personality, or behavior. **2.** The psychological origin of a specific psychic process or event. **—psy′cho·ge·net′ic** (-jə-nĕt′ĭk) *adj.* **—psy′cho·ge·net′i·cal·ly** *adv.*

psy·cho·gen·ic (sī′kə-jĕn′ĭk) *adj.* Originating in the mind or in mental activities and conditions. **—psy′cho·gen′i·cal·ly** *adv.*

psy·chog·no·sis (sī′kŏg-nō′sĭs, -kəg-) *n. Psychiat.* The diagnosis of psychic disorders. **—psy′chog·nos′tic** (-nŏs′tĭk) *adj.*

psy·cho·graph (sī′kə-grăf′) *n.* **1.** A psychological profile of an individual or group. **2.** A psychobiography. **—psy′cho·graph′ic** *adj.*

psy·cho·his·to·ry (sī′kō-hĭs′tə-rē) *n.* A psychoanalytic interpretation or study of a historical event or person. **—psy′cho·his·tor′i·an** (-hĭ-stôr′ē-ən, -stŏr′-) *n.* **—psy′cho·his·tor′i·cal** (-stôr′ĭ-kəl, -stŏr′-) *adj.*

psy·cho·ki·ne·sis (sī′kō-kĭ-nē′sĭs, -kī-) *n.* **1.** The production of motion, esp. in inanimate and remote objects, by the exercise of psychic powers. **2.** *Psychiat.* Uninhibited, maniacal motor response. **—psy′cho·ki·net′ic** (-kĭ-nĕt′ĭk, -kī-) *adj.* **—psy′cho·ki·net′i·cal·ly** *adv.*

psy·cho·lin·guis·tics (sī′kō-lĭng-gwĭs′tĭks) *n. (used with a sing. verb).* The study of the interaction between psychological factors and linguistic behavior. **—psy′cho·lin′guist** *n.* **—psy′cho·lin·guis′tic** *adj.*

psy·cho·log·i·cal (sī′kə-lŏj′ĭ-kəl) *adj.* **1.** Of or pertaining to psychology. **2.** Of, pertaining to, or derived from the mind or emotions. **3.** Capable of influencing the mind or emotions. **—psy′cho·log′i·cal·ly** *adv.*

psychological moment *n.* The time when the mental state of a person is most likely to produce the desired response.

psy·chol·o·gize (sī-kŏl′ə-jīz′) *v.* **-gized, -giz·ing, -giz·es.** *—tr.* To explain (behavior) psychologically. *—intr.* **1.** To investigate psychologically. **2.** To reason or speculate psychologically.

ptarmigan

psy·chol·o·gy (sī-kŏl′ə-jē) *n., pl.* **-gies. 1.** The science of mental processes and behavior. **2.** The emotional and behavioral characteristics of an individual, group, or activity: *the psychology of war.* **3.** Subtle tactical action or argument: *used poor psychology on his employer.* **—psy·chol′o·gist** *n.*

psy·cho·met·rics (sī′kə-mĕt′rĭks) *n. (used with a sing. verb).* **1.** The measurement of psychological variables, such as intelligence, aptitude, and emotional disturbance. **2.** The mathematical and esp. statistical design of psychological tests and measures. **—psy′cho·met′ric, psy′cho·met′ri·cal** *adj.* **—psy′cho·met′ri·cal·ly** *adv.* **—psy·chom′e·tri′cian** (sī-kŏm′ĭ-trĭsh′ən), **psy·chom′e·trist** (sī-kŏm′ĭ-trĭst) *n.*

psy·cho·mo·tor (sī′kə-mō′tər) *adj.* Of or pertaining to muscular activity associated with mental processes.

psy·cho·neu·ro·sis (sī′kō-no͝o-rō′sĭs, -nyo͝o-) *n.* Neurosis. **—psy′cho·neu·rot′ic** (-rŏt′ĭk) *adj. & n.*

psy·cho·path (sī′kə-păth′) *n.* A person with a personality disorder, esp. one manifested in aggressively antisocial behavior. [< PSYCHOPATHY.] **—psy′cho·path′ic** *adj.* **—psy′cho·path′i·cal·ly** *adv.*

psy·cho·pa·thol·o·gy (sī′kō-pə-thŏl′ə-jē, -pă-) *n.* The study of pathological mental conditions. **—psy′cho·path′o·log′i·cal** (-păth′ə-lŏj′ĭ-kəl), **psy′cho·path′o·log′ic** *adj.* **—psy′cho·pa·thol′o·gist** *n.*

psy·chop·a·thy (sī-kŏp′ə-thē) *n.* Mental disorder, esp. when of unknown origin.

psy·cho·phys·ics (sī′kō-fĭz′ĭks) *n. (used with a sing. verb).* The psychological study of the relationships between physical stimuli and sensory response. **—psy′cho·phys′i·cal** *adj.* **—psy′cho·phys′i·cal·ly** *adv.* **—psy′cho·phys′i·cist** (-fĭz′ĭ-sĭst) *n.*

psy·cho·phys·i·ol·o·gy (sī′kō-fĭz′ē-ŏl′ə-jē) *n.* The study of correlations between behavior and physiology. **—psy′cho·phys′i·o·log′i·cal** (-fĭz′ē-ə-lŏj′ĭ-kəl), **psy′cho·phys′i·o·log′ic** *adj.* **—psy′cho·phys′i·ol′o·gist** *n.*

psy·cho·sis (sī-kō′sĭs) *n., pl.* **-ses** (-sēz′). Severe mental disorder, with or without organic damage, characterized by deterioration of normal intellectual and social functioning and by partial or complete withdrawal from reality.

psy·cho·so·cial (sī′kō-sō′shəl) *adj.* Involving aspects of both social and psychological behavior: *a child's psychosocial development.* **—psy′cho·so′cial·ly** *adv.*

psy·cho·so·mat·ic (sī′kə-sō-măt′ĭk) *adj.* **1.** Of or pertaining to phenomena that are both physiological and psychological; somatic and psychic. **2.** Of or pertaining to a partially or wholly psychogenic disease or physiological disorder. *—n.* One who experiences bodily symptoms as a result of mental conflict. **—psy′cho·so·mat′i·cal·ly** *adv.*

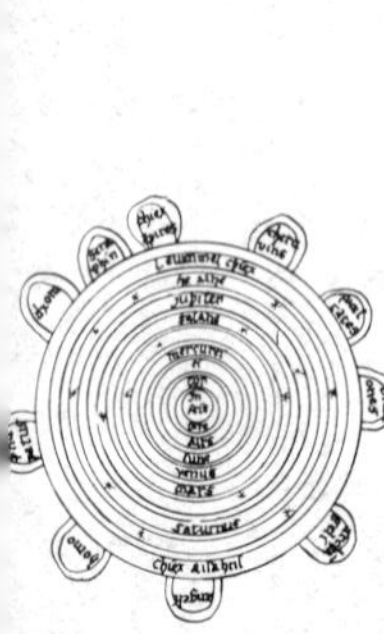

Ptolemaic system

psy·cho·sur·ger·y (sī′kō-sûr′jə-rē) *n.* Brain surgery when used to treat mental disorders. **—psy′cho·sur′geon** *n.* **—psy′cho·sur′gi·cal** *adj.*

psy·cho·tech·nics (sī′kō-tĕk′nĭks) *n. (used with a sing. verb).* The practical or technological use of psychology, as in analysis of social or industrial problems. **—psy′cho·tech′ni·cal** *adj.* **—psy′cho·tech·ni′cian** (-tĕk-nĭsh′ən) *n.*

psy·cho·ther·a·peu·tics (sī′kō-thĕr′ə-pyo͞o′tĭks) *n. (used with a sing. or pl. verb).* Psychotherapy.

psy·cho·ther·a·py (sī′kō-thĕr′ə-pē) *n.* The psychological treatment of mental, emotional, and nervous disorders. **—psy′cho·ther′a·peu′tic** (-pyo͞o′tĭk) *adj.* **—psy′cho·ther′a·peu′ti·cal·ly** *adv.* **—psy′cho·ther′a·pist** *n.*

psy·chot·ic (sī-kŏt′ĭk) *n.* One afflicted with a psychosis. *—adj.* Of, pertaining to, or caused by psychosis. [< PSYCHOSIS.] **—psy·chot′i·cal·ly** *adv.*

psy·chot·o·mi·met·ic (sī-kŏt′ō-mə-mĕt′ĭk, -mī-) *adj.* Pertaining to or inducing symptoms of a psychotic state. *—n.* A psychotomimetic agent. [PSYCHOT(IC) + MIMETIC.] **—psy·chot′o·mi·met′i·cal·ly** *adv.*

psy·cho·tro·pic (sī′kə-trō′pĭk, -trŏp′ĭk) *adj.* Having an altering effect on the mind.

psych-out (sīk′out′) *n. Informal.* An act or instance of undermining someone's confidence by psychological means.

psychro- *pref.* Cold: *psychrometer.* [< Gk. *psukhros,* cold.]

psy·chrom·e·ter (sī-krŏm′ĭ-tər) *n.* A hygrometer that uses the difference in readings between two thermometers, one having a wet bulb ventilated to cause evaporation and the other having a dry bulb, as a measure of atmospheric moisture.

psy·chro·phil·ic (sī′krō-fĭl′ĭk) *adj. Biol.* Thriving at relatively low temperatures, usually at or below 15°C. Used of certain bacteria.

psyl·la (sĭl′ə) also **psyl·lid** (sĭl′ĭd) *n.* Any of various plant lice of the family Chermidae (or Psyllidae), esp. *Psylla pyricola,* a pest that infests pear trees. [NLat. *Psylla,* genus name < Gk. *psulla,* flea.]

Pt The symbol for the element platinum.

ptar·mi·gan (tär′mĭ-gən) *n., pl.* **ptarmigan** or **-gans.** Any of various birds of the genus *Lagopus,* of the arctic and subarctic regions of the Northern Hemisphere, having feathered feet and plumage that is brownish in summer and white in winter. [Alteration of Sc. Gael. *tarmachan.*]

PT boat (pē-tē′) *n.* A fast, maneuverable, lightly armed vessel used to torpedo enemy shipping. [P(ATROL) + T(ORPEDO) BOAT.]

-pter *suff.* Wing; winglike part: *ornithopter.* [< Gk. *pteron,* wing.]

pter·i·dol·o·gy (tĕr′ĭ-dŏl′ə-jē) *n.* The study of ferns. [Gk. *pteris, pterid-,* fern (< *pteron,* feather) + -LOGY.] **—pter′i·do·log′i·cal** (-də-lŏj′ĭ-kəl) *adj.* **—pter′i·dol′o·gist** *n.*

pte·rid·o·phyte (tə-rĭd′ə-fīt′, tĕr′ĭ-dō-) *n.* Any of various plants of the division Pteridophyta, including the ferns, club mosses, and horsetails. [NLat. *Pteridophyta,* division name : Gk. *pteris,* fern (< *pteron,* feather) + Gk. *phuton,* plant.] **—pte·rid′o·phyt′ic** (tə-rĭd′ə-fĭt′ĭk, tĕr′ĭ-dō-), **pter′i·doph′y·tous** (tĕr′ĭ-dŏf′ĭ-təs) *adj.*

pter·o·cer·coid (tĕr′ə-sûr′koid′) *n.* The infective larva of some tapeworms, characterized by its solid elongated body. [Gk. *pteron,* wing + *kerkos,* tail + -OID.]

pter·o·dac·tyl (tĕr′ə-dăk′təl) *n.* Any of various extinct flying reptiles of the family Pterodactylidae. [NLat. *Pterodactylus,* reptile genus : Gk. *pteron,* wing + Gk. *daktulos,* finger.] **—pter′o·dac′ty·loid′** *adj.* **—pter′o·dac′ty·lous** *adj.*

pter·o·pod (tĕr′ə-pŏd′) *n.* Any of various small marine gastropod mollusks of the order Pteropoda that swim with winglike expanded lobes of the foot. [NLat. *Pteropoda,* order name < Gk. *pteropous,* wing-footed : *pteron,* wing + *pous,* foot.] **—pter′o·pod′** *adj.* **—pte·rop′o·dan** (tə-rŏp′ə-dən) *adj. & n.*

pter·o·saur (tĕr′ə-sôr′) *n.* Any of various extinct flying reptiles of the order Pterosauria, including the pterodactyls, of the Jurassic and Cretaceous periods, characterized by wings consisting of a flap of skin supported by the very long fourth digit on each front leg. [NLat. *Pterosauria,* order name : Gk. *pteron,* wing + Gk. *sauros,* lizard.]

pter·o·yl·glu·tam·ic acid (tĕr′ō-ĭl-glo͞o-tăm′ĭk) *n.* Folic acid. [E. *pteroic acid,* an amino acid + -YL + GLUTAMIC ACID.]

pter·y·goid (tĕr′ĭ-goid′) *adj. Anat.* Of or denoting either of two processes in the skull that are attached like wings to the body of the sphenoid bone. *—n.* Either of the pterygoid anatomical processes. [< Gk. *pterugoeidēs,* winglike : *pterux,* wing (< *pteron*) + *-eidēs,* -oid.]

ptis·an (tĭz′ən, tĭ-zăn′) *n.* A slightly medicinal infusion, such as barley water. [ME *tisan* < OFr. *tisane* < Lat. *ptisana* < Gk. *ptisanē* < *ptissein,* to crush.]

Ptol·e·ma·ic (tŏl′ə-mā′ĭk) *adj.* **1.** Of or pertaining to the astronomer Ptolemy. **2.** Of or pertaining to the Ptolemies or to Egypt during their rule (323–30 B.C.).

Ptolemaic system *n.* The astronomical system of Ptolemy, having the earth at the center of the universe, with the moon, planets, and stars revolving about it.

Ptol·e·ma·ist (tŏl′ə-mā′ĭst) *n.* An adherent of or believer in the Ptolemaic system.

pto·maine also **pto·main** (tō′mān′, tō-mān′) *n.* Any of various basic nitrogenous materials, some poisonous, produced by the putrefaction and decomposition of protein. [Ital. *ptomaina* < Gk. *ptōma,* corpse < *piptein,* to fall.]

ptomaine poisoning *n.* Food poisoning caused by bacteria or bacterial toxins.

pto·sis (tō′sĭs) *n., pl.* **-ses** (-sēz′). Abnormal and permanent lowering of an organ, esp. drooping of the upper eyelid caused by muscle failure. [Gk. *ptōsis,* fall < *piptein,* to fall.] **—pto′tic** *adj.*

pty·a·lin (tī′ə-lĭn) *n.* A salivary enzyme in man and some lower animals that hydrolyzes starch into maltose and various dextrins. [Gk. *ptualon,* saliva (< *ptuein,* to spit) + -IN.]

pty·a·lism (tī′ə-lĭz′əm) *n.* Excessive flow of saliva. [< Gk. *ptualon,* saliva < Gk. *ptuein,* to spit.]

Pu The symbol for the element plutonium.

pub (pŭb) *n.* A tavern; inn. [Short for PUBLIC HOUSE.]

pub-crawl (pŭb′krôl′) *intr.v.* **-crawled, -crawl·ing, -crawls.** *Slang.* To make the rounds of a series of bars.

pu·ber·ty (pyo͞o′bər-tē) *n.* **1.** The stage of maturation in which an individual becomes physiologically capable of sexual reproduction. **2.** The approach to maturity: *"Mankind will not reach puberty for another hundred thousand years"* (René Dubos). [ME *puberte* < Lat. *pubertas* < *puber,* adult < *pubes,* pubic hair.] **—pu′ber·tal, pu′ber·al** (pyo͞o′bər-əl) *adj.*

pu·ber·u·lent (pyo͞o-bĕr′yə-lənt, -bĕr′ə-) also **pu·ber·u·lous** (-bĕr′yə-ləs, -bĕr′ə-) *adj.* Covered with minute hairs or very fine down; finely pubescent. [< Lat. *puber,* downy < *pubes,* pubic hair.]

pu·bes (pyo͞o′bēz) *n., pl.* **pubes. 1.** The pubic region. **2.** The pubic hair. **3.** Plural of **pubis.** [Lat.]

pu·bes·cence (pyo͞o-bĕs′əns) *n.* **1. a.** A covering of soft down or short hairs, as on certain plants and insects. **b.** The state of being pubescent. **2.** The attainment or onset of puberty.

pu·bes·cent (pyo͞o-bĕs′ənt) *adj.* **1.** Covered with short hairs or soft down. **2.** Reaching or having reached puberty. [Fr. < Lat. *pubescens,* pr.part of *pubescere,* to reach puberty < *puber,* adult < *pubes,* pubic hair.]

pu·bic (pyo͞o′bĭk) *adj.* Of or in the region of the lower part of the abdomen, the pubis, or the pubes. [< PUBES.]

pu·bis (pyo͞o′bĭs) *n., pl.* **-bes** (-bēz). The forward portion of either of the hipbones, at the juncture forming the front arch of the pelvis. [NLat. *(os) pubis,* (bone) of the groin < *pubes,* groin.]

pub·lic (pŭb′lĭk) *adj.* **1.** Of, concerning, or affecting the community or the people: *the public good.* **2.** Maintained for or used by the people or community: *a public park.* **3.** Participated in or attended by the people or community: *a public lecture.* **4.** Connected with or acting on behalf of the people, community, or government rather than private matters or interests: *public office.* **5.** Open to the knowledge or judgment of all: *a public scandal.* —*n.* **1.** The community or the people as a whole. **2.** A group of people sharing a common interest: *the reading public.* **3.** Admirers or followers, esp. of a celebrity. [ME *publyk* < OFr. *public* < Lat. *publicus* < *populus,* people.] **—pub′lic·ness** *n.*

public access *n.* The availability of television or radio broadcast facilities, as provided by law, for use by the public for presentation of programs, as those of community interest.

pub·lic-ad·dress system (pŭb′lĭk-ə-drĕs′) *n.* An electronic amplification apparatus installed and used for broadcasting in public areas.

pub·li·can (pŭb′lĭ-kən) *n.* **1.** *Chiefly Brit.* The keeper of a public house; tavernkeeper. **2.** A collector of public taxes or tolls in the ancient Roman Empire. **3.** A collector of taxes or tribute from the public. [ME, tax collector < OFr. *publicain* < Lat. *publicanus* < *publicum,* public revenue < *publicus,* public < *populus,* people.]

public assistance *n.* Relief (sense 3).

pub·li·ca·tion (pŭb′lĭ-kā′shən) *n.* **1.** The act or process of publishing printed matter. **2.** An issue of printed material offered for sale or distribution. **3.** The communication of information to the public. [ME *publicacioun* < OFr. < LLat. *publicatio* < *publicare,* to make public < Lat. *publicus,* public < *populus,* people.]

public defender *n.* An attorney or staff of attorneys, usually publicly appointed, having responsibility for the legal defense of those unable to afford or obtain legal assistance.

public domain *n.* **1.** Land owned and controlled by the state or federal government. **2.** The status of publications, products, and processes that are not protected under patent or copyright.

public health *n.* The art and science of protecting and improving community health by means of preventive medicine, health education, communicable disease control, and the application of the social and sanitary sciences.

public house *n.* *Chiefly Brit.* A place, as a tavern or bar, licensed to sell alcoholic beverages.

pub·li·cist (pŭb′lĭ-sĭst) *n.* A person who publicizes, esp. a press or publicity agent.

pub·lic·i·ty (pŭ-blĭs′ĭ-tē) *n.* **1. a.** Information that concerns a person, group, event, or product and that is disseminated through various communications media to attract public notice. **b.** Public interest, notice, or notoriety achieved by the spreading of such information. **c.** The act, process, or occupation of disseminating information to gain public interest. **2.** The condition of being public. [Fr. *publicité* < *public,* public < OFr. —see PUBLIC.]

pub·li·cize (pŭb′lĭ-sīz′) *tr.v.* **-cized, -ciz·ing, -ciz·es.** To give publicity to.

public law *n.* **1.** The branch of law dealing with the state or government and its relationships with individuals or other governments. **2.** A law affecting the public.

public library *n.* A noncommercial library for the use of the general public, often supported by public funds.

pub·lic·ly (pŭb′lĭk-lē) *adv.* **1.** In a public manner; openly. **2.** By or with consent of the public.

public prosecutor *n.* A government official who prosecutes criminal actions on behalf of the state or community.

public relations *pl.n.* **1.** The methods and activities employed to promote a favorable relationship with the public. **2.** The degree of success obtained in achieving a favorable relationship with the public. **3.** The staff employed to promote a favorable relationship with the public. **4.** The art or science of establishing a favorable relationship with the public.

public sale *n.* An auction (sense 1).

public school *n.* **1.** In the United States, an elementary or secondary school supported by public funds and providing free education for children of a community or district. **2.** In Great Britain, a private boarding school for pupils between the ages of thirteen and eighteen.

public servant *n.* A person who holds a government position by election or by appointment.

public service *n.* **1.** Employment within a governmental system, esp. within the civil services. **2.** A service performed for the benefit of the public.

pub·lic-serv·ice corporation (pŭb′lĭk-sûr′vĭs) *n.* A corporation providing utilities for the public.

public speaking *n.* The art or process of making speeches before an audience. **—public speaker** *n.*

pub·lic-spir·it·ed (pŭb′lĭk-spĭr′ĭ-tĭd) *adj.* Motivated by or showing devotion to the public welfare. **—pub′lic-spir′it·ed·ness** *n.*

public television *n.* Noncommercial television that provides programs, esp. of an educational nature, for the public.

public utility *n.* **1.** A private business organization, subject to governmental regulation, that provides an essential service or commodity, such as water, electricity, transportation, or communication, to the public. **2.** Often **public utilities.** Stock shares issued by a company providing essential public services.

public works *pl.n.* Construction projects, such as highways or dams, financed by public funds and constructed by a government for the benefit or use of the general public.

pub·lish (pŭb′lĭsh) *v.* **-lished, -lish·ing, -lish·es.** —*tr.* **1.** To prepare and issue (printed material) for public distribution or sale. **2.** To bring to the public attention; announce. —*intr.* **1.** To issue a publication. **2.** To be the author of a published work or works. [ME *publishen* < OFr. *publier* < LLat. *publicare,* to make public. —see PUBLICATION.] **—pub′lish·a·ble** *adj.*

pub·lish·er (pŭb′lĭ-shər) *n.* One that is engaged in publishing printed material.

puc·coon (pə-ko͞on′) *n.* **1. a.** Any of several North American plants of the genus *Lithospermum,* yielding a red or yellow dye, esp. *L. canescens,* having orange flowers. **b.** Any of several other plants yielding a reddish dye, as the bloodroot. **2.** The dye from a puccoon. [Algonquian *pocoon.*]

puce (pyo͞os) *n.* A deep red to dark grayish purple. [Fr. *(couleur) puce,* flea (color) < Lat. *pulex,* flea.] **—puce** *adj.*

puck (pŭk) *n.* A hard rubber disk used in ice hockey as the playing and scoring medium. [Prob. < dial. *puck,* to strike, var. of POKE[1].]

Puck (pŭk) *n.* A mischievous sprite in English folklore. [ME *pouke* < OE *pūca.*]

puck·a (pŭk′ə) *n.* Variant of **pukka.**

puck·er (pŭk′ər) *v.* **-ered, -er·ing, -ers.** —*tr.* To gather into small wrinkles or folds. —*intr.* To become contracted and wrinkled. —*n.* A wrinkle or wrinkled part, as in tightly stitched cloth. [Perh. < POCKET.]

puck·ish (pŭk′ĭsh) *adj.* Mischievous; impish: *a puckish grin.* **—puck′ish·ly** *adv.* **—puck′ish·ness** *n.*

pud·ding (po͝od′ĭng) *n.* **1. a.** A sweet dessert, usually containing flour or a cereal product, that has been boiled, steamed, or baked. **b.** A mixture with a soft, puddinglike consistency. **2.** A sausagelike preparation made with minced meat or various other ingredients stuffed into a bag or skin and boiled. [ME < OFr. *boudin* < Lat. *botulus,* sausage.]

pudding stone *n.* A conglomerate (sense 2).

pud·dle (pŭd′l) *n.* **1. a.** A small pool of water. **b.** A small pool of a liquid. **2.** A tempered paste of wet clay and sand used as waterproofing. —*v.* **-dled, -dling, -dles.** —*tr.* **1.** To make muddy. **2.** To work (clay or sand) into a thick, watertight paste. **3.** To process (impure metal) by puddling. —*intr.* To splash or dabble in or as if in a puddle. [ME *podel,* dim. of OE *pudd,* ditch.] **—pud′dly** *adj.*

puddle duck *n.* A dabbler.

pud·dler (pŭd′lər) *n.* One who puddles iron or clay.

pud·dling (pŭd′lĭng) *n.* **1.** The purification of impure metal, esp. pig iron, by agitation of a molten bath of the metal in an oxidizing atmosphere. **2.** Compaction of wet material, as clay, to make a watertight paste.

pu·den·cy (pyo͞od'n-sē) *n.* Modesty. [LLat. *pudentia* < Lat. *pudēre,* to be ashamed.]

pu·den·dum (pyo͞o-dĕn'dəm) *n., pl.* **-da** (-də). **1.** A woman's external genital organs; vulva. **2. pudenda.** The external genital organs of either sex. [Lat., neuter gerund. of *pudēre,* to be ashamed.] **—pu·den'dal** *adj.*

pudg·y (pŭj'ē) *adj.* **-i·er, -i·est.** Short and fat; chubby: *pudgy fingers.* [Orig. unknown.] **—pudg'i·ness** *n.*

pueb·lo (pwĕb'lō) *n., pl.* **-los. 1.** A community dwelling, up to five stories high, built of stone or adobe by Indian tribes of the southwestern United States. **2. Pueblo** *pl.* **Pueblo** or **-los.** A member of a tribe, such as the Hopi or Zuñi, inhabiting pueblos. **3.** An Indian village of the southwestern United States. [Sp., pueblo, people < Lat. *populus,* people.]

pu·er·ile (pyo͞o'ər-əl, pyo͝or'əl, -īl') *adj.* **1.** Belonging to childhood; juvenile. **2.** Immature; childish. [Fr. *puéril* < Lat. *puerilis* < *puer,* child.] **—pu'er·ile·ly** *adv.* **—pu'er·ile·ness, pu'er·il'i·ty** (-ĭl'ĭ-tē) *n.*

puffball

pu·er·per·al (pyo͞o-ûr'pər-əl) *adj.* Connected with, resulting from, or following childbirth. [< Lat. *puerperus,* bearing children : *puer,* child + *parēre,* to bear.]

puerperal fever *n.* Infection of the endometrium and of the bloodstream following childbirth.

pu·er·pe·ri·um (pyo͞o'ər-pîr'ē-əm) *n., pl.* **-ri·a** (-ē-ə). **1.** The state of a woman while bearing a child or immediately thereafter. **2.** The approximate six-week period from childbirth to return of normal uterine size. [Lat., childbirth < *puerperus,* bearing children. —see PUERPERAL.]

puff (pŭf) *n.* **1. a.** A short, forceful exhalation of breath. **b.** A short, sudden gust of wind. **c.** A brief, sudden emission of air, vapor, or smoke. **d.** A short, sibilant sound produced by a puff. **2.** An amount of vapor, smoke, or similar material released in a puff. **3.** An act of drawing in and expelling the breath, as in smoking tobacco. **4.** A swelling or rounded protuberance. **5.** A light, inflated pastry, often filled with custard or cream. **6.** A light, soft pad for applying cosmetic powder. **7.** A soft roll of hair forming part of a coiffure. **8.** A gathered and protruding portion of fabric. **9.** A light, padded bed covering. **10.** An approving or flattering recommendation. *—v.* **puffed, puff·ing, puffs.** *—intr.* **1.** To blow in puffs. **2.** To come forth in puffs. **3.** To breathe forcefully and rapidly. **4.** To emit puffs. **5.** To take puffs on a cigarette, pipe, or cigar. **6.** To swell or seem to swell, as with air or pride. *—tr.* **1.** To emit or give forth in puffs. **2.** To impel with puffs. **3.** To smoke (a cigar, for example). **4.** To inflate or distend. **5.** To fill with pride or conceit. **6.** To publicize with exaggerated praise. [ME *puffen* < OE *pyffan.*] **—puff'i·ly** *adv.* **—puff'i·ness** *n.* **—puff'y** *adj.*

puffin

puff adder *n.* **1.** A venomous African viper, *Bitis arietans,* having crescent-shaped yellowish markings. **2.** The hognose snake. [So called because it inflates its body when excited.]

puff·ball (pŭf'bôl') *n.* **1.** Any of various fungi of the genus *Lycoperdon* and related genera, having a ball-shaped fruiting body that when broken open releases the enclosed spores in puffs of dust. **2.** *Informal.* The rounded head of a dandelion that has gone to seed.

puffed-up (pŭft'ŭp') *adj.* Characterized by an exaggerated show of dignity or self-importance; pompous.

puff·er (pŭf'ər) *n.* **1.** One that puffs. **2.** Any of various marine fishes of the family Tetraodontidae that are capable of swelling up.

puff·er·y (pŭf'ə-rē) *n.* Favorable and often exaggeratedly flattering publicity, esp. for promotional purposes.

puf·fin (pŭf'ĭn) *n.* Any of several sea birds of the genera *Fratercula* and *Lunda,* of northern regions, characteristically having black and white plumage and a vertically flattened, brightly colored bill. [ME *poffoun.*]

puff pastry *n.* Dough that is rolled and folded in layers and that expands in baking to form light, flaky pastry.

pug[1] (pŭg) *n.* **1.** A small dog of a breed originating in China, having a snub nose, a wrinkled face, a square body, short smooth hair, and a curled tail. **2.** A pug nose. [Orig. unknown.]

pug[2] (pŭg) *n.* **1.** Clay ground and kneaded with water into a plastic consistency for forming bricks or pottery. **2.** A machine for grinding and mixing clay. *—tr.v.* **pugged, pug·ging, pugs. 1.** To work or knead (clay) with water. **2.** To fill in with clay or mortar. **3.** To make soundproof by covering or packing with clay, mortar, sawdust, or felt. [Orig. unknown.]

pug[1]

pug[3] (pŭg) *n.* A footprint, track, or trail, esp. of an animal. [Hindi *pag,* prob. < Skt. *padakam,* step, pace < *padam,* foot.]

pug[4] (pŭg) *n. Slang.* A boxer. [Short for PUGILIST.]

pug·gree (pŭg'rē) also **pug·ga·ree** or **pug·a·ree** (pŭg'ə-rē) *n.* A cloth band or scarf wrapped around the crown of a hat or sun helmet. [Hindi *pagṛī.*]

pu·gi·lism (pyo͞o'jə-lĭz'əm) *n.* The skill or practice of fighting with the fists; boxing. [< Lat. *pugil,* boxer.] **—pu'gi·list** *n.* **—pu'gi·lis'tic** *adj.*

pu·gil stick (pyo͞o'jəl) *n.* A long pole with padded ends used in the armed forces to simulate bayonet fighting. [Lat. *pugil,* boxer + STICK.]

pug·mark (pŭg'märk') *n.* Pug[3].

pug·na·cious (pŭg-nā'shəs) *adj.* Eager to fight; having a quarrelsome disposition. [Lat. *pugnax, pugnac-* < *pugnare,* to fight < *pugnus,* fist.] **—pug·na'cious·ly** *adv.* **—pug·na'cious·ness, pug·nac'i·ty** (-năs'ĭ-tē) *n.*

pug nose *n.* A short nose that is somewhat flattened and turned up at the end. [Prob. < PUG[1].] **—pug'-nosed'** *adj.*

puis·ne (pyo͞o'nē) *Chiefly Brit. Law.* Lower in rank; junior. *—n.* One of lesser rank, esp. an associate judge. [Norman Fr. *puisne* < OFr. : *puis,* afterward (< Lat. *post*) + *ne,* born < Lat. *nasci,* to be born.]

puis·sance (pwĭs'əns, pyo͞o'ĭ-səns, pyo͞o-ĭs'əns) *n.* Power; might. **—puis'sant** *adj.* **—puis'sant·ly** *adv.*

puke (pyo͞ok) *intr. & tr.v.* **puked, puk·ing, pukes.** To vomit or vomit up. *—n.* **1.** Vomit. **2.** The act of vomiting. [Prob. imit.]

puk·ka also **puck·a** (pŭk'ə) *adj.* **1.** Genuine; authentic. **2.** Superior; first-class. [Hindi *pakkā,* cooked, ripe, firm < Skt. *pakva-,* p.part. of *pacati,* he cooked.]

pul (po͞ol) *n., pl.* **puls** or **pu·li** (po͞o'lē). See table at **currency.** [Pers. *pūl.*]

pul·chri·tude (pŭl'krĭ-to͞od', -tyo͞od') *n.* Physical beauty and appeal. [ME *pulcritude* < Lat. *pulchritūdō* < *pulcher,* beautiful.]

pul·chri·tu·di·nous (pŭl'krĭ-to͞od'n-əs, -tyo͞od'-) *adj.* Characterized by or having pulchritude.

pule (pyo͞ol) *intr.v.* **puled, pul·ing, pules.** To whine; whimper. [Perh. < Fr. *piauler.*] **—pul'er** *n.*

pu·li[1] (po͞ol'ē, pyo͞o'lē) *n., pl.* **pu·lis** or **pu·lik** (po͞ol'ĕk, pyo͞o'lĕk). A long-haired sheep dog of a Hungarian breed. [Hung.]

pu·li[2] (po͞o'lē) *n.* A plural of **pul.**

pu·li·cide (pyo͞o'lĭ-sīd') *n.* An agent that destroys fleas. [Lat. *pulex, pulic-,* flea + -CIDE.]

pu·lik (po͞ol'ĕk, pyo͞o'lĕk) *n.* A plural of **puli[1].**

Pu·lit·zer Prize (po͝ol'ĭt-sər, pyo͞o'lĭt-) *n.* Any of several awards established by Joseph Pulitzer and conferred annually for accomplishment in various fields of American journalism, literature, and music.

pull (po͝ol) *v.* **pulled, pull·ing, pulls.** *—tr.* **1.** To apply force to so as to cause or tend to cause motion toward the source of the force. **2.** To remove from a fixed position; extract: *pull teeth.* **3.** To tug at; jerk or tweak. **4.** To rip or tear; rend. **5.** To stretch (taffy, for example) repeatedly. **6.** To strain (a muscle, for example) injuriously. **7.** *Informal.* To attract; draw: *a performer who pulls large crowds.* **8.** *Slang.* To draw out (a knife or gun) in readiness for use. **9.** *Informal.* To use less than full force in delivering (a punch); soften. **10.** *Baseball.* To hit (a ball) in the direction one is facing when the swing is carried through. **11. a.** To operate (an oar) in rowing. **b.** To transport or propel by rowing. **c.** To be rowed by: *That boat pulls six oars.* **12.** To rein in (a horse) to keep it from winning a race. **13.** *Printing.* To produce (a print or impression) from type. *—intr.* **1.** To exert force in pulling something. **2.** To move: *The bus pulled away from the curb.* **3.** To drink or inhale deeply. **4.** To row a boat. ***—phrasal verbs.*** **pull away. 1.** To move backward or away; withdraw. **2.** To move ahead: *The horse pulled away and took the lead in the race.* **pull down. 1.** To demolish; destroy: *pull down an old house.* **2.** To reduce to a lower level. **3.** To depress, as in spirits or health. **4.** *Informal.* To draw (money) as wages: *pulled down a fine salary.* **pull for.** To work, hope, or cheer for the success of. **pull in. 1.** To arrive at a destination: *We pulled in at midnight.* **2.** To rein in; restrain. **3.** *Informal.* To arrest: *The police pulled in three suspects for questioning.* **pull off.** *Informal.* To perform in spite of difficulties or obstacles; bring off: *pulled off a last-minute win.* **pull out.** To withdraw from a situation or commitment. **pull over.** To bring a vehicle to a stop at a curb or at the side of a road. **pull round.** To restore or be restored to sound health. **pull through.** To come or bring successfully through trouble or illness. **pull up. 1.** To bring or come to a halt. **2.** To move to a position or place ahead, as in a race. *—n.* **1.** The action or process of pulling. **2.** Force exerted in pulling or required to overcome resistance in pulling. **3.** A sustained effort: *a long pull across the mountains.* **4.** Something used for pulling, as a knob on a drawer. **5.** A deep inhalation or draft, as on a cigar. **6.** *Slang.* A means of gaining special advantage; influence: *He has pull with the boss.* **7.** *Informal.* Ability to draw or attract; appeal: *a star with pull at the box office.* ***—idioms.*** **pull a fast one.** *Informal.* To play a trick or perpetrate a fraud. **pull (one's) punch (or punches).** To refrain from utilizing all the force and resources at one's disposal: *didn't pull any punches during the negotiations.* **pull (oneself) together.** To regain one's composure. **pull (one's) weight.** To do one's own share, as of work. **pull (someone's) leg.** To play a joke on; tease. **pull strings (or wires).** To exert secret control or influence in order to gain an end. **pull the rug (out) from under.** To remove all support and assistance from, usually suddenly. **pull the wool over (someone's) eyes.** To deceive; hoodwink. **pull together.** To make a joint effort; cooperate. **pull up stakes.** To leave; move out: *pulled up stakes and moved to the West.* [ME *pullen* < OE *pullian.*] **—pull'er** *n.*

pull·back (po͝ol'băk') *n.* **1.** The act or process of pulling something back, esp. an orderly troop withdrawal. **2.** A device for holding or drawing something back.

pull date *n.* A date stamped on a packaged food product after which it should not be sold.

pul·let (pōōl′ĭt) *n.* A young hen, esp. of the common domestic fowl, usually less than one year old. [ME *pulet* < OFr. *poulet,* dim. of *poul,* cock and *poule,* hen, both < Lat. *pullus,* chicken.]

pul·ley (pōōl′ē) *n., pl.* **-leys. 1.** A simple machine used to change the direction and point of application of a pulling force, esp. for lifting weight, consisting essentially of a wheel with a grooved rim in which a pulled rope or chain is run. **2.** A wheel turned by or driving a belt. [ME *poley* < OFr. *polie,* ult. < Gk. *polos,* axis.]

pulley

Pull·man (pōōl′mən) *n.* **1.** A railroad parlor car or sleeping car. **2.** A large suitcase. [After George M. *Pullman* (1831–1897).]

pull-on (pōōl′ŏn′, -ôn′) *n.* A garment, as a sweater or pants, designed to be pulled on.

pul·lo·rum disease (pə-lôr′əm, -lōr′-) *n.* A severe contagious diarrhea of young poultry, caused by the bacterium *Salmonella pullorum.* [NLat. *pullorum,* specific epithet of *Salmonella pullorum* < Lat., genitive pl. of *pullus,* chicken.]

pull·out (pōōl′out′) *n.* **1.** A withdrawal, esp. of troops. **2.** The change from a dive to level flight in aviation. **3.** Something designed to be pulled out.

pull·o·ver (pōōl′ō′vər) *n.* A garment, such as a sweater, that must be put on by being drawn over the head.

pul·lu·late (pŭl′yə-lāt′) *intr.v.* **-lat·ed, -lat·ing, -lates. 1.** To put forth sprouts; germinate. **2.** To breed rapidly or abundantly. **3.** To teem; swarm. [Lat. *pullulare, pullulat-* < *pullulus,* dim. of *pullus,* chicken.] **—pul′lu·la′tion** *n.* **—pul′lu·la′tive** *adj.*

pull-up (pōōl′ŭp′) *n.* An exercise for strengthening the arms, performed by hanging by the hands from an overhead bar and pulling the body upward until the chin is even with or above the bar.

pul·mo·nar·y (pōōl′mə-nĕr′ē, pŭl′-) *adj.* **1.** Of or pertaining to the lungs. **2.** Having lungs or lunglike organs. [Lat. *pulmonarius* < *pulmo,* lung.]

pulmonary artery *n.* An artery in which blood travels directly from the heart to the lungs.

pulmonary vein *n.* One of four veins in which blood travels directly from the lungs to the heart.

pul·mo·nate (pōōl′mə-nāt′, pŭl′-) *adj.* **1.** Having lungs or lunglike organs. **2.** Relating to the Pulmonata, an order of gastropods including snails and slugs, in which the mantle cavity is modified to function as a lung. *—n.* A member of the Pulmonata. [NLat. *pulmonatus* < Lat. *pulmo,* lung.]

pul·mon·ic (pōōl-mŏn′ĭk, pŭl-) *adj.* Of or pertaining to the lungs; pulmonary.

pulp (pŭlp) *n.* **1.** A soft, moist, shapeless mass of matter. **2.** The soft, moist part of fruit. **3.** A mass of pressed vegetable matter: *apple pulp.* **4.** The soft pith forming the contents of the stem of a plant. **5.** A mixture of cellulose material, such as wood, paper, and rags, ground up and moistened to make paper. **6.** The soft inner structure of a tooth, consisting of nerve and blood vessels. **7.** A mixture of powdered ore and water. **8.** A magazine or book containing lurid subject matter. *—v.* **pulped, pulp·ing, pulps.** *—tr.* **1.** To reduce to pulp. **2.** To remove the pulp from. *—intr.* To become reduced to a pulpy consistency. [Lat. *pulpa,* flesh.] **—pulp′i·ness** *n.* **—pulp′ous** (pŭl′pəs), **pulp′y** *adj.*

pul·pit (pōōl′pĭt, pŭl′-) *n.* **1.** An elevated platform, lectern, or stand used in preaching or conducting a religious service. **2.** A raised platform, such as one used by harpooners in a whaling boat. **3. a.** Clergymen collectively. **b.** The ministry of preaching. [ME < Lat. *pulpitum,* platform.]

pulp·wood (pŭlp′wōōd′) *n.* Soft wood, such as spruce, aspen, or pine, used in making paper.

pul·que (pōōl′kā′, -kē, pōōl′-) *n.* A fermented, milky beverage made in Mexico from various species of agave. [Mex. Sp. < Nahuatl *poliuhqui,* decomposed.]

pul·sar (pŭl′sär′) *n. Astron.* Any of several very short-period variable galactic radio sources generally believed to be rotating neutron stars. [PULSE + (STELL)AR.]

pul·sate (pŭl′sāt′) *intr.v.* **-sat·ed, -sat·ing, -sates. 1.** To expand and contract rhythmically; throb. **2.** To quiver. [Lat. *pulsare, pulsat-,* freq. of *pellere,* to beat.]

Synonyms: *pulsate, beat, palpitate, throb.* These verbs refer to recurrent, rhythmical movement such as that involved in the action of the heart. *Pulsate,* which is largely technical in application, and *beat* imply regular and vigorous movement. *Beat* often also suggests rhythmical sound. *Palpitate* applies to excessively rapid movement or pulsation; usually it also implies irregular movement, such as fluttering. *Throb* emphasizes both rapidity and strength of pulsation; the term is especially associated with physical or emotional stress.

pul·sa·tile (pŭl′sə-təl, -tīl′) *adj.* Pulsating; vibrating. [Med. Lat. *pulsatilis* < Lat. *pulsare,* freq. of *pellere,* to beat.]

pul·sa·tion (pŭl-sā′shən) *n.* **1.** The act of pulsating. **2.** A single beat, throb, or vibration.

pul·sa·tor (pŭl′sā′tər, pŭl-sā′-) *n.* A pulsating device or machine.

pul·sa·to·ry (pŭl′sə-tôr′ē, -tōr′ē) *adj.* Having rhythmical vibration or movement; pulsating.

pulse[1] (pŭls) *n.* **1.** *Physiol.* The rhythmical throbbing of arteries produced by the regular contractions of the heart. **2.** A regular or rhythmical beating. **3.** A single throb or beat. **4.** *Physics & Electronics.* A transient amplification or intensification of a characteristic of a system, esp. of a wave characteristic, followed by return to equilibrium or steady state: *a signal pulse; beam pulse.* **5.** The perceptible emotions or sentiments of a group of people: *the pulse of the electorate.* *—intr.v.* **pulsed, puls·ing, puls·es.** To pulsate. [ME *pous* < OFr. < Lat. *pulsus* < *pellere,* to beat.] **—pulse′less** *adj.*

pulse[2] (pŭls) *n.* **1.** The edible seeds of certain pod-bearing plants, such as peas and beans. **2.** A plant yielding pulse. [ME *pols* < OFr. < Lat. *puls,* pottage of meal and pulse.]

pulse·jet (pŭls′jĕt′) *n.* A jet engine in which air intake and combustion occur intermittently, producing rapid periodic bursts of thrusts.

pulse modulation *n.* Modulation by coded variation of the amplitude or other characteristic of wave pulses.

pul·sim·e·ter (pŭl-sĭm′ĭ-tər) also **pul·som·e·ter** (-sŏm′-) *n. Med.* An instrument that measures the frequency or strength of the pulse.

pul·som·e·ter (pŭl-sŏm′ĭ-tər) *n.* **1.** A pump for raising water by the pulsed condensation of steam. **2.** Variant of **pulsimeter.**

pul·ver·a·ble (pŭl′vər-ə-bəl) *adj.* Capable of being pulverized.

pul·ver·ize (pŭl′və-rīz′) *v.* **-ized, -iz·ing, -iz·es.** *—tr.* **1.** To pound, crush, or grind to a powder or dust. **2.** To demolish. *—intr.* To be ground or reduced to powder or dust. [LLat. *pulverizare* < Lat. *pulvis,* dust.] **—pul′ver·iz′a·ble** *adj.* **—pul′ver·i·za′tion** *n.* **—pul′ver·iz′er** *n.*

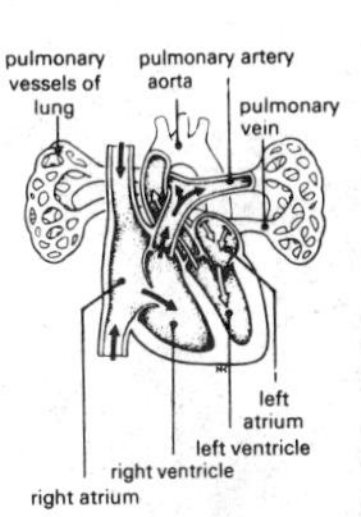

pulmonary
Pulmonary circulation

pul·ver·u·lent (pŭl-vĕr′yə-lənt, -vĕr′ə-) *adj.* **1.** Made of, covered with, or crumbling to fine powder or dust. **2.** Dusty; crumbly. [Lat. *pulverulentus,* dusty < *pulvis,* dust.]

pul·vil·lus (pŭl-vĭl′əs) *n., pl.* **-vil·li** (-vĭl′ī′). One of the soft, cushionlike pads between the claws of an insect's foot. [Lat., dim. of *pulvinus,* cushion.]

pul·vi·nate (pŭl′və-nāt′) also **pul·vi·nat·ed** (-nā′tĭd) *adj.* **1.** Cushion-shaped. **2.** *Bot.* Having a swelling at the base. Used of a leafstalk. [Lat. *pulvinatus* < *pulvinus,* cushion.]

pul·vi·nus (pŭl-vī′nəs, -vē′-) *n., pl.* **-ni** (nī′). *Bot.* A swelling of the stem at the base of a leafstalk. [Lat., cushion.]

pu·ma (pyōō′mə, pōō′-) *n.* The mountain lion. [Sp. < Quechua *poma.*]

pum·ice (pŭm′ĭs) *n.* A porous, lightweight volcanic rock used in solid form as an abrasive and in powdered form as a polish and abrasive. *—tr.v.* **-iced, -ic·ing, -ic·es.** To clean, polish, or smooth with pumice. [ME *pomys* < OFr. *pomis* < Lat. *pumex.*] **—pu·mi′ceous** (pyōō-mĭsh′əs, pə-) *adj.* **—pum′ic·er** *n.*

pum·mel (pŭm′əl) *tr.v.* **-meled, -mel·ing, -mels** also **-melled, -mel·ling, -mels.** To beat; pommel. *—n.* An act of pummeling; pommel.

pump[1] (pŭmp) *n.* **1.** A machine or device for transferring a liquid or gas from a source or container through tubes or pipes to another container or receiver. **2. a.** *Biochem.* A biochemical mechanism for transporting ions, atoms, or molecules against a concentration gradient by an expenditure of energy. **b.** The process of such transport. **3.** *Physics.* Electromagnetic radiation used to raise atoms or molecules to a higher energy level. *—v.* **pumped, pump·ing, pumps.** *—tr.* **1.** To raise or cause to flow by means of a pump. **2.** To inflate with gas by means of a pump: *pump up a tire.* **3.** To remove the water from: *pump out a flooded basement.* **4.** To cause to operate with the up-and-down motion of a pump handle. **5.** To propel, eject, or insert with or as if with a pump. **6.** *Physics.* To supply (a laser) with sufficient energy to achieve population inversion. **7.** *Physics.* To raise atoms or molecules to a higher energy level by exposing them to electromagnetic radiation at a resonant frequency. **8.** *Biochem.* To transport ions, atoms, or molecules against a concentration gradient by the expenditure of chemically stored energy. **9.** To question closely or persistently: *pump a witness.* *—intr.* **1.** To operate a pump. **2.** To raise or move gas or liquid with a pump. **3.** To move up and down in the manner of a pump handle. [ME *pumpe.*] **—pump′er** *n.*

pump[2] (pŭmp) *n.* A low-cut shoe without fastenings. [Orig. unknown.]

pumped storage *n.* A system of generating electricity using hydroelectric power in which electricity is generated during the hours of peak consumption by using water that has been pumped into an elevated reservoir during the hours of low consumption.

pum·per·nick·el (pŭm′pər-nĭk′əl) *n.* A dark, sourish bread made from whole, coarsely ground rye. [G.]

pump·kin (pŭmp′kĭn, pŭm′-, pŭng′-) *n.* **1. a.** A coarse, trailing vine, *Cucurbita pepo,* widely cultivated for its fruit. **b.** The large, pulpy round fruit of this vine, having a thick, orange-yellow rind and numerous seeds. **c.** Either of two similar vines, *C. maxima* or *C. moschata,* bearing large, pumpkinlike squashes. **2.** A moderate to strong orange. [Alteration of obs. *pumpion* < OFr. *pompon* < Lat. *pepo* < Gk. *pepōn,* large melon < *pepōn,* ripe < *peptein,* to ripen.]

pump·kin·seed (pŭmp′kĭn-sēd′, pŭm′-, pŭng′-) *n.* **1.** The seed of the pumpkin. **2.** A North American sunfish, *Lepomis gibbosus,* having brightly colored markings.

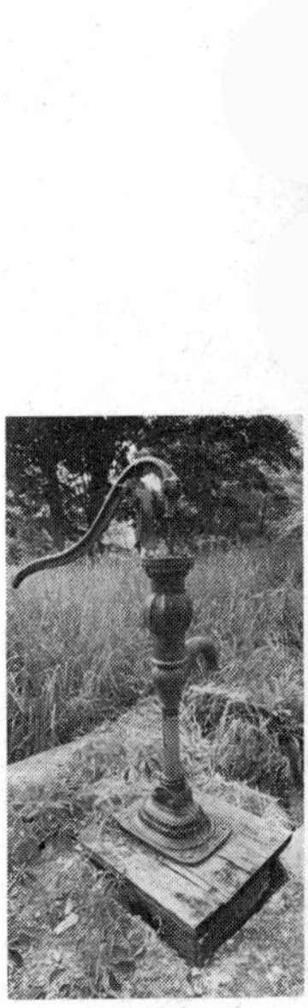
pump[1]

pun (pŭn) *n.* A play on words, sometimes on different senses of the same word and sometimes on the similar sense or sound of different words. —*intr.v.* **punned, pun·ning, puns.** To make a pun. [Orig. unknown.] —**pun'ning·ly** *adv.*

punch[1] (pŭnch) *n.* **1.** A tool for circular or other shaped piercing: *a leather punch.* **2.** A tool for forcing a pin, bolt, or rivet in or out of a hole. **3.** A tool for stamping a design on a surface. **4.** A countersink. —*v.* **punched, punch·ing, punch·es.** —*tr.* To use a punch on; perforate or mark. —*intr.* To use a punch. [Short for PUNCHEON[1].]

punch[2] (pŭnch) *tr.v.* **punched, punch·ing, punch·es. 1.** To hit with a sharp blow of the fist. **2.** To poke or prod with a stick. —***phrasal verbs.* punch in.** To check in formally at a job before a day's work. **punch out. 1.** To check out formally at a job before leaving after a day's work. **2.** *Slang.* To eject from a military aircraft. **3.** *Western U.S.* To herd (cattle). —*n.* **1.** A blow with the fist. **2.** Vigor or drive. —***idiom.* beat to the punch.** To make the first decisive move. [ME *punchen.*] —**punch'er** *n.* —**punch'less** *adj.*

punch[3] (pŭnch) *n.* A sweetened beverage of fruit juices, often spiced, usually with a wine or liquor base. [Perh. < Hindi *pānch* < Skt. *pañca-*, five (from its originally having been prepared from five ingredients).]

Punch (pŭnch) *n.* The quarrelsome hook-nosed husband of Judy in the comic puppet show *Punch and Judy.* —***idiom.* pleased as Punch.** Highly pleased; gratified. [Short for PUNCHINELLO.]

punch·board (pŭnch'bord', -bōrd') *n.* A small, usually rectangular board, used as a game of chance, that contains many holes each filled with a folded slip of paper that when punched out indicates a designated prize, win, or loss.

punch bowl *n.* A large bowl used for serving a beverage, as punch.

punch card also **punched card** *n.* A card punched with holes or notches to represent letters and numbers or with a pattern of holes to represent related data, for use in a computer.

punch-drunk (pŭnch'drŭngk') *adj.* **1.** Behaving in a bewildered, confused, or dazed manner. **2.** Showing signs of brain damage caused by repeated blows to the head in boxing.

pun·cheon[1] (pŭn'chən) *n.* **1.** A short, wooden upright used in structural framing. **2.** A piece of broad, heavy timber, roughly dressed, with one face finished flat. **3.** A punching, perforating, or stamping tool, esp. one used by a goldsmith. [ME *ponson,* a sharp tool < OFr. *poinçon* < Lat. *pungere,* to prick.]

pun·cheon[2] (pŭn'chən) *n.* **1.** A cask with a capacity of approximately 318 liters, or 84 U.S. gallons. **2.** The amount of liquid contained in a puncheon. [OFr. *poinçon.*]

punch·er (pŭn'chər) *n.* **1.** One that punches. **2.** A cowboy; cowpuncher.

Pun·chi·nel·lo (pŭn'chə-nĕl'ō) *n., pl.* **-los** or **-loes. 1.** The short, fat buffoon or clown in an Italian puppet show. **2.** Someone thought to resemble a short, fat puppet. [Orig. unknown.]

punching bag *n.* A stuffed or inflated leather bag that is usually suspended so that it can be punched with the fists for exercise.

punch line *n.* The climax of a joke or humorous story.

punch-out (pŭnch'out') *n.* A section of material, as cardboard, that is scored or perforated so that it may easily be pushed out.

punch press *n.* A power press that can be fitted with various dies, as for metalworking.

punch tape *n.* Paper tape in which holes representing data to be processed by computer are punched.

punch-up (pŭnch'ŭp') *n.* *Chiefly Brit.* A fist fight.

punch·y (pŭn'chē) *adj.* **-i·er, -i·est.** Groggy or dazed from or as if from a punch or series of punches; punch-drunk. —**punch'i·ly** *adv.* —**punch'i·ness** *n.*

punc·tate (pŭngk'tāt') also **punc·tat·ed** (-tā'tĭd) *adj.* Having tiny spots, points, or depressions. [NLat. *punctatus* < Lat. *punctum,* prick mark < *pungere,* to prick.] —**punc·ta'tion** *n.*

punc·til·i·o (pŭngk-tĭl'ē-ō') *n., pl.* **-os. 1.** A fine point of etiquette. **2.** Precise observance of formalities. [Ital. *punctiglio,* dim. of *punto,* point < Lat. *punctum* < *pungere,* to prick.]

punc·til·i·ous (pŭngk-tĭl'ē-əs) *adj.* **1.** Attentive to the finer points of etiquette and formal conduct. **2.** Precise; scrupulous. —**punc·til'i·ous·ly** *adv.* —**punc·til'i·ous·ness** *n.*

punc·tu·al (pŭngk'cho͞o-əl) *adj.* **1.** Acting or arriving exactly at the time appointed; prompt. **2.** Paid or accomplished at or by the appointed time. **3.** Precise; exact. **4.** Confined to or having the nature of a point in space. [Med. Lat. *punctualis* < Lat. *punctum,* point < *pungere,* to prick.] —**punc'tu·al'i·ty** (-ăl'ĭ-tē), **punc'tu·al·ness** *n.* —**punc'tu·al·ly** *adv.*

punc·tu·ate (pŭngk'cho͞o-āt') *v.* **-at·ed, -at·ing, -ates.** —*tr.* **1.** To provide (a text) with punctuation marks. **2.** To interrupt periodically: *"lectures punctuated by questions and discussions"* (Gilbert Highet). **3.** To stress or emphasize. —*intr.* To use punctuation. [Med. Lat. *punctuare, punctuat-* < Lat. *punctum,* point < *pungere,* to prick.] —**punc'tu·a'tive** *adj.* —**punc'tu·a'tor** *n.*

punc·tu·a·tion (pŭngk'cho͞o-ā'shən) *n.* **1. a.** The use of standard marks and signs in writing and printing to separate words into sentences, clauses, and phrases in order to clarify meaning. **b.** The marks so used. **2.** An act or instance of punctuating.

punctuation mark *n.* One of a set of marks or signs used to punctuate texts, as the comma (,) or the period (.).

punc·ture (pŭngk'chər) *v.* **-tured, -tur·ing, -tures.** —*tr.* **1.** To pierce with a pointed object. **2.** To make (a hole) by piercing. **3.** To cause to collapse by piercing. **4.** To depreciate or deflate: *cutting remarks that punctured his ego.* —*intr.* To be pierced or punctured. —*n.* **1.** An act or instance of puncturing. **2.** A hole or depression made by a sharp object, esp. a hole in a pneumatic tire. [< Lat. *punctura,* a pricking < *pungere,* to prick.] —**punc'tur·a·ble** *adj.*

puncture weed *n.* A prostrate weed, *Tribulus terrestris,* native to Europe, bearing fruit with stout, divergent spines.

pun·dit (pŭn'dĭt) *n.* **1.** A Brahmanic scholar. **2.** A learned person. **3.** An authority or critic: *a political pundit.* [Hindi *paṇḍit* < Skt. *paṇḍitaḥ,* a learned man, of Dravidian orig.] —**pun'dit·ry** *n.*

pung (pŭng) *n.* *New England.* A low box sleigh drawn by one horse. [Short for *tompong,* of Algonquian orig.]

pun·gent (pŭn'jənt) *adj.* **1.** Affecting the organs of taste or smell with a sharp, acrid sensation. **2.** Penetrating; biting; caustic: *pungent satire.* **3.** Pointed: *a pungent leaf.* [Lat. *pungens, pungent-,* pr. part. of *pungere,* to sting.] —**pun'gen·cy** *n.* —**pun'gent·ly** *adv.*

Pu·nic (pyo͞o'nĭk) *adj.* **1.** Of or pertaining to ancient Carthage or its people. **2.** Having the character of treachery attributed to the Carthaginians by the Romans. —*n.* The dialect of Phoenician spoken in ancient Carthage. [Lat. *Punicus* < *Poenus,* a Carthaginian < Gk. *Phoinix,* Phoenician.]

pun·ish (pŭn'ĭsh) *v.* **-ished, -ish·ing, -ish·es.** —*tr.* **1.** To subject (someone) to a penalty for a crime, fault, or misbehavior. **2.** To inflict a penalty on a criminal or wrongdoer for (an offense). **3.** To handle roughly; injure; hurt. **4.** *Informal.* To deplete (a stock or supply) heavily. —*intr.* To give punishment. [ME *punissen* < OFr. *punir* < Lat. *poenire* < *poena,* punishment < Gk. *poinē.*] —**pun'ish·a·bil'i·ty** *n.* —**pun'ish·a·ble** *adj.* —**pun'ish·er** *n.*

Synonyms: *punish, chastise, discipline, castigate, penalize.* These verbs refer to different ways of causing pain or loss to someone for wrong behavior. *Punish* usually means subjecting someone to loss of freedom or money or to physical pain for wrongdoing. *Chastise* usually refers to corporal punishment as a means of improving behavior. *Discipline* stresses punishment designed to control an offender and to eliminate or reform unacceptable conduct. *Castigate,* now always verbal, means to berate or censure, often in public. *Penalize,* weaker than *punish,* usually involves a demand for money or forfeiture of a privilege or gain because the rules of fair play or established conduct have been broken: *penalized for late payment of taxes.*

pun·ish·ment (pŭn'ĭsh-mənt) *n.* **1. a.** An act of punishing. **b.** The condition of being punished. **2.** A penalty imposed for wrongdoing. **3.** *Informal.* Rough handling; mistreatment.

pu·ni·tive (pyo͞o'nĭ-tĭv) *adj.* Inflicting or aiming to inflict punishment; punishing. [Fr. *punitif* < Med. Lat. *punitivus* < Lat. *punire,* to punish, var. of *poenire.* —see PUNISH.] —**pu'ni·tive·ly** *adv.* —**pu'ni·tive·ness** *n.*

punitive damages *pl.n.* *Law.* Damages awarded by a court to a plaintiff as additional punishment to a defendant for a serious wrong.

pu·ni·to·ry (pyo͞o'nĭ-tôr'ē, -tōr'ē) *adj.* Inflicting or aiming to inflict punishment. [Lat. *punitus,* punished (< p.part. of *punire*) + -ORY.]

Pun·ja·bi also **Pan·ja·bi** (pŭn-jä'bē, -jăb'ē) *n.* **1.** A native of the Punjab. **2.** An Indic language spoken in the Punjab.

punk[1] (pŭngk) *n.* **1.** Dry, decayed wood, used as tinder. **2.** Any of various substances that smolder when ignited, used to light fireworks. **3.** Chinese incense. [Orig. unknown.]

punk[2] (pŭngk) *n.* **1.** *Slang.* **a.** An inexperienced or callow youth. **b.** A young tough. **c.** A passive homosexual; catamite. **2.** *Slang.* Punk rock. **3.** *Slang.* A punk rocker. **4.** *Archaic.* A whore. —*adj.* *Slang.* **1.** Of poor quality; worthless. **2.** Weak in spirits or health. **3.** Of or relating to a style of dress worn by punk rockers and characterized by bizarre make-up and outlandish, shocking clothing. [Orig. unknown.]

pun·ka or **pun·kah** (pŭng'kə) *n.* A fan used esp. in India, made of a palm frond or strip of cloth hung from the ceiling and moved by a servant. [Hindi *pankhá* < Skt. *pakṣakaḥ,* fan < *pakṣaḥ,* wing.]

punk·ie also **punk·y** or **punk·ey** (pŭng'kē) *n., pl.* **-ies** also **-eys.** Any of various tiny, winged, biting insects of the genus *Culicoides* and related genera. [< PUNK[1].]

pun·kin (pŭng'kĭn) *n.* *Regional.* A pumpkin.

punk rock *n.* A form of hard-driving rock music characterized by an extremely bitter treatment of alienation and social unrest.

punk rocker *n.* *Slang.* **1.** One who performs punk rock music. **2.** One who wears punk fashions.

punk·y (pŭng'kē) *n.* Variant of **punkie.**

pun·ster (pŭn'stər) *n.* A maker of puns.

punt[1] (pŭnt) *n.* An open, flat-bottomed boat with squared ends, propelled by a long pole and used in shallow waters. —*v.* **punt·ed, punt·ing, punts.** —*tr.* **1.** To propel (a boat)

punt[1]

with a pole. **2.** To carry in a punt. *—intr.* To go in a punt. [MLG *punte,* ferryboat < Lat *ponto,* pontoon < *pons,* bridge.] **—punt'er** *n.*

punt² (pŭnt) *Football.* *—n.* A kick in which a football is dropped from the hands and kicked before it touches the ground. *—v.* **punt·ed, punt·ing, punts.** *—tr.* To propel (a football) by means of a punt. *—intr.* To execute a punt. [Orig. unknown.] **—punt'er** *n.*

punt³ (pŭnt) *intr.v.* **punt·ed, punt·ing, punts. 1.** In games such as roulette, to lay a bet against the bank. **2.** *Chiefly Brit.* To gamble. [Fr. *ponter* < *ponte,* point < Sp. *punto* < Lat. *punctum* < *pungere,* to prick.] **—punt'er** *n.*

pun·ty (pŭn'tē) *n., pl.* **-ties.** In glassmaking, an iron rod on which molten glass is handled. [Var. of PONTIL.]

pu·ny (pyo͞o'nē) *adj.* **-ni·er, -ni·est.** Of inferior size, strength, or significance; weak. [OFr. *puisne.* —see PUISNE.] **—pu'ni·ly** *adv.* **—pu'ni·ness** *n.*

pup (pŭp) *n.* **1.** A young dog; puppy. **2.** The young of certain animals such as the seal. **3.** A puppy (sense 2). *—intr.v.* **pupped, pup·ping, pups.** To give birth to pups. [Back-formation < PUPPY.]

pu·pa (pyo͞o'pə) *n., pl.* **-pae** (-pē) or **-pas.** The inactive stage in the metamorphosis of many insects, following the larval stage and preceding the adult form. [Lat., girl.] **—pu'pal** *adj.*

pu·pate (pyo͞o'pāt') *intr.v.* **-pat·ed, -pat·ing, -pates.** To become a pupa. **—pu·pa'tion** *n.*

pu·pil¹ (pyo͞o'pəl) *n.* **1.** A student under the direct supervision of a teacher. **2.** *Law.* A minor under the supervision of a guardian. [ME *pupille,* orphan < OFr. < Lat. *pupillus,* dim. of *pupus,* boy.]

pu·pil² (pyo͞o'pəl) *n.* The apparently black circular aperture in the center of the iris of the eye. [ME *pupilla* < Lat.] **—pu'pi·lar** *adj.*

pu·pil·age also **pu·pil·lage** (pyo͞o'pə-lĭj) *n.* The state or period of being a pupil.

pu·pil·lar·y¹ (pyo͞o'pə-lĕr'ē) *adj.* Of or pertaining to a ward or a student.

pu·pil·lar·y² (pyo͞o'pə-lĕr'ē) *adj.* Of or affecting the pupil of the eye.

pu·pip·a·rous (pyo͞o-pĭp'ər-əs) *adj.* Producing well-developed young that are ready to pupate, as certain parasitic flies.

pup·pet (pŭp'ĭt) *n.* **1.** A small figure of a person or animal, having jointed parts animated from above by strings or wires; marionette. **2.** A figure having a cloth body and hollow head, designed to be fitted over and manipulated by the hand. **3.** A toy representing a human figure; doll. **4.** One whose behavior is determined by the will of others: *a political puppet.* **—modifier:** *a puppet show; a puppet leader.* [ME *popet,* doll, ult. < Lat. *pupa.*]

pup·pet·eer (pŭp'ĭ-tîr') *n.* One who operates and entertains with puppets or marionettes.

pup·pet·ry (pŭp'ĭ-trē) *n., pl.* **-ries. 1.** The art of making puppets and presenting puppet shows. **2.** The actions of puppets. **3.** Stilted or artificial dramatic performance.

Pup·pis (pŭp'ĭs) *n.* A constellation in the Southern Hemisphere near Canis Major and Pyxis. [Lat. < *puppis,* stern.]

pup·py (pŭp'ē) *n., pl.* **-pies. 1.** A young dog; pup. **2.** A conceited or inexperienced youth. [ME *popi* < OFr. *popee,* doll < Lat. *pupa.*]

pup·py·ish (pŭp'ē-ĭsh) *adj.* Resembling or characteristic of a puppy.

puppy love *n.* Adolescent love or infatuation.

pup tent *n.* A shelter tent.

pur·blind (pûr'blīnd') *adj.* **1.** Having poor vision; nearly or partly blind. **2.** Slow in understanding or discernment; dull. [ME *pur blind,* totally blind.] **—pur'blind'ly** *adv.* **—pur'blind'ness** *n.*

pur·chas·a·ble (pûr'chĭ-sə-bəl) *adj.* **1.** Capable of being bought. **2.** Capable of being bribed; venal: *a purchasable congressman.* **—pur'chas·a·bil'i·ty** *n.*

pur·chase (pûr'chĭs) *tr.v.* **-chased, -chas·ing, -chas·es. 1.** To obtain in exchange for money or its equivalent; buy. **2.** To acquire by effort; earn. **3.** *Law.* To acquire (property) legally by means other than inheritance. **4.** To move or hold with a mechanical device such as a lever or wrench. *—n.* **1.** Something that is bought. **2. a.** The act of buying. **b.** Acquisition through the payment of money or its equivalent. **3.** *Law.* The acquisition of property other than by inheritance. **4.** A grip applied manually or mechanically to move something or prevent it from slipping. **5.** A tackle, lever, or other device used to obtain mechanical advantage. **6.** A position, as of a lever or one's feet, affording means to move or secure a weight. **7.** A means of increasing power, influence, or advantage. [ME *pourchasen* < OFr. *pourchacier,* to pursue : *pour-,* for (< Lat. *pro-*) + *chacier,* to chase. —see CHASE¹.] **—pur'chas·er** *n.*

purchasing power *n.* **1.** The ability to purchase, generally measured by income. **2.** The value of a particular monetary unit in terms of the goods or services that can be purchased with it.

pur·dah (pûr'də) *n.* **1.** In India, a curtain used to screen women from men or strangers. **2.** The Hindu practice of secluding women. [Hindi *parda,* veil < Pers. *pardah.*]

pure (pyo͝or) *adj.* **pur·er, pur·est. 1.** Having a homogeneous or uniform composition; not mixed: *pure oxygen.* **2.** Free from adulterants or impurities; full-strength: *pure chocolate.* **3.** Free from dirt, defilement, or pollution; clean. **4.** Free from foreign elements. **5.** Containing nothing inappropriate or extraneous: *a pure literary style.* **6.** Complete; utter: *pure folly.* **7.** Without faults; perfect; sinless. **8.** Chaste; virgin. **9.** Of unmixed blood or ancestry. **10.** *Genetics.* Breeding true to parental type; homozygous. **11.** *Mus.* Free from discordant qualities: *pure tones.* **12.** Articulated with a single unchanging speech sound; monophthongal: *a pure vowel.* **13.** Theoretical rather than applied: *pure science.* **14.** *Philos.* Free from empirical elements: *pure reason.* [ME *pur* < OFr. < Lat. *purus,* clean.] **—pure'ly** *adv.* **—pure'ness** *n.*

pure·blood (pyo͝or'blŭd') also **pure·blood·ed** (-blŭd'ĭd) *adj.* Of pure breeding stock; purebred. **—pure'blood'** *n.*

pure·bred (pyo͝or'brĕd') *adj.* Of a strain established through breeding many generations of unmixed stock. *—n.* (pyo͝or'brĕd'). A purebred animal.

pure democracy *n.* A democracy in which the power to govern lies directly in the hands of the people rather than being exercised through their representatives.

pu·rée (pyo͝o-rā', pyo͝or'ā) *tr.v.* **-réed, -rée·ing, -rées.** To rub (food) through a strainer. *—n.* Food prepared by puréeing. [Fr. < OFr. *purer,* to strain < Lat. *purare,* to purify < *purus,* clean.]

pur·fle (pûr'fəl) *tr.v.* **-fled, -fling, -fles.** To finish or decorate the border or edge of. *—n.* Also **pur·fling** (-flĭng). An ornamental border or edging. [ME *purfilen* < OFr. *porfiler* < VLat. **profilare* : Lat. *pro-,* forth + Lat. *filum,* thread.]

pur·ga·tion (pûr-gā'shən) *n.* The act of purging or purifying.

pur·ga·tive (pûr'gə-tĭv) *adj.* Tending to cleanse or purge, esp. tending to cause evacuation of the bowels. *—n.* A purgative agent or medicine; cathartic.

pur·ga·to·ri·al (pûr'gə-tôr'ē-əl, -tōr'-) *adj.* **1.** Serving to purify of sin; expiatory. **2.** Of, pertaining to, or resembling purgatory.

pur·ga·to·ry (pûr'gə-tôr'ē, -tōr'ē) *n., pl.* **-ries. 1.** *Rom. Cath. Ch.* A state in which the souls of those who have died in grace must expiate their sins. **2.** A place or condition of expiation, suffering, or remorse. *—adj.* Tending to cleanse or purge. [ME *purgatorie* < Med. Lat. *purgatorium* < Lat. *purgare,* to cleanse < *purus,* clean.]

purge (pûrj) *v.* **purged, purg·ing, purg·es.** *—tr.* **1. a.** To free from impurities; purify. **b.** To remove (impurities and other elements) by or as if by cleansing. **2.** To rid of sin, guilt, or defilement. **3.** *Law.* To clear (a person) of a charge or imputation. **4.** To rid (a nation, political party, or other group) of persons considered to be undesirable. **5.** *Med.* **a.** To cause evacuation of (the bowels). **b.** To induce evacuation of the bowels in (a patient). *—intr.* **1.** To become pure or clean. **2.** To undergo or cause an emptying of the bowels. *—n.* **1.** The act or process of purging. **2.** Something that purges, esp. a medicinal purgative. [ME *purgen* < OFr. *purger* < Lat. *purgare,* to cleanse < *purus,* clean.] **—purg'er** *n.*

pu·ri (po͝or'ē) *n.* Variant of **poori.**

pu·ri·fi·ca·tion (pyo͝or'ə-fĭ-kā'shən) *n.* The act or process of cleansing or purifying.

pu·ri·fi·ca·tor (pyo͝or'ə-fĭ-kā'tər) *n.* **1.** *Eccles.* A cloth used to clean the chalice after the celebration of the Eucharist. **2.** One that purifies.

pu·ri·fy (pyo͝or'ə-fī') *v.* **-fied, -fy·ing, -fies.** *—tr.* **1.** To rid of impurities; cleanse. **2.** To rid of foreign or objectionable elements. **3.** To free from sin, guilt, or other defilement. *—intr.* To become clean or pure. [ME *purifien* < OFr. *purifier* < Lat. *purificare* : *purus,* clean + *facere,* to make.] **—pu·rif'i·ca·to'ry** (pyo͝o-rĭf'ĭ-kə-tôr'ē, -tōr'ē) *adj.* **—pu'ri·fi'er** *n.*

Pu·rim (po͝or'ĭm, po͝o-rēm') *n.* A Jewish holiday in the month of Adar, celebrating the deliverance of the Jews from massacre by Haman. [Heb. *pūrīm,* pl. of *pūr,* lot (from the lots Haman cast to decide the day of the massacre), perh. < Akkadian *pūru,* stone.]

pu·rine (pyo͝or'ēn') *n.* **1.** A colorless crystalline compound, $C_5H_4N_4$, used in organic synthesis and metabolism studies. **2.** Any of a group of naturally occurring organic compounds derived from or having molecular structures related to purine, including uric acid, adenine, guanine, and caffeine. [G. *Purin,* a blend of Lat. *purus,* clean and NLat. *uricus, uricum,* uric (acid).]

pur·ism (pyo͝or'ĭz'əm) *n.* **1.** Strict observance of or insistence upon traditional correctness, esp. of language: *"By purism is to be understood a needless & irritating insistence on purity or correctness of speech"* (H.W. Fowler). **2.** An example of purism.

pur·ist (pyo͝or'ĭst) *n.* One who practices or urges strict correctness, esp. in the use of words. **—pu·ris'tic** (pyo͝o-rĭs'tĭk) *adj.* **—pu·ris'ti·cal·ly** *adv.*

Pu·ri·tan (pyo͝or'ĭ-tn) *n.* **1.** A member of a group of English Protestants who in the 16th and 17th centuries advocated simplification of the ceremonies and creeds of the Church of England and strict religious discipline. **2. puritan.** One who lives in accordance with Protestant precepts, esp. one who regards luxury or pleasure as sinful. *—adj.* **1.** Of or pertaining to the Puritans or Puritanism. **2. puritan.** Characteristic of a puritan; puritanical. [< LLat. *puritas,* purity < Lat. *purus,* pure.]

pu·ri·tan·i·cal (pyo͝or'ĭ-tăn'ĭ-kəl) *adj.* **1.** Rigorous in religious observance; marked by stern morality. **2. Puritanical.**

puppet

Of, pertaining to, or characteristic of the Puritans. **—pu'ri·tan'i·cal·ly** *adv.* **—pu'ri·tan'i·cal·ness** *n.*

Pu·ri·tan·ism (pyo͝or'ĭ-tn-ĭz'əm) *n.* **1.** The practices and doctrines of the Puritans. **2. puritanism.** Scrupulous moral rigor, esp. hostility to social pleasures and indulgences.

pu·ri·ty (pyo͝or'ĭ-tē) *n.* **1.** The quality or condition of being pure. **2.** A quantitative assessment of homogeneity or uniformity. **3.** Freedom from sin or guilt; innocence; chastity. **4.** The absence in speech or writing of foreign words, slang, or other elements deemed inappropriate to good style. **5.** The proportion of a single-frequency spectral component in a mixture of achromatic and spectral colors.

Pur·kin·je cell (pûr-kĭn'jē) *n.* Any of numerous nerve cells of the cerebellar cortex distinguished by a large rounded cell body. [After Johannes E. *Purkinje* (1787–1869).]

Purkinje fiber *n.* Any of the large modified cardiac muscle fibers that comprise the cardiac impulse conducting system of the heart.

purl[1] (pûrl) *intr.v.* **purled, purl·ing, purls.** To flow or ripple with a murmuring sound. *—n.* The sound made by rippling water. [Prob. of Scand. orig.]

purl[2] also **pearl** (pûrl) *—v.* **purled, purl·ing, purls** also **pearled, pearl·ing, pearls.** *—tr.* **1.** To knit with a purl stitch. **2.** To edge or finish with lace or embroidery. *—intr.* **1.** To do knitting with a purl stitch. **2.** To edge or finish with lace or embroidery. *—n.* **1.** The inversion of a knit stitch; purl stitch. **2.** A decorative edging of lace or embroidery. **3.** Gold or silver wire used in embroidery. [Orig. unknown.]

pur·lieu (pûrl'yo͞o, pûr'lo͞o) *n.* **1.** An outlying or neighboring area. **2. purlieus.** Outskirts; environs. **3.** A place that one frequents. [ME *perlew,* alteration of Norman Fr. *puralée,* perambulation < OFr. *poraler,* to traverse : *por-,* forth (< Lat. *pro-*) + *aler,* to go.]

pur·lin also **pur·line** (pûr'lĭn) *n.* One of several horizontal timbers supporting the rafters of a roof. [ME *purlyn.*]

pur·loin (pər-loin', pûr'loin') *v.* **-loined, -loin·ing, -loins.** *—tr.* To steal; filch. *—intr.* To commit theft. [ME *purloynen,* to remove < Norman Fr. *purloigner* : *pur-,* away (< Lat. *pro-*) + *loign,* far < Lat. *longē* < *longus,* long.] **—pur·loin'er** *n.*

purl stitch *n.* An inverted knitting stitch, often alternated with the plain stitch to produce a ribbed effect.

pu·ro·my·cin (pyo͝or'ə-mī'sĭn) *n.* A broad-spectrum antibiotic, $C_{22}H_{29}N_7O_5$, obtained from the adinomycete *Streptomyces alboniger.* [PUR(INE) + -MYCIN.]

pur·ple (pûr'pəl) *n.* **1.** Any of a group of colors with a hue between that of violet and red. **2.** Cloth of a color between violet and red, formerly worn as a symbol of royalty or high office. **3.** Imperial power; high rank: *born to the purple.* **4.** The rank or office of a cardinal. **5.** The rank or office of a bishop. *—adj.* **1.** Of the color purple. **2.** Royal or imperial; regal. **3.** Elaborate and ornate: *purple prose.* *—tr. & intr.v.* **-pled, -pling, -ples.** To make or become purple. [ME *purpel* < OE *purple* < *purpura,* purple cloth < Lat., purple < Gk. *porphura,* a shellfish yielding purple dye.]

pur·ple·heart (pûr'pəl-härt') *n.* **1.** Any of several tropical American trees of the genus *Peltogyne,* valued for their decorative wood. **2.** The purple heartwood of the purpleheart.

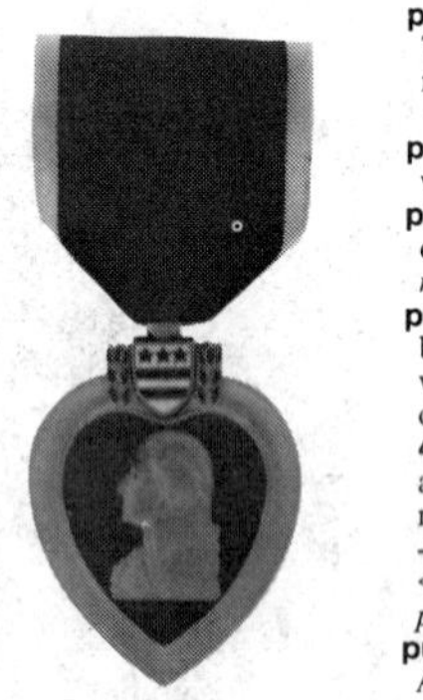

Purple Heart

Purple Heart *n.* A U.S. military decoration awarded to servicemen wounded in action.

purple loosestrife *n.* A marsh plant, *Lythrum salicaria,* having long spikes of purple flowers.

purple martin *n.* A North American bird, *Progne subis,* related to the swallows, having a glossy, blue-black back and, in the male, a dark breast.

purple salt *n.* Potassium permanganate.

pur·plish (pûr'plĭsh) *adj.* Somewhat purple.

pur·port (pər-pôrt', -pōrt') *tr.v.* **-port·ed, -port·ing, -ports.** **1.** To have or present the appearance, often false, of being or intending; profess: *selfish behavior that purports to be altruistic.* **2.** To have the intention of doing; purpose. *—n.* (pûr'pôrt', -pōrt'). **1.** Meaning presented, intended, or implied; import. **2.** Intention; purpose. [ME *purporten* < OFr. *purporter,* to contain < Med. Lat. *proportare,* to extend : Lat. *pro-,* forth + Lat. *portare,* to carry.]

pur·port·ed (pər-pôr'tĭd, -pōr'-) *adj.* Assumed to be such; supposed. **—pur·port'ed·ly** *adv.*

pur·pose (pûr'pəs) *n.* **1.** The object toward which one strives or for which something exists; goal; aim. **2.** A result or effect that is intended or desired; intention. **3.** Determination; resolution. **4.** The matter at hand; point at issue. *—tr.v.* **-posed, -pos·ing, -pos·es.** To intend or resolve to perform or accomplish. ***—idioms.* on purpose.** Intentionally; deliberately. **to good purpose.** With good results. **to little** (or **no**) **purpose.** With few or no results. [ME *purpos* < OFr. < *purposer,* to intend < Lat. *proponere,* to put forward. —see PROPOSE.]

pur·pose·ful (pûr'pəs-fəl) *adj.* **1.** Having a purpose; intentional. **2.** Having or manifesting purpose; determined. **—pur'pose·ful·ly** *adv.* **—pur'pose·ful·ness** *n.*

pur·pose·less (pûr'pəs-lĭs) *adj.* Without purpose; aimless; pointless. **—pur'pose·less·ly** *adv.* **—pur'pose·less·ness** *n.*

pur·pose·ly (pûr'pəs-lē) *adv.* With specific purpose.

pur·po·sive (pûr'pə-sĭv) *adj.* **1.** Having or serving a purpose. **2.** Purposeful as opposed to aimless or random: *purposive behavior.* **—pur'po·sive·ly** *adv.* **—pur'po·sive·ness** *n.*

pur·pu·ra (pûr'pə-rə, -pyə-) *n.* A condition characterized by purplish discolorations of the skin and mucous membranes caused by hemorrhages into the affected tissues. [NLat. < Lat., purple.] **—pur·pu'ric** (-pyo͝or'ĭk) *adj.*

purr (pûr) *n.* **1.** The softly vibrant sound made by a cat to express pleasure or contentment. **2.** A sound similar to that made by a contented cat: *the purr of an engine.* *—v.* **purred, purr·ing, purrs.** *—intr.* To make or utter a soft, vibrant sound: *The sewing machine purred.* *—tr.* To express by a soft, vibrant sound. [Imit.]

purse (pûrs) *n.* **1.** A small bag or pouch for carrying money. **2.** A woman's pocketbook or handbag. **3.** Something that resembles a bag or pouch. **4.** Available wealth or resources; money. **5.** A sum of money collected as a present or offered as a prize. *—tr.v.* **pursed, purs·ing, purs·es.** To gather or contract (the lips or brow) into wrinkles or folds; pucker. [ME *purs* < OE < LLat. *bursa,* bag < Gk., leather.] **—purse'like'** *adj.*

purs·er (pûr'sər) *n.* The officer in charge of money matters on board a ship. [ME < *purs,* purse.]

purse seine (sān) *n.* A fishing seine that is pursed or drawn into the shape of a bag to enclose the catch.

purse strings *pl.n.* Financial support or resources.

purs·lane (pûrs'lĭn, -lān') *n.* A trailing weed, *Portulaca oleracea,* having small yellow flowers, reddish stems, and fleshy leaves that are sometimes used in salads. [ME < OFr. *porcelaine,* cowrie shell. —see PORCELAIN.]

pur·su·ance (pər-so͞o'əns) *n.* The carrying out or putting into effect of something; prosecution.

pur·su·ant (pər-so͞o'ənt) *adj.* Proceeding from and conformable to; in accordance with. *—adv.* Also **pur·su·ant·ly** (-lē). Accordingly; consequently. [ME *poursuiant* < OFr., pr.part. of *poursuivre,* to pursue < Lat. *prosequi.* —see PROSECUTE.]

pur·sue (pər-so͞o') *v.* **-sued, -su·ing, -sues.** *—tr.* **1.** To follow in an effort to overtake or capture; chase. **2.** To strive to gain or accomplish. **3.** To proceed along the course of; follow. **4.** To carry further; advance. **5.** To be engaged in (a vocation or hobby, for example). **6.** To harass; persecute. *—intr.* **1.** To follow in an effort to overtake or capture; chase. **2.** To carry on; continue. [ME *pursuen* < Norman Fr. *pursuer* < Lat. *prosequi.* —see PROSECUTE.] **—pur·su'a·ble** *adj.* **—pur·su'er** *n.*

pur·suit (pər-so͞ot') *n.* **1.** The act or an instance of chasing or pursuing. **2.** The act of striving: *the pursuit of success.* **3.** A vocation, hobby, or other activity regularly engaged in. [ME *pursuite* < OFr. *poursuite* < *poursuivre,* to pursue < Lat. *prosequi.* —see PROSECUTE.]

pursuit plane *n.* A high-speed fighter plane designed and equipped to pursue and attack enemy aircraft.

pur·sui·vant (pûr'swĭ-vənt) *n.* **1.** In the British Colleges of Heralds, an officer ranking below a herald. **2.** A follower or attendant. [ME *pursevant,* attendant < OFr. *poursuivant,* follower < pr.part. of *poursuivre,* to follow < Lat. *prosequi.* —see PROSECUTE.]

pur·te·nance (pûr'tn-əns) *n.* An animal's viscera or inner organs, esp. the heart, liver, and lungs. [ME *portenaunce* < OFr. *partenance,* accessory < *partenir,* to pertain. —see PERTAIN.]

pu·ru·lence (pyo͝or'ə-ləns, pyo͝or'yə-) *n.* **1.** The condition of secreting or containing pus. **2.** Pus.

pu·ru·lent (pyo͝or'ə-lənt, pyo͝or'yə-) *adj.* Containing or secreting pus. [Lat. *purulentus* < *pus,* pus.] **—pu'ru·lent·ly** *adv.*

pur·vey (pər-vā', pûr'vā') *tr.v.* **-veyed, -vey·ing, -veys.** **1.** To supply (food, for example); furnish. **2.** To advertise or circulate. [ME *purveien* < OFr. *porveioir* < Lat. *providēre.* —see PROVIDE.] **—pur·vey'ance** *n.*

pur·vey·or (pər-vā'ər) *n.* **1.** A person who furnishes provisions, esp. food. **2.** A distributor; dispenser: *a purveyor of lies.*

pur·view (pûr'vyo͞o') *n.* **1.** The extent or range of function, power, or competence; scope. **2.** Range of vision, comprehension, or experience; outlook. **3.** *Law.* The body, scope, or limit of a statute. [ME *purveu,* proviso < Norman Fr. *purveu,* it is provided (from the use of this word to introduce a proviso) < OFr. *porveu* < *porveioir,* to provide. —see PURVEY.]

pus (pŭs) *n.* A viscous, yellowish-white fluid formed in infected tissue, consisting chiefly of leucocytes, cellular debris, and liquefied tissue elements. [Lat.]

Pu·sey·ism (pyo͞o'zē-ĭz'əm, pyo͞o'sē-) *n.* Tractarianism. [After Edward B. *Pusey* (1800–1882).] **—Pu'sey·ite'** (-īt') *n.*

push (po͝osh) *v.* **pushed, push·ing, push·es.** *—tr.* **1.** To exert force against (an object) to move it away. **2.** To move (an object) by exerting force against it; thrust; shove. **3.** To force (one's way): *He pushed his way through the crowd.* **4.** To urge forward. **5.** To urge insistently to do something; pressure. **6.** To bear hard upon; press. **7.** To extend or enlarge: *push civilization past the frontier.* **8.** *Slang.* **a.** To promote or sell (a product). **b.** To sell (a narcotic) illegally. *—intr.* **1.** To exert outward force against something. **2.** To advance despite difficulty or opposition; press forward. **3.** To expend great or vigorous effort. ***—phrasal verbs.* push around.** *Informal.* To treat or threaten to treat roughly; intimidate. **push off.** *Informal.* To depart; set out. **push on.** To proceed; continue. *—n.* **1.** The act of pushing; thrust. **2.** A vigorous or insistent effort toward an end;

drive. **3.** A provocation to action; stimulus. **4.** *Informal.* Persevering energy; enterprise. **—*idiom.* push (one's) luck.** To take an ever-increasing risk or risks. [ME *pusshen* < OFr. *poulser* < Lat. *pulsare,* freq. of *pellere,* to beat.]
push·ball (po͝osh′bôl′) *n.* **1.** A game in which two opposing teams attempt to push a heavy ball, six feet in diameter, across a goal. **2.** The ball used in the game of pushball.
push broom *n.* A broom having a wide brush that is perpendicular to the end of a long handle and is designed to be pushed in sweeping.
push button *n.* A small button that activates an electric circuit.
push·cart (po͝osh′kärt′) *n.* A light cart pushed by hand.
push·down (po͝osh′doun′) *n.* *Computer Sci.* A section of stored data from which the most recently stored material must be the first to be utilized.
push·er (po͝osh′ər) *n.* **1.** One that pushes. **2.** *Slang.* A person who sells drugs illegally.
push·ful (po͝osh′fo͝ol′) *adj.* Pushing. **—push′ful·ness** *n.*
push·ing (po͝osh′ĭng) *adj.* **1.** Energetic; enterprising. **2.** Aggressive; forward; presuming. **—push′ing·ly** *adv.*
push·o·ver (po͝osh′ō′vər) *n.* **1.** Something that is easily accomplished. **2.** One that is easily defeated or taken advantage of.
push·pin (po͝osh′pĭn′) *n.* **1.** A tacklike pin with a large head that is easily inserted into a wall or board. **2.** A game played by children with pins.
push·rod also **push rod** (po͝osh′rŏd′) *n.* A rod moved by a cam to operate the valves in an internal-combustion engine.
Push·tu (pŭsh′to͞o) *n.* Variant of **Pashto.**
push·up (po͝osh′ŭp′) *n.* **1.** An exercise for strengthening arm muscles, performed by lying with the face and palms to the floor and by pushing the body up and down with the arms. **2.** *Computer Sci.* A section of stored data from which the earliest stored material must be the first to be utilized.
push·y (po͝osh′ē) *adj.* **-i·er, -i·est.** *Informal.* Disagreeably forward or aggressive. **—push′i·ly** *adv.* **—push′i·ness** *n.*
pu·sil·la·nim·i·ty (pyo͞o′sə-lə-nĭm′ĭ-tē) *n.* The state or quality of being pusillanimous; faint-hearted cowardice.
pu·sil·lan·i·mous (pyo͞o′sə-lăn′ə-məs) *adj.* Lacking courage; cowardly. [LLat. *pusillanimis* : Lat. *pusillus,* weak (< *pusus,* boy) + *animus,* spirit.] **—pu′sil·lan′i·mous·ly** *adv.*
puss[1] (po͝os) *n.* *Informal.* **1.** A cat. **2.** A girl or young woman. [Prob. of Germanic orig.]
puss[2] (po͝os) *n.* *Slang.* **1.** The mouth. **2.** The face. [Ir. Gael. *bus,* mouth < OIr., lip.]
puss·ley (pŭs′lē) *n.* Purslane. [Alteration of PURSLANE.]
puss·y[1] (po͝os′ē) *n., pl.* **-ies.** *Informal.* **1.** A cat. **2.** A fuzzy catkin, esp. of the pussy willow.
pus·sy[2] (pŭs′ē) *adj.* **-si·er, -si·est.** Resembling or containing pus.
puss·y[3] (po͝os′ē) *n.* *Vulgar Slang.* **1.** The vulva. **2. a.** A woman. **b.** A sexually attractive woman. [Perh. of Scand. orig.]
puss·y·cat (po͝os′ē-kăt′) *n.* **1.** A cat. **2.** *Informal.* One who is easygoing, mild-mannered, or amiable.
puss·y·foot (po͝os′ē-fo͝ot′) *intr.v.* **-foot·ed, -foot·ing, -foots. 1.** To move stealthily or cautiously. **2.** *Slang.* To act or proceed cautiously or timidly to avoid committing oneself. **—puss′y·foot′er** *n.*
puss·y·toes (po͝os′ē-tōz′) *pl.n. (used with a sing. or pl. verb).* Any of several low-growing plants of the genus *Antennaria,* having leaves with whitish down and clusters of small white flowers. [From the cluster's resemblance to a cat's paw.]
pussy willow *n.* **1.** A North American shrub or small tree, *Salix discolor,* having silky catkins. **2.** Any of several willows similar to the pussy willow.
pus·tu·lant (pŭs′chə-lənt, pŭs′tyə-) *adj.* Causing pustules to form. *—n.* An agent that produces pustules.
pus·tu·lar (pŭs′chə-lər, pŭs′tyə-) *adj.* Of, pertaining to, or having pustules.
pus·tu·late (pŭs′chə-lāt′, pŭs′tyə-) *intr. & tr.v.* **-lat·ed, -lat·ing, -lates.** To form or cause to form pustules. *—adj.* Covered with pustules or pustulelike blisters.
pus·tu·la·tion (pŭs′chə-lā′shən, pŭs′tyə-) *n.* **1.** The formation or appearance of pustules. **2.** A pustule.
pus·tule (pŭs′cho͞ol, pŭs′tyo͞ol) *n.* **1.** A slight, inflamed elevation of the skin filled with pus. **2.** A small swelling similar to a blister or pimple. [ME < OFr. < Lat. *pustula,* blister.]
put (po͝ot) *v.* **put, put·ting, puts.** *—tr.* **1.** To place in a specified location; set. **2.** To cause to be in a specified condition: *put one's room in order.* **3.** To cause to undergo something; subject: *put a prisoner to torture.* **4.** To assign; attribute: *put a false interpretation on events.* **5.** To estimate: *He put the time at five o'clock.* **6.** To impose or levy: *put a tax on cigarettes.* **7.** To wager (a stake); bet: *put $10 on a horse.* **8.** To hurl with an overhand pushing motion: *put the shot.* **9.** To bring up for consideration or judgment: *put a question to the judge.* **10.** To express; state: *putting it bluntly.* **11.** To render in a specified language or literary form: *put prose into verse.* **12.** To adapt: *lyrics put to music.* **13.** To urge or force to some action: *put an outlaw to flight.* **14.** To apply: *We must put our minds to it.* *—intr.* **1.** To begin to move, esp. in a hurry. **2.** *Naut.* To proceed: *The ship put into the harbor.* **—*phrasal verbs.* put about.** *Naut.* To change or cause to change direction; go or cause to go from one tack to another. **put across. 1.** To state so as to be understood clearly or accepted readily. **2.** To attain or carry through by deceit or trickery. **put away. 1.** To renounce; discard: *put all negative thoughts away.* **2.** *Informal.* To consume (food or drink) readily and quickly. **3. a.** *Informal.* To confine to a mental institution. **b.** *Informal.* To kill. **c.** To bury. **put by.** To save for later use: *put by supplies for the winter.* **put down. 1. a.** To write down. **b.** To enter in a list. **2. a.** To bring to an end; repress: *put down a rebellion.* **b.** To render ineffective: *put down rumors.* **3.** *Slang.* **a.** To criticize: *put her down for being late.* **b.** To belittle; disparage: *She put down his attempts to ski.* **c.** To humiliate: *The teacher put the student down with a caustic retort.* **4. a.** To assign to a category: *Just put him down as a sneak.* **b.** To attribute: *Let's put this down to experience.* **5.** To consume (food or drink) readily; put away. **put forth. 1.** To grow: *The plant put forth leaves.* **2.** To exert; bring to bear. **3.** To offer for consideration. **put forward.** To propose for consideration: *put forward an idea.* **put in. 1.** To make a formal offer of: *put in a plea of guilty.* **2.** To interpose: *He put in a word for me with the boss.* **3.** To spend (time) at a given location or at a job: *a convict who had put in six years at hard labor; put in eight hours behind a desk.* **4.** To plant: *We put in 20 apple trees.* **5.** *Naut.* To enter a port or harbor: *The freighter puts in at noon.* **6.** To enter a request, application, or offer: *put in for a day off.* **put off. 1. a.** To delay; postpone: *put off paying the bills.* **b.** To persuade to wait: *managed to put off the creditors for another week.* **2.** To discard; take off. **3.** To repel or repulse, as from bad manners: *His attitude put us off.* **4.** To pass (money) or sell (merchandise) fraudulently. **put on. 1.** To clothe oneself with; don. **2.** To apply; activate: *put on the brake.* **3.** To assume affectedly: *put on an English accent.* **4.** *Slang.* To tease or mislead (another): *You're putting me on!* **5.** To add: *put on weight.* **6.** To produce; perform: *put on a variety show.* **put out. 1.** To extinguish: *put out a fire.* **2.** *Naut.* To leave, as a port or harbor; depart. **3.** To expel: *put out a drunk.* **4.** To publish: *put out a book.* **5.** To inconvenience: *Did our early arrival put you out?* **6.** To irritate: *I was put out by his sloppiness.* **7.** *Baseball.* To retire (a runner). **put over. 1.** To postpone; delay. **2.** To put across, esp. to deceive: *put a lie over on me.* **put through. 1.** To bring to a successful end: *put the project through on time.* **2.** To cause to undergo: *He put me through a lot of trouble.* **3. a.** To make a telephone connection for: *She put me through on the office line.* **b.** To obtain a connection for (a telephone call). **put to.** *Naut.* To head for shore. **put together. 1.** To construct; build. **2.** To add; combine. **put up. 1.** To erect; build. **2.** To preserve; can: *put up jam.* **3.** To nominate. **4.** To provide (funds) in advance. **5.** To provide lodgings for: *put someone up for the night.* **6.** To incite to an action: *put the child up to a prank.* **7.** To start (game animals) from cover: *put up grouse.* **8.** To offer for sale: *put up his antiques at auction.* **9. a.** To make a display or the appearance of: *put up a bluff.* **b.** To engage in; carry on: *put up a good fight.* **put upon.** To impose on; overburden: *He was put upon by his friends.* *—n.* **1.** An act of putting the shot. **2.** An option to sell a stipulated amount of stock or securities within a specified time and at a fixed price. *—adj. Informal.* Fixed; stationary: *stay put.* **—*idioms.* put down roots.** To establish a permanent residence. **put in mind.** To remind. **put (one's) finger on.** To identify. **put (one's) foot down.** To take a firm stand. **put (one's) foot in (one's) mouth.** To make a tactless remark. **put (one's) house in order.** To organize one's affairs. **put on the dog.** *Slang.* To give oneself airs. **put the arm (or bite) on.** *Slang.* To ask (someone) for money. **put the finger on.** *Slang.* To inform on; snitch on. **put the make on.** *Slang.* To make sexual advances to. **put the screws to (or on).** To pressure (another) in an extreme manner. **put to bed.** To make final preparations for the printing of (a newspaper, for example). **put to it.** To give extreme difficulty to: *was put to it to finish on time.* **put two and two together.** To draw the proper conclusion from given evidence or indications. **put up or shut up.** *Slang.* To endure (something unpleasant) without complaining. **put up to.** To instigate; incite. **put up with.** To endure without complaint: *had to put up with the inconvenience.* [ME *putten.*]
pu·ta·men (pyo͞o-tā′mən) *n., pl.* **-tam·i·na** (-tăm′ə-nə). A hard, shell-like covering, such as that enclosing the kernel of a peach. [Lat., husk < *putare,* to prune.] **—pu·tam′i·nous** (-tăm′ə-nəs) *adj.*
pu·ta·tive (pyo͞o′tə-tĭv) *adj.* Generally regarded as such; supposed; reputed. [ME < OFr. *putatif* < LLat. *putativus* < Lat. *putare,* to consider.] **—pu′ta·tive·ly** *adv.*
put-down (po͝ot′doun′) *n.* *Slang.* A dismissal or rejection, esp. in the form of a critical or slighting remark.
put·log (po͝ot′lôg′, -lŏg′, pŭt′-) *n.* One of the short pieces of lumber that support a scaffolding floor. [Alteration of obs. *pullock,* perh. < PUT.]
put·off (po͝ot′ôf′, -ŏf′) *n.* A pretext for inaction; excuse.
put-on (po͝ot′ŏn′, -ôn′) *adj.* Pretended; feigned. *—n. Slang.* **1.** The act of teasing or misleading someone, esp. for amusement. **2.** Something, as a prank or book, intended as a hoax or joke; spoof. **3.** A deceptive outward appearance.
Pu·tong·hua (po͞o′tông′hwä′, -wä′, -tŏng′-) *n.* Mandarin (sense 3). [Chin. (Mandarin) *pu[3] tong[1] hua[4]* : *pu[3],* common + *tong[1],* through + *hua[4],* words.]

pushup

pussy willow

put·out (po͝ot′out′) *n. Baseball.* A play in which a batter or base runner is retired.

put-put (pŭt′pŭt′) *n. Slang.* **1.** A small gasoline engine. **2.** A boat or vehicle operated by a put-put. [Imit. of a running engine.]

pu·tre·fac·tion (pyo͞o′trə-făk′shən) *n.* **1.** The partial decomposition of organic matter by microorganisms, producing foul-smelling matter. **2.** Putrefied matter. **3.** The condition of being putrefied. [ME *putrefaccioun* < LLat. *putrefactio* < Lat. *putrefacere,* to make rotten. —see PUTREFY.]

pu·tre·fac·tive (pyo͞o′trə-făk′tĭv) *adj.* **1.** Bringing about putrefaction. **2.** Of or pertaining to putrefaction.

pu·tre·fy (pyo͞o′trə-fī′) *v.* **-fied, -fy·ing, -fies.** —*tr.* **1.** To decompose (something); cause to decay. **2.** To make gangrenous. —*intr.* **1.** To decompose. **2.** To become gangrenous. [ME *putrefien* < OFr. *putrefier* < Lat. *putrefacere* : *puter,* rotten + *facere,* to make.]

pu·tres·cence (pyo͞o-trĕs′əns) *n.* **1.** Putrescent character or condition. **2.** Putrid matter.

pu·tres·cent (pyo͞o-trĕs′ənt) *adj.* **1.** Becoming putrid; putrefying. **2.** Of or pertaining to putrefaction. [Lat. *putrescens, putrescent-,* pr.part. of *putrescere,* to rot, inceptive of *putrēre,* to be rotten < *puter,* rotten.]

pu·tres·ci·ble (pyo͞o-trĕs′ə-bəl) *adj.* Subject to putrefaction. [Fr. < Lat. *putrescere,* to rot. —see PUTRESCENT.]

pu·trid (pyo͞o′trĭd) *adj.* **1.** Decomposed and foul-smelling; rotten. **2.** Proceeding from, pertaining to, or displaying putrefaction. **3.** Corrupt; morally rotten. **4.** Extremely objectionable; vile. [Lat. *putridus* < *putrere,* to be rotten < *puter,* rotten.] **—pu·trid′i·ty** (-trĭd′ĭ-tē), **pu′trid·ness** *n.* **—pu′trid·ly** *adv.*

putsch also **Putsch** (po͝och) *n.* A sudden attempt by a group to overthrow a government. [G.] **—putsch′ist** *n.*

putt (pŭt) *Sports.* —*n.* A light golf stroke made on the putting green in an effort to place the ball into the hole. —*v.* **putt·ed, putt·ing, putts.** —*tr.* To hit (a golf ball) with a light stroke on the green. —*intr.* To putt a golf ball. [Var. of *put.*]

put·tee (pŭ-tē′, pŭt′ē) also **put·ty** (pŭt′ē) *n., pl.* **-tees** also **-ties. 1.** A strip of cloth wound spirally around the leg from ankle to knee. **2.** A gaiter covering the lower leg. [Hindi *paṭṭī* < Skt. *paṭṭikā,* fem. of *paṭṭakaḥ,* bandage, ribbon < *paṭṭaḥ,* strip of cloth.]

puttee

put·ter[1] (pŭt′ər) *n. Sports.* **1.** A short, stiff-shafted golf club used for putting. **2.** A golfer who is putting.

put·ter[2] (pŭt′ər) *v.* **-tered, -ter·ing, -ters.** —*intr.* To occupy oneself in an aimless or desultory manner. —*tr.* To waste (time) in idling: *puttered away the hours in the garden.* [Var. of dial. *potler,* perh. < *pote,* to push.] **—put′ter·er** *n.*

putting green *n. Sports.* **1.** The area at the end of a fairway on a golf course in which the hole is placed, having more closely mowed turf than the rest of the course. **2.** An area for practicing putting.

put·ty[1] (pŭt′ē) *n., pl.* **-ties. 1. a.** A doughlike cement made by mixing whiting and linseed oil, used to fill holes in woodwork and secure panes of glass. **b.** A substance with a similar consistency or function. **2.** A fine lime cement used as a finishing coat on plaster. **3.** A yellowish or light brownish gray to grayish yellow or light grayish brown. —*tr.v.* **-tied, -ty·ing, -ties.** To fill, cover, or secure with putty. [Fr. *potée* < OFr., a potful < *pot,* pot.]

put·ty[2] (pŭt′ē) *n.* Variant of **puttee.**

put·ty·root (pŭt′ē-ro͞ot′, -ro͝ot′) *n.* A North American orchid, *Aplectrum hyemale,* bearing a single leaf and yellowish-brown or purplish flowers. [From the use of the sticky substance in its corm as a cement.]

put-up (po͝ot′ŭp′) *adj. Informal.* Planned or prearranged secretly.

puz·zle (pŭz′əl) *v.* **-zled, -zling, -zles.** —*tr.* **1.** To cause uncertainty and indecision in; perplex. **2.** To clarify or solve (something confusing) by reasoning or study: *He puzzled out the significance of her statement.* —*intr.* **1.** To be perplexed. **2.** To ponder over a problem in an effort to solve or understand it. —*n.* **1.** Something that puzzles. **2.** A toy, game, or testing device that tests ingenuity. **3.** The condition of being perplexed; bewilderment. [Orig. unknown.] **—puz′zler** *n.*

Synonyms: *puzzle, perplex, mystify, bewilder, confound, baffle.* These verbs refer to various degrees of mental challenge or confusion. *Puzzle* implies presenting an intricate, difficult, but solvable problem. *Perplex* stresses uncertainty or anxiety over reaching a decision or solution. To *mystify* is to puzzle by purposely obscuring or concealing facts. *Bewilder* emphasizes not only perplexity, but extreme confusion of the mind. *Confound* strongly implies astonishment. To *baffle* is to outwit or frustrate by puzzling.

puz·zle·ment (pŭz′əl-mənt) *n.* The state of being confused or baffled; perplexity.

py– *pref.* Variant of **pyo-.**

py·a (pē-ä′) *n.* See table at **currency.** [Burmese.]

pyramid

pyc·nid·i·um (pĭk-nĭd′ē-əm) *n., pl.* **-i·a** (-ē-ə). A rounded or flask-shaped asexual fruiting body containing spores that occurs in certain fungi. [NLat. : Gk. *puknos,* thick + Gk. *-idion,* dim. suffix.] **—pyc·nid′i·al** *adj.*

pyc·nom·e·ter (pĭk-nŏm′ĭ-tər) *n.* A standard vessel used in measuring the density or specific gravity of materials. [Gk. *puknos,* dense + METER.]

py·e·li·tis (pī′ə-lī′tĭs) *n.* Pyelonephritis. [Gk. *puelos,* basin + -ITIS.]

py·e·lo·ne·phri·tis (pī′ə-lō-nĭ-frī′tĭs) *n.* Inflammation of both the kidney and its pelvis. [Gk. *puelos,* basin + NEPHRITIS.] **—py′e·lo·ne·phrit′ic** (-frĭt′ĭk) *adj.*

py·e·mi·a (pī-ē′mē-ə) *n.* The presence of pus in the blood. **—py·e′mic** *adj.*

py·gid·i·um (pī-jĭd′ē-əm) *n., pl.* **-i·a** (-ē-ə). The posterior body region of certain arthropods. [Gk. *pugidion,* dim. of *pugē,* buttocks.] **—py·gid′i·al** *adj.*

pyg·mae·an or **pyg·me·an** (pĭg-mē′ən, pĭg′mē-) *adj.* Pygmy. [< Lat. *pygmaeus.*]

Pyg·ma·lion (pĭg-māl′yən, -mā′lē-ən) *n. Gk. Myth.* A king of Cyprus who carved and then fell in love with a statue of a woman, which Aphrodite brought to life as Galatea. [Lat. < Gk. *Pugmaliōn.*]

pyg·moid (pĭg′moid′) *adj.* Resembling or characteristic of a Pygmy.

Pyg·my also **Pig·my** (pĭg′mē) —*n., pl.* **-mies. 1.** *Gk. Myth.* A member of a race of dwarfs. **2.** A member of any of several African and Asian peoples with a hereditary stature of from four to five feet. **3. pygmy.** An individual of unusually small size or significance. —*adj.* **1.** Of or pertaining to the Pygmies. **2. pygmy. a.** Unusually or atypically small. **b.** Unimportant; trivial. [ME *pigmie* < Lat. *pygmaeus,* dwarfish < Gk. *pugmaios* < *pugmē,* the length from the elbow to the knuckles.]

py·ja·mas (pə-jä′məz, -jăm′əz) *n. Chiefly Brit.* Variant of **pajamas.**

pyk·nic (pĭk′nĭk) *adj. Anthropol.* Characterized by short, stocky, and powerful stature; endomorphic. [< Gk. *puknos,* compact.] **—pyk′nic** *n.*

py·lon (pī′lŏn′) *n.* **1.** A monumental gateway in the form of a pair of truncated pyramids serving as the entrance to an ancient Egyptian temple. **2.** A large structure or structures marking an entrance or approach. **3.** A tower marking a turning point in a race among aircraft. **4.** A steel tower supporting high-tension wires. **5.** A temporary artificial leg. [Gk. *pulōn,* gateway < *pulē,* gate.]

py·lo·rus (pī-lôr′əs, -lōr′-, pĭ-) *n., pl.* **-lo·ri** (-lôr′ī′, -lōr′ī′). The passage connecting the stomach and the duodenum. [LLat. *pylorus* < Gk. *pulōros* : *pulē,* gate + *ouros,* watcher < *horan,* to see.] **—py·lo′ric** (-ĭk) *adj.*

pyo– or **py–** *pref.* Pus: *pyoderma.* [< Gk. *puon,* pus.]

py·o·der·ma (pī′ə-dûr′mə) *n.* A pus-causing skin disease. **—py′o·der′mic** *adj.*

py·o·gen·e·sis (pī′ə-jĕn′ĭ-sĭs) *n.* Pyosis. **—py′o·gen′ic** *adj.*

py·or·rhe·a or **py·or·rhoe·a** (pī′ə-rē′ə) *n.* **1.** A discharge of pus. **2.** Inflammation of the gum and tooth sockets leading to loosening of the teeth. **—py′or·rhe′al** *adj.*

py·o·sis (pī-ō′sĭs) *n.* The formation of pus.

pyr– *pref.* Variant of **pyro-.**

py·ra·can·tha (pī′rə-kăn′thə) *n.* A shrub of the genus *Pyracantha*; the fire thorn. [Gk. *purakantha,* a shrub : *pur,* fire + *akantha,* thorn.]

py·ral·id (pī-răl′ĭd) also **py·ral·i·did** (pī-răl′ĭ-dĭd) *n.* Any of various small or medium-sized moths of the large, widely distributed family Pyralididae. —*adj.* Of or belonging to the Pyralididae. [NLat. *Pyralididae,* family name < Gk. *puralis,* an insect said to live in fire < *pur,* fire.]

pyr·a·mid (pĭr′ə-mĭd) *n.* **1.** A polyhedron with a polygonal base and triangular faces meeting in a common vertex. **2.** Something shaped like a pyramid. **3.** A massive monument found esp. in Egypt, having a rectangular base and four triangular faces culminating in a single apex, and serving as a tomb or temple. **4.** The transactions involved in pyramiding stock. —*v.* **-mid·ed, -mid·ing, -mids.** —*tr.* **1.** To place or build in the shape of a pyramid. **2.** To build (an argument or thesis, for example) progressively from a basic general premise. **3.** To speculate in (stock) by making a series of buying and selling transactions in which paper profits are used as margin for buying more stock. —*intr.* **1.** To assume the shape of a pyramid. **2.** To increase rapidly and on a widening base. **3.** To pyramid stocks. [Lat. *pyramis, pyramid-* < Gk. *puramis.*] **—py·ram′i·dal** (pĭ-răm′ĭ-dəl), **pyr′a·mid′ic, pyr′a·mid′i·cal** *adj.* **—py·ram′i·dal·ly** *adv.*

Pyr·a·mus (pĭr′ə-məs) *n. Rom. Myth.* The legendary youth of Babylon who committed suicide when he mistakenly thought his lover Thisbe was dead. [Lat.]

py·rar·gy·rite (pī-rär′jə-rīt′, pĭ-) *n.* A deep red to black silver ore with composition Ag_3SbS_3. [G. *Pyrargyrit* : Gk. *pur,* fire + Gk. *arguros,* silver + *-it,* -ite.]

pyre (pīr) *n.* **1.** A heap of combustibles for burning a corpse as a funeral rite. **2.** A pile of combustibles. [Lat. *pyra* < Gk. *pura* < *pur,* fire.]

py·rene (pī′rēn′, pī-rēn′) *n.* The stone of certain fruits. [NLat. *pyrena* < Gk. *purēn.*]

py·re·noid (pī-rē′noid′, pī′rə-) *n.* One of the protein granules of certain algae and similar plants in which starch is formed. [NLat. *pyrena,* fruit stone + -OID.]

py·re·thrin (pī-rē′thrĭn, -rĕth′rĭn) *n.* Either of two viscous liquid esters, $C_{21}H_{28}O_3$ or $C_{22}H_{28}O_5$, that are extracted from pyrethrum flowers and are used as insecticides. [PYRETHR(UM) + -IN.]

py·re·thrum (pī-rē′thrəm, -rĕth′rəm) *n.* **1.** Any of several Old World plants of the genus *Chrysanthemum* and related genera, such as *C. coccineum,* cultivated for its showy flowers. **2.** The dried flowers of *C. cinerariaefolium* or *C. coccineum,* used as an insecticide. [Lat., pellitory < Gk. *purethron,* feverfew, ult. < *pur,* fire.]

py·ret·ic (pī-rĕt′ĭk) *adj.* Characterized or affected by fever; feverish. [Gk. *puretikos* < *puretos,* fever < *pur,* fire.]

Py·rex (pī′rĕks′). A trademark for any of various types of heat-resistant and chemical-resistant glass.

py·rex·i·a (pī-rĕk′sē-ə) *n.* Fever. [NLat. < Gk. *purexis* < *puressein,* to have a fever < *puretos,* fever < *pur,* fire.] —**py·rex′i·al, py·rex′ic** *adj.*

pyr·he·li·om·e·ter (pīr′hē-lē-ŏm′ĭ-tər, pĭr′-) *n.* Any of various devices that measure all or restricted components of incident solar radiation. —**pyr′he·li·o·met′ric** (-ə-mĕt′rĭk) *adj.*

py·ric (pī′rĭk, pĭr′ĭk) *adj.* Of, pertaining to, or resulting from burning. [Fr. *pyrique* < Gk. *pur,* fire.]

pyr·i·dine (pĭr′ĭ-dēn′) *n.* A flammable, colorless or yellowish liquid base, C_5H_5N, used to synthesize vitamins and drugs, as a solvent, and as a denaturant for alcohol. —**py·rid′ic** (pī-rĭd′ĭk) *adj.*

pyr·i·dox·a·mine (pĭr′ĭ-dŏk′sə-mēn′) *n.* An amine, $C_8H_{12}N_2O_2$, of the vitamin B_6 group. [PYRIDOX(INE) + -AMINE.]

pyr·i·dox·ine (pĭr′ĭ-dŏk′sēn′, -sĭn) also **pyr·i·dox·in** (-dŏk′sĭn) *n.* A pyridine derivative, $C_8H_{11}O_3N$, occurring in plant and animal tissues and active in various metabolic processes. [PYRID(INE) + OX- + -INE.]

pyr·i·form (pĭr′ə-fôrm′) *adj.* Pear-shaped. [Med. Lat. *pyrum,* pear (alteration of Lat. *pirum*) + -FORM.]

py·rim·i·dine (pī-rĭm′ĭ-dēn′, pĭ-) *n.* **1.** A liquid and crystalline organic base, $C_4H_4N_2$. **2.** Any of several basic compounds, such as uracil, having a molecular structure similar to pyrimidine and found in living matter as a nucleotide component. [Alteration of PYRIDINE.]

py·rite (pī′rīt′) *n.* A yellow to brown, widely occurring mineral sulfide, FeS_2, used as an iron ore and to produce sulfur dioxide for sulfuric acid. [< Lat. *pyrites,* flint. —see PYRITES.] —**py·rit′ic** (-rĭt′ĭk), **py·rit′i·cal** *adj.*

py·ri·tes (pī-rī′tēz, pī′rīts′) *n., pl.* **pyrites.** Any of various natural metallic sulfides, esp. of iron. [Lat., flint < Gk. *puritēs (lithos),* fire (stone) < *pur,* fire.]

pyro– or **pyr–** *pref.* **1.** Fire; heat: *pyrotechnic.* **2.** Resulting from or as if from the action of fire or heat: *pyrography.* **3.** Fever: *pyrogen.* **4.** Derived from an acid by the loss of a water molecule: *pyrosulfuric acid.* [< Gk. *pur,* fire.]

py·ro·cat·e·chol (pī′rō-kăt′ĭ-kôl′, -kōl′) *n.* A colorless, crystalline organic compound, $C_6H_4(OH)_2$, used as an antiseptic and photographic developer. [PYRO- + CATECH(U) + -OL.]

py·ro·cel·lu·lose (pī′rō-sĕl′yə-lōs′, -lōz′) *n.* A cellulose nitrate used as a component of smokeless powder.

py·ro·chem·i·cal (pī′rō-kĕm′ĭ-kəl) *adj.* Designating or pertaining to chemical activity at elevated temperatures. —**py′ro·chem′i·cal·ly** *adv.*

py·ro·clas·tic (pī′rō-klăs′tĭk) *adj.* Formed by rock fragmentation resulting from volcanic ejection.

py·ro·e·lec·tric (pī′rō-ĭ-lĕk′trĭk) *adj.* Exhibiting or pertaining to pyroelectricity. —*n.* A pyroelectric material.

py·ro·e·lec·tric·i·ty (pī′rō-ĭ-lĕk-trĭs′ĭ-tē) *n.* The generation of electric charge on a crystal by change of temperature.

py·ro·gal·lic acid (pī′rō-găl′ĭk, -gô′lĭk) *n.* Pyrogallol.

py·ro·gal·lol (pī′rō-găl′ôl′, -ōl′, -gô′lôl′, -lōl′) *n.* A white lustrous crystalline compound, $C_6H_3(OH)_3$, used as a photographic developer and to treat skin diseases. [PYRO- + GALL(IC) + -OL¹.] —**py′ro·gal′lic** (-găl′ĭk, -gô′lĭk) *adj.*

py·ro·gen (pī′rə-jən) *n.* A substance that produces fever.

py·ro·gen·ic (pī′rō-jĕn′ĭk) also **py·rog·e·nous** (pī-rŏj′ə-nəs) *adj.* **1.** Producing or produced by fever. **2.** Caused by or generating heat. **3.** Igneous (sense 2.b.). —**py′ro·ge·nic′i·ty** (-rō-jə-nĭs′ĭ-tē) *n.*

py·rog·ra·phy (pī-rŏg′rə-fē) *n.* **1.** The art or process of producing designs on wood, leather, or other material by using heated tools or a fine flame. **2.** A design made by pyrography. —**py′ro·graph′** (pī′rə-grăf′) *n.* —**py·rog′ra·pher** *n.* —**py′ro·graph′ic** *adj.*

py·ro·lig·ne·ous (pī′rō-lĭg′nē-əs) *adj.* Made by the destructive distillation of wood.

pyroligneous acid *n.* A reddish-brown wood distillate containing acetic acid, methyl alcohol, acetone, and a tarry residue.

py·ro·lu·site (pī′rō-lo͞o′sīt′) *n.* A soft, black to dark-gray ore of manganese, consisting essentially of manganese dioxide. [G. *Pyrolusit* : Gk. *pur,* fire + Gk. *lousis,* a washing (< *louein,* to wash) + *-it,* -ite.]

py·rol·y·sis (pī-rŏl′ĭ-sĭs) *n.* Chemical change caused by heat. —**py′ro·lyt′ic** (-rə-lĭt′ĭk) *adj.* —**py′ro·lyt′i·cal·ly** *adv.*

py·ro·lyze (pī′rə-līz′) *tr.v.* **-lyzed, -lyz·ing, -lyz·es.** To subject (something) to pyrolysis.

py·ro·man·cy (pī′rə-măn′sē) *n.* Divination by fire or flames. [ME *piromance* < OFr. *pyromancie* < LLat. *pyromantia* < Gk. *puromanteia* : *pur-,* fire + *manteia,* divination. —see -MANCY.] —**py′ro·man′tic** (-măn′tĭk) *adj.*

py·ro·ma·ni·a (pī′rō-mā′nē-ə, -mān′yə) *n.* The uncontrollable impulse to start fires. —**py′ro·ma′ni·ac′** (-mā′nē-ăk′) *adj.* & *n.* —**py′ro·ma·ni′a·cal** (-mə-nī′ə-kəl) *adj.*

py·ro·met·al·lur·gy (pī′rō-mĕt′l-ûr′jē) *n.* Metallurgy that depends on the action of heat, as smelting. —**py′ro·met′al·lur′gi·cal** (-mĕt′l-ûr′jĭ-kəl) *adj.*

py·rom·e·ter (pī-rŏm′ĭ-tər) *n.* An electrical thermometer used for measuring high temperatures. —**py′ro·met′ric** (-rə-mĕt′rĭk), **py′ro·met′ri·cal** *adj.* —**py′ro·met′ri·cal·ly** *adv.* —**py·rom′e·try** *n.*

py·ro·mor·phite (pī′rə-môr′fīt′) *n.* A lead ore with composition $Pb_5(PO_4,AsO_4)_3Cl$, occurring in green, brown, or yellow crystals. [G. *Pyromorphit* : Gk. *pur,* fire + Gk. *morphē,* form + *-it,* -ite.]

py·rope (pī′rōp′) *n.* A deep-red garnet, $Mg_3Al_2Si_3O_{12}$, used as a gem. [ME *pirope* < OFr. < Lat. *pyropus,* gold-bronze < Gk. *purōpos* : *pur,* fire + *ōps,* eye.]

py·ro·phor·ic (pī′rə-fôr′ĭk, -fōr′-) *adj.* **1.** Spontaneously igniting in air. **2.** Producing sparks by friction. [< Gk. *purophoros,* fire-bearing : *pur,* fire + *pherein,* to carry.]

py·ro·phos·phate (pī′rə-fŏs′făt′) *n.* A salt or ester of pyrophosphoric acid. —**py′ro·phos·phat′ic** (-făt′ĭk) *adj.*

py·ro·phos·phor·ic acid (pī′rō-fŏs-fôr′ĭk, -fōr′-) *n.* A syrupy viscous liquid, $H_4P_2O_7$, used as a catalyst and in organic chemical manufacture.

py·ro·phyl·lite (pī′rō-fĭl′īt′, pī-rŏf′ə-līt′) *n.* A silvery white or pale-green mineral aluminum silicate, $Al_2Si_4O_{10}(OH)_2$, occurring naturally in soft, compact masses.

py·ro·sis (pī-rō′sĭs) *n.* Heartburn. [Gk. *purōsis,* a burning < *puroun,* to burn < *pur,* fire.]

py·ro·stat (pī′rə-stăt) *n.* **1.** An automatic sensing device that activates an alarm or extinguisher in case of fire. **2.** A high-temperature thermostat.

py·ro·sul·fate (pī′rō-sŭl′făt′) *n.* A salt of pyrosulfuric acid. [PYROSULF(URIC ACID) + -ATE².]

py·ro·sul·fu·ric acid (pī′rō-sŭl-fyo͝or′ĭk) *n.* A heavy, oily, colorless to dark-brown liquid, $H_2S_2O_7$, produced by adding sulfur trioxide to concentrated sulfuric acid and used in petroleum refining and explosives.

py·ro·tech·nic (pī′rə-tĕk′nĭk) also **py·ro·tech·ni·cal** (-nĭ-kəl) *adj.* **1.** Of or pertaining to fireworks. **2.** Resembling fireworks; brilliant: *a pyrotechnic wit.* —**py′ro·tech′ni·cal·ly** *adv.*

py·ro·tech·nics (pī′rə-tĕk′nĭks) *n.* **1.** *(used with a sing. verb).* The art of manufacturing or setting off fireworks. **2.** A fireworks display. **3.** A brilliant display, as of rhetoric or wit, or of virtuosity in the performing arts. —**py′ro·tech′nist** *n.*

py·ro·tech·ny (pī′rə-tĕk′nē) *n.* Pyrotechnics (sense 1).

py·rox·ene (pī-rŏk′sēn′) *n.* Any of a group of crystalline mineral silicates common in igneous and metamorphic rocks and containing two metallic oxides, as of magnesium, iron, calcium, or sodium. [Fr. *pyroxène* : Gk. *pur,* fire + Gk. *xenos,* stranger.] —**py′rox·en′ic** (pī′rŏk-sē′nĭk, -sĕn′ĭk) *adj.*

py·rox·e·nite (pī-rŏk′sə-nīt′) *n.* An igneous rock consisting chiefly of pyroxenes. —**py·rox′e·nit′ic** (-nĭt′ĭk) *adj.*

py·rox·y·lin (pī-rŏk′sə-lĭn) also **py·rox·y·line** (-lēn′, -lĭn) *n.* A highly flammable nitrocellulose used in the manufacture of collodion, plastics, and lacquers.

pyr·rhic (pĭr′ĭk) *n.* A Greek metrical foot composed of two short syllables. —*adj.* Of or characterized by pyrrhics. [Gk. *purrhikhios* < *purrhikhē,* a war dance.]

Pyr·rhic victory (pĭr′ĭk) *n.* A victory that is offset by staggering losses. [From the victory of *Pyrrhus* (319–272 B.C.), king of Epirus, over the Romans at Asculum in 279 B.C.]

pyr·rho·tite (pĭr′ə-tīt′) also **pyr·rho·tine** (-tīn′) *n.* A naturally occurring brownish-bronze iron sulfide, FeS, characterized by weak magnetic properties and used as an iron ore and in the manufacture of sulfuric acid. [G. *Pyrrhotin* < Gk. *purrhotēs,* redness < *purrhos,* fiery < *pur,* fire.]

pyr·rhu·lox·i·a (pĭr′ə-lŏk′sē-ə, pĭr′yə-) *n.* A crested gray and red bird, *Pyrrhuloxia sinuata,* of the southwestern United States and Mexico, having a short, thick bill. [NLat. *Pyrrhuloxia,* genus name : *Pyrrhula,* finch genus (< Gk. *purrhoulas,* red bird < *purrhos,* red < *pur,* fire) + *Loxia,* crossbill genus < Gk. *loxos,* oblique.]

pyr·role (pîr′ōl′) *n.* A yellowish or brown liquid, C_4H_5N, having a characteristic odor similar to chloroform and used to manufacture a wide variety of drugs. [Gk. *purrhos,* red (< *pur,* fire) + -OLE.] —**pyr·ro′lic** (pĭ-rō′lĭk) *adj.*

py·ru·vic acid (pī-ro͞o′vĭk, pĭ-) *n.* A colorless liquid, CH_3CO-$COOH$, formed as a fundamental intermediate in protein and carbohydrate metabolism. [PYR(O)- + Lat. *uva,* grape.]

Py·thag·o·re·an·ism (pĭ-thăg′ə-rē′ə-nĭz′əm) *n.* The syncretistic philosophy expounded by Pythagoras, chiefly distinguished by its description of reality in terms of arithmetical relationships. —**Py·thag′o·re′an** (-rē′ən) *n.* & *adj.*

Pythagorean theorem *n.* The theorem that the sum of the squares of the lengths of the sides of a right triangle is equal to the square of the length of the hypotenuse.

Pyth·i·an (pĭth′ē-ən) *adj.* **1.** Of or pertaining to Delphi, the temple of Apollo at Delphi, or its oracle. **2.** Of or pertaining to the Pythian games. [Lat. *Pythius* < Gk. *Puthios* < *puthō,* ancient name of Delphi, Greece.] —**Pyth′ic** *adj.*

Pythian games *pl.n.* In ancient Greece, a pan-Hellenic festival of athletic tournaments held every four years at Delphi in honor of Apollo.

Pyth·i·as (pĭth′ē-əs) *n.* *Rom. Myth.* A Greek who narrowly escaped being executed while held as a voluntary hostage in place of his condemned friend Damon. [Lat., alteration of Gk. *Phintias.*]

Py·thon (pī′thŏn′, -thən) *n.* **1.** *Gk. Myth.* A dragon or serpent that was the tutelary demon of the oracular cult at Delphi until killed and expropriated by Apollo. **2. python.** Any of various nonvenomous Old World snakes of the family Pythonidae that coil around and suffocate their prey. **3. python. a.** A soothsaying spirit or demon. **b.** A person possessed by such a spirit. [Gk. *Puthōn.*]

py·tho·ness (pī′thə-nĭs, pĭth′ə-) *n.* **1.** The priestess of Apollo at Delphi. **2.** A prophetess. [ME *phitonesse* < OFr. *phitonise* < LLat. *pythonissa* < Gk. *Puthōn,* Python.]

py·thon·ic (pī-thŏn′ĭk) *adj.* **1.** Of, pertaining to, or resembling a python. **2.** Of or like an oracle; prophetic. **3.** Of extraordinary size and power.

py·u·ri·a (pī-yo͝or′ē-ə) *n.* The abnormal condition of pus in the urine.

pyx also **pix** (pĭks) *n.* **1.** *Eccles.* **a.** A container in which supplies of wafers for the Eucharist are kept. **b.** A container in which the Eucharist is carried to the sick. **2.** A chest in a mint in which specimen coins are placed to await assay. [ME *pyxe* < Lat. *pyxis,* box < Gk. *puxis.*]

pyx·i·des (pĭk′sĭ-dēz′) *n.* Plural of **pyxis.**

pyx·id·i·um (pĭk-sĭd′ē-əm) *n., pl.* **-i·a** (-ē-ə). A pyxis. [NLat. < Gk. *puxidion,* dim. of *puxis,* box.]

pyx·ie (pĭk′sē) *n.* A creeping evergreen shrub, *Pyxidanthera barbulata,* native to pine barrens of the eastern United States, having small white or pinkish flowers. [NLat. *Pyxidanthera,* genus name : PYXIS + Med. Lat. *anthera,* pollen. —see ANTHER.]

pyx·is (pĭk′sĭs) *n., pl.* **pyx·i·des** (-sĭ-dēz′). *Bot.* A seed capsule having a circular lid that falls off to release the seeds. [Gk. *puxis,* box.]

Pyx·is (pĭk′sĭs) *n.* A constellation in the Southern Hemisphere, near Antlia and Puppis. [NLat. *Pyxis (nautica),* (mariner's) compass < Gk. *puxis,* box.]

Q

Around 1000 B.C. the Phoenicians and other Semitic peoples began to use graphic signs to represent individual speech sounds instead of syllables or words. They used this symbol (1) to represent a velar consonant that is not found in English or any other Indo-European language and called it *qōph,* their word for "monkey." The Greeks, adapting the Phoenician alphabet, used *qōph* to represent the sound of the consonant "k" and altered its name to *qoppa* (2,3). Since they also used *kappa* to represent the same sound, they eventually dropped *qoppa* from the alphabet. The Romans borrowed the alphabet from the Greeks via the Etruscans. Like the Greeks, the Romans already had a symbol for the sound of "k," but they retained Q to represent that sound when it was followed by U. They also adapted the alphabet for monumental inscriptions, and their monumental script (6) is the prototype of modern capital letters (9,10). Medieval scribes adapted the Roman capitals to being quickly written on paper, parchment, and vellum. These uncial and cursive minuscules (7,8) are the prototypes of modern lower-case letters, both written and printed (12,11).

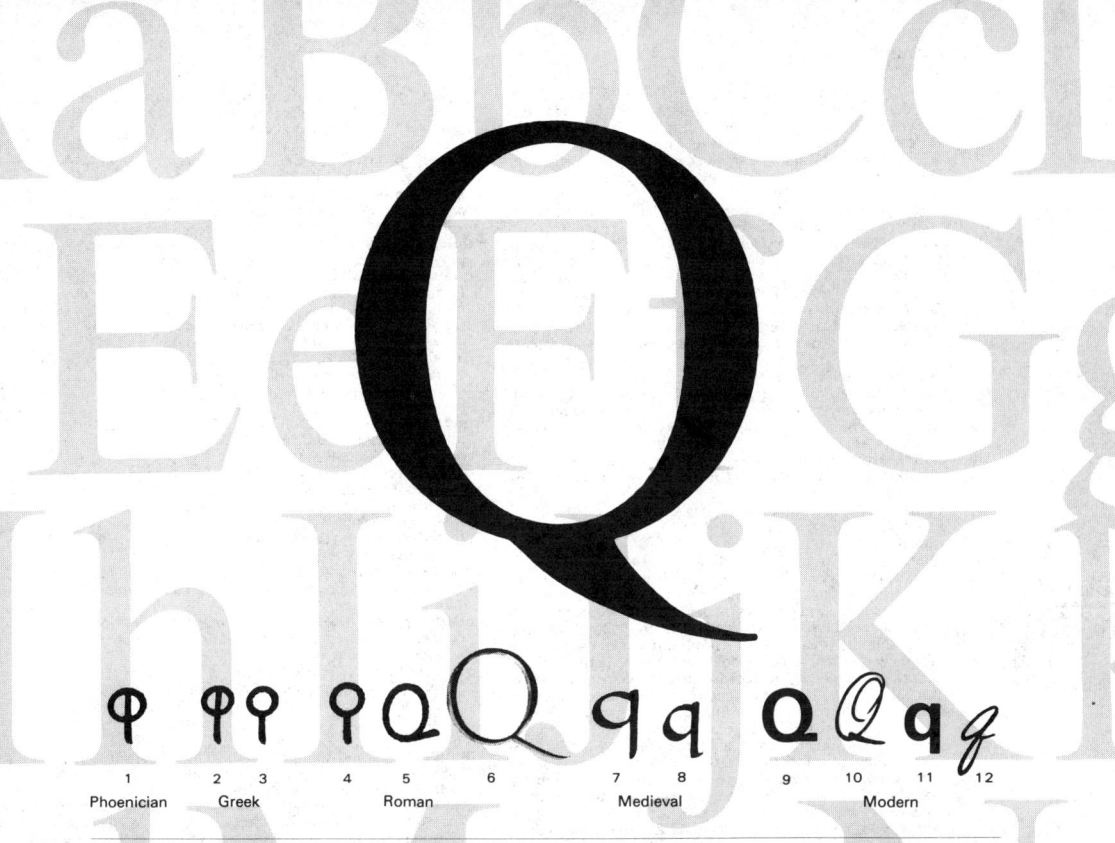

q

q or **Q** (kyo͞o) *n., pl.* **q's** or **Q's.** **1.** The 17th letter of the modern English alphabet. **2.** Any of the speech sounds represented by this letter. **3.** The 17th in a series.
Q fever *n.* An infectious disease caused by the rickettsia *Coxiella burnetii* that is characterized by fever, malaise, and muscular pains. [Q(UERY) + FEVER.]
qin·tar (kĭn-tär′) *n.* Variant of **quintar.**
qoph (kôf) *n.* The 19th letter of the Hebrew alphabet. See table at **alphabet.** [Heb. *qōph.*]
q.t. (kyo͞o′tē′) *n. Slang.* Quiet: *on the q.t.* [Short for QUIET.]
qua (kwā, kwä) *prep.* In the capacity or character of; as: *The President qua head of his party mediated the dispute.* [Lat., ablative fem. sing. of *qui,* who.]
Quaa·lude (kwā′lo͞od′). A trademark for methaqualone.
quack[1] (kwăk) *n.* The characteristic sound uttered by a duck. —*intr.v.* **quacked, quack·ing, quacks.** To utter a quack. [Imit.]
quack[2] (kwăk) *n.* **1.** An untrained person who pretends to have medical knowledge. **2.** A charlatan; mountebank. —***modifier:*** *a quack cure.* —*intr.v.* **quacked, quack·ing, quacks.** To act as a quack. [Short for QUACKSALVER.] —**quack′er·y** *n.*
quack grass *n.* Couch grass. [Var. of QUITCH GRASS.]
quack·sal·ver (kwăk′săl′vər) *n. Archaic.* A quack[2]. [Obs. Du.]
quad[1] (kwŏd) *n.* A quadrangle (sense 2).
quad[2] (kwŏd) *n.* A quadrat.
quad[3] (kwŏd) *n.* A quadruplet.
quadr– *pref.* Variant of **quadri–.**
quad·ran·gle (kwŏd′răng′gəl) *n.* **1.** *Math.* A plane figure consisting of four points, no three of which are collinear, connected by straight lines. **2. a.** A rectangular area surrounded on all four sides by buildings. **b.** The buildings bordering this area. **3.** The area of land shown on one atlas sheet charted by the U.S. Geological Survey. [ME < OFr. < LLat. *quadrangulum,* neuter of *quadrangulus,* four-cornered, var. of Lat. *quadriangulus* : *quadri-,* four + *angulus,* angle.]

quadrangle

quad·rant (kwŏd′rənt) *n.* **1.** *Math.* **a.** A circular arc subtending a central angle of 90 degrees; one fourth of the circumference of a circle. **b.** The plane area bounded by two perpendicular radii and the arc they subtend. **c.** Any of the four areas into which a plane is divided by the reference axes in a Cartesian coordinate system, designated *first, second, third,* and *fourth,* counting clockwise from the area in which both coordinates are positive. **2.** A machine part or other mechanical device that is shaped like a quarter circle. **3.** An early instrument for measuring altitudes, consisting of a 90-degree graduated arc with a movable radius for measuring angles. [Lat. *quadrans, quadrant-,* quarter.]
quad·ra·phon·ic (kwŏd′rə-fŏn′ĭk) *adj.* Of or for an extension of stereophonic sound reproduction in which two additional channels are used at the rear of the listening space, reproducing signals that are independent of or derived from the front channels. —**qua·draph′o·ny** (kwŏ-drăf′ə-nē) *n.*

quagga

quad·ra·son·ic (kwŏd′rə-sŏn′ĭk) *adj.* Quadraphonic.
quad·rat (kwŏd′rət, -răt′) *n. Printing.* A piece of type metal lower than the raised typeface, used for filling spaces and blank lines. [Var. of QUADRATE.]
quad·rate (kwŏd′rāt′, -rĭt) *n.* **1. a.** A square or cube. **b.** An approximately square or cubic area, space, or object. **2.** *Zool.* A bone or cartilaginous structure of the skull, joining the upper and lower jaws in birds, fish, reptiles, and amphibians. —*adj.* **1.** Having four sides and four angles; square or rectangular. **2.** *Zool.* Designating the quadrate bone or cartilage. —*intr.v.* **-rat·ed, -rat·ing, -rates.** *Archaic.* To correspond; agree. [ME < Lat. *quadratus,* p.part. of *quadrare,* to make square < *quadrus,* square.]
quad·rat·ic (kwŏ-drăt′ĭk) *adj.* Of, pertaining to, or containing mathematical quantities of the second degree or less. [< QUADRATE.] —**quad·rat′ic** *n.* —**quad·rat′i·cal·ly** *adv.*
quadratic equation *n.* An equation of the second degree, having the general form $ax^2 + bx + c = 0$, where *a, b,* and *c* are constants.
quadratic formula *n.* The formula $x = [-b \pm \sqrt{(b^2 - 4ac)}]/2a$, used to compute the roots of a quadratic equation.
quad·rat·ics (kwŏ-drăt′ĭks) *n. (used with a sing. verb).* The algebra of quadratic equations.
quad·ra·ture (kwŏd′rə-cho͝or′) *n.* **1.** The process of making something square. **2.** *Math.* The process of constructing a square equal in area to a given surface. **3.** *Astron.* A configuration in which the angular separation of two celestial bodies, as measured from a third, is 90 degrees.
quad·ren·ni·al (kwŏ-drĕn′ē-əl) *adj.* **1.** Happening once in four years. **2.** Lasting for four years. —*n.* An event occurring every four years. —**quad·ren′ni·al·ly** *adv.*
quad·ren·ni·um (kwŏ-drĕn′ē-əm) *n., pl.* **-ni·ums** or **-ni·a** (-ē-ə). A period of four years. [Lat. *quadriennium* : *quadri-,* four + *annus,* year.]

quahog

quadri– or **quadru–** or **quadr–** *pref.* **1.** Four: *quadrilateral.* **2.** Square: *quadrate.* [ME < Lat.]
quad·ric (kwŏd′rĭk) *adj.* Of or pertaining to geometric surfaces that are defined by quadratic equations.
quad·ri·cen·ten·ni·al (kwŏd′rĭ-sĕn-tĕn′ē-əl) *n.* A 400th anniversary. —**quad′ri·cen·ten′ni·al** *adj.*
quad·ri·ceps (kwŏd′rĭ-sĕps′) *n.* The large four-part extensor muscle at the front of the thigh. [QUADRI- + (BI)CEPS.] —**quad′ri·cip′i·tal** (-sĭp′ĭ-təl) *adj.*
quad·ri·fid (kwŏd′rə-fĭd′) *adj. Bot.* Divided into four parts: *a quadrifid leaf.*
quad·ri·ga (kwŏd′rī-gə) *n., pl.* **-gae** (-gē). A two-wheeled chariot drawn by four horses abreast. [Lat., sing. of *quadrigae,* team of four horses, short for *quadrijugae,* fem. pl. of *quadrijugus,* of a team of four : *quadri-,* four + *jungere,* to yoke.]
quad·ri·lat·er·al (kwŏd′rə-lăt′ər-əl) *n. Math.* A four-sided polygon. —*adj.* Having four sides.
qua·drille[1] (kwŏ-drĭl′, kwə-, kə-) *n.* **1.** A square dance of French origin composed of five figures and performed by four couples. **2.** Music for the quadrille in 6/8 and 2/4 time. [Fr. < *quadrille,* one of four divisions of an army < Sp. *cuadrilla,* dim. of *cuadra,* square < Lat. *quadra.*]
qua·drille[2] (kwŏ-drĭl′, kwə-, kə-) *n.* A card game popular during the 18th century, played by 4 people with a deck of 40 cards. [Fr., perh. < Sp. *cuartillo* < *cuarto,* fourth < Lat. *quartus.*]
quad·ril·lion (kwŏ-drĭl′yən) *n.* **1.** The cardinal number equal to 10^{15}. **2.** *Chiefly Brit.* Septillion (sense 1). [QUADR(I)- + (M)ILLION.] —**quad·ril′lion** *adj.*
quad·ril·lionth (kwŏ-drĭl′yənth) *n.* The ordinal number that matches quadrillion in a series. —**quad·ril′lionth** *adj. & adv.*
quad·ri·par·tite (kwŏd′rə-pär′tīt′) *adj.* **1.** Consisting of or divided into four parts. **2.** Involving four participants.
quad·ri·phon·ic (kwŏd′rə-fŏn′ĭk) *adj.* Quadraphonic. —**quad′ri·phon′y** *n.*
quad·ri·ple·gi·a (kwŏd′rə-plē′jē-ə, -jə) *n.* Complete paralysis of the body from the neck down. —**quad′ri·ple′gic** (-jĭk) *adj. & n.*
quad·ri·va·lent (kwŏd′rə-vā′lənt) *adj. Chem.* **1.** Having four valences. **2.** Having a valence of four; tetravalent. —**quad′ri·va′lence, quad′ri·va′len·cy** *n.*
quad·riv·i·um (kwŏ-drĭv′ē-əm) *n., pl.* **-i·a** (-ē-ə). The higher division of the seven liberal arts in the Middle Ages, composed of geometry, astronomy, arithmetic, and music. [LLat. < Lat., place where four roads meet : *quadri-,* four + *via,* road.]
quad·roon (kwŏ-dro͞on′) *n.* A person having one quarter Negro ancestry. [Sp. *cuarteron* < *cuarto,* quarter < Lat. *quartus.*]
quadru– *pref.* Variant of **quadri–.**
quad·ru·ma·nous (kwŏ-dro͞o′mə-nəs) also **quad·ru·ma·nal** (-nəl) *adj. Zool.* Having four feet with opposable first digits, as primates other than man. [QUADRU- + Lat. *manus,* hand.]
quad·rum·vi·rate (kwŏd·rŭm-və-rĭt) *n.* A group of four persons joined in authority or office, esp. a government of four persons. [QUADR(I)- + (TRI)UMVIRATE.] —**quad′rum·vir** *n.*
quad·ru·ped (kwŏd′rə-pĕd′) *n.* A four-footed animal. —**quad·ru′pe·dal** (kwŏ-dro͞o′pə-dəl, kwŏd′rə-pĕd′l) *adj.*
quad·ru·ple (kwŏ-dro͞o′pəl, -drŭp′əl, kwŏd′ro͞o-pəl) *adj.* **1.** Having four parts or members. **2.** Multiplied by four; fourfold. **3.** *Mus.* Having four beats to the measure. —*n.* A number four times as great as another. —*v.* **-pled, -pling, -ples.** —*tr.* To multiply or increase by four. —*intr.* To become quadrupled. [Fr. < Lat. *quadruplus.*]
quad·ru·plet (kwŏ-drŭp′lĭt, -dro͞o′plĭt, kwŏd′rə-plĭt) *n.* **1.** A group or combination of four associated by common properties or behavior. **2.** One of four offspring born in a single birth.
quad·ru·pli·cate (kwŏ-dro͞o′plĭ-kĭt) *adj.* **1.** Multiplied by four; quadruple. **2.** Fourth in a group of four identical things. —*n.* One of a group of four identical things. —*v.* (-kāt′) **-cat·ed, -cat·ing, -cates.** —*tr.* To multiply four times. —*intr.* To become quadruplicated. [Lat. *quadruplicatus,* p.part. of *quadruplicare,* to multiply by four < *quadruplex,* fourfold : *quadru-,* four + *-plex,* -fold.] —**quad·ru′pli·cate·ly** (-kĭt-lē) *adv.* —**quad·ru′pli·ca′tion** *n.*
quaes·tor (kwĕs′tər, kwē′stər) *n.* Any of various public officials in ancient Rome responsible for finance and administration in various areas of government and the military. [ME *questor* < Lat. *quaestor* < *quaerere,* to inquire.] —**quaes·to′ri·al** (kwĕ-stôr′ē-əl, -stōr′-, kwē-) *adj.* —**quaes′tor·ship′** *n.*
quaff (kwŏf, kwăf, kwôf) *v.* **quaffed, quaff·ing, quaffs.** —*tr.* To drink heartily. —*intr.* To drink something heartily. —*n.* A hearty draft. [Orig. unknown.] —**quaff′er** *n.*
quag (kwăg, kwôg) *n.* A quagmire. [Orig. unknown.]
quag·ga (kwăg′ə, kwŏg′ə) *n.* A zebralike mammal, *Equus quagga,* of southern Africa, that has been extinct since the late 19th century. [Afr. < Xhosa *i-qwara,* perh. < Hottentot *quăgga.*]
quag·gy (kwăg′ē, kwŏg′ē) *adj.* **-gi·er, -gi·est. 1.** Like a marsh; soggy. **2.** Soft; flabby.
quag·mire (kwăg′mīr′, kwŏg′-) *n.* **1.** Land with a soft, muddy surface that yields when stepped on. **2.** A difficult or precarious situation; predicament.
qua·hog also **qua·haug** (kwô′hôg′, -hŏg′, kwō′-, kō′-) *n.* An edible clam, *Venus mercenaria,* of the Atlantic coast of North America, having a hard, rounded shell. [Narraganset *poquaûhock.*]
quai (kā, kē) *n.* A quay.
quaich also **quaigh** (kwāKH) *n.* A two-handled Scottish drinking cup of varying size. [Sc. Gael. *cuach.*]

quail[1] (kwāl) *n., pl.* **quail** or **quails. 1.** Any of various chickenlike Old World birds of the genus *Coturnix,* esp. *C. coturnix,* a small bird having mottled brown plumage and a short tail. **2.** Any of various New World birds similar or related to the quail, such as the bobwhite. [ME *quaille* < OFr. < Med. Lat. *quaccula.*]

quail[2] (kwāl) *intr.v.* **quailed, quail·ing, quails.** To shrink back in fear; cower: "*When his eyes beheld the Mountain and the desert, he quailed*" (J.R.R. Tolkien). [ME *quailen,* to give way.]

quaint (kwānt) *adj.* **-er, -est. 1.** Charmingly curious, esp. in an old-fashioned way: *a quaint old inn.* **2.** Unfamiliar or unusual in character; strange: *quaint island customs.* [ME *coint,* strange < OFr. < Lat. *cognitus,* p.part of *cognoscere,* to learn. —see COGNITION.] **—quaint'ly** *adv.* **—quaint'ness** *n.*

quake (kwāk) *intr.v.* **quaked, quak·ing, quakes. 1.** To shake or tremble with instability or shock. **2.** To shiver or tremble, as with cold or strong emotion. *—n.* **1.** An instance of quaking. **2.** An earthquake. [ME *quaken* < OE *cwacian.*] **—quak'y** *adj.*

Quak·er (kwā'kər) *n. Informal.* Friend (sense 6). [< QUAKE.] **—Quak'er·ism** *n.* **—Quak'er·ly** *adv. & adj.*

Quaker gun *n.* A dummy gun made of wood. [From the *Quakers'* opposition to war.]

Quak·er-la·dies (kwā'kər-lā'dēz) *pl.n.* Bluets.

qua·le (kwä'lē) *n., pl.* **-li·a** (-lē-ə). A property, such as whiteness, considered independently from things having the property. [Lat., neuter of *qualis,* of what kind.]

qual·i·fi·ca·tion (kwŏl'ə-fĭ-kā'shən) *n.* **1. a.** The act of qualifying. **b.** The condition of being qualified. **2.** A quality or ability that suits a person to a specific position or task. **3.** A condition or circumstance that must be met or complied with. **4.** A restriction or modification.

qual·i·fied (kwŏl'ə-fīd') *adj.* **1.** Competent, suited, or having met the requirements for a specific position or task. **2.** Limited, restricted, or modified: *a qualified plan for expansion.* **—qual'i·fied'ly** (-fīd'lē, -fī'ĭd-lē) *adv.*

qual·i·fi·er (kwŏl'ə-fī'ər) *n.* **1.** One that qualifies. **2.** *Gram.* A word or phrase that qualifies, limits, or modifies the meaning of another word or phrase.

qual·i·fy (kwŏl'ə-fī') *v.* **-fied, -fy·ing, -fies.** *—tr.* **1.** To describe by enumerating the characteristics of; characterize. **2.** To make competent or eligible for an office, position, or task. **3. a.** To declare competent or capable; certify. **b.** To make legally capable; license. **4.** To modify, limit, or restrict, as by giving exceptions. **5.** To make less harsh or severe; moderate. **6.** *Gram.* To modify the meaning of (a noun, for example). *—intr.* To be or to become qualified. [OFr. *qualifier* < Med. Lat. *qualificare,* to attribute a quality to : Lat. *qualis,* of such a kind + Lat. *facere,* to make.]

qual·i·ta·tive (kwŏl'ĭ-tā'tĭv) *adj.* Of, pertaining to, or concerning quality. [LLat. *qualitativus* < Lat. *qualitas,* quality < *qualis,* of what kind.] **—qual'i·ta'tive·ly** *adv.*

qualitative analysis *n.* Chemical determination of the constituents of a substance without regard to quantity.

qual·i·ty (kwŏl'ĭ-tē) *n., pl.* **-ties. 1.** The essential character of something; nature. **2. a.** An inherent or distinguishing characteristic; property. **b.** A personal trait, esp. a character trait: *has few redeeming qualities.* **3. a.** Superiority of kind: *an intellect of unquestioned quality.* **b.** Degree or grade of excellence: *yard goods of low quality.* **4.** High social position. **5.** *Mus.* Timbre, as determined by overtones. **6.** The character of a vowel sound determined by the size and shape of the oral cavity and the amount of resonance with which the sound is produced. **7.** *Logic.* The positive or negative character of a proposition. [ME *qualite* < OFr. < Lat. *qualitas* < *qualis,* of what kind.]

Synonyms: *quality, property, attribute, character, trait.* The most inclusive of these terms, *quality,* is any feature that distinguishes or identifies someone or something. *Property* designates a specific quality that is basic to a thing and often makes it act in a certain way. An *attribute,* unlike a *property,* is a quality that is less precisely known and is only ascribed to someone or something: *properties of iron; attributes of God. Character* and *trait* stress distinctive features, but *character* usually applies to what distinguishes the whole of a thing, or a group, whereas *trait* refers to one particular feature, and is usually restricted to persons.

quality control *n.* A system for ensuring the maintenance of proper standards in manufactured goods, esp. by periodic inspection of the product.

qualm (kwäm, kwôm) *n.* **1.** A sudden feeling of sickness, faintness, or nausea. **2.** A sensation of doubt or misgiving; uneasiness. **3.** A pang of conscience. [Orig. unknown.]

Synonyms: *qualm, scruple, compunction, misgiving, reservation.* These nouns denote varying degrees of uncertainty felt by a person about his judgment in taking action. *Qualm* can be as slight as a feeling of uneasiness or as strong as a queasy sensation in its implication of self-doubt. *Scruple* adds the idea of conscience. *Compunction* increases the importance of conscience in deciding the rightness or wrongness of one's acts. *Misgiving* implies mistrust or misapprehension as to one's ability, or fear that one has made a mistake. *Reservation* also connotes doubt about the fitness or correctness of an action, but refers to a rather well-defined limiting condition that one has arrived at.

qualm·ish (kwä'mĭsh, kwôm'-ĭsh) *adj.* **1.** Feeling qualms. **2.** Of or producing qualms. **—qualm'ish·ly** *adv.*

quam·ash (kwŏm'ăsh') *n.* Variant of **camas.**

quan·da·ry (kwŏn'də-rē, -drē) *n., pl.* **-ries.** A state of uncertainty or perplexity; dilemma. [Orig. unknown.]

quan·ta (kwŏn'tə) *n.* Plural of **quantum.**

quan·ta·some (kwŏn'tə-sōm') *n.* One of numerous granules located on the inner lamellar surface of a chloroplast.

quan·ti·fy (kwŏn'tə-fī') *tr.v.* **-fied, -fy·ing, -fies. 1.** To determine or express the quantity of. **2.** *Logic.* To limit the variables of (a proposition) by prefixing an operator such as *all* or *some.* [Med. Lat. *quantificare* : Lat. *quantus,* how great + Lat. *facere,* to make.] **—quan'ti·fi'a·ble** *adj.* **—quan'ti·fi·ca'tion** (-fĭ-kā'shən) *n.* **—quan'ti·fi'er** *n.*

quan·ti·tate (kwŏn'tĭ-tāt') *tr.v.* **-tat·ed, -tat·ing, -tates.** To determine or measure the quantity of. **—quan'ti·ta'tion** *n.*

quan·ti·ta·tive (kwŏn'tĭ-tā'tĭv) *adj.* **1. a.** Expressed or capable of expression as a quantity. **b.** Of, pertaining to, or susceptible of measurement. **c.** Of or pertaining to number or quantity. **2.** Pertaining to syllables in classical verse that are based upon duration of sound rather than stress. [Med. Lat. *quantitativus* < Lat. *quantitas,* quantity < *quantus,* how great.] **—quan'ti·ta'tive·ly** *adv.* **—quan'ti·ta'tive·ness** *n.*

quantitative analysis *n.* Chemical determination of the amounts or proportions of constituents in a substance.

quantitative gene *n. Genetics.* A polygene.

quan·ti·ty (kwŏn'tĭ-tē) *n., pl.* **-ties. 1. a.** A specified or indefinite number or amount. **b.** A considerable amount or number: *sell wholesale drugs in quantity.* **c.** An exact amount or number. **2.** The measurable, countable, or comparable property or aspect of a thing. **3.** *Math.* Something serving as the object of a mathematical operation. **4.** The length of a vowel or consonant sound expressed in terms of the time needed to produce it. **5.** *Logic.* The exact character of a proposition in reference to its universality, singularity, or particularity. [ME *quantite* < OFr. < Lat. *quantitas* < *quantus,* how great.]

quan·tize (kwŏn'tīz') *tr.v.* **-tized, -tiz·ing, -tiz·es.** *Physics.* **1.** To limit the possible values of (a magnitude or quantity) to a discrete set of values by quantum mechanical rules. **2.** To replace the dynamic variables of a system by the corresponding quantum mechanical operators in order to calculate the behavior of the system. **—quan'ti·za'tion** *n.*

quan·tum (kwŏn'təm) *n., pl.* **-ta** (-tə). **1.** A quantity or amount of something. **2.** A specified portion of something. **3.** Something that may be counted or measured. **4.** *Physics.* **a.** An indivisible unit of energy, equal for radiation of frequency ν to the product hν, where h is Planck's constant. **b.** The particle mediating a specific type of fundamental interaction. [Lat., neuter of *quantus,* how great.]

quantum chromodynamics *n.* Chromodynamics.

quantum electrodynamics *n. Physics.* The quantum mechanical theory of the properties and interactions of charged elementary particles, esp. of the electron, with the electromagnetic field.

quantum fluid *n. Physics.* Quantum liquid.

quantum jump *n.* **1.** *Physics.* The transition of an atomic or molecular system from one discrete energy level to another with concomitant absorption or emission of radiation having energy equal to the difference between the two levels. **2.** An abrupt change or step, esp. in knowledge or information.

quantum liquid *n. Physics.* A fluid exhibiting thermal, conductive, or kinetic behavior attributable to the quantum statistics obeyed by the particles of the fluid, esp. a superfluid.

quantum mechanics *n. (used with a sing. or pl. verb). Physics.* Quantum theory, esp. the quantum theory of the structure and behavior of atoms and molecules.

quantum number *n. Physics.* Any of a set of real numbers that individually characterize the properties and collectively specify the state of a particle or of an atomic system.

quantum state *n. Physics.* Any of the possible states of a system described by quantum theory.

quantum theory *n. Physics.* A mathematical theory of dynamic systems in which dynamic variables are represented by abstract mathematical operators having properties that specify the behavior of the system.

quar·an·tine (kwôr'ən-tēn', kwŏr'-) *n.* **1. a.** A period of time during which a vehicle, a person, or material suspected of carrying a contagious disease is detained at a port of entry under enforced isolation to prevent disease from entering a country. **b.** A place for such detention. **2.** Enforced isolation or restriction of free movement imposed to prevent a contagious disease from spreading. **3.** A condition of enforced isolation. **4.** A period of 40 days. *—tr.v.* **-tined, -tin·ing, -tines. 1.** To isolate in or as if in quarantine. **2.** To isolate politically or economically. [Ital. *quarantine* < *quaranta,* forty < Lat. *quadraginta.*]

quark (kwôrk) *n. Physics.* Any of a group of hypothetical subatomic particles having electric charges of magnitude one-third or two-thirds that of the electron, proposed as the fundamental units of matter. [Poss. < *Three quarks for Muster Mark!,* a line in *Finnegans Wake,* by James Joyce (1882–1941).]

quar·rel[1] (kwôr'əl, kwŏr'-) *n.* **1.** An angry dispute; argument. **2.** A cause for a dispute or argument: *We have no*

George Miksch Sutton

quail[1]

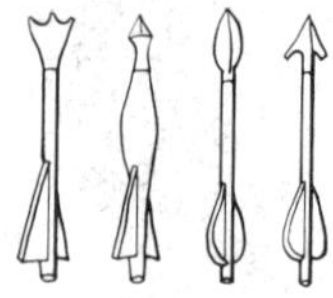

quarrel[2]

quarry[2]

quarter-deck

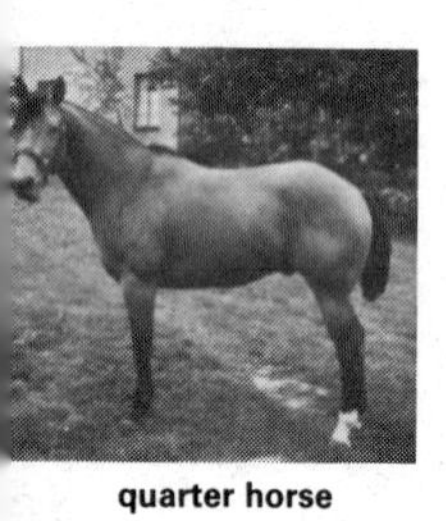

quarter horse

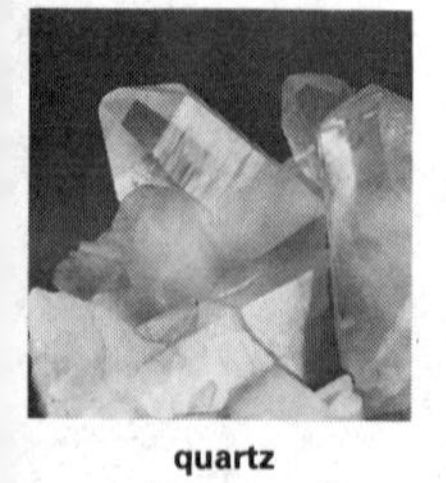

quartz

quarrel with the findings. —*intr.v.* **-reled, -rel·ing, -rels** or **-relled, -rel·ling, -rels. 1.** To engage in a quarrel; argue angrily: *never quarrels with his wife.* **2.** To disagree; differ. **3.** To find fault in something; complain. [ME *querele,* complaint < OFr. < Lat. *querela* < *queri,* to complain.] **—quar'rel·er, quar'rel·ler** *n.*

quar·rel[2] (kwôr'əl, kwŏr'-) *n.* **1.** A bolt for a crossbow. **2.** A tool having a squared head, as a stonemason's chisel. **3.** A small diamond-shaped or square pane of glass in a latticed window. [ME *quarel* < OFr. < VLat. **quadrellus,* dim. of Lat. *quadrus,* square.]

quar·rel·some (kwôr'əl-səm, kwŏr'-) *adj.* Tending to quarrel; contentious.

quar·ry[1] (kwôr'ē, kwŏr'ē) *n., pl.* **-ries. 1.** A hunted animal; prey. **2.** The object of a hunt or pursuit. [ME *querre,* entrails of a deer given to hounds as a reward < OFr. *cuiree* < LLat. *corata,* viscera < Lat. *cor,* heart.]

quar·ry[2] (kwôr'ē, kwŏr'ē) *n., pl.* **-ries. 1.** An open excavation or pit from which stone is obtained by digging, cutting, or blasting. **2.** A rich or productive source. —*tr.v.* **-ried, -ry·ing, -ries. 1.** To obtain (stone) from a quarry, as by cutting, digging, or blasting. **2.** To use (land) as a quarry. [ME *quarey* < OFr. *quarriere* < Lat. *quadrus,* square.] **—quar'ri·er** *n.*

quar·ry[3] (kwôr'ē, kwŏr'ē) *n., pl.* **-ries.** A square or diamond shape. [Var. of QUARREL[2]]

quart (kwôrt) *n.* **1. a.** A unit of volume or capacity in the U.S. Customary System, used in liquid measure, equal to 2 pints or .946 liter. **b.** A unit of volume or capacity in the U.S. Customary System, used in dry measure, equal to 2 pints or 1.101 liters. **c.** A unit of volume or capacity in the British Imperial System, used in liquid and dry measure, equal to 1.201 U.S. liquid quarts, 1.032 U.S. dry quarts, or 69.354 cubic inches. **2.** A container having a capacity of one quart. [ME < OFr. *quarte* < Lat. *quartus,* fourth.]

quar·tan (kwôrt'n) *adj.* Occurring every fourth day, counting inclusively, or every 72 hours. Used of a fever. —*n.* A recurrent malarial fever, occurring every 72 hours. [ME *quartain* < OFr. *quartaine* < Lat. *quartana* < *quartanus,* of the fourth < *quartus,* fourth.]

quar·ter (kwôr'tər) *n.* **1.** One of four equal parts of something. **2.** A coin equal to one-fourth of the dollar of the United States and Canada. **3.** One-fourth of an hour; 15 minutes. **4. a.** One-fourth of a year; three months: *Sales were up in the second quarter.* **b.** An academic term lasting for approximately three months. **5.** *Astron.* **a.** One-fourth of the period of the moon's revolution around the earth. **b.** Either of two of the visible phases of the moon: *the first quarter; the third quarter.* **6.** *Sports.* One of four equal periods of playing time into which some games are divided. **7.** One-fourth of a yard; nine inches. **8.** One-fourth of a mile; two furlongs. **9.** One-fourth of a pound; four ounces. **10.** One-fourth of a ton; 500 pounds. Used as a measure of grain. **11.** *Chiefly Brit.* A measure of grain equal to approximately eight bushels. **12. a.** One-fourth of a hundredweight; 25 pounds. **b.** One-fourth of a British hundredweight; 28 pounds. **13. a.** One of the four major divisions of the compass. **b.** One-fourth of the distance between any two of the 32 divisions of the compass. **c.** *Naut.* The general direction on either side of a ship located 45 degrees off the stern. **d.** One of the four major divisions of the horizon as determined by the four major points of the compass. **e.** A region or area of the earth thought of as falling into such a specific division of the compass. **14.** *Naut.* **a.** The upper portion of the after side of a ship, usually between the aftermost mast and the stern. **b.** The part of a yard between the slings and the yardarm. **15.** Any of four equal divisions of a shield in heraldry. **16.** One leg of a carcass of an animal, usually including the adjoining parts. **17.** Either side of a horse's hoof. **18.** The part of the side of a shoe between the heel and the vamp. **19. quarters.** A place of residence, esp. the buildings or barracks housing military personnel or their dependents. **20.** Often **quarters.** A proper or assigned station or place, as for officers and crew on a warship. **21.** Often **Quarter.** A specific district or section, as of a city: *the Latin Quarter.* **22.** Often **quarters.** An unspecified person or group: *information from the highest quarters.* **23.** Mercy or clemency, esp. when shown to an enemy. —*v.* **-tered, -ter·ing, -ters.** —*tr.* **1. a.** To cut or otherwise divide into four equal or equivalent parts. **b.** To quartersaw. **2.** To divide or separate into a number of parts. **3.** To dismember (a human body) into four parts. **4.** To divide (a heraldic shield) into four equal areas with vertical and horizontal lines. **5. a.** To mark or place (holes, for example) a fourth of a circle apart. **b.** To locate and adjust (one machine part) at right angles to its connecting part within the machine. **6.** To furnish with housing. **7.** To traverse (an area of ground) laterally back and forth while slowly advancing forward. —*intr.* **1.** To take up or be assigned lodgings. **2.** To cover an area of ground by ranging over it from side to side. —*adj.* **1.** Being one of four equal or equivalent parts. **2.** Being one-fourth of a standard or usual value. **—*idiom.* at close quarters.** At close range. [ME < OFr. *quartier* < Lat. *quartarius* < *quartus,* fourth.]

Usage: With reference to the time of day, *a* in the following phrases is optional: *(a) quarter of* (or *to* or *before*) *ten; (a) quarter past* (or *after*) *ten.*

quar·ter·age (kwôr'tər-ĭj) *n.* A monetary allowance, wage, or payment made or received quarterly.

quar·ter·back (kwôr'tər-băk') *n. Football.* The backfield player whose position is behind the line of scrimmage and who usually calls the signals for the plays. —*v.* **-backed, -back·ing, -backs.** —*tr.* **1.** To direct the offense of. **2.** To lead or direct the operations of. —*intr.* To play quarterback.

quarter day *n.* Any of the four days of the year regarded as the beginning of a new season or quarter, when most quarterly payments are due.

quar·ter-deck (kwôr'tər-dĕk') *n.* The after part of the upper deck of a sailing ship, usually reserved for officers.

quar·ter·fi·nal (kwôr'tər-fī'nəl) *adj.* Designating one of four competitions in a tournament, whose winners go on to play in semifinal competitions. —*n.* **1. quarterfinals.** A quarterfinal round. **2.** A quarterfinal match. **—quar'ter·fi'nal·ist** *n.*

quarter horse *n.* One of a breed of strong saddle horses developed in the western United States. [So called because it was formerly trained for races up to a quarter mile.]

quar·ter-hour also **quarter hour** (kwôr'tər-our') *n.* **1.** Fifteen minutes. **2.** The point on a clock's face marking either 15 minutes after or 15 minutes before an hour.

quar·ter·ly (kwôr'tər-lē) *adj.* **1.** Made up of four parts. **2.** Being one of four parts. **3.** Occurring or appearing at three-month intervals. —*n., pl.* **-lies.** A publication issued regularly every three months. —*adv.* In or by quarters.

quar·ter·mas·ter (kwôr'tər-măs'tər) *n.* **1.** A military officer responsible for the food, clothing, and equipment of troops. **2.** A petty officer responsible for the navigation of a ship.

quar·tern (kwôr'tərn) *n.* One-fourth of something. [ME *quartron* < OFr. < *quartier,* quarter. —see QUARTER.]

quarter note *n. Mus.* A note having one fourth the time value of a whole note.

quar·ter-phase (kwôr'tər-fāz') *adj.* Two-phase.

quar·ter·saw (kwôr'tər-sô') *tr.v.* **-sawed, -sawed** or **-sawn, -saw·ing, -saws.** To saw (a log) into quarters lengthwise along its axis.

quarter section *n.* A quarter of a square mile of land.

quarter sessions *pl.n. Law.* **1.** A British local court of limited jurisdiction that sits quarterly. **2.** In the United States, a local court with criminal jurisdiction, and sometimes administrative functions, that sits quarterly.

quar·ter·staff (kwôr'tər-stăf') *n., pl.* **-staves** (-stāvz'). A long wooden staff, formerly used as a weapon.

quar·ter·tone (kwôr'tər-tōn') *n. Mus.* Half a semitone.

quar·tet also **quar·tette** (kwôr-tĕt') *n.* **1.** A musical composition for four voices or instruments. **2.** A group of four performing musicians. **3.** A set of four persons or things. [Ital. *quartetto,* dim. of *quarto,* fourth < Lat. *quartus.*]

quar·tic (kwôr'tĭk) *adj. Math.* Of or designating the fourth degree. [< Lat. *quartus,* fourth.] **—quar'tic** *n.*

quar·tile (kwôr'tīl', -tĭl) *n.* The value of the boundary at the 25th, 50th, or 75th percentiles of a frequency distribution divided into four parts, each containing a quarter of the population. [< Lat. *quartus,* fourth.]

quar·to (kwôr'tō) *n., pl.* **-tos. 1.** The page size obtained by folding a whole sheet into four leaves. **2.** A book composed of quarto pages. [< Lat. *quartus,* fourth.]

quartz (kwôrts) *n.* A hard, crystalline, vitreous mineral silicon dioxide, SiO_2, found worldwide as a component of sandstone and granite, or as pure crystals in such varieties as agate, chalcedony, chert, flint, opal, and rock crystal. [G. *Quarz* < MHG, of Slav. orig.] **—quartz'ose'** (kwôrt'sōs') *adj.*

quartz glass *n.* A pure silica glass, highly transparent to ultraviolet radiations.

quartz·if·er·ous (kwôrt-sĭf'ər-əs) *adj.* Containing quartz.

quartz·ite (kwôrt'sīt') *n.* A metamorphic rock resulting from the recrystallization of quartz sandstone.

quartz lamp *n.* An incandescent lamp enclosed by a quartz envelope containing mercury vapor that emits ultraviolet radiation when heated by a filament.

qua·sar (kwā'zär', -sär', -zər, -sər) *n.* A quasi-stellar object. [QUAS(I) + (STELL)AR.]

quash (kwŏsh) *tr.v.* **quashed, quash·ing, quash·es. 1.** To set aside or annul, esp. by judicial action. **2.** To put down or suppress forcibly and completely: *quash a rebellion.* [ME *quassen*< OFr. *casser* < LLat. *cassare* < Lat. *cassus,* void.]

qua·si (kwā'zī', -sī', kwä'zē, -sē) *adj.* Having a likeness to something; resembling: *a quasi success.* [Lat., as if.]

quasi– *pref.* To some degree; in some manner: *quasi-scientific.* [Lat. *quasi,* as if.]

qua·si-stel·lar object (kwā'zī-stĕl'ər, -sī'-, kwä'zē-, -sē-) *n.* A member of any of several classes of starlike objects having exceptionally large red shifts that are often emitters of radio frequency as well as visible radiation and have apparently immense speeds, energies, and distances from earth.

quasi-stellar radio source *n.* A quasi-stellar object.

quas·sia (kwŏsh'ə) *n.* **1.** A tree, *Quassia amara,* of tropical America, having bright scarlet flowers. **2.** A bitter substance obtained from the wood and bark of the quassia and related trees, used in medicine and as an insecticide. [NLat., after Graman *Quassi,* an 18th-cent. Surinamian.]

qua·ter·nar·y (kwŏt'ər-nĕr'ē, kwə-tûr'nə-rē) *adj.* **1.** Consisting of four; in fours. **2.** *Chem.* **a.** Designating a compound having four alkyl groups connected to a nitrogen or phosphorus atom. **b.** Designating a compound consisting of four different atoms or radicals. **3. Quaternary.** *Geol.* Of, belonging to, or designating the geologic time, system of rocks, and sedimentary deposits of the second period of the Cenozoic era, from the end of the Tertiary through the present, characterized by the appearance and development of man, and including the Pleistocene and Holocene epochs. —*n., pl.* **-nar·ies. 1.** The number four. **2.** That member of a group which is fourth in order. **3. Quaternary.** *Geol.* The Quaternary period or system of deposits. [Lat. *quaternarius* < *quaterni,* by four < *quater,* four times.]

quaternary ammonium compound *n.* Any of a group of compounds in which the hydrogen atoms of the ammonium radical are replaced by organic radicals, used as antiseptics, solvents, and emulsifying agents.

qua·ter·ni·on (kwə-tûr′nē-ən) *n.* **1.** A set of four persons or items. **2.** *Math.* An element of a system of four dimensional vectors obeying laws similar to those of complex numbers. [ME *quaternioun* < LLat. *quaternio* < Lat. *quaterni,* by four < *quater,* four times.]

quat·rain (kwŏt′rān′, kwŏ-trān′) *n.* A stanza or poem of four lines. [Fr. < OFr. < *quatre,* four < Lat. *quattuor.*]

quat·re·foil (kăt′ər-foil′, kăt′rə-) *n.* **1.** A representation of a flower with four petals or a leaf with four leaflets, esp. in heraldry. **2.** *Archit.* An ornament or tracery with four foils or lobes. [ME *quaterfoile* : *quater-,* four (< OFr. *quatre* < Lat. *quattuor*) + *foil,* leaf < OFr. < Lat. *folium.*]

quat·tro·cen·to (kwŏt′rō-chĕn′tō) *n.* The 15th-century period of Italian art and literature. [Ital., short for *millequattrocento,* one thousand four hundred.]

qua·ver (kwā′vər) *v.* **-vered, -ver·ing, -vers.** —*intr.* **1.** To quiver, as from weakness; tremble. **2.** To speak in a quivering voice or utter a quivering sound. **3.** To produce a trill on a musical instrument or with the voice. —*tr.* To utter or sing in a trilling voice. —*n.* **1.** A quivering sound. **2.** A trill. **3.** *Chiefly Brit.* An eighth note. [ME *quaveren,* freq. of *quaren,* to tremble, of Germanic orig.] **—qua′ver·ing·ly** *adv.* **—qua′ver·y** *adj.*

quay (kē, kā) *n.* A wharf or reinforced bank where ships are loaded or unloaded. [ME *keye* < OFr. *quai,* of Celt. orig.]

quay·age (kē′ĭj) *n.* **1.** A charge for the use of a quay. **2.** The space available on a system of quays. **3.** Quays collectively.

quean (kwēn) *n.* **1.** A disreputable woman, esp. a prostitute. **2.** *Chiefly Scot.* A young woman. [ME *quen* < OE *cwene,* woman.]

quea·sy also **quea·zy** (kwē′zē) *adj.* **-si·er, -si·est** also **-zi·er, -zi·est. 1.** Nauseated. **2.** Easily nauseated. **3.** Causing nausea; sickening. **4. a.** Causing uneasiness. **b.** Uneasy; troubled. **5. a.** Easily troubled. **b.** Ill at ease; squeamish. [ME *coisy.*] **—quea′si·ly** *adv.* **—quea′si·ness** *n.*

Qué·be·cois (kā′bĕ-kwä′) *n., pl.* **Québecois.** A native or resident of Quebec, esp. a French-speaking one. [Fr. < *Québec,* Quebec.]

que·bra·cho (kā-brä′chō) *n., pl.* **-chos. 1.** Any of several South American trees having very hard wood, esp. *Aspidosperma quebracho-blanco,* whose bark is used in medicine, and *Schinopsis lorentzii,* whose wood yields tannin. **2.** The bark or wood of a quebracho tree. [Am. Sp., var. of *quiebrahacha* : *quebrar,* to break (< Lat. *crepare,* to crack) + *hacha,* ax < Fr. *hache* < OFr., of Germanic orig.]

Quech·ua (kĕch′wə, -wä′) *n., pl.* **Quechua** or **-uas. 1.** A tribe or a member of a tribe of South American Indians originally constituting the ruling class of the Incan Empire. **2. a.** The language of the Quechua that is also spoken by other Indian peoples of Peru, Ecuador, Bolivia, Chile, and Argentina. **b.** A language family consisting of the Quechua language. [Sp. < Quechua *kkechúwa,* robber.] **—Quech′uan** *adj.*

queen (kwēn) *n.* **1.** The wife or widow of a king. **2.** A female monarch or ruler. **3.** A goddess or a thing personified as a woman, and having eminence or supremacy in a given domain: *Paris is the queen of cities.* **4.** The most powerful chess piece, able to move in any direction in a straight line. **5.** A playing card bearing the figure of a queen, next above the jack and below the king in each suit. **6.** The fertile, fully developed female in a colony of social bees, ants, or termites. **7.** *Offensive Slang.* A male homosexual, esp. one with marked female characteristics. —*v.* **queened, queen·ing, queens.** —*tr.* **1.** To make (a woman) a queen. **2.** *Chess.* To raise (a pawn) to queen. —*intr.* **1.** To reign as queen. **2.** To act like a queen; domineer: *queens it over the whole family.* [ME *quene* < OE *cwēn.*] **—queen′like** *adj.*

Queen Anne *n.* The style in English architecture and furniture typical of the reign of Queen Anne (1702–14). **—*modifier:*** *a Queen Anne chair.*

Queen Anne's lace *n.* A widely distributed plant, *Daucus carota,* native to Eurasia, having finely divided leaves and flat clusters of small white flowers.

queen consort *n., pl.* **queens consort.** The wife of a reigning king.

queen-cup (kwēn′kŭp′) *n.* A plant, *Clintonia uniflora,* of northwestern North America, bearing a solitary white flower and a blue berry.

queen·ly (kwēn′lē) *adj.* **-li·er, -li·est. 1.** Of or resembling a queen. **2.** Pertaining to or befitting a queen. **—queen′li·ness** *n.*

queen mother *n.* A dowager queen who is the mother of the reigning monarch.

queen of the prairie *n.* A plant, *Filipendula rubra,* of prairies and meadows of the central United States, having compound leaves and clusters of small pink flowers.

queen olive *n.* A variety of olive having large fruit, used for eating rather than as a source of oil.

queen post *n.* One of two upright supporting posts set vertically between the rafters and the tie beam at equal distances from the apex of a roof.

queen regnant *n., pl.* **queens regnant.** A queen reigning in her own right.

Queen's Bench *n.* A division of the British superior courts system that hears criminal and civil cases. Used when the monarch is a female.

Queen's Counsel *n.* A barrister appointed as counsel to the British crown when the monarch is a female.

queen·ship (kwēn′shĭp′) *n.* **1.** The rank or state of being a queen. **2.** A noble or regal quality, as of a queen.

queen-size (kwēn′sīz′) *adj.* **1.** Relating to, used for, or being a bed approximately 60 inches by 80 inches in dimension: *queen-size sheets.* **2.** Extra large in size: *queen-size pantyhose.*

queen truss *n.* A building truss having queen posts.

queer (kwîr) *adj.* **-er, -est. 1.** Deviating from the expected or normal; strange. **2.** Odd or unconventional in behavior; eccentric. **3.** Of a questionable nature or character; suspicious. **4.** *Slang.* Fake; counterfeit. **5.** Feeling slightly ill; queasy. **6.** *Offensive Slang.* Homosexual. —*n.* *Offensive Slang.* A homosexual. —*tr.v.* **queered, queer·ing, queers.** *Slang.* **1.** To ruin or thwart. **2.** To put into a bad position. [Orig. unknown.] **—queer′ish** *adj.* **—queer′ly** *adv.* **—queer′ness** *n.*

quell (kwĕl) *tr.v.* **quelled, quell·ing, quells. 1.** To put down forcibly; suppress. **2.** To pacify; quiet. [ME *quellen,* to kill < OE *cwellan.*]

quench (kwĕnch) *tr.v.* **quenched, quench·ing, quench·es. 1.** To put out (a fire, for example); extinguish. **2.** To suppress; squelch: *quenched my enthusiasm.* **3.** To put an end to; destroy. **4.** To slake; satisfy. **5.** To cool (hot metal) by thrusting in water or other liquid. [ME *quenchen* < OE *ācwencan.*] **—quench′a·ble** *adj.* **—quench′er** *n.* **—quench′less** *adj.*

que·nelle (kə-nĕl′) *n.* A ball or dumpling of forcemeat bound with eggs and poached in stock or water. [Fr.]

quer·ce·tin (kwûr′sĭ-tĭn) *n.* A yellow, powdered crystalline compound, $C_{15}H_{10}O_7$, synthesized or occurring as a glycoside in the rind and bark of numerous plants, and used medicinally to treat abnormal capillary fragility. [< Lat. *quercus,* oak.]

quer·ci·tron (kwûr′sĭ-trən, -trŏn′, kwər-sĭt′rən) *n.* **1.** The black oak. **2. a.** The bright-orange inner bark of the black oak, from which a yellow dye is obtained. **b.** This dye. [Lat. *quercus,* oak + CITRON.]

que·rist (kwîr′ĭst) *n.* One who questions or inquires. [< Lat. *quaerere,* to ask.]

quern (kwûrn) *n.* A primitive hand-turned grain mill. [ME *querne* < OE *cweorn.*]

quer·u·lous (kwĕr′ə-ləs, kwĕr′yə-) *adj.* **1.** Given to complaining; peevish. **2.** Expressing or showing a complaint; fretful: *a querulous voice.* [Lat. *querulus* < *queri,* to complain.] **—quer′u·lous·ly** *adv.* **—quer′u·lous·ness** *n.*

que·ry (kwîr′ē) *n., pl.* **-ries. 1.** A question; inquiry. **2.** A doubt in the mind. **3.** A notation, usually a question mark, calling attention to an item to question its validity or accuracy. —*tr.v.* **-ried, -ry·ing, -ries. 1.** To express doubt or uncertainty about; question. **2.** To put a question to (a person). **3.** To mark (an item) with a notation in order to question its validity or accuracy. [Alteration of obs. *quaere* < Lat., imper. of *quaerere,* to ask.] **—que′ri·er** *n.*

quest (kwĕst) *n.* **1.** The act or instance of seeking or pursuing something; search. **2.** In medieval romance, an expedition undertaken by a knight in order to perform a prescribed feat. **3.** *Archaic.* A jury of inquest. —*v.* **quest·ed, quest·ing, quests.** —*intr.* **1.** To go on a quest. **2.** To search for game. —*tr.* To search for; seek. [ME *queste* < OFr. < Lat. *questa,* fem. p.part. of *quaerere,* to seek.] **—quest′er** *n.*

ques·tion (kwĕs′chən) *n.* **1. a.** An expression of inquiry that invites or calls for a reply. **b.** An interrogative sentence, phrase, or gesture. **2.** A subject or point open to controversy; issue. **3.** A difficult matter; problem: *a question of ethics.* **4.** A point or subject under discussion or being considered. **5. a.** A proposition brought up for consideration by an assembly. **b.** The act of bringing such a proposal to vote. **6.** Uncertainty; doubt: *no question about its validity.* **7.** Possibility; chance: *out of the question.* —*v.* **-tioned, -tion·ing, -tions.** —*tr.* **1.** To put a question to. **2.** To interrogate, as a witness or suspect. **3.** To express doubt about; dispute. **4.** To analyze; examine. —*intr.* To ask questions. [ME < OFr. < Lat. *quaestio* < *quaerere,* to ask.] **—ques′tion·er** *n.* **—ques′tion·ing·ly** *adv.*

ques·tion·a·ble (kwĕs′chə-nə-bəl) *adj.* **1. a.** Open to doubt or challenge; problematic. **b.** Not yet determined or specified; uncertain. **2.** Of dubious morality or respectability. **—ques′tion·a·ble·ness, ques′tion·a·bil′i·ty** *n.* **—ques′tion·a·bly** *adv.*

question mark *n.* A punctuation symbol (?) written at the end of a sentence or phrase to indicate a direct question.

ques·tion·naire (kwĕs′chə-nâr′) *n.* A printed form containing a set of questions, esp. one addressed to a statistically

quatrefoil

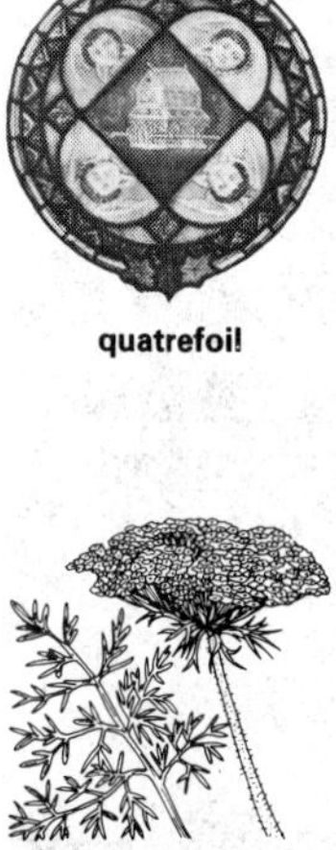

Queen Anne's lace

queen post

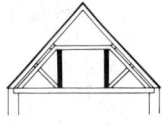

quill
A flight feather

quillwort

quilt

quince

significant number of subjects by way of gathering information, as for a survey. [Fr. < *questionner,* to ask < *question,* question < OFr.]

quet·zal (kĕt-sälʹ) *n., pl.* **-zals** or **-za·les** (-säʹlās). **1.** A Central American bird, *Pharomacrus mocino,* having brilliant bronze-green and red plumage and, in the male, long, flowing tail feathers. **2.** See table at **currency.** [Am. Sp. < Nahuatl *quetzalli,* large brilliant tail feather.]

Quet·zal·co·a·tl (kĕt-sälʹkō-ätʹl) *n.* A god of the Toltecs and Aztecs, represented as a plumed serpent. [Nahuatl.]

queue (kyo͞o) *n.* **1.** A waiting line of people or vehicles. **2.** A long braid of real or artificial hair worn hanging down the back of the neck; pigtail. **3.** A sequence of stored computer data or programs awaiting processing. —*intr.v.* **queued, queu·ing, queues.** To get in line: *queue up at the box office.* [Fr. < OFr. *cue,* tail < Lat. *cauda.*]

quib·ble (kwĭbʹəl) *intr.v.* **-bled, -bling, -bles.** To avoid acknowledging the truth or importance of something by raising trivial distinctions and objections. —*n.* **1.** A petty distinction or irrelevant objection. **2.** *Archaic.* A pun. [Prob. < obs. *quib,* perh. < Lat. *quibus,* pl. of *qui,* who, from its frequent use in legal documents.] —**quibʹbler** *n.*

quiche (kēsh) *n.* A rich unsweetened custard baked in a pastry shell often with other ingredients, as vegetables or seafood. [Fr. < dial. G. *Küche,* dim. of *Kuchen,* cake < OHG *kuocho.*]

Qui·ché (kē-chāʹ) *n.* **1.** An Indian people of Guatemala. **2.** The Mayan language of the Quiché.

quiche Lor·raine (lə-rānʹ, lô-) *n.* A quiche containing cheese and pieces of bacon. [Fr., after *Lorraine,* a region of northeastern France.]

quick (kwĭk) *adj.* **-er, -est. 1.** Moving or functioning rapidly and energetically; speedy. **2.** Learning, thinking, or understanding with speed and dexterity; bright: *a quick mind.* **3. a.** Perceiving or responding with speed and sensitivity; keen. **b.** Reacting immediately and sharply: *a quick temper.* **4. a.** Occurring or achieved in a relatively brief period of time: *a quick rise up through the ranks.* **b.** Done or occurring immediately: *a quick inspection.* **5.** Tending to react hastily: *quick to find fault.* **6.** *Archaic.* Alive. **7.** *Archaic.* Pregnant. —*n.* **1.** Sensitive or raw exposed flesh, as under the fingernails. **2.** The most personal and sensitive aspect of the emotions: *cut to the quick.* **3.** The living: *the quick and the dead.* **4.** The vital core of a thing; essence: *the quick of the matter.* —*adv.* Quickly; promptly. [ME *quicke,* swift, alive < OE *cwicu,* alive.] —**quickʹly** *adv.* —**quickʹness** *n.*

Usage: Both *quick* and *quickly* can be used as adverbs. *Quick* is more frequent in speech: *Come quick!* In writing the slightly more formal *quickly* is preferred: *When he heard the news, John returned quickly.* In the latter example, *quick* would be unacceptable to a large majority of the Usage Panel.

quick-and-dirt·y (kwĭkʹən-dûrʹtē) *adj.* Cheaply made or done; of inferior quality: *a quick-and-dirty housing project.*

quick assets *pl.n.* Liquid assets, including cash on hand and assets readily convertible to cash.

quick bread *n.* A bread made with a leavening agent, such as baking powder, that expands during baking and does not require a leavening period beforehand.

quick·en (kwĭkʹən) *v.* **-ened, -en·ing, -ens.** —*tr.* **1.** To make more rapid; accelerate. **2.** To make alive; vitalize. **3.** To excite and stimulate; stir. **4.** To make steeper. —*intr.* **1.** To become more rapid. **2.** To come or return to life. **3.** To reach the stage of pregnancy when the fetus can be felt to move. —**quickʹen·er** *n.*

quick-freeze (kwĭkʹfrēzʹ) *tr.v.* **-froze** (-frōzʹ), **-froz·en** (-frōʹzən), **-freez·ing, -freez·es.** To freeze (food) by a process sufficiently rapid to retain natural flavor, nutritional value, or other properties.

quick grass *n.* Couch grass. [Var. of QUITCHGRASS.]

quick·ie (kwĭkʹē) *n. Informal.* Something made or done rapidly.

quick·lime (kwĭkʹlīmʹ) *n.* Calcium oxide. [ME *quykke lyme,* transl. of Lat. *calx viva.*]

quick·sand (kwĭkʹsăndʹ) *n.* A bed of loose sand mixed with water forming a soft, shifting mass that yields easily to pressure and tends to suck down any object resting on its surface.

quick·set (kwĭkʹsĕtʹ) *n. Chiefly Brit.* **1.** Cuttings or slips of a plant suitable for hedges. **2.** A hedge consisting of quickset.

quick·sil·ver (kwĭkʹsĭlʹvər) *n.* Mercury (sense 2). —*adj.* Unpredictable; mercurial. [ME < OE *cwicseolfor,* transl. of Lat. *argentum vivum.*]

quick·step (kwĭkʹstĕpʹ) *n. Mus.* A march for accompanying military quick time.

quick-tem·pered (kwĭkʹtĕmʹpərd) *adj.* Easily aroused to anger.

quick time *n.* A military marching pace of 120 steps per minute.

quick-wit·ted (kwĭkʹwĭtʹĭd) *adj.* Mentally alert and sharp; keen. —**quickʹ-witʹted·ly** *adv.* —**quickʹ-witʹted·ness** *n.*

quid[1] (kwĭd) *n.* A cut of something to be chewed, such as tobacco. [ME *quide,* cud < OE *cwidu.*]

quid[2] (kwĭd) *n., pl.* **quid** or **quids.** *Chiefly Brit. Slang.* A pound sterling. [Orig. unknown.]

quid·di·ty (kwĭdʹĭ-tē) *n., pl.* **-ties. 1.** The real nature of a thing; essence. **2.** A hairsplitting distinction; quibble. [Med. Lat. *quidditas* < Lat. *quid,* what.]

quid·nunc (kwĭdʹnŭngkʹ) *n.* A nosy person; busybody. [Lat. *quid nunc?* what now?]

quid pro quo (kwĭdʹ prō kwōʹ) *n.* An equal exchange or substitution. [Lat., something for something.]

qui·es·cent (kwī-ĕsʹənt, kwē-) *adj.* Inactive or still; dormant. [Lat. *quiescens, quiescent-,* pr. part. of *quiescere,* to rest < *quies,* rest.] —**qui·esʹcence** *n.* —**qui·esʹcent·ly** *adv.*

qui·et (kwīʹĭt) *adj.* **-er, -est. 1.** Making no noise; silent. **2.** Free of noise; hushed. **3.** Calm and unmoving; still: *floating on quiet waters.* **4.** Free of turmoil and agitation; untroubled. **5.** Restful; soothing. **6.** Characterized by tranquillity; serene; peaceful. **7.** Not showy or garish; restrained: *a room decorated in quiet colors.* —*n.* The quality or condition of being quiet; tranquillity. —*v.* **-et·ed, -et·ing, -ets.** —*tr.* **1.** To cause to become quiet. **2.** *Law.* To make (a title) secure by freeing from all questions or challenges. —*intr.* To become quiet: *The child wouldn't quiet down.* [ME < OFr. *quiete* < Lat. *quietus,* p.part. of *quiescere,* to rest < *quies,* rest.] —**quiʹet·ly** *adv.* —**quiʹet·ness** *n.*

qui·et·ism (kwīʹĭ-tĭzʹəm) *n.* **1.** A form of Christian mysticism enjoining passive contemplation and the beatific annihilation of the will. **2.** A state of quietness and passivity. —**quiʹet·ist** *n.* —**quiʹet·isʹtic** *adj.*

qui·e·tude (kwīʹĭ-to͞odʹ, -tyo͞odʹ) *n.* A condition of tranquillity. [LLat. *quietudo* < Lat. *quietus,* p.part. of *quiescere,* to rest < *quies,* rest.]

qui·e·tus (kwī-ēʹtəs) *n.* **1.** Something that serves to suppress, check, or eliminate. **2.** Release from life; death. **3.** A final discharge, as of a duty or debt. [Short for Med. Lat. *quietus est,* he is discharged (of an obligation).]

quiff (kwĭf) *n. Chiefly Brit.* A tuft of hair, esp. a forelock. [Orig. unknown.]

quill (kwĭl) *n.* **1.** The hollow, stemlike main shaft of a feather. **2.** Any of the larger wing or tail feathers of a bird. **3.** A writing pen made from a quill. **4.** A plectrum for a stringed musical instrument of the clavichord type. **5.** A toothpick made from the stem of a feather. **6.** One of the sharp hollow spines of a porcupine or hedgehog. **7.** A musical pipe having a hollow stem. **8.** A spindle or bobbin around which yarn is wound in weaving. **9.** A hollow shaft that rotates on a solid shaft when gears are engaged. —*tr.v.* **quilled, quill·ing, quills. 1.** To wind (thread or yarn) onto a quill. **2.** To make or press small ridges in (fabric). [ME *quil,* of Germanic orig.]

quill·back (kwĭlʹbăkʹ) *n., pl.* **-backs** or **quillback.** A North American freshwater fish, *Carpiodes cyprinus,* having one ray of the dorsal fin extending conspicuously beyond the others.

quill·wort (kwĭlʹwûrtʹ, -wôrtʹ) *n.* Any of several aquatic or marsh plants of the genus *Isoetes,* having short, fleshy stems and grasslike leaves.

quilt (kwĭlt) *n.* **1.** A bed coverlet made of two layers of fabric with a layer of cotton, wool, feathers, or down in between, all stitched firmly together, usually in a crisscross design. **2.** A thick protective cover similar to or suggestive of a quilt. —*v.* **quilt·ed, quilt·ing, quilts.** —*tr.* **1.** To make into a quilt by stitching together (layers of fabric). **2.** To construct like a quilt: *quilt a skirt.* **3.** To pad and stitch ornamentally. —*intr.* **1.** To make a quilt. **2.** To do quilted work. [ME *quilte* < OFr. *cuilte* < Lat. *culcita,* mattress.]

quilt·ing (kwĭlʹtĭng) *n.* **1.** The process of doing quilted work. **2. a.** Material used to make quilts. **b.** Quilted material.

quin- *pref.* Variant of **quino-.**

quin·a·crine hydrochloride (kwĭnʹə-krēnʹ) *n.* A bright-yellow, bitter, crystalline compound, used primarily to treat malaria. [QUIN- + ACR(ID)INE.]

quin·a·liz·a·rin (kwĭnʹə-lĭzʹə-rĭn) *n.* A red crystalline compound, $C_{14}H_8O_6$.

qui·nate (kwīʹnātʹ) *adj.* Arranged in groups of five: *quinate leaflets.* [< Lat. *quini,* five each.]

quince (kwĭns) *n.* **1.** A tree, *Cydonia oblonga,* native to western Asia, having white flowers and applelike fruit. **2.** The aromatic, many-seeded fruit of the quince, edible only when cooked. [ME *quynce,* pl. of *quyn,* quince < OFr. *coin* < Lat. *cotoneum,* var. of *cydoneum,* after *Cydonia,* an ancient town in Crete.]

quin·cun·cial also **quin·cunx·ial** (kwĭn-kŭnʹshəl) *adj.* Of, pertaining to, or forming a quincunx. —**quin·cunʹcial·ly** *adv.*

quin·cunx (kwĭnʹkŭngksʹ) *n.* An arrangement of five objects with one at each corner of a rectangle or square and one at the center. [Lat., five twelfths : *quinque,* five + *uncia,* twelfth < *unus,* unit.]

quin·cunx·ial (kwĭn-kŭnʹshəl) *adj.* Variant of **quincuncial.**

quin·de·cen·ni·al (kwĭnʹdĭ-sĕnʹē-əl) *adj.* **1.** Occurring once every 15 years. **2.** Lasting 15 years. —*n.* A 15th anniversary. [Lat. *quindecim,* fifteen (*quinque,* five + *decem,* ten) + *annus,* year.]

qui·nel·la (kwĭ-nĕlʹə, kē-) or **qui·nie·la** (kĕn-yĕlʹə) *n.* A system of betting in which the bettor, in order to win, must pick the first two finishers of a race, but not necessarily in the correct sequence. [Am. Sp., a lottery-like game.]

quin·i·dine (kwĭnʹĭ-dēnʹ) *n.* A colorless crystalline alkaloid, $C_{20}H_{24}N_2O_2$, resembling quinine and used in treating certain heart disorders and malaria.

qui·nie·la (kēn-yĕl'ə) *n.* Variant of **quinella**.
qui·nine (kwī'nīn') *n.* **1.** A bitter, colorless, amorphous powder or crystalline alkaloid, $C_{20}H_{24}N_2O_2 \cdot 3H_2O$, derived from certain cinchona barks and used in medicine to treat malaria. **2.** Any of various compounds or salts of quinine.
quinine water *n.* A carbonated beverage flavored with quinine.
quin·nat salmon (kwĭn'ăt') *n.* The chinook salmon. [Salish *t'kwinnat.*]
quino– or **quin–** *pref.* **1.** Cinchona; cinchona bark: *quinoidine.* **2.** Quinone: *quinoid.* [Sp. *quina,* cinchona bark, short for *quinaquina* < Quechua.]
quin·oid (kwĭn'oid') *n.* A substance resembling quinone in structure or physical properties.
qui·noi·dine (kwĭ-noi'dēn', -dĭn) *n.* A brownish-black mixture of alkaloids remaining after extraction of crystalline alkaloids from cinchona bark, used as a quinine substitute.
quin·o·line (kwĭn'ə-lēn', -lĭn) *n.* An aromatic organic base, C_9H_7N, having a pungent tarlike odor, synthesized or obtained from coal tar, and used as a food preservative and in making antiseptics and dyes.
qui·none (kwĭ-nōn', kwĭn'ōn') *n.* Any of a class of aromatic compounds found widely in plants, esp. the yellow crystalline form, $C_6H_4O_2$, used in making dyes, in tanning hides, and in photography.
quin·o·noid (kwĭn'ə-noid', kwĭ-nō'noid') *adj.* Of, containing, or resembling quinone, in structure or properties.
quin·qua·ge·nar·i·an (kwĭng'kwə-jə-nâr'ē-ən) *n.* A person 50 years old, or in his fifties. *—adj.* Of or characteristic of a person in his fifties. [< Lat. *quinquagenarius,* containing fifty < *quinquageni,* fifty each < *quinquaginta,* fifty : *quinque,* five + *-ginta,* times ten.]
Quin·qua·ges·i·ma (kwĭng'kwə-jĕs'ə-mə) *n.* Shrove Sunday, about 50 days before Easter. [Med. Lat. < Lat., fiftieth < *quinquaginta,* fifty. —see QUINQUAGENARIAN.]
quinque– *pref.* Five: *quinquevalent.* [< Lat. *quinque,* five.]
quin·que·fo·li·ate (kwĭng'kwə-fō'lē-ĭt, -āt') *adj.* Having five leaves, leaflets, or leaflike parts.
quin·quen·ni·al (kwĭn-kwĕn'ē-əl, kwĭng-) *adj.* **1.** Happening once every five years. **2.** Lasting for five years. *—n.* **1.** A fifth anniversary. **2.** A period of five years. **—quin·quen'ni·al·ly** *adv.*
quin·quen·ni·um (kwĭn-kwĕn'ē-əm, kwĭng-) *n., pl.* **-quen·ni·ums** or **-quen·ni·a** (-kwĕn'ē-ə). A period of five years. [Lat. : *quinque,* five + *annus,* year.]
quin·que·va·lent (kwĭng'kwə-vā'lənt) *adj.* Pentavalent. **—quin'que·va'lence** *n.*
quin·sy (kwĭn'zē) *n.* Acute inflammation of the tonsils and the surrounding tissue, often leading to the formation of an abscess. [ME *quinesye* < Med. Lat. *quinancia* < Gk. *kunankhē* : *kuōn, dog* + *ankhein,* to strangle.]
quint[1] (kwĭnt) *n.* In piquet, a sequence of five cards of the same suit in one hand. [Fr. < Lat. *quintus,* fifth.]
quint[2] (kwĭnt) *n.* A quintuplet.
quin·tain (kwĭnt'n) *n.* A post, or a target mounted on a post, to be tilted at by horsemen or footmen. [ME *quintaine* < OFr., prob. < Lat. *quintana,* a street in a Roman camp < *quintus,* fifth.]
quin·tal (kwĭnt'l) *n.* **1.** A unit of mass in the metric system equal to 100 kilograms. **2.** A hundredweight (sense 2). [ME, a unit of weight < OFr. < Med. Lat. *quintale* < Ar. *qinṭār* < LGk. *kentēnarion* < LLat. *centenarium* < Lat. *centum,* hundred.]
quin·tar (kēn-tär') also **qin·tar** (kĭn-) *n.* See table at **currency.** [Albanian *qintar.*]
quin·tes·sence (kwĭn-tĕs'əns) *n.* **1.** The pure, highly concentrated essence of something. **2.** The purest or most typical instance: *the quintessence of evil.* **3.** In ancient and medieval philosophy, the fifth and highest essence (after the four elements of earth, air, fire, and water), thought to be the substance of the heavenly bodies and latent in all things. [ME < OFr. *quinte essence,* fifth essence < Med. Lat. *quinta essentia,* transl. of Gk. *pemptē ousia.*] **—quin'tes·sen'tial** (kwĭn'tĭ-sĕn'shəl) *adj.* **—quin'tes·sen'tial·ly** *adv.*
quin·tet also **quin·tette** (kwĭn-tĕt') *n.* **1.** A musical composition for five voices or instruments. **2.** A group of five performing musicians. **3.** A set of five persons or things. [Ital. *quintetto* < *quinto,* fifth < Lat. *quintus.*]
quin·tile (kwĭn'tīl', kwĭnt'l) *n.* **1.** The astrological aspect of planets distant from each other by 72 degrees or one fifth of the zodiac. **2.** The portion of a frequency distribution containing one fifth of the total sample. [< Lat. *quintus,* fifth.]
quin·til·lion (kwĭn-tĭl'yən) *n.* **1.** The cardinal number equal to 10^{18}. **2.** *Chiefly Brit.* The cardinal number equal to 10^{30}. [Lat. *quintus,* fifth + (M)ILLION.] **—quin·til'lion** *adj.*
quin·til·lionth (kwĭn-tĭl'yənth) *n.* The ordinal number that matches the number quintillion in a series. **—quin·til'lionth** *adj.*
quin·tu·ple (kwĭn-tōō'pəl, -tyōō'-, -tŭp'əl, kwĭn'tə-pəl) *adj.* **1.** Consisting of five parts or units. **2.** Five times as much, as many, or as large. *—n.* A fivefold amount or number. *—v.* **-pled, -pling, -ples.** *—tr.* To multiply by five. *—intr.* To be multiplied fivefold. [OFr. < Lat. *quintus,* fifth.]
quin·tu·plet (kwĭn-tŭp'lĭt, -tōō'plĭt, -tyōō'plĭt, kwĭn'tə-plĭt) *n.* **1.** A group or combination of five associated by common properties or behavior. **2.** One of five offspring born in a single birth. [< QUINTUPLE.]
quin·tu·pli·cate (kwĭn-tōō'plĭ-kĭt, -tyōō'-) *adj.* **1.** Multiplied by five; fivefold. **2.** Being the fifth of a set of five identical copies. *—n.* **1.** One of a set of five identical things. **2.** A set of five copies. *—tr.v.* (-kāt') **-cat·ed, -cat·ing, -cates.** To make five copies of. [Prob. < QUINTUPLE.]
quip (kwĭp) *n.* **1.** A brief, witty remark delivered offhand. **2.** A cleverly sarcastic remark; gibe. **3.** A quibble (sense 1). **4.** Something curious or odd. *—intr.v.* **quipped, quip·ping, quips.** To make quips. [Alteration of obs. *quippy,* perh. < Lat. *quippe,* indeed < *quid,* what.]
quip·ster (kwĭp'stər) *n.* One known for making quips.
qui·pu (kē'pōō) *n.* A device consisting of variously colored and knotted cords attached to a base rope, used by the Incas of Peru for calculating and recording numbers. [Sp. *quipo* < Quechua *quipu.*]
quire[1] (kwīr) *n.* A set of 24 or sometimes 25 sheets of paper of the same size and stock; one twentieth of a ream. [ME *quayer,* four doubled sheets of paper < OFr. *quaer* < Lat. *quaterni,* set of four < *quater,* four times.]
quire[2] (kwīr) *n. & v. Archaic.* Variant of **choir.**
quirk (kwûrk) *n.* **1.** A sudden sharp turn or twist. **2.** A peculiarity of behavior; idiosyncrasy. **3.** An unpredictable or unaccountable act or event; vagary. **4.** An equivocation; quibble. **5.** *Archit.* A lengthwise groove on a molding between the convex upper part and the soffit. [Orig. unknown.] **—quirk'i·ly** *adv.* **—quirk'i·ness** *n.* **—quirk'y** *adj.*
quirt (kwûrt) *n.* A riding whip with a short handle and a lash of braided rawhide. [Perh. < Sp. *cuerda,* whip < Lat. *chorda,* cord < Gk. *khordē.*]

quirt

quis·ling (kwĭz'lĭng) *n.* A traitor who serves as the puppet of the enemy occupying his country. [After Vidkun *Quisling* (1887–1945).]
quit (kwĭt) *v.* **quit** or **quit·ted** (kwĭt'ĭd), **quit·ting, quits.** *—tr.* **1.** To depart from; leave. **2.** To leave the company of. **3.** To give up; relinquish: *quit a job.* **4.** To abandon or put aside; forsake: *told him to quit his low-down ways.* **5.** To discontinue; cease. **6.** To rid oneself of by paying: *quit a debt.* **7.** To release from a burden or responsibility. **8.** To conduct (oneself) in a specified way: *Quit yourselves like gentlemen.* *—intr.* **1.** To cease to perform. **2.** To give up as in defeat; stop. **3.** To leave a job. *—adj.* Absolved of a duty or obligation; free. [ME *quiten,* to release < OFr. *quiter* < Med. Lat. *quietare* < Lat. *quietus,* at rest.]
quitch grass (kwĭch) *n.* Couch grass. [Ult. < OE *cwice.*]
quit·claim (kwĭt'klām') *Law.* *—n.* The transfer of a title, right, or claim to another. *—tr.v.* **-claimed, -claim·ing, -claims.** To renounce all claim to (a possession or right). [AN *quiteclame* < *quiteclamer,* to release < OFr. : *quite,* free (< Lat. *quietus,* freed of) + *clamer,* to proclaim < Lat. *clamare.*]
quite (kwīt) *adv.* **1.** To the greatest extent; completely: *not quite finished.* **2.** Actually; really: *He's quite positive about it.* **3.** To a degree; rather: *quite soon.* [< ME, rid of < OFr. < Lat. *quietus,* freed of.]
quit·rent (kwĭt'rĕnt') *n.* A rent paid by a freeman in lieu of services required of him by feudal custom. [ME *quiterent* : *quite,* free + *rent,* rent.]
quits (kwĭts) *adj.* Even with, as by payment or requital. [ME, prob. < Med. Lat. *quittus,* alteration of Lat. *quietus,* freed of.]
quit·tance (kwĭt'ns) *n.* **1. a.** Release from a debt, obligation, or penalty. **b.** A document or receipt certifying such a release. **2.** Something given as requital or recompense; repayment. [ME *quitance* < OFr. < *quiter,* to free. —see QUIT.]
quit·ter (kwĭt'ər) *n.* One who gives up easily.
quit·tor (kwĭt'ər) *n.* An inflammation of the hoof cartilage of horses and other solid-hoofed animals, characterized by degeneration of hoof tissue, formation of a slough, and fistulous sores. [ME *quiture,* perh. < OFr., decoction < Lat. *coctura* < *coquere,* to cook.]
quiv·er[1] (kwĭv'ər) *intr.v.* **-ered, -er·ing, -ers.** To shake with a rapid slight motion; tremble. *—n.* The act or motion of quivering. [ME *quiveren,* perh. < *quiver,* nimble.]
quiv·er[2] (kwĭv'ər) *n.* **1.** A portable case for arrows. **2.** A case full of arrows. [ME < AN *quiveir,* var. of OFr. *cuivre,* of Germanic orig.]

quiver[2]

qui vive (kē vēv') *n.* A sentinel's challenge. **—*idiom.* on the qui vive.** On the alert; vigilant. [Fr., (long) live who? (a sentry's challenge to determine a person's political sympathies).]
quix·ot·ic (kwĭk-sŏt'ĭk) also **quix·ot·i·cal** (-ĭ-kəl) *adj.* Idealistic without regard to practicality. [After *Don Quixote,* hero and title of a romance by Miguel de Cervantes (1547–1616).] **—quix·ot'i·cal·ly** *adv.* **—quix'o·tism** (kwĭk'sə-tĭz'əm) *n.*
quiz (kwĭz) *tr.v.* **quizzed, quiz·zing, quiz·zes.** **1.** To question closely or repeatedly; interrogate. **2.** To test the knowledge of by posing questions. **3.** *Chiefly Brit.* To poke fun at; mock. *—n., pl.* **quiz·zes.** **1.** A questioning or inquiry. **2.** A short oral or written test. **3.** A practical joke. [Orig. unknown.] **—quiz'zer** *n.*
quiz·mas·ter (kwĭz'măs'tər) *n.* One who asks the contestants questions in a quiz show.

quiz show *n.* A radio or television show in which contestants answer questions, usually for prizes.
quiz·zi·cal (kwĭz'ĭ-kəl) *adj.* **1.** Suggesting puzzlement; questioning. **2.** Teasing; mocking: *"his face wore a somewhat quizzical almost impertinent air"* (Lawrence Durrell). **3.** Eccentric; odd. **—quiz'zi·cal'i·ty** (-kăl'ĭ-tē) *n.* **—quiz'zi·cal·ly** *adv.*
quod (kwŏd) *n. Chiefly Brit. Slang.* Prison. [Orig. unknown.]
quod·li·bet (kwŏd'lə-bĕt') *n.* **1. a.** A theological or philosophical issue presented for formal argument or disputation. **b.** The disputation itself. **2.** A usually humorous musical medley. [Lat., anything at all : *quod,* what + *libet,* it pleases < *libere,* to please.]
quoin (koin, kwoin) *n.* **1. a.** An exterior angle of a wall or other masonry. **b.** A stone serving to form such an angle; cornerstone. **2.** A keystone. **3.** *Printing.* A wedge-shaped block used to lock type in a chase. **4.** A wedge used to raise the level of a gun. *—tr.v.* **quoined, quoin·ing, quoins.** To provide, secure, or raise with a quoin or quoins. [Var. of COIN.]
quoit (kwoit, koit) *n.* **1. quoits** *(used with a sing. verb).* A game in which flat rings of iron or rope are pitched at a stake, with points awarded for encircling it. **2.** One of the rings used in quoits. [ME *coite.*]
quon·dam (kwŏn'dəm, -dăm') *adj.* That once was; former: *"the quondam drunkard, now perfectly sober"* (Bret Harte). [Lat. < *quom,* when.]
Quon·set (kwŏn'sĭt). A trademark for a prefabricated portable hut having a semicircular roof of corrugated metal that curves down to form walls.
quo·rum (kwôr'əm, kwōr'-) *n.* **1.** The minimum number of officers and members of a committee or organization, usually a majority, who must be present for the valid transaction of business. **2.** A select group. [ME, quorum of justices of the peace < Lat., of whom, from the wording of a commission naming certain persons as members of a body (as the bench).]
quo·ta (kwō'tə) *n.* **1. a.** A proportional share, as of goods, assigned to a group or to each member of a group; allotment. **b.** A production assignment. **2.** The maximum number, esp. of people, that may be admitted, as to a nation, group, or institution. [Med. Lat. < Lat., fem. of *quotus,* of what number < *quot,* how many.]
quot·a·ble (kwō'tə-bəl) *adj.* Suitable for or worthy of quoting. **—quot'a·bil'i·ty** *n.*
quo·ta·tion (kwō-tā'shən) *n.* **1.** The act of quoting. **2.** A passage that is quoted. **3. a.** The quoting of current prices and bids for securities and goods. **b.** The prices or bids cited. **—quo·ta'tion·al** *adj.* **—quo·ta'tion·al·ly** *adv.*
quotation mark *n.* Either of a pair of punctuation marks (" ") or (' ') used to mark the beginning and end of a passage attributed to another and repeated word for word.
quote (kwōt) *v.* **quot·ed, quot·ing, quotes.** *—tr.* **1.** To repeat or copy the words of (another), usually with acknowledgment of the source. **2.** To cite or refer to for illustration or proof. **3.** To state (a price) for securities, goods, or services. *—intr.* To give a quotation, as from a book. *—n. Informal.* **1.** A quotation. **2.** A quotation mark. [ME *coten,* to mark a book with numbers or marginal references < Med. Lat. *quotare* < Lat. *quotus,* of what number < *quot,* how many.] **—quot'er** *n.*

Usage: *Quote* (transitive verb) is appropriate when words are being given exactly as they were originally written or spoken. When the reference is less exact, *cite* is preferable. • *Quote* (noun) as a substitute for *quotation* is considered unacceptable in writing by a large majority of the Usage Panel.

quoth (kwōth) *v. Archaic.* Uttered; said. Used only in the first and third persons, with the subject following: *"Quoth the raven 'Nevermore!'"* (Poe). [ME < OE *cwæð,* he said < *cwæðan,* to say.]
quo·tha (kwō'thə) *interj. Archaic.* Used to express surprise or sarcasm, after quoting the word or phrase of another. [Contraction of *quoth he.*]
quo·tid·i·an (kwō-tĭd'ē-ən) *adj.* **1.** Recurring daily. **2.** Everyday; commonplace. [ME *cotidian* < OFr. *cotidien* < Lat. *quotidianus* < *quotidie,* each day : *quot,* as many as + *dies,* day.]
quo·tient (kwō'shənt) *n.* The quantity resulting from division of one quantity by another. [ME *quocient* < Lat. *quotiens,* how many times < *quot,* how many.]
qu·rush (kōō'rəsh) *n., pl.* **qurush** or **-es.** See table at **currency.** [Ar. *qurūš.*]

R

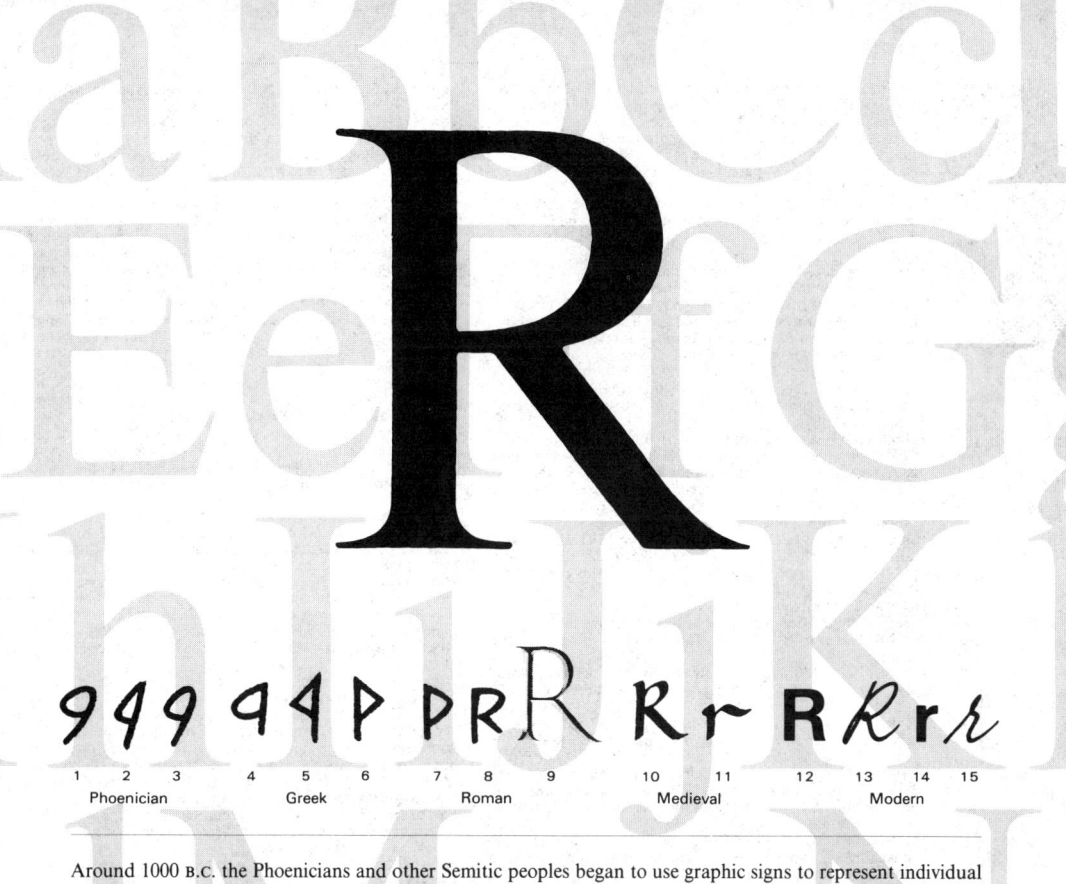

1 2 3 4 5 6 7 8 9 10 11 12 13 14 15

Phoenician Greek Roman Medieval Modern

Around 1000 B.C. the Phoenicians and other Semitic peoples began to use graphic signs to represent individual speech sounds instead of syllables or words. They used a symbol in the forms (1,2,3) to represent the sound of the consonant "r" and called it *rēsh,* their word for "head." The Greeks, adapting the Phoenician alphabet, kept the phonetic value of *rēsh* but changed its shape and orientation (4,5,6) and altered its name to *rhō.* The Romans borrowed the alphabet from the Greeks via the Etruscans, adding a tail to *rhō* in order to distinguish it from their letter P. They also adapted the alphabet for monumental inscriptions. Their monumental script (9) is the prototype of modern capital letters (12,13). Medieval scribes adapted the Roman capitals to being quickly written on paper, parchment, and vellum. These uncial and cursive minuscules (10,11) are the prototypes of modern lower-case letters, both written and printed (15,14).

---

r

---

p **pop** / r **roar** / s **sauce** / sh **ship, dish** / t **tight** / th **thin, path** / *th* **this, bathe** / ŭ **cut** / ûr **urge** / v **valve** / w **with** / y **yes** / z **zebra, size** / zh **vision** / ə **about, item, edible, gallop, circus** / œ *Fr.* **feu**, *Ger.* **schön** / ü *Fr.* **tu**, *Ger.* **über** / KH *Ger.* **ich**, *Scot.* **loch** / N *Fr.* **bon.**

rabbit

r or **R** (är) *n., pl.* **r's** or **R's. 1.** The 18th letter of the modern English alphabet. **2.** Any of the speech sounds represented by the letter *r.* **3.** The 18th in a series.

R (är) *adj.* Indicating a motion-picture rating of such nature that no one under a certain age (17) can be admitted unless accompanied by a parent or guardian. [Short for RESTRICTED.]

Ra[1] (rä) also **Re** (rā) *n.* The sun god, the supreme deity of the ancient Egyptians, represented as a man with the head of a hawk crowned with a solar disk and uraeus. [Of Egyptian orig.]

Ra[2] The symbol for the element radium.

ra·ba·to (rə-bä′tō) *n.* Variant of **rebato.**

rab·bet (răb′ĭt) also **re·bate** (rē′bāt′, răb′ĭt) *n.* **1.** A cut or groove along or near the edge of a piece of wood that allows another piece to fit into it to form a joint. **2.** A joint made with a rabbet. —*v.* **-bet·ed, -bet·ing, -bets** also **-bat·ed, -bat·ing, -bates.** —*tr.* **1.** To cut a rabbet in. **2.** To join by a rabbet. —*intr.* To be joined by a rabbet. [ME *rabet* < OFr. *rabat,* act of beating down < *rabattre,* to beat down again. —see REBATE[1].]

rab·bi (răb′ī) also **rab·bin** (răb′ĭn) *n., pl.* **-bis** also **-bins. 1.** The ordained spiritual leader of a Jewish congregation. **2.** A person formerly authorized to interpret Jewish law. [LLat. < Gk. *rhabbi* < Heb. *rabbi* : *rabh,* master + *-ī,* my.]

rab·bin·ate (răb′ĭn-āt′, -ĭt) *n.* **1.** The office or function of a rabbi. **2.** Rabbis collectively.

rab·bin·i·cal (rə-bĭn′ĭ-kəl) also **rab·bin·ic** (-ĭk) *adj.* Of, pertaining to, or characteristic of rabbis, or their views, learning, writings, or language. [< Fr. *rabbin,* rabbi.] **—rab·bin′i·cal·ly** *adv.*

Rab·bin·ic Hebrew (rə-bĭn′ĭk) *n.* The Hebrew language as used in the learned writings of esp. medieval rabbis.

rab·bin·ism (răb′ĭn-ĭz′əm) *n.* Rabbinical teachings and traditions.

rab·bin·ist (răb′ĭn-ĭst) *n.* A strict observer of the Talmud and of rabbinical traditions. **—rab·bin·is′tic, rab·bin·it′ic** (-ĭt′ĭk) *adj.*

rab·bit (răb′ĭt) *n., pl.* **rabbit** or **-bits. 1.** Any of various long-eared, short-tailed, burrowing mammals of the family Leporidae, such as the commonly domesticated Old World species *Oryctolagus cuniculus* or the cottontail. **2.** A hare. **3.** The fur of a rabbit or hare. **4.** Welsh rabbit. —*intr.v.* **-bit·ed, -bit·ing, -bits.** To hunt rabbits or hares. [ME *rabet.*] **—rab′bit·er** *n.*

rabbit ears *pl.n. Informal.* An indoor television antenna consisting of two usually adjustable rods connected to a base and swiveling apart at a V-shaped angle.

rabbit fever *n.* Tularemia.

rab·bit-foot clover (răb′ĭt-fo͝ot′) *n.* A clover, *Trifolium arvense,* native to the Old World, having pinkish-gray, furlike flowers resembling rabbits' paws.

rabbit punch *n.* A chopping blow to the back of the neck.

rab·ble[1] (răb′əl) *n.* **1.** A tumultuous mob. **2.** A group of persons of the lowest class, often regarded with contempt. [ME, pack of animals.]

rab·ble[2] (răb′əl) *n. Metallurgy.* **1.** An iron bar with one end bent like a rake, used to stir and skim molten iron in puddling. **2.** Any of various tools or mechanically operated devices similar to a rabble used in roasting or refining furnaces. —*tr.v.* **-bled, -bling, -bles.** To stir or skim (molten iron) with a rabble. [Fr. *râble,* fire shovel < OFr. *roable* < Med. Lat. *rotabulum* < Lat. *rutabulum* < *ruere,* to rake up.]

rab·bler (răb′lər) *n.* A rabble[2].

rab·ble-rous·er (răb′əl-rou′zər) *n.* A demagogue.

Rab·e·lai·si·an (răb′ə-lā′zē-ən, -zhən) *adj.* **1.** Of or relating to Francois Rabelais or to his works. **2.** Characterized by lusty humor and bold caricature.

Ra·bi (rŭ′bē) also **Ra·bi·a** (rə-bē′ə) *n.* Either the third or the fourth month of the Moslem calendar. See table at **calendar.** [Ar. *rabī‘,* spring.]

rab·id (răb′ĭd) *adj.* **1.** Of or afflicted with rabies. **2.** Overzealous; fanatical: *a rabid football fan.* **3.** Raging; uncontrollable: *rabid thirst.* [Lat. *rabidus* < *rabere,* to rave.] **—ra·bid′i·ty** (rə-bĭd′ə-tē, rā-), **rab′id·ness** *n.* **—rab′id·ly** *adv.*

ra·bies (rā′bēz) *n.* An acute, infectious, often fatal viral disease of most warm-blooded animals, esp. wolves, cats, and dogs, that attacks the central nervous system and is transmitted by the bite of infected animals. [NLat. < Lat. *rabies,* rage < *rabere,* to rave.] **—ra′bi·et′ic** (-ĕt′ĭk) *adj.*

rac·coon (ră-ko͞on′) *n., pl.* **-coons** or **raccoon. 1.** A carnivorous North American mammal, *Procyon lotor,* having grayish-brown fur, black, masklike facial markings, and a bushy, black-ringed tail. **2.** The fur of the raccoon. **3.** Any of various animals similar or related to the raccoon. [Algonquian (Virginia) *arathkone.*]

race[1] (rās) *n.* **1.** A local geographic or global human population distinguished as a more or less distinct group by genetically transmitted physical characteristics. **2.** Mankind as a whole. **3.** A group of people united or classified together on the basis of common history, nationality, or geographical distribution: *the German race.* **4.** A genealogical line; lineage. **5.** *Biol.* **a.** A plant or animal population that differs from others of the same species in the frequency of hereditary traits; subspecies. **b.** A breed or strain, as of domestic animals. **6.** A distinguishing or characteristic quality, such as the flavor of a wine. [Fr., generation < OItal. *razza.*]

race[2]
Horse race

race[2] (rās) *n.* **1. a.** A competition of speed, as in running or riding. **b. races.** A series of such competitions held at a specified time on a regular course. **2.** A contest or pursuit of supremacy: *the Presidential race.* **3.** Steady or rapid onward movement: *the race of time.* **4. a.** A strong or swift current of water. **b.** The channel of such a current. **c.** An artificial channel built to transport water and utilize its energy: *a mill race.* **5.** A groovelike part of a machine in which a moving part slides or rolls. **6.** A slipstream. —*v.* **raced, rac·ing, rac·es.** —*intr.* **1.** To compete in a contest of speed. **2.** To move rapidly or at top speed. **3.** To run too rapidly because of decreased resistance or a lighter load: *an engine that was racing.* —*tr.* **1.** To compete against in a contest of speed. **2.** To cause to compete in such a contest. **3.** To cause (an engine with the gears disengaged, for example) to run swiftly or too swiftly. [ME *ras* < ON *rās.*]

race[3] (rās) *n.* A root, esp. of ginger. [OFr. *rais,* root < Lat. *radix.*]

race·course (rās′kôrs′) *n.* A racetrack.

race·horse (rās′hôrs′) *n.* A horse bred and trained to race.

ra·ceme (rā-sēm′, rə-) *n. Bot.* An inflorescence in which stalked flowers are arranged singly along a common main axis, as in the lily of the valley. [Lat. *racemus,* a bunch of grapes.]

ra·ce·mic (rā-sē′mĭk, -sĕm′ĭk, rə-) *adj.* Of or pertaining to a chemical compound containing equal quantities of dextrorotatory and levorotatory isomers so that it does not rotate the plane of incident polarized light.

racemic acid *n.* An optically inactive form of tartaric acid, $C_4H_6O_6 \cdot H_2O$, that can be separated into dextrorotatory and levorotatory components and is sometimes found in grape juice during wine-making.

ra·ce·mi·form (rā-sē′mə-fôrm′) *adj. Bot.* Racemelike in form.

rac·e·mism (răs′ə-mĭz′əm, rā-sē′-) *n. Chem.* The condition or state of being racemic.

rac·e·mi·za·tion (răs′ə-mĭ-zā′shən) *n. Chem.* The conversion of an optically active substance to a racemic form.

rac·e·mose (răs′ə-mōs′) *adj.* **1.** *Bot.* Resembling or growing in a raceme. **2.** *Anat.* Having a structure of clustered parts. Used of glands. [Lat. *racemosus,* full of clusters < *racemus,* bunch of grapes.] **—rac′e·mose′ly** *adv.*

rac·er (rā′sər) *n.* **1.** One that engages in races or is capable of great speed. **2.** Any of various fast-moving North American snakes of the genus *Coluber.*

race riot *n.* A riot caused by racial hatred or dissensions.

race·run·ner (rās′rŭn′ər) *n.* Any of several fast-moving New World lizards of the genus *Cnemidophorus.*

race·track (rās′trăk′) *n.* A course laid out for racing.

race·way (rās′wā′) *n.* **1.** A race[2] (sense 4.c.). **2.** A usually rectangular tube for enclosing and protecting electric wires. **3.** A racetrack.

Ra·chel (rā′chəl) *n.* In the Old Testament, the second wife of Jacob and mother of his sons Joseph and Benjamin. [Heb. *Rāḥēl.*]

ra·chis (rā′kĭs) *n., pl.* **-chis·es** or **-chi·des** (-kə-dēz′). *Biol.* A main axis or shaft, as the main stem of an inflorescence or the spinal column. [NLat. < Gk. *rhakhis,* backbone.] **—ra′chi·al** *adj.*

ra·chi·tis (rə-kī′tĭs) *n.* Rickets. [Gk. *rhakhitis,* disease of the spine < *rhakhis,* spine.] **—ra·chit′ic** (-kĭt′ĭk) *adj.*

ra·cial (rā′shəl) *adj.* **1.** Of, pertaining to, or typical of an ethnic group. **2.** Arising from or based upon differences between ethnic groups. **—ra′cial·ly** *adv.*

ra·cial·ism (rā′shə-lĭz′əm) *n. Chiefly Brit.* Variant of **racism.**

racing form *n.* An information sheet about horse races.

ra·cism (rā′sĭz′əm) *n.* **1.** The notion that one's own ethnic stock is superior. **2.** Discrimination or prejudice based on racism. **—rac′ist** *n.*

rack[1] (răk) *n.* **1.** A framework or stand in which to hold or display various articles, esp.: **a.** A triangular frame for arranging billiard balls at the start of a game. **b.** A receptacle for livestock feed. **c.** A frame for holding bombs in an airplane. **d.** *Printing.* An upright framework for holding cases of type or galley proof. **2.** A toothed bar that meshes with another toothed machine part, as a pinion or gearwheel. **3.** An instrument of torture on which the victim's body was stretched. **4. a.** A state of intense anguish. **b.** A cause of intense anguish. **5.** The stress of storm. **6.** A pair of antlers. —*tr.v.* **racked, rack·ing, racks. 1.** To place (billiard balls, for example) in a rack. **2.** To torture by means of the rack. **3.** To torment: *Pain racked his entire body.* **4.** To strain with great effort: *rack one's brain.* **—phrasal verb. rack up.** *Slang.* To accumulate or score: *rack up points.* **—idiom. on the rack.** Under great strain or stress. [ME *rakke,* prob. < MDu., framework.] **—rack′er** *n.*

rack[2] (răk) *n.* Either of two gaits of horses, the single-foot or the pace. —*intr.v.* **racked, rack·ing, racks.** To go or move in a rack. [Orig. unknown.]

rack[3] (răk) *n.* A thin mass of wind-driven clouds. —*intr.v.* **racked, rack·ing, racks.** To be driven by the wind, as clouds. [ME *rak,* prob. of Scand. orig.]

rack[4] (răk) *n.* Destruction: *rack and ruin.* [Var. of WRACK[1].]

Usage: The choice of *rack* or *wrack* in certain set

phrases is sometimes puzzling. *Rack,* in a term such as *nerve-racking,* derives from the medieval instrument of torture and thus carries the intended sense of strain or torture. *Wrack* refers to violent destruction or wreckage. In modern usage, however, *rack* is accepted as a variant spelling of *wrack.* Therefore, it is correct to write either *rack and ruin* or *wrack and ruin,* either *storm-wracked* or *storm-racked.*

rack[5] (răk) *tr.v.* **racked, rack·ing, racks.** To drain (wine or cider) from the dregs. [ME *rakken* < OProv. *arracar* < *raca,* stems and husks of grapes.]

rack[6] (răk) *n.* **1.** A wholesale rib cut of lamb between the shoulder and the loin. **2.** A crown roast of lamb. [Prob. < RACK[1].]

rack and pinion *n.* A device for the interconversion of rotary and linear motion, consisting of a pinion and a mated rack.

rack·et[1] also **rac·quet** (răk′ĭt) *n.* **1.** A device consisting of an oval frame with a tight interlaced network of strings and a handle, used to strike a ball or shuttle-cock. **2.** A wooden paddle, such as one used in table tennis. **3. rackets** *(used with a sing. verb).* A game similar to tennis, played in a four-walled court. [OFr. *raquette* < Ar. *râḥet,* palm of the hand.]

rack·et[2] (răk′ĭt) *n.* **1.** A clamor; uproar. **2.** A dishonest business or practice, esp. one that obtains money through fraud or extortion. **3.** *Slang.* A business or job. **4.** An easy and profitable means of livelihood. *—intr.v.* **-et·ed, -et·ing, -ets.** To lead an active social life. [Orig. unknown.]

rack·et·eer (răk′ĭ-tîr′) *n.* A person engaged in an illegal business. *—intr.v.* **-eered, -eer·ing, -eers.** To engage in a racket.

rack·et·y (răk′ĭ-tē) *adj.* Noisy; raucous.

rack railway *n.* A cog railway.

rack-rent (răk′rĕnt′) *n.* Exorbitant rent. *—tr.v.* **-rent·ed, -rent·ing, -rents.** To exact exorbitant rent for or from. [< RACK[1].] **—rack′-rent′er** *n.*

ra·clette (rä-klĕt′, ră-) *n.* **1.** A Swiss dish consisting of cheese melted and served on boiled potatoes or bread. **2.** A firm cheese used in making raclette. [Fr. < *racler,* to scrape.]

rac·on·teur (răk′ŏn-tûr′) *n.* A person who tells stories and anecdotes with skill and wit. [Fr. < OFr. < *raconter,* to tell : *re-,* again (< Lat.) + *cunter,* to tell, to reckon. —see ACCOUNT.]

ra·coon (ră-ko͞on′) *n.* A raccoon.

rac·quet (răk′ĭt) *n.* Variant of **racket[1]**.

rac·quet·ball (răk′ĭt-bôl′) *n.* A court game that is identical to handball but utilizes a short racquet and a larger, softer ball.

rac·y (rā′sē) *adj.* **-i·er, -i·est. 1.** Having a distinctive quality or taste. **2. a.** Piquant or pungent. **b.** Risqué; ribald. **c.** Vigorous; lively. [< RACE[1].] **—rac′i·ly** *adv.* **—rac′i·ness** *n.*

rad (răd) *n. Physics.* A unit of energy absorbed from ionizing radiation, equal to 100 ergs per gram of irradiated material. [Short for RADIATION.]

ra·dar (rā′där) *n.* **1.** A method of detecting distant objects and determining their position, velocity, or other characteristics by analysis of very high frequency radio waves reflected from their surfaces. **2.** The equipment used in radar detection. [RA(DIO) D(ETECTING) A(ND) R(ANGING).]

radar astronomy *n.* Astronomy of the solar system using reflected radio waves to determine celestial characteristics.

radar beacon *n.* A fixed device that sends or receives, amplifies, alters, and returns a radar signal, permitting a distant receiver to determine its bearing and sometimes its range.

ra·dar·scope (rā′där-skōp′) *n.* The oscilloscope viewing screen of a radar receiver. [RADAR + (OSCILLO)SCOPE.]

radar telescope *n.* A large radar antenna used in radar astronomy.

rad·dle[1] (răd′l) *tr.v.* **-dled, -dling, -dles.** To twist together or interweave. [< dial. *raddle,* stick interwoven with others in a fence < OFr. *reddalle,* poss. < MHG *reidel.*]

rad·dle[2] (răd′l) *n. & v.* Variant of **ruddle.**

rad·dled (răd′ld) *adj.* Worn-out and broken-down. [Orig. unknown.]

radi– *pref.* Variant of **radio-.**

ra·di·al (rā′dē-əl) *adj.* **1. a.** Of, pertaining to, or arranged like rays or radii. **b.** Radiating from or converging to a common center. **c.** Having or characterized by parts so arranged or so radiating. **2.** Moving or directed along a radius. **3.** *Anat.* Of, pertaining to, or near the radius or forearm. **4.** Developing symmetrically about a central point. *—n.* **1.** A radial part, as a ray, spoke, or radius. **2.** A radial tire. [Med. Lat. < Lat. *radius,* ray.] **—ra′di·al·ly** *adv.*

radial engine *n.* An internal-combustion engine, as formerly used in propeller-driven aircraft, with radially arrayed cylinders.

radial symmetry *n.* Symmetrical arrangement of constituents, esp. of radiating parts, about a central point.

radial tire also **radial ply tire** *n.* A pneumatic tire in which the ply cords extending to beads are laid at approximately right angles to the center line of the tread.

ra·di·an (rā′dē-ən) *n.* A unit of angular measure equal to the angle subtended at the center of a circle by an arc of length equal to the radius of the circle, equal to $360/2\pi$ degrees, or approximately 57°17′44.6″. [RADI(US) + -AN.]

ra·di·ance (rā′dē-əns) also **ra·di·an·cy** (-ən-sē) *n.* **1.** The quality or state of being radiant. **2.** *Physics.* The radiant energy emitted per unit time in a specified direction by a unit area of an emitting surface.

ra·di·ant (rā′dē-ənt) *adj.* **1.** Emitting heat or light. **2.** Consisting of or emitted as radiation: *radiant heat.* **3.** Filled with happiness, joy, or love. **4.** Glowing; bright: *a radiant diamond.* *—n.* **1.** An object or point from which light or heat rays are emitted. **2.** *Astron.* The apparent celestial origin of a meteoric shower. [Lat. *radians, radiant-,* pr.part. of *radiare,* to radiate.] **—ra′di·ant·ly** *adv.*

radiant energy *n. Physics.* Energy transferred by radiation, esp. by an electromagnetic wave.

radiant flux *n.* The rate of flow of radiant energy.

ra·di·ate (rā′dē-āt′) *v.* **-at·ed, -at·ing, -ates.** *—intr.* **1.** To emit radiation. **2.** To issue or emerge in rays. **3.** To spread out or converge radially, as the spokes of a wheel. *—tr.* **1.** To emit (light, for example). **2.** To diffuse or disseminate from or as if from a center. **3.** To irradiate or illuminate (an object). **4.** To manifest in a glowing manner: *He radiated confidence.* *—adj.* (rā′dē-ĭt). **1.** *Bot.* Having rays or raylike parts: *radiate flowers.* **2.** *Zool.* Characterized by radial symmetry. **3.** Surrounded with rays, as a head represented on a coin. [Lat. *radiare, radiat-,* to emit beams < *radius,* ray.] **—ra′di·a′tive** *adj.*

ra·di·a·tion (rā′dē-ā′shən) *n.* **1.** The act or process of radiating. **2.** *Physics.* **a.** The emission and propagation of waves or particles. **b.** The propagating waves or particles, such as light, sound, radiant heat, or particles, emitted by radioactivity. **3.** *Anat.* Radial arrangement of parts, as of a group of nerve fibers connecting different areas of the brain. **4.** *Biol.* Adaptive radiation.

radiation sickness *n.* Illness induced by ionizing radiation, ranging in severity from nausea, vomiting, headache, and diarrhea to loss of hair and teeth, reduction in red and white blood cell count, extensive hemorrhaging, sterility, and death.

ra·di·a·tor (rā′dē-ā′tər) *n.* **1.** A heating device consisting of a series of connected pipes for the circulation of steam or hot water. **2.** A cooling device, as in automotive engines, through which water or other fluids circulate as a coolant. **3.** *Physics.* A body that emits radiation. **4.** A transmitting antenna.

rad·i·cal (răd′ĭ-kəl) *adj.* **1.** Arising from or going to a root or source; basic. **2.** Carried to the utmost limit; extreme: *radical social change.* **3.** Favoring or effecting extreme or revolutionary changes, as in political organization. **4.** Of or designating a word root. **5.** *Bot.* Of, pertaining to, or growing from the root. *—n.* **1.** One who advocates political and social revolution. **2.** *Math.* The root of a quantity as indicated by the radical sign. **3.** *Chem.* An atom or group of atoms with at least one unpaired electron. **4.** *Ling.* Root[1] (sense 8). [ME, of a root < LLat. *radicalis,* having roots < Lat. *radix,* root.] **—rad′i·cal·ly** *adv.* **—rad′i·cal·ness** *n.*

radical expression *n.* A mathematical expression or form in which radical signs appear.

rad·i·cal·ism (răd′ĭ-kə-lĭz′əm) *n.* The doctrines or practices of esp. political radicals.

rad·i·cal·ize (răd′ĭ-kə-līz′) *tr.v.* **-ized, -iz·ing, -iz·es.** To make radical or more radical. **—rad′i·cal·i·za′tion** *n.*

radical sign *n.* **1.** The sign $\sqrt{}$ placed before a quantity, indicating extraction of the root designated by a raised integral index. When extracting a square root, the index is customarily omitted. **2.** The radical sign together with a horizontal bar extending from its top to the end of the expression from which a root is to be extracted.

rad·i·cand (răd′ĭ-kănd′) *n.* The quantity under a radical sign: *3 is the radicand of* $\sqrt{3}$. [Lat. *radicandum,* neuter gerund. of *radicare,* to take root < *radix,* root.]

rad·i·ces (răd′ĭ-sēz′) *n.* A plural of **radix.**

rad·i·cle (răd′ĭ-kəl) *n.* **1.** *Bot.* The part of the plant embryo that develops into the primary root. **2.** *Anat.* A small structure resembling a root, as a fibril of a nerve. [Lat. *radicula,* dim. of *radix,* root.]

ra·di·i (rā′dē-ī′) *n.* A plural of **radius.**

ra·di·o (rā′dē-ō) *n., pl.* **-os. 1.** The use of electromagnetic waves in the approximate frequency range from 10 kilocycles/second to 300,000 megacycles/second to transmit or receive electric signals without wires connecting the points of transmission and reception. **2.** Communication of audible signals encoded in electromagnetic waves transmitted and received by radio. **3.** Transmission of programs for the public by radio broadcast. **4. a.** The equipment used to transmit radio signals; transmitter. **b.** The equipment used to receive radio signals; receiver. **c.** A complex of equipment capable of both transmitting and receiving radio signals. **5. a.** A station for radio transmitting. **b.** A radio broadcasting organization or network of affiliated organizations. **c.** The radio broadcasting industry. **6.** A message sent by radio. *—v.* **-oed, -o·ing, -os.** *—tr.* To transmit or communicate by radio. *—intr.* To transmit a message by radio. [Short for RADIOTELEGRAPHY.]

radio– or **radi–** *pref.* **1.** Radiation; radiant energy: *radiometer.* **2.** Radioactive: *radiochemistry.* **3.** Radio: *radiotelephone.* [< RADIATION.]

ra·di·o·ac·tive (rā′dē-ō-ăk′tĭv) *adj.* Of or exhibiting radioactivity. **—ra′di·o·ac′tive·ly** *adv.*

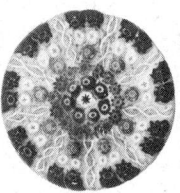

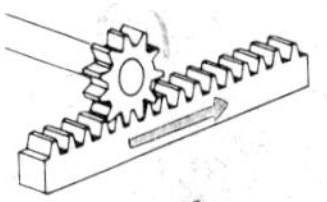

rack[1]

radial symmetry

radiometer

radioactive decay *n.* A progressive decrease in the number of radioactive atoms in a substance by spontaneous nuclear disintegration or transformation.
radioactive series *n.* A group of isotopes related by a sequence of radioactive decay processes in which the heavier members of the group are transformed into successively lighter ones, the lightest being stable.
ra·di·o·ac·tiv·i·ty (rā'dē-ō-ăk'tĭv'ĭ-tē) *n.* **1.** The radiation, including alpha particles, nucleons, electrons, and gamma rays, that is emitted as a consequence of a nuclear reaction. **2.** The radiation emitted by radioactivity, including alpha particles, nucleons, electrons, and gamma rays.
radio astronomy *n.* The study of celestial objects and phenomena by observation and analysis of emitted or reflected radio-frequency waves.
radio beacon *n.* A fixed radio transmitter that broadcasts distinctive signals as a navigational aid.
radio beam *n.* A focused beam of radio signals transmitted by a radio beacon to guide aircraft or ships.
ra·di·o·bi·ol·o·gy (rā'dē-ō-bī-ŏl'ə-jē) *n.* **1.** The study of the effects of radiation on living organisms. **2.** The use of radioactive tracers to study biological processes. **—ra'di·o·bi'o·log'i·cal** (-ə-lŏj'ĭ-kəl) *adj.* **—ra'di·o·bi·ol'o·gist** *n.*
ra·di·o·broad·cast (rā'dē-ō-brôd'kăst') *v.* **-cast** or **-cast·ed, -cast·ing, -casts.** *—tr.* To broadcast (a program, for example) by radio. *—intr.* To broadcast by radio. **—ra'di·o·broad'cast'er** *n.*
ra·di·o·car·bon (rā'dē-ō-kär'bən) *n.* Radioactive carbon, esp. carbon 14.
radiocarbon dating *n.* Carbon dating.
ra·di·o·cast (rā'dē-ō-kăst') *tr. & intr.v.* **-cast** or **-cast·ed, -cast·ing, -casts.** To radiobroadcast. [RADIO + (BROAD)-CAST.] **—ra'di·o·cast'er** *n.*
ra·di·o·chem·is·try (rā'dē-ō-kĕm'ĭ-strē) *n.* The chemistry of radioactive materials. **—ra'di·o·chem'i·cal** *adj.*
radio compass *n.* A navigational aid consisting of an automatic radio receiver that determines the transmission direction of incoming radio waves.
ra·di·o·el·e·ment (rā'dē-ō-ĕl'ə-mənt) *n.* A naturally occurring or artificially produced radioactive element.

radish

radio frequency *n.* **1.** The frequency of the waves transmitted by a specific radio station. **2.** A frequency in the range within which radio waves may be transmitted, from about 10 kilocycles/second to about 300,000 megacycles/second. Radio frequency groups are: *very low frequency* (vlf), 10 to 30 kilocycles/second; *low frequency* (lf), 30 to 300 kilocycles/second; *medium frequency* (mf), 300 to 3,000 kilocycles/second; *high frequency* (hf), 3,000 to 30,000 kilocycles/second; *very high frequency* (vhf), 30 to 300 megacycles/second; *ultrahigh frequency* (uhf), 300 to 3,000 megacycles/second; *superhigh frequency* (shf), 3,000 to 30,000 megacycles/second; *extremely high frequency* (ehf), 30,000 to 300,000 megacycles/second.
radio galaxy *n.* A galaxy emitting large amounts of radio energy.
ra·di·o·ge·nic (rā'dē-ō-jĕn'ĭk) *adj.* Caused by radioactivity.
ra·di·o·gram (rā'dē-ō-grăm') *n.* **1.** A message transmitted by wireless telegraphy. **2.** A radiograph.
ra·di·o·graph (rā'dē-ō-grăf') *n.* An image produced on a radiosensitive surface, as a photographic film, by radiation other than visible light, esp. by x rays passed through an object or by photographing a fluoroscopic image. *—tr.v.* **-graphed, -graph·ing, -graphs.** To make a radiograph of. **—ra'di·og'ra·pher** (-ŏg'rə-fər) *n.* **—ra'di·o·graph'ic** *adj.* **—ra'di·o·graph'i·cal·ly** *adv.* **—ra'di·og'ra·phy** *n.*
ra·di·o·im·mu·no·as·say (rā'dē-ō-ĭm'yə-nō-ăs'ā, -ĭm-yōō'-) *n.* The immunoassay of a radioactively labeled substance, as a hormone or enzyme.
ra·di·o·i·so·tope (rā'dē-ō-ī'sə-tōp') *n.* A naturally or artificially produced radioactive isotope of an element.

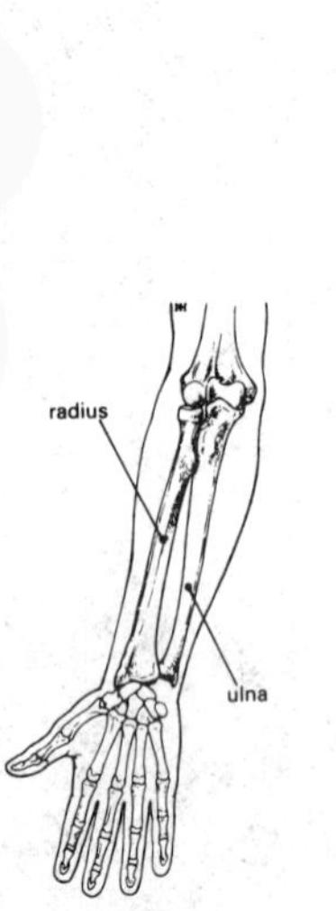

radius

ra·di·o·lar·i·an (rā'dē-ō-lâr'ē-ən) *n.* Any of various marine protozoans of the order Radiolaria, having rigid siliceous skeletons and spicules. [< NLat. *Radiolaria,* order name < LLat. *radiolus,* dim. of *radius,* ray.]
ra·di·o·lo·ca·tion (rā'dē-ō-lō-kā'shən) *n.* The detection of distant objects by radar.
ra·di·ol·o·gy (rā'dē-ŏl'ə-jē) *n.* **1.** The use of ionizing radiation for medical diagnosis, esp. the use of x-rays in medical radiography or fluoroscopy. **2.** The use of radiation for the scientific examination of material structures; radioscopy. **—ra'di·o·log'i·cal** (-ə-lŏj'ĭ-kəl) *adj.* **—ra'di·o·log'i·cal·ly** *adv.* **—ra'di·ol'o·gist** *n.*
ra·di·ol·y·sis (rā'dē-ŏl'ĭ-sĭs) *n.* Chemical dissociation of molecules as a result of radiation. **—ra'di·o·lyt'ic** (-ə-lĭt'ĭk) *adj.*
ra·di·o·man (rā'dē-ō-măn') *n.* A radio technician or operator.
ra·di·om·e·ter (rā'dē-ŏm'ĭ-tər) *n.* A device that detects and measures radiation, consisting of a partially evacuated glass bulb containing lightweight vertical vanes, each blackened on one side, suspended radially about a central vertical axis to permit their revolution about the axis as a measure of incident radiation. **—ra'di·o·met'ric** (-ō-mĕt'rĭk) *adj.* **—ra'di·om'e·try** *n.*
ra·di·o·nu·clide (rā'dē-ō-nōō'klīd', -nyōō'-) *n.* A radioactive nuclide.
ra·di·o·paque (rā'dē-ō-pāk') *adj.* Not allowing the penetration of radiation, as x rays.
ra·di·o·phone (rā'dē-ō-fōn') *n.* A radiotelephone. **—ra'di·o·phon'ic** (-fŏn'ĭk) *adj.*
ra·di·o·pho·to·graph (rā'dē-ō-fō'tə-grăf') also **ra·di·o·pho·to** (rā'dē-ō-fō'tō) *n.* A photograph transmitted by radio waves, each image point being reproduced by a received electric impulse. **—ra'di·o·pho·tog'ra·phy** (rā'dē-ō-fə-tŏg'rə-fē) *n.*
ra·di·os·co·py (rā'dē-ŏs'kə-pē) *n.* The examination of the inner structure of optically opaque objects by x-rays or other penetrating radiation; radiology. **—ra'di·o·scop'ic** (-ō-skŏp'ĭk), **ra'di·o·scop'i·cal** *adj.*
ra·di·o·sen·si·tive (rā'dē-ō-sĕn'sĭ-tĭv) *adj.* Sensitive to radiation. Used esp. of living structures.
ra·di·o·sonde (rā'dē-ō-sŏnd') *n.* An instrument carried aloft, chiefly by balloon, to gather and transmit meteorological data. [RADIO- + Fr. *sonde,* sounding line < OFr., prob. of Germanic orig.]
radio spectrum *n.* The entire range of electromagnetic communications frequencies, including those used for radio, radar, and television; radio-frequency spectrum.
ra·di·o·tel·e·graph (rā'dē-ō-tĕl'ĭ-grăf') *n.* The sending of messages by radiotelegraphy. **—ra'di·o·tel'e·graph'ic** *adj.*
ra·di·o·te·leg·ra·phy (rā'dē-ō-tə-lĕg'rə-fē) *n.* Wireless telegraphy in which messages are sent by radio.
ra·di·o·tel·e·phone (rā'dē-ō-tĕl'ə-fōn') *n.* A telephone in which audible communication is established by radio. **—ra'di·o·tel'e·phon'ic** (-ə-fŏn'ĭk) *adj.* **—ra'di·o·te·leph'o·ny** (-tə-lĕf'ə-nē) *n.*
radio telescope *n.* A sensitive, directional radio-antenna system used to detect and analyze radio waves of extraterrestrial origin.
ra·di·o·ther·a·py (rā'dē-ō-thĕr'ə-pē) *n.* The treatment of disease with radiation, esp. by selective irradiation with x rays or other ionizing radiation and by ingestion of radioisotopes.
ra·di·o·tho·ri·um (rā'dē-ō-thôr'ē-əm, -thōr'-) *n.* A radioactive isotope of thorium with mass number 228.
ra·di·o·trac·er (rā'dē-ō-trā'sər) *n.* A radioactive tracer.
radio wave *n.* A radio-frequency electromagnetic wave.
rad·ish (răd'ĭsh) *n.* **1.** Any of various plants of the genus *Raphanus,* esp. *R. sativus,* having a thickened, edible root. **2.** The pungent root of the radish, eaten raw as an appetizer and in salads. [ME *radiche* < OE *rædic* < Lat. *radix,* root.]
ra·di·um (rā'dē-əm) *n. Symbol* **Ra** A rare brilliant-white, luminescent, highly radioactive metallic element having 13 isotopes with mass numbers between 213 and 230, of which radium 226 with a half-life of 1,622 years is the most common. It is used in cancer radiotherapy, as a neutron source for some research purposes, and as a constituent of luminescent paints. Atomic number 88; melting point 700°C; boiling point 1,737°C; valence 2. [< Lat. *radius,* ray.]
radium therapy *n.* The use of radium in radiotherapy, esp. in treating cancer.
ra·di·us (rā'dē-əs) *n., pl.* **-di·i** (-dē-ī') or **-di·us·es. 1. a.** A line segment that joins the center of a circle with any point on its circumference. **b.** A line segment that joins the center of a sphere with any point on its surface. **c.** A line segment that joins the center of a regular polygon to any of its vertices. **d.** The length of any such line segment. **2.** A measure of circular area or extent: *every family within a radius of 25 miles.* **3.** A measure of range of activity or influence. **4.** A radial part or structure, as a mechanically pivoted arm or the spoke of a wheel. **5.** *Anat.* **a.** A long, prismatic, slightly curved bone, the shorter and thicker of the two forearm bones, located on the lateral side of the ulna. **b.** A similar bone in many vertebrates. [Lat., ray.]
radius vector *n.* **1.** *Math.* **a.** A line segment that joins a variable point to the origin of polar or spherical coordinates. **b.** The length of such a line segment. **2.** *Astron.* A line segment that joins the center of a satellite to the focus of its orbit.
ra·dix (rā'dĭks) *n., pl.* **rad·i·ces** (răd'ə-sēz', rā'də-) or **ra·dix·es. 1.** *Biol.* A root or point of origin. **2.** *Math.* The base of a system of numbers, as are 2 of the binary system and 10 of the decimal system. [Lat.]
ra·dome (rā'dōm) *n.* A domelike protective housing for a radar antenna used esp. in certain aircraft. [RA(DAR) + DOME.]
ra·don (rā'dŏn) *n. Symbol* **Rn** A colorless, radioactive, inert gaseous element formed by disintegration of radium. It is used as a radiation source in radiotherapy and to produce neutrons for research. Atomic number 86; atomic weight 222; melting point –71°C; boiling point –61.8°C; specific gravity (solid) 4; valence 0; half-life 3.823 days. [RAD(IUM) + -ON[2].]
rad·u·la (răj'ōō-lə) *n., pl.* **-lae** (-lē'). *Zool.* In mollusks, a flexible, tonguelike organ with rows of horny teeth on the surface. [NLat. < Lat., scraper < *radere,* to scrape.] **—rad'u·lar** *adj.*
raf·fi·a also **raph·i·a** (răf'ē-ə) *n.* **1.** An African palm tree, *Raphia ruffia,* having large leaves that yield a useful fiber. **2.** The fiber of the leaves of the raffia, used for mats, baskets, and other products. [Malagasy *rafia.*]
raf·fi·nose (răf'ə-nōs') *n.* A white crystalline sugar,

$C_{18}H_{32}O_{16}\cdot 5H_2O$, obtained from cottonseed meal and sugar beets. [Fr. < *raffiner,* to refine : *re-,* again + *affiner,* to refine (*a-,* to + *fin,* fine).]

raff·ish (răf′ĭsh) *adj.* **1.** Vulgar; showy. **2.** Rakish. [Prob. < dial. *raff,* rubbish < ME *raf.*] **—raff′ish·ly** *adv.* **—raff′ish·ness** *n.*

raf·fle[1] (răf′əl) *n.* A lottery in which a number of persons buy chances on a prize. *—v.* **-fled, -fling, -fles.** *—tr.* To offer as a prize in a raffle: *raffle off a new car.* *—intr.* To conduct or take part in a raffle. [ME *rafle,* a game using dice < OFr. *raffle,* act of seizing.] **—raf′fler** *n.*

raf·fle[2] (răf′əl) *n.* Rubbish; debris. [Prob. < Fr. *rafle,* act of seizing < OFr.]

raf·fle·sia (ră-flē′zhə) *n.* Any of various parasitic leafless plants of the genus *Rafflesia,* of tropical Asia, having very large, often malodorous flowers. [NLat., genus name, after Sir Stamford *Raffles* (1781–1826).]

raft[1] (răft) *n.* **1.** A flat structure, typically made of planks, logs, or barrels, that floats on water and is used for transport or as a platform for swimmers. **2.** A life raft. *—v.* **raft·ed, raft·ing, rafts.** *—tr.* **1.** To convey on a raft. **2.** To make into a raft. *—intr.* To travel by raft. [ME < ON *raptr,* beam.]

raft[2] (răft) *n. Informal.* A great number, amount, or collection. [Alteration of dial. *raff,* rubbish < ME *raf.*]

raft·er (răf′tər) *n.* One of the sloping beams that supports a pitched roof. [ME < OE *ræfter.*]

rag[1] (răg) *n.* **1.** A scrap of cloth. **2.** Cloth converted to pulp for papermaking: *the rag content of bond paper.* **3.** A scrap; fragment. **4.** *Slang.* **a.** A newspaper. **b.** A magazine or newspaper specializing in sensationalism or gossip. **5. rags.** Threadbare or tattered clothing. **6.** The stringy central portion and membranous walls of citrus fruits. [ME *ragge* < OE *ragg < ON *rögg.*]

rag[2] (răg) *tr.v.* **ragged, rag·ging, rags. 1.** *Slang.* To tease; taunt. **2.** To scold. **3.** *Chiefly Brit.* To play a joke on. *—n. Chiefly Brit.* A practical joke; prank. [Orig. unknown.]

rag[3] (răg) *n.* **1.** A roofing slate with one rough surface. **2.** *Chiefly Brit.* A coarsely textured rock. [Orig. unknown.]

rag[4] (răg) *tr.v.* **ragged, rag·ging, rags.** To compose or play (a piece of music) in ragtime. *—n.* A piece of music written in ragtime. [Short for RAGTIME.]

ra·ga (rä′gə) *n.* A traditional form in Hindu music, consisting of a theme that expresses some aspect of religious feeling and sets forth a tonal system on which variations are improvised within a prescribed framework of typical progressions, melodic formulas, and rhythmic patterns. [Skt. *rāgaḥ,* color, musical mode.]

rag·a·muf·fin (răg′ə-mŭf′ĭn) *n.* A dirty or unkempt child. [After *Ragamoffyn,* demon in *Piers Plowman,* a 14th-cent. allegorical poem.]

rag·bag (răg′băg′) *n.* **1.** A bag for storing rags. **2.** A motley collection; mixture.

rage (rāj) *n.* **1. a.** Violent anger. **b.** A fit of anger. **2.** Furious intensity, as of a storm or disease. **3.** Burning desire or passion. **4.** A fad; craze. *—intr.v.* **raged, rag·ing, rag·es. 1.** To speak or act furiously. **2.** To move with great violence or intensity: *The storm raged through several states.* **3.** To spread or prevail unchecked: *The plague raged throughout Europe.* [ME < OFr. < LLat. *rabia* < Lat. *rabies* < *rabere,* to be mad.]

rag·ged (răg′ĭd) *adj.* **1.** Tattered, frayed, or torn. **2.** Dressed in tattered or threadbare clothes. **3.** Unkempt or shaggy. **4.** Having a rough surface or edges. **5.** Imperfect; sloppy: *a ragged performance.* **6.** Harsh; rasping: *a ragged cry.* [ME < *ragge,* rag.] **—rag′ged·ly** *adv.* **—rag′ged·ness** *n.*

ragged robin *n.* A plant, *Lychnis flos-cuculi,* native to Eurasia, having reddish or white flowers with deeply lobed petals.

ra·gi (răg′ē) *n.* A grass, *Eleusine coracana,* of Africa and Asia, cultivated for its edible grain. [Hindi *rāgī* < Skt.]

rag·lan (răg′lən) *n.* A loose garment with slanted shoulder seams and with the sleeves extending in one piece to the neckline. ***—modifier:*** *a raglan sleeve.* [After Fitzroy James Henry Somerset (1788–1855), 1st Baron *Raglan.*]

rag·man (răg′măn′) *n.* A seller of rags.

ra·gout (ră-go͞o′) *n.* A meat and vegetable stew. [Fr. *ragoût* < *ragoûter,* to revive the taste : *re-,* again (< Lat.) + *à,* to (< Lat. *ad*) + *goût,* taste (< Lat. *gustus*).]

rag picker *n.* A ragman.

rag·tag (răg′tăg′) *adj.* **1.** Shaggy or unkempt; ragged. **2.** Falling apart; ramshackle.

ragtag and bobtail *n.* Rabble; riffraff.

rag·time (răg′tīm′) *n. Mus.* A style of jazz characterized by elaborately syncopated rhythm in the melody and a steadily accented accompaniment. [Prob. < RAGGED TIME.]

rag·weed (răg′wēd′) *n.* **1.** A weed of the genus *Ambrosia,* esp. *A. artemisiifolia* or *A. trifida,* whose profuse pollen is one of the chief causes of hay fever. **2.** *Chiefly Brit.* The ragwort. [From the ragged shape of its leaves.]

rag·wort (răg′wûrt′, -wôrt′) *n.* Any of several plants of the genus *Senecio,* having yellow flowers, esp. *S. aureus,* the golden ragwort of eastern North America, and *S. jacobaea,* of Europe. [From the ragged shape of its leaves.]

rah (rä) *interj.* Hurrah. Used to express approval or pleasure. [Short for HURRAH.]

raid (rād) *n.* **1.** A surprise attack, as one made by a commando force. **2.** A sudden and forcible entry of a place by police. **3.** A daring, predatory operation mounted against a competition, esp. in business. **4.** An attempt by speculators to drive stock prices down by mutual selling. *—v.* **raid·ed, raid·ing, raids.** *—tr.* To make a raid on. *—intr.* To conduct or participate in a raid. [Sc., raid on horseback < ME *rade* < OE *rād,* ride, raid.] **—raid′er** *n.*

rail[1] (rāl) *n.* **1.** A horizontal bar supported by vertical posts, as in a fence. **2.** A railing or balustrade. **3.** A steel bar used, usually in pairs, as a track for railroad cars and similar vehicles. **4.** The railroad as a means of transportation: *goods transported by rail.* **5. rails.** The stocks and bonds issued by railroads: *Rails are up two points today.* **6.** A horizontal piece of wood in a door or in paneling. *—tr.v.* **railed, rail·ing, rails.** To supply or enclose with a rail or rails. [ME *raile* < OFr. *reille* < Lat. *regula,* rod, ruler < *regere,* to rule.]

rail[2] (rāl) *n.* Any of various marsh birds of the family Rallidae, characteristically having brownish plumage and short wings adapted for only short flights. [ME *raile* < OFr. *raale.*]

rail[3] (rāl) *intr.v.* **railed, rail·ing, rails.** To condemn or attack in bitter, harsh, or abusive language: *railed against the proposed budget cuts.* [ME *railen* < OFr. *railler* < VLat. **ragulare* < LLat. *ragere,* to bray.] **—rail′er** *n.*

rail fence *n.* A fence of split logs secured to posts.

rail·head (rāl′hĕd′) *n.* **1.** The farthest point on a railroad to which rails have been laid. **2.** The section of a railroad where military supplies are unloaded.

rail·ing (rā′lĭng) *n.* **1. a.** A banister, balustrade, or fence made of rails. **b.** The upper, longitudinal part of a balustrade. **2.** Rails collectively. **3.** Material for making rails.

rail·ler·y (rā′lə-rē) *n., pl.* **-ies.** Good-natured teasing or ridicule; banter. [Fr. *raillerie* < OFr. *railler,* to rail.]

rail·road (rāl′rōd′) *n.* **1.** A road composed of parallel steel rails supported by ties and providing a track for locomotive-drawn trains and other rolling stock. **2.** The entire system of railroad track, together with the land, stations, rolling stock, and other property used in rail transportation. *—v.* **-road·ed, -road·ing, -roads.** *—tr.* **1.** To transport by railroad. **2.** To supply (an area) with railroads. **3.** *Informal.* **a.** To rush or push through quickly in order to prevent careful consideration: *railroad a law through Congress.* **b.** To cause (someone) to be imprisoned or condemned without a fair trial or on trumped-up charges. *—intr.* To work for a railroad company.

railroad flat *n.* An apartment in which the rooms are connected in a line, with windows at the front and rear.

rail·road·ing (rāl′rō′dĭng) *n.* The operation or construction of railroads.

rail-split·ter (rāl′splĭt′ər) *n.* One that splits logs for fences.

rail·way (rāl′wā′) *n.* **1.** A railroad, esp. one operated over a limited area, as a street railway. **2.** A track providing a runway for wheeled equipment.

rai·ment (rā′mənt) *n.* Clothing; garments. [ME *rayment,* short for *arrayment* < OFr. *araiement,* array < *arrayer,* to array.]

rain (rān) *n.* **1. a.** Water condensed from atmospheric vapor, falling to earth in drops. **b.** A fall of such water; rainstorm. **c.** The descent of such water. **d.** Rainy weather. **2.** A rapid or heavy fall of something: *hit by a rain of criticisms.* **3. rains.** The rainy season or seasonal rainfalls, as in certain tropical areas. *—v.* **rained, rain·ing, rains.** *—intr.* **1.** To fall in drops of water from the clouds. **2.** To fall like rain: *Praise rained down on him.* **3.** To release rain. *—tr.* **1.** To send or pour down. **2.** To offer or give abundantly. ***—phrasal verb.*** **rain out.** To force the postponement of (an outdoor event) because of rain. [ME < OE *rēn.*]

rain·bow (rān′bō′) *n.* **1. a.** An arc of spectral colors appearing in the sky opposite the sun as a result of the refractive dispersion of sunlight in drops of rain or mist. **b.** A similar arc, as in a waterfall mist or graded display of colors. **2.** An illusory hope. [ME < OE *rēnboga* : *rēn,* rain + *boga,* bow.]

rainbow cactus *n.* A tall, spiny, cylindrical cactus, *Echinocereus rigidissimus,* of the southwestern United States and Mexico, having showy pink flowers.

rainbow trout *n.* A North American food fish, *Salmo gairdneri,* having a reddish longitudinal band and black spots.

rain check *n.* **1.** A ticket stub for an outdoor event entitling the holder to admission at a future date if the original event is canceled because of rain. **2.** A postponement of the acceptance of an offer, esp. an assurance to a customer that a sale item sold out or out of stock can be purchased later at the sale price.

rain·coat (rān′kōt′) *n.* A waterproof or water-resistant coat.

rain date *n.* A second date scheduled for an outdoor event in case rain forces cancellation of the first date.

rain·drop (rān′drŏp′) *n.* A drop of rain.

rain·fall (rān′fôl′) *n.* **1.** A shower or fall of rain. **2.** The quantity of water, expressed in inches, precipitated as rain, snow, hail, or sleet in a specified area and time interval.

rain forest *n.* A dense evergreen forest occupying a tropical region with an annual rainfall of at least 100 inches.

rain gauge also **rain gage** *n.* A device for measuring rainfall.

rain·mak·er (rān′mā′kər) *n.* A person supposedly capable of producing rain.

raft[1]

ragged robin

ragweed

George Miksch Sutton

rail[2]

rain·mak·ing (rān′mā′kĭng) *n.* **1.** The ceremony and rituals observed by a rainmaker. **2.** *Informal.* Cloud seeding.
rain·spout (rān′spout′) *n.* A spout draining a roof gutter.
rain·squall (rān′skwôl′) *n.* A squall accompanied by rain.
rain·storm (rān′stôrm) *n.* A storm accompanied by rain.
rain-wash (rān′wŏsh′) *Geol.* —*n.* **1.** Rock debris transported downhill by rain. **2.** Decomposed rock and similar matter washed down into the soil by rain. —*tr.v.* **-washed, -wash·ing, -wash·es.** To wash (material) down a slope by rain.
rain·wat·er (rān′wô′tər, -wŏt′ər) *n.* Water precipitated as rain with little dissolved mineral matter.
rain·wear (rān′wâr′) *n.* Waterproof clothing.
rain·y (rā′nē) *adj.* **-i·er, -i·est.** Characterized by, full of, or bringing rain. —**rain′i·ness** *n.*
rainy day *n.* A time of need or trouble.
raise (rāz) *v.* **raised, rais·ing, rais·es.** —*tr.* **1.** To move or cause to move upward or to a higher position; lift. **2.** To place or set upright; make erect. **3.** To erect or build. **4. a.** To cause to arise, appear, or exist: *The slap raised a welt.* **b.** To awaken from or as if from death. **5.** To increase in size, quantity, or worth. **6.** To increase in intensity, degree, strength, or pitch: *raised his voice.* **7.** To improve in rank or dignity; promote. **8. a.** To grow or breed: *raise German shepherds.* **b.** To bring up; rear: *raise children.* **9.** To put forward for consideration: *raised an important question.* **10.** *Law.* To begin or set (a lawsuit) in operation. **11.** To express or utter (a shout, for example). **12. a.** To bring about; provoke: *raise a laugh.* **b.** To arouse or stir up: *raise a revolt.* **13.** To gather together; collect: *raise money.* **14.** To cause (dough) to puff up. **15.** To end (a siege) by withdrawing troops or forcing the enemy troops to withdraw. **16.** To remove or withdraw (an order). **17. a.** To increase (a poker bet). **b.** To bet more than (a preceding bettor in poker). **c.** To increase the bid of (one's bridge partner). **18.** *Naut.* To bring into sight by approaching nearer. **19.** To alter and increase illegally the written value of (a check, for example). **20.** To cough up (phlegm). **21.** *Scot.* To make angry; enrage. **22.** To make contact with by radio: *couldn't raise him on our* CB. —*intr.* To increase the stakes in poker or gambling. —*n.* **1.** An act of raising or increasing. **2.** An increase in salary. —***idioms.*** **raise cain** (or **hell**). **1.** To behave in a rowdy or unruly fashion. **2.** To reprimand someone severely and loudly. **raise eyebrows.** To cause surprise or amazement. [ME *raisen* < ON *reisa.*]
Usage: *Raise* is properly used as a transitive verb: *He raised the window.* For intransitive uses, *rise* is standard: *The curtain rises.* However, *raise* is sometimes used as an intransitive verb: *The window raises easily* (acceptable to almost half the Usage Panel). • *Raise* (noun), rather than *rise,* is now standard in the United States for an increase in salary, though one still speaks of a *rise in prices.*
raised (rāzd) *adj.* **1.** Represented in relief, as a surface design; embossed. **2.** Made light and high by yeast or other leaven.
rai·sin (rā′zən) *n.* A sweet grape of several varieties, dried either in the sun or artificially. [ME < OFr., grape < Lat. *racemus,* bunch of grapes.]
rai·son d'ê·tre (rĕ-zôɴ′ dĕ′tr) *n.* Reason or justification for existing. [Fr.]
raj (räj) *n.* Dominion; sovereignty. [Hindi *rāj* < Skt. *rājan,* king < *rājati,* he rules.]
ra·ja (rä′jə) *n.* Variant of **rajah.**
Raj·ab (rŭj′əb) *n.* The seventh month of the Moslem calendar. See table at **calendar.** [Ar.]
ra·jah or **ra·ja** (rä′jə) *n.* A prince, chief, or ruler in India or the East Indies. [Hindi *rājā* < Skt. *rājan,* king < *rājati,* he rules.]
Raj·put also **Raj·poot** (räj′po͝ot) *n.* One of a Hindu people claiming descent from the warlike and powerful rulers of northern India from the 8th to the 13th century.

rake[1]

rake[1] (rāk) *n.* **1.** A long-handled implement with a row of projecting teeth at its head, used esp. to gather leaves or to loosen or smooth earth. **2.** An implement that resembles a rake. —*v.* **raked, rak·ing, rakes.** —*tr.* **1.** To gather or move with or as if with a rake. **2.** To smooth, scrape, or loosen with a rake or similar implement. **3.** To gain in abundance: *suddenly began raking in the money.* **4.** To search or examine thoroughly. **5.** To scrape; scratch. **6.** To aim heavy gunfire along the length of. —*intr.* **1.** To use a rake. **2.** To conduct a search: *raked through his drawer for clean socks.* **3.** To make one's way rapidly or roughly: *raked through the crowd.* —***phrasal verb.*** **rake up.** To revive or bring to light; uncover: *rake up old gossip.* [ME < OE *raca.*] —**rak′er** *n.*
rake[2] (rāk) *n.* A libertine; roué. [Short for RAKEHELL.]
rake[3] (rāk) *v.* **raked, rak·ing, rakes.** —*intr.* To slant or incline from the vertical, as a ship's mast. —*tr.* To cause to lean or slant. —*n.* **1.** Inclination from the vertical or from the horizontal. **2.** The angle between the cutting edge of a tool and a plane perpendicular to the working surface to which the tool is applied. [Orig. unknown.]
rak·ee (răk′ē, rä′kē, rä′kə) *n.* Variant of **raki.**
rake·hell (rāk′hĕl′) *n.* A rake; roué. [Poss. by folk etymology < obs. *rackle,* headstrong.] —**rake′hell′y** *adj.*
rake-off (rāk′ôf′, -ŏf′) *n. Slang.* A percentage or share of the profits of an enterprise, esp. one given or accepted as a bribe. [From the rake used by a croupier in a gambling house.]
rak·i also **rak·ee** (răk′ē, rä′kē, rä′kə) *n.* A brandy of Turkey and the Balkan Peninsula, distilled from grapes or plums and flavored with anise. [Turk. *rāqī.*]
rak·ish[1] (rā′kĭsh) *adj.* **1.** *Naut.* Having a trim, streamlined appearance. **2.** Showy or jaunty in appearance. [Prob. < RAKE[3] (from the raking masts of pirate ships).] —**rak′ish·ly** *adv.* —**rak′ish·ness** *n.*
rak·ish[2] (rā′kĭsh) *adj.* Like a rake; dissolute. —**rak′ish·ly** *adv.* —**rak′ish·ness** *n.*
rale also **râle** (räl) *n.* An abnormal or pathological respiratory sound. [Fr. *râle* < *râler,* to make a rattling sound in the throat.]
ral·len·tan·do (răl′ən-tăn′dō, räl′lĕn-tän′dō) *Mus.* —*adj.* Gradually slackening in tempo; ritardando. Used as a direction. —*n., pl.* **-dos.** A passage or movement performed with a gradual reduction in tempo. [Ital., pr.part. of *rallentare,* to slow down : *re-,* (intensive < Lat.) + *allentare,* to slow down < LLat. (Lat. *ad-,* to + Lat. *lentus,* slow).] —**ral′len·tan′do** *adv.*
ral·li·form (răl′ə-fôrm′) *adj.* Pertaining to or resembling the rail, a marsh bird. [< Med. Lat. *rallus,* rail < OFr. *raale.*]
ral·ly[1] (răl′ē) *v.* **-lied, -ly·ing, -lies.** —*tr.* **1.** To call together for a common purpose; assemble. **2.** To reassemble and restore to order. **3.** To rouse or revive (one's strength, for example) from inactivity or decline. —*intr.* **1.** To meet for a common purpose. **2.** To join in an effort for a common cause. **3.** To recover abruptly from a setback or disadvantage: *the stock market rallied; rallied back to win by scoring four runs in the bottom of the ninth inning.* **4.** To show sudden improvement in health or spirits. **5.** *Sports.* To exchange several strokes in net games. —*n., pl.* **-lies. 1.** An assembly, esp. one intended to inspire enthusiasm for a cause: *a political rally.* **2. a.** A reassembling, as of dispersed troops. **b.** The signal ordering this. **3.** A sharp improvement in health, vigor, or spirits. **4.** A notable rise in stock market prices and active trading after a decline. **5.** An abrupt recovery from a setback or disadvantage. **6.** *Sports.* An exchange of several strokes in net games before one side scores a point. **7.** A competition in which automobiles are driven over public roads and under normal traffic regulations but with specified rules as to speed, time, and route. [Fr. *rallier* < OFr. *ralier* : *re-,* again + *alier,* to unite, ally. —see ALLY.] —**ral′li·er** *n.*
ral·ly[2] (răl′ē) *v.* **-lied, -ly·ing, -lies.** —*tr.* To tease good-humoredly; banter. —*intr.* To banter or jest. [Fr. *railler* < OFr., to rail. —see RAIL[3].] —**ral′li·er** *n.*
ralph (rălf) *intr.v.* **ralphed, ralph·ing, ralphs.** *Slang.* To vomit. [Imit.]
ram (răm) *n.* **1.** A male sheep. **2. Ram.** A constellation and sign of the zodiac, Aries. **3.** Any of several devices used to drive, batter, or crush by forceful impact, esp.: **a.** A battering-ram. **b.** The weight that drops in a pile driver or steam hammer. **c.** The plunger or piston of a force pump or hydraulic press. **4. a.** A projection on the prow of a warship, used to batter or cut into an enemy vessel. **b.** A ship having such a projection. **5.** A hydraulic ram. —*tr.v.* **rammed, ram·ming, rams. 1.** To strike or drive against with a heavy impact; butt. **2.** To force or press into place. **3.** To cram; stuff. **4.** To force passage or acceptance of: *rammed the project through to completion.* [ME < OE *ramm.*] —**ram′mer** *n.*
Ra·ma (rä′mə) *n. Hinduism.* A deified hero worshiped as an incarnation of Vishnu. [Skt. *Ramaḥ* < *rāma-,* dark, beautiful.]
Ram·a·dan (răm′ə-dän′) *n.* **1.** The ninth month of the Moslem year, spent in fasting from sunrise to sunset. See table at **calendar. 2.** The fast engaged in during Ramadan. [Ar. *Ramaḍān* < *ramaḍ,* dryness.]
Ra·man effect (rä′mən) *n. Physics.* The alteration in frequency and random alteration in phase of light scattered in a material medium. [After Sir Chandrasekhara Venkata *Raman* (1888–1970), its discoverer.]
ra·mate (rā′māt′) *adj.* Having branches; branched. [< Lat. *ramus,* branch.]
ram·ble (răm′bəl) *intr.v.* **-bled, -bling, -bles. 1.** To walk or wander aimlessly. **2.** To follow an irregularly winding course of motion or growth. **3.** To speak or write at length and with many digressions. —*n.* A leisurely stroll. [Prob. < ME *romblen* < *romen,* to roam.]
ram·bler (răm′blər) *n.* **1.** One that rambles. **2.** A type of climbing rose having numerous red, pink, or white flowers.
ram·bling (răm′blĭng) *adj.* **1.** Roaming; wandering. **2.** Extended over an irregular area; sprawling: *a large rambling country estate.* **3.** Lengthy and aimless: *a rambling speech.* —**ram′bling·ly** *adv.*
Ram·bouil·let (răm′bo͞o-lā, räm′bo͞o-yā′) *n.* Any of a breed of merino sheep of French origin, raised for wool and meat. [After *Rambouillet,* town in northern France.]
ram·bunc·tious (răm-bŭngk′shəs) *adj.* Boisterous; disorderly. [Prob. alteration of E. *rumbustious,* alteration of *robustious* < Lat. *robustus,* strong < *robur,* oak, strength.]
ram·bu·tan (răm-bo͞ot′ən) *n.* **1.** A tree, *Nephelium lappaceum,* of southeastern Asia, bearing edible, oval red fruit with soft spines. **2.** The fruit of the rambutan. [Malay < *rambut,* hair.]
ram·e·kin also **ram·e·quin** (răm′ĭ-kĭn) *n.* **1.** A cheese prepa-

ration made with eggs and bread crumbs or unsweetened puff pastry, baked and served in individual dishes. **2.** A small individual dish used for both baking and serving. [Fr. *ramequin* < LG *ramken,* dim. of *ram,* cream < MLG *rōme.*]

ra·mi (rā′mī′) *n.* Plural of **ramus.**

ram·ie (răm′ē) *n.* **1.** A woody Asian plant, *Boehmeria nivea,* having broad leaves. **2.** The flaxlike fiber from the stem of the ramie, used in making fabrics and cordage. [Malay *rami.*]

ram·i·fi·ca·tion (răm′ə-fĭ-kā′shən) *n.* **1.** The act or process of branching out or dividing into branches. **2.** A branch or other subordinate part extending from a main body. **3.** An arrangement of branches or branching parts. **4.** A development or consequence growing out of and often complicating a problem, plan, or statement: *the ramifications of court decisions.*

ram·i·form (răm′ə-fôrm′) *adj.* Branchlike or branching. [Lat. *ramus,* branch + -FORM.]

ram·i·fy (răm′ə-fī′) *v.* **-fied, -fy·ing, -fies.** —*tr.* To divide into or cause to extend in branches or branchlike parts. —*intr.* To branch out. [OFr. *ramifier* : Lat. *ramus,* branch + Lat. *facere,* to make.]

ram·jet (răm′jĕt′) *n.* A jet engine that propels aircraft by igniting fuel with air taken and compressed by the engine in a fashion that produces greater exhaust than intake velocity.

ra·mose (rā′mōs′, rə-mōs′) *adj.* Having many branches. [Lat. *ramosus* < *ramus,* branch.]

ra·mous (rā′məs) *adj.* **1.** Of or resembling branches. **2.** Branching; ramose. [Lat. *ramosus,* ramose.]

ramp¹ (rămp) *n.* **1.** An inclined passage or roadway connecting different levels, as of a building or road. **2.** *Archit.* A concave bend of a handrail where a sharp change in level or direction occurs, as at a stair landing. **3.** A mobile staircase for entering and leaving an airplane. [Fr. *rampe* < *ramper,* to slope < OFr., to ramp.]

ramp² (rămp) *intr.v.* **ramped, ramp·ing, ramps. 1.** To stand in the rampant position. **2.** To assume a threatening stance. **3.** To act threateningly or violently; rage. —*n.* The act of ramping. [ME *rampen* < OFr. *ramper,* to rear up, of Germanic orig.]

ram·page (răm′pāj′) *n.* A course of violent, frenzied action or behavior. —*intr.v.* (răm-pāj′). **-paged, -pag·ing, -pag·es.** To move about wildly or violently. [Sc., poss. < RAMP².] **—ram·pag′er** *n.*

ram·pa·geous (răm-pā′jəs) *adj.* Raging; frenzied. **—ram·pa′geous·ly** *adv.* **—ram·pa′geous·ness** *n.*

ram·pant (răm′pənt) *adj.* **1.** Extending unchecked; unrestrained: *a rampant growth of vegetation.* **2.** Characterized by uncontrolled violence, extravagance, or lack of restraint: *rampant political corruption.* **3. a.** Rearing or ramping on the hind legs. **b.** *Heraldry.* Rearing on the left hind leg with the forelegs elevated, the right above the left, and usually with the head in profile. **4.** *Archit.* Springing from a support or abutment higher at one side than at the other: *a rampant arch.* [ME *rampaunt* < OFr. *rampant,* pr.part. of *ramper,* to ramp.] **—ram′pan·cy** *n.* **—ram′pant·ly** *adv.*

ram·part (răm′pärt′, -pərt) *n.* **1.** A fortification consisting of an elevation or embankment, often provided with a parapet. **2.** Something that serves to protect or defend. —*tr.v.* **-part·ed, -part·ing, -parts.** To defend with a rampart. [OFr. < *ramparer,* to fortify : *re-* (intensive < Lat.) + *emparer,* to take possession of < OProv. *amparar* (Lat. *ante-,* before + Lat. *parare,* to prepare).]

ram·pike (răm′pīk′) *n.* A standing dead tree or tree stump, esp. one killed by fire. [Orig. unknown.]

ram·pi·on (răm′pē-ən) *n.* **1.** A Eurasian plant, *Campanula rapunculus,* having clusters of bluish flowers and an edible root used in salads. **2.** Any of various plants of the genus *Phyteuma* similar to the rampion. [Prob. < OFr. *raiponce* < OItal. *raponzo,* prob. < *rapa,* turnip < Lat. *rapum.*]

ram·rod (răm′rŏd′) *n.* **1.** A metal rod used to force the charge into a muzzle-loading firearm. **2.** A rod used to clean the barrel of a firearm.

ram·shack·le (răm′shăk′əl) *adj.* Likely to fall apart because of shoddy construction or upkeep; rickety. [Back-formation < E. *ramshackled,* ramshackle < *ransackled,* p.part. of obs. *ransackle,* to ransack, freq. of ME *ransaken,* to ransack. —see RANSACK.]

ram's horn *n. Judaism.* A shofar.

ram·son (răm′zən, -sən) *n.* Often **ramsons.** A broad-leaved Eurasian garlic, *Allium ursinum,* having a bulbous root used in salads and relishes. [ME *ramsyn* < OE *hramsan,* ramsons, pl. of *hransa.*]

ram·til (răm′tĭl) *n.* An African plant, *Guizotia abyssinica,* grown for its oil-rich seeds. [Hindi *rāmtil* : Skt. *rāma-,* dark + Skt. *tilaḥ,* sesame.]

ram·u·lose (răm′yə-lōs′) *adj.* Having numerous small branches. [Lat. *ramulosus* < *ramulus,* dim. of *ramus,* branch.]

ra·mus (rā′məs) *n., pl.* **-mi** (-mī′). *Biol.* A branchlike part of a structure. [NLat. < Lat., ramus.]

ran (răn) *v.* Past tense of **run.**

Ran (răn) *n.* The Norse goddess of the sea and of drowning persons. [ON *Rān.*]

ranch (rănch) *n.* **1.** An extensive farm, esp. in the American West, on which large herds of cattle, sheep, or horses are raised. **2.** A large farm on which a particular crop or kind of animal is raised. —*intr.v.* **ranched, ranch·ing, ranch·es.** To work on or manage a ranch. [Mex. Sp. *rancho,* small ranch < Sp., hut < OSp. *rancher,* to be billeted < OFr. *ranger,* to put in place < *renc,* place, line.]

ranch·er (răn′chər) *n.* **1.** One who owns or manages a ranch. **2.** A ranch house (sense 2).

ran·che·ri·a (răn′chə-rē′ə) *n. Southwestern U.S.* **1. a.** A Mexican herdsman's hut. **b.** A village of such huts. **2.** An Indian village. [Mex. Sp. < *ranchero,* ranchero.]

ran·che·ro (răn-châr′ō) *n., pl.* **-ros.** *Southwestern U.S.* A rancher. [Mex. Sp. < *rancho,* small ranch. —see RANCH.]

ranch house *n.* **1.** The building on a ranch occupied by its operator. **2.** A rectangular, one-story house with a low-pitched roof.

ranch·man (rănch′mən) *n.* A rancher.

ranch mink *n.* A mink bred in captivity from Alaskan and Labrador strains for special pelt colors and qualities.

ran·cho (răn′chō) *n., pl.* **-chos.** *Southwestern U.S.* **1.** A hut or group of huts in which ranch workers live. **2.** A ranch. [Mex. Sp., small ranch. —see RANCH.]

ran·cid (răn′sĭd) *adj.* **1.** Having the disagreeable odor or taste of decomposed oils or fats; rank. **2.** Offensive: *rancid remarks.* [Lat. *rancidus* < *rancēre,* to stink.] **—ran·cid′i·ty, ran′cid·ness** *n.*

ran·cor (răng′kər) *n.* Bitter, long-lasting resentment; ill will. [ME *rancour* < OFr. < Lat. *rancor,* rancid smell < *rancēre,* to stink.] **—ran′cor·ous** *adj.* **—ran′cor·ous·ly** *adv.* **—ran′cor·ous·ness** *n.*

ran·cour (răng′kər) *n. Chiefly Brit.* Variant of **rancor.**

rand (rănd, ränd) *n.* See table at **currency.** [Afr. < Du., edge.]

ran·dan (răn′dăn′) *n.* **1.** A boat designed to be rowed by three persons. **2.** The method of rowing a randan, in which the persons fore and aft use one oar each, and the person amidships uses two. [Orig. unknown.]

ran·dom (răn′dəm) *adj.* **1.** Having no specific pattern or objective; haphazard. **2.** *Statistics.* **a.** Of or designating a phenomenon that does not produce the same outcome or consequences every time it occurs under identical circumstances. **b.** Of or designating an event having a relative frequency of occurrence that approaches a stable limit as the number of observations of the event increases to infinity. **c.** Of or designating a sample drawn from a population so that each member of the population has an equal chance to be drawn. **d.** Of or pertaining to a member of such a sample: *a random number.* **—idiom. at random.** Without definite method or purpose; unsystematically. [ME *randoun* < OFr. *randon* < *randir,* to run, of Germanic orig.] **—ran′dom·ly** *adv.*

ran·dom-ac·cess (răn′dəm-ăk′sĕs′) *adj.* Allowing access to stored computer data without regard to data sequence.

ran·dom·ize (răn′də-mīz′) *tr.v.* **-ized, -iz·ing, -iz·es.** To make random, esp. for scientific experimentation. **—ran′dom·i·za′tion** *n.*

random variable *n. Statistics.* A variable having numerical values determined by the results of a chance experiment.

random walk *n. Math.* A series of sequential movements in which the direction and size of each move is randomly determined.

ran·dy (răn′dē) *adj.* **-di·er, -di·est. 1. a.** Lascivious; lecherous. **b.** Of or characterized by frank, uninhibited sexuality. **2.** *Chiefly Scot.* Ill-mannered. [Poss. < obs. *rand,* alteration of RANT.]

ra·nee (rä′nē) *n.* Variant of **rani.**

rang (răng) *v.* Past tense of **ring².**

range (rānj) *n.* **1. a.** The extent of perception, knowledge, experience, or ability. **b.** The area or sphere in which an activity takes place. **c.** The full extent covered by something: *within the range of possibilities.* **2. a.** An amount or extent of variation: *a wide price range.* **b.** *Mus.* The gamut of tones within the capacity of a voice or instrument. **3. a.** The maximum or effective distance that can be traversed, as by bullets, sound, or radio signal. **b.** The distance to a target. **4.** The maximum distance that a ship or other vehicle can travel before exhausting its fuel supply. **5.** A place for shooting at targets. **6.** *Aerospace.* A testing area in which rockets and missiles are fired and flown. **7.** An extensive area of open land on which livestock wander and graze. **8.** The geographical region in which a kind of plant or animal normally lives or grows. **9.** The act of wandering or roaming over a large area. **10.** *Math.* The totality of points in a set established by a mapping. **11.** *Statistics.* A measure of dispersion equal to the difference or interval between the smallest and largest of a set of quantities. **12.** A class, rank, or order. **13.** An extended group or series, esp. one of mountains. **14.** One of a series of double-faced bookcases in a library stack room. **15.** A single series or row of townships, each six miles square, extending parallel to and numbered east and west from a survey base meridian line. **16.** A stove with spaces for cooking a number of things at the same time. —*v.* **ranged, rang·ing, rang·es.** —*tr.* **1.** To arrange or dispose in a particular order, esp. in rows or lines. **2.** To assign to a particular category; classify. **3.** To align (a gun, for example) with a target. **4. a.** To determine the distance of (a target). **b.** To be capable of reaching (a maximum distance). **5.** To move or travel over or through (a region), as in exploration. **6.** To turn (livestock) on a range

rampant
A lion rampant

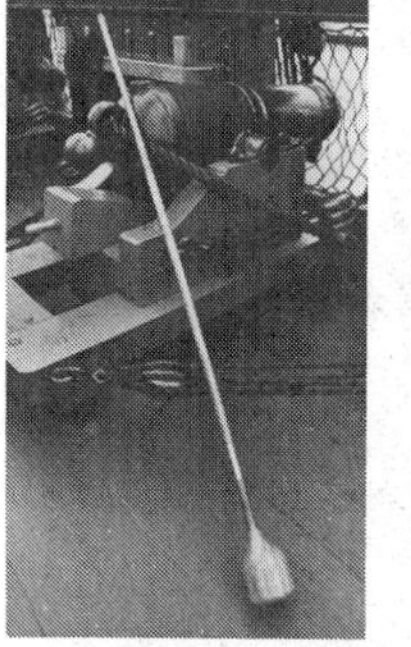
ramrod

to graze. **7.** *Naut.* To uncoil (an anchor cable) on deck so the anchor may descend easily. —*intr.* **1.** To vary within specified limits: *ages ranging from two to ten.* **2.** To extend in a particular direction: *a river ranging to the east.* **3.** To extend in the same direction. **4.** To move over or through a given area, as in exploration. **5.** To roam or wander. **6.** To live or grow within a particular region. [ME, series < OFr. *renge* < *rengier,* to put in a row < *renc,* line, of Germanic orig.]

range finder *n.* Any of various optical, electronic, or acoustical instruments used to determine the distance of an object.

range•land (rānj′lănd′, -lənd) *n.* An expanse of land suitable for range.

rang•er (rān′jər) *n.* **1.** A wanderer; rover. **2.** One of an armed troop employed in patrolling a specific region. **3. Ranger.** A member of a group of U.S. soldiers specially trained for making raids. **4. a.** A person employed to patrol and guard a forest. **b.** *Chiefly Brit.* The keeper of a royal forest or park. **5.** One of a cattle herd that grazes on a range.

rang•y (rān′jē) *adj.* **-i•er, -i•est. 1.** Inclined to rove. **2.** Having slender, long limbs. **3.** Providing ample range; roomy.

ra•ni also **ra•nee** (rä′nē) *n., pl.* **-nis. 1.** The wife of a rajah. **2.** A reigning Hindu princess or queen. [Hindi *rānī* < Skt. *rājñī,* fem. of *rājān,* rajah. —see RAJAH.]

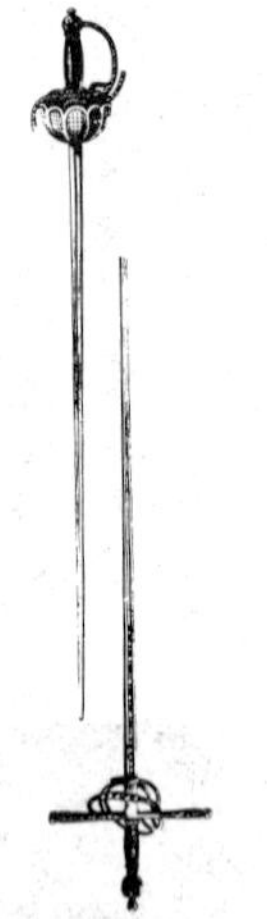
rapier

rank[1] (răngk) *n.* **1. a.** A relative position in society. **b.** An official position or grade: *the rank of sergeant.* **c.** A relative position or degree of value in a graded group. **d.** High or eminent station or position: *persons of rank.* **2.** A row, line, series, or range. **3. a.** A line of soldiers, vehicles, or other military equipment standing side by side in close order. **b. ranks.** The armed forces. **c. ranks.** Personnel, esp. enlisted military personnel. **4. ranks.** A body of people classed together; numbers: *joined the ranks of the unemployed.* **5.** Any of the horizontal lines of squares on a chessboard. —*v.* **ranked, rank•ing, ranks.** —*tr.* **1.** To place in a row or rows. **2.** To give a particular order or position to; classify. **3.** To outrank or take precedence over. —*intr.* **1.** To hold a particular rank: *rank first.* **2.** To form or stand in a row or rows. —***idiom.*** **pull rank.** *Slang.* To use one's superior rank to gain an advantage. [OFr. *renc,* of Germanic orig.]

rank[2] (răngk) *adj.* **-er, -est. 1.** Growing profusely or with excessive vigor: *rank weeds.* **2.** Yielding a profuse, often excessive, crop; highly fertile: *rank earth.* **3.** Strong and offensive in odor or flavor. **4.** Indecent; disgusting. **5.** Absolute; complete: *a rank amateur.* [ME < OE *ranc,* strong, full-grown.] —**rank′ly** *adv.* —**rank′ness** *n.*

rank and file *n.* **1.** The common soldiers of an army. **2.** Those who form the major portion of a group or organization, excluding the leaders and officers.

rank•er (răng′kər) *n. Chiefly Brit.* **1.** An enlisted soldier. **2.** A commissioned officer who has been promoted from enlisted status.

Ran•kine scale (răng′kĭn) *n.* The scale of absolute temperature using Fahrenheit degrees, in which the freezing point of water is 491.69° and the boiling point of water is 671.69°. [After William J.M. *Rankine* (1820–1872).]

rank•ing (răng′kĭng) *adj.* Of the highest rank; pre-eminent.

ran•kle (răng′kəl) *v.* **-kled, -kling, -kles.** —*intr.* **1.** To cause persistent irritation or resentment. **2.** To become sore or inflamed; fester. —*tr.* To embitter; irritate. [ME *ranclen* < OFr. *rancler,* alteration of *draoncler* < *draoncle,* festering sore < LLat. *dracunculus,* small serpent, dim. of Lat. *draco,* serpent.]

ran•sack (răn′săk′) *tr.v.* **-sacked, -sack•ing, -sacks. 1.** To search or examine thoroughly. **2.** To search carefully for plunder; pillage. [ME *ransaken* < ON *rannsaka* : *rann,* house + *-saka,* to search.] —**ran′sack′er** *n.*

ran•som (răn′səm) *n.* **1. a.** The release of a person or property in return for payment of a demanded price. **b.** The price or payment demanded or paid. **2.** *Theol.* A redemption from sin and its consequences. —*tr.v.* **-somed, -som•ing, -soms. 1. a.** To obtain the release of by paying a certain price. **b.** To release after receiving such a payment. **2.** *Theol.* To deliver from sin and its consequences. [ME *ransoun* < OFr. *rançon* < Lat. *redemptio,* a buying back < *redimere,* to redeem. —see REDEEM.] —**ran′som•er** *n.*

rant (rănt) *v.* **rant•ed, rant•ing, rants.** —*intr.* To speak or declaim in a violent, loud, or vehement manner; rave. —*tr.* To exclaim with violence or extravagance. —*n.* **1.** Violent, loud, or extravagant speech. **2.** *Chiefly Brit. Regional.* Wild or uproarious merriment. [Prob. < Du. *ranten.*] —**rant′er** *n.*

ran•u•la (răn′yə-lə) *n.* A cyst on the underside of the tongue caused by the obstruction of a duct of a salivary gland. [NLat. < Lat., swelling on the tongue, dim. of *rana,* frog.]

ra•nun•cu•lus (rə-nŭng′kyə-ləs) *n., pl.* **-lus•es** or **-li** (-lī′). A plant of the genus *Ranunculus,* including the buttercups. [NLat., *Ranunculus,* genus name < Lat., a kind of medicinal plant, dim. of *rana,* frog.]

rap[1] (răp) *v.* **rapped, rap•ping, raps.** —*tr.* **1.** To hit sharply and swiftly; strike: *rapped the table with his fist.* **2.** To utter sharply: *rap out a complaint.* **3.** To criticize or blame. —*intr.* To strike a quick, light blow: *rapped on the door.* —*n.* **1.** A quick, light blow or knock. **2.** A knocking or tapping sound. **3.** *Slang.* **a.** A reprimand or censure. **b.** A legal sentence to serve in prison. **4.** *Slang.* A negative quality or characteristic associated with a person or object. —***idioms.*** **beat the rap.** *Slang.* To escape punishment or be acquitted of a charge. **take the rap.** *Slang.* To accept punishment for a crime, esp. when innocent. [ME *rappen.*]

rap[2] (răp) *tr.v.* **rapt** or **rapped, rap•ping, raps. 1.** *past participle* **rapt.** To enchant or seize with rapture. **2.** To snatch. [Back-formation < RAPT.]

rap[3] (răp) *n. Informal.* The least bit: *I don't care a rap.* [< obs. *rap,* 18th-cent. Irish counterfeit halfpenny.]

rap[4] (răp) *Slang.* —*intr.v.* **rap•ped, rap•ping, raps.** To discuss freely and at length. —*n.* A talk, conversation, or discussion. [Poss. < RAPPORT.]

ra•pa•cious (rə-pā′shəs) *adj.* **1.** Taking by force; plundering. **2.** Greedy; ravenous. **3.** Subsisting on live prey. [< Lat. *rapax, rapac-* < *rapere,* to seize.] —**ra•pa′cious•ly** *adv.* —**ra•pa′cious•ness, ra•pac′i•ty** (rə-păs′ĭ-tē) *n.*

rape[1] (rāp) *n.* **1.** The crime of forcing another person to submit to sexual intercourse. **2.** The act of seizing and carrying off by force; abduction. **3.** Abusive or improper treatment; violation: *a rape of justice.* —*tr.v.* **raped, rap•ing, rapes. 1.** To force (another person) to submit to sexual intercourse. **2.** To seize and carry off by force. **3.** To plunder or pillage. [ME < *rapen,* to rape < OFr. *raper* < Lat. *rapere,* to seize.] —**rap′er, rap′ist** *n.*

rape[2] (rāp) *n.* A Eurasian plant, *Brassica napus,* cultivated as fodder and for its seed, which yields a useful oil. [ME < Lat. *rapa,* turnip.]

rape[3] (rāp) *n.* The refuse of grapes left after the extraction of the juice in wine-making. [Fr. *râpe,* grape stalk < OFr. < *rasper,* to scrape, of Germanic orig.]

rape oil *n.* The edible oil extracted from rapeseed, also used as a lubricant and in the manufacture of various products.

rape•seed (rāp′sēd′) *n.* The seed of the rape plant.

Raph•a•el (răf′ē-əl, rä′fē-) *n.* One of the archangels. [Heb. *Rĕphā′ēl.*]

ra•phe also **rha•phe** (rā′fē) *n., pl.* **-phae** (-fē′). *Biol.* A seamlike line or ridge between two similar parts, as in the scrotum, the coat of certain seeds, or the valves of a diatom. [NLat. < Gk. *rhaphē,* seam < *rhaptein,* to sew.]

raph•i•a (răf′ē-ə) *n.* Variant of **raffia.**

ra•phide (rā′fīd) also **ra•phis** (-fĭs) *n., pl.* **raph•i•des** (răf′ĭ-dēz′). *Bot.* One of a bundle of needle-shaped crystals, composed chiefly of calcium oxalate, occurring in many plant cells. [Back-formation < *rapides,* pl. < NLat. < Gk. *rhaphides,* pl. of *rhaphis,* needle < *rhaptein,* to sew.]

rap•id (răp′ĭd) *adj.* **-er, -est.** Moving, acting, or occurring with great speed; swift. —*n.* Often **rapids.** An extremely fast-moving part of a river, caused by a steep descent in the riverbed. [Lat. *rapidus* < *rapere,* to seize.] —**rap′id•ly** *adv.* —**ra•pid′i•ty** (rə-pĭd′ĭ-tē), **rap′id•ness** *n.*

rapid eye movement *n.* The rapid, periodic, jerky movement of the eyes during certain stages of the sleep cycle when dreaming takes place.

rap•id-fire (răp′ĭd-fīr′) *adj.* **1.** Designed to fire shots in rapid succession. **2.** Marked by continuous, rapid occurrence: *rapid-fire questions.*

rapid transit *n.* An urban passenger transportation system using elevated or underground trains or a combination of both.

ra•pi•er (rā′pē-ər, rāp′yər) *n.* **1.** A long, slender, two-edged sword with a cuplike hilt, used in the 16th and 17th centuries. **2.** A light, sharp-pointed sword lacking a cutting edge and used only for thrusting. [Fr. *rapière* < OFr. *(espee) rapiere,* rapier (sword).]

rap•ine (răp′ĭn) *n.* Forcible seizure of another's property; plunder. [ME *rapyne* < Lat. *rapina* < *rapere,* to seize.]

rap•pa•ree (răp′ə-rē′) *n.* **1.** A freebooting soldier of 17th-century Ireland. **2.** A bandit or robber. [Ir. Gael. *rapaire.*]

rap•pee (ră-pē′) *n.* A strong snuff made from a dark, coarse tobacco. [Fr. *(tabac) râpé,* grated (tobacco) < *râper,* to grate < OFr. *rasper,* to scrape, of Germanic orig.]

rap•pel (ră-pĕl′) *n.* The act or method of descending from a mountainside or cliff by means of a double rope passed under one thigh and over the opposite shoulder. —*intr.v.* **-pelled, -pel•ling, -pels.** To descend from a steep height by rappel. [Fr. < OFr., recall < *rapeler,* to recall : *re-,* back + *appeler,* to summon.]

rap•pen (rä′pən) *n., pl.* **rappen.** See table at **currency.** [G. < MHG *rappe,* raven.]

rap•per (răp′ər) *n.* One that raps, esp. a doorknocker.

rap•port (ră-pôr′, -pōr′, rə-) *n.* Relationship, esp. one of mutual trust or emotional affinity. [Fr. < *rapporter,* to bring back < OFr. *raporter* : *re-,* back + *aporter,* to bring < Lat. *apportare* (*ad-,* to + *portare,* to carry).]

rap•proche•ment (ră′prôsh-mäN′) *n.* **1.** A reestablishing of cordial relations, as between two countries. **2.** The state of reconciliation or of cordial relations. [Fr. < *rapprocher,* to bring together : *re-* (intensive < Lat.) + *approcher,* to approach (Lat. *ad-,* to + Lat. *prope,* near).]

rap•scal•lion (răp-skăl′yən) *n.* A rascal; scamp. [Alteration of E. *rascallion* < RASCAL.]

rap session *n. Slang.* An informal discussion held by a group of people.

rap sheet *n. Informal.* A police arrest record.

rapt (răpt) *v.* A past tense and past participle of **rap**[2]. —*adj.* **1.** Deeply moved or delighted; enraptured: *listening with*

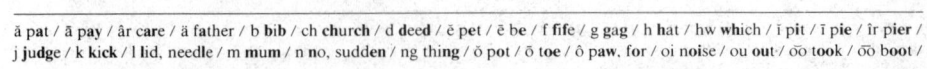

rapt admiration. **2.** Deeply absorbed; engrossed: *rapt in thought.* [ME, carried away < Lat. *raptus,* p.part. of *rapere,* to seize.]

rap·tor (răp′tər) *n.* A bird of prey. [Lat., one who seizes < *rapere,* to seize.]

rap·to·ri·al (răp-tôr′ē-əl, -tōr′-) *adj.* **1.** Subsisting by seizing prey; predatory. **2.** Adapted for the seizing of prey. **3.** Of, relating to, or characteristic of birds of prey.

rap·ture (răp′chər) *n.* **1.** The state of being transported by a lofty emotion; ecstasy. **2.** An expression of ecstatic feeling. **3.** The transporting of a person from one place to another, esp. to heaven. *—tr.v.* **-tured, -tur·ing, -tures.** To enrapture. [Med. Lat. *raptura,* ecstasy < Lat. *rapere,* to seize.]

rap·tur·ous (răp′chər-əs) *adj.* Filled with great joy or rapture; ecstatic. **—rap′tur·ous·ly** *adv.* **—rap′tur·ous·ness** *n.*

ra·ra a·vis (râr′ə ā′vĭs) *n., pl.* **rara a·vis·es** or **ra·rae a·ves** (râr′ē ā′vēz). A rare or unique person or thing. [Lat., rare bird.]

rare[1] (râr) *adj.* **rar·er, rar·est. 1.** Infrequently occurring; uncommon. **2.** Highly valued owing to uncommonness; special: *a rare gold coin.* **3.** Thin in density; rarefied. Used of gases. [ME < Lat. *rarus.*] **—rare′ness** *n.*

Usage: *Rare* and *scarce* are sometimes interchangeable, but *scarce* carries an additional implication that the quantities involved are insufficient or inadequate. Thus, we speak of *rare books* or of the *rare qualities* of someone we admire, but of *increasingly scarce reserves of coal.*

rare[2] (râr) *adj.* **rar·er, rar·est.** Cooked a short time to retain juice and redness: *rare steak.* [ME *rere,* lightly boiled < OE *hrēr.*] **—rare′ness** *n.*

rare·bit (râr′bĭt) *n.* Welsh rabbit. [Prob. alteration of (WELSH) RABBIT.]

rare earth *n.* **1.** Any of various oxides of the rare-earth elements. **2.** A rare-earth element.

rare-earth element (râr′ûrth′) *n.* Any of the abundant metallic elements of atomic number 57 through 71. [So called because they were originally thought to be rare.]

rar·ee show (râr′ē) *n.* **1.** A peepshow. **2.** A street show. [Alteration of *rare show.*]

rar·e·fac·tion (râr′ə-făk′shən) also **rar·e·fi·ca·tion** (-fĭ-kā′shən) *n.* **1.** The act or process of rarefying. **2.** The state of being rarefied. **—rar′e·fac′tive** *adj.*

rar·e·fied (râr′ə-fīd) *adj.* **1.** Belonging to or reserved for a small and select group; esoteric. **2.** Elevated in character or style; lofty.

rar·e·fy (râr′ə-fī′) *v.* **-fied, -fy·ing, -fies.** *—tr.* **1.** To make thin, less compact, or less dense. **2.** To purify or refine. *—intr.* To become thin, purer, or less dense. [ME *rarefien* < OFr. *rarefier* < Lat. *rarefacere* : *rarus,* rare + *facere,* to make.] **—rar′e·fi′a·ble** *adj.*

rare·ly (râr′lē) *adv.* **1.** Not often; infrequently: *"The truth is rarely pure and never simple"* (Oscar Wilde). **2.** In an unusual degree; exceptionally. **3.** With uncommon excellence.

Usage: Strictly speaking, the use of *ever* after *rarely* or *seldom* is redundant. Thus, the example *he rarely* (or *seldom*) *ever watches television* is unacceptable in speech to a majority of the Usage Panel and in writing to a large majority. The following constructions, using either *rarely* or *seldom,* are standard, however: *rarely if ever; rarely or never* (but not *rarely or ever*).

rare·ripe (râr′rīp′) *adj.* Ripening early. *—n.* A fruit or vegetable that ripens early. [Dial. *rare,* early + RIPE.]

rar·ing (râr′ĭng) *adj. Informal.* Full of eagerness; enthusiastic: *raring to get started.* [< pr.part. of dial. *rare,* var. of REAR[2].]

rar·i·ty (râr′ĭ-tē) *n., pl.* **-ties. 1.** Something that is rare. **2.** The quality or state of being rare; infrequency of occurrence.

ras·bo·ra (răz-bôr′ə, -bōr′ə) *n.* Any of various tropical fishes of the genus *Rasbora,* of which several brightly colored species are kept in home aquariums. [NLat. *Rasbora,* genus name < a native word in the East Indies.]

ras·cal (răs′kəl) *n.* **1.** An unscrupulous, dishonest person; scoundrel. **2.** One that is playfully mischievous. [ME, man of low station < OFr. *rascaille,* prob. < OFr. *rasque,* mud.] **—ras′cal·ly** *adj.*

ras·cal·i·ty (răs-kăl′ĭ-tē) *n., pl.* **-ties. 1.** The behavior or character of a rascal. **2.** A base or mischievous act.

rase (rāz) *tr.v.* **rased, ras·ing, ras·es. 1.** To erase. **2.** Variant of **raze.**

rash[1] (răsh) *adj.* **-er, -est. 1.** Characterized by ill-considered haste or boldness; impetuous. **2.** *Obs.* Quick in producing an effect. [ME *rasche,* active.] **—rash′ly** *adv.* **—rash′ness** *n.*

rash[2] (răsh) *n.* **1.** A skin eruption. **2.** An outbreak of many instances within a brief period: *a rash of burglaries.* [Poss. < obs. Fr. *rache* < OFr. *rasche* < *raschier,* to scratch < VLat. **rasciare* < Lat. *radere.*]

rash·er (răsh′ər) *n.* **1.** A thin slice of bacon fried or broiled. **2.** A dish or order of thin slices of fried or broiled bacon. [Orig. unknown.]

ra·so·ri·al (rə-zôr′ē-əl, -zōr′-, -sôr′-, -sōr′-) *adj.* Characteristically scratching the ground for food. Used of chickens and similar birds. [< LLat. *rasor,* scraper < Lat. *radere,* to scrape.]

rasp (răsp) *v.* **rasped, rasp·ing, rasps.** *—tr.* **1.** To file or scrape with a coarse file with sharp projections. **2.** To utter in a grating voice. **3.** To grate upon (nerves or feelings). *—intr.* **1.** To scrape harshly; grate. **2.** To make a harsh, grating sound. *—n.* **1.** A coarse file with sharp, raised, pointed projections. **2.** The act of filing with a rasp. **3.** A harsh, grating sound. [ME *raspen* < OFr. *rasper,* of Germanic orig.] **—rasp′er** *n.* **—rasp′ing·ly** *adv.*

rasp·ber·ry (răz′bĕr′ē) *n.* **1.** Any of various shrubby, usually prickly plants of the genus *Rubus,* bearing edible berries, such as *R. strigosus,* of eastern North America, and *R. idaeus,* of Europe. **2.** The fruit of the raspberry, consisting of a mass of small, fleshy, usually red drupelets. **3.** A moderate to dark or deep purplish red. **4.** *Slang.* A derisive or contemptuous sound made by vibrating the extended tongue and the lips while exhaling. [Obs. *raspit,* raspberry + BERRY.]

rasp·y (răs′pē) *adj.* **-i·er, -i·est.** Grating; rough.

Ras·ta·fa·ri·an·ism (rä′stə-făr′ē-ə-nĭz′əm, răs′tə-fâr′-) *n.* A black Jamaican religious cult whose members worship Haile Selassie. [After *Ras Tafari,* former name of Haile Selassie (1892–1975).] **—Ras′ta** (rä′stə, răs′tə), **Ras′ta·fa′ri·an** *n.*

rat (răt) *n.* **1.** Any of various long-tailed rodents resembling mice, but larger, esp. one of the genus *Rattus.* **2.** Any of various animals similar to a rat. **3.** *Slang.* A despicable, sneaky person, esp. one who betrays or informs upon his associates. **4.** *Informal.* A pad of hair or other material worn as part of a woman's coiffure to puff out the hair. *—intr.v.* **rat·ted, rat·ting, rats. 1.** To hunt for or catch rats, esp. with the aid of dogs. **2.** *Slang.* To desert or betray one's comrades by giving information: *ratted to the police on his best friend.* [ME < OE *ræt.*]

rat·a·ble (rā′tə-bəl) *adj.* **1.** Capable of being rated, estimated, or appraised. **2.** Proportional. **3.** *Chiefly Brit.* Liable to assessment; taxable. **—rat′a·bil′i·ty, rat′a·ble·ness** *n.* **—rat′a·bly** *adv.*

rat·a·fi·a (răt′ə-fē′ə) also **rat·a·fee** (-ə-fē′) *n.* **1.** A sweet cordial flavored with fruit kernels or almonds. **2.** A biscuit flavored with ratafia. [Fr.]

rat·a·plan (răt′ə-plăn′) *n.* A tattoo, as of a drum, the hoofs of a galloping horse, or machine-gun fire. [Fr.]

rat-a-tat-tat (răt′ə-tăt′tăt′) *n.* A series of short, sharp sounds, as those made by knocking on a door. [Imit.]

rat-bite fever (răt′bīt′) *n.* Either of two infectious diseases contractible from the bite of a rat: **a.** That arising from *Streptobacillus moniliformis* and characterized by skin inflammation, back and joint pains, headache, and vomiting. **b.** That from *Spirillum minus,* with ulceration at the site of the bite, a purplish rash, and recurrent fever.

rat cheese *n.* Cheddar.

ratch·et (răch′ĭt) *n.* **1.** A mechanism consisting of a pawl, or hinged catch, that engages the sloping teeth of a wheel or bar, permitting motion in one direction only. **2.** The pawl, wheel, or bar of a ratchet. [Fr. *rochet* < OFr. *rocquet,* head of a lance, of Germanic orig.]

rate[1] (rāt) *n.* **1.** A quantity measured with respect to another measured quantity: *a rate of speed of 60 miles an hour.* **2.** A measure of a part with respect to a whole; proportion: *the birth rate; a tax rate.* **3.** The cost per unit of a commodity or service: *postal rates.* **4.** A charge or payment calculated in relation to a particular sum or quantity: *interest rates.* **5.** Level of quality. **6. rates.** *Chiefly Brit.* A property tax assessed locally. *—v.* **rat·ed, rat·ing, rates.** *—tr.* **1.** To calculate the value of; appraise. **2.** To place in a particular rank or grade: *rate cuts of meat.* **3.** To regard or account: *rated the movie excellent.* **4.** To value for purposes of taxation. **5.** To set a rate for (goods to be shipped). **6.** To specify the performance limits of (a machine, for example). **7.** *Informal.* To merit or deserve: *rate special treatment.* *—intr.* **1.** To be ranked in a particular class. **2.** *Informal.* To have status, importance, or influence. *—idiom.* **at any rate. 1.** Whatever the case may be. **2.** At least. [ME < OFr. < Med. Lat. *rata,* proportion, short for *pro rata parte,* according to an estimated part.]

rate[2] (rāt) *v.* **rat·ed, rat·ing, rates.** *—tr.* To berate. *—intr.* To express reproof. [ME *raten.*]

ra·tel (rāt′l, răt′l) *n.* The honey badger. [Afr. < MDu., rattle.]

rate of exchange *n.* The ratio at which the unit of currency of one country is or may be exchanged for the unit of currency of another country.

rate·pay·er (rāt′pā′ər) *n. Chiefly Brit.* A person who pays rates.

rat·er (rā′tər) *n.* **1.** One that rates, esp. one that establishes a rating. **2.** One having an indicated rank or rating: *a third-rater.*

rat·fink (răt′fĭngk′) *n. Slang.* A contemptible, obnoxious, or otherwise undesirable person.

rat·fish (răt′fĭsh′) *n., pl.* **ratfish** or **-fish·es.** A fish, *Hydrolagus colliei,* of Pacific waters, having a long, narrow tail.

rathe (rāth, răth) *adj. Archaic.* Appearing or ripening early in the year. [ME, quick < OE *hraðe.*]

rath·er (răth′ər, rä′thər) *adv.* **1.** More readily; preferably: *I'd rather go to the movies.* **2.** With more reason, logic, wisdom, or other justification. **3.** More exactly; more accurately: *He's my friend, or rather he was my friend.* **4.** To a certain extent; somewhat: *rather nice.* **5.** On the contrary. **6.** (ră′thûr′, rä′-). *Chiefly Brit.* Most certainly. Used as an emphatic affirmative reply. [ME < OE *hraðor,* comp. of *hrað,* quickly.]

rasp

raspberry

ratchet
Wheel and pawl

rattle[1]
Child's rattle with whistle

rattlesnake

rattlesnake flag

Usage: *Rather* is usually preceded by *should* or *would* in expressing preference: *He would rather not go.* But *had* is equally acceptable: *I had rather be dead than be a slave.* In a contraction such as *he'd,* either *would* or *had* can be understood.

raths·kel·ler (rät'skĕl'ər, răt'-, răth'-) *n.* A restaurant in the style of the cellar of a German city hall that features the serving of beer. [Obs. G., restaurant in the city hall basement : *Rat,* council + *Keller,* cellar < Lat. *cellarium.*]

rat·i·fi·ca·tion (răt'ə-fĭ-kā'shən) *n.* The act of ratifying or the condition of being ratified.

rat·i·fy (răt'ə-fī') *tr.v.* **-fied, -fy·ing, -fies.** To give formal sanction to; approve and so make valid. [ME *ratifien* < OFr. *ratifier* < Med. Lat. *ratificare* : Lat. *ratus,* fixed (< *reri,* to reckon) + Lat. *facere,* to make.] **—rat'i·fi'er** *n.*

rat·i·né (răt'ə-nā') *n.* A loosely woven fabric with a nubby texture. [Fr., p.part. of *ratiner,* to adorn.]

rat·ing[1] (rā'tĭng) *n.* **1.** A position assigned on a scale; standing. **2.** A classification according to specialty or proficiency, as of a member of the armed forces. **3.** An evaluation of the financial status of a business or an individual: *a credit rating.* **4.** A specified performance limit, as of capacity, range, or operational capability: *power rating.* **5.** The popularity of a television or radio program as estimated by a poll of segments of the audience. **6.** *Chiefly Brit.* An enlisted man in the navy.

rat·ing[2] (rā'tĭng) *n.* A scolding.

ra·tio (rā'shō, rā'shē-ō') *n., pl.* **-tios. 1.** Relation in degree or number between two similar things. **2.** The relative value of silver and gold in a currency system that is bimetallic. **3.** *Math.* The relative size of two quantities expressed as the quotient of one divided by the other: *The ratio of 7 to 4 is written 7:4 or 7/4.* [Lat., calculation < *reri,* to reckon.]

ra·ti·oc·i·nate (răsh'ē-ŏs'ə-nāt') *intr.v.* **-nat·ed, -nat·ing, -nates.** To reason methodically and logically. [Lat. *ratiocinari, ratiocinat-* < *ratio,* calculation < *reri,* to reckon.] **—ra'ti·oc'i·na'tive** *adj.* **—ra'ti·oc'i·na'tion** *n.* **—ra'ti·oc'i·na'tor** *n.*

ra·tion (răsh'ən, rā'shən) *n.* **1.** A fixed portion, esp. an amount of food allotted to persons in military service or to civilians in times of scarcity. **2. rations.** Food issued or available to members of a group. *—tr.v.* **-tioned, -tion·ing, -tions. 1.** To supply with rations. **2.** To distribute as rations: *rationed out flour and sugar.* **3.** To restrict to limited amounts. [Fr. < Lat. *ratio,* calculation < *reri,* to reckon.]

ra·tion·al (răsh'ən-əl) *adj.* **1.** Having or exercising the ability to reason. **2.** Of sound mind; sane. **3.** Consistent with or based on reason; logical: *rational behavior.* **4.** *Math.* Designating an algebraic expression no variable of which appears in an irreducible radical or with a fractional exponent. [Lat. *rationalis* < *ratio,* reason < *reri,* to reckon.] **—ra'tion·al·ly** *adv.* **—ra'tion·al·ness** *n.*

ra·tion·ale (răsh'ə-năl') *n.* **1.** The fundamental reasons for something; basis. **2.** An exposition of principles or reasons. [Lat. *rationale,* neuter of *rationalis,* rational.]

rational function *n.* A function that is a quotient of polynomials.

ra·tion·al·ism (răsh'ə-nə-lĭz'əm) *n.* The theory that the exercise of reason, rather than the acceptance of empiricism, authority, or spiritual revelation, provides the only valid basis for action or belief, and that reason is the prime source of knowledge and of spiritual truth. **—ra'tion·al·ist** *n.* **—ra'tion·al·is'tic** *adj.* **—ra'tion·al·is'ti·cal·ly** *adv.*

ra·tion·al·i·ty (răsh'ə-năl'ĭ-tē) *n., pl.* **-ties. 1.** The quality or condition of being rational. **2.** A rational belief or practice.

ra·tion·al·i·za·tion (răsh'ən-əl-ə-zā'shən) *n.* **1.** The act, process, or practice of rationalizing. **2.** An instance of rationalizing.

ra·tion·al·ize (răsh'ə-nə-līz') *v.* **-ized, -iz·ing, -iz·es.** *—tr.* **1.** To make rational. **2.** To interpret from a rational standpoint. **3.** To devise self-satisfying but incorrect reasons for (one's behavior). **4.** *Math.* To remove radicals without changing the value of (an expression) or roots of (an equation). **5.** *Chiefly Brit.* To bring modern, efficient methods to (an industry, for example). *—intr.* **1.** To think in a rational or rationalistic way. **2.** To devise self-satisfying but incorrect reasons for one's behavior. **—ra'tion·al·iz'er** *n.*

rational number *n.* A number capable of being expressed as an integer or quotient of integers.

rat·ite (răt'īt') *adj.* Designating any of a group of flightless birds having a flat breastbone without the keellike prominence characteristic of most flying birds. *—n.* A ratite bird, as the ostrich or emu. [< Lat. *ratitus,* marked with the figure of a raft < *ratis,* raft.]

rat·line also **rat·lin** (răt'lĭn) *n. Naut.* **1.** Any of the small ropes fastened horizontally to the shrouds of a ship and forming a ladder for going aloft. **2.** The rope used for ratline. [Orig. unknown.]

ra·toon also **rat·toon** (ră-to͞on') *n.* A basal shoot sprouting from a plant such as the banana, pineapple, or sugar cane. *—v.* **-tooned, -toon·ing, -toons.** *—intr.* To produce or grow as a ratoon. *—tr.* To propagate (a crop) from ratoons. [Sp. *retoño,* sprout < *retoñar* : *re-,* again (< Lat.) + *otoñar,* to grow in autumn < Lat. *autumnus,* autumn.]

rat race *n. Slang.* A difficult, tiring, often competitive activity or rush.

rats·bane (răts'bān') *n.* Rat poison, esp. arsenic trioxide.

rat snake *n.* Any of several nonvenomous snakes of the genus *Elaphe.*

rat·tail (răt'tāl') also **rat·tailed** (-tāld') *adj.* Shaped like a rat's tail: *a rat-tail file.* *—n.* The grenadier (sense 2).

rat-tail cactus *n.* A tropical American cactus, *Aporocactus flagelliformis,* having thin, creeping or hanging stems and brilliant crimson flowers.

rat·tan (ră-tăn', rə-) *n.* **1.** Any of various climbing palms of the genera *Calamus, Daemonorops,* or *Plectomia,* of tropical Asia, having long, tough, slender stems. **2.** The stems of the rattan, used to make wickerwork. **3.** A switch or cane made from rattan. [Malay *rotan.*]

rat·teen (ră-tēn') *n. Archaic.* A thick, twilled woolen cloth. [Fr. *ratine.*]

rat·ter (răt'ər) *n.* **1.** One that catches or kills rats. **2.** *Slang.* A deserter, betrayer, or traitor.

rat·tle[1] (răt'l) *v.* **-tled, -tling, -tles.** *—intr.* **1. a.** To make or emit a quick succession of short, sharp sounds. **b.** To move with such sounds: *a train rattling along the track.* **2.** To talk rapidly and at length, usually without much thought: *rattled on about this and that.* *—tr.* **1.** To cause to rattle. **2.** To utter or perform rapidly or effortlessly: *rattle off a list of names.* **3.** *Informal.* To fluster, unnerve: *The accident really rattled her.* *—n.* **1.** Short, percussive sounds produced in rapid succession. **2.** A device, such as a baby's toy, that produces short percussive sounds. **3.** A rattling sound in the throat caused by obstructed breathing, esp. near the time of death. **4.** The series of horny structures at the end of a rattlesnake's tail. **5.** Loud or rapid talk; chatter. [ME *rattelen* < MLG *rattelen.*]

rat·tle[2] (răt'l) *tr.v.* **-tled, -tling, -tles.** *Naut.* To secure ratlines to (shrouds). [Back-formation < *rattling,* var. of RATLINE.]

rat·tle·box (răt'l-bŏks') *n.* Any of various plants or shrubs of the genus *Crotalaria,* having inflated pods within which the seeds rattle.

rat·tle·brained (răt'l-brānd') *adj.* Giddy and talkative; foolish. **—rat'tle·brain'** *n.*

rat·tler (răt'lər) *n.* **1.** One that rattles. **2.** A rattlesnake. **3.** *Informal.* A freight train.

rat·tle·snake (răt'l-snāk') *n.* Any of various venomous New World snakes of the genera *Crotalus* and *Sistrurus,* having at the end of the tail a series of loosely attached, horny segments that can be vibrated to produce a rattling or buzzing sound.

rattlesnake flag *n.* Any of several U.S. flags bearing the motto "Don't Tread on Me" and a picture of a rattlesnake, used during the French and Indian War and the Revolutionary War.

rattlesnake master *n.* Any of several plants supposedly effective against the venom of rattlesnakes, as *Eryngium yuccifolium,* of the southeastern United States, having narrow leaves with spiny margins and pale-blue or white flowers.

rattlesnake plantain *n.* Any of various small orchids of the genus *Goodyera,* having mottled or striped leaves and spikes of whitish flowers. [From the resemblance of its leaves to a rattlesnake's skin.]

rattlesnake root *n.* Any of various plants of the genus *Prenanthes,* having thick, bitter-tasting roots. [From the belief that the root cured a rattlesnake's bite.]

rattlesnake weed *n.* A plant, *Hieracium venosum,* having red-veined or purple-veined leaves and yellow flowers.

rat·tle·trap (răt'l-trăp') *n.* A rickety, worn-out vehicle.

rat·tling (răt'lĭng) *Informal.* *—adj.* **1.** Animated; brisk: *rattling conversation.* **2.** Very good. *—adv.* Especially; very: *a rattling good party.*

rat·tly (răt'lē) *adj.* Rattling or apt to rattle; clattering.

rat·toon (ră-to͞on) *n.* Variant of **ratoon.**

rat·trap (răt'trăp') *n.* **1.** A device for trapping rats. **2.** A dilapidated or unsanitary dwelling.

rat trap cheese *n.* Cheddar.

rat·ty (răt'ē) *adj.* **-ti·er, -ti·est. 1.** Of or characteristic of rats. **2.** Infested by rats. **3.** *Slang.* Dilapidated; shabby. **4.** Annoyed; irritable.

rau·cous (rô'kəs) *adj.* **1.** Rough-sounding and harsh: *raucous laughter.* **2.** Boisterous; disorderly: *a raucous party.* [Lat. *raucus.*] **—rau'cous·ly** *adv.* **—rau'cous·ness, rau'ci·ty** (rô'sə-tē) *n.*

raun·chy (rôn'chē, rän'-) *adj.* **-chi·er, -chi·est.** *Slang.* **1.** Grimy; unkempt. **2. a.** Vigorously or loudly obscene; vulgar: *raunchy jokes.* **b.** Sexually explicit: *a raunchy novel.* **c.** Lustful; randy. [Orig. unknown.] **—raun'chi·ly** *adv.* **—raun'chi·ness** *n.*

rau·wol·fi·a (rou-wo͝ol'fē-ə, rô-) *n.* Any of various tropical trees and shrubs of the genus *Rauwolfia,* esp. *R. serpentina,* of southeastern Asia. The root of this species is the source of tranquilizing alkaloid drugs such as reserpine. [NLat. *Rauwolfia,* genus name, after Leonhard *Rauwolf* (d. 1596).]

rav·age (răv'ĭj) *v.* **-aged, -ag·ing, -ag·es.** *—tr.* **1.** To bring heavy destruction on; devastate: *A tornado ravaged the countryside.* **2.** To pillage; sack. *—intr.* To wreak destruction. *—n.* **1.** The act or practice of ravaging. **2.** Grievous damage; havoc: *the ravages of disease.* [Fr. *ravager* < *ravir,* to ravish.] **—rav'ag·er** *n.*

rave (rāv) *v.* **raved, rav·ing, raves.** *—intr.* **1.** To speak wildly, irrationally, or incoherently: *raving like a madman.* **2.** To roar; rage: *The storm raved in the forest.* **3.** To speak with

wild enthusiasm: *He raved about her scheme.* —*tr.* To utter frenziedly. —*n.* **1.** The state or act of raving. **2.** *Informal.* An extravagantly enthusiastic opinion or review: *The play got raves.* **—modifier:** *rave reviews.* [ME *raven* < ONFr. *raver.*]
rav·el (răv′əl) *v.* **-eled, -el·ing, -els** also **-elled, -el·ling, -els.** —*tr.* **1.** To separate the fibers or threads of (cloth, for example); unravel. **2.** To clarify by separating the aspects of. **3.** To tangle or complicate. —*intr.* **1.** To become separated into its component threads; unravel; fray. **2.** To become tangled or confused. —*n.* **1.** A raveling. **2.** A broken or discarded thread. **3.** A tangle. [Du. *rafelen* < *rafel,* loose thread.] **—rav′el·er** *n.*
rav·el·ing also **rav·el·ling** (răv′ə-lĭng) *n.* A thread or fiber that has become separated from a woven material.
rav·el·ment (răv′əl-mənt) *n.* Confusion or complexity; tangle.
ra·ven[1] (rā′vən) *n.* A large bird, *Corvus corax,* having black plumage and a croaking cry. —*adj.* Black and shiny. [ME < OE *hræfn.*]
rav·en[2] (răv′ən) *v.* **-ened, -en·ing, -ens.** —*tr.* **1.** To consume greedily; devour. **2.** To seek or seize as prey or plunder. —*intr.* **1.** To seek or seize prey or plunder. **2.** To eat ravenously. —*n.* Variant of **ravin.** [OFr. *raviner,* to take by force < VLat. **rapinare* < Lat. *rapina,* rapine < *rapere,* to seize.] **—rav′en·er** *n.*
rav·en·ous (răv′ə-nəs) *adj.* **1.** Extremely hungry; voracious. **2.** Predatory. **3.** Greedy for gratification: *ravenous for power.* [ME < OFr. *ravineux* < *raviner,* to take by force. — see RAVEN[2].] **—rav′en·ous·ly** *adv.* **—rav′en·ous·ness** *n.*
ra·vi·gote (ră-vē-gôt′) *n.* A vinegar sauce spiced with minced onion, capers, and herbs, used with boiled meats or fish. [Fr. < *ravigoter,* to add new vigor : *re-,* again (< Lat.) + *a-,* to (< Lat. *ad-*) + *vigeur,* vigor < Lat. *vigor.*]
rav·in also **rav·en** (răv′ən) *n.* **1.** Voracity; rapaciousness. **2.** Something taken as prey. **3.** The act or practice of preying. [ME *ravine* < OFr., rapine < Lat. *rapina* < *rapere,* to seize.]
ra·vine (rə-vēn′) *n.* A deep, narrow cleft or gorge in the earth's surface, esp. one worn by the flow of water. [Fr. < OFr., violent rush < Lat. *rapina,* rapine < *rapere,* to seize.]
rav·ing (rā′vĭng) *adj.* **1.** Talking or behaving irrationally; wild: *a raving maniac.* **2.** *Informal.* Exciting admiration: *a raving beauty.* —*n.* Delirious, irrational speech. **—rav′ing·ly** *adv.*
ra·vi·o·li (răv′ē-ō′lē, ră′vē-) *pl.n.* **1.** Small casings of pasta with various fillings, such as chopped meat or cheese. **2.** A dish made with ravioli. [Ital., pl. of dial. *raviolo,* dim. of *rava,* turnip < Lat. *rapa.*]
rav·ish (răv′ĭsh) *tr.v.* **-ished, -ish·ing, -ish·es. 1.** To seize and carry away by force. **2.** To rape; violate. **3.** To overwhelm with emotion; enrapture. [ME *ravisshen* < OFr. *ravir, raviss-* < VLat. **rapire* < Lat. *rapere,* to seize.] **—rav′ish·er** *n.*
rav·ish·ing (răv′ĭ-shĭng) *adj.* Entrancing. **—rav′ish·ing·ly** *adv.*
rav·ish·ment (răv′ĭsh-mənt) *n.* **1.** The act of seizing by force. **2.** Rape. **3.** Rapture; entrancement.
raw (rô) *adj.* **-er, -est. 1.** Uncooked: *raw meat.* **2. a.** Being in a natural condition; not processed or refined: *raw wool.* **b.** Not finished, covered, or coated: *raw wood.* **3.** Untrained and inexperienced: *raw recruits.* **4.** Recently finished; fresh: *raw plaster.* **5.** Having subcutaneous tissue exposed: *a raw wound.* **6.** Inflamed; sore: *a raw throat.* **7.** Unpleasantly damp and chilly: *raw weather.* **8.** Cruel and unfair: *a raw punishment.* **9.** Outspoken; crude: *a raw portrayal of truth.* **—*idiom.* in the raw. 1.** In a crude or unrefined state: *nature in the raw.* **2.** *Informal.* Nude; naked. [ME < OE *hrēaw.*] **—raw′ly** *adv.* **—raw′ness** *n.*
raw·boned (rô′bōnd′) *adj.* Having a lean, gaunt frame with prominent bones.
raw deal *n. Slang.* An instance of unjust or cruel treatment.
raw·hide (rô′hīd′) *n.* **1.** The untanned hide of cattle or other animals. **2.** A whip or rope made of rawhide. —*tr.v.* **-hid·ed, -hid·ing, -hides.** To beat with a rawhide whip.
ra·win·sonde (rā′wĭn-sŏnd′) *n.* A radiosonde used to observe upper-air wind velocity and direction that is tracked by a radio direction-finding instrument or radar. [RA(DAR) + WIN(D) + (RADIO)SONDE.]
raw material *n.* **1.** Unprocessed natural products used in manufacture. **2.** Unprocessed data of any kind.
raw sienna *n.* **1.** A brownish-yellow pigment. **2.** A brownish orange to light brown.
raw silk *n.* **1.** Untreated silk as reeled from the cocoon. **2.** Fabric woven from raw silk.
ray[1] (rā) *n.* **1. a.** A thin line or narrow beam of radiation, esp. one of visible light. **b.** A graphic or other representation of such a line. **2.** A small amount; trace: *a ray of hope.* **3.** A straight line extending from a point. **4.** A structure having the form of a straight line extending from a given point. **5.** *Bot.* A ray flower. **6.** *Zool.* One of the bony spines supporting the membrane of a fish's fin. —*tr.v.* **rayed, ray·ing, rays. 1.** To send out as rays; emit. **2.** To supply with rays or radiating lines. **3.** To cast rays upon; irradiate. [ME < OFr. *rai* < Lat. *radius.*]
ray[2] (rā) *n.* Any of various marine fishes of the order Rajiformes or Batoidei, having cartilaginous skeletons, horizontally flattened bodies, and narrow tails. [ME *raye* < OFr. *raie* < Lat. *raia.*]
ray flower *n.* Any of the flat, strap-shaped marginal flowers around the head of certain flowers, as the daisy.
Ray·leigh scattering (rā′lē) *n.* The scattering of light waves by particles with dimensions much smaller than their wavelengths, resulting in angular separation of colors and responsible for the reddish color of sunset and the blue of the sky. [After John William Strutt (1842–1919), 3rd Baron *Rayleigh.*]
ray·less (rā′lĭs) *adj.* **1.** Lacking rays: *a rayless flower.* **2.** Lacking light: *a rayless dungeon.*
ray·on (rā′ŏn) *n.* **1.** Any of several similar synthetic textile fibers produced by forcing a cellulose solution through fine spinnerets and solidifying the resulting filaments. **2.** A fabric woven or knit from rayon. [< RAY[1].]
raze also **rase** (rāz) *tr.v.* **razed, raz·ing, raz·es** also **rased, ras·ing, ras·es. 1.** To tear down or demolish; level to the ground. **2.** To scrape or shave off. **3.** *Archaic.* To erase. [ME *rasen,* to scrape < OFr. *raser* < VLat. **rasare* < Lat. *radere.*]
ra·zor (rā′zər) *n.* A sharp-edged cutting instrument used esp. for shaving the face. [ME *rasor* < OFr. < *raser,* to scrape. — see RAZE.]
ra·zor·back (rā′zər-băk′) *n.* **1.** A semiwild hog of the southeastern United States, having a narrow body with a ridged back. **2.** The rorqual. **3.** A sharp, ridged hill.
ra·zor·bill (rā′zər-bĭl′) *n.* The razor-billed auk.
ra·zor-billed auk (rā′zər-bĭld′) *n.* A sea bird, *Alca torda,* of the northern Atlantic, having black-and-white plumage and a flattened, white-ringed bill.
razor clam *n.* Any of various clams of the family Solenidae, characteristically having long, narrow shells.
razz (răz) *n. Slang.* A raspberry (sense 4). —*tr.v.* **razzed, razz·ing, razz·es.** *Slang.* To deride, heckle, or tease. [Shortening and alteration of RASPBERRY.]
raz·zle-daz·zle (răz′əl-dăz′əl) *n. Slang.* An act, display, or condition of confusion, dazzling excitement, or bewilderment. [Redup. of DAZZLE.]
razz·ma·tazz (răz′mə-tăz′) *n. Slang.* **1.** A flashy action or display intended to bewilder, confuse, or deceive. **2.** Ambiguous or evasive language; double talk. **3.** Ebullient energy; vim. [Prob. alteration of RAZZLE-DAZZLE.]
Rb The symbol for the element rubidium.
re[1] (rā) *n. Mus.* A solmization syllable representing the second tone of the diatonic scale. [ME < Med. Lat. —see GAMUT.]
re[2] (rē) *prep.* Concerning; in reference to; in the case of. [Lat., ablative of *res,* thing.]
Re[1] The symbol for the element rhenium.
Re[2] (rē) *n.* Variant of **Ra.**
re– *pref.* **1.** Again; anew: *rebuild.* **2.** Backwards; back: *react.* **3.** Used as an intensive: *refine.* [ME < OFr. < Lat.]
Usage: Many compounds other than those entered here may be formed with *re-.* In forming compounds *re-* is normally joined with the following element without space or hyphen: *reopen.* If the second element begins with *e,* it is preferable to separate it with a hyphen: *re-entry.* However, such compounds may often be found written solid and are indicated here as fully acceptable variants. If a compound that resembles a familiar word is intended in a special sense, the hyphen is necessary to make the distinction: *re-creation,* meaning "creation anew." The hyphen may also be necessary to clarify an unusual nonce formation: *re-realignment,* or a compound that produces a series of three or more vowels: *re-aerify.*
–'re *suff.* Are: *They're not at home.*
reach (rēch) *v.* **reached, reach·ing, reach·es.** —*tr.* **1.** To stretch out or put forth (a bodily part); extend: *reached out her arms.* **2.** To touch or grasp by stretching out or extending: *couldn't reach the shelf.* **3.** To arrive at; attain: *reach a conclusion.* **4. a.** To succeed in communicating with: *They reached him by telephone.* **b.** To succeed in having an effect on: *No one seems able to reach her anymore.* **5. a.** To extend as far as: *The property reached the shore.* **b.** To carry as far as: *Her cry reached our ears.* **6.** To aggregate or amount to: *Sales reached the thousands.* **7.** *Informal.* To give or hand over to someone: *Reach me the sugar.* **8.** To score a hit, as with a weapon. —*intr.* **1.** To extend or thrust out something. **2.** To try to grasp or touch something: *reach for a gun.* **3. a.** To have coextension in time or space. **b.** To be extensive in influence or effect. **4.** *Naut.* To sail with the wind abeam. —*n.* **1.** The act or power of stretching or thrusting out. **2.** The extent or distance something can reach. **3. a.** The range of a person's understanding; comprehension: *a subject beyond her reach.* **b.** The range or scope of influence or effect. **4.** An unbroken expanse: *a reach of prairie.* **5.** A pole connecting the rear axle of a vehicle with the front. **6.** *Naut.* The tack of a sailing vessel with the wind abeam. **7.** The stretch of water visible between bends in a river or channel. [ME *rechen* < OE *rǣcan.*] **—reach′er** *n.*
Synonyms: *reach, achieve, attain, gain, compass, accomplish.* These terms presuppose attainment of certain objectives. *Reach* connotes arriving at a goal through effort and progress. *Achieve* suggests the successful executing of an important enterprise through skill or initiative. *Attain* may imply great effort and pride in reaching a level or goal.

raven[1]

rawhide
Drawing by
Frederic Remington
of cowboy
wielding rawhide

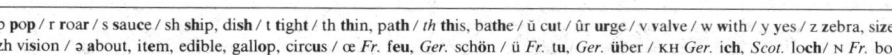

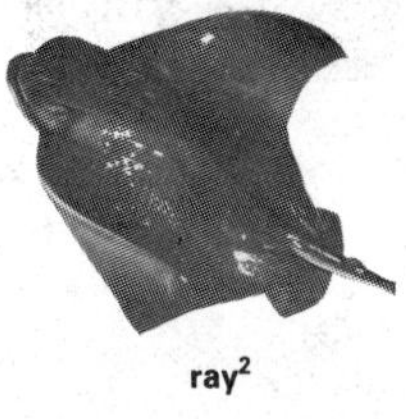
ray[2]

Gain connotes arriving at a goal despite considerable effort in surmounting obstacles, often with the implication of deserved satisfaction. *Compass* implies mental rather than physical effort in attaining goals. *Accomplish* connotes successful completion.

re·act (rē-ăkt') *intr.v.* **-act·ed, -act·ing, -acts. 1.** To act in response to a stimulus or prompting: *reacted to his sarcastic tone.* **2.** To act in opposition to some former condition or act: *composers who reacted against romanticism.* **3.** *Chem.* To undergo chemical change.

re·ac·tance (rē-ăk'təns) *n.* Opposition to the flow of alternating electric current caused by the inductance and capacitance in a circuit.

re·ac·tant (rē-ăk'tənt) *n.* A substance participating in a chemical reaction, esp. a directly reacting substance present at the initiation of the reaction.

re·ac·tion (rē-ăk'shən) *n.* **1. a.** A response to a stimulus. **b.** The state resulting from such a response. **2.** A reverse or opposing action. **3. a.** A tendency to revert to a former state. **b.** Opposition to progress or liberalism. **4.** A chemical change or transformation in which a substance decomposes, combines with other substances, or interchanges constituents with other substances. **5.** *Physics.* A nuclear reaction.

re·ac·tion·ar·y (rē-ăk'shə-nĕr'ē) *adj.* Characterized by reaction, esp. opposing progress or liberalism. *—n., pl.* **-ar·ies.** An opponent of progress or liberalism.

reaction engine *n.* An engine that develops thrust by the focused expulsion of matter, esp. ignited fuel gases.

reaction time *n.* The time interval between the application of a stimulus and the detection of a response.

re·ac·ti·vate (rē-ăk'tə-vāt') *tr.v.* **-vat·ed, -vat·ing, -vates. 1.** To make active again. **2.** To restore effectiveness or the ability to function of. **—re·ac'ti·va'tion** *n.*

re·ac·tive (rē-ăk'tĭv) *adj.* **1.** Tending to be responsive or to react to a stimulus. **2.** Characterized by reaction. **3.** *Chem. & Physics.* Tending to participate in reactions.

re·ac·tor (rē-ăk'tər) *n.* **1.** One that reacts. **2.** *Elect.* A circuit element, such as a coil, used to introduce reactance. **3.** *Physics.* A nuclear reactor.

read (rēd) *v.* **read** (rĕd), **read·ing, reads.** *—tr.* **1.** To examine and grasp the meaning of (written or printed characters, words, or sentences). **2.** To utter or render aloud (written or printed material): *read her poems to the students.* **3.** To interpret the nature or meaning of through close examination or observation: *read what was in her heart.* **4.** To determine the intent or mood of: *can read her mind like a book.* **5. a.** To attribute a certain interpretation or meaning to: *read a different meaning into what he said.* **b.** To consider (something written or printed) as having a particular meaning or significance: *read the novel as a parable.* **6.** To foretell or predict (the future). **7.** To receive or comprehend (a radio message, for example). **8.** To study or make a study of: *read the law.* **9.** To learn or get knowledge of from something written or printed: *He read that interest rates would continue to rise.* **10.** To proofread. **11.** To have or use as a preferred reading in a particular passage: *For "colour" read "color."* **12.** To indicate, register, or show: *The dial reads 32°.* *—intr.* **1.** To read printed or written characters, as of words or music. **2.** To speak aloud the words that one is reading: *read to his children every night.* **3.** To learn by reading: *he read about UFOs.* **4.** To study. **5.** To have a particular wording: *The line reads thus.* **6.** To contain a specific meaning: *As the law reads, he is guilty.* **7.** To have a specified character or quality for the reader: *His poems read well.* *—n.* Something that is read: *The novel is a good read.* **—*phrasal verb.* read out. 1.** To read aloud. **2.** To expel by proclamation from a social, political, or other group. *—adj.* (rĕd). Informed by reading; learned. **—*idioms.* read between the lines.** To perceive or detect a meaning or implication that is obscure or unexpressed. **read the riot act. 1.** To reprimand scathingly. **2.** To object strongly. **3.** To order a mob to break up. —See Usage note at **see.** [ME *reden* < OE *rǣdan,* to advise.]

read·a·ble (rē'də-bəl) *adj.* **1.** Capable of being read easily; legible. **2.** Pleasurable or interesting to read. **—read'a·bil'i·ty, read'a·ble·ness** *n.* **—read'a·bly** *adv.*

read·er (rē'dər) *n.* **1.** One who reads. **2.** A professional reciter of literary works. **3.** A minor cleric or layperson who recites lessons or prayers in church services. **4.** A person employed by a publisher to read and evaluate manuscripts. **5.** A corrector of printers' proofs. **6.** A teaching assistant who reads and grades examination papers. **7.** *Chiefly Brit.* A university lecturer. **8. a.** A textbook of reading exercises. **b.** An anthology, esp. a literary anthology.

read·er·ship (rē'dər-shĭp') *n.* **1.** The readers collectively of a publication. **2.** *Chiefly Brit.* The office of a reader.

read·i·ly (rĕd'ə-lē) *adv.* **1.** Promptly. **2.** Willingly. **3.** Easily.

read·ing (rē'dĭng) *n.* **1.** The act or practice of a reader. **2.** Written or printed material. **3.** The act of rendering aloud written or printed matter. **4.** An official or public recitation of written material: *the reading of a will.* **5.** A personal interpretation or appraisal: *gave us his reading of the situation.* **6.** The specific form of a particular passage in a text. **7.** The information indicated by a gauge or graduated instrument.

re·ad·just (rē'ə-jŭst') *tr.v.* **-just·ed, -just·ing, -justs.** To adjust or arrange again. **—re'ad·just'er** *n.* **—re'ad·just'ment** *n.*

realism
Detail from
Gustave Courbet's
"Young Ladies
from the Village"

read-only memory (rēd'ōn'lē) *n.* A small computer memory that allows fast access to permanently stored data.

read-out (rēd'out') *n.* Presentation of computer data, usually in digital form, from calculations or storage.

read·y (rĕd'ē) *adj.* **-i·er, -i·est. 1.** Prepared or available for service or action. **2.** Mentally disposed; willing: *He was ready to believe them.* **3.** Liable or about to do something: *ready to quit.* **4.** Prompt in apprehending or reacting: *a ready intelligence; a ready response.* **5.** Available: *ready money.* *—tr.v.* **read·ied, read·y·ing, read·ies.** To cause to be ready. **—*idiom.* at the ready.** Designating or describing a firearm in position for aiming and firing. [ME *redy* < OE *rǣde.*] **—read'i·ness** *n.*

read·y-made (rĕd'ē-mād') *adj.* **1.** Already made, prepared, or available: *ready-made clothes.* **2.** Preconceived: *a ready-made excuse.*

re·af·firm (rē'ə-fûrm') *tr.v.* **-firmed, -firm·ing, -firms.** To affirm or assert again. **—re'af·fir·ma'tion** (rē'ăf-ər-mā'shən) *n.*

re·a·gent (rē-ā'jənt) *n.* A substance used in a chemical reaction to detect, measure, examine, or produce other substances.

re·a·gin (rē-ā'jĭn) *n.* **1.** An antibody found in the blood of individuals that have a genetic predisposition to such allergies as asthma and hay fever. **2.** A substance present in the blood of individuals that have a positive serological test for syphilis. [REAG(ENT) + -IN.] **—re'a·gin'ic** (rē'ə-jĭn'ĭk) *adj.* **—re'a·gin'i·cal·ly** *adv.*

re·al[1] (rē'əl, rēl) *adj.* **1.** Not imaginary, fictional, or pretended; actual. **2.** Authentic or genuine: *a real diamond.* **3.** Essential; basic: *The real problem is poverty.* **4.** Being no less than what is stated; worthy of the name: *a real friend.* **5.** Serious; not to be taken lightly: *in real trouble.* **6.** *Philos.* Existing actually and objectively. **7.** Of, pertaining to, or designating an image formed by light rays that converge in space. **8.** *Math.* Of, pertaining to, or designating the nonimaginary part of a complex quantity. **9.** *Law.* Of or pertaining to stationary or fixed property, as buildings or land. *—adv. Informal.* Very: *real sorry.* [ME, of property or things < AN < Med. Lat. *realis* < LLat., real < Lat. *res,* thing.] **—real'ness** *n.*

Synonyms: *real, actual, true, authentic, concrete, existent, genuine, tangible, veritable. Real,* although frequently used interchangeably with the terms that follow, pertains basically to that which is not imaginary but is existent and identifiable as a thing, state, or quality. *Actual* connotes that which is demonstrable. *True* implies belief in that which conforms to fact. *Authentic* implies acceptance of historical or attributable reliability rather than visible proof. *Concrete* implies the reality of actual things. *Existent* applies to concepts or objects existing either in time or space: *existent tensions. Genuine* presupposes evidence or belief that a thing or object is what it is claimed to be. *Tangible* stresses the mind's acceptance of that which can be touched or seen. *Veritable,* which should be used sparingly, applies to persons and things having all the qualities claimed for them.

re·al[2] (rā-äl') *n., pl.* **-als** or **-al·es** (-ä'lās). A former Spanish silver monetary unit. [Sp. < *real,* royal < Lat. *regalis* < *rex,* king.]

re·al[3] (rā-äl') *n., pl.* **reals** or **reis** (rās). Either of two former monetary units of Portugal and Brazil. [Port. < *real,* royal < Lat. *regalis* < *rex,* king.]

real estate *n.* Land, including all the natural resources and permanent buildings on it.

re·al·gar (rē-ăl'gär', -gər) *n.* A soft orange-red arsenic ore, As_2S_2, used in pyrotechnics, tanning, and as a pigment. [ME < Med. Lat. < Catalan < Ar. *rajh alghār,* powder of the mine.]

re·a·lign (rē'ə-līn') *tr.v.* **-ligned, -lign·ing, -ligns. 1.** To put back into proper order or condition, as tires. **2.** To make new groupings of or working arrangements between. **—re'a·lign'ment** *n.*

re·al·ism (rē'ə-lĭz'əm) *n.* **1.** An inclination toward literal truth and pragmatism. **2.** Artistic representation or treatment that aims or is felt to be visually accurate. **3.** *Philos.* **a.** The doctrine that universal principles are more real than objects as sensed. **b.** The doctrine that names somehow denote the essences of things or categories of things. **c.** The doctrine that the objects of perception exist independently of the perceiver.

re·al·ist (rē'ə-lĭst) *n.* **1.** A person inclined to literal truth and pragmatism. **2.** A practitioner of artistic or philosophic realism.

re·al·is·tic (rē'ə-lĭs'tĭc) *adj.* **1.** Tending to or expressing an awareness of things as they really are: *a realistic appraisal of his chances.* **2.** Accurately representing what is depicted or described: *a realistic novel about ghetto life.* **—re'al·is'ti·cal·ly** *adv.*

re·al·i·ty (rē-ăl'ĭ-tē) *n., pl.* **-ties. 1.** The quality or state of being actual or true. **2.** A person, entity, or event that is actual. **3.** The totality of all things possessing actuality, existence, or essence. **4.** That which exists objectively and in fact. **5.** *Philos.* The sum of all that is real, absolute, and unchangeable.

reality principle *n. Psychoanal.* Awareness of and adjustment to environmental demands in a manner that assures ultimate satisfaction of instinctual needs.

re·al·i·za·tion (rē′ə-lĭ-zā′shən) *n.* **1.** The act of realizing or the condition of being realized. **2.** The result of realizing.

re·al·ize (rē′ə-līz′) *v.* **-ized, -iz·ing, -iz·es.** —*tr.* **1.** To comprehend completely or correctly. **2.** To make real or actualize; make happen: *realized his lifelong ambition to play the piano.* **3.** To make realistic. **4.** To obtain or achieve, as gain or profit: *realize a return on an investment.* **5.** To bring in (a sum) as profit by sale. —*intr.* To exchange holdings or goods for money. [Fr. *réaliser* < OFr. *realiser* < *real,* real < LLat. *realis* < Lat. *res,* thing.] **—re′al·iz′a·ble** *adj.* **—re′al·iz′er** *n.*

re·al·ly (rē′ə-lē, rē′lē) *adv.* **1.** In actual truth or fact: *The horseshoe crab isn't really a crab at all.* **2.** Truly: *That was a really enjoyable evening.* **3.** Indeed: *Really, you shouldn't have done it.*

realm (rĕlm) *n.* **1.** A kingdom. **2.** A field, sphere, or province: *the realm of science.* [ME *realme* < OFr. < Lat. *regimen,* government < *regere,* to rule.]

real number *n.* A rational or irrational number.

re·al·po·li·tik (rā-äl′pō′lĭ-tēk′) *n.* A usually expansionist national policy having as its sole principle the advancement of the national interest. [G. : *real,* practical + *Politik,* politics.] **—re·al′po′li·tik′er** *n.*

real time *n.* **1.** The actual time in which a physical process under computer study or control occurs. **2.** The time required for a computer to solve a problem, measured from the time data are fed in to the time a solution is received.

Re·al·tor (rē′əl-tər, -tôr′). A collective mark for a real-estate agent affiliated with the National Association of Realtors.

re·al·ty (rē′əl-tē) *n., pl.* **-ties.** Real estate.

ream[1] (rēm) *n.* **1.** A quantity of paper, formerly 480 sheets, now 500 sheets or, in a printer's ream, 516 sheets. **2.** Often **reams.** Very much: *reams of work to do.* [ME *reme* < OFr. *remme* < Ar. *rizmah,* bundle.]

ream[2] (rēm) *tr.v.* **reamed, ream·ing, reams. 1.** To form, shape, taper, or enlarge (a hole) with or as if with a reamer. **2.** To remove (material) by reaming. **3.** To squeeze the juice out of (fruit) with a reamer. [Orig. unknown.]

ream·er (rē′mər) *n.* **1.** Any of various tools used to shape or enlarge holes. **2.** A utensil with a conical, ridged projection, used for extracting citrus-fruit juice. **3.** One that reams.

reap (rēp) *v.* **reaped, reap·ing, reaps.** —*tr.* **1.** To cut (grain or pulse) for harvest with a scythe, sickle, or reaper. **2.** To harvest (a crop). **3.** To harvest a crop from: *reap a field.* **4.** To obtain as a result of effort: *reaped profits from his invention.* —*intr.* **1.** To cut or harvest grain or pulse. **2.** To obtain a return or reward. [ME *repen* < OE *rīpan.*]

reap·er (rē′pər) *n.* **1.** One that reaps. **2.** A machine for harvesting grain or pulse crops.

re·ap·por·tion (rē′ə-pôr′shən) *tr.v.* **-tioned, -tion·ing, -tions.** To distribute anew.

re·ap·por·tion·ment (rē′ə-pôr′shən-mənt) *n.* **1.** The act of reapportioning or the state of being reapportioned. **2.** The redistribution of representation in a legislative body, esp. the periodic reallotment of U.S. Congressional seats according to changes in the census figures as required by the Constitution.

re·ap·prais·al (rē′ə-prā′zəl) *n.* A new appraisal or evaluation.

rear[1] (rîr) *n.* **1.** The hind part of something. **2.** The point or area farthest from the front of something: *the rear of the hall.* **3.** The part of a military deployment usually farthest from the fighting front. **4.** *Informal.* The buttocks. —*adj.* Of, at, or located in the rear. [Prob. short for REARGUARD or REARWARD[2].]

rear[2] (rîr) *v.* **reared, rear·ing, rears.** —*tr.* **1.** To care for (a child) during the early stages of life; bring up. **2.** To lift upright; raise. **3.** To build; erect. **4.** To tend (growing plants or animals). —*intr.* **1.** To rise on the hind legs, as a horse. **2.** To rise high in the air; tower. [ME *reren,* to raise < OE *rǣran.*] **—rear′er** *n.*

rear admiral *n.* A naval officer ranking below a vice admiral and above a captain.

rear guard *n.* A detachment of troops that protects the rear of a military force. [ME *reregarde* < OFr. : *rere,* backward (< Lat. *retro*) + *garde,* guard < *garder,* to defend, of Germanic orig.]

rear-guard (rîr′gärd′) *adj.* Of or pertaining to resistance, either military or social: *fought rear-guard actions against the invading army.*

re·arm (rē-ärm′) *v.* **-armed, -arm·ing, -arms.** —*tr.* **1.** To arm again. **2.** To equip with better weapons. —*intr.* To arm oneself again. **—re·ar′ma·ment** (rē-är′mə-mənt) *n.*

rear·most (rîr′mōst′) *adj.* Farthest in the rear; last.

re·ar·range (rē′ə-rānj′) *tr.v.* **-ranged, -rang·ing, -rang·es.** To change the arrangement of. **—re′ar·range′ment** *n.*

rear·view mirror (rîr′vyōō′) *n.* A mirror, such as one attached to a motor vehicle, that gives a view of what is behind.

rear·ward[1] (rîr′wərd) *adj. & adv.* At or toward the rear. —*n.* A position or place at the rear. **—rear′wards** *adv.*

rear·ward[2] (rîr′wôrd′) *n.* The rear guard of an armed force. [ME *rerewarde* < AN : *rere,* behind (< Lat. *retro*) + *warde,* guard, of Germanic orig.]

rea·son (rē′zən) *n.* **1.** The basis or motive for an action, decision, or conviction. **2.** A declaration made to explain or justify an action, decision, or conviction: *asked her reason for leaving.* **3.** An underlying fact or cause that provides logical sense for a premise or occurrence: *There is reason to believe he didn't commit the crime.* **4.** The capacity for rational thought, inference, or discrimination. **5.** Good judgment; sound sense. **6.** Normal mental state; sanity: *lost his reason.* **7.** *Logic.* A premise, usually the minor premise, of an argument. —*v.* **-soned, -son·ing, -sons.** —*intr.* **1.** To use the faculty of reason; think logically. **2.** To talk or argue logically and persuasively. **3.** *Archaic.* To engage in conversation or discussion. —*tr.* **1.** To determine or conclude by logical thinking: *reasoned out a solution.* **2.** To persuade or dissuade (someone) with reasons. **3.** To discuss; debate. **—*idioms.* by reason of.** Because of. **in reason.** With good sense or justification; reasonably. **within reason.** Within the bounds of good sense or practicality. **with reason.** With good cause; justifiably. —See Usage note at **because.** [ME < OFr. *raison* < Lat. *ratio* < *reri,* to think.] **—rea′son·er** *n.*

Synonyms: *reason, intuition, understanding, discernment, judgment. Reason* in this comparison is the intellectual process of seeking truth or knowledge by inferring from either fact or logic. *Intuition* is instinctive knowing or perception without reference to the rational process. *Understanding* is the apprehension or comprehension of knowledge resulting from reason or thinking. *Discernment* is the faculty of discriminating, often through selection, what is apprehensible, relevant, or worthwhile. *Judgment* is the faculty of making sound conclusions.

rea·son·a·ble (rē′zə-nə-bəl) *adj.* **1.** Capable of reasoning; rational. **2.** Governed by or in accordance with reason or sound thinking. **3.** Within the bounds of common sense: *arrive home at a reasonable hour.* **4.** Not excessive or extreme; fair: *reasonable prices.* **—rea′son·a·bil′i·ty, rea′son·a·ble·ness** *n.* **—rea′son·a·bly** *adv.*

rea·son·ing (rē′zə-nĭng) *n.* **1.** The use of reason, esp. to form conclusions, inferences, or judgments. **2.** The evidence or arguments used in reasoning.

re·as·sure (rē′ə-shŏŏr′) *tr.v.* **-sured, -sur·ing, -sures. 1.** To restore confidence to. **2.** To assure again. **3.** To reinsure. **—re′as·sur′ance** *n.* **—re′as·sur′ing·ly** *adv.*

re·a·ta (rē-ä′tə) *n.* Variant of **riata.**

Ré·au·mur or **Re·au·mur** (rā′ō-myŏŏr′) *adj.* Denoting or indicating on a thermometer scale that registers the freezing point of water as 0° and the boiling point as 80°. [After René Antoine de *Réaumur* (1683–1757).]

reave[1] (rēv) *v.* **reaved** or **reft** (rĕft), **reav·ing, reaves.** *Archaic.* —*tr.* **1.** To seize and carry off forcibly. **2.** To deprive of; bereave. —*intr.* To rob, plunder, or pillage. [ME *reven* < OE *rēafian.*]

reave[2] (rēv) *tr.v.* **reaved** or **reft** (rĕft), **reav·ing, reaves.** *Archaic.* To break or tear apart. [ME *reven,* poss. alteration of ON *rifa,* to rive.]

Reb[1] also **reb** (rĕb) *n. Informal.* A Confederate soldier in the Civil War. [Short for REBEL.]

Reb[2] (rĕb) *n.* A Jewish title of respect, approximately equivalent to "Mr." or "Sir," but used with the given name rather than the surname. [Yiddish < Heb. *rabbi,* my master. —see RABBI.]

re·bar·ba·tive (rē-bär′bə-tĭv) *adj.* Tending to irritate; repellent. [Fr. *rébarbatif* < OFr. *rebarber,* to be repellent : *re-,* against (< Lat.) + *barbe,* beard < Lat. *barba.*]

re·bate[1] (rē′bāt′) *n.* A deduction from an amount to be paid or a return of part of an amount given in payment. —*tr.v.* (rē′bāt′, rĭ-bāt′) **-bat·ed, -bat·ing, -bates. 1.** To deduct or return (an amount) from a payment or bill. **2.** To dull or blunt (a weapon, for example). **3.** To lessen; diminish. [ME *rebaten* < OFr. *rebattre,* to reduce, to beat down again : *re-,* again (< Lat.) + *abattre,* to beat down (*a-,* to + *battre,* to batter).] **—re′bat·er** *n.*

re·bate[2] *n. & v.* Variant of **rabbet.**

re·ba·to (rĭ-bä′tō) also **ra·ba·to** (rə-) *n., pl.* **-tos.** A stiff, flaring collar of lace or other fabric, worn by both sexes early in the 17th century. [OFr. *rabat* < *rabattre,* to turn down again, reduce. —see REBATE[1].]

re·bec also **re·beck** (rē′bĕk′) *n.* A pear-shaped, two- or three-stringed musical instrument of medieval times, played with a bow. [OFr., alteration of *rebebe* < OProv. *rebab* < Ar. *rebāb.*]

Re·bec·ca also **Re·bek·ah** (rĭ-bĕk′ə) *n.* In the Old Testament, the wife of Isaac and the mother of Jacob and Esau. [Heb. *Ribqāh.*]

re·bel (rĭ-bĕl′) *intr.v.* **-belled, -bel·ling, -bels. 1.** To refuse allegiance to and oppose by force an established government or ruling authority. **2.** To resist or defy an authority or generally accepted convention. **3.** To feel or express strong unwillingness or repugnance: *She rebelled at the unwelcome suggestion.* —*n.* **reb·el** (rĕb′əl). A person who rebels or is in rebellion. **—*modifier:*** *rebel soldiers; a rebel movement.* [ME *rebellen* < OFr. *rebeller* < Lat. *rebellare* : *re-,* against + *bellare,* to make war < *bellum,* war.]

re·bel·lion (rĭ-bĕl′yən) *n.* **1.** An uprising or organized opposition intended to change or overthrow an existing government or ruling authority. **2.** An act or show of defiance toward an authority or established convention. [ME < OFr. < Lat. *rebellio* < *rebellare,* to rebel.]

Synonyms: *rebellion, revolution, revolt, riot, mutiny, in-*

reamer
Above: Wood reamer
Below: Fruit reamer

reaper

surrection, uprising, coup d'état, putsch. These terms pertain in varying degree to opposition to an existing order or authority. *Rebellion* is defiance of authority in general or open but unorganized disobedience: *the teen-age rebellion;* also, it is open, armed, and organized insurrection against constituted political authority that usually fails of its purpose, as *Shay's Rebellion. Revolution* is a radical alteration in a system or in social conditions, such as the *Industrial Revolution;* also, it is the overthrowing by open, organized armed force of a government and replacing it with another, such as the *American Revolution. Revolt* is widespread opposition to prevailing standards: *a taxpayers' revolt;* also, it is an armed attempt to change authority. *Riot* is a sudden, violent, disorganized uprising, frequently unarmed and unplanned. *Mutiny* is forcible resistance to constituted authority, especially by subordinates in the armed forces. *Insurrection* and *uprising* are armed attempts to change authority. *Coup d'état* is a sudden, violent overthrow of a government. *Putsch* is an attempted *coup d'état.*

re·bel·lious (rĭ-bĕl'yəs) *adj.* **1.** Participating in or tending toward a rebellion. **2.** Of or characteristic of a rebel. **3.** Resisting management or control; unruly. **—re·bel'lious·ly** *adv.* **—re·bel'lious·ness** *n.*

re·bind (rē-bīnd') *tr.v.* **-bound** (-bound'), **-bind·ing, -binds.** To bind again, esp. to put a new binding on (a book). *—n.* (rē'bīnd'). A book that has been rebound.

re·birth (rē-bûrth', rē'bûrth') *n.* **1.** A second or new birth; reincarnation. **2.** A renaissance; revival.

re·born (rē-bôrn') *adj.* Emotionally or spiritually revived or regenerated.

re·bound¹ (rē'bound', rĭ-) *v.* **-bound·ed, -bound·ing, -bounds.** *—intr.* **1.** To spring or bounce back after hitting or colliding with something. **2.** To recover, as from depression or disappointment. **3.** To re-echo; resound. **4.** *Basketball.* To retrieve and gain possession of the ball as it bounces off the backboard or rim after an unsuccessful shot. *—tr.* To cause to rebound. *—n.* (rē'bound', rĭ-bound'). **1.** A springing or bounding back; recoil. **2. a.** *Sports.* A rebounding or caroming ball or hockey puck. **b.** *Basketball.* The act or an instance of taking possession of a rebounding ball. **3.** A quick recovery from or reaction to disappointment or depression. [ME *rebounden* < OFr. *rebondir* : *re-*, back (< Lat.) + *bondir,* to resound. —see BOUND¹.]

re·bound² (rē-bound') *v.* Past tense and past participle of **rebind. —re·bound'er** *n.*

re·bo·zo (rĭ-bō'sō) *n., pl.* **-zos.** A long scarf worn over the head and shoulders chiefly by Mexican women. [Sp. < *rebosar,* to muffle with a shawl.]

re·broad·cast (rē-brôd'kăst') *tr.v.* **-cast** or **-cast·ed, -cast·ing, -casts. 1.** To repeat the broadcast of (a program). **2.** To receive and send out (a broadcast) again. *—n.* A broadcast that is repeated or that is relayed from another station.

re·buff (rĭ-bŭf') *n.* **1.** A blunt or abrupt repulse or refusal, as to an offer. **2.** A check or abrupt setback to progress or action. *—tr.v.* **-buffed, -buff·ing, -buffs. 1.** To refuse bluntly or contemptuously; snub. **2.** To repel or drive back. [OFr. *rebuffer* < OItal. *ribuffare* < *ribuffo,* reprimand : *ri-*, back (< Lat. *re-*) + *buffo,* gust.]

re·build (rē-bĭld') *tr.v.* **-built** (-bĭlt'), **-build·ing, -builds. 1.** To build again. **2.** To make extensive structural repairs on. **3.** To remodel or make extensive changes in: *rebuilding society.*

re·buke (rĭ-byo͞ok') *tr.v.* **-buked, -buk·ing, -bukes. 1.** To criticize or reprove sharply; reprimand. **2.** To check or repress. *—n.* A sharp reproof. [ME *rebuken* < ONFr. *rebuker.*]

re·bus (rē'bəs) *n., pl.* **-bus·es.** A puzzle composed of words or syllables that appear in the form of pictures. [Lat., ablative pl. of *res,* thing.]

rebus
The first lines of the poem "A Visit from St. Nicholas" presented as a rebus

re·but (rĭ-bŭt') *v.* **-but·ted, -but·ting, -buts.** *—tr.* **1.** To refute, esp. by offering opposing evidence or arguments, as in a legal case. **2.** To repel. *—intr.* To present opposing evidence or arguments. [ME *rebuten* < OFr. *reboter* : *re-*, back (< Lat.) + *boter,* to butt, of Germanic orig.]

re·but·tal (rĭ-bŭt'l) *n.* **1.** The act of rebutting. **2.** A statement made in rebutting.

re·but·ter (rĭ-bŭt'ər) *n.* **1.** A person who refutes or rebuts. **2.** *Law.* The defendant's answer to the plaintiff's surrejoinder.

re·cal·ci·trant (rĭ-kăl'sĭ-trənt) *adj.* Stubbornly resistant to authority, domination, or guidance; refractory. *—n.* A recalcitrant person. [Lat. *recalcitrans, recalcitrant-*, pr.part. of *recalcitrare,* to be disobedient : *re-*, back + *calcitrare,* to kick < *calx,* heel.] **—re·cal'ci·trance, re·cal'ci·tran·cy** *n.*

re·ca·les·cence (rē'kə-lĕs'əns) *n.* A sudden increase of heat in a cooling metal caused by an exothermic structural change. [< Lat. *recalescere,* to grow warm again : *re-*, again + *calescere,* to become warm < *calēre,* to be warm.] **—re'ca·les'cent** *adj.*

re·call (rĭ-kôl') *tr.v.* **-called, -cal·ling, -calls. 1.** To ask or order to return: *recalled all workers who had been laid off.* **2.** To summon back to awareness of or concern with the subject or situation at hand. **3.** To remember; recollect. **4.** To cancel, take back, or revoke. **5.** To bring back; restore. *—n.* (*also* rē'kôl'). **1.** The act of recalling or summoning back, esp. an official order to return. **2.** A signal, as a bugle call, used to summon servicemen back to their posts. **3.** The ability to remember information or experiences. **4.** The act of revoking. **5. a.** The procedure by which a public official may be removed from office by popular vote. **b.** The right to employ this procedure. **6.** A request by the manufacturer of a product specified as defective for its return to the dealer for necessary repairs or adjustments. **—re·call'a·ble** *adj.*

re·cant (rĭ-kănt') *v.* **-cant·ed, -cant·ing, -cants.** *—tr.* To make a formal retraction or disavowal of (a statement or belief to which one has previously committed oneself). *—intr.* To make a formal retraction or disavowal of a previously held belief. [Lat. *recantare* : *re-*, back + *cantare,* to sing < *canere.*] **—re'can·ta'tion** *n.* **—re·cant'er** *n.*

re·cap¹ (rē-kăp') *tr.v.* **-capped, -cap·ping, -caps. 1.** To replace a cap or caplike covering on: *recap a bottle.* **2.** To restore (a used automobile tire) to usable condition by bonding new rubber onto the worn tread and lateral surface. *—n.* (rē'kăp'). A tire that has been recapped.

re·cap² (rē'kăp') *tr.v.* **-capped, -capping, -caps.** To recapitulate. *—n.* A recapitulation, as of a news report.

re·cap·i·tal·ize (rē-kăp'ĭ-tl-īz') *tr.v.* **-ized, -iz·ing, -iz·es.** To change the capital structure of (a corporation). **—re·cap'i·tal·i·za'tion** *n.*

re·ca·pit·u·late (rē'kə-pĭch'ə-lāt') *v.* **-lat·ed, -lat·ing, -lates.** *—tr.* **1.** To repeat in concise form. **2.** *Biol.* To appear to repeat (the evolutionary stages of the species) during the embryonic development of the individual organism. *—intr.* To summarize. [LLat. *recapitulare, recapitulat-* : *re-*, again + *capitulare,* to put under headings < Lat. *capitulum,* heading, dim. of *caput,* head.] **—re·ca·pit'u·la'tive, re·ca·pit'u·la·to'ry** (-lə-tôr'ē, -tōr'ē) *adj.*

re·ca·pit·u·la·tion (rē'kə-pĭch'ə-lā'shən) *n.* **1.** The act or process of recapitulating. **2.** A summary or concise review. **3.** *Biol.* The apparent repetition of some of the evolutionary stages of the species during embryonic development of the individual organism. **4.** *Mus.* The restatement of the exposition that constitutes the third section of the typical sonata form.

re·cap·ture (rē-kăp'chər) *n.* **1. a.** The act of retaking or recovering something. **b.** The condition of being retaken or recovered. **2.** *Law.* The act or an instance of retaking booty or goods. **3.** Something recaptured. **4.** The lawful taking by a government of a fixed amount of the profits of a public-service corporation in excess of a stipulated rate of return. *—tr.v.* **-tured, -tur·ing, -tures. 1.** To capture again. **2.** To recall: *an attempt to recapture the past.* **3.** To acquire by the government procedure of recapture.

re·cast (rē-kăst') *tr.v.* **-cast, -cast·ing, -casts. 1.** To mold again: *recast a bell.* **2.** To set down or present (ideas, for example) in a new or different arrangement. **3.** To change the cast of (a theatrical production). *—n.* (rē'kăst'). **1.** The act or process of recasting. **2.** Something produced by recasting.

re·cede (rĭ-sēd') *intr.v.* **-ced·ed, -ced·ing, -cedes. 1.** To move back or away from a limit, point, or mark: *The flood waters receded.* **2.** To slope backward. **3.** To become or seem to become more distant. **4.** To withdraw or retreat. [Lat. *recedere* : *re-*, back + *cedere,* to go away.]

re·cede (rē-sēd') *tr.v.* **-ced·ed, -ced·ing, -cedes.** To cede back; yield or grant to one formerly in possession.

re·ceipt (rĭ-sēt') *n.* **1. a.** The act of receiving something. **b.** The fact of being received. **2.** Often **receipts.** The quantity or amount of something received: *cash receipts.* **3.** A written acknowledgment that a specified article, sum of money, or delivery of merchandise has been received. **4.** *Regional.* A recipe. *—v.* **-ceipt·ed, -ceipt·ing, -ceipts.** *—tr.* **1.** To mark (a bill) as having been paid. **2.** To give or write a receipt for (money paid or goods delivered). *—intr.* To give a receipt. [ME *receite* < ONFr. < Med. Lat. *recepta* < Lat. *recipere,* to receive.]

re·ceiv·a·ble (rĭ-sē'və-bəl) *adj.* **1.** Suitable for being received or accepted, esp. as payment. **2.** Awaiting or requiring payment; due or collectable: *accounts receivable.* *—n.* **receivables.** Business assets representing the total amounts due from others.

re·ceive (rĭ-sēv') *v.* **-ceived, -ceiv·ing, -ceives.** *—tr.* **1.** To take or acquire (something given, offered, or transmitted); get. **2.** To acquire knowledge of or information about: *receive bad news.* **3.** To have bestowed on oneself, as a title. **4.** To meet with; experience: *receive sympathetic treatment.* **5.** To have inflicted or imposed on oneself: *receive a penalty.* **6.** To bear the weight or force of; support. **7.** To take or intercept the impact of, as a blow. **8.** To take in, hold, or contain: *a tank receiving rainwater.* **9.** To admit: *receive new members.* **10.** To greet or welcome: *receive guests.* **11.** To perceive or acquire mentally: *receive a bad impression.* **12.** To regard with approval or disapproval: *theories well received.* **13.** To listen to and formally and authoritatively acknowledge: *receive an oath of allegiance.* *—intr.* **1.** To acquire or get something; be a recipient. **2.** To admit or welcome guests or visitors. **3.** To partake of the Eucharist. **4.** *Electronics.* To convert incoming electromagnetic waves into visible or audible signals. **5.** *Football.* To catch or take possession of a kicked ball. [ME *receiven* < ONFr. *receivre* < Lat. *recipere* : *re-*, again + *capere,* to take.]

Received Pronunciation *n.* The pronunciation of British

English that reflects the social and cultural predominance of southern English speech, that was at one time characteristic of the English spoken at the public schools and Oxford and Cambridge Universities, and that was accepted as the standard form of English used in broadcasting.

Received Standard English *n.* British English characterized esp. by Received Pronunciation.

re·ceiv·er (rĭ-sē′vər) *n.* **1.** One that receives something. **2.** An official appointed to receive and account for money due. **3.** *Law.* A person appointed by a court administrator to take into custody the property or funds of others, pending litigation. **4.** A person who knowingly buys or receives stolen goods. **5.** A receptacle intended for a specific purpose. **6.** *Electronics.* A device, such as a part of a radio, television set, or telephone, that receives incoming electromagnetic signals and converts them to perceptible forms. **7.** *Football.* **a.** A member of the offensive team eligible to catch a forward pass. **b.** *Baseball.* The catcher.

re·ceiv·er·ship (rĭ-sē′vər-shĭp′) *n.* *Law.* **1.** The office or functions of a receiver. **2.** The state of being held by a receiver.

receiving blanket *n.* A lightweight blanket used to wrap a baby esp. after a bath.

receiving line *n.* A group of people who form a line to individually greet arriving guests, as at a formal affair.

re·cen·sion (rĭ-sĕn′shən) *n.* **1.** A critical revision of a text incorporating the most plausible elements found in varying sources. **2.** A text revised through recension. [Lat. *recensio,* a reviewing < *recensēre,* to review : *re-,* again + *censēre,* to estimate.]

re·cent (rē′sənt) *adj.* **1.** Of, belonging to, or occurring at a time immediately prior to the present. **2.** Modern; new. **3. Recent.** *Geol.* Of, belonging to, or designating the Holocene epoch. [Lat. *recens.*] **—re′cen·cy, re′cent·ness** *n.* **—re′cent·ly** *adv.*

re·cept (rē′sĕpt′) *n.* A mental image formed from what is common to successive perceptions. [RE- + (PER)CEPT.]

re·cep·ta·cle (rĭ-sĕp′tə-kəl) *n.* **1.** Something that holds or contains; container. **2.** *Bot.* The part of a flower stalk that bears and supports the floral organs. **3.** *Elect.* A fitting connected to a power supply and equipped to receive a plug. [Lat. *receptaculum* < *receptare,* to receive again, freq. of *recipere,* to receive.]

re·cep·tion (rĭ-sĕp′shən) *n.* **1.** The act or process of receiving or of being received. **2.** A welcome, greeting, or acceptance: *a friendly reception.* **3.** A social function: *a wedding reception.* **4.** Mental approval or acceptance: *the reception of a new theory.* **5.** *Electronics.* **a.** The action of receiving electromagnetic signals. **b.** The condition or quality of received signals. [Lat. *receptio* < *recipere,* to receive.]

re·cep·tion·ist (rĭ-sĕp′shə-nĭst) *n.* An office worker employed chiefly to receive callers and answer the telephone.

re·cep·tive (rĭ-sĕp′tĭv) *adj.* **1.** Capable of or qualified for receiving. **2.** Ready or willing to receive favorably: *receptive to their proposals.* **—re·cep′tive·ly** *adv.* **—re′cep·tiv′i·ty, re·cep′tive·ness** *n.*

re·cep·tor (rĭ-sĕp′tər) *n.* A nerve ending specialized to sense or receive stimuli.

re·cer·ti·fi·ca·tion (rē′sûr-tə-fĭ-kā′shən) *n.* Renewal of certification, esp. by a licensing board. **—re·cer′ti·fy** *v.* **(-fied, -fy·ing, -fies).**

re·cess (rē′sĕs′, rĭ-sĕs′) *n.* **1. a.** A temporary cessation of the customary activities of an engagement, occupation, or pursuit. **b.** The period of such cessation. **2.** Often **recesses.** A remote, secret, or secluded place. **3. a.** An indentation or small hollow. **b.** An alcove. *—v.* **-cessed, -ces·sing, -ces·ses.** *—tr.* **1.** To place in a recess. **2.** To create or fashion a recess in. **3.** To suspend for a recess. *—intr.* To take a recess. [Lat. *recessus* < *recedere,* to recede. —see RECEDE[1].]

re·ces·sion (rĭ-sĕsh′ən) *n.* **1.** The act of withdrawing or going back. **2.** The filing out of clergy and choir members after a church service. **3.** A moderate and temporary decline in economic activity. [Lat. *recessio* < *recessus,* recess.]

re-ces·sion (rē-sĕsh′ən) *n.* The act of restoring possession to a former owner.

re·ces·sion·al (rĭ-sĕsh′ə-nəl) *adj.* Of or pertaining to recession. *—n.* **1.** A hymn that accompanies the exit of the clergy and choir after a service. **2.** A recession from a church.

re·ces·sive (rĭ-sĕs′ĭv) *adj.* **1.** Tending to go backward or recede. **2.** *Genetics.* Of, pertaining to, or designating an allele that does not produce a phenotypic effect when heterozygous with a dominant allele. *—n.* *Genetics.* **1.** A recessive allele or trait. **2.** An organism having a recessive trait. **—re·ces′sive·ly** *adv.*

re·charge (rē-chärj′) *tr.v.* **-charged, -charg·ing, -charg·es.** To charge again, esp. to re-energize a storage battery. **—re′charge′** *n.* **—re·charge′a·ble** *adj.* **—re·charg′er** *n.*

ré·chauf·fé (rā′shō-fā′) *n.* **1.** Warmed leftover food. **2.** Old material reworked or rehashed. [Fr. < *réchauffer,* to reheat : *re-,* again (< Lat.) + *chauffer,* to warm < OFr. —see CHAFE.]

re·cher·ché (rə-shĕr′shā′) *adj.* **1.** Uncommon; rare. **2.** Exquisite or choice. **3.** Overrefined; forced. **4.** Pretentious; overblown. [Fr. < *rechercher,* to research < OFr. *recercher.* —see RESEARCH.]

re·cid·i·vism (rĭ-sĭd′ə-vĭz′əm) *n.* A tendency to relapse into a former pattern of behavior, esp. a tendency to return to criminal habits. [< Fr. *récidiviste,* recidivist < *récidiver,* to relapse < Med. Lat. *recidivare* < Lat. *recidivus,* returning < *recidere,* to fall back : *re-,* back + *cadere,* to fall.] **—re·cid′i·vist** *n.* **—re·cid′i·vis′tic, re·cid′i·vous** *adj.*

rec·i·pe (rĕs′ə-pē′) *n.* **1.** A set of directions with a list of ingredients for making or preparing something, esp. food. **2.** A medical prescription. **3.** A formula for or means to a desired end: *a recipe for success.* [Lat., imper. of *recipere,* to take, receive. —see RECEIVE.]

re·cip·i·ence (rĭ-sĭp′ē-əns) also **re·cip·i·en·cy** (-ən-sē) *n.* The capacity to receive; receptivity.

re·cip·i·ent (rĭ-sĭp′ē-ənt) *adj.* Functioning as a receiver; receptive. *—n.* One that receives or is receptive. [Lat. *recipiens, recipient-* pr.part. of *recipere,* to receive.]

re·cip·ro·cal (rĭ-sĭp′rə-kəl) *adj.* **1.** Concerning each of two or more persons or things. **2.** Interchanged, given, or owed mutually: *reciprocal funds.* **3.** Performed, experienced, or felt by both sides: *reciprocal respect.* **4.** Interchangeable; complementary. **5.** *Gram.* Expressing mutual action or relationship. Used of some verbs and compound pronouns. **6.** *Math.* Of or pertaining to a quantity divided into 1. *—n.* **1.** Something that is reciprocal to something else. **2.** *Math.* The quotient of a specific quantity divided into 1. For example, the reciprocal of 7 is $^1/_7$; the reciprocal of $^2/_3$ is $^3/_2$. —See Usage note at **mutual.** [Lat. *reciprocus,* alternating.] **—re·cip′ro·cal′i·ty** (-kăl′ĭ-tē), **re·cip′ro·cal·ness** *n.* **—re·cip′ro·cal·ly** *adv.*

reciprocal pronoun *n.* *Gram.* A pronoun or pronominal phrase expressing mutual action or relationship.

re·cip·ro·cate (rĭ-sĭp′rə-kāt′) *v.* **-cat·ed, -cat·ing, -cates.** *—tr.* **1.** To give or take mutually; interchange. **2.** To show or feel in response or return. *—intr.* **1.** To move back and forth alternately. **2.** To give and take something mutually. **3.** To make a return for something given or done. **4.** To be complementary or equivalent. [Lat. *reciprocare, reciprocat-,* to move back and forth < *reciprocus,* alternating.] **—re·cip′ro·ca′tive** *adj.* **—re·cip′ro·ca′tor** *n.*

reciprocating engine *n.* An engine having a crankshaft turned by linearly reciprocating pistons.

re·cip·ro·ca·tion (rĭ-sĭp′rə-kā′shən) *n.* **1.** An alternating back-and-forth movement. **2.** The act or fact of reciprocating; interchange.

rec·i·proc·i·ty (rĕs′ə-prŏs′ĭ-tē) *n., pl.* **-ties. 1.** A reciprocal condition or relationship. **2.** A mutual or cooperative interchange of favors or privileges, esp. the exchange of rights or privileges of trade between nations.

re·ci·sion (rĭ-sĭzh′ən) *n.* The act of rescinding; annulment or cancellation. [OFr. < Lat. *recidere,* to cut away : *re-,* back + *caedere,* to cut.]

re·cit·al (rĭ-sīt′l) *n.* **1.** The act of reading or reciting in a public performance. **2.** A very detailed account or report of something; narration. **3.** A performance of music or dance, esp. by a solo performer.

rec·i·ta·tion (rĕs′ĭ-tā′shən) *n.* **1.** The act of reciting memorized materials in a public performance. **2. a.** The oral delivery of prepared lessons by a pupil. **b.** The class period within which this recitation occurs. **3.** The material presented in a recitation.

rec·i·ta·tive[1] (rĕs′ĭ-tā′tĭv, rĭ-sī′tə-tĭv) *adj.* Of, pertaining to, or having the character of a recital or recitation.

rec·i·ta·tive[2] (rĕs′ĭ-tə-tēv′) *n.* **1.** A musical style used in opera and oratorio in which the text is declaimed in the rhythm of natural speech with slight melodic variation. **2.** A passage rendered in recitative. [Ital. *recitativo* < Lat. *recitare,* to recite.]

re·ci·ta·ti·vo (rĕs′ĭ-tə-tē′vō, rä′chē-tä-) *n., pl.* **-vi** (-vē) or **-vos** (-vōz). A recitative[2]. [Ital.]

re·cite (rĭ-sīt′) *v.* **-cit·ed, -cit·ing, -cites.** *—tr.* **1.** To repeat or utter aloud something rehearsed or memorized, esp. to do so before an audience. **2.** To relate in detail. **3.** To list or enumerate. *—intr.* **1.** To deliver a recitation. **2.** To repeat lessons prepared or memorized. [ME *reciten* < OFr. *reciter* < Lat. *recitare,* to read out : *re-* (intensive) + *citare,* to quote < *ciēre,* to call.] **—re·cit′er** *n.*

reck (rĕk) *tr. & intr.v.* **recked, reck·ing, recks.** To take heed of or to have caution. [ME *recken* < OE *reccan.*]

reck·less (rĕk′lĭs) *adj.* **1. a.** Heedless or careless. **b.** Headstrong; rash. **2.** Having no regard for consequences; wild: *a reckless driver.* [ME *reckeles* < OE *rēceléas.*] **—reck′less·ly** *adv.* **—reck′less·ness** *n.*

Synonyms: *reckless, adventurous, rash, precipitate, foolhardy, audacious, daring, venturous, venturesome. Reckless* suggests heedlessness or thoughtlessness in action or decision. *Adventurous* implies willingness to incur risk and danger, but usually not mindlessly. *Rash* and *precipitate* connote haste and lack of deliberation in deed or decision. *Foolhardy* implies absence of sound judgment. *Audacious* and *daring* suggest fearlessness and confidence. *Venturous* and *venturesome* imply inclination to take risk that is recognized as such.

reck·on (rĕk′ən) *v.* **-oned, -on·ing, -ons.** *—tr.* **1.** To count or compute: *reckon the cost.* **2.** To consider as being; regard as. **3.** *Informal.* To think or assume. *—intr.* **1.** To make a calculation; figure. **2.** To depend: *reckon on financial aid.*

—*idiom.* **reckon with.** To come to terms or settle accounts with. [ME *reknen* < OE *gerecenian,* to explain.]
reck·on·er (rĕk′ə-nər) *n.* **1.** One that reckons. **2.** A handbook of mathematical tables to facilitate computation.
reck·on·ing (rĕk′ə-nĭng) *n.* **1.** The act of counting. **2.** An itemized bill or statement of a sum due. **3.** A settlement of accounts: *a day of reckoning.* **4. a.** The act or process of calculating the position of a ship or aircraft. **b.** The position so calculated.
re·claim (rĭ-klām′) *tr.v.* **-claimed, -claim·ing, -claims. 1.** To make suitable for cultivation or habitation, as by filling, irrigating, or fertilizing: *reclaim marshlands.* **2.** To procure (usable substances) from refuse or waste products. **3.** To turn from error, evil, or barbarism; reform. **4.** To tame (a falcon, for example). [ME *reclamen,* to call back < OFr. *reclamer,* to entreat < Lat. *reclamare* : *re-,* against + *clamare,* call out.] **—re·claim′a·ble** *adj.* **—re·claim′ant, re·claim′er** *n.*
re-claim (rē-klām′) *tr.v.* **-claimed, -claim·ing, -claims.** To demand the restoration or return of; claim again or back.
rec·la·ma·tion (rĕk′lə-mā′shən) *n.* **1.** The act or process of reclaiming. **2.** A restoration, as to productivity, usefulness, or morality. [OFr. < Lat. *reclamatio,* cry of opposition < *reclamare,* to exclaim against. —see RECLAIM.]
ré·clame (rā-kläm′) *n.* **1.** Public acclaim. **2.** A taste or flair for publicity. [Fr., advertising < *réclamer,* to claim < OFr. *reclamer,* to exclaim against. —see RECLAIM.]
rec·li·nate (rĕk′lə-nāt′) *adj. Bot.* Bent or turned downward toward the base. [Lat. *reclinatus,* p.part. of *reclinare,* to recline.]
re·cline (rĭ-klīn′) *v.* **-clined, -clin·ing, -clines.** —*tr.* To cause to assume a leaning or prone position. —*intr.* To lie back or down. [ME *reclinen* < OFr. *recliner* < Lat. *reclinare* : *re-,* back + *clinare,* to bend.] **—rec′li·na′tion** (rĕk′lə-nā′shən) *n.* **—re·clin′er** *n.*
re·cluse (rĕk′lo͞os′, rĭ-klo͞os′) *n.* A person who withdraws from the world to live in solitude and seclusion. —*adj.* Withdrawn from the world; solitary. [ME < OFr. *reclus* < Lat. *reclusus,* p.part. of *recludere,* to close up : *re-* (intensive) + *claudere,* to close.]
re·clu·sion (rĭ-klo͞o′zhən) *n.* **1.** The condition of being a recluse. **2.** The state of being in solitary confinement.
re·clu·sive (rĭ-klo͞o′sĭv, -zĭv) *adj.* **1.** Seeking or preferring seclusion or isolation. **2.** Providing seclusion: *a reclusive hut.*
rec·og·ni·tion (rĕk′əg-nĭsh′ən) *n.* **1.** The act of recognizing or condition of being recognized. **2.** An awareness that something perceived has been perceived before. **3.** An acknowledgment, as of a claim: *a recognition of their civil rights.* **4.** Attention or favorable notice: *recognition for his many achievements.* **5.** An acknowledgment or acceptance of the national status of a new government by another nation. [Lat. *recognitio* < *recognoscere,* to recognize.] **—re·cog′ni·to′ry** (rĭ-kŏg′nə-tôr′ē, -tōr′ē), **re·cog′ni·tive** *adj.*
re·cog·ni·zance (rĭ-kŏg′nĭ-zəns, -kŏn′ĭ-) *n.* **1.** *Law.* **a.** An obligation of record entered into before a court or magistrate with the condition to perform a particular act, as to appear in court. **b.** A sum of money pledged to assure the performance of such an act. **2.** A recognition. **3.** *Archaic.* A pledge; token. [ME < OFr. *reconoissance* < *reconoistre,* to recognize.] **—re·cog′ni·zant** *adj.*
rec·og·nize (rĕk′əg-nīz′) *tr.v.* **-nized, -niz·ing, -niz·es. 1.** To know to be something that has been perceived before: *recognize a face.* **2.** To know or identify from past experience or knowledge: *recognize hostility.* **3.** To perceive or acknowledge the validity or reality of: *recognize a demand.* **4.** To acknowledge as a speaker. **5.** To acknowledge or accept the national status of as a new government. **6.** To acknowledge, approve of, or appreciate: *recognize services rendered.* **7.** To admit the acquaintance of, as by salutation: *recognize an old friend with a cheerful greeting.* **8.** *Law.* To enter into a recognizance. [OFr. *reconoistre, reconoiss-* < Lat. *recognoscere* : *re-,* again + *cognoscere,* to know.] **—rec′og·niz′a·ble** *adj.* **—rec′og·niz′a·bly** *adv.* **—rec′og·niz′er** *n.*
re·coil (rĭ-koil′) *intr.v.* **-coiled, -coil·ing, -coils. 1.** To kick or spring back, as upon firing. **2.** To shrink back in fear or repugnance. **3.** To fall back; return. —*n.* (*also* rē′koil′). **1.** The backward action or kick of a firearm upon firing. **2.** The act or state of recoiling; reaction. [ME *recoilen* < OFr. *reculer* : *re-,* back (< Lat.) + *cul,* buttocks < Lat. *culus.*] **—re·coil′er** *n.*

Synonyms: *recoil, blench, cower, quail, shrink, cringe, flinch. Recoil* implies instinctive, involuntary drawing back, as from something dangerous or repulsive. *Blench* applies to the act of shying back or turning away. *Cower, quail,* and *shrink* imply fear or despair, involving avoidance of that which is difficult by shying away, sinking downward, or huddling. *Cringe* suggests crouching or slinking resulting from cowardice or servility: *He cringed before the bully. Flinch* connotes instinctive drawing back from something painful: *He flinched from the blow.*

rec·ol·lect (rĕk′ə-lĕkt′) *v.* **-lect·ed, -lect·ing, -lects.** —*tr.* To recall to mind. —*intr.* To have a recollection. [Med. Lat. *recolligere, recollect-* < Lat., to gather up : *re-,* again + *colligere,* to collect. —see COLLECT.] **—rec′ol·lec′tive** *adj.* **—rec′ol·lec′tive·ly** *adv.*
re-col·lect (rē′kə-lĕkt′) *tr.v.* **-lect·ed, -lect·ing, -lects. 1.** To collect again. **2.** To calm or control (oneself). **—re′-col·lec′tion** *n.*
rec·ol·lec·tion (rĕk′ə-lĕk′shən) *n.* **1.** The act or power of recollecting. **2.** Something recollected.
re·com·bi·nant (rē-kŏm′bə-nənt) *n.* An organism in which genetic recombination has taken place. **—re·com′bi·nant** *adj.*
recombinant DNA *n.* DNA prepared through laboratory manipulation in which genes from one species of an organism are transplanted or spliced to another organism.
re·com·bi·na·tion (rē′kŏm-bə-nā′shən) *n.* The formation in offspring of genetic combinations not present in parents.
rec·om·mend (rĕk′ə-mĕnd′) *tr.v.* **-mend·ed, -mend·ing, -mends. 1.** To praise or commend to another as being worthy or desirable; endorse: *recommended him for the job.* **2.** To make attractive or acceptable: *Honesty recommends any person.* **3.** To commit to the charge of another; entrust. **4.** To counsel or advise (that something be done). [ME *recommenden* < Med. Lat. *recommendare* : Lat. *re-* (intensive) + Lat. *commendare,* to entrust (*com-,* together + *mandare,* to order).] **—rec′om·mend′a·ble** *adj.* **—rec′om·mend′er** *n.*
rec·om·men·da·tion (rĕk′ə-mĕn-dā′shən) *n.* **1.** The act of recommending. **2.** Something that recommends, esp. a favorable statement concerning the character or qualifications of someone. **—rec′om·men′da·to′ry** (-də-tôr′ē, -tōr′ē) *adj.*
re·com·mit (rē′kə-mĭt′) *tr.v.* **-mit·ted, -mit·ting, -mits. 1.** To commit again. **2.** To refer (proposed legislation, for example) to a committee again. **—re′com·mit′ment, re′com·mit′tal** (-mĭt′l) *n.*
rec·om·pense (rĕk′əm-pĕns′) *tr.v.* **-pensed, -pens·ing, -pens·es. 1.** To award compensation to. **2.** To award compensation for; make a return for. —*n.* **1.** Amends made for something, as damage or loss. **2.** Payment in return for something given or done, as services. [ME *recompensen* < OFr. *recompenser* < LLat. *recompensare* : Lat. *re-,* back + Lat. *compensare,* to compensate. —see COMPENSATE.]
re·com·pose (rē′kəm-pōz′) *tr.v.* **-posed, -pos·ing, -pos·es. 1.** To compose again; reorganize or rearrange. **2.** To restore to composure; calm. **—re′com·po·si′tion** (rē′kŏm-pə-zĭsh′ən) *n.*
re·con (rē′kŏn′) *n.* The smallest genetic unit that is capable of recombination. [REC(OMBINATION) + -ON¹.]
rec·on·cil·a·ble (rĕk′ən-sī′lə-bəl, rĕk′ən-sī′-) *adj.* Capable of or qualified for reconciliation. **—rec′on·cil′a·bil′i·ty, rec′on·cil′a·ble·ness** *n.* **—rec′on·cil′a·bly** *adv.*
rec·on·cile (rĕk′ən-sīl′) *tr.v.* **-ciled, -cil·ing, -ciles. 1.** To reestablish friendship between. **2.** To settle or resolve, as a dispute. **3.** To bring (oneself) to accept. **4.** To make compatible or consistent: *reconcile my way of thinking with yours.* [ME *reconcilen* < OFr. *reconcilier* < Lat. *reconciliare* : *re-,* back + *conciliare,* to conciliate < *concilium,* meeting.] **—rec′on·cile′ment, rec′on·cil′i·a′tion** (-sĭl′ē-ā′shən) *n.* **—rec′on·cil′er** *n.* **—rec′on·cil′i·a·to′ry** (-sĭl′ē-ə-tôr′ē, -tōr′ē) *adj.*
rec·on·dite (rĕk′ən-dīt′, rĭ-kŏn′dīt′) *adj.* **1.** Not easily understood; abstruse. **2.** Concerned with or treating something abstruse or obscure: *recondite scholarship.* **3.** Concealed; hidden. [Lat. *reconditus,* p.part. of *recondere,* to put away : *re-,* back + *condere,* to hide (*com-,* together + *dare,* to give).] **—rec′on·dite′ly** *adv.* **—rec′on·dite′ness** *n.*
re·con·di·tion (rē′kən-dĭsh′ən) *tr.v.* **-tioned, -tion·ing, -tions.** To restore by repairing, renovating, or rebuilding.
re·con·firm (rē′kən-fûrm′) *tr.v.* **-firmed, -firm·ing, -firms.** To confirm again, esp. to establish or support more firmly. **—re′con·fir·ma′tion** (rē′kŏn-fər-mā′shən) *n.*
re·con·nais·sance also **re·con·nois·sance** (rĭ-kŏn′ə-səns, -zəns) *n.* An inspection or exploration of an area, esp. one made to gather military information. [Fr. < OFr. *reconoissance* < *reconnoistre,* to recognize < Lat. *recognoscere.* —see RECOGNIZE.]
re·con·noi·ter (rē′kə-noi′tər, rĕk′ə-) *v.* **-tered, -ter·ing, -ters.** —*tr.* To make a preliminary inspection of. —*intr.* To make a reconnaissance. [Obs. Fr. *reconnoître* < OFr. *reconoistre,* to recognize. —see RECONNAISSANCE.] **—re′con·noi′ter·er** *n.*
re·con·sid·er (rē′kən-sĭd′ər) *v.* **-ered, -er·ing, -ers.** —*tr.* **1.** To consider again, esp. with intent to alter or modify a previous decision. **2.** To take up for reconsideration, as a matter previously acted on by a legislature. —*intr.* To consider again. **—re′con·sid′er·a′tion** *n.*
re·con·struct (rē′kən-strŭkt′) *tr.v.* **-struct·ed, -struct·ing, -structs.** To construct again.
re·con·struc·tion (rē′kən-strŭk′shən) *n.* **1.** The act or result of reconstructing. **2. Reconstruction.** The period (1865–77) during which the states of the Southern Confederacy were controlled by the Federal government before being readmitted to the Union. **—re′con·struc′tive** *adj.*
re·con·vert (rē′kən-vûrt′) *v.* **-vert·ed, -vert·ing, -verts.** —*tr.* To cause to undergo conversion to a previous state or condition. —*intr.* To undergo conversion to a previous state or condition. **—re′con·ver′sion** (-vûr′zhən, -shən) *n.*
re·con·vey (rē′kən-vā′) *tr.v.* **-veyed, -vey·ing, -veys.** To convey back to a former owner or place. **—re′con·vey′ance** *n.*
re·cord (rĭ-kôrd′) *v.* **-cord·ed, -cord·ing, -cords.** —*tr.* **1.** To set down for preservation in writing or other permanent form. **2.** To register or indicate: *The clerk recorded the votes.* **3.** To register (sound) in permanent form by mechanical or

electrical means for reproduction. —*intr.* To record something. —*n.* **rec·ord** (rĕk′ərd). **1. a.** An account, as of information or facts, set down esp. in writing as a means of preserving knowledge. **b.** Something on which such an account is made. **c.** Something that records: *a fossil record.* **2.** Information or data on a particular subject collected and preserved: *the coldest day on record.* **3.** The known history of performance or achievement: *your high-school record.* **4.** The best performance known, as in a sport: *the world record in weightlifting.* **5.** *Law.* **a.** An account officially written and preserved as evidence or testimony. **b.** An account of judicial or legislative proceedings written and preserved as evidence. **c.** The documents or volumes containing such evidence. **6. a.** A disk designed to be played on a phonograph. **b.** Something, as magnetic tape, on which sound or visual images have been recorded. —***idioms.*** **off the record.** Not for publication: *told me that his remarks were strictly off the record.* **on record.** Known to have stated or taken a certain position: *wanted to go on record as opposing the new legislation.* [ME *recorden* < OFr. *recorder* < Lat. *recordari,* to remember : *re-,* again + *cor,* heart.]

re·cord·er (rĭ-kôr′dər) *n.* **1.** One that records, as a tape recorder. **2.** A judge who has criminal jurisdiction in a city. **3.** A flute with eight finger holes and a whistlelike mouthpiece.

re·cord·ing (rĭ-kôr′dĭng) *n.* **1.** Something on which sound or visual images have been recorded. **2.** A recorded sound or picture.

re·count (rĭ-kount′) *tr.v.* **-count·ed, -count·ing, -counts. 1.** To narrate the facts or particulars of. **2.** To enumerate. [ME *recounten* < OFr. *reconter* : *re-,* again + *conter,* relate. —see COUNT[1].] **—re·count′al** *n.*

re-count (rē-kount′) *tr.v.* **-count·ed, -count·ing, -counts.** To count again. —*n.* (*also* rē′kount′). An additional count, esp. a second count of votes cast in an election.

re·coup (rĭ-ko͞op′) *v.* **-couped, -coup·ing, -coups.** —*tr.* **1.** To receive an equivalent for; make up for: *recoup a loss.* **2.** To return as an equivalent for; reimburse. **3.** *Law.* To deduct or withhold (part of something due) for an equitable reason. —*intr.* To regain a former favorable position. —*n.* The act of recouping. [ME *recoupen* < OFr. *recouper,* to cut back : *re-,* back (< Lat.) + *couper,* to cut < *coup,* blow. —see COUP.] **—re·coup′a·ble** *adj.* **—re·coup′ment** *n.*

re·course (rē′kôrs′, -kōrs′, rĭ-kôrs′, -kōrs′) *n.* **1.** The act or instance of turning or applying to a person or thing for aid or security: *have recourse to the courts.* **2.** One that is turned or applied to for aid or security: *His only recourse was the police.* **3.** *Law.* The right to demand payment from the endorser of a commercial paper when the first party liable fails to pay. [ME *recours* < OFr. < Lat. *recursus,* a running back < *recurrere,* to run back : *re-,* back + *currere,* to run.]

re·cov·er (rĭ-kŭv′ər) *v.* **-ered, -er·ing, -ers.** —*tr.* **1.** To get back; regain. **2.** To restore (oneself) to a normal state. **3.** To compensate for. —*intr.* **1.** To regain a normal or usual condition, as of health. **2.** To receive a favorable judgment in a lawsuit. [ME *recoveren* < OFr. *recoverer* < Lat. *recuperare.* —see RECUPERATE.] **—re·cov′er·a·ble** *adj.* **—re·cov′er·er** *n.*

Synonyms: *recover, reclaim, regain, recoup, retrieve. Recover* refers to the getting back of something lost. *Reclaim* applies both to the act of demanding the return of something and to the restoration of a thing to good condition. *Regain* suggests effort in getting back something lost or taken from one, usually a quality or status rather than an object. *Recoup* means getting back the equivalent of something lost or damaged. *Retrieve* pertains either to the physical recovery of a thing or to the repair or remedy of the consequences of an act.

re-cov·er (rē-kŭv′ər) *tr.v.* **-ered, -er·ing, -ers.** To cover anew.

re·cov·er·y (rĭ-kŭv′ə-rē) *n., pl.* **-ies. 1.** An act, instance, process, or duration of recovering. **2.** A return to a normal condition. **3.** Something gained or restored in recovering. **4.** The act of obtaining usable substances from unusable sources, as waste material.

recovery room *n.* A hospital room equipped for the care and observation of patients immediately following surgery.

rec·re·ant (rĕk′rē-ənt) *adj.* **1.** Unfaithful or disloyal to a belief, duty, or cause. **2.** Craven or cowardly. —*n.* **1.** A faithless or disloyal person. **2.** A coward. [ME < OFr., pr.part. of *recroire,* to remember < Med. Lat. *recredere* : Lat. *re-,* back + Lat. *credere,* to entrust.] **—rec′re·ance, rec′re·an·cy** *n.* **—rec′re·ant·ly** *adv.*

rec·re·ate (rĕk′rē-āt′) *v.* **-at·ed, -at·ing, -ates.** —*tr.* To impart fresh life to; refresh mentally or physically. —*intr.* To take recreation. [Lat. *recreare, recreat-* : *re-,* anew + *creare,* to create.] **—rec′re·a′tive** *adj.*

re-cre·ate (rē′krē-āt′) *tr.v.* **-at·ed, -at·ing, -ates.** To create anew.

rec·re·a·tion (rĕk′rē-ā′shən) *n.* Refreshment of one's mind or body after work through some activity that amuses or stimulates; play. **—rec′re·a′tion·al** *adj.*

recreational vehicle *n.* A vehicle, as a camper or a motor home, used for traveling and recreational activities.

rec·re·ment (rĕk′rə-mənt) *n.* Waste matter; dross. [Lat. *recrementum* : *re-,* back + *cernere,* to separate.] **—rec′re·men′tal** (-mĕn′tl) *adj.*

re·crim·i·nate (rĭ-krĭm′ə-nāt′) *v.* **-nat·ed, -nat·ing, -nates.** —*tr.* To accuse in return. —*intr.* To counter one accusation with another. [Med. Lat. *recriminare, recriminat-* : Lat. *re-,* against + *criminare,* to accuse < *crimen,* accusation.] **—re·crim′i·na′tive, re·crim′i·na·to′ry** (-nə-tôr′ē, -tōr′ē) *adj.* **—re·crim′i·na′tor** *n.*

re·crim·i·na·tion (rĭ-krĭm′ə-nā′shən) *n.* **1.** The act of recriminating. **2.** A countercharge.

re·cru·desce (rē′kro͞o-dĕs′) *intr.v.* **-desced, -desc·ing, -desc·es.** To break out anew after a dormant or inactive period. [Lat. *recrudescere,* to grow raw again : *re-,* again + *crudescere,* to get worse < *crudus,* raw.] **—re′cru·des′cence** *n.* **—re′cru·des′cent** *adj.*

re·cruit (rĭ-kro͞ot′) *v.* **-cruit·ed, -cruit·ing, -cruits.** —*tr.* **1.** To engage (persons) for military service. **2.** To strengthen or raise (an armed force) by enlistment. **3.** To supply with new members or employees. **4.** To enroll or seek to enroll: *colleges recruiting minority students.* **5.** To replenish. **6.** To renew or restore the health, vitality, or intensity of. —*intr.* **1.** To raise a military force. **2.** To obtain replacements for or new supplies of something lost, wasted, or needed. **3.** To regain lost health or strength; recover. —*n.* **1.** A newly engaged member of a military force, esp. one of the lowest rank or grade. **2.** A new member of an organization or body. [Fr. *recruter* < obs. *recrute,* recruit < OFr. *recroistre,* to grow again < Lat. *recrescere* : *re-,* again + *crescere,* to grow.] **—re·cruit′er** *n.* **—re·cruit′ment** *n.*

recorder

rec·ta (rĕk′tə) *n.* A plural of **rectum.**

rec·tal (rĕk′təl) *adj.* Of, pertaining to, or near the rectum.

rec·tan·gle (rĕk′tăng′gəl) *n.* A parallelogram with a right angle. [Med. Lat. *rectangulum* : Lat. *rectus,* right + Lat. *angulus,* angle.]

rec·tan·gu·lar (rĕk-tăng′gyə-lər) *adj.* **1.** Having the shape of a rectangle. **2.** Having right angles. **3.** Designating a geometric coordinate system with mutually perpendicular axes. **—rec·tan′gu·lar′i·ty** (-lăr′ĭ-tē) *n.* **—rec·tan′gu·lar·ly** *adv.*

rectangular coordinate *n. Math.* A coordinate in a rectangular Cartesian coordinate system.

rec·ti (rĕk′tī′) *n.* Plural of **rectus.**

rec·ti·fi·er (rĕk′tə-fī′ər) *n.* **1.** One that rectifies. **2.** *Elect.* A device, as a diode, that converts alternating current to direct current. **3.** A worker who blends or dilutes whiskey or other alcoholic beverages.

rec·ti·fy (rĕk′tə-fī′) *tr.v.* **-fied, -fy·ing, -fies. 1.** To set right; correct. **2.** To correct by calculation or adjustment. **3.** *Chem.* To refine or purify, esp. by distillation. **4.** *Elect.* To convert (alternating current) into direct current. **5.** To adjust (the proof of alcoholic beverages) by adding water or other liquids. [ME *rectifien* < OFr. *rectifier* < Med. Lat. *rectificare* : *rectus,* right + *facere,* to make.] **—rec′ti·fi′a·ble** *adj.* **—rec′ti·fi·ca′tion** (-fə-kā′shən) *n.*

rec·ti·lin·e·ar (rĕk′tə-lĭn′ē-ər) *adj.* Moving in, consisting of, bounded by, or characterized by a straight line or lines. [LLat. *rectilineus* : Lat. *rectus,* right + Lat. *linea,* line.] **—rec′ti·lin′e·ar·ly** *adv.*

rec·ti·tude (rĕk′tĭ-to͞od′, -tyo͞od′) *n.* **1.** Moral uprightness; righteousness. **2.** The quality or condition of being correct in intellectual judgment. **3.** Straightness. [ME < OFr. < LLat. *rectitudo* < Lat. *rectus,* straight.]

rec·to (rĕk′tō) *n., pl.* **-tos.** The right-hand page of a book or the front side of a leaf, as opposed to the verso. [Lat. *recto* (*folio*), (the page) being right.]

rec·tor (rĕk′tər) *n.* **1.** A clergyman in charge of a parish in the Protestant Episcopal Church. **2.** An Anglican clergyman who has charge of a parish and owns the tithes from it. **3.** A Roman Catholic priest appointed to be managerial as well as spiritual head of a church or other institution such as a seminary or university. **4.** The principal of certain schools, colleges, and universities. [Lat., director < *regere,* to rule.] **—rec′tor·ate** (-ĭt) *n.* **—rec·to′ri·al** (rĕk-tôr′ē-əl, -tōr′-) *adj.*

rec·to·ry (rĕk′tə-rē) *n., pl.* **1.** The house in which a parish priest or minister lives. **2. a.** An Anglican rector's dwelling. **b.** An Anglican rector's office and benefice.

rec·trix (rĕk′trĭks) *n., pl.* **rec·tri·ces** (rĕk′trə-sēz′, rĕk-trī′sēz). One of the stiff main feathers of a bird's tail. [NLat. < Lat., fem. of *rector,* director < *regere,* to rule.]

rec·tum (rĕk′təm) *n., pl.* **-tums** or **-ta** (-tə). The portion of the large intestine extending from the sigmoid flexure to the anal canal. [NLat. *rectum* (*intestinum*), straight (intestine).]

rec·tus (rĕk′təs) *n., pl.* **-ti** (-tī′). Any of various straight muscles, as of the abdomen, eye, neck, and thigh. [NLat. < Lat., straight.]

re·cum·bent (rĭ-kŭm′bənt) *adj.* **1.** Lying down; reclining: *a recumbent statue of Aphrodite.* **2.** Resting; idle. **3.** *Biol.* Resting upon the surface from which it arises: *a recumbent organ.* [Lat. *recumbens,* pr.part. of *recumbere,* to lie down : *re-,* back + *cumbere,* to lie.] **—re·cum′bence, re·cum′ben·cy** *n.* **—re·cum′bent·ly** *adv.*

re·cu·per·ate (rĭ-ko͞o′pə-rāt′, -kyo͞o′-) *v.* **-at·ed, -at·ing, -ates.** —*intr.* **1.** To return to health or strength; recover. **2.** To recover from financial loss. —*tr.* **1.** To restore to health or strength. **2.** To regain. [Lat. *recuperare, recuperat-* : *re-,* back + *capere,* to take.] **—re·cu′per·a′tion** *n.* **—re·cu′per·a′tive** (-pə-rā′tĭv, -pər-ə-tĭv, -kyo͞o′-), **re·cu′per·a·to′ry** (-pər-ə-tôr′ē, -tōr′ē) *adj.*

re·cur (rĭ-kûr′) *intr.v.* **-curred, -cur·ring, -curs. 1.** To happen or come up again or repeatedly. **2.** To return to one's atten-

tion or memory. **3.** To return in thought or discourse. **4.** To have recourse: *recur to the use of force.* [Lat. *recurrere* : *re-*, back + *currere,* to run.] **—re·cur'rence** *n.*
re·cur·rent (rĭ-kûr'ənt, -kŭr'-) *adj.* **1.** Occurring or appearing again or repeatedly. **2.** *Anat.* Running in a reverse direction. Used of arteries and nerves. **—re·cur'rent·ly** *adv.*
recurrent fever *n.* Relapsing fever.
recurring decimal *n. Math.* A repeating decimal.
re·cur·sion (rĭ-kûr'zhən) *n.* **1.** A mathematical expression, as a polynomial, each term of which is determined by application of a formula to preceding terms. **2.** A formula that generates the successive terms of a recursion. [LLat. *recursio,* a running back < Lat. *recurrere,* to run back, recur.] **—re·cur'sive** *adj.*
re·cur·vate (rĭ-kûr'vāt', -vĭt) *adj.* Bent or curved backward. [Lat. *recurvatus,* p.part. of *recurvare,* to recurve.]
re·curve (rē-kûrv') *tr. & intr.v.* **-curved, -curv·ing, -curves.** To curve backward or downward or to become curved backward or downward. [Lat. *recurvare* : Lat. *re-*, back + *curvare,* to curve.] **—re'cur·va'tion** (rē'kûr-vā'shən) *n.*
rec·u·sant (rĕk'yə-zənt, rĭ-kyōō'-) *n.* **1.** A Roman Catholic who refused to attend the services of the Church of England between the reigns of Henry VIII and George II. **2.** A dissenter; nonconformist. [Lat. *recusans,* pr.part. *recusare,* to refuse : *re-*, against + *causa,* cause.] **—rec'u·san·cy** *n.* **—rec'u·sant** *adj.*
re·cy·cle (rē-sī'kəl) *tr.v.* **-cled, -cling, -cles. 1.** To put or pass through a cycle again, as for further treatment. **2.** To start a different cycle in. **3. a.** To extract useful materials from (garbage or waste). **b.** To extract and reuse (useful substances found in waste). **4. a.** To use again, esp. to reprocess in order to use again: *recycle aluminum cans.* **b.** To recondition and adapt to a new use or function: *recycling old warehouses into condominiums.*
red (rĕd) *n.* **1.** Any of a group of colors that may vary in lightness and saturation and whose hue resembles that of blood; the hue of the long-wave end of the spectrum; one of the additive or light primaries; one of the psychological primary hues, evoked in the normal observer by the long-wave end of the spectrum. **2.** A pigment or dye having a red hue. **3.** Something that has a red hue. **4. a.** Often **Red.** A Communist. **b.** A revolutionary activist. ***—modifier:*** *red propaganda; a red government. —adj.* **red·der, red·dest. 1.** Having a color resembling that of blood. **2.** Reddish in color or having parts that are reddish in color: *a red dog; a red oak.* **3.** Having a coppery skin tone. **4.** Having a ruddy or flushed complexion: *red with embarrassment.* ***—idioms.*** **in the red.** Operating at a loss; in debt. **see red.** To be or become furious. [ME < OE *rēad.*] **—red'ly** *adv.* **—red'ness** *n.*
re·dact (rĭ-dăkt') *tr.v.* **-dact·ed, -dact·ing, -dacts. 1.** To draw up or frame (a proclamation, for example). **2.** To make ready for publication; edit or revise. [Lat. *redigere, redact-*, to drive back : *re-*, *red-*, back + *agere,* to drive.] **—re·dac'tion** *n.* **—re·dac'tor** (-dăk'tər, -tôr') *n.*
red algae *n.* Any of the algae of the division Rhodophyta, characteristically red or reddish in color.
red·bait (rĕd'bāt') *tr.v.* **-bait·ed, -bait·ing, -baits.** To attack or denounce (a person or group) as Communist. **—red'bait'er** *n.* **—red'bait'ing** *n.*
red·bird (rĕd'bûrd') *n.* Any of various birds with red plumage, as the cardinal or scarlet tanager.
red blood cell *n.* An erythrocyte.
red-blood·ed (rĕd'blŭd'ĭd) *adj.* Strong or virile.
red·breast (rĕd'brĕst') *n.* **1.** A bird with a red breast, as the robin. **2.** A freshwater sunfish, *Lepomis auritus,* of eastern North America.
red·brick (rĕd'brĭk') *adj.* Of, pertaining to, or being the British universities other than Oxford and Cambridge. [So-called because many of the buildings of such universities were built of red bricks.]
red·bud (rĕd'bŭd') *n.* Any of several shrubs or small trees of the genus *Cercis,* having pinkish flowers that bloom before the leaves appear.
red·cap (rĕd'kăp') *n.* A porter, usually in a railroad station.
red carpet *n.* A carpet laid down for important visitors. ***—idiom.*** **roll out the red carpet.** To welcome with great hospitality or ceremony.
red cedar *n.* **1.** An evergreen tree, *Juniperus virginiana,* of eastern North America. **2.** A tall evergreen tree, *Thuja plicata,* of western North America. **3.** The reddish, aromatic, durable wood of the red cedar or similar trees.
red cent *n. Informal.* Something of insignificant value: *not worth a red cent.*
red clover *n.* A Eurasian plant, *Trifolium pratense,* widely naturalized in North America and frequently planted as a forage or cover crop, having leaflets in groups of three and globular heads of fragrant, rose-purple flowers.
red·coat (rĕd'kōt') *n.* A British soldier during the American Revolution and the War of 1812.
Red Cross *n.* **1.** An international organization, formed according to the terms of the Geneva Convention of 1864, for the care of the wounded, sick, and homeless in wartime and now also during and following natural disasters. **2.** A national branch of the Red Cross. **3.** The emblem of the Red Cross, a Geneva cross or a red Greek cross on a white background.

red clover

Red Cross
Emblem of the organization

redd (rĕd) *tr.v.* **redd·ed** or **redd, redd·ing, redds.** *Chiefly Regional.* To put in order: *redded up the room.* [ME *redden,* to clear, prob. alteration of *ridden,* to rid< ON *ryðja.*]
red deer *n.* A common European deer, *Cervus elaphus,* having a reddish-brown coat and many-branched antlers.
red·den (rĕd'n) *tr. & intr.v.* **-dened, -den·ing, -dens.** To make or become red.
red·dish (rĕd'ĭsh) *adj.* Mixed or tinged with red; somewhat red. **—red'dish·ness** *n.*
red·dle (rĕd'l) *n. & v.* Variant of **ruddle.**
red-dog (rĕd'dôg', -dŏg') *Football. —v.* **-dogged, -dog·ging, -dogs.** *—intr.* To charge across the line of scrimmage in an attempt to overwhelm the opposing quarterback before he can throw a forward pass. Used of linebackers and sometimes of defensive backs. *—tr.* To charge (the passer) in football. *—n.* The act or an instance of reddogging.
red drum *n.* A food fish, *Sciaenops ocellata,* of southern Atlantic coastal waters.
rede (rēd) *tr.v.* **red·ed, red·ing, redes.** *Regional.* **1.** To give advice to; counsel. **2.** To interpret; explain. *—n.* **1.** *Regional.* Advice or counsel. **2.** *Archaic.* A narration. [ME *reden* < OE *rǣdan.*]
re·dec·o·rate (rē-dĕk'ə-rāt') *v.* **-rat·ed, -rat·ing, -rates.** *—tr.* To change the appearance or décor of; refurbish. *—intr.* To change a decorative scheme. **—re·dec'o·ra'tion** *n.* **—re·dec'o·ra'tor** *n.*
re·deem (rĭ-dēm') *tr.v.* **-deemed, -deem·ing, -deems. 1.** To recover ownership of by paying a specified sum. **2.** To pay off, as a promissory note. **3.** To turn in (coupons, for example) and receive something in exchange. **4.** To fulfill (a pledge, for example). **5.** To convert into cash: *redeem stocks.* **6.** To set free; rescue or ransom. **7.** To save from a state of sinfulness and its consequences. **8.** To make up for. [ME *redemen* < Lat. *redimere* : *re-*, *red-*, back + *emere,* to buy.] **—re·deem'a·ble** *adj.*
re·deem·er (rĭ-dē'mər) *n.* **1.** One who redeems. **2. Redeemer.** Christ.
re·de·liv·er (rē'dĭ-lĭv'ər) *tr.v.* **-ered, -er·ing, -ers. 1.** To deliver again. **2.** To deliver in return; give back.
re·demp·tion (rĭ-dĕmp'shən) *n.* **1.** The act of redeeming or the condition of being redeemed. **2.** A recovery of something pawned or mortgaged. **3.** The payment of an obligation, as a government's payment of the value of its bonds. **4.** Deliverance upon payment of ransom; rescue. **5.** *Theol.* Salvation from sin through Christ's sacrifice. [ME *redempcioun* < OFr. *redemption* < Lat. *redemptio* < *redimere,* to redeem.] **—re·demp'tion·al, re·demp'tive, re·demp'to·ry** (-tə-rē) *adj.*
re·demp·tion·er (rĭ-dĕmp'shə-nər) *n.* A colonial emigrant from Europe to America who paid for his voyage by serving as a bondservant for a specified period.
Re·demp·tor·ist (rĭ-dĕmp'tər-ĭst) *n.* A member of the Congregation of the Most Holy Redeemer, a Roman Catholic order, founded by St. Alphonsus de Liguori in 1732.
re·de·ploy (rē'dĭ-ploi') *tr.v.* **-ployed, -ploy·ing, -ploys.** To move (military forces) from one combat zone to another. **—re'de·ploy'ment** *n.*
re·de·sign (rē'dĭ-zīn') *tr.v.* **-signed, -sign·ing, -signs.** To make a revision in the appearance or function of. **—re'de·sign'** *n.*
re·de·vel·op (rē'dĭ-vĕl'əp) *v.* **-oped, -op·ing, -ops.** *—tr.* **1.** To develop (something) again. **2.** To tone or intensify (a developed photographic negative) by a second developing process. **3.** To restore to a better condition: *redeveloping the waterfront. —intr.* To develop again. **—re'de·vel'op·er** *n.* **—re'de·vel'op·ment** *n.*
red·eye (rĕd'ī') *n.* **1.** *Informal.* A danger signal on a railroad. **2.** *Slang.* Whiskey of an inferior grade. **3.** Any of several red-eyed fishes, as the rock bass. **4.** *Slang.* A late-night or overnight flight: *caught the redeye to New York.*
redeye gravy *n.* Gravy made from the juices of a cooked ham.
red fir *n.* **1.** An evergreen tree, *Abies magnifica,* of California and Oregon, having reddish wood valued as timber. **2.** The wood of the red fir or similar trees.
red fire *n.* Any of various combustible compounds, esp. salts of lithium or strontium, that burn bright red and are used in flares and fireworks.
red·fish (rĕd'fĭsh') *n., pl.* **redfish** or **-fish·es.** Any of several fishes that are reddish in color.
red fox *n.* Any of several foxes of the genus *Vulpes,* characteristically having reddish fur, esp. *V. fulva,* of North America.
Red Guard *n.* **1.** A member of an activist youth movement in China that espouses Maoist principles. **2.** A member of a radical political group with Maoist leanings.
red gum[1] *n.* Any of several Australian trees of the genus *Eucalyptus,* esp. *E. rostrata,* which has been naturalized in California.
red gum[2] *n.* Strophulus.
red-hand·ed (rĕd'hăn'dĭd) *adv. & adj.* In the act of committing something wrong: *The thief was caught red-handed with the loot.* **—red'-hand'ed·ly** *adv.*
red·head (rĕd'hĕd') *n.* **1.** A person with red hair. **2.** A North American duck, *Aythya americana,* the male of which has black and gray plumage and a reddish head.

red heat *n.* **1.** The temperature of a red-hot substance. **2.** The physical condition of a red-hot substance.
red herring *n.* **1.** A smoked herring having a reddish color. **2.** Something that draws attention from the matter or issue at hand. [From its use to distract hunting dogs from the trail.]
red-hot (rĕd′hŏt′) *adj.* **1.** Glowing hot; very hot. **2.** Heated, as with excitement, anger, or enthusiasm: *a red-hot speech.* **3.** New; very recent: *red-hot information.* —*n.* **1.** A hot dog. **2.** A small usually round red candy strongly flavored with cinnamon.
re·di·a (rē′dē-ə) *n., pl.* **-di·ae** (-dē-ē′). A larva of certain trematodes that is produced within the sporocyst and that can give rise to additional rediae or to cercariae. [NLat., after Francesco *Redi,* 17th-cent. Italian naturalist.]
Red Indian *n.* A North American Indian.
red·in·gote (rĕd′ĭng-gōt′) *n.* **1.** A man's long double-breasted topcoat with full skirt. **2.** A woman's full-length unlined coat or dress open down the front to show a dress or underdress. [Fr. < E. *riding coat.*]
red ink *n.* **1.** A financial loss in business. **2.** The condition of showing a deficit in business operations. [From the use of red ink to record debits and losses in financial records.]
re·di·rect (rē′dĭ-rĕkt′, -dī-) *tr.v.* **-rect·ed, -rect·ing, -rects.** To change the direction or course of. **—re′di·rec′tion** *n.*
re·dis·count (rē-dĭs′kount′) *tr.v.* **-count·ed, -count·ing, -counts.** To discount again. —*n.* **1.** The act of rediscounting. **2.** Often **rediscounts.** Commercial paper that is discounted a second time.
re·dis·trib·ute (rē′dĭ-strĭb′yo͞ot) *tr.v.* **-ut·ed, -ut·ing, -utes.** To distribute again in a different way; reallocate. **—re·dis′tri·bu′tion** *n.* **—re′dis·trib′u·tive** *adj.*
re·dis·trict (rē-dĭs′trĭkt) *tr.v.* **-trict·ed, -trict·ing, -tricts.** To divide again into districts, esp. to give new boundaries to administrative or election districts.
red lead *n.* A bright-red powder, Pb_3O_4, used in paints, glass, pottery, and pipe-joint packing.
red-let·ter (rĕd′lĕt′ər) *adj.* Memorably happy: *a red-letter day.* [From the practice of marking in red the holy days in church calendars.]
red light *n.* **1.** A red traffic or danger signal indicating stop. **2.** A sign of caution; deterrent.
red-light district (rĕd′līt′) *n.* A neighborhood containing many brothels.
red·line (rĕd′līn′) *v.* **-lined, -lin·ing, -lines.** *intr.* To refuse home mortgages or insurance to areas or neighborhoods deemed poor financial risks. —*tr.* To discriminate against by refusing to grant loans, mortgages, or insurance to. **—red′lin′ing** *n.*
red maple *n.* A medium-sized American maple, *Acer rubrum,* with reddish twigs and buds.
red mulberry *n.* A tree, *Morus rubra,* of eastern and central North America, having irregularly lobed leaves and edible, blackberrylike fruit.
red mullet *n.* A fish of the family Mullidae; goatfish.
red·neck (rĕd′nĕk′) *n. Slang.* **1.** A member of the white rural laboring class, esp. in the southern United States. **2.** *Offensive Slang.* A person who advocates a provincial, conservative, often bigoted sociopolitical attitude considered characteristic of a redneck.
re·do (rē-do͞o′) *tr.v.* **-did** (-dĭd′), **-done** (-dŭn′), **-do·ing, -does** (-dŭz′). **1.** To do over again. **2.** To redecorate.
red ocher *n.* **1.** A natural red mixture of clay and iron oxide. **2.** A refined form of red ocher used as pigment.
red·o·lent (rĕd′ə-lənt) *adj.* **1.** Having or emitting fragrance; aromatic. **2.** Suggestive; reminiscent: *a campaign redolent of machine politics.* [ME < OFr. < Lat. *redolens,* pr. part. of *redolēre,* to smell : *re-, red-* (intensive) + *olēre,* to smell.] **—red′o·lence, red′o·len·cy** *n.* **—red′o·lent·ly** *adv.*
red osier *n.* A North American shrub, *Cornus stolonifera,* often forming dense clumps and having red branches, white flowers, and bluish-white, berrylike fruit.
re·dou·ble (rē-dŭb′əl) *v.* **-bled, -bling, -bles.** —*tr.* **1.** To double. **2.** To repeat. **3.** To double the doubling bid of (an opponent) in bridge. —*intr.* **1.** To become twice as great. **2.** To double a double in bridge.
re·doubt (rĭ-dout′) *n.* **1.** A small, often temporary defensive fortification. **2.** A reinforcing earthwork or breastwork within a permanent rampart. **3.** A protected place of refuge or defense. [OFr. *redoute* < OItal. *ridotto* < Med. Lat. *reductus,* concealed place < Lat. *reducere,* to withdraw : *re-,* back + *ducere,* to lead.]
re·doubt·a·ble (rĭ-dou′tə-bəl) *adj.* **1.** Arousing fear or awe; formidable. **2.** Worthy of respect or honor. [ME < OFr. *redoutable* < *redouter,* to dread : *re-* (intensive < Lat.) + *douter,* to doubt < Lat. *dubitare.*] **—re·doubt′a·bly** *adv.*
re·dound (rĭ-dound′) *intr.v.* **-dound·ed, -dound·ing, -dounds.** **1.** To have an effect or consequence: *deeds that redound to one's discredit.* **2.** To return; recoil: *Glory redounds upon the brave.* **3.** To contribute; accrue. [ME *redounden,* to abound < OFr. *redonder* < Lat. *redundare,* to overflow. —see REDUNDANT.]
red·out (rĕd′out′) *n.* A reddening of the visual field caused by blood that is forced into the head when an individual is subjected to a negative force of gravity.
re·dox (rē′dŏks′) *n. Chem.* Oxidation-reduction. [RED(UCTION) + OX(IDATION).]
red-pen·cil (rĕd′pĕn′səl) *tr.v.* **-ciled, -cil·ing, -cils.** To censor, cut, revise, or correct with or as if with a red pencil.
red pepper *n.* **1.** The pungent, red, podlike fruit of any of several varieties of the pepper plant, *Capsicum frutescens.* **2.** Cayenne pepper.
red pine *n.* An evergreen timber tree, *Pinus resinosa,* of northeastern North America.
red·poll (rĕd′pōl′) *n.* Any of several finches of the genus *Acanthis,* having brownish plumage and a red crown.
Red Poll *n.* Any of a breed of reddish, hornless cattle developed in England and raised for dairy and meat products.
red puccoon *n.* The bloodroot.
re·dress (rĭ-drĕs′) *tr.v.* **-dressed, -dress·ing, -dress·es.** **1.** To set right; remedy or rectify. **2.** To make amends to. **3.** To make amends for. **4.** To adjust (a balance, for example). —*n.* (*also* rē′drĕs). **1.** Satisfaction or amends for wrong done. **2.** Correction or reformation. [ME *redressen* < OFr. *redresser* : *re-,* back (< Lat.) + *dresser,* to arrange. —see DRESS.] **—re·dress′er, re·dres′sor** *n.*
red·root (rĕd′ro͞ot′) *n.* **1.** A bog plant, *Lachnanthes tinctoria,* of eastern North America, having red roots and woolly yellow flowers. **2.** The pigweed (sense 2).
red salmon *n.* The sockeye salmon.
red·shank (rĕd′shăngk′) *n.* An Old World wading bird, *Tringa totanus,* having long red legs.
red shift *n.* **1.** An apparent increase in the wavelength of radiation emitted by a receding celestial body as a consequence of the Doppler effect. **2.** An increase in wavelength resulting from loss of energy by radiation moving against a gravitational field.
red·shirt (rĕd′shûrt′) *n.* A college athlete who does not participate in varsity competition for one year in order to extend his four-year period of eligibility. [From the red jersey worn by such athletes to distinguish them from the regular players.] **—red′shirt′** *v.* **(-shirt·ed, -shirt·ing, -shirts).**
red·skin (rĕd′skĭn′) *n. Offensive Slang.* A North American Indian.
red snapper *n.* Any of several marine food fishes of the genus *Lutjanus,* of tropical and semitropical waters, having red or reddish bodies.
red spider *n.* Any of various small red mites of the family Tetranychidae that feed on vegetation.
red squill *n.* **1.** The sea onion (sense 1). **2.** A powder prepared from the bulbs of the red squill and used as a rat poison.
red squirrel *n.* A North American squirrel, *Tamiasciurus hudsonicus,* having reddish or tawny fur.
red·start (rĕd′stärt′) *n.* **1.** A small North American bird, *Setophaga ruticilla,* the male of which has black plumage with orange patches on the wings and tail. **2.** A European bird, *Phoenicurus phoenicurus,* having grayish plumage and a rust-red breast and tail. [RED + obs. *start,* tail < ME *stert* < OE *steort.*]
red tape *n.* Official forms and procedures, esp. when oppressively complex and time consuming. [From its former use in tying British official documents.]
red tide *n.* Ocean waters colored by the proliferation of red, one-celled, plantlike animals in sufficient numbers to kill fish.
red·top (rĕd′tŏp′) *n.* A widely cultivated grass, *Agrostis alba,* native to Europe, having reddish flower clusters.
re·duce (rĭ-do͞os′, -dyo͞os′) *v.* **-duced, -duc·ing, -duc·es.** —*tr.* **1.** To lessen in extent, amount, number, degree, or price. **2.** To gain control of; conquer. **3.** To put in order or arrange systematically. **4.** To separate into orderly components by analysis. **5.** To bring to a certain state or condition: *Enemy bombers reduced the city to rubble.* **6.** To powder or pulverize. **7.** To thin (paint) with a solvent. **8.** *Chem.* **a.** To decrease the valence of (an atom) by adding electrons. **b.** To deoxidize. **c.** To add hydrogen to. **d.** To change to a metallic state by removing nonmetallic constituents; smelt. **9.** *Math.* To change the form of (an expression) without changing the value. **10.** *Med.* To restore (a fractured or displaced body part) to a normal condition. —*intr.* **1.** To become diminished. **2.** To lose weight, as by dieting. [ME *reducen,* to bring back < Lat. *reducere* : *re-,* back + *ducere,* to lead.] **—re·duc′er** *n.* **—re·duc′i·bil′i·ty** *n.* **—re·duc′i·ble** *adj.* **—re·duc′i·bly** *adv.*
reducing agent *n.* A substance that chemically reduces other substances.
re·duc·tant (rĭ-dŭk′tənt) *n.* A reducing agent.
re·duc·tase (rĭ-dŭk′tās′, -tāz′) *n.* An enzyme that catalyzes biochemical reduction reactions. [REDUCT(ION) + -ASE.]
re·duc·ti·o ad ab·sur·dum (rĭ-dŭk′tē-ō ăd əb-sûr′dəm) *n.* Disproof of a proposition by showing the absurdity of its inevitable conclusion. [Lat., reduction to absurdity.]
re·duc·tion (rĭ-dŭk′shən) *n.* **1.** The act or process of reducing. **2.** The result of reducing. **3.** The amount by which something is lessened or diminished. **4.** *Biol.* The first meiotic division, in which the chromosome number is reduced. **5.** *Chem.* A decrease in positive valence or an increase in negative valence by the gaining of electrons. **6.** *Math.* **a.** The canceling of common factors in the numerator and denominator of a fraction. **b.** The converting of a fraction

red mulberry

to its decimal equivalent. [ME *reduccion,* restoration < OFr. *reduction* < Lat. *reductio* < *reducere,* to bring back : *re-,* back + *ducere,* to lead.] **—re·duc'tion·al, re·duc'tive** *adj.*

reduction division *n. Biol.* **1.** Reduction (sense 4). **2.** Meiosis (sense 1).

re·duc·tiv·ism (rĭ-dŭk'tə-vĭz'əm) *n.* Minimal art. **—re·duc'tiv·ist** *n.*

reel[1]

re·dun·dan·cy (rĭ-dŭn'dən-sē) *n., pl.* **-cies. 1.** The state of being redundant. **2.** Superfluity or excess. **3.** Unnecessary repetition. **4. a.** Duplication or repetition of elements in electronic or mechanical equipment to provide alternative functional channels in case of failure. **b.** Repetition of parts or all of a message to circumvent transmission errors.

re·dun·dant (rĭ-dŭn'dənt) *adj.* **1.** Exceeding what is necessary or natural; superfluous. **2.** Needlessly repetitive; verbose. [Lat. *redundans,* pr.part. of *redundare,* to overflow : *re-, red-* (intensive) + *undare,* to surge < *unda,* wave.] **—re·dun'dant·ly** *adv.*

re·du·pli·cate (rĭ-do͞o'plə-kāt', -dyo͞o'-) *v.* **-cat·ed, -cat·ing, -cates.** *—tr.* **1.** To repeat over and again; redouble. **2.** *Ling.* **a.** To double (the initial syllable or all of a root word) to produce an inflectional or derivational form. **b.** To form (a new word) by doubling all or part of a word. *—intr.* To be doubled. *—adj.* (rĭ-do͞o'plə-kĭt, -dyo͞o'-). Doubled. [LLat. *reduplicare, reduplicat-* : *re-,* again + *duplicare,* to duplicate.]

re·du·pli·ca·tion (rĭ-do͞o'plĭ-kā'shən, -dyo͞o'-) *n.* **1.** The act of reduplicating or the state of being reduplicated. **2.** A product or result of reduplicating. **3. a.** A word formed by or containing a reduplicated element. **b.** The added element in a word form that is reduplicated. **—re·du'pli·ca'tive** *adj.* **—re·du'pli·ca'tive·ly** *adv.*

re·du·vi·id (rĭ-do͞o'vē-ĭd, -dyo͞o'-) *n.* Any of various hemipterous insects of the family Reduviidae that have curved beaks adapted for sucking blood. [< NLat. *Reduviidae,* family name < *Reduvius,* type genus < Lat. *reduvia,* hangnail, fragment.]

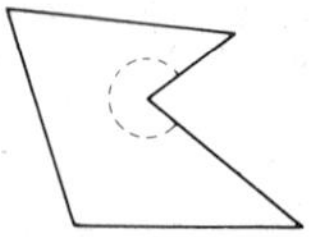

re-entrant angle

red·wing (rĕd'wĭng') *n.* **1.** A North American blackbird, *Agelaius phoeniceus,* the male of which has scarlet patches on the wings. **2.** A European thrush, *Turdus iliacus,* having reddish feathers under the wings.

red-winged black·bird (rĕd'wĭngd' blăk'bûrd') *n.* The redwing (sense 1).

red·wood (rĕd'wo͝od') *n.* **1.** A very tall evergreen tree, *Sequoia sempervirens,* of coastal and northern California. **2.** The soft, reddish wood of the redwood tree. **3.** Any of various woods having reddish color or yielding red dye.

re·ech·o (rĭ-ĕk'ō) *v.* **-oed, -o·ing, -oes.** *—intr.* To sound back or reverberate again. *—tr.* To echo back; repeat.

reed (rēd) *n.* **1. a.** Any of various tall grasses having jointed, hollow stalks, esp. one of the genera *Phragmites* or *Arundo.* **b.** The stalk of one of these plants. **2.** A primitive wind instrument made of a hollow reed stalk. **3.** *Mus.* **a.** A flexible strip of cane or metal set into the mouthpiece of certain musical instruments to produce tone by vibrating in response to a stream of air. **b.** An instrument, as an oboe or clarinet, fitted with a reed. **4.** A narrow, movable frame fitted with reed or metal strips that separate the warp threads in weaving. **5.** *Archit.* A reeding. [ME *rede* < OE *hrēod.*]

reed·bird (rēd'bûrd') *n.* The bobolink.

reed·buck (rēd'bŭk') *n.* Any of several African antelopes of the genus *Redunca.* [Transl. of Afr. *rietbok.*]

reed·ing (rē'dĭng) *n. Archit.* A convex decorative molding having parallel strips resembling thin reeds.

reed·ling (rēd'lĭng) *n.* A small Eurasian marsh bird, *Panurus biarmicus,* the male of which has mustachelike black markings.

reed mace *n.* The cattail.

reed organ *n.* A keyboard instrument in which free-beating reeds produce tones when acted upon by currents of air.

reed pipe *n.* An organ pipe with a reed that vibrates and produces a tone when air is forced through it.

reed stop *n.* A stop on an organ made up of reed pipes having any of various tonal characteristics.

re·ed·u·cate (rē-ĕj'ə-kāt') *tr.v.* **-cat·ed, -cat·ing, -cates. 1.** To instruct again. **2.** To retrain (a person) to function effectively; rehabilitate. **—re-ed'u·ca'tion** *n.*

reed·y (rē'dē) *adj.* **-i·er, -i·est. 1.** Full of reeds. **2.** Made of reeds. **3.** Resembling a reed. **4.** Having a tone like that of a reed instrument. **—reed'i·ness** *n.*

reef[1] (rēf) *n.* **1.** *Geol.* A strip or ridge of rocks, sand, or coral that rises to or near the surface of a body of water. **2.** A vein of ore. [MDu. *rif,* poss. < ON, ridge.] **—reef'y** *adj.*

referee

reef[2] (rēf) *Naut. —n.* A portion of a sail rolled and tied down to lessen the area exposed to the wind. *—tr.v.* **reefed, reef·ing, reefs. 1.** To reduce the size of (a sail) by tucking in a part and tying it to or rolling it around a yard. **2.** To shorten (a topmast or bowsprit) by taking part of it in. [ME *riff* < ON *rif,* ridge.]

reef·er[1] (rē'fər) *n.* **1.** A person who reefs, as a midshipman. **2.** A short, heavy, close-fitting, double-breasted jacket.

reef·er[2] (rē'fər) *n. Slang.* Marijuana, esp. a marijuana cigarette. [Prob. < REEF[2].]

reef knot *n.* A square knot.

reek (rēk) *v.* **reeked, reek·ing, reeks.** *—intr.* **1.** To smoke, steam, or fume. **2.** To be pervaded by something unpleasant: *a situation that reeked of scandal.* **3.** To give off or become permeated with a strong and unpleasant odor. *—tr.* **1.** To emit or exude (smoke, for example). **2.** To process or treat by exposing to the action of smoke. *—n.* **1.** A strong and offensive odor; stench. **2.** Vapor; steam. [ME *reken* < OE *rēocan.*] **—reek'er** *n.* **—reek'y** *adj.*

reel[1] (rēl) *n.* **1.** A device, as a cylinder, spool, or frame, that turns on an axis and is used for winding rope, tape, or other flexible materials. **2.** A cylindrical device attached to a fishing rod to let out or wind up the line. **3.** The quantity of wire, film, or other material wound on one reel. **4.** A fast dance of Scottish origin. **5.** The Virginia reel. **6.** The music for a reel. *—tr.v.* **reeled, reel·ing, reels. 1.** To wind upon a reel. **2.** To recover by winding on a reel: *reel in a large fish.* **—phrasal verb. reel off.** To recite fluently and usually at length: *reeled off dates and names.* [ME < OE *hrēol.*] **—reel'a·ble** *adj.*

reel[2] (rēl) *v.* **reeled, reel·ing, reels.** *—intr.* **1.** To be thrown off balance or fall back. **2.** To stagger, lurch, or sway, as from drunkenness. **3.** To go round and round in a whirling motion. **4.** To feel dizzy. *—tr.* To cause to reel. *—n.* A staggering, swaying, or whirling movement. [ME *relen,* prob. < *reel,* spool < OE *hrēol.*] **—reel'er** *n.*

re-e·lect or **re·e·lect** (rē'ĭ-lĕkt') *tr.v.* **-lect·ed, -lect·ing, -lects.** To elect again. **—re'-e·lec'tion** *n.*

re-en·act (rē'ĕn-ăkt', -ə-năkt') *tr.v.* **-act·ed, -act·ing, -acts. 1.** To enact again: *re-enact a law.* **2.** To perform again: *re-enact the first two scenes.* **3.** To go through a second time; recreate: *re-enact the events leading up to the accident.* **—re'-en·act'ment** *n.*

re-en·force or **re·en·force** (rē'ĭn-fôrs', -fōrs') *v.* Variants of **reinforce.**

re-en·ter or **re·en·ter** (rē-ĕn'tər) *v.* **-tered, -ter·ing, -ters.** *—intr.* To come in or enter again. *—tr.* To record again on a list or ledger. **—re-en'trance** *n.*

re-en·trant or **re·en·trant** (rē-ĕn'trənt) *adj.* Re-entering; pointing inward. *—n.* A re-entrant angle or part.

re-entrant angle *n.* An interior angle of a polygon greater than 180 degrees.

re-en·try or **re·en·try** (rē-ĕn'trē) *n., pl.* **-tries. 1.** The act of re-entering. **2.** *Law.* The recovery of possession under a right reserved in a previous property transaction. **3. a.** In bridge and whist, the act of regaining the lead by taking a trick. **b.** The card that will take a trick and thus regain the lead. **4.** *Aerospace.* The return of a missile or spacecraft into the earth's atmosphere.

reeve[1] (rēv) *n.* **1.** A high officer of local administration appointed by the Anglo-Saxon kings. **2.** In the later medieval period, a bailiff or steward of a manor. **3.** Any of various minor officers of parishes or other local authorities. **4.** The elected president of a town council in some parts of Canada. [ME < OE *gerēfa.*]

reeve[2] (rēv) *tr.v.* **reeved** or **rove** (rōv), **reev·ing, reeves.** *Naut.* **1.** To pass (a rope or rod) through a hole, ring, pulley, or block. **2.** To fasten by passing through or around. [Orig. unknown.]

reeve[3] (rēv) *n.* The female ruff[1] (sense 3). [Prob. alteration of RUFF[1].]

re-ex·am·ine or **re·ex·am·ine** (rē'ĭg-zăm'ĭn) *tr.v.* **-ined, -in·ing, -ines. 1.** To examine again or anew; review. **2.** *Law.* To question (a witness) again after cross-examination. **—re'-ex·am'i·na'tion** *n.*

re·fect (rĭ-fĕkt') *tr.v.* **-fect·ed, -fect·ing, -fects.** *Archaic.* To refresh with food and drink. [Lat. *reficere, refect-,* to refresh : *re-,* back + *facere,* to make.]

re·fec·tion (rĭ-fĕk'shən) *n.* **1.** Refreshment with food and drink. **2.** A light meal or repast. [ME *refeccioun* < OFr. *refection* < Lat. *refectio* < *reficere,* to refresh. —see REFECT.]

re·fec·to·ry (rĭ-fĕk'tə-rē) *n., pl.* **-ries.** A room where meals are served. [LLat. *refectorium* < Lat. *reficere,* to refresh. —see REFECT.]

refectory table *n.* A long table with straight, heavy legs.

re·fer (rĭ-fûr') *v.* **-ferred, -fer·ring, -fers.** *—tr.* **1.** To direct to a source for help or information: *referred her to a heart specialist.* **2.** To assign or attribute to; regard as originated by. **3.** To assign to or regard as belonging within a particular kind or class. **4.** To submit (a matter in dispute) to an authority for arbitration, decision, or examination. **5.** To direct the attention of: *refer him to his duties.* *—intr.* **1.** To pertain; concern: *questions referring to yesterday's lecture.* **2.** To allude or make reference: *referred to Pennsylvania as the Keystone State.* **3.** To turn to, as for information or authority. —See Usage note at **allude.** [ME *referen* < OFr. *referer* < Lat. *referre* : *re-,* back + *ferre,* to carry.] **—ref'er·a·ble** (rĕf'ər-ə-bəl, rĭ-fûr'-) *adj.* **—re·fer'ral** (rĭ-fûr'əl) *n.* **—re·fer'rer** *n.*

ref·e·ree (rĕf'ə-rē') *n.* **1.** One to whom something is referred, esp. for settlement or decision. **2.** *Sports.* An official supervising the play; umpire. **3.** *Law.* A person appointed by a court to examine and report on a case. *—v.* **-reed, -ree·ing, -rees.** *—tr.* To judge as referee. *—intr.* To act as referee.

ref·er·ence (rĕf'ər-əns, rĕf'rəns) *n.* **1.** An act of referring. **2. a.** One that is referred to. **b.** Significance in a specified context. **c.** Meaning or denotation. **3.** The state of being related or referred: *with reference to; in reference to.* **4.** An allusion to an occurrence or situation: *made frequent refer-*

ences to his promotion. **5. a.** A note in a publication referring the reader to another passage or source. **b.** The passage or source so referred to. **c.** A mark or footnote used to direct a reader elsewhere for additional information. **6.** *Law.* **a.** The submission of a case to a referee. **b.** Legal actions conducted before or by a referee. **7. a.** A person who is in a position to recommend another or to vouch for his fitness, as for a job. **b.** A written statement about a person's qualifications, character, and dependability. **—ref'er·enc·er** *n.* **—ref'er·en'tial** (-ə-rĕn'shəl) *adj.*

ref·er·en·dum (rĕf'ə-rĕn'dəm) *n., pl.* **-dums** or **-da** (-də). **1. a.** The submission of a proposed public measure or actual statute to a direct popular vote. **b.** Such a vote. **2.** A note from a diplomat to his government requesting instructions. [Lat., neuter gerund. of *referre,* to refer.]

ref·er·ent (rĕf'ər-ənt, rĭ-fûr'ənt) *n.* **1.** Something that refers, esp. a linguistic item in its capacity of referring to a meaning. **2.** Something referred to.

re·fill (rē-fĭl') *tr.v.* **-filled, -fill·ing, -fills.** To fill again. *—n.* (rē'fĭl'). **1.** A product packaged to replace the used contents of a container. **2.** A second or subsequent filling.

re·fine (rĭ-fīn') *v.* **-fined, -fin·ing, -fines.** *—tr.* **1.** To reduce to a pure state; purify. **2.** To remove by purifying. **3.** To free from coarse characteristics: *refined his manners.* *—intr.* **1.** To become free of impurities. **2.** To acquire polish or elegance. **3.** To use subtlety and precise distinctions in thought or speech. **—re·fin'er** *n.*

re·fined (rĭ-fīnd') *adj.* **1.** Free from coarseness or vulgarity; polite. **2.** Free of impurities; purified. **3.** Precise to a fine degree.

re·fine·ment (rĭ-fīn'mənt) *n.* **1. a.** An act of refining. **b.** The state of being refined. **2.** The result of refining; an improvement or elaboration. **3.** Fineness of thought or expression; polish; cultivation. **4.** A keen or precise phrasing; subtle distinction.

re·fin·er·y (rĭ-fī'nə-rē) *n., pl.* **-ies.** An industrial plant for purifying a crude substance, as petroleum or sugar.

re·fin·ish (rē-fĭn'ĭsh) *tr.v.* **-ished, -ish·ing, -ish·es.** To put a new finish on (furniture). **—re·fin'ish·er** *n.*

re·fit (rē-fĭt') *v.* **-fit·ted, -fit·ting, -fits.** *—tr.* To prepare and equip for additional use. *—intr.* To be made fit again. *—n.* (rē'fĭt', rē-fĭt'). **1.** The repair of damage or wear. **2.** A secondary or subsequent preparation of supplies and equipment.

re·flect (rĭ-flĕkt') *v.* **-flect·ed, -flect·ing, -flects.** *—tr.* **1.** To throw or bend back (light, for example) from a surface. **2.** To form an image of (an object); mirror. **3.** To manifest as a result of one's actions: *Her work reflects intelligence.* **4.** *Archaic.* To bend back. *—intr.* **1.** To be bent back. **2.** To give back a likeness. **3.** To think or consider seriously. **4.** To bring blame or reproach. [ME *reflecten* < OFr. *reflecter* < Lat. *reflectere,* to bend back : *re-,* back + *flectere,* to bend.]

re·flec·tance (rĭ-flĕk'təns) *n.* The ratio of the total radiant flux, as of light, reflected by a surface to the total incident on the surface.

reflecting telescope *n.* An optical telescope in which the principal image-forming element is a parabolic or spherical mirror.

re·flec·tion (rĭ-flĕk'shən) *n.* **1.** An instance of reflecting or the state of being reflected. **2.** Something reflected, as light, radiant heat, sound, or an image. **3. a.** Concentration of the mind; careful consideration. **b.** The results of such consideration. **4.** An imputation of censure or discredit. **—re·flec'tion·al** *adj.*

re·flec·tive (rĭ-flĕk'tĭv) *adj.* **1.** Of, pertaining to, produced by, or resulting from reflection. **2.** Meditative; pensive. **—re·flec'tive·ly** *adv.*

re·flec·tiv·i·ty (rē'flĕk-tĭv'ĭ-tē) *n., pl.* **-ties.** **1.** The quality of being reflective. **2.** The ability to reflect. **3.** *Physics.* The ratio of the intensity of the total radiation, as of light, reflected from a surface to the total incident on the surface.

re·flec·tom·e·ter (rē'flĕk-tŏm'ĭ-tər) *n.* An instrument for measuring the reflectance of a surface.

re·flec·tor (rĭ-flĕk'tər) *n.* **1.** Something that reflects. **2.** A surface that reflects radiation. **3.** A reflecting telescope.

re·flex (rē'flĕks') *adj.* **1.** Turned, thrown, or bent backward. **2.** *Physiol.* Designating an involuntary action or response, such as a sneeze, blink, or hiccup. *—n.* (rē'flĕks'). **1.** Reflection or an image produced by reflection. **2.** *Physiol.* An involuntary response to a stimulus. **3.** *Psychol.* An unlearned or instinctive response to a stimulus. **4.** *Ling.* A form or feature that reflects or represents an earlier (often reconstructed) form or feature having undergone phonetic or other change. *—tr.v.* (rĭ-flĕks') **-flexed, -flex·ing, -flex·es.** **1.** To bend, turn back, or reflect. **2.** To cause to undergo a reflex process. [Lat. *reflexus,* p.part. of *reflectere,* to bend back. —see REFLECT.]

reflex angle *n.* An angle greater than 180 degrees and less than 360 degrees.

reflex arc *n. Physiol.* The neural path of a simple reflex.

reflex camera *n.* A camera fitted with a mirror to reflect the exact focused image that can be recorded onto a coupled viewing screen.

re·flex·ion (rĭ-flĕk'shən) *n. Chiefly Brit.* Variant of **reflection.**

re·flex·ive (rĭ-flĕk'sĭv) *adj.* **1.** *Gram.* **a.** Designating a verb having an identical subject and direct object, as *dressed* in the sentence *She dressed herself.* **b.** Designating the pronoun used as direct object of a reflexive verb, as *herself* in *She dressed herself.* **2.** Of or pertaining to a reflex. *—n.* A reflexive verb or pronoun. **—re·flex'ive·ly** *adv.* **—re·flex'ive·ness, re'flex·iv'i·ty** (rē'flĕk-sĭv'ĭ-tē) *n.*

ref·lu·ent (rĕf'lo͞o-ənt) *adj.* Flowing back; ebbing. [Lat. *refluens,* pr.part. of *refluere,* to flow back : *re-,* back + *fluere,* to flow.] **—ref'lu·ence** *n.*

re·flux (rē'flŭks') *n.* A flowing back; ebb. [ME < Med. Lat. *refluxus* : Lat. *re-,* back + *fluxus,* flow < *fluere,* to flow.]

re·for·est (rē-fôr'ĭst, -fŏr'ĭst) *tr.v.* **-est·ed, -est·ing, -ests.** To replant (an area) with forest trees. **—re'for·es·ta'tion** *n.*

re·form (rĭ-fôrm') *v.* **-formed, -form·ing, -forms.** *—tr.* **1.** To improve by alteration, correction of error, or removal of defects. **2.** To abolish abuse or malpractice in: *reform the government.* **3.** To cause (a person) to abandon irresponsible or immoral practices. *—intr.* To give up irresponsible or immoral practices. *—n.* **1.** A change for the better; correction of evils or abuses. **2.** A movement that attempts to institute improved social and political conditions without revolutionary change. **3.** Moral improvement. [ME *reformen* < OFr. *reformer* < Lat. *reformare* : *re-,* again + *formare,* to form < *forma,* form.] **—re·for'ma·tive** *adj.* **—re·form'er** *n.*

re-form (rē-fôrm') *v.* **-formed, -for·ming, -forms.** *—tr.* To form again. *—intr.* To become formed again.

ref·or·ma·tion (rĕf'ər-mā'shən) *n.* **1.** The act of reforming or state of being reformed. **2. Reformation.** The 16th-century movement resulting in the separation of the Protestant churches from the Roman Catholic Church. **—ref'or·ma'tion·al** *adj.*

re·for·ma·to·ry (rĭ-fôr'mə-tôr'ē, -tōr'ē) *n., pl.* **-ries.** A penal institution for the discipline, reformation, and training of young offenders. *—adj.* Serving or intending to reform.

re·formed (rĭ-fôrmd') *adj.* **1.** Improved by the removal of faults. **2.** Improved in conduct or character. **3. Reformed.** Of, pertaining to, or denoting the Protestant churches that follow the teachings of Calvin and Zwingli. **4. Reformed.** Of, pertaining to, or denoting Reform Judaism.

re·form·ism (rĭ-fôr'mĭz'əm) *n.* A doctrine or movement of reform. **—re·form'ist** *n.*

Reform Judaism *n.* A branch of Judaism introduced in the 19th century that seeks to reconcile historical Judaism with present-day life and does not require strict observance of traditional law.

reform school *n.* A reformatory.

re·fract (rĭ-frăkt') *tr.v.* **-fract·ed, -fract·ing, -fracts.** To deflect (light, for example) from a straight path by refraction. [Lat. *refringere, refract-,* to break up : *re-,* back + *frangere,* to break.]

refracting telescope *n.* A telescope in which the final image is produced entirely by lenses.

re·frac·tion (rĭ-frăk'shən) *n.* **1.** *Physics.* The deflection of a propagating wave, as of light or sound, at the boundary between two mediums with different refractive indices or in passage through a medium of nonuniform density. **2.** *Astron.* The apparent positional elevation of celestial objects caused by deflection of light entering the earth's atmosphere. **—re·frac'tion·al, re·frac'tive** *adj.* **—re·frac'tive·ly** *adv.* **—re·frac'tive·ness, re'frac·tiv'i·ty** (rē'frăk-tĭv'ĭ-tē) *n.*

refractive index *n. Physics.* Index of refraction.

re·frac·tom·e·ter (rē'frăk-tŏm'ĭ-tər) *n.* Any of several instruments that measure indices of refraction.

re·frac·tor (rĭ-frăk'tər) *n.* **1.** One that refracts. **2.** A refracting telescope.

re·frac·to·ry (rĭ-frăk'tə-rē) *adj.* **1.** Obstinate; unmanageable: *a refractory child.* **2.** Difficult to melt or work; resistant to heat. **3.** Not responsive to treatment: *a refractory disease.* *—n., pl.* **-ries.** **1.** One that is refractory. **2.** Ceramic material that is resistant to high temperatures. [Obs. *refractary* < Lat. *refractarius* < *refringere,* to break up. —see REFRACT.] **—re·frac'to·ri·ly** *adv.* **—re·frac'to·ri·ness** *n.*

re·frain¹ (rĭ-frān') *v.* **-frained, -frain·ing, -frains.** *—intr.* To hold oneself back; forbear: *refrained from swearing.* *—tr. Archaic.* To restrain or hold back; curb. [ME *refrenen* < OFr. *refrener* < Lat. *refrenare,* to restrain : *re-,* back + *frenum,* bridle.] **—re·frain'er** *n.* **—re·frain'ment** *n.*

re·frain² (rĭ-frān') *n.* **1. a.** A phrase or verse repeated at intervals throughout a song or poem, esp. at the end of each stanza. **b.** Music for the refrain of a poem. **2.** A repeated theme. [ME *refreyn* < OFr. *refrain* < *refraindre,* to resound < Lat. *refringere,* to break up. —see REFRACT.]

re·fran·gi·ble (rĭ-frăn'jə-bəl) *adj.* Capable of being refracted. **—re·fran'gi·bil'i·ty, re·fran'gi·ble·ness** *n.*

re·fresh (rĭ-frĕsh') *v.* **-freshed, -fresh·ing, -fresh·es.** *—tr.* **1.** To revive (a person) with or as if with rest, food, or drink. **2.** To make cool, clean, or damp; freshen. **3.** To renew by stimulation: *refresh one's memory.* *—intr.* **1.** To take refreshment. **2.** To become revived; reinvigorate. [ME *refresshen* < OFr. *refreschir* : *re-,* anew (< Lat.) + *fres,* fresh, of Germanic orig.]

re·fresh·en (rĭ-frĕsh'ən) *tr. & intr.v.* **-fresh·ened, -fresh·en·ing, -fresh·ens.** To refresh.

re·fresh·er (rĭ-frĕsh'ər) *n.* One that refreshes. *—adj.* Serving to reacquaint one with material previously studied: *a refresher course.*

reflection

regalia
Coronation of Queen Elizabeth II of England, 1953

re·fresh·ing (rĭ-frĕsh′ĭng) *adj.* **1.** Serving to refresh. **2.** Pleasantly fresh and different. **—re·fresh′ing·ly** *adv.*

re·fresh·ment (rĭ-frĕsh′mənt) *n.* **1.** The act of refreshing or state of being refreshed. **2.** Something, such as food or drink, that refreshes. **3. refreshments. a.** Assorted light foods. **b.** A light meal or snack.

re·frig·er·ant (rĭ-frĭj′ər-ənt) *adj.* **1.** Cooling or freezing; refrigerating. **2.** *Med.* Reducing fever. *—n.* **1.** A substance, such as air, ammonia, water, or carbon dioxide, used to produce refrigeration, either as the working substance of a refrigerator or by direct absorption of heat. **2.** *Med.* An agent used to reduce fever.

re·frig·er·ate (rĭ-frĭj′ə-rāt′) *tr.v.* **-at·ed, -at·ing, -ates. 1.** To cool or chill (a substance). **2.** To preserve (food) by chilling. [Lat. *refrigerare, refrigerat-* : *re-*, anew + *frigerare*, to make cool < *frigus*, cool.] **—re·frig′er·a′tion** *n.* **—re·frig′er·a′tive** *adj. & n.* **—re·frig′er·a·to′ry** (-ər-ə-tôr′ē, -tōr′ē) *adj.*

re·frig·er·a·tor (rĭ-frĭj′ə-rā′tər) *n.* A room or cabinet used to store substances, such as food, at a low temperature.

re·frin·gence (rĭ-frĭn′jəns) *n.* Refractive power.

re·frin·gent (rĭ-frĭn′jənt) *adj.* Of, pertaining to, or producing refraction; refractive. [Lat. *refringens*, pr.part. of *refringere*, to break up. —see REFRACT.]

reft[1] (rĕft) *v. Archaic.* A past tense and past participle of **reave**[1].

reft[2] (rĕft) *v. Archaic.* A past tense and past participle of **reave**[2].

re·fu·el (rē-fyo͞o′əl) *v.* **-eled, -el·ing, -els** also **-elled, -el·ling, -els.** *—tr.* To supply again with fuel. *—intr.* To take on a fresh supply of fuel.

ref·uge (rĕf′yo͞oj) *n.* **1.** Protection or shelter, as from danger or hardship. **2.** A place providing protection or shelter; haven. **3.** Something to which one may turn for help, relief, or escape: *Silence was his only refuge.* *—v.* **-uged, -ug·ing, -ug·es.** *Archaic.* *—tr.* To give refuge to. *—intr.* To take refuge. [ME < OFr. < Lat. *refugium* < *refugere*, to run away : *re-*, back + *fugere*, to flee.]

ref·u·gee (rĕf′yo͞o-jē′) *n.* A person who flees usually to another country for refuge, esp. from invasion, oppression, or persecution. —See Usage note at **-ee**[1]. [Fr. *réfugié* < p.part. of *réfugier*, to take refuge < OFr. *refuge*, refuge.]

re·ful·gent (rĭ-fo͝ol′jənt, -fŭl′-) *adj.* Shining radiantly; resplendent. [Lat. *refulgens* < pr.part. of *refulgere*, to flash back : *re-*, back + *fulgere*, to flash.] **—re·ful′gence, re·ful′gen·cy** *n.* **—re·ful′gent·ly** *adv.*

re·fund (rĭ-fŭnd′, rē′fŭnd′) *v.* **-fund·ed, -fund·ing, -funds.** *—tr.* **1.** To return or give back. **2.** To repay (money). *—intr.* To make repayment. *—n.* (rē′fŭnd′). **1.** A repayment of funds. **2.** An amount repaid. [ME *refunden*, to pour back < OFr. *refunder* < Lat. *refundere* : *re-*, back + *fundere*, to pour.] **—re·fund′a·ble** *adj.* **—re·fund′er** *n.* **—re·fund′ment** *n.*

re-fund (rē-fŭnd′) *tr.v.* **-fund·ed, -fund·ing, -funds. 1.** To fund anew. **2.** To pay back (a debt) with new borrowing, esp. to replace (a bond issue) with a new bond issue.

re·fur·bish (rē-fûr′bĭsh) *tr.v.* **-bished, -bish·ing, -bish·es.** To make clean, bright, or fresh again. **—re·fur′bish·ment** *n.*

re·fus·al (rĭ-fyo͞o′zəl) *n.* **1.** The act of refusing. **2.** The opportunity or right to accept or reject.

re·fuse[1] (rĭ-fyo͞oz′) *v.* **-fused, -fus·ing, -fus·es.** *—tr.* **1.** To decline to do, accept, give, or allow. **2.** To decline to jump (an obstacle). Used of a horse. *—intr.* To decline to do, accept, allow, or give something. [ME *refusen* < OFr. *refuser* < VLat. **refusare* < Lat. *refundere*, to pour back. —see REFUND.] **—re·fus′er** *n.*

Synonyms: *refuse, decline, reject, spurn, rebuff, ignore.* These verbs imply negation or denial in varying manner. *Refuse* is used of a positive, unyielding, sometimes brusque decision not to act, accept, or do something. *Decline* involves withholding consent but usually doing so courteously: *decline an invitation.* *Reject* applies to a blunt, even hostile, refusal to do something. *Spurn* is to reject scornfully or contemptuously. *Rebuff* pertains to the disdainful refusal to accept something offered. *Ignore* implies affront in not recognizing the presence or existence of a person or proposal.

ref·use[2] (rĕf′yo͞os) *n.* Anything discarded or rejected as useless or worthless; trash. [ME < OFr. *refus*, rejection < *refuser*, to refuse.]

ref·u·ta·tion (rĕf′yo͞o-tā′shən) also **re·fut·al** (rĭ-fyo͞ot′l) *n.* **1.** The act of refuting. **2.** Something that refutes.

re·fute (rĭ-fyo͞ot′) *tr.v.* **-fut·ed, -fut·ing, -futes. 1.** To prove to be false or erroneous; disprove: *refute an argument.* **2.** To deny the accuracy or truth of. [Lat. *refutare* : *re-*, back + *-futare*, to beat.] **—re·fut′a·bil′i·ty** (rĭ-fyo͞o′tə-bĭl′ĭ-tē, rĕf′yə-tə-) *n.* **—re·fut′a·ble** *adj.* **—re·fut′a·bly** *adv.* **—re·fut′er** *n.*

re·gain (rē-gān′) *tr.v.* **-gained, -gain·ing, -gains. 1.** To recover possession of. **2.** To reach again. **—re·gain′er** *n.*

re·gal (rē′gəl) *adj.* **1.** Of or pertaining to a king; royal. **2.** Belonging to or befitting a king: *regal attire.* **3.** Of great magnificence; splendid. [ME < OFr. < Lat. *regalis* < *rex*, king.] **—re·gal′i·ty** (rĭ-găl′ĭ-tē) *n.* **—re′gal·ly** *adv.*

re·gale (rĭ-gāl′) *v.* **-galed, -gal·ing, -gales.** *—tr.* **1.** To delight or entertain; give pleasure to. **2.** To entertain sumptuously with food and drink; provide a feast for. *—intr.* To feast oneself. *—n.* **1.** A great feast; sumptuous repast. **2.** A choice food or drink; delicacy. **3.** Refreshment. [Fr. *régaler* < OFr. *regaler* : *re-* (intensive < Lat.) + *gale*, pleasure.] **—re·gale′ment** *n.*

re·ga·lia (rĭ-gāl′yə, -gā′lē-ə) *pl.n.* *(used with a sing. or pl. verb).* **1.** The emblems and symbols of royalty, as the crown and scepter. **2.** The rights and privileges of royalty. **3.** The distinguishing symbols of a rank, office, order, or society. **4.** Magnificent attire; finery. [Med. Lat. < Lat., neuter pl. of *regalis*, regal.]

re·gard (rĭ-gärd′) *v.* **-gard·ed, -gard·ing, -gards.** *—tr.* **1.** To look at attentively; observe closely. **2.** To look upon or consider in a particular way: *I regard him as a fool.* **3.** To have great esteem or admiration for. **4.** *Archaic.* To relate, concern, or refer to. **5.** To consider or take into account. **6.** *Obs.* To take care of. *—intr.* **1.** To look; gaze. **2.** To give heed; pay attention. *—n.* **1.** A look or gaze. **2.** Careful thought or attention; heed: *gives little regard to his appearance.* **3.** Respect, affection, or esteem: *won the regard of all.* **4. regards.** Greetings that show respect or affection; good wishes: *send one's regards.* **5.** A particular point or respect: *I agree in this regard.* **6.** Basis for action; motive. **7.** *Obs.* Appearance or aspect. ***—idioms.* as regards.** Concerning. **in** (or **with**) **regard to.** With respect to; concerning. [ME *regarden* < OFr. *regarder* : *re-*, back + *guarder*, to guard, of Germanic orig.]

Synonyms: *regard, esteem, admiration, approbation.* These nouns refer in varying degree to the appreciation of the worth of a person or thing. *Regard* is the least forceful, a general term implying affection and recognition of worth; in the plural it is often used as a courteous close to a letter or message: *with best regards.* *Esteem* connotes measured, considered, and pleasurable appraisal of worth: *esteem for a distinguished scholar.* *Admiration* is undisguised pleasure, delight, and wonder in contemplating something unusual, beautiful, or skillful. *Approbation* is the approval or commendation of something after careful consideration of its worth.

Usage: *Regard* is traditionally used as a singular in the phrase *in* (or *with*) *regard to* (not *in regards to*). *Regarding* and *as regards* are used in the same sense of "with reference to" but are not acceptable to a majority of the Usage Panel. In the same sense *with respect to* is acceptable, but *respecting* is not. • *Respects* is sometimes held preferable to *regards* in the sense of "particulars": *In some respects* (not *regards*) *the books are alike.*

re·gar·dant (rĭ-gär′dnt) *adj. Heraldry.* With the face turned backward in profile. [ME < OFr., pr.part. of *regarder*, to regard.]

re·gard·ful (rĭ-gärd′fəl) *adj.* **1.** Showing attention; heedful. **2.** Showing deference; respectful. **—re·gard′ful·ly** *adv.* **—re·gard′ful·ness** *n.*

re·gard·ing (rĭ-gär′dĭng) *prep.* In reference to; concerning. —See Usage note at **regard.**

re·gard·less (rĭ-gärd′lĭs) *adj.* Heedless; unmindful. *—adv.* In spite of everything; anyway. **—re·gard′less·ly** *adv.* **—re·gard′less·ness** *n.*

re·gard·less of *prep.* In spite of.

re·gat·ta (rĭ-gä′tə, -găt′ə) *n.* A boat race or an organized series of boat races. [Ital.]

re·ge·late (rē′jə-lāt′, rē′jə-lāt′) *intr.v.* **-lat·ed, -lat·ing, -lates.** To undergo regelation. [RE- + Lat. *gelare, gelat-*, to freeze.]

re·ge·la·tion (rē′jə-lā′shən) *n.* **1.** The fusion of two blocks of ice by pressure. **2.** Successive melting under pressure and freezing when pressure is relaxed at the interface of two blocks of ice.

re·gen·cy (rē′jən-sē) *n., pl.* **-cies. 1.** A person or group selected to govern in place of a king or other ruler in case of minority, absence, incompetence, or sickness. **2.** The period during which a regent governs. **3.** The office, area of jurisdiction, or government of a regent or regents. *—adj.* Also **Re·gen·cy.** Of, relating to, or characteristic of the style, esp. in furniture, prevalent during the regency (1811–20) of George, Prince of Wales.

re·gen·er·a·cy (rĭ-jĕn′ər-ə-sē) *n.* The state of being regenerated.

re·gen·er·ate (rĭ-jĕn′ə-rāt′) *v.* **-at·ed, -at·ing, -ates.** *—tr.* **1.** To reform spiritually or morally. **2.** To form, construct, or create anew. **3.** *Biol.* To replace (a lost or damaged organ or part) by formation of new tissue. *—intr.* **1.** To become formed or constructed again. **2.** To undergo spiritual conversion or rebirth. **3.** To effect regeneration. *—n.* (rĭ-jĕn′ər-ĭt). One who is spiritually reborn or reformed. *—adj.* (rĭ-jĕn′ər-ĭt). **1.** Spiritually or morally revitalized. **2.** Restored; refreshed; renewed. [Lat. *regenerare, regenerat-*, to reproduce : *re-*, again + *generare*, to beget < *genus*, birth.] **—re·gen′er·a·ble** (-rə-bəl) *adj.* **—re·gen′er·ate·ly** *adv.* **—re·gen′er·a′tor** *n.*

re·gen·er·a·tion (rĭ-jĕn′ə-rā′shən) *n.* **1.** The act or process of regenerating or the state of being regenerated. **2.** Spiritual or moral revival or rebirth. **3.** *Biol.* The regrowth of lost or destroyed parts or organs.

re·gen·er·a·tive (rĭ-jĕn′ə-rā′tĭv, -ər-ə-tĭv) *adj.* **1.** Of, pertaining to, or marked by regeneration. **2.** Liable to regenerate. **—re·gen′er·a′tive·ly** *adv.*

re·gent (rē′jənt) *n.* **1.** One who rules during the absence or disability of a sovereign. **2.** One acting as a ruler or governor. **3.** A person serving on a board that governs an institution, such as a university. [ME < OFr., ruling < Lat. *regens,* pr.part. of *regere,* to rule.] **—re'gent·al** (-jən'tl) *adj.*

reg·gae (rĕg'ā) *n.* Popular music of Jamaican origin having elements of calypso, soul, and rock'n'roll and characterized by a simple, syncopated rhythm. [Orig. unknown.]

reg·i·cide (rĕj'ĭ-sīd') *n.* **1.** The killing of a king. **2.** One who kills a king. [Lat. *rex, regi-,* king + -CIDE.] **—reg'i·ci'dal** (-sīd'l) *adj.*

re·gime also **ré·gime** (rā-zhēm', rĭ-) *n.* **1. a.** A system of management. **b.** A government that is in power; administration. **2.** A social system or pattern. **3.** A regimen. [Fr. *régime* < Lat. *regimen* < *regere,* to rule.]

reg·i·men (rĕj'ə-mən, -mĕn') *n.* **1.** Governmental rule or control. **2.** The systematic procedure of a natural phenomenon or process. **3.** A system, as of therapy or diet. [ME < Lat., regime.]

reg·i·ment (rĕj'ə-mənt) *n.* A military unit of ground troops consisting of at least two battalions. *—tr.v.* (rĕj'ə-mĕnt') **-ment·ed, -ment·ing, -ments. 1.** To organize or form into a regiment. **2.** To appoint to a regiment. **3.** To put into order; systematize. **4.** To impose uniformity and rigid order upon. [ME < OFr. < LLat. *regimentum,* rule < Lat. *regere,* to rule.] **—reg'i·men'tal** (-mĕn'tl) *adj.* **—reg'i·men'tal·ly** *adv.* **—reg'i·men·ta'tion** *n.*

reg·i·men·tals (rĕj'ə-mĕn'tlz) *pl.n.* **1.** The uniform and insignia characteristic of a particular regiment. **2.** Military dress.

re·gion (rē'jən) *n.* **1.** A large, usually continuous segment of a surface or space; area. **2.** A large and indefinite portion of the earth's surface. **3.** A specified district or territory. **4.** A field of interest or activity; sphere. **5.** A part of the earth characterized by distinctive animal or plant life. **6.** An area of the body having natural or arbitrarily assigned boundaries: *the abdominal region.* [ME *regioun* < OFr. *region* < Lat. *regio* < *regere,* to direct.]

re·gion·al (rē'jə-nəl) *adj.* **1.** Of, pertaining to, or characteristic of a large geographic region. **2.** Of, pertaining to, or characteristic of a particular region or district; localized. **3.** Of, belonging to, or characteristic of a form of a language that is distributed in identifiable geographic areas and has identifiable phonetic, structural, and other differences from the standard form of the language; dialectal. *—n.* **1.** Something that serves a region, as a branch of an organization. **2.** Someone or something regional. **—re'gion·al·ly** *adv.*

ré·gis·seur (rā'zhē-sûr') *n., pl.* **-seurs** (-sûr'). The director of a ballet. [Fr. < *régir,* to direct < Lat. *regere* < *rex,* king.]

reg·is·ter (rĕj'ĭ-stər) *n.* **1. a.** A formal or official recording of items, names, or actions. **b.** A book for such entries. **2.** An entry in a register. **3.** A device that automatically registers a quantity or number. **4.** An adjustable, grill-like device through which heated or cooled air is released into a room. **5.** A state of proper alignment or positioning. **6.** Registration; registry. **7.** *Mus.* **a.** The range of an instrument or voice. **b.** A part of such a range that has similar quality. **c.** A group of matched organ pipes; stop. *—v.* **-tered, -ter·ing, -ters.** *—tr.* **1. a.** To enter in an official register. **b.** To enroll officially or formally. **2.** To indicate, as on an instrument or scale. **3.** To show (emotion). **4.** To cause (mail) to be officially recorded by payment of a fee. *—intr.* **1.** To place or cause placement of one's name in a register. **2.** To have one's name officially placed on a list of eligible voters. **3.** To create an impression. **4.** To be in correct alignment. [ME *registre* < OFr. < Med. Lat. *registrum* < LLat. *regesta* < Lat., neuter pl. of *regestus,* p.part. of *regerere,* to record: *re-,* back + *gerere,* to carry.] **—reg'is·ter·er** *n.* **—reg'is·tra·ble** (-ĭ-strə-bəl) *adj.*

reg·is·tered (rĕj'ĭ-stərd) *adj.* **1.** Having the owner's name listed in a register: *registered bonds.* **2.** Having a pedigree recorded in a breed association studbook: *a registered poodle.* **3.** Officially qualified: *a registered pharmacist.*

registered mail *n.* Mail that is recorded by the post office when sent and at each point on its route so as to assure safe delivery.

registered nurse *n.* A graduate trained nurse who has passed a state registration examination.

reg·is·trant (rĕj'ĭ-strənt) *n.* One who registers or is registered.

reg·is·trar (rĕj'ĭ-strär', rĕj'ĭ-strär') *n.* **1.** An officer in a college or university who keeps records on the enrollment and academic standing of students. **2.** An officer of a corporation responsible for maintaining records of ownership of its securities. **3.** An admitting officer in a hospital.

reg·is·tra·tion (rĕj'ĭ-strā'shən) *n.* **1.** The act of registering. **2.** The number of persons registered; enrollment. **3.** An entry in a register. **4.** A document certifying an act of registering. **5.** *Mus.* **a.** A combination of organ stops selected to be used in playing a piece. **b.** The technique of selecting and adjusting organ stops.

reg·is·try (rĕj'ĭ-strē) *n., pl.* **-tries. 1.** Registration. **2.** A ship's registered nationality; flag. **3.** A place for registering. **4.** A book for official records.

re·gius professor (rē'jəs, -jē-əs) *n.* One holding a professorship established by royal subsidy at certain British universities. [< Lat. *regius,* royal < *rex,* king.]

reg·let (rĕg'lĭt) *n.* **1.** *Archit.* A narrow, flat molding. **2.** *Printing.* A flat piece of wood used to separate lines of type. [OFr. < *regle,* ruler < Lat. *regula* < *regere,* to rule.]

reg·nal (rĕg'nəl) *adj.* Designating a specified year of a monarch's reign calculated from the date of accession. [Med. Lat. *regnalis,* royal < Lat. *regnum,* reign < *rex,* king.]

reg·nant (rĕg'nənt) *adj.* **1.** Reigning; ruling. **2.** Predominant. **3.** Widespread; prevalent. [Lat. *regnans,* pr.part. of *regnare,* to reign < *regnum,* reign < *rex,* king.]

reg·o·lith (rĕg'ə-lĭth') *n.* The layer of loose rock material resting on bedrock, constituting the surface of most land. [Gk. *rhēgos,* blanket + -LITH.]

re·gorge (rē-gôrj') *tr.v.* **-gorged, -gorg·ing, -gorg·es.** To disgorge. [Fr. *regorger* < OFr. : *re-,* back + *gorger,* to gorge < *gorge,* throat.]

re·gress (rĭ-grĕs') *v.* **-gressed, -gress·ing, -gress·es.** *—intr.* **1.** To revert or return to a previous and usually worse condition. **2.** To have a tendency to approach or go back to a statistical mean. *—tr.* To induce a state of regression in. *—n.* (rē'grĕs'). **1.** Return or withdrawal. **2.** The act of reasoning backward from an effect to a cause. [Lat. *regredi, regress-* : *re-,* back + *gradi,* to go.] **—re·gres'sor** *n.*

re·gres·sion (rĭ-grĕsh'ən) *n.* **1.** Reversion; retrogression. **2.** Relapse to a less perfect or developed state. **3.** *Psychoanal.* Reversion to a more primitive or less mature behavior pattern. **4.** *Statistics.* The tendency for the expected value of one of two jointly correlated random variables to approach more closely the mean value of its set than the other. **5.** *Astron.* Retrogradation.

re·gres·sive (rĭ-grĕs'ĭv) *adj.* **1.** Tending to return or revert. **2.** Characterized by regression or a tendency to regress. **3.** Having the rate lessen as the amount taxed increases. **—re·gres'sive·ly** *adv.* **—re·gres'sive·ness** *n.*

re·gret (rĭ-grĕt') *v.* **-gret·ted, -gret·ting, -grets.** *—tr.* **1.** To feel sorry, disappointed, or distressed about. **2.** To feel sorrow or grief over; mourn. *—intr.* To feel regret. *—n.* **1.** A sense of loss and longing for someone gone. **2.** Distress over a desire unfulfilled or an action performed or not performed. **3.** An expression of grief or disappointment. **4. regrets.** A courteous declining to accept an invitation. [ME *regretten* < OFr. *regretter,* to lament.] **—re·gret'ta·ble** *adj.* **—re·gret'ta·bly** *adv.* **—re·gret'ter** *n.*

Synonyms: *regret, sorrow, grief, anguish, woe, heartache.* These nouns relate to mental distress. *Regret* has the broadest range of meanings, from mere disappointment in not being able to do something to painful sense of loss, bitterness, or longing for something lost or done or left undone. *Sorrow* connotes sadness caused by misfortune or the loss of a loved one and also implies contrition for something one regrets having done. *Grief* is deep, acute personal sorrow arising as from irreplaceable loss. *Anguish* implies an agonizing grief so painful as to be excruciating. *Woe* is intense, prolonged unhappiness or misery. *Heartache* implies longing for something out of reach.

re·gret·ful (rĭ-grĕt'fəl) *adj.* Full of regret or sorrow. **—re·gret'ful·ly** *adv.* **—re·gret'ful·ness** *n.*

re·group (rē-gro͞op') *v.* **-grouped, -group·ing, -groups.** *—tr.* To arrange in a new grouping. *—intr.* **1.** To change or reassemble a military formation, as after a battle. **2.** To reorganize for renewed effort, as after a temporary defeat.

reg·u·lar (rĕg'yə-lər) *adj.* **1.** Customary, usual, or normal. **2.** Orderly or symmetrical. **3.** Conforming to set procedure, principle, or discipline. **4.** Methodical; well-ordered. **5.** Occurring at fixed intervals; periodic. **6.** Constant; not varying. **7.** Formally correct; proper. **8.** Having the required qualifications for an occupation. **9.** Perfect; complete; thorough: *a regular villain.* **10.** *Informal.* Good; nice: *a regular guy.* **11.** *Bot.* Having symmetrically arranged parts of similar size and shape: *regular flowers.* **12.** *Gram.* Belonging to a standard mode of inflection or conjugation. **13.** Belonging to a religious order and bound by its rules: *the regular clergy.* **14. a.** Having equal sides and equal angles. Used of polygons. **b.** Having faces that are congruent regular polygons and congruent polyhedral angles. Used of polyhedra. **15.** Belonging to or constituting the permanent army of a nation. *—n.* **1.** A member of the clergy or of a religious order. **2.** A soldier belonging to a regular army. **3.** A dependable and loyal person: *one of the party regulars.* **4.** A clothing size designed for persons of average height. **5.** *Informal.* A habitual customer. [ME, under religious rule < OFr. *reguler* < Lat. *regularis,* of a bar, according to rule < *regula,* bar, ruler < *regere,* to rule.] **—reg'u·lar'i·ty** (-lăr'ĭ-tē) *n.* **—reg'u·lar·ly** *adv.*

regular army *n.* The permanent standing army of a nation or state.

reg·u·lar·ize (rĕg'yə-lə-rīz') *tr.v.* **-ized, -iz·ing, -iz·es.** To make regular or cause to conform. **—reg'u·lar·i·za'tion, reg'u·lar·iz'er** *n.*

regular year *n.* In the Jewish calendar: **a.** An ordinary year of 354 days. **b.** A leap year of 384 days.

reg·u·late (rĕg'yə-lāt') *tr.v.* **-lat·ed, -lat·ing, -lates. 1.** To control or direct according to a rule. **2.** To adjust in conformity to a specification or requirement. **3.** To adjust (a mechanism) for accurate and proper functioning. [Lat. *regulare, regulat-* < Lat. *regula,* a rule.] **—reg'u·la'tive, reg'u·la·to'ry** (-lə-tôr'ē, -tōr'ē) *adj.*

reg·u·la·tion (rĕg'yə-lā'shən) *n.* **1.** The act of regulating. **2.** A principle, rule, or law designed to control or govern behavior. **3.** A governmental order having the force of law.

regiment
Soldiers storming Fort Wagner on July 18, 1863

register
Cash register

reindeer

reg·u·la·tor (rĕg′yə-lā′tər) *n.* **1.** One that regulates. **2. a.** The mechanism in a watch by which its speed is governed. **b.** An accurate clock used as a standard for timing other clocks. **3. a.** A device to maintain uniform speed in a machine; governor. **b.** A device to control the flow of gases, liquids, or electric current.

regulator gene *n.* A gene that represses the activity of another gene in an operon.

Reg·u·lus (rĕg′yə-ləs) *n., pl.* **-li** (-lī′) or **-lus·es. 1.** A bright double star in the constellation Leo. **2. regulus.** *Metallurgy.* **a.** The relatively pure metallic part of a charge that sinks to the bottom of a furnace or crucible. **b.** A relatively impure product of various ores in smelting. [Lat., ruler of a small country, dim. of *rex,* king.] **—reg′u·line** (rĕg′yə-lĭn, -līn′) *adj.*

re·gur·gi·tate (rē-gûr′jĭ-tāt′) *v.* **-tat·ed, -tat·ing, -tates.** *—intr.* To rush or surge back; regorge. *—tr.* To cause to pour back, esp. to cast up (partially digested food); vomit. [Med. Lat. *regurgitare, regurgitat-* : *re-,* back + LLat. *gurgitare,* to engulf < Lat. *gurges,* whirlpool.] **—re·gur′gi·ta′tion** *n.* **—re·gur′gi·ta·tive** *adj.*

re·hab (rē′hăb′) *n.* Something, esp. a building, that has undergone structural rehabilitation. *—v.* **-habbed, -hab·bing, -habs.** *—tr.* To rehabilitate (a building, for example) structurally. *—intr.* To undergo structural rehabilitation.

re·ha·bil·i·tate (rē′hə-bĭl′ĭ-tāt′) *tr.v.* **-tat·ed, -tat·ing, -tates. 1.** To restore (a handicapped person, for example) to useful life through education and therapy. **2.** To reinstate the good name of. **3.** To restore the former rank, privileges, or rights of. **4.** To restore to a former state or condition. [Med. Lat. *rehabilitare, rehabilitat-* : Lat. *re-,* again + LLat. *habilitare,* to habilitate. —see HABILITATE.] **—re′ha·bil′i·ta′tion** *n.* **—re′ha·bil′i·ta′tive** *adj.*

re·hash (rē-hăsh′) *tr.v.* **-hashed, -hash·ing, -hash·es.** To go over, repeat, or rework (old material). *—n.* (rē′hăsh′). **1.** The process or action of rehashing. **2.** Something that is the result of rehashing.

re·hear (rē-hîr′) *tr.v.* **-heard** (-hûrd′), **-hear·ing, -hears. 1.** To hear again. **2.** *Law.* To give a second or new judicial hearing to.

re·hear·ing (rē-hîr′ĭng) *n. Law.* A second or new hearing of a case, plea, or suit in the same court.

re·hears·al (rĭ-hûr′səl) *n.* **1.** The act or process of practicing in preparation for a performance, esp. for a public performance. **2.** A verbal repetition or recital.

re·hearse (rĭ-hûrs′) *v.* **-hearsed, -hears·ing, -hears·es.** *—tr.* **1.** To practice or give a rehearsal of, esp. in preparation for a public performance. **2.** To perfect or cause to perfect (an action) by repetition. **3.** To retell or recite. *—intr.* To rehearse a song, play, or dance. [ME *rehercen,* to repeat < OFr. *rehercer* : *re-,* again (< Lat.) + *hercer,* to harrow < *herce,* harrow < Lat. *hirpex.*] **—re·hears′er** *n.*

re·house (rē-houz′) *tr.v.* **-housed, -hous·ing, -hous·es.** To put or re-establish in a new, usually improved, dwelling or shelter.

reichs·mark (rīks′märk′) *n., pl.* **reichsmark** or **-marks.** A monetary unit of Germany from 1925–1948. [G. : *Reichs,* genitive of *Reich,* realm + *Mark,* unit of currency < MHG *marke.*]

re·i·fy (rē′ə-fī′, rā′-) *tr.v.* **-fied, -fy·ing, -fies.** To regard or treat (an abstraction) as if it had concrete or material existence. [Lat. *res,* thing + -FY.] **—re′i·fi·ca′tion** (-fĭ-kā′shən) *n.* **—re′i·fi′er** *n.*

reign (rān) *n.* **1.** The exercise of sovereign power, as by a monarch. **2.** The term during which a sovereign rules. **3.** Dominance or widespread influence: *the reign of reason.* *—intr.v.* **reigned, reign·ing, reigns. 1.** To exercise sovereign power. **2.** To hold the title of sovereign, but with limited authority. **3.** To be predominant or prevalent. [ME *reigne* < OFr. < Lat. *regnum* < *rex,* king.]

Reign of Terror *n.* **1.** The period (1793–94) of the French Revolution during which thousands of persons were executed. **2. reign of terror.** A period of violence committed esp. by those in power that results in widespread terror.

re·im·burse (rē′ĭm-bûrs′) *tr.v.* **-bursed, -burs·ing, -burs·es. 1.** To repay: *He reimbursed their expenses.* **2.** To pay back or compensate (a person) for money spent, or losses or damages incurred. [RE- + obs. *imburse,* to pay < Med. Lat. *imbursare,* to appropriate (Lat. *in-,* in + Lat. *bursa,* bag < Gk., skin).] **—re′im·burs′a·ble** *adj.* **—re′im·burse′ment** *n.*

re·im·port (rē′ĭm-pôrt′, -pōrt′, rē-ĭm′pôrt′, -pōrt′) *tr.v.* **-port·ed, -port·ing, -ports.** To bring back into a country (goods made from raw materials originally exported from that country). *—n.* (rē-ĭm′pôrt′, -pōrt′). **1.** The act of reimporting. **2.** Goods reimported. **—re′im·por·ta′tion** *n.*

re·im·pres·sion (rē′ĭm-prĕsh′ən) *n.* A reprint (sense 1.a.).

rein (rān) *n.* **1.** Often **reins.** A long, narrow leather strap attached to the bit of a bridle and used by a rider or driver to control a horse or other animal. **2.** A means of restraint, check, or guidance. *—v.* **reined, rein·ing, reins.** *—tr.* **1.** To check or hold back. **2.** To guide or control. **3.** To equip with reins. *—intr.* **1.** To control a horse with reins. **2.** To exert control over oneself as if with reins. ***—idioms.*** **draw in the reins. 1.** To exert pressure on the reins. **2.** To slow or stop. **give (free) rein to.** To release from restraints. **tight rein.** Close control. [ME *reine* < OFr. *resne* < VLat. **retina* < Lat. *retinēre,* to retain.]

re·in·car·nate (rē′ĭn-kär′nāt′) *tr.v.* **-nat·ed, -nat·ing, -nates.** To be reborn in another body; incarnate again. **—re′in·car·na′tion** *n.* **—re′in·car·na′tion·ist** *n.*

rein·deer (rān′dîr′) *n., pl.* **reindeer** or **-deers.** A large deer, *Rangifer tarandus,* of arctic regions of the Old World and Greenland, having branched antlers in both sexes. [ME *reyndere* < ON *hreindýri* : *hreinn,* reindeer + *dyr,* deer.]

reindeer moss *n.* An erect, grayish, branching lichen, *Cladonia rangiferina,* of arctic regions, forming the chief source of food for reindeer.

re·in·fec·tion (rē′ĭn-fĕk′shən) *n.* A second infection that follows recovery from a previous infection by the same causative agent.

re·in·force also **re-en·force** (rē′ĭn-fôrs′, -fōrs′) *tr.v.* **-forced, -forc·ing, -forc·es. 1.** To give more force or effectiveness to; strengthen. **2.** To strengthen militarily with additional manpower or equipment. **3.** To strengthen, as by adding extra support or padding. **4.** To increase in number. **5.** *Psychol.* **a.** To reward (an experimental subject, for example) with a reinforcer subsequent to a desired response or performance. **b.** To stimulate (a response) by means of a reinforcer. [RE- + *inforce,* var. of ENFORCE.] **—re′in·force′a·ble** *adj.*

reinforced concrete *n.* Poured concrete containing steel bars or metal netting to increase its tensile strength.

re·in·force·ment (rē′ĭn-fôrs′mənt, -fōrs′-) *n.* **1.** The act or process of reinforcing or the condition of being reinforced. **2.** Something that reinforces. **3.** Often **reinforcements.** Additional troops, vessels, or equipment sent to support a military action. **4.** *Psychol.* **a.** The occurrence or experimental introduction of an unconditioned stimulus along with a conditioned stimulus. **b.** The strengthening of a conditioned response by such means. **c.** The strengthening of an instrumental or operant conditioned response leading to satisfaction. **d.** An event, circumstance, or condition that increases the likelihood that a given response will recur in a situation like that in which the reinforcing condition originally occurred.

re·in·forc·er (rē′ĭn-fôr′sər, -fōr′-) *n. Psychol.* A stimulus, such as a reward, that in operant conditioning strengthens a desired response.

reins (rānz) *pl.n.* **1.** The kidneys, loins, or lower back region. **2.** The seat of affections and passions. [ME < OFr. < Lat. *renes.*]

re·in·state (rē′ĭn-stāt′) *tr.v.* **-stat·ed, -stat·ing, -states. 1.** To bring back into use or existence. **2.** To restore to a previous condition or position. **—re′in·state′ment** *n.*

re·in·sure (rē-ĭn-sho͝or′) *tr.v.* **-sured, -sur·ing, -sures. 1.** To insure again. **2.** To insure by contracting to transfer in whole or in part a risk or contingent liability already covered under an existing contract. **—re′in·sur′ance** *n.* **—re′in·sur′er** *n.*

re·in·te·grate (rē-ĭn′tĭ-grāt′) *tr.v.* **-grat·ed, -grat·ing, -grates.** To restore to a condition of integration or unity. **—re′in·te·gra′tion** *n.* **—re·in′te·gra′tive** *adj.*

re·in·ter·pret (rē′ĭn-tûr′prĭt) *tr.v.* **-pret·ed, -pret·ing, -prets.** To interpret again or anew. **—re′in·ter′pre·ta′tion** (-tûr′-prĭ-tā′shən) *n.*

re·in·vest (rē′ĭn-vĕst′) *tr.v.* **-vest·ed, -vest·ing, -vests.** To invest (capital or earnings) again. Used esp. of receipts derived from securities. **—re′in·vest′ment** *n.*

re·in·vig·o·rate (rē′ĭn-vĭg′ə-rāt′) *tr.v.* **-rat·ed, -rat·ing, -rates.** To make vigorous again. **—re′in·vig′o·ra′tion** *n.* **—re′in·vig′o·ra′tor** *n.*

reis (rās) *n.* A plural of **real**[3].

re·is·sue (rē-ĭsh′o͞o) *v.* **-sued, -su·ing, -sues.** *—tr.* To issue again. *—intr.* To come forth again. *—n.* **1.** A second or subsequent issue, as of a book. **2.** A reprinting of postage stamps from unchanged plates.

re·it·er·ate (rē-ĭt′ə-rāt′) *tr.v.* **-at·ed, -at·ing, -ates.** To say over again. [Lat. *reiterare, reiterat-* : *re-,* again + *iterare,* to iterate < *iterum,* again.] **—re·it′er·a′tion, re·it′er·a′tive·ness** *n.* **—re·it′er·a′tor** *n.* **—re·it′er·a′tive** *adj.* **—re·it′er·a′tive·ly** *adv.*

re·ject (rĭ-jĕkt′) *tr.v.* **-ject·ed, -ject·ing, -jects. 1.** To refuse to accept, recognize, or make use of; repudiate. **2.** To refuse to consider or grant; deny. **3.** To refuse affection or recognition to (a person). **4.** To discard as defective or useless; throw away. **5.** To spit out or vomit. *—n.* (rē′jĕkt). Something or someone that has been rejected. [ME *rejecten* < Lat. *reicere,* to throw back : *re-,* back + *jacere,* to throw.] **—re·ject′er, re·jec′tor** *n.* **—re·jec′tive** *adj.*

re·jec·tion (rĭ-jĕk′shən) *n.* **1.** The act or process of rejecting. **2.** The condition of being rejected. **3.** Something rejected.

rejection slip *n.* A printed form or note accompanying an author's manuscript that has been rejected for publication.

rejective art *n.* Minimal art. **—re·jec′tiv·ist** (rĭ-jĕk′tĭ-vĭst′) *adj.*

re·joice (rĭ-jois′) *v.* **-joiced, -joic·ing, -joic·es.** *—intr.* To feel or be joyful. *—tr.* To fill with joy; gladden. ***—phrasal verb.*** **rejoice in.** To have or possess. [ME *rejoicen* < OFr. *rejoir, rejoiss-* : *re-* (intensive) + *joir,* to be joyful < Lat. *gaudēre.*] **—re·joic′er** *n.*

re·joic·ing (rĭ-joi′sĭng) *n.* The feeling or expressing of joy or an instance of this; joyful celebration. **—re·joic′ing·ly** *adv.*

re·join (rĭ-join′) *v.* **-joined, -join·ing, -joins.** *—tr.* To say as a reply. *—intr.* **1.** To respond; answer. **2.** *Law.* To answer a plaintiff's replication. [ME *rejoinen* < OFr. *rejoindre* : *re-*, back (< Lat.) + *joindre,* to join < Lat. *jungere.*]

re-join (rē-join′) *v.* **-joined, -join·ing, -joins.** —*tr.* **1.** To come together again in company with. **2.** To join or put together again; reunite. —*intr.* To be or become joined again.

re·join·der (rĭ-join′dər) *n.* **1.** An answer, esp. to a reply. **2.** *Law.* A second pleading by a defendant, in answer to a plaintiff's replication. [ME *rejoyner* < OFr. *rejoindre,* to answer, rejoin.]

re·ju·ve·nate (rĭ-jo͞o′və-nāt′) *tr.v.* **-nat·ed, -nat·ing, -nates.** **1.** To restore the youthful vigor or appearance of. **2. a.** To stimulate (a stream) to renewed erosive activity, as by uplift. **b.** To develop youthful topographical features in (a previously leveled area). [RE- + Lat. *juvenis,* a youth.] **—re·ju′ve·na′tion** *n.* **—re·ju′ve·na′tor** (-tər) *n.*

re·ju·ve·nes·cence (rĭ-jo͞o′və-nĕs′əns) *n.* A renewal of youthful appearance or character. **—re·ju′ve·nes′cent** *adj.*

re-laid (rē-lād′, rē′lād′) *v.* Past tense and past participle of **re-lay.**

re·lapse (rĭ-lăps′) *intr.v.* **-lapsed, -laps·ing, -laps·es.** **1.** To fall back or revert to a former state. **2.** To regress after partial recovery from illness. **3.** To slip back into bad ways; backslide. —*n.* (rē′lăps, rĭ-lăps′). The act or result of relapsing. [Lat. *relabi, relaps-* : *re-,* back + *labi,* to slide.] **—re·laps′er** *n.*

relapsing fever *n.* Any of several infectious diseases characterized by chills and fever, and caused by spirochetes transmitted by lice and ticks.

re·late (rĭ-lāt′) *v.* **-lat·ed, -lat·ing, -lates.** —*tr.* **1.** To narrate or tell. **2.** To bring into logical or natural association. —*intr.* **1.** To have connection, relation, or reference. **2.** To interact with others in a meaningful or coherent fashion: *couldn't relate well with her peers.* **3.** To respond, esp. in a favorable manner. [Lat. *referre, relat-* : *re-,* back + *ferre,* to bear.] **—re·lat′a·ble** *adj.* **—re·lat′er** *n.*

re·lat·ed (rĭ-lā′tĭd) *adj.* **1.** Connected; associated. **2.** Connected by kinship, marriage, or common origin. **3.** Having a close harmonic connection. **—re·lat′ed·ly** *adv.* **—re·lat′ed·ness** *n.*

re·la·tion (rĭ-lā′shən) *n.* **1.** A logical or natural association between two or more things; connection. **2.** The connection of people by blood or marriage; kinship. **3.** A person connected to another by blood or marriage; relative. **4.** The mode in which a person or thing is connected with another: *the relation of parent to child.* **5. relations.** The connections, dealings, or associations drawing together persons, groups, or nations in personal, business, or diplomatic affairs. **6.** Reference; regard. **7. a.** The act of telling or narrating. **b.** A narrative; account. **8.** *Law.* The assumption that an act or proceeding has taken place prior to its completion or official enactment. **9. relations.** Sexual intercourse.

Usage: Although *relation* and *relative* are interchangeable in the sense of "one related by kinship," *relative* is now more common.

re·la·tion·al (rĭ-lā′shə-nəl) *adj.* **1.** Of or arising from kinship. **2.** Indicating or constituting relations. **3.** Expressing a syntactic relation. **—re·la′tion·al·ly** *adv.*

re·la·tion·ship (rĭ-lā′shən-shĭp′) *n.* **1.** The condition or fact of being related. **2.** Connection by blood or marriage; kinship. **3.** A specified state of affairs existing among people related to or dealing with one another: *has a close relationship with his sisters.*

rel·a·tive (rĕl′ə-tĭv) *adj.* **1.** Having pertinence or relevance; connected; related. **2.** Considered in comparison to or relationship with something else. **3.** Dependent upon or interconnected with something else for intelligibility or significance; not absolute. **4.** *Gram.* Referring to or qualifying an antecedent: *a relative pronoun.* **5.** *Mus.* Having the same key signature. Used of major and minor scales and keys. —*n.* **1.** One related by kinship. **2.** One that is relative. **3.** A relative term. [ME *relatif* < LLat. *relativus* < Lat. *referre,* to relate.] **—rel′a·tive·ly** *adv.* **—rel′a·tive·ness** *n.*

Usage: *Relatively* is appropriate when a comparison is stated or implied: *The first question on the examination was relatively easy* (that is, in comparison to the others). In formal style *relatively* should not be used to mean simply "fairly," as in *I am relatively sure of it.* —See also Usage note at **relation.**

relative biological effectiveness *n. Physics.* A measure of the capacity of a specific ionizing radiation to produce a specific biological effect, usually expressed as the dose of radium gamma rays or 200-kilovolt x-rays relative to the dose of the ionization in question required to produce the effect.

relative clause *n. Gram.* A dependent clause introduced by a relative pronoun.

relative humidity *n.* The ratio of the amount of water vapor in the air at a specific temperature to the maximum capacity of the air at that temperature.

relative permittivity *n.* Permittivity.

relative pitch *n.* **1.** The pitch of a tone as determined by its position in a scale. **2.** The ability to recognize or produce a tone by mentally establishing a relationship between its pitch and that of a recently heard tone.

relative pronoun *n. Gram.* A pronoun that introduces a relative clause and has reference to an antecedent.

relative to *prep.* With regard to: *discussed matters relative to the divorce.*

rel·a·tiv·ism (rĕl′ə-tĭ-vĭz′əm) *n. Philos.* The theory that truth is an ethical relative to the individual or group that holds it.

rel·a·tiv·ist (rĕl′ə-tĭ-vĭst) *n.* **1.** A proponent of relativism. **2.** A physicist specializing in the theories of relativity.

rel·a·tiv·is·tic (rĕl′ə-tĭ-vĭs′tĭk) *adj.* **1.** Of or pertaining to relativism. **2.** *Physics.* **a.** Of, pertaining to, or resulting from speeds that are large with respect to the speed of light: *relativistic increase in mass.* **b.** Of or pertaining to phenomena explicable by special or general relativity: *relativistic mechanics.*

rel·a·tiv·i·ty (rĕl′ə-tĭv′ĭ-tē) *n.* **1.** The quality or state of being relative. **2.** *Philos.* Existence dependent solely upon relation to a thinking mind. **3.** A state of dependence in which the existence or significance of one entity is solely dependent upon that of another. **4.** *Physics.* **a.** Special relativity. **b.** General relativity.

re·la·tor (rĭ-lā′tər) *n.* One who relates or narrates.

re·lax (rĭ-lăks′) *v.* **-laxed, -lax·ing, -lax·es.** —*tr.* **1.** To make lax or loose: *relax one's grip.* **2.** To make less severe or strict. **3.** To reduce in intensity; slacken. **4.** To relieve from effort or strain. —*intr.* **1.** To take one's ease; rest. **2.** To become lax or loose. **3.** To become less severe or strict. **4.** To become less formal, aloof, or tense. [ME *relaxen* < Lat. *relaxare* : *re-,* back + *laxare,* to loosen < *laxus,* loose.] **—re·lax′a·ble** *adj.* **—re·lax′er** *n.*

re·lax·ant (rĭ-lăk′sənt) *n.* Something, such as a drug or therapeutic treatment, that relaxes or relieves muscular or nervous tension. —*adj.* Tending to relax or to relieve tension.

re·lax·a·tion (rē′lăk-sā′shən) *n.* **1. a.** The act of relaxing. **b.** The state of being relaxed. **2.** Refreshment of body or mind; recreation: *play golf for relaxation.* **3.** A loosening or slackening. **4.** A reduction in strictness or severity. **5.** *Physiol.* The lengthening of inactive muscle or muscle fibers. **6.** *Physics.* The return or adjustment of a system to equilibrium following displacement or abrupt change. **7.** *Math.* A numerical method in which the errors, or residuals, resulting from an initial approximation are reduced by succeeding approximations until all errors are within specified limits. **—re·lax′a·tive** *adj.* & *n.*

relaxation time *n. Physics.* The time required for an exponential variable to decrease to $1/e$ (0.368) of its initial value.

re·laxed (rĭ-lăkst′) *adj.* **1.** Not rigorous or strict. **2.** Not tense or rigid. **3.** Being easy and informal in manner.

re·lax·in (rĭ-lăk′sən) *n.* A female hormone secreted by the corpus luteum that helps soften the cervix and relax the pelvic ligaments in childbirth.

re·lay (rē′lā, rĭ-lā′) *n.* **1.** A fresh team, as of horses or dogs, to relieve weary animals in a hunt, task, or journey. **2.** A crew of laborers who relieve another crew at work; shift. **3.** The act of passing something along from one person, group, or station to another. **4. a.** A relay race. **b.** A division of a relay race. **5.** *Elect.* An automatic electromagnetic or electromechanical device that responds to a small current or voltage change by activating switches or other devices in an electric circuit. —*tr.v.* **-layed -lay·ing, -lays.** **1.** To pass or send along by or as if by relay: *relay a message.* **2.** To supply with fresh relays. **3.** *Elect.* To control or retransmit by means of a relay. [ME *relai* < OFr. < *relaier,* to relay : *re-,* back + *laier,* to leave, alteration of *laissier* < Lat. *laxare,* to loosen < *laxus,* loose.]

re-lay (rē-lā′) *tr.v.* **-laid** (-lād′), **-lay·ing, -lays.** To lay again.

relay race *n.* A race between two or more teams, in which each team member runs only a set part of the race, and then is relieved by another member of his team.

re·leas·a·ble (rĭ-lē′sə-bəl) *adj.* **1.** Capable of being released. **2.** Intended or designed to release: *releasable ski bindings.* **—re·leas·a·bil′i·ty** *n.* **—re·leas′a·bly** *adv.*

re·lease (rĭ-lēs′) *tr.v.* **-leased, -leas·ing, -leas·es.** **1.** To set free from confinement, restraint, or bondage; liberate. **2.** To free, unfasten, or let go of. **3.** To relieve from debt or obligation. **4.** To allow performance, sale, publication, or circulation of. **5.** To relinquish (a right, for example). —*n.* **1.** A deliverance; liberation. **2.** An authoritative discharge, as from an obligation or from prison. **3.** An unfastening or letting go of something caught or held fast. **4.** A device or catch for locking or releasing a mechanism. **5. a.** A freeing of something for general publication, use, or circulation. **b.** Something thus released: *a press release.* **6.** *Law.* **a.** The relinquishment of a right, title, or claim to another. **b.** The document granting such a relinquishment. [ME *relesen* < OFr. *relaissier* < Lat. *relaxare,* to relax.] **—re·leas′er** *n.*

re-lease (rē-lēs′) *tr.v.* **-leased, -leas·ing, -leas·es.** To lease again.

released time *n.* In some U.S. public schools, a part of a regular school day during which children are excused from class attendance to receive outside religious instruction.

rel·e·gate (rĕl′ə-gāt′) *tr.v.* **-gat·ed, -gat·ing, -gates.** **1.** To send or consign, esp. to an obscure place, position, or condition. **2.** To assign to a particular class or category; classify. **3.** To refer or assign (a task, for example) for decision or performance. **4.** To banish; exile. [Lat. *relegare, relegat-,* to send away : *re-,* back + *legare,* to send.] **—rel′e·ga′tion** *n.*

re·lent (rĭ-lĕnt′) *v.* **-lent·ed, -lent·ing, -lents.** —*intr.* To become softened or gentler in attitude, temper, or determination. —*tr.* To cause to slacken or abate. [ME *relenten* < Med. Lat. **relentare* : *re-* (intensive < Lat.) + *lentare,* to soften < Lat., to bend < *lentus,* flexible.]

re·lent·less (rĭ-lĕnt′lĭs) *adj.* **1.** Unyielding; pitiless: *relentless persecution.* **2.** Steady and persistent; unremitting: *relentless rain.* **—re·lent′less·ly** *adv.* **—re·lent′less·ness** *n.*

relief
Detail from Buddhist temple, Katmandu, Nepal

rel·e·vance (rĕl′ə-vəns) also **rel·e·van·cy** (-vən-sē) *n.* **1. a.** Pertinence to the matter at hand. **b.** Social applicability: *a government with no relevance.* **2.** The capability of an information retrieval system to select and retrieve data appropriate to a user's needs.

rel·e·vant (rĕl′ə-vənt) *adj.* Related to the matter at hand; pertinent. [Med. Lat. *relevans, relevant-* < Lat., pr.part. of *relevare,* to relieve.] **—rel′e·vant·ly** *adv.*

Synonyms: *relevant, pertinent, germane, material, apt, apposite, apropos.* These terms are related by their varying degree of appropriateness to a subject. *Relevant* is that which has a bearing on the matter at hand. *Pertinent* implies a logical and precise bearing. *Germane* is that which is so closely akin to the subject as to reinforce it. *Material* has the sense of being needed to complete the subject: *material evidence. Apt* is that which is fitting, to the point. *Apposite* is strikingly appropriate or pertinent. *Apropos* is both relevant and opportune, frequently used with *of: apropos of the discussion.*

re·li·a·ble (rĭ-lī′ə-bəl) *adj.* That can be relied upon; dependable. **—re·li′a·bil′i·ty, re·li′a·ble·ness** *n.* **—re·li′a·bly** *adv.*

re·li·ance (rĭ-lī′əns) *n.* **1.** The act of relying. **2.** Confidence; dependence; trust. **3.** One that can be depended on.

re·li·ant (rĭ-lī′ənt) *adj.* Having or demonstrating reliance. **—re·li′ant·ly** *adv.*

rel·ic (rĕl′ĭk) *n.* **1. a.** Something that has survived decay or deterioration. **b.** A belief or custom remaining as a trace of an earlier culture or an outmoded practice. *"Corporal punishment was a relic of barbarism"* (Cyril Connolly). **2.** Something cherished for its age or associations with a person, place, or event; keepsake. **3.** An object of religious veneration, esp. an article reputed to be associated with a saint or martyr. **4. relics.** A corpse; remains. [ME *relik* < OFr. *relique* < LLat. *reliquiae,* sacred relics < Lat., remains < *relinquere,* to leave behind. —see RELINQUISH.]

reliquary
12th-century Spanish

rel·ict (rĕl′ĭkt, rĭ-lĭkt′) *n.* **1.** *Ecol.* An organism or species of an earlier time surviving in an environment that has undergone considerable change. **2.** A widow. —*adj. Geol.* Pertaining to something that has survived, such as structures or minerals after destructive processes. [Lat. *relictus,* p.part. of *relinquere,* to leave behind. —see RELINQUISH.]

re·lic·tion (rĭ-lĭk′shən) *n. Geol.* The gradual recession of water, leaving permanently dry land.

re·lief (rĭ-lēf′) *n.* **1.** Ease from or lessening of pain or discomfort. **2.** Something that lessens pain, discomfort, fear, or anxiety. **3.** Assistance, such as money or food, given to the needy, aged, or to the inhabitants of a disaster-stricken region. **4. a.** A release from a job, post, or duty, as of a sentinel. **b.** The person or persons taking over the duties of another. **5. a.** The projection of figures or forms from a flat background, or such a projection that is apparent only, as in painting. **b.** An art work fashioned in this manner. **6.** The variations in elevation of an area of the earth's surface. **7.** Distinction or prominence resulting from contrast: *"the light brought the white church . . . into relief from the flat ledges"* (Willa Cather). **8.** In feudal law, a payment made by the heir of a deceased tenant to a lord for the privilege of succeeding to the tenant's estate. ***—idiom.* on relief.** Receiving government funds because of need or poverty. [ME < OFr. < *relever,* to relieve.]

relief map *n.* A map that depicts land configuration, as with contour lines, shading, or colors.

relief pitcher *n. Baseball.* A pitcher who regularly stands ready to replace another pitcher during a game.

re·lieve (rĭ-lēv′) *tr.v.* **-lieved, -liev·ing, -lieves. 1.** To cause a lessening or alleviation of: *relieved all his symptoms.* **2.** To free from pain or trouble. **3.** To furnish assistance or aid to. **4.** To release (a person) from an obligation, restriction, or burden, as by law or legislation. **5.** To free from a specified duty by providing or acting as a substitute. **6.** To make less unpleasant, monotonous, or tiresome. **7.** To make distinct or more effective through contrast; set off: *A black sash relieves a white gown.* **8.** To eliminate the bodily wastes of (oneself). **9. a.** To take away from. **b.** To rob: *relieved him of his money.* [ME *releven* < OFr. *relever* < Lat. *relevare* : *re-* (intensive) + *levare,* to raise < *levis,* light.] **—re·liev′a·ble** *adj.* **—re·liev′er** *n.*

Synonyms: *relieve, allay, alleviate, assuage, comfort, lighten, soothe, mitigate.* These terms have in common the sense of lessening a burden. *Relieve* implies making that which causes discomfort or distress more endurable by some positive action. *Allay* suggests giving comfort by laying at rest for the time being that which is causing distress: *allay one's fears. Alleviate* connotes temporary lessening of distress by some action without removing its cause. *Assuage, comfort, lighten,* and *soothe* imply the employment of moral or spiritual means to lessen distress, as through words or acts of cheer, consolation, or reassurance. *Mitigate* connotes moderating the severity of that which is distressing.

re·lie·vo (rĭ-lē′vō) *n., pl.* **-vos.** A relief (sense 5). [Ital. < *rilievare,* to raise < Lat. *relevare.* —see RELIEVE.]

re·lig·ion (rĭ-lĭj′ən) *n.* **1. a.** Belief in and reverence for a supernatural power recognized as the creator and governor of the universe. **b.** A particular integrated system of this expression: *the Hindu religion.* **2.** The spiritual or emotional attitude of one who recognizes the existence of a superhuman power or powers. **3.** An objective pursued with zeal or conscientious devotion: *A collector might make a religion of his hobby.* [ME *religioun* < OFr. *religion* < Lat. *religio.*]

re·lig·ion·ism (rĭ-lĭj′ən-ĭz′əm) *n.* Excessive or affected religious zeal. **—re·lig′ion·ist** *n.*

re·li·gi·ose (rĭ-lĭj′ē-ōs′) *adj.* Overly religious, esp. in a conspicuous or sentimental manner. [< RELIGIOUS.]

re·lig·i·os·i·ty (rĭ-lĭj′ē-ŏs′ĭ-tē) *n., pl.* **-ties. 1.** The state of being religious. **2.** Excessive or affected piety.

re·lig·ious (rĭ-lĭj′əs) *adj.* **1.** Of, pertaining to, or teaching religion. **2.** Adhering to or manifesting religion; pious. **3.** Extremely faithful; conscientious: *religious devotion to duty.* —*n., pl.* **religious.** A person, such as a nun or monk, belonging to a monastic order. [ME < OFr. < Lat. *religiosus* < *religio,* religion.] **—re·lig′ious·ly** *adv.* **—re·lig′ious·ness** *n.*

Synonyms: *religious, devout, saintly, pious, sanctimonious, puritanical.* These terms have in common the sense of a mental, emotional, or reverential attitude about religion. *Religious* implies adherence to religion in both belief and practice. *Devout* connotes inward faith and outward sincere observance of rituals and requirements. *Saintly* implies an exceptional, exemplary quality of spiritual and religious integrity. *Pious* suggests basically a godly and reverential observance of religion, but when referring to ostentatious conduct, the term may imply derogation. *Sanctimonious,* in its modern usage, connotes sustained religious hypocrisy. *Puritanical* applies to a religious person who seeks to impose on others his own strict moral code.

re·line (rē-līn′) *tr.v.* **-lined, -lin·ing, -lines. 1.** To make new lines on. **2.** To put a new lining in.

re·lin·quish (rĭ-lĭng′kwĭsh) *tr.v.* **-quished, -quish·ing, -quish·es. 1.** To retire from; leave; abandon. **2.** To put aside or desist from (something practiced, professed, or intended). **3.** To surrender; renounce: *"the papacy did not relinquish its claims for political power"* (George L. Mosse). **4.** To cease holding physically; release. [ME *relinquisshen* < OFr. *relinquir, relinquiss-* < Lat. *relinquere,* to leave behind : *re-,* behind + *linquere,* to leave.] **—re·lin′quish·er** *n.* **—re·lin′quish·ment** *n.*

Synonyms: *relinquish, yield, resign, abandon, surrender, cede, waive, forgo, renounce.* These terms have in common the sense of giving up something either voluntarily or involuntarily. *Relinquish* connotes giving up something desirable or prized unwillingly and regretfully. *Yield* implies giving way under contest or pressure with the hope that such action will be temporary. *Resign* suggests submission out of hopelessness. It may also refer to the giving up of office. *Abandon* and *surrender* agree in implying the giving up of something with no expectation of returning to it or recovering it, but differ in that the former action usually is voluntary and the latter the result of force. *Cede* connotes formal transfer of rights or territory. *Waive* implies a voluntary decision to dispense with a claim or a right. *Forgo* suggests abstaining or refraining from something mildly desirable or pleasurable: *forgo dessert. Renounce* means to turn down something or to dissociate oneself from it formally, usually as a matter of principle.

rel·i·quar·y (rĕl′ə-kwĕr′ē) *n., pl.* **-ies.** A receptacle, such as a coffer or shrine, for keeping or displaying sacred relics. [Fr. *reliquaire* < Med. Lat. *reliquiarium* < LLat. *reliquiae,* sacred relics. —see RELIC.]

rel·ique (rĕl′ĭk) *n. Archaic.* Variant of **relic.**

re·liq·ui·ae (rĭ-lĭk′wĭ-ē′) *pl.n.* Remains, esp. of fossil organisms. [Lat., remains. —see RELIC.]

rel·ish (rĕl′ĭsh) *n.* **1.** An appetite for something; appreciation or liking: *"a relish for luxury and splendor"* (Henry James). **2. a.** Pleasure; zest. **b.** Something that lends pleasure or zest. **3.** A spicy or savory condiment served with food. **4.** The flavor of a food, esp. when appetizing. **5.** A trace or suggestion of some important quality. —*v.* **-ished, -ish·ing, -ish·es.** —*tr.* **1.** To enjoy; take pleasure in. **2.** To like the flavor of. **3.** To give spice or flavor to. —*intr.* To have a pleasing or distinctive taste. [ME *reles,* taste < OFr., something remaining < *relaissier,* to leave behind < Lat. *relaxare,* to relax.] **—rel′ish·a·ble** *adj.*

re·live (rē-lĭv′) *v.* **-lived, -liv·ing, -lives.** —*tr.* To undergo again, esp. by means of the imagination. —*intr.* To live again.

re·lo·cate (rē-lō′kāt′) *v.* **-cat·ed, -cat·ing, -cates.** —*tr.* To establish in a new place. —*intr.* To become established in a new residence or place of business: *relocated in the suburbs.* **—re′lo·ca′tion** *n.*

re·lu·cent (rĭ-lo͞o′sənt) *adj.* Reflecting light; shining. [Lat. *relucens,* pr.part. of *relucēre,* to shine back : *re-,* back + *lucēre,* to shine.]

re·luct (rĭ-lŭkt′) *intr.v.* **-luct·ed, -luct·ing, -lucts.** To show reluctance or repugnance. [Lat. *reluctari* : *re-,* against + *luctari,* to struggle.]

re·luc·tance (rĭ-lŭk′təns) also **re·luc·tan·cy** (-tən-sē) *n.*

1. The state of being reluctant; disinclination. 2. *Physics.* A magnetic quantity analogous to electric resistance and equal in a closed magnetic circuit to the ratio of circuit length to the product of cross-sectional area and permeability.

re·luc·tant (rĭ-lŭk′tənt) *adj.* **1.** Unwilling; averse: *reluctant to help.* **2.** Marked by unwillingness. **3.** Offering resistance; opposing. [Lat. *reluctans, reluctant-,* pr.part. of *reluctari,* to reluct.] **—re·luc′tant·ly** *adv.*

rel·uc·tiv·i·ty (rĕl′ək-tĭv′ĭ-tē) *n., pl.* **-ties.** *Physics.* A measure of the resistance of a material to the establishment of a magnetic field within it, equal to the reciprocal of magnetic permeability. [RELUCT(ANCE) + (CONDUCT)IVITY.]

re·lume (rĭ-lo͞om′) *tr.v.* **-lumed, -lum·ing, -lumes.** To make bright or clear again; illuminate again. [RE- + (IL)LUME.]

re·ly (rĭ-lī′) *intr.v.* **-lied, -ly·ing, -lies. 1.** To depend: *rely on one's parents for love and support.* **2.** To trust confidently: *rely on the children to behave.* [ME *relien,* to rally < OFr. *relier* < Lat. *religare,* to bind fast : *re-* (intensive) + *ligare,* to bind.] **—re·li′er** *n.*

Synonyms: *rely, trust, depend, bank, count, reckon. Rely* implies having complete confidence in the ability or veracity of another. *Trust* has the sense of belief based on inconclusive evidence. *Depend* implies confidence in the strength or support of another. *Bank* and *count,* informal terms, suggest assurance of the fulfillment of a promise. *Reckon* implies a sense of expectancy in the fulfillment of a promise or action.

rem (rĕm) *n. Physics.* The amount of ionizing radiation required to produce the same biological effect as one roentgen of high-penetration x-rays. [R(OENTGEN) E(QUIVALENT IN) M(AN).]

REM (rĕm) *n.* The rapid, periodic, jerky movement of the eyes during certain stages of the sleep cycle when dreaming takes place. [R(APID) E(YE) M(OVEMENT).]

re·made (rē-mād′) *v.* Past tense and past participle of **remake.**

re·main (rĭ-mān′) *intr.v.* **-mained, -main·ing, -mains. 1.** To continue without change of condition, quality, or place. **2.** To stay or be left over after the removal, departure, loss, or destruction of others. **3.** To be left as still to be dealt with: *A cure remains to be found.* **4.** To endure or persist. [ME *remaynen* < OFr. *remaindre* < Lat. *remanere* : *re-,* back + *manere,* to stay.]

re·main·der (rĭ-mān′dər) *n.* **1.** Something that is left over after other parts have been taken away. **2.** *Math.* **a.** In division, the dividend minus the product of the divisor and quotient. **b.** In subtraction, the difference. **3.** *Law.* An estate effective and enjoyable only after the determination of another estate. **4.** A book remaining with a publisher after sales have fallen off, sold at a reduction. *—tr.v.* **-dered, -der·ing, -ders.** To sell (books) as remainders. [ME < AN < OFr. *remaindre,* to remain.]

Synonyms: *remainder, rest, residue, residuum, residuals, balance, remnant, leavings, tailings, remains, relic. Remainder,* the most general of these terms, is that which is left when something is taken away. *Rest* is used virtually interchangeably with *remainder* in its general meaning. *Residue* and *residuum* refer to what is left after something has undergone dissolution or diminution, as by combustion; also, both terms refer to what is left of an estate after probate costs and bequests have been satisfied. *Residuals* in modern usage refers to royalty payments made to artists on the remainder of the life of an artistic production after the original production or edition has run its course. *Balance* implies that which is left at a bank after withdrawals; also, the unpaid amount on a charge account. *Remnant* is any small piece or quantity remaining after the major part has been used. *Leavings* and *tailings* are the culls remaining after that which is valuable has been taken away: *the tailings of a gold mine. Remains* specifically refers to a corpse, although it also applies to monuments of the past. *Relic* is a treasured memento, cherished in memory of a person, event, or place.

re·mains (rĭ-mānz′) *pl.n.* **1.** All that is left after other parts have been taken away, used up, or destroyed. **2.** A corpse. **3.** The unpublished writings of a deceased author. **4.** Ancient ruins or fossils.

re·make (rē-māk′) *tr.v.* **-made** (-mād′), **-mak·ing, -makes.** To make anew; reconstruct. *—n.* **1.** An instance of making anew. **2.** Something made again: *a remake of a motion picture.*

re·man (rē-măn′) *tr.v.* **-manned, -man·ning, -mans. 1.** To supply with a new contingent of men, as for work or defense. **2.** To renew the manliness or courage of.

re·mand (rĭ-mănd′) *tr.v.* **-mand·ed, -mand·ing, -mands. 1.** To send or order back. **2.** *Law.* **a.** To send back (one in custody) to prison, to another court, or to another agency for further proceedings. **b.** To send back (a case) to a lower court with instructions about further proceedings. *—n.* **1.** The state of being remanded. **2.** The act of remanding. **3.** A person remanded. [ME *remaunden* < OFr. *remander* < LLat. *remandere,* to send back : *re-,* back + *mandare,* to order.] **—re·mand′ment** *n.*

rem·a·nence (rĕm′ə-nəns) *n. Physics.* The magnetic induction that remains in a material after removal of the magnetizing force. [< ME *remanent,* remaining < Lat. *remanens,* pr.part. of *remanēre,* to remain.] **—rem′a·nent** *adj.*

re·mark (rĭ-märk′) *v.* **-marked, -mark·ing, -marks.** *—tr.* **1.** To say or write briefly and casually as a comment. **2.** To take notice of; observe. *—intr.* To make a comment or observation. *—n.* **1.** The act of noticing and mentioning: *a place worthy of remark.* **2.** A casual or brief expression of opinion; comment. [Fr. *remarquer* < OFr. : *re-* (intensive < Lat.) + *marquer,* to mark, ult. of Germanic orig.] **—re·mark′er** *n.*

re·mark·a·ble (rĭ-mär′kə-bəl) *adj.* **1.** Worthy of notice. **2.** Extraordinary; uncommon. **—re·mark′a·ble·ness** *n.* **—re·mark′a·bly** *adv.*

re·marque (rĭ-märk′) *n.* **1.** A mark made in the margin of an engraving plate to indicate its stage of development prior to completion. **2.** A print or proof from a plate carrying such a mark. [Fr., remark < *remarquer,* to remark.]

re·match (rē-măch′, rē′măch′) *n.* A second contest between the same opponents.

re·me·di·a·ble (rĭ-mē′dē-ə-bəl) *adj.* Capable of being remedied. **—re·me′di·a·ble·ness** *n.* **—re·me′di·a·bly** *adv.*

re·me·di·al (rĭ-mē′dē-əl) *adj.* **1.** Supplying a remedy. **2.** Intended to correct, esp. poor study or reading habits. **—re·me′di·al·ly** *adv.*

re·me·di·ate (rĭ-mē′dē-āt′) *tr.v.* **-at·ed, -at·ing, -ates.** To provide remedial aid for (a learning disability, for example). **—re·me′di·a′tion** *n.*

rem·e·dy (rĕm′ə-dē) *n., pl.* **-dies. 1.** Something, such as medicine or therapy, that relieves pain, cures disease, or corrects a disorder. **2.** Something that corrects an evil, fault, or error: *tried to find a remedy for poverty.* **3.** *Law.* A legal means of preventing or correcting a wrong or enforcing a right. **4.** A mint's allowance for deviation from the standard weight or quality of coins. *—tr.v.* **-died, -dy·ing, -dies. 1.** To relieve or cure (a disease or disorder). **2.** To set right or rectify (an error). [ME < AN *remedie* < Lat. *remedium* : *re-,* against + *mederi,* to heal.]

re·mem·ber (rĭ-mĕm′bər) *v.* **-bered, -ber·ing, -bers.** *—tr.* **1.** To recall to the mind; think of again. **2.** To recall to the mind with effort or determination. **3.** To retain in the mind; keep carefully in memory: *remember a poem.* **4.** To keep (someone) in mind as worthy of affection or recognition. **5.** To reward with a gift or tip. **6.** To give greetings from. **7.** *Archaic.* To remind. *—intr.* To have or use the faculty of memory. [ME *remembren* < OFr. *remembrer* < LLat. *rememorari,* to remember again : Lat. *re-,* again + LLat. *memorari,* to be mindful of < Lat. *memor,* mindful.] **—re·mem′ber·a·bil′i·ty** *n.* **—re·mem′ber·a·ble** *adj.* **—re·mem′ber·er** *n.*

re·mem·brance (rĭ-mĕm′brəns) *n.* **1.** The act of remembering. **2.** The state of being remembered. **3.** Something serving to celebrate or honor the memory of a person or event; memorial. **4.** The length of time over which one's memory extends. **5.** Something remembered; reminiscence. **6.** A memento; souvenir. **7.** A greeting. [ME < OFr. < *remembrer,* to remember.]

re·mem·branc·er (rĭ-mĕm′brən-sər) *n.* **1.** One that causes another to remember; reminder. **2. Remembrancer. a.** One of several officers of the Court of Exchequer in England. **b.** An officer of the British judiciary responsible for collecting debts due to the Crown.

re·mex (rē′mĕks′) *n., pl.* **rem·i·ges** (rĕm′ə-jēz′). A quill or flight feather of a bird's wing. [NLat. < Lat., rower : *remus,* oar + *agere,* to drive.] **—re·mig′i·al** (rĭ-mĭj′ē-əl) *adj.*

re·mil·i·ta·rize (rē-mĭl′ĭ-tə-rīz′) *tr.v.* **-rized, -riz·ing, -riz·es.** To militarize again, as with forces or equipment. **—re·mil′i·ta·ri·za′tion** *n.*

re·mind (rĭ-mīnd′) *tr.v.* **-mind·ed, -mind·ing, -minds.** To cause to remember; make mindful. **—re·mind′er** *n.*

rem·i·nisce (rĕm′ə-nĭs′) *intr.v.* **-nisced, -nisc·ing, -nisc·es.** To recollect and tell of past experiences or events. [Back-formation < REMINISCENT.]

rem·i·nis·cence (rĕm′ə-nĭs′əns) *n.* **1.** The act or process of recalling the past. **2.** A thing remembered; memory. **3.** Often **reminiscences.** A narration of past experiences. **4.** An event that brings to mind a similar, former event.

rem·i·nis·cent (rĕm′ə-nĭs′ənt) *adj.* **1.** Having the quality of or containing reminiscence. **2.** Tending to recall or talk of the past. [Lat. *reminiscens, reminiscent-,* pr.part. of *reminisci,* to recollect.] **—rem′i·nis′cent·ly** *adv.*

re·mint (rē-mĭnt′) *tr.v.* **-mint·ed, -mint·ing, -mints.** To make into new coin by melting down and reprocessing.

re·mise (rĭ-mīz′) *tr.v.* **-mised, -mis·ing, -mis·es.** *Law.* To relinquish a claim to; surrender by deed. [ME *remisen* < OFr. *remis,* p.part. of *remettre,* to remit < Lat. *remittere.* —see REMIT.]

re·miss (rĭ-mĭs′) *adj.* **1.** Lax in attending to duty; negligent. **2.** Exhibiting carelessness or slackness. [ME < Lat. *remissus,* slack, p.part. of *remittere,* to remit.] **—re·miss′ly** *adv.* **—re·miss′ness** *n.*

re·mis·si·ble (rĭ-mĭs′ə-bəl) *adj.* Capable of being remitted or forgiven. **—re·mis′si·bil′i·ty** *n.* **—re·mis′si·bly** *adv.*

re·mis·sion (rĭ-mĭsh′ən) *n.* **1. a.** The act of remitting. **b.** The condition or period in which something, such as the symptoms of a disease, is remitted. **2.** Release, as from a debt or obligation. **3.** A lessening of intensity or degree; abatement.

re·mit (rĭ-mĭt′) *v.* **-mit·ted, -mit·ting, -mits.** *—tr.* **1.** To send (money); transmit. **2. a.** To cancel (a penalty, for example). **b.** To pardon; forgive. **3.** To restore to an original condition; put back. **4.** *Law.* To refer (a case) back to a lower court for further consideration. **5.** To relax; slacken. **6.** To defer; postpone. *—intr.* **1.** To transmit money. **2.** To diminish; abate. [ME *remitten* < Lat. *remittere* : *re-*, back + *mittere,* to send.] **—re·mit'ta·ble** *adj.* **—re·mit'ter** *n.*

re·mit·tal (rĭ-mĭt'l) *n.* Remission.

re·mit·tance (rĭ-mĭt'ns) *n.* **1.** Money or credit sent to someone. **2.** The act of sending money or credit.

remittance man *n.* A person who lives abroad on funds sent from home.

re·mit·tent (rĭ-mĭt'nt) *adj.* Characterized by temporary abatements in severity. Used esp. of diseases. **—re·mit'tence, re·mit'ten·cy** *n.* **—re·mit'tent·ly** *adv.*

rem·nant (rĕm'nənt) *n.* **1.** Something left over; remainder. **2.** A leftover piece of fabric remaining after the rest of the bolt has been sold. **3.** A surviving trace or small part that remains. **4.** Often **remnants.** A small, remaining group of people. [ME *remanent.* —see REMANENCE.]

re·mod·el (rē-mŏd'l) *tr.v.* **-eled, -el·ing, -els** also **-elled, -el·ling, -els.** To remake with a new structure; reconstruct.

re·mon·e·tize (rē-mŏn'ə-tīz', rē-mŭn'-) *tr.v.* **-tized, -tiz·ing, -tiz·es.** To restore (silver, for example) to use as legal tender. **—re·mon'e·ti·za'tion** *n.*

re·mon·strance (rĭ-mŏn'strəns) *n.* **1.** The act of remonstrating. **2.** An expression of protest, opposition, or reproof.

re·mon·strant (rĭ-mŏn'strənt) *adj.* Characterized by remonstrance; expostulatory. *—n.* **1.** Someone who remonstrates or opposes. **2. Remonstrant. a.** One of the Dutch Arminians who, in 1610, formally stated the grounds of their dissent from strict Calvinism. **b.** A member of the Protestant denomination founded by these dissenters. **—re·mon'strant·ly** *adv.*

re·mon·strate (rĭ-mŏn'strāt') *v.* **-strat·ed, -strat·ing, -strates.** *—tr.* To say in protest, objection, or reproof. *—intr.* To make objections; argue against an action. [Med. Lat. *remonstrare, remonstrat-,* to demonstrate : Lat. *re-* (intensive) + Lat. *monstrare,* to show < *monstrum,* portent.] **—re'mon·stra'tion** (rē'mŏn-strā'shən, rĕm'ən-) *n.* **—re·mon'stra·tive** (rĭ-mŏn'strə-tĭv) *adj.* **—re·mon'stra·tive·ly** *adv.* **—re·mon'stra'tor** *n.*

re·mon·tant (rĭ-mŏn'tənt) *adj.* Blooming more than once during a season. *—n.* A remontant rose. [Fr., pr.part. of *remonter,* to rise again < OFr. —see REMOUNT.]

remora

rem·o·ra (rĕm'ər-ə) *n.* Any of several marine fishes of the family Echeneidae, having on the head a sucking disk with which they attach themselves to sharks, whales, sea turtles, or the hulls of ships. [Lat., delay < *remorari,* to delay : *re-*, back + *morari,* to delay < *mora,* delay.]

re·morse (rĭ-môrs') *n.* **1.** Moral anguish arising from repentance for past misdeeds; bitter regret. **2.** *Obs.* Compassion. [ME < OFr. *remors* < Med. Lat. *remorsus* < Lat. *remordēre,* to torment : *re-* (intensive) + *mordēre,* to bite.] **—re·morse'ful** *adj.* **—re·morse'ful·ly** *adv.* **—re·morse'ful·ness** *n.*

re·morse·less (rĭ-môrs'lĭs) *adj.* Having no pity or compassion; merciless. **—re·morse'less·ly** *adv.* **—re·morse'less·ness** *n.*

re·mote (rĭ-mōt') *adj.* **-mot·er, -mot·est. 1.** Located far away; relatively distant in space. **2.** Distant in time: *the remote past.* **3.** Barely discernible; slight: *a very remote possibility.* **4.** Being distantly related by blood or marriage: *a remote cousin.* **5.** Distant in manner; aloof. [Lat. *remotus,* p.part. of *removere,* to remove.] **—re·mote'ly** *adv.* **—re·mote'ness** *n.*

remote control *n.* The direction of a remote activity, process, or machine, as by radioed instructions or coded signals.

re·mo·tion (rĭ-mō'shən) *n.* **1.** The act of removing; a removal. **2.** *Obs.* Departure. [ME *remocion* < Lat. *remotio* < *removēre,* to remove.]

ré·mou·lade (rā'mo͞o-läd') *n.* A piquant cold sauce for cold poultry, meat, and shellfish, made of mayonnaise with chopped pickles, capers, anchovies, and herbs. [Fr.]

re·mount (rē-mount') *tr.v.* **-mount·ed, -mount·ing, -mounts. 1.** To mount again. **2.** To supply with fresh horses. *—n.* (rē'-mount', rē-mount'). A fresh horse. [ME *remounten* < OFr. *remonter,* to remount, to rise again : *re-*, again (< Lat.) + *monter,* to mount. —see MOUNT[1].]

re·mov·a·ble (rĭ-mo͞o'və-bəl) *adj.* Capable of being removed. **—re·mov'a·bil'i·ty, re·mov'a·ble·ness** *n.* **—re·mov'a·bly** *adv.*

re·mov·al (rĭ-mo͞o'vəl) *n.* **1. a.** The act of removing. **b.** The fact of being removed. **2.** Relocation, as of a residence or business. **3.** Dismissal, as from office.

re·move (rĭ-mo͞ov') *v.* **-moved, -mov·ing, -moves.** *—tr.* **1.** To move from a position occupied: *remove the dishes.* **2.** To convey from one place to another. **3.** To take from one's person; doff: *remove one's hat.* **4.** To take away: *remove stains.* **5.** To do away with; eliminate. **6.** To dismiss from office. *—intr.* **1.** To change one's place of residence or business; move: *"In 1751, I removed from the country to the town"* (Hume). **2.** To depart; go away. *—n.* **1.** The act of removing; removal. **2.** The distance or degree of space, time, or status that separates persons or things: *were at a safe remove from the scene of battle.* [ME *removen* < OFr. *removoir* < Lat. *removēre,* to move back : *re-*, back + *movēre,* to move.] **—re·mov'er** *n.*

re·moved (rĭ-mo͞ovd') *adj.* **1.** Distant in space, time, or nature; remote. **2.** Separated in relationship by a given degree of descent: *My first cousin's child is my first cousin once removed.* **—re·mov'ed·ly** (-mo͞o'vĭd-lē) *adv.* **—re·mov'ed·ness** (-mo͞o'vĭd-nĭs) *n.*

re·mu·da (rĭ-mo͞o'də) *n.* A herd of horses from which ranch hands select their mounts. [Mex. Sp., change of horses < Sp., exchange < *remudar,* to exchange : *re-*, in return (< Lat.) + *mudar,* to change < Lat. *mutare.*]

re·mu·ner·ate (rĭ-myo͞o'nə-rāt') *tr.v.* **-at·ed, -at·ing, -ates. 1.** To pay to (a person) for goods provided, services rendered, or losses incurred. **2.** To compensate for; make payment for: *remunerate his efforts.* [Lat. *remunerare, remunerat-* : *re-*, in response + *munerare,* to give < *munus,* gift.] **—re·mu'ner·a·bil'i·ty** (-nər-ə-bĭl'ĭ-tē) *n.* **—re·mu'ner·a·ble** *adj.* **—re·mu'ner·a'tor** *n.*

re·mu·ner·a·tion (rĭ-myo͞o'nə-rā'shən) *n.* **1.** An act of remunerating. **2.** Something that remunerates; payment.

re·mu·ner·a·tive (rĭ-myo͞o'nə-rā'tĭv) *adj.* **1.** Likely to be well remunerated; profitable. **2.** Serving to remunerate. **—re·mu'ner·a'tive·ly** *adv.* **—re·mu'ner·a'tive·ness** *n.*

Re·mus (rē'məs) *n. Rom. Myth.* The twin brother of Romulus. [Lat.]

ren·ais·sance (rĕn'ĭ-säns', -zäns', rĭ-nā'səns) *n.* **1.** A rebirth; revival. **2. Renaissance. a.** The humanistic revival of classical art, literature, and learning that originated in Italy in the 14th century and later spread through Europe. **b.** The period of this revival, roughly from the 14th through the 16th century. **3.** Often **Renaissance.** A period of revived intellectual or artistic achievement or enthusiasm: *the Celtic Renaissance.* *—adj.* **Renaissance. 1.** Of, pertaining to, or characteristic of the Renaissance or its artistic and intellectual works and styles. **2.** Of or designating the style of architecture and decoration prevalent during the Renaissance. [Fr. < OFr. < *renaistre,* to be born again < Lat. *renasci* : *re-*, again + *nasci,* to be born.]

Renaissance man *n.* A man who has diverse interests and expertise in a number of areas.

re·nal (rē'nəl) *adj.* Of, pertaining to, or in the region of the kidneys. [Fr. *rénal* < LLat. *renalis* < Lat. *renes,* kidneys.]

re·nas·cence (rĭ-năs'əns, -nā'səns) *n.* **1.** A new birth or life; rebirth. **2. Renascence.** Renaissance.

re·nas·cent (rĭ-năs'ənt, -nā'sənt) *adj.* Coming into being again; showing renewed growth or vigor. [Lat. *renascens, renascent-,* pr.part. of *renasci,* to be born again : *re-*, again + *nasci,* to be born.]

ren·coun·ter (rĕn-koun'tər) *n.* An unplanned meeting. *—v.* **-tered, -ter·ing, -ters.** *—tr.* To meet unexpectedly. *—intr.* To have an unexpected meeting. [OFr. *rencontre* < *rencontrer,* to meet : *re-*, again (< Lat.) + *encontrer,* to meet.]

rend (rĕnd) *v.* **rent** (rĕnt) or **rend·ed, rend·ing, rends.** *—tr.* **1.** To tear apart or into pieces violently; split. **2.** To remove forcibly; wrest. **3.** To penetrate and disturb as if by tearing: *screams that rend the silence.* **4.** To distress (the heart, for example) painfully. *—intr.* To burst; come apart. [ME *renden* < OE *rendan.*]

ren·der (rĕn'dər) *tr.v.* **-dered, -der·ing, -ders. 1.** To submit or present, for consideration or approval: *render a bill.* **2.** To give or make available: *render assistance.* **3.** To give what is due or proper: *rendered homage.* **4.** To give in return or retribution: *render an apology for his rudeness.* **5.** To surrender or relinquish; yield. **6.** To represent in a verbal or artistic form; depict: *"Joyce has attempted . . . to render . . . what our participation in life is like"* (Edmund Wilson). **7.** To perform an interpretation of (a musical piece, for example). **8.** To express in another language or form; translate. **9.** To pronounce formally: *The jury rendered its verdict.* **10.** To cause to become; make: *"This study renders men acute, inquisitive"* (Burke). **11.** To reduce, convert, or melt down (fat) by heating. **12.** To coat (brick, for example) with plaster or cement. *—n.* A payment in kind, services, or cash from a tenant to a feudal lord. [ME *rendren,* to give in return < OFr. *rendre,* to give back < VLat. **rendere* < Lat. *reddere* : *re-*, *red-*, back + *dare,* to give.] **—ren'der·a·ble** *adj.* **—ren'der·er** *n.*

ren·dez·vous (rän'dā-vo͞o', -də-) *n., pl.* **-vous** (-vo͞oz'). **1.** A prearranged meeting place. **2.** A prearranged meeting. **3.** A popular gathering place. **4.** The process of bringing two spacecraft together. *—tr. & intr.v.* **-voused** (-vo͞od'), **-vous·ing** (-vo͞o'ĭng), **-vous** (-vo͞oz'). To bring or meet together at a specified time and place. [Fr. < OFr. < the phrase *rendez vous,* present yourselves.]

ren·di·tion (rĕn-dĭsh'ən) *n.* **1.** The act of rendering. **2.** An interpretation of a musical score or dramatic piece. **3.** A performance of a musical or dramatic work. **4.** An often interpretive translation. **5.** A surrender. [Obs. Fr. < OFr. *rendre,* to give back. —see RENDER.]

ren·e·gade (rĕn'ĭ-gād') *n.* **1.** One who rejects his religion, cause, allegiance, or group for another; traitor. **2.** An outlaw. *—intr.v.* **-gad·ed, -gad·ing, -gades.** To become a renegade. [Sp. *renegado* < Med. Lat. *renegatus* < p.part. of *renegare,* to deny : Lat. *re-* (intensive) + *negare,* to deny.]

re·nege (rĭ-nĭg', -nĕg', -nēg') *v.* **-neged, -neg·ing, -neges.** *—intr.* **1.** To fail to carry out a promise or commitment. **2.** In card games, to fail to follow suit when able and required by the rules to do so. *—tr.* To renounce; disown. *—n.* The act of reneging. [Med. Lat. *renegare,* to deny. —see RENEGADE.] **—re·neg'er** *n.*

re·ne·go·ti·ate (rē'nĭ-gō'shē-āt') *tr.v.* **-at·ed, -at·ing, -ates.** To negotiate anew, esp. to revise the terms of (a contract) so as to limit or get back excess profits gained by the contractor. —**re′ne·go′ti·a·ble** *adj.* —**re′ne·go·ti·a′tion** *n.*

re·new (rĭ-no͞o′, -nyo͞o′) *v.* **-newed, -new·ing, -news.** —*tr.* **1.** To make new or as if new again; restore. **2.** To take up again; resume. **3.** To repeat so as to reaffirm. **4.** To regain (vigor); revive. **5.** To arrange for the extension of: *renew a contract.* **6.** To replenish. **7.** To bring into being again; reestablish. —*intr.* **1.** To become new again. **2.** To start over. [ME *renewen* : *re-*, again + *new,* new.] —**re·new′a·bil′i·ty** (-ə-bĭl′ĭ-tē) *n.* —**re·new′a·ble** *adj.* —**re·new′a·bly** *adv.* —**re·new′er** *n.*

re·new·al (rĭ-no͞o′əl, -nyo͞o′-) *n.* **1. a.** The act of renewing. **b.** The state of being renewed. **2.** Something renewed.

re·new·ed·ly (rĭ-no͞o′ĭd-lē, -nyo͞o′-) *adv.* Over again; anew.

ren·i·form (rĕn′ə-fôrm′, rē′nə-) *adj.* Shaped like a kidney. [Lat. *renes,* kidneys + -FORM.]

ren·in (rĕn′ĭn) *n.* A protein-digesting enzyme released by the kidney that acts to raise blood pressure. [Lat. *renes,* kidneys + -IN.]

ren·i·tent (rĕn′ĭ-tənt, rĭ-nīt′nt) *adj.* **1.** Resistant to physical pressure; not pliant. **2.** Reluctant to yield or be swayed; recalcitrant. [Lat. *renitens, renitent-,* pr.part. of *reniti,* to resist : *re-*, against + *niti,* to press forward.] —**ren′i·tence, ren′i·ten·cy** *n.*

ren·min·bi (rĕn′mĭn-bē′) *n.* See table at **currency.** [Chin. (Mandarin) *ren[2] min[2] bi[4]* : *ren[2] min[2],* the people (*ren[2],* human being + *min[2],* people) + *bi[4],* money.]

ren·nase (rĕn′ās) *n.* Rennin.

ren·net (rĕn′ĭt) *n.* **1.** The inner lining of the fourth stomach of calves and other young ruminants. **2.** A dried extract made from the stomach lining of a ruminant, used to curdle milk. **3.** Rennin. [ME.]

ren·nin (rĕn′ĭn) *n.* A milk-coagulating enzyme that is produced from rennet and used in making cheeses and junkets. [RENN(ET) + -IN.]

ren·nin·o·gen (rĕ-nĭn′ə-jən) *n.* The zymogenic precursor of rennin.

re·nom·i·nate (rē-nŏm′ə-nāt′) *tr.v.* **-nat·ed, -nat·ing, -nates.** To nominate again esp. for a subsequent term. —**re′nom·i·na′tion** *n.*

re·nounce (rĭ-nouns′) *v.* **-nounced, -nounc·ing, -nounc·es.** —*tr.* **1.** To give up, esp. by formal announcement. **2.** To reject; disown. —*intr. Games.* To revoke in cards. —*n. Games.* A revoke in cards. [ME *renouncen* < OFr. *renoncer* < Lat. *renuntiare,* to report : *re-*, back + *nuntiare,* to announce < *nuntius,* messenger.] —**re·nounce′ment** *n.* —**re·nounc′er** *n.*

ren·o·vate (rĕn′ə-vāt′) *tr.v.* **-vat·ed, -vat·ing, -vates. 1.** To restore to an earlier condition, as by repairing or remodeling. **2.** To impart new vigor to; revive. [Lat. *renovare, renovat-* : *re-*, again + *novare,* to make new < *novus,* new.] —**ren′o·va′tion** *n.* —**ren′o·va′tor** *n.*

re·nown (rĭ-noun′) *n.* **1.** The quality of being widely honored and acclaimed; fame. **2.** *Obs.* Report; rumor. [ME *renowne* < OFr. *renon* < *renomer,* to make famous : *re-*, again (< Lat.) + *nomer,* to name < Lat. *nominare* < *nomen,* name.]

re·nowned (rĭ-nound′) *adj.* Having renown; famous.

rent[1] (rĕnt) *n.* **1.** Payment, usually of an amount fixed by contract, made by a tenant at specified intervals in return for the right to occupy or use the property of another. **2.** *Econ.* **a.** The return derived from cultivated or improved land after deduction of all production costs. **b.** The revenue yielded by a piece of land in excess of that yielded by the poorest or least favorably located land, under equal market conditions. —*v.* **rent·ed, rent·ing, rents.** —*tr.* **1.** To obtain occupancy or use of (another's property) in return for regular payments. **2.** To grant temporary occupancy or use of (one's own property) in return for regular payments. —*intr.* To be for rent: *The cottage rents for $200 a month.* —**idiom. for rent.** Available for use or service in return for payment. [ME < OFr. *rente* < VLat. **rendita,* fem. p.part. of **rendere.* —see RENDER.] —**rent·a·bil·i·ty** *n.* —**rent′a·ble** *adj.*

rent[2] (rĕnt) *v.* A past tense and past participle of **rend.** —*n.* **1.** An opening made by rending; rip. **2.** A breach of relations between persons.

rent·al (rĕn′tl) *n.* **1.** An amount paid out or taken in as rent. **2.** A list of tenants and schedule of rents. **3.** Property available for renting. **4.** The act of renting. **5.** An agency that rents something. —*adj.* Of, concerning, or available for rent.

rent control *n.* Official, esp. governmental, control and regulation of the amount charged for rented housing.

rente (ränt) *n., pl.* **rentes** (ränt). **1.** In French law, an annual income; annuity. **2. a.** Often **rentes.** The securities representing the national debt of France. **b.** The interest paid on this debt. [Fr. < OFr., income, rent.]

rent·er (rĕn′tər) *n.* One who pays rent for the use of another's property; tenant.

ren·tier (rän-tyā′) *n.* In France, one who derives a fixed income from property rentals or returns on investments. [Fr. < OFr. < *rente,* income, rent.]

rent strike *n.* An agreement among tenants to refuse to pay rent, as in protest of poor services.

re·num·ber (rē-nŭm′bər) *tr.v.* **-bered -ber·ing, -bers.** To number again or in a different order.

re·nun·ci·a·tion (rĭ-nŭn′sē-ā′shən) *n.* **1.** The act or practice of renouncing: *"Reality imposes on human beings the necessity of renunciation of pleasures"* (Norman O. Brown). **2.** A declaration in which something is renounced. [ME < Lat. *renuntiatio* < *renuntiare,* to renounce.] —**re·nun′ci·a′tive, re·nun′ci·a·to′ry** (-ə-tôr′ē, -tōr′ē) *adj.*

re·o·pen (rē-ō′pən) *v.* **-pened, -pen·ing, -pens.** —*tr.* To open or take up again. —*intr.* To start over; resume.

re·or·der (rē-ôr′dər) *v.* **-dered, -der·ing, -ders.** —*tr.* **1.** To order again. **2.** To straighten out or put in order again. **3.** To rearrange. —*intr.* To order the same goods again. —*n.* An order of goods like a previous one from the same supplier.

re·or·gan·i·za·tion (rē-ôr′gə-nĭ-zā′shən) *n.* **1.** The act or process of organizing again or differently. **2.** A thorough alteration of the structure of a business corporation. —**re·or′gan·i·za′tion·al** *adj.*

re·or·gan·ize (rē-ôr′gə-nīz′) *v.* **-ized, -iz·ing, -iz·es.** —*tr.* To organize again or anew. —*intr.* To undergo or effect changes in organization. —**re·or′gan·iz′er** *n.*

re·o·vi·rus (rē′ō-vī′rəs) *n.* Any of a group of RNA-containing animal viruses that are sometimes found in the respiratory and digestive tracts of healthy individuals. [R(ESPIRATORY) + E(NTERIC) + O(RPHAN) + VIRUS.]

rep[1] also **repp** (rĕp) *n.* A ribbed or corded fabric of various materials, such as cotton, wool, or silk. [Fr. *reps.*]

rep[2] (rĕp) *n. Informal.* A representative.

rep[3] (rĕp) *n. Physics.* A unit of absorbed radiation dose, equal to the absorbed dose in water that has been exposed to one roentgen. [R(OENTGEN) + E(QUIVALENT) + P(HYSICAL).]

rep[4] (rĕp) *n. Informal.* A repertory theater.

re·pack·age (rē-păk′ĭj) *tr.v.* **-aged, -ag·ing, -ag·es.** To package again or anew, esp. to put in a more attractive package. —**re·pack′ag·er** *n.*

re·paid (rē-pād′) *v.* Past tense and past participle of **repay.**

re·pair[1] (rĭ-pâr′) *v.* **-paired, -pair·ing, -pairs.** —*tr.* **1.** To restore to sound condition after damage or injury; fix. **2.** To set right; remedy: *repair an error.* **3.** To renew or refresh. **4.** To make up for or compensate for (a loss or wrong, for example). —*intr.* To make repairs. —*n.* **1.** The work, act, or process of repairing. **2.** General condition after use or repairing: *in good repair.* **3.** An instance of repairing. [ME *repairen* < OFr. *reparer* < Lat. *reparare* : *re-*, back + *parare,* to put in order.] —**re·pair′er** *n.*

re·pair[2] (rĭ-pâr′) *intr.v.* **-paired, -pair·ing, -pairs.** To betake oneself; go: *repair to the parlor.* —*n.* **1.** An act of repairing. **2.** A place to which one goes frequently or habitually; haunt. [ME *reparen,* to return < OFr. *repairer* < LLat. *repatriare,* to return to one's country. —see REPATRIATE.] —**re·pair′a·ble** *adj.*

re·pair·man (rĭ-pâr′măn′, -mən) *n.* A person whose occupation is making repairs.

re·pand (rĭ-pănd′) *adj. Bot.* Having a somewhat wavy margin: *a repand leaf.* [Lat. *repandus,* bent backward : *re-*, back + *pandus,* bent < *pandere,* to spread.]

rep·a·ra·ble (rĕp′ər-ə-bəl) *adj.* Capable of being repaired. —**rep′a·ra·bil′i·ty** *n.* —**rep′a·ra·bly** *adv.*

rep·a·ra·tion (rĕp′ə-rā′shən) *n.* **1. a.** The act or process of repairing. **b.** The condition of being repaired. **2.** The act or process of making amends; expiation. **3.** Something done or paid as amends; compensation. **4. reparations.** Compensation or remuneration required from a defeated nation as indemnity for damage or injury during a war. [ME < OFr. < LLat. *reparatio* < Lat. *reparare,* to repair. —see REPAIR[1].]

Synonyms: *reparation, redress, amends, restitution, indemnity. Reparation* implies giving compensation to satisfy one who has suffered injury, loss, or wrong at the hands of another; in the plural form it applies to the compensation a defeated nation must make for damage to the enemy, especially to civilians. *Redress* involves reparation without good will necessarily resulting, since it presupposes an act of retaliation to right a wrong: *He sought redress in the courts. Amends* does not have the force of *redress* or *reparation,* connoting the giving of satisfaction for a minor grievance or lesser injury, often apologetically. *Restitution* means returning to the rightful owner what has been taken illegally from him or giving back something of equal worth: *The thief made restitution by returning the stolen goods. Indemnity* implies repayment or reimbursement for loss or damage.

re·par·a·tive (rĭ-păr′ə-tĭv) also **re·par·a·to·ry** (-tôr′ē, -tōr′ē) *adj.* **1.** Tending to repair. **2.** Of, pertaining to, or of the nature of reparations.

rep·ar·tee (rĕp′ər-tē′, -tā′, -är-) *n.* **1. a.** A swift, witty reply; a ready or spirited retort. **b.** Witty and spirited conversation characterized by such replies. **2.** Skill and cleverness in conversational repartee. [Fr. *repartie* < *repartir,* to retort < OFr., to retort, to depart again : *re-*, again (< Lat.) + *partir,* to depart < Lat. *partire,* to divide < *pars,* part.]

re·par·ti·tion (rē′pär-tĭsh′ən) *n.* **1.** Distribution; apportionment. **2.** A partitioning again or in a different way. —*tr.v.* **-tioned, -tion·ing, -tions.** To partition again; redivide.

re·pass (rē-păs′) *v.* **-passed, -pass·ing, -pass·es.** —*tr.* **1.** To pass (something) again. **2.** To cause to pass again in the opposite direction. —*intr.* To pass again; go by again. —**re·pas′sage** (-ĭj) *n.*

re·past (rĭ-păst′) *n.* **1.** A meal. **2.** The food eaten or provided at a meal. —*v.* **-past·ed, -past·ing, -pasts.** —*intr.* To take food. —*tr. Obs.* To give food to. [ME < OFr. < *repaistre,* to

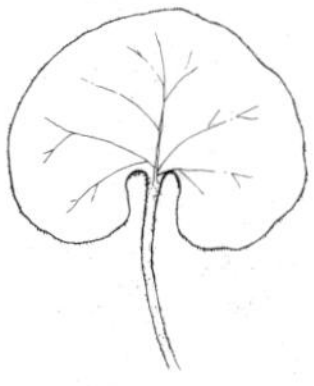

reniform
Reniform leaf of wild ginger

feed < LLat. *repascere* : *re-* (intensive) + *pascere,* to feed.]

re·pa·tri·ate (rē-pā′trē-āt′) *tr.v.* **-at·ed, -at·ing, -ates.** To restore or return to the country of birth or citizenship: *repatriate war refugees.* —*n.* (-ĭt, -āt′). Someone who has been repatriated. [LLat. *repatriare,* to return to one's country : *re-,* back + *patria,* native country.] **—re·pa′tri·a′tion** *n.*

re·pay (rĭ-pā′) *v.* **-paid** (-păd′), **-pay·ing, -pays.** —*tr.* **1.** To pay back: *repaid a debt.* **2.** To give back, either in return or in requital: *repay malice with malice.* **3.** To make compensation or a return for: *a company that repays hard work with bonuses.* **4.** To make or do in return: *repay a call.* —*intr.* To make repayment or requital. **—re·pay′a·ble** *adj.* **—re·pay′ment** *n.*

re·peal (rĭ-pēl′) *tr.v.* **-pealed, -peal·ing, -peals.** **1.** To revoke or rescind, esp. by an official or formal act. **2.** *Obs.* To summon back or recall, esp. from exile. —*n.* The act or process of repealing. [ME *repelen* < AN *repeler* < OFr. *rapeler* : *re-,* back (< Lat.) + *apeler,* to appeal. —see APPEAL.] **—re·peal′a·ble** *adj.* **—re·peal′er** *n.*

re·peat (rĭ-pēt′) *v.* **-peat·ed, -peat·ing, -peats.** —*tr.* **1.** To utter or state again. **2.** To utter in duplication of another's utterance. **3.** To recite from memory. **4.** To tell to another. **5.** To do, experience, or produce again. **6.** To express (oneself) in the same way or words: *repeats himself constantly.* —*intr.* **1.** To do or say something again. **2.** To commit the fraudulent offense of voting more than once in a single election. —*n.* **1.** The act of repeating. **2.** Something repeated: *a repeat of a television program.* **3.** *Mus.* **a.** A passage or section that is repeated. **b.** A sign usually consisting of two vertical dots, indicating a passage to be repeated. [ME *repeten* < OFr. *repeter* < Lat. *repetere,* to seek again : *re-,* again + *petere,* to seek.] **—re·peat′a·bil′i·ty** *n.* **—re·peat′a·ble** *adj.*

re·peat·ed (rĭ-pē′tĭd) *adj.* Said, done, or occurring again and again. **—re·peat′ed·ly** *adv.*

re·peat·er (rĭ-pē′tər) *n.* **1.** One that repeats. **2.** A watch or clock with a pressure-activated mechanism that strikes the hour. **3.** A repeating firearm. **4.** A student who repeats a course, usually one that has been failed. **5.** Someone who fraudulently votes more than once in a single election. **6.** Someone who has been convicted of wrongdoing more than once, esp. for the same offense.

repeating decimal *n. Math.* A decimal in which after a certain digit a pattern of one or more digits is repeated indefinitely.

repeating firearm *n.* A firearm capable of firing several times without reloading.

re·pel (rĭ-pĕl′) *v.* **-pelled, -pel·ling, -pels.** —*tr.* **1.** To drive back; ward off or keep away: *repel insects.* **2.** To offer resistance to; fight against: *repel an invasion.* **3.** To refuse to accept; reject: *repel an offer.* **4.** To turn away from; spurn. **5.** To cause aversion or distaste in: *His rudeness repels everyone.* **6.** To be resistant to; be incapable of absorbing or mixing with. **7.** To present an opposing force to; push back or away by a force: *Electric charges of the same sign repel one another.* —*intr.* **1.** To offer a resistant force to something. **2.** To cause aversion or distaste. [ME *repellen* < Lat. *repellere* : *re-,* back + *pellere,* to drive.] **—re·pel′ler** *n.*

Usage: The verbs *repel* and *repulse* both have the physical sense of driving back or off. *Repulse* also may apply to rebuffing or rejecting discourteously, but only *repel* is used in the sense of causing distaste or aversion: *His arrogance repelled us. He repulsed with rudeness all attempts to help him.*

re·pel·lent (rĭ-pĕl′ənt) *adj.* **1. a.** Serving or tending to repel. **b.** Capable of repelling. **2.** Inspiring aversion or distaste; repulsive. **3.** Resistant or impervious to a substance: *a water-repellent fabric.* —*n.* Something that repels, esp.: **a.** A substance used to repel insects. **b.** A substance or treatment for making a fabric or surface impervious or resistant to something. **—re·pel′lence, re·pel′len·cy** *n.* **—re·pel′lent·ly** *adv.*

re·pent[1] (rĭ-pĕnt′) *v.* **-pent·ed, -pent·ing, -pents.** —*intr.* **1.** To feel remorse, contrition, or self-reproach. **2.** To feel such regret for past conduct as to change one's mind regarding it: *He repented of his severity.* **3.** To make a change for the better as a result of remorse or contrition for one's sins. —*tr.* **1.** To feel regret or self-reproach for. **2.** To cause to feel remorse or regret. [ME *repenten* < OFr. *repentir* : *re-,* in response (< Lat.) + *pentir,* to be sorry < Lat. *paenitēre.*] **—re·pent′er** *n.*

re·pent[2] (rē′pənt) *adj. Biol.* Creeping along the ground; prostrate. [Lat. *repens, repent-,* pr.part. of *repere,* to creep.]

re·pen·tance (rĭ-pĕn′təns) *n.* **1.** Remorse or contrition for past conduct or sin. **2.** The act or process of repenting.

re·pen·tant (rĭ-pĕn′tənt) *adj.* Characterized by or demonstrating repentance; penitent. **—re·pen′tant·ly** *adv.*

re·per·cus·sion (rē′pər-kŭsh′ən, rĕp′ər-) *n.* **1.** An indirect effect, influence, or result produced by an event or action. **2.** A recoil, rebounding, or reciprocal motion after impact. **3.** A reflection, esp. of sound. [Lat. *repercussio* < *repercutere,* to cause to rebound : *re-,* back + *percutere,* to strike.] **—re′per·cus′sive** *adj.*

rep·er·toire (rĕp′ər-twär′) *n.* **1.** The stock of songs, plays, operas, readings, or other pieces that a player or company is prepared to perform. **2.** The range or number of skills, aptitudes, or special accomplishments, as of a person or group. [Fr. < LLat. *repertorium.* —see REPERTORY.]

rep·er·to·ry (rĕp′ər-tôr′ē, -tōr′ē) *n., pl.* **-ries.** **1.** A repertoire. **2.** A theater in which a resident company presents plays from a specified repertoire, usually in alternation. **3.** A place, as a storehouse, where a stock of things is kept; repository. [LLat. *repertorium* < Lat. *repertus,* p.part. of *reperire,* to find out : *re-,* again + *parire,* to produce.] **—rep′er·to′ri·al** *adj.*

rep·e·tend (rĕp′ĭ-tĕnd′, rĕp′ĭ-tĕnd′) *n.* **1.** A word, sound, or phrase that is repeated; refrain. **2.** *Math.* The digit or group of digits that repeats infinitely in a repeating decimal. [Lat. *repetendum,* neuter gerund. of *repetere,* to repeat.]

rep·e·ti·tion (rĕp′ĭ-tĭsh′ən) *n.* **1.** The act or process or an instance of repeating or being repeated. **2.** A recitation or recital, esp. of prepared or memorized material. [Lat. *repetitio* < *repetere,* to repeat.] **—rep′e·ti′tion·al** *adj.*

rep·e·ti·tious (rĕp′ĭ-tĭsh′əs) *adj.* Characterized by or filled with repetition, esp. needless or tedious repetition. **—rep′e·ti′tious·ly** *adv.* **—rep′e·ti′tious·ness** *n.*

re·pet·i·tive (rĭ-pĕt′ĭ-tĭv) *adj.* Repetitious. **—re·pet′i·tive·ly** *adv.* **—re·pet′i·tive·ness** *n.*

re·phrase (rē-frāz′) *tr.v.* **-phrased, -phras·ing, -phras·es.** To phrase again, esp. to state in a new or different way.

re·pine (rĭ-pīn′) *intr.v.* **-pined, -pin·ing, -pines.** **1.** To be discontented or low in spirits; complain or fret. **2.** To yearn after something. **—re·pin′er** *n.*

re·place (rĭ-plās′) *tr.v.* **-placed, -plac·ing, -plac·es.** **1.** To put back in a former position or place. **2.** To take or fill the place of. **3.** To be or provide a substitute for. **4.** To pay back or return; refund. **—re·place′a·ble** *adj.* **—re·plac′er** *n.*

Synonyms: *replace, supplant, displace, supersede. Replace* applies both to substituting something new or workable for that which is lost, depleted, or worn out and to placing another in the stead of one who leaves or is dismissed from a position. *Supplant,* in literal usage, suggests intrigue but is now often used without such implication. It emphasizes the loss of prestige or power by what or who is replaced. *Displace* implies the involuntary yielding of a place to another or simply to mechanical movement: *Gas displaced the water. Supersede* pertains to the replacement of a person or thing by another held to be superior or more recent.

re·place·ment (rĭ-plās′mənt) *n.* **1.** The act or process of replacing or of being replaced; substitution. **2.** One that replaces, esp. a person assigned to a vacant military position.

re·plant (rē-plănt′) *tr.v.* **-plant·ed, -plant·ing, -plants.** **1.** To plant something again or in a new place. **2.** To supply with new plants: *replant a window box.* —*n.* (rē′plănt′). Something that has been replanted.

re·play (rē-plā′) *tr.v.* **-played, -play·ing, -plays.** To play over again. —*n.* (rē′plā′). **1.** The act or process of replaying something, esp. by such means as a videotape. **2.** Something replayed.

re·plead·er (rĭ-plē′dər) *n. Law.* **1.** A court order requiring parties to plead their case again because of some prior erroneous or miscarried pleading. **2.** The right of pleading again.

re·plen·ish (rĭ-plĕn′ĭsh) *v.* **-ished, -ish·ing, -ish·es.** —*tr.* **1.** To fill or make complete again; add a new stock or supply to: *replenish the larder.* **2.** To inspire or nourish: *The music will replenish my weary soul.* —*intr.* To become full again. [ME *replenisshen* < OFr. *replenir, repleniss-* : *re-,* again (< Lat.) + *plenir,* to fill < *plein,* full < Lat. *plenus.*] **—re·plen′ish·er** *n.* **—re·plen′ish·ment** *n.*

re·plete (rĭ-plēt′) *adj.* **1.** Plentifully supplied; abounding. **2.** Filled to satiation; gorged. [ME *replet* < OFr. < Lat. *repletus,* p.part. of *replēre,* to refill : *re-,* again + *plēre,* to fill.] **—re·plete′ness** *n.*

Usage: *Replete* means "abundantly supplied": *a sports-car race replete with thrills, chills, and spills.* It should not be used to mean simply "complete" or "equipped": *an estate replete with pool, tennis courts, and golf course* (better, *complete with*).

re·ple·tion (rĭ-plē′shən) *n.* **1.** The condition of being fully supplied or completely filled. **2.** A state of excessive fullness.

re·plev·i·a·ble (rĭ-plĕv′ē-ə-bəl) *adj. Law.* Capable of being recovered by replevin.

re·plev·in (rĭ-plĕv′ĭn) *n.* **1.** An action to recover personal property said or claimed to be unlawfully taken. **2.** The writ or procedure of replevin. —*tr.v.* **-ined, -in·ing, -ins.** To replevy. [ME < AN *replevine* < *replevir,* to give as a security < OFr. : *re-,* back + *plevir,* to pledge.]

re·plev·y (rĭ-plĕv′ē) *tr.v.* **-ied, -y·ing, -ies.** To regain possession of by a writ of replevin. —*n., pl.* **-ies.** Replevin. [AN *replevir* < OFr., to give as a security. —see REPLEVIN.]

rep·li·ca (rĕp′lĭ-kə) *n.* **1.** A copy or reproduction of a work of art, esp. one made by the original artist. **2.** A copy or reproduction. [Ital. < *replicare,* to repeat < Lat., to fold back. —see REPLICATE.]

rep·li·cate (rĕp′lĭ-kāt′) *v.* **-cat·ed, -cat·ing, -cates.** —*tr.* **1.** To duplicate, copy, or repeat. **2.** To fold over or bend back upon itself. —*intr.* To become replicated. —*adj.* (-kĭt). Folded over or bent back upon itself: *a replicate leaf.* [Lat. *replicare, replicat-,* to fold back : *re-,* back + *plicare,* to fold.] **—rep′li·ca′tive** *adj.*

rep·li·ca·tion (rĕp′lĭ-kā′shən) *n.* **1.** A fold or a folding back.

2. A reply to an answer; rejoinder. **3.** *Law.* The plaintiff's response to the defendant's answer or plea. **4.** An echo or reverberation. **5.** A copy or reproduction. **6.** The act or process of duplicating or reproducing something.

re·ply (rĭ-plī′) *v.* **-plied, -ply·ing, -plies.** —*intr.* **1.** To give an answer in speech or writing. **2.** To respond by an action or gesture: *He replied by shrugging his shoulders.* **3. a.** To echo. **b.** To return gunfire or an attack: *The big guns replied.* **4.** *Law.* To answer a defendant's plea. —*tr.* To say or give as an answer: *He replied that he was unable to help them.* —*n., pl.* **-plies. 1.** An answer in speech or writing. **2.** A response by action or gesture. **3.** *Law.* A plaintiff's speech or argument in answer to that of a defendant. [ME *replien* < OFr. *replier* < Lat. *replicare,* to fold back. —see REPLICATE.] **—re·pli′er** *n.*

re·po (rē′pō′) *n. Informal.* A repurchase agreement. [Shortening and alteration of REPURCHASE AGREEMENT.]

re·po·lar·i·za·tion (rē-pō′lər-ĭ-zā′shən) *n.* The restoration of a polarized state in a muscle fiber or membrane following contraction.

re·port (rĭ-pôrt′, -pōrt′) *n.* **1.** An account presented usually in detail. **2.** A formal account of the proceedings or transactions of a group. **3.** An account of a court case or judicial decision. **4.** Common talk; rumor or gossip: *According to report, they eloped.* **5.** Reputation; repute: *a man of bad report.* **6.** An explosive noise: *the rifle's report.* —*v.* **-port·ed, -port·ing, -ports.** —*tr.* **1.** To make or present an account of, often officially, formally, or regularly. **2.** To relate or tell about; present: *report one's findings.* **3.** To write or provide an account or summation of for publication or broadcast. **4.** To submit or relate the results of considerations concerning: *The committee reported the bill.* **5.** To carry back and repeat to another. **6.** To complain about or denounce: *Report him to the police.* —*intr.* **1.** To make a report. **2.** To serve as a reporter for a newspaper or similar publication. **3.** To present oneself: *report for duty.* **—phrasal verb. report out.** To return after deliberation to a legislative body for action: *The committee reported the new tax bill out.* **—idiom. on report.** Subject to disciplinary action. [ME *reporten* < OFr. *reporter* < Lat. *reportare* : *re-,* back + *portare,* to carry.] **—re·port′a·ble** *adj.*

re·port·age (rĕp′ər-täzh′, rĭ-pôr′tĭj, -pōr′-) *n.* **1.** The reporting of news or information of general interest. **2.** Something that is reported.

report card *n.* A report of a student's progress presented periodically to a parent or guardian.

re·port·ed·ly (rĭ-pôr′tĭd-lē, -pōr′-) *adv.* By report; supposedly.

re·port·er (rĭ-pôr′tər, -pōr′-) *n.* **1.** A person who reports. **2.** A writer of news stories. **3.** A person authorized to write and issue official accounts of judicial or legislative proceedings. **—rep′or·to′ri·al** (rĕp′ər-tôr′ē-əl, -tōr′-, rē′pər-) *adj.* **—rep′or·to′ri·al·ly** *adv.*

re·pose[1] (rĭ-pōz′) *n.* **1. a.** The act of resting; rest. **b.** The state of being at rest. **2.** Poise; composure. **3.** Calmness; tranquillity. —*v.* **-posed, -pos·ing, -pos·es.** —*tr.* To lay (oneself) down. —*intr.* **1.** To lie at rest. **2.** To lie supported by something. [< ME *reposen* < OFr. *reposer* < LLat. *repausare* : Lat. *re-* (intensive) + Lat. *pausare,* to rest < *pausa,* rest. —see PAUSE.] **—re·pos′al** *n.* **—re·pos′er** *n.*

re·pose[2] (rĭ-pōz′) *tr.v.* **-posed, -pos·ing, -pos·es.** To place (trust, for example) in: *The nation had reposed its hopes in a single man.* [ME *reposen* < Lat. *reponere* : *re-,* back + *ponere,* to place.]

re·pose·ful (rĭ-pōz′fəl) *adj.* Marked by or conducive to repose. **—re·pose′ful·ly** *adv.* **—re·pose′ful·ness** *n.*

re·pos·it (rĭ-pŏz′ĭt) *tr.v.* **-it·ed, -it·ing, -its.** To put away; store. [Lat. *reponere, reposit-* : *re-,* back + *ponere,* to place.] **—re′po·si′tion** (rē′pə-zĭsh′ən, rĕp′ə-) *n.*

re·pos·i·to·ry (rĭ-pŏz′ĭ-tôr′ē, -tōr′ē) *n., pl.* **-ries. 1.** A place where things may be put for safekeeping. **2.** A warehouse. **3.** A museum. **4.** A burial vault; tomb. **5.** A person who receives a confidence.

re·pos·sess (rē′pə-zĕs′) *tr.v.* **-sessed, -sess·ing, -sess·es. 1. a.** To regain possession of. **b.** To reclaim possession of for failure to pay installments due. **2.** To give back possession to. **—re′pos·ses′sion** *n.*

re·pous·sé (rə-po͞o-sā′) *adj.* **1.** Shaped or decorated with patterns in relief formed by hammering and pressing on the reverse side. Used esp. of metal. **2.** Raised in relief. —*n.* **1.** A repoussé design. **2.** The technique of hammering and pressing repoussé designs. [Fr., p.part. of *repousser,* to push back < OFr. : *re-,* back (< Lat.) + *pousser,* to push < Lat. *pulsare,* to beat, freq. of *pellere,* to push.]

repp (rĕp) *n.* Variant of **rep**[1].

rep·re·hend (rĕp′rĭ-hĕnd′) *tr.v.* **-hend·ed, -hend·ing, -hends.** To reprove; censure. [ME *reprehenden* < Lat. *reprehendere* : *re-* (intensive) + *prehendere,* to seize.]

rep·re·hen·si·ble (rĕp′rĭ-hĕn′sə-bəl) *adj.* Deserving of rebuke or censure; blameworthy. [LLat. *reprehensibilis* < Lat. *reprehendere,* to reprehend.] **—rep′re·hen′si·bil′i·ty, rep′re·hen′si·ble·ness** *n.* **—rep′re·hen′si·bly** *adv.*

rep·re·hen·sion (rĕp′rĭ-hĕn′shən) *n.* The act of reprehending; reproval.

rep·re·sent (rĕp′rĭ-zĕnt′) *tr.v.* **-sent·ed, -sent·ing, -sents. 1.** To stand for; symbolize: *The eagle represents the United States.* **2.** To depict in art; portray. **3.** To present clearly to the mind. **4.** To draw attention to by way of remonstrance or protest. **5.** To describe as an embodiment of a specified quality. **6. a.** To serve as the official and authorized delegate or agent for. **b.** To act as a spokesman for. **7.** To serve as an example of: *a mammal represented by seven species.* **8.** To be the equivalent of. **9. a.** To stage (a play, for example); produce. **b.** To act the part or role of. [ME *representen* < Lat. *repraesentare,* to show : *re-,* again + *praesentare,* to present.] **—rep′re·sent′a·bil′i·ty** *n.* **—rep′re·sent′a·ble** *adj.* **—rep′re·sent′er** *n.*

rep·re·sen·ta·tion (rĕp′rĭ-zĕn-tā′shən, -zən-) *n.* **1. a.** The act of representing. **b.** The state of being represented. **2.** Something that represents. **3. a.** An account or statement, as of facts, allegations, or arguments. **b.** An expostulation; protest. **4.** A presentation or production, as of a play. **5.** The state or condition of serving as an official delegate, agent, or spokesman. **6.** The right or privilege of being represented by delegates having a voice in a legislative body. **7.** *Law.* A statement of fact made by one party in order to induce another party to enter into a contract.

rep·re·sen·ta·tion·al (rĕp′rĭ-zĕn-tā′shə-nəl, -zən-) *adj.* Of or pertaining to representation, esp. to realistic graphic representation. **—rep′re·sen·ta′tion·al·ism** *n.*

rep·re·sen·ta·tive (rĕp′rĭ-zĕn′tə-tĭv) *n.* **1.** One that serves as an example or type for others of the same classification. **2.** One that serves as a delegate or agent for another. **3. a.** A member of a governmental body, usually legislative, chosen by popular vote. **b.** In the United States, a member of the House of Representatives or of a state legislature. —*adj.* **1.** Representing or capable of representing, depicting, or portraying. **2.** Authorized to act as an official delegate or agent. **3.** Of, pertaining to, or characteristic of government by representation. **4.** Typical of others of the same class. **—rep′re·sen′ta·tive·ly** *adv.* **—rep′re·sen′ta·tive·ness** *n.*

re·press (rĭ-prĕs′) *v.* **-pressed, -press·ing, -press·es.** —*tr.* **1.** To hold back; restrain: *repress a laugh.* **2.** To suppress; quell: *repress a rebellion.* **3.** *Psychoanal.* To exclude (memories, for example) from the conscious mind. —*intr.* To take repressive action. [ME *repressen* < Lat. *reprimere* : *re-,* back + *premere,* to press.] **—re·press′er** *n.* **—re·press′i·bil′i·ty** *n.* **—re·press′i·ble** *adj.*

re·pres·sion (rĭ-prĕsh′ən) *n.* **1. a.** The act of repressing. **b.** The state of being repressed. **2.** *Psychoanal.* The unconscious exclusion of painful impulses, desires, or fears from the conscious mind. **—re·pres′sion·ist** *adj.*

re·pres·sive (rĭ-prĕs′ĭv) *adj.* Causing or inclined to cause repression: *a repressive dictatorship.* **—re·pres′sive·ly** *adv.* **—re·pres′sive·ness** *n.*

re·pres·sor (rĭ-prĕs′ər) *n.* **1.** One that represses. **2.** *Biol.* A chemical compound that prevents the synthesis of a protein by interfering with the action of DNA.

re·prieve (rĭ-prēv′) *tr.v.* **-prieved, -priev·ing, -prieves. 1.** To postpone the punishment of. **2.** To give temporary relief to. —*n.* **1. a.** The postponement of a punishment. **b.** A warrant for such a postponement. **2.** Temporary relief, as from danger or pain. [ME *repryen* < OFr. *reprendre,* to take back < Lat. *reprehendere,* to hold back. —see REPREHEND.] **—re·priev′a·ble** *adj.*

rep·ri·mand (rĕp′rə-mănd′) *tr.v.* **-mand·ed, -mand·ing, -mands.** To rebuke or censure severely or formally. —*n.* A severe or formal rebuke or censure. [OFr. *reprimander* < *reprimende,* a reprimand < Lat. *reprimenda,* neuter pl. gerund. of *reprimere,* to repress.]

re·print (rē′prĭnt′) *n.* **1.** Something that has been printed again, esp.: **a.** A new printing identical to an original. **b.** A separately printed excerpt. **2.** A facsimile of a stamp printed after the original issue of the stamp has ceased. —*tr.v.* (rē-prĭnt′) **-print·ed, -print·ing, -prints.** To print again. **—re·print′er** *n.*

re·pri·sal (rĭ-prī′zəl) *n.* **1.** The forcible seizure of an enemy's goods or subjects in retaliation for injuries inflicted. **2.** The practice of using political or military force without actually resorting to war. **3.** Retaliation for an injury with the intent of inflicting at least as much injury in return. [ME *reprisail* < AN *reprisaille* < Med. Lat. *reprisalia,* reprisals < Lat. *reprehendere,* to reprehend.]

re·prise (rĭ-prēz′) *n.* **1.** *Mus.* **a.** A repetition of a phrase or verse. **b.** A return to an original theme. **2.** A recurrence or resumption of an action. **3.** An annual charge or deduction made out of an estate. [ME < OFr. < fem. p.part. of *reprendre,* to take back. —see REPRIEVE.]

re·pro (rē′prō) *n., pl.* **-pros.** *Printing.* A reproduction proof.

re·proach (rĭ-prōch′) *tr.v.* **-proached, -proach·ing, -proach·es. 1.** To blame for something; rebuke. **2.** To bring shame upon; disgrace. —*n.* **1.** Blame; rebuke. **2.** Something that causes rebuke or blame. **3.** Disgrace; shame. [ME *reprochen* < OFr. *reprochier* < VLat. **repropiare* : Lat. *re-,* back + Lat. *prope,* near.] **—re·proach′a·ble** *adj.* **—re·proach′a·ble·ness** *n.* **—re·proach′a·bly** *adv.* **—re·proach′er** *n.*

re·proach·ful (rĭ-prōch′fəl) *adj.* Expressing reproach or blame. **—re·proach′ful·ly** *adv.* **—re·proach′ful·ness** *n.*

rep·ro·bate (rĕp′rə-bāt′) *n.* **1.** A morally unprincipled person. **2.** *Theol.* One who is predestined to damnation. —*adj.* **1.** Morally unprincipled; profligate. **2.** *Theol.* Rejected by God and without hope of salvation. —*tr.v.* **-bat·ed, -bat·ing,**

-bates. **1.** To disapprove of; condemn. **2.** *Theol.* To abandon to eternal damnation. [LLat. *reprobatus,* p.part. of *reprobare,* to reprove.] **—rep'ro·ba'tion** *n.* **—rep'ro·ba'tive** *adj.*

re·proc·ess (rē-prŏs'ĕs', -prō'sĕs') *tr.v.* **-essed, -ess·ing, -ess·es.** To cause to undergo special or additional processing before reuse.

re·pro·duce (rē'prə-do͞os', -dyo͞os') *v.* **-duced, -duc·ing, -duc·es.** —*tr.* **1.** To produce a counterpart, image, or copy of. **2.** *Biol.* To generate (offspring) by sexual or asexual means. **3.** To produce again or anew; re-create. **4.** To bring (a memory, for example) to mind again. —*intr.* **1.** To generate offspring. **2.** To undergo copying. **—re'pro·duc'er** *n.* **—re'pro·duc'i·bil'i·ty** *n.* **—re'pro·duc'i·ble** *adj.*

re·pro·duc·tion (rē'prə-dŭk'shən) *n.* **1.** The act of reproducing or process of being reproduced. **2.** Something reproduced. **3.** *Biol.* The sexual or asexual process by which organisms generate others of the same kind.

reproduction proof *n. Printing.* A proof of typeset material made for reproduction through a photographic process such as photo-offset lithography.

re·pro·duc·tive (rē'prə-dŭk'tĭv) *adj.* **1.** Of or pertaining to reproduction. **2.** Tending to reproduce. **—re'pro·duc'tive·ly** *adv.* **—re'pro·duc'tive·ness** *n.*

re·prog·ra·phy (rĭ-prŏg'rə-fē) *n.* The exact reproduction, as by photocopying or offset printing, of graphic material. [RE-PRO(DUCTION) + -GRAPHY.] **—re·prog'ra·pher** *n.* **—re'pro·graph'ic** (rē'prə-grăf'ĭk, rĕp'rə-) *adj.* **—re'pro·graph'ics** *n.*

re·proof (rĭ-pro͞of') *n.* An act or expression of reproving.

re·prove (rĭ-pro͞ov') *tr.v.* **-proved, -prov·ing, -proves.** **1.** To rebuke for a fault or misdeed; scold. **2.** To find fault with. [ME *reproven* < OFr. *reprover* < LLat. *reprobare,* to disapprove : Lat. *re-* (reversal) + Lat. *probare,* to approve.] **—re·prov'a·ble** *adj.* **—re·prov'er** *n.* **—re·prov'ing·ly** *adv.*

reptile
A chameleon

rep·tile (rĕp'tĭl, -tīl') *n.* **1.** Any of various cold-blooded, usually egg-laying vertebrates of the class Reptilia, as a snake, lizard, crocodile, turtle, or dinosaur, having an external covering of scales or horny plates and breathing by means of lungs. **2.** A despicable or treacherous person. [ME *reptil* < OFr. *reptile* < Lat. *reptilis,* creeping < *repere,* to creep.]

rep·til·i·an (rĕp-tĭl'ē-ən, -tĭl'yən) *adj.* **1.** Of or pertaining to reptiles. **2.** Resembling or characteristic of a reptile. —*n.* A reptile.

re·pub·lic (rĭ-pŭb'lĭk) *n.* **1. a.** A political order whose head of state is not a monarch and in modern times is usually a president. **b.** A nation having such a political order. **2. a.** A political order in which the supreme power lies in a body of citizens who are entitled to vote for officers and representatives responsible to them. **b.** A nation having such a political order. **3.** A specific republican government of a nation: *the Fourth Republic of France.* **4.** A group of people working as equals in the same sphere or field: *the republic of letters.* [OFr. *republique* < Lat. *respublica* : *res,* thing + *publica,* fem. of *publicus,* of the people.]

re·pub·li·can (rĭ-pŭb'lĭ-kən) *adj.* **1.** Of, pertaining to, or characteristic of a republic. **2.** In favor of a republican form of government. **3. Republican.** Of, pertaining to, characteristic of, or belonging to the Republican Party of the United States. —*n.* **1.** A person who favors a republican form of government. **2. Republican.** A member of the Republican Party of the United States. **—re·pub'li·can·ism** *n.*

re·pub·li·can·ize (rĭ-pŭb'lĭ-kə-nīz') *tr.v.* **-ized, -iz·ing, -iz·es.** To make republican. **—re·pub'li·can·i·za'tion** *n.*

Republican Party *n.* **1.** One of the two primary political parties of the United States, organized in 1854 to oppose slavery. **2.** The Democratic-Republican Party, a political party of the United States, organized in 1792 by Thomas Jefferson.

re·pub·li·ca·tion (rē-pŭb'lĭ-kā'shən) *n.* **1.** The act or process of republishing. **2.** Something that is republished.

re·pub·lish (rē-pŭb'lĭsh) *tr.v.* **-lished, -lish·ing, -lish·es.** **1.** To publish again. **2.** *Law.* To revive (a canceled will). **—re·pub'lish·er** *n.*

reredos
Open-hearth reredos from the Shetland Islands

re·pu·di·ate (rĭ-pyo͞o'dē-āt') *tr.v.* **-at·ed, -at·ing, -ates.** **1.** To reject the validity of. **2.** To refuse to recognize or pay. **3.** To reject as untrue. **4.** To disown (a child, for example). [Lat. *repudiare, repudiat-* < *repudium,* divorce.] **—re·pu'di·a'tive** *adj.* **—re·pu'di·a'tor** *n.*

re·pu·di·a·tion (rĭ-pyo͞o'dē-ā'shən) *n.* **1. a.** The act of repudiating. **b.** The state of being repudiated. **2.** The refusal, esp. by public authorities, to acknowledge a contract or debt. **—re·pu'di·a'tion·ist** *n.*

re·pugn (rĭ-pyo͞on') *v.* **-pugned, -pugn·ing, -pugns.** —*tr.* To oppose or resist. —*intr. Archaic.* To be opposed; conflict. [ME *repugnen* < OFr. *repugner* < Lat. *repugnare,* to fight against : *re-,* against + *pugnare,* to fight.]

re·pug·nance (rĭ-pŭg'nəns) also **re·pug·nan·cy** (-nən-sē) *n.* **1.** The state of feeling extreme dislike or aversion. **2.** *Logic.* The relationship of contradictory terms; inconsistency.

re·pug·nant (rĭ-pŭg'nənt) *adj.* **1.** Arousing disgust or aversion; offensive or repulsive. **2.** *Logic.* Contradictory; inconsistent. [ME, resisting < OFr. < Lat. *repugnans,* pr.part. of *repugnare,* to fight against. —see REPUGN.] **—re·pug'nant·ly** *adv.*

re·pulse (rĭ-pŭls') *tr.v.* **-pulsed, -puls·ing, -puls·es.** **1.** To drive back; repel. **2.** To rebuff or reject with rudeness, coldness, or denial. —*n.* **1. a.** The act of repulsing. **b.** The state of being repulsed. **2.** Rejection; refusal. —See Usage note at **repel.** [Lat. *repellere, repuls-* : *re-,* back + *pellere,* to drive.] **—re·puls'er** *n.*

re·pul·sion (rĭ-pŭl'shən) *n.* **1. a.** The act of repulsing. **b.** The condition of being repulsed. **2.** Extreme aversion.

re·pul·sive (rĭ-pŭl'sĭv) *adj.* **1.** Causing extreme aversion; disgusting. **2.** Tending to repel or drive off. **—re·pul'sive·ly** *adv.* **—re·pul'sive·ness** *n.*

re·pur·chase agreement (rē-pûr'chĭs) *n.* A contract giving the seller of property the right or obligation to buy back the property under specified terms.

rep·u·ta·ble (rĕp'yə-tə-bəl) *adj.* **1.** Having a good reputation; honorable. **2.** In correct usage. Used of words. **—rep'u·ta·bil'i·ty** *n.* **—rep'u·ta·bly** *adv.*

rep·u·ta·tion (rĕp'yə-tā'shən) *n.* **1.** The general estimation in which a person is held by the public. **2.** The state or situation of being held in high repute. **3.** A specific characteristic or trait ascribed to one: *a reputation for courtesy.* [ME *reputacion* < Lat. *reputatio,* a reckoning < *reputare,* to think over. —see REPUTE.]

re·pute (rĭ-pyo͞ot') *tr.v.* **-put·ed, -put·ing, -putes.** **1.** To ascribe a particular fact or characteristic to. **2.** To consider or suppose. —*n.* **1.** Reputation. **2.** A good reputation. [ME *reputen* < OFr. *reputer* < Lat. *reputare,* to think over : *re-,* again + *putare,* to think.]

re·put·ed (rĭ-pyo͞o'tĭd) *adj.* Generally considered, assumed, or supposed. **—re·put'ed·ly** *adv.*

re·quest (rĭ-kwĕst') *tr.v.* **-quest·ed, -quest·ing, -quests.** **1.** To ask for; express a desire for. **2.** To ask (a person) to do something. —*n.* **1.** The act of asking. **2.** Something requested. **3.** The fact or condition of being requested. —***idioms.* by request.** In response to an expressed desire. **in request.** In great demand. [OFr. *requester* < *requeste,* a request < VLat. **requaestia* < Lat. *requirere,* to ask for. —see REQUIRE.] **—re·quest'er** *n.*

req·ui·em (rĕk'wē-əm, rē'kwē-) *n.* **1. Requiem.** *Rom. Cath. Ch.* **a.** A mass for a deceased person. **b.** A musical composition for such a mass. **2.** A hymn, composition, or service for the dead. [ME < Lat., accusative of *requies,* rest, the first word of the mass for the dead.]

req·ui·es·cat (rĕk'wē-ĕs'kăt', -kät') *n.* A prayer for the repose of the souls of the dead. [Lat., may he rest.]

re·quire (rĭ-kwīr') *tr.v.* **-quired, -quir·ing, -quires.** **1.** To have as a requisite; need. **2.** To call for as fitting; demand. **3.** To impose an obligation on; compel. **4.** To command; order. [ME *requiren* < OFr. *requere* < VLat. **requaerere* < Lat. *requirere* : *re-,* again + *quaerere,* to seek.] **—re·quir'a·ble** *adj.* **—re·quir'er** *n.*

re·quire·ment (rĭ-kwīr'mənt) *n.* **1.** Something that is required; necessity. **2.** Something obligatory; prerequisite.

req·ui·site (rĕk'wĭ-zĭt) *adj.* Required; essential. —*n.* Something that is requisite. [ME < Lat. *requisitus,* p.part. of *requirere,* to require.] **—req'ui·site·ly** *adv.* **—req'ui·site·ness** *n.*

req·ui·si·tion (rĕk'wĭ-zĭsh'ən) *n.* **1.** A formal written request for something that is needed. **2.** A necessity; requirement. **3.** The state or condition of being needed. **4.** A formal request of one government to another demanding the return of a criminal or fugitive. —*tr.v.* **-tioned, -tion·ing, -tions.** **1.** To demand, as for military needs. **2.** To make demands of.

re·quit·al (rĭ-kwīt'l) *n.* **1.** The act of requiting. **2.** Return, as for an injury or a friendly act.

re·quite (rĭ-kwīt') *tr.v.* **-quit·ed, -quit·ing, -quites.** **1.** To make repayment or return for: *requite another's love.* **2.** To avenge. [RE- + obs. *quite,* to pay, var. of QUIT.] **—re·quit'a·ble** *adj.* **—re·quit'er** *n.*

re·ra·di·a·tion (rē-rā'dē-ā'shən) *n. Physics.* Radiation emission resulting from radiation absorption.

rere·dos (rĕr'ĭ-dŏs', rîr'-, rîr'dŏs') *n.* **1.** A retable. **2.** The back of an open hearth of a fireplace. [ME < OFr. *areredos* : *arere,* behind (Lat. *ad,* to + *retro,* backward) + *dos,* back < Lat. *dorsum.*]

re·re·lease (rē'rĭ-lēs') *tr.v.* **-leased, -leas·ing, -leas·es.** To release (a motion picture, for example) again. **—re're·lease'** *n.*

re·run (rē'rŭn') *n.* A repetition of a recorded motion-picture or television performance. —*tr.v.* (rē-rŭn') **-ran** (-răn'), **-run, run·ning, -runs.** To present a rerun of.

res ad·ju·di·ca·ta (rēz' ə-jo͞o'dĭ-kä'tə) *n.* Variant of **res judicata.**

re·sale (rē'sāl', rē-sāl') *n.* The act of selling again. **—re·sal'a·ble** *adj.*

re·scind (rĭ-sĭnd') *tr.v.* **-scind·ed, -scind·ing, -scinds.** To make void; repeal or annul. [Lat. *rescindere* : *re-* (intensive) + *scindere,* to cut.] **—re·scind'a·ble** *adj.* **—re·scind'er** *n.* **—re·scind'ment** *n.*

re·scis·sion (rĭ-sĭzh'ən) *n.* The act of rescinding. [LLat. *rescissio* < Lat. *rescindere,* to rescind.]

re·scis·so·ry (rĭ-sĭz'ə-rē, -sĭs'-) *adj.* Of or pertaining to rescission.

re·script (rē'skrĭpt') *n.* **1.** *Rom. Cath. Ch.* A response from the pope or another ecclesiastical superior to a question regarding discipline or doctrine. **2.** A formal decree or edict. **3.** An act of rewriting. **4.** A reply from a Roman emperor to a magistrate's query on a point of law. [Lat. *rescriptum* < neuter p.part. of *rescribere,* to write back : *re-,* back + *scribere,* to write.]

res·cue (rĕs′kyo͞o) *tr.v.* **-cued, -cu·ing, -cues. 1.** To save, as from danger or imprisonment. **2.** *Law.* To take from legal custody by force. *—n.* **1.** An act of rescuing; deliverance. **2.** *Law.* Removal from legal custody by force. [ME *rescuen* < OFr. *rescourre* : *re-*, back (< Lat.) + *escourre,* to shake < Lat. *escutere* (*ex-*, out + *quatere,* to shake).] **—res′cu·a·ble** *adj.* **—res′cu·er** *n.*

rescue grass *n.* A tall grass, *Bromus catharticus,* native to tropical America, cultivated in warm regions for hay. [Prob. alteration of FESCUE GRASS.]

rescue mission *n.* An esp. urban religious mission that aids and seeks to convert destitute individuals.

re·search (rĭ-sûrch′, rē′sûrch′) *n.* **1.** Scholarly or scientific investigation or inquiry. **2.** Close and careful study. *—v.* **-searched, -search·ing, -search·es.** *—intr.* To engage in or perform research. *—tr.* To study thoroughly. [OFr. *recerche* < *recercher,* to research : *re-*, again (< Lat. *re-*) + *cerchier,* to search. —see SEARCH.] **—re·search′a·ble** *adj.* **—re·search′er, re·search′ist** *n.*

ré·seau or **re·seau** (rā-zō′, rĭ-) *n., pl.* **-seaus** or **-seaux** (-zōz′). **1.** A net or mesh foundation for lace. **2.** *Astron.* A reference grid of fine lines forming uniform squares on a photographic plate or print, used to aid in measurement. **3.** A mosaic screen of fine lines of three colors, used in color photography. [Fr. < OFr. *reseuil,* dim. of *raiz,* net < Lat. *rete.*]

re·sect (rĭ-sĕkt′) *tr.v.* **-sect·ed, -sect·ing, -sects.** To perform a resection on. [Lat. *resecare, resect-,* to cut off : *re-*, back + *secare,* to cut.] **—re·sect′a·bil′i·ty** *n.* **—re·sect′a·ble** *adj.*

re·sec·tion (rĭ-sĕk′shən) *n.* The surgical removal of part of an organ or structure.

re·se·da (rĭ-sē′də, -sĕd′ə) *n.* **1.** A plant of the genus *Reseda,* which includes the mignonette. **2.** A grayish or dark green to yellow green or light olive. [NLat. *Reseda,* genus name < Lat. *reseda,* a kind of plant.] **—re·se′da** *adj.*

re·seg·re·ga·tion (rē-sĕg′rĭ-gā′shən) *n.* A renewal of segregation, as in a school system, after a period of desegregation.

re·sem·blance (rĭ-zĕm′bləns) *n.* **1.** The condition or quality of resembling; similarity in nature, form, or appearance. **2.** Something that resembles another; likeness.

re·sem·ble (rĭ-zĕm′bəl) *tr.v.* **-bled, -bling, -bles.** To have a similarity or likeness to. [ME *resemblen* < OFr. *resembler* : *re-* (intensive < Lat.) + *sembler,* to be like < Lat. *simulare,* to imitate < *similis,* like.] **—re·sem′bler** *n.*

re·sent (rĭ-zĕnt′) *tr.v.* **-sent·ed, -sent·ing, -sents.** To feel indignantly aggrieved at. [Obs. Fr. *resentir,* to feel strongly : *re-* (intensive) + *sentir,* to feel < Lat. *sentire.*]

re·sent·ful (rĭ-zĕnt′fəl) *adj.* Full of, characterized by, or inclined to feel resentment. **—re·sent′ful·ly** *adv.* **—re·sent′ful·ness** *n.*

re·sent·ment (rĭ-zĕnt′mənt) *n.* Indignation or ill will felt as a result of a real or imagined offense.

re·ser·pine (rĭ-sûr′pēn′, -pĭn, rĕs′ər-pĭn, -pēn′, rĕz′-) *n.* A white to yellowish powder, $C_{33}H_{40}N_2O_9$, isolated from the roots of certain species of rauwolfia and used as a sedative and tranquilizer. [G. *Reserpin* < NLat. *Rauwolfia serpentina,* species of snakeroot : RAUWOLFIA + LLat. *serpentina,* fem. of *serpentinus,* serpentine < Lat. *serpere,* to creep.]

res·er·va·tion (rĕz′ər-vā′shən) *n.* **1.** The act of reserving. **2.** Something that is reserved. **3.** A limiting qualification, condition, or exception: *has reservations about the proposal.* **4.** A tract of land set apart by the federal government for a special purpose, esp. one for the use of an American Indian people or tribe. **5. a.** An arrangement by which accommodations are secured in advance, as in a hotel or on an airplane. **b.** The accommodations so secured. **c.** The record or promise of such an arrangement.

re·serve (rĭ-zûrv′) *tr.v.* **-served, -serv·ing, -serves. 1.** To keep back or save for future use or a special purpose. **2.** To set apart for a particular person or use. **3.** To keep or secure for oneself; retain: *I reserve the right to disagree.* *—n.* **1.** Something kept back or saved for future use or a special purpose. **2.** The act of reserving. **3.** The keeping of one's feelings, thoughts, or affairs to oneself. **4.** Self-restraint in expression; reticence. **5.** Lack of enthusiasm; skeptical caution. **6.** An amount of capital held back from investment by a bank or company in order to meet probable or possible demands. **7.** A reservation of public land: *a forest reserve.* **8.** Often **reserves. a.** A fighting force kept uncommitted until strategic need arises. **b.** The part of a country's armed forces not on active duty but subject to call in an emergency. ***—modifier:** a reserve supply of food.* ***—idiom.*** **in reserve.** Kept back, set aside, or saved. [ME *reserven* < OFr. *reserver* < Lat. *reservare,* to keep back : *re-*, back + *servare,* to keep.] **—re·serv′a·ble** *adj.* **—re·serv′er** *n.*

reserve bank *n.* A central bank that holds the reserves of other banks.

re·served (rĭ-zûrvd′) *adj.* **1.** Held in reserve; kept back or set aside. **2.** Marked by self-restraint in action and expression. **—re·serv′ed·ly** (-zûr′vĭd-lē) *adv.* **—re·serv′ed·ness** *n.*

re·serv·ist (rĭ-zûr′vĭst) *n.* One who is a member of a military reserve.

res·er·voir (rĕz′ər-vwär′, -vwôr′, -vôr′) *n.* **1.** A body of water collected and stored for future use in a natural or artificial lake. **2.** A receptacle or chamber for storing a fluid. **3.** *Anat.* A cisterna. **4.** A large supply; reserve: *a reservoir of gratitude.* [Fr. *réservoir* < *réserver,* to reserve.]

re·set (rē-sĕt′) *tr.v.* **-set, -set·ting, -sets. 1.** To set again: *reset a broken bone.* **2.** To change the reading of: *reset a clock.* *—n.* (rē′sĕt′). **1.** The act of resetting. **2.** Something that is reset. **—re·set′ta·ble** *adj.* **—re·set′ter** *n.*

res ges·tae (rās′ gĕs′tī′, rēz′ jĕs′tē) *pl.n.* **1.** Things done; deeds. **2.** *Law.* The facts of a case that are admissible in evidence. [Lat., things done.]

resh (rĕsh) *n.* The 20th letter of the Hebrew alphabet. See table at **alphabet.** [Heb. *rēsh* < *rōsh,* head.]

re·shape (rē-shāp′) *tr.v.* **-shaped, -shap·ing, -shapes.** To shape, form, or organize again or anew. **—re·shap′er** *n.*

re·shuf·fle (rē-shŭf′əl) *tr.v.* **-fled, -fling, -fles. 1.** To shuffle again: *reshuffle cards.* **2.** To arrange or organize anew: *The president reshuffled his advisory committee.* **—re·shuf′fle** *n.*

re·sid (rĭ-zĭd′) *n. Informal.* Residual oil.

re·side (rĭ-zīd′) *intr.v.* **-sid·ed, -sid·ing, -sides. 1.** To live in a place for an extended or permanent period of time. **2.** To be inherently present; exist. **3.** To be vested, as a power or right. [ME *residen* < OFr. *resider* < Lat. *residēre,* to sit back : *re-*, back + *sedēre,* to sit.] **—re·sid′er** *n.*

res·i·dence (rĕz′ĭ-dəns, -dĕns′) *n.* **1.** The place in which one lives; dwelling. **2.** The act or a period of residing somewhere. **3.** A medical residency. **4.** The official home or location of a corporation. ***—idiom.*** **in residence.** Committed to live and work in a specific place, often for a certain length of time: *an artist in residence at a college.*

res·i·den·cy (rĕz′ĭ-dən-sē, -dĕn′-) *n., pl.* **-cies. 1.** The period during which a physician receives specialized clinical training. **2. a.** The house of a colonial resident. **b.** The sphere of authority of a colonial resident. **3.** Residence.

res·i·dent (rĕz′ĭ-dənt, -dĕnt′) *n.* **1.** One who makes his home in a particular place. **2.** A colonial official acting as adviser to the ruler of a protected state, often having quasi-gubernatorial powers. **3.** A nonmigratory bird or other animal. **4.** A physician serving a period of residency. *—adj.* **1.** Dwelling in a particular place; residing. **2.** Living somewhere in connection with duty or work. **3.** Inherently present. **4.** Nonmigratory, as a bird or other animal.

reseda

res·i·den·tial (rĕz′ĭ-dĕn′shəl) *adj.* **1.** Of, relating to, or having residence. **2.** Of, suitable for, or limited to residences. **—res′i·den′tial·ly** *adv.*

res·i·den·ti·ar·y (rĕz′ĭ-dĕn′shē-ĕr′ē, -shə-rē) *adj.* **1.** Having a residence, esp. an official one. **2.** Involving or requiring official residence. *—n., pl.* **-ies. 1.** A resident. **2.** A clergyman required to have an official residence.

re·sid·u·a (rĭ-zĭj′o͞o-ə) *n.* Plural of **residuum.**

re·sid·u·al (rĭ-zĭj′o͞o-əl) *adj.* **1.** Of, pertaining to, or characteristic of a residue. **2.** Remaining as a residue. *—n.* **1.** The quantity left over at the end of a process; remainder. **2.** Often **residuals.** A payment made to a performer for each repeat showing of a recorded television show. **—re·sid′u·al·ly** *adv.*

residual oil *n.* The low-grade oil products that remain after the distillation of petroleum.

re·sid·u·ar·y (rĭ-zĭj′o͞o-ĕr′ē) *adj.* **1.** Of, pertaining to, or constituting a residue. **2.** *Law.* Entitled to the residue of an estate.

res·i·due (rĕz′ĭ-do͞o′, -dyo͞o′) *n.* **1.** The remainder of something after removal of a part. **2.** Matter remaining after completion of an abstractive chemical or physical process, such as evaporation, combustion, distillation, or filtration; residuum. **3.** *Law.* The remainder of a testator's estate after all claims, debts, and bequests are satisfied. [ME < OFr. *residu* < Lat. *residuum,* neuter of *residuus,* remaining < *residēre,* to sit back. —see RESIDE.]

re·sid·u·um (rĭ-zĭj′o͞o-əm) *n., pl.* **-u·a** (-o͞o-ə). **1.** Something remaining after removal of a part; residue. **2.** *Law.* Residue (sense 3). [Lat., residue.]

re·sign (rĭ-zīn′) *v.* **-signed, -sign·ing, -signs.** *—tr.* **1.** To submit (oneself) passively; accept as inevitable. **2.** To give up (a position), esp. by formal notification; quit. **3.** To relinquish (a privilege, right, or claim). *—intr.* To give up one's job or office; quit, esp. by formal notification: *resign from the army.* [ME *resigner* < OFr. *resigner* < Lat. *resignare,* to unseal : *re-* (reversal) + *signare,* to seal < *signum,* mark.] **—re·sign′er** *n.*

re-sign (rē-sīn′) *tr.v.* **-signed, -sign·ing, -signs.** To sign again.

res·ig·na·tion (rĕz′ĭg-nā′shən) *n.* **1.** The act or an instance of resigning. **2.** An oral or written statement that one is resigning a position or office. **3.** Unresisting acceptance; passive submission.

re·signed (rĭ-zīnd′) *adj.* Feeling or marked by resignation; acquiescent. **—re·sign′ed·ly** (-zī′nĭd-lē) *adv.* **—re·sign′ed·ness** *n.*

re·sile (rĭ-zīl′) *intr.v.* **-siled, -sil·ing, -siles.** To spring back, esp. to resume a prior position or form after being stretched or pressed. [Lat. *resilire,* to leap back : *re-*, back + *salire,* to leap.]

re·sil·ience (rĭ-zĭl′yəns) also **re·sil·ien·cy** (-yən-sē) *n.* **1.** The ability to recover quickly from illness, change, or misfortune; buoyancy. **2.** The property of a material that enables it to resume its original shape or position after being bent, stretched, or compressed; elasticity. **—re·sil'ient** *adj.* **—re·sil'ient·ly** *adv.*

res·in (rĕz'ĭn) *n.* **1.** Any of numerous clear to translucent yellow or brown solid or semisolid viscous substances of plant origin, such as copal, rosin, and amber, used principally in lacquers, varnishes, inks, adhesives, synthetic plastics, and pharmaceuticals. **2.** Any of numerous physically similar polymerized synthetics or chemically modified natural resins including thermoplastic materials, such as polyvinyl, polystyrene, and polyethylene, and thermosetting materials, such as polyesters, epoxies, and silicones, that are used with fillers, stabilizers, pigments, and other components to form plastics. *—tr.v.* **-ined, -in·ing, -ins.** To treat or rub with resin. [ME < OFr. *resine* < Lat. *resina.*] **—res'in·ous** (rĕz'ə-nəs) *adj.*

res·in·ate (rĕz'ə-nāt') *tr.v.* **-at·ed, -at·ing, -ates.** To impregnate, permeate, or flavor with resin.

resin canal *n.* A tubular intercellular space containing secretory cells that secrete resin, often found in gymnosperms.

res·in·if·er·ous (rĕz'ə-nĭf'ər-əs) *adj.* Yielding resin.

res·in·oid (rĕz'ə-noid') *adj.* Characteristic of, pertaining to, or containing resin. *—n.* A resinoid synthetic, esp. a thermosetting resin.

re·sist (rĭ-zĭst') *v.* **-sist·ed, -sist·ing, -sists.** *—tr.* **1.** To strive or work against; oppose actively. **2.** To remain firm against the action or effect of; withstand. **3.** To keep from giving in to or enjoying. *—intr.* To offer resistance; act in opposition. *—n.* A substance that can cover and protect a surface, as from corrosion. [ME *resisten* < Lat. *resistere* : *re-*, against + *sistere,* to place.] **—re·sist'er** *n.*

re·sis·tance (rĭ-zĭs'təns) *n.* **1. a.** The act of resisting. **b.** The capacity to resist. **2.** A force that tends to oppose or retard motion. **3.** *Elect.* The opposition to electric current characteristic of a medium, substance, or circuit element. **4.** An underground organization engaged in a struggle for national liberation in a country under military or totalitarian occupation. **5.** *Psychoanal.* A process in which the ego opposes the conscious recall of unpleasant experiences. **—re·sis'tant** *adj.*

re·sist·i·ble (rĭ-zĭs'tə-bəl) *adj.* Capable of being resisted. **—re·sist'i·bil'i·ty** *n.* **—re·sist'i·bly** *adv.*

re·sis·tive (rĭ-zĭs'tĭv) *adj.* Capable of, tending toward, or marked by resistance: *a person resistive to changes.* **—re·sis'tive·ly** *adv.* **—re·sis'tive·ness** *n.*

re·sis·tiv·i·ty (rē'zĭs-tĭv'ĭ-tē) *n.* **1.** The capacity for or tendency toward resistance. **2.** *Elect.* The resistance per unit length of a substance with uniform cross section.

re·sist·less (rĭ-zĭst'lĭs) *adj.* **1.** Incapable of being resisted; irresistible. **2.** Powerless to resist; unresisting. **—re·sist'less·ly** *adv.* **—re·sist'less·ness** *n.*

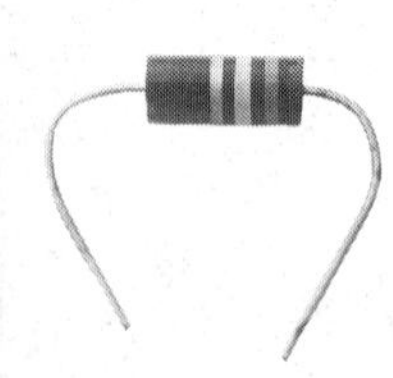

resistor

re·sis·tor (rĭ-zĭs'tər) *n.* An electric circuit element used to provide resistance.

res ju·di·ca·ta (rēz' jo͞o'dĭ-kä'tə) also **res ad·ju·di·ca·ta** (rēz' ə-jo͞o'-) *n.* An adjudicated precedent in law. [Lat., thing decided.]

re·sole (rē-sōl') *tr.v.* **-soled, -sol·ing, -soles.** To put a new sole on (a shoe).

re·sol·u·ble (rĭ-zŏl'yə-bəl) *adj.* Capable of being resolved. [LLat. *resolubilis* < Lat. *resolvere,* to resolve.] **—re·sol'u·bil'i·ty, re·sol'u·ble·ness** *n.*

res·o·lute (rĕz'ə-lo͞ot') *adj.* Characterized by firmness or determination; unwavering. [Lat. *resolutus,* p.part. of *resolvere,* to resolve.] **—res'o·lute'ly** *adv.* **—res'o·lute'ness** *n.*

res·o·lu·tion (rĕz'ə-lo͞o'shən) *n.* **1.** The state or quality of being resolute; firm determination. **2.** The act of resolving to do something. **3.** A course of action determined or decided upon. **4.** A formal statement of a decision or expression of opinion put before or adopted by an assembly such as the U.S. Congress. **5.** The action or process of separating or reducing something into its constituent parts: *the prismatic resolution of sunlight into its spectral colors.* **6.** *Med.* The subsiding or termination of an abnormal condition, as a fever or inflammation. **7.** A decision made by a court of law. **8.** An explanation, as of a problem or puzzle; solution. **9.** *Mus.* **a.** The progression of a dissonant tone or chord to a consonant tone or chord. **b.** The tone or chord to which such a progression is made.

re·solve (rĭ-zŏlv') *v.* **-solved, -solv·ing, -solves.** *—tr.* **1.** To make a firm decision about. **2.** To cause (a person) to reach a decision. **3.** To decide or express by formal vote. **4.** To separate (something) into constituent parts. **5.** To change or convert: *His resentment resolved itself into resignation.* **6.** To find a solution to; solve. **7.** To remove or dispel (doubts); explain away. **8.** To bring to a usually successful conclusion: *resolve a conflict.* **9.** *Med.* To cause reduction of (an inflammation, for example). **10.** *Mus.* To cause (a tone or chord) to progress from dissonance to consonance. **11.** *Chem.* To separate (a racemic compound or mixture) into its optically active constituents. **12.** To render visible and distinguish parts of (an image). **13.** *Math.* To separate (a vector, for example) into coordinate components. **14.** To melt or dissolve (something). *—intr.* **1.** To reach a decision or make a determination: *resolve on a proposal.* **2.** To become separated or reduced to constituents. **3.** *Mus.* To undergo resolution. *—n.* **1.** Firmness of purpose; resolution. **2.** A determination or decision; fixed purpose. **3.** A formal resolution made by a deliberative body. [ME *resolven,* to dissolve < Lat. *resolvere,* to untie : *re-*, back + *solvere,* to untie.] **—re·solv'a·bil'i·ty, re·solv'a·ble·ness** *n.* **—re·solv'a·ble** *adj.* **—re·solv'er** *n.*

re·sol·vent (rĭ-zŏl'vənt) *adj.* Causing or capable of causing separation into constituents; solvent. *—n.* A resolvent substance, esp. a medicine that reduces inflammation or swelling.

res·o·nance (rĕz'ə-nəns) *n.* **1.** The quality or condition of being resonant. **2.** *Physics.* **a.** The enhancement of the response of an electric or mechanical system to a periodic driving force when the driving frequency is equal to the natural undamped frequency of the system. **b.** The condition of a system of subatomic particles in which the probability of a particular reaction, as for nuclear capture of a neutron, is a maximum; the occurrence of a cross-section maximum. **c.** The event corresponding to such a maximum, esp. the formation of a particle state having only a few possible modes of decay and characterized by a lifetime considerably longer than neighboring states. **3.** *Acoustics.* The intensification and prolongation of sound, esp. of a musical tone, produced by sympathetic vibration. **4.** *Med.* The sound produced by diagnostic percussion of the normal chest. **5.** *Chem.* The phenomenon of interrelated alternative bond structures in certain molecules, produced by redistribution of valence electrons without change in the relative positions of bound atoms and resulting in highly stable compounds. **6.** The intensification of vocal tones during articulation.

res·o·nant (rĕz'ə-nənt) *adj.* **1.** Of, pertaining to, or exhibiting resonance. **2.** Producing resonance: *resonant frequency excitation.* **3.** Resulting from or as if from resonance: *resonant amplification; a resonant voice.* [Lat. *resonans, resonant-,* pr.part. of *resonare,* to resound.] **—res'o·nant·ly** *adv.*

resonant circuit *n.* An electric circuit with inductance and capacitance chosen to produce a specified value of the natural frequency of the circuit.

res·o·nate (rĕz'ə-nāt') *v.* **-nat·ed, -nat·ing, -nates.** *—intr.* **1.** To exhibit or produce resonance or resonant effects. **2.** To resound. *—tr.* To subject to resonating. [Lat. *resonare, resonat-.* —see RESOUND.] **—res'o·na'tion** *n.*

res·o·na·tor (rĕz'ə-nā'tər) *n.* **1.** A resonating system. **2. a.** A hollow chamber or cavity with dimensions chosen to permit internal resonant oscillation of electromagnetic or acoustical waves of specific frequencies. **b.** *Electronics.* Any of various microwave generating tubes or devices containing such resonant chambers or cavities. **c.** *Electronics.* A resonant circuit.

re·sorb (rē-sôrb', -zôrb') *v.* **-sorbed, -sorb·ing, -sorbs.** *—tr.* **1.** To absorb again. **2.** *Biol.* To dissolve and assimilate (bone tissue, for example). *—intr.* To undergo resorption. [Lat. *resorbere,* to suck back : *re-*, back + *sorbere,* to suck up.]

res·or·cin·ol (rə-zôr'sə-nôl', -nōl') also **res·or·cin** (rə-zôr'sĭn) *n.* A white crystalline compound, $C_6H_4(OH)_2$, used to treat certain skin diseases and in dyes, resin adhesives, and pharmaceuticals. [RES(IN) + ORC(HIL) + -IN + -OL.]

re·sorp·tion (rē-sôrp'shən, -zôrp'-) *n.* The act or process of resorbing.

re·sort (rĭ-zôrt') *intr.v.* **-sort·ed, -sort·ing, -sorts.** **1.** To have recourse: *The government resorted to censorship of the press.* **2.** To go customarily or frequently; repair. *—n.* **1.** A place frequented by people for relaxation or recreation: *a winter resort.* **2.** A customary or frequent going or gathering: *a popular place of resort.* **3.** Recourse. **4.** A person or thing turned to for aid or relief. [ME *resorten,* to return < OFr. *resortir,* to go out again : *re-*, again + *sortir,* to go out.]

re·sound (rĭ-zound') *v.* **-sound·ed, -sound·ing, -sounds.** *—intr.* **1.** To be filled with sound; reverberate. **2.** To make a loud, long, or reverberating sound. **3.** To sound loudly; ring. **4.** To become famous, celebrated, or extolled. *—tr.* **1.** To send back (sound). **2.** To utter or emit loudly. **3.** To proclaim widely; celebrate. [ME *resounen* < OFr. *resoner* < Lat. *resonare* : *re-*, again + *sonare,* to sound.] **—re·sound'ing** *adj.* **—re·sound'ing·ly** *adv.*

re·source (rē'sôrs', -sōrs', -zôrs', -zōrs', rĭ-sôrs', -sōrs', -zôrs', -zōrs') *n.* **1.** Something that can be turned to for support or help. **2.** An available supply that can be drawn upon when needed. **3.** An ability to deal with a situation effectively. **4.** Often **resources.** Means that can be used to advantage. **5.** Often **resources.** Available capital; assets. **6.** A way of spending one's leisure time. [Fr. *ressource* < OFr. *ressourse* < *resourdre,* to rise again < Lat. *resurgere* : *re-*, again + *surgere,* to rise.]

re·source·ful (rĭ-sôrs'fəl, -sōrs'-, -zôrs'-, -zōrs'-) *adj.* Capable of acting effectively or imaginatively, esp. in difficult situations. **—re·source'ful·ly** *adv.* **—re·source'ful·ness** *n.*

re·spect (rĭ-spĕkt') *tr.v.* **-spect·ed, -spect·ing, -spects.** **1.** To feel or show deferential regard for; esteem. **2.** To avoid violation of or interference with. **3.** To relate or refer to; concern. *—n.* **1.** A feeling of deferential regard; esteem. **2.** The state of being regarded with honor or esteem. **3.** Willingness to show consideration or appreciation. **4. respects.** Polite expressions of consideration or deference: *pay one's respects.* **5.** A particular aspect, feature, or detail. **6.** Relation;

reference. —See Usage note at **regard.** [Lat. *respicere, respect-* : *re-,* back + *specere,* to look.] **—re·spect'er** *n.*

re·spect·a·bil·i·ty (rĭ-spĕk'tə-bĭl'ĭ-tē) *n.* The quality, state, or characteristic of being respectable.

re·spect·a·ble (rĭ-spĕk'tə-bəl) *adj.* **1.** Meriting respect or esteem; worthy. **2.** Of or appropriate to good or proper behavior or conventional conduct. **3.** Of moderately good quality: *respectable work.* **4.** Considerable in amount, number, or size: *a respectable sum of money.* **5.** Acceptable in appearance; presentable: *a respectable hat.* **—re·spect'a·ble·ness** *n.* **—re·spect'a·bly** *adv.*

re·spect·ful (rĭ-spĕkt'fəl) *adj.* Showing or marked by proper respect. **—re·spect'ful·ly** *adv.* **—re·spect'ful·ness** *n.*

re·spect·ing (rĭ-spĕk'tĭng) *prep.* With respect to; concerning. —See Usage note at **regard.**

re·spec·tive (rĭ-spĕk'tĭv) *adj.* Relating or pertaining to two or more persons or things regarded individually; particular: *their respective fields.* **—re·spec'tive·ness** *n.*

re·spec·tive·ly (rĭ-spĕk'tĭv-lē) *adv.* Singly in the order designated or mentioned: *I'm referring to each of you respectively.*

re·spell (rē-spĕl') *tr.v.* **-spelled** or **-spelt** (-spĕlt'), **-spell·ing, -spells.** To spell again or in a new way, esp. by using a phonetic alphabet.

res·pi·ra·ble (rĕs'pər-ə-bəl, rĭ-spīr'-) *adj.* **1.** Fit for breathing. **2.** Capable of being inhaled. **—res'pi·ra·bil'i·ty** *n.*

res·pi·ra·tion (rĕs'pə-rā'shən) *n.* **1.** The act or process of inhaling and exhaling; breathing. **2.** The metabolic process by which an organism assimilates oxygen and releases carbon dioxide and other products of oxidation. **—res'pi·ra'tion·al** *adj.*

res·pi·ra·tor (rĕs'pə-rā'tər) *n.* **1.** An apparatus used in administering artificial respiration. **2.** A screenlike device worn over the mouth or nose or both to protect the respiratory tract.

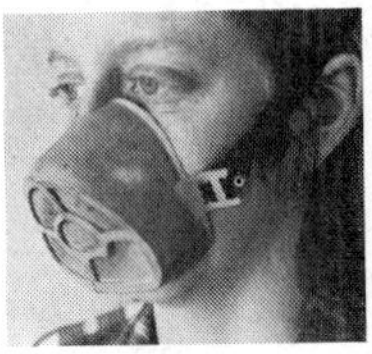

respirator

res·pi·ra·to·ry (rĕs'pər-ə-tôr'ē, -tōr'ē, rĭ-spīr'ə-) *adj.* Of, pertaining to, affecting, or used in respiration.

respiratory pigment *n.* Any of various conjugated colored proteins, such as hemoglobin, that occur in living organisms and function in oxygen transfer in cellular respiration.

respiratory system *n.* The integrated system of organs involved in the intake and exchange of oxygen and carbon dioxide between an organism and the atmosphere.

re·spire (rĭ-spīr') *v.* **-spired, -spir·ing, -spires.** *—intr.* **1.** To breathe in and out; inhale and exhale. **2.** To undergo the metabolic process of respiration. **3.** To breathe easily again, as after a period of exertion or trouble. *—tr.* To inhale and exhale (air); breathe. [ME *respiren,* to breathe again < Lat. *respirare* : *re-,* again + *spirare,* to breathe.]

res·pite (rĕs'pĭt) *n.* **1.** A usually short interval of rest or relief. **2.** *Law.* The temporary suspension of a death sentence; reprieve. *—tr.v.* **-pit·ed, -pit·ing, -pites. 1.** To delay; postpone. **2.** To grant a reprieve from (a punishment or sentence). [ME < OFr. *respit* < Lat. *respectus,* refuge < *respicere,* to respect.]

re·splen·dent (rĭ-splĕn'dənt) *adj.* Filled with splendor; brilliant. [ME < Lat. *resplendens,* pr.part. of *resplendēre,* to shine brightly : *re-* (intensive) + *splendēre,* to shine.] **—re·splen'dence, re·splen'den·cy** *n.* **—re·splen'dent·ly** *adv.*

re·spond (rĭ-spŏnd') *v.* **-spond·ed, -spond·ing, -sponds.** *—intr.* **1.** To make a reply; answer. **2.** To act in return or in answer. **3.** To react positively or favorably. *—tr.* To say in reply; answer. *—n. Archit.* A pilaster supporting an arch. [Lat. *respondēre* : *re-,* in return + *spondēre,* to promise.]

re·spon·dent (rĭ-spŏn'dənt) *adj.* **1.** Giving or given as an answer; responsive. **2.** *Law.* Being a defendant. *—n.* **1.** A person who responds. **2.** *Law.* A defendant, esp. in divorce or equity cases. **—re·spon'dence, re·spon'den·cy** *n.*

re·spond·er (rĭ-spŏn'dər) *n.* One that responds.

re·sponse (rĭ-spŏns') *n.* **1.** The act of responding. **2.** A reply or answer. **3.** A reaction, as that of an organism or mechanism, to a specific stimulus. **4. a.** Something that is spoken or sung by a congregation or choir in answer to the officiating minister or priest. **b.** An anthem that is sung after a reading; responsory. [ME *respons* < OFr. < Lat. *responsum* < *respondēre,* to respond.]

re·spon·si·bil·i·ty (rĭ-spŏn'sə-bĭl'ĭ-tē) *n., pl.* **-ties. 1.** The state, quality, or fact of being responsible. **2.** Something for which one is responsible; duty, obligation, or burden.

re·spon·si·ble (rĭ-spŏn'sə-bəl) *adj.* **1.** Legally or ethically accountable for the care or welfare of another. **2.** Involving personal accountability or ability to act without guidance or superior authority. **3.** Being the source or cause of something. **4.** Capable of making moral or rational decisions on one's own and therefore answerable for one's behavior. **5.** Capable of being trusted or depended upon; reliable. **6.** Based upon or characterized by good judgment or sound thinking. **7.** Having the means to pay debts or fulfill obligations. **8.** Required to render account; answerable: *The cabinet is responsible to the parliament.* [Obs. Fr., corresponding to < Lat. *respondēre,* to respond.] **—re·spon'si·ble·ness** *n.* **—re·spon'si·bly** *adv.*

Synonyms: *responsible, answerable, liable, accountable, amenable.* These adjectives relate to obligations, usually to a superior authority. *Responsible* implies trustworthy performance of fixed duties and consequent awareness of the penality for failure to do them. It may also refer to obligation for things or possessions. *Answerable* suggests a moral or contractual commitment subject to resolution by a higher authority. *Liable* may refer to legal responsibility, as in the payment of damages, or to obligation to perform service, such as military service. *Accountable* emphasizes liability for something of value either contractually or because of one's position of responsibility. *Amenable* refers to the condition of being subject to control or review.

Usage: Some usage experts say that *responsible* should be used only with reference to persons, not things, since only persons can be held accountable. The word is commonly used, however, with reference to things: *Defective construction was responsible for the crash* (acceptable to a majority of the Usage Panel).

re·spon·sive (rĭ-spŏn'sĭv) *adj.* **1.** Answering or replying; responding. **2.** Readily reacting to suggestions, influences, appeals, or efforts. **3.** Containing or using responses: *responsive reading.* **—re·spon'sive·ly** *adv.* **—re·spon'sive·ness** *n.*

re·spon·so·ry (rĭ-spŏn'sə-rē) *n., pl.* **-ries.** A responsive reading or anthem in a church service. [ME < LLat. *responsoria* < Lat. *respondēre,* to respond.]

res pub·li·ca (rās pōō'blē-kä') *n.* **1.** A state, republic, or commonwealth. **2.** The general public good or welfare. [Lat. —see REPUBLIC.]

res·sen·ti·ment (rə-säɴ'tē-mäɴ) *n.* A generalized feeling of resentment and often hostility harbored by one individual or group against another, esp. chronically and with no means of direct expression. [G. < Fr., resentment.]

rest[1] (rĕst) *n.* **1.** The act or state of ceasing from work, activity, or motion; quiet. **2.** Peace, ease, or refreshment resulting from sleep or the cessation of an activity. **3.** Sleep. **4.** Death. **5.** Relief or freedom from disquiet or disturbance. **6.** Mental or emotional tranquillity. **7.** Termination or absence of motion. **8.** *Mus.* **a.** An interval of silence corresponding to one of the possible time values within a measure. **b.** The mark or symbol indicating such a pause and its length. **9.** A short pause in a line of poetry; caesura. **10.** A device used as a support. *—v.* **rest·ed, rest·ing, rests.** *—intr.* **1.** To cease motion, work, or activity. **2.** To lie down, esp. to sleep. **3.** To be at peace or ease; be tranquil. **4.** To be, become, or remain temporarily still, quiet, or inactive. **5.** To be supported or based; lie, lean, or sit. **6.** To be imposed or placed, as a responsibility: *The burden rests with me.* **7.** To depend or rely. **8.** To be located or be in a specified place. **9.** To be fixed or directed on something: *"His brown eyes rested on her for a moment"* (John LeCarré). **10.** To remain; linger. **11.** *Law.* To cease voluntarily the presentation of evidence in a case. *—tr.* **1.** To give rest or repose to. **2.** To place, lay, or lean for ease, support, or repose. **3.** To base or ground. **4.** To fix or direct (the gaze, for example). **5.** To bring to rest; halt. **6.** *Law.* To cease voluntarily the introduction of evidence in (a case). ***—idioms.* at rest. 1.** In a state or condition of repose, esp.: **a.** Asleep. **b.** Dead. **2.** Motionless; inactive. **3.** Free from anxiety or distress. **lay to rest. 1.** To bury (the dead). **2.** To quell or put down (a false assertion, for example): *lay a rumor to rest.* [ME < OE.] **—rest'er** *n.*

Synonyms: *rest, relaxation, repose, leisure, ease, comfort. Rest* refers to inactivity following work or other exertion and suggests mental and physical recuperation. *Relaxation* implies the seeking of release from tension, fatigue, or worry in something pleasurable. *Repose* connotes peace of mind, a complete absence of worry or effort. *Leisure* applies to a person's free time when he can do what pleases him. *Ease* implies effortless enjoyment of freedom from work or worry. *Comfort* suggests well-being and satisfaction with one's condition.

rest[2] (rĕst) *n.* **1.** The part that is left over after something has been removed; remainder. **2.** Those remaining: *The rest are coming later.* *—intr.v.* **rest·ed, rest·ing, rests. 1.** To be or continue to be; remain: *rest easy.* **2.** To remain or be left over. ***—idiom.* for the rest.** With respect to the remaining. [ME < OFr. *reste* < *rester,* to remain < Lat. *restare,* to stay behind : *re-,* back + *stare,* to stay.]

rest[3] (rĕst) *n.* A support for a lance on the side of the breastplate of medieval armor. [ME < *arest* < OFr. < *arester,* to arrest. —see ARREST.]

re·start (rē-stärt') *v.* **-start·ed, -start·ing, -starts.** *—tr.* To start again or anew. *—intr.* To begin operation again. **—re'start'** *n.* **—re·start'a·ble** *adj.*

re·state (rē-stāt') *tr.v.* **-stat·ed, -stat·ing, -states.** To state again or in a new form. **—re·state'ment** *n.*

res·tau·rant (rĕs'tər-ənt, -tə-ränt') *n.* A place where meals are served to the public. [Fr. < pr.part. of *restaurer,* to restore < OFr. *restorer.* —see RESTORE.]

res·tau·ra·teur (rĕs'tər-ə-tûr') also **res·tau·ran·teur** (-tə-rän-tûr') *n.* The manager or owner of a restaurant. [Fr. < *restaurer,* to restore.]

rest energy *n.* The energy equivalent of the rest mass of a body, equal to the rest mass multiplied by the speed of light squared.

rest·ful (rĕst'fəl) *adj.* **1.** Affording, marked by, or suggesting rest; tranquil. **2.** At rest; quiet. **—rest'ful·ly** *adv.* **—rest'ful·ness** *n.*

rest·har·row (rĕst'hăr'ō) *n.* Any of several Old World plants of the genus *Ononis,* having tough, woody stems and roots and pink or purplish flowers. [Obs. *rest,* to check, short for ARREST + HARROW.]

rest home *n.* An establishment where elderly or sick people are housed and cared for.

rest·ing (rĕs'tĭng) *adj.* **1. a.** In a state of inactivity or rest. **b.** Dead. **2.** *Bot.* Dormant. Used esp. of spores that germinate after a prolonged period.

resting cell *n.* A cell that is not actively in the process of dividing.

res·ti·tute (rĕs'tĭ-to͞ot', -tyo͞ot') *v.* **-tut·ed, -tut·ing, -tutes.** —*tr.* **1.** To bring back to a former condition; restore. **2.** To refund. —*intr.* To undergo restitution. [Lat. *restituere, restitut-* : *re-,* back + *statuere,* to set up < *stare,* to stand.]

res·ti·tu·tion (rĕs'tĭ-to͞o'shən, -tyo͞o'-) *n.* **1.** The act of restoring to the rightful owner something that has been taken away, lost, or surrendered. **2.** The act of making good or compensating for loss, damage, or injury; indemnification. **3.** A return to or restoration of a previous state or position.

res·tive (rĕs'tĭv) *adj.* **1.** Impatient or nervous under restriction, delay, or pressure; uneasy. **2.** Difficult to control; refractory. **3.** Refusing to move, as a horse or other animal. [ME *restyf,* stationary < OFr. *restif* < VLat. **restivus* < Lat. *restare,* to keep back : *re-,* back + *stare,* to stand.] —**res'tive·ly** *adv.* —**res'tive·ness** *n.*

Usage: *Restive* and *restless* are now commonly used as equivalent terms. *Restive,* however, implies more than simply "nervous" or "fidgety"; it implies resistance to some sort of restraint. Thus, a child may be *restless* if he is sleeping poorly but *restive* only if he is being kept in bed.

rest·less (rĕst'lĭs) *adj.* **1.** Without quiet, repose, or rest: *a restless night.* **2.** Incapable of resting, relaxing, or being still: *a restless child.* **3.** Never still or motionless: *the restless sea.* —See Usage note at **restive.** —**rest'less·ly** *adv.* —**rest'less·ness** *n.*

rest mass *n.* The physical mass of a body as observed in a reference system with respect to which the body is at rest.

re·stock (rē-stŏk') *tr.v.* **-stocked, -stock·ing, -stocks.** To stock again; furnish new stock for.

res·to·ra·tion (rĕs'tə-rā'shən) *n.* **1. a.** The action of restoring: *damage too great for restoration.* **b.** A particular act of restoring: *Restoration of the sculpture was expensive.* **2.** The state of being restored. **3.** Something, as a renovated building, that has been restored. **4. Restoration. a.** The return of Charles II to the British throne in 1660. **b.** The period between the return of Charles II and the Revolution of 1688.

re·stor·a·tive (rĭ-stôr'ə-tĭv, -stōr'-) *adj.* **1.** Of or pertaining to restoration. **2.** Tending or having the power to restore. —*n.* Something that restores. —**re·stor'a·tive·ly** *adv.* —**re·stor'a·tive·ness** *n.*

re·store (rĭ-stôr', -stōr') *tr.v.* **-stored, -stor·ing, -stores. 1.** To bring back into existence or use; re-establish: *restore law and order.* **2.** To bring back to an original condition: *restore a building.* **3.** To put (someone) back in a prior position: *restore the emperor to the throne.* **4.** To give make restitution of; give back: *restore the stolen funds.* [ME *restoren* < OFr. *restorer* < Lat. *restaurare.*] —**re·stor'er** *n.*

re·strain (rĭ-strān') *tr.v.* **-strained, -strain·ing, -strains. 1.** To control; check. **2.** To deprive of freedom or liberty. **3.** To limit or restrict. [ME *restreyer* < OFr. *restraindre* < Lat. *restringere,* to bind back : *re-,* back + *stringere,* to bind.] —**re·strain'a·ble** *adj.* —**re·strain'ed·ly** (-strā'nĭd-lē) *adv.* —**re·strain'er** *n.*

Synonyms: *restrain, restrict, curb, check, snaffle, bridle, inhibit. Restrain* implies restriction of one's freedom of action by either moral or physical force, frequently for one's own good: *The groom restrained the frightened horse. Restrict* means to set bounds: *He restricted his son's allowance. Curb* and *check* imply a sudden or abrupt stoppage of an advance or forward motion. *Snaffle* applies to a gentler, less forcible stoppage. *Bridle* means holding in or governing one's emotions or passions. *Inhibit* usually connotes a self-imposed check on one's actions or emotions.

re·straint (rĭ-strānt') *n.* **1. a.** The act of restraining. **b.** The condition of being restrained. **2.** Loss or abridgment of freedom. **3.** An influence that inhibits or restrains; limitation. **4.** An instrument or means of restraining. **5.** Control or repression of feelings; constraint. [ME *restreinte* < OFr. *restreinte* < p.part. of *restraindre,* to restrain.]

re·strict (rĭ-strĭkt') *tr.v.* **-strict·ed, -strict·ing, -stricts.** To keep within limits; confine. [Lat. *restringere, restrict-,* to restrain.]

re·strict·ed (rĭ-strĭk'tĭd) *adj.* **1.** Confined; limited. **2.** Excluding or unavailable to members of certain groups: *a restricted neighborhood.* —**re·strict'ed·ly** *adv.*

re·stric·tion (rĭ-strĭk'shən) *n.* **1.** The act of restricting. **2.** The state of being restricted. **3.** Something that restricts; limitation.

re·stric·tive (rĭ-strĭk'tĭv) *adj.* **1.** Tending or serving to restrict. **2.** *Gram.* Denoting a subordinate clause, phrase, or term considered to limit the use of the word or word group that it modifies, thus being essential to the meaning of the sentence. —**re·stric'tive·ly** *adv.* —**re·stric'tive·ness** *n.*

rest room *n.* A public lavatory.

re·struc·ture (rē-strŭk'chər) *v.* **-tured, -tur·ing, -tures.** —*tr.* To alter the make-up of. —*intr.* To alter the structure of something.

re·sult (rĭ-zŭlt') *intr.v.* **-sult·ed, -sult·ing, -sults. 1.** To occur or exist as a consequence of a particular cause. **2.** To end in a particular way. —*n.* The consequence of a particular action, operation, or course; outcome. [ME *resulten* < Med. Lat. *resultare* < Lat., to leap back : *re-,* back + *saltare,* to dance, freq. of *salire,* to leap.] —**re·sult'ful** *adj.* —**re·sult'ful·ness** *n.* —**re·sult'less** *adj.*

re·sul·tant (rĭ-zŭl'tənt) *adj.* Issuing or following as a consequence or result. —*n.* **1.** Something that results; outcome. **2.** *Math.* A vectorial sum. —**re·sul'tant·ly** *adv.*

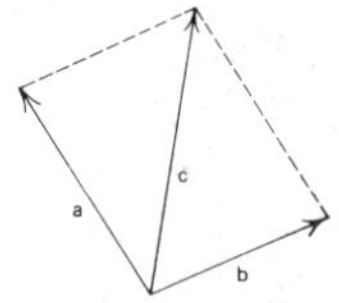

resultant
c is the resultant of vectors *a* and *b*

re·sume (rĭ-zo͞om') *v.* **-sumed, -sum·ing, -sumes.** —*tr.* **1.** To begin or take up again after interruption. **2.** To assume or take again. **3.** To take on or take back again. —*intr.* To begin again or continue after interruption. [ME *resumer* < OFr. *resumer* < Lat. *resumere* : *re-,* again + *sumere,* to take up.] —**re·sum'a·ble** *adj.* —**re·sum'er** *n.*

rés·u·mé (rĕz'o͞o-mā', rĕz'o͞o-mā') *n.* A summary, esp. a brief record of one's personal history and experience submitted with a job application. [Fr. < p.part. of *résumer,* to summarize < OFr. *resumer,* to resume.]

re·sump·tion (rĭ-zŭmp'shən) *n.* The act of resuming. [ME < OFr. < LLat. *resumptio* < Lat. *resumere,* to resume.]

re·su·pi·nate (rĭ-so͞o'pə-nāt', -nĭt) *adj. Biol.* Inverted or seemingly turned upside-down. [Lat. *resupinatus,* bent back, p.part. of *resupinare,* to bend back : *re-,* back + *supinus,* supine.] —**re·su'pi·na'tion** *n.*

re·su·pine (rĕs'ə-pīn') *adj.* Lying on the back; supine. [Lat. *resupinus* < *resupinare,* to bend back. —see RESUPINATE.]

re·sur·face (rē-sûr'fəs) *v.* **-faced, -fac·ing, -fac·es.** —*tr.* To cover with a new surface. —*intr.* To come to the surface again; reappear.

re·surge (rĭ-sûrj') *intr.v.* **-surged, -surg·ing, -surg·es. 1.** To rise again. **2.** To sweep or surge back again. [Lat. *resurgere* : *re-,* again + *surgere,* to rise.]

re·sur·gent (rĭ-sûr'jənt) *adj.* **1.** Rising or tending to rise again. **2.** Sweeping or surging back again. —**re·sur'gence** *n.*

res·ur·rect (rĕz'ə-rĕkt') *v.* **-rect·ed, -rect·ing, -rects.** —*tr.* **1.** To bring back to life; raise from the dead. **2.** To bring back into practice, notice, or use. —*intr.* To rise from the dead; return to life. [Back-formation < RESURRECTION.]

res·ur·rec·tion (rĕz'ə-rĕk'shən) *n.* **1.** The act of rising from the dead or returning to life. **2.** The state of those who have returned to life. **3.** The act of bringing back to practice, notice, or use; revival. **4. Resurrection. a.** The rising again of Christ on the third day after the Crucifixion. **b.** The rising again of the dead at the Last Judgment. [ME < OFr. < LLat. *resurrectio* < Lat. *resurgere,* to rise again. —see RESURGE.] —**res'ur·rec'tion·al** *adj.*

resurrection fern *n.* An American fern, *Polypodium polypoides,* of warm regions, having fronds that curl up and apparently die in prolonged dry weather and expand under moist conditions.

res·ur·rec·tion·ist (rĕz'ə-rĕk'shə-nĭst) *n.* **1.** One who steals bodies from the grave in order to sell them for dissection; body snatcher. **2.** One who resurrects.

resurrection plant *n.* Any of several plants, esp. the rose of Jericho, that appear dead during dry periods and expand and continue to grow under moist conditions.

re·sur·vey (rē'sər-vā', rē-sûr'vā') *tr.v.* **-veyed, -vey·ing, -veys.** To survey or study anew. —*n.* (rē-sûr'vā'). A new survey or study.

re·sus·ci·tate (rĭ-sŭs'ĭ-tāt') *v.* **-tat·ed, -tat·ing, -tates.** —*tr.* To restore consciousness, vigor, or life to. —*intr.* To return to consciousness, vigor, or life; revive. [Lat. *resuscitare, resuscitat-* : *re-,* again + *suscitare,* to stir up (*sub-,* up from below + *citare,* to move violently, freq. of *ciēre,* to put in motion).] —**re·sus'ci·ta·ble** (-tə-bəl) *adj.* —**re·sus'ci·ta'tion** *n.* —**re·sus'ci·ta'tive** *adj.* —**re·sus'ci·ta'tor** *n.*

ret (rĕt) *v.* **ret·ted, ret·ting, rets.** —*tr.* To moisten or soak (flax, for example) to soften and separate the fibers by partial rotting. —*intr.* To become retted. [ME *reten.*]

re·ta·ble (rē'tā'bəl, rĕt'ə-) *n.* A structure forming the back of an altar, esp.: **a.** An overhanging shelf for lights and ornaments. **b.** A frame enclosing painted panels. [Fr. < Sp. *retablo* : Lat. *retro-,* back + *tabulum,* table.]

retable
Detail from "The Retable of Saint Peter" by Martin de Soria, 15th-century Spanish

re·tail (rē'tāl') *n.* The sale of goods or commodities in small quantities to the consumer. —*adj.* Of, pertaining to, or engaged in the sale of goods or commodities at retail. —*v.* **-tailed, -tail·ing, -tails.** —*tr.* **1.** To sell in small quantities directly to consumers. **2.** (*also* rĭ-tāl'). To tell and retell. —*intr.* To sell at retail. —***idiom.* at retail.** At a retail price. [ME < OFr. *retaille,* piece cut off < *retailler,* to cut up : *re-* (intensive) + *tailler,* to cut. —see TAILOR.] —**re'tail'** *adv.* —**re'tail'er** *n.*

re·tail·ing (rē'tā'lĭng) *n.* The functions and activities involved in the selling of commodities to the consumer.

re·tain (rĭ-tān') *tr.v.* **-tained, -tain·ing, -tains. 1.** To keep or hold in one's possession. **2.** To keep or hold in a particular place, condition, or position. **3.** To keep in mind; remember. **4.** To hire (a lawyer, for example) by the payment of a fee. **5.** To keep in one's service or pay. [ME *reteinen* < OFr. *retenir* < Lat. *retinēre* : *re-,* back + *tenēre,* to hold.] —**re·tain'a·ble** *adj.* —**re·tain'ment** *n.*

retained object *n. Gram.* An object in a passive construction that is identical to the object in the corresponding active construction, as *story* in *Susan was told the story by John.*

re·tain·er[1] (rĭ-tā′nər) *n.* **1.** One that retains. **2. a.** One who served in a noble household, as in the feudal period, but who ranked higher than a servant; attendant. **b.** A domestic servant. **c.** An employee. **3.** A device, frame, or groove that restrains or guides something.

re·tain·er[2] (rĭ-tā′nər) *n.* **1.** The act of retaining a professional adviser, as a lawyer. **2.** The fee paid to engage the services of a professional adviser.

re·take (rē-tāk′) *tr.v.* **-took** (-to͝ok′), **-tak·en** (-tā′kən), **-tak·ing, -takes. 1.** To take again. **2.** To photograph again. —*n.* (rē′tāk′). **1.** A taking again. **2.** A rephotographed scene.

re·tal·i·ate (rĭ-tăl′ē-āt′) *v.* **-at·ed, -at·ing, -ates.** —*intr.* To return like for like, esp. to return evil for evil. —*tr.* To pay back (an injury) in kind. [Lat. *retaliare, retaliat-* : *re-*, back + *talio*, punishment in kind.] **—re·tal′i·a′tion** *n.* **—re·tal′i·a′tive** (-ā′tĭv), **re·tal′i·a·to′ry** (-ə-tôr′ē, -tōr′ē) *adj.*

re·tard (rĭ-tärd′) *v.* **-tard·ed, -tard·ing, -tards.** —*tr.* To slow the progress of; impede or delay. —*intr.* To become delayed. —*n.* **1.** Delay. **2.** *Mus.* A slackening of tempo. [ME *retarden* < OFr. *retarder* < Lat. *retardare* : *re-*, back + *tardare*, to delay < *tardus*, slow.] **—re·tar′dant** *adj.* & *n.* **—re·tard′er** *n.*

re·tar·date (rĭ-tär′dāt′, -dĭt) *n.* A mentally retarded person.

re·tar·da·tion (rē′tär-dā′shən) *n.* **1.** The act or process of retarding. **2.** The condition of being retarded. **3.** Something that retards; delay or hindrance. **4.** *Mus.* A diminishing of tempo; retard. **5.** *Psychol.* Mental deficiency.

re·tard·ed (rĭ-tär′dĭd) *adj.* Relatively slow or backward in mental or emotional development or in academic achievement.

retch (rĕch) *v.* **retched, retch·ing, retch·es.** —*intr.* To try to vomit; heave. —*tr.* To vomit. [Alteration of obs. *reach*, ult. < OE *hrǣcan*.] **—retch** *n.*

re·te (rē′tē) *n., pl.* **re·ti·a** (rē′tē-ə, rē′shə). An anatomical mesh or network, as of veins, arteries, or nerves. [NLat. < Lat., net.]

re·tell (rē-tĕl′) *tr.v.* **-told** (-tōld′), **-tell·ing, -tells. 1.** To relate or tell again. **2.** To count again.

re·tell·ing (rē-tĕl′ĭng) *n.* A new account or adaptation of a story: *a retelling of a Roman myth.*

re·tene (rē′tēn′, rĕt′ēn′) *n.* A crystalline compound, $C_{18}H_{18}$, derived from pine tar, fossil resins, and tar oils. [Gk. *rhētinē*, resin.]

re·ten·tion (rĭ-tĕn′shən) *n.* **1.** The act of retaining. **2.** The condition of being retained. **3.** The ability to retain. **4.** The capacity to remember; memory. **5.** Something that is retained. **6.** *Pathol.* Involuntary withholding of normally eliminated wastes or secretions. [ME *retencion* < OFr. < Lat. *retentio* < *retinēre*, to retain : *re-*, back + *tenēre*, to hold.]

re·ten·tive (rĭ-tĕn′tĭv) *adj.* Having the ability or capacity to retain: *a retentive memory.* **—re·ten′tive·ly** *adv.* **—re·ten′tive·ness** *n.*

re·ten·tiv·i·ty (rē′tĕn-tĭv′ĭ-tē) *n.* The quality or state of being retentive.

re·think (rē-thĭngk′) *tr.* & *intr.v.* **-thought** (-thôt′), **-think·ing, -thinks.** To reconsider or involve oneself in reconsideration. **—re′think′** *n.* **—re·think′er** *n.*

re·ti·a (rē′tē-ə, rē′shə) *n.* Plural of **rete.**

re·ti·ar·y (rē′shē-ĕr′ē) *adj.* Of, resembling, or forming a net or web. [< Lat. *rete*, net.]

ret·i·cence (rĕt′ĭ-səns) *n.* **1.** The state or quality of being reticent; reserve. **2.** An instance of being reticent.

ret·i·cent (rĕt′ĭ-sənt) *adj.* **1.** Characteristically hesitant or disinclined to speak out; reserved. **2.** Restrained or reserved in style. [Lat. *reticens, reticent-*, to keep silent : *re-* (intensive) + *tacēre*, to be silent.] **—ret′i·cent·ly** *adv.*

ret·i·cle (rĕt′ĭ-kəl) *n.* A grid or pattern used to establish scale or position in the eyepiece of an optical instrument. [Lat. *reticulum*, dim. of *rete*, net.]

re·tic·u·la (rĭ-tĭk′yə-lə) *n.* Plural of **reticulum.**

re·tic·u·lar (rĭ-tĭk′yə-lər) *adj.* **1.** Netlike. **2.** Marked by complexity; intricate. [NLat. *reticularis* < Lat. *reticulum*, dim. of *rete*, net.]

re·tic·u·late (rĭ-tĭk′yə-lĭt, -lāt′) *adj.* Resembling or forming a network: *reticulate veins of a leaf.* —*v.* (-lāt′) **-lat·ed, -lat·ing, -lates.** —*tr.* **1.** To make a net or network of. **2.** To mark with lines resembling a network. —*intr.* To form a net or network. [Lat. *reticulatus* < *reticulum*, dim of *rete*, net.] **—re·tic′u·late·ly** *adv.* **—re·tic′u·la′tion** *n.*

ret·i·cule (rĕt′ĭ-kyo͞ol′) *n.* **1.** A woman's drawstring handbag or purse. **2.** A reticle. [Fr. *réticule* < Lat. *reticulum*, dim. of *rete*, net.]

re·tic·u·lo·cyte (rĭ-tĭk′yə-lō-sīt′) *n.* An immature erythrocyte that contains a network of basophilic filaments. [RETICUL(UM) + -CYTE.] **—re·tic′u·lo·cyt′ic** (-sĭt′ĭk) *adj.*

re·tic·u·lo·en·do·the·li·al system (rĭ-tĭk′yə-lō-ĕn′də-thē′lē-əl) *n.* The widely diffused bodily system comprising all phagocytic cells except the leukocytes. [< RETICUL(UM) + ENDOTHELIAL.]

re·tic·u·lum (rĭ-tĭk′yə-ləm) *n., pl.* **-la** (-lə). **1.** A netlike formation or structure; network. **2.** *Zool.* The second compartment of the stomach of ruminant mammals, lined with a membrane having honeycombed ridges. **3. Reticulum.** A constellation in the Southern Hemisphere near Dorado and Horologium. [Lat., net, dim. of *rete*, net.]

re·ti·form (rē′tə-fôrm′, rĕt′ə-) *adj.* Arranged like a net; reticulate. [Lat. *rete*, net + -FORM.]

retin- *pref.* Variant of **retino-.**

ret·i·na (rĕt′n-ə) *n., pl.* **ret·i·nas** or **ret·i·nae** (rĕt′n-ē′). A delicate multilayer light-sensitive membrane lining the inner eyeball and connected by the optic nerve to the brain. [ME *rethina* < Med. Lat. *retina*, prob. < Lat. *rete*, net.] **—ret′i·nal** *adj.*

ret·i·nac·u·lum (rĕt′n-ăk′yə-ləm) *n., pl.* **-la.** *Biol.* A band or bandlike structure that holds an organ or part in place. [NLat. < Lat., band, tether < *retinēre*, to restrain. —see RETAIN.] **—ret′i·nac′u·lar** *adj.*

ret·i·nae (rĕt′n-ē′) *n.* A plural of **retina.**

ret·i·nene (rĕt′n-ēn′) *n.* A crystalline retinal pigment, $C_{19}H_{27}CHO$, a component of rhodopsin.

ret·i·ni·tis (rĕt′n-ī′tĭs) *n.* Inflammation of the retina.

retino- or **retin-** *pref.* Retina: *retinoscopy.* [< RETINA.]

ret·i·nol (rĕt′n-ôl′, -ōl′) *n.* Vitamin A.

ret·i·nop·a·thy (rĕt′n-ŏp′ə-thē) *n.* A pathological disorder of the retina. **—ret′i·no·path′ic** (-ō-păth′ĭk) *adj.*

ret·i·no·scope (rĕt′n-ə-skōp′) *n., pl.* **-pies.** An optical instrument for examining refraction of light in the eye.

ret·i·nos·co·py (rĕt′n-ŏs′kə-pē) *n., pl.* **-pies.** Medical examination and analysis of the refractive properties of the eye. **—ret′i·no·scop′ic** (-ə-skŏp′ĭk) *adj.*

ret·i·nue (rĕt′n-o͞o′, rĕt′n-yo͞o′) *n.* The retainers accompanying a high-ranking person. [ME *retenue* < OFr. < fem. p.part. of *retenir*, to retain.]

re·tire (rĭ-tīr′) *v.* **-tired, -tir·ing, -tires.** —*intr.* **1.** To withdraw, as for rest, seclusion, or shelter. **2.** To go to bed. **3.** To withdraw from business or public life and live on one's income, savings, or pension. **4.** To fall back; retreat. —*tr.* **1.** To remove from active service: *retire an old career officer.* **2.** To lead (troops, for example) away from action; withdraw. **3.** To take out of circulation: *retire bonds.* **4.** *Baseball.* To put out (a batter). [OFr. *retirer* : *re-*, back + *tirer*, to draw.]

re·tired (rĭ-tīrd′) *adj.* **1.** Withdrawn; secluded. **2.** Withdrawn from business or public life. **3.** Received by a person in retirement: *retired pay.* **—re·tired·ly** *adv.* **—re·tired′ness** *n.*

re·tir·ee (rĭ-tīr′ē′) *n.* A person who has retired from his occupation.

re·tire·ment (rĭ-tīr′mənt) *n.* **1.** The act of retiring. **2.** The state of being retired from one's occupation **3.** Seclusion or privacy. **4.** A place of seclusion or privacy; retreat.

re·tir·ing (rĭ-tī′rĭng) *adj.* Shy and reserved; modest. **—re·tir′ing·ly** *adv.* **—re·tir′ing·ness** *n.*

re·tool (rē-to͞ol′) *tr.v.* **-tooled, -tool·ing, -tools. 1.** To fit out anew with tools. **2.** To revise and reorganize.

re·tort[1] (rĭ-tôrt′) *v.* **-tort·ed, -tort·ing, -torts.** —*tr.* **1.** To return in kind; pay back. **2. a.** To reply, esp. in a quick, direct manner. **b.** To present a counterargument to. —*intr.* **1.** To make a reply, esp. one that is marked by sharpness or wit. **2.** To present a counterargument. —*n.* **1.** A quick, incisive reply, esp. one that turns the first speaker's words to his own disadvantage. **2.** An act of retorting. [Lat. *retorquere, retort-*, to bend back : *re-*, back + *torquere*, to bend.] **—re·tort′er** *n.*

re·tort[2] (rĭ-tôrt′, rē′tôrt′) *n.* A closed laboratory vessel with an outlet tube, used for distillation, sublimation, or decomposition by heat. [OFr. *retorte* < Med. Lat. *retorta*, fem. of Lat. *retortus*, p.part. of *retorquere*, to bend back. —see RETORT[1].]

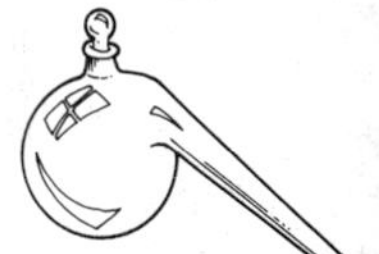
retort[2]

re·touch (rē-tŭch′) *v.* **-touched, -touch·ing, -touch·es.** —*tr.* **1.** To add new details or touches to for correction or improvement. **2.** To improve or change (a photographic negative or print) by adding details or removing flaws. —*intr.* To give retouches. —*n.* (rē′tŭch′, rē-tŭch′). The act or process of retouching. **—re·touch′er** *n.*

re·trace (rē-trās′) *tr.v.* **-traced, -trac·ing, -trac·es. 1.** To trace again. **2.** To go back over, as one's steps. **—re·trace′a·ble** *adj.*

re·tract (rĭ-trăkt′) *v.* **-tract·ed, -tract·ing, -tracts.** —*tr.* **1.** To take back; disavow: *refused to retract his statement.* **2.** To draw back or in: *a plane retracting its landing gear.* **3. a.** To utter (a sound) with the tongue drawn back. **b.** To draw back (the tongue). —*intr.* **1.** To take back or disavow something. **2.** To draw back. [ME *retracten* < OFr. *retracter* < Lat. *retractare*, to handle again, freq. of *retrahere*, to draw back : *re-*, back + *trahere*, to draw.] **—re·tract′a·ble, re·tract′i·ble** *adj.* **—re′trac·ta′tion** (rē′trăk-tā′shən) *n.*

re·trac·tile (rĭ-trăk′tĭl, -tīl′) *adj.* Capable of being drawn back or in: *Cats have retractile claws.* **—re′trac·til′i·ty** (rē′trăk-tĭl′ĭ-tē) *n.*

re·trac·tion (rĭ-trăk′shən) *n.* **1. a.** The act of recanting. **b.** Something retracted. **2.** The power of drawing back or of being drawn back.

re·trac·tive (rĭ-trăk′tĭv) *adj.* Tending to retract.

re·trac·tor (rĭ-trăk′tər) *n.* **1.** One that retracts. **2.** *Anat.* A muscle, such as a flexor, that retracts an organ or part. **3.** *Med.* An instrument that holds back the edges of a wound.

re·train (rē-trān′) *tr.* & *intr.v.* **-trained, -train·ing, -trains.** To train or undergo training again. **—re·train′a·ble** *adj.*

re·tral (rē′trəl, rĕt′rəl) *adj.* **1.** At, close to, or toward the back. **2.** Backward; reverse. [< Lat. *retro,* back.] **—re'tral·ly** *adv.*

re·tread (rē-trĕd') *tr.v.* **-tread·ed, -tread·ing, -treads.** To fit (a worn automobile tire) with a new tread. *—n.* (rē'trĕd'). **1.** A retreaded tire. **2.** *Informal.* A person who is retrained for work.

re-tread (rē-trĕd') *tr.v.* **-trod** (-trŏd'), **-trod·den** (-trŏd'n), **-tread·ing, -treads.** To tread again.

re·treat (rĭ-trēt') *n.* **1.** The act of going backward or of withdrawing. **2.** A quiet, private, or secure place; refuge. **3. a.** A period of seclusion, retirement, or solitude. **b.** A period of group withdrawal for prayer, meditation, and study: *a religious retreat.* **4. a.** The withdrawal of a military force from a dangerous position or from an enemy attack. **b.** The signal for such withdrawal, made on a drum or trumpet. **c.** A trumpet call signaling the lowering of the flag at sunset, as on a military base. *—v.* **-treat·ed, -treat·ing, -treats.** *—intr.* **1.** To fall back or withdraw in the face of danger or an enemy attack. **2.** To slope backward. *—tr.* To move (a chess piece) back. [ME *retret* < OFr. *retrait* < p.part. of *retraire,* to draw back < *retrahere.* —see RETRACT.] **—re·treat'er** *n.*

re·trench (rĭ-trĕnch') *v.* **-trenched, -trench·ing, -trench·es.** *—tr.* **1.** To cut down; reduce. **2.** To remove, delete, or omit. *—intr.* To curtail expenses; economize. [Obs. Fr. *retrencher* < OFr. *retrenchier* : *re-* (intensive) + *trenchier,* to cut. —see TRENCH.] **—re·trench'ment** *n.*

re·tri·al (rē-trī'əl, -trīl', rē'trī'əl, -trīl') *n.* A second trial, as of a legal case.

ret·ri·bu·tion (rĕt'rə-byōō'shən) *n.* **1.** Something given or demanded in repayment, esp. punishment. **2.** *Theol.* Punishment or reward distributed in a future life based on performance in this one. [ME *retribucion* < OFr. *retribution* < LLat. *retributio* < Lat. *retribuere,* to pay back : *re-,* back + *tribuere,* to grant.]

re·trib·u·tive (rĭ-trĭb'yə-tĭv) *adj.* Of, involving, or characterized by retribution. **—re·trib'u·tive·ly** *adv.*

re·trib·u·to·ry (rĭ-trĭb'yə-tôr'ē, -tōr'ē) *adj.* Retributive.

re·triev·al (rĭ-trē'vəl) *n.* **1.** The act or process of retrieving. **2.** The possibility of being retrieved or restored: *lost possessions beyond retrieval.*

re·trieve (rĭ-trēv') *v.* **-trieved, -triev·ing, -trieves.** *—tr.* **1.** To get back; regain. **2.** To revive; restore. **3.** To put right; rectify. **4.** To recall to mind; remember. **5.** To find and carry back; fetch. *—intr.* To find and bring back game. *—n.* The act of retrieving. [ME *retreven* < OFr. *retrover* : *re-,* again + *trover,* to find.] **—re·triev'a·bil'i·ty** *n.* **—re·triev'a·ble** *adj.* **—re·triev'a·bly** *adv.*

retriever
Golden retriever

re·triev·er (rĭ-trē'vər) *n.* **1.** One that retrieves. **2.** Any of several breeds of dog developed and trained to retrieve game.

retro– *pref.* **1.** Backward; back: *retrorocket.* **2.** Situated behind: *retrolental.* [< Lat. *retro,* backward, behind.]

ret·ro·ac·tion (rĕt'rō-ăk'shən) *n.* **1.** A retroactive action. **2.** An opposing or reciprocal action; reaction.

ret·ro·ac·tive (rĕt'rō-ăk'tĭv) *adj.* Influencing or applying to a period prior to enactment: *a retroactive pay increase.* [Fr. *rétroactif* < Lat. *retroagere,* to drive back : *retro,* back + *agere,* to drive.] **—ret'ro·ac'tive·ly** *adv.* **—ret'ro·ac·tiv'i·ty** (-ĭ-tē) *n.*

ret·ro·cede (rĕt'rō-sēd') *v.* **-ced·ed, -ced·ing, -cedes.** *—intr.* To go back; recede. *—tr.* To cede or give back; return. [Lat. *retrocedere* : *retro,* back + *cedere,* to go.] **—ret'ro·ces'sion** (-sĕsh'ən) *n.*

ret·ro·flex (rĕt'rə-flĕks') also **ret·ro·flexed** (-flĕkst') *adj.* **1.** Bent, curved, or turned backward. **2.** Pronounced with the tip of the tongue turned back against the roof of the mouth. [NLat. *retroflexus* < LLat. *retroflectere,* to bend back : *retro,* back + *flectere,* to bend.] **—ret'ro·flex'ion, ret'ro·flec'tion** *n.*

ret·ro·grade (rĕt'rə-grād') *adj.* **1.** Moving or tending backward. **2.** Inverted or reversed. **3.** Reverting to an earlier or inferior condition. **4.** *Astron.* Having a direction of motion opposite to that of the earth on its axis or of the planets around the sun. **5.** *Archaic.* Opposed; contrary. *—intr.v.* **-grad·ed, -grad·ing, -grades. 1.** To move or seem to move backward. **2.** To decline; degenerate. [ME < Lat. *retrogradus* : *retro-,* back + *gradus,* step.] **—ret'ro·gra·da'tion** (-rō-grā-dā'shən) *n.* **—ret'ro·grade'ly** *adv.*

ret·ro·gress (rĕt'rə-grĕs', rĕt'rə-grĕs') *intr.v.* **-gressed, -gress·ing, -gress·es. 1.** To return to an earlier, inferior, or less complex condition. **2.** To go or move backward. [Lat. *retrogradi, retrogress-* : *retro,* back + *gradi,* to go.] **—ret'ro·gres'sive** *adj.* **—re'tro·res'sive·ly** *adv.*

ret·ro·gres·sion (rĕt'rə-grĕsh'ən) *n.* **1.** The act or process of deteriorating or declining. **2.** *Biol.* A return to a less complex or more primitive state or stage.

ret·ro·len·tal (rĕt'rō-lĕn'tl) *adj.* Behind a lens. [RETRO- + NLat. *lens,* lens + -AL.]

ret·ro·oc·u·lar (rĕt'rō-ŏk'yə-lər) *adj.* Situated behind the edge.

ret·ro·pha·ryn·ge·al (rĕt'rō-fə-rĭn'jē-əl, -jəl, -făr'ĭn-jē'əl) *adj.* Behind the pharynx.

ret·ro·rock·et (rĕt'rō-rŏk'ĭt) *n.* A rocket engine used to retard, arrest, or reverse the motion of an aircraft, missile, spacecraft, or other vehicle.

re·trorse (rĭ-trôrs', rē'trôrs') *adj.* Directed or turned backward or downward. [Lat. *retrorsus,* contraction of *retroversus* : *retro,* back + *versus,* p.part. of *vertere,* to turn.] **—re·trorse'ly** *adv.*

ret·ro·spect (rĕt'rə-spĕkt') *n.* A review, survey, or contemplation of things in the past. *—v.* **-spect·ed, -spect·ing, -spects.** *—intr.* **1.** To contemplate the past. **2.** To refer back. *—tr.* To look back on or contemplate (things past). **—*idiom.* in retrospect.** Looking backward or reviewing the past. [< Lat. *retrospectus,* p.part. of *retrospicere,* to look back at : *retro,* back + *specere,* to look at.] **—ret'ro·spec'tion** *n.*

ret·ro·spec·tive (rĕt'rə-spĕk'tĭv) *adj.* **1.** Looking back on, contemplating, or directed to the past. **2.** Looking or directed backward. **3.** Applying to or influencing the past; retroactive. **4.** Of or pertaining to a show exhibiting the work of an artist or school over a period of years. *—n.* A retrospective art exhibition. **—ret'ro·spec'tive·ly** *adv.*

re·trous·sé (rə-trōō-sā', rĕt'rōō-sā') *adj.* Turned up at the end. Used of the nose. [Fr., p.part. of *retrousser,* to turn back < OFr. : *re-,* back + *trousser,* to tie in a bundle.]

ret·ro·ver·sion (rĕt'rō-vûr'zhən, -shən) *n.* **1.** A turning or tilting backward. **2.** The state of being turned or tilted back. [< Lat. *retroversus,* retrorse.]

re·try (rē-trī') *tr.v.* **-tried, -try·ing, -tries.** To try again.

ret·si·na (rĕt'sĭ-nə, rĕt-sē'nə) *n.* A resinated Greek wine. [Mod. Gk., prob. < Ital. *retsina,* resin.]

re·turn (rĭ-tûrn') *v.* **-turned, -turn·ing, -turns.** *—intr.* **1.** To go or come back, as to an earlier condition or place. **2.** To revert in speech, thought, or practice. **3.** To revert to a former owner. **4.** To answer; respond. *—tr.* **1.** To send, put, or carry back: *return bottles to the store.* **2. a.** To give or send back in reciprocation: *She returned his praise.* **b.** To reflect: *return an echo.* **3.** To produce or yield (profit or interest) as a payment for labor, investment, or expenditure. **4.** To reflect or send back (light or sound). **5.** To submit (a report, for example) to a judge or other person in authority. **6.** To render or deliver (a verdict). **7.** To re-elect, as to a legislative body. **8.** In certain card games, to respond to (a partner's lead) by leading the same suit. **9.** To turn away from or place at an angle to the previous line of direction. *—n.* **1.** The act or condition of going, coming, bringing, or sending back. **2. a.** Something that is brought or sent back. **b.** Something that goes or comes back. **3.** A recurrence, as of a periodic occasion or event. **4.** Something exchanged for that received; repayment. **5.** A reply; response. **6. a.** The profit made on an exchange of goods. **b.** Often **returns.** A profit or yield, as from labor or investments. **c.** Output or yield per unit rather than cost per unit, as in the manufacturing of a particular product. **7. a.** A report, list, or set of statistics, esp. one that is formal or official. **b.** Often **returns.** A report on the vote in an election. **c.** *Chiefly Brit.* An election. **8.** A lead in certain card games that responds to the lead of one's partner. **9.** *Sports.* In tennis and certain other sports: **a.** The act of sending the ball back to one's opponent. **b.** The ball so returned. **10.** *Football.* **a.** The act of running back the ball after a kickoff, punt, interception, or fumble. **b.** The yardage gained in a return. **11.** *Archit.* **a.** The extension of a molding, projection, or other part at an angle (usually 90 degrees) to the main part. **b.** A part of a building set at an angle to the façade. **12.** A round-trip ticket. **13.** *Law.* **a.** The bringing or sending back of a writ, subpoena, or other document, generally with a short written report on it, by a sheriff or other officer, to the court from which it was issued. **b.** A certified report by an assessor, election officer, collector, or other official. **14.** A formal statement on the required official form indicating taxable income, allowed deductions, exemptions, and the computed tax that is due. **—*modifier:*** *the return voyage; a return visit; a return boxing match.* **—*idiom.* in return.** in repayment or reciprocation. [ME *retornen* < OFr. *retourner* : *re-,* back (< Lat.) + *tourner,* to turn. —see TURN.] **—re·turn'er** *n.*

Synonyms: *return, revert, recur, recrudesce. Return* denotes going back or coming back to a former place, position, or condition. *Revert* refers to returning to an earlier and less desirable condition. *Recur* applies to repeated occurrences of the same thing. *Recrudesce* is said of that which becomes active after a period of quiescence.

re·turn·a·ble (rĭ-tûr'nə-bəl) *adj.* **1.** Capable of being returned or brought back. **2.** Legally required to be returned.

re·turn·ee (rĭ-tûr'nē') *n.* One that has returned, as from a voyage. —See Usage note at **-ee**[1].

re·tuse (rĭ-tōōs', -tyōōs') *adj.* Having a rounded or blunt apex with a shallow notch. Used chiefly of leaves. [Lat. *retusus,* p.part. of *retundere,* to beat back : *re-,* back + *tundere,* to beat.]

Reu·ben[1] (rōō'bən) *n.* **1.** In the Old Testament, Jacob's eldest son, the ancestor of one of the tribes of Israel. **2.** The tribe of Israel descended from Reuben. [Heb. *Re'ū-bēn.*]

Reu·ben[2] (rōō'bən) *n.* A hot sandwich consisting of corned beef, Swiss cheese, and sauerkraut usually served on rye bread. [< the name *Reuben.*]

re·u·ni·fy (rē-yōō'nə-fī') *tr.v.* **-fied, -fy·ing, -fies.** To restore unity to. **—re·u'ni·fi·ca'tion** (-fĭ-kā'shən) *n.*

re·un·ion (rē-yōōn'yən) *n.* **1.** The act of reuniting. **2.** The state of being reunited. **3.** A gathering of the members of a group who have been separated.

re·u·nite (rē'yōō-nīt') *v.* **-nit·ed, -nit·ing, -nites.** *—tr.* To bring together again. *—intr.* To come together again. [Med. Lat.

reunire, reunit- : Lat. *re-,* again + LLat. *unire,* to unite < Lat. *unus,* one.]

re-up (rē-ŭp′) *intr.v. Informal.* **-upped, -up·ping, -ups.** To enlist again.

re·use (rē-yo͞oz′) *tr.v.* **-used, -us·ing, -us·es.** To use again, esp. after special treatment or processing. **—re·us′a·ble** *adj.* **—re·use′** (-yo͞os′) *n.*

rev (rĕv) *Informal.* —*n.* A revolution, as of a motor. —*v.* **revved, rev·ving, revs.** —*tr.* **1.** To increase the speed of (a motor). **2.** To rouse or excite as preparation for action: *revving himself up for the game.* —*intr.* **1.** To operate at an increased speed. **2.** To be roused or excited about something.

re·val·i·date (rē-văl′ĭ-dāt′) *tr.v.* **-dat·ed, -dat·ing, -dates.** To declare valid again. **—re·val′i·da′tion** *n.*

re·val·u·ate (rē-văl′yo͞o-āt′) *tr.v.* **-at·ed, -at·ing, -ates.** To make a new valuation of. **—re·val′u·a′tion** *n.*

re·vamp (rē-vămp′) *tr.v.* **-vamped, -vamp·ing, -vamps. 1.** To patch up or restore; renovate. **2.** To revise or reconstruct (a manuscript, for example). **3.** To vamp (a shoe) anew.

re·vanch·ism (rĭ-vănch′ĭz′əm) *n.* A foreign policy motivated by a desire to regain territory lost earlier to an enemy. [< Fr. *revanche,* revenge < *revancher,* to revenge < OFr. *revencher.* —see REVENGE.] **—re·vanch′ist** *n.*

re·veal (rĭ-vēl′) *tr.v.* **-vealed, -veal·ing, -veals. 1.** To divulge or disclose; make known. **2.** To bring to view; show. [ME *revelen* < OFr. *reveler* < Lat. *revelare* : *re-* (reversal) + *velare,* to cover < *velum,* veil.] **—re·veal′a·ble** *adj.* **—re·veal′er** *n.* **—re·veal′ment** *n.*

Synonyms: *reveal, expose, disclose, divulge, impart, betray. Reveal* is to make known what has heretofore been kept secret. *Expose* is a stronger term referring to making public something reprehensible, such as a crime or conspiracy. *Disclose* means to make known something that has been under consideration but for valid reasons has been kept from public knowledge. *Divulge* implies making known what has been a secret to a small circle. *Impart* refers to sharing knowledge or information with another. *Betray* implies making known and thereby breaking a trust or pledge.

rev·eil·le (rĕv′ə-lē) *n.* **1.** The sounding of a bugle early in the morning to awaken and summon persons in a camp or garrison. **2.** The first military formation of the day. [Alteration of Fr. *réveillez,* imper. pl. of *réveiller,* to wake < OFr. *reveiller* : *re-,* again (< Lat.) + *eveiller,* to awake < Lat. *evigilare* (*ex-,* out + *vigilare,* to stay awake < *vigil,* awake).]

rev·el (rĕv′əl) *intr.v.* **-eled, -el·ing, -els** also **-elled, -el·ling, -els. 1.** To take great pleasure or delight: *He reveled in his work.* **2.** To engage in uproarious festivities; make merry. —*n.* Often **revels.** A noisy festivity. [ME *revelen* < OFr. *reveler,* to make noise, to rebel < Lat. *rebellare,* to rebel.] **—rev′el·er** *n.*

rev·e·la·tion (rĕv′ə-lā′shən) *n.* **1.** Something revealed. **2.** An act of revealing, esp. a dramatic disclosure of something not previously known or realized. **3.** *Theol.* A manifestation of divine will or truth. **4. Revelation.** See table at **Bible.** [ME < OFr. < LLat. *revelatio* < Lat. *revelare,* to reveal.]

rev·e·la·to·ry (rĕv′ə-lə-tôr′ē, -tōr′ē, rĭ-vĕl′ə-) *adj.* Of, pertaining to, or containing a revelation.

rev·el·ry (rĕv′əl-rē) *n., pl.* **-ries.** Boisterous merrymaking. **—rev′el·rous** (-rəs) *adj.*

rev·e·nant (rĕv′ə-nənt) *n.* **1.** One that returns after an absence. **2.** One who returns after death. [Fr. < pr.part. of *revenir,* to return < Lat. *revenire* : *re-,* back + *venire,* to come.]

re·venge (rĭ-vĕnj′) *tr.v.* **-venged, -veng·ing, -veng·es. 1.** To inflict punishment in return for (injury or insult); avenge. **2.** To seek or take vengeance for (oneself or another person). —*n.* **1.** Vengeance; retaliation. **2.** The act of taking vengeance. **3.** A desire for revenge; vindictiveness. [ME *revenger* < OFr. *revenger,* var. of *revencher* < LLat. *revindicare* : *re-,* in response + *vindicare,* to avenge < *vindex,* avenger.] **—re·veng′er** *n.*

re·venge·ful (rĭ-vĕnj′fəl) *adj.* Full of or tending to revenge. **—re·venge′ful·ly** *adv.* **—re·venge′ful·ness** *n.*

rev·e·nue (rĕv′ə-no͞o, -nyo͞o) *n.* **1.** The income of a government from all sources appropriated for the payment of the public expenses. **2.** Yield from property or investment; income. **3.** A single source of income. **4.** A governmental department set up to collect public funds. [ME < OFr. < fem. p.part. of *revenir,* to return < Lat. *revenire.* —see REVENANT.]

rev·e·nu·er (rĕv′ə-no͞o′ər, -nyo͞o′-) *n.* **1.** A revenue agent. **2.** A lightly armed motorboat used in collecting revenue.

re·ver·ber·ate (rĭ-vûr′bə-rāt′) *v.* **-at·ed, -at·ing, -ates.** —*intr.* **1.** To re-echo; resound. **2.** To be repeatedly reflected. **3.** To rebound or recoil; redound. —*tr.* **1.** To re-echo (a sound). **2.** To reflect (heat or light) repeatedly. [Lat. *reverberare, reverberat-,* to cause to rebound : *re-,* back + *verbarare,* to beat < *verber,* whip.] **—re·ver′ber·a′tion** *n.* **—re·ver′ber·a·to′ry** (-bə-rə-tôr′ē, -tōr′ē), **re·ver′ber·ant, re·ver′ber·a′tive** *adj.* **—re·ver′ber·ant·ly** *adv.*

re·vere[1] (rĭ-vîr′) *tr.v.* **-vered, -ver·ing, -veres.** To regard with awe, great respect, or devotion. [Lat. *revereri* : *re-* (intensive) + *vereri,* to respect.]

Synonyms: *revere, worship, venerate, adore, sanctify, idolize, idolatrize.* These terms imply the deepest respect and esteem for a person, an object, or a deity. *Revere* has a sense of treasuring with profound respect: *to revere the memory of Lincoln. Worship* implies intense, unquestioning esteem, love, and adoration, sometimes manifested in set forms. *Venerate* has the quality of love added to esteem. *Adore* is to love with rapturous and complete devotion. *Sanctify* connotes giving something a sacred character. *Idolize* or *idolatrize* implies worship of an object to which attributes of a deity are ascribed.

re·vere[2] (rĭ-vîr′, -vâr′) *n.* Variant of **revers.**

rev·er·ence (rĕv′ər-əns) *n.* **1.** A feeling of profound awe and respect and often love; veneration. **2.** An act of showing respect, esp. an obeisance. **3.** The state of being revered. **4. Reverence.** A title of respect for a clergyman. —*tr.v.* **-enced, -enc·ing, -enc·es.** To venerate. **—rev′er·enc·er** *n.*

rev·er·end (rĕv′ər-ənd) *adj.* **1.** Deserving of reverence. **2.** Pertaining to or characteristic of the clergy; clerical. **3.** Often **Reverend.** Designating a member of the clergy: *the Reverend John Doe.* —*n. Informal.* A cleric or minister. [ME < OFr. < Lat. *reverendus,* gerund. of *revereri,* to revere.]

rev·er·ent (rĕv′ər-ənt) *adj.* Feeling or showing reverence. [ME < Lat. *reverens,* pr.part. of *revereri,* to revere.] **—rev′er·ent·ly** *adv.*

rev·er·en·tial (rĕv′ə-rĕn′shəl) *adj.* **1.** Expressing reverence; reverent. **2.** Inspiring reverence. **—rev′er·en′tial·ly** *adv.*

rev·er·ie (rĕv′ər-ē) *n.* **1.** Abstracted musing; daydreaming. **2.** A daydream: *"I felt caught up in a reverie of years long past"* (William Styron). [ME < OFr. < *rever,* to dream.]

re·vers also **re·vere** (rĭ-vîr′, -vâr′) *n., pl.* **revers** also **-veres** (-vîrz′, -vârz′). A part of a garment turned back to show the reverse side, as a lapel. [Fr. < OFr., reverse.]

re·ver·sal (rĭ-vûr′səl) *n.* **1.** An act or instance of reversing. **2.** The state of being reversed. **3.** *Law.* The act or an instance of changing or setting aside a lower court's decision by a higher court.

re·verse (rĭ-vûrs′) *adj.* **1.** Turned backward in position, direction, or order. **2.** Moving or acting in a manner contrary to the usual. **3.** Causing backward movement: *a reverse gear.* —*n.* **1.** The opposite or contrary of something. **2.** The back or rear part of something. **3.** A change to an opposite position, condition, or direction. **4.** A change in fortune from better to worse; setback: *suffered financial reverses.* **5. a.** A mechanism for reversing movement, as a gear in an automobile. **b.** The reverse position or operating condition of such a mechanism. —*v.* **-versed, -vers·ing, -vers·es.** —*tr.* **1.** To turn to the opposite direction or tendency. **2.** To turn inside out or upside down. **3.** To exchange the positions of; transpose. **4.** *Law.* To revoke or annul (a decision or decree). —*intr.* **1.** To turn or move in the opposite direction. **2.** To reverse the action of an engine. ***—idioms.* in reverse.** In an opposite direction. **reverse one's field.** To turn and proceed in the opposite direction. [ME *revers* < OFr. < Lat. *reversus,* turned back, p.part. of *revertere,* to revert.] **—re·verse′ly** *adv.* **—re·vers′er** *n.*

Synonyms: *reverse, invert, transpose. Reverse* implies a complete turning about to a contrary position with reference to action, direction, or policy. *Invert* basically means to turn something upside down or inside out but may imply placing something in a contrary order. *Transpose* applies to altering position in a sequence by reversing or changing the order.

reverse discrimination *n.* Discrimination against members of a dominant group, esp. discrimination against whites or males in employment.

re·vers·i·ble (rĭ-vûr′sə-bəl) *adj.* **1.** Capable of being reversed. **2.** *Chem. & Physics.* Capable of successively assuming or producing either of two states: *a reversible cell; a reversible reaction.* —*n.* A reversible item of clothing. **—re·vers′i·bil′i·ty, re·vers′i·ble·ness** *n.* **—re·vers′i·bly** *adv.*

re·ver·sion (rĭ-vûr′zhən) *n.* **1.** A return to a former condition, belief, or interest. **2.** A turning away or in the opposite direction; reversal. **3.** *Genetics.* Atavism. **4.** *Law.* **a.** The return of an estate to the grantor or to his estate after the grant has expired. **b.** The estate thus returned. **c.** The right to succeed to an estate.

re·ver·sion·ar·y (rĭ-vûr′zhə-nĕr′ē) also **re·ver·sion·al** (-zhən-əl) *adj. Law.* Of or connected with the reversion of an estate.

re·ver·sion·er (rĭ-vûr′zhə-nər) *n. Law.* A person entitled to receive an estate in reversion.

re·vert (rĭ-vûrt′) *intr.v.* **-vert·ed, -vert·ing, -verts. 1.** To return to a former condition, practice, subject, or belief. **2.** *Law.* To return to the former owner or his heirs. Used of money or property. **3.** To return to an ancestral type. [ME *reverten* < OFr. *revertir* < Lat. *revertere* : *re-,* back + *vertere,* to turn.] **—re·vert′er** *n.* **—re·vert′i·ble** *adj.* **—re·ver′tive** *adj.*

Usage: *Revert back* is held to be redundant, since *revert* has the sense of going back.

re·vest (rē-vĕst′) *tr.v.* **-vest·ed, -vest·ing, -vests. 1.** To invest (someone) again with power or ownership; reinstate. **2.** To vest (power, for example) once again in a person or agency. [ME *revesten,* to clothe < OFr. *revestir* < LLat. *revestire,* to clothe again : Lat. *re-,* again + *vestire,* to clothe < *vestis,* garment.]

re·vet (rĭ-vĕt′) *v.* **-vet·ted, -vet·ting, -vets.** —*tr.* To retain (a wall of earth) with a layer of stone or other suitable mate-

revetment

rial. —*intr.* To construct a revetment. [Fr. *revêtir* < OFr. *revestir,* to clothe again. —see REVEST.]

re·vet·ment (rĭ-vĕt′mənt) *n.* **1.** A facing, as of masonry, used to support an embankment. **2.** A barricade against explosives.

re·view (rĭ-vyo͞o′) *v.* **-viewed, -view·ing, -views.** —*tr.* **1.** To look over, study, or examine again. **2.** To consider retrospectively; look back on. **3.** To examine with an eye to criticism or correction. **4.** To write or give a critical report on (a new work or performance). **5.** *Law.* To examine (an action or determination), esp. in a higher court, in order to correct possible errors. **6.** To subject to a formal inspection, esp. a military inspection. —*intr.* **1.** To go over or restudy material. **2.** To act as a reviewer, esp. for a newspaper or magazine. —*n.* **1.** A re-examination or reconsideration. **2.** A retrospective view or survey. **3.** A restudying of subject matter. **4.** An inspection or examination for the purpose of evaluating something. **5. a.** A report or essay giving a critical estimate of a work or performance. **b.** A periodical publication devoted primarily to such reports. **6.** A formal military inspection. **7.** *Law.* An examination of an action or determination, esp. by a higher court, in order to correct possible errors. **8.** A revue. [OFr. *revoir* : *re-,* again (< Lat.) + *voir,* to see < Lat. *vidēre.*] **—re·view′a·ble** *adj.*

re·view·er (rĭ-vyo͞o′ər) *n.* One who reviews, esp. a newspaper or magazine critic.

Revolutionary War
Detail from
"The Spirit of '76" by
Archibald M. Willard

re·vile (rĭ-vīl′) *v.* **-viled, -vil·ing, -viles.** —*tr.* To denounce with abusive language. —*intr.* To use abusive language. [ME *revilen* < OFr. *reviler* : *re-* (intensive < Lat.) + *vil,* vile < Lat. *vilis.*] **—re·vile′ment** *n.* **—re·vil′er** *n.* **—re·vil′ing·ly** *adv.*

re·vis·al (rĭ-vī′zəl) *n.* The act of revising; revision.

re·vise (rĭ-vīz′) *tr.v.* **-vised, -vis·ing, -vis·es.** **1.** To prepare a newly edited version of (a text). **2.** To change or modify: *revise an earlier opinion.* —*n.* (rē′vīz′, rĭ-vīz′). *Printing.* A proof made from an earlier proof on which corrections have been made. [Lat. *revisere,* to visit again : *re-,* again < *visere,* freq. of *vidēre,* to see.] **—re·vis′a·ble** *adj.* **—re·vis′er, re·vi′sor** *n.*

Revised Standard Version *n.* A modern American version of the English Bible in the King James tradition.

Revised Version *n.* A British and American revision of the King James Version of the Bible.

re·vi·sion (rĭ-vĭzh′ən) *n.* **1.** The act or procedure of revising. **2.** A revised or new version. **—re·vi′sion·ar′y** *adj.*

re·vi·sion·ism (rĭ-vĭzh′ə-nĭz′əm) *n.* **1.** Advocacy of the revision of an accepted, usually long-standing view, theory, or doctrine, esp. a revision of historical events and movements. **2.** A recurrent tendency within the Communist movement to revise Marxist theory in such a way as to provide justification for a retreat from the revolutionary to the reformist position. **—re·vi′sion·ist** *n.*

revolver

re·vis·it (rē-vĭz′ĭt) *tr.v.* **-it·ed, -it·ing, -its.** To visit again. —*n.* A second or repeated visit. **—re′vis·i·ta′tion** *n.*

re·vi·so·ry (rĭ-vī′zə-rē) *adj.* Of, pertaining to, effecting, or having the power of revision.

re·vi·tal·ize (rē-vīt′l-īz′) *tr.v.* **-ized, -iz·ing, -iz·es.** To impart new life or vigor to: *plans to revitalize inner-city neighborhoods.* **—re·vi′tal·i·za′tion** *n.*

re·viv·al (rĭ-vī′vəl) *n.* **1.** The act of reviving or the condition of being revived. **2.** A restoration to use, acceptance, activity, or vigor after a period of obscurity or quiescence. **3.** A new presentation of an old play, motion picture, opera, ballet, or similar theatrical vehicle. **4.** A reawakening of interest in religion. **5.** A meeting or series of meetings for the purpose of reawakening religious faith, often characterized by impassioned preaching and public professions of faith.

re·viv·al·ism (rĭ-vī′və-lĭz′əm) *n.* **1.** The spirit or activities characteristic of religious revivals. **2.** A desire to revive.

re·viv·al·ist (rĭ-vī′və-lĭst) *n.* **1.** A person who promotes or leads religious revivals. **2.** A person who revives practices or ideas of an earlier time. **—re·viv′al·is′tic** *adj.*

re·vive (rĭ-vīv′) *v.* **-vived, -viv·ing, -vives.** —*tr.* **1.** To bring back to life or consciousness; resuscitate. **2.** To impart new health, vigor, or spirit to. **3.** To restore to use, currency, activity, or notice. **4.** To restore the validity or effectiveness of. **5.** To renew in the mind; recall. **6.** To present (an old play, for example) again. —*intr.* **1.** To return to life or consciousness. **2.** To regain health, vigor, or good spirits. **3.** To return to use, currency, or notice. **4.** To return to validity, effectiveness, or operative condition. [ME *reviven* < OFr. *revivre* < LLat. *revivere,* to live again : Lat. *re-,* again + Lat. *vivere,* to live.] **—re·viv′er** *n.*

re·viv·i·fy (rē-vĭv′ə-fī′) *tr.v.* **-fied, -fy·ing, -fies.** To impart new life, energy, or spirit to. [OFr. *revivifier* < LLat. *revivificare* : Lat. *re-,* again + LLat. *vivificare,* to vivify. —see VIVIFY.] **—re·viv′i·fi·ca′tion** *n.*

rev·o·ca·ble (rĕv′ə-kə-bəl) also **re·vok·a·ble** (rĭ-vō′-) *adj.* Capable of being revoked.

rev·o·ca·tion (rĕv′ə-kā′shən) *n.* The act or an instance of revoking. **—rev′o·ca·to′ry** (rĕv′ə-kə-tôr′ē, -tōr′ē) *adj.*

re·vok·a·ble (rĭ-vō′kə-bəl) *adj.* Variant of **revocable.**

re·voke (rĭ-vōk′) *v.* **-voked, -vok·ing, -vokes.** —*tr.* To void or annul by recalling, withdrawing, or reversing: *revoke a license.* —*intr.* To fail to follow suit in a card game when one is required and able to do so. —*n.* A failure to follow suit in a card game. [ME *revoken* < OFr. *revoquer* < Lat. *revocare,* to call back : *re-,* back + *vocare,* to call.] **—re·vok′er** *n.*

re·volt (rĭ-vōlt′) *v.* **-volt·ed, -volt·ing, -volts.** —*intr.* **1.** To attempt to overthrow the authority of the state; rebel. **2.** To oppose or refuse to accept something: *revolt against high taxes.* —*tr.* To fill with disgust or abhorrence; repel. —*n.* **1.** An uprising, esp. against state authority; rebellion. **2.** An act of protest or rejection. **3.** The state of a person or persons in rebellion: *seems like half the population is in revolt.* [OFr. *revolter* < OItal. *rivoltare,* to overthrow < VLat. **revolvitare* < Lat. *revolvere,* to turn over. —see REVOLVE.] **—re·volt′er** *n.*

re·volt·ing (rĭ-vōl′tĭng) *adj.* Causing disgust; abhorrent. **—re·volt′ing·ly** *adv.*

rev·o·lute (rĕv′ə-lo͞ot′) *adj. Bot.* Rolled back on the undersurface from the tip or margins, as some leaves before they are expanded. [Lat. *revolutus,* p.part. of *revolvere,* to roll back. —see REVOLVE.]

rev·o·lu·tion (rĕv′ə-lo͞o′shən) *n.* **1. a.** Orbital motion about a point, esp. as distinguished from axial rotation: *the planetary revolution about the sun.* **b.** A turning or rotational motion about an axis. **c.** A single complete cycle of such orbital or axial motion. **2.** A sudden or momentous change in any situation: *the revolution in physics.* **3. a.** A sudden political overthrow or seizure of power brought about from within a given system. **b.** Activities directed toward bringing about basic changes in the socioeconomic structure, as of a minority or cultural segment of the population. [ME *revolucioun* < OFr. *revolution* < LLat. *revolutio* < Lat. *revolvere,* to turn over. —see REVOLVE.]

rev·o·lu·tion·ar·y (rĕv′ə-lo͞o′shə-nĕr′ē) *adj.* **1.** Of, pertaining to, or bringing about a political or social revolution. **2.** Characterized by or resulting in radical change: *a revolutionary discovery.* —*n., pl.* **-ies.** A militant in the struggle for revolution.

Revolutionary calendar *n.* The calendar officially adopted in France during the French Revolution.

Revolutionary War *n.* The American Revolution.

rev·o·lu·tion·ist (rĕv′ə-lo͞o′shə-nĭst) *n.* One who favors or is engaged in a revolution.

rev·o·lu·tion·ize (rĕv′ə-lo͞o′shə-nīz′) *tr.v.* **-ized, -iz·ing, -iz·es.** **1.** To bring about a radical change in. **2.** To cause (a country) to undergo a political or social revolution. **3.** To fill with revolutionary principles.

re·volve (rĭ-vŏlv′) *v.* **-volved, -volv·ing, -volves.** —*intr.* **1.** To orbit a central point. **2.** To turn on an axis; rotate. **3.** To recur in cycles or at periodic intervals. **4.** To be held in the mind and considered in turn. —*tr.* **1.** To cause to revolve. **2.** To ponder or reflect on. [ME *revolven* < Lat. *revolvere,* to turn over, to roll back : *re-,* back + *volvere,* to roll.] **—re·volv′a·ble** *adj.*

re·volv·er (rĭ-vŏl′vər) *n.* **1.** A pistol having a revolving cylinder with several cartridge chambers. **2.** One that revolves.

re·vue (rĭ-vyo͞o′) *n.* A musical show consisting of skits, songs, and dances, often satirizing current events, trends, and personalities. [Fr. < OFr., p.part. of *revoir,* to review.]

re·vul·sion (rĭ-vŭl′shən) *n.* **1.** A sudden and strong change or reaction in feeling, esp. a feeling of violent disgust or loathing. **2.** A withdrawing or turning away from something. [Lat. *revulsio* < *revellere,* to tear back : *re-,* back + *vellere,* to tear.] **—re·vul′sive** *adj.*

re·ward (rĭ-wôrd′) *n.* **1.** Something, as money, given or offered esp. for a special service, such as the return of a lost article or the capture of a criminal. **2.** A satisfying return or result. —*tr.v.* **-ward·ed, -ward·ing, -wards.** **1.** To give a reward to or for. **2.** To satisfy or gratify; recompense. [ME *rewarden* < ONFr. *rewarder* : *re-* (intensive < Lat.) + *warder,* to watch over, of Germanic orig.] **—re·ward′er** *n.*

re·wind (rē-wīnd′) *tr.v.* **-wound** (-wound′), **-wind·ing, -winds.** To wind again or anew. —*n.* (rē′wīnd′, rē-wīnd′). The act or process of rewinding something. **—re·wind′er** *n.*

re·wire (rē-wīr′) *tr.v.* **-wired, -wir·ing, -wires.** To provide with new wiring.

re·word (rē-wûrd′) *tr.v.* **-word·ed, -word·ing, -words.** **1.** To state or express again in different words. **2.** To state or express again in the same words; repeat.

re·work (rē-wûrk′) *tr.v.* **-worked, -work·ing, -works.** **1.** To work over again; revise. **2.** To subject to a repeated or new process. —*n.* (rē′wûrk′). Something that has been reworked: *just a rework of an old speech.*

re·write (rē-rīt′) *tr.v.* **-wrote** (-rōt′), **-writ·ten** (-rĭt′n), **-writ·ing, -writes.** **1.** To write again, esp. in a different or improved form. **2.** To write (an account given by a reporter) in a form suitable for publishing. —*n.* (rē′rīt′). Something rewritten. **—re·writ′er** *n.*

Reye's syndrome (rāz) *n.* An acute encephalopathy characterized by fever, vomiting, fatty infiltration of the liver, disorientation, and coma that usually follows a viral infection (as influenza) and occurs mainly in children. [After R.D.K. *Reye* (d. 1977).]

Rey·nard (rā′nərd, -närd′, rĕn′ərd) *n.* A fox. [ME *Reynard* < OFr. *Renart,* the fox in *Roman de Renart,* the Romance of Reynard.]

re·zone (rē-zōn′) *tr.v.* **-zoned, -zon·ing, -zones.** To change the zoning of.

R factor *n.* A genetic factor of bacteria that transmits resistance to antibiotics from one bacterium to another by conjugation. [R(ESISTANCE) FACTOR.]

Rh The symbol for the element rhodium.

rhab·do·man·cy (răb′də-măn′sē) *n.* Divination by means of a wand or a rod, esp. for discovering underground water or ores. [LGk. *rhabdomanteia* : Gk. *rhabdos,* rod + Gk. *-manteia,* -mancy.] —**rhab′do·man′cer** *n.*

rhab·do·my·o·ma (răb′dō-mī-ō′mə) *n., pl.* **-mas** or **-ma·ta** (-mə-tə). *Pathol.* A tumor in striated muscular fibers. [Gk. *rhabdos,* rod + MYOMA.]

rhab·do·vi·rus (răb′də-vī′rəs) *n.* Any of a group of RNA-containing plant and animal viruses that include the rabies virus. [Gk. *rhabdos,* rod + VIRUS.]

Rhad·a·man·thine (răd′ə-măn′thĭn, -thīn′) *adj.* Strictly and uncompromisingly just. [< Gk. *Rhadamanthos,* a judge in the underworld.]

Rhae·to-Ro·man·ic (rē′tō-rō-măn′ĭk) also **Rhae·to-Ro·mance** (-rō-măns′) *n.* A Romance language of southern Switzerland, northern Italy, and the Tyrol. [Lat. *Rhaetus,* of Rhaetia, a Roman province + ROMANIC.] —**Rhae′to-Ro·man′ic, Rhae′to-Ro·mance′** *adj.*

rha·phe (rā′fē) *n.* Variant of **raphe.**

rhap·sod·ic (răp-sŏd′ĭk) also **rhap·sod·i·cal** (-ĭ-kəl) *adj.* **1.** Of, resembling, or characteristic of a rhapsody. **2.** Immoderately impassioned or enthusiastic; ecstatic. —**rhap·sod′i·cal·ly** *adv.*

rhap·so·dist (răp′sə-dĭst) *n.* **1.** In ancient Greece, an epic singer. **2.** A person who uses extravagantly enthusiastic or impassioned language.

rhap·so·dize (răp′sə-dīz′) *v.* **-dized, -diz·ing, -diz·es.** —*intr.* To express oneself in an immoderately enthusiastic manner. —*tr.* To recite (something) in the manner of a rhapsody.

rhap·so·dy (răp′sə-dē) *n., pl.* **-dies. 1.** Exalted or excessively enthusiastic expression of feeling in speech or writing. **2.** A literary work written in an impassioned or exalted style. **3.** *Mus.* A composition of irregular form and an often improvisatory character. **4.** In ancient Greece, an epic poem or a portion of one suitable for uninterrupted recitation. [Lat. *rhapsodia,* epic poem < Gk. *rhapsōidia* < *rhapsōidos,* singer of epic poems : *rhaptein,* to sew together + *ōidē,* song.]

rhat·a·ny (răt′n-ē) *n., pl.* **-nies. 1.** Either of two South American shrubs, *Krameria triandra* or *K. argentea,* having thick, fleshy roots. **2.** The dried root of the rhatany, formerly used as an astringent. [Am. Sp. *ratania* < Quechua *ratanya.*]

rhe·a (rē′ə) *n.* Any of several flightless South American birds of the genus *Rhea,* resembling the ostrich but somewhat smaller and having three toes instead of two. [NLat. *Rhea,* genus name < Lat., the mother of Romulus and Remus.]

Rhe·a (rē′ə) *n. Gk. Myth.* The wife of Cronus. [Gk. *Rhēa.*]

Rhen·ish (rĕn′ĭsh) *adj.* Of or pertaining to the river Rhine or the lands bordering on it. —*n.* Rhine wine (sense 1). [< Lat. *Rhenus,* the Rhine.]

rhe·ni·um (rē′nē-əm) *n. Symbol* **Re** A rare dense silvery-white metallic element with a very high melting point. It is used for electrical contacts and with tungsten for high-temperature thermocouples. Atomic number 75; atomic weight 186.2; melting point 3,180°C; boiling point 5,627°C; specific gravity 21.02; valences 1, 2, 3, 4, 5, 6, 7. [< Lat. *Rhenus,* the Rhine.]

rheo– *pref.* Current; flow: *rheotaxis.* [< Gk. *rheos,* stream < *rhein,* to flow.]

rhe·ol·o·gy (rē-ŏl′ə-jē) *n.* The study of the deformation and flow of matter. —**rhe′o·log′i·cal** (rē′ə-lŏj′ĭ-kəl) *adj.* —**rhe·ol′o·gist** *n.*

rhe·om·e·ter (rē-ŏm′ĭ-tər) *n.* An instrument for measuring the flow of viscous liquids, as of blood.

rhe·o·stat (rē′ə-stăt′) *n.* A continuously variable electrical resistor used to regulate current. —**rhe′o·stat′ic** *adj.*

rhe·o·tax·is (rē′ə-tăk′sĭs) *n.* The movement of an organism in response to the flow of a current. —**rhe′o·tac′tic** (-tăk′tĭk) *adj.*

rhe·sus monkey (rē′səs) *n.* A brownish monkey, *Macaca mulatta,* of India, used extensively in biological experimentation. [< NLat. *Rhesus* < Gk. *Rhēsos,* a mythical king of Thrace.]

rhe·tor (rē′tôr′, -tər) *n. Obs.* **1.** A teacher of rhetoric. **2.** An orator. [ME *rether* < Med. Lat. < Lat. *rhetor* < Gk. *rhētōr.*]

rhet·o·ric (rĕt′ər-ĭk) *n.* **1.** The study of the elements, as structure or style, used in writing and speaking. **2.** The art of effective expression and the persuasive use of language. **3.** Affected or pretentious language: *political rhetoric.* **4.** Verbal communication; discourse. [ME *rethorik* < OFr. *rethorique* < Lat. *rhetorica* < Gk. *rhētorikē* (*tekhnē*), rhetorical (art) < *rhētorikos,* rhetorical < *rhētōr,* rhetor.]

rhe·tor·i·cal (rĭ-tôr′ĭ-kəl, -tŏr′-) *adj.* **1.** Concerned primarily with style or effect; showy or overelaborate. **2.** Resembling rhetoric; oratorical. —**rhe·tor′i·cal·ly** *adv.*

rhetorical question *n.* A question to which no answer is expected.

rhet·o·ri·cian (rĕt′ə-rĭsh′ən) *n.* **1.** An expert in or teacher of rhetoric. **2.** An eloquent speaker or writer. **3.** A person given to verbal extravagance.

rheum (ro͞om) *n.* A watery or thin mucous discharge from the eyes or nose. [ME *reume* < OFr. < Lat. *rheuma* < Gk. < *rhein,* to flow.] —**rheum′y** *adj.*

rheu·mat·ic (ro͞o-măt′ĭk) *adj.* Of, pertaining to, or afflicted with rheumatism. —*n.* **1.** A person afflicted with rheumatism. **2. rheumatics.** *Informal.* Pains due to rheumatism. [ME *rhewmatyk,* of rheum < Lat. *rheumaticus,* a person suffering from rheum < Gk. *rheumatikos,* subject to rheum < *rheuma,* stream < *rhein,* to flow.]

rheumatic fever *n.* A severe infectious disease occurring chiefly in children, characterized by fever and painful inflammation of the joints and frequently resulting in permanent damage to the valves of the heart.

rheu·ma·tism (ro͞o′mə-tĭz′əm) *n.* **1.** Any of several pathological conditions of the muscles, tendons, joints, bones, or nerves, characterized by discomfort and disability. **2.** Rheumatoid arthritis. [Lat. *rheumatismus,* rheum < Gk. *rheumatismos* < *rheumatizesthai,* to suffer from rheum < *rheuma,* rheum < *rhein,* to flow.]

rheu·ma·toid (ro͞o′mə-toid′) also **rheu·ma·toi·dal** (ro͞o′mə-toid′l) *adj.* **1.** Of or resembling rheumatism. **2.** Afflicted with rheumatism. —**rheu′ma·toi′dal·ly** *adv.*

rheumatoid arthritis *n.* A chronic disease marked by stiffness and inflammation of the joints, weakness, loss of mobility, and deformity.

rheumatoid factor *n.* An immunoglobulin present in the blood serum of many individuals afflicted with rheumatoid arthritis, used as a means of diagnosing the disease.

Rh factor (är′āch′) *n.* Any of several substances on the surface of red blood cells that induce antigenic reactions with Rh negative blood cells. [< RH(ESUS MONKEY), from its being first detected in the blood of this animal.]

rhin– *pref.* Variant of **rhino–.**

rhi·nal (rī′nəl) *adj.* Of or pertaining to the nose; nasal.

rhi·nen·ceph·a·lon (rī′nĕn-sĕf′ə-lŏn′, -lən) *n., pl.* **-la** (-lə). The olfactory region of the brain, located in the cerebrum. —**rhi′nen·ce·phal′ic** (-sə-făl′ĭk) *adj.*

rhine·stone (rīn′stōn′) *n.* A colorless, artificial gem of paste or glass, often with facets that sparkle in imitation of diamond. [After the *Rhine,* a river in Europe.]

Rhine wine (rīn) *n.* **1.** Any of several dry, white wines produced in the Rhine valley. **2.** A light, dry wine similar to Rhine wine.

rhi·ni·tis (rī-nī′tĭs) *n.* Inflammation of the nasal mucous membranes.

rhi·no[1] (rī′nō) *n., pl.* **-nos.** *Informal.* A rhinoceros.

rhi·no[2] (rī′nō) *n. Chiefly Brit. Slang.* Money; cash. [Orig. unknown.]

rhino– or **rhin–** *pref.* Nose; nasal: *rhinitis.* [< Gk. *rhis, rhin-,* nose.]

rhi·noc·er·os (rī-nŏs′ər-əs) *n., pl.* **rhinoceros** or **-os·es.** Any of several large, thick-skinned, herbivorous mammals of the family Rhinocerotidae, of Africa and Asia, having one or two upright horns on the snout. [ME *rinoceros* < Lat. *rhinoceros* < Gk. *rhinokerōs* : *rhis,* nose + *keras,* horn.]

rhi·nol·o·gy (rī-nŏl′ə-jē) *n.* The anatomy, physiology, and pathology of the nose. —**rhi·nol′o·gist** *n.*

rhi·no·phar·yn·gi·tis (rī′nō-făr′ĭn-jī′tĭs) *n.* Inflammation of the nasal and pharyngeal mucous membrane.

rhi·no·plas·ty (rī′nō-plăs′tē, -nə-) *n.* Plastic surgery of the nose. —**rhi′no·plas′tic** *adj.*

rhi·nos·co·py (rī-nŏs′kə-pē) *n.* Examination of the nasal passages.

rhi·no·vi·rus (rī′nō-vī′rəs) *n.* Any of a group of picornaviruses that are causative agents of disorders of the respiratory tract, such as the common cold.

rhiz– *pref.* Variant of **rhizo–.**

rhi·zan·thous (rī-zăn′thəs) *adj.* Bearing flowers directly from the root.

rhizo– or **rhiz–** *pref.* Root: *rhizogenic.* [< Gk. *rhiza,* root.]

rhi·zo·bi·um (rī-zō′bē-əm) *n., pl.* **-bi·a** (-bē-ə). Any of various nitrogen-fixing bacteria of the genus *Rhizobium* that form nodules on the roots of leguminous plants such as clover and beans. [NLat. *Rhizobium,* genus name : RHIZO- + Gk. *bios,* life.]

rhi·zo·ceph·a·lan (rī′zō-sĕf′ə-lən) *n.* Any of various small aquatic crustaceans of the order Rhizocephala that are parasitic on other crustaceans. [< NLat. *Rhizocephala,* order name : RHIZO- + Gk. *kephalē,* head.] —**rhi′zo·ceph′a·lous** *adj.*

rhi·zo·gen·ic (rī′zō-jĕn′ĭk) also **rhi·zo·ge·net·ic** (-jə-nĕt′ĭk) *adj. Bot.* Giving rise to roots: *rhizogenic tissue.*

rhi·zoid (rī′zoid′) *n.* **1.** A slender, rootlike filament by which mosses, liverworts, and ferns attach to the substratum and absorb nourishment. **2.** A rootlike extension of the thallus of a fungus. —**rhi′zoid′, rhi·zoi′dal** (-zoid′l) *adj.*

rhi·zome (rī′zōm′) *n.* A rootlike, usually horizontal stem growing under or along the ground that sends out roots from its lower surface and leaves or shoots from its upper surface. [NLat. *rhizoma* < Gk. *rhizōma,* mass of roots < *rhizoun,* to cause to take root < *rhiza,* root.] —**rhi·zom′a·tous** (-zŏm′ə-təs, -zō′mə-təs) *adj.*

rhi·zo·morph (rī′zō-môrf′) *n.* A rootlike part, such as a threadlike structure in fungi, consisting of strands of hyphae.

rhi·zo·mor·phous (rī′zō-môr′fəs) *adj. Bot.* Having the form of a root.

rhi·zoph·a·gous (rī-zŏf′ə-gəs) *adj.* Feeding on roots.

rhi·zo·pod (rī′zō-pŏd′) *n.* A protozoan of the class or subclass Rhizopoda, such as an amoeba or radiolarian, charac-

George Miksch Sutton

rhea

rhesus monkey

rhinoceros

teristically moving and taking in food by means of pseudopodia. [< NLat. *Rhizopoda,* class name : RHIZO- + Gk. *pous,* foot.] **—rhi·zop′o·dan** (-zŏp′ə-dən) *adj. & n.* **—rhi·zop′o·dous** *adj.*

rhi·zo·pus (rī′zō-pəs) *n.* Any of various often destructive fungi of the genus *Rhizopus,* such as *R. nigricans,* the common bread mold. [NLat. *Rhizopus,* genus name : RHIZO- + Gk. *pous,* foot.]

rhi·zo·sphere (rī′zə-sfîr′) *n.* The soil zone of increased microbial growth and activity that surrounds the roots of a plant.

rhi·zot·o·my (rī-zŏt′ə-mē) *n., pl.* **-mies.** Surgical severance of spinal nerve roots to relieve pain or hypertension.

Rh-neg·a·tive (är′ăch-nĕg′ə-tĭv) *adj.* Lacking an Rh factor.

rho (rō) *n.* The 17th letter of the Greek alphabet. See table at **alphabet.** [Gk. *rhō,* of Phoenician orig.; akin to Heb. *rēsh.*]

rhod– *pref.* Variant of **rhodo-.**

rho·da·mine (rō′də-mēn′) *n.* Any of several synthetic red to pink dyes.

Rhode Island Red (rōd) *n.* Any of an American breed of domestic fowls having dark reddish-brown feathers.

Rho·de·sian man (rō-dē′zhən) *n.* A fossil man, *Homo rhodesiensis* or *Cyphanthropus rhodesiensis,* found in south-central Africa, having a large, low skull with massive brow ridges and skeletal bones similar to modern man.

Rhodesian ridgeback

Rhodesian ridge·back (rĭj′băk′) *n.* A large dog of a breed developed in Africa, having short, yellowish-tan hair that forms a ridge along the back.

Rhodes scholar (rōdz) *n.* A British Commonwealth or U.S. student who holds a scholarship established by the will of Cecil J. Rhodes that permits attendance at Oxford University for a period of two or three years. **—Rhodes scholarship** *n.*

rho·di·um (rō′dē-əm) *n. Symbol* **Rh** A hard, durable, silvery-white metallic element that is used to form high-temperature alloys with platinum and is plated on other metals to produce a durable corrosion-resistant coating. Atomic number 45; atomic weight 102.905; melting point 1,966°C; boiling point 3,727°C; specific gravity 12.41; valences 2, 3, 4, 5. [Gk. *rhodon,* rose + -IUM.]

rhodo– or **rhod–** *pref.* Rose; rosy; red: *rhodolite.* [< Gk. *rhodon,* rose.]

rho·do·chro·site (rō′də-krō′sīt′) *n.* A naturally occurring impure manganese carbonate, $MnCO_3$, light-pink to rose-red in color with a pearly or vitreous luster, used as a manganese ore. [G. *Rhodochrosit* : Gk. *rhodon,* rose + Gk. *khrōs,* color + G. *-it,* -ite.]

rhododendron

rho·do·den·dron (rō′də-dĕn′drən) *n.* Any of various evergreen shrubs of the genus *Rhododendron,* of the North Temperate Zone, having clusters of variously colored flowers. [NLat. *Rhododendron,* genus name < Lat., oleander < Gk. : *rhodon,* rose + *dendron,* tree.]

rho·do·lite (rō′də-līt′) *n.* A rose-red or pink variety of garnet, a silicate mineral used as a gem.

rho·do·mon·tade (rŏd′ə-mŏn-tād′, -täd′) *n.* Variant of **rodomontade.**

rho·do·nite (rō′də-nīt′) *n.* A pink to rose-red mineral, essentially a glassy crystalline manganese silicate, $MnSiO_3$, used as an ornamental stone. [G. *Rhodonit* < Gk. *rhodon,* rose.]

rho·do·plast (rō′də-plăst′) *n.* A reddish chromatophore found in red algae.

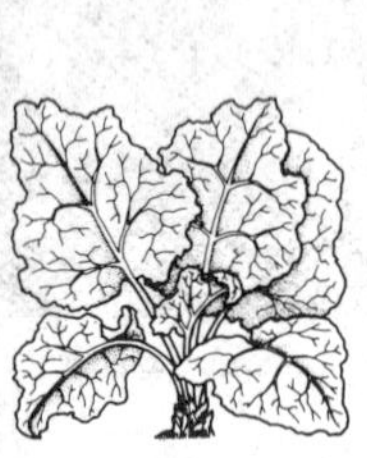

rhubarb

rho·dop·sin (rō-dŏp′sĭn) *n.* The pigment sensitive to red light in the retinal rods of the eyes, consisting of opsin and retinene.

rho·do·ra (rō-dôr′ə, -dōr′ə) *n.* A shrub, *Rhododendron canadense,* of eastern North America, having rose-purple flowers that bloom before the leaves appear. [NLat. *Rhodora,* genus name < Lat., a kind of plant.]

rhomb– *pref.* Variant of **rhombo-.**

rhom·ben·ceph·a·lon (rŏm′bĕn-sĕf′ə-lŏn′, -lən) *n.* The portion of the embryonic brain from which the metencephalon, myelencephalon, and subsequently the cerebellum, pons, and medulla oblongata develop.

rhom·bi (rŏm′bī′) *n.* A plural of **rhombus.**

rhom·bic (rŏm′bĭk) *adj.* **1.** Having the shape of a rhombus. **2.** Orthorhombic.

rhombo– or **rhomb–** *pref.* Rhombus: *rhombohedron.* [< RHOMBUS.]

rhom·bo·he·dron (rŏm′bō-hē′drən) *n., pl.* **-drons** or **-dra** (-drə). A prism with six faces, each a rhombus. **—rhom′bo·he′dral** *adj.*

rhom·boid (rŏm′boid′) *n.* A parallelogram with unequal adjacent sides. *—adj.* Shaped like a rhomboid. [LLat. *rhomboides* < Gk. *rhomboeidēs,* resembling a rhombus : *rhombos,* rhombus + *-eidēs,* -oid.] **—rhom·boi′dal** (-boid′l) *adj.*

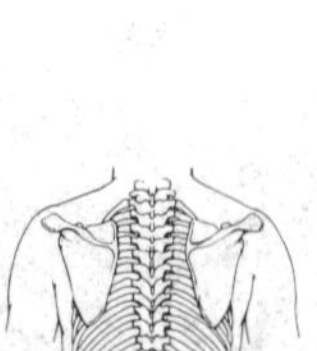

rib

rhom·bus (rŏm′bəs) *n., pl.* **-bus·es** or **-bi** (-bī′). An equilateral parallelogram. [Lat. < Gk. *rhombos.*]

rhon·chus (rŏng′kəs) *n., pl.* **-chi** (-kī′). A coarse rattling sound somewhat like snoring, usually caused by secretion in the bronchial tube. [LLat., a snoring < Gk. *rhonkos* < *rhenkein,* to snore.] **—rhon′chal, rhon′chi·al** (-kē-əl) *adj.*

Rh-pos·i·tive (är′ăch-pŏz′ĭ-tĭv) *adj.* Containing an Rh factor.

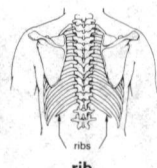

rhu·barb (rōō′bärb′) *n.* **1.** Any of several plants of the genus *Rheum,* characterized by large, long-stalked leaves, esp. *R. rhaponticum,* the common garden rhubarb, having long green or reddish acid leafstalks that are edible when sweetened and cooked. **2.** The dried, bitter-tasting rhizome and roots of *R. palmatum* or *R. officinale,* of central Asia, used as a laxative. **3.** *Slang.* A heated discussion, quarrel, or fight. [ME *rubarbe* < OFr. < Med. Lat. *rubarbum,* prob. < LLat. *rha barbarum,* barbarian rhubarb.]

rhumb (rŭm, rŭmb) *n.* **1.** A rhumb line. **2.** One of the points of the mariner's compass. [Sp. *rumbo.*]

rhum·ba (rŭm′bə, rōōm′-) *n.* Variant of **rumba.**

rhumb line *n.* The path of a ship that maintains a fixed compass direction, shown on a map as a line crossing all meridians at the same angle.

rhyme also **rime** (rīm) *—n.* **1.** Correspondence of terminal sounds of words or of lines of verse. **2. a.** A poem or verse having a regular correspondence of sounds, esp. at the ends of lines. **b.** Poetry or verse of this kind. **3.** A word that corresponds with another in terminal sound, such as *baboon* and *harpoon.* *—v.* **rhymed, rhym·ing, rhymes** also **rimed, rim·ing, rimes.** *—intr.* **1.** To form a rhyme. **2.** To compose rhymes or verse. **3.** To make use of rhymes in composing verse. *—tr.* **1.** To put into rhyme or compose with rhymes. **2.** To use (a word or words) as a rhyme. [ME *rime* < OFr. < Med. Lat. *rithmus,* rhythm < Lat. *rhythmos* < Gk. *rhuthmos.*]

rhym·er also **rim·er** (rī′mər) *n.* A person who composes rhyming verses, esp. a rhymester.

rhyme scheme *n.* The arrangement of rhymes in a poem or stanza.

rhyme·ster also **rime·ster** (rīm′stər) *n.* **1.** A person who composes light verse. **2.** An inferior poet.

rhyn·cho·ce·pha·lian (rĭng′kō-sə-făl′yən) *adj.* Of or belonging to the Rhynchocephalia, an order of mostly extinct lizardlike reptiles. *—n.* A rhynchocephalian reptile. [< NLat. *Rhynchocephalia,* order name : Gk. *rhunkhos,* beak + *kephalē,* head.]

rhy·o·lite (rī′ə-līt′) *n.* A glassy volcanic rock, similar to granite in composition and usually exhibiting flow lines. [G. *Rhyolit* < Gk. *rhuax,* stream < *rhein,* to flow.]

rhythm (rĭth′əm) *n.* **1.** Movement or variation characterized by the regular recurrence or alternation of different quantities or conditions: *the rhythm of the tides.* **2.** The patterned, recurring alternations of contrasting elements of sound or speech. **3.** *Mus.* **a.** A regular pattern formed by a series of notes of differing duration and stress. **b.** A specific kind of such a pattern: *a waltz rhythm.* **c.** A group of instruments in a band supplying the rhythm. **4. a.** The metrical flow of sound with a regulated pattern of long and short or accented and unaccented syllables in poetry. **b.** A specific kind of such a metrical flow: *iambic rhythm.* **5.** In painting, sculpture, and other visual arts, a regular or harmonious pattern created by lines, forms, and colors. [OFr. *rhythme* < Lat. *rhythmus* < Gk. *rhuthmos.*]

Synonyms: *rhythm, meter, cadence, beat. Rhythm* denotes the regular patterned flow, the ebb and rise, of sounds and movement in speech, music, writing, dance, and other physical activities, and in natural phenomena: *the rhythm of the heart. Meter* basically means measure, and applies to a system or pattern of measured recurrence of length, beat, or numbers in poetry and music. *Cadence* refers specifically to the pleasing rise and fall of the voice in speech or singing and to the harmonic sequence of chords in music indicating conclusion. *Beat* is the heavy stress in rhythm; it may also be used loosely for rhythm.

rhythm and blues *n.* A kind of music developed by black Americans that combines blues and jazz, characterized by a strong simple rhythm.

rhyth·mi·cal (rĭth′mĭ-kəl) also **rhyth·mic** (-mĭk) *adj.* Of, pertaining to, or having rhythm; recurring with measured regularity. **—rhyth′mi·cal·ly** *adv.*

rhyth·mics (rĭth′mĭks) *n. (used with a sing. verb).* The study of rhythm.

rhyth·mist (rĭth′mĭst) *n.* **1.** One who is expert in or has a keen sense of rhythm. **2.** One who studies or produces rhythm.

rhythm method *n.* A birth-control method dependent on continence during the period of female ovulation.

ri·al[1] (rē-ôl′, -äl′) *n.* See table at **currency.** [Pers. < Ar. *riyāl.*]

ri·al[2] (rē-ôl′, -äl′) *n.* Variant of **riyal.**

ri·al·to (rē-ăl′tō, rā-äl′). **1.** A theatrical district. **2.** A marketplace. [After *Rialto,* an island in Venice on which a market was situated.]

ri·a·ta also **re·a·ta** (rē-ä′tə) *n.* A lariat; lasso. [Sp., rope.]

rib (rĭb) *n.* **1.** *Anat.* **a.** One of a series of long, curved bones, occurring in 12 pairs in human beings and extending from the spine to or toward the sternum. **b.** A similar bone in most vertebrates. **2.** A part or piece similar to a rib and serving to shape or support: *the rib of an umbrella.* **3.** A cut of meat enclosing one or more ribs. **4.** One of many curved members attached to a boat or ship's keel and extending upward and outward to form the framework of the hull. **5.** One of many formed transverse pieces along the length of an airplane wing used to establish shape. **6.** *Archit.* **a.** An arch or a projecting arched member of a vault. **b.** One of the curved pieces of an arch. **7.** A raised ridge or wale in knitted material or in cloth. **8.** *Bot.* One of the main veins of a leaf or other plant organ. **9.** *Slang.* A joke. *—tr.v.* **ribbed, rib·bing, ribs. 1.** To shape, support, or provide with a rib or ribs. **2.** To make with ridges or raised markings. **3.** *Slang.* To tease or make fun of. [ME < OE.]

rib·ald (rĭb′əld) *adj.* Pertaining to or indulging in vulgar, lewd humor. *—n.* A ribald person. [ME *ribaud,* ribald person < OFr. *ribauld* < *riber,* to be wanton, of Germanic orig.]

rib·ald·ry (rĭb′əl-drē) *n., pl.* **-ries.** Ribald language or joking.

rib·and (rĭb′ənd) *n.* A ribbon, esp. one used as a decoration. [ME *riban* < OFr. —see RIBBON.]

rib·band (rĭb′ănd, -ənd, -ən) *n.* A length of flexible wood or metal used to hold the ribs of a ship in place while the exterior planking or plating is being applied.

rib·bing (rĭb′ĭng) *n.* **1.** Ribs collectively. **2.** An arrangement of ribs, as in a boat. **3.** *Slang.* An instance of joking or teasing.

rib·bon (rĭb′ən) *n.* **1.** A narrow strip or band of fine fabric, as satin or velvet, finished at the edges and used for trimming or tying. **2.** Something that resembles a ribbon, as a measuring tape. **3. ribbons.** Tattered or ragged strips: *a dress torn to ribbons.* **4.** An inked strip of cloth used for making the impression, as in a typewriter. **5. a.** A band of colored cloth signifying membership in an order or the award of a prize. **b.** A strip of colored cloth worn on the left breast of a uniform to indicate the award of a medal or decoration. **6. ribbons.** *Informal.* Reins for driving horses. *—tr.v.* **-boned, -bon·ing, -bons. 1.** To decorate or tie with ribbons. **2.** To tear into ribbons or shreds. [ME *riban* < OFr., of Germanic orig.]

rib·bon·fish (rĭb′ən-fĭsh′) *n., pl.* **ribbonfish** or **-fish·es.** Any of several marine fishes, chiefly of the genus *Trachipterus,* having long, narrow, compressed bodies.

ribbon snake *n.* A nonvenomous North American snake, *Thamnophis sauritus,* having yellow or reddish stripes along the body.

ribbon worm *n.* A nemertean.

rib cage *n.* The enclosing structure formed by the ribs and the bones to which they are attached.

rib eye *n.* A cut of meat taken from the outside of the rib.

rib·grass (rĭb′grăs′) *n.* A weedy plant, *Plantago lanceolata,* having lancelike, ribbed leaves and a dense spike of small whitish flowers.

ri·bo·fla·vin (rī′bō-flā′vĭn) *n.* A crystalline orange-yellow pigment, $C_{17}H_{20}O_6N_4$, the principal growth-promoting factor in the vitamin B complex, found in milk, leafy vegetables, fresh meat, and egg yolks, and produced synthetically. [RIBO(SE) + FLAVIN.]

ri·bo·nu·cle·ase (rī′bō-no͞o′klē-ās, -nyo͞o′-, -āz) *n.* Any of various enzymes that decompose ribonucleic acids.

ri·bo·nu·cle·ic acid (rī′bō-no͞o-klē′ĭk, -nyo͞o-) *n.* A universal polymeric constituent of all living cells, consisting of a single-stranded chain of alternating phosphate and ribose units with the bases adenine, guanine, cytosine, and uracil bonded to the ribose, the structure and base sequence of which are determinants of protein synthesis. [RIBO(SE) + NUCLEIC ACID.]

ri·bo·nu·cle·o·pro·tein (rī′bō-no͞o′klē-ō-prō′tēn, -tē-ĭn, -nyo͞o′-) *n.* A nucleoprotein that contains RNA. [RIBONUCLE(IC ACID) + PROTEIN.]

ri·bo·nu·cle·o·side (rī′bō-no͞o′klē-ə-sīd′, -nyo͞o′-) *n.* A nucleoside that contains ribose as its sugar component. [RIBO(SE) + NUCLEOSIDE.]

ri·bose (rī′bōs′) *n.* A pentose sugar, $C_5H_{10}O_5$, occurring as a component of nucleic acids. [< G. *Ribonsäure,* a tetrahydroxyl acid from which ribose is obtained.]

ribosomal RNA *n.* The RNA that is a permanent structural part of a ribosome.

ri·bo·some (rī′bə-sōm) *n.* A spherical cytoplasmic RNA-containing particle active in the synthesis of protein. [RIBO(SE) + -SOME[3].] **—ri·bo·so′mal** (-sō′məl) *adj.*

rib roast *n.* A cut of beef containing the sizable piece located along the outside of the rib.

rib·wort (rĭb′wûrt′, -wôrt′) *n.* Ribgrass.

rice (rīs) *n.* **1.** A cereal grass, *Oryza sativa,* that is cultivated extensively in warm climates and is a staple food throughout the world. **2.** The starchy edible seed of rice. *—tr.v.* **riced, ric·ing, ric·es.** To sieve (food) to the consistency of rice. [ME *ryce* < OFr. *ris* < OItal. *riso* < Lat. *oryza* < Gk. *oruza.*]

rice·bird (rīs′bûrd′) *n.* **1.** *Southern U.S.* The bobolink. **2.** Any of various birds that frequent rice fields.

rice paper *n.* A thin paper made chiefly from the pith of the rice-paper tree.

rice-pa·per plant (rīs′pā′pər) *n.* Rice-paper tree.

rice-paper tree *n.* A shrub or small tree, *Tetrapanax papyriferum,* of eastern Asia, grown as a source of fiber for rice paper.

ric·er (rī′sər) *n.* A kitchen utensil used for ricing soft foods by extrusion through small holes.

rice weevil *n.* A small destructive insect, *Sitophilus oryzae,* that infests stored grain and cereal products.

rich (rĭch) *adj.* **-er, -est. 1.** Possessing great material wealth. **2.** Having great worth or value. **3.** Magnificent; sumptuous: *a rich brocade.* **4. a.** Having an abundant supply of something: *rich in ideas.* **b.** Abounding, esp. in natural resources: *rich land.* **5.** Extremely productive. **6.** Containing a large amount of choice ingredients, as butter, sugar, or eggs: *a rich dessert.* **7. a.** Pleasantly full and mellow: *a rich tenor voice.* **b.** Warm and strong in color. **8.** Containing a large proportion of fuel to air: *a rich gas mixture.* **9.** *Informal.* Highly amusing. [ME *riche* < OE *rīce.*] **—rich′ly** *adv.* **—rich′ness** *n.*

Rich·ard Roe (rĭch′ərd) *n.* A name used in legal proceedings to designate a fictitious or unidentified person.

rich·en (rĭch′ən) *tr.v.* **-ened, -en·ing, -ens.** To make rich.

rich·es (rĭch′ĭz) *pl.n.* **1.** Abundant wealth. **2.** Valuable or precious possessions. [ME < *richesse,* wealth < OFr. < *riche,* rich, of Germanic orig.]

Rich·ter scale (rĭk′tər) *n.* A logarithmic scale ranging from 1 to 10, used to express the magnitude or total energy of an earthquake. In this scale an increase of 1 represents a 60-fold increase in energy. [After Charles F. *Richter* (b. 1900).]

ri·cin (rī′sĭn, rĭs′ĭn) *n.* A poisonous protein extracted from the castor bean and used as a biochemical reagent. [Lat. *ricinus,* castor-oil plant.]

ri·cin·o·le·ic acid (rĭs′ĭn-ō-lē′ĭk) *n.* An unsaturated fatty acid, $C_{18}H_{34}O_3$, prepared from castor oil and used in making soaps and in textile finishing. [Lat. *ricinus,* castor-oil plant + OLEIC.]

rick (rĭk) *n.* A stack of hay, straw, or similar material, esp. when covered or thatched for protection from the weather. *—tr.v.* **ricked, rick·ing, ricks.** To pile in ricks. [ME *reke* < OE *hrēac.*]

rick·ets (rĭk′ĭts) *n.* *(used with a sing. verb).* A deficiency disease resulting from a lack of vitamin D and from insufficient exposure to sunlight, characterized by defective bone growth and occurring chiefly in children. [Orig. unknown.]

rick·ett·si·a (rĭ-kĕt′sē-ə) *n., pl.* **-si·ae** (-sē-ē′). Any of various microorganisms of the genus *Rickettsia,* carried as parasites by many ticks, fleas, and lice, that cause diseases such as typhus, scrub typhus, and Rocky Mountain spotted fever in human beings. [NLat. *Rickettsia,* genus name, after Howard T. *Ricketts* (1871–1910).] **—rick·ett′si·al** *adj.*

rick·ett·si·o·sis (rĭ-kĕt′sē-ō′sĭs) *n., pl.* **-ses** (-sēz′). Infection with or disease caused by rickettsiae.

rick·et·y (rĭk′ĭt-ē) *adj.* **-i·er, -i·est. 1.** Likely to break or fall apart; shaky. **2.** Feeble with age; infirm. **3.** Of, having, or resembling rickets. [From RICKETS.] **—rick′et·i·ness** *n.*

rick·ey (rĭk′ē) *n., pl.* **-eys.** A drink of soda water, lime juice, sugar, and usually gin. [Prob. < the name *Rickey.*]

rick·rack (rĭk′răk′) *n.* A flat, narrow braid in zigzag form, used as a trimming. [Redup. of RACK[1].]

rick·sha or **rick·shaw** (rĭk′shô) *n.* A small, two-wheeled oriental carriage drawn by one or two persons. [Short for JINRIKSHA.]

ric·o·chet (rĭk′ə-shā′, -shĕt′) *intr.v.* **-cheted** (-shād′), **-chet·ing** (-shā′ĭng), **-chets** also **-chet·ted** (-shĕt′ĭd), **-chet·ting** (-shĕt′ĭng), **-chets.** To rebound at least once from a surface. *—n.* An instance of ricocheting. [Fr.]

ri·cot·ta (rē-kôt′tä, rĭ-kŏt′ə) *n.* **1.** An Italian soft cheese that resembles cottage cheese. **2.** A cheese similar to ricotta made in the United States. [Ital. < Lat. *recocta,* fem. p.part. of *recoquere,* to cook again : *re-,* again + *coquere,* to cook.]

ric·tus (rĭk′təs) *n.* **1. a.** The expanse of an open mouth, a bird's beak, or similar structure. **b.** A gaping grimace: *Her face contorted into a rictus of pain.* **2.** A cleft, split, or gap. [Lat. < p.part. of *ringi,* to open the mouth wide.] **—ric′tal** *adj.*

rid (rĭd) *tr.v.* **rid** or **rid·ded, rid·ding, rids.** To free from: *finally rid himself of financial worries.* [ME < *ridden* < ON *ryðja.*] **—rid′der** *n.*

rid·dance (rĭd′ns) *n.* **1.** An act of ridding. **2.** A deliverance from or removal of something.

rid·den (rĭd′n) *v.* Past participle of **ride.** *—adj.* Dominated: *disease-ridden; grief-ridden.*

rid·dle[1] (rĭd′l) *tr.v.* **-dled, -dling, -dles. 1.** To pierce with numerous holes; perforate: *riddle a tank with bullets.* **2.** To put through a coarse sieve. **3.** To spread throughout: *a theory riddled with flaws.* *—n.* A coarse sieve, as for gravel. [ME *riddlen,* to sift < *riddil,* sieve < OE *hriddel.*] **—rid′dler** *n.*

rid·dle[2] (rĭd′l) *n.* **1.** A question or statement requiring thought to answer or understand; conundrum. **2.** Something or someone perplexing; enigma. *—v.* **rid·dled, -dling, -dles.** *—tr.* To solve or explain. *—intr.* **1.** To solve or propound riddles. **2.** To speak in riddles. [ME *redeles* < OE *rǣdelse.*] **—rid′dler** *n.*

ride (rīd) *v.* **rode** (rōd), **rid·den** (rĭd′n), **rid·ing, rides.** *—intr.* **1.** To be carried or conveyed, as in a vehicle or on horseback. **2. a.** To travel over a surface: *This car rides well.* **b.** To move or proceed. **3.** To float or move on or as if on water: *rode into office on a tide of discontent.* **4.** To lie at anchor. **5.** To seem to float: *the moon riding among the clouds.* **6.** To be sustained or supported. **7.** To depend: *The outcome rides on the election.* **8.** To continue without interference: *Let it ride.* **9.** To work or move from the proper place, esp. on the body: *shorts that ride up.* *—tr.* **1.** To sit on and drive. **2.** To be supported or carried upon: *a swimmer riding the waves.* **3.** To travel over, along, or through: *ride the highways.* **4.** To rest upon by overlapping; overlie. **5.** To take part in or do by riding: *He rode his last race.* **6.** To control or dominate. **7.** To cause to ride, esp. to cause to be carried: *ride him out of town on a rail.* **8.** To keep (a vessel) at anchor. **9.** *Informal.* To tease or ridicule. **10.** To dominate the mind or thoughts of: *ridden with guilt.* **11.** To keep partially engaged by slightly depressing a pedal with the foot: *riding the clutch.* **—*phrasal verb.* ride out.** To survive or outlast: *rode out the storm.* *—n.* **1.** An act of riding, as on an animal or in a vehicle. **2.** A path made for riding on horseback, esp. through woodlands. **3.** A device, as at an amusement park, that one rides for pleasure or excitement. **4.** A means of transportation: *waiting for his ride to come.* **—*idioms.* ride for a fall.** To court danger or disaster. **ride herd on.** To keep watch or control over. **ride high.** To experience success. **ride roughshod over.** To take a course of action without regard for the feeling, opinions, or welfare of others. **ride shotgun. 1.** To guard a person or a thing while in transit. **2.** To ride in the passenger seat of a car or truck. **take for a ride.** *Slang.* **1.** To transport to a place and kill (someone). **2.** To deceive or swindle. [ME *riden* < OE *ridan.*]

ridgepole

rid·er (rī′dər) *n.* **1.** One that rides. **2.** A person who rides horses. **3.** A clause, usually having little relevance to the main issue, added to a legislative bill. **4.** An amendment or addition to a document or record. **5.** Something, as the top rail of a fence, that rests upon or is supported by something else.

rid·er·ship (rī′dər-shĭp′) *n.* The number of passengers who ride a particular public transit system.

ridge (rĭj) *n.* **1.** The long, narrow upper section or crest of something: *ridge of a wave.* **2.** A long, narrow land elevation. **3.** A long, narrow, or crested part of the body: *the ridge of the nose.* **4.** The horizontal line formed by the juncture of two sloping planes, esp. the line formed by the surfaces of a roof. **5.** A narrow raised strip, as in cloth or on plowed ground. *—v.* **ridged, ridg·ing, ridg·es.** *—tr.* To mark with, form into, or provide with ridges. *—intr.* To form ridges. [ME *rigge* < OE *hrycg.*]

ridge·back (rĭj′băk′) *n.* A Rhodesian ridgeback.

ridge·ling also **ridg·ling** (rĭj′lĭng) *n.* A male animal with one or two undescended testicles. [Orig. unknown.]

ridge·pole (rĭj′pōl′) *n.* **1.** A horizontal beam at the ridge of a roof to which the rafters are attached. **2.** The horizontal pole at the top of a tent.

ridg·y (rĭj′ē) *adj.* **-i·er, -i·est.** Having or forming ridges.

rid·i·cule (rĭd′ə-kyo͞ol′) *n.* Words or actions intended to evoke contemptuous laughter at or feelings toward a person or thing. *—tr.v.* **-culed, -cul·ing, -cules.** To deride, mock, or make fun of. [Fr. < Lat. *ridiculum,* joke < *ridiculus,* laughable, ridiculous.] **—rid′i·cul′er** *n.*

Synonyms: *ridicule, mock, taunt, twit, deride, gibe.* These verbs concern the efforts of one to find amusement or delight at the expense of another; they vary from mere mischief to sheer malice. *Ridicule* refers to the attempt to arouse laughter or merriment at another's expense by making fun of or belittling him. *Mock* implies contempt through caricature. *Taunt* suggests reproach through sarcasm. *Twit* applies to an effort to ridicule by calling attention to something embarrassing. *Deride* implies scorn and contempt in demeaning another. *Gibe* refers to light taunting of someone over something trivial or humorous.

rifle[1]
Automatic rifle

ri·dic·u·lous (rĭ-dĭk′yə-ləs) *adj.* Deserving or inspiring ridicule; absurd or preposterous; laughable. [Lat. *ridiculus,* laughable < *ridēre,* to laugh.] **—ri·dic′u·lous·ly** *adv.* **—ri·dic′u·lous·ness** *n.*

rid·ing[1] (rī′dĭng) *n.* **1.** The action of riding. **2.** Horseback riding. **—*modifier:* *riding gear.***

rid·ing[2] (rī′dĭng) *n.* **1.** Any one of three former administrative divisions of Yorkshire, England. **2.** An administrative division or electoral division in Canada. [ME *rithing* < OE **ðriðing* < ON *ðriðjungr,* third part < *ðriði,* third.]

riding habit *n.* The costume worn by a horseback rider.

rid·ley (rĭd′lē) *n., pl.* **-leys.** A marine turtle, *Lepidochelys kempi,* of the Gulf of Mexico and Atlantic coastal waters. [Prob. < the name *Ridley.*]

ri·el (rē-ĕl′) *n.* See table at **currency.** [Orig. unknown.]

Rie·mann·ian geometry (rē-män′ē-ən) *n.* A non-Euclidean geometry based on the postulate that there are no parallel lines. [After Bernhard *Riemann* (1826–1866).]

Ries·ling (rēs′lĭng) *n.* A dry white wine similar to Rhine wine. [G.]

rigging

ri·fam·pi·cin (rĭ-făm′pĭ-sĭn) *n.* An antibiotic that has both antibacterial and antiviral action. [Blend of E. *rifamycin,* an antibiotic + AMPICILLIN.]

rife (rīf) *adj.* **rif·er, rif·est. 1.** Common or frequent in occurrence; widespread: *Fatal disease was rife in the village.* **2.** Abounding; full: *an administration rife with corruption.* [ME *rif* < OE *ryfe.*]

riff (rĭf) *n. Mus.* A short rhythmic phrase repeated constantly. [Orig. unknown.]

Riff (rĭf) also **Rif·fi·an** (rĭf′ē-ən) *n.* A Berber tribesman of the Rif country in northern Morocco, Africa.

rif·fle (rĭf′əl) *n.* **1. a.** A rocky shoal or sandbar lying just below the surface of a waterway. **b.** A stretch of choppy water caused by such a shoal or sandbar; rapid. **2. a.** In mining, the sectional stone or wood bottom lining of a sluice, arranged to trap mineral particles, as of gold. **b.** A groove or block in such a lining. **3.** The act of shuffling cards. *—v.* **-fled, -fling, -fles.** *—tr.* **1.** To shuffle (playing cards) by holding part of a deck in each hand and raising up the edges before releasing them to fall alternately in one stack. **2.** To thumb through (the pages of a book, for example). *—intr.* **1.** To shuffle cards. **2.** To become choppy, as water. [Orig unknown.]

rif·fler (rĭf′lər) *n.* A file with curved ends suitable for scraping. [OFr. *riffloir* < *riffler,* to scratch.]

riff·raff (rĭf′răf′) *n.* **1.** Worthless or disreputable persons. **2.** Rubbish; trash. [ME *rif and raf,* one and all < OFr. *rif et raf.*]

ri·fle[1] (rī′fəl) *n.* **1. a.** A firearm with a rifled bore designed to be fired from the shoulder. **b.** An artillery piece or naval gun with such spiral grooves. **2. rifles.** Troops armed with rifles. *—tr.v.* **-fled, -fling, -fles.** To cut spiral grooves within (a gun barrel, for example). [< *rifle,* to cut spiral grooves < OFr., to scratch.]

ri·fle[2] (rī′fəl) *tr.v.* **-fled, -fling, -fles. 1.** To search with intent to steal. **2.** To ransack or plunder; pillage. **3.** To rob: *rifle a safe.* [ME *riflen,* to plunder < OFr. *rifler.*] **—ri′fler** *n.*

ri·fle·bird (rī′fəl-bûrd′) *n.* Any of several birds of paradise of the genera *Craspedophora* and *Ptiloris,* of Australia and New Guinea.

ri·fle·man (rī′fəl-mən) *n.* **1.** A soldier equipped with a rifle. **2.** One who shoots a rifle skillfully.

ri·fle·ry (rī′fəl-rē) *n.* **1.** The art and practice of marksmanship. **2.** Rifle fire: *the sound of distant riflery.*

ri·fle·scope (rī′fəl-skōp′) *n.* A telescopic sight for a rifle.

ri·fling (rī′flĭng) *n.* **1.** The process or operation of cutting spiral grooves in a rifle barrel. **2.** Grooves cut in a rifle barrel.

rift[1] (rĭft) *n.* **1. a.** *Geol.* A fault (sense 3). **b.** A narrow fissure in rock. **2.** A break in friendly relations. *—v.* **rift·ed, rift·ing, rifts.** *—intr.* To split open; break. *—tr.* To cause to split open or break. [ME, of Scand. orig.]

rift[2] (rĭft) *n.* **1.** A shallow area in a waterway. **2.** The backwash of a wave that has broken upon a beach. [Prob. alteration of dial. *riff,* reef.]

rift valley *n.* A long, narrow depression in the earth's surface formed when the land sinks between two fairly parallel faults.

rig (rĭg) *tr.v.* **rigged, rig·ging, rigs. 1.** To provide with harness or equipment; fit out. **2. a.** To equip (a ship) with sails, shrouds, and yards. **b.** To fit (sails or shrouds, for example) to masts and yards. **3.** *Informal.* To dress, clothe, or adorn: *rigged out in her best dress.* **4.** To make or construct in haste or in a makeshift manner: *rig up a tent for the night.* **5.** To manipulate dishonestly for personal gain: *rig a prize fight.* *—n.* **1.** The arrangement of masts, spars, and sails on a sailing vessel. **2.** Special equipment or gear for a particular purpose. **3.** A vehicle with one or more horses harnessed to it. **4.** The special apparatus used for drilling oil wells. **5.** *Western U.S.* A saddle. **6.** *Informal.* A costume or dress: *wore an outlandish rig to the office.* **7.** Fishing tackle. [ME *riggen,* prob. of Scand orig.]

rig·a·doon (rĭg′ə-do͞on′) *n.* **1.** A lively jumping quickstep for one couple. **2.** Music for the rigadoon, usually in rapid duple meter. [Fr. *rigaudon.*]

rig·a·ma·role (rĭg′ə-mə-rōl′) *n.* Variant of **rigmarole.**

rig·a·to·ni (rĭg′ə-tō′nē) *n.* Large, ribbed, macaroni tubes, slightly curved and cut into short lengths. [Ital, pl. < *regato,* p.part. of *regare,* to draw a line < *riga,* line, of Germanic orig.]

Ri·gel (rī′jəl) *n.* A bright double star in the constellation Orion. [Ar. *rijl,* foot.]

rig·ger (rĭg′ər) *n.* **1.** A person who rigs. **2.** A ship with a specific kind of rigging: *a square rigger.*

rig·ging (rĭg′ĭng) *n.* **1.** The system of ropes, chains, and tackle used to support and control the masts, sails, and yards of a sailing vessel. **2.** The supporting material for construction work.

right (rīt) *adj.* **-er, -est. 1.** Conforming with or conformable to justice, law, or morality. **2.** In accordance with fact, reason, or truth; correct: *the right answer.* **3.** Fitting, proper, or appropriate: *It is not right to lie.* **4.** Most favorable, desirable, or convenient: *the right time to act.* **5.** In a satisfactory state or condition: *put things right.* **6.** Being in good mental or physical health or order. **7.** Intended to be worn facing outward or toward an observer: *the right side of the dress.* **8.** *Archaic.* Genuine; not spurious. **9. a.** Of, pertaining to, or toward that side of the human body away from the heart. **b.** Of or located on the side opposite the left. **c.** Toward this side: *a right turn.* **10.** Of or tending toward conservative or reactionary political policies or views. **11.** *Math.* **a.** Formed by or in reference to a line or plane that is perpendicular to another line or plane. **b.** Having the axis perpendicular to the base: *right cone.* **12.** Straight; uncurved; direct: *a right line.* *—n.* **1.** That which is just, morally good, legal, proper, or fitting. **2. a.** The right-hand side or direction. **b.** Something that is on or toward the right-hand side. **3.** A faction, party, or other political group whose policies are conservative or reactionary. **4. a.** The right hand. **b.** A blow given by the right hand: *knocked him out with a right to the jaw.* **5.** Something that is due to a person by law, tradition, or nature. **6.** A just or legal claim or title. **7. a.** A stockholder's privilege of buying additional stock in a corporation at a special price, usually at par or at a price below the current market value. **b.** The negotiable certificate on which this privilege is indicated. **c.** Often **rights.** A privilege of subscribing for a particular stock or bond. *—adv.* **1.** In a straight line; directly: *came right by the door.* **2.** Properly; well: *The suit doesn't fit right.* **3.** Exactly; just: *It happened right over there.* **4.** Immediately: *right after dinner.* **5.** Completely; quite: *The wind blew right through him.* **6.** According to law, morality, or justice. **7.** Accurately; correctly. **8.** On or toward the right side or direction: *looked left and then looked right.* **9.** To a high degree; very: *a right pleasant home.* **10.** Used as an intensive: *kept right on going.* **11.** Very: *The Right Honorable Winston S. Churchill.* *—v.* **right·ed, right·ing, rights.** *—tr.* **1.** To put in or restore to an upright or proper position: *They righted their boat.* **2.** To put in order or set right; correct: *judicial measures designed to right generations of unfair labor practices.* **3.** To make reparation or amends for; redress: *right a wrong.* *—intr.* To regain an upright or proper position. ***—idioms.*** **by rights.** Justly; properly. **in one's own right.** Through the force of one's own skills or qualifications. **to rights.** In a satisfactory or orderly condition: *set the place to rights.* [ME < OE *riht.*] **—right'er** *n.*

Synonyms: *right, privilege, prerogative, perquisite, franchise, birthright, title.* These nouns apply to powers and possession and one's established claim to them. *Right* refers to a just claim, legally, morally, or traditionally: *the right of free speech. Privilege* usually suggests an advantage not enjoyed by everyone: *his privilege to sit at the head table. Prerogative* connotes a prior right or privilege based on custom, law, office, sex, or recognition of precedence: *the President's prerogative to veto. Perquisite* applies to advantage accorded one by virtue of one's position or the needs of one's employment: *His perquisites included the use of an automobile. Franchise* denotes specific rights formally and legally granted. *Birthright* applies to heritable rights as a result of birth. *Title* refers to that which establishes the right to ownership of property.

right angle *n.* An angle formed by the perpendicular intersection of two straight lines; an angle of 90 degrees.

right-an·gled (rīt'ăng'gəld) *adj.* Forming or containing one or more right angles: *a right-angled bend.*

right ascension *n.* The angular distance of a celestial body or point on the celestial sphere, measured eastward from the vernal equinox along the celestial equator to the hour circle of the body or point and expressed in degrees or in hours.

right away *adv.* At once; without delay.

right circular cone *n.* A cone (sense 1.b.).

right·eous (rī'chəs) *adj.* **1.** Meeting the standards of what is right and just; morally right: *a righteous action.* **2.** *Slang.* Authentic; true. *—n.* Righteous individuals collectively. [ME *ryghtuous* < OE *rihtwīs* : *rihgt,* right + *wīs,* wise, manner.] **—right'eous·ly** *adv.* **—right'eous·ness** *n.*

right face *n.* A military command to turn 90 degrees to the right.

right field *n. Baseball.* The part of the outfield that is to the right as viewed from home plate.

right fielder *n. Baseball.* An outfielder who defends right field.

right·ful (rīt'fəl) *adj.* **1.** Right or proper; just. **2.** Having a just or proper claim: *Return this dog to its rightful owner.* **3.** Held or owned by just or proper claim: *This dog is my rightful property.* **—right'ful·ly** *adv.* **—right'ful·ness** *n.*

right-hand (rīt'hănd') *adj.* **1.** Located on the right side. **2.** Directed toward the right side: *a right-hand turn.* **3.** Of, for, or done by the right hand. **4.** Helpful; reliable: *my right-hand man.* **—right'-hand'er** *n.*

right-hand·ed (rīt'hăn'dĭd) *adj.* **1.** Using the right hand more easily or skillfully than the left. **2.** Done with the right hand. **3.** Made to be used by the right hand. **4.** Turning or spiraling from left to right; clockwise. **—right'-hand'ed, right'-hand'ed·ly** *adv.* **—right'-hand'ed·ness** *n.*

right·ism also **Right·ism** (rī'tĭz'əm) *n.* Reactionary or conservative political activities or ideas. **—right'ist** *n.*

right·ly (rīt'lē) *adv.* **1.** In a correct manner; properly: *act rightly.* **2.** With honesty; justly. **3.** *Informal.* Really: *I don't rightly know.*

right-mind·ed (rīt'mīn'dĭd) *adj.* Having ideas and views based on what is right. **—right'-mind'ed·ness** *n.*

right·ness (rīt'nĭs) *n.* The state or quality of being right.

right of asylum *n. Law.* The right of receiving protection within a foreign embassy or other place recognized by custom, law, or treaty.

right off *adv.* Immediately; right away. ***—idiom.*** **right off the bat.** Right off.

right of search *n. Law.* The right of a warring nation to stop a neutral vessel on the high seas and search it for contraband.

right of way also **right-of-way** (rīt'əv-wā') *n., pl.* **rights-of-way** or **right-of-ways. 1.** *Law.* **a.** The right to pass over property owned by another party. **b.** The path or thoroughfare on which such passage is made. **2.** The strip of land over which facilities such as highways, railroads, or power lines are built. **3.** The customary or legal right of a person, vessel, or vehicle to pass in front of another.

right on *interj. Slang.* Used as an exclamation of encouragement, approval, or support.

right-on (rīt'ŏn', -ôn') *adj. Slang.* **1.** Up-to-date and sophisticated; trendy. **2.** Absolutely right; perfectly true.

right-to-life (rīt'tə-līf') *adj.* Of, relating to, or advocating laws that forbid abortion on demand; antiabortion. **—right'-to-lif'er** *n.*

right-to-work law (rīt'tə-wûrk') *n.* A state law that prohibits the union shop.

right triangle *n.* A triangle containing an angle of 90 degrees.

right whale *n.* Any of several whales of the family Balaenidae, characterized by a large head, absence of a dorsal fin, and whalebone plates in the mouth.

right wing *n.* A division holding relatively conservative views within a larger political group. **—right winger** *n.*

rig·id (rĭj'ĭd) *adj.* **1.** Not bending; inflexible. **2.** Not moving; fixed. **3.** Rigorous; severe: *a rigid examination.* **4.** Scrupulously strict; undeviating: *a rigid social structure.* [OFr. *rigide* < Lat. *rigidus* < *rigēre,* to be stiff.] **—rig'id·ly** *adv.* **—rig'id·ness** *n.*

ri·gid·i·ty (rĭ-jĭd'ĭ-tē) *n., pl.* **-ties. 1.** The state or quality of being rigid. **2.** An instance of being rigid.

rig·ma·role (rĭg'mə-rōl) also **rig·a·ma·role** (-ə-mə-rōl) *n.* **1.** Confused, rambling, or incoherent discourse; nonsense. **2.** A complicated and petty set of procedures. [Alteration of obs. *ragman roll,* catalog < ME *rageman rolle,* scroll used in Ragman, a game of chance.]

rig·or (rĭg'ər) *n.* **1.** Strictness or severity, as in temperament, action, or judgment. **2.** A harsh or trying circumstance; hardship. **3.** A severe or cruel act. **4.** *Med.* Shivering or trembling, as caused by a chill. **5.** *Physiol.* A state of rigidity in living tissues or organs that prevents response to stimuli. **6.** *Obs.* Stiffness or rigidity. [ME *rigour* < OFr. < Lat. *rigor* < *rigēre,* to be stiff.]

rig·or·ism (rĭg'ə-rĭz'əm) *n.* Severity or strictness in conduct, judgment, or practice. **—rig'or·ist** *n.* **—rig'or·is'tic** *adj.*

rig·or mor·tis (rĭg'ər môr'tĭs) *n.* Muscular stiffening following death. [Lat., stiffness of death.]

rig·or·ous (rĭg'ər-əs) *adj.* **1.** Characterized by or acting with rigor. **2.** Full of rigors; harsh: *a rigorous climate.* **3.** Precisely accurate; strict. **—rig'or·ous·ly** *adv.* **—rig'or·ous·ness** *n.*

rig·our (rĭg'ər) *n. Chiefly Brit.* Variant of **rigor.**

Rig-Ve·da (rĭg-vā'də, -vē'də) *n.* The most ancient collection of Hindu sacred verses. [Skt. *ṛgvedaḥ* : *ṛc,* verse, sacred text + *vedaḥ,* veda.]

Riks·mal (rēks'mōl) *n.* An official literary form of Norwegian based on written Danish. [Norw. : *rik,* kingdom + *mål,* speech.]

rile (rīl) *tr.v.* **riled, ril·ing, riles. 1.** To vex; irritate. **2.** To stir up (liquid); roil. [Alteration of ROIL.]

ril·ey (rī'lē) *adj.* **1.** Riled; upset. **2.** Roiled; turbid.

rill also **rille** (rĭl) *n.* **1.** A small brook; rivulet. **2.** Any of various long, narrow, straight depressions on the moon's surface. [LG *rille.*]

rill·et (rĭl'ĭt) *n.* A small rill.

rim (rĭm) *n.* **1.** The border, edge, or margin of an object. **2.** The circular outer part of a wheel, furthest from the axle. **3.** A circular metal structure around which a wheel tire is fitted. *—tr.v.* **rimmed, rim·ming, rims. 1.** To furnish with a rim. **2.** *Sports.* To roll around the rim of (a basket, for example) without falling in. [ME *rym* < OE *rima,* of Germanic orig.]

rime[1] (rīm) *n.* A frost or granular ice coating, as on grass and trees; hoarfrost. *—tr.v.* **rimed, rim·ing, rimes.** To cover with or as if with rime. [ME *rim* < OE *hrīma.*] **—rim'y** *adj.*

rime[2] (rīm) *n. & v.* Variant of **rhyme.**

rim·er (rī'mər) *n.* Variant of **rhymer.**

rime riche (rēm rēsh') *n., pl.* **rimes riches** (rēm rēsh'). Rhyme using words or parts of words that are pronounced identically but have different meanings, for example, *write-right* or *port-deport.* [Fr. : *rime,* rhyme + *riche,* rich.]

rime·ster (rīm'stər) *n.* Variant of **rhymester.**

ri·mose (rī'mōs', rī-mōs') *adj.* Full of chinks, cracks, or crevices. [Lat. *rimosus* < *rima,* fissure.] **—ri'mose·ly** *adv.* **—ri·mos'i·ty** (-mŏs'ĭ-tē) *n.*

rim·ple (rĭm'pəl) *n.* A fold; wrinkle. *—v.* **-pled, -pling, -ples.** *—tr.* To wrinkle; rumple. *—intr.* To form wrinkles or creases. [ME *rymple* < OE *hrympel.*]

rind (rīnd) *n.* A tough outer covering, as bark, the skin of some fruits, or the coating on cheese or bacon. [ME < OE.]

rin·der·pest (rĭn'dər-pĕst') *n.* An acute, contagious virus disease, chiefly of cattle, characterized by ulceration of the intestinal tract. [G. : *Rinder,* cattle + *Pest,* plague < Lat. *pestis.*]

rin·for·zan·do (rēn'fôr-tsän'dō) *adj. Mus.* With a sudden increase of emphasis. Used as a direction. [Ital., pr.part. of *rinforzare,* to reinforce: *ri-,* again (< Lat. *re-*) + *inforzare,* to enforce (< OFr. *enforcier*). —see ENFORCE.]

ring[1] (rĭng) *n.* **1.** A circular object, form, or arrangement with a vacant circular center. **2.** A small circular band, generally made of precious metal and often set with jewels, worn on a finger. **3.** A circular band used for carrying, holding, or containing something: *a napkin ring.* **4.** A circular movement or course, as in dancing. **5.** An enclosed, usually circular area in which exhibitions, sports, or contests take place: *a circus ring.* **6. a.** A rectangular arena set off by stakes and ropes in which boxing or wrestling is held. **b.** The sport of boxing. **7. a.** An enclosed area in which bets are placed at a racetrack. **b.** Bookmakers collectively. **8.** An

ring[1]
Napkin ring

exclusive group of persons acting privately or illegally to advance their own gain: *a drug ring.* **9.** A political contest; race. **10.** *Bot.* An annual ring. **11.** *Math.* The planar area between two concentric circles; annulus. **12.** *Math.* An algebraic system consisting of a set with two binary operations in the set such that the set together with one operation, usually denoted *addition,* is a commutative group, together with the second, usually denoted *multiplication,* is a semigroup, and multiplication is distributive over addition. **13.** Any of the turns comprising a spiral or helix. **14.** *Chem.* A group of atoms chemically bound in a manner graphically representable as a circular form. *—v.* **ringed, ring·ing, rings.** *—tr.* **1.** To surround with a ring; encircle. **2.** To form into a ring or rings. **3.** To ornament or supply with a ring or rings. **4.** To remove a circular strip of bark around the circumference of (a tree trunk or branch); girdle. **5.** To put a ring in the nose of (an animal). **6.** To hem in (animals) by riding in a circle around them. **7.** To toss a ring over (a peg), as in horseshoes. *—intr.* **1.** To form a ring or rings. **2.** To move, run, or fly in a spiral or circular course. [ME < OE *hring.*]

ringmaster
Drawing of a ringmaster with clown, by A. B. Frost

ring[2] (rĭng) *v.* **rang** (răng), **rung, ring·ing, rings.** *—intr.* **1.** To give forth a clear, resonant sound. **2.** To cause something to ring. **3.** To sound a bell in order to summon someone. **4.** To have a sound or character suggestive of a particular quality: *a story that rings true.* **5.** To be filled with sound; resound: *The room rang with laughter.* **6.** To hear a persistent humming or buzzing: *ears ringing from the blast.* **7.** To be filled with talk or rumor: *The whole town rang with the news.* *—tr.* **1.** To cause (a bell, for example) to ring. **2.** To produce (a sound) by or as if by ringing. **3.** To announce, proclaim, or signal by or as if by ringing: *a clock that rings the hour.* **4.** To call (someone) on the telephone. **5.** To test (a coin, for example) for quality by the sound it produces when struck against something. ***—phrasal verb.*** **ring up.** To record, esp. by means of a cash register: *ring up a sale.* *—n.* **1.** The sound created by a bell or other sonorous, vibrating object. **2.** A loud sound, esp. one that is repeated or continued. **3.** A telephone call. **4.** A suggestion of a particular quality: *His offer has a suspicious ring.* **5.** A set of bells. **6.** An act or instance of sounding a bell. ***—idiom.*** **ring a bell.** *Informal.* To arouse a memory, often indistinct. [ME *ringen* < OE *hringan.*]

ring-billed gull (rĭng′bĭld′) *n.* A North American gull, *Larus delawarensis,* having a black ring around its bill.

ring·bolt (rĭng′bōlt′) *n.* A bolt having a ring fitted through an eye at its head.

ring·bone (rĭng′bōn′) *n.* A bony growth on the fetlock, pastern, or coffin bone of a horse's foot, usually causing lameness.

ring·dove (rĭng′dŭv′) *n.* **1.** An Old World pigeon, *Streptopelia risoria,* having black markings forming a half circle on the neck. **2.** The wood pigeon.

ring-necked pheasant

ringed (rĭngd) *adj.* **1.** Wearing or marked with a ring or rings. **2.** Encircled or surrounded by bands or rings.

rin·gent (rĭn′jənt) *adj. Biol.* Having gaping liplike parts, as the corolla of some flowers or the shells of certain bivalves. [Lat. *ringens, ringent-,* pr.part. of *ringi,* to open the mouth wide]

ring·er[1] (rĭng′ər) *n.* A horseshoe or quoit thrown so that it encircles the peg.

ring·er[2] (rĭng′ər) *n.* **1.** One that sounds a bell or chime. **2.** *Slang.* A contestant entered dishonestly into a competition. **3.** *Slang.* A person who bears a striking resemblance to another.

Ring·er's solution (rĭng′ərz) also **Ring·er solution** (rĭng′ər) *n.* An aqueous solution of the chlorides of sodium, potassium, and calcium that is isotonic to animal tissue and is used topically as a physiological saline. [After Sydney *Ringer* (1835–1910).]

ring finger *n.* The third finger of the left hand.

ring·hals (rĭng′hăls′) *n.* An African snake, *Haemachates haemachatus,* that spits forth its venom at its victims. [Afr. : *ring,* ring (< MDu. *rinc*) + *hals,* neck < MDu.]

ring·lead·er (rĭng′lē′dər) *n.* A person who leads others, esp. in unlawful or improper activities.

ring·let (rĭng′lĭt) *n.* **1.** A long, spirally curled lock of hair. **2.** A small circle or ring. **—ring′let·ed** *adj.*

ring·mas·ter (rĭng′măs′tər) *n.* A person in charge of the performances in a circus ring.

Ring Nebula *n.* A planetary nebula in the constellation Lyra.

ring-necked pheasant (rĭng′nĕkt′) *n.* A widely distributed bird, *Phasianus colchicus,* native to the Old World, of which the male has a long pointed tail, brightly colored plumage, and a white ring around the neck.

ring·side (rĭng′sīd′) *n.* **1.** The area or seats immediately outside an arena or ring, as at a prize fight. **2.** A place providing a close view of a spectacle.

ring·tail (rĭng′tāl′) *n.* A ring-tailed animal, as the cacomistle.

ring-tailed (rĭng′tāld′) *adj.* **1.** Having a tail with ringlike markings. **2.** Having a tail that curls to form a ring.

ring·worm (rĭng′wûrm′) *n.* Any of a number of contagious skin diseases caused by several related fungi, characterized by ring-shaped, scaly, itching patches on the skin.

rink

rink (rĭngk) *n.* **1.** An area surfaced with smooth ice for skating, hockey, or curling. **2.** A smooth floor suited for roller-skating. **3.** A building that houses a surface prepared for skating. **4.** A section of a bowling green large enough for holding a match. **5.** A team of players in quoits, bowling, or curling. [ME *renk,* race course < OFr. *renc,* line, of Germanic orig.]

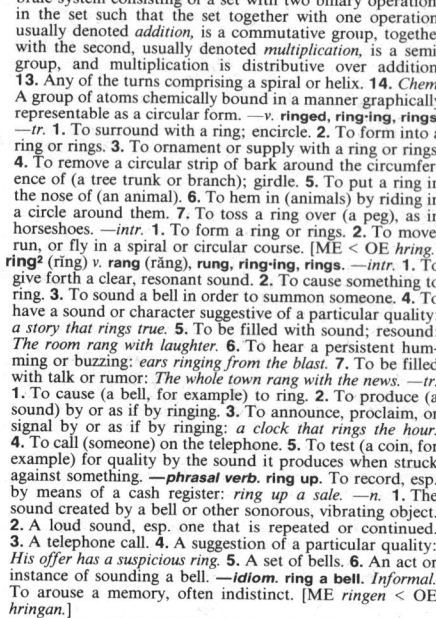

rin·ky-dink (rĭng′kē-dĭngk′) *adj. Slang.* **1.** Old-fashioned; worn-out. **2.** Insignificant; unimportant. *—n. Slang.* One that is rinky-dink. [Orig. unkown.]

rinse (rĭns) *tr.v.* **rinsed, rins·ing, rins·es. 1.** To wash lightly with water. **2.** To remove (soap, for example) by washing lightly in water. *—n.* **1.** The act of washing lightly. **2.** The water or other solution used in rinsing. **3.** A cosmetic solution used in conditioning or tinting the hair. [ME *ryncen* < OFr. *rincer* < VLat. **recentiare* < Lat. *recens,* fresh.] **—rins′a·ble, rins′i·ble** *adj.* **—rins′er** *n.*

ri·ot (rī′ət) *n.* **1.** A wild or turbulent disturbance created by a large number of people. **2.** *Law.* A violent disturbance of the public peace by three or more persons assembled for a common private purpose. **3.** An unrestrained outbreak, as of laughter or passions. **4.** A profusion, as of colors. **5. a.** Unrestrained merrymaking; revelry. **b.** Debauchery. **6.** *Slang.* An irresistibly funny person or thing. *—v.* **-ot·ed, -ot·ing, -ots.** *—intr.* **1.** To take part in a riot. **2.** To live wildly or engage in uncontrolled revelry. *—tr.* To waste (money or time) in wild or wanton living. ***—idiom.*** **run riot. 1.** To move or act with wild abandon. **2.** To grow luxuriantly. [ME < OFr., dispute < *rioter,* to quarrel, poss. < *ruire,* to roar < Lat. *rugire.*] **—ri′ot·er** *n.*

Riot Act *n.* **1.** An English law, enacted in 1715, providing that if 12 or more persons unlawfully assemble and disturb the public peace, they must disperse upon proclamation or be considered guilty of felony. **2. riot act.** An energetic or forceful warning or reproach.

ri·ot·ous (rī′ət-əs) *adj.* **1.** Of, pertaining to, or resembling a riot. **2.** Taking part in or inciting to riot or uproar. **3.** Uproarious; boisterous. **4.** Dissolute; wanton. **5.** Abundant or luxuriant: *a riotous growth.* **—ri′ot·ous·ly** *adv.* **—ri′ot·ous·ness** *n.*

rip[1] (rĭp) *v.* **ripped, rip·ping, rips.** *—tr.* **1.** To cut or tear apart roughly or energetically; slash. **2.** To remove by cutting or tearing roughly. **3.** To split or saw (wood) along the grain. **4.** *Informal.* To produce, display, or exclaim suddenly: *ripped out a vicious oath.* *—intr.* **1.** To become torn or split apart. **2.** *Informal.* To move quickly or violently. ***—phrasal verb.*** **rip off.** *Slang.* **1.** To steal from; rob: *ripped off a liquor store.* **2.** To steal: *ripped off a leather jacket.* **3.** To exploit, swindle, cheat, or defraud: *a con man who ripped us off.* *—n.* **1.** A torn or split place, esp. along a seam. **2.** The act of ripping. **3.** A ripsaw. ***—idiom.*** **rip into.** To attack vehemently; censure: *ripped into his opponent's record.* [ME *rippen.*] **—rip′per** *n.*

rip[2] (rĭp) *n.* **1.** A stretch of broken water in a river, estuary, or tidal channel. **2.** A rip current. [Prob. < RIP[1].]

rip[3] (rĭp) *n.* **1.** A dissolute person. **2.** An old or worthless horse. [Poss. shortening and alteration of REPROBATE.]

ri·par·i·an (rĭ-pâr′ē-ən) *adj.* Of, on, or pertaining to the bank of a natural course of water. [Lat. *riparius* < *ripa,* bank.]

riparian right *n. Law.* The right, as to fishing or to the use of a river bed, of one who owns riparian land.

rip·cord (rĭp′kôrd′) *n.* **1.** A cord pulled to release the pack of a parachute. **2.** A cord pulled to release gas from a balloon.

rip current *n.* A current of water disturbed by an opposing current, esp. in tidal waters or by passage over an irregular bottom.

ripe (rīp) *adj.* **rip·er, rip·est. 1.** Fully developed; mature. **2.** Resembling matured fruit, as in fullness: *a ripe figure.* **3.** Sufficiently advanced in preparation or aging to be used: *ripe cheese.* **4.** Thoroughly matured, as by study or experience; seasoned: *ripe judgment.* **5.** Advanced in years: *the ripe age of 85.* **6.** Fully prepared to do or undergo something; ready. **7.** Sufficiently advanced; opportune: *The time is ripe.* [ME < OE *rīpe.*] **—ripe′ly** *adv.* **—ripe′ness** *n.*

rip·en (rī′pən) *tr. & intr.v.* **-ened, -en·ing, -ens.** To make or become ripe; mature. **—rip′en·er** *n.*

rip-off (rĭp′ôf′, -ŏf′) *n. Slang.* **1.** A theft. **2.** A thief. **3.** An act of exploitation. **4.** Something, as a film or a story, that is clearly imitative of or based on something else.

ri·poste (rĭ-pōst′) *n.* **1.** A quick thrust given after parrying an opponent's lunge in fencing. **2.** A retaliatory action, maneuver, or retort. *—intr.v.* **-post·ed, -post·ing, -postes. 1.** To make a return thrust. **2.** To retort quickly. [Fr. < Ital. *risposta,* answer, fem. p.part. of *rispondere,* to answer < Lat. *respondēre* : *re-,* in return + *spondēre,* to promise.]

rip·ping (rĭp′ĭng) *adj. Informal.* Excellent; marvelous: *had a ripping time at the party.* [Prob. < RIP[1].]

rip·ple[1] (rĭp′əl) *v.* **-pled, -pling, -ples.** *—intr.* **1. a.** To form or display little undulations or waves on the surface, as does disturbed water. **b.** To flow with such undulations or waves on the surface. **2.** To rise and fall gently in tone or volume. *—tr.* To cause to form small waves or undulations. *—n.* **1.** A small wave. **2.** A wavelike motion; undulation: *the ripple of muscles.* **3.** A sound like rippling water: *a ripple of laughter.* [Poss. freq. of RIP[1].] **—rip′pler** *n.* **—rip′pling·ly** *adv.*

rip·ple[2] (rĭp′əl) *n.* A comblike, toothed instrument for removing seeds from flax and other fibers. *—tr.v.* **-pled,**

-pling, -ples. To remove seeds from with a ripple. [ME *ripelen,* to remove seeds.]
ripple effect *n.* A gradually spreading effect or influence: *"warned of a far-reaching ripple effect inflating the economy"* (Newsweek).
rip·plet (rĭp′lĭt) *n.* A little wave or ripple.
rip·ply (rĭp′lē) *adj.* **-pli·er, -pli·est.** Characterized by or sounding in ripples.
rip·rap (rĭp′răp′) *n.* **1.** A loose assemblage of broken stones erected in water or on soft ground as a foundation. **2.** The broken stones used for a riprap. *—tr.v.* **-rapped, -rap·ping, -raps. 1.** To construct a riprap in or upon. **2.** To strengthen with a riprap. [Redup. of RAP[1].]
rip-roar·ing (rĭp′rôr′ĭng, -rō′rĭng) also **rip-roar·i·ous** (rĭp′-rôr′ē-əs, -rōr′ē-əs) *adj.* Noisy, lively, and exciting. [RIP[1] + (UP)ROAR(IOUS) + -ING.]
rip·saw (rĭp′sô′) *n.* A coarse-toothed saw for cutting wood along the grain.
rip·snort·er (rĭp′snôr′tər) *n. Slang.* One that is remarkable for strength, intensity, or excellence. **—rip′snort′ing** *adj.*
rip tide *n.* A rip current.
Rip·u·ar·i·an (rĭp′yo͞o-âr′ē-ən) *adj.* Of or designating a group of Franks who lived along the Rhine, near Cologne, in the 4th century. [Med. Lat. *Ripuarius.*] **—Rip′u·ar′i·an** *n.*
rise (rīz) *v.* **rose** (rōz), **ris·en** (rĭz′ən), **ris·ing, ris·es.** *—intr.* **1.** To assume a standing position after lying, sitting, or kneeling. **2.** To get out of bed. **3.** To move from a lower to a higher position; ascend: *Hot air rises.* **4.** To increase in size, volume, or level: *The river rises every spring.* **5.** To increase in number, amount, or value: *Prices are rising.* **6.** To increase in intensity, force, or speed: *The wind has risen.* **7.** To increase in pitch or volume. **8.** To appear above the horizon: *The sun rises later in the fall.* **9.** To extend upward; be prominent: *The tower rose above the hill.* **10.** To slant or slope upward: *Mount McKinley rises to 20,320 feet.* **11.** To originate; come into existence: *a storm rising in the north.* **12.** To be erected: *New buildings are rising in the city.* **13.** To appear at the surface of the water or the earth; emerge. **14.** To puff up or become larger; swell up: *Bread dough rises.* **15.** To become stiff and erect. **16.** To attain a higher status: *an officer who rose through the ranks.* **17.** To become apparent to the mind or senses: *Fears rose to haunt him.* **18.** To uplift oneself to meet a demand or challenge. **19.** To return to life. **20.** To rebel: *"the right to rise up, and shake off the existing government"* (Lincoln). **21.** To close a session of an official assembly; adjourn. *—tr.* **1.** To cause to rise. **2.** To cause (a distant object at sea) to become visible above the horizon by advancing closer. *—n.* **1.** The act of rising; ascent. **2.** The degree of elevation or ascent. **3.** The appearance of the sun or other heavenly body above the horizon. **4.** An increase in height, as of the level of water. **5.** A gently sloped hill. **6.** An origin, beginning, or source: *the rise of a river.* **7.** Occasion or opportunity: *give rise to doubt.* **8.** The emergence of a fish seeking food or bait at the water's surface. **9.** An increase in price, worth, quantity, or degree. **10.** An increase in intensity, volume, or pitch. **11.** Elevation in social status, prosperity, or importance. **12.** The height of a flight of stairs or of a single riser. **13.** *Chiefly Brit.* An increase in salary or wages; raise. **14.** *Informal.* An angry or irritated reaction: *finally got a rise out of her.* [ME *risen* < OE *rīsan.*]

Synonyms: *rise, ascend, climb, soar, tower, mount, surge, spring.* These verbs all denote a moving upward but differ widely in their connotations and metaphorical senses. *Rise* is applied to a great range of acts, chiefly involving steady or customary upward movement. *Ascend* connotes a rising step by step; *climb,* a steady progress against gravity or other resistance; *soar,* the effortless attainment of great height; and *tower,* admirable height or supremacy relative to the surroundings. With *mount,* the idea of a level or limit to be achieved is present. *Surge* implies ponderous, irresistible forward momentum, while to *spring* is to rise in a single, swift movement.

Usage: Either *rise* or *arise* may be used in the sense of "to get out of bed." —See also Usage note at **raise.**

ris·er (rī′zər) *n.* **1.** A person who rises, esp. from sleep: *a late riser.* **2.** The vertical part of a stair step.
ris·i·bil·i·ty (rĭz′ə-bĭl′ĭ-tē) *n., pl.* **-ties. 1.** The ability or tendency to laugh. **2. risibilities.** A sense of the ludicrous or amusing. **3.** Laughter; hilarity.
ris·i·ble (rĭz′ə-bəl) *adj.* **1.** Capable of laughing or inclined to laugh. **2.** Pertaining to or used in laughter. **3.** Apt to excite laughter; ludicrous. [LLat. *risibilis* < Lat. *rīdēre,* to laugh.] **—ris′i·bly** *adv.*
ris·ing (rī′zĭng) *adj.* **1.** Ascending, sloping upward, or advancing: *a rising tide.* **2.** Coming to maturity; emerging: *the rising generation.* *—n.* **1.** The act of someone or something that rises. **2.** An uprising; insurrection. **3.** A prominence or projection. **4.** The leaven or yeast used to make dough rise in baking.
risk (rĭsk) *n.* **1.** The possibility of suffering harm or loss; danger. **2.** A factor, element, or course involving uncertain danger; hazard. **3. a.** The danger or probability of loss to an insurer. **b.** The amount that an insurance company stands to lose. **c.** A person or thing considered with respect to the possibility of loss to an insurer: *a poor risk.* *—tr.v.* **risked, risk·ing, risks. 1.** To expose to a chance of loss or damage; hazard. **2.** To incur the risk of: *His action risked a sharp reprisal.* [Fr. *risque* < Ital. *risco.*] **—risk′er** *n.*
risk·y (rĭs′kē) *adj.* **-i·er, -i·est.** Accompanied by or involving risk or danger; hazardous. **—risk′i·ness** *n.*
Ri·sor·gi·men·to (rē-sôr′jē-mĕn′tō) *n.* The period of or the movement for the liberation and political unification of Italy, beginning about 1750 and lasting until 1870. [Ital., resurrection < *risorgere,* to rise again < Lat. *resurgere* : *re-,* again + *surgere,* to rise (*sub-,* up from under + *regere,* to direct).]
ri·sot·to (rē-sôt′ō, rĭ-sŏt′ō) *n.* Rice cooked in broth with grated cheese and seasonings. [Ital.]
ris·qué (rĭs-kā′) *adj.* Suggestive of or bordering on indelicacy or impropriety: *a risqué joke.* [Fr. < *risquer,* to risk < *risque,* risk.]
ris·sole (rĭ′sōl, rē-sōl′) *n.* A small, pastry-enclosed croquette with a minced meat or fish filling, usually fried in deep fat. [Fr. < OFr. *ruissole* < VLat. **russeola* (pasta), reddish paste < fem. of LLat. *russeolus,* reddish < Lat. *russus,* red.]
ris·so·lé (rē-sô-lā′) *adj.* Browned by frying. [Fr. < *rissoler,* to brown < *rissole,* rissole.]
ri·tar·dan·do (rē′tär-dän′dō) *adj. & adv. Mus.* Gradually slowing in tempo; retarding. Used as a direction. [Ital., pr.part. of *ritardare,* to slow down < Lat. *retardare,* to retard. —see RETARD.]

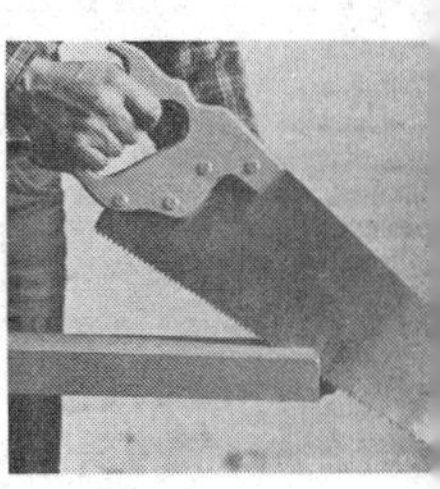
ripsaw

rite (rīt) *n.* **1.** The prescribed or customary form for conducting a religious or other solemn ceremony: *the rite of baptism.* **2.** A ceremonial act or series of acts: *fertility rites.* **3. Rite.** A branch of the Christian church distinguished by its own liturgy. [ME < Lat. *ritus.*]
rite of passage *n.* A significant event in an individual's life that indicates a transition from one stage to another, as from adolescence to adulthood, and that may be marked by a ritual or ceremony.
ri·tor·nel·lo (rē′tôr-nĕl′lō) *n., pl.* **-li** (-lē) or **-los.** *Mus.* **1.** An instrumental interlude recurring after each stanza in a vocal work. **2.** A passage for full orchestra in a baroque concerto grosso. **3.** An instrumental interlude in early 17th-century opera. **4.** The refrain of a rondo. [Ital., dim. of *ritorno,* return < *ritornare,* to return.]
rit·ter (rĭt′ər) *n., pl.* **ritter.** A knight. [G. < MHG *riter* < MDu. *ridder.*]
rit·u·al (rĭch′o͞o-əl) *n.* **1.** The prescribed form or order of conducting a religious or solemn ceremony. **2.** A body of ceremonies or rites, as those used in a church or fraternal organization. **3.** A book of rites or ceremonial forms. **4. rituals. a.** A ceremonial act or a series of such acts. **b.** The performance of such acts. **5.** A detailed method of procedure faithfully or regularly followed: *Her household chores have become a ritual with her.* [Lat. *ritualis,* of rites < *ritus,* rite.] **—rit′u·al·ly** *adv.*
rit·u·al·ism (rĭch′o͞o-ə-lĭz′əm) *n.* **1.** The practice or observance of religious ritual. **2.** Insistence upon or adherence to ritual.
rit·u·al·ist (rĭch′o͞o-ə-lĭst) *n.* **1.** An authority on or student of ritual. **2.** A person who practices or advocates the observance of ritual.
rit·u·al·is·tic (rĭch′o͞o-ə-lĭs′tĭk) *adj.* **1.** Pertaining to ritual or ritualism. **2.** Advocating or practicing ritual. **—rit′u·al·is′ti·cal·ly** *adv.*
rit·u·al·ize (rĭch′o͞o-ə-līz′) *v.* **-ized, -iz·ing, -iz·es.** *—intr.* To engage in ritualism. *—tr.* **1.** To make a ritual of. **2.** To force a ritual upon. **—rit′u·al·i·za′tion** *n.*
ritz·y (rĭt′sē) *adj.* **-i·er, -i·est.** *Slang.* Elegant; fancy. [After the *Ritz* hotels.]
riv·age (rĭv′ĭj) *n. Archaic.* A coast, shore, or bank. [ME < OFr. < *rive,* bank < Lat. *ripa.*]
ri·val (rī′vəl) *n.* **1.** One who attempts to equal or surpass another, or who pursues the same object as another; competitor. **2.** One that equals or almost equals another in a particular respect. **3.** *Obs.* A companion or associate in a particular duty. *—v.* **-valed** or **-valled, -val·ing** or **-val·ling, -vals.** *—tr.* **1.** to attempt to equal or surpass. **2.** To be the equal of; match. *—intr.* To be a competitor or rival; compete. [OFr. < Lat. *rivalis,* a rival, one using the same stream as another < *rivus,* stream.]

Synonyms: *rival, compete, vie, emulate, match.* These verbs apply to the act of seeking to equal or surpass another. *Rival* is the most general, connoting an attempt to reach the same level of proficiency or recognition as another. *Compete* and the less forceful *vie* imply a common aim in attainment and usually a satisfaction in the effort involved: *They competed with each other for the honor. Emulate* connotes conscious imitation of excellence. *Match* is said of attainment of equality with a competitor in gradual steps.

ri·val·ry (rī′vəl-rē) *n., pl.* **-ries. 1.** The act of competing or emulating. **2.** The state or condition of being a rival.
rive (rīv) *v.* **rived, rived** or **riv·en** (rĭv′ən), **riv·ing, rives.** *—tr.* **1.** To rend or tear apart. **2.** To break into pieces, as by a blow; cleave or split asunder. **3.** To break or distress (the spirit, for example). *—intr.* To be or become split. [ME *riven* < ON *rīfa.*]
riv·er (rĭv′ər) *n.* **1.** A large natural stream of water emptying into an ocean, lake, or other body of water and usually fed

along its course by converging tributaries. **2.** A stream or abundant flow resembling a river: *a river of tears.* **—idiom. up the river.** *Slang.* In or to prison. [ME < OFr. *rivere* < VLat. **riparia* < fem. of Lat. *riparius,* of a bank < *ripa,* bank.]

riv·er·bank (rĭv′ər-băngk′) *n.* The bank of a river.

river basin *n.* The land area drained by a river and its tributaries.

riv·er·bed (rĭv′ər-bĕd′) *n.* The area between the banks of a river covered or once covered by water.

riv·er·boat (rĭv′ər-bōt′) *n.* A boat suitable for use on a river.

riv·er·head (rĭv′ər-hĕd′) *n.* The source of a river.

river horse *n.* The hippopotamus (sense 1).

riv·er·ine (rĭv′ə-rīn′, -rēn′) *adj.* **1.** Pertaining to or resembling a river. **2.** Located on or inhabiting the banks of a river; riparian.

riv·er·side (rĭv′ər-sīd′) *n.* The bank or side of a river.

riv·er·ward (rĭv′ər-wərd) also **riv·er·wards** (-wərdz) *adv.* Toward a river.

riv·er·weed (rĭv′ər-wēd′) *n.* A North American plant, *Podostemum ceratophyllum,* growing on rocks in rapidly flowing streams and resembling seaweed.

riv·et (rĭv′ĭt) *n.* A metal bolt or pin having a head on one end, used to fasten metal plates or other objects together by inserting the shank through a hole in each piece and hammering down the plain end so as to form a new head. *—tr.v.* **-et·ed, -et·ing, -ets. 1.** To fasten or secure with or as if with a rivet. **2.** To hammer the headless end of so as to form a head and fasten something. **3.** To fasten or secure firmly; fix. **4.** To engross or hold (the attention, for example). [ME *ryvette* < OFr. *river,* to attach.] **—riv′et·er** *n.*

ri·vière (rē-vyâr′) *n.* A necklace of diamonds or other precious stones, generally in one strand. [Fr., river < OFr. *rivere.* —see RIVER.]

riv·u·let (rĭv′yə-lĭt) *n.* A small brook or stream; streamlet. [Ital. *rivoletto,* dim. of *rivolo,* small stream < Lat. *rivulus,* dim. of *rivus,* stream.]

ri·yal also **ri·al** (rē-ôl′, -äl′) *n.* See table at **currency.** [Ar. *riyāl.*]

ri·yal-o·man·i (rē-ôl′ō-mä′nē, rē-äl′-) *n.* See table at **currency.** [Ar. *riyāl 'umānīy,* riyal of Oman.]

RK galaxy (är′kā′) *n.* A ring galaxy composed of a ring structure with a large bright knot of incandescent material on the ring itself.

Rn The symbol for the element radon.

RNA (är′ĕn-ā′) *n.* Ribonucleic acid.

RN·ase (är′ĕn-ās′) also **RNA·ase** (är′ĕn-ā′ās′, -āz′) *n.* Ribonuclease.

roach[1] (rōch) *n., pl.* **roach** or **roach·es. 1.** A freshwater fish, *Rutilus rutilus,* of northern Europe. **2.** Any of various fishes similar or related to the roach, as some North American sunfishes. [ME *roche* < OFr.]

roach[2] (rōch) *n.* The cockroach.

roach[3] (rōch) *n.* **1.** A roll of hair brushed up from the forehead or temple. **2.** *Naut.* A cut on the edge of a sail to prevent chafing. **3.** *Slang.* The butt of a marijuana cigarette. *—tr.v.* **roached, roach·ing, roach·es. 1.** To brush (hair) in a roach. **2.** To shave (the mane of a horse) to a short bristle. [Orig. unknown.]

roach clip *n.* A device used to hold the butt of a marijuana cigarette.

road (rōd) *n.* **1. a.** An open way, generally public, for the passage of vehicles, persons, and animals. **b.** The surface of a road; roadbed. **2.** A course or path. **3.** A railroad. **4.** Often **roads.** A roadstead. **—idiom. on the road. 1.** On tour, as a theatrical company. **2.** Traveling, esp. as a salesman. **3.** Wandering, as a vagabond. [ME *rood,* act of riding < OE *rād.*]

road agent *n.* A bandit who robbed stagecoaches.

road·bed (rōd′bĕd′) *n.* **1. a.** The foundation upon which the ties, rails, and ballast of a railroad are laid. **b.** A layer of ballast directly under the ties. **2.** The foundation and surface of a road.

road·block (rōd′blŏk′) *n.* **1.** A barricade or obstruction across a road set up by the police to prevent the escape of a fugitive or by the military to prevent the passage of enemy troops. **2.** An obstruction in a road, as rocks or a fallen tree. **3.** Something, as a situation or condition, that prevents further progress toward an accomplishment.

road hog *n.* A driver whose vehicle overlaps another's traffic lane.

road·house (rōd′hous′) *n.* An inn, restaurant, or nightclub located on a road outside a city.

road metal *n.* Crushed or broken stone, cinders, or similar material used in the construction and repair of roads and roadbeds.

roadrunner

road·run·ner (rōd′rŭn′ər) *n.* A swift-running, crested bird, *Geococcyx californianus,* of southwestern North America, having streaked, brownish plumage and a long tail.

road show *n.* **1.** A show presented by a troupe of theatrical performers on tour. **2.** A new motion picture shown at selected theaters usually for higher ticket prices.

road·side (rōd′sīd′) *n.* The area bordering on the side of a road.

road·stead (rōd′stĕd′) *n. Naut.* A sheltered offshore anchorage area for ships.

road·ster (rōd′stər) *n.* **1.** An open automobile having a single seat in the front for two or three people and a rumble seat or luggage compartment in the back. **2.** A horse for riding on a road.

road test *n.* **1.** A test of a motor vehicle's operating capability under actual road conditions. **2.** A test of driving ability on the road required of a candidate for a driver's license.

road·way (rōd′wā′) *n.* A road, esp. the part over which vehicles travel.

road·work (rōd′wûrk′) *n.* Outdoor long-distance running as a form of physical exercise or conditioning.

roam (rōm) *v.* **roamed, roam·ing, roams.** *—intr.* To move or travel without purpose or plan; wander. *—tr.* To wander over or through: *roamed the streets.* *—n.* The act of roaming. [ME *romen.*] **—roam′er** *n.*

roan (rōn) *adj.* Having a chestnut, bay, or sorrel coat thickly sprinkled with white or gray: *a roan horse.* *—n.* **1.** The characteristic coloring of a roan horse. **2.** A roan horse or other animal. **3.** A soft, flexible sheepskin leather, often treated to resemble morocco and used in bookbinding. [OFr. < OSp. *roano.*]

roar (rôr) *v.* **roared, roar·ing, roars.** *—intr.* **1.** To utter a loud, deep, prolonged sound, esp. in distress, rage, or excitement. **2.** To laugh loudly or excitedly. **3.** To make or produce a loud noise or din: *The engines roared.* **4.** To be disorderly or rowdy. **5.** To breathe with a rasping sound. Used of a horse. *—tr.* **1.** To utter or express with a loud, deep, and prolonged sound. **2.** To put, bring, or force into a specified state by roaring: *The crowd roared itself hoarse.* *—n.* **1.** A loud, deep, prolonged sound or cry, as of a person in distress or rage. **2.** The loud, deep cry of a wild animal. **3.** A loud, prolonged noise, such as that produced by waves. **4.** A loud burst of laughter. [ME *roren* < OE *rārian.*] **—roar′er** *n.*

roar·ing (rôr′ĭng) *adj.* Very lively or successful; thriving: *a roaring trade.* *—adv.* Extremely; very: *roaring drunk.*

roast (rōst) *v.* **roast·ed, roast·ing, roasts.** *—tr.* **1.** To cook with dry heat, as in an oven or near hot coals. **2.** To dry, brown, or parch by exposing to heat. **3.** To expose to great or excessive heat. **4.** *Metallurgy.* To heat (ores) in a furnace in order to dehydrate, purify, or oxidize. **5.** *Informal.* To ridicule or criticize harshly. *—intr.* **1.** To cook meat or other food in an oven. **2.** To undergo roasting. *—n.* **1.** Something roasted. **2.** A cut of meat suitable or prepared for roasting. **3. a.** The act or process of roasting. **b.** The state of being roasted. **4.** Harsh ridicule or criticism. [ME *rosten* < OFr. *rostir,* of Germanic orig.]

roast·er (rō′stər) *n.* **1.** One that roasts. **2.** A special pan or apparatus for roasting. **3.** Something, esp. a young chicken, that is fit for roasting.

rob (rŏb) *v.* **robbed, rob·bing, robs.** *—tr.* **1.** To take property from (a person or persons) illegally by using or threatening to use violence or force; commit robbery upon. **2.** To take valuable or desired articles unlawfully from: *rob a bank.* **3. a.** To deprive (a person) unjustly of something belonging to, desired by, or legally due to him: *rob a person of his reputation.* **b.** To deprive of something injuriously: *a parasite that robs a tree of its sap.* **4.** To take as booty; steal. *—intr.* To commit or engage in robbery. [ME *robben* < OFr. *rober,* of Germanic orig.] **—rob′ber** *n.*

Synonyms: *rob, burglarize, filch, pilfer, plunder, loot, ransack, steal, thieve.* All these verbs mean to take property from another or valuables from a place. *Rob* in its most common usage means to take property from another through fear, force, or violence; the term may also imply depriving another by fraud or stealth of property legally his. *Burglarize* connotes entering a place to commit theft or another felony. *Filch* and *pilfer* both imply stealth in taking small sums of money or petty objects. *Plunder* in modern usage refers to robbery on a large scale; it also applies to pillaging by victorious troops in conquered areas. *Loot* suggests in its primary sense the carrying away of property by undisciplined troops or mobs; the term also applies to the systematic pilfering of funds or property by trusted persons. *Ransack* pertains to a thorough search of a house or building by persons seeking to take valuable or desired articles. *Steal* and *thieve* both apply to the practice of taking property or belongings surreptitiously and without permission; *steal* also can mean to appropriate another's ideas as one's own or to plagiarize.

ro·ba·lo (rō-bä′lō) *n., pl.* **-los** or **robalo.** Any of various chiefly tropical marine food fishes of the family Centropomidae, as the snook. [Sp. *róbalo.*]

robber baron *n.* **1.** A feudal lord who robbed travelers passing through his domain. **2.** One of the American industrial or financial magnates of the latter 19th century who became wealthy by unethical means, such as questionable stock-market operations or exploitation of labor or political connections.

robber fly *n.* Any of various predatory flies of the family Asilidae, characteristically having long, bristly legs.

rob·ber·y (rŏb′ə-rē) *n., pl.* **-ies.** An act or an instance of unlawfully taking the property of another by the use of violence or intimidation.

robe (rōb) *n.* **1.** A long, loose, flowing outer garment, esp.: **a.** An official garment worn on formal occasions to show office or rank, as by a judge or high church official. **b.** An academic gown. **c.** A dressing gown or bathrobe. **2. robes.** Clothes in general; apparel. **3.** A blanket or covering made of fur, cloth, or other material: *a lap robe.* —*tr. & intr.v.* **robed, rob·ing, robes.** To dress in or put on a robe. [ME < OFr., of Germanic orig.]

rob·in (rŏb′ĭn) *n.* **1.** A North American songbird, *Turdus migratorius,* having a rust-red breast and gray and black upper plumage. **2.** A small Old World bird, *Erithacus rubecula,* having an orange breast and a brown back. **3.** Any of various birds resembling a robin. [From the name *Robin.*]

Robin Good·fel·low (go͝od′fĕl′ō) *n.* Puck.

Robin Hood (ho͝od) *n.* A legendary English outlaw of the 12th century, famous for his courage, chivalry, and practice of robbing the rich to aid the poor.

rob·in's-egg blue (rŏb′ĭnz-ĕg′) *n.* A pale to green to light bluish green to greenish or grayish blue.

Rob·in·son Cru·soe (rŏb′ĭn-sən kro͞o′sō) *n.* The hero of Daniel Defoe's novel *Robinson Crusoe* (1719), a shipwrecked English sailor who lived for years on a small tropical island.

Robin's plantain *n.* A plant, *Erigeron pulchellus,* of eastern North America, having many-rayed purplish flowers.

ro·ble (rō′blā) *n.* **1.** An oak, *Quercus lobata,* of California, having leathery leaves and slender, pointed acorns. **2.** Any of various trees that are similar or related to the roble. [Sp., oak < Lat. *robur.*]

rob·o·rant (rŏb′ər-ənt) *adj.* Restoring vigor or strength. —*n.* A roborant drug; tonic. [Lat. *roborans, roborant-,* pr.part. of *roborare,* to strengthen < *robur,* strength, oak.]

ro·bot (rō′bət, -bŏt′) *n.* **1.** A mechanical device that resembles a human being and is capable of performing human tasks or behaving in a human manner. **2.** A person who works mechanically without original thought. **3.** A machine or device that works automatically or by remote control. [Czech < *robota,* work.] **—ro′bot·is′tic** (-bə-tĭs′tĭk) *adj.*

robot bomb *n.* A small explosive-carrying jet-propelled gyroscopically guided winged missile.

ro·bot·ics (rō-bŏt′ĭks) *n. (used with a sing. verb).* The study and application of the technology of robots.

robot pilot *n.* An automatic pilot.

rob roy (rŏb roi′) *n.* A cocktail made with Scotch whisky, sweet vermouth, and bitters. [< *Rob Roy,* nickname of Robert Macgregor (1671–1734).]

ro·bust (rō-bŭst′, rō′bŭst′) *adj.* **1.** Full of health and strength; vigorous. **2.** Powerfully built; sturdy. **3.** Requiring or suited to physical strength or endurance: *robust labor.* **4.** Boisterous; rough. **5.** Marked by richness and fullness; full-bodied: *a robust wine.* [Lat. *robustus* < *robur,* strength, oak.] **—ro·bust′ly** *adv.* **—ro·bust′ness** *n.*

roc (rŏk) *n.* A legendary bird of prey of enormous size and strength. [Ar. *rukkh.*]

roc·am·bole (rŏk′əm-bōl′) *n.* **1.** A European plant, *Allium scorodoprasum,* having a garliclike bulb. **2.** The bulb of the rocambole, used as a seasoning. [Fr. < G. *Rockenbolle* : *Rocken,* distaff (< OHG *rocko*) + *Bolle,* bulb < OHG *bolla,* ball.]

Ro·chelle powder (rō-shĕl′) *n.* Seidlitz powder.

Rochelle salt *n.* A colorless efflorescent crystalline compound, $KNaC_4H_4O_6{\cdot}4H_2O$, used in making mirrors, in electronics, and as a laxative. [After La *Rochelle,* France.]

roche mou·ton·née (rôsh′ mo͞ot′n-ā′) *n., pl.* **roches mou·ton·nées** (rôsh′ mo͞ot′n-ā′, -āz′). A bedrock outcrop worn smooth by glacial abrasion. [Fr., fleecy rock.]

roch·et (rŏch′ĭt) *n.* A ceremonial vestment made of linen or lawn, worn by bishops and other church dignitaries. [ME < OFr., of Germanic orig.]

rock¹ (rŏk) *n.* **1.** A relatively hard naturally formed mass of mineral or petrified matter; stone. **2. a.** A relatively small piece or fragment of rock. **b.** A relatively large body of such material, as a cliff or peak. **3.** *Geol.* A naturally formed mineral mass or aggregate that constitutes a significant part of the earth's crust. **4.** Someone or something that is very firm, stable, or dependable. **5. rocks.** *Slang.* Money. **6.** *Slang.* A large gem, esp. a diamond. **7. a.** A varicolored stick candy. **b.** Rock candy. **—*idiom.* on the rocks. 1.** In a state of destruction or ruin: *Their marriage is on the rocks.* **2.** Without money; bankrupt. **3.** Served over ice cubes without water or mix: *Scotch on the rocks.* [ME < ONFr. *roque.*]

rock² (rŏk) *v.* **rocked, rock·ing, rocks.** —*intr.* **1.** To move back and forth or from side to side, esp. gently or rhythmically. **2.** To sway violently, as from a blow or shock; shake. **3.** To be washed and panned in a cradle or in a rocker. Used of ores. —*tr.* **1.** To sway back and forth or from side to side, esp. so as to soothe or lull to sleep. **2.** To cause to shake or sway violently. **3.** To disturb the emotions or mind of; upset: *The juicy scandal rocked the town.* **4.** To wash or pan (ore) in a cradle or rocker. **5.** In mezzotint engraving, to roughen (a metal plate) with various rockers and roulettes. —*n.* **1.** The act of rocking. **2.** A rocking motion. **3.** Rock 'n' roll. **—*idiom.* rock the boat.** *Slang.* To disturb the balance of a situation. [ME *rokken* < OE *roccian.*] **—rock′ing·ly** *adv.*

rock·a·bil·ly (rŏk′ə-bĭl′ē) *n.* A form of popular music combining rock 'n' roll and country and western styles. [ROCK ('N' ROLL) + (HILL)BILLY.]

rock·a·by also **rock·a·bye** or **rock-a-bye** (rŏk′ə-bī′) *interj.* Used to lull an infant to sleep. [ROCK + (LULL)ABY.]

rock-and-roll (rŏk′ən-rōl′) *n.* Variant of **rock 'n' roll.**

rock and rye *n.* A rye whiskey bottled commercially with rock candy and fruit.

rock·a·way (rŏk′ə-wā′) *n.* A four-wheeled carriage with two seats and a standing top. [After *Rockaway,* a town in New Jersey where it was first made.]

rock bass *n.* **1.** A freshwater food fish, *Ambloplites rupestris,* of eastern and central North America. **2.** Any of various fishes similar or related to the rock bass.

rock bottom *n.* The lowest level or absolute bottom: *Prices have reached rock bottom.* **—rock′-bot′tom** (rŏk′bŏt′əm) *adj.*

rock-bound (rŏk′bound′) *adj.* Hemmed in by or bordered with rocks: *a rock-bound lake.*

rock candy *n.* Sugar in the form of large, hard, clear crystals.

Rock Cornish hen *n.* A small fowl of a breed developed by crossing white Plymouth Rock and Cornish strains, used esp. as a roasting chicken.

rock crystal *n.* Transparent quartz, esp. when colorless.

rock dove *n.* A bird, *Columba livia,* native to Europe but widely distributed elsewhere, having variously colored plumage with iridescent neck markings. It is the common pigeon seen in cities and frequently domesticated.

rock·er (rŏk′ər) *n.* **1.** A person who rocks something, such as a cradle. **2.** A rocking chair. **3.** A rocking horse. **4.** One of the two curved pieces upon which a cradle, rocking chair, or similar device rocks. **5.** A cradle used for washing or panning ores. **6.** A small steel plate with a curved, toothed edge used to roughen a copper plate for a mezzotint. **7.** An ice skate with a curved blade. **8.** A curved stripe at the bottom part of a chevron worn by noncommissioned officers below the rank of sergeant. **9. a.** A rock song, singer, or musician. **b.** A fan of rock music. **—*idiom.* off (one's) rocker.** *Slang.* Out of one's mind; crazy.

rocker arm *n.* A pivoted lever, as in an automobile engine, used to transfer cam or pushrod motion to a valve stem.

rocker cam *n.* A cam on a rockshaft.

rock·er·y (rŏk′ə-rē) *n., pl.* **-ies.** A rock garden.

rock·et¹ (rŏk′ĭt) *n.* **1. a.** A device propelled by ejection of matter, esp. by the high-velocity ejection of the gaseous combustion products produced by internal ignition of solid or liquid fuels. **b.** An engine that propels in this manner. **2. a.** A weapon carrying an explosive or other warhead and using rocket power. **b.** An incendiary weapon with a rounded hollow warhead filled with explosives and formerly fired from a ship. **3.** A firework for aerial display. —*v.* **-et·ed, -et·ing, -ets.** —*intr.* **1.** To move swiftly, as a rocket does. **2.** To fly swiftly straight up, as a frightened game bird. **3.** To rise rapidly or unexpectedly; skyrocket. —*tr.* **1.** To assault with rockets. **2.** To carry by means of a rocket. [Ital. *rochetta,* dim. of *rocca,* distaff, of Germanic orig.]

rock·et² (rŏk′ĭt) *n.* **1.** A plant, *Eruca sativa,* native to Eurasia, having yellowish-white flowers and leaves that are sometimes used in salads. **2.** Any of several plants, esp. one of the genus *Hesperis,* that are related to the rocket. [OFr. *roquette* < Ital. *ruchetta,* dim. of *ruca* < Lat. *eruca,* a kind of cabbage.]

rock·et·eer (rŏk′ĭ-tîr′) *n.* A person who designs, launches, studies, or pilots rockets.

rocket engine *n.* An engine that propels by means of rockets, esp. one that propels spacecraft or aircraft.

rocket motor *n.* A rocket engine, esp. one using solid propellants.

rock·et·ry (rŏk′ĭ-trē) *n.* The science and technology of rocket design, construction, and flight.

rock·et·sonde (rŏk′ĭt-sŏnd′) *n.* A rocket used for observation in the upper atmosphere. [ROCKET + Fr. *sonde,* sounding line < OFr., prob. of Germanic orig.]

rock·fish (rŏk′fĭsh′) *n., pl.* **rockfish** or **-fish·es. 1.** Any of various fishes living among rocks. **2.** Any of various fishes, chiefly of the genus *Sebastodes,* of Pacific waters. **3.** The striped bass.

rock flour *n.* Pulverized rock produced by glacial abrasion.

rock garden *n.* A rocky area in which plants particularly adapted to such terrain are cultivated.

rock hound *n.* **1.** One who specializes in geology. **2.** One who collects rocks and minerals as a hobby.

rocking chair *n.* A chair mounted on rockers or springs.

rocking horse *n.* A toy horse large enough for a child to ride, mounted upon rockers or springs.

rock·ling (rŏk′lĭng) *n., pl.* **rockling** or **-lings.** Any of various small marine fishes of the family Gadidae, of North Atlantic coastal waters.

rock lobster *n.* The spiny lobster.

rock maple *n.* **1.** The sugar maple. **2.** The tough, close-grained wood of the sugar maple.

rock 'n' roll (rŏk′ ən rōl′) also **rock-and-roll** (rŏk′ən-rōl′) *n.* Popular music combining elements of rhythm and blues with country and western music and having a heavily accented beat.

rock oil *n. Chiefly Brit.* Petroleum.

rock·oon (rŏ-ko͞on′) *n.* A device used for high-altitude research sounding, composed of a small, solid-propellant rocket carried aloft by a balloon. [ROCK(ET) + (BALL)OON.]

robin

robot

roc
Illustration by
Edward W. Lane

rockaway

rocking chair

rock-ribbed (rŏk′rĭbd′) *adj.* **1.** Having rocks or rock outcroppings. **2.** Stern and unyielding.
rock·rose (rŏk′rōz′) *n.* Any of various plants or shrubs of the genus *Helianthemum* and related genera, having roselike yellow, white, or reddish flowers.
rock salt *n.* Common salt, essentially sodium chloride, occurring in large solid masses.
rock·shaft (rŏk′shăft′) *n.* A shaft that oscillates or rocks upon its bearings but does not revolve.
rock·weed (rŏk′wēd′) *n.* Any of several coarse, brownish seaweeds of the genera *Fucus* and *Ascophyllum* that grow on rocks in coastal areas.
rock·work (rŏk′wûrk′) *n.* **1.** A natural mass of rocks. **2.** Stonework imitating the irregular surface of natural rocks.
rock·y[1] (rŏk′ē) *adj.* **-i·er, -i·est. 1.** Consisting of, containing, or abounding in rock or rocks. **2.** Resembling or suggesting rock; firm or hard. **3.** Marked by obstructions or difficulties: *the rocky road to success.* **—rock′i·ness** *n.*
rock·y[2] (rŏk′ē) *adj.* **-i·er, -i·est. 1.** Inclined or prone to sway or totter; unsteady or shaky. **2.** Weak, dizzy, or nauseated. **—rock′i·ness** *n.*
Rocky Mountain goat *n.* The mountain goat.
Rocky Mountain sheep *n.* The bighorn.
Rocky Mountain spotted fever *n.* An acute infectious disease caused by a microorganism, *Rickettsia rickettsii,* transmitted by ticks, characterized by muscular pains, high fever, and skin eruptions, and endemic throughout North America.
ro·co·co (rə-kō′kō, rō′kə-kō′) *adj.* **1.** Of or relating to an artistic style originating in 18th-century France and characterized by fanciful asymmetric ornamentation. **2.** Excessively elaborate; ornate. **3.** *Mus.* Of or relating to an 18th-century style immediately following the baroque in Europe. *—n.* Rococo style or work. [Fr., alteration of *rocaille,* rockwork < *roc,* rock, var. of *roche* < OFr.]
rod (rŏd) *n.* **1.** A straight, thin piece or bar of material such as metal or wood. **2.** A shoot or stem cut from or growing as part of a woody plant. **3. a.** A stick or bundle of sticks used for whipping. **b.** Punishment; correction. **4.** A fishing rod. **5.** A scepter or staff symbolizing power or authority; wand. **6.** Power or dominion, esp. of a tyrannical nature. **7.** A metal bar in a machine: *a piston rod.* **8.** A measuring stick. **9.** A leveling rod. **10.** A lightning rod. **11.** A divining rod. **12. a.** A linear measure equal to 5.5 yards, 16.5 feet, or 5.03 meters. **b.** A unit of measure equal to 30.25 square yards. **13.** *Anat.* Any of various rod-shaped cells in the retina that respond to dim light. **14.** *Microbiol.* An elongated microorganism. **15.** *Slang.* A pistol or revolver. **16.** A drawbar under a freight car. [ME *rodd* < OE.]
rode (rōd) *v.* Past tense of **ride.**
ro·dent (rōd′nt) *n.* Any of various mammals of the order Rodentia, such as a mouse, rat, squirrel, or beaver, characterized by large incisors adapted for gnawing or nibbling. *—adj.* **1.** Gnawing. **2.** Of or pertaining to rodents. [< NLat. *Rodentia,* order name < Lat. *rodens,* pr.part. of *rodere,* to gnaw.]
ro·den·ti·cide (rō-dĕn′tĭ-sīd′) *n.* An agent used to kill rodents.

rodeo

ro·de·o (rō′dē-ō′, rō-dā′ō) *n., pl.* **-os. 1.** A cattle roundup. **2.** An enclosure for keeping cattle that have been rounded up. **3.** A competition in which cowboys display skills such as riding broncos or lassoing. [Sp. < *rodear,* to surround < Lat. *rotare,* to rotate < *rota,* wheel.]
rod·o·mon·tade also **rhod·o·mon·tade** (rŏd′ə-mŏn-tād′, -täd′, rō′də-) *n.* Pretentious boasting or bragging; bluster. *—adj.* Pretentiously boastful or bragging. *—intr.v.* **-tad·ed, -tad·ing, -tades.** To boast or brag; bluster. [OFr. < OItal. *rodomontada* < *Rodomonte,* a character in *Orlando Innamorata,* by Matteo Boiardo (1434–1494).]
roe[1] (rō) *n.* **1.** The egg-laden ovary of a fish. **2.** The egg mass of certain crustaceans, such as the lobster. **3.** Soft roe. [ME *row.*]
roe[2] (rō) *n.* The roe deer. [ME *ro* < OE *rā.*]
roe·buck (rō′bŭk′) *n.* A male roe deer.
roe deer *n.* A rather small, delicately formed Eurasian deer, *Capreolus capreolus,* having a brownish coat and short, branched antlers in the male.
roent·gen also **rönt·gen** (rĕnt′gən, -jən, rŭnt′-) *n. Physics.* An obsolete unit of radiation dosage equal to the quantity of ionizing radiation that will produce one electrostatic unit of electricity in one cubic centimeter of dry air at 0°C and standard atmospheric pressure. [After Wilhelm Konrad *Roentgen* (1845–1923).] **—roent′gen** *adj.*
roent·gen·ize (rĕnt′gə-nīz′, -jə-, rŭnt′-) *tr.v.* **-ized, -iz·ing, -iz·es.** To subject to the action of x-rays.
roentgeno– *pref.* X-ray: *roentgenography.* [< ROENTGEN.]
roent·gen·o·gram (rĕnt′gə-nə-grăm′, -jə-, rŭnt′-) also **roent·gen·o·graph** (-grăf′) *n.* A photograph made with x-rays.
roent·gen·o·graph (rĕnt′gə-nə-grăf′, -jə-, rŭnt′-) *n.* A roentgenogram.
roent·gen·og·ra·phy (rĕnt′gə-nŏg′rə-fē, -jə-, rŭnt′-) *n.* Photography with the use of x-rays. **—roent′gen·o·graph′ic** (-nə-grăf′ĭk) *adj.* **—roent′gen·o·graph′ic·al·ly** *adv.*
roent·gen·ol·o·gy (rĕnt′gə-nŏl′ə-jē, -jə-, rŭnt′-) *n.* Radiology with x-rays. **—roent′gen·o·log′ic** (-ə-lŏj′ĭk), **roent′gen·o·log′i·cal** *adj.* **—roent′gen·o·log′i·cal·ly** *adv.* **—roent′gen·ol′o·gist** *n.*
roent·gen·o·scope (rĕnt′gə-nə-skōp′, -jə-, rŭnt′-) *n.* A fluoroscope. **—roent′gen·o·scop′ic** (-skŏp′ĭk) *adj.* **—roent′gen·os′co·py** (-nŏs′kə-pē) *n.*
roent·gen·o·ther·a·py (rĕnt′gə-nə-thĕr′ə-pē, -jə-, rŭnt′-) *n.* The therapeutic use of x-rays in treating disease.
Roentgen ray *n.* An x-ray (sense 1.b.).
ro·ga·tion (rō-gā′shən) *n.* **1.** Often **rogations.** *Eccles.* Solemn prayer or supplication, esp. as chanted during the rites of Rogation Day. **2. a.** The proposal of a law by tribune or consul to the people of ancient Rome for acceptance or rejection. **b.** A law proposed in this manner. [ME *rogacioun* < Lat. *rogatio* < *rogare,* to ask.]
Rogation Day *n. Eccles.* One of the three days of prayer preceding Ascension Day.
ro·ga·to·ry (rō′gə-tôr′ē, -tōr′ē) *adj.* Requesting information; questioning. [Fr. *rogatoire* < Med. Lat. *rogatorius* < Lat. *rogare,* to ask.]
rog·er (rŏj′ər) *interj.* Used in radio communications to indicate that a message has been received. [< the name *Roger,* code word for the letter *r.*]
rogue (rōg) *n.* **1.** An unprincipled person; scoundrel. **2.** A person who is playfully mischievous; scamp. **3.** *Archaic.* A wandering beggar; vagrant. **4.** A vicious and solitary animal, esp. an elephant that has separated itself from its herd. **5.** An organism, esp. a plant, that shows an undesirable variation from a standard. *—v.* **rogued, rogu·ing, rogues.** *—tr.* **1.** To defraud. **2.** To remove (diseased or abnormal specimens) from a group of plants of the same variety. *—intr.* To remove undesired plant specimens. [Orig. unknown.]
rogu·er·y (rō′gə-rē) *n., pl.* **-ies. 1.** Behavior characteristic of a rogue. **2.** A mischievous act.
rogues' gallery *n.* A collection of pictures of criminals maintained in police files and used for making identifications.
rogu·ish (rō′gĭsh) *adj.* **1.** Dishonest; unprincipled. **2.** Playfully mischievous. **—rogu′ish·ly** *adv.* **—rogu′ish·ness** *n.*
roil (roil) *v.* **roiled, roil·ing, roils.** *—tr.* **1.** To make (a liquid) muddy or cloudy by stirring up sediment. **2.** To displease or disturb; vex. *—intr.* To be in a state of turbulence or agitation. [Orig. unknown.]
roil·y (roi′lē) *adj.* **-i·er, -i·est. 1.** Muddy; cloudy. **2.** Agitated.
rois·ter (roi′stər) *intr.v.* **-tered, -ter·ing, -ters. 1.** To engage in boisterous merrymaking; revel noisily. **2.** To behave in a blustering manner; swagger. [< obs. *roister,* roisterer, prob. < OFr. *rustre,* ruffian, alteration of *ruste* < Lat. *rusticus,* rustic < *rus,* country.] **—rois′ter·er** *n.* **—rois′ter·ous** *adj.*
ro·la·mite (rō′lə-mīt′) *n.* A device consisting of two or more hard cylindrical rollers fitted between two parallel constraints with a flexible nonstretching band looped around them in which the rollers move against each other within the constraints with very little friction to perform various functions. [ROL(L) + *-amite,* of unknown orig.]
Ro·land (rō′lənd, rô-läɴ′) *n.* A legendary defender of the Christians and nephew of Charlemagne killed in the battle against the Saracens at Roncesvalles (A.D. 778).
role also **rôle** (rōl) *n.* **1.** A character or part played by an actor in a dramatic performance. **2.** The characteristic and expected social behavior of an individual. **3.** A function or position. [Fr. *rôle* < OFr. *rolle,* roll of parchment < Lat. *rotula,* little wheel, dim. of *rota,* wheel.]
role model *n.* An individual who serves as a model in a particular behavioral role for another individual to emulate.
role-play (rōl′plā′) *v.* **-played, -play·ing, -plays.** *—tr.* To play the part of; act out. *—intr.* To play a role.
rolf·ing (rôl′fĭng, rŏl′-) *n.* A technique of deep, often painful muscular manipulation and massage designed to relieve both bodily and emotional tension. [After Ida *Rolf* (d. 1979).]
roll (rōl) *v.* **rolled, roll·ing, rolls.** *—intr.* **1.** To move forward along a surface by revolving on an axis or by repeatedly turning over. **2.** To travel or be moved on wheels or rollers. **3.** To travel around or wander: *roll from town to town.* **4. a.** To travel or be carried in a vehicle. **b.** To be carried on a stream: *The logs rolled down the cascading river.* **5.** To gain momentum: *The political campaign began to roll.* **6.** To go by; elapse: *The days rolled by.* **7.** To recur periodically; move as if in cycles: *Summer has rolled around again.* **8.** To move in a periodic revolution, as a planet in its orbit. **9.** To turn over and over: *The puppy rolled in the mud.* **10.** To shift the eyes usually quickly and continually: *Her eyes rolled with fright.* **11.** To turn around or revolve on or as if on an axis. **12.** To advance with a rising and falling motion; undulate: *The waves rolled toward shore.* **13.** To extend or appear to extend in gentle rises and falls: *The hills roll to the sea.* **14.** To move or rock from side to side, as a ship. **15.** To walk with a swaying, unsteady motion. **16.** To take the shape of a ball or cylinder: *Yarn rolls easily.* **17.** To become flattened by or as if by pressure applied by a roller. **18.** To make a deep, prolonged, surging sound, as thunder. **19.** To make a sustained, trilling sound, as certain birds. **20.** To beat a drum in a continuous series of short blows. **21.** To pour or flow in a continual stream: *tourists rolling in.* **22.** To

enjoy ample amounts: *rolling in money.* —*tr.* **1.** To cause to move forward along a surface by revolving on an axis or by repeatedly turning over. **2.** To move or push along on wheels or rollers: *roll the plane out of the hangar.* **3.** To impel or send onward in a steady, swelling motion: *The sea rolls its waves onto the sand.* **4.** To impart a swaying, rocking motion to: *Heavy seas rolled the ship.* **5.** To turn around or partly turn around; rotate: *rolled his head toward the door.* **6.** To cause to begin moving or operating: *roll the cameras.* **7.** To extend or lay out: *rolled out a long rope.* **8.** To pronounce or utter with a trill: *You must roll your "r's" in Spanish.* **9.** To utter or emit in full, swelling tones. **10.** To beat (a drum) with a continuous series of short blows. **11.** To wrap (something) round and round upon itself or around something else: *roll up a scroll.* **12. a.** To envelop or enfold in a covering: *roll laundry in a sheet.* **b.** To make by shaping into a ball or cylinder: *roll a cigarette.* **13.** To spread, compress, or flatten by applying pressure with a roller: *roll dough.* **14.** *Printing.* To apply ink to (type) with a roller or rollers. **15.** To throw (dice) in craps or other games. **16.** *Slang.* To rob (a drunken, sleeping, or otherwise helpless person). —***phrasal verbs.*** **roll back. 1.** To reduce (prices or wages) to a previous lower level. **2.** To cause to retreat; turn back. **roll out.** To get out of bed. **roll up. 1.** *Informal.* To arrive in a vehicle. **2.** To amass; accumulate: *roll up a fortune.* —*n.* **1.** The act or an instance of rolling. **2.** Something rolled up in the form of a cylinder: *a roll of tape.* **3.** A quantity of something, such as cloth or wallpaper, rolled into a cylinder and often considered as a unit of measure. **4.** A piece of parchment or paper that may be or is rolled up; scroll. **5.** A register or catalogue. **6.** A list of names of persons belonging to a given group. **7.** A mass of something in cylindrical or rounded form: *a roll of tobacco.* **8. a.** A small rounded portion of bread. **b.** A portion of food shaped like a tube with a filling. **9.** A rolling, swaying, or rocking motion. **10.** A gentle swell or undulation of a surface: *the roll of the plains.* **11.** A deep reverberation or rumble. **12.** A rapid succession of short sounds: *the roll of a drum.* **13.** A trill: *the roll of his "r's."* **14.** A resonant, rhythmical flow of words. **15.** A roller, esp. a cylinder on which to roll something up or with which to flatten something. **16.** A maneuver in which an airplane makes a single complete rotation about its longitudinal axis without changing direction or losing altitude. **17.** *Slang.* Money, esp. a wad of paper money. —***idiom.*** **roll the bones.** To cast dice, esp. in craps. [ME *rollen* < OFr. *roler* < VLat. **rotulare* < Lat. *rotula,* little wheel, dim. of *rota,* wheel.]

roll·a·way (rōl′ə-wā′) *adj.* Set upon rollers for easy moving and storing: *a rollaway bed.*

roll·back (rōl′băk′) *n.* A reduction of prices or wages to a previous lower level by governmental action or direction.

roll bar *n.* A sturdy metal bar built into the inside roof of an automobile to prevent or reduce injury in case of a rollover.

roll call *n.* **1.** The reading aloud of a list of names of people, as in a classroom or military post, to determine who is absent. **2.** The time fixed for a roll call.

roll·er (rō′lər) *n.* **1.** One that rolls. **2.** Any of various cylindrical devices, esp.: **a.** A small, spokeless wheel, such as that of a roller skate or caster. **b.** An elongated cylinder upon which something such as a window shade or towel is wound. **c.** A heavy cylinder used to perform leveling or crushing operations. **d.** *Printing.* A cylinder, usually of hard rubber, used to ink the type before the paper is impressed. **e.** A cylinder of wire mesh, foam rubber, or other material around which a strand of hair is wound to produce a soft curl or wave. **3.** A long, rolled bandage. **4.** A heavy, swelling wave that breaks on a coast. **5.** Any of various African, Far Eastern, and Australian birds of the family Coraciidae, having bright-blue wings, stocky bodies, and hooked bills and noted for their aggressiveness.

roller bearing *n.* A bearing using rollers to reduce friction between machine parts.

roller coaster *n.* A steep, sharply banked elevated railway with small open passenger cars, operated as an amusement-park entertainment.

roller skate *n.* A shoe with four small wheels attached to it for skating on sidewalks and hard floors.

roll·er-skate (rō′lər-skāt′) *intr.v.* **-skat·ed, -skat·ing, -skates.** To skate on roller skates. **—roller skater** *n.*

Rolle's theorem (rôlz, rōlz) *n.* A theorem in mathematics stating that if a curve is continuous, has two x-intercepts, and has a tangent at every point between the intercepts, at least one of these tangents is parallel to the x-axis. [After Michel *Rolle* (d. 1719).]

roll film *n.* Photographic film rolled on a spool.

rol·lick (rŏl′ĭk) *intr.v.* **-licked, -lick·ing, -licks.** To behave or move in a carefree, frolicsome manner; romp. —*n.* A carefree escapade; lark. [Orig. unknown.] **—rol′lick·some, rol′lick·y** *adj.*

rol·lick·ing (rŏl′ĭ-kĭng) *adj.* Carefree and high-spirited; boisterous. **—rol′lick·ing·ly** *adv.*

rolling mill *n.* **1.** A factory in which metal is rolled into sheets, bars, or other forms. **2.** A machine used for rolling metal.

rolling pin *n.* A smooth cylinder, usually of wood, with a handle at each end, used for rolling out dough.

rolling stock *n.* A railroad's wheeled vehicles.

roll·mops (rōl′mŏps′) *n., pl.* **rollmops.** A marinated fillet of herring wrapped around a gherkin or onion and served as an hors d'oeuvre. [G. : *rollen,* to roll + *Mops,* pug dog.]

roll·o·ver (rōl′ō′vər) *n.* **1.** The act or process of rolling over. **2.** An accident in which a motor vehicle overturns.

roll-top desk (rōl′tŏp′) *n.* A desk fitted with a flexible sliding top made of parallel slats.

roll·way (rōl′wā′) *n.* A surface along which cylinders or objects on rollers may be moved.

ro·ly-po·ly (rō′lē-pō′lē) *adj.* Short and plump; pudgy. —*n., pl.* **-lies. 1.** A roly-poly creature. **2.** *Chiefly Brit.* A pudding made by rolling up jam or fruit in pastry dough and cooking it. [Redup. of *roly* < ROLL.]

Ro·ma·ic (rō-mā′ĭk) *n.* Modern vernacular Greek. [Mod. Gk. *Rhōmaikos* < Gk., Roman < *Rhōmē,* Rome < Lat. *Roma.*] **—Ro·ma′ic** *adj.*

ro·maine (rō-mān′) *n.* A variety of lettuce, *Lactuca sativa longifolia,* having long crisp leaves forming a slender head. [Fr. < fem. of *Romain,* Roman < OFr. < Lat. *Romanus* < *Roma,* Rome.]

ro·man (rō-mäN′) *n.* A metrical narrative of medieval France derived from the ancient epic poems. [Fr. < OFr. *romans,* romance.]

Ro·man (rō′mən) *adj.* **1.** Of, pertaining to, derived from, or characteristic of Rome and its people, esp. ancient Rome. **2.** Of, pertaining to, composed in, or characteristic of the Latin language. **3.** Of or pertaining to the Roman Catholic Church. **4.** Of or designating an architectural style developed by the ancient Romans and characterized by great round arches and barrel vaults, concrete masonry construction, and classical orders as decorative features. **5. roman.** Of, set, or printed in type characterized by upright letters. —*n.* **1.** A native, resident, or citizen of Rome, esp. ancient Rome. **2.** The Italian language as spoken in Rome. **3.** One belonging to the Roman Catholic Church. **4. roman.** Roman type or letters. [ME < OE *Rōmān* < Lat. *Romanus* < *Roma,* Rome.]

ro·man à clef (rō-mäN′ ä klā′) *n., pl.* **ro·mans à clef** (rō-mäN′ ä klā′). A novel in which actual persons or places are depicted in fictional guise. [Fr. : *roman,* novel + *à,* with + *clef,* key.]

Roman alphabet *n.* The Latin alphabet.

Roman calendar *n.* The lunar calendar used by the ancient Romans until the introduction of the Julian calendar in 46 B.C.

Roman candle *n.* A firework consisting of a tube from which balls of fire are ejected.

Roman Catholic *adj.* Of, designating, or pertaining to the Roman Catholic Church. —*n.* A member of the Roman Catholic Church.

Roman Catholic Church *n.* The Christian church that is characterized by a hierarchic structure of bishops and priests in which doctrinal and disciplinary authority are dependent upon apostolic succession, with the pope as head of the episcopal college.

Roman Catholicism *n.* The doctrines, practices, and organization of the Roman Catholic Church.

ro·mance (rō-măns′, rō′măns′) *n.* **1. a.** A long medieval narrative in prose or verse telling of the adventures of chivalric heroes. **b.** A long, fictitious tale of heroes and extraordinary or mysterious events. **c.** The class of literature of such tales. **d.** A quality suggestive of the adventure and idealized exploits found in such tales: *"These fine old guns often have a romance clinging to them"* (Richard Jefferies). **2.** A novel, story, or film dealing with a love affair. **3.** The class or style of fictional works about idealized love. **4. a.** A love affair. **b.** Romantic involvement; love. **c.** A strong, usually short-lived attachment or enthusiasm. **5.** Inclination toward the romantic or adventurous; romantic spirit. **6.** A fictitiously embellished account or explanation. **7.** A short lyrical song or instrumental piece. **8. Romance.** The Romance languages. —*adj.* **Romance.** Of, pertaining to, or constituting the languages that developed from Latin. —*v.* (rō-măns′) **-manced, -manc·ing, -manc·es.** —*intr.* **1.** To invent, write, or tell romances. **2.** To think or behave in a romantic manner. —*tr. Informal.* **1.** To make romantic love to; woo. **2.** To have a love affair with. [ME < OFr. *romans,* romance, work written in French < Lat. *Romanicus,* Roman < *Romanus* < *Roma,* Rome.] **—ro·manc′er** *n.*

Ro·man·esque (rō′mə-nĕsk′) *adj.* **1.** Of, pertaining to, or designating a transitional style of European architecture prevalent from the 9th to the 12th century. **2.** Of, pertaining to, or designating styles in painting and sculpture corresponding to Romanesque. —*n.* A Romanesque style of architecture, painting, or sculpture.

ro·man-fleuve (rō-mäN′flœv′) *n., pl.* **ro·mans-fleuves** (rō-mäN′flœv′). A long novel, often in many volumes, chronicling the history of several generations of a family, community, or other group. [Fr. : *roman,* novel + *fleuve,* river.]

Roman holiday *n.* **1.** A time of debauchery or of often sadistic enjoyment. **2.** A violent disturbance; riot. [From the bloody gladiatorial contests staged as entertainment for the ancient Romans.]

George Miksch Sutton

roller

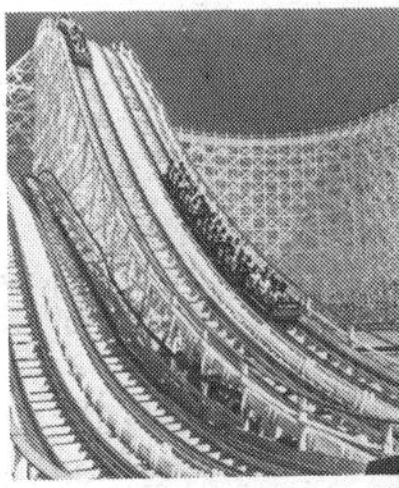

roller coaster

roller-skate

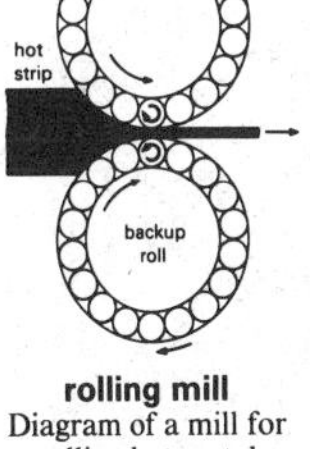

rolling mill
Diagram of a mill for rolling hot metal

I	1
II	2
III	3
IV	4
V	5
VI	6
VII	7
VIII	8
IX	9
X	10
XI	11
XII	12
XIII	13
XIV	14
XV	15
XVI	16
XVII	17
XVIII	18
XIX	19
XX	20
XXI	21
XXIX	29
XXX	30
XL	40
XLVIII	48
IL	49
L	50
LX	60
XC	90
XCVIII	98
IC	99
C	100
CI	101
CC	200
D	500
DC	600
CM	900
M	1,000
MDCLXVI	1666
MCMLXXX	1980

Roman numeral

Ro·ma·ni·an (rō-mā′nē-ən, -mān′yən) *adj. & n.* Variant of **Rumanian.**

Ro·man·ic (rō-măn′ĭk) *adj.* **1.** Of or derived from the ancient Romans. **2.** Romance. —**Ro·man′ic** *n.*

Ro·man·ism (rō′mə-nĭz′əm) *n.* Roman Catholicism.

Ro·man·ist (rō′mə-nĭst) *n.* **1.** One who professes Roman Catholicism. **2.** A student of or authority on Roman law, culture, and institutions.

Ro·man·ize (rō′mə-nīz′) *tr.v.* **-ized, -iz·ing, -iz·es. 1.** To convert (someone) to Roman Catholicism. **2.** To make Roman in character, allegiance, or style. **3.** To write or transliterate in the Latin alphabet. —**Ro′man·i·za′tion** *n.*

Roman law *n.* The system of laws of ancient Rome, upon which the legal systems of many countries are based.

Roman nose *n.* A nose with a high, prominent bridge.

Roman numeral *n.* Any of the numerals formed with the characters I, V, X, L, C, D, and M in the ancient system of numeration.

Ro·ma·no (rə-mä′nō, rō-) *n.* A hard, dry Italian cheese similar to but sharper than Parmesan. [Ital., Roman < Lat. *Romanus.*]

Ro·mans (rō′mənz) *pl.n. (used with a sing. verb).* See table at **Bible.**

Ro·mansch also **Ro·mansh** (rō-mänsh′, -mănsh′) *n.* The Rhaeto-Romanic dialects of eastern Switzerland and neighboring parts of Italy. [Romansch *Romantsch* < Lat. *Romanicus,* Roman. —see ROMANCE.]

ro·man·tic (rō-măn′tĭk) *adj.* **1.** Of, pertaining to, or characteristic of romance. **2.** Given to thoughts or feelings of romance. **3.** Conducive to romance. **4.** Imaginative but impractical: *romantic notions.* **5.** Not based on fact; imaginary. **6.** Of or characteristic of romanticism in the arts. —*n.* **1.** A romantic person. **2.** A romanticist. [Fr. *romantique* < OFr. *romans,* romance.] —**ro·man′ti·cal·ly** *adv.*

ro·man·ti·cism (rō-măn′tĭ-sĭz′əm) *n.* **1.** An artistic and intellectual movement that originated in the late 18th century and stressed strong emotion, imagination, freedom from classical correctness in art forms, and rebellion against social conventions. **2.** The spirit and attitudes characteristic of romantic thought. —**ro·man′ti·cist** *n.*

ro·man·ti·cize (rō-măn′tĭ-sīz′) *v.* **-cized, -ciz·ing, -ciz·es.** —*tr.* To interpret romantically. —*intr.* To think in a romantic way. —**ro·man′ti·ci·za′tion** *n.*

Rom·a·ny (rŏm′ə-nē, rō′mə-) *n., pl.* **Romany** or **-nies. 1.** A Gypsy. **2.** The Indic language of the Gypsies. [Romany *romani,* pl. of *romano,* gypsy < *rom,* man < Skt. *ḍomaḥ,* man of a low caste.] —**Rom′a·ny** *adj.*

ro·maunt (rō-mônt′, -mŏnt′) *n. Archaic.* A verse romance. [ME < OFr. *romant,* romance < Lat. *Romanicus,* Roman. —see ROMANCE.]

Ro·me·o (rō′mē-ō′) *n., pl.* **-os.** A male lover. [After *Romeo,* the hero of *Romeo and Juliet* by William Shakespeare (1564–1616).]

Rom·ish (rō′mĭsh) *adj.* Of or pertaining to the Roman Catholic Church. —**Rom′ish·ly** *adv.* —**Rom′ish·ness** *n.*

romp (rŏmp) *intr.v.* **romped, romp·ing, romps. 1.** To play or frolic boisterously. **2.** *Slang.* To win easily. —*n.* **1.** Lively, merry play; frolic. **2.** One, esp. a girl, that sports and frolics. **3.** *Slang.* An easy win. [Alteration of RAMP[2].]

romp·er (rŏm′pər) *n.* **1.** One that romps. **2. rompers.** A loose-fitting playsuit with short bloomers worn esp. by small children.

Rom·u·lus (rŏm′yə-ləs) *n. Rom. Myth.* The son of Mars and legendary founder of Rome. [Lat.]

ron·deau (rŏn′dō, rŏn-dō′) *n., pl.* **-deaux** (-dōz, -dōz′). **1.** A lyrical poem of French origin having 13 or sometimes 10 lines with two rhymes throughout and with the opening phrase repeated twice as a refrain. **2.** *Mus.* A monophonic trouvère song. [OFr., alteration of *rondel.* —see RONDEL.]

ron·del (rŏn′dəl, rŏn-dĕl′) *n.* A rondeau that usually has 14 lines. [ME < OFr., dim. of *ronde,* circle, round. —see ROUND.]

ron·de·let (rŏn′dl-ĕt′, -dl-ā′) *n.* A short rondeau having five or seven lines and one refrain in one stanza. [OFr., dim. of *rondel,* rondel.]

ron·do (rŏn′dō, rŏn-dō′) *n., pl.* **-dos.** A musical composition having a refrain that occurs at least three times in its original key between contrasting couplets. [Ital. *rondò* < OFr. *rondeau,* rondeau.]

ron·dure (rŏn′jər, -dyŏŏr′) *n.* Something circular or gracefully rounded. [OFr. *rondeur,* roundness < *ronde,* round. —see ROUND.]

ron·nel (rŏn′əl) *n.* **1.** A solid, light-brown compound, $C_8H_8Cl_3O_3PS$, used as an insecticide, esp. against flies and cockroaches. **2. Ronnel.** A trademark for ronnel outside the United States. [< *Ronnel,* a non-U.S. trademark.]

rönt·gen (rĕnt′gən, -jən, rŭnt′-) *n.* Variant of **roentgen.**

rood (rōōd) *n.* **1. a.** A crucifix symbolizing the cross on which Christ was crucified. **b.** A large crucifix or the representation of one over the altar screen of a medieval church. **2.** *Chiefly Brit.* A measure of length that varies from 5½ to 8 yards. **3.** A measure of land equal to ¼ acre, or 40 square rods. [ME < OE *rōd.*]

rood screen *n.* An ornamented altar screen, usually surmounted by a crucifix, separating the choir of a church from the nave.

roof (rōōf, rŏŏf) *n.* **1.** The exterior surface and its supporting structures on the top of a building. **2.** The top covering of something: *the roof of a car.* **3. a.** A vaulted inner structure: *the roof of the mouth.* **b.** The highest point; summit: *the roof of the world.* **4.** A house or home. —*tr.v.* **roofed, roof·ing, roofs.** To furnish or cover with or as if with a roof. —*idiom.* **raise the roof.** *Slang.* **1.** To be extremely noisy and boisterous. **2.** To complain loudly and bitterly. [ME < OE *hrōf.*]

roof·er (rōō′fər, rŏŏf′ər) *n.* One who lays or repairs roofs.

roof garden *n.* **1.** A garden on the roof of an urban building. **2.** A restaurant at the top or on the roof of a building that often features music and dancing.

roof·ing (rōō′fĭng, rŏŏf′ĭng) *n.* Materials used in building a roof.

roof·less (rōōf′lĭs, rŏŏf′-) *adj.* **1.** Lacking a roof. **2.** Having no home or shelter; homeless.

roof·top (rōōf′tŏp′, rŏŏf′-) *n.* The surface of a roof, esp. of a flat roof.

roof·tree (rōōf′trē′, rŏŏf′-) *n.* **1.** A long horizontal beam extending along the ridge of a roof; ridgepole. **2.** A roof.

rook[1] (rŏŏk) *n.* A crowlike Old World bird, *Corvus frugilegus,* that nests in colonies near the tops of trees. —*tr.v.* **rooked, rook·ing, rooks.** *Slang.* To swindle. [ME *rok* < OE *hrōc.*]

rook[2] (rŏŏk) *n.* A chess piece that may move in a straight line over any number of empty squares in a rank or file. [ME *rok* < OFr. *roc* < Ar. *rukh* < Pers.]

rook·er·y (rŏŏk′ə-rē) *n., pl.* **-ies. 1. a.** A place where rooks nest and breed. **b.** The breeding ground of certain other birds and animals, such as seals. **2.** *Informal.* A crowded and run-down tenement.

rook·ie (rŏŏk′ē) *n. Slang.* **1.** An untrained recruit. **2.** A novice player in sports. **3.** An inexperienced person. [Alteration of RECRUIT.]

room (rōōm, rŏŏm) *n.* **1.** A space that is or may be occupied by something: *a desk that takes up too much room.* **2. a.** An area separated by walls or partitions from other similar parts of the structure or building in which it is located. **b.** The people present in such an area: *The whole room laughed.* **3. rooms.** Living quarters. **4.** Suitable opportunity: *room for error.* —*intr.v.* **roomed, room·ing, rooms.** To occupy a room; lodge. [ME *roum* < OE *rūm.*]

room and board *n.* Lodging and meals either earned or provided.

room·er (rōō′mər, rŏŏm′ər) *n.* A lodger.

room·ette (rōō-mĕt′, rŏŏm-ĕt′) *n.* A small private compartment in a railroad sleeping car.

room·ful (rōōm′fŏŏl′, rŏŏm′-) *n., pl.* **-fuls. 1.** As much or as many as a room will hold. **2.** The number of people in a room.

rooming house *n.* A house where lodgers may rent rooms.

room·mate (rōōm′māt′, rŏŏm′-) *n.* A person with whom one shares a room or apartment.

room·y (rōō′mē, rŏŏm′ē) *adj.* **-i·er, -i·est.** Having plenty of room; spacious. —**room′i·ly** *adv.* —**room′i·ness** *n.*

roor·back (rŏŏr′băk′) *n.* A false or slanderous story used for political advantage. [After Baron von *Roorback,* imaginary author of an imaginary book, *Roorback's Tour Through the Western and Southern States,* from which a passage was purportedly quoted in an attempt to disparage presidential candidate James K. Polk in 1844.]

roost (rōōst) *n.* **1.** A perch on which domestic fowl or other birds rest or sleep. **2.** A place with perches for fowl or other birds. **3.** A place for temporary rest or sleep. —*intr.v.* **roost·ed, roost·ing, roosts.** To rest or sleep on or as if on a perch or roost. —*idiom.* **rule the roost.** To be in charge; dominate. [ME *rooste* < OE *hrōst.*]

roost·er (rōō′stər) *n.* **1. a.** The adult male of the common domestic fowl. **b.** The adult male of other birds; cock. **2.** A pugnacious and cocky person.

root[1] (rōōt, rŏŏt) *n.* **1. a.** The usually underground portion of a plant that serves as support, draws food and water from the surrounding soil, and stores food. **b.** A similar underground plant part such as a rhizome, corm, or tuber. **c.** One of many small, hairlike growths that serve to attach and support plants such as the ivy and other vines. **2.** The embedded part of an organ or structure such as a hair, tooth, or nerve. **3.** A base or support. **4.** An essential part or element; basic core: *finally got to the root of the problem.* **5.** A primary source; origin. **6.** An antecedent or ancestor. **7.** Often **roots.** The condition of being settled and of belonging to a particular place or society: *put down roots in a new town.* **8.** *Ling.* An element that constitutes the basis from which a word is derived by phonetic change or by the addition of other elements, such as inflectional endings or affixes. **9.** *Math.* **a.** A number that when multiplied by itself an indicated number of times forms a product equal to a specified number: *a fourth root of 4 is* $\sqrt{2}$. **b.** A number that reduces a polynomial equation in one variable to an identity when it is substituted for the variable. **c.** A root *a* of the polynomial equation $f(x) = 0$ in which $(x-a)$ occurs at least twice as a factor of $f(x)$. **10.** *Mus.* **a.** The note from which a chord is built. **b.** The first or lowest note of a triad or chord. —*v.* **root·ed, root·ing, roots.** —*intr.* **1.** To grow a root or roots. **2.** To become firmly established, settled, or entrenched. —*tr.* **1.** To cause to put out roots and grow. **2.** To implant by or as if by the roots. **3.** To furnish a primary source or origin to. **4.** To remove by or as if by the roots: *rooting out members of the opposition.* [ME *rot* < OE *rōt* < ON.] **—root'er** *n.*

root[2] (ro͞ot, ro͝ot) *v.* **root·ed, root·ing, roots.** *—tr.* To dig with or as if with the snout or nose. *—intr.* **1.** To dig in the earth with or as if with the snout or nose. **2.** To rummage for something. [ME *wroten* < OE *wrōtan.*] **—root'er** *n.*

root[3] (ro͞ot, ro͝ot) *intr.v.* **root·ed, root·ing, roots. 1.** To give encouragement to a contestant or team; cheer. **2.** To lend support to someone or something. [Poss. alteration of ROUT[3].] **—root'er** *n.*

root·age (ro͞o'tĭj, ro͝ot-ĭj) *n.* **1.** A system or growth of roots. **2.** Establishment by or as if by roots.

root beer *n.* A carbonated soft drink made from extracts of the roots of certain plants.

root canal *n.* A pulp-filled cavity in a root of a tooth.

root cap *n. Bot.* A thimble-shaped mass of cells that covers and protects the tip of a growing root.

root cellar *n.* A cellar, usually covered with earth, used for the storage of root crops and other vegetables.

root hair *n. Bot.* A thin, hairlike outgrowth of a plant root that absorbs water and minerals from the soil.

root knot *n.* A disease of plants caused by a nematode and characterized by protuberant enlargements on the roots.

root·less (ro͞ot'lĭs, ro͝ot'-) *adj.* **1.** Having no roots. **2.** Not belonging to a particular place or society: *rootless refugees in a strange country.* **—root'less·ness** *n.*

root·let (ro͞ot'lĭt, ro͝ot'-) *n.* A small root or division of a root.

root mean square *n.* The square root of the arithmetic mean of the squares of a set of numbers.

root·stalk (ro͞ot'stôk', ro͝ot'-) *n.* A rhizome.

root·stock (ro͞ot'stŏk', ro͝ot'-) *n.* **1.** A rhizome. **2.** A source or origin.

root·y (ro͞o'tē, ro͝ot'ē) *adj.* **-i·er, -i·est. 1.** Full of roots. **2.** Consisting of a root or roots. **3.** Resembling roots. **—root'i·ness** *n.*

rope (rōp) *n.* **1.** A flexible, heavy cord of twisted hemp or other fiber. **2.** A cord with a noose at one end for hanging a person. **3.** Death by hanging. **4.** A lasso or lariat. **5. ropes.** Several cords strung between poles to enclose a boxing or wrestling ring. **6.** A string of items attached in one line by twisting or braiding: *a rope of onions.* **7.** A sticky glutinous formation of stringy matter in a liquid. **8. ropes.** *Informal.* Specialized procedures or techniques: *learning the ropes.* *—v.* **roped, rop·ing, ropes.** *—tr.* **1.** To tie or fasten with or as if with rope. **2.** To enclose with a rope: *rope off the scene of the crime.* **3.** To catch with a rope or lasso. **4.** *Informal.* To trick or deceive: *An unscrupulous salesman roped him into buying worthless property.* *—intr.* To become ropy and sticky. [ME < OE *rāp.*] **—rop'er** *n.*

rope tow *n.* A ski tow consisting of an endless rope.

rope·walk (rōp'wôk') *n.* **1.** A long, usually covered path or alley where ropes are made. **2.** A long, narrow building containing a ropewalk.

rop·y (rō'pē) *adj.* **-i·er, -i·est. 1.** Resembling a rope or ropes. **2.** Forming sticky glutinous strings or threads, as some liquids. **—rop'i·ly** *adv.* **—rop'i·ness** *n.*

roque (rōk) *n.* A difficult form of croquet played on a hard court. [Alteration of CROQUET.]

Roque·fort (rōk'fərt). A trademark for a cheese that is made from ewes' milk and ripened in caves.

ro·que·laure (rō'kə-lôr', -lōr', rŏk'ə-) *n.* A man's knee-length cloak popular during the 18th and early 19th century. [After Antoine Gaston Jean-Baptiste (1656–1738), Duc de *Roquelaure.*]

ror·qual (rôr'kwəl) *n.* Any of several whalebone-bearing whales of the genus *Balaenoptera,* having longitudinal grooves on the throat and a small, pointed dorsal fin. [Fr. < Norw. *rørhval* < ON *reytharhvalr* : *reythr,* rorqual + *hvalr,* whale.]

Ror·schach test (rôr'shäk', -shäкн') *n.* A psychological projective test of personality in which a subject's interpretations of ten standard abstract designs are analyzed as a measure of emotional and intellectual functioning and integration. [After Hermann *Rorschach* (1884–1922).]

ro·sa·ceous (rō-zā'shəs) *adj.* **1.** *Bot.* Of or belonging to the Rosaceae, the plant family that includes the roses. **2.** Resembling the flower of a rose. [< NLat. *Rosaceae,* family name < Lat. *rosaceus,* made of roses < *rosa,* rose.]

ros·an·i·line also **ros·an·i·lin** (rō-zăn'ə-lĭn) *n.* A brownish-red crystalline organic compound, $C_{20}H_{21}N_3O$, derived from aniline and used in the manufacture of dyes. [ROS(E) + ANILINE.]

ro·sa·ry (rō'zə-rē) *n., pl.* **-ries. 1.** *Rom. Cath. Ch.* **a.** A form of devotion to the Virgin Mary, consisting of three sets of five decades each of the "Hail Mary," each decade preceded by an "Our Father" and ending with a "Glory Be to the Father." **b.** A string of beads on which these prayers are counted. **2.** Beads similar to a rosary used by other religious groups. [Med. Lat. *rosarium* < Lat., rose garden < neuter of *rosarius,* of roses < *rosa,* rose.]

rosary pea *n.* A woody vine, *Abrus precatorius,* of tropical Asia, having scarlet, black-spotted, poisonous seeds that are used as beads.

rose[1] (rōz) *n.* **1. a.** Any of numerous shrubs or vines of the genus *Rosa,* usually having prickly stems, compound leaves, and variously colored, often fragrant flowers. **b.** The flower of any of these plants, occurring in a wide variety of colors such as pink, red, yellow, and white. **2.** Any of various plants related to or resembling the rose. **3.** A dark pink to purplish pink to moderate red or purplish red. It covers a variable range of medium lightness and moderate saturation. **4.** A rosy color of the cheeks. **5.** An ornament resembling a rose in form; rosette. **6.** A perfume obtained from or having the odor of roses. **7.** A perforated nozzle for spraying water from a hose or sprinkling can. **8. a.** A form of gem cut marked by a flat base and a faceted, hemispheric upper surface. **b.** A gem, esp. a diamond, with a rose cut. **9.** A rose window. **10.** A compass card. *—adj.* Of the color rose. [ME < OE < Lat. *rosa.*]

rose[2] (rōz) *v.* Past tense of **rise.**

ro·sé (rō-zā') *n.* A pink, light wine made from red grapes from which the skins are removed during fermentation. [Fr., pink < OFr. *rose,* rose < Lat. *rosa.*]

rose acacia *n.* A shrub, *Robinia hispida,* of the southern United States, having brittle, bristly branches and clusters of rose-colored flowers.

ro·se·ate (rō'zē-ĭt, -āt') *adj.* **1.** Rose-colored. **2.** Cheerful; optimistic. [< Lat. *roseus,* rosy < *rosa,* rose.] **—ro'se·ate·ly** *adv.*

rose·bay (rōz'bā') *n.* **1.** Any of several shrubs of the genus *Rhododendron,* esp. *R. maximum,* of northeastern North America, having large, glossy leaves and clusters of white or pink flowers. **2.** The oleander. **3.** *Chiefly Brit.* The willow herb.

rose beetle *n.* The rose chafer.

rose-breast·ed grosbeak (rōz'brĕs'tĭd) *n.* A North American bird, *Pheucticus ludovicianus,* the male of which is black and white with a rose-red patch on the breast.

rose·bud (rōz'bŭd') *n.* The bud of a rose.

rose·bush (rōz'bo͝osh') *n.* A shrub that bears roses.

rose campion *n.* A European plant, *Lychnis coronaria,* naturalized in northeastern North America, that is covered with white, woolly down and has rose-red flowers.

rose chafer *n.* A long-legged gray beetle, *Macrodactylus subspinosus,* that causes damage to garden plants, esp. roses and grapes.

rose-col·ored (rōz'kŭl'ərd) *adj.* **1.** Having the color rose. **2.** Seeing or seen overoptimistically.

rose fever *n.* A spring or early summer hay fever.

rose·fish (rōz'fĭsh') *n., pl.* **rosefish** or **-fish·es.** A bright-red marine food fish, *Sebastes marinus,* of North Atlantic waters.

rose geranium *n.* A woody plant, *Pelargonium graveolens,* having rose-pink flowers and fragrant leaves used for flavoring and in perfumery.

ro·selle (rō-zĕl') *n.* A tropical Old World plant, *Hibiscus sabdariffa,* with yellow flowers, whose floral bracts when immature have a pleasantly acid flavor and are used to make jelly and beverages. [Orig. unknown.]

rose mallow *n.* A tall plant, *Hibiscus moscheutos,* growing in brackish marshes of eastern North America and having leaves covered with whitish down and white or pink flowers.

rose·mar·y (rōz'mĕr'ē) *n., pl.* **-ies.** An aromatic evergreen shrub, *Rosmarinus officinalis,* of southern Europe, having light-blue flowers and grayish-green leaves that are used in cooking and perfume manufacture. [Alteration of ME *rosmarine* < Lat. *ros marinus,* sea dew.]

rose moss *n.* **1.** A moss of the genus *Rhodobryum,* esp. *R. roseum,* characterized by conspicuous terminal leaf rosettes. **2.** Portulaca.

rose of Jer·i·cho (jĕr'ĭ-kō') *n.* A fernlike desert plant, *Anastatica hierochuntica,* that forms a tight ball when dry and unfolds and blooms under moist conditions.

rose of Shar·on (shăr'ən, shâr'-) *n.* **1.** A tall shrub, *Hibiscus syriacus,* having large reddish, purple, or white flowers. **2.** A shrubby plant, *Hypericum calycinum,* native to Eurasia, having evergreen leaves and yellow flowers.

ro·se·o·la (rō-zē'ə-lə, rō'zē-ō'lə) *n.* A rose-colored skin rash. [NLat. < Lat. *roseus,* rosy < *rosa,* rose.] **—ro·se'o·lar** *adj.*

rose pink *n.* A light purplish pink to moderate or strong pink. **—rose'-pink'** (rōz'pĭngk') *adj.*

rose quartz *n.* A pinkish quartz used as a gemstone.

rose·root (rōz'ro͞ot', -ro͝ot') *n.* A plant, *Sedum roseum,* of the Northern Hemisphere, having fleshy leaves and greenish-yellow or purple flowers.

Ro·set·ta stone (rō-zĕt'ə) *n.* A basalt tablet bearing an inscription in Greek, Egyptian hieroglyphic, and Demotic that was discovered in 1799 near the town of Rosetta, Egypt, and provided the key to the decipherment of hieroglyphics.

ro·sette (rō-zĕt') *n.* **1.** An ornament or badge made of ribbon or silk that is pleated or gathered to resemble a rose and is used to decorate clothing or is worn in the buttonhole of civilian dress to indicate the possession of certain medals or honors. **2.** A roselike marking or formation, such as one of the clusters of spots on a leopard's fur. **3.** *Archit.* A painted, carved, or sculptured ornament having a circular arrangement of parts resembling the petals of a rose. **4.** *Bot.* A circular cluster of leaves or other plant parts. [Fr. < OFr. < dim. of *rose,* rose < Lat. *rosa.*]

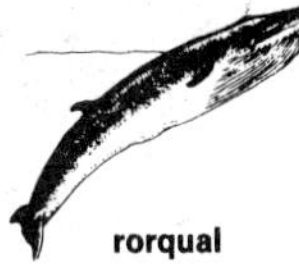
rorqual

Rorschach test

rose[1]

rose window

rotisserie

rose water *n.* A fragrant preparation made by steeping or distilling rose petals in water, used in cosmetics and in cookery.

rose window *n.* A circular window usually of stained glass with radiating tracery in the form of a rose.

rose·wood (rōz'wo͝od') *n.* **1.** Any of various tropical or semi-tropical trees, chiefly of the genus *Dalbergia,* having hard reddish or dark wood with a strongly marked grain. **2.** The wood of a rosewood tree, used in cabinetwork.

Rosh Ha·sha·nah also **Rosh Ha·sha·na** or **Rosh Ha·sho·na** or **Rosh Ha·sho·nah** (rŏsh' hə-shä'nə, -shō'-, rōsh') *n.* The Jewish New Year, a solemn occasion celebrated by Orthodox and Conservative Jews on the first and second of Tishri and by Reform Jews on the first of Tishri only. [Heb. *rōsh hasshānāh,* beginning of the year.]

Ro·si·cru·cian (rō'zĭ-kro͞o'shən, rŏz'ĭ-) *n.* **1.** A member of an international fraternity of religious mysticism devoted to the application of esoteric religious doctrine to modern life. **2.** A member of any of several secret religious organizations similar to the Rosicrucian fraternity and active in the 17th and 18th centuries. *—adj.* Of or pertaining to Rosicrucians or their philosophy. [< Med. Lat. *Rosae Crucis,* transl. of G. *Rosenkreutz,* surname of the reputed founder of the society in the 15th cent.] **—Ro'si·cru'cian·ism** *n.*

ros·in (rŏz'ĭn) *n.* A translucent yellowish to dark-brown resin derived from the sap of various pine trees and used to increase sliding friction on the bows of certain stringed instruments and in a wide variety of manufactured products including varnishes, inks, linoleum, and soldering compounds. *—tr.v.* **-ined, -in·ing, -ins.** To coat or rub with rosin. [ME, var. of *resin,* resin.] **—ros'in·y** *adj.*

rosin oil *n.* A white to brown viscous liquid obtained by fractional distillation of rosin and used in lubricants, electrical insulation, and printing inks.

ros·in·ol (rŏz'ĭ-nôl', -nōl') *n.* Rosin oil.

ros·in·weed (rŏz'ĭn-wēd') *n.* Any of several North American plants of the genus *Silphium* and related genera, esp. the compass plant, the cup plant, and the gum plant, having a resinous juice.

ros·tel·la (rŏ-stĕl'ə) *n.* Plural of **rostellum.**

ros·tel·late (rŏs'tə-lāt', rŏ-stĕl'ĭt) *adj.* Having a rostellum. [NLat. *rostellatus* < *rostellum,* rostellum.]

ros·tel·lum (rŏ-stĕl'əm) *n., pl.* **ros·tel·la** (rŏ-stĕl'ə). *Biol.* A small, beaklike part, as a projection on the stigma of an orchid, a tubular mouth part on some insects, or the hooked projection on the head of a tapeworm. [NLat. < Lat., dim. of *rostrum,* beak.] **—ros·tel'lar** *adj.*

ros·ter (rŏs'tər, rô'stər) *n.* **1.** A list of names. **2.** A list of the names of military officers and enlisted personnel enrolled for active duty. [Du. *rooster,* roster, gridiron < *rooster,* to roast.]

ros·tra (rŏs'trə, rô'strə) *n.* A plural of **rostrum.**

ros·trate (rŏs'trāt', -trĭt, rô'strāt', -strĭt) *adj.* Having a rostrum or beaklike part. [Lat. *rostratus* < *rostrum,* beak.]

ros·trum (rŏs'trəm, rô'strəm) *n., pl.* **ros·trums** or **ros·tra** (rŏs'trə, rô'strə). **1.** A dais, platform, or similar raised place for public speaking. **2.** In ancient Rome: **a.** The curved, beaklike prow of a ship. **b.** The speakers' platform in the Forum, which was decorated with the prows of captured enemy ships. **3.** *Biol.* A beaklike or snoutlike projection. [Lat., beak.] **—ros'tral** *adj.*

ros·y (rō'zē) *adj.* **-i·er, -i·est. 1.** Having the characteristic pink or red color of a rose. **2.** Consisting of, decorated with, or suggestive of roses. **3.** Flushed with a healthy glow. **4.** Cheerful; optimistic. **—ros'i·ly** *adv.* **—ros'i·ness** *n.*

rot (rŏt) *v.* **rot·ted, rot·ting, rots.** *—intr.* **1.** To undergo decomposition, esp. organic decomposition; decay. **2.** To become damaged or useless because of decay: *The beams had rotted away.* **3.** To decay morally; become degenerate. *—tr.* To cause to decompose or decay. *—n.* **1. a.** The process of rotting. **b.** The condition of being rotten. **2. a.** Foot rot. **b.** Liver fluke. **3.** Any of several plant diseases characterized by the breakdown of tissue and caused by various bacteria, fungi, or microorganisms. **4.** *Archaic.* A disease causing the decay of flesh. **5.** Pointless talk. *—interj.* Used to express contempt or impatience. [ME *roten* < OE *rotian.*]

ro·ta (rō'tə) *n.* **1.** *Chiefly Brit.* A roll call or roster of names. **2.** *Chiefly Brit.* A round or rotation of duties. **3. Rota.** *Rom. Cath. Ch.* A tribunal of prelates, called in full the Sacred Roman Rota, that serves as an ecclesiastical court. [Lat., wheel.]

Ro·tar·i·an (rō-târ'ē-ən) *n.* A member of the Rotary Club, a major national and international service club.

ro·ta·ry (rō'tə-rē) *adj.* Of, pertaining to, causing, or characterized by rotation, esp. axial rotation. *—n., pl.* **-ries. 1.** A part or device that rotates around an axis. **2.** A traffic circle. [Med. Lat. *rotarius* < Lat. *rota,* wheel.]

rotary engine *n.* An engine, such as a turbine, in which power is supplied directly to vanes or other rotary parts.

rotary harrow *n.* A harrow consisting of a series of freely turning wheels rimmed with spikes.

rotary plow *n.* A plow having a series of hoes arranged on a revolving power-driven shaft.

rotary press *n.* A printing press having a cylinder to which curved plates are attached so that when they revolve they will print onto a continuous roll of paper.

rotary tiller *n.* A rotary plow.

ro·tate (rō'tāt') *v.* **-tat·ed, -tat·ing, -tates.** *—intr.* **1.** To turn or spin on an axis. **2.** To proceed in sequence; alternate. *—tr.* **1.** To cause rotation. **2.** To plant or grow (crops) in a fixed order of succession. *—adj.* Having radiating parts; wheel-shaped. [Lat. *rotare, rotat-* < *rota,* wheel.] **—ro'tat'a·ble** *adj.*

ro·ta·tion (rō-tā'shən) *n.* **1. a.** Motion in which the path of every point in the moving object is a circle or circular arc centered on a specified axis, esp. on an internal axis: *the axial rotation of the earth.* **b.** A single complete cycle of such motion; revolution. **2.** *Math.* A coordinate transformation consisting of an angular displacement or successive angular displacements of coordinate axes with the origin remaining fixed. **3.** Uniform sequential variation. **—ro·ta'tion·al** *adj.*

ro·ta·tive (rō'tā'tĭv) *adj.* **1.** Of, pertaining to, causing, or characterized by rotation. **2.** Characterized by or occurring in alternation or succession. **—ro'ta'tive·ly** *adv.*

ro·ta·tor (rō'tā'tər) *n.* One that rotates.

ro·ta·to·ry (rō'tə-tôr'ē, -tōr'ē) *adj.* **1.** Of, pertaining to, causing, or characterized by rotation. **2.** Occurring in or proceeding in alternation or succession.

rote[1] (rōt) *n.* **1.** A memorizing process using routine or repetition without full comprehension: *learn by rote.* **2.** Mechanical routine marked by unthinking repetition. [ME.]

rote[2] (rōt) *n.* The sound of surf breaking on the shore. [Prob. of Scand. orig.]

rote[3] (rōt) *n.* A medieval stringed instrument. [ME < OFr., of Germanic orig.]

ro·te·none (rōt'ə-nōn') *n.* A white crystalline compound, $C_{23}H_{22}O_6$, extracted from the roots of derris and cubé and used as an insecticide. [J. *rōten,* derris + -ONE.]

rot·gut (rŏt'gŭt') *n. Slang.* Inferior liquor.

ro·ti·fer (rō'tə-fər) *n.* Any of various minute multicellular aquatic organisms of the phylum Rotifera, having at the anterior end a wheellike ring of cilia. [< NLat. *Rotifera,* phylum name < Lat. *rota,* wheel.] **—ro·tif'er·al** (-tĭf'ər-əl), **ro·tif'er·ous** *adj.*

ro·ti·form (rō'tə-fôrm') *adj.* Shaped like a wheel. [Lat. *rota,* wheel + -FORM.]

ro·tis·se·rie (rō-tĭs'ə-rē) *n.* **1.** A cooking device equipped with a rotating spit on which meat or other food is roasted. **2.** A shop or restaurant where meats are roasted to order. [Fr. *rôtisserie* < OFr. *rostisserie* < *rostir,* to roast, of Germanic orig.]

rot·l (rŏt'l) *n.* A unit of weight used in countries bordering on the Mediterranean and in nearby areas, varying in different regions from about one to five pounds. [Ar. *raṭl.*]

ro·to·gra·vure (rō'tə-grə-vyo͝or') *n.* **1.** An intaglio printing process in which letters and pictures are transferred from an etched copper cylinder to a web of paper, plastic, or similar material in a rotary press. **2.** Printed material, as a newspaper section, produced by rotogravure. [Lat. *rota,* wheel + GRAVURE.]

ro·tor (rō'tər) *n.* **1.** A rotating part of an electrical or mechanical device. **2.** An assembly of rotating horizontal airfoils, such as that of a helicopter. [Contraction of ROTATOR.]

rotor ship *n.* A ship propelled by one or more tall cylindrical rotors operated by wind power.

ro·to·till (rō'tə-tĭl') *tr.v.* **-tilled, -till·ing, -tills.** To turn over with a rotary plow: *rototill the garden.* [Back-formation < ROTOTILLER.]

Ro·to·till·er (rō'tə-tĭl'ər). A trademark for a rotary cultivator.

rot·ten (rŏt'n) *adj.* **-er, -est. 1.** In a state of putrefaction or decay; decomposed. **2.** Having a foul odor resulting from or suggestive of decay; putrid. **3.** Made weak or unsound by rot. **4.** Morally corrupt or despicable. **5.** Very bad; wretched: *rotten weather.* [ME *roten* < ON *rotinn.*] **—rot'ten·ly** *adv.* **—rot'ten·ness** *n.*

rotten borough *n.* An election district having only a few voters but the same voting power as other more populous districts.

rot·ten·stone (rŏt'n-stōn') *n.* A friable variety of tripoli, the product of decomposed siliceous limestone, used for polishing.

rott·wei·ler (rŏt'wī'lər, rôt'vī'-) *n.* A German breed of dog having a stocky body, short black fur, and tan face markings. [G. < *Rottweil,* city in southwestern Germany where it was orig. bred.]

ro·tund (rō-tŭnd') *adj.* **1.** Rounded; plump. **2.** Sonorous. [Lat. *rotundus* < *rota,* wheel.] **—ro·tund'ly** *adv.* **—ro·tund'ness** *n.*

ro·tun·da (rō-tŭn'də) *n.* **1.** A circular building or hall, esp. one with a dome. **2.** A large room with a high ceiling, as a lobby of a hotel. [Ital. < Lat., fem. of *rotundus,* rotund.]

ro·tun·di·ty (rō-tŭn'dĭ-tē) *n., pl.* **-ties. 1.** The condition of being round or plump. **2.** A rotund protrusion or object.

ro·tu·rier (rō-to͝or'ē-ā', -tyo͝or'-) *n.* A commoner. [Fr. < OFr. < *roture,* newly cultivated land < Lat. *ruptura,* action of breaking < *rumpere,* to break.]

rou·ble or **ru·ble** (ro͞o'bəl) *n.* See table at **currency.** [R. *rubl'.*]

rou·é (ro͞o-ā') *n.* A lecherous and dissipated man. [Fr. < p.part. of *rouer,* to break on a wheel < Lat. *rotare,* to rotate < *rota,* wheel.]

rouge (ro͞ozh) *n.* **1.** A red or pink cosmetic for coloring the cheeks or lips. **2.** A reddish powder, chiefly ferric oxide, used to polish metals or glass. —*v.* **rouged, roug·ing, roug·es.** —*tr.* **1.** To put rouge on. **2.** To color with rouge. —*intr.* To use rouge as a cosmetic. [Fr. < OFr., of red color < Lat. *rubeus.*]

rouge et noir (ro͞ozh' ā nwär') *n.* A gambling card game played at a table marked with two red and two black diamond-shaped spots on which bets are placed. [Fr., red and black.]

rough (rŭf) *adj.* **-er, -est. 1.** Having a bumpy, uneven surface; not smooth or even. **2.** Coarse or shaggy to the touch: *a rough, scratchy blanket.* **3.** Characterized by violent motion; turbulent: *rough waters.* **4.** Severely inclement; stormy: *a rough winter.* **5.** Boisterous, unruly, or rowdy in manner or behavior. **6.** Not gentle or careful; violent: *rough handling.* **7.** Savage; brutal: *a rough temper.* **8.** Rude; uncouth. **9.** *Informal.* Difficult or unpleasant to endure or do; trying: *a rough time.* **10.** Harsh to the ear: *a rough, raspy sound.* **11.** Harsh or sharp to the taste: *a rough wine.* **12.** Lacking polish or finesse. **13.** In a natural state: *rough diamonds.* **14.** Not perfected, completed, or fully detailed: *a rough drawing.* **15.** Requiring physical strength rather than intelligence: *rough work.* —*n.* **1.** Rugged, overgrown ground. **2.** The part of a golf course left unmowed and uncultivated as distinguished from the fairway and the greens. **3.** A rough, irregular, or difficult part or condition. **4.** Something in an unfinished or hastily worked-out state. **5.** A crude, unmannerly person; rowdy. —*tr.v.* **roughed, rough·ing, roughs. 1.** To make rough; roughen. **2.** To treat roughly or with physical violence; manhandle: *roughed up his opponent.* **3.** To prepare or indicate in a rough or unfinished form: *rough out a house plan.* —*adv.* In a rough manner; roughly. —***idioms.*** **in the rough.** In a crude or unfinished state. **rough it.** To get along without the usual comforts and conveniences: *roughed it on our camping trip.* [ME < OE *rūh.*] —**rough'er** *n.* —**rough'ly** *adv.* —**rough'ness** *n.*

Synonyms: *rough, harsh, jagged, rugged, scabrous, uneven. Rough* describes any surface that to the sight or touch has inequalities, irregularities, projections, ridges, or breaks: *a rough path. Harsh* in this context implies discordance to the senses, as grating to the ear. *Jagged* refers to an edge with irregular projections and depressions: *a jagged ridge. Rugged* refers to strength or endurance in persons and to irregularity of terrain. *Scabrous* connotes that which is scaly or rough to the tactile sense and often repulsive or obscene in nature. *Uneven* refers to a fluctuation in line or, figuratively, in standards of production: *The quality was uneven.*

rough·age (rŭf'ĭj) *n.* The relatively coarse, indigestible parts of certain foods and fodder that contain cellulose and stimulate peristalsis.

rough-and-read·y (rŭf'ən-rĕd'ē) *adj.* Rough or crude but effective for a purpose or use.

rough-and-tum·ble (rŭf'ən-tŭm'bəl) *adj.* Characterized by roughness and disregard for order or rules: *a rough-and-tumble scuffle.*

rough breathing *n.* **1.** An aspirate sound in Greek like that of the letter *h* in English. **2.** The mark (ʽ) placed over initial sounds in Greek to indicate a preceding aspirate.

rough·cast (rŭf'kăst') *n.* **1.** A coarse plaster used for outside wall surfaces. **2.** A rough preliminary model or form. —*tr.v.* **-cast, -cast·ing, -casts. 1.** To plaster (a wall, for example) with roughcast. **2.** To shape or work into a rough or preliminary form. —**rough'cast'er** *n.*

rough·dry (rŭf'drī') *tr.v.* **-dried, -dry·ing, -dries.** To dry (something laundered) without ironing or smoothing out.

rough·en (rŭf'ən) *tr. & intr.v.* **-ened, -en·ing, -ens.** To make or become rough.

rough·hew (rŭf'hyo͞o') *tr.v.* **-hewed** or **-hewn** (-hyo͞on'), **-hew·ing, -hews. 1.** To hew or shape (timber, for example) roughly, without finishing. **2.** To make in rough form.

rough·house (rŭf'hous') *n.* Rowdy, uproarious play or behavior. —*v.* **-housed, -hous·ing, -hous·es.** —*intr.* To engage in roughhouse. —*tr.* To handle or treat roughly, usually in fun.

rough-leg·ged hawk (rŭf'lĕg'ĭd) *n.* A hawk, *Buteo lagopus,* having dark plumage and whitish feathers covering the legs.

rough·neck (rŭf'nĕk') *n.* **1.** An uncouth person. **2.** A rowdy.

rough·rid·er (rŭf'rī'dər) *n.* **1.** A skilled rider of little-trained horses, esp. one who breaks horses for riding. **2. Rough-rider.** A member of the 1st U.S. Volunteer Cavalry regiment under Theodore Roosevelt in the Spanish-American War.

rough·shod (rŭf'shŏd') *adj.* **1.** Shod with horseshoes having projecting nails or points to prevent slipping. **2.** Marked by brutal force.

rou·lade (ro͞o-läd') *n.* **1. a.** A musical embellishment consisting of a rapid run of several notes sung to one syllable. **b.** A roll on a drum. **2.** A slice of meat rolled around a filling and cooked. [Fr. < *rouler,* to roll < OFr. *roler.* —see ROLL.]

rou·leau (ro͞o-lō') *n., pl.* **-leaux** or **-leaus** (-lōz'). **1.** A small roll, esp. of coins wrapped in paper. **2.** A roll or fold of ribbon used for piping. [Fr. < OFr. *rolel,* dim. of *role,* roll < Lat. *rotula,* little wheel, dim. of *rota,* wheel.]

rou·lette (ro͞o-lĕt') *n.* **1.** A gambling game in which the players bet on which slot of a rotating disk a small ball will come to rest in. **2.** A small, toothed disk of tempered steel attached to a handle and used to make rows of dots, slits, or perforations, as in engraving or on a sheet of postage stamps. **3.** Short consecutive incisions made between individual stamps in a sheet for easy separation. —*tr.v.* **-lett·ed, -lett·ing, -lettes.** To mark or divide with a roulette. [Fr. < OFr. < *rouelle,* dim. of *roue,* wheel < Lat. *rota.*]

Rou·ma·ni·an (ro͞o-mā'nē-ən, -mān'yən) *adj. & n.* Variant of **Rumanian.**

round¹ (round) *adj.* **1.** Ball-shaped; spherical. **2.** Circular or circular in cross section. **3.** Having a curved edge or surface; not flat or angular. **4.** Formed or articulated with the lips in a rounded shape: *a round vowel.* **5.** Whole or complete; full: *a round dozen.* **6. a.** Expressed or designated as a whole number or integer; not fractional. **b.** Not exact; approximate: *a round estimate.* **7.** Large; considerable: *a round sum.* **8.** Brought to a satisfying perfection; finished: *a round, polished writing style.* **9.** Full in tone; sonorous. **10.** Brisk; rapid: *a round pace.* **11.** Outspoken; blunt: *a round scolding.* **12.** Done with full force; unrestrained: *a round thrashing.* —*n.* **1.** The state of being round. **2. a.** Something, as a circle, disk, globe, or ring, that is round. **b.** A curved or rounded form or part. **3.** A rung or crossbar, as on a ladder or chair. **4.** A cut of beef from the part of the thigh between the rump and the shank. **5.** An assembly of people; group. **6.** Movement around a circle or about an axis. **7.** A round dance. **8.** A complete course, succession, or series: *a round of parties.* **9.** Often **rounds.** A course of customary or prescribed actions, duties, or places. **10.** A complete range or extent. **11.** One drink for each person in a gathering or group. **12.** A single outburst of applause or cheering. **13. a.** A single shot or volley. **b.** Ammunition for a single shot. **14.** A rounded slice of bread. **15.** A specified number of arrows shot from a specified distance to a target in archery. **16.** An interval of play in various games and sports that occupies a specified time, comprises a certain number of plays, or allows each player a turn. **17.** *Mus.* A composition for two or more voices in which each voice enters at a different time with the same melody. —*v.* **round·ed, round·ing, rounds.** —*tr.* **1.** To make round. **2.** To pronounce with rounded lips; labialize. **3.** To fill out; make plump. **4.** To bring to completion or perfection; finish. **5.** To express as a round number. **6.** To make a complete circuit of; go or pass around. **7.** To make a turn about or to the other side of: *rounded a bend in the road.* **8.** To encompass; surround. **9.** To move or cause to proceed in a circular course. —*intr.* **1.** To become round. **2.** To take a circular course; complete or partially complete a circuit. **3.** To turn about, as on an axis; reverse. **4.** To become curved, filled out, or plump. **5.** To come to completion or perfection. —***phrasal verbs.*** **round on.** To turn on; assail. **round up. 1.** To seek out and bring together; gather. **2.** To herd (cattle) together from various places. —*adv.* Around. —*prep.* **1.** Around. **2.** From the beginning to the end of; throughout: *a plant that grows round the year.* —***idiom.*** **in the round. 1.** With the stage in the center of the audience. **2.** Fully shaped so as to stand free of a background: *a sculpture in the round.* [ME < OFr. *ronde* < Lat. *rotundus* < *rota,* wheel.] —**round'ness** *n.*

round² (round) *tr.v.* **round·ed, round·ing, rounds.** *Archaic.* To whisper. [ME *rounden* < OE *rūnian.*]

round·a·bout (round'ə-bout') *adj.* Indirect; circuitous. —*n.* **1.** A short, close-fitting jacket. **2.** *Chiefly Brit.* A merry-go-round. **3.** *Chiefly Brit.* A traffic circle.

round clam *n.* The quahog.

round dance *n.* **1.** A folk dance performed with the dancers arranged in a circle. **2.** A ballroom dance in which couples proceed in a circular direction around the room.

round·ed (roun'dĭd) *adj.* **1.** Made round; shaped in a circle or sphere. **2.** Pronounced with the lips shaped ovally; labialized. **3.** Complete; balanced. —**round'ed·ness** *n.*

roun·del (roun'dəl) *n.* **1.** A curved form, esp. a semicircular panel, window, or recess. **2. a.** A rondel. **b.** A rondeau. **c.** An English variation of the rondeau consisting of three triplets with a refrain after the first and third. [ME < OFr. *rondel,* dim. of *ronde,* circle, round. —see ROUND.]

roun·de·lay (roun'də-lā') *n.* A poem or song with a regularly recurring refrain. [OFr. *rondelet,* dim. of *rondel,* roundel.]

round·er (roun'dər) *n.* **1.** One that rounds, esp. a tool for rounding corners and edges. **2.** A person who makes rounds, as a watchman. **3. Rounder.** *Chiefly Brit.* A Methodist preacher who travels a circuit among his congregations. **4.** *Informal.* A dissolute or dishonest person. **5. rounders** *(used with a sing. verb).* An English ball game similar to baseball.

round hand *n.* A style of handwriting in which the letters are rounded and full rather than angular.

Round·head (round'hĕd') *n.* A member or supporter of the Parliamentary or Puritan party during the English Civil War. [From the close-cropped hair of the Puritans.]

round·house (round'hous') *n.* **1.** A circular building for housing and switching locomotives. **2.** A cabin on the after part of the quarter-deck of a ship. **3.** A meld of four kings and four queens in pinochle. **4.** *Slang.* A punch or swing delivered with a sweeping sidearm movement.

round·ish (roun'dĭsh) *adj.* Somewhat round. —**round'ish·ness** *n.*

round·let (round'lĭt) *n.* **1.** A little circle. **2.** A small circular object. [ME < OFr. *rondelet,* dim. of *rondel,* roundel.]

round·ly (round'lē) *adv.* **1.** In the form of a circle or sphere. **2.** With full force or vigor; thoroughly: *roundly applauded; was roundly criticized.*

round robin *n.* **1.** A tournament in which each contestant is matched in turn against every other contestant. **2.** A petition or protest on which the signatures are arranged in the form of a circle in order to conceal the order of signing. **3.** A letter sent among members of a group, often with comments added by each person in turn.

round-shoul·dered (round'shōl'dərd) *adj.* Having the shoulders and upper back rounded.

rounds·man (roundz'mən) *n.* **1.** A police officer in charge of several patrolmen. **2.** A person who makes rounds, as a deliveryman.

Round Table
15th-century French manuscript illustration

round steak *n.* A lean, oval cut of beef from between the rump and shank.

Round Table *n.* **1. a.** The circular table of King Arthur and his knights. **b.** The knights of King Arthur as a group. **2. round table.** A conference or discussion with several participants.

round-the-clock (round'*th*ə-klŏk') *adj.* Lasting or continuing throughout the entire 24 hours of the day; continuous.

round trip *n.* A trip from one place to another and back, usually over the same route.

round·up (round'ŭp') *n.* **1. a.** The herding together of cattle for inspection, branding, or shipping. **b.** The cattle that are herded together. **c.** The cowboys and horses employed in such herding. **2.** A gathering up, as of persons under suspicion by the police. **3.** A summary: *a news roundup.*

round·worm (round'wûrm') *n.* A nematode.

roup (ro͞op) *n.* An infectious disease of poultry and pigeons characterized by inflammation and discharge from the mouth and eyes. [Orig. unknown.]

rouse (rouz) *v.* **roused, rous·ing, rous·es.** *—tr.* **1.** To arouse from sleep, unconsciousness, or inactivity. **2.** To stir up, as to anger or action; excite. *—intr.* **1.** To awaken. **2.** To become active. *—n.* The act or an instance of rousing. [ME *rowsen,* to shake feathers.] **—rous'er** *n.*

rous·ing (rou'zĭng) *adj.* **1.** Inducing enthusiasm or excitement; stirring: *a rousing sermon.* **2.** Lively; vigorous: *a rousing march tune.* **3.** *Informal.* Extraordinary; exceptional: *a rousing good time; a rousing lie.* **—rous'ing·ly** *adv.*

rowan

Rous sarcoma (rous) *n.* A malignant sarcoma that can be produced in chickens by inoculation with the specific viral causative agent. [After Francis P. *Rous* (1879–1970).]

roust (roust) *tr.v.* **roust·ed, roust·ing, rousts.** To rout, esp. out of bed. [Alteration of ROUSE.]

roust·a·bout (rous'tə-bout') *n.* **1.** A deck or wharf laborer, esp. on the Mississippi River. **2.** A laborer in a circus. **3.** A laborer employed for temporary or unskilled jobs, as in an oil field.

rout[1] (rout) *n.* **1.** A disorderly retreat or flight following defeat. **2.** An overwhelming defeat. **3. a.** A disorderly crowd of persons; mob. **b.** Low-class people; rabble. **4.** A public disturbance; riot. **5.** *Archaic.* A company of people or animals, esp. of knights or wolves. **6.** *Archaic.* A wild party. *—tr.v.* **rout·ed, rout·ing, routs. 1.** To put to disorderly flight or retreat. **2.** To defeat overwhelmingly. [ME *route* < OFr. < Lat. *rumpere,* to break.]

rout[2] (rout) *v.* **rout·ed, rout·ing, routs.** *—intr.* **1.** To dig with the snout; root. **2.** To poke around; rummage. *—tr.* **1.** To dig up with the snout. **2.** To expose to view; uncover. **3.** To hollow, scoop, or gouge out. **4.** To drive or force out; eject. [Var. of ROOT[2].]

rout[3] (rout, ro͞ot) *intr.v.* **rout·ed, rout·ing, routs.** *Chiefly Brit.* To make a loud noise or clamor. [ME *routen* < ON *rauta,* to roar.]

route (ro͞ot, rout) *n.* **1. a.** A road, course, or way for travel from one place to another. **b.** A highway. **c.** A means of reaching a goal. **2.** A customary line of travel. **3.** A fixed course or territory assigned to a salesman or deliveryman. *—tr.v.* **rout·ed, rout·ing, routes. 1.** To send along; forward. **2.** To schedule the order of (a sequence of procedures). [ME < OFr. < Lat. *ruptus,* p.part. of *rumpere,* to break.]

rout·er[1] (ro͞o'tər, rou'tər) *n.* One that routes.

rout·er[2] (rou'tər) *n.* One that routs.

rou·tine (ro͞o-tēn') *n.* **1.** A prescribed and detailed course of action to be followed regularly; standard procedure. **2.** A set of customary and often mechanically performed procedures or activities. **3.** A set piece of entertainment, esp. in a nightclub or theater. **4.** *Slang.* A particular kind of behavior or activity: *went into her hurt routine.* *—adj.* **1.** In accordance with established procedure: *a routine check of passports.* **2.** Habitual; regular. **3.** Not special; ordinary: *a routine day.* [Fr. < OFr. < *route,* route.] **—rou·tine'ly** *adv.* **—rou·tin'ism** *n.* **—rou·tin'ist** *n.*

rou·tin·ize (ro͞o-tē'nīz', ro͞ot'n-īz') *tr.v.* **-ized, -iz·ing, -iz·es. 1.** To establish a routine for. **2.** To reduce to a routine. **—rou·tin'i·za'tion** *n.*

roux (ro͞o) *n.* A mixture of flour and fat cooked together and used as a thickening. [Fr. *(beurre) roux,* browned (butter) < *roux,* reddish brown < OFr. *rous* < Lat. *russus,* red.]

rove[1] (rōv) *v.* **roved, rov·ing, roves.** *—intr.* To wander about at random, esp. over a wide area; roam. *—tr.* To roam or wander around, over, or through. *—n.* An act of roving. [ME *roven,* to shoot arrows at a mark.]

rove[2] (rōv) *tr.v.* **roved, rov·ing, roves. 1.** To card (wool). **2.** To put (fibers) through an eye or opening. **3.** To stretch and twist (fibers) before spinning; ravel out. *—n.* A slightly twisted and extended fiber or sliver. [Orig. unknown.]

rove[3] (rōv) *v.* A past tense and past participle of **reeve.**

rove beetle *n.* Any of numerous beetles of the family Staphylinidae, often found in decaying matter and having slender bodies and short wing covers. [Poss. < ROVE[1].]

rov·er[1] (rō'vər) *n.* **1.** One that roves; wanderer. **2.** A mark in archery selected by chance.

ro·ver[2] (rō'vər) *n.* **1.** A pirate. **2.** A pirate vessel. [ME < MDu., robber < *roven,* to rob.]

row[1] (rō) *n.* **1.** A series of objects placed next to each other, usually in a straight line. **2.** A succession without a break or gap in time: *won the title for three years in a row.* **3.** A continuous line of buildings along a street. *—tr.v.* **rowed, row·ing, rows.** To place in a row. [ME < OE *rāw.*]

row[2] (rō) *v.* **rowed, row·ing, rows.** *—intr.* To propel a boat with or as if with oars. *—tr.* **1.** To propel (a boat) with or as if with oars. **2.** To carry in or on a boat propelled by oars. **3.** To propel or convey in a manner resembling rowing. **4.** To employ (a specified number of oars or oarsmen). **5.** To pull (an oar) as part of a racing crew. **6.** To race against by rowing. *—n.* **1. a.** An act or instance of rowing. **b.** A shift at the oars of a boat. **2.** A trip or excursion in a rowboat. [ME *rowen* < OE *rōwan.*] **—row'er** *n.*

row[3] (rou) *n.* **1.** A boisterous disturbance or quarrel; brawl. **2.** An uproar; noise. *—intr.v.* **rowed, row·ing, rows.** To take part in a row. [Orig. unknown.]

row·an (rou'ən) *n.* A small deciduous tree, *Sorbus aucuparia,* native to Europe, having clusters of white flowers and orange-red berries. [Of Scand. orig.]

row·boat (rō'bōt') *n.* A small boat propelled by oars.

row·dy (rou'dē) *n., pl.* **-dies.** A rough, disorderly person. *—adj.* **-di·er, -di·est.** Disorderly; rough. [Prob. < ROW[3].] **—row'di·ly** *adv.* **—row'di·ness** *n.* **—row'dy·ism** *n.*

row·el (rou'əl) *n.* A sharp-toothed wheel inserted into the end of the shank of a spur. *—tr.v.* **-eled, -el·ing, -els** or **-elled, -el·ling, -els.** To spur or urge with or as if with a rowel. [ME *rowelle* < OFr. *rouelle,* dim. of *roue,* wheel < Lat. *rota.*]

row·en (rou'ən) *n.* A second crop, as of hay, in a season. [ME *rewain* < OFr. *regain* : *re-,* again + *gaaignier,* to till.]

row house *n.* One of a series of identical houses situated side by side and joined by common walls.

row·lock (rō'lŏk') *n. Chiefly Brit.* An oarlock.

roy·al (roi'əl) *adj.* **1.** Of or pertaining to a king, queen, or other monarch. **2.** Of the rank of a king or queen. **3.** Of, pertaining to, or in the service of a kingdom. **4.** Issued or performed by a sovereign: *a royal warrant; a royal visit.* **5.** Founded, chartered, or authorized by a sovereign. **6.** Befitting royalty; stately. **7.** Superior in size or quality. *—n.* **1.** A sail set on the royalmast. **2.** A paper size, 20 by 25 inches for printing, 19 by 24 inches for writing. **3.** *Informal.* A member of a monarch's family. **—*idiom.* the royal road.** A way or method that presents no difficulties: *the royal road to success.* [ME < OFr. *roial* < Lat. *regalis* < *rex,* king.] **—roy'al·ly** *adv.*

royal blue *n.* A deep to strong blue. **—roy'al-blue'** *adj.*

royal fern *n.* A deep-rooted fern, *Osmunda regalis,* of worldwide distribution, having tall, upright fronds.

royal flush *n.* A poker hand consisting of the five highest cards of one suit.

roy·al·ism (roi'ə-lĭz'əm) *n.* Support of or adherence to the principle of rule by a monarch.

roy·al·ist (roi'ə-lĭst) *n.* **1.** A supporter of government by a king or queen. **2. Royalist. a.** A Cavalier. **b.** An American loyal to British rule during the American Revolution; Tory.

royal jelly *n.* A nutritious substance secreted in the pharyngeal glands of worker bees, serving as food for the young larvae and as the only food for those that develop into queen bees.

roy·al·mast also **royal mast** (roi'əl-măst') *n. Naut.* The small mast immediately above the topgallant mast.

royal palm *n.* Any of several palm trees of the genus *Roystonea,* having a tall, naked trunk surmounted by a large tuft of pinnate leaves.

royal poinciana *n.* A tropical and semitropical tree, *Delonix regia,* native to Madagascar, having clusters of large scarlet and yellow flowers and long pods.

royal purple *n.* A moderate or strong violet to deep purple or dark reddish purple. **—roy'al-pur'ple** *adj.*

roy·al·ty (roi'əl-tē) *n., pl.* **-ties. 1. a.** A person of royal rank or lineage. **b.** Monarchs and their families collectively. **2.** The lineage or rank of a monarch. **3.** The power, status, or authority of a monarch. **4.** Royal quality or bearing. **5.** A kingdom or possession ruled by a monarch. **6.** A right or prerogative of the crown, as that of receiving a percentage of the proceeds from mines in the royal domain. **7. a.** The granting of a right by a sovereign to a corporation or individual to exploit specified natural resources. **b.** The payment for such a right. **8. a.** A share paid to an author or composer out of the proceeds resulting from the sale or performance of his work. **b.** A share in the proceeds paid to an inventor or proprietor for the right to use his invention or services. **c.** A share of the profit or product reserved by the grantor, esp. of an oil or mining lease.

RPG (är′pē-jē′) *n.* A computer programming language designed for business reporting that generates specific programs from the user's specifications. [R(EPORT) P(ROGRAM) G(ENERATOR).]

-rrhagia *suff.* Abnormal or excessive flow or discharge: *menorrhagia.* [NLat. < Gk. < *rhēgnunai,* to burst forth.]

-rrhea or **-rrhoea** *suff.* Flow; discharge: *seborrhea.* [ME *-ria* < LLat. *-rrhoea* < Gk. *-rrhoia* < *rhoia,* a flowing < *rhein,* to flow.]

Ru The symbol for the element ruthenium.

rub (rŭb) *v.* **rubbed, rub·bing, rubs.** —*tr.* **1. a.** To subject to the action of something that moves back and forth with friction and pressure. **b.** To cause to move along a surface with friction and pressure. **2.** To irritate; annoy: *His laziness was beginning to rub me.* —*intr.* **1. a.** To move along a surface with friction and pressure. **b.** To chafe with friction. **c.** To cause irritation or annoyance. **2.** *Informal.* To continue in a given situation, usually with some difficulty. **3.** To admit rubbing: *a blackboard that rubs clean easily.* **4.** To be transferred by contact or proximity: *wished some of her luck would rub off on him.* —**phrasal verbs. rub in.** To harp on (an unpleasant matter). **rub out. 1.** To obliterate by or as if by rubbing. **2.** *Slang.* To kill; murder. **rub up. 1.** To refresh one's knowledge of. **2.** To improve or increase the keenness of (a mental faculty). —*n.* **1.** The act of rubbing. **2.** The application of friction and pressure: *a back rub.* **3.** An unevenness on a surface. **4.** An act or remark that annoys or hurts another. **5.** Difficulty: *"Aye, there's the rub"* (Shakespeare). —**idioms. rub elbows (or shoulders).** To mix or socialize closely. **rub the wrong way.** To annoy or irritate. [ME *rubben.*]

ru·basse (ro͞o-băs′, ro͞o′băs′) *n.* A quartz colored ruby red by its iron-oxide content. [Fr. *rubace* < *rubis,* ruby.]

ru·ba·to (ro͞o-bä′tō) *Mus.* —*n., pl.* **-tos.** Rhythmic flexibility within a phrase or measure. —*adj.* Containing or characterized by rubato. [Ital. *(tempo) rubato,* stolen (time) < *rubare,* to rob, of Germanic orig.]

rub·ber[1] (rŭb′ər) *n.* **1.** A light-cream to dark-amber, amorphous, elastic, solid polymer of isoprene, $(C_5H_8)_n$, generally prepared by coagulation and drying of the milky sap or latex of various tropical plants, esp. the rubber tree, and subsequently vulcanized, pigmented, and otherwise modified for finishing as any of a wide variety of manufactured products including electric insulation, elastic bands and belts, tires, and containers. **2.** Any of numerous synthetic elastic materials of varying chemical composition with properties similar to those of natural rubber. **3.** A low overshoe made of rubber. **4.** *Baseball.* The oblong piece of hard rubber on which the pitcher must stand when he delivers the ball. **5. a.** One who rubs. **b.** One who gives a massage. **6.** Something made of rubber, as: **a.** An eraser. **b.** A tire. **c.** A set of tires on a vehicle. **7.** *Slang.* A condom.

rub·ber[2] (rŭb′ər) *n.* **1.** A series of games of which two out of three or three out of five must be won to terminate the play. **2.** An odd game played to break a tie. [Orig. unknown.]

rubber band *n.* An elastic loop of natural or synthetic rubber used to hold objects together.

rub·ber-base paint (rŭb′ər-bās′) *n.* Latex paint.

rubber check *n.* A check returned by a bank because of insufficient funds in the account on which it is drawn.

rub·ber·ize (rŭb′ə-rīz′) *tr.v.* **-ized, -iz·ing, -iz·es.** To coat, treat, or impregnate with rubber.

rub·ber·neck (rŭb′ər-nĕk′) *Slang.* —*n.* A gawking tourist or sightseer. —*intr.v.* **-necked, -neck·ing, -necks.** To look about or survey with unsophisticated wonderment or curiosity.

rubber plant *n.* **1.** Any of several tropical plants yielding sap that can be coagulated to form crude rubber. **2.** A small tree, *Ficus elastica,* that has large, glossy, leathery leaves and is popular as a house plant.

rubber stamp *n.* **1.** A piece of rubber affixed to a handle and bearing raised characters used to make ink impressions, as of names or dates. **2.** A person or body that gives perfunctory approval or endorsement of a policy without assessing its merit. **3.** A perfunctory approval or endorsement.

rub·ber-stamp (rŭb′ər-stămp′) *tr.v.* **-stamped, -stamp·ing, -stamps. 1.** To mark with the imprint of a rubber stamp. **2.** To endorse, vote for, or approve without question or deliberation.

rubber tree *n.* A tree, *Hevea brasiliensis,* native to tropical America but widely cultivated throughout the tropics, yielding a milky juice, or latex, that is a major source of commercial rubber.

rub·ber·y (rŭb′ə-rē) *adj.* Of or like rubber; elastic.

rub·bing (rŭb′ĭng) *n.* **1.** The act of polishing, cleaning, or drying. **2.** A representation of a raised or indented surface made by placing paper over the surface and rubbing the paper gently with a marking agent such as charcoal or chalk.

rub·bish (rŭb′ĭsh) *n.* **1.** Something discarded as refuse; garbage. **2.** Worthless material. **3.** Foolish discourse; nonsense. [ME *robishe* < AN *robbous.*]

rub·bish·y (rŭb′ĭ-shē) *adj.* **1.** Littered with rubbish. **2.** Of no value; worthless.

rub·ble (rŭb′əl) *n.* **1.** Fragments of rock or masonry crumbled by natural or manmade forces. **2. a.** Irregular fragments or pieces of rock used in masonry. **b.** The masonry made with such rocks. [ME *rubel.*] —**rub′bly** *adj.*

rub·ble·work (rŭb′əl-wôrk′) *n.* Masonry made with rubble.

rub·down (rŭb′doun′) *n.* An energetic massage of the body.

rube (ro͞ob) *n. Slang.* An unsophisticated country fellow. [Prob. < *Rube,* nickname for *Reuben.*]

ru·be·fa·cient (ro͞o′bə-fā′shənt) *adj.* Producing redness, as of the skin. —*n.* A substance that irritates the skin, causing redness. [Lat. *rubefaciens, rubefacient-,* pr.part. of *rubefacere,* to make red : *rubeus,* red + *facere,* to make.] —**ru′be·fac′tion** (-făk′shən) *n.*

Rube Gold·berg (ro͞ob-gōld′bûrg′) *adj.* Of, pertaining to, or being a contrivance that brings about by complicated means what apparently could be accomplished simply. [After Reuben (*Rube*) L. *Goldberg* (1883–1970), inventor of such contrivances.]

ru·bel·la (ro͞o-bĕl′ə) *n.* German measles. [NLat., fem. of Lat. *rubellus,* red < *ruber.*]

ru·bel·lite (ro͞o′bə-līt′, ro͞o-bĕl′īt′) *n.* A red tourmaline used as a gemstone. [Lat. *rubellus,* red (< *ruber*) + -ITE.]

ru·be·o·la (ro͞o-bē′ə-lə, ro͞o′bē-ō′lə) *n.* **1.** Measles. **2.** German measles. [NLat., neuter pl. dim. of Lat. *rubeus,* red.] —**ru·be′o·lar** *adj.*

ru·bes·cent (ro͞o-bĕs′ənt) *adj.* Reddening. [Lat. *rubescens, rubescent-,* pr.part. of *rubescere,* to grow red < *rubēre,* to be red.] —**ru·bes′cence** *n.*

Ru·bi·con (ro͞o′bĭ-kŏn′) *n.* A limit that when passed or exceeded permits of no return. [Lat. *Rubico, Rubicon-,* a river in Italy the crossing of which by Julius Caesar and his army in 49 B.C. began a civil war.]

ru·bi·cund (ro͞o′bĭ-kənd) *adj.* Inclined to a healthy rosiness; ruddy. [Lat. *rubicundus* < *rubēre,* to be red.] —**ru′bi·cun′di·ty** (-kŭn′dĭ-tē) *n.*

ru·bid·i·um (ro͞o-bĭd′ē-əm) *n. Symbol* **Rb** A soft silvery-white alkali element that ignites spontaneously in air and reacts violently with water, used in photocells and in the manufacture of vacuum tubes. Atomic number 37; atomic weight 85.47; melting point 38.89°C; boiling point 688°C; specific gravity (solid) 1.532; valences 1, 2, 3, 4. [NLat. < Lat. *rubidus,* red < *rubēre,* to be red.]

ru·big·i·nous (ro͞o-bĭj′ə-nəs) also **ru·big·i·nose** (-nōs′) *adj.* Rust-colored; reddish-brown. [Lat. *rubiginosus* < *rubigo,* rust.]

ru·bi·ous (ro͞o′bē-əs) *adj.* Of the color of a ruby; red.

ru·ble (ro͞o′bəl) *n.* Variant of **rouble.**

ru·bric (ro͞o′brĭk) *n.* **1.** A part of a manuscript or book, such as a title, heading, or initial letter, that appears in decorative red lettering or is otherwise distinguished from the rest of the text. **2.** A title or heading of a statute or chapter in a code of law. **3. a.** A class or category. **b.** A title; name. **4.** *Eccles.* A direction in a missal, hymnal, or other liturgical book. **5.** An authoritative rule or direction. **6.** A short commentary or explanation covering a broad subject. **7.** Red ocher. —*adj.* **1.** Red or reddish. **2.** Written in red. [ME *rubrike* < OFr. *rubriche* < Lat. *rubrica,* rubric, red chalk < *ruber,* red.] —**ru′bri·cal** *adj.*

ru·bri·cate (ro͞o′brĭ-kāt′) *tr.v.* **-cat·ed, -cat·ing, -cates. 1.** To arrange, write, or print as a rubric. **2.** To provide with rubrics. **3.** To establish rules for. [Lat. *rubricare, rubricat-,* to color red < *rubrica,* rubric.] —**ru′bri·ca′tion** *n.* —**ru′bri·ca′tor** *n.*

ru·bri·cian (ro͞o-brĭsh′ən) *n.* A person learned in the rubrics of ecclesiastical ritual.

ru·by (ro͞o′bē) *n., pl.* **-bies. 1.** A deep-red, translucent corundum highly valued as a precious stone. **2.** Something made from a ruby, as a watch bearing. **3.** A dark or deep red to deep purplish red. —*adj.* Of the color ruby. [ME < OFr. *rubi, rubis* < Med. Lat. *rubinus (lapis),* red (stone) < Lat. *rubeus,* red.]

ruby laser *n.* A laser utilizing a ruby crystal to produce an intense beam of coherent red light, used in light-transmission communication and for localized heating.

ru·by-throat·ed hummingbird (ro͞o′bē-thrō′tĭd) *n.* A small bird, *Archilochus colubris,* of eastern North America, having metallic-green upper plumage and in the male a brilliant red throat.

ruche (ro͞osh) *n.* A ruffle or pleat of lace, muslin, or other fine fabric used for trimming women's garments. [Fr. < OFr. < Med. Lat. *rusca,* bark of a tree, of Celt. orig.]

ruch·ing (ro͞o′shĭng) *n.* **1.** A ruche. **2.** Fabric for ruches.

ruck[1] (rŭk) *n.* **1.** A large number mixed together; jumble. **2.** The multitude of ordinary people. [ME *ruke.*]

ruck[2] (rŭk) *v.* **rucked, ruck·ing, rucks.** —*tr.* **1.** To make a fold in; crease. **2.** To disturb or ruffle; irritate. —*intr.* **1.** To become creased. **2.** To become irritated. —*n.* A crease or pucker, as in cloth. [Ult. < ON *hrukka,* wrinkle.]

ruck·sack (rŭk′săk′, ro͝ok′-) *n.* A knapsack. [G. : *Ruck,* back (< OHG *hrukki*) + *Sack,* sack < OHG *sac* < Lat. *saccus.*]

ruck·us (rŭk′əs) *n. Informal.* A noisy disturbance; commotion. [Blend of RUCTION and RUMPUS.]

ruc·tion (rŭk′shən) *n. Informal.* **1.** A riotous disturbance. **2.** A noisy quarrel. [Poss. alteration of INSURRECTION.]

rudd (rŭd) *n.* A European freshwater fish, *Scardinius ery-*

rubber plant

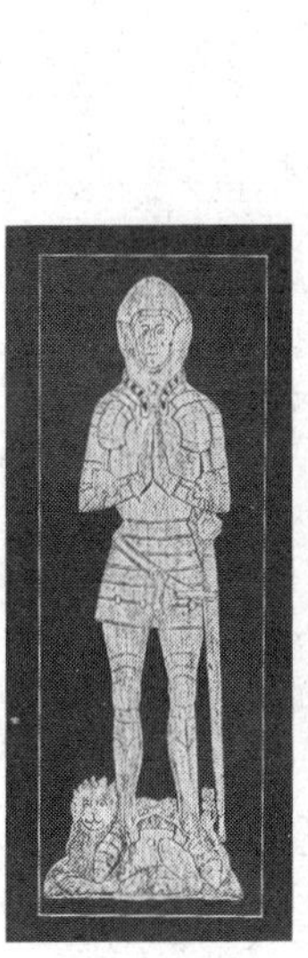

rubbing
Rubbing of a
15th-century brass figure

ruby-throated hummingbird

rug
Bukhara rug

throphthalmus, having a brownish body and red fins. [Prob. < E. *rud,* red. —see RUDDLE.]

rud·der (rŭd′ər) *n.* **1. a.** A vertically hinged plate of metal or wood mounted at the stern of a vessel for directing its course. **b.** A similar structure at the tail of an aircraft, used for effecting horizontal changes in course. **2.** Something that controls direction; guide. [ME *rodyr* < OE *rōðer.*]

rud·der·post (rŭd′ər-pōst′) *n.* A rudderstock.

rud·der·stock (rŭd′ər-stŏk′) *n.* The vertical shaft of a rudder that allows it to pivot when the tiller or steering gear is operated.

rud·dle (rŭd′l) *n.* Red ocherous iron ore, used in dyeing and marking. —*tr.v.* **-dled, -dling, -dles.** To dye or mark with or as if with red ocher: *ruddle sheep.* [Dim. of E. *rud,* red < ME *rudde* < OE *rudu.*]

rud·dle·man (rŭd′l-mən) *n.* A man who sells ruddle.

rud·dock (rŭd′ək) *n. Chiefly Brit. Regional.* The Old World robin. [ME *ruddok* < OE *rudduc.*]

rud·dy (rŭd′ē) *adj.* **-di·er, -di·est. 1.** Having a healthy, reddish color. **2.** Reddish; rosy. **3.** *Chiefly Brit.* Used as an intensive: *a ruddy shame.* [ME *rudie* < OE *rudig* < *rudu,* red.] **—rud′di·ly** *adv.* **—rud′di·ness** *n.*

ruddy duck *n.* A North American duck, *Oxyura jamaicensis,* having stiff, pointed tail feathers and in the male brownish-red upper plumage and a black and white head.

rude (ro͞od) *adj.* **rud·er, rud·est. 1.** Primitive; uncivilized: *a rude and savage land.* **2.** Lowly; humble: *a rude thatched hut.* **3. a.** Lacking the graces of civilized life; uncouth. **b.** Without education or knowledge; unlearned. **c.** Ill-mannered; discourteous. **4.** Formed without skill or precision; crude: *A log formed a rude footbridge.* **5.** Vigorous; robust. **6.** Sudden and jarring: *a rude shock.* [ME < OFr. < Lat. *rudis,* unformed.] **—rude′ly** *adv.* **—rude′ness** *n.*

ru·der·al (ro͞o′dər-əl) *Bot.* —*adj.* Growing in rubbish, poor land, or waste. —*n.* A ruderal plant. [NLat. *ruderalis* < Lat. *rudus,* rubbish.]

rudes·by (ro͞odz′bē) *n., pl.* **-bies.** *Archaic.* An ill-bred, insolent, or ill-tempered person. [RUDE + *-sby,* as in such names as *Grimsby.*]

ru·di·ment (ro͞o′də-mənt) *n.* **1.** Often **rudiments.** A fundamental element, principle, or skill, as of a field of learning. **2.** Often **rudiments.** Something in an incipient or undeveloped form; beginning: *the rudiments of social behavior in children.* **3.** *Biol.* An imperfectly or incompletely developed organ or part. [OFr. < Lat. *rudimentum* < *rudis,* rough, unformed.] **—ru′di·men′tal** (-mĕn′tl) *adj.*

ru·di·men·ta·ry (ro͞o′də-mĕn′tə-rē, -mĕn′trē) *adj.* **1.** Of or relating to basic facts or principles that must be learned first; elementary. **2.** In the earliest stages of development; incipient. **3.** *Biol.* Imperfectly or incompletely developed; vestigial: *a rudimentary organ.* **—ru′di·men·tar′i·ly** (-târ′ə-lē) *adv.* **—ru′di·men′ta·ri·ness** *n.*

rue[1] (ro͞o) *v.* **rued, ru·ing, rues.** —*tr.* To feel regret, remorse, or sorrow for. —*intr.* To feel regret, remorse, or sorrow; be penitent. —*n. Archaic.* Sorrow; regret. [ME *ruen* < OE *hrēowan.*] **—ru′er** *n.*

rue[2] (ro͞o) *n.* An aromatic Eurasian plant of the genus *Ruta,* esp. *R. graveolens,* having evergreen leaves that yield an acrid, volatile oil formerly used in medicine. [ME < OFr. < Lat. *ruta* < Gk. *rhutē.*]

rue anemone *n.* A small North American woodland plant, *Anemonella thalictroides,* having white or pinkish flowers.

rue·ful (ro͞o′fəl) *adj.* **1.** Inspiring pity or compassion. **2.** Causing, feeling, or expressing sorrow or regret. **—rue′ful·ly** *adv.* **—rue′ful·ness** *n.*

ru·fes·cent (ro͞o-fĕs′ənt) *adj.* Tinged with red. [Lat. *rufescens, rufescent-,* pr.part. of *rufescere,* to become red < *rufus,* red.] **—ru·fes′cence** *n.*

ruff[1] (rŭf) *n.* **1.** A stiffly starched frilled or pleated circular collar of lace, muslin, or other fine fabric, worn by men and women in the 16th and 17th centuries. **2.** A distinctive collarlike projection around the neck, as of feathers on a bird or of fur on a mammal. **3.** The male of a Eurasian sandpiper, *Philomachus pugnax,* having collarlike, erectile feathers around the neck during the breeding season. [Perh. short for RUFFLE[1].] **—ruffed** *adj.*

ruff[2] (rŭf) *n.* **1.** The playing of a trump card when one cannot follow suit. **2.** An old game resembling whist. —*tr. & intr.v.* **ruffed, ruff·ing, ruffs.** To trump or play a trump. [OFr. *roffle.*]

ruff[3] (rŭf) *n.* A European freshwater fish, *Acerina cernua,* related to the perches. [ME *ruf,* poss. < *ruch,* rough < OE *rūh.*]

ruffed grouse *n.* A chickenlike North American game bird, *Bonasa umbellus,* having mottled brownish plumage.

ruf·fi·an (rŭf′ē-ən, rŭf′yən) *n.* **1.** A tough or rowdy fellow. **2.** A thug or gangster. [OFr.] **—ruf′fi·an·ism** *n.* **—ruf′fi·an·ly** *adj.*

ruf·fle[1] (rŭf′əl) *n.* **1.** A strip of frilled or closely pleated fabric used for trimming or decoration. **2.** A bird's ruff. **3. a.** A ruckus or fray. **b.** Annoyance; vexation. **4.** An irregularity or slight disturbance of a surface. —*v.* **-fled, -fling, -fles.** —*tr.* **1.** To disturb the smoothness or regularity of; ripple. **2.** To pleat or gather (fabric) into a ruffle. **3.** To erect (the feathers). **4.** To discompose; fluster. **5.** To flip through (the pages of a book). **6.** To shuffle (cards). —*intr.* **1.** To become irregular or rough. **2.** To flutter. **3.** To become flustered. [< ME *ruffelen,* to roughen.]

ruf·fle[2] (rŭf′əl) *n.* A low continuous beating of a drum that is not as loud as a roll. —*tr.v.* **-fled, -fling, -fles.** To beat a ruffle on (a drum). [Freq. of obs. *ruff,* a drum roll.]

ruf·fle[3] (rŭf′əl) *intr.v.* **-fled, -fling, -fles.** To behave arrogantly or roughly; swagger. [ME *ruffelen.*] **—ruf′fler** *n.*

ru·fous (ro͞o′fəs) *adj.* Strong yellowish pink to moderate orange. [Lat. *rufus,* red.]

rug (rŭg) *n.* **1.** A piece of heavy fabric used to cover a portion of a floor. **2.** An animal skin used as a floor covering. **3.** *Chiefly Brit.* A piece of thick, warm fabric or fur used as a coverlet or lap robe. [Of Scand. orig.]

ru·ga (ro͞o′gə) *n., pl.* **-gae** (-gē′, -gī′). Often **rugae.** *Biol.* A fold, crease, or wrinkle, as in the lining of the stomach. [Lat.] **—ru′gate′** (-gāt′) *adj.*

Rug·by (rŭg′bē) *n.* A form of football in which players on two competing teams may kick, dribble, or run with the ball, and forward passing, substitution of players, and time-outs are not permitted. [After *Rugby* School, England.]

rug·ged (rŭg′ĭd) *adj.* **1.** Having a rough, irregular surface: *rugged terrain.* **2.** Having strong features marked with furrows or wrinkles. **3.** Tempestuous; stormy. **4.** Demanding great effort, ability, or endurance. **5.** Lacking culture or polish. **6.** Vigorously healthy; hardy. [ME, shaggy, of Scand. orig.] **—rug′ged·ly** *adv.* **—rug′ged·ness** *n.*

rug·ger (rŭg′ər) *n. Chiefly Brit.* Rugby.

ru·gose (ro͞o′gōs′) also **ru·gous** (-gəs) *adj.* **1.** Having many wrinkles or creases. **2.** *Bot.* Having a rough and ridged surface, as certain prominently veined leaves do. [Lat. *rugosus* < *ruga,* wrinkle.] **—ru′gose′ly** *adv.* **—ru·gos′i·ty** (-gŏs′ĭ-tē) *n.*

ru·in (ro͞o′ĭn) *n.* **1.** Total destruction or disintegration rendering something formless, useless, or valueless. **2.** The cause of total destruction: *A single flaw is the ruin of a diamond.* **3.** A condition of total destruction or collapse: *The city fell into ruin.* **4.** Often **ruins.** The remains of something destroyed, disintegrated, or decayed. **5. a.** Total loss of one's health, fortune, position, or honor. **b.** The cause of such loss: *Drinking was his ruin.* **6.** A ruined person, object, or building. —*v.* **-ined, -in·ing, -ins.** —*tr.* **1.** To destroy or demolish completely. **2.** To harm irreparably. **3.** To reduce to poverty or bankruptcy. **4.** To deprive of chastity. —*intr.* To fall into ruin. [ME *ruine* < OFr. < Lat. *ruina,* ruin, a falling down < *ruere,* to rush.] **—ru′in·a·ble** *adj.* **—ru′in·er** *n.*

Synonyms: *ruin, raze, demolish, destroy, devastate, damage, wreck.* These verbs mean to cause serious injury to a thing or, less often, to a person. *Ruin* implies depriving of usefulness, soundness, or integrity without altogether doing away with the object injured. *Raze* means to level to the ground, and *demolish,* to pull down or break into pieces. *Destroy* is less specific but stresses an end to usefulness if not utter elimination of something. *Devastate* means to lay waste and implies severe and widespread injury and desolation. *Damage* is nonspecific with respect to extent of injury but in general is the weakest of these terms. *Wreck* suggests severe, usually irreparable injury, often incurred violently or willfully.

ru·in·ate (ro͞o′ə-nāt′) *adj.* Ruined. [Med. Lat. *ruinatus,* p.part. of *ruinare,* to ruin < Lat. *ruina,* ruin.]

ru·in·a·tion (ro͞o′ə-nā′shən) *n.* **1. a.** The act of ruining. **b.** The condition of being ruined. **2.** The cause of ruin.

ru·in·ous (ro͞o′ə-nəs) *adj.* **1.** Causing or apt to cause ruin; destructive. **2.** Falling to ruin; dilapidated or decayed. **—ru′in·ous·ly** *adv.* **—ru′in·ous·ness** *n.*

rule (ro͞ol) *n.* **1. a.** Governing power or its possession or use; authority. **b.** The duration of such power. **2.** An authoritative direction for conduct, esp. one of the regulations governing procedure in a legislative body or a regulation observed by the players in a game, sport, or contest. **3.** A usual or customary course of action or behavior: *Violence is the rule in that area.* **4.** A statement that describes what is true in most or all cases. **5.** A standard method or procedure for solving a class of mathematical problems. **6.** *Law.* **a.** A court order limited in application to a specific case. **b.** A subordinate regulation governing a particular matter. **7.** A ruler (sense 2). **8.** *Printing.* A thin metal strip of various widths and designs, used to print borders or lines, as between columns. —*v.* **ruled, rul·ing, rules.** —*tr.* **1.** To exercise control over; govern. **2.** To dominate by powerful influence; hold sway over. **3.** To keep within proper limits; restrain. **4.** To decide or declare judicially; decree. **5. a.** To mark with straight parallel lines: *ruled note paper.* **b.** To mark (a straight line), as with a ruler. —*intr.* **1.** To exercise authority; be in control or command. **2.** To formulate and issue a decree or decision. **3.** To maintain a specified rate or level: *Prices ruled low.* **—phrasal verb. rule out.** To remove from consideration; exclude: *The snowstorm ruled out their weekly meeting.* **—idioms. as a rule.** In general; for the most part: *As a rule, we take the bus.* **rule of thumb.** A useful principle that has wide application but is not intended to be strictly accurate. [ME *reule* < OFr. < Lat. *regula* < *regere,* to rule.] **—rul′a·ble** *adj.*

ruled surface *n.* A surface, such as a cone or a cylinder, generated by the motion of a straight line.

rul·er (ro͞o′lər) *n.* **1.** One that rules or governs, as a sovereign.

2. A straight-edged strip, as of wood or metal, for drawing straight lines and measuring lengths.

rul·ing (ro͞o′lĭng) *adj.* **1.** Exercising control or authority. **2.** Predominant. *—n.* **1.** The act of governing or controlling. **2.** An authoritative or official decision: *a court ruling.*

rum[1] (rŭm) *n.* **1.** An alcoholic liquor distilled from fermented molasses or sugar cane. **2.** Intoxicating beverages. [Prob. short for obs. *rumbullion.*]

rum[2] (rŭm) *adj.* **rum·mer, rum·mest.** *Chiefly Brit.* Odd; queer. [Orig. unknown.]

ru·ma·ki (rə-mä′kē) *n.* An appetizer of Japanese origin consisting of a marinated piece of chicken liver and a water chestnut that are wrapped in a slice of bacon and grilled or broiled. [Perh. of J. orig.]

Ru·ma·ni·an (ro͞o-mā′nē-ən, -mān′yən) also **Ro·ma·ni·an** (rō-) or **Rou·ma·ni·an** (ro͞o-) *—adj.* Of or pertaining to Rumania, its people, or their language. *—n.* **1.** A native or inhabitant of Rumania. **2.** The Romance language of the Rumanians.

rum·ba also **rhum·ba** (rŭm′bə, ro͝om′-, ro͞om′-) *n.* **1.** A complex rhythmical dance that originated in Cuba. **2.** A modern ballroom adaptation of the rumba. [Am. Sp. < *rumbo,* revelry < Sp., pomp.]

rum·ble (rŭm′bəl) *v.* **-bled, -bling, -bles.** *—intr.* **1.** To make a deep, long rolling sound. **2.** To move or proceed with a rumbling sound. **3.** *Slang.* To engage in a gang fight. *—tr.* **1.** To utter with a rumbling sound. **2.** To polish or mix (metal parts) in a tumbling box. *—n.* **1.** A deep, long rolling sound. **2.** A tumbling box. **3.** A luggage compartment or servant's seat in the rear of a carriage. **4.** *Slang.* **a.** Pervasive, widespread expression of unrest or dissatisfaction. **b.** A gang fight. [ME *romblen,* prob. < MDu. *rommeler.*] **—rum′bler** *n.* **—rum′bling·ly** *adv.* **—rum′bly** *adj.*

rumble seat *n.* An uncovered passenger seat that opens out from the rear of an automobile.

ru·men (ro͞o′mən) *n., pl.* **-mi·na** (-mə-nə) or **-mens.** The first division of the stomach of a ruminant animal, in which food is partly digested before being regurgitated for further chewing. [Lat., throat.]

ru·mi·nant (ro͞o′mə-nənt) *n.* Any of various hoofed, even-toed, usually horned mammals of the suborder Ruminantia, such as cattle, sheep, goats, deer, and giraffes, characteristically having a stomach divided into four compartments and chewing a cud consisting of regurgitated, partially digested food. *—adj.* **1.** Characterized by the chewing of cud. **2.** Of or belonging to the Ruminantia. **3.** Meditative; contemplative. [< NLat. *Ruminantia,* suborder name < Lat. *ruminare,* to ruminate.]

ru·mi·nate (ro͞o′mə-nāt′) *v.* **-nat·ed, -nat·ing, -nates.** *—intr.* **1.** To chew cud. **2.** To meditate at length; muse. *—tr.* To meditate or reflect on. [Lat. *ruminare, ruminat-* < *rumen,* throat.] **—ru′mi·na′tive** *adj.* **—ru′mi·na′tive·ly** *adv.* **—ru′mi·na′tor** *n.*

ru·mi·na·tion (ro͞o′mə-nā′shən) *n.* **1.** The act or process of chewing cud. **2.** The act of pondering; meditation.

rum·mage (rŭm′ĭj) *v.* **-maged, -mag·ing, -mag·es.** *—tr.* **1.** To search thoroughly by handling, turning over, or disarranging the contents of. **2.** To discover by searching thoroughly. *—intr.* To make an energetic, usually hasty search. *—n.* **1.** A thorough search among a number of things. **2.** A confusion of miscellaneous articles. [Obs. *rummage,* act of packing cargo < OFr. *arrumage* < *arumer,* to stow : *a-,* to (< Lat. *ad-*) + *run,* ship's hold, of Germanic orig.] **—rum′mag·er** *n.*

rummage sale *n.* **1.** A sale of assorted secondhand objects contributed by donors to raise money for a charity. **2.** A sale, esp. of unclaimed or excess goods, as at a warehouse or wharf.

rum·mer (rŭm′ər) *n.* A large drinking cup or glass. [G. *Römer* < Du. *roemer* < *roemen,* to praise.]

rum·my[1] (rŭm′ē) *n.* A card game, played in many variations, in which the object is to obtain sets of three or more cards of the same rank or suit. [Orig. unknown.]

rum·my[2] (rŭm′ē) *n., pl.* **-mies.** *Slang.* A drunkard.

rum·my[3] (rŭm′ē) *adj.* **-mi·er, -mi·est.** *Chiefly Brit.* Rum[2].

ru·mor (ro͞o′mər) *n.* Unverified information of uncertain origin usually spread by word of mouth; hearsay. *—tr.v.* **-mored, -mor·ing, -mors.** To spread or tell by rumor. [ME < OFr. < Lat.]

ru·mor·mon·ger (ro͞o′mər-mŭng′gər, -mŏng′-) *n.* A person who spreads rumors.

ru·mour (ro͞o′mər) *n. & v. Chiefly Brit.* Variant of **rumor.**

rump (rŭmp) *n.* **1.** The fleshy hindquarters of an animal. **2.** A cut of beef or veal from the rump. **3.** The human buttocks. **4.** The part of a bird's back nearest the tail. **5.** The last or inferior part. **6.** A legislature having only a small part of its original membership and so being unrepresentative or lacking authority. [ME *rumpe,* of Scand. orig.]

rum·ple (rŭm′pəl) *v.* **-pled, -pling, -ples.** *—tr.* To wrinkle or form into folds or creases. *—intr.* To become wrinkled or creased. *—n.* An irregular or untidy crease. [Du. *rompelen* < MDu.] **—rum′ply** *adj.*

rum·pus (rŭm′pəs) *n.* A noisy clamor. [Orig. unknown.]

rumpus room *n.* A room for play and parties.

rum·run·ner (rŭm′rŭn′ər) *n.* **1.** A person who illegally transports liquor across a border. **2.** A boat used to transport liquor illegally across a border.

run (rŭn) *v.* **ran** (răn), **run, run·ning, runs.** *—intr.* **1. a.** To move swiftly on foot so both feet leave the ground during each stride. **b.** To move at a fast gallop. Used of a horse. **2.** To retreat rapidly; flee: *grabbed the money and ran.* **3. a.** To move without hindrance or restraint: *dogs running loose.* **b.** To keep company: *ran with a wild crowd.* **c.** To go or move about from place to place; roam: *always running around without her glasses.* **4.** To migrate, esp. to move in a shoal in order to spawn. **5. a.** To move or go quickly; hurry: *run for the police.* **b.** To go when in trouble or distress: *always running to his lawyer.* **c.** To make a short, quick trip or visit. **6. a.** To take part in a race or contest: *ran in the Boston Marathon.* **b.** To compete in a race for elected office: *ran for mayor.* **c.** To finish a race or contest in a specified position: *ran second.* **7.** To move freely, as by rolling or sliding: *The car ran downhill.* **8.** To be in operation: *The engine is running.* **9.** To go back and forth esp. on a regular basis; ply: *The ferry runs every hour.* **10.** *Naut.* To sail or steer before the wind or on an indicated course: *run before a storm.* **11. a.** To flow in a steady stream. **b.** To emit pus or serous fluid. **12.** To melt and flow: *A hot flame will make the solder run.* **13.** To spread or dissolve, as dyes in fabric: *Colorfast garments do not run.* **14.** To extend, stretch, or reach in a certain direction or to a particular point: *This road runs to the next town.* **15.** To extend, spread, or climb as a result of growing: *ivy running up the wall.* **16.** To spread rapidly: *disease that ran rampant.* **17. a.** To be valid in a given area: *The speed limit runs only to the town line.* **b.** To be present as a valid accompaniment: *Fishing rights run with ownership of the land.* **18.** To unravel along a line: *Her stocking ran.* **19.** To continue in effect or operation: *a lease with one year to run.* **20.** To pass: *Days ran into weeks.* **21.** To tend to persist or recur: *Stinginess runs in that family.* **22. a.** To accumulate or accrue: *The interest runs from the first of the month.* **b.** To become payable. **23.** To take a particular form or order: *His reasoning runs thus.* **24.** To tend or incline: *Her tastes run to the bizarre.* **25.** To occupy or exist in a certain range: *The sizes run from small to large.* **26.** To be presented or performed for a continuous period of time: *The play ran for six months.* **27.** To pass into a specified condition: *We ran into debt.* *—tr.* **1. a.** To travel over on foot at a pace faster than the walk: *run the entire distance.* **b.** To cause (an animal) to move quickly or rapidly. **2.** To allow to move without restraint. **3.** To do or accomplish by or as if by running: *run errands.* **4.** To hunt or pursue; chase: *dogs running deer.* **5.** To bring to a given condition by or as if by running: *She ran him ragged.* **6.** To cause to move quickly: *He ran his fingers along the keyboard.* **7. a.** To cause to compete in or as if in a race: *He ran two horses in the Derby.* **b.** To present or nominate for elective office: *They ran him for mayor.* **8.** To cause to move or progress freely. **9.** To cause to function; operate: *run a machine.* **10.** To convey or transport: *Run me into town.* **11.** *Naut.* To cause to move on a course: *We ran our boat into a cove.* **12. a.** To smuggle: *run guns.* **b.** To evade and pass through: *run a roadblock.* **13.** To pass over or through: *run the rapids.* **14.** To cause to flow: *run water into a tub.* **15.** To stream with: *The fountains ran wine.* **16. a.** To melt, fuse, or smelt (metal). **b.** To mold or cast (molten metal): *run gold into ingots.* **17.** To cause to extend or pass: *run a rope between the poles.* **18.** To mark or trace on a surface: *run a pencil line between two points.* **19.** To sew with a continuous line of stitches: *run a seam.* **20.** To cause to unravel along a line: *ran her stocking on a splinter.* **21. a.** To cause to crash or collide: *ran the car into a fence.* **b.** To cause to penetrate: *She ran a pin into her thumb.* **22.** To continue to present or perform: *ran the film for a month.* **23.** To publish in a periodical: *run an advertisement.* **24.** To subject or be subjected to: *run a risk.* **25. a.** To score (balls or points) consecutively in billiard games: *run 15 balls.* **b.** To clear (the table) in pool by consecutive scores. **26.** To conduct or perform: *run an experiment.* **27.** To control, manage, or direct: *ran the campaign by herself.* **—phrasal verbs. run across.** To find by chance; come upon. **run after. 1.** To pursue; chase. **2.** To seek the company or attention of: *got tired of running after her.* **run against. 1.** To encounter unexpectedly; run into. **2.** To work against; oppose: *found public sentiment running against him.* **run along.** To go away; leave. **run away. 1. a.** To flee; escape. **b.** To leave one's home, esp. to elope. **2.** To stampede. **run away with. 1. a.** To make off with hurriedly. **b.** To steal. **2.** To be greater or better than others in (a performance, for example). **run down. 1.** To stop because of lack of force or power. **2.** To become tired. **3. a.** To collide with and knock down. **b.** To collide with and cause to sink. **4.** To chase and capture. **5.** To trace the source of: *ran down all possible leads.* **6.** To disparage. **7.** To run over; review: *run down a list once more.* **8.** *Baseball.* To put a runner out after trapping him between two bases. **run in. 1.** To insert or include as something extra. **2.** *Printing.* To make a solid body of text without a paragraph or other break. **3.** *Slang.* To take into legal custody. **4.** To go to or seek out the company of in order to socialize; visit. **run into. 1.** To meet or find by chance: *ran into an old friend.* **2.** To encounter: *ran into trouble.* **3.** To collide with. **4.** To amount to:

rumble seat

runabout

runcinate
Runcinate leaf of dandelion

basic Germanic runic alphabet

ð ȝ
edh yogh

two later runes used in English

rune¹

rung¹

running board

His net worth ran into seven figures. **run off. 1.** To print, duplicate, or copy: *ran off 200 copies.* **2.** To run away; elope. **3.** To spill over; overflow. **4.** To decide a contest or competition by a run-off. **5.** To force or drive off (trespassers, for example). **run off with.** To steal or carry away. **run on. 1. a.** To keep going; continue. **b.** To talk volubly, persistently, and usually inconsequentially: *He ran on about his tax problems.* **2.** *Printing.* To continue a text without a formal break. **run out. 1.** To become used up; be exhausted: *The supplies ran out.* **2.** To put out by force; compel to leave: *ran him out of town.* **3.** To become void, esp. through the passage of time or an omission: *an insurance policy that had run out.* **run out of.** To exhaust the supply of: *ran out of gas.* **run out on.** To abandon: *ran out on his wife; ran out on the liberal party.* **run over. 1.** To collide with, knock down, and often pass over: *The car ran over a child.* **2.** To read or review quickly. **3.** To flow over. **4.** To go beyond a limit: *The meeting ran over by 30 minutes.* **run through. 1.** To pierce: *was run through by a dagger.* **2.** To use up quickly: *ran through all her money.* **3.** To rehearse quickly. **4.** To go over the salient facts of: *run through preflight procedures.* **run up.** To make or become greater or larger: *ran up huge bills.* —*n.* **1. a.** A pace faster than a walk. **b.** A gait faster than a canter. **2.** An act of running. **3. a.** A distance covered by or as if by running. **b.** The time taken to cover such a distance: *a two minutes' run from the subway.* **4.** A running race: *won the mile run.* **5.** A quick trip or visit: *a run into town.* **6.** *Baseball.* A point scored by advancing around the bases and reaching home plate safely. **7.** *Football.* A player's attempt to carry the ball past or through the opposing team, usually for a specified distance: *a 30-yard run.* **8. a.** The migrating of fish, esp. in order to spawn. **b.** A group or school of fish ascending a river in order to spawn. **9.** Unrestricted freedom or use: *I had the run of their library.* **10.** A stretch or period of riding, as in a race or to hounds. **11.** A track or slope along or down which something can travel: *a ski run.* **12.** The distance a golf ball rolls after hitting the ground. **13. a.** A scheduled or regular route. **b.** The territory of a news reporter. **14. a.** A continuous period of operation, esp. of a machine or factory. **b.** The production achieved during such a period: *a run of 5,000 copies of a book.* **15. a.** A movement or flow. **b.** The duration of such a flow. **c.** The amount of such a flow. **16.** A pipe or channel through which something flows: *a mill run.* **17.** A small, fast-flowing stream or brook. **18.** A fall or slide, as of sand or mud. **19.** A continuous length or extent of something: *a ten-foot run of tubing.* **20.** A vein or seam, as of ore or rock. **21.** The direction, configuration, or lie of something: *the run of the grain in leather.* **22. a.** A trail or way made or frequented by animals. **b.** An outdoor enclosure for domestic animals or poultry. **23. a.** A length of torn or unraveled stitches in a knitted fabric. **b.** A blemish caused by excessive paint flow. **24.** An unbroken series or sequence: *a run of dry summers.* **25.** An unbroken sequence of theatrical performances. **26.** *Mus.* A rapid sequence of notes; roulade. **27.** A series of unexpected and urgent demands, as by depositors or customers: *a run on a bank.* **28. a.** A continuous set or sequence, as of playing cards in one suit. **b.** A successful sequence of shots or points. **29.** A sustained state or condition: *a run of good luck.* **30.** A trend or tendency: *the run of events.* **31.** The average type, group, or category; majority: *The broad run of voters want him to win.* **32.** *Slang.* Diarrhea. —***idioms.*** **a run for (one's) money.** Strong competition. **in the long run.** In the final analysis or outcome. **in the short run.** In the immediate future. **on the run. 1. a.** In rapid retreat. **b.** In hiding, as a fugitive. **2.** Hurrying busily from place to place. **run a temperature.** To have a fever. **run rings around.** To be markedly superior to. **run short. 1.** To become scanty or insufficient in supply: *Fuel oil ran short during the winter.* **2.** To use up so that a supply becomes insufficient or scanty: *ran short of paper clips.* [ME *runnen* < OE *rinnan.*]

run·a·bout (rŭn'ə-bout') *n.* **1. a.** A small, open automobile or carriage. **b.** A small motorboat. **c.** A light aircraft. **2.** A vagabond or wanderer.

run·a·gate (rŭn'ə-gāt') *n. Archaic.* **1.** A renegade or deserter. **2.** A vagabond. [Alteration of RENEGADE.]

run-a·round (rŭn'ə-round') *n.* **1.** Deception, usually in the form of evasive excuses. **2.** *Printing.* Type set in a column narrower than the body of the text, as on either side of a picture.

run·a·way (rŭn'ə-wā') *n.* **1.** A person who has run away, as a fugitive. **2.** Something that has escaped from control or proper confinement. **3.** *Informal.* An easy victory. —*adj.* **1.** Escaping or having escaped from captivity or control. **2.** Out of control or proper confinement: *a runaway car.* **3.** Easily won: *a runaway victory.* **4.** Of or pertaining to a rapid price rise.

run·back (rŭn'băk') *n. Football.* **1.** The act of returning a kickoff, punt, or intercepted forward pass. **2.** The distance covered in a runback.

run·ci·ble spoon (rŭn'sə-bəl) *n.* A three-pronged fork, as a pickle fork, curved like a spoon and having a cutting edge. [Coined by Edward Lear (1812–1888).]

run·ci·nate (rŭn'sə-nāt') *adj. Bot.* Having saw-toothed divisions directed backward: *runcinate leaves.* [Lat. *runcinatus,* p.part. of *runcinare,* to plane < *runcina,* carpenter's plane.]

run-down (rŭn'doun') *n.* **1.** A point-by-point summary. **2.** *Baseball.* A play in which a runner is put out when he is trapped between bases. —*adj.* (rŭn'doun'). **1.** In poor physical condition; weak or exhausted. **2.** Unwound and not running.

rune¹ (ro͞on) *n.* **1.** One of the letters of an alphabet used by ancient Germanic peoples, esp. by the Scandinavians and Anglo-Saxons. **2.** A magic charm. [ME < OE *rūn.*] —**run'ic** *adj.*

rune² (ro͞on) *n.* A Finnish poem or canto. [Finn. *runo,* of Germanic orig.]

rung¹ (rŭng) *n.* **1.** A rod or bar forming a step of a ladder. **2.** A crosspiece between the legs of a chair. **3.** The spoke in a wheel. **4.** *Naut.* One of the spokes or handles on a ship's steering wheel. [ME < OE *hrung.*]

rung² (rŭng) *v.* Past participle of **ring²**.

run-in (rŭn'ĭn') *n.* **1.** A quarrel or an argument. **2.** *Printing.* Matter added to a text. —*adj.* (rŭn'ĭn). *Printing.* Added or inserted in a text.

run·let (rŭn'lĭt) *n.* A rivulet.

run·nel (rŭn'əl) *n.* **1.** A rivulet; brook. **2.** A narrow channel or course, as for water. [ME *rynel* < OE < *rinnan,* to run.]

run·ner (rŭn'ər) *n.* **1.** A person who competes in a race. **2. a.** *Baseball.* A person who runs the bases. **b.** *Football.* A person who carries the ball. **3.** A fugitive. **4.** A messenger or errand boy. **5.** An agent or collector, as for a bank or brokerage house. **6.** A person who solicits business, as for a hotel or store. **7.** A smuggler. **8.** A vessel engaged in smuggling. **9.** A person who operates or manages something. **10.** A device in or on which a mechanism slides or moves, as: **a.** The blade of a skate. **b.** The supports on which a drawer slides. **11.** A long narrow carpet. **12.** A long narrow tablecloth. **13.** A roller towel. **14.** *Metallurgy.* A channel along which molten metal is poured into a mold; gate. **15.** *Bot.* **a.** A slender, creeping stem that puts forth roots from nodes spaced at intervals along its length. **b.** A plant, such as the strawberry, having such a stem. **c.** A twining vine, such as the scarlet runner. **16.** Any of several marine fishes of the family Carangidae, such as the blue runner, *Caranx crysos,* of temperate waters of the American Atlantic coast.

run·ner-up (rŭn'ər-ŭp') *n.* One that takes second place.

run·ning (rŭn'ĭng) *n.* **1.** The act or action of one that runs. **2.** The power or ability to run. **3.** The sport or exercise of someone who runs. —*adv.* Consecutively: *four years running.* —***idioms.*** **in the running. 1.** Entered as a contender in a competition. **2.** Having the possibility of winning or placing well in a competition. **out of the running. 1.** Not entered as a contender in a competition. **2.** Having no possibility of winning a contest.

running board *n.* A narrow footboard extending under and beside the doors of some automobiles and other conveyances.

running gear *n.* The working parts of an automobile, locomotive, or other vehicle.

running hand *n.* Handwriting done rapidly without lifting the pen from the paper.

running head *n. Printing.* A title printed at the top of every page or every other page, as in a book.

running knot *n.* A slipknot.

running light *n.* One of several lights on a vehicle, as a ship, kept lighted between dusk and dawn to indicate position and size.

running mate *n.* **1.** A horse used to set the pace in a race for another horse. **2.** The candidate or nominee for the lesser of two closely associated political offices. **3.** A companion.

running start *n.* A flying start.

running stitch *n.* One of a series of small, even stitches.

running title *n.* A running head.

run·ny (rŭn'ē) *adj.* **-ni·er, -ni·est.** Inclined to run or flow.

run-off (rŭn'ôf', -ŏf') *n.* **1. a.** The overflow of a fluid from a container. **b.** Rainfall that is not absorbed by the soil. **2.** Eliminated waste products from manufacturing processes. **3.** An extra competition held to break a tie.

run-of-the-mill (rŭn'əv-*th*ə-mĭl') *adj.* Not special or outstanding; average.

run-on (rŭn'ŏn', -ôn') *n. Printing.* Matter that is appended or added without a formal break. —**run'-on'** *adj.*

runt (rŭnt) *n.* **1.** An undersized animal, esp. the smallest animal of a litter. **2.** A person of small stature. [Orig. unknown.] —**runt'i·ness** *n.* —**runt'y** *adj.*

run-through (rŭn'thro͞o') *n.* A complete but rapid review or rehearsal of something, such as a theatrical work.

run-up (rŭn'ŭp') *n.* An often sudden and rapid increase: *a run-up in interest rates; a run-up in food prices.*

run·way (rŭn'wā') *n.* **1.** A path, channel, or track over which something runs. **2.** The bed of a water course. **3.** A chute down which logs are skidded. **4.** A narrow track in a bowling lane on which balls are returned after they are bowled. **5.** A smooth ramp for wheeled vehicles. **6.** A narrow walkway extending from a stage into an auditorium. **7.** A strip of level ground, usually paved, on which aircraft take off and land.

ru·pee (ro͞o-pē', ro͞o'pē) *n.* See table at **currency.** [Hindi *rupaīyā* < Skt. *rupyam,* silver < *rūpam,* shape.]

ru·pi·ah (ro͞o-pē′ə) *n., pl.* **rupiah** or **-ahs.** See table at **currency.** [Hindi *rupaīyā.* —see RUPEE.]
ru·pic·o·lous (ro͞o-pĭk′ə-ləs) *adj.* Thriving among or inhabiting rocks. [Lat. *rupes,* rock + -COLOUS.]
rup·ture (rŭp′chər) *n.* **1. a.** The process of breaking open or bursting. **b.** The state of being broken open or burst. **2.** A break in friendly relations. **3.** *Pathol.* **a.** A hernia, esp. of the groin or intestines. **b.** A tear in bodily tissue. —*v.* **-tured, -tur·ing, -tures.** —*tr.* To break open; burst. —*intr.* To undergo or suffer a rupture. [ME *ruptur* < OFr. *rupture* < Lat. *ruptura* < *rumpere,* to break.] **—rup′tur·a·ble** *adj.*
ru·ral (ro͝or′əl) *adj.* **1.** Of or pertaining to the country as opposed to the city; rustic. **2.** Of or pertaining to people who live in the country. **3.** Of or relating to farming; agricultural. [ME < OFr. < Lat. *ruralis* < *rus,* country.] **—ru′ral·ly** *adv.*

Synonyms: *rural, arcadian, bucolic, rustic, pastoral, sylvan.* These adjectives are all descriptive of existence or environment that is close to nature; those with a literary flavor are often used facetiously. *Rural* applies to sparsely settled or agricultural country as distinct from settled communities. *Arcadian* implies ideal or simple country living. *Bucolic* is often used derisively of country people or manners. *Rustic,* sometimes uncomplimentary, applies to country people who seem unsophisticated but may also apply favorably to living conditions or to natural environments that are pleasingly primitive. *Pastoral* implies the supposed peace of rural living and the shepherd's life, with a suggestion of artificiality. *Sylvan* refers to wooded as opposed to cultivated country and carries the sense of unspoiled beauty.

rural free delivery *n.* Free government delivery of mail in rural areas.
ru·ral·ism (ro͝or′ə-lĭz′əm) *n.* Rurality.
ru·ral·ist (ro͝or′ə-lĭst) *n.* **1.** One who resides in a rural area. **2.** An advocate of rural life.
ru·ral·i·ty (ro͞o-răl′ĭ-tē) *n., pl.* **-ties. 1.** The state or quality of being rural. **2.** A rural trait or characteristic.
ru·ral·ize (ro͝or′ə-līz′) *tr. & intr.v.* **-ized, -iz·ing, -iz·es.** To make or become rural. **—ru′ral·i·za′tion** *n.*
rural route *n.* A rural mail route.
ruse (ro͞os, ro͞oz) *n.* An action or device meant to confuse or mislead. [ME, detour < OFr. < *ruser,* to drive back. —see RUSH.]
rush¹ (rŭsh) *v.* **rushed, rush·ing, rush·es.** —*intr.* **1.** To move or act swiftly; hurry. **2.** To make a sudden or swift attack or charge. **3.** To flow or surge rapidly, often with noise: *Tons of water rushed over the falls.* **4.** *Football.* To move the ball by running. —*tr.* **1.** To cause to move or act with unusual haste or violence. **2.** To perform with great haste. **3.** To attack swiftly and suddenly. **4.** To carry or transport hastily: *rushed her to the hospital.* **5.** To entertain or pay great attention to: *They rushed him for their fraternity.* —*n.* **1.** A sudden forward motion. **2.** An anxious and eager movement to get to or from a place. **3.** General haste or busyness. **4.** A sudden attack; onslaught. **5.** A rapid, often noisy flow or passage. **6.** *Football.* An attempt to move the ball by running. **7.** Often **rushes.** The first, unedited print of a motion-picture scene. **8.** A great flurry of activity or press of business. **9.** The intensely pleasurable sensation experienced immediately after use of a narcotic. [ME *rushen* < OFr. *ruser,* to drive back < Lat. *recusare,* to reject : *re-,* back + *causari,* to give as a reason < *causa,* cause.] **—rush′er** *n.*
rush² (rŭsh) *n.* **1. a.** Any of various grasslike marsh plants of the family Juncaceae, having pliant hollow or pithy stems. **b.** Any of various similar, usually aquatic plants. **2.** The stem of a rush, used in making baskets, mats, and chair seats. [ME < OE *rysc.*]
rush candle *n.* A rushlight.
rush hour *n.* A period of heavy traffic. **—rush′-hour′** *adj.*
rush·light (rŭsh′līt′) *n.* A candle consisting of a rush wick in tallow.
rush·y (rŭsh′ē) *adj.* **-i·er, -i·est. 1.** Resembling or characteristic of rushes; rushlike. **2.** Abounding in rushes: *a rushy marsh.*
rusk (rŭsk) *n.* **1.** A light, soft-textured sweetened biscuit. **2.** Sweet raised bread dried and browned in an oven. [Sp. *rosca,* coil.]
rus·set (rŭs′ĭt) *n.* **1.** A moderate to strong brown. **2.** A coarse reddish-brown to brown homespun cloth. **3.** A winter apple with a rough reddish-brown skin. —*adj.* Moderate brown to strong brown. [ME < OFr. *rousset* < *rous,* red < Lat. *russus.*]
Rus·sian (rŭsh′ən) *n.* **1.** A native or inhabitant of Russia. **2.** A person who is of Russian descent. **3.** The Slavic language of the Russians that is the official language of the U.S.S.R. [Med. Lat. *Russi* < OR *Rus′.*] **—Rus′sian** *adj.*
Russian dressing *n.* Salad dressing, as mayonnaise, with chili sauce, chopped pickles, and pimientos.
Rus·sian·ize (rŭsh′ə-nīz′) *tr.v.* **-ized, -iz·ing, -iz·es.** To make Russian. **—Rus′sian·i·za′tion** *n.*
Russian olive *n.* The oleaster.
Russian Orthodox Church *n.* An independent branch of the Eastern Orthodox Church headed by the Patriarch of Moscow.
Russian roulette *n.* **1.** A stunt in which a person spins the cylinder of a revolver loaded with one bullet, aims the muzzle at his head, and pulls the trigger. **2.** An act of reckless bravado.
Russian thistle *n.* A red-stemmed, prickly plant, *Salsola kali tenuifolia,* native to Asia, that is a troublesome weed in western North America.
Russian wolfhound *n.* The borzoi.
Russo– *pref.* Russia; Russian: *Russophobe.* [< RUSSIA.]
Rus·so·phil·i·a (rŭs′ə-fĭl′ē-ə) *n.* Interest in or enthusiasm for Russia and its culture, people, government, or language. **—Rus′so·phile′** (-fīl′, -fĭl) *n.*
Rus·so·pho·bi·a (rŭs′ə-fō′bē-ə) *n.* Dislike or fear of Russia or its policies. **—Rus′so·phobe′** (-fōb′) *n.*
rust (rŭst) *n.* **1.** Any of various powdery or scaly reddish-brown or reddish-yellow hydrated ferric oxides formed on iron and iron-containing materials by low-temperature oxidation in the presence of water. **2.** Any of various metallic coatings, esp. oxides, formed by corrosion. **3.** A stain or coating resembling iron rust. **4.** Deterioration, as of ability, resulting from inactivity or neglect. **5. a.** Any of various parasitic fungi of the order Uredinales that are injurious to a wide variety of plants. **b.** A plant disease caused by such fungi, characterized by reddish or brownish spots on leaves, stems, and other parts. **6.** A strong brown. —*v.* **rust·ed, rust·ing, rusts.** —*intr.* **1.** To become corroded. **2.** To deteriorate or degenerate through inactivity or neglect. **3.** To become the color of rust. **4.** To develop a disease caused by a rust fungus. —*tr.* **1.** To corrode or subject (a metal) to rust formation. **2.** To impair or spoil, as by misuse or inactivity. **3.** To color something strong brown. [ME < OE *rūst.*] **—rust** *adj.* **—rust′a·ble** *adj.*
rus·tic (rŭs′tĭk) *adj.* **1.** Of, pertaining to, or typical of country life. **2.** Simple and unsophisticated. **3.** Made of rough tree branches: *rustic furniture.* —*n.* **1.** A rural person. **2.** A crude, coarse, or simple person. [ME *rustyk* < OFr. *rustique* < Lat. *rusticus* < *rus,* country.] **—rus′ti·cal·ly** *adv.*
rus·ti·cate (rŭs′tĭ-kāt′) *v.* **-cat·ed, -cat·ing, -cates.** —*intr.* To go to or live in the country. —*tr.* **1.** To send to the country. **2.** *Chiefly Brit.* To suspend (a student) from a university. **3.** To construct (masonry) with conspicuous, often beveled points. [Lat. *rusticari, rusticat-,* to live in the country < *rus,* country.] **—rus′ti·ca′tion** *n.* **—rus′ti·ca′tor** *n.*
rus·tic·i·ty (rŭ-stĭs′ĭ-tē) *n., pl.* **-ties. 1.** The state or condition of being rustic. **2.** A rustic trait or mannerism.
rus·tle (rŭs′əl) *v.* **-tled, -tling, -tles.** —*intr.* **1.** To move with soft fluttering or crackling sounds. **2.** To move or act energetically or with speed. **3.** To forage food. **4.** To steal cattle. —*tr.* **1.** To cause to rustle. **2.** To obtain by rustling. **3.** To steal (cattle). [ME *rustlen.*] **—rus′tler** *n.* **—rus′tling·ly** *adv.*
rust·less (rŭst′lĭs) *adj.* Free from rust.
rust·proof (rŭst′pro͞of′) *adj.* Incapable of rusting.
rust·y (rŭs′tē) *adj.* **-i·er, -i·est. 1.** Covered with rust; corroded. **2.** Consisting of or produced by rust. **3.** Having a yellowish-red or brownish-red color. **4.** Working or operating stiffly or incorrectly because of or as if because of rust. **5.** Weakened or impaired by neglect, disuse, or lack of practice. **—rust′i·ly** *adv.* **—rust′i·ness** *n.*
rut¹ (rŭt) *n.* **1.** A sunken track or groove made by the passage of vehicles. **2.** A fixed and usually boring routine. —*tr.v.* **rut·ted, rut·ting, ruts.** To furrow. [Poss. < OFr. *route,* way. —see ROUTE.]
rut² (rŭt) *n.* **1.** A cyclically recurring condition of sexual excitement and reproductive activity in male mammals, such as deer. **2.** A periodic condition of mammalian sexual activity; estrus. —*intr.v.* **rut·ted, rut·ting, ruts.** To be in rut. [ME *rutte* < OFr. *rut,* bellowing < LLat. < Lat. *rugire,* to roar.]
ru·ta·ba·ga (ro͞o′tə-bā′gə, ro͝ot′ə-) *n.* **1.** A plant, *Brassica napobrassica,* native to Eurasia, having a thick, bulbous root used as food and livestock feed. **2.** The edible root of the rutabaga. [Dial. Swed. *rotabagge* : *rot,* root (< ON *rōt*) + *bagge,* bag (< ON *baggi*).]
ruth (ro͞oth) *n.* **1.** Compassion or pity for another. **2.** Sorrow or misery about one's own misdeeds or flaws. [ME < *rewen,* to rue < OE *hrēowan.*]
Ruth (ro͞oth) *n.* **1.** In the Old Testament, a Moabite widow who left home with her mother-in-law and went to Bethlehem, where she later married Boaz. **2.** See table at **Bible.** [Heb. *Rūth,* poss. < *rē′ūth,* companion.]
Ru·the·ni·an (ro͞o-thē′nē-ən, -thēn′yən) *n.* **1.** A member of a group of Ukrainians living in Ruthenia. **2.** The Ukrainian dialect of the Ruthenians. **—Ru·the′ni·an** *adj.*
ru·then·ic (ro͞o-thĕn′ĭk, -thē′nĭk) *adj.* Pertaining to or containing ruthenium with a high valence.
ru·the·ni·ous (ro͞o-thē′nē-əs) *adj.* Pertaining to or containing ruthenium with a low valence. [RUTHENI(UM) + -OUS.]
ru·the·ni·um (ro͞o-thē′nē-əm) *n.* *Symbol* **Ru** A hard white acid-resistant metallic element that is found in platinum ores and is used to harden platinum and palladium for jewelry and in alloys for nonmagnetic wear-resistant instrument pivots and electrical contacts. Atomic number 44; atomic weight 101.07; melting point 2,250°C; boiling point 3,900°C; specific gravity 12.41; valences 0, 1, 2, 3, 4, 5, 6, 7, 8. [< Med. Lat. *Ruthenia,* Russia.]
ruth·er·ford (rŭth′ər-fərd) *n.* A unit of radioactivity equal to

the quantity of radioactive material that undergoes one million disintegrations per second. [After Ernest *Rutherford* (1871–1937), 1st Baron Rutherford.]
Rutherford scattering (rŭth′ər-fərd) *n.* The scattering undergone by a stream of heavy charged particles fired at a sample of a heavy metal, due to exposure to coulombic forces in the atomic nuclei of the sample.
ruth·ful (ro͞oth′fəl) *adj.* **1.** Full of sorrow; rueful. **2.** Causing sorrow or pity. **—ruth′ful·ly** *adv.* **—ruth′ful·ness** *n.*
ruth·less (ro͞oth′lĭs) *adj.* Having no compassion or pity; merciless. **—ruth′less·ly** *adv.* **—ruth′less·ness** *n.*
ru·ti·lant (ro͞ot′l-ənt) *adj.* Bright red in color. [ME *rutilaunt* < Lat. *rutilans,* pr.part. of *rutilare,* to make red < *rutilus,* red.]
ru·tile (ro͞o′tēl′, -tīl′) *n.* The lustrous red, reddish-brown, or black natural mineral form of titanium dioxide, TiO_2, used as a gemstone, as a source of titanium, and in paints and fillers. [G. *Rutil* < Lat. *rutilus,* red.]
rut·tish (rŭt′ĭsh) *adj.* Lustful; libidinous. **—rut′tish·ly** *adv.* **—rut′tish·ness** *n.*
rut·ty (rŭt′ē) *adj.* **-ti·er, -ti·est.** Full of ruts. **—rut′ti·ness** *n.*
R-val·ue (är′văl′yo͞o) *n.* A measure of the capacity of a material, such as insulation, to impede heat flow with increasing values indicating a greater capacity. [R(ESISTANCE) VALUE.]
Rx (är′ĕks′) *n.* **1.** A prescription for medicine or medical appliances. **2.** A remedy, cure, or solution for a disorder or a problem. [Alteration of ℞, symbol used in prescriptions, abbr. of Lat. *recipe,* imper. of *recipere,* to take. —see RECEIVE.]
-ry *suff.* Variant of **-ery.**
ry·a (rē′ə) *n.* **1.** A handwoven Scandinavian rug with a thick pile and usually very colorful abstract designs. **2.** The weaving pattern characteristic of rya rugs. [After *Rya,* a village in Sweden.]
rye[1] (rī) *n.* **1.** A widely cultivated cereal grass, *Secale cereale,* whose seeds are valued as grain. **2.** The grain of the rye, used in making flour and whiskey and for livestock feed. **3.** Whiskey made from rye. [ME < OE *ryge.*]
rye[2] (rī) *n.* A male Gypsy. [Romany *rai* < Skt. *rājan,* king. —see RAJAH.]
rye bread *n.* Bread made partially or entirely from rye flour.
rye grass *n.* Any of several pasture or meadow grasses of the genus *Lolium,* native to Eurasia.
rynd (rĭnd, rīnd) *n.* An iron bar supporting an upper millstone. [ME.]
ry·ot (rī′ət) *n.* A peasant or tenant farmer in India. [Hindi *ra‘īyat* < Ar. *ra‘īyah,* herd.]

S

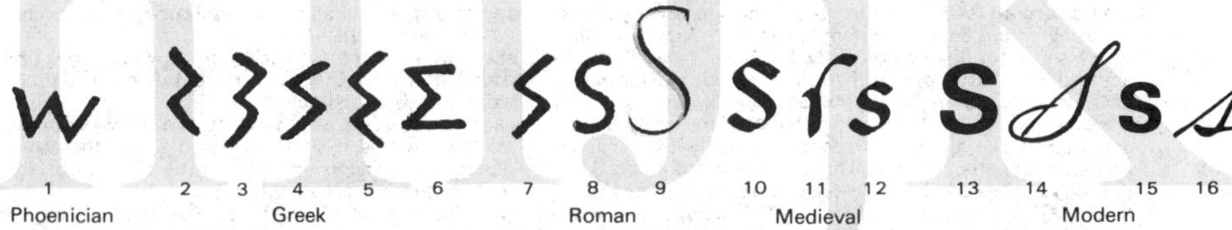

Around 1000 B.C. the Phoenicians and other Semitic peoples began to use graphic signs to represent individual speech sounds instead of syllables or words. They used this symbol (1) to represent the sound of the consonant represented in English orthography by "sh" and called it *shin,* their word for "tooth." The Greeks, adapting the Phoenician alphabet, used *shin* to represent the sound of the consonant "s." They varied its orientation (2,3,4, 5,6) and altered its name to *sigma.* The Romans borrowed the alphabet from the Greeks via the Etruscans and adapted it for carving in stone. Monumental script (9) is the prototype of modern capital letters (13,14). Medieval scribes adapted the Roman capitals to being quickly written on paper, parchment, and vellum. These uncial and cursive minuscules (10,11,12) are the prototypes of modern lower-case letters, both written and printed (16,15).

s

s or **S** (ĕs) *n., pl.* **s's** or **S's.** **1.** The 19th letter of the modern English alphabet. **2.** Any of the speech sounds represented by the letter *s.* **3.** Something shaped like the letter S. **4.** The 19th in a series.

S The symbol for the element sulfur.

-s¹ or **-es** *suff.* Used to form plural nouns: *letters.* [ME < OE *-as,* nominative and accusative pl. suffix.]

-s² or **-es** *suff.* Used to form the 3rd person singular present of all regular and most irregular verbs: *looks; holds.* [ME < OE *-es, -as.*]

-s³ *suff.* Used to form adverbs: *They were caught unawares. He works nights.* [ME *-es,* genitive sing. suffix < OE.]

-'s¹. Used to form the possessive case of singular nouns, plural nouns that do not end in *s,* certain pronouns, and phrases that function as nouns or pronouns: *nation's; women's; another's; the girl next door's cat.* [ME *-es,* genitive sing. suffix < OE.]

-'s² *suff.* **1.** Is: *She's here.* **2.** Has: *He's arrived.* **3.** Does: *What's he want?* **4.** Us: *Let's go.*

Saa·nen (sä'nən, zä'-) *n.* A dairy goat of a breed developed in Switzerland, having a white, short-haired coat and no horns. [After *Saanen,* Switzerland.]

sab·a·dil·la (săb'ə-dĭl'ə, -dē'ə) *n.* **1.** A tropical American plant, *Schoenocaulon officinale,* having poisonous seeds used in insecticides. **2.** The dry, ripe seeds of the sabadilla. [Sp. *cebadilla,* dim. of *cebada,* barley < *cebo,* feed < Lat. *cibus,* food.]

Sab·a·oth (săb'ā-ŏth', sə-bā'ōth') *pl.n.* Hosts; armies: *the Lord of Sabaoth.* [Lat. *sabaoth* < Gk. *sabaōth* < Heb. *ṣĕbhā'oth* < *ṣābhā',* army.]

sab·bat (săb'ət) *n.* The witches' Sabbath. [Fr., sabbat, Sabbath < OFr., Sabbath.]

Sab·ba·tar·i·an (săb'ə-târ'ē-ən) *n.* **1.** A person who observes Saturday as the Sabbath, as in Judaism. **2.** A person who believes in strict observance of the Sabbath. *—adj.* Pertaining to the Sabbath or to Sabbatarians. [LLat. *sabbatarius* < Lat. *sabbatum,* Sabbath.] **—Sab'ba·tar'i·an·ism** *n.*

Sab·bath (săb'əth) *n.* **1.** The seventh day of the week, Saturday, observed as the day of rest and worship by the Jews and some Christian sects. **2.** The first day of the week, Sunday, observed as the day of rest and worship by most Christians. [ME *sabath* < OFr. *sabbat* and OE *sabat,* both < Lat. *sabbatum* < Gk. *sabbaton* < Heb. *shabbāth* < *shābhath,* he rested.]

sab·bat·i·cal (sə-băt'ĭ-kəl) also **sab·bat·ic** (-ĭk) *adj.* **1. Sabbatical** also **Sabbatic.** Pertaining or appropriate to the Sabbath as the day of rest. **2.** Pertaining to a sabbatical year. *—n.* A sabbatical year. [LLat. *sabbaticus* < Gk. *sabbatikos* < *sabbaton,* Sabbath.]

sabbatical year *n.* **1.** Often **Sabbatical year.** A year during which land remained fallow, observed every seven years by the ancient Jews. **2.** A leave of absence, often with pay, usually granted every seventh year, as to a college professor, for travel, research, or rest.

Sa·bel·li·an (sə-bĕl'ē-ən) *n.* **1.** A group of extinct Italic languages that includes Sabine. **2.** A speaker of one of these languages. [< Lat. *Sabellus,* Sabine.] **—Sa·bel'li·an** *adj.*

sa·ber (sā'bər) *n.* **1.** A heavy cavalry sword with a one-edged, slightly curved blade. **2.** A light dueling or fencing sword having an arched guard covering the hand and a tapered flexible blade with a cutting edge on one side and on the tip. *—tr.v.* **-bered, -ber·ing, -bers.** To hit, injure, or kill with a saber. [Fr. *sabre* < obs. G. *sabel.*]

saber rattling *n.* A flamboyant display of military power.

sa·ber-toothed tiger (sā'bər-to͞otht') *n.* Any of various extinct cats of the Oligocene to the Pleistocene epoch, esp. one of the larger members of the genus *Smilodon,* characterized by long upper canine teeth.

sa·bin (sā'bĭn) *n.* A unit of acoustic absorption equivalent to the absorption by one square foot of a surface that absorbs all incident sound. [After Wallace Clement Ware *Sabine* (1868–1919).]

Sa·bine (sā'bīn') *n.* **1.** A member of an ancient tribe of central Italy, conquered and assimilated by the Romans in 290 B.C. **2.** The Italic language of the Sabines. *—adj.* Of or pertaining to the Sabine people or their language. [ME *Sabyn* < Lat. *Sabinus.*]

Sa·bin vaccine (sā'bĭn) *n.* An oral vaccine consisting of a live attenuated virus that is taken to immunize against poliomyelitis. [After Albert B. *Sabin* (b. 1906), its developer.]

sa·ble (sā'bəl) *n.* **1. a.** A carnivorous mammal, *Martes zibellina,* of northern Europe and Asia, having soft, dark fur. **b.** The pelt or fur of this animal. **c.** The similar fur of other species of martens. **2. a.** The color black, esp. in heraldry. **b. sables.** Black garments worn in mourning. **3.** A grayish yellowish brown. **4.** A sablefish. *—**modifier:** a sable coat.* *—adj.* **1.** Of the color black, as in heraldry or mourning. **2.** Dark; somber. [ME < OFr., of Slavic orig.]

sable antelope *n.* A large African antelope, *Hippotragus niger,* having a usually dark coat and backward-curving horns.

sa·ble·fish (sā'bəl-fĭsh') *n., pl.* **sablefish** or **-fish·es.** A dark-colored marine food fish, *Anoplopoma fimbria,* of North American Pacific waters.

sabot

sa·bot (să-bō', săb'ō) *n.* **1.** A wooden shoe worn in several European countries. **2.** (*also* săb'ət). A sandal or shoe having a band of leather or other material across the instep. [Fr. < OFr.]

sab·o·tage (săb'ə-täzh') *n.* **1.** The destruction of property or obstruction of normal operations, as by enemy agents in time of war. **2.** Treacherous action to defeat or hinder a cause or an endeavor; deliberate subversion. *—tr.v.* **-taged, -tag·ing, -tag·es.** To commit sabotage against. [Fr. < *saboter,* to sabotage < *sabot,* sabot.]

sab·o·teur (săb'ə-tûr') *n.* A person who commits sabotage. [Fr. < *saboter,* to sabotage.]

sa·bra (sä'brə) *n.* A native-born Israeli. [Heb. *ṣabēr,* sabra, prickly pear.]

sa·bre (sā'bər) *n. & v. Chiefly Brit.* Variant of **saber.**

sab·u·lous (săb'yə-ləs) also **sab·u·lose** (-lōs') *adj.* Gritty; sandy. [Lat. *sabulosus* < *sabulum,* coarse sand.] **—sab'u·los'i·ty** (-lŏs'ĭ-tē) *n.*

sac (săk) *n.* A pouch or pouchlike structure in a plant or animal, sometimes filled with fluid. [Fr., bag < Lat. *saccus.* —see SACK¹.]

Sac (săk, sôk) *n.* Variant of **Sauk.**

sac·a·ton (săk'ə-tōn') *n.* A grass, *Sporobolus wrightii,* of the southwestern United States, used for pasture and hay in saline areas. [Am. Sp. *zacatón* < *zacate,* coarse grass < Nahuatl, grass.]

sac·cade (să-käd', sə-) *n.* A rapid intermittent eye movement, such as that which occurs when the eye fixes on one point after another in the visual field. [Fr., twitch < OFr. < *saquer,* to pull.] **—sac·cad'ic** *adj.*

sac·cate (săk'āt') *adj.* Shaped like or having a pouch or sac. [< Lat. *saccus,* bag. —see SACK¹.]

sacchar- *pref.* Variant of **saccharo-.**

sac·cha·rase (săk'ə-rās', -rāz') *n.* Invertase.

sac·cha·rate (săk'ə-rāt') *n.* A salt or ester of saccharic acid. [SACCHAR(IC ACID) + -ATE².]

sac·char·ic acid (sə-kăr'ĭk) *n.* A white crystalline acid, $COOH(CHOH)_4COOH$, formed by the oxidation of glucose, sucrose, or starch.

sac·cha·ride (săk'ə-rīd') *n.* Any of a series of compounds of carbon, hydrogen, and oxygen in which the atoms of the latter two elements are in the ratio of 2:1, esp. those containing the group $C_6H_{10}O_5$.

sac·char·i·fy (sə-kăr'ə-fī', să-) *tr.v.* **-fied, -fy·ing, -fies.** To convert (starch, for example) into sugar. **—sac·char'i·fi·ca'tion** *n.*

sac·cha·rim·e·ter (săk'ə-rĭm'ĭ-tər) *n.* **1.** A polarimeter that indicates the concentration of sugar in a solution. **2.** An instrument that determines the sugar content of a fermenting sample from carbon dioxide measurements. **—sac'cha·rim'e·try** *n.*

sac·cha·rin (săk'ər-ĭn) *n.* A white crystalline powder, $C_7H_5NO_3S$, having a taste about 500 times sweeter than cane sugar, used as a calorie-free sweetener.

sac·cha·rine (săk'ər-ĭn, -ə-rēn', -ə-rīn') *adj.* **1.** Of, relating to, or characteristic of sugar or saccharin; sweet. **2.** Having a cloyingly sweet attitude, tone, or character: *a saccharine smile.* **—sac'cha·rine·ly** *adv.* **—sac'cha·rin'i·ty** (-ə-rĭn'ĭ-tē) *n.*

saccharo- or **sacchar-** *pref.* Sugar: *saccharide.* [< Lat. *saccharum,* sugar < Gk. *sakkharon* < Pali *sakkharā* < Skt. *śarkarā.*]

sac·cha·roid (săk'ə-roid') or **sac·cha·roi·dal** (săk'ə-roid'l) *adj.* Designating rocks and minerals having a granular structure similar to that of loaf sugar.

sac·cha·rom·e·ter (săk'ə-rŏm'ĭ-tər) *n.* A hydrometer that determines the amount of sugar in a solution from density measurements.

sac·cha·ro·my·cete (săk'ə-rō-mī'sēt') *n.* Any of various yeast fungi, esp. of the genus *Saccharomyces,* many of which ferment sugar. **—sac'cha·ro·my·ce'tic** (-mī-sē'tĭk), **sac'cha·ro·my·ce'tous** (-mī-sē'təs) *adj.*

sac·cha·rose (săk'ə-rōs') *n.* Sucrose.

sac·cu·late (săk'yə-lāt') or **sac·cu·lat·ed** (-lā'tĭd) also **sac·cu·lar** (-lər) *adj.* Formed of or divided into a series of saclike dilations or pouches.

sac·cule (săk'yo͞ol) also **sac·cu·lus** (-yə-ləs) *n., pl.* **-cules** also **-cu·li** (-yə-lī'). **1.** A small sac. **2.** The smaller of two membranous sacs in the vestibule of the labyrinth of the ear. [Lat., dim. of *saccus,* bag. —see SACK¹.]

sac·er·do·tal (săs'ər-dōt'l, săk'-) *adj.* **1.** Of or pertaining to priests or the priesthood; priestly. **2.** Of or pertaining to sacerdotalism. [ME < OFr. < Lat. *sacerdotalis* < *sacerdos,* priest < *sacer,* sacred.] **—sac'er·do'tal·ly** *adv.*

sac·er·do·tal·ism (săs'ər-dōt'l-ĭz'əm, săk'-) *n.* The belief that priests act as mediators between God and man.

sa·chem (sā'chəm) *n.* **1.** The chief of a North American Indian tribe or confederation, esp. an Algonquian chief. **2.** A high official of the Tammany Society. [Narraganset *sâchim,* chief.]

sa·cher torte (sä'kər tôrt', zä'KHər tôr'tə) *n.* A rich chocolate cake filled with jam and topped with chocolate icing. [G. *Sachertorte* : *Sacher,* surname of a family of 19th- and 20th-cent. hoteliers + *Torte,* torte.]

sa·chet (să-shā') *n.* A small packet of perfumed powder used to scent clothes, as in trunks or closets. [Fr. < OFr., dim. of *sac,* bag < Lat. *saccus.* —see SACK¹.]

sack¹ (săk) *n.* **1. a.** A large bag of strong, coarse material for holding objects in bulk. **b.** A similar container of paper or

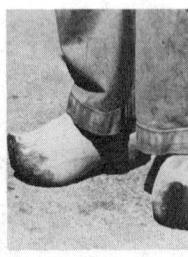

plastic. **c.** The amount held in a sack. **2.** Also **sacque.** A short, loose-fitting garment for women and children. **3.** *Slang.* A dismissal from employment: *finally got the sack.* **4.** *Slang.* A bed, mattress, or sleeping bag. **5.** A baseball base. —*tr.v.* **sacked, sack·ing, sacks. 1.** To place in a sack. **2.** *Slang.* To discharge from employment. —***phrasal verb.* sack out.** *Slang.* To sleep. [ME < OE *sæcc* < Lat. *saccus* < Gk. *sakkos,* of Semitic orig.]

sack² (săk) *tr.v.* **sacked, sack·ing, sacks.** To rob of goods or valuables, esp. after capture. —*n.* **1.** The looting or pillaging of a captured town. **2.** Plunder; loot. [< OFr. *(mettre a) sac,* (to put in) a sack.]

sack³ (săk) *n.* Any of various light, dry, strong wines from Spain and the Canary Islands, imported to England in the 16th and 17th centuries. [< OFr. *(vin) sec,* dry (wine) < Lat. *siccus,* dry.]

sack·but (săk′bŭt′) *n.* **1.** A medieval musical instrument resembling the trombone. **2.** A triangular stringed instrument. [OFr. *saqueboute* : *saquer,* to pull + *bouter,* to push, of Germanic orig.]

sack·cloth (săk′klôth′, -klŏth′) *n.* **1.** Sacking. **2. a.** A rough cloth of camel's hair, goat hair, hemp, cotton, or flax. **b.** Garments made of this cloth, worn as a symbol of mourning or penitence.

sack·ing (săk′ĭng) *n.* A coarse, stout woven cloth, such as burlap or gunny, used for making sacks.

sacque (săk) *n.* Variant of **sack¹** (sense 2).

sa·cra (sā′krə, săk′rə) *n.* Plural of **sacrum.**

sa·cral¹ (sā′krəl) *adj.* Of, near, or pertaining to the sacrum.

sa·cral² (sā′krəl) *adj.* Pertaining to sacred rites or observances. [< Lat. *sacer, sacr-,* sacred.]

sac·ra·ment (săk′rə-mənt) *n.* **1.** A formal Christian rite, such as baptism and matrimony, esp. one considered to have been instituted by Jesus as a means of grace. **2.** Often **Sacrament. a.** The Eucharist. **b.** The consecrated elements of the Eucharist, esp. the bread or host. [ME < OFr. *sacrement* < LLat. *sacramentum* < Lat., oath < *sacrare,* to consecrate < *sacer,* sacred.]

sac·ra·men·tal (săk′rə-mĕn′tl) *adj.* **1.** Of, pertaining to, or used in a sacrament. **2.** Consecrated or bound by or as if by a sacrament: *a sacramental duty.* **3.** Having the force or efficacy of a sacrament. —*n.* A rite, action, or sacred object used by some Christian churches in worship. **—sac′ra·men′tal·ly** *adv.*

sac·ra·men·tal·ism (săk′rə-mĕn′tl-ĭz′əm) *n.* **1.** The doctrine that observance of the sacraments is necessary for salvation and that such participation can confer grace. **2.** Emphasis on the efficacy of a sacramental. **—sac′ra·men′tal·ist** *n.*

Sac·ra·men·tar·i·an (săk′rə-mĕn-târ′ē-ən) *n.* A person who regards the sacraments merely as symbols and not as a corporeal manifestation of Christ. —*adj.* **1.** Of or pertaining to Sacramentarians. **2.** Of or pertaining to sacramentalism or sacramentalists. **—Sac′ra·men·tar′i·an·ism** *n.*

sa·crar·i·um (sə-krâr′ē-əm, să-, sā-) *n., pl.* **-i·a** (-ē-ə). *Eccles.* **1.** The sanctuary or sacristy of a church. **2.** A piscina. [Med. Lat. < Lat., shrine < *sacer,* sacred.]

sa·cred (sā′krĭd) *adj.* **1.** Dedicated to or set apart for the worship of a deity. **2.** Worthy of religious veneration: *the sacred teachings of Buddha.* **3.** Made or declared holy: *sacred bread and wine.* **4.** Dedicated or devoted exclusively to a single use, purpose, or person: *a private office sacred to the President.* **5.** Worthy of respect; venerable. **6.** Of or pertaining to religious objects, rites, or practices. [ME, p.part. of *sacren,* to consecrate < OFr. *sacrer* < Lat. *sacrare* < *sacer,* sacred.] **—sa′cred·ly** *adv.* **—sa′cred·ness** *n.*

Sacred College *n.* The College of Cardinals.

sacred cow *n.* One that is immune from criticism. [From the veneration of the cow by the Hindus.]

sac·ri·fice (săk′rə-fīs′) *n.* **1. a.** The act of offering something to a deity in propitiation or homage, esp. the ritual slaughter of an animal or person. **b.** A victim offered in this way. **2. a.** The forfeiture of something highly valued for the sake of one considered to have a greater value or claim. **b.** Something so forfeited. **3. a.** The relinquishment of something at less than its presumed value. **b.** Something so relinquished. **c.** A loss so sustained. **4.** *Baseball.* A sacrifice hit. —*v.* **-ficed, -fic·ing, -fic·es.** —*tr.* **1.** To offer as a sacrifice to a deity. **2.** To forfeit (one thing) for another thing considered to be of greater value. **3.** To sell or give away at a loss. —*intr.* **1.** To make or offer a sacrifice. **2.** *Baseball.* To make a sacrifice hit. [ME < OFr. < Lat. *sacrificium* : *sacer,* sacred + *facere,* to make.] **—sac′ri·fic′er** *n.*

sacrifice fly *n. Baseball.* A fly ball enabling a runner to score after it is caught by a fielder.

sacrifice hit *n. Baseball.* A bunt that allows a runner to advance a base while the batter is retired.

sac·ri·fi·cial (săk′rə-fĭsh′əl) *adj.* Of, pertaining to, or concerned with a sacrifice: *a sacrificial lamb.* **—sac′ri·fi′cial·ly** *adv.*

sac·ri·lege (săk′rə-lĭj) *n.* The desecration, profanation, misuse, or theft of something sacred. [ME < OFr. < Lat. *sacrilegium* < *sacrilegus,* one who steals sacred things : *sacer,* sacred + *legere,* to gather.] **—sac′ri·le′gist** (săk′rə-lē′jĭst) *n.*

sac·ri·le·gious (săk′rə-lē′jəs, -lĭj′əs) *adj.* **1.** Disrespectful or irreverent toward something sacred; profane. **2.** Having committed sacrilege. **—sac′ri·le′gious·ly** *adv.* **—sac′ri·le′gious·ness** *n.*

Usage: *Sacrilegious,* the adjective of *sacrilege,* is often misspelled through confusion with *religious.*

sac·ris·tan (săk′rĭ-stən) *n.* **1.** A person in charge of a sacristy. **2.** A sexton. [ME < Med. Lat. *sacristanus* < *sacrista* < Lat. *sacer,* sacred.]

sac·ris·ty (săk′rĭ-stē) *n., pl.* **-ties.** A room in a church housing the sacred vessels and vestments; vestry. [Fr. *sacristie* < Med. Lat. *sacristia* < *sacrista,* sacristan.]

sac·ro·il·i·ac (săk′rō-ĭl′ē-ăk′, sā′krō-) *adj.* Of, pertaining to, or affecting the sacrum and ilium and their articulation or associated ligaments. —*n.* The sacroiliac region or cartilage. [SACR(UM) + ILI(UM) + -AC.]

sac·ro·lum·bar (săk′rō-lŭm′bər, -bär′, sā′krō-) *adj.* Of, pertaining to, or affecting the sacrum and the lumbar region. [SACR(UM) + LUMBAR.]

sac·ro·sanct (săk′rō-săngkt′) *adj.* Regarded as sacred and inviolable. [Lat. *sacrosanctus,* consecrated with religious ceremonies : *sacrum,* religious rite (< *sacer,* sacred) + *sanctus,* p.part. of *sancire,* to consecrate.] **—sac′ro·sanc′ti·ty** (-săngk′tĭ-tē) *n.*

sa·crum (sā′krəm, săk′rəm) *n., pl.* **sa·cra** (sā′krə, săk′rə). A triangular bone made up of five fused vertebrae and forming the posterior section of the pelvis. [NLat. < LLat. *(os) sacrum,* transl. of Gk. *(hieron) osteron,* sacred bone.]

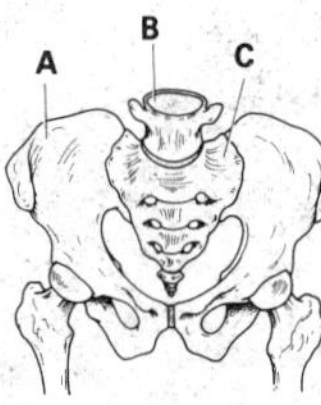

sacrum
A. Pelvis
B. Vertebra
C. Sacrum

sad (săd) *adj.* **sad·der, sad·dest. 1.** Affected or characterized by sorrow or unhappiness. **2.** Expressive of sorrow or unhappiness. **3.** Causing sorrow or gloom; depressing. **4.** Deplorable; sorry: *a sad state of affairs.* **5.** Dark-hued; somber. [ME, serious < OE *sæd,* sated.] **—sad′ly** *adv.* **—sad′ness** *n.*

Synonyms: *sad, melancholy, depressed, blue, dejected, downcast, sorrowful, doleful, woebegone, desolate, miserable, wretched.* These adjectives all indicate low spirits. *Sad* is the most general. *Melancholy* can refer to a lingering state resulting from temperament or to a condition marked merely by somber thoughts. The first of these senses is often described by *depressed. Blue* less formally applies to lowness of spirits. *Dejected* and *downcast* suggest dark moods of rather short duration, often triggered abruptly by something external and marked by disheartenment. *Sorrowful* applies broadly to manifestation of extreme sadness. *Doleful* describes what is mournful, gloomy, or dismal; especially with reference to appearance or nature, it sometimes suggests unintentionally comic effects. *Woebegone* suggests the appearance of one overcome by woe. *Desolate* implies extreme sorrow due to an irreparable loss. *Miserable* and *wretched* pertain to any state of profound unhappiness.

sad·den (săd′n) *tr. & intr.v.* **-dened, -den·ing, -dens.** To make or become sad.

sad·dhu (sä′do͞o) *n.* Variant of **sadhu.**

sad·dle (săd′l) *n.* **1. a.** A leather seat for a rider, secured on an animal's back by a girth. **b.** Similar tack used for attaching a pack to an animal. **c.** The padded part of a driving harness fitting over a horse's back. **d.** The seat of a bicycle, motorcycle, or similar vehicle. **e.** Something that resembles a saddle in shape. **2. a.** A cut of meat consisting of part of the backbone and both loins. **b.** The lower part of a male fowl's back. **3 a.** A saddle-shaped depression in the ridge of a hill. **b.** A ridge between two peaks. —*v.* **-dled, -dling, -dles.** —*tr.* **1.** To put a saddle on. **2.** To load or burden; encumber: *saddled with ten children.* —*intr.* **1.** To saddle a horse. **2.** To get into a saddle. **—*idiom.* in the saddle.** In control; dominant. [ME *sadel* < OE *sadol.*]

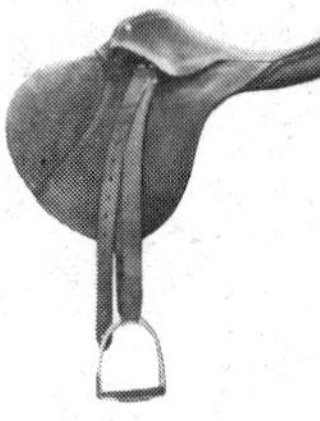
saddle
English saddle

sad·dle·bag (săd′l-băg′) *n.* **1.** One of a pair of pouches hanging across the back of a horse behind the saddle. **2.** A pouch hanging from a saddle or over the rear wheel of a motorcycle or bicycle.

saddle blanket *n.* A blanket placed between a saddle and a horse's back to prevent galling.

sad·dle·bow (săd′l-bō′) *n.* The arched upper front part of a saddle.

sad·dle·cloth (săd′l-klôth′, -klŏth′) *n.* A cloth placed under the saddle of a racehorse and bearing its number.

saddle horse *n.* A horse bred or schooled for riding.

sad·dler (săd′lər) *n.* One that makes, repairs, or sells equipment for horses.

saddle roof *n.* A roof having a ridge and two gables.

sad·dler·y (săd′lə-rē) *n., pl.* **-ies. 1.** Equipment, as saddles and harnesses, for horses. **2.** A shop selling saddlery. **3.** The craft or business of a saddler.

saddle shoe *n.* A flat casual shoe, usually white, having a band of leather in a contrasting color across the instep.

saddle soap *n.* A preparation containing mild soap and neat's-foot oil, used for cleaning and softening leather.

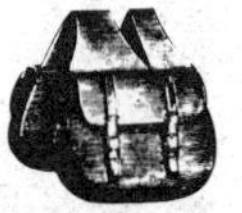
saddlebag
Pair of U.S. Army leather saddlebags

saddle sore *n.* **1.** A sore on a horse's back caused by an improperly fitted saddle. **2.** A sore on a rider caused by saddle chafing.

saddle stitch *n.* **1.** A simple overcasting stitch, usually of a thread contrasting in color with the fabric, that is used primarily as ornament on clothing. **2.** A stitch used in sewing together the leaves of a book at the fold lines, either with thread or wire.

sad·dle·tree (săd′l-trē′) *n.* The frame of a saddle.

Sad·du·cee (săj′ə-sē′, săd′yə-) *n.* A member of a Jewish sect of the 2nd century B.C. through the 1st century A.D. that

safety net

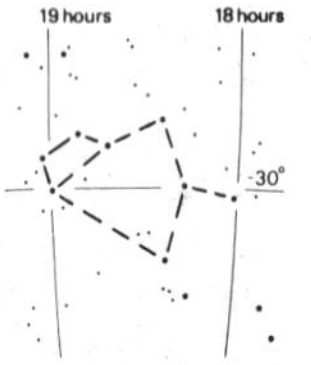

Sagittarius

saguaro

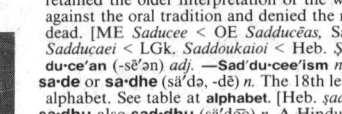

retained the older interpretation of the written Mosaic law against the oral tradition and denied the resurrection of the dead. [ME *Saducee* < OE *Sadducēas,* Sadducees < LLat. *Sadducaei* < LGk. *Saddoukaioi* < Heb. *Ṣĕddūqīm.*] **—Sad′du·ce′an** (-sē′ən) *adj.* **—Sad′du·cee′ism** *n.*

sa·de or **sa·dhe** (sä′də, -dē) *n.* The 18th letter of the Hebrew alphabet. See table at **alphabet.** [Heb. *ṣadhe.*]

sa·dhu also **sad·dhu** (sä′do͞o) *n.* A Hindu ascetic holy man. [Skt. *sādhu-,* right, holy.]

sad·i·ron (săd′ī′ərn) *n.* A heavy flatiron having points at both ends and a removable handle. [SAD, heavy (obs.) + IRON.]

sa·dism (sā′dĭz′əm, săd′ĭz′-) *n.* **1.** *Psychol.* The perversion of deriving sexual satisfaction from the infliction of pain on others. **2.** Delight in cruelty. **3.** Extreme cruelty. [After Comte Donatien de *Sade* (1740–1814).] **—sa′dist** *n.* **—sa·dis′tic** (sə-dĭs′tĭk) *adj.* **—sa·dis′ti·cal·ly** *adv.*

sa·do·mas·o·chism (sā′dō-măs′ə-kĭz′əm, săd′ō-) *n. Psychol.* The perversion of taking pleasure, esp. sexual gratification, from simultaneous sadism and masochism. [SAD(ISM) + MASOCHISM.] **—sa′do·mas′o·chist** *n.* **—sa′do·mas′o·chis′tic** (-kĭs′tĭk) *adj.*

sad sack *n. Informal.* An extremely inept or clumsy person.

Sa·far also **Sa·phar** (sə-fär′) *n.* The second month of the Moslem calendar. See table at **calendar.** [Ar.]

sa·fa·ri (sə-fä′rē) *n.* **1.** An overland expedition, esp. for hunting or exploring in eastern Africa. **2.** *Informal.* A journey or trip: *a sightseeing safari.* [Ar. *safarīy,* journey < *safara,* he traveled.]

safe (sāf) *adj.* **saf·er, saf·est. 1.** Secure from danger, harm, or evil. **2.** Free from danger or injury; unhurt: *safe and sound.* **3.** Free from risk; sure: *a safe bet.* **4.** Affording protection: *a safe place.* **5.** *Baseball.* Having reached a base without being put out, as a batter or base runner. *—n.* **1.** A metal container usually having a lock, used for storing valuables. **2.** A repository for protecting stored items, esp. a cooled compartment for perishable foods. **3.** *Slang.* A condom. [ME *sauf* < OFr. < Lat. *salvus,* healthy.] **—safe′ly** *adv.* **—safe′ness** *n.*

safe-con·duct (sāf′kŏn′dŭkt) *n.* **1.** An official document or an escort assuring unmolested passage, as through enemy territory. **2.** The protection afforded by a safe-conduct.

safe·crack·er (sāf′krăk′ər) *n.* One that breaks into safes in order to steal. **—safe′crack′ing** *n.*

safe-de·pos·it box (sāf′dĭ-pŏz′ĭt) *n.* A fireproof metal box, usually in a bank vault, for the safe storage of valuables.

safe·guard (sāf′gärd′) *n.* **1. a.** One that serves as a guard or protection. **b.** A mechanical device designed to prevent accidents. **c.** A safe-conduct. **2. a.** A protective stipulation, as in a contract. **b.** A precautionary measure. *—tr.v.* **-guard·ed, -guard·ing, -guards.** To guard; protect.

safe·keep·ing (sāf′kē′pĭng) *n.* The act of keeping safe or the state of being kept safe; protection.

safe·light (sāf′līt′) *n.* A lamp having one or more color filters capable of permitting moderate darkroom illumination without exposure of photosensitive film or paper.

safe·ty (sāf′tē) *n., pl.* **-ties. 1.** The condition of being safe; freedom from danger, risk, or injury. **2.** A device designed to prevent accidents, as a lock on a firearm preventing accidental firing. **3.** *Football.* **a.** A play in which a member of the offensive team downs the ball, willingly or unwillingly, behind his own goal line, resulting in two points for the defensive team. **b.** One of two defensive football backs. **4.** *Slang.* A condom.

safety circuit *n.* An electronic circuit that prevents malfunction by either sounding an alert or activating a trip circuit on a protective device.

safety glass *n.* A composite of two sheets of glass with an intermediate layer of transparent plastic used to prevent shattering.

safety island *n.* An area marked off within a roadway from which traffic is banned, esp. for pedestrian safety.

safety lamp *n.* A miner's lamp with a protective wire gauze surrounding the flame to prevent ignition of flammable gases.

safety match *n.* A match that can be lighted only by being struck against a chemically prepared friction surface.

safety net *n.* **1.** A large net for catching one that falls or jumps, as from a circus trapeze. **2.** A guarantee, esp. of financial security.

safety pin *n.* **1.** A pin in the form of a clasp, having a sheath to cover and hold the point. **2.** A pin that prevents the premature or accidental detonation of an explosive device, such as a bomb or grenade.

safety razor *n.* A razor in which the blade is fitted into a holder with guards to prevent cutting of the skin.

safety valve *n.* **1.** A valve in a pressure container, as in a steam boiler, that automatically opens when pressure reaches a dangerous level. **2.** An outlet for the release of repressed energy or emotion.

saf·flow·er (săf′lou′ər) *n.* **1.** A plant, *Carthamus tinctorius,* native to Asia, having orange flowers that yield a dyestuff and seeds that are the source of an oil used in cooking, cosmetics, paints, and medicine. **2.** The dried flowers of the safflower. [Du. *saffloer* < OFr. *saffleur* < OItal. *saffiore,* saffron < Ar. *aṣfar,* a yellow plant.]

saf·fron (săf′rən) *n.* **1. a.** A plant, *Crocus sativus,* native to the Old World, having purple or white flowers with orange stigmas. **b.** The dried stigmas of this plant, used to color foods and as a cooking spice and a dyestuff. **2.** A moderate or strong orange-yellow to moderate orange. [ME *saffran* < OFr. *safran* < Med. Lat. *safranum* < Ar. *za'farān.*]

saf·ra·nine (săf′rə-nēn′, -nĭn) also **saf·ra·nin** (-nĭn) *n.* Any of a family of dyes based on phenazine, used in the textile industry and as a biological stain. [< Fr. *safran,* saffron.]

saf·role (săf′rōl′) *n.* A colorless or pale-yellow oily liquid, $C_{10}H_{10}O_2$, derived from oil of sassafras and other essential oils and used in making perfume and soap. [< Fr. *safran,* saffron.]

sag (săg) *v.* **sagged, sag·ging, sags.** *—intr.* **1.** To sink, droop, or settle from pressure or weight. **2.** To lose vigor, firmness, or resilience: *My spirits sagged after the job rejection.* **3.** To decline, as in value or price. **4.** *Naut.* To drift to leeward. *—tr.* To cause to sag. *—n.* **1.** The act of sagging. **2.** An instance or extent of sagging. **3.** A sagging area; depression. **4.** A temporary decline in monetary value. **5.** *Naut.* A drift to leeward. [ME *saggen,* prob. of Scand. orig.]

sa·ga (sä′gə) *n.* **1. a.** A prose narrative of the 12th and 13th centuries recounting historical and legendary events and exploits in Iceland or Norway. **b.** A modern prose narrative that resembles a saga. **2.** A long, detailed report: *the saga of their family problems.* [ON.]

sa·ga·cious (sə-gā′shəs) *adj.* Possessing or showing sound judgment and keen perception; wise. [< Lat. *sagax, sagac-,* quick-witted.] **—sa·ga′cious·ly** *adv.* **—sa·ga′cious·ness** *n.*

sa·gac·i·ty (sə-găs′ĭ-tē) *n.* The quality of being sagacious; wisdom.

sag·a·more (săg′ə-môr′, -mōr′) *n.* A subordinate chief among the Algonquian Indians of North America. [Abnaki *sàkama.*]

saga novel *n.* A roman-fleuve.

sage¹ (sāj) *n.* A person who is venerated for his experience, judgment, and wisdom. *—adj.* **sag·er, sag·est. 1.** Having or showing wisdom and calm judgment. **2.** Proceeding from or marked by wisdom and calm judgment: *sage advice.* **3.** *Archaic.* Serious; solemn. [ME < OFr. < VLat. **sapius* < Lat. *sapere,* to be wise.] **—sage′ly** *adv.* **—sage′ness** *n.*

sage² (sāj) *n.* **1.** Any of various plants and shrubs of the genus *Salvia,* esp. *S. officinalis,* having aromatic grayish-green leaves used as a cooking herb. **2.** The leaves of the sage. [ME *sauge* < OFr. < Lat. *salvia* < *salvus,* healthy.]

sage·brush (sāj′brŭsh′) *n.* Any of several aromatic plants of the genus *Artemisia,* esp. *A. tridentata,* a shrub of arid regions of western North America, having silver-green leaves and large clusters of small white flowers.

sage grouse *n.* A chickenlike bird, *Centrocercus urophasianus,* of western North America, having long, pointed tail feathers that can be spread fanwise.

sag·ger also **sag·gar** (săg′ər) *n.* **1.** A protective casing of fire clay in which delicate ceramic articles are fired. **2.** Clay used to make ceramic casings. [Perh. alteration of SAFEGUARD.]

Sa·git·ta (sə-jĭt′ə) *n.* A constellation in the Northern Hemisphere near Aquila and Vulpecula. [Lat. < *sagitta,* arrow.]

sag·it·tal (săj′ĭ-tl) *adj.* **1.** *Anat.* Of or relating to the suture uniting the two parietal bones of the skull. **2.** *Zool.* Of or pertaining to the sagittal plane. [< Lat. *sagitta,* arrow.] **—sag′it·tal·ly** *adv.*

sagittal plane *n.* The longitudinal vertical plane that divides the body of a bilaterally symmetrical animal into right and left halves.

Sag·it·tar·i·us (săj′ĭ-târ′ē-əs) *n.* **1.** A constellation in the Southern Hemisphere near Scorpius and Capricornus. **2.** The ninth sign of the zodiac. [ME < Lat. < *sagittarius,* archer < *sagitta,* arrow.]

sag·it·tate (săj′ĭ-tāt′) *adj. Bot.* Having the shape of an arrowhead: *sagittate leaves.* [< Lat. *sagitta,* arrow.]

sa·go (sā′gō) *n., pl.* **-gos.** A powdery starch obtained from the trunks of the sago palm and used in Asia as a food thickener and textile stiffener. [Malay *sagu.*]

sago palm *n.* **1.** Any of various palm trees of the genera *Metroxylon, Arenga,* and *Caryota,* of tropical Asia. **2.** A palmlike cycad, *Cycas revoluta,* of southeastern Asia.

sa·gua·ro (sə-gwär′ō, -wär′ō) also **sa·hua·ro** (sə-wär′ō) *n., pl.* **-ros. 1.** A very large cactus, *Carnegiea gigantea,* of the southwestern United States and northern Mexico, having upward-curving branches, white flowers, and edible red fruit. **2.** The fruit of the saguaro. [Mex. Sp.]

Sa·hap·tin (sä-hăp′tĭn) *n., pl.* **Sahaptin** or **-tins. 1.** A member of a North American Indian people of Idaho, Washington, and Oregon. **2.** The language of the Sahaptin.

Sa·hel (sə-hāl′, -hēl′) *n.* A steppe or savanna that borders on a desert. [Fr. < Ar. *sāhil,* shore.] **—Sa·hel′i·an** *adj.*

sa·hib (sä′ĭb) *n.* Master; sir. Used as a title of respect when addressing Europeans in colonial India. [Hindi *ṣāḥib,* master < Ar.]

sa·hua·ro (sə-wär′ō) *n.* Variant of **saguaro.**

said (sĕd) *v.* Past tense and past participle of **say.** *—adj. Law.* Named or mentioned before; aforementioned.

Usage: The adjective *said* is seldom appropriate to any but legal or business writing, where it is equivalent to *afore-*

said: the said tenant (named in a lease); *said property.* In general usage, in similar contexts, *said* is usually unnecessary and *the tenant* or *the property* will suffice.

sai·ga (sī'gə) *n.* Either of two small antelopes, *Saiga tatarica* or *S. mongolia,* of the plains of northern Eurasia, having a stubby, proboscislike nose. [R. *saĭga,* of Turkic orig.]

sail (sāl) *n.* **1. a.** A length of triangular or rectangular fabric attached to a ship to catch the wind and propel it. **b.** The sails of a ship or boat. **2.** *pl.* **sail** or **sails.** A sailing vessel. **3.** A trip or voyage in a sailing craft. **4.** Something resembling a sail in form or function, such as the blade of a windmill. —*v.* **sailed, sail·ing, sails.** —*intr.* **1.** To move across the surface of water, esp. by means of a sailing vessel. **2.** To travel by water in a vessel. **3.** To start out on a voyage or journey. **4.** To operate a sailing craft, esp. for sport. **5.** To move swiftly, smoothly, or effortlessly. —*tr.* **1.** To navigate or manage (a vessel). **2.** To voyage upon or across: *sail the Pacific.* ***—phrasal verb.*** **sail into.** To attack or criticize vigorously. [ME < OE *segl.*]

Sail·board (sāl'bôrd', -bōrd'). A trademark for a small light sailboat with a flat hull.

sail·boat (sāl'bōt') *n.* A small boat propelled partly or wholly by sail.

sail·cloth (sāl'klôth', -klŏth') *n.* A strong fabric, as cotton canvas, suitable for making sails or tents.

sail·fish (sāl'fĭsh') *n., pl.* **sailfish** or **-fish·es.** Any of various large marine fishes of the genus *Istiophorus,* having the upper jaw prolonged into a spearlike bone and a large, saillike dorsal fin.

sail·ing (sā'lĭng) *n.* **1.** The skill required to operate and navigate a vessel; navigation. **2.** The sport of operating or riding in a sailboat. **3.** Departure or time of departure from a port.

sail·or (sā'lər) *n.* **1.** One that serves in a navy or works on a ship, esp. an ordinary seaman. **2.** A person who travels by water. **3.** A low-crowned straw hat with a flat top and flat brim.

sail·or's-choice (sā'lərz-chois') *n., pl.* **sailor's-choice.** Any of various fishes of the North American Atlantic coast, such as the pinfish or *Haemulon parrai* of more southerly waters.

sail·plane (sāl'plān') *n.* A light glider that is used esp. for soaring. **—sail'plane'** *v.* **(-planed, -plan·ing, -planes).** **—sail'plan'er** *n.*

sain·foin (sān'foin', săn'-) *n.* A plant, *Onobrychis viciaefolia,* native to Eurasia, that has compound leaves and pink or white flowers and is often used as fodder. [Fr. < OFr. < Med. Lat. *sanum faenum* : Lat. *sanus,* healthy + Lat. *faenum,* hay.]

saint (sānt) *n.* **1.** *Theol.* **a.** A person officially recognized, esp. by canonization, as being entitled to public veneration and capable of interceding for people on earth. **b.** A person who has died and gone to heaven. **c. Saint.** A member of any of various religious groups, esp. a Latter-Day Saint. **2.** An extremely virtuous person. —*tr.v.* **saint·ed, saint·ing, saints.** To name, recognize, or venerate as a saint; canonize. [ME < OFr. < Lat. *sanctus,* holy, p.part. of *sancire,* to consecrate.]

Saint Ag·nes' Eve (ăg'nĭs, -nĭ-sĭz) *n.* The night of January 20th, when, according to legend, a woman will dream of her future husband. [After *St. Agnes* (d. A.D. 304).]

Saint An·tho·ny's cross (ăn'thə-nēz) *n.* A tau cross.

Saint Ber·nard (bər-närd') *n.* A large, strong dog of a breed developed in Switzerland, having a thick brown and white coat, originally used by monks of the hospice of Saint Bernard in the Swiss Alps to help patrol the snow-covered region.

saint·dom (sānt'dəm) *n.* The condition or quality of being a saint.

saint·ed (sān'tĭd) *adj.* **1.** Considered a saint; canonized. **2.** Of saintly character; holy.

Saint El·mo's fire (ĕl'mōz) *n.* A visible electric discharge emanating from a pointed object, as the mast of a ship or wing of an airplane, during an electrical storm. [After *St. Elmo* (d. A.D. 303), patron saint of sailors.]

saint·hood (sānt'ho͝od') *n.* **1.** The status, character, or condition of being a saint. **2.** Saints collectively.

Saint Lo·uis encephalitis (lo͞o'ĭs) *n.* A viral encephalitis transmitted by a culex mosquito that occurs in parts of North America. [After *St. Louis,* Missouri, where an epidemic of the disease occurred in 1933.]

saint·ly (sānt'lē) *adj.* **-li·er, -li·est.** Resembling, pertaining to, or befitting a saint. **—saint'li·ness** *n.*

Saint Nich·o·las (nĭk'ə-ləs) or **Saint Nick** (nĭk) *n.* Santa Claus. [After *St. Nicholas* of Myra (d. A.D. 352?).]

Saint Pat·rick's Day (păt'rĭks) *n.* March 17, observed in honor of Saint Patrick, the patron saint of Ireland.

saint's day *n.* A day in a liturgical calendar that is observed in honor of a saint.

Saint Val·en·tine's Day (văl'ən-tīnz') *n.* February 14, on which valentines are traditionally exchanged. [After *St. Valentine* (d. A.D. 270?).]

saith (sĕth, sā'ĭth) *v. Archaic.* Third person singular present tense of **say.**

Sai·va (sī'və, shī'-) *n. Hinduism.* A member of the cult of the god Shiva. [Skt. *śaiva-,* belonging to Shiva < *śivaḥ,* Shiva.] **—Sai'vism** *n.*

sake[1] (sāk) *n.* **1.** Purpose; motive: *a quarrel only for the sake of argument.* **2.** Advantage; good: *for the sake of his health.* **3.** Personal benefit or interest; welfare: *for his own sake.* [ME, lawsuit, guilt < OE *sacu.*]

sailfish

sa·ke[2] also **sa·ki** (sä'kē, -kĕ) *n.* A Japanese liquor made from fermented rice. [J., alcoholic drink.]

sa·ker (sā'kər) *n.* A Eurasian falcon, *Falco cherrug,* having brown plumage and often trained for falconry. [ME *sagre* < OFr. *sacre* < Ar. *ṣaqr.*]

sa·ki (sä'kē, -kĕ) *n.* Variant of **sake**[2].

sal (săl) *n.* Salt. [Lat.]

sa·laam (sə-läm') *n.* **1.** A ceremonious act of deference or obeisance, esp. a low bow performed while placing the right palm on the forehead. **2.** A respectful ceremonial greeting performed esp. in the East. —*tr. & intr.v.* **-laamed, -laam·ing, -laams.** To greet with or perform a salaam. [Ar. *salām,* peace.]

Saint Bernard

sal·a·ble also **sale·a·ble** (sā'lə-bəl) *adj.* Offered or suitable for sale; marketable. **—sal'a·bil'i·ty, sal'a·ble·ness** *n.* **—sal'a·bly** *adv.*

sa·la·cious (sə-lā'shəs) *adj.* **1.** Sexually appealing or stimulating; lascivious. **2.** Lustful; bawdy. [< Lat. *salax, salac-,* lustful, fond of leaping < *salire,* to leap.] **—sa·la'cious·ly** *adv.* **—sa·la'cious·ness, sa·lac'i·ty** (sə-lăs'ĭ-tē) *n.*

sal·ad (săl'əd) *n.* **1. a.** A dish consisting of green, leafy raw vegetables, often with radish, cucumber, or tomato, tossed with a dressing. **b.** The course consisting of this dish. **2.** A cold dish of chopped fruit, meat, fish, eggs, or other food, usually prepared with a dressing, such as mayonnaise. **3.** A green vegetable or herb used in salad, esp. lettuce. [ME < OFr. *salade* < OProv. *salada* < VLat. **salata,* p.part. of **salare* < Lat. *sal,* salt.]

salad bar *n.* A counter in a restaurant from which customers may serve themselves a variety of salad ingredients and dressings.

salad days *pl.n.* A time of youth, innocence, and inexperience: *"my salad days when I was green in judgment, cold in blood"* (Shakespeare).

salad dressing *n.* A sauce, as of mayonnaise or oil and vinegar, served on salad.

salad oil *n.* An edible vegetable oil, as corn oil, that may be used in salad dressings.

sal·a·man·der (săl'ə-măn'dər) *n.* **1.** Any of various small, lizardlike amphibians of the order Caudata, having porous, scaleless skin and four legs that are often weak or rudimentary. **2.** A mythical creature, generally resembling a lizard, believed capable of living in or withstanding fire. **3.** An object, such as a poker, used in fire or capable of withstanding heat. **4.** *Metallurgy.* A mass of solidified material, largely metallic, left in a blast-furnace hearth. **5.** A portable stove used to heat or dry buildings under construction. [ME *salamandre* < OFr. < Lat. *salamandra* < Gk.] **—sal'a·man'drine** (-drĭn) *adj.*

salamander
Western tiger salamander

sa·la·mi (sə-lä'mē) *n.* A highly spiced and salted sausage, either hard or soft in consistency. [Ital., pl. of *salame,* salami < *salare,* to salt < VLat. **salare* < Lat. *sal,* salt.]

sal ammoniac *n.* Ammonium chloride. [ME *sal armoniak* < Lat. *sal ammoniacum,* salt of Ammon. —see AMMONIA.]

sal·a·ry (săl'ə-rē, săl'rē) *n., pl.* **-ries.** A fixed compensation for services, paid to a person on a regular basis. [ME *salarie* < Lat. *salarium,* money given to Roman soldiers to buy salt < *sal,* salt.] **—sal'a·ried** *adj.*

sale (sāl) *n.* **1.** The exchange of goods or services for an amount of money or its equivalent; the act of selling. **2.** An instance of selling property. **3.** An opportunity for selling or being sold; demand. **4.** Availability for purchase: *a store where pets are for sale.* **5.** A selling of property to the highest bidder; auction. **6.** A special disposal of goods at lowered prices: *coats on sale this week.* **7. sales. a.** Activities involved in selling goods or services. **b.** Gross receipts. [ME < OE *sala* < ON.]

sale·a·ble (sā'lə-bəl) *adj.* Variant of **salable.**

sal·ep (săl'əp, sə-lĕp') *n.* A starchy meal ground from the dried roots of various Old World orchids of the genera *Orchis* and *Eulophia,* used for food and formerly as medicine. [Fr. or Sp., both < Turk. *sālep* < Ar. *saḥleb,* a kind of orchid.]

sal·er·a·tus (săl'ə-rā'təs) *n.* Sodium or potassium bicarbonate used as a leavening agent; baking soda. [NLat. *sal aeratus,* aerated salt.]

sales check *n.* A slip of paper given by a store to serve as a record or receipt of a purchase or sale.

sales·clerk (sālz'klûrk') *n.* A person employed to sell goods in a store.

sales·girl (sālz'gûrl') *n.* A saleswoman.

Sa·le·sian (sə-lē'zhən, sā-) *n.* A member of the Society of St. Francis de Sales, a Roman Catholic congregation founded in Turin in 1845 and dedicated chiefly to education and missionary work. —*adj.* Of or pertaining to the Salesians.

sales·la·dy (sālz'lā'dē) *n.* A saleswoman.

sales·man (sālz'mən) *n.* A man employed to sell merchandise in a store or in a designated territory. **—sales'man·ship'** (-shĭp') *n.*

sales·peo·ple (sālz'pē'pəl) *pl.n.* Persons engaged in selling merchandise or services.

sales tax *n.* A tax levied on the retail price of merchandise and collected by the retailer.

sales·wom·an (sālz′wo͝om′ən) *n.* A woman employed to sell merchandise in a store or in a designated territory.

sali– *pref.* Salt: *salimeter.* [< Lat. *sal,* salt.]

Sa·li·an (sā′lē-ən, sāl′yən) *adj.* Of or pertaining to a tribe of Franks who settled in the Rhine region of the Netherlands in the 4th century A.D. *—n.* A Salian Frank. [< LLat. *Salii,* the Salian Franks.]

sal·ic (săl′ĭk) *adj.* Pertaining to igneous rocks, such as quartz and the feldspars, containing large amounts of silica and alumina. [S(ILICA) + AL(UMINA) + -IC.]

Sa·lic (sā′lĭk, săl′ĭk) also **Sa·lique** (sā′lĭk, săl′ĭk, sā-lēk′, sā-) *adj.* **1.** Designating or pertaining to the Salian Franks. **2.** Of or pertaining to the Salic law or to the legal code of the Salian Franks. [OFr. *salique* < Med. Lat. *Salicus* < LLat. *Salii,* the Salian Franks.]

sal·i·cin (săl′ĭ-sĭn) *n.* A bitter glucoside, $C_{13}H_{18}O_7$, obtained mainly from the bark of poplar and willow trees and formerly used as an analgesic. [Fr. *salicine* < Lat. *salix,* willow.]

Salic law *n.* **1.** The legal code of the Salian Franks. **2.** A law, thought to derive from the code of laws of the Salian Franks, prohibiting a woman from succeeding to a throne.

sa·lic·y·late (sə-lĭs′ə-lāt′, -lĭt, săl′ə-sĭl′ĭt) *n.* A salt or ester of salicylic acid. [SALICYL(IC ACID) + -ATE[2].]

sal·i·cyl·ic acid (săl′ĭ-sĭl′ĭk) *n.* A white crystalline acid, $C_7H_6O_3$, used in making aspirin, as a preservative and flavoring agent, and in the external treatment of certain skin conditions such as eczema. [< Fr. *salicyle,* the radical of salicylic acid < *salicine,* salicin.]

sal·i·cyl·ism (săl′ĭ-sə-lĭz′əm) *n.* A toxic syndrome caused by excessive doses of salicylic acid or salicylates. [SALICYL(IC ACID) + -ISM.]

sa·li·ence (sā′lē-əns, sāl′yəns) also **sa·li·en·cy** (sā′lē-ən-sē, sāl′yən-) *n.* **1.** The quality or condition of being salient. **2.** A pronounced feature or part; highlight.

sa·li·ent (sā′lē-ənt, sāl′yənt) *adj.* **1.** Projecting or jutting beyond a line or surface; protruding. **2.** Strikingly conspicuous; prominent. **3.** Springing; jumping: *salient tree toads.* *—n.* **1.** The area of a military defense, such as a battle line, that projects closest to the enemy. **2.** A projecting angle or part. [Lat. *saliens, salient-,* pr.part. of *salire,* to leap.] **—sa′li·ent·ly** *adv.* **—sa′li·ent·ness** *n.*

sa·li·en·tian (sā′lē-ĕn′shən) *n.* An amphibian of the order Salientia (formerly Anura or Batrachia), which includes the frogs and toads. *—adj.* Of or belonging to the Salientia. [NLat. *Salientia,* order name < Lat. *saliens,* pr.part. of *salire,* to leap.]

sa·lif·er·ous (sə-lĭf′ər-əs) *adj.* Containing or yielding salt.

sa·lim·e·ter (sə-lĭm′ĭ-tər) *n.* A specially graduated hydrometer that indicates directly the percentage of a salt in a salt solution. **—sal′i·met′ric** (săl′ə-mĕt′rĭk) *adj.* **—sa·lim′e·try** *n.*

sa·li·na (sə-lī′nə, -lē′-) *n.* **1.** A salt marsh, spring, pond, or lake. **2.** A land area encrusted with salt. [Sp. < Lat. *salinae,* salt pits < *salinus,* saline.]

sa·line (sā′lēn′, -līn′) *adj.* **1.** Of, relating to, or containing salt; salty. **2.** Pertaining to mineral salts having the characteristics of common salt. *—n.* **1.** A salt of magnesium or of the alkalis, used in medicine as a cathartic. **2.** A saline solution, esp. one that is isotonic with blood and is used in medicine and surgery. [Lat. *salinus* < *sal,* salt.] **—sa·lin′i·ty** (sə-lĭn′ĭ-tē) *n.*

sal·i·nize (săl′ə-nīz′) *tr.v.* **-nized, -niz·ing, -niz·es.** To treat with salt. **—sal′i·ni·za′tion** *n.*

sal·i·nom·e·ter (săl′ə-nŏm′ĭ-tər) *n.* An instrument, esp. a salimeter, used to measure the amount of salt in a solution. **—sal′i·no·met′ric** (-nə-mĕt′rĭk) *adj.* **—sal′i·nom′e·try** *n.*

Sa·lique (sā′lĭk, săl′ĭk, sā-lēk′, sā-) *adj.* Variant of **Salic.**

Salis·bur·y steak (sôlz′bĕr′ē, -brē, sălz′-) *n.* A patty of ground beef mixed with various seasonings and broiled or fried. [After J. H. *Salisbury,* 19th-cent. English nutritionist.]

Sa·lish (sā′lĭsh) also **Sa·lish·an** (-lĭ-shən) *n.* **1.** A family of North American Indian languages of the northwestern United States and British Columbia. **2.** The Indians speaking languages of the Salish family. **—Sa′lish·an** *adj.*

sa·li·va (sə-lī′və) *n.* The watery, tasteless liquid mixture of salivary and oral mucous gland secretions that lubricates chewed food, moistens the oral walls, and contains the enzyme ptyalin, which functions in the predigestion of starches. [Lat.]

sal·i·var·y (săl′ə-vĕr′ē) *adj.* **1.** Of, pertaining to, or producing saliva. **2.** Of or pertaining to a salivary gland.

salivary gland *n.* A gland that secretes saliva, esp. any of three pairs of large glands, the parotid, submandibular, and sublingual, whose secretions enter the mouth and mingle in saliva.

sal·i·vate (săl′ə-vāt′) *v.* **-vat·ed, -vat·ing, -vates.** *—intr.* To secrete or produce saliva. *—tr.* To produce excessive salivation in.

sal·i·va·tion (săl′ə-vā′shən) *n.* **1.** The act or process of secreting saliva. **2.** An abnormally abundant flow of saliva.

Salk vaccine (sôlk, sôk) *n.* A killed-virus vaccine used to immunize actively against poliomyelitis. [After Jonas *Salk* (b.1914).]

sal·let (săl′ĭt) *n.* A light medieval helmet with a brim flaring in the back, sometimes fitted with a visor. [ME < OFr. *salade.*]

sal·low[1] (săl′ō) *adj.* **-er, -est.** Of a sickly yellowish hue or complexion. *—tr.v.* **-lowed, -low·ing, -lows.** To make sallow. [ME *salowe* < OE *salo.*] **—sal′low·ly** *adv.* **—sal′low·ness** *n.*

sal·low[2] (săl′ō) *n.* Any of several European willows, esp. *Salix caprea,* whose wood is a source of charcoal. [ME *salwe* < OE *sealh.*]

sal·ly (săl′ē) *intr.v.* **-lied, -ly·ing, -lies. 1.** To rush out or leap forth suddenly. **2.** To issue suddenly from a defensive or besieged position to make an attack upon an enemy. **3.** To set out on a trip or excursion: *sallied forth to see the world.* *—n., pl.* **-lies. 1.** A sudden rush forward; leap. **2.** An assault from a defensive position; sortie. **3.** A sudden emergence into action or expression; outburst. **4.** A witticism; quip. **5.** A venturing forth; jaunt. [< OFr. *saillie,* a sally < *sallir,* to rush forward < Lat. *salire,* to leap.]

sal·ly lunn (săl′ē lŭn′) *n.* A somewhat sweet bread leavened with yeast. [After *Sally Lunn,* 18th-cent. English baker.]

sally port *n.* A gate in a fortification designed for sorties.

sal·ma·gun·di (săl′mə-gŭn′dē) *n.* **1.** A salad of chopped meat, anchovies, eggs, and onions, often arranged in rows on lettuce and served with vinegar and oil. **2.** A mixture or assortment; potpourri. [Fr. *salmigondis.*]

sal·mi (săl′mē) *n.* A highly spiced dish consisting of roasted game birds minced and stewed in wine. [Fr. *salmis,* short for *salmigondis,* salmagundi.]

salm·on (săm′ən, sä′mən) *n., pl.* **salmon** or **-ons. 1.** Any of various large food and game fishes of the genera *Salmo* and *Oncorhynchus,* of northern waters, characteristically swimming from salt to fresh water to spawn and having delicate pinkish flesh. **2.** A moderate, light, or strong yellowish pink to a moderate reddish orange or light orange. [ME < OFr. *saumon* < Lat. *salmo.*]

salm·on·ber·ry (săm′ən-bĕr′ē, sä′mən-) *n.* **1.** A prickly shrub, *Rubus spectabilis,* of western North America, having compound leaves and fragrant reddish flowers. **2.** The edible salmon-colored, raspberrylike fruit of the salmonberry.

sal·mo·nel·la (săl′mə-nĕl′ə) *n., pl.* **-nel·lae** (-nĕl′ē) or **-nel·las** or **-nel·la.** Any of various rod-shaped bacteria of the genus *Salmonella,* many of which are pathogenic. [NLat. *Salmonella,* genus name, after Daniel E. *Salmon* (1850–1914).]

sal·mo·nel·lo·sis (săl′mə-nĕ-lō′sĭs) *n., pl.* **-ses** (-sēz′). Infection with salmonellae.

salm·o·nid (săm′ə-nĭd, săl′mə-) *adj.* Salmonoid. **—salm′o·nid** *n.*

salm·o·noid (săm′ə-noid′, sä′mə-) *adj.* **1.** Resembling or characteristic of a salmon. **2.** Of or belonging to the family Salmonidae, which includes the salmon, trout, and whitefishes. *—n.* A salmonoid fish.

sal·ol (săl′ôl′, -ōl′) *n.* A white crystalline powder, $C_{13}H_{10}O_3$, derived from salicylic acid and used in the manufacture of plastics and sun-tan oils and medicinally as an analgesic and antipyretic. [Orig. a trademark.]

Sa·lo·me (sə-lō′mē, săl′ə-mā′) *n.* Daughter of Herodias and niece of Herod Antipas, who granted her the head of John the Baptist in return for her dancing. [LLat. < Gk. *Salōmē.*]

sa·lom·e·ter (sā-lŏm′ĭ-tər, sə-) *n.* A salimeter.

sa·lon (sə-lŏn′, săl′ŏn′, sā-lôɴ′) *n.* **1.** A large room, such as a drawing room, used for receiving and entertaining guests. **2.** A periodic gathering of persons of social or intellectual distinction. **3.** A hall or gallery for the exhibition of works of art. **4.** Often **Salon.** An annual exhibition of art works in France. **5.** A commercial establishment offering a product or service related to fashion: *a beauty salon.* [Fr. < Ital. *salone,* aug. of *sala,* hall, of Germanic orig.]

sa·loon (sə-lo͞on′) *n.* **1.** A place where alcoholic drinks are sold and drunk; tavern. **2.** A large room or hall for receptions, public entertainment, or exhibitions. **3. a.** The officers' dining and social room on a cargo ship. **b.** A large social lounge on a passenger ship. **4.** *Chiefly Brit.* A sedan automobile. [Fr. *salon,* salon.]

sa·loon·keep·er (sə-lo͞on′kē′pər) *n.* One that owns or operates a saloon for drinking.

sa·loop (sə-lo͞op′) *n.* A hot drink, formerly used medicinally, made from salep, sassafras, or similar aromatic herbs. [Alteration of SALEP.]

salp (sălp) also **sal·pa** (săl′pə) *n.* Any of various free-swimming chordates of the genus *Salpa,* of warm seas, having a translucent, somewhat flattened, keglike body. [NLat. *Salpa,* genus name < Lat., a kind of stockfish < Gk. *salpē.*] **—sal′pi·form′** (săl′pə-fôrm′) *adj.*

salping– *pref.* Salpinx: *salpingitis.* [< Gk. *salpinx, salping-,* trumpet.]

sal·pin·gec·to·my (săl′pĭn-jĕk′tə-mē) *n., pl.* **-mies.** The surgical removal of the Fallopian tube.

sal·pin·ges (săl-pĭn′jēz) *n.* Plural of **salpinx.**

sal·pin·gi·tis (săl′pĭn-jī′tĭs) *n.* Inflammation of the Fallopian or Eustachian tube.

sal·pinx (săl′pĭngks) *n., pl.* **sal·pin·ges** (săl-pĭn′jēz). **1.** The Fallopian tube. **2.** The Eustachian tube. [Gk. *salpinx,* trumpet.] **—sal·pin′gi·an** (-pĭn′jē-ən, -jən) *adj.*

sal·sa (säl′sə) *n.* A popular form of Latin American dance music, characterized by elements of jazz, blues, and rock. [Am. Sp. < Sp., sauce < Lat. *salsa.* —see SAUCE.]

sal·si·fy (săl′sə-fē, -fī′) *n.* **1.** A plant, *Tragopogon porrifolius,* native to Europe, having grasslike leaves, purple flowers, and an edible taproot. **2.** The root of the salsify, eaten as a vegetable. [Fr. *salsifis* < obs. Ital. *salsifica.*]

saltbox

sal soda *n.* A hydrated sodium carbonate used as a general cleanser.

salt (sôlt) *n.* **1.** A colorless or white crystalline solid, chiefly sodium chloride, extensively used as a food seasoning and preservative. **2.** A chemical compound formed by replacing all or part of the hydrogen ions of an acid with one or more cations of a base. **3. salts.** Any of various mineral salts used as a laxative or cathartic. **4. salts.** Smelling salts. **5. salts.** Epsom salts. **6.** An element that gives flavor or zest. **7.** Sharp, lively wit. **8.** *Informal.* A sailor, esp. when old or experienced. **9.** A saltcellar. —*tr.v.* **salt·ed, salt·ing, salts. 1.** To add, treat, season, or sprinkle with salt. **2.** To cure or preserve by treating with salt or a salt solution. **3.** To provide salt for (deer or cattle). **4.** To add zest or liveliness to: *salt a lecture with anecdotes.* **5.** To give an appearance of value to by fraudulent means, esp. to place valuable minerals in (a mine) for the purpose of deceiving. ***—phrasal verbs.* salt away.** To put aside; save. **salt out.** To separate (a dissolved substance) by adding salt to the solution. ***—idiom.* worth (one's) salt.** Efficient and capable. [ME < OE *sealt.*]

salt-and-pep·per (sôlt′ən-pĕp′ər) *adj.* Pepper-and-salt.

sal·ta·rel·lo (săl′tə-rĕl′ō, sôl′-) *n., pl.* **-rel·los** or **-rel·li** (-rĕl′ē). A lively Italian dance with a skipping step at the beginning of each measure. [Ital. < *saltare,* to leap < Lat. —see SALTATION.]

sal·ta·tion (săl-tā′shən, sôl-) *n.* **1.** The act of leaping, jumping, or dancing. **2.** Discontinuous movement, transition, or development; advancement by leaps. **3.** *Biol.* A mutation or discontinuous variation. [Lat. *saltatio* < *saltatus,* p.part. of *saltare,* to leap < freq. of *salire,* to jump.]

sal·ta·to·ri·al (săl′tə-tôr′ē-əl, -tōr′-, sôl′-) *adj.* **1.** Of or relating to leaping or dancing. **2.** Adapted for or characterized by leaping.

sal·ta·to·ry (săl′tə-tôr′ē, -tōr′ē, sôl′-) *adj.* **1.** Of, pertaining to, or adapted for leaping or dancing. **2.** Proceeding by leaps rather than by smooth, gradual transitions.

salt·box (sôlt′bŏks′) *n.* A frame house with two stories in front and one in back, topped by a roof with a long rear slope.

salt·bush (sôlt′bo͝osh′) *n.* Any of several salt-tolerant plants of the genus *Atriplex,* esp. *A. hortensis.*

salt cake *n.* Impure sodium sulfate used in making paper pulp, soaps and detergents, glass, ceramic glazes, and dyes.

salt·cel·lar (sôlt′sĕl′ər) *n.* A small dish for holding and dispensing salt. [Alteration of ME *salt saler* : *salt,* salt + *saler,* saltcellar < OFr. *saliere* < Lat. *salarius,* of salt < *sal,* salt.]

salt·er (sôl′tər) *n.* **1.** One that manufactures or sells salt. **2.** One that treats meat, fish, or other foods with salt.

salt·ern (sôl′tərn) *n.* A building or place of salt manufacture; saltworks. [OE *sealtærn* : *sealt,* salt + *ærn,* house.]

salt grass *n.* Any of various grasses, such as those of the genus *Distichlis,* that grow in salt marshes and alkaline regions.

salt hay *n.* **1.** The wiry, tough stems of several species of salt-marsh rushes, esp. *Juncus gerardi,* used as a garden mulch and packing material. **2.** Hay prepared from salt grass.

sal·tine (sôl-tēn′) *n.* A thin, crisp cracker sprinkled with coarse salt.

sal·tire (sôl′tîr′, săl′-) *n. Heraldry.* An ordinary in the shape of a St. Andrew's cross, formed by the crossing of a bend and a bend sinister. [ME *sawtire* < OFr. *saultoir,* stile < *saulter,* to jump < Lat. *saltare.* —see SALTATION.]

salt·ish (sôl′tĭsh) *adj.* Somewhat salty.

salt lick *n.* **1.** A natural deposit of exposed salt that animals lick. **2.** A block of salt or an artificial medicated saline preparation set out for cattle, sheep, or deer to lick.

salt marsh *n.* Low coastal grassland frequently overflowed by the tide.

salt·pe·ter (sôlt′pē′tər) *n.* **1.** Potassium nitrate. **2.** Sodium nitrate. **3.** Niter. [ME *salpetre* < OFr. < Med. Lat. *salpetra* : Lat. *sal,* salt + *petra,* rock < Gk.]

salt rheum *n.* Eczema.

salt·shak·er (sôlt′shā′kər) *n.* A container with a perforated top for sprinkling table salt.

salt·works (sôlt′wûrks′) *pl.n. (used with a sing. or pl. verb).* A place or building where salt is manufactured commercially.

salt·wort (sôlt′wûrt′, -wôrt′) *n.* Any of several plants of the genus *Salsola,* esp. *S. kali,* native to the Old World, having stiff, prickly leaves and growing on sandy seashores.

salt·y (sôl′tē) *adj.* **-i·er, -i·est. 1.** Of, containing, or seasoned with salt. **2.** Suggestive of the sea or sailing life. **3.** Witty; pungent: *salty humor.* **—salt′i·ly** *adv.* **—salt′i·ness** *n.*

sa·lu·bri·ous (sə-lo͞o′brē-əs) *adj.* Conducive or favorable to health or well-being. [< Lat. *salubris* < *salus,* health.] **—sa·lu′bri·ous·ly** *adv.* **—sa·lu′bri·ous·ness, sa·lu′bri·ty** (-brĭ-tē) *n.*

sa·lu·ki (sə-lo͞o′kē) *n.* A tall, slender dog of an ancient breed developed in Arabia and Egypt, having a smooth, silky, variously colored coat. [Ar. *salūqīy,* of Saluq, an ancient Arabian city.]

sal·u·tar·y (săl′yə-tĕr′ē) *adj.* **1.** Effecting or designed to effect an improvement; remedial: *salutary advice.* **2.** Favorable to health; wholesome: *a salutary climate.* [OFr. *salutaire* < Lat. *salutaris* < *salus,* health.] **—sal′u·tar′i·ly** (-târ′ə-lē) *adv.* **—sal′u·tar′i·ness** *n.*

sal·u·ta·tion (săl′yə-tā′shən) *n.* **1.** A polite expression of greeting or good will. **2.** A gesture of greeting, as a bow or kiss. **3.** A word or phrase of greeting, as *Dear Sir* in a letter.

sa·lu·ta·to·ri·an (sə-lo͞o′tə-tôr′ē-ən, -tōr′-) *n.* The student who delivers the salutatory at graduation exercises, usually the one ranking second highest in the class.

sa·lu·ta·to·ry (sə-lo͞o′tə-tôr′ē, -tōr′ē) *n., pl.* **-ries.** An opening or welcoming address. —*adj.* Of, relating to, or expressing a salutation.

sa·lute (sə-lo͞ot′) *v.* **-lut·ed, -lut·ing, -lutes.** —*tr.* **1.** To greet or address with an expression of welcome, good will, or respect. **2.** To recognize (a military superior) with a gesture prescribed by regulations, as by raising the hand to the cap. **3.** To honor formally and ceremoniously. **4.** To come forth as if to greet. —*intr.* To make a gesture of greeting or respect. —*n.* **1.** An act or gesture of welcome, honor, or courteous recognition. **2.** A formal military display of honor or greeting, as the firing of cannon. [ME *saluten* < Lat. *salutare* < *salus,* health.] **—sa·lut′er** *n.*

sal·va·ble (săl′və-bəl) *adj.* Capable of being saved or salvaged. [< LLat. *salvare,* to save < Lat. *salvus,* safe.]

Sal·va·do·ri·an (săl′və-dôr′ē-ən, -dōr′-) also **Sal·va·do·ran** (-dôr′ən, -dōr′-) *n.* A native or inhabitant of El Salvador. **—Sal′va·do′ri·an** *adj.*

sal·vage (săl′vĭj) *n.* **1. a.** The rescue of a ship, its crew, or its cargo from fire or shipwreck. **b.** The ship, crew, or cargo so rescued. **c.** Compensation given to those who voluntarily aid in such a rescue. **2. a.** The act of saving imperiled property from loss. **b.** The property so saved. —*tr.v.* **-vaged, -vag·ing, -vag·es. 1.** To save from loss or destruction. **2.** To save (discarded or damaged material) for further use. [< Fr., act of saving < OFr. *salver,* to save < LLat. *salvare* < Lat. *salvus,* safe.] **—sal′vage·a·ble** *adj.* **—sal′vag·er** *n.*

sal·var·san (săl′vər-săn′) *n.* Arsphenamine. [G.; orig. a trademark.]

sal·va·tion (săl-vā′shən) *n.* **1. a.** Preservation or deliverance from evil or difficulty. **b.** A source, means, or cause of such preservation or deliverance. **2. a.** *Theol.* The deliverance of man or his soul from the power or penalty of sin; redemption. **b.** *Christian Science.* The realization and demonstration of Life, Truth, and Love as supreme over all, carrying with it the destruction of the illusions of sin, sickness, and death. [ME < OFr. < LLat. *salvatio* < *salvare,* to save < Lat. *salvus,* safe.] **—sal·va′tion·al** *adj.*

Salvation Army *n.* An international evangelical and charitable organization founded in 1865 by William Booth.

sal·va·tion·ist (săl-vā′shə-nĭst) *n.* **1.** Often **Salvationist.** A member of the Salvation Army. **2.** An evangelist.

salve[1] (săv, säv) *n.* **1.** An analgesic or medicinal ointment. **2.** Something that soothes or heals; balm. **3.** Flattery or commendation. —*tr.v.* **salved, salv·ing, salves.** To soothe or heal with or as if with salve. [ME < OE *sealf.*]

salve[2] (sălv) *tr.v.* **salved, salv·ing, salves.** To salvage. [Back-formation < SALVAGE.] **—sal′vor** *n.*

sal·ver (săl′vər) *n.* A tray for serving food or drinks. [Alteration of Fr. *salve* < Sp. *salva,* tasting of food to detect poison < *salvar,* to save, taste food to detect poison < LLat. *salvare,* to save < Lat. *salvus,* safe.]

sal·vi·a (săl′vē-ə) *n.* Any of various plants and shrubs of the genus *Salvia,* esp. scarlet sage. [NLat. *Salvia,* genus name < Lat. *salvia,* sage. —see SAGE[2].]

sal·vo (săl′vō) *n., pl.* **-vos** or **-voes. 1. a.** A simultaneous discharge of firearms. **b.** The simultaneous release of a rack of bombs from an aircraft. **c.** The projectiles or bombs thus released. **2.** A sudden outburst: *a salvo of cheers.* **3.** A salute; tribute: *salvos of praise from the reviewers.* [Ital. *salva,* salute < Lat. *salve,* hail, imper. of *salvēre,* to be in good health < *salvus,* safe.]

sal volatile *n.* A solution of ammonium carbonate in alcohol or ammonia water. [NLat., volatile salt.]

sam·a·ra (săm′ər-ə, sə-mâr′ə, -mär′ə) *n.* A winged, usually one-seeded fruit that does not split open, as of the ash or maple. [Lat., elm seed.]

Sa·mar·i·tan (sə-măr′ĭ-tn, -mâr′-) *n.* **1.** A native or inhabitant of Samaria. **2.** A Good Samaritan. —*adj.* Of or relating to Samaria or to Samaritans. [ME < LLat. *Samaritanus* < Gk. *Samaritēs* < *Samareia,* Samaria.]

sa·mar·i·um (sə-mâr′ē-əm, -măr′-) *n. Symbol* **Sm** A silvery or pale-gray metallic rare-earth element found in monazite and bastnaesite and used as a dopant for laser materials, in infrared absorbing glass, and as a neutron absorber in certain nuclear reactors. Atomic number 62; atomic weight 150.35; melting point 1,072°C; boiling point 1,900°C; specific gravity (approximately) 7.50; valences 2, 3. [SAMAR(SKITE) + -IUM.]

sa·mar·skite (sə-mär′skīt′, săm′ər-) *n.* A velvet-black mineral oxide with red-brown streaks that is a source of several rare-earth metals. [Fr., after Col. von *Samarski,* 19th-cent. Russian mine official.]

sam·ba (săm′bə, säm′-) *n.* **1.** An African dance modified in Brazil as a ballroom dance. **2.** Music in 4/4 time for dancing the samba. —*intr.v.* **-baed, -ba·ing, -bas.** To dance the samba. [Port.]

sam·bar also **sam·bur** (săm′bər, säm′-) *n.* A large deer, *Cervus unicolor,* of southeastern Asia, having a reddish-brown coat. [Hindi *sāmbar* < Skt. *śambaraḥ.*]

Sam Browne belt (săm′ broun′) *n.* A belt worn as part of a

saltire

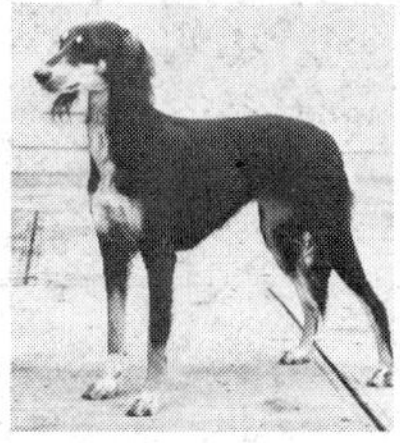

saluki

salute

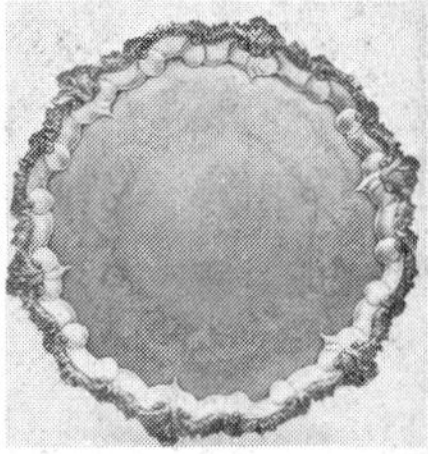

salver

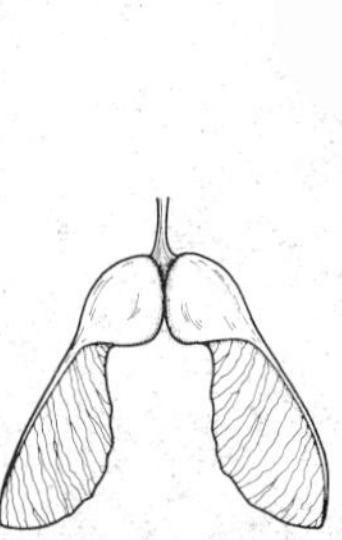

samara
Of a sugar maple

samovar

sampan

sampler

sand
Sand castle

military or police uniform, having a shoulder strap that runs diagonally across the chest. [After Sir *Samuel* James *Browne* (1824–1901).]

sam·bur (săm′bər, säm′-) *n.* Variant of **sambar.**

same (sām) *adj.* **1.** Being the very one; identical. **2.** Similar in kind, quality, quantity, or degree. **3.** Conforming in every detail: *according to the same rules as before.* **4.** Being the one previously mentioned or indicated; aforesaid. —*adv.* In the same way. —*pron.* **1.** Someone or something identical with another. **2.** Someone or something previously mentioned or described. [ME < ON *samr.*]

Synonyms: *same, selfsame, identical, equal, equivalent.* These adjectives refer to the absence of difference or disparity. *Same, selfsame,* and *identical* are all applicable, when only one object is under consideration, in the sense of one and the same: *the same* (or *selfsame* or *identical*) *man I saw this morning. Same* and *identical* are also used when two or more objects are considered. In this sense *same* implies absence of difference with respect to kind, quality, quantity, or the like; *identical* specifies strict agreement in every respect and detail. *Equal* refers more generally to absence of difference between two or more with respect to extent, amount, value, force, or the like. *Equivalent,* referring to two or more, means not identical but having the same worth, effect, force, or meaning.

Usage: Only in legal language is *the same* or just *same* used as a substitute for *it* or *them.* In general writing, one should avoid sentences like *The charge is $5; please remit same. When I have finished the books, I will return the same.*

sa·mekh (sä′mĕk′) *n.* The 15th letter of the Hebrew alphabet. See table at **alphabet.** [Heb. *sāmekh.*]

same·ness (sām′nĭs) *n.* **1.** The condition of being the same; identity. **2.** A lack of variety or change; monotony.

sam·i·sen (săm′ĭ-sĕn′) *n.* A Japanese musical instrument resembling a banjo, having a very long neck and three strings played with a plectrum. [J. : *sami,* three + *sen,* string.]

sam·ite (săm′īt′, sā′mīt′) *n.* A heavy silk fabric, often interwoven with gold or silver, worn in the Middle Ages. [ME *samit* < OFr. < Med. Lat. *examitum* < Med. Gk. *hexamiton* < Gk. *hexamitos,* of six threads : *hexa-,* six + *mitos,* warp thread.]

sa·miz·dat (sä′mēz-dät′) *n.* **1. a.** The secret publication and distribution of government-banned literature in the U.S.S.R. **b.** The literature produced by this system. **2.** An underground press. [R. : *sam,* self + *izdatel′stvo,* publisher < *izdat′,* to publish.]

sam·let (săm′lĭt) *n.* A young salmon. [Blend of SALMON + -LET.]

Sa·mo·an (sə-mō′ən) *adj.* Of or pertaining to Samoa, its Polynesian inhabitants, or their language. —*n.* **1.** A native or inhabitant of Samoa. **2.** The Polynesian language of Samoa.

sam·o·var (săm′ə-vär′) *n.* A metal urn with a spigot, used to boil water for tea. [R. : *samo-,* self + *varit′,* to boil.]

Sam·o·yed also **Sam·o·yede** (săm′ə-yĕd′, -oi-ĕd′) *n.* **1.** A member of a Ural-Altaic people inhabiting the tundra lands of the northeastern European Soviet Union and northwestern Siberia. **2.** A branch of the Uralic language family that comprises the languages of the Samoyeds. **3.** A dog of a breed originally developed in northern Eurasia, having a thick, long white coat. [R. *samoed* < Lapp *Sāme-Ǟednàma,* of Lapland.] **—Sam′o·yed′ic** (-yĕd′ĭk) *adj.*

samp (sămp) *n.* A coarse hominy or a porridge made from it. [Narraganset *nasàump,* corn mush.]

sam·pan (săm′păn′) *n.* A flat-bottomed Oriental skiff propelled usually by two oars. [Chin. *san*^{1} *ban*^{3} : *san*^{1}, small + *ban*^{3}, board.]

sam·phire (săm′fīr′) *n.* **1.** The glasswort. **2.** Any of several Old World plants of coastal areas, esp. *Crithmium maritimum,* having fleshy divided leaves and small white flowers. [Alteration of OFr. (*herbe de*) *Saint Pierre,* St. Peter's herb.]

sam·ple (săm′pəl) *n.* **1. a.** A portion, piece, or segment that is representative of a whole. **b.** An entity that is representative of a class; specimen. **2.** *Statistics.* A set of elements drawn from and analyzed to estimate the characteristics of a population. —*tr.v.* **-pled, -pling, -ples.** To take a sample of, esp. to test or examine by a sample. [ME < OFr. *essample.* —see EXAMPLE.]

sam·pler (săm′plər) *n.* **1.** One that is employed to take and appraise samples, as of a food product. **2.** A mechanical device for obtaining and analyzing samples. **3.** A piece of cloth embroidered with various designs or mottoes.

sam·pling (săm′plĭng) *n.* **1.** *Statistics.* A sample (sense 2). **2.** The process of selecting a sample.

sampling circuit *n.* A circuit that yields an output suitable for use as an error or negative signal in a controller program that uses sampling action.

sampling distribution *n.* The distribution of a statistic, such as occurs when a number of sample means are calculated for a given population.

sampling gate *n.* A circuit that produces an output only when first activated by a preliminary pulse.

sam·sa·ra (səm-sä′rə) *n.* *Hinduism & Buddhism.* The eternal cycle of birth, suffering, death, and rebirth. [Skt. *samsārah* : *sam-,* together + *sarati,* it flows.]

Sam·son (săm′sən) *n.* An Israelite judge of extraordinary strength, betrayed to the Philistines by Delilah. [LLat. *Sampson* < Gk. *Sampsōn* < Heb. *shimshōn,* like the sun < *shemesh,* sun.]

Sam·u·el (săm′yo͞o-əl) **1.** A Hebrew judge and prophet of the 11th century B.C. **2.** See table at **Bible.** [LLat. < Gk. *Samouel* < Heb. *Shĕmū′ēl.*]

sam·u·rai (săm′ə-rī′, -yə-) *n., pl.* **samurai** or **-rais. 1.** The feudal military aristocracy of Japan. **2.** A professional warrior belonging to the samurai. [J., warrior.]

san·a·to·ri·um (săn′ə-tôr′ē-əm, -tōr′-) also **san·a·tar·i·um** (-târ′ē-əm) *n., pl.* **-to·ri·ums** or **-to·ri·a** (-tôr′ē-ə, -tōr′-) also **-tar·i·ums** or **-tar·i·a** (-târ′ē-ə). **1.** An institution for the treatment of chronic diseases or for medically supervised recuperation. **2.** A sanitarium. [NLat., neuter of LLat. *sanatorius,* curative < Lat. *sanatus,* p.part. of *sanare,* to heal < *sanus,* healthy.]

san·be·ni·to (săn′bə-nē′tō) *n., pl.* **-tos.** A garment of sackcloth worn at an auto-da-fé of the Spanish Inquisition by condemned heretics, being yellow with red crosses for the penitent and black with painted flames and devils for the impenitent. [Sp. *sambenito* < *San Benito,* St. Benedict.]

sanc·ta (săngk′tə) *n.* A plural of **sanctum.**

sanc·ti·fy (săngk′tə-fī′) *tr.v.* **-fied, -fy·ing, -fies. 1.** To set apart for sacred use; consecrate. **2.** To make holy; purify. **3.** To give religious sanction to, as with an oath: *sanctify a marriage.* **4.** To give social or moral sanction to. **5.** To make productive of holiness or blessing. [ME *sanctifien* < OFr. *sanctifier* < LLat. *sanctificare* : Lat. *sanctus,* p.part. of *sancire,* to consecrate + Lat. *facere,* to make.] **—sanc′ti·fi·ca′tion** *n.* **—sanc′ti·fi′er** *n.*

sanc·ti·mo·ni·ous (săngk′tə-mō′nē-əs) *adj.* Feigning piety or righteousness. **—sanc′ti·mo′ni·ous·ly** *adv.* **—sanc′ti·mo′ni·ous·ness** *n.*

sanc·ti·mo·ny (săngk′tə-mō′nē) *n.* Feigned piety or righteousness; hypocritical high-mindedness. [OFr. *sanctimonie* < Lat. *sanctimonia,* sacredness < *sanctus,* holy. —see SANCTIFY.]

sanc·tion (săngk′shən) *n.* **1.** Authoritative permission or approval that makes a course of action valid. **2.** Support or encouragement, as from public opinion or established custom. **3.** A consideration, influence, or principle that dictates an ethical choice. **4.** A law or decree. **5.** The penalty for noncompliance specified in a law or decree. **6.** A penalty, specified or in the form of moral pressure, that acts to ensure compliance or conformity. **7.** A coercive measure adopted usually by several nations acting together against a nation violating international law. —*tr.v.* **-tioned, -tion·ing, -tions. 1.** To authorize; legitimize. **2.** To maintain or encourage by an indication of approval. [OFr. < Lat. *sanctio,* an ordaining < *sanctus,* holy. —see SANCTIFY.]

sanc·ti·ty (săngk′tĭ-tē) *n., pl.* **-ties. 1.** Holiness of life; saintliness. **2.** The quality or condition of being considered sacred; inviolability. **3.** Something considered sacred. [ME *saunctite* < OFr. *sainctite* < Lat. *sanctitas* < *sanctus,* sacred. —see SANCTIFY.]

sanc·tu·ar·y (săngk′cho͞o-ĕr′ē) *n., pl.* **-ies. 1. a.** A sacred place, such as a church, temple, or mosque. **b.** The most holy part of a sacred place. **2. a.** A place that provides refuge, asylum, or immunity from arrest. **b.** The immunity provided by a sanctuary. **3.** A reserved area in which animals or birds are protected from hunting or molestation. [ME *sanctuarie* < OFr. *sainctuarie* < LLat. *sanctuarium* < Lat. *sanctus,* sacred. —see SANCTIFY.]

sanc·tum (săngk′təm) *n., pl.* **-tums** or **-ta** (-tə). **1.** A sacred or holy place. **2.** A private place where one is free from intrusion. [Lat., neuter of *sanctus,* sacred. —see SANCTIFY.]

sanctum sanc·to·rum (săngk-tôr′əm, -tōr′-) *n.* **1.** The holy of holies. **2.** An inviolably private place. [LLat. (transl. of Gk. *to hagion tōn hagiōn,* transl. of Heb. *qōdesh haqqodashīm*).]

Sanc·tus (săngk′təs) *n.* A hymn of praise sung at the end of the Preface in many eucharistic liturgies. [ME < Med. Lat. < Lat. *sanctus,* holy (from the first word of the hymn). —see SANCTIFY.]

sand (sănd) *n.* **1. a.** Loose, granular, gritty particles of worn or disintegrated rock, finer than gravel and coarser than dust. **b.** Often **sands.** A tract of land covered with sand, as a beach or desert. **c.** The sand in an hourglass. **2. sands.** Moments of allotted time or duration: "*The sands are number'd that make up my life*" (Shakespeare). **3.** *Slang.* Grit; courage. **4.** A light grayish brown to yellowish gray. —*tr.v.* **sand·ed, sand·ing, sands. 1.** To sprinkle or cover with or as if with sand. **2.** To polish or scrape with sand or sandpaper. **3.** To mix with sand. **4.** To fill up (a harbor) with sand. [ME < OE.]

san·dal^1 (săn′dl) *n.* **1.** A shoe consisting of a sole fastened to the foot by thongs or straps. **2.** A light slipper or low-cut shoe fastened to the foot by an ankle strap. **3.** A rubber overshoe cut very low and covering little more than the sole of the shoe. **4.** A strap or band for fastening a low shoe or slipper on the foot. [ME *sandalie* < Lat. *sandalium* < Gk. *sandalion,* dim. of *sandalon,* sandal.]

san·dal^2 (săn′dl) *n.* Sandalwood. [ME < OFr. < Med. Lat. *sandalum, santalum* < Gk. *santalon, sandanon.*]

san·dal·wood (săn′dl-wo͝od′) *n.* **1. a.** Any of several Asian trees of the genus *Santalum,* esp. *S. album,* having aromatic yellowish heartwood that is used in cabinetmaking and wood carving and that yields an oil used in perfumery. **b.** The wood of this tree or of similar trees. **2.** A light to moderate or grayish brown.

san·da·rac (săn′də-răk′) *n.* **1.** A tree, *Tetraclinis articulata* or *Callitris quadrivalvis,* of northern Africa, having wood yielding a brittle, translucent resin used in varnishes. **2.** The resin of the sandarac. [Lat., red pigment < Gk. *sandarakē,* realgar.]

sand·bag (sănd′băg′) *n.* A bag filled with sand, used as ballast, to form protective walls, or as a weapon. —*tr.v.* **-bagged, -bag·ging, -bags. 1.** To put sandbags in or around. **2. a.** To hit with or as if with a sandbag. **b.** To force by crude means; coerce.

sand·bank (sănd′băngk′) *n.* A large mass of sand, as on a hillside or in a river.

sand·bar (sănd′bär′) *n.* An offshore shoal of sand built up by the action of waves or currents.

sand·blast (sănd′blăst′) *n.* **1. a.** A blast of air or steam carrying sand at high velocity to etch glass or to clean stone or metal surfaces. **b.** A machine used to apply such a blast. **2.** A strong wind carrying sand along. —*tr.v.* **-blast·ed, -blast·ing, -blasts.** To apply a sandblast to (a building, for example). **—sand′blast′er** *n.*

sand-blind (sănd′blīnd′) *adj.* Partially blind. [ME < OE **sāmblind* : *sam-,* half + *blind,* blind.]

sand·box (sănd′bŏks′) *n.* A low box filled with sand for children to play in.

sandbox tree *n.* A tropical American tree, *Hura crepitans,* having a spiny trunk and woody seed capsules that split explosively when ripe. [So called because the capsules were formerly used to hold sand for drying ink.]

sand·bur (sănd′bûr′) *n.* **1.** Any of several grasses of the genus *Cenchrus,* esp. *C. tribuloides,* of the eastern United States and tropical America, having burlike, spiny fruiting clusters. **2.** A plant, *Solanum rostratum,* of the western United States and Mexico, having prickly fruit.

sand-cast (sănd′kăst′) *tr.v.* **-cast, -cast·ing, -casts.** To make (a casting) by pouring molten metal into a sand mold.

sand crack *n.* A fissure in the side of a horse's hoof, often causing lameness.

sand dab *n.* Any of several small food fishes of the genus *Citharichthys,* of Pacific waters, related to and resembling the flounders.

sand dollar *n.* Any of various thin, circular echinoderms of the order Exocycloida or Clypeasteroidea, esp. *Echinarachnius parma,* of sandy ocean bottoms of the northern Atlantic and Pacific.

sand eel *n.* The sand lance.

sand·er (săn′dər) *n.* **1. a.** One that spreads sand. **b.** One that sands surfaces, as of wood. **2.** A sanding machine.

sand·er·ling (săn′dər-lĭng) *n.* A small shore bird, *Crocethia alba,* having predominantly gray and white plumage. [Perh. < SAND + -LING.]

sand flea *n.* **1.** Any of various small crustaceans living on sandy beaches. **2.** The chigoe.

sand fly *n.* Any of various small biting flies of the genus *Phlebotomus,* of tropical areas, some of which transmit diseases.

sand-fly fever (sănd′flī′) *n.* A mild virus disease transmitted by the bite of a sand fly, *Phlebotomus papatasil,* characterized by fever, malaise, eye pain, and headache.

sand grouse *n.* Any of various pigeonlike birds of the genus *Pterocles* and related genera, of arid and semiarid regions of the Old World.

san·dhi (săn′dē, săn′-) *n. Ling.* The modification of the sound of a morpheme in certain phonetic contexts. The difference between the pronunciation of *the* in *the house* and in *the other house* is an instance of sandhi. [Skt. *saṃdhiḥ,* union : *sam-,* together + *dadhāti,* he places.]

sand·hog (sănd′hôg′, -hŏg′) *n.* A laborer who works inside a caisson, as in the construction of underwater tunnels.

sand hopper *n.* A beach flea.

sanding machine *n.* A machine having a powered abrasive-covered disk or belt, used for smoothing, polishing, or refinishing.

sand lance *n.* Any of several small marine fishes of the genus *Ammodytes,* having a slender body with a forked tail fin and often burrowing in the sand of tidelands.

sand lily *n.* A low-growing plant, *Leucocrinum montanum,* of the western United States, having grasslike leaves and fragrant white, star-shaped flowers.

sand·lot (sănd′lŏt′) *n.* A vacant lot used esp. by children for unorganized sports. —***modifier:*** *sandlot baseball.*

sand·man (sănd′măn′) *n.* A character in fairy tales and folklore who puts children to sleep by sprinkling sand in their eyes.

sand painting *n.* **1.** A ceremonial design of the Navaho Indians made by trickling fine colored sand onto a base of neutral sand. **2.** The art of making designs with colored sand.

sand·pa·per (sănd′pā′pər) *n.* Heavy paper coated on one side with sand or other abrasive material, used for smoothing. —*tr.v.* **-pered, -per·ing, -pers.** To rub with sandpaper.

sand·pi·per (sănd′pī′pər) *n.* Any of various small wading birds of the family Scolopacidae, usually having a long, straight bill.

sand·stone (sănd′stōn′) *n.* Variously colored sedimentary rock composed predominantly of sandlike quartz grains cemented by lime, silica, or other materials.

sand·storm (sănd′stôrm′) *n.* A strong wind carrying clouds of sand through the air.

sand table *n.* **1.** A table with raised edges, used for holding sand with which children play. **2.** A table on which a relief model of terrain is built out of sand for the study of military maneuvers.

sand trap *n.* A hazard on a golf course consisting of a depression filled with sand.

sand verbena *n.* Any of several plants of the genus *Abronia,* of western North America, having fragrant, usually pink flowers.

sand·wich (sănd′wĭch, săn′-) *n.* **1.** Two or more slices of bread with a filling such as meat or cheese placed between them. **2.** Something resembling a sandwich. —*tr.v.* **-wiched, -wich·ing, -wich·es. 1.** To make (something) into or as if into a sandwich. **2.** To insert (one thing) tightly between two other things of differing character or quality. **3.** To make room or time for: *sandwiched lunch between the two meetings.* [After John Montagu (1718–1792), 4th Earl of Sandwich.]

sandwich board *n.* Two large boards bearing placards, hinged at the top by straps for hanging over the shoulders with one board in front and other behind, used for picketing or advertising.

sandwich man *n.* A man who pickets or advertises by carrying a sandwich board.

sand·worm (sănd′wûrm′) *n.* Any of various segmented worms, esp. of the genera *Nereis* and *Arenicola,* generally inhabiting coastal mud or sand and often used as fishing bait.

sand·wort (sănd′wûrt′, -wôrt′) *n.* Any of numerous low-growing plants of the genus *Arenaria,* having small, usually white flowers.

sand·y (săn′dē) *adj.* **-i·er, -i·est. 1.** Covered with, full of, or consisting of sand. **2.** Having characteristics similar to sand. **3.** Of the color of sand; yellowish red. **—sand′i·ness** *n.*

sane (sān) *adj.* **san·er, san·est. 1.** Mentally healthy; of sound mind. **2.** Having or showing sound judgment; reasonable. [Lat. *sanus,* healthy.] **—sane′ly** *adv.* **—sane′ness** *n.*

San·for·ized (săn′fə-rīzd′). A trademark for fabric preshrunk by a patented mechanical process so as to minimize later shrinkage.

sang (săng) *v.* Past tense of **sing.**

san·ga·ree (săng′gə-rē′) *n.* A sweet, chilled beverage made of wine or other alcoholic liquor and grated nutmeg. [Sp. *sangría,* act of bleeding < *sangre,* blood < Lat. *sanguis.*]

sang-froid (säN-frwä′) *n.* Composure; imperturbability. [Fr. : *sang,* blood + *froid,* cold.]

san·gri·a (săng-grē′ə, săn-) *n.* A cold drink made of red or white wine mixed with brandy, sugar, fruit juice, and soda water. [Sp. *sangría,* act of bleeding < *sangre,* blood < Lat. *sanguis.*]

san·gui·nar·i·a (săng′gwə-nâr′ē-ə, -nĕr′-) *n.* Bloodroot. [NLat. *Sanguinaria,* genus name < Lat., a plant that stanches blood, fem. of *sanguinarius,* sanguinary.]

san·gui·nar·y (săng′gwə-nĕr′ē) *adj.* **1.** Accompanied by carnage. **2.** Bloodthirsty. **3.** Consisting of blood. [Lat. *sanguinarius* < *sanguis,* blood.] **—san′gui·nar′i·ly** (-nâr′ə-lē) *adv.*

san·guine (săng′gwĭn) *adj.* **1. a.** Of the color of blood; red. **b.** Ruddy: *a sanguine complexion.* **2. a.** *Archaic.* Having blood as the dominant humor in terms of medieval physiology. **b.** Having the temperament and ruddy complexion formerly thought to be characteristic of a person dominated by this humor; passionate. **3.** Cheerfully confident; optimistic. [ME *sanguin* < OFr. < Lat. *sanguineus* < *sanguis,* blood.] **—san′guine·ly** *adv.* **—san′guine·ness, san·guin′i·ty** (săng-gwĭn′ĭ-tē) *n.*

san·guin·e·ous (săng-gwĭn′ē-əs) *adj.* **1.** Pertaining to or involving blood or bloodshed. **2.** Blood-red. [Lat. *sanguineus* < *sanguis,* blood.]

san·guin·o·lent (săng-gwĭn′ə-lənt) *adj.* Mixed or tinged with blood. [Lat. *sanguinolentus,* full of blood < *sanguis,* blood.]

San·hed·rin (săn-hĕd′rĭn, -hē′drĭn, sän-) *n.* The highest judicial and ecclesiastical council of the ancient Jewish nation, composed of from 70 to 72 members. [Heb. *sanhedhrīn* < Gk. *sunedrion,* council < *sunedros,* sitting in council : *sun-,* together + *hedra,* seat.]

san·i·cle (săn′ĭ-kəl) *n.* Any of various plants of the genus *Sanicula,* having clusters of small, greenish flowers and reputedly having medicinal value as an astringent. [ME < OFr. < Med. Lat. *sanicula,* prob. < Lat. *sanus,* healthy.]

sa·ni·es (sā′nē-ēz′) *n., pl.* **sanies.** A thin, fetid, greenish fluid consisting of serum and pus discharged from a wound, ulcer, or fistula. [Lat.] **—sa′ni·ous** (-əs) *adj.*

san·i·tar·i·a (săn′ĭ-târ′ē-ə) *n.* A plural of **sanitarium.**

san·i·tar·i·an (săn′ĭ-târ′ē-ən) *n.* A public health or sanitation expert.

san·i·tar·i·um (săn′ĭ-târ′ē-əm) *n., pl.* **-i·ums** or **-i·a** (-ē-ə). **1.** A health resort. **2.** A sanatorium.

san·i·tar·y (săn′ĭ-tĕr′ē) *adj.* **1.** Of or relating to health.

sandal[1]

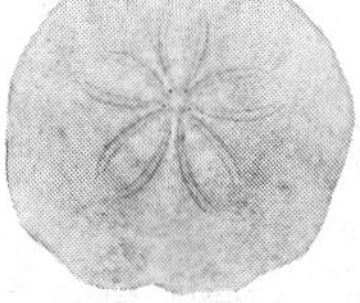

sand dollar

George Miksch Sutton

sand grouse

sandwich man

2. Free from elements, as filth or bacteria, that endanger health; hygienic. [Fr. *sanitaire* < Lat. *sanitas,* health < *sanus,* healthy.] **—san′i·tar′i·ly** (-târ′ə-lē) *adv.*

sanitary engineer *n.* An engineer specializing in the maintenance of urban environmental conditions conducive to the preservation of public health. **—sanitary engineering** *n.*

sanitary landfill *n.* Landfill.

sanitary napkin *n.* A disposable pad of absorbent material worn to absorb menstrual flow.

san·i·ta·tion (săn′ĭ-tā′shən) *n.* **1.** The formulation and application of measures designed to protect public health. **2.** The disposal of sewage.

san·i·tize (săn′ĭ-tīz′) *tr.v.* **-tized, -tiz·ing, -tiz·es. 1.** To make sanitary. **2.** To make more acceptable by removing unpleasant or offensive features from: *sanitized the language in adapting the novel for television.*

san·i·ty (săn′ĭ-tē) *n.* **1.** The condition of being sane. **2.** Soundness of judgment or reason. [ME *sanite* < OFr. < Lat. *sanitas,* health < *sanus,* healthy.]

San Jo·se scale (săn′ hō-zā′) *n.* A destructive scale insect, *Aspidiotus perniciosus,* that does considerable damage to fruit trees and fruit-bearing plants. [After *San Jose,* California.]

sank (săngk) *v.* Past tense of **sink.**

San·khya (säng′kyə) *n.* A system of Hindu philosophy based on a dualism involving the ultimate principles of soul and potential matter. [Skt. *sāṁkhya-,* based on enumeration < *saṁkhyā,* enumeration : *sam-,* with + *khyāti,* he says.]

san·nup (săn′əp) *n.* A married American Indian man. [Of Algonquian orig.]

sans (sănz) *prep.* Without. [ME < OFr. < Lat. *sine.*]

sans-cu·lotte (sănz′kyo͞o-lŏt′) *n.* **1.** An extreme radical republican during the French Revolution. **2.** A revolutionary extremist. [Fr. : *sans,* without + *culotte,* breeches.] **—sans′-cu·lot′tic** (-lŏt′ĭk) *adj.* **—sans′-cu·lot′tism** *n.*

san·sei (sän′sā′, sän-sā′) *n., pl.* **sansei** or **-seis.** The U.S.-born grandchild of Japanese immigrants to America. [J. : *san,* three + *sei,* generation.]

sansevieria

san·se·vie·ri·a (săn′sə-vîr′ē-ə) *n.* Any of various tropical Old World plants of the genus *Sansevieria,* having thick, lance-shaped leaves and often cultivated as a house plant. [NLat. *Sansevieria,* genus name, after Raimondo di Sangro (1710–1771), Prince of *San Severo,* Italy.]

San·skrit (săn′skrĭt′) *n.* An ancient Indic language that is the language of Hinduism and the Vedas and is the classical literary language of India. [Skt. *saṁskṛta-,* elegant : *sam-,* together + *karoti,* he makes.] **—San′skrit′ist** *n.*

San·skrit·ic (săn-skrĭt′ĭk) *n.* Indic. **—San·skrit′ic** *adj.*

sans ser·if (săn sĕr′ĭf) *n.* A typeface without serifs.

San·ta Claus (săn′tə klôz′) *n.* The personification of the spirit of Christmas, usually represented as a jolly, fat old man with a white beard and a red suit. [Alteration of dial. Du. *Sinterklaas* < MDu. *Sinterclaes,* St. Nicholas.]

san·ta·lol (săn′tə-lôl′, -lōl′) *n.* A colorless liquid, $C_{15}H_{24}O$, obtained from sandalwood and used in perfumes. [NLat. *Santalum,* sandalwood genus + -OL[2].]

san·ton·i·ca (săn-tŏn′ĭ-kə) *n.* **1.** A wormwood, *Artemisia maritima,* of the Old World, having flowers that yield santonin. **2.** The dried unopened flowers of the santonica. [NLat. < Lat. *(herba) santonica,* fem. of *santonicus,* of the Santoni, a people of Aquitania.]

san·to·nin (săn′tə-nĭn) *n.* A colorless crystalline compound, $C_{15}H_{18}O_3$, obtained from species of wormwood, esp. santonica, and used as an anthelmintic. [SANTON(ICA) + -IN.]

sap[1]
Sap buckets on a sugar maple tree

sap[1] (săp) *n.* **1. a.** The watery fluid that circulates through a plant, carrying food and other substances to the tissues. **b.** A plant juice or fluid. **2.** An essential bodily fluid. **3.** Health and energy; vitality. **4.** *Slang.* A gullible person; dupe. **5.** A blackjack[1] (sense 1). *—tr.v.* **sapped, sap·ping, saps.** To hit or knock out with a sap. [ME < OE *sæp.*]

sap[2] (săp) *n.* A covered trench or tunnel dug to a point within an enemy position. *—v.* **sapped, sap·ping, saps.** *—tr.* **1.** To undermine the foundations of (a fortification). **2.** To deplete or weaken gradually; devitalize. *—intr.* To dig a sap. [OFr. *sappe* or OItal. *zappa.*]

sap·a·jou (săp′ə-jo͞o) *n.* A capuchin monkey. [Fr. < Tupi.]

Sa·phar (sə-fär′) *n.* Variant of **Safar.**

sap·head (săp′hĕd′) *n. Slang.* A fool. **—sap′head′ed** *adj.*

sa·phe·na (sə-fē′nə) *n., pl.* **-nae** (-nē′). Either of two large superficial veins of the leg. [ME < Med. Lat. < Ar. *ṣāfīn.*] **—sa·phe′nous** *adj.*

sap·id (săp′ĭd) *adj.* **1. a.** Having flavor. **b.** Pleasantly flavorful; savory. **2.** Pleasing to the mind; engaging. [Lat. *sapidus* < *sapere,* to taste.] **—sa·pid′i·ty** (să-pĭd′ĭ-tē, sə-) *n.*

sa·pi·ent (sā′pē-ənt) *adj.* Having great wisdom and discernment. [ME < OFr. < Lat. *sapiens,* pr.part. of *sapere,* to taste, be wise.] **—sa′pi·ence** *n.* **—sa′pi·ent·ly** *adv.*

sap·less (săp′lĭs) *adj.* **1.** Devoid of sap; dry. **2.** Lacking spirit or energy. **—sap′less·ness** *n.*

sap·ling (săp′lĭng) *n.* **1.** A young tree. **2.** A youth.

sap·o·dil·la (săp′ə-dĭl′ə, -dē′yə) *n.* **1.** An evergreen tree, *Achras zapota,* of tropical America, having latex that yields chicle. **2.** The edible russet fruit of the sapodilla. [Sp. *zapotillo,* dim. of *zapote,* sapodilla fruit < Nahuatl *tzapotl.*]

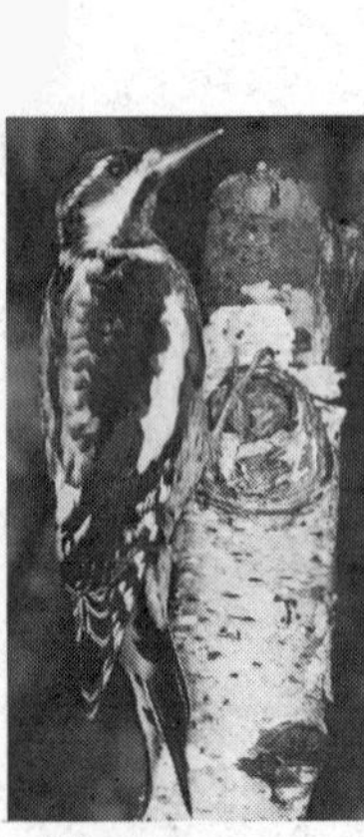

sapsucker
Yellow-bellied sapsucker

sap·o·na·ceous (săp′ə-nā′shəs) *adj.* Having the qualities of soap. [Lat. *sapo, sapon-,* soap + -ACEOUS.] **—sap′o·na′ceous·ness** *n.*

sap·o·na·ted (săp′ə-nā′tĭd) *adj.* Combined or treated with a soap. [< Lat. *sapo, sapon-,* soap.]

sa·pon·i·fi·ca·tion (sə-pŏn′ə-fĭ-kā′shən) *n.* The hydrolysis of an ester by an alkali, producing a free alcohol and an acid salt, esp. alkaline hydrolysis of fats to make soap.

sa·pon·i·fy (sə-pŏn′ə-fī′) *v.* **-fied, -fy·ing, -fies.** *—tr.* **1.** To convert (an ester) by saponification. **2.** To convert (fats) into soap. *—intr.* To undergo saponification. [Fr. *saponifier* < Lat. *sapo,* soap.] **—sa·pon′i·fi′a·ble** *adj.* **—sa·pon′i·fi′er** *n.*

sap·o·nin (săp′ə-nĭn, sə-pō′-) *n.* Any of various plant glucosides that form soapy colloidal solutions when mixed and agitated with water, used in detergents, foaming agents, and emulsifiers. [Fr. *saponine* < Lat. *sapo,* soap.]

sap·o·nite (săp′ə-nīt′) *n.* An amorphous, hydrous silicate of magnesium occurring as a soaplike mass in the cavities of certain rocks, such as diabase. [Swed. *saponit* < Lat. *sapo,* soap.]

sa·por (sā′pər, -pôr′) *n.* A quality perceptible to the sense of taste; flavor. [ME < Lat. < *sapere,* to taste.] **—sa′po·rif′ic** (sā′pə-rĭf′ĭk, săp′ə-), **sa′po·rous** (sā′pər-əs, săp′ər-) *adj.*

sa·po·ta (sə-pō′tə) *n.* The sapodilla (sense 2). [Sp. *zapota* < Nahuatl *tzapotl.*]

sap·pan·wood (sə-păn′wo͝od′, săp′ăn-, -ən-) *n.* **1.** A tree, *Caesalpina sappan,* of tropical Asia, having wood that yields a red dye. **2.** The wood of the sappanwood. [Malay *sapang,* sappanwood + WOOD.]

sap·per (săp′ər) *n.* **1.** A military engineer who specializes in sapping and other field fortification activities. **2.** A military engineer who lays, detects, and disarms mines. [< SAP[2].]

Sap·phic (săf′ĭk) *adj.* **1.** Of or pertaining to the Greek poet Sappho. **2. a.** Designating a verse of dactyls combined with trochees or anapests with iambs, esp. one of 11 syllables. **b.** Designating a stanza of three such verses followed by an Adonic. **c.** Designating an ode made up of such stanzas. **3.** Often **sapphic.** Of or pertaining to lesbianism. *—n.* A Sapphic meter, verse, stanza, or ode.

sap·phire (săf′īr′) *n.* **1.** Any of several relatively pure forms of corundum, esp. a blue form used as a gemstone. **2.** A corundum gem. **3.** The blue color of a gem sapphire. ***—modifier:*** *a sapphire ring.* *—adj.* Having the color of a blue sapphire. [ME *saphir* < OFr. *safir* < Lat. *sapphirus* < Gk. *sappheiros,* of Semitic orig.]

sap·phi·rine (săf′ə-rīn′, -rēn′, sə-fīr′ĭn) *adj.* Of or resembling sapphire. *—n.* A rare light-blue or green aluminum-magnesium silicate mineral.

sap·py (săp′ē) *adj.* **-pi·er, -pi·est. 1.** Full of sap; juicy. **2.** *Slang.* Excessively sentimental; mawkish. **3.** *Slang.* Silly or foolish. **—sap′pi·ly** *adv.* **—sap′pi·ness** *n.*

sapr– *pref.* Variant of **sapro-.**

sa·pre·mia also **sa·prae·mia** (să-prē′mē-ə) *n.* Septicemia. **—sa·pre′mic** *adj.*

sapro– or **sapr–** *pref.* **1.** Decay; putrefaction: *saprogenic.* **2.** Dead or decaying organic material: *saprophyte.* [< Gk. *sapros,* rotten.]

sap·robe (săp′rōb′) *n.* An organism that derives its nourishment from nonliving or decaying organic matter. [SAPRO- + Gk. *bios,* life.] **—sa·pro′bic** (să-prō′bĭk) *adj.* **—sa·pro′bi·cal·ly** *adv.*

sap·ro·gen·ic (săp′rə-jĕn′ĭk) *adj.* Of, producing, or resulting from putrefaction. **—sap′ro·ge·nic′i·ty** (-jə-nĭs′ĭ-tē) *n.*

sap·ro·lite (săp′rə-līt′) *n.* Clay, silt, or other rock remnants remaining at the site of disintegration.

sap·ro·pel (săp′rə-pĕl′) *n.* **1.** An aquatic sludge rich in organic matter. **2.** A fluid slime found in swamps as a product of putrefaction. [SAPRO- + Gk. *pēlos,* mud.] **—sap′ro·pel′ic** (-pĕl′ĭk, -pē′lĭk) *adj.*

sa·proph·a·gous (să-prŏf′ə-gəs) *adj.* Feeding on decaying matter.

sap·ro·phyte (săp′rə-fīt′) *n.* A plant that lives on and derives its nourishment from dead or decaying organic matter. **—sap′ro·phyt′ic** (-fĭt′ĭk) *adj.* **—sap′ro·phyt′ic·al·ly** *adv.*

sap·ro·zo·ic (săp′rə-zō′ĭk) *adj.* **1.** Pertaining to or designating nutrition by absorption of dissolved organic and inorganic materials, as in protozoans and some fungi. **2.** Feeding on dead or decaying animal matter.

sap·sa·go (săp-să′gō, săp′sə-gō′) *n.* A hard cheese made from skim-milk curd, colored and flavored with sweet clover. [Alteration of G. *Schabzieger* : *schaben,* to scrape + *Zieger,* whey.]

sap·suck·er (săp′sŭk′ər) *n.* Either of two small North American woodpeckers, *Sphyrapicus varius* or *S. thyrsoides,* that drill holes in and drink the sap of certain trees.

sap·wood (săp′wo͝od′) *n.* Newly formed outer wood that lies just inside the cambium of a tree or woody plant and is usually lighter in color and more active in nutrition than the heartwood.

sar·a·band also **sar·a·bande** (săr′ə-bănd′) *n.* **1.** A stately court dance of the 17th and 18th centuries, in slow triple time. **2.** The music for the saraband. [Fr. *sarabande* < Sp. *zarabanda.*]

Sar·a·cen (săr′ə-sən) *n.* **1.** A member of a pre-Islamic nomadic people of the Syrian-Arabian deserts. **2.** An Arab. **3.** A Moslem, esp. of the time of the Crusades. [ME < OFr.

Saracin < LLat. *Saracenus* < LGk. *Sarakēnos,* perh. of Ar. orig.] —**Sar′a·cen′ic** (-sĕn′ĭk) *adj.*

Sar·ah (sâr′ə) *n.* In the Old Testament, the wife of Abraham and mother of Isaac. [Heb. *Sārāh,* princess.]

sa·ran (sə-răn′) *n.* **1.** Any of various thermoplastic resins derived from vinyl compounds and used to make packaging films, fittings, and bristles and as a fiber in various heavy fabrics. **2. Saran.** A trademark for saran outside the U.S. [< *Saran,* a former U.S. trademark.]

sa·ra·pe (sə-rä′pē) *n.* Variant of **serape.**

Sar·a·to·ga trunk (săr′ə-tō′gə) *n.* A large traveling trunk having a rounded top. [After *Saratoga* Springs, New York.]

sarc– *pref.* Variant of **sarco-.**

sar·casm (sär′kăz′əm) *n.* **1.** A sharply mocking or contemptuously ironic remark intended to wound another. **2.** The use of sarcasm. [Gk. *sarkasmos* < *sarkazein,* to bite the lips in rage < *sarx,* flesh.]

sar·cas·tic (sär-kăs′tĭk) *adj.* **1.** Expressing sarcasm. **2.** Given to using sarcasm. [SARC(ASM) + *-astic,* as in *enthusiastic.*] —**sar·cas′ti·cal·ly** *adv.*

Synonyms: *sarcastic, ironic, caustic, satirical, sardonic.* These adjectives apply to personal expression that is bitter, cutting, or derisive. *Sarcastic* and *ironic* both pertain to a form of expression in which meanings are conveyed obliquely. *Sarcastic* suggests open taunting and ridicule; *ironic* suggests a milder and subtler form of mockery. *Caustic* can apply to any expression that is biting or corrosive. *Satirical* refers to expression that seeks to expose wrong or folly to ridicule, often by means of sarcasm or irony. *Sardonic* can describe both the content and manner of expression and is associated with scorn, derision, mockery, and cynicism.

sarce·net (särs′nĭt) *n.* A fine, soft silk cloth. [ME *sarsenet* < AN *sarzinett.*]

sarco– or **sarc–** *pref.* **1.** Flesh: *sarcophagic.* **2.** Striated muscle: *sarcolemma.* [Gk. *sarko-* < *sarx,* flesh.]

sar·co·carp (sär′kə-kärp′) *n.* The fleshy pulp surrounding the seed of a drupaceous fruit, as a peach or plum.

sar·coid (sär′koid′) *adj.* Pertaining to or resembling flesh.

sar·coid·o·sis (sär′koi-dō′sĭs) *n.* A disease of unknown origin characterized by the formation of granulomatous lesions that appear esp. in the liver, lungs, skin, and lymph nodes.

sar·co·lem·ma (sär′kə-lĕm′ə) *n.* A thin membrane surrounding a striated muscle fiber. [SARCO- + Gk. *lemma,* husk.] —**sar′co·lem′mal** *adj.*

sar·co·ma (sär-kō′mə) *n., pl.* **-ma·ta** (-mə-tə) or **-mas.** A malignant tumor arising from nonepithelial connective tissues. —**sar·co′ma·toid′, sar·co′ma·tous** *adj.*

sar·co·mere (sär′kə-mîr′) *n.* A structural unit of a striated muscle fiber.

sar·coph·a·gi (sär-kŏf′ə-jī′) *n.* A plural of **sarcophagus.**

sar·co·phag·ic (sär′kə-făj′ĭk) also **sar·coph·a·gous** (sär-kŏf′ə-gəs) *adj.* Carnivorous.

sar·coph·a·gus (sär-kŏf′ə-gəs) *n., pl.* **-gi** (-jī′) or **-gus·es.** A stone coffin. [Lat. *sarcophagus* < Gk. *sarkophagos,* flesh-eating : *sarx,* flesh + *phagein,* to eat.]

sar·co·plasm (sär′kə-plăz′əm) *n.* The cytoplasm of muscle cells. —**sar′co·plas′mic** *adj.*

sar·cop·tic mange (sär-kŏp′tĭk) *n.* Mange caused by the mite *Sarcoptes scabiei.* [< NLat. *Sarcoptes,* genus name : SARCO- + Gk. *koptein,* to cut.]

sar·cous (sär′kəs) *adj.* Of, pertaining to, or consisting of flesh or muscle.

sard (särd) *n.* A clear or translucent deep orange-red to brownish red chalcedony. [Fr. *sarde* < Lat. *sarda,* a kind of precious stone, perh. < Gk. *sardion* < *Sardeis,* Sardis, an ancient city in Asia Minor.]

sar·dine (sär-dēn′) *n.* **1.** Any of various small or half-grown edible herrings or related fishes of the family Clupeidae, frequently canned in oil. **2.** Any of numerous edible small, silvery freshwater or marine fishes unrelated to the sardine. [ME *sardeyn* < OFr. *sardine* < Lat. *sardina* < *sarda,* a kind of fish.]

sar·don·ic (sär-dŏn′ĭk) *adj.* Scornfully mocking and derisive. [Fr. *sardonique* < Gk. *sardonios,* alteration of *sardanios,* bitter, scornful.] —**sar·don′i·cal·ly** *adv.* —**sar·don′i·cism** (-ĭ-sĭz′əm) *n.*

sar·don·yx (sär-dŏn′ĭks, sär′dn-ĭks′) *n.* An onyx with alternating brown and white bands of sard and other minerals. [ME *sardonix* < Lat. *sardonyx* < Gk. *sardonux* : *sardion,* sard + *onux,* onyx.]

sar·gas·so (sär-găs′ō) *n.* Gulfweed. [Port. *sargaço.*]

sar·gas·sum (sär-găs′əm) *n.* Gulfweed. [NLat. *Sargassum,* genus name < SARGASSO.]

sarge (särj) *n. Informal.* Sergeant.

sa·ri (sä′rē) *n.* An outer garment worn chiefly by women of India and Pakistan, consisting of a length of lightweight cloth with one end wrapped about the waist to form a skirt and the other draped over the shoulder or covering the head. [Hindi *sāṛī* < Skt. *śāṭī.*]

sar·men·tose (sär-mĕn′tōs′) *adj.* Having slender, prostrate stems that root at intervals, as in the strawberry. [Lat. *sarmentosus,* full of twigs < *sarmentum,* twigs.]

sa·rong (sə-rông′, -rŏng′) *n.* A skirt consisting of a length of brightly colored cloth wrapped about the waist that is worn by both men and women in Malaysia, Indonesia, and the Pacific islands. [Malay.]

sar·sa·pa·ril·la (săs′pə-rĭl′ə, särs′-) *n.* **1. a.** The dried roots of any of several tropical American plants of the genus *Smilax,* esp. *S. aristolochiaefolia,* of Mexico, used as a flavoring. **b.** A sweet soft drink flavored with sarsaparilla. **2.** Either of two North American plants, *Aralia hispida* or *A. nudicaulis,* having clusters of small white flowers. [Sp. *zarzaparrilla* : *zarza,* bramble (< Ar. *sharaṣ*) + *parrilla,* dim. of *parra,* vine.]

sar·to·ri·al (sär-tôr′ē-əl, -tōr′-) *adj.* Of or relating to a tailor, tailoring, or tailored clothing. [< Lat. *sartor,* tailor. —see SARTORIUS.] —**sar·to′ri·al·ly** *adv.*

sar·to·ri·us (sär-tôr′ē-əs, -tōr′-) *n.* A flat, narrow thigh muscle, the longest of the human anatomy, crossing the front of the thigh obliquely from the hip to the inner side of the tibia. [NLat. < Lat. *sartor,* tailor < *sartus,* p.part. of *sarcire,* to mend.]

sash[1] (săsh) *n.* A band or ribbon worn about the waist, as for ornament, or over the shoulder as a symbol of rank. [Ar. *shāsh,* muslin.]

sash[2] (săsh) *n.* A frame in which the panes of a window or door are set. —*tr.v.* **sashed, sash·ing, sash·es.** To furnish with a sash. [Alteration of Fr. *châssis,* frame. —see CHASSIS.]

sa·shay (să-shā′) *Informal.* —*intr.v.* **-shayed, -shay·ing, -shays. 1.** To strut or flounce. **2.** To perform the chassé in dancing. —*n.* An excursion; sally. [Alteration of CHASSÉ.]

sa·shi·mi (sä-shē′mē) *n.* A Japanese dish consisting of very thin slices of raw fish. [J.]

sas·ka·toon (săs′kə-to͞on′) *n.* A shrub, *Amelanchier alnifolia,* of northwestern North America, having white flowers and edible dark-purple fruit. [Cree *misāskwatomin,* saskatoon berry.]

Sas·quatch (săs′kwŏch′) *n.* A hairy, manlike creature said to inhabit the Pacific Northwest and Canada.

sass (săs) *Informal.* —*n.* Impertinent, disrespectful speech; back talk. —*tr.v.* **sassed, sass·ing, sass·es.** To talk impudently to. [Back-formation < SASSY[1].]

sas·sa·by (săs′ə-bē) *n., pl.* **-bies.** An African antelope, *Damaliscus lunatus,* having curved, ridged horns. [Of Bantu orig.]

sas·sa·fras (săs′ə-frăs′) *n.* **1.** A North American tree, *Sassafras albidum,* having irregularly lobed leaves and aromatic bark. **2.** The dried root bark of the sassafras, used as flavoring and as a source of a volatile oil. [Sp. *sasafrás.*]

Sas·sa·nid (săs′ə-nĭd, sə-sä′nĭd, -săn′-) also **Sas·sa·ni·an** (sə-sā′nē-ən, să-) or **Sas·sa·nide** (săs′ə-nīd′) *n.* A member of the dynasty of Persian kings ruling from the 3rd through the middle of the 17th century A.D. [Med. Lat. *Sassanidae,* the Sassanids < *Sassanus,* Sassan, grandfather of the founder of the dynasty.] —**Sas′sa·nid** *adj.*

sass·wood (săs′wo͝od′) *n.* Sassy[2]. [SASSY[2] + WOOD.]

sas·sy[1] (săs′ē) *adj.* **-si·er, -si·est. 1.** Impudent. **2.** Jaunty. [Alteration of SAUCY.] —**sas′si·ly** *adv.* —**sas′si·ness** *n.*

sas·sy[2] (săs′ē) *n., pl.* **-sies.** A tree, *Erythrophloeum guineense,* of western Africa, having bark that yields a poison. [Prob. of African orig.]

sas·tru·ga (să-stro͞o′gə) *n.* A long, wavelike ridge of snow found on the polar plains, formed by the wind. [R. *zastruga,* groove : *za,* by + *struga,* deep place.]

sat (săt) *v.* Past tense and past participle of **sit.**

Sa·tan (sāt′n) *n.* The Devil. [ME < OE < LLat. < Gk. < Heb. *śāṭān,* devil, adversary < *śāṭan,* he accused.]

sa·tang (sə-tăng′) *n., pl.* **satang.** See table at **currency.** [Thai *satāṅ.*]

sa·tan·ic (sə-tăn′ĭk, sā-) or **sa·tan·i·cal** (-ĭ-kəl) *adj.* **1.** Pertaining to or suggestive of Satan or evil. **2.** Profoundly cruel or evil; fiendish. —**sa·tan′i·cal·ly** *adv.*

Sa·tan·ism (sāt′n-ĭz′əm) *n.* **1.** The worship of Satan characterized by a travesty of the Christian rites. **2. satanism.** Profound wickedness. —**Sa′tan·ist** *n.*

satch·el (săch′əl) *n.* A small bag, often having a shoulder strap, used for carrying books or clothing. [ME *sachel* < OFr. < Lat. *saccellus,* dim. of *saccus,* bag. —see SACK[1].]

sate[1] (sāt) *tr.v.* **sat·ed, sat·ing, sates. 1.** To satisfy (an appetite) fully. **2.** To indulge to excess; glut. [Prob. alteration of obs. *sade,* to satiate < ME *saden* < OE *sadian.*]

sate[2] (săt, sāt) *v. Archaic.* Past tense of **sit.**

sa·teen (să-tēn′) *n.* A cotton fabric with a satinlike finish. [Alteration of SATIN.]

sat·el·lite (săt′l-īt′) *n.* **1.** *Astron.* A relatively small body orbiting a planet; moon. **2.** *Aerospace.* A manmade object intended to orbit a celestial body. **3.** One who attends a powerful dignitary. **4.** A subservient follower. **5.** A nation that is dominated politically by another. **6.** An urban or suburban community located near a big city. [OFr. < Lat. *satelles,* attendant.]

satellite station *n.* A radio or television station that rebroadcasts a received transmission immediately on a different wavelength.

sa·tem (sä′təm) *adj.* Designating those Indo-European languages, including the Indo-Iranian, Armenian, Albanian, and Balto-Slavic subfamilies, in which original velar stops became fricatives (as $k > s$ or *š*) and labiovelar stops became velars (as $kw > k$). [Avestan *satəm,* hundred (a word whose initial sound illustrates the sound change).]

sarcophagus
Above: 16th-century B.C. Egyptian
Below: 1st-century Roman

sari

sassafras

sa·tia·ble (sā'shə-bəl, -shē-ə-) *adj.* Capable of being satiated. **—sa'tia·bil'i·ty** *n.* **—sa'tia·bly** *adv.*

sa·ti·ate (sā'shē-āt') *tr.v.* **-at·ed, -at·ing, -ates. 1.** To satisfy (an appetite or desire) fully. **2.** To gratify to excess; sate. *—adj.* (-ĭt). Filled to satisfaction. [Lat. *satiare, satiat-* < *satis,* sufficient.] **—sa'ti·a'tion** *n.*

Synonyms: *satiate, sate, cloy, glut, gorge, surfeit.* These verbs mean to fill or supply to the utmost or, more often, to excess. *Satiate* and *sate* are generally interchangeable. Although they can mean merely to satisfy fully, both usually imply satisfaction beyond natural desire, or overindulgence. *Cloy* invariably stresses the discomfort or ennui produced by gratification beyond desire. *Glut* emphasizes the sheer volume of oversupply more than its effects, especially with respect to overeating or flooding a market with goods. *Gorge* refers principally to greedy overstuffing with food. *Surfeit* implies oversupply and consequent dissatisfaction, though less strongly than *cloy.*

Saturn
Detail of Saturn's rings

sa·ti·e·ty (sə-tī'ĭ-tē) *n.* The condition of being full or gratified beyond the point of satisfaction; surfeit. [OFr. *satiete* < Lat. *satietas,* sufficiency < *satis,* sufficient.]

sat·in (săt'n) *n.* A smooth fabric, as of silk or rayon, woven with a glossy face and a dull back. ***—modifier:*** *a satin blouse.* [ME *satyn* < OFr. *satin.*]

sat·in·et (săt'n-ĕt') *n.* A thin inferior satin or an imitation satin, esp. one containing cotton.

sat·in·flow·er (săt'n-flou'ər) *n.* A plant, *Godetia grandiflora,* of California, having showy red-blotched flowers.

sat·in·pod (săt'n-pŏd') *n.* Honesty (sense 4).

satin stitch *n.* An embroidery stitch worked in close parallel lines to give a solid satinlike finish.

satin weave *n.* A basic weave construction with the interlacing of the threads so arranged that the face of the cloth is covered with warp yarn or filling yarn and no twill line is distinguishable.

sat·in·wood (săt'n-wo͝od') *n.* **1. a.** A tree, *Chloroxylon swietenia,* of southern Asia, having hard, yellowish, close-grained wood. **b.** The wood of this tree. **2. a.** Any of several trees having wood similar to satinwood. **b.** The wood of any of these trees.

sat·in·y (săt'n-ē) *adj.* Lustrous and smooth like satin.

sat·ire (săt'īr') *n.* **1. a.** A literary work in which human vice or folly is attacked through irony, derision, or wit. **b.** The branch of literature comprising such works. **2.** Irony or caustic wit used to attack or expose folly, vice, or stupidity. [OFr. < Lat. *satira,* alteration of *satura,* mixture, poem treating various subjects < fem. of *satur,* sated.]

satyr
5th-century B.C. Greek vase

sa·tir·i·cal (sə-tĭr'ĭ-kəl) or **sa·tir·ic** (-ĭk) *adj.* Of, relating to, or characterized by satire. **—sa·tir'i·cal·ly** *adv.*

sat·i·rist (săt'ər-ĭst) *n.* A writer of satirical works.

sat·i·rize (săt'ə-rīz') *tr.v.* **-rized, -riz·ing, -riz·es.** To ridicule or attack by means of satire.

sat·is·fac·tion (săt'ĭs-făk'shən) *n.* **1. a.** The fulfillment or gratification of a desire, need, or appetite. **b.** Pleasure derived from such gratification. **2.** Compensation for injury or loss; reparation. **3.** A source of gratification. [ME < OFr. < LLat. < Lat., amends < *satisfacere,* to satisfy.]

sat·is·fac·to·ry (săt'ĭs-făk'tə-rē) *adj.* Giving satisfaction sufficient to meet a demand or requirement; adequate. **—sat'is·fac'to·ri·ly** *adv.* **—sat'is·fac'to·ri·ness** *n.*

sat·is·fi·a·ble (săt'ĭs-fī'ə-bəl) *adj.* Capable of being satisfied.

sat·is·fy (săt'ĭs-fī') *v.* **-fied, -fy·ing, -fies.** *—tr.* **1.** To gratify the need, desire, or expectation of. **2.** To fulfill (a need or desire). **3. a.** To free from doubt or question; assure. **b.** To dispel (a doubt). **4. a.** To discharge (an obligation, for example). **b.** To discharge an obligation to (a creditor). **5.** To conform to the requirements of (a standard or rule). **6.** To make reparation for; redress. **7.** *Math.* To make the left and right sides of an equation equal after substituting equivalent quantities for the unknown variables in the equation. *—intr.* To give satisfaction. [ME *satisfien* < OFr. *satisfier* < Lat. *satisfacere* : *satis,* sufficient + *facere,* to make.] **—sat'is·fi'er** *n.* **—sat'is·fy'ing·ly** *adv.*

sa·to·ri (sä-tôr'ē, -tōr'ē, sə-) *n.* A state of spiritual enlightenment sought in Zen Buddhism. [J., insight.]

sa·trap (sā'trăp', săt'răp') *n.* **1.** A governor of a province in ancient Persia. **2.** A subordinate ruler. [ME *satrape* < OFr. < Lat. *satrapes* < Gk. < OPers. *khshathrapāvā,* protector of the people.]

sa·tra·py (sā'trə-pē, -trăp'ē, săt'rə-pē) *n., pl.* **-pies.** The territory or sphere under the rule of a satrap.

sat·u·rant (săch'ər-ənt) *adj.* Serving to saturate; impregnating. *—n.* A substance used to saturate.

sat·u·rate (săch'ə-rāt') *tr.v.* **-rat·ed, -rat·ing, -rates. 1.** To imbue or impregnate thoroughly: *"The recollection was saturated with sunshine"* (Vladimir Nabokov). **2.** To soak, fill, or load to capacity. **3.** *Chem.* **a.** To cause (a solution) to be saturated. **b.** To cause (a compound) to be saturated. *—adj.* (-rĭt). Saturated. [Lat. *saturare, saturat-,* to fill < *satur,* sated.] **—sat'u·ra·ble** (săch'ər-ə-bəl) *adj.* **—sat'u·ra'tor** *n.*

sat·u·rat·ed (săch'ə-rā'tĭd) *adj.* **1.** Unable to hold or contain more; full. **2.** Soaked with moisture; drenched. **3.** *Chem.* **a.** Containing all the solute that can normally be dissolved at a given temperature. Used of solutions. **b.** Having all available valence bonds filled. Used esp. of organic compounds. **4.** *Geol.* Of or pertaining to minerals that can crystallize from magmas even in the presence of excess silica.

sat·u·ra·tion (săch'ə-rā'shən) *n.* **1. a.** The act or process of saturating. **b.** The condition of being saturated. **2.** *Physics.* A state of a ferromagnetic substance in which an increase in applied magnetic field strength does not produce an increase in magnetic intensity. **3.** *Chem.* The state of a compound or solution that is fully saturated. **4.** *Meteorol.* A condition in which air at a specific temperature contains all the moisture vapor possible without precipitating; 100 per cent relative humidity. **5.** Vividness of hue; degree of difference from a gray of the same lightness or brightness. **6.** Intensive shelling or bombing of a military target to achieve total destruction. **7.** The flooding of a market with all of a commodity that consumers can purchase.

Sat·ur·day (săt'ər-dē, -dā') *n.* The seventh day of the week. [ME *Saterday* < OE *Sæternesdæg,* transl. of Lat. *dies Saturni,* Saturn's day.]

Saturday night special *n. Informal.* A cheap handgun.

Sat·urn (săt'ərn) *n.* **1.** *Rom. Myth.* The god of agriculture, identified with the Greek god Cronus. **2.** The sixth planet from the sun and the second-largest in the solar system, having a diameter of 119,000 kilometers, or 74,000 miles, a mass 95 times that of Earth, and an orbital period of 29.5 years at a mean distance of about 1,425,000,000 kilometers, or 886,000,000 miles. [ME *Saturnus* < OE < Lat. *Saturnus.*]

sat·ur·na·li·a (săt'ər-nā'lē-ə, -nāl'yə) *pl.n.* **1. Saturnalia.** The ancient Roman seven-day festival of Saturn, which began on December 17. **2.** *(used with a sing. verb).* An unrestrained celebration. [Lat. *saturnalia,* the festival of Saturn < neuter pl. of *Saturnalis,* Saturnian < *Saturnus,* Saturn.]

Sa·tur·ni·an (să-tûr'nē-ən, sə-) *adj.* **1.** Of or pertaining to the planet Saturn or to its supposed astrological influence. **2.** *Archaic.* Of or pertaining to the god Saturn or his reign.

sa·tur·ni·id (să-tûr'nē-ĭd, sə-) *n.* Any of various often large and colorful moths of the family Saturniidae. *—adj.* Of or belonging to the Saturniidae. [NLat. *Saturniidae,* family name < *Saturnia,* type genus < Lat., daughter of Saturn < *Saturnus,* Saturn.]

sat·ur·nine (săt'ər-nīn') *adj.* **1.** Having the temperament of one born under the supposed astrological influence of Saturn. **2. a.** Melancholy or sullen in disposition. **b.** Sarcastic: *a saturnine expression on his face.* **3. a.** Pertaining to or resembling lead. **b.** Produced by the absorption of lead. **—sat'ur·nine'ly** *adv.*

sat·urn·ism (săt'ər-nĭz'əm) *n.* Lead poisoning. [< SATURN, lead (obs.).]

Sa·tya·gra·ha (sə-tyä'grə-hə) *n.* The policy of nonviolent resistance initiated in India by Mahatma Gandhi as a means of pressing for political reform. [Skt. *satyāgraha* : *satyam,* truth + *graha,* the act of seizing < *gṛhṇāti,* he seizes.]

sa·tyr (sā'tər, săt'ər) *n.* **1.** Often **Satyr.** *Gk. Myth.* A woodland god depicted as having the pointed ears, legs, and short horns of a goat. **2.** A lecher. **3.** A man who has satyriasis. **4.** Any of various butterflies of the family Satyridae, having brown wings marked with eyelike spots. [ME < Lat. *satyrus* < Gk. *saturos.*] **—sa·tyr'ic** (sā-tĭr'ĭk, sə-, să-), **sa·tyr'i·cal** *adj.*

sa·ty·ri·a·sis (sā'tə-rī'ə-sĭs, săt'ə-) *n.* Excessive and often uncontrollable sexual desire in a male. [LLat. < Gk. *saturiasis* < *saturos,* satyr.]

sauce (sôs) *n.* **1.** A flavorful liquid dressing or relish served as an accompaniment to food. **2.** Stewed fruit, usually served with other foods. **3.** Something that adds zest, flavor, or piquancy to something else. **4.** *Informal.* Impudence; sauciness. **5.** *Slang.* Alcoholic liquor. *—tr.v.* **sauced, sauc·ing, sauc·es. 1.** To season or flavor with sauce. **2.** To add piquancy or zest to. **3.** *Informal.* To be impertinent or impudent to. [ME < OFr. < Lat. *salsa,* fem. of *salsus,* salted, p.part. of *sallere,* to salt < *sal,* salt.]

sauce bé·ar·naise (bā'är-nāz') *n.* A sauce similar to hollandaise but flavored with tarragon, shallots, and chervil. [Fr. < *Béarn,* a region in southwestern France.]

sauce·box (sôs'bŏks') *n. Informal.* An impertinent person.

sauce·pan (sôs'păn') *n.* A deep cooking pan with a handle.

sau·cer (sô'sər) *n.* **1.** A small, shallow dish having a slight circular depression in the center for holding a cup. **2.** An object similar to a saucer in shape. [ME, sauce dish < OFr. *saussier* < *sausse, sauce,* sauce.]

sauc·y (sô'sē) *adj.* **-i·er, -i·est. 1.** Impertinent or disrespectful. **2.** Piquant; pert. **—sau'ci·ly** *adv.* **—sau'ci·ness** *n.*

sau·er·bra·ten (sour'brät'n) *n.* A pot roast of beef marinated in vinegar, water, wine, and spices before being cooked. [G. : *sauer,* sour + *Braten,* roast meat.]

sau·er·kraut (sour'krout') *n.* Chopped or shredded cabbage that is salted and fermented in its own juice. [G. : *sauer,* sour + *Kraut,* cabbage.]

sau·ger (sô'gər) *n.* A small North American freshwater fish, *Stizostidion canadense,* having a spotted, spiny dorsal fin. [Orig. unknown.]

Sauk (sôk) also **Sac** (săk, sôk) *n., pl.* **Sauk** or **Sauks** also **Sac** or **Sacs. 1. a.** A tribe of Algonquian-speaking North American Indians living originally in Michigan, Wisconsin, and Illinois and now settled in Iowa and Oklahoma. **b.** A member of this tribe. **2.** The Algonquian language of the Sauk. [Fr., of Algonquian orig.]

sau·na (sou'nə, sô'-) *n.* **1.** A steam bath in which the steam is usually produced by pouring water over heated rocks. **2.** A room for taking a sauna. [Finn.]

saun·ter (sôn′tər) *intr.v.* **-tered, -ter·ing, -ters.** To walk at a leisurely pace; stroll. *—n.* A leisurely pace; stroll. [Prob. < ME *santren,* to muse.]

sau·rel (sôr′əl, sô-rĕl′) *n.* **1.** A marine fish, *Trachurus trachurus,* of eastern Atlantic waters. **2.** The jack mackerel. [Fr. < NLat. *saurus,* lizard < Gk. *sauros.*]

sau·ri·an (sôr′ē-ən) *n.* Any of various reptiles of the suborder Sauria, which includes the true lizards. *—adj.* Of, belonging to, or characteristic of the Sauria. [< NLat. *Sauria,* suborder name < *saurus,* lizard < Gk. *sauros.*]

sau·ro·pod (sôr′ə-pŏd′) *n.* Any of various large semiaquatic dinosaurs of the suborder Sauropoda, of the Jurassic and Cretaceous periods. *—adj.* Of or belonging to the Sauropoda. [NLat. *Sauropoda,* suborder name : *saurus,* lizard (< Gk. *sauros*) + Gk. *pous,* foot.] **—sau·rop′o·dous** (sô-rŏp′ə-dəs) *adj.*

sau·ry (sôr′ē) *n., pl.* **-ries.** Any of several offshore marine fishes of the family Scomberesocidae, related to the needlefishes. [NLat. *saurus,* lizard < Gk. *sauros.*]

sau·sage (sô′sĭj) *n.* Finely chopped and seasoned meat, esp. pork, usually stuffed into a prepared animal intestine or other casing and cooked or cured. [ME *sausige* < ONFr. *saussiche* < LLat. *salsicia* < *salsicius,* prepared by salting < *salsus,* salted. —see SAUCE.]

sau·té (sō-tā′, sô-) *tr.v.* **-téed, -té·ing, -tés.** To fry lightly in fat in a shallow, open pan. *—n.* Sautéed food. [Fr., tossed < p.part. of *sauter,* to leap < Lat. *saltare.* —see SALTATION.]

sau·terne or **Sau·terne** (sō-tûrn′, sô-) *n.* A delicate, sweet white wine. [Fr. < *Sauternes,* a commune in France.]

sav·age (săv′ĭj) *adj.* **1.** Not domesticated or cultivated; wild. **2.** Not civilized; barbaric. **3.** Ferocious; fierce. **4.** Vicious or merciless; brutal. **5.** Lacking polish or manners; rude. *—n.* **1.** A primitive or uncivilized person. **2.** A brutal, fierce, or vicious person. **3.** A rude person; boor. *—tr.v.* **-aged, -ag·ing, -ag·es. 1.** To attack violently. **2.** To make angry or fierce. **3.** To bite or trample ferociously. [ME *sauvage* < OFr. < Lat. *silvaticus,* of the woods, wild < *silva,* forest.] **—sav′age·ly** *adv.* **—sav′age·ness** *n.*

sav·age·ry (săv′ĭj-rē) *n., pl.* **-ries. 1.** The quality or condition of being savage. **2.** A savage act. **3.** Savage behavior or nature; barbarity.

sa·van·na also **sa·van·nah** (sə-văn′ə) *n.* A flat, treeless grassland of tropical or subtropical regions. [Sp. *zavana* < Taino *zabana.*]

sa·vant (să-vänt′) *n.* A learned scholar. [Fr. < pr.part. of *savoir,* to know < VLat. **sapēre* < Lat. *sapere,* to be wise.]

save[1] (sāv) *v.* **saved, sav·ing, saves.** *—tr.* **1.** To rescue from harm, danger, or loss. **2.** To keep in a safe condition; safeguard. **3.** To prevent the waste or loss of; conserve. **4.** To set aside for future use; store. **5.** To treat with care in order to avoid fatigue, wear, or damage; spare. **6.** To make unnecessary; obviate: *saved me an extra trip.* **7. a.** *Sports.* To prevent an opponent from scoring or winning, esp. in hockey. **b.** *Baseball.* To preserve (a victory) by protecting a team's lead. Used of a relief pitcher. **8.** *Theol.* To deliver from sin; redeem. *—intr.* **1.** To avoid waste or expense; economize. **2.** To accumulate money or goods. **3.** To preserve a person or thing from harm or loss. *—n.* **1.** *Sports.* An act that prevents an opponent from scoring. **2.** *Baseball.* A game in which a relief pitcher preserves a victory by protecting a team's lead. [ME *saven* < OFr. *sauver* < LLat. *salvare* < Lat. *salvus,* safe.] **—sav′a·ble, save′a·ble** *adj.* **—sav′er** *n.*

Synonyms: *save, rescue, reclaim, redeem, deliver.* These verbs are compared in the sense of freeing a person or thing from danger, evil, confinement, or servitude. *Save,* the most general, applies to any act of preserving from the consequences of danger or evil, including sin. *Rescue* usually implies saving from immediate harm or danger by direct action. *Reclaim,* applied to persons, usually means to restore to an earlier state of moral and physical soundness or to reform after a lapse; it can also mean to return or convert a thing to usefulness or productivity. *Redeem* refers to freeing from captivity, pawn, or the consequences of sin, error, or misuse, in every case by the expenditure of money or effort. *Deliver* applies chiefly to freeing persons from confinement, restraint, or evil.

save[2] (sāv) *prep.* With the exception of; except: *"No man enjoys self-reproach save a masochist"* (Philip Wylie). *—conj.* **1.** Were it not. **2.** *Archaic.* Unless. [ME < OFr. *sauf* < Lat. *salvo,* ablative sing. of *salvus,* safe.]

save-all (săv′ôl′) *n.* **1.** A device that prevents the waste, damage, or loss of something. **2.** A receptacle for catching the waste products of a process for further use in manufacture.

sav·e·loy (săv′ə-loi′) *n.* A highly seasoned smoked pork sausage. [Alteration of obs. Fr. *cervelat* < Ital. *cervellato* < *cervello,* brain < Lat. *cerebellum,* dim. of *cerebrum,* brain.]

sav·in or **sav·ine** (săv′ĭn) *n.* **1.** An evergreen Eurasian shrub, *Juniperus sabina,* whose young shoots yield an oil formerly used medicinally. **2.** Any of several shrubs or trees related to the savin. [ME < OE *safine* and OFr. *savine,* both < Lat. *(herba) Sabina,* Sabine (plant).]

sav·ing (sā′vĭng) *n.* **1.** Preservation or rescue from harm, danger, or loss. **2.** Avoidance of excess expenditure; economy. **3.** A reduction in expenditure or cost. **4. savings.** Sums of money saved. **5.** Something that is saved. **6.** *Law.* An exception or reservation. *—prep.* With the exception of. *—conj.* Except; save.

Usage: Many maintain that the singular *a* and the plural *savings* should not be used together: *The price represents a saving* (not *savings*) *of ten dollars.* In this example the plural form, though sometimes used, is unacceptable to a large majority of the Usage Panel.

savings account *n.* An account that draws interest at a bank.

savings bank *n.* A bank that receives and invests the savings of private depositors and pays interest on the deposits.

savings bond *n.* A nontransferable registered bond issued by the U.S. Government in denominations of $25 to $1,000.

sav·ior (sāv′yər) *n.* **1.** A person who rescues someone or something from dire circumstances. **2. Savior.** Christ. [ME *saviour* < OFr. *sauveour* < LLat. *salvator* < *salvare,* to save < *salvus,* safe.]

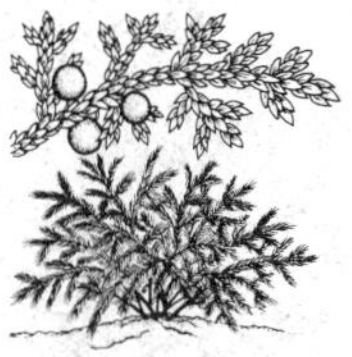

savin

sav·iour (sāv′yər) *n. Chiefly Brit.* Variant of **savior.**

sa·voir-faire (săv′wär-fâr′) *n.* The ability to say and do the right thing in any situation. [Fr. : *savoir,* to know + *faire,* to do.]

sa·vor (sā′vər) *n.* **1.** The taste or smell of something. **2.** A specific taste or smell. **3.** A distinctive or typical quality. *—v.* **-vored, -vor·ing, -vors.** *—intr.* **1.** To have a particular savor. **2.** To exhibit a specified quality or characteristic: *actions that savored of vanity.* *—tr.* **1.** To impart a flavor or scent to. **2.** To taste or enjoy with zest; relish. **3.** To have or show the savor of. [ME *savour* < OFr. < Lat. *sapor* < *sapere,* to taste.] **—sa′vor·er** *n.* **—sa′vor·ous** *adj.*

sa·vor·y[1] (sā′və-rē) *adj.* **1.** Appetizing to the taste or smell. **2.** Piquant, pungent, or salty to the taste; not sweet. **3.** Morally respectable; inoffensive. *—n., pl.* **-ies.** A dish of pungent taste, such as anchovies on toast or pickled fruit, sometimes served in Britain as an hors d'oeuvre or instead of a sweet dessert. **—sa′vor·i·ly** *adv.* **—sa′vor·i·ness** *n.*

sa·vor·y[2] (sā′və-rē) *n., pl.* **-ies. 1.** Either of two aromatic herbs, *Satureja hortensis* or *S. montana,* native to the Old World. **2.** The leaves of the savory, used as seasoning. [ME *saverey,* perh. alteration of OE *sætherie* < Lat. *satureia.*]

sa·vour (sā′vər) *n. & v. Chiefly Brit.* Variant of **savor.**

sa·vour·y (sā′və-rē) *adj. & n. Chiefly Brit.* Variant of **savory**[1].

Sa·voy·ard (sə-voi′ärd′, săv′oi-yärd′, săv′wä-yär′) *n.* A performer or devoted admirer of Gilbert and Sullivan operas, most of which were first staged at London's Savoy Theatre.

sav·vy (săv′ē) *Slang. —intr.v.* **-vied, -vy·ing, -vies.** To understand or know; comprehend. *—n.* Practical understanding or know-how; common sense. *—adj.* **-vi·er, -vi·est.** Practical and perceptive. [< Sp. *sabe (usted),* (you) know < *saber,* to know < Lat. *sapere,* to be wise.]

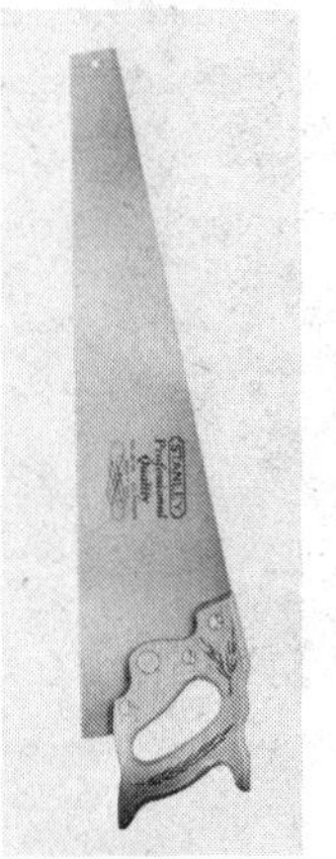

saw[1]

saw[1] (sô) *n.* **1.** A portable tool, either hand-operated or power-operated, having a thin metal blade or disk with a sharp-toothed edge, used for cutting wood, metal, or other hard materials. **2.** A powered disk tool lacking teeth, used for cutting metal. **3.** A fixed machine for the operation of a saw or series of saws. *—v.* **sawed, sawed** or **sawn** (sôn), **saw·ing, saws.** *—tr.* **1.** To cut or divide with or as if with a saw. **2.** To produce or shape with or as if with a saw. **3.** To handle with a sawlike motion: *sawed at the ball with the bat.* *—intr.* **1.** To use a saw. **2.** To cut or be cut with or as if with a saw. [ME *sawe* < OE *sagu.*] **—saw′er** *n.*

saw[2] (sô) *n.* A familiar saying, esp. one worn out through repetition. [ME *sawe* < OE *sagu,* speech.]

saw[3] (sô) *v.* Past tense of **see**[1].

saw·bones (sô′bōnz′) *n., pl.* **sawbones** or **saw·bones·es** (-bōn′zĭz). *Slang.* A physician, esp. a surgeon.

saw·buck (sô′bŭk′) *n.* **1.** A sawhorse. **2.** *Slang.* A ten-dollar bill.

saw·dust (sô′dŭst′) *n.* The small particles of wood or other material that fall from an object as a result of sawing.

sawed-off (sôd′ôf′, -ŏf′) *adj.* **1.** Having one end sawed off: *a sawed-off shotgun.* **2.** *Slang.* Short; runty.

saw·fish (sô′fĭsh′) *n., pl.* **sawfish** or **-fish·es.** Any of various marine fishes of the genus *Pristis,* related to the rays and skates and having a bladelike snout with teeth along both sides.

saw·fly (sô′flī′) *n.* Any of various destructive insects, chiefly of the family Tenthredinidae, the females of which have sawlike ovipositors used for cutting into plant tissue to deposit their eggs.

saw grass *n.* Any of several grasses or sedges, esp. *Cladium jamaicense,* having leaves with minutely toothed margins.

saw·horse (sô′hôrs′) *n.* A rack or trestle, esp. one with X-shaped legs, used to support a piece of wood being sawed.

sawhorse

saw log *n.* A log of a size large enough for sawing into boards.

saw·mill (sô′mĭl′) *n.* **1.** A plant where lumber is machine-cut into boards. **2.** A large machine for sawing lumber.

sawn (sôn) *v.* A past participle of **saw**[1].

saw palmetto *n.* Any of several low-growing, prickly palms of the genus *Sabal,* of the southeastern United States.

saw set *n.* An instrument used to give set to the teeth of a saw by bending each alternate tooth slightly outward.

saxophone

scabbard
16th-century German

scaffold

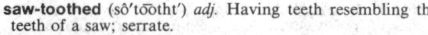

saw-toothed (sô′to͞otht′) *adj.* Having teeth resembling the teeth of a saw; serrate.
saw-whet owl (sô′hwĕt′, -wĕt′) *n.* A small brown and white owl, *Aegolius acadicus,* of western North America, having no ear tufts. [From the resemblance of its call to the sound made in sharpening a saw.]
saw·yer (sô′yər) *n.* **1.** One employed at sawing wood. **2.** Any of several longicorn beetles having larvae that bore large holes in living or dead wood. [ME *sawier* < *sawen,* to saw < *sawe,* saw.]
sax (săks) *n. Informal.* A saxophone.
sax·a·tile (săk′sə-tīl′, -tĭl) *adj. Ecol.* Saxicolous. [Lat. *saxatilis* < *saxum,* rock.]
sax·horn (săks′hôrn′) *n.* Any of a family of valved brass wind instruments that resemble the bugle and have a full, even tone and wide compass. [After Adolphe *Sax* (1814–1894), its inventor.]
sax·ic·o·lous (săk-sĭk′ə-ləs) also **sax·ic·o·line** (-līn′) *adj. Ecol.* Growing on or living among rocks. [Lat. *saxum,* rock + -COLOUS.]
sax·i·frage (săk′sə-frĭj, -frāj′) *n.* Any of numerous plants of the genus *Saxifraga,* of temperate regions, having small flowers and leaves often forming a basal rosette. [ME < OFr. < LLat. *saxifraga* < *saxifragus,* rock-breaking (from its being found growing in rock crevices) : Lat. *saxum,* rock + Lat. *frangere,* to break.]
sax·i·tox·in (săk′sĭ-tŏk′sĭn) *n.* A poisonous substance, $C_{10}H_{17}N_7O_4 \cdot 2HCl$, produced by an organism that causes red tide and found in some species of mollusks. [NLat. *Saxidomus giganteus,* clam species + TOXIN.]
Sax·on (săk′sən) *n.* **1.** A member of a West Germanic tribal group that inhabited northern Germany and invaded England in the 5th century with the Angles and Jutes. **2.** An Englishman as distinguished from an Irishman, Welshman, or Scot. **3.** A native or inhabitant of Saxony. **4. a.** The West Germanic language of any of the Saxon peoples. **b.** The Germanic elements of English as distinguished from the French and Latin elements. [ME < OFr. < LLat. *Saxo,* of Germanic orig.] **—Sax′on** *adj.*
Sax·on·ism (săk′sə-nĭz′əm) *n.* An English word, phrase, or idiom of Anglo-Saxon origin.
sax·o·ny also **Sax·o·ny** (săk′sə-nē) *n.* **1.** A high-grade wool fabric, originally made from the wool of sheep raised in Saxony. **2.** A fine soft woolen fabric similar in weave to tweed.
sax·o·phone (săk′sə-fōn′) *n.* A wind instrument with a single-reed mouthpiece and a usually curved conical metal tube, available in a variety of sizes. [After Adolphe *Sax* (1814–1894), its inventor.] **—sax′o·phon′ist** *n.*
sax·tu·ba (săks′to͞o′bə, -tyo͞o′-) *n.* A large bass saxhorn. [SAX(HORN) + TUBA.]
say (sā) *v.* **said** (sĕd), **say·ing, says** (sĕz). *—tr.* **1.** To utter aloud; pronounce. **2.** To express in words. **3.** To state; declare. **4.** To repeat or recite: *say grace.* **5.** To report or maintain; allege: *"They say that falling in love is wonderful"* (Irving Berlin). **6.** To indicate; show: *The clock says it's 5:00 P.M.* **7.** To estimate or suppose; assume: *Let's say that you're right.* *—intr.* To make a statement or express an opinion. *—n.* **1.** A positive assertion or assurance: *We're risking this on your say.* **2.** A turn or chance to speak. **3.** The right or power to influence a decision; voice: *have one's say.* *—adv.* **1.** Approximately: *There were, say, 500 people present.* **2.** For instance: *a woodwind, say an oboe.* **—*idiom.* that is to say.** In other words. [ME *sayen* < OE *secgan.*]
say·ing (sā′ĭng) *n.* A familiar expression or sentiment.
Synonyms: *saying, maxim, adage, saw, motto, epigram, proverb, aphorism.* These nouns denote concise, familiar expressions believed to contain truth or wisdom. *Saying,* the most general, is any such expression that is often repeated. *Maxim* refers particularly to a rule of conduct grounded in practical experience. *Adage* is applicable to a saying whose wisdom has gained credit through long use. *Saw* usually refers to a saying that is discredited through frequent repetition. *Motto* is usually a moral maxim that expresses the aims or principles of a person, group, or institution. *Epigram* is a terse, witty expression, often paradoxical or satirical and neatly or brilliantly phrased. *Proverb* refers to an old and unpretentious statement that illustrates something such as a basic truth. *Aphorism,* an expression of a truth or principle, implies depth of content and stylistic distinction. *Aphorisms* and *epigrams* are frequently of known authorship; the other terms in this group are more often of anonymous origin.
say-so (sā′sō′) *n., pl.* **-sos.** *Informal.* **1.** An unsupported statement or assurance. **2.** An authoritative assertion. **3.** The right or authority to decide.
say·yid (sā′yĭd) *n.* Lord; sir. Used as a title of respect for an Islamic dignitary. [Ar.]
Sb The symbol for the element antimony. [Lat. *stibium.*]
'sblood (zblŭd) *interj. Archaic.* Used as an oath. [Contraction of *God's blood.*]
Sc The symbol for the element scandium.
scab (skăb) *n.* **1.** The crustlike exudate that covers a healing wound. **2.** Scabies or mange in domestic animals or livestock. **3. a.** Any of various plant diseases caused by fungi or bacteria and resulting in crustlike spots on fruit, leaves, or roots. **b.** The spots caused by such a disease. **4. a.** A worker who refuses membership in a labor union. **b.** An employee who works while others are on strike; strikebreaker. **c.** A person hired to replace a striking worker. **d.** A low or contemptible person. *—intr.v.* **scabbed, scab·bing, scabs. 1.** To become covered with a scab. **2.** To take a job held by a worker on strike. [ME *scabbe* < ON *skabb.*]
scab·bard (skăb′ərd) *n.* A sheath or container, as for a dagger or sword. *—tr.v.* **-bard·ed, -bard·ing, -bards.** To put into or furnish with a scabbard. [ME *scauberc* < AN *escaubers* (pl.), of Germanic orig.]
scab·ble (skăb′əl) *tr.v.* **-bled, -bling, -bles.** To work or dress (stone) to a stage prior to that of fine tooling. [ME *scaplen* < OFr. *eschapler,* to dress timber : *es-,* off (< Lat. ex-) + *chapler,* to cut < LLat. *capulare.*]
scab·by (skăb′ē) *adj.* **-bi·er, -bi·est. 1.** Having, consisting of, or covered with scabs. **2.** Afflicted with scabies. **3.** *Informal.* Low; vile: *a scabby trick.* **—scab′bi·ly** *adv.* **—scab′bi·ness** *n.*
sca·bies (skā′bēz) *n., pl.* **scabies. 1.** A contagious skin disease caused by a mite, *Sarcoptes scabiei,* and characterized by intense itching. **2.** A disease in animals, esp. sheep, that is similar to scabies. [Lat., itch < *scabere,* to scratch.]
sca·bi·o·sa (skā′bē-ō′sə, -zə, skăb′ē-) *n.* Scabious². [NLat. *Scabiosa,* genus name < Med. Lat. *scabiosa (herba),* (herb) for scabies < Lat. *scabies,* itch < *scabere,* to scratch.]
sca·bi·ous¹ (skā′bē-əs, skăb′ē-) *adj.* **1.** Of or pertaining to scabies. **2.** Having scabs.
sca·bi·ous² (skā′bē-əs) *n.* Any of various plants of the genus *Scabiosa,* esp. *S. pratensis* or *S. atropurpureus,* having opposite leaves and variously colored flower heads. [ME *scabiose* < Med. Lat. *scabiosa (herba),* (herb) for scabies < Lat. *scabies,* itch < *scabere,* to scratch.]
scab·rous (skăb′rəs, skā′brəs) *adj.* **1.** Rough to the touch; scaly. **2.** Difficult to handle; knotty. **3.** Salacious; off-color: *a scabrous novel.* [Lat. *scabrosus* < *scaber,* scurfy.] **—scab′rous·ly** *adv.* **—scab′rous·ness** *n.*
scad (skăd) *n., pl.* **scad** or **scads.** Any of several marine fishes of the family Carangidae, related to the jacks and pompanos. [Orig. unknown.]
scads (skădz) *pl.n. Informal.* A large number or amount: *scads of people.* [Orig. unknown.]
scaf·fold (skăf′əld, -ōld′) *n.* **1.** A temporary platform used by workers in the construction or repair of a building. **2.** A raised wooden framework or platform. **3.** A platform used in the execution of condemned prisoners. *—tr.v.* **-fold·ed, -fold·ing, -folds. 1.** To provide or support with a scaffold. **2.** To place on a scaffold. [ME < ONFr. *escafaut.*]
scaf·fold·ing (skăf′əl-dĭng, skăf′ōl′-) *n.* **1.** A scaffold or system of scaffolds. **2.** The materials for scaffolds.
scag (skăg) *n. Slang.* Heroin. [Orig. unknown.]
scagl·io·la (skăl-yō′lə, -yô′-) *n.* Plasterwork in imitation of ornamental marble, consisting of ground gypsum and glue colored with marble or granite dust. [Ital., dim. of *scaglia,* chip, of Germanic orig.]
sca·lade (skə-lăd′, -läd′) also **sca·la·do** (skə-lā′dō, -lä′-) *n., pl.* **-lades** also **-la·dos.** An escalade. [Ital. *scalada, scalata.* — see ESCALADE.]
scal·age (skā′lĭj) *n.* **1.** The percentage by which a deduction from listed weights or prices of goods is figured to compensate for loss, as by shrinkage. **2.** The estimated amount of lumber in logs being scaled.
sca·lar (skā′lər, -lär′) *n.* **1.** A quantity, such as mass, length, time, or temperature, completely specified by a number on an appropriate scale. **2.** A device that yields an output equal to the input multiplied by a constant, as in a linear amplifier. [Lat. *scalaris,* of a staircase < *scalae,* ladder.] **—sca′lar** *adj.*
sca·la·re (skə-lâr′ē, -lär′ē) *n.* The angelfish. [NLat. < Lat. *scalaris,* of a ladder < *scalae,* ladder.]
sca·lar·i·form (skə-lăr′ə-fôrm′) *adj.* Having rungs; ladderlike. Used of certain vessels and tissues. [Lat. *scalaris,* of a ladder (< *scalae,* ladder) + -FORM.] **—sca·lar′i·form′ly** *adv.*
scalar product *n.* The numerical product of the lengths of two vectors and the cosine of the angle between them.
scal·a·wag (skăl′ə-wăg′) also **scal·ly·wag** (skăl′ē-) *n.* **1.** *Informal.* A reprobate; rascal. **2.** A white Republican Southerner during Reconstruction. [Orig. unknown.]
scald¹ (skôld) *v.* **scald·ed, scald·ing, scalds.** *—tr.* **1.** To burn with or as if with hot liquid or steam. **2.** To subject to or treat with boiling water. **3.** To heat (a liquid) almost to the boiling point. *—intr.* To be or become scalded. *—n.* **1.** A bodily injury caused by scalding. **2. a.** A superficial discoloration on fruit, vegetables, leaves, or tree trunks caused by sudden exposure to intense sunlight or the action of gases. **b.** A disease of some cereal grasses caused by a fungus of the genus *Rhynchosporium.* [ME *scalden* < ONFr. *escalder* < LLat. *excaldare,* to wash in hot water : Lat. *ex-,* from + Lat. *calidus,* warm.]
scald² (skôld) *n.* Variant of **skald.**
scald³ (skôld, skäld) *n.* Variant of **scall.**
scald·ing (skôl′dĭng) *adj.* **1.** Causing a burning sensation, as from contact with hot liquid. **2.** Boiling. **3.** Scorching; searing: *scalding sunlight.* **4.** Extremely harsh; biting: *a scalding review.*
scale¹ (skāl) *n.* **1. a.** A small, platelike dermal or epidermal structure characteristically forming the external covering of fishes, reptiles, and certain mammals. **b.** A similar part,

such as one of the minute structures overlapping to form the covering on the wings of butterflies and moths. **2.** *Pathol.* A dry, thin flake of epidermis shed from the skin. **3.** A small, thin piece. **4.** *Bot.* Any of various thin, often overlapping parts, such as one of the protective rudimentary leaves covering the buds of certain trees. **5. a.** A scale insect. **b.** A plant disease or infestation caused by scale insects. **6. a.** A flaky oxide film formed on a metal, as on iron, heated to high temperatures. **b.** A flake of rust. **7.** A coating or incrustation formed inside boilers, kettles, and other similar containers after extensive use. *—v.* **scaled, scal·ing, scales.** *—tr.* **1.** To clear or strip of scale or scales. **2.** To remove in layers or scales. **3.** To cover with scales; encrust. **4.** To throw (a thin, flat object) so that it soars through the air or skips along the surface of a body of water. *—intr.* **1.** To come off in layers or scales; flake. **2.** To become encrusted. [ME < OFr. *escale,* shell, of Germanic orig.]

scale[2] (skāl) *n.* **1. a.** A system of ordered marks at fixed intervals used as a reference standard in measurement. **b.** An instrument or device bearing such marks. **2. a.** The proportion used in determining the relationship of a representation to that which it represents. **b.** A calibrated line, as on a map or architectural plan, to indicate such a proportion. **3.** A progressive classification, as of size, amount, importance, or rank. **4.** A relative level or degree: *entertain on a lavish scale.* **5.** *Math.* A system of notation in which the value of numbers is determined by their place relative to the fixed constant of the system: *decimal scale.* **6.** *Mus.* An ascending or descending series of tones proceeding by a specified scheme of intervals and varying in pitch arrangement and interval size. *—v.* **scaled, scal·ing, scales.** *—tr.* **1.** To climb up or over; ascend. **2.** To make in accordance with a particular proportion or scale. **3.** To adjust according to a proportion; regulate. **4.** To estimate or measure the quantity of lumber in (logs or uncut trees). *—intr.* **1.** To climb; ascend. **2.** To ascend in steps or stages. [ME, ladder < LLat. *scala* < Lat. *scalae.*]

scale[3] (skāl) *n.* **1.** An instrument or machine for weighing. **2.** Either of the pans, trays, or dishes of a balance. *—v.* **scaled, scal·ing, scales.** *—tr.* To weigh with scales. *—intr.* To have as a weight, as determined by a scale. [ME < ON *skāl,* bowl.]

scale insect *n.* Any of various destructive sucking insects of the family Coccidae, the females of which secrete and remain under waxy scales on plant tissue.

scale moss *n.* Any of various leafy liverworts of the order Jungermanniales.

sca·lene (skā'lēn', skā-lēn') *adj.* Having three unequal sides. Used of triangles. [LLat. *scalenus* < Gk. *skalēnos,* uneven.]

scal·er (skā'lər) *n.* An electronic circuit that records the aggregate of a specific number of signals that occur too rapidly to be recorded individually. [< SCALE[2].]

scall (skôl) also **scald** (skôld) *n.* A scaly eruption of the skin or scalp. [ME < ON *scalli,* a bald head.]

scal·lion (skăl'yən) *n.* **1.** A young onion before the enlargement of the bulb. **2.** Any of several onionlike plants, such as a leek or shallot. [ME *scaloun* < AN < VLat. **escalonia,* alteration of Lat. *Ascalonia (caepa),* Ascalonian (onion) < *Ascalo,* Ascalon, a port in Palestine.]

scal·lop (skŏl'əp, skăl'-) also **scol·lop** (skŏl'-) *n.* **1.** Any of various free-swimming marine mollusks of the family Pectinidae, having fan-shaped bivalve shells with a radiating fluted pattern. **2.** The edible adductor muscle of a scallop. **3.** A scallop shell or a similarly shaped dish, used for baking and serving seafood. **4.** One of a series of semicircular curved projections forming an ornamental border. **5.** A thin, boneless slice of meat. *—tr.v.* **-loped, -lop·ing, -lops. 1.** To design or border (cloth) with scallops. **2.** To bake in a casserole with milk or a sauce and often with bread crumbs. **3.** To cut (meat) into scallops. [ME *scalop* < OFr. *escalope,* shell, of Germanic orig.] **—scal'lop·er** *n.*

scal·ly·wag (skăl'ē-wăg') *n.* Variant of **scalawag.**

sca·lop·pi·ne also **sca·lop·pi·ni** (skăl'ə-pē'nē, skä'lə-) *pl.n.* Small, thinly sliced pieces of meat, esp. veal, dredged in flour and sautéed in a sauce of wine or tomatoes and seasonings. [Ital., pl. of *scaloppina,* dim. of *scaloppa,* fillet of beef < OFr. *escalope,* shell, of Germanic orig.]

scalp (skălp) *n.* **1.** *Anat.* The skin covering the top of the human head. **2.** The skin covering the top of the human head with attached hair, formerly cut or torn from an enemy as a battle trophy by certain North American Indians. **3.** A piece of hide from the skull of certain animals, such as the fox, shown as proof of killing in order to collect a bounty. **4.** A trophy of victory. **5.** *Informal.* The profit made by a ticket scalper. *—v.* **scalped, scalp·ing, scalps.** *—tr.* **1.** To cut or tear the scalp from. **2.** To deprive of top growth or of a top layer. **3.** *Informal.* To sell (tickets) at a price higher than the established value. **4.** *Informal.* To buy and sell (stocks or bonds) quickly in order to make many small profits. *—intr. Informal.* To scalp bonds or tickets. [ME, of Scand. orig.] **—scalp'er** *n.*

scal·pel (skăl'pəl, skăl-pĕl') *n.* A small straight knife with a thin, sharp blade used in surgery and dissection. [Lat. *scalpellum,* dim. of *scalper,* knife < *scalpere,* to cut.]

scalp lock *n.* A long lock of hair left on the top of the shaven head by certain North American Indians.

scal·y (skā'lē) *adj.* **-i·er, -i·est. 1.** Covered or partially covered with scales. **2.** Shedding scales or flakes; flaking. **3.** *Slang.* Mean; despicable. **—scal'i·ness** *n.*

scaly anteater *n.* The pangolin.

scam (skăm) *n. Slang.* A fraudulent business scheme; swindle. [Orig. unknown.]

scam·mo·ny (skăm'ə-nē) *n., pl.* **-nies. 1.** A plant, *Convolvulus scammonia,* of the eastern Mediterranean region, having large roots formerly used as a cathartic. **2.** A preparation made from the scammony. [ME *scamonie* < Lat. *scammonea* < Gk. *skammōnia.*]

scamp[1] (skămp) *n.* **1.** A rogue; rascal. **2.** A mischievous youngster. [< obs. *scamp,* to go about idly.]

scamp[2] (skămp) *tr.v.* **scamped, scamp·ing, scamps.** To perform in a careless, superficial way. [Poss. of Scand. orig.]

scam·per (skăm'pər) *intr.v.* **-pered, -per·ing, -pers.** To run or go hurriedly. *—n.* A hasty run or departure. [Prob. < Flem. *scamperen,* to decamp < OFr. *escamper* < VLat. **excampare* : Lat. *ex-,* away + Lat. *campus,* field.]

scam·pi (skăm'pē, skäm'-) *n.* A dish consisting of shrimp cooked in a garlic and butter sauce. [Ital., pl. of *scampo,* a kind of lobster.]

scan (skăn) *v.* **scanned, scan·ning, scans.** *—tr.* **1.** To examine closely. **2.** To look over quickly but thoroughly by moving from one point to another. **3.** To look over or leaf through hastily. **4.** To analyze (verse) into metrical patterns. **5.** *Electronics.* **a.** To move a finely focused beam of light or electrons in a systematic pattern over (a surface) in order to reproduce or sense and subsequently transmit an image. **b.** To move a radar beam over (a sector of sky) in search of a target. **c.** To search (a series of punched cards or a magnetic tape) automatically for specific data. *—intr.* **1.** To analyze verse into metrical patterns. **2.** To conform to a metrical pattern. **3.** *Electronics.* To undergo electronic scanning. *—n.* **1.** An act of scanning. **2.** A scope or field of vision. [ME *scannen* < LLat. *scandere* < Lat., to climb.] **—scan'na·ble** *adj.* **—scan'ner** *n.*

scan·dal (skăn'dl) *n.* **1.** An act or circumstance that brings about disgrace or offends the morality of the social community. **2.** Talk damaging to the character; malicious gossip. **3.** Damage to reputation or character caused by offensive or grossly improper behavior. **4.** A person whose conduct brings about disgrace or shame. *—tr.v.* **-daled, -dal·ing, -dals. 1.** *Archaic.* To defame. **2.** *Obs.* To disgrace or dishonor. [Fr. *scandale* < LLat. *scandalum* < Gk. *skandalon,* trap, scandal.]

scan·dal·ize (skăn'dl-īz') *tr.v.* **-ized, -iz·ing, -iz·es. 1.** To shock the propriety or moral sense of. **2.** *Archaic.* To dishonor; disgrace. **—scan'dal·i·za'tion** *n.* **—scan'dal·iz'er** *n.*

scan·dal·ous (skăn'dl-əs) *adj.* **1.** Causing scandal; shocking. **2.** Containing defamatory or shocking information. **—scan'dal·ous·ly** *adv.* **—scan'dal·ous·ness** *n.*

scandal sheet *n.* A newspaper or other periodical that habitually prints gossip or scandalous stories.

scan·dent (skăn'dənt) *adj. Bot.* Climbing: *a scandent vine.* [Lat. *scandens, scandent-,* pr.part. of *scandere,* to climb.]

scan·di·a (skăn'dē-ə) *n. Chem.* Scandium oxide. [< SCANDIUM.]

Scan·di·an (skăn'dē-ən) *adj.* Scandinavian. [< Lat. *Scandia,* Scandinavia.]

Scan·di·na·vi·an (skăn'də-nā'vē-ən, -nāv'yən) *adj.* Of or relating to Scandinavia, its inhabitants, culture, or languages. *—n.* **1.** A native or inhabitant of Scandinavia. **2.** The North Germanic languages.

scan·di·um (skăn'dē-əm) *n. Symbol* **Sc** A silvery-white, very lightweight metallic element found in various rare minerals and separated as a by-product in the processing of certain uranium ores. An artificially radioactive isotope is used as a tracer in oil-well and pipeline studies. Atomic number 21; atomic weight 44.956; melting point 1,539°C; boiling point 2,727°C; specific gravity 2.992; valence 3. [< Lat. *Scandia,* Scandinavia, where it was discovered.] **—scan'dic** *adj.*

scandium oxide *n.* A white amorphous powder, Sc_2O_3, used as a source of scandium and in the manufacture of ceramics.

scan·ning (skăn'ĭng) *n.* Any of various electronic or optical techniques by which images or recorded information are sensed for subsequent modification, integration, or transmission.

scanning electron microscope *n.* An electron microscope that forms a three-dimensional image on a cathode-ray tube by moving a beam of focused electrons across an object and reading both the electrons scattered by the object and the secondary electrons produced by it.

scan·sion (skăn'shən) *n.* The analysis of verse into metrical patterns. [LLat. *scansio* < Lat., act of climbing < *scandere,* to climb.]

scan·so·ri·al (skăn-sôr'ē-əl, -sōr'-) *adj.* Adapted to or specialized for climbing. [< Lat. *scansorius* < *scandere,* to climb.]

scant (skănt) *adj.* **-er, -est. 1.** Deficient in quantity or amount; meager. **2.** Being just short of a specific measure: *a scant three miles.* **3.** Inadequately supplied: *scant of breath.* *—tr.v.* **scant·ed, scant·ing, scants. 1.** To provide with an inadequate portion or allowance; skimp. **2.** To limit, as in amount or share; stint. **3.** To reduce the size or amount of;

scale[3]

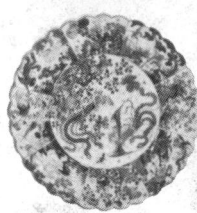

scallop
Above: Shell
Below: Scalloped border on a dish

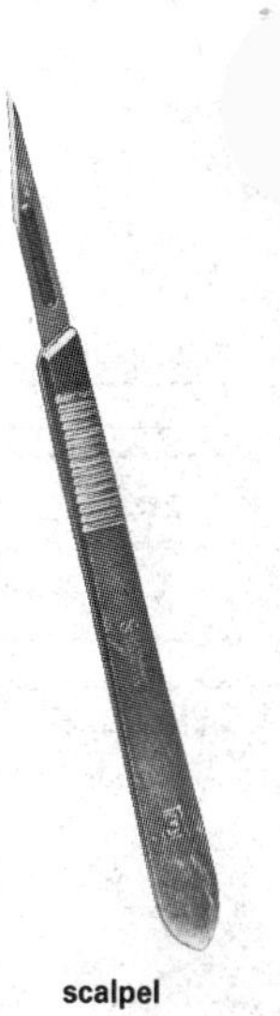

scalpel

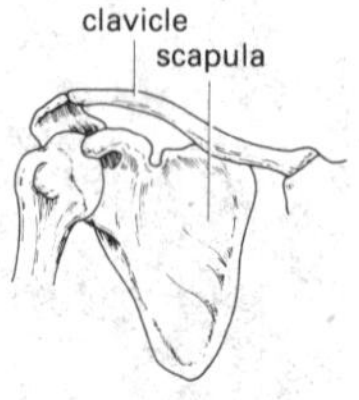

scapula

scarab
Detail of bracelet from the tomb of Tutankhamen

Scaramouch

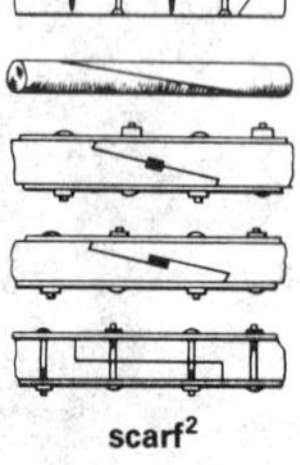

scarf²

cut down. **4.** To deal with or treat inadequately or neglectfully. [ME < ON *skamt,* neuter of *skammr,* short.] **—scant'ly** *adv.* **—scant'ness** *n.*

scant·ling (skănt'lĭng, -lĭn) *n.* **1.** A small piece of timber, as an upright in the frame of a house. **2.** The dimensions of building materials such as stone or timber, esp. in breadth and thickness. **3.** Often **scantlings.** *Naut.* The dimensions of the structural parts of a vessel. **4.** A very small amount. [Alteration of obs. *scantlon,* carpenter's gauge < ME *scantilon* < OFr. *escantillon.*]

scant·y (skăn'tē) *adj.* **-i·er, -i·est. 1.** Barely sufficient or adequate. **2.** Deficient; small. **—scant'i·ly** *adv.* **—scant'i·ness** *n.*

scape¹ (skāp) *n.* **1.** *Bot.* A leafless flower stalk growing directly from the ground. **2.** A stalklike part, such as a feather shaft or a segment of an insect's antenna. **3.** *Archit.* The shaft of a column. [Lat. *scapus,* stalk.]

scape² (skāp) *v.* & *n. Archaic.* Variant of **escape.**

-scape *suff.* Scene; view: *seascape.* [< LANDSCAPE.]

scape·goat (skāp'gōt') *n.* **1.** In the Old Testament, a live goat over whose head Aaron confessed all the sins of the children of Israel and which was sent into the wilderness symbolically bearing their sins on the Day of Atonement. **2.** A person or group bearing blame for others. *—tr.v.* **-goat·ed, -goat·ing, -goats.** To make a scapegoat of. [(E)SCAPE + GOAT, as transl. of Heb. *azāzēl,* goat of Azazel, construed as *ēz-ōzēl,* goat that escapes.]

scape·grace (skāp'grās') *n.* An unprincipled or incorrigible person; reprobate. [SCAPE² + GRACE.]

scaph·oid (skăf'oid') *adj.* Boat-shaped. *—n. Anat.* The navicular. [NLat. *scaphoides* < Gk. *skaphoeidēs* : *skaphē,* boat + *-eidēs,* -oid.]

scap·o·lite (skăp'ə-līt') *n.* Any of a series of variously colored, often fluorescent mineral silicates of aluminum, calcium, and sodium. [Fr. : Lat. *scapus,* stalk + Gk. *lithos,* stone (from the prismatic shape of its crystals).]

sca·pose (skā'pōs') *adj.* Resembling or consisting of a scape.

scap·u·la (skăp'yə-lə) *n., pl.* **-las** or **-lae** (-lē'). Either of two large, flat, triangular bones forming the back part of the shoulder. [Lat.]

scap·u·lar (skăp'yə-lər) *n.* **1.** A monk's sleeveless outer garment that hangs from the shoulders and sometimes has a cowl. **2.** A badge worn by members of certain religious orders, consisting of two pieces of cloth joined by strings and worn under the clothing about the shoulders. **3.** One of the feathers covering the shoulder of a bird. *—adj. Anat.* Of or pertaining to the shoulder or scapula. [ME *scapulare* < Med. Lat. *scapulare* < Lat. *scapula,* shoulder.]

scap·u·lo·cla·vic·u·lar (skăp'yə-lō-klə-vĭk'yə-lər) *adj.* Of, pertaining to, or affecting both the scapula and the clavicle.

scar¹ (skär) *n.* **1.** A mark left on the skin following the healing of a surface injury or wound. **2.** A lingering sign of damage or injury, either mental or physical. **3.** *Bot.* A mark indicating a former attachment, as of a leaf to a stem. **4.** A mark, dent, or other blemish resulting from use or contact. *—v.* **scarred, scar·ring, scars.** *—tr.* **1.** To mark with a scar. **2.** To do lingering damage to. *—intr.* **1.** To form a scar. **2.** To become scarred. [ME < OFr. *escare,* scab < LLat. *eschara* < Gk. *eskhara,* hearth, scab caused by burning.]

scar² (skär) *n.* **1.** A protruding, isolated rock. **2.** A bare, rocky place on a mountain side or other steep slope. [ME *skerre* < ON *sker,* low reef.]

scar·ab (skăr'əb) *n.* **1.** A scarabaeid beetle, esp. *Scarabaeus sacer,* regarded as sacred by the ancient Egyptians. **2.** A representation of a scarab beetle, as a ceramic or stone sculpture, used in ancient Egypt as a talisman and a symbol of the soul. [OFr. *scarabee* < Lat. *scarabaeus.*]

scar·a·bae·i (skăr'ə-bē'ī') *n.* A plural of **scarabaeus.**

scar·a·bae·id (skăr'ə-bē'ĭd) *n.* Any of the numerous beetles of the family Scarabaeidae, which includes the June bugs and dung beetles. *—adj.* Of or belonging to the Scarabaeidae. [NLat. *Scarabaeidae,* family name < Lat. *scarabaeus,* beetle.]

scar·a·bae·us (skăr'ə-bē'əs) *n., pl.* **-bae·us·es** or **-bae·i** (-bē'ī'). A scarab. [Lat.]

scar·a·bi·a·sis (skăr'ə-bī'ə-sĭs) *n.* Infestation of the intestine with the dung beetle. [SCARAB(AEID) + -IASIS.]

scar·a·boid (skăr'ə-boid') *adj.* Resembling or characteristic of a scarabaeid beetle.

Scar·a·mouch also **Scar·a·mouche** (skăr'ə-mo͞osh', -mo͞och', -mouch') *n.* A stock character in old Italian comedy and pantomime, depicted as a boastful, cowardly braggart or buffoon. [Fr. *Scaramouche* < Ital. *Scaramuccia.*]

scarce (skârs) *adj.* **scarc·er, scarc·est. 1.** Infrequently seen or found; rare. **2.** Insufficient to meet a demand or requirement. —See Usage note at **rare.** [ME *scars* < ONFr. *escars* < VLat. **excarpsus,* p.part. of **excarpere,* alteration of Lat. *excerpere,* to pick out. —see EXCERPT.] **—scarce'ness** *n.*

scarce·ly (skârs'lē) *adv.* **1.** By a small margin; barely. **2.** Almost not; hardly. **3.** Certainly not.

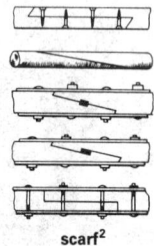

Usage: *Scarcely* has the force of a negative; therefore it is not properly used with another negative: *I could scarcely believe it* (not *I couldn't scarcely believe it*). A clause following *scarcely* is introduced by *when* or, less often, by *before* but not by *than: The meeting had scarcely begun when* (or *before* but not *than*) *it was interrupted.* See also Usage note at **hardly.**

scar·ci·ty (skâr'sĭ-tē) *n., pl.* **-ties. 1.** Insufficient amount or supply; shortage. **2.** Rarity of appearance or occurrence.

scare (skâr) *v.* **scared, scar·ing, scares.** *—tr.* To startle with fear; frighten. *—intr.* To become frightened. ***—phrasal verb.*** **scare up.** *Informal.* To gather or prepare with considerable difficulty and effort: *managed to scare up the needed data.* *—n.* **1.** A condition or sensation of sudden fear. **2.** A general state of alarm or panic. [ME *skerren* < ON *skirra* < *skjarr,* timid.] **—scar'er** *n.* **—scar'ing·ly** *adv.*

scare·crow (skâr'krō') *n.* **1.** A crude figure of a person set up in a field to scare birds away from growing crops. **2.** Something frightening but not dangerous. **3.** A gaunt or haggard person.

scare·mon·ger (skâr'mŭng'gər, -mŏng'-) *n.* A person who spreads frightening rumors; alarmist.

scarf¹ (skärf) *n., pl.* **scarfs** or **scarves** (skärvz). **1.** A wide piece of cloth worn about the head, neck, or shoulders. **2.** A runner, as for a bureau or table. **3.** A sash denoting military rank. *—tr.v.* **scarfed, scarf·ing, scarfs. 1.** To dress, cover, or decorate with or as if with a scarf. **2.** To wrap around loosely. [ONFr. *escarpe,* sash, sling.]

scarf² (skärf) *n., pl.* **scarfs. 1.** A joint made by cutting and notching the ends of two timbers and strapping or bolting them together to make a continuous piece. **2.** The end of a timber notched to form a scarf. *—tr.v.* **scarfed, scarf·ing, scarfs. 1.** To join by means of a scarf joint. **2.** To cut a scarf in. [ME *skarf.*]

scarf·skin (skärf'skĭn') *n.* The epidermis or outermost layer of skin, esp. the cuticle.

scar·i·fi·ca·tor (skăr'ə-fĭ-kā'tər) *n.* A surgical instrument with several spring-operated lancets used for skin scarification.

scar·i·fy¹ (skăr'ə-fī') *tr.v.* **-fied, -fy·ing, -fies. 1.** To make superficial incisions in (the skin), as when vaccinating. **2.** To break up the surface of (topsoil). **3.** To criticize severely. **4.** *Bot.* To slit or soften the outer coat of (seeds) in order to speed germination. [ME *scarifien* < OFr. *scarifier* < LLat. *scarificare,* alteration of *scarifare* < Gk. *skariphasthai,* to scratch, sketch < *skariphos,* pencil.] **—scar'i·fi·ca'tion** *n.* **—scar'i·fi'er** *n*

scar·i·fy² (skăr'ə-fī') *tr.v.* **-fied, -fy·ing, -fies.** To scare.

scar·i·ous (skâr'ē-əs) also **scar·i·ose** (-ōs') *adj.* Thin, membranous, and dry: *scarious bracts.* [NLat. *scariosus.*]

scar·la·ti·na (skär'lə-tē'nə) *n.* Scarlet fever. [NLat. < Med. Lat. *scarlata,* scarlet.] **—scar'la·ti'nal** *adj.*

scar·la·ti·noid (skär'lə-tē'noid') *adj.* Resembling scarlet fever or its rash. [NLat. *scarlatina,* scarlet fever + -OID.]

scar·let (skär'lĭt) *n.* **1.** A strong to vivid red or reddish orange. **2.** Scarlet-colored clothing or cloth. *—adj.* **1.** Having a scarlet color. **2.** Sinful or unchaste; whorish. [ME < OFr. *escarlate* < Med. Lat. *scarlata,* scarlet cloth < Pers. *sāqalāt,* a kind of rich cloth.]

scarlet fever *n.* An acute contagious disease caused by a hemolytic streptococcus, occurring predominantly among children and characterized by a scarlet skin eruption and high fever.

scarlet pimpernel *n.* Pimpernel.

scarlet runner *n.* A climbing bean plant, *Phaseolus coccineus,* native to tropical America, having scarlet flowers and long pods containing edible seeds.

scarlet sage *n.* A species of salvia, *Salvia splendens,* with showy scarlet flowers.

scarlet tanager *n.* A New World bird, *Piranga olivacea,* of which the male has bright scarlet plumage with a black tail and wings.

scarp (skärp) *n.* **1.** A steep slope; cliff. **2.** A steep slope at the outer edge of a fortification. *—tr.v.* **scarped, scarp·ing, scarps.** To cut or make into a scarp. [Ital. *scarpa,* perh. of Germanic orig.]

scar tissue *n.* A dense, often hard layer of connective tissue formed over a healing wound or cut.

scarves (skärvz) *n.* A plural of **scarf¹.**

scar·y (skâr'ē) *adj.* **-i·er, -i·est. 1.** Frightening; alarming. **2.** Easily scared; very timid.

scat¹ (skăt) *intr.v.* **scat·ted, scat·ting, scats.** *Informal.* To go away hastily; leave at once. [Orig. unknown.]

scat² (skăt) *n.* Jazz singing in which improvised, meaningless syllables are sung to a melody. *—intr.v.* **scat·ted, scat·ting, scats.** To sing scat. [Perh. imit.]

scat³ (skăt) *n.* The excremental droppings of an animal. [Gk. *skōr, skat-,* excrement.]

scathe (skāth) *tr.v.* **scathed, scath·ing, scathes. 1.** To harm or injure severely, esp. by fire. **2.** To criticize severely. *—n.* Harm; injury. [ME *skathen* < ON *skaða.*]

scath·ing (skā'*th*ĭng) *adj.* **1.** Extremely severe or harsh; bitterly denunciatory: *"a scathing tract on the uselessness of war"* (Pierre Brodin). **2.** Harmful or painful; injurious.

scato- *pref.* Excrement: *scatology.* [Gk. *skato-* < *skōr,* ordure.]

sca·tol·o·gy (skă-tŏl'ə-jē, skə-) *n.* **1.** The study of fecal excrement, as in medicine or paleontology. **2. a.** An obsession with excrement or excretory functions. **b.** The psychiatric study of such an obsession. **3.** Interest in or preoccupation with obscenity, as in literature. **—scat'o·log'i·cal** (skăt'l-ŏj'ĭ-kəl), **scat'o·log'ic** *adj.* **—sca·tol'o·gist** *n.*

scat·ter (skăt'ər) *v.* **-tered, -ter·ing, -ters.** *—tr.* **1.** To cause to separate and go in various directions; disperse. **2.** To distribute loosely by or as if by sprinkling or strewing. **3.** *Physics.* To deflect (radiation or particles). *—intr.* **1.** To separate and go in several directions. **2.** To occur or fall at widely spaced intervals. *—n.* **1.** The act of scattering. **2.** The condition of being scattered. **3.** Something scattered. [ME *scateren.*] **—scat'ter·er** *n.*

Synonyms: *scatter, disperse, dissipate, dispel.* These verbs are compared as they mean to cause something considered as a mass or aggregate to break up. *Scatter* usually refers to widespread and often haphazard distribution of components, as persons fleeing a storm or physical objects blown by wind. *Disperse* makes a stronger implication of complete breaking up of the mass, as a crowd of persons routed by police or a mass of clouds acted on by sunlight. *Dissipate* usually implies reduction to nothing, as by squandering (a fortune, time, or energy) or causing something (such as fog or mist) to evaporate. *Dispel* suggests making disappear as if by scattering; often it takes as its object something nonphysical, as a rumor, fear, joy, or doubt.

scat·ter·brain (skăt'ər-brān') *n.* A flighty, disorganized, or thoughtless person. **—scat'ter·brained'** *adj.*

scat·ter·good (skăt'ər-gŏŏd') *n.* A spendthrift; wastrel.

scat·ter·gun (skăt'ər-gŭn') *n.* A shotgun.

scat·ter·ing (skăt'ər-ĭng) *n.* **1. a.** The act or process of one that scatters. **b.** The state of being scattered. **2.** A small, irregularly occurring amount or quantity of something: *a scattering of applause.* **3.** *Physics.* The dispersal of a beam of particles or of radiation into a range of directions resulting from physical interactions. *—adj.* Placed at intervals or occurring irregularly. **—scat'ter·ing·ly** *adv.*

scattering matrix *n.* An S matrix.

scatter pin *n.* A woman's small decorative brooch often worn in groups of two or three.

scatter rug *n.* A small rug for carpeting a part of a floor.

scat·ter·shot (skăt'ər-shŏt') *adj.* Covering a wide range in a random way: *scattershot testimony.*

scat·ter-site (skăt'ər-sīt') *adj.* Of or designating publicly funded low-income housing units scattered throughout middle-income residential areas.

scat·ty (skăt'ē) *adj.* **-ti·er, -ti·est.** *Chiefly Brit. Slang.* Crazy; foolish. [Prob. SCATT(ERBRAIN) + -Y[1].]

scaup (skôp) *n., pl.* **scaup** or **scaups.** Either of two diving ducks, *Aythya marila* or *A. affinis,* having predominantly black and white plumage. [Perh. alteration of Sc. *scalp,* bed of mussels (from its feeding on shellfish).]

scav·enge (skăv'ənj) *v.* **-enged, -eng·ing, -eng·es.** *—tr.* **1.** To collect and remove refuse from. **2.** To search through for salvageable material. **3.** To collect (salvageable material) by searching. **4.** To expel (exhaust gases) from a cylinder of an internal-combustion engine. **5.** *Metallurgy.* To clean (molten metal) by chemically removing impurities. *—intr.* To search through discarded material or refuse for something useful. [Back-formation < SCAVENGER.]

scav·en·ger (skăv'ən-jər) *n.* **1.** An animal that feeds on dead or decaying matter. **2.** A person who scavenges. **3.** *Chem.* A substance added to a mixture to remove impurities or to counteract the undesirable effects of other constituents. [Alteration of obs. *scavager,* street cleaner < ME *skawager,* toll collector < AN *scawager* < *scawage,* a tax on the goods of foreign merchants < Flem. *scawen,* to look at, show.]

sce·nar·i·o (sĭ-nâr'ē-ō', -när'-, -năr'-) *n., pl.* **-os. 1.** An outline of the plot of a dramatic or literary work. **2.** A screenplay. **3.** An outline of a hypothesized or projected chain of events. [Ital. < LLat. *scaenarius,* of the stage < Lat. *scaena,* stage. —see SCENE.]

sce·nar·ist (sĭ-nâr'ĭst, -när'-, -năr'-) *n.* A writer of screenplays.

scend also **send** (sĕnd) *intr.v.* **scend·ed, scend·ing, scends** also **send·ed, send·ing, sends.** To heave upward on a wave or swell. *—n.* The rising movement of a ship on a wave or swell. [Prob. alteration of SEND.]

scene (sēn) *n.* **1.** A picture or prospect as seen by a viewer; view. **2.** The place where an action or event occurs. **3.** The place in which the action of a narrative occurs; setting. **4.** A subdivision of an act in a dramatic presentation in which the setting is fixed and the time continuous. **5.** A shot or series of shots in a film constituting a unit of continuous related action. **6.** The scenery and properties for a dramatic presentation. **7.** *Archaic.* A theater stage. **8.** A real or fictitious episode, esp. when described. **9.** A public display of passion or temper. **10.** *Slang.* **a.** A sphere of activity: *the drug scene.* **b.** A given situation: *a bad scene.* **—idiom. behind the scenes. 1.** Backstage. **2.** In private. [OFr., stage < Lat. *scaena* < Gk. *skēnē,* stage, tent.]

scen·er·y (sē'nə-rē) *n., pl.* **-ies. 1.** A landscape. **2.** The painted backdrops on a theatrical stage. **—sce'nic** *adj.* **—sce'ni·cal·ly** *adv.*

scene-steal·er (sēn'stē'lər) *n.* An actor who draws attention to himself when he is not meant to be the focus of attention.

scent (sĕnt) *n.* **1.** A distinctive odor. **2.** A perfume. **3.** An odor left by the passing of an animal. **4.** The trail of a hunted animal or fugitive. **5.** The sense of smell. **6.** A hint of something imminent; suggestion. *—v.* **scent·ed, scent·ing, scents.** *—tr.* **1.** To perceive or identify by the sense of smell. **2.** To suspect or detect as if by smelling: *scent danger.* **3.** To perfume. *—intr.* To hunt prey by means of the sense of smell. Used of hounds. [ME *sent* < *senten,* to scent < OFr. *sentir* < Lat. *sentire,* to feel.]

scent gland *n.* A specialized apocrine gland in many mammals that produces odorous substances.

scep·ter (sĕp'tər) *n.* **1.** A staff held by a sovereign on ceremonial occasions as an emblem of authority. **2.** Sovereign office or power. *—tr.v.* **-tered, -ter·ing, -ters.** To invest with royal authority. [ME *sceptre* < OFr. < Lat. *sceptrum* < Gk. *skēptron,* staff.]

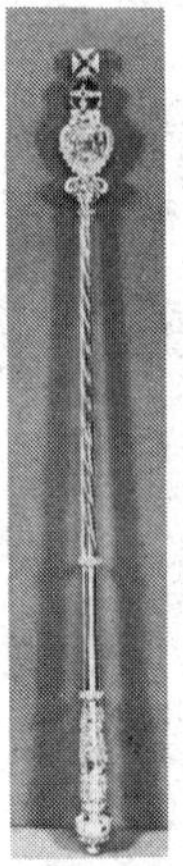

scepter

scep·tic (skĕp'tĭk) *n.* Variant of **skeptic.**

scep·ti·cal (skĕp'tĭ-kəl) *adj.* Variant of **skeptical.**

scep·ti·cism (skĕp'tĭ-sĭz'əm) *n.* Variant of **skepticism.**

scep·tre (sĕp'tər) *n. & v. Chiefly Brit.* Variant of **scepter.**

scha·den·freu·de (shäd'n-froi'də) *n.* Pleasure derived from the misfortunes of others. [G. : *schaden,* damage + *freude,* joy.]

schav (shäv) *n.* A chilled soup made with sorrel, onions, lemon juice, eggs, and sugar and served with sour cream. [Pol. *szczaw,* sorrel.]

sched·ule (skĕj'o͞ol, -əl; *Brit.* shĕd'yo͞ol) *n.* **1.** A printed or often written list of items in tabular form. **2. a.** A program of forthcoming events or appointments. **b.** A student's program of classes. **3.** A timetable of departures and arrivals. **4.** A production plan allotting work to be done and specifying deadlines. **5.** A supplemental statement of details appended to a document. *—tr.v.* **-uled, -ul·ing, -ules. 1.** To enter on a schedule. **2.** To make up a schedule for. **3.** To plan or appoint for a certain time or date. [ME *sedule,* slip of parchment or paper, note < OFr. *cedule* < LLat. *schedula,* dim. of Lat. *scheda,* papyrus leaf, of Gk. orig.]

schee·lite (shā'līt') *n.* A variously colored natural form of calcium tungstate, $CaWO_4$, found in igneous rocks and used as a source of tungsten. [After Karl *Scheele* (1742–1786), its discoverer.]

sche·ma (skē'mə) *n., pl.* **-ma·ta** (-mə-tə). A diagrammatic representation; outline. [Gk. *skhēma, skhēmat-,* form.]

sche·mat·ic (skē-măt'ĭk) *adj.* Of, pertaining to, or in the form of a scheme or diagram. *—n.* A structural or procedural diagram, esp. of an electrical or mechanical system. [NLat. *schematicus* < Gk. *skhēma,* form.] **—sche·mat'i·cal·ly** *adv.*

sche·ma·tism (skē'mə-tĭz'əm) *n.* The patterned disposition of constituents within a given system.

sche·ma·tize (skē'mə-tīz') *tr.v.* **-tized, -tiz·ing, -tiz·es.** To form into a scheme. [Gk. *skhēmatizein,* to give form to < *skhēma,* form.] **—sche'ma·ti·za'tion** *n.*

scheme (skēm) *n.* **1.** A systematic plan of action. **2.** An orderly combination of related parts or elements. **3.** A plan, esp. a secret or devious one; plot. **4.** A chart, diagram, or outline of a system or object. **5.** A visionary plan. *—v.* **schemed, schem·ing, schemes.** *—tr.* **1.** To contrive a plan or scheme for. **2.** To plot. *—intr.* To make plans, esp. secret or devious ones. [Lat. *schema,* figure, manner < Gk. *skhēma,* form.] **—schem'er** *n.*

scher·zan·do (skĕrt-sän'dō) *Mus. —adv.* In a light, playful manner. Used as a direction. *—n., pl.* **-dos.** A passage to be performed scherzando. [Ital., gerund. of *scherzare,* to joke < *scherzo,* joke. —see SCHERZO.] **—scher·zan'do** *adj.*

scher·zo (skĕr'tsō) *n., pl.* **-zos** or **-zi** (-tsē). *Mus.* A lively movement commonly in $^3/_4$ time. [Ital., joke, scherzo < MHG *scherz,* joke < *scherzen,* to leap with joy.]

Schick test (shĭk) *n.* An intracutaneous skin test of susceptibility to diphtheria. [After Bela *Schick* (1877–1967), its inventor.]

Schiff's reagent (shĭfs) *n.* An aqueous solution of rosaniline and sulfurous acid used to test for the presence of aldehydes. [After Hugo *Schiff* (1834–1915).]

schil·ler (shĭl'ər) *n.* A lustrous, almost metallic reflection from certain planes in a mineral grain. [G.]

schil·ling (shĭl'ĭng) *n.* See table at **currency.** [G.]

schip·per·ke (skĭp'ər-kē, -kə) *n.* A small dog of a breed developed in Belgium, having dense, long black fur. [Flem., dim. of *schipper,* skipper (from the dog's use as a watchdog on a boat) < MDu. —see SKIPPER[1].]

schism (sĭz'əm, skĭz'-) *n.* **1. a.** A separation or division into factions, esp. a formal breach of union within a Christian church. **b.** The offense of attempting to produce such a split. **2.** A body or sect that participates in or creates a schism. [ME *scisme* < OFr. < LLat. *schisma* < Gk. *skhisma,* division < *skhizein,* to split.] **—schis·mat'ic** (sĭz-măt'ĭk, skĭz-) *adj.* **—schis·mat'i·cal·ly** *adv.*

schist (shĭst) *n.* Any of various medium- to coarse-grained metamorphic rocks composed of laminated, often flaky parallel layers of chiefly micaceous minerals. [Fr. *schiste* < Lat. *(lapis) schistos,* fissile (stone) < Gk. *skhistos,* split, divisible < *skhizein,* to split.] **—schis'tose'** (shĭs'tōs'), **schis'tous** (shĭs'təs) *adj.*

schis·to·some (shĭs'tə-sōm') *n.* Any of several chiefly tropical trematode worms of the genus *Schistosoma,* many of which are parasitic in the blood of man and other mammals. [NLat. *Schistosoma,* genus name : Gk. *skhistos,* split + Gk. *soma,* body.] **—schis'to·som'al** (-sō'məl) *adj.*

schnauzer

schis·to·so·mi·a·sis (shĭs′tō-sə-mī′ə-sĭs) *n.* Any of various generally tropical diseases caused by infestation with schistosomes.

schiz– *pref.* Variant of **schizo-.**

schiz·o (skĭt′sō) *n., pl.* **-os.** *Slang.* A schizophrenic person.

schizo– or **schiz–** *pref.* **1.** Split; cleft: *schizocarp.* **2.** Cleavage; fission: *schizogenesis.* **3.** Schizophrenia: *schizoid.* [Gk. *skhizo-* < *skhizein,* to split.]

schiz·o·carp (skĭz′ə-kärp′, skĭt′sə-) *n.* A dry seed that splits at maturity into two or more closed carpels, each usually containing one seed, as in the fruit of the carrot or mallow. **—schiz′o·car′pous, schiz′o·car′pic** *adj.*

schiz·o·gen·e·sis (skĭz′ō-jĕn′ĭ-sĭs, skĭt′sō-) *n.* Reproduction by fission.

schi·zog·o·ny (skĭ-zŏg′ə-nē, skĭt-sŏg′-) *n.* Reproduction by multiple asexual fission, characteristic of many sporozoans. **—schi·zog′o·nous** *adj.*

schiz·oid (skĭt′soid′) *adj.* Characteristic of or resembling schizophrenia. *—n.* A schizophrenic person.

schiz·o·my·cete (skĭz′ō-mī′sēt′, -mī-sēt′, skĭt′sō-) *n.* Any of numerous one-celled microorganisms of the class Schizomycetes, which includes the bacteria. [NLat. *Schizomycetes,* class name : SCHIZO- + Gk. *mukētes,* pl. of *mukēs,* fungus.] **—schiz′o·my·ce′tous** (-mī-sē′təs) *adj.*

schiz·o·my·co·sis (skĭz′ō-mī-kō′sĭs, skĭt′sō-) *n.* A disease caused by bacteria. [SCHIZO(MYCETE) + MYCOSIS.]

schiz·ont (skĭz′ŏnt′, skĭt′sŏnt′) *n.* A protozoan cell produced by schizogony in the life cycle of a sporozoan.

schiz·o·phrene (skĭt′sə-frēn′) *n.* An individual afflicted with schizophrenia. [Back-formation < SCHIZOPHRENIA.]

schiz·o·phre·ni·a (skĭt′sə-frē′nē-ə) *n.* Any of a group of psychotic reactions characterized by withdrawal from reality with highly variable accompanying affective, behavioral, and intellectual disturbances. **—schiz′o·phren′ic** (-frĕn′ĭk) *adj. & n.*

schiz·o·phyte (skĭz′ə-fīt′, skĭt′sə-) *n.* Any of various one-celled or simple colonial organisms of the division Schizophyta, including bacteria, that reproduce asexually, usually by fission. [NLat. *Schizophyta,* division name : SCHIZO- + Gk. *phuton,* plant.] **—schiz′o·phyt′ic** (-fĭt′ĭk, skĭt′sə-) *adj.*

schiz·o·pod (skĭz′ə-pŏd′) *n.* Any of various shrimplike crustaceans of the orders Euphausiacea and Mysidacea (formerly included in the single order Schizopoda). [NLat. *Schizopoda,* former order name : SCHIZO- + Gk. *pous,* foot.] **—schiz·op′o·dous** (skĭ-zŏp′ə-dəs, skĭt-sŏp′-) *adj.*

schiz·o·thy·mi·a (skĭt′sə-thī′mē-ə) *n.* Schizoid behavior that resembles schizophrenia in the tendency to autistic thinking but remains within the limits of normality. **—schiz′o·thy′mic** (-thī′mĭk) *adj.*

schiz·y (skĭt′sē) *adj.* **-i·er, -i·est.** *Slang.* Schizoid. [Shortening and alteration of SCHIZOID.]

schle·miel (shlə-mēl′) *n. Slang.* A habitual bungler; dolt. [Yiddish *shlumiel,* perh. < Heb. *Shelūmīel,* Shelumiel, a character in the Bible.]

schlep (shlĕp) *Slang.* *—v.* **schlepped, schlep·ping, schleps.** *—tr.* To carry clumsily or with difficulty; lug. *—intr.* To move slowly or laboriously: *schlepped all around town looking for wallpaper.* *—n.* **1.** An arduous journey. **2.** A clumsy or stupid person. [Yiddish *shleppen,* to drag < MLG *slēpen.*] **—schlep′per** *n.*

schlie·ren (shlîr′ən) *pl.n.* **1.** *Geol.* Irregular tabular bodies occurring as essential components of plutonic rock but differing in texture or composition from the principal mass. **2.** Regions of a transparent medium, as of a flowing gas, that exhibit densities different from that of the bulk of the medium. [G. < dial. G., pl. of *Shlier,* ulcer < MHG *slier.*]

schli·ma·zel (shlĭ-mä′zəl) *n. Slang.* An extremely unlucky or inept person; a habitual failure. [Yiddish *shlimazel,* bad luck : *shlim,* bad (< MHG *slimp)* + Heb. *mazāl,* luck.]

schlock also **shlock** (shlŏk) *n. Slang.* Merchandise of meretricious or obviously inferior quality. [Yiddish < G. *Schlag,* a blow.] **—schlock′y** *adj.*

schmaltz also **schmalz** (shmälts) *n.* **1.** Excessively sentimental art or music. **2.** Maudlin sentimentality. [Yiddish *shmalts,* melted fat < MHG *smalz* < OHG.] **—schmaltz′y** *adj.*

schmeer also **schmear** (shmîr) *n. Slang.* **1.** An aggregate of persons or things: *bought the whole schmeer.* **2.** A bribe. [Yiddish *shmir* < G. *Schmiere,* grease.]

Schmidt system (shmĭt) *n.* A system consisting of a concave spherical mirror and a transparent plate of glass at its center of curvature, used in reflecting telescopes to offset spherical aberration, coma, and astigmatism. [After Bernhard *Schmidt* (1879–1935), its inventor.]

schmo also **schmoe** (shmō) *n., pl.* **schmoes.** *Slang.* A stupid person; jerk. [Yiddish *shmok* < Slovene *šmok.*]

schmoose also **schmooze** (shmo͞oz) *Slang.* *—intr.v.* **schmoosed, schmoos·ing, schmoos·es** also **schmoozed, schmooz·ing, schmooz·es.** To chat idly. *—n.* A chat. [Yiddish *shmuesn,* to chat < *shmues,* a chat < Heb. *shemu'ōth,* pl. of *shemu'āh,* rumor < *shāmō'a,* he heard.] **—schmoos′er** *n.*

schmuck (shmŭk) *n. Slang.* A clumsy or stupid person. [Yiddish *shmok,* penis, fool < G. *Schmuck,* ornament < MLG *smuck.*]

schnapps (shnäps, shnăps) *n., pl.* **schnapps.** Any of various strong liquors. [G. *Schnaps* < LG *snaps,* mouthful < *snappen,* to snap < MLG, to speak hastily.]

schnau·zer (shnou′zər, shnout′ser) *n.* A dog of a breed developed in Germany, having a wiry gray coat and a blunt muzzle and ranging in size from fairly small to quite large. [G. < *Schnauze,* snout.]

schnit·zel (shnĭt′səl) *n.* A thin cutlet of veal fried lightly in butter. [G., dim. of *Schnitz,* slice.]

schnook (shno͝ok) *n.* A stupid or easily victimized person; dupe. [Yiddish *shnok.*]

schnor·rer (shnôr′ər, shnōr′-) *n. Slang.* One who takes advantage of the generosity of friends; parasite. [Yiddish *shnorer* < *shnoren,* to beg < MHG *snurren,* to hum, whir.]

schnoz·zle (shnŏz′əl) also **schnozz** (shnŏz) *n. Slang.* The nose. [Prob. alteration of Yiddish *shnoitsl,* dim of *shnoits,* snout < G. *Schnauze.*]

schol·ar (skŏl′ər) *n.* **1. a.** A learned or erudite person. **b.** A specialist in a given branch of the humanities. **2. a.** One who attends school or studies with a teacher. **b.** One considered in the light of his aptness at learning: *a poor scholar.* **3.** A student who holds or has held a particular scholarship. [ME *scoler* < OFr. *escoler* < LLat. *scholaris,* of a school < Lat. *schola, scola,* school. —see SCHOOL.]

schol·ar·ly (skŏl′ər-lē) *adj.* Of, pertaining to, or characteristic of scholars or scholarship. **—schol′ar·li·ness** *n.*

schol·ar·ship (skŏl′ər-shĭp′) *n.* **1.** The methods, discipline, and attainments of a scholar. **2.** Knowledge resulting from study and research in a particular field. **3.** Financial aid awarded to a student, as by a college.

scho·las·tic (skə-lăs′tĭk) *adj.* **1.** Of or pertaining to schools; academic. **2.** Often **Scholastic.** Of or characteristic of the Medieval Schoolmen. **3.** Pedantic; dogmatic. *—n.* **1.** Often **Scholastic.** A Medieval Schoolman. **2.** A dogmatist; pedant. [Lat. *scholasticus* < Gk. *skholastikos* < *skholazein,* to study < *skholē,* school.] **—scho·las′ti·cal·ly** *adv.*

scho·las·ti·cism (skə-lăs′tĭ-sĭz′əm) *n.* **1.** Often **Scholasticism.** The dominant theological and philosophical school of the High Middle Ages, based on the authority of the Latin Fathers and of Aristotle and his commentators. **2. a.** Close adherence to the methods, traditions, and teachings of a given sect or school. **b.** A pedantic adherence to scholarly methodology.

scho·li·a (skō′lē-ə) *n.* A plural of **scholium.**

scho·li·ast (skō′lē-ăst′) *n.* One of the ancient commentators who annotated the classical authors. [LGk. *skholiastēs* < *skholiazein,* to comment on < Gk. *skholion,* scholium.]

scho·li·um (skō′lē-əm) *n., pl.* **-li·ums** or **-li·a** (-lē-ə). **1.** An explanatory note or commentary, as on a Greek or Latin text. **2.** A note amplifying a proof or process, as in mathematics. [NLat. < Gk. *skholion,* dim. of *skholē,* lecture, school.]

school¹ (sko͞ol) *n.* **1.** An institution for the instruction of children. **2.** An institution for instruction in a skill or business. **3. a.** A college or university. **b.** An institution within or associated with a college or university for instruction in a specialized field. **c.** The student body of an educational institution. **d.** The building or group of buildings in which instruction is given or in which students work and live. **4.** The process of being educated formally, esp. education comprising a planned series of courses over a number of years. **5.** A session of instruction. **6.** A group of persons, esp. philosophers, artists, or writers, whose thought, work, or style demonstrates a common influence or unifying belief. **7.** A class of people distinguished by a convention of manners, customs, or opinions. **8.** Education provided by a set of circumstances or experiences: *the school of hard knocks.* **9.** A division comprising several grades or classes in a private school. **10.** The prescribed regulations and drill instructions applying to individuals or to a unit of an army or navy. *—tr.v.* **schooled, school·ing, schools. 1.** To instruct; educate. **2.** To train; discipline. [ME *scole* < OE *scōl* < Med. Lat. *scola* < Lat. *schola* < Gk. *skholē.*]

school² (sko͞ol) *n.* A large group of aquatic animals, esp. fish, swimming together; shoal. *—intr.v.* **schooled, school·ing, schools.** To swim in or form into a school. [ME *scole* < MDu. *schōle,* troop.]

school age *n.* The period of childhood during which a child is considered able to attend school and is usually legally required to do so.

school bag *n.* A usually cloth bag for carrying textbooks and school supplies.

school board *n.* A local board that oversees public schools.

school·book (sko͞ol′bo͝ok′) *n.* A textbook for use in school.

school·boy (sko͞ol′boi′) *n.* A boy attending school.

school bus *n.* A publicly or privately owned vehicle that is used for taking schoolchildren to and from school or school-related activities.

school·child (sko͞ol′chīld′) *n.* A child attending school.

school committee *n.* A school board.

school district *n.* A limited area within a state often comprising several towns that functions as the administrative unit of a public-school system.

school edition *n.* A simplified, abridged, or emended edition of a book issued esp. for use in schools.

school·girl (sko͞ol′gûrl′) *n.* A girl attending school.

school·house (sko͞ol′hous′) *n.* A building used as a school.

school·ing (sko͞o'lĭng) *n.* **1.** Formal instruction or training given at school. **2.** Training or instruction obtained through experience or exposure. **3.** The training of a horse or of a horse and rider in specific techniques.
school·ma'am (sko͞ol'mäm', -măm') *n.* Variant of **schoolmarm.**
school·man (sko͞ol'mən) *n.* **1.** Often **Schoolman.** A philosopher or theologian of a medieval university. **2.** A professional educator or scholar.
school·marm (sko͞ol'märm') also **school·ma'am** (-mäm', -măm') *n. Informal.* A female teacher, esp. one who is pedantic, old-fashioned, or prudish. [SCHOOL + dial. *marm,* var. of MA'AM.]
school·mas·ter (sko͞ol'măs'tər) *n.* **1.** A male teacher. **2.** A headmaster of a school. **3.** A reddish-brown food fish, the snapper *Lutjanus apodus,* of the tropical Atlantic and the Gulf of Mexico.
school·mate (sko͞ol'māt') *n.* A school companion or associate.
school·mis·tress (sko͞ol'mĭs'trĭs) *n.* **1.** A female teacher. **2.** A headmistress of a school.
school·room (sko͞ol'ro͞om', -ro͝om') *n.* A classroom.
school·teach·er (sko͞ol'tē'chər) *n.* A person who teaches in a school below the college level.
school·work (sko͞ol'wûrk') *n.* Lessons done at school or assigned as homework.
school year *n.* The period of the year that constitutes a complete annual session of school.
schoo·ner (sko͞o'nər) *n.* **1.** A ship with two or more masts, all of which are fore-and-aft-rigged. **2.** A large beer glass, generally holding a pint or more. **3.** A prairie schooner. [Orig. unknown.]
schorl (shôrl) *n.* Tourmaline, esp. black tourmaline. [G. *Schörl.*] **—schor·la'ceous** (shôr-lā'shəs) *adj.*
schot·tische (shŏt'ĭsh, shŏ-tēsh') *n.* **1.** A round dance in 2/4 time. **2.** Music for the schottische. [G. < *schottisch,* Scottish.]
schtick (shtĭk) *n.* Variant of **shtick.**
schuss (sho͝os, sho͞os) *intr.v.* **schussed, schuss·ing, schuss·es.** To make a fast straight run in skiing. *—n.* **1.** A straight, steep course for skiing. **2.** The act of schussing. [G. < OHG *scuz,* shot.]
schuss·boom·er (sho͝os'bo͞o'mər, sho͞os'-) *n.* One who schusses very proficiently.
schwa (shwä) *n.* **1.** A vowel sound that in English often occurs in an unstressed syllable, as the sound of *a* in *alone* or *e* in *linen.* **2.** The symbol ə often used to represent schwa. [G. < Heb. *shĕwā'.*]
Schwann cell (shwän) *n.* One of the cells of the neurilemma of a nerve fiber. [After Theodor *Schwann* (1810–1882).]
Schwarz·schild radius (shwôrts'chīld', shfärts'shĭld) *n.* The radius of a collapsing celestial object at which gravitational forces exceed the ability of matter and energy to escape, resulting in a black hole. [After Karl *Schwarzschild* (d. 1916).]
sci·at·ic (sī-ăt'ĭk) *adj.* **1.** Of or pertaining to the ischium. **2.** Of or pertaining to sciatica. [OFr. *sciatique* < LLat. *sciaticus* < Lat. *ischiadicus* < Gk. *iskhiadikos* < *iskhion,* hip.]
sci·at·i·ca (sī-ăt'ĭ-kə) *n.* **1.** Neuralgia of the sciatic nerve. **2.** Chronic neuralgic pain in the area of the hip or thigh. [ME < Med. Lat. < LLat., fem. of *sciaticus,* of the hip. —see SCIATIC.]
sciatic nerve *n.* A sensory and motor nerve originating in the sacral plexus and running through the pelvis and upper leg.
sci·ence (sī'əns) *n.* **1. a.** The observation, identification, description, experimental investigation, and theoretical explanation of natural phenomena. **b.** Such activity restricted to a class of natural phenomena. **c.** Such activity applied to any class of phenomena. **2.** Methodological activity, discipline, or study. **3.** An activity that appears to require study and method. **4.** Knowledge, esp. knowledge gained through experience. [ME, knowledge, learning < OFr. < Lat. *scientia* < *sciens,* pr.part. of *scire,* to know.]
science fiction *n.* Fiction in which actual or potential scientific discoveries and developments form part of the plot.
sci·en·tial (sī-ĕn'shəl) *adj.* **1.** Of or producing knowledge or science. **2.** Capable; skillful.
sci·en·tif·ic (sī'ən-tĭf'ĭk) *adj.* Of, relating to, or employing the methodology of science. [Med. Lat. *scientificus,* producing knowledge : Lat. *scientia,* knowledge + Lat. *facere,* to make.] **—sci'en·tif'i·cal·ly** *adv.*
scientific empiricism *n.* The philosophical view that there are no ultimate differences among the various sciences.
scientific method *n.* The totality of principles and processes regarded as characteristic of or necessary for scientific investigation, including rules for concept formation, conduct of observations and experiments, and validation of hypotheses by observations or experiments.
scientific notation *n.* A method of writing or displaying numbers in terms of powers of ten; for example, the number 10,492 would be represented as 1.0492×10^4.
sci·en·tism (sī'ən-tĭz'əm) *n.* The theory that investigational methods used in the natural sciences should be applied in all fields of inquiry. **—sci'en·tis'tic** *adj.*
sci·en·tist (sī'ən-tĭst) *n.* **1.** A person having expert knowledge of one or more sciences. **2. Scientist.** A Christian Scientist.
sci-fi (sī'fī') *n. Informal.* Science fiction.
scil·i·cet (sĭl'ĭ-sĕt', skē'lĭ-kĕt') *adv.* That is to say; namely. [Lat., contraction of *scire licet,* it is permitted to know.]
scim·i·tar (sĭm'ĭ-tər, -tär') *n.* A curved Oriental sword with a single edge on its convex side. [Ital. *scimitarra.*]
scin·til·la (sĭn-tĭl'ə) *n.* A minute amount; iota. [Lat., spark.]
scin·til·late (sĭn'tl-āt') *v.* **-lat·ed, -lat·ing, -lates.** *—intr.* **1.** To throw off sparks; flash. **2.** To sparkle or shine. **3.** To be animated and brilliant. *—tr.* To give off (sparks or flashes). [Lat. *scintillare, scintillat-* < *scintilla,* spark.] **—scin'til·lat'ing·ly** *adv.*
scin·til·la·tion (sĭn'tl-ā'shən) *n.* **1.** The action of scintillating. **2.** A spark; flash. **3.** *Astron.* Rapid variation in the light of a celestial body caused by turbulence in the earth's atmosphere; twinkling. **4.** *Physics.* A flash of light produced in certain media by absorption of an ionizing particle or photon.
scintillation counter *n.* A device for detecting and counting scintillations produced by ionizing radiation.
scin·ti·scan (sĭn'tĭ-skăn') *n.* A two-dimensional representation of radiation emitted from a radioisotope introduced into a bodily organ. [SCINTI(LLATION) + SCAN.]
sci·o·lism (sī'ə-lĭz'əm) *n.* A pretentious attitude of scholarship; superficial knowledgeability. [< Lat. *sciolus,* smatterer, dim. of *scius,* knowing < *scire,* to know.] **—sci'o·list** *n.* **—sci'o·lis'tic** *adj.*
sci·on (sī'ən) *n.* **1.** A descendant or heir. **2.** A detached shoot or twig containing buds from a woody plant, used in grafting. [ME < OFr. *cion,* of Germanic orig.]
sci·re fa·ci·as (sī'rē fā'shē-əs, fā'shəs) *n. Law.* **1.** A writ requiring the party against whom it is issued to appear and show cause why a judicial record should not be enforced, repealed, or annulled. **2.** A judicial proceeding under a scire facias. [< Lat., you should cause (him) to know, a phrase that occurs in the writ.]
sci·roc·co (shə-rŏk'ō, sə-) *n.* Variant of **sirocco.**
scir·rhus (skĭr'əs, sĭr'-) *n., pl.* **scir·rhi** (skĭr'ī', sĭr'ī') or **scir·rhus·es.** A hard cancerous growth usually associated with connective tissue. [NLat. < Gk. *skirrhos, skiros* < *skiros,* hard.] **—scir'rhous, scir'rhoid'** *adj.*
scis·sile (sĭs'əl, -īl') *adj.* Capable of being cut or split easily. [Fr. < Lat. *scissilis* < *scindere,* to cut.]
scis·sion (sĭzh'ən, sĭsh'-) *n.* The act of cutting or severing; division. [Fr. < LLat. *scissio* < Lat. *scindere,* to cut.]
scis·sor (sĭz'ər) *tr.v.* **-sored, -sor·ing, -sors.** To cut or clip with scissors or shears. *—n.* Scissors.
scis·sors (sĭz'ərz) *pl.n. (used with a sing. or pl. verb).* **1.** A cutting implement consisting of two blades joined by a swivel pin that allows the cutting edges to be opened and closed. **2.** A wrestling hold in which the legs are locked about the head or body of the opponent. **3.** Any of various gymnastic exercises or jumps in which the movement of the legs suggests the opening and closing of scissors. [ME *sisoures* < OFr. *cisoires* < Med. Lat. *cisoria,* pl. of LLat. *cisorium,* cutting instrument < Lat. *caedere,* to cut.]
scissors kick *n.* A swimming kick in which the legs are opened and closed like scissors.
scis·sor·tail (sĭz'ər-tāl') *n.* A bird, *Muscivora forficata,* of the southwestern United States, Mexico, and Central and South America, having a long, forked tail.
sclaff (sklăf) *v.* **sclaffed, sclaff·ing, sclaffs.** *—intr.* To scrape or strike the ground with a golf club behind the ball before hitting it. *—tr.* **1.** To hit (a golf club) against the ground before striking the ball. **2.** To strike (the ground) with a golf club before hitting the ball. *—n.* An act of sclaffing. [Sc., to strike with a flat surface.] **—sclaff'er** *n.*
scler– *pref.* Variant of **sclero-.**
scle·ra (sklîr'ə) *n.* The tough, white, fibrous outer envelope of tissue covering all of the eyeball except the cornea. [NLat. < Gk. *sklēros,* hard.] **—scle'ral** *adj.*
scler·e·id (sklĕr'ē-ĭd) *n.* A thick-walled lignified sclerenchyma cell. [SCLERE(NCHYMA) + -ID.]
scle·ren·chy·ma (sklə-rĕng'kə-mə) *n.* Supportive or protective plant tissue consisting of thick-walled, usually lignified cells. **—scle'ren·chym'a·tous** (sklîr'ən-kĭm'ə-təs, -kī'mə-) *adj.*
scle·rite (sklîr'īt') *n.* One of the hard outer plates forming part of the exoskeleton of an arthropod, esp. an insect.
scle·ri·tis (sklə-rī'tĭs) *n.* Inflammation of the sclera. **—scle·rit'ic** (-rĭt'ĭk) *adj.*
sclero– or **scler–** *pref.* **1.** Hard: *sclerite.* **2.** Hardness: *sclerometer.* **3.** Sclera: *scleritis.* [< Gk. *sklēros,* hard.]
scle·ro·der·ma (sklîr'ə-dûr'mə) *n.* Pathological thickening and hardening of the skin.
scle·ro·der·ma·tous (sklîr'ə-dûr'mə-təs) *adj.* **1.** Characterizing or afflicted with scleroderma. **2.** *Zool.* Having an outer covering of hard plates or bony scales.
scle·roid (sklîr'oid') *adj. Biol.* Hard or hardened; indurated.
scle·ro·ma (sklə-rō'mə) *n., pl.* **-ma·ta** (-mə-tə). An abnormally hard patch of bodily tissue. [NLat. < Gk. *sklērōma,* hardening < *sklēroun,* to harden < *sklēros,* hard.]
scle·rom·e·ter (sklə-rŏm'ĭ-tər) *n.* An instrument used to determine relative hardness by measurement of the pressure

schooner

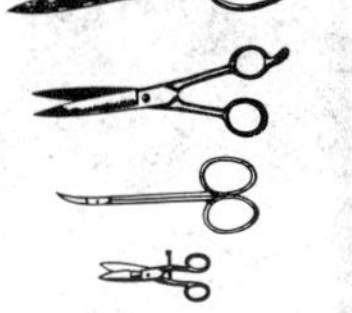

scissors
From top: Trimming scissors; barber scissors; manicure scissors; buttonhole scissors

scissortail

required on a standard diamond stylus to achieve penetration.
scle·ro·pro·tein (sklîr′ō-prō′tēn′, -tē-ĭn) *n.* Any of a large class of proteins found in skeletal and connective tissue.
scle·rosed (sklə-rōzd′, -rōst′) *adj.* **1.** Affected with sclerosis; hardened. **2.** Lignified. [< SCLEROSIS.]
scle·ro·sis (sklə-rō′sĭs) *n., pl.* **-ses** (-sēz′). **1. a.** A thickening or hardening of a body part, as of an artery, esp. from tissue overgrowth or disease. **b.** A disease characterized by sclerosis. **2.** *Bot.* The hardening of an outer cell wall by formation or deposit of lignin. [ME *sclirosis* < Med. Lat. < Gk. *sklērōsis* < *sklēroun,* to harden. —see SCLEROMA.]
scle·ro·ti·a (sklə-rō′shē-ə, -shə) *n.* Plural of **sclerotium.**
scle·rot·ic (sklə-rŏt′ĭk) *adj.* **1.** Affected with or marked by sclerosis. **2.** *Anat.* Of or pertaining to the sclera. —*n.* Sclera.
scle·ro·ti·um (sklə-rō′shē-əm, -shəm) *n., pl.* **-ti·a** (-shē-ə, -shə). A dense mass of branching filaments, or hyphae, in certain fungi, containing stored food and capable of remaining dormant for long periods. [NLat. < Gk. *sklērotēs,* hardness < *sklēros,* hard.]
scler·o·ti·za·tion (sklĕr′ə-tĭ-zā′shən) *n.* The process by which the cuticle of an insect is hardened by the cross linkage of chitin protein molecules. [Gk. *sklērotēs,* hardness (< *sklēros,* hard) + -IZATION.] **—scler′o·tized′** (sklĕr′ə-tīzd′) *adj.*
scle·rot·o·my (sklə-rŏt′ə-mē) *n., pl.* **-mies.** Surgical incision of the sclera.
scle·rous (sklîr′əs) *adj.* Hardened; toughened. [Gk. *sklēros,* hard.]
scoff (skŏf, skôf) *v.* **scoffed, scoff·ing, scoffs.** —*tr.* To mock at or treat with derision. —*intr.* To treat or express derisively; mock. —*n.* An expression of derision or scorn. [ME *scoffen* < *scof,* mockery, poss. of Scand. orig.] **—scoff′er** *n.* **—scoff′ing·ly** *adv.*
scoff·law (skŏf′lô′, skôf′-) *n.* A person who habitually violates the law or fails to answer court summonses.
scold (skōld) *v.* **scold·ed, scold·ing, scolds.** —*tr.* To reprimand or criticize harshly. —*intr.* To reprove or criticize openly. —*n.* A person who habitually scolds others. [ME *scolden,* to rail at < *scolde,* an abusive person, prob. of Scand. orig.] **—scold′er** *n.* **—scold′ing·ly** *adv.*

Synonyms: *scold, upbraid, berate, revile, nag, rail.* These verbs mean to express criticism or disfavor. *Scold* implies anger or irritation and the tone and manner of one correcting a child at fault. *Upbraid* is stronger and generally implies rather formal criticism, such as that made by an official or a superior. *Berate* suggests scolding or rebuking angrily and abusively at length. *Revile* especially stresses the idea of abusive language; usually it implies deliberate and prolonged verbal assault. *Nag* refers to complaining and faultfinding, usually prolonged and persistent. *Rail* also suggests persistent criticism but is much stronger through its implication of scorn and abuse.

scold·ing (skōl′dĭng) *n.* A harsh reprimand.
sco·lex (skō′lĕks′) *n., pl.* **-li·ces** (-lĭ-sēz′). The knoblike anterior end of a tapeworm, having suckers or hooklike parts that in the adult stage serve as organs of attachment to the host on which the tapeworm is parasitic. [NLat. < Gk. *skōlēx,* worm.]
sco·li·o·sis (skō′lē-ō′sĭs, skŏl′ē-) *n.* Abnormal lateral curvature of the spine. [Gk. *skolios,* crooked + -OSIS.] **—sco′li·ot′ic** (-ŏt′ĭk) *adj.*
scol·lop (skŏl′əp) *n.* & *v.* Variant of **scallop.**
scol·o·pen·drid (skŏl′ə-pĕn′drĭd) *n.* Any of numerous arthropods of the family Scolopendridae, which includes the centipedes. [NLat. *Scolopendridae,* family name < Lat. *scolopendra,* millipede < Gk. *skolopendra.*] **—scol′o·pen′drine′** (-drīn′, -drĭn) *adj.*
scom·broid (skŏm′broid′) *adj.* Of or belonging to the suborder Scombroidei, which includes marine fishes such as the mackerel. —*n.* A scombroid fish. [NLat. *Scombroidei,* suborder name < Lat. *scomber,* mackerel < Gk. *skombros.*]
sconce[1] (skŏns) *n.* A small defensive earthwork or fort. [Du. *schans* < G. *Schanze.*]
sconce[2] (skŏns) *n.* **1.** A decorative wall bracket for candles or lights. **2.** *Informal.* The head or skull. [ME < OFr. *esconse,* lantern, hiding place < Med. Lat. *sconsa* < Lat. *absconsus,* p.part. of *abscondere,* to hide away : *ab-,* away + *condere,* to hide.]
scone (skōn, skŏn) *n.* A small biscuitlike pastry or quickbread, sometimes baked on a griddle. [Perh. < Du. *schoonbrood,* fine white bread < MDu. *schoonbroot* : *schoon,* bright + *broot,* bread.]
scoop (sko͞op) *n.* **1. a.** A shovellike utensil, usually having a deep, curved dish and a short handle: *a flour scoop.* **b.** The amount a scoop holds. **2.** A ladle; dipper. **3. a.** A thick-handled utensil for dispensing balls of ice cream or other soft food, often having a sweeping band in the dish that is levered by the thumb to free the contents. **b.** A portion of food gathered with this utensil. **4.** An implement for bailing water from a boat. **5.** A narrow, spoon-shaped instrument for surgical extraction in cavities or cysts. **6.** The bucket or shovel of a steam shovel or dredge. **7.** A scooping movement or action. **8.** *Slang.* An exclusive news story acquired by luck or initiative. —*tr.v.* **scooped, scoop·ing, scoops. 1.** To take up or dip into with or as if with a scoop. **2.** To hollow out by digging. **3.** To gather or collect swiftly; grab: *scoop up a handful of jelly beans.* **4.** *Slang.* To top or outmaneuver (a competitor) in acquiring and publishing an important news story. [ME < MDu. *schope,* shovel.] **—scoop′er** *n.*
scoot (sko͞ot) *intr.v.* **scoot·ed, scoot·ing, scoots.** To go suddenly and speedily. [Prob. of Scand. orig.] **—scoot** *n.*
scoot·er (sko͞o′tər) *n.* **1.** A child's vehicle consisting of a long footboard between two small end wheels, controlled by an upright steering handle attached to the front wheel. **2.** A motor scooter. **3.** A flat-bottomed sailboat with runners that can skim over water or ice. [< SCOOT.]
scop (skŏp) *n.* An Anglo-Saxon bard or minstrel. [OE.]
scope (skōp, shōp) *n.* **1.** The range of one's perceptions, thoughts, or actions. **2.** Breadth or opportunity to function. **3.** The area covered by a given activity or subject. **4.** The length or sweep of a mooring cable. **5.** *Informal.* A viewing instrument such as a microscope, periscope, or telescope. [Ital. *scopo,* aim, purpose < Gk. *skopos,* target, aim.]
-scope *suff.* An instrument for viewing or observing: *bronchoscope.* [Lat. *-scopium* < Gk. *-skopion* < *skopein,* to see.]
sco·pol·a·mine (skō-pŏl′ə-mēn′, -mĭn) *n.* A thick, syrupy, colorless alkaloid, $C_{17}H_{21}NO_4$, extracted from such plants as henbane and used as a mydriatic, sedative, and truth serum. [G. *Scopolamin* : NLat. *Scopolia,* plant genus (after Giovanni *Scopoli,* 1723–1788) + G. *Amin,* amine.]
sco·po·line (skō′pə-lēn′, -lĭn) *n.* A crystalline alkaloid, $C_8H_{13}O_2N$, derived from scopolamine and used as a narcotic. [SCOPOL(AMINE) + -INE.]
scop·u·la (skŏp′yə-lə) *n., pl.* **-lae** (-lē′). A dense, brushlike tuft of hairs, as in certain insects. [LLat., dim. of Lat. *scopa,* twigs.] **—scop′u·late′** (-lāt′) *adj.*
-scopy *suff.* Viewing; seeing; observation: *microscopy.* [Gk. *-skopia* < *skopein,* to see.]
scor·bu·tic (skôr-byo͞o′tĭk) *adj.* Of, pertaining to, resembling, or afflicted with scurvy. [NLat. *scorbuticus* < LLat. *scorbutus,* scurvy, perh. of Germanic orig.] **—scor·bu′ti·cal·ly** *adv.*
scorch (skôrch) *v.* **scorched, scorch·ing, scorch·es.** —*tr.* **1.** To burn slightly so as to alter in color or taste. **2.** To wither or parch with intense heat. **3.** To subject to severe censure. —*intr.* To become scorched or singed. —*n.* **1.** A slight or surface burn. **2.** A discoloration caused by heat. **3.** Brown spotting on plant leaves caused by fungi, heat, or lack of water. [ME *scorchen,* prob. of Scand. orig.] **—scorch′ing·ly** *adv.*
scorched-earth policy (skôrcht′ûrth′) *n.* A military policy of devastating all land and buildings in the course of an advance or retreat so as to leave nothing salvageable to the enemy.
scorch·er (skôr′chər) *n.* **1.** One that scorches. **2.** *Informal.* An extremely hot day.
score (skôr, skōr) *n.* **1.** A notch or incision, esp. one made to keep a tally. **2.** A record, usually numerical, of a competitive event: *keeping score.* **3. a.** The total number of points made by each competitor or side in a contest, either final or at a given stage. **b.** The number of points attributed to a competitor or team. **4.** A result, usually expressed numerically, of a test or examination. **5. a.** An amount due; debt. **b.** A grievance that is harbored and requires satisfaction: *settle an old score.* **6.** A ground; reason. **7.** A group of 20 items. **8. scores.** Large numbers. **9.** The written form of a musical composition for orchestral or vocal parts, either complete or for a particular instrument or voice. **10.** The music composed for a stage show or film. **11.** *Informal.* **a.** The act of securing an advantage, esp. a surprising or significant gain. **b.** The act of buying illicit drugs. **c.** A successful robbery; heist. **d.** A sexual conquest. —*v.* **scored, scor·ing, scores.** —*tr.* **1.** To mark with lines or notches, esp. for the purpose of keeping a record. **2.** To cancel or eliminate by or as if by superimposing lines. **3.** To mark the surface of (meat, for example) with usually parallel cuts. **4. a.** To gain (a point) in a game or contest. **b.** To count or be worth as points. **5.** To achieve; win. **6.** To evaluate and assign a grade to. **7.** *Mus.* **a.** To orchestrate. **b.** To arrange for a specific instrument. **8.** To criticize cuttingly; berate. **9.** *Informal.* To succeed in acquiring: *scored two tickets to the play.* —*intr.* **1.** To make a point in a game or contest. **2.** To keep the score of a game or contest. **3.** *Informal.* **a.** To achieve a purpose or advantage, esp. to make a surprising gain or coup. **b.** To succeed in seducing someone sexually. [ME *scor* < OE **scoru* < ON *skor,* notch, twenty.] **—scor′er** *n.*
score·board (skôr′bôrd′, skōr′bōrd′) *n.* A large board for indicating the score of a game.
score·card (skôr′kärd′, skōr′-) *n.* **1.** A printed program or card enabling a spectator to identify players and record the progress of a game. **2.** A small card used, as in golf, to record one's own performance.
score·keep·er (skôr′kē′pər, skōr′-) *n.* An official who records the score throughout a game or competition.
score·less (skôr′lĭs, skōr′-) *adj.* Having no points scored.
sco·ri·a (skôr′ē-ə, skōr′-) *n., pl.* **sco·ri·ae** (skôr′ē-ē′, skōr′-). **1.** *Geol.* Rough fragments of burnt, crustlike lava. **2.** *Metallurgy.* The refuse of a smelted metal or ore; slag. [ME, dross < Lat. < Gk. *skōria* < *skōr,* excrement.] **—sco′ri·a′ceous** (skôr′ē-ā′shəs, skōr′-) *adj.*

sconce[2]
18th-century English

scoop

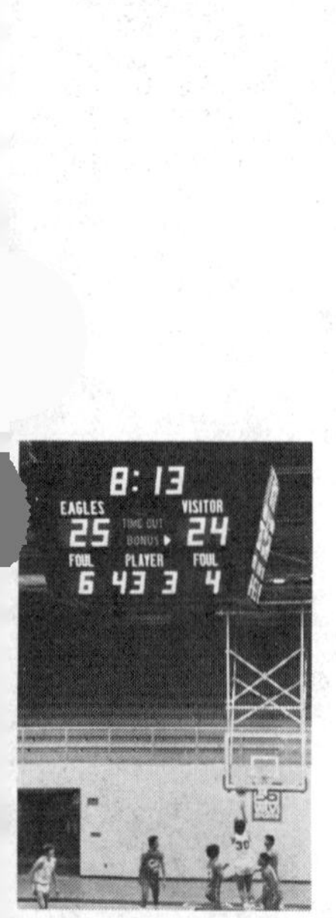

score

sco·ri·fy (skôr′ə-fī′, skōr′-) *tr.v.* **-fied, -fy·ing, -fies.** To separate (an ore) into scoria and a precious metal.

scorn (skôrn) *n.* **1. a.** Contempt or disdain felt toward a person or object considered despicable or inferior. **b.** The expression of such an attitude in behavior or speech; derision. **2.** One treated or spoken of with contempt. —*v.* **scorned, scorn·ing, scorns.** —*tr.* **1.** To consider or treat as contemptible or unworthy. **2.** To reject or refuse with derision. —*intr.* To express contempt; scoff. [ME *scorne* < OFr. *escarn,* of Germanic orig.] **—scorn′er** *n.* **—scorn′ful** *adj.* **—scorn′ful·ly** *adv.* **—scorn′ful·ness** *n.*

scor·pae·noid (skôr-pē′noid′) *adj.* Of or belonging to the suborder Scorpaenoidei, which includes the scorpion fishes and rockfishes. —*n.* A scorpaenoid fish. [NLat. *Scorpaenoidei,* suborder name < *Scorpaena,* type genus < Lat., a kind of fish < Gk. *skorpaina,* fem. of *skorpios,* a sea fish, scorpion.]

Scor·pi·o (skôr′pē-ō′) *n.* **1.** Variant of **Scorpius. 2.** The eighth sign of the zodiac. [Lat. < *scorpio,* scorpion.]

scor·pi·oid (skôr′pē-oid′) *adj.* **1.** Pertaining to or resembling a scorpion. **2.** *Bot.* Curved or curled like the tail of a scorpion: *a scorpioid inflorescence.* [Gk. *skorpioeides,* scorpionlike : *skorpios,* scorpion + *-eidēs,* -oid.]

scor·pi·on (skôr′pē-ən) *n.* **1.** Any of various arachnids of the order Scorpionida, of warm, dry regions, having a segmented body and an erectile tail tipped with a venomous sting. **2. Scorpion.** The constellation and sign of the zodiac Scorpius. [ME *scorpioun* < OFr. *scorpion* < Lat. *scorpio* < Gk. *skorpios.*]

scorpion fish *n.* Any of numerous small, often brilliantly colored marine fishes of the family Scorpaenidae, most species of which have poisonous spines in the dorsal fin.

scorpion fly *n.* An insect of the order Mecoptera, having in the male of most species a curved genital structure that resembles the sting of a scorpion.

Scor·pi·us (skôr′pē-əs) also **Scor·pi·o** (-pē-ō′) *n.* A constellation in the Southern Hemisphere near Libra and Sagittarius, containing the star Antares. [Lat. *scorpius, scorpio,* scorpion, Scorpius < Gk. *skorpios.*]

scot (skŏt) *n.* Money that is assessed or paid. [ME, tax, partly < ON *skot,* and partly < OFr. *escot,* of Germanic orig.]

Scot (skŏt) *n.* **1.** A native or inhabitant of Scotland. **2.** A member of the ancient Gaelic tribe that migrated to the northern part of Great Britain from Ireland in about the 6th century A.D. —See Usage note at **Scotsman.** [ME *Scottes,* Scotsmen < OE *Scottas,* Scotsmen, Irishmen < LLat. *Scotti.*]

scot and lot (skŏt) *n.* A municipal tax formerly levied in Great Britain on the members of a community in proportion to their ability to pay. **—*idiom.* pay scot and lot.** To pay in full.

scotch[1] (skŏch) *tr.v.* **scotched, scotch·ing, scotch·es. 1.** To cut or score. **2.** To injure so as to render harmless. **3.** To put an abrupt end to. —*n.* **1.** A surface cut or abrasion. **2.** A line drawn on the ground, such as one used in playing hopscotch. [ME *scocchen,* perh. < AN *escocher,* to notch : *es-* (intensive < Lat. *ex-*) + OFr. *coche,* notch.]

scotch[2] (skŏch) *tr.v.* **scotched, scotch·ing, scotch·es.** To block (a wheel, for example) with a prop to prevent rolling or slipping. —*n.* A block or wedge used as a prop behind or under an object likely to roll. [Orig. unknown.]

Scotch (skŏch) *n.* **1.** *(used with a pl. verb).* The people of Scotland. **2.** Scots. **3.** Scotch whisky. —*adj.* **1.** Of or pertaining to the people, language, or culture of Scotland. **2.** Tight with one's money; frugal. —See Usage note at **Scotsman.** [Contraction of SCOTTISH.]

Scotch-I·rish (skŏch′ī′rĭsh) *adj.* Of, relating to, or characteristic of the people of northern Ireland who are of Scottish descent, esp. those who emigrated to America.

Scotch·man (skŏch′mən) *n.* A Scot. —See Usage note at **Scotsman.**

Scotch terrier *n.* A Scottish terrier.

Scotch verdict *n.* **1.** *Law.* A verdict permissible in certain criminal cases indicating only that guilt is not proven. **2.** An inconclusive judgment or pronouncement.

Scotch whisky *n.* A whiskey distilled in Scotland from malted barley.

Scotch woodcock *n.* A savory dish consisting of scrambled eggs on toast with anchovies or anchovy paste.

sco·ter (skō′tər) *n.* Any of several dark-colored diving ducks of the genera *Oidemia* and *Melanitta,* of northern coastal areas. [Orig. unknown.]

scot-free (skŏt′frē′) *adj.* Free from obligation, punishment, or penalty.

scot·o·bi·ot·ic (skŏt′ō-bī-ŏt′ĭk) *adj.* Capable of thriving in darkness. [Gk. *skotos,* darkness + BIOTIC.]

sco·to·ma (skə-tō′mə) *n., pl.* **-mas** or **-ma·ta** (-mə-tə). An area of pathologically diminished vision within the visual field. [NLat. < Med. Lat., dim sight < Gk. *skotōma,* dizziness < *skotoun,* to darken < *skotos,* darkness.] **—sco·to′ma·tous** *adj.*

sco·to·pi·a (skə-tō′pē-ə) *n.* Ability to see in dim light; night-adaptive vision. [Gk. *skotos,* darkness + -OPIA.] **—sco·to′·pic** (-tō′pĭk, -tŏp′ĭk) *adj.*

Scots (skŏts) *adj.* Scottish. —*n.* The dialect of English used in Scotland. [ME *scottis,* var. of *scottisc,* Scottish.]

Scots·man (skŏts′mən) *n.* A Scot.

Usage: *Scotsman, Scot,* and *Scotchman* are all employed to designate one of the people of Scotland; *Scotchman* and *Scotch* are sometimes considered mildly offensive. *Scots* and (*the*) *Scotch* are the usual collective plural forms. Of the corresponding adjectives *Scottish* and *Scots* are generally preferred to *Scotch* in Scotland for general usage. But each has become an established form in certain well-known combinations, such as *Scotch broth, Scotch whisky, Scottish rite, Scots Guards. Scot* is not an adjective.

Scot·ti·cism (skŏt′ĭ-sĭz′əm) *n.* An idiom or other expression characteristic of Scottish English.

Scot·tie (skŏt′ē) *n.* **1.** A Scotsman. **2.** A Scottish terrier.

Scot·tish (skŏt′ĭsh) *adj.* Of or characteristic of Scotland, its people, or its language. —*n.* **1.** Scots. **2.** The people of Scotland. [ME *scottisc* < *Scottes,* Scots. —see SCOT.]

Scottish deerhound *n.* A deerhound.

Scottish Gaelic *n.* The Goidelic language of Scotland.

Scottish rite *n.* A ceremonial rite in a Masonic system.

Scottish terrier *n.* A terrier of a breed originating in Scotland, having a heavy-set body, short legs, a blunt muzzle, and a dark, wiry coat.

scoun·drel (skoun′drəl) *n.* A villain. [Orig. unknown.] **—scoun′drel·ly** *adj.*

scour[1] (skour) *v.* **scoured, scour·ing, scours.** —*tr.* **1. a.** To clean, polish, or wash by scrubbing vigorously. **b.** To remove by scrubbing. **2.** To remove dirt or grease from (cloth or fibers) by means of a detergent. **3.** To clean (wheat) before the milling process. **4.** To clear (an area) by freeing of weeds or other vegetation. **5.** To clear (a channel or pipe) by flushing. —*intr.* **1.** To scrub something in order to clean or polish it. **2.** To have diarrhea. Used of livestock. —*n.* **1.** A scouring action or effect. **2.** A place that has been scoured, as by flushing with water. **3.** A cleansing agent for wool. **4. scours** *(used with a sing. or pl. verb).* Diarrhea in livestock. [ME *scouren* < MDu. *scūren* < OFr. *escurer* < LLat. *excurare,* to clean out : *ex-,* out < Lat. + *curare,* to clean < Lat. *cura,* care.]

scour[2] (skour) *v.* **scoured, scour·ing, scours.** —*tr.* **1.** To range over (an area) quickly and energetically. **2.** To search through or over thoroughly. —*intr.* **1.** To range over or about an area, esp. in a search. **2.** To move swiftly; run. [ME *scouren,* prob. of Scand. orig.]

scour·er (skour′ər) *n.* One that scours.

scourge (skûrj) *n.* **1.** A whip used to inflict punishment. **2.** A means of inflicting severe suffering, vengeance, or punishment. **3.** A cause of widespread and dreaded affliction, such as pestilence or war. —*tr.v.* **scourged, scourg·ing, scourg·es. 1.** To flog. **2.** To chastise severely; excoriate. **3.** To ravage; devastate. [ME < AN *escorge* < OFr. *escorgier,* to whip < VLat. **excorrigiare* : Lat. *ex-* (intensive) + Lat. *corrigia,* thong.] **—scourg′er** *n.*

scouring rush *n.* Any of several species of horsetail, esp. *Equisetum hyemale,* having rough-ridged stems formerly used for scouring utensils.

scour·ings (skour′ĭngz) *pl.n.* **1.** The refuse that remains after scouring grain. **2.** Dregs; scum.

scouse (skous) *n.* Lobscouse. [Short for LOBSCOUSE.]

scout[1] (skout) *v.* **scout·ed, scout·ing, scouts.** —*tr.* **1.** To spy upon or explore carefully in order to obtain information; reconnoiter. **2.** To observe and evaluate (a talented person) for possible hiring. —*intr.* **1.** To search: *scout around for some gossip.* **2.** To search for talented persons: *He scouts for the Boston Celtics.* —*n.* **1. a.** A person, aircraft, or ship dispatched from a main body to gather information, esp. in preparation for military action. **b.** The action of reconnoitering. **2.** A watchman or sentinel. **3.** A person employed to discover and recruit persons with talent, as in sports or entertainment. **4. a.** A member of the Boy Scouts. **b.** A member of the Girl Scouts. **5.** *Chiefly Brit.* A student's servant at Oxford University. **6.** *Informal.* A fellow: *a good scout.* [< ME *scoute,* act of watching or spying < OFr. *escoute* < *escouter,* to listen < Lat. *auscultare.*] **—scout′er** *n.*

scout[2] (skout) *v.* **scout·ed, scout·ing, scouts.** —*tr.* To reject with disdain or derision. —*intr.* To scoff. [Of Scand. orig.]

scout·ing (skou′tĭng) *n.* Participation in the activities of the Boy Scouts or Girl Scouts.

scout·mas·ter (skout′măs′tər) *n.* The adult leader in charge of a troop of Boy Scouts.

scow (skou) *n.* A large flat-bottomed boat with square ends, used chiefly for transporting freight. [Du. *schouw.*]

scowl (skoul) *v.* **scowled, scowl·ing, scowls.** —*intr.* To wrinkle or contract the brow as an expression of anger or disapproval. —*tr.* To express with a scowl. —*n.* A look of anger or strong disapproval. [ME *scoulen,* of Scand. orig.] **—scowl′er** *n.* **—scowl′ing·ly** *adv.*

scrab·ble (skrăb′əl) *v.* **-bled, -bling, -bles.** —*intr.* **1.** To scrape or grope about frenetically with the hands. **2.** To climb with scrambling, disorderly haste. **3.** To make hasty, disordered markings; scribble. —*tr.* **1.** To make or obtain by scraping together hastily. **2.** To scribble on or over. —*n.* **1.** The act or an instance of scrabbling. **2.** A scribble. [MDu. *schrabbelen,* freq. of *schrabben,* to scrape.]

scrag (skrăg) *n.* **1.** A bony or scrawny person or animal. **2.** A piece of lean or bony meat, esp. a neck of mutton. **3.** *Slang.* The human neck. —*tr.v.* **scragged, scrag·ging,**

scorpion

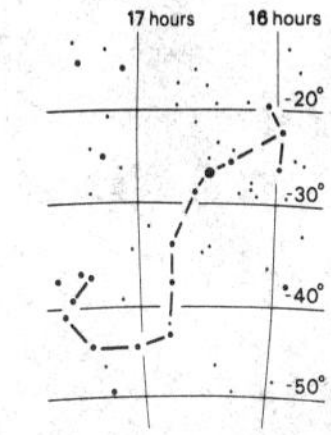

Scorpius

Scottish deerhound

Scottish terrier

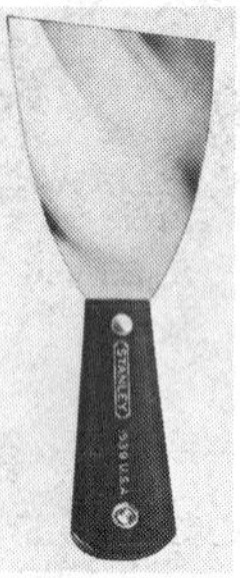

scrape
A scraper

screech owl

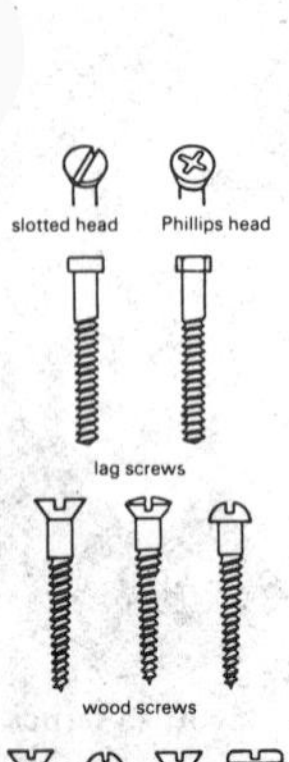

screw

scrags. *Informal.* To wring the neck of; strangle. [ME *cragge,* neck < MDu. *crāghe.*]

scrag·gly (skrăg′lē) *adj.* **-gli·er, -gli·est.** Ragged; unkempt. [< SCRAG.]

scrag·gy (skrăg′ē) *adj.* **-gi·er, -gi·est. 1.** Jagged; rough. **2.** Bony and lean. **—scrag′gi·ly** *adv.* **—scrag′gi·ness** *n.*

scram (skrăm) *intr.v.* **scrammed, scram·ming, scrams.** *Slang.* To leave at once. [Short for SCRAMBLE.]

scram·ble (skrăm′bəl) *v.* **-bled, -bling, -bles.** *—intr.* **1.** To move or climb hurriedly, esp. on the hands and knees. **2.** To struggle or contend frantically. **3.** To take off with all possible haste in order to intercept enemy aircraft. *—tr.* **1.** To mix or throw together haphazardly. **2.** To gather together in a hurried or disorderly fashion. **3.** *Electronics.* To distort or garble (a signal) so as to render it unintelligible without a special receiver. *—n.* **1.** The act or an instance of scrambling. **2.** An arduous hike or climb over rough terrain. **3.** An unceremonious scuffle or struggle. **4.** A swift takeoff of military aircraft in response to attack. [Perh. blend of obs. *scamble,* to struggle for, and *cramble,* to crawl.]

scrambled eggs *pl.n.* **1.** Eggs fried with the yolks and whites mixed together. **2.** *Slang.* The gold braid worn on the bill of the cap of a field grade officer in the armed services.

scram·bler (skrăm′blər) *n.* **1.** One that scrambles. **2.** An electronic device that scrambles telecommunication signals to make them unintelligible to an eavesdropper.

scram·jet (skrăm′jĕt′) *n.* A ramjet airplane engine that burns fuel in the supersonic airstream produced by the plane after reaching supersonic speeds by conventional means. [S(UPERSONIC) + C(OMBUSTION) + RAMJET.]

scrap¹ (skrăp) *n.* **1.** A small piece or bit; fragment. **2. scraps.** Leftover bits of food. **3.** Discarded waste material, esp. metal suitable for reprocessing. **4. scraps.** Crisp pieces of rendered animal fat; cracklings. *—tr.v.* **scrapped, scrap·ping, scraps. 1.** To break down into parts for disposal or salvage. **2.** To discard as worthless; junk. [ME < ON *skrap,* trifles.]

scrap² (skrăp) *Slang.* *—intr.v.* **scrapped, scrap·ping, scraps.** To fight, often with the fists. *—n.* A fight or scuffle. [Orig. unknown.] **—scrap′per** *n.*

scrap·book (skrăp′bo͝ok′) *n.* A book with blank pages for the mounting and preserving of pictures or other mementos.

scrape (skrāp) *v.* **scraped, scrap·ing, scrapes.** *—tr.* **1.** To rub (a surface) with considerable pressure. **2.** To draw (a hard or abrasive object) forcefully over a surface. **3.** To remove from a surface by or as if by rubbing. **4.** To abrade or smooth by rubbing with a sharp or rough instrument. **5.** To injure the surface of by rubbing against something rough or sharp. **6.** To amass or produce with difficulty: *scrape together some cash.* *—intr.* **1.** To come into sliding, abrasive contact. **2.** To rub or move with a harsh grating noise. **3.** To give forth a harsh grating noise. **4.** To practice petty economies; scrimp. **5.** To succeed or manage with difficulty: *scraped through by a narrow margin.* *—n.* **1.** The act of scraping. **2.** The sound of scraping. **3.** An abrasion on the skin. **4.** *Slang.* **a.** An embarrassing predicament. **b.** A fight; scuffle. [ME *scrapen* < ON *skrapa.*] **—scrap′er** *n.*

scrap heap *n.* **1.** A heap of scrapped metal. **2.** A place for discarding useless or worthless material.

scra·pie (skrā′pē, skrăp′ē) *n.* A usually fatal virus disease of sheep marked by progressive degeneration of the central nervous system. [< SCRAPE.]

scrap·ple (skrăp′əl) *n.* A mush of pork scraps and cornmeal that is allowed to set and is then sliced and fried. [Dim. of SCRAP¹.]

scrap·py¹ (skrăp′ē) *adj.* **-pi·er, -pi·est.** Composed of scraps; fragmentary. **—scrap′pi·ly** *adv.* **—scrap′pi·ness** *n.*

scrap·py² (skrăp′ē) *adj.* **-pi·er, -pi·est. 1.** Quarrelsome; contentious. **2.** Full of fighting spirit. **—scrap′pi·ly** *adv.* **—scrap′pi·ness** *n.*

scratch (skrăch) *v.* **scratched, scratch·ing, scratch·es.** *—tr.* **1.** To make a thin, shallow cut or mark on (a surface) with a sharp instrument. **2.** To use the nails or claws to dig or scrape at. **3.** To rub or scrape (the skin) to relieve itching. **4.** To scrape or strike on an abrasive surface. **5.** To write or draw hurriedly. **6.** To strike out or cancel (a word, for example) by or as if by drawing lines through. **7.** To withdraw (an entry) from a contest. *—intr.* **1.** To use the nails or claws to dig, scrape, or wound. **2.** To rub or scrape the skin to relieve itching. **3.** To make a harsh, scraping sound. **4.** To gather funds or produce a living with difficulty. **5.** To withdraw from a contest. **6.** To make a shot in billiards that results in a penalty, as when the cue ball falls into a pocket or jumps the cushion. *—n.* **1. a.** A linelike mark produced by scratching. **b.** A slight wound. **2.** A hasty scribble. **3.** A sound made by scratching. **4.** The starting line for a race. **5.** A contestant who has been withdrawn from the running. **6. a.** The act of scratching in billiards. **b.** A fluke or chance shot in billiards. **7.** Poultry feed. **8.** *Slang.* Money. *—adj.* **1.** Done by chance. **2.** Assembled at random; haphazard. **3.** *Sports.* Without a golf handicap. **—idioms. from scratch.** From the beginning. **up to scratch.** *Informal.* **1.** Meeting the requirements. **2.** In fit condition. [ME *scracchen,* prob. blend of *scratten,* to scratch, and *cracchen,* to scratch < MDu. *cratsen,* to scrape.] **—scratch′er** *n.*

scratch hit *n.* *Baseball.* A batted ball that is not squarely struck or cleanly fielded but is counted as a hit.

scratch line *n.* **1.** A starting line for a race. **2.** A line beyond which a contestant must not step.

scratch·pad (skrăch′păd′) *n.* A usually high-speed internal register used for temporary storage in a computer memory.

scratch sheet *n.* A dope sheet.

scratch test *n.* A test for allergy performed by scratching the skin and applying an allergen to the wound.

scratch·y (skrăch′ē) *adj.* **-i·er, -i·est. 1.** Marked by or consisting of scratches. **2.** Making a harsh, scratching noise. **3.** Irregular; rough. **4.** Harsh and irritating: *a scratchy fabric.* **—scratch′i·ly** *adv.* **—scratch′i·ness** *n.*

scrawl (skrôl) *v.* **scrawled, scrawl·ing, scrawls.** *—tr.* To write hastily or illegibly. *—intr.* To write in a sprawling, irregular manner. *—n.* Irregular, often illegible handwriting. [Perh. < obs. *scrawl,* to gesticulate.] **—scrawl′er** *n.* **—scrawl′y** *adj.*

scraw·ny (skrô′nē) *adj.* **-ni·er, -ni·est.** Gaunt and bony. [Orig. unknown.] **—scraw′ni·ness** *n.*

screak (skrēk) *intr.v.* **screaked, screak·ing, screaks.** To screech; shriek. *—n.* A screech. [ME *skricken* < ON *skrækja.*] **—screak′y** *adj.*

scream (skrēm) *v.* **screamed, scream·ing, screams.** *—intr.* **1.** To utter a long, loud, piercing cry, as of pain. **2.** To make a loud, piercing sound. **3.** To speak or write in a heated, hysterical manner. **4.** To have or produce a startling effect. *—tr.* To utter or say in or as if in a screaming voice. *—n.* **1.** A long, loud, piercing cry or sound. **2.** *Slang.* One that is hilariously or ridiculously funny. [ME *scremen,* perh. of Scand. orig.]

Synonyms: *scream, shriek, screech, yell.* These verbs mean to make a loud, piercing sound, usually vocal. *Scream* generally implies sudden, piercing, prolonged sound indicative of intense pain, anger, or surprise. *Shriek* differs principally in its rather stronger implication of shrillness, inarticulateness, and lack of control. *Screech* stresses shrill, raucous, rasping sound. Both *screech* and *shriek* chiefly express pain, terror, or anger, or they can apply to violent laughter. *Yell* suggests a vigorous outcry expressive of any of the emotional conditions mentioned in the foregoing but also, more specifically, of joy.

scream·er (skrē′mər) *n.* **1.** One that screams. **2.** *Slang.* A sensational headline. **3.** *Slang.* Something that evokes screams or laughter. **4.** Any of several large aquatic birds of the family Anhimidae, of South America, having a harsh, resonant call.

scree (skrē) *n.* **1.** Loose rock debris. **2.** A slope of scree at the base of a steep incline or cliff. [Prob. ult. < ON *skriða,* landslide.]

screech (skrēch) *v.* **screeched, screech·ing, screech·es.** *—intr.* **1.** To scream in a high-pitched, strident voice. **2.** To make a prolonged shrill, grating noise. *—tr.* To say or utter in or as if in a screeching voice. *—n.* A high-pitched, harsh, piercing cry; shriek. [ME *scrichen,* to screech < ON *skrækja.*] **—screech′er** *n.* **—screech′y** *adj.*

screech owl *n.* Any of various small owls of the genus *Otus,* esp. *O. asio,* of North America, having ear tufts and a quavering, whistlelike call.

screed (skrēd) *n.* **1.** A long, monotonous harangue or piece of writing. **2.** A strip of wood, plaster, or metal placed on a wall or pavement as a guide for the even application of plaster or concrete. [ME *screde,* fragment < OE *scrēade.*]

screen (skrēn) *n.* **1.** A movable device, as a panel, designed to divide, conceal, or protect. **2.** Something that serves to divide, conceal, or protect. **3. a.** A coarse sieve used for sifting out fine particles, as of sand, gravel, or coal. **b.** A system for appraising and selecting personnel. **4.** A window insertion of framed wire or plastic mesh used to keep out insects. **5.** The surface upon which a picture is projected for viewing. **6.** *Electronics.* The phosphorescent surface upon which the image is formed in a cathode-ray tube. **7.** *Printing.* A glass plate marked off with crossing lines, placed before the lens of a camera when photographing for halftone reproduction. *—tr.v.* **screened, screen·ing, screens. 1.** To provide with a screen: *screen a porch.* **2. a.** To conceal from view. **b.** To protect, guard, or shield. **3. a.** To separate or sift out by means of a sieve or screen. **b.** To examine systematically in order to determine suitability. **4.** To show or project (a motion picture, for example) on a screen. [ME *screne* < OFr. *escren* < MDu. *scherm,* shield.] **—screen′er** *n.*

screen·ing (skrē′nĭng) *n.* **1. screenings** *(used with a sing. or pl. verb).* Refuse, such as waste coal, separated out by a screen. **2.** The mesh material used to make door or window screens. **3.** A presentation of a motion picture.

screen·land (skrēn′lănd′) *n.* The motion-picture industry.

screen·play (skrēn′plā′) *n.* The script for a motion picture.

screen test *n.* A brief motion-picture sequence filmed to test the ability of an aspiring actor. **—screen′-test′** *v.* **(-test·ed, -test·ing, -tests).**

screen·writ·er (skrēn′rī′tər) *n.* A writer of screenplays.

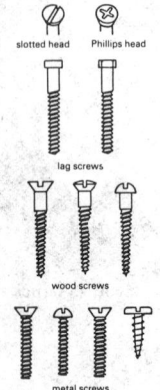

screw (skro͞o) *n.* **1. a.** A cylindrical rod incised with one or more helical or advancing spiral threads, as a lead screw or worm screw. **b.** The tapped collar or socket that receives this. **2.** A metal pin with incised threads and a broad slotted head that can be driven as a fastener by turning with a screwdriver, esp.: **a.** A tapered and pointed wood screw. **b.** A cylindrical and flat-tipped machine screw. **3.** A device having a helical form, as a corkscrew. **4.** A propeller. **5.** A twist or turn of or as if of a screw. **6.** *Vulgar Slang.* The act or an instance of having sexual intercourse. **7.** *Chiefly Brit. Slang.* Salary; wages. **8.** *Chiefly Brit.* A small paper packet, as of tobacco. **9.** *Chiefly Brit.* An old broken-down horse. **10.** *Chiefly Brit.* A stingy or crafty bargainer. **11.** *Slang.* **a.** A prison guard. **b.** The turnkey of a jail. *—v.* **screwed, screw·ing, screws.** *—tr.* **1.** To drive or tighten (a screw). **2. a.** To fasten, tighten, or attach by or as if by means of a screw. **b.** To attach (a tapped or threaded fitting or cap) by twisting into place. **c.** To rotate (a part) on a threaded axis. **3.** To contort (one's face). **4.** *Slang.* To take advantage of; cheat. **5.** *Vulgar Slang.* To have sexual intercourse with. *—intr.* **1.** To turn or twist. **2. a.** To become attached by means of screw threads. **b.** To be capable of such attachment. **3.** *Vulgar Slang.* To have sexual intercourse. ***—phrasal verb.*** **screw up.** *Slang.* To make a mess of (an undertaking). [ME *skrewe* < OFr. *escrove,* female screw, nut < Med. Lat. *scrofa* < Lat., sow.] **—screw'er** *n.*

screw·ball (skro͞o'bôl') *n.* **1.** *Baseball.* A pitched ball that curves in the direction opposite to that of a normal curve ball. **2.** *Slang.* An eccentric, impulsively whimsical, or irrational person.

screw bean *n.* **1.** A mesquite, *Prosopis pubescens,* of the southwestern United States, having compound leaves, tiny yellowish-white flowers, and twisted pods used as fodder. **2.** The pod of the screw bean.

screw cap *n.* A cap that screws onto the threaded mouth of a container.

screw·driv·er (skro͞o'drī'vər) *n.* **1.** A tool used for turning screws. **2.** A cocktail of vodka and orange juice.

screw eye *n.* A wood screw with an eyelet in place of a head.

screw jack *n.* A jackscrew.

screw pine *n.* The pandanus.

screw propeller *n.* A propeller.

screw thread *n.* **1.** The continuous helical groove on a screw or on the inner surface of a nut. **2.** One complete turn of a screw thread.

screw-up (skro͞o'ŭp') *n. Slang.* **1.** One who screws up. **2.** A blunder; mess.

screw·worm (skro͞o'wûrm') *n.* The larva of the screwworm fly.

screwworm fly *n.* A blue-green fly, *Cochliomyia hominivorax,* of the New World, that breeds in the living tissue of mammals, having penetrated chiefly through open wounds, and whose parasitic larvae cause serious injury or death to livestock.

screw·y (skro͞o'ē) *adj.* **-i·er, -i·est.** *Slang.* **1.** Eccentric; crazy. **2.** Ludicrously odd, unlikely, or inappropriate. **—screw'i·ness** *n.*

scrib·ble (skrĭb'əl) *v.* **-bled, -bling, -bles.** *—tr.* **1.** To write hurriedly without heed to legibility or style. **2.** To cover with scribbles, doodles, or meaningless marks. *—intr.* To write or draw in a hurried, careless way. *—n.* **1.** Careless, hurried writing. **2.** Meaningless marks and lines. [ME *scriblen* < Med. Lat. *scribillare,* freq. of Lat. *scribere,* to write.]

scrib·bler (skrĭb'lər) *n.* **1.** A person who scribbles. **2.** A very minor or disreputable author.

scribe (skrīb) *n.* **1.** A public clerk or secretary. **2.** A professional copyist of manuscripts and documents. **3.** A writer or journalist. **4.** A scriber. *—v.* **scribed, scrib·ing, scribes.** *—tr.* **1.** To mark with a scriber. **2.** To write or inscribe. *—intr.* To work as a scribe. [ME < Lat. *scriba* < *scribere,* to write.] **—scrib'al** *adj.*

scrib·er (skrī'bər) *n.* A sharply pointed tool used for marking lines, as on wood, metal, or ceramic.

scrim (skrĭm) *n.* **1.** A durable, loosely woven cotton or linen fabric used for curtains or upholstery lining or in industry. **2.** A transparent fabric used as a drop in the theater. [Orig. unknown.]

scrim·mage (skrĭm'ĭj) *n.* **1. a.** A rough-and-tumble struggle; tussle. **b.** A skirmish. **2.** *Football.* **a.** The contest between two teams from the time the ball is snapped back until it becomes out of play. **b.** A team's practice session. **3.** A Rugby scrummage. *—intr.v.* **-maged, -mag·ing, -mag·es.** *Football.* To engage in a scrimmage. [Obs. *scrimish,* alteration of SKIRMISH.]

scrimp (skrĭmp) *v.* **scrimped, scrimp·ing, scrimps.** *—intr.* To economize severely. *—tr.* **1.** To be excessively sparing with or of. **2.** To cut or make too small or scanty. [Perh. of Scand. orig.] **—scrimp'i·ness** *n.* **—scrimp'y** *adj.*

scrim·shaw (skrĭm'shô') *n.* **1.** The art of carving or incising intricate designs on whalebone or whale ivory. **2.** A decorative article made by scrimshaw. *—v.* **-shawed, -shaw·ing, -shaws.** *—tr.* To decorate (whale ivory or whalebone) with intricate carvings or designs. *—intr.* To make scrimshaw. [Orig. unknown.]

scrip[1] (skrĭp) *n.* **1.** A small scrap of paper, esp. a short list or schedule. **2.** Paper money issued for temporary emergency use. [Alteration of SCRIPT.]

scrip[2] (skrĭp) *n.* **1.** A provisional certificate entitling the holder to a fractional share of stock or of other jointly owned property. **2.** Scrip certificates collectively. [Short for *subscription receipt,* receipt for a portion of a loan.]

scrip[3] (skrĭp) *n. Archaic.* A wallet, small satchel, or bag. [ME *scrippe* < Med. Lat. *scrippa.*]

script (skrĭpt) *n.* **1. a.** Handwriting as distinguished from print. **b.** A style of writing with cursive characters. **c.** Alphabet. **2.** A printer's type that imitates handwriting. **3.** *Law.* An original document. **4.** The text of a play, broadcast, or motion picture. *—tr.v.* **script·ed, script·ing, scripts.** To prepare (a text) for filming. [ME *skript,* a piece of writing < OFr. *escript* < Lat. *scriptum,* neuter p.part. of *scribere,* to write.]

scrip·to·ri·um (skrĭp-tôr'ē-əm, -tōr'-) *n., pl.* **-to·ri·ums** or **-to·ri·a** (-tôr'ē-ə, -tōr'-). A room in a monastery set aside for the copying, writing, or illuminating of manuscripts and records. [Med. Lat. < Lat. *scriptus,* p.part. of *scribere,* to write.]

scrip·tur·al (skrĭp'chər-əl) *adj.* **1.** Of or pertaining to writing; written. **2. Scriptural.** Of, relating to, based upon, or contained in the Scriptures. **—scrip'tur·al·ly** *adv.*

Scrip·ture (skrĭp'chər) *n.* **1. a.** A sacred writing or book. **b.** A passage from such a writing or book. **2.** Often **Scriptures.** The Holy Scriptures. **3. scripture.** A statement regarded as authoritative. [ME < LLat. *scriptura* < Lat., act of writing < *scriptus,* p.part. of *scribere,* to write.]

script·writ·er (skrĭpt'rī'tər) *n.* A person who writes copy to be used by an announcer, performer, or director.

scriv·en·er (skrĭv'ə-nər, skrĭv'nər) *n. Archaic.* **1.** A scribe. **2.** A notary. [ME *scriveiner* < *scrivein* < OFr. *escrevein* < LLat. *scribanus* < Lat. *scriba,* scribe.]

scro·bic·u·late (skrō-bĭk'yə-lĭt, -lāt') *adj. Biol.* Marked with many shallow depressions, grooves, or pits. [< Lat. *scrobiculus,* dim. of *scrobis,* trench.]

scrod (skrŏd) *n.* A young cod or haddock, esp. one split and boned for cooking. [Poss. < obs. Du. *schrood,* shred.]

scrof·u·la (skrŏf'yə-lə) *n.* A constitutional condition affecting the tissues of the young and characterized by predisposition to tuberculosis, lymphatism, glandular swellings, and respiratory catarrhs. [Med. Lat. < Lat. *scrofulae* (pl.), swelling of the glands < *scrofa,* sow.]

scrof·u·lous (skrŏf'yə-ləs) *adj.* **1.** Pertaining to, affected with, or resembling scrofula. **2.** Morally degenerate; corrupt. **—scrof'u·lous·ly** *adv.* **—scrof'u·lous·ness** *n.*

scroll (skrōl) *n.* **1.** A roll, as of parchment or papyrus, used esp. for writing a document. **2. a.** *Archaic.* A piece of writing, as a letter. **b.** A list or schedule of names. **3.** An ornament or ornamental design that resembles a partially rolled scroll of paper. **4.** The curved head on an instrument of the violin family. [ME *scrowle,* alteration of *scrowe* < OFr. *escroue,* strip of parchment, of Germanic orig.]

scroll saw *n.* A hand or power saw with a narrow ribbonlike blade for cutting curved or irregular shapes.

scroll·work (skrōl'wûrk') *n.* Embellishment with a scroll motif, esp. ornamentation executed in wood with a scroll saw.

Scrooge (skro͞oj) *n.* A mean-spirited miser. [After Ebenezer *Scrooge,* a miserly character in *A Christmas Carol* by Charles Dickens (1812–1870).]

scro·tum (skrō'təm) *n., pl.* **-ta** (-tə) or **-tums.** The external sac of skin enclosing the testes in most mammals. [Lat.] **—scro'tal** (skrōt'l) *adj.*

scrounge (skrounj) *v.* **scrounged, scroung·ing, scroung·es.** *Slang.* *—tr.* **1.** To obtain by salvaging or foraging. **2.** To wheedle; cadge. *—intr.* **1.** To forage about in an effort to acquire something at no cost. **2.** To wheedle. [Alteration of dial. *scrunge,* to steal.] **—scroung'er** *n.*

scrub[1] (skrŭb) *v.* **scrubbed, scrub·bing, scrubs.** *—tr.* **1. a.** To rub hard in order to clean. **b.** To remove (dirt or stains) by such rubbing. **2.** To cleanse (a gas). **3.** *Slang.* To cancel; drop. *—intr.* To clean or wash something by hard rubbing. *—n.* An act of scrubbing. [ME *scrobben,* to currycomb a horse < MDu. *schrobben,* to clean by rubbing.]

scrub[2] (skrŭb) *n.* **1.** A straggly, stunted tree or shrub. **2.** A growth or tract of stunted vegetation. **3.** An undersized or poorly developed domestic animal. **4.** An undersized or insignificant person. **5.** *Sports.* A player not on the varsity or first team. [ME, prob. of Scand. orig.]

scrub·ber (skrŭb'ər) *n.* **1.** One that scrubs. **2.** An apparatus for removing impurities from a gas.

scrub·by (skrŭb'ē) *adj.* **-bi·er, -bi·est.** **1.** Covered with or consisting of scrub or underbrush. **2.** Straggly or stunted. **3.** Paltry; wretched. **—scrub'bi·ness** *n.*

scrub pine *n.* Any of several small, straggling pine trees, esp. *Pinus virginiana,* of the eastern United States, having prickly cones.

scrub typhus *n.* An acute infectious disease common in Asia, transmitted by a mite and characterized by sudden fever, painful swelling of the lymphatic glands, skin lesions, and skin rash.

scrub·wom·an (skrŭb'wo͝om'ən) *n.* A woman hired to clean; charwoman.

scruff (skrŭf) *n.* The back of the neck; nape. [Orig. unknown.]

scruf·fy (skrŭf'ē) *adj.* **-fi·er, -fi·est.** **1.** Shabby. **2.** *Chiefly Brit.* Scaly; scabby. [< obs. *scruff,* scurf.]

scrum (skrŭm) *Informal.* *—n.* A scrummage. *—intr.v.*

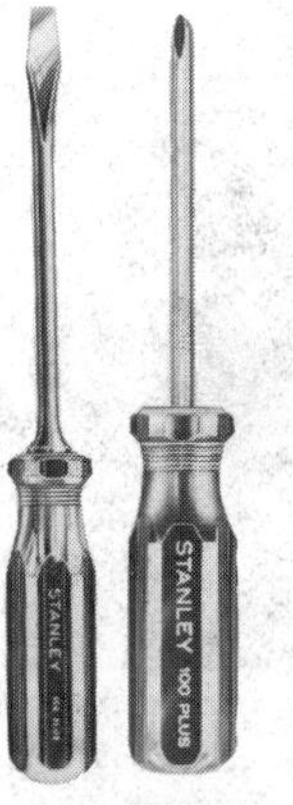

screwdriver
Square-bar standard (*left*) and Phillips (*right*)

scrimshaw

scuba diver

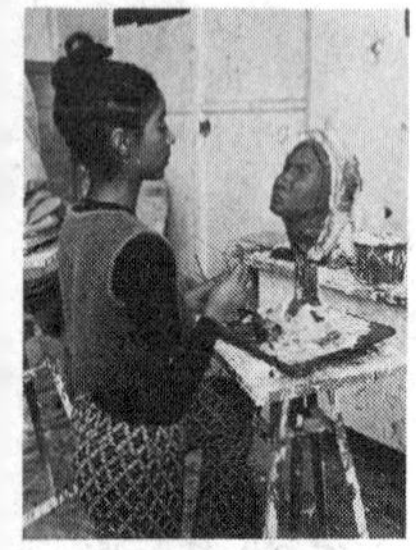
sculptress

scuttle[2]
Coal scuttle

scythe

scrummed, scrum·ming, scrums. To engage in a scrummage.
scrum·mage (skrŭm′ĭj) *n.* A Rugby formation in which the two sets of forwards mass together around the ball and, with their heads down, try to shoulder their opponents off the ball and kick it to their own team. —*intr.v.* **-maged, -mag·ing, -mag·es.** To engage in a scrummage. [Alteration of SCRIMMAGE.] —**scrum′mag·er** *n.*
scrump·tious (skrŭmp′shəs) *adj. Slang.* Splendid; delectable. [Perh. alteration of SUMPTUOUS.] —**scrump′tious·ly** *adv.*
scrunch (skrŭnch, skrŏŏnch) *v.* **scrunched, scrunch·ing, scrunch·es.** —*tr.* **1.** To crush or crunch. **2.** To hunch: *scrunched up his shoulders against the wind.* —*intr.* **1.** To hunch. **2.** To move with or make a crunching sound. —*n.* A crunching sound. [Alteration of CRUNCH.]
scru·ple (skrōō′pəl) *n.* **1.** An ethical objection that inhibits action. **2.** A unit of apothecary weight equal to about 1.3 grams, or 20 grains. **3.** A minute part or amount. —*intr.v.* **-pled, -pling, -ples.** To hesitate as a result of conscience or principle. [OFr. *scrupule* < Lat. *scrupulus,* small stone, scruple < *scrupus,* rough stone.]
scru·pu·lous (skrōō′pyə-ləs) *adj.* **1.** Having scruples; principled. **2.** Very conscientious and exacting. [ME < Lat. *scrupulosus* < *scrupulus,* scruple.] —**scru′pu·los′i·ty** (-lŏs′ĭ-tē), **scru′pu·lous·ness** *n.* —**scru′pu·lous·ly** *adv.*
scru·ta·ble (skrōō′tə-bəl) *adj.* Capable of being understood through study and observation; comprehensible. [Med. Lat. *scrutabilis,* searchable < Lat. *scrutari,* to search. —see SCRUTINY.]
scru·ti·nize (skrōōt′n-īz′) *tr.v.* **-nized, -niz·ing, -niz·es.** To examine or observe with great care; inspect critically. —**scru′ti·niz′er** *n.* —**scru′ti·niz′ing·ly** *adv.*
scru·ti·ny (skrōōt′n-ē) *n., pl.* **-nies. 1.** A close, careful examination or study. **2.** Close observation; surveillance. [Lat. *scrutinium* < *scrutari,* to search, examine < *scruta,* trash.]
scu·ba (skōō′bə, skyōō′-) *n.* An apparatus containing compressed air and used for breathing under water while swimming. [S(ELF) + C(ONTAINED) + U(NDERWATER) + B(REATHING) + A(PPARATUS).]
scuba diver *n.* One who uses scuba gear in underwater swimming.
scud (skŭd) *intr.v.* **scud·ded, scud·ding, scuds. 1.** To run or skim along swiftly and easily. **2.** *Naut.* To run before a gale with little or no sail set. —*n.* **1.** The act of scudding. **2. a.** Wind-driven clouds, mist, or rain. **b.** A sudden light shower. [Prob. of Scand. orig.]
scu·do (skōō′dō) *n., pl.* **-di** (-dē). A monetary unit and coin formerly used in Italy and Sicily. [Ital. < Lat. *scutum,* shield.]
scuff (skŭf) *v.* **scuffed, scuff·ing, scuffs.** —*intr.* To scrape the feet while walking; shuffle. —*tr.* **1.** To scrape with the feet. **2.** To shuffle or shift (the feet), as in embarrassment. **3.** To scrape and roughen the surface of. —*n.* **1.** The act or sound of scuffing. **2.** A worn or rough spot resulting from scuffing. **3.** A flat, backless house slipper. [Prob. of Scand. orig.]
scuf·fle[1] (skŭf′əl) *intr.v.* **-fled, -fling, -fles. 1.** To fight or struggle confusedly at close quarters. **2. a.** To shuffle. **b.** To scoot with shuffling steps. —*n.* A rough, disorderly struggle at close quarters. [Prob. of Scand. orig.] —**scuf′fler** *n.*
scuf·fle[2] (skŭf′əl) *n.* A hoe manipulated by pushing rather than pulling. [Du. *schoffel,* hoe for weeding.]
scull (skŭl) *n.* **1.** A long oar twisted from side to side over the stern of a boat to propel it. **2.** One of a pair of short-handled oars used by a single rower. **3.** A small, light racing boat for one, two, or four oarsmen. —*v.* **sculled, scull·ing, sculls.** —*tr.* To propel (a boat) with a scull. —*intr.* To use a scull to propel a boat. [ME *sculle.*] —**scull′er** *n.*
scul·ler·y (skŭl′ə-rē) *n., pl.* **-ies.** A room adjoining the kitchen for dishwashing and other kitchen chores. [ME < OFr. *escuelerie* < *escuelier,* keeper of dishes < *escuele,* dish < Lat. *scutella,* salver, dim. of *scutra,* platter.]
scul·lion (skŭl′yən) *n. Archaic.* A servant employed to do menial tasks in a kitchen. [ME *sculyon,* prob. < OFr. *escovillon,* dishcloth, dim. of *escouvee,* broom < Lat. *scopa.*]
scul·pin (skŭl′pĭn) *n., pl.* **-pins** or **sculpin. 1.** Any of various marine and freshwater fishes of the family Cottidae, having a large, flattened head and prominent spines. **2.** A scorpion fish, *Scorpaena guttata,* of California coastal waters. [Orig. unknown.]
sculpt (skŭlpt) *tr.v.* **sculpt·ed, sculpt·ing, sculpts.** To sculpture. [Fr. *sculpter, sculper* < Lat. *sculpere,* to carve.]
sculp·tor (skŭlp′tər) *n.* **1.** A person who produces sculptural artwork. **2. Sculptor.** A constellation in the Southern Hemisphere near Cetus and Phoenix. [Lat. < *sculptus,* p.part. of *sculpere,* to carve.]
sculp·tress (skŭlp′trĭs) *n.* A woman who sculptures.
sculp·ture (skŭlp′chər) *n.* **1.** The art or practice of shaping figures or designs in the round or in relief, as by chiseling marble, modeling clay, or casting in metal. **2. a.** A work of art created by sculpture. **b.** Such works collectively. **3.** Ridges, indentations, or other markings, as on a shell, formed by natural processes. —*tr.v.* **-tured, -tur·ing, -tures. 1.** To fashion into a three-dimensional figure. **2.** To represent in sculpture. **3.** To ornament with sculpture. **4.** To change the shape or contour of, as by erosion. [ME < Lat. *sculptura* < *sculptus,* p.part. of *sculpere,* to carve.] —**sculp′tur·al** *adj.* —**sculp′tur·al·ly** *adv.*
sculp·tur·esque (skŭlp′chə-rĕsk′) *adj.* Suggestive of or having the qualities of sculpture. —**sculp′tur·esque′ly** *adv.*
scum (skŭm) *n.* **1.** A filmy layer of extraneous or impure matter that forms on or rises to the surface of a liquid or body of water. **2.** The refuse or dross of molten metals. **3.** Refuse or worthless matter. —*v.* **scummed, scum·ming, scums.** —*tr.* To remove the scum from. —*intr.* To become covered with scum. [ME < MDu. *schūm.*] —**scum′mer** *n.*
scum·ble (skŭm′bəl) *tr.v.* **-bled, -bling, -bles.** To soften the colors or outlines of (a painting) by covering with a film of opaque or semiopaque color or by rubbing. —*n.* **1.** The effect produced by scumbling. **2.** Material used for scumbling. [Freq. of SCUM.]
scun·ner (skŭn′ər) *n.* A strong dislike; aversion. [ME *skunner.*]
scup (skŭp) *n., pl.* **scup** or **scups.** A food fish, *Stenotomus chrysops,* of western Atlantic waters, related to and resembling the porgies. [Narraganset *mishcùp.*]
scup·per (skŭp′ər) *n. Naut.* An opening in the side of a ship at deck level to allow water to run off. [ME *skopper.*]
scup·per·nong (skŭp′ər-nông′, -nŏng′) *n.* **1.** The muscadine grape, esp. a cultivated variety having sweet, yellowish fruit. **2.** A wine made from scuppernongs. [After the *Scuppernong* River, North Carolina.]
scurf (skûrf) *n.* **1.** Scaly or shredded dry skin, such as dandruff. **2.** A loose, scaly crust coating a surface, esp. of a plant. [ME, of Scand. orig.] —**scurf′i·ness** *n.* —**scurf′y** *adj.*
scur·rile also **scur·ril** (skûr′əl, skŭr′-) *adj. Archaic.* Scurrilous. [Fr. < Lat. *scurrilis,* jeering < *scurra,* buffoon.]
scur·ril·i·ty (skə-rĭl′ĭ-tē) *n., pl.* **-ties. 1.** The quality of being scurrilous. **2.** A scurrilous remark or passage.
scur·ri·lous (skûr′ə-ləs, skŭr′-) *adj.* **1.** Given to the use of vulgar or low abusive language; foul-mouthed. **2.** Expressed in coarse and abusive language. —**scur′ri·lous·ly** *adv.* —**scur′ri·lous·ness** *n.*
scur·ry (skûr′ē, skŭr′ē) *intr.v.* **-ried, -ry·ing, -ries. 1.** To go with light running steps; scamper. **2.** To flurry or swirl about. —*n., pl.* **-ries.** An act or noise of scurrying. [Prob. short for HURRY-SCURRY.]
scur·vy (skûr′vē) *n.* A disease caused by deficiency of vitamin C, characterized by spongy and bleeding gums, bleeding under the skin, and extreme weakness. —*adj.* **-vi·er, -vi·est. 1.** Mean; contemptible. **2.** *Obs.* Scurfy. [< SCURF.] —**scur′vi·ly** *adv.* —**scur′vi·ness** *n.*
scurvy grass *n.* A plant, *Cochlearia officinalis,* of northern regions, having bitter foliage and formerly used to cure scurvy.
scut (skŭt) *n.* A stubby erect tail, as that of a hare. [ME, hare.]
scu·tage (skyōō′tĭj) *n.* A feudal tax paid in lieu of military service. [ME < Med. Lat. *scutagium* < Lat. *scutum,* shield.]
scutch (skŭch) *tr.v.* **scutched, scutch·ing, scutch·es.** To separate the valuable fibers of (flax, for example) from the woody parts by beating. —*n.* An implement for scutching. [Obs. Fr. *escoucher* < OFr. *escousser* < VLat. **excussare,* freq. of Lat. *excutere,* to shake out : *ex-,* out + *quatere,* to shake.] —**scutch′er** *n.*
scutch·eon (skŭch′ən) *n.* **1.** Variant of **escutcheon. 2.** A shield-shaped object, such as a scute.
scutch grass *n.* Bermuda grass.
scu·ta (skyōō′tə) *n.* Plural of **scutum.**
scute (skyōōt) *n.* A horny, chitinous, or bony external plate or scale, such as one of those on the shell of a turtle. [Lat. *scutum,* shield.]
scu·tel·la (skyōō-tĕl′ə) *n.* Plural of **scutellum.**
scu·tel·late (skyōō-tĕl′ĭt, skyōōt′l-āt′) also **scu·tel·lat·ed** (skyōōt′l-ā′tĭd) *adj.* **1.** *Zool.* **a.** Covered with bony plates or scales. **b.** Having a scutellum. **2.** *Bot.* Shaped like a shield or platter.
scu·tel·la·tion (skyōōt′l-ā′shən) *n.* An arrangement or covering of scales, as on a bird's leg.
scu·tel·lum (skyōō-tĕl′əm) *n., pl.* **-tel·la** (-tĕl′ə). **1.** *Zool.* A shieldlike bony plate or scale, as on the thorax of some insects. **2.** *Bot.* Any of several shield-shaped structures, such as the cotyledon of a grass. [NLat., dim. of Lat. *scutum,* shield.] —**scu·tel′lar** *adj.*
scut·ter (skŭt′ər) *intr.v.* **-tered, -ter·ing, -ters.** *Chiefly Brit.* To bustle about; scuttle. [Alteration of SCUTTLE[3].]
scut·tle[1] (skŭt′l) *n.* **1.** A small opening or hatch with a movable lid in the deck or hull of a ship or in the roof or floor of a house. **2.** The lid or hatch of a scuttle. —*tr.v.* **-tled, -tling, -tles. 1. a.** To cut or open a hole or holes in (a ship's hull). **b.** To sink (a ship) by this means. **2.** *Informal.* To scrap; discard. [ME *skottell* < OFr. *escoutille.*]
scut·tle[2] (skŭt′l) *n.* **1.** A metal pail for carrying coal. **2.** A shallow open basket for carrying vegetables, flowers, or grain. [ME *scutel,* basket < OE, dish < Lat. *scutella.*]
scut·tle[3] (skŭt′l) *intr.v.* **-tled, -tling, -tles.** To run hastily; scurry. —*n.* A hurried run. [Prob. alteration of dial. *scuddle,* freq. of SCUD.]
scut·tle·butt (skŭt′l-bŭt′) *n.* **1.** A drinking fountain on a ship. **2.** *Archaic.* A cask on a ship used to hold the day's supply of drinking water. **3.** *Slang.* Gossip; rumor. [SCUTTLE[1] + BUTT[5].]

scu·tum (skyo͞o′təm) *n., pl.* **-ta** (-tə). *Zool.* A bony, calcareous, chitinous, or horny scale or plate, as on certain barnacles. [Lat., shield.]
scuz·zy (skŭz′ē) *adj.* **-zi·er, -zi·est.** *Slang.* Dirty; grimy. [Orig. unknown.]
Scyl·la (sĭl′ə) *n. Gk. Myth.* A female sea monster who devoured sailors. **—*idiom.* between Scylla and Charybdis.** In a spot where avoiding one danger exposes a person to another. [Lat. < Gk. *Skulla.*]
scy·phis·to·ma (sī-fĭs′tə-mə) *n., pl.* **-mae** (-mē) or **-mas.** A larva of a scyphozoan that produces free-swimming medusae. [NLat. : Gk. *skuphos,* cup + Gk. *stoma,* mouth.]
scy·pho·zo·an (sī′fə-zō′ən) *n.* Any of various marine coelenterates of the class Scyphozoa, including the jellyfishes, usually having a well-developed medusoid stage. [< NLat. *Scyphozoa,* class name : Gk. *skuphos,* cup + Gk. *zōia,* pl. of *zōion,* animal.]
scythe (sīth) *n.* An implement consisting of a long, curved single-edged blade with a long, bent handle, used for mowing or reaping. *—tr.v.* **scythed, scyth·ing, scythes.** To cut with a scythe. [ME *sithe* < OE *siðe.*]
Scyth·i·an (sĭth′ē-ən, sĭ*th*′-) *n.* **1.** A member of the ancient nomadic people inhabiting Scythia. **2.** The extinct Iranian language of the Scythians. *—adj.* Of or pertaining to the Scythians, their land, or their language.
Scyth·o-Dra·vid·i·an (sĭth′ō-drə-vĭd′ē-ən, sĭ*th*′-) *adj.* Of or pertaining to an ethnic group of northwestern India having mixed Iranian and Dravidian characteristics. [SCYTH(IAN) + DRAVIDIAN.]
Se The symbol for the element selenium.
sea (sē) *n.* **1. a.** The continuous body of salt water covering most of the earth's surface, esp. this body regarded as a geophysical entity distinct from earth and sky. **b.** A tract of water within an ocean. **c.** A relatively large body of salt water completely or partly landlocked. **d.** A body of fresh water. **2.** The condition of the ocean's surface with regard to its course, flow, swell, or turbulence: *a high sea.* **3.** Something that suggests the sea in its overwhelming sweep or vastness: *a sea of advancing troops.* **4.** Seafaring as a way of life. **5.** A lunar mare. **—*idiom.* at sea. 1.** On the open waters of the ocean. **2.** At a loss; perplexed. [ME *see* < OE *sǣ.*]
sea anchor *n. Naut.* A drag, usually a canvas-covered conical frame, floating behind a vessel to prevent drifting or to maintain a heading into the wind.
sea anemone *n.* Any of numerous flowerlike marine coelenterates of the class Anthozoa (or Actinozoa), having a flexible, cylindrical body and tentacles surrounding a central mouth.
sea bass *n.* Any of various marine food fishes of the genus *Centropristes* and related genera, esp. *C. striatus,* of coastal Atlantic waters of the United States.
sea·bed (sē′bĕd′) *n.* The bottom of a sea or ocean.
Sea·bee (sē′bē′) *n.* A member of one of the U.S. Navy's construction battalions for building naval aviation bases and facilities. [Alteration of *cee bee,* pronunciation of the initial letters of *construction battalion.*]
sea bird *n.* A bird, such as a petrel or albatross, that frequents the ocean, esp. far from shore.
sea biscuit *n.* Hardtack.
sea·board (sē′bôrd′, -bōrd′) *n.* **1.** A seacoast. **2.** The land near the sea.
sea·borne (sē′bôrn′, -bōrn′) *adj.* **1.** Conveyed by sea; transported by ship. **2.** Carried on or over the sea.
sea bread *n.* Hardtack.
sea bream *n.* Any of various marine food fishes of the family Sparidae, esp. *Archosargus rhomboidalis,* of western Atlantic coastal waters.
sea breeze *n.* A cool breeze blowing inland from the sea.
sea butterfly *n.* A pteropod.
sea captain *n.* The captain of a ship, esp. of a merchant ship.
sea change *n.* **1.** A change caused by the sea: *"Of his bones are coral made/ Those are pearls that were his eyes/ Nothing of him that doth fade/ But doth suffer a sea change"* (Shakespeare). **2.** A marked transformation: *"The script suffered considerable sea changes, particularly in structure"* (Harold Pinter).
sea·coast (sē′kōst′) *n.* Land bordering the sea.
sea coconut *n.* The double coconut.
sea cow *n.* Any of several marine mammals of the order Sirenia, such as a manatee or dugong.
sea cradle *n.* The chiton.
sea crayfish *n.* The spiny lobster.
sea cucumber *n.* Any of various cucumber-shaped echinoderms of the class Holothuroidea, having a flexible body with tentacles surrounding the mouth.
sea·dog (sē′dôg′, -dŏg′) *n.* A fogbow.
sea dog *n.* **1.** Any of various seals or similar marine mammals. **2.** A sailor with long experience of the sea.
sea duck *n.* Any of various diving ducks, such as the eider or scoter, of coastal areas.
sea duty *n.* Duty undertaken in the U.S. Navy outside the continental United States.
sea eagle *n.* Any of various fish-eating eagles or similar birds, such as the bald eagle or the osprey.
sea elephant *n.* The elephant seal.
sea fan *n.* Any of various yellowish to reddish fan-shaped corals of the genus *Gorgonia,* esp. *G. flabellum,* of coastal waters of Florida and the West Indies.
sea·far·er (sē′fâr′ər) *n.* A sailor or mariner.
sea·far·ing (sē′fâr′ĭng) *n.* A sailor's calling. *—adj.* Following a life at sea.
sea feather *n.* Any of several anthozoans of the family Pennatulidae, having a featherlike shape.
sea·floor (sē′flôr′, -flōr′) *n.* Seabed.
sea·food (sē′fo͞od′) *n.* Edible fish or shellfish from the sea.
sea·fowl (sē′foul′) *n.* **1.** A sea bird. **2.** Sea birds collectively.
sea front *n.* A strip of land at the very edge of the sea, esp. land desirable for a resort.
sea·girt (sē′gûrt′) *adj.* Surrounded by the sea.
sea·go·ing (sē′gō′ĭng) *adj.* **1.** Made or used for ocean voyages. **2.** Seafaring.
sea gooseberry *n.* A marine organism of the genus *Pleurobrachia,* having two tentacles and a round, iridescent body.
sea grant college *n.* A state college or university that receives government grants for oceanographic research.
sea grape *n.* A tropical American shrub or small tree, *Coccolobis uvifera,* of sandy beaches, having broad, rounded leaves and hard, purplish fruit in grapelike clusters.
sea green *n.* **1.** A medium green or bluish green. **2.** A medium yellow green.
sea gull *n.* A gull, esp. one appearing near coastal areas.
sea holly *n.* An Old World plant, *Eryngium maritimum,* growing on seashores and having prickly leaves and clusters of blue or purplish flowers.
sea horse *n.* **1.** A small marine fish of the genus *Hippocampus,* characteristically swimming in an upright position and having a prehensile tail, a horselike head, and a body covered with bony plates. **2.** A walrus. **3.** A mythical animal, half fish and half horse, ridden by Neptune and other sea gods. **4.** A large white-capped wave.
Sea Island cotton *n.* A species of cotton, *Gossypium barbadense,* native to tropical America and widely cultivated for its fine, long-staple fibers. [After the *Sea Islands,* an island chain off the coasts of South Carolina, Georgia, and Florida.]
sea kale *n.* A European plant, *Crambe maritima,* having edible, cabbagelike leaves.
sea king *n.* A Viking pirate chief of the early Middle Ages.
seal¹ (sēl) *n.* **1. a.** A die or signet having a raised or incised emblem used to stamp an impression upon a receptive substance such as wax or lead. **b.** The impression made. **c.** The design or emblem itself, belonging exclusively to the user: *the king's seal.* **d.** A small disk or wafer of wax, lead, or paper bearing such an imprint and affixed to a document to prove authenticity or to secure it. **2.** Something, as a commercial hallmark, that serves to authenticate, confirm, or attest. **3.** An adhesive agent, as wax or putty, used to close or secure something or to prevent seepage of moisture or air. **4.** A device or fluid in a drainpipe that prevents the upward passage of gas. **5.** An airtight closure. **6.** A small decorative paper sticker: *a Christmas seal.* *—tr.v.* **sealed, seal·ing, seals. 1.** To affix a seal to in order to prove authenticity or attest to accuracy, legal weight, quality, or another standard. **2. a.** To close with or as if with a seal. **b.** To close hermetically. **c.** To make fast or fill up, as with plaster or cement. **3.** To grant, certify, or designate under seal or authority. **4.** To establish or determine irrevocably: *His fate was sealed.* **5.** *Mormon Ch.* To make (a marriage, for example) binding for life; solemnize forever. **—*phrasal verb.* seal off.** To close tightly. [ME *seel* < OFr. < Lat. *sigillum,* dim. of *signum,* sign.] **—seal′a·ble** *adj.*
seal² (sēl) *n.* **1.** Any of various aquatic, carnivorous mammals of the families Phocidae and Otariidae, having a sleek, torpedo-shaped body and limbs that are modified into paddlelike flippers. **2.** The pelt or fur of a seal, esp. a fur seal. **3.** Leather made from the hide of a seal. *—intr.v.* **sealed, seal·ing, seals.** To hunt seals. [ME *seel* < OE *seolh.*]
sea lamprey *n.* A large marine lamprey, *Petromyzon marinus,* that is common in the Great Lakes and is parasitic to freshwater fish.
sea-lane (sē′lān′) *n.* A permanent or commonly used sea route.
seal·ant (sē′lənt) *n.* A sealing agent.
sea lavender *n.* Any of several salt-marsh plants of the genus *Limonium,* having clusters of small lavender or pinkish flowers.
sea legs *pl.n. Informal.* The ability to walk on board ship with steadiness, esp. in rough seas.
seal·er¹ (sē′lər) *n.* **1.** One that seals. **2.** An undercoat of paint or varnish used to size a surface. **3.** An officer who inspects, tests, and certifies weights and measures.
seal·er² (sē′lər) *n.* One that is engaged in seal hunting.
seal·er·y (sē′lə-rē) *n., pl.* **-ies. 1.** The occupation of hunting seals. **2.** A place where seals are hunted.
sea lettuce *n.* Any of several green seaweeds of the genus *Ulva,* having thin, leaflike, irregularly shaped fronds sometimes used as food.
sea level *n.* The level of the ocean's surface, esp. the mean level halfway between high and low tide, used as a standard in reckoning land elevation or sea depths.
sea lily *n.* Any of various marine crinoids, usually anchored

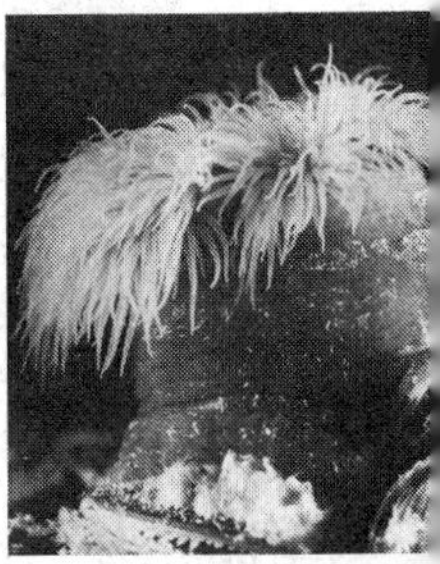
sea anemone

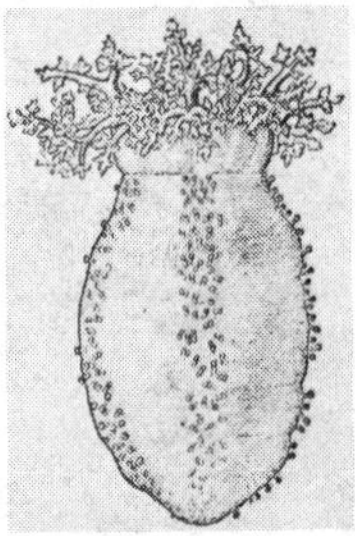
sea cucumber

sea gull

sea horse

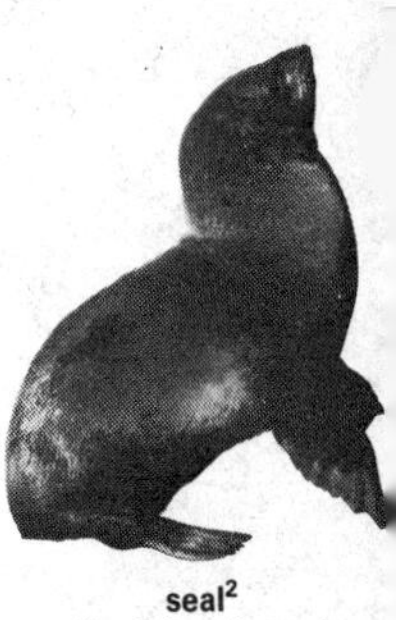
seal²
Guadalupe fur seal

to the ocean floor in deep water, having a flowerlike body supported by a long stalk.

sea lion
Zalophus californianus

sealing wax *n.* A resinous preparation of shellac and turpentine that is soft and fluid when heated but solidifies upon cooling, used to seal letters, batteries, or jars.

sea lion *n.* Any of several seals of the family Otariidae, having small but distinct external ears, esp. *Zalophus californianus,* of the Northern Pacific.

seal ring *n.* A signet ring.

seal·skin (sēl′skĭn′) *n.* **1.** The pelt or fur of a fur seal, esp. the underfur. **2.** A coat or other garment made of sealskin.

Sea·ly·ham terrier (sē′lē-hăm′, -lē-əm) *n.* A terrier of a breed developed in Wales, having a wiry white coat, a long head, and short legs. [After *Sealyham,* Wales.]

seam (sēm) *n.* **1. a.** A line of junction formed by sewing together two pieces of material along their margins. **b.** A similar line, ridge, or groove made by fitting, joining, or lapping together two sections along their edges. **c.** A suture. **d.** A scar. **2.** A line across a surface, as a crack, fissure, or wrinkle. **3.** A thin layer or stratum, as of coal or rock. —*v.* **seamed, seam·ing, seams.** —*tr.* **1.** To put together with or as if with a seam. **2.** To mark with a groove, wrinkle, scar, or other seamlike line. **3.** To form ridges in by purling. —*intr.* **1.** To crack open; become fissured or furrowed. **2.** To purl. [ME *seem* < OE *sēam.*] —**seam′er** *n.*

sea-maid·en (sē′mād′n) also **sea-maid** (-mād′) *n.* A mermaid or a sea nymph.

sea otter

sea·man (sē′mən) *n.* **1.** A mariner or sailor. **2.** An enlisted man in the U.S. Navy or Coast Guard ranking above seaman apprentice and below petty officer.

seaman apprentice *n.* An enlisted man in the U.S. Navy or Coast Guard ranking above a seaman recruit and below a seaman.

seaman recruit *n.* An enlisted man of the lowest rank in the U.S. Navy or Coast Guard.

sea·man·ship (sē′mən-shĭp′) *n.* Skill in managing or navigating a boat or ship.

sea·mark (sē′märk′) *n.* **1.** A landmark visible from the sea, used as a guide in navigation. **2.** The mark along a coastline indicating the upper tidal limits.

sea mew *n.* Any of various gulls frequenting coastal areas, esp. *Larus canus,* of Europe.

sea mile *n.* A nautical mile.

sea milkwort *n.* A fleshy plant, *Glaux maritima,* of shores and brackish marshes, having pink or white flowers.

seam·less (sēm′lĭs) *adj.* **1.** Without seams. **2.** Perfectly consistent. —**seam′less·ness** *n.*

sea·mount (sē′mount′) *n.* A submarine mountain rising to more than 3,000 feet above the ocean floor but having a summit at least 1,000 feet below sea level.

sea mouse *n.* Any of various segmented marine worms of the genus *Aphrodite,* esp. *A. aculeata,* having a flattened elliptical body with overlapping scales covered by long hairs.

seam·ster (sēm′stər) *n.* A tailor. [ME *semester* < OE *sēamestre* < *sēam,* seam.]

seam·stress (sēm′strĭs) *n.* A woman who sews, esp. one who makes her living by sewing.

sea robin

seam·y (sē′mē) *adj.* **-i·er, -i·est. 1.** Having, marked with, or showing a seam. **2.** Sordid; base: *the seamy side of life.* —**seam′i·ness** *n.*

sé·ance (sā′äns′, -äɴs′) *n.* **1.** A meeting of persons to receive spiritualistic messages. **2.** A meeting, session, or sitting. [Fr. < OFr., a sitting < *seoir,* to sit < Lat. *sedēre.*]

sea oats *pl.n.* (*used with a sing. or pl. verb*). A tall grass, *Uniola panicolata,* common along the coast of the southern United States.

sea onion *n.* **1.** A plant, *Urginea maritima,* of the Mediterranean area, cultivated for its bulb that yields a powder used medicinally and as a rat poison. **2.** A small European bulbous plant, *Scilla verna,* having fragrant blue flowers.

sea otter *n.* A large, nearly extinct marine otter, *Enhydra lutris,* of northern Pacific coasts, having a soft dark-brown coat valued as fur.

sea pen *n.* Any of various marine anthozoans of the families Stylatulidae and Funiculinidae, resembling and related to the sea feathers. [From its resemblance to a quill pen.]

sea·plane (sē′plān′) *n.* An aircraft equipped with floats for landing on or taking off from a body of water.

sea·port (sē′pôrt′, -pōrt′) *n.* A harbor or town having facilities for seagoing ships.

sea power *n.* **1.** A nation having significant naval strength. **2.** Naval strength.

sea purse *n.* The purse-shaped egg case of skates or of certain sharks.

sea·quake (sē′kwāk′) *n.* An earthquake under the sea floor.

sear[1] (sîr) *v.* **seared, sear·ing, sears.** —*tr.* **1.** To cause to wither or dry up. **2.** To char, scorch, or burn the surface of with or as if with a hot instrument. —*intr.* To become withered or dried up. —*n.* A condition, as a scar, produced by searing. [ME *seren* < OE *sēarian* < *sēar,* withered.]

sear[2] (sîr) *n.* The catch in a gunlock that keeps the hammer halfcocked or fully cocked. [Prob. < OFr. *serre,* lock < *serrer,* to grasp < LLat. *serare,* to bolt < Lat. *sera,* bar, bolt.]

sear[3] (sîr) *adj.* Variant of **sere[1]**.

sea raven *n.* A large sculpin, *Hemitripterus americanus,* of the western Atlantic.

search (sûrch) *v.* **searched, search·ing, search·es.** —*tr.* **1.** To make a thorough examination of or look over carefully in order to find something; explore. **2.** To make a careful examination or investigation of; probe: *search one's conscience.* **3.** To make a thorough check of (a legal document); scrutinize: *search a title.* **4. a.** To examine in order to find something lost or concealed. **b.** To examine the person or personal effects of in order to find something lost or concealed. **5.** To come to know; learn. —*intr.* To conduct a thorough investigation; seek: *searching for clues.* —*n.* **1.** An act of searching. **2.** The exercise of right of search. [ME *serchen* < OFr. *cerchier* < LLat. *circare,* to go around < Lat. *circus,* circle.] —**search′a·ble** *adj.* —**search′er** *n.*

search·ing (sûr′chĭng) *adj.* **1.** Examining closely or thoroughly: *a searching investigation of their stock-market dealings.* **2.** Keenly observant: *searching insights.*

search·less (sûrch′lĭs) *adj.* Mysterious; impenetrable.

search·light (sûrch′līt′) *n.* **1. a.** An apparatus containing a light source and a reflector for projecting a bright beam of approximately parallel rays of light. **b.** The beam of light so projected. **2.** A flashlight.

search warrant *n.* A warrant giving legal authorization for a search.

sea robin *n.* Any of various marine fishes of the family Triglidae, having a bony head and extremely long pectoral fins with fingerlike rays.

sea room *n.* Space at sea adequate for maneuvering a ship.

sea·scape (sē′skāp′) *n.* A view or picture of the sea.

Sea Scout *n.* A member of a program designed to train Boy Scouts in seamanship.

sea serpent *n.* A large snakelike marine animal often reported by mariners since antiquity but never positively identified.

sea·shell (sē′shĕl′) *n.* The calcareous shell of a marine mollusk or similar marine organism.

sea·shore (sē′shôr′, -shōr′) *n.* **1.** Land by the sea. **2.** *Law.* Ground lying between high-water and low-water marks; foreshore.

sea·sick·ness (sē′sĭk′nĭs) *n.* Nausea and other malaise provoked by the motion of a vessel at sea. —**sea′sick′** *adj.*

sea·side (sē′sīd′) *n.* The seashore.

sea slug *n.* Any of various shell-less marine gastropods of the suborder Nudibranchia, having a colorful body with fringelike projections.

sea snake *n.* Any of various venomous tropical marine snakes of the family Hydrophidae, chiefly of the Pacific and Indian oceans.

sea·son (sē′zən) *n.* **1. a.** One of the four natural divisions of the year, spring, summer, autumn, and winter, indicated by the passage of the sun through an equinox or solstice and derived from the apparent north-south movement of the sun caused by the fixed direction of the earth's axis in solar orbit. **b.** The two divisions of the year, rainy and dry, in tropical climates. **2.** A recurrent period that is characterized by certain occupations, festivities, or crops. **3.** A suitable, natural, or convenient time. **4.** A period of time. —*v.* **-soned, -son·ing, -sons.** —*tr.* **1.** To improve or enhance the flavor of (food) by adding salt, spices, herbs, or other flavorings. **2.** To add zest, piquancy, or interest to: *seasoned his lectures with jokes.* **3.** To dry (lumber) until it is usable; cure. **4.** To render competent through trial and experience. **5.** To accustom; inure. **6.** To moderate; temper. —*intr.* To become usable, competent, or tempered. —***idioms.* in season. 1.** Available or ready for eating or other use. **2.** Legally available to the hunter, fisherman, or trapper. **3.** At the right moment; opportunely. **4.** In heat. Used of animals. **out of season. 1.** Not available or ready for eating or hunting. **2.** Not at the right or proper moment; inopportunely. [ME *sesoun* < OFr. *seson* < Lat. *satio,* act of sowing < *satus,* p.part. of *serere,* to plant.]

sea·son·a·ble (sē′zə-nə-bəl, sēz′nə-) *adj.* **1.** In keeping with the time or the season. **2.** Occurring or performed at the proper time; timely. —See Usage note at **seasonal.** —**sea′son·a·bly** *adv.*

sea·son·al (sē′zə-nəl, sēz′nəl) *adj.* Of or dependent upon a particular season. —**sea′son·al·ly** *adv.*

Usage: *Seasonal* and *seasonable,* though closely related, are differentiated in usage. *Seasonal* applies to what depends on or is controlled by the season of the year: *a seasonal rise in employment. Seasonable* applies to what is appropriate to the season (*seasonable clothing*) or timely (*a seasonable intervention in the dispute*). Rains are *seasonal* if they occur at a certain time of the year. They are *seasonable* at any time if they save the crops.

sea·son·er (sē′zə-nər, sēz′nər) *n.* **1.** One that uses seasonings. **2.** Seasoning.

sea·son·ing (sē′zə-nĭng, sēz′nĭng) *n.* **1.** Something, as a spice or herb, used to flavor food. **2.** The act or process by which something is seasoned.

season ticket *n.* A ticket valid for a specified period of time.

sea spider *n.* Any of various marine arachnids of the class Pycnogonida, having long legs and a relatively small body.

sea squirt *n.* Any of various sedentary marine animals of the class Ascidiacea, having a transparent, sac-shaped body with two siphons. [From its habit of squirting water when disturbed.]

sea·strand (sē′strănd′) *n.* A seashore.

seat (sēt) *n.* **1.** Something that may be sat upon, as a chair or bench. **2.** A place in which one may sit. **3.** The part of something on which one rests in sitting: *a bicycle seat.* **4. a.** The buttocks. **b.** That part of a garment covering the buttocks. **5. a.** A part serving as the base of something. **b.** The surface or part upon which another part sits or rests. **6. a.** The place where something is located or based. **b.** A center of authority; capital: *the county seat.* **7.** A place of abode or residence, esp. a large house that is part of an estate. **8.** Membership in a legislative body, stock exchange, or other organization, obtained by purchase, appointment, or election. **9.** The manner of sitting on a horse. —*tr.v.* **seat·ed, seat·ing, seats. 1. a.** To place in or on a seat. **b.** To cause or assist to sit down: *seat an elderly woman.* **2.** To provide with a particular seat. **3.** To have or provide seats for: *We can seat 300 in the auditorium.* **4.** To install in a position of authority or eminence. **5.** To fix firmly in place. [ME *sete* < ON *sæti.*]

sea tangle *n.* Any of various brown seaweeds, esp. of the genus *Laminaria.*

seat belt *n.* A safety strap or harness designed to hold a person securely in a seat, as in an automobile or aircraft.

seat·ing (sē′tĭng) *n.* **1.** The act of providing or furnishing with a seat or seats. **2.** The arrangement of seats in a room, auditorium, or banquet hall. **3.** The member or part upon or within which another part is seated. **4.** Material for upholstering seats.

sea·train (sē′trān′) *n.* A seagoing vessel capable of carrying a train of railroad cars.

sea trout *n.* **1.** Any of several marine fishes of the genus *Cynoscion,* esp. the weakfish. **2.** Any of several trouts or similar fishes that live in the sea but migrate to fresh water to spawn.

sea urchin *n.* Any of various echinoderms of the class Echinoidea, having a soft body enclosed in a round, symmetrical, limy shell covered with long spines.

sea wall *n.* An embankment to prevent erosion of a shoreline.

sea walnut *n.* Any of several ctenophores of the genus *Mnemiopsis* and related genera, having a translucent, ovoid body with lengthwise ridges and rows of hairlike cilia.

sea·ward (sē′wərd) *adj. & adv.* At or toward the sea. —**sea′wards** (-wərdz) *adv.*

sea·ware (sē′wâr′) *n.* Sea wrack used as fertilizer. [SEA + dial. *ware,* seaweed < ME < OE *wār.*]

sea·wa·ter (sē′wô′tər, -wŏt′ər) *n.* Water in or coming from the sea.

sea·way (sē′wā′) *n.* **1.** A sea route. **2.** An inland waterway for ocean shipping. **3.** The headway of a ship. **4.** A rough sea.

sea·weed (sē′wēd′) *n.* **1.** Any of numerous marine algae, such as a kelp, rockweed, or gulfweed. **2.** Any of various marine plants.

sea·wor·thy (sē′wûr′*th*ē) *adj.* **-thi·er, -thi·est.** Designating a vessel that is fit to sail. —**sea′wor′thi·ness** *n.*

sea wrack *n.* Material cast ashore, esp. seaweed.

se·ba·ceous (sĭ-bā′shəs) *adj. Physiol.* **1.** Of, pertaining to, or resembling fat or sebum; fatty. **2.** Secreting fat or sebum. [Lat. *sebaceus* < *sebum,* tallow.]

sebaceous gland *n.* Any of various glands in the corium of the skin that open into a hair follicle and produce and secrete sebum.

se·bac·ic acid (sĭ-băs′ĭk, -bā′sĭk, sē-) *n.* A white crystalline acid, $C_{10}H_{18}O_4$, used in the manufacture of certain synthetic resins and fibers, various plasticizers, and polyester rubbers. [< SEBACEOUS.]

sebi– or **sebo–** *pref.* Fat; sebum: *sebiferous.* [< Lat. *sebum,* tallow.]

se·bif·er·ous (sĭ-bĭf′ər-əs) also **se·bip·a·rous** (-bĭp′-). Producing or secreting fatty, oily, or waxy matter; sebaceous.

sebo– *pref.* Variant of **sebi-.**

seb·or·rhe·a also **seb·or·rhoe·a** (sĕb′ə-rē′ə) *n.* A disease of the sebaceous glands characterized by excessive secretion of sebum or an alteration in its quality, resulting in an oily coating, crusts, or scales on the skin. —**seb′or·rhe′ic** *adj.*

se·bum (sē′bəm) *n.* The semifluid secretion of the sebaceous glands. [Lat., tallow.]

sec (sĕk) *adj.* Dry. Used of wines, esp. champagne. [Fr.]

sec·a·lose (sĕk′ə-lōs′) *n.* A fructose polysaccharide. [NLat. *Secale,* grass genus (< Lat. *secale,* rye) + -OSE.]

se·cant (sē′kănt′, -kənt) *n.* **1. a.** A straight line intersecting a curve at two or more points. **b.** The straight line drawn from the center through one end of a circular arc and intersecting the tangent to the other end of the arc. **2. a.** The reciprocal of the cosine of an angle. **b.** For an acute angle, the ratio of the hypotenuse to the side of a right triangle adjacent to the acute angle. [< Lat. *secans, secant-,* cutting, pr.part. of *secare,* to cut.]

sec·co (sĕk′ō) *n., pl.* **-cos.** The art or an example of painting on dry plaster. [Ital. < Lat. *siccus,* dry.]

se·cede (sĭ-sēd′) *intr.v.* **-ced·ed, -ced·ing, -cedes.** To withdraw formally from membership in an organization, association, or alliance. [Lat. *secedere,* to separate : *se-,* apart + *cedere,* to go.]

se·cern (sĭ-sûrn′) *tr.v.* **-cerned, -cern·ing, -cerns. 1.** To discern as separate; discriminate. **2.** *Physiol.* To secrete. Used of a gland or follicle. [Lat. *secernere,* to sever : *se-,* apart + *cernere,* to separate.] —**se·cern′ment** *n.*

se·ces·sion (sĭ-sĕsh′ən) *n.* **1.** The act of seceding. **2.** Often **Secession.** The withdrawal of 11 Southern states from the Federal Union in 1860–61, precipitating the Civil War. [Lat. *secessio* < *secessus,* p.part. of *secedere,* to secede.] —**se·ces′sion·al** *adj.*

se·ces·sion·ism (sĭ-sĕsh′ə-nĭz′əm) *n.* The policy of those maintaining the right of secession. —**se·ces′sion·ist** *n.*

Seck·el pear (sĕk′əl, sĭk′-) *n.* A variety of pear having small, sweet, reddish-brown fruit. [Perh. < the name *Seckel.*]

se·clude (sĭ-klo͞od′) *tr.v.* **-clud·ed, -clud·ing, -cludes. 1.** To remove or set apart from others. **2.** To screen from view; make private. [ME *secluden,* to shut off < Lat. *secludere* : *se-,* apart + *claudere,* to shut.]

se·clud·ed (sĭ-klo͞o′dĭd) *adj.* **1.** Removed or remote from others; solitary. **2.** Screened from view; sequestered. —**se·clud′ed·ly** *adv.* —**se·clud′ed·ness** *n.*

se·clu·sion (sĭ-klo͞o′zhən) *n.* **1. a.** The act of secluding. **b.** The state of being secluded. **2.** A secluded place or abode. [Med. Lat. *seclusio* < Lat. *seclusus,* p.part. of *secludere,* to seclude.]

se·clu·sive (sĭ-klo͞o′sĭv, -zĭv) *adj.* Of, fond of, or seeking seclusion. —**se·clu′sive·ly** *adv.* —**se·clu′sive·ness** *n.*

sec·o·bar·bi·tal (sĕk′ō-bär′bĭ-tôl′) *n.* A barbiturate, $C_{12}H_{18}N_2O_3$, that is used as a sedative and hypnotic in the form of its sodium salt. [*Seconal,* a trademark for secobarbital + BARBITAL.]

sec·ond[1] (sĕk′ənd) *n.* **1.** A unit of time equal to 1/60 of a minute. **2.** *Informal.* A brief period of time; moment. **3.** *Math.* A unit of angular measure equal to 1/60 of a minute of arc. [ME *seconde,* one-sixtieth of a minute of arc < OFr. < Med. Lat. *(pars minuta) secunda,* second (small part), fem. of Lat. *secundus,* second, following.]

sec·ond[2] (sĕk′ənd) *adj.* **1.** Coming next after the first in order, place, rank, time, or quality. **2.** Repeating an initial instance; another: *a second chance.* **3.** Inferior to another; subordinate: *second to none.* **4.** *Mus.* **a.** Having a lower pitch. **b.** Singing or playing a part having a lower range. **5.** Having the second-highest ratio. Used of gears in a sequence. —*n.* **1. a.** The ordinal number that matches the number 2 in a series. **b.** One of two equal parts. **2.** One that is next in order, place, time, or quality after the first. **3.** Often **seconds.** An article of merchandise of inferior quality. **4.** The official attendant of a contestant in a duel or boxing match. **5.** *Mus.* **a.** The interval between consecutive tones on the diatonic scale. **b.** A tone separated by this interval from another tone. **c.** A combination of two such tones in notation or in harmony. **d.** The second part, instrument, or voice in a harmonized composition. **6.** An utterance of endorsement. **7.** The forward gears in an automobile transmission having the second-highest ratio. —*tr.v.* **-ond·ed, -ond·ing, -onds. 1.** To attend (a duelist, for example) as an aide or assistant. **2.** To promote or encourage; reinforce. **3.** To endorse (a motion or nomination) as a required preliminary to discussion or vote. —*adv.* **1.** In the second order, place, or rank: *finished second.* **2.** But for one other; save one: *the second-highest peak.* [ME < OFr. < Lat. *secundus,* following.]

Second Advent *n.* The Second Coming.

sec·ond·ar·y (sĕk′ən-dĕr′ē) *adj.* **1. a.** Of the second rank; not primary. **b.** Inferior. **c.** Minor; lesser. **2.** Derived from what is primary or original: *a secondary source.* **3.** Of, pertaining to, or designating the shorter flight feathers projecting along the inner part of the edge of a bird's wing. **4.** *Elect.* Having an induced current that is generated by an inductively coupled primary. Used of a circuit or coil. **5.** *Chem.* Formed by replacement of two atoms or radicals within a molecule. Used of a compound. **6.** *Geol.* Resulting from changes in the pre-existing minerals. **7.** Of or relating to a secondary school: *secondary education.* —*n., pl.* **-ies. 1.** One that acts in an auxiliary, subordinate, or inferior capacity. **2.** One of the shorter flight feathers projecting along the inner part of the edge of a bird's wing. **3.** *Elect.* A coil or circuit having an induced current. **4.** *Astron.* A body that orbits a primary; satellite. **5.** *Football.* The defensive backfield. —**sec′ond·ar′i·ly** (-dâr′ə-lē) *adv.* —**sec′ond·ar′i·ness** *n.*

secondary battery *n. Elect.* A storage battery.

secondary cell *n.* A rechargeable electric cell that converts chemical energy into electrical energy by a reversible chemical reaction.

secondary color *n.* A color produced by mixing two primary colors in approximately equal proportions.

secondary electron *n.* An electron produced in secondary emission.

secondary emission *n.* Emission of electrons from the surface of a substance bombarded by electrons or ions.

secondary offering *n.* The sale of a large block of outstanding stock through dealers but outside of a stock exchange.

secondary school *n.* A school that is intermediate in level between elementary school and college and that usually of-

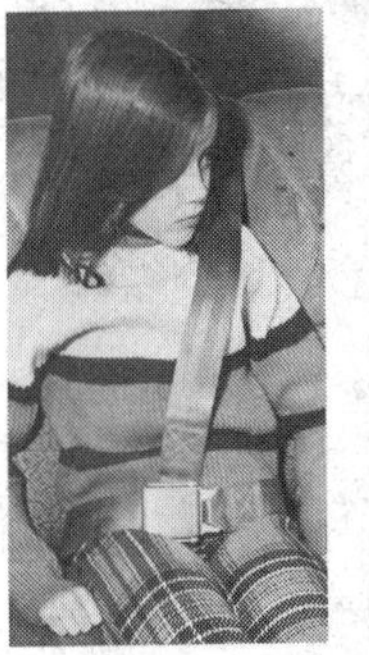

seat belt

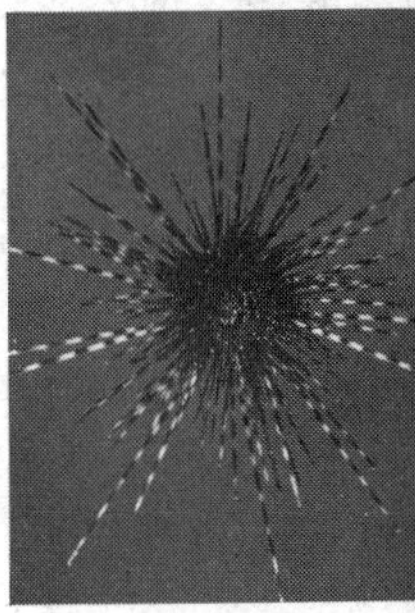

sea urchin

secretary

George Miksch Sutton

secretary bird

fers general, technical, vocational, or college-preparatory curricula.
secondary sex characteristic *n.* Any of various genetically transmitted anatomical, physiological, or behavioral characteristics, as voice quality, abundance of facial hair, or breast development, that first appear in humans at puberty and differentiate between the sexes without having a direct reproductive function.
second base *n. Baseball.* **1.** The base across the diamond from home plate, to be touched second by a runner. **2.** The position played by a second baseman.
second baseman *n. Baseball.* The infielder who is positioned near and to the first-base side of second base.
second best *n.* One that is next to the best. *—adv.* Next to the best.
sec·ond-best (sĕk′ənd-bĕst′) *adj.* Next to the best.
second childhood *n.* Senility; dotage.
second class *n.* **1.** Second-class travel accommodations. **2.** Second-class mail.
sec·ond-class (sĕk′ənd-klăs′) *adj.* **1.** Of secondary status; inferior. **2.** Of or pertaining to travel accommodations ranking next below the highest or first class. **3.** Of or pertaining to a class of U.S. and Canadian mail consisting of newspapers and periodicals. *—adv.* By means of second-class mail or second-class travel accommodations.
Second Coming *n.* The return of Christ as judge upon the last day; millennium.
sec·ond-de·gree burn (sĕk′ənd-dĭ-grē′) *n.* A burn that blisters the skin.
Second Empire *n.* A heavily ornate style of furniture, architecture, and decoration that was developed in mid-19th-century France.
second fiddle *n.* **1.** A secondary role. **2.** One who plays a secondary role.
second generation *n. Computer Sci.* Of, relating to, or being the period of computer technology that made use of solid-state circuitry and off-line storage and extensively developed software.
second growth *n.* Trees that cover an area after the removal of the original stand, as by cutting or fire.
sec·ond-guess (sĕk′ənd-gĕs′) *v.* **-guessed, -guess·ing, -guess·es.** *—tr.* **1.** To criticize after an outcome is known. **2.** To anticipate the actions or intentions of; outguess. *—intr.* To criticize a decision after its outcome is known. **—sec′ond-guess′er** *n.*
sec·ond·hand (sĕk′ənd-hănd′) *adj.* **1.** Previously used by another; not new. **2.** Dealing in previously used merchandise. **3.** Obtained, derived, or borrowed from another; not original. *—adv.* In an indirect manner; indirectly.
second hand[1] *n.* The hand of a timepiece that marks the seconds.
second hand[2] *n.* An intermediary person or source: *heard at second hand.*
se·con·di (sĭ-kôn′dē) *n.* Plural of **secondo.**
second lieutenant *n.* An officer in the U.S. Army, Air Force, and Marine Corps of the lowest commissioned grade, ranking below a first lieutenant.
sec·ond·ly (sĕk′ənd-lē) *adv.* In the second place; second.
second mortgage *n.* A mortgage on property that is already mortgaged.
second nature *n.* A deeply ingrained habit.
se·con·do (sĭ-kôn′dō) *n., pl.* **-di** (-dē). *Mus.* The second part in a concert piece, esp. the lower part in a piano duet. [Ital. < Lat. *secundus,* second, following.]
second person *n. Gram.* The form of a pronoun or verb used in referring to the person addressed, as *you* and *shall* in *you shall not enter.*
sec·ond-rate (sĕk′ənd-rāt′) *adj.* Of inferior or mediocre quality or value. **—sec′ond-rate′ness** *n.* **—sec′ond-rat′er** *n.*
second sight *n.* Clairvoyance.
sec·ond-sto·ry man (sĕk′ənd-stôr′ē, -stōr′ē) *n.* A burglar adept at entering through upstairs windows.
sec·ond-strike (sĕk′ənd-strīk′) *adj.* Of, relating to, or constituting a nuclear-weapons force able to withstand nuclear attack and therefore capable of delivering a retaliatory attack.
sec·ond-string (sĕk′ənd-strĭng′) *adj.* Of, pertaining to, or being a substitute, as on a ball team.
second thought *n.* A reconsideration of a decision or opinion previously made.
second wind *n.* Restored energy or strength.
Second World *n.* The Communist nations of the world, esp. as an economic and political bloc.
Second World War *n.* World War II.
se·cre·cy (sē′krĭ-sē) *n., pl.* **-cies. 1.** The quality or condition of being secret or hidden; concealment. **2.** The ability or habit of keeping secrets; closeness. [Alteration of obs. *secretie* < ME *secretee* < *secret,* secret.]
se·cret (sē′krĭt) *adj.* **1.** Concealed from general knowledge or view; kept hidden. **2.** Dependably close-mouthed; discreet. **3.** Operating in a hidden or confidential manner: *a secret agent.* **4.** Not visibly expressed; inward. **5.** Not frequented; secluded. **6.** Known or shared only by the initiated: *secret rites.* **7.** Beyond ordinary understanding; mysterious. **8.** Designating the security classification below top-secret and above confidential. *—n.* **1.** Something kept hidden from others or known only to oneself or to a few. **2.** Something that remains beyond understanding or explanation; mystery. **3.** A method or formula on which success is based. **4. Secret.** A variable prayer said after the Offertory and before the Preface in the liturgy of the Mass. [ME < OFr. < Lat. *secretus,* p.part. of *secernere,* to sever : *se-,* apart + *cernere,* to separate.] **—se′cret·ly** *adv.*
Synonyms: *secret, stealthy, covert, clandestine, furtive, surreptitious, underhand.* These adjectives apply to what is purposely concealed from view or knowledge. *Secret* is the most general and therefore least strong in suggesting anything beyond this basic sense. *Stealthy* is most often applied to action designed to achieve an end without attracting notice. *Covert* describes any act not taken openly. *Clandestine* implies secrecy for the purpose of concealing illegal or improper actions. *Furtive* applies to action and suggests the slyness and evasiveness of a thief. *Surreptitious* usually describes quick, secret, often nefarious action. *Underhand* describes action or means involving unfairness, deceit, or fraud as well as concealment.
se·cre·ta·gogue (sə-krē′tə-gôg′, -gŏg′) *n.* An agent that stimulates secretion. [SECRET(ION) + -AGOGUE.]
sec·re·tar·i·at (sĕk′rĭ-târ′ē-ĭt) *n.* **1. a.** The department administered by a governmental secretary, esp. for an international organization. **b.** The office occupied by such a department. **2.** The office or position of a governmental secretary. [Fr. *secrétariat* < Med. Lat. *secretariatus* < *secretarius,* secretary.]
sec·re·tar·y (sĕk′rĭ-tĕr′ē) *n., pl.* **-ies. 1.** A person employed to handle correspondence, keep files, and do clerical work for an individual or company. **2.** An officer who keeps records of the meetings, stock transfers, and legal transactions of a company or other organization. **3.** An official presiding over an administrative department of state. **4.** A desk with a small bookcase on top. [ME *secretarie,* confidant < Med. Lat. *secretarius,* confidential officer < Lat. *secretus,* secret.] **—sec′re·tar′i·al** (-târ′ē-əl) *adj.*
secretary bird *n.* A large African bird of prey, *Sagittarius serpentarius,* with long legs and a crest of quills at the back of the head.
sec·re·tar·y-gen·er·al (sĕk′rĭ-tĕr′ē-jĕn′ər-əl) *n., pl.* **sec·re·tar·ies-gen·er·al.** A principal executive officer, as in certain political parties or governmental bodies such as the United Nations.
secret ballot *n.* An Australian ballot.
se·crete[1] (sĭ-krēt′) *tr.v.* **-cret·ed, -cret·ing, -cretes.** To generate and separate out (a substance) from cells or bodily fluids. [Back-formation < SECRETION.] **—se·cre′tor** *n.*
se·crete[2] (sĭ-krēt′) *tr.v.* **-cret·ed, -cret·ing, -cretes.** To conceal in a hiding place; cache. [Obs. *secret,* to conceal < SECRET.]
se·cre·tin (sĭ-krēt′n) *n.* A hormone secreted in the duodenum to stimulate the flow of pancreatic juice. [SECRET(ION) + -IN.]
se·cre·tion (sĭ-krē′shən) *n.* **1.** The process of secreting a substance, esp. one that is not a waste, from blood or cells. **2.** A substance secreted. [Fr. *sécrétion* < Lat. *secretio,* separation < *secernere,* to sever. —see SECERN.] **—se·cre′tion·ar′y** (-shə-nĕr′ē) *adj.*
se·cre·tive (sē′krĭ-tĭv, sĭ-krē′tĭv) *adj.* Tending to secrecy; not given to openness, as of purpose or action. **—se′cre·tive·ly** *adv.* **—se′cre·tive·ness** *n.*
se·cre·to·ry (sĭ-krē′tə-rē) *adj.* Pertaining to or performing the function of secretion.
secret partner *n.* A partner whose participation in a business partnership is kept hidden from the public.
secret police *n.* A police force operating largely in secret and often using terrorism to suppress political opposition.
secret service *n.* **1. a.** Intelligence-gathering activities conducted secretly by a government agency. **b.** A government agency that is engaged in intelligence-gathering activities. **2. Secret Service.** A branch of the U.S. Treasury Department concerned with the suppression of counterfeiting and esp. the protection of the President.
sect (sĕkt) *n.* **1.** A group of people forming a distinct unit within a larger group by virtue of certain refinements or distinctions of belief or practice. **2.** A religious body, esp. one that has separated from a larger denomination. **3.** A small faction united by common interests or beliefs. [ME *secte* < OFr. < Lat. *secta,* faction < *sequi,* to follow.]
-sect *suff.* **1.** To cut; divide: *trisect.* **2.** Cut; divided: *pinnatisect.* [< Lat. *sectus,* p.part. of *secare,* to cut.]
sec·tar·i·an (sĕk-târ′ē-ən) *adj.* **1.** Of, pertaining to, or characteristic of a sect. **2.** Adhering or confined to the dogmatic limits of a sect; partisan. **3.** Narrow-minded; parochial. *—n.* **1.** A member of a sect. **2.** One characterized by bigoted adherence to a factional viewpoint. **—sec·tar′i·an·ism** *n.*
sec·ta·ry (sĕk′tə-rē) *n., pl.* **-ries. 1.** A sectarian. **2.** A dissenter from an established church, esp. a Protestant nonconformist. [Med. Lat. *sectarius* < Lat. *secta,* sect.]
sec·tile (sĕk′təl, -tīl′) *adj.* Capable of being cut or severed smoothly by a knife. [Lat. *sectilis* < *secare,* to cut.] **—sec·til′i·ty** (-tĭl′ĭ-tē) *n.*
sec·tion (sĕk′shən) *n.* **1.** One of several components of something; piece. **2.** A subdivision of a written work. **3.** A division of a statute or legal code. **4.** A distinct portion of a

newspaper: *the sports section.* **5.** A distinct area of a town, county, or country: *a residential section.* **6.** A land unit of 640 acres or one square mile, equal to $^1/_{36}$ of a township. **7.** The act or process of separating or cutting, esp. the surgical separation of tissue. **8.** A thin slice, as of tissue, suitable for microscopic examination. **9.** A segment of a fruit, esp. a citrus fruit. **10.** The representation of a solid object as it would appear if cut by an intersecting plane, so that the internal structure is displayed. **11.** *Math.* The planar configuration formed by the intersection of a solid by a plane. **12. a.** A portion of a railroad track maintained by a single crew. **b.** An area in a sleeping car containing an upper and lower berth. **13.** An army tactical unit smaller than a platoon and larger than a squad. **14.** A unit of vessels or aircraft within a military division. **15. a.** The character (§) used in printing to mark the beginning of a section. **b.** This character used as the fourth in a series of reference marks for footnotes. —*tr.v.* **-tioned, -tion·ing, -tions. 1.** To separate or divide into parts. **2.** To separate (tissue) surgically. **3.** To shade or crosshatch (part of a drawing) to indicate sections. [Lat. *sectio,* act of cutting < *sectus,* p.part. of *secare,* to cut.]

sec·tion·al (sĕk′shə-nəl) *adj.* **1.** Of, pertaining to, or characteristic of a particular district. **2.** Composed of or divided into component sections. —*n.* A piece of furniture made up of sections that can be used separately or together. **—sec′tion·al·ly** *adv.*

sec·tion·al·ism (sĕk′shə-nə-lĭz′əm) *n.* Excessive devotion to local interests and customs. **—sec′tion·al·ist** *n.*

sec·tion·al·ize (sĕk′shə-nə-līz′) *tr.v.* **-ized, -iz·ing, -iz·es.** To divide into sections, esp. into geographical sections. **—sec′tion·al·i·za′tion** *n.*

Section Eight *n.* **1.** A U.S. Army discharge based on military unfitness or undesirable character traits. **2.** A soldier discharged under a Section Eight. [After *Section VIII,* Army Regulation 615-360, which provided for the discharge of psychopaths and neurotics.]

section gang *n.* A work crew assigned to a section of railroad track.

section hand *n.* A laborer assigned to a section gang.

sec·tor (sĕk′tər, -tôr′) *n.* **1.** *Math.* The portion of a circle bounded by two radii and one of the intercepted arcs. **2. a.** A division of a defensive position for which one military unit is responsible. **b.** A division of an offensive position. **3.** A part or division of something, such as a city, resembling a military sector. **4.** *Computer Sci.* A bit or a set of bits on a magnetic storage system making up the smallest addressable unit of information. —*tr.v.* **-tored, -tor·ing, -tors.** To divide into sectors. [LLat. < Lat., cutter < *secare,* to cut.] **—sec·to′ri·al** (-tôr′ē-əl, -tōr′-) *adj.*

sec·u·lar (sĕk′yə-lər) *adj.* **1.** Worldly rather than spiritual. **2.** Not specifically pertaining to religion or to a religious body: *secular music.* **3.** Pertaining to or advocating secularism. **4.** Not bound by monastic restrictions, esp. not belonging to a religious order. Used of the clergy. **5.** Occurring or observed once in an age or century. **6.** Lasting from century to century. —*n.* **1.** A secular clergyman. **2.** A layman. [ME *seculer* < OFr. < Lat. *saecularis* < *saeculum,* generation, age.] **—sec′u·lar·ly** *adv.*

sec·u·lar·ism (sĕk′yə-lə-rĭz′əm) *n.* The view that consideration of the present well-being of mankind should predominate over religious considerations in civil affairs or public education. **—sec′u·lar·ist** *n.* **—sec′u·lar·is′tic** *adj.*

sec·u·lar·i·ty (sĕk′yə-lăr′ĭ-tē) *n., pl.* **-ties. 1.** The condition or quality of being secular. **2.** Something secular.

sec·u·lar·ize (sĕk′yə-lə-rīz′) *tr.v.* **-ized, -iz·ing, -iz·es. 1.** To convert from ecclesiastical or religious to civil or lay use or ownership. **2.** To cause to draw away from religious orientation; make worldly. **3.** To lift the monastic restrictions from (a member of the clergy). **—sec′u·lar·i·za′tion** *n.*

se·cund (sē′kŭnd′, sĭ-kŭnd′) *adj.* Arranged on or turned to one side of an axis. [Lat. *secundus,* following.]

se·cun·dines (sē-kŭn′dīnz′, sĕk′ən-dīnz′) *pl.n.* Afterbirth. [ME *secundine* < LLat. *secundinae* < *secundus,* following.]

se·cure (sĭ-kyŏŏr′) *adj.* **-cur·er, -cur·est. 1.** Free from danger or risk of loss; safe. **2.** Free from fear or doubt. **3. a.** Not likely to fail or give way; stable. **b.** Well-fastened. **4.** Assured; guaranteed. **5.** *Archaic.* Careless or overconfident. —*tr.v.* **-cured, -cur·ing, -cures. 1.** To guard from danger or risk of loss. **2.** To make firm or tight; fasten. **3.** To make certain; guarantee. **4.** To make a pledge on (a loan, for example). **5.** To get possession of; acquire. **6.** To bring about; effect. [Lat. *securus* : *se-,* without + *cura,* care.] **—se·cur′a·ble** *adj.* **—se·cure′ly** *adv.* **—se·cure′ment** *n.* **—se·cure′ness** *n.* **—se·cur′er** *n.*

Securities and Exchange Commission *n.* A U.S. governmental agency that supervises the exchange of securities so as to protect investors against malpractice.

se·cu·ri·ty (sĭ-kyŏŏr′ĭ-tē) *n., pl.* **-ties. 1.** Freedom from risk or danger; safety. **2.** Freedom from doubt, anxiety, or fear; confidence. **3.** Something that gives or assures safety. **4.** *Computer Sci.* **a.** The level to which a program or device is safe from unauthorized use. **b.** Prevention of unauthorized use of a program or device. **5.** Something deposited or given as assurance of the fulfillment of an obligation; pledge. **6.** One who undertakes to fulfill the obligation of another; surety. **7.** Written evidence of ownership or creditorship, esp. a stock certificate. **8.** Measures adopted to guarantee freedom or secrecy of action or communication, as in wartime. [ME *securite* < Lat. *securitas* < *securus,* secure.]

security blanket *n.* **1.** A blanket or toy carried by a child to reduce anxiety. **2.** Something that dispels anxiety.

Security Council *n.* The permanent peace-keeping organ of the United Nations, composed of five permanent members and ten elected members.

security guard *n.* A person hired by a private organization to guard a physical plant and maintain order.

se·dan (sĭ-dăn′) *n.* **1.** A closed automobile having two or four doors and a front and rear seat. **2.** A portable enclosed chair for one person, having poles in the front and rear and carried by two men. [Orig. unknown.]

Se·dar·im (sĭ-där′ĭm) *n.* A plural of **Seder.**

se·date¹ (sĭ-dāt′) *adj.* Serenely deliberate in character or manner; composed. [Lat. *sedatus,* p.part. of *sedare,* to settle, calm.] **—se·date′ly** *adv.* **—se·date′ness** *n.*

se·date² (sĭ-dāt′) *tr.v.* **-dat·ed, -dat·ing, -dates.** To administer a sedative to. [Back-formation < SEDATIVE.]

se·da·tion (sĭ-dā′shən) *n.* **1.** The reduction of stress or excitement by administration of a sedative. **2.** The state or condition induced by a sedative.

sed·a·tive (sĕd′ə-tĭv) *adj.* Having a soothing, calming, or tranquilizing effect. —*n.* A sedative agent or drug. [Fr. *sédatif* < Med. Lat. *sedativus* < Lat. *sedare,* to calm.]

sed·en·tar·y (sĕd′n-tĕr′ē) *adj.* **1.** Characterized by or requiring much sitting: *a sedentary job.* **2.** Accustomed to sitting or to taking little exercise. **3.** Remaining in one area; not migratory. **4.** *Zool.* Attached to a surface and not free-moving, as a barnacle. [Fr. *sédentaire* < Lat. *sedentarius* < *sedens,* pr.part. of *sedēre,* to sit.] **—sed′en·tar′i·ly** (-târ′ə-lē) *adv.* **—sed′en·tar′i·ness** *n.*

Se·der (sā′dər) *n., pl.* **Se·ders** or **Se·dar·im** (sĭ-där′ĭm). *Judaism.* The feast commemorating the exodus of the Israelites from Egypt, celebrated on the eve of the first two days of Passover. [Heb. *sēdher,* order.]

se·der·unt (sə-dĭr′ənt, -dĕr′-) *n.* A prolonged session, as for discussion. [Lat., they sat.]

sedge (sĕj) *n.* Any of numerous plants of the family Cyperaceae, resembling grasses but having solid rather than hollow stems. [ME *segge* < OE *secg.*]

se·dil·ia (sĭ-dēl′yə, -dĭl′-) *pl.n.* A set of seats, usually three, built into the wall on the south side of the choir near the altar in Gothic-style churches for the use of the celebrant and his ministers. [Lat. *sedilia,* pl. of *sedile,* seat < *sedēre,* to sit.]

sed·i·ment (sĕd′ə-mənt) *n.* **1.** Material that settles to the bottom of a liquid; lees. **2. a.** Material suspended in water or in the air. **b.** The deposition of such material onto the surface underlying this water or air. **c.** The material so deposited. [Fr. *sédiment* < Lat. *sedimentum,* act of settling < *sedēre,* to sit, settle.]

sed·i·men·ta·ry (sĕd′ə-mĕn′tə-rē, -mĕn′trē) also **sed·i·men·tal** (-mĕn′tl) *adj.* **1.** Of, containing, resembling, or derived from sediment. **2.** *Geol.* Of or pertaining to rocks formed from sediment or from transported fragments deposited in water.

sed·i·men·ta·tion (sĕd′ə-mən-tā′shən, -mĕn-) *n.* The act or process of depositing sediment.

sed·i·men·tol·o·gy (sĕd′ə-mən-tŏl′ə-jē, -mĕn-) *n.* The science that deals with the description, classification, and origin of sedimentary rock. **—sed′i·men·to·log′ic** (-tə-lŏj′ĭk), **sed′i·men·to·log′i·cal** *adj.* **—sed′i·men·tol′o·gist** *n.*

se·di·tion (sĭ-dĭsh′ən) *n.* **1.** Conduct or language inciting rebellion against the authority of a state. **2.** Insurrection; rebellion. [ME *sedicioun* < OFr. *sedition* < Lat. *seditio,* separation : *se-,* apart + *itio,* act of going < *itus,* p.part. of *ire,* to go.] **—se·di′tion·ist** *n.*

se·di·tious (sĭ-dĭsh′əs) *adj.* **1.** Constituting or having the nature of sedition. **2.** Engaged in sedition. **—se·di′tious·ly** *adv.* **—se·di′tious·ness** *n.*

se·duce (sĭ-dōōs′, -dyōōs′) *tr.v.* **-duced, -duc·ing, -duc·es. 1.** To lead (a person) away from duty or proper conduct; corrupt. **2.** To induce to have sexual intercourse. **3. a.** To entice or beguile into a desired state or position. **b.** To win over; attract. [ME *seduisen* < OFr. *seduire, seduis-* < Lat. *seducere,* to lead away : *se-,* apart + *ducere,* to lead.] **—se·duce′a·ble, se·duc′i·ble** *adj.* **—se·duc′er** *n.*

se·duce·ment (sĭ-dōōs′mənt, -dyōōs′-) *n.* **1.** Seduction. **2.** Something that seduces.

se·duc·tion (sĭ-dŭk′shən) *n.* **1. a.** The act of seducing. **b.** The condition of being seduced. **2.** Something that seduces or has the qualities to seduce; enticement.

se·duc·tive (sĭ-dŭk′tĭv) *adj.* Tending to seduce. **—se·duc′tive·ly** *adv.* **—se·duc′tive·ness** *n.*

se·duc·tress (sĭ-dŭk′trĭs) *n.* A woman who seduces.

sed·u·lous (sĕj′ə-ləs) *adj.* Diligent; painstaking. [Lat. *sedulus.*] **—sed′u·lous·ly** *adv.* **—sed′u·lous·ness, se·du′li·ty** (sĭ-dōō′lĭ-tē, -dyōō′-) *n.*

se·dum (sē′dəm) *n.* Any of numerous plants of the genus *Sedum,* having thick, fleshy leaves. [NLat. *Sedum,* genus name < Lat. *sedum,* houseleek.]

see¹ (sē) *v.* **saw** (sô), **seen** (sēn), **see·ing, sees.** —*tr.* **1.** To perceive with the eye. **2.** To apprehend as if by the sense of

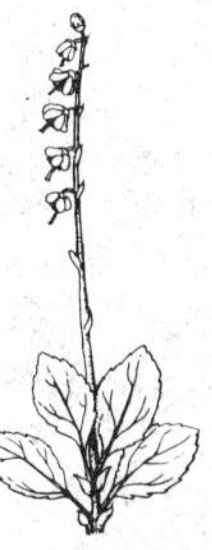

secund
Secund raceme of *Pyrola secunda*

sedan
19th-century English

sedilia

sight: *see with one's fingers.* **3.** To have a mental image of; visualize: *could still see his hometown as it once was.* **4.** To understand; comprehend. **5.** To regard; view. **6.** To believe possible; imagine: *I don't see her as a teacher.* **7.** To foresee. **8.** To know through first-hand experience; undergo: *"He saw some service on the king's side"* (Tucker Brooke). **9.** To be characterized by or bring forth: *"Her long reign saw the heyday of verbal humor"* (Richard Kain). **10.** To find out; ascertain. **11.** To refer to; read: *asked the reader to see page one of the preface.* **12.** To take note of. **13.** To meet or be in the company of. **14.** To socialize together often or regularly. **15.** To visit socially or for consultation: *see a doctor.* **16.** To receive socially or for consultation: *an attorney who sees many clients.* **17.** To attend; view. **18.** To escort; attend: *see someone off.* **19.** To make sure; take care: *See that it gets done right away.* **20. a.** To meet (a bet) in card games. **b.** To meet the bet of (another player). *—intr.* **1.** To have the power of sight. **2.** To understand; comprehend. **3.** To consider: *Let's see, which should we take?* **4.** To wait and ascertain how things go: *We probably can do it, but we'll have to see.* **5.** To have foresight: *"No man can see to the end of time"* (John F. Kennedy). **6.** To take note. ***—phrasal verbs.*** **see about. 1.** To attend to. **2.** To investigate. **see through.** To understand the true character or nature of. **see to.** To attend to. [ME *seen* < OE *sēon.*]

Synonyms: *see, behold, note, notice, espy, descry, observe, contemplate, survey, view, perceive, discern, remark, scan, skim.* These verbs refer to being visually or mentally aware of something. *See,* the most general, can mean merely to look at but more often implies recognition, understanding, or appreciation. *Behold,* usually in literary or other formal contexts, is stronger in implying real awareness of what is seen. *Note* and *notice* go further by suggesting close attention and rather detailed visual or mental impression. *Note,* in particular, implies careful and systematic recording in the mind of what is seen. *Espy* and *descry* both stress acuteness of sight that permits detection of something distant or obscure. *Observe* emphasizes attention that is both careful and closely directed. *Contemplate* implies looking attentively and meditatively. *Survey* stresses detailed examination of something on a wide or full scale. *View* usually also implies close attention but suggests examination in a special way or with a particular purpose in mind. *Perceive* and *discern* both imply not only visual recognition but mental observation and understanding. *Perceive* is especially associated with insight, and *discern* with the mental capacity for distinguishing, discriminating, and making judgments. *Remark* suggests directing the attention closely, usually to some specific detail. *Scan* usually refers to quick visual inspection of something but can also mean to examine closely. *Skim* is limited to the sense of looking quickly to get the gist of something.

seesaw

Usage: The phrase *see where* sometimes occurs in speech as an informal equivalent of *see that* as in the sentence: *I see that he is running for mayor.* The same applies to *read where.* The informal usage, permissible in speech, should be avoided in formal writing.

see² (sē) *n.* **1.** The official seat, center of authority, jurisdiction, or office of a bishop. **2.** *Obs.* A cathedra. [ME < OFr. *se* < Lat. *sedes,* seat.]

see·catch (sē'kăch') *n., pl.* **-catch·ie** (-kăch'ē). An adult male Alaskan fur seal. [R. *sekach.*]

seed (sēd) *n., pl.* **seeds** or **seed. 1.** A fertilized and ripened plant ovule containing an embryo capable of germinating to produce a new plant. **2.** A propagative part of a plant, as a tuber or spore. **3.** Seeds collectively. **4.** The seed-bearing stage of a plant. **5.** A source or beginning; germ. **6.** Offspring; progeny. **7.** Family stock; ancestry. **8.** Sperm; semen. **9.** A young oyster or oysters used for propagating a new oyster bed. *—v.* **seed·ed, seed·ing, seeds.** *—tr.* **1.** To plant seeds in (land); sow. **2.** To plant in soil. **3.** To remove the seeds from (fruit). **4.** To sprinkle (a cloud) with particles, as of silver iodide, in order to disperse it or produce rain. **5.** *Sports.* **a.** To arrange (the drawing for positions in a tournament) so that the more skilled contestants meet in the later rounds. **b.** To rank (a contestant) in this way. *—intr.* **1.** To sow seed. **2.** To go to seed. ***—idiom.*** **go** (or **run**) **to seed. 1.** To pass into the seed-bearing stage. **2.** To become weak or devitalized; deteriorate. [ME < OE *sǣd.*]

seed·bed (sēd'bĕd') *n.* **1.** A bed of soil cultivated for planting seeds. **2.** An area or source of growth or gradual manifestation.

seed cake *n.* A sweet cake or cookie containing aromatic seeds.

seed coat *n.* The outer protective covering of a seed.

seed·er (sē'dər) *n.* **1.** A machine or implement used for planting seeds. **2.** A machine or implement used to remove the seeds from fruit.

seed leaf *n.* A cotyledon (sense 1).

seed·ling (sēd'lĭng) *n.* A young plant that is grown from a seed.

seed money *n.* Money needed or provided to start a new project.

seed oyster *n.* A young oyster, esp. one suitable for transplanting to another bed.

seed pearl *n.* A very small, often imperfect pearl.

seed plant *n.* A seed-bearing plant.

seed·pod (sēd'pŏd') *n.* A pod¹ (sense 1).

seed stock *n.* **1.** A supply of seed for planting. **2.** A source of new entities: *a seed stock of salmon in the river.*

seed·time (sēd'tīm') *n.* **1.** A time for planting seeds. **2.** A time of new growth or development.

seed vessel *n. Bot.* A pericarp.

seed·y (sē'dē) *adj.* **-i·er, -i·est. 1.** Having many seeds. **2.** Seedlike. **3.** Worn and shabby in appearance; unkempt: *"He was soiled and seedy and fragrant with gin"* (Mark Twain). **4.** Tired or sick; unwell. **5.** Somewhat disreputable; squalid: *a seedy hotel.* **—seed'i·ly** *adv.* **—seed'i·ness** *n.*

see·ing (sē'ĭng) *conj.* Inasmuch as.

Seeing Eye. A trademark for a dog trained to lead a blind person.

seek (sēk) *v.* **sought** (sôt), **seek·ing, seeks.** *—tr.* **1.** To try to locate or discover; search for. **2.** To endeavor to obtain or reach. **3.** To go to or toward: *Water seeks its own level.* **4.** To inquire for; request. **5.** To try; endeavor. **6.** *Obs.* To explore. *—intr.* To make a search or investigation. *—n. Computer Sci.* A serial inspection of the data in storage to produce a desired item of data. [ME *seken* < OE *sēcan.*] **—seek'er** *n.*

seel (sēl) *tr.v.* **seeled, seel·ing, seels.** To stitch closed the eyes of (a falcon). [ME *silen* < OFr. *ciller* < Med. Lat. *cilare* < Lat. *cilium,* eyelid.]

seem (sēm) *intr.v.* **seemed, seem·ing, seems. 1.** To give the impression of being; appear. **2.** To appear to one's own opinion or mind: *I can't seem to get the story straight.* **3.** To appear to be evident: *It seems you object to the plan.* **4.** To appear to exist: *There seems no reason to postpone it.* [ME *semen* < ON *sœma,* to conform to < *sœmr,* fitting.]

seem·ing (sē'mĭng) *adj.* Apparent; ostensible. *—n.* Outward appearance; semblance. **—seem'ing·ly** *adv.* **—seem'ing·ness** *n.*

seem·ly (sēm'lē) *adj.* **-li·er, -li·est. 1.** Conforming to standards of conduct and good taste; suitable: *seemly behavior.* **2.** Of pleasing appearance; handsome. *—adv.* In a seemly manner; suitably. [ME *semely* < ON *sœmiligr* < *sœmr,* fitting.] **—seem'li·ness** *n.*

seen (sēn) *v.* Past participle of **see.**

seep (sēp) *intr.v.* **seeped, seep·ing, seeps. 1.** To pass slowly through small openings or pores; ooze. **2.** To enter, depart, or become diffused gradually. *—n.* A spot where water or petroleum trickles out of the ground to form a pool. [Alteration of dial. *sipe* < ME *sipen* < OE *sipian.*]

seep·age (sē'pĭj) *n.* **1.** The act or process of seeping. **2.** A quantity of something that has seeped.

seer (sîr, sē'ər) *n.* **1.** One that sees. **2.** A prophet. **3.** A clairvoyant. [ME < *seen,* to see.]

seer·ess (sîr'ĭs) *n.* A female prophet or clairvoyant.

seer·suck·er (sîr'sŭk'ər) *n.* A light, thin fabric, generally cotton or rayon, with a crinkled surface and a usually striped pattern. [Urdu *sīrsakar* < Pers. *shīr-o-shakar* : *shīr,* milk + *o,* and + *shakar,* sugar < Skt. *śarkarā.*]

see·saw (sē'sô') *n.* **1.** A long plank balanced on a central fulcrum so that with a person riding on each end, one end goes up as the other goes down. **2.** The act or game of riding a seesaw. **3.** A back-and-forth or up-and-down movement. *—intr.v.* **-sawed, -saw·ing, -saws. 1.** To play on a seesaw. **2.** To move back and forth or up and down. [Redup. of SAW¹.]

seethe (sēth) *v.* **seethed, seeth·ing, seethes.** *—intr.* **1.** To churn and foam as if boiling. **2.** To move in confusion; ferment. **3.** To be violently excited or agitated. **4.** *Archaic.* To come to a boil. *—tr.* **1.** To soak in liquid. **2.** *Archaic.* To boil. *—n.* The act of seething. [ME *sethen,* to boil < OE *sēothan.*]

see-through (sē'thrōō') *adj.* Transparent.

seg·ment (sĕg'mənt) *n.* **1.** Any of the parts into which something can be divided. **2.** *Math.* A portion of a figure cut off by a line or plane, esp.: **a.** The area bounded by a chord and the arc of a curve subtended by the chord. **b.** The portion of a curve between any two points on the curve. **c.** The portion of a sphere bounded by two parallel planes intersecting or tangent to the sphere. **3.** *Biol.* A clearly differentiated subdivision of an organism or part, such as a metamere. *—tr. & intr.v.* (sĕg-mĕnt') **-ment·ed, -ment·ing, -ments.** To divide or become divided into segments. [Lat. *segmentum* < *secare,* to cut.] **—seg'men·tar'y** (-mən-tĕr'ē) *adj.*

seg·men·tal (sĕg-mĕn'tl) *adj.* **1.** Of or relating to segments. **2.** Divided or organized into segments. **—seg·men'tal·ly** *adv.*

seg·men·ta·tion (sĕg'mən-tā'shən, -mĕn-) *n.* **1.** Division into segments. **2.** *Biol.* Cleavage.

segmentation cavity *n. Biol.* A blastocoel.

seg·ment·ed (sĕg'mĕn'tĭd, sĕg-mĕn'-) *adj.* Divided into distinct segments.

se·gno (sā'nyō) *n., pl.* **-gnos.** *Mus.* A notational sign, esp. the sign marking the beginning or end of a repeat. [Ital., sign < Lat. *signum.*]

se·go (sē'gō) *n., pl.* **-gos.** The succulent, edible bulb of the sego lily. [Of Ute orig.]

sego lily *n.* A plant, *Calochortus nuttallii,* of western North America, having showy, variously colored flowers.

seg·re·gate (sĕg'rĭ-gāt') *v.* **-gat·ed, -gat·ing, -gates.** *—tr.* **1.** To separate or isolate from others or from a main body or group. **2.** To impose the separation of (a race or class) from the rest of society. —*intr.* **1.** To become separated from a main body or mass. **2.** To practice a policy of racial segregation. **3.** *Genetics.* To undergo genetic segregation. —*adj.* (-gĭt, -gāt′). Separated; isolated. [Lat. *segregare, segregat-* : *se-*, apart + *grex,* flock.] **—seg′re·ga′tive** *adj.* **—seg′re·ga′tor** *n.*

seg·re·ga·tion (sĕg′rĭ-gā′shən) *n.* **1. a.** The act or process of segregating. **b.** The condition of being segregated. **2.** The policy and practice of imposing the social separation of races, as in schools, housing, and industry, esp. discriminatory practices against nonwhites in a predominantly white society. **3.** *Genetics.* The separation of paired alleles in meiosis.

seg·re·ga·tion·ist (sĕg′rĭ-gā′shə-nĭst) *n.* One who advocates or practices a policy of racial segregation.

se·gue (sĕg′wā′, sā′gwā′) *intr.v.* **-gued, -gu·ing, -gues.** To make a transition directly from one section or theme, as of music, to another. [Ital., there follows < *seguire,* to follow < Lat. *sequi.*]

se·gui·di·lla (sĕg′ə-dē′yə, -dēl′yə) *n.* **1.** A Spanish stanza form of four to seven short verses. **2. a.** A lively Spanish dance. **b.** The music for this dance, in 3/4 time. [Sp. < *seguida,* fem. p.part. of *seguir,* to follow < VLat. **sequere* < Lat. *sequi.*]

sei·cen·to (sā-chĕn′tō) *n.* The 17th century with reference to Italian literature and art. [Ital., short for *milleseicento,* one thousand six hundred.]

seiche (sāsh, sĕch) *n.* A wave that oscillates in lakes, bays, or gulfs from a few minutes to a few hours as a result of seismic or atmospheric disturbances. [Dial. Fr.]

sei·del (sīd′l, zīd′l) *n.* A beer mug. [G. < MHG *sīdel* < Lat. *situla,* bucket.]

Seid·litz powder also **Seid·litz powders** (sĕd′lĭts) *n.* A cathartic consisting of Rochelle salts, sodium bicarbonate, and tartaric acid. [So called from its laxative properties, which are similar to those of the spring water at *Seidlitz,* a village in Bohemia.]

seign·ior (sān-yôr′, sān′yôr′) *n.* A man of rank, esp. a feudal lord. [ME *seignour* < OFr. *seigneur* < Med. Lat. *senior* < Lat., older, comp. of *senex,* old.] **—sei·gnio′ri·al** *adj.*

seign·ior·age (sān′yər-ĭj) *n.* A profit or revenue taken from the minting of coins, usually the difference between the value of the bullion used and the face value of the coin. [ME *seigneurage* < OFr. < *seigneur,* seignior.]

seign·ior·y (sān′yə-rē) *n., pl.* **-ies. 1.** The feudal estate of a lord; manor. **2.** The authority and power of a feudal lord.

seine (sān) *n.* A large fishing net made to hang vertically in the water by weights at the lower edge and floats at the top. —*v.* **seined, sein·ing, seines.** —*intr.* To fish with a seine. —*tr.* To fish for or catch with a seine. [ME < OE *segne* < Lat. *sagena* < Gk. *sagēnē.*] **—sein′er** *n.*

seise (sēz) *v.* Variant of **seize** (sense 6).

sei·sin also **sei·zin** (sē′zĭn) *n. Law.* **1.** Legal possession of land, as a freehold estate. **2. a.** The act of taking legal possession of land. **b.** Property thus legally possessed. [ME *seisine* < OFr. < *seisir,* to seize.]

seism (sī′zəm) *n.* An earthquake. [Gk. *seismos* < *seiein,* to shake.]

seism- *pref.* Variant of **seismo-.**

seis·mic (sīz′mĭk) *adj.* Of, subject to, or caused by an earthquake or earth vibration. **—seis′mi·cal·ly** *adv.* **—seis·mic′i·ty** (-mĭs′ĭ-tē) *n.*

seis·mism (sīz′mĭz′əm) *n.* The collective phenomena involved in earthquakes.

seismo- or **seism-** *pref.* Earthquake: *seismograph.* [< Gk. *seismos,* earthquake.]

seis·mo·gram (sīz′mə-grăm′) *n.* The record of an earth tremor made by a seismograph.

seis·mo·graph (sīz′mə-grăf′) *n.* An instrument for automatically detecting and recording the intensity, direction, and duration of a movement of the ground, esp. of an earthquake. **—seis·mog′ra·pher** (sīz-mŏg′rə-fər) *n.* **—seis′mo·graph′ic** *adj.* **—seis·mog′ra·phy** *n.*

seis·mol·o·gy (sīz-mŏl′ə-jē) *n.* The geophysical science of earthquakes and of the mechanical properties of the earth. **—seis′mo·log′ic** (-mə-lŏj′ĭk), **seis′mo·log′i·cal** *adj.* **—seis′mo·log′i·cal·ly** *adv.* **—seis·mol′o·gist** *n.*

seis·mom·e·ter (sīz-mŏm′ĭ-tər) *n.* A detecting device that receives seismic impulses. **—seis′mo·met′ric** (-mə-mĕt′rĭk), **seis′mo·met′ri·cal** *adj.*

seis·mom·e·try (sīz-mŏm′ĭ-trē) *n.* The study of earthquakes.

seis·mo·scope (sīz′mə-skōp′) *n.* An instrument that indicates the occurrence or time of occurrence of an earthquake. **—seis′mo·scop′ic** (-skŏp′ĭk) *adj.*

sei·sor (sē′zər, -zôr′) *n.* Variant of **seizor.**

seize (sēz) *v.* **seized, seiz·ing, seiz·es.** —*tr.* **1.** To grasp suddenly and forcibly; take or grab. **2.** To grasp with the mind; comprehend. **3.** To have a sudden effect upon. **4.** To take into custody; capture. **5.** To take quick and forcible possession of: *seize a cache of arms.* **6.** Also **seise. a.** *Law.* To take into legal custody; confiscate. **b.** *Obs.* To put in possession of a feudal property. **7.** To put to immediate advantage, as an opportunity; act swiftly upon. **8.** *Naut.* To bind with turns of small line. —*intr.* **1.** To lay sudden or forcible hold: *seize on an opportunity.* **2.** To cohere or fuse with another part as a result of high pressure or temperature, restricting or preventing further motion. [ME *seisen* < OFr. *seisir,* to take possession, of Germanic orig.] **—seiz′a·ble** *adj.* **—seiz′er** *n.*

sei·zin (sē′zĭn) *n.* Variant of **seisin.**

seiz·ing (sē′zĭng) *n. Naut.* A binding of larger lines made with multiple turns of smaller line.

seiz·or also **sei·sor** (sē′zər, -zôr′) *n. Law.* One that takes seisin.

sei·zure (sē′zhər) *n.* **1. a.** The act of seizing. **b.** The condition of being seized. **2.** A sudden paroxysm, as an epileptic convulsion or heart attack. **3.** A sudden onset, cognition, or sensation of a subjective nature: "*His mother had sudden strange seizures of uneasiness about him*" (D.H. Lawrence).

se·la·chi·an (sĭ-lā′kē-ən) *adj.* Of or belonging to the order Selachii (or Squaliformes), which includes the sharks and rays. —*n.* A member of the Selachii. [< NLat. *Selachi,* order name < Gk. *selakhē,* pl. of *selakhos,* a cartilaginous fish.]

se·lag·i·nel·la (sə-lăj′ə-nĕl′ə) *n.* Any of numerous fernlike, usually prostrate plants of the genus *Selaginella,* having small scalelike leaves and bearing spores. [NLat. *Selaginella,* genus name < Lat. *selago,* a plant resembling the savin.]

se·lah (sē′lə, -lä′) *n.* A Hebrew word of unknown meaning often marking the end of a verse in the Psalms and thought to be a term indicating a pause or rest. [Heb. *selāh.*]

sel·dom (sĕl′dəm) *adv.* Not often; infrequently. —*adj. Archaic.* Infrequent; rare. —See Usage note at **rarely.** [ME *selden* < OE *seldan.*] **—sel′dom·ness** *n.*

se·lect (sĭ-lĕkt′) *v.* **-lect·ed, -lect·ing, -lects.** —*tr.* To choose from among several; pick out. —*intr.* To make a choice or selection. —*adj.* Also **se·lect·ed** (-lĕk′tĭd). **1.** Singled out in preference; chosen. **2.** Of special value or quality; preferred. —*n.* One that is select. [Lat. *seligere, select-* : *se-*, apart + *legere,* to choose.] **—se·lect′ness** *n.*

se·lect·ee (sĭ-lĕk′tē′) *n.* One who is selected, esp. for military service.

se·lec·tion (sĭ-lĕk′shən) *n.* **1. a.** The act of selecting or the fact of being selected. **b.** One that is selected. **2.** A carefully chosen or representative collection of persons or things. **3.** A literary or musical text chosen for reading or performance. **4.** *Biol.* A process that favors or induces the survival and perpetuation of one kind of organism in competition with others.

se·lec·tive (sĭ-lĕk′tĭv) *adj.* **1.** Of or characterized by selection; discriminating. **2.** Empowered or tending to select. **3.** *Electronics.* Capable of rejecting frequencies other than that selected or tuned. **—se·lec′tive·ly** *adv.* **—se·lec′tive·ness** *n.*

selective service *n.* A system for calling up individuals for compulsory military service.

se·lec·tiv·i·ty (sĭ-lĕk′tĭv′ĭ-tē, sē′lĕk-) *n.* **1.** The state or quality of being selective. **2.** The degree to which an electronic receiver is selective.

se·lect·man (sĭ-lĕkt′măn′, -mən) *n.* One of a board of town officers chosen annually in New England communities to manage local affairs.

se·lec·tor (sĭ-lĕk′tər) *n.* One that selects.

selen- *pref.* Variant of **seleno-.**

sel·e·nate (sĕl′ə-nāt′) *n.* A salt or ester of selenic acid. [SELEN(IC ACID) + -ATE[2].]

se·le·nic (sə-lē′nĭk, -lĕn′ĭk) *adj.* Of, pertaining to, or containing selenium.

selenic acid *n.* A highly corrosive hygroscopic white solid acid with composition H_2SeO_4.

se·le·ni·ous acid (sĭ-lē′nē-əs) *n.* Selenous acid.

sel·e·nite (sĕl′ə-nīt′) *n.* Gypsum in the form of colorless clear crystals. [Lat. *selenites* < Gk. *selēnitēs (lithos),* moon (stone) < *selēnē,* moon, from the belief that it waxed and waned with the moon.]

se·le·ni·um (sĭ-lē′nē-əm) *n. Symbol* **Se** A nonmetallic element, red in powder form, black in vitreous form, and metallic gray in crystalline form, resembling sulfur and obtained primarily as a by-product of electrolytic copper refining. It is widely used in rectifiers, as a semiconductor, and in xerography, and certain forms exhibit photovoltaic and photoconductive action, making it useful in photocells, photographic exposure meters, and solar cells. Atomic number 34; atomic weight 78.96; melting point (of gray selenium) 217°C; boiling point (gray) 684.9°C; specific gravity (gray) 4.79; (vitreous) 4.28; valence 2, 4, or 6. [Gk. *selēnē,* moon + -IUM.]

selenium cell *n.* A photoconductive cell consisting of an insulated selenium strip between two suitable electrodes.

seleno- or **selen-** *pref.* **1.** Moon: *selenography.* **2.** Selenium: *selenosis.* [< Gk. *selenē,* moon.]

sel·e·nod·e·sy (sĕl′ə-nŏd′ĭ-sē) *n.* The mathematical study of the exact size and shape of the moon. [SELENO- + (GEO)DESY.]

sel·e·nog·ra·phy (sĕl′ə-nŏg′rə-fē) *n.* The study of the physical features of the moon. **—sel′e·nog′ra·pher, sel′e·nog′ra·phist** *n.* **—sel′e·no·graph′ic** (-nə-grăf′ĭk), **sel′e·no·graph′i·cal** *adj.* **—sel′e·no·graph′i·cal·ly** *adv.*

sel·e·nol·o·gy (sĕl′ə-nŏl′ə-jē) *n.* The astronomical study of the moon. **—sel′e·no·log′i·cal** (-nə-lŏj′ĭ-kəl) *adj.* **—sel′e·nol′o·gist** *n.*

sel·e·no·sis (sĕl′ə-nō′sĭs) *n.* Selenium poisoning.

seismograph

seismometer

se·le·nous acid (sĭ-lē′nəs) *n.* A transparent, colorless crystalline acid, H_2SeO_3, used as a chemical reagent.

self (sĕlf) *n., pl.* **selves** (sĕlvz). **1.** The total, essential, or particular being of a person; the individual. **2.** The essential qualities distinguishing one individual from another; individuality. **3.** An individual's consciousness of his own being or identity; ego. **4.** One's own interests, welfare, or advantage: *thinking of self alone.* —*pron.* Myself, yourself, himself, or herself: *a living wage for self and family.* —*adj.* **1.** *Obs.* Same or identical. **2.** Of the same character throughout. **3.** Of the same material as the article with which it is used: *a dress with a self belt.* [ME < OE *self* (pronoun).]

self– *pref.* **1.** Oneself; itself: *self-control.* **2.** Automatic; automatically: *self-loading.* [ME < OE < *self,* self.]

self-a·ban·doned (sĕlf′ə-băn′dənd) *adj.* Abandoned by oneself, esp. having completely yielded to one's impulses. —**self′a·ban′don·ment** *n.*

self-a·base·ment (sĕlf′ə-bās′mənt) *n.* Degradation or humiliation of oneself, esp. because of feelings of inferiority or guilt.

self-ab·ne·ga·tion (sĕlf′ăb′nĭ-gā′shən) *n.* The setting aside of self-interest for the sake of others or for a belief or principle. —**self′-ab′ne·gat′ing** *adj.*

self-a·buse (sĕlf′ə-byo͞os′) *n.* **1.** Abuse of oneself or one's abilities. **2.** Masturbation.

self-act·ing (sĕlf′ăk′tĭng) *adj.* Capable of acting automatically.

self-ac·tu·al·ize (sĕlf′ăk′cho͞o-ə-līz′) *intr.v.* **-ized, -iz·ing, -iz·es.** To achieve one's full potential. —**self′-ac′tu·al·i·za′tion** *n.* —**self′-ac′tu·al·iz′er** *n.*

self-ad·dressed (sĕlf′ə-drĕst′) *adj.* Addressed to oneself: *a self-addressed envelope.*

self-ag·gran·dize·ment (sĕlf′ə-grăn′dĭz-mənt) *n.* The act or practice of enhancing one's own importance, power, or reputation. —**self′-ag·gran′diz′ing** (-ə-grăn′dī′zĭng) *adj.*

self-a·nal·y·sis (sĕlf′ə-năl′ĭ-sĭs) *n.* An independent methodical attempt by an individual to study and comprehend his own personality or emotions. —**self′-an′a·lyt′i·cal** (-ăn′ə-lĭt′ĭ-kəl), **self′-an′a·lyt′ic** *adj.*

self-an·ni·hi·la·tion (sĕlf′ə-nī′ə-lā′shən) *n.* **1.** Self-destruction. **2.** Loss of self-awareness, as in a mystical state.

self-ap·point·ed (sĕlf′ə-poin′tĭd) *adj.* Designated or chosen by oneself rather than by due authority: *a self-appointed arbiter.*

self-as·sert·ing (sĕlf′ə-sûr′tĭng) *adj.* **1.** Asserting oneself or one's own rights or views. **2. a.** Self-confident. **b.** Overbearing; arrogant.

self-as·ser·tion (sĕlf′ə-sûr′shən) *n.* Determined advancement of one's own personality, wishes, or views. —**self′-as·ser′tive** *adj.* —**self′-as·ser′tive·ly** *adv.*

self-as·sured (sĕlf′ə-sho͝ord′) *adj.* Having or showing confidence and sureness. —**self′-as·sur′ance** *n.*

self-a·ware (sĕlf′ə-wâr′) *adj.* Aware of oneself as an individual entity or personality. —**self′-a·ware′ness** *n.*

self-cen·tered (sĕlf′sĕn′tərd) *adj.* Engrossed in oneself and one's affairs; selfish. —**self′-cen′tered·ly** *adv.* —**self′-cen′tered·ness** *n.*

self-col·ored (sĕlf′kŭl′ərd) *adj.* **1.** In the natural or original color. **2.** Of only one color.

self-com·mand (sĕlf′kə-mănd′) *n.* Full presence of mind; self-control.

self-com·pla·cent (sĕlf′kəm-plā′sənt) *adj.* Characterized by self-satisfaction. —**self′-com·pla′cen·cy** *n.* —**self′-com·pla′cent·ly** *adv.*

self-con·cep·tion (sĕlf′kən-sĕp′shən) *n.* Self-image.

self-con·cern (sĕlf′kən-sûrn′) *n.* A selfish or unwholesome concern for oneself. —**self′-con·cerned′** *adj.*

self-con·fessed (sĕlf′kən-fĕst′) *adj.* According to one's own admission.

self-con·fi·dence (sĕlf′kŏn′fĭ-dəns) *n.* Confidence in oneself or one's abilities. —**self′-con′fi·dent** *adj.* —**self′-con′fi·dent·ly** *adv.*

self-con·scious (sĕlf′kŏn′shəs) *adj.* **1.** Excessively conscious of one's appearance or manner. **2.** Socially ill at ease. **3.** Showing the effects of self-consciousness; stilted: *self-conscious prose.* **4.** Aware of oneself as an individual or of one's own being, actions, or thoughts. —**self′-con′scious·ly** *adv.* —**self′-con′scious·ness** *n.*

self-con·tained (sĕlf′kən-tānd′) *adj.* **1.** Possessing within oneself or itself all that is necessary; self-sufficient. **2.** Keeping to oneself; reserved.

self-con·tent (sĕlf′kən-tĕnt′) *adj.* Satisfied with oneself; complacent. —*n.* Also **self-con·tent·ment** (-tĕnt′mənt). Self-satisfaction; complacency. —**self′-con·tent′ed** *adj.* —**self′-con·tent′ed·ly** (-tĕn′tĭd-lē) *adv.*

self-con·tra·dic·tion (sĕlf′kŏn′trə-dĭk′shən) *n.* **1.** The act, state, or fact of contradicting oneself or itself. **2.** An idea or statement containing contradictory elements. —**self′-con′tra·dic′to·ry** (-dĭk′tə-rē) *adj.*

self-con·trol (sĕlf′kən-trōl′) *n.* Control of one's emotions, desires, or actions by one's own will. —**self′-con·trolled′** *adj.*

self-cor·rect·ing (sĕlf′kə-rĕk′tĭng) *adj.* Of or comprising a typewriter mechanism that automatically allows for correction of a typing error.

self-crit·i·cal (sĕlf′krĭt′ĭ-kəl) *adj.* Watchful for one's own faults and weaknesses. —**self′-crit′i·cal·ly** *adv.* —**self′-crit′i·cism** *n.*

self-de·ceit (sĕlf′dĭ-sēt′) *n.* Self-deception.

self-de·ceived (sĕlf′dĭ-sēvd′) *adj.* Deceived by one's own illusion or error.

self-de·ceiv·ing (sĕlf′dĭ-sē′vĭng) *adj.* Given to or promoting mistaken notions about oneself.

self-de·cep·tion (sĕlf′dĭ-sĕp′shən) *n.* **1.** The act of deceiving oneself. **2.** The state of being deceived by oneself. —**self′-de·cep′tive** *adj.*

self-de·feat·ing (sĕlf′dĭ-fē′tĭng) *adj.* Injurious to one's or its own purposes or welfare.

self-de·fense (sĕlf′dĭ-fĕns′) *n.* **1.** Defense of oneself when physically attacked. **2.** Defense of what belongs to oneself, as one's works or reputation. **3.** *Law.* The right to protect oneself against violence or threatened violence with whatever force or means are reasonably necessary. —**self′-de·fen′sive** *adj.*

self-de·ni·al (sĕlf′dĭ-nī′əl) *n.* Sacrifice or restraint of one's own comfort or gratification. —**self′-de·ny′ing** *adj.* —**self′-de·ny′ing·ly** *adv.*

self-dep·re·cat·ing (sĕlf′dĕp′rĭ-kā′tĭng) *adj.* Disparaging or detracting from oneself. —**self′-dep′re·cat′ing·ly** *adv.*

self-dep·re·ca·to·ry (sĕlf′dĕp′rĭ-kə-tôr′ē, -tōr′ē) *adj.* Self-deprecating.

self-de·pre·ci·a·tion (sĕlf′dĭ-prē′shē-ā′shən) *n.* Disparagement of oneself.

self-de·struct (sĕlf′dĭ-strŭkt′) *n.* A mechanism for causing a device to destroy itself. —*intr.v.* **-struct·ed, -struct·ing, -structs.** To destroy oneself or itself. [Back-formation < SELF-DESTRUCTION.]

self-de·struc·tion (sĕlf′dĭ-strŭk′shən) *n.* **1.** The act or process of destroying oneself. **2.** Suicide.

self-de·struc·tive (sĕlf′dĭ-strŭk′tĭv) *adj.* **1.** Tending to do harm to oneself. **2.** Marked by an impulse to harm or kill oneself. —**self′-de·struc′tive·ly** *adv.* —**self′-de·struc′tive·ness** *n.*

self-de·ter·mi·na·tion (sĕlf′dĭ-tûr′mə-nā′shən) *n.* **1.** Determination of one's own fate or course of action without compulsion; free will. **2.** Freedom of the people of a given area to determine their own political status; independence.

self-de·vel·op·ment (sĕlf′dĭ-vĕl′əp-mənt) *n.* Development of one's capabilities or potentialities.

self-de·vo·tion (sĕlf′dĭ-vō′shən) *n.* Devotion or dedication of oneself esp. to a service or ideal. —**self′-de·vot′ed·ly** (-tĭd-lē) *adv.* —**self′-de·vot′ed·ness** *n.*

self-di·ges·tion (sĕlf′dĭ-jĕs′chən, -dī-) *n.* Autolysis.

self-di·rect·ed (sĕlf′dĭ-rĕk′tĭd, -dī-) *adj.* Directed or guided by oneself, esp. as an independent agent. —**self′-di·rect′ing** *adj.* —**self′-di·rec′tion** *n.*

self-dis·ci·pline (sĕlf′dĭs′ə-plĭn) *n.* Training and control of oneself and one's conduct, usually for personal improvement.

self-dis·cov·er·y (sĕlf′dĭ-skŭv′ə-rē) *n.* The act or process of achieving understanding or knowledge of oneself.

self-dis·trust (sĕlf′dĭs-trŭst′) *n.* A lack of confidence in one's abilities. —**self′-dis·trust′ful** *adj.*

self-doubt (sĕlf′dout′) *n.* A lack of faith or belief in oneself. —**self′-doubt′ing** *adj.*

self-driv·en (sĕlf′drĭv′ən) *adj.* Driven by itself; automotive.

self-ed·u·cat·ed (sĕlf′ĕj′ə-kā′tĭd) *adj.* Educated by one's own efforts without the benefits of formal instruction. —**self′-ed′u·ca′tion** *n.*

self-ef·fac·ing (sĕlf′ĭ-fā′sĭng) *adj.* Not drawing attention to oneself; humble. —**self′-ef·face′ment** *n.*

self-e·lect·ed (sĕlf′ĭ-lĕk′tĭd) *adj.* Self-appointed.

self-em·ployed (sĕlf′ĕm-ploid′) *adj.* Working for oneself, rather than for an employer. —**self′-em·ploy′ment** *n.*

self-en·forc·ing (sĕlf′ĕn-fôr′sĭng, -fōr′-) *adj.* Holding within itself the means or a guarantee of its enforcement: *a self-enforcing order.*

self-en·rich·ment (sĕlf′ĕn-rĭch′mənt) *n.* The act or process of developing or augmenting one's intellectual powers or spiritual resources.

self-es·teem (sĕlf′ĭ-stēm′) *n.* Pride in oneself.

self-ev·i·dent (sĕlf′ĕv′ĭ-dənt) *adj.* Requiring no proof or explanation. —**self′-ev′i·dence** *n.* —**self′-ev′i·dent·ly** *adv.*

self-ex·am·i·na·tion (sĕlf′ĭg-zăm′ə-nā′shən) *n.* An introspective consideration of one's own thoughts or emotions.

self-ex·ile (sĕlf′ĕg′zīl′, -ĕk′sīl′) *n.* One exiled by his own decision or volition. —**self′-ex′iled′** *adj.*

self-ex·plan·a·to·ry (sĕlf′ĭk-splăn′ə-tôr′ē, -tōr′ē) *adj.* Needing no explanation; obvious.

self-ex·pres·sion (sĕlf′ĭk-sprĕsh′ən) *n.* Expression of one's own personality, as through speech or art. —**self′-ex·pres′sive** (-sprĕs′ĭv) *adj.*

self-fer·til·i·za·tion (sĕlf′fûr′tl-ĭ-zā′shən) *n.* Fertilization by sperm from the same animal, as in some hermaphrodites, or by pollen from the same flower. —**self′-fer′til·ized′** *adj.*

self-flag·el·la·tion (sĕlf′flăj′ə-lā′shən) *n.* The act of severely censuring oneself.

self-for·get·ful (sĕlf′fər-gĕt′fəl, -fôr-) *adj.* Characterized by a lack of selfish interests; selfless. —**self′-for·get′ful·ly** *adv.* —**self′-for·get′ful·ness** *n.*

self-ful·fill·ing (sĕlf′fo͝ol-fĭl′ĭng) *adj.* **1.** Achieving self-fulfill-

ment. **2.** Achieving fulfillment as a result of having been expected or foretold: *a self-fulfilling prophecy.*
self-ful·fill·ment (sĕlf′fo͝ol-fĭl′mənt) *n.* Fulfillment of oneself.
self-giv·en (sĕlf′gĭv′ən) *adj.* **1.** Originating or derived from itself: *a self-given entity.* **2.** Given by oneself; self-appointed: *a self-given role.*
self-giv·ing (sĕlf′gĭv′ĭng) *adj.* Characterized by self-sacrificing behavior; unselfish.
self-gov·erned (sĕlf′gŭv′ərnd) *adj.* **1.** Not swayed or controlled by others. **2.** Characterized by self-discipline or self-control.
self-gov·ern·ing (sĕlf′gŭv′ər-nĭng) *adj.* **1.** Exercising control or rule over oneself or itself. **2.** Having the right or power of self-government; autonomous.
self-gov·ern·ment (sĕlf′gŭv′ərn-mənt) *n.* **1.** Political independence; autonomy. **2.** Popular or representative government; democracy. **3.** *Archaic.* Self-control.
self-grat·i·fi·ca·tion (sĕlf′grăt′ə-fĭ-kā′shən) *n.* The act of giving oneself pleasure or gratification.
self-hard·en·ing (sĕlf′här′dn-ĭng) *adj.* Of or pertaining to materials, as certain steels, that harden without special treatment.
self-heal (sĕlf′hēl′) *n.* Any of several plants reputed to have healing powers, esp. *Prunella vulgaris,* a low-growing plant native to Europe, having tightly clustered violet-blue flowers.
self-help (sĕlf′hĕlp′) *n.* The act or an instance of helping or improving oneself.
self·hood (sĕlf′ho͝od′) *n.* **1.** The state of having a distinct identity; individuality. **2.** The fully developed self; an achieved personality. **3.** Self-centeredness. [Transl. of G. *Selbheit.*]
self-hyp·no·sis (sĕlf′hĭp-nō′sĭs) *n.* The act or process of hypnotizing oneself.
self-i·den·ti·fi·ca·tion (sĕlf′ī-dĕn′tə-fĭ-kā′shən) *n.* Identification with one that exists outside oneself.
self-i·den·ti·ty (sĕlf′ī-dĕn′tĭ-tē) *n.* **1.** Oneness of a thing with itself. **2.** Awareness of and identification with oneself as a separate individual.
self-im·age (sĕlf′ĭm′ĭj) *n.* One's concept of oneself or one's status.
self-im·mo·la·tion (sĕlf′ĭm′ə-lā′shən) *n.* Deliberate sacrifice of oneself.
self-im·por·tance (sĕlf′ĭm-pôr′tns) *n.* Excessively high opinion of one's own importance or station; conceit. **—self′-im·por′tant** *adj.* **—self′-im·por′tant·ly** *adv.*
self-im·posed (sĕlf′ĭm-pōzd′) *adj.* Voluntarily assumed or endured.
self-im·prove·ment (sĕlf′ĭm-pro͞ov′mənt) *n.* Improvement of one's condition through one's own efforts.
self-in·clu·sive (sĕlf′ĭn-klo͞o′sĭv, -zĭv) *adj.* **1.** Enclosing or including itself. **2.** Whole or complete in itself.
self-in·crim·i·na·tion (sĕlf′ĭn-krĭm′ə-nā′shən) *n.* Incrimination of oneself, esp. by one's own testimony in a criminal prosecution. **—self′-in·crim′i·nat′ing** *adj.* **—self′-in·crim′i·na·to′ry** (-nə-tôr′ē, -tōr′ē) *adj.*
self-in·duced (sĕlf′ĭn-do͞ost′, -dyo͞ost′) *adj.* **1.** Induced by oneself or itself: *a self-induced wound.* **2.** *Elect.* Produced by self-induction.
self-in·duc·tion (sĕlf′ĭn-dŭk′shən) *n.* The generation by a changing current of an electromotive force in the same circuit tending to counteract such change. **—self′-in·duc′tive** *adj.*
self-in·dul·gence (sĕlf′ĭn-dŭl′jəns) *n.* Excessive indulgence of one's own appetites and desires. **—self′-in·dul′gent** *adj.* **—self′-in·dul′gent·ly** *adv.*
self-in·flict·ed (sĕlf′ĭn-flĭk′tĭd) *adj.* Inflicted or imposed upon oneself: *a self-inflicted punishment.*
self-in·struct·ed (sĕlf′ĭn-strŭk′tĭd) *adj.* Self-taught.
self-in·struc·tion·al (sĕlf′ĭn-strŭk′shə-nəl) *adj.* Relating to or designed for independent study.
self-in·sur·ance (sĕlf′ĭn-sho͝or′əns) *n.* Insurance of oneself or one's possessions against possible loss by regularly setting aside funds. **—self′-in·sured′** *adj.*
self-in·ter·est (sĕlf′ĭn′trĭst, -ĭn′tər-ĭst) *n.* **1.** Personal advantage or interest. **2.** Selfish regard for one's personal advantage or interest. **—self′-in′ter·est·ed** *adj.*
self-in·volved (sĕlf′ĭn-vŏlvd′) *adj.* Absorbed in one's own interests or activities.
self·ish (sĕl′fĭsh) *adj.* **1.** Concerned chiefly or only with oneself without regard for the well-being of others; egotistic. **2.** Arising from, characterized by, or showing selfishness: *a selfish whim.* **—self′ish·ly** *adv.* **—self′ish·ness** *n.*
self-jus·ti·fy·ing (sĕlf′jŭs′tə-fī′ĭng) *adj.* **1.** Making excuses for oneself. **2.** Justifying itself automatically: *a self-justifying typewriter.* **—self′-jus′ti·fi·ca′tion** (-jŭs′tə-fĭ-kā′shən) *n.*
self-knowl·edge (sĕlf′nŏl′ĭj) *n.* Knowledge of one's own nature, abilities, and limitations.
self·less (sĕlf′lĭs) *adj.* Without concern for oneself; unselfish. **—self′less·ly** *adv.* **—self′less·ness** *n.*
self-lim·it·ing (sĕlf-lĭm′ĭ-tĭng) *adj.* Limiting oneself or itself. **—self′-lim′i·ta′tion** (-tā′shən) *n.*
self-liq·ui·dat·ing (sĕlf′lĭk′wĭ-dā′tĭng) *adj.* **1.** Involving goods convertible into cash in a short time. Used of business transactions. **2.** Producing a return equal to the sum invested to create or maintain something: *a self-liquidating toll-bridge project.*
self-load·ing (sĕlf′lō′dĭng) *adj.* Automatically ejecting the shell and chambering the next round from the magazine. Used of firearms.
self-love (sĕlf′lŭv′) *n.* The instinct or desire to promote one's own well-being. **—self′-lov′ing** *adj.*
self-made (sĕlf′măd′) *adj.* **1.** Having achieved success unaided: *a self-made man.* **2.** Made by oneself or itself.
self-mail·er (sĕlf′mā′lər) *n.* A folder that can be mailed without being enclosed in an envelope. **—self′-mail′ing** *adj.*
self-mas·ter·y (sĕlf′măs′tə-rē) *n.* Self-command.
self·ness (sĕlf′nĭs) *n.* **1.** The quality or state of being self-centered; selfishness. **2.** Selfhood (sense 1).
self-ob·ser·va·tion (sĕlf′ŏb′zər-vā′shən) *n.* **1.** Observation of one's own countenance or appearance. **2.** Examination of one's own thoughts or emotions.
self-o·pin·ion (sĕlf′ə-pĭn′yən) *n.* A high or conceited opinion of oneself.
self-o·pin·ion·at·ed (sĕlf′ə-pĭn′yə-nā′tĭd) *adj.* **1.** Vain; conceited. **2.** Obstinately insistent upon one's own opinion.
self-or·dained (sĕlf′ôr-dānd′) *adj.* Ordained by oneself rather than by others; practicing by one's own authority.
self-per·cep·tion (sĕlf′pər-sĕp′shən) *n.* Self-concept.
self-per·pet·u·at·ing (sĕlf′pər-pĕch′o͞o-ā′tĭng) *adj.* Having the power to renew or perpetuate oneself or itself for an indefinite length of time. **—self′-per·pet′u·a′tion** *n.*
self-pit·y (sĕlf′pĭt′ē) *n.* Pity for oneself. **—self′-pit′y·ing** *adj.* **—self′-pit′y·ing·ly** *adv.*
self-poised (sĕlf′poizd′) *adj.* **1.** Being in a state of balance without need of support. **2.** Being in command of oneself.
self-pol·li·na·tion (sĕlf′pŏl′ə-nā′shən) *n.* The transfer of pollen from an anther to a stigma of the same flower. **—self′-pol′li·nat′ed** *adj.*
self-por·trait (sĕlf′pôr′trĭt, -trāt′, -pōr′-) *n.* A portrait, pictorial or verbal, of oneself created by oneself.
self-pos·ses·sion (sĕlf′pə-zĕsh′ən) *n.* Full command of one's faculties, feelings, and behavior; poise. **—self′-pos·sessed′** *adj.*
self-pres·er·va·tion (sĕlf′prĕz′ər-vā′shən) *n.* **1.** Protection of oneself from harm or destruction. **2.** The instinct for individual preservation.
self-pro·claimed (sĕlf′prō-klāmd′, -prə-) *adj.* Self-styled.
self-pro·pelled (sĕlf′prə-pĕld′) *adj.* Containing its own means of propulsion: *a self-propelled howitzer.*
self-pro·tec·tive (sĕlf′prə-tĕk′tĭv) *adj.* Serving to protect oneself. **—self′-pro·tec′tive·ly** *adv.*
self-pu·ri·fi·ca·tion (sĕlf′pyo͝or′ə-fĭ-kā′shən) *n.* **1.** Purification produced by nature: *self-purification of water.* **2.** Purification of oneself.
self-re·al·i·za·tion (sĕlf′rē′ə-lĭ-zā′shən) *n.* The complete development or fulfillment of one's own potential.
self-re·cord·ing (sĕlf′rĭ-kôr′dĭng) *adj.* Automatically recording its own functions or operations. Used of a machine or instrument.
self-re·crim·i·na·tion (sĕlf′rĭ-krĭm′ə-nā′shən) *n.* The act of blaming oneself.
self-re·flec·tion (sĕlf′rĭ-flĕk′shən) *n.* Self-examination. **—self′-re·flec′tive** *adj.* **—self′-re·flec′tive·ly** *adv.*
self-re·gard (sĕlf′rĭ-gärd′) *n.* **1.** Consideration of oneself or one's interests. **2.** Self-respect.
self-reg·u·lat·ing (sĕlf′rĕg′yə-lā′tĭng) *adj.* **1.** Regulating oneself or itself. **2.** Regulating itself automatically. **—self′-reg·u·la′tion** *n.*
self-re·li·ance (sĕlf′rĭ-lī′əns) *n.* Reliance upon one's own capabilities, judgment, or resources. **—self′-re·li′ant** *adj.* **—self′-re·li′ant·ly** *adv.*
self-rep·li·cat·ing (sĕlf′rĕp′lĭ-kā′tĭng) *adj.* Reproducing itself.
self-re·proach (sĕlf′rĭ-prōch′) *n.* The act or an instance of charging oneself with a fault or mistake. **—self′-re·proach′ful** *adj.* **—self′-re·proach′ful·ly** *adv.*
self-re·spect (sĕlf′rĭ-spĕkt′) *n.* Due respect for oneself, one's character, and one's conduct. **—self′-re·spect′ing** *adj.*
self-re·straint (sĕlf′rĭ-strānt′) *n.* Restraint of one's emotions, desires, or inclinations; self-control.
self-rev·e·la·tion (sĕlf′rĕv′ə-lā′shən) *n.* Revelation of one's own thoughts, emotions, or attitudes, esp. unintentionally. **—self′-re·veal′ing** (-rĭ-vē′lĭng) *adj.*
self-righ·teous (sĕlf′rī′chəs) *adj.* Piously sure of one's own righteousness; moralistic. **—self′-righ′teous·ly** *adv.* **—self′-righ′teous·ness** *n.*
self-right·ing (sĕlf′rī′tĭng) *adj.* Capable of righting itself when overturned: *a self-righting boat.*
self-ris·ing flour (sĕlf′rī′zĭng) *n.* A commercially produced mixture of flour and leavening.
self-rule (sĕlf′ro͞ol′) *n.* Self-government.
self-sac·ri·fice (sĕlf′săk′rə-fīs′) *n.* Sacrifice of one's personal interests or well-being for the sake of others or for a cause. **—self′-sac′ri·fic′ing** *adj.*
self·same (sĕlf′sām′) *adj.* Exactly identical; the very same. [ME *selve same* : *self,* same + *same,* same.] **—self′same′·ness** *n.*
self-sat·is·fac·tion (sĕlf′săt′ĭs-făk′shən) *n.* Satisfaction with oneself or with one's accomplishments.
self-seal·ing (sĕlf′sē′lĭng) *adj.* **1.** Capable of sealing itself, as

self-heal

semaphore

after being pierced: *a self-sealing tire.* **2.** Capable of being sealed without moisture: *a self-sealing envelope.*

self-seek·ing (sĕlf′sē′kĭng) *adj.* Pursuing only one's own interests. —*n.* The characteristics or activities of a self-seeking person. —**self′-seek′er** *n.*

self-se·lec·tion (sĕlf′sĭ-lĕk′shən) *n.* **1.** Selection of or by oneself. **2.** Selection of merchandise by oneself from a display counter or rack in a store.

self-serv·ice (sĕlf′sûr′vĭs) *adj.* Being a retail commercial enterprise in which the customers serve themselves and pay a cashier.

self-serv·ing (sĕlf′sûr′vĭng) *adj.* Serving one's own interests, esp. without concern for the needs or interests of others.

self-slaugh·ter (sĕlf′slô′tər) *n.* Suicide.

self-start·er (sĕlf′stär′tər) *n.* **1.** A starter (sense 3). **2.** An individual with initiative.

self-stud·y (sĕlf′stŭd′ē) *n.* **1.** Study of oneself. **2.** Independent or self-instructional study.

self-styled (sĕlf′stīld′) *adj.* As characterized by oneself: *"poets, real or self-styled"* (Constantine Fitzgibbon).

self-suf·fi·cient (sĕlf′sə-fĭsh′ənt) also **self-suf·fic·ing** (-fī′sĭng) *adj.* **1.** Capable of providing for oneself without the help of others; not dependent. **2.** Having undue confidence; smug. —**self′-suf·fi′cien·cy** *n.*

self-sup·port (sĕlf′sə-pôrt′, -pōrt′) *n.* The act of or capacity for supporting oneself financially without the help of others. —**self′-sup·port′ed, self′-sup·port′ing** *adj.*

self-sus·tain·ing (sĕlf′sə-stā′nĭng) *adj.* Capable of sustaining oneself or itself independently.

self-taught (sĕlf′tôt′) *adj.* Having taught oneself without formal instruction or the help of others.

self-treat·ment (sĕlf′trēt′mənt) *n.* The act of treating one's own illness without professional assistance.

self-trust (sĕlf′trŭst′) *n.* Self-confidence.

self-un·der·stand·ing (sĕlf′ŭn′dər-stăn′dĭng) *n.* Self-knowledge.

self-will (sĕlf′wĭl′) *n.* Willfulness, esp. in satisfying one's own desires; obstinacy. —**self′-willed′** *adj.*

self-wind·ing (sĕlf′wīn′dĭng) *adj.* Not requiring to be wound manually. Used of clocks and watches.

Sel·juk (sĕl′jo͞ok′, sĕl-jo͞ok′) *n.* A member of one of several Turkish dynasties ruling over central and western Asia from the 11th to the 13th century. [< Turk. *Seljūk,* the eponymous ancestor of the dynasties.]

sell (sĕl) *v.* **sold** (sōld), **sell·ing, sells.** —*tr.* **1.** To exchange or deliver for money or its equivalent. **2.** To offer for sale, as for one's business or livelihood: *He sells textiles.* **3.** To give up or surrender in exchange for a price or reward: *sold his soul to the devil.* **4.** To be responsible for the sale of; promote successfully: *Publicity sold that product.* **5.** To convince of: *They sold him on the idea.* **6.** *Slang.* To cheat or dupe. —*intr.* **1.** To exchange ownership for money or its equivalent; engage in selling. **2.** To be sold or be on sale. **3.** To attract prospective buyers; be popular on the market: *an item that sells well.* **4.** To be approved of; gain acceptance. —*n.* **1.** The activity of selling. **2.** *Slang.* A hoax or swindle. —***phrasal verbs.* sell off.** To get rid of by selling, often at reduced prices. **sell out. 1.** To sell all one's goods or possessions. **2.** *Slang.* To betray one's cause or colleagues: *He sold out to the other side.* —***idioms.* sell a bill of goods.** To take unfair advantage of. **sell down the river.** To betray the true trust or faith of. **sell short. 1.** To contract for the sale of securities or commodities one expects to own at a later date and at more advantageous terms. **2.** To underestimate the true value or worth of. [ME *sellen* < OE *sellan,* to give.] —**sell′a·ble** *adj.*

sell·er (sĕl′ər) *n.* **1.** A person who sells; vender. **2.** An item that sells in a particular manner: *a best seller.*

selling climax *n.* A sharp decline in stock prices on a heavy volume of trading followed by a rally.

selling point *n.* An aspect of something that is stressed or played up, as in advertising or selling.

sell·out (sĕl′out′) *n.* **1.** The act of selling out. **2.** An event for which all the tickets are sold. **3.** *Slang.* One who has betrayed his principles or an espoused cause.

sel·syn (sĕl′sĭn′) *n.* A device for the instantaneous transmission and reception, from a generator to a motor, of the angular movement of rotating parts. [SEL(F) + SYN(CHRONOUS).]

selt·zer (sĕlt′sər) *n.* **1.** A natural effervescent spring water of high mineral content. **2.** Soda water (sense 1). [G. *Selterser (Wasser),* (water) of Nieder Selters, a district in West Germany.]

sel·vage also **sel·vedge** (sĕl′vĭj) *n.* **1. a.** The edge of a fabric woven so that it will not ravel, esp. an ornamental fringe at either end of an oriental carpet. **b.** An edge similar to this, usually a tapelike one. **2.** The edge plate of a lock with a slot for a bolt. [ME, prob. < MDu. *selfegghe* : *self,* self + *egge,* edge.]

selves (sĕlvz) *n.* Plural of **self.**

se·man·teme (sĭ-măn′tēm′) *n.* An irreducible linguistic unit of meaning. [SEMANT(IC) + -EME.]

se·man·tic (sĭ-măn′tĭk) *adj.* **1.** Of or pertaining to meaning, esp. meaning in language. **2.** Of, relating to, or according to the science of semantics. [Gk. *sēmantikos,* significant < *sēmainein,* to signify < *sēma,* sign.] —**se·man′ti·cal·ly** *adv.*

se·man·ti·cist (sĭ-măn′tĭ-sĭst) *n.* A specialist in semantics.

se·man·tics (sĭ-măn′tĭks) *n. (used with a sing. verb).* **1.** *Ling.* The study or science of meaning in language forms, esp. with regard to its historical change. **2.** *Logic.* The study of relationships between signs and symbols and what they represent.

sem·a·phore (sĕm′ə-fôr′, -fōr′) *n.* **1.** A visual signaling apparatus with flags, lights, or mechanically moving arms, as on a railroad. **2.** A system for signaling using two flags that are held one in each hand. —*v.* **-phored, -phor·ing, -phores.** —*tr.* To send (a message) by semaphore. —*intr.* To signal with a semaphore. [Gk. *sēma,* sign + -PHORE.]

se·ma·si·ol·o·gy (sĭ-mā′sē-ŏl′ə-jē, -zē-) *n. Logic.* Semantics. [Gk. *sēmasia,* meaning (< *sēmainein,* to signify < *sēma,* sign) + -LOGY.] —**se·ma′si·o·log′i·cal** (-ə-lŏj′ĭ-kəl) *adj.* —**se·ma′si·ol′o·gist** *n.*

se·mat·ic (sĭ-măt′ĭk) *adj.* Serving as a warning or signal of danger. Used esp. of the coloring of certain animals. [< Gk. *sēma, sēmat-,* sign.]

sem·bla·ble (sĕm′blə-bəl) *adj.* **1.** Resembling; like. **2.** Seeming; apparent. —*n.* Something that closely resembles something else. [ME < OFr. < *sembler,* to resemble < Lat. *simulare,* to simulate < *similis,* like.] —**sem′bla·bly** *adv.*

sem·blance (sĕm′bləns) *n.* **1.** An outward or token appearance; form: *"Foolish men mistake transitory semblance for eternal fact"* (Carlyle). **2.** A representation; copy. **3.** The barest trace; modicum: *not a semblance of truth.* [ME < OFr. < *semblant,* pr.part. of *sembler,* to resemble. —see SEMBLABLE.]

se·mé (sĕ-mā′, sə-) *adj. Heraldry.* Having a design embellished with small, delicate figures, such as a lacing of stars or flowers. [Fr., p.part. of *semer,* to sow, scatter < Lat. *seminare* < *semen,* seed.]

se·mei·ol·o·gy (sē′mī-ŏl′ə-jē) *n.* Variant of **semiology.**

se·mei·ot·ic (sē′mī-ŏt′ĭk) *adj.* Variant of **semiotic.**

se·mei·ot·ics (sē′mī-ŏt′ĭks) *n.* Variant of **semiotics.**

se·meme (sĕ′mēm′) *n.* The meaning expressed by a morpheme. [Gk. *sēmainein,* to signify (< *sēma,* sign) + -EME.]

se·men (sē′mən) *n.* A viscous whitish secretion of the male reproductive organs, the transporting medium for spermatozoa. [ME < Lat. *semen,* seed.]

se·mes·ter (sə-mĕs′tər) *n.* One of two divisions of 15 to 18 weeks each of an academic year. [G. < Lat. *(cursus) semestris,* (period) of six months : *sex,* six + *mensis,* month.]

sem·i (sĕm′ē, sĕm′ī) *n.* A semitrailer.

semi– *pref.* **1.** Half: *semicircle.* **2.** Partial; partially: *semiconscious.* **3.** Resembling or having some of the characteristics of: *semiofficial.* **4.** Occurring twice during: *semimonthly.* [Lat. *semi-,* half.]

sem·i·ab·stract (sĕm′ē-ăb-străkt′, -ăb′străkt′) *adj.* Of or relating to an art form characterized by recognizable but stylized subject matter. —**sem′i·ab·strac′tion** *n.*

sem·i·an·nu·al (sĕm′ē-ăn′yo͞o-əl, sĕm′ī-) *adj.* Happening or issued twice a year. —**sem′i·an′nu·al·ly** *adv.*

sem·i·a·quat·ic (sĕm′ē-ə-kwŏt′ĭk, -kwăt′-, sĕm′ī-) *adj.* Adapted for living or growing in or near water; not entirely aquatic.

sem·i·ar·id (sĕm′ē-ăr′ĭd, sĕm′ī-) *adj.* Characterized by light annual rainfall and capable of sustaining only short grasses and shrubs. —**sem′i·a·rid′i·ty** (-ə-rĭd′ĭ-tē, -ă-rĭd′-) *n.*

sem·i·au·to·mat·ed (sĕm′ē-ô′tə-mā′tĭd, sĕm′ī-) *adj.* Partially automated.

sem·i·au·to·mat·ic (sĕm′ē-ô′tə-măt′ĭk, sĕm′ī-) *adj.* **1.** Partially automatic. **2.** Ejecting the shell and loading the next round of ammunition automatically after each shot has been fired. Used of firearms. —*n.* A semiautomatic firearm.

sem·i·au·ton·o·mous (sĕm′ē-ô-tŏn′ə-məs, sĕm′ī-) *adj.* Having the powers of self-government within a larger organization or structure.

sem·i·breve (sĕm′ē-brĕv′, -brēv′, sĕm′ī-) *n. Chiefly Brit. Mus.* A whole note.

sem·i·cen·ten·ni·al (sĕm′ē-sĕn-tĕn′ē-əl, sĕm′ī-) *adj.* Marking the 50th anniversary of an event. —*n.* A 50th anniversary or its celebration.

sem·i·cir·cle (sĕm′ĭ-sûr′kəl) *n.* **1.** A half of a circle as divided by a diameter. **2.** An object or arrangement of objects in the shape of a half-circle. —**sem′i·cir′cu·lar** (-kyə-lər) *adj.*

semicircular canal *n.* Any of the three tubular and looped structures in the labyrinth of the inner ear, together functioning in the maintenance of a sense of balance and orientation.

sem·i·civ·i·lized (sĕm′ē-sĭv′ə-līzd′, sĕm′ī-) *adj.* Partly civilized.

sem·i·clas·si·cal (sĕm′ē-klăs′ĭ-kəl, sĕm′ī-) *adj.* **1.** Of, relating to, or being a musical work that in style or form falls between classical and popular music. **2.** Of, relating to, or being classical music that has acquired popular appeal.

sem·i·co·lon (sĕm′ĭ-kō′lən) *n.* A mark of punctuation (;) indicating a degree of separation intermediate in value between the comma and the period.

sem·i·co·ma (sĕm′ē-kō′mə, sĕm′ī-) *n.* A partial or mild comatose state. —**sem′i·co′ma·tose′** (-mə-tōs′, -kŏm′ə-) *adj.*

sem·i·con·duc·tor (sĕm′ē-kən-dŭk′tər, sĕm′ī-) *n.* Any of various solid crystalline substances, such as germanium or silicon, having electrical conductivity greater than insulators but less than good conductors.

sem·i·con·scious (sĕm′ē-kŏn′shəs, sĕm′ī-) *adj.* Half-conscious. **—sem′i·con′scious·ly** *adv.* **—sem′i·con′scious·ness** *n.*
sem·i·dark·ness (sĕm′ē-därk′nĭs, sĕm′ī-) *n.* Partial darkness.
sem·i·des·ert (sĕm′ē-dĕz′ərt, sĕm′ī-) *n.* An area often located between a desert and a grassland or woodland.
sem·i·de·tached (sĕm′ē-dĭ-tăcht′, sĕm′ī-) *adj.* Attached to something on one side only: *a semidetached house.*
sem·i·di·am·e·ter (sĕm′ē-dī-ăm′ĭ-tər, sĕm′ī-) *n.* The apparent radius of a celestial body when viewed as a disk from Earth.
sem·i·di·ur·nal (sĕm′ē-dī-ûr′nəl, sĕm′ī-) *adj.* **1.** Of, pertaining to, occurring, or performed during a half-day. **2.** Occurring or coming approximately once every 12 hours, as the tides. **3.** Designating the arc described by a celestial body between its meridian passage and its points of rising or setting.
sem·i·di·vine (sĕm′ē-dĭ-vīn′, sĕm′ī-) *adj.* Not fully divine but more than mortal, as a demigod in Greek mythology.
sem·i·doc·u·men·ta·ry (sĕm′ē-dŏk′yə-mĕn′tə-rē, -mĕn′trē, sĕm′ī-) *n.* A film presenting a fictional story that incorporates many factual details or actual events. **—sem′i·doc′u·men′ta·ry** *adj.*
sem·i·dome (sĕm′ē-dōm′, sĕm′ī-) *n.* A roof covering a semicircular space; half a dome.
sem·i·el·lip·ti·cal (sĕm′ē-ĭ-lĭp′tĭ-kəl, sĕm′ī-) *adj.* Having the form or shape of half of an ellipse, esp. when divided along the major axis.
sem·i·fi·nal (sĕm′ē-fī′nəl, sĕm′ī-) *adj.* Immediately preceding the final, as in a series of competitions or examinations. *—n.* (sĕm′ē-fī′nəl, sĕm′ī-). **1.** An event, as a match or competition, that precedes a final event. **2.** One of the two competitions of the next to the last round in an elimination tournament. **—sem′i·fi′nal·ist** *n.*
sem·i·flu·id (sĕm′ē-flo͞o′ĭd, sĕm′ī-) *adj.* Intermediate in flow properties between solids and liquids; highly viscous. *—n.* (sĕm′ē-flo͞o′ĭd, sĕm′ī-). A semifluid substance.
sem·i·for·mal (sĕm′ē-fôr′məl, sĕm′ī-) *adj.* **1.** Moderately formal: *a semiformal dance.* **2.** Suitable for a moderately formal occasion: *semiformal clothes.*
sem·i·group (sĕm′ē-gro͞op′, sĕm′ī-) *n. Math.* A nonempty set with an associative binary multiplication.
sem·i·in·de·pend·ent (sĕm′ē-ĭn′dĭ-pĕn′dənt, sĕm′ī-) *adj.* **1.** Partially independent. **2.** Semiautonomous.
sem·i·in·fi·nite (sĕm′ē-ĭn′fə-nĭt, sĕm′ī-) *adj.* Unbounded in one direction or dimension.
sem·i·liq·uid (sĕm′ē-lĭk′wĭd, sĕm′ī-) *adj.* Intermediate in properties, esp. in flow properties, between liquids and solids. *—n.* (sĕm′ē-lĭk′wĭd, sĕm′ī-). A semiliquid substance.
sem·i·lit·er·ate (sĕm′ē-lĭt′ər-ĭt, sĕm′ī-) *adj.* **1.** Having achieved an elementary level of reading and writing ability. **2.** Having limited understanding, as of a technical subject.
sem·i·log (sĕm′ē-lôg′, -lŏg′, sĕm′ī-) *adj.* Semilogarithmic.
sem·i·log·a·rith·mic (sĕm′ē-lô′gə-rĭ*th*′mĭk, -lŏg′ə-, sĕm′ī-) *adj.* Having one logarithmic and one arithmetic scale: *semilogarithmic graph paper.*
sem·i·lu·nar (sĕm′ē-lo͞o′nər, sĕm′ī-) also **sem·i·lu·nate** (-lo͞o′nāt′) *adj.* Shaped like a half-moon; crescent.
semilunar bone *n. Anat.* The lunate bone.
semilunar valve *n.* Either of two crescent-shaped valves, each having three cusps, located in the aorta and in the pulmonary artery and preventing blood from flowing back into the heart.
sem·i·lu·nate (sĕm′ē-lo͞o′nāt′, sĕm′ī-) *adj.* Variant of **semilunar.**
sem·i·month·ly (sĕm′ē-mŭnth′lē, sĕm′ī-) *adj.* Occurring or issued twice a month. *—n., pl.* **-lies.** A semimonthly publication. *—adv.* Twice monthly; at half-monthly intervals.
sem·i·nal (sĕm′ə-nəl) *adj.* **1.** Of, relating to, or containing semen or seed. **2.** Of, pertaining to, or having the power to originate; creative. [ME < OFr. < Lat. *seminalis* < *semen,* seed.] **—sem′i·nal·ly** *adv.*
sem·i·nar (sĕm′ə-när′) *n.* **1. a.** A small group of advanced students in a college or graduate school engaged in original research under the guidance of a professor who meets regularly with them for reports and discussions. **b.** A course of study so pursued. **c.** A scheduled meeting of such a group. **2.** A meeting for an exchange of ideas in an area; conference. [G. < Lat. *seminarium,* seed plot < *semen,* seed.]
sem·i·nar·i·an (sĕm′ə-nâr′ē-ən) *n.* A seminary student.
sem·i·nar·y (sĕm′ə-nĕr′ē) *n., pl.* **-ies. 1. a.** A school, esp. a theological school for the training of priests, ministers, or rabbis. **b.** A school of higher education, esp. a private school for girls. **2.** A place or environment in which something is developed or nurtured. [ME, seed plot < Lat. *seminarium* < *semen,* seed.]
sem·i·na·tion (sĕm′ə-nā′shən) *n.* The dispersal or production of seed. [Lat. *seminatio,* propagation < *seminatus,* propagation < *seminatus,* p.part. of *seminare,* to sow < *semen,* seed.]
sem·i·nif·er·ous (sĕm′ə-nĭf′ər-əs) *adj. Biol.* **1.** Conveying or producing semen. **2.** Bearing seed. [Lat. *semen, semin-,* seed, semen + -FEROUS.]
Sem·i·nole (sĕm′ə-nōl′) *n., pl.* **Seminole** or **-noles. 1. a.** A tribe of North American Indians, a late Creek offshoot, originally living in Alabama, later in Florida, but now chiefly in Oklahoma. **b.** A member of this tribe. **2.** The Muskhogean language of the Seminole. [Creek *simanóli* < Am. Sp. *cimarrón,* wild.] **—Sem′i·nole′** *adj.*
sem·i·no·mad (sĕm′ē-nō′măd′, sĕm′ī-) *n.* One of a people whose living habits are largely nomadic but who plant some crops at a base point. **—sem′i·no·mad′ic** (-nō-măd′ĭk) *adj.*
sem·i·of·fi·cial (sĕm′ē-ə-fĭsh′əl, sĕm′ī-) *adj.* Having some official authority or sanction. **—sem′i·of·fi′cial·ly** *adv.*
se·mi·ol·o·gy (sē′mē-ŏl′ə-jē, -mī-) also **se·mei·ol·o·gy** (sē′mī-) *n.* **1. a.** The science dealing with signs or sign language. **b.** The use of signs in signaling, as with a semaphore. **2.** Symptomatology. [Gk. *sēmion,* sign + -LOGY.]
sem·i·o·paque (sĕm′ē-ō-pāk′, sĕm′ī-) *adj.* Partially opaque.
se·mi·ot·ic (sē′mē-ŏt′ĭk, -mī-) also **se·mi·ot·i·cal** (-ĭ-kəl) or **se·mei·ot·ic** (sē′mī-) also **se·mei·ot·i·cal** (-ĭ-kəl) *adj.* **1.** *Logic.* Of or relating to semantics. **2.** *Med.* Relating to symptomatology. [Gk. *sēmeiōtikos,* observant of signs < *sēmeioun,* to note < *sēmeion,* sign.]
se·mi·ot·ics (sē′mē-ŏt′ĭks, -mī-) also **se·mei·ot·ics** (sē′mī-) *n. (used with a sing. verb).* **1.** *Logic.* Semantics. **2.** *Med.* Symptomatology. **—se′mi·o·ti′cian** (-ə-tĭsh′ən) *n.*
sem·i·pal·mate (sĕm′ē-păl′māt′, -pä′māt′, -päl′māt′, sĕm′ī-) also **sem·i·pal·mat·ed** (-mā′tĭd) *adj.* Having partial or reduced webbing between the toes, as some wading birds do.
sem·i·par·a·site (sĕm′ē-păr′ə-sīt′, sĕm′ī-) *n. Biol.* A hemiparasite. **—sem′i·par′a·sit′ic** (-sĭt′ĭk) *adj.*
sem·i·per·me·a·ble (sĕm′ē-pûr′mē-ə-bəl, sĕm′ī-) *adj.* **1.** Partially permeable. **2.** Of or relating to a natural or artificial membrane that is permeable to some molecules in a mixture but not to all. **—sem′i·per′me·a·bil′i·ty** (-bĭl′ĭ-tē) *n.*
sem·i·po·lit·i·cal (sĕm′ē-pə-lĭt′ĭ-kəl, sĕm′ī-) *adj.* Political in some aspects or activities.
sem·i·por·ce·lain (sĕm′ē-pôr′sə-lĭn, -pōr′-, sĕm′ī-) *n.* Any of several glazed ceramic wares resembling porcelain but having little or no translucency.
sem·i·post·al (sĕm′ē-pō′stəl, sĕm′ī-) *n.* A postage stamp sold for more than its postal value, esp. to raise money for a charitable purpose.
sem·i·pre·cious (sĕm′ē-prĕsh′əs, sĕm′ī-) *adj.* Of less value than a precious stone.
sem·i·pri·vate (sĕm′ē-prī′vĭt, sĕm′ī-) *adj.* Shared with usually one to three other hospital patients: *a semiprivate room.*
sem·i·pro (sĕm′ē-prō′, sĕm′ī-) *adj. Informal.* Semiprofessional. **—sem′i·pro′** *n.*
sem·i·pro·fes·sion·al (sĕm′ē-prə-fĕsh′ə-nəl, sĕm′ī-) *adj.* **1.** Taking part in a sport for pay but not on a full-time basis. **2.** Composed of or engaged in by semiprofessional players. **3.** Designating an apartment that may be used by a resident professionally but for only part of his income. *—n.* **1.** A semiprofessional player. **2.** One whose occupation or work has some of the characteristics of a profession or of a professional. **—sem′i·pro·fes′sion·al·ly** *adv.*
sem·i·qua·ver (sĕm′ē-kwā′vər) *n. Mus. Chiefly Brit.* A sixteenth note.
sem·i·re·tired (sĕm′ē-rĭ-tīrd′, sĕm′ī-) *adj.* Working on a part-time basis only, esp. for reasons of ill health or advanced age. **—sem′i·re·tire′ment** *n.*
sem·i·rig·id (sĕm′ē-rĭj′ĭd, sĕm′ī-) *adj.* Having some rigid components.
sem·i·round (sĕm′ē-round′, sĕm′ī-) *adj.* Having a round side and a flat side. *—n.* (sĕm′ē-round′, sĕm′ī-). Something that is semiround.
sem·i·skilled (sĕm′ē-skĭld′, sĕm′ī-) *adj.* **1.** Possessing some skills but not enough to do specialized work. **2.** Requiring limited skills: *a semiskilled job.*
sem·i·soft (sĕm′ē-sôft′, -sŏft′, sĕm′ī-) *adj.* **1.** Of medium softness. **2.** Firm but easily sliced: *semisoft cheese.*
sem·i·sol·id (sĕm′ē-sŏl′ĭd, sĕm′ī-) *adj.* Intermediate in properties, esp. in rigidity, between solids and liquids. *—n.* (sĕm′ē-sŏl′ĭd, sĕm′ī-). A semisolid substance, such as a stiff dough or firm gelatin.
sem·i·sweet (sĕm′ē-swēt′, sĕm′ī-) *adj.* Having a small amount of sweetening: *semisweet chocolate.*
Sem·ite (sĕm′īt′) *n.* **1.** One of a people of Caucasian stock comprising chiefly Jews and Arabs but in ancient times also including Babylonians, Assyrians, Phoenicians, and others of the eastern Mediterranean area. **2.** One of the people descended from Shem. [NLat. *semita* < LLat. *Sem,* Shem, eponymous ancestor of the Semites < Gk. < Heb. *Shem.*]
Se·mit·ic (sə-mĭt′ĭk) *adj.* **1.** Of or relating to the Semites, esp. Jewish or Arabic. **2.** Of, relating to, or comprising a subfamily of the Afro-Asiatic language family that includes Arabic, Hebrew, Amharic, and Aramaic. *—n.* **1.** The Semitic languages. **2.** Any one of the Semitic languages.
Se·mit·ics (sə-mĭt′ĭks) *n. (used with a sing. verb).* The study of the history, languages, and cultures of the Semitic peoples. **—Se·mit′i·cist** (-ĭ-sĭst) *n.*
Sem·i·tism (sĕm′ĭ-tĭz′əm) *n.* **1.** A Semitic word or idiom. **2.** Semitic traits, attributes, or customs. **3.** A policy or a predisposition in favor of the Jews.
sem·i·tone (sĕm′ē-tōn′, sĕm′ī-) *n. Mus.* An interval equal to a half tone in the standard diatonic scale. **—sem′i·ton′ic** (-tŏn′ĭk) *adj.* **—sem′i·ton′i·cal·ly** *adv.*
sem·i·trail·er (sĕm′ē-trā′lər, sĕm′ī-) *n.* A trailer with a set or

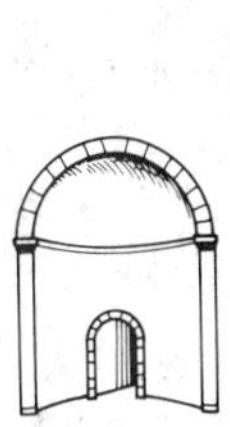

semidome

semipalmate
Semipalmate foot of a plover

Seneca snakeroot

senna

sets of wheels at the rear only, the forward portion supported by the truck tractor or towing vehicle.

sem·i·trans·par·ent (sĕm′ē-trăns-pâr′ənt, -păr′-, sĕm′ī-) *adj.* Partially transparent.

sem·i·trop·i·cal (sĕm′ē-trŏp′ĭ-kəl, sĕm′ī-) *adj.* Partly tropical; subtropical.

sem·i·vow·el (sĕm′ĭ-vou′əl) *n.* A letter or vocal sound having the sound of a vowel but used as a consonant, as *w, y,* and *r.*

sem·i·week·ly (sĕm′ē-wēk′lē, sĕm′ī-) *adj.* Issued or happening twice a week. —*n., pl.* **-lies.** A semiweekly event or publication. —*adv.* Twice weekly.

sem·i·year·ly (sĕm′ē-yîr′lē, sĕm′ī-) *adj.* Issued or happening twice a year or once every half year. —*n., pl.* **-lies.** A semiyearly event or publication. —*adv.* Every half year.

sem·o·li·na (sĕm′ə-lē′nə) *n.* The gritty, coarse particles of wheat left after the finer flour has passed through the bolting machine, used for pasta. [Ital. *semolino,* dim. of *semola,* bran < Lat. *simila,* fine flour.]

sem·pi·ter·nal (sĕm′pĭ-tûr′nəl) *adj.* Eternal; perpetual. [ME < OFr. *sempiternel* < LLat. *sempiternalis* < Lat. *sempiternus* : *semper,* always + *aeternus,* eternal.] **—sem′pi·ter′ni·ty** (-nĭ-tē) *n.*

sem·pli·ce (sĕm′plĭ-chā′) *adv. Mus.* Simply; plainly. Used as a direction. [Ital. < Lat. *simplex,* simple.] **—sem′pli·ce′** *adj.*

sem·pre (sĕm′prā) *adv. Mus.* In the same manner throughout. Used as a direction. [Ital., always < Lat. *semper.*]

semp·stress (sĕmp′strĭs, sĕm′-) *n.* A seamstress. [Var. of SEAMSTRESS.]

sen[1] (sĕn) *n., pl.* **sen.** See table at **currency.** [J. < Chin. (Mandarin) *qian*[2], money.]

sen[2] (sĕn) *n., pl.* **sen.** See table at **currency.** [Indonesian *sén* < E. CENT.]

se·nar·i·us (sə-nâr′ē-əs) *n., pl.* **-nar·i·i** (-nâr′ē-ī′). A Greek or Latin verse consisting of six feet. [Lat. —see SENARY.]

sen·a·ry (sĕn′ə-rē) *adj.* **1.** Of or relating to the number six. **2.** Having six things or parts. [Lat. *senarius* < *seni,* six each < *sex,* six.]

sen·ate (sĕn′ĭt) *n.* **1.** An assembly or council of citizens having the highest deliberative and legislative functions in a government, specifically: **a. Senate.** The upper house of the U.S. Congress, to which two members are elected from each state by popular vote for a six-year term. **b.** Often **Senate.** The upper house in the bicameral legislature of many states in the United States. **c. Senate.** The upper legislative house in Canada, France, and some other countries. **d.** The supreme council of state of the ancient Roman republic and later of the empire. **2.** The building or hall in which a senate meets. **3.** A governing, advisory, or disciplinary body of some colleges and universities composed of faculty members and sometimes student representatives. [ME *senat* < OFr. < Lat. *senatus* < *senex,* old man.]

sen·a·tor (sĕn′ə-tər) *n.* A member of a senate. **—sen′a·tor·ship′** *n.*

sen·a·to·ri·al (sĕn′ə-tôr′ē-əl, -tōr′-) *adj.* **1.** Of, concerning, or befitting a senator or a senate. **2.** Composed of senators. **—sen′a·to′ri·al·ly** *adv.*

senatorial courtesy *n.* The custom in the U.S. Senate of refusing to confirm a presidential appointment to office opposed by both senators from the state of the appointee or by the senior senator of the President's party.

senatorial district *n.* A territorial district from which a senator is elected.

send[1] (sĕnd) *v.* **sent** (sĕnt), **send·ing, sends.** —*tr.* **1.** To cause to be conveyed by an intermediary to a destination: *send goods by plane.* **2.** To dispatch, as by a communications medium. **3. a.** To direct to go on a mission. **b.** To require or enable to go: *sent his daughter to college.* **c.** To direct (a person) to a source of information; refer. **4.** To give off (heat, for example); emit. **5.** To direct or propel with force; drive: *The batter sent the ball to left field.* **6.** To cause to take place or befall; inflict. **7. a.** To put or drive into a given state or condition: *news that sent them into a frenzy.* **b.** *Slang.* To transport with delight; carry away: *That music really sends me.* —*intr.* **1.** To dispatch someone to do an errand or convey a message: *send out for hamburgers.* **2.** To dispatch a request or order, esp. by mail: *send away for a new catalog.* **—idioms. send down.** *Chiefly Brit.* To suspend or dismiss from a university. **send flying.** To scatter or knock in all directions with great force or violence. **send for.** To request to come by means of a message or messenger; summon. **send up.** *Informal.* **1.** To send to jail. **2.** *Chiefly Brit. Slang.* To amuse oneself at the expense of; parody. [ME *senden* < OE *sendan.*] **—send′er** *n.*

send[2] (sĕnd) *v. & n.* Variant of **scend.**

sen·dal (sĕn′dl) *n.* A light, thin silk used in the Middle Ages for fine garments, church vestments, and banners. [ME *cendal* < OFr.]

send·off (sĕnd′ôf′, -ŏf′) *n.* A demonstration of affection and good wishes for the beginning of a new undertaking.

send-up (sĕnd′ŭp′) *n. Informal.* An amusing imitation or parody; takeoff.

se·ne (sā′nā) *n., pl.* **sene.** See table at **currency.** [Samoan < E. CENT.]

Sen·e·ca (sĕn′ĭ-kə) *n., pl.* **Seneca** or **-cas. 1. a.** A tribe of North American Indians formerly inhabiting western New York. **b.** A member of this tribe. **2.** The Iroquoian language of the Seneca. [Du. *Sennecaas,* perh. of Algonquian orig.]

Seneca snakeroot *n.* A North American plant, *Polygala senega,* having a terminal cluster of small white flowers.

se·nec·ti·tude (sĭ-nĕk′tĭ-to͞od′, -tyo͞od′) *n.* Old age. [Med. Lat. *senectitudo* < Lat. *senectus* < *senex,* old.]

sen·e·ga (sĕn′ĭ-gə) *n.* The dried roots of the Seneca snakeroot, used medicinally as an expectorant. [Alteration of SENECA.]

se·nes·cent (sĭ-nĕs′ənt) *adj.* Growing old; aging. [Lat. *senescens, senescent-,* pr.part. of *senescere,* to grow old, inchoative of *senēre,* to be old < *senex,* old.] **—se·nes′cence** *n.*

sen·e·schal (sĕn′ə-shəl) *n.* An official in a medieval noble household in charge of domestic arrangements and the administration of servants; steward. [ME < OFr. < Med. Lat. *siniscalcus,* of Germanic orig.]

se·nile (sē′nīl′, sĕn′īl′) *adj.* **1.** Pertaining to, characteristic of, or proceeding from old age. **2.** Exhibiting senility. **3.** *Geol.* Worn away nearly to the base level, as at the end of an erosion cycle. [OFr. < Lat. *senilis* < *senex,* old.] **—se′nile′ly** *adv.*

senile dementia *n.* Progressive, abnormally accelerated deterioration of mental faculties and emotional stability in old age.

se·nil·i·ty (sĭ-nĭl′ĭ-tē) *n.* **1.** The state of being senile. **2.** The mental and physical deterioration of old age.

sen·ior (sēn′yər) *adj.* **1.** Of or designating the older of two, esp. denoting the older of two persons having the same name, as father and son. **2. a.** Above others in rank or length of service. **b.** Having precedence in making certain decisions. **3.** Of or pertaining to the fourth and last year of high school or college. —*n.* **1.** A senior person. **2.** A student in the fourth year of high school or college. [Lat., comp. of *senex,* old.]

senior citizen *n.* A person of or over the age of retirement.

senior high school *n.* A high school usually comprising grades 10, 11, and 12.

sen·ior·i·ty (sēn-yôr′ĭ-tē, -yŏr′-) *n.* **1.** The state of being older or higher in rank. **2.** Precedence of position, esp. precedence over others of the same rank by reason of a longer span of service.

sen·i·ti (sĕn′ĭ-tē) *n., pl.* **seniti.** See table at **currency.** [Tongan < E. CENT.]

sen·na (sĕn′ə) *n.* **1.** Any of various plants of the genus *Cassia,* having compound leaves and usually yellow flowers. **2.** The dried leaves of *C. angustifolia* or *C. acutifolia,* used medicinally as a cathartic. [NLat. < Ar. *sanā′.*]

sen·net[1] (sĕn′ĭt) *n.* A call on a trumpet or cornet signaling the ceremonial exits and entrances of actors in Elizabethan drama. [Perh. var. of SIGNET.]

sen·net[2] (sĕn′ĭt) *n.* Any of several barracudas, esp. *Sphyraena borealis,* of the western Atlantic. [Orig. unknown.]

sen·night (sĕn′īt′) *n. Archaic.* A week. [ME *seoveniht* < OE *seofon nihta,* seven nights.]

sen·nit (sĕn′ĭt) *n.* **1.** *Naut.* Braided cordage formed by plaiting several strands of rope fiber or similar material. **2.** Plaited straw, grass, or palm leaves for making hats. [Orig. unknown.]

se·no·pi·a (sĭ-nō′pē-ə) *n.* Improvement of near vision sometimes occurring in the aged because of swelling of the crystalline lens in incipient cataract. [Lat. *senex,* old + -OPIA.]

se·ñor (sān-yôr′) *n., pl.* **se·ño·res** (sān-yôr′ās). **1.** The Spanish title of courtesy for a man, equivalent to the English *Mr.* or *sir.* **2.** A Spanish or Spanish-speaking man. [Sp. < Med. Lat. *senior,* lord < Lat., senior.]

se·ño·ra (sān-yôr′ə) *n.* **1.** The Spanish title of courtesy for a married woman, equivalent to the English *Mrs.* or *madam.* **2.** A Spanish or Spanish-speaking woman. [Sp., fem. of *señor,* señor.]

se·ño·res (sān-yôr′ās) *n.* Plural of **señor.**

se·ño·ri·ta (sān′yə-rē′tə) *n.* **1.** The Spanish title of courtesy for an unmarried young woman or a girl, equivalent to the English *Miss.* **2.** A Spanish or Spanish-speaking unmarried woman or girl. [Sp., dim. of *señora,* señora.]

sen·sate (sĕn′sāt′) also **sen·sat·ed** (-sā′tĭd) *adj.* Perceived by the senses. [LLat. *sensatus,* gifted with sense < Lat. *sensus,* sense.] **—sen′sate′ly** *adv.*

sen·sa·tion (sĕn-sā′shən, sən-) *n.* **1. a.** A perception associated with stimulation of a sense organ or with a specific bodily condition: *the sensation of heat.* **b.** The faculty to feel or perceive; physical sensibility: *He had little sensation left in his leg.* **2.** A state of heightened interest or emotion: *"The anticipation produced in me a sensation somewhat between bliss and fear"* (James Weldon Johnson). **3. a.** A condition of intense public interest and excitement: *"The purser made a sensation as sailors like to do, by predicting a storm"* (Evelyn Waugh). **b.** An event or object causing such public excitement. [Med. Lat. *sensatio* < LLat. *sensatus,* gifted with sense < *sensus,* sense.]

sen·sa·tion·al (sĕn-sā′shə-nəl, sən-) *adj.* **1.** Of or pertaining to sensation. **2.** Arousing or intended to arouse strong curiosity, interest, or reaction, esp. by exaggerated or lurid details. **3.** Outstanding; spectacular. **—sen·sa′tion·al·ly** *adv.*

sen·sa·tion·al·ism (sĕn-sā′shə-nə-lĭz′əm, sən-) *n.* **1. a.** The use of sensational matter or methods, esp. in writing, journalism, or politics. **b.** Sensational subject matter. **c.** Interest in or the effect of such subject matter. **2.** *Philos.* The theory that sensation is the only source of knowledge. **3.** The ethical doctrine that feeling is the only criterion of good. **—sen·sa'tion·al·ist** *n.* **—sen·sa'tion·al·is'tic** *adj.*

sense (sĕns) *n.* **1. a.** Any of the animal functions of hearing, sight, smell, touch, and taste. **b.** The faculty of self-perception exemplified by these functions. **2. senses.** The faculties of sensation as means of providing physical gratification and pleasure. **3. a.** Intuitive or acquired perception or ability to estimate: *a sense of timing.* **b.** A capacity to appreciate or understand: *a sense of humor.* **c.** A vague feeling, as of coming danger. **d.** Recognition or perception either through the senses or through the intellect; consciousness: *a sense of guilt.* **4. a.** Often **senses.** Normal ability to think or reason soundly; correct judgment: *Come to your senses.* **b.** Something that is sound or reasonable: *There's no sense in waiting.* **5. a.** Import; significance. **b.** Lexical meaning: *"Let us take 'useful,' as Locke takes it, in its proper and popular sense"* (John Henry Newman). **c.** The meaning of a word in a particular context. **6.** Judgment; consensus: *sounding out the sense of the electorate on capital punishment.* —*tr.v.* **sensed, sens·ing, sens·es. 1.** To become aware of; perceive. **2.** To grasp; understand. **3.** To detect automatically: *sense radioactivity.* [Lat. *sensus,* the faculty of perceiving < p.part. of *sentire,* to feel.]

sense datum *n.* A basic unanalyzable experience resulting from the stimulation of a sense organ.

sense·less (sĕns'lĭs) *adj.* **1.** Without sense or meaning; meaningless: *a senseless attack.* **2.** Lacking sense; foolish: *a senseless plan.* **3.** Insensate; unconscious. **—sense'less·ly** *adv.* **—sense'less·ness** *n.*

sense organ *n.* A specialized organ or structure, such as the eye or ear, the stimulation of which initiates a process of sensory perception.

sense perception *n.* Perception by the bodily senses.

sen·si·bil·i·ty (sĕn'sə-bĭl'ĭ-tē) *n., pl.* **-ties. 1.** The ability to feel or perceive. **2. a.** Keen intellectual perception: *the sensibility of a painter to color.* **b.** Mental or emotional responsiveness toward something, as the feelings of another. **3.** Often **sensibilities.** Receptiveness to impression, whether pleasant or unpleasant; acuteness of feeling: *"The sufferings of the Cuban people shocked our sensibilities"* (George F. Kennan). **4.** Refined awareness and appreciation in matters of feeling. **5.** The aptness of plant organisms and instruments to be affected by environment.

sen·si·ble (sĕn'sə-bəl) *adj.* **1.** Perceptible by the senses or by the mind. **2.** Readily perceived; appreciable. **3.** Having the faculty of sensation; able to feel or perceive. **4.** Having a perception of something; cognizant. **5.** Acting with or showing good sense: *a sensible man; a sensible choice.* [ME < OFr. < Lat. *sensibilis* < *sensus,* sense.] **—sen'si·ble·ness** *n.* **—sen'si·bly** *adv.*

sen·sil·lum (sĕn-sĭl'əm) *n., pl.* **-sil·la** (-sĭl'ə). An epithelial sense organ consisting of one cell or a few cells. [NLat., dim. of Med. Lat. *sensus,* sense organ < Lat., sense.]

sen·si·tive (sĕn'sĭ-tĭv) *adj.* **1.** Capable of perceiving with a sense or senses. **2.** Responsive to external conditions or stimulation. **3.** Susceptible to the attitudes, feelings, or circumstances of others. **4.** Quick to take offense; touchy. **5.** Easily irritated: *sensitive skin.* **6.** Readily altered by the action of an agent: *film that is sensitive to light.* **7.** Registering very slight differences or changes of condition. Used of an instrument. **8.** Fluctuating or tending to fluctuate, as stock prices. **9.** Of or relating to classified information: *a sensitive post in the State Department; sensitive data.* [ME < OFr. *sensitif* < Med. Lat. *sensitivus* < Lat. *sensus,* sense.] **—sen'si·tive·ly** *adv.* **—sen'si·tive·ness** *n.*

sensitive plant *n.* **1.** A woody tropical American plant, *Mimosa pudica,* having leaflets and stems that fold and droop when touched. **2.** Any of various plants similar to the sensitive plant, such as *Cassia nictitans,* of eastern North America.

sen·si·tiv·i·ty (sĕn'sĭ-tĭv'ĭ-tē) *n., pl.* **-ties. 1.** The quality or condition of being sensitive. **2.** Organic or organismic responsiveness to stimulation. **3.** *Electronics.* The minimum input signal required to produce a specified output signal. **4.** The degree of response of a plate or film to light, esp. to light of a specified wavelength.

sensitivity training *n.* Training in small-group interaction in which individuals are taught how to develop a sensitive awareness and understanding of themselves and of their relationships with others.

sen·si·tize (sĕn'sĭ-tīz') *v.* **-tized, -tiz·ing, -tiz·es.** —*tr.* **1.** To make sensitive. **2.** To make (a film or plate) sensitive to light, esp. to light of a specific wavelength. —*intr.* To become sensitive. **—sen'si·ti·za'tion** *n.* **—sen'si·tiz'er** *n.*

sen·si·tom·e·ter (sĕn'sĭ-tŏm'ĭ-tər) *n.* **1.** A device used for measuring the sensitivity of photographic film to light. **2.** A device similar to a sensitometer for measuring the sensitivity of eyes to light. [SENSIT(IVE) + -METER.] **—sen'si·to·met'ric** (-tə-mĕt'rĭk) *adj.* **—sen'si·tom'e·try** *n.*

sen·sor (sĕn'sər, -sôr') *n.* A device, such as a photoelectric cell, that receives and responds to a signal or stimulus. [< Lat. *sensus,* sense.]

sen·so·ri·a (sĕn-sôr'ē-ə, -sōr'-) *n.* A plural of **sensorium.**

sen·so·ri·al (sĕn-sôr'ē-əl, -sōr'-) *adj.* Sensory.

sen·so·ri·mo·tor (sĕn'sə-rē-mō'tər) *adj.* Of, pertaining to, or combining the functions of the sensing and motor activities. Used of nerves. [SENSOR(Y) + MOTOR.]

sen·so·ri·neu·ral (sĕn'sə-rē-no͝or'əl, -nyo͝or'-) *adj.* Of, pertaining to, or involving the neural aspects of sensory perception.

sen·so·ri·um (sĕn-sôr'ē-əm, -sōr'-) *n., pl.* **-so·ri·ums** or **-so·ri·a** (-sôr'ē-ə, -sōr'-). **1.** The part of the brain that receives and correlates the impressions conveyed to various sensory areas. **2.** The entire sensory system. [LLat. *sensorium,* organ of sensation < Lat. *sensus,* sense.]

sen·so·ry (sĕn'sə-rē) *adj.* **1.** Of or pertaining to the senses or sensation. **2.** Transmitting impulses from sense organs to nerve centers; afferent.

sensory deprivation *n.* Deprivation of sensory stimulation, as by prolonged immersion in a tank of water, in order to observe physical and esp. psychological reactions.

sen·su·al (sĕn'sho͞o-əl) *adj.* **1.** Pertaining to or affecting any of the senses or a sense organ. **2. a.** Pertaining to or given to the gratification of the physical appetites, esp. the sexual appetite. **b.** Suggesting sexuality; voluptuous. **c.** Physical rather than spiritual or intellectual. **d.** Lacking in moral or spiritual interests; worldly. **3.** Sensory. **—sen'su·al·ly** *adv.* **—sen'su·al·ness** *n.*

sen·su·al·ism (sĕn'sho͞o-ə-lĭz'əm) *n.* **1.** Sensuality. **2.** The ethical doctrine that the pleasures of the senses are the highest good. **3.** *Philos.* Sensationalism (sense 2). **—sen'su·al·ist** *n.* **—sen'su·al·is'tic** *adj.*

sen·su·al·i·ty (sĕn'sho͞o-ăl'ĭ-tē) *n.* **1.** The quality or state of being sensual. **2. a.** Excessive devotion to sensual pleasures. **b.** Lasciviousness.

sen·su·al·ize (sĕn'sho͞o-ə-līz') *tr.v.* **-ized, -iz·ing, -iz·es.** To make sensual. **—sen'su·al·i·za'tion** *n.*

sen·su·ous (sĕn'sho͞o-əs) *adj.* **1.** Of, pertaining to, or derived from the senses. **2.** Having qualities that appeal to the senses: *the sensuous beauty of a spring day.* **3.** Readily susceptible through the senses; highly appreciative of the pleasures of sensation. **—sen'su·os'i·ty** (-ŏs'ĭ-tē) *n.* **—sen'su·ous·ly** *adv.* **—sen'su·ous·ness** *n.*

Synonyms: *sensuous, sensual, luxurious, voluptuous, sybaritic, epicurean.* These adjectives refer to satisfaction of the senses. *Sensuous* can refer to any of the senses but more often applies to those involved in aesthetic enjoyment of art, music, nature, and the like. *Sensual* specifically applies to gratification of the physical senses, particularly those associated with sexual pleasure. *Luxurious* in this comparison is applicable to gratification of physical comfort, aesthetic fulfillment, or sense of extreme well-being. *Voluptuous* refers principally to satisfaction of the physical senses and stresses indulgence in pleasure. *Sybaritic* suggests devotion to luxury and pleasure even more strongly. *Epicurean* stresses gratification of a taste for good food and drink.

Sen·sur·round (sĕn'sə-round'). A trademark for a motion-picture sound effect consisting of low-frequency sound signals felt by the audience as vibrations.

sent (sĕnt) *v.* Past tense and past participle of **send**[1].

sen·tence (sĕn'təns) *n.* **1.** A grammatical unit comprising a word or a group of words that is separate from any other grammatical construction and usually consists of at least one subject with its predicate and contains a finite verb or verb phrase. **2. a.** A court judgment, esp. a judicial decision of what punishment is to be inflicted on a convicted person. **b.** The penalty meted out. **3.** An opinion, esp. one given formally after deliberation. **4.** *Archaic.* An aphorism. —*tr.v.* **-tenced, -tenc·ing, -tenc·es.** To pass sentence on (a convicted person). [ME, opinion < OFr. < Lat. *sententia* < *sentire,* to feel.] **—sen·ten'tial** (sĕn-tĕn'shəl) *adj.* **—sen·ten'tial·ly** *adv.*

sen·tenc·er (sĕn'tən-sər) *n.* One that pronounces sentence.

sentence stress *n.* The variation in emphasis or vocal stress on the syllables of words within a sentence.

sen·ten·tia (sĕn-tĕn'shə, -shē-ə) *n., pl.* **-ti·ae** (-shē-ē'). An adage or an aphorism. [Lat. —see SENTENCE.]

sen·ten·tious (sĕn-tĕn'shəs) *adj.* **1.** Terse and energetic in expression; pithy. **2. a.** Abounding in aphorisms. **b.** Given to aphoristic utterances. **3. a.** Abounding in pompous moralizing. **b.** Given to pompous moralizing. [Lat. *sententiosus,* full of meaning < *sententia,* opinion < *sentire,* to feel.] **—sen·ten'tious·ly** *adv.* **—sen·ten'tious·ness** *n.*

sen·tience (sĕn'shəns, -shē-əns, -tē-əns) *n.* **1.** The quality or state of being sentient; consciousness. **2.** Feeling as distinguished from perception or thought.

sen·tient (sĕn'shənt, -shē-ənt, -tē-ənt) *adj.* **1.** Having sense perception; conscious: *"The living knew themselves just sentient puppets on God's stage"* (T.E. Lawrence). **2.** Experiencing sensation or feeling. —*n.* **1.** A sentient person or thing. **2.** The mind. [Lat. *sentiens, sentient-,* pr.part. of *sentire,* to feel.] **—sen'ti·ent·ly** *adv.*

sen·ti·ment (sĕn'tə-mənt) *n.* **1. a.** A general cast of mind regarding something: *Anti-American sentiment was running high in some countries.* **b.** A specific view. **2.** A thought, view, or attitude based on feeling or emotion rather than reason. **3.** The emotional import of a passage as distinguished from the words used. **4.** Susceptibility to tender, romantic, or nostalgic feeling. **5. a.** Emotion. **b.** Romantic, nostalgic feeling verging on sentimentality. **6.** The expression of delicate and sensitive feeling, as in art and literature. **7.** A vague feeling or awareness; sensation: *"overpowered by an intense sentiment of horror"* (Poe). [ME *sentement* < OFr. < Med. Lat. *sentimentum* < Lat. *sentire,* to feel.]

sen·ti·men·tal (sĕn′tə-mĕn′tl) *adj.* **1. a.** Characterized by or swayed by sentiment. **b.** Affectedly or extravagantly emotional. **2.** Resulting from or colored by emotion rather than reason or realism. **3.** Appealing to the sentiments, esp. to romantic feelings: *sentimental music.* **—sen′ti·men′tal·ly** *adv.*

sen·ti·men·tal·ism (sĕn′tə-mĕn′tl-ĭz′əm) *n.* **1.** A predilection for the sentimental. **2.** An idea or expression marked by excessive sentiment. **—sen′ti·men′tal·ist** *n.*

sen·ti·men·tal·i·ty (sĕn′tə-mĕn-tăl′ĭ-tē) *n., pl.* **-ties. 1.** The condition or quality of being excessively or affectedly sentimental. **2.** A sentimental idea or an expression of it.

sen·ti·men·tal·ize (sĕn′tə-mĕn′tl-īz′) *v.* **-ized, -iz·ing, -iz·es.** *—tr.* To regard with sentiment; be sentimental about. *—intr.* To behave in a sentimental manner. **—sen′ti·men′tal·i·za′tion** *n.*

sen·ti·nel (sĕn′tə-nəl) *n.* One that keeps guard; sentry. *—tr.v.* **-neled, -nel·ing, -nels** or **-nelled, -nel·ling, -nels. 1.** To watch over as a sentinel. **2.** To provide with a sentinel. **3.** To post as a sentinel. [Fr. *sentinelle* < Ital. *sentinella,* prob. < *sentire,* to watch < Lat. *sentire,* to feel.]

sen·try (sĕn′trē) *n., pl.* **-tries. 1.** A guard, esp. a soldier posted at a given spot to prevent the passage of unauthorized persons. **2.** The duty of a sentry; watch. [Perh. alteration of obs. *sentery,* sanctuary.]

sentry box

sentry box *n.* A small shelter for a sentry on his post.

se·pal (sē′pəl) *n.* One of the usually green segments forming the calyx of a flower. [NLat. *sepalum* < *sepa,* sepal < Gk. *skepē,* covering.] **—se′paled, sep′a·lous** (sĕp′ə-ləs) *adj.*

se·pal·oid (sē′pə-loid′, sĕp′ə-) also **se·pal·ine** (-līn′, -lĭn) *adj.* Resembling or characteristic of a sepal.

-sepalous *suff.* Having a specified kind or number of sepals: *gamosepalous.* [SEPAL + -OUS.]

sep·a·ra·ble (sĕp′ər-ə-bəl, sĕp′rə-) *adj.* Capable of being separated. [OFr. < Lat. *separabilis* < *separare,* to separate.] **—sep′a·ra·bil′i·ty** *n.* **—sep′a·ra·bly** *adv.*

sep·a·rate (sĕp′ə-rāt′) *v.* **-rat·ed, -rat·ing, -rates.** *—tr.* **1. a.** To set or keep apart; disunite. **b.** To space apart; scatter. **c.** To sort. **2.** To differentiate or discriminate between; distinguish. **3.** To remove from a mixture or combination; isolate. **4.** To part (a married couple), often by decree: *He was separated from his wife last March.* **5.** To terminate a contractual relationship, as military service, with; discharge. *—intr.* **1.** To become disconnected or severed; come apart. **2.** To withdraw: *The state threatened to separate from the Union.* **3.** To part company; disperse. **4.** To stop living together as husband and wife. **5.** To become divided into components or parts: *Oil and water tend to separate.* *—adj.* (sĕp′ər-ĭt, sĕp′rĭt). **1.** Set apart from others; detached. **2.** *Archaic.* Withdrawn from others; solitary. **3.** Existing as an entity; independent. **4.** Dissimilar; distinct. **5.** Not shared; individual. *—n.* (sĕp′ər-ĭt, sĕp′rĭt). A garment, such as a skirt, jacket, or pair of slacks, that may be purchased separately and worn in various combinations with other garments. [ME *separaten* < Lat. *separare* : *se-,* apart + *parare,* to make ready.] **—sep′a·rate·ly** *adv.* **—sep′a·rate·ness** *n.*

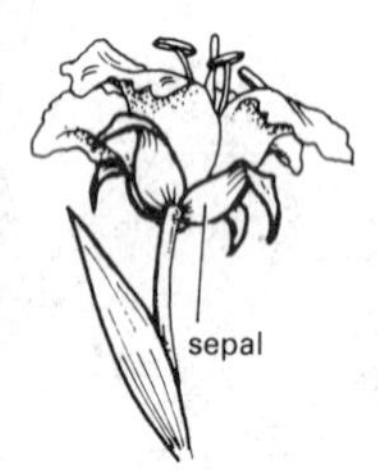

sepal

Synonyms: *separate, divide, part, sever, sunder, divorce, diverge, segregate.* These verbs refer to disjoining or disuniting. *Separate* applies both to putting apart by removing one or more components from a mass or by the act of dissociating and to keeping apart by occupying a position between things: *The Pyrenees separate France and Spain. Divide* also has both these senses. With respect to putting apart *divide* usually implies separation into predetermined portions or groups. The term can also refer to voluntary splitting or branching off. With respect to keeping apart *divide* often implies separation into opposing or hostile groups. *Part* refers most often to separation of persons or of segments: *The curtains parted. Sever* usually applies to cutting a part from the whole or cutting a whole into sections, or it can refer figuratively to ending a relationship. In every case abruptness and force are implied. *Sunder* stresses violent separation by tearing or wrenching apart. *Divorce* most often refers to the dissolution of a marriage or other close union. *Diverge* involves disjoining by going off in different directions from a common starting point or norm. *Segregate* principally refers to setting a group of persons apart from the mass or community at large; usually it implies discriminatory action against a racial group or social class thus isolated.

sep·a·ra·tion (sĕp′ə-rā′shən) *n.* **1. a.** The act or process of separating. **b.** The state of being separated. **2.** The place where a division or parting occurs. **3.** An interval or space that separates; gap. **4. a.** *Law.* An agreement or court decree terminating the conjugal relationship of a husband and wife. **b.** Discharge, as from employment or military service. [ME *separacion* < OFr. < Lat. *separatio* < *separare,* to separate.]

sep·a·ra·tion·ist (sĕp′ə-rā′shə-nĭst) *n.* A separatist.

sep·a·ra·tist (sĕp′ər-ə-tĭst, sĕp′rə-tĭst, sĕp′ə-rā′tĭst) *n.* One who secedes or advocates separation, esp. from an established church; sectarian. **—sep′a·ra·tism** (-tĭz′əm) *n.* **—sep′a·ra·tis′tic** *adj.*

sep·a·ra·tive (sĕp′ə-rā′tĭv, sĕp′ər-ə-tĭv, sĕp′rə-tĭv) *adj.* Tending to separate or to cause separation.

sep·a·ra·tor (sĕp′ə-rā′tər) *n.* **1.** One that separates. **2.** A device for separating cream from milk.

Se·phar·di (sə-fär′dē) *n., pl.* **-dim** (-dĭm). A member of the branch of European Jews who settled primarily in Spain, Portugal, and northern Africa. [Modern Heb. *Sĕphāradhī* < *Sĕphārad,* Spain.] **—Se·phar′dic** (-dĭk) *adj.*

se·pi·a (sē′pē-ə) *n.* **1. a.** A dark-brown ink or pigment originally prepared from the secretion of the cuttlefish. **b.** A drawing or picture done in this pigment. **c.** A photograph in a brown tint. **2.** A dark grayish yellowish brown to dark or moderate olive brown. *—adj.* **1.** Of the color sepia. **2.** Done or made in sepia. [Ital. *seppia* < Lat. *sepia* < Gk., cuttlefish.]

se·pi·o·lite (sē′pē-ə-līt′) *n. Mineral.* Meerschaum (sense 1). [G. *Sepiolith* : Gk. *sēpion,* cuttlebone (< *sēpia,* cuttlefish) + Gk. *lithos,* stone.]

se·poy (sē′poi′) *n.* In some Middle Eastern countries, a native regular soldier, esp. a native Indian soldier formerly serving under British command. [Prob. < Port. *sipae* < Urdu *sipāhī* < Pers. < *sipāh,* army.]

sep·pu·ku (sĕp′o͞o-ko͞o) *n.* Hara-kiri. [J., self-disembowelment : *seppu,* to cut + *ku,* abdomen.]

sep·sis (sĕp′sĭs) *n., pl.* **-ses** (-sēz′). The presence of pathogenic organisms or their toxins in the blood or tissues. [Gk. *sēpsis,* putrefaction < *sēpein,* to make rotten.]

sept (sĕpt) *n.* A division of a tribe, esp. in ancient and medieval Ireland; clan. [Prob. alteration of SECT.]

sep·ta (sĕp′tə) *n.* Plural of **septum.**

sep·tal (sĕp′təl) *adj.* Of or pertaining to a septum.

sep·tar·i·um (sĕp-târ′ē-əm) *n., pl.* **-i·a** (-ē-ə). An irregular polygonal system of calcite-filled cracks occurring in certain rock concretions. [SEPT(UM) + -ARIUM.] **—sep·tar′i·an** *adj.*

sep·tate (sĕp′tāt′) *adj.* Having a septum or septa.

Sep·tem·ber (sĕp-tĕm′bər) *n.* The ninth month of the year according to the Gregorian calendar. See table at **calendar.** [ME *Septembre* < OFr. < Lat. *September,* the seventh month < *septem,* seven.]

Sep·tem·brist (sĕp-tĕm′brĭst) *n.* **1.** One of the mob that massacred the imprisoned royalists in Paris, France, in September, 1792. **2.** A bloodthirsty revolutionist.

sep·te·nar·i·us (sĕp′tə-nâr′ē-əs) *n., pl.* **-i·i** (-ē-ī′). A Greek or Latin verse containing seven feet. [Lat. *septenarius,* of seven < *septeni,* seven each < *septem,* seven.]

sep·ten·ni·al (sĕp-tĕn′ē-əl) *adj.* **1.** Occurring every seven years. **2.** Consisting of or continuing for seven years. *—n.* An event that occurs every seven years. [< Lat. *septennium,* period of seven years < *septennis,* of seven years : *septem,* seven + *annus,* year.] **—sep·ten′ni·al·ly** *adv.*

sep·ten·tri·on (sĕp-tĕn′trē-ŏn′, -ən) *n. Obs.* The north; northern regions. [ME *septemtrioun* < OFr. *septentrion* < Lat. *septentriones,* seven plow oxen, the seven principal stars of Ursa Major or Ursa Minor : *septem,* seven + *triones,* pl. of *trio,* plow ox.] **—sep·ten′tri·o·nal** (-trē-ə-nəl) *adj.*

sep·tet also **sep·tette** (sĕp-tĕt′) *n.* **1.** A group of seven. **2.** *Mus.* **a.** A composition for seven voices or instruments. **b.** The musicians performing such a composition. [G. < Lat. *septem,* seven.]

sep·tic (sĕp′tĭk) *adj.* **1.** Of, pertaining to, or having the nature of sepsis. **2.** Causing sepsis; putrefactive. *—n.* A putrefactive substance. [Lat. *septicus,* putrefying < Gk. *sēptikos* < *sēptos,* rotten < *sēpein,* to make rotten.] **—sep·tic′i·ty** (-tĭs′ĭ-tē) *n.*

sep·ti·ce·mi·a (sĕp′tĭ-sē′mē-ə) *n.* A systemic disease caused by pathogenic organisms or their toxins in the blood stream. **—sep′ti·ce′mic** (-mĭk) *adj.*

sep·ti·ci·dal (sĕp′tĭ-sīd′l) *adj. Bot.* Splitting along or through the septa. Used of a seed capsule. [SEPT(UM) + -CID(E) + -AL.] **—sep′ti·ci′dal·ly** *adv.*

septic sore throat *n.* An infection of the throat, often epidemic, caused by hemolytic streptococci and characterized by fever and inflammation of the tonsils.

septic tank *n.* A sewage-disposal tank in which a continuous flow of waste material is decomposed by anaerobic bacteria.

sep·tif·ra·gal (sĕp-tĭf′rə-gəl) *adj. Bot.* Characterized by the breaking away of certain parts of the plant from its dividing walls. [SEPTUM + Lat. *frangere,* to break.]

sep·ti·lat·er·al (sĕp′tə-lăt′ər-əl) *adj.* Seven-sided. [Lat. *septem,* seven + LATERAL.]

sep·til·lion (sĕp-tĭl′yən) *n.* **1.** The cardinal number that is written 10^{24}. **2.** *Chiefly Brit.* The cardinal number that is written 10^{42}. [Fr. : *septi-,* seven + *million,* million.] **—sep·til′lion** *adj.*

sep·til·lionth (sĕp-tĭl′yənth) *n.* **1.** The ordinal number that matches the number one septillion in a series. **2.** One of a septillion equal parts. **—sep·til′lionth** *adj. & adv.*

sep·tu·a·ge·nar·i·an (sĕp′to͞o-ə-jə-nâr′ē-ən, -tyo͞o-) *n.* A person who is seventy years old or between the ages of seventy and eighty. *—adj.* **1.** Being seventy years old or between the ages of seventy and eighty. **2.** Of or pertaining to a septuagenarian. [< Lat. *septuagenarius,* of the number seventy < *septuageni,* seventy each < *septuaginta,* seventy < *septem,* seven.]

Sep·tu·a·ges·i·ma (sĕp′to͞o-ə-jĕs′ə-mə, -jā′zə-) *n.* The third Sunday before Lent. [ME < OFr. < LLat. *septuagesima* <

Lat. *septuagesimus,* seventieth < *septuaginta,* seventy < *septem,* seven.]

Sep·tu·a·gint (sĕp′tōō-ə-jĭnt′, sĕp-tōō′ə-jənt, -tyōō′-) *n.* A Greek translation of the Old Testament made in the 3rd century B.C. [Lat. *septuaginta,* seventy (from the traditional number of its translators) < *septem,* seven.]

sep·tum (sĕp′təm) *n., pl.* **-ta** (-tə). A thin partition or membrane between two cavities or soft masses of tissue in a plant or animal. [Lat. *saeptum,* partition < *saepire,* to enclose < *saepes,* fence.]

septum pel·lu·ci·dum (pə-lōō′sĭ-dəm) *n. Anat.* A thin membrane of nervous tissue that forms the medial wall of the lateral ventricles in the brain. [NLat., transparent partition.]

sep·tu·ple (sĕp-tōō′pəl, -tyōō′-) *adj.* **1.** Consisting of or containing seven. **2.** Multiplied by seven. *—tr.v.* **-pled, -pling, -ples.** To multiply by seven. [LLat. *septuplus,* sevenfold < Lat. *septem,* seven.]

sep·ul·cher (sĕp′əl-kər) *n.* **1.** A burial vault. **2.** A receptacle for sacred relics, esp. in an altar. *—tr.v.* **-chered, -cher·ing, -chers.** To place in a sepulcher; inter. [ME *sepulcre* < OFr. < Lat. *sepulcrum* < *sepultus,* p.part. of *sepelire,* to bury.]

se·pul·chral (sə-pŭl′krəl, -pōōl′-) *adj.* **1.** Of or pertaining to a sepulcher. **2.** Suggestive of the grave; funereal. **—se·pul′chral·ly** *adv.*

sep·ul·chre (sĕp′əl-kər) *n. & v. Chiefly Brit.* Variant of **sepulcher.**

sep·ul·ture (sĕp′əl-chŏŏr′, -chər) *n. Archaic.* **1.** The act of interment; burial. **2.** A sepulcher. [ME < OFr. < Lat. *sepultura* < *sepultus,* p.part. of *sepelire,* to bury.]

se·qua·cious (sĭ-kwā′shəs) *adj.* **1.** *Archaic.* Disposed to follow any leader; dependent. **2.** Following in logical sequence and regularity. [< Lat. *sequax, sequac-,* pursuing < *sequi,* to follow.] **—se·qua′cious·ly** *adv.* **—se·quac′i·ty** (-kwăs′ĭ-tē) *n.*

se·quel (sē′kwəl, -kwĕl′) *n.* **1.** Something that follows; continuation. **2.** A literary work complete in itself but continuing the narrative of an earlier work. **3.** A result or consequence. [ME *sequele* < OFr. *sequelle* < Lat. *sequela* < *sequi,* to follow.]

se·quel·a (sĭ-kwĕl′ə) *n., pl.* **-quel·ae** (-kwĕl′ē). Something that follows, esp. a pathological condition resulting from a disease. [Lat., sequel.]

se·quence (sē′kwəns, -kwĕns′) *n.* **1.** A following of one thing after another; succession. **2.** An order of succession; arrangement. **3.** A related or continuous series. **4.** Three or more playing cards in consecutive order; run. **5.** A series of single movie shots so edited as to constitute an aesthetic or dramatic unit; episode. **6.** *Mus.* A melodic or harmonic pattern successively repeated at different pitches with or without a key change. **7.** *Rom. Cath. Ch.* A hymn read between the gradual and the gospel. **8.** *Math.* An ordered set of quantities, as x, $2x^2$, $3x^3$, $4x^4$. *—tr.v.* **-quenced, -quenc·ing, -quenc·es.** To organize or arrange in a sequence. [LLat. *sequentia* < Lat. *sequens,* pr.part. of *sequi,* to follow.]

se·quenc·er (sē′kwən-sər, -kwĕn′-) *n.* A device that sorts cards, data, or programs in a prearranged sequence.

se·quent (sē′kwənt) *adj.* **1.** Following in order or time; subsequent. **2.** Following as a result; consequent. *—n.* A result; consequence. [Lat. *sequens, sequent-,* pr.part. of *sequi,* to follow.]

se·quen·tial (sĭ-kwĕn′shəl) *adj.* **1.** Forming or characterized by a sequence, as of notes or units. **2.** Sequent. **—se·quen′ti·al′i·ty** (-shē-ăl′ĭ-tē) *n.* **—se·quen′tial·ly** *adv.*

se·ques·ter (sĭ-kwĕs′tər) *v.* **-tered, -ter·ing, -ters.** *—tr.* **1.** To remove or set apart; segregate. **2.** *Law.* To take temporary possession of (property) as security against legal claims. **3.** *Law.* To requisition and confiscate (enemy property). **4.** To cause to withdraw into seclusion. *—intr. Chem.* To undergo sequestration. [ME *sequestren* < LLat. *sequestrare,* to give up for safekeeping < Lat. *sequester,* depository.]

se·ques·tra (sĭ-kwĕs′trə) *n.* Plural of **sequestrum.**

se·ques·trant (sĭ-kwĕs′trənt) *n.* A chemical that promotes sequestration.

se·ques·trate (sē′kwĭ-strāt′, sĕk′wĭ-, sĭ-kwĕs′trāt′) *tr.v.* **-trat·ed, -trat·ing, -trates.** **1.** *Law.* To seize; confiscate. **2.** *Archaic.* To sequester. [LLat. *sequestrare, sequestrat-,* to give up for safekeeping < Lat. *sequester,* depository.]

se·ques·tra·tion (sē′kwĭ-strā′shən, sĕk′wĭ-) *n.* **1.** The act of sequestering; segregation. **2.** *Law.* **a.** Seizure of property. **b.** A writ authorizing seizure of property. **3.** *Chem.* The inhibition or prevention of normal ion behavior by combination with added materials, esp. the prevention of metallic ion precipitation from solution by formation of a coordination complex with a phosphate. [ME *sequestracioun,* excommunication < LLat. *sequestratio,* separation < *sequestrare,* to give up for safekeeping < Lat. *sequester,* depository.]

se·ques·trum (sĭ-kwĕs′trəm) *n., pl.* **-tra** (-trə). A dead bone fragment separated from healthy bone. [NLat. < Lat., deposit < *sequester,* depository.]

se·quin (sē′kwĭn) *n.* **1.** A small shiny ornamental disk, often sewn on cloth; spangle. **2.** A gold coin of the Venetian Republic. [Fr. < Ital. *zecchino,* a coin < *zecca,* the mint < Ar. *sikkah,* coin die.]

se·quoi·a (sĭ-kwoi′ə) *n.* A very large evergreen tree of the genus *Sequoia,* which includes the redwood and the giant sequoia. [NLat. *Sequoia,* genus name, after *Sequoya* (George Guess), d.1843.]

se·ra (sîr′ə) *n.* A plural of **serum.**

sé·rac (sə-răk′, sā-) *n.* A large mass of ice broken off the main body of a glacier and remaining behind in a crevasse after glacial movement or melting. [Fr. < Med. Lat. *seracium,* whey < Lat. *serum.*]

se·ra·glio (sə-răl′yō, -räl′-) *n., pl.* **-glios.** **1.** A large harem. **2.** A sultan's palace. [Ital. *serraglio,* prob. partly < VLat. **serraculum,* enclosure (< Lat. *serare,* to lock up < *sera,* lock), and partly < Turk. *serai,* palace.]

se·ra·pe also **sa·ra·pe** (sə-rä′pē, -răp′ē) *n.* A woolen cloak or poncho worn by Latin-American men. [Mex. Sp. *sarape.*]

ser·aph (sĕr′əf) *n., pl.* **-a·phim** (-ə-fĭm) or **-aphs.** **1.** A celestial being having three pairs of wings. **2.** One of the nine orders of angels. [Back-formation < *seraphim* (pl.) < ME *seraphin* < OE < LLat. < Heb. *sĕrāphīm,* pl. of *sārāph.*] **—se·raph′ic** (sə-răf′ĭk), **se·raph′i·cal** *adj.* **—se·raph′i·cal·ly** *adv.*

Se·ra·pis (sə-rā′pĭs) *n.* An ancient Egyptian god of the lower world, also worshiped in ancient Greece and Rome.

Serb (sûrb) *n.* A Serbian. [Serbian *Srb.*]

Ser·bi·an (sûr′bē-ən) *n.* **1.** A member of a southern Slavic people that is the dominant ethnic group of Serbia and adjacent republics of Yugoslavia. **2.** A Serbo-Croatian. **3.** Serbo-Croatian as spoken in Serbia. *—adj.* Of or relating to Serbia or the Serbians.

Ser·bo-Cro·a·tian (sûr′bō-krō-ā′shən) *n.* **1.** The Slavic language of the Serbs and the Croats. **2.** A native speaker of Serbo-Croatian. *—adj.* Of or pertaining to Serbo-Croatian or those who speak it.

sere[1] also **sear** (sîr) *adj.* Withered; dry. [ME < OE *sēar.*]

sere[2] (sîr) *n.* The entire sequence of ecological communities successively occupying an area. [< SERIES.]

ser·e·nade (sĕr′ə-nād′, sĕr′ə-nād′) *n.* **1.** A complimentary musical performance given to honor or express love for someone. **2.** An instrumental composition written for a small ensemble and comprising characteristics of the suite and the sonata. *—v.* **-nad·ed, -nad·ing, -nades.** *—tr.* To perform a serenade for. *—intr.* To perform a serenade. [Fr. *sérénade* < Ital. *serenata* < *sereno,* serene < Lat. *serenus.*] **—ser′e·nad′er** *n.*

sequoia
Sequoia through which a road has been cut

ser·en·dip·i·ty (sĕr′ən-dĭp′ĭ-tē) *n.* The faculty of making fortunate and unexpected discoveries by accident. [From its possession by the characters in the Persian fairy tale *The Three Princes of Serendip.*] **—ser′en·dip′i·tous** *adj.*

se·rene (sə-rēn′) *adj.* **1.** Unruffled; tranquil. **2.** Unclouded; fair. **3.** Often **Serene.** August. Used as part of a title of respect for certain royal personages: *Her Serene Highness.* [Lat. *serenus,* serene, clear.] **—se·rene′ly** *adv.* **—se·rene′ness, se·ren′i·ty** (-rĕn′ĭ-tē) *n.*

serf (sûrf) *n.* **1.** A slave, esp. a member of the lowest feudal class in medieval Europe, bound to the land and owned by a lord. **2.** A person in servitude. [ME < OFr. < Lat. *servus,* slave.] **—serf′dom** *n.*

serge (sûrj) *n.* A twilled cloth of worsted or worsted and wool, often used for suits. [ME *sarge* < OFr. < VLat. **sarica* < Lat. *serica,* silks < *sericus,* silken < *Seres,* a people of Eastern Asia.]

ser·geant (sär′jənt) *n.* **1. a.** Any of several ranks of noncommissioned officers in the U.S. Army, Air Force, or Marine Corps. **b.** One that holds any of these ranks. **2. a.** The rank of police officer next below a captain, lieutenant, or inspector. **b.** A police officer holding this rank. **3.** A sergeant at arms. [ME *sergeaunte,* a common soldier < OFr. *sergent* < Lat. *serviens,* pr.part. of *servire,* to serve < *servus,* slave.] **—ser′gean·cy, ser′geant·ship′** *n.*

sergeant at arms *n.* An officer appointed to keep order within an organization, such as a legislative, judicial, or social body.

sergeant first class *n.* A noncommissioned officer next below master sergeant in the U.S. Army.

sergeant fish *n.* The cobia.

sergeant major *n.* **1.** A noncommissioned officer serving as chief administrative assistant of a headquarters unit of the U.S. Army, Air Force, or Marine Corps. **2.** *Chiefly Brit.* A noncommissioned officer of the highest rank. **3.** A fish, *Abudefduf saxatilis,* of warm seas, having a flattened body with dark vertical stripes.

se·ri·al (sîr′ē-əl) *adj.* **1.** Of, forming, or arranged in a series. **2. a.** Published or produced in installments, as a novel or television drama. **b.** Pertaining to such publication or production. **3.** *Mus.* Pertaining to or based on a 12-tone row. *—n.* A literary or dramatic work published or produced in installments. **—se′ri·al·ly** *adv.*

se·ri·al·ism (sîr′ē-ə-lĭz′əm) *n.* **1.** Serial music. **2.** The theory or composition of serial music. **—se′ri·al·ist** *n.*

se·ri·al·ize (sîr′ē-ə-līz′) *tr.v.* **-ized, -iz·ing, -iz·es.** To write or publish in serial form. **—se′ri·al·i·za′tion** *n.*

serial number *n.* A number that is one of a series and is used for identification, as of a machine.

se·ri·ate (sîr′ē-āt′, -ĭt) *adj.* Arranged or occurring in a series or in rows. **—se′ri·ate′ly** *adv.*

se·ri·a·tim (sîr′ē-ā′tĭm, -ăt′ĭm) *adv.* One after another; in a series. [Med. Lat. < Lat. *series,* series.]

se·ri·ceous (sĭ-rĭsh′əs) *adj.* **1.** Silky. **2.** *Bot.* Covered with soft, silky hairs. [LLat. *sericeus,* silken < Lat. *sericus.* —see SERGE.]

George Miksch Sutton

seriema

serif

serpent
18th-century Belgian

serrate
Serrate leaf

ser·i·cin (sĕr′ĭ-sĭn) *n.* A viscous, gelatinous protein that forms on the surface of raw-silk fibers. [< Lat. *sericus,* silken.]

ser·i·cul·ture (sĕr′ĭ-kŭl′chər) *n.* The production of raw silk and the raising of silkworms for this purpose. [Lat. *sericum,* silk (< *Seres,* a people of Eastern Asia) + CULTURE.] **—ser′i·cul′tur·al** *adj.* **—ser′i·cul′tur·ist** *n.*

ser·i·e·ma (sĕr′ĭ-ē′mə) *n.* Either of two cranelike South American birds, *Cariama cristata* or *Chunga burmeisteri,* having a tuftlike crest at the base of the bill. [Tupi, crested.]

se·ries (sîr′ēz) *n., pl.* **series. 1.** A group of things of the same class coming one after the other in succession: *a series of accidents; a series of novels.* **2.** A group of objects related by a linearly varying morphological or configurational characteristic: *a radioactive decay series; the paraffin series.* **3.** *Math.* The indicated sum of a finite or of a sequentially ordered infinite set of terms. **4.** *Gram.* A succession of coordinate elements in a sentence. **5.** A succession of usually continuously numbered issues or volumes of a publication, published with related authors or subjects and similar formats. **6. a.** *Sports.* A number of games played one after the other by the same opposing teams. **b.** *Baseball.* The World Series. **—*idiom.* in series.** In an arrangement that forms a series. [Lat. *series* < *serere,* to join.]

Synonyms: *series, succession, progression, sequence, chain, train, string, set.* These nouns denote groups of things considered from the standpoint of order or arrangement. *Series* refers to like or related things or events arranged or occurring in order. *Succession* applies to like or related things or events that follow each other, generally in order of time and without interruption. A *progression* is a series that reveals a definite pattern of advance. In a *sequence* things follow one another in chronological or numerical order or in order that indicates causal or logical relationship or a recurrent pattern. *Chain* suggests a series of things closely linked or a sequence of closely related ideas or events. *Train* can apply to a procession of persons or vehicles or to a sequence of ideas or events. *String* refers to a continuous series or succession of like things or events, sometimes with the suggestion of impressive length. *Set* applies to a number of matching or similar things that have a common function or purpose or that form a whole. It can also denote a group of persons closely associated.

series circuit *n.* An electric circuit connected so that current passes through each circuit element in turn without branching.

se·ries-wound (sîr′ēz-wound′) *adj.* Designating an electric motor or dynamo in which the armature circuit and the field circuit are connected in series with the external circuit.

ser·if (sĕr′ĭf) *n. Printing.* A fine line finishing off the main strokes of a letter, as at the top and bottom of *M.* [Perh. < Du. *schreef,* line < MDu. *scrēve* < *scriven,* to write < Lat. *scribere.*]

ser·i·graph (sĕr′ĭ-grăf′) *n.* A print made by the silk-screen process. [Lat. *sericum,* silk (< *Seres,* a people of Eastern Asia) + -GRAPH.] **—se·rig′ra·pher** (sə-rĭg′rə-fər) *n.* **—se·rig′ra·phy** (-fē) *n.*

ser·in (sĕr′ĭn) *n.* Any of several Old World finches of the genus *Serinus,* having yellowish plumage. [Fr.]

ser·ine (sĕr′ēn′) *n.* An amino acid, $C_3H_7NO_3$, that is a common constituent of many proteins. [SER(ICIN) + -INE.]

se·ri·o·com·ic (sîr′ē-ō-kŏm′ĭk) *adj.* Both serious and comic. [SERIO(US) + COMIC.] **—se′ri·o·com′i·cal·ly** *adv.*

se·ri·ous (sîr′ē-əs) *adj.* **1.** Grave in character, quality, or manner. **2.** Said or done in earnest; sincere. **3.** Concerned with important rather than trivial matters; weighty. **4.** Marked by considerable effort or devotion. **5.** Causing anxiety. [ME *seryous* < OFr. *serieux* < LLat. *seriosus* < Lat. *serius.*] **—se′ri·ous·ly** *adv.* **—se′ri·ous·ness** *n.*

Synonyms: *serious, sober, grave, solemn, earnest, sedate, staid.* These adjectives are compared as they refer to the appearance, air, manner, or disposition of persons. *Serious* applies broadly to one whose main concern is with responsibility and work as opposed to play. *Sober* strengthens the implications of dedication to purpose, circumspect behavior, and self-control. *Grave* suggests dignity and somberness associated with weighty affairs, especially those that give cause for deep concern. *Solemn* adds to the foregoing the suggestion of formality and impressiveness. *Earnest* implies manifest sincerity and intensity of purpose. *Sedate* implies a calm, dignified manner. *Staid* emphasizes unvarying dignity and observance of propriety.

ser·jeant (sär′jənt) *n. Chiefly Brit.* Variant of **sergeant** (senses 2 and 3).

ser·mon (sûr′mən) *n.* **1.** A religious discourse delivered as part of a church service. **2.** An often lengthy and tedious speech of reproof or exhortation. [ME < OFr. < Lat. *sermo,* discourse.] **—ser·mon′ic** (-mŏn′ĭk), **ser·mon′i·cal** *adj.*

ser·mon·ize (sûr′mə-nīz′) *v.* **-ized, -iz·ing, -iz·es.** *—tr.* To deliver a sermon to (someone). *—intr.* To deliver or speak as though delivering a sermon. **—ser′mon·iz′er** *n.*

Sermon on the Mount *n.* In the New Testament, a discourse of Jesus, delivered on the Mount of Olives.

sero– *pref.* Serum: *serotherapy.* [< SERUM.]

se·ro·di·ag·no·sis (sîr′ō-dī′əg-nō′sĭs, sĕr′ō-) *n.* Diagnosis by use of blood serum reactions. **—se′ro·di′ag·nos′tic** (-nŏs′tĭk) *adj.*

se·rol·o·gy (sĭ-rŏl′ə-jē) *n.* The medical science that deals with serums. **—se′ro·log′ic** (sîr′ə-lŏj′ĭk), **se′ro·log′i·cal** *adj.* **—se·rol′o·gist** *n.*

se·ro·pu·ru·lent (sîr′ō-pyo͝or′ə-lənt, -pyo͝or′yə-, sĕr′-) *adj.* Consisting of serum and pus.

se·ro·sa (sĭ-rō′sə, -zə) *n., pl.* **-sas** or **-sae** (-sē′). A serous membrane. [NLat., fem. of *serosus,* serous < Lat. *serum,* serum.] **—se·ro′sal** (-zəl) *adj.*

se·ro·ther·a·py (sîr′ō-thĕr′ə-pē, sĕr′-) *n.* The treatment of disease by administration of a serum or antitoxin.

se·rot·i·nal (sĭ-rŏt′n-əl, sĕr′ə-tī′nəl) *adj.* Serotinous.

se·rot·i·nous (sĭ-rŏt′n-əs, sĕr′ə-tī′nəs) *adj. Biol.* Late in developing or blooming. [Lat. *serotinus,* coming late < *sero,* at a late hour < *serus,* late.]

se·ro·to·nin (sîr′ə-tō′nĭn, sĕr′-) *n.* An organic compound, $C_{10}H_{12}N_2O$, found in animal and human tissue, esp. the brain, blood serum, and gastric mucosa, and capable of raising the blood pressure. [SERO- + TON(IC) + -IN.]

se·ro·type (sîr′ə-tīp′, sĕr′-) *n.* A group of related microorganisms distinguished by its antigenic composition.

se·rous (sîr′əs) *adj.* Containing, secreting, or resembling serum.

serous membrane *n.* A thin membrane lining a closed bodily cavity.

se·row (sə-rō′) *n.* Any of several goatlike antelopes of the genus *Capricornis,* of mountainous regions of eastern Asia, having short horns and a dark coat. [Lepcha *să-ro.*]

Ser·pens (sûr′pənz, -pĕnz′) *n.* A constellation in the equatorial region of the northern sky, made up of two parts: *Serpens Cauda,* the "tail," and *Serpens Caput,* the "head," both near Hercules and Ophiuchus. [Lat. *Serpens* < *serpens,* serpent.]

ser·pent (sûr′pənt) *n.* **1.** A snake. **2.** Often **Serpent. a.** The creature that tempted Eve. **b.** Satan. **3.** A subtle, sly, or treacherous person. **4.** A firework that writhes while burning. **5.** *Mus.* A deep-voiced wind instrument of serpentine shape, used principally in the 18th century, approximately eight feet in length and made of brass or wood. **6. Serpent.** Serpens. [ME < OFr. < Lat. *serpens* < pr.part. of *serpere,* to creep.]

ser·pen·tine (sûr′pən-tēn′, -tīn′) *adj.* **1.** Of or resembling a serpent, as in form or movement; sinuous. **2.** Subtly sly and tempting. *—n.* (-tēn′). A greenish, brownish, or spotted mineral, $3MgO{\cdot}2SiO_2{\cdot}2H_2O$, used as a source of magnesium and in architecture as a decorative stone. [ME < OFr. *serpentin* < LLat. *serpentinus* < Lat. *serpens,* serpent.]

serpent star *n.* A brittle star.

ser·pi·go (sər-pī′gō) *n.* A spreading skin eruption or lesion, such as ringworm. [ME < Med. Lat. < Lat. *serpere,* to creep.] **—ser·pig′i·nous** (sər-pĭj′ə-nəs) *adj.*

ser·ran·id (sə-răn′ĭd, sĕr′ə-nĭd) *adj.* Of or belonging to the family Serranidae, which includes the sea basses and groupers. [NLat. *Serranidae,* family name < Lat. *serra,* saw.] **—ser·ran′id** *n.*

ser·rate (sĕr′āt′) also **ser·rat·ed** (-ā′tĭd) *adj.* **1.** Having notched, toothlike projections. **2.** Having the edge or margin notched with toothlike projections: *serrate leaves.* [Lat. *serratus,* saw-shaped < Lat. *serra,* saw.]

ser·ra·tion (sə-rā′shən, sĕ-) *n.* **1.** The state of being serrate. **2.** A series or set of teeth or notches. **3.** A single tooth or notch in a serrate edge.

ser·ried (sĕr′ēd) *adj.* Pressed or crowded together, esp. in rows: *troops in serried ranks.* [P.part. of obs. *serry,* to close ranks < OFr. *serre,* p.part. of *serrer,* to crowd, grasp. —see SEAR[2].] **—ser′ried·ly** *adv.*

ser·ru·late (sĕr′yə-lĭt, -lāt′, sĕr′ə-) also **ser·ru·lat·ed** (-lā′tĭd) *adj.* Having small, toothlike notches along the edge; minutely serrate. [NLat. *serrulatus* < Lat. *serrula,* dim. of *serra,* saw.]

ser·tu·lar·i·an (sûr′chə-lâr′ē-ən, sûr′tl-âr′-) *n.* Any of various colonial hydroids of the genus *Sertularia,* having stalkless polyps arranged in pairs along a long, branching stem. [< NLat. *Sertularia,* genus name < Lat. *sertula,* dim. of *serta,* garland < *serere,* to entwine.]

se·rum (sîr′əm) *n., pl.* **se·rums** or **se·ra** (sîr′ə). **1.** The clear yellowish fluid obtained upon separating whole blood into its solid and liquid components. **2.** The fluid from the tissues of immunized animals, used esp. as an antitoxin. **3.** Watery fluid from animal tissue, such as that found in edema. **4.** Whey. [Lat., whey, serum.]

serum albumin *n.* A protein fraction of blood serum involved in maintaining osmotic pressure and used in the treatment of shock.

serum globulin *n.* A protein fraction of blood serum chiefly containing antibodies.

serum sickness *n.* A hypersensitive reaction to the administration of serum, characterized by fever, swelling, skin rash, and enlargement of the lymph nodes.

ser·val (sûr′vəl, sər-văl′) *n.* A long-legged wild cat, *Felis serval,* of Africa, having a yellowish coat with black spots. [Fr. < Port. *(lobo) cerval,* deerlike (wolf), lynx < *cervo,* deer < Lat. *cervus.*]

ser·vant (sûr′vənt) *n.* **1.** One who is privately employed to perform domestic services. **2.** One who is publicly employed to perform services, as for a government. **3.** One who expresses submission, recognizance, or debt to another: *your obedient servant.* [ME < OFr. < pr.part. of *servir,* to serve.]

serve (sûrv) *v.* **served, serv·ing, serves.** —*tr.* **1. a.** To work for. **b.** To be a servant to. **2. a.** To prepare and offer (food, for example): *serve tea.* **b.** To place food before (someone); wait on. **3. a.** To provide goods and services for (customers): *served the public at the same location for 30 years.* **b.** To supply (goods or services) to customers. **c.** To assist (the celebrant) during Mass. **4.** To be of assistance to or promote the interests of; aid: *"Both major parties today seek to serve the national interest"* (John F. Kennedy). **5.** To spend or complete (time): *serve four terms in Congress.* **6.** To fight or undergo military service for: *served his country as an airman.* **7.** To give homage and obedience to: *served God and country.* **8.** To requite: *Punish him; it will serve him right.* **9.** To copulate with. Used of male animals: *The buck served the doe.* **10.** To meet the needs or requirements of; satisfy: *serve the purpose.* **11.** *Law.* **a.** To deliver or present (a legal writ or summons). **b.** To present such a writ to. **12.** *Sports.* To put (a ball or shuttlecock) in play, as in tennis, badminton, and jai alai. **13.** To bind or whip (a rope) with fine cord or wire. —*intr.* **1.** To be employed as a servant. **2.** To do a term of duty: *serve in the U.S. Air Force.* **3.** To act in a particular capacity: *serve as a clerk.* **4.** To be of service or use; function: *serve as a reminder.* **5.** To meet requirements or needs; satisfy: *a device that will serve well.* **6.** To wait on table: *serve at luncheon.* **7.** *Sports.* To put a ball or shuttlecock into play, as in court games. **8.** To assist the celebrant during Mass. —*n. Sports.* The right, manner, or act of serving in many court games. —See Usage note at **service.** [ME *serven* < OFr. *servir* < Lat. *servire* < *servus,* slave.]

serv·er (sûr′vər) *n.* **1.** One that serves. **2.** Something, such as a tray, used in serving. **3.** An attendant to the celebrant at a Mass. **4.** *Sports.* The player who serves, as in court games.

serv·ice (sûr′vĭs) *n.* **1.** The occupation or duties of a servant. **2.** Employment in duties or work for another, esp. for a government. **3.** A government branch or department and its employees: *the diplomatic service.* **4. a.** The armed forces of a nation. **b.** A branch of the armed forces of a nation. **5.** Work or duties performed for a superior. **6.** Work done for others as an occupation or business: *provides full catering service.* **7.** Installation, maintenance, or repairs provided or guaranteed by a dealer or manufacturer. **8.** A facility providing the public with the use of something, such as water or transportation. **9.** Acts of devotion to God; witness. **10.** A religious rite. **11.** An act of assistance or benefit to another or others; favor. **12.** The serving of food or the manner in which it is served. **13.** A set of dishes or utensils: *a silver tea service.* **14.** *Sports.* The act, manner, or right of serving in many court games; serve. **15.** Copulation with a female. Used of male animals. **16.** *Law.* The serving of a writ or summons. **17.** The material, as cord, used in binding or wrapping rope. ***—modifier:*** *a service entrance; a service guarantee.* —*tr.v.* **-iced, -ic·ing, -ic·es. 1.** To make fit for use; adjust, repair, or maintain: *service a car.* **2.** To provide services to. **3.** To make interest payments on (a debt). **4.** To copulate with. Used of male animals. [ME *servise* < OFr. *service* < Lat. *servitum,* slavery < *servus,* slave.]

Usage: Aside from specialized senses in finance (*service a debt*) and animal breeding (*service a mare*), *service* is used principally in the sense "to repair or maintain": *service the electric dishwasher.* In the sense "to supply goods or services to," *serve* is the most frequent or only choice: *One radio network serves three states.*

serv·ice·a·ble (sûr′vĭs-ə-bəl) *adj.* **1.** Ready for service; usable. **2.** Able to give long service; durable. **—serv′ice·a·bil′i·ty, serv′ice·a·ble·ness** *n.* **—serv′ice·a·bly** *adv.*

serv·ice·ber·ry (sûr′vĭs-bĕr′ē, sär′-) *n.* The shadbush or one of its fruit. [SERVICE (TREE) + BERRY.]

service break *n. Sports.* A game won on an opponent's serve, as in tennis.

service cap *n.* A visored flat-topped military cap.

service charge *n.* An additional charge for a service for which there is already a basic fee.

service line *n. Sports.* A boundary line, as in tennis or handball, that must not be overstepped in serving.

serv·ice·man (sûr′vĭs-măn′, -mən) *n.* **1.** A member of the armed forces. **2.** Also **service man.** A man whose work is the maintenance and repair of equipment.

service mark *n.* A device that identifies a service offered to the public, as by an airline or insurance company.

service station *n.* **1.** A filling station. **2.** A business or branch of a business where services, esp. repairs, can be obtained.

serv·ice tree (sûr′vĭs, sär′-) *n.* Either of two Old World trees, *Sorbus domestica* or *S. torminalis,* having clusters of white flowers and brownish, edible fruit. [ME *serves,* pl. of *serve,* the service tree < OE *syrfe* < Lat. *sorbus.*]

ser·vi·ette (sûr′vē-ĕt′) *n.* A table napkin. [Fr. < OFr., towel, napkin < *servir,* to serve.]

ser·vile (sûr′vəl, -vīl′) *adj.* **1.** Slavish in character or attitude; abjectly submissive. **2.** Of or suitable to a slave or servant: *servile tasks.* [ME < Lat. *servilis* < *servus,* slave.] **—ser′vile·ly** *adv.* **—ser′vile·ness, ser·vil′i·ty** (sər-vĭl′ĭ-tē) *n.*

serv·ing (sûr′vĭng) *n.* **1.** The act of one that serves. **2.** An individual portion or helping of food or drink.

ser·vi·tor (sûr′vĭ-tər, -tôr′) *n.* One that performs the duties of a servant to another; attendant. [ME < OFr. < Lat. *servitor* < *servire,* to serve < *servus,* slave.] **—ser′vi·tor·ship′** *n.*

ser·vi·tude (sûr′vĭ-to͞od′, -tyo͞od′) *n.* **1.** Submission to a master. **2.** Forced labor imposed as a punishment for crime: *penal servitude.* **3.** *Law.* A right that grants use of another's property. [ME *servytude* < OFr. < Lat. *servitudo* < *servus,* slave.]

Synonyms: *servitude, bondage, slavery.* These nouns state a condition of being involuntarily under the power of another. *Servitude* sometimes refers broadly to the absence of liberty but generally implies involuntary service. *Bondage* emphasizes being bound to the service of another with virtually no hope of freedom. To be held in *slavery* is to be owned bodily by the person one serves and treated as his property. Less literally, *slavery* and *bondage* can refer to subjection to any person, economic system, or vice.

ser·vo (sûr′vō) *n., pl.* **-vos. 1.** A servomechanism. **2.** A servomotor.

ser·vo·mech·a·nism (sûr′vō-mĕk′ə-nĭz′əm) *n.* A feedback system that consists of a sensing element, an amplifier, and a servomotor, used in the automatic control of a mechanical device. [SERVO(MOTOR) + MECHANISM.]

ser·vo·mo·tor (sûr′vō-mō′tər) *n.* An electric motor or hydraulic piston that supplies power to a servomechanism. [Fr. *servomoteur* : Lat. *servus,* slave + Fr. *moteur,* motor.]

ses·a·me (sĕs′ə-mē) *n.* **1.** A plant, *Sesamum indicum,* of tropical Asia, bearing small, flat seeds used as food and as a source of oil. **2.** The seeds of the sesame. [Lat. *sesamum* < Gk. *sēsamon, sēsamē,* of Semitic orig.]

ses·a·moid (sĕs′ə-moid′) *adj.* Of or designating a small bone, such as the kneecap, that develops in a tendon or in the capsule of a joint. [Gk. *sēsamoeidēs,* shaped like a sesame seed < *sēsamon, sēsamē,* sesame.] **—ses′a·moid′** *n.*

sesqui– *pref.* One and a half: *sesquicentennial.* [Lat. : *semis,* half + *-que,* and.]

ses·qui·cen·ten·ni·al (sĕs′kwĭ-sĕn-tĕn′ē-əl) *adj.* Of or pertaining to a period of 150 years. —*n.* A 150th anniversary or its celebration.

ses·qui·pe·da·lian (sĕs′kwĭ-pĭ-dāl′yən) also **ses·quip·e·dal** (sĕ-skwĭp′ĭ-dl) *adj.* **1.** Long and ponderous; polysyllabic. **2.** Given to using long words. —*n.* **sesquipedalian.** A long word. [Lat. *sesquipedalis,* of a foot and a half in length : *sesqui-,* one half more + *pes,* foot.]

ses·sile (sĕs′īl′, -əl) *adj.* **1.** *Bot.* Stalkless and attached directly at the base: *sessile leaves.* **2.** *Zool.* Permanently attached or fixed; not free-moving. [Lat. *sessilis,* low, of sitting < *sessus,* p.part. of *sedēre,* to sit.] **—ses·sil′i·ty** (sĕ-sĭl′ĭ-tē) *n.*

sessile
Sessile leaf

ses·sion (sĕsh′ən) *n.* **1. a.** A meeting of a legislative or judicial body for the purpose of transacting business. **b.** A series of such meetings. **c.** The term or duration of time that is taken by such a series of meetings. **2.** The part of a year or of a day during which a school holds classes. **3.** A group of persons assembled for a common purpose or with a common interest: *a gossip session.* **4.** A court of criminal jurisdiction in the United States: *the court of sessions.* **5.** A period of time devoted to a specific activity. [ME < OFr. < Lat. *sessio,* act of sitting < *sessus,* p.part. of *sedēre,* to sit.] **—ses′sion·al** *adj.* **—ses′sion·al·ly** *adv.*

ses·terce (sĕs′tûrs′) *n.* A silver or bronze coin of ancient Rome equivalent to 1/4 denarius. [Lat. *sestertius,* a coin worth two and a half asses : *semis,* half + *tertius,* third.]

ses·ter·tium (sĕ-stûr′shəm, -shē-əm) *n., pl.* **-tia** (-shə, -shē-ə). A monetary unit of ancient Rome equivalent to 1,000 sesterces. [Lat. *(mille) sestertium,* (a thousand) sesterces.]

ses·tet (sĕ-stĕt′) *n.* A stanza constituting the last six lines of a sonnet. [Ital. *sestetto* < *sesto,* sixth < Lat. *sextus.*]

ses·ti·na (sĕ-stē′nə) *n.* An originally Provençal verse form consisting of six six-line stanzas and a three-line envoi, repeating the end words of the first stanza throughout according to a scheme of cruciate retrogradation. [Ital. < *sesto,* sixth < Lat. *sextus.*]

set[1] (sĕt) *v.* **set, set·ting, sets.** —*tr.* **1.** To put in a specified position; place: *set a book on a table.* **2.** To put into a specified state: *set him at liberty.* **3.** To put into a stable position; fix. **4.** To restore to a proper and normal state when dislocated or broken: *set a broken arm.* **5. a.** To adjust for proper functioning. **b.** To adjust (a saw) by deflecting the teeth. **c.** To spread open to the wind: *set the sails.* **6.** To adjust according to a standard. **7.** To adjust (an instrument) to a specific point or calibration: *set an alarm clock.* **8.** To arrange properly for use: *set a place for a dinner guest; set a table.* **9.** To apply equipment, as curlers and clips, to (hair) in order to style. **10.** *Printing.* **a.** To arrange (type) into words and sentences preparatory to printing; compose. **b.** To transpose into type. **11. a.** To compose (music) to fit a given text. **b.** To write (words) to fit a given melodic line. **12.** To arrange scenery on (a theater stage). **13.** To prescribe or establish: *set a precedent.* **14.** To prescribe the unfolding of (a scene) in a specific place: *a play set in Venice.* **15.** To prescribe as a time for: *set June 6 as the day of the invasion.* **16.** To detail or assign (someone) to a particular duty, service, or station: *set the boy to cleaning closets; set guards around the perimeter.* **17.** To incite to hostile action:

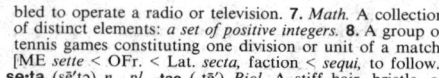

a war that set families against one another. **18. a.** To establish as the highest level of performance: *set a world aviation record.* **b.** To establish as a model: *set a good example for the children.* **19. a.** To put in a mounting; mount: *set an emerald in a pendant.* **b.** To apply jewels to; stud: *a tiara set with diamonds.* **20.** To cause to sit. **21. a.** To put (a hen) on eggs for the purpose of hatching them. **b.** To put (eggs) beneath a hen or in an incubator. **22.** To position (oneself) to start an action, as running a race. **23. a.** To value or regard something at the rate of: *sets a great deal by good nutrition.* **b.** To fix at a given amount: *set bail for the criminal at $50,000.* **c.** To make as an estimate of worth: *We set a high value on human life.* **24.** To point to the location of (game) by holding a fixed attitude. Used of a hunting dog. **25.** To produce, as after pollination: *set seed.* **26. a.** To prepare (a trap) for catching prey. **b.** To fix (a hook) firmly into a fish's jaw. —*intr.* **1.** To disappear below the horizon: *The sun set at seven that evening.* **2.** To diminish or decline; wane. **3.** To sit on eggs. Used of fowl. **4.** To become fixed; harden. **5.** To become whole; knit. Used of a broken bone. **6.** To mature or develop, as after pollination. **7.** *Regional.* To sit. **8.** To position oneself preparatory to an action, as running a race. —***phrasal verbs.*** **set about.** To begin or start: *set about solving the problem.* **set apart. 1.** To reserve for a specific use. **2.** To make noticeable. **set aside. 1.** To separate and reserve for a special purpose. **2.** To discard or reject. **3.** To declare invalid; annul or overrule. **set at.** To attack or assail. **set back. 1.** To slow down the progress of; hinder. **2.** *Informal.* To cost: *That coat set me back $1,000.* **set down. 1.** *Informal.* To cause to sit; seat: *Set the baby down here.* **2.** To put in writing; record: *He set down the facts.* **3. a.** To regard; consider: *Just set him down as a sneak.* **b.** To assign to a cause; attribute: *Let's set the error down to inexperience.* **4.** To land (an aircraft). **set forth. 1.** To present for consideration; propose. **2.** To express in words: *set forth her ideas.* **set in. 1.** To insert: *set in the sleeve of a gown.* **2.** To begin to happen or be apparent: *Infection set in.* **3.** To move toward the shore. Used of wind or water. **set off. 1. a.** To give rise to; cause to occur: *set off a chemical reaction.* **b.** To cause to explode. **2.** To indicate as being different; distinguish: *features setting him off from the crowd.* **3.** To direct attention to by contrast; accentuate: *set off a passage with italics.* **4.** To start on a journey: *set off for Europe.* **set out. 1.** To begin an earnest attempt; undertake: *set out to understand why the plan had failed.* **2.** To lay out systematically and graphically: *set out a terrace.* **3.** To display for exhibition or sale. **4.** To plant: *set out seedlings.* **5.** To start a journey: *set out at dawn for town.* **set to. 1.** To begin working energetically; start in. **2.** To begin fighting. **set up. 1.** To place in an upright position. **2. a.** To elevate; raise. **b.** To raise in authority or power; invest with power: *set the general up as a dictator.* **c.** To put (oneself) forward as; claim to be: *set himself up as an authority on language.* **3.** To assemble and erect: *set up a new machine.* **4.** To establish; found: *set up a charity.* **5.** To cause; create: *set up howls of protest.* **6.** To establish in business by providing capital, equipment, or other backing. **7.** *Informal.* **a.** To treat (someone) to drinks. **b.** To pay for (drinks). **8.** *Informal.* To stimulate or exhilarate: *a victory that really set the team up.* **9.** To lay plans for: *set up a kidnapping.* —*adj.* **1.** Fixed or established by agreement: *a set time for the launching.* **2.** Established by convention: *followed set procedures for filing a grievance.* **3.** Established deliberately; intentional. **4.** Fixed and rigid: *a set, grim face.* **5.** Not willing to change: *was set in his ways.* **6.** Ready: *We're set to go.* —*n.* **1. a.** The act or process of setting. **b.** The condition resulting from setting. **2.** A permanent firming or hardening of a substance, as by cooling. **3.** The deflection of the teeth of a saw. **4.** The manner in which something is positioned: *the set of her cap.* **5.** The carriage or bearing of a part of the body. **6.** A descent below the horizon. **7.** The direction or course of wind or water. **8.** A seedling, slip, or cutting that is ready for planting. **9.** The act of arranging hair by waving and curling it. —***idioms.*** **set eyes on.** To catch sight of; see. **set foot in.** To enter. **set foot on.** To step on. **set in motion.** To give impetus to: *The indictment set the judicial process in motion.* **set (one's) heart on.** To be determined to do something. **set (or put) (one's) house in order.** To arrange one's affairs in an orderly manner. **set (one's) sights on.** To have as a goal: *She set her sights on medical school.* **set (someone) straight.** To inform fully. **set store by.** To regard as valuable or worthwhile. [ME *setten* < OE *settan.*]

Usage: Originally *set* meant "to cause (something) to sit," so that it is now in most cases a transitive verb: *She sets the book on the table. He sets the table. Sit* is generally an intransitive verb: *He sits at the table.* There are some exceptions: *The sun sets* (not *sits*). *A hen sets* (or *sits*) *on her eggs.*

settee
18th-century English

settle
18th-century American

set² (sĕt) *n.* **1.** A group of things of the same kind that belong together and are so used: *a chess set.* **2.** A group of persons sharing a common interest: *the high-school set.* **3.** A group of books or periodicals published as a unit. **4. a.** A number of couples required for participation in a square dance. **b.** The movements constituting a square dance. **5. a.** The scenery constructed for a theatrical performance. **b.** The entire enclosure in which a motion picture is filmed; sound stage. **6.** The collective receiving apparatus assembled to operate a radio or television. **7.** *Math.* A collection of distinct elements: *a set of positive integers.* **8.** A group of tennis games constituting one division or unit of a match. [ME *sette* < OFr. < Lat. *secta,* faction < *sequi,* to follow.]

se·ta (sē′tə) *n., pl.* **-tae** (-tē′) *Biol.* A stiff hair, bristle, or bristlelike process. [NLat. < Lat. *saeta,* bristle.] —**se′tal** (sēt′l) *adj.*

se·ta·ceous (sī-tā′shəs) *adj.* **1.** Having or consisting of bristles; bristly. **2.** Resembling a bristle or bristles; bristlelike. [SET(A) + -ACEOUS.]

se·tae (sē′tē′) *n.* Plural of **seta.**

set·back (sĕt′băk′) *n.* **1.** An unanticipated or sudden check in progress; reverse. **2. a.** A steplike recession in a wall. **b.** Any of a series of such recessions in the rise of a tall building.

set back *n. Football.* An offensive back who lines up behind the quarterback.

set chisel *n.* A chisel with a cutting edge on a tapered shaft.

Seth (sĕth) *n.* In the Old Testament, the third son of Adam. [Heb., appointed.]

se·ti·form (sē′tə-fôrm′) *adj.* Having the shape of a seta or bristle.

set·line (sĕt′līn′) *n.* A long fishing line towed by a boat and supporting many smaller lines bearing baited hooks.

set·off (sĕt′ôf′, -ŏf′) *n.* **1.** Something, such as a decoration, that sets off something else by contrast. **2.** Something that offsets or compensates for something else; counterbalance. **3. a.** A counterclaim. **b.** The settlement of a debt by a debtor's establishing such a claim against his creditor. **4.** *Archit.* A flat projection, as from a wall; ledge.

se·tose (sē′tōs′) *adj.* Bristly or bristlelike; setaceous.

set piece *n.* **1.** A realistic piece of stage scenery constructed to stand by itself. **2.** An often brilliantly executed artistic or literary work characterized by a formal pattern. **3.** A carefully planned and executed operation, esp. a military operation.

set·screw (sĕt′skro͞o′) *n.* **1.** A screw, often without a head, used to hold two parts in a position relative to each other without motion. **2.** A screw used to regulate the tension of a spring.

set·tee (sĕ-tē′) *n.* **1.** A long wooden bench with a back. **2.** A small sofa. [Perh. alteration of SETTLE.]

set·ter (sĕt′ər) *n.* **1.** One that sets. **2.** Any of several breeds of long-haired dogs originally trained to indicate the presence of game by crouching in a set position.

set theory *n.* The study of the mathematical properties of sets.

set·ting (sĕt′ĭng) *n.* **1. a.** The context and environment in which a situation is set. **b.** The time and place in which a literary or a dramatic work is set. **2.** The scenery constructed for a theatrical performance. **3.** Music composed or arranged to fit a text. **4.** A mounting, as for a jewel. **5.** A set of eggs in a hen's nest.

set·tle (sĕt′l) *v.* **-tled, -tling, -tles.** —*tr.* **1.** To put into order; arrange or fix definitely as desired. **2.** To put firmly in a desired position or place; establish. **3.** To establish as a resident or residents: *settled her family in Ohio.* **4.** To establish residence in: *Pioneers settled the West.* **5.** To establish in a residence, business, or profession. **6.** To restore calmness or comfort to. **7. a.** To cause to come to rest, sink, or become compact. **b.** To cause (a liquid) to become clear by forming a sediment. **8.** To subdue or make orderly. **9.** To establish on a permanent basis; stabilize. **10. a.** To make compensation for (a claim). **b.** To pay (a debt). **11.** To conclude (a dispute, for example) by a final decision. **12.** To decide (a lawsuit) by mutual agreement of the involved parties without court action. **13.** *Law.* To secure or assign (property or title) by legal action. —*intr.* **1.** To discontinue moving and come to rest in one place. **2.** To descend or subside gradually. **3.** To sink and become more compact: *The dust settled.* **4. a.** To become clear. Used of liquids. **b.** To be separated from a solution or mixture as a sediment. **5.** To establish one's residence. **6.** To reach a decision; determine. **7. a.** To compensate for a claim. **b.** To pay a debt. —***phrasal verbs.*** **settle down. 1.** To begin living a more orderly life: *He settled down as a farmer with a family.* **2.** To become less nervous or restless. **settle for.** To accept in spite of incomplete satisfaction. —*n.* A long wooden bench with a high back, often including storage space beneath the seat. [ME *setlen,* to seat < OE *setlan* < *setl,* seat.]

set·tle·ment (sĕt′l-mənt) *n.* **1.** The act or process of settling. **2. a.** Establishment, as of a person in a business or of people in a new region. **b.** A newly colonized region. **3.** A small community. **4.** An adjustment or other understanding reached, as in financial or business proceedings. **5. a.** The transfer of property to provide for the future needs of a person. **b.** Property thus transferred. **6.** A welfare center providing community services in an underprivileged area.

set·tler (sĕt′lər) *n.* **1.** One that settles or decides something. **2.** A person who settles in a new region.

set·tlings (sĕt′lĭngz) *pl.n.* Sediment; dregs.

set-to (sĕt′to͞o′) *n., pl.* **-tos.** A brief but usually heated contest.

set·up (sĕt′ŭp′) *n.* **1.** *Informal.* The way in which something is constituted, arranged, or planned. **2.** Bodily carriage, esp. when erect. **3.** Physical make-up; physique. **4.** Often **setups.**

Informal. The collective ingredients and mixers, as ice and soda water, necessary for serving a variety of alcoholic drinks. **5.** *Slang.* **a.** A contest prearranged to result in an easy or faked victory. **b.** An endeavor that is intentionally made easy. **c.** A fraud, hoax, or deceptive scheme.

sev·en (sĕv′ən) *n.* **1.** The cardinal number that is next after the number 6 and equal to the sum of 6 + 1. **2.** The seventh in a set or sequence. [ME < OE *seofon*; akin to G. *sieben,* Lat. *septem,* Gk. *hepta,* and Skt. *sapta.*] **—sev′en** *adj. & pron.*

sev·en·fold (sĕv′ən-fōld′) *adj.* **1.** Consisting of seven parts or members. **2.** Having seven times as many or as much. **—sev′en·fold′** *adv.*

seven seas also **Seven Seas** *pl.n.* All the oceans of the world.

sev·en·teen (sĕv′ən-tēn′) *n.* **1.** The cardinal number that is next after the number 16 and equal to the sum of 16 + 1. **2.** The seventeenth in a set or sequence. [ME *seventene* < OE *seofontīne* < *seofon,* seven.] **—sev′en·teen′** *adj. & pron.*

sev·en·teenth (sĕv′ən-tēnth′) *n.* **1.** The ordinal number that matches the number 17 in a series. **2.** One of 17 equal parts. **—sev′en·teenth′** *adj. & adv.*

sev·en·teen-year locust (sĕv′ən-tēn′yîr′) *n.* A cicada, *Magicicada septendecim,* of the eastern United States, having a nymphal stage in which it remains underground for 17 or sometimes 13 years.

sev·enth (sĕv′ənth) *n.* **1.** The ordinal number that matches the number seven in a series. **2.** One of seven equal parts. **3.** A musical interval encompassing seven diatonic degrees. [ME < *seven,* seven.] **—sev′enth** *adj. & adv.*

Sev·enth-day Adventist (sĕv′ənth-dā′) *n.* A member of a sect of Adventism distinguished chiefly for its observance of the Sabbath on Saturday.

seventh heaven *n.* **1.** The farthest of the concentric spheres containing the stars and comprising the dwelling place of God and the angels in the Moslem and cabalist systems. **2.** A state of great joy and satisfaction.

sev·en·ti·eth (sĕv′ən-tē-ĭth) *n.* **1.** The ordinal number that matches the number 70 in a series. **2.** One of 70 equal parts. **—sev′en·ti·eth** *adj. & adv.*

sev·en·ty (sĕv′ən-tē) *n.* The cardinal number equal to 7 × 10. [ME < OE *hundseofontig* : *hund,* hundred + *seofon,* seven + *-tig,* -ty.] **—sev′en·ty** *adj. & pron.*

sev·en-up (sĕv′ən-ŭp′) *n.* A card game requiring seven points to win.

sev·er (sĕv′ər) *v.* **-ered, -er·ing, -ers.** *—tr.* **1.** To divide or separate into parts; keep apart or make distinct. **2.** To cut or break forcibly into two or more parts. **3.** To break off, as a relationship; dissolve. *—intr.* **1.** To become cut or broken apart. **2.** To separate or go apart; divide. [ME *severen* < OFr. *severer* < Lat. *separare.* —see SEPARATE.] **—sev′er·a·ble** *adj.*

sev·er·al (sĕv′ər-əl, sĕv′rəl) *adj.* **1.** Being of a number more than two or three but not many: *several miles away.* **2.** Single; distinct: "*Pshaw! said I, with an air of carelessness, three several times*" (Sterne). **3.** Respectively different; various: *They parted and went their several ways.* **4.** *Law.* Pertaining separately to each party of a bond or note. *—n.* Several persons or things; a few. [ME *severall,* separate < AN *several* < Med. Lat. *separalis* < Lat. *separ* < *separare,* to separate. —see SEPARATE.] **—sev′er·al·ly** *adv.*

sev·er·ance (sĕv′ər-əns, sĕv′rəns) *n.* **1. a.** The act or process of severing. **b.** The condition of being severed. **2.** Separation; partition.

severance pay *n.* A sum of money usually based on length of employment for which an employee is eligible upon termination.

se·vere (sə-vîr′) *adj.* **-ver·er, -ver·est. 1.** Unsparing and harsh in treating others: *a severe taskmaster.* **2.** Corresponding strictly to established rule; maintained rigidly: *severe accuracy.* **3.** Austere or dour in appearance, manner, or temperament; forbidding: *spoke in a severe voice.* **4.** Extremely plain in substance or style: *a severe black dress.* **5.** Extremely intense: *severe pain; a severe storm.* **6.** Extremely difficult to perform or accomplish; trying: *a severe test of our loyalty.* [OFr. < Lat. *severus.*] **—se·vere′ly** *adv.* **—se·vere′ness** *n.*

Synonyms: *severe, stern, austere, ascetic, strict, exacting.* These adjectives mean to be unsparing, especially with respect to discipline or control. *Severe* is broadly applicable to persons or things that adhere rigidly to established, often rigorous standards or high principles or that impose harsh or taxing conditions. *Stern* is often interchangeable with *severe* but especially suggests unyielding disposition, unshakable resolution, and forbidding appearance or nature. *Austere* implies, in persons, self-restraint or self-denial, extreme reserve, and often rigid moral standards. In things it implies severe simplicity. *Ascetic* applies principally to the character and life of a person who practices extreme self-denial and who usually renounces worldly interests for spiritual or intellectual pursuits. *Strict* stresses the idea of rigid observance of rules or standards. *Exacting* applies to persons or things that make rigorous demands on one's time, labor, or attention.

se·ver·i·ty (sə-vĕr′ĭ-tē) *n.* The state or quality of being severe.

Sè·vres (sĕv′rə) *n.* A fine French porcelain, often elaborately decorated. [After *Sèvres,* France.]

sew (sō) *v.* **sewed, sewn** (sōn) or **sewed, sew·ing, sews.** *—tr.* **1.** To make, repair, or fasten with a needle and thread: *sew a dress; sew on a button.* **2.** To furnish with stitches for the purpose of closing, fastening, or attaching: *sew an incision closed.* *—intr.* To work with a needle and thread or with a sewing machine. ***—phrasal verb.* sew up.** *Informal.* **1.** To complete successfully: *a happy salesman who had sewn up a deal.* **2.** To control; monopolize. [ME *sewen* < OE *seowian.*]

sew·age (so͞o′ĭj) *n.* Liquid and solid waste carried off with ground water in sewers or drains. [SEW(ER) + -AGE.]

sew·er[1] (so͞o′ər) *n.* An artificial, usually underground conduit for carrying off sewage or rainwater. [ME < OFr. *sewiere* < VLat. **exaquaria* : Lat. *ex-,* out of + Lat. *aqua,* water.]

sew·er[2] (so͞o′ər) *n.* A medieval servant who supervised the serving of meals. [ME < AN *asseour* < OFr. *asseoir,* to seat < Lat. *assidēre,* to sit down : *ad-,* to + *sedēre,* to sit.]

sew·er[3] (sō′ər) *n.* One that sews.

sew·er·age (so͞o′ər-ĭj) *n.* **1.** A system of sewers. **2.** The removal of waste materials by means of a sewer system. **3.** Sewage.

sew·ing (sō′ĭng) *n.* **1.** The act, occupation, or hobby of a person who sews. **2.** The article upon which one is working with needle and thread; needlework.

sewing circle *n.* A group of women who meet regularly for the purpose of sewing, often for charitable causes.

sewing machine *n.* A machine for sewing, often having additional attachments for special stitching.

sewn (sōn) *v.* A past participle of **sew.**

sex (sĕks) *n.* **1. a.** The property or quality by which organisms are classified according to their reproductive functions. **b.** Either of two divisions, designated male and female, of this classification. **2.** Males or females collectively. **3.** The condition or character of being male or female; the physiological, functional, and psychological differences that distinguish the male and the female. **4.** The sexual urge or instinct as it manifests itself in behavior. **5.** Sexual intercourse. **6.** The genitalia. *—tr.v.* **sexed, sex·ing, sex·es.** To determine the sex of (young chickens). [ME < Lat. *sexus.*]

sex– *pref.* Six: *sexpartite.* [Lat. *sex,* six.]

sex·a·ge·nar·i·an (sĕk′sə-jə-nâr′ē-ən) *n.* A person who is sixty years old or between the ages of sixty and seventy. *—adj.* **1.** Being sixty years old or between the ages of sixty and seventy. **2.** Of or pertaining to a sexagenarian. [< Lat. *sexagenarius,* sexagenary.]

sex·ag·e·nar·y (sĕk-săj′ə-nĕr′ē) *adj.* **1.** Pertaining to or proceeding by sixties. **2.** Sexagenarian. *—n., pl.* **-ies.** A sexagenarian. [Lat. *sexagenarius* < *sexageni,* sixty each < *sexaginta,* sixty < *sex,* six.]

Sex·a·ges·i·ma (sĕk′sə-jĕs′ə-mə, -jā′zə-) *n.* The second Sunday before Lent. [LLat. *sexagesima* < Lat. *sexagesimus,* sixtieth < *sexaginta,* sixty < *sex,* six.]

sex·a·ges·i·mal (sĕk′sə-jĕs′ə-məl) *adj.* Of, relating to, or based on the number 60. [< Lat. *sexagesimus,* sixty. —see SEXAGESIMA.]

sex appeal *n.* Physical attractiveness or personal qualities that arouse sexual interest in another person.

sex cell *n.* A gamete.

sex·cen·te·nar·y (sĕk-sĕn′tə-nĕr′ē, sĕk′sĕn-tĕn′ə-rē) *adj.* Pertaining to 600 or to a 600-year period. *—n., pl.* **-ies.** A 600th anniversary or its commemoration. [< Lat. *sexcenteni,* six hundred each : *sex,* six + *centeni,* a hundred each < *centum,* hundred.]

sex chromosome *n.* Either of a pair of chromosomes, usually designated X or Y, in the germ cells of man, most animals, and some plants, that combine to determine the sex of an individual, XX resulting in a female and XY in a male.

sex·en·ni·al (sĕk-sĕn′ē-əl) *adj.* **1.** Occurring every six years. **2.** Relating to or lasting six years. *—n.* An event that occurs every six years. [< Lat. *sexennium,* of six years : *sex,* six + *annus,* year.] **—sex·en′ni·al·ly** *adv.*

sex gland *n.* A testis or ovary; gonad.

sex hormone *n.* Any of various animal hormones, such as estrogen and androgen, affecting the growth or function of the reproductive organs and the development of secondary sex characteristics.

sex·ism (sĕk′sĭz′əm) *n.* **1.** Discrimination based on sex, esp. discrimination against women. **2.** Attitudes or conditions that promote stereotyping of social roles based on gender. **—sex′ist** *adj. & n.*

sex·less (sĕks′lĭs) *adj.* **1.** Lacking sexual characteristics; neuter. **2.** Arousing or exhibiting no sexual interest or desire; asexual **—sex′less·ly** *adv.* **—sex′less·ness** *n.*

sex linkage *n.* The condition in which a gene responsible for a specific phenotypic trait is located on the X chromosome, resulting in sexually dependent inheritance of the trait.

sex-linked (sĕks′lĭngkt′) *adj.* **1.** Carried by a sex chromosome, esp. an X chromosome. Used of genes. **2.** Sexually determined. Used esp. of inherited traits.

sex·ol·o·gy (sĕk-sŏl′ə-jē) *n.* The study of human sexual behavior. **—sex′o·log′ic** (-sə-lŏj′ĭk), **sex′o·log′i·cal** *adj.* **—sex·ol′o·gist** *n.*

sex·par·tite (sĕks-pär′tīt′) *adj.* Composed of or divided into six parts, as a groined vault.

Sèvres
18th-century urn-shaped vase

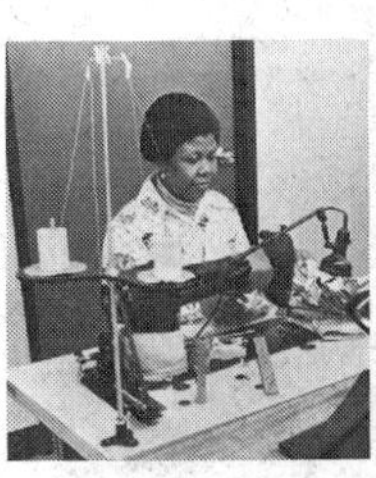

sewing machine

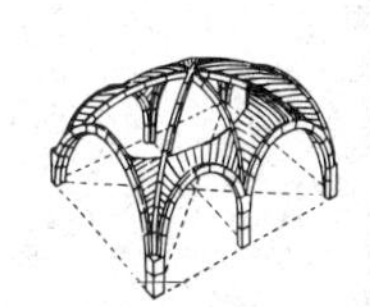

sexpartite
Sexpartite vault

sextant

sex·pot (sĕks′pŏt′) *n. Informal.* A strikingly sexy person.

sext also **Sext** (sĕkst) *n. Eccles.* **1.** The fourth of the seven canonical hours. **2.** The time of day set aside for sext, usually the sixth hour, or noon. [ME *sexte* < Lat. *sexta (hora),* sixth (hour) < *sextus,* sixth.]

sex·tan (sĕks′tən) *n.* A malarial fever with paroxysms recurring every six days. *—adj.* Occurring or recurring every six days. [NLat. *sextana (febris),* sextan (fever) < Lat. *sextus,* sixth.]

Sex·tans (sĕks′tənz) *n.* A constellation in the equatorial region of the sky near Leo and Hydra. [NLat., sextant.]

sex·tant (sĕk′stənt) *n.* **1.** A navigational instrument used for measuring the altitudes of celestial bodies. **2. Sextant.** Sextans. [NLat. *sextans, sextant-* < Lat., sixth part (from its being graduated in sixths of a circle) < *sextus,* sixth.]

sex·tet (sĕk-stĕt′) *n.* **1.** *Mus.* **a.** A group composed of six vocalists or musicians. **b.** A musical composition written for six performers. **2.** A group of six persons or things. [Alteration of SESTET.]

sex·tile (sĕk′stīl′, -stəl) *adj.* Designating the position of two celestial bodies when they are 60 degrees apart. [Lat. *sextilis,* one sixth < *sextus,* sixth.]

sex·til·lion (sĕk-stĭl′yən) *n.* **1.** The cardinal number written 10^{21}. **2.** *Chiefly Brit.* The cardinal number written 10^{36}. [Fr. : *sex-,* six (< Lat. *sex*) + *million,* million.] **—sex·til′lion** *adj. & pron.*

sex·til·lionth (sĕk-stĭl′yənth) *n.* **1.** The ordinal number that matches the number sextillion in a series. **2.** One of sextillion equal parts. **—sex·til′lionth** *adj. & adv.*

sex·to·dec·i·mo (sĕk′stō-dĕs′ə-mō′) *n., pl.* **-mos. 1.** The page size of a book composed of printer's sheets folded into 16 leaves or 32 pages. **2.** A book composed of sextodecimo pages. [Lat. *sextodecimo,* ablative of *sextusdecimus,* one sixteenth : *sextus,* sixth + *decimus,* tenth < *decem,* ten.]

sex·ton (sĕk′stən) *n.* An employee or officer of a church who is responsible for the care and upkeep of church property and sometimes for ringing bells and digging graves. [ME *segerstone* < AN *segerstaine* < Med. Lat. *sacristanus,* sacristan. —see SACRISTAN.]

sexton beetle *n.* The burying beetle.

sex·tu·ple (sĕk-sto͞o′pəl, -styo͞o′-, -stŭp′əl, sĕk′stŭp′əl) *tr. & intr.v.* **-pled, -pling, -ples.** To multiply or be multiplied by six. *—adj.* **1.** Containing or consisting of six parts; sixfold. **2.** Larger or greater by sixfold; multiplied by six. **3.** *Mus.* Having six beats to the measure. *—n.* A number six times larger than another. [Prob. SEX- + (QUIN)TUPLE.] **—sex·tu′ply** *adv.*

shackle
Illustration by Gustave Doré for *Don Quixote,* showing prisoners in shackles

sex·tu·plet (sĕk-stŭp′lĭt, -sto͞o′plĭt, -styo͞o′-, sĕk′stŭp′lĭt) *n.* **1.** One of six offspring delivered at one birth. **2. sextuplets.** The six offspring of one birth. **3.** A group of six similar persons or things; sextet. [SEXTU(PLE) + (TRI)PLET.]

sex·tu·pli·cate (sĕk-sto͞o′plĭ-kĭt, -styo͞o′-) *adj.* **1.** Six times as many or as much; sixfold. **2.** Raised to the sixth power. *—tr.v.* (-kāt′) **-cat·ed, -cat·ing, -cates.** To sextuple. *—n.* (-kĭt). One of six similar things. [SEXTU(PLE) + (DU)PLICATE.] **—sex·tu′pli·cate·ly** *adv.* **—sex·tu′pli·ca′tion** *n.*

sex·u·al (sĕk′sho͞o-əl) *adj.* **1.** Of, pertaining to, affecting, or characteristic of sex, the sexes, or the sex organs and their functions. **2.** Implying or symbolizing erotic desires or activity. **3.** Of, pertaining to, or designating reproduction involving the union of male and female gametes. [LLat. *sexualis* < Lat. *sexus,* sex.] **—sex′u·al·ly** *adv.*

sexual intercourse *n.* Coitus, esp. between humans.

sex·u·al·i·ty (sĕk′sho͞o-ăl′ĭ-tē) *n.* **1.** The condition of being characterized and distinguished by sex. **2.** Concern with or interest in sexual activity. **3.** The quality of possessing a sexual character or potency.

sex·u·al·ize (sĕk′sho͞o-ə-līz′) *tr.v.* **-ized, -iz·ing, -iz·es.** To make sexual in character or quality.

sexual selection *n.* A Darwinian adjunct of natural selection hypothesizing the preferred hereditary selection of characteristics involved in male courtship displays and combat.

sex·y (sĕk′sē) *adj.* **-i·er, -i·est.** Arousing or tending to arouse sexual desire or interest. **—sex′i·ly** *adv.* **—sex′i·ness** *n.*

Sey·fert galaxy (sē′fərt, sī′-) *n.* A spiral galaxy with a small, compact, bright nucleus that exhibits variable light intensity and radio-wave emission. [After Carl K. *Seyfert* (d. 1960).]

sfer·ics also **spher·ics** (sfîr′ĭks, sfĕr′-) *n. (used with a sing. verb).* **1.** The study of atmospherics, esp. using electronic detectors. **2.** Atmospherics. [Short for ATMOSPHERICS.]

sfor·zan·do (sfôrt-sän′dō, -săn′-) *adj. Mus.* Suddenly and strongly accented. Used as a direction. *—n., pl.* **-dos** or **-di** (-dē). A sforzando tone or chord. [Ital., pr.part of *sforzare,* to use force.] **—sfor·zan′do** *adv.*

sgraf·fi·to (zgrə-fē′tō, skrä-) *n., pl.* **-ti** (-tē). **1.** Decoration produced on pottery or ceramic by scratching through a surface of plaster or glazing to reveal a different color beneath. **2.** Ware decorated with sgraffito. [Ital. < p.part. of *sgraffire,* to scratch.]

sh (sh) *interj.* Used to urge silence.

Sha·ban also **Shaa·ban** (shə-bän′) *n.* The eighth month of the year in the Moslem calendar. See table at **calendar.** [Ar. *sha'bān.*]

Shab·bat (shə-bät′, shä′bəs) *n.* The Jewish Sabbath. [Heb. *shabbāth,* sabbath.]

shab·by (shăb′ē) *adj.* **-bi·er, -bi·est. 1.** Threadbare; worn-out. **2.** Wearing worn garments; seedy. **3.** Dilapidated; deteriorated. **4.** Despicable; mean. [< obs. *shab,* scab < ME *schab* < OE *sceabb.*] **—shab′bi·ly** *adv.* **—shab′bi·ness** *n.*

Sha·bu·oth (shə-vo͞o′ōt′, -ōth′, -əs) *n.* Variant of **Shavuot.**

shack (shăk) *n.* A small, crudely built cabin; shanty. **—*idiom.* shack up.** *Slang.* **1.** To live, room, or stay at a place: *I'm shacking up with my cousin till I find a place.* **2.** To live in sexual intimacy with another person. [Mex. Sp. *jacal* < Nahuatl *xacalli,* adobe hut : *xàmitl,* adobe + *calli,* house.]

shack·le (shăk′əl) *n.* **1.** A metal fastening, usually one of a pair, for encircling and confining the ankle or wrist of a prisoner or captive; fetter or manacle. **2.** A hobble for an animal. **3.** Any of several devices, as a clevis, used to fasten or couple. **4.** Often **shackles.** A restraint or a check to action or progress: *economic shackles that precluded further investment.* *—tr.v.* **-led, -ling, -les. 1.** To put shackles on; fetter. **2.** To fasten or connect with a shackle. **3.** To restrict, confine, or hamper. [ME *schackle* < OE *sceacel,* fetter.] **—shack′ler** *n.*

shack·o (shăk′ō, shā′kō, shä′-) *n.* Variant of **shako.**

shad (shăd) *n., pl.* **shad** or **shads.** Any of several food fishes of the genus *Alosa,* related to the herrings but atypical in swimming up streams from marine waters to spawn. [ME < OE *sceadd.*]

shad·ber·ry (shăd′bĕr′ē) *n.* The fruit of the shadbush.

shad·blow (shăd′blō′) *n.* A shadbush.

shad·bush (shăd′bo͝osh′) *n.* Any of various North American shrubs or trees of the genus *Amelanchier,* having white flowers and edible blue-black or purplish fruit.

shad·dock (shăd′ək) *n.* **1.** A tropical tree, *Citrus maxima* (or *C. grandis*), closely related to the grapefruit. **2.** The edible yellow, pear-shaped fruit of the shaddock. [After Captain *Shaddock,* 17th-cent. English ship commander.]

shade (shād) *n.* **1.** Light diminished in intensity as a result of the interception of the rays; partial darkness. **2.** An area or space of partial darkness. **3.** Cover or shelter provided by an object's interception of the sun or its rays. **4.** Any of various devices used to reduce or screen light or heat: *window shades.* **5. shades.** *Slang.* Sunglasses. **6.** Relative obscurity. **7. shades.** Dark shadows gathering at dusk. **8.** The part of a picture or photograph depicting darkness or shadow. **9.** The degree to which a color is mixed with black or is decreasingly illuminated; gradation of darkness. **10.** A slight difference or variation; nuance: *shades of meanings.* **11.** A small amount; trace. **12.** A disembodied spirit; ghost. **13. shades.** *Informal.* Reminders; echoes: *seeing her again roused shades of the past.* **—*modifier:* *a shade tree.*** *—tr.v.* **shad·ed, shad·ing, shades. 1.** To screen from light or heat. **2.** To obscure or darken. **3.** To cause shade in or on. **4. a.** To represent degrees of darkness in: *shade a drawing.* **b.** To produce (gradations of light or color) in. **5.** To change or vary by slight degrees: *shade the meaning.* **6.** *Informal.* To make a slight reduction in: *shade prices.* [ME *schade* < OE *sceadu.*]

shad·fly (shăd′flī′) *n.* The mayfly.

shad·ing (shā′dĭng) *n.* **1.** Screening against light or heat. **2.** The lines or other marks used to fill in outlines of a sketch, engraving, or painting to represent gradations of colors or darkness. **3.** A small variation, gradation, or difference.

shad·ow (shăd′ō) *n.* **1.** An area that is not or is only partially irradiated or illuminated because of the interception of radiation by an opaque object between the area and the source of radiation. **2.** The rough image cast by an object blocking rays of illumination. **3.** An imperfect imitation or copy. **4. shadows.** The darkness following sunset. **5. a.** Gloom; unhappiness. **b.** An influence that causes such feeling. **6.** A shaded area in a picture or photograph. **7.** A mirrored image or reflection. **8.** A phantom; ghost. **9. a.** A detective. **b.** A spy. **10.** A faint indication; premonition. **11.** A vestige; remnant. **12.** An insignificant portion or amount; slight trace. **13.** Shelter; protection. *—tr.v.* **-owed, -ow·ing, -ows. 1.** To cast a shadow upon; shade. **2.** To make gloomy or dark; cloud. **3.** To represent vaguely, mysteriously, or prophetically. **4.** To darken in a painting or drawing; shade in. **5.** To follow after, esp. in secret; trail. *—adj.* Not having official status: *a shadow government of exiled leaders.* [ME *schadow* < OE *sceaduwe* < *sceadu,* shade, shadow.] **—shad′ow·er** *n.*

shad·ow·box (shăd′ō-bŏks′) *intr.v.* **-boxed, -box·ing, -box·es.** To spar with an imaginary opponent, as for exercise.

shadow cabinet *n.* A group of leaders of a parliamentary opposition who are expected to hold positions in the official cabinet when their party is returned to power.

shadow dance *n.* A dance presented by casting shadows of dancers on a screen.

shad·ow·graph (shăd′ō-grăf′) *n.* An image produced by casting a shadow on a screen.

shadow play *n.* A play presented by casting shadows of puppets or actors on a screen.

shad·ow·y (shăd′ō-ē) *adj.* **-i·er, -i·est. 1.** Pertaining to or resembling a shadow. **2.** Full of shadows; dark. **3.** Vague; indistinct. **4.** Of dubious character or honesty; shady. **—shad′ow·i·ness** *n.*

shad·y (shā′dē) *adj.* **-i·er, -i·est. 1.** Full of shade; shaded. **2.** Casting shade. **3.** Quiet, dark, or concealed; hidden. **4.** Of dubious character or honesty; questionable. **—shad′i·ly** *adv.* **—shad′i·ness** *n.*

shaft (shăft) *n.* **1.** The long, narrow stem or body of a spear or arrow. **2.** A spear or arrow. **3. a.** A projectile suggestive of a spear or arrow in appearance or configuration. **b.** *Informal.* A scornfully satirical comment; barb. **c.** *Slang.* Harsh, unfair treatment: *really gave them the shaft.* **4.** A ray or beam of light. **5.** The handle of any of various tools or implements. **6.** The rib of a feather. **7.** *Anat.* **a.** The midsection of a long bone; diaphysis. **b.** The section of a hair projecting from the surface of the body. **8. a.** A column or obelisk. **b.** The section of a column between the capital and the base. **9.** One of two parallel poles between which an animal is harnessed to a vehicle. **10.** A long, generally cylindrical bar, esp. one that rotates and transmits power: *a drive shaft.* **11.** A long, narrow passage sunk into the earth; tunnel. **12.** A vertical passage housing an elevator. **13.** A duct or conduit for the passage of air, as for ventilation or heating. *—tr.v.* **shaft·ed, shaft·ing, shafts. 1.** To equip with a shaft. **2.** *Slang.* To treat in a harsh, unfair way. [ME < OE *sceaft.*]

shaft·ing (shăf′tĭng) *n.* **1.** A system of shafts, as in a mechanical device, for transmitting motion or power. **2.** Material from which shafts are made.

shag¹ (shăg) *n.* **1.** A tangle or mass, esp. of rough, matted hair. **2. a.** A coarse long nap, as on a woolen cloth. **b.** Cloth having such a nap. **3.** Coarse shredded tobacco. *—tr.v.* **shagged, shag·ging, shags. 1.** To make shaggy; roughen. **2. a.** To chase and bring back; fetch. **b.** *Baseball.* To chase and catch (fly balls) in practice. [ME *shagge < OE *sceagga,* matted hair.]

shag² (shăg) *n.* A dance step of the 1930's consisting of a hop on each foot in turn. *—intr.v.* **shagged, shag·ging, shags.** To dance the shag. [Orig. unknown.]

shag³ (shăg) *n.* The cormorant (sense 1). [Perh. from its shaggy crest.]

shag·bark (shăg′bärk′) *n.* A North American hickory tree, *Carya ovata,* having shaggy bark, compound leaves, and edible nuts with a hard shell.

shag·gy (shăg′ē) *adj.* **-gi·er, -gi·est. 1.** Having, covered with, or resembling long, rough hair or wool. **2.** Bushy and matted: *shaggy hair.* **3.** Poorly groomed; unkempt. **—shag′gi·ly** *adv.* **—shag′gi·ness** *n.*

shaggy cap *n.* The shaggy mane.

shag·gy-dog story (shăg′ē-dôg′, -dŏg′) *n.* A long, drawn-out anecdote ending with an absurd or anticlimactic punch line.

shaggy mane *n.* An edible mushroom, *Coprinus comatus,* having shaggy scales covering the cap.

sha·green (shə-grēn′) *n.* **1.** The rough hide of a shark or ray, covered with numerous bony denticles and used as an abrasive and as leather. **2.** An untanned leather with a granular surface that is often dyed green. [Fr. *chagrin* < Turk. *sağri,* leather.] **—sha·green′** *adj.*

shah (shä) *n.* The title of the former hereditary monarchs of Iran. [Pers. *shāh,* king.]

Sha·hap·tin (shä-hăp′tĭn) or **Sha·hap·ti·an** (-tē-ĭn) *n.* Variants of **Sahaptin.**

shai·tan (shī-tän′, shā-) *n.* **1.** Often **Shaitan.** *Islam.* The Devil; Satan. **2.** An evil spirit; fiend. [Ar. *shaiṭān* < Heb. *śāṭān* < *śāṭan,* he accused.]

shake (shāk) *v.* **shook** (shŏŏk), **shak·en** (shā′kən), **shak·ing, shakes.** *—tr.* **1.** To cause to move to and fro with jerky movements. **2.** To cause to quiver or tremble; vibrate or rock: *A severe tremor shook the ground.* **3.** To cause to stagger or waver. **4.** To remove or dislodge by jerky movements: *shake the dust from the cushions.* **5.** To bring to a specified condition by or as if by shaking: *"It is not easy to shake one's heart free of the impression"* (John Middleton Murry). **6.** To disturb or agitate; unnerve: *was shaken by the news of the disaster.* **7.** To brandish or wave: *shake one's fist.* **8.** To clasp (hands) in greeting or leave-taking or as a sign of agreement. **9.** *Mus.* To trill (a note). **10.** To rattle and mix (dice) before casting. *—intr.* **1.** To move to and fro in jerky movements. **2.** To tremble, as from cold or in anger. **3.** To become unsteady; totter or waver. **4.** *Mus.* To trill. **5.** To shake hands. ***—phrasal verbs.*** **shake down. 1.** *Informal.* To extort money from. **2.** *Informal.* To make a thorough search of. **3.** To subject (a vessel) to a shakedown cruise. **shake off.** To free oneself of; get rid of: *shook off his pursuers.* **shake up.** *Informal.* To rearrange or reorganize drastically. *—n.* **1.** An act of shaking. **2.** A trembling or quivering movement. **3.** *Informal.* An earthquake. **4.** A fissure in rock. **5.** A crack in timber caused by wind or frost. **6.** *Slang.* A moment or instant; trice: *I'll do it in a shake.* **7.** *Mus.* A trill. **8.** A beverage in which the ingredients are mixed by shaking: *a milk shake.* **9.** A rough shingle used to cover barns and other rustic buildings. **10. shakes.** *Informal.* Uncontrollable trembling, as in a sick person. **11.** *Slang.* Bargain; deal: *getting a fair shake.* ***—idioms.*** **give (someone) the shake.** *Slang.* To escape from or get rid of. **no great shakes.** *Slang.* Unexceptional; ordinary. **shake a leg.** *Informal.* **1.** To dance. **2.** To move quickly; hurry up. [ME *schaken* < OE *sceacan.*] **—shak′a·ble, shake′a·ble** *adj.*

Synonyms: *shake, tremble, quake, quiver, shiver, shudder, wobble.* These verbs mean to give evidence of agitation in the form of involuntary vibratory movement. *Shake,* the most general, applies to any such pronounced movement in a thing or a person, especially one moved by strong emotion. *Tremble* implies quick and rather slight movement like that of a person affected by fear, anger, or awe. *Quake* refers to violent convulsive movement caused by physical or emotional upheaval. *Quiver* suggests rather slight movement, as of a person experiencing chill or fear. Whereas *trembling* implies localized movement in persons, *shivering* affects a wide area of the body. *Shudder* chiefly applies to sudden strong, convulsive shaking in a person, caused by fear, horror, or a revolting sight or thought. *Wobble* refers to pronounced and very unsteady movement.

shake·down (shāk′doun′) *n.* **1.** *Informal.* Extortion of money, as by blackmail. **2.** *Informal.* A thorough search of a place or person. **3.** A period of appraisal followed by adjustments to improve efficiency or functioning. *—adj.* Designed to test the performance of a ship or airplane and familiarize the crew with the operation: *a shakedown cruise.*

shak·er (shā′kər) *n.* **1.** One that shakes. **2.** A container used for shaking: *a pepper shaker.* **3.** A container used to mix or blend by shaking: *a cocktail shaker.* **4. Shaker.** A member of a religious sect originating in England in 1747, practicing communal living and observing celibacy.

Shake·spear·e·an or **Shake·spear·i·an** (shāk-spîr′ē-ən) *adj.* Of, pertaining to, or like Shakespeare, his works, or his style. *—n.* A scholar of Shakespeare or his works.

Shake·spear·e·an·a or **Shake·spear·i·an·a** (shāk-spîr′ē-ăn′ə, -ä′nə) *n.* A collection of items by or relating to Shakespeare.

Shakespearean sonnet *n.* The sonnet form perfected by Shakespeare, composed of three quatrains and a terminal couplet with the rhyme pattern *abab cdcd efef gg* and retaining the break or pause in theme that falls between the octave and sestet in earlier sonnet forms.

shake·up (shāk′ŭp′) *n.* A thorough, often drastic reorganization, as in the personnel of a business or government.

shaking palsy *n.* Parkinson's disease.

shak·o also **shack·o** (shăk′ō, shā′kō, shä′-) *n., pl.* **-os** or **-oes.** A stiff, cylindrical military dress hat with a metal plate in front, a short visor, and a plume. [Fr. *schako* < Hung. *csákó* < *csákó (süveg),* pointed (cap) < *csák,* peak < G. *Zacken,* point.]

Shak·ta (shäk′tə, säk′-) *n.* A member of a Hindu sect that worships Shakti. [Skt. *śākta* < *śaktiḥ,* Shakti.] **—Shak′tism** *n.* **—Shak′tist** *n.*

Shak·ti (shŭk′tē, shäk′-) *n.* *Hinduism.* The wife of the god Shiva, the personification of nature and generative power. [Skt. *śaktiḥ* < *śaknoti,* he is strong.]

shak·y (shā′kē) *adj.* **-i·er, -i·est. 1.** Trembling or quivering; tremulous. **2.** Unsteady or unsound; weak: *a shaky table.* **3.** Not to be depended upon; precarious: *a shaky alliance.* **—shak′i·ly** *adv.* **—shak′i·ness** *n.*

shale (shāl) *n.* A fissile rock composed of laminated layers of claylike, fine-grained sediments. [Prob. < ME, shell < OE *scealu.*]

shale oil *n.* A crude oil that is obtained from oil shale by heating and distillation.

shall (shăl) *aux.v.* past **should** (shŏŏd). **1.** Used to indicate simple futurity: *I shall be 28 tomorrow.* **2.** Used to express: **a.** Determination or promise: *He shall answer for his misdeeds.* **b.** Inevitability: *That day shall come.* **c.** Command: *Students shall report weekly to their tutors.* **d.** A directive or requirement: *The penalty shall not exceed two years in prison.* **3.** *Archaic.* **a.** To be able to. **b.** To have to; must. [ME *schal* < OE *sceal.*]

Usage: In formal writing, as indicated above, *shall* is employed in the first person to indicate futurity: *I shall leave tomorrow.* In the second and third persons, the same sense of futurity is expressed by *will: He will come this afternoon.* Use of the auxiliaries *shall* and *will* is reversed when the writer wants to indicate such conditions as determination, promise, obligation, command, compulsion, permission, or inevitability; *will* is then employed in the first person and *shall* in the second and third. Thus, *I will leave tomorrow* (meaning, "I am determined, or obligated, or compelled, or fated to leave"). *He shall come this afternoon* likewise can express any of the conditions enumerated, such as promise, permission, command, or compulsion. Such, at least, are the rules of traditional grammar. However, these distinctions are only rarely observed in American English, even in formal writing. In general usage, *will* is widely employed in all three persons to indicate futurity: *We will be in New York next week* (acceptable to a majority of the Usage Panel as an example in writing on all levels). *Shall* is largely neglected, except in some interrogatives, such as *Shall we go? Where shall we take our vacation this year?* and in a few set phrases: *We shall overcome. Will,* in all three persons, is employed more often than *shall* in expressing any of the forms of emphatic futurity. In speech, the degree of stress of the auxiliary verb is usually more indicative of the intended meaning than the choice of *shall* or *will.* In writing, a condition other than mere futurity is often expressed more clearly by an alternative to *shall* or *will,* such as *must* or *have to* (indicating determination, compulsion, or obligation) or by

shagbark
Shagbark hickory

use of an intensifying word, such as *certainly* or *surely,* with *shall* or *will.* Informally, contractions such as *I'll, we'll,* and *you'll* are generally employed without distinction between the functions of *shall* and *will* as formally defined.

shal·loon (shə-lo͞on′, shă-) *n.* A lightweight wool or worsted twill fabric, used chiefly for coat linings. [Fr. *chalon,* after *Châlons*-sur-Marne, France.]

shal·lop (shăl′əp) *n.* An open boat fitted with oars or sails or both. [Fr. *chaloupe* < Du. *sloep,* sloop.]

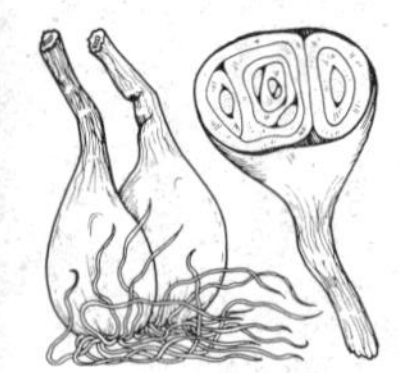

shallot

shal·lot (shə-lŏt′, shăl′ət) *n.* **1.** A plant, *Allium ascalonicum,* closely related to the onion, cultivated for its edible bulb that divides into smaller sections. **2.** The mild-flavored bulb of the shallot, used in cookery. [Obs. Fr. *eschalotte* < OFr. *eschaloigne* <VLat. **escalonia.* —see SCALLION.]

shal·low (shăl′ō) *adj.* **-er, -est. 1.** Measuring little from bottom to top or surface; not deep. **2.** Lacking depth, as in intellect or significance: *"His intellect was of the shallowest order . . . his mind was in its original state of white paper"* (Lamb). *—n.* A shallow part of a body of water; shoal. *—tr. & intr.v.* **-lowed, -low·ing, -lows.** To make or become shallow. [ME *schalowe.*] **—shal′low·ly** *adv.* **—shal′low·ness** *n.*

sha·lom (shä-lōm′, shə-) *interj.* Used as a greeting or farewell among Jews. [Heb. *shālōm,* peace.]

sha·lom a·lei·chem (shô′ləm ə-lā′KHəm, -kəm, shō′-) *interj.* Used as a greeting or farewell among Jews. [Heb. *shālōm 'alēkhem,* peace be with you.]

shalt (shălt) *aux.v. Archaic.* A second person singular present tense of **shall.**

sham (shăm) *n.* **1.** Something false or empty that is purported to be genuine; a spurious imitation. **2.** The quality of deceitfulness; empty pretense. **3.** A person who assumes a false character; impostor: *"He a man! Hell! He was a hollow sham!"* (Conrad). **4.** A decorative cover made to simulate an article of household linen and used over or in place of it: *a pillow sham.* *—adj.* Not genuine; fake: *sham modesty.* *—v.* **shammed, sham·ming, shams.** *—tr.* To put on the false appearance of; feign. *—intr.* To assume a false appearance or character; dissemble. [Perh. dial. var. of SHAME.] **—sham′mer** *n.*

shamrock

sha·man (shä′mən, shā′-) *n.* **1.** A priest of shamanism. **2.** A medicine man among certain North American Indians. [R. < Tungus *šaman,* ult. < Skt. *śramaṇas.*]

sha·man·ism (shä′mə-nĭz′əm, shā′-) *n.* **1.** The religious practices of certain native peoples of northern Asia who believe that good and evil spirits pervade the world and can be summoned or heard through inspired priests acting as mediums. **2.** A form of primitive spiritualism, such as that practiced among certain North American Indian tribes. **—sha′man·ist** *n.* **—sha′man·is′tic** *adj.*

Sha·mash (shä′măsh′) *n.* The sun god of Assyro-Babylonian religion, worshiped as the author of justice and compassion. [Akkadian.]

sham·ble (shăm′bəl) *intr.v.* **-bled, -bling, -bles.** To walk in an awkward, lazy, or unsteady manner, shuffling the feet. *—n.* A shuffling gait. [< E. *shamble,* awkward, ungainly.]

sham·bles (shăm′bəlz) *pl.n. (used with a sing. verb).* **1.** A scene or condition of complete disorder or ruin: *"The economy was in shambles"* (W. Bruce Lincoln). **2.** A place or scene of bloodshed or carnage. **3.** A slaughterhouse. **4.** *Chiefly Brit.* A meat market or butcher shop. [< dial. *shamble,* a table for selling meat < ME *shamel* < OE *sceamel,* table.]

shame (shām) *n.* **1. a.** A painful emotion caused by a strong sense of guilt, embarrassment, unworthiness, or disgrace. **b.** Capacity for such a feeling: *Have you no shame?* **2.** A person or thing that brings dishonor, disgrace, or condemnation. **3.** A condition of disgrace or dishonor; ignominy. **4.** A great disappointment. *—tr.v.* **shamed, sham·ing, shames. 1.** To cause to feel shame; put to shame. **2.** To bring dishonor or disgrace upon. **3.** To force by making ashamed: *He was shamed into an apology.* **—*idiom.* put to shame. 1.** To fill with shame; disgrace. **2.** To outdo thoroughly; surpass. [ME < OE *sceamu.*]

shame·faced (shām′fāst′) *adj.* **1.** Indicative of shame; ashamed: *a shamefaced explanation.* **2.** Extremely modest or shy; bashful. [Alteration of obs. *shamefast,* bashful, ashamed < ME < OE *sceamfæst* : *sceamu,* shame + *fæst,* fixed.] **—shame′fac′ed·ly** (-fā′sĭd-lē) *adv.* **—shame′fac′ed·ness** *n.*

shame·ful (shām′fəl) *adj.* **1. a.** Causing shame; disgraceful. **b.** Deserving shame; indecent. **2.** *Archaic.* Full of shame; ashamed. **—shame′ful·ly** *adv.* **—shame′ful·ness** *n.*

shame·less (shām′lĭs) *adj.* **1.** Not subject to shame; brazen. **2.** Exhibiting a lack of shame: *a shameless lie.* **—shame′less·ly** *adv.* **—shame′less·ness** *n.*

Synonyms: *shameless, brazen, barefaced, brash, bold, impudent, unblushing, forward.* These adjectives describe personal behavior that is in defiance of social and moral proprieties. *Shameless* implies lack of both modesty and sense of decency, together with contempt for the rights of others. *Brazen* is somewhat stronger in its suggestion of open display of conscienceless behavior. *Barefaced* specifies absence of any attempt to conceal misconduct. *Brash* stresses impetuousness, lack of tact and forethought, and reckless indifference to consequences of action. *Bold,* as compared here, implies undue presumption. *Impudent* suggests pertness that verges on insolence. *Unblushing* implies lack of embarrassment where grounds for it clearly exist. *Forward* applies less forcefully to one who is unduly self-assertive.

sham·mes (shä′məs) *n., pl.* **sham·mo·sim** (shä-mô′sĭm). *Judaism.* **1.** A sexton in a synagogue. **2.** The candle used to light the other eight candles of a Chanukah menorah. [Yiddish *shames* < Heb. *shammāsh.*]

sham·mo·sim (shä-mô′sĭm) *n.* Plural of **shammes.**

sham·my (shăm′ē) *n. & v.* Variant of **chamois.**

sham·poo (shăm-po͞o′) *n., pl.* **-poos. 1.** Any of various liquid or cream preparations of soap or detergent used to wash the hair and scalp. **2.** Any of various cleaning agents for rugs, upholstery, or cars. **3.** The act or process of washing or cleaning with shampoo. *—v.* **-pooed, -poo·ing, -poos.** *—tr.* To wash or clean with shampoo. *—intr.* To wash or clean something with shampoo. [< Hindi *cā̃pō,* imper. of *cā̃pna,* to press.]

sham·rock (shăm′rŏk′) *n.* Any of several plants, such as a clover or wood sorrel, having compound leaves with three small leaflets, considered the national emblem of Ireland. [Ir. *seamrog,* dim. of *seamar,* clover.]

sha·mus (shä′məs, shā′-) *n. Slang.* **1.** A policeman. **2.** A private detective. [Perh. var. of SHAMMES.]

Shan (shän, shăn) *n., pl.* **Shan** or **Shans. 1. a.** One of a group of Mongoloid tribes living in Burma, Thailand, and southern China. **b.** A member of one of these tribes. **2.** The Tai language of the Shan. **—Shan** *adj.*

shan·dy·gaff (shăn′dē-găf′) *n.* A drink made of beer or ale mixed with ginger beer, ginger ale, or lemonade. [Orig. unknown.]

shang·hai (shăng-hī′) *tr.v.* **-haied, -hai·ing, -hais. 1.** To kidnap (a man) for compulsory service aboard a ship, esp. after rendering him insensible. **2.** To induce or compel (someone) to do something, esp. by fraud or force. [After *Shanghai,* China, from the former custom of kidnaping sailors to man ships going to China.]

Shang·hai (shăng-hī′) *n.* A red and black domestic fowl of a breed said to have been imported from Asia. [After *Shanghai,* China.]

Shan·gri-la (shăng′grĭ-lä′) *n.* An imaginary, remote paradise on earth; utopia. [After *Shangri-La,* the imaginary land in the novel *Lost Horizon* by James Hilton (1900–1954).]

shank (shăngk) *n.* **1.** *Anat.* **a.** The part of the human leg between the knee and ankle. **b.** A corresponding part in other vertebrates. **2.** The whole leg of a human being. **3.** A cut of meat from the leg of a steer, calf, sheep, or lamb. **4.** The long, narrow part of a nail or pin. **5.** A stem, stalk, or similar part. **6.** The stem of an anchor. **7.** The long shaft of a fishhook. **8.** The part of a tobacco pipe between the bowl and stem. **9.** The shaft of a key. **10.** The narrower section of a spoon's handle. **11. a.** The narrow part of a shoe's sole under the instep. **b.** A piece of metal or other material used to reinforce or shape this part. **12.** A ring or other projection on the back of a button by which it is sewn to cloth. **13. a.** The part of a drill or other tool that connects the functioning head to the handle. **b.** A tang (sense 4.b.). **14. a.** The latter part of a period of time. **b.** The early part of a period of time. [ME *schank* < OE *sceanca.*]

shank·piece (shăngk′pēs′) *n.* An arch support inserted into the shank of a shoe.

shan't or **sha'nt** (shănt, shänt). Shall not.

shan·tey (shăn′tē) *n.* Variant of **chantey.**

shan·tung (shăn-tŭng′) *n.* **1.** A heavy fabric, made of spun wild silk, with a rough, nubby surface. **2.** An imitation of shantung, made of rayon or cotton. [After *Shandong* (Shantung), China.]

shan·ty[1] (shăn′tē) *n., pl.* **-ties.** A roughly built, often ramshackle cabin; shack. [Prob. Canadian Fr. *chantier* < Fr., timberyard < OFr., gantry < Lat. *cantherius,* rafter.]

shan·ty[2] (shăn′tē) *n.* Variant of **chantey.**

shan·ty·man (shăn′tē-mən, -măn′) *n.* A man who lives in a shanty, esp. a lumberjack.

shan·ty·town (shăn′tē-toun′) *n.* A town or a section of a town consisting of ramshackle huts.

shape (shāp) *n.* **1. a.** The characteristic surface configuration of a thing; form. **b.** Something distinguished from its surroundings by its outline. **2.** The contour of a person's body; figure. **3. a.** A definite form. **b.** A desirable form: *a fabric that holds its shape.* **4.** A form or condition in which something may exist or appear; embodiment: *a god in the shape of a swan.* **5.** Assumed or false appearance; guise. **6.** A ghostly form; phantom. **7.** Something, as a mold or pattern, that is used to give or determine form. **8.** Proper condition for action, effectiveness, or use: *an athlete in excellent shape.* *—tr.v.* **shaped, shap·ing, shapes. 1.** To give a particular form to; create. **2.** To cause to conform to a particular form or pattern; adapt to fit. **3. a.** To plan; devise. **b.** To embody in a definite form: *shaped a folk legend into a full-scale opera.* **—*phrasal verb.* shape up.** *Informal.* **1.** To turn out; develop. **2.** To improve so as to meet a standard. [ME < OE *gesceap,* a creation.] **—shap′er** *n.*

shape·less (shāp′lĭs) *adj.* **1.** Having no distinct shape. **2.** Lacking symmetrical or attractive form; not shapely. **—shape′less·ly** *adv.* **—shape′less·ness** *n.*

shape·ly (shāp′lē) *adj.* **-li·er, -li·est.** Having a pleasing shape; well-proportioned: *a shapely figure.* **—shape′li·ness** *n.*

shap·en (shā′pən) *v. Archaic.* Past participle of **shape.**

shape·up (shāp′ŭp′) *n.* An assembled group of longshoremen from which the day's work crew is chosen by a representative of the union.

shard (shärd) also **sherd** (shûrd) *n.* **1.** A piece of broken pottery; potsherd. **2.** A fragment of a brittle substance, as of glass or metal. **3.** *Zool.* A tough sheath, esp. the outer wing covering of a beetle. [ME *sherd* < OE *sceard.*]

share[1] (shâr) *n.* **1.** A part or portion belonging to, distributed to, contributed by, or owed by a person or group. **2.** An equitable portion: *do one's share of the work.* **3.** Any of the equal parts into which the capital stock of a corporation or company is divided. —*v.* **shared, shar·ing, shares.** —*tr.* **1.** To divide and parcel out in shares; apportion. **2.** To participate in, use, or experience in common: *share responsibilities; share an apartment.* —*intr.* To have or take a part; participate: *share in an effort.* **—idioms. go shares.** To be concerned or partake equally or jointly, as in a business venture. **on shares.** With each individual concerned taking a share, usually equal, of any profit or loss. Used of an enterprise. [ME < OE *scearu,* division.] **—shar′er** *n.*

Synonyms: *share, participate, partake.* These verbs refer to forms of joint activity, such as having, using, or experiencing something with others. *Share* applies both to possession, use, and enjoyment of physical things and to division of what is nonphysical, such as responsibility or work. *Participate* implies taking an active part in activities or experiences with others. *Partake,* a less common term, usually refers to having a portion of something, especially food or drink, but can be applied to involvement in intangible things, such as emotional experiences.

share[2] (shâr) *n.* A plowshare. [ME < OE *scēar.*]

share·crop (shâr′krŏp′) *intr.v.* **-cropped, -crop·ping, -crops.** To work as a sharecropper.

share·crop·per (shâr′krŏp′ər) *n.* A tenant farmer who gives a share of his crop to the landlord in lieu of rent.

share·hold·er (shâr′hōl′dər) *n.* One that owns or holds a share or shares of stock; stockholder.

sha·rif (shə-rēf′) *n.* Variant of **sherif.**

shark (shärk) *n.* **1.** Any of numerous chiefly marine fishes of the order Squaliformes (or Selachii), which are sometimes large and voracious and have a cartilaginous skeleton and tough skin covered with small, toothlike scales. **2.** A ruthless, greedy, or dishonest person, esp. a vicious usurer. **3.** *Slang.* A person who is unusually skilled in a particular activity: *a card shark.* —*intr.v.* **sharked, shark·ing, sharks.** To live by fraud and trickery. [Orig. unknown.]

shark·skin (shärk′skĭn′) *n.* **1.** The skin of a shark. **2.** Leather made from the skin of a shark. **3.** A rayon and acetate fabric having a smooth, somewhat shiny surface.

shark sucker *n.* A remora.

sharp (shärp) *adj.* **-er, -est. 1.** Having a thin, keen edge or a fine, acute point; suitable for or capable of cutting or piercing: *a sharp knife.* **2. a.** Having clear form and detail: *a sharp photographic image.* **b.** Terminating in an edge or point: *sharp, angular cliffs.* **c.** Clearly and distinctly set forth: *sharp contrasts in behavior.* **3.** Abrupt or acute: *a sharp drop.* **4.** Shrewd; astute: *a sharp observation.* **5.** Artful; underhand: *sharp selling practices.* **6.** Vigilant; alert. **7.** Brisk; vigorous. **8.** Harsh; biting: *sharp criticism.* **9.** Fierce or impetuous; violent. **10.** Intense; severe: *a sharp pain.* **11.** Sudden and shrill. **12.** Strongly affecting the senses of smell and taste: *a sharp, pungent odor; a sharp cheese.* **13.** Composed of hard, angular particles: *sharp sand.* **14.** *Mus.* **a.** Raised in pitch by a semitone. **b.** Above the proper pitch. **c.** Having the key signature in sharps. **15.** Voiceless. Used of a consonant. **16.** *Slang.* Attractive or stylish: *a sharp jacket.* —*adv.* **1.** In a sharp manner. **2.** Punctually; exactly: *at three o'clock sharp.* **3.** *Mus.* Above the true or proper pitch. —*n.* **1.** *Mus.* **a.** A musical note or tone raised one semitone above its normal pitch. **b.** A sign (♯) indicating this. **2.** A slender sewing needle with a very fine point. **3.** *Informal.* A shrewd cheater; sharper. —*v.* **sharped, sharp·ing, sharps.** *Mus.* —*tr.* To raise in pitch by a semitone. —*intr.* To play or sing above the proper pitch. [ME *scharp* < OE *scearp.*] **—sharp′ly** *adv.* **—sharp′ness** *n.*

Synonyms: *sharp, keen, acute.* These adjectives describe edges or points that are not dull; they may also indicate degrees of mental awareness. *Sharp* applies to a point or an edge that can easily pierce or cut. *Keen* usually specifies a long, sharp cutting edge. *Acute* applies both to what has a pointed tip or end and to an angle of less than 90 degrees. Figuratively *sharp* suggests quickness of perception or cleverness. *Keen* implies both mental vigor and discernment. *Acute* implies even more strongly a penetrating analytical ability.

sharp·en (shär′pən) *tr. & intr.v.* **-ened, -en·ing, -ens.** To make or become sharp or sharper. **—sharp′en·er** *n.*

sharp·er (shär′pər) *n.* One that deals dishonestly with others, esp. a gambler who cheats.

sharp-eyed (shärp′īd′) *adj.* **1.** Having keen eyesight. **2.** Keenly perceptive or observant; alert.

sharp·ie (shär′pē) *n.* **1.** A long, narrow, flat-bottomed fishing boat that has a centerboard and one or two masts, each rigged with a triangular sail. **2.** *Informal.* An alert, quick-witted person. [< SHARP.]

sharpie

sharp-set (shärp′sĕt′) *adj.* **1.** Set at a sharp angle or presenting a sharp edge. **2.** Having an avid appetite or desire. **—sharp′set′ness** *n.*

sharp-shinned hawk (shärp′shĭnd′) *n.* A small North American hawk, *Accipiter striatus,* having short, rounded wings and a long tail.

sharp·shoot·er (shärp′sho͞o′tər) *n.* **1.** An expert marksman. **2. a.** The second military grade of proficiency in the use of rifles and other small arms. **b.** A person having this grade of proficiency.

sharp·shoot·ing (shärp′sho͞o′tĭng) *n.* **1.** Expert marksmanship. **2.** Accurate and often unexpected verbal or written attack.

sharp-sight·ed (shärp′sī′tĭd) *adj.* Sharp-eyed.

sharp-tongued (shärp′tŭngd′) *adj.* Harsh, critical, or sarcastic in speech.

sharp-wit·ted (shärp′wĭt′ĭd) *adj.* Having a keenly perceptive mind. **—sharp′-wit′ted·ness** *n.*

shash·lik or **shash·lick** (shäsh-lĭk′, shäsh′lĭk) *n.* A dish consisting of marinated cubes of mutton or veal grilled or roasted on a spit, often with slices of eggplant, onion, and tomato; shish kebab. [R. *shashlyk,* of Turkic orig.]

Shas·ta daisy (shăs′tə) *n.* A cultivated variety of *Chrysanthemum maximum,* of the Pyrenees, having large, white, daisylike flowers. [After Mt. *Shasta* in California.]

shat (shăt) *v. Obscene.* A past tense and past participle of **shit.**

shat·ter (shăt′ər) *v.* **-tered, -ter·ing, -ters.** —*tr.* **1.** To cause to break or burst suddenly into pieces, as with a violent blow. **2.** To damage seriously; disable. —*intr.* To break into pieces; smash or burst. —*n.* **1.** The act of shattering. **2.** Often **shatters.** A splintered or fragmented condition: *a once beautiful vase now in shatters.* [ME *schateren* < OE *sceaterian.*]

shatter cone *n.* A conical fragment of rock that is formed from the high pressure in volcanism or meteorite impact and has striations radiating from the apex.

shat·ter·proof glass (shăt′ər-pro͞of′) *n.* Safety glass.

shave (shāv) *v.* **shaved, shaved** or **shav·en** (shā′vən), **shav·ing, shaves.** —*tr.* **1.** To remove the beard or other body hair from, as with a razor. **2.** To cut (the beard, for example) at the surface of the skin with a razor. **3.** To crop, trim, or mow closely: *shave a meadow.* **4.** To remove thin slices from: *shave a board.* **5.** To cut or scrape into thin slices; shred: *shave cheese.* **6.** To come close to or graze in passing. **7.** *Informal.* To purchase (a note) at a reduction greater than the legal or customary rate. **8.** *Informal.* To cut (a price) by a slight margin. —*intr.* To remove a beard or hair with a razor. —*n.* **1.** The act, process, or result of shaving. **2.** A thin slice or scraping; shaving. **3.** Any of various tools used for shaving. **—idiom. close shave.** *Informal.* A narrow escape. [ME *shaven,* to scrape < OE *sceafan.*]

shav·er (shā′vər) *n.* **1. a.** One that shaves. **b.** A device used in shaving. **2.** *Informal.* A small child, esp. a boy.

shav·ing (shā′vĭng) *n.* **1.** A thin slice; sliver. **2.** The action of one that shaves.

Sha·vu·ot also **Sha·bu·oth** (shə-vo͞o′ōt′, -ōth′, -əs) *n.* A Jewish holiday commemorating the revelation of the Law on Mount Sinai and the celebration of the wheat festival in ancient times, observed on the sixth and seventh of Sivan. [Heb. *shābhūʿōth* < *shābhūaʿ,* week.]

shawl (shôl) *n.* A square or oblong piece of cloth worn as a covering for the head, neck, and shoulders. —*tr.v.* **shawled, shawl·ing, shawls.** To cover with or as if with a shawl. [Pers. *shāl.*]

shawl

shawm (shôm) *n.* Any of various early double-reed wind instruments, forerunners of the modern oboe. [ME *schallemele* < OFr. *chalemel* < VLat. **calamellus,* dim. of Lat. *calamus,* reed < Gk. *kalamos.*]

Shaw·nee (shô-nē′) *n., pl.* **Shawnee** or **-nees. 1. a.** A tribe of Algonquian-speaking North American Indians, formerly living in the Tennessee Valley and adjacent areas, now surviving in Oklahoma. **b.** A member of this tribe. **2.** The Algonquian language of the Shawnee. [Obs. *Shawanese* < Delaware *šāonu* < Shawnee *šāwanwa,* a Shawnee.]

Shaw·wal (shə-wäl′) *n.* The tenth month of the year in the Moslem calendar. See table at **calendar.** [Ar. *Shawwāl.*]

shay (shā) *n. Informal.* A chaise. [Back-formation < CHAISE, taken as pl.]

she (shē) *pron.* **1.** Used to represent the female person or animal last mentioned or implied. **2.** Used traditionally of certain objects and institutions such as ships and nations. —*n.* A female animal or person: *a she-cat; Is the cat a she?* —See Usage notes at **be, everyone,** and **I.** [ME *sche,* prob. alteration of OE *hēo,* she, or *sēo,* fem. demonstrative pronoun.]

shea butter (shē, shā) *n.* A whitish or yellowish fat obtained from the nut of the shea tree, used as food and for making soap and candles.

sheaf (shēf) *n., pl.* **sheaves** (shēvz). **1.** A bundle of cut stalks of grain or similar plants bound with straw or twine. **2.** A collection of items held or bound together. **3.** An archer's quiver. —*tr.v.* **sheafed, sheaf·ing, sheafs.** To bind into a sheaf. [ME *sheef* < OE *scēaf.*]

shear
Shearing sheep

shear (shîr) *v.* **sheared, sheared** or **shorn** (shôrn, shōrn), **shear·ing, shears.** —*tr.* **1.** To remove (fleece or hair) by cutting or clipping. **2.** To remove the hair or fleece from. **3.** To cut with or as if with shears: *shearing a hedge.* **4.** To strip, divest, or deprive of. —*intr.* **1.** To use a cutting tool such as shears. **2.** To move or proceed by or as if by cutting: *shear through the wheat.* **3.** *Physics.* To become deformed by forces tending to produce a shearing strain. —*n.* **1.** The act, process, or result of shearing. **2.** Something cut off by shearing. **3.** The act, process, or fact of shearing. Used to indicate a sheep's age: *a two-shear ram.* **4.** *Physics.* **a.** An applied force or system of forces that tends to produce a shearing strain. **b.** A shearing strain. [ME *scheren* < OE *sceran.*] **—shear'er** *n.*

shearing strain *n.* A condition in or deformation of an elastic body caused by forces that tend to produce an opposite but parallel sliding motion of the body's planes.

shearing stress *n. Physics.* Shear (sense 4.a.).

shear legs also **sheer·legs** (shîr'lĕgz') *n.* An apparatus used to lift heavy weights, consisting of two or more spars joined at the top and spread at the base, the tackle being suspended from the top.

shear·ling (shîr'lĭng) *n.* **1.** A year-old sheep that has been shorn once. **2.** The skin of a shearling or of a newly shorn sheep, tanned and with the wool on.

shears (shîrz) *pl.n.* **1. a.** Large scissors. **b.** Any of various implements or machines that cut with a scissorlike action. **2.** Also **sheers.** A shear legs. [ME *schere,* scissors < OE *scēar.*]

shear stress *n. Physics.* Shear (sense 4.a.).

shear·wa·ter (shîr'wô'tər, -wŏt'ər) *n.* Any of various oceanic birds of the family Procellariidae, esp. of the genus *Puffinus,* having long wings and a hooked bill.

sheat·fish (shēt'fĭsh') *n., pl.* **sheatfish** or **-fish·es.** A large freshwater catfish, *Silurus glanis,* of Eurasia. [Alteration of obs. *sheathfish* : SHEATH + FISH.]

sheath (shēth) *n., pl.* **sheaths** (shē*th*z, shēths). **1.** A case for a blade, as of a sword. **2.** Any of various coverings resembling or used like a sheath. **3.** *Biol.* An enveloping structure or part, such as the tubular base of a leaf surrounding a stem. **4.** A close-fitting dress. —*tr.v.* **sheathed, sheath·ing, sheaths.** To sheathe. [ME *schethe* < OE *scēath.*]

sheath·bill (shēth'bĭl') *n.* Either of two shore birds, *Chionia alba* or *C. minor,* of Antarctic regions, having white plumage and a horny covering on the base of the bill.

sheathe (shē*th*) *tr.v.* **sheathed, sheath·ing, sheathes. 1.** To insert into or provide with a sheath. **2.** To retract (a claw) into a sheath. **3.** To enclose; encase. **—sheath'er** *n.*

shed²

sheath·ing (shē'*th*ĭng) *n.* **1.** A layer of boards or of other wood or fiber materials applied to the outer studs, joists, and rafters of a building to strengthen the structure and serve as a base for an exterior weatherproof cladding. **2.** An exterior covering on the underwater part of a ship's hull that protects it against marine growths. **3.** The act of providing sheathing for something.

sheath knife *n.* A knife that has a fixed blade and fits into a sheath.

shea tree (shē, shā) *n.* An African tree, *Butyrospermum parkii,* having fruit containing oily seeds that yield shea butter. [Mandekan *si.*]

sheave¹ (shēv) *tr.v.* **sheaved, sheav·ing, sheaves.** To collect and bind into a sheaf.

sheave² (shēv, shĭv) *n.* A wheel or disk with a grooved rim, esp. one used as a pulley. [ME *sheve.*]

sheaves (shēvz) *n.* Plural of **sheaf.**

she·bang (shə-băng') *n. Informal.* A situation, organization, contrivance, or set of facts or things: *organized and ran the whole shebang.* [Orig. unknown.]

She·bat (shə-bät', -vät') *n.* Variant of **Shevat.**

she·been (shə-bēn') *n. Chiefly Ir.* An unlicensed drinking establishment. [Ir. Gael. *sībīn,* bad ale.]

shed¹ (shĕd) *v.* **shed, shed·ding, sheds.** —*tr.* **1.** To cause to pour forth: *shed tears.* **2.** To send forth; diffuse or radiate: *shed light.* **3.** To repel without allowing penetration: *A duck's feathers shed water.* **4.** To lose by natural process: *"He was a middle-aged child that had never shed its baby fat"* (Truman Capote). —*intr.* **1.** To lose a natural growth or covering by natural process. **2.** To pour forth, fall off, or drop out: *All the leaves have shed.* —*n.* **1.** Something that sheds, esp. an elevation in the earth's surface from which water flows in two directions; watershed. **2.** Something that has been shed. **—*idiom.* shed blood.** To take life, esp. with violence; kill. [ME *sheden* < OE *scēadan,* to divide.]

sheet bend

shed² (shĕd) *n.* **1.** A small structure, either freestanding or attached to a larger structure, serving for storage or shelter. **2.** A large low structure often open on all sides. [Alteration of obs. *shadde,* var. of SHADE.]

she'd (shēd). **1.** She had. **2.** She would.

shed·der (shĕd'ər) *n.* One that sheds, as a long-haired animal or a molting snake.

shed dormer *n.* A dormer having a roof that slopes in the same direction as the one in which the dormer is located.

she-dev·il (shē'dĕv'əl) *n.* A malicious or cruel woman.

sheen (shēn) *n.* **1.** Glistening brightness; shininess: *the sheen of old satin in candlelight.* **2.** Splendid attire. [ME *shene,* beautiful < OE *scīene.*]

shee·ny (shē'nē) *n., pl.* **-nies.** *Offensive Slang.* A Jew. [Orig. unknown.]

sheep (shēp) *n., pl.* **sheep. 1.** Any of various usually horned ruminant mammals of the genus *Ovis,* esp. the domesticated species *O. aries,* raised in many breeds for its wool, edible flesh, or skin. **2.** Leather made from the skin of a sheep. **3. a.** One who is meek and submissive. **b.** One who is easily swayed or led. [ME < OE *scēap.*]

sheep·ber·ry (shēp'bĕr'ē) *n.* A North American shrub or tree, *Viburnum lentago,* having clusters of white flowers and blue-black edible berries.

sheep·cote (shēp'kōt', -kŏt') *n. Chiefly Brit.* A sheepfold.

sheep dip *n.* Any of various liquid disinfectants used to destroy parasites in the wool of sheep prior to shearing.

sheep dog also **sheep·dog** (shēp'dôg', -dŏg') *n.* A dog trained to guard and herd sheep.

sheep·fold (shēp'fōld') *n.* A pen for sheep.

sheep·herd·er (shēp'hûr'dər) *n.* One that herds a large flock of sheep, esp. in open range; shepherd. **—sheep'herd'ing** *n.*

sheep·ish (shē'pĭsh) *adj.* **1.** Embarrassed, as by consciousness of a fault: *a sheepish grin.* **2.** Resembling a sheep in meekness or stupidity. **—sheep'ish·ly** *adv.* **—sheep'ish·ness** *n.*

sheep ked (kĕd) *n.* Sheep tick. [SHEEP + *ked,* sheep ked, of unknown orig.]

sheep laurel *n.* An evergreen shrub, *Kalmia angustifolia,* of eastern North America, having rose-pink flowers and poisonous foliage.

sheep's eyes *pl.n.* Shyly amorous glances.

sheep·shank (shēp'shăngk') *n.* A knot used to shorten a line.

sheeps·head (shēps'hĕd') *n.* A food fish, *Archosargus probatocephalus,* of north Atlantic waters, having dark, vertical markings.

sheep·shear·ing (shēp'shîr'ĭng) *n.* **1.** The act of shearing sheep. **2. a.** The time when sheep are sheared. **b.** The festivities held at this time. **—sheep'shear'er** *n.*

sheep·skin (shēp'skĭn') *n.* **1.** The skin of a sheep either tanned with the fleece left on or in the form of leather or parchment. **2.** A diploma. **—*modifier:*** *a sheepskin coat.*

sheep tick *n.* A wingless fly, *Melophagus ovinus,* that is parasitic to sheep.

sheer¹ (shîr) *intr. & tr.v.* **sheered, sheer·ing, sheers.** To swerve or cause to swerve from a course. —*n.* **1.** A swerving or deviating course. **2.** *Naut.* **a.** The upward curve or amount of upward curve of the longitudinal lines of a ship's hull as viewed from the side. **b.** The position in which a ship is placed to enable it to keep clear of a single bow anchor. [Perh. alteration of SHEAR.]

sheer² (shîr) *adj.* **-er, -est. 1.** Thin, fine, and transparent: *sheer curtains; sheer chiffon.* **2. a.** Undiluted; pure: *sheer happiness.* **b.** Free from admixture or adulterants; unmixed: *sheer alcohol.* **3.** Almost perpendicular; steep: *sheer rock cliffs.* —*adv.* Almost perpendicularly. [Obs. *shere,* thin, clear < ME *schir,* free from service or guilt, prob. < ON *skærr,* bright, pure.] **—sheer'ly** *adv.* **—sheer'ness** *n.*

sheer·legs (shîr'lĕgs') *n.* Variant of **shear legs.**

sheers (shîrz) *n.* Variant of **shears** (sense 2).

sheet¹ (shēt) *n.* **1.** A broad rectangular piece of fabric serving as a basic article of bedding. **2.** A broad, thin, usually rectangular mass or piece of material, as paper, metal, glass, or plywood. **3.** A broad, flat, continuous surface or expanse: *a sheet of ice.* **4.** A newspaper, esp. a tabloid. **5.** *Geol.* A broad, relatively thin deposit or layer of igneous or sedimentary rock. **6.** A large block of stamps printed by a single impression of a plate before the individual stamps have been separated. —*v.* **sheet·ed, sheet·ing, sheets.** —*tr.* To cover with, wrap in, or provide with a sheet. —*intr.* To flow or fall in a sheet: *rain sheeting on the roof.* [ME *schete,* cloth < OE *scēte.*]

sheet² (shēt) *Naut.* —*n.* **1.** A rope or chain attached to one or both of the lower corners of a sail, serving to move or extend it. **2. sheets.** The spaces at either end of an open boat in front of and behind the seats. —*intr.v.* **sheet·ed, sheet·ing, sheets.** To extend in a certain direction. Used of the sheets of a sail. **—*idiom.* three sheets to the wind.** *Informal.* Drunk. [ME *schete* < OE *scēata,* corner of a sail.]

sheet anchor *n.* **1.** *Naut.* A large extra anchor intended for use in an emergency. **2.** One that can be turned to in time of emergency. [Perh. SHEET² + ANCHOR.]

sheet bend *n.* A knot in which one rope or piece of yarn is made fast to the bight of another.

sheet glass *n.* Molten glass drawn into a wide sheet that is cut into required lengths after annealing and hardening.

sheet·ing (shē'tĭng) *n.* Material, as metal or cloth, used to make a sheet.

sheet lightning *n.* Lightning that appears as a broad, sheetlike illumination of parts of a thundercloud, caused by the reflection of a lightning flash.

sheet music *n.* Music printed on unbound sheets of paper.

Sheet·rock (shēt'rŏk'). A trademark for plasterboard.

she·getz (shā'gĭts) *n., pl.* **shkotz·im** (shkôt'sĭm). *Offensive.* A non-Jewish boy or young man. [Yiddish *sheygets* < Heb. *sheqeṣ,* blemish.]

sheik also **sheikh** (shēk) *n.* **1.** (*also* shāk). **a.** A Moslem religious official. **b.** The leader of an Arab family, village, or tribe. **2.** *Slang.* A romantically alluring man. [Ar. *shaik,* old man < *shākha,* he grew old.]

sheik·dom (shēk′dəm, shāk′-) *n.* The area ruled by a sheik.

shek·el (shĕk′əl) *n.* **1.** See table at **currency. 2. a.** Any of several ancient units of weight, esp. a Hebrew unit equal to about a half ounce. **b.** A gold or silver coin equal in weight to one of these units, esp. the chief silver coin of the Hebrews. **3.** *Slang.* **a.** A coin. **b. shekels.** Money. [Heb. *sheqel* < *shāqal,* he weighed.]

She·ki·nah (shĭ-kē′nə, -KHē′-, -kī′-) *n.* A visible manifestation of the divine presence as described in Jewish theology. [Heb. *shĕkhīnāh* < *shākhan,* to dwell.]

shel·drake (shĕl′drāk′) *n.* **1.** Any of various large Old World ducks of the genus *Tadorna,* esp. *T. tadorna,* having predominantly black and white plumage. **2.** The merganser. [ME *sheldedrake* : *sheld-,* variegated + *drake,* drake.]

shel·duck (shĕl′dŭk′) *n.* A sheldrake (sense 1). [SHEL(DRAKE) + DUCK.]

shelf (shĕlf) *n., pl.* **shelves** (shĕlvz). **1. a.** A flat, usually rectangular structure of a rigid material, as wood, glass, or metal, fixed at right angles to a wall or other vertical surface and used to hold or store objects. **b.** The contents or capacity of such a structure. **2.** Something, as a balcony, that resembles a shelf. **3.** A reef, sandbar, or shoal. **4.** Bedrock. ***—idiom.* on the shelf. 1.** In a state of disuse. **2. a.** Unemployed. **b.** Out of circulation. **c.** Retired. [ME, prob. < MLG *schelf.*]

shelf ice *n.* An extension of glacial ice into coastal waters that is in contact with the bottom near the shore but not toward the outer edge of the shelf.

shelf life *n.* The length of time a product may be stored, as on a supermarket shelf, without deteriorating.

shell (shĕl) *n.* **1. a.** The usually hard outer covering that encases certain organisms. **b.** A similar outer covering on an egg, fruit, or nut. **c.** The material composing such a covering. **2.** Something resembling or having the form of a shell, esp.: **a.** A framework or exterior, as of a building. **b.** A thin layer of pastry. **c.** The hull of a ship. **d.** The external part of the ear. **e.** A long, narrow racing boat propelled by oarsmen. **3. a.** A projectile or piece of ammunition, esp. the hollow tube containing explosives used to propel such a projectile. **b.** A metal or cardboard case containing the charge, primer, and shot fired from a shotgun. **4.** An attitude or manner adopted to mask one's true feelings. **5.** *Physics.* **a.** Any of the set of hypothetical spherical surfaces centered on the nucleus of an atom that contain the orbits of electrons having the same principal quantum number; hence, all the electrons in an atom that have the same principal quantum number. **b.** Any of a set of groupings of nucleon energy states in a nucleus or of nucleons occupying such states in which the binding energies of states differ from one another by much less than from the binding energies of states in another grouping. **6.** A usually sleeveless and collarless knit blouse. ***—modifier:*** *shell beads; a shell case.* —*v.* **shelled, shell·ing, shells.** —*tr.* **1. a.** To remove the shell of; shuck. **b.** To remove from a shell. **2.** To separate the kernels of (corn) from the cob. **3.** To fire shells at; bombard. **4. a.** To defeat decisively. **b.** *Baseball.* To hit the pitches of hard and with regularity: *shelled the pitcher for 8 runs in the first inning.* —*intr.* **1.** To shed or become free of a shell. **2.** To look for or collect shells. ***—phrasal verb.* shell out.** *Informal.* To pay. [ME < OE *scell.*] **—shell′er** *n.*

she'll (shēl). **1.** She will. **2.** She shall.

shel·lac (shə-lăk′) *n.* **1.** A purified lac formed into thin yellow or orange flakes, often bleached white and widely used in varnishes, paints, stains, inks, and sealing wax, as a binder, and in phonograph records. **2.** A thin varnish made by dissolving flake shellac in denatured alcohol, used as a wood coating and sealer and for finishing floors. —*v.* **-lacked, -lack·ing, -lacs.** —*tr.* **1.** To apply shellac to. **2.** *Slang.* To defeat decisively. **3.** *Slang.* To administer blows to; batter mercilessly. —*intr.* To apply shellac. [SHEL(L) + LAC[1]]

shell·back (shĕl′băk′) *n.* A veteran sailor, esp. one who has crossed the equator.

shell bean *n.* Any of various beans cultivated for their edible seeds rather than for their pods.

shell·fire (shĕl′fīr′) *n.* The firing or shooting of shells.

shell·fish (shĕl′fĭsh′) *n., pl.* **shellfish** or **-fish·es.** An aquatic animal, as a mollusk or crustacean, having a shell or shell-like exoskeleton.

shell·flow·er (shĕl′flou′ər) *n.* **1.** A tall plant, *Molucella laevis,* native to Asia, having tiny flowers and conspicuous green calyxes. **2.** A tall plant, *Alpina speciosa,* native to tropical Asia, having showy, variously colored flowers.

shell game *n.* **1.** Thimblerig (sense 1). **2.** A scheme in which the customer cannot win; swindle.

shell jacket *n.* **1.** A tight-fitting short military jacket worn buttoned up the front. **2.** A mess jacket.

shell pink *n.* A pinkish white to strong yellowish pink, including grayish and light yellowish pinks. **—shell′-pink′** *adj.*

shell·proof (shĕl′pro͞of′) *adj.* Capable of withstanding shellfire.

shell shock *n.* **1.** Any of various usually acute, often hysterical neuroses originating in trauma suffered under fire in modern warfare. **2.** Combat fatigue. **—shell′-shocked′** *adj.*

shel·ter (shĕl′tər) *n.* **1. a.** Something that provides cover or protection, as from the weather. **b.** A refuge; haven. **2.** The state of being covered or protected. —*v.* **-tered, -ter·ing, -ters.** —*tr.* To provide cover or protection for. —*intr.* To take cover; find refuge. [Orig. unknown.] **—shel′ter·er** *n.*

Synonyms: *shelter, cover, retreat, refuge, asylum, sanctuary, haven.* These nouns refer to places that afford protection or to the condition of being protected. *Shelter* usually implies an enclosed area that protects temporarily against a specific threat, such as a storm or air raid. *Cover* suggests a concealed place resorted to hastily for temporary protection. *Retreat* applies chiefly to a place of seclusion to which one retires for meditation or to escape the demands of worldly affairs. *Refuge* suggests a place of escape, real or figurative, from actual pursuit or from harassment. *Asylum* adds to *refuge* the idea of legal protection against a pursuer or of immunity to prosecution. *Sanctuary* denotes a sacred or inviolable place of refuge. *Haven* can apply to an anchorage or broadly to any sheltered place.

shel·ter·belt (shĕl′tər-bĕlt′) *n.* A barrier consisting of trees and shrubs that reduces erosion and protects against the effects of wind and storms.

shelter tent *n.* A small tent usually formed of two or more pieces of waterproof material.

shel·tie also **shel·ty** (shĕl′tē) *n., pl.* **-ties. 1.** A Shetland pony. **2.** A Shetland sheepdog. [Prob. < ON *Hjalti,* Shetlander.]

shelve (shĕlv) *v.* **shelved, shelv·ing, shelves.** —*tr.* **1.** To place or arrange on a shelf. **2.** To put away as though on a shelf; put aside: *"as usual, Dixon shelved this question"* (Kingsley Amis). **3.** To cause to retire from service; dismiss. **4.** To furnish or outfit with shelves. —*intr.* To slope gradually; incline. **—shelv′er** *n.*

shelves (shĕlvz) *n.* Plural of **shelf.**

shelv·ing (shĕl′vĭng) *n.* **1.** Shelves collectively. **2.** Material for shelves. **3.** An incline; slope.

Shem (shĕm) *n.* The eldest son of Noah in the Old Testament. [Heb. *Shēm.*]

she·nan·i·gan (shə-năn′ĭ-gən) *n. Informal.* **1.** Often **shenanigans.** Prankishness; mischief. **2.** Treachery; deceit. [Orig. unknown.]

she-oak (shē′ōk′) *n.* The beefwood.

she·ol (shē′ōl′, shē-ōl′) *n.* **1.** Hell. **2. Sheol.** A place described in the Old Testament as the abode of the dead. [Heb. *shĕōl.*]

shep·herd (shĕp′ərd) *n.* **1.** One who herds, guards, and tends sheep. **2.** One who cares for and guides a group of people, as a minister or teacher. —*tr.v.* **-herd·ed, -herd·ing, -herds.** To herd, guard, tend, or guide as or in the manner of a shepherd. [ME *sheepherde* < OE *scēaphirde* : *scēap,* sheep + *hirde,* herdsman.]

shepherd dog *n.* Any of various dogs trained to tend sheep.

shep·herd·ess (shĕp′ər-dĭs) *n.* A girl or woman who tends sheep.

shepherd's pie *n.* A casserole consisting of cooked meat with gravy, topped by a layer or surrounded by a border of mashed potatoes.

shep·herd's-purse (shĕp′ərdz-pûrs′) *n.* A common weed, *Capsella bursa-pastoris,* having small white flowers and flat, heart-shaped fruit. [From its pouchlike pods.]

Sher·a·ton (shĕr′ə-tən) *adj.* Of, pertaining to, or being a style of English furniture that originated about 1800 and that is characterized by straight lines and graceful proportions. [After Thomas *Sheraton* (1751–1806), its originator.]

sher·bet (shûr′bĭt) *n.* **1.** A sweet-flavored water ice to which milk, egg white, or gelatin has been added. **2.** A beverage made of sweetened diluted fruit juice. [Turk. < Pers. *sharbat* < Ar. *sharbah,* drink < *shariba,* he drank.]

sherd (shûrd) *n.* Variant of **shard.**

she·rif also **sha·rif** (shə-rēf′) *n.* **1.** A descendant of the prophet Mohammed through his daughter Fatima. **2.** The chief magistrate of Mecca. **3.** A Moroccan prince or ruler. [Ar. *sharīf,* noble < *sharafa,* he was exalted.]

sher·iff (shĕr′ĭf) *n.* **1.** The chief executive of the courts of superior jurisdiction in a U.S. county. **2.** An officer of a shire or county in England, Scotland, and Northern Ireland. [ME *schirreff,* the representative of royal authority in a shire < OE *scīrgerēfa* : *scīr,* shire + *gerēfa,* reeve.]

she·root (shə-ro͞ot′) *n.* Variant of **cheroot.**

Sher·pa (shûr′pə) *n., pl.* **Sherpa** or **-pas.** A member of a Tibetan people living in northern Nepal.

sher·ry (shĕr′ē) *n., pl.* **-ries.** An amber-colored fortified Spanish wine ranging from very dry to sweet. [Alteration of obs. *sherris* (taken as pl.), after *Xeres,* Jerez, Spain.]

Shet·land (shĕt′lənd) *n.* **1.** A fine, loosely twisted yarn made from the wool of sheep raised in the Shetland Islands and used for knitting and weaving. **2.** A garment, esp. a sweater, made of Shetland. [After the *Shetland* Islands.]

Shetland pony *n.* A small, compactly built pony of a breed originating in the Shetland Islands.

Shetland sheepdog *n.* A dog of a breed developed in the Shetland Islands, having a rough coat and resembling a small collie.

She·vat (shə-vät′) also **She·bat** (-bät′, -vät′) *n.* The fifth month of the Hebrew calendar. See table at **calendar.** [Heb. *shĕbhāt.*]

shell
Above: Racing shell
Below: Ammunition

shepherd's-purse

Sheraton
18th-century American

Shetland pony

shillelagh

shew·bread (shō′brĕd′) *n. Archaic.* Variant of **showbread.**
Shi·ah also **Shi·a** (shē′ə) *n.* **1.** The principal minority sect of Islam, composed of the followers of Ali, the cousin and son-in-law of Mohammed, who regard the heirs of Ali as the legitimate successors to the Prophet and reject the other caliphs and the Sunnite legal and political institutions. **2.** A Shiite. [Ar. *shī'ah,* a following < *shā'a,* he followed.]
shi·at·su (shē-ät′so͞o) *n.* A massage in which finger pressure is applied to those areas of the body used in acupuncture. [Short for J. *shiatsuryōhō* : *shi,* finger + *atsu-,* pressure + *ryōhō,* treatment.]
shib·ah (shĭv′ə) *n..* Variant of **shiva.**
shib·bo·leth (shĭb′ə-lĭth, -lĕth′) *n.* **1.** A language usage that distinguishes the members of one group or class from another. **2. a.** A slogan; catchword. **b.** A common saying or idea. [Heb. *shibbōleth,* an ear of corn, stream, from the use of this word to distinguish Gileadites from Ephraimites, who pronounced it *sibbōleth.*]
shield (shēld) *n.* **1.** An article of protective armor made of leather, metal, or wood and carried on the forearm. **2.** A means of defense; protection. **3. a.** An escutcheon. **b.** A police officer's badge. **c.** A decorative emblem that often serves to identify. **4.** A steel sheet attached to a gun to protect the gunners from small-arms fire. **5.** *Zool.* A protective plate or similar hard outer covering. **6.** A piece of rubberized or absorbent cloth worn, as at the armpits, to protect a garment from perspiration. **7.** *Physics.* A mass of material, such as lead or cement, that encloses a nuclear reactor in order to reduce the amount of radiation that escapes into the surrounding area. —*v.* **shield·ed, shield·ing, shields.** —*tr.* **1.** To protect or defend with or as if with a shield; guard. **2.** To cover up; conceal. —*intr.* To act or serve as a shield or safeguard. [ME *sheeld* < OE *scield.*] **—shield′er** *n.*
shield law *n.* A law that protects journalists from being compelled to reveal confidential sources of information.
Shield of David *n.* The Magen David.
shiel·ing (shē′lĭng, -lĭn) *n. Scot.* A shepherd's hut. [< Sc. *shiel,* hut < ME *schele,* prob. of Scand. orig.]
shi·er (shī′ər) *adj.* A comparative of **shy**[1].
shies[1] (shīz) *v.* Third person singular present tense of **shy**[1]. —*n.* Plural of **shy**[1].
shies[2] (shīz) *v.* Third person singular present tense of **shy**[2]. —*n.* Plural of **shy**[2].
shi·est (shī′ĭst) *adj.* A superlative of **shy**[1].
shift (shĭft) *v.* **shift·ed, shift·ing, shifts.** —*tr.* **1.** To move or transfer from one place or position to another. **2.** To exchange (one thing) for another; switch: *shift tactics.* **3.** To change (gears) in an automobile. **4.** *Ling.* To alter phonetically or as part of a systematic change. —*intr.* **1.** To change position, direction, place, or form. **2. a.** To provide for one's own needs; get along: *shifts for himself.* **b.** To get along by tricky or evasive means. **3.** To change gears, as when driving an automobile. —*n.* **1.** A change from one individual, position, or configuration to another; transfer. **2.** A change of direction or form. **3. a.** A group of workers on duty at the same time, as at a factory. **b.** The working period of such a group: *worked the night shift.* **4.** *Mus.* A change of the position of the hand in playing the violin or a similar instrument. **5.** *Ling.* **a.** A systematic change of the phonetic or phonemic structure of a language. **b.** Functional shift. **6.** *Sports.* A lateral movement of the offensive backfield from one formation to another just prior to putting a football in play. **7. a.** A loosely fitting dress that hangs straight from the shoulder; chemise. **b.** A woman's undergarment; slip or chemise. **8. a.** A means to an end; expedient. **b.** A stratagem; trick. [ME *shiften,* to arrange < OE *sciftan.*] **—shift′er** *n.*
shift character *n.* A data control character that determines the shift of character codes in a message.
shift·less (shĭft′lĭs) *adj.* **1.** Lacking ambition or purpose; lazy. **2.** Lacking resourcefulness or efficiency; incapable. [SHIFT, resourcefulness (obs.) + -LESS.] **—shift′less·ly** *adv.* **—shift′less·ness** *n.*
shift register *n.* A computer memory device in which data can be moved to the left or to the right.
shift·y (shĭf′tē) *adj.* **-i·er, -i·est. 1.** Tricky; crafty. **2.** Suggesting craft or guile; furtive. **3.** Full of expedients; resourceful. **—shift′i·ly** *adv.* **—shift′i·ness** *n.*
shi·gel·la (shĭ-gĕl′ə) *n., pl.* **-gel·lae** (-gĕl′ē). Any of various nonmotile rod-shaped bacteria of the genus *Shigella,* which includes some species that cause dysentery. [NLat. *Shigella,* genus name, after Kiyoshi *Shiga* (1870–1957).]
Shi·ism (shē′ĭz′əm) *n.* The religion or doctrines of the Shiah.
Shi·ite (shē′īt′) *n.* A member of the Shiah branch of Islam. **—Shi·it′ic** (-ĭt′ĭk) *adj.*
shi·ka·ri (shĭ-kär′ē, -kăr′ē) *n.* A big-game hunting guide. [Hindi < Pers. *shikārī* < *shikār,* hunting.]
shik·sa also **shik·se** (shĭk′sə) *n. Offensive.* A non-Jewish girl or young woman. [Yiddish *shikse,* fem. of *sheygets.* —see SHEGETZ.]
shi·ling·i (shĭ-lĭng′ē) *n., pl.* **shilingi.** See table at **currency.** [Swahili < E. SHILLING.]
shill (shĭl) *Slang.* —*n.* One who works as a decoy, as in a confidence game, by posing as a customer or an innocent bystander. —*intr.v.* **shilled, shill·ing, shills.** To act as a shill. [Orig. unknown.]
shil·le·lagh also **shil·la·lah** (shə-lā′lē, -lə) *n.* A club or cudgel, esp. one of oak or blackthorn. [After *Shillelagh,* Ireland.]
shil·ling (shĭl′ĭng) *n.* **1.** See table at **currency. 2.** *Printing.* A virgule. [ME < OE *scilling.*]
shil·ly-shal·ly (shĭl′ē-shăl′ē) *intr.v.* **-lied, -ly·ing, -lies. 1.** To put off acting; hesitate or waver. **2.** To idle or poke; dawdle. —*adj.* Hesitant; vacillating. —*n., pl.* **-lies.** Procrastination; hesitation. —*adv.* In a hesitant manner; irresolutely. [Redup. of the phrase *shall I.*] **—shil′ly-shal′li·er** *n.*
shim (shĭm) *n.* A thin, often tapered piece of material, as metal, wood, or stone, used as leveler or filler between materials such as stone or metal or between pieces of furniture and the floor. —*tr.v.* **shimmed, shim·ming, shims.** To level or fill in by using a shim. [Orig. unknown.]
shim·mer (shĭm′ər) *intr.v.* **-mered, -mer·ing, -mers.** To shine with a flickering light. —*n.* A flickering or tremulous light; glimmer. [ME *schimeren* < OE *scimerian.*] **—shim′mer·y** *adj.*
shim·my (shĭm′ē) *n., pl.* **-mies. 1.** A dance popular in the 1920's, characterized by rapid shaking of the body. **2.** Abnormal vibration or wobbling, as in the chassis of an automobile. **3.** *Regional.* A chemise. —*intr.v.* **-mied, -my·ing, -mies. 1.** To vibrate or wobble abnormally. **2.** To shake the body in or as if in dancing the shimmy. [Short for *shimmy-shake* < *shimmy,* alteration of CHEMISE.]
shin[1] (shĭn) *n.* **1.** *Anat.* **a.** The front part of the leg below the knee and above the ankle. **b.** The tibia. **2.** The lower part of the foreleg in beef cattle as opposed to the upper foreleg or shank. Used of cuts of meat. —*v.* **shinned, shin·ning, shins.** —*tr.* **1.** To climb (a rope, for example) by gripping and pulling alternately with the hands and legs. **2.** To kick or hit in the shins. —*intr.* To climb something by shinning. [ME *shine* < OE *scinu.*]
shin[2] (shēn, shĭn) *n.* The 22nd letter of the Hebrew alphabet. See table at **alphabet.** [Heb. *shīn.*]
shin·bone (shĭn′bōn′) *n.* The tibia.
shin·dig (shĭn′dĭg′) *n. Slang.* A festive party or celebration. [Prob. alteration of SHINDY.]
shin·dy (shĭn′dē) *n., pl.* **-dies.** *Slang.* **1.** A commotion; uproar. **2.** A shindig. [Alteration of SHINNY[1].]
shine (shīn) *v.* **shone** (shōn) or **shined, shin·ing, shines.** —*intr.* **1.** To emit light; beam. **2.** To reflect light; glint or glisten. **3.** To distinguish oneself in an activity or field; excel. **4.** To become clearly apparent. —*tr.* **1.** To aim or cast the beam or glow of: *Shine that light over here.* **2.** *past tense and past participle* **shined.** To make glossy or bright by polishing. —*n.* **1.** Brightness; radiance. **2.** A shoeshine. **3.** Fair weather: *rain or shine.* **4. shines.** *Informal.* Foolish pranks or tricks. **5.** *Slang.* Whiskey; moonshine. ***—idiom.* take a shine to.** To like spontaneously. [ME *shinen* < OE *scīnan.*]
shin·er (shī′nər) *n.* **1.** One that shines. **2.** *Slang.* A black eye. **3. a.** Any of numerous small, often silvery North American freshwater fishes of the family Cyprinidae, esp. one of the genus *Notropis.* **b.** Any of various other small silvery fishes.
shin·gle[1] (shĭng′gəl) *n.* **1.** A thin oblong piece of material, as wood or asbestos, that is laid in overlapping rows to cover the roofs and sides of houses. **2.** *Informal.* A small signboard, as one indicating a doctor's office: *hang out a shingle.* **3.** A woman's close-cropped haircut. —*tr.v.* **-gled, -gling, -gles. 1.** To cover (a roof or building) with shingles. **2.** To cut (hair) short and close to the head. [ME *schyngle* < Lat. *scindula,* alteration of *scandula.*] **—shin′gler** *n.*
shin·gle[2] (shĭng′gəl) *n.* **1. a.** Beach gravel consisting of large smooth pebbles unmixed with finer material. **b.** A stretch of shore or beach covered with coarse, smooth gravel. **2.** Gravel that is coarser than ordinary gravel. [Sc. *chyngill,* perh. of MLG orig.] **—shin′gly** *adj.*
shin·gles (shĭng′gəlz) *pl.n. (used with a sing. or pl. verb). Pathol.* Herpes zoster. [ME *schingles,* by folk ety. < Med. Lat. *cingulus* < Lat., belt < *cingere,* to gird.]
shin·leaf (shĭn′lēf′) *n.* A North American woodland plant, *Pyrola elliptica,* having rounded basal leaves and white flowers. [From the use of its leaves in plasters for sore legs.]
shin·ny[1] (shĭn′ē) *n., pl.* **-nies. 1.** A simple form of hockey played by schoolboys. **2.** The curved stick used in shinny. [Prob. < the phrase *shin ye,* a cry used in the game.]
shin·ny[2] (shĭn′ē) *intr.v.* **-nied, -ny·ing, -nies.** To climb by shinning.
shin·plas·ter (shĭn′plăs′tər) *n.* Paper currency issued privately, esp. such currency devalued by lack of backing or by inflation. [From its resemblance to paper used in plasters for sore legs.]
Shin·to (shĭn′tō) *n.* The aboriginal religion of Japan, marked by the veneration of nature spirits and of ancestors. [J. *shintō* : *shin,* gods (< Chin. *shen²*) + *dō,* way (< Chin. *dao⁴*).] **—Shin′to·ism** *n.* **—Shin′to·ist** *n.* **—Shin′to·is′tic** *adj.*
shin·y (shī′nē) *adj.* **-i·er, -i·est. 1.** Bright; glistening. **2.** Clear; shining. **—shin′i·ness** *n.*
ship (shĭp) *n.* **1.** A vessel of considerable size adapted for deep-water navigation. **2.** A three-masted sailing vessel with square mainsails on all masts. **3.** *Law.* A vessel intended for marine transportation, without regard to form, rig, or means of propulsion. **4.** The crew of a ship. **5.** An aircraft. —*v.* **shipped, ship·ping, ships.** —*tr.* **1.** To place or take on board a ship. **2.** To send or cause to be transported: *shipped the goods by mail to Europe.* **3.** To hire for work on a ship.

shinleaf

4. To take in (water) over the side of a ship. —*intr.* **1.** To go aboard or travel by means of a ship. **2.** To hire oneself out or enlist for service on a ship. [ME *schipp* < OE *scip.*]

-ship *suff.* **1. a.** Quality, state, or condition: *scholarship.* **b.** One that shows or possesses a quality, state, or condition: *township.* **2.** Rank, status, or office: *professorship.* **3.** Art, skill, or craft: *penmanship.* [ME < OE *-scipe.*]

ship biscuit *n.* Hardtack.

ship·board (shĭp′bôrd′, -bōrd′) *n.* The side of a ship. **—*idiom.* on shipboard.** On board a ship.

ship·build·ing (shĭp′bĭl′dĭng) *n.* The business of constructing ships. **—ship′build′er** *n.*

ship canal *n.* A canal deep enough to serve ships.

ship fever *n.* Typhus.

ship·load (shĭp′lōd′) *n.* The amount a ship carries or is able to carry.

ship·man (shĭp′mən) *n. Archaic.* **1.** A sailor. **2.** A shipmaster.

ship·mas·ter (shĭp′măs′tər) *n.* The officer in command of a merchant ship.

ship·mate (shĭp′māt′) *n.* A sailor serving on the same ship as another; fellow sailor.

ship·ment (shĭp′mənt) *n.* **1.** The act of shipping goods. **2.** The goods or cargo shipped.

ship money *n.* A tax once levied on English maritime towns and shires to provide revenue for the construction of warships.

ship of the line *n.* A warship large enough to take a position in the line of battle.

ship·per (shĭp′ər) *n.* One that consigns or receives goods for transportation; shipping agent.

ship·ping (shĭp′ĭng) *n.* **1.** The act or business of transporting goods. **2.** The body of ships belonging to one port, industry, or country, often referred to in aggregate tonnage. **3.** Passage on a ship.

shipping clerk *n.* A person employed to manage the shipment or receipt of goods.

ship-rigged (shĭp′rĭgd′) *adj. Naut.* Rigged with three or more masts and square sails.

ship·shape (shĭp′shāp′) *adj.* Neatly arranged; tidy. [Short for obs. *shipshapen,* arranged as a ship should be : SHIP + obs. *shapen,* p.part. of SHAPE.] **—ship′shape′** *adv.*

ship's papers *pl.n.* The documents that international law requires a ship to carry and provide on demand for inspection.

ship·way (shĭp′wā′) *n.* **1.** The structure supporting a ship during construction or in dry dock. **2.** A ship canal.

ship·worm (shĭp′wûrm′) *n.* Any of various wormlike marine mollusks of the genera *Teredo* and *Bankia,* having rudimentary bivalve shells with which they bore into wood, often doing extensive damage.

ship·wreck (shĭp′rĕk′) *n.* **1. a.** The destruction of a ship, as by storm or collision. **b.** The remains of a wrecked ship. **2.** Complete failure or ruin. —*tr.v.* **-wrecked, -wreck·ing, -wrecks. 1.** To cause (a ship or its passengers) to suffer shipwreck. **2.** To ruin utterly. [Alteration of obs. *shipwrack* < ME *shipwrak* < OE *scipwræc,* jetsam : *scip,* ship + *wræc,* something driven by the sea.]

ship·wright (shĭp′rīt′) *n.* A carpenter employed in the construction or maintenance of ships.

ship·yard (shĭp′yärd′) *n.* A yard where ships are built or repaired.

shire (shīr) *n.* One of the counties of Great Britain. [ME < OE *scīr,* region, district.]

shire horse *n.* A large, powerful draft horse of a breed originating in the shires or midland region of England.

shire town *n.* A county town.

shirk (shûrk) *v.* **shirked, shirk·ing, shirks.** —*tr.* To avoid discharging: *"A number of high civil servants shirked their duty to preserve their jobs"* (Nevil Shute). —*intr.* To avoid work or duty. [Orig. unknown.] **—shirk′er** *n.*

Shir·ley poppy (shûr′lē) *n.* A variety of the corn poppy having scarlet, pink, or salmon flowers. [After *Shirley* vicarage in Croydon, England.]

shirr (shûr) *tr.v.* **shirred, shirr·ing, shirrs. 1.** To gather (cloth) into three or more decorative parallel rows. **2.** To cook (unshelled eggs) by baking until set. —*n.* A gathering of cloth into three or more decorative parallel rows. [Orig. unknown.]

shirt (shûrt) *n.* **1.** A garment for the upper part of the body, typically having a collar, sleeves, and a front opening. **2.** An undershirt. **3.** A night shirt. **4.** A protective cloth casing, as for use in shipping perishable goods. **—*idioms.* keep (one's) shirt on.** *Slang.* To remain calm or patient. **lose (one's) shirt.** *Slang.* To lose everything one has or owns. [ME *sherte* < OE *scyrte.*]

shirt·dress (shûrt′drĕs′) *n.* A usually simple dress styled like a shirt with a collar and buttons down the front.

shirt·ing (shûr′tĭng) *n.* Fabric suitable for making shirts.

shirt-sleeve (shûrt′slēv′) also **shirt-sleeves** (-slēvz′) or **shirt-sleeved** (-slēvd′) *adj.* **1. a.** Being dressed casually, esp. being without a coat: *shirt-sleeve spectators.* **b.** Calling for the removal of a coat: *shirt-sleeve weather.* **2.** Marked by informality or straightforwardness: *shirt-sleeve politics; a shirt-sleeve biography.*

shirt·tail (shûrt′tāl′) *n.* **1.** The part of a shirt that extends below the waist, esp. in the back. **2.** Something small, inadequate, or of little value. **3.** A brief addition at the conclusion of a newspaper article. —*adj.* **1.** Very young: *shirttail kids.* **2.** Distantly related: *a shirttail cousin.* **3.** Of little value; inadequate: *a shirttail cabin in the woods.*

shirt·waist (shûrt′wāst′) *n.* **1.** A woman's tailored shirt with details copied from men's shirts. **2.** A woman's dress with the bodice styled like a tailored shirt.

shirt·y (shûr′tē) *adj.* **-i·er, -i·est.** Ill-tempered; angry.

shish ke·bab also **shish ke·bob** or **shish ka·bob** (shĭsh′ kə-bŏb′) *n.* A dish consisting of pieces of seasoned meat roasted on skewers and served with condiments. [Turk. *şiş kebabiu* : *şiş,* skewer + *kebap,* roast meat.]

shist (shĭst) *n.* Variant of **schist.**

shit (shĭt) *Obscene.* —*v.* **shit** also **shat** (shăt), **shit·ting, shits.** —*intr.* To defecate. —*tr.* To defecate in. —*n.* **1.** Excrement. **2.** An act or instance of defecating. **3.** Foolishness; nonsense. [ME *shiten* < OE *scītan.*]

shit·head (shĭt′hĕd′) *n. Vulgar Slang.* A highly contemptible or objectionable person.

shit·tah (shĭt′ə) *n.* A tree, probably a species of acacia, that was a source of a wood mentioned frequently in the Bible. [Heb. *shiṭṭāh.*]

shit·tim·wood (shĭt′ĭm-wo͝od′) *n.* The wood of the shittah, used to make the ark of the Hebrew tabernacle. [Heb. *shiṭṭim,* pl. of *shiṭṭāh,* shittah + WOOD.]

shiv (shĭv) *n. Slang.* A knife or razor, used esp. as a weapon. [Romany *chiv,* blade.]

shiv·a also **shiv·ah** or **shib·ah** (shĭv′ə) *n. Judaism.* A seven-day period of formal mourning observed after the funeral of a close relative. [Yiddish < Heb. *shiv'āh,* seven.]

Shi·va (shē′və, shĭv′ə) also **Si·va** (shē′və, sē′-, shĭv′ə, sĭv′ə) *n. Hinduism.* The god of destruction and reproduction, a member of the Hindu triad along with Brahma and Vishnu. [Skt. *śivaḥ* < *śiva-,* gracious.] **—Shi′va·ism** *n.* **—Shi′va·ist** *n.*

Shiva

shiv·ah (shĭv′ə) *n.* Variant of **shiva.**

shiv·a·ree (shĭv′ə-rē′, shĭv′ə-rē′) *n.* Variant of **charivari.**

shiv·er[1] (shĭv′ər) *v.* **-ered, -er·ing, -ers.** —*intr.* **1.** To shudder or shake from or as if from cold; tremble. **2.** To quiver or vibrate, as by the force of the wind. —*tr.* To cause (a sail) to flutter in the wind. —*n.* An act of shivering; tremble. [ME *shiveren, chiveren.*]

shiv·er[2] (shĭv′ər) *intr. & tr.v.* **-ered, -er·ing, -ers.** To break or cause to break into fragments or splinters; shatter. [ME *schiveren* < *schivere,* fragment.]

shiv·er·y[1] (shĭv′ə-rē) *adj.* **1.** Trembling, as from cold or fear. **2.** Causing shivers; chilling.

shiv·er·y[2] (shĭv′ə-rē) *adj.* Easily broken; brittle.

shkotz·im (shkôt′sĭm) *n.* Plural of **shegetz.**

shle·miel (shlə-mēl′) *n.* Variant of **schlemiel.**

shlep (shlĕp) *v.* Variant of **schlep.**

shlock (shlŏk) *n.* Variant of **schlock.**

shmear (shmîr) *n.* Variant of **schmeer.**

shmuck (shmŭk) *n.* Variant of **schmuck.**

shoal[1] (shōl) *n.* **1.** A place in a body of water where the water is particularly shallow. **2.** A sandy elevation of the bottom of a body of water, constituting a hazard to navigation; sandbank or sandbar. —*v.* **shoaled, shoal·ing, shoals.** —*intr.* To become shallow. —*tr.* **1.** To make shallow. **2.** To come or sail into a shallower part of. —*adj.* Having little depth; shallow. [ME *schald* < OE *sceald,* shallow.]

Synonyms: *shoal, reef, bar, bank.* These nouns have reference to elevations of ground under water. A *shoal* is an elevation of land coming close to but not above the surface of the water. The term also is applied to the shallow area thus formed. A *reef* is a ridge, usually of rock or coral, extending near or slightly above the water's surface. A *bar* is a ridge, usually of sand, near the surface and often exposed at low water. A *bank* in this comparison is a large, totally submerged plateau that rises from the floor of the sea or another large body of water but that is well below the water level.

shoal[2] (shōl) *n.* **1.** A large group; crowd. **2.** A school of fish or other marine animals. —*intr.v.* **shoaled, shoal·ing, shoals.** To come together in large numbers; throng. [Prob. < MLG *schōle.*]

shoat also **shote** (shōt) *n.* A young pig just after weaning. [ME *shote.*]

shock[1] (shŏk) *n.* **1.** A violent collision or impact; heavy blow. **2. a.** Something that jars the mind or emotions as if with a violent, unexpected blow. **b.** The disturbance of function, equilibrium, or mental faculties caused by such a blow; violent agitation. **3.** A severe offense to one's sense of propriety or decency; outrage. **4.** *Pathol.* A generally temporary state of massive physiological reaction to bodily trauma, usually characterized by marked loss of blood pressure and the depression of vital processes. **5.** The sensation and muscular spasm caused by an electric current passing through the body or through a bodily part. **6.** Shock therapy. —*v.* **shocked, shock·ing, shocks.** —*tr.* **1.** To strike with great surprise and agitation. **2.** To strike with disgust; offend. **3.** To induce a state of shock in (a person). **4.** To subject (an animal or person) to an electric shock. —*intr.* To come into contact violently, as in battle; collide. [OFr. *choc* < *choquer,* to strike.]

shock[2] (shŏk) *n.* **1.** A number of sheaves of grain stacked

p **pop** / r **roar** / s **sauce** / sh **ship, dish** / t **tight** / th **thin, path** / *th* **this, bathe** / ŭ **cut** / ûr **urge** / v **valve** / w **with** / y **yes** / z **zebra, size** / zh **vision** / ə **about, item, edible, gallop, circus** / œ *Fr.* **feu,** *Ger.* **schön** / ü *Fr.* **tu,** *Ger.* **über** / KH *Ger.* **ich,** *Scot.* **loch** / N *Fr.* **bon.**

upright in a field for drying. **2.** A thick, heavy mass: *a shock of white hair.* *—tr.v.* **shocked, shock·ing, shocks.** To gather (grain) into shocks. [ME *schock,* perh. of LG orig.]

shock absorber *n.* Any of various devices used to absorb mechanical shocks, esp. a hydraulically damped coupling used to absorb impulsive forces generated by the contact of automotive wheels with irregular road surfaces.

shock·er (shŏk′ər) *n.* One that startles, shocks, or horrifies, as a sensational story or novel.

shock·ing (shŏk′ĭng) *adj.* **1.** Highly disturbing emotionally. **2.** Highly offensive; indecent or distasteful. **3.** Very vivid or intense in tone: *shocking pink.* **—shock′ing·ly** *adv.*

shock therapy *n.* The inducing of shock by electric current or drugs, sometimes with convulsions, as a therapy for mental illness.

shock treatment *n.* Shock therapy.

shock troops *pl.n.* Highly experienced and capable troopers who are specially trained to lead attacks.

shock wave *n.* **1.** A large-amplitude compression wave, such as that produced by an explosion, caused by supersonic motion of a body in a medium. **2.** A violent disruption, disturbance, or reaction: *Shock waves of revolution shattered the nation.*

shod (shŏd) *v.* Past tense and a past participle of **shoe.**

shod·den (shŏd′n) *v.* A past participle of **shoe.**

shod·dy (shŏd′ē) *n., pl.* **-dies. 1. a.** Wool fibers obtained by shredding unfelted woolen or worsted rags or worn garments. **b.** Yarn, fabric, or garments made from or containing such reclaimed wool fibers. **2.** Inferior or imitation goods. *—adj.* **-di·er, -di·est. 1.** Made of or containing shoddy or other inferior material. **2.** Of poor quality or workmanship. **3.** Dishonest: *shoddy business practices.* **4.** Transparently and cheaply imitative. **5.** Shabby; rundown. [Orig. unknown.] **—shod′di·ly** *adv.* **—shod′di·ness** *n.*

shoe (sho͞o) *n.* **1.** A durable covering for the human foot, esp. one of a matched pair made of leather or similar material reaching about to the ankle and having a rigid sole and heel. **2.** A horseshoe. **3.** A part or device placed at an end, foot, or bottom, esp.: **a.** A strip of metal fitted onto the bottom of a sled runner. **b.** A skid placed under the wheel of a vehicle to retard its motion. **c.** The outer covering, casing, or tread of a pneumatic rubber tire. **4.** The part of a brake that presses against the wheel or drum to retard its motion. **5.** The sliding contact plate on an electric train or streetcar that conducts electricity from the third rail. **6. shoes.** *Informal.* **a.** Position; status. **b.** Plight: *I wouldn't want to be in his shoes.* *—tr.v.* **shod** (shŏd), **shod** or **shod·den** (shŏd′n), **shoe·ing, shoes. 1.** To furnish or fit with shoes. **2.** To cover with a wooden or metal guard to protect against wear. [ME *shoo* < OE *scōh.*]

shoe·bill (sho͞o′bĭl′) *n.* A tall wading bird, *Balaeniceps rex,* native to swampy regions of eastern tropical Africa and having slaty plumage, long black legs, a stubby neck, and a large shoelike bill with a hook on the upper mandible.

shoe·horn (sho͞o′hôrn′) *n.* A curved implement, often of horn or smooth metal, used at the heel to help slip on a shoe. *—tr.v.* **-horned, -horn·ing, -horns.** To squeeze into an insufficient space.

shoe·lace (sho͞o′lās′) *n.* A string or cord used for lacing and fastening shoes.

shoe·mak·er (sho͞o′mā′kər) *n.* One that makes or repairs shoes. **—shoe′mak′ing** *n.*

shoe·string (sho͞o′strĭng′) *n.* **1.** A shoelace. **2.** A small sum of money; barely adequate capital: *a company that started on a shoestring.* *—adj.* **1.** Cut to or in the shape of a shoestring; long and slender: *shoestring potatoes.* **2.** Marked by or consisting of a small amount of money: *a shoestring budget.*

shoe·tree (sho͞o′trē′) *n.* A foot-shaped form inserted into a shoe to preserve its shape.

sho·far (shō′fär′, -fər) *n., pl.* **sho·fars** or **sho·froth** (shō-frōt′, -frōth′, -frōs′). *Judaism.* A trumpet made of a ram's horn, blown for warning, summoning, and ritual purposes by the ancient Hebrews and now sounded in the synagogue at Rosh Hashanah and Yom Kippur. [Heb. *shōphār,* ram's horn.]

sho·gun (shō′gən) *n.* Any of a line of military leaders of Japan who until 1868 exercised absolute rule under the nominal leadership of the emperor. [J. *shōgun,* general, of Chin. orig.]

sho·gun·ate (shō′gə-nĭt, -nāt′) *n.* The government of a shogun.

sho·ji (shō′jē) *n., pl.* **shoji** or **-jis.** A translucent paper screen forming a sliding door or partition in a Japanese house. [J. *shōji* < Chin. (Mandarin) *zhang*^{4} *zi*^{3}.]

shone (shōn) *v.* A past tense and past participle of **shine.**

shoo (sho͞o) *interj.* Used to frighten away animals or birds. *—tr.v.* **shooed, shoo·ing, shoos.** To drive or frighten away by or as if by crying "shoo."

shoo·fly (sho͞o′flī′) *n.* **1.** A child's rocker having the seat built between two sides cut in the shape of an animal. **2.** *Slang.* An undercover policeman who checks on the honesty and performance of other policemen.

shoofly pie *n.* A pie with a filling of molasses and brown sugar.

shoemaker

shofar

shooting star

shoo-in (sho͞o′ĭn′) *n. Informal.* One that seems certain of winning.

shook[1] (sho͝ok) *n.* **1.** A set of parts for assembling a barrel or packing box. **2.** A shock of grain. [Orig. unknown.]

shook[2] (sho͝ok) *v.* Past tense of **shake.**

shook-up (sho͝ok-ŭp′) *adj. Slang.* Emotionally upset; shaken.

shoon (sho͞on) *n. Archaic.* A plural of **shoe.**

shoot (sho͞ot) *v.* **shot** (shŏt), **shoot·ing, shoots.** *—tr.* **1.** To hit, wound, or kill with a missile fired from a weapon. **2.** To fire or let fly (a missile) from a weapon. **3.** To discharge (a weapon). **4. a.** To send forth suddenly, intensely, or swiftly: *shooting angry looks at her.* **b.** To utter (sounds or words) forcefully, rapidly, or suddenly: *She shot a retort to the insult.* **5.** To pass over or through swiftly: *shoot the rapids.* **6.** To cover (country) in hunting for game. **7.** To record (a motion picture, for example) on film. **8.** To cause to project or protrude; extend. **9.** To begin to grow or produce; put forth. **10.** To pour, empty out, or discharge down or as if down a chute. **11.** To variegate with streaks or threads of a different color: *a black coat shot with gray.* **12. a.** To move or propel (a marble or ball) toward its objective. **b.** To score (a point or goal). **c.** To play (golf, craps, or pool). **13.** To slide into or out of a fastening: *shoot a door bolt.* **14.** To measure the altitude of with a sextant or other instrument: *shoot a star.* *—intr.* **1.** To discharge a missile from a weapon. **2.** To discharge fire; go off. **3.** To move swiftly; dart. **4.** To protrude; project. **5.** To hunt with a weapon, esp. for sport. **6.** To put forth new growth; germinate. **7.** To take pictures; film. **8.** To propel a ball or other object toward the goal. **9.** To take one's turn at play. ***—phrasal verbs.*** **shoot down. 1.** To bring down (an aircraft, for example) by hitting and damaging with cannon fire or a missile. **2.** *Slang.* To ruin the aspirations of; disappoint. **3. a.** *Informal.* To put an end to; defeat: *shot down the proposal.* **b.** To expose as false; discredit: *shot down his theory.* **shoot for** (or **at**). To strive or aim for; have as a goal. **shoot up. 1.** *Informal.* To grow or get taller rapidly. **2.** *Slang.* To inject (a narcotic drug) directly into a vein. *—n.* **1.** The motion or movement of something that is shot; a forward or upward advance. **2. a.** The young growth arising from a germinating seed; sprout. **b.** A bud or young leaf on a plant. **3.** A new growing part. **4.** A narrow, swift, or turbulent section of a stream; rapid. **5.** An inclined channel through which something, such as timber, can be shot; chute. **6.** An organized shooting activity, as a skeet tournament or a hunt. **7.** *Informal.* The launching of a rocket or similar missile. **8.** The distance a shot travels; range. **9.** The interval between strokes in rowing. *—interj.* **1.** Used to express surprise or mild annoyance. **2.** Used to express readiness to listen. ***—idioms.*** **shoot from the hip.** To act or speak with no thought of the consequences. **shoot (one's) bolt.** To exhaust completely all of one's resources or capabilities. **shoot the breeze.** To talk idly. **shoot the works. 1.** To expend all of one's efforts. **2.** To expend all of one's capital. [ME *schoten* < OE *scēotan.*] **—shoot′er** *n.*

shoot-'em-up (sho͞ot′əm-ŭp′) *Informal.* A movie or television show featuring much physical violence, esp. shooting and killing.

shooting gallery *n.* An enclosed target range for firearms practice or competition.

shooting iron *n. Informal.* A six-shooter.

shooting star *n.* **1.** A meteor (sense 1). **2.** Any of several North American plants of the genus *Dodecatheon,* having nodding flowers with reflexed petals.

shooting stick *n.* A stick pointed at one end and opening into a seat at the other, typically used by spectators at races.

shoot-out also **shoot·out** (sho͞ot′out′) *n.* A confrontation in which armed opponents shoot guns at one another.

shoot-up (sho͞ot′ŭp′) *n. Slang.* An act of shooting up a narcotic drug.

shop (shŏp) *n.* **1.** Also **shoppe** (shŏp). A small retail store or a specialty department in a large store. **2.** An atelier; studio. **3.** A place for manufacturing or repairing, as of machinery: *a machine shop.* **4. a.** A commercial or industrial establishment. **b.** A business establishment: *set up shop.* **5.** A home workshop. **6. a.** A schoolroom fitted with machinery and tools for instruction in the manual arts. **b.** The manual arts as a technical science or course of study. ***—modifier:*** *a shop window.* *—v.* **shopped, shop·ping, shops.** *—intr.* **1.** To visit stores for the purpose of inspecting and buying merchandise. **2.** To look for something with the intention of acquiring it. *—tr.* To visit or buy from (a particular store). ***—idiom.*** **talk shop.** To talk about one's business. [ME *shoppe* < OE *sceoppa,* booth, stall.]

shop·keep·er (shŏp′kē′pər) *n.* One who owns or manages a shop.

shop·lift·er (shŏp′lĭf′tər) *n.* One who steals goods on display in a store. **—shop′lift′ing** *n.*

shoppe (shŏp) *n.* Variant of **shop** (sense 1).

shop·per (shŏp′ər) *n.* **1.** One that shops. **2.** A commercial agent who compares the merchandise and prices of competing merchants. **3.** A commercial employee who fills mail or telephone orders. **4.** A usually free paper carrying chiefly advertising and some local news.

shopping bag *n.* A strong bag with handles that is designed for carrying a shopper's purchases.

shop·ping-bag lady (shŏp′ĭng-băg′) *n.* A bag lady.
shopping center *n.* A group of stores and shops forming a central retail market within a given area.
shopping mall *n.* **1.** An urban shopping area limited to pedestrians. **2.** A shopping center with stores facing an enclosed walkway for pedestrians.
shop steward *n.* A union member elected to represent the union in its dealings with management.
shop·talk (shŏp′tôk′) *n.* Talk or conversation concerning one's business.
shop·worn (shŏp′wôrn′, -wōrn′) *adj.* **1.** Tarnished, frayed, faded, or otherwise defective from being on display in a store. **2.** Stale because of overuse or familiarity: *shopworn anecdotes.*
sho·ran (shôr′ăn′, shōr′-) *n.* A relatively short-range navigation system by which a ship or aircraft can determine its position with high precision by measuring the times required for a radar signal to reach each of two ground stations of known position and to return. [SHO(RT) RA(NGE) N(AVIGATION).]
shore[1] (shôr, shōr) *n.* **1.** The land along the edge of an ocean, sea, lake, or river; coast. **2.** Often **shores.** Land: *native shores.* [ME *schore,* prob. of LG orig.]
shore[2] (shôr, shōr) *tr.v.* **shored, shor·ing, shores.** To prop up, as with an inclined timber: *shore up sagging floors.* —*n.* A beam or timber propped against a structure to provide usually temporary support. [ME *schoren* < *schore,* prop, prob. of LG orig.]
shore[3] (shôr, shōr) *v. Archaic.* A past tense of **shear.**
shore bird *n.* Any of various birds, such as a sandpiper, plover, or snipe, that frequent the shores of coastal or inland waters.
shore·line (shôr′līn′, shōr′-) *n.* The line marking the edge of a body of water.
shore patrol *n.* A detail of the U.S. Navy, Marine Corps, or Coast Guard serving as military police ashore.
shore·ward (shôr′wərd, shōr′-) also **shore·wards** (-wərdz) *adv.* Toward the shore.
shor·ing (shôr′ĭng, shōr′-) *n.* **1.** The act or operation of propping with shores. **2.** A system of supporting shores.
shorl (shôrl) *n.* Variant of **schorl.**
shorn (shôrn, shōrn) *v.* A past participle of **shear.**
short (shôrt) *adj.* **-er, -est. 1.** Having little length; not long. **2.** Having little height; not tall. **3. a.** Lasting a small extent in time; brief: *a short holiday.* **b.** Appearing to pass quickly: *finished the job in a few short months.* **4.** Inadequate; insufficient: *oil in short supply; were short on experience.* **5.** Lacking in length or amount: *a board short two inches.* **6.** Lacking in breadth or scope. **7.** Not lengthy; succinct: *short and to the point.* **8. a.** Not owning the stocks or commodities one is selling. **b.** Pertaining to or designating a sale of stocks or goods that the seller does not yet own but must produce to meet the terms of a contract. **9.** Lacking in retentiveness: *a short memory.* **10.** Rudely brief; abrupt. **11.** Containing a large amount of shortening; flaky: *a short pie crust.* **12. a.** In Greek and Latin verse, indicating a syllable of relatively brief duration. **b.** In English prosody, unstressed. **13. a.** Designating a particular pronunciation of the letters for the vowel sounds, such as the sound of (ă) in *pan* as distinguished from the sound of (ā) in *pane.* **b.** Describing a speech sound of relatively brief duration as opposed to the same or a similar sound of relatively long duration. **14.** *Slang.* Being near the end of a tour of military duty. —*adv.* **1.** Abruptly; quickly: *stop short.* **2.** Rudely; curtly. **3.** At a point before a given limit or goal: *an arrow that fell short.* **4.** At a disadvantage: *caught short by the play.* **5.** Without owning what one is selling: *sell short.* —*n.* **1.** Something that is short, esp.: **a.** A briefly articulated or unaccented syllable. **b.** A short vowel. **c.** A short sale. **d.** A person who sells short. **e. shorts.** Short trousers extending to the knee or above. **f. shorts.** Men's undershorts. **g.** A short subject. **2. shorts.** A by-product of wheat processing, consisting of bran mixed with coarse meal or flour. **3. shorts.** Clippings or trimmings that remain as by-products in various manufacturing processes, often used to make an inferior variety of the product. **4.** *Elect.* **a.** A short circuit. **b.** A malfunction caused by a short circuit. **5.** *Baseball.* A shortstop. —*v.* **short·ed, short·ing, shorts.** —*tr.* **1.** To cause a short circuit in. **2.** *Informal.* To give (a person) less than he is entitled to; shortchange. —*intr.* To short-circuit. —***idioms.*** **for short.** As an abbreviation: *He's called Ed for short.* **in short.** In summary; briefly. **short for.** An abbreviation of: *Ed is short for Edward.* [ME <OE *sceort.*] —**short′ness** *n.*
short account *n.* **1.** The account of a person who sells short. **2.** The total open short sales of a particular commodity or security or on the market as a whole.
short·age (shôr′tĭj) *n.* A deficiency in amount; insufficiency.
short·bread (shôrt′brĕd′) *n.* A kneaded dough of flour, sugar, and butter, rolled thickly, cut into cookies, and baked.
short·cake (shôrt′kāk′) *n.* A dessert consisting of a cake made usually with rich biscuit dough split and filled with fruit and topped with cream.
short·change (shôrt′chānj′) *tr.v.* **-changed, -chang·ing, -chang·es.** *Informal.* **1.** To give (someone) less change than is due. **2.** To swindle, cheat, or trick. —**short′chang′er** *n.*
short circuit *n.* An accidentally established low-resistance connection between two points in an electric circuit.
short-cir·cuit (shôrt′sûr′kĭt) *v.* **-cuit·ed, -cuit·ing, -cuits.** —*tr.* **1.** To cause to have a short circuit. **2.** *Informal.* To hamper the progress of; impede. —*intr.* To become affected with a short circuit.
short·com·ing (shôrt′kŭm′ĭng) *n.* A deficiency; flaw.
short covering *n.* The buying of securities, stocks, or commodities in order to close out a short sale.
short cut *n.* **1.** A more direct route than the customary one. **2.** A means of saving time or effort.
short division *n.* A division of one number by another, usually no more than two digits, without writing out the remainders.
short·en (shôr′tn) *v.* **-ened, -en·ing, -ens.** —*tr.* **1.** To make short or shorter. **2.** To take in (a sail) so that less canvas is exposed to the wind. **3.** To reduce in force, efficacy, or intensity. **4.** To add shortening to (dough) so as to make flaky. —*intr.* To become short or shorter. —**short′en·er** *n.*
shortened form *n.* An abbreviated form of a polysyllabic word, as *auto* for *automobile.*
short·en·ing (shôr′tn-ĭng, shôrt′nĭng) *n.* **1.** A fat, such as butter or lard, used to make cake or pastry light or flaky. **2.** A shortened form of something, as an abbreviation. **3.** The act of one that shortens.
short·fall (shôrt′fôl′) *n.* **1.** A failure to attain a specified amount or level; shortage. **2.** The amount by which a supply falls short of expectation, need, or demand. **3.** A monetary deficit.
short fuse *n.* A quick temper.
short·hand (shôrt′hănd′) *n.* **1.** A system of rapid handwriting employing symbols to represent words, phrases, and letters; stenography. **2.** A system, form, or instance of abbreviated or formulaic reference: *"The classical error is to regard a scientific law as only a shorthand for its instances"* (J. Bronowski).
short-hand·ed (shôrt′hăn′dĭd) *adj.* Lacking the usual or necessary number of workmen, employees, or assistants.
short·horn (shôrt′hôrn′) *n.* One of a breed of beef or dairy cattle originating in northern England and having short, curved horns.
short hundredweight *n.* A hundredweight (sense 1).
short·leaf pine (shôrt′lēf′) *n.* A pine, *Pinus echinata,* that has short flexible leaves and is common in the southern United States.
short-lived (shôrt′līvd′, -lĭvd′) *adj.* Living or lasting only a short time; ephemeral.
short·ly (shôrt′lē) *adv.* **1.** In a short time; soon. **2.** In a few words; concisely. **3.** In an abrupt manner; curtly.
short order *n.* Food quickly prepared and served, as in a diner.
short rib *n.* A cut of meat consisting of the area between the rib roast and the plate.
short shrift *n.* **1. a.** A short respite, as from death. **b.** The short space of time granted a condemned prisoner for his confession before execution. **2.** Summary and unsympathetic treatment.
short sight *n.* Myopia.
short·sight·ed (shôrt′sī′tĭd) *adj.* **1.** Near-sighted; myopic. **2.** Lacking foresight. —**short′sight′ed·ly** *adv.* —**short′sight′ed·ness** *n.*
short-spo·ken (shôrt′spō′kən) *adj.* Given to shortness or abruptness in manner or speech; curt.
short·stop (shôrt′stŏp′) *n.* *Baseball.* **1.** The field position between second and third bases. **2.** The player who occupies shortstop.
short story *n.* A short piece of prose fiction aiming at unity of characterization, theme, and effect.
short subject *n.* A brief motion picture often shown between showings of longer motion pictures.
short-tem·pered (shôrt′tĕm′pərd) *adj.* Easily or quickly moved to anger; irascible.
short-term (shôrt′tûrm′) *adj.* **1.** Involving or lasting a relatively short time. **2.** Payable or reaching maturity within a relatively short time, as a year: *a short-term loan.*
short ton *n.* A ton (sense 1.b.).
short wave *n.* An electromagnetic wave with wavelength in the short-wave region.
short-wave (shôrt′wāv′) *adj.* **1.** Having a wavelength of less than approximately 80 meters. **2.** Capable of receiving or transmitting at wavelengths of less than approximately 80 meters.
short-wind·ed (shôrt′wĭn′dĭd) *adj.* **1.** Having or marked by shortness of breath. **2.** Choppy; disconnected.
Sho·sho·ne also **Sho·sho·ni** (shō-shō′nē) *n., pl.* **Shoshone** or **-nes** also **Shoshoni** or **-nis. 1. a.** A tribe of Uto-Aztecan-speaking North American Indians formerly occupying parts of Nevada, Oregon, Idaho, Utah, Wyoming, and Texas. **b.** A member of this tribe. **2.** The Uto-Aztecan language of the Shoshone.
Sho·sho·ne·an (shō-shō′nē-ən) *n.* A group of Uto-Aztecan languages that includes most of the Uto-Aztecan languages found in the United States. —**Sho·sho′ne·an** *adj.*
Sho·sho·ni (shō-shō′nē) *n.* Variant of **Shoshone.**
shot[1] (shŏt) *n.* **1.** The firing or discharge of a weapon, as of a

shore[1]

shoreline

shorthorn

p **p**op / r **r**oar / s **s**auce / sh **sh**ip, di**sh** / t **t**ight / th **th**in, pa**th** / *th* **th**is, ba**th**e / ŭ c**u**t / ûr **ur**ge / v **v**alve / w **w**ith / y **y**es / z **z**ebra, si**z**e / zh vi**s**ion / ə **a**bout, it**e**m, ed**i**ble, gall**o**p, circ**u**s / œ *Fr.* **feu**, *Ger.* **schön** / ü *Fr.* **tu**, *Ger.* **über** / KH *Ger.* **ich**, *Scot.* **loch** / N *Fr.* **bon**.

gun. **2.** *pl.* **shot.** A projectile, such as a pellet or bullet, from a firearm. **3.** *Informal.* **a.** Something, as a throw, hit, or drive in any of several games, that resembles the directed discharge of a weapon in force and carry. **b.** A home run. **4.** One who shoots: *a good shot.* **5.** The distance over which something is shot; range. **6.** An attempt to hit or land on something with a missile or rocket: *a moon shot.* **7. a.** An attempt. **b.** A guess. **c.** An opportunity. **8.** The heavy metal ball that is put for distance in the shot-put. **9.** A charge of explosives used in blasting mine shafts. **10. a.** A photograph or one in a series of photographs. **b.** A single cinematic view or take. **11.** A hypodermic injection. **12.** A drink, esp. a jigger, of liquor. **13.** *Naut.* A unit designating chain length, in the United States 15 fathoms, in Great Britain $12\frac{1}{2}$ fathoms. —*tr.v.* **shot·ted, shot·ting, shots. 1.** To load or weight with shot. **2.** To clean (bottles) by shaking when full of shot. —***idioms.*** **like a shot.** Very quickly. **shot in the arm.** Something that boosts one's spirits. **shot in the dark. 1.** A wild, unsubstantiated guess. **2.** An attempt that has little chance of succeeding. [ME *schot* < OE *sceot.*]

shovel

shot[2] (shŏt) *adj.* **1.** Of changeable or variegated color, as fabric having different-colored warp and weft; iridescent. **2.** *Informal.* Worn-out or ruined.

shot[3] (shŏt) *v.* Past tense and past participle of **shoot.**

shote (shōt) *n.* Variant of **shoat.**

shot·gun (shŏt′gŭn′) *n.* **1.** A shoulder-held firearm that fires multiple pellets through a smooth bore. **2.** *Football.* An offensive formation in which the quarterback positions himself a few yards behind the scrimmage line and the remaining backs play in various scattered positions.

shotgun marriage also **shotgun wedding** *n.* A marriage that is forced or necessitated because of pregnancy.

shot-put (shŏt′po͝ot′) *n.* **1. a.** An athletic event in which the contestants attempt to throw or put a shot or heavy ball as far as possible. **b.** The standard ball used in this competition. **2.** A throw; heave. —**shot′-put′ter** *n.*

shott (shŏt) *n.* Variant of **chott.**

shot·ten (shŏt′n) *adj.* Having recently spawned and thus being less desirable as food. Used of fish, esp. herring. [ME *schotyn,* p.part. of *schoten,* to shoot.]

should (sho͝od) *aux.v.* Past tense of **shall. 1.** Used to express obligation or duty: *You should send her a note.* **2.** Used to express probability or expectation: *They should arrive at noon.* **3.** Used to express conditionality or contingency: *If he should fall, then so would I.* **4.** Used to moderate the directness or bluntness of a statement: *I should think he would like to go.*

Usage: In traditional grammar the rules governing the use of *should* and *would* were based on the rules governing the use of *shall* and *will.* In modern times and especially in American usage, these rules have been greatly eroded, even more in the case of *should* and *would* than in the case of *shall* and *will.* Either *should* or *would* is now used in the first person to express conditional futurity: *If I had known that, I should* (or *would*) *have made a different reply.* In that example either *should* or *would* is acceptable to a great majority of the Usage Panel. But in the second and third persons only *would* is used: *If he had known that, he would have made a different reply. Would* cannot always be substituted for *should,* however. *Should* is used in all three persons in a conditional clause: *if I* (or *you* or *he*) *should decide to go. Should* is also used in all three persons to express duty or obligation (the equivalent of *ought to*): I (or *you* or *he*) *should go.* On the other hand, *would* is used to express volition or promise: *I agreed that I would do it.* Either *would* or *should* is possible as an auxiliary with *like, be inclined, be glad, prefer,* and related verbs: *I would* (or *should*) *like to call your attention to an oversight.* Here *would* is acceptable on all levels to a large majority of the Panel and is more common in American usage than *should. Should have* is sometimes incorrectly written *should of* by writers who have mistaken the source of the spoken contraction *should've.*

shoul·der (shōl′dər) *n.* **1.** *Anat.* **a.** The part of the human body between the neck and upper arm. **b.** The joint connecting the arm with the trunk. **2.** The part of an animal that corresponds to the human shoulder. **3.** Often **shoulders.** The two shoulders and the area of the back between them. **4.** The forequarter of some animals. **5.** The portion of a garment that covers the shoulder. **6.** The angle between the face and the flank of a bastion in a fortification. **7.** *Printing.* The extended flat surface on the body of type beyond the letter or character. **8. a.** The edge or ridge running on either side of a roadway. **b.** A shoulderlike projection or slope. —*v.* **-dered, -der·ing, -ders.** —*tr.* **1.** To carry or place (a burden, for example) on the shoulders. **2.** To take on; assume: *shouldering the blame for his friends.* **3.** To push or apply force to with or as if with the shoulder: *shouldered her way through the mob.* —*intr.* To push with the shoulders. [ME *shulder* < OE *sculdor.*]

shoulder bag *n.* An often large handbag carried by a strap that is looped over the shoulder.

shoulder belt *n.* An automobile safety belt worn diagonally across the body and over the shoulder.

shoulder blade *n.* The scapula.

shoulder girdle *n.* The pectoral girdle.

shoulder harness *n.* A shoulder belt.

shoulder patch *n.* An identification patch worn on the upper portion of the sleeve of a uniform.

should·n't (sho͝od′nt). Should not.

shouldst (sho͝odst) also **should·est** (sho͝od′ĭst) *aux.v. Archaic.* Second person singular past tense of **shall.**

shout (shout) *n.* A loud cry. —*tr. & intr.v.* **shout·ed, shout·ing, shouts.** To say with or utter a shout. [ME *shoute.*] —**shout′er** *n.*

shouting distance *n.* A short distance: *lived within shouting distance of each other.*

shove (shŭv) *v.* **shoved, shov·ing, shoves.** —*tr.* To prod or give thrust to, as forward or along a surface; push rudely or roughly. —*intr.* To push someone or something with force. —***phrasal verb.*** **shove off.** *Informal.* To leave. —*n.* The act of shoving; a rude or rough push. [ME *schouven* < OE *scūfan.*] —**shov′er** *n.*

shov·el (shŭv′əl) *n.* **1.** A tool with a handle and a somewhat flattened scoop for picking up material, as dirt or snow. **2.** A large mechanical device or vehicle for heavy digging or excavation. **3.** A shovelful. —*v.* **-eled, -el·ing, -els** or **-elled, -el·ling, -els.** —*tr.* **1.** To move or remove with a shovel. **2.** To clear or make with a shovel. **3.** To convey or throw in a rough or hasty way, as if with a shovel. —*intr.* To dig or work with a shovel. [ME *schovel* < OE *scofl.*]

shov·el·er also **shov·el·ler** (shŭv′ə-lər, shŭv′lər) *n.* **1.** One that shovels. **2.** A widely distributed duck, *Spatula clypeata* (or *Anas clypeata*), having a long, broad bill.

shov·el·ful (shŭv′əl-fo͝ol′) *n.* The amount a shovel will hold.

shovel hat *n.* A stiff, broad-brimmed, low-crowned hat, turned up at the sides and projecting in front, worn by some English clergymen.

shov·el·head (shŭv′əl-hĕd′) *n.* A shark, *Sphyrna tiburo,* of Atlantic and Pacific waters.

shov·el·nose (shŭv′əl-nōz′) *n.* A sturgeon, *Scaphirhynchus platorynchus,* of the Mississippi River, having a broad, flat snout.

shov·el-nosed (shŭv′əl-nōzd′) *adj.* Having a broad, flattened snout, bill, or head.

show (shō) *v.* **showed, shown** (shōn) or **showed, show·ing, shows.** —*tr.* **1. a.** To cause or allow to be seen or viewed; make visible. **b.** To present in public exhibition or competition. **2.** To conduct; guide. **3.** To point out; demonstrate. **4. a.** To manifest; reveal. **b.** To indicate; register. **5.** To grant; bestow. **6.** *Law.* To plead; allege: *show cause.* —*intr.* **1.** To be or become visible or evident. **2.** *Informal.* To put in an appearance. **3.** To appear; seem. **4.** To be exhibited publicly; run. **5.** *Sports.* To finish third or better for betting purposes. —***phrasal verbs.*** **show off.** To display or behave in an ostentatious or conspicuous way. **show up. 1.** To expose or reveal the true character or nature of. **2.** To be clearly visible. **3.** To put in an appearance; arrive. —*n.* **1.** A display; manifestation: *made a show of strength.* **2.** A false appearance: *a show of kindness.* **3.** A striking appearance or display; spectacle. **4.** A pompous or ostentatious display. **5. a.** A public exhibition or entertainment. **b.** A troupe or company. **6.** *Informal.* An affair or undertaking: *ran the whole show.* **7.** *Sports.* Third place or better for betting purposes: *win, place, and show.* —***idioms.*** **show (one's) hand. 1.** To display one's cards with faces up. **2.** To state one's intentions or reveal one's resources. **show (someone) the door.** *Informal.* To tell another to leave. [ME *showen* < OE *scēawian,* to look at.]

Synonyms: *show, display, expose, parade, exhibit, flaunt.* These verbs mean to present something to view. *Show* is the most general, since it makes no clear implication as to manner or method of presentation. *Display* usually suggests an attempt to present something to best advantage, but it can imply ostentation or even the making obvious of something better concealed, such as ignorance. *Expose* usually involves uncovering or bringing from concealment or unmasking. *Parade* generally suggests a blatant or boastful presentation. *Exhibit* implies open, rather formal presentation that invites inspection. *Flaunt* implies a prideful, arrogant attempt to gain attention.

show bill *n.* An advertising poster.

show biz (bĭz) *n. Slang.* Show business.

show·boat (shō′bōt′) *n.* **1.** A river steamboat having a troupe of actors and a theater aboard for performances on the river. **2.** One who seeks attention by ostentatious behavior; show-off.

show·bread (shō′brĕd′) *n.* The 12 loaves of blessed unleavened bread placed every Sabbath in the sanctuary of the Tabernacle by the Hebrew priests of ancient Israel. [Transl. of G. *Schaubrot,* transl. of Heb. *leḥem pānim,* bread of the Divine Presence.]

show business *n.* The entertainment industry.

show·case (shō′kās′) *n.* **1.** A display case or cabinet, as in a store or museum. **2.** A setting in which something may be displayed to advantage. —*tr.v.* **-cased, -cas·ing, -cas·es.** To display prominently and to advantage.

show·down (shō′doun′) *n.* **1.** The laying down of the players' hands of cards to determine the winner of the pot in poker. **2.** An event or circumstance that forces an issue to a conclusion.

show·er[1] (shou′ər) *n.* **1. a.** A brief fall of precipitation, as rain, hail, or sleet. **b.** A fall of a group of objects, esp. of a large group, from the sky: *a meteor shower.* **2.** A brief or sudden downpour: *a shower of leaves.* **3.** An abundant flow; outpouring: *a shower of abuse.* **4.** A party held to honor and present gifts to someone: *a bridal shower.* **5.** A shower bath. *—v.* **-ered, -er·ing, -ers.** *—tr.* **1.** To sprinkle; spray. **2.** To bestow abundantly. *—intr.* **1.** To fall or pour down in a shower. **2.** To take a shower bath. [ME *shour* < OE *scūr.*] **—show′er·y** *adj.*

show·er² (shō′ər) *n.* One that shows.

shower bath *n.* A bath in which water is sprayed on the bather from an overhead nozzle.

show·girl (shō′gûrl′) *n.* A chorus girl or similar entertainer.

show·ing (shō′ĭng) *n.* **1.** The act of presenting or displaying. **2.** Performance, as in a competition or test of skill: *a poor showing.* **3.** A presentation of evidence, facts, or figures.

show·man (shō′mən) *n.* **1.** A theatrical producer. **2.** A person having a flair for dramatic or visual effectiveness. **—show′man·ship′** *n.*

shown (shōn) *v.* A past participle of **show.**

show·off (shō′ôf′, -ŏf′) *n.* **1.** The act of showing off. **2.** Someone who shows off; exhibitionist.

show·piece (shō′pēs′) *n.* Something exhibited, esp. as an outstanding example of its kind.

show place also **show·place** (shō′plās′) *n.* A place that is viewed and frequented for its beauty or excellence.

show room *n.* A room in which merchandise is on display.

show·stop·per (shō′stŏp′ər) *n.* One, as an act or a performer, that evokes so much audience applause that a performance is temporarily interrupted.

show·y (shō′ē) *adj.* **-i·er, -i·est. 1.** Making a conspicuous display; striking: *showy flowers.* **2.** Displaying brilliance and virtuosity of ability or performance. **3.** Gaudy; flashy. **—show′i·ly** *adv.* **—show′i·ness** *n.*

shrank (shrăngk) *v.* A past tense of **shrink.**

shrap·nel (shrăp′nəl) *n., pl.* **shrapnel. 1. a.** An artillery shell containing metal balls fused to explode in the air above enemy troops. **b.** The metal balls in such a weapon. **2.** Shell fragments from a high-explosive shell. [After General Henry *Shrapnel* (1761–1842), its inventor.]

shred (shrĕd) *n.* **1.** A long, irregular strip cut or torn off. **2.** A small amount; particle. *—tr.v.* **shred·ded** or **shred, shred·ding, shreds.** To cut or tear into shreds. [ME *shrede* < OE *screade.*] **—shred′der** *n.*

shrew (shro͞o) *n.* **1.** Any of various small, chiefly insectivorous mammals of the family Soricidae, having a long, pointed nose and small, often poorly developed eyes. **2.** A woman with a violent, scolding, or nagging temperament; scold. [ME *shrewe,* villain < OE *scrēawa,* shrewmouse.]

shrewd (shro͞od) *adj.* **-er, -est. 1.** Having keen insight; astute. **2.** Artful; cunning. **3.** Sharp; penetrating. [ME *shrewed,* wicked < *shrew,* rascal.] **—shrewd′ly** *adv.*

Synonyms: *shrewd, sagacious, astute, quick-witted.* These adjectives refer to the possession of a keen, searching intelligence combined usually with sound judgment. *Shrewd* stresses perceptiveness, hardheadedness, cunning, and an intuitive knack in practical matters. *Sagacious* emphasizes more profound wisdom based on wide experience and a gift for discernment and farsightedness. *Astute* suggests qualities associated with practical wisdom, such as acute understanding, insight, discernment, and immunity to being deceived. *Quick-witted,* the narrowest term, refers to alertness and mental adroitness.

shrewd·ness (shro͞od′nĭs) *n.* **1.** The quality of being shrewd. **2.** An aggregation of apes.

shrew·ish (shro͞o′ĭsh) *adj.* Ill-tempered; nagging. **—shrew′ish·ly** *adv.* **—shrew′ish·ness** *n.*

shrew mole *n.* Any of several shrewlike moles of the family Talpidae, esp. *Neurotrichus gibbsi,* of western North America, or *Uropsilus soricipes,* of eastern Asia.

shrew·mouse (shro͞o′mous′) *n.* A shrew (sense 1).

shriek (shrēk) *n.* **1.** A loud, shrill outcry; screech. **2.** A sound suggestive of a shriek. *—v.* **shrieked, shriek·ing, shrieks.** *—intr.* **1.** To utter a shriek. **2.** To make a sound similar to a shriek. *—tr.* To utter with a shriek: *shrieked a warning.* [< ME *shriken,* to shriek.] **—shriek′er** *n.*

shrie·val (shrē′vəl) *adj.* Of or pertaining to a sheriff. [< obs. *shrieve,* var. of SHERIFF.] **—shrie′val·ty** *n.*

shrift (shrĭft) *n. Archaic.* **1.** The act of shriving. **2.** Confession to a priest. **3.** Absolution given by a priest. [ME < OE *scrift* < *scrīfan,* to shrive < Lat. *scribere,* to write.]

shrike (shrīk) *n.* Any of various carnivorous birds of the family Laniidae, having a hooked bill and often impaling its prey on sharp-pointed thorns or barbs of wire fencing. [Prob. < ME **shrik* < OE *scrīc,* thrush.]

shrill (shrĭl) *adj.* **-er, -est. 1.** High-pitched and piercing in tone or sound. **2.** Producing a shrill tone or sound. **3.** Sharp or keen to the senses. *—v.* **shrilled, shrill·ing, shrills.** *—tr.* To utter in a shrill manner; scream. *—intr.* To produce a shrill cry or sound. [ME *shrille* < *shrillen,* to shriek.] **—shrill′ness** *n.* **—shril′ly** *adv.*

shrimp (shrĭmp) *n., pl.* **shrimp** or **shrimps. 1. a.** Any of various small, slender-bodied, chiefly marine decapod crustaceans of the suborder Natantia, many species of which are edible. **b.** Any of various similar crustaceans. **2.** *Slang.* A small or unimportant person. *—intr.v.* **shrimped, shrimp·ing, shrimps.** To catch or fish for shrimp. [ME *shrimpe,* perh. of LG orig.]

shrimp·fish (shrĭmp′fĭsh′) *n., pl.* **shrimpfish** or **-fish·es.** Any of various small, slender tropical marine fishes of the family Centriscidae, related to the sea horses and pipefish.

shrimp plant *n.* A shrubby plant, *Beloperone guttata,* having inconspicuous flowers borne between a series of reddish bracts.

shrine (shrīn) *n.* **1.** A container or receptacle for sacred relics; reliquary. **2.** The tomb of a saint or other venerated person. **3.** A site hallowed by a venerated object or its associations. *—tr.v.* **shrined, shrin·ing, shrines.** To enshrine. [ME *shrine* < OE *scrīn,* box < Lat. *scrinium,* case for books or papers.]

Shrin·er (shrī′nər) *n.* A member of a U.S. secret fraternal order that is not Masonic but that admits only Knights Templars and 32nd-degree Masons as members. [After the Ancient Arabic Order of Nobles of the Mystic *Shrine,* their fraternal order.]

shrink (shrĭngk) *v.* **shrank** (shrăngk) or **shrunk** (shrŭngk), **shrunk** or **shrunk·en** (shrŭng′kən), **shrink·ing, shrinks.** *—intr.* **1.** To become constricted from heat, moisture, or cold; contract. **2.** To become reduced in amount or value; dwindle: *His savings quickly shrank.* **3.** To draw back; recoil. **4.** To be reluctant to do or say something. *—tr.* To cause to shrink. *—n.* **1. a.** The act of shrinking. **b.** Shrinkage. **2.** *Slang.* A psychiatrist or psychologist. [ME *shrinken* < OE *scrincan.*] **—shrink′a·ble** *adj.* **—shrink′er** *n.*

shrink·age (shrĭng′kĭj) *n.* **1.** The process of shrinking. **2.** A reduction in value; depreciation. **3.** The total weight loss sustained by livestock in shipment to a market. **4.** The amount of a loss by shrinkage.

shrinking violet *n. Informal.* A shy or retiring person.

shrink package *n.* A transparent form-fitting plastic wrapping, esp. of polyethylene or polyvinyl chloride, used to protect a commodity from dust, moisture, and abrasion.

shrink-pack·age (shrĭngk′păk′ĭj) *tr.v.* **-aged, -ag·ing, -ag·es.** To enclose (a commodity) in a shrink package.

shrink wrap *n.* A shrink package.

shrink-wrap (shrĭngk′răp′) *tr.v.* **-wrapped, -wrap·ping, -wraps.** To shrink-package.

shrive (shrīv) *v.* **shrove** (shrōv) or **shrived, shriv·en** (shrĭv′ən) or **shrived, shriv·ing, shrives.** *—tr.* **1.** To hear the confession of and give absolution to (a penitent). **2.** To obtain absolution for (oneself) by confessing and doing penance. *—intr.* **1.** To make or go to confession. **2.** To hear confessions. [ME *schriven* < OE *scrīfan* < Lat. *scribere,* to write.] **—shriv′er** *n.*

shriv·el (shrĭv′əl) *v.* **-eled, -el·ing, -els** or **-elled, -el·ling, -els.** *—intr.* **1.** To shrink and wrinkle, often in drying. **2.** To lose vitality or intensity: *"Their spirits shrivelled in the numbing breath of a military government"* (T.E. Lawrence). *—tr.* To cause to become shriveled. [Orig. unknown.]

shriv·en (shrĭv′ən) *v.* A past participle of **shrive.**

Shrop·shire (shrŏp′shîr′, -shər, -shīr′) *n.* A large, hornless, black-faced sheep of a breed developed in Shropshire, England, and raised for meat and wool.

shroud (shroud) *n.* **1.** A cloth used to wrap a body for burial; winding sheet. **2.** Something that conceals, protects, or screens in the manner of a garment. **3. a.** One of a set of ropes or wire cables stretched from the masthead to a vessel's sides to support the mast. **b.** A similar support for a smokestack or comparable structure. **c.** One of the ropes connecting the harness and canopy of a parachute. *—v.* **shroud·ed, shroud·ing, shrouds.** *—tr.* **1.** To wrap (a corpse) in burial clothing. **2.** To screen; hide. **3.** *Archaic.* To shelter; protect. *—intr. Archaic.* To take cover; find shelter. [ME *schrud,* garment < OE *scrūd.*]

shrove (shrōv) *v.* A past tense of **shrive.**

Shrove·tide (shrōv′tīd′) *n.* The three days, Shrove Sunday, Shrove Monday, and Shrove Tuesday, preceding Ash Wednesday. [ME *schroftyde* : *schrof-,* shriving (< *schriven,* to shrive) + *tyde,* time < OE *tīd.*]

shrub¹ (shrŭb) *n.* A woody plant of relatively low height, distinguished from a tree by having several stems rather than a single trunk; bush. [ME *schrubbe* < OE *scrybb.*]

shrub² (shrŭb) *n.* A beverage made from fruit juice, sugar, and a liquor such as rum or brandy. [Ar. *shurb,* a drink < *shariba,* to drink.]

shrub·ber·y (shrŭb′ə-rē) *n., pl.* **-ies. 1.** Shrubs collectively. **2.** A group or planting of shrubs.

shrub·by (shrŭb′ē) *adj.* **-bi·er, -bi·est. 1.** Consisting of, planted with, or covered with shrubs. **2.** Of or resembling a shrub; shrublike. **—shrub′bi·ness** *n.*

shrug (shrŭg) *v.* **shrugged, shrug·ging, shrugs.** *—tr.* To raise (the shoulders) as a gesture esp. of doubt, disdain, or indifference. *—intr.* To raise the shoulders as a gesture esp. of doubt, disdain, or indifference. ***—phrasal verb.*** **shrug off. 1.** To minimize the importance of. **2.** To get rid of. **3.** To wriggle out of (clothing). *—n.* **1.** The expressive gesture of shrugging. **2.** A woman's short jacket or sweater open down the front. [ME *shruggen.*]

George Miksch Sutton

shrike

shrunk (shrŭngk) *v.* A past tense and past participle of **shrink.**

shrunk·en (shrŭng′kən) *v.* A past participle of **shrink.**

shtetl (shtĕt′l, shtāt′l) *n.* A small Eastern European Jewish community of former times. [Yiddish < MHG *stetel,* dim. of *stat,* town < OHG, place.]

shtick also **schtick** (shtĭk) *n. Slang.* **1.** A characteristic attribute, talent, or trait. **2.** A striking portion or detail. **3.** The method of doing something. **4.** An entertainment routine. [Yiddish *shtik* < MHG *stücke,* piece < OHG *stucki.*]

shuck (shŭk) *n.* **1.** The outer covering of something such as a pea pod, corn husk, or oyster shell. **2.** *Slang.* A deception or sham. —*v.* **shucked, shuck·ing, shucks.** —*tr.* **1.** To remove the husk or shell from. **2.** *Informal.* To cast off (clothing, for example). **3.** *Slang.* To deceive. —*intr. Slang.* To talk or behave in a deceptive manner. —*interj.* **shucks.** Used to express mild disappointment, disgust, or annoyance. [Orig. unknown.] **—shuck'er** *n.*

shutter

shud·der (shŭd'ər) *intr.v.* **-dered, -der·ing, -ders. 1.** To tremble or shiver convulsively, as from fear or aversion: *"They shuddered at the thought of hard work"* (Conrad). **2.** To vibrate; quiver. —*n.* A convulsive shiver, as from fear or cold; tremor. [ME *shoddren.*] **—shud'der·ing·ly** *adv.*

shuf·fle (shŭf'əl) *v.* **-fled, -fling, -fles.** —*tr.* **1.** To drag (the feet) along the floor or ground while walking; scuffle. **2.** To move (something) from one place to another. **3.** To mix together or otherwise handle in a disordered, haphazard fashion. **4.** To put aside or conceal hastily; cover up. **5.** To mix together (playing cards, tiles, or dominoes) to change their order of arrangement. —*intr.* **1.** To move with a shuffling gait. **2.** To dance the shuffle. **3.** To shift about from place to place. **4.** To act in a shifty or deceitful manner; equivocate. **5.** To mix playing cards, tiles, or dominoes together to change their order of arrangement. —*n.* **1.** A shuffling gait or movement. **2.** A dance in which the feet scrape along the floor at each step. **3.** An evasive or deceitful action; equivocation. **4. a.** The act of mixing cards, dominoes, or tiles. **b.** A player's right or turn to do this. [Prob. < LG *schüffeln,* to walk clumsily.] **—shuf'fler** *n.*

shuf·fle·board (shŭf'əl-bôrd', -bōrd') *n.* **1.** A game in which disks are pushed or slid along a smooth, level surface toward numbered squares with a pronged cue. **2.** The surface on which shuffleboard is played. [Alteration of obs. *shove-board* : SHOVE + BOARD.]

shul (sho͝ol, sho͞ol) *n.* A synagogue. [Yiddish < MHG *schuol,* school < OHG *scuola* < Lat. *scola.* —see SCHOOL[1].]

shun (shŭn) *tr.v.* **shunned, shun·ning, shuns.** To avoid deliberately and esp. consistently: *shunned his neighbor.* [ME *shunnen* < OE *scunian,* to abhor.] **—shun'ner** *n.*

shun·pike (shŭn'pīk') *n.* A side road taken to avoid the tollgates on a major artery. —*intr.v.* **-piked, -pik·ing, -pikes.** To travel on a shunpike, esp. for pleasure. **—shun'pik'er** *n.*

shunt (shŭnt) *n.* **1.** The act or process of turning aside or moving to an alternate course. **2.** A railroad switch. **3.** *Elect.* A low-resistance connection between two points in an electric circuit that forms an alternative path for a portion of the current. —*v.* **shunt·ed, shunt·ing, shunts.** —*tr.* **1.** To turn or move aside or onto another course: *shunting traffic around a bottleneck.* **2.** To shift or switch (a train or car) from one track to another. **3.** *Elect.* To provide or divert (current) by means of a shunt. **4.** To evade or avoid (a task, for example) by refusing or putting aside. —*intr.* **1.** To move or turn aside. **2.** *Elect.* To become diverted by means of a shunt. Used of a circuit. **3.** To shift one's views or direction. [ME *shunten,* to flinch.] **—shunt'er** *n.*

shunt-wound (shŭnt'wound') *adj.* Of or pertaining to a direct-current motor or generator in which the field coil is connected in parallel with the armature so that the same voltage appears across each.

shush (shŭsh) *interj.* Used to express a demand for silence. —*tr.v.* **shushed, shush·ing, shush·es.** To demand silence from by saying "shush."

shut (shŭt) *v.* **shut, shut·ting, shuts.** —*tr.* **1.** To move (a door, for example) into closed position over or within a conjoined aperture. **2.** To block passage or access to; close. **3.** To fasten or secure with a lock, catch, or latch. **4.** To prevent or forbid access to; bar. **5.** To close (a business establishment). —*intr.* To move or become moved to a closed position; close. ***—phrasal verbs.* shut down. 1.** To halt the operation of. **2.** To stop operating, esp. automatically. **shut in.** To prevent egress from; confine. **shut off. 1.** To halt operation. **2.** To stop operating: *a switch that shuts off automatically.* **3.** To close off: *shut himself off from the rest of the world.* **shut out. 1.** To keep from entering. **2.** *Sports.* To prevent (a team) from scoring any runs or points. **shut up. 1.** To silence (a person). **2.** To stop speaking. —*n.* **1.** The act or time of closing or shutting. **2.** The line of connection between welded pieces of metal. [ME *shutten* < OE *scyttan.*]

shut·down (shŭt'doun') *n.* A cessation of operations or activity, as work in an industrial plant.

shut·eye (shŭt'ī') *n. Slang.* Sleep.

shut-in (shŭt'ĭn') *n.* A person confined indoors by illness or disability. —*adj.* (shŭt-ĭn'). **1.** Confined to a house or hospital, as by illness. **2.** *Psychiat.* Disposed to avoid other people; excessively introverted.

shut·off (shŭt'ôf', -ŏf') *n.* **1.** A device that shuts something off. **2.** A stoppage; cessation.

Siamese cat

shut·out (shŭt'out') *n.* **1.** A lockout. **2.** *Sports.* A game in which one side does not score.

shut·ter (shŭt'ər) *n.* **1.** One that shuts. **2.** A hinged cover or screen for a window, usually fitted with louvers. **3. shutters.** The movable louvers on a pipe organ, controlled by pedals, that open and close the swell box. **4.** A mechanical device that opens and shuts the lens aperture of a camera to expose a plate or film. —*tr.v.* **-tered, -ter·ing, -ters.** To furnish or close with shutters.

shut·ter·bug (shŭt'ər-bŭg') *n. Informal.* An amateur photographer.

shut·tle (shŭt'l) *n.* **1.** A device used in weaving to carry the woof thread back and forth between the warp threads. **2.** A device for holding the thread in tatting, in netting, and in a sewing machine. **3. a.** Regular travel back and forth over an established, often short route by a vehicle, such as an airplane. **b.** The route used by a vehicle that shuttles. **c.** A vehicle that frequently travels back and forth between points. —*v.* **-tled, -tling, -tles.** —*intr.* To go, move, or travel back and forth by or as if by a shuttle. —*tr.* **1.** To move or cause to move back and forth frequently. **2.** To transport by or as if by a shuttle. [ME *schutylle* < OE *scytel,* dart.]

shut·tle·cock (shŭt'l-kŏk') *n.* A small rounded piece of cork or rubber with a crown of feathers or plastic, used in badminton. —*tr.v.* **-cocked, -cock·ing, -cocks.** To throw or send back and forth like a shuttlecock.

shuttle diplomacy *n.* Diplomatic negotiations conducted by an official intermediary who travels frequently between the nations involved. **—shuttle diplomat** *n.*

shy[1] (shī) *adj.* **shi·er** or **shy·er, shi·est** or **shy·est. 1.** Easily startled; timid. **2.** Bashful; reserved. **3.** Distrustful; wary. **4.** *Informal.* Not having paid an amount due, as one's ante in poker. **5.** *Informal.* Short; lacking: *Eleven is one shy of a dozen.* —*intr.v.* **shied, shy·ing, shies. 1.** To move suddenly, as if startled. **2.** To draw back, as from fear or caution. —*n., pl.* **shies.** A sudden movement, as from fright. [ME *schey* < OE *scēoh.*] **—shy'er** *n.* **—shy'ly** *adv.* **—shy'ness** *n.*

Synonyms: *shy, bashful, diffident, modest, coy, demure.* These adjectives describe persons who are markedly unobtrusive. *Shy* implies either a retiring or withdrawn nature or timidity resulting from lack of social experience. *Bashful* suggests obvious embarrassment or awkwardness in the presence of others. *Diffident* implies lack of self-confidence. *Modest* is associated with a retiring nature, absence of vanity, and a dislike of personal ostentation. *Coy* usually implies false modesty or feigned shyness that may be calculated to stimulate attention or attract the interest of others. *Demure* implies a sedate, modest manner or decorous appearance.

shy[2] (shī) *v.* **shied, shy·ing, shies.** —*tr.* To throw (something) with a swift sideways motion. —*intr.* To throw something with a swift sideways motion. —*n., pl.* **shies. 1.** A quick throw; fling. **2.** *Informal.* A gibe; sneer. **3.** *Informal.* An experiment; try. [Perh. < SHY.]

shy·lock (shī'lŏk') *n.* **1. Shylock.** The ruthless usurer in Shakespeare's play *The Merchant of Venice.* **2.** A ruthless creditor; loan shark. —*intr.v.* **-locked, -lock·ing, -locks.** To lend money at exorbitant interest rates.

shy·ster (shī'stər) *n. Slang.* An unethical, unscrupulous practitioner, esp. of law or politics. [Perh. after *Scheuster,* an unscrupulous 19th-cent. lawyer.]

si (sē) *n. Mus.* Ti. [Med. Lat. —see GAMUT.]

Si The symbol for the element silicon.

si·al (sī'ăl') *n.* A layer of rock rich in silica and alumina underlying all continental land masses. [SI(LICON) + AL(UMINUM).]

si·a·lad·en·i·tis (sī'ə-lăd'n-ī'tĭs) *n.* Inflammation of a salivary gland. [Gk. *sialon,* saliva + *adēn,* gland + -ITIS.]

si·al·a·gogue (sī-ăl'ə-gôg', -gŏg') *n.* An agent that increases the flow of saliva. [Gk. *sialon,* saliva + -AGOGUE.]

si·al·ic acid (sī-ăl'ĭk) *n.* Any of a group of amino carbohydrates that are found as components of mucoproteins, lipids, and polysaccharides in bacteria and animal tissue. [Gk. *sialon,* saliva + -IC.]

si·a·mang (sē'ə-măng', sē-ăm'əng) *n.* A large black gibbon, *Symphalangus syndactylus* (or *Hylobates syndactylus*), of Sumatra and the Malay Peninsula, having an inflatable throat sac. [Malay.]

Si·a·mese (sī'ə-mēz', -mēs') *adj.* **1.** Thai. **2.** Closely connected or very similar; twin. **3. siamese.** Connecting two hoses or pipes to a larger hose or pipe. —*n., pl.* **Siamese.** Thai. [After *Siam* (Thailand).]

Siamese cat *n.* A short-haired cat of a breed developed in the Orient, having blue eyes and a pale fawn or gray coat with darker ears, face, tail, and feet.

Siamese fighting fish *n.* A small, often brightly colored freshwater fish, *Betta splendens,* native to tropical Asia and popular in home aquariums.

Siamese twin *n.* One of a pair of twins born with their bodies joined together. [After Chang and Eng (1811–1874), joined Chinese twins born in *Siam* (Thailand).]

sib (sĭb) *n.* **1. a.** A blood relation; kinsman. **b.** Relatives collectively; kinfolk. **2.** A brother or sister; sibling. —*adj.* Related by blood; akin. [ME *sibbe* < OE *sibb.*]

Si·be·ri·an husky (sī-bîr'ē-ən) *n.* A husky[3] (sense 1).

sib·i·lant (sĭb'ə-lənt) *adj.* Of, characterized by, or producing a hissing sound, as the sound of (s) or (sh). —*n.* **1.** A speech sound, as (s), (sh), (z), or (zh), that suggests hissing. **2.** A sibilant consonant. [Lat. *sibilans, sibilant-,* pr.part. of *sibi-*

lare, to hiss.] **—sib'i·lance, sib'i·lan·cy** *n.* **—sib'i·lant·ly** *adv.*
sib·i·late (sĭb'ə-lāt') *intr. & tr.v.* **-lat·ed, -lat·ing, -lates.** To utter or pronounce with a hissing sound. [Lat. *sibilare, sibilat-,* to hiss.] **—sib'i·la'tion** *n.*
sib·ling (sĭb'lĭng) *n.* One of two or more persons having one or esp. both parents in common; brother or sister. [ME *siblyng* < OE *sibling* < *sibb,* kinsman.]
sib·yl (sĭb'əl) *n.* **1.** One of a number of women regarded as oracles or prophetesses by the ancient Greeks and Romans. **2.** A female prophet. [ME *Sibile* < OFr. < Lat. *Sibylla* < Gk. *Sibulla.*]
sib·yl·line (sĭb'ə-līn', -lēn') also **si·byl·ic** or **si·byl·lic** (sĭ-bĭl'ĭk) *adj.* **1.** Pertaining to, coming from, or characteristic of a sibyl. **2.** Prophetic; oracular.
sic[1] (sĭk) *adv.* Thus; so. Used in written texts to indicate that a surprising or paradoxical word, phrase, or fact is not a mistake and is to be read as it stands. [Lat.]
sic[2] also **sick** (sĭk) *tr.v.* **sicced, sic·cing, sics** also **sicked, sick·ing, sicks. 1.** To urge to attack or chase. **2.** To set upon or chase: *"Sic him," he commanded his dog.* [Dial. var. of SEEK.]
sic·ca·tive (sĭk'ə-tĭv) *n.* A substance added to paints and some medicines to promote drying; drier. [Lat. *siccativus,* drying < *siccare,* to dry < *siccus,* dry.]
sick[1] (sĭk) *adj.* **-er, -est. 1. a.** Suffering from or affected with a physical illness; ailing. **b.** Nauseated. **2.** Of or for sick persons: *sick wards.* **3. a.** Mentally ill or disturbed. **b.** Morbid or unwholesome: *a sick joke.* **c.** Defective; unsound: *a sick economy.* **4. a.** Deeply distressed; upset. **b.** Disgusted; revolted. **c.** Weary; tired: *sick of it all.* **d.** Pining; longing: *sick for his native land.* **5.** In need of repairs. Used of a ship. **6.** Unable to produce a profitable yield of crops. ***—idiom.*** **sick and tired.** Thoroughly weary, discouraged, or bored. [ME *sek* < OE *sēoc.*]

Synonyms: *sick, ill, indisposed, unwell.* These adjectives describe persons not in good health. *Sick* applies to such a condition of any nature or severity. It sometimes specifies nausea and may also suggest an alien attitude toward society. *Ill* can be used as a polite equivalent of *sick* or as a term intended to emphasize the severity of a condition. *Indisposed* refers to minor sickness. *Unwell,* sometimes considered euphemistic, has the wide range of *sick.*

sick[2] (sĭk) *v.* Variant of **sic**[2].
sick·bay (sĭk'bā') *n.* **1.** The hospital and dispensary of a ship. **2.** A place where the sick or injured are treated.
sick·bed (sĭk'bĕd') *n.* A sick person's bed.
sick call *n.* **1.** The daily line-up of military personnel requiring medical attention. **2.** The signal announcing sick call.
sick·ee (sĭk'ē) *n.* Variant of **sickie.**
sick·en (sĭk'ən) *tr. & intr.v.* **-ened, -en·ing, -ens.** To make or become sick. **—sick'en·er** *n.*
sick·en·ing (sĭk'ə-nĭng) *adj.* **1.** Causing sickness. **2.** Revolting or disgusting; loathsome. **—sick'en·ing·ly** *adv.*
sick headache *n.* A headache accompanied by nausea.
sick·ie also **sick·ee** (sĭk'ē) *n. Slang.* One who is emotionally or morally sick.
sick·ish (sĭk'ĭsh) *adj.* **1.** Somewhat sick. **2.** Somewhat nauseated. **3.** Somewhat revolting or nauseating. **—sick'ish·ly** *adv.* **—sick'ish·ness** *n.*
sick·le (sĭk'əl) *n.* **1.** An implement having a semicircular blade attached to a short handle, used for cutting grain or tall grass. **2.** The cutting mechanism of a reaper or mower. *—tr.v.* **-led, -ling, -les.** To cut with a sickle. [ME *sikel* < OE *sicol* < Lat. *secula.*]
sick leave *n.* Paid absence from work allowed an employee because of sickness.
sick·le·bill (sĭk'əl-bĭl') *n.* Any of several birds having sharply curved bills, esp. *Falculea palliata,* of Madagascar.
sickle cell *n.* An abnormal crescent-shaped red blood cell.
sickle cell anemia *n.* A hereditary anemia characterized by the presence of oxygen-deficient sickle cells, episodic pain, and leg ulcers.
sickle feather *n.* Any of the long, curving feathers in the tail of a cock.
sick·le·mi·a (sĭk'ə-lē'mē-ə) *n.* The presence of sickle cells in the blood.
sick list *n.* A list of sick personnel, as in the armed forces.
sick·ly (sĭk'lē) *adj.* **-li·er, -li·est. 1.** Prone to sickness; ailing. **2.** Of, caused by, or associated with sickness: *a sickly pallor.* **3.** Conducive to sickness; unhealthful. **4.** Nauseating; sickening. **5.** Feeble; weak: *a sickly handshake.* *—tr.v.* **-lied, -ly·ing, -lies.** To make sickly: *"timidity . . . sicklies the whole cast of thought in action"* (Henry Adams). **—sick'li·ness** *n.* **—sick'ly, sick'li·ly** *adv.*
sick·ness (sĭk'nĭs) *n.* **1.** The condition of being sick; illness. **2.** A disease; malady. **3.** Nausea.
sick-out (sĭk'out') *n.* An organized action by employees who claim illness and absent themselves from work, usually to force the granting of demands or to avoid being penalized for striking formally.
sick pay *n.* Wages paid to an employee who is absent on sick leave.
sick·room (sĭk'rŏŏm', -rōōm') *n.* A room occupied by a sick person.
sic pas·sim (sĭk păs'ĭm) *adv.* Thus everywhere. Used to indicate that a term or idea is to be found throughout a text. [Lat.]
sid·dur (sĭd'ər, -ŏŏr') *n., pl.* **sid·du·rim** (sĭ-dŏŏr'ĭm). A Jewish prayer book containing prayers for the various days of the year. [Heb. *siddūr,* arrangement < *siddēr,* he arranged.]
side (sīd) *n.* **1.** *Math.* **a.** A line bounding a plane figure. **b.** A surface bounding a solid figure. **2.** A surface of an object, esp. a surface joining a top and bottom. **3.** A surface of an object that extends more or less perpendicularly from an observer standing in front: *the side of the ship.* **4.** Either of the two surfaces of a flat object, such as a piece of paper. **5. a.** The part within an object or area to the left or right of the observer or of its vertical axis. **b.** The left or right half of the trunk of a human or animal body. **6.** The space immediately next to someone or something: *stood at her side.* **7.** One of two or more contrasted parts or places within an area, identified by its location with respect to a center: *the north side of the park.* **8.** An area separated from another area by an intervening feature, as a line or barrier: *on this side of the Atlantic.* **9. a.** One of two or more opposing groups, teams, or sets of opinions. **b.** One of the positions maintained in a dispute or debate. **10.** A distinct aspect: *the cruel side of her nature.* **11.** Line of descent: *my aunt on my mother's side.* **12.** *Chiefly Brit. Slang.* Nerve; swagger. *—adj.* **1.** Located on a side: *a side door.* **2.** From or to one side; oblique: *a side view.* **3.** Minor; incidental: *a side interest.* **4.** In addition to the main part; supplementary: *a side benefit.* *—v.* **sid·ed, sid·ing, sides.** *—tr.* **1.** To be in agreement with; support. **2.** To be positioned next to. **3.** To provide sides or siding for: *side a barn.* *—intr.* To align oneself with a particular side: *sided with his wife in the argument.* ***—idioms.*** **on the side. 1.** In addition to the main portion. **2.** In addition to the main occupation or arrangement. **side by side.** Next to each other; close together. [ME < OE *sīde.*]

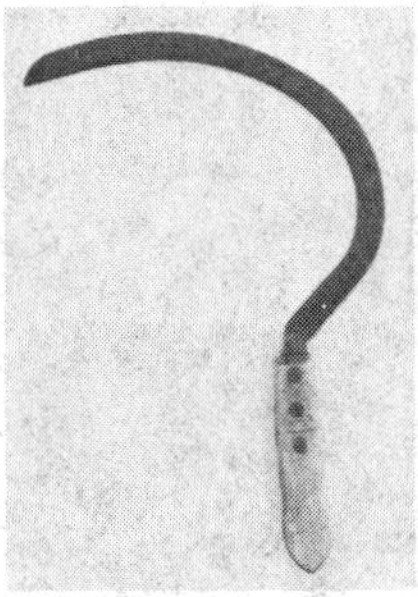
sickle

side·arm (sīd'ärm') *adj. Baseball.* Thrown with or marked by a sweep of the arm between shoulder and hip height: *a sidearm curve ball.* **—side'arm** *adv.*
side arm *n.* A small weapon, as a sword, bayonet, or pistol, carried at the side or waist.
side·band also **side band** (sīd'bănd') *n.* Either of the two bands of frequencies, one just above and one just below a carrier frequency, that result from modulation of a carrier wave.
side·bar (sīd'bär') *n.* A short news story that accompanies and presents sidelights of a major news story.
side·board (sīd'bôrd', -bōrd') *n.* A piece of dining-room furniture having drawers and shelves for linens and tableware.
side·burns (sīd'bûrnz') *pl.n.* Growths of hair down the sides of a man's face in front of the ears, esp. when worn with the rest of the beard shaved off. [Alteration of BURNSIDES.]
side·car (sīd'kär') *n.* **1.** A one-wheeled car for a single passenger, attached to the side of a motorcycle. **2.** A cocktail combining brandy, an orange-flavored liqueur, and lemon juice.

sidecar

sid·ed (sī'dĭd) *adj.* Having sides usually of a specified number or kind: *many-sided; marble-sided.* **—sid'ed·ness** *n.*
side dish *n.* A dish served as an accompaniment to the main course.
side drum *n.* A snare drum.
side effect *n.* A peripheral or secondary effect, esp. an undesirable secondary effect of a drug or therapy.
side-glance (sīd'glăns') *n.* **1.** A glance cast to the side. **2.** An indirect or casual reference; allusion.
side issue *n.* An issue aside from the primary point or issue.
side·kick (sīd'kĭk') *n. Slang.* A close friend and follower.
side·light (sīd'līt') *n.* **1.** A light coming from the side. **2.** *Naut.* Either of two lights, red to port, green to starboard, shown by ships at night. **3.** Incidental information.
side·line also **side line** (sīd'līn') *n.* **1. a.** A line along either of the two sides of a playing court or field, marking its limits. **b. sidelines.** The space outside such limits, occupied by spectators and inactive players. **c. sidelines.** The position or point of view of those who observe rather than participate in an activity. **2.** A subsidiary line of merchandise. **3.** An activity pursued in addition to one's regular occupation. *—tr.v.* **-lined, -lin·ing, -lines.** To remove or keep from active participation, as in athletic contests.
side·lin·er (sīd'lī'nər) *n.* One that remains on the sidelines, as during a game or an activity.
side·ling (sīd'lĭng) *adj.* **1.** Directed to one side; oblique. **2.** Sloping; inclined. *—adv.* Obliquely; sideways. [ME *sideling* < *side,* side.]
side·long (sīd'lông', -lŏng') *adj.* **1.** Directed to one side; sideways: *a sidelong glance.* **2.** Slanting; sloping. *—adv.* **1.** On or toward the side; sideways. **2.** Obliquely. [Alteration of SIDELING.]
side·man (sīd'măn') *n.* An instrumentalist in a jazz band.
sider– *pref.* Variant of **sidero-.**
si·de·re·al (sī-dîr'ē-əl) *adj.* **1.** Of, pertaining to, or concerned with the stars or constellations; stellar. **2.** Measured or determined by means of the stars: *sidereal time.* **3.** Relative to the stars. [< Lat. *siderus* < *sidus,* constellation.]
sidereal day *n.* The time required for a complete rotation of the earth, measured as the interval between two successive meridian transits of the vernal equinox, or 23 hours, 56 minutes, 4.09 seconds in units of mean solar time.

side-wheeler
The steamer *Nantucket*

sieve
Used in an archaeological excavation

sight
On a gun

sidereal hour *n.* A 24th part of a sidereal day.
sidereal month *n.* A month (sense 1).
sidereal time *n.* Time based upon the axial and orbital rotation of the earth with reference to the background of stars.
sidereal year *n.* The time required for one complete revolution of the earth about the sun, relative to the fixed stars, or 365 days, 6 hours, 9 minutes, 9.54 seconds in units of mean solar time.
sid·er·ite (sĭd′ə-rīt′) *n.* **1.** An impure yellowish-brown iron carbonate mineral. **2.** An iron meteorite. **—sid′er·it′ic** (-rĭt′ĭk) *adj.*
sidero– or **sider–** *pref.* Iron: *siderolite.* [< Gk. *sidēros,* iron.]
sid·er·o·lite (sĭd′ər-ə-līt′) *n.* A meteorite that contains iron, nickel, silicon, magnesium, and small amounts of other elements.
sid·er·o·sil·i·co·sis (sĭd′ə-rō-sĭl′ĭ-kō′sĭs) *n.* Pneumoconiosis caused by excessive inhalation of silica and iron dust.
sid·er·o·sis (sĭd′ə-rō′sĭs) *n.* Chronic inflammation of the lungs caused by excessive inhalation of dust containing iron salts or particles.
sid·er·o·stat (sĭd′ər-ə-stăt′) *n.* An optical system consisting of a rotating clock-driven mirror that reflects light from a celestial body in a relatively fixed direction to a fixed telescope or other bulky astronomical instrument. [Lat. *sidus, sider-,* constellation + -STAT.]
side·sad·dle (sīd′săd′l) *n.* A saddle designed so that a woman may sit with both legs on one side of the horse. *—adv.* On a sidesaddle.
side show *n.* **1.** A small show offered in addition to the main attraction, as at a circus. **2.** A diverting incident or spectacle.
side·slip (sīd′slĭp′) *intr.v.* **-slipped, -slip·ping, -slips. 1.** To slip or skid to one side. **2.** To slide sideways and downward in skiing. **3.** To fly sideways and downward in an airplane along the lateral axis to reduce altitude without gaining speed or as the result of banking too deeply.
side·spin (sīd′spĭn′) *n.* A rotary motion that spins a ball horizontally.
side·split·ting (sīd′splĭt′ĭng) *adj.* Very funny. **—side′split′ting·ly** *adv.*
side·step (sīd′stĕp′) *v.* **-stepped, -step·ping, -steps.** *—intr.* **1.** To step aside. **2.** To dodge an issue or responsibility. *—tr.* **1.** To step out of the way of. **2.** To evade; skirt. **—side′step′per** *n.*
side step *n.* **1.** A step to one side. **2.** A sideways step.
side-strad·dle hop (sīd′străd′l) *n.* A jumping jack (sense 2).
side stroke *n.* A swimming stroke in which a person swims on one side and thrusts his arms forward alternately while performing a scissors kick.
side·swipe (sīd′swīp′) *tr.v.* **-swiped, -swip·ing, -swipes.** To strike along the side of in passing. *—n.* A glancing blow on or along the side.
side·track (sīd′trăk′) *v.* **-tracked, -track·ing, -tracks.** *—tr.* **1.** To switch from a main track to a siding. **2.** To divert from a main issue or course. *—intr.* **1.** To run into a siding. **2.** To deviate from a main issue or course. *—n.* A railroad siding.
side·walk (sīd′wôk′) *n.* A walk or raised path for pedestrians along the side of a road.
sidewalk artist *n.* An artist who draws pictures, usually with chalk, on a sidewalk surface as a means of acquiring money from passers-by.
sidewalk superintendent *n. Informal.* A pedestrian who stops to watch construction or demolition work.
side wall *n.* A side surface of an automobile tire.
side·ward (sīd′wərd) *adj. & adv.* At or toward one side. **—side′wards** (-wərdz) *adv.*
side·ways (sīd′wāz′) also **side·way** (-wā′) or **side·wise** (-wīz′) *adv.* **1.** From one side. **2.** Toward one side; in a sideward direction. **3.** Presenting the side instead of the front or back. *—adj.* Toward or from one side.
side-wheel (sīd′hwēl′, -wēl′) *adj.* Of, pertaining to, or being a steamboat with a paddle wheel on each side.
side-wheel·er (sīd′hwē′lər, -wē′-) *n.* A side-wheel steamboat.
side-whis·kers (sīd′hwĭs′kərz, -wĭs′-) *pl.n.* Whiskers worn usually long on the sides of a man's face.
side·wind·er (sīd′wīn′dər) *n.* **1.** A small rattlesnake, *Crotalus cerastes,* of the southwestern United States and Mexico, that moves by a distinctive lateral looping motion of its body. **2.** A powerful blow by the fist delivered from the side. **3.** A short-range supersonic air-to-air missile.
side·wise (sīd′wīz′) *adv. & adj.* Variant of **sideways.**
sid·ing (sī′dĭng) *n.* **1.** A short section of railroad track connected by switches with a main track. **2.** Material, such as boards or shingles, used for surfacing a frame building.
si·dle (sīd′l) *v.* **-dled, -dling, -dles.** *—intr.* To move sideways; edge along esp. furtively or indirectly. *—tr.* To cause to move sidewise. *—n.* A sidelong step or movement. [Back-formation < SIDELING.] **—si′dling·ly** *adv.*
siege (sēj) *n.* **1.** The surrounding and blockading of a town or fortress by an army bent on capturing it. **2.** A prolonged period, as of illness. **3.** *Obs.* **a.** A seat. **b.** A seat of rule. *—tr.v.* **sieged, sieg·ing, sieg·es.** To besiege. [ME *sege* < OFr., seat < VLat. **sedicum* < Lat. *sedēre,* to be seated.]
Siege Perilous *n.* A seat at King Arthur's Round Table kept for the knight destined to find the Holy Grail and fatal for any other occupant.
Sieg·fried (sēg′frēd′, sĭg′-) *n.* A principal character of the *Nibelungenlied* and other medieval epics. [G. < OHG *Sigifrith* : *sigu,* victory + *fridu,* peace.]
sie·mens (sē′mənz) *n.* A unit of conductance equal to one ampere per volt. [After Werner von *Siemens* (1816–1892).]
si·en·na (sē-ĕn′ə) *n.* **1.** A special clay containing iron and manganese oxides, used as a pigment for oil and water-color painting. **2.** Raw sienna (sense 2). **3.** Burnt sienna. [Short for *terra-sienna* < Ital. *terra di Sienna,* earth of Siena < *Sienna,* Siena, a city in Italy.]
si·er·o·zem (sī-ĕr′ə-zĕm′, sē-ĕr′ə-zhôm′) *n.* Any of a group of soils found in cool to temperate arid regions that is brownish-gray at the surface with a lighter layer below and is based in a carbonate or hardpan layer. [R. *serozem* : *seryĭ,* gray + *zemlya,* earth.]
si·er·ra (sē-ĕr′ə) *n.* **1.** A rugged range of mountains having an irregular or serrated profile. **2.** Any of several mackerel-like fishes of the genus *Scomberomorus,* of tropical seas. [Sp. < Lat. *serra,* saw.] **—si·er′ran** *adj.*
si·es·ta (sē-ĕs′tə) *n.* A rest or nap, usually taken after the midday meal. [Sp. < Lat. *sexta (hora),* sixth (hour) < *sextus,* sixth.]
sieve (sĭv) *n.* A utensil of wire mesh or closely perforated metal used for straining, sifting, ricing, or puréeing. *—v.* **sieved, siev·ing, sieves.** *—tr.* To pass through a sieve. *—intr.* To sift. [ME *sive* < OE *sife.*]
sieve tube *n.* A series of cells joined end to end, forming a tube through which food is conducted in vascular plants.
sift (sĭft) *v.* **sift·ed, sift·ing, sifts.** *—tr.* **1.** To put through a sieve or other straining device in order to separate the fine from the coarse particles. **2.** To distinguish as if separating with a sieve: *sifted the candidates for the job.* **3.** To apply by scattering with or as if with a sieve. **4.** To examine closely and carefully: *sift the evidence.* *—intr.* **1.** To sift something. **2.** To pass through or as if through a sieve. **3.** To make a careful and critical examination: *sifted through the evidence.* [ME *siften* < OE *siftan.*] **—sift′er** *n.*
sift·ing (sĭf′tĭng) *n. Computer Sci.* An internal sorting technique in which data are displaced to permit the insertion of new data.
sift·ings (sĭf′tĭngz) *pl.n.* Material removed or separated with or as if with a sieve.
sigh (sī) *v.* **sighed, sigh·ing, sighs.** *—intr.* **1. a.** To exhale audibly in a long, deep breath, as in weariness or relief. **b.** To emit a similar sound: *willows sighing in the wind.* **2.** To feel yearning, longing, or grief; mourn. *—tr.* **1.** To express with or as if with an audible exhalation. **2.** *Archaic.* To lament. *—n.* The act or sound of sighing. [ME *sighen,* alteration of *siken,* to sigh < OE *sīcan.*] **—sigh′er** *n.*
sight (sīt) *n.* **1.** The ability to see. **2.** The act or fact of seeing. **3.** The field of one's vision. **4.** The foreseeable future; prospect: *no solution in sight.* **5.** Something that is seen. **6.** Something worth seeing: *the sights of London.* **7.** *Informal.* Something unsightly: *Her hair was a sight.* **8. a.** A device used to assist aim by guiding the eye, as on a firearm or surveying instrument. **b.** An aim or observation taken with such a device. **9.** An opportunity to observe or inspect. **10.** *Regional.* A large number or quantity. *—tr.v.* **sight·ed, sight·ing, sights. 1.** To see or observe within one's field of vision: *sight land.* **2.** To observe or take a sight of with an instrument: *sight a target.* **3.** To adjust the sights of (a rifle, for example). **4.** To take aim with (a firearm). ***—idioms.*** **out of sight.** *Slang.* Remarkable; incredible. **sight for sore eyes.** *Informal.* A person whose arrival or appearance is a cause for relief or joy. **sight unseen.** Without seeing the object in question: *buy a car sight unseen.* [ME < OE *gesihð,* something seen.]
sight draft *n.* A draft or bill that is payable upon demand or presentation.
sight·ed (sī′tĭd) *adj.* **1.** Having sight. **2.** Having eyesight of a specified kind: *keen-sighted.*
sight gag *n.* A comic bit or effect that depends on action rather than words.
sight·less (sīt′lĭs) *adj.* **1.** Blind. **2.** Invisible. **—sight′less·ly** *adv.* **—sight′less·ness** *n.*
sight·ly (sīt′lē) *adj.* **-li·er, -li·est. 1.** Pleasing to see; handsome. **2.** Affording a fine view. **—sight′li·ness** *n.*
sight-read (sīt′rēd′) *v.* **-read** (-rĕd′), **-read·ing, -reads.** *—tr.* To read or perform (music, for example) without preparation or prior acquaintance. *—intr.* To read or perform something at sight. **—sight′-read′er** *n.*
sight rhyme *n.* An eye rhyme.
sight·see (sīt′sē′) *intr.v.* **-saw** (-sô′), **-seen** (-sēn′), **-see·ing, -sees.** To engage in sightseeing. **—sight′se′er** *n.*
sight·see·ing (sīt′sē′ĭng) *n.* The act or pastime of touring places of interest. *—adj.* Used or engaged in sightseeing.
sig·il (sĭj′əl, sĭg′ĭl) *n.* **1.** A seal; signet. **2.** A sign or image considered magical. [Lat. *sigillum,* dim. of *signum,* sign.]
sig·ma (sĭg′mə) *n.* **1.** The 18th letter of the Greek alphabet, written Σ,σ. See table at **alphabet. 2.** *Physics.* Any of three subatomic particles in the baryon family. [Gk., of Phoenician orig; akin to Heb. *sāmehk,* samek.] **—sig′mate′** (-māt′) *adj.*
sig·moid (sĭg′moid′) also **sig·moi·dal** (sĭg-moid′l) *adj.*

1. Having the shape of the letter S. **2.** Of or pertaining to the sigmoid flexure of the colon. [Gk. *sigmoeidēs* : *sigma,* sigma + *-eidēs,* -oid.]

sigmoid flexure *n.* An S-shaped bend in the colon between the descending section and the rectum.

sign (sīn) *n.* **1.** Something that suggests the presence or existence of a fact, condition, or quality. **2.** An action or gesture used to convey an idea, a desire, information, or a command: *gave the go-ahead sign.* **3.** A board, poster, or placard displayed in a public place to advertise or to convey information or a direction. **4.** A conventional figure or device that stands for a word, phrase, or operation; a symbol, as in mathematics or musical notation. **5.** *pl.* **sign.** An indicator, such as a spoor or scent, of the presence or trail of an animal: *a deer sign.* **6.** A trace or vestige: *no sign of life.* **7.** A portentous incident or event; presage: *signs of a long cold winter.* **8.** A bodily manifestation that serves to indicate the presence of a malfunction or disease. **9.** One of the 12 divisions of the zodiac, each named for a constellation and represented by a symbol. —*v.* **signed, sign·ing, signs.** —*tr.* **1.** To affix one's signature to. **2.** To write (one's signature). **3.** To approve or ratify (a document) by affixing a signature, seal, or other mark: *sign a bill into law.* **4.** To relinquish or transfer title to by signature: *signed away all her claims to the estate.* **5.** To express or signify with a sign. **6.** To consecrate with the sign of the cross. —*intr.* **1.** To make a sign or signs; signal. **2.** To write one's signature. ***—phrasal verbs.*** **sign in.** To record the arrival of by signing. **sign off.** To stop transmission after identifying the broadcasting station. **sign on. 1.** To enlist oneself: *I signed on as a deck hand.* **2.** To start transmission after identifying the broadcasting station. **sign out.** To record the departure of by signing. **sign up.** To volunteer one's services; enlist. [ME *signe* < OFr. < Lat. *signum.*] **—sign'er** *n.*

Synonyms: *sign, badge, mark, token, indication, symptom, note.* These nouns are compared as they denote outward evidence of something. *Sign,* the most general, can mean virtually any such manifestation. *Badge* usually refers to something worn that denotes membership in a group or rank, achievement, or condition: *Her mink coat was a badge of success. Mark* can refer to a personal characteristic or indication of character: *Intolerance is the mark of a bigot.* It can also denote evidence of an experience: *Poverty had left its mark on him. Token* usually refers to a symbol, pledge, or proof of something intangible: *a token of affection. Indication* refers to evidence of a condition. *Symptom* suggests visible evidence of an adverse condition, such as a disease. *Note* applies to a distinguishing characteristic or feature: *the note of mysticism in his novels.*

sig·nal (sĭg'nəl) *n.* **1. a.** An indicator, as a gesture or mechanical device, serving as a means of communication. **b.** A message communicated by such means. **2.** Something that incites action: *The execution was the signal for mass protests.* **3.** *Electronics.* An impulse or fluctuating electric quantity, such as voltage, current, or electric field strength, whose variations represent coded information. **4.** The sound, image, or message transmitted or received in telegraphy, telephony, radio, television, or radar. ***—modifier:*** *a signal flare.* —*adj.* Out of the ordinary; conspicuous: *a signal feat.* —*v.* **-naled, -nal·ing, -nals** or **-nalled, -nal·ling, -nals.** —*tr.* **1.** To make a signal to. **2.** To relate or make known by signals. —*intr.* To make a signal or signals. [Fr. < OFr. < Med. Lat. *signale* < Lat. *signalis,* of a sign < *signum,* sign.] **—sig'nal·er** *n.*

sig·nal·ize (sĭg'nə-līz') *tr.v.* **-ized, -iz·ing, -iz·es. 1.** To make remarkable or conspicuous. **2.** To point out particularly. **—sig'nal·i·za'tion** *n.*

sig·nal·ly (sĭg'nə-lē) *adv.* Conspicuously.

sig·nal·ment (sĭg'nəl-mənt) *n.* A detailed description of the appearance of a person, as for police files. [Fr. *signalement* < *signaler,* to mark out < *signal,* signal.]

sig·na·to·ry (sĭg'nə-tôr'ē, -tōr'ē) *adj.* Bound by signed agreement. —*n., pl.* **-ries.** One that has signed a treaty or other document. [Lat. *signatorius* < *signare,* to mark < *signum,* sign.]

sig·na·ture (sĭg'nə-chər) *n.* **1.** The name of a person as written by himself. **2.** A distinctive mark, characteristic, or sound effect indicating identity. **3.** The act of signing one's name. **4.** The part of a physician's prescription containing directions to the patient. **5.** *Mus.* **a.** A sign used to indicate key. **b.** A sign used to indicate tempo. **6.** *Printing.* **a.** A letter, number, or symbol placed at the bottom of the first page of each form of printed pages of a book as a guide to the proper sequence of the sheets in binding. **b.** A large sheet printed with four or a multiple of four pages that when folded becomes a section of the book. [OFr. < *signer,* to sign < Lat. *signare,* to mark < *signum,* sign.]

sign·board (sīn'bôrd', -bōrd') *n.* A board bearing a sign.

sig·net (sĭg'nĭt) *n.* **1.** A seal, esp. one used on a document. **2.** The impression made with a signet. —*tr.v.* **-net·ed, -net·ing, -nets.** To mark or endorse with a signet. [ME < OFr., dim. of *signe,* sign.]

signet ring *n.* A finger ring bearing an engraved signet.

sig·ni·fi·a·ble (sĭg'nə-fī'ə-bəl) *adj.* Capable of being depicted by a sign or symbol.

sig·nif·i·cance (sĭg-nĭf'ĭ-kəns) also **sig·nif·i·can·cy** (-kən-sē) *n.* **1.** The state or quality of being significant. **2.** Meaning; import. **3.** Implied meaning; suggestiveness.

significance level *n.* Level of significance.

sig·nif·i·cant (sĭg-nĭf'ĭ-kənt) *adj.* **1.** Having or expressing a meaning; meaningful. **2.** Having or expressing a covert meaning; suggestive: *a significant glance.* **3.** Notable; valuable. [Lat. *significans, significant-,* pr.part. of *significare,* to signify.] **—sig·nif'i·cant·ly** *adv.*

significant digits *pl.n. Math.* The digits of the decimal form of a number beginning with the leftmost nonzero digit and extending to the right to include all digits warranted by the accuracy of measuring devices used to obtain the numbers.

sig·ni·fi·ca·tion (sĭg'nə-fĭ-kā'shən) *n.* **1.** The intended meaning; sense. **2.** The act of signifying; indication.

sig·nif·i·ca·tive (sĭg-nĭf'ĭ-kā'tĭv) *adj.* **1.** Indicative; significant. **2.** Suggestive; symbolic. **—sig·nif'i·ca'tive·ness** *n.*

sig·ni·fy (sĭg'nə-fī') *v.* **-fied, -fy·ing, -fies.** —*tr.* **1.** To serve as a sign of; betoken. **2.** To make known; intimate. —*intr.* To have meaning or importance. [ME *signifien* < OFr. *signifier* < Lat. *significare* : *signum,* sign + *facere,* to make.] **—sig'ni·fi'er** *n.*

si·gnior (sēn-yôr', -yōr') *n.* Signor.

si·gnio·ry (sēn'yə-rē) *n.* Variant of **signory.**

sign language *n.* A system of communication by means of hand gestures, used esp. by deaf people.

sign manual *n., pl.* **signs manual.** A signature, esp. that of a monarch at the top of a royal decree.

sign of the cross *n.* A gesture describing the form of a cross, made in token of faith in Christ or as an invocation of blessing, esp. in the Roman Catholic Church.

si·gnor (sēn-yôr', -yōr') *n., pl.* **si·gno·ri** (sēn-yôr'ē, -yōr'ē) or **si·gnors.** Used as a title of courtesy for an Italian man, equivalent to the English *Mr.* or *Sir.* [Ital. *signor,* var. of *signore.*]

si·gno·ra (sēn-yôr'ə, -yōr'ə) *n., pl.* **si·gno·re** (sēn-yôr'ā, -yōr'ā) or **si·gno·ras.** Used as title of courtesy for a married Italian woman, equivalent to the English *Mrs.* or *madam.* [Ital., fem. of *signore,* signore.]

si·gno·re (sēn-yôr'ā, -yōr'ā) *n., pl.* **si·gno·ri** (sēn-yôr'ē, -yōr'ē). Used as a title of courtesy for an Italian man, equivalent to the English *Mr.* or *sir.* [Ital. < Med. Lat. *senior,* lord < Lat., elder. —see SENIOR.]

si·gno·ri (sēn-yôr'ē, -yōr'ē) *n.* **1.** A plural of **signor. 2.** A plural of **signore.**

si·gno·ri·na (sēn'yə-rē'nə) *n., pl.* **-ne** (-nā) or **-nas.** Used as a title of courtesy for an unmarried Italian woman, equivalent to the English *Miss.* [Ital., dim. of *signora,* signora.]

si·gno·ry or **si·gnio·ry** (sēn'yə-rē) *n., pl.* **-ries.** A seigniory. [ME *signorie* < OFr. *seigneurie* < *seigneur,* seignior. —see SEIGNIOR.]

sign·post (sīn'pōst') *n.* **1.** A post supporting a sign that has information or directions for travelers. **2.** Something that serves as an indication, sign, or guide.

Sig·urd (sĭg'ərd) *n. Myth.* A Norse hero who slays the dragon Fafnir. [ON *Sigurðr.*]

Sikh (sēk) *n.* An adherent of Sikhism. —*adj.* Of or pertaining to the Sikhs or to Sikhism. [Hindi < Skt. *śiṣyaḥ,* pupil < *śikṣati,* he wishes to learn, desiderative of *śaknōti,* he is able.]

Sikh·ism (sēk'ĭz'əm) *n.* The doctrines and practices of a monotheistic Hindu religious sect founded in the 16th century.

si·lage (sī'lĭj) *n.* Fodder prepared by storing and fermenting green forage plants in a silo.

sil·ane (sĭl'ān', sī'lān') *n.* Any of a group of silicon hydrides with the general formula SiH that are analogous to the paraffin hydrocarbons. [SIL(ICON) + (METH)ANE.]

sild (sĭld) *n.* A young herring other than a sprat that is processed as a sardine in Norway. [Norw.]

si·lence (sī'ləns) *n.* **1.** The condition or quality of being or keeping silent. **2.** The absence of sound; stillness. **3.** A period of time without speech or noise. **4.** Refusal or failure to speak out; secrecy. —*tr.v.* **-lenced, -lenc·ing, -lenc·es. 1.** To make silent or bring to silence. **2.** To curtail the expression of; suppress: *silencing all criticism.* [ME < OFr. < Lat. *silentium* < *silēre,* to be silent.]

si·lenc·er (sī'lən-sər) *n.* **1.** One that silences. **2.** A device attached to the muzzle of a firearm to muffle the sound of firing.

si·le·ni (sī-lē'nī') *n.* Plural of **silenus.**

si·lent (sī'lənt) *adj.* **1.** Making no sound or noise; quiet. **2.** Not disposed to speak; taciturn. **3.** Unable to speak; mute. **4.** Refusing or failing to give information or an opinion; secretive. **5.** Not voiced or expressed; tacit: *silent admissions of guilt.* **6.** Inactive or undisturbed; quiescent: *a silent volcano.* **7.** Having no phonetic value; unpronounced, as the *b* in *subtle.* **8.** Having no sound track. Used of some motion pictures. [Lat. *silens, silent-,* pr.part. of *silēre,* to be silent.] **—si'lent·ly** *adv.* **—si'lent·ness** *n.*

Synonyms: *silent, reticent, reserved, taciturn, secretive, uncommunicative, noncommittal, tightlipped.* These adjectives describe persons who are sparing with speech. *Silent* can refer to literal speechlessness but more often merely implies habitual reluctance to speak. *Reticent* does not necessarily imply silence as a trait but rather suggests reluctance to speak out at a given time, particularly about one's personal

signal

affairs. *Reserved* suggests aloofness and habitual restraint in communicating. *Taciturn* also implies unsociableness and a characteristic tendency to be untalkative. *Secretive* implies an unwillingness to speak about matters that could be openly discussed and suggests deliberate concealment. *Uncommunicative* suggests the deliberate withholding of information. *Noncommittal* describes one who abstains from taking a stand or from committing himself in a discussion. *Tightlipped* implies rigid self-restraint in speech.

silent butler *n.* A small receptacle with a handle and a hinged cover, used for collecting ashes and crumbs.

silent partner *n.* One that makes financial investments in a business enterprise but does not participate in its management.

silent treatment *n.* The act or an instance of totally disregarding the object of one's contempt or disapproval as a means of expressing one's attitude: *gave her boss the silent treatment.*

si·le·nus (sī-lē'nəs) *n., pl.* **-ni** (-nī'). *Gk. Myth.* Any of various minor woodland deities or spirits and companions of Dionysus. [Lat. < Gk. *silēnos* < *Silēnos,* Silenus.]

Si·le·nus (sī-lē'nəs). *Gk. Myth.* A satyr, the foster father of Dionysus. [Lat. < Gk. *Silēnos.*]

si·le·sia (sī-lē'zhə, -shə) *n.* **1.** A smooth linen fabric first produced in Silesia. **2.** A twilled cotton fabric used for linings.

si·lex (sī'lĕks') *n.* **1.** *Obs.* Silica. **2.** Finely ground tripoli used as an inert paint filler. [Lat., hard stone, flint.]

silhouette

sil·hou·ette (sĭl'o͞o-ĕt') *n.* **1.** A drawing consisting of the outline of something, esp. a human profile, filled in with a solid color. **2.** An outline of something that appears dark against a light background. —*tr.v.* **-et·ted, -et·ting, -ettes.** To cause to be seen as a silhouette; outline. [Fr. < Étienne de *Silhouette* (1709–1767).]

silic– *pref.* Variant of **silici-**.

sil·i·ca (sĭl'ĭ-kə) *n.* A white or colorless crystalline compound, SiO_2, occurring abundantly as quartz, sand, flint, agate, and many other minerals and used to manufacture a wide variety of materials, notably glass and concrete. [NLat. < Lat. *silex,* hard stone, flint.]

silica gel *n.* Amorphous silica that resembles white sand and is used as a drying and dehumidifying agent, a catalyst and catalyst carrier, an anticaking agent in cosmetics, and in chromatography.

silo

sil·i·cate (sĭl'ĭ-kāt', -kĭt) *n.* Any of numerous compounds containing silicon, oxygen, and a metallic or organic radical, occurring in most rocks except limestone and dolomite, and forming the basis of common glass and bricks.

si·li·ceous (sĭ-lĭsh'əs) *adj.* Containing, resembling, pertaining to, or consisting of silica. [Lat. *siliceus,* of flint < *silex,* flint.]

silici– or **silic–** *pref.* **1.** Silicon: *silicate.* **2.** Silica: *silicify.* [< SILICON and SILICA.]

si·lic·ic (sĭ-lĭs'ĭk) *adj.* Pertaining to, resembling, or derived from silica or silicon.

silicic acid *n.* A jellylike substance, $SiO_2.nH_2O$, produced when sodium silicate solution is acidified.

sil·i·cic·o·lous (sĭl'ĭ-sĭk'ə-ləs) *adj.* Thriving in soil containing a high silica content.

sil·i·cide (sĭl'ĭ-sīd') *n.* A compound of silicon with another element or radical.

sil·i·cif·er·ous (sĭl'ĭ-sĭf'ər-əs) *adj.* Bearing, producing, or in partial combination with silica.

si·lic·i·fy (sĭ-lĭs'ə-fī') *tr. & intr.v.* **-fied, -fy·ing, -fies.** To convert or become converted into silica. **—si·lic'i·fi·ca'tion** *n.*

sil·i·cle (sĭl'ĭ-kəl) *n. Bot.* A short, flat silique. [Lat. *silicula,* dim. of *siliqua,* seed pod.]

sil·i·con (sĭl'ĭ-kən, -kŏn') *n. Symbol* **Si** A nonmetallic element occurring extensively in the earth's crust in silica and silicates, having both an amorphous and a crystalline allotrope, and used doped or in combination with other materials in glass, semiconducting devices, concrete, brick, refractories, pottery, and silicones. Atomic number 14; atomic weight 28.086; melting point 1,410°C; boiling point 2,355°C; specific gravity 2.33; valence 4. [< SILICA.]

silicon carbide *n.* A bluish-black crystalline compound, SiC, one of the hardest known substances, used as an abrasive and heat-refractory material and in single crystals as semiconductors, esp. in high-temperature applications.

silicon dioxide *n. Chem.* Silica.

sil·i·cone (sĭl'ĭ-kōn') *n.* Any of a group of semi-inorganic polymers based on the structural unit R_2SiO, where R is an organic group, characterized by wide-range thermal stability, high lubricity, extreme water repellence, and physiochemical inertness, used in adhesives, lubricants, protective coatings, paints, electrical insulation, synthetic rubber, and prosthetic replacements for bodily parts.

sil·i·co·sis (sĭl'ĭ-kō'sĭs) *n.* Fibrosis of the lungs caused by long-term inhalation of silica dust and resulting in a chronic shortness of breath.

si·lique (sĭ-lēk') *n.* A long pod that is divided by a membranous partition and splits at both seams, characteristic of fruit of the mustards and related plants. [Fr. < Lat. *siliqua,* seed pod.] **—sil'i·quous** (sĭl'ĭ-kwəs), **sil'i·quose'** (-kwōs') *adj.*

silk (sĭlk) *n.* **1. a.** The fine, lustrous fiber produced by certain insect larvae and spiders, esp. that produced by a silkworm to form its cocoon. **b.** Thread or fabric made from this fiber. **c.** A garment made from this fabric. **2. silks.** The brightly colored identifying garments of a jockey or harness driver. **3.** A silky, filamentous material, such as the styles forming a tuft on an ear of corn. —*intr.v.* **silked, silk·ing, silks.** To develop silk. Used of corn. [ME < OE *sioloc,* prob. of Slav. orig.]

silk cotton *n.* A silky fiber, such as kapok, attached to the seeds of certain trees.

silk-cot·ton tree (sĭlk'kŏt'n) *n.* Any of several trees of the family Bombacaceae, esp. *Ceiba pentandra,* native to tropical America and cultivated for its leathery fruit containing the silklike fiber kapok.

silk·en (sĭl'kən) *adj.* **1.** Made of silk. **2.** Resembling silk in texture or appearance; smooth and lustrous. **3.** Delicately pleasing or caressing in effect: *a silken voice.* **4.** Luxurious.

silk hat *n.* A man's silk-covered top hat.

silk oak *n.* A tree, *Grevillea robusta,* native to Australia, having divided leaves and showy clusters of orange flowers.

silk-screen process (sĭlk'skrēn') *n.* A method of producing a stencil in which a design is imposed upon a screen of silk or other fine fabric, with blank areas coated with an impermeable substance, and ink is forced through the cloth onto the printing surface. **—silk'-screen'** *v.* **(-screened, -screen·ing, -screens).**

silk-stock·ing (sĭlk'stŏk'ĭng) *n.* **1.** An aristocratic or wealthy person. **2.** *Informal.* A member or supporter of the Whig party formed during the early 19th century in the United States.

silk tree *n.* A tree, *Albizzia julibrissin,* native to the eastern Mediterranean area, having feathery compound leaves and clusters of pinkish flowers.

silk·weed (sĭlk'wēd') *n.* The milkweed (sense 1).

silk·worm (sĭlk'wûrm') *n.* Any of various caterpillars that produce silk cocoons, esp. the larva of a moth, *Bombyx mori,* native to Asia, that spins a cocoon of fine, lustrous fiber that is the source of commercial silk.

silk·y (sĭl'kē) *adj.* **-i·er, -i·est. 1.** Resembling silk; lustrous. **2.** Made of silk; silken. **3.** Having long, silklike hairs or a silky covering. **4.** Ingratiating; seductive. **—silk'i·ly** *adv.* **—silk'i·ness** *n.*

sill (sĭl) *n.* **1.** *Archit.* The horizontal member that bears the upright portion of a frame, esp. the base of a window. **2.** *Geol.* A relatively thin sheet of igneous rock intruded between beds of other rock. [ME *sille* < OE *sylle,* threshold.]

sil·la·bub (sĭl'ə-bŭb') *n.* Variant of **syllabub.**

sil·ly (sĭl'ē) *adj.* **-li·er, -li·est. 1.** Showing a lack of good sense; stupid. **2.** Frivolous. **3.** Semiconscious; dazed. [ME *syly,* defenseless, pitiable, alteration of *sely,* fortunate, holy < OE *gesælig,* blessed.] **—sil'li·ly** (sĭl'ə-lē) *adv.* **—sil'li·ness** *n.*

si·lo (sī'lō) *n., pl.* **-los. 1. a.** A tall, cylindrical structure in which fodder is stored. **b.** A pit dug for the same purpose. **2.** An underground shelter for a missile. —*tr.v.* **-loed, -lo·ing, -los.** To store in a silo. [Sp. < Lat. *sirus* < Gk. *siros,* pit for storing grain.]

si·lox·ane (sĭ-lŏk'sān', sī-) *n.* Any of a class of organic or inorganic chemical compounds of silicon, oxygen, and usually carbon and hydrogen, based on the structural unit R_2SiO, where R is CH_3, H, C_2H_5, or a more complex group. [SIL(ICON) + OX(YGEN) + (METH)ANE.]

silt (sĭlt) *n.* A sedimentary material consisting of fine mineral particles intermediate in size between sand and clay. —*v.* **silt·ed, silt·ing, silts.** —*intr.* To become filled with silt. —*tr.* To fill, cover, or obstruct with silt. [ME *cylte,* prob. of Scand. orig.]

silt·stone (sĭlt'stōn') *n.* Stone composed of hardened silt.

Sil·u·res (sĭl'yə-rēz') *pl.n.* A people described by Tacitus as occupying southwestern Britain at the time of the Roman invasion. [Lat.]

Si·lu·ri·an (sĭ-lo͝or'ē-ən, sī-) *adj.* **1.** *Geol.* Of, belonging to, or designating the geologic time, system of rocks, or sedimentary deposits of the third period of the Paleozoic era, characterized by the appearance of land plants. **2.** Of or relating to the Silures or their culture. —*n. Geol.* The Silurian period or system of deposits. [< SILURES (so called because the Silures lived in the part of Wales where the rocks were first identified).]

si·lu·rid (sĭ-lo͝or'ĭd, sī-) *adj.* Of or belonging to the family Siluridae, which includes various freshwater catfishes of Europe and Asia. —*n.* A silurid fish. [NLat. *Siluridae,* family name < Lat. *silurus,* a large freshwater fish < Gk. *silouros.*]

sil·va also **syl·va** (sĭl'və) *n.* **1.** The trees or forests of a region. **2.** A written work on the trees or forests of a region. [Lat., forest.]

sil·van (sĭl'vən) *adj. & n.* Variant of **sylvan.**

Sil·va·nus also **Syl·va·nus** (sĭl-vā'nəs) *n. Rom. Myth.* A god of forests, fields, and herding. [Lat. < *silva,* forest.]

sil·ver (sĭl'vər) *n.* **1.** *Symbol* **Ag** A lustrous white, ductile, malleable metallic element, occurring both uncombined and in ores such as argentite, having the highest thermal and electrical conductivity of the metals. It is highly valued for jewelry, tableware, and other ornamental use and is widely used in coinage, photography, dental and soldering alloys, electrical contacts, and printed circuits. Atomic number 47; atomic weight 107.870; melting point 960.8°C; boiling point 2,212°C; specific gravity 10.50; valences 1, 2. **2.** Silver as a commodity or medium of exchange. **3.** Coins made of silver. **4. a.** Domestic articles, such as tableware, made of or plated with silver. **b.** Tableware made of other metals, such as stainless steel. **5.** The color medium gray. **6.** A silver salt, esp. silver nitrate, used to sensitize paper. —***modifier:*** *silver buttons.* —*adj.* **1.** Having a lustrous medium-gray color: *silver hair.* **2.** Having a bell-like sound. **3.** Eloquent; persuasive: *a silver tongue.* **4.** Favoring the adoption of silver as a standard of currency. **5.** Of or designating a 25th anniversary. —*v.* **-vered, -ver·ing, -vers.** —*tr.* **1.** To cover, plate, or adorn with silver or a similar lustrous substance. **2.** To cause to resemble silver. **3.** To coat (photographic paper) with a film of silver nitrate or other silver salt. —*intr.* To become silvery. [ME < OE *siolfor.*]

silver age *n.* A period of history secondary in achievement to that of a golden age.

sil·ver-bell tree (sĭl′vər-bĕl′) *n.* Any of several trees or shrubs of the genus *Halesia,* esp. *H. carolina,* of the southeastern United States, having drooping, bell-shaped white flowers.

sil·ver·ber·ry (sĭl′vər-bĕr′ē) *n.* A North American shrub, *Elaeagnus commutata,* with silvery flowers, leaves, and berries.

silver bromide *n.* A pale-yellow crystalline compound, AgBr, that turns black on exposure to light and is used as the light-sensitive component on ordinary photographic films and plates.

silver certificate *n.* A paper money bill formerly issued as legal tender by the U.S. government in representation of deposited silver bullion.

silver chloride *n.* A white granular powder, AgCl, that turns dark on exposure to light and is used in photography, photometry, and optics.

silver cord *n.* The emotional bond between a mother and her offspring. [After *The Silver Cord,* a play by Sidney Howard (1891–1939).]

sil·ver·fish (sĭl′vər-fĭsh′) *n., pl.* **silverfish** or **-fish·es. 1.** Any of various fishes having silvery scales, such as a tarpon. **2.** A silvery, wingless insect, *Lepisma saccharina,* that often causes extensive damage to bookbindings and starched clothing.

silver fox *n.* **1.** A color phase of the North American red fox, *Vulpes fulva,* having black fur tipped with white. **2.** The fur of the silver fox.

silver iodide *n.* A pale-yellow, odorless powder, AgI, that darkens on exposure to light and is used in artificial rainmaking, in photography, and as an antiseptic.

sil·ver·ly (sĭl′vər-lē) *adv.* With a silvery appearance or tone.

sil·vern (sĭl′vərn) *adj.* Like silver; silvery.

silver nitrate *n.* A poisonous, colorless crystalline compound, $AgNO_3$, that becomes grayish black when exposed to light in the presence of organic matter and is used in photography, mirror manufacturing, hair dyeing, and silver plating and as an external medicine.

silver perch *n.* The mademoiselle.

silver plate *n.* Tableware, such as flatware or hollowware, made of or coated with silver.

silver protein *n.* A preparation of silver and protein, usually in the form of gelatin, used as an antibacterial agent.

sil·ver·rod (sĭl′vər-rŏd′) *n.* A North American plant, *Solidago bicolor,* related to the goldenrods but having white rather than yellow flowers.

silver salmon *n.* The coho salmon.

silver screen *n.* **1.** A screen for showing motion pictures. **2.** Motion pictures (sense 2).

sil·ver·side (sĭl′vər-sīd′) also **sil·ver·sides** (-sīdz′) *n.* Any of various marine and freshwater fishes of the family Atherinidae, characteristically having a silvery band along each side.

sil·ver·smith (sĭl′vər-smĭth′) *n.* A person who makes, repairs, or replates articles of silver.

silver spoon *n.* Inherited wealth: *born with a silver spoon in his mouth.*

silver standard *n.* A monetary standard under which a specified quantity of silver constitutes the basic unit of currency.

Silver Star *n.* A U.S. military decoration awarded for gallantry in action.

sil·ver-tongued (sĭl′vər-tŭngd′) *adj.* Having the power of fluent and persuasive speech; eloquent.

sil·ver·ware (sĭl′vər-wâr′) *n.* Articles, esp. tableware, made of or plated with silver.

sil·ver·weed (sĭl′vər-wēd′) *n.* A plant, *Potentilla anserina,* having yellow flowers and leaves that are silvery beneath.

sil·ver·y (sĭl′və-rē) *adj.* **1.** Containing or coated with silver. **2.** Like silver in luster; glittering: *"a fountain threw high its silvery water"* (Harriet Beecher Stowe). **3.** Having a clear, ringing sound. —**sil′ver·i·ness** *n.*

sil·vex (sĭl′vĕks′) *n.* A solid, toxic, selective herbicide, $C_9H_7O_3Cl_3$, used primarily against woody plants. [Lat. *silva,* forest + EX(TERMINATOR).]

sil·vi·chem·i·cal (sĭl′vĭ-kĕm′ĭ-kəl) *n.* Any of various chemicals derived from wood. [Lat. *silva,* forest + CHEMICAL.]

sil·vic·o·lous (sĭl-vĭk′ə-ləs) *adj.* Inhabiting forests. [< Lat. *silvicola,* inhabitant of the forest : *silva,* forest + *colere,* to dwell.]

sil·vi·cul·ture (sĭl′vĭ-kŭl′chər) *n.* The care and cultivation of forest trees; forestry. [Fr. : Lat. *silva,* forest + *culture,* culture.] —**sil′vi·cul′tur·al** *adj.* —**sil′vi·cul′tur·ist** *n.*

si·ma (sī′mə) *n.* The lower layer of the earth's outer crust, rich in silica, iron, and magnesium, that underlies the sial. [SI(LICA) + MA(GNESIUM).]

Sim·chas To·rah (sĭm′KHəs tôr′ə, tōr′ə) *n.* A Jewish holiday celebrated on the 23rd day of Tishri, marking the end of the Feast of Tabernacles. [Heb. *shimḥath tōrāh,* rejoicing over the Law.]

Sim·e·on (sĭm′ē-ən) *n.* **1.** In the Old Testament, the second son of Jacob and Leah and ancestor of the tribe of Israel descended from him. **2.** The man who, upon seeing the infant Jesus, spoke the Nunc Dimittis. [LLat. < Gk. *Symeōn* < Heb. *Shim'ōn* < *shāma',* he heard.]

sim·i·an (sĭm′ē-ən) *adj.* Pertaining to, characteristic of, or resembling an ape or monkey. —*n.* An ape or monkey. [< Lat. *simia,* ape < *simus,* snub-nosed < Gk. *simos.*]

sim·i·lar (sĭm′ə-lər) *adj.* **1.** Related in appearance or nature; alike though not identical. **2.** *Math.* Designating figures having corresponding angles equal and corresponding line segments proportional. [Fr. *similaire* < Lat. *similis,* like.] —**sim′i·lar·ly** *adv.*

sim·i·lar·i·ty (sĭm′ə-lăr′ĭ-tē) *n., pl.* **-ties. 1.** The condition or quality of being similar; resemblance. **2.** An instance in which objects are similar.

sim·i·le (sĭm′ə-lē) *n.* A figure of speech in which two essentially unlike things are compared, often in a phrase introduced by *like* or *as* as in: *He was as strong as a bull.* [Lat., neuter of *similis,* like.]

si·mil·i·tude (sĭ-mĭl′ĭ-to͞od′, -tyo͞od′) *n.* **1.** Similarity. **2.** Something closely resembling another; counterpart. **3.** *Archaic.* A simile, allegory, or parable. [ME < OFr. < Lat. *similitudo* < *similis,* like.]

sim·mer (sĭm′ər) *v.* **-mered, -mer·ing, -mers.** —*intr.* **1.** To cook gently just at or below the boiling point. **2.** To be filled with barely controlled anger or resentment; seethe. —*tr.* To cook (food, for example) gently just at or below the boiling point. —***phrasal verb.*** **simmer down. 1.** To reduce the liquid volume of by simmering. **2.** To become calm after excitement or anger. —*n.* The state or process of simmering. [Alteration of obs. *simper,* to simmer < ME *simperen.*]

sim·nel (sĭm′nəl) *n. Chiefly Brit.* **1.** A crisp bread made of fine wheat flour. **2.** A fruitcake eaten on festive occasions. [ME *simenel* < OFr. < Lat. *simila,* fine flour.]

si·mo·le·on (sĭ-mō′lē-ən) *n. Slang.* A dollar. [Orig. unknown.]

si·mo·ni·ac (sĭ-mō′nē-ăk′, sī-) *n.* A person who practices simony. —**si·mo′ni·ac′, si′mo·ni′a·cal** (sī′mə-nī′ə-kəl, sĭm′ə-) *adj.* —**si′mo·ni′a·cal·ly** *adv.*

Si·mon Le·gree (sī′mən lə-grē′) *n.* A brutal taskmaster. [After *Simon Legree,* a cruel slave dealer in the novel *Uncle Tom's Cabin* by Harriet Beecher Stowe.]

si·mon-pure (sī′mən-pyo͝or′) *adj.* **1.** Genuinely and thoroughly pure. **2.** Superficially or hypocritically virtuous. [< the phrase *the real Simon Pure,* after *Simon Pure,* a character impersonated by a rival in the play *A Bold Stroke for a Wife* by Susanna Centlivre.]

si·mo·ny (sī′mə-nē, sĭm′ə-) *n.* The buying or selling of ecclesiastical pardons, offices, or emoluments. [ME *simonie* < OFr. < LLat. *simonia,* after *Simon* Magus, a sorcerer who tried to buy spiritual powers from the Apostle Peter.] —**si′mo·nist** *n.*

si·moom (sĭ-mo͞om′) also **si·moon** (-mo͞on′) *n.* A strong, hot, sand-laden wind of the Sahara and Arabian deserts. [Ar. *samūm,* poisonous < *samma,* he poisoned.]

simp (sĭmp) *n. Slang.* A simpleton; fool.

sim·pa·ti·co (sĭm-pä′tĭ-kō′, -păt′ĭ-) *adj.* **1.** Of like mind or temperament; compatible. **2.** Having attractive qualities; pleasing. [Ital. < *simpatia,* sympathy < Lat. *sympathia.* —see SYMPATHY.]

sim·per (sĭm′pər) *v.* **-pered, -per·ing, -pers.** —*intr.* To smile in a silly or self-conscious manner. —*tr.* To utter or express with a simper. —*n.* A silly or self-conscious smile. [Of Scand. orig.] —**sim′per·er** *n.* —**sim′per·ing·ly** *adv.*

sim·ple (sĭm′pəl) *adj.* **-pler, -plest. 1.** Having or composed of one thing or part only. **2.** Not involved or complicated; easy: *a simple task.* **3.** Without additions or modifications; mere: *a simple "yes" or "no."* **4.** Without embellishment; not ornate or adorned: *a simple dress.* **5.** Not elaborate, elegant, or luxurious. **6.** Unassuming or unpretentious; not affected. **7.** Not guileful or deceitful; sincere. **8.** Humble or lowly in condition or rank: *a simple peasant.* **9.** Ordinary or common: *a simple head cold.* **10.** Not important or significant; trivial. **11.** Having or manifesting little sense or intellect; silly. **12.** *Biol.* Having no divisions or subdivisions; not compound: *a simple leaf.* **13.** *Mus.* Without overtones: *a simple tone.* —*n.* **1.** A single component of a complex, esp. one that is unanalyzable. **2.** A fool; simpleton. **3.** A person of humble birth or condition. **4.** A medicinal plant or the medicine obtained from it. [ME < OFr. < Lat. *simplus.*]

simple closed curve *n.* A Jordan curve.

simple equation *n.* A linear equation.

simple fraction *n.* A fraction in which both the numerator and the denominator are integers.

simple fruit *n.* A fruit, such as a pea pod, grape, or almond, that develops from a single pistil.

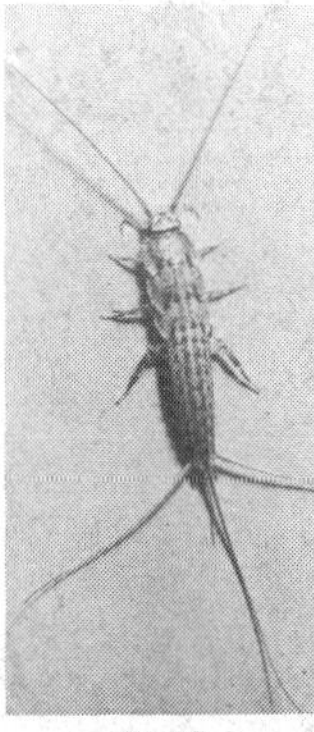

silverfish

simple harmonic motion *n. Physics.* A periodic motion that may be described as a sinusoidal function of time; specifically, the motion of a particle that obeys the equation $x = A\cos(kt + \phi)$, where x is the displacement of the particle from the origin at any time t, A is the maximum displacement, ϕ is the initial phase or angular displacement at $t = 0$, and k is a constant equal to 2π times the frequency of the oscillation.
simple honors *pl.n.* Three honors in trump or three aces at no-trump held by the same side in bridge.
simple interest *n.* Interest paid only on the original principal, not on the interest accrued.
simple machine *n.* A machine (sense 1.b.).
simple microscope *n.* A microscope having one lens or lens system, as a magnifying glass or hand lens.
sim·ple-mind·ed (sĭm′pəl-mīn′dĭd) *adj.* **1.** Not sophisticated; artless. **2.** Stupid or silly. **3.** Mentally defective. **—sim′ple-mind′ed·ly** *adv.* **—sim′ple-mind′ed·ness** *n.*
simple pendulum *n.* A pendulum (sense 1).
simple sentence *n.* A sentence having no coordinate or subordinate clauses, as *The cat purred.*
Simple Simon *n.* A foolish fellow; simpleton. [After *Simple Simon,* a character in a nursery rhyme.]
simple sugar *n.* A monosaccharide.
sim·ple·ton (sĭm′pəl-tən) *n.* A silly or stupid person; fool. [< SIMPLE.]
sim·plex (sĭm′plĕks′) *adj.* Denoting a system of telegraphy in which only one message may be sent in either direction at one time. [Lat. *simplex,* simple.]
sim·plic·i·ty (sĭm-plĭs′ĭ-tē) *n., pl.* **-ties. 1.** The property, condition, or quality of being simple. **2.** Absence of luxury or showiness; plainness. **3.** Absence of affectation or pretense. **4.** Lack of good sense or intelligence; foolishness. [ME *symplicite* < OFr. < Lat. *simplicitas* < *simplex,* simple.]
sim·pli·fy (sĭm′plə-fī′) *tr.v.* **-fied, -fy·ing, -fies.** To make simple or simpler; render less complex or intricate. [Fr. *simplifier* < Med. Lat. *simplificare* : Lat. *simplus,* simple + *facere,* to make.] **—sim′pli·fi·ca′tion** *n.* **—sim′pli·fi′er** *n.*
sim·plism (sĭm′plĭz′əm) *n.* The tendency to oversimplify an issue or problem by ignoring complexities or complications. [Fr. *simplisme* < OFr. *simple,* simple.] **—sim·plis′tic** (sĭm-plĭs′tĭk) *adj.* **—sim·plis′ti·cal·ly** *adv.*
sim·ply (sĭm′plē) *adv.* **1.** In a simple manner; plainly. **2.** Foolishly. **3.** Merely; only: *We knew him simply as Bill.* **4.** Absolutely; altogether: *simply delicious.* **5.** Frankly; candidly: *You are, quite simply, inadequate for this job.*
simply connected *adj.* Of, being, or characterized by a mathematical surface that is divided into two separate parts by every simple closed curve within it.
simply ordered *adj.* Having any three mathematical elements transitively related and any two elements equal or connected by an asymmetric relationship.
sim·u·la·cra (sĭm′yə-lā′krə, -lăk′rə) *n.* Plural of **simulacrum.**
sim·u·la·cre (sĭm′yə-lā′kər, -lăk′ər) *n. Archaic.* A simulacrum.
sim·u·la·crum (sĭm′yə-lā′krəm, -lăk′rəm) *n., pl.* **-la·cra** (-lā′krə, -lăk′rə). **1.** An image or representation of something. **2.** An unreal or vague semblance of something. [Lat. < *simulare,* to simulate < *similis,* like.]
sim·u·lar (sĭm′yə-lər, -lär′) *Archaic. —n.* One that simulates; simulator. *—adj.* Simulated; sham.
sim·u·late (sĭm′yə-lāt′) *tr.v.* **-lat·ed, -lat·ing, -lates. 1.** To have or take on the appearance, form, or sound of; imitate. **2.** To make a pretense of; feign: *simulate an interest.* *—adj.* (-lĭt, -lāt′). Simulated; assumed. [Lat. *simulare, simulat-* < *similis,* like.] **—sim′u·la′tive** *adj.*
sim·u·la·tion (sĭm′yə-lā′shən) *n.* **1.** The act or process of simulating. **2.** An imitation. **3.** The assumption of a false appearance.
sim·u·la·tor (sĭm′yə-lā′tər) *n.* One that simulates, esp. an apparatus that generates test conditions approximating actual or operational conditions.
si·mul·cast (sī′məl-kăst′, sĭm′əl-) *tr.v.* **-cast·ed, -cast·ing, -casts.** To broadcast simultaneously by FM and AM radio or by radio and television. *—n.* A simulcasted broadcast. [SIMUL(TANEOUS) + (BROAD)CAST.]
si·mul·ta·ne·ous (sī′məl-tā′nē-əs, sĭm′əl-) *adj.* **1.** Happening, existing, or done at the same time. **2.** *Math.* Collectively restricting the values of a set of variables: *simultaneous equations.* [Lat. *simul,* at the same time + E. *-aneous,* as in *instantaneous.*] **—si′mul·ta′ne·ous·ly** *adv.* **—si′mul·ta′ne·ous·ness, si′mul·ta·ne′i·ty** (-tə-nē′ĭ-tē, -nā′-) *n.*
sin¹ (sĭn) *n.* **1.** A transgression of a religious or moral law, esp. when deliberate. **2.** *Theol.* A condition of estrangement from God as a result of breaking God's law. **3.** An offense, violation, fault, or error. *—intr.v.* **sinned, sin·ning, sins. 1.** To violate a religious or moral law. **2.** To commit an offense or violation. [ME *sinne* < OE *synn.*]
sin² (sēn, sĭn) *n.* The 21st letter of the Hebrew alphabet. See table at **alphabet.** [Heb., var. of *shīn,* the letter shin.]
sin·an·thro·pus (sī-năn′thrə-pəs, sī-, sī′năn-thrō′pəs, sĭn′-ăn-) *n.* An extinct manlike primate of the genus *Sinanthropus,* which includes Peking man. [NLat. *Sinanthropus,* genus name : SINO- + *anthropus,* human being.]
sin·a·pism (sĭn′ə-pĭz′əm) *n.* A mustard plaster. [Fr. *sinapisme* < LLat. *sinapismus* < Gk. *sinapismos,* use of a mustard plaster < *sinapizein,* to apply a mustard plaster < *sinapi,* mustard.]
since (sĭns) *adv.* **1.** From then until now or between then and now: *He left town and hasn't been here since.* **2.** Before now; ago: *long since forgotten.* *—prep.* From a specified time in the past: *He has not been home since Easter.* *—conj.* **1.** During the time after which: *He hasn't been home since he graduated.* **2.** Continuously from the time when: *He hasn't spoken since he sat down.* **3.** As a result of the fact that; inasmuch as: *Since you're not interested, I won't tell you about it.* —See Usage notes at **ago** and **because.** [ME *sinnes,* contraction of *sithenes* < OE *siððan.*]
sin·cere (sĭn-sîr′) *adj.* **-cer·er, -cer·est. 1.** Not feigned or affected; true: *a sincere apology.* **2.** Presenting no false appearance; honest: *a sincere believer.* **3.** *Archaic.* Pure; unadulterated. [Lat. *sincerus.*] **—sin·cere′ly** *adv.* **—sin·cere′ness** *n.*

Synonyms: *sincere, natural, unaffected, unfeigned, wholehearted, hearty, heartfelt.* These adjectives describe what is genuine and free from dissimulation or artifice. *Sincere* emphasizes honesty of expression or behavior. It implies freedom from hypocrisy and usually a disposition to be constructive. *Natural* and *unaffected* stress absence of artificiality. *Natural* usually applies to appearance or behavior thought to express one's true nature, whereas *unaffected* may imply genuineness where the opposite could be expected. *Unfeigned* especially suggests freedom from falseness or deceit. *Wholehearted* and *hearty* imply not only genuineness of feeling but also its expression in convincing terms. *Wholehearted* suggests total commitment and unstinting devotion to a cause or the like. *Hearty* especially stresses convincing expression of feeling openly displayed. *Heartfelt,* in contrast, emphasizes depth of feeling rather than its display.

sin·cer·i·ty (sĭn-sĕr′ĭ-tē) *n.* The quality or condition of being sincere.
sin·ci·put (sĭn′sə-pət) *n., pl.* **sin·ci·puts** or **sin·cip·i·ta** (sĭn-sĭp′ĭ-tə). **1.** The upper half of the cranium, esp. the anterior portion above and including the forehead. **2.** The forehead. [Lat. : *semi-,* half + *caput,* head.] **—sin·cip′i·tal** (-sĭp′ĭ-tl) *adj.*
Sin·dhi (sĭn′dē) *n., pl.* **Sindhi** or **-dhis. 1. a.** The predominantly Moslem people of Sind. **b.** A member of this people. **2.** The Indic language of Sind. [Ar. *Sindī.*] **—Sin′dhi** *adj.*
sine (sīn) *n.* **1.** The ordinate of the endpoint of an arc of a unit circle centered at the origin of a Cartesian coordinate system, the arc being of length x and measured counterclockwise from the point (1, 0) if x is positive or clockwise if x is negative. **2.** In a right triangle, the function of an acute angle that is the ratio of the opposite side to the hypotenuse. [Med. Lat. *sinus* < Lat., curve.]
si·ne·cure (sī′nĭ-kyo͝or′, sĭn′ĭ-) *n.* **1.** An ecclesiastical benefice not attached to the spiritual duties of a parish. **2.** A position or office that requires little or no work but provides a salary. [< Med. Lat. *sine cura,* without cure of souls.] **—si′ne·cur·ism** *n.* **—si′ne·cur·ist** *n.*
sine curve *n.* The graph of the equation $y = \sin x$.
si·ne di·e (sī′nĭ dī′ē, sĭn′ā dē′ā′) *adv.* Without a day specified for a future meeting; indefinitely: *Parliament was dismissed sine die.* [Lat., without a day.]
si·ne qua non (sĭn′ĭ kwä nŏn′, nōn′, sī′nĭ kwā nŏn′) *n.* An essential element or condition. [Lat., without which not.]
sin·ew (sĭn′yo͞o) *n.* **1.** A tendon. **2.** Vigorous strength; muscular power. **3.** Often **sinews.** The source or mainstay of vitality and strength: *"Good company and good discourse are the very sinews of virtue"* (Walton). [ME *sinewe* < OE *sinu.*]
sine wave *n. Physics.* A waveform with deviation that can be expressed as the sine or cosine of a linear function of time or space or both.
sin·ew·y (sĭn′yo͞o-ē) *adj.* **1.** Like or consisting of sinew. **2.** Lean and muscular. **3.** Strong; vigorous.
sin·ful (sĭn′fəl) *adj.* Marked by or full of sin; wicked. **—sin′ful·ly** *adv.* **—sin′ful·ness** *n.*
sing (sĭng) *v.* **sang** (săng), **sung** (sŭng), **sing·ing, sings.** *—intr.* **1.** To utter a series of words or sounds in musical tones. **2.** To vocalize songs or musical selections. **3.** To give or have the effect of melody; lilt. **4.** To produce musical sounds when played. **5.** To make a high whine or hum: *The machine sang.* **6.** To be filled with a buzzing sound. **7.** To proclaim or extol something in verse. **8.** *Slang.* To give information or evidence against someone. *—tr.* **1.** To render in tones with musical inflections of the voice: *She sang the message.* **2.** To produce the musical sound of. **3.** To intone; chant. **4.** To proclaim or extol, esp. in verse: *sang his praises.* **5.** To bring to a specified state by singing: *sang the baby to sleep.* **—*phrasal verb.* sing out.** To call out loudly. *—n.* A gathering of people for group singing. [ME *singen* < OE *singan.*] **—sing′a·ble** *adj.*
sing-a·long (sĭng′ə-lông′, -lŏng′) *n.* A songfest.
singe (sĭnj) *tr.v.* **singed, singe·ing, sing·es. 1.** To burn superficially; scorch. **2.** To burn the ends of. **3.** To burn off the feathers or bristles of by subjecting briefly to flame. *—n.* A scorch. [ME *sengen* < OE *sengan.*] **—sing′er** (sĭn′jər) *n.*
sing·er (sĭng′ər) *n.* **1.** A person who sings, esp. a trained or professional vocalist. **2.** A poet. **3.** A songbird.
Sin·gha·lese (sĭng′gə-lēz′, -lēs′) also **Sin·ha·lese** (sĭn′-

"Simple Simon went a poaching/For to shoot some game./A mantrap caught him by the leg/Which gave poor Simon pain."

"He went for water with a sieve/But soon it all ran through . . ."

Simple Simon
Woodcut illustrations

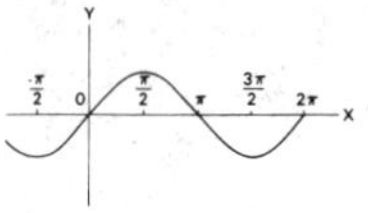

sine curve

hə-lēz′, -lēs′) *n., pl.* **Singhalese** also **Sinhalese. 1.** A people constituting the major portion of the population of Sri Lanka. **2.** The Indic language of the Singhalese that is the chief language of Sri Lanka. *—adj.* Of or pertaining to the Singhalese or their language. [Skt. *Simhala,* Sri Lanka + -ESE.]

sin·gle (sĭng′gəl) *adj.* **1.** Not accompanied by another or others; sole: *a single survivor.* **2. a.** Consisting of one form or part: *a single thickness; a single standard of excellence for all.* **b.** Consisting of one alone: *He had but a single thought, which was to escape.* **3.** Not divided; unbroken. **4.** Separate from others; distinct: *Every single person is different.* **5.** Designed to accommodate one person: *a single bed.* **6. a.** Unmarried. **b.** Of or relating to celibacy. **7.** *Bot.* Having only one rank or row of petals: *a single flower.* *—n.* **1.** A separate unit; individual. **2.** An accommodation for one person. **3.** An unmarried person. **4.** A one-dollar bill. **5. a.** *Baseball.* A one-base hit. **b.** A hit for one run in cricket. **c.** A golf match between two players. **d.** Often **singles.** A tennis match between two players. *—v.* **-gled, -gling, -gles.** *—tr.* **1.** To choose or distinguish from among others: *singled her out from the list of applicants.* **2.** *Baseball.* To cause (a baserunner) to score or advance by making a one-base hit: *singled him to second.* *—intr. Baseball.* To make a one-base hit. [ME *sengle* < OFr. < Lat. *singulus.*] **—sin′gle·ness** *n.*

Synonyms: *single, sole, unique, solitary, individual, separate.* These adjectives refer in various ways to the condition of being one in number. *Single* means one only, that is, not in accompaniment or association or combination with another or others. *Sole* stresses the idea of one and only, either in the sense of being the only one in existence or the only one involved in what is under consideration. *Unique* applies to what is the only one of its kind in existence. *Solitary* applies to what stands alone or to the condition of isolation. *Individual* makes specific reference to one person or thing distinguished from the mass to which it belongs or from all others. *Separate,* as compared here, implies the condition of being one and distinct by reason of being disunited from all others under consideration.

sin·gle-blind (sĭng′gəl-blīnd′) *adj.* Of, relating to, or being an experimental procedure in which the experimenters know the composition of the test and control groups but the subjects do not.

sin·gle-breast·ed (sĭng′gəl-brĕs′tĭd) *adj.* Closing with a narrow overlap and fastened down the front with a single row of buttons: *a single-breasted suit.*

single combat *n.* Combat between two individuals.

single entry *n.* A system of bookkeeping in which a business keeps only a single account showing amounts due and amounts owed.

single file *n.* A line of people, animals, or things standing or moving one behind the other. **—single file** *adv.*

sin·gle-foot (sĭng′gəl-fo͝ot′) *n.* A rapid gait of a horse in which each foot strikes the ground separately. *—intr.v.* **-foot·ed, -foot·ing, -foots.** To go at the single-foot.

sin·gle-hand·ed (sĭng′gəl-hăn′dĭd) *adj.* **1.** Working or done without help; unassisted. **2.** Designed for use with one hand. **3.** Having or using only one hand. **—sin′gle-hand′ed·ly** *adv.* **—sin′gle-hand′ed·ness** *n.*

sin·gle-heart·ed (sĭng′gəl-här′tĭd) *adj.* Characterized by sincerity and dedication. **—sin′gle-heart′ed·ly** *adv.* **—sin′gle-heart′ed·ness** *n.*

single knot *n.* An overhand knot.

sin·gle-mind·ed (sĭng′gəl-mīn′dĭd) *adj.* **1.** Having one overriding purpose or opinion. **2.** Steadfast. **—sin′gle-mind′ed·ly** *adv.* **—sin′gle-mind′ed·ness** *n.*

sin·gle-phase (sĭng′gəl-fāz′) *adj.* Producing, carrying, or powered by a single alternating voltage.

singles bar *n.* A bar patronized esp. by unmarried men and women.

sin·gle-space (sĭng′gəl-spās′) *v.* **-spaced, -spac·ing, -spac·es.** *—tr.* To type (copy) without leaving a blank line between lines. *—intr.* To type copy without line spaces.

sin·gle·stick (sĭng′gəl-stĭk′) *n.* **1.** A one-handed fencing stick fitted with a hand guard. **2.** The art, sport, or exercise of fencing with a singlestick.

sin·gle·stick·er (sĭng′gəl-stĭk′ər) *n. Informal.* A sailboat with one mast; sloop.

sin·glet (sĭng′glĭt) *n.* **1.** *Chiefly Brit.* A man's jersey undershirt. **2.** *Physics.* A multiplet with a single member.

single tax *n.* A system by which all revenue is derived from a tax on one object, esp. on land.

sin·gle·ton (sĭng′gəl-tən) *n.* **1.** A playing card that is the only one of its suit in a player's hand. **2.** An individual separated or distinguished from two or more of its group. [< SINGLE.]

single-track (sĭng′gəl-trăk′) *adj.* **1.** Having just one track. **2.** Lacking range or flexibility; one-track.

sin·gle·tree (sĭng′gəl-trē) *n.* A whiffletree.

sin·gly (sĭng′glē) *adv.* **1.** Without company or help; alone. **2.** One by one; individually.

sing·song (sĭng′sông′, -sŏng′) *n.* **1.** Verse characterized by mechanical regularity of rhythm and rhyme. **2.** A monotonously rising and falling speech cadence.

sing·spiel (sĭng′spēl′, zĭng′shpēl′) *n.* An 18th-century German musical comedy featuring folk songs interspersed with dialogue. [G. : *singen,* to sing + *Spiel,* play.]

sin·gu·lar (sĭng′gyə-lər) *adj.* **1. a.** Being only one; individual. **b.** Deviating strongly from a norm; rare. **2.** *Gram.* Of or being a word form denoting a single person or thing or several considered as a single unit. **3.** *Logic.* Of or relating to the specific as distinguished from the general; individual. **4.** Peculiar; eccentric. *—n. Gram.* **1.** The singular number or a form denoting it. **2.** A word having a singular number. [ME *singuler* < OFr. < Lat. *singularis* < *singulus,* single.] **—sin′gu·lar·ly** *adv.* **—sin′gu·lar·ness** *n.*

sin·gu·lar·i·ty (sĭng′gyə-lăr′ĭ-tē) *n., pl.* **-ties. 1.** The condition or quality of being singular. **2.** A trait marking one as distinct from others; peculiarity. **3.** Something uncommon or unusual. **4.** A black hole. **5.** *Math.* A point at which the derivative does not exist for a given function of a random variable but every neighborhood of which contains points for which the derivative exists.

sin·gu·lar·ize (sĭng′gyə-lə-rīz′) *tr.v.* **-ized, -iz·ing, -iz·es.** To make conspicuous; distinguish.

singular point *n.* A singularity (sense 5).

Sin·ha·lese (sĭn′hə-lēz′, -lēs′) *n. & adj.* Variant of **Singhalese.**

Si·ni·cism (sī′nĭ-sĭz′əm, sĭn′ĭ-) *n.* A custom or trait peculiar to the Chinese. [< Med. Lat. *Sinicus,* Chinese < LLat. *Sinae,* the Chinese. —see SINO-.]

Si·ni·cize (sī′nĭ-sīz′, sĭn′ĭ-) *tr.v.* **-cized, -ciz·ing, -ciz·es.** To change or modify by Chinese influence. [< Med. Lat. *Sinicus,* Chinese < LLat. *Sinae.* —see SINO-.]

sin·is·ter (sĭn′ĭ-stər) *adj.* **1.** Suggesting or threatening evil: *a sinister smile.* **2.** Presaging trouble; ominous: *sinister storm clouds.* **3.** On the left side; left. **4.** *Heraldry.* On the left of the bearer and hence on the right of the observer. [ME *sinistre* < OFr. < Lat. *sinister,* on the left, unlucky.] **—sin′is·ter·ly** *adv.* **—sin′is·ter·ness** *n.*

Synonyms: *sinister, baleful, malign, dire.* These adjectives apply to what is indicative of or threatens disaster or evil. *Sinister* usually implies impending or lurking danger that makes its presence felt indirectly by signs or portents. *Baleful* intensifies the sense of menace by suggesting a direct threat. The term can also refer to evil already present. *Malign* is generally applied to what is present and is either causing harm or exercising a great potential for evil. *Dire* describes what is in itself disastrous or the cause of great suffering or what represents a grave and direct threat of calamity.

sinister
Bend sinister

sin·is·tral (sĭn′ĭ-strəl, sĭ-nĭs′trəl) *adj.* **1.** Of or facing the left side. **2.** Left-handed. **3.** *Zool.* Designating or pertaining to a gastropod shell that has its aperture to the left when facing the observer with the apex upward. **—sin′is·tral·ly** *adv.*

sin·is·trorse (sĭn′ĭ-strôrs′) *adj.* Growing upward in a spiral that turns from right to left: *a sinistrorse vine.* [NLat. *sinistrorsus* < Lat., turned toward the left : *sinister,* left + *versus,* p.part. of *vertere,* to turn.] **—sin′is·trorse′ly** *adv.*

sin·is·trous (sĭn′ĭ-strəs, sĭ-nĭs′trəs) *adj. Archaic.* Sinister; ill-omened. **—sin′is·trous·ly** *adv.*

Si·nit·ic (sī-nĭt′ĭk, sĭ-) *n.* The branch of Sino-Tibetan that comprises Chinese. [SIN(O)- + *-itic,* as in *Semitic.*] **—Si·nit′ic** *adj.*

sink (sĭngk) *v.* **sank** (săngk) or **sunk** (sŭngk), **sunk, sink·ing, sinks.** *—intr.* **1.** To descend to the bottom. **2.** To move to a lower level, esp. to go down slowly or in stages. **3.** To appear to move downward. **4.** To slope downward; incline. **5.** To pass into a specified condition: *sank into a deep sleep.* **6.** To pass into a worsened physical condition: *The patient is sinking fast.* **7.** To become weaker, quieter, or less forceful: *His voice sank to a whisper.* **8.** To diminish, as in value. **9.** To feel great disappointment or discouragement. **10.** To seep; penetrate: *water sinking into the ground.* **11.** To make an impression; become understood: *The meaning finally sank in.* *—tr.* **1.** To cause to descend beneath a surface: *sink a ship.* **2.** To cause to drop or lower: *sank the bucket into the well.* **3.** To force into the ground: *sink a piling.* **4.** To dig or drill (a mine or well) in the earth. **5.** To make weaker, quieter, or less forceful. **6.** To debase the nature of; degrade. **7.** To suppress; hide. **8.** *Informal.* To defeat, as in a game. **9. a.** To invest. **b.** To invest without any prospect of return. **10.** To pay off (a debt). **11.** *Sports.* To get (the ball) into a hole or basket. *—n.* **1.** A water basin fixed to a wall or floor and having a drainpipe and generally a piped supply of water. **2.** A cesspool. **3.** A sinkhole. **4.** A place regarded as wicked and corrupt. [ME *sinken* < OE *sincan.*] **—sink′a·ble** *adj.*

sink·er (sĭng′kər) *n.* **1.** One that sinks. **2.** A weight used for sinking fishing lines or nets. **3.** *Slang.* A doughnut.

sink·hole (sĭngk′hōl′) *n.* A natural depression in a land surface communicating with a subterranean passage, generally occurring in limestone regions and formed by solution or by collapse of a cavern roof.

sinking fund *n.* A fund accumulated to pay off a public or corporate debt.

sin·less (sĭn′lĭs) *adj.* Free from sin. **—sin′less·ly** *adv.* **—sin′less·ness** *n.*

sin·ner (sĭn′ər) *n.* **1.** One who sins. **2.** A scamp.

Sinn Fein (shĭn fān′) *n.* An Irish political and cultural society founded in about 1905 to promote political and economic independence and the renewal of culture in Ireland. [Ir. Gael. : *sinn,* we + *féin,* self.]

Sino– *pref.* Chinese: *Sinology.* [Fr. < LLat. *Sinae,* the Chinese < Gk. *Sinai* < Ar. *Sīn,* China.]

si·no·a·tri·al (sī′nō-ā′trē-əl) *adj.* Of or pertaining to the sinoatrial node. [SIN(US) + ATRIAL.]

sinoatrial node *n.* A small mass of specialized cardiac muscle fibers located in the posterior wall of the right atrium of the heart that generates the initiating impulses of the heartbeat.

Si·no·logue also **Sin·o·log** (sī′nə-lôg′, -lŏg′, sĭn′ə-) *n.* A student of Sinology. [Fr., back-formation < *Sinologie,* Sinology.]

Si·nol·o·gy (sī-nŏl′ə-jē, sĭ-) *n.* The study of Chinese language, literature, or civilization. [Fr. *Sinologie* < *Sino-,* Sino- + *-logie,* -logy.] **—Si′no·log′i·cal** (sī′nə-lŏj′ĭ-kəl, sĭn′ə-) *adj.* **—Si·nol′o·gist** *n.*

Si·no·phile (sī′nə-fīl′, sĭn′ə-) *n.* One friendly to the Chinese and their interests.

Si·no-Ti·bet·an (sī′nō-tĭ-bĕt′n, sĭn′ō-) *n.* A language family that includes the Sinitic and Tibeto-Burman branches. **—Si′no-Ti·bet′an** *adj.*

sin·ter (sĭn′tər) *n.* **1.** *Geol.* A chemical sediment or crust, as of porous silica, deposited by a mineral spring. **2.** A mass formed by sintering. *—v.* **-tered, -ter·ing, -ters.** *—tr.* To weld together (metallic powder, for example) partially and without melting. *—intr.* To form a homogeneous mass by heating without melting. [G., iron dross.]

sin·u·ate (sĭn′yo͞o-ĭt, -āt′) also **sin·u·at·ed** (-ā′tĭd) *adj.* Having a wavy indented margin, as a leaf. [Lat. *sinuatus,* p.part. of *sinuare,* to bend < *sinus,* curve.] **—sin′u·ate·ly** *adv.* **—sin′u·a′tion** (-ā′shən) *n.*

sin·u·os·i·ty (sĭn′yo͞o-ŏs′ĭ-tē) *n., pl.* **-ties. 1.** The quality of being sinuous. **2.** A bending or curving shape or movement.

sin·u·ous (sĭn′yo͞o-əs) *adj.* **1.** Characterized by many curves or turns; winding. **2.** Supple and lithe. **3.** Sinuate. [Lat. *sinuosus* < *sinus,* curve.] **—sin′u·ous·ly** *adv.* **—sin′u·ous·ness** *n.*

si·nus (sī′nəs) *n.* **1.** A depression or cavity formed by a bending or curving. **2.** *Anat.* **a.** A dilated channel for the passage of chiefly venous blood. **b.** Any of various air-filled cavities in the cranial bones, esp. one communicating with the nostrils. **3.** *Pathol.* A fistula or channel to a suppurating cavity. **4.** *Bot.* A notch or indentation between lobes of a leaf or corolla. [Lat. *sinus,* curve, hollow.]

si·nus·i·tis (sī′nə-sī′tĭs) *n.* Inflammation of a sinus membrane, esp. in the nasal region.

si·nu·soid (sī′nə-soid′, -nyə-) *n.* A sine curve. [Med. Lat. *sinus,* sine < Lat., curve + -OID.] **—si′nu·soi′dal** (-soid′l) *adj.*

sinusoidal projection *n.* A map projection in which areas are equal to corresponding areas on a globe, the parallels and the prime meridian being straight lines and the other meridians being increasingly curved outward from the prime meridian.

Si·on (sī′ən) *n.* Variant of **Zion.**

Siou·an (so͞o′ən) *n.* A large North American Indian language family spoken from Lake Michigan to the Rocky Mountains and southward to Arkansas. [SIOU(X) + -AN.] **—Siouan** *adj.*

Sioux (so͞o) *n., pl.* **Sioux** (so͞o, so͞oz). **1. a.** Any of the various groups of Siouan-speaking North American Indian peoples formerly occupying parts of the Great Plains in the Dakotas, Minnesota, and Nebraska. **b.** An individual member of one of the Sioux groups. **2.** Any of the languages of the Sioux. [Fr., short for *Nadowessioux* < Ojibwa *nātowēssiwak,* the Dakota.] **—Sioux** *adj.*

sip (sĭp) *v.* **sipped, sip·ping, sips.** *—tr.* **1.** To drink delicately and in small quantities. **2.** To drink from in sips. *—intr.* To drink in sips. *—n.* **1.** The act of sipping. **2.** A small quantity of liquid sipped. [ME *sippen.*] **—sip′per** *n.*

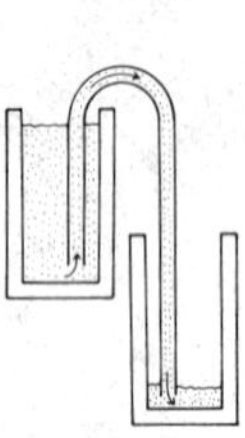

siphon

si·phon also **sy·phon** (sī′fən) *n.* **1.** A pipe or tube fashioned or deployed in an inverted U shape and filled until atmospheric pressure is sufficient to force a liquid from a reservoir in one end of the tube over a barrier higher than the reservoir and out the other end. **2.** *Zool.* A tubular organ, esp. of aquatic invertebrates such as squids or clams, by which water is taken in or expelled. *—v.* **-phoned, -phon·ing, -phons.** *—tr.* To draw off or convey through or as if through a siphon. *—intr.* To pass through a siphon. [Fr. < Lat. *sipho* < Gk. *siphōn,* tube.] **—si′phon·al, si·phon′ic** (sī-fŏn′ĭk) *adj.*

si·phon·o·phore (sī-fŏn′ə-fôr′, -fōr′, sī′fə-nə-) *n.* Any of various colonial marine coelenterates of the order Siphonophora, which includes the Portuguese man-of-war. [NLat. *Siphonophora,* order name : Lat. *sipho,* siphon + Gk. *pherein,* to bear.]

si·phon·o·stele (sī-fŏn′ə-stēl′, sī′fə-nə-stē′lē) *n.* A vascular tube surrounding the pith in the stems of certain plants. [SIPHON + STELE.] **—si·phon′o·ste′lic** (-stē′lĭk) *adj.*

si·phun·cle (sī′fŭng′kəl) *n.* **1.** A tubelike structure in the body of a shelled cephalopod, such as a chambered nautilus, extending through each chamber of the shell. **2.** A dorsal tube in an aphid, secreting a waxy fluid. [Lat. *siphunculus,* dim. of *sipho,* siphon.]

sip·pet (sĭp′ĭt) *n.* A small piece of toast or bread soaked in gravy or other juice. [< *sip,* alteration of SOP.]

sir (sûr) *n.* **1.** Often **Sir.** A respectful form of address used instead of a man's name. **2. Sir.** A title of honor used before the given name or the full name of baronets and knights. **3.** A gentleman of rank. [ME, var. of *sire.* —see SIRE.]

sir·dar (sûr′där′, sər-där) *n.* A person of high rank, esp. in India. [Hindi *sardār* < Pers. : *sar,* head + *-dār,* holder.]

sire (sīr) *n.* **1. a.** A father. **b.** *Archaic.* A male ancestor; forefather. **2.** The male parent of an animal, esp. a domesticated mammal such as a horse. **3.** *Archaic.* A gentleman of rank. **4.** *Archaic.* A title and form of address to a superior, used esp. in addressing a king. *—tr.v.* **sired, sir·ing, sires.** To beget. [ME < OFr. < Lat. *senior,* older, comp. of *senex,* old.]

sir·ee (sə-rē′) *n.* Variant of **sirree.**

si·ren (sī′rən) *n.* **1.** Often **Siren.** *Gk. Myth.* One of a group of sea nymphs who by their sweet singing lured mariners to destruction on the rocks surrounding their island. **2.** A beautiful, seductive woman; temptress. **3. a.** A device in which compressed air or steam is driven against a rotating perforated disk to create a loud, penetrating whistle, wailing, or other sound as a signal or warning. **b.** An instrument producing a similar sound as a signal or warning. **4.** Any of several North American amphibians of the family Sirenidae, having an eellike body and no hind limbs. [ME < OFr. *sereine* < LLat. *sirena* < Lat. *Siren* < Gk. *Seirēn.*]

si·re·ni·an (sī-rē′nē-ən) *n.* A herbivorous aquatic mammal of the order Sirenia, which includes the manatee and the dugong. *—adj.* Of or belonging to the Sirenia. [< NLat. *Sirenia,* order name < Lat. *Siren,* siren.]

siren song *n.* An enticing plea or appeal, esp. one that is deceptively alluring.

Sir·i·us (sĭr′ē-əs) *n.* A star in the constellation Canis Major, the brightest star in the sky, approximately 8.7 light years distant from Earth. [Lat. < Gk. *Seirios* < *seirios,* burning.]

sir·loin (sûr′loin′) *n.* A cut of meat, esp. of beef, from the upper part of the loin between the rump and the porterhouse. [OFr. *surlonge* : *sur,* above (< Lat. *super*) + *longe,* loin < Lat. *lumbus.*]

si·roc·co (sə-rŏk′ō) also **sci·roc·co** (shə-) *n., pl.* **-cos. 1.** A hot, humid south or southeast wind of southern Italy, Sicily, and the Mediterranean islands, originating in the Sahara as a dry, dusty wind but becoming moist as it passes over the Mediterranean. **2.** A hot or warm southerly wind, esp. one moving toward a low barometric pressure center. [Ital. < Ar. *sharq,* east.]

sir·rah (sĭr′ə) *n. Obs.* Mister; fellow. Used as a contemptuous form of address. [Alteration of SIR.]

sir·ree also **sir·ee** (sə-rē′) *n. Informal.* Sir. Used after *yes* or *no* for emphasis.

sir·up (sĭr′əp, sûr′-) *n.* Variant of **syrup.**

sir·vente (sîr-vänt′) also **sir·ven·tes** (-vĕn′təs) *n., pl.* **-ventes** (-vänt′, -vänts′) also **-ven·tes** (-vĕn′təs). A form of lyric verse of the Provençal troubadours satirizing political, social, or moral themes. [Fr. < Prov. *sirventes* < *sirvent,* servant < Lat. *serviens,* pr.part. of *servire,* to serve < *servus,* servant.]

sis (sĭs) *n. Informal.* Sister.

si·sal (sī′səl, -zəl) *n.* **1.** A fleshy plant, *Agave sisalana,* native to Mexico, widely cultivated for its large leaves that yield a stiff fiber used for cordage and rope. **2. a.** The fiber of the sisal. **b.** The fiber of certain similar or related plants. [Mex. Sp., after *Sisal,* a town in Yucatán.]

sis·kin (sĭs′kĭn) *n.* Any of several small birds of the family Fringillidae, esp. *Carduelis spinus,* of Eurasia, or the pine siskin. [MDu. *sīseken,* dim. of MLG *sīsek,* of Slav. orig.]

sis·si·fied (sĭs′ə-fīd′) *adj.* Of, relating to, or having the characteristics of a sissy; effeminate.

sis·sy (sĭs′ē) *n., pl.* **-sies. 1.** An effeminate boy or man; milksop. **2.** A timid or cowardly person. **3.** *Informal.* Sister. [< *sis,* short for SISTER.] **—sis′sy** *adj.*

sissy bar *n. Informal.* A narrow, inverted bar shaped like a U that rises from behind the seat of a motorcycle or bicycle and that supports the driver or a passenger.

sis·ter (sĭs′tər) *n.* **1. a.** A female having the same mother and father as another. **b.** A female having one parent in common with another. **2.** A female who shares a common ancestry, allegiance, character, or purpose with another or others, specifically: **a.** A kinswoman. **b.** A female fellow member, as of a sorority. **c.** A fellow woman, friend, or companion. **3.** *Informal.* A girl or woman. Used as a form of direct address. **4. Sister.** *Eccles.* **a.** A member of a religious order of women; nun. **b.** A form of address for such a person. **5.** *Chiefly Brit.* A nurse, esp. the head nurse in a ward. **6.** One identified as female and closely related to another: *"the sisters Death and Night"* (Walt Whitman). [ME, partly < OE *sweostor,* and partly of Scand. orig.]

sis·ter·hood (sĭs′tər-ho͝od′) *n.* **1.** The state or relationship of being a sister or sisters. **2.** The quality of being sisterly. **3.** A society, esp. a religious society, of women. **4.** Association or unification of women in a common cause: *the sisterhood of feminists.*

sis·ter-in-law (sĭs′tər-ĭn-lô′) *n., pl.* **sis·ters-in-law. 1.** The sister of one's husband or wife. **2.** The wife of one's brother. **3.** The wife of the brother of one's spouse.

sis·ter·ly (sĭs′tər-lē) *adj.* Characteristic of or befitting a sister or sisters. *—adv.* As a sister. **—sis′ter·li·ness** *n.*

Sis·tine (sĭs′tēn′, sĭ-stēn′) also **Six·tine** (sĭk′stēn′, -stīn′) *adj.*

1. Of or concerning one of the popes named Sixtus. **2.** Of or relating to the Sistine Chapel in the Vatican. [Ital. *sistino* < NLat. *sixtinus* < *Sixtus,* the name of several popes.]

sis·trum (sĭs'trəm) *n., pl.* **-trums** or **-tra** (-trə). A percussion instrument of ancient Egypt consisting of metal rods or loops attached to a metal frame. [ME < Lat. < Gk. *seistron* < *seiein,* to shake.]

Sis·y·phus (sĭs'ə-fəs) *n. Gk. Myth.* A cruel king of Corinth condemned forever to roll a huge stone up a hill in Hades only to have it roll down again on nearing the top. **—Sis'y·phe'an** (-fē'ən) *adj.*

sit (sĭt) *v.* **sat** (săt), **sit·ting, sits.** *—intr.* **1.** To rest with the torso vertical and the body supported upon the buttocks. **2.** To rest with the hindquarters lowered onto a supporting surface. Used of animals. **3.** To perch. Used of birds. **4.** To cover eggs for hatching; brood. **5.** To be situated; lie: *a house that sits on a hill.* **6.** To pose for an artist or photographer. **7. a.** To occupy a seat as a member of a body of officials: *sit in Congress.* **b.** To be in session. **8.** To remain inactive or unused. **9.** To lie or rest in a specified manner: *sit idle.* **10.** To affect one with or as if with a burden; weigh: *Official duties sat heavily on him.* **11.** To fit, fall, or drape in a specified manner: *The jacket sits perfectly on you.* **12.** To be agreeable to one; please: *The idea didn't sit well with him.* **13.** *Chiefly Brit.* To take an examination, as for a degree. **14.** To blow from a particular direction. Used of the wind. **15.** To baby-sit or keep watch. *—tr.* **1.** To cause to sit; seat: *Sit yourself over there.* **2.** To keep one's seat upon (an animal). ***—phrasal verbs.*** **sit down.** To take a seat. **sit in. 1.** To attend or participate in as a visitor: *sat in on the discussion.* **2.** To take part in a sit-in. **sit on** (or **upon**). *Informal.* **1.** To suppress or repress: *sat on the evidence.* **2.** To rebuke sharply; reprimand. **sit out. 1.** To stay until the end of. **2.** To refrain from taking part in: *sit out a dance.* **sit up. 1.** To stay up later than the customary bedtime. **2.** To become suddenly alert: *sit up and take notice.* ***—idioms.*** **sit on (one's) hands.** To fail to act. **sit pretty.** *Informal.* To be in a very favorable position. **sit tight.** *Informal.* To be patient and await the next move. —See Usage note at **set.** [ME *sitten* < OE *sittan.*]

si·tar (sĭ-tär') *n.* A Hindu stringed instrument made of seasoned gourds and teak and having a track of 20 metal frets with 6 or 7 main playing strings above and 13 sympathetic resonating strings below. [Hindi *sitār* < Pers. : *si,* three + *tār,* string.] **—si·tar'ist** *n.*

sit·com also **sit-com** (sĭt'kŏm') *n. Informal.* A situation comedy.

sit-down (sĭt'doun') *n.* **1.** A work stoppage in which the workers refuse to leave their place of employment pending agreement. **2.** An obstruction of normal activity, as of an office, by the act of a large group sitting down to express a grievance or protest. *—adj.* Performed or accomplished while sitting down: *a sit-down dinner.*

site (sīt) *n.* **1.** The place where something was, is, or is to be located. **2.** The place or setting of an event. *—tr.v.* **sit·ed, sit·ing, sites.** To situate or locate on a site: *sited the power plant by the river.* [ME < OFr. < Lat. *situs,* place < p.part. of *sinere,* to allow, put.]

sith (sĭth) *conj. Archaic.* Since. [ME *sithe* < OE *siððan,* since.] **—sith** *adv. & prep.*

sit-in (sĭt'ĭn') *n.* **1.** A protest demonstration in which participants seat themselves in an appropriate place and refuse to move until their demands are considered or met. **2.** An act of occupying the seats or an area of a segregated establishment to protest racial discrimination.

si·tol·o·gy (sī-tŏl'ə-jē) *n.* The science of foods, nutrition, and diet. [Gk. *sitos,* food, grain + -LOGY.]

si·tos·ter·ol (sī-tŏs'tə-rôl', -rōl', sĭ-) *n.* Any of a group of sterols that occur in plants and are used in the synthesis of steroid hormones. [Gk. *sitos,* food, grain + STEROL.]

sit·ter (sĭt'ər) *n.* **1.** One that sits, esp. a baby sitter. **2.** A brooding hen.

sit·ting (sĭt'ĭng) *n.* **1.** The act or position of one that sits. **2.** A period during which one is seated and occupied with a single activity, as posing for a portrait or reading a book. **3.** A session, as of a legislature or court. **4. a.** An incubation period. **b.** The number of eggs under a brooding bird.

sitting duck *n. Informal.* An easy target or victim.

sitting room *n.* A living room.

sit·u·ate (sĭch'o͞o-āt') *tr.v.* **-at·ed, -at·ing, -ates. 1.** To place in a certain spot or position; locate. **2.** To place under particular circumstances or in a given condition. *—adj.* (-ĭt, -āt'). *Archaic.* Situated. [Med. Lat. *situare, situat-,* to put < Lat. *situs,* place.]

sit·u·a·tion (sĭch'o͞o-ā'shən) *n.* **1. a.** The way in which something is positioned vis-à-vis its surroundings. **b.** The place in which something is situated; location. **2.** Position with regard to surrounding conditions and attendant circumstances; status. **3.** A combination of circumstances at a given moment; state of affairs: *the international situation.* **4.** A critical or problematic combination of circumstances. **5.** A position of employment; post. **—sit'u·a'tion·al** *adj.*

situation comedy *n.* A humorous radio or television series with a continuing cast of characters.

situation ethics *n. (used with a pl. verb).* A system of ethics based on brotherly love in which acts are morally evaluated within a situational context rather than by application of moral absolutes.

sit-up (sĭt'ŭp') *n.* A physical exercise in which one uses the abdominal muscles to raise the torso from a supine to a sitting position with or without bending the knees and then returns to the original position.

si·tus (sī'təs) *n., pl.* **situs.** Position, esp. normal position, as of a bodily organ. [Lat., place.]

sitz bath (sĭts) *n.* **1.** A tub in which one bathes in a sitting position. **2.** A bath taken in a sitz bath, esp. for therapeutic reasons. [Partial transl. of G. *Sitzbad* : *Sitz,* act of sitting + *Bad,* bath.]

sitz·krieg (sĭt'skrēg', zĭt'-) *n.* Warfare marked by a lack of aggression or progress. [G. : *sitz,* act of sitting + *Krieg,* war.]

sitz·mark (sĭt'smärk', zĭt'-) *n.* A hollow made in the snow by a skier falling backward. [Partial transl. of G. *sitzmarke* : *sitz,* act of sitting + *Marke,* mark.]

Si·va (shē'və, sē'-, shĭv'ə, sĭv'ə) *n.* Variant of **Shiva.**

Si·van (sĭv'ən) *n.* The ninth month of the Hebrew year. See table at **calendar.** [Heb. *Sīwān.*]

six (sĭks) *n.* **1.** The cardinal number that is next after the number 5 and equal to the sum of 5 + 1. **2.** The sixth in a set or sequence. **3.** Something having six parts, units, or members, esp. a motor vehicle having six cylinders. ***—idiom.*** **at sixes and sevens.** In a state of confusion or disorder. [ME < OE *siex,* akin to G. *sechs,* Lat. *sex,* Gk. *hex,* and Skt. *ṣaṣ.*] **—six** *adj. & pron.*

six-gun (sĭks'gŭn') *n.* A six-shooter.

six-pack (sĭks'păk') *n.* **1.** Six units of a commodity, esp. six cans or bottles of a beverage sold in a pack. **2.** The contents of a six-pack.

six·pence (sĭks'pəns) *n. Chiefly Brit.* **1.** A former coin worth six pennies. **2.** The sum of six pennies.

six·pen·ny (sĭks'pə-nē) *adj.* **1.** Valued at, selling for, or worth sixpence. **2.** Of little worth; paltry. **3.** (sĭks'pĕn'ē). Denoting a size of nails, generally two inches.

six-shoot·er (sĭks'sho͞o'tər) *n. Informal.* A six-chambered revolver.

six·teen (sĭk-stēn') *n.* **1.** The cardinal number that is next after the number 15 and equal to the sum of 15 + 1. **2.** The sixteenth in a set or sequence. [ME *sixtene* < OE *sixtyne.*] **—six·teen'** *adj. & pron.*

six·teen·mo (sĭk-stēn'mō) *n., pl.* **-mos.** Sextodecimo.

six·teenth (sĭk-stēnth') *n.* **1.** The ordinal number that matches the number 16 in a series. **2.** One of 16 equal parts. **—six·teenth'** *adj. & adv.*

sixteenth note *n. Mus.* A note having $^1/_{16}$ the time value of a whole note.

sixth (sĭksth) *n.* **1.** The ordinal number that matches the number 6 in a series. **2.** One of six equal parts. **3.** *Mus.* **a.** An interval of six degrees in a diatonic scale. **b.** A tone separated by this interval from a given tone. **c.** The harmonic combination of two tones separated by this interval. **d.** The sixth tone of a scale; submediant. **—sixth** *adj. & adv.*

sixth sense *n.* A power of perception seemingly independent of the five senses; intuition.

six·ti·eth (sĭk'stē-ĭth) *n.* **1.** The ordinal number that matches the number 60 in a series. **2.** One of 60 equal parts. **—six'ti·eth** *adj. & adv.*

Six·tine (sĭk'stēn', -stīn') *adj.* Variant of **Sistine.**

six·ty (sĭks'tē) *n.* The cardinal number equal to 6 × 10. [ME < OE *siextig* : *siex,* six + *-tig,* -ty.] **—six'ty** *adj. & pron.*

six·ty-fourth note (sĭk'stē-fôrth', -fōrth') *n. Mus.* A note having $^1/_{64}$ the time value of a whole note.

siz·a·ble also **size·a·ble** (sī'zə-bəl) *adj.* Of considerable size; fairly large. **—siz'a·ble·ness** *n.* **—siz'a·bly** *adv.*

size[1] (sīz) *n.* **1.** The physical dimensions, proportions, magnitude, or extent of something. **2.** Any of a series of graduated categories of dimension whereby manufactured articles are classified. **3.** Considerable extent, amount, or dimensions. **4.** Moral or mental qualities, rank, or status with reference to relative importance or the capacity to meet given requirements. **5.** The actual state of affairs: *That's about the size of the situation.* *—tr.v.* **sized, siz·ing, siz·es. 1.** To arrange, classify, or distribute according to size. **2.** To make, cut, or shape to a required size. ***—phrasal verb.*** **size up. 1.** To make an estimate, opinion, or judgment of: *sized up her opponent.* **2.** To meet given specifications or requirements. [ME *syse* < OFr. *sise* < *assise,* act of sitting. —see ASSIZE.]

size[2] (sīz) *n.* Any of several gelatinous or glutinous substances usually made from glue, wax, or clay and used as a glaze or filler for porous materials such as paper, cloth, or wall surfaces. *—tr.v.* **sized, siz·ing, siz·es.** To treat or coat with size or a similar substance. [ME *syse.*] **—siz'y** *adj.*

size·a·ble (sī'zə-bəl) *adj.* Variant of **sizable.**

sized (sīzd) *adj.* Having a particular or specified size: *medium-sized.*

siz·ing (sī'zĭng) *n.* **1.** A glaze or filler; size. **2.** The treatment of a fabric or other surface with size.

siz·zle (sĭz'əl) *intr.v.* **-zled, -zling, -zles. 1.** To make the hissing sound characteristic of frying fat. **2.** To seethe with anger or indignation. **3.** To be very hot. *—n.* A hissing sound. [Imit.]

siz·zler (sĭz'lər) *n. Informal.* A very hot day.

sitar

skateboard

skald also **scald** (skôld, skäld) *n.* An ancient Scandinavian poet; bard. [ON *skāld.*] **—skald'ic** *adj.*
skat (skăt) *n.* **1.** A card game for three persons played with 32 cards, sevens through aces. **2.** One of the combinations of cards occurring in skat. [G. < Ital. *scarto,* a discarded card < *scartare,* to reject : *s-,* out (< Lat. *ex-*) + *carta,* card < Lat. *charta,* leaf of papyrus. —see CARD[1].]
skate[1] (skāt) *n.* **1. a.** A shoe having a bladelike metal runner fixed to its sole, enabling the wearer to glide easily over ice. **b.** Such a runner having clamps and straps for attaching it to a shoe or boot. **2.** A roller skate. *—intr.v.* **skat·ed, skat·ing, skates.** To glide or move along on or as if on skates. [< Du. *schaats* (taken as pl.), stilt, skate < ONFr. *escace,* stilt, perh. of Germanic orig.] **—skat'ing** *n.*
skate[2] (skāt) *n.* Any of various marine fishes of the family Rajidae, having a cartilaginous skeleton and a flattened body with the pectoral fins forming winglike lateral extensions. [ME *scate* < ON *skata.*]
skate[3] (skāt) *n.* A chap; fellow. [Perh. alteration of dial. *skite,* contemptible person.]

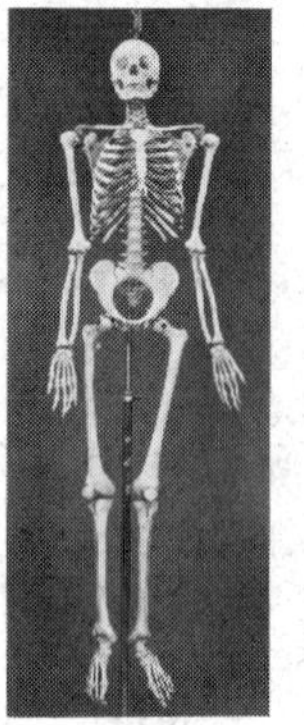

skeleton

skate·board (skāt'bôrd', -bōrd') *n.* A short, narrow board having a set of four roller-skate wheels mounted under it.
skat·er (skā'tər) *n.* **1.** One who skates. **2.** The water strider.
skat·ole (skăt'ōl', skā'tōl') also **skat·ol** (skăt'ôl', skā'tōl') *n.* A white crystalline organic compound, C_9H_9N, having a strong fecal odor, found naturally in feces, beets, and coal tar and used as a fixative in the manufacture of perfume. [Gk. *skōr, skat-,* dung + -OLE.]
skean (skēn) *n.* A type of double-edged dagger formerly used in Ireland and Scotland. [Ir. Gael. *scian* < OIr. *scīan.*]
ske·dad·dle (skĭ-dăd'l) *intr.v.* **-dled, -dling, -dles.** *Informal.* To leave hastily; flee. [Orig. unknown.] **—ske·dad'dler** *n.*
skeet (skēt) *n.* A form of trapshooting in which clay targets are thrown from traps to simulate birds in flight and are shot at from different stations. [Ult. < ON *skjōta,* to shoot.]
skeg (skĕg) *n. Naut.* **1.** A timber that connects the keel and the sternpost of a ship. **2.** An arm extending to the rear of the keel to support the rudder and protect the propeller. **3.** A series of timbers attached to the stern of a small boat, serving as a keel to keep the boat on course. [Du. *scheg* < ON *skegg,* beard.]
skein (skān) *n.* **1. a.** A length of thread or yarn wound in a loose, elongated coil. **b.** Something suggestive of this: *a twisted skein of lies.* **2.** A flock of geese or similar birds in flight. [ME *skeyne* < OFr. *escaigne.*]

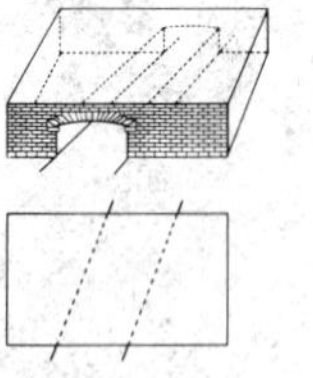

skew arch

skel·e·tal (skĕl'ĭ-tl) *adj.* Of, pertaining to, forming, or of the nature of a skeleton. **—skel'e·tal·ly** *adv.*
skel·e·ton (skĕl'ĭ-tn) *n.* **1. a.** The internal vertebrate structure composed of bone and cartilage that protects and supports the soft organs, tissues, and parts. **b.** The hard external supporting and protecting structure in many invertebrates and certain vertebrates, such as turtles; exoskeleton. **2.** A supporting structure or framework. **3.** An outline or sketch. **4.** One that is very thin or emaciated. ***—modifier:*** *a skeleton staff.* [NLat. < Gk., neuter of *skeletos,* dried up.]
skeleton key *n.* A key with a large portion of the bit filed away so that it can open different locks.
skelp (skĕlp) *v.* **skelped, skelp·ing, skelps.** *Chiefly Brit. —tr.* To strike or slap. *—intr.* To move quickly; hurry. *—n.* A forceful slap. [ME *skelpen.*]
skep (skĕp) *n.* A beehive, esp. one of straw. [ME, basket, basketful < OE *sceppe* < ON *skeppa,* basket.]

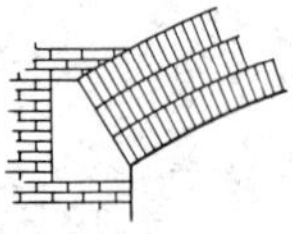

skewback

skep·tic also **scep·tic** (skĕp'tĭk) *n.* **1.** One who instinctively or habitually doubts, questions, or disagrees with assertions or generally accepted conclusions. **2.** One inclined to skepticism in religious matters. **3. a.** Often **Skeptic.** An adherent of a philosophical school of skepticism. **b. Skeptic.** A member of an ancient Greek school of philosophical skepticism, esp. that of Pyrrho of Elis. [Lat. *Scepticus,* disciple of Pyrrho < Gk. *Skeptikos* < *skeptesthai,* to examine.]
skep·ti·cal also **scep·ti·cal** (skĕp'tĭ-kəl) *adj.* **1.** Doubting; questioning. **2.** Pertaining to or characteristic of skeptics or skepticism. **—skep'ti·cal·ly** *adv.*
skep·ti·cism also **scep·ti·cism** (skĕp'tĭ-sĭz'əm) *n.* **1.** A doubting or questioning attitude or state of mind; dubiety. **2.** The philosophical doctrine that absolute knowledge is impossible and that inquiry must be a process of doubting in order to acquire approximate or relative certainty. **3.** Doubt or disbelief of religious tenets.
sker·ry (skĕr'ē) *n., pl.* **-ries.** A small rocky reef or island. [Of Scand. orig.]
sketch (skĕch) *n.* **1.** A hasty or undetailed drawing or painting made as a preliminary study. **2.** A brief, incomplete delineation or presentation, as of a book to be completed; outline. **3. a.** A brief, light, or informal short story, essay, or other literary composition. **b.** *Mus.* A brief composition, esp. for the piano. **c.** A short, often satirical scene or play in a revue or variety show; skit. **4.** *Informal.* An amusing person. *—v.* **sketched, sketch·ing, sketch·es.** *—tr.* To make a sketch of; outline. *—intr.* To make a sketch. [Du. *schets* < Ital. *schizzo* < *schizzare,* to fizz.] **—sketch'er** *n.*

skewer

sketch·book (skĕch'bo͝ok') *n.* **1.** A pad of paper used for sketching. **2.** A book of literary sketches.
sketch·y (skĕch'ē) *adj.* **-i·er, -i·est. 1.** Resembling a sketch; giving only major points or parts. **2. a.** Incomplete. **b.** Slight; superficial. **—sketch'i·ly** *adv.* **—sketch'i·ness** *n.*
skew (skyo͞o) *v.* **skewed, skew·ing, skews.** *—intr.* **1.** To take an oblique course or direction. **2.** To look obliquely or sideways. *—tr.* **1.** To turn or place at an angle. **2.** To give a bias to; distort. *—adj.* **1.** Placed or turned to one side; asymmetric. **2.** Distorted or biased in meaning or effect. **3.** Having a part that diverges, as gearing. **4. a.** *Math.* Neither parallel nor intersecting. Used of straight lines in space. **b.** *Statistics.* Not symmetric about the mean. Used of distributions. *—n.* An oblique or slanting movement, position, or direction. [ME *skewen,* to move sideways, escape < ONFr. *eskiuer,* of Germanic orig.] **—skew'ness** *n.*
skew arch *n. Archit.* An arch having sides not at right angles to the face of its abutments.
skew·back (skyo͞o'băk') *n. Archit.* Either of two inset abutments sloped to support a segmental arch.
skew·bald (skyo͞o'bôld') *adj.* Having spots or patches of white on a coat of a color other than black: *a skewbald horse.* [Obs. *skewed,* skewbald + BALD.]
skew·er (skyo͞o'ər) *n.* **1.** A long metal or wooden pin used to secure or suspend food during cooking; spit. **2.** Any of various picks or rods having a function or shape similar to a skewer. *—tr.v.* **-ered, -er·ing, -ers.** To hold together or pierce with or as if with a skewer. [Var. of dial. *skiver.*]
skew field *n.* A mathematical field in which commutativity does not hold for multiplication.
skew lines *pl.n.* Straight lines that are not in the same plane and do not intersect.
ski (skē) *n., pl.* **skis. 1. a.** One of a pair of long, flat runners of wood, metal, or plastic that curve upward in front and may be attached to a boot for gliding or traveling over snow. **b.** A waterski. **2.** Something shaped like a ski that is used as a runner on a vehicle. *—v.* **skied, ski·ing, skis.** *—intr.* To travel on skis, esp. as a sport. *—tr.* To travel over on skis. [Norw. < ON *skīð.*] **—ski'er** *n.* **—ski'ing** *n.*
ski·a·gram (skī'ə-grăm') also **ski·a·graph** (-grăf', -gräf') *n.* A picture or photograph made up of shadows or outlines. [Gk. *skia,* shadow + -GRAM.]
ski·ag·ra·phy (skī-ăg'rə-fē) *n.* The art or technique of making skiagrams. [SKIA(GRAM) + -GRAPHY.]
ski·a·scope (skī'ə-skōp') *n.* A retinoscope. [Gk. *skia,* shadow + -SCOPE.]
ski·as·co·py (skī-ăs'kə-pē) *n.* Retinoscopy.
ski·bob (skē'bŏb') *n. Sports.* A vehicle for gliding downhill over snow consisting of two skis one behind the other on a metal frame, steering handlebars connected to the shorter forward ski, and a low seat attached to the longer rear ski for the rider, who wears small skis for balance. **—ski'bob·ber** *n.*
ski boot *n.* A stiff padded leather or plastic low boot that is fastened to the foot with strong buckles or laces and locked into place in a ski binding.
skid (skĭd) *n.* **1.** The act of sliding or slipping over a surface, often sideways. **2. a.** A plank, log, or timber, usually one of a pair, used as a support or as a track for sliding or rolling heavy objects. **b.** A small platform for stacking merchandise to be moved or temporarily stored. **c.** One of several logs or timbers forming a skid road. **3. skids.** *Naut.* A wooden framework attached to the side of a ship to prevent damage, as when unloading. **4.** A shoe or drag applying pressure to a wheel to brake a vehicle. **5.** A runner in the landing gear of certain aircraft. *—v.* **skid·ded, skid·ding, skids.** *—intr.* **1.** To slip or slide sideways while moving because of loss of traction, as a vehicle. **2.** To slide without revolving: *wheels skidding on oily pavement.* **3.** To move sideways in a turn because of insufficient banking. Used of an airplane. *—tr.* **1.** To brake (a wheel) with a skid. **2.** To haul on a skid or skids. ***—idiom.* on the skids.** *Slang.* On a path to ruin or failure. [Orig. unknown.]
skid fin *n.* An upright auxiliary airfoil formerly placed above the upper wing in biplanes to increase lateral stability.
skid road *n.* **1.** A track made of logs laid transversely about five feet apart that is used to haul logs to a loading platform or a mill. **2.** *Slang.* Skid row.
skid row *n. Slang.* A squalid district inhabited by derelicts and vagrants. [Alteration of SKID ROAD.]
skied (skīd) *v.* Past tense and past participle of **sky.**
skiff (skĭf) *n. Naut.* A flat-bottomed open boat of shallow draft, having a pointed bow and a square stern and propelled by oars, sail, or motor. [Fr. *esquif* < Ital. *schifo,* of Germanic orig.]
skif·fle (skĭf'əl) *n.* Folk or country music played by performers who use unconventional instruments or percussion, as kazoos, washboards, or jugs. [Perh. imit.]
ski·jor·ing (skē'jôr'ĭng, -jōr'-) *n.* A sport in which a skier is drawn over ice or snow by a horse or vehicle. [Norw. *skikjoring : ski,* ski + *kjoring,* driving < *kjore,* to drive < ON *keyra.*]
ski jump *n.* **1.** A jump or leap made by a skier. **2.** A course or chute prepared for a ski jump.
skil·ful (skĭl'fəl) *adj.* Variant of **skillful.**
ski lift *n.* A power-driven conveyor, usually with attached towing bars, suspended chairs, or gondolas, used to carry skiers to the top of a trail or slope.
skill (skĭl) *n.* **1.** Proficiency, ability, or dexterity; expertness. **2.** An art, trade, or technique, particularly one requiring use

of the hands or body. **3.** *Obs.* A reason; cause. [ME *skile* < ON *skil,* discernment.]

skilled (skĭld) *adj.* **1.** Having or showing skill; expert. **2.** Requiring specialized ability or training: *a skilled trade.*

skil·let (skĭl′ĭt) *n.* **1.** A frying pan. **2.** *Chiefly Brit.* A long-handled stewing pan or saucepan sometimes having legs. [ME *skelet.*]

skill·ful also **skil·ful** (skĭl′fəl) *adj.* **1.** Possessing or exercising skill; expert. **2.** Characterized by, showing, or requiring skill. **—skill′ful·ly** *adv.* **—skill′ful·ness** *n.*

skim (skĭm) *v.* **skimmed, skim·ming, skims.** *—tr.* **1.** To remove floating matter from (a liquid). **2.** To remove (floating matter) from a liquid. **3.** To coat or cover with or as if with a thin layer, as of scum. **4. a.** To hurl across and close to the surface of, so as to bounce on water or slide on ice: *skimming stones.* **b.** To glide or pass quickly and lightly over. **5.** To read or glance through quickly or superficially: *skimmed the book.* *—intr.* **1.** To move or pass swiftly and lightly over or near a surface; glide. **2.** To give a quick and superficial reading, scrutiny, or consideration; glance: *skimmed through the newspaper.* **3.** To become coated with a thin layer. *—n.* **1.** The act of skimming. **2.** Something that has been skimmed, as skim milk. **3.** A thin layer or film. [ME *skymmen.*]

ski mask *n.* A knitted mask worn esp. by skiers for protection from the cold.

skim·mer (skĭm′ər) *n.* **1.** One that skims. **2.** A flat utensil, usually perforated and resembling a ladle, used in skimming liquids. **3.** A wide-brimmed hat with a flat shallow crown. **4.** Any of several chiefly coastal birds of the genus *Rynchops,* having long narrow wings and a long bill with a longer lower mandible for skimming the water's surface for food.

skim milk *n.* Milk from which the cream has been removed.

skim·ming (skĭm′ĭng) *n.* **1.** Often **skimmings.** That which is skimmed off a liquid. **2.** The action of skimming.

ski·mo·bile (skē′mō-bēl′, -mə-) *n.* A snowmobile.

skimp (skĭmp) *v.* **skimped, skimp·ing, skimps.** *—tr.* **1.** To do hastily, carelessly, or with poor material. **2.** To be extremely sparing with; scrimp. *—intr.* To be very or unduly thrifty: *skimp on the budget.* *—adj.* Scanty; skimpy. [Perh. alteration of SCRIMP.]

skimp·y (skĭm′pē) *adj.* **-i·er, -i·est.** **1.** Inadequate in size, fullness, or amount; scanty: *a skimpy meal.* **2.** Unduly thrifty; niggardly. **—skimp′i·ly** *adv.* **—skimp′i·ness** *n.*

skin (skĭn) *n.* **1.** The membranous tissue forming the external covering of the animal body; integument. **2.** An animal pelt, esp. the comparatively pliable pelt of a small or young animal. **3.** An outer layer resembling skin in function or appearance, as the rind of fruit or the plating on a ship or rocket. **4.** A liquid container made of animal skin. *—v.* **skinned, skin·ning, skins.** *—tr.* **1.** To remove skin from. **2.** To cover with or as if with skin. **3.** To remove or peel off (an outer covering). **4.** *Slang.* To fleece; swindle. **5.** To bruise, cut, or injure the skin or surface of: *skinned her knee.* *—intr.* **1.** To become covered with or as if with skin. **2.** To pass by or through with little room to spare. **3.** To go hurriedly. ***—idioms.* by the skin of one's teeth.** By the smallest margin. **get under one's skin.** **1.** To anger or irritate. **2.** To be or become an obsession. **have a thick skin.** To be unperturbed by criticism or insults. **have a thin skin.** To be easily hurt by criticism, unkindness, or rebuke. [ME < ON *skinn.*]

skin-deep (skĭn′dēp′) *adj.* Superficial; shallow. *—adv.* In a shallow manner; superficially.

skin-dive (skĭn′dīv′) *intr.v.* **-dived, -div·ing, -dives.** To participate in skin diving.

skin diving *n.* Underwater swimming, exploration, or fishing, often with flippers, a face mask, and a snorkel or scuba. **—skin diver** *n.*

skin drag *n.* Skin friction.

skin effect *n.* The tendency of electric current density in a conductor carrying alternating current to be greater at the surface than at the center.

skin flick *n. Slang.* A pornographic film.

skin·flint (skĭn′flĭnt′) *n.* A miser.

skin friction *n.* Friction caused by air crossing the surface of aircraft or rockets at high speeds.

skin game *n.* **1.** A crooked gambling game. **2.** A swindle.

skin graft *n.* A surgical graft of skin from one part of the body to another or from one individual to another.

skin grafting *n.* The process of making a skin graft.

skin·head (skĭn′hĕd′) *n. Slang.* A young British working-class tough with close-cropped hair.

skink (skĭngk) *n.* Any of numerous smooth, shiny lizards of the family Scincidae, having a cylindrical body and short or rudimentary legs. [Lat. *scincus* < Gk. *skinkos.*]

skinned (skĭnd) *adj.* Having skin of a specified kind: *fair-skinned.*

skin·ner (skĭn′ər) *n.* **1.** A person who flays, dresses, or sells animal skins. **2.** *Western U.S.* A mule driver.

Skin·ner box (skĭn′ər) *n.* An apparatus which is used in laboratories for animal experiments in operant conditioning and which usually contains a bar or lever to be pressed by the animal to gain a reward, as food, or to avoid a painful stimulus, as shock. [After B.F. *Skinner* (b.1904).]

skin·ny (skĭn′ē) *adj.* **-ni·er, -ni·est.** **1.** Of, pertaining to, or resembling skin. **2.** Very thin. **—skin′ni·ness** *n.*

skin·ny-dip (skĭn′ē-dĭp′) *intr.v.* **-dipped, -dip·ping, -dips.** *Informal.* To swim in the nude. **—skin′ny-dip′per** *n.* **—skin·ny-dip·ping** *n.*

skin-pop (skĭn′pŏp′) *tr.v.* **-popped, -pop·ping, -pops.** *Slang.* To inject, as a narcotic drug, beneath the skin rather than into a vein. **—skin′-pop′ping** *n.*

skin test *n.* A test for an allergy or infectious disease, performed by means of a patch test, scratch test, or an intracutaneous injection of an allergen or extract of the disease-causing organism.

skin·tight (skĭn′tīt′) *adj.* Fitting or clinging closely to the skin.

skip (skĭp) *v.* **skipped, skip·ping, skips.** *—intr.* **1. a.** To move by springing or hopping on one foot and then the other. **b.** To leap lightly about. **2.** To bounce over or be deflected from a surface; skim or ricochet. **3. a.** To pass from point to point omitting or disregarding what intervenes: *skipping over the television channels.* **b.** To be promoted in school beyond the next regular class or grade. **4.** *Informal.* To leave hastily; abscond. **5.** To misfire: *The engine skipped and choked.* *—tr.* **1.** To leap or jump lightly over: *skip rope.* **2.** To pass over, omit, or disregard: *skipped the minor details of the story.* **3.** To cause to ricochet or skim. **4.** To be promoted beyond (the next grade or level). **5. a.** *Informal.* To leave hastily: *He skipped town.* **b.** To fail to attend: *skipped school.* *—n.* **1.** A leaping or jumping movement, esp. a gait in which hops and steps alternate. **2.** A passing over or omission. [ME *skippen.*]

skip distance *n.* The smallest separation between a transmitter and a receiver that permits radio signals of a specific frequency to travel from one to the other by reflection from the ionosphere.

skip·jack (skĭp′jăk′) *n., pl.* **skipjack** or **-jacks.** **1.** Any of several marine food fishes of the genus *Euthynnus,* related to and resembling the tuna. **2.** Any of various fishes, as certain herrings.

skip·per[1] (skĭp′ər) *n.* The master of a ship. [ME *skypper* < MDu. *schipper* < *schip,* ship.] **—skip′per** *v.* **(-pered, -per·ing, -pers).**

skip·per[2] (skĭp′ər) *n.* **1.** One that skips. **2.** Any of numerous butterflies of the families Hesperiidae and Megathymidae, having a hairy, mothlike body and a darting flight pattern. **3.** Any of several related marine fishes, esp. a saury, *Cololabis saira,* of Pacific waters.

skirl (skûrl) *v.* **skirled, skirl·ing, skirls.** *—intr.* To produce a shrill, piercing tone. Used of a bagpipe. *—tr.* To play on the bagpipe. *—n.* **1.** The shrill sound made by a bagpipe. **2.** A shrill, piercing sound. [ME *skrillen,* prob. of Scand. orig.]

skir·mish (skûr′mĭsh) *n.* **1.** A minor encounter in war between small bodies of troops, often as part of larger movements. **2.** A minor or preliminary conflict or dispute. *—intr.v.* **-mished, -mish·ing, -mish·es.** To engage in a skirmish. [ME *skirmisshe* < OFr. *eskermir, eskirmiss-,* to fight with a sword, of Germanic orig.] **—skir′mish·er** *n.*

skir·ret (skûr′ĭt) *n.* An Old World plant, *Sium sisarum,* having a sweetish, edible root. [ME *skirwhit,* alteration of OFr. *eschervi,* prob. < Ar. *alkarawyā,* caraway.]

skirt (skûrt) *n.* **1.** That part of a garment, such as a dress or gown, that hangs from the waist down. **2.** A separate garment hanging from the waist and worn by women and girls. **3. a.** One of the leather flaps hanging from the side of a saddle. **b.** The lower outer section of a rocket vehicle. **4.** A border, margin, or outer edge. **5. skirts.** The edge or outskirts, as of a town. **6.** *Slang.* A woman or girl. *—v.* **skirt·ed, skirt·ing, skirts.** *—tr.* **1.** To lie along, form the border of, or surround; bound. **2.** To move or pass around rather than across or through. **3.** To evade or elude (as a topic of conversation) by circumlocution: *skirted the issue.* *—intr.* To be near or move along the edge or border of something. [ME < ON *skyrta,* shirt.]

ski run *n.* A slope or trail for skiing.

skit (skĭt) *n.* **1.** A short, usually comic theatrical sketch. **2.** A short humorous or satirical piece of writing. [Orig. unknown.]

ski touring *n. Sports.* Cross-country skiing for pleasure rather than competition. **—ski tourer** *n.*

ski tow *n.* **1.** A type of ski lift in which skiers cling to a continuous rope as they are hauled up a slope. **2.** A ski lift.

skit·ter (skĭt′ər) *v.* **-tered, -ter·ing, -ters.** *—intr.* **1.** To skip, glide, or move lightly or rapidly along a surface; flit. **2.** To fish by drawing a lure or baited hook over the surface of the water with a skipping movement. *—tr.* To cause to skitter. [Prob. freq. of dial. *skite,* to run rapidly.]

skit·tish (skĭt′ĭsh) *adj.* **1.** Excitable or nervous. **2.** Shy, coy, or timid. **3. a.** Extremely lively or frivolous in action or character. **b.** Undependable or fickle. [ME.] **—skit′tish·ly** *adv.* **—skit′tish·ness** *n.*

skit·tle (skĭt′l) *n. Chiefly Brit.* **1. skittles.** *(used with a sing. verb).* The game of ninepins, in which a wooden disk or ball is thrown to knock down the pins. **2.** One of the pins used in skittles. [Orig. unknown.]

skive (skīv) *tr.v.* **skived, skiv·ing, skives.** To shave or cut off the surface of (leather or rubber); pare. [Of Scand. orig.]

skiv·er (skī′vər) *n.* **1.** A soft, thin leather split off the outside

skid

skimmer

skink

of sheepskin and used for bookbinding. **2.** One that skives. **3.** A knife or other cutting device used in skiving.
Skiv·vies (skĭv′ēz). A trademark for underwear.
ski·wear (skē′wâr′) *n.* Clothing that is appropriate to wear for skiing.
skoal (skōl) *interj.* Used as a drinking toast. [Dan. and Norw. *skaal,* cup.]
sku·a (skyo͞o′ə) *n.* **1.** A predatory gull-like sea bird, *Catharacta skua,* of northern regions, having brownish plumage. **2.** *Chiefly Brit.* A jaeger. [NLat. < Faroese *skūvur* < ON *skūfr.*]
skul·dug·ger·y (skŭl-dŭg′ə-rē) *n.* Variant of **skullduggery.**
skulk (skŭlk) *intr.v.* **skulked, skulk·ing, skulks. 1.** To lie in hiding; lurk. **2.** To move about stealthily. **3.** To evade work or obligation; malinger. —*n.* **1.** One who skulks. **2.** A group of foxes. [ME *skulken,* of Scand. orig.] **—skulk′er** *n.*
skull (skŭl) *n.* **1.** The framework of the head of vertebrates, made up of the bones of the brain case and face. **2.** The head, esp. regarded as the seat of thought or intelligence. **3.** A death's-head. [ME *skulle.*]

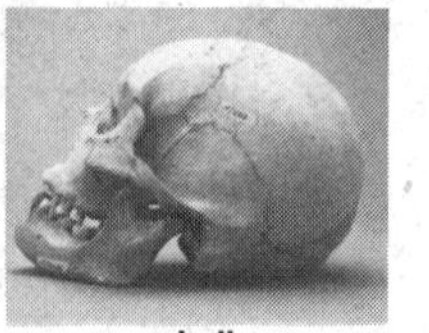
skull

skull and crossbones *n.* A representation of a human skull above two long crossed bones, a symbol of death once used by pirates and now used as a warning label on poisons.
skull·cap (skŭl′kăp′) *n.* **1. a.** A light, close-fitting, brimless cap sometimes worn indoors. **b.** A yarmulke. **2.** Any of various plants of the genus *Scutellaria,* having clusters of two-lipped flowers.
skull·dug·ger·y also **skul·dug·ger·y** (skŭl-dŭg′ə-rē) *n., pl.* **-ger·ies.** Crafty deception or trickery. [Orig. unknown.]
skunk (skŭngk) *n.* **1.** Any of several small, carnivorous New World mammals of the genus *Mephitis* and related genera, having a bushy tail and black fur with white markings and ejecting a malodorous secretion from glands near the anus. **2.** The glossy black and white fur of the skunk. **3.** *Slang.* A mean or despicable person. —*tr.v.* **skunked, skunk·ing, skunks.** *Slang.* **1.** To defeat overwhelmingly, esp. by keeping from scoring. **2. a.** To cheat. **b.** To fail to pay. [Massachuset *squnck.*]

skunk

skunk cabbage *n.* **1.** An ill-smelling swamp plant, *Symplocarpus foetidus,* of eastern North America, having minute flowers enclosed in a mottled greenish or purplish spathe. **2.** A plant, *Lysichitum americanum,* of western North America similar to skunk cabbage.
skunkweed (skŭngk′wēd) *n.* Skunk cabbage.
sky (skī) *n., pl.* **skies. 1.** The upper atmosphere, appearing as a hemisphere above the earth. **2.** The highest level or degree: *reaching for the sky.* **3.** The celestial or heavenly regions. **4.** Often **skies.** The appearance of the upper atmosphere, esp. with respect to weather: *threatening skies.* —*tr.v.* **skied, sky·ing, skies. 1.** To hit or throw (a ball, for example) high in the air. **2.** To hang (a painting, for example) high up on the wall, above the line of vision, esp. in an exhibition. [ME < ON *sky̅,* cloud.]
sky blue *n.* A light to pale blue, from a light greenish to light purplish blue.
sky·borne (skī′bôrn′, -bōrn′) *adj.* Airborne.
sky·cap (skī′kăp′) *n.* An airport employee who carries luggage. [SKY + (RED)CAP.]

skyline
New York City

sky·dive (skī′dīv′) *intr.v.* **-dived, -div·ing, -dives.** *Sports.* To jump from an airplane, performing various maneuvers before pulling the ripcord of a parachute. **—sky′div′er** *n.* **—sky′div′ing** *n.*
Skye terrier (skī) *n.* A small terrier of a breed native to the Isle of Skye, having a long, low body, short legs, and shaggy hair.
sky·ey (skī′ē) *adj.* Of or resembling the sky.
sky-high (skī′hī′) *adv.* **1.** To a very high level: *garbage piled sky-high.* **2.** In a lavish or enthusiastic manner. **3.** In pieces or to pieces; apart: *blew the bridge sky-high.* —*adj.* **1.** High up in the air. **2.** Exorbitantly high: *sky-high prices.*
sky·jack (skī′jăk′) *tr.v.* **-jacked, -jack·ing, -jacks.** To hijack (an airplane, esp. one in flight) through the use or threat of force. [SKY + (HI)JACK.] **—sky′jack′er** *n.* **—sky′jack′ing** *n.*
sky·lark (skī′lärk′) *n.* An Old World bird, *Alauda arvensis,* having brownish plumage and noted for its singing while in flight. —*intr.v.* **-larked, -lark·ing, -larks.** To indulge in frolic.
sky·light (skī′līt′) *n.* An overhead window admitting daylight.
sky·line (skī′līn′) *n.* **1.** The line along which the surface of the earth and sky appear to meet; horizon. **2.** The outline of a group of buildings or a mountain range seen against the sky.
sky·lounge (skī′lounj′) *n.* A vehicle that collects passengers and then is carried by a helicopter between a downtown terminal and an airport.
sky marshal *n.* An armed federal law-enforcement officer assigned to prevent skyjackings.
sky pilot *n.* *Slang.* A clergyman; chaplain.
sky·rock·et (skī′rŏk′ĭt) *n.* A firework that ascends high into the air where it explodes in a brilliant cascade of flares and starlike sparks. —*intr. & tr.v.* **-et·ed, -et·ing, -ets.** To rise or cause to rise rapidly and suddenly, as in amount, position, or reputation.
sky·sail (skī′səl, -sāl′) *n.* A small square sail above the royal in a square-rigged vessel.
sky·scrap·er (skī′skrā′pər) *n.* A very tall building.

skyscraper

sky·walk (skī′wôk′) *n.* An elevated usually enclosed walkway between two buildings.
sky·ward (skī′wərd) *adj. & adv.* At or toward the sky. **—sky′wards** *adv.*
sky wave *n.* A radio wave.
sky·way (skī′wā′) *n.* **1.** An airline route; air lane. **2.** An elevated highway.
sky·writ·ing (skī′rī′tĭng) *n.* **1.** The process of writing in the sky by releasing a visible vapor from an airplane. **2.** The letters or words formed in skywriting. **—sky′writ′er** *n.*
slab[1] (slăb) *n.* **1.** A broad, flat, somewhat thick piece, as of cake, stone, or cheese. **2.** An outside piece cut from a log when squaring it for lumber. **3.** *Baseball.* The pitcher's rubber. —*tr.v.* **slabbed, slab·bing, slabs. 1.** To make or shape into a slab. **2.** To cover or pave with slabs. **3.** To dress (a log) by cutting slabs. [ME *slabbe.*]
slab[2] (slăb) *adj.* *Archaic.* Viscid. Used in the phrase *thick and slab.* [Prob. of Scand. orig.]
slab-sid·ed (slăb′sī′dĭd) *adj.* *Informal.* **1.** Having flat sides. **2.** Tall and slim; lanky.
slack[1] (slăk) *adj.* **1.** Not lively or moving; sluggish. **2.** Not busy; lacking in work: *a slack business season.* **3.** Not tense or taut; loose: *a slack rope.* **4.** Lacking firmness: *a slack grip.* **5.** Lacking in diligence; negligent: *a slack worker.* **6.** Flowing or blowing with little speed. Used of the wind or tide. —*v.* **slacked, slack·ing, slacks.** —*tr.* **1.** To slacken. **2.** To be remiss about. **3.** To slake (lime). —*intr.* To be or become slack. ***—phrasal verb.*** **slack off.** To decrease in activity or intensity; abate. —*n.* **1.** A loose or slack part or portion of something, such as a rope or sail. **2.** A lack of tension; looseness. **3.** A period of little activity; lull. **4. a.** A cessation of movement in a current of air or water. **b.** An area of still water. **5. slacks.** Separate trousers not part of a suit. —*adv.* In a slack manner: *"His mouth hung slack between laughter and surprise"* (Ivan Gold). [ME *slak* < OE *slæc.*] **—slack′ly** *adv.* **—slack′ness** *n.*
slack[2] (slăk) *n.* A mixture of coal fragments, coal dust, and dirt that remains after screening coal. [ME *sleck.*]
slack[3] (slăk) *n.* *Chiefly Brit.* **1.** A small dell or hollow. **2.** A bog; morass. [ME *slak* < ON *slakki.*]
slack-baked (slăk′bākt′) *adj.* **1.** Not perfectly baked; underdone; half-baked. Used chiefly of bread. **2.** Imperfectly made.
slack·en (slăk′ən) *v.* **-ened, -en·ing, -ens.** —*tr.* **1.** To make slower; slow down: *The runners slackened their pace.* **2.** To make less vigorous, intense, firm, or severe. **3.** To reduce the tension or tautness of; loosen. —*intr.* **1.** To slow down. **2.** To become less energetic, active, firm, or strict. **3.** To become less tense or taut; loosen.
slack·er (slăk′ər) *n.* A person who shirks work or responsibility, esp. one who tries to evade military service in wartime.
slack water *n.* **1.** The period at high or low tide when there is no visible flow of water. **2.** An area in a sea or river unaffected by currents; still water.
slag (slăg) *n.* **1.** The vitreous mass left as a residue by the smelting of metallic ore. **2.** Scoria (sense 1). —*v.* **slagged, slag·ging, slags.** —*tr.* To change into slag. —*intr.* To form slag; become slaglike. [MLG *slagge.*] **—slag′gy** *adj.*
slain (slān) *v.* Past participle of **slay.**
slake (slāk) *v.* **slaked, slak·ing, slakes.** —*tr.* **1.** To quench or satisfy: *slaked her thirst.* **2.** To lessen the force or activity of; moderate: *slaking his anger.* **3.** To cool or refresh by wetting or moistening. **4.** To combine (lime) chemically with water or moist air. —*intr.* To undergo a slaking process; crumble or disintegrate, as lime. [ME *slaken,* to abate < OE *slacian* < *slæc,* slack, sluggish.]
sla·lom (slä′ləm) *n.* **1.** Skiing in a zigzag course. **2.** A race along such a course, laid out with flag-marked poles. [Norw. : *slad,* sloping + *lom,* path.] **—sla′lom** *v.* **(-lomed, -lom·ing, -loms).**
slam[1] (slăm) *v.* **slammed, slam·ming, slams.** —*tr.* **1.** To shut with force and loud noise: *slammed the door.* **2.** To put, throw, or otherwise forcefully move so as to produce a loud noise: *slammed the book on the desk.* **3.** To hit or strike with great force. **4.** *Slang.* To criticize harshly; attack verbally. —*intr.* **1.** To close or swing into place with force so as to produce a loud noise. **2.** To hit something with force; crash. —*n.* **1. a.** A forceful movement that produces a loud noise. **b.** The noise so produced. **2.** *Slang.* A harsh or devastating criticism. [Perh. of Scand. orig.]
slam[2] (slăm) *n.* In bridge and other whist-derived card games, the winning of all the tricks or all but one during the play of one hand. [Orig. unknown.]
slam-bang (slăm′băng′) *adv.* **1.** Swiftly and noisily. **2.** Recklessly.
slam·mer (slăm′ər) *n.* *Slang.* A jail: *"If he doesn't wind up in the slammer, he's likely to get a job teaching journalism"* (Nat Hentoff). [< SLAM[1].]
slan·der (slăn′dər) *n.* **1.** *Law.* The utterance of defamatory statements injurious to the reputation or well-being of a person. **2.** A malicious statement or report. —*v.* **-dered, -der·ing, -ders.** —*tr.* To utter damaging reports about. —*intr.* To utter or spread slander. [ME *slaundre* < OFr. *esclandre* < Lat. *scandalum,* scandal < Gk. *skandalon,* trap.] **—slan′der·er** *n.* **—slan′der·ous** *adj.* **—slan′der·ous·ly** *adv.*

slang (slăng) *n.* **1.** The nonstandard vocabulary of a given culture or subculture, consisting typically of arbitrary and often ephemeral coinages and figures of speech characterized by spontaneity and sometimes by raciness. **2.** Language peculiar to a group; argot or jargon. **—*modifier:*** *a slang term.* [Orig. unknown.] **—slang'i·ly** *adv.* **—slang'i·ness** *n.* **—slang'y** *adj.*
slant (slănt) *v.* **slant·ed, slant·ing, slants.** —*tr.* **1.** To give an oblique direction to. **2.** To present so as to conform to a particular bias: *slanted the story in favor of the strikers.* —*intr.* To incline obliquely. —*n.* **1. a.** A sloping direction, plane, or course; incline. **b.** Slope; obliquity. **2.** A bias or point of view. [Alteration of obs. *slent* < ME *slenten,* to lie aslant, of Scand. orig.] **—slant'ing·ly** *adv.*
slant·ways (slănt'wāz) *adv.* Slantwise.
slant·wise (slănt'wīz') *adv.* At a slant or slope; obliquely. —*adj.* Slanting; oblique.
slap (slăp) *n.* **1. a.** A smacking blow made with the open hand or with any flat thing. **b.** The sound so made. **2.** An injury, as to one's pride. —*v.* **slapped, slap·ping, slaps.** —*tr.* **1.** To strike with a flat object, as the palm of the hand. **2.** To criticize or insult sharply. **3.** To put or place with a slapping sound: *slapped a silver dollar on the bar.* —*intr.* To strike or beat with the force and sound of a slap. **—*phrasal verb.*** **slap down. 1.** To prohibit from acting in a specific way by means of a sharp blow or emphatic censure. **2.** To put a sudden end to; squelch; suppress. —*adv. Informal.* Directly and with force. [LG *slapp.*] **—slap'per** *n.*
slap·dash (slăp'dăsh') *adj.* Characterized by haste or carelessness: *slapdash work.* —*adv.* In a reckless, haphazard manner.
slap·hap·py (slăp'hăp'ē) *adj.* **-pi·er, -pi·est.** *Slang.* **1.** Dazed, silly, or incoherent from or as if from blows to the head. **2.** Happy-go-lucky.
slap·jack (slăp'jăk') *n.* **1.** A pancake; flapjack. **2.** A simple card game. [SLAP + (FLAP)JACK.]
slap shot *n.* A shot made in ice hockey that consists of a swinging stroke.
slap·stick (slăp'stĭk') *n.* **1.** A paddle designed to produce a loud whacking sound, formerly used by actors in farces. **2.** A form of comedy marked by many chases, collisions, crude practical jokes, and similar boisterous actions.
slash (slăsh) *v.* **slashed, slash·ing, slash·es.** —*tr.* **1.** To cut or form by cutting with violent sweeping strokes. **2.** To lash violently with sweeping strokes. **3.** To make a gash or gashes in. **4.** To cut a slit or slits in. **5.** To criticize sharply. **6.** To reduce or curtail drastically: *slash prices.* —*intr.* **1.** To make violent and sweeping strokes with or as if with a sharp instrument. **2.** To cut one's way with such strokes: *We slashed through the dense jungle.* —*n.* **1.** A sweeping stroke made with a sharp instrument. **2.** A cut or other injury made by such a stroke; gash; slit. **3.** An ornamental slit in a fabric or article of clothing. **4.** Branches and other residue left on a forest floor after the cutting of timber. **5.** Often **slashes.** Wet or swampy ground overgrown with bushes and trees. **6.** *Printing.* A virgule. **—*modifier:*** *slash sleeves.* [ME *slashen.*] **—slash'er** *n.*
slash·ing (slăsh'ĭng) *adj.* **1.** Bitingly critical or satiric: *slashing wit.* **2.** Dashing; pelting: *slashing hailstorm.* **3.** Brilliant; intense: *slashing colors.*
slash pine *n.* Any of several pine trees of the southeastern United States and adjacent regions that grow in swampy coastal areas.
slat (slăt) *n.* **1.** A narrow strip of metal or wood, as in a Venetian blind. **2.** A movable auxiliary airfoil running along the leading edge of the wing of an airplane. **3. slats.** *Slang.* The ribs. —*tr.v.* **slat·ted, slat·ting, slats.** To provide or make with slats. [ME *sclat* < OFr. *esclat,* splinter.]
slatch (slăch) *n. New England.* **1.** A momentary lull between breaking waves, favorable for launching a boat. **2.** A lull in a high windstorm. [Var. of SLACK[1].]
slate (slāt) *n.* **1.** A fine-grained metamorphic rock that splits into thin, smooth-surfaced layers. **2. a.** A piece of slate cut for use as roofing material or a writing surface. **b.** A writing tablet made of any material similar to slate. **3.** A record of past performance or activity: *a clean slate.* **4.** A list of the candidates of a particular political party running for various offices. **5.** A dark gray to bluish gray, to dark bluish or dark purplish gray. **—*modifier:*** *a slate roof.* —*tr.v.* **slat·ed, slat·ing, slates. 1.** To cover (a roof, for example) with slate. **2.** To put on a list of candidates. **3.** To designate or destine: *"I was slated to amass wealth beyond the dreams of avarice"* (S.J. Perelman). [ME *sclate* < OFr. *esclate,* splinter, fem. of *esclat.*]
slate black *n.* A purplish black. **—slate'-black'** (slāt'blăk') *adj.*
slate blue (slāt'blōō') *n.* A grayish blue to dark bluish gray. **—slate'-blue'** *adj.*
slat·er (slā'tər) *n.* **1.** One employed to lay slate roofs. **2.** Any of several small isopod crustaceans, as a sow bug.
slath·er (slăth'ər) *tr.v.* **-ered, -er·ing, -ers.** *Informal.* **1.** To use great amounts of; lavish. **2. a.** To spread thickly with. **b.** To spread thickly on. —*n.* Often **slathers.** *Slang.* A great amount; lots: *slathers of money.* [Orig. unknown.]
slat·ing (slā'tĭng) *n.* **1.** The act, process, or occupation of laying slates. **2.** Slates collectively.
slat·tern (slăt'ərn) *n.* An untidy woman; slut. [Perh. < dial. *slattering,* slovenly, pr.part. of dial. *slatter,* to slop.]
slat·tern·ly (slăt'ərn-lē) *adj.* **1.** Slovenly; untidy: *"electricity took the place of candles and slatternly hearth-fires"* (Sinclair Lewis). **2.** Characteristic of or befitting a slattern. **—slat'tern·li·ness** *n.*
slaugh·ter (slô'tər) *n.* **1.** The killing of animals for food. **2.** The killing of a large number of persons; carnage; massacre. —*tr.v.* **-tered, -ter·ing, -ters. 1.** To kill (animals) for food; butcher. **2. a.** To kill (persons) in large numbers; massacre. **b.** To kill in a violent or brutal manner. [ME, of Scand. orig.] **—slaugh'ter·er** *n.* **—slaugh'ter·ous** *adj.*
slaugh·ter·house (slô'tər-hous') *n.* **1.** A place where animals are butchered. **2.** A scene of massacre or carnage.
Slav (släv) *n.* A member of one of the Slavic-speaking peoples of eastern Europe. [ME *Sclave* < Med. Lat. *Sclavus* < LGk. *Sklabos.*]
slave (slāv) *n.* **1.** One bound in servitude to a person or household as an instrument of labor. **2.** One who is submissive or subject to a specified person or influence. **3.** A person who works extremely hard. **4.** A machine or component that is controlled by another machine or component. **—*modifier:*** *slave labor.* —*intr.v.* **slaved, slav·ing, slaves.** To work like a slave; drudge. [ME *sclave* < OFr. *esclave* < Med. Lat. *sclavus* < *Sclavus,* Slav.]
slave driver *n.* **1.** A severely exacting employer or supervisor. **2.** An overseer of slaves at work.
slav·er[1] (slăv'ər) *intr.v.* **-ered, -er·ing, -ers. 1.** To slobber. **2.** To fawn; drivel. —*n.* **1.** Saliva drooling from the mouth. **2.** Slobbering flattery or drivel. [ME *slaveren,* prob. < ON *slafra.*]
slav·er[2] (slā'vər) *n.* **1.** A ship engaged in slave traffic. **2.** A person who traffics in slaves.
slav·er·y (slā'və-rē, slāv'rē) *n., pl.* **-ies. 1.** Bondage to a master or household. **2.** A mode of production in which slaves constitute the principal work force. **3.** The condition of being subject or addicted to a specified influence. **4.** A condition of hard work and subjection: *wage slavery.*
slave state *n.* **1. Slave State.** Any of the 15 states of the Union in which slavery was legal before the Civil War, including Alabama, Arkansas, Delaware, Florida, Georgia, Kentucky, Louisiana, Maryland, Mississippi, Missouri, North Carolina, South Carolina, Tennessee, Texas, and Virginia. **2.** Any country that is under totalitarian rule.
slave trade *n.* Traffic in slaves.
Slav·ic (slä'vĭk) *adj.* Of or pertaining to the Slavs or their languages. —*n.* A branch of the Indo-European language family that includes Bulgarian, Byelorussian, Czech, Polish, Russian, Serbo-Croatian, Slovak, Slovene, and Ukrainian.
slav·ish (slā'vĭsh) *adj.* **1.** Pertaining to or characteristic of a slave; servile: *slavish devotion.* **2.** Pertaining to or characteristic of the institution of slavery; oppressive. **3.** Showing no originality; blindly imitative: *a slavish copy of the original.* **—slav'ish·ly** *adv.* **—slav'ish·ness** *n.*
slav·oc·ra·cy (slā-vŏk'rə-sē) *n., pl.* **-cies.** The power structure formed by the advocates of slavery in the United States before the Civil War. **—slav'o·crat'** (slā'və-krăt') *n.* **—slav'o·crat'ic** *adj.*
Sla·von·ic (slə-vŏn'ĭk) *n.* Slavic. **—Sla·von'ic** *adj.*
Slav·o·phile (slăv'ə-fīl') also **Slav·o·phil** (-fĭl) *n.* **1.** A person who admires the Slavs. **2.** A person who advocates the supremacy of the Slavic, and esp. Russian, culture. **—Sla·voph'i·lism** (slə-vŏf'ə-lĭz'əm) *n.*
slaw (slô) *n.* Coleslaw.
slay (slā) *tr.v.* **slew** (slōō), **slain** (slān), **slay·ing, slays. 1. a.** To kill violently. **b.** To kill deliberately. **2.** *Slang.* To overwhelm, as with laughter or love: *Her jokes slay me.* [ME *sleen* < OE *slēan.*] **—slay'er** *n.*
sleave (slēv) *tr.v.* **sleaved, sleav·ing, sleaves.** To separate or disentangle, as a twisted mass of threads. —*n.* **1.** A tangled or knotted thread or ravel. **2.** A thin thread. [ME **sleven* < OE *slǣfan,* to cut.]
sleave silk *n.* Raw untwisted silk; floss, as for embroidery.
sleaze (slēz) *n. Informal.* A sleazy condition, quality, or appearance. [Back-formation < SLEAZY.]
slea·zy (slē'zē) *adj.* **-zi·er, -zi·est. 1.** Thin and loosely woven; flimsy: *a coat with a sleazy lining.* **2.** Made of low-quality materials; cheap; shoddy. **3.** Vulgar; disreputable: *sleazy bars.* [Orig. unknown.] **—slea'zi·ly** *adv.* **—slea'zi·ness** *n.*
sled (slĕd) *n.* **1.** A vehicle mounted on runners, used for carrying people or loads over ice and snow; sledge. **2.** A light wooden frame on runners, used by children for coasting over snow or ice. —*v.* **sled·ded, sled·ding, sleds.** —*tr.* To carry on or convey by a sled. —*intr.* To ride or use a sled. [ME *sledde* < MLG.] **—sled'der** *n.*
sled·ding (slĕd'ĭng) *n.* **1.** The act of using a sled for hauling, transportation, or sport. **2.** The weather or snow conditions under which one may use a sled. **3.** *Informal.* Progress or existence; the going: *The sledding gets tougher every year in this business.*
sledge (slĕj) *n.* A vehicle on low runners drawn by horses, dogs, or other work animals and used for transporting loads across ice and snow. —*tr. & intr.v.* **sledged, sledg·ing, sledg·es.** To convey or travel on a sledge. [MDu. *sleedse.*]
sledge·ham·mer (slĕj'hăm'ər) *n.* A long, heavy hammer, often wielded with both hands, used for driving wedges and

sled
Woodcut of children coasting on sleds

sledge

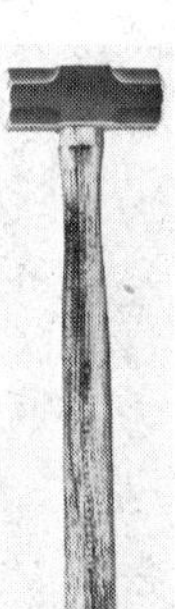

sledgehammer

posts and for other heavy work. —*tr.v.* **-mered, -mer·ing, -mers.** To strike with or as if with a sledgehammer. —*adj.* Ruthlessly severe; crushing. [ME *slegge,* sledgehammer (< OE *slecg)* + HAMMER.]

sleek (slēk) *adj.* **-er, -est. 1.** Smooth and lustrous as if polished; glossy: *sleek dark hair.* **2.** Well-groomed and neatly tailored. **3.** Healthy or well-fed; thriving. **4.** Polished or smooth in behavior, esp. in an unctuous way; slick. —*tr.v.* **sleeked, sleek·ing, sleeks. 1.** To make lustrous or smooth; polish. **2.** To gloss over; conceal. [Var. of SLICK.] **—sleek'ly** *adv.* **—sleek'ness** *n.*

sleep (slēp) *n.* **1. a.** A natural, periodically recurring physiological state of rest, characterized by relative physical and nervous inactivity, unconsciousness, and lessened responsiveness to external stimuli. **b.** A period of this form of rest. **c.** A similar condition of inactivity, such as unconsciousness, dormancy, hibernation, or death. **2.** *Bot.* The folding together of leaves or petals at night or in the absence of light. —*v.* **slept** (slĕpt), **sleep·ing, sleeps.** —*intr.* **1.** To be in the state of sleep or to fall asleep. **2.** To be in a condition resembling sleep, such as hibernation, dormancy, or death. —*tr.* **1.** To pass or get rid of by sleeping: *slept away the day; went home to sleep it off.* **2.** To provide with accommodations for sleeping. ***—phrasal verbs.* sleep around.** *Informal.* To be sexually promiscuous. **sleep in. 1.** To sleep at one's place of employment. **2. a.** To oversleep. **b.** To sleep late on purpose. **sleep out. 1.** To sleep outside. **2.** To sleep at one's own home, not at one's place of employment. **3.** To sleep away from one's home. **sleep with.** To have sexual intercourse with. ***—idiom.* sleep on it.** To consider something overnight before deciding what to do. [ME *slepe* < OE *slæp.*]

sleigh

sleep·er (slē'pər) *n.* **1.** One that sleeps. **2.** A sleeping car. **3.** Any of various usually small marine and freshwater fishes of the family Eleotridae. **4.** *Football.* An offensive player who is stationed in an obscure field position with the hope that he will not be noticed by the other team until after he has performed his function in the play. **5.** *Chiefly Brit.* A heavy beam used as a support for rails in a railroad track; crosstie. **6.** *Informal.* One that achieves unexpected recognition or success, as a race horse, book, or marketed product. **7.** An earmarked unbranded calf.

sleep-in (slēp'ĭn') *adj.* Being one that lives where employed: *a sleep-in housekeeper.*

sleeping bag *n.* A large, warmly lined, usually zippered bag in which a person may sleep outdoors.

sleeping car *n.* A railroad car having accommodations to sleep passengers.

slide

sleeping pill *n.* A sedative, esp. a barbiturate, in the form of a pill or capsule used to relieve insomnia.

sleeping sickness *n.* **1.** An often fatal, endemic infectious disease of man and animals in tropical Africa, caused by either of two protozoans of the genus *Trypanosoma,* transmitted by the tsetse fly, and characterized by fever and lethargy. **2.** *Pathol.* Encephalitis lethargica.

sleep·less (slēp'lĭs) *adj.* **1. a.** Without sleep: *a sleepless night.* **b.** Unable to sleep. **2.** Never resting; always alert or active. **—sleep'less·ly** *adv.* **—sleep'less·ness** *n.*

sleep·walk·ing (slēp'wô'kĭng) *n.* Somnambulism. **—sleep'walk'er** *n.*

sleep·wear (slēp'wâr') *n.* Nightclothes, esp. for women.

sleep·y (slē'pē) *adj.* **-i·er, -i·est. 1.** Ready for or needing sleep; drowsy. **2.** Inactive; dull. **3.** Inducing sleep. **4.** Quiet: *a sleepy little town.* **—sleep'i·ly** *adv.* **—sleep'i·ness** *n.*

sleep·y·head (slē'pē-hĕd') *n. Informal.* A sleepy person.

sleet (slēt) *n.* **1.** Precipitation consisting of generally transparent frozen or partially frozen raindrops. **2.** A mixture of rain and snow or hail. **3.** A thin icy coating that forms when rain or sleet freezes, as on trees or streets. —*intr.v.* **sleet·ed, sleet·ing, sleets.** To shower sleet. [ME *slete.*] **—sleet'y** *adj.*

sleeve (slēv) *n.* **1.** The part of a garment that covers all or a part of the arm. **2.** An encasement into which an object or device fits: *a record sleeve.* —*tr.v.* **sleeved, sleev·ing, sleeves.** To furnish or fit with a sleeve or sleeves. ***—idiom.* up one's sleeve.** Hidden but ready to be used. [ME *sleve* < OE *slēf.*] **—sleeve'less** *adj.*

sleeve coupling *n.* A thin steel cylinder uniting two lengths of shafting or pipe.

sleigh (slā) *n.* A light vehicle mounted on runners for use on snow or ice, having one or more seats and usually drawn by a horse. —*intr.v.* **sleighed, sleigh·ing, sleighs.** To ride in or drive a sleigh. [Du. *slee,* alteration of *slede* < MDu. *slēde.*] **—sleigh'er** *n.*

sleight (slīt) *n.* **1.** Deftness; dexterity. **2.** A clever or skillful trick or deception; an artifice; stratagem. [ME < ON *slægð* < *slægr,* sly.]

sleight of hand *n.* **1.** Tricks or feats performed by jugglers or magicians so quickly that their manner of execution cannot be observed; legerdemain. **2.** Skill in performing sleight of hand. **3.** The performance of sleight of hand.

slen·der (slĕn'dər) *adj.* **-er, -est. 1.** Having little width in proportion to the height or length; gracefully slim: *"She was slender as a willow shoot is slender—and equally graceful, equally erect"* (Frank Norris). **2.** Spare or small in amount or extent; meager: *slender wages.* **3.** Having little force or justification; feeble; frail: *only a slender chance for success.* [ME *sclendre.*] **—slen'der·ly** *adv.* **—slen'der·ness** *n.*

slen·der·ize (slĕn'də-rīz') *v.* **-ized, -iz·ing, -iz·es.** —*intr.* To become slender or more slender. —*tr.* **1.** To make slender or slim. **2.** To cause to appear slender.

slept (slĕpt) *v.* Past tense and past participle of **sleep.**

sleuth (slōōth) *n.* **1.** *Informal.* A detective. **2.** A sleuthhound (sense 1). —*v.* **sleuthed, sleuth·ing, sleuths.** —*tr.* To track or follow. —*intr.* To act as a detective. [Short for SLEUTHHOUND.]

sleuth·hound (slōōth'hound') *n.* **1.** A dog used for tracking or pursuing, as a bloodhound. **2.** A detective. [ME : *sleuth,* animal track (< ON *slōð*) + *hound,* hound.]

slew[1] also **slue** (slōō) *n. Informal.* A large amount or number; lot: *a whole slew of her friends.* [Ir. Gael. *sluag* < OIr. *slúag.*]

slew[2] (slōō) *v.* Past tense of **slay.**

slew[3] (slōō) *n.* Variant of **slough**[1].

slew[4] (slōō) *v. & n.* Variant of **slue**[1]

slice (slīs) *n.* **1.** A thin, broad piece cut from a larger object. **2.** A portion or share: *a slice of the profits.* **3. a.** A knife with a broad, thin, flexible blade, used for cutting and serving food. **b.** A similar implement for spreading printing ink. **4.** *Sports.* **a.** A stroke that causes a ball to curve off course to the right or, if the player is left-handed, to the left. **b.** The course followed by such a ball. —*v.* **sliced, slic·ing, slic·es.** —*tr.* **1.** To cut or divide into slices. **2.** To cut or remove from a larger piece: *slice off a piece of salami.* **3.** To cut through or across with or as if with a knife. **4.** To divide into portions or shares; parcel out. **5.** To spread, work at, or clear away with a bladed tool such as a slice bar. **6.** *Sports.* To hit (a ball) with a slice. —*intr.* **1.** To move like a knife: *The destroyer sliced through the water.* **2.** *Sports.* To hit a ball with a slice. [ME *sclice,* splinter < OFr. *esclice* < *esclicer,* to splinter, of Germanic orig.] **—slice'a·ble** *adj.* **—slic'er** *n.*

slice bar *n.* An iron tool with a flat, broad end, used to loosen and clear out clinkers from furnace grates.

slice-of-life (slīs'əv-līf') *adj.* Of, relating to, or being a dramatic work that accurately portrays a segment of actual life experience.

slick (slĭk) *adj.* **1.** Smooth, glossy, and slippery: *sidewalks slick with ice.* **2.** Deftly executed; adroit; facile. **3.** Shrewd; wily. **4.** Superficially attractive or skillful but without depth or sound quality: *a slick writing style.* —*n.* **1.** A smooth or slippery surface or area. **2.** An implement used to make a surface slick, esp. a chisel used for smoothing and polishing. **3.** *Informal.* A magazine printed on glossy, high-quality paper, featuring articles and fiction of popular appeal but small literary merit. **4.** A racing automobile tire with a smooth tread. —*tr.v.* **slicked, slick·ing, slicks. 1.** To make smooth, glossy, or oily. **2.** *Informal.* To make neat, trim, or tidy; spruce. [ME *slike.*]

slick·en·side (slĭk'ən-sīd') *n.* A polished and striated rock surface caused by one rock mass sliding over another in a fault plane. [Dial. *slicken,* glossy < SLICK + SIDE.]

slick·er (slĭk'ər) *n.* **1.** A glossy raincoat, esp. one made of plastic or oilskin. **2.** A tool for dressing hides. **3.** *Informal.* A cheat; swindler. **4.** *Informal.* A person with stylish clothing and manners.

slid·den *v. Archaic.* Past participle of **slide.**

slide (slīd) *v.* **slid** (slĭd), **slid·ing, slides.** —*intr.* **1.** To move over a surface while maintaining smooth, continuous contact. **2.** To coast on a slippery surface, such as ice or snow. **3.** To pass smoothly and quietly; glide: *a cat burglar sliding from room to room.* **4.** To go unattended or unacted upon: *Let it slide.* **5.** To lose one's balance or intended direction on a slippery surface. **6.** To move downward: *Prices began to slide.* **7.** To move accidentally out of place; slip: *The cup slid out of his hand.* **8.** To return to a less favorable or less worthy condition. **9.** *Baseball.* To drop down and skid, usually feet first, into a base to avoid being tagged out. —*tr.* To cause to slide or slip. —*n.* **1.** A sliding movement or action. **2.** A smooth surface or track for sliding, usually inclined: *a water slide.* **3.** A playground apparatus for children to slide upon, typically consisting of a smooth chute mounted by means of a ladder. **4.** A part that operates by sliding, as the U-shaped section of tube on a trombone that is moved to produce various tones. **5.** An image on a transparent plate for projection on a screen. **6.** A small glass plate for mounting specimens to be examined under a microscope. **7.** An avalanche. **8.** *Mus.* **a.** A portamento. **b.** An ornamentation consisting of two grace notes approaching the main note. [ME *sliden* < OE *slīdan.*] **—slid'er** *n.*

Synonyms: *slide, slip, glide, coast, skid.* These verbs mean to move smoothly over a surface. *Slide* usually implies rapid and easy movement without loss of contact with the surface. *Slip* more often is applied to accidental movement causing a fall, or threat of a fall, to the surface. *Glide* refers to smooth, free-flowing, and seemingly effortless movement. *Coast* applies specifically to effortless movement due to gravity or inertia. *Skid* generally implies involuntary and uncontrolled movement with much friction.

slide rule *n.* A device consisting essentially of two logarithmically scaled rules mounted to slide along each other so that multiplication, division, and sometimes more complex computations may be reduced to the mechanical equivalent of addition or subtraction.

slide valve *n.* A valve that slides back and forth over ports in the cylinder wall of a steam engine, permitting the intake and outflow of steam to move the piston.

sliding scale *n.* A scale in which indicated prices, taxes, or wages vary in accordance with another factor, as wages with the cost-of-living index or medical charges with a patient's income.

sli·er (slī'ər) *adj.* A comparative of **sly**.

sli·est (slī'ĭst) *adj.* A superlative of **sly**.

slight (slīt) *adj.* **-er, -est. 1.** Small in size, degree, or amount; meager. **2.** Of small importance or consideration; trifling. **3.** Slender or frail; delicate: *"Slight are her arms, yet they have bound me straitly"* (Ezra Pound). *—tr.v.* **slight·ed, slight·ing, slights. 1.** To treat with discourteous reserve or inattention. **2.** To do negligently or thoughtlessly; shirk. **3.** To give insufficient weight or consideration to. *—n.* An act of pointed disrespect or discourtesy. [ME, slender, of Scand. orig.] **—slight'ness** *n.*

slight·ing (slī'tĭng) *adj.* Constituting or conveying a slight; disrespectful; discourteous. **—slight'ing·ly** *adv.*

slight·ly (slīt'lē) *adv.* **1.** Carelessly. **2.** To a small degree or extent; somewhat.

slim (slĭm) *adj.* **slim·mer, slim·mest. 1.** Small in girth or thickness in proportion to height or length; slender. **2.** Small in quality or amount; scant; meager. *—tr. & intr.v.* **slimmed, slim·ming, slims.** To make or become slim or thin. [Du., inferior, < MDu. *slimp,* bad.] **—slim'ly** *adv.* **—slim'ness** *n.*

slime (slīm) *n.* **1.** A thick, sticky, slippery substance. **2.** A mucous substance secreted by certain animals, as fish or slugs. *—tr.v.* **slimed, slim·ing, slimes. 1.** To smear with slime. **2.** To remove slime from, as from fish to be canned. [ME < OE *slīm.*]

slime fungus *n.* Slime mold.

slime mold *n.* Any of various fungi of the class Myxomycetes, having a vegetative body consisting of a slimy, motile, multinucleate mass of protoplasm.

slim·nas·tics (slĭm-năs'tĭks) *pl.n.* Physical exercises designed to facilitate weight loss. [SLIM + (GYM)NASTICS.]

slim·sy (slĭm'zē) also **slimp·sy** (slĭmp'sē) *adj.* **-si·er, -si·est.** *Informal.* Frail; flimsy. [Blend of SLIM and FLIMSY.]

slim·y (slī'mē) *adj.* **-i·er, -i·est. 1.** Consisting of or resembling slime; viscous. **2.** Covered with or exuding slime. **3.** Vile; foul. **—slim'i·ly** *adv.* **—slim'i·ness** *n.*

sling¹ (slĭng) *n.* **1. a.** A weapon consisting of a looped strap in which a stone is whirled and then let fly. **b.** A slingshot. **2.** A looped rope, strap, or chain for supporting, cradling, or hoisting something, esp.: **a.** A strap over the heel to hold a shoe in place. **b.** A strap used to carry a rifle over the shoulder. **c.** *Naut.* A rope or chain for supporting a yard. **d.** A band suspended from the neck to support an injured arm or hand. **3.** The act of slinging. *—tr.v.* **slung** (slŭng), **sling·ing, slings. 1.** To hurl from or as if from a sling; fling. **2.** To place or carry in a sling. **3.** To move by means of a sling; raise or lower in a sling. **4.** To hang loosely or freely; let swing. [ME.] **—sling'er** *n.*

sling² (slĭng) *n.* A drink of brandy, whiskey, or gin, sweetened and usually lemon-flavored. [Orig. unknown.]

sling·shot (slĭng'shŏt') *n.* A Y-shaped stick with an elastic strap attached to the prongs, used for flinging small stones.

slink (slĭngk) *v.* **slunk** (slŭngk), **slink·ing, slinks.** *—intr.* To move in a quiet, furtive manner; sneak. *—tr.* To give birth to prematurely. Used esp. of cows. *—n.* An animal, esp. a calf, born prematurely. *—adj.* Born prematurely. [ME *slynken* < OE *slincan.*] **—slink'ing·ly** *adv.*

slink·y (slĭng'kē) *adj.* **-i·er, -i·est. 1.** Stealthy; furtive; sneaking. **2.** *Informal.* Graceful, sinuous, and sleek: *a slinky evening gown.*

slip¹ (slĭp) *v.* **slipped, slip·ping, slips.** *—intr.* **1. a.** To move quietly and smoothly; glide. **b.** To move stealthily. **2.** To pass gradually, easily, or imperceptibly: *The days slipped by.* **3. a.** To slide unexpectedly and by accident; lose one's balance. **b.** To slide out of place; shift position: *The gear slipped.* **c.** To escape, as from a fastening or grip: *The dog slipped out of its collar.* **4.** To get away completely. **5.** *Informal.* To decline in physical or mental ability, strength, or keenness. **6.** *Informal.* To decline; fall off: *His work is slipping.* **7.** To fall behind a scheduled production rate. **8.** To fall into fault or error. *—tr.* **1.** To cause to move in a smooth, easy, or sliding motion: *slipped the bolt into place.* **2.** To place or insert smoothly and quietly. **3.** To put on or remove (clothing) easily or quickly: *slip on a sweater; slip off shoes.* **4.** To free oneself or itself from; get loose from. **5.** To bring forth (young) prematurely. Used of animals. **6.** To unleash or free (a dog or hawk) to pursue game. **7.** To release; loose; unfasten: *slip the knot.* **8.** To dislocate (a bone). **9.** To pass (a knitting stitch) from one needle to another without knitting it. *—n.* **1.** The act of slipping or sliding. **2.** An accident or mishap, esp. a falling down. **3. a.** An error in conduct or thinking; deviation. **b.** A slight error or oversight, as in speech or writing: *a slip of the tongue.* **4. a.** A docking place for a ship; pier. **b.** A space for a ship between two docks or wharves. **c.** A slipway. **5.** The difference between a vessel's actual speed through water and the speed at which the vessel would move if the screw were propelling against a solid. **6.** A woman's undergarment, serving as a lining for a dress. **7.** A pillowcase. **8.** *Geol.* **a.** A smooth crack at which rock strata have moved on each other. **b.** A small fault. **9.** The difference between optimal and actual output in a mechanical device. **10.** Movement between two parts where none should exist, as between a pulley and belt. **11.** The sliding movement of an airplane in certain attitudes of the plane. *—idioms.* **give (someone) the slip.** *Slang.* To escape the pursuit of. **let slip.** To say inadvertently. **slip one over on.** *Informal.* To hoodwink; trick. [ME *slippen,* prob. < MLG.]

slip² (slĭp) *n.* **1.** A part of a plant cut or broken off for grafting or planting; a scion or cutting. **2.** A long, narrow piece; strip. **3.** A youthful, slender person: *a slip of a girl.* **4.** A small piece of paper, esp. a small form or list: *a sales slip.* **5.** A narrow pew in a church. *—tr.v.* **slipped, slip·ping, slips.** To make a slip from (a plant or plant part). [ME *slippe,* scion.]

slip³ (slĭp) *n.* Thinned potter's clay used for decorating or coating ceramics. [ME *slyppe,* slime < OE *slypa,* a soft mass.]

slip·case (slĭp'kās') *n.* An open-ended protective box for a book.

slip·cov·er (slĭp'kŭv'ər) *n.* A fitted, removable cover of cloth or other material for a piece of upholstered furniture. *—tr.v.* **-ered, -er·ing, -ers.** To provide with a slipcover.

slip·knot (slĭp'nŏt') *n.* **1.** A knot made with a loop so that it slips easily along the rope or cord around which it is tied. **2.** A knot made so that it can readily be untied by pulling one free end.

slip-on (slĭp'ŏn', -ôn') *n.* A garment easily donned or removed. *—modifier: a slip-on blouse.*

slip·o·ver (slĭp'ō'vər) *n.* A garment designed to be put on or taken off over the head. *—modifier: a slipover sweater.*

slip·page (slĭp'ĭj) *n.* **1.** A slipping. **2.** The amount or extent of slipping. **3.** Loss of motion or power due to slipping.

slipped disk *n.* A herniation of an intervertebral disk that results in back pain or sciatica.

slip·per (slĭp'ər) *n.* A light, low shoe that may be slipped on and off easily.

slip·per·wort (slĭp'ər-wûrt', -wôrt') *n.* The calceolaria.

slip·per·y (slĭp'ə-rē) *adj.* **-i·er, -i·est. 1.** Causing or tending to cause sliding or slipping. **2.** Tending to slip or slide, as from one's grasp: *a slippery bar of soap.* **3.** Elusive; evasive: *"how extraordinarily slippery a liar the camera is"* (James Agee). [Alteration of obs. *slipper,* slippery < ME < OE *slipor.*] **—slip'per·i·ly** *adv.* **—slip'per·i·ness** *n.*

slippery elm *n.* A tree, *Ulmus rubra,* of eastern North America, having twigs and leaves with a mucilaginous, aromatic juice formerly used medicinally.

slippery elm

slip ring *n.* A metal ring mounted on a rotating part of a machine to provide a continuous electrical connection through brushes on stationary contacts.

slip-sheet (slĭp'shēt') *Printing.* *—n.* A blank sheet of paper slipped between newly printed sheets to prevent offsetting. *—tr.v.* **-sheet·ed, -sheet·ing, -sheets.** To insert blank sheets between (printed sheets).

slip·shod (slĭp'shŏd') *adj.* **1.** Poorly made or done; careless. **2.** Slovenly in appearance; shabby; seedy.

slip·slop (slĭp'slŏp') *n.* **1.** *Archaic.* Unappetizing liquid or watery food; slops. **2.** Trivial conversation or writing; twaddle. [Redup. of SLOP.]

slip·stitch (slĭp'stĭch') *n.* A stitch used wherever stitching must be invisible on the right side of a garment, as on hems and facings, made by picking up one or two threads of fabric and then loosely catching the needle in the hem edge.

slip·stream (slĭp'strēm') *n.* **1.** The turbulent flow of air driven backward by the propeller or propellers of an aircraft. **2.** The region of reduced air pressure and forward suction produced by and immediately behind a fast-moving ground vehicle. *—intr.v.* **-streamed, -stream·ing, -streams.** To drive in the slipstream of a ground vehicle.

slip-up (slĭp'ŭp') *n.* *Informal.* An error; oversight.

slip·way (slĭp'wā') *n.* A sloping incline leading down to the water on which ships are built or repaired.

slit (slĭt) *n.* A long, narrow cut, tear, or opening. *—tr.v.* **slit, slit·ting, slits. 1.** To make a long, narrow incision in. **2.** To cut lengthwise into strips; split. [ME *slitte.*]

slith·er (slĭ*th*'ər) *v.* **-ered, -er·ing, -ers.** *—intr.* **1.** To slip and slide, as on a loose or uneven surface: *"I tried mechanically to get my body on its feet but they slithered under me"* (William Golding). **2.** To move along by gliding. *—tr.* To cause to slither or glide. *—n.* A slithering movement or gait. [ME *sliddren* < OE *slidrian,* freq. of *slīdan,* to slide.] **—slith'er·y** *adj.*

slit trench *n.* A narrow, shallow trench dug during combat for the protection of a single soldier or a small group.

sliv·er (slĭv'ər) *n.* **1.** A slender piece cut, split, or broken off; splinter. **2.** (*also* slī'vər). A continuous strand of loose wool, flax, or cotton, ready for drawing and twisting. *—tr. & intr.v.* **-ered, -er·ing, -ers.** To split or become split into slivers. [ME *slifere* < *slyven,* to split.]

sliv·o·vitz (slĭv'ə-vĭts) *n.* A dry, colorless plum brandy. [Serbo-Croatian *šljivovica* < *šljiva,* plum.]

slob (slŏb) *n.* *Informal.* An obnoxious, crude, or slovenly person. [Ir. Gael. *slab,* mud.]

slob·ber (slŏb'ər) *v.* **-bered, -ber·ing, -bers.** *—intr.* **1.** To let saliva dribble from the mouth; slaver. **2.** To spill (liquid or food) from the mouth while eating or drinking. **3.** To indulge in mawkish sentimentality in speech or writing. *—tr.* To wet or smear with or as if with saliva or food dribbled from the mouth. *—n.* **1.** Saliva or liquid running from the mouth; drivel. **2.** Oversentimental speech or writing; drivel. [ME *sloberen.*] **—slob'ber·er** *n.* **—slob'ber·y** *adj.*

sloe (slō) *n.* **1.** The blackthorn. **2.** The tart, blue-black, plumlike fruit of the sloe. [ME *sloo* < OE *slā.*]

sloe-eyed (slō'īd') *adj.* Having soft, slanted, dark eyes.

sloe gin *n.* A liqueur having a gin base, flavored with fresh sloes.

slog (slŏg) *v.* **slogged, slog·ging, slogs.** *—tr.* To strike with heavy blows, as in boxing. *—intr.* **1.** To walk with a slow, plodding gait. **2.** To work diligently for long hours. *—n.* **1.** Long, hard work. **2.** A long, exhausting march or hike. [Orig. unknown.] **—slog'ger** *n.*

slo·gan (slō'gən) *n.* **1.** A phrase expressing the aims or nature of an enterprise or organization; motto. **2.** A battle cry of the Scottish clans. **3.** A catch phrase used in advertising or promotion. [Sc. *slogorne,* battle cry < Gael. *sluagh-ghairm* : *sluagh,* host + *gairm,* shout.]

slo·gan·eer (slō'gə-nîr') *n.* One that invents or uses slogans. **—slo'gan·eer'** *v.* **(-eered, -eer·ing, -eers).**

slo·gan·ize (slō'gə-nīz') *tr.v.* **-ized, -iz·ing, -iz·es.** To express in slogan form.

sloop

sloop (slo͞op) *n. Naut.* A single-masted, fore-and-aft-rigged sailing boat with a short standing bowsprit or none at all and a single headsail set from the forestay. [Du. *sloep.*]

sloop of war *n.* A small, armed vessel larger than a gunboat, carrying guns on one deck only.

slop[1] (slŏp) *n.* **1.** Liquid spilled or splashed. **2.** Soft mud or slush. **3.** Unappetizing, watery food or soup. **4.** Often **slops.** Waste food used to feed pigs or other animals; swill. **5.** Often **slops.** Mash remaining after the process of alcohol distillation. **6.** Often **slops.** Human excrement. **7.** Repulsively effusive writing or speech. *—v.* **slopped, slop·ping, slops.** *—intr.* **1.** To spill or splash, as a liquid. **2.** To spill over; overflow. **3.** To gush with excessive sentimentality. **4.** To plod or tramp awkwardly as if walking through mud: *"he slopped along in broken slippers, hands in pockets, whistling"* (Alan Sillitoe). *—tr.* **1.** To spill (liquid). **2.** To spill liquid upon. **3.** To dish out or serve unappetizingly or clumsily. **4.** To feed slops to (animals). [ME *sloppe,* a muddy place.]

slop[2] (slŏp) *n.* **1. slops.** Articles of clothing and bedding issued to sailors from a ship's stores. **2. slops.** Short, full trousers or breeches worn in the 16th century. **3.** A loose outer garment, as a smock or overalls. **4. slops.** *Chiefly Brit.* Cheap, ready-made garments. [ME *sloppe,* a kind of garment.]

slot machine

slope (slōp) *v.* **sloped, slop·ing, slopes.** *—intr.* **1.** To incline upward or downward; lie on a slant. **2.** To move on a slant; ascend or descend. *—tr.* To cause to slope. *—n.* **1.** An inclined line, surface, plane, position, or direction. **2.** A stretch of ground forming a natural or artificial incline: *ski slopes.* **3. a.** A deviation from the horizontal. **b.** The amount or degree of such deviation. **4.** *Math.* The rate at which an ordinate of a point of a line on a coordinate plane changes with respect to a change in the abscissa. **5.** *Math.* The slope of the line tangent to a plane curve at a given point. [< ME *slope,* sloping.] **—slop'er** *n.* **—slop'ing·ly** *adv.*

slo-pitch (slō'pĭch') *n.* Variant of **slow-pitch.**

slop·py (slŏp'ē) *adj.* **-pi·er, -pi·est. 1.** Of, resembling, or covered with slop; muddy: *sloppy ground.* **2.** Watery and unappetizing: *a sloppy stew.* **3.** Spotted or splashed with liquid or slop. **4.** *Informal.* Untidy; messy: *a sloppy house.* **5.** *Informal.* Careless; slipshod: *sloppy work.* **6.** *Informal.* Oversentimental; gushy. **—slop'pi·ly** *adv.* **—slop'pi·ness** *n.*

Synonyms: *sloppy, slovenly, slatternly, blowzy, frowzy, dowdy, unkempt, untidy.* These adjectives refer principally to appearance and indicate lack of care and of qualities that constitute neatness. *Sloppy* informally describes persons or things deficient in cleanliness or orderliness or both. Applied to things, it can also describe inferior quality caused by careless or slipshod work. *Slovenly* is often interchangeable with *sloppy* but applies more often to personal appearance and habits. *Slatternly* refers to lack of cleanliness and neatness in women. *Blowzy* suggests the appearance of a stout, coarse, ruddy-faced woman with disheveled attire. *Frowzy* implies disordered personal appearance and, often, uncleanliness that is offensive. *Dowdy* suggests drabness and tasteless dress in women. *Unkempt* applies to appearance of both persons and things and implies marked lack of care or maintenance. *Untidy,* the least forceful of these terms, refers to persons and things in the broad sense of being deficient in orderliness and care.

sloppy joe (jō) *n.* Ground cooked meat in a usually spicy sauce served on a bun.

slop·work (slŏp'wûrk') *n.* **1. a.** The manufacture of cheap ready-made clothes. **b.** Such clothes themselves. **2.** Work of inferior quality.

slosh (slŏsh) *v.* **sloshed, slosh·ing, slosh·es.** *—tr.* **1.** To stir or splash (a liquid). **2.** To agitate in a liquid: *slosh clothes in a bleach solution.* *—intr.* To splash or flounder in water or another liquid. *—n.* **1.** Slush. **2.** The sound of splashing liquid. [Alteration of SLUSH.] **—slosh'y** *adj.*

sloshed (slŏsht) *adj. Slang.* Drunk. [< p.part. of SLOSH.]

slot[1] (slŏt) *n.* **1.** A long, narrow groove, opening, or notch, as for receiving coins in a vending machine. **2.** A gap between a main and an auxiliary airfoil to provide space for airflow and facilitate the smooth passage of air over the wing. **3.** *Informal.* A suitable position or niche. *—tr.v.* **slot·ted, slot·ting, slots. 1.** To cut or make a slot or slots in. **2.** *Informal.* To put into or assign to a slot. [ME, indentation running down the middle of the breast < OFr. *esclot.*]

slot[2] (slŏt) *n.* The track or trail of an animal, esp. a deer. [OFr. *esclot,* horse's hoofprint, perh. < ON *slōð,* track.]

slot car *n.* An electric toy racing car that fits into a slotted track and is controlled by a rheostat held by the operator.

sloth (slôth, slōth, slŏth) *n.* **1.** Aversion to work or exertion; laziness; indolence. **2.** Any of various slow-moving, arboreal mammals of the family Bradypodidae of tropical America, esp.: **a.** A member of the genus *Bradypus,* having three long-clawed toes on each foot. **b.** A member of the genus *Choloepus,* having two toes on the forefeet and three on the hind feet. **3.** A company of bears. [ME *slowth* < *slow,* slow < OE *slāw.*]

sloth bear *n.* A bear, *Melursus ursinus,* of south-central Asia, having a long snout and dark, shaggy hair.

sloth·ful (slôth'fəl, slōth'-, slŏth'-) *adj.* Lazy; sluggish: *"If we seek merely swollen, slothful ease. . .then bolder and stronger peoples will pass us by"* (Theodore Roosevelt). **—sloth'ful·ly** *adv.* **—sloth'ful·ness** *n.*

slot machine *n.* A vending or gambling machine operated by the insertion of coins into a slot.

slot racing *n.* The game or sport of racing slot cars. **—slot racer** *n.*

slouch (slouch) *v.* **slouched, slouch·ing, slouch·es.** *—intr.* **1.** To sit, stand, or walk with an awkward, drooping posture; assume an excessively relaxed position. **2.** To droop or hang carelessly, as a hat. *—tr.* To cause to droop. *—n.* **1.** A drooping posture or position. **2.** An awkward, lazy, or inept person. [Orig. unknown.] **—slouch'i·ly** *adv.* **—slouch'i·ness** *n.* **—slouch'y** *adj.*

slouch hat *n.* A soft hat with a broad, flexible brim.

slough[1] (slo͞o, slou) also **slew** (slo͞o) *n.* **1.** A depression or hollow, usually filled with deep mud or mire. **2.** Also **slue** (slo͞o). A stagnant swamp, marsh, bog, or pond, esp. as part of a bayou, inlet, or backwater. **3.** A state of deep despair or moral degradation. [ME *slogh* < OE *slōh.*]

slough[2] (slŭf) *n.* **1.** The dead outer skin shed by a snake or amphibian. **2.** *Med.* Dead tissue separated from a living structure. **3.** Any outer layer or covering that is shed. *—v.* **sloughed, slough·ing, sloughs.** *—intr.* **1.** To be cast off or shed; come off. **2.** To shed a slough. **3.** *Med.* To separate from surrounding tissue. Used of dead tissue. *—tr.* To discard as undesirable or unfavorable; get rid of. [ME *slughe.*] **—slough'y** *adj.*

Slo·vak (slō'väk', -văk') also **Slo·va·ki·an** (slō-vä'kē-ən, -văk'ē-ən) *n.* **1.** A member of a Slavic people living in Slovakia. **2.** The Slavic language of the Slovaks. *—adj.* Of or pertaining to Slovakia, the Slovaks, or their language. [Slovak *Slovák.*]

slov·en (slŭv'ən) *n.* One who is careless in personal appearance or work. [ME *sloveyn.*]

Slo·vene (slō'vēn') *n.* **1.** A native or inhabitant of Slovenia. **2.** The Slavic language of Slovenia. **—Slo'vene'** *adj.*

slov·en·ly (slŭv'ən-lē) *adj.* **1.** Having the habits or appearance of a sloven. **2. a.** Untidy; messy. **b.** Careless; slipshod. **—slov'en·li·ness** *n.* **—slov'en·ly** *adv.*

slow (slō) *adj.* **-er, -est. 1. a.** Not moving or able to move quickly; proceeding at a low speed: *a slow boat.* **b.** Marked by a retarded tempo: *a slow waltz.* **2. a.** Taking or requiring a long time: *the slow job of making bread.* **b.** Taking more time than is usual: *a slow worker; slow progress in peace negotiations.* **3. a.** Registering a time or rate behind or below the correct one: *a slow clock.* **b.** Not on time; tardy: *The train is slow today.* **4.** Lacking in promptness or willingness; not precipitate: *slow to accept.* **5.** Sluggish; inactive: *Business was slow.* **6.** *Informal.* Lacking in liveliness or interest; boring: *a slow party.* **7.** Not quick to understand; obtuse: *a slow student.* **8.** Only moderately warm; low: *a slow oven.* *—adv.* **1.** So as to fall behind: *The watch runs slow.* **2.** At a low speed: *Go slow!* *—v.* **slowed, slow·ing, slows.** *—tr.* **1.** To make slow or slower. **2.** To delay; retard. *—intr.* To become slow or slower. [ME < OE *slāw.*] **—slow'ly** *adv.* **—slow'ness** *n.*

Synonyms: *slow, dilatory, leisurely, laggard, deliberate.* These adjectives describe persons or their actions that in general take more time than is necessary. *Slow* is the least specific and not necessarily unfavorable in its implication. *Dilatory* implies fault, such as waste of time, procrastination, or indifference. *Leisurely* suggests lack of pressure or of awareness of a deadline. *Laggard* implies loitering or falling behind through indifference or lack of effort. *Deliberate* applies to one whose lack of speed in acting traces to self-restraint, careful consideration of each move, desire to avoid error, or the like.

Usage: *Slow* may sometimes be used as a variant form of the adverb *slowly,* when it comes after the verb: *We drove the car slow.* In formal writing *slowly* is generally preferred. *Slow* is often used in speech and informal writing, especially when brevity and forcefulness are sought: *Drive slow! Slow* is also the established idiomatic form with certain senses of common verbs: *The watch runs slow. Take it slow.*

slow burn *n.* A gradual increase or accumulation of anger: *doing a slow burn while waiting in line.*

slow·down (slō′doun′) *n.* A slackening of pace, esp. an intentional slowing down of production.

slow-foot·ed (slō′fo͝ot′ĭd) *adj.* Proceeding at a tediously slow pace: *a slow-footed story.*

slow match *n.* A fuse that burns slowly and is used to set off explosives.

slow motion *n.* A motion-picture technique in which the action as projected is slower than the original action.

slow neutron *n.* A neutron in thermal equilibrium with the surrounding medium, esp. one produced by fission, slowed by a moderator, and having an average speed of approximately 2,200 meters per second.

slow-pitch also **slo-pitch** (slō′pĭch′) *n. Sports.* A softball game in which there are ten players to a team and in which a pitch, in order to be legal, must travel in an arc from three to ten feet high.

slow·poke (slō′pōk′) *n. Informal.* One who moves, works, or acts slowly.

slow virus *n.* Any of a group of animal viruses, such as the one that causes multiple sclerosis, characterized by prolonged incubation periods in which the virus remains dormant in the body prior to the development of symptoms.

slow-wit·ted (slō′wĭt′ĭd) *adj.* Slow to comprehend; dull. **—slow′wit′ted·ly** *adv.* **—slow′wit′ted·ness** *n.*

slow·worm (slō′wûrm′) *n.* A limbless European lizard, *Anguis fragilis,* having a smooth, snakelike body. [ME *slowurm* < OE *slāwyrm.*]

sloyd (sloid) *n.* A system of manual training developed in Sweden, based upon woodcarving and joinery as exercises in the use of tools. [Swed. *slöjd,* skill, skilled labor.]

slub (slŭb) *tr.v.* **slubbed, slub·bing, slubs.** To draw out and twist (a sliver of silk or other textile fiber) in preparation for spinning. *—n.* **1.** A soft, thick nub in yarn that is either an imperfection or purposely set for a desired effect. **2.** A slightly twisted roll of fiber, as of silk or cotton. [Orig. unknown.]

sludge (slŭj) *n.* **1.** Mud, mire, or ooze covering the ground or forming a deposit, as on a river bed. **2.** Slushy matter or sediment such as that precipitated by the treatment of sewage or collected in a boiler. **3.** Finely broken or half-formed ice on a body of water. [Perh. alteration of dial. *slutch,* mire.] **—sludg′y** *adj.*

slue[1] also **slew** (slo͞o) *v.* **slued, slu·ing, slues** also **slewed, slew·ing, slews.** *—tr.* **1.** To turn or twist (something) sideways. **2.** To twist (a mast or boom) around on its axis. *—intr.* To turn, twist, move, or skid to the side. *—n.* **1.** The act of sluing. **2.** The position to which something has slued. [Orig. unknown.]

slue[2] *n.* Variant of **slew[1]**.

slue[3] *n.* A variant of **slough[1]** (sense 2).

slug[1] (slŭg) *n.* **1.** A round bullet larger than buckshot. **2.** *Informal.* A shot of liquor. **3.** A small metal disk for use in a slot machine, esp. one used illegally. **4.** A lump of metal or glass ready to be processed. **5.** *Printing.* **a.** A strip of type metal, less than type-high and thicker than a lead, used for spacing. **b.** A line of cast type in a single strip of metal. **c.** A compositor's type line of identifying marks or instructions, inserted temporarily in copy. **6.** *Physics.* The unit of mass that is accelerated at the rate of one foot per second per second when acted upon by a force of one pound weight. *—tr.v.* **slugged, slug·ging, slugs.** *Printing.* To add slugs to. [Prob. < SLUG[2].]

slug[2] (slŭg) *n.* **1.** Any of various terrestrial gastropod mollusks of the genus *Limax* and related genera, having an elongated body with no external shell. **2.** The smooth, soft larva of certain insects, such as the sawfly. **3.** *Informal.* A sluggard. [ME *slugge,* sluggard, prob. of Scand. orig.]

slug[3] (slŭg) *tr.v.* **slugged, slug·ging, slugs.** To strike heavily, esp. with the fist. *—n.* A hard, heavy blow, as with the fist or a baseball bat. [Perh. < SLUG[1].]

slug·a·bed (slŭg′ə-bĕd′) *n.* One inclined to stay in bed out of laziness.

slug·fest (slŭg′fĕst′) *n. Slang.* **1.** A fight marked by a vicious exchange of blows. **2.** *Baseball.* A game in which many hits and runs are scored.

slug·gard (slŭg′ərd) *n.* A slothful person; idler. *—adj.* Lazy. [ME *sluggart,* prob. < *sluggen,* to be lazy, prob. of Scand. orig.] **—slug′gard·ly** *adj.* **—slug′gard·ness** *n.*

slug·ger (slŭg′ər) *n.* **1.** One that slugs, as a fighter who swings out with his fists. **2.** *Baseball.* A hard hitter.

slug·gish (slŭg′ĭsh) *adj.* **1.** Displaying little movement or activity; slow; inactive. **2.** Lacking in alertness, vigor, or energy; dull; lazy. **3.** Slow to perform or respond to stimulation. [ME, prob. < *sluggen,* to be lazy. —see SLUGGARD.] **—slug′gish·ly** *adv.* **—slug′gish·ness** *n.*

sluice (slo͞os) *n.* **1. a.** A manmade channel for conducting water with a valve or gate to regulate the flow. **b.** The body of water so regulated or held back. **2.** The valve or gate used in a sluice. **3.** An artificial channel, esp. one for carrying off excess water. **4.** A long inclined trough, as for carrying logs or separating gold ore. *—v.* **sluiced, sluic·ing, sluic·es.** *—tr.* **1. a.** To flood or drench by means of a sluice. **b.** To wash with a sudden flow of water; flush. **2.** To draw off or let out by a sluice. **3.** To send (logs) down a sluice. *—intr.* To flow out from or as if from a sluice. [ME *scluse* < OFr. *excluse* < Lat. *exclusa,* fem. p.part. of *excludere,* to shut out. —see EXCLUDE.]

slum (slŭm) *n.* Often **slums.** A heavily populated urban area characterized by poor housing and squalor. ***—modifier:*** *slum housing.* *—intr.v.* **slummed, slum·ming, slums.** To visit a slum, esp. from curiosity or for amusement. Usually used in the phrase *go slumming.* [Orig. unknown.]

slum·ber (slŭm′bər) *v.* **-bered, -ber·ing, -bers.** *—intr.* **1.** To sleep. **2.** To be dormant or quiescent. *—tr.* To pass (time) in sleep. *—n.* **1.** Sleep. **2.** A state of inactivity or dormancy. [ME *slumeren,* freq. of *slumen,* to doze < *slume,* sleep < OE *sluma.*] **—slum′ber·er** *n.* **—slum′ber·ing·ly** *adv.*

slum·ber·ous (slŭm′bər-əs) also **slum·ber·y** (-bə-rē) or **slum·brous** (-brəs) *adj.* **1.** Sleepy; drowsy. **2. a.** Suggestive of or resembling sleep. **b.** Quiet; tranquil. **3.** Causing or inducing sleep; soporific. **—slum′ber·ous·ly** *adv.* **—slum′ber·ous·ness** *n.*

slumber party *n.* An overnight party in which young teenage girls wear nightclothes, socialize, and sometimes sleep.

slum·gul·lion (slŭm′gŭl′yən) *n.* **1.** *Slang.* A watery meat stew. **2.** *Chiefly Brit. Slang.* A weak beverage. [Perh. dial. *slum,* slime + dial. *gullion,* mud.]

slum·lord (slŭm′lôrd′) *n. Informal.* A landlord of slum property, esp. one that allows the property to deteriorate.

slump (slŭmp) *intr.v.* **slumped, slump·ing, slumps. 1.** To fall or sink suddenly, as into a bog or through a crust of snow or ice. **2.** To decline suddenly; sink: *Business slumped.* **3.** To slide down suddenly. **4.** To droop, as in sitting or standing; slouch. *—n.* A sudden falling off or decline, as in interest, activity, prices, or business. [Prob. of Scand. orig.]

slung (slŭng) *v.* Past tense and past participle of **sling[1]**.

slung·shot (slŭng′shŏt′) *n.* A small, heavy weight attached to a thong, used as a weapon.

slunk (slŭngk) *v.* Past tense and past participle of **slink**.

slur (slûr) *tr.v.* **slurred, slur·ring, slurs. 1.** To pass over lightly or carelessly; treat without due consideration. **2.** To pronounce indistinctly. **3.** To speak slightingly of; disparage. **4.** *Mus.* **a.** To glide over (a series of notes) smoothly without a break. **b.** To mark with a slur. **5.** *Printing.* To blur or smear. *—n.* **1.** A disparaging remark; aspersion. **2.** A slurred utterance or sound. **3.** *Mus.* **a.** A curved line connecting notes on a score to indicate that they are to be played or sung legato. **b.** A passage played or sung in this manner. **4.** *Printing.* A smeared or blurred impression. [< ME *sloor,* mud.]

slurb (slûrb) *n. Informal.* An unsightly suburban area marked by inferior and often tiresomely similar dwellings. [SL(OVENLY) + (SUB)URB.]

slurp (slûrp) *v.* **slurped, slurp·ing, slurps.** *—tr.* To eat or drink in a noisy manner. *—intr.* To eat or drink something noisily. [Du. *slurpen.*]

slur·ry (slûr′ē) *n., pl.* **-ries.** A thin mixture of a liquid, esp. water, and any of several finely divided substances, such as cement, plaster of Paris, or clay particles. [ME *slory,* perh. < *sloor,* mud.]

slush (slŭsh) *n.* **1.** Partially melted snow or ice. **2.** Soft mud; slop; mire. **3.** Refuse grease or fat from a ship's galley. **4.** A greasy compound used as a lubricant for machinery. **5.** Maudlin speech or writing; sentimental drivel. *—v.* **slushed, slush·ing, slush·es.** *—tr.* **1.** To daub (machinery) with slush. **2.** To fill (joints in masonry) with mortar. **3.** To wash down (a deck) by dashing water upon. **4.** To splash or soak with slush or mud. *—intr.* **1.** To walk or proceed through slush. **2.** To make a splashing or slushy sound. [Perh. of Scand. orig.] **—slush′i·ness** *n.* **—slush′y** *adv.*

slush fund *n.* **1.** A fund raised for undesignated purposes, esp.: **a.** A fund used by a group, as office employees, for entertainment or the like. **b.** A fund raised by a group for corrupt practices, as bribery or graft. **2.** Money formerly raised by the sale of garbage from a warship to buy small items of luxury for the crew.

slut (slŭt) *n.* **1.** A slovenly, dirty woman; slattern. **2. a.** A woman of loose morals. **b.** A prostitute. **3.** A bold, brazen girl. **4.** A female dog. [ME *slutte.*] **—slut′tish** *adj.* **—slut′tish·ly** *adv.* **—slut′tish·ness** *n.*

sly (slī) *adj.* **sli·er, sli·est** also **sly·er, sly·est. 1.** Stealthily clever; crafty; cunning. **2.** Secretive rather than open; underhand; deceitful. **3.** Playfully mischievous; roguish: arch: *a sly wink.* [ME *sleih* < ON *slœgr,* clever.] **—sly′ly** *adv.* **—sly′ness** *n.*

Synonyms: *sly, cunning, tricky, crafty, wily, foxy, artful, guileful.* These adjectives describe persons disposed to be indirect or devious in dealing with others. *Sly* usually implies stealth and absence of candor but in general suggests roguishness more strongly than outright deceit. *Cunning* stresses mental acuteness and practical skill in gaining an end, often at the expense of moral principles. *Tricky* emphasizes shiftiness, deception, and general absence of scruples. *Crafty* suggests one who is a master of devious methods in general. *Wily* suggests subterfuge or stratagem intended to trap another. *Foxy* implies shrewdness and usually long experience in the use of trickery, but is often less derogatory than most of these terms. *Artful* emphasizes adroitness and

sluice
Hells Canyon Dam in Idaho

ingenuity, but not necessarily deceit, in maneuvering to gain an advantage. *Guileful,* in contrast, implies a designing, deceitful, and often treacherous nature.

sly·boots (slī'bo͞ots') *n. Informal.* A sly person.

slype (slīp) *n. Archit.* A covered passage, esp. one between the transept and chapter house of a cathedral. [Orig. unknown.]

Sm The symbol for the element samarium.

smack[1] (smăk) *v.* **smacked, smack·ing, smacks.** *—tr.* **1.** To make a sound by pressing together the lips and pulling them apart quickly. **2.** To kiss noisily. **3.** To strike heartily and noisily. *—intr.* To make or give a smack. *—n.* **1.** The loud, sharp sound of smacking. **2.** A noisy kiss. **3.** A sharp blow or slap. *—adv.* **1.** With a smack: *fell smack on her head.* **2.** Directly: *went smack against the rules.* [Prob. of MLG orig.]

smack[2] (smăk) *n.* **1. a.** A distinctive flavor or taste. **b.** A suggestion or trace. **2.** A small amount; smattering. *—intr.v.* **smacked, smack·ing, smacks. 1.** To have a distinctive flavor or taste. **2.** To give an indication; suggest: *This smacks of foul play.* [ME < OE *smæc.*]

smack[3] (smăk) *n.* A sloop-rigged boat used chiefly in fishing, esp. to transport the catch to a market. [Du. *smak.*]

smack[4] (smăk) *n. Slang.* Heroin. [Orig. unknown.]

smack-dab (smăk'dăb') *adv. Slang.* Squarely; directly.

smack·er (smăk'ər) *n.* **1.** A loud kiss. **2.** A resounding blow. **3.** *Slang.* A dollar.

smack·ing (smăk'ĭng) *adj.* Brisk; vigorous; spanking: *a smacking breeze.*

small (smôl) *adj.* **-er, -est. 1.** Characterized by relatively little size or slight dimensions. **2.** Limited in importance or significance; trivial: *a small matter.* **3.** Limited in degree or scope: *small farm operations.* **4.** Lacking position, influence, or status; minor: *"A crowd of small writers had vainly attempted to rival Addison"* (Macaulay). **5.** Unpretentious; modest. **6.** Not fully grown; very young. **7.** Petty: *a small mind.* **8.** Belittled; humiliated. **9.** Diluted; weak. Used of alcoholic beverages. **10.** Lacking strength: *a small voice.* *—adv.* **1.** In small pieces: *Cut it up small.* **2.** Softly. **3.** In a small manner. *—n.* **1.** Something smaller than the rest: *the small of the back.* **2. smalls. a.** Small things collectively. **b.** *Chiefly Brit.* Smallclothes. [ME < OE *smæl.*] **—small'ness** *n.*

Synonyms: *small, little, diminutive, minute, miniature, minuscule, tiny, wee, petite.* These adjectives describe persons or things whose physical size is markedly below that of the average. *Small* and *little* can often be used interchangeably. In general, *small* has the wider application; with reference to physical size, *little* is usually more emphatic in implying sharp reduction from the average. *Little* is sometimes used also to add a sense of charm, endearment, or pathos to the term modified. *Diminutive* means very, often abnormally, small. *Minute* describes what is small to the point of being difficult to see. *Miniature* applies to a representation of something on a greatly reduced scale. *Minuscule* refers to what is very small, and is occasionally used in the sense of miniature. *Tiny* and *wee* both mean exceptionally small and are often interchangeable, though *wee* generally implies endearment or humor. *Petite* is applied principally to the feminine figure in the sense of small and trim.

small arm *n.* A firearm that can be carried in the hand.

small beer *n.* **1.** Beer that is weak or of inferior quality. **2.** Trivia.

small calorie *n.* A calorie (sense 1).

small capital *n.* A smaller letter having the form of a capital letter, for example: SMALL CAPITALS.

small change *n.* **1.** Coins of low denomination. **2.** Something of little value or significance.

small-claims court (smôl'klāmz') *n.* A special court established for the simplified and efficient handling of small claims on debts.

small·clothes (smôl'klō*th*z', -klōz') *pl.n.* **1.** Men's close-fitting knee breeches worn in the 18th century. **2.** *Chiefly Brit.* Small items of clothing, such as underclothes or handkerchiefs.

smallclothes
Viennese dandy of the 18th century

small fry *n.* **1.** Young or small fish. **2.** Small children. **3.** Unimportant or insignificant persons or things.

small hours *pl.n.* The early postmidnight hours.

small intestine *n.* The part of the intestine in which digestion is completed, extending from the pylorus to the cecum and consisting of the duodenum, the jejunum, and the ileum.

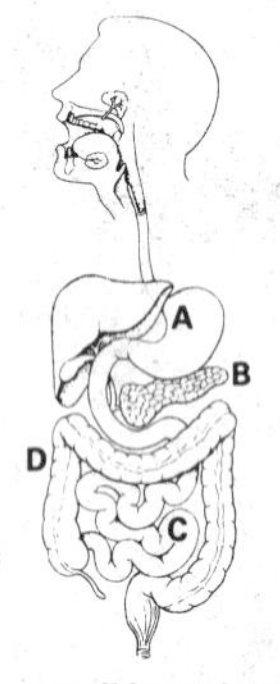

small intestine
A. Stomach
B. Pancreas
C. Small intestine
D. Large intestine

small-mind·ed (smôl'mīn'dĭd) *adj.* **1.** Having a narrow or selfish attitude. **2.** Characterized by pettiness or selfishness. **—small'-mind'ed·ly** *adv.* **—small'-mind'ed·ness** *n.*

small·mouth bass (smôl'mouth') *n.* A North American freshwater food and game fish, *Micropterus dolomieui.*

small potatoes *pl.n. Informal.* Unimportant persons or things.

small·pox (smôl'pŏks') *n.* An acute, highly infectious disease caused by a virus and initially characterized by chills, high fever, headache, and backache, with subsequent widespread eruption of pimples that eventually blister, produce pus, and form pockmarks.

small-scale (smôl'skāl') *adj.* **1.** Limited in scope or extent; modest: *a small-scale plan.* **2.** Created on a small scale.

small talk *n.* Casual or trivial conversation.

small·time (smôl'tīm') *adj. Informal.* Insignificant or unimportant; minor: *a smalltime comedian.* **—small'tim'er** *n.*

smalt (smôlt) *n.* A deep-blue paint and ceramic pigment produced by pulverizing a glass made of silica, potash, and cobalt oxide. [Fr. < Ital. *smalto,* of Germanic orig.]

smalt·ite (smôl'tīt') also **smalt·ine** (smôl'tĭn, -tēn') *n.* A white to silver-gray ore of nickel and cobalt, essentially $(Co,Ni)As_2$. [Alteration of *smaltine* < Fr. < *smalt,* smalt.]

sma·rag·dite (smə-răg'dīt') *n.* A thin, foliated, light-green amphibole mineral. [Fr. < Lat. *smaragdus,* a kind of precious stone < Gk. *smaragdos.*]

smarm·y (smär'mē) *adj.* **-i·er, -i·est. 1.** Sleek. **2.** Gushingly or unctuously flattering: *"He is a smarmy, obsequious sort"* (New Yorker). **—smarm·i·ness** *n.* [< dial. *smarm,* to gush, slobber.]

smart (smärt) *adj.* **-er, -est. 1 a.** Characterized by sharp, quick thought; intelligent; bright. **b.** Amusingly clever; witty: *a smart remark.* **c.** Impertinent: *a smart answer.* **2.** Characterized by sharp, quick movement; energetic: *a smart pace.* **3.** Characterized by sharpness and shrewdness in dealings: *a smart businessman.* **4.** Fashionable; elegant: *a smart suit; a smart restaurant; the smart set.* **5.** Of, relating to, or being a device that imitates human intelligence. *—intr.v.* **smart·ed, smart·ing, smarts. 1. a.** To cause a sharp usually superficial, stinging pain, as an acrid liquid or a slap. **b.** To be the source of such a pain, as a wound. **c.** To feel such a pain. **2.** To suffer acutely, as from mental distress, wounded feelings, or remorse: *"No creature smarts so little as a fool"* (Pope). **3.** To suffer or pay a heavy penalty. *—n.* **1.** Sharp mental or physical pain. **2. smarts.** *Slang.* Intelligence; expertise. [ME, causing pain < OE *smeart.*] **—smart'ly** *adv.* **—smart'ness** *n.*

smart al·eck (ăl'ĭk) *n. Informal.* One who is obnoxiously self-assertive and arrogant. [SMART + *Aleck,* nickname for *Alexander.*] **—smart'-al'eck·y** *adj.*

smart bomb *n.* A bomb that can be guided by radio waves or a laser beam to its target.

smart·en (smär'tn) *v.* **-ened, -en·ing, -ens.** *—tr.* **1.** To improve in appearance or stylishness; spruce up. **2.** To make quicker: *smarten the pace.* *—intr.* To make oneself smart or smarter.

smart money *n.* **1.** Compensation beyond the value of actual harm, awarded by jury in cases of gross negligence or willful misconduct. **2.** A bet or bets placed by experienced gamblers or those having privileged information.

smart·weed (smärt'wēd') *n.* Any of various marsh plants of the genus *Polygonum* (or *Persicaria*), having small, densely clustered pink, white, or green flowers.

smartweed

smar·ty-pants (smär'tē-pănts') *pl.n. Informal.* A smart aleck.

smash (smăsh) *v.* **smashed, smash·ing, smash·es.** *—tr.* **1.** To break into pieces suddenly, noisily, and violently; shatter. **2. a.** To throw or dash (something) violently so as to shatter or crush. **b.** To strike with a heavy blow; batter. **3.** *Sports.* To hit (a ball or shuttlecock) in a violent overhand stroke. **4.** To crush or destroy completely: *smashed all resistance.* *—intr.* **1.** To move or be moved suddenly, noisily, and violently. **2.** To break into pieces, as from a violent blow or collision. **3.** *Sports.* To hit a ball or shuttlecock in a violent overhand stroke. **4.** To be crushed or destroyed. **5.** To go bankrupt. *—n.* **1. a.** The act or sound of smashing. **b.** The condition of having been smashed. **2. a.** Total defeat or destruction; ruin. **b.** Financial failure; bankruptcy. **3.** A collision or crash. **4. a.** A drink made of mint, sugar, soda water, and alcoholic liquor, usually brandy. **b.** A soft drink made of crushed fruit. **5.** *Sports.* A violent overhand stroke as in tennis or badminton. **6.** *Informal.* A resounding success. *—adj. Informal.* Of, relating to, or being a resounding success. *—adv.* With a sudden, violent crash. [Perh. blend of SMACK and CRASH.] **—smash'er** *n.*

smash·ed (smăsht) *adj. Slang.* Intoxicated; drunk.

smash·ing (smăsh'ĭng) *adj. Informal.* Extraordinarily impressive or fine; wonderful.

smash·up (smăsh'ŭp') *n.* **1.** A total collapse or defeat. **2.** A serious collision between vehicles; wreck.

smat·ter (smăt'ər) *v.* **-tered, -ter·ing, -ters.** *—tr.* **1.** To speak (a language) without fluency. **2.** To study or approach superficially; dabble in. *—intr.* To prattle. *—n.* A smattering. [ME *smateren.*] **—smat'ter·er** *n.*

smat·ter·ing (smăt'ər-ĭng) *n.* **1.** Superficial or piecemeal knowledge: *"A smattering of everything, and a knowledge of nothing"* (Dickens). **2.** A small, scattered amount or number: *a smattering of raindrops.*

smaze (smāz) *n.* A relatively dry atmospheric mixture of smoke and haze. [SM(OKE) + (H)AZE.]

smear (smîr) *v.* **smeared, smear·ing, smears.** *—tr.* **1.** To spread or daub with a sticky, greasy, or dirty substance. **2.** To stain by or as if by spreading or daubing with a sticky, greasy, or dirty substance. **3.** To stain or attempt to destroy the reputation of; vilify: *political enemies smearing his name.* **4.** *Slang.* To defeat utterly; smash. *—intr.* To be or become stained or dirtied. *—n.* **1.** A mark made by smearing; spot; blot. **2.** A substance to be spread on a surface. **3.** A sub-

stance or preparation placed on a slide for microscopic examination. **4.** An attempt to destroy a reputation; vilification; slander. [ME *smeren,* to anoint < OE *smerian.*]
smear·case (smîr'kās') *n.* Cottage cheese. [G. *Schmierkäse* : *schmieren,* to smear + *Käse,* cheese < Lat. *caseus.*]
smear word *n.* An abusive or disparaging word or phrase intended to denigrate a person or group.
smear·y (smîr'ē) *adj.* **-i·er, -i·est. 1.** Smeared. **2.** Tending to smear or soil. **—smear'i·ness** *n.*
smell (smĕl) *v.* **smelled** or **smelt** (smĕlt), **smell·ing, smells.** *—tr.* **1.** To perceive the scent of (something) by means of the olfactory nerves. **2.** To sense the presence of by or as if by the olfactory nerves; detect; discover: *We smelled trouble ahead.* *—intr.* **1.** To use the sense of smell; perceive the scent of something. **2.** To have or emit an odor. **3.** To be suggestive; have a touch of something: *a cave that smells of terror.* **4.** To have or emit an unpleasant odor; stink. **5.** To appear to be dishonest; suggest evil or corruption. *—n.* **1.** The sense by which odors are perceived; the olfactory sense. **2.** That quality of something that may be perceived by the olfactory sense; odor; scent. **3.** The act or an instance of smelling. **4.** A distinctive quality enveloping or characterizing something; aura; trace: *the smell of success.* ***—idiom.*** **smell a rat.** *Slang.* To suspect that something is wrong. [ME *smellen.*]
smelling salts *pl.n. (used with a sing. or pl. verb).* Any of several preparations based on spirits of ammonia, sniffed as a restorative.
smell·y (smĕl'ē) *adj.* **-i·er, -i·est.** *Informal.* Having an unpleasant or offensive odor.
smelt[1] (smĕlt) *v.* **smelt·ed, smelt·ing, smelts.** *—tr.* To melt or fuse (ores), separating the metallic constituents. *—intr.* To melt or fuse. Used of ores. [MLG *smelten.*]
smelt[2] (smĕlt) *n., pl.* **smelts** or **smelt.** Any of various small silvery marine and freshwater food fishes of the family Osmeridae, esp. *Osmerus mordax,* of North America and *O. eperlanus,* of Europe. [ME < OE.]
smelt[3] (smĕlt) *v.* A past tense and past participle of **smell.**
smelt·er (smĕl'tər) *n.* **1. a.** An apparatus for smelting. **b.** Also **smelt·er·y** (smĕl'tə-rē). An establishment for smelting. **2.** A person engaged in the smelting industry.
smew (smyōō) *n.* A small, crested Old World duck, *Mergus albellus,* having a narrow bill and white and black plumage in the male. [Orig. unknown.]
smid·gen also **smid·geon** or **smid·gin** (smĭj'ən) *n. Informal.* A very small quantity or portion; bit; mite. [Prob. alteration of dial. *smitch,* particle.]
smi·lax (smī'lăks') *n.* **1.** Any plant of the genus *Smilax,* which includes climbing vines such as the catbrier. **2.** A vine, *Asparagus asparagoides,* that has glossy foliage and is popular as a floral decoration. [NLat. *Smilax,* genus name < Lat. *smilax,* bindweed < Gk.]
smile (smīl) *n.* **1.** A facial expression characterized by an upward curving of the corners of the mouth and indicating pleasure, amusement, or derision. **2.** A pleasant or favorable disposition or aspect. *—v.* **smiled, smil·ing, smiles.** *—intr.* **1.** To have or form a smile. **2.** To express or appear to express approval or beneficence. *—tr.* **1.** To express with a smile. **2.** To effect or accomplish with or as if with a smile. [< ME *smilen,* to smile.] **—smil'er** *n.* **—smil'ing·ly** *adv.* **—smil'ing·ness** *n.*
Synonyms: *smile, grin, simper, smirk.* These nouns denote facial expressions in which the mouth is widened and curved upward slightly at the corners. *Smile* is the most general, since it can cover a wide range of feeling, from affection to malice, and can even refer to a mask for one's true feelings. A *grin* is a broad smile that exposes the teeth. Usually it is a spontaneous expression of good humor, approval, or triumph. A *simper* is a tight-lipped, affected, silly smile expressing self-indulgence. A *smirk* is an affected but bolder smile that expresses derision or suggests smugness or conceit.
smirch (smûrch) *tr.v.* **smirched, smirch·ing, smirch·es. 1.** To soil, stain, or dirty with a smearing agent: *"their tough, hostile faces, smirched by the grime and rust"* (Henry Roth). **2.** To dishonor; defame. *—n.* Something that smirches; a blot, smear, or stain. [ME *smorchen.*]
smirk (smûrk) *intr.v.* **smirked, smirk·ing, smirks.** To smile in a self-conscious, knowing, or simpering manner. *—n.* A self-conscious, knowing, or simpering smile. [ME *smirken* < OE *smearcian,* to smile.] **—smirk'er** *n.* **—smirk'ing·ly** *adv.*
smite (smīt) *v.* **smote** (smōt), **smit·ten** (smĭt'n) or **smote, smit·ing, smites.** *—tr.* **1. a.** To inflict a heavy blow on with or as if with the hand, a tool or a weapon. **b.** To drive or strike (a weapon, for example) forcefully onto or into something else. **2.** To attack, damage, or destroy by or as if by blows. **3. a.** To afflict: *smitten with the plague.* **b.** To afflict retributively; chasten or chastise. **4.** To affect sharply with deep feeling: *smitten with love.* *—intr.* To strike or beat. [ME *smiten* < OE *smītan.*] **—smit'er** *n.*
smith (smĭth) *n.* **1.** A metalworker, esp. one who works metal when it is hot and malleable. Often used in combination: *silversmith, goldsmith.* **2.** A blacksmith. [ME < OE *smið.*]
smith·er·eens (smĭth'ə-rēnz') *pl.n. Informal.* Fragments or splintered pieces; bits: *The dish broke into smithereens.* [Ir. Gael. *smidirīn,* dim. of *smiodar,* small fragment.]
smith·er·y (smĭth'ə-rē) *n., pl.* **-ies. 1.** The occupation or craft of a smith. **2.** A smithy.
smith·son·ite (smĭth'sə-nīt') *n.* A white or yellow-to-brown mineral, chiefly $ZnCO_3$, used as a source of zinc. [After James *Smithson* (1765–1829).]
smith·y (smĭth'ē, smĭ*th*'ē) *n., pl.* **-ies.** A blacksmith's shop; forge. [ME < ON *smiðja.*]
smit·ten (smĭt'n) *v.* A past participle of **smite.**
smock (smŏk) *n.* A loose coatlike outer garment, often worn to protect the clothes while working. *—tr.v.* **smocked, smock·ing, smocks. 1.** To clothe in a smock. **2.** To decorate (fabric) with smocking. [ME *smok,* woman's undergarment < OE *smoc.*]

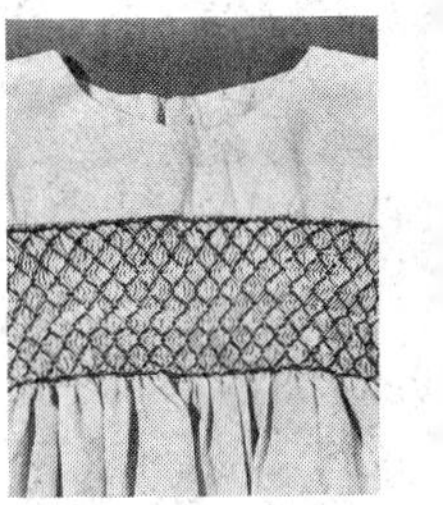
smocking

smock·ing (smŏk'ĭng) *n.* Needlework decoration of small regularly spaced gathers stitched into a honeycomb pattern.
smog (smŏg, smôg) *n.* Fog that has become mixed and polluted with smoke. [SM(OKE) + (F)OG.] **—smog'gy** *adj.* **—smog'less** *adj.*
smoke (smōk) *n.* **1.** The vaporous system made up of small particles of carbonaceous matter in the air, resulting mainly from the incomplete combustion of organic material, such as wood or coal. **2.** A suspension of particles in a gaseous medium. **3.** A cloud of fine particles. **4.** Something insubstantial, unreal, or transitory. **5. a.** The act of smoking any form of tobacco. **b.** The duration of this act. **6.** *Informal.* Tobacco in any form that can be smoked, esp. a cigarette. **7.** A substance used in warfare to produce a smoke screen. **8.** A pale to grayish blue to bluish gray or dark gray. ***—modifier:*** *a smoke shop; a smoke bomb.* *—v.* **smoked, smok·ing, smokes.** *—intr.* **1.** To emit smoke or a smokelike substance. **2.** To emit smoke excessively. **3.** To draw in and exhale smoke from a cigarette, cigar, or pipe. *—tr.* **1.** To draw in and exhale the smoke of (tobacco, for example). **2.** To preserve (meat or fish) by exposure to the aromatic smoke of burning hardwood, usually after pickling in salt or brine. **3.** To fumigate (a house, for example). **4.** To expose (glass) to smoke in order to darken or change its color. ***—phrasal verb.*** **smoke out. 1.** To force out of a place of hiding or concealment by or as if by the use of smoke. **2.** To detect and bring to public view; expose; reveal. [ME < OE *smoca.*]
smoke·chas·er (smōk'chā'sər) *n.* A forest firefighter, esp. one whose light equipment permits quick arrival at a fire.
smoke detector *n.* An alarm device that automatically detects the presence of smoke.
smoke·house (smōk'hous') *n.* A structure in which meat or fish is cured with smoke.
smoke·jack (smōk'jăk') *n.* A device for turning a roasting spit in a chimney, activated by the current of rising gases.
smoke·jump·er (smōk'jŭm'pər) *n.* A firefighter who drops by parachute into a forest fire.
smoke·less (smōk'lĭs) *adj.* Emitting little or no smoke.
smokeless powder *n.* A propellant charge composed mainly of nitrocellulose, which produces little or no smoke, used in projectiles and small artillery rockets.
smok·er (smō'kər) *n.* **1.** One that smokes. **2.** A railroad car in which smoking is permitted. **3.** An informal social gathering for men.
smoke screen *n.* **1.** A mass of dense artificial smoke used to conceal military areas or operations from an enemy. **2.** An action or statement used to conceal actual plans or intentions.
smoke·stack (smōk'stăk') *n.* A large chimney or vertical pipe through which combustion vapors, gases, and smoke are discharged.
smoke tree *n.* Either of two trees, *Cotinus obovatus,* of the southern United States, or *C. coggygria,* of Eurasia, having plumelike clusters of small yellowish flowers. [From the resemblance of the flower clusters to puffs of smoke.]
Smok·ey (smō'kē) *n. Slang.* A law-enforcement officer on highway patrol. [From the resemblance of some state troopers' hats to that of *Smokey* the Bear, an animal who warns against fires in U.S. Forest Service posters.]
smoking car *n.* A smoker (sense 2).
smoking gun *n. Informal.* Something that serves as indisputable evidence or proof, esp. of a crime.
smoking jacket *n.* A man's evening jacket, often made of a fine fabric, elaborately trimmed, and usually worn at home.
smoking room *n.* A room, as in a hotel or private club, set aside for smokers.
smok·ing-room (smō'kĭng-rōōm', -rŏŏm') *adj.* Marked by indecency; obscene: *smoking-room humor.*
smok·y (smō'kē) *adj.* **-i·er, -i·est. 1.** Emitting smoke in profuse volume. **2.** Mixed or filled with smoke. **3.** Resembling or similar to smoke. **4.** Discolored or soiled with smoke. **5.** Tasting of smoke. **—smok'i·ly** *adv.* **—smok'i·ness** *n.*
smoky quartz *n.* Cairngorm.
smol·der also **smoul·der** (smōl'dər) *intr.v.* **-dered, -der·ing, -ders. 1.** To burn with little smoke and no flame. **2.** To exist in a suppressed state. **3.** To manifest repressed anger or hatred. *—n.* Thick smoke resulting from a slow fire. [ME *smolderen* < *smolder,* smolder.]
smolt (smōlt) *n.* A young salmon at the stage at which it migrates from fresh water to the sea. [ME.]

smooch (smo͞och) *n. Slang.* A kiss. —*intr.v.* **smooched, smooch·ing, smooch·es.** *Slang.* To kiss. [Perh. imit. of the sound of a kiss.]

smooth (smo͞o*th*) *adj.* **-er, -est. 1.** Having a surface free from irregularities, roughness, or projections; even. **2.** Having a fine texture. **3.** Having an even consistency: *a smooth pudding.* **4.** Having an even or gentle motion or movement: *a smooth ride.* **5.** Having no obstructions or difficulties: *a smooth operation.* **6.** Serene. **7.** Bland: *a smooth wine.* **8.** Artfully suave; ingratiating: *smooth talk.* **9.** Having no grossness or coarseness in dress or manner. —*v.* **smoothed, smooth·ing, smoothes.** —*tr.* **1.** To make (something) even, level, or unwrinkled. **2.** To rid of obstructions, hindrances, or difficulties. **3.** To soothe or tranquilize; make calm. **4.** To make less harsh or crude; refine. —*intr.* To become smooth. —*n.* **1.** A smooth part of something; a smooth surface. **2.** The act of smoothing. [ME *smothe* < OE *smōð.*] **—smooth'er** *n.* **—smooth'ly** *adv.* **—smooth'ness** *n.*

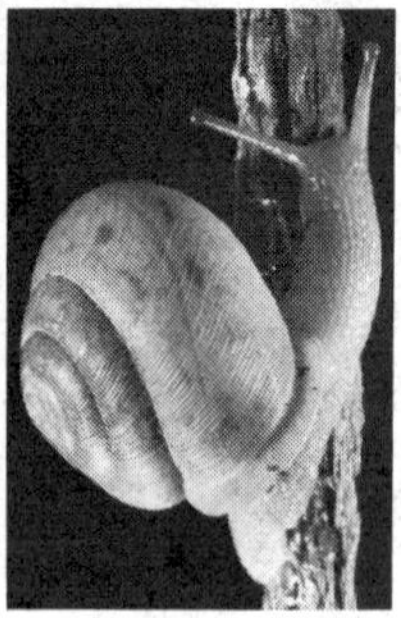

snail

smooth·bore also **smooth bore** (smo͞o*th*'bôr', -bōr') —*adj.* Having no rifling within the barrel. Used of a firearm. —*n.* A firearm having no rifling.

smooth breathing *n.* The symbol (') written over some initial vowels in classical Greek to indicate that they are not aspirated.

smooth·en (smo͞o'*th*ən) *tr. & intr.v.* **-ened, -en·ing, -ens.** To make or become smooth.

smooth·ie also **smooth·y** (smo͞o'*th*ē) *n. Slang.* **1.** An assured, artfully ingratiating person. **2.** A person who is smooth-tongued.

smooth muscle *n.* The unstriated involuntary muscle of the internal organs, as of the intestine, bladder, and blood vessels, excluding the heart.

smooth-tongued (smo͞o*th*'tŭngd') *adj.* Speaking in a pleasing, esp. flattering manner.

smooth·y (smo͞o'*th*ē) *n.* Variant of **smoothie.**

smor·gas·bord (smôr'gəs-bôrd', -bōrd') *n.* A buffet meal featuring a varied number of dishes. [Swed. *smörgåsbord* : *smörgås,* sandwich + *bord,* table.]

smote (smōt) *v.* Past tense and a past participle of **smite.**

smoth·er (smŭ*th*'ər) *v.* **-ered, -er·ing, -ers.** —*tr.* **1. a.** To suffocate (another). **b.** To deprive (a fire) of the oxygen necessary for combustion. **2.** To conceal, suppress, or hide: *smothered the facts of the case.* **3.** To cover (a foodstuff) thickly with another foodstuff: *smother chicken in sauce.* **4.** To lavish a surfeit of a given emotion upon (someone): *smothered me with affection.* —*intr.* **1. a.** To suffocate. **b.** To be extinguished. **2.** To be concealed or suppressed. **3.** To be surfeited with a given emotion. —*n.* Anything that smothers, as a dense cloud of smoke or dust. [ME *smotheren* < *smorther,* dense smoke.] **—smoth'er·y** *adj.*

snake
Red Diamond rattlesnake

smoul·der (smōl'dər) *v. & n.* Variant of **smolder.**

smudge (smŭj) *v.* **smudged, smudg·ing, smudg·es.** —*tr.* **1.** To make dirty, esp. in one small area. **2.** To smear or blur. **3.** To fill (an orchard or other planted area) with dense smoke from a smudge pot in order to prevent damage from insects or frost. —*intr.* **1.** To smear, as with dirt, soot, or ink. **2.** To be smudged. —*n.* **1.** A blotch or smear. **2.** A smoky fire used as a protection against insects or frost. [ME *smogen.*] **—smudg'i·ly** *adv.* **—smudg'i·ness** *n.* **—smudg'y** *adj.*

smudge pot *n.* A receptacle in which oil or other smoky fuel is burned, as to protect an orchard from insects or frost or to indicate wind direction.

smug (smŭg) *adj.* **smug·ger, smug·gest.** Complacent or self-righteous. [Prob. < LG *smuck,* neat < MLG < *smucken,* to adorn.] **—smug'ly** *adv.* **—smug'ness** *n.*

smug·gle (smŭg'əl) *v.* **-gled, -gling, -gles.** —*tr.* **1.** To import or export without paying lawful customs charges or duties. **2.** To bring in or take out illicitly or by stealth. —*intr.* To engage in smuggling. [LG *smuggeln.*] **—smug'gler** *n.*

smut (smŭt) *n.* **1. a.** A particle of dirt. **b.** A smudge made by soot, smoke, or dirt. **2.** Obscenity in speech or writing. **3. a.** Any of various plant diseases caused by fungi of the order Ustilaginales that result in the formation of black, powdery masses of spores on the affected parts. **b.** A fungus causing such a disease. —*v.* **smut·ted, smut·ting, smuts.** —*tr.* **1.** To blacken or smudge, as with smoke or grime. **2.** To affect (a plant) with smut. **3.** To free (grain, for example) from smut. **4.** To make obscene. —*intr.* **1.** To emit smut. **2.** To be or become blackened or smudged. **3.** To become affected with smut, as a plant. [Alteration of *smot,* stain < ME *smotten,* to besmirch.] **—smut'ti·ly** *adv.* **—smut'ti·ness** *n.* **—smut'ty** *adj.*

smutch (smŭch) *tr.v.* **smutched, smutch·ing, smutch·es.** To soil or stain. —*n.* A stain or spot of dirt. [Perh. alteration of SMUDGE.] **—smutch'y** *adj.*

Sn The symbol for the element tin. [< Lat. *stannum,* tin.]

snack (snăk) *n.* **1.** A hurried or light meal. **2.** Food eaten between meals. —*intr.v.* **snacked, snack·ing, snacks.** To eat a hurried or light meal. [ME *snake,* a bite < *snaken,* to bite.]

snack bar *n.* A lunch counter where light meals are served.

snaf·fle (snăf'əl) *n.* A bit for a horse, consisting of two bars jointed at the center. —*tr.v.* **-fled, -fling, -fles.** To put on or control with a snaffle. [Orig. unknown.]

sna·fu (snă-fo͞o') *Slang.* —*adj.* In a state of complete confusion. —*tr.v.* **-fued, -fu·ing, -fus.** To make chaotic or confused. —*n., pl.* **-fus.** Any chaotic or confused situation. [S(ITUATION) + N(ORMAL) + A(LL) + F(UCKED) + U(P).]

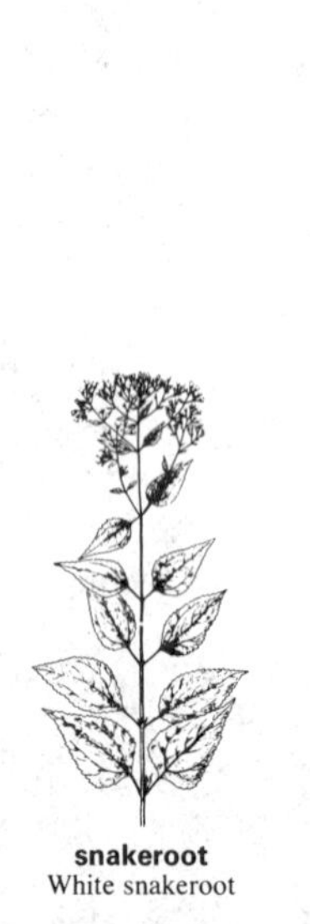

snakeroot
White snakeroot

snag (snăg) *n.* **1.** Any rough, sharp, or jagged protuberance. **2.** A tree or a part of a tree that protrudes above the surface in a body of water. **3.** A snaggletooth. **4.** A break, pull, or tear in a fabric. **5.** An unforeseen or hidden obstacle. —*v.* **snagged, snag·ging, snags.** —*tr.* **1.** To hinder, break, tear, or destroy by or as if by a snag. **2.** To free of snags. **3.** *Informal.* To catch unexpectedly and quickly. —*intr.* To be damaged by a snag. [Of Scand. orig.] **—snag'gy** *adj.*

snag·gle·tooth (snăg'əl-to͞oth') *n.* A tooth that is broken or not in alignment with the others. [Dial. *snaggled,* irregular (< SNAG) + TOOTH.]

snail (snāl) *n.* **1.** Any of numerous aquatic or terrestrial mollusks of the class Gastropoda, characteristically having a spirally coiled shell, a broad retractile foot, and a distinct head. **2.** A slow-moving, lazy, or sluggish person. [ME < OE *snægl.*]

snail fever *n.* Schistosomiasis.

snail-paced (snāl'pāst') *adj.* Moving with extreme slowness.

snake (snāk) *n.* **1.** Any of various scaly, legless, sometimes venomous reptiles of the suborder Serpentes, having a long, tapering, cylindrical body. **2. Snake.** Hydra (sense 3). **3.** A treacherous person. **4.** A long, highly flexible metal wire used for cleaning drains. **5.** *Econ.* The concept of fixing the value of currencies to each other within defined parameters, which when graphed visually show these currencies remaining parallel in value to each other as a unit despite fluctuations with other currencies. —*v.* **snaked, snak·ing, snakes.** —*tr.* **1.** To drag or pull lengthwise, esp. to drag with a rope or chain. **2.** To pull with quick jerks. **3.** To move in the manner of a snake. —*intr.* To move with a snakelike motion; crawl. [ME < OE *snaca.*]

snake·bird (snāk'bûrd') *n.* Any of several long-necked, long-billed birds of the genus *Anhinga,* as the water turkey.

snake·bite (snāk'bīt') *n.* **1.** The bite of a snake. **2.** Poisoning resulting from the bite of a venomous snake.

snake charmer *n.* One who utilizes rhythmic music and bodily movements to control snakes.

snake dance *n.* **1.** A dance performed as part of a biennial religious ceremony of the Hopi Indians, in which the dancers carry live rattlesnakes in their mouths. **2.** A procession of persons who join hands and move forward in a zigzag line.

snake fence *n.* A worm fence.

snake·head (snāk'hĕd') *n.* The turtlehead.

snake in the grass *n.* One that is treacherous.

snake·mouth (snāk'mouth') *n.* An orchid, *Pogonia ophioglossoides,* of eastern North America, having a solitary rose-purple flower with a fringed lip.

snake oil *n.* A worthless preparation fraudulently peddled as a cure for many ills.

snake pit *n. Slang.* **1.** A place of disorder and chaos. **2.** A mental institution.

snake plant *n.* Any of several tropical Old World plants of the genus *Sansevieria,* having narrow, rigid, often mottled leaves and widely cultivated as a house plant.

snake·root (snāk'ro͞ot', -ro͝ot') *n.* Any of various plants having roots reputed to cure snakebite, esp. a plant of the genus *Eupatorium* or the genus *Rauwolfia.*

snake·skin (snāk'skĭn') *n.* The skin of a snake, esp. when prepared as leather.

snake·stone (snāk'stōn') *n.* **1.** A small stone or piece of porous substance reputed to cure snakebite. **2.** A whetstone.

snake·weed (snāk'wēd') *n.* Any of various plants having reputed power to cure snakebite.

snak·y (snā'kē) *adj.* **-i·er, -i·est. 1.** Pertaining to or characteristic of snakes. **2.** Having the form or movement of a snake; serpentine. **3.** Overrun with snakes. **4.** Treacherous; sly. **—snak'i·ly** *adv.* **—snak'i·ness** *n.*

snap (snăp) *v.* **snapped, snap·ping, snaps.** —*intr.* **1.** To make a brisk, sharp cracking sound. **2.** To break suddenly with a brisk, sharp cracking sound. **3.** To give way abruptly under pressure or tension. **4.** To bring the jaws briskly together, often with a clicking sound; bite. **5.** To snatch or grasp suddenly and with eagerness: *snap at a chance to go to Europe.* **6.** To speak abruptly or sharply: *snapped at the child.* **7.** To move swiftly and smartly: *snap to attention.* **8.** To flash or appear to flash light; sparkle: *eyes that snapped with anger.* **9.** To open or close with a click: *The lock snapped shut.* —*tr.* **1.** To snatch at with or as if with the teeth; bite. **2.** To come apart or break with a snapping sound. **3.** To utter abruptly or sharply. **4. a.** To cause to emit a snapping sound: *snap a whip.* **b.** To close or latch with a snapping sound. **5.** To cause to move abruptly and smartly: *"His head was snapped back by a sudden scream from the bed"* (James Michener). **6.** To take (a photograph). **7.** *Sports.* To center (a football). ***—phrasal verb.* snap back.** To recover quickly. —*n.* **1.** A sudden, sharp cracking sound or the action producing such a sound. **2.** A sudden breaking of something. **3.** A clasp, catch, or other fastening device that operates with a snapping sound. **4.** A sudden attempt to bite, snatch, or grasp. **5. a.** The sound produced by rapid movement of the second finger from the thumb tip to the base of the thumb. **b.** The act of producing this sound. **6.** The sudden release of anything held under pressure or tension. **7.** A thin, crisp, usually circular cooky: *a ginger snap.* **8.** *Informal.* Briskness, liveliness, or energy. **9.** A brief spell of brisk, cold weather. **10.** *Informal.* An effortless task. **11. a.** A snapshot. **b.** The taking of a snapshot. **12.** A snap bean. **13.** *Sports.* The passing of a football from the center to a back that initiates each play. *—adj.* **1.** Made or done on the spur of the moment: *a snap decision.* **2.** Fastening with a snap. **3.** *Informal.* Simple; easy. *—adv.* With a snap. [MLG *snappen,* to seize.]

snap bean *n.* A bean, as the string bean, cultivated for its crisp, edible pods.

snap-brim (snăp′brĭm′) *n.* A hat having a flexible brim, usually turned down in front and up at the back.

snap·drag·on (snăp′drăg′ən) *n.* Any of several plants of the genus *Antirrhinum,* esp. a widely cultivated species, *A. majus,* of the Mediterranean region, having showy clusters of two-lipped, variously colored flowers. [From the imagined resemblance of the flowers to the mouth of a dragon.]

snap·per (snăp′ər) *n.* **1.** One that snaps. **2.** *pl.* **snapper** or **-pers.** Any of numerous widely distributed marine fishes of the family Lutjanidae, many of which are prized as food and game fishes. **3.** A snapping turtle.

snapping beetle *n.* The click beetle.

snapping turtle *n.* Any of several New World freshwater turtles of the family Chelydridae, esp., *Chelydra serpentina* or *Macrochelys temmincki,* of North America, having a rough shell and powerful hooked jaws.

snap·pish (snăp′ĭsh) *adj.* **1.** Liable to snap or bite, as a dog. **2.** Liable to speak sharply or curtly; irritable; curt. **—snap′pish·ly** *adv.* **—snap′pish·ness** *n.*

snap·py (snăp′ē) *adj.* **-pi·er, -pi·est. 1.** *Informal.* Lively or energetic; brisk. **2.** *Informal.* Smart or chic in appearance. **3.** Snappish. **—snap′pi·ly** *adv.* **—snap′pi·ness** *n.*

snap roll *n.* An aerial maneuver in which an aircraft is put through a sharp roll of 360 degrees about its longitudinal axis.

snap·shoot (snăp′sho͞ot′) *tr.v.* **-shot** (shŏt), **-shoot·ing, -shoots.** To take a snapshot of. [Back-formation < SNAPSHOT.] **—snap′shoot′er** *n.*

snap·shot (snăp′shŏt′) *n.* A photograph taken with a small hand-held camera.

snare[1] (snâr) *n.* **1.** A trapping device, often consisting of a noose, used for capturing birds and small animals. **2.** Anything that serves to entangle the unwary. **3.** A surgical instrument with a wire loop controlled by a mechanism in the handle, used to remove growths, such as tumors and polyps. *—tr.v.* **snared, snar·ing, snares. 1.** To trap with a snare. **2.** To entrap (someone). [ME < OE *sneare* < ON *snara.*] **—snar′er** *n.*

snare[2] (snâr) *n.* **1.** Any of the wires or cords stretched across the lower skin of a snare drum to increase reverberation. **2.** A snare drum. [Prob. < Du. *snaar,* string.]

snare drum *n.* A small double-headed drum having a snare or snares stretched across the bottom head to increase reverberation.

snarl[1] (snärl) *v.* **snarled, snarl·ing, snarls.** *—intr.* **1.** To growl viciously while baring the teeth. **2.** To speak angrily or threateningly. *—tr.* To utter with anger or hostility. *—n.* **1.** A vicious growl. **2.** A vicious, hostile utterance. [Freq. of obs. *snar,* to growl.] **—snarl′er** *n.* **—snarl′ing·ly** *adv.* **—snarl′y** *adj.*

snarl[2] (snärl) *n.* **1.** A tangled mass, as of hair or yarn. **2.** A confused, complicated, or tangled situation; predicament. *—v.* **snarled, snarl·ing, snarls.** *—intr.* To become tangled or confused. *—tr.* **1.** To tangle or knot (hair, for example). **2.** To confuse; complicate. [ME *snarle,* trap < *snare.* —see SNARE[1].] **—snarl′er** *n.* **—snarl′y** *adj.*

snatch (snăch) *v.* **snatched, snatch·ing, snatch·es.** *—tr.* **1.** To grasp or seize hastily, eagerly, or suddenly. **2.** To grasp or seize illicitly. *—intr.* To make grasping or seizing motions. *—n.* **1.** The act of snatching; a quick grasp or grab. **2.** A brief period of time: *"At the end we preferred to travel all night, sleeping in snatches"* (T.S. Eliot). **3.** A small amount; bit; fragment: *a snatch of dialogue.* **4.** *Slang.* A kidnaping. **5.** A lift in weightlifting in which the weight is raised in one uninterrupted motion from the floor to an overhead position. [ME *snacchen,* to snap at.] **—snatch′er** *n.*

snatch block *n. Naut.* A block that can be opened on one side to receive the looped part of a rope.

snatch·y (snăch′ē) *adj.* **-i·er, -i·est.** Occurring in snatches; intermittent.

snaz·zy (snăz′ē) *adj.* **-zi·er, -zi·est.** *Slang.* Fashionable or flashy. [Perh. a blend of SNAPPY and JAZZY.]

sneak (snēk) *v.* **sneaked, sneak·ing, sneaks.** *—intr.* **1.** To go or move in a quiet, stealthy way. **2.** To behave in a cowardly or servile manner. *—tr.* To move, give, take, or put in a quiet, stealthy manner: *sneak candy into one's mouth.* *—n.* **1.** A stealthy, cowardly, or underhand person. **2.** An instance of sneaking; a quiet, stealthy movement. ***—modifier:*** *a sneak attack.* [Orig. unknown.]

sneak·er (snē′kər) *n.* **1.** One that sneaks. **2.** A sports shoe usually made of canvas and having soft rubber soles.

sneak·ing (snē′kĭng) *adj.* **1.** Acting in a stealthy, furtive way. **2.** Unavowed; secret. **3.** Gradually growing or persistent. **—sneak′ing·ly** *adv.*

sneak preview *n.* A single public showing of a motion picture prior to its general release.

sneak thief *n.* A burglar who enters without breaking in.

sneak·y (snē′kē) *adj.* **-i·er, -i·est.** Furtive; surreptitious. **—sneak′i·ly** *adv.* **—sneak′i·ness** *n.*

sneer (snîr) *n.* **1.** A scornful facial expression characterized by a slight raising of one corner of the upper lip. **2.** A contemptuous facial expression, sound, or statement. *—v.* **sneered, sneer·ing, sneers.** *—tr.* To utter with a sneer or in a sneering manner. *—intr.* **1.** To assume a scornful, contemptuous, or derisive facial expression. **2.** To speak in a scornful, contemptuous, or derisive manner. [Perh. of LG orig.] **—sneer′er** *n.* **—sneer′ful** *adj.* **—sneer′ing·ly** *adv.*

sneeze (snēz) *intr.v.* **sneezed, sneez·ing, sneez·es.** To expel air forcibly from the mouth and nose in an explosive, spasmodic involuntary action resulting from irritation of the nasal mucosa. *—n.* An instance of sneezing. [ME *snesen,* alteration of *fnesen* < OE *fnēosan.*] **—sneez′er** *n.* **—sneez′y** *adj.*

sneeze·weed (snēz′wēd′) *n.* **1.** Any of several North American plants of the genus *Helenium,* having yellow, rayed flowers. **2.** The sneezewort.

sneeze·wort (snēz′wûrt′, -wôrt′) *n.* A plant, *Achillea ptarmica,* native to Europe, having clusters of white flowers.

snell (snĕl) *n.* A length of fine, threadlike material, such as monofilament or gut, that connects a fishhook to a heavier line; leader. [Orig. unknown.]

snib (snĭb) *tr.v.* **snibbed, snib·bing, snibs.** *Chiefly Brit.* To latch (a door). [Orig. unknown.]

snick·er (snĭk′ər) *intr.v.* **-ered, -er·ing, -ers.** To utter a partly stifled laugh. *—n.* A snide, slightly stifled laugh. [Imit.] **—snick′er·ing·ly** *adv.*

snick·er·snee (snĭk′ər-snē′) *n.* **1.** A knife resembling a sword. **2.** *Archaic.* The act of fighting with knives. [Alteration of obs. *stick or snee,* to cut and thrust in fighting with a knife : Du. *steken,* to stab + Du. *snijden,* to cut.]

snide (snīd) *adj.* **snid·er, snid·est.** Derogatory in a malicious, superior way; sarcastic. [Orig. unknown.] **—snide′ly** *adv.* **—snide′ness** *n.*

sniff (snĭf) *v.* **sniffed, sniff·ing, sniffs.** *—intr.* **1.** To inhale a short, audible breath through the nose, as in smelling something. **2.** To indicate ridicule, contempt, or doubt by or as if by sniffing: *sniffed at her protestations of regret.* **3.** To savor an odor by sniffing. *—tr.* **1.** To inhale forcibly through the nose. **2.** To smell or try to smell by sniffing. **3.** To perceive or detect by or as if by sniffing: *sniffed trouble ahead.* *—n.* **1.** An instance or the sound of sniffing. **2.** Something that is sniffed or perceived by sniffing; whiff. [ME *sniffen.*] **—sniff′er** *n.*

snif·fle (snĭf′əl) *intr.v.* **-fled, -fling, -fles. 1.** To breathe audibly through a congested nose. **2.** To weep or whimper lightly with spasmodic sniffing. *—n.* **1.** An act or sound of sniffling. **2. sniffles.** *Informal.* A condition, such as a head cold, accompanied by sniffles. [Freq. of SNIFF.]

sniff·y (snĭf′ē) *adj.* **-i·er, -i·est.** *Informal.* Disposed to showing arrogance or contempt; haughty.

snif·ter (snĭf′tər) *n.* **1.** A pear-shaped goblet with a narrow top, used in serving brandy or other aromatic liquors. **2.** *Slang.* A small portion of liquor. [Dial. *snifter,* sniff < ME *sniftеren,* to sniff.]

snig·ger (snĭg′ər) *n.* A snicker. *—intr.v.* **-gered, -ger·ing, -gers.** To snicker. [Alteration of SNICKER.]

snip (snĭp) *v.* **snipped, snip·ping, snips.** *—tr.* To cut, clip, or separate in a short, quick stroke with scissors or shears. *—intr.* To cut or clip with short, quick strokes. *—n.* **1.** An instance of snipping or the sound produced by snipping. **2. a.** A small cut made with scissors or shears. **b.** A small piece cut or clipped off. **3.** *Informal.* **a.** A small or slight person or thing. **b.** A small person who is mischievous or annoying. **4. snips.** Small hand shears used in cutting sheet metal. **5.** *Slang.* Something easily accomplished. [LG *snippen,* to snap.]

snipe (snīp) *n., pl.* **snipe** or **snipes. 1. a.** Any of various long-billed wading birds of the genus *Capella,* esp. the common, widely distributed species *C. gallinago.* **b.** Any of various similar or related birds. **2.** A shot, esp. a gunshot, from a concealed place. *—intr.v.* **sniped, snip·ing, snipes. 1.** To shoot at individuals from a concealed place. **2.** To shoot snipe. **3.** To make malicious, underhanded remarks or attacks. [ME *snype,* prob. of Scand. orig.]

snip·er (snī′pər) *n.* **1.** A skilled military rifleman detailed to spot and pick off enemy soldiers from a concealed place. **2.** One who shoots at other people from a concealed place.

snip·pet (snĭp′ĭt) *n.* **1.** A tidbit or morsel. **2.** *Informal.* A small or mischievous person; snip.

snip·pet·y (snĭp′ĭ-tē) *adj.* **-i·er, -i·est. 1.** Made up of snippets. **2.** *Informal.* Snippy.

snip·py (snĭp′ē) *adj.* **-pi·er, -pi·est.** *Informal.* **1.** Impertinent. **2.** Fragmentary.

snit (snĭt) *n. Slang.* A state of agitation or irritation: *She is in a snit because of the delay.* [Orig. unknown.]

snitch (snĭch) *v.* **snitched, snitch·ing, snitch·es.** *Slang.* *—tr.* To steal (something of little or no value). *—intr.* To turn informer: *snitched on his friends.* *—n.* **1.** A thief. **2.** An informer; squealer. [Orig. unknown.] **—snitch′er** *n.*

sniv·el (snĭv′əl) *intr.v.* **-eled, -el·ing, -els** or **-elled, -el·ling,**

snapdragon

snapping turtle

snare[1]
Rabbit snares

George Miksch Sutton
snipe

snout

George Miksch Sutton

snow goose

snow leopard

snowmobile

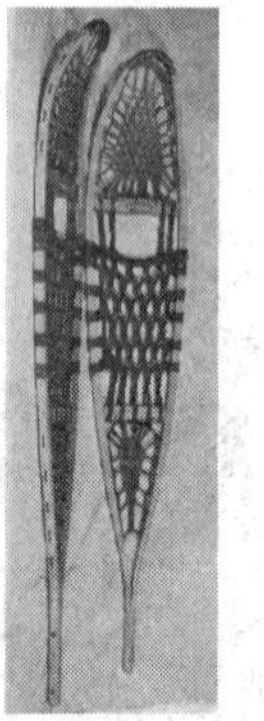

snowshoe

-els. **1.** To cry or weep with sniffling. **2.** To complain or whine tearfully. **3.** To run at the nose. **4.** To sniffle. *—n.* **1.** An act of sniffling or sniveling. **2.** Nasal mucus. [ME *snyvelen,* to run at the nose, of OE orig.] **—sniv'el·er** *n.*

snob (snŏb) *n.* **1.** A person who is convinced of and flaunts his social superiority. **2.** A person who despises his inferiors and whose condescension arises from social or intellectual pretension. [Obs. *snob,* person of the lower classes < dial. *snob,* cobbler.]

snob·ber·y (snŏb'ə-rē) *n., pl.* **-ies.** Snobbish behavior.

snob·bish (snŏb'ĭsh) *adj.* Of, characteristic of, befitting, or resembling a snob; pretentious. **—snob'bish·ly** *adv.* **—snob'bish·ness** *n.*

snob·bism (snŏb'ĭz'əm) *n.* Snobbery.

snood (sno͞od) *n.* **1.** A small netlike cap worn by women to keep the hair in place. **2.** A headband or fillet. *—tr.v.* **snood·ed, snood·ing, snoods.** To hold (the hair) in place with a snood. [ME **snood* < OE *snōd.*]

snook (sno͝ok, sno͞ok) *n., pl.* **snook** or **snooks.** Any of several chiefly marine fishes of the family Centropomidae, esp. *Centropomus undecimalis,* of warm Atlantic waters. [Du. *snoek,* pike < MDu. *snoec.*]

snook·er (sno͝ok'ər) *n.* A pocket billiards game in which 15 red and 6 nonred balls are used. [Orig. unknown.]

snoop (sno͞op) *Informal.* *—intr.v.* **snooped, snoop·ing, snoops.** To pry into the private affairs of others, esp. by prowling about. *—n.* One who snoops. [Du. *snoepen,* to eat on the sly.] **—snoop'er** *n.*

snoop·y (sno͞o'pē) *adj.* **-i·er, -i·est.** *Informal.* Inclined or known to snoop. **—snoop'i·ly** *adv.* **—snoop'i·ness** *n.*

snoot (sno͞ot) *Slang.* **1.** A snout or nose. **2.** A snob. [ME *snute,* snout.]

snoot·y (sno͞o'tē) *adj.* **-i·er, -i·est.** *Slang.* **1.** Snobbishly aloof; haughty. **2.** High-class; exclusive. **—snoot'i·ly** *adv.* **—snoot'i·ness** *n.*

snooze (sno͞oz) *Informal.* *—intr.v.* **snoozed, snooz·ing, snooz·es.** To take a light nap; doze. *—n.* A brief light sleep. [Orig. unknown.]

snore (snôr, snōr) *intr.v.* **snored, snor·ing, snores.** To breathe through the nose and mouth while sleeping, making snorting noises caused by the vibration of the soft palate. *—n.* **1.** An instance of snoring. **2.** The noise produced by snoring. [ME *snoren,* to snort.] **—snor'er** *n.*

snor·kel (snôr'kəl) *n.* **1.** A retractable vertical tube in a submarine that contains air-intake and exhaust pipes for the engines and for ventilation and that permits extended periods of submergence at periscope depth. **2.** A breathing apparatus used by skin divers, consisting of a long tube held in the mouth. *—intr.v.* **-keled, -kel·ing, -kels.** To dive using a skin-diving snorkel. [G. *Schnorchel,* snorkel, snout < *schnarchen,* to snore.] **—snor'kel·er** *n.*

snort (snôrt) *n.* **1. a.** A rough, noisy sound made by breathing forcefully through the nostrils, as a horse or pig does. **b.** A sound resembling this: *the snort of a steam engine.* **2.** *Slang.* **a.** A drink of liquor, esp. when swallowed in one gulp. **b.** The inhalation of a drug. **c.** The liquor or drug taken. *—v.* **snort·ed, snort·ing, snorts.** *—intr.* **1.** To breathe noisily and forcefully through the nostrils. **2.** To make an abrupt noise expressive of scorn, ridicule, or contempt. **3.** *Slang.* To inhale a drug. *—tr.* **1.** To express with a snort: *snorted his disapproval.* **2.** *Slang.* To inhale (a drug): *snorted cocaine.* [< ME *snorten,* to snort.] **—snort'er** *n.*

snot (snŏt) *n. Slang.* **1.** Nasal mucus; phlegm. **2.** An untrustworthy, devious, or malicious person. [ME < OE *gesnot.*]

snot·ty (snŏt'ē) *adj.* **-ti·er, -ti·est.** **1.** *Slang.* Dirtied with nasal mucus. **2.** *Vulgar Slang.* Mean and nasty.

snout (snout) *n.* **1. a.** The projecting nose, jaws, or anterior facial part of an animal's muzzle. **b.** A similar prolongation of the anterior portion of the head in certain insects, such as weevils. **2.** A spout or nozzle likened to a snout. **3.** *Slang.* The human nose. [ME *snute,* prob. of MLG orig.]

snout beetle *n.* Any of numerous weevils of the family Curculionidae, having the front of the head elongated to form a snout.

snow (snō) *n.* **1.** Solid precipitation in the form of white or translucent ice crystals of various shapes originating in the upper atmosphere as frozen particles of water vapor. **2. a.** Something resembling snow. **b.** The white specks on a television screen resulting from weak reception. **c.** *Slang.* Cocaine. **d.** *Slang.* Heroin. **3.** A falling of snow; snowstorm. *—v.* **snowed, snow·ing, snows.** *—intr.* To fall as or in snow. *—tr.* **1.** To cover, shut off, or close off with snow: *snowed in by the blizzard.* **2.** *Slang.* To overwhelm with insincere talk, esp. with flattery. ***—phrasal verb.*** **snow under.** **1.** To overwhelm: *was snowed under with work.* **2.** To defeat by a very large margin. [ME < OE *snāw.*]

snow apple *n.* The Fameuse.

snow·ball (snō'bôl') *n.* **1.** A mass of soft, wet snow packed into a ball that can be thrown, as in play. **2.** Any of several plants or shrubs having rounded clusters of white flowers, esp. a cultivated variety of *Viburnum opulus.* *—v.* **-balled, -ball·ing, -balls.** *—intr.* **1.** To throw snowballs. **2.** To grow rapidly in significance, importance, or size: *problems that snowballed by the hour.* *—tr.* **1.** To throw snowballs at. **2.** To cause to grow or increase rapidly.

snow·bell (snō'bĕl') *n.* Either of two shrubs, *Styrax grandifolia* or *S. americana,* of the southeastern United States, having bell-shaped white flowers.

snow·ber·ry (snō'bĕr'ē) *n.* Any of various shrubs of the genus *Symphoricarpos,* esp. *S. albus,* having small pinkish flowers and white berries.

snow·bird (snō'bûrd') *n.* Any of several birds, such as the junco, seen under snowy winter conditions.

snow blindness *n.* Conjunctivitis and deteriorated vision caused by sunlight reflected from snow or ice. **—snow'-blind', snow'blind'ed** *adj.*

snow·blink (snō'blĭngk') *n.* A white sky glow reflected from snowfields.

snow·bound (snō'bound') *adj.* Confined in one place by heavy snow.

snow bunting *n.* A bird, *Plectrophenax nivalis,* of northern regions, having predominantly white winter plumage.

snow·bush (snō'bo͝osh') also **snow·brush** (-brŭsh') *n.* A shrub, *Ceanothus velutinus,* of western North America, having large clusters of small white flowers.

snow·cap (snō'kăp') *n.* A cap of snow, as on a mountaintop. **—snow'capped'** *adj.*

snow·drift (snō'drĭft') *n.* Snow banked up by the wind.

snow·drop (snō'drŏp') *n.* Any of several bulbous plants of the genus *Galanthus,* native to Eurasia, having solitary, nodding white flowers that bloom early in spring.

snowdrop tree *n.* The silverbell tree.

snow·fall (snō'fôl') *n.* **1.** A fall of snow. **2.** The amount of snow that falls during a given period or in a specified area.

snow fence *n.* Temporary fencing composed of thin upright slats, used to prevent snow from drifting onto walks or roads.

snow·flake (snō'flāk') *n.* **1.** A single flake or crystal of snow. **2.** Any of several bulbous plants of the genus *Leucojum,* native to Europe, having white or whitish flowers.

snow goose *n.* A goose, *Chen hyperborea,* that breeds in northern regions, having white plumage with black wing tips.

snow job *n. Slang.* An effort to deceive, overwhelm, or persuade with insincere talk, esp. flattery.

snow leopard *n.* A large feline mammal, *Uncia uncia,* of the highlands of central Asia, having long, thick, whitish fur with dark markings.

snow lily *n.* The fawn lily.

snow line *n.* **1.** The lower altitudinal boundary of a snow-covered area, esp. of one that is perennially covered, as the snowcap of a mountain. **2.** The fluctuating latitudinal boundaries around the polar regions marking the extent of snow cover.

snow·mo·bile (snō'mō-bēl') *n.* A small vehicle with skilike runners in front and tanklike treads, used for driving in or traveling on snow. **—snow'mo·bil'er** *n.* **—snow'mo·bil'ing** *n.*

snow-on-the-moun·tain (snō'ŏn-*thə*-moun'tən, -ôn-) *n.* A widely cultivated plant, *Euphorbia marginata,* of central North America, having white-margined leaves and showy white bracts.

snow pellets *n.* Graupel.

snow plant *n.* A saprophytic plant, *Sarcodes sanguinea,* of the mountains of western North America, having a fleshy, scaly, reddish stalk and scarlet flowers.

snow·plow (snō'plou') *n.* **1.** A plowlike device or vehicle used to remove snow, esp. from roads and railroad tracks. **2.** A maneuver in skiing in which the tips of the skis are brought together in order to slow or stop progress. **—snow'plow'** *v.* **(-plowed, -plow·ing, -plows).**

snow·shed (snō'shĕd') *n.* A roofing built over portions of a railroad track to protect them from snowslides.

snow·shoe (snō'sho͞o') *n.* A racket-shaped frame containing interlaced leather strips that can be attached to the foot to facilitate walking on deep snow. **—snow'shoe'** *v.* **(-shoed, -shoe·ing, -shoes).**

snowshoe rabbit *n.* A hare, *Lepus americanus,* of northern North America, having large, heavily furred feet and fur that is white in winter and brown in summer.

snow·storm (snō'stôrm') *n.* A storm marked by heavy snowfall and often high winds.

snow·suit (snō'so͞ot') *n.* A child's zippered winter coverall.

snow tire *n.* A tire with a deep tread to give added traction on snow.

snow-white (snō'hwīt', -wīt') *adj.* White as snow.

snow·y (snō'ē) *adj.* **-i·er, -i·est.** **1. a.** Abounding in or covered with snow. **b.** Subject to snow: *a snowy climate.* **2.** Resembling or suggesting snow. **—snow'i·ly** *adv.* **—snow'i·ness** *n.*

snub (snŭb) *tr.v.* **snubbed, snub·bing, snubs.** **1.** To slight by ignoring or behaving coldly toward; scorn. **2.** To dismiss, turn down, or frustrate the expectations of. **3. a.** To check suddenly the movement of (a rope or cable running out) by turning it about a post. **b.** To secure (a vessel, for example) in this manner. *—n.* **1.** A deliberate slight or affront. **2.** A sudden checking, as of a rope or cable running out. [ME *snubben,* to rebuke < ON *snubba.*] **—snub'ber** *n.*

snub-nosed (snŭb'nōzd') *adj.* **1.** Having a short, turned-up nose. **2.** Having an extremely short barrel: *a snub-nosed pistol.*

snuck (snŭk) *v. Nonstandard.* A past tense and past participle of **sneak.**

snuff[1] (snŭf) *v.* **snuffed, snuff·ing, snuffs.** *—tr.* **1.** To inhale through the nose; sniff. **2.** To sense or examine by smelling; sniff at. *—intr.* To sniff; inhale. *—n.* An act of snuffing or the sound produced in snuffing; sniff. [Prob. < MDu. *snuffen.*]

snuff[2] (snŭf) *n.* The charred portion of a candlewick. *—tr.v.* **snuffed, snuff·ing, snuffs. 1.** To cut off the charred portion of (a candlewick). **2.** To extinguish: *snuffed out the candles.* **3.** To put a sudden end to; destroy. [ME *snoffe.*]

snuff[3] (snŭf) *n.* **1. a.** A preparation of finely pulverized tobacco that can be drawn up into the nostrils by inhaling. **b.** The quantity of this inhaled at a single time; pinch. **2.** A powdery substance, such as a medicine, taken by inhaling. *—intr.v.* **snuffed, snuff·ing, snuffs.** To use or inhale snuff. ***—idiom.*** **up to snuff.** *Informal.* **1.** Normal in health. **2.** Up to standard. [Du. *snuf,* short for *snuftabak* < MDu. *snuffen,* to sniff.]

snuff·box (snŭf′bŏks′) *n.* A small, often highly decorative box with a hinged lid used for carrying snuff.

snuff·er[1] (snŭf′ər) *n.* One who uses snuff.

snuff·er[2] (snŭf′ər) *n.* **1.** One that snuffs out candles. **2. snuffers.** An instrument resembling a pair of shears that is used for cutting the snuff from or for extinguishing candles.

snuf·fle (snŭf′əl) *v.* **-fled, -fling, -fles.** *—intr.* **1.** To breathe noisily, as through a blocked nose. **2.** To sniff. **3.** To talk or sing nasally; whine. *—tr.* To utter (something) in a snuffling tone. *—n.* **1.** An act of snuffling. **2.** The sound produced in snuffling. **3. snuffles.** *Informal.* The sniffles. [Prob. < LG *snuffelen.*] **—snuf′fler** *n.*

snug[1] (snŭg) *adj.* **snug·ger, snug·gest. 1.** Comfortably sheltered; cozy. **2.** Small but well-arranged: *a snug apartment.* **3. a.** Closely secured and well-built; compact: *a snug little sailboat.* **b.** Seaworthy. **c.** Close-fitting: *a snug jacket.* *—v.* **snugged, snug·ging, snugs.** *—tr.* To make snug or secure. *—intr.* To nestle; snuggle. ***—phrasal verb.*** **snug down.** *Naut.* To prepare (a vessel) to weather a storm, as by taking in sail or securing movable gear. [Perh. of Scand. orig.] **—snug, snug′ly** *adv.* **—snug′ness** *n.*

snug[2] *n. Chiefly Brit.* A very small private room in a pub. [Short for SNUGGERY.]

snug·ger·y (snŭg′ə-rē) *n., pl.* **-ies.** *Chiefly Brit.* A snug position or place.

snug·gle (snŭg′əl) *v.* **-gled, -gling, -gles.** *—intr.* To lie or press close together; cuddle. *—tr.* To draw close or hold closely, as for comfort or in affection; hug. [Freq. of SNUG.]

so[1] (sō) *adv.* **1.** In the condition or manner expressed or indicated; thus: *Why does he think so?* **2.** To the amount or degree expressed or understood; to such an extent: *He was so weary that he fell.* **3.** To a great extent; to such an evident degree: *But the idea is so obvious.* **4.** Because of the reason given; consequently: *He was weary and so he fell.* **5.** Approximately; thereabouts: *The ticket costs ten dollars or so.* **6.** In the same way; likewise: *You were on time and so was I.* **7.** Then; apparently. Used in expressing astonishment, disapproval, or sarcasm: *So you think you've got troubles?* **8.** In truth; indeed: *"You aren't right." "I am so!"* *—adj.* True; factual: *I wouldn't have told you this if it weren't so.* *—conj.* With the result or consequence that: *He failed to appear, so we went on without him.* *—pron.* Such as has already been suggested or specified; the same: *became a loyal friend and remained so.* *—interj.* Used to express surprise or comprehension. ***—idioms.*** **so as to.** In order to: *Mail your package so as to ensure its timely arrival.* **so that.** In order that: *I stopped so that you could catch up.* [ME < OE *swā.*]

Usage: In formal writing the conjunction *so* is preferably followed by *that* when it introduces a clause stating the purpose of or reason for an action: *He stayed a day longer so that he could avoid the holiday traffic.* If *that* were omitted in the preceding example, the sentence would be unacceptable to a majority of the Usage Panel. • *So* generally stands alone, however, when it is used to introduce a clause that states the result or consequence of something: *The traffic was unusually heavy, so he stayed a day longer.* • New England speakers often use expressions like *so didn't I* where others would say *so did I,* as in *John has gone to college and so hasn't Sandy.* This usage is apt to confuse a speaker who has not encountered it and should be avoided in writing.

so[2] (sō) *n. Mus.* Variant of **sol.**

soak (sōk) *v.* **soaked, soak·ing, soaks.** *—tr.* **1. a.** To make thoroughly wet or saturated by or as if by placing in liquid. **b.** To immerse in liquid for a period of time. **2.** To absorb (liquid) through pores or interstices. **3.** *Informal.* To take in or accept mentally, esp. eagerly and easily: *soaked up the gossip.* **4.** *Informal.* **a.** To drink (alcoholic liquor), esp. to excess. **b.** To make (a person) drunk. **5.** *Slang.* To overcharge (a person) for something. *—intr.* **1.** To be immersed until thoroughly saturated. **2.** To penetrate or permeate; seep. **3.** *Slang.* To drink to excess. *—n.* **1. a.** The act or process of soaking. **b.** The condition of being soaked. **2.** Liquid in which something may be soaked. **3.** *Slang.* A drunkard. [ME *soken* < OE *socian.*] **—soak′er** *n.*

soak·age (sō′kĭj) *n.* **1. a.** The process of soaking. **b.** The condition of being soaked. **2.** The amount of liquid that soaks into, through, or out of an object.

so-and-so (sō′ən-sō′) *n., pl.* **-sos. 1.** An unnamed or unspecified person or thing. **2.** *Informal.* A son of a gun.

soap (sōp) *n.* **1.** A cleansing agent, manufactured in bars, granules, flakes, or liquid form, made from a mixture of the sodium salts of various fatty acids of natural oils and fats. **2.** A metallic salt of a fatty acid, as of aluminum or iron. **3.** *Slang.* Money, esp. money used for bribery. **4.** *Slang.* A soap opera. *—tr.v.* **soaped, soap·ing, soaps. 1.** To treat or cover with or as if with soap. **2.** *Slang.* To bribe. ***—idiom.*** **no soap.** *Slang.* **1.** Not possible or permissible. **2.** Unsuccessful; futile. [ME *sope* < OE *sāpe.*]

soap·bark (sōp′bärk′) *n.* **1. a.** A tree, *Quillaja saponaria,* of western South America, having bark used as soap and as a source of saponin. **b.** The bark of this tree. **2.** Any of several trees or shrubs having bark similar to that of the soapbark.

soap·ber·ry (sōp′bĕr′ē) *n.* **1.** Any of various chiefly tropical New World trees of the genus *Sapindus,* having pulpy fruit that lathers like soap. **2.** The fruit of a soapberry tree.

soap·box also **soap box** (sōp′bŏks′) *n.* **1.** A carton in which soap is packed. **2.** A temporary platform used while making an impromptu or nonofficial public speech.

Soapbox Derby. A service mark for a downhill race using children's homemade racing cars without motors or pedals.

soap bubble *n.* **1.** A bubble, esp. a large one, formed from soapy water. **2.** Something beautiful but transient, insubstantial, or illusory.

soap opera *n.* A daytime radio or television serial drama characterized by stock characters and situations, sentimentality, and melodrama. [From its orig. having been sponsored by soap companies.]

soap plant *n.* **1.** A plant, *Chlorogalum pomeridianum,* of California, having small white flowers and a bulbous root formerly used as soap. **2.** Any of various plants having parts used as soap.

soap·stone (sōp′stōn′) *n.* Steatite. [From its soapy texture.]

soap·suds (sōp′sŭdz′) *pl.n.* Suds from soapy water.

soap·wort (sōp′wûrt′, -wôrt′) *n.* The bouncing Bet. [From its yielding a soapy substance when the leaves are bruised.]

soap·y (sō′pē) *adj.* **-i·er, -i·est. 1.** Containing or consisting of soap. **2.** Covered with soap. **3.** Pertaining to or resembling soap. **4.** *Slang.* Unctuous; oily. **—soap′i·ly** *adv.* **—soap′i·ness** *n.*

soar (sôr, sōr) *intr.v.* **soared, soar·ing, soars. 1.** To rise, fly, or glide high and with little apparent effort. **2.** To climb swiftly or powerfully. **3.** To glide in an aircraft while maintaining altitude. **4.** To ascend suddenly above the normal or usual level: *Our spirits soared.* *—n.* **1.** The act of soaring. **2.** The altitude or scope attained in soaring. [ME *soren* < OFr. *esorer* < VLat. **exaurare* : Lat *ex-,* out of + Lat. *aura,* air < Gk., breeze.] **—soar′er** *n.* **—soar′ing·ly** *adv.*

soar·ing (sôr′ĭng, sōr′-) *n.* The act of gliding while maintaining altitude, esp. the sport of flying a heavier-than-air craft by utilizing ascending currents of air.

so·a·ve (sō-ä′vā) *n.* A dry white Italian table wine. [Ital. < Lat. *suāvis,* sweet.]

sob (sŏb) *v.* **sobbed, sob·bing, sobs.** *—intr.* **1.** To weep aloud with convulsive gasping; cry uncontrollably. **2.** To make a sound resembling that of sobbing. *—tr.* **1.** To utter with sobs. **2.** To put or bring (oneself) into a specified condition by sobbing: *sob oneself to sleep.* *—n.* The act or sound of sobbing. [ME *sobben.*] **—sob′bing·ly** *adv.*

so·ber (sō′bər) *adj.* **-er, -est. 1.** Habitually abstemious in the use of alcoholic liquors; temperate. **2.** Not intoxicated. **3.** Straightforward in character; serious. **4.** Plain or subdued; not garish: *sober attire.* **5.** Devoid of frivolity, excess, exaggeration, or speculative imagination: *gave a sober assessment of the situation.* **6.** Characterized by self-control or sanity; reasonable. *—tr. & intr.v.* **-bered, -ber·ing, -bers.** To make or become sober. [ME < OFr. *sobre* < Lat. *sobrius.*] **—so′ber·ly** *adv.* **—so′ber·ness** *n.*

sober-sided (sō′bər-sī′dĭd) *adj.* Devoid of extreme qualities, such as exaggeration; sober. **—so′ber-sid′ed·ness** *n.*

so·ber·sides (sō′bər-sīdz′) *pl.n. (used with a sing. or pl. verb).* A sober-sided person.

so·bri·e·ty (sō-brī′ĭ-tē) *n.* **1.** Seriousness or gravity in bearing, manner, or treatment; solemnity. **2.** Absence of alcoholic intoxication.

so·bri·quet (sō′brĭ-kā′, sō′brĭ-kā′) also **sou·bri·quet** (so͞o′brĭ-kā′, so͞o′brĭ-kā′) *n.* **1.** An affectionate or humorous nickname. **2.** An assumed name. [Fr.]

sob sister *n.* **1.** A journalist, esp. a woman, employed as a writer or editor of sob stories. **2.** A sentimental and ineffective person who seeks to do good.

sob story *n.* **1.** A tale of personal hardship or misfortune intended to arouse pity. **2.** A maudlin plea given as an explanation or rationalization.

soc·age (sŏk′ĭj, sō′kĭj) *n.* Feudal tenure of land by a tenant not a knight, in return for agricultural or other nonmilitary services or for payment of rent in money. [ME *sokage* < *soke,* soke.] **—soc′ag·er** *n.*

so-called (sō′kôld′) *adj.* **1.** Commonly called: *a so-called four-power summit.* **2.** Incorrectly or falsely termed: *a so-called teetotaler.*

soc·cer (sŏk′ər) *n.* A game played on a rectangular field with net goals at either end in which two teams of 11 players each maneuver a round ball mainly by kicking or butting or

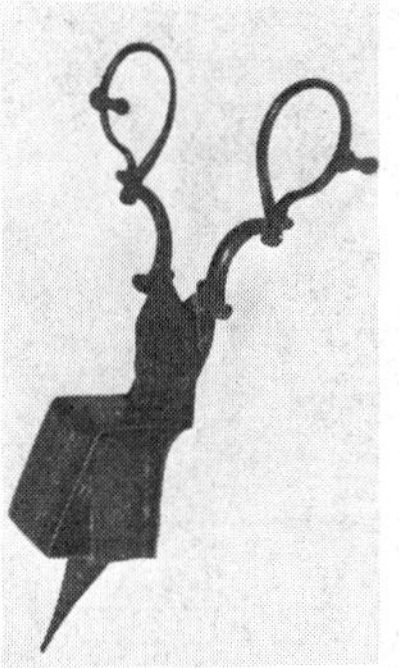

snuffer[2]

soccer

p **pop** / r **roar** / s **sauce** / sh **ship, dish** / t **tight** / th **thin, path** / *th* **this, bathe** / ŭ **cut** / ûr **urge** / v **valve** / w **with** / y **yes** / z **zebra, size** / zh **vision** / ə **about, item, edible, gallop, circus** / œ *Fr.* **feu,** *Ger.* **schön** / ü *Fr.* **tu,** *Ger.* **über** / KH *Ger.* **ich,** *Scot.* **loch** / N *Fr.* **bon.**

by using any part of the body except the arms and hands in attempts to score points. [Shortening and alteration of *association football.*]

so·cia·bil·i·ty (sō′shə-bĭl′ĭ-tē) *n., pl.* **-ties. 1.** The disposition or quality of being sociable. **2.** An instance of being sociable.

so·cia·ble (sō′shə-bəl) *adj.* **1.** Pleasant, friendly, or affable. **2.** Providing occasion for conversation and conviviality. *—n.* A social. [OFr. < Lat. *sociabilis* < *sociare,* to share < *socius,* partner.] **—so′cia·ble·ness** *n.* **—so′cia·bly** *adv.*

so·cial (sō′shəl) *adj.* **1. a.** Living together in communities. **b.** Of or pertaining to communal living. **c.** Of or pertaining to society. **2.** Living in an organized group or similar close aggregate: *social insects.* **3.** Involving allies or members of a confederacy. **4.** Of or pertaining to the upper classes. **5.** Fond of the company of others; sociable. **6.** Intended for convivial activities. **7.** Of, pertaining to, or occupied with welfare work. *—n.* An informal social gathering, as of the members of a church congregation. [Lat. *socialis,* of companionship < *socius,* partner.]

social climber *n.* A person who strives for acceptance in fashionable society.

social contract *n.* An agreement among the members of an organized society or between the governed and the government defining and limiting the rights and duties of each.

social disease *n.* **1.** Venereal disease. **2.** A disease having its highest incidence among social classes predisposed to it by a given set of adverse living or working conditions.

so·cial·ism (sō′shə-lĭz′əm) *n.* **1. a.** A social system in which the producers possess both political power and the means of producing and distributing goods. **b.** The theory or practice of those who support such a social system. **2.** In Marxist-Leninist theory, the building of the material base for communism under the dictatorship of the proletariat.

so·cial·ist (sō′shə-lĭst) *n.* **1.** An advocate of socialism. **2.** A member of a socialist party. *—adj.* **1.** Of, promoting, or practicing socialism. **2. Socialist.** Of, belonging to, or constituting a socialist party.

so·cial·is·tic (sō′shə-lĭs′tĭk) *adj.* Of, advocating, or tending toward socialism. **—so′cial·is′ti·cal·ly** *adv.*

socialist party *n.* Any of certain political parties advocating socialism to be achieved by democratic process.

socialist realism *n.* A Marxist aesthetic doctrine that seeks to promote the development of social consciousness through the didactic use of literature, art, and music.

so·cial·ite (sō′shə-līt′) *n.* One prominent in fashionable society.

so·ci·al·i·ty (sō′shē-ăl′ĭ-tē) *n., pl.* **-ties. 1. a.** The state or quality of being sociable; sociability. **b.** An instance of sociableness. **2.** The tendency to form communities and societies.

so·cial·ize (sō′shə-līz′) *v.* **-ized, -iz·ing, -iz·es.** *—tr.* **1.** To place under government or group ownership or control. **2.** To fit for companionship with others; make sociable. **3.** To convert or adapt to the needs of society. *—intr.* To take part in social activities. **—so′cial·i·za′tion** *n.* **—so′cial·iz′er** *n.*

socialized medicine *n.* The provision of medical and hospital care for the people at nominal cost by means of government regulation of health services and subsidies derived from taxation.

so·cial·ly (sō′shə-lē) *adv.* **1.** In a social way. **2.** With regard to society: *socially important.* **3.** By society: *socially accepted behavior.*

social register *n.* A directory listing persons of social prominence in a community.

social science *n.* The study of society and of individual relationships in and to society, generally regarded as including sociology, psychology, anthropology, economics, political science, and history.

social secretary *n.* A personal secretary who handles social correspondence and appointments.

social security *n.* **1.** A government program that provides economic assistance to persons faced with unemployment, disability, or old age, financed by assessment of employers and employees. **2.** The economic assistance provided by social security.

social service *n.* **1.** Organized efforts to advance human welfare; social work. **2.** Often **social services.** Welfare services, such as free school lunches, provided by a government for its needy citizens.

social studies *pl.n.* A course of study including geography, history, government, and sociology, taught in secondary and elementary schools.

social work *n.* Welfare work usually involving casework. **—social worker** *n.*

so·ci·e·tal (sə-sī′ĭ-təl) *adj.* Of or pertaining to the structure, organization, or functioning of society. **—so·ci′e·tal·ly** *adv.*

so·ci·e·ty (sə-sī′ĭ-tē) *n., pl.* **-ties. 1. a.** The totality of social relationships among human beings. **b.** A group of human beings broadly distinguished from other groups by mutual interests, participation in characteristic relationships, shared institutions, and a common culture. **c.** The institutions and culture of a distinct self-perpetuating group. **2. a.** The rich, privileged, and fashionable social class. **b.** The socially dominant members of a community. **3.** Companionship; company. **4.** *Biol.* A colony or community of organisms, usually of the same species. [OFr. *societe* < Lat. *societas,* fellowship < *socius,* partner.]

soda fountain

Society of Friends *n.* A Christian sect, founded in about 1650 in England, that rejects ritual, formal sacraments, a formal creed, a priesthood, and violence.

Society of Jesus *n.* The Jesuits.

So·cin·i·an (sō-sĭn′ē-ən) *n.* An adherent of a 16th-century Italian sect holding unitarian views, including denial of the divinity of Jesus. *—adj.* Of or pertaining to the Socinians or their doctrines. [NLat. *Socinianus,* after Laelius *Socinus* and Faustus *Socinus,* 16th-cent. Italian theologians.] **—So·cin′i·an·ism** *n.*

socio– *pref.* **1.** Society: *sociometry.* **2.** Social: *socioeconomic.* [Fr. < Lat. *socius,* fellow.]

so·ci·o·cul·tur·al (sō′sē-ō-kŭl′chər-əl, -shē-) *adj.* Both social and cultural. **—so′ci·o·cul′tur·al·ly** *adv.*

so·ci·o·ec·o·nom·ic (sō′sē-ō-ĕk′ə-nŏm′ĭk, -ē′kə-, -shē-) *adj.* Both social and economic.

so·ci·o·lin·guis·tics (sō′sē-ō-lĭng-gwĭs′tĭks) *n.* *(used with a sing. verb).* The study of linguistic behavior as influenced by social and cultural factors. **—so·ci·o·lin·guist** *n.* **—so·ci·o·lin·guis·tic** *adj.*

so·ci·ol·o·gy (sō′sē-ŏl′ə-jē, -shē-) *n.* **1.** The study of human social behavior, esp. the study of the origins, organization, institutions, and development of human society. **2.** The analysis of a social institution or societal segment as a self-contained entity or in relation to society as a whole. [Fr. *sociologie* : *socio-,* socio- + *-logie,* -logy.] **—so′ci·o·log′ic** (-ə-lŏj′ĭk), **so′ci·o·log′i·cal** *adj.* **—so′ci·o·log′i·cal·ly** *adv.* **—so′ci·ol′o·gist** *n.*

so·ci·om·e·try (sō′sē-ŏm′ĭ-trē, -shē-) *n.* The quantitative study of interpersonal relationships in populations, esp. the study and measurement of preferences.

so·ci·o·path (sō′sē-ə-păth′, -shē-) *n.* An individual with asocial or antisocial behavior or character traits. **—so′ci·o·path′ic** *adj.*

so·ci·o·po·li·ti·cal (sō′sē-ō-pə-lĭt′ĭ-kəl, -shē-) *adj.* Both social and political.

so·ci·o·re·lig·ious (sō′sē-ō-rĭ-lĭj′əs, -shē-) *adj.* Both social and religious.

sock[1] (sŏk) *n.* **1.** *pl.* **socks** or **sox.** A short stocking reaching a point between the ankle and the knee. **2. a.** A light shoe worn by comic actors in ancient Greek and Roman plays. **b.** Comic drama; comedy. **3.** A windsock. *—tr.v.* **socked, sock·ing, socks.** To provide with socks. ***—phrasal verbs.*** **sock away.** *Informal.* To put away (money); stash. **sock in.** To close to air traffic: *fog that socked in the airport.* [ME *socke* < OE *socc,* a kind of light shoe < Lat. *soccus.*]

sock[2] (sŏk) *Slang.* *—v.* **socked, sock·ing, socks.** *—tr.* To hit or strike forcefully; punch. *—intr.* To deliver a blow. *—n.* A hard blow or punch. [Orig. unknown.]

sock·dol·a·ger also **sock·dol·o·ger** (sŏk-dŏl′ə-jər) *n.* *Slang.* **1.** A conclusive blow or remark. **2.** Something outstanding. [Orig. unknown.]

sock·et (sŏk′ĭt) *n.* **1.** An opening or cavity into which an inserted part is designed to fit: *a light-bulb socket.* **2.** *Anat.* **a.** The hollow part of a joint that receives the end of a bone. **b.** A hollow or concavity into which a part, such as the eye, fits. *—tr.v.* **-et·ed, -et·ing, -ets.** To furnish with or insert into a socket. [ME *soket* < AN, spearhead, dim. of OFr. *soc,* plowshare, prob. of Celtic orig.]

sock·eye salmon (sŏk′ī′) *n.* A salmon, *Oncorhynchus nerka,* of northern Pacific coastal waters, that is a commercially valuable food fish. [By folk ety. < Salish *sukkegh.*]

so·cle (sō′kəl) *n.* *Archit.* **1.** A plain square block higher than a plinth, serving as a pedestal for sculpture, a vase, or a column. **2.** A plain plinth supporting a wall. [Fr. < Ital. *zoccolo,* wooden shoe < Lat. *socculus,* dim. of *soccus,* a kind of light shoe.]

sod[1] (sŏd) *n.* **1.** A section of grass-covered surface soil held together by matted roots; turf. **2.** The ground, esp. when covered with grass. *—tr.v.* **sod·ded, sod·ding, sods.** To cover with sod. [ME < MLG *sode.*]

sod[2] (sŏd) *n.* *Chiefly Brit. Slang.* An obnoxious or contemptible person. [Short for SODOMITE.]

so·da (sō′də) *n.* **1. a.** Any of various forms of sodium carbonate. **b.** Chemically combined sodium. **2.** Carbonated water or a soft drink containing it. **3.** A refreshment made from carbonated water, ice cream, and usually a flavoring. **4.** The card turned face up at the beginning of faro. [Med. Lat., barilla.]

soda ash *n.* Crude anhydrous sodium carbonate used esp. as an industrial chemical.

soda biscuit *n.* **1.** A breadlike biscuit leavened with baking soda. **2.** A soda cracker.

soda cracker *n.* A thin, usually square cracker leavened slightly with baking soda.

soda fountain *n.* **1.** An apparatus with faucets for dispensing soda water. **2.** A counter equipped for preparing and serving soft drinks, ice-cream dishes, or sandwiches.

soda jerk *n.* *Slang.* One who works at a soda fountain. [Short for *soda jerker.*]

soda lime *n.* A mixture of calcium hydroxide and sodium or potassium hydroxide, used as a drying agent and carbon dioxide absorbent.

so·da·list (sō′də-lĭst, sō-dăl′ĭst) *n.* A member of a sodality.

so·da·lite (sō′də-līt′) *n.* A blue-white vitreous mineral, essentially $Na_4Al_3Si_3O_{12}Cl$, found in igneous rocks.

so·dal·i·ty (sō-dăl′ĭ-tē) *n., pl.* **-ties. 1.** A society or association, esp. a devotional or charitable society in the Roman Catholic Church. **2.** Fellowship. [Lat. *sodalitas,* fellowship < *sodalis,* fellow.]

so·da·mide (sō′də-mīd′) *n.* Sodium amide.

soda niter *n.* Sodium nitrate.

soda pop *n. Informal.* A soft drink; soda.

soda water *n.* **1.** Effervescent water charged under pressure with purified carbon dioxide gas, used as a beverage or mixer. **2.** A solution of water, sodium bicarbonate, and acid.

sod·den (sŏd′n) *adj.* **1.** Thoroughly soaked; saturated. **2.** Soggy and heavy from improper cooking; doughy. **3.** Bloated and dull, esp. from drink. **4.** Unimaginative; torpid. —*tr. & intr.v.* **-dened, -den·ing, -dens.** To make or become sodden. [ME *soden,* boiled, p.part. of *sethen,* to boil. —see SEETHE.] **—sod′den·ly** *adv.* **—sod′den·ness** *n.*

so·di·um (sō′dē-əm) *n. Symbol* **Na** A soft, light, extremely malleable silver-white metallic element that reacts explosively with water, is naturally abundant in combined forms, esp. in common salt, and is used in the production of a wide variety of industrially important compounds. Atomic number 11; atomic weight 22.99; melting point 97.8°C; boiling point 892°C; specific gravity 0.971; valence 1. [SOD(A) + -IUM.]

sodium ammonium phosphate *n.* A colorless, odorless crystalline compound, $NaNH_4HPO_4{\cdot}4H_2O$, used as an analytical reagent.

sodium benzoate *n.* The sodium salt of benzoic acid, C_6H_5COONa, used as a food preservative, antiseptic, and intermediate in dye manufacture and in the production of pharmaceuticals.

sodium bicarbonate *n.* A white crystalline compound, $NaHCO_3$, with a slightly alkaline taste, used in making effervescent salts and beverages, artificial mineral water, baking soda and pharmaceuticals and in fire extinguishers.

sodium borate *n.* A crystalline compound, $Na_2B_4O_7{\cdot}10H_2O$, used in the manufacture of glass, detergents, and pharmaceuticals.

sodium carbonate *n.* **1.** A white powdery compound, Na_2CO_3, used in the manufacture of sodium bicarbonate, sodium nitrate, glass, ceramics, detergents, and soap. **2.** Any of various hydrated carbonates of sodium, such as sal soda.

sodium chlorate *n.* A colorless crystalline compound, $NaClO_3$, used as a bleaching and oxidizing agent and in explosives.

sodium chloride *n.* A colorless crystalline compound, NaCl, used in the manufacture of chemicals and as a food preservative and seasoning.

sodium cyanide *n.* A poisonous white crystalline compound, NaCN, used in extracting gold and silver from ores and in dye manufacture.

sodium cyclamate *n.* A soluble white crystalline powder, $C_6H_{11}NHSO_3Na$, 30 times as sweet as sugar and formerly a major constituent of low-calorie sweetening agents.

sodium dichromate *n.* A red-orange crystalline compound, $Na_2Cr_2O_7{\cdot}2H_2O$, used as an oxidizing agent.

sodium glutamate *n.* A white crystalline compound, $COOH\text{-}(CH_2)_2CH(NH_2)COONa$, having a meatlike taste, used in cooking.

sodium hydrosulfite *n.* A yellowish powder, $Na_2S_2O_4$, used as a bleaching and reducing agent.

sodium hydroxide *n.* A strongly alkaline compound, NaOH, used in the manufacture of chemicals and soaps and in petroleum refining.

sodium hypochlorite *n.* An unstable salt, NaOCl, usually stored in solution and used as a fungicide and an oxidizing bleach.

sodium hyposulfite *n.* **1.** Sodium hydrosulfite. **2.** Sodium thiosulfate.

sodium nitrate *n.* A white crystalline compound, $NaNO_3$, used in solid rocket propellants and in the manufacture of explosives and tobacco.

sodium perborate *n.* A white odorless crystalline compound, $NaBO_2{\cdot}H_2O_2{\cdot}3H_2O$, used as a mild alkaline oxidizing agent in dentifrices, as a topical antiseptic and deodorant, and as an industrial reagent.

sodium peroxide *n.* A yellowish-white powder, Na_2O_2, employed industrially as an oxidizing and bleaching agent and medically as a germicide, antiseptic, and disinfectant.

sodium phosphate *n.* Any of the three sodium salts of phosphoric acid, NaH_2PO_4, Na_2HPO_4, and Na_3PO_4, widely used in industry, pharmaceutical manufacturing, medicine, and chemistry.

sodium propionate *n.* A clear crystalline compound, C_2H_5COONa, capable of retarding the growth of molds and bacteria and used to prevent food spoilage.

sodium silicate *n.* Any of various water-soluble silicate glass compounds used as a preservative for eggs, in plaster and cement, and in various purification and refining processes.

sodium sulfate *n.* A white crystalline compound, Na_2SO_4, used to manufacture paper, glass, dyes, and pharmaceuticals.

sodium sulfide *n.* A hygroscopic yellow compound, Na_2S, used as a metal ore reagent and in photography, engraving, and printing.

sodium sulfite *n.* A white crystalline or powdered compound, Na_2SO_3, used in preserving foods, silvering mirrors, developing photographs, and making dyes.

sodium thiosulfate *n.* A white, translucent crystalline compound, $Na_2S_2O_3{\cdot}5H_2O$, used as a photographic fixing agent and as a bleach.

so·di·um-va·por lamp (sō′dē-əm-vā′pər) *n.* An electric lamp containing a small amount of sodium and neon gas, used in generating yellow light for lighting streets and highways.

Sod·om or **sod·om** (sŏd′əm) *n.* A place well known for vice and corruption. [After *Sodom,* a wicked city in ancient Palestine.]

sod·om·ite (sŏd′ə-mīt′) *n.* One who engages in sodomy.

sod·om·y (sŏd′ə-mē) *n.* **1.** Anal copulation of one male with another. **2.** Anal or oral copulation with a member of the opposite sex. **3.** Copulation with an animal. [ME < OFr. *sodomie* < LLat. *Sodoma,* Sodom.]

so·ev·er (sō-ĕv′ər) *adv.* At all; in any way: *"Space to breathe, how short soever"* (B. Jonson).

so·fa (sō′fə) *n.* A long upholstered seat with a back and arms. [Ar. *sufah,* dais.]

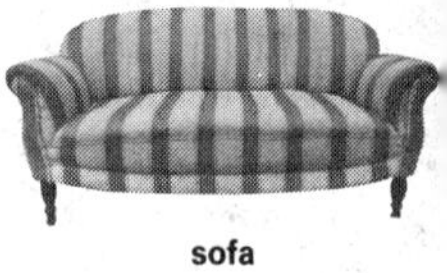
sofa

sofa bed *n.* A sofa whose seat unfolds to form a bed.

so·far (sō′fär′) *n.* A system for detecting and locating underwater explosions propagated over long distances through deep ocean layers, used to find survivors lost at sea. [SO(UND) F(IXING) A(ND) R(ANGING).]

sof·fit (sŏf′ĭt) *n.* The underside of a structural component, such as a beam, arch, staircase, or cornice. [Fr. *soffite* < Ital. *soffito* < VLat. **suffictus* < *Lat. suffixus,* p.part. of *suffigere,* to fasten beneath. —see SUFFIX.]

soft (sôft, sŏft) *adj.* **-er, -est. 1. a.** Easily molded, cut, or worked. **b.** Yielding readily to pressure or weight. **2.** Out of condition; flabby. **3.** Smooth or fine to the touch: *soft velvet.* **4. a.** Not loud, harsh, or irritating: *a soft voice.* **b.** Not brilliant or glaring; subdued: *soft colors.* **5.** Not sharply drawn or delineated: *soft charcoal shading.* **6.** Mild; balmy: *a soft breeze.* **7. a.** Of a gentle disposition; tender. **b.** Affectionate: *a soft glance.* **c.** Attracted or emotionally involved: *He has been soft on her for years.* **d.** Not stern; lenient. **e.** Lacking strength of character; weak. **f.** *Informal.* Simple; feeble: *soft in the head.* **g.** Gradually declining in trend; not firm: *a soft economy.* **8. a.** *Informal.* Easy: *a soft job.* **b.** Based on conciliation or negotiation rather than on threats or power plays: *took a soft line toward their opponents.* **9.** Of or pertaining to a paper currency as distinct from a hard currency backed by gold. **10.** Having low dissolved mineral content. **11. a.** Sibilant rather than guttural, as *c* in *certain* and *g* in *gem.* **b.** Voiced and weakly articulated: *a soft consonant.* **c.** Palatalized, as certain consonants in Slavic languages. **12.** Occurring under such circumstances and at such a speed as to preclude destructive impact: *The airplane made a soft landing on the runway.* **13.** Unprotected against enemy attack: *soft launching sites.* —*n.* A soft object or part. —*adv.* In a soft manner; gently. [ME, pleasant, calm < OE *sōfte.*] **—soft′ly** *adv.* **—soft′ness** *n.*

soft·ball (sôft′bôl′, sŏft′-) *n.* **1.** A variation of baseball played on a smaller diamond with a larger, softer ball that is pitched underhand. **2.** The ball used in softball.

soft-boiled (sôft′boild′, sŏft′-) *adj.* **1.** Boiled in the shell to a soft consistency. Used of an egg. **2.** *Informal.* **a.** Softhearted; lenient. **b.** Sentimental.

soft·bound (sôft′bound′, sŏft′-) *adj.* Not bound between hard covers: *softbound books.*

soft clam *n.* The soft-shell clam.

soft coal *n.* Bituminous coal.

soft-core (sôft′kôr′, -kōr′, sŏft′-) *adj.* **1.** Being less explicit than hard-core material in depicting or describing sexual activity: *soft-core pornography.* **2.** Moderate: *a soft-core sports fan.*

soft drink *n.* A nonalcoholic, usually carbonated beverage.

soft drug *n.* A drug, such as marijuana, that is nonaddictive and considered less damaging to the health than a hard drug.

soft·en (sô′fən, sŏf′ən) *v.* **-ened, -en·ing, -ens.** —*tr.* **1.** To make soft or softer. **2.** To weaken the strength, morale, or resistance of by preliminary harassment. —*intr.* To become soft or softer. **—soft′en·er** *n.*

soft-finned (sôft′fĭnd′, sŏft′-) *adj. Zool.* Having fins supported by flexible cartilaginous rays.

soft goods *pl.n.* Dry goods.

soft hail *n.* Graupel.

soft·head (sôft′hĕd′, sŏft′-) *n.* A foolish or feeble-minded person; simpleton.

soft·head·ed (sôft′hĕd′ĭd, sŏft′-) *adj.* Lacking judgment, realism, or firmness. **—soft′head′ed·ly** *adv.* **—soft′head′ed·ness** *n.*

soft·heart·ed (sôft′här′tĭd, sŏft′-) *adj.* Easily moved; tender. **—soft′heart′ed·ly** *adv.* **—soft′heart′ed·ness** *n.*

soft-land (sôft′lănd′, sŏft′-) *intr. & tr.v.* **-land·ed, -land·ing, -lands.** To make or cause to make a soft landing.

soft landing *n.* The landing of a space vehicle on a celestial body in such a way as to prevent damage or destruction.
soft-lin·er (sôft'lī'nər, sŏft'-) *n.* One that takes a moderate or flexible approach, esp. on a political issue.
soft palate *n.* The movable fold, consisting of muscular fibers enclosed in mucous membrane, that is suspended from the rear of the hard palate and closes off the nasal cavity from the oral cavity during swallowing or sucking.
soft paste also **soft-paste** (sôft'pāst', sŏft'-) *n.* Any of various ceramics containing frit and refined clay.
soft pedal *n.* A pedal used to mute tone, as on a piano.
soft-ped·al (sôft'pĕd'l, sŏft'-) *tr.v.* **-aled, -al·ing, -als** or **-alled, -al·ling, -als. 1.** To soften or mute the tone of by depressing the soft pedal. **2.** *Informal.* To make less emphatic or obvious; play down.
soft rock *n.* A style of rock 'n' roll characterized by the predominance of melody and minimal use of electronic modulations.
soft roe *n.* The spermatozoa or testes of a fish; milt.
soft sculpture *n.* A sculpture made of pliant materials, such as cloth or foam rubber.
soft sell *n. Informal.* A subtly persuasive and low-pressure method of selling or advertising.
soft-shell (sôft'shĕl', sŏft'-) also **soft-shelled** (-shĕld') *adj.* Having a soft, brittle, or unhardened shell.
soft-shell clam *n.* A common edible clam, *Mya arenaria,* having a thin, elongated shell.
soft-shell crab *n.* A marine crab before its shell has hardened after molting, esp. the edible species, *Callinectes sapidus,* of eastern North America, in this stage.
soft-shelled turtle *n.* Any of various freshwater turtles of the family Trionychidae, having a flat carapace covered with leathery skin.
soft-shoe (sôft'sho͞o', sŏft'-) *n.* A type of tap dancing performed without metal taps on the shoes.
soft shoulder *n.* A border of soft earth running along the edge of a road.
soft soap *n.* **1.** A fluid or semifluid soap. **2.** *Informal.* Flattery; cajolery.
soft-soap (sôft'sōp', sŏft'-) *tr.v.* **-soaped, -soap·ing, -soaps.** *Informal.* To flatter in order to gain something; cajole. **—soft'-soap'er** *n.*
soft-spo·ken (sôft'spō'kən, sŏft'-) *adj.* **1.** Speaking with a soft or gentle voice. **2.** Smooth; ingratiating.
soft spot *n.* **1.** A tender or sentimental feeling. **2.** In the skull of an infant, either of the points of juncture of the sagittal and lambdoid or sagittal and coronal sutures.
soft touch *n.* One who is easily persuaded or taken advantage of.
soft·ware (sôft'wâr', sŏft'-) *n.* **1.** Written or printed data, such as programs, routines, and symbolic languages, essential to the operation of computers. **2.** Documents containing information on the operation and maintenance of computers.
soft water *n.* Water containing little or no dissolved salts of calcium or magnesium, esp. water containing less than 85.5 parts per million of calcium carbonate.
soft·wood (sôft'wo͝od', sŏft'-) *n.* **1.** The wood of a coniferous tree. **2.** A coniferous tree.
soft·y (sôf'tē, sŏf'-) *n., pl.* **-ies.** *Informal.* **1.** A weak or sentimental person. **2.** A person who finds it difficult to punish or be strict.
sog·gy (sŏg'ē, sôg'ē) *adj.* **-gi·er, -gi·est. 1.** Saturated or sodden with moisture; soaked. **2.** Lacking spirit; dull. **3.** Humid; sultry. [< dial. *sog,* to soak.] **—sog'gi·ly** *adv.* **—sog'gi·ness** *n.*
soi-di·sant (swä'dē-zäN') *adj.* Self-styled; so-called. [Fr.]
soi·gné also **soi·gnée** (swän-yā') *adj.* **1.** Showing sophisticated elegance; fashionable: *a soigné little club.* **2.** Well-groomed; polished. [Fr. < p.part. of *soigner,* to take care of < Med. Lat. *soniare.*]
soil[1] (soil) *n.* **1.** The top layer of the earth's surface, suitable for the growth of plant life. **2.** A particular kind of earth or ground: *sandy soil.* **3.** Country; land: *native soil.* **4.** The agricultural life: *a man of the soil.* **5.** A place or condition favorable to growth. [ME < AN, a piece of ground < Lat. *solium,* seat.]
soil[2] (soil) *v.* **soiled, soil·ing, soils.** *—tr.* **1.** To make dirty, particularly on the surface. **2.** To disgrace; tarnish: *a reputation soiled by scandal.* **3.** To corrupt; defile. **4.** To dirty with excrement. *—intr.* To become dirty, stained, or tarnished. *—n.* **1. a.** The state of being soiled. **b.** A stain. **2.** Filth, sewage, or refuse matter. **3.** Manure, esp. human excrement, used as fertilizer. [ME *soilen* < OFr. *souiller* < VLat. **suculare* < Lat. *suculus,* dim. of *sus,* pig.]
soil[3] (soil) *tr.v.* **soiled, soil·ing, soils. 1.** To feed (livestock) with soilage. **2.** To purge (livestock) by feeding with green food. [Orig. unknown.]
soil·age (soi'lĭj) *n.* Green crops cut for feeding penned livestock.
soil pipe *n.* A drain pipe that carries off wastes from a plumbing fixture, esp. from a toilet.
soil·ure (soil'yər) *n.* **1.** Soiling or the condition of being soiled. **2.** A blot, stain, or smudge.
soi·ree also **soi·rée** (swä-rā') *n.* An evening party or reception. [Fr. *soirée* < *soir,* evening < Lat. *serus,* late.]

solar panel

so·journ (sō'jûrn', sō-jûrn') *intr.v.* **-journed, -journ·ing, -journs.** To stay for a time; reside temporarily. *—n.* A temporary stay; brief residence. [ME *sojournen* < OFr. *sojorner* < VLat. **subdiurnare* : Lat. *sub-,* under + LLat. *diurnum,* day < Lat. *diurnus,* daily < *dies,* day.] **—so'journ'er** *n.*
soke (sōk) *n.* **1.** In early English law, the right of local jurisdiction, generally one of the feudal rights of lordship. **2.** The district over which soke jurisdiction was exercised. [ME < Med. Lat. *soca* < OE *socn,* act of seeking.]
sol[1] (sōl) also **so** (sō) *n. Mus.* **1.** The syllable used to represent the fifth tone of a diatonic scale. **2.** The tone G. [ME < Med. Lat. —see GAMUT.]
sol[2] (sŏl) *n.* **1.** A former monetary unit of France, equal to 12 deniers. **2.** An old French coin worth 12 deniers. [ME < OFr. < Lat. *solidus,* solidus.]
sol[3] (sōl) *n., pl.* **so·les** (sō'lās). See table at **currency.** [Sp. < Lat. *sol,* sun.]
sol[4] (sôl, sōl) *n.* A liquid colloidal dispersion. [Short for HYDROSOL.]
Sol (sŏl, sōl) *n.* The sun. [ME < Lat.]
so·la[1] (sō'lə) *n.* A plural of **solum.**
so·la[2] (sō'lə) *adj.* Feminine of **solus.**
sol·ace (sŏl'ĭs) also **sol·ace·ment** (-mənt) *n.* **1.** Comfort in sorrow, misfortune, or distress; consolation. **2.** Something that furnishes comfort or consolation. *—tr.v.* **-aced, -ac·ing, -ac·es. 1.** To comfort, cheer, or console, as in trouble or sorrow. **2.** To allay or assuage: *He solaced his misery in work.* [ME *solas* < OFr. < Lat. *solacium* < *solari,* to console.] **—sol'ac·er** *n.*
so·la·nine (sō'lə-nēn', -nĭn) *n.* A bitter poisonous alkaloid, $C_{45}H_{73}NO_{15}$, derived from potato sprouts, tomatoes, and nightshade, formerly used to treat epilepsy. [Fr. < Lat. *solanum,* nightshade < *sol,* sun.]
so·lar (sō'lər) *adj.* **1.** Of, pertaining to, or proceeding from the sun: *solar rays.* **2.** Utilizing or operated by energy derived from the sun: *a solar heating system.* **3.** Determined or measured with respect to the sun: *the solar year.* [ME < Lat. *solaris* < *sol,* sun.]
solar battery *n.* A system consisting of a large number of connected solar cells.
solar cell *n.* A semiconductor device that converts the energy of sunlight into electric energy, used mainly as a power supply in space vehicles.
solar constant *n.* The amount of solar radiation perpendicularly impinging on a surface of unit area at a distance of one astronomical unit from the sun in a unit interval of time, having an average value of 1.94 calories per minute per square centimeter.
solar day *n.* The interval between two successive meridian passages of the sun.
solar flare *n.* A temporary outburst of solar gases from a small area of the sun's surface, a source of intense radiation.
solar furnace *n.* A parabolic reflector that focuses solar radiation at a point to obtain temperatures as high as 4,000°C.
solar house *n.* A house having large quantities of heat-absorbing material behind large glass areas, designed to supplement or replace conventional heating methods.
so·lar·i·a (sō-lâr'ē-ə) *n.* A plural of **solarium.**
so·lar·im·e·ter (sō'lə-rĭm'ĭ-tər) *n.* An instrument used to measure the flux of solar radiation through a surface.
so·lar·i·um (sō-lâr'ē-əm) *n., pl.* **-i·a** (-ē-ə) or **-i·ums.** A room, gallery, or glassed-in porch exposed to the sun. [Lat., terrace < *sol,* sun.]
so·lar·ize (sō'lə-rīz') *v.* **-ized, -iz·ing, -iz·es.** *—tr.* To affect by exposing to the sun's rays. *—intr.* To be overexposed. Used of photographic film. **—so'lar·i·za'tion** *n.*
solar month *n.* A month (sense 6).
solar panel *n.* A panel of connected solar cells.
solar plexus *n.* **1.** The large network of sympathetic nerves and ganglia located in the peritoneal cavity behind the stomach and having branching tracts that supply nerves to the abdominal viscera. **2.** *Informal.* The pit of the stomach. [From its radially branching ganglia.]
solar system *n.* The sun together with the nine planets and all other celestial bodies that orbit the sun.
solar wind *n.* The plasma ejected at high speeds from the surface of the sun.
solar year *n.* A tropical year.
so·la·ti·um (sō-lā'shē-əm) *n., pl.* **-ti·a** (-shē-ə). *Law.* Compensation for damage to the feelings as distinct from financial loss or physical suffering. [LLat., solace < Lat. *solari,* to console.]
sold *v.* Past tense and past participle of **sell.**
sol·dan (sŏl'dən, sōl'-) also **sou·dan** (so͞od'n) *n. Archaic.* A sultan. [ME < OFr. < Ar. *sulṭān.* —see SULTAN.]
sol·der (sŏd'ər) *n.* **1.** Any of various fusible alloys, usually tin and lead, used to join metallic parts when applied in the melted state to the solid metal. **2.** Something that joins or cements. *—v.* **-dered, -der·ing, -ders.** *—tr.* To serve as a bond between; join. *—intr.* **1.** To unite or repair things with solder. **2.** To be joined by or as if by solder. [ME *soudur* < OFr. *soudure* < *souder,* to solder < Lat. *solidare,* to make solid < *solidus,* solid.] **—sol'der·er** *n.*
sol·dier (sōl'jər) *n.* **1.** One who serves in an army. **2.** An enlisted person or a noncommissioned officer as distin-

ă pat / ā pay / âr care / ä father / b bib / ch church / d deed / ĕ pet / ē be / f fife / g gag / h hat / hw which / ĭ pit / ī pie / îr pier / j judge / k kick / l lid, needle / m mum / n no, sudden / ng thing / ŏ pot / ō toe / ô paw, for / oi noise / ou out / o͝o took / o͞o boot /

guished from a commissioned officer. **3.** An active, loyal, and militant follower. **4.** A sexually undeveloped form of certain ants and termites, having the jaws specialized to serve as fighting weapons. *—intr.v.* **-diered, -dier·ing, -diers. 1.** To be or serve as a soldier. **2.** To make a show of working in order to escape punishment. [ME *soudeour,* mercenary < OFr. *soudier* < *soude,* pay < Lat. *solidus,* solidus.]

sol·dier·ly (sōl′jər-lē) *adj.* Of, pertaining to, or befitting a soldier.

soldier of fortune *n.* One who will serve in any army for personal gain or love of adventure.

soldiers' home *n.* A government-funded institution for the care of armed forces veterans.

sol·dier·y (sōl′jə-rē) *n., pl.* **-ies. 1.** Soldiers collectively. **2.** A body of soldiers. **3.** The military profession.

sold-out (sōld′out′) *adj.* Having all tickets or accommodations completely sold, esp. ahead of time.

sole[1] (sōl) *n.* **1.** The undersurface of the foot. **2.** The undersurface of a shoe or boot. **3.** The part on which something rests while standing, esp.: **a.** The bottom surface of a plow. **b.** The bottom surface of the head of a golf club. *—tr.v.* **soled, sol·ing, soles. 1.** To furnish (a shoe or boot) with a sole. **2.** To put the sole of (a golf club) on the ground, as in preparing to make a stroke. [ME < OFr. *solea,* sandal < *solum,* bottom.]

sole[2] (sōl) *adj.* **1.** Being the only one; single: *His sole purpose was to succeed.* **2.** Of or pertaining to only one individual or group; exclusive: *The court has the sole right to decide.* **3.** *Law.* Single or unmarried. [ME, alone < OFr. *sol* < Lat. *solus.*]

sole[3] (sōl) *n., pl.* **sole** or **soles. 1.** Any of various chiefly marine flatfishes of the family Soleidae, related to and resembling the flounders, esp. any of several European species, such as *Solea solea,* valued as food fishes. **2.** Any of various flatfishes. [ME < OFr. < Lat. *solea,* sandal, flatfish < *solum,* bottom.]

sol·e·cism (sŏl′ĭ-sĭz′əm, sō′lĭ-) *n.* **1.** A nonstandard usage or grammatical construction. **2.** A violation of etiquette. **3.** An impropriety, mistake, or incongruity. [Lat. *soloecismus* < Gk. *soloikismos* < *soloikos,* speaking incorrectly, after *Soloi,* an Athenian colony in Cilicia where a substandard dialect was spoken.] **—sol′e·cist** *n.* **—sol′e·cis′tic** *adj.*

sole·ly (sōl′lē, sō′lē) *adv.* **1.** Alone; singly: *solely responsible.* **2.** Entirely; exclusively: *did it solely for love.*

sol·emn (sŏl′əm) *adj.* **1.** Marked by deep earnestness; grave: *a solemn voice.* **2.** Of impressive and serious nature: *a solemn occasion.* **3.** Performed with full ceremony: *a solemn High Mass.* **4.** Invoking the force of religion; sacred: *a solemn vow.* **5.** Gloomy; somber. [ME *solempne* < OFr. < Lat. *sollemnis,* established, customary.] **—sol′emn·ly** *adv.* **—sol′emn·ness** *n.*

so·lem·ni·ty (sə-lĕm′nĭ-tē) *n., pl.* **-ties. 1.** The condition or quality of being solemn. **2.** A solemn observance or proceeding.

sol·em·nize (sŏl′əm-nīz′) *tr.v.* **-nized, -niz·ing, -niz·es. 1.** To celebrate or observe (a religious occasion, for example) with formal ceremonies or rites. **2.** To perform with formal ceremony. **3.** To make serious or grave. **—sol′em·ni·za′tion** *n.*

so·le·noid (sō′lə-noid′) *n.* **1.** A cylindrical coil of insulated wire in which an axial magnetic field is established by a flow of electric current. **2.** An assembly often used as a switch, consisting essentially of a coil and a metal core free to slide along the coil axis under the influence of the magnetic field. [Fr. *solénoïde* < Gk. *sōlēnoeidēs,* pipe-shaped : *sōlēn,* pipe + *-eidēs,* -oid.] **—so′le·noi′dal** (-noid′l) *adj.* **—so′le·noi′dal·ly** *adv.*

sole·plate (sōl′plāt′) *n.* The undersurface of a clothes iron.

sole·print (sōl′prĭnt′) *n.* **1.** A print of the sole of the foot. **2.** A soleprint made for identification, as of an infant.

so·les (sō′lās) *n.* Plural of **sol[3]**.

sol-fa (sōl-fä′) *n. Mus.* **1.** The set of syllables *do, re, mi, fa, sol, la,* and *ti,* used to represent the tones of the scale. **2.** The use of the sol-fa syllables. *—v.* **-faed, -fa·ing, -fas.** *—intr.* To use the sol-fa syllables. *—tr.* To sing using the sol-fa syllables. [SOL[1] + FA.]

sol·fa·ta·ra (sōl′fə-tär′ə) *n.* A volcanic fissure that emits sulfurous vapors, steam, and at times hot mud. [Ital., sulfurous volcano < *solfo,* sulfur < Lat. *sulfur.*] **—sol′fa·ta′ric** *adj.*

sol·fège (sōl-fĕzh′) *n.* Solfeggio. [Fr. < Ital. *solfeggio.*]

sol·feg·gio (sōl-fĕj′ē-ō′, -fĕj′ō) *n. Mus.* **1.** The use of the sol-fa syllables to note the tones of the scale; solmization. **2.** A singing exercise in which the sol-fa syllables are used. [Ital. < *sol-fa,* sol-fa.]

sol·fe·ri·no (sŏl′fə-rē′nō) *n.* A moderate purplish red. [After *Solferino,* Italy, from the discovery of a dye of this color in the same year that a battle was fought there.] **—sol′fe·ri′no** *adj.*

so·lic·it (sə-lĭs′ĭt) *v.* **-it·ed, -it·ing, -its.** *—tr.* **1.** To seek to obtain by persuasion, entreaty, or formal application: *solicit votes.* **2.** To petition persistently; importune: *solicited the neighbors for donations.* **3.** To entice or incite to evil or illegal action. **4.** To approach or accost with an offer of sexual services. *—intr.* To make solicitation or petition for something desired. [ME *soliciten,* to disturb < OFr. *solliciter* < Lat. *sollicitare* < *sollicitus,* solicitous.] **—so·lic′i·ta′tion** *n.*

so·lic·i·tor (sə-lĭs′ĭ-tər) *n.* **1.** One that solicits, esp. one that seeks trade or contributions. **2.** The chief law officer of a city, town, or government department. **3.** *Chiefly Brit.* A lawyer who is not a member of the bar and who may be heard only in the lower courts.

solicitor general *n., pl.* **solicitors general. 1.** A law officer assisting an attorney general. **2.** The chief law officer in a state not having an attorney general.

so·lic·i·tous (sə-lĭs′ĭ-təs) *adj.* **1.** Concerned; attentive: *a solicitous parent.* **2.** Full of desire; eager. **3.** Anxious; worried: *solicitous about her daughter's future.* **4.** Extremely careful; meticulous: *solicitous in matters of behavior.* **5.** Expressing solicitude: *a solicitous inquiry about her family.* [Lat. *sollicitus,* troubled : *sollus,* entire + *citus,* p.part. of *ciere,* to move.] **—so·lic′i·tous·ly** *adv.* **—so·lic′i·tous·ness** *n.*

so·lic·i·tude (sə-lĭs′ĭ-to͞od′, -tyo͞od′) *n.* **1.** The state or quality of being solicitous. **2.** Often **solicitudes.** Something that causes anxiety or concern.

sol·id (sŏl′ĭd) *adj.* **1.** Of definite shape and volume; not liquid or gaseous. **2.** Not hollowed out: *a solid block of wood.* **3.** Being the same substance or color throughout: *solid gold.* **4.** Of or pertaining to three-dimensional geometric figures or bodies. **5.** Without gaps or breaks; continuous: *a solid line of people.* **6.** Of good quality and substance; well-made: *a solid foundation.* **7.** Substantial; hearty: *a solid meal.* **8.** Sound; reliable: *solid facts.* **9.** Financially sound. **10.** Upstanding and dependable: *a solid citizen.* **11.** Written without a hyphen or space: *The word "software" is a solid compound.* **12.** *Printing.* Without leads between the lines. **13.** Acting together; unanimous: *a solid voting bloc.* *—n.* **1.** A substance that is neither liquid nor gaseous. **2.** A geometric figure having three dimensions. [ME *solide,* not hollow < OFr. < Lat. *solidus.*] **—sol′id·ly** *adv.* **—sol′id·ness** *n.*

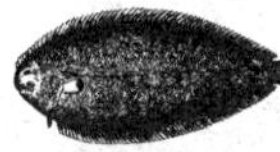

sole[3]
European sole

solid angle *n.* An angle subtended at a point by a surface, measured in steradians with respect to the area delimited on the unit sphere centered on that point by the locus of points of intersection of the sphere with the lines joining the point to the perimeter of the surface.

sol·i·dar·i·ty (sŏl′ĭ-dăr′ĭ-tē) *n.* A union of interests, purposes, or sympathies among members of a group; fellowship.

solid geometry *n.* The geometry of three-dimensional figures and surfaces.

sol·i·di (sŏl′ĭ-dī′) *n.* Plural of **solidus.**

so·lid·i·fy (sə-lĭd′ə-fī′) *v.* **-fied, -fy·ing, -fies.** *—tr.* **1.** To make solid, compact, or hard. **2.** To make strong or united. *—intr.* To become solid or united. **—so·lid′i·fi·ca′tion** *n.*

so·lid·i·ty (sə-lĭd′ĭ-tē) *n.* **1.** The condition or property of being solid. **2.** Soundness of mind, moral character, or finances.

solid of revolution *n.* A volume generated by the rotation of a plane figure about an axis in its plane.

solid propellant *n.* A rocket propellant in solid form, combining both fuel and oxidizer in the form of a compact, cohesive grain.

solid solution *n. Chem.* A homogeneous crystalline structure in which one or more types of atoms or molecules may be partly substituted for the original atoms and molecules without changing the structure.

sol·id-state (sŏl′ĭd-stāt′) *adj.* **1.** Characteristic of or pertaining to the physical properties of solid materials, esp. to the electromagnetic, thermodynamic, and structural properties of crystalline solids. **2.** Based on or consisting chiefly or exclusively of semiconducting materials, components, and related devices.

sol·i·dus (sŏl′ĭ-dəs) *n., pl.* **-di** (-dī′). **1.** An ancient Roman coin used until the fall of the Byzantine Empire. **2.** A virgule; slash. [ME < Lat. < *solidus,* solid.]

so·lil·o·quize (sə-lĭl′ə-kwīz′) *intr. & tr.v.* **-quized, -quiz·ing, -quiz·es.** To utter or put into the form of a soliloquy. **—so·lil′o·quist, so·lil′o·quiz′er** *n.*

so·lil·o·quy (sə-lĭl′ə-kwē) *n., pl.* **-quies. 1.** A literary or dramatic form of discourse in which a character talks to himself or reveals his thoughts in the form of a monologue without addressing a listener. **2.** The act of speaking to oneself. [LLat. : Lat. *solus,* alone + Lat. *loqui,* to speak.]

sol·ip·sism (sŏl′ĭp-sĭz′əm, sō′lĭp-) *n. Philos.* **1.** The theory that the self is the only thing that can be known and verified. **2.** The theory or view that the self is the only reality. [Lat. *solus,* alone + Lat. *ipse,* self + -ISM.] **—sol′ip·sist** *n.* **—sol′ip·sis′tic** *adj.*

sol·i·taire (sŏl′ĭ-târ′) *n.* **1.** A gem, such as a diamond, set alone. **2.** Any of a number of card games played by one person. [Fr. < OFr., solitary < Lat. *solitarius* < *solus,* alone.]

sol·i·tar·y (sŏl′ĭ-tĕr′ē) *adj.* **1.** Existing, living, or going without others; alone: *a solitary traveler.* **2.** Happening, done, or made alone: *a solitary evening.* **3.** Remote from civilization; secluded: *a solitary retreat.* **4.** Single; sole: *a solitary pine standing on the hill.* *—n., pl.* **-ies. 1.** A person who lives alone; recluse. **2.** *Informal.* Solitary confinement. [ME < Lat. *solitarius* < *solus,* alone.] **—sol′i·tar′i·ly** (-târ′ə-lē) *adv.* **—sol′i·tar′i·ness** *n.*

solitary confinement *n.* The confinement of a prisoner in a cell in which he is isolated from all others.

sol·i·tude (sŏl′ĭ-to͞od′, -tyo͞od′) *n.* **1.** The state of being alone or remote from others; isolation. **2.** A lonely or secluded place. [ME < OFr. < Lat. *solitudo* < *solus,* alone.]
Synonyms: *solitude, isolation, seclusion, retirement.*

These nouns denote the state of being alone or of being withdrawn or remote from society. *Solitude* implies the absence of all other persons but is otherwise not very specific. *Isolation* can refer to the condition of one person, a group, or even a unit such as a country. In every case it emphasizes total detachment from others. *Seclusion* can apply to one person or a group and suggests being removed or apart from others though not necessarily completely inaccessible. Sometimes it implies surroundings that conceal. *Retirement* usually refers to the condition of one person who withdraws from regular activity or from society. The term does not necessarily imply physical detachment.

sol·i·tud·i·nar·i·an (sŏl′ĭ-to͞od′n-âr′ē-ən, -tyo͞od′-) *n.* One that leads a solitary or secluded life. [Lat. *solitudo, solitudin-,* solitude + -ARIAN.]

sol·ler·et (sŏl′ə-rĕt′) *n.* A steel shoe made of overlapping plates, forming a part of a medieval suit of armor. [OFr., dim. of *soller,* shoe.]

sol·mi·za·tion (sŏl′mĭ-zā′shən) *n. Mus.* The act or a system of using syllables, such as *do, re,* and *mi,* to represent the tones of the scale. [Fr. *solmisation* < *solmiser,* to sol-fa.]

so·lo (sō′lō) *n., pl.* **-los. 1.** A musical composition or passage for an individual voice or instrument, with or without accompaniment. **2.** A performance accomplished by a single individual. **3.** Any of various card games in which one player singly opposes others. *—adj.* **1.** Composed, arranged for, or performed by a single voice or instrument. **2.** Made or done by a single individual. *—adv.* Unaccompanied; alone. *—intr.v.* **-loed, -lo·ing, -los.** To perform alone, esp. to fly an airplane without a companion or instructor. [Ital. < Lat. *solus,* alone.]

so·lo·ist (sō′lō-ĭst) *n.* One who performs a solo.

Solomon's seal

Sol·o·mon (sŏl′ə-mən) *n.* A son of David and king of Israel in the 10th century B.C. who was noted for his wealth and wisdom. [Heb. *Shĕlōmōh* < *shālōm,* peace.]

Solomon's seal *n.* **1.** A six-pointed star or hexagram supposed to possess mystical powers. **2.** Any of several plants of the genus *Polygonatum,* having paired, drooping, greenish or yellowish flowers.

so·lon (sō′lən, -lŏn′) *n.* A wise lawgiver. [After *Solon,* Athenian statesman of the 7th to 6th cent. B.C.]

so long *interj. Informal.* Used to express farewell.

sol·stice (sŏl′stĭs, sōl′-, sôl′-) *n.* **1.** *Astron.* Either of two times of the year when the sun has no apparent northward or southward motion, at the most northern or most southern point of the ecliptic. The summer solstice, when the sun is in the zenith at the tropic of Cancer, occurs about June 22, and the winter solstice, when it is over the tropic of Capricorn, occurs about December 22. **2.** A highest point or culmination. [ME < OFr. < Lat. *solstitium* : *sol,* sun + *sistere,* to stand.] **—sol·sti′tial** (-stĭsh′əl) *adj.*

sol·u·bil·i·ty (sŏl′yə-bĭl′ĭ-tē) *n., pl.* **-ties. 1.** The quality or condition of being soluble. **2.** The amount of a substance that can be dissolved in a given amount of solvent.

sol·u·bi·lize (sŏl′yə-bə-līz′) *tr.v.* **-lized, -liz·ing, -liz·es.** To make (substances such as fats and lipids, which are not appreciably soluble under standard conditions) soluble in water by the action of a detergent or similar agent.

sol·u·ble (sŏl′yə-bəl) *adj.* **1.** Capable of being dissolved, esp. easily dissolved. **2.** Capable of being solved or explained. [ME < OFr. < LLat. *solubilis* < *solvere,* to loosen.] **—sol′u·ble·ness** *n.* **—sol′u·bly** *adv.*

soluble glass *n.* Sodium silicate.

so·lum (sō′ləm) *n., pl.* **-la** (-lə) or **-lums.** The surface layers of a soil profile in which topsoil formation occurs. [NLat. < Lat., foundation.]

so·lus (sō′ləs) *adj. & adv.* By oneself; alone. Used as a stage direction. [Lat., alone.]

sol·ute (sŏl′yo͞ot′) *n.* A substance dissolved in another substance, usually the component of a solution present in the lesser amount. *—adj.* In solution; dissolved. [< Lat. *solutus,* p.part. of *solvere,* to loosen.]

so·lu·tion (sə-lo͞o′shən) *n.* **1. a.** A spontaneously forming homogeneous mixture of two or more substances, retaining its constitution in subdivision to molecular volumes, displaying no settling, and having various possible proportions of the constituents, which may be solids, liquids, gases, or intercombinations. **b.** The process of forming such a mixture. **2.** The state of being dissolved. **3.** The method or process of solving a problem. **4.** The answer to or disposition of a problem. **5.** *Law.* The payment or satisfaction of a claim or debt. **6.** The action of separating or breaking up; dissolution. [ME < OFr. < Lat. *solutio* < *solutus,* p.part. of *solvere,* to loosen.]

So·lu·tre·an also **So·lu·tri·an** (sə-lo͞o′trē-ən) *adj.* Of or relating to the Old World Upper Paleolithic culture that succeeded the Aurignacian and was characterized by improved flint implements and stylized symbolic forms of art. [After *Solutré,* France.]

solv·a·ble (sŏl′və-bəl, sôl′-) *adj.* Capable of being solved. **—solv′a·bil′i·ty, solv′a·ble·ness** *n.*

sol·va·tion (sŏl-vā′shən, sôl-) *n.* Any of a class of chemical reactions, such as the formation of hydrated copper sulfate in aqueous solution, in which solute and solvent molecules combine with relatively weak covalent bonds. [SOLV(ENT) + -ATION.]

Sol·vay process (sŏl′vā′) *n.* A process used to produce large quantities of sodium bicarbonate from salt, ammonia, carbon dioxide, and limestone. [After Ernest *Solvay* (1838–1932).]

solve (sŏlv, sôlv) *tr.v.* **solved, solv·ing, solves. 1.** To find a solution to. **2.** To work out a correct solution to (a problem). [ME *solven,* to loosen < Lat. *solvere.*] **—solv′er** *n.*

sol·vent (sŏl′vənt, sôl′-) *adj.* **1.** Capable of meeting financial obligations. **2.** Capable of dissolving another substance. *—n.* **1.** *Chem.* **a.** The component of a solution that is present in excess or that undergoes no change of state. **b.** A liquid capable of dissolving another substance. **2.** Something that solves. [Lat. *solvens, solvent-,* pr.part. of *solvere,* to loosen.] **—sol′ven·cy** *n.*

sol·vol·y·sis (sŏl-vŏl′ĭ-sĭs, sôl-) *n.* Any of a class of ionic chemical reactions, such as hydrolysis, in which solute and solvent react and alter the acidity or relative ionic concentrations of the solution. [SOLV(ENT) + -LYSIS.] **—sol′vo·lyt′ic** (-və-lĭt′ĭk) *adj.*

so·ma (sō′mə) *n., pl.* **-ma·ta** (-mə-tə) or **-mas.** *Biol.* The physical entity of an organism, exclusive of the germ cells. [NLat. < Gk. *sōma,* body.]

So·ma·li (sō-mä′lē) *n., pl.* **Somali** or **-lis. 1.** A member of one of a group of Hamitic tribes of Somaliland. **2.** The Cushitic language of the Somali.

so many *adj.* **1.** Forming an unspecified number: *issued so many memos each week.* **2.** Forming a group: *fought like so many tigers.*

so·ma·ta (sō′mə-tə) *n.* A plural of **soma.**

so·mat·ic (sō-măt′ĭk) *adj.* **1.** Of or pertaining to the body, esp. as distinguished from a bodily part, the mind, or the environment; physical. **2.** Of or pertaining to the wall of the body cavity, esp. as distinguished from the head, limbs, or viscera. **3.** Of or pertaining to somatoplasm. [Gk. *sōmatikos* < *sōma,* body.] **—so·mat′i·cal·ly** *adv.*

somatic cell *n.* A bodily cell other than a germ cell.

somato– *pref.* **1.** Body: *somatology.* **2.** Soma: *somatoplasm.* [< Gk. *sōma, sōmat-,* body.]

so·mat·o·gen·ic (sō-măt′ə-jĕn′ĭk) also **so·mat·o·ge·net·ic** (-jə-nĕt′ĭk) *adj.* Arising within the body in response to environment.

so·ma·tol·o·gy (sō′mə-tŏl′ə-jē) *n.* **1.** The physiological and anatomical study of the body. **2.** Physical anthropology. **—so′ma·to·log′i·cal** (sō′mə-tə-lŏj′ĭ-kəl, sō-măt′ə-) *adj.*

so·mat·o·plasm (sō-măt′ə-plăz′əm) *n.* **1.** The entirety of specialized protoplasm, other than germ plasm, constituting the body. **2.** The protoplasm of a somatic cell.

so·mat·o·pleure (sō-măt′ə-plo͝or′) *n.* A complex sheet of embryonic cells in certain vertebrates, formed by association of part of the mesoderm with the ectoderm and developing as the internal body wall. [NLat. *somatopleura* : SOMATO- + Gk. *pleura,* side.] **—so·mat′o·pleu′ric** (-plo͝or′ĭk) *adj.*

so·mat·o·type (sō-măt′ə-tīp′) *n.* The morphological type of a human body; physique. **—so·mat′o·typ′ic** (-tĭp′ĭk) *adj.*

som·ber (sŏm′bər) *adj.* **1.** Dark; gloomy. **2.** Melancholy; dismal: *a somber mood.* [Fr. *sombre.*] **—som′ber·ly** *adv.* **—som′ber·ness** *n.*

som·bre (sŏm′bər) *adj. Chiefly Brit.* Variant of **somber.**

som·bre·ro (sŏm-brâr′ō, səm-) *n., pl.* **-ros.** A large straw or felt hat with a broad brim and tall crown, worn esp. in Mexico and the American southwest. [Sp. < *sombra,* shade, of Lat. orig.]

som·brous (sŏm′brəs) *adj. Archaic.* Somber.

some (sŭm) *adj.* **1.** Being an unspecified number or quantity: *some people; some sugar.* **2.** Unknown or unspecified by name: *Some woman called.* **3.** *Logic.* Being part and perhaps all of a class. **4.** *Informal.* Remarkable: *He is some skier.* *—pron.* **1.** An indefinite or unspecified number or portion. **2.** An indefinite additional quantity: *did the assigned work and then some.* *—adv.* **1.** Approximately; about: *some 40 people.* **2.** *Informal.* Somewhat. [ME < OE *sum,* a certain one.]

-some[1] *suff.* Characterized by a specified quality, condition, or action: *bothersome.* [ME *-som* < OE *-sum.*]

-some[2] *suff.* A group of a specified number of members: *threesome.* [ME *-sum* < *sum,* some.]

-some[3] *suff.* **1.** Body: *centrosome.* **2.** Chromosome: *monosome.* [< Gk. *sōma,* body.]

some·bod·y (sŭm′bŏd′ē, -bə-dē) *pron.* An unspecified or unknown person; someone. *—n., pl.* **-ies.** *Informal.* A person of importance: *thinks he's a real somebody.* —See Usage note at **everyone.**

some·day (sŭm′dā′) *adv.* At a time in the future.

some·how (sŭm′hou′) *adv.* In a way not specified, understood, or known.

some·one (sŭm′wŭn′, -wən) *pron.* Some person; somebody. *—n. Informal.* A somebody. —See Usage note at **everyone.**

some·place (sŭm′plās′) *adv.* Somewhere.

som·er·sault also **sum·mer·sault** (sŭm′ər-sôlt′) *—n.* **1.** An acrobatic stunt in which the body rolls in a complete circle, heels over head. **2.** A complete reversal, as of sympathies or opinions. *—intr.v.* **-sault·ed, -sault·ing, -saults.** To execute a somersault. [OFr. *sombresault,* var. of *sobresault* : *sobre-,* above (< Lat. *supra*) + *sault,* leap (< Lat. *saltus* < *salire,* to leap).]

som·er·set also **sum·mer·set** (sŭm′ər-sĕt′) *n.* A somersault. —*intr.v.* **-set·ted, -set·ting, -sets.** To somersault.
some·thing (sŭm′thĭng) *pron.* An undetermined or unspecified thing. —*n. Informal.* A remarkable or important thing or person. —*adv.* **1.** A little; somewhat: *looks something like her mother.* **2.** *Informal.* To an extreme degree: *drinks something fierce.* —***idioms.*** **something else.** *Informal.* One that is special or remarkable: *Her new film is something else.* **something of.** To some extent: *He's something of an eccentric.*
some·time (sŭm′tīm′) *adv.* **1.** At an indefinite or unstated time: *I'll meet you sometime this afternoon.* **2.** At an indefinite time in the future: *Let's get together sometime.* **3.** Sometimes. **4.** *Archaic.* Formerly. —*adj.* **1.** Having been at some prior time; former: *a sometime secretary.* **2.** *Nonstandard.* Occasional.
Usage: *Sometime* as an adjective is properly employed to mean "former." It is also used colloquially with the meaning "occasional": *the team's sometime star and sometime problem child.* This latter use, however, is unacceptable to a majority of the Usage Panel.
some·times (sŭm′tīmz′) *adv.* **1.** At times; now and then. **2.** *Obs.* At some prior time; formerly.
some·way (sŭm′wā′) also **some·ways** (-wāz′) *adv.* In some way or another; somehow.
some·what (sŭm′hwŏt′, -wŏt′, -hwət, -wət) *adv.* To some extent or degree; rather. —*pron. Archaic.* Something.
some·where (sŭm′hwâr′, -wâr′) *adv.* **1.** At, in, or to a place not specified or known: *found it somewhere in the woods.* **2.** To a place or state of further development or progress: *finally getting somewhere.* **3.** Approximately; roughly: *somewhere about halfway through.* —*n.* An unknown or unspecified place.
some·wheres (sŭm′hwârz′, -wârz′) *adv. Informal.* Somewhere.
so·mite (sō′mīt′) *n.* **1.** *Zool.* A metamere. **2.** A segmental mass of mesoderm in the vertebrate embryo, occurring in pairs along the notochord. [Gk. *sōma,* body + -ITE[1].]
som·me·lier (sŭm′əl-yā′) *n.* A wine steward in a restaurant. [Fr. < OFr., officer in charge of provisions, pack-animal driver < *somme,* pack < LLat. *sagma* < Gk., packsaddle.]
somn– *pref.* Variant of **somni-.**
som·nam·bu·late (sŏm-năm′byə-lāt′) *intr.v.* **-lat·ed, -lat·ing, -lates.** To walk while asleep. —**som·nam′bu·lar** (-lər) *adj.*
som·nam·bu·lism (sŏm-năm′byə-lĭz′əm) *n.* Walking while asleep or in a sleeplike condition. —**som·nam′bu·list** *n.* —**som·nam′bu·lis′tic** *adj.*
somni– or **somn–** *pref.* Sleep: *somnambulate.* [< Lat. *somnus,* sleep.]
som·ni·fa·cient (sŏm′nə-fā′shənt) *adj.* Tending to produce sleep; hypnotic. —**som′ni·fa′cient** *n.*
som·nif·er·ous (sŏm-nĭf′ər-əs) also **som·nif·ic** (-nĭf′ĭk) *adj.* Inducing sleep. —**som·nif′er·ous·ly** *adv.*
som·no·lence (sŏm′nə-ləns) *n.* Drowsiness; sleepiness.
som·no·lent (sŏm′nə-lənt) *adj.* **1.** Drowsy; sleepy. **2.** Inducing or tending to induce sleep; soporific. [ME *sompnolent* < OFr. < Lat. *somnolentus* < *somnus,* sleep.] —**som′no·lent·ly** *adv.*
so much *adv.* By the amount or degree expressed or indicated: *If he wins the award, so much the better for the team.* —*adj.* Used as an intensive: *The report sounded like so much baloney.* —*pron.* **1.** Something unspecified: *charged so much a yard.* **2.** Everything that can be said or done: *so much for the story behind the trial.*
so much as *adv.* Even: *wouldn't so much as look at her.*
son (sŭn) *n.* **1.** A male offspring. **2.** A male descendant. **3. a.** An adopted male child. **b.** A son-in-law. **4.** A man or boy strongly influenced by or associated with a place, cause, race, or school. **5.** A young man. Used as a familiar term of address. [ME < OE *sunu.*]
so·nance (sō′nəns) *n.* Sound.
so·nant (sō′nənt) *adj.* Voiced, as a speech sound. —*n.* **1.** A voiced speech sound. **2.** A syllabic consonant. [Lat. *sonans, sonant-,* pr.part. of *sonare,* to sound.]
so·nar (sō′när′) *n.* **1.** A system using transmitted and reflected acoustic waves to detect and locate submerged objects. **2.** An apparatus, as in a submarine, using sonar. [SO(UND) NA(VIGATION) R(ANGING).]
so·na·ta (sə-nä′tə) *n.* An instrumental musical composition, as for the piano, consisting of three or four independent movements varying in key, mood, and tempo. [Ital. < fem. p.part. of *sonare,* to sound < Lat. *sonare.*]
sonata form *n.* A musical form consisting of three sections, the exposition, development, and recapitulation, often followed by a coda.
son·a·ti·na (sŏn′ə-tē′nə) *n.* A sonata having shorter movements than the typical sonata. [Ital., dim. of *sonata,* sonata.]
sone (sōn) *n.* A subjective unit of loudness, equal to the loudness of a pure tone having a frequency of 1,000 hertz at 40 decibels above the listener's threshold of audibility. [< Lat. *sonus,* a sound.]
son et lu·mière (sôɴ′ ā lüm-yâr′) *n.* A dramatic spectacle using special light and sound effects, often held at a historic site. [Fr.: *son,* sound + *et,* and + *lumière,* light.]
song (sông, sŏng) *n.* **1.** A brief musical composition written or adapted for singing. **2.** The act or art of singing. **3.** A melodious utterance, such as a bird call. **4. a.** Poetry; verse. **b.** A lyric poem or ballad. —***idiom.*** **for a song.** At a low price. [ME < OE *sang.*]
song and dance *n.* **1.** A theatrical performance that combines singing and dancing. **2.** *Slang.* **a.** An excessively elaborate effort to explain or justify. **b.** An elaborate story or explanation intended to deceive or mislead.
song·bird (sông′bûrd′, sŏng′-) *n.* A bird, esp. one of the suborder Passeres, having a melodious song or call.
song·fest (sông′fĕst′, sŏng′-) *n.* A casual gathering for group singing.
song·ful (sông′fəl, sŏng′-) *adj.* Melodious; tuneful. —**song′ful·ly** *adv.* —**song′ful·ness** *n.*
Song of Solomon *n.* See table at **Bible.**
song·smith (sông′smĭth′, sŏng′-) *n.* A songwriter.
song sparrow *n.* A North American songbird, *Melospiza melodia,* having streaked brownish plumage.
song·ster (sông′stər, sŏng′-) *n.* **1.** A singer. **2.** A songwriter.
song thrush *n.* An Old World songbird, *Turdus philomelos,* having brown upper plumage and a spotted breast.
song·writ·er (sông′rī′tər, sŏng′-) *n.* One who writes lyrics or composes tunes for songs.
son·ic (sŏn′ĭk) *adj.* **1.** Of or relating to audible sound: *a sonic wave.* **2.** Having a speed approaching or being that of sound in air, approximately 738 miles per hour at sea level. [< Lat. *sonus,* a sound.]
sonic barrier *n.* The sudden sharp increase in aerodynamic drag experienced by aircraft approaching the speed of sound.
sonic boom *n.* A loud transient explosive sound caused by the shock wave preceding an aircraft traveling at supersonic speeds.
son-in-law (sŭn′ĭn-lô′) *n., pl.* **sons-in-law.** The husband of one's daughter.
son·net (sŏn′ĭt) *n.* A 14-line poetic form usually made up of an octave and a sestet embodying the statement and the resolution of a single theme. [Fr. < Ital. *sonetto* < OProv. *sonet,* dim. of *son,* song < Lat. *sonus,* a sound.]
son·net·eer (sŏn′ĭ-tîr′) *n.* **1.** A composer of sonnets. **2.** An inferior poet.
son·ny (sŭn′ē) *n., pl.* **-nies.** A little boy. Used as a familiar form of address. [Dim. of SON.]
son of a gun *n. Informal.* A fellow: *That son of a gun is quite a hustler.*
son of God *n.* Christ.
so·no·rant (sə-nôr′ənt, -nōr′-, sŏn′ər-) *n.* A voiced consonant regarded as a syllabic sound, as the last sound in the word *sudden.* [SONOR(OUS) + -ANT.]
so·nor·i·ty (sə-nôr′ĭ-tē, -nŏr′-) *n., pl.* **-ties.** **1.** The quality or state of being sonorous; resonance. **2.** A sound.
so·no·rous (sə-nôr′əs, -nōr′-, sŏn′ər-) *adj.* **1.** Having or producing sound. **2.** Having or producing a full, deep, or rich sound. **3.** Impressive; grandiloquent. [Lat. *sonorus* < *sonor,* sound < *sonare,* to sound.] —**so·no′rous·ly** *adv.* —**so·no′rous·ness** *n.*
son·ship (sŭn′shĭp′) *n.* The fact or relationship of being a son.
soo·chong (so͞o′chông′, -shông′) *n.* Variant of **souchong.**
soon (so͞on) *adv.* **-er, -est.** **1.** In the near future; shortly. **2.** Without hesitation; promptly: *came as soon as possible.* **3.** Before the usual or appointed time; early. **4.** With willingness; readily: *I'd as soon leave right now.* **5.** *Obs.* Immediately. —***idioms.*** **no sooner than.** As soon as: *No sooner was the frost off the ground than the work began.* **sooner or later.** Sometime; eventually. [ME *sone* < OE *sōna,* immediately.]
Usage: *No sooner,* as a comparative adverb, should be followed by *than,* not *when,* as in these typical examples: *No sooner had she come than the maid knocked. I had no sooner left than she called.*
soon·er (so͞o′nər) *n. Slang.* **1.** A person who settled homestead land in the early West before it was officially made available, in order to have first choice of location. **2. Sooner.** A native or resident of Oklahoma. [< SOON.]
soot (so͝ot, sŭt, so͞ot) *n.* A fine dispersion of black particles, chiefly carbon, produced by the incomplete combustion of coal, oil, wood, or other fuels. —*tr.v.* **soot·ed, soot·ing, soots.** To cover or smudge with soot. [ME < OE *sōt.*]
sooth (so͞oth) *adj. Archaic.* **1.** Real; true. **2.** Soft; sweet. —*n. Archaic.* Truth; reality. [ME < OE *sōð.*] —**sooth′ly** *adv.*
soothe (so͞o*th*) *v.* **soothed, sooth·ing, soothes.** —*tr.* **1.** To calm or placate. **2.** To ease or relieve the pain of. —*intr.* To bring comfort, composure, or relief. [ME *sothen,* to verify < OE *sōðian* < *sōð,* truth.] —**sooth′er** *n.*
sooth·fast (so͞oth′făst′) *adj. Archaic.* **1.** Truthful; honest. **2.** True; real. [ME *sothfast* < OE *sōðfæst* : *sōð,* truth + *fæst,* fixed, fast.]
sooth·ing (so͞o′*th*ĭng) *adj.* Tending to soothe: *a soft, soothing voice.* —**sooth′ing·ly** *adv.* —**sooth′ing·ness** *n.*
sooth·say (so͞oth′sā′) *intr.v.* **-said** (-sĕd′), **-say·ing, -says** (-sĕz′). To foretell future events; predict. [Back-formation < SOOTHSAYER.]
sooth·say·er (so͞oth′sā′ər) *n.* A person who claims to be able to foretell events or predict the future; seer.
sooth·say·ing (so͞oth′sā′ĭng) *n.* **1.** The art or practice of foretelling events. **2.** A prediction; prophecy.
soot·y (so͝ot′ē, sŭt′ē, so͞o′tē) *adj.* **-i·er, -i·est.** **1.** Covered with

soot. **2.** Of or producing soot. **3.** Black or dark like soot. **—soot'i·ness** *n.*

sooty grouse *n.* The blue grouse.

sooty mold *n.* A black fungus of the genus *Capnodium,* growing on plants in the droppings of sucking insects such as aphids.

sop (sŏp) *v.* **sopped, sop·ping, sops.** *—tr.* **1.** To dip, soak, or drench in a liquid; saturate. **2.** To take up by absorption: *sop up water with a paper towel.* *—intr.* To be or become thoroughly soaked or saturated. *—n.* **1.** A piece of food soaked or dipped in a liquid. **2. a.** Something yielded to placate or soothe. **b.** A bribe. [< ME *soppe,* dipped bread < OE *sopp.*]

soph·ism (sŏf'ĭz'əm) *n.* **1.** A plausible but fallacious argument. **2.** Deceptive or fallacious argumentation. [ME *sophime* < OFr. < Lat. *sophisma* < Gk., clever device < *sophos,* clever.]

soph·ist (sŏf'ĭst) *n.* **1. Sophist. a.** A member of a pre-Socratic school of philosophy in ancient Greece. **b.** Any of a class of later Greek teachers of rhetoric and philosophy known for their over subtle and often misleading arguments. **2.** A scholar or thinker, esp. one skillful in devious argumentation. [Lat. *sophistes* < Gk. *sophistēs,* expert < *sophizesthai,* to play tricks < *sophos,* clever.]

so·phis·tic (sə-fĭs'tĭk) or **so·phis·ti·cal** (-tĭ-kəl) *adj.* **1.** Of, pertaining to, or characteristic of sophists. **2.** Specious; fallacious. **—so·phis'ti·cal·ly** *adv.*

so·phis·ti·cate (sə-fĭs'tĭ-kāt') *v.* **-cat·ed, -cat·ing, -cates.** *—tr.* **1.** To cause to become less natural, esp. to make less naive and cause to be worldly-wise. **2.** To corrupt or pervert; adulterate. **3.** To make more complex or inclusive; refine. *—intr.* To use sophistry. *—n.* (-kĭt). A sophisticated person. [Med. Lat. *sophisticare, sophisticat-* < Lat. *sophisticus,* sophistic < Gk. *sophistikos* < *sophistēs,* sophist.] **—so·phis'ti·ca'tion** *n.* **—so·phis'ti·ca'tor** *n.*

so·phis·ti·cat·ed (sə-fĭs'tĭ-kā'tĭd) *adj.* **1.** Having acquired worldly knowledge or refinement; lacking natural simplicity or naiveté. **2.** Very complex or complicated: *employs the latest and most sophisticated technology.* **3.** Suitable for or appealing to the tastes of sophisticates: *a sophisticated drama.* **—so·phis'ti·cat'ed·ly** *adv.*

soph·is·try (sŏf'ĭ-strē) *n., pl.* **-tries. 1.** A plausible but misleading or fallacious argument. **2.** Plausible but fallacious argumentation.

soph·o·more (sŏf'ə-môr', -mōr') *n.* **1.** A second-year student in an American college or high school. **2.** A person in his second year of an endeavor. [Gk. *sophos,* wise + Gk. *mōros,* foolish.]

soph·o·mor·ic (sŏf'ə-môr'ĭk, -mōr'-, -mŏr'-) *adj.* **1.** Of or characteristic of a sophomore. **2.** Immature and overconfident. **—soph'o·mor'i·cal·ly** *adv.*

So·phy (sō'fē) *n., pl.* **-phies.** A title formerly given to kings of Persia. [Pers. *Safi,* surname of a Persian dynasty (1500–1736) < Ar. *Ṣafiuddin,* purity of religion.]

so·por (sō'pər, -pôr') *n.* An abnormally deep sleep; stupor. [Lat., sleep.]

sop·o·rif·er·ous (sŏp'ə-rĭf'ər-əs, sō'pə-) *adj.* Inducing or tending to induce sleep; soporific. **—sop'o·rif'er·ous·ly** *adv.* **—sop'o·rif'er·ous·ness** *n.*

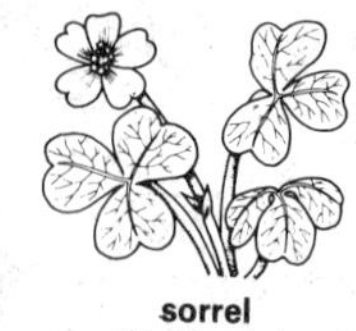

sorrel
Wood sorrel

sop·o·rif·ic (sŏp'ə-rĭf'ĭk, sō'pə-) *adj.* **1.** Inducing or tending to induce sleep. **2.** Drowsy. *—n.* A sleep-inducing drug.

sop·ping (sŏp'ĭng) *adj.* Thoroughly soaked; drenched. *—adv.* Extremely: *sopping wet.*

sop·py (sŏp'ē) *adj.* **-pi·er, -pi·est. 1.** Soaked; sopping. **2.** Rainy. **3.** *Slang.* Mawkish.

so·pra·ni·no (sō'prə-nē'nō, sŏp'rə-) *n., pl.* **-nos.** A musical instrument, as a recorder, that is higher in pitch than the soprano of its family. [Ital., dim. of *soprano,* soprano.]

so·pran·o (sə-prăn'ō, -prä'nō) *n., pl.* **-os. 1.** The highest singing voice of a woman or young boy. **2.** A singer having a soprano voice. **3.** A part written in the range of the soprano voice. **4.** The tonal range characteristic of a soprano. ***—modifier:*** *a soprano aria.* [Ital. < *sopra,* above < Lat. *supra.*]

so·ra (sôr'ə, sōr'ə) *n.* A North American marsh bird, *Porzana carolina,* having grayish-brown plumage. [Prob. of American Indian orig.]

sorb¹ (sôrb) *tr.v.* **sorbed, sorb·ing, sorbs.** To take up and hold, as by absorption or adsorption. [Back-formation < ADSORB and ABSORB.]

sorb² (sôrb) *n.* **1.** Any of several Old World trees of the genus *Sorbus* or related genera, such as the service tree or the rowan. **2.** The fruit of the sorb. [Fr. *sorbe* < Lat. *sorbus,* service tree.]

Sorb (sôrb) *n.* A Wend. [G. *Sorbe.*]

sor·bet (sôr'bĭt) *n.* **1.** Sherbet. **2.** A frozen dessert similar to a frappé and having a mushy consistency. [Fr. < Ital. *sorbetto* < Turk. *sherbet.* —see SHERBET.]

Sor·bi·an (sôr'bē-ən) *n.* **1.** A Wend. **2.** Wendish. [< SORB.] **—Sor'bi·an** *adj.*

sor·bic acid (sôr'bĭk) *n.* A white crystalline solid, $C_6H_8O_2$, found in the berries of the mountain ash and also synthesized, used as a food preservative and fungicide. [< SORB².]

Sor·bon·ist (sôr-bŏn'ĭst, -bŭn'-) *n.* A professor or a student at the Sorbonne. [Fr. *sorboniste* < *Sorbonne,* the Sorbonne, a university in Paris, France.]

sor·bose (sôr'bōs') *n.* A white sweetish crystalline sugar, $C_6H_{12}O_6$, used in the manufacture of ascorbic acid. [SORB² + -OSE.]

sor·cer·er (sôr'sər-ər) *n.* A person who practices sorcery; wizard. [ME *sorser* < OFr. *sorcier* < VLat. **sortiarius* < Lat. *sors,* lot, chance.]

sor·cer·ess (sôr'sər-ĭs) *n.* A woman who practices sorcery.

sor·cer·y (sôr'sə-rē) *n.* The use of supernatural power over others through the assistance of evil spirits; witchcraft. [ME *sorcerie* < OFr. < *sorcier,* sorcerer.] **—sor'cer·ous** *adj.* **—sor'cer·ous·ly** *adv.*

sord (sôrd) *n.* A flight of mallards. [ME *sorde* < *sorden,* to rise up in flight < OFr. *sordre* < Lat. *surgere,* to rise.]

sor·did (sôr'dĭd) *adj.* **1.** Filthy or dirty; foul. **2.** Depressingly squalid; wretched: *sordid shantytowns.* **3.** Morally degraded; base: *"the sordid details of his orgies stank under his very nostrils"* (James Joyce). **4.** Exceedingly mercenary; grasping. [Fr. *sordide* < Lat. *sordidus* < *sordēre,* to be dirty.] **—sor'did·ly** *adv.* **—sor'did·ness** *n.*

sor·di·no (sôr-dē'nō) *n., pl.* **-ni** (-nē). A mute for a musical instrument. [Ital. < *sordo,* deaf, mute < Lat. *surdus.*]

sore (sôr, sōr) *adj.* **sor·er, sor·est. 1.** Painful to the touch; tender. **2.** Feeling physical pain; hurting: *sore all over.* **3.** Causing misery, sorrow, or distress; grievous: *in sore need.* **4.** Causing embarrassment or irritation: *a sore subject.* **5.** Full of distress; sorrowful. **6.** *Informal.* Angry; offended. *—adv. Archaic.* Sorely. *—n.* **1.** An open skin lesion, wound, or ulcer. **2.** A source of pain, distress, or irritation. [ME < OE *sār.*] **—sore'ness** *n.*

sore·head (sôr'hĕd', sōr'-) *n. Slang.* A person who is easily offended, annoyed, or angered.

sore·ly (sôr'lē, sōr'-) *adv.* **1.** Painfully; grievously. **2.** Extremely; greatly: *His skill was sorely needed.*

sore throat *n.* Any of various inflammations of the tonsils, pharynx, or larynx characterized by pain in swallowing.

sor·gho (sôr'gō) *n.* Variant of **sorgo.**

sor·ghum (sôr'gəm) *n.* **1.** An Old World grass, *Sorghum vulgare,* several varieties of which are widely cultivated as grain and forage or as a source of syrup. **2.** Syrup made from the juice of the sorghum. [NLat. < Ital. *sorgo.*]

sor·go also **sor·gho** (sôr'gō) *n., pl.* **-gos** also **-ghos.** Any of various sorghums, esp. *Sorghum vulgare saccharatum,* cultivated as a source of syrup. [Ital.]

so·ri (sôr'ī', sōr'ī') *n.* Plural of **sorus.**

sor·i·cine (sôr'ĭ-sīn', sōr'-, sŏr'-) *adj.* Of or belonging to the family Soricidae, which includes the shrews. [Lat. *soricinus* < *sorex,* shrew.]

so·ri·tes (sə-rī'tēz) *n., pl.* **sorites.** *Logic.* A form of argument in which a series of incomplete syllogisms is so arranged that the predicate of each premise forms the subject of the next until the subject of the first is joined with the predicate of the last in the conclusion. [Lat. *sorites* < Gk. *sōreitēs* < *sōros,* heap.]

so·ro·ral (sə-rôr'əl, -rōr'-) *adj.* Of, pertaining to, or like a sister; sisterly. [< Lat. *soror,* sister.]

so·ror·ate (sə-rôr'ĭt, -rōr'-) *n.* The custom of marriage of a man to his wife's sister or sisters, usually after the wife has died or proved sterile. [< Lat. *soror,* sister.]

so·ror·i·cide (sə-rôr'ĭ-sīd', -rōr'-) *n.* **1.** The killing of one's sister. **2.** A person who kills his own sister. [Lat. *soror,* sister + -CIDE.] **—so·ror'i·cid'al** (-sīd'l) *adj.*

so·ror·i·ty (sə-rôr'ĭ-tē, -rōr'-) *n., pl.* **-ties.** A social club or civic club for women, esp. one at a college. [Med. Lat. *sororitas* < Lat. *soror,* sister.]

sorp·tion (sôrp'shən) *n.* **1.** The process of sorbing. **2.** The state of being sorbed. [Back-formation < ABSORPTION and ADSORPTION.] **—sorp'tive** *adj.*

sor·rel¹ (sôr'əl, sŏr'-) *n.* **1.** Any of several plants of the genus *Rumex,* having acid-flavored leaves sometimes used as salad greens, esp. *R. acetosella,* a widely naturalized species native to Eurasia. **2.** Any of various plants of the genus *Oxalis.* [ME *sorel* < OFr. *surele* < *sur,* sour, of Germanic orig.]

sor·rel² (sôr'əl, sŏr'-) *n.* **1.** A brownish orange to light brown. **2.** A sorrel-colored horse. [< ME *sorelle,* sorrel-colored < OFr. *sorel* < *sor,* red-brown.]

sorrel tree *n.* Sourwood.

sor·row (sŏr'ō, sôr'ō) *n.* **1.** Mental suffering or pain caused by injury, loss, or despair. **2.** Something that causes sorrow; misfortune. **3.** The expression of sorrow; grieving. *—intr.v.* **-rowed, -row·ing, -rows.** To feel or display sorrow; grieve. [ME *sorow* < OE *sorg.*] **—sor'row·er** *n.*

sor·row·ful (sŏr'ō-fəl, -ə-fəl, sôr'-) *adj.* **1.** Causing or feeling sorrow. **2.** Marked by or expressing sorrow. **—sor'row·ful·ly** *adv.* **—sor'row·ful·ness** *n.*

sor·ry (sŏr'ē, sôr'ē) *adj.* **-ri·er, -ri·est. 1.** Feeling or expressing sympathy, pity, or regret: *I'm sorry I'm late.* **2.** Worthless or inferior; paltry: *a sorry excuse.* **3.** Causing sorrow, grief, or misfortune; grievous: *a sorry development.* [ME *sory* < OE *sārig,* painful < *sār,* sore.] **—sor'ri·ly** *adv.* **—sor'ri·ness** *n.*

sort (sôrt) *n.* **1.** A group or collection of similar persons or things; kind. **2.** The character or nature of something; type: *a likable sort of person.* **3.** A method of acting or behaving. **4.** Often **sorts.** *Printing.* One of the characters in a font of type. *—tr.v.* **sort·ed, sort·ing, sorts. 1.** To arrange according to class, kind, or size; classify. **2.** To separate from others: *sort out the wheat from the chaff.* **3.** To clarify by going over mentally: *tried to sort out her problems.* —**idioms. after a sort.** In a haphazard or imperfect way. **of sorts. 1.** Of a mediocre or inferior kind. **2.** Of one kind or another. **out of sorts.** *Informal.* **1.** Slightly sick. **2.** Irritable; cross. **sort of.** *Informal.* Somewhat; rather: *sort of silly.* —See Usage note at **kind**[2]. [ME < OFr. *sorte,* prob. < Lat. *sors,* lot.] —**sort'a·ble** *adj.* —**sort'er** *n.*

sor·tie (sôr'tē, sôr-tē') *n.* **1.** An armed attack made from a place surrounded by enemy forces. **2.** A flight of a warplane on a combat mission. —*intr.v.* **-tied, -tie·ing, -ties.** To go on a sortie. [Fr. < OFr. *sortir,* to go out.]

sor·ti·lege (sôr'tl-ĭj) *n.* **1.** The act or practice of foretelling the future by drawing lots. **2.** Sorcery; witchcraft. [ME < OFr. < Med. Lat. *sortilegium* < *sortilegus,* diviner : Lat. *sors,* lot + Lat. *legere,* to read.]

so·rus (sôr'əs, sōr'-) *n., pl.* **so·ri** (sôr'ī', sōr'ī'). **1.** A cluster of spore cases borne by ferns on the undersides of the fronds. **2.** A structure in certain fungi and lichens similar to a sorus. [NLat. < Gk. *sōros,* heap.]

S O S (ĕs'ō-ĕs', ĕs'ō-ĕs') *n.* **1.** The letters represented by the signal • • • — — — • • •, used internationally as a distress signal, esp. by ships and aircraft. **2.** A call or signal for help.

so-so (sō'sō') *adj.* Mediocre; passable. —*adv.* Tolerably; passably.

so·ste·nu·to (sō'stə-no͞o'tō, sô'-) *Mus.* —*adv.* In a sustained or prolonged manner. Used as a direction. —*n., pl.* **-tos** or **-ti** (-tē). A passage played or sung sostenuto. [Ital., p.part. of *sostenere,* to sustain < Lat. *sustinēre.* —see SUSTAIN.] —**so'ste·nu'to** *adj.*

sot (sŏt) *n.* A chronic drunkard. [ME, fool < OE *sott* < Lat. *sottus.*]

so·te·ri·ol·o·gy (sō-tîr'ē-ŏl'ə-jē) *n.* The theological doctrine of salvation as effected by Christ. [Gk. *sōtērion,* deliverance (< *sōtēr,* savior < *saos,* safe) + -LOGY.] —**so·te'ri·o·log'ic** (-ə-lŏj'ĭk), **so·te'ri·o·log'i·cal** *adj.*

So·thic (sō'thĭk, sŏth'ĭk) *adj.* **1.** Of, pertaining to, or deriving from the name of Sothis. **2.** Designating the ancient Egyptian year, consisting of $365\frac{1}{4}$ days. **3.** Designating a cycle consisting of 1,460 years of 365 days in the ancient Egyptian calendar. [< Gk. *Sōthis,* the star Sirius.]

So·this (sō'thĭs) *n.* Sirius. [Gk. *Sōthis.*]

So·tho (sō'tō) *n.* **1.** A group of Bantu languages spoken in southern Africa. **2.** Any of the Sotho languages.

so·tol (sō'tōl') *n.* Any of several tall, woody plants of the genus *Dasylirion,* of the southwestern United States and adjacent Mexico, having prickly-margined leaves and a large cluster of whitish flowers. [Mex. Sp. *sotole* < Nahuatl *tzotolli.*]

sot·tish (sŏt'ĭsh) *adj.* **1.** Stupefied from or as if from drink. **2.** Tending to drink excessively; drunken. —**sot'tish·ly** *adv.* —**sot'tish·ness** *n.*

sot·to vo·ce (sŏt'ō vō'chē) *adv.* **1.** Softly, so as not to be overheard; in an undertone. **2.** *Mus.* Very softly. Used as a direction. [Ital., under the voice.]

sou (so͞o) *n.* A former French coin. [Fr. < obs. *sol* < Lat. *solidus,* solidus.]

sou·a·ri nut (so͞o-är'ē) *n.* **1.** A South American tree, *Caryocar nuciferum,* bearing nuts used as food and a source of cooking oil. **2.** The nut of the souari nut tree. [Fr. *saouari* < Galibi *sawarra.*]

sou·bise (so͞o-bēz') *n.* A sauce made with onions or onion purée. [Fr., after Charles de Rohan, Prince de *Soubise* (1715–1787).]

sou·brette (so͞o-brĕt') *n.* **1. a.** A saucy, coquettish, and intriguing lady's maid in comedies or comic opera. **b.** An actress or singer taking such a part. **2.** A flirtatious or frivolous young woman. [Fr. < Prov. *soubreto,* fem. of *soubret,* conceited < *soubra,* to leave aside < OProv. *sobras,* to be excessive < Lat. *superare* < *super,* above.]

sou·bri·quet (so͞o'brĭ-kā', so͞o'brĭ-kā') *n.* Variant of **sobriquet.**

sou·chong also **soo·chong** (so͞o'chông', -shông') *n.* One of several varieties of black tea native to China and adjacent regions. [Chin. (Mandarin) *xiao*^{3} *zhong*^{3} : *xiao*^{3}, small + *zhong*^{3}, kind.]

sou·dan (so͞od'n) *n.* Variant of **soldan.**

souf·flé (so͞o-flā') *n.* A light, fluffy baked dish made with egg yolks and beaten egg whites combined with various other ingredients and served as a main dish or sweetened as a dessert. —*adj.* Made light and puffy by beating and baking or cooking. [Fr. < p.part. of *souffler,* to puff up < Lat. *sufflare* : *sub-,* under + *flare,* to blow.] —**souf·fléd'** *adj.*

sough (sŭf, sou) *intr.v.* **soughed, sough·ing, soughs.** To make a soft murmuring or rustling sound. —*n.* A soft murmuring or rustling sound, as of the wind or a gentle surf. [ME *swoghen* < OE *swōgan.*]

sought (sôt) *v.* Past tense and past participle of **seek.**

soul (sōl) *n.* **1.** The animating and vital principle in man, credited with the faculties of thought, action, and emotion and often conceived as an immaterial entity. **2.** The spiritual nature of man, regarded as immortal, separable from the body at death, and susceptible to happiness or misery in a future state. **3.** The disembodied spirit of a dead human being; shade. **4. Soul.** *Christian Science.* God. **5.** A human being: *not a soul in sight.* **6.** The central or integral part of something; vital core: *She's the soul of the movement.* **7.** A person considered as the perfect embodiment of an intangible quality; personification: *the very soul of discretion.* **8.** A person's emotional or moral nature. **9. a.** An awareness of and pride in the physical and cultural aspects of the African heritage. **b.** A strong, deeply-felt emotion conveyed by a performer or artist. [ME < OE *sāwol.*]

soul brother *n. Slang.* A fellow black male.

soul food *n.* Food, as ham hocks and collard greens, traditionally eaten by southern American blacks.

soul·ful (sōl'fəl) *adj.* Full of or expressing deep feeling; profoundly emotional. —**soul'ful·ly** *adv.* —**soul'ful·ness** *n.*

soul kiss *n.* A French kiss.

soul·less (sōl'lĭs) *adj.* Devoid of sensitivity or the capacity for deep feeling. —**soul'less·ly** *adv.* —**soul'less·ness** *n.*

soul mate *n.* One of two persons compatible with each other in disposition, point of view, or sensitivity.

soul music *n.* A kind of music developed by American blacks, combining elements of gospel music and rhythm and blues.

soul-search·ing (sōl'sûr'chĭng) *n.* The penetrating examination of one's motives, convictions, and emotional attitudes.

soul sister *n. Slang.* A fellow black female.

sound[1] (sound) *n.* **1. a.** A vibratory disturbance in the pressure and density of a fluid or in the elastic strain in a solid, with frequency in the approximate range between 20 and 20,000 hertz, capable of being detected by the organs of hearing. **b.** A disturbance of any frequency. **c.** The sensation stimulated in the organs of hearing by such a disturbance. **d.** Such sensations collectively. **2.** A distinctive noise: *a hollow sound.* **3.** The distance over which something can be heard: *within sound of hearing.* **4. a.** An articulation made by the vocal apparatus. **b.** The distinctive character of such an articulation: *The words "bear" and "bare" have the same sound.* **5.** A mental impression conveyed; implication: *didn't like the sound of the invitation.* **6.** Auditory material that is recorded, as for a motion picture. **7.** Meaningless noise. **8.** *Archaic.* Rumor; report. —*v.* **sound·ed, sound·ing, sounds.** —*intr.* **1.** To make or give forth a sound. **2.** To present a particular impression: *That argument sounds reasonable.* —*tr.* **1.** To cause to give forth or produce a sound: *sounded the gong.* **2.** To summon, announce, or signal by a sound: *sound a warning.* **3.** To articulate; pronounce: *sound a vowel.* **4.** To make known; celebrate. **5.** To examine (a bodily organ or part) by causing to emit sound; auscultate. —***phrasal verb.* sound off. 1.** To count cadence when marching in military formation. **2.** To express one's views vigorously: *was always sounding off about the cost of living.* [ME *soun* < OFr. *son* < Lat. *sonus.*]

sound[2] (sound) *adj.* **-er, -est. 1.** Free from defect, decay, or damage; in good condition. **2.** Free from disease or injury; healthy. **3.** Having a firm basis; unshakable: *a sound foundation.* **4.** Financially secure or safe: *a sound economy.* **5. a.** Based on valid reasoning; sensible and correct: *a sound observation.* **b.** Founded on thorough experience or knowledge: *sound research.* **6.** Thorough; complete: *a sound flogging.* **7.** Deep and unbroken; undisturbed: *a sound sleep.* **8.** Free from moral defect; upright. **9.** Worthy of confidence; trustworthy. **10.** Marked by or showing common sense and good judgment; levelheaded: *a sound approach to the problem.* **11.** Compatible with an accepted point of view; conservative. **12.** *Law.* Valid; legal. [ME *sund* < OE *gesund.*] —**sound'ly** *adv.* —**sound'ness** *n.*

sound[3] (sound) *n.* **1.** A long, relatively wide body of water, larger than a strait or a channel, connecting larger bodies of water. **2.** A long, wide ocean inlet. **3.** The air bladder of a fish. [ME, partly from OE *sund,* swimming, sea, and partly < ON *sund,* strait, channel < *sundr,* asunder.]

sound[4] (sound) *v.* **sound·ed, sound·ing, sounds.** —*tr.* **1.** To measure the depth of (water), esp. by means of a weighted line; fathom. **2.** To try to learn the attitudes or opinions of: *sounded out her feelings.* **3.** To probe (a bodily cavity) with a sound. —*intr.* **1.** To measure depth. **2.** To dive swiftly downward. Used of a whale or fish. **3.** To look into; investigate. —*n.* An instrument used to examine bodily cavities. [ME *sounden* < OFr. *sonder* < *sonde,* sounding line, prob. of Germanic orig.] —**sound'a·ble** *adj.*

sound barrier *n.* The sonic barrier.

sound·board (sound'bôrd', -bōrd') *n.* A sounding board (sense 1).

sound box *n.* A hollow chamber in the body of a musical instrument, such as a violin or cello, that intensifies the resonance of the tone.

sound camera *n.* A motion-picture camera equipped to record sound and image synchronously.

sound effects *pl.n.* Imitative sounds, as of thunder or an explosion, produced artificially for theatrical purposes.

sound·er (soun'dər) *n.* One that sounds, esp. a device for making soundings of the sea.

sound·ing[1] (soun'dĭng) *n.* **1.** The act of one that sounds. **2.** An environmental probe for scientific observation. **3. a.** A measured depth of water. **b.** Often **soundings.** Water shallow enough for depth measurements to be taken by a hand line.

sound·ing[2] (soun'dĭng) *adj.* **1.** Emitting a full sound; resonant. **2.** Noisy but with little significance; high-sounding.

sounding board *n.* **1.** A thin board forming the upper portion of the resonant chamber in a musical instrument, such as a violin or piano, and serving to increase resonance. **2.** A structure suspended behind or over a podium or platform to reflect the speaker's voice to the audience. **3.** A person or group whose reactions to an idea, opinion, or point of view will serve as a measure of its effectiveness or acceptability. **4.** A device or means serving to spread or popularize an idea or point of view.

sounding lead *n.* The metal weight at the end of a sounding line.

soursop

sounding line *n.* A line marked at intervals of fathoms and weighted at one end, used to determine the depth of water.

sounding rocket *n.* A rocket used to make observations anywhere within the earth's atmosphere.

sound·less (sound′lĭs) *adj.* Having or making no sound. **—sound′less·ly** *adv.* **—sound′less·ness** *n.*

sound pollution *n.* Noise pollution.

sound·proof (sound′pro͞of′) *adj.* Not penetrable by audible sound. *—tr.v.* **-proofed, -proof·ing, -proofs.** To make soundproof.

sound ranging *n.* The electronic location of a sound source, as of enemy weapons, by checking time intervals indicated by microphones of known position.

sound stage *n.* A room or studio, usually soundproof, used for the production of motion pictures.

sound·track (sound′trăk′) *n.* **1.** The narrow strip at one side of a motion-picture film that carries the sound recording. **2. a.** The music that accompanies a motion picture. **b.** A commercial phonograph record or tape of such music.

sound truck *n.* A truck or other vehicle having one or more loud-speakers, usually on top, for area broadcasting.

sound wave *n.* A wave of sound.

sousaphone

soup (so͞op) *n.* **1.** A liquid food prepared from meat, fish, or vegetable stock with various other ingredients added and often containing pieces of solid food. **2.** *Slang.* Something suggestive of the consistency of soup, esp.: **a.** Dense fog. **b.** Nitroglycerine. **3.** A chaotic or unfortunate situation. ***—phrasal verb.*** **soup up.** *Slang.* To add horsepower or greater speed potential to (an engine or vehicle). ***—idiom.*** **in the soup.** *Slang.* In trouble; having difficulties. [Fr. *soupe* < OFr., broth, of Germanic orig.]

soup·çon (so͞op-sôɴ′, so͞op′sŏn′) *n.* A very small amount; trace. [Fr. < VLat. **suspectio* < Lat. *suspectus,* p.part. of *suspicere,* to suspect. —see SUSPECT.]

soup du jour (so͞op′ də zho͝or′) *n.* A soup featured by a restaurant on a given day. [Fr., soup of the day.]

soup kitchen *n.* A place where food is offered free or at very low cost to the needy.

soup·spoon (so͞op′spo͞on′) *n.* A spoon somewhat larger than a teaspoon, used for eating soup.

soup·y (so͞o′pē) *adj.* **-i·er, -i·est. 1.** Having the consistency or appearance of soup. **2.** Foggy. **3.** *Informal.* Sentimental.

sour (sour) *adj.* **-er, -est. 1.** Having a taste characteristic of that produced by acids; sharp, tart, or tangy. **2.** Made acid or rancid by fermentation. **3.** Having the characteristics of fermentation or rancidity; tasting or smelling of decay. **4.** Bad-tempered and morose; peevish: *a sour temper.* **5.** Not up to the expected or usual ability or quality; bad: *His pitching went sour.* **6.** Designating soil that is excessively acid and damaging to crops. **7.** Containing an excess of sulfur compounds. Used of gasoline. *—n.* **1.** The sensation of sour taste, one of the four primary tastes. **2.** Something that is sour. **3.** A mixed drink made esp. with whiskey, lemon or lime juice, sugar, and sometimes soda water. *—tr. & intr.v.* **soured, sour·ing, sours. 1.** To make or become sour. **2.** To make or become disagreeable, disillusioned, or disenchanted. [ME < OE *sūr.*] **—sour′ly** *adv.* **—sour′ness** *n.*

sour·ball (sour′bôl′) *n.* A round piece of hard, tart candy.

source (sôrs, sōrs) *n.* **1.** A place or thing from which something comes or derives; point of origin. **2.** A spring, lake, or other body of water at which a stream or river originates. **3.** One that causes, creates, or initiates something; maker. **4.** One that supplies information. **5.** A book, document, or other record supplying primary or firsthand information. [ME *sourse* < OFr. < fem. p.part. of *sourdre,* to rise < Lat. *surgere.* —see SURGE.]

source book *n.* **1.** A primary document, as of history, literature, or religion, upon which secondary writings are based. **2.** A collection of source books.

sour cherry *n.* **1.** A tree, *Prunus cerasus,* native to Eurasia, having white flowers and tart red fruit. **2.** The edible fruit of the sour cherry.

sour cream *n.* **1.** Cream that has soured naturally by the action of lactic-acid bacteria, used in baking certain breads and cakes. **2.** A smooth, thick, artificially soured cream, widely used as an ingredient in soups, salads, and various meat dishes.

sour·dine (so͞or-dēn′) *n.* **1.** An obsolete double-reed instrument with a soft tone. **2.** A mute, esp. one for a violin. **3.** A stop on an organ producing a low, soft, muted tone. [Fr. < Ital. *sordina* < *sordo,* deaf, mute < Lat. *surdus.*]

sour·dough (sour′dō′) *n.* **1.** Sour fermented dough used as leaven in making bread. **2.** *Slang.* An old-time settler or prospector, esp. in Alaska and northwestern Canada.

sour gum *n.* A tree, *Nyssa sylvatica,* of eastern North America, having glossy, somewhat leathery leaves and soft wood.

sour mash *n.* **1.** A mixture of new mash and mash from a preceding run used to distill certain malt whiskeys. **2.** Whiskey distilled from sour mash.

sour·puss (sour′po͝os′) *n.* *Slang.* A habitually gloomy or sullen person. [SOUR + PUSS[2].]

sour salt *n.* Crystals of citric acid used in cooking.

sour·sop (sour′sŏp′) *n.* **1.** A tropical American tree, *Annona muricata,* bearing spiny fruit with tart, edible pulp. **2.** The fruit of the soursop.

sour·wood (sour′wo͝od′) *n.* A tree, *Oxydendrum arboreum,* of the southeastern United States, having clusters of small white flowers. [So called from its sour-tasting leaves.]

sou·sa·phone (so͞o′zə-fōn′, -sə-) *n.* A large brass wind instrument, similar to the tuba, having a flaring bell. [After John Philip *Sousa* (1854–1932).]

souse[1] (sous) *v.* **soused, sous·ing, sous·es.** *—tr.* **1.** To plunge in a liquid. **2.** To make soaking wet; drench. **3.** To steep in a mixture, as in pickling. **4.** *Slang.* To make intoxicated. *—intr.* To become immersed or soaking wet. *—n.* **1.** The act or process of sousing. **2. a.** Food steeped in pickle, esp. pork trimmings. **b.** The liquid used in pickling; brine. **3.** *Slang.* A drunkard. [ME *sousen,* to pickle < *souse,* pickled meat < OFr. *sous,* of Germanic orig.]

souse[2] (sous) *v.* **soused, sous·ing, sous·es.** *Archaic.* *—tr.* To pounce upon; attack. *—intr.* To swoop down, as an attacking hawk does. *—n.* *Obs.* A swooping motion of attack. [ME *souce,* swooping motion, perh. alteration of *sourse,* source. —see SOURCE.]

sou·tache (so͞o-tăsh′) *n.* A narrow flat braid in a herringbone pattern, used for trimming and embroidery. [Fr. < Hung. *sujtá.*]

sou·tane (so͞o-tän′, -tăn′) *n.* A cassock worn by Roman Catholic priests. [Fr. < Ital. *sottana* < *sotto,* under < Lat. *subtus* < *sub.*]

south (south) *n.* **1. a.** The direction along a meridian to the right of an observer facing in the direction of the earth's rotation; the direction to the right of sunrise. **b.** The cardinal point on the mariner's compass 180 degrees clockwise from north. **c.** An area or region lying in this direction. **2.** Often **South. a.** The southern part of the earth. **b.** The southern part of a country or region. **3. South.** The southern part of the United States, esp. the states that fought for the Confederacy in the Civil War. *—adj.* **1.** Moving to or toward or situated in the south. **2.** Coming from or originating in the south: *a dry south wind.* **3. South.** Officially designating the southern part of a country, continent, or other geographic area: *South America.* *—adv.* In, from, or toward the south. [ME < OE *sūð.*]

south·bound (south′bound′) *adj.* Going toward the south.

south by east *n.* The direction or point on the mariner's compass halfway between due south and south-southeast; 168 degrees 45 minutes east of due north. *—adv. & adj.* Toward or from a south by east direction or point.

south by west *n.* The direction or point on the mariner's compass halfway between due south and south-southwest; 168 degrees 45 minutes west of due north. *—adv. & adj.* Toward or from a south by west direction or point.

South·down (south′doun′) *n.* Any of a breed of small, hornless sheep of English origin, having dense, short, fine-textured wool. [After the *South Downs,* a range of hills in southeastern England.]

south·east (south-ēst′, sou-ēst′) *n.* **1.** The direction or point on the mariner's compass halfway between south and east; 135 degrees east of due north. **2.** An area or region lying in the southeast. *—adj.* **1.** Situated toward, facing, or in the southeast. **2.** Coming from or originating in the southeast, as a wind. *—adv.* In, from, or toward the southeast. **—south·east′ern** *adj.*

southeast by east *n.* The direction or point on the mariner's compass halfway between southeast and east-southeast; 123 degrees 45 minutes east of due north. *—adv. & adj.* Toward or from a southeast by east direction or point.

southeast by south *n.* The direction or point on the mariner's compass halfway between southeast and south-southeast; 146 degrees 15 minutes east of due north. *—adv. & adj.* Toward or from a southeast by south direction or point.

south·east·er (south-ē′stər, sou-ē′-) *n.* A storm or gale blowing from the southeast.

south·east·er·ly (south-ē′stər-lē, sou-ē′-) *adj.* **1.** Toward or in the southeast. **2.** From the southeast. **—south·east′er·ly** *adv.*

south·east·ward (south-ēst′wərd, sou-ēst′-) *adj. & adv.* At or toward the southeast. *—n.* **1.** A direction or point toward the southeast. **2.** A region or part situated in or toward the southeast. **—south·east′ward·ly** *adj. & adv.* **—south·east′wards** *adv.*

south·er (sou′*th*ər) *n.* A strong wind coming from the south.

south·er·ly (sŭ*th*′ər-lē) *adj.* **1.** Situated toward the south. **2.** From the south: *a strong southerly wind.* *—n., pl.* **-lies.** A storm or wind from the south. **—south′er·ly** *adv.*

south·ern (sŭ*th*′ərn) *adj.* **1.** Situated toward, in, or facing the south. **2.** Coming from the south: *a southern breeze.* **3.** Native to or growing in the south. **4.** Often **Southern.** Of, pertaining to, or characteristic of southern regions or the

South. **5.** South of the equator. [ME *southerne* < OE *sūðerne.*]
Southern Cross *n.* Crux.
Southern Crown *n.* Corona Australis.
south·ern·er (sŭ*th*′ər-nər) *n.* **1.** A native or inhabitant of the south. **2.** Often **Southerner.** A native or inhabitant of the southern United States.
Southern Hemisphere *n.* The half of the earth south of the equator.
South·ern·ism (sŭ*th*′ər-nĭz′əm) *n.* **1.** An expression or a pronunciation characteristic of the southern United States. **2.** A trait, attitude, or practice characteristic of the South or Southerners, esp. in the United States.
southern lights *pl.n.* The aurora australis.
south·ern·most (sŭ*th*′ərn-mōst′) *adj.* Farthest south.
south·ern·wood (sŭ*th*′ərn-wŏŏd′) *n.* An aromatic woody plant, *Artemisia abrotanum,* native to Europe, having finely divided grayish foliage.
south·ing (sou′*th*ĭng) *n.* **1.** The difference in latitude between two positions as a result of a movement to the south. **2.** Progress toward the south.
south·land or **South·land** (south′lănd′, -lənd) *n.* A region in the south of a country or area.
south·paw (south′pô′) *n. Slang.* A left-handed person, esp. a left-handed baseball pitcher.
South Pole *n.* **1.** The southern end of the earth's axis of rotation. **2.** The celestial zenith of the heavens as viewed from the south terrestrial pole. **3. south pole.** The south-seeking magnetic pole of a magnet.
south·ron (sŭ*th*′rən) *n.* **1.** Often **Southron.** *Chiefly Scot.* A person who lives in the south, esp. an Englishman as called by a Scotsman. **2.** A native or inhabitant of the American South. Used by the Confederate side in the Civil War. *—adj. Chiefly Scot.* Southern. [ME < *southerne,* southern.]
south-south·east (south′south-ēst′, sou′sou-ēst′) *n.* The direction or point on the mariner's compass halfway between due south and southeast; 157 degrees 30 minutes east of due north. *—adj.* Situated toward, facing, or in the south-southeast. *—adv.* In, from, or toward the south-southeast.
south-south·west (south′south-wĕst′, sou′sou-wĕst′) *n.* The direction or point on the mariner's compass halfway between due south and southwest; 157 degrees 30 minutes west of due north. *—adj.* Situated toward, facing, or in the south-southwest. *—adv.* In, from, or toward the south-southwest.
south·ward (south′wərd, sŭ*th*′ərd) *adj. & adv.* At or toward the south. *—n.* **1.** A direction toward the south. **2.** A region situated in or toward the south. **—south′ward·ly** *adj. & adv.* **—south′wards** *adv.*
south·west (south-wĕst′, sou-wĕst′) *n.* **1. a.** The direction or point on the mariner's compass halfway between south and west; 135 degrees west of due north. **b.** An area or region lying in this direction. **2. Southwest.** A region of the southwestern United States generally considered to include New Mexico, Arizona, Texas, California, Nevada, Utah, and Colorado. *—adj.* **1.** To, toward, of, facing, or in the southwest. **2.** Coming from or originating in the southwest: *a southwest wind.* *—adv.* In, from, or toward the southwest. **—south·west′ern** *adj.*
southwest by south *n.* The direction or point on the mariner's compass halfway between southwest and south-southwest; 146 degrees 15 minutes west of due north. *—adv. & adj.* Toward or from a southwest by south direction or point.
southwest by west *n.* The direction or point on the mariner's compass halfway between southwest and west-southwest; 123 degrees 45 minutes west of due north. *—adv. & adj.* Toward or from a southwest by west direction or point.
south·west·er (south-wĕs′tər, sou-wĕs′-) *n.* **1. a.** A storm from the southwest. **b.** A strong wind from the southwest. **2.** A waterproof hat of material such as plastic, oilskin, or canvas with a broad brim behind to protect the neck.
south·west·er·ly (south-wĕs′tər-lē, sou-wĕs′-) *adj.* **1.** Toward or in the southwest. **2.** From the southwest. **—south·west′er·ly** *adv.*
south·west·ward (south-wĕst′wərd) *adj. & adv.* At or toward the southwest. *—n.* **1.** A direction or point toward the southwest. **2.** A region or part situated in or toward the southwest. **—south·west′ward·ly** *adj. & adv.* **—south·west′wards** *adv.*
sou·ve·nir (sōō′və-nîr′, sōō′və-nîr′) *n.* Something serving as a token of remembrance; memento. [Fr., memory < *souvenir,* to recall < Lat. *subvenire,* to come to mind : *sub-,* under + *venire,* to come.]
sov·er·eign (sŏv′ər-ĭn, sŏv′rĭn) *n.* **1.** The chief of state in a monarchy. **2.** A gold coin formerly used in Great Britain. *—adj.* **1.** Paramount; supreme. **2.** Having supreme rank or power. **3.** Self-governing; independent: *a sovereign state.* **4. a.** Of superlative strength or efficacy: *a sovereign remedy.* **b.** Unmitigated: *sovereign contempt.* [ME *souverein* < OFr. < VLat. **superanus* < Lat. *super,* above.] **—sov′er·eign·ly** *adv.*
sov·er·eign·ty (sŏv′ər-ĭn-tē, sŏv′rĭn-) *n., pl.* **-ties. 1.** Supremacy of authority or rule as exercised by a sovereign or a sovereign state. **2.** Royal rank, authority, or power. **3.** Complete independence and self-government. **4.** A territory existing as an independent state.
so·vi·et (sō′vē-ĕt′, -ĭt, sŏv′ē-) *n.* **1.** In the Soviet Union, one of the popularly elected legislative assemblies that exist at local, regional, and national levels. **2. Soviets.** The people and government of the Soviet Union. *—adj.* **1.** Often **Soviet.** Of or pertaining to the Union of Soviet Socialist Republics. **2.** Of or pertaining to a soviet. [R. *sovet,* council.]
so·vi·et·ize also **So·vi·et·ize** (sō′vē-ĭ-tīz′, sŏv′ē-) *tr.v.* **-ized, -iz·ing, -iz·es. 1.** To cause to come under Soviet control. **2.** To cause to conform to Soviet political, social, and cultural policy. **—so′vi·et·i·za′tion** *n.*
sov·khoz (sŏf-kôz′, -KHôz′) *n.* A state-owned farm in the USSR that pays wages to its workers. [R., short for *sovetskoe khozyaĭstvo,* soviet farm.]
sow[1] (sō) *v.* **sowed, sown** (sōn) or **sowed, sow·ing, sows.** *—tr.* **1.** To scatter (seed) over the ground for growing. **2.** To impregnate (a growing medium) with seed. **3.** To propagate; disseminate: *sow rumors and dissension.* **4.** To strew or cover with something; spread thickly. *—intr.* To scatter seed for growing. [ME *sowen* < OE *sāwan.*] **—sow′er** *n.*
sow[2] (sou) *n.* **1.** An adult female hog. **2. a.** A channel that conducts molten iron to the molds in a pig bed. **b.** The mass of metal solidified in such a channel or mold. [ME < OE *sugu.*]
sow·bel·ly (sou′bĕl′ē) *n. Informal.* Salt pork.
sow·bread (sou′brĕd′) *n.* The cyclamen.
sow bug *n.* Any of various small terrestrial crustaceans, chiefly of the genera *Oniscus* and *Porcellio,* commonly found under logs or stones and having an oval, segmented body. [From its piglike shape.]
sown (sōn) *v.* A past participle of **sow**[1].
sow thistle *n.* Any of various plants of the genus *Sonchus,* esp. *S. oleraceus,* native to Europe, having prickly leaves and yellow flowers.

sow thistle

sox (sŏks) *n.* A plural of **sock**[1] (sense 1).
soy (soi) *n.* **1.** The soybean. **2.** A salty brown liquid condiment made by fermenting soybeans in brine. [J. *shō-yu* < Chin. (Mandarin) *jiang*[4] *you*[2] : *jiang*[4], soy paste + *you*[2], sauce.]
soy·a (soi′ə) *n.* The soybean (sense 2). [Du. *soja* < J. *shō-yu,* soy.]
soy·bean (soi′bēn′) *n.* **1.** A leguminous Asiatic plant, *Glycine max,* widely cultivated for forage and soil improvement and for its nutritious, edible seeds. **2.** The seed of the soybean.

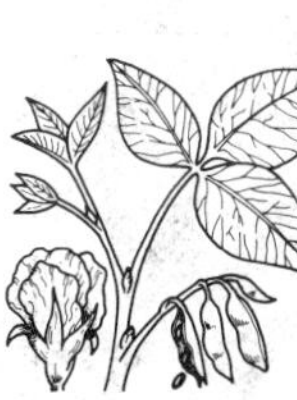

soybean

soy·milk (soi′mĭlk′) *n.* A substitute for milk that is made from soybeans and often supplemented with vitamins.
spa (spä) *n.* **1.** A mineral spring. **2.** A resort area having mineral springs. **3.** A fashionable hotel or resort. **4.** *Regional.* A soda fountain (sense 2). [After *Spa,* a resort town in Belgium.]
space (spās) *n.* **1. a.** A set of elements or points satisfying specified geometric postulates: *non-Euclidean space.* **b.** The infinite extension of the three-dimensional field of everyday life. **2.** The expanse in which the solar system, stars, and galaxies exist; universe. **3.** A blank or empty area: *the spaces between words.* **4.** An area provided for a particular purpose: *a parking space.* **5.** Reserved or available accommodation on a public transportation vehicle. **6. a.** A period or interval of time. **b.** A little while: *for a space.* **7.** *Informal.* Sufficient freedom from external pressure to develop or explore one's needs, interests, and individuality. **8.** *Mus.* One of the intervals between the lines of a staff. **9.** *Printing.* One of the blank pieces of type or other means used for separating words or characters. **10.** One of the intervals during the telegraphic transmission of a message when the key is open or not in contact. **11.** Broadcast time or areas in printed material that is available esp. for use by advertisers. *—tr.v.* **spaced, spac·ing, spac·es. 1.** To organize or arrange with spaces between. **2.** To separate or keep apart. [ME, distance < OFr. *espace* < Lat. *spatium.*] **—spac′er** *n.*
space biology *n.* Exobiology.
space·borne (spās′bôrn′) *adj.* Operating in or involving equipment operating in outer space: *a spaceborne satellite.*
space capsule *n. Aerospace.* A capsule (sense 6).
space charge *n.* An electric charge in a vacuum or region of low gas pressure, as in a vacuum tube, carried by a stream of electrons or ions.
space·craft (spās′krăft′) *n., pl.* **spacecraft.** A vehicle designed to be launched into space.
spaced (spāst) *adj. Slang.* Spaced-out.
spaced-out (spāst′out′) *adj. Slang.* Stupefied from or as if from a drug.
space flight *n.* Flight beyond the atmosphere of the earth.
space lattice *n.* Any of the 14 possible geometric arrangements of points at which the atoms of a crystal may occur.
space·less (spās′lĭs) *adj.* Having no limits or boundaries.
space·man (spās′măn′, -mən) *n.* **1.** A person who travels in outer space. **2.** A visitor that comes to Earth from outer space.
space medicine *n.* The medical science of the biological, physiological, and psychological effects of space flight upon human beings.
space·port (spās′pôrt′, -pōrt′) *n.* An installation for testing and launching spacecraft.

space shuttle

space walk

spade[2]

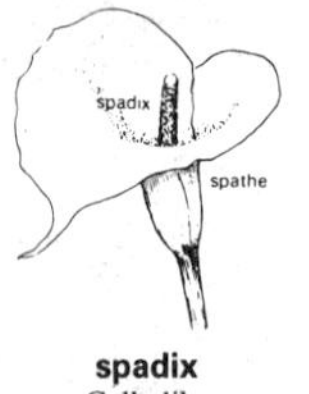

spadix
Calla lily

spanker
On the barque *Hesper*

space probe *n.* A spacecraft carrying instruments designed to explore the physical properties of outer space or of celestial bodies other than Earth.

space science *n.* **1.** Any of several scientific disciplines, such as exobiology, that study phenomena occurring in the upper atmosphere, in space, or on celestial bodies other than Earth. **2.** A discipline related to or dealing with the problems of space flight.

space·ship or **space ship** (spās′shĭp′) *n.* A spacecraft.

space shuttle *n.* A space vehicle designed to transport astronauts between Earth and an orbiting space station.

space sickness *n.* Any of various ailments resulting from manned space flight.

space station *n.* A large manned satellite designed for permanent orbit around Earth and used for scientific research and military reconnaissance or as an assembly point for long-range spacecraft.

space suit *n.* A protective pressure suit having an independent air supply and other devices designed to permit the wearer relatively free movement in space.

space-time (spās′tīm′) *n.* The four-dimensional continuum of one temporal and three spatial coordinates in which any event or physical object is located.

space vehicle *n.* A spacecraft.

space walk *n.* An excursion by an astronaut outside a spacecraft in space; extravehicular activity. **—space walk** *v.* **—space walker** *n.*

space·ward (spās′wərd) *adv.* Toward outer space.

space writer *n.* A writer, as a journalist, paid according to the amount of space his material occupies in print.

spac·ey (spā′sē) *adj.* Variant of **spacy.**

spa·cial (spā′shəl) *adj.* Variant of **spatial.**

spac·ing (spā′sĭng) *n.* **1. a.** The act or result of arranging by spaces. **b.** A system of or allowance for intervals. **2.** A space or spaces, as in printed matter.

spa·cious (spā′shəs) *adj.* **1.** Providing or having much space or room; extensive. **2.** Vast in range or scope: *a spacious view.* **—spa′cious·ly** *adv.* **—spa′cious·ness** *n.*

Spack·le (spăk′əl). A trademark for a powder to be mixed with water or a ready-to-use plastic paste designed to fill cracks and holes in plaster before painting or papering.

spac·y or **spac·ey** (spā′sē) *adj.* **-i·er, -i·est.** *Slang.* **1.** Spaced-out. **2.** Eccentric; offbeat.

spade[1] (spād) *n.* **1.** A sturdy digging tool having a thick handle and a heavy, flat iron blade that can be pressed into the ground with the foot. **2.** Any of various digging or cutting tools resembling the spade. *—tr.v.* **spad·ed, spad·ing, spades.** To dig or cut with a spade. **—*idiom.* call a spade a spade.** To speak frankly and truly. [ME < OE *spadu.*] **—spad′er** *n.*

spade[2] (spād) *n.* **1.** The black figure, shaped like an inverted heart with a short stalk at the bottom, on a playing card. **2. spades.** The suit of cards identified by a spade. **3.** A card bearing a spade. **4.** *Offensive.* A black person. [Ital. *spada,* broadsword < Lat. *spatha* < Gk. *spathē,* broad blade.]

spade·fish (spād′fĭsh′) *n., pl.* **spadefish** or **-fish·es.** Any of several marine food fishes of the family Ephippidae, esp. *Chaetodipterus faber,* of the Atlantic, or *C. zonatus,* of the Pacific. [From its shape.]

spade·work (spād′wûrk′) *n.* **1.** Work requiring a spade. **2.** Preparatory work necessary to a project or activity.

spa·dix (spā′dĭks) *n., pl.* **spa·di·ces** (spā′dĭ-sēz′). A clublike spike bearing minute flowers, usually enclosed within a sheathlike spathe, as in the calla and the jack-in-the-pulpit. [Lat., broken-off palm branch < Gk.]

spa·ghet·ti (spə-gĕt′ē) *n.* **1.** A pasta made into long, solid strings and cooked by boiling. **2.** *Elect.* A slender tube of insulating material into which bare wire is inserted, esp. in radio circuits. [Ital., pl. dim. of *spago,* string.]

spa·ghet·ti·ni (spăg′ĭ-tē′nē) *n.* A form of pasta that is thinner than spaghetti but not as thin as vermicelli. [Ital., dim. of *spaghetti,* spaghetti.]

spaghetti Western *n.* A low-budget Western film made by the Italian film industry.

spa·gyr·ic (spə-gîr′ĭk) also **spa·gyr·i·cal** (-ĭ-kəl) *adj.* Pertaining to or resembling alchemy; alchemical. [NLat. *spagiricus.*]

spake (spāk) *v. Archaic.* A past tense of **speak.**

spall (spôl) *n.* A chip, fragment, or flake from a piece of stone or ore. *—v.* **spalled, spall·ing, spalls.** *—tr.* To break up into chips or fragments. *—intr.* To chip or crumble. [ME *spalle.*]

spal·la·tion (spô-lā′shən) *n.* A nuclear reaction in which many particles are ejected from an atomic nucleus by an incident particle of sufficiently high energy.

Spam (spăm). A trademark for spiced pork products, luncheon meat, and deviled luncheon-meat spread.

span[1] (spăn) *n.* **1.** The extent or measure of space between two points or extremities, as of a bridge or roof; breadth. **2.** The distance between the tips of an airplane's wings. **3.** The section between two intermediate supports of a bridge. **4.** Something that spans, as a railroad trestle or bridge. **5.** The distance from the tip of the thumb to the tip of the little finger when the hand is fully extended, formerly used as a unit of measure equal to about nine inches. **6.** A period of time: *a life span.* *—tr.v.* **spanned, span·ning, spans. 1.** To measure by or as if by the fully extended hand. **2.** To encircle with the hand or hands in or as if in measuring. **3.** To extend across: *a career that spanned 40 years.* **4.** To form a span over: *The footbridge spanned the gorge.* [ME, unit of measurement < OE *spann.*]

span[2] (spăn) *tr.v.* **spanned, span·ning, spans.** To bind or fetter. *—n.* **1.** *Naut.* A stretch of rope made fast at either end. **2.** A pair of animals, such as oxen, matched in size, strength, or color. [MDu. *spannen.*]

span[3] (spăn) *v. Archaic.* A past tense and past participle of **spin.**

span·drel also **span·dril** (spăn′drəl) *n. Archit.* **1.** The triangular space between the left or right exterior curve of an arch and the rectangular framework surrounding it. **2.** The space between two arches and a horizontal molding or cornice above them. [ME *spaundrell* < AN *spaundre* < OFr. *espandre,* to spread out < Lat. *expandere.* —see EXPAND.]

spang (spăng) *adv.* Precisely; squarely: *right spang in the middle of the table.* [Orig. unknown.]

span·gle (spăng′gəl) *n.* **1.** A small, often circular piece of sparkling metal or plastic sewn esp. on garments for decoration. **2.** A small sparkling object, drop, or spot: *spangles of sunlight.* *—v.* **-gled, -gling, -gles.** *—tr.* To adorn or cause to sparkle by covering with or as if with spangles: *Lights spangled the night skyline.* *—intr.* To sparkle in the manner of spangles. [ME *spangele,* dim. of *spange,* perh. < MDu., buckle.] **—span′gly** *adj.*

Span·iard (spăn′yərd) *n.* A native or inhabitant of Spain.

span·iel (spăn′yəl) *n.* **1.** Any of several breeds of small to medium-sized dogs, usually having drooping ears, short legs, and a silky, wavy coat. **2.** A docile or servile person. [ME *spanyel* < OFr. *espaignol,* Spaniard, Spanish dog < Lat. *Hispaniolus,* Spanish < *Hispania,* Spain.]

Span·ish (spăn′ĭsh) *adj.* Of or pertaining to Spain, its inhabitants, or their language or culture. *—n.* **1.** The Romance language of Spain and most of Central and South America. **2.** The inhabitants of Spain.

Span·ish-A·mer·i·can (spăn′ĭsh-ə-mĕr′ĭ-kən) *adj.* **1.** Of or pertaining to the countries or people of Spanish America. **2.** Of or pertaining to people of Spanish descent residing in the United States. *—n.* **1.** A native or inhabitant of a Spanish-American country. **2.** A person of Spanish descent who lives in the United States.

Spanish bayonet *n.* **1.** Any of several New World plants of the genus *Yucca,* esp. *Y. aloifolia,* having a tall, woody stem, stiff, pointed leaves, and a large cluster of white flowers. **2.** A plant similar to the Spanish bayonet, *Y. filamentosa.*

Spanish cedar *n.* **1.** Any of several tropical American trees of the genus *Cedrela,* esp. *C. odorata,* having reddish, aromatic wood used for cabinetwork and cigar boxes. **2.** The wood of the Spanish cedar.

Spanish chestnut *n.* **1.** A tree, *Castanea sativa,* of the Mediterranean area, bearing edible nuts. **2.** The nut of the Spanish chestnut.

Spanish fly *n.* **1.** A European blister beetle, *Lytta vesicatoria.* **2.** Cantharides.

Spanish mackerel *n.* Any of various marine food fishes of the genus *Scomberomorus,* esp. a commercially important species, *S. maculatus,* of American Atlantic coastal waters.

Spanish moss *n.* An epiphytic plant, *Tillandsia usneoides,* growing on trees of the southeastern United States and tropical America, having gray, threadlike stems drooping in long, densely matted clusters.

Spanish needles *pl.n. (used with a sing. or pl. verb).* A North American plant, *Bidens bipinnata,* having yellowish flowers and slender, barbed fruit.

Spanish omelet *n.* An omelet served with an often spicy sauce of tomatoes, onions, and peppers.

Spanish onion *n.* A mild-flavored, yellow-skinned onion, probably derived from *Allium fistulosum.*

Spanish paprika *n.* A mild seasoning made from pimientos.

Spanish rice *n.* A dish consisting of rice cooked with tomatoes, spices, chopped onions, and green peppers.

spank (spăngk) *v.* **spanked, spank·ing, spanks.** *—tr.* To slap on the buttocks with a flat object or with the open hand as punishment. *—intr.* To move briskly or spiritedly. *—n.* A slap on the buttocks. [Perh. imit.]

spank·er (spăng′kər) *n.* **1.** One that spanks. **2.** *Naut.* A quadrilateral gaff sail set abaft the after mast of a square-rigged sailing ship.

spank·ing (spăng′kĭng) *adj.* **1.** *Informal.* Exceptional of its kind; remarkable. **2.** Brisk and fresh: *a spanking breeze.* *—adv.* Exceedingly: *a spanking clean shirt.* [Orig. unknown.]

span·ner (spăn′ər) *n.* **1.** One that spans. **2.** *Chiefly Brit.* A wrench. **3.** A measuring worm. [G., winding tool < *spannen,* to stretch.]

span-new (spăn′no͞o′, -nyo͞o′) *adj. Regional.* Entirely new. [ME *spannewe,* partial transl. of ON *spānnȳr* : *spānn,* chip + *nȳr,* new.]

span·worm (spăn′wûrm′) *n.* A measuring worm. [< SPAN[2].]

spar[1] (spär) *n.* **1.** *Naut.* A wooden or metal pole, as a mast, boom, yard, or bowsprit, used to support rigging. **2.** A usually metal pole used as part of a crane or derrick. **3.** A principal structural member in an airplane wing that runs from tip to tip or from root to tip. *—tr.v.* **sparred, spar·ring,**

spars. **1.** To supply with spars. **2.** *Archaic.* To fasten with a bolt. [ME *sparre,* rafter < ON *sperra,* beam.]

spar[2] (spär) *intr.v.* **sparred, spar·ring, spars.** **1.** To box, esp. for practice. **2.** To bandy words about in argument; dispute. **3.** To fight by striking with the feet and spurs. Used of cocks. *—n.* **1.** The act of sparring. **2.** A boxing match. [ME *sparren,* to thrust or strike rapidly.]

spar[3] (spär) *n.* Any of various nonmetallic, readily cleavable minerals with a vitreous luster, as feldspar. [MLG.]

Spar also **SPAR** (spär) *n.* A member of the women's reserve of the U.S. Coast Guard. [Contraction of Lat. *semper paratus,* always prepared, the motto of the U.S. Coast Guard.]

spare (spâr) *v.* **spared, spar·ing, spares.** *—tr.* **1. a.** To treat mercifully or leniently. **b.** To refrain from harming or destroying. **2.** To save or relieve from experiencing or doing something: *spared herself the trouble of going.* **3.** To use with restraint: *Don't spare the mustard.* **4.** To give or grant out of one's resources; afford: *Can you spare ten minutes? —intr.* **1.** To be frugal. **2. a.** To be merciful or lenient. **b.** To refrain or forbear. *—adj.* **spar·er, spar·est. 1. a.** Kept in reserve: *a spare tire.* **b.** In excess of what is needed; extra: *spare cash.* **c.** Free for other use; unoccupied: *spare time.* **2. a.** Economical; meager: *a spare budget.* **b.** Thin or lean: *a tall, spare man. —n.* **1.** A replacement, such as a tire, reserved for future need. **2. a.** The act of knocking down all ten pins with two successive rolls of a bowling ball. **b.** The score made by doing this. *—idiom.* **to spare.** In addition to what is needed: *paid his bills and had money to spare.* [ME *sparen,* to leave unharmed < OE *sparian.*] **—spare'ly** *adv.* **—spare'ness** *n.* **—spar'er** *n.*

spare·ribs (spâr'rĭbz') *pl.n.* A cut of pork consisting of the ribs with most of the meat trimmed off. [By folk ety. < MLG *ribbespēr : ribbe,* rib + *spēr,* spit.]

sparge (spärj) *tr.v.* **sparged, sparg·ing, sparg·es. 1.** To spray or sprinkle. **2.** To introduce air or gas into (a liquid). *—n.* A sprinkle. [OFr. *espargier* < Lat. *spargere.*]

spar·id (spăr'ĭd, spâr'-) *adj.* Of or belonging to the family Sparidae, which includes the porgies and similar fishes. *—n.* A member of the Sparidae. [NLat. *Sparidae,* family name < *Sparus,* type genus < Lat., a kind of fish < Gk. *sparos.*]

spar·ing (spâr'ĭng) *adj.* **1.** Thrifty; frugal. **2.** Forbearing; lenient. **—spar'ing·ly** *adv.* **—spar'ing·ness** *n.*

spark[1] (spärk) *n.* **1.** An incandescent particle, esp.: **a.** One thrown off from a burning substance. **b.** One resulting from friction. **c.** One remaining in an otherwise extinguished fire; ember. **2.** A glistening particle of something, as metal. **3. a.** A flash of light, esp. a flash produced by electric discharge. **b.** A short pulse or flow of electric current. **4.** A trace or suggestion, as: **a.** A quality or feeling with latent potential; seed: *the spark of genius.* **b.** A vital, animating, or activating factor: *the spark of revolt.* **5. sparks** *(used with a sing. verb). Informal.* A ship's radio operator. **6.** *Elect.* **a.** The luminous phenomenon resulting from a disruptive discharge through an insulating material. **b.** The discharge itself. *—v.* **sparked, spark·ing, sparks.** *—intr.* **1.** To give off sparks. **2.** To operate correctly. Used of the ignition system of an internal-combustion engine. *—tr.* **1.** To set in motion; activate. **2.** To rouse to action. [ME *sparke* < OE *spærca.*] **—spark'er** *n.*

spark[2] (spärk) *n.* **1.** A young dandy or gallant. **2.** A lover; suitor. *—v.* **sparked, spark·ing, sparks.** *—tr.* To court or woo. *—intr.* To play the suitor. [Perh. of Scand. orig.] **—spark'er** *n.*

spark arrester *n.* **1.** A device to keep sparks from escaping, as at a chimney opening. **2.** A device to control electric sparking at a point where a circuit is made or broken.

spark chamber *n.* A device consisting of electrically charged parallel metal plates in a chamber filled with inert gas, used to detect and measure charged subatomic particles as they pass from one plate to another, leaving a trail of sparks.

spark coil *n.* An induction coil used to produce a spark, as in an internal-combustion engine.

spark gap *n.* A gap in an otherwise complete electric circuit across which a discharge occurs at some prescribed voltage.

spark generator *n.* A spark transmitter (sense 1).

sparking plug *n. Chiefly Brit.* Variant of **spark plug.**

spar·kle (spär'kəl) *intr.v.* **-kled, -kling, -kles. 1.** To give off sparks. **2.** To give off or reflect flashes of light; glitter. **3.** To shine with animation. **4.** To flash with wit. **5.** To release gas bubbles; effervesce: *Champagne sparkles. —n.* **1.** A small spark or gleaming particle. **2.** A glittering quality. **3.** Shining animation; vivacity. **4.** Effervescence. [ME *sparklen,* freq. of *sparken,* to spark.]

spar·kler (spär'klər) *n.* **1.** One that sparkles. **2.** A firework that burns slowly and gives off a shower of sparks. **3.** *Informal.* A diamond.

sparkling wine *n.* Any of various effervescent wines, such as champagne, produced by a process that involves fermentation in the bottle.

spark plug *n.* **1.** A device inserted in the head of an internal-combustion-engine cylinder that ignites the fuel mixture by means of an electric spark. **2.** *Informal.* A person who gives life or energy to an undertaking.

spark·plug (spärk'plŭg') *tr.v.* **-plugged, -plug·ging, -plugs.** *Informal.* To inspire or energize (an undertaking, for example).

spark transmitter *n.* **1.** A source of alternating current that derives its output from the discharge of a condenser across a spark gap. **2.** A now obsolete radio transmitter using a discharge across a spark gap to create a signal.

spark·y (spär'kē) *adj.* Animated; lively.

spar·ling (spär'lĭng) *n.* **1.** The European smelt. **2.** A young herring. [ME *sperlinge* < OFr. *esperlinge,* of Germanic orig.]

sparring partner *n.* A person who serves as a boxer's opponent during practice sessions.

spar·row (spăr'ō) *n.* **1.** Any of various small New World birds of the genera *Spizella, Zonotrichia, Melospiza,* and other closely related genera within the family Fringillidae, having grayish or brownish plumage. **2.** Any of several birds similar or related to the sparrow, such as the common house sparrow. [ME *sparowe* < OE *spearwe.*]

spar·row·grass (spăr'ə-grăs', -grəs) *n. Regional.* Asparagus. [By folk ety. < ASPARAGUS.]

sparrow hawk *n.* **1.** A small North American falcon, *Falco sparverius,* that preys on small birds and animals. **2.** A European hawk, *Accipiter nisus,* similar to the sparrow hawk.

sparse (spärs) *adj.* **spars·er, spars·est.** Occurring and esp. growing or settled at widely spaced intervals: *a sparse crop; a sparse population.* [Lat. *sparsus,* p.part. of *spargere,* to scatter.] **—sparse'ly** *adv.* **—sparse'ness, spar'si·ty** (spär'sĭ-tē) *n.*

Spar·tan (spär'tn) *adj.* **1.** Of or pertaining to the ancient Greek city-state Sparta or its people. **2.** Characterized by self-discipline; austere: *a Spartan diet. —n.* **1.** A citizen of Sparta. **2.** One of Spartan character. **—Spar'tan·ism** *n.*

spar varnish *n.* A waterproof varnish.

spasm (spăz'əm) *n.* **1.** A sudden, involuntary contraction of a muscle or group of muscles. **2.** A sudden burst of energy, activity, or emotion. [ME *spasme* < OFr. < Lat. *spasmus* < Gk. *spasmos* < *span,* to pull.]

spas·mod·ic (spăz-mŏd'ĭk) *adj.* **1.** Pertaining to, affected by, or having the character of a spasm; convulsive. **2.** Happening intermittently; fitful: *spasmodic rifle fire.* **3.** Given to sudden outbursts of energy or feeling; excitable. [NLat. *spasmodicus* < Gk. *spasmodikos* < *spasmos,* spasm.] **—spas·mod'i·cal·ly** *adv.*

spas·tic (spăs'tĭk) *adj.* Of, pertaining to, or characterized by spasms. *—n.* **1.** A person suffering from muscular spasms. **2.** A person afflicted with spastic paralysis. [Lat. *spasticus* < Gk. *spastikos* < *span,* to pull.] **—spas'ti·cal·ly** *adv.* **—spas·tic'i·ty** (spă-stĭs'ĭ-tē) *n.*

spastic paralysis *n.* A chronic pathological condition involving exaggerated tendon reflexes and muscular spasms accompanying sclerosis of the spinal cord.

spat[1] (spăt) *v.* A past tense and past participle of **spit[1].**

spat[2] (spăt) *n., pl.* **spat** or **spats.** An oyster or similar bivalve mollusk in the larval stage, esp. when it settles to the bottom and begins to develop a shell. *intr.v.* **spat·ted, spat·ting, spats.** To spawn. Used of oysters and similar mollusks. [Orig. unknown.]

spat[3] (spăt) *n.* Often **spats.** A cloth or leather gaiter covering the shoe upper and the ankle and fastening under the shoe with a strap. [Short for E. *spatterdash* : SPATTER + DASH.]

spat[4] (spăt) *n.* **1.** A brief, petty quarrel. **2.** *Informal.* A slap or smack. **3.** A spattering sound, as of raindrops. *—v.* **spat·ted, spat·ting, spats.** *—intr.* **1.** To engage in a brief, petty quarrel. **2.** To strike with a light spattering sound; slap. *—tr. Informal.* To slap. [Orig. unknown.]

spate (spāt) *n.* **1.** A sudden flood, rush, or outpouring: *a spate of angry words.* **2.** *Chiefly Brit.* **a.** A flash flood. **b.** A freshet resulting from a downpour of rain or melting of snow. **c.** A sudden heavy fall of rain. [ME.]

spathe (spāth) *n. Bot.* A leaflike organ that encloses or spreads from the base of the spadix of certain plants, such as the jack-in-the-pulpit or the calla. [Lat. *spatha,* broadsword < Gk. *spathē,* broad blade.]

spath·ic (spăth'ĭk) *adj.* Having good cleavage. Used of minerals. [< G. *spath, spat,* spar.]

spa·tial also **spa·cial** (spā'shəl) *adj.* Of, pertaining to, involving, or having the nature of space. [< Lat. *spatium,* space.] **—spa'ti·al'i·ty** (spā'shē-ăl'ĭ-tē) *n.* **—spa'tial·ly** *adv.*

spa·ti·o·tem·po·ral (spā'shē-ō-tĕm'pər-əl) *adj.* **1.** Of, pertaining to, or existing in both space and time. **2.** Of or relating to space-time. [Lat. *spatium,* space + TEMPORAL.] **—spa'ti·o·tem'po·ral·ly** *adv.*

spat·ter (spăt'ər) *v.* **-tered, -ter·ing, -ters.** *—tr.* **1.** To scatter (a liquid) in drops or small splashes. **2.** To spot, splash, or soil. **3.** To sully the reputation of; defame. *—intr.* **1.** To spit off drops or small splashes; splatter. **2.** To fall with a splash or a splashing sound. *—n.* **1.** The act of spattering. **2.** A spattering sound. **3.** A drop or splash of something spattered. [Perh. of LG orig.]

spat·ter·dock (spăt'ər-dŏk') *n.* An aquatic plant, *Nuphar advena,* of eastern North America, having broad leaves and globe-shaped yellow flowers. [SPATTER + DOCK[4].]

spat·u·la (spăch'ə-lə) *n.* **1.** A small implement having a broad, flat, flexible blade that is used esp. to mix, spread, or lift soft material. **2.** An implement, such as a small wooden paddle, used to press down the tongue. [Lat., dim. of *spatha,* broadsword < Gk. *spathē,* broad blade.] **—spat'u·lar** *adj.*

spat·u·late (spăch'ə-lĭt) *adj.* Shaped like a spatula.

spark plug

sparrow hawk

spat[3]
Canvas gaiters

spear

spearfish
Tetrapturus belone

spearmint

spav·in (spăv′ĭn) *n.* Either of two diseases affecting the hock joint of horses: *bog spavin,* an infusion of lymph that enlarges the joint, and *bone spavin,* a bony deposit that stiffens the joint. [ME *spaveyne* < OFr. *espavin.*] **—spav′ined** *adj.*

spawn (spôn) *n.* **1.** The eggs of aquatic animals such as bivalve mollusks, fishes, and amphibians. **2.** Offspring occurring in numbers; brood. **3.** A person regarded as the issue of a parent or family: *the spawn of a tyrant.* **4.** A product or an outcome. **5.** Fragments of mycelia used to start a mushroom culture. *—v.* **spawned, spawn·ing, spawns.** *—intr.* **1.** To deposit eggs; produce spawn. **2.** To produce offspring in numbers like spawn. *—tr.* **1.** To produce (spawn). **2.** To give birth to: *a family that had spawned a monster.* **3.** To give rise to; engender: *tyranny that spawned revolt.* **4.** To bring forth; produce. **5.** To plant with mycelia. [ME *spawne* < *spawnen,* to spawn < AN *espaundre* < OFr. *espandre,* to spread < Lat. *expandere.* —see EXPAND.]

spay (spā) *tr.v.* **spayed, spay·ing, spays.** To excise the ovaries of (a female animal). [ME *spayen* < OFr. *espeer,* to cut with a sword < *espee,* sword < Lat. *spatha.* —see SPATHE.]

speak (spēk) *v.* **spoke** (spōk), **spo·ken** (spō′kən), **speak·ing, speaks.** *—intr.* **1.** To utter words with ordinary speech modulation; talk. **2. a.** To express oneself. **b.** To be on good terms: *They are no longer speaking.* **3.** To deliver an address or lecture. **4.** To convey a message: *Actions speak louder than words.* **5.** To be expressive. **6. a.** To produce a characteristic sound: *The drums spoke.* **b.** To give off a sound on firing: *The cannons spoke.* **7.** To make communicative sounds. *—tr.* **1.** To articulate in a speaking voice. **2.** To converse in or be able to converse in (a language): *speak German.* **3. a.** To express aloud; tell: *spoke the truth.* **b.** To express in writing. **4.** To show to be; reveal. **5.** *Naut.* To hail and communicate with (another vessel) at sea. ***—phrasal verbs.*** **speak down to.** To speak condescendingly to: *never spoke down to his audience.* **speak out.** To talk freely and fearlessly. **speak up.** To speak without fear or hesitation. ***—idioms.*** **so to speak.** In a manner of speaking. **speak (one's) mind.** To express one's opinion. **to speak of.** Worthy of mention: *There's nothing new to speak of.* [ME *speken* < OE *specan.*] **—speak′a·ble** *adj.*

Synonyms: *speak, talk, converse, discourse, chatter, gossip.* These verbs mean to express oneself or to communicate orally. *Speak* and *talk,* the most general, are often interchangeable. *Speak,* however, can refer to rather formal or authoritative utterance; *talk,* more often than *speak,* implies an ordinary or even idle exchange involving two or more persons. *Converse* stresses interchange of thoughts and ideas. *Discourse* usually refers to formal, extended, well-organized speech. *Chatter* refers to incessant and idle talk. *Gossip* is sometimes interchangeable with *chatter* but especially applies to unflattering or malicious talk about someone not present.

speak·eas·y (spēk′ē′zē) *n., pl.* **-ies.** A place for the illegal sale of alcoholic drinks, as during U.S. Prohibition.

speak·er (spē′kər) *n.* **1. a.** One who speaks. **b.** A spokesperson. **2.** One who delivers a public speech. **3.** Often **Speaker.** The presiding officer of a legislative assembly. **4.** A loudspeaker.

speak·ing (spē′kĭng) *adj.* **1.** Expressive or telling; eloquent. **2.** True to life; striking: *a speaking likeness.*

speaking tube *n.* A tube used for speaking from one room or building to another.

spear (spîr) *n.* **1.** A weapon consisting of a long shaft with a sharply pointed head. **2.** A shaft with a sharp point and barbs for spearing fish. **3.** A spearman. **4.** A slender stalk, as of asparagus. *—v.* **speared, spear·ing, spears.** *—tr.* **1.** To pierce with or as if with a spear. **2.** To catch with a thrust of the arm: *spear the football.* *—intr.* **1.** To stab with or as if with a spear. **2.** To sprout like a spear. [ME *spere* < OE.] **—spear′er** *n.*

spear·fish (spîr′fĭsh′) *n., pl.* **spearfish** or **-fish·es.** Either of two large marine game fishes, *Tetrapturus angustirostris* or *T. belone,* having the upper jaw elongated into a spearlike projection.

spear·head (spîr′hĕd′) *n.* **1.** The sharpened head of a spear. **2. a.** The leading forces in a military thrust. **b.** The driving force in a given action or endeavor: *He was the spearhead of the project.* *—tr.v.* **-head·ed, -head·ing, -heads.** To be the leader of (an endeavor, for example).

spear·man (spîr′mən) *n.* A soldier armed with a spear.

spear·mint (spîr′mĭnt′) *n.* An aromatic plant, *Mentha spicata,* native to Europe, having clusters of small purplish flowers and yielding an oil widely used as flavoring.

spear·wort (spîr′wûrt′, -wôrt′) *n.* Any of several plants related to the buttercups, esp. *Ranunculus flammula,* native to Eurasia, having lance-shaped leaves and yellow flowers.

spe·cial (spĕsh′əl) *adj.* **1.** Surpassing what is common or usual; exceptional: *a special occasion.* **2. a.** Distinct among others of a kind; singular. **b.** Primary: *one's special interest.* **3.** Peculiar to a specific person or thing; particular: *his own special chair.* **4. a.** Having a limited or specific function, application, or scope: *a special role in the mission.* **b.** Arranged for a particular occasion or purpose: *a special audience.* **5.** Esteemed; close: *special friends.* **6.** Additional; extra: *a special holiday flight.* *—n.* **1.** Something arranged, issued, or appropriated to a particular service or occasion: *rode to work on the commuter special.* **2.** A featured attraction, such as a reduced price: *a special on lamb chops.* **3.** A single television production that features a specific work, a given topic, or a particular performer. [ME < OFr. *especial* < Lat. *specialis* < *species,* kind. —see SPECIES.] **—spe′cial·ly** *adv.*

Usage: *Special* and *specially* have wider application than *especial* and *especially.* In the senses that it shares with *especial,* the adjective *special* is now much more commonly used. *Especial* is increasingly rare and is used chiefly to stress pre-eminence or outstanding quality: *a work of especial ingenuity.* The adverb *especially,* on the other hand, has not been similarly displaced by *specially. Specially* is used with reference to a particular purpose: *specially trained; specially arranged. Especially* is used in the sense of "particularly" or "pre-eminently": *He's especially talented. Jones especially is implicated. Prudence is the best policy, especially now.*

special act *n.* A legislative act that applies only to a particular person or area.

special court-martial *n., pl.* **special courts-martial.** A court-martial consisting of at least three officers for trying intermediate offenses.

special delivery *n.* The delivery of a piece of mail, for an additional charge, by a special messenger rather than by scheduled delivery.

special effects *pl.n.* Visual or sound effects added to a motion picture or taped television show during processing.

Special Forces *pl.n.* A division of the U.S. Army composed of soldiers specially trained in guerrilla fighting.

special handling *n.* The handling of fourth-class or parcel-post mail as first-class mail for an extra charge.

spe·cial·ism (spĕsh′ə-lĭz′əm) *n.* **1.** Confinement or limitation to a given field of study or occupation. **2.** A field of specialization.

spe·cial·ist (spĕsh′ə-lĭst) *n.* **1. a.** A person who has devoted himself to a particular branch of study or research. **b.** A physician certified to practice in a specified field. **2.** Any of several enlisted ranks in the U.S. Army that correspond to those of corporal through sergeant first class. **—spe′cial·is′tic** *adj.*

spe·ci·al·i·ty (spĕsh′ē-ăl′ĭ-tē) *n., pl.* **-ties.** **1.** A distinguishing mark or feature. **2. specialities.** Special points of consideration; particulars. **3.** *Chiefly Brit.* A specialty.

spe·cial·i·za·tion (spĕsh′ə-lĭ-zā′shən) *n.* The act of specializing or the process of becoming specialized.

spe·cial·ize (spĕsh′ə-līz′) *v.* **-ized, -iz·ing, -iz·es.** *—intr.* **1.** To train or employ oneself in a special study or activity. **2.** *Biol.* To develop so as to become adapted to a specific environment or function. **3.** To concentrate on a particular activity or product: *The shop specializes in mountain-climbing gear.* *—tr.* **1.** To make specific mention of; particularize. **2.** To give a particular character or function to. **3.** *Biol.* To adapt by specialization. **4.** To specify the payee in endorsing (a check).

special jury *n.* A jury chosen by the court upon request from a list of presumably better-qualified candidates for a case involving unusually complex issues of fact.

special pleading *n.* **1.** *Law.* The assertion of new or special matter to offset the opposing party's allegations, as an alternative to direct denial. **2.** A presentation of an argument that emphasizes only a favorable or a single aspect of the question at issue.

special relativity *n.* The physical theory of space and time developed by Albert Einstein that is based on the postulates that all the laws of physics are equally valid in all nonaccelerated frames of reference and that light is propagated rectilinearly in all directions at a constant speed and that has as consequences the relativistic mass increase of rapidly moving objects, the Lorentz contraction, time dilatation, and the principle of mass-energy equivalence.

special session *n.* An extraordinary session of a court or of a legislative body.

special theory of relativity *n.* Special relativity.

spe·cial·ty (spĕsh′əl-tē) *n., pl.* **-ties.** **1.** A special pursuit, occupation, aptitude, or skill. **2.** An aspect of medicine to which physicians confine their practice. **3.** A special feature or characteristic; peculiarity. **4.** The state or quality of being special. **5.** *Law.* A special contract or agreement, esp. a deed kept under seal.

spe·ci·a·tion (spē′shē-ā′shən, -sē-) *n.* The evolutionary process by which new species are formed. [SPECI(ES) + -ATION.]

spe·cie (spē′shē, -sē) *n.* Coined money; coin. ***—idiom.*** **in specie.** **1.** In coin. **2.** *Law.* In kind; in the same kind or shape. [Lat. *(in) specie,* (in) kind < ablative of *species.* —see SPECIES.]

spe·cies (spē′shēz, -sēz) *n., pl.* **species.** **1.** *Biol.* **a.** A fundamental category of taxonomic classification, ranking after a genus and consisting of organisms capable of interbreeding. **b.** An organism belonging to such a category, represented in taxonomic nomenclature by a Latin adjective or epithet following a genus name. **2.** *Logic.* A class of individuals or objects grouped by virtue of their common attributes and assigned a common name; a division subordinate to a genus. **3.** A kind, variety, or type. **4.** *Obs.* An outward form or appearance. 5. *Rom. Cath. Ch.* **a.** The outward appearance or form of the Eucharistic elements that is retained after their consecration. **b.** Either of the consecrated elements of the Eucharist. **6.** *Obs.* Specie. [Lat. *species,* appearance, kind < *specere,* to look at.]

spec·i·fi·a·ble (spĕs′ə-fī′ə-bəl) *adj.* Capable of being specified.

spe·cif·ic (spĭ-sĭf′ĭk) *adj.* **1.** Explicitly set forth; definite. **2.** Pertaining to, characterizing, or distinguishing a species. **3.** Special, distinctive, or unique, as a quality or attribute. **4.** Intended for, applying to, or acting upon a particular thing. **5.** Denoting a disease produced by a particular microorganism or condition. **6. a.** Denoting a customs charge levied upon merchandise by unit or weight rather than according to value. **b.** Denoting a commodity rate applicable to the transportation of a single commodity between named points. —*n.* **1.** Something specific, as a quality, statement, or attribute. **2.** A remedy intended for a particular ailment or disorder. [Med. Lat. *specificus* < Lat. *species,* kind, species.] **—spe·cif′i·cal·ly** *adv.* **—spec′i·fic′i·ty** (spĕs′ə-fĭs′ĭ-tē) *n.*

spec·i·fi·ca·tion (spĕs′ə-fĭ-kā′shən) *n.* **1.** An act of specifying. **2. a. specifications.** A detailed and exact statement of particulars, esp. a statement prescribing materials, dimensions, and workmanship for something to be built, installed, or manufactured. **b.** A single item or article that has been specified. **3.** An exact written description of an invention by an applicant for a patent.

specific gravity *n.* The ratio of the mass of a solid or liquid to the mass of an equal volume of distilled water at 4°C or of a gas to an equal volume of air or hydrogen under prescribed conditions of temperature and pressure.

specific heat *n.* **1.** The ratio of the amount of heat required to raise the temperature of a unit mass of a substance by one unit of temperature to the amount of heat required to raise the temperature of a similar mass of a reference material, usually water, by the same amount. **2.** The amount of heat, measured in calories, required to raise the temperature of one gram of a substance by one centigrade degree.

specific impulse *n.* A performance measure for rocket propellants that is equal to units of thrust per unit weight of propellant consumed per unit time.

specific performance *n. Law.* The performance of a legal contract as specified in its terms.

specific resistance *n. Elect.* Resistivity (sense 2).

specific thrust *n.* Specific impulse.

spec·i·fy (spĕs′ə-fī′) *tr.v.* **-fied, -fy·ing, -fies. 1.** To state explicitly. **2.** To include in a specification. [ME *specifien* < OFr. *specifier* < Med. Lat. *specificare* < *specificus,* specific.]

spec·i·men (spĕs′ə-mən) *n.* **1.** An individual, item, or part taken as representative of an entire set or whole; sample. **2.** A sample, as of tissue, blood, or urine, used for analysis and diagnosis. [Lat., example < *specere,* to look at.]

spe·cious (spē′shəs) *adj.* **1.** Deceptively attractive. **2.** Having the ring of truth or plausibility but actually fallacious: *a specious argument.* [ME, attractive < Lat. *speciosus* < *species,* appearance < *specere,* to look at.] **—spe′cious·ly** *adv.* **—spe′cious·ness** *n.*

speck (spĕk) *n.* **1.** A small spot, mark, or discoloration. **2.** A very small bit; particle. —*tr.v.* **specked, speck·ing, specks.** To mark with specks. [ME *specke* < OE *specca.*]

speck·le (spĕk′əl) *n.* A speck or small spot, esp. a natural dot of color on skin, plumage, or foliage. —*tr.v.* **-led, -ling, -les.** To mark or cover with or as if with speckles. [ME *spakle,* perh. of MLG orig.]

speck·led (spĕk′əld) *adj.* **1.** Dotted or covered with speckles, esp. flecked with small spots of contrasting color. **2.** Of a mixed character; motley.

speckled trout *n.* The brook trout.

specs (spĕks) *pl.n. Informal.* **1.** Also **specks.** Eyeglasses; spectacles. **2.** Specifications (sense 2.a.).

spec·ta·cle (spĕk′tə-kəl) *n.* **1.** A public performance or display. **2. a.** An object of interest. **b.** A regrettable public display, as of bad behavior: *made a spectacle of himself.* **3. a.** Something seen or capable of being seen. **b.** The sight of something. **4. spectacles. a.** Glasses (sense 4.b.). **b.** Something resembling eyeglasses in shape or suggesting them in function. [ME < OFr. < Lat. *spectaculum* < *spectare,* to watch, freq. of *specere,* to look at.]

spec·ta·cled (spĕk′tə-kəld) *adj.* **1.** Wearing spectacles. **2.** Having markings suggesting spectacles. Used of animals.

spec·tac·u·lar (spĕk-tăk′yə-lər) *adj.* Of the nature of a spectacle; sensational. —*n.* A single theatrical production of unusual length or lavishness. **—spec·tac′u·lar′i·ty** (-lăr′ĭ-tē) *n.* **—spec·tac′u·lar·ly** *adv.*

spec·ta·tor (spĕk′tā′tər) *n.* An observer of an event. [Lat. *spectator* < *spectare,* to watch. —see SPECTACLE.]

spec·ter (spĕk′tər) *n.* **1.** A phantom; apparition. **2.** A threatening or haunting possibility: *the terrible specter of nuclear war.* [Fr. *spectre* < Lat. *spectrum,* appearance < *specere,* to look at.]

spec·tra (spĕk′trə) *n.* A plural of **spectrum.**

spec·tral (spĕk′trəl) *adj.* **1.** Of or resembling a specter; ghostly. **2.** Of, pertaining to, or produced by a spectrum. **—spec·tral′i·ty** (-trăl′ĭ-tē), **spec′tral·ness** *n.* **—spec′tral·ly** *adv.*

spectral line *n.* An isolated peak of intensity in a spectrum, esp. one of the visible dispersed images of the slit through which light enters the collimator of a spectroscope, produced by light of a single wavelength.

spec·tre (spĕk′tər) *n. Chiefly Brit.* Variant of **specter.**

spectro– *pref.* Spectrum: *spectrograph.* [< SPECTRUM.]

spec·tro·gram (spĕk′trə-grăm′) *n.* A graph or photograph of a spectrum.

spec·tro·graph (spĕk′trə-grăf′) *n.* **1.** A spectroscope equipped to photograph spectra. **2.** A spectrogram. **—spec′tro·graph′ic** *adj.* **—spec′tro·graph′i·cal·ly** *adv.* **—spec·trog′ra·phy** (-trŏg′rə-fē) *n.*

spec·tro·he·li·o·gram (spĕk′trō-hē′lē-ə-grăm′) *n.* A photograph of the sun taken in a narrow wavelength band centered on a selected wavelength.

spec·tro·he·li·o·graph (spĕk′trō-hē′lē-ə-grăf′) *n.* An instrument used to make spectroheliograms. **—spec′tro·he′li·o·graph′ic** *adj.* **—spec′tro·he′li·og′ra·phy** (-ŏg′rə-fē) *n.*

spec·tro·he·li·o·scope (spĕk′trō-hē′lē-ə-skōp′) *n.* An instrument used to observe solar radiation. **—spec′tro·he′li·o·scop′ic** (-skŏp′ĭk) *adj.*

spec·trom·e·ter (spĕk-trŏm′ĭ-tər) *n.* A spectroscope equipped with scales for measuring the positions of spectral lines. [SPECTRO(SCOPE) + -METER.] **—spec′tro·met′ric** (-trə-mĕt′rĭk) *adj.* **—spec·trom′e·try** *n.*

spec·tro·pho·tom·e·ter (spĕk′trō-fō-tŏm′ĭ-tər) *n. Physics.* An instrument used to determine the distribution of energy in a spectrum of luminous radiation. **—spec′tro·pho′to·met′ric** (-fō′tə-mĕt′rĭk) *adj.* **—spec′tro·pho·tom′e·try** *n.*

spec·tro·scope (spĕk′trə-skōp′) *n.* Any of various instruments for resolving and observing or recording spectra. **—spec′tro·scop′ic** (-skŏp′ĭk), **spec′tro·scop′i·cal** *adj.* **—spec′tro·scop′i·cal·ly** *adv.*

spectroscopic analysis *n.* The analysis of a spectrum to determine characteristics of its source, as the analysis of the optical spectrum of an incandescent body to determine its composition or motion.

spec·tros·co·py (spĕk-trŏs′kə-pē) *n.* The study of spectra, esp. the experimental observation of optical spectra. **—spec·tros′co·pist** *n.*

spec·trum (spĕk′trəm) *n., pl.* **-tra** (-trə) or **-trums. 1.** *Physics.* The distribution of a characteristic of a physical system or phenomenon, esp.: **a.** The distribution of energy emitted by a radiant source, as by an incandescent body, arranged in order of wavelengths. **b.** The distribution of atomic or subatomic particles in a system, as in a magnetically resolved molecular beam, arranged in order of masses. **c.** A graphic or photographic representation of such a distribution. **2. a.** A range of values of a quantity or set of related quantities. **b.** A broad sequence or range of related qualities, ideas, or activities: *the whole spectrum of 20th-century thought.* [Lat., appearance < *specere,* to look at.]

spec·u·la (spĕk′yə-lə) *n.* A plural of **speculum.**

spec·u·lar (spĕk′yə-lər) *adj.* Of, resembling, or produced by a mirror or speculum.

spec·u·late (spĕk′yə-lāt′) *intr.v.* **-lat·ed, -lat·ing, -lates. 1.** To meditate on a given subject; reflect. **2.** To engage in the buying or selling of a commodity with an element of risk on the chance of profit. [Lat. *speculari, speculat-,* to observe < *specula,* watchtower < *specere,* to look at.]

spec·u·la·tion (spĕk′yə-lā′shən) *n.* **1. a.** The act of speculating. **b.** Contemplation of a profound nature. **c.** A conclusion, opinion, or theory reached by speculating. **2. a.** Engagement in risky business transactions on the chance of quick or considerable profit. **b.** An instance of speculating.

spec·u·la·tive (spĕk′yə-lə-tĭv, -lā′-) *adj.* **1.** Of, characterized by, or based upon contemplative speculation. **2. a.** Given to speculation or conjecture. **b.** Spent in speculation. **3. a.** Engaging in, given to, or involving financial speculation. **b.** Characteristic of speculation in the involvement of chance; risky. **—spec′u·la·tive·ly** *adv.* **—spec′u·la·tive·ness** *n.*

spec·u·la·tor (spĕk′yə-lā′tər) *n.* One that speculates.

spec·u·lum (spĕk′yə-ləm) *n., pl.* **-la** (-lə) or **-lums. 1.** A mirror or polished metal plate used as a reflector in optical instruments. **2.** An instrument for dilating the opening of a body cavity for medical examination. **3.** *Biol.* **a.** A bright, often iridescent patch of color on the wings of certain birds, esp. ducks. **b.** A transparent spot in the wings of some butterflies or moths. [Lat., mirror < *specere,* to look at.]

sped (spĕd) *v.* A past tense and past participle of **speed.**

speech (spēch) *n.* **1. a.** The faculty or act of speaking. **b.** The faculty or act of expressing or describing thoughts, feelings, or perceptions by the articulation of words. **2.** Something that is spoken; utterance. **3.** Vocal communication; conversation. **4. a.** A talk or public address. **b.** A printed copy of an address. **5.** A person's habitual manner or style of speaking. **6.** The language or dialect of a nation or region. **7.** The sounding of a musical instrument. **8.** The study of oral communication, speech sounds, and vocal physiology. **9.** *Archaic.* Rumor. [ME *speche* < OE *spǣc, sprǣc.*]

speech community *n.* All speakers of a particular language or dialect, whether located in one area or scattered.

speech·i·fy (spē′chə-fī′) *intr.v.* **-fied, -fy·ing, -fies.** To give a speech. **—speech′i·fi′er** *n.*

speech·less (spēch′lĭs) *adj.* **1.** Lacking the faculty of speech; dumb. **2.** Temporarily unable to speak, as through astonishment. **3.** Refraining from speech; silent. **4.** Unexpressed or inexpressible in words: *speechless admiration.* **—speech′less·ly** *adv.* **—speech′less·ness** *n.*
speech·mak·er (spēch′mā′kər) *n.* One who makes a speech. **—speech′mak′ing** *n.*
speed (spēd) *n.* **1.** *Math. & Physics.* The rate or a measure of the rate of motion, esp.: **a.** Distance traveled divided by the time of travel. **b.** The limit of this quotient as the time of travel becomes vanishingly small; the first derivative of distance with respect to time. **c.** The magnitude of a velocity. **2.** Swiftness of action. **3.** The act or state of moving rapidly; rapidity. **4.** A transmission gear or set of gears in a motor vehicle. **5. a.** A numerical expression of the sensitivity of a photographic film, plate, or paper to light. **b.** The capacity of a lens to accumulate light at an appropriate aperture. **c.** The length of time required or permitted for a camera shutter to open and admit light. **6.** *Slang.* Amphetamine. **7.** *Archaic.* Prosperity; luck. *—v.* **sped** (spĕd) or **speed·ed, speed·ing, speeds.** *—tr.* **1. a.** To hasten. **b.** To send or dispatch with haste. **2. a.** To increase the speed or rate of; accelerate: *speed up production.* **b.** To set the speed of (a machine). **3.** To drive (a motor vehicle) at a high or illegal rate of speed. **4. a.** To wish Godspeed to. **b.** *Archaic.* To help to succeed or prosper; aid. **c.** To further, promote, or expedite (a legal action, for example). *—intr.* **1.** To go or move rapidly. **2. a.** To drive fast. **b.** To exceed a traffic speed limit. **3.** To pass quickly: *The days sped by.* **4.** To move, perform, or happen at a faster rate; accelerate. **5.** *Obs.* **a.** To prove successful; prosper. **b.** To go well or poorly with a person; fare. [ME *spede* < OE *spēd,* success.]
Synonyms: *speed, hurry, hasten, quicken, accelerate, precipitate, expedite.* These verbs mean to move or cause to move rapidly or to increase the pace of a person or thing. *Speed* refers directly to very rapid movement. *Hurry* implies movement or action at a rate markedly faster than usual, sometimes accompanied by commotion or confusion. *Hasten* refers to stepped-up activity that increases progress or brings a desired result much closer to fulfillment. Even more than *hurry,* it stresses urgency. *Quicken* and especially *accelerate* refer to increase in rate of activity, growth, or progress. *Precipitate* implies sudden or impetuous action that causes or impels rapid movement or that causes something to happen suddenly or prematurely. *Expedite* refers to action that furthers the quick and efficient accomplishment of something or accelerates its fulfillment.
speed·ball (spēd′bôl′) *n. Slang.* An intravenous dose of cocaine and heroin.
speed·boat (spēd′bōt′) *n.* A fast motorboat.
speed·boat·ing (spēd′bō′tĭng) *n.* The act or sport of controlling a speedboat. **—speed′boat′er** *n.*
speed·er (spē′dər) *n.* One that speeds, esp. a driver who exceeds a legal or safe speed.
speed freak *n. Slang.* A habitual user of amphetamines and esp. of methamphetamine.
speed·ing (spē′dĭng) *adj.* Moving with speed. *—n.* The act of driving esp. a motor vehicle faster than is allowed by law.
speed limit *n.* The maximum speed legally permitted on a given stretch of road.
speed·om·e·ter (spĭ-dŏm′ĭ-tər, spē-) *n.* **1.** An instrument for indicating speed. **2.** An odometer.
speed-read (spēd′rēd′) *intr.v.* **-read** (-rĕd′), **-read·ing, -reads.** To practice or engage in speed-reading. **—speed′-read′er** *n.*
speed-read·ing (spēd′rē′dĭng) *n.* A method of reading rapidly by assimilating several words or phrases at a glance or by skimming.
speed shop *n.* An automotive shop that caters to hot rodders.
speed·ster (spēd′stər) *n.* **1.** A speeder. **2.** A fast car.
speed trap *n.* The deployment of concealed police officers or electronic devices on a stretch of road to catch speeders.
speed·up (spēd′ŭp′) *n.* Acceleration of production without increase in pay.
speed·way (spēd′wā′) *n.* **1.** A course for automobile racing. **2.** A road designed for fast-moving traffic; expressway.
speed·well (spēd′wĕl′) *n.* Any of various plants of the genus *Veronica,* having clusters of small, usually blue flowers.
speed·y (spē′dē) *adj.* **-i·er, -i·est. 1.** Characterized by rapid motion; swift. **2.** Accomplished or arrived at without delay; prompt. **3.** *Slang.* Of, containing, or affecting like an amphetamine. **—speed′i·ly** *adv.* **—speed′i·ness** *n.*
speiss (spīs) *n.* A basic arsenic or antimony compound of iron, often with nickel, copper, or other metals, having a metallic luster and a strong tendency to crystallize, produced during the smelting of various ores. [G. *Speise,* food < OHG *spīsa* < Med. Lat. *spesa,* provisions < Lat. *expensa,* p.part. of *expendere,* to pay out. —see EXPEND.]
spe·le·ol·o·gy (spē′lē-ŏl′ə-jē) *n.* **1.** The study of the physical, geologic, and biological aspects of caves. **2.** The exploration of caves. [Lat. *speleum,* cave (< Gk. *spēlaion*) + -LOGY.] **—spe′le·o·log′i·cal** (-ə-lŏj′ĭ-kəl) *adj.* **—spe′le·ol′o·gist** *n.*
spell[1] (spĕl) *v.* **spelled** or **spelt** (spĕlt), **spell·ing, spells.** *—tr.* **1.** To name or write in order the letters constituting (a word or part of a word). **2.** To be the letters of (a word). **3.** To mean; signify. *—intr.* To form a word or words correctly by means of letters. ***—phrasal verbs.* spell down.** To defeat in a spelldown. **spell out. 1.** To make perfectly clear and understandable. **2.** To puzzle out; comprehend by study. [ME *spellen,* to read letter by letter < OFr. *espelir,* of Germanic orig.]
spell[2] (spĕl) *n.* **1.** An incantational word or formula. **2.** A state of compelling attraction; fascination. **3.** A bewitched state; trance. *—tr.v.* **spelled, spell·ing, spells.** To put under a spell. [ME, discourse < OE, story.]
spell[3] (spĕl) *n.* **1.** A short, indefinite period of time. **2.** *Informal.* A period of weather of a particular kind: *a dry spell.* **3.** A period of work; shift. **4.** *Informal.* A period, bout, or fit of illness, indisposition, or irritability. **5.** *Informal.* A short distance. *—v.* **spelled, spell·ing, spells.** *—tr.* **1.** To relieve (someone) from work temporarily by taking a turn. **2.** To allow to rest a while. *—intr.* To rest for a time from an activity. [< ME *spelen,* to spare < OE *spelian,* to represent.]
spell·bind (spĕl′bīnd′) *tr.v.* **-bound** (-bound′), **-bind·ing, -binds.** To hold under or as if under a spell; enchant.
spell·bind·er (spĕl′bīn′dər) *n.* One that holds others spellbound, esp. a speaker or performer who enthralls an audience.
spell·bound (spĕl′bound′) *adj.* Entranced; fascinated.
spell·down (spĕl′doun′) *n.* A contest in which competitors are eliminated as they fail to spell a given word correctly.
spell·er (spĕl′ər) *n.* **1.** One who spells words. **2.** An elementary textbook that teaches spelling.
spell·ing (spĕl′ĭng) *n.* **1. a.** The forming of words with letters in an accepted order; orthography. **b.** The art or study of orthography. **2.** The way in which a word is spelled.
spelling bee *n.* A spelldown.
spelt[1] (spĕlt) *n.* A hardy wheat, *Triticum spelta,* grown mostly in Europe. [ME < OE < LLat. *spelta,* of Germanic orig.]
spelt[2] (spĕlt) *v.* A past tense and past participle of **spell[1]**.
spel·ter (spĕl′tər) *n.* Zinc, esp. in the form of ingots, slabs, or plates. [Prob. of MLG orig.]
spe·lunk·er (spĭ-lŭng′kər, spē′lŭng′-) *n.* A person who explores and studies caves; speleologist. [< obs. *spelunk,* cave < ME < Lat. *spelunca* < Gk. *spēlunx.*] **—spe′lunk′ing** *n.*
spen·cer[1] (spĕn′sər) *n. Naut.* A trysail. [Perh. < the name *Spencer.*]
spen·cer[2] (spĕn′sər) *n.* **1.** A short double-breasted overcoat worn by men in the early 19th century. **2.** A close-fitting, waist-length jacket worn by women. [After George John *Spencer* (1758–1834), 2nd Earl Spencer.]
Spen·ce·ri·an[1] (spĕn-sîr′ē-ən) *adj.* Of or pertaining to Herbert Spencer or to his philosophy. *—n.* A follower of Herbert Spencer.
Spen·ce·ri·an[2] (spĕn-sîr′ē-ən) *adj.* Of or relating to an ornate style of penmanship employing rounded letters slanted to the right. [After Platt Rogers *Spencer* (1800–1864), its inventor.]
Spen·cer·ism (spĕn′sə-rĭz′əm) also **Spen·ce·ri·an·ism** (spĕn-sîr′ē-ə-nĭz′əm) *n.* The system of logical positivism developed by Herbert Spencer, setting forth the idea that evolution is the passage from the simple, indefinite, and incoherent to the complex, definite, and coherent.
spend (spĕnd) *v.* **spent** (spĕnt), **spend·ing, spends.** *—tr.* **1.** To use up or put out; expend: *spent an hour each day exercising.* **2.** To pay out (money). **3.** To deprive of force or strength; wear out: *The storm finally spent itself.* **4.** To pass (time) in a specified manner or place: *spent her summer at the beach.* **5. a.** To throw away; squander: *spent his creativity on worthless projects.* **b.** To sacrifice. *—intr.* **1.** To pay out or expend money. **2.** *Obs.* To be exhausted or consumed. [ME *spenden,* partly < OE *spendan* (< Lat. *expendĕre,* to expend) and partly < OFr. *despendre,* to dispend.] **—spend′a·ble** *adj.* **—spend′er** *n.*
spending money *n.* Cash for small personal needs.
spend·thrift (spĕnd′thrĭft′) *n.* One who squanders money. *—adj.* Wasteful or extravagant. [SPEND + THRIFT, accumulated wealth (obs.).]
Spen·se·ri·an (spĕn-sîr′ē-ən) *adj.* Of, pertaining to, or resembling Edmund Spenser, his poetry, or his style. *—n.* A scholar of Spenser's poetry or life.
Spenserian sonnet *n.* A sonnet form comprising three interlocking quatrains and a couplet with the rhyme pattern *abab bcbc cdcd ee.* [After Edmund *Spenser* (1552–1599).]
Spenserian stanza *n.* A stanza consisting of eight lines of iambic pentameter and a final Alexandrine, rhymed *ababbcbcc,* used by Edmund Spenser in *The Faerie Queene.*
spent (spĕnt) *v.* Past tense and past participle of **spend.** *—adj.* **1.** Consumed; used up. **2.** Passed; come to an end. **3.** Depleted of energy, force, or strength; exhausted. **4.** *Naut.* Of or relating to a vessel at the end of a voyage, with fuel, stores, and water consumed and cargo discharged.
sperm[1] (spûrm) *n., pl.* **sperm** or **sperms. 1.** Spermatozoon. **2.** The male fluid of fertilization; semen. [ME *sperme,* semen < OFr. *esperme* < LLat. *sperma* < Gk.] **—sperm′ous** *adj.*
sperm[2] (spûrm) *n.* A substance, such as spermaceti, associated with the sperm whale. [Short for SPERMACETI.]
sperm- *pref.* Variant of **spermi-**.
-sperm *suff.* Seed: *endosperm.* [< Gk. *sperma,* seed.]

sperma– *pref.* Variant of **spermi-.**
sper·ma·ce·ti (spûr′mə-sē′tē, -sĕt′ē) *n.* A white, waxy substance consisting of various esters of fatty acids, obtained from the head of the sperm whale and used for making candles, ointments, and cosmetics. [ME < Med. Lat. *spermaceti* : Lat. *sperma,* semen (< Gk.) + Lat. *ceti,* genitive of *cetus,* whale (< Gk. *kētos).*]
sper·ma·ry (spûr′mə-rē) *n., pl.* **-ries.** An organ in which male gametes are formed, esp. in invertebrate animals. [NLat. *spermarium* < LLat. *sperma,* semen.]
spermat– *pref.* Variant of **spermato-.**
sper·ma·the·ca (spûr′mə-thē′kə) *n.* A receptacle for storing spermatozoa in certain female invertebrates, esp. insects. [LLat. *sperma,* semen + THECA.] **—sper′ma·the′cal** *adj.*
sper·ma·ti·a (spər-mā′shē-ə, -shə) *n.* Plural of **spermatium.**
sper·mat·ic (spər-măt′ĭk) *adj.* **1.** Of, pertaining to, or resembling sperm; spermous. **2.** Of or pertaining to a spermary.
spermatic cord *n.* A cordlike structure consisting of the vas deferens and its accompanying arteries, veins, nerves, and lymphatic vessels that passes from the abdominal cavity through the inguinal canal down into the scrotum to the back of the testicle.
spermatic fluid *n.* Semen.
sper·ma·tid (spûr′mə-tĭd) *n.* One of four haploid cells formed during mitosis in the male that develop into spermatozoa without further division.
sper·ma·ti·um (spər-mā′shē-əm, -shəm) *n., pl.* **-ti·a** (-shē-ə, -shə). A nonmotile, sporelike structure in red algae and certain fungi, generally acting as a male gamete. [NLat. < Gk. *spermation,* dim. of *sperma,* semen.] **—sper·ma′tial** (-shəl) *adj.*
spermato– or **spermat–** *pref.* **1.** Seed: *spermatophyte.* **2. a.** Sperm: *spermatic.* **b.** Spermatozoon: *spermatophore.* [< Gk. *sperma, spermat-,* seed.]
sper·mat·o·cide (spər-măt′ə-sīd′) *n.* An agent that kills sperm. **—sper·mat′o·cid′al** (-sīd′l) *adj.*
sper·mat·o·cyte (spər-măt′ə-sīt′) *n.* A diploid cell that is converted by meiotic division into four spermatids.
sper·mat·o·gen·e·sis (spər-măt′ə-jĕn′ĭ-sĭs) *n.* The generation of sperm by male meiosis and spermiogenesis. **—sper·mat′o·ge·net′ic** (-jə-nĕt′ĭk), **sper·mat′o·gen′ic** (-jĕn′ĭk) *adj.*
sper·mat·o·go·ni·um (spər-măt′ə-gō′nē-əm) *n., pl.* **-ni·a** (-nē-ə). Any of the cells of the gonads in male animals that are the progenitors of primary spermatocytes. **—sper·mat′o·go′ni·al** *adj.*
sper·ma·toid (spûr′mə-toid′) *adj.* Resembling sperm.
sper·mat·o·phore (spər-măt′ə-fôr′, -fōr′) *n.* An extruded mass or capsule of spermatozoa in certain invertebrates and primitive vertebrates. **—sper′ma·toph′o·ral** (spûr′mə-tŏf′ər-əl) *adj.*
sper·mat·o·phyte (spər-măt′ə-fīt′) *n.* Any of a group of plants of the division Spermatophyta, which includes all seed-bearing plants. **—sper·mat′o·phyt′ic** (-fĭt′ĭk) *adj.*
sper·mat·or·rhe·a also **sper·mat·or·rhoe·a** (spər-măt′ə-rē′ə) *n.* Involuntary seminal discharge without orgasm.
sper·mat·o·zo·a (spər-măt′ə-zō′ə, spûr′mə-tə-) *n.* Plural of **spermatozoon.**
sper·mat·o·zo·id (spər-măt′ə-zō′ĭd, spûr′mə-tə-) *n.* A ciliated male gamete produced in an antheridium. *—adj.* Resembling a spermatozoon. [SPERMATOZO(ON) + -ID.]
sper·mat·o·zo·on (spər-măt′ə-zō′ŏn′, -ən, spûr′mə-tə-) *n., pl.* **-zo·a** (-zō′ə). The fertilizing gamete of a male animal, usually a long nucleated cell with a thin, motile tail. **—sper·mat′o·zo′al, sper·mat′o·zo′an, sper·mat′o·zo′ic** *adj.*
spermi– or **sperma–** or **spermo–** or **sperm–** *pref.* **1.** Seed: *spermophile.* **2.** Sperm: *spermine.* [Gk. *sperm-, spermo-* < *sperma,* seed.]
sper·mi·cide (spûr′mĭ-sīd′) *n.* A spermatocide. **—sper′mi·cid′al** (-sīd′l) *adj.*
sper·mine (spûr′mēn′) *n.* A crystalline compound, $C_{10}H_{26}N_4$, found as a phosphate in semen, yeast, and ox pancreas.
sper·mi·o·gen·e·sis (spûr′mē-ō-jĕn′ĭ-sĭs) *n.* The transformation of a spermatid into a spermatozoon. [NLat. *spermium,* spermatozoon, prob. < Lat. *sperma,* semen + -GENESIS.]
spermo– *pref.* Variant of **spermi-.**
sper·mo·go·ni·um (spûr′mə-gō′nē-əm) *n., pl.* **-ni·a** (-nē-ə). *Bot.* A hollow structure in which spermatia are formed.
sperm oil *n.* A yellow, waxy oil obtained chiefly from the head of the sperm whale and used as an industrial lubricant.
sperm·o·phile (spûr′mə-fīl′) *n.* Any of various North American ground squirrels of the genus *Citellus* (or *Spermophilus*).
sperm whale *n.* A whale, *Physeter catodon,* having a very large head with cavities containing sperm oil and spermaceti and a long, narrow, toothed lower jaw.
sper·ry·lite (spĕr′ĭ-līt′) *n.* A white crystalline platinum mineral, essentially $PtAs_2$. [After F.L. *Sperry,* 19th-cent. Canadian mineralogist.]
spes·sar·tite (spĕs′ər-tīt′) also **spes·sar·tine** (-tēn′) *n.* A mineral silicate of manganese and aluminum, usually containing some iron. [Fr., after *Spessart,* a hilly area in West Germany.]
spew (spyo͞o) *v.* **spewed, spew·ing, spews.** *—tr.* **1.** To vomit or cast out through the mouth. **2.** To force out in a stream; eject: *a volcano spewing molten lava; spewed invective upon his opponent.* *—intr.* To vomit. *—n.* Something that is spewed; vomit. [ME *spewen* < OE *spiwan.*]
sphag·num (sfăg′nəm) *n.* Any of various pale or ashy mosses of the genus *Sphagnum,* whose decomposed remains form peat. [NLat. < Lat. *sphagnos,* a kind of moss < Gk.] **—sphag′nous** *adj.*
sphal·er·ite (sfăl′ə-rīt′) *n.* A yellow, brown, black, or red zinc ore, essentially ZnS with some cadmium, iron, and manganese. [G. *Sphalerit* < Gk. *sphaleros,* slippery < *sphallein,* to trip.]
sphen– *pref.* Variant of **spheno-.**
sphene (sfēn) *n.* A titanium ore, chiefly $CaTiSiO_5$, sometimes used as a gemstone. [Fr. *sphène* < Gk. *sphēn,* wedge.]
sphe·nic (sfē′nĭk) *adj.* Shaped like a wedge.
spheno– or **sphen–** *pref.* Wedge; wedge-shaped: *sphenodon.* [< Gk. *sphēn,* wedge.]
sphe·no·don (sfē′nə-dŏn′, sfĕn′ə-) *n.* The tuatara.
sphe·no·gram (sfē′nə-gram′, sfĕn′ə-) *n.* A cuneiform character.
sphe·noid (sfē′noid′) *n.* The sphenoid bone. *—adj.* **1.** Wedge-shaped. **2.** Of or pertaining to the sphenoid bone. **—sphe·noi′dal** (-noid′l) *adj.*
sphenoid bone *n.* A compound bone with winglike processes, situated at the base of the skull.
spher– *pref.* Variant of **sphero-.**
spher·al (sfîr′əl) *adj.* **1.** Of, pertaining to, or having the shape of a sphere; spherical. **2.** Symmetrical.
sphere (sfîr) *n.* **1.** *Math.* A three-dimensional surface all points of which are equidistant from a fixed point. **2.** A spherical object or figure. **3.** A planet, star, or other heavenly body. **4.** The sky, appearing as a hemisphere to an observer: *the sphere of the heavens.* **5.** Any of a series of concentric, transparent, revolving globes that together were once thought to contain the moon, sun, planets, and stars. **6.** The extent of a person's knowledge, interests, or social position. **7.** An area of power, control, or influence; domain. *—tr.v.* **sphered, spher·ing, spheres. 1.** To form into a sphere. **2.** To put in or within a sphere. **3.** To surround or encompass. [ME *spere* < OFr. *espere* < Lat. *sphaera,* ball < Gk. *sphaira.*] **—sphe·ric′i·ty** (sfĭ-rĭs′ĭ-tē) *n.*
sphere of influence *n.* A territorial area over which political or economic influence is wielded by one nation.
spher·i·cal (sfîr′ĭ-kəl, sfĕr′-) also **spher·ic** (sfîr′ĭk, sfĕr′-) *adj.* **1. a.** Having the shape of a sphere; globular. **b.** Having a shape approximating that of a sphere. **2.** Of or pertaining to a sphere. **3.** Of or pertaining to heavenly bodies; celestial. **—spher′i·cal·ly** *adv.* **—spher′i·cal·ness** *n.*
spherical aberration *n.* An optical defect of refracting and reflecting spherical surfaces in which light rays from one axial point, incident on the surface at different distances from the optical axis, do not come to a common focus.
spherical angle *n.* The angle formed at the intersection of the arcs of two great circles.
spherical astronomy *n.* The branch of astronomy dealing with positions on the celestial sphere.
spher·i·cal-co·or·di·nate system (sfîr′ĭ-kəl-kō-ôr′dn-ĭt, -āt′, sfĕr′-) *n.* A three-dimensional system for locating points in space by means of a radius vector and two angles measured from the center of a sphere with respect to two arbitrary, fixed, perpendicular directions.
spherical excess *n.* The difference between the sum of the angles of a spherical triangle and the sum of the angles of a plane triangle.
spherical geometry *n.* The geometry of circles, angles, and figures on the surface of a sphere.
spherical polygon *n.* A part of a spherical surface that is bounded by arcs of three or more great circles.
spherical triangle *n.* A triangle the three sides of which are arcs of great circles.
spherical trigonometry *n.* The modified form of trigonometry applied to spherical triangles.
spher·ics (sfîr′ĭks, sfĕr′-) *n.* *(used with a sing. verb).* **1. a.** Spherical geometry. **b.** Spherical trigonometry. **2.** Variant of **sferics.**
sphero– or **spher–** *pref.* Sphere: *spherometer.* [Lat. *sphaero-* < Gk. *sphairo-,* sphere.]
sphe·roid (sfîr′oid′, sfĕr′-) *n.* An ellipsoid that is generated by revolving an ellipse around one of its axes. **—sphe·roi′dal** (-oid′l), **sphe·roi′dic** (-oi′dĭk) *adj.* **—sphe·roi′dal·ly** *adv.* **—sphe′roi·dic′i·ty** (-oi-dĭs′ĭ-tē) *n.*
sphe·rom·e·ter (sfĭ-rŏm′ĭ-tər) *n.* An instrument for measuring the curvature of a surface, as of a sphere or cylinder.
spher·ule (sfîr′o͞ol, -yo͞ol, sfĕr′-) *n.* A miniature sphere; globule. [LLat. *sphaerula,* dim. of Lat. *sphaera,* ball < Gk. *sphaira.*] **—spher′u·lar** (sfîr′yə-lər, sfĕr′-) *adj.*
spher·u·lite (sfîr′yə-līt′, -ə-līt′, sfĕr′-) *n.* A small, usually spheroid crystalline body having a radiating structure and found in obsidian and other silicic lava flows. [SPHERUL(E) + -ITE.] **—spher′u·lit′ic** (-lĭt′ĭk) *adj.*
spher·y (sfîr′ē) *adj.* **-i·er, -i·est. 1.** Of or pertaining to the celestial spheres. **2.** Resembling a heavenly body; starlike.
sphinc·ter (sfĭngk′tər) *n.* A ringlike muscle that normally maintains constriction of a bodily passage or orifice and that relaxes as required by normal physiological function-

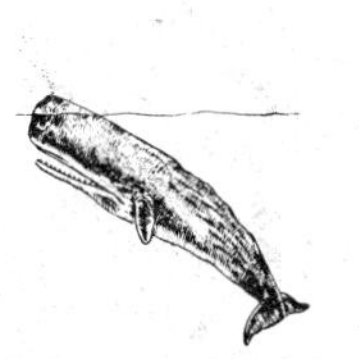

sperm whale

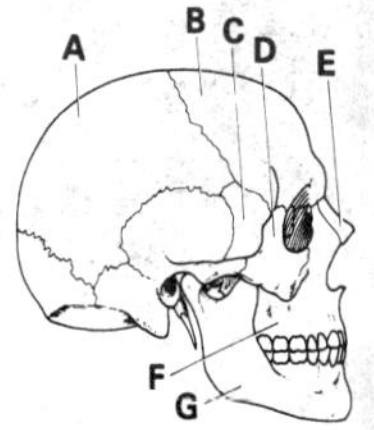

sphenoid
A. Parietal
B. Frontal
C. Sphenoid
D. Zygomatic
E. Nasal
F. Maxilla
G. Mandible

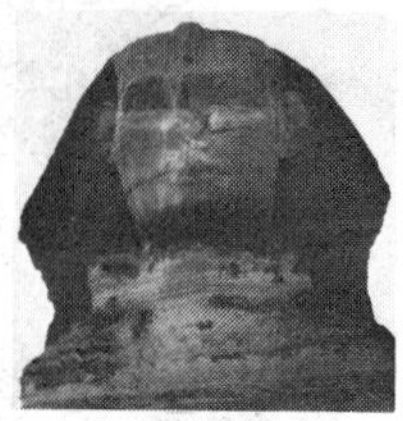

sphinx

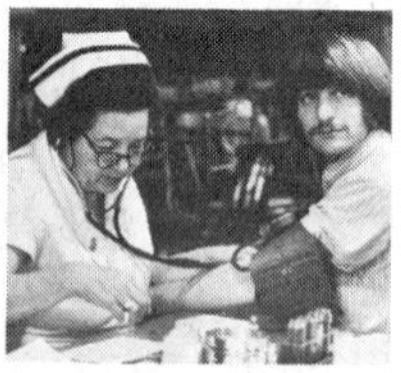

sphygmomanometer

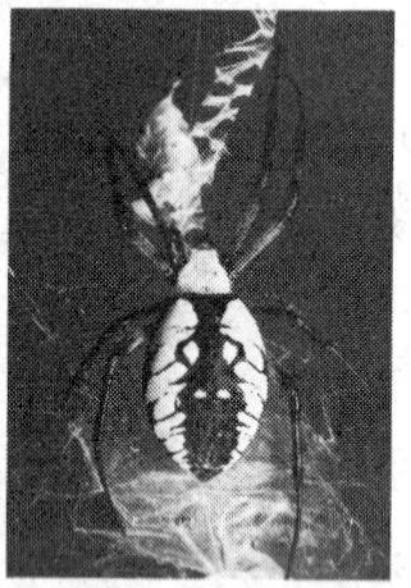

spider
Argiope

spider monkey

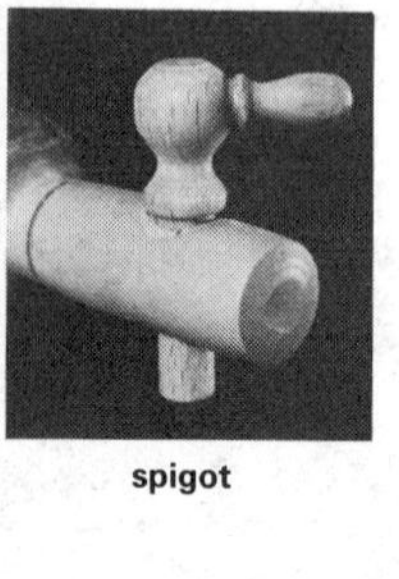

spigot

ing. [LLat. < Gk. *sphinkter* < *sphingein,* to bind tight.] **—sphinc'ter·al** *adj.*

sphinx (sfĭngks) *n., pl.* **sphinx·es** or **sphin·ges** (sfĭn'jēz'). **1.** *Egyptian Myth.* A figure having the body of a lion and the head of a man, ram, or hawk. **2.** *Gk. Myth.* A winged monster having the head of a woman and the body of a lion that destroyed all who could not answer its riddle. **3.** An enigmatic person. [ME *spynx* < Lat. *sphinx* < Gk.]

sphinx moth *n.* The hawk moth.

sphra·gis·tics (sfrə-jĭs'tĭks) *n. (used with a sing. verb).* The study of seals and signets. [Fr. *sphragistique* < LGk. *sphragistikos* < Gk. *sphragis,* seal.]

sphygm– *pref.* Variant of **sphygmo-**.

sphyg·mic (sfĭg'mĭk) *adj. Physiol.* Of or pertaining to the pulse. [Gk. *sphugmikos* < *sphugmos,* pulsation < *sphuzein,* to throb.]

sphygmo– or **sphygm–** *pref.* Pulse: *sphygmograph.* [< Gk. *sphugmos,* pulsation.]

sphyg·mo·gram (sfĭg'mə-grăm') *n.* The record or tracing produced by a sphygmograph.

sphyg·mo·graph (sfĭg'mə-grăf') *n.* An instrument for graphically recording the character and variations of the arterial pulse. **—sphyg'mo·graph'ic** *adj.* **—sphyg·mog'ra·phy** (-mŏg'rə-fē) *n.*

sphyg·moid (sfĭg'moid') *adj. Physiol.* Resembling a pulse; pulselike.

sphyg·mo·ma·nom·e·ter (sfĭg'mō-mə-nŏm'ĭ-tər) also **sphyg·mom·e·ter** (sfĭg-mŏm'ĭ-tər) *n.* An instrument for measuring blood pressure in the arteries. **—sphyg'mo·man'o·met'ric** (-măn'ə-mĕt'rĭk) *adj.* **—sphyg'mo·man'o·met'ri·cal·ly** *adv.* **—sphyg'mo·ma·nom'e·try** *n.*

spic also **spick** (spĭk) *n. Offensive Slang.* A Spanish-speaking person. [Alteration of obs. *spig,* Mexican.]

spi·ca (spī'kə) *n., pl.* **-cae** (-kē') or **-cas**. A bandage applied in overlapping opposite spirals to immobilize a digit or limb. [Lat., ear of grain.]

Spi·ca (spī'kə) *n.* The brightest star in the constellation Virgo, 212 light-years distant from Earth. [Lat. < *spica,* ear of grain.]

spi·cae (spī'kē') *n.* A plural of **spica**.

spic-and-span (spĭk'ən-spăn') *adj.* Variant of **spick-and-span**.

spi·cate (spī'kāt') *adj.* Borne in or forming a spike. [Lat. *spicatus,* p.part. of *spicare,* to provide with spikes < *spica,* ear of grain.]

spic·ca·to (spĭ-kä'tō) *Mus.* —*n., pl.* **-tos**. A technique of bowing in which the bow is made to bounce slightly from the string. —*adj.* Of or employing spiccato. [Ital., p.part. of *spiccare,* to separate.]

spice (spīs) *n.* **1. a.** Any of various aromatic and pungent vegetable substances, such as cinnamon or nutmeg, used to flavor foods or beverages. **b.** These substances as a group. **2.** Something that adds zest or flavor. **3.** A pungent aroma; perfume. —*tr.v.* **spiced, spic·ing, spic·es. 1.** To season with spices. **2.** To add zest or flavor to. [ME < OFr. *espice* < LLat. *species,* wares, spices < Lat., kind < *specere,* to look at.]

spice·ber·ry (spīs'bĕr'ē) *n.* Any of various plants or shrubs having spicy berries, such as the wintergreen.

spice·bush (spīs'bo͝osh') *n.* **1.** An aromatic shrub, *Lindera benzoin,* of eastern North America, having clusters of small, early-blooming yellow flowers. **2.** An aromatic shrub, *Calycanthus occidentalis,* of California, having fragrant, brownish flowers.

spic·er·y (spī'sə-rē) *n., pl.* **-ies**. **1.** Spices as a group. **2.** The aromatic or pungent quality of spices. **3.** *Obs.* A place where spices are stored.

spick (spĭk) *n.* Variant of **spic**.

spick-and-span also **spic-and-span** (spĭk'ən-spăn') *adj.* **1.** Neat and clean; spotless. **2.** Brand-new; fresh. [Short for obs. *spick and spannew* : *spick,* spike + SPANNEW.]

spic·u·la[1] (spĭk'yə-lə) *n.* Plural of **spiculum**.

spic·u·la[2] (spĭk'yə-lə) *n.* Variant of **spicule**.

spic·ule (spĭk'yo͞ol) also **spic·u·la** (-yə-lə) *n., pl.* **-ules** also **-u·lae** (-yə-lē'). A small needlelike structure or part, such as one of the silicate or calcium carbonate processes supporting the soft tissue of certain invertebrates, esp. sponges. [Lat. *spiculum,* spiculum.] **—spic'u·lar** (-yə-lər), **spic'u·late** (-yə-lĭt, -lāt') *adj.*

spic·u·lum (spĭk'yə-ləm) *n., pl.* **-la** (-lə). A spicule or similar needlelike structure. [Lat. *spiculum,* dim. of *spica,* point.]

spic·y (spī'sē) *adj.* **-i·er, -i·est. 1.** Having the characteristics of spice, such as flavor and aroma. **2.** Piquant; zesty. **3.** Slightly scandalous; risqué: *spicy stories.* **—spic'i·ly** *adv.* **—spic'i·ness** *n.*

spi·der (spī'dər) *n.* **1.** Any of numerous arachnids of the order Araneae, having eight legs, a body divided into a cephalothorax and an abdomen, and several spinnerets that produce silk used to make nests, cocoons, or webs for trapping insects. **2.** One that is considered similar to a spider, as in appearance, character, or movement. **3.** A cast-iron frying pan with a long handle, originally equipped with short legs. **4.** A trivet. [ME *spither* < OE *spīðra.*]

spider crab *n.* Any of various crabs, such as those of the genera *Libinia* and *Macrocheira,* having long legs and a relatively small body.

spi·der·flow·er (spī'dər-flou'ər) *n.* The cleome.

spider lily *n.* Any of various chiefly tropical American plants of the genus *Hymenocallis,* having narrow leaves and clusters of white flowers.

spider monkey *n.* Any of several tropical American monkeys of the genus *Ateles,* having long legs and a long prehensile tail.

spi·der·wort (spī'dər-wûrt', -wôrt') *n.* Any of various New World plants of the genus *Tradescantia,* esp. *T. virginiana,* having three-petaled blue or purple flowers.

spi·der·y (spī'də-rē) *adj.* **1.** Resembling a spider. **2. a.** Resembling a spider's legs; long and slender. **b.** Resembling a spider's web; very fine. **3.** Infested with spiders.

spied (spīd) *v.* Past tense and past participle of **spy**.

spie·gel (spē'gəl) *n.* Spiegeleisen. [Short for SPIEGELEISEN.]

spie·gel·ei·sen (spē'gə-lī'zən) *n.* An alloy of iron with approximately 15 per cent manganese and small quantities of carbon and silicon, used in the Bessemer process. [G. *Spiegel,* mirror (< Lat. *speculum*) + *Eisen,* iron.]

spiel (spēl) *Slang.* —*n.* A lengthy, usually extravagant speech or argument intended to persuade. —*v.* **spieled, spiel·ing, spiels.** —*intr.* To talk at length or extravagantly. —*tr.* To say at length or extravagantly. [G., play.] **—spiel'er** *n.*

spies (spīz) *v.* Third person singular present tense of **spy**. —*n.* Plural of **spy**.

spif·fy (spĭf'ē) *adj.* **-fi·er, -fi·est.** *Slang.* Smart in appearance or dress; stylish. [Orig. unknown.] **—spif'fi·ness** *n.*

spig·ot (spĭg'ət) *n.* **1.** A faucet. **2.** The vent plug of a cask. **3.** A wooden faucet placed in the bunghole of a cask. [ME.]

spike[1] (spīk) *n.* **1. a.** A long, thick, sharp-pointed piece of wood or metal. **b.** A heavy nail. **2. a.** A sharp-pointed projection along the top of a fence or wall. **b.** One of several sharp metal projections set in the sole or sole and heel of an athletic shoe for grip. **c. spikes.** A pair of athletic shoes having spikes. **3. spikes.** Shoes having spike heels. **4.** An unbranched antler of a young deer. **5.** A small young mackerel. **6. a.** The act of driving a volleyball at a sharp angle into the opponent's court by jumping near the net and hitting the ball down hard from above. **b.** *Informal.* The act of excitedly slamming a football to the ground after scoring a touchdown or making a big play. —*tr.v.* **spiked, spik·ing, spikes. 1.** To secure or provide with a spike. **2.** To impale, pierce, or injure with a spike. **3.** To render (a muzzleloading gun) useless by driving a spike into the vent. **4.** To put an end to; block: *spike a scheme.* **5.** *Slang.* To add alcoholic liquor to. **6.** To drive (a volleyball or football) in a spike. [ME *spyk,* perh. of Scand. or MLG orig.]

spike[2] (spīk) *n.* **1.** An ear of grain. **2.** *Bot.* A usually elongated inflorescence with stalkless or nearly stalkless flowers arranged along an axis. [ME *spik* < Lat. *spica,* ear of grain.]

spike heel *n.* A very high thin heel used on a woman's shoe.

spike lavender *n.* An aromatic plant, *Lavandula latifolia,* of southern Europe, yielding an oil similar to that of true lavender.

spike·let (spīk'lĭt) *n.* A small or secondary spike, esp. one of those forming the inflorescence of grasses or similar plants.

spike·nard (spīk'närd') *n.* **1.** An aromatic plant, *Nardostachys jatamansi,* of India, having rose-purple flowers. **2.** A costly ointment of antiquity, probably prepared from the spikenard. **3.** A North American plant, *Aralia racemosa,* having small, greenish flowers and an aromatic root. [ME < Med. Lat. *spica nardi,* spike of a nard.]

spik·y (spī'kē) *adj.* **-i·er, -i·est.** Having a projecting sharp point. **—spik'i·ly** *adv.* **—spik'i·ness** *n.*

spile (spīl) *n.* **1.** A post used as a foundation; pile. **2.** A wooden plug; bung. **3.** A spigot used in taking sap from a tree. —*tr.v.* **spiled, spil·ing, spiles.** To support, plug, or tap with a spile. [MLG *spīle,* wooden peg.]

spill[1] (spĭl) *v.* **spilled** or **spilt** (spĭlt), **spill·ing, spills.** —*tr.* **1.** To cause or allow (a substance) to run or fall out of a container. **2.** To shed (blood). **3.** To let the wind out of (a sail). **4.** To cause to fall: *The horse spilled its rider.* **5.** *Informal.* To divulge: *spilled all he knew about her.* —*intr.* **1.** To run or fall out of a container. **2.** To come to the ground suddenly and involuntarily. **3.** To pour out or spread beyond limits: *The fans spilled onto the playing field.* —*n.* **1.** An act of spilling. **2.** The amount spilled. **3.** A fall, as from a horse. —***idiom.*** **spill the beans.** *Informal.* To divulge all. [ME *spillen,* to kill < OE *spillan.*] **—spill'er** *n.*

spill[2] (spĭl) *n.* **1.** A piece of wood or rolled paper used to light a fire. **2.** A small peg used as a plug; spile. [MLG *spīle,* wooden peg.]

spill·age (spĭl'ĭj) *n.* **1.** An act of spilling. **2.** The amount spilled.

spil·li·kin (spĭl'ĭ-kĭn) *n.* **1.** A jackstraw. **2. spillikins.** Jackstraws. [Perh. < obs. Du. *spelleken,* small peg.]

spill·way (spĭl'wā') *n.* A channel for an overflow of water, as from a reservoir.

spilt (spĭlt) *v.* A past tense and past participle of **spill**[1].

spilth (spĭlth) *n.* Spillage. [< SPILL.]

spin (spĭn) *v.* **spun** (spŭn), **spin·ning, spins.** —*tr.* **1. a.** To draw out and twist (fibers) into thread. **b.** To form (thread or yarn) in this manner. **2.** To form (a web, for example) by extruding viscous filaments. **3.** To make or produce by or as if by drawing out and twisting. **4.** To prolong or extend.

5. To relate, esp. imaginatively: *spun tales for the children.* **6.** To cause to rotate swiftly; twirl. —*intr.* **1.** To make thread or yarn by drawing out and twisting fibers. **2.** To extrude viscous filaments, forming thread. Used of an insect. **3.** To rotate rapidly; whirl. **4.** To seem to be whirling, as from dizziness; reel. **5.** To ride or drive rapidly. **6.** To fish with spinning tackle. ***—phrasal verb.* spin off.** To derive (a product, for example) from something larger and more or less unrelated. —*n.* **1.** The act of spinning. **2.** A swift whirling motion. **3.** A state of mental confusion. **4.** *Informal.* A short drive in a vehicle. **5.** The flight condition of an aircraft in a nose-down, spiraling, stalled descent. **6.** *Physics.* **a.** The intrinsic angular momentum of a subatomic particle. **b.** The total angular momentum of an atomic nucleus. **c.** A nonnegative integral or half-integral quantum number that specifies the value of such momenta in units of Planck's constant divided by 2π. [ME *spinnen* < OE *spinnan.*]

spin·ach (spĭn′ĭch) *n.* **1.** A widely cultivated plant, *Spinacia oleracea,* native to Asia, having succulent, edible leaves. **2.** The leaves of the spinach, eaten as a vegetable. [OFr. *espinache* < OSp. *espinaca* < Ar. *isfānākh.*]

spi·nal (spī′nəl) *adj.* **1.** Of, pertaining to, or situated near the spine or spinal cord; vertebral. **2.** Resembling a spine or spinous part. —*n.* A spinal anesthetic. **—spi′nal·ly** *adv.*

spinal anesthesia *n.* Partial or complete anesthesia produced by injecting an anesthetic substance into the spinal canal.

spinal canal *n.* The canal formed by the successive openings in the vertebrae through which the spinal cord and its membranes pass.

spinal column *n.* The columnar assemblage of articulated vertebrae extending from the cranium to the coccyx or the end of the tail, encasing the spinal cord and forming the supporting axis of the body; backbone.

spinal cord *n.* The part of the central nervous system contained within the spinal canal and continuous at its cranial end with the medulla oblongata.

spinal meningitis *n. Pathol.* Cerebrospinal meningitis.

spin·dle (spĭn′dl) *n.* **1. a.** A notched stick for spinning fibers into thread by hand. **b.** A pin or rod holding a bobbin or spool on which thread is wound on a spinning wheel or spinning machine. **2.** Any of various slender mechanical parts that revolve or serve as axes for larger revolving parts, as in a lock or an axle. **3.** *Biol.* The axis between cytoplasm centers, along which the chromosomes are distributed in mitosis. —*v.* **-dled, -dling, -dles.** —*tr.* To impale or perforate on the spike of a spindle: *Do not fold, spindle, or mutilate this card.* —*intr.* To grow into a thin, elongated, or weakly form. [ME *spindel* < OE *spinel.*]

spin·dle-legs (spĭn′dl-lĕgz′) *pl.n.* Long, thin legs.

spindle tree *n.* Any of various shrubs or trees of the genus *Euonymus,* many species of which have brightly colored fruit. [So called because the wood is often used to make spindles.]

spin·dling (spĭnd′lĭng) *adj.* Spindly.

spin·dly (spĭnd′lē) *adj.* **-dli·er, -dli·est. 1.** Slender and elongated. **2.** Of weak growth.

spin·drift (spĭn′drĭft′) *n.* Wind-blown sea spray. [Var. of SPOONDRIFT.]

spine (spīn) *n.* **1.** The spinal column of a vertebrate. **2.** *Zool.* Any of various pointed projections, processes, or appendages of animals. **3.** *Bot.* A sharp-pointed, usually woody process arising from the stem of a plant; thorn. **4.** The hinged back of a book. **5.** Something that resembles a spine. [ME < OFr. *espine* < Lat. *spina.*]

spi·nel also **spi·nelle** (spĭ-nĕl′) *n.* Any of several hard white, orange, red, green, blue, or black minerals with composition $MgAl_2O_4$, the red variety being valued as a gem. [Ital. *spinella,* dim. of *spina,* thorn (from its sharply pointed crystals) < Lat. *spina.*]

spine·less (spīn′lĭs) *adj.* **1.** Lacking a vertebral column. **2.** Having no spiny processes. **3.** Lacking in courage or will power. **—spine′less·ly** *adv.* **—spine′less·ness** *n.*

spi·nelle (spĭ-nĕl′). Variant of **spinel.**

spi·nes·cent (spī-nĕs′ənt) *adj. Biol.* **1.** Having a spine. **2.** Having or tending toward the form of a spine. [LLat. *spinescens, spinescent-,* pr.part. of *spinescere,* to become thorny < Lat. *spina,* thorn.] **—spi·nes′cence** *n.*

spin·et (spĭn′ĭt) *n.* **1.** A small, compact upright piano. **2.** A small harpsichord with a single keyboard. [Obs. Fr. *espinette* < Ital. *spinetta.*]

spi·nif·er·ous (spī-nĭf′ər-əs) *adj.* Spine-bearing; spiny. [< Lat. *spinifer* < *spina,* thorn.]

spi·ni·fex (spī′nə-fĕks′) *n.* Any of various Australian grasses, chiefly of the genus *Spinifex,* growing in arid regions and having spiny leaves or seeds. [NLat. *Spinifex,* genus name : Lat. *spina,* thorn + Lat. *facere,* to make.]

spin·na·ker (spĭn′ə-kər) *n.* A large triangular sail set on a spar that swings out opposite the mainsail, used on racing yachts when running before the wind. [Orig. unknown.]

spin·ner (spĭn′ər) *n.* **1.** One that spins. **2.** An angler's lure that spins rapidly. **3.** A fairing fitted over the hub of the propeller in some aircraft. **4.** A device consisting of a dial and an arrow that is spun to indicate the next move in a board game.

spin·ner·et (spĭn′ə-rĕt′) *n.* **1.** *Zool.* A posterior structure in spiders and certain insect larvae, containing passages through which silky filaments are secreted. **2.** A device for making rayon, nylon, and other synthetic fibers, consisting of a plate pierced with holes through which plastic material is extruded in filaments.

spin·ner·y (spĭn′ə-rē) *n., pl.* **-ies.** A spinning mill.

spin·ney (spĭn′ē) *n., pl.* **-neys.** *Chiefly Brit.* A small grove; copse. [OFr. *espinei,* thicket < Lat. *spinetum,* thorn hedge < *spina,* thorn.]

spin·ning (spĭn′ĭng) *n.* The process of making fibrous material into yarn or thread.

spinning frame *n.* A machine that draws and twists fibers into yarn and winds it on spindles.

spinning jenny *n.* An early form of spinning machine having several spindles.

spinning wheel *n.* An apparatus for making yarn or thread, consisting of a foot- or hand-driven wheel and a single spindle.

spin-off (spĭn′ôf′, -ŏf′) *n.* **1.** Something, as a product, derived from something larger and more or less unrelated; by-product. **2.** Something derived from an earlier work, esp. a television show starring a character who had a popular minor role in an earlier show.

spi·nose (spī′nōs′) *adj.* Bearing spines; spiny: *a spinose plant.* [Lat. *spinosus* < *spina,* thorn.] **—spi′nose′ly** *adv.* **—spi·nos′i·ty** (-nŏs′ĭ-tē) *n.*

spi·no·tec·tal (spī′nō-tĕk′təl) *adj.* Of or pertaining to the spinal cord and the tectum.

spi·nous (spī′nəs) *adj.* **1.** Resembling a spine or thorn. **2.** Having spines or similar projections; spiny.

spinous process *n.* The rearward projection from the arch of a vertebra, that with those of the other vertebrae forms the spine.

spin·ster (spĭn′stər) *n.* **1.** A woman who has remained single beyond the conventional age for marrying. **2.** A single woman. **3.** A woman whose occupation is spinning. [ME *spinnester* < *spinnen,* to spin.] **—spin′ster·hood′** *n.* **—spin′ster·ish** *adj.*

spin·thar·i·scope (spĭn-thăr′ĭ-skōp′) *n.* A device for observing individual scintillations produced by ionizing radiation, consisting of a tube with a magnifying lens at one end and a phosphorescent screen and a speck of radioactive salt at the other. [Gk. *spintharis,* spark + SCOPE.] **—spin·thar′i·scop′ic** (-skŏp′ĭk) *adj.*

spin-the-bot·tle (spĭn′*th*ə-bŏt′l) *n.* A game in which a spinning bottle is used to determine one's partner, as for kissing.

spi·nule (spĭn′yo͞ol) *n.* A small spine or thorn. [Lat. *spinula,* dim. of *spina,* thorn.]

spi·nu·lose (spĭn′yə-lōs′) also **spi·nu·lous** (spī′nyə-ləs) *adj.* **1.** Having spinules; minutely spiny. **2.** Shaped like a spinule.

spin wave *n.* A sinusoidal wave of quantized energy propagated through a substance as a result of shifts in atomic magnetic fields as a response to outside stimuli.

spin·y (spī′nē) *adj.* **-i·er, -i·est. 1.** Bearing or covered with spines, thorns, or similar stiff projections. **2.** Shaped like a spine. **3.** Difficult; troublesome. **—spin′i·ness** *n.*

spiny anteater *n.* The echidna.

spin·y-finned (spī′nē-fĭnd′) *adj.* Having fins supported by sharp, spiny, inflexible rays.

spin·y-head·ed worm (spī′nē-hĕd′ĭd) *n.* Any of various worms of the phylum Acanthocephala that are endoparasitic to vertebrates and are characterized by an anterior cylindrical retractile proboscis that bears many rows of hooks.

spiny lobster *n.* Any of various edible marine decapod crustaceans of the family Palinuridae, having a spiny carapace and lacking the large pincers characteristic of true lobsters.

spin·y-rayed (spī′nē-rād′) *adj.* Spiny-finned.

spir·a·cle (spĭr′ə-kəl, spī′rə-) *n.* **1.** *Zool.* A respiratory aperture, esp.: **a.** Any of several tracheal openings in the exoskeleton of an insect or spider. **b.** A small respiratory opening behind the eye of fishes, such as sharks, rays, and skates. **c.** The blowhole of a cetacean. **2.** *Geol.* A small volcanic vent formed by gases on a lava flow. **3.** An aperture or opening through which air is admitted and expelled. [Lat. *spiraculum,* breathing hole < *spirare,* to breathe.] **—spi·rac′u·lar** (spī-răk′yə-lər, spĭ-) *adj.*

spi·rae·a (spī-rē′ə) *n.* Variant of **spirea.**

spi·ral (spī′rəl) *n.* **1.** The locus in a plane of a point moving around a fixed center at a monotonically increasing or decreasing distance from the center. **2. a.** The three-dimensional locus of a point moving parallel to and about a central axis at a constant or continuously varying distance; helix. **b.** Something having the form of such a curve: *spirals of smoke.* **3.** The course or flight path of an object rotating on its longitudinal axis. **4.** A continuously accelerating increase or decrease: *the wage-price spiral.* —*adj.* **1.** Of or resembling a spiral. **2.** Coiling in a constantly changing plane; helical. **3.** Circling around to form a series of constantly changing planes. —*v.* **-raled, -ral·ing, -rals** or **-ralled, -ral·ling, -rals.** —*intr.* **1.** To take a spiral form or course. **2.** To rise or fall with steady acceleration. —*tr.* To cause to take a spiral form or course. [Med. Lat. *spiralis* < Lat. *spira,* coil < Gk. *speira.*] **—spi·ral′i·ty** (spī-răl′ĭ-tē) *n.* **—spi′ral·ly** *adv.*

spiral binding *n.* A binding for notebooks and booklets in which a cylindrical spiral of wire or plastic is passed

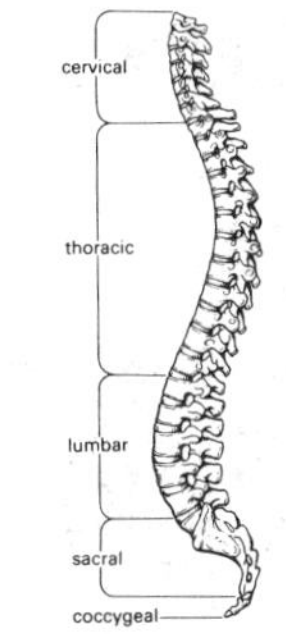

spine
Side view of the human spine

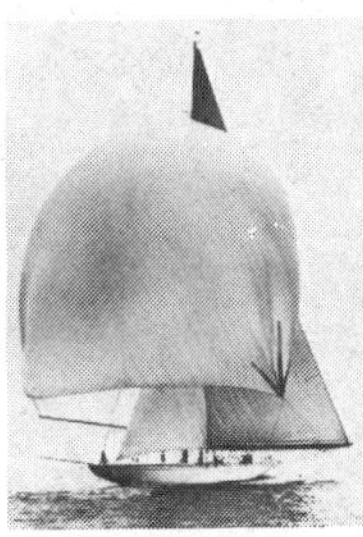
spinnaker

spinning wheel

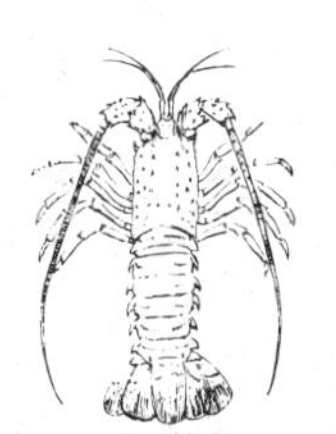
spiny lobster

spiral

through a row of punched holes at the edge of each sheet.
spiral galaxy *n.* A galaxy having a spiral structure with spiral arms consisting mainly of gas, dust, and stars.
spi·rant (spī′rənt) *n.* A fricative. —*adj.* Fricative. [Lat. *spirans, spirant-,* pr.part. of *spirare,* to breathe.]
spire¹ (spīr) *n.* **1.** A top part or point that tapers upward; pinnacle. **2.** A formation or structure that tapers to a point at the top, as a steeple. **3.** A slender, tapering part, such as a newly sprouting blade of grass. —*v.* **spired, spir·ing, spires.** —*tr.* To furnish with a spire. —*intr.* To rise taperingly, as a spire. [ME < OE *spīr.*]
spire² (spīr) *n.* **1.** A spiral, esp. a single turn of a spiral; whorl. **2.** *Zool.* The area farthest from the aperture and nearest the apex on a coiled gastropod shell. [Fr. < Lat. *spira,* coil < Gk. *speira.*]
spi·re·a also **spi·rae·a** (spī-rē′ə) *n.* Any of various plants or shrubs of the genus *Spiraea,* including the bridal wreath, hardhack, and meadowsweet, having clusters of small white or pink flowers. [Lat. *spiraea,* meadowsweet < Gk. *speiraia* < *speira,* coil.]
spi·reme (spī′rēm′) also **spi·rem** (-rĕm′) *n. Biol.* **1.** The tangle of filaments that appears at the beginning of the prophase portion of meiosis or mitosis. **2.** One of these filaments. [G. *Spirem* < Gk. *speirēma,* coil < *speira.*]
spi·rif·er·ous (spī-rĭf′ər-əs) *adj.* Having a spiral structure or spiral parts. [SPIR(E) + -FEROUS.]
spi·ril·lum (spī-rĭl′əm) *n., pl.* **-ril·la** (-rĭl′ə). Any of various flagellated aerobic bacteria of the genus *Spirillum,* having an elongated spiral form. [NLat. *Spirillum,* genus name, dim. of Lat. *spira,* coil < Gk. *speira.*]
spir·it (spĭr′ĭt) *n.* **1.** The vital principle or animating force traditionally believed to be within living beings. **2.** The soul, considered as departing from the body of a person at death. **3. Spirit.** The Holy Ghost. **4. Spirit.** *Christian Science.* God. **5.** A supernatural being, such as a ghost. **6. a.** The part of a human being associated with the mind and feelings as distinguished from the physical body: *still with us in spirit.* **b.** The essential nature of a person. **7.** A person as characterized by a stated quality: *He is a proud spirit.* **8.** An inclination or tendency of a specified kind. **9. spirits.** A mood or emotional state. **10.** A particular mood or emotional state characterized by vigor and animation. **11.** Strong loyalty or dedication. **12.** The predominant mood of an occasion or period: *"The spirit of 1776 is not dead"* (Thomas Jefferson). **13.** The real sense or significance of something: *the spirit of the law.* **14.** Often **spirits.** An alcohol solution of an essential or volatile substance. **15. spirits.** An alcoholic beverage. —*tr.v.* **-it·ed, -it·ing, -its. 1.** To carry off mysteriously or secretly. **2.** To impart courage, animation, or determination to; inspirit. [ME < AN < Lat. *spiritus,* breath < *spirare,* to breathe.]
spir·it·ed (spĭr′ĭ-tĭd) *adj.* **1.** Full of or characterized by animation, vigor, or courage: *a spirited debate.* **2.** Having a specified mood or nature: *high-spirited.* —**spir′it·ed·ly** *adv.* —**spir′it·ed·ness** *n.*
spir·it·ism (spĭr′ĭ-tĭz′əm) *n.* Spiritualism. —**spir′it·ist** *n.* —**spir′it·is′tic** *adj.*
spirit lamp *n.* A lamp using alcohol or other liquid fuel.
spir·it·less (spĭr′ĭt-lĭs) *adj.* Lacking energy or enthusiasm; listless. —**spir′it·less·ly** *adv.* —**spir′it·less·ness** *n.*
spirit level *n.* A level (sense 7.a.).
spirit of ammonia *n.* Variant of **spirits of ammonia.**
spirit of turpentine *n.* Variant of **spirits of turpentine.**
spirit of wine *n.* Variant of **spirits of wine.**
spir·it·ous (spĭr′ĭ-təs) *adj.* **1.** Spirituous. **2.** *Archaic.* Highly refined; pure.
spirit rapping *n.* Communication by rapping, held to be produced by spirits of the dead, as at a séance.
spirits of ammonia also **spirit of ammonia** *n.* A colorless aromatic solution made from ammonium carbonate, ammonia water, alcohol, and water, with small amounts of various aromatic agents, used as a remedy for faintness.
spirits of turpentine also **spirit of turpentine** *n.* Turpentine (sense 1).
spirits of wine also **spirit of wine** *n.* Rectified ethyl alcohol.
spir·i·tu·al (spĭr′ĭ-cho͞o-əl) *adj.* **1.** Of, relating to, consisting of, or having the nature of spirit; not tangible or material. **2.** Of, concerned with, or affecting the soul. **3.** Of, from, or pertaining to God; deific. **4.** Of or belonging to a church or religion; sacred. **5.** Pertaining to or having the nature of spirits; supernatural. —*n.* **1. a.** A religious folk song of black American origin. **b.** A work composed in imitation of a spiritual. **2.** Often **spirituals.** Religious, spiritual, or ecclesiastical matters. —**spir′i·tu·al·ly** *adv.* —**spir′i·tu·al·ness** *n.*
spiritual bouquet *n.* A card sent by a Roman Catholic indicating that certain devotional acts will be undertaken on behalf of a person, as in honor of a special occasion or as a memorial.
spir·i·tu·al·ism (spĭr′ĭ-cho͞o-ə-lĭz′əm) *n.* **1. a.** The belief that the dead communicate with the living, usually through a medium. **b.** The practices or doctrines of those holding such a belief. **2.** A philosophy, doctrine, or religion emphasizing the spiritual rather than the material. —**spir′i·tu·al·ist** *n.* —**spir′i·tu·al·is′tic** *adj.*
spir·i·tu·al·i·ty (spĭr′ĭ-cho͞o-ăl′ĭ-tē) *n., pl.* **-ties. 1.** The state, quality, or fact of being spiritual. **2.** Ecclesiastics collectively; the clergy. **3.** Often **spiritualities.** Something, as property or revenue, belonging to the church or to an ecclesiastic.
spir·i·tu·al·ize (spĭr′ĭ-cho͞o-ə-līz′) *tr.v.* **-ized, -iz·ing, -iz·es. 1.** To impart a spiritual nature to; purify. **2.** To invest with or treat as having a spiritual sense or meaning. —**spir′i·tu·al·i·za′tion** *n.* —**spir′i·tu·al·iz′er** *n.*
spir·i·tu·al·ty (spĭr′ĭ-cho͞o-əl-tē) *n., pl.* **-ties.** Spirituality.
spir·i·tu·el also **spir·i·tu·elle** (spĭr′ĭ-cho͞o-ĕl′, spē′rē-to͞o-ĕl′, -tü-) *adj.* Having or evidencing a refined mind and wit. [Fr., spiritual.]
spir·i·tu·ous (spĭr′ĭ-cho͞o-əs) *adj.* Having the nature of or containing alcohol; alcoholic. —**spir′i·tu·os′i·ty** (-ŏs′ĭ-tē), **spir′i·tu·ous·ness** *n.*
spiro– *pref.* Respiration: *spirometer.* [< Lat. *spirare,* to breathe.]
spi·ro·chete also **spi·ro·chaete** (spī′rə-kēt′) *n.* Any of various slender, nonflagellated, twisted microorganisms of the order Spirochaetales, many of which are pathogenic, causing syphilis, relapsing fever, yaws, and other diseases. [NLat. *Spirochaeta,* genus name : Lat. *spira,* coil + Lat. *chaeta,* bristle < Gk. *khaitē,* long hair.] —**spi′ro·chet′al** (-kēt′l) *adj.*
spi·ro·che·to·sis (spī′rə-kē-tō′sĭs) *n.* Any of various diseases, such as syphilis, caused by a spirochete. [SPIROCHET(E) + -OSIS.]
spi·ro·graph (spī′rə-grăf′) *n.* An instrument for registering the depth and rapidity of respiratory movements. —**spi′ro·graph′ic** *adj.* —**spi′ro·graph′i·cal·ly** *adv.* —**spi·rog′ra·phy** (spī-rŏg′rə-fē) *n.*
spi·ro·gy·ra (spī′rə-jī′rə) *n.* Any of various green, filamentous freshwater algae of the genus *Spirogyra,* having chloroplasts in spirally twisted bands. [NLat. *Spirogyra,* genus name : Lat. *spira,* coil + Gk. *guros,* ring.]
spi·roid (spī′roid′) *adj.* Resembling a spiral.
spi·rom·e·ter (spī-rŏm′ĭ-tər) *n.* An instrument for measuring the volume of air entering and leaving the lungs. —**spi′ro·met′ric** (-rə-mĕt′rĭk) *adj.* —**spi·rom′e·try** *n.*
spi·ro·no·lac·tone (spə-rō′nō-lăk′tōn′, spī-rŏn′ə-) *n.* A steroid, $C_{24}H_{32}O_4S$, used medically as a diuretic. [SPIR(O)- + *-no-* (of unknown orig.) + LACTONE.]
spirt (spûrt) *n. & v. Chiefly Brit.* Variant of **spurt.**
spir·u·la (spĭr′yə-lə, spĭr′ə-) *n., pl.* **-lae** (-lē′). A small cephalopod mollusk of the genus *Spirula,* having a spirally coiled, partitioned internal shell. [NLat. *Spirula,* genus name, dim. of Lat. *spira,* coil < Gk. *speira.*]
spit¹ (spĭt) *n.* **1.** Saliva, esp. when expectorated; spittle. **2.** The act of expectorating. **3.** Something resembling saliva, as the frothy secretion of certain insects. **4.** A brief, scattered fall of rain or snow. —*v.* **spat** (spăt) or **spit, spit·ting, spits.** —*tr.* **1.** To eject from the mouth. **2.** To eject as if by spitting: *spat out an insult; a fire spitting sparks.* —*intr.* **1.** To expectorate. **2.** To express contempt or animosity by or as if by spitting. **3.** To make a hissing or sputtering noise. **4.** To rain or snow in light, scattered drops or flakes. [ME *spitten* < OE *spittan.*]
spit² (spĭt) *n.* **1.** A slender, pointed rod on which meat is impaled for broiling. **2.** A narrow point of land extending into a body of water. —*tr.v.* **spit·ted, spit·ting, spits.** To impale on or as if on a spit. [ME < OE *spitu.*]
spit·al (spĭt′l) *n.* A hospital, esp. one for contagious diseases. [ME *spitel* < Med. Lat. *hospitale.* —see HOSPITAL.]
spit·ball (spĭt′bôl′) *n.* **1.** A piece of paper chewed and shaped into a lump for use as a projectile. **2.** *Baseball.* An illegal pitch in which the ball is moistened on one side with spit.
spit curl *n.* A spiral curl pressed flat against the cheek or forehead. [From the use of saliva to fix the curl.]
spite (spīt) *n.* **1.** Malicious ill will prompting an urge to hurt or humiliate. **2.** An instance of malicious feeling. —*tr.v.* **spit·ed, spit·ing, spites. 1. a.** To show spite toward. **b.** To vent spite upon. **2. a.** To fill with spite. **b.** To annoy. —***idiom.* in spite of.** Regardless of; despite. [ME, outrage, insult, ill will < OFr. *despite.* —see DESPITE.]
spite·ful (spīt′fəl) *adj.* Filled with, prompted by, or showing spite; malicious. —**spite′ful·ly** *adv.* —**spite′ful·ness** *n.*
spit·fire (spĭt′fīr′) *n.* A quick-tempered or highly excitable person.
spit·ter (spĭt′ər) *n.* **1.** One that spits. **2.** *Baseball.* A spitball (sense 2). **3.** A young deer with unbranched horns; pricket.
spitting image *n.* A perfect likeness or counterpart. [Alteration of *spit and image* < *spit,* an exact likeness.]
spit·tle (spĭt′l) *n.* **1.** Spit; saliva. **2.** The frothy liquid secreted by spittlebugs. [ME *spyttle,* alteration of *spatel* < OE *spatl.*]
spit·tle·bug (spĭt′l-bŭg′) *n.* Any of various insects of the family Cercopidae, the nymphs of which form frothy masses of liquid on plant stems.
spittle insect *n.* The spittlebug.
spit·toon (spĭ-to͞on′) *n.* A bowl-shaped, usually metal vessel for spitting into. [SPIT + *-oon,* as in *balloon.*]
spitz (spĭts) *n.* A dog of a breed originating in Germany, having a long, thick, usually white coat and a tail curled over the back. [G. < *spitz,* pointed.]
spiv (spĭv) *n. Chiefly Brit. Slang.* **1.** A usually unemployed

person who lives by his wits. **2.** A person who shirks work or responsibility; slacker. [Dial. *spiff,* dandy.]

splanch·nic (splăngk′nĭk) *adj.* Of or relating to the viscera; visceral: *a splanchnic nerve.* [Gk. *splankhnikos,* of the bowels < *splankhna,* inward parts.]

splash (splăsh) *v.* **splashed, splash·ing, splash·es.** —*tr.* **1.** To dash or scatter (a liquid) about in flying masses. **2.** To dash liquid upon; wet or soil by splashing. **3.** To cause to splash. —*intr.* **1. a.** To cause a liquid to fly in scattered masses. **b.** To fall into or move through liquid with this effect. **2.** To move, spill, or fly about in scattered masses. ***—phrasal verb.*** **splash down.** To land on water. Used of a spacecraft or missile. —*n.* **1.** The act or sound of splashing. **2.** A flying mass of liquid. **3.** A marking produced by or as if by scattered liquid: *a splash of light.* **4.** A great though often short-lived impression; stir. [Alteration of PLASH.] **—splash′er** *n.*

splash·board (splăsh′bôrd′, -bōrd′) *n.* **1.** A structure that protects a vehicle from splashes of mud. **2.** A screen on a boat to keep water from splashing on the deck. **3.** A board for closing a spillway or sluice.

splash·down (splăsh′doun′) *n.* The landing of a missile or spacecraft on water.

splash·y (splăsh′ē) *adj.* **-i·er, -i·est. 1.** Making or liable to make splashes. **2.** Covered with splashes of color. **3.** Showy; ostentatious. **—splash′i·ly** *adv.* **—splash′i·ness** *n.*

splat[1] (splăt) *n.* A slat of wood, such as one in the middle of a chair back. [Orig. unknown.]

splat[2] (splăt) *n.* A slapping noise. —*adv.* With a splat. [Imit.]

splat·ter (splăt′ər) *v.* **-tered, -ter·ing, -ters.** —*tr.* To spatter (something), esp. to soil with splashes of liquid. —*intr.* To spatter, esp. to move or fall so as to cause heavy splashes. —*n.* A splash of liquid. [Blend of SPLASH and SPATTER.]

splay (splā) *adj.* **1.** Spread or turned out. **2.** Clumsy or clumsily formed; awkward. —*n.* **1.** Expansion; spread. **2.** *Archit.* An oblique slope given to the sides of an opening in a wall so that the opening is wider at one face than at the other. —*v.* **splayed, splay·ing, splays.** —*tr.* **1.** To spread (the limbs, for example) out or apart, esp. clumsily. **2.** To make slanting or sloping; bevel. **3.** To dislocate (a bone). Used of an animal. —*intr.* **1.** To be spread out or apart. **2.** To slant or slope. [< ME *splayen,* to spread out, short for *displayen.* —see DISPLAY.]

splay·foot (splā′fo͝ot′) *n.* **1.** A physical deformity characterized by abnormally flat and turned-out feet. **2.** A foot afflicted with splayfoot. **—splay′foot′ed** *adj.*

spleen (splēn) *n.* **1. a.** One of the largest lymphoid structures in human beings, a visceral organ composed of a white pulp of lymphatic nodules and tissue and a red pulp of venous sinusoids in a framework of fibrous partitions lying on the left side below the diaphragm, functioning as a blood filter and to store blood. **b.** A homologous organ or tissue in other vertebrates. **2.** *Obs.* **a.** The seat of emotions or passions. **b.** A whim; caprice. **3.** *Archaic.* Melancholy. **4.** Ill temper. [ME *splene* < OFr. *esplen* < Lat. *splen* < Gk *splēn.*] **—spleen′y** *adj.*

spleen·ful (splēn′fəl) *adj.* Affected by or filled with spleen; irritable.

spleen·wort (splēn′wûrt′, -wôrt′) *n.* Any of various ferns of the genus *Asplenium,* having featherlike, often evergreen fronds. [So called because it was thought to cure spleen disorders.]

splen– *pref.* Variant of **spleno-.**

splen·dent (splĕn′dənt) *adj.* **1.** Shining or lustrous; brilliant. **2.** Celebrated; illustrious. [ME < Lat. *splendens,* pr.part. of *splendēre,* to shine.]

splen·did (splĕn′dĭd) *adj.* **1.** Brilliant with light or color; radiant. **2.** Imposing by reason of showiness or grandeur; magnificent. **3.** Glorious; illustrious. **4.** Admirable for boldness or purity; transcendent. **5.** Very good or satisfying; praiseworthy. [Fr. *splendide* < Lat. *splendidus* < *splendēre,* to shine.] **—splen′did·ly** *adv.* **—splen′did·ness** *n.*

splen·dif·er·ous (splĕn-dĭf′ər-əs) *adj.* Splendid. [ME < Med. Lat. *splendiferus* : Lat. *splendor,* splendor + *ferre,* to bear.]

splen·dor (splĕn′dər) *n.* **1.** Great light or luster; brilliance. **2. a.** Magnificent appearance or display; grandeur. **b.** Something grand or magnificent. **3.** Illustriousness; glory. [ME *splendure* < OFr. *splendeur* < Lat. *splendor* < *splendēre,* to shine.] **—splen′dor·ous, splen′drous** (splĕn′drəs) *adj.*

splen·dour (splĕn′dər) *n. Chiefly Brit.* Variant of **splendor.**

sple·nec·to·my (splĭ-nĕk′tə-mē) *n., pl.* **-mies.** The surgical removal of the spleen.

sple·net·ic (splĭ-nĕt′ĭk) also **sple·net·i·cal** (-ĭ-kəl) *adj.* **1.** Of or pertaining to the spleen. **2.** Affected or marked by spleen; ill-humored and irritable. —*n.* An ill-humored person. [LLat. *spleneticus* < Lat. *splen,* spleen <Gk.] **—sple·net′i·cal·ly** *adv.*

splen·ic (splĕn′ĭk) *adj.* Of, in, near, or pertaining to the spleen.

sple·ni·i (splē′nē-ī′) *n.* Plural of **splenius.**

sple·ni·tis (splĭ-nī′tĭs) *n.* Inflammation of the spleen.

sple·ni·us (splē′nē-əs) *n., pl.* **-ni·i** (-nē-ī′). Either of two muscles of the back of the neck, extending from the vertebral column to the skull, that rotate and extend the head and neck. [NLat. < Lat. *splenius,* patch, plaster < Gk. *splēnion* < *splēn,* spleen.] **—sple′ni·al** *adj.*

spleno– or **splen–** *pref.* Spleen: *splenitis.* [Gk. *splēno-* < *splēn,* spleen.]

sple·no·meg·a·ly (splē′nō-mĕg′ə-lē, splĕn′ō-) *n.* Enlargement of the spleen.

splice (splīs) *tr.v.* **spliced, splic·ing, splic·es. 1. a.** To join (film, for example) at the ends. **b.** To join (ropes) by interweaving strands. **2.** To join (pieces of wood) by overlapping and binding at the ends. **3.** *Informal.* To unite in marriage. —*n.* **1.** A joint made by splicing. **2.** A place where parts have been spliced. [MDu. *splissen.*] **—splic′er** *n.*

spline (splīn) *n.* **1. a.** Any of a series of projections on a shaft that fit into slots on a corresponding shaft, enabling both to rotate together. **b.** The groove or slot for such a projection. **2.** A flexible piece of wood, hard rubber, or metal used in drawing curves. **3.** A wooden or metal strip; slat. [Orig. unknown.]

splint (splĭnt) *n.* **1.** A thin piece split off from a larger piece; splinter. **2.** A rigid device used to prevent motion of a joint or of the ends of a fractured bone. **3.** A thin, flexible wooden strip, such as one used in the making of baskets and chair bottoms. **4.** A plate or strip of metal. **5.** A bony enlargement of the cannon bone or splint bone of a horse. —*tr.v.* **splint·ed, splint·ing, splints.** To support or restrict with or as if with a splint. [ME < MLG *splinte.*]

splint bone *n.* Either of two small metacarpal or metatarsal bones in horses or related animals.

splin·ter (splĭn′tər) *n.* **1.** A sharp, slender piece, as of wood, bone, glass, or metal, split or broken off from a main body. **2.** A group, as a religious sect or a political faction, that has broken away from a parent group. —*v.* **-tered, -ter·ing, -ters.** —*intr.* To split or break into sharp, slender pieces; form splinters. —*tr.* To cause to splinter. [ME < MDu.] **—splin′ter·y** *adj.*

split (splĭt) *v.* **split, split·ting, splits.** —*tr.* **1.** To divide sharply or cleanly, esp. into lengthwise sections or into two parts of approximately equal size. **2.** To break, burst, or rip apart with force; rend. **3.** To separate (persons or groups); disunite. **4.** To divide and share: *split a meal.* **5.** To separate (leather, for example) into layers. **6.** To mark (a vote or ballot) in favor of candidates from different parties. **7.** *Sports.* To win half the games of (a series or doubleheader). **8.** *Slang.* To depart from; leave: *They split the party early.* —*intr.* **1.** To become separated into parts, esp. to divide lengthwise. **2.** To become broken or ripped apart, esp. from internal pressure. **3.** To become divided or part company as a result of discord or disagreement. **4.** To divide or share something with others. **5.** *Slang.* To depart; leave: *All the kids split from home.* —*n.* **1.** The act or result of splitting. **2.** A breach or rupture in a group. **3.** A splinter. **4.** Something divided and portioned out; share. **5.** A split strip of flexible wood used in basketmaking. **6. a.** A bottle of an alcoholic or carbonated beverage half the usual size, usually about six ounces. **b.** A drink of half the usual quantity. **c.** A half pint. **7.** A dessert of sliced fruit, ice cream, and toppings: *a banana split.* **8.** Often **splits.** An acrobatic feat in which the legs are stretched out in opposite directions at right angles to the trunk. **9.** A single thickness of a split hide. **10.** *Sports.* An arrangement of bowling pins left standing after the first bowl with one or more intermediate pins knocked down. —*adj.* **1.** Divided or separated. **2.** Fissured longitudinally; cleft. **3.** Quoted in 16ths rather than in 8ths. Used of stocks. ***—idiom.*** **split hairs.** To see or make trivial distinctions; quibble. [Du. *splitten* < MDu.] **—split′ter** *n.*

split infinitive *n. Gram.* An infinitive verb form with an element, usually an adverb, interposed between *to* and the verb form, as in *to deeply disapprove.*

Usage: The split infinitive, as in *to readily accept,* is not a grammatical error, and it has ample precedent in literature. But many writers and editors still consider that it should be avoided, especially in its more extreme form. It is least desirable, according to a majority of the Usage Panel, when *to* and its verb are separated by a succession of modifying words that slow the reader's comprehension and produce a clumsy effect: *We are seeking a plan to gradually, systematically, and economically relieve the burden.* In this example, termed unacceptable by a large majority of the Usage Panel, placing the adverbs at the end would improve the clarity and style without changing the desired sense: *We are seeking a plan to relieve the burden gradually, systematically, and economically.* Most splits are not so extreme, and in such cases opinion of the Panel is divided: *If you want to really help a patient, you must respect his feelings. To better understand the miners' plight, he went to live in their district.* These examples are acceptable to about half of the Usage Panel. The split infinitive has greatest acceptance when it expresses concisely and clearly a sense that could not be expressed so concisely by another phrasing: *We expect our output to more than double in a year* (acceptable to a large majority of the Usage Panel). Many writers feel also that it is better to split an infinitive than to displace an adverb from what is felt to be its natural position in the sentence, a practice that can make the sentence appear stilted or ambiguous. If the sentence *she wanted to really help her daughter* is rewritten as either *she wanted really to help her*

splat[1]
18th-century American

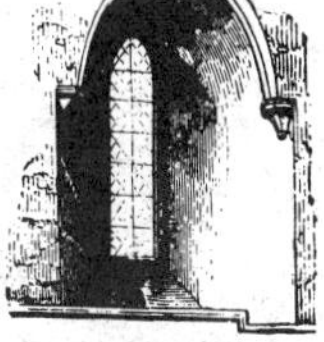

splay

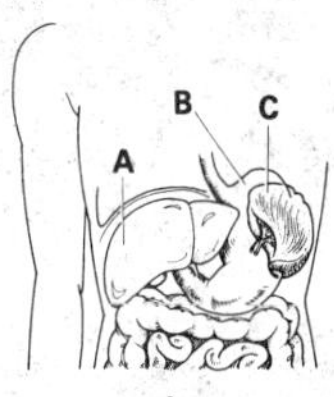

spleen
A. Liver
B. Stomach
C. Spleen

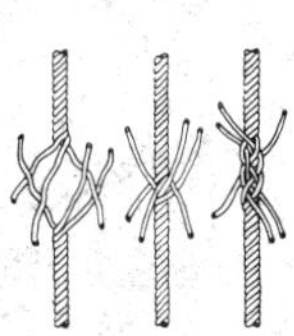

splice
Left to right: Three steps in making a splice

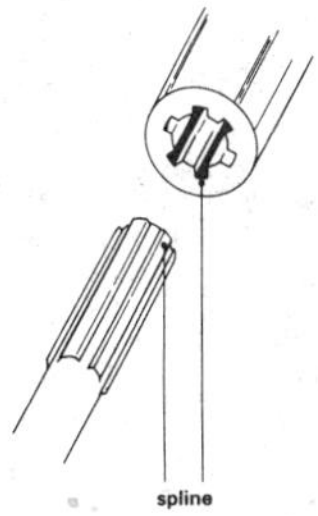

spline

spoke[1]

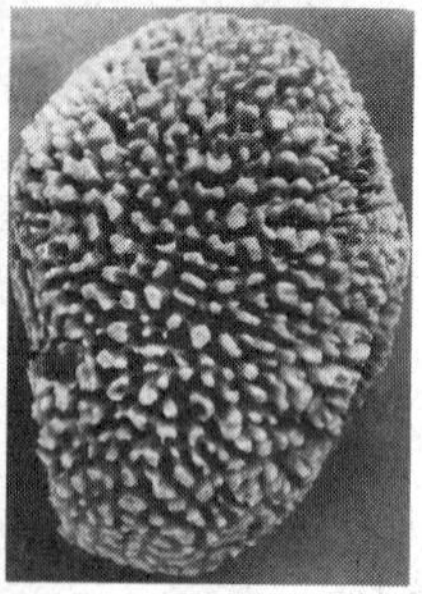

sponge
Two types of ocean sponge

daughter or *she wanted to help her daughter really,* it is unclear whether *really* modifies *wanted* or *help.* Expressions involving the verbs *be* and *have,* such as *to be really sure* and *to have just seen,* are often taken to be split infinitives. They are not, because *to* is not separated from the infinitive *have* or *be.*

split-lev·el (splĭt′lĕv′əl) *adj.* Having the floor levels of adjoining rooms separated by about a half story: *a split-level ranch house.*

split personality *n.* A form of hysteria in which an individual manifests two or more relatively distinct identities.

split rail *n.* A fence rail split lengthwise from a log.

split second *n.* An instant; flash.

split shift *n.* A working shift divided into several time periods, as mornings and evenings, with a break of several hours between.

split ticket *n.* **1.** A ballot cast for candidates of two or more political parties. **2.** A ballot that includes the names of candidates of more than one party.

split·ting (splĭt′ĭng) *adj.* **1.** Acute; piercing. **2.** Very severe, as a headache.

splotch (splŏch) *n.* An irregularly shaped stain, spot, or discolored area. *—tr.v.* **splotched, splotch·ing, splotch·es.** To mark with a splotch or splotches. [Perh. blend of SPOT and BLOTCH.] **—splotch′i·ness** *n.* **—splotch′y** *adj.*

splurge (splûrj) *v.* **splurged, splurg·ing, splurg·es.** *—intr.* **1.** To indulge in an extravagant expense or luxury. **2.** To be showy or ostentatious. *—tr.* To spend extravagantly or wastefully. *—n.* **1.** An extravagant display. **2.** An expensive indulgence; spree. [Orig. unknown.] **—splurg′y** *adj.*

splut·ter (splŭt′ər) *v.* **-tered, -ter·ing, -ters.** *—intr.* **1.** To make a spitting sound. **2.** To speak incoherently, as when confused or angry. *—tr.* To utter or express hastily and incoherently. *—n.* A spluttering noise. [Perh. alteration of SPUTTER.] **—splut′ter·er** *n.*

Spode (spōd). A trademark for porcelain or chinaware of fine quality.

spod·u·mene (spŏj′ə-mēn′) *n.* A greenish to pinkish or lilac mineral, essentially $LiAlSi_2O_6$, used as a source of lithium and in transparent varieties as a gemstone. [Fr. *spodumène* < Gk. *spodoumenos,* pr.part. of *spodousthai,* to be burned to ashes < *spodos,* wood ashes.]

spoil (spoil) *v.* **spoiled** or **spoilt** (spoilt), **spoil·ing, spoils.** *—tr.* **1.** To impair the value or quality of; damage. **2.** To impair the completeness, perfection, or unity of; flaw grievously. **3.** To disrupt; disturb. **4.** To overindulge or overpraise so as to do harm to the character. **5.** *Obs.* **a.** To plunder; despoil. **b.** To take by force. *—intr.* **1.** To become tainted, rotten, or otherwise unfit for use; decay. **2.** *Obs.* To pillage. ***—phrasal verb.*** **spoil for.** To be eager for: *spoiling for a fight.* *—n.* **1. spoils.** Goods or property seized from a victim after a conflict, esp. after a military victory. **2. spoils.** Incidental benefits reaped by a winner, esp. political patronage enjoyed by a successful party or candidate. **3.** *Archaic.* The act of plundering; spoliation. **4.** An object of plunder; prey. **5.** Refuse material removed from an excavation. [ME *spoilen,* to plunder < OFr. *espoillier* < Lat. *spoliare* < *spolium,* booty.]

spoil·age (spoi′lĭj) *n.* **1.** The condition or process of becoming spoiled. **2. a.** Something that has been spoiled. **b.** The degree to which something has been spoiled.

spoil·er (spoi′lər) *n.* **1.** One who seizes spoils or booty. **2.** Something that causes spoilage. **3.** A long, narrow hinged plate on the upper surface of an airplane wing, whose position affects the lift. **4.** A candidate for office whose chances of winning are slight but who may garner enough votes to prevent one of the leading candidates from winning.

spoil·sport (spoil′spôrt′, -spōrt′) *n.* One who mars the pleasure of others.

spoils system *n.* The practice after an election of rewarding loyal supporters of the winning candidates and party with appointive public offices.

spoilt (spoilt) *v.* A past tense and past participle of **spoil.**

spoke[1] (spōk) *n.* **1.** One of the rods or braces that connects the hub and the rim of a wheel. **2.** One of the handles that projects from the rim of a ship's steering wheel. **3.** A rod or stick that may be inserted into a wheel to prevent it from turning. **4.** A rung of a ladder. *—tr.v.* **spoked, spok·ing, spokes. 1.** To equip with spokes. **2.** To impede (a wheel) by inserting a rod. [ME < OE *spāca.*]

spoke[2] (spōk) *v.* **1.** Past tense of **speak. 2.** *Archaic.* Past participle of **speak.**

spo·ken (spō′kən) *v.* Past participle of **speak.** *—adj.* **1.** Expressed orally; uttered. **2.** Speaking or using speech in a specified manner or voice: *soft-spoken.*

spoke·shave (spōk′shāv′) *n.* A drawknife.

spokes·man (spōks′mən) *n.* A person who speaks on behalf of another or others. [Prob. < *spoke,* obs. p.part. of SPEAK + MAN.]

spokes·per·son (spōks′pûr′sən) *n.* A spokesman.

spokes·wom·an (spōks′wo͝om′ən) *n.* A woman who speaks on behalf of another or others. [SPOKES(MAN) + WOMAN.]

spo·li·a·tion (spō′lē-ā′shən) *n.* **1.** The act of despoiling or plundering, esp. the seizure of neutral vessels at sea by a belligerent power in time of war. **2.** *Law.* The intentional alteration or destruction of a document. [ME *spoliacioun* < Lat. *spoliatio* < *spoliare,* to despoil. —see SPOIL.] **—spo′li·a′tor** *n.*

spon·da·ic (spŏn-dā′ĭk) *adj.* Of, pertaining to, or consisting of spondees. [Fr. *spondaïque* < Lat. *spondaicus* < Gk. *spondeiakos* < *spondeios,* spondee.]

spon·dee (spŏn′dē′) *n.* A metric foot consisting of two long or stressed syllables. [ME *sponde* < OFr. *spondee* < Lat. *spondeum* < Gk. *spondeios* < *spondē,* libation, from its use in songs performed at libations.]

spon·dy·li·tis (spŏn′də-lī′tĭs) *n.* Inflammation of one or more of the vertebrae. [Gk. *spondulos,* vertebra + -ITIS.]

sponge (spŭnj) *n.* **1. a.** Any of numerous primitive, chiefly marine animals of the phylum Porifera, characteristically having a porous skeleton composed of fibrous material or siliceous or calcareous spicules and often forming irregularly shaped colonies attached to an underwater surface. **b.** The light, fibrous, absorbent connective structure of certain of these organisms, used for bathing, cleaning, and other purposes. **2.** Any of various substances, such as certain forms of plastics, rubber, or cellulose, that have spongelike qualities. **3.** A gauze pad used to absorb blood and other fluids, as in surgery and wound dressing. **4.** Dough that is leavened or in the process of being leavened. **5.** Any of various light cakes, such as sponge cake. **6.** A sponge bath. **7. a.** *Informal.* A glutton. **b.** *Slang.* A drunkard. **8.** One who habitually depends on others for his maintenance. *—v.* **sponged, spong·ing, spong·es.** *—tr.* **1.** To moisten, wipe, or clean with or as if with a sponge. **2.** To wipe out; erase. **3.** *Informal.* To obtain free: *sponge a meal.* *—intr.* **1.** To fish for sponges. **2.** *Informal.* To live by relying on the generosity of others. ***—idiom.*** **throw (or toss) in the sponge.** *Informal.* To abandon an effort; give up. [ME < OE < Lat. *spongia* < Gk. *sphongos.*]

sponge bath *n.* A washing of the body with a sponge or cloth, without immersion.

sponge cake *n.* A very light, porous cake made of flour, sugar, beaten eggs, and flavoring and containing no shortening.

sponge mushroom *n.* The morel.

spong·er (spŭn′jər) *n.* **1.** One that gathers sponges. **2.** *Informal.* A person who sponges on others; parasite.

sponge rubber *n.* A soft, porous rubber used in toys, cushions, gaskets, weather stripping, and as a vibration dampener.

spon·gin (spŭn′jĭn) *n.* The fibrous material that forms the skeletal structure of sponges. [G. < Lat. *spongia,* sponge.]

spon·gi·o·blast (spŭn′jĭ-ə-blăst′) *n.* Embryonic epithelial cells that give rise to the neuroglia cells. [Lat. *spongia,* sponge + -BLAST.]

spon·gi·o·cyte (spŭn′jĭ-ə-sīt′) *n.* A neuroglia cell. [Lat. *spongia,* sponge + -CYTE.]

spon·go·coel (spŏng′gə-sēl′) *n.* *Zool.* The central cavity of a sponge that opens to the outside by way of the osculum. [SPONG(E) + -COEL.]

spong·y (spŭn′jē) *adj.* **-i·er, -i·est.** Like a sponge in elasticity, absorbency, or porousness. **—spong′i·ness** *n.*

spon·son (spŏn′sən) *n.* **1.** Any of several structures that project from the side of a boat or ship, esp. a gun platform. **2.** A short, curved, air-filled projection on the hull of a seaplane, imparting stability in the water. [Orig. unknown.]

spon·sor (spŏn′sər) *n.* **1.** One who assumes responsibility for a person or group during a period of instruction, apprenticeship, or probation. **2.** One who vouches for the suitability of a candidate for admission. **3.** A legislator who proposes and urges the adoption of a bill. **4.** One who presents a candidate for baptism or confirmation; godparent. **5.** A business enterprise that pays for a radio or television program, usually in return for advertising time. *—tr.v.* **-sored, -sor·ing, -sors.** To act as a sponsor for. [Lat. < *spondēre,* to pledge.] **—spon·so′ri·al** (-sôr′ē-əl, -sōr′-) *adj.* **—spon′sor·ship′** *n.*

spon·ta·ne·i·ty (spŏn′tə-nē′ĭ-tē, -nā′-) *n., pl.* **-ties. 1.** The condition or quality of being spontaneous. **2.** Spontaneous behavior, impulse, or movement.

spon·ta·ne·ous (spŏn-tā′nē-əs) *adj.* **1.** Happening or arising without apparent external cause; self-generated. **2.** Voluntary and impulsive; unpremeditated: *spontaneous applause.* **3.** Unconstrained and unstudied in manner or behavior. **4.** Growing without cultivation or human labor; indigenous. [LLat. *spontaneus* < Lat. *sponte,* voluntarily.] **—spon·ta′ne·ous·ly** *adv.* **—spon·ta′ne·ous·ness** *n.*

Synonyms: *spontaneous, impulsive, instinctive, involuntary, automatic.* These adjectives describe response, in actions or words, either uninfluenced by forethought or seemingly so. *Spontaneous* applies to what comes naturally to a person by reason of temperament or native tendency and not from constraint or external stimulus. *Impulsive* refers to action prompted by a sudden urge not governed by reason and sometimes contrary to reason. *Instinctive* implies behavior guided not by one's reason but by natural consequence of being a member of a given species. Usually the term suggests behavior that promotes one's welfare or that traces to reflex action. *Involuntary* refers to what is not subject to the control of the will, as does *automatic.* The latter also suggests unvarying mechanical response.

spontaneous abortion *n.* A miscarriage (sense 2).

spontaneous combustion *n.* Ignition in a thermally isolated substance, as in oily rags or hay, caused by a localized heat-increasing reaction between the oxidant and the fuel.
spontaneous generation *n. Biol.* Abiogenesis.
spon·toon (spŏn-to͞on′) *n.* A short pike carried by infantry officers in the 18th century. [Fr. *sponton* < Ital. *spuntone* < *spuntare,* to blunt : *s-,* off (< Lat. *dis-*) + *punto,* point < Lat. *punctum* < *pungere,* to pierce.]
spoof (spo͞of) *n.* **1.** Nonsense; tomfoolery. **2.** A hoax. **3.** A gentle satirical imitation; light parody. —*tr.v.* **spoofed, spoof·ing, spoofs. 1.** To deceive. **2.** To do a spoof of; satirize gently. [< *Spoof,* a trademark for a card game characterized by nonsense and hoaxing.]
spook (spo͝ok) *Informal.* —*n.* **1.** A ghost; specter. **2.** A secret agent; spy. —*tr.v.* **spooked, spook·ing, spooks. 1.** To haunt. **2.** To frighten, esp. to startle and cause nervous activity among (cattle). [Du.]
spook·y (spo͞o′kē) *adj.* **-i·er, -i·est.** *Informal.* **1.** Ghostly; eerie. **2.** Easily startled; skittish. —**spook′i·ly** *adv.* —**spook′i·ness** *n.*
spool (spo͞ol) *n.* **1.** A wood or cardboard cylinder upon which wire, thread, or string is wound. **2.** The amount of thread or other material on a particular spool. **3.** A reel for magnetic paper or plastic tape. **4.** Something similar to a spool in shape or function. —*tr.v.* **spooled, spool·ing, spools.** To wind on a spool. [ME *spole* < OFr. *espole* < MDu. *spoele.*]
spool·ing (spo͞o′lĭng) *n. Computer Sci.* A procedure that involves storing information temporarily on a file while awaiting further processing.
spoon (spo͞on) *n.* **1.** A utensil consisting of a small, shallow bowl on a handle, used in preparing, serving, or eating food. **2.** Something similar to a spoon or its bowl, esp.: **a.** A shiny, curved metallic fishing lure. **b.** A paddle or oar with a curved blade. **3.** The three wood golf club. —*v.* **spooned, spoon·ing, spoons.** —*tr.* **1.** To lift, scoop up, or carry with or as if with a spoon. **2.** To shove or scoop (a ball) into the air, as in certain games. —*intr.* **1.** To fish with a spoon lure. **2.** To give the ball an upward scoop in certain games. **3.** *Informal.* To make love, as by kissing or caressing. [ME < OE *spōn,* chip of wood.]
spoon·bill (spo͞on′bĭl′) *n.* **1.** Any of several long-legged wading birds of the subfamily Plataleinae, having a long, flat bill with a broadly spatulate tip. **2.** Any of various broad-billed ducks, such as the shoveler. **3.** The paddlefish.
spoon bread *n.* A soft, custardlike bread made with corn meal, eggs, and milk.
spoon·drift (spo͞on′drĭft′) *n.* Spindrift. [Obs. *spoon,* to drive back and forth + DRIFT.]
spoon·er·ism (spo͞o′nə-rĭz′əm) *n.* An unintentional transposition of sounds of two or more words, as *Let me sew you to your sheet* for *Let me show you to your seat.* [After William A. Spooner (1844–1930).]
spoon·ey (spo͞o′nē) *adj.* Variant of **spoony.**
spoon-fed (spo͞on′fĕd′) *adj.* **1.** Fed with a spoon. **2.** Overindulged; coddled. **3.** Given no chance to think or act independently.
spoon·ful (spo͞on′fo͝ol′) *n., pl.* **-fuls.** The amount a spoon holds.
spoon·y also **spoon·ey** (spo͞o′nē) *adj.* **-i·er, -i·est. 1.** Enamored in a silly or sentimental way. **2.** Feebly sentimental; gushy.
spoor (spo͝or) *n.* The track or trail of an animal, esp. a wild animal. —*v.* **spoored, spoor·ing, spoors.** —*tr.* To track by following a spoor. —*intr.* To track an animal by its spoor. [Afr. < MDu.]
spor– *pref.* Variant of **sporo–.**
spo·rad·ic (spə-răd′ĭk, spô-) also **spo·rad·i·cal** (-ĭ-kəl) *adj.* **1.** Occurring at irregular intervals; having no pattern or order. **2.** Appearing singly or at widely scattered localities, as a plant. **3.** Not widespread; isolated: *a sporadic disease.* [Med. Lat. *sporadicus* < Gk. *sporadikos,* isolated < *sporas,* scattered.] —**spo·rad′i·cal·ly** *adv.* —**spo·rad′i·cal·ness** *n.*
spo·ran·gi·a (spə-răn′jē-ə) *n.* Plural of **sporangium.**
spo·ran·gi·o·phore (spə-răn′jē-ə-fôr′, -fōr′) *n.* A specialized branch or filament bearing sporangia. [SPORANGI(UM) + -PHORE.]
spo·ran·gi·um (spə-răn′jē-əm) *n., pl.* **-gi·a** (-jē-ə). A spore-bearing structure in certain plants, such as fungi, mosses, and ferns. [NLat. : SPOR(O)- + Gk. *angeion,* vessel.] —**spo·ran′gi·al** *adj.*
spore (spôr, spōr) *n.* **1.** An asexual, usually single-celled reproductive organ characteristic of nonflowering plants such as fungi, mosses, or ferns. **2.** A microorganism, as a bacterium, in a dormant or resting state. —*intr.v.* **spored, spor·ing, spores.** To produce spores. [NLat. *spora* < Gk., seed.] —**spo·ra′ceous** (spə-rā′shəs, spô-) *adj.*
spore case *n.* A structure containing spores; sporangium.
spo·ri·cide (spôr′ĭ-sīd′, spōr′-) *n.* An agent used to kill spores. —**spo′ri·cid′al** (-sīd′l) *adj.*
spo·rif·er·ous (spə-rĭf′ər-əs, spô-, spō-) *adj.* Producing spores.
sporo– or **spor–** *pref.* Spore: *sporocyte.* [< NLat. *spora,* spore < Gk., seed.]
spo·ro·carp (spôr′ə-kärp′, spōr′-) *n.* A multicellular structure in which spores are formed.
spo·ro·cyst (spôr′ə-sĭst′, spōr′-) *n.* **1.** A resting cell that produces asexual plant spores. **2.** A protective case containing spores of certain protozoans. **3.** A saclike larval stage in many trematode worms.
spo·ro·cyte (spôr′ə-sīt′, spōr′-) *n.* A cell that produces haploid spores during meiosis.
spo·ro·gen·e·sis (spôr′ə-jĕn′ĭ-sĭs, spōr′-) *n.* The production or formation of spores. —**spo′ro·gen′ic** (-jĕn′ĭk), **spo·rog′e·nous** (spə-rŏj′ə-nəs, spô-) *adj.*
spo·ro·go·ni·um (spôr′ə-gō′nē-əm, spōr′-) *n., pl.* **-ni·a** (-nē-ə). A structure in mosses that produces asexual spores.
spo·rog·o·ny (spə-rŏg′ə-nē, spô-) *n.* The production of spores resulting from sexual fusion of gametes prior to multiple fission, characteristic of certain protozoans. —**spo′ro·gon′ic** (spôr′ə-gŏn′ĭk, spōr′-), **spo·rog′o·nous** (spə-rŏg′ə-nəs, spô-) *adj.*
spo·ro·phore (spôr′ə-fôr′, spōr′ə-fōr′) *n.* A spore-bearing structure, esp. in fungi.
spo·ro·phyll (spôr′ə-fĭl′, spōr′-) *n.* A leaf or leaflike organ that bears spores.
spo·ro·phyte (spôr′ə-fīt′, spōr′-) *n.* The spore-producing phase in plants that reproduce by metagenesis. —**spo′ro·phyt′ic** (-fĭt′ĭk) *adj.*
spo·ro·pol·len·in (spôr′ə-pŏl′ə-nĭn, spōr′-) *n.* A polymer that comprises the exine of spores and pollen grains.
–sporous *suff.* Having a specified number or kind of spores: *heterosporous.* [< SPOR(E) + -OUS.]
spo·ro·zo·an (spôr′ə-zō′ən, spōr′-) *n., pl.* **-zo·a** (-zō′ə). Any of numerous parasitic protozoans of the class Sporozoa, many of which have complex reproductive processes. [< NLat. *Sporozoa,* class name : SPORO- + Gk. *zōia,* pl. of *zōion,* animal.] —**spo′ro·zo′an** *adj.*
spo·ro·zo·ite (spôr′ə-zō′īt′, spōr′-) *n.* A sporozoan that has been released from a spore and is ready to penetrate a new host cell. [SPOROZO(A) + -ITE.]
spor·ran (spôr′ən, spŏr′-) *n.* A leather or fur pouch worn at the front of the kilt by Scottish Highlanders. [Sc. Gael. *sporan* < LLat. *bursa,* bag < Gk., leather.]
sport (spôrt, spōrt) *n.* **1.** An active pastime; recreation. **2.** A specific diversion, usually involving physical exercise and having a set form and body of rules; game. **3.** Mockery; jest: *made sport of his handicap.* **4.** A person known for the manner of his acceptance of the rules of a game or of a difficult situation: *a poor sport.* **5.** *Informal.* A person who lives a gay, extravagant life. **6.** *Genetics.* An organism that shows a marked change from the parent stock; mutation. **7.** *Archaic.* Amorous dalliance; lovemaking. —*v.* **sport·ed, sport·ing, sports.** —*intr.* **1.** To play or frolic. **2.** To joke or trifle. **3.** To mutate. —*tr.* To display or show off: *"His shoes sported elevated heels"* (Truman Capote). —*adj.* Of, relating to, or appropriate for sports: *a sport shirt.* —**idiom. in sport.** In jest; jokingly. [ME *sporten,* to amuse < *disporten.* —see DISPORT.] —**sport′ful** *adj.* —**sport′ful·ly** *adv.* —**sport′ful·ness** *n.*
sport·ing (spôr′tĭng, spōr′-) *adj.* **1.** Used in or appropriate for sports. **2.** Characterized by sportsmanship. **3.** Of or associated with gambling. —**sport′ing·ly** *adv.*
sporting chance *n. Informal.* A fair chance for success.
spor·tive (spôr′tĭv, spōr′-) *adj.* **1.** Playful; frolicsome. **2.** Pertaining to or interested in sports. **3.** *Obs.* Amorous; wanton. —**spor′tive·ly** *adv.* —**spor′tive·ness** *n.*
sports car *n.* An automobile equipped for racing, esp. an aerodynamically shaped one- or two-passenger vehicle having a low center of gravity and steering and suspension designed for precise control at high speeds on curving roads.
sports·cast (spôrts′kăst′, spōrts′-) *n.* A radio or television broadcast of a sports event or of sports news. [SPORTS + (BROAD)CAST.] —**sports′cast′er** *n.*
sports·man (spôrts′mən, spōrts′-) *n.* **1.** A man who is active in sports. **2.** One who abides by the rules of a contest and accepts victory or defeat graciously. —**sports′man·ly** *adj.*
sports·man·ship (spôrts′mən-shĭp′, spōrts′-) *n.* The qualities and conduct befitting a sportsman.
sports medicine *n.* Medicine dealing with the diseases and injuries resulting from participation in sports.
sports·wear (spôrts′wâr′, spōrts′-) *n.* Clothes designed for comfort and casual wear.
sports·wom·an (spôrts′wo͝om′ən, spōrts′-) *n.* A woman who is active in sports.
sports·writ·er (spôrts′rī′tər, spōrts′-) *n.* A person who writes about sports, esp. for a newspaper or a magazine.
sport·y (spôr′tē, spōr′-) *adj.* **-i·er, -i·est.** *Informal.* **1.** Appropriate to sport or participation in sports. **2.** Casual in style. Used of clothes. **3.** Gay; carefree. —**sport′i·ly** *adv.* —**sport′i·ness** *n.*
spor·u·late (spôr′yə-lāt′, spōr′-) *intr.v.* **-lat·ed, -lat·ing, -lates.** To produce or release spores. [< NLat. *sporula,* small spore, dim. of *spora,* spore.] —**spor′u·la′tion** *n.*
spot (spŏt) *n.* **1.** A particular place of relatively small and definite limits. **2. a.** A mark on a surface differing sharply in color from the surroundings, esp. a stain or blot. **b.** A mark on a playing card indicating its value: *a ten spot.* **3.** A position; location. **4.** *Informal.* A situation, esp. a troublesome one. **5.** A personal defect or injury, as in one's reputation. **6.** *pl.* **spots** or **spot.** An edible marine fish, *Leiostomus xanthurus,* of North American Atlantic waters, having a

spoonbill

sporran

spread eagle

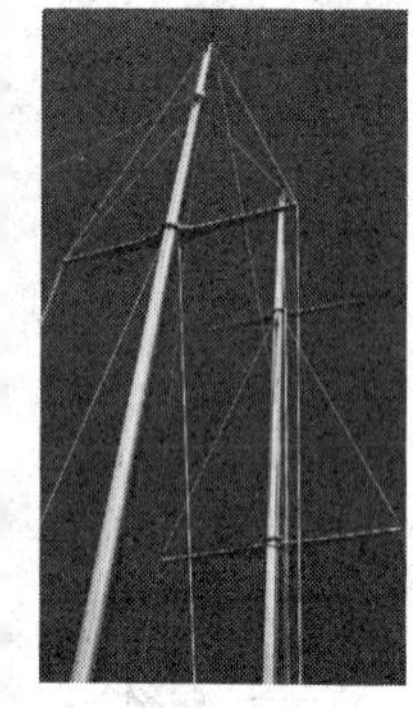

spreader

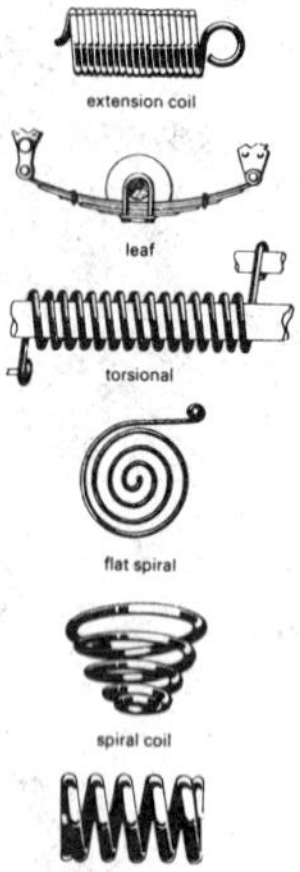

spring

dark spot above each pectoral fin. **7.** *Chiefly Brit. Informal.* A small amount; bit: *a spot of tea.* **8.** *Informal.* A spotlight. **9.** A short presentation or commercial on radio or television between major programs, esp. by a local station on a network broadcast. —*v.* **spot·ted, spot·ting, spots.** —*tr.* **1.** To cause a spot or spots to appear upon, esp.: **a.** To soil with spots. **b.** To decorate with spots; dot. **2.** To place in a particular location; situate precisely. **3.** To detect; discern. **4.** *Sports.* To yield as a handicap: *spotted their opponents 11 points.* —*intr.* **1.** To become marked with spots. **2.** To cause a discoloration or make a stain. **3.** To locate targets from the air during combat or training missions. —*adj.* **1.** Made, paid, or delivered immediately: *spot cash.* **2.** Presented between major radio or television programs: *a spot announcement.* —**idioms. hit the spot.** *Informal.* To be just what is needed; be quite satisfying. **in spots.** Now and then; here and there; occasionally. **on the spot. 1.** Without delay or movement; at once. **2.** At the scene of action. **3.** Under pressure or attention; in a pressed position. [ME.] —**spot'ta·ble** *adj.*

spot check *n.* An inspection or investigation that is carried out at random or limited to a few instances.

spot-check (spŏt'chĕk') *v.* **-checked, -check·ing, -checks.** —*tr.* To subject to a spot check. —*intr.* To make a spot check.

spot·less (spŏt'lĭs) *adj.* **1.** Perfectly clean. **2.** Free from blemish; impeccable. —**spot'less·ly** *adv.* —**spot'less·ness** *n.*

spot·light (spŏt'līt') *n.* **1. a.** A strong beam of light that illuminates only a small area, used esp. to center attention on a stage actor. **b.** A lamp that produces such a light. **2.** Public notoriety or prominence. **3.** An artificial source of light with a strongly focused beam, as on an automobile. —*tr.v.* **-light·ed** or **-lit** (-lĭt), **-light·ing, -lights. 1.** To illuminate with a spotlight. **2.** To focus attention on.

spot price *n.* The market price of a commodity.

spot·ted (spŏt'ĭd) *adj.* Marked or stained with spots.

spotted cranesbill *n.* The wild geranium.

spotted fever *n.* **1.** Any of various often fatal infectious diseases, such as typhus and Rocky Mountain spotted fever, caused by *Rickettsiae,* that are transmitted by ticks and mites and are characterized by skin eruptions. **2.** An epidemic form of cerebrospinal meningitis.

spotted sandpiper *n.* A small brownish-gray North American shore bird, *Actitis macularia.*

spot·ter (spŏt'ər) *n.* **1.** One that applies spots. **2.** One that looks for, locates, and reports something, esp.: **a.** A military or civil-defense lookout. **b.** *Informal.* A person hired to detect dishonest acts by employees, as in a bank. **3.** *Sports.* **a.** One who identifies players on the field, as for a radio or television announcer. **b.** One who is responsible for watching and guarding a performer during practice to prevent injury, as in gymnastics or water-skiing. **4.** One employed by a dry cleaner to remove spots.

spot·ty (spŏt'ē) *adj.* **-ti·er, -ti·est. 1.** Lacking or marked with spots; spotted. **2.** Lacking consistency; uneven. —**spot'ti·ly** *adv.* —**spot'ti·ness** *n.*

spou·sal (spou'zəl, -səl) *adj.* Of or pertaining to marriage; nuptial. —*n.* Often **spousals.** Marriage; nuptials.

spouse (spous, spouz) *n.* A marriage partner; husband or wife. —*tr.v.* (spouz, spous) **spoused, spous·ing, spous·es.** *Archaic.* To marry; wed. [ME < OFr. *espous* < Lat. *sponsus,* betrothal < p.part. of *spondēre,* to pledge.]

spout (spout) *v.* **spout·ed, spout·ing, spouts.** —*intr.* **1.** To gush forth in a rapid stream or in spurts. **2.** To discharge a liquid or other substance continuously or in spurts. **3.** *Informal.* To speak volubly and tediously. —*tr.* **1.** To cause to flow or spurt out. **2.** To utter pompously and volubly. **3.** *Chiefly Brit. Slang.* To pawn. —*n.* **1.** A tube, mouth, or pipe through which liquid is released or discharged. **2.** A continuous stream of liquid. **3.** *Chiefly Brit. Slang.* A pawnbroker's shop. [ME *spouten.*] —**spout'er** *n.*

sprach·ge·fühl (shpräĸʜ'gə-fül') *n.* A feeling for language; an ear for the idiomatically correct or appropriate. [G.]

sprag (străg) *n.* **1. a.** A piece of wood or metal wedged beneath a wheel or between spokes to keep a vehicle from rolling. **b.** A pointed stake lowered at an angle into the ground from a vehicle to prevent movement. **2.** A prop to support a mine roof. [Perh. of Scand. orig.]

sprain (sprān) *n.* **1.** A painful wrenching or laceration of the ligaments of a joint. **2.** The condition resulting from a sprain. —*tr.v.* **sprained, sprain·ing, sprains.** To cause a sprain in (a muscle or joint). [Orig. unknown.]

sprang (sprăng) *v.* A past tense of **spring.**

sprat (sprăt) *n.* **1.** A small marine food fish, *Clupea sprattus,* of northeastern Atlantic waters. **2.** Any of various fish similar to the sprat, as a young herring. [Alteration of ME *sprotte* < OE *sprott.*]

sprawl (sprôl) *v.* **sprawled, sprawl·ing, sprawls.** —*intr.* **1.** To sit or lie with the body and limbs spread out awkwardly. **2.** To spread out in a straggling or disordered fashion: *untidy tenements sprawling toward the river.* —*tr.* To cause to spread out in a straggling or disordered fashion. —*n.* **1.** A sprawling position or posture. **2.** Haphazard growth or extension outward, esp. that resulting from new housing on the outskirts of a city: *urban sprawl.* [ME *sprawlen* < OE *sprēawlian.*] —**sprawl'er** *n.*

spray[1] (sprā) *n.* **1.** Water or other liquid moving in a mass of dispersed droplets, as from a wave. **2. a.** A fine jet of liquid discharged from a pressurized container. **b.** A pressurized container; atomizer. **c.** Any of numerous commercial products, including paints, cosmetics, and insecticides, that are dispensed from containers in this manner. —***modifier:*** *a spray paint; a spray can.* —*v.* **sprayed, spray·ing, sprays.** —*tr.* **1.** To disperse (a liquid) in a mass or jet of droplets. **2.** To apply a spray to (a surface). —*intr.* **1.** To discharge sprays of liquid. **2.** To move in the form of a spray. [< MDu. *sprayen,* to sprinkle.] —**spray'er** *n.*

spray[2] (sprā) *n.* **1.** A small branch bearing buds, flowers, or berries. **2.** Something that resembles a spray. [ME.]

spray gun *n.* A gunlike device for applying sprays.

spread (sprĕd) *v.* **spread, spread·ing, spreads.** —*tr.* **1.** To open to a fuller extent or width; stretch: *spread the tablecloth.* **2.** To make wider the gap between; move farther apart: *spread her fingers.* **3. a.** To distribute over a surface in a layer; apply. **b.** To cover with a layer: *spread a cracker with butter.* **4.** To distribute widely: *The tornado spread destruction.* **5.** To cause to become widely known; disseminate. **6. a.** To prepare (a table) for eating; set. **b.** To arrange (food or a meal) on a table. —*intr.* **1.** To be extended or enlarged. **2.** To become distributed or widely dispersed. **3.** To increase in range of occurrence; become known or prevalent over a wide area: *The word spread fast.* **4.** To become distributed in a layer. **5.** To become separated; be forced farther apart. —*n.* **1. a.** The act of spreading. **b.** Dissemination, as of news; diffusion. **2. a.** An open area of land; expanse. **b.** A ranch or farmland. **3.** The extent or limit to which something is or can be spread; range. **4.** A cloth covering for a bed, table, or other piece of furniture. **5.** *Informal.* An abundant meal laid out on a table. **6.** A food to be spread on bread or crackers. **7. a.** Facing pages of a magazine or newspaper with related matter extending across the fold. **b.** A story or advertisement running across two or more columns. **8.** A difference, as between two figures or totals. [ME *spreden* < OE *sprǣdan.*]

spread eagle *n.* **1. a.** The figure of an eagle with wings and legs spread. **b.** The emblem on the Great Seal of the United States. **2.** A posture or design resembling a spread eagle.

spread-ea·gle (sprĕd'ē'gəl) *adj.* **1.** With the arms and legs stretched out. **2.** *Informal.* Full of patriotic or jingoistic rhetoric. —*v.* **-gled, -gling, -gles.** —*tr.* To place in a spread-eagle position, esp. as a means of punishment. —*intr.* To make a grandiloquent, patriotic speech.

spread·er (sprĕd'ər) *n.* One that spreads, esp.: **a.** A butter knife. **b.** A farm implement for scattering fertilizer or seed. **c.** A device, such as a bar, for keeping wires or stays apart.

spree (sprē) *n.* **1.** A gay, lively outing. **2.** A drinking bout. **3.** An overindulgence in an activity: *a buying spree.* [Perh. alteration of Sc. *spreath,* cattle raid < Ir. Gael. *sprēidh* < Lat. *praeda,* booty.]

spri·er (sprī'ər) *adj.* Comparative of **spry.**

spri·est (sprī'ĭst) *adj.* Superlative of **spry.**

sprig (sprĭg) *n.* **1. a.** A small shoot or twig of a plant. **b.** An ornament in this shape. **2.** A small brad without a head. **3.** A young, immature person. —*tr.v.* **sprigged, sprig·ging, sprigs. 1.** To decorate with a design of sprigs. **2.** To remove a sprig or sprigs from (a bush or tree). **3.** To fasten with a small headless brad. [ME *sprigge.*] —**sprig'ger** *n.*

spright (sprīt) *n.* Variant of **sprite.**

spright·ly (sprīt'lē) *adj.* **-li·er, -li·est.** Buoyant or animated; full of life. —*adv.* With briskness; gaily. —**spright'li·ness** *n.*

spring (sprĭng) *v.* **sprang** (sprăng) or **sprung** (sprŭng), **sprung, spring·ing, springs.** —*intr.* **1.** To move upward or forward in a single quick motion. **2.** To appear or emerge suddenly. **3.** To shift position suddenly: *The door sprang shut.* **4.** To arise from a source; develop. **5.** To become warped, bent, or cracked. Used of wood. **6.** To move out of place; come loose, as a part of a machine. —*tr.* **1.** To cause to leap, dart, or come forth suddenly. **2.** To jump over; vault. **3.** To release from a checked or inoperative position; actuate: *Motion will spring the trap.* **4.** To cause to warp, bend, or crack, as by force. **5.** To present unexpectedly: *spring a surprise.* **6.** *Slang.* To cause to be released, esp. from prison. —*n.* **1.** An elastic device, such as a coil of wire, that regains its original shape after being compressed or extended. **2.** An actuating force or factor; impetus. **3.** The quality of elasticity; resilience. **4. a.** The act of springing, esp. a jump or leap. **b.** The distance covered by a leap. **5.** A flock of teal. **6.** A usually rapid return to normal shape after removal of stress; recoil. **7.** A natural fountain or flow of water. **8.** A source, origin, or beginning. **9.** The season of the year, occurring between winter and summer, during which the weather becomes warmer and plants revive, extending in the Northern Hemisphere from the vernal equinox to the summer solstice and popularly considered to comprise March, April, and May. **10.** A warping, bending, or cracking, such as that caused by excessive force. [ME *springen* < OE *springan.*]

spring beauty *n.* Any of several plants of the genus *Claytonia,* esp. *C. virginica,* of eastern North America, having narrow leaves and white or pinkish flowers.

spring·board (sprĭng'bôrd', -bōrd') *n.* **1.** A flexible board mounted on a fulcrum with one end secured, used by gymnasts to gain momentum at the start of an exercise. **2.** A diving board. **3.** A starting-off place.

spring·bok (sprĭng′bŏk′) *n., pl.* **springbok** or **-boks.** A small brown and white gazelle, *Antidorcas marsupialis,* of southern Africa, that is capable of leaping high into the air. [Afr. : *spring,* to leap up + *bok,* male deer.]

spring chicken *n.* **1.** A young chicken, esp. one from two to ten months old, having tender meat. **2.** *Slang.* A young or naive person.

spring-clean·ing (sprĭng′-klē′nĭng) *n.* An extensive cleaning, esp. of a home after winter.

springe (sprĭnj) *n.* **1.** A device for snaring small game, made by attaching a noose to a branch under tension. **2.** A trap; snare. [ME.]

spring·er (sprĭng′ər) *n.* **1.** One that springs. **2.** A springer spaniel. **3.** *Western U.S.* A cow about to give birth. **4.** *Archit.* **a.** The impost of an arch. **b.** The bottom stone of an arch resting on the impost.

springer spaniel *n.* A dog of a breed originating in England or Wales, having drooping ears and a silky brown and white or black and white coat.

spring fever *n.* The feelings of languor, rejuvenation, or yearning that may affect people at the advent of spring.

Spring·field rifle (sprĭng′fēld′) *n.* A magazine-fed breech-loading bolt-action .30-caliber U.S. Army rifle. [After *Springfield,* Massachusetts, where it was first made.]

spring·form pan (sprĭng′fôrm′) *n.* A baking pan with an upright removable rim fastened to the bottom with a spring.

spring·halt (sprĭng′hôlt′) *n.* A stringhalt. [Alteration of STRINGHALT.]

spring·head (sprĭng′hĕd′) *n.* A fountainhead or source.

spring·house (sprĭng′hous′) *n.* A small house constructed over a spring and used to keep food cool.

spring·let (sprĭng′lĭt) *n.* A small spring of water; rill.

spring lock *n.* A lock in which the bolt shoots automatically by means of a spring.

spring peeper *n.* A small, brownish tree frog, *Hyla crucifer,* of eastern North America, having a characteristic shrill, high-pitched call.

spring roll *n.* An egg roll.

spring·tail (sprĭng′tāl′) *n.* Any of various small wingless insects of the order Collembola, having abdominal appendages that act as springs to catapult them through the air.

spring tide *n.* **1.** The tide generally having the greatest rise and fall, occurring at or shortly after the new moon or the full moon when the sun, moon, and earth are approximately aligned. **2.** A great flood or rush, as of emotion.

spring·time (sprĭng′tīm′) *n.* The season of spring.

spring·wood (sprĭng′wo͝od′) *n.* Young, usually soft wood that lies directly beneath the bark and develops in early spring.

spring·y (sprĭng′ē) *adj.* **-i·er, -i·est.** **1.** Resilient; elastic. **2.** Abounding with freshwater springs. **—spring′i·ly** *adv.* **—spring′i·ness** *n.*

sprin·kle (sprĭng′kəl) *v.* **-kled, -kling, -kles.** *—tr.* **1.** To scatter or release in drops or small particles. **2.** To scatter drops or particles upon. *—intr.* **1.** To scatter small drops or particles of something. **2.** To fall or rain in small or infrequent drops. *—n.* **1.** The act of sprinkling. **2.** A light, sparse rainfall. **3.** A small amount. [ME *sprenklen,* perh. of MLG orig.]

sprin·kler (sprĭng′klər) *n.* **1.** One that sprinkles, esp.: **a.** An outlet on a sprinkler system. **b.** A device attached to the end of a water hose, used for sprinkling water on lawns. **2.** A sprinkler system.

sprinkler system *n.* A fire-extinguishing system consisting of a network of water pipes equipped to release water automatically when temperatures rise above a predetermined limit.

sprin·kling (sprĭng′klĭng) *n.* **1.** Something that is sprinkled. **2.** A small amount or quantity; modicum. **3.** A small quantity tossed or sparsely distributed.

sprint (sprĭnt) *n.* A short race run at top speed. *—intr.v.* **sprint·ed, sprint·ing, sprints.** To run at top speed. [Of Scand. orig.] **—sprint′er** *n.*

sprit (sprĭt) *n.* **1.** A pole extending diagonally across a fore-and-aft sail from the lower part of the mast to the peak of the sail. **2.** A bowsprit. [ME *sprytt* < OE *sprēot,* pole.]

sprite also **spright** (sprīt) *n.* **1. a.** A small or elusive supernatural being. **b.** An elflike person. **2. a.** A specter or ghost. **b.** *Archaic.* A soul. [ME *spreit* < OFr. *esprit* < Lat. *spiritus.* —see SPIRIT.]

sprit·sail (sprĭt′səl, -sāl′) *n.* A sail extended by a sprit.

sprock·et (sprŏk′ĭt) *n.* Any of various toothlike projections arranged on a wheel rim to engage the links of a chain. [Orig. unknown.]

sprocket wheel *n.* A wheel rimmed with sprockets, used to engage the links of a chain in a pulley or drive system.

sprout (sprout) *v.* **sprout·ed, sprout·ing, sprouts.** *—intr.* **1.** To begin to grow; give off shoots or buds. **2.** To grow or develop quickly; burgeon. *—tr.* To cause to grow. *—n.* **1.** A young plant growth, as a bud or shoot. **2.** Something resembling or suggestive of a sprout. **3. sprouts.** Brussels sprouts. [ME *spruten* < OE *sprūtan.*]

spruce[1] (spro͞os) *n.* **1. a.** Any of various coniferous evergreen trees of the genus *Picea,* having needlelike foliage, drooping cones, and soft wood often used for paper pulp. **b.** Any of various similar or related trees. **c.** The wood of any of these trees. **2.** A grayish or dark grayish to greenish black. [Short for obs. *Spruce fir,* Prussian fir < *Spruce,* Prussia < ME *Sprewse,* alteration of *Pruce* < OFr. < Med. Lat. *Prussia.*]

spruce[2] (spro͞os) *adj.* **spruc·er, spruc·est.** Neat, trim, or dapper in appearance. *—v.* **spruced, spruc·ing, spruc·es.** *—tr.* To make spruce; dress neatly. *—intr.* To become spruce: *He spruced up for the dance.* [Perh. < obs. *spruce leather,* Prussian leather. —see SPRUCE[1].] **—spruce′ly** *adv.* **—spruce′ness** *n.*

spruce beer *n.* A slightly fermented beverage made with an extract of spruce needles and twigs with molasses or sugar.

spruce pine *n.* The black spruce.

sprue (spro͞o) *n.* A chronic, chiefly tropical disease characterized by diarrhea, emaciation, and anemia. [Du. *spruw* < MDu. *sprouwe.*]

sprung (sprŭng) *v.* A past tense and the past participle of **spring.**

sprung rhythm *n.* A forcefully accentual verse rhythm in which a stressed syllable is followed by an irregular number of unstressed or slack syllables to form a foot having a metrical value equal to that of the other feet in the line. [Coined by Gerard Manley Hopkins (1844–1889).]

spry (sprī) *adj.* **spri·er** or **spry·er, spri·est** or **spry·est.** Briskly active; lively. [Perh. of Scand. orig.] **—spry′ly** *adv.* **—spry′ness** *n.*

spud (spŭd) *n.* **1.** A sharp tool resembling a spade for rooting or digging out weeds. **2.** *Slang.* A potato. *—tr.v.* **spud·ded, spud·ding, spuds.** To remove (weeds, for example) with a spud. [ME *spudde,* short knife.]

spue (spyo͞o) *v. & n. Obs.* Variant of **spew.**

spume (spyo͞om) *n.* Foam or froth on a liquid. *—intr.v.* **spumed, spum·ing, spumes.** To froth or foam. [ME < OFr. *espume* < Lat. *spuma.*] **—spu′mous, spum′y** *adj.*

spu·mo·ne also **spu·mo·ni** (spo͞o-mō′nē) *n.* An Italian frozen dessert of ice cream containing fruit, nuts, or candies. [Ital. < *spuma,* foam < Lat.]

spun (spŭn) *v.* Past tense and past participle of **spin.**

spun glass *n.* **1.** Fiber glass. **2.** Fine blown glass having delicate, often spiral threading or filigree.

spunk (spŭngk) *n.* **1.** Punk, touchwood, or other tinder. **2.** *Informal.* Spirit; pluck. [Sc. Gael. *spong,* tinder < Lat. *spongia,* sponge.]

spunk·y (spŭng′kē) *adj.* **-i·er, -i·est.** Spirited; plucky. **—spunk′i·ly** *adv.* **—spunk′i·ness** *n.*

spun silk *n.* A yarn made from short-fibered silk.

spun sugar *n.* Sugar threaded into a confectionary fluff.

spun yarn *n.* A lightweight line made of several rope yarns loosely wound together, used for seizings on board ship.

spur (spûr) *n.* **1.** One of a pair of spikes or spiked wheels attached to a rider's heels and used to urge a horse forward. **2.** An incentive; stimulus. **3.** A spurlike attachment or projection, as: **a.** A spinelike process on the leg of some birds. **b.** A climbing iron; crampon. **c.** The gaff attached to the leg of a gamecock. **d.** A short or stunted branch of a tree. **e.** An ergot growing on rye. **4.** A lateral ridge projecting from a mountain or mountain range. **5.** An oblique reinforcing prop or stay of timber or masonry. **6.** *Bot.* A tubular extension of the corolla or calyx of a flower, as in a columbine or larkspur. **7.** A spur track. *—v.* **spurred, spur·ring, spurs.** *—tr.* **1.** To urge (a horse) on by the use of spurs. **2.** To incite; prompt. *—intr.* To ride quickly on horseback by making use of spurs. ***—idiom.* on the spur of the moment.** On a sudden impulse. [ME *spure* < OE *spura.*]

spurge (spûrj) *n.* Any of various chiefly tropical plants of the genus *Euphorbia,* characteristically having milky juice and small flowers that in some species are surrounded by showy bracts. [ME < OFr. *espurge* < *espurgier,* to purge (from its use as a purgative) < Lat. *expurgare.* —see EXPURGATE.]

spur gear *n.* A gear with teeth radially arrayed on the rim parallel to its axis.

spurge laurel *n.* A low-growing shrub, *Daphne laureola,* of southern Europe, having glossy evergreen leaves and small yellowish-green flowers.

spu·ri·ous (spyo͝or′ē-əs) *adj.* **1.** Lacking authenticity or validity; false. **2.** Constituting a forgery or interpolation. **3.** Illegitimate; bastard. **4.** *Bot.* Similar in appearance but unlike in structure or function. [LLat. *spurius,* false < Lat., illegitimate.] **—spu′ri·ous·ly** *adv.* **—spu′ri·ous·ness** *n.*

spurn (spûrn) *v.* **spurned, spurn·ing, spurns.** *—tr.* **1.** To reject or refuse disdainfully; scorn. **2.** *Archaic.* **a.** To kick disdainfully. **b.** To tread on; trample. *—intr.* To refuse something contemptuously. *—n.* **1.** A contemptuous rejection. **2.** *Archaic.* A kick. [ME *spurnen* < OE *spurnan.*] **—spurn′er** *n.*

spurred (spûrd) *adj.* **1.** Wearing spurs. **2.** Having a spur or spurs: *spurred flowers.*

spur·rey (spûr′ē) *n.* Variant of **spurry.**

spur·ri·er (spûr′ē-ər) *n.* One that makes spurs. [ME *sporior* < *spore, spure,* spur.]

spur·ry also **spur·rey** (spûr′ē) *n., pl.* **-ries** also **-reys.** Any of several weedy, low-growing plants of the genera *Spergula* or *Spergularia,* esp. *Spergula arvensis,* native to Europe, having whorled leaves and small white flowers. [Du. *spurrie* <

springer spaniel

sprinkler

sprit

sprocket

MDu. *speurie,* prob. < Med. Lat. *spergula,* prob. < Lat. *spargere,* to scatter.]

spurt (spûrt) *n.* **1.** A sudden and forcible gush. **2.** A sudden outbreak or short burst of energy or activity. —*v.* **spurt·ed, spurt·ing, spurts.** —*intr.* To gush forth. —*tr.* To force out in a jet or squirt. [ME *sprutten,* to sprout < OE *sprytten.*]

spur track *n.* A short side track that connects with the main track of a railroad system.

spu·ta (spyo͞o'tə) *n.* Plural of **sputum.**

sput·nik (spo͝ot'nĭk, spŭt'-, spo͞ot'-) *n.* Any of the artificial earth satellites launched by the USSR, esp. the first, launched October 4, 1957. [R. *sputnik (zemlyi),* fellow traveler (of Earth).]

sput·ter (spŭt'ər) *v.* **-tered, -ter·ing, -ters.** —*intr.* **1. a.** To spit out small particles in short bursts, often with corresponding sounds or noises. **b.** To make the sporadic coughing noise characteristic of such activity. **2.** To speak in a hasty or confused fashion; stammer. —*tr.* **1.** To spit out (saliva, for example) in short bursts. **2.** To utter in a hasty or confused fashion. —*n.* **1.** The act of sputtering. **2.** The sound of sputtering. **3.** The particles that are emitted during sputtering. **4.** Hasty or confused utterances. [Prob. of LG orig.] —**sput'ter·er** *n.*

spu·tum (spyo͞o'təm) *n., pl.* **-ta** (-tə). **1.** Expectorated saliva; spittle. **2.** Expectorated matter, including saliva, substances from the respiratory tract, and foreign material. [Lat. *sputum* < *sputus,* p.part. of *spuere,* to spit.]

spy (spī) *n., pl.* **spies. 1.** A clandestine agent employed by a state to obtain intelligence relating to its eventual or actual enemies at home or abroad. **2.** One who secretly watches another or others. **3.** The act of watching covertly or secretly. —*v.* **spied, spy·ing, spies.** —*tr.* **1.** To keep under surveillance with hostile intent. **2.** To catch sight of; see. —*intr.* **1. a.** To observe secretly and closely. **b.** To engage in espionage. **2.** To investigate: *spying into their activities.* [ME *spie* < OFr. *espie* < *espier,* to watch, of Germanic orig.]

spy·glass (spī'glăs') *n.* **1.** A small telescope. **2. spyglasses.** Binoculars.

squab (skwŏb) *n.* **1.** A young, unfledged pigeon. **2.** A short, fat person. **3.** A soft cushion. **4.** A couch; sofa. —*adj.* **1.** Short and broad; squat. **2.** Newly hatched or unfledged. [Prob. of Scand. orig.]

squab·ble (skwŏb'əl) *intr.v.* **-bled, -bling, -bles.** To engage in a trivial quarrel; bicker. —*n.* A trivial quarrel. [Prob. of Scand. orig.] —**squab'bler** *n.*

squab·by (skwŏb'ē) *adj.* **-bi·er, -bi·est.** Short and fat; squat.

squad (skwŏd) *n.* **1.** A small group of persons organized for a specific purpose. **2.** The smallest unit of military personnel, frequently designated as a line or rank in formation. **3.** An athletic team. [OFr. *esquadre* < OSp. *escuadra* and OItal. *squadra,* both < VLat. **exquadrare,* to make square. —see SQUARE.]

squad car *n.* A police patrol car connected by radiotelephone with headquarters.

squad·ron (skwŏd'rən) *n.* **1.** A group of naval vessels constituting two or more divisions of a fleet. **2.** An armored cavalry unit consisting of two to four troops, a headquarters, and certain auxiliary units. **3.** The basic tactical air force unit, subordinate to a group and consisting of two or more flights. **4.** An organized multitude; legion: *"squadrons of flies like particles of dust danced up and down"* (T.E. Lawrence). [Ital. *squadrone* < *squadra,* squad. —see SQUAD.]

squash[1]
Different types of squash

squad room *n.* A room in a police station where officers assemble, as for assignment or briefing.

squa·lene (skwā'lēn') *n.* A natural unsaturated aliphatic hydrocarbon, $C_{30}H_{50}$, found in human sebum and other fatty deposits, that is an intermediate in the biosynthesis of cholesterol and is used in biochemical research. [< NLat. *Squalus,* shark genus (from its occurrence in the liver oil of sharks) < Lat. *squalus,* a sea fish + -ENE.]

squal·id (skwŏl'ĭd) *adj.* **1.** Having a dirty or wretched appearance. **2.** Morally repulsive; sordid. [Lat. *squalidus* < *squalere,* to be filthy < *squalus,* filthy.] —**squa·lid'i·ty** (skwŏ-lĭd'ĭ-tē), **squal'id·ness** *n.* —**squal'id·ly** *adv.*

squall[1] (skwôl) *n.* A loud, harsh outcry. —*intr.v.* **squalled, squall·ing, squalls.** To scream or cry loudly and harshly. [Prob. of Scand. orig.] —**squall'er** *n.*

squall[2] (skwôl) *n.* **1.** A brief, sudden, and violent windstorm, often accompanied by rain or snow. **2.** *Informal.* A disturbance or commotion. —*intr.v.* **squalled, squall·ing, squalls.** To blow strongly for a brief period. [Prob. of Scand. orig.]

squall line *n.* A zone of squalls and other violent changes in weather that marks the replacement of a warm air current by cold air.

squall·y (skwô'lē) *adj.* **-i·er, -i·est. 1.** Characterized by squalls; gusty. **2.** *Informal.* Marked by disturbance or trouble.

squal·or (skwŏl'ər) *n.* The state or quality of being squalid; filth and misery. [Lat.]

squa·ma (skwā'mə, skwä'-) *n., pl.* **-mae** (-mē'). **1.** A scale or scalelike structure. **2.** A thin plate of bone. [Lat.] —**squa'mate'** (-māt') *adj.*

squa·ma·tion (skwə-mā'shən) *n.* **1.** The condition of being scaly. **2.** An arrangement of scales, as on a fish.

Squa·mish (skwä'mĭsh) *n.* Variant of **Suquamish.**

squa·mo·sal (skwə-mō'səl, -zəl) *adj.* Of or pertaining to the squamous area of the temporal bone. —*n.* A squamosal bone. [< Lat. *squamosus,* squamous.]

squa·mous (skwā'məs, skwä'-) also **squa·mose** (-mōs') *adj.* **1.** Covered with or formed of scales; scaly. **2.** Resembling a scale or scales. [Lat. *squamosus* < *squama,* scale.] —**squa'mous·ly** *adv.* —**squa'mous·ness** *n.*

squamous cell *n.* An epithelial cell that is flat and scaly.

squamous epithelium *n.* Epithelium that is single-layered and composed of flat scaly cells.

squa·mu·lose (skwā'myə-lōs', skwä'-) *adj.* Having or consisting of minute scales. [< NLat. *squamula,* dim. of Lat. *squama,* scale.]

squan·der (skwŏn'dər) *tr.v.* **-dered, -der·ing, -ders. 1.** To spend wastefully or extravagantly; dissipate. **2.** *Obs.* To scatter. —*n.* Extravagant expenditure; prodigality. [Orig. unknown.] —**squan'der·er** *n.* —**squan'der·ing·ly** *adv.*

square (skwâr) *n.* **1.** A rectangle having four equal sides. **2.** Something characterized by an equal-sided rectangular form. **3.** A T-shaped or L-shaped instrument for drawing or testing right angles. **4.** The product of a number or quantity multiplied by itself. **5.** Any of the quadrilateral spaces dividing a checkerboard. **6. a.** An open, often quadrilateral area at the intersection of two or more streets. **b.** A rectangular space enclosed by streets and occupied by buildings. **7.** *Slang.* One characterized by rigid conventionality or lack of sophistication. —*adj.* **squar·er, squar·est. 1.** Having four equal sides and four right angles. **2.** Forming a right angle. **3. a.** Expressed in units measuring area: *square feet.* **b.** Having a specified length in each of two equal dimensions. **4.** *Naut.* Set at right angles to the mast and keel, as the yards of a square-rigged ship. **5. a.** Of more or less quadrate dimensions: *a square house.* **b.** Characterized by blocklike solidity or sturdiness. **6.** Honest; direct: *a square answer.* **7.** Just; equitable: *a square deal.* **8.** Paid-up; settled. **9.** In golf, even; tied. **10.** *Slang.* Rigidly conventional; straight. —*v.* **squared, squar·ing, squares.** —*tr.* **1.** To cut to a square or rectangular shape. **2.** To test for conformity to a desired plane, straight line, or right angle. **3.** To test by comparison. **4.** To bring into conformity or agreement. **5.** To set straight or at right angles: *square one's cap.* **6.** To bring into balance; settle: *square a debt.* **7.** In golf, to even the score of; tie. **8.** To raise (a number or quantity) to the second power. **9.** To find a square equal in area to (the area of a given figure). —*intr.* **1.** To be at right angles. **2.** To agree or conform; balance. —***phrasal verbs.*** **square away. 1.** To square the yards of a sailing vessel. **2.** To put away or in order. **square off.** To assume a fighting stance. —*adv.* **1.** At right angles. **2.** In a square shape. **3.** Solidly. **4.** Directly; straight. **5.** In an honest manner; straightforwardly. [ME < OFr. *esquare* < VLat. **exquadra* < **exquadrare,* to square : Lat. *ex-* (intensive) + *quadrare,* to square < *quadrus,* a square.] —**square'ly** *adv.* —**square'ness** *n.* —**squar'er** *n.*

square bracket *n.* A bracket (sense 4.a.).

square dance *n.* **1.** A dance in which sets of four couples form squares. **2.** Any of various group dances of English rural origin.

square-dance (skwâr'dăns') *intr.v.* **-danced, -danc·ing, -danc·es.** To perform a square dance. —**square'-danc'er** *n.*

square knot *n.* A common double knot with the loose ends parallel to the standing parts.

square matrix *n.* *Math.* A matrix with equal numbers of rows and columns.

square measure *n.* A system of units used in measuring area.

square rig *n.* A sailing-ship rig with sails of rectangular cut set approximately at right angles to the keel line from horizontal yards. —**square'-rigged'** *adj.*

square-rig·ger (skwâr'rĭg'ər) *n.* A square-rigged vessel.

square root *n.* A divisor of a quantity that when squared gives the quantity.

square sail *n.* A four-sided sail bent to a yard set athwart the mast.

squar·rose (skwăr'ōs', skwär'-) *adj.* **1.** *Biol.* Having rough or spreading scalelike processes. **2.** *Bot.* Spreading or recurved at the tip: *squarrose bracts.* [Lat. *squarrosus,* scabby.]

squash[1] (skwŏsh, skwôsh) *n.* **1.** Any of various plants of the genus *Cucurbita,* having fleshy edible fruit with a hard rind. **2.** The fruit of a squash, used as a vegetable. [Short for obs. *isquoutersquash* < Massachuset *askōōtasquash.*]

squash[2] (skwŏsh, skwôsh) *v.* **squashed, squash·ing, squash·es.** —*tr.* **1.** To beat, squeeze, or flatten to a pulp; crush. **2.** To put down or suppress; quash: *squash a revolt.* **3.** To silence (a person), as with crushing words. —*intr.* **1.** To be crushed or flattened. **2.** To move with a squelching sound. —*n.* **1.** The impact or sound of a soft body dropping against a surface. **2.** The sound of water being squeezed out, as from spongy ground or wet shoes. **3.** A crush; press: *a squash of people.* **4.** *Chiefly Brit.* A citrus-base soft drink. **5. a.** A game played in a walled court with a racket and a hard rubber ball. **b.** A similar game played with an inflated rubber ball. —*adv.* With a squashing sound. [OFr. *esquasshe* < VLat. **exquassare* : Lat. *ex-* (intensive) + *quassare,* to shatter, freq. of *quatere,* to shake.] —**squash'er** *n.*

squash bug *n.* A blackish North American insect, *Anasa tristis,* that is destructive to squash, pumpkins, and other crops.

squash·y (skwŏ′shē, skwô′shē) *adj.* **-i·er, -i·est. 1.** Easily squashed. **2.** Overripe and soft; pulpy. **3.** Boggy; squishy. **—squash′i·ly** *adv.* **—squash′i·ness** *n.*
squat (skwŏt) *v.* **squat·ted, squat·ting, squats.** —*intr.* **1.** To sit on one's heels. **2.** To settle on unoccupied land without legal claim. **3.** To occupy a given piece of public land in order to acquire title to it. —*tr.* **1.** To put (oneself) in a crouching posture. **2.** To occupy as a squatter. —*adj.* **squat·ter, squat·test. 1.** Seated in a squatting position. **2.** Short and thick. —*n.* **1. a.** A squatting or crouching posture. **b.** The act of squatting or crouching. **2.** The lair of a hare. **3.** The land occupied by a squatter. [ME *squatten* < OFr. *esquatir,* to crush : *es-* (intensive < Lat. *ex-*) + *quatir,* to press flat < VLat. **coactire* < Lat. *cogere,* to compress (*co-,* together + *agere,* to drive).] **—squat′ter** *n.*
squaw (skwô) *n.* A North American Indian woman. [Massachuset *squa.*]
squaw·fish (skwô′fĭsh′) *n., pl.* **squawfish** or **-fish·es.** Any of several large freshwater fishes of the genus *Ptychocheilus,* of western North America.
squawk (skwôk) *v.* **squawked, squawk·ing, squawks.** —*intr.* **1.** To utter a harsh scream; screech. **2.** To make a loud, angry, or peevish protest. —*tr.* To utter with or as if with a squawk. —*n.* **1.** A loud screech; squall. **2.** A protest or complaint. [Perh. blend of SQUALL and SQUEAK.] **—squawk′er** *n.*
squaw man *n.* A frontiersman having an Indian wife and usually living with her tribe.
squaw·root (skwô′rōōt′, -rŏŏt′) *n.* A plant, *Conopholis americana,* of eastern North America, that has yellowish flowers and a stem covered with brownish scales and is parasitic on the roots of oaks and other trees.
squeak (skwēk) *v.* **squeaked, squeak·ing, squeaks.** —*intr.* **1.** To utter or make a brief thin, shrill cry or sound. **2.** To pass or win by a slight margin: *squeaked through the driving test.* **3.** *Slang.* To turn informer. —*tr.* To utter in a squeaky voice. —*n.* **1.** A brief thin, shrill cry or sound. **2.** An escape: *a close squeak.* [ME *squeken.*] **—squeak′er** *n.*
squeak·y (skwē′kē) *adj.* **-i·er, -i·est.** Characterized by squeaking tones; tending to squeak. **—squeak′i·ly** *adv.* **—squeak′i·ness** *n.*
squeal (skwēl) *v.* **squealed, squeal·ing, squeals.** —*intr.* **1.** To utter or produce a loud, shrill cry or sound. **2.** *Slang.* To betray a friend or a secret. —*tr.* To utter or produce with a squeal. —*n.* A loud, shrill cry or noise. [ME *squelen.*] **—squeal′er** *n.*
squea·mish (skwē′mĭsh) *adj.* **1. a.** Easily nauseated or sickened. **b.** Nauseated. **2.** Easily offended or disgusted; prudish. **3.** Excessively fastidious; oversensitive. [ME *squaymisch,* alteration of AN *escoymous.*] **—squea′mish·ly** *adv.* **—squea′mish·ness** *n.*
squee·gee (skwē′jē′) *n.* **1.** A T-shaped implement having a crosspiece edged with rubber or leather, used to remove water from a surface, as a window. **2.** An implement or a rubber roller used in printing and photography. —*tr.v.* **-geed, -gee·ing, -gees.** To wipe or smooth with a squeegee. [Perh. < E. *squeege,* to press, alteration of SQUEEZE.]
squeeze (skwēz) *v.* **squeezed, squeez·ing, squeez·es.** —*tr.* **1.** To press hard upon or together; compress. **2.** To exert pressure on, as by way of extracting liquid: *squeeze an orange.* **3.** To extract from by applying pressure: *squeeze juice from a lemon.* **4.** To extract by dishonest means; extort. **5.** To obtain room or passage for by pressure; cram. **6.** To oppress with burdensome exactions. **7.** In bridge, to force (an opponent) to use a potentially winning card in a trick he cannot take. —*intr.* **1.** To give way under pressure. **2.** To exert pressure. **3.** To force one's way, as through a crowd. ***—phrasal verb.* squeeze off.** To fire (a round of bullets) by squeezing the trigger of a gun. —*n.* **1.** An act or instance of compressing. **2.** A handclasp or brief embrace. **3.** A group crowded together. **4. a.** An amount squeezed out of something. **b.** A minor ingredient; pinch. **5. a.** *Informal.* A squeeze play. **b.** Financial pressure caused by shortages or narrowing economic margins. **6.** A forced discard of a potentially winning card in bridge. [Alteration of obs. *quease,* to press < ME *queysen* < OE *cwȳsan.*] **—squeez′er** *n.*
squeeze play *n.* **1.** *Baseball.* A play in which the batter attempts to bunt so that a runner on third base may score. **2.** *Informal.* Pressure exerted to obtain a concession or achieve a goal.
squelch (skwĕlch) *v.* **squelched, squelch·ing, squelch·es.** —*tr.* **1.** To crush by or as if by trampling; squash. **2.** To put down or silence, as with a crushing remark. **3.** To cause to make a squishing sound. —*intr.* To make or move with a splashing, squashing, or sucking sound. —*n.* **1.** A squishing sound. **2.** A crushing reply. **3.** An electric circuit that cuts off a radio receiver when the signal is too weak for reception of anything but noise. [Imit.] **—squelch′er** *n.*
sque·teague (skwĭ-tēg′) *n., pl.* **squeteague. 1.** The weakfish. **2.** Any of several fishes related to the weakfish. [Prob. of Algonquian orig.]
squib (skwĭb) *n.* **1. a.** A firecracker. **b.** A broken firecracker that burns but does not explode. **2.** A brief, sometimes witty literary effort, such as a lampoon. —*v.* **squibbed, squib·bing, squibs.** —*intr.* To write squibs. —*tr.* **1.** To write squibs about. **2.** *Football.* To kick (the ball) low on a kickoff so that it bounces along the ground. [Prob. imit.]
squib kick *n. Football.* A kind of kickoff in which the ball is kicked low so that it will bounce along the ground, making it difficult to field and return.
squid (skwĭd) *n., pl.* **squids** or **squid.** Any of various marine cephalopod mollusks of the genera *Loligo, Rossia,* and related genera, having a usually elongated body, ten arms surrounding the mouth, a vestigial internal shell, and a pair of triangular or rounded fins. [Orig. unknown.]

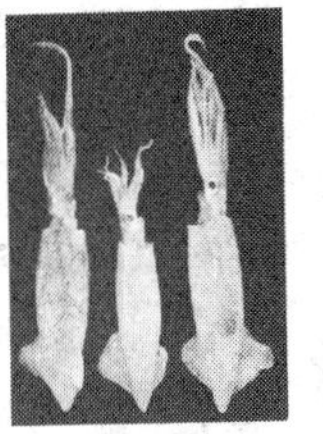

squid

squiffed (skwĭft) or **squif·fy** (skwĭf′ē) *adj. Slang.* Drunk. [Orig. unknown.]
squig·gle (skwĭg′əl) *n.* A small wiggly mark or scrawl. —*intr.v.* **-gled, -gling, -gles.** To squirm and wriggle. [Blend of SQUIRM and WRIGGLE.] **—squig′gly** *adj.*
squill (skwĭl) *n.* **1.** Any of several bulbous plants of the genus *Scilla,* native to Eurasia, having narrow leaves and bell-shaped blue, white, or pink flowers. **2. a.** The sea onion. **b.** The dried inner scales of the bulbs of the squill, used as rat poison and formerly as a cardiac stimulant, expectorant, and diuretic. [ME < Lat. *squilla* < Gk. *skilla.*]
squil·la (skwĭl′ə) *n., pl.* **squil·las** or **squil·lae** (skwĭl′ē′). Any of various burrowing marine crustaceans of the order Stomatopoda, having a pair of jointed grasping appendages. [NLat. *Squilla,* type genus < Lat. *squilla,* shrimp.]
squinch (skwĭnch) *n.* A quarter-spherical segment of masonry vaulting or corbeling used across the upper inside corners of a square tower as the transition to a circular or octagonal superstructure. [Shortening and alteration of SCUNCHEON.]
squint (skwĭnt) *v.* **squint·ed, squint·ing, squints.** —*intr.* **1.** To look with the eyes partly open. **2.** To look or glance to the side. **3.** To suffer from strabismus. **4.** To have an indirect or implicit tendency. —*tr.* **1.** To cause to squint. **2.** To close (the eyes) partly. —*n.* **1.** The act of squinting. **2.** An inclination; tendency. **3.** Strabismus. —*adj.* **1.** Looking obliquely or askance. **2.** Affected with strabismus. [Short for ASQUINT.] **—squint′er** *n.*
squint-eyed (skwĭnt′īd′) *adj.* **1.** Having strabismus. **2.** With narrowed or squinting eyes. **3.** Looking askance; biased.
squir·ar·chy (skwīr′är′kē) *n.* Variant of **squirearchy.**
squire (skwīr) *n.* **1.** A young nobleman attendant upon a knight and ranked next below a knight in feudal hierarchy. **2.** An English country gentleman. **3.** A judge or other local dignitary. **4.** A man who attends or escorts a woman; gallant. —*tr.v.* **squired, squir·ing, squires.** To attend as a squire or escort. [ME *squier* < OFr. *esquier.* —see ESQUIRE.]
squire·ar·chy or **squir·ar·chy** (skwīr′är′kē) *n., pl.* **-chies. 1.** Squires collectively. **2.** Government by landed proprietors.
squirm (skwûrm) *intr.v.* **squirmed, squirm·ing, squirms. 1.** To twist about in a wriggling, snakelike motion; writhe. **2.** To feel or exhibit signs of humiliation or embarrassment. —*n.* **1.** The act of squirming. **2.** A squirming movement. [Perh. imit.] **—squirm′er** *n.* **—squirm′y** *adj.*
squir·rel (skwûr′əl, skwŭr′-) *n.* **1.** Any of various arboreal rodents of the genus *Sciurus* and related genera, usually with gray or reddish-brown fur and a long, flexible, bushy tail. **2.** Any of various animals of the family Sciuridae, such as the ground squirrel or the flying squirrel. **3.** The fur of a squirrel. [ME *squirel* < AN *esquirel* < VLat. **scuriolus* < Lat. *sciurus* < Gk. *skiouros* : *skia,* shadow + *oura,* tail.]

squirrel

squirrel corn *n.* A low-growing North American plant, *Dicentra canadensis,* having finely divided leaves, cream-colored flowers, and tubers resembling grains of corn.
squir·rel·fish (skwûr′əl-fĭsh′, skwŭr′-) *n., pl.* **squirrelfish** or **-fish·es.** Any of various fishes of the genus *Holocentrus* and related genera, of warm marine waters, having large eyes and a usually reddish body.
squir·rel·ly (skwûr′ə-lē, skwŭr′-) *adj. Slang.* Crazy; eccentric.
squirrel monkey *n.* Either of two tropical American monkeys, *Saimiri sciureus* or *S. örstedii,* having short, thick fur and a long, nonprehensile tail.
squirt (skwûrt) *v.* **squirt·ed, squirt·ing, squirts.** —*intr.* **1.** To be ejected in a thin swift stream. **2.** To eject a thin swift stream. —*tr.* **1.** To eject (liquid) in a thin swift stream. **2.** To wet with liquid ejected in a thin swift stream. —*n.* **1.** The act of squirting. **2.** A device used to squirt. **3.** A stream squirted. **4.** *Informal.* **a.** An impudent youngster. **b.** A child; kid. [ME *squirten.*] **—squirt′er** *n.*
squirt gun *n.* A toy designed to squirt a stream of water.
squirting cucumber *n.* A hairy vine, *Ecballium elaterium,* of the Mediterranean region, having fruit that when ripe discharges its seeds and juice explosively.
squish (skwĭsh) *v.* **squished, squish·ing, squish·es.** *Informal.* —*tr.* To squash noisily. —*intr.* To emit a sound like that of soft mud being compressed. —*n.* The sound made by squishing. [Alteration of SQUASH.] **—squish′y** *adj.*
Sr The symbol for the element strontium.
sRNA *n.* Transfer RNA. [S(OLUBLE) RNA.]
-st *suff.* Variant of **-est**[2].
stab (stăb) *v.* **stabbed, stab·bing, stabs.** —*tr.* **1.** To pierce or wound with or as if with a pointed object. **2.** To plunge (a weapon) into a body. —*intr.* **1.** To lunge with or as if with a pointed weapon. **2.** To inflict a wound by stabbing. —*n.* **1.** A thrust made with a pointed instrument or weapon. **2.** A

staff¹
Detail from an ancient Greek vase painting

stag

wound inflicted by or as if by stabbing. **3.** An attempt; effort. [< ME *stabbe,* a stab wound.] **—stab'ber** *n.*

sta·bile (stā'bĭl, -bīl') *adj.* Immobile; unchangeable. *—n.* (-bēl'). An abstract sculpture, usually of sheet metal, with no moving parts. [Lat. *stabilis,* stable.]

sta·bil·i·ty (stə-bĭl'ĭ-tē) *n., pl.* **-ties. 1.** Resistance to sudden change, dislodgment, or overthrow. **2. a.** Constancy of character or purpose; steadfastness. **b.** Reliability; dependability. **3.** A vow committing a monk to one monastery for life.

sta·bi·lize (stā'bə-līz') *v.* **-lized, -liz·ing, -liz·es.** *—tr.* **1.** To make stable. **2.** To maintain the stability of. *—intr.* To become stable. **—sta'bi·li·za'tion** *n.*

sta·bi·liz·er (stā'bə-lī'zər) *n.* **1.** One that stabilizes. **2.** *Naut.* A device in a ship or boat, as a gyroscopically controlled fin, used to prevent excessive rolling. **3.** An airfoil used to stabilize an aircraft in flight. **4.** *Chem.* A substance that renders or maintains a solution, mixture, suspension, or state resistant to chemical change.

sta·ble¹ (stā'bəl) *adj.* **-bler, -blest. 1. a.** Resistant to sudden change of position or condition. **b.** Maintaining equilibrium; self-restoring. **2.** *Physics.* Having no known mode of decay; indefinitely long-lived. Used of atomic particles. **3.** Immutable and permanent; enduring. **4.** *Chem.* Not easily decomposed or otherwise modified chemically. **5. a.** Consistently dependable. **b.** Not subject to mental illness or irrationality: *a stable person.* [ME < OFr. *estable* < Lat. *stabilis.*] **—sta'ble·ness** *n.* **—sta'bly** *adv.*

sta·ble² (stā'bəl) *n.* **1. a.** A building for the shelter and feeding of domestic animals, esp. horses and cattle. **b.** The animals lodged in such a building. **2.** All of the racehorses belonging to a single owner or racing establishment. **3.** The personnel employed to keep and train a collection of racehorses. **4.** A group that serves under a single authority: *a stable of prizefighters.* *—v.* **-bled, -bling, -bles.** *—tr.* To put or keep (an animal) in a stable. *—intr.* To live or be kept in a stable. [ME < OFr. *estable* < Lat. *stabulum.*]

sta·bling (stā'blĭng) *n.* **1.** Stables collectively. **2.** Accommodations in a stable for animals.

stab·lish (stăb'lĭsh) *v. Archaic.* Variant of **establish.**

stac·ca·to (stə-kä'tō) *adj.* **1.** *Mus.* Cut short crisply; disconnected: *a staccato passage.* **2.** Composed of abrupt, distinct parts or sounds: *staccato applause.* *—n., pl.* **-tos** or **-ti** (-tē). An abrupt, distinct manner or sound. [Ital., p.part. of *staccare,* to detach < OFr. *destachier.* —see DETACH.] **—stac·ca'to** *adv.*

stack (stăk) *n.* **1.** A large, usually conical pile of straw or fodder arranged for outdoor storage. **2.** An orderly pile, esp. one arranged in layers. **3.** *Computer Sci.* A section of memory and its associated registers used for temporary storage of information, operating on a last-in-first-out principle. **4.** A group of three or more unslung rifles supporting each other butt downward and forming a cone. **5. a.** A chimney or flue. **b.** A group of chimneys. **6.** A vertical exhaust pipe, as on a ship or locomotive. **7.** Several rows of enclosed bookshelves. **8. stacks.** The area of a library in which most of the books are shelved. **9.** An English measure of coal or cut wood, equal to 108 cubic feet. **10.** *Informal.* A large quantity. *—tr.v.* **stacked, stack·ing, stacks. 1.** To arrange in a stack; pile. **2.** To load with stacks of material. **3.** To prearrange the order of (playing cards, for example); cheat. ***—phrasal verb.*** **stack up.** To measure up; compare. [ME < ON *stakkr.*] **—stack'er** *n.*

stacked heel *n.* A shoe heel made of several layers of material, as leather.

stack·up (stăk'ŭp') *n.* An arrangement of airplanes circling an airport at prescribed levels, awaiting instructions to land.

stac·te (stăk'tē) *n.* A spice used by the ancient Jews in making incense. [Lat. *stacte* < Gk. *staktē* < *staktos,* oozing < *stazein,* to ooze.]

stad·dle (stăd'l) *n.* A foundation, esp. a platform upon which hay or straw is stacked. [ME *stathel* < OE *staðol.*]

stad·hold·er (stăd'hōl'dər) also **stadt·hold·er** (stăt'-) *n.* **1.** A governor or viceroy formerly stationed in a province of the Netherlands. **2.** The chief magistrate of the Netherlands. [Partial transl. of Du. *stadhouder* : *stad,* place + *houder,* holder.]

sta·di·a (stā'dē-ə) *n.* **1. a.** A method of surveying distances with a telescopic instrument having two parallel lines used to intercept intervals on a calibrated rod, the intervals being proportional to the intervening distance. **b.** The graduated rod used. **2.** The parallel lines in a telescope. **3.** A plural of **stadium.** [Ital., prob. < Lat., pl. of *stadium,* a unit of length. —see STADIUM.]

sta·di·um (stā'dē-əm) *n., pl.* **-di·a** (-dē-ə). **1.** In ancient Greece, a course on which foot races were held, usually semicircular and having tiers of seats for spectators. **2.** An ancient Greek measure of distance, based on the length of such a course and equal to about 185 kilometers, or 607 feet. **3.** *pl.* **-di·ums.** A large, often unroofed structure in which athletic events are held. **4.** A stage in the progress of a disease. [ME, unit of length < Lat. < Gk. *stadion,* alteration of *spadion,* racetrack < *span,* to pull.]

stadium coat *n.* A medium-length, usually heavy coat for casual wear.

stadt·hold·er (stăt'hol'dər) *n.* Variant of **stadholder.**

staff¹ (stăf) *n.* **1.** *pl.* **staffs** or **staves** (stāvz). A pole, rod, or stick used for various purposes, esp.: **a.** A stick or cane carried as an aid in walking or climbing. **b.** A stick used as a weapon; cudgel. **c.** A pole upon which a flag is displayed. **d.** A rod or baton carried as a symbol of authority. **2.** *pl.* **staffs.** A rule or similar graduated stick used for testing or measuring, as in surveying. **3.** *pl.* **staffs. a.** A group of assistants who aid an executive or other person in authority. **b.** A group of military or naval officers who serve a commanding officer but do not participate in combat and have no authority to command. **c.** The personnel who carry out a specific enterprise: *the nursing staff of a hospital.* **4.** *pl.* **staffs** or **staves.** *Mus.* The set of horizontal lines and their intermediate spaces upon which notes are written or printed. *—tr.v.* **staffed, staff·ing, staffs. 1.** To provide with a staff of employees. **2.** To serve as a member of the staff of. [ME *staf* < OE *stæf.*]

staff² (stăf) *n.* A building material that resembles stucco, composed of plaster and fiber and used as a wall covering over the skeleton of temporary buildings, as at expositions. [Prob. < G. *staffen,* to adorn.]

staff·er (stăf'ər) *n. Informal.* A member of a staff.

staff of life *n.* A staple or necessary food, esp. bread.

Staf·ford·shire terrier (stăf'ərd-shîr') *n.* A dog of a breed developed in England, having a short, variously colored coat and widely set forelegs. [After *Staffordshire,* a county in England.]

staff sergeant *n.* **1.** A noncommissioned army officer of the rank above a sergeant and below a sergeant first class. **2.** A noncommissioned air force officer of the rank above an airman first class and below a technical sergeant. **3.** A noncommissioned marine corps officer of the rank above a sergeant and below a gunnery sergeant.

staff tree *n.* Any of various dicotyledonous, shrubby plants of the genus *Celastrus,* which includes the bittersweet.

stag (stăg) *n.* **1.** The adult male of various deer, esp. the red deer. **2.** An animal, esp. a pig, castrated after reaching sexual maturity. **3.** A man who attends a social affair without escorting a woman. **4.** A social affair for men only. *—adj.* For or attended by men only: *a stag party.* *—adv.* As a single male; alone: *go stag.* *—intr.v.* **stagged, stag·ging, stags.** To attend a social affair without escorting a woman. [ME < OE *stagga.*]

stag beetle *n.* Any of numerous large beetles of the family Lucanidae, having long, powerful, antlerlike mandibles.

stage (stāj) *n.* **1.** A raised and level floor or platform. **2.** A platform on a microscope on which slides to be viewed are mounted. **3.** A worker's scaffold. **4. a.** The raised platform upon which theatrical performances are presented. **b.** An area in which actors perform. **c.** The acting profession. **d.** Dramatic literature or performance; the theater. **5.** The scene or setting of an event or series of events. **6.** A resting place on a journey, esp. one providing overnight accommodations. **7.** The distance between stopping places on a journey. **8.** A stagecoach. **9.** A level or story of a building. **10.** The level of the surface of a river or other fluctuating body of water in relation to some datum: *at flood stage.* **11.** A level, degree, or period of time in the course of a process; step. **12.** One of two or more successive propulsion units of a rocket vehicle that fires after the preceding one has been jettisoned. **13.** *Geol.* A subdivision in the classification of stratified rocks, ranking just below a series and representing rock formed during a chronological age. **14.** *Electronics.* An element or group of elements in a complex arrangement of parts, esp. a single tube or transistor and its accessory components in an amplifier. *—v.* **staged, stag·ing, stag·es.** *—tr.* **1.** To exhibit, present, or perform on or as if on a stage: *stage a boxing match.* **2.** To produce or direct (a theatrical performance). **3.** To arrange and carry out: *stage an invasion.* *—intr.* To be adaptable to or suitable for theatrical presentation. [ME < OFr. *estage* < VLat. **staticum* < Lat. *stare,* to stand.]

stage·coach (stāj'kōch') *n.* A four-wheeled horse-drawn vehicle formerly used to transport mail, parcels, and passengers.

stage·craft (stāj'krăft') *n.* Skill in the use of theatrical techniques or devices.

stage fright *n.* The fear or nervousness some people experience when performing or speaking before an audience.

stage·hand (stāj'hănd') *n.* A person who works backstage in a theater.

stage-man·age (stāj'măn'ĭj) *tr.v.* **-aged, -ag·ing, -ag·es. 1.** To serve as overall supervisor of the stage and actors for (a theatrical production). **2.** To supervise (a political campaign, for example) from behind the scenes. **—stage management** *n.* **—stage manager** *n.*

stag·er (stā'jər) *n.* One who possesses the wisdom of long experience; veteran.

stage-struck (stāj'strŭk') *adj.* Enthralled with the stage or with hopes of becoming an actor.

stage whisper *n.* **1.** The conventional whisper of an actor, intended to be heard by the audience but not by one or more of the other performers. **2.** A whisper intended to be overheard.

stag·ey (stā'jē) *adj.* Variant of **stagy.**

stag·fla·tion (stăg-flā'shən) *n.* A condition in which a high rate of price and wage inflation is coupled with stagnant consumer demand and high unemployment. [STAG(NATION) + (IN)FLATION.] **—stag·fla'tion·ar'y** (-shə-nĕr'ē) *adj.*

stag·ger (stăg'ər) *v.* **-gered, -ger·ing, -gers.** *—intr.* **1.** To move or stand unsteadily, as if under a great weight; totter. **2.** To lose strength or confidence. *—tr.* **1.** To cause to totter, sway, or reel: *The blow staggered him.* **2.** To overwhelm with emotion or surprise. **3.** To place regularly on alternating sides of a midline; set in a zigzag row or rows: *theater seats staggered for clear viewing.* **4.** To arrange in alternating or overlapping time periods. *—n.* **1.** The act of staggering. **2.** A staggered pattern, arrangement, or order. **3. staggers** *(used with a sing. verb).* **a.** Any of various diseases marked by vertigo, confusion, and weakness. **b.** Any of various diseases of the nervous system in animals, esp. a cerebrospinal disease of horses in which the animal loses coordination, staggers, and often falls. [Alteration of ME *stakeren* < ON *stakra,* freq. of *staka,* to push.] **—stag'ger·er** *n.* **—stag'ger·ing·ly** *adv.*

stag·ger·bush (stăg'ər-bo͝osh') *n.* A shrub, *Lyonia mariana,* of the eastern United States, having poisonous foliage.

stag·horn fern (stăg'hôrn') *n.* Any of several tropical epiphytic ferns of the genus *Platycerium,* having large divided fronds that resemble antlers.

stag·hound (stăg'hound') *n.* Any of several dogs, such as a deerhound, formerly used in hunting deer.

stag·ing (stā'jĭng) *n.* **1.** A temporary platform; scaffold. **2. a.** The operation of stagecoaches as an enterprise. **b.** Travel by stagecoach. **3.** The process of producing and directing a stage play. **4.** The act of jettisoning a stage of a multistage rocket.

staging area *n.* A place where armed forces and military supplies are gathered before departure for another locale.

stag·nant (stăg'nənt) *adj.* **1.** Not moving or flowing; motionless. **2.** Foul from standing still; stale: *stagnant ponds.* **3.** Lacking liveliness or briskness; sluggish: *a stagnant period for sales.* [Lat. *stagnans, stagnant-,* pr.part. of *stagnare,* to be stagnant < *stagnum,* swamp.] **—stag'nan·cy** *n.* **—stag'nant·ly** *adv.*

stag·nate (stăg'nāt') *intr.v.* **-nat·ed, -nat·ing, -nates. 1.** To be or become stagnant. **2.** To fail to progress or develop. [Lat. *stagnare, stagnat-* < *stagnum,* swamp.] **—stag·na'tion** *n.*

St. Ag·nes' Eve (sānt ăg'nĭs) *n.* Variant of **Saint Agnes' Eve.**

stag·y also **stag·ey** (stā'jē) *adj.* **-i·er, -i·est.** Having a theatrical character or quality, esp. artificial and affected. **—stag'i·ly** *adv.* **—stag'i·ness** *n.*

staid (stād) *adj.* **1.** Prudently reserved and colorless in style, manner, or behavior; sober. **2.** Fixed; permanent: *"There is nothing settled, nothing staid in this universe"* (Virginia Woolf). [< obs. *staid,* p.part. of STAY.] **—staid'ly** *adv.* **—staid'ness** *n.*

stain (stān) *v.* **stained, stain·ing, stains.** *—tr.* **1.** To discolor, soil, or spot. **2.** To taint; corrupt. **3.** To color with a coat of penetrating liquid dye or tint. **4.** To treat (specimens for the microscope) with a reagent or dye that makes visible certain parts without affecting others. *—intr.* To produce or receive discolorations. *—n.* **1.** A spot or smudge of foreign matter. **2.** A blemish upon one's moral character or reputation. **3.** A liquid substance applied esp. to wood that penetrates the surface and imparts a rich color. **4.** A colored solution used for staining microscopic specimens. [ME *steynen,* partly < OFr. *desteindre,* to deprive of color (Lat. *dis-,* apart + *tingere,* to dye), and partly < ON *steina,* to paint.] **—stain'a·ble** *adj.* **—stain'er** *n.*

stained glass *n.* Glass colored by mixing pigments inherently in the glass, by fusing colored metallic oxides onto the glass, or by painting and baking transparent colors on the glass surface.

stained glass

stain·less (stān'lĭs) *adj.* **1.** Without stain or blemish. **2.** Resistant to stain or corrosion. **—stain'less·ly** *adv.*

stainless steel *n.* Any of various steels alloyed with sufficient chromium to resist corrosion, oxidation, or rusting associated with exposure of ordinary steel to water and moist air.

stair (stâr) *n.* **1. stairs.** A series or flight of steps; staircase. **2.** One of a flight of steps. [ME < OE *stæger.*]

stair·case (stâr'kās') *n.* A flight or series of flights of steps and a supporting structure connecting separate levels.

stair·way (stâr'wā') *n.* A staircase.

stair·well (stâr'wĕl') *n.* A vertical shaft around which a staircase has been built.

stake (stāk) *n.* **1.** A piece of wood or metal sharpened at one end for driving into the ground, such as a marker, fence pole, or tent peg. **2. a.** A vertical post to which an offender is bound for execution by burning. **b.** Execution by burning. **3.** A vertical post secured at the edge of a platform, as on a truck. **4.** A territorial division in the Mormon Church consisting of a group of wards under the jurisdiction of a president. **5.** Often **stakes. a.** Money or property risked in a wager or gambling game. **b.** The reward or prize awarded the winner of a contest or race; purse. **6.** A race offering a reward or prize to the winner. **7.** A share or interest in an enterprise, esp. a financial share. **8.** A grubstake. *—tr.v.* **staked, stak·ing, stakes. 1.** To indicate the location or limits of with or as if with stakes: stake out a claim. **2.** To attach or support with a stake. **3.** To tether or tie to a stake. **4.** To gamble or risk; hazard. **5.** To provide working capital for; finance. ***—phrasal verb.* stake out. 1.** To assign (a police officer) to a given area in order to conduct surveillance. **2.** To conduct a stakeout. ***—idioms.* at stake.** In jeopardy. **pull up stakes.** To conclude one's affairs and move on. [ME < OE *staca.*]

stake·out (stāk'out') *n.* Surveillance of an area, building, or person esp.by the police.

Sta·kha·nov·ite (stə-kä'nə-vīt') *n.* A Soviet worker whose diligence and zeal earn him high governmental esteem. [After Alexei *Stakhanov* (1905–1977).]

sta·lac·tite (stə-lăk'tīt', stăl'ək-) *n.* A cylindrical or conical deposit, usually of calcite or aragonite, projecting downward from the roof of a cavern as a result of the dripping of mineral-rich water. [NLat. *stalactites* < Gk. *stalaktos,* dripping < *stalassein,* to drip.] **—sta·lac'ti·form'** *adj.* **—stal'ac·tit'ic** (stăl'ăk-tĭt'ĭk, stə-lăk'-) *adj.*

sta·lag (stä'läg', stăl'ăg') *n.* A German prisoner-of-war camp for noncommissioned and enlisted personnel. [G., short for *Stammlager,* base camp.]

sta·lag·mite (stə-lăg'mīt', stăl'əg-) *n.* A cylindrical or conical deposit, usually of calcite or aragonite, projecting upward from the floor of a cavern as a result of the dripping of mineral-rich water. [NLat. *stalagmites* < Gk. *stalagma,* a drop < *stalagmos,* dripping < *stalassein,* to drip.] **—stal'ag·mit'ic** (stăl'əg-mĭt'ĭk, stə-lăg'-) *adj.*

stalactite
Stalactites and stalagmites in the Luray Caverns of northern Virginia

stale¹ (stāl) *adj.* **stal·er, stal·est. 1.** Having lost freshness, effervescence, or palatability. **2.** Lacking in originality or spontaneity: *a stale joke.* **3.** Impaired in efficacy or strength. **4.** Having lost legal efficacy or force through lack of exercise or action. *—tr. & intr.v.* **staled, stal·ing, stales.** To make or become stale. [ME, well-aged (as beer).] **—stale'ly** *adv.* **—stale'ness** *n.*

stale² (stāl) *intr.v.* **staled, stal·ing, stales.** To urinate. Used of horses and camels. *—n.* The urine of horses or camels. [ME *stalen.*]

stale·mate (stāl'māt') *n.* **1.** A drawing position in chess in which only the king can move and although not in check can move only into check. **2.** A situation in which further action by either of two opponents is impossible; deadlock. *—tr.v.* **-mat·ed, -mat·ing, -mates.** To bring into a stalemate. [Obs. *stale,* stalemate (< ME < AN *estale*) + MATE².]

Sta·lin·ism (stä'lə-nĭz'əm) *n.* The bureaucratic and authoritarian exercise of state power and mechanistic application of Marxist-Leninist principles associated with the period of Stalin's leadership, esp. in the Soviet Union and the socialist states of central Europe. **—Sta'lin·ist** *n.*

stalk¹ (stôk) *n.* **1. a.** A stem or main axis of a herbaceous plant. **b.** A stem or similar structure that supports a plant part such as a flower, flower cluster, or leaf. **2.** A slender or elongated support or structure. [ME.] **—stalk'y** *adj.*

stalk² (stôk) *v.* **stalked, stalk·ing, stalks.** *—intr.* **1.** To walk with a stiff, haughty, or angry gait. **2.** To move threateningly or menacingly. **3.** To track game. *—tr.* **1.** To pursue by tracking. **2.** To go through (a tract of country) in pursuit of game or other quarry. [ME *stalken* < OE *(be)stealcian,* to walk softly.] **—stalk'er** *n.*

stalk·ing-horse (stô'kĭng-hôrs') *n.* **1. a.** A horse trained to conceal the hunter while stalking. **b.** A canvas screen made in the figure of a horse, used for similar concealment. **2.** Something used to cover one's true purpose; decoy. **3.** A sham candidate put forward to conceal the candidacy of another or to divide the opposition.

stall (stôl) *n.* **1.** A compartment for one domestic animal in a barn or shed. **2.** A small compartment, booth, or cubicle. **3. a.** An enclosed seat in the chancel of a church. **b.** A pew in a church. **4.** *Chiefly Brit.* A seat in the front part of the orchestra in a theater. **5.** A parking space for an automobile. **6.** A protective sheath of rubber or similar material for a finger or thumb. **7.** A ruse or delaying tactic employed to mislead interrogators or postpone action. **8.** A sudden, unintended loss of power or effectiveness in an engine. **9.** A condition in which an airplane or airfoil experiences an interruption of airflow resulting in loss of lift and a tendency to drop. *—v.* **stalled, stall·ing, stalls.** *—tr.* **1.** To put or lodge (an animal) in a stall. **2.** To maintain (an animal) in a stall for fattening. **3.** To check the motion or progress of. **4.** To employ delaying tactics against: *stall off creditors.* **5.** To cause (an engine) accidentally to stop running. **6.** To cause (an airplane) to go into a stall. *—intr.* **1.** To live or be lodged in a stall. **2.** To stick fast in mud or snow. **3.** To come to a standstill. **4.** To employ delaying tactics. **5.** To stop running from mechanical failure. Used of an engine. **6.** To lose forward flying speed causing a stall. [ME < OE *steall,* cattle stall.]

stall-feed (stôl'fēd') *tr.v.* **-fed** (-fĕd'), **-feed·ing, -feeds.** To lodge and feed (an animal) in a stall for the purpose of fattening.

stal·lion (stăl'yən) *n.* An adult male horse that has not been castrated. [ME *stalyone* < OFr. *estalon,* of Germanic orig.]

stal·wart (stôl'wərt) *adj.* **1.** Having physical strength; robust. **2.** Resolute; uncompromising. *—n.* **1.** One who is physically and morally strong. **2.** One who actively supports an organization or cause. [ME, alteration of *stalworth* < OE *stælwierthe,* serviceable.] **—stal'wart·ly** *adv.* **—stal'wart·ness** *n.*

sta·men (stā'mən) *n., pl.* **sta·mens** or **sta·mi·na** (stă'mə-nə,

stamen
Stamens of a lily

stăm′ə-). The pollen-producing reproductive organ of a flower, usually consisting of a filament and an anther. [Lat. *stamen, stamin-,* thread.]

stamin– *pref.* Stamen: *staminate.* [Lat. *stamen, stamin-,* thread.]

stam·i·na[1] (stăm′ə-nə) *n.* The physical or moral strength required to resist or withstand disease, fatigue, or hardship; endurance. [Lat., pl. of *stamen,* thread.]

sta·mi·na[2] (stā′mə-nə, stăm′ə-) *n.* A plural of **stamen.**

stam·i·nal[1] (stăm′ə-nəl) *adj.* Pertaining to, showing, or producing stamina.

sta·mi·nal[2] (stā′mə-nəl, stăm′ə-) *adj.* Pertaining to a stamen or stamens.

sta·mi·nate (stā′mə-nĭt, -nāt′, stăm′ə-) *adj. Bot.* **1.** Having a stamen or stamens. **2.** Bearing stamens but lacking pistils: *staminate flowers.*

stam·i·node (stā′mə-nōd′, stăm′ə-) also **stam·i·no·di·um** (stā′mə-nō′dē-əm, stăm′ə-) *n., pl.* **-nodes** also **-no·di·a** (-nō′dē-ə). *Bot.* A sterile functionless stamen. [NLat. *staminodium* < Lat. *stamen,* thread.]

sta·mi·no·dy (stā′mə-nō′dē, stăm′ə-) *n.* The transformation of a floral organ into a stamen. [STAMIN- + Gk. *-ōdēs,* like.]

stam·mel (stăm′əl) *n.* **1.** *Obs.* A coarse, red woolen cloth formerly used for undergarments. **2.** *Archaic.* The red color of stammel. *—adj. Obs.* Dull-red. [Prob. alteration of *stamin* < ME *stamyn* < Lat. *stamineus,* consisting of threads < *stamen,* thread.]

stam·mer (stăm′ər) *v.* **-mered, -mer·ing, -mers.** *—intr.* To intrude involuntary pauses and sometimes syllabic repetitions into one's speaking. *—tr.* To utter or say with a stammer. *—n.* An instance or the habit of stammering. [ME *stameren* < OE *stamerian.*] **—stam′mer·er** *n.* **—stam′mer·ing·ly** *adv.*

Synonyms: *stammer, stutter.* These verbs apply to hesitant, stumbling, or repetitive speech. *Stammer* generally refers to involuntary pauses or breaks in speech. *Stutter* usually refers to spasmodic repetition or exaggeration of sounds or syllables, especially initial consonants.

stamp (stămp) *v.* **stamped, stamp·ing, stamps.** *—tr.* **1.** To bring down (the foot) forcibly. **2.** To bring the foot down upon (an object or surface) forcibly. **3.** To bring into a specified condition by or as if by thrusting downward forcibly with the foot. **4.** To form or cut out by application of a mold, form, or die. **5.** To imprint or impress with a mark, design, or seal. **6.** To impress forcibly or permanently. **7.** To affix an adhesive stamp to. **8.** To identify, characterize, or reveal: *stamped her a traitor to the cause. —intr.* **1.** To thrust the foot forcibly downward. **2.** To walk with forcible, heavy steps. *—n.* **1.** The act of stamping. **2. a.** An implement or device used to impress, cut out, or shape something to which it is applied. **b.** The impression or shape thus formed. **3.** A mark, design, or seal, whose impression indicates ownership, approval, or completion. **4. a.** A small piece of gummed paper sold by a government for attachment to an article that is to be mailed; postage stamp. **b.** A similar piece of gummed paper issued for a specific purpose: *trading stamps.* **5.** An identifying or characterizing mark or impression. **6.** Characteristic nature or quality. —See Usage note at **stomp.** [ME *stampen.*]

stam·pede (stăm-pēd′) *n.* **1.** A sudden headlong rush of startled animals. **2.** A sudden headlong rush of a crowd of people. **3.** A precipitous mass movement. *—v.* **-ped·ed, -ped·ing, -pedes.** *—tr.* **1.** To cause (animals) to move in a headlong rush. **2.** To cause (a group of people) to act on impulse. *—intr.* **1.** To move in a headlong rush. **2.** To act on impulse. [Sp. *estampida,* uproar < Prov. < *estampier,* to stamp, of Germanic orig.] **—stam·ped′er** *n.*

stamping ground *n.* One's customary environment or favorite gathering place.

stamp mill *n.* **1.** A machine that crushes ore. **2.** A building in which ore is crushed.

stance (stăns) *n.* **1.** The attitude or position of a standing person or animal, esp. the position assumed by an athlete or sportsman directly preparatory to action. **2.** One's emotional or intellectual attitude or position. [OFr. *estance,* position < Ital. *stanza* < VLat. **stantia* < Lat. *stare,* to stand.]

stanch[1] also **staunch** (stônch, stänch) *tr.v.* **stanched, stanch·ing, stanch·es** also **staunched, staunch·ing, staunch·es. 1.** To stop or check the flow of (a bodily fluid, esp. blood). **2.** To check the flow of blood from (a wound). —See Usage note at **staunch[1].** [ME *stanchen* < OFr. *estanchier* < VLat. **stanticare* < Lat. *stans,* pr.part. of *stare,* to stand.] **—stanch′er** *n.*

stanch[2] (stônch, stänch) *adj.* Variant of **staunch[1].**

stan·chion (stăn′chən, -shən) *n.* **1.** An upright pole, post, or support. **2.** One of the vertical posts used to secure cattle in a stall. *—tr.v.* **-chioned, -chion·ing, -chions. 1.** To equip with stanchions. **2.** To confine (cattle) in stanchions. [ME *stanchon* < OFr. *estanchon* < *estance,* prop. —see STANCE.]

stand (stănd) *v.* **stood** (stŏŏd), **stand·ing, stands.** *—intr.* **1. a.** To take or maintain an upright position on the feet. **b.** To be placed in or maintain an erect position. **c.** To grow in a vertical direction. **2.** To assume a standing position in a manner specified: *stand straight.* **3.** To point or range in hunting. **4.** To measure or equal a specified height when in a standing position: *stand five feet tall.* **5. a.** To remain stable, valid, intact, or unchanged: *The law still stands.* **b.** To be or remain sure of or committed to: *stands on his position.* **6.** To have a specified position, expectation, or opportunity: *stand to gain.* **7.** To be situated or placed. **8.** To be in a specified class or degree; rank: *stands third in her class.* **9.** To remain in a stationary position. **10. a.** To remain without flowing or being disturbed. **b.** To stagnate. **11.** To assume or maintain an attitude, conviction, or course: *He stands on his earlier offer.* **12.** *Chiefly Brit.* To be a candidate for public office. **13.** To take or hold a particular course or direction; steer: *a ship standing to windward. —tr.* **1.** To cause to stand; place upright. **2.** To encounter; meet: *stand battle.* **3. a.** To resist; withstand: *stand siege.* **b.** To tolerate; endure. **4.** To be subjected to; undergo: *stand trial.* **5.** *Informal.* To pick up the check for; treat: *stand someone to a drink.* **—phrasal verbs. stand down.** To leave a witness stand. **stand for.** To represent; symbolize. **stand in.** To act as a stand-in. **stand off. 1.** To maintain a distance from; avoid. **2.** To fail in or deny compliance or agreement. **3.** To put off; evade. **4.** To take or maintain a course away from shore. **stand out. 1.** To protrude; stick out. **2.** To be conspicuous. **3.** To refuse compliance; maintain opposition: *stand out against a verdict.* **4.** To take or maintain a course away from shore. **stand up. 1.** To assume a standing position; rise. **2.** To prove valid, satisfactory, or durable. **3.** *Informal.* To fail to keep an appointment with someone: *stood his date up. —n.* **1.** The act of standing. **2.** A halt. **3.** A ceasing of work or activity; standstill. **4.** A stop on a performance tour: *one-night stands in summer stock.* **5.** The place where a person stands. **6.** A booth, stall, or counter for the display of goods for sale. **7.** A parking space reserved for taxis. **8.** A desperate or decisive halt for defense or resistance, as in a battle. **9.** A position or opinion one is prepared to defend: *take a stand.* **10. stands.** The bleachers at a playing field or stadium. **11.** A witness stand. **12.** A small rack, prop, or table for holding various articles: *a music stand.* **13.** A group or growth of tall plants or trees: *a stand of pine.* **—idioms. stand a chance.** To have a chance of gaining or accomplishing. **stand one's ground.** To hold one's position. **stand on one's own (two) feet.** To act or think in an independent way. **stand to reason.** To be consistent with reason. **stand up with.** To act as best man or maid of honor for. [ME *standen* < OE *standan.*] **—stand′er** *n.*

stand-a·lone (stănd′ə-lōn′) *adj.* Of, pertaining to, or being a device that can complete its function without further dependence on another device: *a stand-alone terminal.*

stan·dard (stăn′dərd) *n.* **1.** A flag, banner, or ensign, specifically: **a.** The ensign of a chief of state, nation, or city. **b.** A long, tapering flag bearing heraldic devices distinctive of a person or corporation. **c.** The colors of a mounted or motorized military unit. **2. a.** An acknowledged measure of comparison for quantitative or qualitative value; criterion. **b.** An object that under specified conditions defines, represents, or records the magnitude of a unit **3.** The set proportion by weight of gold or silver to alloy metal prescribed for use in coinage. **4.** The commodity or commodities used to back a monetary system. **5. a.** A degree or level of requirement, excellence, or attainment. **b.** Often **standards.** A requirement of moral conduct: *maintains his high standards in all his dealings.* **6.** *Chiefly Brit.* A grade level in elementary schools. **7.** A pedestal, stand, or base. **8.** *Bot.* **a.** The large upper petal of the flower of a pea or related plant. **b.** One of the narrow, upright petals of an iris. **9.** A shrub or small tree that through grafting or training has a single stem of limited height with a crown of leaves and flowers at its apex. *—adj.* **1. a.** Serving as a standard of measurement or value. **b.** Commonly used and accepted as an authority: *a standard atlas.* **c.** Of average but acceptable quality. **d.** Of normal or prescribed size or quantity. **2.** *Ling.* Conforming to established educated usage in speech or writing. [ME < OFr. *estandard,* rallying place, of Germanic orig.]

stan·dard-bear·er (stăn′dərd-bâr′ər) *n.* **1.** One that bears the colors of a military unit. **2.** One that is in the vanguard of a political or religious movement.

stan·dard·bred (stăn′dərd-brĕd′) *n.* One of an American breed of horses developed for harness racing.

standard candle *n.* A candela.

standard deviation *n. Statistics.* **1.** The square root of the variance. **2.** A statistic used as a measure of dispersion in a distribution, the square root of the arithmetic average of the squares of the deviations from the mean.

standard gauge *n.* **1.** A railroad track having a width of $56\frac{1}{2}$ inches. **2.** A railroad or railroad car built to standard gauge specification.

stan·dard·ize (stăn′dər-dīz′) *tr.v.* **-ized, -iz·ing, -iz·es.** To make, cause, adjust, or adapt to fit a standard. **—stan′dard·i·za′tion** *n.*

standard of living *n.* A measure of the goods and services affordable by and available to a person or a country.

standard operating procedure *n.* An established procedure to be followed for a given operation or situation.

standard time *n.* The time in any of 24 time zones, usually the mean solar time at the central meridian of each zone. In the continental United States, there are four standard time zones: Eastern, using the 75th meridian; Central, using the

90th meridian; Mountain, using the 105th meridian; and Pacific, using the 120th meridian.
stand·by (stănd′bī′) *n., pl.* **-bys. 1.** One that can always be depended upon. **2.** A favorite or frequent choice. **3. a.** One kept in readiness to serve as a substitute. **b.** The condition of being in readiness to serve as a substitute.
stand·ee (stăn-dē′) *n.* One using standing room. —See Usage note at **-ee**[1].
stand-in (stănd′ĭn′) *n.* **1.** One who substitutes for an actor during lights and camera adjustments. **2.** A substitute.
stand·ing (stăn′dĭng) *n.* **1.** The act or position of one that stands. **2.** Standing room. **3. a.** Status with respect to credit, rank, or reputation. **b.** High reputation; esteem. **4.** Length of time; duration. —*adj.* **1.** Remaining upright; erect. **2.** Made or performed from an upright position: *standing jumps.* **3.** Permanent and unchanging. **4.** Not movable; stationary. **5.** Not flowing or circulating; stagnant.
standing army *n.* A permanent army of paid soldiers.
standing crop *n.* The total amount of living organisms in a specific area at a given time.
standing room *n.* Space in which to stand, as in a public place where all seats are filled.
standing wave *n.* A wave in which the amplitude of the resultant of a transmitted and a reflected wave is stationary in time and in which some of the energy of the transmitted wave is absorbed by the reflecting boundary.
stand·off (stănd′ôf′, -ŏf′) *n.* A stand-off insulator.
stand-off (stănd′ôf′, -ŏf′) *n.* **1.** A tie, as in a contest; draw. **2.** An effect that neutralizes or counterbalances.
standoff insulator *n.* An insulator used to support a conductor a specified distance from a surface.
stand·off·ish (stănd-ô′fĭsh, -ŏf′ĭsh) *adj.* Unsociable; aloof.
stand oil *n.* A drying oil, as linseed, tung, or soya, heated with minimum oxidation until thickened and used in oil enamel paints.
stand·out (stănd′out′) *n.* One that is outstanding or excellent.
stand·pipe (stănd′pīp′) *n.* A large vertical pipe into which water is pumped in order to produce a desired pressure.
stand·point (stănd′point′) *n.* A position from which things are considered or judged; point of view. [Transl. of G. *Standpunkt.*]
St. An·drew's cross (sānt′ ăn′dro͞oz) *n.* **1.** A cross shaped like the letter X. **2.** A shrubby New World plant, *Ascyrum hypericoides,* having four-petaled yellow flowers. [After the apostle *St. Andrew* (d. ca. A.D. 60).]
stand·still (stănd′stĭl′) *n.* A halt: *traffic came to a standstill.*
stand·up or **stand-up** (stănd′ŭp′) *adj.* **1.** Erect; upright. **2.** Taken standing: *a stand-up supper.* **3.** Designating a fist fight confined largely to heavy blows with little maneuvering. **4.** Of or designating a performance done without costume, props, or assisting persons: *a standup comedian.*
Stan·ford-Bi·net scale (stăn′fərd-bĭ-nā′) *n.* A revision of the Binet-Simon scale used in one form or another since 1916. [After *Stanford* University, California.]
stang (stăng) *v. Obs.* A past tense of **sting.**
stan·hope (stăn′hōp′, stăn′əp) *n.* A light open carriage with one seat and two or four wheels. [After the Rev. Fitzroy *Stanhope* (1787–1864).]
stank (stăngk) *v.* A past tense of **stink.**
stan·nic (stăn′ĭk) *adj.* Of, pertaining to, or containing tin, esp. with valence 4. [Prob. < Fr. *stannique* < LLat. *stannum,* tin < Lat., an alloy of silver and lead.]
stannic chloride *n.* A colorless caustic liquid, $Na_2SnCl_6 \cdot H_2O$, made from tin treated with chlorine and used in the manufacture of textiles, sensitized papers, and perfumes.
stan·nite (stăn′īt′) *n.* A gray to black mineral, chiefly Cu_2FeSnS, having a metallic luster. [G. *Stannit* < LLat. *stannum,* tin. —see STANNIC.]
stan·nous (stăn′əs) *adj.* Of or pertaining to tin, esp. with valence 2. [< LLat. *stannum,* tin.]
stannous fluoride *n.* A white powder, SnF_2, used to fluoridate toothpaste.
St. An·tho·ny's fire (sānt′ ăn′thə-nēz) *n.* Erysipelas. [After *St. Anthony* (d. ca. A.D. 350).]
stan·za (stăn′zə) *n.* One of the divisions of a poem, composed of two or more lines usually characterized by a common pattern of meter, rhyme, and number of lines. [Ital.—see STANCE.] —**stan·za′ic** (-zā′ĭk) *adj.*
sta·pe·dec·to·my (stā′pĭ-dĕk′tə-mē, -pē-) *n., pl.* **-mies.** The surgical removal of the stapes. [NLat. *stapes, staped-,* stapes + -ECTOMY.]
sta·pes (stā′pēz) *n., pl.* **stapes** or **sta·pe·des** (stā′pĭ-dēz′). A small bone of the inner ear, shaped somewhat like a stirrup. [NLat. *stapes, staped-* < Med. Lat., stirrup.] —**sta·pe′di·al** (stā-pē′dē-əl) *adj.*
staph (stăf) *n.* Staphylococcus.
staphylo– *pref.* **1.** Cluster; resembling a cluster: *staphylococcus.* **2.** The uvula: *staphyloplasty.* [NLat. < Gk. *staphulē,* bunch of grapes.]
staph·y·lo·coc·cus (stăf′ə-lō-kŏk′əs) *n., pl.* **-coc·ci** (-kŏk′sī′, -kŏk′ī′). Any of various Gram-positive, spherical parasitic bacteria of the genus *Staphylococcus,* occurring in grapelike clusters and causing boils, septicemia, and other infections. —**staph′y·lo·coc′cal** (-kŏk′əl), **staph′y·lo·coc′cic** (-kŏk′sĭk, -kŏk′ĭk) *adj.*
staph·y·lo·plas·ty (stăf′ə-lō-plăs′tē) *n.* Corrective surgery of the uvula and the soft palate. —**staph′y·lo·plas′tic** *adj.*
staph·y·lor·rha·phy also **staph·y·lôr·a·phy** (stăf′ə-lôr′ə-fē) *n.* The correction of a cleft palate or divided uvula by plastic surgery. [STAPHYLO- + Gk. *rhaptein,* to sew.]
sta·ple[1] (stā′pəl) *n.* **1.** A major commodity grown or produced in a region. **2.** A major item of trade that is in steady demand. **3.** A major part, element, or feature. **4.** Raw material. **5.** The fiber of cotton, wool, or flax, graded as to length and fineness. —***modifier:*** *a staple crop; staple exports.* —*tr.v.* **-pled, -pling, -ples.** To grade (fibers) according to length and fineness. [ME, market town < OFr. *estaple* < MDu. *stapel,* pillar, emporium.]
sta·ple[2] (stā′pəl) *n.* **1.** A U-shaped metal loop with pointed ends, driven into a surface to hold a bolt, hook, or hasp, or to hold wiring in place. **2.** A thin piece of wire having the shape of a square bracket, used as a fastening for papers, cloth, and similar materials. —*tr.v.* **-pled, -pling, -ples.** To fasten by means of a staple or staples. [ME *stapel* < OE *stapol,* post.]
sta·pler[1] (stā′plər) *n.* A person who deals in staple goods or staple fibers.
sta·pler[2] (stā′plər) *n.* A device used to bind material together by means of staples.
star (stär) *n.* **1.** *Astron.* A self-luminous, self-containing mass of gas in which the energy generated by nuclear reactions in the interior is balanced by the outflow of energy to the surface, and the inward-directed gravitational forces are balanced by the outward-directed gas and radiation pressures. **2.** Any of the celestial bodies visible at night from Earth as relatively stationary, usually twinkling points of light. **3.** Something regarded as resembling a star. **4.** A graphic design having five or more radiating points, often used as a symbol. **5.** An artistic performer or athlete whose leading role or superior performance is acknowledged. **6.** An asterisk (*). **7.** A white spot on the forehead of a horse. **8. stars. a.** The constellations of the zodiac believed to influence personal destiny. **b.** The planets in relation to the constellations. **9. stars.** The future; destiny. —*v.* **starred, star·ring, stars.** —*tr.* **1. a.** To ornament with stars. **b.** To award or mark with a star for excellence. **2.** To mark with an asterisk. **3.** To present or feature (a performer) in a leading role. —*intr.* **1.** To play the leading role in a theatrical production. **2.** To do an outstanding job; perform excellently. [ME *sterre* < OE *steorra.*] —**star′less** *adj.*
star anise *n.* **1.** An aromatic tree, *Illicium verum,* of eastern Asia, having purple-red flowers and starlike clusters of anise-scented fruit. **2.** The fruit of the star anise, used in Oriental cooking.
star apple *n.* **1.** A tropical American tree, *Chrysophyllum cainito,* bearing smooth-skinned greenish-purple fruit. **2.** The edible fruit of the star apple.
star·board (stär′bərd) *n.* The right-hand side of a ship or aircraft as one faces forward. —*adj.* On the right-hand side. —*adv.* To or toward the right-hand side. [ME *sterbord* < OE *stēorbord* : *stēor,* rudder + *bord,* side of a ship.]
starch (stärch) *n.* **1.** A naturally abundant nutrient carbohydrate, $(C_6H_{10}O_5)n$, found chiefly in the seeds, fruits, tubers, roots, and stem pith of plants, notably in corn, potatoes, wheat, and rice, varying widely in appearance according to source but commonly prepared as a white, amorphous, tasteless powder. **2.** Any of various substances, including natural starch, used to stiffen fabrics. **3.** Foods having a high content of starch. **4.** Stiff behavior. **5.** Vigor; mettle. —*tr.v.* **starched, starch·ing, starch·es.** To stiffen with starch. [ME *starche* < *starchen,* to stiffen, of OE orig.]
Star Chamber *n.* **1.** A 15th- to 17th-century English court consisting of judges who were appointed by the Crown and sat in closed session on cases involving the security of the state. **2. star chamber.** A court or group characterized by secret, harsh, or arbitrary procedures. [So called because the ceiling of the original courtroom was decorated with stars.]
star-cham·ber (stär′chām′bər) *adj.* Characterized by secret, harsh, or arbitrary procedures. [< STAR CHAMBER.]
starch·y (stär′chē) *adj.* **-i·er, -i·est. 1.** Of or resembling starch. **2.** Containing starch. **3.** Stiffened with starch. **4.** *Informal.* Stiff; formal. —**starch′i·ly** *adv.* —**starch′i·ness** *n.*
star·dom (stär′dəm) *n.* **1.** The status of an actor or entertainer acknowledged as a star. **2.** Stars collectively.
stare (stâr) *v.* **stared, star·ing, stares.** —*intr.* **1.** To look with a steady, often wide-eyed gaze. **2.** *Chiefly Brit.* To stand out; be conspicuous. **3.** To stand on end; bristle, as hair or feathers. —*tr.* To look at intently. —***phrasal verb.*** **stare down.** To cause to waver or give in by or as if by staring. —*n.* An intent gaze. [ME *staren* < OE *starian.*] —**star′er** *n.*
sta·rets (stär′yəts) *n., pl.* **star·tsy** (stärt′sē). A respected spiritual adviser, often a monk or religious hermit, in the Eastern Orthodox Church. [R. < *staryĭ,* old.]
star facet *n.* One of the eight small triangular facets in the crown of a brilliant-cut gem.
star·fish (stär′fĭsh′) *n., pl.* **starfish** or **-fish·es.** Any of various marine echinoderms of the class Asteroidea, characteristically having a radially symmetrical form with five arms extending from a central disk.
star·flow·er (stär′flou′ər) *n.* **1.** Any of several small North American plants of the genus *Trientalis,* having white, star-

star anise

star apple

starfish

stargazer

George Miksch Sutton

starling[1]

like flowers. **2.** Any of several plants having starlike flowers.

star·gaze (stär′gāz′) *intr.v.* **-gazed, -gaz·ing, -gaz·es. 1.** To gaze at the stars. **2.** To daydream.

star·gaz·er (stär′gā′zər) *n.* **1. a.** *Informal.* An astronomer. **b.** An astrologer. **2.** Any of various marine bottom-dwelling fishes of the families Uranoscopidae and Dactyloscopidae, having eyes on the top of the head.

star grass *n.* **1.** Any of various plants of the genus *Hypoxis,* having grasslike leaves and star-shaped flowers. **2.** Any of various plants similar to the star grass, as the colicroot.

stark (stärk) *adj.* **-er, -est. 1.** Bare; blunt: *stark truth.* **2.** Complete or utter; extreme: *stark poverty.* **3.** Harsh in appearance; grim: *stark cliffs.* —*adv.* Utterly; entirely: *stark raving mad.* [ME < OE *stearc,* hard, severe.] **—stark′ly** *adv.* **—stark′ness** *n.*

stark·ers (stär′kərz) *adj. Chiefly Brit. Slang.* Stark naked.

star·let (stär′lĭt) *n.* **1.** A small star. **2.** A young motion-picture actress publicized as a future star.

star·light (stär′līt′) *n.* The light given by the stars.

star·ling[1] (stär′lĭng) *n.* Any of various Old World birds of the family Sturnidae, characteristically having dark, often iridescent plumage, esp. *Sturnus vulgaris,* widely naturalized in North America. [ME < OE *stærlinc* : *stær,* starling + *-linc,* -ling.]

star·ling[2] (stär′lĭng) *n.* A protective structure of pilings surrounding a pier of a bridge. [Perh. alteration of ME *stadelinge* < ME *stathel,* foundation < OE *staðol.*]

star·lit (stär′lĭt′) *adj.* Illuminated by starlight.

star-nosed mole (stär′nōzd′) *n.* A mole, *Condylura cristata,* of eastern North America, having 22 small fleshy tentacles encircling the end of its nose.

star-of-Beth·le·hem (stär′əv-bĕth′lĭ-hĕm′) *n.* **1.** A plant, *Ornithogalum umbellatum,* native to Europe, having narrow leaves and a cluster of star-shaped white flowers. **2.** Any of several plants similar or related to the star-of-Bethlehem. [After the star that guided the Magi to Bethlehem.]

Star of David *n.* The Magen David.

star·quake (stär′kwāk′) *n.* A seismological occurrence on a star.

star·ry (stär′ē) *adj.* **-ri·er, -ri·est. 1.** Marked or set with stars or starlike objects. **2.** Shining or glittering like stars. **3.** Shaped like a star. **4.** Lighted by stars; starlit. **5.** Of, pertaining to, or from the stars; stellar. **—star′ri·ness** *n.*

star·ry-eyed (stär′ē-īd′) *adj.* Naively enthusiastic or visionary.

Stars and Bars *n. (used with a sing. or pl. verb).* The first Confederate flag.

Stars and Stripes *n. (used with a sing. or pl. verb).* The flag of the United States.

star sapphire *n.* A sapphire with a polished convex surface exhibiting asterism.

star shell *n.* An artillery shell that explodes in midair with a shower of lights, used for illumination and signaling.

Star-Spangled Banner (stär′spăng′gəld) *n.* **1.** The flag of the United States. **2.** The national anthem of the United States, written by Francis Scott Key in 1814.

start (stärt) *v.* **start·ed, start·ing, starts.** —*intr.* **1.** To begin an activity or movement; set out. **2.** To have a beginning; commence. **3.** To move suddenly or involuntarily: *started at the loud noise.* **4.** To come quickly into view, life, or activity; spring forth. **5.** *Sports.* To be in the line-up for a race or game. **6.** To protrude or bulge. **7.** To become loosened or disengaged. —*tr.* **1.** To commence; begin. **2.** To set into motion, operation, or activity. **3.** To introduce; originate. **4.** *Sports.* **a.** To cause to enter into a race or game. **b.** To put (a player) into the starting line-up for a game. **5.** To help (someone) in beginning an activity or venture. **6.** To found; establish: *start a business.* **7.** To tend in an early stage of development: *start seedlings.* **8.** To rouse (game) from its hiding place or lair; flush. **9.** To displace or loosen. ***—phrasal verb.* start up.** To start an engine or motor. —*n.* **1.** A beginning; commencement. **2.** A startled reaction or movement. **3. starts.** Quick, brief spurts of effort or activity: *The project progressed by fits and starts.* **4.** A part that has become dislocated or loosened. **5.** A place or time of beginning. **6. a.** A starting line for a race. **b.** A signal to begin a race. **7.** A position of advantage over others, as in a race or endeavor; lead. **8.** An opportunity granted to pursue a career or course of action. ***—idioms.* start something.** *Informal.* To cause trouble. **to start with. 1.** At the beginning; initially. **2.** In any case. [ME *sterten* < OE *styrtan,* to leap up.]

start·er (stär′tər) *n.* **1.** One that starts. **2.** A worker who supervises departures of public transportation vehicles. **3.** An attachment for starting an internal-combustion engine without hand cranking. **4.** *Sports.* **a.** One who signals the start of a race. **b.** A person or animal that starts in a race or game.

star thistle *n.* Any of several plants of the genus *Centaurea,* esp. *C. calcitrapa,* native to Eurasia, having spiny purplish flower heads.

star·tle (stär′tl) *v.* **-tled, -tling, -tles.** —*tr.* **1.** To cause to make a quick involuntary movement or start. **2.** To alarm, frighten, or surprise. —*intr.* To become startled. —*n.* A sudden mild shock; start. [ME *stertlen* < OE *steartlian,* to kick.] **—star′tling·ly** *adv.* **—star′tling·ness** *n.*

star tracker *n.* A telescopic instrument, used chiefly on rockets, that provides a guidance reference by remaining fixed on a celestial body.

star thistle

star·tsy (stärt′sē) *n.* Plural of **starets.**

star·va·tion (stär-vā′shən) *n.* **1.** The act or process of starving. **2.** The condition of being starved.

starve (stärv) *v.* **starved, starv·ing, starves.** —*intr.* **1.** To suffer or die from extreme or prolonged lack of food. **2.** To suffer from deprivation. **3.** *Informal.* To be hungry. **4.** *Archaic.* To suffer or die from cold. —*tr.* **1.** To cause to starve. **2.** To compel or force to a specified state by starving. [ME *sterven,* to die < OE *steorfan.*]

starve·ling (stärv′lĭng) *n.* One that is starving or being starved. —*adj.* **1.** Starving. **2.** Poor in quality; inadequate.

star·wort (stär′wûrt′, -wôrt′) *n.* Any of various plants having star-shaped flowers.

stash (stăsh) *tr.v.* **stashed, stash·ing, stash·es.** To hide or store away in a secret place. —*n.* **1.** A store or cache of money or valuables. **2.** Something hidden away. [Orig. unknown.]

sta·sis (stā′sĭs) *n., pl.* **-ses** (-sēz′). **1.** *Pathol.* Stagnation of a bodily fluid, esp. of blood. **2.** A condition of balance among various forces; motionlessness. [NLat. < Gk., standstill.]

-stasis *suff.* **1.** Slowing; stoppage: *bacteriostasis.* **2.** Stable state: *homeostasis.* [< Gk. *stasis,* standstill.]

-stat *suff.* **1.** Something that stabilizes: *rheostat.* **2.** A device for reflecting something specified in a constant direction: *heliostat.* [NLat. *-stata* < Gk. *-statēs,* one that causes to stand.]

state (stāt) *n.* **1.** A condition or mode of being with regard to a set of circumstances; position. **2.** A condition of being in a stage or form, as of structure, growth, or development: *the fetal state.* **3.** A mental or emotional condition or disposition. **4.** *Informal.* A condition of excitement or distress. **5.** *Physics.* The condition of a physical system as specified by a set of appropriate macroscopic or quantum variables: *the proton state of the nucleon.* **6.** A social position or rank; estate. **7.** Ceremony; pomp: *foreign leaders dining in state at the White House.* **8. a.** The supreme public power within a sovereign political entity. **b.** The sphere of supreme civil power within a given polity: *matters of state.* **9.** A specific mode of government: *a socialist state.* **10.** A body politic, esp. one constituting a nation: *the states of eastern Europe.* **11.** One of the more or less internally autonomous territorial and political units composing a federation under a sovereign government: *the United States of America.* —*tr.v.* **stat·ed, stat·ing, states.** To set forth in words; declare. [ME < OFr. *estat* < Lat. *status,* position, p.part. of *stare,* to stand.]

Synonyms: *state, condition, situation, status.* These nouns denote the mode of being or form of existence of a person or thing. *State* and *condition* are the most general and are largely interchangeable. *Situation* more narrowly refers to a state or condition at a particular time, determined by a combination of circumstances that have special bearing on the person or thing in question. *Status* usually applies to a person or thing considered in relation to others of the same class. With reference to persons, it implies relative standing in a group. With respect to things, it implies a state or condition, as of a specified time.

State attorney or **State's attorney** *n.* A prosecuting attorney for the state.

state·craft (stāt′krăft′) *n.* The art of leading a country.

state·hood (stāt′ho͝od′) *n.* The status of being a state (rather than a territory or dependency) of the United States.

state house also **State House** *n.* A building in which a state legislature holds sessions; state capitol.

state·ly (stāt′lē) *adj.* **-li·er, -li·est. 1.** Dignified; formal. **2.** Majestic; lofty. —*adv.* In a ceremonious or imposing manner. [ME *statly,* suitable to a person of rank < *state,* state, rank.] **—state′li·ness** *n.*

state·ment (stāt′mənt) *n.* **1.** The act of stating or declaring. **2.** Something stated; declaration. **3.** *Law.* A formal pleading. **4.** An abstract of a commercial or financial account showing an amount due; bill. **5.** A monthly report sent to a debtor or bank depositor. **6.** *Computer Sci.* An elementary instruction in a computer's source language.

state of the art *n.* The highest level of development, as of a device, technique, or scientific field, achieved at any particular time.

state prison *n.* A prison maintained by a state for the confinement of persons convicted of felonies.

state·room (stāt′ro͞om′) *n.* A private cabin or compartment with sleeping accommodations on a ship or train.

state's evidence also **State's evidence** *n.* **1.** Evidence for the prosecution in U.S. state or Federal trials. **2.** A person who gives evidence for the state in criminal proceedings.

States-Gen·er·al (stāts′jĕn′ər-əl) *n.* **1.** A legislative assembly of representatives from the estates of the nation, as opposed to a provincial assembly. **2.** The legislative assembly in France before the Revolution. [Transl. of Fr. *états généraux.*]

state·side (stāt′sīd′) *adj.* Of or in the continental United States. —*adv. Informal.* To, toward, or in the continental United States.

states·man (stāts′mən) *n.* **1.** One who is a leader in national or international affairs. **2.** A political leader regarded as a disinterested promoter of the public good. **—states'man·like'**, **states'man·ly** *adj.* **—states'man·ship'** *n.*

States' rights also **State rights** *pl.n.* **1.** All rights not delegated to the Federal Government by the Constitution nor denied by it to the states. **2.** The political position advocating strict interpretation of the Constitution with regard to the limitation of Federal powers and the extension of the autonomy of the individual state to the greatest possible degree. **—States' righter** *n.*

States' Rights Party *n.* A former political party founded in 1948 by Southern Democrats to consolidate opposition to civil rights policies of the regular Democratic Party.

states·wom·an (stāts'wo͝om'ən) *n.* A woman who is a leader in national or international affairs.

state university *n.* A university that is maintained as part of the public education system of a state.

state·wide (stāt'wīd') *adj.* Occurring throughout a state. **—state'wide'** *adv.*

stat·ic (stăt'ĭk) also **stat·i·cal** (-ĭ-kəl) *adj.* **1.** Having no motion; at rest; quiescent. **2.** *Elect.* Of, pertaining to, or producing stationary charges; electrostatic. **3.** Of, pertaining to, or produced by random radio noise. *—n.* **1.** Random noise, as crackling, in a receiver or specks on a television screen produced by atmospheric disturbances. **2.** *Slang.* **a.** Back talk. **b.** Interference; obstruction. **c.** Angry criticism. [NLat. *staticus* < Gk. *statikos,* causing to stand < *statos,* standing.] **—stat'i·cal·ly** *adv.*

static dump *n.* A printout of the contents of a computer memory that is consistently performed at a particular point in the machine's run.

stat·i·ce (stăt'ĭ-sē') *n.* Sea lavender. [NLat. *Statice,* genus name < Lat., an astringent plant < Gk. *statikē* < fem. of *statikos,* causing to stand, astringent. —see STATIC.]

static electricity *n.* **1.** An accumulation of electric charge on an insulated body. **2.** Electric discharge resulting from the accumulation of electric charge on an insulated body.

static memory *n.* A computer memory with no moving parts.

static routine *n.* A computer subroutine with the addresses of the operands involved as the only parameters.

stat·ics (stăt'ĭks) *n. (used with a sing. verb).* The equilibrium mechanics of stationary bodies.

static tube *n.* A specialized tube that is used to measure the static pressure in a stream of fluid.

sta·tion (stā'shən) *n.* **1.** The place or position where a person or thing stands or is assigned to stand; post: *a sentry station.* **2.** The place, building, or establishment from which a service is provided or operations are directed: *a police station.* **3.** A stopping place along a route, esp. a stop for refueling or for taking on passengers; depot. **4.** Social position; rank. **5.** An establishment equipped for observation and study: *a radar station.* **6.** An establishment equipped for radio or television transmission. **7.** An input or output point along a communications system. *—tr.v.* **-tioned, -tion·ing, -tions.** To assign to a position; post. [ME *stacioun* < OFr. *estation* < Lat. *statio* < *status,* p.part. of *stare,* to stand.]

sta·tion·ar·y (stā'shə-nĕr'ē) *adj.* **1. a.** Not moving. **b.** Not capable of being moved; fixed. **2.** Unchanging: *a stationary sound.* *—n., pl.* **-ries.** One that is stationary. [ME *stacionarye* < Lat. *stationarius* < *statio,* station.]

stationary front *n.* A transition zone between two nearly stationary air masses of different density.

stationary orbit *n.* Synchronous orbit.

stationary satellite *n.* An artificial satellite in a synchronous orbit.

stationary wave *n.* A standing wave.

station break *n.* An intermission in a radio or television program for identification of the network or station.

sta·tion·er (stā'shə-nər) *n.* **1.** A person who sells stationery. **2.** *Obs.* **a.** A publisher. **b.** A bookseller. [ME *staciouner* < Med. Lat. *stationarius,* shopkeeper < *statio,* shop < Lat., station.]

sta·tion·er·y (stā'shə-nĕr'ē) *n.* **1.** Writing paper and envelopes. **2.** Writing materials and office supplies. **3.** A retail establishment that sells stationery and related items.

station house *n.* **1.** A police station. **2.** A fire station.

sta·tion·mas·ter (stā'shən-măs'tər) *n.* An official in charge of a railroad or bus station.

Stations of the Cross *pl.n. Eccles.* **1.** A devotion consisting of meditating before each of 14 crosses set up in a church or along a path commemorating 14 events in the Passion of Jesus. **2.** The 14 crosses, often accompanied by images or pictures representing the stages of Christ's passion.

station wagon *n.* An automobile having an extended interior with a third seat or luggage platform and a tailgate.

sta·tis·tic (stə-tĭs'tĭk) *n.* **1.** A numerical datum. **2.** An estimate of a parameter, as of the population mean or variance, obtained from a sample. **3.** A random variable that takes on the characteristics of a statistic. [Back-formation < STATISTICS.]

sta·tis·ti·cal (stə-tĭs'tĭ-kəl) *adj.* Of, pertaining to, or employing statistics or the principles of statistics. **—sta·tis'ti·cal·ly** *adv.*

stat·is·ti·cian (stăt-ĭ-stĭsh'ən) *n.* **1.** A mathematician specializing in statistics. **2.** A compiler of statistical data.

sta·tis·tics (stə-tĭs'tĭks) *n.* **1.** *(used with a sing. verb).* The mathematics of the collection, organization, and interpretation of numerical data, esp. the analysis of population characteristics by inference from sampling. **2.** *(used with a pl. verb).* A collection of numerical data. [G. *Statistik,* political science < NLat. *statisticus,* of state affairs < Lat. *status,* state. —see STATE.]

sta·tive (stā'tĭv) *adj.* Belonging to or designating a class of verbs which express a state or condition. *—n.* A verb of the stative class.

stato– *pref.* **1.** Resting; remaining: *statoblast.* **2.** Equilibrium; balance: *statocyst.* [< Gk. *statos,* standing, placed.]

stat·o·blast (stăt'ə-blăst') *n.* An asexually produced encapsulated bud of a freshwater bryozoan from which new individuals develop after the parent colony has disintegrated.

stat·o·cyst (stăt'ə-sĭst') *n.* A small organ of balance in many invertebrates, consisting of a fluid-filled sac containing statoliths that help indicate position when the animal moves.

stat·o·lith (stăt'l-ĭth') *n.* A small, movable concretion of calcium carbonate found in statocysts.

sta·tor (stā'tər) *n.* The stationary part of a motor, dynamo, turbine, or other working machine about which a rotor turns. [Lat., one that stands < *status,* p.part of *stare,* to stand.]

stat·o·scope (stăt'ə-skōp') *n.* **1.** A barometer for recording small variations in atmospheric pressure. **2.** A device for indicating small changes in an airplane's altitude.

stat·u·ar·y (stăch'o͞o-ĕr'ē) *n., pl.* **-ies. 1.** Statues collectively. **2.** A sculptor. **3.** The art of making statues. *—adj.* Of, pertaining to, or suitable for a statue. [Partly < Lat. *statuaria,* art of making statues, and partly < Lat. *statuarius,* sculptor, both < *statuarius,* of a statue < *statua,* statue.]

statuary
The Vatican

stat·ue (stăch'o͞o) *n.* A form or likeness sculpted, modeled, carved, or cast in material such as stone, clay, wood, or bronze. [ME < OFr. < Lat. *statua* < *statuere,* to set up. —see STATUTE.]

Statue of Liberty *n.* A statue representing liberty as a woman with a torch upraised in one hand and a book in the other arm, located on Liberty Island in New York harbor.

stat·u·esque (stăch'o͞o-ĕsk') *adj.* Suggestive of a statue, as in proportion, grace, or dignity; stately. **—stat'u·esque'ly** *adv.*

stat·u·ette (stăch'o͞o-ĕt') *n.* A small statue.

stat·ure (stăch'ər) *n.* **1.** The natural height of a human or animal body in an upright position. **2.** A level achieved; status. [ME < OFr. < Lat. *statura* < *status,* p.part. of *stare,* to stand.]

stat·us (stā'təs, stăt'əs) *n.* **1.** The legal character or condition of a person or thing: *the status of a minor.* **2.** A stage of progress or development. **3. a.** A relative position in a ranked group or in a social system: *the high status of professional people.* **b.** A high relative position. **4.** A state of affairs; situation. [Lat., condition, p.part of *stare,* to stand.]

statue
"The Appeal to the Great Spirit" by Cyrus E. Dallin

sta·tus quo (stā'təs kwō', stăt'əs) *n.* The existing condition or state of affairs. [Lat., state in which.]

status word *n.* A computer storage location which provides data to restore an interrupted program.

stat·u·ta·ble (stăch'ə-tə-bəl) *adj.* **1.** Enacted, regulated, or authorized by statute; statutory. **2.** Legally punishable; recognized by statute: *a statutable offense.*

stat·ute (stăch'o͞ot) *n.* **1.** A law enacted by a legislature. **2.** A decree or edict, as of a ruler. **3.** An established law or rule, as of a corporation. [ME < OFr. *estatut* < LLat. *statutum* < Lat. *statutus,* p.part. of *statuere,* to set up < *status,* p.part of *stare,* to stand.]

statute law *n.* A law established by legislative enactment.

statute mile *n.* A mile (sense 1).

statute of limitations *n. Law.* A statute setting a time limit on legal action in certain cases.

stat·u·to·ry (stăch'ə-tôr'ē, -tōr'ē) *adj.* **1.** Of or pertaining to a statute. **2.** Enacted, regulated, or authorized by statute.

statutory offense *n.* A legal offense declared by statute.

statutory rape *n.* Sexual intercourse with a female who has not reached the statutory age of consent.

staunch[1] (stônch, stänch) also **stanch** (stänch, stănch) *adj.* **-er, -est. 1.** Firm and steadfast; true. **2.** Having a strong or substantial construction or constitution. [ME *staunche,* watertight < OFr. *estanche* < *estanchier,* to stanch. —see STANCH.] **—staunch'ly** *adv.* **—staunch'ness** *n.*

Usage: *Staunch* is more common than *stanch* as the spelling of the adjective. *Stanch* is more common than *staunch* as the spelling of the verb.

staunch[2] (stônch, stänch) *v.* Variant of **stanch**[1]. —See Usage note at **staunch**[1].

stau·ro·lite (stôr'ə-līt') *n.* A brownish-black mineral, chiefly $FeAl_4Si_2O_{10}(OH)_2$, often having crossed intergrown crystals and sometimes used as a gem. [Fr. < Gk. *stauros,* cross.] **—stau'ro·lit'ic** (-lĭt'ĭk) *adj.*

stave (stāv) *n.* **1.** A narrow strip of wood forming part of the sides of a barrel, tub, or similar structure. **2.** A rung of a ladder or chair. **3.** A staff or cudgel. **4.** A musical staff. **5.** A set of verses; stanza. *—v.* **staved** or **stove** (stōv), **stav·ing, staves.** *—tr.* **1.** To break in or puncture the staves of. **2.** To break or smash a hole in. **3.** To crush or smash inward. **4.** To furnish with staves. *—intr.* To be or become crushed in. ***—phrasal verb.* stave off.** To keep or hold off; repel. [Back-formation < *staves,* pl. of STAFF.]

staves (stāvz) *n.* A plural of **staff**[1] (senses 1, 2, 4).

staves·a·cre (stāvz'ā'kər) *n.* **1.** A larkspur, *Delphinium staphisagria,* of southern Europe, with greenish-white flowers. **2.** The poisonous seeds of the stavesacre, formerly used externally as a parasiticide. [By folk ety. < ME *staphisagre* < Lat. *staphis agria* < Gk., wild raisin.]

stay[1] (stā) *v.* **stayed, stay·ing, stays.** —*intr.* **1.** To remain or continue in a given place or condition: *stay awake.* **2.** To remain or sojourn as a guest or lodger. **3.** To stop moving; cease. **4.** To wait; pause. **5.** To hold on; endure. **6.** To keep up in a race or contest. **7.** To meet a bet in poker without raising it. —*tr.* **1.** To stop or halt; check. **2.** To postpone; delay. **3.** To delay or stop the effect of (an order, for example) by legal action or mandate. **4.** To satisfy or appease temporarily: *stayed his anger.* **5.** To wait for; await. —*n.* **1.** The action of halting; check. **2.** The action of coming to a halt. **3.** A brief period of residence or visiting. **4.** A suspension or postponement of a legal action or execution. [ME *steyen,* to halt < OFr. *ester,* to stop < Lat. *stare,* to stand.]

Synonyms: *stay, remain, wait, abide, tarry, linger, sojourn.* These verbs mean to continue in a given place. *Stay* often suggests nothing beyond that, though it can imply that the person involved is a guest or visitor, as *remain* usually does not. *Remain* sometimes implies continuing residence after others have gone, but often it, like *stay,* is employed in the general sense of continuing. *Wait* suggests continuing for a purpose, often as a prelude to activity or in expectation of something. *Abide* implies continuing for a lengthy period, as *wait* generally does not. *Tarry* and *linger* both imply delaying departure beyond an indicated time, but *linger* is somewhat stronger in suggesting reluctance to leave. *Sojourn* implies temporary residence in a place, as that of a person in a foreign country.

stay[2] (stā) *tr.v.* **stayed, stay·ing, stays. 1.** To brace, support, or prop up. **2.** To strengthen or sustain mentally or spiritually. **3.** To rest or fix on for support. —*n.* **1.** A support or brace. **2.** A strip of bone, plastic, or metal, used to stiffen a garment or part, as a corset or shirt collar. **3. stays.** A corset. [OFr. *estayer,* to support < *estaie,* a support, of Germanic orig.]

stay[3] (stā) *n.* **1.** A heavy rope or cable, usually of wire, used as a brace or support for a mast or spar. **2.** A rope used to steady, guide, or brace something. —*v.* **stayed, stay·ing, stays.** —*tr.* **1.** To brace or support with a stay. **2.** To put (a ship) on the opposite tack. —*intr.* To come about. [ME < OE *stæg.*]

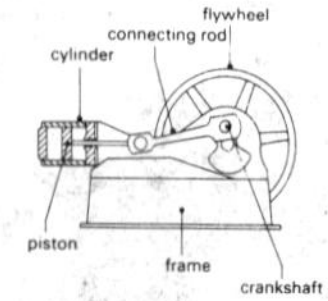

steam engine

staying power *n.* The ability to endure or last.

stay-in strike (stā'ĭn') *n.* A job action that consists of a slowdown or work stoppage by employees who remain at their work place.

stay·sail (stā'səl, -sāl') *n. Naut.* A triangular sail hoisted on a stay.

St. Ber·nard (sānt' bər-närd') *n.* The Saint Bernard.

stead (stĕd) *n.* The place, position, or function properly or customarily occupied by another. —*tr.v.* **stead·ed, stead·ing, steads.** To be of advantage or service to; benefit. [ME *stede* < OE.]

stead·fast also **sted·fast** (stĕd'făst', -fəst) *adj.* **1.** Fixed or unchanging; steady. **2.** Firmly loyal or constant. [ME *stedefast* < OE *stedefæst* : *stede,* place + *fæst,* fixed, fast.] **—stead'fast'ly** *adv.* **—stead'fast'ness** *n.*

stead·y (stĕd'ē) *adj.* **-i·er, -i·est. 1.** Firm in position or place; stable. **2.** Direct and unfaltering; sure. **3.** Having a continuous movement, quality, or pace: *a steady breeze.* **4.** Not easily excited or upset: *steady nerves.* **5.** Reliable; dependable. **6.** Temperate; sober. —*v.* **stead·ied, stead·y·ing, stead·ies.** —*tr.* To make steady; stabilize. —*intr.* To become steady. —*interj.* **1.** Used to urge self-control. **2.** *Naut.* Used to direct the helmsman to keep the ship's head in the same direction: *Steady as she goes!* —*n., pl.* **-ies.** *Slang.* The boy or girl whom one dates regularly and exclusively. —***idiom.* go steady.** To date regularly and exclusively. **—stead'i·er** *n.* **—stead'i·ly** *adv.* **—stead'i·ness** *n.*

Synonyms: *steady, even, equable, uniform, constant.* These adjectives refer to things or persons that show stability or lack of change. *Steady* can imply continuity of activity, regularity of movement or behavior, or the manifestation of firmness or self-control. *Even* suggests the maintenance of a level of activity or behavior and the consequent absence of irregularity or fluctuation. *Equable* implies an inherent tendency to be regular in movement or activity, to avoid extremes, or (in persons) to be tranquil. *Uniform* emphasizes sameness in form, character, degree, regularity of occurrence, or the like. This sameness can apply to one thing that shows no variation within itself, or it can refer to a group that reveals no diversity. *Constant* describes a thing incapable of, or not given to, change or a person who is firm and steadfast in purpose. It also can imply continuity or regularity of activity or occurrence.

steady state *n.* A stable condition that does not change over time or in which change in one direction is continually balanced by change in another.

stead·y-state theory (stĕd'ē-stāt') *n.* A cosmological theory that assumes that the large-scale view of the universe is independent of the position of the observer in space and time and that the expansion of the universe, required on other grounds, is compensated for by the continuous creation of matter.

steak (stāk) *n.* **1.** A slice of meat, usually beef, typically cut thick and across the muscle grain and usually broiled or fried. **2.** A thick slice of a large fish cut across the body. **3.** A patty of ground meat broiled or fried. [ME *steyke* < ON *steik.*]

steak au poiv·re (ō pwäv'rə) *n.* Steak studded with coarsely ground pepper before cooking and often flambéed with cognac. [Fr. *au poivre,* with pepper.]

steak house *n.* A restaurant that specializes in beefsteak dishes.

steak knife *n.* A table knife with a sharp often serrated steel blade.

steak tar·tare (tär'-tär') *n.* Raw ground beef mixed with onion, seasoning, and raw egg, eaten as an appetizer. [STEAK + Fr. *tartare,* Tartar.]

steal (stēl) *v.* **stole** (stōl), **sto·len** (stō'lən), **steal·ing, steals.** —*tr.* **1.** To take (the property of another) without right or permission. **2.** To get or effect secretly or artfully. **3.** To move, carry, or place surreptitiously. **4.** *Baseball.* To advance to (another base) without the ball being batted, by running during the delivery of a pitch. —*intr.* **1.** To commit theft. **2.** To move, happen, or elapse stealthily or unobtrusively. **3.** *Baseball.* To steal a base. —*n.* **1.** The act of stealing; theft. **2.** *Baseball.* The act of stealing a base. **3.** *Slang.* A bargain. [ME *stelen* < OE *stelan.*] **—steal'er** *n.*

stealth (stĕlth) *n.* **1.** The act of moving, proceeding, or acting in a covert way. **2.** Furtiveness; covertness. **3.** *Archaic.* The act of stealing. [ME *stelth.*]

stealth·y (stĕl'thē) *adj.* **-i·er, -i·est.** Marked by clandestine or secret movement. **—stealth'i·ly** *adv.* **—stealth'i·ness** *n.*

steam (stēm) *n.* **1. a.** The vapor phase of water. **b.** The mist of cooling water vapor. **2.** Steam heating. **3.** Power; energy. —*v.* **steamed, steam·ing, steams.** —*intr.* **1.** To produce or emit steam. **2.** To become or rise up as steam. **3.** To become misted or covered with steam. **4.** To move by means of steam power. **5.** *Informal.* To become very angry; fume. —*tr.* To expose to steam, as in cooking. [ME *steme,* vapor < OE *stēam.*]

steam bath *n.* **1.** The act of bathing through exposure to steam, which induces perspiration. **2.** A room or building equipped to provide bathing with steam.

steam beer *n.* A western U.S. beer of a highly effervescent quality.

steam·boat (stēm'bōt') *n.* A steamship.

steam boiler *n.* A closed tank in which water is converted into steam under pressure.

steam chest *n.* A compartment in a steam engine through which steam is delivered from the boiler to a cylinder.

steam engine *n.* An engine that converts the heat energy of pressurized steam into mechanical energy, esp. one in which steam drives a piston in a closed cylinder.

steam·er (stē'mər) *n.* **1.** A steamship. **2.** A container in which something is steamed. **3.** A soft-shell clam.

steamer rug *n.* A warm blanket used esp. by shipboard passengers while sitting in deck chairs.

steamer trunk *n.* A small trunk originally designed to fit under the bunk of a steamship cabin.

steam·fit·ter (stēm'fĭt'ər) *n.* A person whose occupation is the installation and repair of heating, ventilating, refrigerating, and air-conditioning systems.

steam heating *n.* A heating system by which steam is generated in a boiler and piped to radiators.

steam iron *n.* A pressing iron that holds and heats water to be emitted as steam on the cloth being pressed.

steam radio *n. Chiefly Brit. Slang.* Radio broadcasting considered as being old-fashioned by comparison with television.

steam·rol·ler also **steam roller** (stēm'rō'lər) *n.* **1.** A vehicle equipped with a heavy roller for smoothing road surfaces. **2.** A ruthless or irresistible force or power. —*v.* **-lered, -ler·ing, -lers.** —*tr.* **1.** To smooth or level (a road) with a steamroller. **2.** To overwhelm or suppress ruthlessly; crush. —*intr.* To move or proceed with overwhelming or crushing force.

steam·ship (stēm'shĭp') *n.* A large vessel propelled by one or more steam-driven screws or propellers.

steam shovel *n.* A steam-driven machine for digging.

steam table *n.* A table in which containers of cooked food are kept warm by hot water or steam circulating below.

steam turbine *n.* A turbine operated by highly pressurized steam directed against or through vanes on a rotor.

steam·y (stē'mē) *adj.* **-i·er, -i·est. 1.** Filled with or emitting steam. **2.** *Slang.* Erotic. **—steam'i·ly** *adv.* **—steam'i·ness** *n.*

ste·ap·sin (stē-ăp'sĭn) *n.* An enzyme of pancreatic juice that catalyzes the hydrolysis of fats to fatty acids and glycerol. [Gk. *stear,* tallow + (PE)PSIN.]

ste·a·rate (stē'ə-rāt', stîr'āt') *n.* A salt or ester of stearic acid. [STEAR(IC) + -ATE.]

ste·ar·ic (stē-ăr'ĭk, stîr'ĭk) *adj.* Of, pertaining to, or similar to stearin or fat. [Fr. *stéarique* < Gk. *stear,* tallow.]

stearic acid *n.* A colorless, odorless, waxlike fatty acid, $CH_3(CH_2)_{16}COOH$, occurring in natural animal and vegetable fats.

ste·a·rin (stē'ər-ĭn, stîr'ĭn) *n.* **1.** A colorless, odorless, tasteless ester of glycerol and stearic acid, $C_3H_5(C_{18}H_{35}O_2)_3$, used in the manufacture of soap and candles and for textile sizing. **2.** Stearic acid, esp. as used commercially. **3.** The solid form of fat. [Fr. *stéarine* < Gk. *stear,* tallow.]

ste·a·rop·tene (stē'ə-rŏp'tēn') *n.* The portion of a natural essential oil that separates out as a white, crystalline solid on cooling or standing. [STEAR(IC) + Gk. *ptēnos,* flying.]

ste·a·tite (stē'ə-tīt') *n.* A massive, white-to-green talc used in paints, ceramics, and insulation. [Lat. *steatitis,* a precious stone < Gk. < *stear,* tallow.] **—ste'a·tit'ic** (-tĭt'ĭk) *adj.*

steato– *pref.* Fat: *steatolysis.* [Gk. < *stear,* tallow.]

ste·a·tol·y·sis (stē'ə-tŏl'ĭ-sĭs) *n.* The digestive emulsification of fats prior to assimilation.

ste·at·o·pyg·i·a (stē-ăt'ə-pĭj'ē-ə, -pī'jē-ə) *n.* An excessive accumulation of fat on the buttocks. [STEATO- + Gk. *pugē,* rump.] **—ste'at·o·pyg'ic** (-pĭj'ĭk, -pī'jĭk), **ste'a·to·py'gous** (-pī'gəs) *adj.*

ste·at·or·rhe·a (stē'ə-tə-rē'ə) also **ste·at·or·rhoe·a** (stē-ăt'-ə-rē'ə) *n.* **1.** Overaction of the sebaceous glands. **2.** Excessive discharge of fat in the feces.

sted·fast (stĕd'făst', -fəst) *adj.* Variant of **steadfast.**

steed (stēd) *n.* A horse, esp. one that is spirited. [ME *stede* < OE *stēda,* stallion.]

steel (stēl) *n.* **1.** Any of various generally hard, strong, durable, malleable alloys of iron and carbon, usually containing between 0.2 and 1.5 per cent carbon, often with other constituents such as manganese, chromium, nickel, molybdenum, copper, tungsten, cobalt, or silicon, depending on the desired alloy properties, and widely used as a structural material. **2.** A quality suggestive of steel, esp. a hard, unflinching character. **3.** Something made of steel, as a sword. **4.** A knife sharpener consisting of a handled steel rod. **5.** A slender strip or band of steel used for stiffening. **6.** A dark gray to purplish gray. **—*modifier:*** *steel beams; the steel industry.* —*adj.* Of the color steel. —*tr.v.* **steeled, steel·ing, steels. 1.** To cover, plate, edge, or point with steel. **2.** To make hard, strong, or obdurate; strengthen: *steeled himself for disappointment.* [ME *stel* < OE *stȳle.*]

steel band *n.* A musical band of Trinidadian origin, composed chiefly of percussion instruments fashioned from oil drums.

steel blue *n.* **1.** A medium grayish blue. **2.** One of several blue colors taken on by steel while being tempered.

steel engraving *n.* **1.** The art or process of engraving on a steel plate. **2.** An impression produced with an engraved steel plate.

steel guitar *n.* A Hawaiian guitar.

steel·head (stēl'hĕd') *n.* The rainbow trout when occurring in marine waters or large inland lakes.

steel-trap (stēl'trăp') *adj.* Very quick and keen; trenchant: *a steel-trap intellect.*

steel wool *n.* Fine fibers of steel woven or matted together to form an abrasive for cleaning, smoothing, or polishing.

steel·work (stēl'wûrk') *n.* **1.** Something made of steel. **2. steelworks.** A plant where steel is made; foundry. **—steel'work'er** *n.*

steel·y (stē'lē) *adj.* **-i·er, -i·est. 1.** Made of steel. **2.** Like steel, as in coldness or hardness: *steely eyes.* **—steel'i·ness** *n.*

steel·yard (stēl'yärd') *n.* A balance consisting of a scaled arm suspended off center, a hook at the shorter end on which to hang the object being weighed, and a counterbalance at the longer end that can be moved to find the weight. [STEEL + YARD (rod).]

steen·bok (stēn'bŏk', stān'-) also **stein·bok** (stīn'bŏk') *n.* An African antelope, *Raphicerus campestris,* having a brownish coat and short, pointed horns in the male. [Afr. < MDu. *steenboc,* ibex : *steen,* stone + *boc,* buck.]

steep¹ (stēp) *adj.* **-er, -est. 1.** Having a sharp inclination; precipitous. **2.** Rising or falling rapidly or precipitously: *a steep rise in salaries.* **3. a.** Excessive; stiff: *a steep price.* **b.** Ambitious; difficult: *a steep undertaking.* —*n.* A precipitous slope. [ME *stepe* < OE *stēap,* lofty.] **—steep'ly** *adv.* **—steep'ness** *n.*

steep² (stēp) *v.* **steeped, steep·ing, steeps.** —*tr.* **1.** To soak in liquid in order to cleanse, soften, or extract a given property from. **2.** To infuse or subject thoroughly to. **3.** To make thoroughly wet; saturate. —*intr.* To undergo a soaking in liquid. —*n.* **1. a.** The process of steeping. **b.** The state of being steeped. **2.** A liquid, bath, or solution in which something is steeped. [ME *stepen.*] **—steep'er** *n.*

steep·en (stē'pən) *v.* **-ened, -en·ing, -ens.** —*tr.* To make steeper. —*intr.* To become steeper.

stee·ple (stē'pəl) *n.* **1.** A tall tower forming the superstructure of a building, such as a church or temple, and usually surmounted by a spire. **2.** A spire. [ME *stepel* < OE *stēpel,* tall tower.]

stee·ple·bush (stē'pəl-bŏŏsh') *n.* The hardhack.

stee·ple·chase (stē'pəl-chās') *n.* A horse race across open country or over an obstacle course. [From the use of church steeples as goals.] **—stee'ple·chas'er** *n.*

stee·ple·jack (stē'pəl-jăk') *n.* A worker on steeples or other very high structures.

steer¹ (stîr) *v.* **steered, steer·ing, steers.** —*tr.* **1.** To guide by means of a device such as a rudder, paddle, or wheel. **2. a.** To direct the course of. **b.** To maneuver (a person) into a place or course of action. —*intr.* **1.** To guide a vessel or vehicle. **2.** To follow or move in a set course. **3.** To be capable of being steered or guided: *a craft that steers easily.* —*n.* A piece of advice. [ME *steren* < OE *stīeran.*] **—steer'a·ble** *adj.* **—steer'er** *n.*

steer² (stîr) *n.* A young ox, esp. one castrated before sexual maturity and raised for beef. [ME < OE *stēor.*]

steer·age (stîr'ĭj) *n.* **1.** The action or practice of steering. **2.** The effect of the helm on a ship. **3.** The steering apparatus of a ship. **4.** The section of a passenger ship, originally near the rudder, providing the cheapest accommodations for passengers.

steer·age·way (stîr'ĭj-wā') *n.* The minimum rate of motion required for the helm of a ship or boat to have effect.

steering committee *n.* A committee that sets agendas and schedules of business, as for a legislative body or other assemblage.

steering gear *n.* The mechanism by which dispositions of the steering controls of a vehicle are transferred to the part that interacts with the external medium.

steering wheel *n.* A wheel that controls steering.

steers·man (stîrz'mən) *n.* A helmsman.

steeve¹ (stēv) *n.* A spar or derrick with a block at one end, used for stowing cargo. —*tr.v.* **steeved, steev·ing, steeves.** To stow or pack (cargo) in the hold of a ship. [ME *steven,* to stow < OFr. *estiver* < Sp. *estibar,* to cram < Lat. *stipare.*]

steeve² (stēv) *Naut.* —*n* The angle formed by the bowsprit and the horizon or the keel. —*v.* **steeved, steev·ing, steeves.** —*tr.* To incline (a bowsprit) upward at an angle with the horizon or the keel. —*intr.* To have an upward inclination. Used of a bowsprit. [Orig. unknown.]

steg·o·don also **steg·o·dont** (stĕg'ə-dŏn', -dŏnt') *n.* Any of various extinct elephantlike mammals of the genus *Stegodon* and related genera, of the Pliocene to Pleistocene epoch. [NLat. *Stegodon,* genus name : Gk. *stegos,* roof (< *stegein,* to cover) + Gk. *odous, odont-,* tooth.]

steg·o·saur (stĕg'ə-sôr') also **steg·o·sau·rus** (stĕg'ə-sôr'əs) *n.* Any of several herbivorous dinosaurs of the genus *Stegosaurus* and related genera, of the Triassic to the Cretaceous period, having a double row of upright bony plates along the back. [NLat. *Stegosaurus,* genus name : Gk. *stegos,* roof (< *stegein,* to cover) + *sauros,* lizard.]

stein (stīn) *n.* A mug, esp. one for beer, usually holding about a pint. [G., prob. short for *Steingut,* stoneware : *Stein,* stone + *Gut,* goods.]

stein·bok (stīn'bok') *n.* Variant of **steenbok.**

ste·le (stē'lē) *n., pl.* **-les** or **-lae** (-lē). **1.** An upright stone or slab with an inscribed or sculptured surface, used as a monument or as a commemorative tablet in the face of a building. **2.** *Bot.* The central core of vascular tissue in a plant stem. [Gk. *stēlē,* pillar.] **—ste'lar** (-lər) *adj.*

stel·lar (stĕl'ər) *adj.* **1.** Of, relating to, or consisting of stars. **2. a.** Of or relating to a star performer. **b.** Outstanding; principal. [LLat. *stellaris* < *stella,* star.]

stellar wind *n.* The varying flow of plasma ejected from a star's surface into interstellar space.

stel·late (stĕl'āt') also **stel·lat·ed** (-ā'tĭd) *adj.* Arranged or shaped like a star; radiating from a center. [Lat. *stellatus* < *stella,* star.] **—stel'late·ly** *adv.*

stel·li·form (stĕl'ə-fôrm') *adj.* Star-shaped. [NLat. *stelliformis* < Lat. *stella,* star.]

stel·li·fy (stĕl'ə-fī') *tr.v.* **-fied, -fy·ing, -fies.** To transform into a star. [ME *stellifien* < OFr. *stellifier* < Med. Lat. *stellificare* : Lat. *stella,* star + Lat. *facere,* to make.]

stel·lu·lar (stĕl'yə-lər) *adj.* **1.** Having the form of a small star. **2.** Bespangled with small stars. [< LLat. *stellula,* dim. of Lat. *stella,* star.]

St. El·mo's fire (sānt' ĕl'mōz) *n.* Saint Elmo's fire.

stem¹ (stĕm) *n.* **1. a.** The main ascending axis of a plant; stalk or trunk. **b.** A slender stalk supporting or connecting another plant part, such as a leaf or flower. **2.** A banana stalk bearing several bunches of bananas. **3.** A connecting or supporting part, esp.: **a.** The tube of a tobacco pipe. **b.** The slender upright support of a wine glass or goblet. **c.** The small projecting shaft with an expanded crown by which a watch is wound. **d.** The rounded rod in the center of certain locks about which the key fits and is turned. **e.** The shaft of a feather or hair. **f.** The upright stroke of a typeface or letter. **g.** The vertical line extending from the head of a musical note. **4.** The main line of descent of a family. **5.** The main part of a word to which affixes are added. **6.** The curved upright beam at the fore of a vessel into which the hull timbers are scarfed to form the prow. **7.** The tubular glass structure mounting the filament or electrodes in an incandescent bulb or vacuum tube. —*v.* **stemmed, stem·ming, stems.** —*tr.* **1.** To remove the stem of. **2.** To provide with a stem. **3.** To make headway against. —*intr.* To derive from or originate in: *new projects stemming from his earlier research.* **—*idiom.* from stem to stern.** From one end to another. [ME < OE *stefn,* prow.] **—stem'less** *adj.*

stem² (stĕm) *v.* **stemmed, stem·ming, stems.** —*tr.* **1.** To stop or hold back by or as if by damming; stanch. **2.** To plug or tamp (a blast hole, for example). **3.** To point (skis) inward. —*intr.* To point skis inward in order to slow down or turn. [ME *stemmen* < ON *stemma.*]

stem cell *n.* An unspecialized cell that gives rise to a specific specialized cell, as a blood cell.

stem·ma (stĕm'ə) *n., pl.* **stem·ma·ta** (stĕm'ə-tə) or **stem·mas.**

steeple

steeplechase

stein

1. In ancient Rome, a scroll recording the genealogy of a family; family tree. **2.** The genealogy of the manuscripts of a literary work. [Lat., garland < Gk. < *stephein,* to encircle.]
stemmed (stĕmd) *adj.* **1.** Having the stems removed. **2.** Provided with a stem.
stem·mer (stĕm′ər) *n.* One that removes stems, as from fruit or tobacco.
stem rust *n.* A rust disease affecting the stem of a plant.
stem·son (stĕm′sən) *n. Naut.* A piece of supporting timber bolted to the stem and keelson at their junction near the bow of a wooden vessel. [STEM (prow) + (KEEL)SON.]
stem turn *n.* A skiing turn made by stemming the downhill ski and placing one's weight upon it while bringing the other ski into a parallel position.
stem·ware (stĕm′wâr′) *n.* Glassware mounted on a stem.
stem-wind·er (stĕm′wīn′dər) *n.* A stem-winding watch.
stem-wind·ing (stĕm′wīn′dĭng) *adj.* Wound by turning an expanded crown on the stem.
stench (stĕnch) *n.* A strong and foul odor; stink. [ME < OE *stenc,* odor.]
sten·cil (stĕn′səl) *n.* **1.** A sheet of celluloid, cardboard, or other material in which a desired lettering or design has been cut so that ink or paint applied to the sheet will reproduce the pattern on the surface beneath. **2.** The lettering or design produced by stencil. —*tr.v.* **-ciled, -cil·ing, -cils** or **-cilled, -cil·ling, -cils. 1.** To mark with a stencil. **2.** To produce by stencil. [< ME *stanselen,* to adorn with bright colors < OFr. *estenceler* < *estencele,* spark < VLat. **stincilla,* alteration of Lat. *scintilla,* spark.] **—sten′cil·er** *n.*
stencil paper *n.* Strong tissue-thin paper treated for making stencils.
sten·o (stĕn′ō) *n., pl.* **-os. 1.** A stenographer. **2.** Stenography.
steno– *pref.* Narrow; small : *stenotopic.* [< Gk. *stenos,* narrow.]
sten·o·bath·ic (stĕn′ə-băth′ĭk) *adj.* Of or pertaining to an organism that is able to live only within a narrow range of water depths. **—sten′o·bath′** *n.*
sten·o·graph (stĕn′ə-grăf′) *n.* **1.** A keyboard machine for reproducing letters in a shorthand system. **2.** A particular character in shorthand. —*tr.v.* **-graphed, -graph·ing, -graphs.** To write in shorthand. [Back-formation < STENOGRAPHY.]
ste·nog·ra·pher (stə-nŏg′rə-fər) *n.* A person skilled in shorthand, esp. one employed to take and transcribe dictation.
ste·nog·ra·phy (stə-nŏg′rə-fē) *n.* **1.** The art or process of writing in shorthand. **2.** Material written down in shorthand. **—sten′o·graph′ic** (stĕn′ə-grăf′ĭk), **sten′o·graph′i·cal** *adj.* **—sten′o·graph′i·cal·ly** *adv.*
sten·o·ha·line (stĕn′ə-hā′līn, -hăl′īn) *adj.* Of or pertaining to an organism that is able to live only within a narrow range of water salinity.
ste·noph·a·gous (stə-nŏf′ə-gəs) *adj.* Feeding on a single kind or limited range of food.
ste·nosed (stə-nōzd′, -nōst′) *adj.* Characterized by stenosis. [STENOS(IS) + -ED.]
ste·no·sis (stə-nō′sĭs) *n.* The constriction or narrowing of a duct or passage. [NLat. < Gk. *stenōsis,* a narrowing < *stenoun,* to narrow < *stenos,* narrow.] **—ste·not′ic** (-nŏt′ĭk) *adj.*
sten·o·ther·mal (stĕn′ə-thûr′məl) *adj.* Of or pertaining to organisms adapted to living only within a limited range of temperature.
sten·o·top·ic (stĕn′ə-tŏp′ĭk) *adj.* Having narrow limits of adaptation to environmental conditions. [STENO- + Gk. *topos,* place.]
sten·o·type (stĕn′ə-tīp′) *n.* **1.** A symbol or combination of symbols representing a sound, word, or phrase, esp. in shorthand. **2.** A keyboard machine used to record dictation by a phonetic system. [(STENO)GRAPHY + TYPE.]
sten·tor (stĕn′tôr′) *n.* Any of several trumpet-shaped aquatic microorganisms of the genus *Stentor,* having cilia around the oral cavity. [NLat. *Stentor,* genus name, after *Stentor,* a Greek herald. —see STENTORIAN.]
sten·to·ri·an (stĕn-tôr′ē-ən, -tōr′-) *adj.* Extremely loud: *a stentorian voice.* [After *Stentor,* a loud-voiced Greek herald in the *Iliad,* a Homeric poem.]
step (stĕp) *n.* **1. a.** The single complete movement of raising one foot and putting it down in another spot, as in walking. **b.** A manner of walking; gait. **c.** A fixed rhythm or pace, as in marching: *keep step.* **d.** The sound of a footstep. **e.** A footprint. **2. a.** The distance traversed by moving one foot ahead of the other. **b.** A very short distance: *just a step away.* **c. steps.** Course; path: *followed in his father's steps.* **3. a.** A rest for the foot in ascending or descending. **b. steps.** Stairs. **4. a.** One of a series of actions or measures taken to achieve a goal. **b.** A stage in a process. **5.** A degree in progress or a grade or rank in a scale: *a step ahead of the others.* **6.** *Mus.* The interval that separates two successive tones of a scale. **7.** *Computer Sci.* A single instructor in a computer sequence. **8.** *Naut.* The block in which the heel of a mast is fixed. —*v.* **stepped, step·ping, steps.** —*intr.* **1.** To put or press the foot: *step on the gas.* **2.** To shift or move slightly by taking a step or two: *step back.* **3.** To walk a short distance to a specified place or in a specified direction: *step over to the corner.* **4.** To move with the feet in a particular manner: *step lively.* **5.** To move into a new situation by or as if by taking a single step: *stepping into a life of ease.* **6.** To treat with arrogant indifference: *He's always stepping on people.* —*tr.* **1.** To put or set (the foot) down: *step foot on land.* **2.** To measure by pacing: *step off ten yards.* **3.** To furnish with steps; make steps in. **4.** To cause a computer to execute a single instruction. **5.** *Naut.* To place (a mast) in its step. **—*phrasal verbs.* step down. 1.** To resign from a high post. **2.** To reduce, esp. in stages: *stepping down the electric power.* **step in. 1.** To enter into an activity or situation. **2.** To intervene. **step out. 1.** To walk briskly. **2.** To go outside for a short time. **3.** *Informal.* To go out for a special evening of entertainment. **4.** To withdraw; quit. **step up. 1.** To increase, esp. in stages: *step up production.* **2.** To make oneself known: *step up and be counted.* **—*idioms.* in step. 1.** Moving in rhythm. **2.** *Informal.* In conformity with one's environment: *in step with the times.* **out of step. 1.** Not in step: *recruits marching out of step.* **2.** Not in conformity with one's environment: *out of step with the times.* **step by step.** By degrees. **step on it.** *Informal.* To go faster; hurry. **watch (one's) step.** To move or proceed carefully. [ME < OE *stæp.*]
step– *pref.* Related by means of a remarriage rather than by blood: *stepparent.* [ME < OE *stēop-.*]
step·broth·er (stĕp′brŭth′ər) *n.* The son of a person's stepparent by a previous marriage.
step·child (stĕp′chīld′) *n.* The child of a person's spouse by a former marriage.
step dance *n.* A dance in which the dancer emphasizes certain steps, as clogging or tapping, rather than body position or gesture.
step·daugh·ter (stĕp′dô′tər) *n.* The daughter of a person's spouse by a former marriage.
step-down (stĕp′doun′) *adj.* Decreasing in stages: *a step-down gear.* —*n.* A reduction in amount or size.
step-down transformer *n.* A transformer that has a greater number of turns in the primary winding than in the secondary, used to transform high voltage to low voltage.
step·fa·ther (stĕp′fä′*th*ər) *n.* The husband of a person's mother by a later marriage.
steph·a·no·tis (stĕf′ə-nō′tĭs) *n.* Any of various woody climbing plants of the genus *Stephanotis,* cultivated for its showy, fragrant, white flowers. [NLat. *Stephanotis,* genus name < Gk. *stephanōtis,* deserving a crown < *stephanos,* crown, wreath < *stephein,* to crown.]
step-in (stĕp′ĭn′) *adj.* Put on by stepping into: *a step-in robe.* —*n.* **1. step-ins.** Panties with wide legs. **2.** A step-in garment.
step·lad·der (stĕp′lăd′ər) *n.* A portable ladder with a hinged supporting frame and usually topped with a small platform.

stepladder

step·moth·er (stĕp′mŭ*th*′ər) *n.* The wife of a person's father by a later marriage.
step·par·ent (stĕp′pâr′ənt, -păr′-) *n.* A stepfather or a stepmother.
steppe (stĕp) *n.* A vast semiarid grass-covered plain, usually lightly wooded, as found in southeastern Europe and Siberia. [R. *step′.*]
stepped-up (stĕpt′ŭp′) *adj.* Increased in pace or intensity; heightened: *a stepped-up political campaign.*
step·per (stĕp′ər) *n.* **1.** One that steps, esp. in a spirited manner. **2.** *Slang.* A dancer.
step·ping-off place (stĕp′ĭng-ôf′, -ŏf′) *n.* **1.** The last stop on an outbound line, as of a train. **2.** A place or point from which one leaves for unfamiliar regions.
step·ping·stone (stĕp′ĭng-stōn′) *n.* **1.** A stone that provides a place to step, as in crossing a stream. **2.** An advantageous position for advancement toward some goal.
step rocket *n.* A multistage rocket.
step·sis·ter (stĕp′sĭs′tər) *n.* The daughter of a person's stepparent by a previous marriage.
step·son (stĕp′sŭn′) *n.* The son of a person's spouse by a former marriage.
step turn *n.* A skiing turn made by lifting a ski, putting it down again pointed in the direction of the turn, and placing one's weight on it while bringing the other ski into parallel position.
step-up (stĕp′ŭp′) *adj.* Increasing in steps or by stages. —*n.* An increase in size, amount, or activity.
step-up transformer *n.* A transformer that has fewer turns in the primary winding than in the secondary, used to transform low voltage to high voltage.
step·wise (stĕp′wīz′) *adj.* **1.** Marked by a gradual progression as if step by step. **2.** Moving from one musical tone to an adjacent one. **—step′wise′** *adv.*
–ster *suff.* **1.** One that is associated with, participates in, makes, or does: *songster.* **2.** One that is: *youngster.* [ME < OE *-estre.*]
ste·ra·di·an (stĭ-rā′dē-ən) *n.* A unit of measure equal to the solid angle subtended at the center of a sphere by an area equal to the radius squared on the surface of the sphere: *The total solid angle of a sphere is 4π steradians.* [STE(REO)- + RADIAN.]
ster·co·ra·ceous (stûr′kə-rā′shəs) also **ster·co·rous** (stûr′kər-əs) *adj.* Consisting of or relating to excrement. [Lat. *stercus, stercor-,* dung + -ACEOUS.]
stere (stîr) *n.* A unit of volume equal to one cubic meter. [Fr. *stère* < Gk. *stereos,* solid, hard.]
ster·e·o (stĕr′ē-ō′, stîr′-) *n., pl.* **-os. 1. a.** A stereophonic

sound-reproduction system. **b.** Stereophonic sound. **2.** A stereotype. **3.** A stereoscopic system or photograph.

stereo– *pref.* **1.** Solid; solid body: *stereotropism.* **2.** Three-dimensional: *stereoscope.* [< Gk. *stereos,* solid.]

ster•e•o•bate (stĕr′ē-ō-bāt′, stîr′-) *n. Archit.* **1.** A stylobate. **2.** The foundation of a stone building, its top course sometimes being a stylobate. [Lat. *stereobata* < Gk. *stereobatēs* : *stereos,* solid + *bainein,* to go.]

ster•e•o•chem•is•try (stĕr′ē-ō-kĕm′ĭ-strē, stîr′-) *n.* The chemical study of spatial arrangements of atoms in molecules and of the effects of these arrangements on the molecule's properties. **—ster′e•o•chem′i•cal** *adj.*

ster•e•o•chro•my (stĕr′ē-ō-krō′mē, stîr′-) *n.* The art or process of mural painting with pigments mixed with water glass. **—ster′e•o•chrome′** *n.* **—ster′e•o•chro′mic** *adj.* **—ster′e•o•chro′mi•cal•ly** *adv.*

ster•e•o•gram (stĕr′ē-ō-grăm′, stîr′-) *n.* **1.** A picture or diagram designed to give the impression of solidity. **2.** A stereograph.

ster•e•o•graph (stĕr′ē-ō-grăf′, stîr′-) *n.* Two stereoscopic pictures or one picture with two superposed stereoscopic images, designed to give a three-dimensional effect when viewed through a stereoscope or special glasses. *—tr.v.* **-graphed, -graph•ing, -graphs.** To make (a stereographic picture).

ster•e•og•ra•phy (stĕr′ē-ŏg′rə-fē, stîr′-) *n.* **1.** The art or technique of depicting solid bodies on a plane surface. **2.** Photography that involves the use of stereoscopic equipment. **—ster′e•o•graph′ic** (-ə-grăf′ĭk), **ster′e•o•graph′i•cal** *adj.* **—ster′e•o•graph′i•cal•ly** *adv.*

ster•e•o•i•so•mer (stĕr′ē-ō-ī′sə-mər, stîr′-) *n.* An isomer (sense 1.c.).

ster•e•o•i•som•er•ism (stĕr′ē-ō-ī-sŏm′ə-rĭz′əm, stîr′-) *n.* Isomerism created by differences in the spatial arrangement of atoms in a molecule. **—ster′e•o•i′so•mer′ic** (-ī′-sə-mĕr′ĭk) *adj.*

ster•e•ol•o•gy (stĕr′ē-ŏl′ə-jē) *n.* The study of three-dimensional properties of objects or matter usually observed two-dimensionally. **—ster′e•o•log′ic** (-ə-lŏj′ĭk), **ster′e•o•log′i•cal** *adj.* **—ster′e•o•log′i•cal•ly** *adv.* **—ster′e•ol′o•gist** *n.*

ster•e•o•mi•cro•scope (stĕr′ē-ō-mī′krə-skōp′, stîr′-) *n.* A microscope optically equipped for stereoscopic viewing. **—ster′e•o•mi′cro•scop′ic** *adj.*

ster•e•o•phon•ic (stĕr′ē-ō-fŏn′ĭk, stîr′-) *adj.* Of or used in a sound-reproduction system that uses two or more separate channels to give a more natural distribution of sound. **—ster′e•o•phon′i•cal•ly** *adv.* **—ster′e•oph′on•y** (-ē-ŏf′ə-nē) *n.*

ster•e•op•sis (stĕr′ē-ŏp′sĭs, stîr′-) *n.* Stereoscopic vision.

ster•e•op•ti•con (stĕr′ē-ŏp′tĭ-kŏn′, stîr′-) *n.* A magic lantern, esp. one made double so as to produce dissolving views. [NLat. STEREO- + Greek *optikon,* neuter of *optikos,* optic.]

ster•e•o•scope (stĕr′ē-ə-skōp′, stîr′-) *n.* An optical instrument used to impart a three-dimensional effect to two photographs of the same scene taken at slightly different angles and viewed through two eyepieces.

ster•e•o•scop•ic (stĕr′ē-ə-skŏp′ĭk, stîr′-) *adj.* **1.** Of or pertaining to stereoscopy, esp. three-dimensional. **2.** Of or pertaining to a stereoscope. **—ster′e•o•scop′i•cal•ly** *adv.*

ster•e•os•co•py (stĕr′ē-ŏs′kə-pē, stîr′-) *n.* **1.** The viewing of objects as three-dimensional. **2.** The technique of making or using stereoscopes and stereoscopic slides. **—ster′e•os′co•pist** *n.*

ster•e•o•tax•is (stĕr′ē-ə-tăk′sĭs, stîr′-) also **ster•e•o•tax•y** (stĕr′ē-ə-tăk′sē, stîr′-) *n.* Thigmotaxis. **—ster′e•o•tac′tic** (-tăk′tĭk), **ster′e•o•tac′ti•cal** *adj.* **—ster′e•o•tac′ti•cal•ly** *adv.*

ster•e•ot•ro•pism (stĕr′ē-ŏt′rə-pĭz′əm, stîr′-) *n.* Thigmotropism. **—ster′e•o•trop′ic** (-ē-ə-trŏp′ĭk) *adj.*

ster•e•o•type (stĕr′ē-ə-tīp′, stîr′-) *n.* **1.** A conventional, formulaic, and usually oversimplified conception, opinion, or belief. **2.** A person, group, event, or issue considered to typify or conform to an unvarying pattern or manner, lacking any individuality: *the very stereotype of a college sophomore.* **3.** A metal printing plate cast from a matrix that is molded from a raised printing surface, such as type. *—tr.v.* **-typed, -typ•ing, -types. 1.** To develop a fixed, unvarying idea about. **2.** To make a stereotype of. **3.** To print from a stereotype. [Fr. *stéréotype* : *stéréo-,* stereo- + *-type,* -type.] **—ster′e•o•typ′er** *n.* **—ster′e•o•typ′ic** (-tĭp′ĭk), **ster′e•o•typ′i•cal** *adj.*

ster•e•o•typed (stĕr′ē-ə-tīpt′, stîr′-) *adj.* **1.** Printed or reproduced from stereotype plates. **2.** Not individualized; conventional.

ster•e•o•ty•py (stĕr′ē-ə-tī′pē, stîr′-) *n.* **1.** The process or art of making stereotype plates. **2.** Excessive repetition or lack of variation in movements, ideas, or patterns of speech.

ster•e•o•vi•sion (stĕr′ē-ō-vĭzh′ən, stîr′-) *n.* Visual perception of or exhibition in three dimensions.

ster•ic (stĕr′ĭk, stîr′-) *adj.* Of or pertaining to the spatial arrangement of atoms in a molecule. [STER(EO)- + -IC.] **—ster′i•cal•ly** *adv.*

ste•rig•ma (stə-rĭg′mə) *n., pl.* **-ma•ta.** A slender projection of the basidium of some fungi which bears a basidiospore. [NLat. < Gk. *stērigma,* support < *stērizein,* to support.]

ster•il•ant (stĕr′ə-lənt) *n.* A sterilizing agent.

ster•ile (stĕr′əl, -īl′) *adj.* **1.** Incapable of reproducing sexually; infertile. **2.** Capable of producing little or no vegetation; unfruitful. **3.** Free from bacteria or other microorganisms. **4.** Lacking in imagination or vitality: *sterile prose.* **5.** Lacking any power to function; not productive or effective. [OFr. < Lat. *sterilis,* unfruitful.] **—ster′ile•ly** *adv.* **—ster′ile•ness, ste•ril′i•ty** (stə-rĭl′ĭ-tē) *n.*

Synonyms: *sterile, infertile, barren, unfruitful, impotent.* These adjectives, in literal usage, mean lacking or seemingly lacking in power to produce offspring. Figuratively they suggest absence of a productive result. *Sterile* means being unable to procreate because of some defect in the reproductive organs; by extension it describes any lack of creativity. *Infertile* means *sterile* in the literal sense of the latter term. *Barren* describes, in particular, a woman who has tried and failed to have children. It can also apply to what is devoid of profit, enjoyment, or any other desirable thing. *Unfruitful* literally means not bearing fruit and figuratively means not having a useful result. *Impotent* specifies inability of a male to engage in sexual intercourse; in a general sense, it means powerless to act effectively.

ster•il•i•za•tion (stĕr′ə-lĭ-zā′shən) *n.* **1.** The procedure or act of sterilizing. **2.** The condition of being sterile or sterilized.

ster•il•ize (stĕr′ə-līz′) *tr.v.* **-ized, -iz•ing, -iz•es. 1.** To render sterile. **2.** *Econ.* To place (gold) in safekeeping so as not to affect the supply of money or credit. **—ster′il•iz′er** *n.*

ster•let (stûr′lĭt) *n.* A sturgeon, *Acipenser ruthenus,* of the Black Sea and adjacent waters, used as a source of caviar. [R. *sterlyad′.*]

ster•ling (stûr′lĭng) *n.* **1.** British money, esp. the pound as the basic monetary unit of the United Kingdom. **2.** British coinage of silver or gold, having as a standard of fineness 0.500 for silver and 0.91666 for gold. **3. a.** Sterling silver. **b.** Articles, such as tableware, made of sterling silver. *—adj.* **1.** Consisting of or relating to sterling or British money. **2.** Made of sterling silver. **3.** Of the highest quality: *sterling character.* [ME, silver penny.]

sterling silver *n.* **1.** An alloy of 92.5 per cent silver with copper or another metal. **2.** Objects made of sterling silver.

stern[1] (stûrn) *adj.* **-er, -est. 1.** Firm or unyielding; inflexible: *stern discipline* **2.** Grave or severe in manner or appearance; austere: *a stern teacher.* **3.** Grim, gloomy, or forbidding in appearance or outlook. **4.** Inexorable; relentless: *stern demands on his time.* [ME *sterne* < OE *styrne.*]

stern[2] (stûrn) *n.* **1.** The rear part of a ship or boat. **2.** A rear part or section. [ME *sterne,* perh. of Scand. orig.]

stern[2]
17th-century Dutch engraving

ster•na (stûr′nə) *n.* A plural of **sternum.**

ster•nal (stûr′nəl) *adj.* Of, near, or pertaining to the sternum. [NLat. *sternalis* < *sternum,* sternum.]

stern chaser *n.* A gun or cannon mounted on the stern of a ship for firing at a pursuing vessel.

stern•fore•most (stûrn′fôr′mōst′, -fōr′-) *adv.* With the stern foremost; backward.

stern•most (stûrn′mōst′) *adj.* Farthest astern.

ster•no•cos•tal (stûr′nō-kŏs′təl) *adj.* Of or pertaining to both the sternum and the ribs. [STERN(UM) + Lat. *costa,* rib + -AL.]

stern•post (stûrn′pōst′) *n.* The principal upright post at the stern of a vessel, usually serving to support the rudder.

stern sheets *pl.n.* The stern area of an open boat.

stern•son (stûrn′sən) *n.* A bar of metal or wood set between the keelson and the sternpost to fortify the joint. [STERN + (KEEL)SON.]

ster•num (stûr′nəm) *n., pl.* **-nums** or **-na** (-nə). A long flat bone articulating with the cartilages of and forming the midventral support of most of the ribs in tetrapod vertebrates, and also of the collarbone in man and certain other vertebrates. [NLat. < Gk. *sternon.*]

ster•nu•ta•tion (stûr′nyə-tā′shən) *n.* **1.** The act of sneezing. **2.** A sneeze. [Lat. *sternutatio, sternutation-* < *sternutare,* freq. of *sternuere,* to sneeze.]

ster•nu•ta•tor (stûr′nyə-tā′tər) *n.* A substance that irritates the nasal and respiratory passages and causes coughing, sneezing, lachrimation, and sometimes vomiting.

ster•nu•ta•to•ry (stûr-nyōō′tə-tôr′ē, -tōr′ē, -nōō′-) also **ster•nu•ta•tive** (stûr′nyə-tā′tĭv) *adj.* Causing or tending to cause sneezing. *—n., pl.* **-ries.** A sternutatory substance, such as pepper.

stern•ward (stûrn′wərd) *adj. & adv.* At or in the stern; astern. **—stern′wards** *adv.*

stern•way (stûrn′wā′) *n.* The backward movement of a vessel.

stern-wheel•er (stûrn′hwē′lər, -wē′lər) *n.* A steamboat propelled by a paddle wheel at the stern.

ster•oid (stîr′oid′, stĕr′-) *n.* Any of numerous naturally occurring, fat-soluble organic compounds having a 17-carbon-atom ring as a basis, and including the sterols and bile acids, many hormones, certain natural drugs such as digitalis compounds, and the precursors of certain vitamins. [STER(OL) + -OID.]

ste•roid•o•gen•e•sis (stĭ-roi′də-jĕn′ĭ-sĭs, stîr′oi-, stĕr′-) *n.* The production of steroids. **—ste•roid′o•gen′ic** *adj.*

ster•ol (stîr′ôl′, -ōl′, stĕr′-) *n.* Any of a group of predominantly unsaturated solid alcohols of the steroid group, as cholesterol and ergosterol, occurring in the fatty tissues of plants and animals. [Short for CHOLESTEROL.]

Ster•o•pe (stĕr′ə-pē′) *n.* **1.** *Gk. Myth.* One of the seven

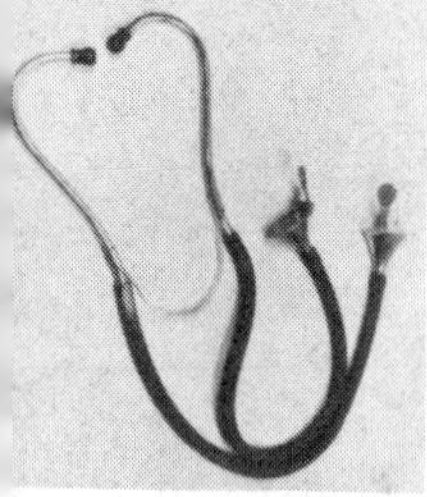

stethoscope

Stetson

Pleiades. **2.** One of the stars in the constellation Pleiades. [Gk. < *asteropē,* lightning.]

ster·son knee (stûr′sən) *n.* A sternson.

ster·tor (stûr′tər) *n.* A heavy snoring sound in respiration. [NLat. < Lat. *stertere,* to snore.] **—ster′to·rous** (stûr′tər-əs) *adj.* **—ster′to·rous·ly** *adv.*

stet (stĕt) *n.* A printer's term directing that a letter, word, or other matter marked for omission or correction is to be retained. *—tr.v.* **stet·ted, stet·ting, stets.** To nullify a correction or omission previously made in (printed matter) by underlining it with dots and writing the word *stet* in the margin. [Lat., let it stand.]

steth·o·scope (stĕth′ə-skōp′) *n.* An instrument used for listening to sounds produced within the body. [Fr. *stéthoscope* : Gk. *stēthos,* chest + Fr. *-scope,* -scope.] **—steth′o·scop′ic** (-skŏp′ĭk), **steth′o·scop′i·cal** *adj.* **—steth′o·scop′i·cal·ly** *adv.* **—ste·thos′co·py** (stĕ-thŏs′kə-pē) *n.*

Stet·son (stĕt′sən). A trademark for a hat having a high crown and wide brim.

ste·ve·dore (stē′və-dôr′, -dōr′) *n.* A person employed in the loading or unloading of ships. *—v.* **-dored, -dor·ing, -dores.** *—tr.* To load or unload the cargo of (a ship). *—intr.* To load or unload a ship. [Sp. *estibador* < *estivar,* to stow < Lat. *stipare,* to pack.]

stevedore's knot also **stevedore knot** *n.* A knot used to prevent a line from coming out of a pulley.

stew (sto͞o, styo͞o) *v.* **stewed, stew·ing, stews.** *—tr.* To cook (food) by simmering or boiling slowly. *—intr.* **1.** To undergo cooking by boiling slowly or simmering. **2.** *Informal.* To suffer with oppressive heat or stuffy confinement; swelter. **3.** *Informal.* To worry; fret. *—n.* **1.** A dish cooked by stewing, esp. a mixture of meat or fish and vegetables with stock. **2.** *Informal.* Mental agitation: *in a stew over her lost keys.* **3.** Often **stews.** *Archaic.* A brothel. [ME *stewen* < OFr. *estuver,* to bathe in hot water.]

stew·ard (sto͞o′ərd, styo͞o′-) *n.* **1.** A person who manages another's property, finances, or other affairs. **2.** A person in charge of the household affairs of a large estate, club, hotel, or resort. **3.** An officer on a ship in charge of provisions and dining arrangements. **4.** An attendant on a ship or airplane. **5.** A shop steward. *—v.* **-ard·ed, -ard·ing, -ards.** *—tr.* To serve as steward of; manage. *—intr.* To serve as a steward. [ME < OE *stigweard* : *stig,* hall + *weard,* keeper.]

stew·ard·ess (sto͞o′ər-dĭs, styo͞o′-) *n.* A woman who works as a steward, esp. one who works as a flight attendant.

stewed (sto͞od, styo͞od) *adj.* **1.** Cooked by stewing: *stewed prunes.* **2.** *Slang.* Drunk; intoxicated.

Sthe·no (sthē′nō) *n. Gk. Myth.* One of the three Gorgons. [Gk. *Sthenō* < *sthenos,* strong.]

stib·ine (stĭb′ēn′) *n.* A colorless, flammable poisonous gas, SbH_3, often used as a fumigant. [< Lat. *stibium,* antimony.]

stib·nite (stĭb′nīt′) *n.* A lead-gray mineral, Sb_2S_3, sometimes containing silver and gold, that is the chief source of antimony. [Fr. *stibine,* stibnite (< Lat *stibium,* antimony < Gk. *stibi,* of Egypt. orig.) + -ITE.]

stich (stĭk) *n.* A line of verse. [Gk. *stikhos.*]

stich·ic (stĭk′ĭk) *adj.* Of or pertaining to verse composed in homogeneous and recurrent lines, as in recitative poetry.

sti·chom·e·try (stĭ-kŏm′ĭ-trē) *n.* The division of a prose piece into lines whose lengths correspond to the natural divisions of sense or to the natural cadences, as in manuscripts written before the adoption of punctuation. [Gk. *stikhos,* stich + -METRY.] **—stich′o·met′ric** (stĭk′ə-mĕt′rĭk) *adj.*

stich·o·myth·i·a (stĭk′ə-mĭth′ē-ə) also **sti·chom·y·thy** (stĭ-kŏm′ə-thē) *n.* An ancient Greek arrangement of dialogue in drama, poetry, and disputation in which single lines of verse are spoken by alternate speakers. [Gk. *stikhomuthia* < *stikhomuthein,* to speak in alternating lines : *stikhos,* stich + *muthos,* speech.] **—stich′o·myth′ic** *adj.*

stick (stĭk) *n.* **1.** A long, slender piece of wood, esp.: **a.** A branch or stem cut from a tree or shrub. **b.** A tree branch or other piece of wood used for fuel, cut for lumber, or shaped for a specific purpose. **c.** A wand, staff, or rod. **d.** Any of various sticklike implements used in games or sports: *a hockey stick.* **2.** A cane or walking stick. **3.** Something slender and often cylindrical in form: *a stick of dynamite.* **4.** *Slang.* A marijuana cigarette. **5.** An airplane control that operates the elevators and ailerons. **6.** *Naut.* A mast or a part of a mast. **7.** *Printing.* **a.** A composing stick. **b.** The type contents of a composing stick. **8.** A group of bombs released to fall across a target in a straight row. **9.** A timber tree. **10.** A poke, thrust, or stab with a stick or similar object: *a stick in the ribs.* **11.** The condition or power of adhering: *a glue with plenty of stick.* **12.** **sticks.** *Informal.* **a.** A remote area; backwoods. **b.** A dull or unsophisticated city or town. **13.** *Informal.* A stiff, spiritless, or boring person. **14.** *Archaic.* A difficulty or obstacle; delay. *—v.* **stuck** (stŭk), **stick·ing, sticks.** *—tr.* **1.** To pierce, puncture, or penetrate with a pointed instrument. **2.** To kill by piercing. **3.** To thrust or push (a pointed instrument) into or through another object. **4.** To fasten into place by forcing an end or point into something: *stick a hook on the wall.* **5.** To fasten or attach with or as if with pins, nails, or similar instruments. **6.** To fasten or attach with an adhesive material, glue, or tape. **7.** To cover or decorate with objects piercing the surface. **8.** To fix, impale, or transfix on a pointed object: *stick an olive on a toothpick.* **9.** To put, thrust, or poke into a specified place or position: *stuck a flower in his lapel.* **10.** To detain or delay. **11.** *past tense and past participle* **sticked.** To prop (a vine or other plant) with sticks or brush on which to grow. **12.** *past tense and past participle* **sticked.** *Printing.* To set (type) in a composing stick. **13.** *Informal.* To confuse, baffle, or puzzle: *Even simple questions stick him.* **14.** To cover or smear with something sticky. **15.** To put blame or responsibility on; burden: *stuck him with the bill.* **16.** *Slang.* To defraud or cheat. *—intr.* **1.** To be or become fixed or embedded in place by having the point thrust in. **2.** To become or remain attached or in close association by or as if by adhesion; cling: *stick together in a crowd.* **3. a.** To remain firm, determined, or resolute: *stuck to her principles.* **b.** To remain loyal or faithful: *stuck by a friend.* **4.** To persist, endure, or persevere. **5.** To scruple or hesitate: *She sticks at nothing.* **6.** To be at or come to a standstill; become fixed, blocked, checked, or obstructed. **7.** To extend, project, or protrude. ***—phrasal verbs.*** **stick around.** *Informal.* To remain; linger. **stick out.** To be prominent. **stick up.** To rob, esp. at gunpoint. ***—idioms.*** **be stuck on.** *Informal.* To be very fond of. **stick it to.** *Slang.* To treat severely or wrongfully. **stick one's neck out.** *Informal.* To voluntarily make oneself vulnerable. **stick to one's knitting.** *Informal.* To mind one's own business. **stick to the ribs.** *Informal.* To be substantial or filling. Used of food. [ME *stykke* < OE *sticca.*]

stick·ball (stĭk′bôl′) *n.* A form of baseball played with a rubber ball and a stick or the handle of a broom for a bat.

stick·er (stĭk′ər) *n.* **1.** One that sticks. **2.** A gummed or adhesive label or patch. **3.** A tenacious, diligent, or persistent person. **4.** A thorn, prickle, or barb.

stick figure *n.* A picture of a human or animal figure showing the head as a circle and the rest of the body as a combination of straight lines.

sticking plaster *n.* Adhesive tape.

sticking point *n.* Something causing or likely to cause an impasse.

stick insect *n.* Any of several insects of the family Phasmidae, resembling sticks or twigs, such as the walking stick.

stick-in-the-mud (stĭk′ĭn-*th*ə-mŭd′) *n. Informal.* A person who lacks initiative, imagination, or enthusiasm.

stick·le (stĭk′əl) *intr.v.* **-led, -ling, -les.** **1.** To argue or contend stubbornly, esp. about trifles. **2.** To have or raise objections; scruple. [ME *stightlen,* to contend, freq. of *stighten,* to arrange < OE *stihtian.*]

stick·le·back (stĭk′əl-băk′) *n.* Any of various small freshwater and marine fishes of the family Gasterosteidae, having erectile spines along the back. [ME *stykylbak* : OE *sticel,* prick + ME *bak,* back.]

stick·ler (stĭk′lər) *n.* **1.** A person who insists on something unyieldingly: *a stickler for neatness.* **2.** Something puzzling or difficult.

stick·pin (stĭk′pĭn′) *n.* A decorative pin worn on a necktie.

stick·seed (stĭk′sēd′) *n.* Any of various plants of the genus *Lappula,* having small prickly fruits that cling to clothing or fur.

stick shift *n.* An automobile gearshift operated by hand.

stick·tight (stĭk′tīt′) *n.* Any of various plants, such as the bur marigold, having barbed, clinging seeds or fruit.

stick-to-it·ive·ness (stĭk-to͞o′ĭ-tĭv-nĭs) *n. Informal.* Unwavering pertinacity; perseverance.

stick·up (stĭk′ŭp′) *n. Slang.* A robbery, esp. at gunpoint.

stick·weed (stĭk′wēd′) *n.* Any of various plants having clinging seeds or fruit.

stick·y (stĭk′ē) *adj.* **-i·er, -i·est.** **1.** Having the property of adhering or sticking to a surface; adhesive. **2.** Covered with an adhesive agent. **3.** Warm and humid; muggy. **4.** *Informal.* Painful or difficult: *a sticky situation.* **—stick′i·ly** *adv.* **—stick′i·ness** *n.*

sticky wicket *n. Informal.* A difficult or embarrassing problem or situation.

stied (stīd) *v.* Past tense and past participle of **sty**[1].

sties[1] (stīz) *n.* Plural of **sty**[1]. *—v.* Third person singular present tense of **sty**[1].

sties[2] (stīz) *n.* A plural of **sty**[2].

stiff (stĭf) *adj.* **-er, -est.** **1.** Difficult to bend or stretch; rigid: *a stiff fabric.* **2.** Not moving or operating easily; not limber: *a stiff joint.* **3.** Drawn tightly; taut. **4.** Rigidly or excessively formal, awkward, or constrained; *stiff manners.* **5.** Not liquid, loose, or fluid; thick. **6.** Firm in purpose or resistance; stubborn. **7.** Having a strong, swift, steady force or movement: *a stiff current.* **8.** Potent or strong: *a stiff drink.* **9.** Difficult, laborious, or arduous: *a stiff hike.* **10.** Difficult to carry through, comprehend, or accept; harsh or severe: *a stiff penalty.* **11.** Excessively high: *a stiff price.* **12.** *Naut.* Not heeling over much in spite of great wind or the press of the sail. *—adv.* **1.** In a stiff manner. **2.** Completely; totally: *bored stiff.* *—n. Slang.* **1.** A corpse. **2.** An overformal, constrained, or priggish person. **3.** A drunk. **4.** A person: *working stiffs.* **5.** A hobo; tramp. **6.** A person who tips poorly. [ME *stiffe* < OE *stīf.*] **—stiff′ly** *adv.* **—stiff′ness** *n.*

Synonyms: *stiff, rigid, inflexible, inelastic, tense, taut.* These adjectives are compared as they relate to physical stress and to human behavior and attitudes. Anything *stiff* cannot easily be bent. In reference to persons, *stiff* suggests firmness of position and either lack of ease in manner or cold formality. *Rigid* and *inflexible* apply to what cannot be bent physically, at least without damage or deformation; figuratively they describe unyielding positions or attitudes. *Inelastic* refers largely to what cannot be stretched, bent, or expanded without marked physical change. *Tense* describes the condition of being stretched tight; it is applied literally to muscles and other bodily structures and figuratively to persons under nervous strain. *Taut* is used both in the physical sense of being tightly drawn or stretched and in the related sense of nervous tension.

stiff-arm (stĭf'ärm') *tr.v. Football.* **-armed, -arm·ing, -arms.** To straight-arm.

stiff·en (stĭf'ən) *tr. & intr.v.* **-ened, -en·ing, -ens.** To make or become stiff or stiffer. **—stiff'en·er** *n.*

stiff-necked (stĭf'nĕkt') *adj.* Stubborn; unyielding.

sti·fle[1] (stī'fəl) *v.* **-fled, -fling, -fles.** *—tr.* **1.** To kill by preventing respiration; smother or suffocate. **2.** To interrupt or cut off (the voice, for example). **3.** To hold back; suppress: *stifle dissent.* *—intr.* **1.** To die of suffocation. **2.** To feel smothered or suffocated by or as if by close confinement in a stuffy room. [ME *stufflen.*] **—sti'fler** *n.* **—sti'fling·ly** *adv.*

sti·fle[2] (stī'fəl) *n.* The joint of the hind leg analogous to the human knee in certain quadrupeds, such as the horse. [ME.]

stig·ma (stĭg'mə) *n., pl.* **stig·ma·ta** (stĭg-mä'tə, stĭg'mə-) or **stig·mas. 1.** *Archaic.* A mark burned into the skin of a criminal or slave; brand. **2.** A mark or token of infamy, disgrace, or reproach. **3.** A small mark; scar or birthmark. **4.** *Med.* **a.** A mark or spot on the skin that bleeds as a symptom of hysteria. **b.** A mark indicative of a history of a disease or abnormality. **5.** *Biol.* A small mark, spot, or pore, such as the respiratory spiracle of an insect or an eyespot in certain algae. **6.** *pl.* **-mas.** *Bot.* The apex of the pistil of a flower, upon which pollen is deposited at pollination. **7. stigmata.** Marks or sores corresponding to and resembling the crucifixion wounds of Jesus, sometimes occurring during religious ecstasy or hysteria. [Lat. < Gk., tattoo mark < *stizein,* to prick.] **—stig'mal** *adj.*

stig·mas·ter·ol (stĭg-măs'tə-rôl', -rōl') *n.* A sterol, $C_{29}H_{48}O$, obtained from soybeans or Calabar beans. [NLat. *(Physo)-stigma,* Calabar bean genus + STEROL.]

stig·ma·ta (stĭg-mä'tə, stĭg'mə-) *n.* A plural of **stigma.**

stig·mat·ic (stĭg-măt'ĭk) *adj.* **1.** Pertaining to, resembling, or having a stigma or stigmata. **2.** Anastigmatic. *—n.* A person marked with religious stigmata. **—stig·mat'i·cal·ly** *adv.*

stig·ma·tism (stĭg'mə-tĭz'əm) *n.* **1.** The state or condition of being affected by stigmata. **2.** The state of a refracting or reflecting system that focuses at a point light rays from an off-axis point.

stig·ma·tist (stĭg'mə-tĭst) *n.* A stigmatic.

stig·ma·tize (stĭg'mə-tīz') *tr.v.* **-tized, -tiz·ing, -tiz·es. 1.** To characterize or brand as disgraceful or ignominious. **2.** To mark with stigmata. **3.** To cause stigmata to appear on. [Med Lat. *stigmatizare,* to brand < Gk. *stigmatizein,* to mark < *stigma,* tattoo mark < *stizein,* to prick.] **—stig'ma·ti·za'tion** *n.* **—stig'ma·tiz'er** *n.*

stil·bene (stĭl'bēn') *n.* A colorless or yellowish crystalline compound, $C_{14}H_{12}$, used in the manufacture of dyes and optical bleaches and as a phosphor. [Gk. *stilbos,* shining < *stilbein,* to shimmer + -ENE.]

stil·bes·trol (stĭl-bĕs'trôl', -trōl') *n.* Diethylstilbestrol. [STIL-B(ENE) + ESTR(US) + -OL.]

stil·bite (stĭl'bīt') *n.* A white or yellow lustrous zeolite mineral, essentially $(Ca,Na)_2Al_2Si_7O_{18}\cdot 7H_2O$. [Fr. < Gk. *stilbos,* shining < *stilbein,* to shimmer.]

stile[1] (stīl) *n.* **1.** A set or series of steps for crossing a fence or wall. **2.** A turnstile. [ME < OE *stigel.*]

stile[2] (stīl) *n.* A vertical member of a panel or frame, as in a door or window sash. [Prob. < Du. *stijl,* doorpost.]

sti·let·to (stĭ-lĕt'ō) *n., pl.* **-tos** or **-toes. 1. a.** A small dagger with a slender, tapering blade. **b.** Something resembling this dagger in shape. **2.** A small, sharp-pointed instrument used for making eyelet holes in needlework. [Ital., dim. of *stilo,* dagger < Lat. *stilus,* stylus.]

stiletto heel *n.* A high heel on women's shoes that is thinner than a spike heel.

still[1] (stĭl) *adj.* **-er, -est. 1.** Silent; quiet. **2.** Hushed; subdued. **3.** Without movement; at rest. **4.** Free from disturbance, commotion, or agitation; tranquil. **5.** Free from a noticeable current, as a body of water. **6.** Not carbonated; lacking effervescence: *a still wine.* **7.** Of or pertaining to a single or static photograph as opposed to a motion picture. *—n.* **1.** Silence; quiet: *the still of the night.* **2.** A still photograph, esp. one from a scene of a motion picture used for advertising purposes. **3.** A still-life picture. *—adv.* **1.** Without movement; motionlessly: *stand still.* **2.** Up to or at the time indicated; yet: *still awake.* **3.** In increasing amount or degree: *still further complaints.* **4.** Nevertheless; all the same. **5.** *Archaic & Regional.* Always; constantly. *—v.* **stilled, still·ing, stills.** *—tr.* **1.** To make still or tranquil. **2.** To make quiet; silence. **3.** To make motionless. **4.** To allay; calm. *—intr.* To become still. [ME < OE.] **—still'ness** *n.*

Synonyms: *still, quiet, silent, noiseless, hushed, tranquil.* These adjectives refer to the relative absence of sound or movement. *Still* can apply to what is without sound or activity or both, as can *quiet. Still* is usually the more emphatic in all senses; *quiet* often implies merely the absence of noise, bustle, or customary activity. *Silent* refers only to what is without sound or noise. Like *noiseless* and *hushed,* it makes no clear indication with respect to movement or the absence thereof. *Noiseless* can mean without sound but usually implies freedom from excessive or disturbing sound. *Hushed* suggests a sudden condition of silence, especially one following noise or excitement. *Tranquil* primarily implies calm and lack of agitated movement.

still[2] (stĭl) *n.* **1.** An apparatus for distilling liquids, esp. alcohols, consisting of a vessel in which the substance is vaporized by heat and a cooling device in which the vapor is condensed. **2.** A distillery. [< ME *stillen,* to distill < *distillen.* —see DISTILL.]

still alarm *n.* A fire alarm transmitted by means, such as the telephone, other than by sounding the conventional signal apparatus.

still·birth (stĭl'bûrth') *n.* **1.** The birth of a dead child or fetus. **2.** A child or fetus dead at birth.

still·born (stĭl'bôrn') *adj.* Dead at birth.

still hunt *n.* The hunting of game by stalking or ambushing.

still-hunt (stĭl'hŭnt') *v.* **-hunt·ed, -hunt·ing, -hunts.** *—tr.* To pursue (game) stealthily. *—intr.* To engage in a still hunt.

still life *n., pl.* **still lifes. 1.** The representation of inanimate objects, such as flowers or fruit, in painting or photography. **2.** A painting or picture of inanimate objects.

still·man (stĭl'măn) *n.* **1.** A person who owns or manages a still or distillery. **2.** A person who operates a distillation apparatus, as in an oil refinery.

still·y (stĭl'ē) *adj.* **-i·er, -i·est.** Quiet; calm. **—stil'ly** *adv.*

Stil·son (stĭl'sən). A trademark for a monkey wrench with serrated jaws.

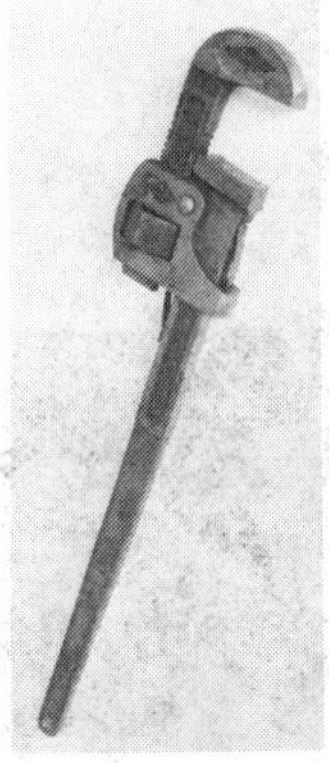
Stilson
Stilson wrench

stilt (stĭlt) *n.* **1.** Either of a pair of long, slender poles each equipped with a raised footrest to permit walking elevated above the ground. **2.** Any of various tall posts or pillars used as support, as for a dock or building. **3.** *pl.* **stilts** or **stilt. a.** A long-legged wading bird, *Himantopus mexicanus* (or *H. himantopus*), having black and white plumage and a long, slender bill. **b.** A related bird, *Cladorhyncus leucocephala,* of Australia. *—tr.v.* **stilt·ed, stilt·ing, stilts.** To place or raise on stilts. [ME *stilte.*]

stilt

stilt·ed (stĭl'tĭd) *adj.* **1.** Stiffly or artificially formal; stiff: *"Standard English must always strike an American as a bit stilted"* (H.L. Mencken). **2.** *Archit.* Having some vertical length between the impost and the beginning of the curve. Used of an arch. **—stilt'ed·ly** *adv.* **—stilt'ed·ness** *n.*

Stil·ton cheese (stĭl'tn) *n.* A rich, waxy cheese with a blue-green mold and a wrinkled rind. [After *Stilton,* a parish in Huntingdon, England.]

stim·u·lant (stĭm'yə-lənt) *n.* **1.** Something that temporarily arouses or accelerates physiological or organic activity. **2.** A stimulus or incentive: *"An age of political excitement is usually a stimulant to literature"* (Will Durant). **3.** An alcoholic beverage.

stim·u·late (stĭm'yə-lāt') *v.* **-lat·ed, -lat·ing, -lates.** *—tr.* To rouse to activity or heightened action, as by spurring or goading; excite. *—intr.* To act or serve as a stimulant or stimulus. [Lat. *stimulare, stimulat-,* to goad on < *stimulus,* goad.] **—stim'u·lat'er, stim'u·la'tor** *n.* **—stim'u·la'tion** *n.* **—stim'u·la'tive** (-lā'tĭv), **stim'u·la·to'ry** (-lə-tôr'ē, -tōr'ē) *adj.*

stim·u·lus (stĭm'yə-ləs) *n., pl.* **-li** (-lī'). **1.** Something causing or regarded as causing a response. **2.** An agent, action, or condition that elicits or accelerates a physiological or psychological activity. **3.** Something that incites or rouses to action; incentive: *"Works which were in themselves poor have often proved a stimulus to the imagination"* (W.H. Auden). [Lat., goad.]

sting (stĭng) *v.* **stung** (stŭng), **sting·ing, stings.** *—tr.* **1.** To pierce or wound painfully with or as if with a sharp-pointed structure or organ, such as that of certain insects. **2.** To cause to feel a sharp, smarting pain by or as if by pricking with a sharp point. **3.** To cause to suffer keenly in the mind or feelings: *Her words stung him bitterly.* **4.** To spur on by or as if by sharp irritation. **5.** *Slang.* To cheat or overcharge. *—intr.* **1.** To have, use, or wound with or as if with a sharp-pointed structure or organ, such as that of certain insects. **2.** To cause or feel a sharp, smarting pain. *—n.* **1.** The act of stinging. **2.** The wound or pain caused by or as if by stinging. **3.** A sharp, piercing organ or part, often ejecting a venomous secretion, such as the modified ovipositor of a bee or wasp or the spine of certain fishes. **4.** A stinging power, quality, or capacity. **5.** A keen stimulus or incitement; goad or spur. **6.** *Informal.* A complicated confidence game planned and executed with great care, esp. one undertaken by undercover agents to catch criminals. [ME *stingen* < OE *stingan.*] **—sting'ing·ly** *adv.*

sting·a·ree (stĭng'ə-rē) *n.* The stingray. [Alteration of STING-RAY.]

sting·er (stĭng'ər) *n.* **1.** One that stings, esp. something, as an insult, that stings or wounds mentally. **2.** A stinging organ or part. **3.** A cocktail of crème de menthe and brandy.

stinging cell *n.* A cnidoblast.

sting·ray (stĭng'rā') *n.* Any of various rays of the family Dasyatidae, having a whiplike tail armed with a venomous spine capable of inflicting severe injury.

stipule

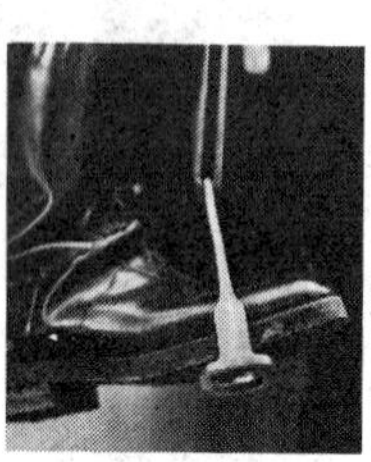

stirrup

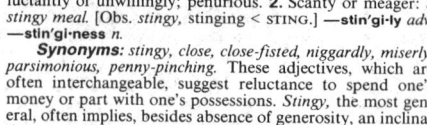

stin·gy (stĭn′jē) *adj.* **-gi·er, -gi·est. 1.** Giving or spending reluctantly or unwillingly; penurious. **2.** Scanty or meager: *a stingy meal.* [Obs. *stingy,* stinging < STING.] **—stin′gi·ly** *adv.* **—stin′gi·ness** *n.*

Synonyms: *stingy, close, close-fisted, niggardly, miserly, parsimonious, penny-pinching.* These adjectives, which are often interchangeable, suggest reluctance to spend one's money or part with one's possessions. *Stingy,* the most general, often implies, besides absence of generosity, an inclination toward meanness in dealings. *Close* and *close-fisted* describe one who is exceedingly and usually annoyingly cautious in money matters. *Niggardly* implies a tendency to be grudging, petty, and covetous. *Miserly* suggests greediness and hoarding of wealth for its own sake. *Parsimonious* emphasizes frugality carried to an extreme. *Penny-pinching* adds to *niggardly* the implication of foolish economy.

stink (stĭngk) *v.* **stank** (stăngk) or **stunk** (stŭngk), **stunk, stink·ing, stinks.** *—intr.* **1.** To emit a strong foul odor. **2. a.** To be highly offensive or abhorrent. **b.** To be in extremely bad repute. **3.** *Slang.* To have something to an extreme or offensive degree: *a deed that stinks of treachery.* **4.** *Slang.* To be of an extremely low or bad quality. *—tr.* To cause to stink: *garbage that stinks up the yard.* *—n.* A strong offensive odor; stench. ***—idiom.* make** (or **raise**) **a stink.** *Slang.* To make a great fuss. [ME *stinken* < OE *stincan.*]

stink·bug (stĭngk′bŭg′) *n.* Any of numerous insects of the family Pentatomidae, having a broad, flattened body and emitting a foul odor.

stink·er (stĭng′kər) *n.* **1.** One that stinks. **2.** *Slang.* A contemptible, disgusting, or irritating person. **3.** *Slang.* Something very difficult: *The interview was a real stinker.*

stink·horn (stĭngk′hôrn′) *n.* Any of several foul-smelling fungi of the order Phallales, such as *Phallus impudicus* or *P. ravenelii,* having a thick, cylindrical stalk and a narrow cap.

stink·ing (stĭng′kĭng) *adj.* **1.** Having a foul smell; fetid. **2.** *Slang.* Very drunk. *—adv. Slang.* To an offensive or extreme degree: *"proceeded to get stinking drunk"* (James Jones). **—stink′ing·ly** *adv.* **—stink′ing·ness** *n.*

stinking chamomile *n.* The mayweed.

stink·pot (stĭngk′pŏt′) *n.* **1.** An earthenware jar containing combustibles emitting a suffocating smoke, formerly used in warfare. **2.** *Slang.* A despised or mean person. **3.** A musk turtle, *Sternotherus odoratus,* of eastern North America.

stink stone also **stink·stone** (stĭngk′stōn′) *n.* A variety of limestone that emits a disagreeable odor when struck or rubbed.

stink·weed (stĭngk′wēd′) *n.* Any of various plants having flowers or foliage with an unpleasant odor.

stink·wood (stĭngk′wo͝od′) *n.* **1. a.** A tree, *Ocotea bullata,* of southern Africa, having wood with an unpleasant odor. **b.** The hard, heavy wood of this tree, used in cabinetwork. **2.** Any of several trees having wood with an unpleasant odor.

stint[1] (stĭnt) *v.* **stint·ed, stint·ing, stints.** *—tr.* **1.** To restrict or limit, as in amount or number; be sparing with. **2.** *Archaic.* To cause to stop. *—intr.* **1.** To subsist on a meager allowance; be frugal. **2.** *Archaic.* To stop or desist. *—n.* **1.** A fixed amount or share of work or duty to be performed within a given period of time. **2.** A limitation or restriction. [ME *stinten,* to cease < OE *styntan,* to blunt.] **—stint′er** *n.*

stint[2] (stĭnt) *n.* Any of several small sandpipers of the genera *Erolia* or *Calidris,* of northern regions. [ME *stynt.*]

stipe (stīp) *n. Bot.* A stalk or stalklike structure, such as the stemlike support of the cap of a mushroom or the main stem of a fern frond. [Fr. < Lat. *stipes,* post.]

sti·pel (stī′pəl, stī-pĕl′) *n.* A minute or secondary stipule at the base of a leaflet. [NLat. *stipella,* dim. of *stipula,* stipule.] **—sti·pel′late** (stī-pĕl′ĭt, stī′pə-lāt′) *adj.*

sti·pend (stī′pĕnd′, -pənd) *n.* A fixed and regular payment, such as a salary for services rendered or an allowance. [ME *stipendie* < OFr. < Lat. *stipendium,* tax : *stips,* contribution + *pendere,* to pay.]

sti·pen·di·ar·y (stī-pĕn′dē-ĕr′ē) *adj.* **1.** Receiving a stipend. **2.** Compensated by stipend: *stipendiary services.* *—n., pl.* **-ies.** A person who receives a stipend, as a clergyman. [Lat. *stipendiarius* < *stipendium,* stipend.]

sti·pes (stī′pēz′) *n., pl.* **stip·i·tes** (stĭp′ĭ-tēz′). **1.** The basal segment of the maxilla of an insect. **2.** A stalklike support or structure. [NLat. < Lat. *stipes,* post.] **—sti′pi·form′** (-pə-fôrm′), **stip′i·ti·form′** (stĭp′ĭ-tə-fôrm′) *adj.*

stip·i·tate (stĭp′ĭ-tāt′) *adj.* Having or supported on a stipe. [< Lat. *stipes, stipit-,* post.]

stip·i·tes (stĭp′ĭ-tēz′) *n.* Plural of **stipes.**

stip·ple (stĭp′əl) *tr.v.* **-pled, -pling, -ples. 1.** To draw, engrave, or paint in dots or short strokes. **2.** To apply (paint, for example) in dots or short strokes. **3.** To dot, fleck, or speckle: *"They crossed a field stippled with purple weeds"* (Flannery O'Connor). *—n.* **1.** The method of drawing, engraving, or painting by stippling. **2.** The effect produced by stippling. [Du. *stippelen,* freq. of *stippen,* to speckle < *stip,* dot.] **—stip′pler** *n.*

stip·u·lar (stĭp′yə-lər) *adj.* Of, pertaining to, or resembling stipules.

stip·u·late[1] (stĭp′yə-lāt′) *v.* **-lat·ed -lat·ing, -lates.** *—tr.* **1.** To specify as a condition of an agreement; require by contract. **2.** To guarantee in an agreement. *—intr.* **1.** To make an express demand or provision in an agreement. **2.** To form an agreement. [Lat. *stipulari, stipulat-,* to bargain.] **—stip′u·la′tor** *n.*

stip·u·late[2] (stĭp′yə-lĭt) *adj.* Having stipules.

stip·u·la·tion (stĭp′yə-lā′shən) *n.* **1.** The act of stipulating. **2.** Something stipulated, esp. a term or condition in an agreement. **—stip′u·la·to′ry** (-lə-tôr′ē, -tōr′ē) *adj.*

stip·ule (stĭp′yo͞ol) *n.* One of the usually small, paired leaflike appendages at the base of a leaf or leafstalk in certain plants. [NLat. *stipula* < Lat., stalk.] **—stip′uled′** *adj.*

stir[1] (stûr) *v.* **stirred, stir·ring, stirs.** *—tr.* **1.** To pass an implement through (a liquid, for example) in circular motions so as to mix or cool the contents. **2.** To alter the placement of slightly; disarrange. **3.** To move briskly or vigorously; bestir. **4.** To rouse (someone), as from sleep or indifference. **5.** To incite, provoke, or instigate: *stir up trouble.* **6.** To excite the emotions of; move or affect strongly. *—intr.* **1.** To change position slightly: *stirred in his sleep.* **2.** To move about actively; venture. **3.** To take place; happen. **4.** To be capable of being stirred. *—n.* **1.** A stirring movement. **2.** A disturbance or commotion. **3.** An excited reaction; ferment. [ME *stiren* < OE *styrian,* to excite.] **—stir′rer** *n.*

stir[2] (stûr) *n. Slang.* Prison. [Orig. unknown.]

stir crazy *adj. Slang.* Distraught or restless from long confinement in or as if in prison.

stir-fry (stûr′frī′) *tr.v.* **-fried, -fry·ing, -fries.** To fry quickly in a small amount of oil over high heat while stirring continuously.

stirk (stûrk) *n.* A yearling heifer or bullock. [ME < OE *stirc.*]

stirps (stûrps) *n., pl.* **stir·pes** (stûr′pēz, -pāz′). **1.** A line of descendants of common ancestry; stock. **2.** *Law.* A person from whom a family is descended. [Lat., stem, lineage.]

stir·ring (stûr′ĭng) *adj.* **1.** Rousing; exciting: *a stirring call to arms.* **2.** Active; lively. **—stir′ring·ly** *adv.*

stir·rup (stûr′əp, stĭr′-) *n.* **1.** A flat-based loop or ring hung from either side of a horse's saddle to support the rider's foot in mounting and riding. **2.** A part or device shaped like a stirrup in which something is supported. **3.** *Naut.* A rope on a ship hanging from a yard and having an eye at the end through which a footrope is passed for support. [ME *stirope* < OE *stigrāp.*]

stir·rup bone *n.* The stapes.

stir·rup-cup (stûr′əp-kŭp′, stĭr′-) *n.* A farewell drink, esp. for a rider who is mounted to depart.

stirrup leather *n.* The strap used to fasten a stirrup to a saddle.

stish·ov·ite (stĭsh′ə-vīt′) *n.* A dense tetragonal form of silicon dioxide that is a polymorph of quartz and that is formed under great pressure. [After S.M. *Stishov,* 20th-cent. Russian mineralogist.]

stitch (stĭch) *n.* **1.** A single complete movement of a threaded needle in sewing or surgical suturing. **2. a.** A single loop of yarn around an implement such as a knitting needle. **b.** The link, loop, or knot made in this way. **3.** A mode of arranging the threads in sewing, knitting, or crocheting: *a purl stitch.* **4.** A sudden sharp pain in the side. **5.** *Informal.* An article of clothing: *not a stitch on.* **6.** *Informal.* The least part; bit: *didn't do a stitch of work.* **7.** A ridge between two furrows. *—v.* **stitched, stitch·ing, stitch·es.** *—tr.* **1.** To fasten or join with or as if with stitches. **2.** To decorate or ornament with or as if with stitches. **3.** To fasten with staples. *—intr.* To make stitches; sew. ***—idiom.* in stitches.** *Informal.* Laughing uncontrollably. [ME *stiche* < OE *stice,* sting.] **—stitch′er** *n.*

stitch·wort (stĭch′wûrt′, -wôrt′) *n.* Any of several low-growing plants of the genus *Stellaria,* having small, white, star-shaped flowers.

stith·y (stĭ*th*′ē, stĭth′ē) *n., pl.* **-ies. 1.** An anvil. **2.** A forge or smithy. [ME *stethy* < ON *steði.*]

sti·ver (stī′vər) *n.* **1.** An obsolete Dutch coin worth $^1/_{20}$ of a guilder. **2.** Something of small value. [Du. *stuiver* < MDu. *stuyver.*]

St. John's bread (sānt′jŏnz′) *n.* The long blackish, sugary, edible pod of the carob. [After *St. John* the Baptist, who lived on honey and locusts (prob. locust beans, or carob) while preaching in the desert.]

St. Johns·wort (sānt jŏnz′wûrt′, -wôrt′) *n.* Any of various plants or shrubs of the genus *Hypericum,* having yellow flowers. [So called because it was gathered on *St. John's* Eve to ward off evil spirits.]

sto·a (stō′ə) *n., pl.* **sto·ae** (stō′ē′) or **sto·as.** An ancient Greek covered walk or colonnade, usually having columns on one side and a wall on the other. [Gk., porch.]

stoat (stōt) *n., pl.* **stoats** or **stoat.** *Chiefly Brit.* The ermine, esp. when in its brown color phase. [ME *stote.*]

sto·chas·tic (stō-kăs′tĭk) *adj.* **1.** Of, denoting, or characterized by conjecture; conjectural. **2. a.** Involving or containing a random variable: *stochastic calculus.* **b.** Involving chance or probability: *a stochastic stimulation.* [Gk. *stokhiastikos* < *stokhazesthai,* to guess at < *stokhos,* aim.] **—sto·chas′ti·cal·ly** *adv.*

stock (stŏk) *n.* **1.** A supply accumulated for future use; store. **2.** The total merchandise kept on hand by a merchant or commercial establishment. **3.** All the animals kept or raised on a farm; livestock. **4.** *Econ.* **a.** The capital or fund that a corporation raises through the sale of shares entitling the holder to dividends and to other rights of ownership. **b.** The number of shares that each stockholder possesses. **c.** A certificate that shows ownership of a stated number of shares. **d.** The part of a tally or record of account formerly given to a creditor. **e.** A debt symbolized by a tally. **5.** The trunk or main stem of a tree or other plant as distinguished from the branches and roots. **6. a.** A plant or stem onto which a graft is made. **b.** A plant or tree from which cuttings and slips are taken. **7. a.** The original progenitor of a family line. **b.** Ancestry or lineage; antecedents. **c.** The type from which a group of animals or plants has descended. **d.** A race, family, or other related group of animals or plants. **e.** An ethnic group or other major division of mankind. **f.** A group of related languages. **g.** A group of related families of languages. **8.** The raw material out of which something is made. **9.** The broth from boiled meat or fish, used as a base in preparing soup, gravy, or sauces. **10. a.** A main upright part, esp. a supporting structure or block. **b. stocks.** The timber frame that supports a ship during construction. **c.** A frame in which a horse or other animal is held for shoeing or for veterinary treatment. **11. stocks.** A former instrument of punishment, consisting of a heavy timber frame with holes for confining the ankles and sometimes the wrists. **12.** *Naut.* A crosspiece at the end of an anchor's shank. **13.** The wooden block from which a bell is suspended. **14. a.** The rear wooden, metal, or plastic handle of a rifle, pistol, or automatic weapon, to which the barrel and mechanism are attached. **b.** The long mooring beam of field-gun carriages that trails along the ground. **15.** A handle, as of a whip or fishing rod. **16.** The frame of a plow, to which the share, handles, colter, and other parts are fastened. **17. a.** A stock company. **b.** The repertoire of such a company. **c.** A theater or theatrical activity, esp. outside of a main theatrical center: *a small role in summer stock.* **18.** Any of several plants of the genus *Mathiola,* native to the Old World, esp. *M. incana,* widely cultivated for its clusters of showy, variously colored flowers. **19.** The portion of a pack of cards or group of dominoes that is not dealt out but is drawn from during a game. **20.** *Geol.* A body of intrusive igneous rock of which less than 40 square miles is exposed. **21. a.** An assessment or estimate: *took stock of the problem.* **b.** Personal reputation or status: *His stock with the students is falling.* **c.** Confidence or credence: *put no stock in his statement.* **22.** A broad scarf worn around the neck. —*v.* **stocked, stock·ing, stocks.** —*tr.* **1.** To provide (a store, for example) with stock; supply. **2.** To keep for future sale or use. **3.** To provide (a rifle, for example) with a stock. **4.** *Obs.* To put (someone) in the stocks as a punishment. —*intr.* **1.** To gather and store a supply of something: *stock up on canned goods.* **2.** To put forth or sprout new shoots. —*adj.* **1.** Kept regularly in stock: *a stock item.* **2.** Commonplace; ordinary: *a stock answer.* **3.** Employed in dealing with or caring for stock or merchandise: *a stock clerk.* **4. a.** Of or pertaining to the raising of livestock: *stock farming.* **b.** Used for breeding: *a stock mare.* **5.** Of or pertaining to a stock company or its repertoire. —*idioms.* **in stock.** Available for sale or use; on hand. **out of stock.** Not available for sale or use. **stock in trade.** A person's resources for any purpose: *Flattery is his stock in trade.* [ME *stok* < OE *stocc,* tree trunk.]

stock·ade (stŏ'kād') *n.* **1.** A defensive barrier made of strong posts or timbers driven upright side by side in the ground. **2.** A fenced or enclosed area, esp. one used for protection or imprisonment. —*tr.v.* **-ad·ed, -ad·ing, -ades.** To fortify, protect, or surround with a stockade. [Fr. *estacade* < Sp. *estacada* < *estaca,* stake, of Germanic orig.]

stock·breed·ing (stŏk'brē'dĭng) *n.* The raising of livestock. —**stock'breed'er** *n.*

stock·bro·ker (stŏk'brō'kər) *n.* A person who acts as an agent in the buying and selling of stocks or other securities. —**stock'bro'ker·age** *n.*

stock car *n.* **1.** An automobile of a standard make modified for racing. **2.** A railroad car carrying livestock.

stock certificate *n.* A certificate establishing ownership of a stated number of shares in a corporation's stock.

stock company *n.* **1.** A company or corporation whose capital is divided into shares. **2.** A company of actors and technicians attached to a single theater and performing in repertory.

stock dove *n.* A common Old World bird, *Columba oenas,* having grayish plumage. [Prob. so called from its living in hollow tree trunks.]

stock exchange *n.* **1.** A place where stocks, bonds, or other securities are bought and sold. **2.** An association of stockbrokers who meet to buy and sell stocks and bonds according to fixed regulations.

stock·fish (stŏk'fĭsh') *n., pl.* **stockfish** or **-fish·es.** A fish, such as cod or haddock, cured by being split and air-dried without salt.

stock·hold·er (stŏk'hōl'dər) *n.* A person who owns a share or shares of stock in a company.

stock·i·net also **stock·i·nette** (stŏk'ə-nĕt') *n.* An elastic knitted fabric used esp. in making undergarments or bandages. [Alteration of *stocking net.*]

stock·ing (stŏk'ĭng) *n.* **1.** A close-fitting, usually knitted covering for the foot and leg. **2.** Something resembling a stocking. [Obs. *stock,* to cover with hose < obs. *stock,* a stocking.]

stocking cap *n.* A knitted cap for casual winter wear that has a long cone-shaped tail usually with a pom-pom attached.

stock·job·ber (stŏk'jŏb'ər) *n.* **1.** *Chiefly Brit.* A stock-exchange operator who deals only with brokers and not with the public. **2.** A stockbroker. Often used as a term of disparagement. —**stock'job'ber·y** *n.*

stock·man (stŏk'mən) *n.* **1.** A person who owns or raises livestock. **2.** A person who is in charge of livestock or works on a stock farm. **3.** A person employed in a stockroom or warehouse.

stock market *n.* **1.** A stock exchange. **2.** The business transacted at a stock exchange. **3.** The prices offered for stocks and bonds in general: *a rising stock market.*

stock·pile also **stock pile** (stŏk'pīl') *n.* A supply stored for future use, usually carefully accrued and maintained. —*tr.v.* **-piled, -pil·ing, -piles.** To accumulate a stockpile of. —**stock'pil'er** *n.*

stock·pot (stŏk'pŏt') *n.* **1.** A pot used for preparing soup stock. **2.** A rich supply or resource.

stock·room also **stock room** (stŏk'ro͞om', -ro͝om') *n.* A room in which a store of goods or materials is kept.

stock-still (stŏk'stĭl') *adj.* Very still; motionless: *stood stock-still.*

stock·tak·ing (stŏk'tā'kĭng) *n.* **1.** The act of inventorying merchandise or supplies on hand. **2.** The act of evaluating a situation at a given point.

stock·y (stŏk'ē) *adj.* **-i·er, -i·est.** **1.** Solidly built; sturdy. **2.** Chubby; plump. —**stock'i·ly** *adv.* —**stock'i·ness** *n.*

stock·yard (stŏk'yärd') *n.* A large enclosed yard, usually with pens or stables, in which cattle, horses, sheep, or pigs are temporarily kept until they are slaughtered or shipped.

stodg·y (stŏj'ē) *adj.* **-i·er, -i·est.** **1. a.** Dull, narrow, and commonplace. **b.** Prim or pompous; stuffy: *"Why is the middle-class so stodgy—so utterly without a sense of humour!"* (Katherine Mansfield). **2.** Heavy; indigestible and starchy: *stodgy food.* **3.** Solidly built; stocky. [< E. *stodge,* thick filling food < *stodge,* to cram.] —**stodg'i·ly** *adv.* —**stodg'i·ness** *n.*

sto·gy or **sto·gie** (stō'gē) *n., pl.* **-gies.** **1.** A long, thin, inexpensive cigar. **2.** A roughly made heavy shoe or boot. [After *Conestoga,* Pennsylvania.]

sto·ic (stō'ĭk) also **sto·i·cal** *adj.* Seemingly indifferent to or unaffected by pleasure or pain; impassive: *"stoic resignation in the face of hunger"* (John F. Kennedy). —*n.* **1. stoic.** A stoic person. **2. Stoic.** A member of a Greek school of philosophy, founded by Zeno about 308 B.C., holding that human beings should be free from passion and calmly accept all occurrences as the unavoidable result of divine will. [< Lat. *Stoicus,* a Stoic < Gk. *Stōikos* < *stoa* (*Poikilē*), (Painted) Porch, where Zeno taught.] —**sto'i·cal·ly** *adv.* —**sto'i·cal·ness** *n.*

stoi·chi·om·e·try (stoi'kē-ŏm'ĭ-trē) *n.* The methodology and technology by which the quantities of reactants and products in chemical reactions are determined. [Gk. *stoicheion,* element + -METRY.] —**stoi'chi·o·met'ric** (-ō-mĕt'rĭk) *adj.* —**stoi'chi·o·met'ri·cal·ly** *adv.*

sto·i·cism (stō'ĭ-sĭz'əm) *n.* **1.** Indifference to pleasure or pain; impassiveness. **2. Stoicism.** The philosophy or doctrines of the Stoics.

stoke (stōk) *v.* **stoked, stok·ing, stokes.** —*tr.* **1.** To stir up and feed amply. **2.** To feed fuel to and tend (a furnace). —*intr.* To feed fuel to and tend a furnace. [Back-formation < STOKER.]

stoke·hold (stōk'hōld') *n. Naut.* The area or compartment into which a ship's furnaces or boilers open.

stoke·hole (stōk'hōl') *n.* **1.** The space about the opening in a furnace or boiler. **2.** A stokehold. [Transl. of Du. *stookgat.*]

stok·er (stō'kər) *n.* **1.** A person who feeds fuel to and tends a furnace, as a fireman on a locomotive. **2.** A mechanical device for feeding coal to a furnace. [Du. < *stoken,* to poke.]

stole[1]

stole[1] (stōl) *n.* **1.** *Eccles.* A long scarf, usually of embroidered silk or linen, worn over the left shoulder by deacons and over both shoulders by priests and bishops while officiating. **2.** A women's long scarf of cloth or fur worn about the shoulders. **3.** A long robe or outer garment worn by matrons in ancient Rome. [ME, long robe < OE *stol* < Lat. *stola* < Gk. *stolē,* garment.]

stole[2] (stōl) *v.* Past tense of **steal.**

sto·len (stō'lən) *v.* Past participle of **steal.**

stol·id (stŏl'ĭd) *adj.* Having or showing little emotion; impassive. [Lat. *stolidus,* stupid.] —**sto·lid'i·ty** (stŏ-lĭd'ĭ-tē, stə-), **stol'id·ness** *n.* —**stol'id·ly** *adv.*

stol·len (stō'lən) *n., pl.* **-len** or **-lens.** A rich yeast bread containing raisins, citron, and chopped nut meats. [G.]

sto·lon (stō'lŏn', -lən) *n.* **1.** *Bot.* A stem growing along or under the ground and taking root at the nodes or apex to form new plants. **2.** *Zool.* A stemlike structure of certain colonial organisms from which new individuals bud. [Lat. *stolo, stolon-,* branch.] —**sto'lon·ate'** (-lə-nāt') *adj.*

sto·lon·if·er·ous (stō'lə-nĭf'ər-əs) *adj.* Bearing or forming stolons. —**sto'lon·if'er·ous·ly** *adv.*

sto·ma (stō'mə) *n., pl.* **-ma·ta** (-mə-tə) or **-mas.** **1.** *Bot.* One of the minute pores in the epidermis of a leaf or stem through which gases and water vapor pass. **2.** *Anat.* **a.** A

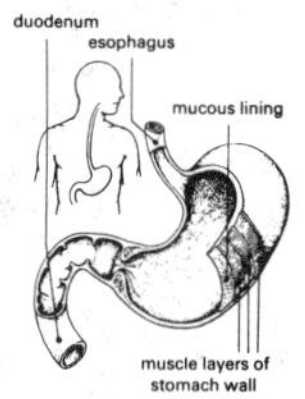

stomach

stonemason

small aperture in the surface of a membrane. **b.** A minute opening in the surface of the peritoneum thought to be for the passage of fluid into the lymphatic vessels. **3.** *Zool.* A mouthlike opening, such as the oral cavity of a nematode. [NLat. < Gk., mouth.]

stom·ach (stŭm′ək) *n.* **1. a.** The enlarged, saclike portion of the alimentary canal, one of the principal organs of digestion, located in vertebrates between the esophagus and the small intestine. **b.** A similar digestive structure of many invertebrates. **2.** The abdomen or belly. **3.** An appetite for food. **4.** A desire or inclination: *had no stomach for quarrels.* **5.** *Obs.* Courage; spirit. **6.** *Obs.* Pride. *—tr.v.* **-ached, -ach·ing, -achs. 1.** To bear; tolerate. **2.** *Obs.* To resent. [ME *stomak* < OFr. *stomaque* < Lat. *stomachus* < Gk. *stomakhos* < *stoma,* mouth.]

stom·ach·ache (stŭm′ək-āk′) *n.* Pain in the abdomen.

stom·ach·er (stŭm′ə-kər) *n.* A decorative, heavily embroidered or jeweled garment formerly worn over the chest and stomach, esp. by women.

sto·mach·ic (stə-măk′ĭk) *adj.* **1.** Of or pertaining to the stomach; gastric. **2.** Beneficial to or stimulating digestion in the stomach. *—n.* A medicine or agent that strengthens or stimulates the stomach. **—sto·mach′i·cal·ly** *adv.*

stomach pump *n.* A suction pump with a flexible tube inserted into the stomach through the mouth and esophagus to empty the stomach in an emergency, as in a case of poisoning.

stomach worm *n.* Any of various parasitic nematode worms that infest the stomachs of animals, esp. *Haemonchus contortus,* a parasite of sheep and other ruminants.

stomat– *pref.* Variant of **stomato–**.

sto·ma·ta (stō′mə-tə) *n.* Plural of **stoma.**

sto·ma·tal (stō′mə-təl) *adj.* Of, pertaining to, or having a stoma.

sto·mat·ic (stō-măt′ĭk) *adj.* **1.** Of or relating to the mouth. **2.** Stomatal.

sto·ma·ti·tis (stō′mə-tī′tĭs) *n.* Inflammation of the mucous tissue of the mouth.

stomato– or **stomat–** *pref.* Mouth; stoma: *stomatitis.* [< Gk. *stoma, stomat-,* mouth.]

sto·ma·tol·o·gy (stō′mə-tŏl′ə-jē) *n.* The medical study of the physiology and pathology of the mouth. **—sto′ma·to·log′i·cal** (-tə-lŏj′ĭ-kəl), **sto′ma·to·log′ic** *adj.* **—sto′ma·tol′o·gist** *n.*

sto·mat·o·pod (stō-măt′ə-pŏd′) *n.* Any of various marine crustaceans of the order Stomatopoda, which includes the squilla. [NLat. *Stomatopoda,* order name : Gk. *stoma,* mouth + Gk. *pous,* foot.]

sto·ma·tous (stō′mə-təs) *adj.* Stomatal.

sto·mo·de·um also **sto·mo·dae·um** (stō′mə-dē′əm) *n., pl.* **-de·a** also **-dae·a** (-dē′ə). The primitive oral cavity of an embryo. [NLat. : Gk. *stoma,* mouth + Gk. *hodaios,* on the way < *hodos,* road.] **—sto′mo·de′al** *adj.*

stomp (stŏmp, stômp) *v.* **stomped, stomp·ing, stomps.** *—tr.* To tread or trample heavily or violently on. *—intr.* To tread or trample heavily or violently. *—n.* **1.** A dance involving a rhythmical and heavy step. **2.** The jazz music for the stomp. [Var. of STAMP.]

Usage: *Stomp* and *stamp* are interchangeable in the sense of "to trample" or "to violently tread on": *stomped to death; stomping horses.* Only *stamp* is used in the sense of "to eliminate": *stamp out a fire; stamp out poverty. Stamp* is also standard in the sense of "to strike the ground with the human foot, as in anger or frustration": *She stamped her foot and began to cry.* Here *stomped* would be unacceptable in writing, according to a large majority of the Usage Panel.

–stomy *suff.* A surgical operation in which an artificial opening is made into a specified organ or part: *colostomy.* [< Gk. *stoma,* opening, mouth.]

stone (stōn) *n.* **1. a.** Concreted earthy or mineral matter; rock. **b.** Stone used for construction. **2.** A small piece of rock. **3.** Rock or a piece of rock shaped or finished for a particular purpose, esp.: **a.** A gravestone or tombstone. **b.** A grindstone, millstone, or whetstone. **c.** A milestone or boundary. **4.** A gem or precious stone. **5.** Something like a stone in shape or hardness, as a hailstone. **6.** *Bot.* The hard covering enclosing the kernel in certain fruits, such as the cherry or plum. **7.** *Pathol.* A mineral concretion in a hollow organ, as in the kidney. **8.** *pl.* **stone.** A unit of weight in Britain, 6.36 kilograms or 14 pounds avoirdupois. **9.** *Printing.* A table with a smooth surface on which page forms are composed. **—*modifier:*** *a stone wall.* *—tr.v.* **stoned, ston·ing, stones. 1.** To hurl or throw stones at, esp. to kill with stones. **2.** To remove the stones or pits from. **3.** To furnish, fit, pave, or line with stones. **4.** To rub on or with a stone in order to polish or sharpen. **5.** *Obs.* To make hard or indifferent. [ME < OE *stān.*] **—ston′er** *n.*

Stone Age *n. Archaeol.* The earliest known period of human culture, characterized by the use of stone tools.

stone-blind (stōn′blīnd′) *adj.* Completely blind.

stone-broke (stōn′brōk′) *adj.* Completely broke; penniless.

stone cell *n.* A nearly isometric sclereid that is found in certain fruits.

stone·chat (stōn′chăt′) *n.* A small Old World bird, *Saxicola torquata,* having dark plumage.

stone·crop (stōn′krŏp′) *n.* **1.** Any of various plants of the genus *Sedum,* having fleshy leaves and variously colored flowers. **2.** Any of various related plants.

stone·cut·ter (stōn′kŭt′ər) *n.* One that cuts or carves stone, esp. a machine that dresses stone. **—stone′cut′ting** *n.*

stoned (stōnd) *adj. Slang.* **1.** Intoxicated; drunk. **2.** Under the influence of a mind-altering drug.

stone-deaf (stōn′dĕf′) *adj.* Completely deaf.

stone·fish (stōn′fĭsh′) *n., pl.* **stonefish** or **-fish·es.** Any of several tropical marine fishes of the family Scorpaenidae, having spines that eject a deadly venom.

stone·fly (stōn′flī′) *n.* Any of numerous winged insects of the order Plecoptera, occurring on banks of streams and used as fishing bait both in the larval and adult stage.

stone fruit *n.* A drupe.

stone-ground (stōn′ground′) *adj.* Ground in a buhrstone mill: *stone-ground flour.*

stone lily *n.* A fossil crinoid.

stone marten *n.* **1.** A Eurasian mammal, *Martes foina,* having brown fur with lighter underfur. **2.** The fur of the stone marten.

stone·ma·son (stōn′mā′sən) *n.* A person who prepares and lays stones in building. **—stone′ma′son·ry** *n.*

stone mint *n.* A North American plant, *Cunila origanoides,* having clusters of small purplish or white flowers.

stone's throw *n.* A short distance.

stone·wall (stōn′wôl′) *v.* **-walled, -wall·ing, -walls.** *—intr.* **1.** To play defensively rather than trying to score in cricket. **2.** *Informal.* **a.** To engage in delaying tactics; stall: *"Stonewalling for a time in order to close the missile gap"* (James Reston). **b.** To refuse to answer or cooperate. *—tr. Informal.* To refuse to answer or cooperate with; resist or rebuff: *"I want you to stonewall it, let them plead the Fifth Amendment. . ."* (Richard M. Nixon). **—stone′wall′er** *n.*

stone·ware (stōn′wâr′) *n.* A heavy, nonporous pottery.

stone·work (stōn′wûrk′) *n.* **1.** The technique or process of working in stone. **2.** Work made of stone; stone masonry. **—stone′work′er** *n.*

stone·wort (stōn′wûrt′, -wôrt′) *n.* Any of various green algae of the genus *Chara* that grow submerged in fresh or brackish water and are frequently encrusted with calcium carbonate deposits.

ston·y also **ston·ey** (stō′nē) *adj.* **-i·er, -i·est. 1.** Covered with or full of stones. **2.** Resembling stone, as in hardness. **3.** Hardhearted; unemotional. **4.** Rigid; impassive: *a stony face.* **5.** Emotionally numbing or paralyzing. **—ston′i·ly** *adv.* **—ston′i·ness** *n.*

ston·y·heart·ed (stō′nē-här′tĭd) *adj.* Devoid of kindness or sympathy; hardhearted. **—ston′y·heart′ed·ness** *n.*

stood (stŏŏd) *v.* Past tense and past participle of **stand.**

stooge (stōōj) *n.* **1.** The straight man to a comedian. **2.** One who allows himself to be used for another's profit; puppet. **3.** A stool pigeon. *—intr.v.* **stooged, stoog·ing, stoog·es.** To be or behave as a stooge. [Orig. unknown.]

stool (stōōl) *n.* **1.** A backless and armless single seat supported on legs or a pedestal. **2.** A low bench or support for the feet or knees in sitting or kneeling, as a footrest. **3.** A toilet seat; privy. **4. a.** A bowel movement. **b.** Fecal matter. **5. a.** A stump or rootstock that produces shoots or suckers. **b.** A shoot or growth from such a stump or rootstock. *—intr.v.* **stooled, stool·ing, stools. 1.** To send up shoots or suckers. **2.** To evacuate the bowels; defecate. **3.** *Slang.* To act as a stool pigeon. [ME *stol* < OE *stōl.*]

stool·ie (stōō′lē) *n.* A stool pigeon (sense 3).

stool pigeon *n.* **1.** A pigeon used as a decoy. **2.** *Slang.* A person acting as a decoy. **3.** *Slang.* An informer or decoy, esp. a spy for the police. [From the practice of tying decoy pigeons to a stool.]

stoop¹ (stōōp) *v.* **stooped, stoop·ing, stoops.** *—intr.* **1.** To bend forward and down from the waist or the middle of the back. **2.** To walk or stand with the head and upper back bent forward. **3.** To bend or sag downward. **4.** To lower oneself; condescend. **5.** To yield; submit. **6.** To swoop down, as a bird in pursuing its prey. *—tr.* **1.** To bend (the head or body) forward and down. **2.** To debase; humble. *—n.* **1.** The act of stooping. **2.** A forward bending of the head and upper back, esp. when habitual. **3.** Self-abasement or condescension. **4.** A descent, as of a bird of prey. [ME *stupen* < OE *stūpian.*]

stoop² (stōōp) *n.* A small porch, platform, or staircase leading to the entrance of a house or building. [Du. *stoep,* front verandah.]

stoop³ (stōōp) *n.* Variant of **stoup.**

stoop·ball (stōōp′bôl′) *n.* A game patterned on baseball in which a player throws a ball against a stoop or wall and then runs to base.

stop (stŏp) *v.* **stopped, stop·ping, stops.** *—tr.* **1.** To close (an opening) by covering, filling in, or plugging up. **2.** To constrict (an opening or orifice). **3.** To obstruct or block passage on (a road, for example). **4.** To prevent the flow or passage of. **5.** To cause to halt, cease, or desist. **6.** To desist from; cease: *stop running.* **7.** To order a bank to withhold payment of: *stopped the check.* **8.** To cause (a motor, for example) to cease operation or function; halt. **9. a.** To press down (a string on a stringed instrument) on the fingerboard to produce a desired pitch. **b.** To close (a hole on a wind instrument) with the finger in sounding a desired pitch.

—intr. **1.** To cease moving, progressing, acting, or operating; come to a halt. **2.** To put an end to what one is doing; cease. **3.** To interrupt one's course or journey for a brief visit or stay: *stop off at the store.* *—n.* **1. a.** The act of stopping. **b.** The condition of being stopped; cessation. **2.** A finish; end. **3.** A stay or visit, as during a trip. **4.** A place stopped at: *a bus stop.* **5.** A device or means that obstructs, blocks, or plugs up. **6.** An order given to a bank to withhold payment on a check. **7. a.** A part in a machine that stops or regulates movement. **b.** A perforated screen or diaphragm that limits the effective aperture of a lens, producing an image of improved definition but lowered intensity. **8.** A mark of punctuation, esp. a period. **9.** *Mus.* **a.** The act of stopping a string or hole on a musical instrument. **b.** A hole on a wind instrument. **c.** A fret on a stringed instrument. **d.** A device such as a key for closing the hole on a wind instrument. **10.** *Mus.* **a.** A tuned set of pipes, as in an organ. **b.** A knob, key, or pull that regulates such a set of pipes. **11.** *Naut.* A line used for securing something temporarily: *a sail stop.* **12.** A consonant, such as English *p, t,* or *k,* characterized by an articulation in which the air passage is completely closed. **13.** The depression between the muzzle and top of the skull of a dog. *—adj.* Of, pertaining to, or being of use at the end of an operation or activity: *a stop code.* [ME *stoppen* < OE *stoppian* < LLat. *stuppare* < Lat. *stuppa,* tow, broken flax < Gk. *stuppē.*]

stop·cock (stŏp′kŏk′) *n.* A valve that regulates the flow of fluid through a pipe; faucet.

stope (stōp) *n.* An excavation in the form of steps made by the mining of ore from steeply inclined or vertical veins. *—tr. & intr.v.* **stoped, stop·ing, stopes.** To remove (ore) from or mine by means of a stope. [Perh. < LG, step.]

stop·gap (stŏp′găp′) *n.* An improvised substitute for something lacking; temporary expedient.

stop·light (stŏp′līt′) *n.* **1.** A traffic signal. **2.** A light on the rear of a vehicle that is activated when the brakes are applied.

stop order *n.* An order to a broker to buy or sell a stock when it reaches a specified level of decline or gain.

stop·o·ver (stŏp′ō′vər) *n.* **1.** An interruption in the course of a journey for stopping or visiting at a certain place. **2.** A place visited briefly in the course of a journey.

stop·page (stŏp′ĭj) *n.* **1.** The act of stopping. **2.** The condition of being stopped.

stop payment *n.* An order to one's bank not to honor a check.

stop·per (stŏp′ər) *n.* **1.** A device, as a cork or plug, inserted to close an opening. **2.** One that causes something to stop. **3.** *Computer Sci.* The topmost memory location in a device or system. *—tr.v.* **-pered, -per·ing, -pers.** To close with or as if with a stopper.

stop·ple (stŏp′əl) *n.* A stopper; plug. *—tr.v.* **-pled, -pling, -ples.** To close with a stopple. [ME *stoppell* < *stoppen,* to stop.]

stop sign *n.* A traffic sign that orders traffic to come to a stop.

stop street *n.* A street intersection at which a vehicle must come to a complete stop before entering a through street.

stop·watch (stŏp′wŏch′) *n.* A timepiece that can be instantly started and stopped by pushing a button.

stopwatch

stor·age (stôr′ĭj, stōr′-) *n.* **1. a.** The act of storing goods. **b.** The state of being stored. **c.** A space for storing goods. **d.** The price charged for keeping goods stored. **2.** The charging or regenerating of a storage battery. **3.** *Computer Sci.* The part of a computer that stores information for subsequent use or retrieval.

storage battery *n.* A group of reversible or rechargeable secondary cells acting as a unit.

storage cell *n.* **1.** A secondary cell. **2.** *Computer Sci.* An elementary unit of storage.

sto·rax (stôr′ăks′, stōr′-) *n.* **1.** Any of various trees of the genus *Styrax,* some of which yield an aromatic resin. **2.** An aromatic resin obtained from a storax tree. **3.** A brownish, aromatic resin used in perfume and medicine and obtained from any of several trees of the genus *Liquidambar,* esp. *L. orientalis,* of Asia Minor. [ME < Lat., alteration of *styrax* < Gk. *sturax,* perh. of Semitic orig.]

store (stôr, stōr) *n.* **1.** A place where merchandise is offered for sale; shop. **2.** A stock or supply reserved for future use. **3. stores.** Supplies, esp. of food, clothing, or arms. **4.** A place where commodities are kept; warehouse or storehouse. **5.** A great quantity or number; abundance. *—tr.v.* **stored, stor·ing, stores. 1.** To reserve or put away for future use. **2.** To fill, supply, or stock. **3.** To deposit or receive in a storehouse or warehouse for safekeeping. ***—idioms.* in store.** Forthcoming. **set store by.** To regard with esteem; value. [ME *stor* < OFr. *estor* < *estorer,* to build < Lat. *instaurare,* to restore.]

store-bought (stôr′bôt′, stōr′-) *adj. Informal.* Manufactured and purchased at retail: *store-bought clothes.*

store cheese *n.* Cheddar cheese.

store·front (stôr′frŭnt′, stōr′-) *n.* **1.** The side of a store facing a street. **2.** A room or suite of rooms in a store building at street level: *a political office in a storefront.* **—store′front′** *adj.*

store·house (stôr′hous′, stōr′-) *n.* **1.** A place or building in which goods are stored; warehouse. **2.** An abundant source or supply: *a storehouse of knowledge.*

store·keep·er (stôr′kē′pər, stōr′-) *n.* **1.** A person who keeps a retail store or shop; shopkeeper. **2.** A person in charge of receiving or distributing stores or supplies, as military or naval supplies.

store·room (stôr′ro͞om′, -ro͝om′, stōr′-) *n.* A room in which things are stored.

sto·rey (stôr′ē, stōr′ē) *n.* Variant of **story[2]**.

sto·ried[1] (stôr′ēd, stōr′-) *adj.* **1.** Celebrated or famous in history or story: *"the storied infamies of the Emperor Tiberius on the Isle of Capri"* (George Marye). **2.** Ornamented with designs representing scenes from history, legend, or story: *storied tapestry.*

sto·ried[2] also **sto·reyed** (stôr′ēd, stōr′-) *adj.* Having or consisting of a specified number of stories: *a three-storied house.*

stork (stôrk) *n.* Any of various large wading birds of the family Ciconiidae, chiefly of warm regions, having long legs and a long straight bill. [ME < OE *storc.*]

George Miksch Sutton

stork

stork's-bill (stôrks′bĭl′) *n.* Any of various plants of the genus *Erodium,* having fruit with a narrow, beaklike point.

storm (stôrm) *n.* **1.** An atmospheric disturbance manifested in strong winds accompanied by rain, snow, or other precipitation and often by thunder and lightning. **2.** *Meteorol.* A wind ranging from 64 to 72 miles per hour. **3.** A heavy shower of objects, such as bullets or missiles. **4.** A strong or violent outburst, as of emotion or excitement. **5.** A violent disturbance or upheaval, as in political, social, or domestic affairs. **6.** A violent, sudden attack on a fortified place. *—v.* **stormed, storm·ing, storms.** *—intr.* **1. a.** To blow forcefully. **b.** To rain, snow, hail, or sleet. **2.** To be extremely angry; rant and rage. **3.** To move or rush tumultuously, violently, or angrily: *stormed into the room.* *—tr.* To capture or try to capture by a violent, sudden attack: *stormed the fortress.* [ME < OE.]

storm·bound (stôrm′bound′) *adj.* Delayed, confined, or cut off from communication by a storm.

storm cellar *n.* A cyclone cellar.

storm center *n.* **1.** The central area covered by a storm, esp. the point of lowest barometric pressure within a storm. **2.** A center of trouble, disturbance, or argument.

storm door *n.* An outer or additional door added for protection against inclement weather.

storm petrel *n.* Any of various small sea birds of the family Hydrobatidae, esp. *Hydrobates pelagicus,* of the North Atlantic and the Mediterranean.

storm trooper *n.* **1.** A member of the Nazi militia noted for brutality and violence. **2.** A person who resembles a Nazi storm trooper.

storm window *n.* A secondary window attached over the usual window to protect against the wind and cold.

storm·y (stôr′mē) *adj.* **-i·er, -i·est. 1.** Subject to, characterized by, or affected by storms; tempestuous. **2.** Characterized by violent emotions, passions, speech, or actions: *a stormy argument.* **—storm′i·ly** *adv.* **—storm′i·ness** *n.*

stormy petrel *n.* **1.** The storm petrel. **2.** A person who brings discord or appears at the onset of trouble; rebel.

sto·ry[1] (stôr′ē, stōr′ē) *n., pl.* **-ries. 1.** The narration of an event or series of events, either true or fictitious. **2.** A prose or verse narrative, usually fictional, intended to interest or amuse the hearer or reader; tale. **3.** A short story. **4.** The plot of a narrative or dramatic work. **5.** A report, statement, or allegation of facts. **6. a.** A news article or broadcast. **b.** The event, situation, or other material for such an article. **7.** An anecdote. **8.** A lie. **9.** Romantic legend or tradition. *—tr.v.* **-ried, -ry·ing, -ries. 1.** To decorate with scenes representing historical or legendary events. **2.** *Archaic.* To tell as a story. [ME *storie* < OFr. *estorie* < Lat. *historia.* —see HISTORY.]

sto·ry[2] also **sto·rey** (stôr′ē, stōr′ē) *n., pl.* **-ries** also **-reys. 1.** A complete horizontal division of a building, comprising the area between two adjacent levels. **2.** The set of rooms on the same level of a building. [ME < Med. Lat. *historia* (prob. from painted windows or sculpture on the front of buildings) < Lat., history. —see HISTORY.]

sto·ry·book (stôr′ē-bo͝ok′, stōr′-) *n.* A book containing a collection of stories, usually for children. *—adj.* Occurring in or resembling the style of a storybook; romantic.

story line *n.* The plot of a story or a dramatic work.

sto·ry·tell·er (stôr′ē-tĕl′ər, stōr′-) *n.* **1.** A person who tells or writes stories. **2.** *Informal.* A person who tells lies; fibber.

stoss (stŏs, stôs, shtōs) *adj.* Facing the direction from which a glacier moves. Used of a rock or slope in its path. [< G. *stossen,* to push < OHG *stōzan.*]

sto·tin·ki (stō-tĭng′kə) *n., pl.* **stotinki.** See table at **currency.** [Bulgarian.]

stound (stound) *n. Obs.* A short time; while. [ME < OE *stund.*]

stoup also **stoop** (sto͞op) *n.* **1.** *Eccles.* A basin or font for holy water at the entrance of a church. **2.** *Scot.* A bucket or pail. **3.** A drinking vessel such as a cup or tankard. [ME *stoup,* bucket < ON *staup.*]

stout (stout) *adj.* **-er, -est. 1.** Determined, bold, or brave: *a stout heart.* **2.** Strong in body; sturdy. **3.** Strong in structure or substance; substantial. **4.** Bulky in figure; corpulent. **5.** Powerful; forceful. **6.** Staunch; firm. *—n.* **1. a.** A stout

stoup

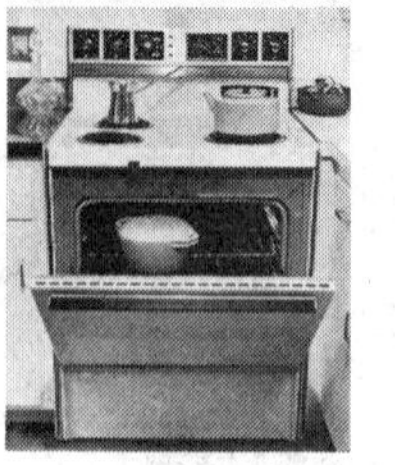

stove¹
Above: 19th-century coal stove
Below: 20th-century electric stove

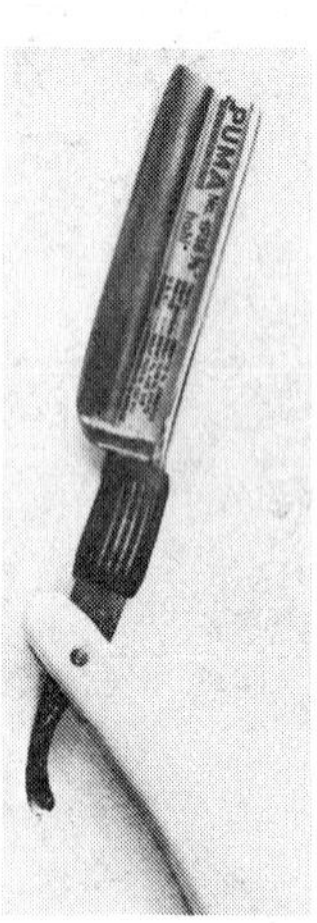

straight razor

strainer

person. **b.** A garment size for a stout person. **2.** A strong, very dark beer or ale. [ME < OFr. *estout,* of Germanic orig.] **—stout'ly** *adv.* **—stout'ness** *n.*

stout·en (stout'n) *tr. & intr.v.* **-ened, -en·ing, -ens.** To make or become stout.

stout·heart·ed (stout'här'tĭd) *adj.* Brave; courageous. **—stout'heart'ed·ly** *adv.* **—stout'heart'ed·ness** *n.*

stove¹ (stōv) *n.* **1.** An apparatus in which electricity or a fuel is used to furnish heat, as for cooking or comfort. **2.** A device used to provide heat for a particular purpose. **3.** A kiln. **4.** A hothouse. [ME, heated room < MLG.]

stove² (stōv) *v.* A past tense and past participle of **stave.**

stove·pipe (stōv'pīp') *n.* **1.** A pipe, usually of thin sheet iron, used to conduct smoke or fumes from a stove into a chimney flue. **2.** A man's tall silk hat.

sto·ver (stō'vər) *n.* The dried stalks and leaves of a cereal crop, used as fodder after the grain has been harvested. [ME, provisions < Norman Fr. *estovers* < OFr. *estovier,* to be necessary < Lat. *est opus,* it is necessary.]

stow (stō) *tr.v.* **stowed, stow·ing, stows. 1.** To place, arrange, or store away, esp. in a neat, compact way: *stow various articles into his knapsack.* **2.** To fill by packing tightly. **3.** *Slang.* To cease; stop. **4.** *Obs.* To provide lodging for; quarter. **5.** *Slang.* To consume (food) greedily. **—*phrasal verb.* stow away.** To be a stowaway. [ME *stowen* < *stow,* place < OE *stōw.*]

stow·age (stō'ĭj) *n.* **1. a.** The act, manner, or process of stowing. **b.** The state of being stowed. **2.** Space or room for storage. **3.** Goods in storage. **4.** A charge for storing goods.

stow·a·way (stō'ə-wā') *n.* A person who hides aboard a ship or other conveyance in order to obtain free passage.

stra·bis·mus (strə-bĭz'məs) *n.* A visual defect in which one eye cannot focus with the other on an objective because of imbalance of the eye muscles. [NLat. < Gk. *strabismos,* condition of squinting < *strabizein,* to squint < *strabos,* squinting.] **—stra·bis'mal, stra·bis'mic** *adj.*

stra·bot·o·my (strə-bŏt'ə-mē) *n., pl.* **-mies.** The cutting of an ocular muscle or tendon to correct strabismus. [Gk. *strabos,* squinting + -TOMY.]

strad·dle (străd'l) *v.* **-dled, -dling, -dles.** *—tr.* **1.** To sit astride of; bestride. **2.** To appear to favor both sides of (an issue). **3.** To fire shots behind and in front of (a target) in order to determine the range. *—intr.* **1.** To sit astride. **2.** To be wide apart; sprawl. **3.** To appear to favor both sides of an issue. *—n.* **1.** The act or posture of sitting astride. **2.** An equivocal or noncommittal position. **3.** The privileged option of either delivering or buying stocks at a specified price within a stated period of time. **—*idiom.* straddle the fence.** To be in an indecisive or neutral position. [< STRIDE.] **—strad'dler** *n.*

Strad·i·var·i·us (străd'ə-vâr'ē-əs, -văr'-) *n.* A stringed instrument, such as a violin, made in the workshop of Antonio Stradivari.

strafe (strāf) *tr.v.* **strafed, straf·ing, strafes.** To attack (ground troops, for example) with machine-gun fire from low-flying aircraft. *—n.* A rake of machine-gun fire from low-flying aircraft. [< G. *(Gott) strafe (England),* (God) punish (England), a common World War I salutation.]

strag·gle (străg'əl) *intr.v.* **-gled, -gling, -gles. 1.** To stray or fall behind. **2.** To proceed or spread out in a scattered or irregular group. [ME *straglen.*] **—strag'gler** *n.*

strag·gly (străg'lē) *adj.* **-gli·er, -gli·est.** Spread out or proceeding irregularly.

straight (strāt) *adj.* **-er, -est. 1.** Extending continuously in the same direction without curving. **2.** Having no waves or bends: *straight hair.* **3.** Erect; upright. **4.** Direct and candid: *a straight answer.* **5.** Uninterrupted; unbroken: *sick for five straight hours.* **6.** Made up of five cards constituting a sequence in poker: *a straight flush.* **7.** Politically undeviating: *always votes a straight party line.* **8.** In correct sequence. **9.** Upright; honorable. **10.** *Slang.* **a.** Conventional, conservative, or law-abiding, esp. relating to or being a member of conventional society. **b.** Heterosexual. **c.** Square (sense 10). **11.** *Slang.* Not being under the influence of alcohol or drugs. **12.** Not deviating from the normal or strict form: *straight Freudian analysis.* **13.** Undiluted or unmixed: *straight whiskey.* **14.** Neatly arranged; orderly. **15.** Sold without discount regardless of the amount purchased. *—adv.* **1.** In a straight line; directly. **2.** In an erect posture; upright. **3.** Without detour or delay: *went straight home.* **4.** Without circumlocution; candidly. **5.** Honestly or virtuously. **6.** Continuously. *—n.* **1.** The straight part of a racecourse between the winning post and the last turn. **2.** A straight line. **3.** A straight part, piece, or position. **4. a.** A numerical sequence of five cards of various suits in poker. **b.** A hand containing a straight. **5.** *Slang.* **a.** A heterosexual person. **b.** A conventional person, esp. one considered a member of established society. **6.** *Slang.* A person who does not use illegal drugs. [ME < *strecchen,* to stretch.] **—straight'ly** *adv.* **—straight'ness** *n.*

straight and narrow *n.* The way of proper conduct and moral integrity: *kept strictly to the straight and narrow.*

straight angle *n.* An angle of 180 degrees.

straight-arm (strāt'ärm') *tr.v.* **-armed, -arm·ing, -arms.** To ward off (a football tackler) by holding the arm out straight.

straight arrow *n. Informal.* An extremely conventional person.

straight-a·way (strāt'ə-wā') *adj.* **1.** Extending in a straight line or course without a curve or turn. **2.** Unhesitating; immediate. *—n.* (strāt'ə-wā'). A straight course, stretch, or track. *—adv.* (strāt'ə-wā'). At once; immediately.

straight chain *n.* An open linear organic molecular structure with no side chains.

straight·edge (strāt'ĕj') *n.* A rigid flat rectangular bar, as of wood or metal, with a straight edge for testing or drawing straight lines. **—straight'edged'** *adj.*

straight·en (strāt'n) *tr. & intr.v.* **-ened, -en·ing, -ens.** To make or become straight. **—*phrasal verb.* straighten out. 1.** To put to rights or restore order to; rectify. **2.** To reform or improve. **—straight'en·er** *n.*

straight face *n.* A face that betrays no sign of emotion. **—straight'-faced'** (strāt'fāst') *adj.*

straight·for·ward (strāt-fôr'wərd) *adj.* **1.** Proceeding in a straight course; direct. **2.** Honest; frank. *—adv.* In a straightforward course or manner. **—straight·for'ward·ly** *adv.* **—straight·for'ward·ness** *n.* **—straight·for'wards** (-wərdz) *adv.*

straight·jack·et (strāt'jăk'ĭt) *n. & v.* Variant of **straitjacket.**

straight-leg (strāt'lĕg') *adj.* Being pants with legs having essentially the same diameter at the top as at the bottom.

straight-line (strāt'līn') *adj.* **1.** Lying in a straight line. **2.** Pertaining to a device whose linkage produces or copies motion in straight lines. **3.** Designating a mode of amortization by equal payments at stated intervals over a given period of time.

straight man *n.* An actor who serves as a foil for a comedian.

straight off *adv.* At once; immediately: *told her straight off the plan wouldn't work.*

straight-out (strāt'out') *adj.* **1.** Straightforward; blunt: *gave them a straight-out "no".* **2.** Complete; unmitigated: *a straight-out error.*

straight razor *n.* A razor consisting of a blade hinged to a handle into which it slips when not in use.

straight ticket *n.* A ballot cast for all the candidates of one party.

straight·way (strāt'wā', -wā') *adv.* Without delay; at once.

strain¹ (strān) *v.* **strained, strain·ing, strains.** *—tr.* **1.** To pull, draw, or stretch tight. **2.** To exert or tax to the utmost. **3.** To injure or impair by overuse or overexertion; wrench: *strain a muscle.* **4.** To stretch or force beyond the proper or legitimate limit: *strain a point.* **5.** To alter (the relations between the parts of a structure or shape) by applying an external force; deform. **6.** To pass (a substance) through a filtering agent such as a strainer. **7.** To draw off or remove by filtration. **8.** To embrace or clasp tightly; hug. *—intr.* **1.** To make violent or steady efforts; strive hard. **2.** To be or become wrenched or twisted. **3.** To be subjected to great stress. **4.** To pull forcibly or violently. **5.** To stretch or exert one's muscles or nerves to the utmost. **6.** To filter, trickle, or ooze. **7.** To be extremely hesitant; balk. *—n.* **1. a.** The act of straining. **b.** The state of being strained. **2.** A great or extreme effort, exertion, or tension. **3.** A wrench or other injury resulting from excessive effort or use. **4.** *Physics.* A deformation produced by stress. **5.** A great or excessive pressure, demand, or stress on one's emotions or resources. [ME *streynen* < OFr. *estreindere,* to bind tightly < Lat. *stringere.*]

strain² (strān) *n.* **1.** The collective descendants of a common ancestor; a race, stock, line, or breed. **2.** Any of the various lines of ancestry united in an individual or family; ancestry; lineage. **3.** *Biol.* A group of organisms of the same species, having distinctive characteristics but not usually considered a separate breed or variety. **4.** A kind; sort. **5. a.** An inborn or inherited tendency or character. **b.** A streak; trace. **6.** The tone or tenor of a verbal utterance. **7.** Often **strains.** A passage of musical expression; tune. **8.** A passage of poetic expression. **9.** An outburst or flow of eloquent or impassioned language. [ME *strene* < OE *strēon.*]

strained (strānd) *adj.* **1.** Passed through a strainer: *strained peaches.* **2.** Done with or marked by excessive effort; forced: *strained humor.* **3.** Antagonized to the verge of open conflict: *strained relations.*

strain·er (strā'nər) *n.* **1.** A device, such as a filter, sieve, or colander, used to separate liquids from solids. **2.** One that strains. **3.** An apparatus for tightening, stretching, or strengthening.

strain gauge *n.* A device in which mechanical motion, as of a thin wire or piezoelectric crystal, is converted into an electric variation that is used as a sensitive measure of strain.

straining beam *n. Archit.* A horizontal tie beam connecting two queen posts in a roof truss.

strain·om·e·ter (strā-nŏm'ĭ-tər) *n.* An extensometer.

strait (strāt) *n.* **1.** Often **straits.** A narrow passage of water joining two larger bodies of water. **2.** Often **straits.** A position of difficulty, perplexity, distress, or need: *in desperate straits.* *—adj. Archaic.* **1.** Narrow or constricted. **2.** Affording little space or room; confined or close. **3.** Strict, rigid, or righteous. [ME *streit* < OFr. *estreit* < Lat. *strictus,* narrow < p.part. of *stringere,* to bind tightly.]

strait·en (strāt'n) *tr.v.* **-ened, -en·ing, -ens. 1.** To make narrow; limit, contract, or restrict. **2.** To put or bring into difficulties or distress, esp. financial hardship: *in straitened circumstances.*

strait·jack·et also **straight·jack·et** (strāt′jăk′ĭt) *—n.* **1.** A long-sleeved jacketlike garment used to bind the arms tightly against the body as a means of restraining a violent patient or prisoner. **2.** A tight restriction. *—tr.v.* **-et·ed, -et·ing, -ets.** To restrict or restrain by or as if by confining in a straitjacket.

strait-laced (strāt′lāst′) *adj.* **1.** Excessively strict in behavior, morality, or opinions. **2.** *Archaic.* Having or wearing a tightly laced garment. **—strait′-lac′ed·ly** (-lā′sĭd-lē, -lāst′lē) *adv.* **—strait′-lac′ed·ness** *n.*

strake (strāk) *n. Naut.* A single continuous line of planking or metal plating extending on a vessel's hull from stem to stern. [ME.]

stra·mo·ni·um (strə-mō′nē-əm) *n.* **1.** The jimsonweed. **2.** The dried poisonous leaves of the jimsonweed, used in the treatment of asthma. [NLat.]

strand[1] (strănd) *n.* Land bordering a body of water; beach. *—v.* **strand·ed, strand·ing, strands.** *—tr.* **1.** To drive or run ashore or aground. **2.** To bring into or leave in a difficult or helpless position: *The troupe was stranded in Peoria. —intr.* **1.** To be driven or run ashore or aground. **2.** To be brought into or left in a difficult or helpless position. [ME < OE.]

strand[2] (strănd) *n.* **1.** Fibers or filaments that are twisted together to form a cable, rope, thread, or yarn. **2.** A single filament such as a fiber or thread: *"She wore her light hair in a bun from which strands slipped"* (Bernard Malamud). **3.** Something that is plaited or twisted into a ropelike length, as a string of pearls. *—tr.v.* **strand·ed, strand·ing, strands. 1.** To make or form (a rope, for example) by twisting strands together. **2.** To break a strand of (a rope, for example). [ME *strond.*]

strand line also **strand·line** (strănd′līn′) *n.* A shore line, esp. one marking an earlier and higher water level.

strange (strānj) *adj.* **strang·er, strang·est. 1.** Previously unknown; unfamiliar. **2.** Unusual; extraordinary. **3.** Peculiar; queer. **4.** Not of one's own or a particular locality, environment, or kind; exotic. **5.** *Archaic.* Alien or foreign. **6.** Lacking experience; unacquainted: *strange to her new duties. —adv.* In a strange manner. [ME *straunge* < OFr. *estrange* < Lat. *extraneus* < *extra,* outside.] **—strange′ly** *adv.*

Synonyms: *strange, peculiar, odd, queer, quaint, outlandish, singular, eccentric.* These adjectives describe persons or things that are notably unusual. *Strange* refers especially to what is unfamiliar, unknown, or inexplicable. *Peculiar,* though often applied to anything unusual, is most applicable to what distinguishes a given person or thing from others. *Odd* suggests the quality of not fitting in, or lack of accord with associates, surroundings, or circumstances. *Queer* implies difference from the norm. *Quaint* often refers to peculiarity that seems old-fashioned but endearing. *Outlandish* suggests alien appearance or manner and often implies uncouthness. *Singular* describes what is unique, unparalleled, or unusual and thus arouses curiosity or wonder. *Eccentric* refers particularly to striking peculiarity of behavior.

strange·ness (strānj′nĭs) *n.* **1.** The quality of being strange. **2.** *Physics.* A quantum number equal to hypercharge minus baryon number, indicating the possible transformations of an elementary particle upon strong interaction with another elementary particle.

strange particle *n.* An unstable elementary particle created in high-energy particle collisions with a short life and a strangeness quantum number other than zero.

strang·er (strān′jər) *n.* **1.** A person who is neither friend nor acquaintance. **2.** A foreigner, newcomer, or outsider. **3.** A person who is unaccustomed to or unacquainted with something specified; novice: *a stranger to our language.* **4.** A visitor or guest. **5.** *Law.* One who is neither privy nor party to a title, act, or contract. [ME *strangere* < OFr. *estrangier* < Lat. *extraneus,* strange < *extra,* outside.]

stran·gle (străng′gəl) *v.* **-gled, -gling, -gles.** *—tr.* **1. a.** To kill by squeezing the throat so as to choke or suffocate; throttle. **b.** To cut off the oxygen supply of; smother. **2.** To suppress, repress, or stifle: *strangle a scream.* **3.** To inhibit the growth or action of; restrict: *"That artist is strangled who is forced to deal with human beings solely in social terms"* (James Baldwin). *—intr.* To die or suffer from suffocation or strangulation; choke. [ME *stranglen* < OFr. *estrangler* < Lat. *strangulare* < Gk. *strangalan* < *strangalē,* halter.] **—stran′gler** *n.*

strangle hold *n.* **1.** *Sports.* An illegal wrestling hold used to choke an opponent. **2.** A force, influence, or action that chokes, restricts, or suppresses freedom or progress.

stran·gles (străng′gəlz) *pl.n. (used with a sing. verb).* An infectious disease of horses and related animals, caused by the bacterium *Streptococcus equi* and characterized by nasal inflammation and abscesses in the mouth. [ME *strangle* (sing.), strangulation < *stranglen,* to strangle.]

stran·gu·late (străng′gyə-lāt′) *v.* **-lat·ed, -lat·ing, -lates.** *—tr.* **1.** To strangle. **2.** *Pathol.* To compress, constrict, or obstruct so as to cut off the flow of blood or other fluid. *—intr.* To be or become strangled or constricted. [Lat. *strangulare, strangulat-,* to strangle.]

stran·gu·la·tion (străng′gyə-lā′shən) *n.* **1.** The act of strangling. **2.** The state of being strangled.

stran·gu·ry (străng′gyə-rē, -gyo͝or′ē) *n.* Slow, painful urination with spasms of the urethra and bladder. [ME < Lat. *stranguria* < Gk. *strangouria* : *stranx,* drop + *-ouria,* -uria.]

strap (străp) *n.* **1. a.** A long, narrow strip of pliant material such as leather. **b.** Such a strip equipped with a buckle or similar fastener for binding or securing objects. **2.** A flat, thin metal or plastic band used for fastening or clamping objects together or into position. **3.** A narrow band formed into a loop for grasping with the hand. **4.** A razor strop. **5.** A strip of leather used in flogging. *—tr.v.* **strapped, strap·ping, straps. 1.** To fasten or secure with a strap. **2.** To beat with a strap. **3.** To strop or sharpen (a razor, for example). [Alteration of STROP.]

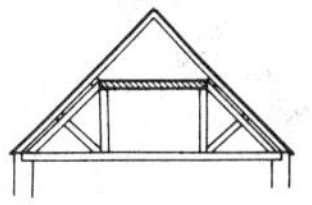

straining beam

strap·hang·er (străp′hăng′ər) *n.* A passenger, as on a bus or subway, who grips a hanging strap for support.

strap·less (străp′lĭs) *adj.* **1.** Without a strap. **2.** Of, pertaining to, or being a dress or undergarment that has no straps and leaves the shoulders bare. *—n.* A strapless garment.

strap·pa·do (stră-pā′dō, -pä′-) *n., pl.* **-does. 1.** A torture in which the victim's hands are tied behind his back and attached to a pulley by means of which he is pulled up off the ground and then dropped halfway down with a jerk. **2.** The apparatus employed in strappado. [Fr. *strapade* < Ital. *strappata* < *strappare,* to drag, prob. of Germanic orig.]

strapped (străpt) *adj. Informal.* Lacking financial resources; penniless. [< STRAP.]

strap·per (străp′ər) *n.* A tall, sturdy person.

strap·ping (străp′ĭng) *adj.* Tall and sturdy.

strass (străs) *n.* Paste[1] (sense 7.b.). [G. or < Fr., after Joseph *Strasser,* an 18th-cent. German jeweler.]

stra·ta (strā′tə, străt′ə) *n.* Plural of **stratum.**

strat·a·gem (străt′ə-jəm) *n.* **1.** A military maneuver designed to deceive or surprise an enemy. **2.** A deception. [Fr. *stratagème* < Lat. *strategema* < Gk. *stratēgēma* < *stratēgein,* to be a general < *stratēgos,* general : *stratos,* army + *agein,* to lead.]

stra·te·gic (strə-tē′jĭk) also **stra·te·gi·cal** (-jĭ-kəl) *adj.* **1.** Of or pertaining to strategy. **2. a.** Important or essential in relation to strategy: *a strategic withdrawal.* **b.** Essential to the effective conduct of war. **c.** Designed to destroy the military potential of an enemy: *strategic bombing.* **—stra·te′gi·cal·ly** *adv.*

stra·te·gics (strə-tē′jĭks) *n. (used with a sing. verb).* The art of strategy.

strat·e·gist (străt′ə-jĭst) *n.* A person who is skilled in strategy.

strat·e·gy (străt′ə-jē) *n., pl.* **-gies. 1.** The science or art of military command as applied to the overall planning and conduct of large-scale combat operations. **2.** A plan of action resulting from the practice of strategy. **3.** The art or skill of using stratagems in endeavors such as politics and business. [Fr. *stratégie* < Gk. *stratēgos,* general. —see STRATAGEM.]

strath (străth) *n. Scot.* A wide, flat river valley. [Sc. Gael. *srath.*]

stra·ti (strā′tī′, străt′ī′) *n.* Plural of **stratus.**

strati– *pref.* Stratum: *stratiform.* [< STRATUM.]

stra·tic·u·late (stră-tĭk′yə-lĭt) *adj.* Having thin strata. [< STRATUM.] **—stra·tic′u·la′tion** *n.*

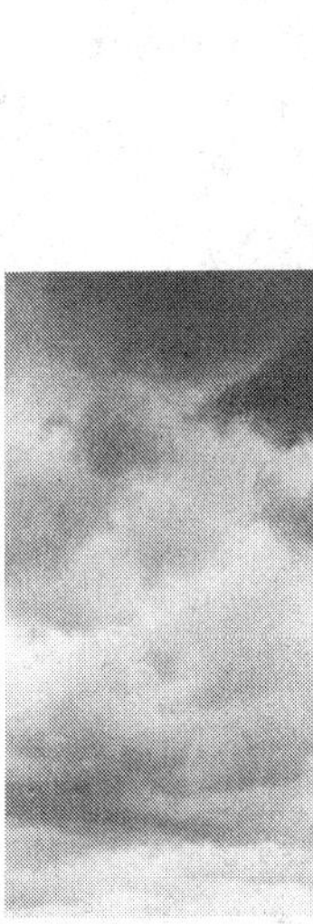

stratocumulus

strat·i·fi·ca·tion (străt′ə-fĭ-kā′shən) *n.* **1.** The act or process of stratifying. **2.** A stratified configuration.

stratified charge engine *n.* An internal-combustion engine that runs on a lean mixture of fuel by means of a divided ignition cylinder that burns rich fuel in a small chamber near the spark plug and a very lean mixture throughout the rest of the cylinder.

strat·i·form (străt′ə-fôrm′) *adj.* Having the form of strata.

strat·i·fy (străt′ə-fī′) *v.* **-fied, -fy·ing, -fies.** *—tr.* **1.** To form, arrange, or deposit in strata. **2.** To preserve (seeds) by placing them between layers of moist sand or similar material. *—intr.* **1.** To become layered; form strata. **2.** To develop different levels of caste, class, privilege, or status. [Fr. *stratifier* < NLat. *stratificare* : STRATUM + Lat. *facere,* to make.]

stra·tig·ra·phy (strə-tĭg′rə-fē) *n.* The study of rock strata, esp. of their distribution, deposition, and age. **—strat′i·graph′ic** (străt′ĭ-grăf′ĭk), **strat′i·graph′i·cal** *adj.* **—strat′i·graph′i·cal·ly** *adv.*

stra·toc·ra·cy (strə-tŏk′rə-sē) *n., pl.* **-cies.** Government by the army. [Gk. *stratos,* army + -CRACY.] **—strat′o·crat′ic** (străt′ə-krăt′ĭk) *adj.*

stra·to·cu·mu·lus (strā′tō-kyo͞om′yə-ləs, străt′ō-) *n., pl.* **-li** (-lī′). A low-lying cloud occurring in extensive horizontal layers with massive, rounded summits. [STRAT(US) + CUMULUS.]

strat·o·sphere (străt′ə-sfîr′) *n.* The relatively isothermal part of the atmosphere above the troposphere and below the mesosphere. [Fr. *stratosphère* : NLat. *stratum,* stratum + *sphère,* sphere < Lat. *sphaera* < Gk. *sphaira.*] **—strat′o·spher′ic** (-sfîr′ĭk, -sfĕr′-) *adj.*

strat·o·vol·ca·no (străt′ō-vŏl-kā′nō, strā′tō-) *n.* A volcano composed of lava and ash deposited in alternating conical layers. [STRAT(UM) + VOLCANO.]

stra·tum (strā′təm, străt′əm) *n., pl.* **-ta** (-tə) or **-tums. 1.** A horizontal layer of any material, esp. one of several parallel layers arranged one on top of another. **2.** *Geol.* **a.** A bed or layer of rock having the same composition throughout. **b.** A formation containing a number of beds or layers of rock of the same kind of material. **3.** A level of society composed of people with similar social, cultural, or economic status. [NLat. < Lat. *stratum,* a covering < *sternere,* to spread.] **—stra'tal** *adj.*

Usage: The standard singular form is *stratum;* the standard plural is *strata* (or sometimes *stratums*) but not *stratas.*

stra·tus (strā'təs, străt'əs) *n., pl.* **stra·ti** (strā'tī', străt'ī'). A low-altitude cloud typically resembling a horizontal layer of fog. [< Lat. p.part. of *sternere,* to spread.]

straw (strô) *n.* **1. a.** Stalks of grain after thrashing, used as bedding and food for animals and for weaving or braiding. **b.** A single stalk of straw. **2.** A slender tube used for sucking up a liquid. **3. a.** Something of minimal value or importance. **b.** Something with too little substance to provide support in a crisis situation: *Near the end he was grasping at straws.* —*tr.v.* **strawed, straw·ing, straws. 1.** To cover (a surface, for example) with straw; strew. **2.** To provide with straw. —*adj.* **1.** Of the color of straw; yellowish. **2.** Having little or no value or substance; unimportant. **—*idioms.* straw in the wind.** A slight hint of something to come. **the last straw.** The final blow to be withstood. [ME < OE *strēaw.*]

strawberry

straw·ber·ry (strô'bĕr'ē) *n.* **1.** Any of various low-growing plants of the genus *Fragaria,* having white flowers and red, fleshy, edible fruit. **2.** The fruit of the strawberry. [ME < OE *strēawberige* : *strēaw,* straw + *berige,* berry.]

strawberry bass *n.* The black crappie.

strawberry blite *n.* A weedy plant, *Chenopodium capitatum,* of northern regions, having minute, petalless flowers and red, berrylike fruit.

strawberry bush *n.* A North American shrub, *Euonymus americanus,* having inconspicuous flowers and showy pinkish fruit.

strawberry mark *n.* A small reddish birthmark.

strawberry roan *n.* A horse having reddish hair mixed with white.

strawberry shrub *n.* Any of several North American shrubs of the genus *Calycanthus,* having aromatic reddish-brown flowers.

strawberry tomato *n.* **1.** A North American plant, *Physalis pruinosa,* having yellow flowers and edible yellowish fruit enclosed in a husk. **2.** The fruit of the strawberry tomato.

strawberry tree *n.* A tree, *Arbutus unedo,* native to southern Europe, having evergreen leaves and strawberrylike fruit.

straw·board (strô'bôrd', -bōrd') *n.* A coarse yellow cardboard made of straw pulp.

straw boss *n. Informal.* A worker who acts as a boss or assistant foreman in addition to his regular duties.

streetcar

straw·flow·er (strô'flou'ər) *n.* A plant, *Helichrysum bracteatum,* native to Australia, having flowers with showy, variously colored bracts that retain their color when dried.

straw-hat (strô'hăt') *adj.* Of or pertaining to summer theater that operates in suburban or resort areas. [From the fashion of wearing straw hats during the summer.]

straw man *n.* **1.** A bundle of straw made into the likeness of a man and often used as a scarecrow. **2.** A person who is set up as cover or front man for a questionable enterprise. **3.** An argument or opponent set up so as to be easily refuted or defeated.

straw vote *n.* An unofficial vote or poll indicating the trend of opinion on a candidate or issue.

straw wine *n.* A dessert wine made from grapes that have been dried on straw.

straw·worm (strô'wûrm') *n.* The destructive larva of a fly, *Harmolita grandis,* of western North America, that infests stalks of grain.

straw yellow *n.* A pale yellow.

stray (strā) *intr.v.* **strayed, stray·ing, strays. 1. a.** To wander from a given place or group or beyond established limits; roam. **b.** To become lost. **2.** To rove, wander about, or meander. **3.** To deviate from a course that is regarded as right or moral; go astray. **4.** To deviate from the subject matter at hand; digress. —*n.* One that has strayed, esp. a domestic animal at large or lost. —*adj.* **1. a.** Straying or having strayed; out of place. **b.** Lost. **2.** Scattered or separate: *"A few stray white bread crumbs lay on the cleanly washed floor"* (Sherwood Anderson). [ME *straien* < OFr. *estraier* < VLat. ***estragare* : Lat. *extra-,* outside + Lat. *vagari,* to wander < *vagus,* wandering.] **—stray'er** *n.*

streak (strēk) *n.* **1.** A line, mark, smear, or band differentiated by color or texture from its surroundings. **2.** A slight trace or tendency; trait: *a mean streak.* **3.** *Informal.* A brief stretch of time; run: *a streak of good luck.* **4.** *Mineral.* The color of the powder of a mineral, used as a distinguishing characteristic. —*v.* **streaked, streak·ing, streaks.** —*tr.* To mark with streaks. —*intr.* **1.** To form streaks. **2.** To be or become streaked. **3. a.** To move at high speed; rush. **b.** To run unclothed through a public place. [ME < OE *strica.*] **—streak'er** *n.*

streak·ing (strē'kĭng) *n.* **1.** The creation of a streaked effect by the chemical lightening of several long strands of hair. **2.** The act of running unclothed through a public place, usually done as a prank.

streak·y (strē'kē) *adj.* **-i·er, -i·est. 1.** Marked with, characterized by, or occurring in streaks. **2.** Variable or uneven in character or quality. **—streak'i·ly** *adv.* **—streak'i·ness** *n.*

stream (strēm) *n.* **1. a.** A body of running water, esp. such a body moving over the earth's surface in a channel or bed, as a brook, rivulet, or river. **b.** A steady current in such a body of water. **2.** A steady current of a fluid. **3.** A steady flow or succession: *a stream of insults.* **4.** A trend, course, or drift, as of opinion, thought, or history. **5.** A beam or ray of light. **6.** *Chiefly Brit.* A track (sense 5). —*v.* **streamed, stream·ing, streams.** —*intr.* **1.** To flow in or as if in a stream. **2.** To pour forth or give off a stream; flow: *eyes streaming with tears.* **3.** To move or proceed in large numbers: *"Hundreds of people were streaming by our house in wild panic"* (James Thurber). **4.** To extend, wave, or float outward: *The banner streamed in the breeze.* **5. a.** To leave a continuous trail of light. **b.** To give forth a continuous stream of light rays or beams; shine. —*tr.* To emit, discharge, or exude. [ME < OE *strēam.*] **—stream'y** *adj.*

stream·bed (strēm'bĕd') *n.* The channel through which a natural stream of water runs or formerly ran.

stream·er (strē'mər) *n.* **1. a.** A long, narrow flag, banner, or pennant. **b.** A long, narrow pendant strip of material. **2.** A shaft or ray of light extending upward from the horizon. **3.** A newspaper headline that runs across a full page.

stream·ing (strē'mĭng) *n. Chiefly Brit.* Tracking.

stream·let (strēm'lĭt) *n.* A small stream.

stream·line (strēm'līn') *n.* **1.** A fluid line having the property that the tangent at every point on the line is aligned with the fluid's local velocity. **2.** The path of one particle in a flowing fluid. **3.** A contour of a body constructed so as to offer minimum resistance to a fluid flow. —*tr.v.* **-lined, -lin·ing, -lines. 1.** To construct or design in a streamlined form. **2.** To improve the appearance or efficiency of; modernize.

stream·lined (strēm'līnd') *adj.* **1.** Designed or arranged to offer the least resistance to fluid flow. **2.** Improved in appearance or efficiency; modernized.

stream·lin·er (strēm'lī'nər) *n.* One that is streamlined, esp. a streamlined passenger train.

stream of consciousness *n.* **1.** *Psychol.* The conscious experience of an individual regarded as a continuous rather than a discrete series of events. **2.** A technique of composition in fiction recording by means of first-person narration a given character's feelings and thoughts.

street (strēt) *n.* **1. a.** A public way or thoroughfare in a city or town, usually including the sidewalks lining one or both sides. **b.** Such a roadway for vehicles. **2.** The people living, working, or habitually gathering in or along a street: *The whole street protested the new regulations.* **3. Street.** A district, such as Wall Street in New York City, that is identified with a specific profession. **4.** The streets of a big city viewed as the scene of crime, poverty, or dereliction. **—*idiom.* on (**or **in) the street. 1.** Without a job; idle. **2.** At liberty; out of prison. [ME < OE *strǣt* < LLat. *strata* < Lat. *sternere,* to cover.]

street Arab *n.* A homeless child; street urchin.

street·car (strēt'kär') *n.* A public passenger car operated on rails along a regular route, usually through the streets of a city.

street·light (strēt'līt') *n.* One of a series of lights that are usually attached to tall poles, are spaced at intervals along a public street or roadway, and are illuminated automatically from dusk to dawn.

street theater *n.* Dramatization of esp. controversial social and political issues, usually presented outside, as on the street or in a park.

street·walk·er (strēt'wô'kər) *n.* A prostitute, esp. one who solicits in the streets. **—street'walk'ing** *n.*

street·wise (strēt'wīz') *adj.* **1.** Experienced in dealing with inner-city dwellers. **2.** Able to survive and satisfy wants and needs on the streets of a big city.

strength (strĕngkth, strĕngth) *n.* **1.** The state, quality, or property of being strong; physical power. **2. a.** The power to resist force, strain, or stress; toughness. **b.** The power to sustain or resist attack; impregnability. **3.** Legal, intellectual, or moral force. **4. a.** A source of power or force. **b.** One that is regarded as the embodiment of protective or supportive power; stay. **5.** Firmness of will, character, mind, or purpose; moral courage or power. **6.** Effective or binding force; efficacy: *the strength of an argument.* **7.** The power or capability of generating a reaction or effect; operative potency: *the strength of a vise.* **8.** Degree of concentration, distillation, or saturation; potency. **9.** Intensity or vehemence, as of emotion, language, or action. **10. a.** A concentration of available numerical force or supportive personnel: *"their strength was in the provinces, particularly Ontario"* (W.L. Morton). **b.** Military force in terms of numbers in personnel or materiel: *a platoon at half strength.* **11.** Firmness of or a continuous rising tendency in prices. **12.** Power derived from the value of playing cards held. **—*idiom.* on the strength of.** On the basis of. [ME < OE *strengðu.*]

Synonyms: *strength, power, might, force, energy, puissance, potency.* These nouns are compared as they relate to the ability to act effectively. *Strength* is the capacity for thus acting, considered especially as the means of physical accomplishment. *Power* is also the source of effective action but has even wider application than *strength*, as in contexts where it implies authority or the ability to control work by superhuman or supernatural means. *Might* implies abundant or overmastering power. *Force* is the application of power or physical strength. *Energy* is power considered either as something expended or as a latent source of action. *Puissance* is approximately equivalent to *might*. *Potency* is power considered as a means of achieving a desired result, and is often used to imply authority, influence, or chemical or medicinal value.

strength·en (strĕngk′thən, strĕng′-) *tr. & intr.v.* **-ened, -en·ing, -ens.** To make or become strong or stronger. **—strength′en·er** *n.*

stren·u·ous (strĕn′yo͞o-əs) *adj.* **1.** Requiring or characterized by great effort, energy, or exertion: *a strenuous task.* **2.** Vigorously active; energetic or zealous. [Lat. *strenuus.*] **—stren′u·os′i·ty** (-ŏs′ĭ-tē), **stren′u·ous·ness** *n.* **—stren′u·ous·ly** *adv.*

strep (strĕp) *adj.* Streptococcal.

strep throat (strĕp) *n.* Septic sore throat.

strepto– *pref.* **1.** Twisted; twisted chain: *streptococcus.* **2.** Streptococcus: *streptolysin.* [< Gk. *streptos,* twisted < *strephein,* to turn.]

strep·to·ba·cil·lus (strĕp′tō-bə-sĭl′əs) *n.* Any of various Gram-negative, rod-shaped, often pathogenic bacteria of the genus *Streptobacillus,* occurring in chains.

strep·to·coc·cal (strĕp′tə-kŏk′əl) also **strep·to·coc·cic** (-kŏk′sĭk, -kŏk′ĭk) *adj.* Of, pertaining to, or caused by a streptococcus.

strep·to·coc·cus (strĕp′tə-kŏk′əs) *n., pl.* **-coc·ci** (-kŏk′sī′, -kŏk′ī′). Any of various round to ovoid, often pathogenic bacteria of the genus *Streptococcus,* occurring in pairs or chains. [NLat. *Streptococcus,* genus name.]

strep·to·kin·ase (strĕp′tō-kĭn′ās′, -āz′, -nās′, -kī′nāz′) *n.* A proteolytic enzyme derived from hemolytic streptococci, capable of dissolving fibrin, and used to dissolve blood clots.

strep·to·ly·sin (strĕp′tə-lī′sĭn) *n.* An antigenic hemolysin derived from some strains of streptococci.

strep·to·my·ces (strĕp′tə-mī′sēz′) *n.* Any of various actinomycetes of the genus *Streptomyces,* including some strains that produce antibiotics. [NLat. *Streptomyces,* genus name : STREPTO- + Gk. *mukēs,* fungus.]

strep·to·my·cin (strĕp′tə-mī′sĭn) *n.* An antibiotic, $C_{21}H_{39}N_7O_{12}$, produced from mold cultures of bacteria of the genus *Streptomyces* and used medicinally to combat various Gram-positive and Gram-negative bacteria and tuberculosis. [< STREPTOMYCES.]

strep·to·thri·cin (strĕp′tə-thrī′sĭn, -thrĭs′ĭn) *n.* An antibiotic isolated from a soil fungus, *Streptomyces lavendulae,* and active against both Gram-positive and Gram-negative bacteria and some fungi. [< NLat. *Streptothrix,* genus of bacteria : Gk. *streptos,* twisted + Gk. *thrix,* hair.]

stress (strĕs) *n.* **1.** Importance, significance, or emphasis placed upon something. **2. a.** The relative force with which a sound or syllable is spoken. **b.** The emphasis placed upon the sound or syllable spoken loudest in a given word or phrase. **3. a.** The relative emphasis given a syllable or word in accordance with a metrical pattern. **b.** A syllable receiving a strong relative emphasis. **4.** *Mus.* An accent (sense 7). **5.** *Physics.* An applied force or system of forces that tends to strain or deform a body. **6.** A mentally or emotionally disruptive or disquieting influence; distress. *—tr.v.* **stressed, stress·ing, stress·es. 1.** To place emphasis on. **2.** To subject to pressure or strain. **3.** To subject to mechanical pressure or force. **4.** To construct so as to withstand a specified stress. [ME *stresse,* hardship < *distresse* OFr. *destresse.* —see DISTRESS.]

STRESS (strĕs) *n.* A computer language designed for use in solving structural analysis problems in civil engineering. [STR(UCTURAL) E(NGINEERING) S(YSTEMS) S(OLVER).]

stres·sor (strĕs′ər) *n.* An agent that causes stress.

stretch (strĕch) *v.* **stretched, stretch·ing, stretch·es.** *—tr.* **1.** To lengthen, widen, or distend by pulling. **2.** To cause to extend from one place to another or across a given space: *stretch the banner across the stage.* **3.** To make taut; tighten. **4.** To reach or put forth; extend: *stretched out his hand.* **5.** To extend (oneself or one's extremities) at full length. **6.** To flex the muscles of: *stretch one's arms.* **7.** To exert to the utmost; strain: *stretch every nerve to win.* **8.** To wrench or strain (a muscle, for example). **9.** *Informal.* To fell by a blow: *He was stretched in the first round.* **10.** To put to torture on the rack. **11. a.** To expand to fulfill a larger function: *stretch a budget.* **b.** To increase the quantity of by admixture or dilution: *stretch a meal by thinning the soup.* **12. a.** To extend the limits of: *stretch the rules.* **b.** To bend or contort: *stretch the truth.* **13.** To prolong: *stretch out an argument.* *—intr.* **1.** To become lengthened, widened, or distended. **2.** To extend or reach over a given distance or area or in a given direction: *"On both sides of us stretched the wet plain"* (Hemingway). **3.** To lie down at full length: *He stretched out on the bed.* **4.** To flex or extend one's muscles or limbs. **5.** To extend over a given period of time: *"This story stretches over a whole generation"* (William Golding). *—n.* **1.** The act of stretching or the state of being stretched. **2.** The extent or scope to which something can be stretched; elasticity. **3.** A continuous or unbroken length, area, or expanse: *an empty stretch of highway.* **4.** A straight section of a racecourse or track, esp. that section leading to the finish line. **5. a.** A continuous period of time. **b.** *Slang.* A term of imprisonment: *served a two-year stretch.* **c.** *Informal.* The last stage of an event, period, or process. [ME *strecchen* < OE *streccan.*] **—stretch′a·ble** *adj.* **—stretch′y** *adj.*

stretch·er (strĕch′ər) *n.* **1.** One that stretches. **2.** A litter, usually of canvas stretched over a frame, used to transport the sick, wounded, or dead. **3.** Any of various devices used for stretching and shaping, such as the wooden framework upon which canvas is stretched for an oil painting. **4. a.** A usually horizontal tie beam or brace serving to support or extend a framework. **b.** A brick or stone laid parallel to the face of a wall.

stretch·er-bear·er (strĕch′ər-bâr′ər) *n.* A person who helps carry a stretcher or litter.

stretch-out (strĕch′out′) *n.* An increase in the work required of industrial workers without a commensurate pay increase.

stretch receptor *n.* A proprioceptor in a muscle or tendon that is stimulated by a stretch.

stret·to (strĕt′ō) *n., pl.* **stret·ti** (strĕt′ē) or **stret·tos.** *Mus.* **1.** A close succession or overlapping of voices in a fugue, esp. in the final section. **2.** A final section, as of an oratorio, performed with an acceleration in tempo to produce a climax. [Ital. < Lat. *strictus,* strict.]

streu·sel (stro͞o′zəl, stroi′-) *n.* A crumblike topping for coffee cakes and rich breads, consisting of flour, sugar, butter, cinnamon, and sometimes chopped nutmeats. [G. < MHG *ströusel,* something strewn < *ströuwen,* to sprinkle < OHG *strowwen.*]

strew (stro͞o) *tr.v.* **strewn** (stro͞on) or **strewed, strew·ing, strews. 1.** To spread here and there; scatter. **2.** To cover (a surface) with things scattered or sprinkled: *"Italy . . . was strewn thick with the remains of Roman buildings"* (Bernard Berenson). **3.** To be or become dispersed over (a surface). [ME *strewen* < OE *strewian.*]

strewn field *n.* An area abundant with tektites.

stri·a (strī′ə) *n., pl.* **stri·ae** (strī′ē′). **1.** A thin, narrow groove or channel. **2.** A thin line or band, esp. one of several that are parallel or close together. [Lat.]

stri·ate (strī′āt′) also **stri·at·ed** (-ā′tĭd) *adj.* **1.** Marked with striae; striped, grooved, or ridged. **2.** Consisting of a stria or striae. *—tr.v.* **-at·ed, -at·ing, -ates.** To mark with striae. [Lat. *striatus,* p.part. of *striare,* to make furrows < *stria,* furrow.]

striated muscle *n.* Skeletal, voluntary, and cardiac muscle, distinguished from smooth muscle by transverse striations of the fibers.

stri·a·tion (strī-ā′shən) *n.* **1.** The state of being striated or having striae. **2.** The form taken by striae. **3.** A stria.

strick·en (strĭk′ən) *adj.* **1.** Struck or wounded, as by a projectile. **2.** Afflicted with something overwhelming, as strong emotion or trouble. **3.** Having the contents made even with the top of a measuring device or container; level: *a stricken measure of flour.* *—v.* A past participle of **strike.** [P.part. of STRIKE.]

strick·le (strĭk′əl) *n.* **1.** An instrument used to level off grain or other material in a measure. **2.** A foundry tool used to shape a mold in sand or loam. **3.** A tool for sharpening scythes. *—tr.v.* **-led, -ling, -les.** To apply a strickle to. [ME *strikelle* < OE *stricel.*]

strict (strĭkt) *adj.* **-er, -est. 1.** Precise; exact: *a strict definition.* **2.** Complete; absolute: *strict loyalty.* **3.** Kept within narrow and specific limits: *a strict application of a law.* **4.** Imposing an exacting discipline; not permissive: *a strict teacher.* **5.** Enforced or maintained rigorously; stringent: *strict standards.* **6.** Rigidly conforming; devout. **7.** *Bot.* Stiff, narrow, and upright. [Lat. *strictus* < p.part. of *stringere,* to bind tightly.] **—strict′ly** *adv.* **—strict′ness** *n.*

stric·ture (strĭk′chər) *n.* **1.** Something that restrains, limits, or restricts. **2.** An adverse remark or criticism; censure. **3.** *Path.* An abnormal narrowing of a duct or passage. [ME < Lat. *strictura* < *stringere,* to bind tightly.]

stride (strīd) *v.* **strode** (strōd), **strid·den** (strĭd′n), **strid·ing, strides.** *—intr.* **1.** To walk with long steps, esp. in a hasty or vigorous manner. **2.** To take a single long step, as in passing over an obstruction. *—tr.* **1.** To stride on, along, or through. **2.** To be astride of; straddle. *—n.* **1.** The act of striding. **2. a.** A single long step. **b.** The distance traveled in such a step. **3. a.** A single coordinated movement of the four legs of a horse or other animal, completed when the legs are returned to their initial relative position. **b.** The distance traveled in a stride. **4.** Often **strides.** A step forward; advance. **—*idiom.* take in (one's) stride.** To handle or accept without disruption of normal routine. [ME *striden* < OE *strīdan.*] **—strid′er** *n.*

stri·dent (strīd′nt) *adj.* Loud, harsh, and grating; shrill: *a strident voice.* [Lat. *stridens, strident-,* pr.part. of *stridēre,* to make harsh sounds.] **—stri′dence, stri′den·cy** *n.* **—stri′dent·ly** *adv.*

stride piano *n.* A style of jazz pianism in which the melody is played by the right hand while a single note is played by the left hand in alternation with a chord that is an octave, or more than an octave, higher.

stri·dor (strī′dər, -dôr′) *n.* **1.** A strident sound. **2.** *Pathol.* A harsh, high-pitched sound in inhalation or exhalation. [Lat. < *stridēre,* to make harsh sounds.]

strid·u·late (strĭj′ə-lāt′) *intr.v.* **-lat·ed, -lat·ing, -lates.** To produce a shrill grating or creaking sound; chirp. [< Lat. *stridulus,* stridulous.] **—strid′u·la′tion** *n.* **—strid′u·la·to′ry** (-lə-tôr′ē, -tōr′ē) *adj.*

strid·u·lous (strĭj′ə-ləs) *adj.* Making or characterized by a strident sound or chirp. [Lat. *stridulus* < *stridēre,* to make harsh sounds.]

strife (strīf) *n.* **1.** Heated, often violent dissension; bitter conflict. **2.** A struggle between rivals; contention. **3.** Earnest endeavor or striving. [ME *strif* < OFr. *estrif* < *estriver,* to fight, of Germanic orig.]

strig·il (strĭj′əl) *n.* An instrument used in ancient Greece and Rome for scraping the skin after a bath. [Lat. *strigilis* < *stringere,* to touch lightly.]

stri·gose (strī′gōs′) *adj.* **1.** Marked with fine, close-set grooves or streaks. **2.** *Bot.* Having stiff, closely pressed hairs or bristles. [NLat. *strigosus* < Lat. *striga,* furrow.]

strike (strīk) *v.* **struck** (strŭk), **struck** or **strick·en** (strĭk′ən), **strik·ing, strikes.** *—tr.* **1. a.** To hit sharply, as with the hand, fist, or a weapon. **b.** To inflict (a blow). **2. a.** To collide with or crash into: *struck the desk with her knee.* **b.** To move into violent contact: *struck her knee against the desk.* **3.** To attack; assault. **4.** To afflict suddenly with a disease or impairment. **5.** To wound by biting. **6.** To hook (a fish) that has taken the bait. **7.** To form by stamping, printing, or punching: *strike a medallion.* **8.** To produce by hitting an agent, such as a key on a musical instrument or a typewriter: *strike a B flat.* **9.** To indicate by a percussive sound: *The clock struck nine.* **10. a.** To produce by friction. **b.** To produce flame, light, or a spark from by friction. **11.** To eliminate or expunge. **12.** To come upon; discover: *struck gold.* **13.** To reach; fall upon: *A bright light struck her face.* **14.** To impress abruptly or freshly, causing an immediate response: *strikes me as a good idea.* **15.** To occur or appear to: *The thought struck me from out of the blue.* **16.** To cause (an emotion) to penetrate deeply: *struck terror into their hearts.* **17. a.** To make or conclude (a bargain). **b.** To achieve (a balance, for example) by careful weighing or reckoning. **18.** To fall into or assume (a pose, for example). **19.** *Naut.* **a.** To haul down (a mast or sail). **b.** To lower (a flag or sail) in salute or surrender. **c.** To lower (cargo) into a hold. **20.** To remove (theatrical properties) from the stage. **21.** To remove or pack up: *strike camp.* **22.** To undertake a strike against (an employer). **23.** To level or smooth; strickle. **24.** To send out or down (roots, for example). *—intr.* **1.** To deal a blow or blows with or as if with the fist or a weapon; hit. **2.** To aim a stroke or blow. **3.** To make contact suddenly or violently; collide. **4.** To begin an attack. **5.** To pierce; penetrate. **6.** To take the bait. **7. a.** To make a percussive sound. **b.** To be indicated by sounds: *The hour has struck.* **8.** To become ignited. **9.** To come suddenly or unexpectedly. **10.** To fall; impinge. **11.** To proceed, esp. in a new direction; set out. **12.** To engage in a strike against an employer. ***—phrasal verbs.*** **strike out. 1.** To begin a course of action. **2.** To undertake enthusiastically. **3.** *Baseball.* **a.** To pitch three strikes to (a batter), putting him out. **b.** To be struck out. **strike up. 1.** To start to play or sound vigorously: *Strike up the band.* **2.** To initiate or begin: *strike up a conversation.* *—n.* **1.** An act or gesture of striking. **2.** An attack, esp. a military air attack upon a single group of targets. **3. a.** A cessation of work by employees in support of demands made upon their employer, as for higher pay or improved conditions. **b.** A temporary stoppage of normal activity undertaken as a protest. **4.** A sudden achievement or valuable discovery, as of a precious mineral. **5. a.** A taking of bait by a fish. **b.** A pull on the line indicating a strike. **6.** A quantity of coins or medals struck at the same time. **7. a.** *Baseball.* A pitched ball that is counted against the batter, typically one that is swung at and missed, fouled off, or judged to have passed through the strike zone. **b.** A perfectly thrown ball. **8.** The knocking down of all the pins in bowling with the first bowl of a frame. **9.** *Geol.* The direction of a horizontal line in the plane of an inclined structural feature such as a rock bed or vein. **10.** A strickle. [ME *striken* < OE *strīcan,* to stroke.]

string bean

stringcourse

strike·bound (strīk′bound′) *adj.* Closed, immobilized, or slowed down by a strike.

strike·break·er (strīk′brā′kər) *n.* A person who works or provides an employer with workers during a strike; scab. **—strike′break′ing** *n.*

strike·out (strīk′out′) *n.* *Baseball.* The act or an instance of striking out.

strik·er (strī′kər) *n.* **1.** One that strikes. **2.** An employee who is on strike against his or her employer. **3.** A device for striking, as the clapper in a bell or the firing pin in a gun. **4. a.** A harpoon. **b.** A harpooner. **5.** An enlisted person in training for a specified naval technical rating.

strike zone *n.* *Baseball.* The area over home plate through which a pitch must pass to be called a strike, defined as being between the batter's armpits and knees.

strik·ing (strī′kĭng) *adj.* Immediately or vividly impressive: *a striking similarity.* **—strik′ing·ly** *adv.* **—strik′ing·ness** *n.*

striking price *n.* The price at which a put or call option may be exercised.

string (strĭng) *n.* **1.** A cord usually made of fiber, used for fastening, tying, or lacing. **2.** Something shaped into a long, thin line: *strings of spaghetti.* **3.** A set of objects threaded together: *a string of beads.* **4.** A series of related acts, events, or items arranged or falling in a line: *a string of victories.* **5.** *Computer Sci.* A set of data arranged in ascending or descending sequence according to a key within the data. **6.** *Informal.* A set of animals, esp. racehorses, belonging to a single owner; a stable. **7.** *Sports.* A group of players constituting a ranked team within a team: *He made the second string.* **8.** *Mus.* **a.** A cord stretched across the sounding board of an instrument that is struck, plucked, or bowed to produce tones. **b. strings.** Instruments having such strings, esp. the instruments of the violin family. **9.** *Archit.* **a.** A stringboard. **b.** A stringcourse. **10.** *Games.* The balk line in billiards. **11.** *Informal.* Often **strings.** A limiting or hidden condition: *a gift with no strings attached.* *—v.* **strung** (strŭng), **string·ing, strings.** *—tr.* **1.** To fit or furnish with a string or strings: *string a guitar.* **2.** To thread on a string. **3.** To arrange in a string or series. **4.** To fasten, tie, or hang with a string or strings. **5.** To extend; stretch out: *string a wire across a room.* **6.** To strip (vegetables) of strings. *—intr.* **1.** To form strings or become stringlike. **2.** To extend or progress in a string, line, or succession. ***—phrasal verbs.*** **string along. 1.** To keep (someone) waiting or dangling. **2.** To cheat; deceive. **string up.** *Informal.* To hang (someone). ***—idiom.*** **pull strings.** To use one's influence, often in secret, to gain an advantage. [ME < OE *streng.*]

string bass *n.* A double bass.

string bean *n.* **1.** A bushy or climbing plant, *Phaseolus vulgaris,* widely cultivated for its narrow, green, edible pods. **2.** The green pod of a bean prepared for cooking by breaking into sections that retain the beans. **3.** *Slang.* A tall, thin person.

string·board (strĭng′bôrd′, -bōrd′) *n.* A board that runs along the side of a staircase to support or cover the ends of the steps.

string·course (strĭng′kôrs′, -kōrs′) *n.* *Archit.* A horizontal band or molding set in the face of a building as a design element.

stringed instrument *n.* A musical instrument played by plucking, striking, or bowing taut strings.

strin·gen·do (strĭn-jĕn′dō) *adj.* *Mus.* Played with an accelerating tempo. Used as a direction. [Ital. < *stringere,* to tighten < Lat.] **—strin·gen′do** *adv.*

strin·gent (strĭn′jənt) *adj.* **1.** Imposing rigorous standards of performance; severe: *stringent safety measures.* **2.** Constricted; tight: *operating under a stringent time limit.* **3.** Characterized by scarcity of money, credit restrictions, or other financial strain: *stringent economic policies.* [Lat. *stringens, stringent-,* pr.part. of *stringere,* to bind tightly.] **—strin′gen·cy** *n.* **—strin′gent·ly** *adv.*

string·er (strĭng′ər) *n.* **1.** One that strings. **2.** *Archit.* **a.** A long, heavy horizontal timber used for any of several connective or supportive purposes. **b.** A stringboard. **3.** A lengthwise timber used to support rails. **4.** A member of a specified string or squad on a team: *a second-stringer.* **5.** A part-time or free-lance correspondent for a news publication.

string·halt (strĭng′hôlt′) *n.* Lameness accompanied by spasmodic movements in the hind legs of a horse. [STRING, tendon (obs.) + HALT².]

string quartet *n.* **1.** A quartet of musicians playing stringed instruments, traditionally including a first and second violinist, a violist, and a cellist. **2.** A composition for a string quartet.

string tie *n.* A narrow necktie, usually tied in a bow.

string·y (strĭng′ē) *adj.* **-i·er, -i·est. 1.** Resembling, forming, or consisting of a string or strings. **2.** Slender and sinewy; wiry. **—string′i·ly** *adv.* **—string′i·ness** *n.*

strip¹ (strĭp) *v.* **stripped, strip·ping, strips.** *—tr.* **1. a.** To remove the clothing or other covering from. **b.** To remove (clothing or other covering). **2.** To deprive of honors, rank, or functions; divest. **3.** To remove all excess detail from. **4.** To remove the leaves from the stalks of. Used esp. of tobacco. **5.** To dismantle (something) piece by piece. **6.** To damage or break the threads or teeth of (a screw, for example). **7.** To milk (a milk-giving creature). **8.** To rob; despoil. *—intr.* **1. a.** To undress completely. **b.** To perform a striptease. **2.** To fall away or be removed; peel. *—n.* A striptease. [ME *stripen* < *strīpan.*]

Synonyms: *strip, divest, denude, bare.* These verbs refer to the act of removing coverings or possessions. *Strip* often suggests force or abrupt action and applies to removal of such diverse things as clothing, natural covering such as bark or foliage, components of machinery, and attributes such as honor, rank, or position. *Divest* more often specifies deprivation of authority or rank or of the physical things that symbolize them. *Denude* generally refers to making land barren by depriving it of natural covering, such as vegetation or topsoil. *Bare* usually implies uncovering, literally or figuratively, and exposing to view.

strip² (strĭp) *n.* **1.** A long, narrow piece, usually of uniform width: *a strip of paper.* **2.** A comic strip. **3.** An airstrip. *—tr.v.* **stripped, strip·ping, strips.** To cut or tear into strips. [Perh. alteration of STRIPE¹.]

strip-crop·ping (strĭp′krŏp′ĭng) *n.* The growing of a cultivated crop, such as cotton, and a sod-forming crop, such as alfalfa, in alternating strips following the contour of the land, in order to minimize erosion.

stripe[1] (strīp) *n.* **1. a.** A long, narrow band distinguished, as by color or texture, from the surrounding material or surface. **b.** A fabric having such a band or bands. **c. stripes.** A garment of such fabric, esp. a prisoner's uniform. **2.** A strip of cloth or braid worn on a uniform to indicate rank, awards received, or length of service; chevron. **3.** Sort; kind: *"All Fascists are not of one mind, one stripe"* (Lillian Hellman). —*tr.v.* **striped, strip·ing, stripes.** To mark with a stripe or stripes. [Poss. < MDu. *strīpe.*]

stripe[2] (strīp) *n.* A stroke or blow, as with a whip. [ME.]

striped (strīpt, strī′pĭd) *adj.* Having a stripe or stripes.

striped bass *n.* A food and game fish, *Roccus saxatilis,* of North American coastal waters, having dark longitudinal stripes along its sides.

striped maple *n.* The moosewood.

strip·er (strī′pər) *n.* **1.** *Slang.* A member of the armed forces who wears stripes designating rank or length of service: *a four-striper.* **2.** *Informal.* A striped bass.

strip·film (strĭp′fĭlm′) *n.* Filmstrip.

strip·ling (strĭp′lĭng) *n.* An adolescent youth. [ME.]

strip mine *n.* An open mine, esp. a coal mine, whose seams or outcrops run close to ground level and are exposed by the removal of topsoil and overburden. —*tr.v.* **strip-mine, -mined, -min·ing, -mines.** To mine (an ore) from a strip mine.

strip·per (strĭp′ər) *n.* **1.** One that strips. **2.** *Slang.* A person who performs a striptease.

strip poker *n.* A poker game in which the losing players in each hand must remove an article of clothing.

strip·tease also **strip tease** (strĭp′tēz′) *n.* A theatrical performance featuring a person who slowly removes clothing to a musical accompaniment. —**strip′teas′er** *n.*

strip·y (strī′pē) *adj.* **-i·er, -i·est.** Suggestive of or marked with stripes; striped.

strive (strīv) *intr.v.* **strove** (strōv), **striv·en** (strĭv′ən) or **strived, striv·ing, strives. 1.** To exert much effort or energy. **2.** To struggle; contend. [ME *striven* < OFr. *estriver,* of Germanic orig.] —**striv′er** *n.*

strobe (strōb) *n.* **1.** Stroboscope. **2.** A strobe light.

strobe light *n.* A flash lamp that produces high-intensity short-duration light pulses by electric discharge in a gas.

stro·bi·la (strō-bī′lə) *n., pl.* **-lae** (-lē). A part or structure that buds to form a series of segments, such as the main body part of a tapeworm or the polyp stage in certain jellyfish. [NLat. < Gk. *strobilē,* twisted plug of lint < *strobilos,* pine cone.] —**stro·bi′lar** *adj.*

stro·bi·la·ceous (strō′bə-lā′shəs) *adj.* Of or resembling a strobile; conelike.

stro·bi·la·tion (strō′bə-lā′shən) *n.* Asexual reproduction by division into body segments, as in tapeworms and jellyfish.

stro·bile (strō′bīl′, -bəl) also **stro·bi·lus** (strō-bī′ləs) *n., pl.* **-biles** or **-bili** (-bī′lī′). A fruiting structure characterized by rows of overlapping scales, such as a pine cone or the fruit of the hop. [NLat. *strobilus* < Gk. *strobilos,* pine cone.]

strob·o·scope (strō′bə-skōp′) *n.* Any of various instruments used to view, calibrate, balance, or otherwise adjust moving, rotating, or vibrating objects by making them appear stationary, esp. with pulsed illumination or mechanical devices that intermittently interrupt observation. [Gk. *strobos,* a whirling round + -SCOPE.] —**stro′bo·scop′ic** (-skŏp′ĭk) *adj.* —**strob′o·scop′i·cal·ly** *adv.*

stro·bo·tron (strō′bə-trŏn′) *n.* A gas-filled cathode tube that produces bright flashes of light for a stroboscope. [STROBO(SCOPE) + -TRON.]

strode (strōd) *v.* Past tense of **stride.**

stroke (strōk) *n.* **1.** An impact; strike. **2.** An act of striking. **3. a.** The striking of a bell or gong. **b.** The sound so produced. **c.** The time so indicated: *the stroke of midnight.* **4.** An event having a powerful immediate effect for good or ill: *a stroke of luck.* **5. a.** The sudden severe onset of a malady, as apoplexy or sunstroke. **b.** *Informal.* Apoplexy. **6.** An inspired or effective idea or act: *a stroke of genius.* **7. a.** A single completed movement of the limbs and body, as in swimming or rowing. **b.** The rate or manner of executing such a movement. **8. a.** The member of a rowing crew who sits nearest the coxswain or the stern and sets the tempo for the oarsmen. **b.** The position this person occupies. **9. a.** A movement of the upper torso and arms for the purpose of striking a ball, as in golf or tennis. **b.** The manner of executing such a movement. **10.** Any of a series of movements of a piston from one end of the limit of its motion to the other. **11. a.** A single mark made by a pen or other marking implement. **b.** The action of making such a mark. **c.** A printed line in a graphic character that resembles such a mark. **12.** A single deft touch, as in literary composition. **13.** A light caressing movement, as of the hand. —*tr.v.* **stroked, strok·ing, strokes. 1.** To rub lightly, with or as if with the hand or something held in the hand; caress. **2.** To set the pace for (a rowing crew). [ME.]

stroll (strōl) *v.* **strolled, stroll·ing, strolls.** —*intr.* To go for a leisurely walk: *stroll in the park.* —*tr.* To walk through at a leisurely pace: *stroll the streets.* —*n.* A leisurely walk. [Prob. < dial. G. *strollen.*]

stroll·er (strō′lər) *n.* **1.** One that strolls. **2.** A strolling player. **3.** A vagabond. **4.** A light four-wheeled chair for transporting small children.

stro·ma (strō′mə) *n., pl.* **-ma·ta** (-mə-tə). The tissue framework, as distinguished from the specific substance, of an organ, gland, or other structure. [NLat. < Lat., covering < Gk. *strōma* < *stornunai,* to spread.] —**stro·mat′ic** (-măt′ĭk) *adj.*

stro·mat·o·lite (strō-măt′l-īt′) *n.* A sedimentary fossil consisting of laminated layers of algal origin. [Gk. *strōma, strōmat-,* bed covering + -LITE.] —**stro·mat′o·lit′ic** (-măt′l-ĭt′ĭk) *adj.*

strong (strông) *adj.* **-er, -est. 1.** Having great physical strength. **2.** In good or sound health; robust. **3.** Economically or financially sound or thriving. **4.** Having force of character, will, morality, or intelligence. **5.** Having or showing ability or achievement in a specified field: *He is strong in chemistry.* **6.** Capable of enduring; solid: *a strong building.* **7.** Capable of being defended: *a strong flank.* **8.** Having a specified number of units or members: *"Marched them along, fifty-score strong"* (Robert Browning). **9.** Having force of motion or action: *a strong current.* **10. a.** Persuasive, effective, and cogent: *a strong argument.* **b.** Forceful and pointed; emphatic: *a strong statement.* **11.** Extreme; drastic: *strong measures.* **12.** Capable of exerting authority effectively: *strong leadership.* **13.** Having force of conviction or feeling: *a strong faith.* **14.** Intense in degree or quality: *a strong emotion.* **15. a.** Having an intense effect on the senses: *a strong smell.* **b.** Containing a considerable percentage of alcohol: *strong punch.* **16.** Characterized by a high degree of saturation. **17.** *Ling.* Designating those verbs in Germanic languages that form a past tense other than by means of a dental suffix; for example, *fly, flew; sing, sang.* —*adv.* In a strong, powerful, or vigorous manner; forcefully. [ME < OE *strang.*] —**strong′ly** *adv.*

Synonyms: *strong, stout, sturdy, tough, stalwart, hale, tenacious.* These adjectives are compared as they relate to vigor, durability, or power of body or spirit. *Strong* is the most general. *Stout* stresses ability to endure by muscular strength, solid construction, or resoluteness. *Sturdy* is closely related to *stout* in its implications of rugged health, solidity, or firmness of spirit or purpose. *Tough* suggests strength of physique or moral fiber that resists opposition or hardship. *Stalwart* implies imposing strength, courage, or unwavering determination, dependability, or loyalty. *Hale* suggests robust health. *Tenacious* stresses ability to hold fast to positions, goals, or opinions.

strong-arm (strông′ärm′) *Informal.* —*adj.* Using physical force or coercion: *strong-arm tactics.* —*tr.v.* **-armed, -arm·ing, -arms.** To use physical force or coercion against.

strong·box (strông′bŏks′) *n.* A stoutly made box or safe in which valuables are deposited.

strong force *n.* Strong interaction.

strong·hold (strông′hōld′) *n.* **1.** A fortress. **2.** An area dominated or occupied by a special group.

strong interaction *n.* A fundamental interaction between elementary particles that causes protons and neutrons to bind together in the atomic nucleus.

strong-mind·ed (strông′mīn′dĭd) *adj.* **1.** Having a determined will. **2.** Having a vigorous mentality. —**strong′-mind′ed·ly** *adv.* —**strong′-mind′ed·ness** *n.*

strong room *n.* A strongly built fireproof room designed for the safekeeping of money or valuables.

strong suit *n.* Long suit.

stron·gyle also **stron·gyl** (strŏn′jīl′, -jəl) *n.* Any of various nematode worms of the family Strongylidae, often parasitic in the gastrointestinal tract of mammals, esp. horses. [NLat. *Strongylus,* type genus < Gk. *strongulos,* compact.]

stron·gy·lo·sis (strŏn′jə-lō′sĭs) *n.* Infestation with strongyles.

stron·ti·an·ite (strŏn′chē-ə-nīt′, -tē-ə-nīt′) *n.* A gray to yellowish-green strontium ore, essentially $SrCO_3$. [*Strontian,* var. of STRONTIUM + -ITE.]

stron·ti·um (strŏn′chē-əm, -tē-əm) *n.* *Symbol* **Sr** A soft, silvery, easily oxidized metallic element that ignites spontaneously in air when finely divided. Strontium is used in pyrotechnic compounds and various alloys. Atomic number 38; atomic weight 87.62; melting point 769°C; boiling point 1,384°C; specific gravity 2.54; valence 2. [After *Strontian,* Scotland.] —**stron′tic** (-tĭk) *adj.*

strontium 90 *n.* The strontium isotope with mass 90, having a half-life of 28 years, used for its high-energy beta emission in certain nuclear electric power sources and constituting a radiation hazard in fallout.

strop (strŏp) *n.* A flexible strip of leather or canvas used for sharpening a razor. —*tr.v.* **stropped, strop·ping, strops.** To sharpen (a razor) on a strop. [ME *stroppe,* band of leather < MLG *strop* < Lat. *stroppus* < Gk. *strophion.*]

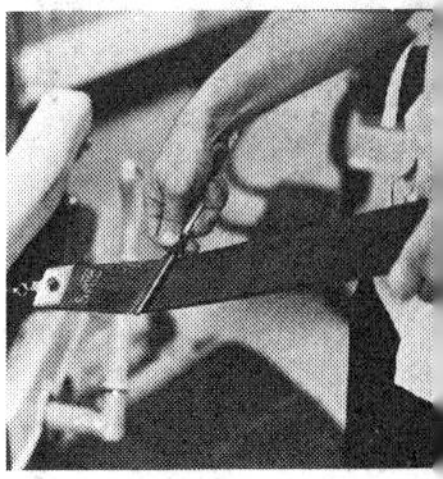

strop

stro·phan·thin (strō-făn′thĭn) *n.* A toxic glycoside or mixture of glycosides, used medicinally as a cardiac tonic. [< NLat. *Strophanthus,* genus of tropical trees or vines : Gk. *strophos,* twisted + Gk. *anthos,* flower.]

stro·phe (strō′fē) *n.* **1. a.** A stanza, esp. the first of a pair of stanzas of alternating form on which the structure of a given poem is based. **b.** A rhythmic system constituting a section of a poem, typically consisting of a series of asymmetric lines. **2.** The first division of the triad (strophe, antistrophe, and epode) constituting a section of a Pindaric ode. **3. a.** The movement of the chorus in classical Greek drama while turning from one side of the orchestra to the other. **b.** The part of a choral ode sung while this movement is executed. [Gk. *strophē,* movement of the chorus < *strephein,* to turn.] **—stro'phic** (strō'fĭk, strŏf'ĭk) *adj.*

stro·phoid (strō'foid') *n.* A plane curve generated by a point that maintains a distance from the y-axis along a straight line equal to the y-intercept. [Gk. *strophos,* twisted (< *strephein,* to twist) + -OID.]

stroph·u·lus (strŏf'yə-ləs) *n.* A disease, esp. common among children, sometimes associated with intestinal disturbances and characterized by a papular eruption of the skin. [NLat. < Gk. *strophos,* twisted cord < *strephein,* to turn.]

stroud (stroud) *n.* A coarse woolen cloth or blanket. [After *Stroud,* England.]

strove (strōv) *v.* A past tense of **strive.**

struck (strŭk) *v.* Past tense and a past participle of **strike.** *—adj.* Affected or shut down by a labor strike.

struck jury *n. Law.* A jury, esp. a special jury, selected from an original panel of 48 members from which each party strikes off names until the list is reduced to 12.

struck measure *n.* A dry measure having the contents leveled off and not heaped.

struc·tur·al (strŭk'chər-əl) *adj.* **1.** Of, relating to, having, or characterized by structure. **2.** Used in or necessary to construction. **3.** *Geol.* Of or pertaining to the structure of rocks and other aspects of the earth's crust. **4.** *Biol.* Of or relating to organic structure; morphological. **—struc'tur·al·ly** *adv.*

structural formula *n.* A chemical formula that represents the configuration of atoms and bonds in a molecule.

structural gene *n.* A gene that determines the amino acid sequence of a protein.

struc·tur·al·ize (strŭk'chər-ə-līz') *tr.v.* **-ized, -iz·ing, -iz·es.** To incorporate into a structure. **—struc'tur·al·i·za'tion** *n.*

structural steel *n.* Steel shaped for use in construction.

struc·ture (strŭk'chər) *n.* **1.** Something made up of a number of parts that are held or put together in a particular way. **2.** The way in which parts are arranged or put together to form a whole. **3.** The interrelation of parts or the principle of organization in a complex entity. **4.** Relatively intricate or extensive organization: *an elaborate electric structure.* **5.** Something constructed, esp. a building or part. *—tr.v.* **-tured, -tur·ing, -tures.** To give form or arrangement to. [ME < OFr. < Lat. *structura* < *struere,* to construct.]

struc·tured (strŭk'chərd) *adj.* **1.** Highly organized: *a structured environment.* **2.** *Psychol.* Having a limited number of correct or nearly correct answers. Used of a test.

stru·del (strōōd'l, shtrōōd'l) *n.* A kind of pastry made with fruit or cheese rolled up in a thin sheet of dough and then baked. [G. < MHG, whirlpool.]

strug·gle (strŭg'əl) *v.* **-gled, -gling, -gles.** *—intr.* **1.** To exert muscular energy, as against a material force or mass; grapple. **2.** To be strenuously engaged with a problem, task, or undertaking. **3.** To make a strenuous effort; strive: *struggling to be polite.* **4. a.** To contend against: *"the human being struggles with his environment"* (Karl A. Menninger). **b.** To compete with. **5.** To progress or penetrate with difficulty. *—tr.* To move or place (something) with an effort: *struggle a trunk into a car.* *—n.* **1.** An act of struggling. **2.** Strenuous effort. **3.** Combat; strife. [ME *struglen.*] **—strug'gler** *n.* **—strug'gling·ly** *adv.*

strut
The Hermes of Praxiteles

strum (strŭm) *v.* **strummed, strum·ming, strums.** *—tr.* To play idly on or as if on (a stringed musical instrument) by plucking the strings with the fingers. *—intr.* To play an instrument by strumming. *—n.* The act or sound of strumming. [Perh. blend of STRING and THRUM[1].] **—strum'mer** *n.*

stru·ma (strōō'mə) *n., pl.* **-mae** (-mē') or **-mas. 1.** *Pathol.* **a.** Scrofula. **b.** Goiter. **2.** *Bot.* A cushionlike swelling at the base of a moss capsule. [Lat.] **—stru·mat'ic** (-măt'ĭk), **stru'mose'** (-mōs'), **stru'mous** (-məs) *adj.*

strum·pet (strŭm'pĭt) *n.* A whore. [ME.]

strung (strŭng) *v.* Past tense and past participle of **string.**

strung-out (strŭng'out') *adj. Slang.* **1. a.** Addicted to a drug. **b.** Stupefied from ingestion of a drug. **2.** Physically or emotionally debilitated from or as if from long-term drug use.

strut (strŭt) *v.* **strut·ted, strut·ting, struts.** *—intr.* To walk with pompous bearing; swagger. *—tr.* To brace with a supporting bar or rod. *—n.* **1.** A stiff, self-important gait. **2.** A bar or rod used to brace a structure against forces applied from the side. [ME *strouten,* to stand out < OE *strūtian,* to stand out stiffly.] **—strut'ter** *n.* **—strut'ting·ly** *adv.*

stru·thi·ous (strōō'thē-əs, -thē-əs) *adj.* Of, pertaining to, or resembling the ostrich or a related bird. [< LLat. *struthio,* ostrich < Gk. *strouthion* < *strouthos.*]

strych·nine (strĭk'nīn', -nĭn, -nēn') *n.* An extremely poisonous white crystalline alkaloid, $C_{21}H_{22}N_2O_2$, derived from nux vomica and related plants, used as a poison for rodents and other pests and medicinally as a stimulant for the central nervous system. [Fr. < NLat., *Strychnos,* genus of tropical trees and vines < Lat. *strychnos,* a kind of nightshade < Gk. *strukhnos.*]

strych·nin·ism (strĭk'nĭ-nĭz'əm, -nī-, -nē-) *n.* Chronic strychnine poisoning.

stub (stŭb) *n.* **1.** The usually short end remaining after something has been used up: *a pencil stub.* **2. a.** The part of a check or receipt retained as a record. **b.** The part of a ticket returned as a voucher of payment. *—tr.v.* **stubbed, stub·bing, stubs. 1.** To pull up (weeds) by the roots. **2.** To clear (a field) of weeds. **3.** To strike (one's toe or foot) against something. **4.** To snuff out (a cigarette butt) by crushing. [ME *stubbe* < OE *stybb.*]

stub·ble (stŭb'əl) *n.* **1.** The short, stiff stalks of a grain or hay crop remaining on a field after the crop has been harvested. **2.** Something resembling stubble, esp. a short stiff growth of beard. [ME *stuble* < OFr. *estuble* < Lat. *stupla,* var. of *stipula,* straw.] **—stub'bly** *adj.*

stub·born (stŭb'ərn) *adj.* **1. a.** Unduly determined to exert one's will; refractory. **b.** Not easily persuaded; obstinate. **2.** Characterized by perseverance; persistent. **3.** Difficult to handle or work; resistant: *stubborn soil.* [ME *stuborn.*] **—stub'born·ly** *adv.* **—stub'born·ness** *n.*

stub·by (stŭb'ē) *adj.* **-bi·er, -bi·est. 1.** Having the nature of a stub; short and stocky. **2.** Covered with or made of stubs. **3.** Short and bristly. **—stub'bi·ly** *adv.* **—stub'bi·ness** *n.*

stub nail *n.* A short, thick nail.

stuc·co (stŭk'ō) *n., pl.* **-coes** or **-cos. 1.** A durable finish for exterior walls, applied wet and usually composed of cement, sand, and lime. **2.** A fine plaster for interior wall ornamentation, such as moldings. **3.** A plaster or cement finish for interior walls. *—tr.v.* **-coed, -co·ing, -coes** or **-cos.** To finish or decorate with stucco. [Ital., of Germanic orig.]

stuck (stŭk) *v.* Past tense and past participle of **stick.**

stuck-up (stŭk'ŭp') *adj. Informal.* Snobbish; conceited.

stud[1] (stŭd) *n.* **1.** An upright post in the framework of a wall for supporting sheets of lath, wallboard, or similar material. **2.** A small knob, nail head, or rivet fixed in and slightly projecting from a surface. **3. a.** A small ornamental button mounted on a short post for insertion through an eyelet, as on a dress shirt. **b.** A buttonlike earring. **4.** Any of various protruding pins or pegs in machinery. **5.** A metal crosspiece used as a brace in a link, as in a chain cable. *—tr.v.* **stud·ded, stud·ding, studs. 1.** To provide with or construct with a stud or studs. **2.** To set with a stud or studs: *stud a bracelet with rubies.* **3.** To be dotted about on, esp. ornamentally; strew: *Daisies studded the meadow.* [ME *stode* < OE *studu.*]

stud[2] (stŭd) *n.* **1. a.** A group of animals, esp. horses, kept for breeding. **b.** A stable or farm where they are kept. **2.** A stallion or other male animal kept for breeding. **3.** Stud poker. **4.** *Slang.* A virile man. **—*idiom.* at stud.** Available or offered for breeding. [ME *stod* < OE *stōd.*]

stud·book (stŭd'bŏŏk') *n.* A book registering the pedigrees of thoroughbred animals, esp. of horses.

stud·ding (stŭd'ĭng) *n.* **1. a.** The wood framework of a wall or partition. **b.** Lumber cut for studs. **2.** Something with which a surface is studded.

stud·ding·sail (stŭn'səl, stŭd'ĭng-sāl') *n. Naut.* A narrow rectangular sail set from extensions of the yards of square-rigged ships. [Orig. unknown.]

stu·dent (stōōd'nt, styōōd'-) *n.* **1.** One who attends a school, college, or university. **2. a.** One who makes a study of something. **b.** An attentive observer: *a student of world affairs.* [ME < Lat. *studens,* pr.part. *studēre,* to study.]

student teacher *n.* A college student who practices teaching under supervision.

student union *n.* A building on a college campus with facilities for social and organizational activities.

stud·fish (stŭd'fĭsh') *n., pl.* **studfish** or **-fish·es.** Either of two small, brightly colored freshwater fishes, *Fundulus catenatus* or *F. stellifer,* of the southeastern United States.

stud·horse also **stud horse** (stŭd'hôrs') *n.* A stallion.

stud·ied (stŭd'ēd) *adj.* **1. a.** Carefully prepared or considered: *a studied effect.* **b.** Lacking spontaneity; contrived: *a studied smile.* **2.** Learned; knowledgeable. **—stud'ied·ly** *adv.* **—stud'ied·ness** *n.*

stu·di·o (stōō'dē-ō, styōō'-) *n., pl.* **-os. 1.** An artist's workroom. **2.** A photographer's establishment. **3.** An establishment where an art is taught or studied: *a dance studio.* **4. a.** A room or building for motion-picture, television, or radio productions. **b.** A room or building where tapes and records are recorded. [Ital. < Lat. *studium,* eagerness.]

studio apartment *n.* A small apartment consisting of one main living space, a small kitchen, and a bathroom.

studio couch *n.* A couch that can be made to serve as a double bed by sliding the frame of a cot from beneath it.

stu·di·ous (stōō'dē-əs, styōō'-) *adj.* **1.** Devoted to study. **2.** Earnest; diligent: *made a studious effort.* **3.** Giving or evincing careful attention; heedful: *"the major . . . was very studious of his appearance"* (H. E. Bates). **4.** Deliberate. **5.** Conducive to study. [ME < Lat. *studiosus* < *studium,* eagerness.] **—stu'di·ous·ly** *adv.* **—stu'di·ous·ness** *n.*

stud poker *n.* Poker in which the first round of cards (and often the last) is dealt face down and the others face up.

stud·work (stŭd'wûrk') *n.* **1.** Work ornamented or covered with studs. **2.** The supportive framework of a wall or partition.

stud·y (stŭd'ē) *n., pl.* **-ies. 1.** The act or process of studying; the pursuit of knowledge, as by reading, observation, or research. **2.** Attentive scrutiny. **3.** A branch of knowledge. **4. studies.** A branch or department of learning: *graduate studies.* **5. a.** A work (as a thesis, for example) resulting from studious endeavor. **b.** A literary work on a particular subject. **c.** A preliminary sketch, as for a work of art. **6.** A musical composition designed as a technical exercise. **7.** A state of mental absorption: *He's in a deep study.* **8.** A room intended or equipped for studying or writing. **9. a.** One who memorizes something, esp. an actor with reference to his ability to memorize a part. **b.** The memorizing of a part in a play. *—v.* **stud·ied, stud·y·ing, stud·ies.** *—tr.* **1.** To apply one's mind purposefully to the acquisition of knowledge or understanding of (a subject): *study a language.* **2.** To read carefully: *study a book.* **3.** To memorize. **4.** To take (a course) at a school. **5.** To inquire into; investigate: *study the mood of the country.* **6.** To examine closely; scrutinize: *study a diagram.* **7.** To give careful thought to; contemplate: *study the next move.* *—intr.* **1.** To apply oneself to learning, esp. by reading. **2.** To pursue a course of study. **3.** To ponder; reflect. [ME *studie* < OFr. *estudie* < Lat. *studium* < *studēre,* to study.]

study hall *n.* **1.** A schoolroom reserved for study. **2.** A period set aside for study.

stuff (stŭf) *n.* **1.** The material out of which something is made or formed; substance. **2.** The basic substance or essential elements; essence: *the stuff heroes are made of.* **3.** Unspecified material: *Put that stuff over there.* **4.** *Informal.* Household or personal articles collectively; belongings. **5.** Worthless objects. **6. a.** *Slang.* Specific talk or actions: *Don't give me that stuff about being tired.* **b.** Special capability: *really showed their stuff and won the game.* **7.** *Chiefly Brit.* Woven material, esp. woolens. **8.** *Slang.* Money; cash. **9.** *Slang.* A habit-forming drug, esp. heroin. *—v.* **stuffed, stuff·ing, stuffs.** *—tr.* **1. a.** To pack tightly; cram: *stuff a Christmas stocking.* **b.** To block (a passage); plug: *stuff a leak with plaster.* **2. a.** To fill with an appropriate stuffing: *stuff a pillow.* **b.** To fill (an animal skin) to restore its natural form. **3.** To cram with food. **4.** To fill (the mind): *His head is stuffed with silly notions.* **5.** To put fraudulent votes into (a ballot box). **6.** To apply a preservative and softening agent to (leather). *—intr.* To overeat; gorge. [ME < OFr. *estoffe* < *estoffer,* to equip.] **—stuff'er** *n.*

stuffed derma *n.* Derma[2].

stuffed shirt *n. Informal.* A stiff, pompous person.

stuff·ing (stŭf'ĭng) *n.* Material used to stuff or fill, esp.: **a.** Padding put in cushions and upholstered furniture. **b.** Food put in the cavity of meat or vegetables.

stuffing box *n.* An enclosure containing packing to prevent leakage around a moving machine part.

stuff shot *n.* A dunk shot.

stuff·y (stŭf'ē) *adj.* **-i·er, -i·est. 1.** Lacking sufficient ventilation. **2.** Having the respiratory passages blocked. **3.** *Informal.* **a.** Dull: *a stuffy dinner party.* **b.** Formal; strait-laced. **—stuff'i·ly** *adv.* **—stuff'i·ness** *n.*

stull (stŭl) *n.* **1.** A timber or other prop supporting the roof of a mine opening. **2.** A platform braced against the sides of a working area in a mine. [Prob. < G. *Stollen,* support < OHG *stollo.*]

stul·ti·fy (stŭl'tə-fī') *tr.v.* **-fied, -fy·ing, -fies. 1.** To render useless or ineffectual; cripple. **2.** To cause to appear stupid, inconsistent, or ridiculous. **3.** *Law.* To allege or prove insane and so not legally responsible. [LLat. *stultificare,* to make foolish : Lat. *stultus,* foolish + Lat. *facere,* to make.] **—stul'ti·fi·ca'tion** *n.* **—stul'ti·fi'er** *n.*

stum (stŭm) *n.* **1.** Unfermented or partly fermented grape juice; must. **2.** Vapid wine renewed by an admixture of stum. *—tr.v.* **stummed, stum·ming, stums.** To ferment (vapid wine) by adding stum. [Du. *stom* < *stom,* dumb < MDu.]

stum·ble (stŭm'bəl) *v.* **-bled, -bling, -bles.** *—intr.* **1. a.** To miss one's step in walking or running. **b.** To act or speak clumsily, unsteadily, or falteringly; flounder: *stumble through a speech.* **2.** To make a mistake; blunder. **3.** To fall into evil ways; err. **4.** To come upon accidentally or unexpectedly: *stumbled on the answer.* *—tr.* To cause to stumble. *—n.* **1.** The act of stumbling. **2.** A mistake, blunder, or sin. [ME *stumblen,* prob. of Scand. orig.] **—stum'bler** *n.* **—stum'bling·ly** *adv.*

stum·ble·bum (stŭm'bəl-bŭm') *n. Slang.* **1.** A blundering or inept person. **2.** A punch-drunk or second-rate prizefighter.

stumbling block *n.* An obstacle or impediment.

stump (stŭmp) *n.* **1.** The part of a tree trunk left protruding from the ground after the tree has fallen or been felled. **2.** A part, as of a branch, limb, or tooth, remaining after the main part has been cut away, broken off, or worn down. **3. a. stumps.** *Informal.* The legs. **b.** An artificial leg. **4.** A short, thickset person. **5.** A heavy footfall. **6.** A place or an occasion used for political or campaign oratory. **7.** A short, pointed roll of leather or paper or wad of rubber for rubbing on a charcoal or pencil drawing to shade or soften it. **8.** *Sports.* In cricket, any one of the three upright sticks in a wicket. *—tr.v.* **stumped, stump·ing, stumps. 1.** To reduce to a stump. **2.** To clear stumps from: *stump a field.* **3.** To stub (a toe or foot). **4.** To traverse (a district) making political speeches: *a candidate stumping the state.* **5.** To shade (a drawing) with a stump. **6.** *Informal.* To challenge (someone); defy. **7.** *Informal.* To bring to a halt; baffle. *—idiom.* **up a stump.** In a quandary. [ME *stumpe* < MLG *stump.*] **—stump'er** *n.* **—stump'i·ness** *n.* **—stump'y** *adj.*

stump·age (stŭm'pĭj) *n.* **1.** Standing timber regarded as a commodity. **2.** The value of standing timber. **3.** The right to cut standing timber.

stun (stŭn) *tr.v.* **stunned, stun·ning, stuns. 1.** To daze or render senseless, as by a blow. **2.** To overwhelm or daze with a loud noise. **3.** To stupefy, as with the emotional impact of an experience; astound. *—n.* A blow or shock that stupefies. [ME *stonen* < OFr. *estoner* < VLat. **extonare* : Lat. *ex-* (intensive) + Lat. *tonare,* to thunder.]

stung (stŭng) *v.* Past tense and past participle of **sting.**

stunk (stŭngk) *v.* Past participle and a past tense of **stink.**

stun·ner (stŭn'ər) *n.* **1.** One that stuns. **2.** *Informal.* An exceptionally good-looking person.

stun·ning (stŭn'ĭng) *adj.* **1.** Causing or capable of causing loss of consciousness or emotional shock. **2.** Of a strikingly attractive appearance. **—stun'ning·ly** *adv.*

stunt[1] (stŭnt) *tr.v.* **stunt·ed, stunt·ing, stunts.** To check the growth or development of. *—n.* **1.** One that stunts. **2.** One that is stunted. **3.** A plant disease that causes dwarfing. [Prob. < dial. *stont,* short in duration, of Scand. orig.] **—stunt'ed·ness** *n.*

stunt[2] (stŭnt) *n.* **1.** A feat displaying unusual strength, skill, or daring. **2.** Something of an unusual nature done for publicity. *—intr.v.* **stunt·ed, stunt·ing, stunts.** To perform a stunt. [Orig. unknown.]

stunt box *n.* An electronic device designed to control the nonprinting functions of a communications terminal.

stunt person *n.* A person who substitutes for an actor in scenes requiring physical prowess or involving physical risk.

stu·pa (sto͞o'pə) *n.* A tope[3]. [Skt. *stūpaḥ,* summit.]

stupe (sto͞op, styo͞op) *n.* A hot medicated compress. [ME < Lat. *stuppa,* tow < Gk. *stuppē.*]

stu·pe·fa·cient (sto͞o'pə-fā'shənt, styo͞o'-) *adj.* Inducing stupor; stupefying. *—n.* A drug that induces stupor, as a narcotic. [Lat. *stupefaciens, stupefacient-,* pr.part. of *stupefacere,* to stupefy.]

stu·pe·fac·tion (sto͞o'pə-făk'shən, styo͞o'-) *n.* **1.** The act of stupefying. **2.** The state of being stupefied. **3.** Great astonishment or consternation.

stu·pe·fac·tive (sto͞o'pə-făk'tĭv, styo͞o'-) *adj. & n.* Stupefacient.

stu·pe·fy (sto͞o'pə-fī', styo͞o'-) *tr.v.* **-fied, -fy·ing, -fies. 1.** To dull the senses of; put into a stupor. **2.** To amaze; astonish. [OFr. *stupefier* < Lat. *stupefacere* : *stupēre,* to be stunned + *facere,* to make.] **—stu'pe·fi'er** *n.*

stu·pen·dous (sto͞o-pĕn'dəs, styo͞o-) *adj.* **1.** Of astounding volume, degree, or size; tremendous. **2.** Eliciting astonishment; amazing. [Lat. *stupendus,* gerund. of *stupēre,* to be stunned.] **—stu·pen'dous·ly** *adv.* **—stu·pen'dous·ness** *n.*

stu·pid (sto͞o'pĭd, styo͞o'-) *adj.* **-er, -est. 1.** Slow to apprehend; dumb. **2.** Showing a lack of intelligence. **3.** Dazed or stunned. **4.** *Informal.* Pointless; worthless: *a stupid job.* *—n. Informal.* A stupid person. [Fr. *stupide* < Lat. *stupidus* < *stupēre,* to be stunned.] **—stu'pid·ly** *adv.* **—stu'pid·ness** *n.*

Synonyms: *stupid, dumb, slow, dull, obtuse, dense, crass.* These adjectives mean lacking in mental acuity. *Slow* and the informal *dumb* imply chronic sluggishness of perception or understanding; *stupid* and *dull* occasionally suggest a merely temporary state. *Stupid* and *dumb* also can refer to individual actions that are extremely foolish. *Obtuse* implies insensitivity or unreceptiveness to instruction. *Dense* suggests a mind that is virtually impenetrable or incapable of grasping even elementary ideas. *Crass* refers especially to stupidity marked by coarseness or tastelessness.

stu·pid·i·ty (sto͞o-pĭd'ĭ-tē, styo͞o-) *n., pl.* **-ties. 1.** The quality or fact of being stupid. **2.** A stupid act, remark, or idea.

stu·por (sto͞o'pər, styo͞o'-) *n.* **1.** A state of reduced sensibility; torpor. **2.** Mental confusion; daze. [ME < Lat. *stupēre,* to be stunned.] **—stu'por·ous** *adj.*

stur·dy (stûr'dē) *adj.* **-di·er, -di·est. 1.** Substantially built; strong. **2.** Stalwart; robust. **3.** Vigorous; lusty: *"We admire Chaucer for his sturdy English wit"* (Thoreau). *—n.* The gid. [ME < OFr. *estourdi,* stunned, p.part. of *estourir,* to stun.] **—stur'di·ly** *adv.* **—stur'di·ness** *n.*

sturgeon

stur·geon (stûr'jən) *n.* Any of various large freshwater and marine fishes of the family Acipenseridae, of the Northern Hemisphere, having edible flesh and roe valued as a source of caviar. [ME < OFr. *estourgeon,* of Germanic orig.]

Sturm und Drang (shto͝orm' o͝ont drăng') *n.* **1.** A late 18th-century German romantic literary movement, the works of which typically depicted the impulsive man struggling against conventional society. **2.** Turmoil; ferment. [G., storm and stress, after *Sturm und Drang,* a drama by Friedrich Maximilian von Klinger (1752–1831).]

stut·ter (stŭt'ər) *v.* **-tered, -ter·ing, -ters.** *—intr.* To speak with a spasmodic hesitation, prolongation, or repetition of sounds. *—tr.* To utter or say with or as if with a stutter. *—n.* The act or habit of stuttering. [Freq. of dial. E. *stut,* to stutter < ME *stutten.*] **—stut'ter·er** *n.* **—stut'ter·ing·ly** *adv.*

St. Vi·tus' dance also **St. Vi·tus's dance** (sānt'vī'təs-ĭz) *n. Pathol.* Chorea. [After *St. Vitus,* a 3rd-cent. child martyr.]

sty[1] (stī) *n., pl.* **sties. 1.** An enclosure for swine. **2.** A filthy place. —*v.* **stied, sty·ing, sties.** —*tr.* To shut up in a sty. —*intr.* To live in a sty. [ME < OE *stig.*]

sty[2] (stī) *n., pl.* **sties.** Inflammation of one or more sebaceous glands of an eyelid. [Short for dial. *styan* < ME **styan* < OE *stīgend* < *stīgan,* to rise.]

styg·i·an also **Styg·i·an** (stĭj'ē-ən) *adj.* **1.** Of or pertaining to the river Styx. **2. a.** Gloomy and dark. **b.** Infernal; hellish. [Lat. *Stygius* < Gk. *Stugios* < *Stux,* Styx.]

styl– *pref.* Variant of **stylo-.**

sty·lar (stī'lər, -lär') *adj.* **1.** Of, pertaining to, or resembling a stylus. **2.** *Biol.* Of or pertaining to a style.

sty·late (stī'lāt') *adj.* Having a style or styles.

style (stīl) *n.* **1.** The way in which something is said, done, expressed, or performed: *a style of speech and writing.* **2.** The combination of distinctive features of literary or artistic expression, execution, or performance characterizing a particular person, group, school, or era. **3.** Sort; type: *a style of furniture.* **4.** A quality of imagination and individuality expressed in one's actions and tastes. **5. a.** A comfortable and elegant mode of existence: *living in style.* **b.** A particular mode of living: *the style of a gentleman.* **6. a.** The fashion of the moment, esp. of dress; vogue: *out of style.* **b.** A particular fashion: *the style of the 1920s.* **7.** A customary manner of presenting printed material, including usage, punctuation, spelling, typography, and arrangement. **8.** Form of address; title. **9.** A slender, pointed writing instrument used by the ancients on wax tablets. **10.** An implement used for etching or engraving. **11.** The needle of a phonograph. **12.** The gnomon of a sundial. **13.** *Bot.* The usually slender part of a pistil, rising from the ovary and tipped by the stigma. **14.** *Zool.* A slender, tubular, or bristlelike process. **15.** *Obs.* A pen. **16.** A surgical probing instrument; stylet. —*tr.v.* **styled, styl·ing, styles. 1.** To call or name; designate: *George VI styled his brother the Duke of Windsor.* **2.** To make consistent with rules of style: *style a manuscript.* **3.** To give style to: *style hair.* [ME < OFr. < Lat. *stilus.*] —**styl'er** *n.*

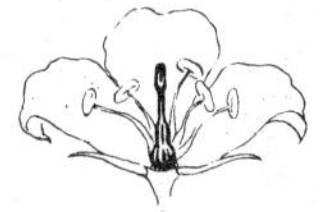

style

style book *n.* A book giving rules and examples of usage, punctuation, and typography, used in the preparation of copy for publication.

sty·let (stī-lĕt', stī'lĭt) *n.* **1.** A slender, pointed instrument or weapon, such as a stiletto. **2.** A surgical probe. **3.** *Zool.* A small, stiff, needlelike process in some invertebrates. [Fr. < Ital. *stiletto,* stiletto. —see STILETTO.]

sty·li (stī'lī') *n.* A plural of **stylus.**

styli– *pref.* Variant of **stylo-.**

sty·li·form (stī'lə-fôrm') *adj.* Having the shape of a style.

styl·ish (stī'lĭsh) *adj.* Conforming to the current fashion; modish. —**styl'ish·ly** *adv.* —**styl'ish·ness** *n.*

styl·ist (stī'lĭst) *n.* **1.** A writer or speaker who cultivates an artful literary style. **2.** A designer of or consultant on styles in decorating, dress, or beauty.

sty·lis·tic (stī-lĭs'tĭk) *adj.* Of or relating to style, esp. literary style. —**sty·lis'ti·cal·ly** *adv.*

sty·lite (stī'līt') *n.* One of a number of early Christian ascetics who lived unsheltered on the tops of high pillars. [LGk. *stulitēs* < Gk. *stulos,* pillar.] —**sty·lit'ic** (-lĭt'ĭk) *adj.* —**sty'lit·ism** (stī'līt'ĭz-əm) *n.*

styl·ize (stī'līz') *tr.v.* **-ized, -iz·ing, -iz·es. 1.** To conform or restrict to a particular style. **2.** To represent conventionally; conventionalize: *"An air of fastidious, stylized melancholy"* (Elizabeth Bowen). —**styl'i·za'tion** *n.* —**styl'iz'er** *n.*

stylo– or **styli–** or **styl–** *pref.* Style: *stylograph.* [< Lat. *stilus,* stake, stem, style.]

sty·lo·bate (stī'lə-bāt') *n. Archit.* The immediate foundation of a row of classical columns. [Lat. *stylobata* < Gk. *stulobatēs* : *stulos,* pillar + *bainein,* to walk.]

sty·lo·graph (stī'lə-grăf') *n.* A fountain pen having a tubular writing point instead of a nib.

sty·log·ra·phy (stī-lŏg'rə-fē) *n.* The art or a method of etching, engraving, or writing with a style. —**sty'lo·graph'ic** (-lə-grăf'ĭk), **sty'lo·graph'i·cal** *adj.*

sty·loid (stī'loid') *adj.* Slender and pointed.

sty·lo·lite (stī'lə-līt') *n.* A small columnar rock development in limestone and other calcareous rocks that is at right angles to the bed, of irregular cross section, and has striated sides. [Gk. *stulos,* pillar + -LITE.]

sty·lo·po·di·um (stī'lə-pō'dē-əm) *n., pl.* **-di·a** (-dē-ə). An enlargement at the base of the style of certain flowers.

sty·lus (stī'ləs) *n., pl.* **-lus·es** or **-li** (-lī'). **1.** A sharp, pointed instrument used for writing, marking, or engraving. **2.** A phonograph needle. **3.** A sharp, pointed tool used for cutting record grooves. [Lat. *stilus.*]

sty·mie also **sty·my** (stī'mē) —*tr.v.* **-mied, -mie·ing, -mies** also **-mied, -my·ing, -mies.** To block; thwart. —*n.* **1.** An obstacle or obstruction. **2.** A situation in golf in which an opponent's ball obstructs the line of play of one's own ball on the putting green. [Orig. unknown.]

styp·sis (stĭp'sĭs) *n.* The action or application of a styptic. [LLat. < Gk. *stupsis* < *stuphein,* to contract.]

styp·tic (stĭp'tĭk) also **styp·ti·cal** (-tĭ-kəl) *adj.* **1.** Contracting the tissues or blood vessels; astringent. **2.** Tending to check bleeding; hemostatic. —*n.* A styptic drug or substance. [ME *stiptik* < LLat. *stypticus* < Gk. *stuptikos* < *stuphein,* to contract.] —**styp·tic'i·ty** (-tĭs'ĭ-tē) *n.*

styptic pencil *n.* A short medicated stick, often of alum, applied to a cut to check bleeding.

sty·rax (stī'răks) *n.* A storax (senses 2, 3).

sty·rene (stī'rēn') *n.* A colorless oily liquid, C_8H_8, the monomer for polystyrene. [< Lat. *styrax,* storax. —see STORAX.]

Sty·ro·foam (stī'rə-fōm'). A trademark for a light, resilient polystyrene plastic.

Styx (stĭks) *n. Gk. Myth.* One of the rivers of Hades, across which the souls of the dead are ferried. [Lat. < Gk. *Stux.*]

su·a·ble (sōō'ə-bəl) *adj.* Legally subject to a court suit. —**su'a·bil'i·ty** *n.*

sua·sion (swā'zhən) *n.* Persuasion: *moral suasion.* [ME < Lat. *suasio* < *suadēre,* to persuade.] —**sua'sive** (-sĭv, -zĭv) *adj.* —**sua'sive·ly** *adv.* —**sua'sive·ness** *n.*

suave (swäv) *adj.* Smoothly gracious in social manner; urbane. [OFr., agreeable < Lat. *suavis.*] —**suave'ly** *adv.* —**suave'ness, suav'i·ty** (swä'vĭ-tē) *n.*

Synonyms: *suave, smooth, urbane, diplomatic, politic.* These adjectives refer to a controlled or refined manner. *Suave* suggests a polished exterior and outward sophistication. *Smooth* stresses conscious, sometimes excessive effort to avoid conflict with others. *Urbane* implies a high degree of refinement together with the assurance that comes from wide social experience. *Diplomatic* especially suggests tact in handling difficult situations, and *politic* adds to this the implication of artful management, sagacity, or shrewdness in gaining an end.

sub (sŭb) *n. Informal.* **1.** A submarine. **2.** A substitute. **3.** *Regional.* A hero (sense 5). —*intr.v.* **subbed, sub·bing, subs.** To act as a substitute.

sub– *pref.* **1.** Below; under; beneath: *subsoil.* **2. a.** Subordinate; secondary: *subplot.* **b.** Subdivision: *subregion.* **3.** Less than completely or normally; nearly; almost: *subhuman.* [Lat. < *sub,* under, below.]

sub·ab·dom·i·nal (sŭb'ăb-dŏm'ə-nəl) *adj.* Located or occurring below the abdomen.

sub·a·cute (sŭb'ə-kyōōt') *adj.* Somewhat acute. Used of a disease. —**sub'a·cute'ly** *adv.*

sub·ad·dress (sŭb'ə-drĕs') *n.* A section of a computer input/output device accessible through an order code.

sub·aer·i·al (sŭb'âr'ē-əl) *adj.* Located or occurring on or near the surface of the earth.

sub·al·pine (sŭb'ăl'pīn') *adj.* **1.** Of or pertaining to regions at or near the foot of the Alps. **2.** Of, designating, or growing or living in mountainous regions just below the timberline.

sub·al·tern (sŭb'ôl'tərn, sŭb'əl-tûrn') *adj.* **1.** Lower in position or rank; secondary. **2.** *Chiefly Brit.* Holding a military rank just below that of captain. **3.** *Logic.* In the relation of a particular proposition to a universal with the same subject, predicate, and quality. —*n.* **1.** A subordinate. **2.** *Chiefly Brit.* A subaltern officer. **3.** *Logic.* A subaltern proposition. [LLat. *subalternus* : Lat. *sub-,* below + Lat. *alternus,* alternate < *alter,* other.]

sub·al·ter·nate (sŭb'ôl'tər-nĭt) *adj.* **1.** Subordinate. **2.** Arranged in an alternating pattern but tending to become opposite. Used of leaves. —**sub·al'ter·na'tion** *n.*

sub·ant·arc·tic (sŭb'ănt-ärk'tĭk, -är'tĭk) *adj.* Of or resembling regions just north of the Antarctic Circle.

sub·a·pi·cal (sŭb'ā'pĭ-kəl) *adj.* Located below or near an apex. —**sub'a'pi·cal·ly** *adv.*

sub·a·que·ous (sŭb'ā'kwē-əs, -ăk'wē-) *adj.* **1.** Formed or adapted for underwater use or operation; submarine. **2.** Found or occurring under water.

sub·arc·tic (sŭb'ärk'tĭk, -är'tĭk) *adj.* Of or resembling regions just south of the Arctic Circle.

sub·ar·id (sŭb'ăr'ĭd) *adj.* Somewhat arid; moderately dry.

sub·a·tom·ic (sŭb'ə-tŏm'ĭk) *adj.* **1.** Of or pertaining to the constituents of the atom. **2.** Having dimensions or participating in reactions characteristic of the constituents of the atom.

sub·au·di·tion (sŭb'ô-dĭsh'ən) *n.* **1.** The act of understanding and mentally supplying a word or thought that has been implied but not expressed. **2.** A word or thought supplied by subaudition. [LLat. *subauditio,* supplying a missing word < *subaudire,* to supply an omitted word : Lat. *sub-,* below + Lat. *audire,* to hear.]

sub·base (sŭb'bās') *n.* The lowermost front strip or molding of a baseboard.

sub·base·ment (sŭb'bās'mənt) *n.* A story or floor beneath a main basement of a building.

sub·bass (sŭb'bās') *n. Mus.* A pedal stop on an organ that produces the lowest tones, having 16 or 32 feet.

sub·cal·i·ber (sŭb'kăl'ə-bər) *adj.* **1.** Smaller in caliber than the barrel of the gun from which it was fired. Used of projectiles. **2.** Of or pertaining to subcaliber projectiles.

sub·car·ri·er (sŭb'kăr'ē-ər) *n.* A section of a transmitted wave used to modify the information-carrying section of the wave.

sub·car·ti·lag·i·nous (sŭb'kär-tə-lăj'ə-nəs) *adj.* **1.** Located beneath a cartilage. **2.** Partly cartilaginous.

sub·ce·les·tial (sŭb'sĭ-lĕs'chəl) *adj.* **1.** Lower than celestial; terrestrial. **2.** Mundane.

sub·chas·er (sŭb'chā'sər) *n.* A submarine chaser.

sub·class (sŭb'klăs') *n.* **1.** A subdivision of a class. **2.** A taxonomic category ranking between a class and an order.

sub·cla·vi·an (sŭb'klā'vē-ən) *adj. Anat.* **1.** Situated beneath the clavicle. **2.** Of or relating to a subclavian part. **3.** Of or

pertaining to the subclavian artery or vein. —*n.* A subclavian structure, as a nerve or muscle. [NLat. *subclavius* : Lat. *sub-*, below + Lat. *clavis*, key.]
subclavian artery *n.* A short part of a major artery originating under the clavicle and continuous with the axillary artery extending to the upper extremities or forelimbs.
subclavian vein *n.* A part of a major vein of the upper extremities or forelimbs that is continuous with the axillary vein and is situated beneath the clavicle.
sub·cli·max (sŭb'klī'măks') *n.* A stage in the ecological succession of a plant or animal community immediately preceding a climax, and often persisting because of the effects of fire, flood, or other conditions. —**sub'cli·mac'tic** (-klī-măk'tĭk) *adj.*
sub·clin·i·cal (sŭb-klĭn'ĭ-kəl) *adj.* Of or pertaining to a disease or condition in which no characteristic symptoms are manifested. —**sub·clin'i·cal·ly** *adv.*
sub·com·mit·tee (sŭb'kə-mĭt'ē) *n.* A subordinate committee composed of members appointed from the main committee.
sub·com·pact (sŭb-kŏm'păkt') *n.* An automobile smaller than a compact.
sub·con·scious (sŭb'kŏn'shəs) *adj.* Not wholly conscious but capable of being made conscious. —**sub·con'scious** *n.* —**sub'con'scious·ly** *adv.* —**sub'con'scious·ness** *n.*
sub·con·ti·nent (sŭb'kŏn'tə-nənt) *n.* A large land mass, as India, that is separate to some degree but still part of a continent.
sub·con·tract (sŭb'kŏn'trăkt') *n.* A contract that assigns some of the obligations of a prior contract to another party. —*v.* (sŭb'kŏn'trăkt', sŭb'kən-trăkt') **-tract·ed, -tract·ing, -tracts.** —*tr.* To make a subcontract for. —*intr.* To make a subcontract.
sub·con·trac·tor (sŭb'kŏn'trăk'tər, sŭb'kən-trăk'tər) *n.* One that enters into a subcontract and assumes some of the obligations of the primary contractor.
sub·cor·tex (sŭb'kôr'tĕks) *n., pl.* **-ti·ces** (-tĭ-sēz'). The portion of the brain immediately below the cerebral cortex. —**sub'cor'ti·cal** (-tĭ-kəl) *adj.* —**sub'cor'ti·cal·ly** *adv.*
sub·cul·ture (sŭb'kŭl'chər) *n.* **1.** One culture of microorganisms derived from another. **2.** A cultural subgroup differentiated by status, ethnic background, residence, religion, or other factors that functionally unify the group and act collectively on each member.
sub·cu·ta·ne·ous (sŭb'kyōō-tā'nē-əs) *adj.* Located or found just beneath the skin. —**sub'cu·ta'ne·ous·ly** *adv.*
sub·cu·tis (sŭb-kyōō'tĭs) *n.* A layer of connective tissue beneath the dermis.
sub·dea·con (sŭb'dē'kən) *n.* **1.** A clergyman ranking just below a deacon. **2.** A cleric who acts as assistant to the deacon at High Mass. [ME < LLat. *subdiaconus*, partial transl. of LGk. *hupodiakonos* : Gk. *hupo-*, below + Gk. *diakonos*, attendant.]
sub·deb (sŭb'dĕb') *n. Informal.* A subdebutante.
sub·deb·u·tante (sŭb'dĕb'yə-tänt') *n.* **1.** A teen-age girl approaching her debut. **2.** A girl in her middle teens.
sub·di·ac·o·nate (sŭb'dī-ăk'ə-nĭt) *n.* The office, order, or rank of subdeacon. [LLat. *subdiaconatus* < *subdiaconus*, subdeacon.] —**sub'di·ac'o·nal** *adj.*
sub·di·vide (sŭb'dĭ-vīd', sŭb'dĭ-vīd') *v.* **-vid·ed, -vid·ing, -vides.** —*tr.* **1.** To divide a part or parts of into smaller parts. **2.** To divide into a number of parts, esp. to divide (land) into lots. —*intr.* To form into subdivisions. [ME *subdividen* < LLat. *subdividere* : Lat. *sub-*, secondary + Lat. *dividere*, to divide.] —**sub'di·vid'er** *n.*
sub·di·vi·sion (sŭb'dĭ-vĭzh'ən, sŭb'dĭ-vĭzh'ən) *n.* **1.** The act or process of subdividing. **2.** A subdivided part. **3.** An area composed of subdivided lots. —**sub'di·vi'sion·al** *adj.*
sub·dom·i·nant (sŭb'dŏm'ə-nənt) *n. Mus.* The fourth tone of a diatonic scale, next below the dominant.
sub·duc·tion (səb-dŭk'shən) *n.* A geological process in which one edge of crustal plate descends below another. [LLat. *subductio*, act of taking away < Lat. *subducere*, to withdraw : *sub-*, under + *ducere*, to lead.] —**sub·duct'** *v.* **(-duct·ed, -duct·ing, -ducts).**
sub·due (səb-dōō', -dyōō') *tr.v.* **-dued, -du·ing, -dues.** **1.** To conquer and subjugate; vanquish. **2.** To quiet or bring under control by physical force or persuasion; make tractable. **3.** To make less intense or prominent; tone down: *A vote of approval subdued his anger.* **4.** To bring (land) under cultivation. [ME *subduen* < OFr. *suduire*, to seduce < Lat. *subducere*, to withdraw : *sub-*, away + *ducere*, to lead.] —**sub·du'a·ble** *adj.* —**sub·du'er** *n.*
sub·dur·al (səb-dŏŏr'əl, -dyŏŏr'-) *adj.* Located or occurring beneath the dura mater.
sub·e·qua·to·ri·al (sŭb'ē-kwə-tôr'ē-əl, -tōr'-, -ĕk-wə-) *adj.* Belonging to a region adjacent to the equatorial area.
su·ber·ic acid (sōō-bĕr'ĭk) *n.* A colorless crystalline dibasic acid, $C_8H_{14}O_4$, used in drug synthesis and plastics manufacture. [Fr. *subérique* (< Lat. *suber*, cork) + ACID.]
su·ber·in (sōō'bər-ĭn) *n.* A waxy waterproof substance present in the cell walls of cork tissue in plants. [Fr. *subérine* < Lat. *suber*, cork.]
su·ber·i·za·tion (sōō'bər-ĭ-zā'shən) *n.* Formation of suberin in the walls of plant cells, thus converting them into cork tissue.
su·ber·ize (sōō'bə-rīz') *tr.v.* **-ized, -iz·ing, -iz·es.** To cause to undergo suberization. [< Lat. *suber*, cork.]
su·ber·ose (sōō'bə-rōs') also **su·ber·ous** (-bər-əs) *adj.* Of, pertaining to, or resembling cork or cork tissue. [NLat. *suberosus* < Lat. *suber*, cork.]
sub·fam·i·ly (sŭb'făm'ə-lē) *n., pl.* **-lies.** **1.** *Biol.* A taxonomic category ranking between a family and a genus. **2.** *Ling.* A division of languages below a family and above a branch.
sub·field (sŭb'fēld') *n.* **1.** A mathematical field that is a subject of another field. **2.** A subdivision of a field of study.
sub·freez·ing (sŭb-frē'zĭng) *adj.* Below freezing.
sub·ge·nus (sŭb'jē'nəs) *n., pl.* **-gen·e·ra** (-jĕn'ər-ə). *Biol.* An occasionally used taxonomic category ranking between a genus and a species. —**sub'ge·ner'ic** (-jə-nĕr'ĭk) *adj.*
sub·gla·cial (sŭb'glā'shəl) *adj.* Formed or deposited beneath a glacier. —**sub'gla'cial·ly** *adv.*
sub·group (sŭb'grōōp') *n.* **1.** A distinct group within a group. **2.** *Math.* A nonempty subset of a group. **3.** A subordinate group. **4.** *Biol.* One of the taxonomic divisions of an order.
sub·gum (sŭb'gŭm') *n.* A Chinese dish of mixed vegetables. [Cantonese *shap kam*, mixture.]
sub·har·mon·ic (sŭb'här-mŏn'ĭk) *adj.* Of, pertaining to, or being a wave with a frequency that is a fraction of a fundamental.
sub·head (sŭb'hĕd') *n.* **1.** Also **sub·head·ing** (-hĕd'ĭng). The heading or title of a subdivision of a printed subject. **2.** A subordinate heading or title.
sub·hu·man (sŭb'hyōō'mən) *adj.* **1.** Below the human race in evolutionary development. **2.** Not fully human.
sub·in·dex (sŭb'ĭn'dĕks) *n., pl.* **-di·ces** (-dĭ-sēz'). *Math.* A subscript.
sub·in·feu·date (sŭb'ĭn-fyōō'dāt') also **sub·in·feud** (-fyōōd') *tr.v.* **-dat·ed, -dat·ing, -dates** also **-feud·ed, -feud·ing, -feuds.** To lease (lands) by subinfeudation.
sub·in·feu·da·tion (sŭb'ĭn-fyōō-dā'shən) *n.* **1.** The sublease of a portion of a feudal estate by a vassal to a subtenant who pays fealty to the vassal. **2.** The lands leased in subinfeudation. —**sub'in·feu'da·to'ry** (-fyōō'də-tôr'ē, -tōr'ē) *adj.*
sub·ir·ri·gate (sŭb'ĭr'ĭ-gāt') *tr.v.* **-gat·ed, -gat·ing, -gates.** To irrigate from beneath, as by underground pipes. —**sub'ir·ri·ga'tion** *n.*
su·bi·to (sōō'bē-tō') *adv. Mus.* Quickly; suddenly. Used as a direction. [Ital. < Lat., unexpectedly < *subire*, to come secretly : *sub-*, below + *ire*, to come.]
sub·ja·cent (sŭb'jā'sənt) *adj.* **1.** Located beneath or below; underlying. **2.** Lying at a lower level but not directly beneath. [Lat. *subjacens*, *subjacent-*, pr.part. of *subjacēre*, to lie beneath : *sub-*, beneath + *jacēre*, to lie] —**sub'ja'cen·cy** *n.*
sub·ject (sŭb'jĭkt) *adj.* **1.** Under the power or authority of another: *subject to the law.* **2.** Prone; disposed: *subject to colds.* **3.** Liable to incur or receive; exposed: *subject to misinterpretation.* **4.** Contingent or dependent: *subject to approval.* —*n.* **1.** A person under the rule of another, esp. one who owes allegiance to a government or ruler: *a subject of the Crown.* **2. a.** A person or thing concerning which something is said or done; topic. **b.** The primary theme of a work of art. **c.** A theme of a musical composition, esp. a fugue. **3.** A course or area of study. **4.** A basis for action; cause. **5. a.** One that experiences or is subjected to something: *made her the subject of ridicule.* **b.** One that is the object of clinical study. **c.** A corpse intended for study and dissection. **6.** *Gram.* A word or phrase in a sentence that denotes the doer of the action, the receiver of the action in passive constructions, or that which is described or identified. **7.** *Logic.* The term of a proposition about which something is affirmed or denied. **8.** *Philos.* **a.** The essential nature or substance of something as distinguished from its attributes. **b.** The mind or thinking part as distinguished from the object of thought. —*tr.v.* (səb-jĕkt') **-ject·ed, -ject·ing, -jects.** **1.** To submit for consideration. **2.** To submit to the authority of. **3.** To render liable to something; expose: *was subjected to infection.* **4.** To cause to experience: *was subjected to torture.* **5.** To subjugate; subdue. [ME < OFr. *subget* < Lat. *subjectus* < *subicere*, to subject : *sub-*, below + *jacere*, to throw.] —**sub·jec'tion** (səb-jĕk'shən) *n.*

Synonyms: *subject, matter, topic, theme.* These nouns relate to the principal idea of any discourse or creative work. *Subject* denotes the thing represented, discussed, or otherwise treated. *Matter* refers somewhat less specifically to the material involved in the work. *Topic* is either interchangeable with *subject* or else denotes a division of it. *Theme* is sometimes used in the sense of any of the foregoing terms but often refers specifically to a basic idea that underlies or unifies the material treated and either summarizes or interprets it.

sub·jec·tive (səb-jĕk'tĭv) *adj.* **1. a.** Proceeding from or taking place within an individual's mind such as to be unaffected by the external world. **b.** Particular to a given individual; personal: *subjective experience.* **2.** Moodily introspective. **3.** Existing only in the mind; illusory. **4.** *Psychol.* Existing only within the experiencer's mind and incapable of external verification. **5.** *Med.* Designating a symptom or condition perceived by the patient and not by the examiner. **6.** Expressing or bringing into prominence the individuality of the artist or author. **7.** *Gram.* Designating the nominative case. **8.** Pertaining to the real nature of something; essential. **—sub·jec'tive·ly** *adv.* **—sub·jec'tive·ness, sub'jec·tiv'i·ty** (sŭb'jĕk-tĭv'ĭ-tē) *n.*

sub·jec·tiv·ism (səb-jĕk'tə-vĭz'əm) *n.* **1.** The quality of being subjective. **2. a.** The doctrine that all knowledge is restricted to the conscious self and its sensory states. **b.** A theory or doctrine that emphasizes the subjective elements in experience. **3.** The theory that individual conscience is the only valid standard of moral judgment. **—sub·jec'tiv·ist** *n.* **—sub·jec'tiv·is'tic** *adj.*

subject matter *n.* Matter under consideration in a written work or speech; theme.

sub·join (səb-join') *tr.v.* **-joined, -join·ing, -joins.** To add at the end; append. [OFr. *subjoindre* < Lat. *subjungere* : *sub-*, under + *jungere,* to join.]

sub·join·der (səb-join'dər) *n.* Something subjoined. [SUBJOIN + *-der,* as in *rejoinder.*]

sub ju·di·ce (sŭb jo͞o'dĭ-sē', yo͞o'dĭ-kā') *adv. Law.* Under judicial deliberation; before a judge or court of law. [Lat.]

sub·ju·gate (sŭb'jə-gāt') *tr.v.* **-gat·ed, -gat·ing, -gates. 1.** To bring under dominion; subdue. **2.** To make subservient; enslave. [ME *subjugaten* < Lat. *subjugare* : *sub-*, under + *jugum,* yoke.] **—sub'ju·ga'tion** *n.* **—sub'ju·ga'tor** *n.*

sub·junc·tion (səb-jŭngk'shən) *n.* **1.** The act of subjoining or the condition of being subjoined. **2.** Something that is subjoined. [LLat. *subjunctio* < *subjungere,* to subjoin.]

sub·junc·tive (səb-jŭngk'tĭv) *adj.* Designating a verb form or set of forms used in English to express a contingent or hypothetical action. *—n.* **1.** The subjunctive mood. **2.** A subjunctive construction. [LLat. *subjunctivus* < Lat. *subjungere,* to subordinate, subjoin.]

sub·king·dom (sŭb'kĭng'dəm) *n. Biol.* A former taxonomic category constituting a major division of a kingdom.

sub·lease (sŭb'lēs') *tr.v.* **-leased, -leas·ing, -leas·es. 1.** To sublet (property). **2.** To rent (property) under a sublease. *—n.* (sŭb'lēs'). A lease of property granted by a lessee.

sub·let (sŭb'lĕt') *tr.v.* **-let, -let·ting, -lets. 1.** To rent (property one holds by lease) to another. **2.** To subcontract (work). *—n.* (sŭb'lĕt'). *Informal.* Property, esp. an apartment, rented by a tenant to another party.

sub·le·thal (sŭb-lē'thəl) *adj.* Less than lethal. **—sub·le'thal·ly** *adv.*

sub·li·mate (sŭb'lə-māt') *v.* **-mat·ed, -mat·ing, -mates.** *—tr.* **1.** *Chem.* To cause (a solid or a gas) to change state without becoming a liquid. **2.** *Psychol.* To modify the natural expression of (an instinctual impulse) in a socially acceptable manner. *—intr.* To transform directly from the solid to the gaseous state or from the gaseous to the solid state without becoming a liquid. [Lat. *sublimare, sublimat-,* to raise < *sublimis,* uplifted.]

submarine

sub·li·ma·tion (sŭb'lə-mā'shən) *n.* **1.** The act or process of sublimating. **2.** That which has been sublimated.

sub·lime (sə-blīm') *adj.* **1.** Characterized by nobility; majestic. **2. a.** Of high spiritual, moral, or intellectual worth. **b.** Not to be excelled; supreme. **3.** Inspiring awe; impressive. **4.** *Obs.* Of lofty appearance or bearing; haughty. **5.** *Archaic.* Raised aloft; set high. *—n.* **1.** Something that is sublime. **2.** The ultimate example of something. *—v.* **-limed, -lim·ing, -limes.** *—tr.* **1.** To render sublime. **2.** *Chem.* To cause to sublimate. *—intr. Chem.* To sublimate. [Lat. *sublimis,* uplifted.] **—sub·lime'ly** *adv.* **—sub·lime'ness, sub·lim'i·ty** (sə-blĭm'ĭ-tē) *n.*

sub·lim·i·nal (sŭb-lĭm'ə-nəl) *adj. Psychol.* **1.** Below the threshold of conscious perception. Used of stimuli. **2.** Inadequate to produce conscious awareness. [SUB- + Lat. *limen, limin-,* threshold.] **—sub·lim'i·nal·ly** *adv.*

sub·lin·gual (sŭb'lĭng'gwəl) *adj.* Situated beneath or on the underside of the tongue.

sub·lit·to·ral (sŭb'lĭt'ər-əl) *adj.* **1.** Near the seashore. **2.** Shallow and lying between the shoreline and the edge of the continental shelf or ranging in depth to about 50 fathoms.

sub·lu·na·ry (sŭb'lo͞o'nə-rē, sŭb'lo͞o-nĕr'ē) also **sub·lu·nar** (-lo͞o'nər) *adj.* **1.** Situated beneath the moon. **2.** Of this world; earthly. [LLat. *sublunaris* : Lat. *sub-*, beneath + Lat. *luna,* moon.]

sub·lux·a·tion (sŭb'lŭk-sā'shən) *n.* An incomplete dislocation of a bone in a joint.

sub·ma·chine gun (sŭb'mə-shēn') *n.* A lightweight automatic or semiautomatic gun fired from the shoulder or hip.

sub·man·dib·u·lar (sŭb'măn-dĭb'yə-lər) *adj.* Submaxillary.

sub·mar·gin·al (sŭb'mär'jə-nəl) *adj.* **1.** Beneath a margin. **2.** Of low productivity; infertile.

sub·ma·rine (sŭb'mə-rēn', sŭb'mə-rēn') *adj.* Beneath the surface of the water; undersea. *—n.* **1.** A ship capable of operating submerged. **2.** *Slang.* A hero (sense 6).

submarine chaser *n.* A small, fast boat equipped to pursue and attack submarines.

sub·ma·rin·er (sŭb'mə-rē'nər, sŭb'măr'ə-nər) *n.* A member of the crew of a submarine.

sub·max·il·lar·y (sŭb'măk'sə-lĕr'ē) *adj.* **1.** Of or relating to the lower jaw. **2.** Situated beneath the maxilla. *—n., pl.* **-ies.** An anatomical part situated beneath the maxilla, as a gland or nerve.

sub·me·di·ant (sŭb'mē'dē-ənt) *n. Mus.* The sixth tone of a diatonic scale.

sub·merge (səb-mûrj') *v.* **-merged, -merg·ing, -merg·es.** *—tr.* **1.** To place or plunge under water or other liquid. **2.** To cover with water; inundate. **3.** To hide from view; obscure. *—intr.* To go under or as if under water. [Lat. *submergere* : *sub-*, under + *mergere,* to plunge.] **—sub·mer'gence** *n.*

sub·merged (səb-mûrjd') *adj.* **1.** *Bot.* Growing or remaining under water: *submerged leaves.* **2.** Living in poverty or misery. **3.** Hidden.

sub·mer·gi·ble (səb-mûr'jə-bəl) *adj.* Able to be plunged into or to remain under water. **—sub·mer'gi·bil'i·ty** *n.*

sub·merse (səb-mûrs') *tr.v.* **-mersed, -mers·ing, -mers·es.** To submerge. [Lat. *submergere, submers-,* to submerge.] **—sub·mer'sion** (-mûr'zhən, -shən) *n.*

sub·mersed (səb-mûrst') *adj. Bot.* Growing or remaining under water.

sub·mers·i·ble (səb-mûr'sə-bəl) *adj.* Submergible. *—n.* A vessel capable of operating or remaining under water.

sub·mi·cro·scop·ic (sŭb'mī-krə-skŏp'ĭk) *adj.* Too small to be resolved by an optical microscope. **—sub'mi·cro·scop'i·cal·ly** *adv.*

sub·min·i·a·ture (sŭb'mĭn'ē-ə-cho͝or', -chər) *adj.* Smaller than miniature; exceedingly small.

sub·min·i·a·tur·ize (sŭb'mĭn'ē-ə-chə-rīz') *tr.v.* **-ized, -iz·ing, -iz·es.** To make subminiature, esp. to manufacture or design (electronic equipment) in subminiature size. **—sub'min'i·a·tur·i·za'tion** *n.*

sub·miss (səb-mĭs') *adj. Archaic.* **1.** Submissive. **2.** Soft in tone. [Lat. *submissus* < p.part. of *submittere,* to set under. — see SUBMIT.]

sub·mis·sion (səb-mĭsh'ən) *n.* **1. a.** The act of submitting to the power of another. **b.** The state of having submitted. **2.** The state of being submissive or compliant; meekness. **3. a.** The act of submitting something for consideration. **b.** Something thus submitted.

sub·mis·sive (səb-mĭs'ĭv) *adj.* Disposed to submit; docile. **—sub·mis'sive·ly** *adv.* **—sub·mis'sive·ness** *n.*

sub·mit (səb-mĭt') *v.* **-mit·ted, -mit·ting, -mits.** *—tr.* **1.** To yield or surrender (oneself) to the will or authority of another. **2.** To subject to a condition or process. **3.** To commit (something) to the consideration or judgment of another. **4.** To offer as a proposition or contention: *I submit that the terms are entirely unreasonable.* *—intr.* **1.** To yield to the opinion or authority of another; give in. **2.** To allow oneself to be subjected; acquiesce. [ME *submitten* < Lat. *submittere,* to set under : *sub-*, under + *mittere,* to cause to go.] **—sub·mit'tal** *n.* **—sub·mit'ter** *n.*

sub·mon·tane (sŭb'mŏn'tān', -mŏn-tān') *adj.* Located under or at the base of a mountain or mountain range. [LLat. *submontanus* : Lat. *sub-*, under + Lat. *montanus,* mountainous < *mons,* mountain.]

sub·mu·co·sa (sŭb'myo͞o-kō'sə) *n.* A layer of loose connective tissue beneath a mucous membrane. **—sub'mu·co'sal** *adj.* **—sub'mu·co'sal·ly** *adv.*

sub·mul·ti·ple (sŭb'mŭl'tə-pəl) *n.* A number that is an exact divisor of another number.

sub·net (sŭb'nĕt') *n.* A system of interconnections within a communications system that allows the component parts to communicate directly with each other.

sub·nor·mal (sŭb'nôr'məl) *adj.* Less than normal; below the average. *—n.* A person who is subnormal in some respect, as in intelligence or coordination. **—sub'nor·mal'i·ty** (-nôr-măl'ĭ-tē) *n.*

sub·o·ce·an·ic (sŭb'ō-shē-ăn'ĭk) *adj.* Formed, situated, or occurring beneath the ocean or the ocean bed.

sub·or·der (sŭb'ôr'dər) *n.* **1.** *Biol.* A taxonomic category ranking after an order and before a family. **2.** A subdivision of any category termed an order.

sub·or·di·nate (sə-bôr'də-nĭt) *adj.* **1.** Belonging to a lower or inferior class or rank; secondary. **2.** Subject to the authority or control of another. *—n.* One that is subordinate. *—tr.v.* (sə-bôr'də-nāt') **-nat·ed, -nat·ing, -nates. 1.** To put in a lower or inferior rank or class. **2.** To make subservient; subdue. [ME *subordinat* < Med. Lat. *subordinatus,* p.part. of *subordinare,* to put in a lower rank : Lat. *sub-*, below + Lat. *ordinare,* to set in order < *ordo,* order.] **—sub·or'di·nate·ly** *adv.* **—sub·or'di·nate·ness, sub·or'di·na'tion** *n.* **—sub·or'di·na'tive** *adj.*

subordinate clause *n. Gram.* A dependent clause.

subordinate conjunction *n. Gram.* A conjunction, as *that, who, which,* and *where,* that introduces a dependent clause.

sub·or·di·na·tion·ism (sə-bôr'də-nā'shə-nĭz'əm) *n. Theol.* The doctrine that the second and third persons of the Trinity are subordinate to the first person. **—sub·or'di·na'tion·ist** *n.*

sub·orn (sə-bôrn') *tr.v.* **-orned, -orn·ing, -orns. 1. a.** To induce (a person) to commit an unlawful act. **b.** To induce (a person) to commit perjury. **2.** To procure (perjured testimony). [Lat. *subornare* : *sub-*, secretly + *ornare,* to equip.] **—sub'or·na'tion** (sŭb'ôr-nā'shən) *n.* **—sub·orn'er** *n.*

sub·ox·ide (sŭb'ŏk'sīd') *n.* An oxide containing a relatively small amount of oxygen.

sub·phy·lum (sŭb'fī'ləm) *n., pl.* **·la** (-lə). *Biol.* A taxonomic category ranking between a phylum and a class.

sub·plot (sŭb'plŏt') *n.* A subordinate literary plot.

sub·poe·na (sə-pē'nə) *n.* A legal writ requiring appearance in court to give testimony. *—tr.v.* **-naed, -na·ing, -nas.** To

serve or summon with such a writ. [ME *suppena* < Lat. *sub poena,* under a penalty.]
sub·prin·ci·pal (sŭb'prĭn'sə-pəl) *n.* **1.** An assistant school principal. **2.** An auxiliary or bracing rafter in a frame. **3.** *Mus.* An open diapason subbass in an organ.
sub·pro·gram (sŭb'prō'grăm, -grəm) *n.* A computer program contained within another program that operates semi-independently of the encasing program.
sub·re·gion (sŭb'rē'jən) *n.* A subdivision of a region, esp. of an ecological region. **—sub're'gion·al** *adj.*
sub·rep·tion (sŭb-rĕp'shən) *n.* **1.** A calculated misrepresentation through concealment of the facts. **2.** An inference drawn from such a misrepresentation. [Lat. *subreptio,* theft < *subrepere,* to take away secretly : *sub-,* secretly + *rapere,* to take away.] **—sub'rep·ti'tious** (sŭb'rĕp-tĭsh'əs) *adj.*
sub·ring (sŭb'rĭng') *n.* A subset of a mathematical ring that is itself a ring.
sub·ro·gate (sŭb'rō-gāt') *tr.v.* **-gat·ed, -gat·ing, -gates.** To substitute (one person) for another. [Lat. *subrogare, subrogat-* : *sub-,* instead of + *rogare,* to ask.]
sub·ro·ga·tion (sŭb'rō-gā'shən) *n.* The substitution of one person for another, esp. the legal doctrine of substituting one creditor for another.
sub ro·sa (sŭb'rō'zə) *adv.* In secret; privately; confidentially: *held the meeting sub rosa.* [Lat., under the rose (from the practice of hanging a rose over a meeting as a symbol of secrecy).]
sub-ro·sa (səb-rō'zā) *adj.* Intended to be secret, private, or confidential: *a sub-rosa agreement.*
sub·rou·tine (sŭb'ro͞o-tēn') *n.* A set of computer instructions that performs a specific task for a main routine, requiring direction back to the proper place in the main routine on completion of the task.
sub·scap·u·lar (sŭb'skăp'yə-lər) *adj. Anat.* Situated below or on the underside of the scapula. *—n.* A subscapular part, such as an artery or nerve.
sub·scribe (səb-scrīb') *v.* **-scribed, -scrib·ing, -scribes.** *—tr.* **1.** To sign (one's name) at the end of a document. **2.** To sign one's name to in attestation, testimony, or consent: *subscribe a will.* **3.** To pledge or contribute (a sum of money). *—intr.* **1.** To sign one's name. **2.** To affix one's signature to a document as a witness or to show consent. **3.** To express concurrence or approval; assent: *subscribe to a belief.* **4.** To promise to pay or contribute money: *subscribe to a charity.* **5.** To contract to receive and pay for a certain number of issues of a publication. [ME *subscriben* < Lat. *subscribere* : *sub-,* under + *scribere,* to write.] **—sub·scrib'er** *n.*
sub·script (sŭb'skrĭpt') *adj.* Written beneath. *—n.* A distinguishing character or symbol written directly beneath or next to and slightly below a letter or number. [Lat. *subscriptus,* p.part. of *subscribere,* to subscribe.]
sub·scrip·tion (səb-skrĭp'shən) *n.* **1.** The signing of one's name, as to a document. **2.** Something subscribed. **3.** A purchase made by signed order, as for a periodical for a specified period of time or for a series of performances. **4.** Acceptance, as of articles of faith, demonstrated by the signing of one's name. **5. a.** The raising of money from subscribers. **b.** A sum of money subscribed. **—sub·scrip'tive** *adj.* **—sub·scrip'tive·ly** *adv.*
sub·se·quence (sŭb'sĭ-kwĕns', -kwəns) *n.* **1.** Something that is subsequent; sequel. **2.** The fact or quality of being subsequent. **3.** *Math.* A sequence that is contained in another sequence.
sub·se·quent (sŭb'sĭ-kwĕnt', -kwənt) *adj.* Following in time or order; succeeding. [ME < OFr. *subsequent* < Lat. *subsequens,* pr.part. of *subsequi,* to follow close after : *sub-,* after + *sequi,* to follow.] **—sub'se·quent'ly** *adv.* **—sub'se·quent'ness** *n.*
sub·sere (sŭb'sîr') *n. Ecol.* A secondary series of communities that succeeds an interrupted climax community.
sub·serve (səb-sûrv') *tr.v.* **-served, -serv·ing, -serves.** To serve to promote (some end); be useful to; further. [Lat. *subservire : sub-,* under + *servire,* to serve.]
sub·ser·vi·ent (səb-sûr'vē-ənt) *adj.* **1.** Useful as a means or instrument; serving to promote an end. **2.** Subordinate in capacity or function. **3.** Obsequious; servile. [Lat. *subserviens, subservient-,* pr.part. of *subservire,* to subserve.] **—sub·ser'vi·ence, sub·ser'vi·en·cy** *n.* **—sub·ser'vi·ent·ly** *adv.*
sub·set (sŭb'sĕt') *n.* A mathematical set contained within a set.
sub·shell (sŭb'shĕl') *n.* Any of the orbitals making up the electron shell of an atom.
sub·shrub (sŭb'shrŭb') *n.* **1.** A herbaceous plant having a woody lower stem. **2.** A low shrub; undershrub.
sub·side (səb-sīd') *intr.v.* **-sid·ed, -sid·ing, -sides. 1.** To sink to a lower or normal level. **2.** To sink or settle down, as into a sofa. **3.** To sink to the bottom, as a sediment; settle. **4.** To become less agitated or active; abate. [Lat. *subsidere* : *sub-,* down + *sidere,* to settle.] **—sub·si'dence** *n.*
sub·sid·i·ar·y (səb-sĭd'ē-ĕr'ē) *adj.* **1.** Serving to assist or supplement; auxiliary. **2.** Secondary in importance; subordinate. **3.** Of, pertaining to, or of the nature of a subsidy. *—n., pl.* **-ries. 1.** One that is subsidiary. **2.** A subsidiary company. **3.** *Mus.* A theme subordinate to a main theme or subject. [Lat. *subsidiarius* < *subsidium,* support < *subsidere,* to subside.] **—sub·sid'i·ar'i·ly** *adv.*
subsidiary company *n.* A company having more than half of its stock owned by another company.
sub·si·dize (sŭb'sĭ-dīz') *tr.v.* **-dized, -diz·ing, -diz·es. 1.** To assist or support with a subsidy. **2.** To secure the assistance of by granting a subsidy. **—sub'si·di·za'tion** *n.* **—sub'si·diz'er** *n.*
sub·si·dy (sŭb'sĭ-dē) *n., pl.* **-dies. 1.** Monetary assistance granted by a government to a person or a private commercial enterprise. **2.** Financial assistance given by one person or government to another. **3.** Money formerly granted to the British Crown by Parliament. [ME *subsidie* < AN < Lat. *subsidium,* support. —see SUBSIDIARY.]
sub·sist (səb-sĭst') *v.* **-sist·ed, -sist·ing, -sists.** *—intr.* **1. a.** To exist; be. **b.** To remain or continue in existence. **2.** To maintain life; live: *subsisted on one meal a day.* **3.** To be logically conceivable. *—tr.* To maintain or support with provisions. [Lat. *subsistere,* to stand up : *sub-,* up + *sistere,* to stand.] **—sub·sist'er** *n.*
sub·sis·tence (səb-sĭs'təns) *n.* **1.** The act or state of subsisting. **2.** A means of subsisting; sustenance. **3.** Something that has real or substantial existence. **4.** *Theol.* Hypostasis. ***—modifier:*** *subsistence wages.* **—sub·sis'tent** *adj.*
sub·soil (sŭb'soil') *n.* The layer or bed of earth beneath the surface soil. *—tr.v.* **-soiled, -soil·ing, -soils.** To plow or turn up the subsoil of. **—sub'soil'er** *n.*
sub·so·lar (sŭb'sō'lər) *adj.* **1.** Situated directly beneath the sun. **2.** Located between the tropics; equatorial.
sub·son·ic (sŭb'sŏn'ĭk) *adj.* **1.** Of less than audible frequency. **2.** Having a speed less than that of sound in a designated medium.
sub·spe·cies (sŭb'spē'shēz, -sēz) *n., pl.* **subspecies.** A subdivision of a taxonomic species, usually based on geographical distribution. **—sub'spe·cif'ic** (-spĭ-sĭf'ĭk) *adj.*
sub·stage (sŭb'stāj') *n.* The part of a microscope located below the stage by which attachments are held in place.
sub·stance (sŭb'stəns) *n.* **1. a.** That which has mass and occupies space; matter. **b.** A material of a particular kind or constitution. **2. a.** Essential nature; essence. **b.** Gist; heart. **3.** Reality; actuality: *a plan without substance.* **4.** Density; body: *Air has little substance.* **5.** Material possessions; goods; wealth: *a person of substance.* [ME < OFr. < Lat. *substantia* < *substans,* pr.part. of *substare,* to be present : *sub,* under + *stare,* to stand.]
sub·stan·dard (sŭb'stăn'dərd) *adj.* **1.** Failing to meet a standard; below standard. **2.** Considered unacceptable usage by the educated members of a speech community.
sub·stan·tial (səb-stăn'shəl) *adj.* **1.** Of, pertaining to, or having substance; material. **2.** Not imaginary; true; real. **3.** Solidly built; strong. **4.** Ample; sustaining: *a substantial breakfast.* **5.** Considerable in importance, value, degree, amount, or extent: *won by a substantial margin.* **6.** Possessing wealth or property; well-to-do. *—pl. n.* **substantials. 1.** The essentials. **2.** Solid things. [ME *substancial* < LLat. *substantialis* < Lat. *substantia,* substance.] **—sub·stan'ti·al'i·ty** (-shē-ăl'ĭ-tē), **sub·stan'tial·ness** *n.* **—sub·stan'tial·ly** *adv.*
sub·stan·ti·ate (səb-stăn'shē-āt') *tr.v.* **-at·ed, -at·ing, -ates. 1.** To support with proof or evidence; verify: *substantiate an accusation.* **2. a.** To give material form to; embody. **b.** To make firm or solid. **3.** To give substance to; make real or actual. [Med. Lat. *substantiare, substantiat-* < Lat. *substantia,* substance.] **—sub·stan'ti·a'tion** *n.*
sub·stan·ti·val (sŭb'stən-tī'vəl) *adj. Gram.* Of, pertaining to, or of the nature of a substantive. **—sub'stan·ti'val·ly** *adv.*
sub·stan·tive (sŭb'stən-tĭv) *adj.* **1.** Substantial; considerable. **2.** Independent in existence or function; not subordinate. **3.** Not imaginary; actual; real. **4.** Of or pertaining to the essence or substance of something; essential: *substantive information.* **5.** Having a solid basis; firm. **6.** *Gram.* Expressing or denoting existence; for example, the verb *to be.* **7.** *Gram.* Denoting a noun or noun equivalent. *—n. Gram.* A word or group of words functioning as a noun. [ME *substantif* < OFr. < LLat. *substantivus* < Lat. *substantia,* substance.] **—sub'stan·tive·ly** *adv.* **—sub'stan·tive·ness** *n.*
sub·sta·tion (sŭb'stā'shən) *n.* A subsidiary or branch station, as of a post office.
sub·stit·u·ent (səb-stĭch'o͞o-ənt) *n.* An atom, radical, or group substituted for another in a compound. *—adj.* Of such an atom or group. [Lat. *substituens, substituent-,* pr. part. of *substituere,* to substitute.]
sub·sti·tute (sŭb'stĭ-to͞ot', -tyo͞ot') *n.* **1.** One that takes the place of another; replacement. **2.** *Gram.* A word or construction used in place of another word, phrase, or clause. ***—modifier:*** *a substitute teacher.* *—v.* **-tut·ed, -tut·ing, -tutes.** *—tr.* To put or use (a person or thing) in place of another. *—intr.* To take the place of another: *"Only art can substitute for nature"* (Leonard Bernstein). [< Lat. *substitutus,* p.part. of *substituere,* to substitute : *sub-,* in place of + *statuere,* to cause to stand.] **—sub'sti·tut'a·bil'it·y** *n.* **—sub'sti·tut'a·ble** *adj.*
sub·sti·tu·tion (sŭb'stĭ-to͞o'shən, -tyo͞o'-) *n.* **1. a.** The act of substituting. **b.** The state of being substituted. **2.** That which is substituted. **—sub'sti·tu'tion·al** *adj.* **—sub'sti·tu'tion·al·ly** *adv.*
sub·sti·tu·tive (sŭb'stĭ-to͞o'tĭv, -tyo͞o'-) *adj.* Serving or capable of serving as a substitute.
sub·strate (sŭb'strāt') *n.* **1.** The material or substance upon

which an enzyme acts. **2.** *Biol.* A surface on which a plant or animal grows or is attached. **3.** A substratum. [< SUBSTRATUM.]

sub·stra·tum (sŭb′strā′təm, -străt′əm) *n., pl.* **-stra·ta** (-strā′tə, -străt′ə) or **-stra·tums. 1. a.** An underlying layer. **b.** A layer of earth beneath the surface soil; subsoil. **2.** The foundation or groundwork for something. **3.** The material upon which another material is coated or fabricated. **4.** *Philos.* The characterless substance that supports attributes of reality. **5.** *Biol.* A substrate. [Med. Lat. < Lat. *substratus,* p.part. of *substernere,* to lay under : *sub-,* under + *sternere,* to spread out.] **—sub′stra′tive** *adj.*

sub·struc·tion (sŭb′strŭk′shən) *n.* A foundation; substructure. [Lat. *substructio* < *substruere,* to build beneath : *sub-,* beneath + *struere,* to build.] **—sub′struc′tion·al** *adj.*

sub·struc·ture (sŭb′strŭk′chər) *n.* **1.** The supporting part of a structure; foundation. **2.** The earth bank or bed supporting railroad tracks. **—sub′struc′tur·al** *adj.*

sub·sume (səb-so͞om′) *tr.v.* **-sumed, -sum·ing, -sumes.** To classify in a more comprehensive category or under a general principle. [Med. Lat. *subsumere* : Lat. *sub-,* from below + Lat. *sumere,* to take up.] **—sub·sum′a·ble** *adj.*

sub·sump·tion (səb-sŭmp′shən) *n.* **1. a.** The act or an instance of subsuming. **b.** Something that is subsumed. **2.** *Logic.* The minor premise of a syllogism. [Med. Lat. *subsumptio,* a subsuming < *subsumere,* to subsume.] **—sub·sump′tive** *adj.*

sub·tem·per·ate (sŭb-tĕm′pər-ĭt, -tĕm′prĭt) *adj.* Of, pertaining to, or occurring within the colder regions of the Temperate Zones.

sub·ten·ant (sŭb-tĕn′ənt) *n.* One that rents property, such as land or a house, from a tenant. **—sub′ten′an·cy** *n.*

sub·tend (səb-tĕnd′) *tr.v.* **-tend·ed, -tend·ing, -tends. 1.** *Math.* To be opposite to and delimit: *The side of a triangle subtends the opposite angle.* **2.** To underlie so as to enclose or surround: *flowers subtended by leafy bracts.* [Lat. *subtendere,* to extend underneath : *sub-,* beneath + *tendere,* to extend.]

sub·ter·fuge (sŭb′tər-fyo͞oj′) *n.* A deceptive stratagem or device: *"the paltry subterfuge of an anonymous signature"* (R.S. Surtees). [Fr. < LLat. *subterfugium* < Lat. *subterfugere,* to escape : *subter,* secretly + *fugere,* to flee.]

sub·ter·mi·nal (sŭb-tûr′mə-nəl) *adj.* Located or occurring near an end.

sub·ter·ra·ne·an (sŭb′tə-rā′nē-ən) *adj.* **1.** Situated or operating beneath the earth's surface; underground. **2.** Hidden; secret. [Lat. *subterraneus* : *sub-,* under + *terra,* earth.] **—sub′ter·ra′ne·an·ly** *adv.*

sub·ter·res·tri·al (sŭb′tə-rĕs′trē-əl) *adj.* Subterranean. *—n.* An animal that lives underground.

subway

sub·tile (sŭt′l, sŭb′təl) *adj.* Subtle. **—sub′tile·ly** *adv.* **—sub·til′i·ty** (səb-tĭl′ĭ-tē), **sub′tile·ness, sub′til·ty** *n.*

sub·ti·lin (sŭb′tə-lĭn) *n.* An antibiotic obtained from the bacterium *Bacillus subtilis* that is active against Gram-positive microorganisms. [NLat. *subtilis,* specific epithet of *Bacillus subtilis* + -IN.]

sub·til·ize (sŭt′l-īz′, sŭb′tə-līz′) *v.* **-ized, -iz·ing, -iz·es.** *—tr.* To render subtle. *—intr.* To argue or discuss with subtlety; make fine distinctions. [Med. Lat. *subtilizare* < Lat. *subtilis,* subtle.] **—sub′til·i·za′tion** *n.*

sub·ti·tle (sŭb′tīt′l) *n.* **1.** A secondary and usually explanatory title, as of a literary work. **2. a.** A printed translation of the dialogue of a foreign-language film shown at the bottom of the screen. **b.** A printed narration or portion of dialogue flashed on the screen between the scenes of a silent film.

sub·tle (sŭt′l) *adj.* **-tler, -tlest. 1. a.** So slight as to be difficult to detect or analyze; elusive. **b.** Not immediately obvious; abstruse. **2.** Able to make fine distinctions: *a subtle mind.* **3. a.** Characterized by skill or ingenuity; clever. **b.** Characterized by craft or slyness; devious. **c.** Operating in a hidden and usually injurious way; insidious. [ME *subtil* < OFr. *sotil* < Lat. *subtilis.*] **—sub′tle·ness** *n.* **—sub′tly** *adv.*

sub·tle·ty (sŭt′l-tē) *n., pl.* **-ties. 1.** The quality or state of being subtle. **2.** Something subtle, esp. a nicety of thought or a fine distinction.

sub·ton·ic (sŭb′tŏn′ĭk) *n. Mus.* The seventh tone of a diatonic scale, immediately below the tonic.

sub·to·pi·a (sŭb-tō′pē-ə) *n. Chiefly Brit.* The suburbs of a city. **—sub·to′pi·an** *adj.* [SUB(URB) + (U)TOPIA.]

sub·top·ic (sŭb′tŏp′ĭk) *n.* One of the divisions into which a main topic may be divided.

sub·tor·rid (sŭb′tôr′ĭd, -tŏr′-) *adj.* Subtropical.

sub·to·tal (sŭb-tōt′l) *adj.* Less than total; incomplete. *—n.* (sŭb′tōt′l). The total of part of a series of numbers. *—v.* (sŭb′tōt′l) **-taled, -tal·ing, -tals** also **-talled, -tal·ling, -tals.** *—tr.* To total part of (a series of numbers). *—intr.* To arrive at a subtotal.

sub·tract (səb-trăkt′) *v.* **-tract·ed, -tract·ing, -tracts.** *—tr.* To take away; deduct. *—intr.* To perform the arithmetic operation of subtraction. [Lat. *substahere, substract-* : *sub-,* away + *trahere,* to draw.] **—sub·tract′er** *n.*

sub·trac·tion (səb-trăk′shən) *n.* **1.** The act or process of subtracting; deduction. **2.** The arithmetic process or operation of finding a quantity that when added to one of two quantities produces the other.

sub·trac·tive (səb-trăk′tĭv) *adj.* **1.** Producing or involving subtraction. **2.** Designating a color produced by light passing through more than one colorant, each of which inhibits certain wavelengths, as in mixtures of pigments. **3.** Designating a photographic process that produces a positive image by superposing or mixing substances that selectively absorb colored light.

sub·tra·hend (sŭb′trə-hĕnd′) *n.* A quantity or number to be subtracted from another. [< Lat. *subtrahendum,* neuter gerund. of *subtrahere,* to subtract.]

sub·trop·i·cal (sŭb-trŏp′ĭ-kəl) *adj.* Of, relating to, or being the geographic areas adjacent to the tropics.

sub·trop·ics (sŭb-trŏp′ĭks) *pl.n.* Subtropical regions.

su·bu·late (so͞o′byə-lĭt, -lāt′, sŭb′yə-) *adj. Biol.* Awl-shaped; tapering to a point. [NLat. *subulatus* < Lat. *subula,* awl.]

sub·um·brel·la (sŭb′ŭm-brĕl′ə) *n. Zool.* The concave undersurface of the body of a jellyfish.

sub·urb (sŭb′ûrb′) *n.* **1.** A usually residential area or community outlying a city. **2. suburbs.** The usually residential region around a major city; environs. [ME < OFr. *suburbe* < Lat. *suburbium* : *sub-,* close to + *urbs,* city.]

sub·ur·ban (sə-bûr′bən) *adj.* **1.** Of, pertaining to, or characteristic of a suburb or life in a suburb. **2.** Located or residing in a suburb. **3.** The culture, manners, and customs typical of life in the suburbs. *—n.* A suburbanite.

sub·ur·ban·ite (sə-bûr′bə-nīt′) *n.* One who lives in a suburb.

sub·ur·ban·ize (sə-bûr′bə-nīz′) *tr.v.* **-ized, -iz·ing, -izes.** To render suburban; impart a suburban character to. **—sub·ur′ban·i·za′tion** *n.*

sub·ur·bi·a (sə-bûr′bē-ə) *n.* **1.** Suburbs. **2. a.** Suburbanites as a group. **b.** Suburbanites as a cultural class.

sub·ven·tion (səb-vĕn′shən) *n.* **1.** The provision of help, aid, or support. **2.** A grant of financial aid; an endowment or subsidy, as that given by a government to an institution for research. [ME *subvencioun* < OFr. *subvention* < LLat. *subventio* < Lat. *subvenire,* to come to help : *sub-,* up + *venire,* to come.] **—sub·ven′tion·ar′y** *adj.*

sub·ver·sion (səb-vûr′zhən, -shən) *n.* **1.** The act of subverting or the condition of being subverted. **2.** *Obs.* A cause of overthrow or ruin. [ME *subversioun* < OFr. *subversion* < LLat. *subversio* < Lat. *subvertere,* to subvert.] **—sub·ver′sion·ar′y** *adj.*

sub·ver·sive (səb-vûr′sĭv, -zĭv) *adj.* Intended or serving to subvert, esp. intended to overthrow or undermine an established government. *—n.* One who advocates or is regarded as advocating subversive means or policies. **—sub·ver′sive·ly** *adv.* **—sub·ver′sive·ness** *n.*

sub·vert (səb-vûrt′) *tr.v.* **-vert·ed, -vert·ing, -verts. 1.** To destroy completely; ruin: *"schemes to subvert the liberties of a great community"* (Alexander Hamilton). **2.** To undermine the character, morals, or allegiance of; corrupt. **3.** To overthrow completely: *"economic assistance . . . must subvert the existing . . . feudal or tribal order"* (Henry A. Kissinger). [ME *subverten* < OFr. *subvertir* < Lat. *subvertere* : *sub-,* from below + *vertere,* to turn.] **—sub·vert′er** *n.*

sub·way (sŭb′wā′) *n.* **1. a.** An underground urban railroad, usually operated by electricity. **b.** A passage for such a railroad. **2.** An underground tunnel or passage, as for a water main.

Su·ca·ryl (so͞o′kə-rĭl′). A trademark for either of two compounds used as low-calorie sweeteners.

suc·ce·da·ne·um (sŭk′sĭ-dā′nē-əm) *n., pl.* **-ne·a** (-nē-ə). A substitute. [NLat. < Lat. *succedaneus,* substituted < *succedere,* to succeed.]

suc·ceed (sək-sēd′) *v.* **-ceed·ed, -ceed·ing, -ceeds.** *—intr.* **1.** To come next in time or succession; follow after, esp. to replace another in an office or position: *She succeeded to the throne.* **2.** To accomplish something desired or intended: *succeeded in having the law repealed.* **3.** *Obs.* To devolve upon a person by way of inheritance. *—tr.* **1.** To follow in time or order; come after. **2.** To follow in office; replace. [ME *succeden* < OFr. *succeder* < Lat. *succedere* : *sub-,* after + *cedere,* to go.] **—suc·ce′dent** (sək-sēd′nt) *adj.* **—suc·ceed′er** *n.*

suc·cès d'es·time (sük-sĕ′ dĕs-tēm′) *n.* A critical but not popular success or achievement. [Fr. : *succès,* success + *de,* of + *estime,* esteem.]

suc·cès fou (sük-sĕ′ fo͞o′) *n.* A wild success. [Fr.]

suc·cess (sək-sĕs′) *n.* **1.** The achievement of something desired, planned, or attempted. **2. a.** The gaining of fame or prosperity. **b.** The extent of such gain. **3.** One that is successful. **4.** *Obs.* A result or outcome. [Lat. *successus* < p.part. of *succedere,* to succeed.]

suc·cess·ful (sək-sĕs′fəl) *adj.* **1.** Having a favorable outcome. **2.** Having obtained something desired or intended. **3.** Having achieved wealth or eminence. **—suc·cess′ful·ly** *adv.*

suc·ces·sion (sək-sĕsh′ən) *n.* **1.** The act or process of following in order or sequence. **2.** A group of persons or things arranged or following in order; sequence. **3. a.** The sequence in which one person after another succeeds to a title, throne, dignity, or estate. **b.** The right of a person or line of persons to so succeed. **c.** The person or line vested with such a right. **4. a.** The act or process of succeeding to the rights or duties of another. **b.** The act or process of becoming entitled as a legal beneficiary to the property of a deceased person. **5.** *Ecol.* The gradual and orderly process of ecosystem development brought about by changes in species populations that culminates in the production of a climax characteristic of a particular geographical region. **—suc·ces′sion·al** *adj.* **—suc·ces′sion·al·ly** *adv.*

suc·ces·sive (sək-sĕs′ĭv) *adj.* **1.** Following in uninterrupted order or sequence. **2.** Of, characterized by, or involving succession. **—suc·ces′sive·ly** *adv.* **—suc·ces′sive·ness** *n.*

successive approximation *n.* A method for estimating the value of an unknown quantity by repeated comparison to a sequence of known quantities.

suc·ces·sor (sək-sĕs′ər) *n.* One that succeeds another.

suc·cinct (sək-sĭngkt′) *adj.* **1.** Clearly expressed in few words; concise; terse. **2.** Characterized by brevity and clarity in speech or writing: *a succinct style.* **3.** *Archaic.* Encircled as if by a girdle; girded. [Lat. *succinctus* < p.part. of *succingere,* to gird from below : *sub-,* below + *cingere,* to gird.] **—suc·cinct′ly** *adv.* **—suc·cinct′ness** *n.*

suc·cin·ic acid (sək-sĭn′ĭk) *n.* A colorless crystalline compound, $C_4H_6O_4$, occurring naturally in amber and synthesized for use in pharmaceuticals and perfumes. [Fr. *succinique* < Lat. *succinum,* amber.]

suc·cor (sŭk′ər) *n.* **1.** Assistance or help in time of distress; relief. **2.** One that affords assistance or relief. *—tr.v.* **-cored, -cor·ing, -cors.** To render assistance to in time of distress. [ME *sucurs* (pl.) < OFr. *secors* < Med. Lat. *succursus* < Lat. *succurere,* to be useful for : *sub-,* up + *currere,* to run.] **—suc′cor·a·ble** *adj.* **—suc′cor·er** *n.*

suc·co·ry (sŭk′ə-rē) *n., pl.* **-ries.** Chicory (sense 2). [Alteration of ME *cicoree.*]

suc·co·tash (sŭk′ə-tăsh′) *n.* Kernels of corn, lima beans, and tomatoes cooked together. [Narraganset *msíckquatash.*]

Suc·coth also **Suk·koth** (so͝ok′ŏt, -əs) *n.* A Jewish harvest festival celebrated for nine days beginning on the eve of the 15th of Tishri. [Heb. *sukkōth* < *sukkāh,* tabernacle.]

suc·cour (sŭk′ər) *n. Chiefly Brit.* Variant of **succor.**

suc·cu·bus (sŭk′yə-bəs) also **suc·cu·ba** (sŭk′yə-bə) *n., pl.* **-bus·es** or **-bi** (-bī′, -bē′) also **-bae** (-bē′, -bī). **1.** A female demon supposed to descend upon and have sexual intercourse with a man while he sleeps. **2.** An evil spirit; demon. [Med. Lat. < LLat. *succuba,* prostitute < Lat. *succubare,* to lie under : *sub-,* under + *cubare,* to lie down.]

suc·cu·lent (sŭk′yə-lənt) *adj.* **1.** Full of juice or sap; juicy. **2.** *Bot.* Having thick, fleshy leaves or stems that conserve moisture. **3.** Interesting or absorbing; not dull or dry. *—n.* A succulent plant, as a sedum or a cactus. [Lat. *succulentus* < *succus,* juice.] **—suc′cu·lence, suc′cu·len·cy** *n.* **—suc′cu·lent·ly** *adv.*

suc·cumb (sə-kŭm′) *intr.v.* **-cumbed, -cumb·ing, -cumbs.** **1.** To yield or submit to an overpowering force or overwhelming desire; give in or give up: *"Meanwhile I had succumbed to the disease of scepticism"* (Cyril Connolly). **2.** To die. [ME *succomben* < OFr. *succomber* < Lat. *succumbere.*]

suc·cus·sion (sə-kŭsh′ən) *n.* **1.** The act or process of shaking violently. **2.** The condition of being shaken violently. [Lat. *succussio* < *succutere,* to shake up : *sub-,* up + *quatere,* to shake.] **—suc·cus′sa·to′ry** (sə-kŭs′ə-tôr′ē, -tōr′ē) *adj.*

such (sŭch) *adj.* **1.** Of this or that kind: *never dreamed that they could do such work.* **2.** Being the same as something implied but left undefined or unsaid: *Such people are never satisfied.* **3.** Of so extreme or great a degree or quality: *Such luck.* *—adv.* **1.** To such a degree: *such good work; such a good job.* **2.** Very; especially: *She has been in such poor health lately.* *—pron.* **1.** Such a person or persons or thing or things. **2.** Someone or something implied or indicated: *Such are the fortunes of war.* **3.** The like: *pins, needles, and such.* **—*idioms.* as such. 1.** As being the person or thing implied or previously mentioned: *A diplomat as such must negotiate.* **2.** In itself or by itself: *Money as such will seldom bring happiness.* **such as. 1.** For example. **2.** Of the stated or implied kind or degree; similar; like: *a statement such as this.* [ME < OE *swylc.*]

such and such *adj.* Not yet specified; undetermined: *They agreed to meet at such and such an hour.*

such·like (sŭch′līk′) *adj.* Of a similar kind; like. *—pron.* Persons or things of such a kind.

suck (sŭk) *v.* **sucked, suck·ing, sucks.** *—tr.* **1.** To draw (liquid) into the mouth by inhalation. **2. a.** To draw in by establishing a partial vacuum. **b.** To draw in by or as if by a current in a fluid. **3.** To draw nourishment through or from. **4.** To hold, moisten, or maneuver (a sweet, for example) in the mouth. **5.** *Vulgar Slang.* To perform fellatio on. *—intr.* **1.** To draw in by or as if by suction. **2.** To draw nourishment; suckle. **3.** To make a sucking sound. **4.** *Vulgar Slang.* To be disgustingly disagreeable or offensive. **—*phrasal verb.* suck in.** *Slang.* To take advantage of; cheat; swindle. *—n.* **1.** The act of sucking. **2.** Suction. **3.** Something drawn in by sucking. [ME *souken* < OE *sūcan.*]

suck·er (sŭk′ər) *n.* **1.** One that sucks. **2.** *Informal.* One who is easily deceived; a gullible person; dupe. **3.** A lollipop. **4. a.** A piston or piston valve, as in a suction pump or syringe. **b.** A tube or pipe, such as a siphon, through which anything is sucked. **5.** Any of numerous chiefly North American freshwater fishes of the family Catostomidae, having a thick-lipped mouth adapted for feeding by suction. **6.** A structure or part adapted for clinging by suction. **7.** *Bot.* A secondary shoot arising from the base of a tree trunk or from the lower part of some shrubs. *—v.* **-ered, -er·ing, -ers.** *—tr.* **1.** To strip suckers or shoots from. **2.** *Informal.* To trick; dupe. *—intr.* To send out suckers or shoots.

suck·er·fish (sŭk′ər-fĭsh′) *n., pl.* **suckerfish** or **-fish·es.** The remora.

suck·ing (sŭk′ĭng) *adj.* Not yet weaned.

sucking louse *n.* Any of various small wingless insects of the order Anoplura that have mouth parts adapted for piercing and sucking.

suck·le (sŭk′əl) *v.* **-led, -ling, -les.** *—tr.* **1.** To cause or allow to take milk at the breast or udder; nurse. **2.** To take in as sustenance; have as nourishment. **3.** To bring up; rear; nourish; foster. *—intr.* To suck at the breast. [Prob. back-formation < SUCKLING.] **—suck′ler** *n.*

suck·ling (sŭk′lĭng) *n.* A young mammal that has not been weaned. [ME *suklinge.*]

su·crase (so͞o′krās′, -krāz′) *n. Chem.* Invertase. [Fr. *sucre,* sugar + -ASE.]

su·cre (so͞o′krā) *n.* See table at **currency.** [Sp., after Antonio José de *Sucre* (1795–1830).]

su·crose (so͞o′krōs′) *n.* A crystalline disaccharide carbohydrate, $C_{12}H_{22}O_{11}$, found in many plants, mainly sugar cane and sugar beet, and used widely as a sweetener, preservative, and in the manufacture of plastics and cellulose. [Fr. *sucre,* sugar + -OSE.]

suc·tion (sŭk′shən) *n.* **1.** The act or process of sucking. **2.** A force that causes a fluid or solid to be drawn into an interior space or to adhere to a surface because of the difference between the external and internal pressures. *—adj.* **1.** Creating suction. **2.** Operating by suction. [LLat. *suctio* < Lat. *sugere,* to suck.]

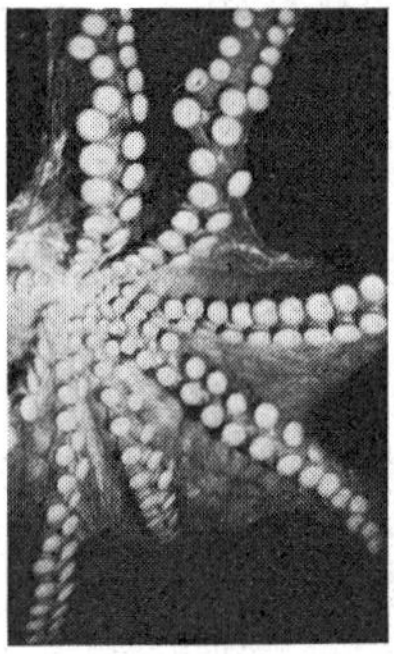

suction
Suction cups on an octopus

suction pump *n.* A pump for drawing up a liquid by means of suction produced by a piston being drawn through a cylinder.

suction stop *n.* A click (sense 3).

suc·to·ri·al (sŭk-tôr′ē-əl, -tōr′-) *adj.* **1.** Adapted for sucking or clinging by suction: *a suctorial organ.* **2.** Having suctorial organs or parts. [NLat. *suctorius* < Lat. *sugere,* to suck.]

Su·dan·ic (so͞o-dăn′ĭk) *n.* The non-Bantu, non-Hamitic languages of the Sudan. **—Su·dan′ic** *adj.*

su·da·to·ri·um (so͞o′də-tôr′ē-əm, -tōr′-) *n., pl.* **-to·ri·a** (-tôr′ē-ə, -tōr′ē-ə). A hot-air room used for sweat baths. [Lat. < *sudatorius,* sweating < *sudare,* to sweat.]

su·da·to·ry (so͞o′də-tôr′ē, -tōr′ē) *adj.* Sudorific. *—n., pl.* **-ries.** **1.** A sudatorium. **2.** A sudorific.

sudd (sŭd) *n.* Floating masses of vegetation that often obstruct navigation on the White Nile. [Ar.]

sud·den (sŭd′n) *adj.* **1.** Happening without warning; unforeseen: *a sudden storm.* **2.** Characterized by hastiness; abrupt; rash: *a sudden departure.* **3.** Characterized by rapidity; quick; swift. **—*idiom.* all of a sudden.** Very quickly and unexpectedly; suddenly. [ME < OFr. *sodein* < Lat. *subitaneus* < *subitus,* sudden < p.part. of *subire,* to approach stealthily : *sub-,* secretly + *ire,* to go.] **—sud′den·ly** *adv.* **—sud′den·ness** *n.*

sudden death *n.* **1.** A death that is not preceded by any condition that would appear fatal. **2.** *Sports.* **a.** A game played to break a tie. **b.** Extra minutes of play added to a tied game, the winning team being the first team to score.

sudden infant death syndrome *n.* The unexpected death of an apparently healthy infant that usually occurs during the first year of life and while the infant is sleeping.

su·dor·if·er·ous (so͞o′də-rĭf′ər-əs) *adj.* Producing or secreting sweat. [LLat. *sudoriferus* : Lat. *sudor,* sweat + Lat. *ferre,* to carry.]

su·dor·if·ic (so͞o′də-rĭf′ĭk) *adj.* Causing or increasing sweat. *—n.* A sudorific medicine. [NLat. *sudorificus* < Lat. *sudor,* sweat.]

Su·dra (so͞o′drə) *n.* **1.** The lowest of the major Hindu castes, the members of which were originally menials but are now largely artisans and laborers. **2.** A member of this caste. [Skt. *śūdraḥ.*]

suds (sŭdz) *pl.n.* **1.** Soapy water. **2.** Foam; lather. **3.** *Slang.* Beer. [Poss. MDu. *sudse,* marsh.]

suds·y (sŭd′zē) *adj.* **-i·er, -i·est.** Full of or resembling suds.

sue (so͞o) *v.* **sued, su·ing, sues.** *—tr.* **1.** To make a petition to; appeal to; beseech. **2.** *Law.* **a.** To petition (a court) for redress of grievances or recovery of a right. **b.** To institute legal proceedings against (a person) for redress of grievances. **c.** To carry (an action) through to a final decision. **3.** To court; woo. *—intr.* **1.** To institute legal proceedings; bring suit. **2.** To make an appeal or entreaty. **3.** To woo. [ME *sewen* < AN *suer* < Lat. *sequi,* to follow.] **—su′er** *n.*

suede also **suède** (swād) *n.* **1.** Leather with a soft napped surface. **2.** Fabric made to resemble suede. [Fr. *suède* < *Suède,* Sweden.]

su·et (so͞o′ĭt) *n.* The hard fatty tissues around the kidneys of cattle and sheep, used in cooking and making tallow. [ME *sewet* < AN **sewet,* dim. of *sue,* tallow < Lat. *sebum.*]

suf·fer (sŭf′ər) *v.* **-fered, -fer·ing, -fers.** *—intr.* **1.** To feel or endure pain or distress. **2.** To sustain loss, injury, harm, or punishment. **3.** To appear at a disadvantage: *"he suffers by comparison with his greater contemporary"* (Albert C. Baugh). *—tr.* **1.** To undergo or sustain (something painful, injurious, or unpleasant). **2.** To experience: *suffer a change* *in staff.* **3.** To endure or bear; stand: *He cannot suffer boredom.* **4.** To permit; allow: *would not suffer impertinence.* [ME *sufferen* < AN *suffrir* < Lat. *sufferre* : *sub-,* from below + *ferre,* to bear.] **—suf′fer·er** *n.* **—suf′fer·ing·ly** *adv.*

suf·fer·a·ble (sŭf′ər-ə-bəl, sŭf′rə-) *adj.* Capable of being suffered, endured, or permitted; tolerable. **—suf′fer·a·bly** *adv.*

suf·fer·ance (sŭf′ər-əns, sŭf′rəns) *n.* **1.** The capacity to tolerate pain or distress. **2.** Sanction or permission implied or given by failure to prohibit; tacit assent; tolerance. **3.** Suffering; misery. **4.** Patient endurance. [ME < OFr. < LLat. *sufferentia* < Lat. *sufferre,* to suffer.]

suf·fer·ing (sŭf′ər-ĭng, sŭf′rĭng) *n.* **1.** The act or condition of one who suffers. **2.** Something that causes pain or distress.

suffragette
Suffragette pickets in front of the White House in 1917

suf·fice (sə-fīs′) *v.* **-ficed, -fic·ing, -fic·es.** *—intr.* **1.** To meet present needs or requirements; be sufficient or adequate: *These rations will suffice until next week.* **2.** To be capable or competent; be equal to a specified task: *No words will suffice to convey his grief.* *—tr.* To be enough or sufficient for; satisfy the needs or requirements of. [ME *suffisen* < OFr. *suffire, suffis-* < Lat. *sufficere* : *sub-,* under + *facere,* to make.] **—suf·fic′er** *n.*

suf·fi·cien·cy (sə-fĭsh′ən-sē) *n.* **1.** The state or quality of being sufficient. **2.** An adequate amount or quantity.

suf·fi·cient (sə-fĭsh′ənt) *adj.* **1.** As much as is needed; enough; adequate: *sufficient food for survival.* **2.** *Archaic.* Competent; qualified. [ME < OFr. < Lat. *sufficiens,* pr.part. of *sufficere,* to suffice.] **—suf·fi′cient·ly** *adv.*

Synonyms: *sufficient, enough, adequate.* These adjectives mean capable of fulfilling a need or requirement. *Sufficient* and *enough* refer to quantity and usually imply equality with the required amount or a slight excess. *Enough* can also be used ironically to indicate a quantity well in excess of what is desired. *Adequate* refers to both quantity and quality. With respect to quantity, it is approximately equivalent to *sufficient* and *enough* in their primary sense. With reference to quality, *adequate* implies capacity for meeting a modest standard and sometimes for barely meeting it.

suf·fix (sŭf′ĭks) *n. Gram.* An affix added to the end of a word or stem, serving to form a new word or as an inflectional ending, such as *-ness* in *gentleness, -ing* in *walking,* or *-s* in *sits.* *—tr.v.* **-fixed, -fix·ing, -fix·es.** To add as a suffix. [< Lat. *suffixus,* p.part. of *suffigere,* to affix : *sub-,* secondary + *figere,* to fix.] **—suf′fix·al** *adj.* **—suf·fix′ion** (sə-fĭk′shən) *n.*

suf·fo·cate (sŭf′ə-kāt′) *v.* **-cat·ed, -cat·ing, -cates.** *—tr.* **1.** To kill or destroy by preventing access of oxygen. **2.** To impair the respiration of; choke; asphyxiate. **3.** To cause discomfort by or as if by cutting off the supply of air. **4.** To suppress the development, imagination, or creativity of; stifle: *"The rigid formality of the place suffocated her"* (Thackeray). *—intr.* **1.** To die from suffocation. **2.** To be stifled; smother. [Lat. *suffocare, suffocat-* : *sub-,* under + *fauces,* throat.] **—suf′fo·ca′tion** *n.* **—suf′fo·ca′tive** *adj.*

sugar beet

Suf·folk (sŭf′ək) *n.* **1.** Any of an English breed of hornless sheep producing high-quality mutton. **2.** Any of a breed of English draft horses with short legs and a thickset, heavy body. [After *Suffolk* County, England.]

suf·fra·gan (sŭf′rə-gən) *n.* **1.** A bishop elected or appointed as an assistant to the bishop or ordinary of a diocese, having administrative and episcopal responsibilities but no jurisdictional functions. **2.** A bishop regarded in his position as subordinate to his archbishop or metropolitan. *—adj.* Of, being, or pertaining to a suffragan; auxiliary; subordinate. [ME < OFr. < Med. Lat. *suffraganeus* < Lat. *suffragium,* suffrage.] **—suf′fra·gan·ship′** *n.*

suf·frage (sŭf′rĭj) *n.* **1.** A vote cast in the procedure used in deciding a disputed question or in electing a person to office. **2. a.** The right or privilege of voting; franchise. **b.** The exercise of such a right. **3.** A short intercessory prayer. [Partly < ME, intercessory prayer (< OFr. < Med. Lat. *suffragium* < Lat., vote), and partly < Lat. *suffragium,* vote.]

suf·fra·gette (sŭf′rə-jĕt′) *n.* A female advocate of suffrage for women. **—suf′fra·get′tism** *n.*

suf·fra·gist (sŭf′rə-jĭst) *n.* An advocate of the extension of political voting rights, esp. to women.

suf·fru·tes·cent (sŭf′rōō-tĕs′ənt) also **suf·fru·ti·cose** (sŭf-rōō′tĭ-kōs′) *adj. Bot.* Having a woody stem or base; somewhat shrubby. [NLat. *suffrutescens, suffrutescent-* : Lat. *sub-,* under + NLat. *frutescens,* frutescent < Lat. *frutex,* shrub.]

suf·fuse (sə-fyōōz′) *tr.v.* **-fused, -fus·ing, -fus·es.** To spread through or over, as with liquid, color, or light: *"The sky above the roof is suffused with deep colors"* (O'Neill). [Lat. *suffundere, suffus-* : *sub-,* below + *fundere,* to pour.] **—suf·fu′sion** *n.* **—suf·fu′sive** (sə-fyōō′sĭv, -zĭv) *adj.*

Su·fi (sōō′fē) *n.* A member of a Moslem mystic sect. [Ar. *sūfīy* < *sūf,* wool.] **—Su′fic** (-fĭk), **Su·fis′tic** (-fĭs′tĭk) *adj.*

Su·fism (sōō′fĭz′əm) *n.* A sect of Islamic mysticism, dating from the 8th century A.D. and developed chiefly in Persia.

sug·ar (shŏŏg′ər) *n.* **1.** A sweet crystalline carbohydrate, sucrose. **2.** Any of a class of water-soluble crystalline carbohydrates, including sucrose and lactose, having a characteristically sweet taste. **3.** A particular amount of sugar, as a cube. **4.** *Slang.* Sweetheart. Used as a form of endearment. *—v.* **-ared, -ar·ing, -ars.** *—tr.* **1.** To coat, cover, or sweeten with sugar. **2.** To make less distasteful or more appealing. *—intr.* To form sugar; granulate. [ME *sugre* < OFr. *sukere* < OItal. *zucchero* < Med. Lat. *succarum* < Ar. *sukkar* < Pers. *shakar* < Skt. *śarkarā.*]

sugar apple *n.* The sweetsop (sense 2).

sugar beet *n.* A form of the common beet, *Beta vulgaris,* having white roots from which sugar is obtained.

sug·ar·ber·ry (shŏŏg′ər-bĕr′ē) *n.* The hackberry.

sugar bush *n.* A grove of sugar maples used as a source of maple syrup or maple sugar.

sugar cane *n.* A tall grass, *Saccharum officinarum,* native to the East Indies, having thick, tough stems that are one of the chief commercial sources of sugar.

sug·ar-coat (shŏŏg′ər-kōt′) *tr.v.* **-coat·ed, -coat·ing, -coats. 1.** To coat with sugar: *sugar-coat a pill.* **2.** To cause to seem more appealing or pleasant.

sugar corn *n.* Sweet corn.

sug·ar-cured (shŏŏg′ər-kyŏŏrd′) *adj.* Cured with a preparation of sugar, salt, and nitrate. Used of meats.

sugar daddy *n. Slang.* A wealthy, usually older man who gives expensive gifts to a young woman in return for her sexual favors or her companionship.

sug·ared (shŏŏg′ərd) *adj.* **1.** Sweetened with sugar. **2.** Made more appealing or pleasant.

sug·ar·house (shŏŏg′ər-hous′) *n.* A sugar refinery or processing plant, esp. a building in which maple sap is boiled down to yield maple syrup and maple sugar.

sugaring off *n.* **1.** The process of boiling down maple sap to yield maple syrup and maple sugar. **2.** An informal social gathering in which the guests help make maple sugar.

sugar loaf *n.* **1.** A large conical loaf of pure concentrated sugar. **2.** Something resembling a loaf of sugar in shape. **—sug′ar-loaf′** (shŏŏg′ər-lōf′) *adj.*

sugar maple *n.* A maple tree, *Acer saccharum,* of eastern North America, having sap that is the source of maple syrup and maple sugar and hard variously grained wood used in cabinetmaking.

sugar of lead *n.* Lead acetate.

sugar of milk *n.* Lactose.

sugar orchard *n.* Sugar bush.

sugar pine *n.* A tall evergreen timber tree, *Pinus lambertiana,* of the Pacific coast of North America.

sug·ar·plum (shŏŏg′ər-plŭm′) *n.* A small piece of sugary candy.

sug·ar·y (shŏŏg′ə-rē) *adj.* **-i·er, -i·est. 1.** Composed of sugar. **2.** Tasting like or resembling sugar. **3.** Deceitfully or cloyingly sweet. **—sug′ar·i·ness** *n.*

sug·gest (səg-jĕst′, sə-jĕst′) *tr.v.* **-gest·ed, -gest·ing, -gests. 1.** To offer for consideration or action; propose. **2. a.** To bring or call to mind by logic or association; evoke: *a cavern that suggests a tomb.* **b.** To serve as or provide a motive for; prompt; demand: *Such a crime suggests apt punishment.* **3.** To make evident indirectly; intimate; imply. [Lat. *suggerere, suggest-* : *sub-,* up + *gerere,* to carry.] **—sug·gest′er** *n.*

Synonyms: *suggest, imply, hint, intimate, insinuate.* These verbs mean to impart thoughts or ideas by indirection. *Suggest,* in this context, usually refers to a process whereby something is called to mind by a listener or viewer as the result of an association of ideas or train of thought. *Imply* refers to conveying an unstated or indirectly stated thought as part of something otherwise more explicit. The implied, or secondary, part is deduced as a seemingly logical consequence of the whole. *Hint* refers to expression that is indirect but contains rather pointed clues. *Intimate* applies to veiled expression that may be the result of discretion or reserve. *Insinuate* refers to covert expression of something, usually unpleasant, in a manner that suggests underhandedness.

sug·gest·i·bil·i·ty (səg-jĕs′tə-bĭl′ĭ-tē, sə-jĕs′-) *n.* Responsiveness or susceptibility to suggestion.

sug·gest·i·ble (səg-jĕs′tə-bəl, sə-jĕs′-) *adj.* Readily influenced by suggestion.

sug·ges·tion (səg-jĕs′chən, sə-jĕs′-) *n.* **1.** The act of suggesting. **2.** Something suggested. **3.** The sequential thought process by which one idea or concept leads to another. **4. a.** The psychological process by which an idea is induced in or adopted without argument, command, or coercion. **b.** An idea or response so induced. **5.** A hint or trace: *not a suggestion of scandal.*

sug·ges·tive (səg-jĕs′tĭv, sə-jĕs′-) *adj.* **1. a.** Tending to suggest thoughts or ideas. **b.** Conveying a hint or suggestion; indicative. **2.** Tending to suggest something improper or indecent. **—sug·ges′tive·ly** *adv.* **—sug·ges′tive·ness** *n.*

su·i·cid·al (sōō′ĭ-sīd′l) *adj.* **1.** Pertaining to, involving, or related to suicide. **2.** Dangerous to oneself or to one's interests; self-destructive; ruinous. **—su′i·cid′al·ly** *adv.*

su·i·cide (sōō′ĭ-sīd′) *n.* **1.** The act or an instance of intentionally killing oneself. **2.** The destruction or ruin of one's own interests. **3.** One who commits suicide. [Lat. *sui,* of oneself + -CIDE.]

su·i·cid·ol·o·gy (sōō′ĭ-sī-dŏl′ə-jē) *n.* The study of suicide, suicidal behavior, and suicide prevention. **—su′i·cid·ol′o·gist** *n.*

su·i ge·ne·ris (sōō′ī jĕn′ər-ĭs, sōō′ē) *adj.* Unique; individual. [< Lat., of its own kind.]

su·i ju·ris (sōō′ī′ jŏŏr′ĭs, sōō′ē) *adj. Law.* Capable of managing one's own affairs. [Lat.]

ă pat / ā pay / âr care / ä father / b **bib** / ch **church** / d **deed** / ĕ pet / ē be / f **fife** / g **gag** / h **hat** / hw **which** / ĭ pit / ī **pie** / îr **pier** / j **judge** / k **kick** / l **lid,** needle / m **mum** / n no, sudden / ng thing / ŏ pot / ō **toe** / ô **paw, for** / oi **noise** / ou **out** / ŏŏ **took** / ōō **boot** /

su·int (so͞o′ĭnt, swĭnt) *n.* A natural grease formed from dried perspiration found in the fleece of sheep, used as a source of potash. [Fr. < OFr. *suer,* to sweat < Lat. *sudare.*]

suit (so͞ot) *n.* **1.** A set of garments consisting of a coat and trousers or skirt that match in color or fabric. **2.** A group of things united into a set or series by having a common form or function. **3.** *Games.* Any of the four sets of playing cards, each with similar spots, that constitute a deck. **4. a.** Attendance required of a vassal at his feudal lord's court or manor. **b.** *Law.* A court proceeding to recover a right or claim. **5.** The act or an instance of courting a woman. —*v.* **suit·ed, suit·ing, suits.** —*tr.* **1.** To meet the requirements of; accommodate: *This candidate does not suit our qualifications.* **2.** To make appropriate or suitable; adapt: *We can suit the building to your specifications.* **3.** To please; satisfy. **4.** To provide with clothing; dress. —*intr.* To be suitable or acceptable. —***idiom.* follow suit. 1.** To play a card of the same suit as the one led. **2.** To do as another has done; follow an example. [ME < AN *suite* < OFr. *sieute* < VLat. **sequita* < **sequere* < Lat. *sequi,* to follow.]

suit·a·ble (so͞o′tə-bəl) *adj.* Appropriate to a given purpose or occasion. —**suit′a·bil′i·ty, suit′a·ble·ness** *n.* —**suit′a·bly** *adv.*

suit·case (so͞ot′kās′) *n.* A usually rectangular piece of luggage for carrying clothing.

suite (swēt) *n.* **1.** A staff of attendants or a train of followers; retinue. **2.** A succession of related things intended to be used together. **3.** A series of connected rooms used as a living unit. **4.** (swēt, so͞ot). A set of matching furniture. **5.** *Mus.* An instrumental composition consisting of a succession of dances in the same or related keys. [Fr. < OFr. *sieute.* —see SUIT.]

suit·ing (so͞o′tĭng) *n.* Fabric from which suits are made.

suit·or (so͞o′tər) *n.* **1.** A person who makes a petition or request. **2.** A person who sues in a court of law; plaintiff; petitioner. **3.** A man who is in the process of courting a woman. [ME < AN *seutor,* follower < Lat. *secutor* < *sequi,* to follow.]

su·ki·ya·ki (so͞o′kē-yä′kē, skē-yä′kē) *n.* A Japanese dish of sliced meat, vegetables, and seasoning fried together. [J.]

Suk·koth (so͝ok′ōt, -əs) *n.* Variant of **Succoth.**

sul·cate (sŭl′kāt′) *adj. Biol.* Having narrow longitudinal indentations; grooved. [Lat. *sulcatus,* p.part. of *sulcare,* to furrow < *sulcus,* furrow.]

sul·cus (sŭl′kəs) *n., pl.* **-ci** (-kī′, -sī′). **1.** A narrow, deep furrow or groove. **2.** *Anat.* Any of the narrow fissures separating adjacent cerebral convolutions. [Lat.] —**sul′cal** *adj.*

sulf– or **sulfo–** *pref.* Sulfur: *sulfate.* [< SULFUR.]

sul·fa·di·a·zine (sŭl′fə-dī′ə-zēn′) *n.* An antibacterial sulfa drug, $C_{10}H_{10}O_2N_4S$, used in the treatment of meningitis and other infections. [SULFA (DRUG) + DIAZINE.]

sul·fa drug (sŭl′fə) *n.* Any of a group of synthetic organic compounds, such as sulfadiazine, chemically similar to sulfonamide and capable of inhibiting bacterial growth and activity. [SULFA(NILAMIDE) + DRUG.]

sul·fa·nil·a·mide (sŭl′fə-nĭl′ə-mīd′, -mĭd) *n.* A white, odorless crystalline sulfonamide, $C_6H_8N_2SO_2$, used in the treatment of various bacterial infections. [SULF- + ANIL(INE) + AMIDE.]

sul·fa·tase (sŭl′fə-tās′) *n.* Any of various esterases that catalyze the hydrolysis of sulfuric esters. [SULFAT(E) + -ASE.]

sul·fate (sŭl′fāt′) *n.* A chemical compound containing the bivalent group SO_4. —*v.* **-fat·ed, -fat·ing, -fates.** —*tr.* **1.** To treat or react with sulfuric acid or a sulfate. **2.** *Elect.* To cause lead sulfate to accumulate on (the plates of a lead-acid storage battery). —*intr.* To become sulfated. [Fr. < Lat. *sulfur,* sulfur.]

sul·fide (sŭl′fīd′) *n.* A compound of bivalent sulfur with an electropositive element or group, esp. a binary compound of sulfur with a metal.

sul·fi·nyl (sŭl′fə-nĭl′) *n.* The bivalent group SO. [SULF- + -IN + -YL.]

sul·fite (sŭl′fīt′) *n.* A salt or ester of sulfurous acid. —**sul·fit′ic** (sŭl-fĭt′ĭk) *adj.*

sulfo– *pref.* Variant of **sulf-.**

sulfon– *pref.* **1.** Sulfonic: *sulfonamide.* **2.** Sulfonyl: *sulfonmethane.* [< SULFONE.]

sul·fon·a·mide (sŭl-fŏn′ə-mīd′, -mĭd) *n.* Any of a group of organic sulfur compounds having the general formula RSO_2NH_2.

sul·fo·nate (sŭl′fə-nāt′) *n.* A compound in which a hydrogen atom is replaced by the sulfonic acid group SO_2OH. —*tr.v.* **-nat·ed, -nat·ing, -nates. 1.** To introduce into (an organic compound) one or more sulfonic-acid groups. **2.** To treat with sulfonic acid. —**sul′fo·na′tion** *n.*

sul·fone (sŭl′fōn′) *n.* Any of various organic sulfur compounds having a sulfonyl group attached to two carbon atoms, esp. such a compound used to treat leprosy or tuberculosis.

sul·fon·ic (sŭl-fŏn′ĭk) *adj.* Of or relating to the chemical group SO_3H.

sul·fon·ic acid (sŭl-fŏn′ĭk, -fō′nĭk) *n.* Any of several organic acids containing one or more sulfonic groups, SO_2OH.

sul·fo·ni·um (sŭl-fō′nē-əm) *n.* The univalent cation H_3S. [SULF- + (AMM)ONIUM.]

sul·fon·meth·ane (sŭl′fōn-mĕth′ān′, -fŏn-) *n.* A colorless crystalline or powdered compound, $C_7H_{16}S_2O_4$, used medicinally as a hypnotic.

sul·fo·nyl (sŭl′fə-nĭl′) *n.* The bivalent radical SO_2.

sulf·ox·ide (sŭl-fŏk′sīd′) *n.* Any of various organic compounds that contain a sulfinyl group.

sul·fur also **sul·phur** (sŭl′fər) —*n. Symbol* **S** A pale-yellow nonmetallic element occurring widely in nature both free and combined in several allotropic forms. It is used in black gunpowder, rubber vulcanization, the manufacture of insecticides and pharmaceuticals, and in the preparation of important sulfur compounds, such as hydrogen sulfide and sulfuric acid. Atomic number 16; atomic weight 32.064; melting point (rhombic) 112.8°C; (monoclinic) 119.0°C; boiling point 444.6°C; specific gravity (rhombic) 2.07; (monoclinic) 1.957; valences 2, 4, 6. —*tr.v.* **-fured, -fur·ing, -furs** also **-phured, -phur·ing, -phurs.** To treat with sulfur or a compound of sulfur. [ME *sulphre* < Lat. *sulfur.*]

sul·fu·rate (sŭl′fə-rāt′, -fyə-) *tr.v.* **-rat·ed, -rat·ing, -rates.** To treat or react with sulfur. —**sul′fu·ra′tion** *n.*

sulfur bacterium *n.* A bacterium that is capable of oxidizing sulfur compounds.

sulfur dioxide *n.* A colorless, extremely irritating gas or liquid, SO_2, used in many industrial processes, esp. the manufacture of sulfuric acid.

sul·fu·re·ous (sŭl-fyo͝or′ē-əs) *adj.* Of or pertaining to sulfur; sulfurous.

sul·fu·ret (sŭl′fə-rĕt′, -fyə-) *tr.v.* **-ret·ed, -ret·ing, -rets** or **ret·ted, -ret·ting, -rets.** To sulfurize. —*n.* A sulfide. [< NLat. *sulfuretum,* sulfide < Lat. *sulfur,* sulfur.]

sul·fu·ric (sŭl-fyo͝or′ĭk) *adj.* Of, relating to, or containing sulfur, esp. with valence 6.

sulfuric acid *n.* A highly corrosive, dense oily liquid, H_2SO_4, colorless to dark-brown depending on its purity and used to manufacture a wide variety of chemicals and materials including fertilizers, paints, detergents, and explosives.

sul·fur·ize (sŭl′fə-rīz′, -fyə-) *tr.v.* **-ized, -iz·ing, -iz·es. 1.** To treat or impregnate with sulfur; sulfuret. **2.** To bleach or fumigate with sulfur or sulfur dioxide. —**sul′fur·i·za′tion** *n.*

sul·fur·ous (sŭl′fər-əs, -fyər-, sŭl-fyo͝or′əs) *adj.* **1.** Of, relating to, derived from, or containing sulfur, esp. in its lower valence. **2.** Characteristic of or emanating from burning sulfur. **3.** Also **sul·phur·ous.** Fiery; hellish.

sulfurous acid *n.* A colorless solution of sulfur dioxide in water, H_2SO_3, characterized by a suffocating sulfurous odor, used as a bleaching agent, preservative, and disinfectant.

sulfur trioxide *n.* A corrosive compound, SO_3, having three solid forms that may coexist in a given sample, used in the sulfonation of organic compounds.

sul·fur·y (sŭl′fə-rē) *adj.* **1.** Similar to or suggesting sulfur. **2.** Also **sul·phur·y.** Fiery; hellish.

sul·fur·yl (sŭl′fə-rĭl′, -fyə-) *n.* Sulfonyl.

sulfuryl chloride *n.* A colorless liquid, SO_2Cl_2, having a pungent odor, used as a chlorinating and dehydrating agent and in the manufacture of pharmaceuticals, dyestuffs, and poison gases.

sulk (sŭlk) *intr.v.* **sulked, sulk·ing, sulks.** To be sullenly aloof or withdrawn, as in silent resentment or protest. —*n.* A mood or display of sulking: *in a sulk; a case of the sulks.* [Back-formation < SULKY.]

sulk·y[1] (sŭl′kē) *adj.* **-i·er, -i·est. 1.** Sullenly aloof or withdrawn. **2.** Gloomy; dismal: *sulky weather.* [Orig. unknown.] —**sulk′i·ly** *adv.* —**sulk′i·ness** *n.*

sulk·y[2] (sŭl′kē) *n., pl.* **-ies.** A light two-wheeled vehicle accommodating one person and drawn by one horse. [< SULKY[1] (from its having a single seat).]

sul·lage (sŭl′ĭj) *n.* **1.** Silt deposited by a current of water. **2.** Waste materials or refuse; sewage. [Perh. < OFr. *souiller,* to soil. —see SOIL[2].]

sul·len (sŭl′ən) *adj.* **-er, -est. 1.** Showing a brooding ill humor or resentment; morose; sulky. **2.** Gloomy or somber in tone, color, or portent: *sullen, gray skies.* **3.** Sluggish; slow: *a sullen march.* [ME *solein* < OFr. *sol,* alone < Lat. *solus.*] —**sul′len·ly** *adv.* —**sul′len·ness** *n.*

sul·ly (sŭl′ē) *tr.v.* **-lied, -ly·ing, -lies. 1.** To mar the cleanness or luster of; soil; stain. **2.** To defile; taint. —*n., pl.* **-lies.** *Archaic.* Something that sullies; stain; spot. [Prob. < OFr. *souiller,* to soil. —see SOIL[2].]

sul·phur[1] (sŭl′fər) *n.* Any of various butterflies of the genus *Colias* and related genera, having yellow or orange wings marked with black. [< SULPHUR[2].]

sul·phur[2] (sŭl′fər) *n. & v.* Variant of **sulfur.**

sul·phur-bot·tom (sŭl′fər-bŏt′əm) *n.* The blue whale.

sulphur butterfly *n.* Sulphur[1].

sul·tan (sŭl′tən) *n.* The ruler of a Moslem country, esp. of the former Ottoman Empire. [OFr. < Med. Lat. *sultanus* < Ar. *sulṭān.*]

sul·tan·a (sŭl-tăn′ə, -tä′nə) *n.* **1.** The wife, mother, sister, or daughter of a sultan. **2.** The mistress of a sultan, king, or prince. **3.** A small, yellow, seedless raisin of a kind originally produced in Asia Minor. [Ital., fem. of *sultano,* sultan < Ar. *sulṭān.*]

sul·tan·ate (sŭl′tə-nāt′) *n.* **1.** The office, power, or reign of a sultan. **2.** The domain of a sultan.

sul·try (sŭl′trē) *adj.* **-tri·er, -tri·est. 1.** Very hot and humid. **2.** Extremely hot; torrid. **3.** Sensual; voluptuous: *a sultry*

sumac

George Miksch Sutton
sunbird

sunburst
Sunburst design on a monstrance

Spanish dance. [< obs. *sulter,* to swelter, var. of SWELTER.] **—sul'tri·ly** *adv.* **—sul'tri·ness** *n.*

Su·lu (so͞o'lo͞o) *n., pl.* **Su·lus** or **Sulu. 1. a.** A Moro people inhabiting the Sulu Archipelago. **b.** A member of the Sulus. **2.** The Austronesian language of the Sulus. [Sulu *sulug,* current.] **—Su'lu·an** *adj. & n.*

sum (sŭm) *n.* **1.** The amount obtained as a result of adding. **2.** The whole amount, quantity, or number; aggregate: *the sum of our knowledge.* **3.** An amount of money: *They paid an enormous sum for their house.* **4.** An arithmetic problem: *a child good at sums.* **5.** A summary; gist. *—tr.v.* **summed, sum·ming, sums.** To add. *—**phrasal verb.*** **sum up.** To summarize. [ME *summe* < OFr. < Lat. *summa* < *summus,* highest.]

su·mac also **su·mach** (so͞o'măk', sho͞o'-) *n.* Any of various shrubs or small trees of the genus *Rhus,* having compound leaves and clusters of small greenish flowers followed by usually red, hairy fruits. Some species cause an acute itching rash on contact. [ME < OFr. < Ar. *summāq.*]

Su·me·ri·an (so͞o-mîr'ē-ən, -mĕr'-) *adj.* Of or pertaining to ancient Sumer, its people, culture, or language. *—n.* **1.** A member of an ancient Babylonian people, probably of non-Semitic origin, who established one of the earliest historic civilizations in Sumer in the fourth millennium B.C. **2.** The language of the Sumerians, of no known linguistic affiliation.

sum·ma cum lau·de (so͝om'ə ko͝om lou'də) *adv.* With the greatest praise. [Lat.]

sum·ma·rize (sŭm'ə-rīz') *tr.v.* **-rized, -riz·ing, -riz·es.** To make a summary of; restate briefly. **—sum'ma·ri·za'tion** *n.* **—sum'ma·ri'zer** *n.*

sum·ma·ry (sŭm'ə-rē) *adj.* **1.** Presenting the substance in a condensed form; concise. **2.** Performed speedily and without ceremony: *summary justice.* *—n., pl.* **-ries.** A condensation of the substance of a larger work; abstract; abridgment. [ME < Med. Lat. *summarius* < Lat. *summa,* sum.] **—sum·mar'i·ly** (sə-mĕr'ə-lē) *adv.* **—sum'ma·ri·ness** *n.*

summary court-martial *n.* A court-martial consisting of one officer for trying relatively minor offenses.

sum·ma·tion (sə-mā'shən) *n.* **1.** The act or process of adding or totaling; addition. **2.** A sum or aggregate. **3.** A concluding statement containing a summary of principal points, esp. of a case before a court of law. [< Med. Lat *summare,* to sum up < Lat. *summa,* sum.]

sum·mer¹ (sŭm'ər) *n.* **1.** The usually warmest season of the year occurring between spring and autumn and comprising in the Northern Hemisphere June, July, and August, or, as calculated astronomically, extending from the summer solstice to the autumnal equinox. **2.** Any period regarded as a time of fruition, fulfillment, happiness, or beauty. **3.** A year: *a girl of twenty summers.* *—**modifier:*** *summer flowers; summer clothes.* *—v.* **-mered, -mer·ing, -mers.** *—tr.* To lodge or keep during the summer: *summering the herd in the south meadow.* *—intr.* To pass the summer: *They summered at the beach.* [ME *sumer* < OE *sumor.*] **—sum'mer·ly** *adj. & adv.*

sum·mer² (sŭm'ər) *n. Archit.* **1.** A heavy horizontal timber that serves as a supporting beam, esp. for the floor above. **2.** A lintel. **3.** A large, heavy stone usually set on the top of a column or pilaster to support an arch or lintel. [ME < Norman Fr. *sumer,* beam, pack animal < VLat. **saumarius* < LLat. *sagmarius,* packhorse < *sagma,* pack-saddle. —see SUMPTER.]

summer cypress *n.* A plant, *Kochia scoparia,* native to Eurasia, having dense foliage that turns bright red.

sum·mer·house (sŭm'ər-hous') *n.* A small, roofed structure in a park or garden affording shade and rest; gazebo.

sum·mer·sault (sŭm'ər-sôlt') *n. & v.* Variant of **somersault.**

summer savory *n.* A European herb, *Satureja hortensis,* used as a seasoning.

summer school *n.* An academic session held during the summer.

summer solstice *n. Astron.* A solstice.

summer squash *n.* Any of several varieties of squash, such as the crookneck or the cymling, that are eaten shortly after being picked rather than kept for storage.

summer stock *n.* The theatrical productions of stock companies presented during the summer.

sum·mer·time (sŭm'ər-tīm') *n.* The summer season.

sum·mer·wood (sŭm'ər-wo͝od') *n.* Wood that develops during the latter part of the growing season and is harder and less porous than springwood.

sum·mer·y (sŭm'ə-rē) *adj.* Pertaining to or suggesting summer.

sum·mit (sŭm'ĭt) *n.* **1.** The highest point or part; the top, as of a mountain. **2.** The highest degree of achievement or status. **3. a.** The highest level, as of government. **b.** A summit conference. [ME *somette* < OFr. *sommette,* dim. of *som,* top < Lat. *summus,* highest.]

Synonyms: *summit, peak, pinnacle, acme, apex, zenith, climax.* Each of these nouns is applicable to the highest point of a thing, physically or figuratively. *Summit* and *peak* refer literally to the top, as of a hill or mountain. Figuratively *summit* suggests the highest level attainable, and *peak* the highest point of achievement. *Pinnacle* refers to a tall, slender mass, such as a spire, that tapers to a point or, figuratively, to a height reached by spectacular achievement. *Acme* is used figuratively, for the most part, to represent perfection. *Apex* is applied to the pointed tip or top of a figure, such as a cone, and figuratively to the focal point or culmination of any concerted effort. *Zenith* is that point in the heavens directly overhead or, by extension, the point of highest achievement, development, or power. *Climax* usually refers to the point of greatest development or intensity, marking the end of an ascending process.

summit conference *n.* A conference, esp. of the highest-ranking officials of a government or governments.

sum·mon (sŭm'ən) *tr.v.* **-moned, -mon·ing, -mons. 1.** To call together; convene. **2.** To send for; request to appear. **3.** To order to appear in court by the issuance of a summons. **4.** To order to do a specific act: *summon the captain to surrender.* **5.** To call forth; evoke: *"He summoned up a smile"* (Colin Turnbull). [ME *somonen* < OFr. *somondre* < VLat. **summonere* < Lat. *summonēre,* to remind privately : *sub-,* secretly + *monēre,* to warn.] **—sum·mon·er** (sŭm'ə-nər) *n.*

sum·mons (sŭm'ənz) *n., pl.* **-mons·es. 1.** A call or order to appear, come, or do something. **2.** *Law.* **a.** A notice summoning a defendant to report to a court. **b.** A notice issued to a person summoning him to report to court as a juror or witness. *—tr.v.* **-monsed, -mons·ing, -mons·es.** To serve a court summons to. [ME *somones* < OFr. *somonse,* p.part. of *somondre,* to summon.]

sum·mum bo·num (so͝om'əm bō'nəm) *n.* The greatest or supreme good. [Lat.]

su·mo (so͞o'mō) *n.* Japanese wrestling in which a fighter loses if forced from the ring or if any part of his body except the soles of his feet touches the ground. [J. *sumō.*]

sump (sŭmp) *n.* **1. a.** Any low area which receives drainage. **b.** A cesspool. **2.** A hole at the lowest point of a mine shaft into which water is drained in order to be pumped out. **3.** The crankcase or oil reservoir of an internal-combustion engine. [ME *sompe,* marsh < MLG *sump.*]

sump·ter (sŭmp'tər) *n.* A pack animal, such as a horse or mule. [ME, driver of a pack-horse < OFr. *sometier* < VLat. **saumatarius* < LLat. *sagma,* pack-saddle < Gk. < *sattein,* to pack.]

sump·tu·ar·y (sŭmp'cho͞o-ĕr'ē) *adj.* **1.** Pertaining to expenditure; regulating or limiting expenses. **2.** Regulating personal behavior on moral or religious grounds: *sumptuary laws.* [Lat. *sumptuarius* < *sumptus,* expense < *sumere,* to spend.]

sump·tu·ous (sŭmp'cho͞o-əs) *adj.* Of a size or splendor suggesting great expense; lavish: *"He likes big meals, so I cook sumptuous ones"* (Anaïs Nin). [ME < OFr. *sumptueux* < Lat. *sumptuosus* < *sumptus,* expense. —see SUMPTUARY.] **—sump'tu·ous·ly** *adv.* **—sump'tu·ous·ness** *n.*

sun (sŭn) *n.* **1.** A star that is the basis of the solar system and that sustains life on Earth, being the source of heat and light. It has a mean distance from Earth of about 150 million kilometers, or 93 million miles, a diameter of approximately 1,390,000 kilometers, or 864,000 miles, and a mass about 330,000 times that of Earth. **2.** A star that is the center of a planetary system. **3.** The radiant energy, esp. heat and visible light, emitted by the sun; sunshine. *—v.* **sunned, sun·ning, suns.** *—tr.* **1.** To expose to the sun's rays. **2.** To warm, dry, or tan (something) in the sun. *—intr.* To bask in the sun. *—**idioms.*** **in the sun.** In the public eye. **place in the sun.** A dominant or favorable position or situation. **under the sun.** On earth; in the world. [ME *sonne* < OE *sunne.*]

sun·bath (sŭn'băth', -bäth') *n.* Exposure of the body to sun.

sun·bathe (sŭn'bā*th*') *intr.v.* **-bathed, -bath·ing, -bathes.** To expose the body to the sun. **—sun'bath'er** (-bā'*th*ər) *n.*

sun·beam (sŭn'bēm') *n.* A ray of sunlight.

sun·belt or **Sun·belt** (sŭn'bĕlt') *n.* The southern and southwestern states of the United States.

sun·bird (sŭn'bûrd') *n.* Any of various small, tropical Old World birds of the family Nectariniidae, having a slender, downward-curving bill and often brightly colored plumage in the male.

sun bittern *n.* A cranelike tropical American bird, *Eurypyga helias,* having mottled brownish plumage and often spreading its wings and tail in a showy display.

sun·bon·net (sŭn'bŏn'ĭt) *n.* A woman's wide-brimmed bonnet with a flap at the back to protect the neck from the sun.

sun·bow (sŭn'bō') *n.* A rainbowlike display of colors resulting from the refraction of sunlight through a spray of water.

sun·burn (sŭn'bûrn') *n.* An inflammation or blistering of the skin caused by overexposure to direct sunlight. *—v.* **-burned** or **-burnt** (-bûrnt'), **-burn·ing, -burns.** *—tr.* To afflict with sunburn. *—intr.* To be afflicted with sunburn.

sun·burst (sŭn'bûrst') *n.* **1.** A sudden burst of sunlight, as through broken clouds. **2. a.** A pattern or design consisting of a central disk with radiating spires projecting in the manner of sunbeams. **b.** A jeweled brooch with such a design.

sun·dae (sŭn'dē, -dā') *n.* A dish of ice cream with a topping such as syrup, fruits, nuts, or whipped cream. [Orig. unknown.]

sun dance *n.* A ritual dance performed by the North American Plains Indians at the summer solstice.

Sun·day (sŭn'dē, -dā') *n.* The first day of the week and the Christian Sabbath. [ME *Soneday* < OE *Sūnnandæg,* transl. of Lat. *dies solis,* day of the sun.]

Sunday school *n.* **1.** A school, generally affiliated with a

church, that offers religious instruction for children on Sundays. **2.** The teachers and pupils of a Sunday school.
sun deck *n.* A roof, balcony, or terrace used for sunbathing.
sun·der (sŭn′dər) *v.* **-dered, -der·ing, -ders.** —*tr.* To break (something) apart; sever: *"an island, not widely sundered from the continent"* (Winston Churchill). —*intr.* To break into parts. —*n.* A division or separation. [ME *sundren* < OE *sundrian.*] **—sun′der·ance** *n.*
sun·dew (sŭn′do͞o, -dyo͞o) *n.* Any of several insectivorous plants of the genus *Drosera,* growing in wet ground and having leaves covered with sticky hairs. [Transl. of Lat. *ros solis.*]
sun·di·al (sŭn′dī′əl) *n.* An instrument that indicates local apparent solar time by measuring the hour angle of the sun with a style that casts a shadow on a calibrated dial.
sun disk *n.* An ancient Near Eastern symbol consisting of a disk set between outspread wings, representing the sun god.
sun·dog (sŭn′dôg′, -dŏg′) *n.* **1.** A parhelion. **2.** A small halo or rainbow near the horizon just off the parhelic circle.
sun·down (sŭn′doun′) *n.* The time of sunset.
sun·down·er (sŭn′dou′nər) *n. Slang.* **1.** In Australia, a tramp who looks for a place to sleep at sundown. **2.** *Chiefly Brit.* A drink taken at sundown.
sun·dries (sŭn′drēz) *pl.n.* Articles too small or numerous to be specified; miscellaneous items. [< SUNDRY.]
sun·drops (sŭn′drŏps′) *pl.n. (used with a sing. or pl. verb).* Any of several New World plants of the genus *Oenothera,* having four-petaled yellow flowers. [So called because the flowers remain open during the hours of sunlight.]
sun·dry (sŭn′drē) *adj.* Various; several; miscellaneous: *sundry items of clothing.* [ME *sundri* < OE *syndrig,* separate.]
sun·fish (sŭn′fĭsh′) *n., pl.* **sunfish** or **-fish·es. 1.** Any of various small North American freshwater fishes of the family Centrarchidae, having laterally compressed, often brightly colored bodies. **2.** Any of several large marine fishes of the family Molidae, esp. the ocean sunfish. [From its roundish body and bright colors.]
sun·flow·er (sŭn′flou′ər) *n.* **1.** Any of several plants of the genus *Helianthus,* esp. *H. annuus,* having tall, coarse stems and large yellow-rayed flowers that produce edible seeds rich in oil. **2.** Brilliant yellow to strong or vivid orange yellow. **—sun′flow′er** *adj.*
sung (sŭng) *v.* Past participle and a past tense of **sing.**
sun·glass (sŭn′glăs′) *n.* A burning glass.
sun·glass·es (sŭn′glăs′ĭz) *pl.n.* Eyeglasses with tinted or polarizing lenses to protect the eyes from the sun's glare.
sun·glow (sŭn′glō′) *n.* A rose or yellow glow in the sky preceding sunrise or following sunset.
sun god *n.* A god that personifies the sun.
sunk (sŭngk) *v.* Past participle and a past tense of **sink.**
sunk·en (sŭng′kən) *v.* A past participle of **sink.** —*adj.* **1.** Depressed, fallen in, or hollowed: *sunken cheeks.* **2.** Situated beneath the surface of the water or ground; submerged. **3.** Below the surrounding level: *a sunken meadow.*
sunk fence *n.* A ditch with a retaining wall set in it to divide lands without marring the landscape.
sun lamp *n.* **1.** A lamp that radiates over a wide range of the spectrum from ultraviolet to infrared and is used in therapeutic and cosmetic treatments. **2.** A high-intensity lamp with parabolic mirrors, used in photography.
sun·less (sŭn′lĭs) *adj.* **1.** Without sunlight; dark or overcast. **2.** Gloomy; cheerless. **—sun′less·ness** *n.*
sun·light (sŭn′līt′) *n.* The light of the sun; sunshine.
sun·lit (sŭn′lĭt′) *adj.* Illuminated by the sun.
sunn (sŭn) *n.* **1.** A plant, *Crotalaria juncea,* of tropical Asia, having clusters of yellow flowers. **2.** A tough fiber from the stems of this plant, used for cordage. [Hindi *san* < Skt. *sāṇa,* hempen.]
Sun·na also **Sun·nah** (so͝on′ə) *n.* The body of traditional Moslem law, observed by the orthodox Moslems and based on the teachings and practices of Mohammed. [Ar. *sunnah.*]
Sun·ni (so͝on′ē) *n.* The great branch of Islam following orthodox tradition and accepting the first four caliphs as rightful successors of Mohammed. [Ar. *sunnīy* < *sunnah,* Sunna.]
Sun·nite (so͝on′īt′) *n.* A Moslem of the Sunni. [< SUNNI.]
sun·ny (sŭn′ē) *adj.* **-ni·er, -ni·est. 1.** Exposed to or abounding in sunshine: *a sunny room.* **2.** Cheerful; genial: *a sunny smile.* **—sun′ni·ly** *adv.* **—sun′ni·ness** *n.*
sun·ny-side up (sŭn′ē-sīd′ ŭp′) *adj.* Fried only on one side. Used of eggs.
sun·rise (sŭn′rīz′) *n.* **1.** The event or time of the daily first appearance of the sun above the eastern horizon. **2.** An outset or emergence.
sun·roof (sŭn′ro͞of′, -ro͝of′) *n.* An automobile roof with a panel that can be slid back or lifted up.
sun·scald (sŭn′skôld′) *n.* An injury to woody plants that is characterized by localized death of plant tissues and that is caused by excessive sun in summer and by the combined effects of sun and low temperatures in winter.
sun·screen (sŭn′skrēn′) *n.* A substance, often in the form of a cream or lotion, used to protect the skin from the damaging ultraviolet rays of the sun. **—sun′screen′ing** *adj.*
sun·seek·er (sŭn′sē′kər) *n.* **1.** A person who travels to a region with a warm, sunny climate. **2.** A photoelectric navigational device on a spacecraft or artificial satellite that maintains a constant fix on the sun.
sun·set (sŭn′sĕt′) *n.* **1.** The event or time of the daily disappearance of the sun below the western horizon. **2.** A decline or final phase: *the sunset of the empire.*
sun·shade (sŭn′shād′) *n.* Something, as an awning or a billed cap, that is used or worn as a protection from the sun's rays.
sun·shine (sŭn′shīn′) *n.* **1.** The light or the direct rays from the sun. **2. a.** Happiness or cheerfulness. **b.** A source of happiness or cheerfulness. **—sun′shin′y** *adj.*
sun·spot (sŭn′spŏt′) *n.* Any of the relatively dark spots that appear in groups on the surface of the sun, that have an approximate 11-year cycle, and are associated with strong magnetic fields.
sun·stone (sŭn′stōn′) *n.* Aventurine.
sun·stroke (sŭn′strōk′) *n.* Heat stroke caused by exposure to the sun and characterized by a rise in temperature, convulsions, and coma.
sun·tan (sŭn′tăn′) *n.* A tan color on the skin resulting from exposure to the sun. **—sun′tanned′** *adj.*
sun·up (sŭn′ŭp′) *n.* The time of sunrise.
sun·ward (sŭn′wərd) *adj. & adv.* At or toward the sun. **—sun·wards** (-wərdz) *adv.*
sun·wise (sŭn′wīz′) *adv.* From left to right, like the sun's course as viewed in the Northern Hemisphere.
sup[1] (sŭp) *v.* **supped, sup·ping, sups.** —*tr.* To take (a liquid) into the mouth by sips. —*intr.* To take liquid into the mouth in small amounts. —*n.* A mouthful or taste of liquid. [ME *soupen* < OE *sūpan.*]
sup[2] (sŭp) *intr.v.* **supped, sup·ping, sups.** To eat the evening meal. [ME *soupen* < OFr. *souper* < *soupe,* soup. —see SOUP.]
supe (so͞op) *n. Slang.* A supernumerary actor; extra. [Short for SUPERNUMERARY.]
su·per (so͞o′pər) *n.* **1.** *Informal.* A superintendent in an apartment or office building. **2.** *Informal.* An extra person, esp. a supernumerary actor. **3.** An article or product of superior size, quality, or grade. **4.** A thin starched cotton mesh used to reinforce books. —*adj. Slang.* Ideal; first-rate. —*tr.v.* **-pered, -per·ing, -pers.** To reinforce or strengthen (a book) with super.
super– *pref.* **1.** Above; over; upon: *superimpose.* **2.** Superior in size, quality, number, or degree: *superfine.* **3. a.** Exceeding a norm: *supersaturate.* **b.** Excessive in degree or intensity: *supersubtle.* **c.** Containing a specified ingredient in an unusually high proportion: *superphosphate.* **4.** More inclusive than a specified category: *superorder.* [< Lat. *super,* over, above.]
su·per·a·ble (so͞o′pər-ə-bəl) *adj.* Capable of being overcome or surmounted. [Lat. *superabilis* < *superare,* to overcome < *super,* over.] **—su′per·a·ble·ness** *n.* **—su′per·a·bly** *adv.*
su·per·a·bound (so͞o′pər-ə-bound′) *intr.v.* **-bound·ed, -bound·ing, -bounds.** To be unusually or excessively abundant. [ME *superabounden* < LLat. *superabundare* : Lat. *super-,* excessively + Lat. *abundare,* to overflow. —see ABOUND.]
su·per·a·bun·dant (so͞o′pər-ə-bŭn′dənt) *adj.* Abundant to excess; more than ample. [ME < LLat. *superabundans,* pr.part. of *superabundare,* to superabound.] **—su′per·a·bun′dance** *n.* **—su′per·a·bun′dant·ly** *adv.*
su·per·al·loy (so͞o′pər-ăl′oi) *n.* Any of several complex temperature-resistant alloys.
su·per·an·nu·ate (so͞o′pər-ăn′yo͞o-āt′) *tr.v.* **-at·ed, -at·ing, -ates. 1.** To allow to retire on a pension because of age or infirmity. **2.** To set aside or discard as old-fashioned or obsolete. [Back-formation from SUPERANNUATED.]
su·per·an·nu·at·ed (so͞o′pər-ăn′yo͞o-ā′tĭd) *adj.* **1.** Retired or ineffective because of advanced age: *"Nothing is more tiresome than a superannuated pedagogue"* (Henry Adams). **2.** Obsolete; antiquated. [Med. Lat. *superannuatus,* p.part. of *superannuari,* to be too old : Lat. *super-,* over + Lat. *annus,* year.]
su·perb (so͞o-pûrb′) *adj.* **1.** Of unusually high quality. **2.** Majestic; imposing. **3.** Rich; luxurious. [Lat. *superbus,* proud < *super,* over.] **—su·perb′ly** *adv.* **—su·perb′ness** *n.*
super band *n.* The range of radio frequencies from 216 to 600 megahertz, used primarily for citizens band and cable television transmission.
su·per·cal·en·der (so͞o′pər-kăl′ən-dər) *n.* A calender with a number of rollers for giving a high finish or gloss to paper. —*tr.v.* **-dered, -der·ing, -ders.** To give high finish to.
su·per·car·go (so͞o′pər-kär′gō) *n., pl.* **-goes** or **-gos.** An officer on board a merchant ship who has charge of the cargo and its sale and purchase. [Sp. *sobrecargo* : *sobre-,* over (< Lat. *super-*) + *cargo,* cargo. —see CARGO.]
su·per·charge (so͞o′pər-chärj′) *tr.v.* **-charged, -charg·ing, -charg·es. 1.** To increase the power of (an engine, for example), as by fitting with a supercharger. **2.** To charge or load excessively; to overload. —*n.* An excess or extra charge.
su·per·charg·er (so͞o′pər-chär′jər) *n.* A blower or compressor, usually driven by the engine, for supplying air under high pressure to the cylinders of an internal-combustion engine.
su·per·cil·i·ar·y (so͞o′pər-sĭl′ē-ĕr′ē) *adj.* **1.** Of or pertaining to the eyebrow. **2.** Located over the eyebrow. [NLat. *superciliaris* < Lat. *supercilium,* eyebrow. —see SUPERCILIOUS.]

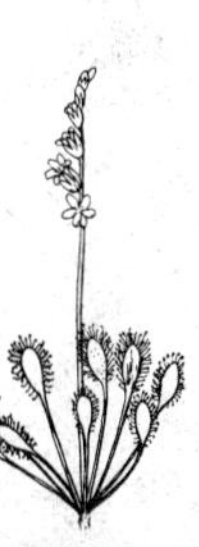
sundew

sundial

sun disk

sunfish

sunflower

su·per·cil·i·ous (so͞o′pər-sĭl′ē-əs) *adj.* Characterized by haughty scorn; disdainful. [Lat. *superciliosus* < *supercilium,* pride, eyebrow : *super-,* above + *cilium,* eyelid.] —**su′per·cil′i·ous·ly** *adv.* —**su′per·cil′i·ous·ness** *n.*
su·per·cil·i·um (so͞o′pər-sĭl′ē-əm) *n.* The eyebrow. [Lat. — see SUPERCILIOUS.]
su·per·class (so͞o′pər-klăs′) *n. Biol.* A taxonomic category ranking between a phylum and a class.
su·per·clus·ter (so͞o′pər-klŭs′tər) *n.* A large group of galaxies in relatively close proximity to each other.
su·per·co·lum·nar (so͞o′pər-kə-lŭm′nər) *adj. Archit.* **1.** Having one order of columns above another. **2.** Situated above a colonnade or column.
su·per·con·duc·tiv·i·ty (so͞o′pər-kŏn′dŭk-tĭv′ĭtē) *n., pl.* **-ties.** The flow of electric current without resistance in certain metals and alloys at temperatures near absolute zero. —**su′per·con·duc′tive** *adj.* —**su′per·con·duc′tor** *n.*
su·per·con·ti·nent (so͞o′pər-kŏn′tə-nənt) *n.* A protocontinent.
su·per·cool (so͞o′pər-ko͞ol′) *v.* **-cooled, -cool·ing, -cools.** —*tr.* To cool (a liquid) below a transition temperature without the transition occurring, esp. to cool below the freezing point without solidification. —*intr.* To become supercooled.
su·per·cur·rent (so͞o′pər-kûr′ənt, -kŭr′-) *n.* An electrical current flowing through a superconductor.
su·per·dom·i·nant (so͞o′pər-dŏm′ə-nənt) *n. Mus.* The submediant.
su·per·du·per (so͞o′pər-do͞o′pər) *adj. Slang.* Great; marvelous. [Redup. of SUPER.]
su·per·e·go (so͞o′pər-ē′gō, -ĕg′ō) *n. Psychoanal.* The division of the psyche that develops by the incorporation of the perceived moral standards of the community, is mainly unconscious, and includes the conscience.
su·per·em·i·nent (so͞o′pər-ĕm′ə-nənt) *adj.* Eminent beyond all others; pre-eminent. [LLat. *supereminens, supereminent-* < Lat., pr.part. of *supereminēre,* to rise above : *super-,* above + *eminēre,* to stand out.] —**su′per·em′i·nence** *n.* —**su′per·em′i·nent·ly** *adv.*
su·per·er·o·gate (so͞o′pər-ĕr′ə-gāt′) *intr.v.* **-gat·ed, -gat·ing, -gates.** To do more than is required, ordered, or expected. [LLat. *supererogare, supererogat-,* to spend more : Lat. *super-,* above + Lat. *erogare,* to spend (*ex-,* out + *rogare,* to ask).]
su·per·er·o·ga·tion (so͞o′pər-ĕr′ə-gā′shən) *n.* The performance of more than is required, demanded, or expected.
su·per·e·rog·a·to·ry (so͞o′pər-ĭ-rŏg′ə-tôr′ē, -tōr′ē) also **su·per·e·rog·a·tive** (-tĭv). *adj.* **1.** Performed or observed beyond the degree required or expected. **2.** Superfluous; unnecessary.
su·per·fam·i·ly (so͞o′pər-făm′ə-lē) *n., pl.* **-lies.** A taxonomic category ranking between an order or its subdivisions and a family.
su·per·fec·ta (so͞o′pər-fĕk′tə) *n.* A method of betting in which the bettor, in order to win, must pick the first four finishers of a race in the correct sequence. [Blend of SUPER- and PERFECTA.]
su·per·fe·cun·da·tion (so͞o′pər-fē′kən-dā′shən, -fĕk′ən-) *n.* The impregnation of more than one ovum within a single menstrual cycle by separate acts of coitus, esp. by different males.
su·per·fe·tate (so͞o′pər-fē′tāt′) *intr.v.* **-tat·ed, -tat·ing, -tates.** To conceive when a fetus is already present in the uterus. [Lat. *superfetare, superfetat-* : *super-,* over + *fetare,* to breed < *fetus,* offspring.]
su·per·fe·ta·tion (so͞o′pər-fē-tā′shən) *n.* The presence of fetuses of different ages resulting from the fertilization and development of two or more ova liberated at different periods of ovulation in the same uterus.
su·per·fi·cial (so͞o′pər-fĭsh′əl) *adj.* **1.** Of, affecting, or being on or near the surface: *a superficial wound.* **2.** Concerned with only what is apparent or obvious; shallow. **3. a.** Apparent rather than actual or substantial. **b.** Trivial; insignificant. [ME < LLat. *superficialis* < Lat. *superficies,* surface. — see SUPERFICIES.] —**su′per·fi′ci·al′i·ty** (-fĭsh′ē-ăl′ĭ-tē), **su′per·fi′cial·ness** *n.* —**su′per·fi′cial·ly** *adv.*
Synonyms: *superficial, shallow, cursory.* These adjectives mean lacking in depth or thoroughness. *Superficial* applies to thought and action concerned largely with the obvious, sometimes implying lack of genuine interest or sincerity. *Shallow* emphasizes lack of intellectual or emotional depth in persons or their works; more strongly than *superficial,* it implies lack of capacity for something better. *Cursory* principally describes action performed speedily and without thoroughness.
su·per·fi·cies (so͞o′pər-fĭsh′ēz, -fĭsh′ē-ēz′) *n., pl.* **superficies. 1.** The surface of an area or body. **2.** The external appearance or aspect of a thing. [Lat. : *super-,* above + *facies,* face.]
su·per·fine (so͞o′pər-fīn′) *adj.* **1.** Of exceptional quality or refinement. **2.** Overdelicate or refined. **3.** Of extra fine texture. —**su′per·fine′ness** *n.*
su·per·flu·id (so͞o′pər-flo͞o′ĭd) *n.* A fluid, as an electric current or a form of helium, exhibiting a frictionless flow at temperatures close to absolute zero. —**su′per·flu·id′i·ty** (-flo͞o-ĭd′ĭ-tē) *n.*
su·per·flu·i·ty (so͞o′pər-flo͞o′ĭ-tē) *n., pl.* **-ties. 1.** The quality or condition of being superfluous. **2.** Something that is superfluous. **3.** Overabundance; excess.
su·per·flu·ous (so͞o-pûr′flo͞o-əs) *adj.* Beyond what is required or sufficient; extra. [ME < Lat. *superfluus* < *superfluere,* to overflow : *super-,* over + *fluere,* to flow.] —**su·per′flu·ous·ly** *adv.* —**su·per′flu·ous·ness** *n.*
su·per·gal·ax·y (so͞o′pər-găl′ək-sē) *n., pl.* **-ies.** A very large group of galaxies.
su·per·gi·ant (so͞o′pər-jī′ənt) *n.* A very large star generally of sufficient rotational speed to flatten from a spherical shape.
su·per·graph·ics (so͞o′pər-grăf′ĭks) *n. (used with a sing. or pl. verb).* Brightly colored and simply designed graphic shapes of billboard proportions.
su·per·heat (so͞o′pər-hēt′) *tr.v.* **-heat·ed, -heat·ing, -heats. 1.** To heat excessively; overheat. **2.** To heat (steam or other vapor not in contact with its own liquid) beyond its saturation point at a given pressure. **3.** To heat (a liquid) above its boiling point at a given pressure without causing vaporization. —*n.* (so͞o′pər-hēt′). **1.** The amount that a vapor is superheated. **2.** The heat imparted in the process of superheating. —**su′per·heat′er** *n.*
su·per·het·er·o·dyne (so͞o′pər-hĕt′ər-ə-dīn′) *adj.* Indicating or pertaining to a form of radio reception in which the frequency of an incoming radio signal is converted to an intermediate frequency, by mixing with a locally generated signal, to facilitate amplification and the rejection of unwanted signals. —*n.* A superheterodyne radio receiver. [SUPER(SONIC) + HETERODYNE.]
su·per·high frequency (so͞o′pər-hī′) *n.* A radio frequency between 3,000 and 30,000 megahertz.
su·per·high·way (so͞o′pər-hī′wā′) *n.* A broad arterial highway, such as an expressway, used for high-speed traffic.
su·per·hu·man (so͞o′pər-hyo͞o′mən) *adj.* **1.** Above or beyond the human; divine. **2.** Beyond ordinary or normal human ability, power, or experience: *"soldiers driven mad by superhuman misery"* (John Reed). —**su′per·hu·man′i·ty** (-măn′ĭ-tĭ) *n.* —**su′per·hu′man·ly** *adv.*
su·per·im·pose (so͞o′pər-ĭm-pōz′) *tr.v.* **-posed, -pos·ing, -pos·es.** To lay or place upon or over something. —**su′per·im′po·si′tion** (-ĭm′pə-zĭsh′ən) *n.*
su·per·in·cum·bent (so͞o′pər-ĭn-kŭm′bənt) *adj.* Lying or resting on or above something. [Lat. *superincumbens, superincumbent-,* pr.part. of *superincumbere,* to lie on top of : *super-,* above + *incumbere,* to lie down. —see INCUMBENT.] —**su′per·in·cum′bence, su′per·in·cum′ben·cy** *n.*
su·per·in·duce (so͞o′pər-ĭn-do͞os′, -dyo͞os′) *tr.v.* **-duced, -duc·ing, -duc·es.** To introduce as an addition. [LLat. *superinducere,* to bring upon : Lat. *super-,* over + Lat. *inducere,* to lead in. —see INDUCE.] —**su′per·in·duc′tion** *n.*
su·per·in·tend (so͞o′pər-ĭn-tĕnd′, so͞o′prĭn-) *tr.v.* **-tend·ed, -tend·ing, -tends.** To have charge of; exercise supervision over. [LLat. *superintendere* : Lat. *super-,* over + Lat. *intendere,* to direct one's attention to. —see INTEND.] —**su′per·in·ten′dence** *n.*
su·per·in·ten·dent (so͞o′pər-ĭn-tĕn′dənt, so͞o′prĭn-) *n.* A person who has the authority to supervise or direct. —**su′per·in·ten′dent** *adj.*
su·pe·ri·or (so͞o-pîr′ē-ər) *adj.* **1.** Higher in rank, station, or authority: *a superior officer.* **2.** Of a higher nature or kind. **3.** Of great value or excellence; extraordinary. **4.** Greater in number or amount: *an army defeated by superior numbers of enemy troops.* **5.** Affecting an attitude of disdain or conceit; haughty; supercilious. **6.** Above being affected or influenced; indifferent or immune: *"Trust magnates were superior to law"* (Gustavus Myers). **7.** Located higher; upper. **8.** *Bot.* Located above and not in contact with the calyx and corolla. Used of an ovary. **9.** *Printing.* Set above the main line of type. **10.** *Logic.* Of wider or more comprehensive application; generic. Used of a term or proposition. —*n.* **1.** One who surpasses another in rank or quality. **2.** The head of a religious community, as a monastery, an abbey, or a convent. **3.** *Printing.* A superior character or letter. [ME < OFr. < Lat., comp. of *superus,* upper < *super,* over.] —**su·pe′ri·or′i·ty** (-ôr′ĭ-tē, -ŏr′-) *n.* —**su·pe′ri·or·ly** *adv.*
superior conjunction *n.* The position of a celestial body when it is on the opposite side of the sun from Earth.
superior court *n.* A court of general jurisdiction, above the inferior courts and below the higher courts of appeal.
superiority complex *n.* **1.** A feeling of being superior to others. **2.** A psychological defense in which feelings of superiority counter feelings of inferiority.
superior planet *n.* A planet whose mean distance from the sun is greater than that of Earth.
su·per·ja·cent (so͞o′pər-jā′sənt) *adj.* Resting or lying immediately above or upon something else. [Lat. *superjacens, superjacent-,* pr.part. of *superjacēre,* to lie over : *super-,* over + *jacēre,* to lie.]
su·per·jet (so͞o′pər-jĕt′) *n.* A supersonic jet airplane.
su·per·la·tive (so͞o-pûr′lə-tĭv) *adj.* **1.** Of the highest order, quality, or degree; superior to all others. **2.** Excessive or exaggerated. **3.** *Gram.* Expressing or involving the extreme degree of comparison of an adjective or adverb. —*n.* **1.** Something of the highest possible excellence. **2.** The highest degree; acme. **3.** *Gram.* **a.** The superlative degree. **b.** An adjective or adverb expressing the superlative degree:

"Brightest" is the superlative of "bright"; "most brightly" is the superlative of "brightly." [ME *superlatyf* < OFr. < LLat. *superlativus* < Lat. *superlatus,* excessive : *super-,* over + *latus,* p.part. of *ferre,* to carry.] **—su·per'la·tive·ly** *adv.*

su·per·lu·na·ry (sōō'pər-lōō'nə-rē) also **su·per·lu·nar** (-nə-r) *adj.* Situated beyond the moon.

su·per·man (sōō'pər-măn') *n.* **1.** A person with more than human powers. **2.** An ideal superior man who, according to Nietzsche, represents the goal of human evolution because of his exercise of creative power and his ability to forgo transient pleasure.

su·per·mar·ket (sōō'pər-mär'kĭt) *n.* A large self-service retail market that sells food and household goods.

su·per·mol·e·cule (sōō'pər-mŏl'ĭ-kyōōl') *n.* Macromolecule.

su·per·nal (sōō-pûr'nəl) *adj.* **1.** Celestial; heavenly. **2.** Of, coming from, or being in the sky or high above. [ME < OFr. < Lat. *supernus* < *super,* over.] **—su·per'nal·ly** *adv.*

su·per·na·tant (sōō'pər-nāt'nt) *adj.* Floating on the surface. [Lat. *supernatans, supernatant-,* pr.part. of *supernatare,* to float : *super-,* above + *natare,* to swim.] **—su'per·na'tant** *n.*

su·per·nate (sōō'pər-nāt') *n.* The clear supernatant fluid over a sediment or precipitate. [Short for SUPERNATANT.]

su·per·nat·u·ral (sōō'pər-năch'ər-əl) *adj.* **1.** Of or pertaining to existence outside the natural world. **2.** Attributed to a power that seems to violate or go beyond natural laws; miraculous. **3.** Of or pertaining to a deity. *—n.* That which is supernatural. **—su'per·nat'u·ral·ly** *adv.* **—su'per·nat'u·ral·ness** *n.*

su·per·nat·u·ral·ism (sōō'pər-năch'ər-ə-lĭz'əm) *n.* **1.** The quality of being supernatural. **2.** Belief in a supernatural agency that intervenes in the course of natural laws. **—su'per·nat'u·ral·ist** *n.* **—su'per·nat'u·ral·is'tic** *adj.*

su·per·nor·mal (sōō'pər-nôr'məl) *adj.* Greatly exceeding the normal or average.

su·per·no·va (sōō'pər-nō'və) *n., pl.* **-vae** (-vē) or **-vas.** A rare celestial phenomenon involving the explosion of most of the material in a star, resulting in an extremely bright, short-lived object that emits vast amounts of energy.

su·per·nu·mer·ar·y (sōō'pər-nōō'mə-rĕr'ē, -nyōō'-) *adj.* **1.** Exceeding a fixed, prescribed, or standard number; extra. **2.** Beyond the required or desired number; superfluous. *—n., pl.* **-ies. 1.** One that is in excess of the regular, necessary, or usual number. **2.** A performer without a speaking part, as one who appears in a crowd scene. [LLat. *supernumerarius* : Lat. *super-,* above + Lat. *numerus,* number.]

su·per·or·der (sōō'pər-ôr'dər) *n.* A taxonomic category ranking between a class or one of its subdivisions and an order.

su·per·o·vu·la·tion (sōō'pər-ō'vyə-lā'shən, -ŏv'yə-) *n.* The production of a large number of ova at one time.

su·per·phos·phate (sōō'pər-fŏs'fāt') *n.* **1.** An acid phosphate. **2.** A fertilizer made by the action of sulfuric acid on phosphate rock that consists chiefly of tribasic calcium phosphate, to form a mixture of gypsum and monobasic calcium phosphate.

su·per·phys·i·cal (sōō'pər-fĭz'ĭ-kəl) *adj.* Exceeding or beyond the purely physical.

su·per·pose (sōō'pər-pōz') *tr.v.* **-posed, -pos·ing, -pos·es. 1.** To set or place over or above something else. **2.** To place (one geometric figure) over another so that all like parts coincide.

su·per·pow·er (sōō'pər-pou'ər) *n.* A powerful and influential nation, esp. one that dominates its satellites and allies in an international power bloc.

su·per·sat·u·rate (sōō'pər-săch'ə-rāt') *tr.v.* **-rat·ed, -rat·ing, -rates.** To cause (a chemical solution) to be more highly concentrated than is normally possible under given conditions of temperature and pressure. **—su'per·sat'u·ra'tion** *n.*

su·per·scribe (sōō'pər-skrīb') *tr.v.* **-scribed, -scrib·ing, -scribes. 1.** To write on the outside or upper part of (a letter, for example). **2.** To write (a name, for example) on the top or outside. [Lat. *superscribere,* to write over : *super-,* over + *scribere,* to write.]

su·per·script (sōō'pər-skrĭpt') *n.* A character set, printed, or written above and immediately to one side of another: *2 is the superscript in* x^2. [< Lat. *superscriptus,* p.part. of *superscribere,* to write over. —see SUPERSCRIBE.] **—su'per·script** *adj.*

su·per·scrip·tion (sōō'pər-skrĭp'shən) *n.* **1.** Something written above or outside something else. **2.** The act of superscribing.

su·per·sede (sōō'pər-sēd') *tr.v.* **-sed·ed, -sed·ing, -sedes. 1.** To take the place of; replace. **2.** To cause to be set aside or displaced. [ME *superceden,* to postpone < OFr. *superceder* < Lat. *supersedēre,* to refrain from : *super-,* above + *sedēre,* to sit.] **—su'per·sed'er** *n.* **—su'per·ses'sion** (-sĕsh'ən) *n.*

su·per·se·de·as (sōō'pər-sē'dē-əs) *n. Law.* A writ containing a command to stay legal proceedings, as in the halting or delaying of the execution of a sentence. [Med. Lat. < Lat., you must desist, the first word of the writ.]

su·per·se·dure (sōō'pər-sē'jər) *n.* **1.** The act or process of superseding. **2.** The replacement of a queen bee by another that is younger or superior.

su·per·sen·si·ble (sōō'pər-sĕn'sə-bəl) *adj.* Beyond or above perception by the senses. **—su'per·sen'si·bly** *adv.*

su·per·son·ic (sōō'pər-sŏn'ĭk) *adj.* Having, caused by, or related to a speed greater than the speed of sound in a specified medium. **—su'per·son'i·cal·ly** *adv.*

su·per·son·ics (sōō'pər-sŏn'ĭks) *n. (used with a sing. verb).* The study of phenomena produced by the motion of a body through a medium at velocities greater than that of sound.

supersonic transport *n.* A large transport airplane engineered to operate at supersonic speeds.

su·per·star (sōō'pər-stär') *n.* **1.** A widely acclaimed star, as in motion pictures or sports, who has great popular appeal. **2.** One that is extremely popular or prominent or that is a major attraction.

su·per·sti·tion (sōō'pər-stĭsh'ən) *n.* **1.** A belief held in spite of evidence to the contrary. **2. a.** A belief, practice, or rite resulting from ignorance of the laws of nature or from faith in magic or chance. **b.** A fearful or abject state of mind resulting from such ignorance or irrationality. [ME *supersticion* < OFr. *superstition* < Lat. *superstitio* < *superstare,* to stand over : *super-,* over + *stare,* to stand.]

su·per·sti·tious (sōō'pər-stĭsh'əs) *adj.* **1.** Inclined to believe in superstition. **2.** Of, characterized by, or proceeding from superstition. **—su'per·sti'tious·ly** *adv.* **—su'per·sti'tious·ness** *n.*

su·per·stra·tum (sōō'pər-strā'təm, -străt'əm) *n., pl.* **-stra·ta** (-strā'tə, -străt'ə). One layer or stratum superimposed upon another.

su·per·struc·ture (sōō'pər-strŭk'chər) *n.* **1.** A structure built on top of something else. **2.** That part of a building or other structure above the foundation. **3.** The rails, sleepers, and other parts of a railway as distinguished from the roadbed. **4.** The parts of a ship's structure above the main deck. **5.** An institution of a society, such as the law, that rests upon a simpler or more fundamental base.

su·per·ton·ic (sōō'pər-tŏn'ĭk) *n. Mus.* The second tone of a diatonic scale.

su·per·vene (sōō'pər-vēn') *intr.v.* **-vened, -ven·ing, -venes. 1.** To come or occur as something extraneous, additional, or unexpected. **2.** To follow immediately after; ensue. [Lat. *supervenire* : *super-,* in addition to + *venire,* to come.] **—su'per·ven'ient** (-vēn'yənt) *adj.* **—su'per·ven'tion** (-vĕn'shən) *n.*

su·per·vise (sōō'pər-vīz') *tr.v.* **-vised, -vis·ing, -vis·es.** To direct and inspect the performance of; superintend. [Med. Lat. *supervidēre, supervis-,* to look over : Lat. *super-,* over + Lat. *vidēre,* to see.] **—su'per·vi'sion** (-vĭzh'ən) *n.*

su·per·vi·sor (sōō'pər-vī'zər) *n.* **1.** A person who supervises. **2.** An elected administrative officer in certain U.S. counties and townships. **3.** A person in charge of a particular department or unit, as in a governmental agency or a school system. **—su'per·vi'so·ry** (-vī'zə-rē) *adj.*

su·pi·nate (sōō'pə-nāt') *v.* **-nat·ed, -nat·ing, -nates.** *—tr.* To turn or place (the hand and forearm) so that the palm is upward. *—intr.* To assume a position with the palm and forearm upward. [Lat. *supinare, supinat-,* to bend backward < *supinus,* backward.] **—su'pi·na'tion** *n.*

su·pi·na·tor (sōō'pə-nā'tər) *n.* A muscle in the forearm that makes supination possible.

su·pine[1] (sōō-pīn', sōō'pīn') *adj.* **1.** Lying on the back or having the face upward. **2.** Having the palm upward. Used of the hand. **3.** Indisposed to act or object; lethargic; passive. **4.** Inclined; sloping. [Lat. *supinus.*] **—su·pine'ly** *adv.* **—su·pine'ness** *n.*

su·pine[2] (sōō'pīn') *n.* A Latin verbal noun having an accusative in *-um* and an ablative in *-ū.* [LLat. *supinum* < Lat. *supinus,* backward.]

sup·per (sŭp'ər) *n.* **1. a.** An evening meal. **b.** A light evening meal when dinner is taken at midday. **2.** A dance or social affair where supper is served. [ME *suppere* < OFr. *souper.* —see SUP[2].]

sup·plant (sə-plănt') *tr.v.* **-plant·ed, -plant·ing, -plants.** To take the place of; supersede. [ME *supplanten* < *supplanter* < Lat. *supplantare,* to trip up : *sub-,* from below + *planta,* sole of the foot.]

sup·ple (sŭp'əl) *adj.* **-pler, -plest. 1.** Readily bent; pliant. **2.** Moving and bending with agility; limber. **3.** Yielding or changing readily; compliant or adaptable. *—v.* **-pled, -pling, -ples.** *—tr.* **1.** To make supple. **2.** To make amiable, friendly, and agreeable. *—intr.* To become supple. [ME *souple* < OFr. < Lat. *supplex,* bending at the knees, humble.] **—sup'ply, sup'ple·ly** *adv.* **—sup'ple·ness** *n.*

sup·ple·ment (sŭp'lə-mənt) *n.* **1.** Something added to complete a thing, make up for a deficiency, or extend or strengthen the whole. **2.** A section added to a book or document to give further information or to correct errors. **3.** A separate section devoted to a special subject inserted into a newspaper or other periodical. **4.** The angle or arc that when added to a given angle or arc makes 180 degrees or a semicircle. *—tr.v.* (sŭp'lə-mĕnt') **-ment·ed, -ment·ing, -ments.** To provide or form a supplement to. [ME < Lat. *supplementum* < *supplēre,* to complete. —see SUPPLY.] **—sup'ple·men'ta·ry** (-tə-rē, -trē), **sup'ple·men'tal** *adj.* **—sup'ple·men·ta'tion** (-mĕn-tā'shən) *n.*

supplementary angle *n.* Supplement (sense 4).

sup·pli·ant (sŭp'lē-ənt) *adj.* Asking humbly and earnestly; beseeching. *—n.* One who supplicates. [ME < OFr., pr.part. of *supplier,* to entreat < Lat. *supplicare.* —see SUPPLICATE.] **—sup'pli·ant·ly** *adv.*

sup·pli·cant (sŭp′lĭ-kənt) *n.* One who supplicates; suppliant. *—adj.* Supplicating.
sup·pli·cate (sŭp′lĭ-kāt′) *v.* **-cat·ed, -cat·ing, -cates.** *—tr.* **1.** To ask for humbly or earnestly, as by praying. **2.** To make a humble entreaty to; beseech. *—intr.* To make a humble and earnest petition; beg. [ME *supplicaten* < Lat. *supplicare,* to kneel down : *sub-,* down + *plicare,* to fold up.] **—sup′pli·ca′tion** *n.* **—sup′pli·ca·to′ry** (-kə-tôr′ē, -tōr′ē) *adj.*
sup·ply (sə-plī′) *v.* **-plied, -ply·ing, -plies.** *—tr.* **1.** To make available for use; provide. **2.** To furnish or equip with: *supplied sheets for every bed.* **3.** To fill sufficiently; satisfy: *supply a need.* **4.** To make up for (a deficiency, for example); compensate for. **5.** To serve temporarily as a substitute in (a church, for example). *—intr.* To fill a position as a substitute. *—n., pl.* **-plies. 1.** The act of supplying. **2.** Something that is or can be supplied. **3.** An amount available or sufficient for a given use; stock. **4.** Often **supplies.** Materials or provisions stored and dispensed when needed. **5.** *Econ.* The amount of a commodity available for meeting a demand or for purchase at a given price. **6.** A clergyman serving as a substitute or temporary pastor. [ME *supplen* < OFr. *soupleer* < Lat. *supplēre* : *sub-,* from below + *plēre,* to fill.] **—sup·pli′er** *n.*
sup·port (sə-pôrt′, -pōrt′) *tr.v.* **-port·ed, -port·ing, -ports. 1.** To bear the weight of, esp. from below. **2.** To hold in position so as to keep from falling, sinking, or slipping. **3.** To be capable of bearing; withstand. **4.** To keep from failing or yielding during stress. **5.** To provide for or maintain, by supplying with money or necessities. **6.** To furnish corroborating evidence for. **7.** To aid the cause of by approving, favoring, or advocating. **8.** To endure; tolerate. **9. a.** To act (a part or role). **b.** To act in a secondary or subordinate role to (a leading actor). *—n.* **1. a.** The act of supporting. **b.** The state of being supported. **2.** One that supports. **3.** Maintenance or subsistence. [ME *supporten* < OFr. *supporter* < Lat. *supportare,* to carry : *sub-,* from below + *portare,* to carry.]

Synonyms: *support, uphold, sustain, maintain, advocate, champion.* These verbs are compared in the sense of giving aid, encouragement, or the like to a person or cause. *Support* refers nonspecifically to any such aid. *Uphold* often implies aid to someone or something faced with strong opposition or a challenge. *Sustain* and *maintain* can refer to material or financial aid or support. In this comparison, however, *sustain* more often suggests keeping up a person's spirits in time of stress, whereas *maintain* applies to the defense of personal rights or a position or cause. *Advocate* implies verbal support, usually in the sense of pleading or arguing. *Champion* suggests aid in the form of defense of what is under attack or protection of what is unable to act in its own behalf.

supreme court
Above: The U.S. Supreme Court Building, Washington, D.C.
Below: Interior of the courtroom

sup·port·a·ble (sə-pôr′tə-bəl, -pōr′-) *adj.* Bearable; endurable. **—sup·port′a·bly** *adv.*
sup·port·er (sə-pôr′tər, -pōr′-) *n.* **1.** One that supports. **2.** One who promotes or advocates; adherent. **3.** An athletic supporter.
sup·por·tive (sə-pôr′tĭv, -pōr′-) *adj.* Furnishing support or assistance.
sup·pos·a·ble (sə-pō′zə-bəl) *adj.* Capable of being supposed or conjectured. **—sup·pos′a·bly** *adv.*
sup·pose (sə-pōz′) *v.* **-posed, -pos·ing, -pos·es.** *—tr.* **1.** To assume to be true or real for the sake of an argument or explanation. **2. a.** To believe, esp. on uncertain or tentative grounds. **b.** To consider to be probable or likely. **3.** To imply as an antecedent condition; presuppose. **4.** To consider as a suggestion: *Suppose we dine together.* *—intr.* To imagine; conjecture. [ME *supposen* < OFr. *supposer* < Med. Lat. *supponere* < Lat., to put under : *sub-,* under + *ponere,* to place.]
sup·posed (sə-pōzd′, -pō′zĭd) *adj.* **1.** Presumed to be true, real, or genuine, esp. on dubious grounds. **2.** Intended: *medication that is supposed to relieve pain.* **3. a.** Required: *He is supposed to go to the store.* **b.** Permitted: *was not supposed to smoke here.* **—sup·pos′ed·ly** (-pō′zĭd-lē) *adv.*
sup·pos·ing (sə-pō′zĭng) *conj.* Assuming that: *Supposing we're right, what should we do?*
sup·po·si·tion (sŭp′ə-zĭsh′ən) *n.* **1.** The act of supposing. **2.** Something supposed; assumption. **—sup′po·si′tion·al** *adj.* **—sup′po·si′tion·al·ly** *adv.*
sup·pos·i·ti·tious (sə-pŏz′ĭ-tĭsh′əs) *adj.* **1.** Substituted with fraudulent intent; spurious. **2.** Hypothetical; supposed. [Lat. *suppositicius* < *supponere,* to substitute. —see SUPPOSE.] **—sup·pos′i·ti′tious·ly** *adv.* **—sup·pos′i·ti′tious·ness** *n.*
sup·pos·i·tive (sə-pŏz′ĭ-tĭv) *adj.* Of the nature of, including, or involving supposition. *—n. Gram.* A conjunction, such as *if* or *providing,* that introduces a supposition. **—sup·pos′i·tive·ly** *adv.*
sup·pos·i·to·ry (sə-pŏz′ĭ-tôr′ē, -tōr′ē) *n., pl.* **-ries.** A solid medication designed to melt within a body cavity other than the mouth. [Med. Lat. *suppositorium* < LLat. *suppositorius,* placed under < *supponere,* to put under. —see SUPPOSE.]
sup·press (sə-prĕs′) *tr.v.* **-pressed, -press·ing, -press·es. 1.** To put an end to forcibly; subdue. **2.** To curtail or prohibit the activities of. **3. a.** To keep from being revealed, published, or circulated. **b.** To keep from the consciousness. **4.** To hold back (an impulse, for example); check. **5.** To reduce the incidence or severity of (a hemorrhage, for example); arrest. [ME *suppressen* < Lat. *supprimere* : *sub-,* down + *premere,* to press.] **—sup·press′er, sup·pres′sor** (-prĕs′ər) *n.* **—sup·press′i·ble** *adj.*

Synonyms: *suppress, stifle.* These verbs refer to the exercise of power or control that either brings about extinction or severely limits force or function. *Suppress* implies crushing or restricting drastically in effectiveness. *Stifle* can refer to physical attack on a person but more often applies to restraining or smothering, as emotions, coughs, or cries.

sup·pres·sion (sə-prĕsh′ən) *n.* **1.** The act of suppressing. **2.** The state of being suppressed. **3.** *Psychoanal.* The conscious exclusion of painful desires or thoughts from awareness.
sup·pres·sive (sə-prĕs′ĭv) *adj.* Tending to suppress; subduing.
sup·pres·sor (sə-prĕs′ər) *n.* **1.** A gene which completely reduces the phenotypic expression of a mutant gene. **2.** The grid between screen and plate in a pentode.
sup·pu·rate (sŭp′yə-rāt′) *intr.v.* **-rat·ed, -rat·ing, -rates.** To form or discharge pus. [Lat. *suppurare, suppurat-* : *sub-,* under + *pus,* pus.]
sup·pu·ra·tion (sŭp′yə-rā′shən) *n.* **1.** The formation or discharge of pus. **2.** Pus. **—sup′pu·ra′tive** *adj.*
supra– *pref.* **1.** Above; over; on top of: *suprarenal.* **2.** Greater than; transcending: *supramolecular.* **3.** Earlier than: *supralapsarian.* [Lat. < *supra,* above, beyond, earlier.]
su·pra·glot·tal (so͞o′prə-glŏt′l) *adj.* **1.** Above or anterior to the glottis. **2.** *Ling.* Designating a phone or phoneme produced by the speech organs anterior to the glottis.
su·pra·lap·sar·i·an (so͞o′prə-lăp-sâr′ē-ən) *n.* A Calvinist who believes that God's determination of the elect preceded the fall of man from grace and the fall itself had been predestined. [SUPRA- + Lat. *lapsus,* fall + -ARIAN.] **—su′pra·lap·sar′i·an** *adj.* **—su′pra·lap·sar′i·an·ism** *n.*
su·pra·lim·i·nal (so͞o′prə-lĭm′ə-nəl) *adj.* Above the threshold of consciousness or of sensation.
su·pra·mo·lec·u·lar (so͞o′prə-mə-lĕk′yə-lər) *adj.* **1.** Consisting of more than one molecule. **2.** Of greater complexity than a molecule.
su·pra·or·bi·tal (so͞o′prə-ôr′bĭ-təl) *adj.* Located above the orbit of the eye.
su·pra·re·nal (so͞o′prə-rē′nəl) *adj.* Located on or above the kidney. *—n.* **1.** A suprarenal part. **2.** An adrenal gland.
suprarenal gland *n.* An adrenal gland.
su·pra·scap·u·lar (so͞o′prə-skăp′yə-lər) *adj.* Located above the scapula.
su·prem·a·cist (so͞o-prĕm′ə-sĭst) *n.* One who believes that a certain group is or should be supreme: *a male supremacist.*
su·prem·a·cy (so͞o-prĕm′ə-sē) *n., pl.* **-cies. 1.** The condition or quality of being supreme. **2.** Supreme power or authority.
su·preme (so͞o-prēm′) *adj.* **1.** Greatest in power, authority, or rank; paramount; dominant. **2.** Greatest in importance, degree, significance, character, or achievement. **3.** Ultimate; final: *the supreme sacrifice.* [Lat. *supremus,* superl. of *superus,* upper < *super,* over.] **—su·preme′ly** *adv.* **—su·preme′ness** *n.*
Supreme Being *n.* God.
supreme court *n.* **1.** The highest federal court in the United States, consisting of nine justices and having jurisdiction over all other courts in the nation. **2.** The highest court in most states within the United States.
Supreme Soviet *n.* The legislature of the Soviet Union, consisting of two houses one of which represents the overall population and the other, the constituent republics.
su·pre·mo (so͞o-prē′mō′, sə-) *n., pl.* **-mos.** *Chiefly Brit.* One who is highest in authority or command, as of an organization. [Sp. and Ital. < *supremo,* supreme < Lat. *supremus.*]
Su·qua·mish (sə-kwä′mĭsh) also **Squa·mish** (skwä′-) *n., pl.* **Suquamish** also **Squamish** or **-mish·es. 1. a.** A tribe of North American Indians of the northwestern Pacific coast, west of Puget Sound. **b.** A member of the Suquamish. **2.** The Salish language of the Suquamish.
sur– *pref.* **1.** Over; above; upon: *surprint.* **2.** Additional: *surtax.* [ME < OFr. < Lat. *super-.* —see SUPER-.]
su·ra (so͝or′ə) *n.* One of the chapters or sections of the Koran. [Ar. *sūrah.*]
su·rah (so͝or′ə) *n.* A soft twilled fabric of silk or of a blend of silk and rayon. [Fr. *surat,* after *Surat,* India, where it was originally made.]
su·ral (so͝or′əl) *adj.* Of or relating to the calf of the leg. [NLat. *suralis* < Lat. *sura,* calf of the leg.]
sur·base (sûr′bās′) *n. Archit.* A molding or border above the base of a structure such as a baseboard.
sur·based (sûr′bāst′) *adj. Archit.* **1.** Having a surbase. **2.** Pertaining to an arch with a rise less than half its span.
sur·cease (sûr′sēs′, sər-sēs′) *Archaic. —tr. & intr.v.* **-ceased, -ceas·ing, -ceas·es.** To bring or come to an end; stop. *—n.* Cessation. [ME *sursesen* < OFr. *sursesoir,* to refrain < Lat. *supersedēre.* —see SUPERSEDE.]
sur·charge (sûr′chärj′) *n.* **1.** An additional sum added to the usual amount or cost. **2.** An overcharge, esp. when unlawful. **3.** An additional or excessive burden; overload. **4. a.** A new value or denomination overprinted on a postage or revenue stamp. **b.** The stamp to which a new value has been applied. **5.** *Law.* The act of surcharging. *—tr.v.* **-charged,**

-charg·ing, -charg·es. 1. To overcharge (a person). **2.** To place an excessive burden upon; overload. **3.** To fill beyond usual capacity; overfill. **4.** To print a surcharge on (a postage or revenue stamp). **5.** *Law.* To show an omission of a credit in (an account). [< ME *surchargen,* to overcharge < OFr. *surcharger* : *sur-,* excessively + *chargier,* to charge. —see CHARGE.]

sur·cin·gle (sûr′sĭng′gəl) *n.* **1.** A girth that binds a saddle, pack, or blanket to the body of a horse. **2.** *Archaic.* The fastening belt on a clerical cassock. —*tr.v.* **-gled, -gling, -gles.** To bind or fasten with a surcingle. [ME *sursengle* < OFr. *surcengle* : *sur-,* over (< Lat. *super-*) + *cengle,* belt < Lat. *cingula* < *cingere,* to gird.]

sur·coat (sûr′kōt′) *n.* **1.** A loose outer coat or gown. **2.** A tunic worn in the Middle Ages by a knight over his armor. [ME *surcote* < OFr. : *sur-,* over + *cote,* coat. —see COAT.]

sur·cu·lose (sûr′kyə-lōs′) *adj. Bot.* Producing suckers: *a surculose shrub.* [Lat. *surculosus,* woody < *surculus,* dim. of *surus,* branch.]

surd (sûrd) *n.* **1.** A sum, as $\sqrt{2} + \sqrt{3}$, containing one or more irrational roots of numbers. **2.** A voiceless sound in speech. —*adj.* Voiceless, as a sound. [< Lat. *surdus,* deaf, trans. of Ar. (*jadhr*) *aṣạm,* deaf (root), transl. of Gk. *alogos,* speechless, irrational.]

sure (sho͝or) *adj.* **sur·er, sur·est. 1.** Incapable of being doubted or disputed; certain: *sure proof of his innocence.* **2.** Not hesitating or wavering; firm: *sure convictions.* **3.** Confident of future possibility; certain in expectation: *sure of victory.* **4. a.** Bound to come about or to happen; inevitable: *sure defeat.* **b.** Having one's course directed; destined; bound: *sure to succeed.* **5.** Certain not to miss or err; steady: *a sure hand on the throttle.* **6.** Worthy of being trusted or depended upon; reliable. **7.** *Obs.* Free from harm or danger; safe. —*adv. Informal.* Surely; certainly. —*idioms.* **for sure.** Certainly; unquestionably: *We'll win for sure.* **make sure.** To establish without doubt; make certain. **to be sure.** Indeed; certainly. [ME < OFr. *sur* < Lat. *securus,* safe. —see SECURE.] —**sure′ness** *n.*

Synonyms: *sure, certain, confident, assured.* These adjectives are compared as they apply to persons who do not doubt their own abilities. *Sure* and *certain* are frequently used interchangeably. *Sure,* however, is the more subjective term, whereas *certain* may imply belief based on experience or established evidence. *Confident* suggests belief founded on faith in or reliance on oneself or others. *Assured* suggests confidence or certainty based on knowledge that doubt has been removed.

sure-fire (sho͝or′fīr′) *adj. Informal.* Bound to be successful or perform as expected: *a sure-fire plan.*

sure-foot·ed (sho͝or′fo͝ot′ĭd) *adj.* Not liable to stumble or fall. —**sure′foot′ed·ly** *adv.* —**sure′foot′ed·ness** *n.*

sure·ly (sho͝or′lē) *adv.* **1.** With confidence; unhesitatingly. **2.** Undoubtedly; certainly: *You surely can't be serious.* **3.** Without fail: *Slowly but surely spring returns.*

sur·e·ty (sho͝or′ĭ-tē) *n., pl.* **-ties. 1.** The condition of being sure, esp. of oneself; self-assurance. **2.** Something beyond doubt; certainty. **3.** A pledge or formal promise made to secure against loss, damage, or default; guarantee or security. **4.** A person who has contracted to be responsible for another, esp. a person who assumes responsibilities or debts in the event of default. [ME *surte* < OFr. < Lat. *securitas* < *securus,* sure. —see SECURE.] —**sur′e·ty·ship′** *n.*

surf (sûrf) *n.* The waves of the sea as they break upon a shore or reef. —*intr.v.* **surfed, surf·ing, surfs.** To engage in surfing. [Orig. unknown.] —**surf′y** *adj.*

sur·face (sûr′fəs) *n.* **1. a.** The outer or the topmost boundary of an object. **b.** A material layer constituting such a boundary. **2.** *Math.* **a.** The boundary of a three-dimensional figure. **b.** The two-dimensional locus of points located in three-dimensional space whose height z above each point (x,y) of a region of a coordinate plane is specified by a function $f(x,y)$ of two arguments. **3.** The superficial or outward appearance of something as distinguished from inner substance or matter. **4.** An airfoil. —*adj.* **1.** Pertaining to, on, or at a surface: *surface algae in the water.* **2. a.** Superficial. **b.** Apparent as opposed to real. —*v.* **-faced, -fac·ing, -fac·es.** —*tr.* **1.** To form the surface of, as by smoothing or leveling. **2.** To provide with a surface. —*intr.* **1.** To rise to the surface. **2.** To emerge after concealment. [Fr. : *sur-,* above + *face,* face < OFr. —see FACE.]

sur·face-ac·tive (sûr′fəs-ăk′tĭv) *adj.* Designating a substance capable of reducing the surface tension of a liquid in which it is dissolved. Used esp. of detergents.

sur·face-ef·fect ship (sûr′fəs-ĭ-fĕkt′) *n.* A ground-effect vehicle that operates over water.

surface of revolution *n.* A surface generated by revolving a plane curve about an axis in its plane.

surface plate *n.* A planometer.

surface tension *n.* A property of liquids arising from unbalanced molecular cohesive forces at or near the surface, as a result of which the surface tends to contract and has properties resembling those of a stretched elastic membrane.

sur·face-to-air missile (sûr′fəs-to͞o-âr′) *n.* A missile, usually guided, launched from the ground against an airborne target.

sur·fac·tant (sər-făk′tənt, sûr′făk′-) *n.* A surface-active substance. [SURF(ACE) + ACT(IVE) + -ANT.]

surf and turf *n.* Seafood and beefsteak served as the main course of a meal, as in a restaurant.

surf·bird (sûrf′bûrd′) *n.* A shore bird, *Aphriza virgata,* of the Pacific coast of North and South America, having dark, spotted plumage.

surf·board (sûrf′bôrd′, -bōrd′) *n.* A long, narrow, somewhat rounded board, used for surfing.

surfboard

surf·boat (sûrf′bōt′) *n.* A strong seaworthy boat that can be launched or landed in heavy surf.

surf·cast·ing (sûrf′kăs′tĭng) *n.* The sport of fishing from shore, casting one's line into the surf. —**surf′cast′er** *n.*

sur·feit (sûr′fĭt) *v.* **-feit·ed, -feit·ing, -feits.** —*tr.* To feed or supply to fullness or excess; satiate. —*intr. Archaic.* To overindulge. —*n.* **1. a.** Overindulgence in food or drink. **b.** The result of such overindulgence; satiety or disgust. **2.** An excessive amount. [ME < OFr. < *surfaire,* to overdo : *sur-,* excessively + *faire,* to do < Lat. *facere.*] —**sur′feit·er** *n.*

surf·er (sûr′fər) *n.* A person who engages in surfing.

surfer's knee *n.* Surfer's knobs.

surfer's knobs *pl.n.* Tumorlike overgrowths of connective tissue just below the knees, on the tops of the feet, and often on the toes, common among surfers who paddle in a kneeling position.

surfer's knot *n.* Surfer's knobs.

sur·fi·cial (sər-fĭsh′əl) *adj.* Of, pertaining to, or occurring on the earth's surface. [SURF(ACE) + (SUPERF)ICIAL.]

surf·ing (sûr′fĭng) *n.* The sport of riding the crests of waves, esp. on a surfboard.

surf·perch (sûrf′pûrch′) *n., pl.* **surfperch** or **-perch·es.** Any of various viviparous marine fishes of the family Embiotocidae, of North American Pacific coastal waters.

surge (sûrj) *v.* **surged, surg·ing, surg·es.** —*intr.* **1.** To move in a billowing or swelling manner in or as if in waves. **2.** To roll or be tossed about on waves, as a boat. **3.** To increase suddenly. **4.** To slip around a windlass. Used of a rope. —*tr.* To loosen or slacken (a cable) gradually. —*n.* **1.** A heavy, billowing, or swelling motion like that of great waves. **2. a.** A wave, ground swell, or billow. **b.** Such waves collectively. **3.** A sudden onrush: *a surge of joy.* **4.** A sudden, transient increase in electric current. **5.** *Naut.* The part of a windlass into which the cable surges. [Prob. < OFr. *sourgir* < Lat. *surgere,* to rise : *sub-,* from below + *regere,* to lead.]

sur·geon (sûr′jən) *n.* A physician specializing in surgery. [ME *surgien* < Norman Fr., short for OFr. *serurgien* < *serurgie,* surgery.]

sur·geon·cy (sûr′jən-sē) *n., pl.* **-cies.** The position, office, rank, or duties of a surgeon.

sur·geon·fish (sûr′jən-fĭsh′) *n., pl.* **surgeonfish** or **-fish·es.** Any of various bright-colored tropical marine fishes of the family Acanthuridae, having a sharp, erectile spine near the base of the tail. [From its lancetlike spines, which resemble surgeons' instruments.]

Surgeon General *n., pl.* **Surgeons General. 1.** The chief general officer in the medical departments of the United States Army, Navy, or Air Force. **2.** The chief medical officer in the United States Public Health Service.

surgeon's knot *n.* Any of several knots used in surgery for tying ligatures or stitching incisions.

sur·ger·y (sûr′jə-rē) *n., pl.* **-ies. 1.** The medical diagnosis and treatment of injury, deformity, and disease by manual and instrumental operations. **2.** An operating room or laboratory of a surgeon or of a hospital's surgical staff. **3.** The skill or work of a surgeon. **4.** *Chiefly Brit.* A physician's office. [ME *surgerie* < OFr. < *serurgie, cerurgie* < Lat. *chirurgia* < Gk. *kheirourgia* < *kheirurgos,* working by hand : *kheir,* hand + *ergon,* work.]

sur·gi·cal (sûr′jĭ-kəl) *adj.* **1.** Of, pertaining to, or characteristic of surgeons or surgery. **2.** Used in surgery. **3.** Resulting from or occurring after surgery. [< SURGEON.] —**sur′gi·cal·ly** *adv.*

su·ri·cate (so͝or′ĭ-kāt′) *n.* A small, gregarious burrowing mammal, *Suricata suricatta,* of southern Africa, having grayish fur and a long tail. [Fr., of African orig.]

sur·ly (sûr′lē) *adj.* **-li·er, -li·est. 1.** Sullenly ill-humored; gruff. **2.** *Obs.* Arrogant; domineering. [Obs. *sirly,* masterful < SIR.] —**sur′li·ly** *adv.* —**sur′li·ness** *n.*

sur·mise (sər-mīz′) *v.* **-mised, -mis·ing, -mis·es.** —*tr.* To infer (something) without sufficiently conclusive evidence; guess. —*intr.* To make a guess or conjecture. —*n.* An idea or opinion based upon insufficiently conclusive evidence; conjecture. [ME *surmysen,* to accuse < OFr. *surmettre, surmis-* < Med. Lat. *supermittere* < Lat., to throw on : *super-,* over + *mittere,* to put.]

sur·mount (sər-mount′) *tr.v.* **-mount·ed, -mount·ing, -mounts. 1.** To overcome (an obstacle, for example); conquer. **2.** To ascend to the top of; climb. **3. a.** To place something above; top. **b.** To be above or on top of: *The church steeple surmounts the square.* **4.** *Obs.* To surpass or exceed in amount. [ME *surmonten,* to excel < OFr. *surmonter* : *sur-,* above + *monter,* to mount. —see MOUNT[1].] —**sur·mount′a·ble** *adj.* —**sur·mount′er** *n.*

sur·mul·let (sər-mŭl′ĭt, sûr′mŭl′-) *n., pl.* **surmullet** or **-lets.** The goatfish. [Fr. *surmulet* < OFr. *sormulet* : prob. *sor,* red-

p **p**op / r **r**oar / s **s**auce / sh **sh**ip, di**sh** / t **t**ight / th **th**in, pa**th** / *th* **th**is, ba**th**e / ŭ c**u**t / ûr **ur**ge / v **v**alve / w **w**ith / y **y**es / z **z**ebra, si**z**e / zh vi**s**ion / ə **a**bout, it**e**m, edib**i**le, gall**o**p, circ**u**s / œ *Fr.* **feu**, *Ger.* **schön** / ü *Fr.* **tu**, *Ger.* **über** / KH *Ger.* **ich**, *Scot.* **loch** / N *Fr.* **bon**.

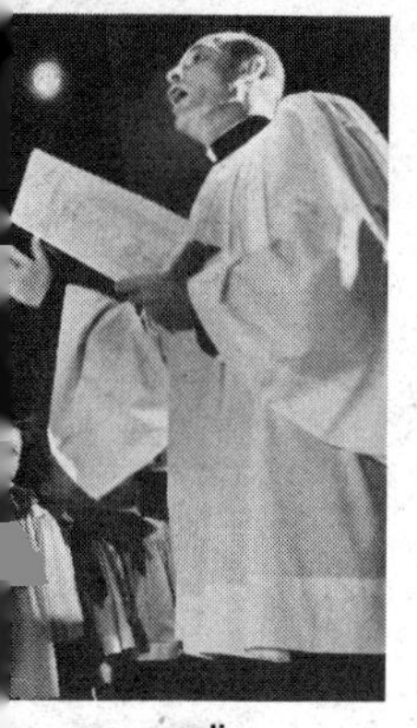

surplice

dish brown (of Germanic orig.) + *mulet,* mullet. —see MULLET.]

sur·name (sûr′nām′) *n.* **1.** A person's family name as distinguished from his given name. **2.** A nickname or epithet added to a person's name. —*tr.v.* **-named, -nam·ing, -names.** To give a surname to. [ME : *sur-*, sur- + *name,* name.]

sur·pass (sər-păs′) *tr.v.* **-passed, -pass·ing, -pass·es. 1.** To go beyond the limit, powers, or extent of; transcend. **2.** To be or go beyond; exceed. [OFr. *surpasser* : *sur-*, over + *passer,* pass. —see PASS.]

sur·pass·ing (sər-păs′ĭng) *adj.* Exceptional; exceeding: *monuments of surpassing splendor.* **—sur·pass′ing·ly** *adv.*

sur·plice (sûr′plĭs) *n.* A loose-fitting white gown with wide sleeves, worn over a cassock by some clergymen. [ME *surplis* < Norman Fr. *surpliz* < OFr. *sourpeliz* < Med. Lat. *superpellicium* : Lat. *super-*, over + *pellicium,* fur coat < Lat. *pellicius,* made of skin < *pellis,* skin.]

sur·plus (sûr′pləs, -plŭs′) *adj.* Being more than or in excess of what is needed or required: *surplus grain.* —*n.* **1.** An amount or quantity in excess of what is needed. **2.** Total assets minus the sum of all liabilities. **3.** Excess of a corporation's net assets over the face value of its capital stock. **4.** Excess of receipts over expenditures. [ME < OFr. < Med. Lat. *superplus* : Lat. *super-*, over + Lat. *plus,* more.]

sur·plus·age (sûr′plə-sĭj) *n.* **1.** Surplus; excess. **2.** An excess of words; verbiage. **3.** Irrelevant matter in a legal pleading.

surplus value *n.* In the Marxian analysis of capitalism, the difference between the value of the product produced by labor and the actual price of labor as paid out in wages.

sur·print (sûr′prĭnt′) *tr.v.* **-print·ed, -print·ing, -prints. 1.** To overprint. **2.** To superimpose (a second negative) upon a previously printed image of the first negative. —*n.* Something that is surprinted.

sur·pris·al (sər-prī′zəl) *n.* **1.** The act of surprising. **2.** The condition of being surprised.

sur·prise also **sur·prize** (sər-prīz′) *tr.v.* **-prised, -pris·ing, -pris·es** also **-prized, -priz·ing, -priz·es. 1.** To encounter suddenly or unexpectedly; take or catch unawares. **2.** To attack or capture suddenly and without warning. **3.** To cause to feel wonder, astonishment, or amazement. **4. a.** To cause (someone) to do or say something unintended. **b.** To elicit or detect through surprise. —*n.* **1.** The act of surprising. **2.** The condition of being surprised; astonishment. **3.** Something that surprises, as an unexpected encounter, event, or gift. [ME *surprysen,* to overcome < OFr. *surprendre, surpris-* : *sur-*, over + *prendre,* to take < Lat. *praehendere,* to seize.] **—sur·pris′er** *n.*

Synonyms: *surprise, astonish, amaze, astound, dumbfound, flabbergast.* These verbs mean to fill a person with wonder or disbelief. All imply a reaction to something that is unexpected. *Surprise* refers to the effect of what is unexpected or unusual. The remaining terms are considerably stronger. *Astonish* implies the condition of being momentarily overwhelmed and often dazed and speechless. *Amaze* suggests wonder and, often, bewilderment. *Astound* implies shock, as from something that seems incredible or has no precedent in one's experience. *Dumbfound* adds to *astound* the implication of speechlessness. *Flabbergast* is used informally, usually in the sense of *astound* or *dumbfound* and sometimes as the equivalent of *astonish* or *amaze.*

sur·re·al (sə-rē′əl) *adj.* Having qualities attributed to surrealism. [Back-formation < SURREALISM.]

sur·re·al·ism (sə-rē′ə-lĭz′əm) *n.* A 20th-century literary and artistic movement that attempts to express the workings of the subconscious by fantastic imagery and incongruous juxtaposition of subject matter. [Fr. *surréalisme* : *sur-*, beyond + *réalisme,* realism < *réel,* real < OFr. *reel* < LLat. *realis* < Lat. *res,* thing.] **—sur·re′al·ist** *n.*

sur·re·al·is·tic (sə-rē′ə-lĭs′tĭk) *adj.* **1.** Of or relating to surrealism. **2.** Having an oddly dreamlike or unreal quality. **—sur·re′al·is′ti·cal·ly** *adv.*

sur·re·but·ter (sûr′rĭ-bŭt′ər) also **sur·re·but·tal** (-bŭt′l) *n. Law.* A plaintiff's reply to a defendant's rebutter.

sur·re·join·der (sûr′rĭ-join′dər) *n. Law.* A plaintiff's reply to a defendant's rejoinder.

sur·ren·der (sə-rĕn′dər) *v.* **-dered, -der·ing, -ders.** —*tr.* **1.** To relinquish possession or control of to another because of demand or compulsion. **2.** To give up in favor of another. **3.** To give up or give back something that has been granted: *surrender a contractual right.* **4.** To give up or abandon: *surrender all hope.* **5.** To give over or resign (oneself) to something, as to an emotion: *surrendered himself to grief.* —*intr.* To give oneself up, as to an enemy. —*n.* **1.** The act or an instance of surrendering. **2.** The delivery of a prisoner, fugitive from justice, or other principal in a legal suit into legal custody. [ME *sorendren* < OFr. *surrendre* : *sur-*, over + *rendre,* to deliver. —see RENDER.]

Synonyms: *surrender, submission, capitulation.* These nouns refer to the act of giving up one's person or possessions into the authority of another or others or of relinquishing one's power, aims, or goals. *Surrender* is the most general. *Submission* makes more explicit the resultant subordination of one side to the other. *Capitulation* involves *surrender* under prearranged conditions.

surrender value *n.* The value of an insurance policy either to the owner or to the beneficiary upon its expiration.

sur·rep·ti·tious (sûr′əp-tĭsh′əs) *adj.* Performed, made, or acquired by secret, clandestine, or stealthy means. [Lat. *surrepticius* < *surripere,* to take away secretly : *sub-*, secretly + *rapere,* to seize.] **—sur′rep·ti′tious·ly** *adv.* **—sur′rep·ti′tious·ness** *n.*

sur·rey (sûr′ē, sŭr′ē) *n., pl.* **-reys.** A horse-drawn four-wheeled carriage having two seats. [Short for *Surrey cart,* after *Surrey,* a county in England where it was first built.]

sur·ro·gate (sûr′ə-gĭt, -gāt′, sŭr′-) *n.* **1.** One that takes the place of another; substitute. **2.** A judge in some U.S. states having jurisdiction over the probate of wills and the settlement of estates. —*adj.* Substitute. —*tr.v.* (-gāt′) **-gat·ed, -gat·ing, -gates. 1.** To put in the place of another, esp. as a successor; replace. **2.** To appoint (another) as a replacement for oneself. [< Lat. *surrogare,* to substitute < *subrogare.* —see SUBROGATE.]

sur·round (sə-round′) *tr.v.* **-round·ed, -round·ing, -rounds. 1.** To extend on all sides of simultaneously; encircle. **2.** To enclose or confine on all sides so as to bar escape or outside communication. [ME *sourrounden,* to inundate < OFr. *suronder* < LLat. *superundare* : Lat. *super-*, over + Lat. *undare,* to rise in waves < *unda,* wave.]

sur·round·ings (sə-roun′dĭngz) *pl.n.* The external circumstances, conditions, and objects that affect the existence and development of something; environment.

sur·sum cor·da (so͝or′səm kôr′də) *n.* **1.** Often **Sursum Corda.** An ecclesiastical versicle offering praise and thanksgiving to God. **2.** Something that instills courage or fervor. [Lat., (lift) up (your) hearts.]

sur·tax (sûr′tăks′) *n.* **1.** An additional tax. **2.** A graduated income tax added to the normal income tax levied on the amount by which a person's net income exceeds a certain sum. —*tr.v.* **-taxed, -tax·ing, -tax·es.** To levy a surtax on.

sur·veil (sər-vāl′) *tr.v.* **-veilled, -veil·ling, -veils.** To keep under surveillance. [Back-formation < SURVEILLANCE.]

sur·veil·lance (sər-vā′ləns) *n.* **1.** Close observation of a person or group, esp. of one under suspicion. **2. a.** The act of observing. **b.** The condition of being observed.

sur·veil·lant (sər-vā′lənt) *adj.* Exercising surveillance. —*n.* One that exercises surveillance. [Fr., pr.part. of *surveiller,* to watch over : *sur-*, over + *veiller,* to watch < Lat. *vigilare* < *vigil,* watchful.]

sur·vey (sər-vā′, sûr′vā′) *v.* **-veyed, -vey·ing, -veys.** —*tr.* **1.** To examine or look at in a comprehensive way. **2.** To inspect carefully; scrutinize. **3.** To determine the boundaries, the area, or the elevations of (land or structures on the earth's surface) by means of measuring angles and distances, using the techniques of geometry and trigonometry. —*intr.* To make a survey. —*n.* (sûr′vā′) *pl.* **-veys. 1.** A detailed inspection or investigation. **2.** A general or comprehensive view. **3. a.** The process of surveying. **b.** A report on or map of what is surveyed. [ME *surveyen* < OFr. *surveeir* < Med. Lat. *supervidēre,* to look over : Lat. *super-*, over + Lat. *vidēre,* to look.] **—sur·vey′or** *n.*

survey course *n.* A course consisting of an overview of a broad topic or field of knowledge.

sur·vey·ing (sər-vā′ĭng) *n.* The measurement of dimensional relationships, as of horizontal distances, elevations, directions, and angles, on the earth's surface esp. for use in locating property boundaries, construction layout, and mapmaking.

surveyor's level *n.* A level having a telescope and attached spirit level mounted on a tripod and rotating around a vertical axis.

sur·viv·a·ble (sər-vī′və-bəl) *adj.* Capable of surviving or being survived. **—sur·viv′a·bil′i·ty** *n.*

sur·viv·al (sər-vī′vəl) *n.* **1. a.** The act or process of surviving. **b.** The fact of having survived. **2.** Something, as an ancient custom or belief, that has survived. ***—modifier:*** *survival techniques.*

survival of the fittest *n.* Natural selection conceived of as a struggle in which only those organisms best adapted to existing conditions survive.

survival value *n.* Usefulness in the struggle for survival: "*emotional activation most clearly has survival value*" (Norman L. Munn).

sur·viv·ance (sər-vī′vəns) *n.* Survival.

sur·vive (sər-vīv′) *v.* **-vived, -viv·ing, -vives.** —*intr.* To remain alive or in existence. —*tr.* **1.** To live longer than; outlive: *survived her husband by five years.* **2.** To live or persist through: *plants surviving a frost.* [ME *surviven* < Norman Fr. *survivre* < OFr. *sourvivre* < LLat. *supervivere* : Lat. *super-*, over + Lat. *vivere,* to live.] **—sur·vi′vor** *n.*

sur·vi·vor·ship (sər-vī′vər-shĭp′) *n.* **1.** *Law.* The right of a person who survives a partner or joint owner to the entire ownership of something that was previously owned jointly. **2.** The condition of being a survivor.

Su·san B. An·tho·ny Day (so͞o′zən-bē-ăn′thə-nē) *n.* February 15 observed in honor of the birthday of Susan B. Anthony.

Su·san·na (so͞o-zăn′ə) *n.* **1.** In the Apocrypha, a captive in Babylon falsely accused of adultery and saved from death by Daniel. **2.** See table at **Bible.** [Heb. *Shōshannāh* < *shōshannāh,* lily.]

sus·cep·tance (sə-sĕp′təns) *n. Elect.* The imaginary part of the complex representation of admittance. [SUSCEPT(IBILITY) + (CONDUCT)ANCE.]

sus·cep·ti·bil·i·ty (sə-sĕp′tə-bĭl′ĭ-tē) *n., pl.* **-ties. 1.** The condition or quality of being susceptible. **2.** The capacity to be affected by deep emotions or strong feelings; sensitivity. **3. susceptibilities.** Sensibilities; feelings.

sus·cep·ti·ble (sə-sĕp′tə-bəl) *adj.* **1.** Easily influenced or affected: *not susceptible to persuasion.* **2.** Liable to be stricken with or by: *susceptible to colds.* **3.** Especially sensitive; highly impressionable. **4.** Capable of accepting or permitting: *susceptible of proof.* [Med. Lat. *susceptibilis,* receivable < Lat. *suscipere,* to receive : *sub-,* from below + *capere,* to take.] **—sus·cep′ti·ble·ness** *n.* **—sus·cep′ti·bly** *adv.*

sus·cep·tive (sə-sĕp′tĭv) *adj.* **1.** Receptive. **2.** Susceptible. **—sus·cep′tive·ness, sus·cep′tiv′i·ty** (sə-sĕp′tĭv′ĭ-tē) *n.*

su·shi (so͞o′shē) *n.* A Japanese dish consisting of thin slices of fresh raw fish or seaweed wrapped around a cake of cooked rice. [J.]

sus·pect (sə-spĕkt′) *v.* **-pect·ed, -pect·ing, -pects.** *—tr.* **1.** To surmise to be true or probable; imagine. **2.** To have doubts about; distrust: *suspected his motives.* **3.** To think (a person) guilty without proof: *suspect her of murder.* *—intr.* To have suspicion. *—n.* (sŭs′pĕkt′). A person who is suspected, esp. of committing a crime. *—adj.* (sŭs′pĕkt′, sə-spĕkt′). Open to or viewed with suspicion. [Lat. *suspectare,* freq. of *suspicere,* to watch : *sub-,* from below + *specere,* to look at.]

sus·pend (sə-spĕnd′) *v.* **-pend·ed, -pend·ing, -pends.** *—tr.* **1.** To bar for a period from a privilege, office, or position, usually as a punishment: *suspend a student from school.* **2.** To cause to stop for a period; interrupt: *suspended a trial.* **3. a.** To hold in abeyance; defer: *suspend judgment.* **b.** To render temporarily ineffective: *suspend a sentence; suspend parking regulations.* **4.** To hang so as to allow free movement. **5.** To support or keep from falling without apparent attachment, as by buoyancy: *suspend oneself in the water.* *—intr.* **1.** To cease for a period; delay. **2.** To fail to make payments or meet obligations. [ME *suspenden* < OFr. *suspendre* < Lat. *suspendere,* to hang up : *sub-,* from below + *pendere,* to hang.]

suspended animation *n.* A dormant condition resembling death and induced by reversible cessation of the vital functions.

sus·pend·er (sə-spĕn′dər) *n.* **1.** One that suspends. **2. suspenders.** A pair of straps, often elastic, worn over the shoulders to support trousers. **3.** *Chiefly Brit.* A garter.

sus·pense (sə-spĕns′) *n.* **1.** The condition of being suspended. **2.** The state or quality of being undecided, uncertain, or doubtful. **3.** Anxiety or apprehension resulting from an uncertain, undecided, or mysterious situation. [ME < Norman Fr. < OFr. < *suspendre,* to suspend.] **—sus·pense′ful** *adj.*

suspense account *n.* A temporary account in which entries of credits or charges are made until their proper disposition can be determined.

sus·pen·sion (sə-spĕn′shən) *n.* **1.** The act of suspending or the condition of being suspended, esp.: **a.** A temporary abrogation or deferment. **b.** A debarment, as from office or privilege. **c.** A postponement of judgment, opinion, or decision. **2.** *Mus.* **a.** The prolongation of one or more tones of a chord into a following chord to create a temporary dissonance. **b.** The tone prolonged by suspension. **3.** A device from which a mechanical part is suspended. **4.** The system of springs and other devices that insulates the chassis of a vehicle from shocks transmitted through the wheels. **5.** *Chem.* A relatively coarse, noncolloidal dispersion of solid particles in a liquid.

suspension bridge *n.* A bridge having the roadway suspended from cables that are usually supported by towers.

suspension points *pl.n.* A series of dots, usually three, used to indicate the omission of a word or words from a written text.

sus·pen·sive (sə-spĕn′sĭv) *adj.* **1.** Serving or tending to suspend or temporarily stop something. **2.** Characterized by or causing suspense. **—sus·pen′sive·ly** *adv.* **—sus·pen′sive·ness** *n.*

sus·pen·soid (sə-spĕn′soid′) *n.* A colloid solution with solid dispersed particles. [SUSPENS(ION) + (COLL)OID.]

sus·pen·sor (sə-spĕn′sər) *n.* **1.** *Bot.* A cell or cellular structure developed from a zygote in seed-bearing plants and connecting the embryo to the embryo sac. **2.** A suspensory. [Med. Lat., one that suspends < Lat. *suspendere,* to suspend. —see SUSPEND.]

sus·pen·so·ry (sə-spĕn′sə-rē) *adj.* **1.** Supporting or suspending: *a suspensory bandage.* **2.** Delaying the completion of something. *—n., pl.* **-ries. 1.** A support or truss. **2.** An athletic supporter.

suspensory ligament *n.* A ligament that supports an organ or bodily part.

sus·pi·cion (sə-spĭsh′ən) *n.* **1.** The act of suspecting the existence of something, esp. of something wrong, without sufficient evidence or proof. **2.** The condition of being suspected, esp. of wrongdoing. **3.** A state of uncertainty; doubt. **4.** A minute amount; trace. *—tr.v.* **-cioned, -cion·ing, -cions.** *Nonstandard.* To suspect. [ME *suspecioun* < Norman Fr., var. of OFr. *sospecon* < Med. Lat. *suspectio* < *suspicere,* to watch. —see SUSPECT.] **—sus·pi′cion·al** *adj.*

sus·pi·cious (sə-spĭsh′əs) *adj.* **1.** Arousing or apt to arouse suspicion; questionable: *suspicious behavior.* **2.** Tending to suspect; distrustful: *a suspicious nature.* **3.** Expressing suspicion: *a suspicious look.* **—sus·pi′cious·ly** *adv.* **—sus·pi′cious·ness** *n.*

sus·pire (sə-spīr′) *intr.v.* **-pired, -pir·ing, -pires. 1.** To breathe. **2.** To sigh. [ME *suspiren* < Lat. *suspirare,* to sigh : *sub,* from below + *spirare,* to breathe.] **—sus′pi·ra′tion** (sŭs′pə-rā′shən) *n.*

Sus·sex spaniel (sŭs′ĭks) *n.* A dog of a breed developed in Sussex, England, having long ears, short legs, and a silky golden-brown coat.

sus·tain (sə-stān′) *tr.v.* **-tained, -tain·ing, -tains. 1.** To keep in existence; maintain. **2.** To supply with necessities or nourishment; provide for. **3.** To support from below; prop. **4.** To support the spirits, vitality, or resolution of; encourage. **5.** To endure or withstand; bear up under: *sustain hardships.* **6.** To experience or suffer (loss or injury). **7.** To affirm the validity or justice of: *sustain an objection.* **8.** To prove or corroborate; confirm. [ME *susteynen* < Norman Fr. *sustein* < OFr. *sustenir* < Lat. *sustinēre,* to hold up : *sub-,* from below + *tenēre,* to hold.] **—sus·tain′a·ble** *adj.* **—sus·tain′er** *n.* **—sus·tain′ment** *n.*

sustaining program *n.* A radio or television program that is supported by the station or network on which it appears and that has no commercial announcements.

sus·te·nance (sŭs′tə-nəns) *n.* **1. a.** The act of sustaining. **b.** The condition of being sustained. **2.** The supporting of life or health; maintenance. **3.** Something, esp. food, that sustains life or health. **4.** Means of livelihood. [ME < Norman Fr. *sustenaunce* < OFr. *soustenance* < *sustenir,* to sustain.]

sus·ten·tac·u·lar (sŭs′tən-tăk′yə-lər, -tĕn-) *adj. Anat.* Serving to support. [< Lat. *sustentaculum,* a support < *sustentare,* to support, freq. of *sustinēre,* to sustain.]

sus·ten·ta·tion (sŭs′tən-tā′shən, -tĕn-) *n.* **1.** Something that sustains; support. **2.** Sustenance. [ME *sustentacion,* maintenance < Norman Fr. < OFr. < Lat. *sustentatio* < *sustentare,* to support. —see SUSTENTACULAR.] **—sus′ten·ta′tive** *adj.*

Su·su (so͞o′so͞o) *n., pl.* **Susu** or **Su·sus. 1.** A West African people residing in Guinea and the Sudan and along the northern border of Sierra Leone. **2.** A member of the Susu. **3.** The Mande language of the Susu.

su·sur·ra·tion (so͞o′sə-rā′shən) also **su·sur·rus** (so͞o-sûr′əs, -sŭr′-) *n.* A soft, whispering or rustling sound; murmur. [ME *susurracyoun* < LLat. *susurratio* < Lat. *susurrare,* to whisper < *susurrus,* whisper.] **—su·sur′rant** (so͞o-sûr′ənt, -sŭr′-), **su·sur′rous** (-sûr′əs, -sŭr′-) *adj.*

sut·ler (sŭt′lər) *n.* A follower of an army camp who peddled provisions to the soldiers. [MDu. *soetler,* of Germanic orig.]

su·tra (so͞o′trə) *n.* **1.** *Hinduism.* Any of various aphoristic doctrinal summaries produced generally between 500 and 200 B.C. and later incorporated into Hindu and Buddhist literature, **2.** *Buddhism.* A scriptural narrative, esp. a text traditionally regarded as a discourse of the Buddha. [Skt. *sūtram.*]

sut·tee (sŭ-tē′, sŭt′ē′) *n.* **1.** The act or practice of a Hindu widow permitting herself to be cremated on her husband's funeral pyre. **2.** A widow cremated by suttee. [Skt. *satī,* virtuous woman, fem. of *sat,* true, pr.part. of *asti,* he is.]

su·ture (so͞o′chər) *n.* **1. a.** The process of joining two surfaces or edges together along a line by or as if by sewing. **b.** The material used in this procedure, as thread, gut, or wire. **c.** The line so formed. **2.** *Anat.* The line of junction or an immovable joint between two bones, esp. of the skull. **3.** *Biol.* A seamlike joint or line of articulation, such as the line of dehiscence in a seed or fruit or the spiral seam marking the junction of whorls of a gastropod shell. *—tr.v.* **-tured, -tur·ing, -tures.** To join by means of sutures. [OFr. < Lat. *sutura* < *suere,* to sew.] **—su′tur·al** *adj.* **—su′tur·al·ly** *adv.*

su·ze·rain (so͞o′zər-ən, -zə-rān′) *n.* **1.** A feudal lord to whom fealty was due. **2.** A nation that controls another nation in international affairs but allows it domestic sovereignty. [Fr. : prob. *sus,* up (< Lat. *sursum,* upward) + *souverain,* sovereign.]

su·ze·rain·ty (so͞o′zər-ən-tē, -zə-rān′tē) *n., pl.* **-ties.** The power or domain of a suzerain.

svelte (svĕlt) *adj.* **svelt·er, svelt·est.** Slender or graceful in figure or outline; slim. [Fr. < Ital. *svelto* < *svellere,* to stretch out < VLat. **exvellere* < Lat. *evellere* : *ex-,* out + *vellere,* to pull.] **—svelte′ly** *adv.* **—svelte′ness** *n.*

swab also **swob** (swŏb) *—n.* **1.** A small piece of absorbent material attached to the end of a stick or wire and used for cleansing or applying medicine. **2.** A specimen of mucus or other material removed with a swab. **3.** A mop used for cleaning floors or decks. **4.** *Slang.* A sailor. **5.** A lout. *—tr.v.* **swabbed, swab·bing, swabs** also **swobbed, swob·bing, swobs. 1.** To use a swab on. **2.** To clean with a swab. [Prob. < MDu. *swabbe,* mop.]

swab·bie also **swab·by** (swŏb′ē) *n., pl.* **-bies.** *Slang.* A sailor.

swad·dle (swŏd′l) *tr.v.* **-dled, -dling, -dles. 1.** To wrap or bind in bandages; swathe. **2.** To wrap (a baby) in swaddling

suspender
Suspenders

suspension bridge
The Golden Gate Bridge

George Miksch Sutton
swallow²

swan

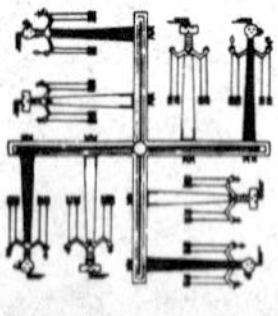

swastika
Above: Navaho Indian swastika with gods of rivers, mountains, and rains
Below: Nazi swastika on the hull of a ship

clothes. **3.** To restrain or restrict. —*n.* A band or cloth used for swaddling. [ME *swadlen,* alteration of *swedlen, swethlen* < *swethel,* swaddling clothes < OE *swæðel.*]

swaddling clothes *pl.n.* **1.** Strips of cloth wrapped around a newborn infant to hold its legs and arms still. **2.** Restrictions imposed upon the immature.

swag (swăg) *n.* **1.** An ornamental hanging draped in a curve between two points. **2.** *Slang.* Stolen property; loot. **3.** *Austral.* The pack or bundle of a swagman. —*intr.v.* **swagged, swag·ging, swags.** *Chiefly Brit.* To lurch or sway. [Prob. of Scand. orig.]

swage (swāj) *n.* **1.** A tool used in bending or shaping cold metal. **2.** A stamp or die for marking or shaping metal with a hammer. **3.** A swage block. —*tr.v.* **swaged, swag·ing, swag·es.** To bend or shape by or as if by using a swage. [ME, ornamental border < OFr. *souage.*]

swage block *n.* A metal block with holes or grooves for shaping metal objects.

swag·ger (swăg′ər) *v.* **-gered, -ger·ing, -gers.** —*intr.* **1.** To walk or conduct oneself with an insolent air; strut. **2.** To brag; boast. —*tr.* To influence or affect by swaggering. —*n.* **1.** A swaggering movement or gait. **2.** Boastful or conceited expression; braggadocio. [Prob. of Scand. orig.] **—swag′ger·er** *n.* **—swag′ger·ing·ly** *adv.*

swagger stick *n.* A short metal-tipped cane carried esp. by military officers.

swag·man (swăg′măn′) *n. Austral.* A man who seeks work while traveling about carrying his swag.

Swa·hi·li (swä-hē′lē) *n., pl.* **Swahili** or **-lis. 1.** A Bantu language that is widely used as a lingua franca in eastern and central Africa. **2.** One of the original speakers of Swahili, a Bantu people of Zanzibar and the neighboring mainland. [Swahili, belonging to the coasts < Ar. *sawāḥil,* pl. of *sāḥil,* coast.] **—Swa·hi′li·an** *adj.*

swain (swān) *n.* **1.** A country youth, esp. a young shepherd. **2.** A lover. [ME *swayn* < ON *sveinn,* boy.]

swale (swāl) *n.* **1.** A low tract of land, esp. moist or marshy ground. **2.** Shade. [Perh. < ME, shade.]

swal·low¹ (swŏl′ō) *v.* **-lowed, -low·ing, -lows.** —*tr.* **1.** To cause (food, for example) to pass through the mouth and throat into the stomach. **2.** To consume or destroy as if by ingestion; devour: *a building that was swallowed up by fire.* **3.** To ingest (something unpleasant) reluctantly. **4. a.** To bear humbly; tolerate: *swallow an insult.* **b.** *Slang.* To believe without question. **5. a.** To refrain from expressing; suppress: *swallow one's feelings.* **b.** To take back; retract: *swallow one's words.* —*intr.* To perform the act of swallowing. —*n.* **1.** The act of swallowing; gulp. **2.** An amount swallowed at one time. **3.** *Naut.* The channel through which a rope runs in a block or a mooring chock. [ME *swalowen* < OE *swelgan.*] **—swal′low·er** *n.*

swal·low² (swŏl′ō) *n.* **1.** Any of various birds of the family Hirundinidae, having long, pointed wings and a usually notched or forked tail. **2.** Any of various birds similar to the swallow, as a swift. [ME *swalowe* < OE *swealwe.*]

swal·low·tail (swŏl′ō-tāl′) *n.* **1. a.** The deeply forked tail of a swallow. **b.** Something similar to the tail of a swallow. **2.** *Informal.* A swallow-tailed coat. **3.** Any of various butterflies of the family Papilionidae, usually having a taillike extension at the end of each hind wing.

swal·low-tailed (swŏl′ō-tāld′) *adj.* **1.** Having a deeply forked tail. Used of various birds. **2.** Resembling the tail of a swallow: *a swallow-tailed kite.*

swallow-tailed coat *n.* A man's black coat worn for formal daytime occasions and having a long rounded and split tail.

swal·low·wort (swŏl′ō-wûrt′, -wôrt′) *n.* **1.** The celandine (sense 1). **2.** Any of several vines of the genus *Cynanchum,* native to Europe, esp. *C. nigrum,* having clusters of small brownish-purple flowers. [From the shape of its pod.]

swam (swăm) *v.* Past tense of **swim.**

swa·mi (swä′mē) *n.* **1.** Lord; master. Used as a Hindu title of respect. **2.** A Hindu religious teacher. **3.** A mystic; yogi. [Hindi *svāmī,* master < Skt. *svāmin.*]

swamp (swŏmp, swômp) *n.* A lowland region saturated with water; marsh. —*v.* **swamped, swamp·ing, swamps.** —*tr.* **1.** To drench in or cover with or as if with water. **2.** To inundate or burden; overwhelm: *swamped with work.* **3.** To fill or sink (a ship) with water. —*intr.* To become full of water or sink, as a ship. [Perh. of LG orig.]

swamp boat *n.* A flat-bottomed boat powered by an airplane propeller projecting above the stern and used in swamps or shallow waters.

swamp·er (swŏm′pər, swôm′-) *n.* **1.** A person who lives in or close to a swamp. **2.** A person who clears a swamp or forest. **3. a.** A menial helper, as in a restaurant. **b.** A truck driver's assistant.

swamp fever *n.* **1.** Malaria (sense 1). **2.** A viral disease in horses, marked by progressive anemia, a staggering gait, and fever.

swamp·land (swŏmp′lănd′, swômp′-) *n.* Land of swampy consistency; marshland.

swamp·y (swŏm′pē, swôm′-) *adj.* **-i·er, -i·est.** Of, pertaining to, or resembling a swamp; marshy. **—swamp′i·ness** *n.*

swan (swŏn) *n.* **1.** Any of various large aquatic birds, chiefly of the genera *Cygnus* and *Olor,* having webbed feet, a long slender neck, and usually white plumage. **2. Swan.** Cygnus. [ME < OE.]

swan dive *n.* A dive performed with the legs straight together, the back arched, and the arms stretched out from the sides.

swank (swăngk) *adj.* **-er, -est. 1.** Imposingly fashionable or elegant; grand. **2.** Ostentatious; pretentious. —*n.* **1.** Smartness in style or bearing; elegance. **2.** Swagger. —*intr.v.* **swanked, swank·ing, swanks.** To act in an ostentatious or pretentious way; swagger. [Perh. < MHG *swanken,* to swing.]

swank·y (swăng′kē) *adj.* **-i·er, -i·est.** Swank. **—swank′i·ly** *adv.* **—swank′i·ness** *n.*

swan·ner·y (swŏn′ə-rē) *n., pl.* **-ies.** A place where swans are raised.

Swan River daisy *n.* An Australian plant, *Brachycome iberidifolia,* cultivated for its showy blue or white flower heads.

swan's-down also **swans·down** (swŏnz′doun′) *n.* **1.** The soft down of a swan. **2.** A soft woolen fabric used esp. for baby clothes. **3.** Canton flannel.

swan·skin (swŏn′skĭn′) *n.* **1.** The skin of a swan with the feathers attached. **2.** Any of several flannel or cotton fabrics with a soft nap.

swan song *n.* **1.** The legendary last utterance of a dying swan. **2.** A farewell or final appearance, action, or work. [Transl. of G. *Schwanenlied.*]

swap also **swop** (swŏp) *Informal.* —*v.* **swapped, swap·ping, swaps** also **swopped, swop·ping, swops.** —*intr.* To trade one thing for another. —*tr.* To exchange. —*n.* An exchange of one thing for another. [Obs. *swap,* to strike hands in closing a bargain < ME *swappen,* to hit.] **—swap′per** *n.*

swap meet *n.* An informal gathering for the barter or sale of used articles or handcrafts.

sward (swôrd) also **swarth** (swôrth) *n.* **1.** Land covered with grassy turf. **2.** A lawn or meadow. [ME < OE *sweard,* skin.]

sware (swâr) *v. Archaic.* A past tense of **swear.**

swarf (swôrf) *n.* Fine metallic filings or shavings removed by a cutting tool. [Prob. of Scand. orig.]

swarm¹ (swôrm) *n.* **1.** A large number of insects or other small organisms, esp. when in motion. **2.** A group of bees with a queen bee in migration to establish a new colony. **3.** An aggregation of persons or animals, esp. when in turmoil or moving in mass: *A swarm of friends congratulated him.* —*v.* **swarmed, swarm·ing, swarms.** —*intr.* **1. a.** To move or emerge in a swarm. **b.** To leave a hive as a swarm. Used of bees. **2.** To move or gather in large numbers. **3.** To be overrun; teem: *a river bank swarming with insects.* —*tr.* To fill with a crowd; throng. [ME, group of bees < OE *swearm.*] **—swarm′er** *n.*

swarm² (swôrm) *tr. & intr.v.* **swarmed, swarm·ing, swarms.** To climb by gripping with the arms and legs. [Orig. unknown.]

swarm spore *n.* A zoospore.

swart (swôrt) *adj. Archaic.* Swarthy. [ME *swarte* < OE *sweart.*] **—swart′ness** *n.*

swarth (swôrth) *n.* Variant of **sward.**

swar·thy (swôr′thē) *adj.* **-thi·er, -thi·est.** Having a dark complexion or color. [Alteration of obs. *swarty* < SWART.] **—swar′thi·ly** *adv.* **—swar′thi·ness** *n.*

swash (swŏsh, swôsh) *n.* **1. a.** A splash of liquid. **b.** The sound of such a splash. **2.** A narrow channel through which tides flow. **3.** A bar over which waves wash freely. **4. a.** Swagger or bluster. **b.** A swaggering or blustering person. —*v.* **swashed, swash·ing, swash·es.** —*intr.* **1.** To strike, move, or wash with a splashing sound. **2.** To swagger. —*tr.* **1.** To splash (a liquid). **2.** To splash a liquid against. [Prob. imit.]

swash·buck·ler (swŏsh′bŭk′lər, swôsh′-) *n.* A flamboyant swordsman or adventurer. [From the striking of bucklers in fighting.] **—swash′buck′ling** *adj.*

swash letter *n.* An ornamental italic letter with elaborate, flowing flourishes and tails. [Orig. unknown.]

swas·ti·ka (swŏs′tĭ-kə) *n.* **1.** An ancient cosmic or religious symbol formed by a Greek cross with the ends of the arms bent at right angles in either a clockwise or a counterclockwise direction. **2.** The emblem of Nazi Germany, officially adopted in 1935. [Skt. *svastikaḥ,* a sign of good luck < *svasti,* success : *su-,* good + *asti,* it is.]

swat (swŏt) *tr.v.* **swat·ted, swat·ting, swats.** To deal a sharp blow to; slap. —*n.* A quick, sharp, or violent blow. [Alteration of SQUAT, to squash (obs.).]

swatch (swŏch) *n.* A sample strip cut from a piece of cloth or other material. [Orig. unknown.]

swath (swŏth, swôth) also **swathe** (swŏth, swôth) *n.* **1. a.** The width of a scythe stroke or a mowing-machine blade. **b.** A path of this width made in mowing. **c.** The mown grass or grain lying on such a path. **2.** Something likened to a swath. **—*idiom.* cut a (wide) swath.** To create a great stir, impression, or display. [ME *swathe* < OE *swæð,* track.]

swathe¹ (swŏth, swôth, swāth) *tr.v.* **swathed, swath·ing, swathes. 1.** To wrap or bind with or as if with bandages. **2.** To enfold or constrict. —*n.* A wrapping, binding, or bandage. [ME *swathen* < OE *swaðian.*] **—swath′er** *n.*

swathe² (swŏth, swôth) *n.* Variant of **swath.**

swat·ter (swŏt′ər) *n.* **1.** One that swats. **2.** A fly swatter. **3.** *Baseball.* A hard-hitting batter.

sway (swā) *v.* **swayed, sway·ing, sways.** —*intr.* **1.** To move back and forth with a swinging motion; oscillate. **2.** To incline or bend to one side; veer: *She swayed and put out a hand to steady herself.* **3. a.** To incline toward change, as in opinion or feeling. **b.** To fluctuate, as in outlook. —*tr.* **1.** To cause to move back and forth. **2.** To cause to incline or bend to one side. **3.** *Naut.* To swing into position, as a mast or a yard. **4. a.** To divert; deflect. **b.** To exert influence on or control over: *His speech swayed the voters.* **5.** *Archaic.* **a.** To rule or govern. **b.** To wield, as a weapon. —*n.* **1.** The act of moving from side to side with a swinging motion. **2.** Power; influence. **3.** Dominion or control. [ME *sweyen.*] **—sway′er** *n.* **—sway′ing·ly** *adv.*

sway·back (swā′băk′) *n.* An excessive inward or downward curvature of the spine. **—sway′backed′** *adj.*

Swa·zi (swä′zē) *n., pl.* **Swazi** or **-zis.** A tribesman of the Bantu people of Swaziland.

swear (swâr) *v.* **swore** (swôr, swōr), **sworn** (swôrn, swōrn), **swear·ing, swears.** —*intr.* **1.** To make a solemn declaration: *I swear to you I spoke the truth.* **2.** To make a solemn promise; vow. **3.** To use profane oaths; curse. **4.** *Law.* To give evidence or testimony under oath. —*tr.* **1.** To declare or affirm solemnly. **2.** To promise or pledge with a solemn oath; vow: *swore his loyalty.* **3.** To utter or bind oneself to (an oath). **4.** To administer a legal oath to. **5.** To say or affirm earnestly and with great conviction. ***—phrasal verbs.*** **swear by.** To have great reliance upon or confidence in. **swear in.** To administer a legal or official oath to: *swear in the mayor.* **swear off.** *Informal.* To pledge to renounce or give up. [ME *swerien* < OE *swerian.*] **—swear′er** *n.*

swear·word (swâr′wûrd′) *n.* An obscene or blasphemous word.

sweat (swĕt) *v.* **sweat·ed** or **sweat, sweat·ing, sweats.** —*intr.* **1.** To excrete perspiration through the pores in the skin; perspire. **2.** To exude in droplets, as moisture from certain cheeses or sap from a tree. **3.** To condense atmospheric moisture. **4. a.** To release moisture, as hay in the swath. **b.** To ferment, as tobacco during curing. **5.** *Informal.* To work long and hard. **6.** *Informal.* To suffer much, as for a misdeed. **7.** *Informal.* To fret or worry. —*tr.* **1.** To excrete (moisture) through a porous surface. **2.** To gather and condense (moisture) on a surface. **3.** To cause to perspire, as by drugs, heat, or strenuous exercise. **4.** To make damp or wet with perspiration. **5.** To cause to work excessively; overwork. **6.** To overwork, esp. at low pay. **7.** *Informal.* **a.** To interrogate (someone) under duress. **b.** To extract (information) from someone under duress. ***—phrasal verb.*** **sweat out.** *Slang.* **1.** To endure anxiously. **2.** To await (something) anxiously. —*n.* **1.** The product of the sweat glands of the skin. **2.** Condensation of moisture in the form of droplets on a surface. **3. a.** The process of sweating. **b.** The condition of being sweated. **4.** Strenuous, exhaustive labor; drudgery. **5.** An exercise run given a horse before a race. **6.** *Informal.* An anxious, fretful condition; impatience. ***—idioms.*** **no sweat.** *Slang.* Easily done or handled. **sweat blood.** *Slang.* **1.** To work diligently or strenuously. **2.** To worry intensely. [ME *sweten* < OE *swǣtan.*] **—sweat′i·ly** *adv.* **—sweat′i·ness** *n.* **—sweat′y** *adj.*

sweat·band (swĕt′bănd′) *n.* **1.** A band of fabric or leather sewn inside the crown of a hat as protection against sweat. **2.** A band of material tied around the forehead or wrist to absorb sweat.

sweat·box (swĕt′bŏks′) *n.* **1.** A box in which something, such as hides or fruit, is fermented by sweating. **2.** A confined place where a person sweats, esp.: **a.** An interrogation room. **b.** A prison cell used for special punishment.

sweat·er (swĕt′ər) *n.* **1.** One that sweats, esp. profusely. **2.** Something, esp. a sudorific, that induces sweating. **3.** A jacket or pullover made esp. of knit, crocheted, or woven wool.

sweat gland *n.* Any of the numerous small, tubular glands that in humans are found nearly everywhere in the skin and that secrete perspiration externally through pores.

sweat pants *pl.n.* Cotton jersey pants usually having a drawstring or elasticized waist and elasticized cuffs that are worn esp. for exercising.

sweat shirt *n.* A usually long-sleeved cotton jersey pullover.

sweat·shop (swĕt′shŏp′) *n.* A shop or factory where employees work long hours for low wages under bad conditions.

sweat suit *n.* A two-piece outfit consisting of cotton jersey pants tightly fitted at the ankles and waist and a sweat shirt.

swede (swēd) *n.* The rutabaga. [From its introduction from Sweden.]

Swede (swēd) *n.* **1.** A native or inhabitant of Sweden. **2.** A person of Swedish descent. [< MLG.]

Swe·den·bor·gi·an·ism (swēd′n-bôr′gē-ə-nĭz′əm, -jē-) *n.* The theological philosophy of Emanuel Swedenborg that forms the basis for the Church of the New Jerusalem. **—Swe′den·bor′gi·an** *n. & adj.*

Swed·ish (swē′dĭsh) *adj.* Of or pertaining to Sweden, the Swedes, or their culture or language. —*n.* The North Germanic language of Sweden.

Swedish massage *n.* A system of massage and exercises for the muscles and joints.

Swedish turnip *n.* The rutabaga.

sweep (swēp) *v.* **swept** (swĕpt), **sweep·ing, sweeps.** —*tr.* **1.** To clean or clear the surface of with or as if with a broom or brush. **2.** To clean or clear away (dirt, for example) with or as if with a broom or brush: *sweep snow from the steps.* **3.** To clear (a space) with or as if with a broom. **4.** To touch or brush lightly with or as if with a trailing garment: *Willow branches swept the ground.* **5. a.** To move or convey with a flowing motion, as by water: *The wind swept tiles from the roof.* **b.** To move or unbalance emotionally: *Love swept him off his feet.* **6.** To remove or destroy: *flood waters sweeping everything in their path.* **7.** To traverse with speed, violence, or intensity; range throughout: *Plague swept Europe.* **8.** To traverse, as when searching: *Searchlights swept the hillside.* **9.** To drag the bottom of (a body of water). **10. a.** To win all the stages of (a game or contest): *swept the World Series.* **b.** To win overwhelmingly in: *a political party that swept the nation.* —*intr.* **1.** To clean or clear a surface with or as if with a broom or brush. **2. a.** To move, surge, or flow with smooth and steady force: *A cool wind swept over the plain.* **b.** To move swiftly or majestically: *She swept by in silence.* **3.** To trail, as a garment: *Her veil swept to the floor.* **4.** To extend gracefully or majestically: *The hills sweep down to the sea.* —*n.* **1.** The act of sweeping; removal with or as if with a broom or brush. **2.** The motion of sweeping: *a sweep of the arm.* **3.** The range or scope encompassed by sweeping: *the sweep of a machine gun.* **4.** A reach or extent: *a sweep of green lawn.* **5.** A curve or contour: *the sweep of her hair.* **6.** A person who sweeps, esp. a chimney sweep. **7. sweeps.** Sweepings. **8. a.** The winning of all stages of a game or contest. **b.** An overwhelming victory or success. **9.** A long oar used to propel a boat. **10.** A long pole attached to a pivot and with a bucket at one end, used to raise water from a well. **11.** *Informal.* A sweepstakes. **12.** *Electronics.* The steady motion of an electron beam across a cathode-ray tube. [ME *swepen.*] **—sweep′er** *n.*

sweep·back (swēp′băk′) *n.* The backward slant of the leading edge of an airfoil.

sweep·ing (swē′pĭng) *adj.* **1.** Influencing or extending over a great area; wide-ranging: *sweeping changes.* **2.** Curving in form or motion: *a sweeping gesture.* —*n.* **1.** The action or occupation of one that sweeps. **2. sweepings.** Things that are swept up; refuse. **—sweep′ing·ly** *adv.*

sweep·stakes (swēp′stāks′) also **sweep·stake** (-stāk′) *n., pl.* **sweepstakes. 1.** A lottery in which the participants' contributions form a fund to be awarded as a prize to the winner or winners. **2.** An event or contest, esp. a horse race, the result of which determines the winner of a sweepstakes. **3.** The prize won in a sweepstakes.

sweet (swēt) *adj.* **-er, -est. 1. a.** Having a sugary taste. **b.** Containing or derived from sugar. **2.** Pleasing to the senses, feelings, or mind; gratifying. **3.** Having a pleasing disposition; lovable: *a sweet child.* **4.** Not saline: *sweet water.* **5.** Not spoiled, sour, or decaying; fresh: *This milk is still sweet.* **6.** Free of acid. **7.** *Mus.* Designating jazz characterized by adherence to a melodic line and to a time signature. **8.** Low in sulfur content: *sweet oil.* —*n.* **1.** The quality of being sweet; sweetness. **2.** Something that is sweet to the taste or that contains sugar. **3.** A candy, preserve, or confection. **4.** *Chiefly Brit.* Something relatively sweet served as a dessert. **5.** A dear or beloved person. [ME *swete* < OE *swēte.*] **—sweet′ly** *adv.* **—sweet′ness** *n.*

sweet alyssum *n.* A widely cultivated plant, *Lobularia maritima,* native to the Mediterranean region, having clusters of small, fragrant white or purplish flowers.

sweet-and-sour (swēt′n-sour′) *adj.* Flavored with a sauce made of sugar and vinegar and often fruit: *sweet-and-sour duck.*

sweet basil *n.* Basil (sense 1).

sweet bay *n.* A small tree, *Magnolia virginiana,* of the southeastern United States, having large, fragrant white flowers.

sweet·bread (swēt′brĕd′) *n.* The thymus gland of a young animal, used for food.

sweet·bri·er also **sweet·bri·ar** (swēt′brī′ər) *n.* A rose, *Rosa eglanteria,* native to Europe, having prickly stems, fragrant leaves, and pink flowers.

sweet cherry *n.* **1.** A widely cultivated tree, *Prunus avium,* native to Eurasia, having white flowers and sweet, edible fruit. **2.** The fruit of the sweet cherry.

sweet chocolate *n.* Chocolate to which sugar has been added.

sweet cicely *n.* **1.** Any of various plants of the genus *Osmorhiza,* having aromatic roots, compound leaves, and clusters of small white flowers. **2.** An aromatic European plant, *Myrrhis odorata,* having compound leaves and clusters of small white flowers.

sweet cider *n.* Unfermented cider.

sweet clover *n.* The melilot.

sweet corn *n.* A variety of corn, *Zea mays rugosa,* having kernels that are sweet when young and that is the common edible corn.

sweet·en (swēt′n) *v.* **-ened, -en·ing, -ens.** —*tr.* **1.** To make sweet or sweeter by or as if by the addition of sugar. **2.** To make more pleasurable or gratifying. **3.** To make bearable;

sweet pea

sweetsop

sweet William

George Miksch Sutton

swift

swing

alleviate. **4.** *Informal.* To increase the value of (collateral for a loan) by adding more securities. **5.** To increase the value of (an unwon poker pot) by adding stakes before reopening. —*intr.* To become sweet. **—sweet'en·er** *n.*

sweet·en·ing (swēt'n-ĭng) *n.* **1.** The act or process of making sweet. **2.** Something used to sweeten.

sweet fern *n.* An aromatic shrub, *Myrica asplenifolia* (or *Comptonia peregrina*), of eastern North America, having narrow, shallowly lobed, fernlike foliage.

sweet flag *n.* A plant, *Acorus calamus,* growing in moist places and having bladelike leaves, minute greenish flowers, and aromatic roots.

sweet gale *n.* A swamp shrub, *Myrica gale,* of northern regions, having aromatic, resinous leaves.

sweet gum *n.* **1.** A New World tree, *Liquidambar styraciflua,* having sharply lobed leaves, prickly, ball-like fruit clusters, and wood used to make furniture. **2.** The aromatic resin obtained from the sweet gum.

sweet·heart (swēt'härt') *n.* **1.** A person who loves and is loved by another. **2.** A lovable person.

swee·tie (swē'tē) *n. Informal.* Sweetheart; dear.

sweet·ing (swē'tĭng) *n.* **1.** A sweet apple. **2.** *Archaic.* A sweetheart.

sweet marjoram *n.* Marjoram (sense 1).

sweet·meat (swēt'mēt') *n.* A piece of candy or other sweet delicacy.

sweet pea *n.* A climbing plant, *Lathyrus odoratus,* native to southern Europe, cultivated for its variously colored, fragrant flowers.

sweet pepper *n.* The bell pepper.

sweet pepperbush *n.* A North American shrub, *Clethra alnifolia,* growing in moist ground and having clusters of small, fragrant white flowers.

sweet potato *n.* **1.** A tropical American vine, *Ipomoea batatas,* cultivated for its thick, orange-colored, edible root. **2.** The root of the sweet potato, eaten cooked as a vegetable. **3.** *Informal.* The ocarina.

sweet·shop (swēt'shŏp') *n. Chiefly Brit.* A candy store.

sweet·sop (swēt'sŏp') *n.* **1.** A tropical American tree, *Annona squamosa,* having yellowish-green fruit with sweet, edible pulp. **2.** The fruit of the sweetsop.

sweet sorghum *n.* Sorgo.

sweet sultan *n.* An Old World plant, *Centaurea moschata,* widely cultivated for its showy, variously colored flowers.

sweet talk *n.* Flattery.

sweet-talk (swēt'tôk') *v.* **-talked, -talk·ing, -talks.** —*tr.* To coax or cajole with flattery. —*intr.* To use flattery.

sweet tooth *n. Informal.* An inordinate fondness for sweets.

sweet William *n.* A widely cultivated plant, *Dianthus barbatus,* native to Eurasia, having flat, dense clusters of varicolored flowers.

swell (swĕl) *v.* **swelled, swelled** or **swol·len** (swō'lən), **swell·ing, swells.** —*intr.* **1.** To increase in size or volume as a result of internal pressure; expand. **2. a.** To increase in force, size, number, or degree: *Membership swelled.* **b.** To grow in loudness or intensity, as a sound: *"the din in front swelled to a tremendous chorus"* (Stephen Crane). **3.** To bulge out; protrude, as a sail. **4.** To rise in billows above the surrounding level, as clouds. **5. a.** To be or become filled with an emotion: *swelled with pride.* **b.** To behave or speak pompously or self-importantly. —*tr.* **1.** To cause to increase in volume, size, number, degree, or intensity. **2.** To fill with emotion. —*n.* **1. a.** The act or process of swelling. **b.** The condition of being swollen. **2.** A swollen part; bulge or protuberance. **3.** A long wave that moves continuously without breaking. **4.** A rounded hill. **5.** *Informal.* A person who is fashionably dressed or prominent in fashionable society. **6.** *Mus.* **a.** A crescendo followed by a gradual diminuendo. **b.** The sign indicating this. **c.** A device on some instruments, such as an organ or harpsichord, for regulating volume. —*adj.* **-er, -est.** *Informal.* **1.** Fashionably elegant; stylish. **2.** Fine; excellent: *"It was swell out, just cool enough"* (James T. Farrell). [ME *swellen* < OE *swellan.*]

swell box *n.* A chamber housing one or more sets of organ pipes and having shutters that can be opened or shut to regulate the volume of tone.

swelled head *n.* An unduly high opinion of oneself; conceit.

swell·fish (swĕl'fĭsh') *n., pl.* **swellfish** or **-fish·es.** The puffer (sense 2).

swell·head (swĕl'hĕd') *n.* One who has a swelled head. **—swell'head'ed** *adj.* **—swell'head'ed·ness** *n.*

swell·ing (swĕl'ĭng) *n.* **1.** The state of being swollen. **2.** Something that is swollen, esp. an abnormally swollen or protuberant bodily part.

swel·ter (swĕl'tər) *v.* **-tered, -ter·ing, -ters.** —*intr.* To be affected by or sweat or feel faint from oppressive heat. —*tr.* **1.** To affect with oppressive heat. **2.** *Archaic.* To exude. —*n.* Oppressive heat. [ME *swelteren,* freq. of *swelten,* to faint from heat < OE *sweltan,* to die.]

swel·ter·ing (swĕl'tər-ing) *adj.* **1.** Oppressively hot and humid. **2.** Suffering from oppressive heat. **—swel'ter·ing·ly** *adv.*

swel·try (swĕl'trē) *adj.* **-tri·er, -tri·est.** Sweltering.

swept (swĕpt) *v.* Past tense and past participle of **sweep.**

swept·back (swĕpt'băk') *adj.* Angled rearward from the points of attachment. Used esp. of aircraft wings.

swerve (swûrv) *tr. & intr.v.* **swerved, swerv·ing, swerves.** To turn aside from a straight course; veer. —*n.* The act of swerving. [ME *swerven* < OE *sweorfan,* to rub.]

swift (swĭft) *adj.* **-er, -est. 1.** Moving or capable of moving with great speed. **2.** Coming, occurring, or accomplished quickly: *a swift retort.* **3.** Quick to act or react; prompt: *swift to take steps.* —*adv.* Quickly: *swift-running.* —*n.* **1. a.** A cylinder on a carding machine. **b.** A reel used to hold yarn as it is being wound off. **2.** Any of various dark-colored birds of the family Apodidae, characteristically having long, narrow wings and a relatively short tail. **3.** Any of various small, fast-moving North American lizards of the genera *Sceloporus* and *Uta.* [ME < OE.] **—swift'ly** *adv.* **—swift'ness** *n.*

swig (swĭg) *Informal.* —*n.* A large swallow, as of a liquid; gulp. —*tr. & intr.v.* **swigged, swig·ging, swigs.** To drink in swigs; gulp. [Orig. unknown.] **—swig'ger** *n.*

swill (swĭl) *v.* **swilled, swill·ing, swills.** —*tr.* **1.** To drink eagerly or greedily: *"Unshaven horsemen swill the great wines of the Chateaux"* (W.H. Auden). **2.** To flood with water, as for washing. **3.** To feed (animals) with slop. —*intr.* To eat or drink eagerly or greedily. —*n.* **1.** A mixture of liquid and solid food, as table scraps, fed to animals, esp. pigs. **2.** Garbage; refuse. **3.** A deep draft of liquor. [ME *swilen* < OE *swilian,* to wash out.] **—swill'er** *n.*

swim (swĭm) *v.* **swam** (swăm), **swum** (swŭm), **swim·ming, swims.** —*intr.* **1.** To propel oneself through water by means of movements of the body. **2.** To move as though gliding through water. **3.** To float on water. **4.** To be immersed: *chicken swimming in gravy.* **5.** To be dizzy; feel faint or giddy: *"His brain still swimming with the effects of the last night's champagne"* (R.S. Surtees). **6.** To appear to spin or reel hazily. —*tr.* **1.** To propel oneself through or across (a body of water) by swimming. **2.** To cause to swim or float on a body of water. —*n.* **1.** The act or an instance of swimming. **2.** A period of swimming. **3.** A state of dizziness. ***—idioms.* in the swim.** *Informal.* Participating in what is current or fashionable. **swim against the stream.** To move in opposition to a prevailing trend. [ME *swimmen* < OE *swimman.*] **—swim'mer** *n.*

swim bladder *n.* An air bladder (sense 1).

swim·mer·et (swĭm'ə-rĕt', swĭm'ə-rĕt') *n.* One of the paired abdominal appendages of certain aquatic crustaceans, such as shrimps, lobsters, and isopods, that function primarily as organs of respiration or locomotion.

swimmer's itch *n.* A form of dermatitis caused by the penetration of the skin by cercariae of certain schistosomes.

swim·ming·ly (swĭm'ĭng-lē) *adv.* With great ease and a high degree of success: *The campaign is proceeding swimmingly.*

swimming pool *n.* A pool constructed for swimming.

swim·suit (swĭm'so͞ot') *n.* A garment worn while swimming.

swin·dle (swĭn'dl) *v.* **-dled, -dling, -dles.** —*tr.* **1.** To cheat or defraud (someone) of money or property. **2.** To obtain (money, for example) by fraudulent means. —*intr.* To practice fraud as a habitual means of obtaining money. —*n.* The act or an instance of swindling; fraud. [Back-formation < *swindler* < G. *Schwindler,* dizzy person < *schwindeln,* to be dizzy < OHG *swintilōn,* freq. of *swintan,* to vanish.] **—swin'dler** *n.*

swine (swīn) *n., pl.* **swine. 1.** Any of the ungulate mammals of the family Suidae, which includes pigs, hogs, and boars. **2.** A contemptible, vicious person. [ME < OE *swīn.*]

swine·herd (swīn'hûrd') *n.* A keeper or tender of swine.

swine·pox (swīn'pŏks') *n.* A disease of domesticated swine caused by a virus similar to that causing cowpox and smallpox and characterized by skin lesions.

swing (swĭng) *v.* **swung, swing·ing, swings.** —*intr.* **1.** To move rhythmically back and forth suspended or as if suspended from above: *a rope swinging from the mast.* **2.** To attempt to strike a ball with a sweeping motion of the arm. **3.** To move laterally or in a curve: *swing over to the curb.* **4.** To turn in place, as on a hinge. **5.** To change from one attitude, position, opinion, or emotion to another; vacillate. **6.** *Slang.* To be executed by hanging. **7. a.** *Mus.* To have a compulsive rhythm. **b.** To play a piece with a compulsive rhythm. **8.** *Slang.* To be spirited and up-to-date. **9.** *Slang.* To engage freely and uninhibitedly in sexual activity. —*tr.* **1.** To cause to move back and forth. **2.** To cause to move in a broad arc: *swing a bat.* **3.** To move with a sweeping motion: *swung his arms.* **4.** To hang or suspend (something) so as to be able to move freely. **5. a.** To suspend on hinges: *swing a shutter.* **b.** To cause to turn on hinges: *swing the door shut.* **6.** To cause to change from one attitude, position, opinion, or emotion to another. **7.** *Slang.* To manipulate or manage successfully: *Can you swing this deal?* **8.** To perform (popular music) in the style of swing. —*n.* **1.** The act of swinging, esp.: **a.** A rhythmic back-and-forth movement. **b.** A single movement or series of movements in one particular direction. **2.** The space traversed while swinging: *The pendulum's swing is 12 inches.* **3.** The manner in which a person or thing swings something, as a baseball bat or golf club. **4.** Freedom and scope of movement or action. **5. a.** A swaying, graceful motion. **b.** A sweep or swoop: *the swing of a bird across the sky.* **6.** A seat suspended from above, on which one may ride back and forth in an arc for recreation. **7.** *Mus.* **a.** An innovation in popular dance music developed about 1935 and based on jazz but employing a larger band and simpler harmonic and rhythmic patterns. **b.** The rhythmic quality of this music. —*adj.* Pertaining to or performing swing. —***idiom.*** **in full swing.** At full speed or intensity. [ME *swingen* < OE *swingan,* to flog.]

Synonyms: *swing, oscillate, sway, rock, vibrate, fluctuate, undulate, waver.* These verbs refer to movement marked in general by a back-and-forth or up-and-down pattern. *Swing* usually applies to arclike movement of something attached at one extremity and free at the other, or to rotating or pivoting movement around an axis. *Oscillate* more specifically refers to regular back-and-forth movement, such as that of a pendulum. *Sway* suggests the movement of something unsteady, light, or flexible. *Rock* can apply both to rhythmic and rather gentle movement and to violent tilting. *Vibrate,* in general usage, usually suggests rhythmic throbbing or pulsating; thus it implies trembling or quivering motion rather than pronounced movement. *Fluctuate* usually applies to movement of nonphysical things, such as prices, and suggests fairly constant change that follows no set course. *Undulate* implies smooth, wavelike movement. *Waver* suggests unsteady and uncertain movement, such as tottering or faltering. In figurative usage it refers to indecisiveness.

swing-by (swĭng'bī') *n., pl.* **-bys.** An interplanetary mission in which a space vehicle utilizes planetary gravitation for course changes.

swinge (swĭnj) *tr.v.* **swinged, swinge·ing, swing·es.** *Archaic.* To strike or beat; swipe. [ME *swengen,* to shake < OE *swengan.*] —**swing'er** (swĭn'jər) *n.*

swing·er (swĭng'ər) *n.* **1.** One that swings. **2.** *Slang.* **a.** A person who actively seeks excitement and moves with the latest trends. **b.** A person who engages freely and uninhibitedly in sexual activity.

swing·ing (swĭng'ĭng) *Slang.* —*n.* The practice of swapping sex partners. —*adj.* **1.** Being spirited and up-to-date. **2.** Being abundant in swingers or swinging activity: *a swinging nightclub.*

swin·gle·tree (swĭng'gəl-trē) *n.* A whiffletree. [< E. *swingle,* wooden instrument < ME < MDu. *swinghel.*]

swing·man (swĭng'mən) *n. Sports.* A team member who has the ability to play effectively in two different positions, as both forward and guard in basketball.

swing shift *n. Informal.* A factory work shift between the day and night shifts, lasting from about 4 P.M. to midnight.

swing-wing (swĭng'wĭng') *adj.* Of or being an airplane with wings constructed to allow the outer portion to fold back along the fusilage to produce streamlining at high speeds.

swin·ish (swī'nĭsh) *adj.* Resembling or befitting swine; bestial.

swipe (swīp) *n.* **1.** A heavy, sweeping blow. **2.** A lever, esp. one that raises the bucket in a well. —*v.* **swiped, swip·ing, swipes.** —*tr.* **1.** To hit with a sweeping blow. **2.** *Slang.* To steal; filch. —*intr.* To make a sweeping blow. [Perh. alteration of SWEEP.]

swirl (swûrl) *v.* **swirled, swirl·ing, swirls.** —*intr.* **1.** To rotate or spin in or as if in a whirlpool or eddy. **2.** To be dizzy or faint. —*tr.* To cause to move with a whirling motion. —*n.* **1.** The motion of whirling or spinning. **2.** Something that swirls; whirlpool or eddy: *"A roaring swirl of white water, sweeping the valley"* (Winston Churchill). **3.** Something that is swirled, such as a line or a curl of hair; whorl. [ME *swyrl,* eddy, prob. of LG orig.] —**swirl'y** *adj.*

swish (swĭsh) *v.* **swished, swish·ing, swish·es.** —*intr.* **1.** To move with a whistle or hiss. **2.** To rustle, as certain fabrics. **3.** *Slang.* To move or act in the manner of an effeminate male. —*tr.* **1.** To cause to make a swishing movement or sound. **2.** To chastise with a rod. —*n.* **1. a.** A sharp whistling or rustling sound: *the swish of scythes.* **b.** A movement making such a sound. **2. a.** A rod used for flogging. **b.** A stroke made with such a rod. **3.** *Slang.* A highly effeminate male. —*adj. Slang.* **1.** *Chiefly Brit.* Fashionable; posh. **2.** Highly effeminate. [Imit.]

swish·y (swĭsh'ē) *adj.* **-i·er, -i·est. 1.** Creating a swishing sound. **2.** *Slang.* Characterized by effeminate manners or traits.

Swiss (swĭs) *adj.* Of, pertaining to, or characteristic of Switzerland, its inhabitants, or its culture. —*n., pl.* **Swiss. 1.** A native or inhabitant of Switzerland. **2.** A person of Swiss descent. **3.** A crisp, sheer cotton cloth used for curtains or light garments. [OFr. *Suisse* < MHG *Swizer* < *Swiz,* Switzerland.]

Swiss chard *n.* Chard.

Swiss cheese *n.* A firm white or pale-yellow cheese with many large holes, originally produced in Switzerland.

Swiss guards *pl.n.* Mercenaries from Switzerland employed as guards at the Vatican.

Swiss steak *n.* A round or shoulder steak that is pounded with flour, braised, and usually served with a seasoned sauce.

switch (swĭch) *n.* **1.** A slender flexible rod, stick, twig, or the like, esp. such a rod used for whipping. **2.** The bushy tip of the tail of certain animals: *a cow's switch.* **3.** A thick bunch of real or synthetic hair used by women in a coiffure. **4.** A flailing or lashing, as with a slender rod. **5.** *Elect.* A device used to break or open an electrical circuit or to divert current from one conductor to another. **6.** A device consisting of two sections of railroad track and the accompanying apparatus, used to transfer rolling stock from one track to another. **7. a.** The act or process of operating a switching device. **b.** The result achieved by such an act. **8.** A transference or shift, as of opinion or attention. —*v.* **switched, switch·ing, switch·es.** —*tr.* **1.** To whip with or as if with a switch. **2.** To jerk or swish abruptly or sharply. **3.** To shift, transfer, change, or divert: *switch the conversation.* **4.** To exchange: *switch sides.* **5.** To connect, disconnect, or divert (an electric current) by operating a switch. **6.** To cause (an electric current or appliance) to begin or cease operation: *switch on the lights; switch off the radio.* **7.** To move (rolling stock) from one track to another; shunt. —*intr.* **1.** To shift or change: *"His Majesty's fleet had recently switched from coal to oil"* (John Dos Passos). **2.** To be shifted or changed. [Perh. < MDu. *swijch,* twig.] —**switch'er** *n.*

switch·back (swĭch'băk') *n.* **1.** A road, roadbed, or trail that ascends a steep incline in a winding course. **2.** *Chiefly Brit.* A roller coaster.

switch·blade knife (swĭch'blād') *n.* A pocket knife having a spring-operated blade that unsheathes when a release on the handle is pressed.

switch·board (swĭch'bôrd', -bōrd') *n.* One or more panels accommodating control switches, indicators, and other apparatus for operating electric circuits.

switch·er·oo (swĭch'ə-ro͞o') *n. Slang.* An unexpected variation or reversal. [Alteration of SWITCH.]

switch hitter *n. Baseball.* An ambidextrous batter.

switch knife *n.* A switchblade knife.

switch·man (swĭch'mən) *n.* A person who operates railroad switches.

switch·yard (swĭch'yärd') *n.* An area where railroad cars are switched and trains assembled.

Swit·zer (swĭt'sər) *n.* A Swiss. [MHG *Swizer.* —see SWISS.]

swiv·el (swĭv'əl) *n.* **1.** A link, pivot, or other fastening so designed that it permits free turning of attached parts. **2.** A pivoted support that allows an attached object, such as a chair or gun, to turn in a horizontal plane. **3.** A cannon that turns on a pivot. —*v.* **-eled, -el·ing, -els** or **-elled, -el·ling, -els.** —*tr.* **1.** To turn or rotate on or as if on a swivel. **2.** To secure, fit, or support with a swivel. —*intr.* To turn on a swivel. [ME *swyvel.*]

swivel chair *n.* A chair that swivels on its base.

swiv·el-hipped (swĭv'əl-hĭpt') *adj.* Characterized by or moving with an exaggerated swinging movement of the hips.

swiv·et (swĭv'ĭt) *n. Informal.* A state of extreme distress or discomposure. [Orig. unknown.]

swiz·zle (swĭz'əl) *n.* Any of various tall mixed drinks, usually made with rum. [Orig. unknown.]

swizzle stick *n.* A rod for stirring mixed drinks.

swob (swŏb) *n.* Variant of **swab.**

swol·len (swō'lən) *v.* A past participle of **swell.**

swoon (swo͞on) *intr.v.* **swooned, swoon·ing, swoons.** To faint. —*n.* A fainting spell; syncope. [ME *swounen,* prob. < OE *swōgan,* to suffocate.]

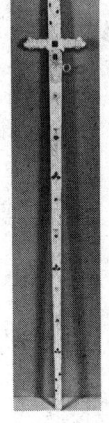

swoop (swo͞op) *v.* **swooped, swoop·ing, swoops.** —*intr.* To make a sudden sweeping movement, as a bird descending upon its prey. —*tr.* To take or snatch suddenly; scoop. —*n.* The act of swooping; a swift, sudden descent. [ME *swopen,* to sweep along < OE *swāpan,* to sweep.]

swoosh (swo͞osh, swo͝osh) *v.* **swooshed, swoosh·ing, swoosh·es.** —*intr.* **1.** To make a rushing sound. **2.** To flow or swirl copiously. —*tr.* To emit or carry with a rushing sound. [Imit.]

swop (swŏp) *v. & n.* Variant of **swap.**

sword (sôrd) *n.* **1.** A weapon having a long blade for cutting or thrusting. **2.** An instrument of death, combat, or destruction. **3. a.** The use of force, as in war. **b.** Power or jurisdiction. **4.** Something that resembles a sword. —***idioms.*** **at swords' points.** Ready for combat; antagonistic. **cross swords. 1.** To fight. **2.** To quarrel violently. **put to the sword.** To kill with a sword. [ME < OE *sweord.*]

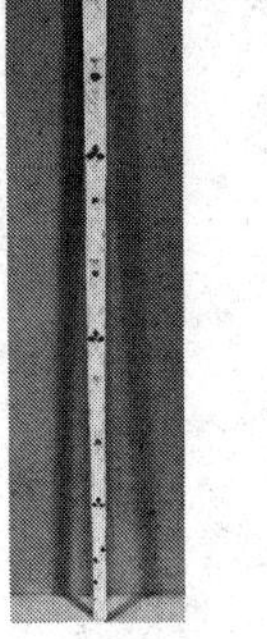

sword

sword bayonet *n.* A short swordlike bayonet.

sword·bill (sôrd'bĭl') *n.* A hummingbird, *Ensifera ensifera,* of tropical South America, having a very long, slender bill.

sword cane *n.* A cane designed to conceal a sword or dagger.

sword dance *n.* A dance performed with swords, esp. one performed around swords laid on the ground.

sword·fish (sôrd'fĭsh') *n., pl.* **swordfish** or **-fish·es.** A large marine game and food fish, *Xiphias gladius,* having a long, swordlike extension of the upper jaw.

sword grass *n.* Any of various grasses or grasslike plants having bladelike, pointed leaves.

sword·knot (sôrd'nŏt') *n.* A decorative loop or tassle attached to the hilt of a sword.

Sword of Damocles *n.* An impending disaster or the permanent threat of it. [After *Damocles,* courtier of Dionysius I, tyrant of Syracuse, who was forced to sit under a sword suspended by a hair to demonstrate the precariousness of a king's fortune.]

swordfish

sword·play (sôrd'plā') *n.* The action or art of using a sword; fencing. —**sword'play'er** *n.*

swords·man (sôrdz'mən) *n.* **1. a.** A person skilled in the use of the sword. **b.** A skilled fencer. **2.** A person armed with a sword. —**swords'man·ship'** *n.*

sword·tail (sôrd'tāl') *n.* A small, brightly colored freshwater fish, *Xiphophorus helleri,* of Central America, that has a long, tapering extension of the caudal fin in the male and is popular in home aquariums.

swore (swôr) *v.* Past tense of **swear.**

sworn (swôrn) *v.* Past participle of **swear.**

swounds or **swouns** *interj.* Variants of **zounds.**

swum (swŭm) *v.* Past participle of **swim.**

swung (swŭng) *v.* A past tense and the past participle of **swing.**

swung dash *n.* A character ~ used in printing to save space by standing for all or part of a previously written out word.

syb·a·rite also **Syb·a·rite** (sĭb'ə-rīt) *n.* A person devoted to pleasure and luxury; voluptuary. [Lat. *Sybarita,* native of Sybaris < Gk. *Subaritēs* < *Subaris,* Sybaris, Italy (from the notorious luxury of the inhabitants of Sybaris).] —**syb'a·rit'ic** (-rĭt'ĭk), **syb'a·rit'i·cal** *adj.* —**syb'a·rit'i·cal·ly** *adv.*

syc·a·mine (sĭk'ə-mīn, -mĭn) *n.* A tree mentioned in the New Testament, thought to be a species of mulberry. [Lat. *sycaminus* < Gk. *sukaminos,* of Semitic orig.]

syc·a·more (sĭk'ə-môr', -mōr') *n.* **1.** A deciduous tree, *Platanus occidentalis,* of eastern North America, having lobed leaves, ball-like seed clusters, and bark that often flakes off in large patches. **2.** A Eurasian tree, *Acer pseudoplatanus,* related to and resembling the maples. **3.** Also *Obs.* **sycomore.** A tree, *Ficus sycomorus,* of northeastern Africa and adjacent Asia, related to the fig and mentioned in the Bible. [ME *sicamour* < OFr. *sicamor* < Lat. *sycomorus* < Gk. *sukomoros.*]

syce (sīs) *n.* A stableman or groom, esp. in India. [Hindi *sā'is* < Ar. < *sāsa,* to administer.]

sy·cee (sī'-sē') *n.* Lumps of pure silver bearing the stamp of a banker or assayer and formerly used in China as money. [Chin. (Cantonese) *sai*^{4} *si*^{1}, fine silk (so called because the pure silver can be spun into fine threads).]

syc·o·more (sĭk'ə-môr', -mōr') *n. Obs.* Variant of **sycamore** (sense 3).

sy·co·ni·um (sī-kō'nē-əm) *n., pl.* **-ni·a** (-nē-ə). The fleshy multiple fruit of the fig, consisting primarily of the enlarged floral receptacle. [NLat. < Gk. *sukon,* fig.]

syc·o·phan·cy (sĭk'ə-fən-sē) *n., pl.* **-cies.** The act, practice, or behavior of a sycophant; servile flattery.

syc·o·phant (sĭk'ə-fənt) *n.* A person who attempts to win favor or advance himself by flattering persons of influence; a servile self-seeker: *"the king appeared . . . with his dogs and sycophants behind him"* (Kathleen Winsor). [Lat. *sycophanta* < Gk. *sukophantēs,* informer : *sukon,* fig + *-phantēs* < *phainein,* to show.] —**syc'o·phan'tic** (-făn'tĭk), **syc'o·phan'ti·cal** *adj.* —**syc'o·phan'ti·cal·ly** *adv.*

Synonyms: *sycophant, toady, flatterer.* These nouns denote persons who lavish praise or attention on others, usually in the hope of gain. *Sycophant* and *toady* both refer to parasites of the rich or powerful and stress self-seeking motives. *Toady* especially implies truckling or adopting a menial attitude. *Flatterer,* less specific and less derogatory, does not always imply hope of gain but may suggest insincerity or servility.

sy·co·sis (sī-kō'sĭs) *n.* A chronic inflammation of the hair follicles, esp. of the beard and scalp. [Gk. *sukōsis,* ulcer resembling a fig < *sukon,* fig.]

sy·e·nite (sī'ə-nīt') *n.* An igneous rock composed primarily of alkali feldspar together with other minerals, such as hornblende. [Lat. *Syenites (lapis),* (stone) of Syene < *Syene,* Syene, ancient city in Egypt < Gk. *Suēnē.*] —**sy'e·nit'ic** (-nĭt'ĭk) *adj.*

sy·li (sĭl'ĭ') *n.* See table at **currency.** [Native word in Guinea.]

syl·la·bar·y (sĭl'ə-bĕr'ē) *n., pl.* **-ies.** A list of syllables, esp. a list or set of written characters, each one representing a syllable. [NLat. *syllabarium* < Lat. *syllaba,* syllable. —see SYLLABLE.]

syl·la·bi (sĭl'ə-bī') *n.* A plural of **syllabus.**

syl·lab·ic (sĭ-lăb'ĭk) *adj.* **1.** Of, pertaining to, or consisting of a syllable or syllables. **2.** Designating a consonant that forms a syllable without a vowel, as the *l* in *riddle* (rĭd'l). **3.** Pronouncing every syllable distinctly: *a syllabic reading of a line of verse.* **4.** Designating a form of verse based on the number of syllables per line rather than on the arrangement of accents or quantities. —*n.* A syllabic sound. [Med. Lat. *syllabicus* < Gk. *sullabikos* < *sullabē,* syllable.] —**syl·lab'i·cal·ly** *adv.*

syl·lab·i·cate (sĭ-lăb'ə-kāt') also **syl·lab·i·fy** (-fī') *tr.v.* **-cat·ed, -cat·ing, -cates** also **-fied, -fy·ing, -fies.** To form or divide into syllables. —**syl·lab'i·ca'tion** *n.*

syl·la·bism (sĭl'ə-bĭz'əm) *n.* **1.** The use of written characters that represent syllables. **2.** Division into syllables. [< Lat. *syllaba,* syllable. —see SYLLABLE.]

syl·la·bize (sĭl'ə-bīz') *tr.v.* **-bized, -biz·ing, -biz·es.** To syllabicate. [Med. Lat. *syllabizare* < Gk. *sullabizein* < *sullabē,* syllable.]

syl·la·ble (sĭl'ə-bəl) *n.* **1.** A unit of spoken language consisting of a single uninterrupted sound formed by a vowel or diphthong alone, of a syllabic consonant alone, or of either with one or more consonants. **2.** One or more letters or phonetic symbols written or printed to approximate a spoken syllable. **3.** The slightest bit or expression. —*tr.v.* **-bled, -bling, -bles.** To pronounce (a line of verse, for example) in syllables. [ME *sillable* < Norman Fr. < OFr. *sillabe* < Lat. *syllaba* < Gk. *sullabē* < *sullambanein,* to combine in pronunciation : *sun-,* together + *lambanein,* to take.]

syl·la·bub also **sil·la·bub** (sĭl'ə-bŭb') *n.* A drink or, with gelatin added, a dessert, consisting of wine or liquor mixed with sweetened milk or cream. [Orig. unknown.]

syl·la·bus (sĭl'ə-bəs) *n., pl.* **-bus·es** or **-bi** (-bī'). **1.** An outline or brief statement of the main points of a text, lecture, or course of study. **2.** *Law.* A short statement preceding a report on an adjudged case and containing the court rulings on the legal points involved. [Med. Lat., prob. alteration of *syllabos,* alteration of Lat. *sittybas* < Gk. *sittubas,* accusative pl. of *sittuba,* title slip.]

syl·lep·sis (sĭ-lĕp'sĭs) *n., pl.* **-ses** (-sēz'). A construction in which a word is used to modify or govern two or more other words although agreeing in number, gender, or case with only one or having different senses, such as literal and figurative, when applied to them, as in *He lost his coat and his temper.* [LLat. < Gk. *sullēpsis* : *sun-,* together + *lēpsis,* a taking < *lambanein,* to take.] —**syl·lep'tic** *adj.*

syl·lo·gism (sĭl'ə-jĭz'əm) *n.* **1.** *Logic.* A form of deductive reasoning consisting of a major premise, a minor premise, and a conclusion; for example, *All men are foolish* (major premise); *Smith is a man* (minor premise); *therefore, Smith is foolish* (conclusion). **2.** Reasoning from the general to the specific; deduction. **3.** A subtle or specious piece of reasoning. [ME *silogisme* < OFr. < Lat. *syllogismus* < Gk. *sullogismos* < *sullogizesthai,* to infer : *sun-,* with + *logizesthai,* to reason < *logos,* reason.]

syl·lo·gist (sĭl'ə-jĭst) *n.* A person who uses or is skilled in syllogistic reasoning.

syl·lo·gis·tic (sĭl'ə-jĭs'tĭk) also **syl·lo·gis·ti·cal** (-tĭ-kəl) *adj.* Of, pertaining to, resembling, or consisting of a syllogism or syllogisms. —**syl'lo·gis'ti·cal·ly** *adv.*

syl·lo·gis·tics (sĭl'ə-jĭs'tĭks) *n. (used with a sing. verb).* **1.** The branch of logic dealing with syllogisms. **2.** The art of reasoning by syllogism.

syl·lo·gize (sĭl'ə-jīz') *v.* **-gized, -giz·ing, -giz·es.** —*intr.* To reason or argue by means of syllogisms. —*tr.* To deduce by syllogism. —**syl'lo·gi·za'tion** *n.* —**syl'lo·giz'er** *n.*

sylph (sĭlf) *n.* **1.** Any of a class of elemental beings without souls that were believed to inhabit the air. **2.** A slim, graceful woman or girl. [NLat. *sylphus.*]

sylph·id (sĭl'fĭd) *n.* A young or diminutive sylph. —*adj.* Pertaining to or resembling a sylph. [Fr. *sylphide* < *sylphe,* sylph < NLat. *sylphus.*]

syl·va (sĭl'və) *n.* Variant of **silva.**

syl·van also **sil·van** (sĭl'vən) *adj.* **1.** Pertaining to or characteristic of woods or forest regions. **2.** Located in or inhabiting a wood or forest. **3.** Abounding in trees; wooded. —*n.* One that lives in or frequents the woods. [Med. Lat. *silvanus* < Lat. *silva, forest.*]

syl·van·ite (sĭl'və-nīt') *n.* A pale brass-yellow to silver-white gold and silver ore, chiefly (Au, Ag)Te_2. [Fr. after *Transylvania,* Rumania, where it was first found.]

Syl·va·nus (sĭl-vā'nəs) *n.* Variant of **Silvanus.**

syl·vat·ic (sĭl-văt'ĭk) *adj.* **1.** Affecting wild animals. **2.** Sylvan. [Lat. *silvaticus,* of the forest, wild < *silva,* forest.]

syl·vite (sĭl'vīt') also **syl·vine** (-vēn') or **syl·vin·ite** (-vĭ-nīt') *n.* A colorless vitreous potassium chloride mineral used as a major source of potassium compounds. [Fr., alteration of *sylvine* < NLat. *(sal digestivus) Sylvii,* (digestive salt) of Sylvius.]

sym- *pref.* Variant of **syn-.**

sym·bi·ont (sĭm'bē-ŏnt', -bī-) *n.* One of the organisms in a symbiotic relationship. [Gk. *sumbiōn, sumbiont-,* pr.part. of *sumbioun,* to live together. —see SYMBIOSIS.] —**sym'bi·on'tic** *adj.*

sym·bi·o·sis (sĭm'bē-ō'sĭs, -bī-) *n. Biol.* The relationship of two or more different organisms in a close association that may be but is not necessarily of benefit to each. [Gk. *sumbiōsis,* companionship < *sumbioun,* to live together : *sun-,* together + *bios,* life.] —**sym'bi·ot'ic** (-ŏt'ĭk), **sym'bi·ot'i·cal** (-ŏt'ĭ-kəl) *adj.* —**sym'bi·ot'i·cal·ly** *adv.*

sym·bi·ote (sĭm'bē-ōt', -bī-) *n.* A symbiont.

sym·bol (sĭm'bəl) *n.* **1.** Something that represents something else by association, resemblance, or convention, esp. a material object used to represent something invisible. **2.** A printed or written sign used to represent an operation, element, quantity, quality, or relation, as in mathematics or music. —*tr.v.* **-boled, -bol·ing, -bols.** To symbolize. [Lat. *symbolum* < Gk. *sumbolon,* token for identification (by comparison with a counterpart) < *sumballein,* to compare : *sun-,* together + *ballein,* to throw.]

sym·bol·ic (sĭm-bŏl'ĭk) also **sym·bol·i·cal** (-ĭ-kəl) *adj.* **1.** Of, pertaining to, or expressed by means of a symbol or symbols. **2.** Serving as a symbol. **3.** Characterized by the use of symbolism, as a work of art. —**sym·bol'i·cal·ly** *adv.* —**sym·bol'i·cal·ness** *n.*

symbolic address *n.* An identification of particular computer data without regard to the location of the data within the device.

symbolic language *n.* A computer programming language

designed for ease of use by human operators rather than computers.

sym·bol·ic logic *n.* A treatment of formal logic in which a calculus or system of symbols is used to represent quantities and relationships.

sym·bol·ism (sĭm'bə-lĭz'əm) *n.* **1.** The practice of representing things by means of symbols or of attributing symbolic meanings or significance to objects, events, or relationships. **2.** A system of symbols or representations. **3.** A symbolic meaning or representation. **4.** The revelation or suggestion of intangible conditions or truths by artistic invention.

sym·bol·ist (sĭm'bə-lĭst) *n.* **1.** A person who uses symbols or symbolism. **2. a.** A person who interprets or represents conditions or truths by the use of symbolism. **b.** Any of a group of chiefly French artists and writers of the late 19th century who expressed their ideas and emotions indirectly through symbols. **—sym'bol·is'tic, sym'bol·is'ti·cal** *adj.*

sym·bol·ize (sĭm'bə-līz') *v.* **-ized, -iz·ing, -iz·es.** *—tr.* **1.** To be or serve as a symbol of: *The dove symbolizes peace.* **2.** To represent or identify by a symbol or symbols. *—intr.* To use symbols. **—sym'bol·i·za'tion** *n.*

sym·bol·o·gy (sĭm-bŏl'ə-jē) *n.* **1.** The study or interpretation of symbols or symbolism. **2.** The art or practice of expression by means of symbols.

sym·met·al·ism (sĭm-mĕt'l-ĭz'əm) *n.* A system of coinage in which a unit of currency consists of a combination of two or more metals in fixed proportions.

sym·met·ric (sĭ-mĕt'rĭk) also **sym·met·ri·cal** (-rĭ-kəl) *adj.* Of or exhibiting symmetry. **—sym·met'ri·cal·ly** *adv.*

symmetric group *n.* A permutation group comprised of all possible permutations of a given number of items.

symmetric matrix *n.* A matrix that is its own transpose.

sym·met·rics (sə-mĕt'rĭks) *n.* *(used with a sing. verb).* An epigrammatic verse form invented (1948) by David McCord, consisting of a quatrain beginning and ending with the same word in which the second rhyming word of the first couplet is repeated at the beginning of the second couplet, the pair forming a third line when printed, being centered between the couplets (of which they are a part) with a colon spaced equally left and right to divide them. [Blend of SYMMETRICAL and METRICS.]

sym·me·trize (sĭm'ĭ-trīz') *tr.v.* **-trized, -triz·ing, -triz·es.** To make symmetrical; impart perfect balance to. **—sym'me·tri·za'tion** *n.*

sym·me·try (sĭm'ĭ-trē) *n., pl.* **-tries. 1.** A relationship of characteristic correspondence, equivalence, or identity among constituents of a system or between different systems: *electric charge symmetry; symmetry in political and religious activism.* **2.** Correspondence of form and arrangement of parts on opposite sides of a boundary, such as a plane or line or around a point or axis. **3.** Structural or functional independence of direction; isotropy. **4.** Beauty as a result of balance or harmonious arrangement. [Obs. Fr. *symmetrie* < Lat. *symmetria* < Gk. *summetria* < *summetros,* of like measure : *sun-,* like + *metron,* measure.]

sym·pa·thec·to·my (sĭm'pə-thĕk'tə-mē) *n., pl.* **-mies.** The removal of a part of a sympathetic nerve or a number of sympathetic ganglia. [SYMPATH(ETIC) + -ECTOMY.]

sym·pa·thet·ic (sĭm'pə-thĕt'ĭk) *adj.* **1.** Of, expressing, feeling, or resulting from sympathy. **2.** In agreement; favorable; inclined: *They were sympathetic to our proposal.* **3.** In accord with one's disposition or mood: *a sympathetic relationship.* **4.** Pertaining to or acting on the sympathetic nervous system. [Gk. *sumpathētikos* < *sumpatheia,* sympathy.] **—sym'pa·thet'i·cal·ly** *adv.*

sympathetic ink *n.* Invisible ink.

sympathetic nervous system *n.* A portion of the autonomic nervous system.

sym·pa·thin (sĭm'pə-thĭn) *n.* A hormone resembling epinephrine, thought to be formed in the muscle cells by sympathetic nerve impulses. [SYMPATH(ETIC) + -IN.]

sym·pa·thize (sĭm'pə-thīz') *intr.v.* **-thized, -thiz·ing, -thiz·es. 1.** To feel or express compassion; commiserate. **2.** To share or understand another's feelings or ideas. **3.** *Obs.* To agree in quality or disposition; correspond. **—sym'pa·thiz'er** *n.* **—sym'pa·thiz'ing·ly** *adv.*

sym·pa·tho·lyt·ic (sĭm'pə-thō-lĭt'ĭk) *adj.* Of or pertaining to an agent that opposes the activity of the sympathetic nervous system. [SYMPATH(ETIC) + -LYTIC.]

sym·pa·tho·mi·met·ic (sĭm'pə-thō-mĭ-mĕt'ĭk, -mī-) *adj.* Of or pertaining to an agent that stimulates the sympathetic nervous system. [SYMPATH(ETIC) + MIMETIC.]

sym·pa·thy (sĭm'pə-thē) *n., pl.* **-thies. 1. a.** A relationship or affinity between persons or things in which whatever affects one correspondingly affects the other. **b.** Mutual understanding or affection arising from this. **2. a.** The act of or capacity for sharing or understanding the feelings of another person. **b.** A feeling or expression of pity or sorrow for the distress of another; compassion; commiseration. **3.** Favor; agreement; accord: *He is in sympathy with their beliefs.* **4.** A feeling of loyalty; devotion; allegiance. [Lat. *sympathia* < Gk. *sumpatheia* < *sumpathēs,* affected by like feelings : *sun-,* like + *pathos,* emotion.]

sympathy strike *n.* A strike by a body of workers for the purpose of supporting a cause or another group of strikers.

SYMBOLS AND SIGNS

The following symbols and signs are among those most commonly used by printers. The designations are also those most commonly used, and do not exhaust the meanings that may be attached to the symbols. Symbols consisting of letters of the alphabet are entered in the regular alphabetical sequence of entries. See also symbols in tables at **element, measurement, particle,** and **proofread,** and foreign letters at **alphabet.**

+ plus
− minus
± plus or minus
∓ minus or plus
× multiplied by
÷ divided by
= equal to
≠ or ≠ not equal to
≈ or ≒ nearly equal to
≡ identical with
≢ not identical with
≎ equivalent
∼ difference
≅ congruent to
> greater than
≯ not greater than
< less than
≮ not less than
≧ or ≥ greater than or equal to
≦ or ≤ less than or equal to
| | absolute value
∪ logical sum or union
∩ logical product or intersection
⊂ is contained in
∊ is a member of; permittivity; mean error
: is to; ratio
:: as; proportion
≐ approaches
⟶ approaches limit of
∝ varies as
∥ parallel
⊥ perpendicular
∠ angle
∟ right angle
△ triangle
□ square
▭ rectangle
▱ parallelogram
○ circle
⌒ arc of circle
≟ equilateral
≙ equiangular
√ radical; root; square root
∛ cube root
∜ fourth root
Σ sum
! or ∟ factorial product
∞ infinity
∫ integral
ƒ function
∂ or δ differential; variation
π pi
∴ therefore
∵ because
— vinculum (above letter)
( ) parentheses
[ ] brackets
{ } braces
° degree
′ minute
″ second
△ increment
ω angular frequency; solid angle
Ω ohm
μΩ microhm
MΩ megohm
Φ magnetic flux
Ψ dielectric flux; electrostatic flux
ρ resistivity
Λ equivalent conductivity
ℜ reluctance
→ direction of flow
⇄ electric current
⌬ benzene ring
→ yields
⇄ reversible reaction
↓ precipitate
↑ gas
‰ salinity
☉ or ☼ sun
● or ◍ new moon
☽ first quarter
○ or ☺ full moon
☾ last quarter
☿ Mercury
♀ Venus
⊖ or ⊕ Earth
♂ Mars
♃ Jupiter
♄ Saturn
♅ Uranus
♆ Neptune
♇ Pluto
♈ Aries
♉ Taurus
♊ Gemini
♋ Cancer
♌ Leo
♍ Virgo
♎ Libra
♏ Scorpius
♐ Sagittarius
♑ Capricornus
♒ Aquarius
♓ Pisces
☌ conjunction
☍ opposition
△ trine
□ quadrature
⚹ sextile
☊ dragon's head, ascending node
☋ dragon's tail, descending node
◍ rain
✱ snow
⊠ snow on ground
⟵ floating ice crystals
▲ hail
△ sleet
∨ frostwork
⊔ hoarfrost
≡ fog
∞ haze; dust haze
⊤ thunder
< sheet lightning
⦶ solar corona
⊕ solar halo
⤡ thunderstorm
⟍ direction
○ or ⊙ or ① annual
⊙⊙ or ② biennial
♃ perennial
♂ or ♂ male
♀ female
□ male (in charts)
○ female (in charts)
℞ take (from Latin *Recipe*)
ĀĀ or Ā or āā of each (doctor's prescription)
℔ pound
℥ ounce
ʒ dram
℈ scruple
ƒ℥ fluid ounce
ƒʒ fluid dram
♏ minim
& or & and; ampersand
⅌ per
number
/ virgule; slash; solidus; shilling
© copyright
% per cent
℅ care of
% account of
@ at
* asterisk
† dagger
‡ double dagger
§ section
☞ index
´ acute
` grave
˜ tilde
ˆ circumflex
¯ macron
˘ breve
¨ dieresis
¸ cedilla
∧ caret

sym·pat·ric (sĭm-păt′rĭk) *adj.* Occupying the same or overlapping geographical areas without interbreeding. Used of populations of closely related species. [SYM- + Gk. *patra,* fatherland (< *patēr,* father) + -IC.] **—sym·pat′ri·cal·ly** *adv.*

sym·pet·al·ous (sĭm-pĕt′l-əs) *adj.* Gamopetalous.

sym·phon·ic (sĭm-fŏn′ĭk) *adj.* **1.** Pertaining to or having the character or form of a symphony. **2.** Harmonious in sound.

symphonic poem *n.* Program music based on an extramusical theme in a single, extended movement for symphony orchestra and typical chiefly of the late 19th century.

sym·pho·ni·ous (sĭm-fō′nē-əs) *adj.* In accord; harmonious. **—sym·pho′ni·ous·ly** *adv.*

sym·pho·nist (sĭm′fə-nĭst) *n.* A person who composes symphonies.

sym·pho·ny (sĭm′fə-nē) *n., pl.* **-nies. 1.** *Mus.* **a.** A usually long sonata for orchestra, consisting of four related movements. **b.** An instrumental passage in a vocal or choral composition. **c.** An instrumental overture or interlude, as in early opera. **2. a.** A symphony orchestra. **b.** *Informal.* An orchestral concert. **3.** Harmony, esp. of sound or color. **4.** Anything characterized by a harmonious combination of elements. [ME *symphonie,* harmony < OFr. < Lat. *symphonia* < Gk. *sumphōnia* < *sumphōnos,* harmonious : *sun-,* together + *phōnē,* sound.]

symphony orchestra *n.* A large orchestra composed of string, wind, and percussion sections, designed for playing symphonic works.

sym·phy·sis (sĭm′fĭ-sĭs) *n., pl.* **-ses** (-sēz′). **1.** *Anat.* Synarthrosis. **2.** The coalescence of similar parts or organs. [Gk. *sumphusis* < *sumphuein,* to cause to grow together : *sun-,* together + *phuein,* to cause to grow.] **—sym′phy·se′al** (sĭm′-fĭ-sē′əl), **sym·phys′i·al** (sĭm-fĭz′ē-əl) *adj.*

sym·po·di·um (sĭm-pō′dē-əm) *n., pl.* **-dia** (-dē-ə). *Bot.* A primary axis that develops from a series of short lateral branches and has a zigzag or irregular form. [NLat. : SYM- + Gk. *podion,* base < *pous,* foot.] **—sym·po′di·al** *adj.* **—sym·po′di·al·ly** *adv.*

sym·po·si·a (sĭm-pō′zē-ə) *n.* A plural of **symposium.**

sym·po·si·ac (sĭm-pō′zē-ăk′) *adj.* Of, of the nature of, appropriate to, or occurring at a symposium. *—n. Archaic.* A meeting or conference; symposium.

sym·po·si·arch (sĭm-pō′zē-ärk′) *n.* **1.** The master or director of an ancient Greek symposium. **2.** A toastmaster. [Gk. *sumposiarkhos* : *sumposion,* symposium + *arkhein,* to rule.]

sym·po·si·um (sĭm-pō′zē-əm) *n., pl.* **-si·ums** or **-si·a** (-zē-ə). **1.** A meeting or conference for discussion of some topic. **2.** A collection of writings on a particular topic, as in a magazine. **3.** A convivial meeting for drinking, music, and intellectual discussion among the ancient Greeks. [Lat. < Gk. *sumposion,* drinking party : *sun-,* together + *posis,* drink.]

symp·tom (sĭm′təm, sĭmp′-) *n.* **1.** A circumstance or phenomenon regarded as an indication or characteristic of a condition or event. **2.** *Med.* A phenomenon experienced by an individual as a departure from normal function, sensation, or appearance, generally indicating disorder or disease. [LLat. *symptoma* < Gk. *sumptōma* < *sumpiptein,* to coincide : *sun-,* together + *piptein,* to fall.] **—symp′to·mat′ic** (-tə-măt′ĭk) *adj.* **—symp′to·mat′i·cal·ly** *adv.*

symp·to·ma·tol·o·gy (sĭm′tə-mə-tŏl′ə-jē, sĭmp′-) *n.* **1.** The medical science of disease symptoms. **2.** The complex of symptoms of a disease. [NLat. *symptomatologia* : Gk. *sumptōma,* symptom + *-logia,* -logy.]

syn– or **sym–** *pref.* **1. a.** Together; with: *synecology.* **b.** United: *syncarp.* **2. a.** Same; similar: *sympatric.* **b.** At the same time: *synesthesia.* [Gk. *sun-* < *sun,* together.]

syn·aer·e·sis (sĭ-nĕr′ĭ-sĭs) *n.* Variant of **syneresis.**

syn·aes·the·sia (sĭn′ĭs-thē′zhə) *n.* Variant of **synesthesia.**

synagogue
Synagogue interior

syn·a·gogue also **syn·a·gog** (sĭn′ə-gŏg′) *n.* **1.** A building or place of meeting for Jewish worship and religious instruction. **2.** A congregation of Jews for worship or religious study. **3.** The Jewish religion as organized or typified in local congregations. [ME *synagoge* < OFr. *sinagoge* < Lat. *synagoga* < Gk. *sunagōgē* < *sunagein,* to bring together : *sun-,* together + *agein,* to lead.] **—syn′a·gog′i·cal** (-gŏj′ĭ-kəl), **syn′a·gog′al** (-gŏg′əl) *adj.*

syn·a·le·pha also **syn·a·loe·pha** (sĭn′ə-lē′fə) *n.* The blending into one syllable of two successive vowels of adjacent syllables; for example, *th' elite* for *the elite.* [NLat. < Gk. *sunaloiphē* < *sunaleiphein,* to unite two syllables : *sun-,* together + *aleiphein,* to smear.]

syn·apse (sĭn′ăps′, sĭ-năps′) *n.* The point at which a nerve impulse passes from an axon of one neuron to the dendrite of another. *—intr.v.* **-apsed, -aps·ing, -aps·es.** To form a synapse. [Gk. *sunapsis,* point of contact < *sunaptein,* to join together : *sun-,* together + *haptein,* to fasten.]

syn·ap·sis (sĭ-năp′sĭs) *n., pl.* **-ses** (-sēz′). **1.** *Biol.* The fusion of similar paternal and maternal chromosome pairs during meiosis. **2.** Synapse. [NLat. < *sunapsis,* point of contact. — see SYNAPSE.] **—syn·ap′tic** *adj.* **—syn·ap′ti·cal·ly** *adv.*

syn·ap·ti·ne·mal complex also **syn·ap·to·ne·mal complex** (sĭ-năp′tə-nēm′əl) *n.* A ribbonlike structure consisting of three protein components that extends across the region of synapsing chromosomes in the first stage of meiosis. [SYNAPTI(C) + Gk. *nēma,* thread + -AL.]

syn·ar·thro·di·a (sĭn′är-thrō′dē-ə) *n., pl.* **-di·ae** (-dē-ē′). Synarthrosis. [SYN- + Gk. *arthrōdia,* a kind of articulation < *arthron,* joint.] **—syn′ar·thro′di·al** *adj.* **—syn′ar·thro′di·al·ly** *adv.*

syn·ar·thro·sis (sĭn′är-thrō′sĭs) *n., pl.* **-ses** (-sēz). *Anat.* Any of several forms of bone articulation in which the bones are rigidly joined without an intervening cavity. [Gk. *sunarthrōsis* : *sun-,* together + *arthrōsis,* articulation < *arthron,* a joint.]

sync or **synch** (sĭngk) *Informal. —n.* **1.** Synchronization. **2.** Synchronism. *—intr. & tr.v.* **synced, sync·ing, syncs** or **synched, synch·ing, synchs.** To synchronize.

syn·carp (sĭn′kärp′) *n.* A fleshy fruit composed of the fruits of several flowers or several carpels of a single flower.

syn·car·pous (sĭn-kär′pəs) *adj.* Having or consisting of united carpels.

syn·chon·dro·sis (sĭng′kŏn-drō′sĭs, sĭn′-) *n.* A synarthrosis in which the surfaces of the bones are connected by cartilage. [NLat. < Gk. *sunkhondrōsis,* cartilaginous joint : *sun-,* together + *khondros,* cartilage + *-ōsis,* -osis.]

syn·chro (sĭng′krō, sĭn′-) *n., pl.* **-chros.** A selsyn. [Short for SYNCHRONOUS.]

synchro– *pref.* Synchronized; synchronous: *synchrotron.* [< SYNCHRONIZED.]

syn·chro·cy·clo·tron (sĭng′krō-sī′klə-trŏn′, sĭn′-) *n.* A proton and positive ion accelerator, the chief components and configuration of which are similar to those of a cyclotron and in which the phase of the accelerating potential is synchronized with the frequency of the accelerated particles by frequency modulation to compensate for relativistic increases in particle mass at high speeds.

syn·chro·flash (sĭng′krō-flăsh′, sĭn′-) *n.* A device on a camera that synchronizes the peak of a flash created by a flash lamp with the opening of the shutter. **—syn′chro·flash′** *adj.*

syn·chro·mesh (sĭng′krō-mĕsh′, sĭn′-) *n.* **1.** An automotive gear-shifting system in which the gears are synchronized at the same speeds before engaging to effect a smooth change. **2.** A gear in such a system. **—syn′chro·mesh′** *adj.*

syn·chron·ic (sĭn-krŏn′ĭk, sĭng-) *adj.* **1.** Synchronous. **2. a.** Descriptive. **b.** Studying the events of a particular time or era without consideration of historical data. **—syn·chron′i·cal·ly** *adv.*

synchronic linguistics *n.* Descriptive linguistics.

syn·chro·nism (sĭng′krə-nĭz′əm, sĭn′-) *n.* **1.** The condition of being synchronous. **2.** A chronological listing of historical personages or events so as to indicate parallel existence or occurrence. **3.** The representation in the same artwork of two or more events that occurred at different times. **—syn′chro·nis′tic, syn′chro·nis′ti·cal** *adj.* **—syn′chro·nis′ti·cal·ly** *adv.*

syn·chro·nize (sĭng′krə-nīz′, sĭn′-) *v.* **-nized, -niz·ing, -niz·es.** *—intr.* **1.** To occur at the same time; be simultaneous. **2.** To operate in unison. *—tr.* **1.** To cause to operate with exact coincidence in time or rate. **2.** To arrange (historical events) so as to indicate parallel existence or occurrence. **3.** To cause (sound effects or dialogue) to coincide with an action. [< SYNCHRONOUS.] **—syn′chro·ni·za′tion** *n.*

syn·chro·niz·er (sĭng′krə-nī′zər, sĭn′-) *n.* **1.** One that synchronizes. **2.** A computer storage device which compensates for a difference in the rate at which information is processed between two or more devices.

syn·chro·nous (sĭng′krə-nəs, sĭn′-) *adj.* **1.** Occurring at the same time. **2.** Moving or operating at the same rate. **3. a.** Having identical periods. **b.** Having identical period and phase. [LLat. *synchronos* < Gk. *sunkhronos* : *sun-,* same + *khronos,* time.] **—syn′chro·nous·ly** *adv.* **—syn′chro·nous·ness** *n.*

synchronous motor *n.* A motor having a speed directly proportional to the frequency of the electric current that operates it.

synchronous orbit *n.* An orbit having a period the same as the period of axial rotation of the earth and so oriented that any body in it maintains a position over one point on the earth's surface.

syn·chro·ny (sĭng′krə-nē, sĭn′-) *n., pl.* **-nies.** A synchronous occurrence, movement, or arrangement. [< SYNCHRONOUS.]

syn·chro·tron (sĭng′krə-trŏn′, sĭn′-) *n.* An accelerator in which charged particles are accelerated around a fixed circular path by a radio-frequency potential and held to the path by a time-varying magnetic field.

synchrotron radiation *n.* Electromagnetic radiation emitted by high-energy particles when accelerated to relativistic speeds by a magnetic field.

syn·cli·nal (sĭn-klī′nəl) *adj.* **1.** Sloping downward from opposite directions to meet in a common point or line. **2.** *Geol.* Pertaining to, formed by, or forming a syncline. *—n.* A syncline. [SYN- + Gk. *klinein,* to lean.]

syn·cline (sĭn′klīn′) *n.* A low, troughlike area in bedrock, in which rocks incline together from opposite sides. [Back-formation < SYNCLINAL.]

syn·com (sĭn′kŏm′) *n.* A communications satellite in a synchronous orbit. [SYN(CHRONOUS) + COM(MUNICATION).]

syn·co·pate (sĭng′kə-pāt′, sĭn′-) *tr.v.* **-pat·ed, -pat·ing, -pates. 1.** *Gram.* **a.** To shorten (a word) by means of syncope. **b.** To drop (a letter or sound) from the spelling or pronunciation of a word. **2.** To modify (musical rhythm) by syncopation. [Med. Lat. *syncopare, syncopat-* < LLat. *syncope,* syncope.] **—syn'co·pa'tor** *n.*

syn·co·pa·tion (sĭng'kə-pā'shən, sĭn'-) *n.* **1.** The act of syncopating or the condition of being syncopated. **2.** Something syncopated. **3.** *Mus.* A shift of accent in a passage or composition that occurs when a normally weak beat is stressed. **4.** *Gram.* Syncope (sense 1).

syn·co·pe (sĭng'kə-pē, sĭn'-) *n.* **1.** *Gram.* The shortening of a word by the omission of a sound, letter, or syllable from the middle of the word; for example, *bos'n* for *boatswain.* **2.** *Pathol.* A brief loss of consciousness caused by transient anemia; swoon. [LLat. < Gk. *sunkopē* < *sunkoptein,* to cut short : *sun-,* together + *koptein,* to strike.] **—syn'co·pal** *adj.*

syn·cre·tism (sĭng'krĭ-tĭz'əm, sĭn'-) *n.* **1.** The attempt or tendency to combine or reconcile differing beliefs, as in philosophy or religion. **2.** *Ling.* The fusion into one of two or more originally different inflectional forms. [Gk. *sunkrētismos,* union < *sunkrētizein,* to unite (in the manner of the Cretan cities) : *sun-,* together + *Krēs,* Cretan.] **—syn'cre·tist** *n.* **—syn'cre·tis'tic** *adj.*

syn·cre·tize (sĭng'krĭ-tīz', sĭn'-) *v.* **-tized, -tiz·ing, -tiz·es.** *—tr.* To reconcile or attempt to reconcile (differing religious beliefs, for example). *—intr.* To combine differing beliefs. [Gk. *sunkrētizein.* —see SYNCRETISM.]

syn·cy·ti·um (sĭn-sĭsh'ē-əm) *n., pl.* **-cy·ti·a** (-sĭsh'ē-ə). A mass of protoplasm with many nuclei but no clear cell boundaries. [NLat. : SYN- + Gk. *kutos,* hollow vessels.] **—syn·cy'ti·al** *adj.*

syn·dac·tyl or **syn·dac·tyle** (sĭn-dăk'təl) also **syn·dac·ty·lous** (-tə-ləs) *adj. Biol.* Having two or more wholly or partially fused digits. *—n.* A syndactyl animal. [Fr. *syndactyle* : Gk. *sun-,* together + Gk. *daktulos,* finger.] **—syn·dac'tyl·ism** *n.*

syn·des·mo·sis (sĭn'dĕz-mō'sĭs, -dĕs-) *n.* The articulation of bones by ligaments. [NLat. < Gk. *sundesmos,* ligament < *sundein,* to bind together. —see SYNDETIC.] **—syn'des·mot'ic** (-mŏt'ĭk) *adj.*

syn·det·ic (sĭn-dĕt'ĭk) *adj.* **1.** Serving to connect, as a conjunction; copulative; conjunctive. **2.** Connected by a conjunction. [Gk. *sundetikos* < *sundetos,* bound together < *sundein,* to bind together : *sun-,* together + *dein,* to bind.] **—syn·det'i·cal·ly** *adv.*

syn·dic (sĭn'dĭk) *n.* **1.** A person appointed to represent a corporation, university, or other organization in business transactions; business agent. **2.** A civil magistrate or similar government official. [Fr. < LLat. *syndicus* < Gk. *sundikos,* public advocate : *sun-,* with + *dikē,* court case.] **—syn'di·cal** *adj.*

syn·di·cal·ism (sĭn'dĭ-kə-lĭz'əm) *n.* A radical political movement that advocates bringing industry and government under the control of labor unions by the use of direct action, such as general strikes and sabotage. [Fr. *syndicalisme* < *chambre syndicale,* trade union.] **—syn'di·cal·ist** *n.* **—syn'di·cal·is'tic** *adj.*

syn·di·cate (sĭn'dĭ-kĭt) *n.* **1. a.** An association of people authorized to undertake some duty or transact some business. **b.** An association of people formed to carry out an enterprise. **2.** An agency that sells articles for publication in a number of newspapers or periodicals simultaneously. **3.** The office, position, or jurisdiction of a syndic or body of syndics. *—v.* (sĭn'dĭ-kāt') **-cat·ed, -cat·ing, -cates.** *—tr.* **1.** To organize into a syndicate. **2.** To sell (an article, for example) through a syndicate for publication. *—intr.* To organize a syndicate. [Fr. *syndicat* < *syndic,* syndic.]

syn·drome (sĭn'drōm') *n.* **1.** A group of signs and symptoms that collectively indicate or characterize a disease, psychological disorder, or other abnormal condition. **2. a.** A complex of symptoms indicating the existence of an undesirable condition or quality. **b.** A distinctive or characteristic pattern of behavior. [Gk. *sundromē,* concurrence of symptoms : *sun-,* together + *dramein,* to run.] **—syn·drom'ic** (-drō'mĭk, -drŏm'ĭk) *adj.*

syn·ec·do·che (sĭ-nĕk'də-kē) *n.* A figure of speech by which a more inclusive term is used for a less inclusive term or vice versa; for example, *head* for *cattle* or *the law* for *a policeman.* [Lat. < Gk. *sunekdokhē* < *sunekdekhesthai,* to take with : *sun-,* with + *ekdekhesthai,* to understand (*ek-,* out of + *dekhesthai,* to take).] **—syn'ec·doch'ic** (sĭn'ĕk-dŏk'ĭk), **syn'ec·doch'i·cal** *adj.*

syn·e·cious (sĭ-nē'shəs) *adj.* Variant of **synoecious.**

syn·e·col·o·gy (sĭn'ĭ-kŏl'ə-jē) *n.* The study of the environmental interrelationships among communities of organisms. **—syn'e·co·log'ic** (-kə-lŏj'ĭk), **syn'e·co·log'i·cal** *adj.*

syn·er·e·sis also **syn·aer·e·sis** (sĭ-nĕr'ĭ-sĭs) *n., pl.* **-ses** (-sēz'). **1.** The drawing together into one syllable of two consecutive vowels ordinarily pronounced separately. **2.** *Chem.* Exudation of the liquid component of a gel. [LLat. *synaeresis* < Gk. *sunairesis* < *sunairein,* to draw together : *sun-,* together + *hairein,* to take.]

syn·er·get·ic (sĭn'ər-jĕt'ĭk) also **syn·er·gic** (sĭ-nûr'jĭk) *adj.* Of or pertaining to synergism.

syn·er·gid (sĭ-nûr'jĭd, sĭn'ər-) *n.* One of two small cells lying near the egg in the mature embryo of a seed plant. [NLat. *synergida* < Gk. *sunergos,* working together. —see SYNERGISM.]

syn·er·gism (sĭn'ər-jĭz'əm) *n.* **1.** Also **syn·er·gy** (-ər-jē) *pl.* **-gies.** The action of two or more substances, organs, or organisms to achieve an effect of which each is individually incapable. **2.** *Theol.* The doctrine that regeneration is effected by a combination of human will and divine grace. [NLat. *synergismus* < Gk. *sunergos,* working together : *sun-,* with + *ergon,* work.]

syn·er·gist (sĭn'ər-jĭst) *n.* **1.** *Theol.* An adherent of synergism. **2.** A synergetic organ, drug, or substance. **—syn'er·gis'tic, syn'er·gis'ti·cal** *adj.* **—syn'er·gis'ti·cal·ly** *adv.*

syn·er·gy (sĭn'ər-jē) *n., pl.* **-gies.** Synergism (sense 1).

syn·e·sis (sĭn'ə-sĭs) *n. Gram.* A construction in which a form differs in number but agrees in meaning with the word governing it; for example, *If anyone arrives, tell them to wait.* [Gk. *sunesis,* understanding < *sunienai,* to understand : *sun-,* together + *hienai,* to send.]

syn·es·the·sia also **syn·aes·the·sia** (sĭn'ĭs-thē'zhə) *n.* A phenomenon in which one type of stimulation evokes the sensation of another, as the hearing of a sound resulting in the sensation of the visualization of a color. [SYN- + (AN)ESTHESIA.] **—syn'es·thet'ic** (-thĕt'ĭk) *adj.*

syn·e·ze·sis (sĭn'ĭ-zē'sĭs) *n.* Variant of **synizesis.**

syn·fu·el (sĭn'fyo͞o'əl) *n.* A liquid, gaseous, or solid hydrocarbon fuel derived from naturally occurring fossil fuels such as coal, shale, or tar sand. [SYN(THETIC) + FUEL.]

syn·ga·my (sĭng'gə-mē) *n.* The fusion of two gametes. **—syn·gam'ic** (sĭn-găm'ĭk), **syn'ga·mous** (sĭng'gə-məs) *adj.*

syn·gen·e·sis (sĭn-jĕn'ĭ-sĭs) *n.* Sexual reproduction. **—syn'ge·net'ic** (-jə-nĕt'ĭk) *adj.*

syn·i·ze·sis also **syn·e·ze·sis** (sĭn'ĭ-zē'sĭs) *n., pl.* **-ses** (-sēz'). **1.** The contraction of two syllables into one by joining in pronunciation two adjacent vowels. **2.** *Biol.* The phase of meiosis in which the chromatin contracts into a mass at one side of the nucleus. [LLat. *synizesis* < Gk. *sunizēsis* < *sunizein,* to collapse : *sun-,* together + *hizein,* to settle down.]

syn·kar·y·on (sĭn-kăr'ē-ŏn', -ē-ən) *n.* The nucleus of a fertilized egg immediately after the male and female nuclei have fused. [SYN- + Gk. *karuon,* nut.] **—syn·kar'y·on'ic** (-ŏn'ĭk) *adj.*

syn·od (sĭn'əd) *n.* **1.** A council or assembly of churches or church officials; ecclesiastical council. **2.** A council or assembly. [ME < LLat. *synodus* < Gk. *sunodos,* meeting : *sun-,* together + *hodos,* road.] **—syn'od·al** (sĭn'ə-dəl) *adj.*

syn·od·i·cal (sĭ-nŏd'ĭ-kəl) also **syn·od·ic** (-nŏd'ĭk) *adj.* **1.** Pertaining to or of the nature of a synod. **2.** Pertaining to the conjunction of celestial bodies, esp. the interval between two successive conjunctions of a planet or the moon with the sun. **—syn·od'i·cal·ly** *adv.*

synodic month *n.* Month (sense 5).

syn·oe·cious also **syn·e·cious** (sĭ-nē'shəs) *adj. Bot.* Having male and female organs in the same structure. [SYN- + (MON)OECIOUS.]

syn·o·nym (sĭn'ə-nĭm') *n.* **1.** A word having a meaning similar to that of another word in the same language. **2.** A word or expression accepted as a figurative or symbolic substitute for another word or expression. **3.** *Biol.* A taxonomic name of an organism that is equivalent to or has been superseded by another designation. [ME *sinonyme* < Lat. *synonymum* < Gk. *sunōnumon* < *sunōnumos,* synonymous.] **—syn'o·nym'ic** (-nĭm'ĭk), **syn'o·nym'i·cal** *adj.* **—syn'o·nym'i·ty** (-nĭm'ĭ-tē) *n.*

syn·on·y·mist (sĭ-nŏn'ə-mĭst) *n.* A person who studies or discriminates synonyms.

syn·on·y·mize (sĭ-nŏn'ə-mīz') *tr.v.* **-mized, -miz·ing, -miz·es.** To provide or analyze the synonyms of (a word).

syn·on·y·mous (sĭ-nŏn'ə-məs) *adj.* Expressing a similar meaning. [Med. Lat. *synonymus* < Gk. *sunōnumos* : *sun-,* same + *onoma* name.] **—syn·on'y·mous·ly** *adv.*

syn·on·y·my (sĭ-nŏn'ə-mē) *n., pl.* **-mies.** **1.** The quality of being synonymous; equivalence of meaning. **2.** The study and classification of synonyms. **3.** A list, book, or system of synonyms. **4.** A chronological list or record of the scientific names that have been applied to a species and its subdivisions.

syn·op·sis (sĭ-nŏp'sĭs) *n., pl.* **-ses** (-sēz'). A brief statement or outline of a subject; abstract. [LLat. < Gk. *sunopsis,* general view : *sun-,* together + *opsis,* view.]

syn·op·size (sĭ-nŏp'sīz') *tr.v.* **-sized, -siz·ing, -siz·es.** To present or write a synopsis of. [LGk. *sunopsizein* < Gk. *sunopsis,* general view. —see SYNOPSIS.]

syn·op·tic (sĭ-nŏp'tĭk) also **syn·op·ti·cal** (-tĭ-kəl) *adj.* **1.** Of or constituting a synopsis; presenting a summary. **2.** Presenting an account from the same point of view. **3.** Often **Synoptic.** Of or designating the first three Gospels of the New Testament, which correspond closely. **—syn·op'ti·cal·ly** *adv.*

syn·os·to·sis (sĭn'ŏs-tō'sĭs) *n., pl.* **-ses** (-sēz'). The fusion of two skeletal bones. [SYN- + Gk. *osteon,* bone + -OSIS.] **—syn'os·tot'ic** (-tŏt'ĭk) *adj.*

syn·o·vi·a (sĭ-nō'vē-ə) *n.* A clear, viscid lubricating fluid secreted by membranes in joint cavities, sheaths of tendons, and bursae. [NLat.] **—syn·o'vi·al** *adj.*

sy·no·vi·tis (sĭ'nə-vī'tĭs) *n.* Inflammation of a synovial membrane. [SYNOV(IAL MEMBRANE) + -ITIS.]

syn·sep·al·ous (sĭn-sĕp′ə-ləs) *adj.* Gamosepalous.

syn·tac·tics (sĭn-tăk′tĭks) *n.* *(used with a sing. or pl. verb).* The branch of semiotics that deals with the formal properties of signs and symbols. [< SYNTACTIC.]

syn·tax (sĭn′tăks′) *n.* **1.** *Gram.* **a.** The way in which words are put together to form phrases and sentences. **b.** The branch of grammar dealing with the formation of phrases and sentences. **2.** *Computer Sci.* The rules governing the construction of a machine language. **3.** Systematic arrangement. [Fr. *syntaxe* < LLat. *syntaxis* < Gk. *suntaxis* < *suntassein,* to combine : *sun-,* together + *tassein,* to arrange.] **—syn·tac′tic** (-tăk′tĭk), **syn·tac′ti·cal** *adj.* **—syn·tac′ti·cal·ly** *adv.*

syn·the·sis (sĭn′thĭ-sĭs) *n., pl.* **-ses** (-sēz′). **1. a.** The combining of separate elements or substances to form a coherent whole. **b.** The whole so formed. **2.** *Chem.* Formation of a compound from its constituents. **3.** *Philos.* **a.** Reasoning from the general to the particular; logical deduction. **b.** The combination of thesis and antithesis in the dialectical process, producing a new and higher form of being. [Lat. < Gk. *sunthesis* < *suntithenai,* to put together : *sun-,* together + *tithenai,* to put.] **—syn′the·sist** *n.*

synthesis gas *n.* A synthetic fuel produced by controlled combustion of coal in the presence of water vapor.

syn·the·size (sĭn′thĭ-sīz′) also **syn·the·tize** (-tīz′) *v.* **-sized, -siz·ing, -siz·es** also **-tized, -tiz·ing, -tiz·es.** *—tr.* **1.** To combine so as to form a new, complex product. **2.** To produce by combining separate elements. *—intr.* To form a synthesis.

syn·the·siz·er (sĭn′thĭ-sī′zər) *n.* **1.** One that synthesizes. **2.** A machine having a simple keyboard and using solid-state circuitry to duplicate the sounds of musical instruments, often up to 12 instruments simultaneously.

syn·thet·ic (sĭn-thĕt′ĭk) also **syn·thet·i·cal** (-ĭ-kəl) *adj.* **1.** Pertaining to, involving, or of the nature of a synthesis. **2.** *Chem.* Produced by synthesis, esp. not of natural origin; manmade. **3.** Not genuine; artificial; devised. **4.** *Ling.* Denoting a language such as Latin or Russian that uses inflectional affixes to express syntactic relationships. *—n.* **synthetic.** A synthetic chemical compound or material. [Gk. *sunthetikos,* component < *suntithenai,* to put together. —see SYNTHESIS.] **—syn·thet′i·cal·ly** *adv.*

synthetic division *n.* A method of dividing a polynomial by another, when the second is of first order, by writing only the coefficients of the terms and changing the sign of the constant term in the divisor.

syn·tro·phism (sĭn-trō′fĭz′əm) *n.* An ecological relationship in which microorganisms are mutually dependent upon one another for nutritional requirements.

sy·pher (sī′fər) *tr.v.* **-phered, -pher·ing, -phers.** To overlap and even (chamfered or beveled plank edges) so that they form a flush surface. [Alteration of CIPHER.]

syphil– *pref.* Variant of **syphilo-.**

syph·i·lis (sĭf′ə-lĭs) *n.* A chronic infectious venereal disease caused by a spirochete, *Treponema pallidum,* transmitted by direct contact, usually in sexual intercourse, and progressing through three stages respectively characterized by local formation of chancres, ulcerous skin eruptions, and systemic infection leading to general paresis. [NLat., alteration of *Syphilus,* protagonist of a poem by Girolamo Fracastoro (1483–1553) in which he is represented as the first victim of the disease.]

syph·i·lit·ic (sĭf′ə-lĭt′ĭk) *adj.* Of, pertaining to, or afflicted with syphilis. *—n.* A person afflicted with syphilis.

syphilo– or **syphil–** *pref.* Syphilis: *syphiloma.* [< SYPHILIS.]

syph·i·loid (sĭf′ə-loid′) *adj.* Characteristic of syphilis.

syph·i·lol·o·gy (sĭf′ə-lŏl′ə-jē) *n.* The sum of knowledge concerning the origin, nature, course, complications, and treatment of syphilis. **—syph′i·lol′o·gist** *n.*

syph·i·lo·ma (sĭf′ə-lō′mə) *n., pl.* **-mas** or **-ma·ta** (-mə-tə). A lesion formed in an advanced stage of syphilis; a gumma. **—syph′i·lom′a·tous** (-lŏm′ə-təs) *adj.*

sy·phon (sī′fən) *n. & v.* Variant of **siphon.**

Syr·ette (sĭ-rĕt′). A trademark for a collapsible tube having an attached hypodermic needle containing a single dose of medicine.

Syr·i·ac (sîr′ē-ăk′) *n.* An ancient Aramaic language spoken in Syria from the 3rd to the 13th century A.D. that survives as the liturgical language of several eastern Christian churches.

Syr·i·an (sîr′ē-ən) *adj.* Of or pertaining to Syria, its culture, or inhabitants. *—n.* **1.** A native or inhabitant of Syria. **2.** A member of a Christian church using the Syriac language.

sy·rin·ga (sə-rĭng′gə) *n.* The mock orange (sense 1). [NLat. < Gk. *surinx,* shepherd's pipe (from the use of its hollow stems to make pipes).]

sy·ringe (sə-rĭnj′, sîr′ĭnj) *n.* **1.** A medical instrument used to inject fluids into the body or draw them from it. **2.** A hypodermic syringe. [ME *syryng* < Med. Lat. *syringa* < Gk. *surinx,* shepherd's pipe.]

sy·rin·go·my·e·li·a (sə-rĭng′gō-mī-ē′lē-ə) *n.* A chronic disease of the spinal cord characterized by the presence of liquid-filled cavities and leading to spasticity and sensory disturbances. [NLat. : Gk. *surinx,* spinal cavity + Gk. *muelos,* marrow < *mus,* muscle, mouse.]

syr·inx (sîr′ĭngks) *n., pl.* **sy·rin·ges** (sə-rĭn′jēz′, -rĭng′gēz′) or **syr·inx·es.** **1.** A panpipe. **2.** *Zool.* The vocal organ of a bird, consisting of thin, vibrating muscles at or close to the division of the trachea. [Lat. < Gk. *surinx.*] **—sy·rin′ge·al** (sə-rĭn′jē-əl) *adj.*

syr·phid (sûr′fĭd) *n.* Any of numerous flies of the family Syrphidae, many of which have a form or coloration mimicking that of bees or wasps. *—adj.* Of or belonging to the Syrphidae. [NLat. *Syrphidae,* family name < Gk. *surphos,* gnat.]

syr·phus fly (sûr′fəs) *n.* Syrphid. [NLat. *Syrphus,* fly genus < Gk. *surphos,* gnat.]

syr·up also **sir·up** (sĭr′əp, sûr′-) *n.* **1.** A thick, sweet, sticky liquid, consisting of a sugar base, natural or artificial flavorings, and water. **2.** The juice of a fruit or plant boiled with sugar until thick and sticky. [ME *sirop* < OFr. < Med. Lat. *siropus* < Ar. *sharāb* < *shariba,* to drink.] **—syr′up·y** *adj.*

sys·sar·co·sis (sĭs′är-kō′sĭs) *n.* The union of bones, as the hyoid bone and lower jaw, by muscle. [Gk. *sussarkōsis,* a being overgrown with flesh < *sussarkousthai,* to be overgrown with flesh : *sun-,* with + *sarkousthai,* passive of *sarkoun,* to cover with flesh < *sarx,* flesh.]

sys·tal·tic (sĭ-stôl′tĭk, -stăl′-) *adj.* Alternately contracting and expanding, as the heart; pulsating. [LLat. *systalticus* < Gk. *sustaltikos* < *sustellein,* to contract : *sun-,* together + *stellein,* to make compact.]

sys·tem (sĭs′təm) *n.* **1.** A group of interacting, interrelated, or interdependent elements forming a complex whole. **2.** A functionally related group of elements, esp.: **a.** The human body regarded as a functional physiological unit. **b.** A group of physiologically complementary organs or parts: *the nervous system.* **c.** A group of interacting mechanical or electrical components. **d.** A network of structures and channels, as for communications, travel, or distribution. **3.** A structurally or anatomically related group of elements or parts. **4.** A set of interrelated ideas or principles. **5.** A social, economic, or political organizational form. **6.** A naturally occurring group of objects or phenomena: *the solar system.* **7.** A set of objects or phenomena grouped together for classification or analysis. **8.** The state or condition of harmonious, orderly interaction. **9.** A method; procedure. **10.** An organized society; establishment. [LLat. *systema, systemat-* < Gk. *sustēma* < *sunistanai,* to combine : *sun-,* together + *histanai,* to make stand.]

sys·tem·at·ic (sĭs′tə-măt′ĭk) also **sys·tem·at·i·cal** (-ĭ-kəl) *adj.* **1.** Of, characterized by, based upon, or constituting a system. **2.** Carried on in a step-by-step procedure. **3.** Characterized by purposeful regularity; methodical. **4.** Of or pertaining to classification or taxonomy. **—sys′tem·at′i·cal·ly** *adv.*

sys·tem·at·ics (sĭs′tə-măt′ĭks) *n.* *(used with a sing. verb).* The classification of organisms in an ordered system designed to indicate natural relationships.

sys·tem·a·tism (sĭs′tə-mə-tĭz′əm, sĭ-stĕm′ə-) *n.* **1.** The practice of classifying or systematizing. **2.** Adherence to a system.

sys·tem·a·tist (sĭs′tə-mə-tĭst, sĭ-stĕm′ə-) *n.* **1.** A person who adheres to or formulates a system. **2.** A taxonomist.

sys·tem·a·tize (sĭs′tə-mə-tīz′) *tr.v.* **-tized, -tiz·ing, -tiz·es.** To formulate into or reduce to a system: *"The aim of science is surely to amass and systematize knowledge"* (V. Gordon Childe). **—sys′tem·a·ti·za′tion** *n.* **—sys′tem·a·tiz′er** *n.*

sys·tem·ic (sĭ-stĕm′ĭk) *adj.* **1.** Of or pertaining to a system or systems. **2.** Of, pertaining to, or affecting the entire body. **—sys·tem′i·cal·ly** *adv.*

sys·tem·ize (sĭs′tə-mīz′) *tr.v.* **-ized, -iz·ing, -iz·es.** To systematize. **—sys′tem·i·za′tion** *n.* **—sys′tem·iz′er** *n.*

systems analysis *n.* **1.** The study of an activity by mathematical means to determine its desired end and the most efficient method of obtaining this. **2.** The act, process, or profession of systems analysis. **—systems analyst** *n.*

sys·to·le (sĭs′tə-lē) *n.* The rhythmic contraction of the heart, esp. of the ventricles, by which blood is driven through the aorta and pulmonary artery after each dilation or diastole. [Gk. *sustolē,* contraction < *sustellein,* to contract. —see SYSTALTIC.] **—sys·tol′ic** (-tŏl′ĭk) *adj.*

syz·y·gy (sĭz′ə-jē) *n., pl.* **-gies.** **1.** *Astron.* **a.** Either of two points in the orbit of a celestial body where the body is in opposition to or in conjunction with the sun. **b.** Either of two points in the orbit of the moon when the moon lies in a straight line with the sun and the earth. **c.** The configuration of the sun, the moon, and the earth lying in a straight line. **2.** The combining of two feet into a single metrical unit in classical prosody. [LLat. *syzygia* < Gk. *suzugia,* conjunction < *suzugos,* paired : *sun-,* together + *zugon,* yoke.] **—sy·zyg′i·al** (sĭ-zĭj′ē-əl) *adj.*

T

Around 1000 B.C. the Phoenicians and other Semitic peoples began to use graphic signs to represent individual speech sounds instead of syllables or words. They used a symbol in the forms (1,2,3) to represent the sound of the consonant "t" and called it *tāw,* their word for "mark." The Greeks, adapting the Phoenician alphabet, kept the phonetic value of *tāw* but changed its shape slightly (4,5) and altered its name to *tau.* The Romans borrowed the alphabet from the Greeks via the Etruscans and adapted it for monumental inscriptions. Monumental script (7) is the prototype of modern capital letters (10,11). Medieval scribes adapted the Roman capitals to being quickly written on paper, parchment, and vellum. These uncial and cursive minuscules (8,9) are the prototypes of modern lower-case letters, both written and printed (13,12).

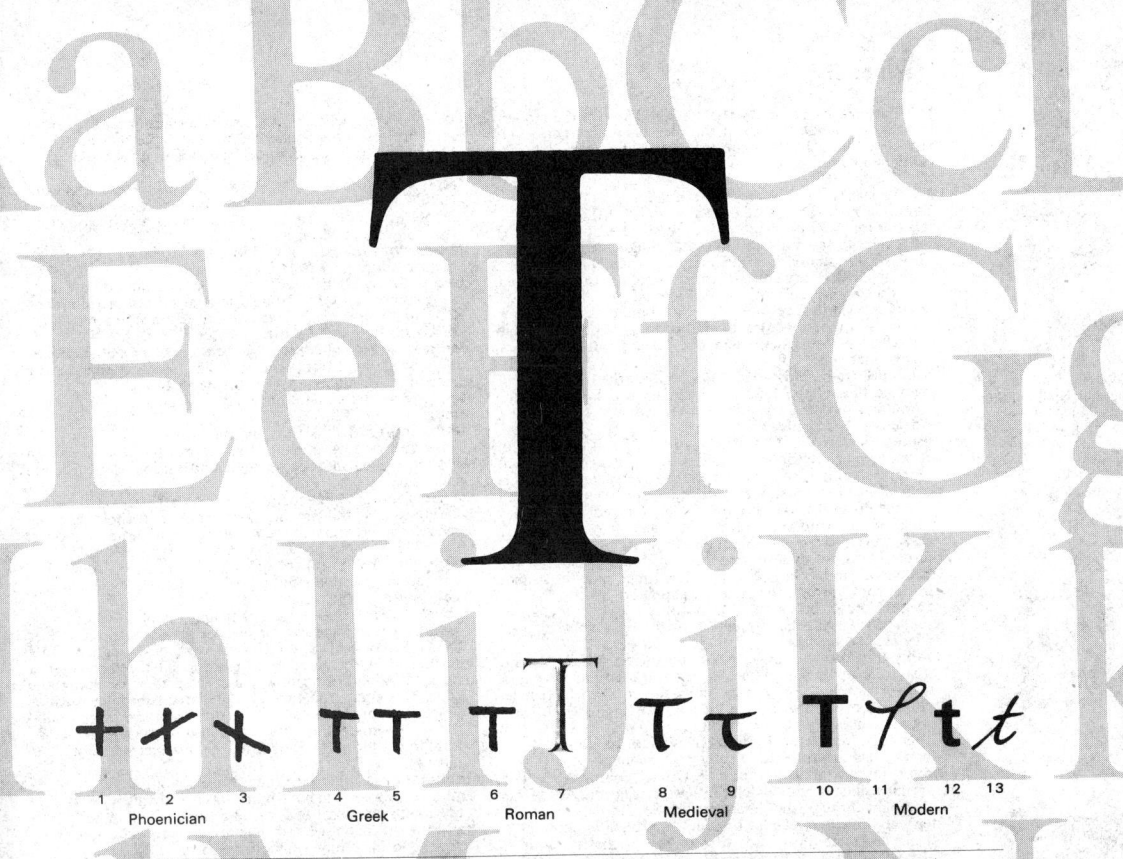

t

tabard
Woodcut of an imperial German herald of the first half of the 16th century

tabernacle

taboret
Carved gilt taboret of Empire style

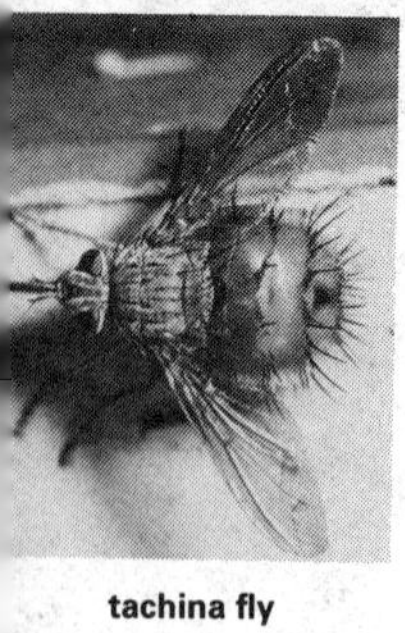

tachina fly

t or **T** (tē) *n., pl.* **t's** or **T's. 1.** The 20th letter of the modern English alphabet. **2.** Any of the speech sounds represented by the letter *t.* **3.** Anything shaped like the letter T. **4.** The 20th in a series. ***—idiom.* to a T.** Perfectly; precisely: *She fits the role to a T.*

Ta The symbol for the element tantalum.

Taal (täl) *n.* Afrikaans. [Du. *taal,* speech < MDu. *tāle.*]

tab (tăb) *n.* **1.** A projection, flap, or short strip attached to an object to facilitate opening, handling, or identification. **2.** A small, usually decorative flap or tongue on a garment. **3.** A small auxiliary control surface attached to a larger one to help stabilize an airplane. **4.** *Informal.* A bill or a check, as for a meal in a restaurant. **5.** A tabulator, as on a typewriter. *—tr.v.* **tabbed, tab·bing, tabs.** To supply with a tab or tabs. ***—idiom.* keep tabs on.** To account for; watch. [Orig. unknown.]

ta·ba·nid (tə-bā′nĭd, -băn′ĭd) *n.* Any of various bloodsucking flies of the family Tabanidae, which includes the horseflies. [NLat. *Tabanidae,* family name < Lat. *tabanus,* horsefly.] **—ta·ba′nid** *adj.*

tab·ard (tăb′ərd) *n.* **1.** A short, heavy cape of coarse cloth formerly worn outdoors. **2. a.** A tunic or capelike garment worn by a knight over his armor and emblazoned with his coat of arms. **b.** A similar garment worn by a herald and bearing his lord's coat of arms. **3.** An embroidered pennant attached to a trumpet. [ME < OFr. *tabart.*]

tab·a·ret (tăb′ə-rĕt′) *n.* A strong upholstery fabric having alternating stripes of satin and moiré. [Prob. < TABBY.]

Ta·bas·co (tə-băs′kō). A trademark for a spicy-hot sauce made from a strong-flavored red pepper.

tab·bou·leh (tə-bo͞o′lə) also **ta·boo·ley** (-lē) *n.* A Lebanese salad made with bulgur wheat, scallions, tomatoes, and parsley. [Ar. *tabbūla.*]

tab·by (tăb′ē) *n., pl.* **-bies. 1.** A rich watered silk. **2.** A plain weave fabric. **3. a.** A domestic cat with a striped coat of a gray or tawny color. **b.** Any domestic cat, esp. a female. **4.** An old maid. **5.** A prying woman; gossip. *—adj.* **1.** Having light and dark striped markings, as a cat. **2.** Made of or resembling watered silk. [Fr. *tabis* < Med. Lat. *attabi* < Ar. *'attābī,* after *Al-'attābīya,* a suburb of Baghdad, Iraq.]

tab·er·na·cle (tăb′ər-năk′əl) *n.* **1.** Often **Tabernacle. a.** The portable sanctuary in which the Jews carried the Ark of the Covenant through the desert. **b.** The Jewish temple. **2.** Often **Tabernacle.** A case or box on a church altar containing the consecrated host and wine of the Eucharist. **3. a.** A place of worship distinguished from a church. **b.** The Mormon temple. **4.** A niche for a statue or relic. **5.** *Naut.* A boxlike support in which the heel of a mast is stepped. *—v.* **-cled, -cling, -cles.** *—tr.* To enshrine. *—intr.* To dwell temporarily. [ME < OFr. < LLat. *tabernaculum* < Lat., tent, dim. of *taberna,* hut.] **—tab′er·nac′u·lar** (-năk′yə-lər) *adj.*

ta·bes (tā′bēz) *n., pl.* **tabes. 1.** Progressive bodily wasting or emaciation. **2.** Tabes dorsalis. [Lat.] **—ta·bet′ic** *adj.*

tabes dor·sa·lis (dôr-sā′lĭs, -săl′ĭs, -sä′lĭs) *n.* A syphilitic disease resulting in a hardening of the dorsal columns of the spinal cord and characterized by shooting pains, unsteadiness, and loss of the ability to coordinate voluntary movements. [NLat., dorsal tabes.]

tab·la (tŭb′lə) *n.* A small hand drum of India. [Hindi < Ar. *ṭabl.*]

tab·la·ture (tăb′lə-cho͝or′) *n.* **1.** *Mus.* An obsolete system of notation using letters and symbols to indicate playing directions rather than tones. **2.** An engraved tablet or surface. [OFr. < Med. Lat. *tabulatus,* tablet < Lat. *tabula.*]

ta·ble (tā′bəl) *n.* **1.** An article of furniture supported by one or more vertical legs and having a flat horizontal surface. **2.** The objects laid out for a meal upon a table. **3.** The food and drink served at meals; fare. **4.** The company of people assembled around a table, as for a meal. **5.** Often **tables.** A gaming table, as for faro, roulette, or dice. **6. a.** Either of the leaves of a backgammon board. **b. tables.** *Obs.* The game of backgammon. **7.** A plateau or tableland. **8. a.** A flat facet cut across the top of a precious stone. **b.** A stone cut in this fashion. **9.** *Mus.* The belly of a stringed instrument. **10.** *Archit.* **a.** A raised or sunken rectangular panel on a wall. **b.** A raised horizontal surface or continuous band on an exterior wall; stringcourse. **11.** *Geol.* A horizontal rock stratum. **12.** In palmistry, a part of the palm framed by four lines. **13.** An orderly arrangement of data, esp. one in which the data are arranged in columns and rows in an essentially rectangular form. **14.** An abbreviated list, as of contents; synopsis. **15.** A slab or tablet, as of stone, bearing an inscription or device. **16. tables.** A system of laws or decrees; code: *the tables of Moses.* *—tr.v.* **-bled, -bling, -bles. 1.** To put or place on a table. **2.** To postpone consideration of (a piece of legislation, for example); shelve. **3.** To enter in a list or table; tabulate. ***—idioms.* on the table.** Postponed or put aside for consideration at a later date. **turn the tables.** To reverse a situation and gain the upper hand. **under the table. 1.** In secret. **2.** Into a completely intoxicated state: *could drink her under the table anytime.* [ME < OFr. < Lat. *tabula,* board.]

tab·leau (tăb′lō′, tă-blō′) *n., pl.* **tab·leaux** or **tab·leaus** (tăb′lōz′, tă-blōz′). **1.** A vivid or graphic description: *The movie was a tableau of a soldier's life.* **2.** A striking incidental scene, as of a picturesque group of people. **3.** An interlude during a scene when all the actors on stage freeze in position and then resume action as before. **4.** A tableau vivant. [Fr. < OFr. *tablel,* dim. of *table,* surface prepared for painting. — see TABLE.]

tab·leau vi·vant (tă-blō′ vē-väɴ′) *n., pl.* **tab·leaux vi·vants** (tă-blō′ vē-väɴ′). A scene presented on stage by costumed actors who remain silent and motionless as if in a picture. [Fr. : *tableau,* tableau + *vivant,* living.]

ta·ble·cloth (tā′bəl-klôth′, -klŏth′) *n.* A cloth to cover a table, esp. during a meal.

ta·ble d'hôte (tä′bəl dōt′) *n., pl.* **ta·bles d'hôte** (tä′bəl dōt′). **1.** A communal table for all guests at a hotel or restaurant. **2.** A full-course meal served at a fixed price in a restaurant or hotel. [Fr. : *table,* table + *de,* of + *hôte,* host.]

ta·ble-hop (tā′bəl-hŏp′) *intr.v.* **-hopped, -hop·ping, -hops.** To move around from table to table greeting friends, as in a restaurant or nightclub. **—ta′ble-hop′per** *n.*

ta·ble·land (tā′bəl-lănd′) *n.* A flat, elevated region; plateau; mesa.

table linen *n.* Tablecloths and napkins.

table salt *n.* **1.** A refined mixture of salts, chiefly sodium chloride, used in cooking and as a seasoning. **2.** Sodium chloride.

ta·ble·spoon (tā′bəl-spo͞on′) *n.* **1.** A large spoon used for eating soups and serving food. **2.** A household cooking measure approximately 15 milliliters, equal to 3 teaspoons, or 1/2 fluid ounce. **3.** The amount a tablespoon holds.

ta·ble·spoon·ful (tā′bəl-spo͞on′fo͝ol′) *n., pl.* **-fuls.** The amount a tablespoon will hold.

table sugar *n.* Sucrose.

tab·let (tăb′lĭt) *n.* **1.** A slab or plaque, as of stone or ivory, with a surface intended for or bearing an inscription. **2.** A thin sheet or leaf, as of clay or ivory, used as a writing surface. **3.** A set of such leaves fastened together, as in a book. **4.** A pad of writing paper glued together along one edge. **5.** A small, flat cake of a prepared substance, such as soap. **6.** A small flat pellet of medication to be taken orally. *—tr.v.* **-let·ed, -let·ing, -lets. 1.** To inscribe on a tablet. **2.** To form into a tablet. [ME *tablette* < OFr. *tablete,* dim. of *table,* table.]

table talk *n.* Casual mealtime conversation.

table tennis *n.* A game similar to lawn tennis, played on a table with wooden paddles and a small celluloid ball.

ta·ble·ware (tā′bəl-wâr′) *n.* The dishes, glassware, and silverware used in setting a table for a meal.

table wine *n.* An unfortified wine served with a meal.

tab·loid (tăb′loid′) *n.* A newspaper of small format giving the news in condensed form, usually with illustrated, often sensational material. [TABL(ET) + -OID.]

ta·boo also **ta·bu** (tə-bo͞o′, tă-) *—n., pl.* **-boos** also **-bus. 1. a.** A prohibition excluding something from use, approach, or mention because of its sacred and inviolable nature. **b.** An object, word, or act protected by such a prohibition. **2.** A ban or inhibition attached to something by social custom or emotional aversion. **3.** Belief in or conformity to religious or social prohibitions. **4.** A proscription devised and observed by any group for its own protection. *—adj.* Excluded or forbidden from use, approach, or mention: *a taboo subject.* *—tr.v.* **-booed, -boo·ing, -boos** also **-bued, -bu·ing, -bus.** To exclude from use, approach, or mention; place under taboo. [Tongan *tabu.*]

ta·bor also **ta·bour** (tā′bər) *n.* A small drum played by a fifer to accompany his fife. [ME *tabur* < OFr.]

tab·o·ret also **tab·ou·ret** (tăb′ə-rĕt′, -rā′) *n.* **1.** A low stool without a back or arms. **2.** A low stand or cabinet. **3.** An embroidery frame. [Fr. *tabouret,* dim. of OFr. *tabur,* tabor.]

ta·bour (tā′bər) *n.* Variant of **tabor.**

tab·ou·ret (tăb′ə-rĕt′, -rā′) *n.* Variant of **taboret.**

ta·bu (tə-bo͞o′, tă-) *n., adj., & v.* Variant of **taboo.**

tab·u·lar (tăb′yə-lər) *adj.* **1.** Having a plane surface; flat. **2.** Organized as a table or list. **3.** Calculated by means of a table. [Lat. *tabularis,* of boards < *tabula,* board.] **—tab′u·lar·ly** *adv.*

tab·u·la ra·sa (tăb′yə-lə rä′sə, rä′zə) *n.* The mind before it receives the impressions gained from experience, esp. the unformed, featureless mind in the philosophy of Locke. [Lat., erased tablet.]

tab·u·lar·ize (tăb′yə-lə-rīz′) *tr.v.* **-ized, -iz·ing, -iz·es.** To put into tabular form; tabulate. **—tab′u·lar·i·za′tion** *n.*

tab·u·late (tăb′yə-lāt′) *tr.v.* **-lat·ed, -lat·ing, -lates. 1.** To arrange in tabular form; condense and list. **2.** To cut or form with a plane surface. *—adj.* (tăb′yə-lĭt, -lāt′). Having a plane surface. [< Lat. *tabula,* writing tablet.] **—tab′u·la′tion** *n.*

tab·u·la·tor (tăb′yə-lā′tər) *n.* **1.** A person who makes tabulations. **2.** A machine into which data can be fed for tabulation. **3.** A mechanism on a typewriter for setting automatic stops or margins for columns.

tac·a·ma·hac (tăk′ə-mə-hăk′) *n.* **1.** Any of several aromatic resinous substances used in ointments and incenses. **2.** The balsam poplar. [Sp. *tacamahaca* < Nahuatl *tecamaca.*]

ta·cet (tā′sĭt, tăs′ĭt, tä′kĕt′) *v. Mus.* Be silent. Used as a direction. [Lat., it is silent < *tacēre,* to be silent.]

tache (tăch) *n. Archaic.* A clasp or buckle. [ME < OFr., of Germanic orig.]

tach·i·na fly (tăk′ə-nə) *n.* Any of several bristly, usually grayish flies of the family Tachinidae, the larvae of which live as parasites within the bodies of other insects. [NLat. *Tachina,* fly genus < Gk. *takhinos,* swift < *takhos,* speed.]

tach·i·nid (tăk′ə-nĭd′) *n.* Tachina fly. [NLat. *Tachinidae,* family name < *Tachina,* fly genus. —see TACHINA FLY.] **—tach′i·nid** *adj.*

tach·ism (tăsh′ĭz′əm) *n.* Action painting. [Fr. *tachisme* < *tache,* stain < OFr., of Germanic orig.] **—tach′ist** *n.*

ta·chis·to·scope (tă-kĭs′tə-skōp′) *n.* An apparatus that projects transient images onto a screen to test visual perception. [Gk. *takhistos,* superl. of *takhus,* swift + -SCOPE.] **—ta·chis′to·scop′ic** (-skŏp′ĭk) *adj.* **—ta·chis′to·scop′i·cal·ly** *adv.*

ta·chom·e·ter (tă-kŏm′ĭ-tər) *n.* An instrument used to determine speed, esp. the rotational speed of a shaft. [Gk. *takhos,* speed + -METER.] **—tach′o·met′ric** (tăk′ə-mĕt′rĭk) *adj.* **—ta·chom′e·try** *n.*

tachy– *pref.* Rapid; accelerated: *tachymeter.* [< Gk. *takhus,* swift.]

tach·y·ar·rhyth·mi·a (tăk′ē-ə-rĭth′mē-ə) *n.* An excessively rapid heartbeat accompanied by arrhythmia.

tach·y·car·di·a (tăk′ĭ-kär′dē-ə) *n.* Excessively rapid heartbeat. [TACHY- + Gk. *kardia,* heart.]

ta·chyg·ra·phy (tă-kĭg′rə-fē) *n.* The art or practice of rapid writing or shorthand, esp. the stenography of the ancient Greeks and Romans.

tach·y·lyte also **tach·y·lite** (tăk′ə-līt′) *n.* A black, glassy basaltic rock. [G. *Tachylyt* : Gk. *takhos* + Gk. *lutos,* soluble < *luein,* to dissolve.] **—tach′y·lyt′ic** (-lĭt′ĭk) *adj.*

ta·chym·e·ter (tă-kĭm′ĭ-tər) *n.* A surveying instrument used for the rapid measurement of distances, elevations, and bearings. **—ta·chym′e·try** *n.*

tach·y·on (tăk′ē-ŏn′) *n.* A hypothetical particle that travels faster than the speed of light. **—tach′y·on′ic** *adj.*

tach·yp·ne·a (tăk′ĭp-nē′ə) *n.* Excessively rapid respiration. [TACHY- + Gk. *pnoiē,* breathing < *pnein,* to breathe.]

tac·it (tăs′ĭt) *adj.* **1.** Not spoken: *Her glance was a tacit invitation.* **2.** Implied by or inferred from actions or statements: *gave tacit approval to the plan.* **3.** *Archaic.* Not speaking; silent. [Lat. *tacitus,* silent < p.part. of *tacēre,* to be silent.] **—tac′it·ly** *adv.* **—tac′it·ness** *n.*

tac·i·turn (tăs′ĭ-tûrn′) *adj.* Habitually untalkative; laconic; uncommunicative. [Fr. *taciturne* < Lat. *taciturnus* < *tacitus,* silent. —see TACIT.] **—tac′i·tur′ni·ty** (-tûr′nĭ-tē) *n.* **—tac′i·turn·ly** *adv.*

tack[1] (tăk) *n.* **1.** A short, light nail with a sharp point and a flat head. **2.** *Naut.* **a.** A rope for holding down the weather clew of a course. **b.** A rope for hauling the outer lower corner of a studdingsail to the boom. **c.** The part of a sail to which a tack is fastened, as the weather clew of a course. **d.** The lower forward corner of a fore-and-aft sail. **3. a.** The position of a vessel relative to the trim of its sails. **b.** The act of changing from one tack to another. **c.** The distance or leg sailed between changes of tack. **4. a.** A course of action meant to minimize opposition to the attainment of a goal. **b.** An approach, esp. one of a series of changing approaches. **5.** A large, loose stitch made as a temporary binding or as a marker. **6.** Stickiness, as of a newly painted surface. *—v.* **tacked, tack·ing, tacks.** *—tr.* **1.** To fasten or attach with or as if with a tack. **2.** To fasten or mark (cloth or a seam, for example) with a loose basting stitch. **3.** To put together loosely and arbitrarily: *He tacked some stories together into a novel.* **4.** To add as an extra item; append: *tacked two dollars onto the bill.* **5.** To bring (a vessel) into the wind in order to change tack. *—intr.* **1 a.** To change the direction or course of a vessel: *ready to tack on the captain's signal.* **b.** To change tack: *The ship tacked to starboard.* **2.** To change one's course of action: *John tacked in midsentence and tried another approach.* [ME *tak,* something that attaches < OFr. *tache,* of Germanic orig.]

tack[2] (tăk) *n.* Food, esp. coarse foodstuffs. [Orig. unknown.]

tack hammer *n.* A light hammer used to drive tacks.

tack·le (tăk′əl) *n.* **1.** The equipment used in a sport or occupation, esp. in fishing; gear. **2.** (tăk′əl, tā′kəl). *Naut.* **a.** A system of ropes and blocks for raising and lowering weights of rigging and pulleys for applying tension. **b.** A rope and its pulley. **3.** *Sports.* **a.** Either of two line players in football positioned between the guard and the end. **b.** The position of this player. **c.** The act of stopping another player by seizing and bringing him down. *—v.* **-led, -ling, -les.** *—tr.* **1.** To take on and wrestle with (an opponent or problem, for example) in order to overcome permanently; come to grips with. **2.** *Sports.* To seize and throw down (another player) in football. **3.** To harness (a horse). *—intr. Sports.* To tackle an opponent in football. [ME *takel.*] **—tack′ler** *n.*

tack·ling (tăk′lĭng) *n.* Gear; tackle.

tack·y[1] (tăk′ē) *adj.* **-i·er, -i·est.** Slightly adhesive or gummy to the touch; sticky. [< TACK[1].] **—tack′i·ness** *n.*

tack·y[2] (tăk′ē) *adj.* **-i·er, -i·est.** *Informal.* **1.** Marked by neglect and disrepair; run-down; shabby. **2. a.** Lacking style or good taste; dowdy. **b.** Vulgar; tawdry: *tacky clothes; a tacky remark.* [< *tacky,* an inferior horse.] **—tack′i·ly** *adv.* **—tack′i·ness** *n.*

ta·co (tä′kō) *n., pl.* **-cos.** A tortilla folded around a filling, as of ground meat or cheese. [Mex. Sp. < Sp., roll < *atacar,* to plug < Ital. *attacare,* to attack, of Germanic orig.]

tac·o·nite (tăk′ə-nīt′) *n.* A fine-grained sedimentary rock of magnetite, hematite, and quartz, mined as a low-grade iron ore. [After the *Taconic* Mountains, New York and western New England.]

tact (tăkt) *n.* **1.** The ability to appreciate the delicacy of a situation and to do or say the kindest or most fitting thing; diplomacy. **2.** *Archaic.* The sense of touch. [Fr. < Lat. *tactus,* touch < p.part. of *tangere,* to touch.]

Synonyms: *tact, address, diplomacy, savoir-faire, finesse, subtlety.* These nouns denote personal qualities conducive to skill in dealing with others. *Tact* involves sensitivity to what is appropriate at any given time in such relationships, together with the ability to speak or act without giving offense. More pointedly, *address* and *diplomacy* imply special talent for approaching and handling such situations adroitly and without offending. *Savoir-faire* involves saying or doing the right or graceful thing, either instinctively or, more often, as a result of social experience. *Finesse* implies artful management of difficult affairs and may suggest cunning or the use of stratagems. *Subtlety* is not limited in meaning to the context of these terms. In this comparison it is in contrast to what is obvious or direct and may imply mental acuteness or ingenuity, a tendency to indirection, or even craftiness.

tact·ful (tăkt′fəl) *adj.* Possessing or showing tact; considerate; discreet: *a tactful person; a tactful remark.* **—tact′ful·ly** *adv.* **—tact′ful·ness** *n.*

tac·tic (tăk′tĭk) *n.* An expedient for achieving a goal; maneuver. *—adj.* Of or pertaining to arrangement or order.

tac·ti·cal (tăk′tĭ-kəl) *adj.* **1.** Of or pertaining to tactics. **2.** Characterized by adroitness in maneuvering.

tac·ti·cian (tăk-tĭsh′ən) *n.* **1.** A person skilled in the planning and execution of military tactics. **2.** A clever maneuverer.

tac·tics (tăk′tĭks) *n. (used with a sing. verb).* The technique or science of securing the objectives designated by strategy, esp. the art of deploying and directing troops, ships, and aircraft in coefficient maneuvers against the enemy. [NLat. *tactica* < Gk. *taktika* < neuter pl. of *taktikos,* of order < *taktos,* arranged < *tassein,* to arrange.]

tac·tile (tăk′təl, -tīl′) *adj.* **1.** Perceptible to the sense of touch; tangible. **2.** Used for feeling: *a tactile organ.* **3.** Of, pertaining to, or proceeding from the sense of touch: *a tactile reflex.* [Lat. *tactilis* < *tangere,* to touch.] **—tac·til′i·ty** (-tĭl′ĭ-tē) *n.*

tac·tion (tăk′shən) *n.* The act of touching; contact. [Lat. *tactio, taction-* < *tangere,* to touch.]

tact·less (tăkt′lĭs) *adj.* Lacking in tact; bluntly inconsiderate. **—tact′less·ly** *adv.* **—tact′less·ness** *n.*

tac·to·re·cep·tor (tăk′tō-rĭ-sĕp′tər) *n.* A receptor that responds to touch. [Lat. *tactus,* touch + RECEPTOR.]

tac·tu·al (tăk′chōō-əl) *adj.* Of, producing, derived from, or pertaining to the sense of touch; tactile. [< Lat. *tactus,* touch.] **—tac′tu·al·ly** *adv.*

tad (tăd) *n. Informal.* **1.** A small boy. **2.** A small amount or degree; bit: *needed a tad more seasoning.* [Perh. < dial. *tad,* toad < ME *tode.*]

tad·pole (tăd′pōl′) *n.* The aquatic larval stage of a frog or toad, having a tail and external gills that disappear as the limbs develop and the adult stage is reached. [ME *taddepol* : *tode,* toad (< OE *tādige*) + *pol,* head (< MLG *poll*).]

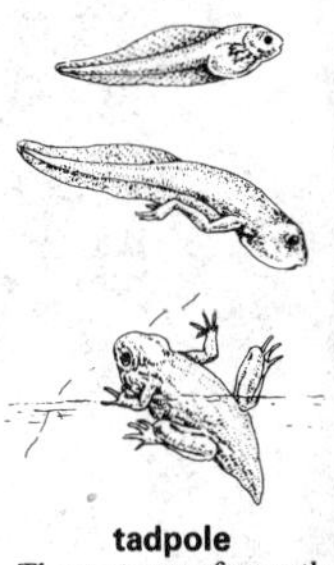
tadpole
Three stages of growth

tae kwon do (tī kwŏn′dō) *n.* A Korean form of karate. [Korean.]

tael (tāl) *n.* **1.** Any of various units of weight used in eastern Asia, roughly equivalent to 38 grams or $1^{1}/_{3}$ ounces. **2.** A Chinese monetary unit formerly in use, equivalent in value to 38 grams or $1^{1}/_{3}$ ounces of standard silver. [Port. < Malay *tahil,* prob. < Hindi *tolā,* a weight < Skt. *tulā.*]

tae·ni·a also **te·ni·a** (tē′nē-ə) *n., pl.* **-ni·ae** (-nē-ē′) or **-ni·as.** **1.** A narrow band or ribbon for the hair worn in ancient Greece. **2.** *Archit.* A band in the Doric order separating the frieze from the architrave. **3.** A ribbonlike anatomical structure. **4.** A flatworm of the genus *Taenia,* which includes many tapeworms. [Lat. < Gk. *tainia.*]

tae·ni·a·cide (tē′nē-ə-sīd′) *n.* Variant of **teniacide.**

tae·ni·a·sis (tē-nī′ə-sĭs) *n.* Variant of **teniasis.**

taf·fe·ta (tăf′ĭ-tə) *n.* A crisp, smooth fabric with a slight sheen, made of various fibers and used esp. for women's garments. *—adj.* Made of or resembling taffeta. [ME < OFr. *taffetas* < OItal. *taffettà* < Turk. *tafta* < Pers. *tāftah,* woven < *tāftan,* to weave.]

taffeta weave *n.* Plain weave.

taf·fi·a (tăf′ē-ə) *n.* Variant of **tafia.**

taff·rail (tăf′rāl′, -rəl) *n.* **1.** The rail around the stern of a vessel. **2.** The flat upper part of the stern of a vessel, made of wood and often richly carved. [Alteration of *tafferel* < Du. *taffereel,* dim. of *tafel,* panel < MDu. *tāvele* < OFr. *tablel* < Lat. *tabula,* board.]

taffrail log *n.* A screw log.

taf·fy (tăf′ē) *n., pl* **-fies.** **1.** A sweet, chewy candy of molasses or brown sugar boiled until very thick and then pulled until the candy is glossy and holds its shape. **2.** *Informal.* Wheedling flattery. [Orig. unknown.]

taffy pull *n.* A social gathering at which taffy is prepared.

taf·i·a also **taf·fi·a** (tăf′ē-ə) *n.* A cheap rum distilled from molasses and refuse sugar in the West Indies. [Native word in the West Indies.]

tag[1] (tăg) *n.* **1.** A strip of leather, paper, metal, or plastic attached to something or hung from a wearer's neck to identify, classify, or label: *a price tag.* **2.** The plastic or metal tip at the end of a shoelace. **3.** The contrastingly colored tip of an animal's tail. **4.** A bright piece of feather, floss, or tinsel surrounding the shank of the hook on a fishing fly. **5. a.** A dirty, matted lock of wool. **b.** A loose lock of hair. **6.** A rag; tatter. **7.** A small, loose fragment: *I have heard tags and snippets of what is being said.* **8.** An ornamental flourish at the end of a signature. **9. a.** A brief quotation used in speaking for added effect. **b.** A cliché, saw, or similar short, conventional idea used in speaking as an embellishment: *These tags of wit and wisdom weary me.* **10. a.** The refrain or last lines of a song or poem. **b.** The closing lines of a speech in a play; cue. **11.** A designation or epithet: *He did not take kindly to the tag of pauper.* —*v.* **tagged, tag·ging, tags.** —*tr.* **1.** To label, identify, or recognize with or as with a tag: *I tagged him as a loser.* **2.** To put a ticket on (an automobile) for a traffic or parking violation. **3.** To charge with a crime: *He was tagged for murder.* **4.** To add as an appendage to: *tagged $20 on the bill for extra labor.* **5.** To follow closely: *The baby tagged her mother around the house.* **6.** To cut the tags from (a sheep). —*intr.* To follow along after; accompany: *tagged after his brother everywhere; insisted on tagging along.* [ME *tagge,* dangling piece of cloth on a garment, poss. of Scand. orig.]

tag[2] (tăg) *n.* **1.** A children's game in which one player pursues the others until he is able to touch one of them, who then in turn becomes the pursuer. **2. a.** *Baseball.* The act of putting another player out by touching him with the ball when he is not on base. **b.** The act of touching a player in touch football. —*tr.v.* **tagged, tag·ging, tags. 1.** To touch (another player) in the game of tag. **2. a.** *Baseball.* To touch (a runner) with the ball in order to put him out. **b.** In touch football, to touch (the runner) as a substitute for tackling him. ***—phrasal verb.*** **tag up.** *Baseball.* To return to and touch a base with one foot before running to the next base after a fielder has caught a flyball. [Orig. unknown.]

Ta·ga·log (tə-gä'lôg') *n., pl.* **Tagalog** or **-logs. 1.** A member of a people native to the Philippines and inhabiting Manila and its adjacent provinces. **2.** The Austronesian language of the Tagalog. [Tagalog : *taga,* belonging to + *ilog,* river.]

tag·a·long (tăg'ə-lông', -lŏng') *n.* One that persistently follows another.

tag day *n.* A day on which collectors for a charitable fund solicit contributions, giving each contributor a tag.

tag·ger (tăg'ər) *n.* **1.** One that tags, esp. the pursuer in the game of tag. **2. taggers.** A very thin sheet iron, usually plated with tin.

tag line *n.* **1.** An ending line, as in a play or joke, that serves to make a point. **2.** An often repeated phrase associated with an individual, organization, or commercial product.

tag sale *n.* A garage sale.

ta·hi·ni (tə-hē'nē) *n.* A usually thick, smooth sauce made from ground sesame seeds. [Turk. *tāhin,* sesame flour or oil.]

Ta·hi·tian (tə-hē'shən) *adj.* Of or pertaining to Tahiti or its people or language. —*n.* **1.** A native or inhabitant of Tahiti. **2.** The Polynesian language of Tahiti.

Ta·hi·ti orange (tə-hē'tē) *n.* The Otaheite orange.

tahr (tär) *n.* Any of several goatlike mammals of the genus *Hemitragus,* of mountainous regions of Asia, having curved horns and a shaggy coat. [Nepalese *thar.*]

tah·sil·dar also **tah·seel·dar** (tə-sēl'där') *n.* A district official in India in charge of revenues and taxation. [Urdu *taḥsīldār* < Pers. < Ar. : *taḥsīl,* collection + Pers. *-dār,* having.]

Tai (tī) *n.* A family of languages spoken in Southeast Asia and southern China that includes Thai, Lao, and Shan. —*adj.* Of or pertaining to this language family.

tai chi (tī' chē', jē') or **tai chi chuan** (chwän', cho͞o-än') *n.* A Chinese system of physical exercises designed esp. for meditation and for the development of self-discipline and a sense of well-being. [Chin. (Mandarin) *tai⁴ ji² quan²* : *tai⁴,* highest + *ji²,* reach + *quan²,* boxing.]

tai·ga (tī'gə) *n.* The subarctic evergreen forest of Siberia and of similar regions elsewhere in Eurasia and North America. [R. *taĭga.*]

tail[1] (tāl) *n.* **1.** The posterior part of an animal, esp. when elongated and extending beyond the trunk or main part of the body. **2.** The bottom, rear, or hindmost part. **3.** The rear end of a wagon or other vehicle. **4. a.** The rear portion of an airplane's fuselage. **b.** An assembly of stabilizing planes and control surfaces in this region. **5.** The vaned rear portion of a bomb or missile. **6.** Any appendage to the rear or bottom of a thing: *the tail of a kite.* **7.** A braid of hair; pigtail. **8.** Something that follows or takes the last place: *the tail of the journey.* **9.** A retinue or train of followers. **10.** The end of a line of persons or things. **11.** The short closing line of certain stanzas. **12.** The refuse or dross remaining from processes as distilling or milling. **13.** *Printing.* The bottom of a page; bottom margin. **14. tails.** The reverse of a coin: *heads or tails.* **15.** *Informal.* The trail of a person or animal in flight: *The hounds were on his tail.* **16.** *Informal.* An agent assigned to follow and report on someone's movements and actions. **17. tails. a.** A formal evening costume worn by men. **b.** A swallow-tailed coat. ***—modifier:*** *tail feathers; the tail section.* —*v.* **tailed, tail·ing, tails.** —*tr.* **1.** To provide with a tail: *tail a kite.* **2.** To deprive of a tail; dock. **3.** To serve as the tail of: *The Santa Claus float tailed the parade.* **4.** To connect (objects often dissimilar or incongruous) by or as by the tail or end: *tail two ideas together.* **5.** *Archit.* To set one end of (a beam, board, or brick) into a wall. **6.** *Informal.* To follow and keep under surveillance. —*intr.* **1.** To become lengthened or spaced when moving in a line: *The patrol tailed out in pairs.* **2.** *Archit.* To be inserted at one end, as a floor timber or beam. **3.** *Informal.* To follow. **4.** *Naut.* **a.** To go aground with the stern foremost. **b.** To be pointed in some direction with the stern when riding at anchor or on a mooring: *She was tailing into the wind.* ***—phrasal verbs.*** **tail down.** To ease a heavy load down a steep slope. **tail off** (or **away**). To diminish gradually; dwindle; subside: *The fireworks tailed off into darkness.* [ME < OE *tægel.*]

tail[2] (tāl). *Law.* —*n.* The limitation of the inheritance of an estate to a particular person or persons. —*adj.* In tail: *a tail estate.* [ME *taille* < OFr., division < *tailler,* to cut. —see TAILOR.]

tail·back (tāl'băk') *n. Football.* The back on the offensive team lining up farthest from the line of scrimmage.

tail beam *n.* A tailpiece (sense 3).

tail·board (tāl'bôrd', -bōrd') *n.* The tailgate of a vehicle.

tail·bone (tāl'bōn') *n.* The coccyx.

tail end *n.* **1.** The rear or hindmost part. **2.** The very end; conclusion.

tail·gate (tāl'gāt') *n.* **1.** One of the pair of gates downstream in a canal lock. **2.** A hinged board or closure at the rear of a vehicle, as a station wagon, that can be lowered during loading and unloading. —*v.* **-gat·ed, -gat·ing, -gates.** —*tr.* To drive so closely behind (another vehicle) that one cannot stop or swerve in an emergency. —*intr.* To follow another car too closely.

tail-heav·y (tāl'hĕv'ē) *adj.* **-i·er, -i·est.** Having too much weight at the rear either from overloading or from poor design and construction.

tail·ing (tā'lĭng) *n.* **1. tailings.** Refuse or dross remaining after processes such as milling, distilling, or mining. **2.** *Archit.* The portion of a tailed beam, brick, or board inside a wall.

tail lamp *n.* A taillight.

taille (tä'yə, tāl) *n.* A form of direct royal taxation that was levied in France before 1789 on nonprivileged subjects and lands and tended to weigh most heavily on the peasants. [Fr. < OFr., division < *tailler,* to cut. —see TAILOR.]

tail·light (tāl'līt') *n.* A red light or one of a pair mounted on the rear end of a vehicle.

tai·lor (tā'lər) *n.* A person who makes, repairs, and alters garments such as suits, coats, and dresses. —*v.* **-lored, -lor·ing, -lors.** —*tr.* **1.** To produce (a garment). **2.** To outfit (someone) with clothes. **3.** To make, alter, or adapt for a particular end: *a speech tailored to a special audience.* —*intr.* To exercise the trade of a tailor. [ME < AN *taillour* < OFr. *tailler,* to cut < VLat. **taliare,* **talliare,* to cut < Lat. *talea,* a cutting.]

tai·lor·bird (tā'lər-bûrd') *n.* Any of several Old World tropical birds of the genus *Orthotomus,* characteristically using plant fibers to stitch leaves together in making its nest.

tai·lored (tā'lərd) *adj.* **1.** Made by a tailor; custom-made. **2.** Simple, trim, or severe in line or design: *a neat, tailored dress; tailored curtains.*

tai·lor-made (tā'lər-mād') *adj.* **1.** Made by a tailor. **2.** Perfectly fitted to a condition, preference, or purpose; made or as if made to order: *a tailor-made job.* —*n.* A garment made by a tailor.

tailor's chalk *n.* A thin piece of hard chalk used in tailoring for making temporary alteration marks on clothing.

tail·piece (tāl'pēs') *n.* **1.** Any piece forming an end to something; appendage. **2.** *Printing.* An engraving or design placed as an ornament at the end of a chapter or at the bottom of a page. **3.** *Archit.* A beam tailed into a wall. **4.** *Mus.* A triangular piece of ebony to which the lower ends of the strings of a violin or cello are attached.

tail pipe *n.* The pipe through which exhaust gases from an engine are discharged.

tail·race (tāl'rās') *n.* **1.** The part of a millrace below the water wheel through which the spent water flows. **2.** A channel for floating away mine tailings and refuse.

tail·skid (tāl'skĭd') *n.* A skid attached to the rear underside of certain airplanes to act as a runner.

tail·spin (tāl'spĭn') *n.* **1.** The descent of an aircraft in a spin, characterized by the rapid spiral movement of the tail section. **2.** An emotional collapse; loss of emotional control.

tail·stock (tāl'stŏk') *n.* The adjustable stock of a lathe supporting the spindle containing the dead center.

tail wind *n.* A wind blowing in the same direction as that of the course of a vehicle.

tain (tān) *n.* **1.** A type of paper-thin tin plate. **2.** Tinfoil used as a backing for mirrors. [Fr. < *étain,* tin.]

Tai·no (tī'nō) *n., pl.* **Taino** or **-nos. 1.** An extinct aboriginal Arawakan Indian people of the West Indies. **2.** The language of the Taino. [Sp., of American Indian orig.]

taint (tānt) *v.* **taint·ed, taint·ing, taints.** —*tr.* **1.** To stain the honor of someone or something: *Her reputation is forever tainted.* **2.** To expose to contagion; infect with or as with a disease: *"such a malady is more likely to taint a particular* *county or district, than an entire state"* (James Madison). **3.** To make poisonous or rotten; infect or spoil. **4.** To infect with moral corruption. *—intr.* To become discolored; rot. *—n.* **1.** A moral defect considered as a stain or spot. **2.** An infecting touch, influence, or tinge. [Partly < ME *tainten,* to color (< AN *teinter* < *teint,* p.part. of OFr. *teindre,* to color < Lat. *tingere,* to dye), and partly < ME *taynten,* to convict (< OFr. *ataint,* p.part of *ataindre,* to attain). —see ATTAIN.]

taj (täzh, täj) *n.* A tall conical cap worn by Moslems as a headdress of distinction. [Ar. *tāj* < Pers.]

ta·ka (tä′kə) *n.* See table at **currency**. [Bengali *ṭākā* < Skt. *ṭaṅkaḥ,* coin.]

ta·ka·he (tə-kī′) *n.* An almost extinct flightless bird, *Notornis mantelli,* of New Zealand, having a large bill and brightly colored plumage. [Maori.]

takahe

take (tāk) *v.* **took** (to͝ok), **tak·en** (tā′kən), **tak·ing, takes.** *—tr.* **1.** To get into one's possession by force, skill, or artifice, esp.: **a.** To capture physically; seize: *take an enemy fortress.* **b.** To kill, snare, or trap (fish or game, for example). **c.** To acquire in a game or competition; win: *take your opponent's queen.* **d.** To seize authoritatively; confiscate. **e.** To catch (a ball in play), esp. in baseball: *He took it on the fly.* **2.** To grasp with the hands; grip: *take your partner's hand.* **3.** To be affected with; come down with; contract: *He had taken the flu.* **4.** To encounter or catch in a particular situation; come upon; discover: *took him by surprise.* **5.** To deal a blow to; strike; hit: *He took his opponent a sharp jab to the ribs.* **6.** To affect favorably or winsomely; charm; captivate: *He was completely taken by the puppy.* **7.** To put (food or drink, for example) into the body; eat, drink, inhale, or draw in: *take a deep breath; took a little soup for dinner.* **8.** To expose one's body to (healthful or pleasurable treatment, for example): *take some sun.* **9.** To bring or receive into a particular relation, association, or other connection: *take a new partner into the firm.* **10.** To have sexual intercourse with: *Abraham took his slave girl.* **11.** To accept and place under one's care or keeping. **12.** To appropriate for one's own or another's use or benefit; obtain by purchase; secure; buy: *We always take season tickets.* **13. a.** To assume for oneself: *take credit.* **b.** To charge or oblige oneself with the fulfillment of (a task or duty, for example); commit oneself to: *He took chairmanship of the committee.* **c.** To pledge one's obedience to; impose (a vow or promise) upon oneself. **d.** To subject oneself to: *We took extra time to do the job properly.* **e.** To accept or adopt for one's own. **f.** To put forth or adopt as a point of argument, defense, or discussion: *Your interpretation of the poem is well taken.* **g.** To require or have as a fitting or proper accompaniment: *Intransitive verbs take no direct object.* **14.** To obtain through competition: *took first place.* **15.** To defeat: *St. Louis took Boston three to one.* **16. a.** To select; pick out; choose: *take any card.* **b.** To choose for one's own use; avail oneself of the use of: *He took a rented car.* **c.** To use, as in operating: *This camera takes 35mm film.* **d.** To use as a means of conveyance or transportation: *take a train to Pittsburgh.* **e.** To use as a means of safety or refuge: *take shelter from the storm.* **17.** To assume occupancy of: *take a seat.* **18.** To have as a requirement or necessity for something; require: *It takes money to live in that town.* **19.** To obtain from a source; derive; draw: *The book takes its title from the Bible.* **20.** To obtain through particular procedures, as through measurement: *take one's temperature.* **21. a.** To put down in writing; write: *take a letter.* **b.** To put down an image, likeness, or representation of by or as by drawing, painting, or photography: *take a picture of us.* **22. a.** To accept (something owed, offered, or given) either reluctantly or willingly: *take criticism.* **b.** To submit to (something inflicted); endure: *didn't take his punishment very well.* **c.** To withstand: *The dam took the heavy flood waters.* **d.** To accept or believe (something put forth) as true: *I'll take your word.* **e.** To follow (advice, a suggestion, or a lead, for example). **f.** To accept, handle, or deal with in a particular way: *He takes things in stride.* **g.** To consider in a particular relation or from a particular viewpoint: *take the bitter with the sweet.* **23.** To indulge in; do, perform, or accomplish: *take precautions.* **24. a.** To allow to come in; give access or admission to; admit: *The boat took in a lot of water but remained afloat.* **b.** To provide room for; accommodate: *We can't take more than 300 guests.* **c.** To become saturated or impregnated with (dye, for example). **25. a.** To understand or interpret: *took her smile as an invitation.* **b.** To consider; assume: *take the matter as settled.* **c.** To consider to be equal to; reckon: *We take their number at a thousand.* **d.** To perceive or feel; experience: *I take pleasure to inform you.* **26.** To carry along or cause to go with one to another place: *Don't forget to take your umbrella.* **27.** To convey to another place: *This bus takes you to New York.* **28.** To remove from a place: *take the dishes from the sink.* **29.** To secure by removing: *The dentist took two molars.* **30.** To cause to die; kill; destroy: *The blight took these tomatoes.* **31.** To subtract: *take 15 from 30.* **32.** To commit oneself to the study of; enroll in: *take a biology course.* **33.** To swindle; defraud; cheat: *You were taken.* **34.** *Baseball.* To refrain from swinging at (a pitched ball). *—intr.* **1.** To acquire possession. **2.** To engage or mesh; catch, as gears or other mechanical parts. **3.** To start growing; root; germinate: *Have the seeds taken?* **4.** To have the intended effect; operate; work: *The transfusion apparently took.* **5.** To gain popularity or favor: *The TV series didn't take and was canceled.* **6.** To detract: *Her stringy hair takes away from her lovely face.* **7.** To become: *He took sick.* ***—phrasal verbs.*** **take back.** To retract something stated or written. **take down. 1.** To bring to a lower position from a higher one. **2.** To dismantle; take apart: *take down the Christmas tree.* **3.** To lower the arrogance or self-esteem of (a person): *took him down a peg or two.* **4.** To put down in writing. **take in. 1.** To grant admittance to; receive as a guest or employee. **2.** To reduce in size; make smaller or shorter: *take in the waist on a pair of pants.* **3.** To include or comprise. **4.** To understand. **5.** To deceive or swindle. **6.** To look at thoroughly; view: *took in the sights.* **7.** To accept (work) to be done in one's house for pay: *took in washing.* **8.** To convey (a prisoner) to a police station. **take off. 1.** To remove, as clothing: *take one's hat off.* **2.** To release: *took the brake off.* **3.** To deduct as a discount: *took 20 per cent off the bill.* **4.** To carry off or away. **5.** *Slang.* **a.** To go off; leave: *took off in a hurry.* **b.** To achieve wide use or popularity. **6.** To rise in flight: *The plane took off on time.* **7.** To discontinue: *took off the commuter special.* **8.** To withhold service due, as from one's work: *took three days off during hunting season.* **take on. 1.** To undertake or begin to handle: *took on extra responsibilities.* **2.** To hire; engage: *took on more workers during harvest.* **3.** To oppose in competition: *a wrestler who took on all comers.* **4.** *Informal.* To display violent or passionate emotion: *Don't take on so!* **5.** To acquire (an appearance, for example) as or as if one's own: *He took on the look of a banker.* **take out. 1.** To extract; remove: *took the splinter out.* **2.** To secure (a license, for example) by application to an authority. **3.** *Informal.* To escort, as a date: *took her out only once.* **4.** To give vent to: *took out his frustration on us.* **5.** To obtain as an equivalent in a different form: *took out the money owed in services.* **6.** *Informal.* To begin a course; set out: *took out after them.* **take over.** To assume the control or management of. **take up. 1.** To raise; lift. **2.** To reduce in size; shorten or tighten: *take up a gown.* **3.** To pay off an outstanding debt, mortgage, or note. **4.** To accept as offered, as an option, a bet, or a challenge. **5.** To begin again; resume: *take up where we left off.* **6.** To use up, consume, or occupy: *The extra duties took up most of her time.* **7. a.** To develop an interest in or devotion to: *take up mountain climbing.* **b.** To deal with: *Let's take up each problem, one at a time.* **c.** To assume: *took up a friendly attitude.* **d.** To absorb or adsorb: *crops taking up nutrients.* **e.** To enter into (a profession or business): *took up engineering.* *—n.* **1. a.** The act or process of taking. **b.** That which is taken. **2.** The number of fish, game birds, or other animals killed or captured at one time. **3.** A quantity of anything collected at one time, esp. the amount of profit or receipts taken on a business arrangement or venture. **4.** *Slang.* The amount of money collected as admission to a sporting event; the gate. **5.** The uninterrupted running of a motion picture or television camera or set of recording equipment in filming a movie or television program or cutting a record. **6. a.** A scene filmed or televised without interrupting the run of the camera. **b.** A recording made in a single session. **7. a.** Any physical reaction, as a rash, indicating a successful vaccination. **b.** A successful graft. **8.** *Slang.* An attempt or try: *He got the answer on the third take.* ***—idioms.*** **on the take. 1.** Seeking to take advantage of another. **2.** Seeking to take or taking bribes or illegal income. **take a bath.** To experience serious financial loss. **take account of.** To take into account. **take advantage of. 1.** To use to one's advantage; derive profit from. **2.** To impose upon (a person) to his or her detriment; exploit. **take after. 1.** To follow as an example. **2.** To resemble in appearance, temperament, or character: *takes after his father.* **take amiss.** To be offended through misunderstanding of. **take apart. 1.** To disassemble or divide into parts. **2.** To dissect or analyze (an object or theory, for example), usually to discover hidden weaknesses or flaws. **3.** *Informal.* To tear into violently; beat up; thrash. **take a powder.** To leave quickly. **take care.** To be careful. **take care of.** To assume responsibility for the maintenance, support, or treatment of. **take charge.** To assume control or command. **take effect. 1.** To become operative, as under law or regulation: *The curfew takes effect at midnight.* **2.** To have the intended effect, as a drug. **take exception.** To express opposition by argument: *took exception to the prosecutor's line of questioning.* **take five (or ten).** To take a short rest or break, as of five or ten minutes. **take for. 1.** To consider or suppose to be; regard as: *Don't take me for a fool.* **2.** To consider mistakenly: *took him for dead.* **take for granted. 1.** To consider as true, real, or forthcoming; anticipate correctly. **2.** To underestimate the value of: *took his employees for granted.* **take heart.** To be confident or courageous. **take hold. 1.** To seize, as by grasping. **2.** To become established: *The newly planted vines took hold.* **take into account.** To make allowances for: *took the peculiar circumstances into account.* **take into consideration.** To make allowances for; take into account. **take in vain.** To use a name, esp. a sacred name, profanely or blasphemously. **take issue.** To assume an opposing position; disagree. **take it. 1.** To understand; assume: *As I take it, he won't accept the proposal.* **2.** *Informal.* To endure abuse, criticism, or other harsh treatment: *If*

talapoin

talaria
5th-century B.C. vase showing Hermes wearing talaria

talisman
Above: Ancient talisman
Below: Lucky rabbit's foot

you can dish it out, you've got to learn to take it. **take it lying down.** *Informal.* To submit to harsh treatment with no resistance. **take it on the chin.** *Informal.* To endure punishment, suffering, or defeat. **take it or leave it.** To accept or reject unconditionally. **take it out on.** *Informal.* To abuse another person in venting one's own anger. **take notice of.** To pay attention to. **take one's time.** To act slowly or at one's leisure. **take part.** To participate in; join. **take place. 1.** To have as a locality. **2.** To happen. **take root. 1.** To become established or fixed. **2.** To become rooted. **take shape.** To take on a distinctive form. **take sides.** To associate with and support a particular faction, group, or cause. **take stock. 1.** To take an inventory. **2.** To make an estimate or appraisal, as of resources. **take stock in.** To trust, believe in, or attach importance to. **take the cake.** To come in first in a contest; to take the prize. **take the count. 1.** To be defeated. **2.** *Sports.* To be counted out in boxing. **take the floor.** To rise to deliver a formal speech, as to an assembly. **take to. 1.** To have recourse to; go to, as for safety: *took to the woods.* **2.** To develop as a habit or steady practice: *take to drink.* **3.** To become fond of or attached to: *"Two keen minds that they are, they took to each other"* (Jack Kerouac). **take to task.** To reprove severely. **take up for.** To support (a person or a group, for example) in an argument. **take up with.** To begin to associate with; consort with. [ME *taken* < OE *tacan* < ON *taka.*]

take·down (tāk′doun′) *adj.* Capable of being taken down or apart, as certain rifles. —*n.* **1.** A takedown article. **2.** The mechanism allowing an article to be easily taken down. **3.** *Informal.* **a.** The act of humiliating a person. **b.** An instance of such humiliation: *That was quite a takedown he gave you.*

take-home pay (tāk′hōm′) *n.* The amount of one's salary remaining after federal, state, and often city income taxes and other various deductions have been withheld.

take-in (tāk′ĭn′) *n.* An act or instance of swindling or cheating; deception.

tak·en (tā′kən) *v.* Past participle of **take.**

take·off (tāk′ôf′, -ŏf′) *n.* **1.** The act of rising in flight. Used of an aircraft or rocket. **2.** The point or place from which one takes off. **3.** *Informal.* An amusing imitative caricature or burlesque of another person.

take-out (tāk′out′) *adj.* **1.** Intended to be consumed away from the premises: *take-out pizza.* **2.** Dealing with or designed for take-out products: *a take-out counter; take-out containers.* **—take′-out** *n.*

take·o·ver also **take-o·ver** (tāk′ō′vər) *n.* The act or an instance of assuming control or management of or responsibility for, esp. the forcible seizure of power, as in a nation or political organization. **—take′o′ver** *adj.*

tak·er (tā′kər) *n.* A person who takes or takes up something, as a wager or purchase.

take-up (tāk′ŭp′) *n.* **1.** A device for reducing slack or taking up lost motion, as in a loom. **2.** The act of taking or tightening up.

ta·kin (tä′kēn′) *n.* A goatlike mammal, *Budorcas taxicolor,* of the mountains of central Asia, having backward-pointing horns and a shaggy coat. [Of Tibeto-Burman orig.]

tak·ing (tā′kĭng) *adj.* **1.** Capturing the interest; fetching; winning: *a taking smile.* **2.** Contagious; catching. Used of an infectious disease. —*n.* **1.** The act of one that takes. **2.** That which is taken, as a catch of fish. **3. takings.** Receipts, esp. of money.

ta·la (tä′lə) *n.* See table at **currency.** [Samoan < E. DOLLAR.]

tal·a·poin (tăl′ə-poin′) *n.* A small African monkey, *Miopithecus talapoin* (or *Cercopithecus talapoin*), having a long tail and greenish fur. [Fr. < Port. *talapão,* monk < Mon *tala pōi.*]

ta·lar·i·a (tə-lâr′ē-ə) *pl.n.* Winged sandals such as those worn by Hermes and Iris as represented in Greco-Roman painting and sculpture. [Lat. < *talaris,* of the ankles < *talus,* ankle.]

talc (tălk) *n.* A fine-grained white, greenish, or gray mineral, essentially $Mg_3Si_4O_{10}(OH)_2$, having a soft soapy texture and used in talcum and face powder, as a paper coating, and as a filler for paint and plastics. —*tr.v.* **talcked, talck·ing, talcs** or **talced, talc·ing, talcs.** To apply talc to (a photographic plate, for example). [OFr. *talc* < Med. Lat. *talcum* < Ar. *ṭalq* < Pers. *talk.*]

talc·ose (tăl′kōs′) also **talc·ous** (tăl′kəs) or **talck·y** (tăl′kē) *adj.* Made of or containing talc.

tal·cum (tăl′kəm) *n.* **1.** Soapstone or talc. **2.** Talcum powder. [Med. Lat., talc.]

talcum powder *n.* A fine, often perfumed powder made from purified talc, for use on the skin.

tale (tāl) *n.* **1.** A report or revelation; recital of events or happenings: *She told us her tale of woe.* **2.** A malicious story; piece of gossip. **3.** A deliberate lie; falsehood. **4.** A diverting or edifying narrative of real or imaginary events. **5.** *Archaic.* A tally or reckoning; total. [ME < OE *talu.*]

tale·bear·er (tāl′bâr′ər) *n.* A person who spreads malicious stories or gossip. **—tale′bear′ing** *adj. & n.*

tal·ent (tăl′ənt) *n.* **1.** A mental or physical aptitude; natural or acquired ability. **2. a.** Natural endowment or ability of a superior quality. **b.** A person or group of persons having such ability: *The company makes good use of talent.* **3.** A variable unit of weight and money used in ancient Greece, Rome, and the Middle East. [ME < OE *talente,* a unit of money < Lat. *talentum* < Gk. *talanton.*] **—tal′ent·ed** *adj.*

talent scout *n.* An agent sent on tour in search of talented people for acting, sports, or business.

talent show *n.* A show that features amateur performers whose talent may win recognition or a special award.

ta·ler also **tha·ler** (tä′lər) *n., pl.* **taler** or **-lers** or **thaler** or **-lers.** Any of numerous silver coins that served as a unit of currency in certain Germanic countries between the 15th and 19th centuries. [G. —see DOLLAR.]

ta·les (tā′lēz) *n., pl.* **tales.** *Law.* **1.** A group of persons summoned to fill vacancies on a jury that has become deficient in number. **2.** The writ allowing for a summons of jurors. [ME < Med. Lat. *tales de circumstantibus,* such (persons) from those standing about (a phrase used in the writ).]

tales·man (tālz′mən, tā′lēz-) *n. Law.* A person summoned under a writ of tales.

tale·tell·er (tāl′tĕl′ər) *n.* **1.** A person who tells stories; storyteller. **2.** A talebearer. **—tale′tell′ing** *adj. & n.*

ta·li (tā′lī′) *n.* Plural of **talus**[1].

tal·i·on (tăl′ē-ən) *n.* A punishment identical to the offense, as the death penalty for murder. [ME *talioun* < OFr. *talion* < Lat. *talio.*]

tal·i·ped (tăl′ə-pĕd′) *adj.* Afflicted with talipes; clubfooted. —*n.* A person with a clubfoot.

tal·i·pes (tăl′ə-pēz′) *n.* Clubfoot. [NLat. *talipes, taliped-* : Lat. *talus,* ankle + Lat. *pes,* foot.]

tal·i·pot (tăl′ə-pŏt′) *n.* A tall palm tree, *Corypha umbraculifera,* of tropical Asia, having a spreading crown of large, fanlike leaves. [Bengali *tālipōt.*]

tal·is·man (tăl′ĭs-mən, tăl′ĭz-) *n., pl.* **-mans. 1.** An object marked with magical signs and believed to confer on its bearer supernatural powers or protection. **2.** Anything having apparently magical power: *Her most powerful talisman was her beauty.* [Fr. *talisman* or Sp. *talismán* or Ital. *talismano,* all < Ar. *ṭilsām* < LGk. *telesma* < Gk., consecration < *telein,* to consecrate < *telos,* result.]

tal·is·man·ic (tăl′ĭs-măn′ĭk, tăl′ĭz-) also **tal·is·man·i·cal** (-ĭ-kəl) *adj.* **1.** Of or pertaining to talismans: *talismanic formulas.* **2.** Possessing magical power: *a talismanic amulet.*

talk (tôk) *v.* **talked, talk·ing, talks.** —*tr.* **1.** To articulate (words): *Those are real words the baby is talking.* **2.** To articulate (something) in words: *talk treason.* **3.** To speak of or discuss (something): *talk business.* **4.** To speak (an idiom): *He talks Pidgin English with the crew.* **5.** To spend (a period of time) by or as if by talking: *talked the evening away.* —*intr.* **1.** To converse by means of spoken language: *We talked for hours.* **2.** To articulate words: *The baby can talk.* **3.** To imitate the sounds of human speech: *The parrot talks.* **4.** To manifest one's thoughts other than by articulate language: *talk with the hands.* **5.** To express one's thoughts in writing: *Voltaire talks about London in this text.* **6.** To parley or negotiate with someone: *Let's talk before fighting.* **7.** To chatter incessantly: *She did nothing but talk.* **8.** To gossip: *People will talk.* **9.** To consult or confer with someone: *I talked with the doctor.* **10.** To yield under coercion information concerning oneself or others: *Has the prisoner talked?* **—phrasal verbs. talk around. 1.** To persuade: *talked them around to his point of view.* **2.** To speak indirectly about something: *talked around the subject but never got to the point.* **talk back. 1.** To make an impertinent reply: *a saucy child who talked back to her parents.* **2.** To make a belligerent response: *heavy guns talking back.* **talk down. 1.** To depreciate: *talked down the importance of the move.* **2.** To address (someone) with insulting condescension: *talked down to his wife.* **3.** To silence (a person): *His boss could talk him down with one word.* **talk out. 1.** To discuss a matter exhaustively: *talked out her problems.* **2.** To speak loudly or clearly. **3.** To exhaust someone by talking. **4.** *Chiefly Brit.* To filibuster proposed legislation. **talk over. 1.** To win someone over by persuasion: *talked her over to our side.* **2.** To discuss a subject: *talked the matter over.* **talk up. 1.** To propagandize in favor of a person or thing: *talked the candidate up; talked up the new cosmetic.* **2.** To speak up impertinently or defiantly, esp. to a superior: *was reprimanded for talking up to the company commander.* —*n.* **1.** The articulation of ideas in conversation: *She knew how to make diverting and intelligent talk.* **2.** An informal speech: *give a talk.* **3.** Any hearsay, rumor, or speculation concerning something: *There is talk of war.* **4.** A subject of conversation: *the talk of the town.* **5.** A conference or negotiation: *a peace talk.* **6.** Jargon; slang: *prison talk.* **7.** Empty speech: *much talk and no action.* **8.** A particular manner of speech: *baby talk.* **9.** Something, as the sounds of animals, resembling talk: *whale talk.* **—idioms. talk at. 1.** To say something intended for a listener without addressing him directly: *talked at his opponent in the debate.* **2.** To address someone without regard to his response: *She talks at people, never with them.* **talk big.** *Slang.* To brag. **talk sense.** To speak rationally and coherently. **talk (someone) into.** To persuade. **talk (someone) out of.** To dissuade. **talk through (one's) hat.** To speak irrationally or illogically. **talk turkey.** To speak forthrightly or bluntly. [ME *talken.*]

talk·a·thon (tôk′ə-thŏn′) *n.* A lengthy session of discussions, speech-making, or debate. [TALK + (MAR)ATHON.]

talk·a·tive (tô′kə-tĭv) *adj.* Having an inclination to talk; loquacious. **—talk′a·tive·ly** *adv.* **—talk′a·tive·ness** *n.*
Synonyms: *talkative, loquacious, wordy, garrulous, voluble, effusive, verbose, glib.* These adjectives describe persons or their style of speech or writing and usually imply excessive use of words. *Talkative* is the most neutral and suggests sociability more often than offensiveness. *Loquacious* stresses fluency or readiness of speech, often in a mildly derogatory sense. *Wordy* applies principally to writing in which point and clarity are dulled by needless repetition. *Garrulous* describes one who talks readily and at too great length and whose speech is usually rambling and diffuse. *Voluble* stresses fluency in speech, often unfavorably in the sense of an unending flow. *Effusive* suggests a gushing forth of oral or written expression that lacks discipline or substance. *Verbose* implies either overwriting or windy speech, characteristically marked by dullness or obscurity. *Glib* refers to one whose speech is fluent and smooth; often the term suggests shallowness, lack of sincerity, or questionable motives.
talk·er (tô′kər) *n.* A person who talks, esp. a loquacious or garrulous person.
talk·ie (tô′kē) *n. Informal.* A motion-picture film with a sound track.
talking book *n.* A phonograph record of a reading of a book, designed for use by the blind.
talking point *n.* Something, as an esp. persuasive point, that helps to support an argument.
talk·ing-to (tô′kĭng-to͞o′) *n., pl.* **-tos.** *Informal.* A scolding; dressing-down.
talk show *n.* A radio or television show in which usually noted individuals or celebrities participate in discussions or are interviewed.
talk·y (tô′kē) *adj.* **-i·er, -i·est. 1.** Talkative; loquacious. **2.** Containing too much talk: *a talky, boring play.*
tall (tôl) *adj.* **-er, -est. 1. a.** Having greater than ordinary height: *a tall woman.* **b.** Having considerable height: *tall trees.* **2.** Having a stated height: *a plant three feet tall.* **3.** *Informal.* Fanciful; boastful: *tall talk.* **4.** *Archaic.* Excellent; comely; fine. **5.** Long: *a tall glass for lemonade.* **6.** Impressively great or difficult: *a tall order to fill.* *—adv.* Straight; with proud bearing: *stand tall.* [ME, brave < OE *getæl,* swift.]
tal·lage (tăl′ĭj) *n.* An occasional tax levied by the Anglo-Norman kings on crown lands and royal towns. *—tr.v.* **-laged, -lag·ing, -lag·es.** To levy a tax on. [ME *taillage* < OFr., feudal fee < *tailler,* to cut. —see TAILOR.]
tall·boy (tôl′boi′) *n. Chiefly Brit.* A highboy.
tall drink *n.* A drink served in a tall glass and consisting typically of a liquor base with any of various diluents and flavorings.
tal·lith (tä′lĭs, -lĭth) *n., pl.* **tal·lith·im** (tä′lĭ-sēm′, -thēm′). A fringed prayer shawl with bands of black or blue, worn by Orthodox and Conservative Jewish men, esp. at prayer. [Heb. *ṭallīth.*]
tall oil (täl, tôl) *n.* An oily resinous liquid composed of a mixture of rosin acids and fatty acids obtained as a by-product in the treatment of pine pulp and used in soaps, emulsions, and lubricants. [Partial transl. of G. *Tallöl* < partial transl. of Swed. *tallojla* : *tall,* pine (< ON *thöll,* young pine tree) + *ojla,* oil.]
tal·low (tăl′ō) *n.* **1.** A mixture of the whitish, tasteless solid or hard fat obtained from parts of the bodies of cattle, sheep, or horses, and used in edibles or to make candles, leather dressing, soap, and lubricants. **2.** Any of various fats similar to tallow, as from plants. *—tr.v.* **-lowed, -low·ing, -lows. 1.** To smear or cover with tallow. **2.** To fatten (animals) for the purpose of obtaining tallow. [ME *talow.*] **—tal′low·y** *adj.*
tal·ly (tăl′ē) *n., pl.* **-lies. 1.** A stick on which notches are made to keep a count or score. **2.** The reckoning or score kept on a piece of wood, a gunstock, blackboard, or score card. **3.** A mark used in recording a number of acts or objects, most often in series of five, consisting of four vertical lines canceled diagonally or horizontally by a fifth line. **4.** A label of identification used in gardens and greenhouses. **5.** Something that is very similar to something else; double. **6.** A metal plate attached to a ship's machinery and bearing instructions for its use. *—v.* **-lied, -ly·ing, -lies.** *—tr.* **1.** To record by making a mark. **2.** To reckon or count. **3.** To label with a tally. **4.** To cause to correspond or agree. *—intr.* **1.** To be alike; agree. **2.** To keep score or a reckoning of a thing. [ME *taly* < Med. Lat. *talea* < Lat., stick.]
tal·ly·ho (tăl′ē-hō′) *interj.* Used to urge hounds in fox hunting. *—v.* **-hoed, -ho·ing, -hos.** *—tr.* To excite (hounds) on a fox hunt by shouting "tallyho" when the fox is sighted. *—intr.* To shout "tallyho" as a hunting cry. *—n., pl.* **-hos. 1.** The cry of "tallyho." **2.** A kind of pleasure coach drawn by four horses. [Prob. < Fr. *taïaut* < OFr. *thialau.*]
tal·ly·man (tăl′ē-mən) *n.* **1.** A recorder or scorekeeper. **2.** *Chiefly Brit.* A merchant whose customers pay him by the week according to a simple reckoning, without regular bookkeeping and billing.
Tal·mi gold (tăl′mē) *n.* A composite metal made of gold and brass, used in making jewelry. [G. *Talmigold.*]
Tal·mud (täl′mo͝od′, tăl′məd) *n.* The collection of ancient Rabbinic writings consisting of the Mishnah and the Gemara, constituting the basis of religious authority for traditional Judaism. [Heb. *talmūd.*] **—Tal·mu′dic** (tăl-mo͞o′dĭk, -myo͞o′-, tăl-), **Tal·mu′di·cal** *adj.* **—Tal′mud·ist** (tăl′mo͝od-ĭst, tăl′məd-) *n.*
tal·on (tăl′ən) *n.* **1. a.** The claw of a bird of prey. **b.** The similar claw of a predatory animal. **2.** Something similar to or suggestive of a claw. **3.** The part of a lock which the key presses in order to shoot the bolt. **4.** The part of the deck of cards in certain card games left on the table after the deal. [ME < OFr., heel < Lat. *talus,* ankle.] **—tal′oned** *adj.*
ta·lus[1] (tā′ləs) *n., pl.* **-li** (-lī′). **1.** A tarsal bone that articulates with the tibia and fibula to form the anklebone. **2.** The ankle. [NLat. < Lat., ankle.]
ta·lus[2] (tā′ləs) *n., pl.* **-lus·es. 1.** A slope formed by the accumulation of debris. **2.** A sloping mass of debris at the base of a cliff. [OFr., sloping side of an earthwork.]
tam (tăm) *n.* A tam-o'-shanter.
ta·ma·le (tə-mä′lē) *n.* An often highly seasoned Mexican dish made of fried chopped meat and crushed peppers rolled in cornmeal dough, wrapped in corn husks, and steamed. [Mex. Sp. *tamales,* pl. of *tamal* < Nahuatl *tamalli.*]
ta·man·du·a (tə-măn′do͞o-ə) *n.* A chiefly arboreal anteater, *Tamandua tetradactyla,* of tropical America, having a dense, furry coat. [Port. *tamanduá* < Tupi.]
tam·a·rack (tăm′ə-răk′) *n.* Any of several North American larch trees, esp. *Larix laricina,* having short deciduous needles. [Of Algonquian orig.]
tam·a·rau also **ta·ma·rao** (tăm′ə-rou′) *n.* A small, short-horned buffalo, *Anoa mindorensis,* of the island of Mindoro in the Philippines. [Tagalog *tamaráw.*]
tam·a·rin (tăm′ə-rĭn, -răn′) *n.* Any of various small, long-tailed monkeys of the genus *Saguinus,* of tropical South America. [Fr. < Galibi.]
tam·a·rind (tăm′ə-rĭnd′) *n.* **1.** A tropical Old World tree, *Tamarindus indica,* with compound leaves and red-striped yellow flowers. **2.** The fruit of the tamarind, consisting of a long pod with seeds embedded in an edible pulp. [Med. Lat. *tamarindus* < Ar. *tamr hindī* : *tamr,* date + *hindī,* of India.]
tam·a·risk (tăm′ə-rĭsk′) *n.* Any of numerous shrubs or small trees of the genus *Tamarix,* native to Eurasia, having small, scalelike leaves and clusters of pink flowers. [ME *tamarisc* < LLat. *tamariscus* < Lat. *tamarix.*]
tam·bac or **tam·bak** (tŏm′băk) *n.* Variants of **tombac.**
tam·ba·la (tăm-bä′lə) *n.* See table at **currency.** [Native word in Malawi.]
tam·bour (tăm′bo͝or′, tăm-bo͝or′) *n.* **1.** A drum or drummer. **2. a.** A small wooden embroidery frame consisting of two concentric hoops between which fabric is stretched. **b.** Embroidery made on such a frame. **3.** A rolling front or top for a desk, consisting of narrow strips of wood glued to canvas. **4. a.** The wall of a circular building surrounded with columns. **b.** The vertical part of a cupola. *—v.* **-boured, -bour·ing, -bours.** *—tr.* To do (embroidery) on a tambour. *—intr.* To embroider at a tambour frame. [ME < OFr.]
tam·bou·ra also **tam·bu·ra** (tŭm-bo͝or′ə) *n.* An unfretted lute of India, used as a harmonic drone. [Pers. *ṭanbūr.*]
tam·bou·rin (tăm′bo͞o-rĭn, täN-bo͞o-răN′) *n.* **1. a.** A long, narrow drum used in Provence. **b.** One who plays this drum. **2.** A style of dance in lively two-beat rhythm, accompanied by the tambourin. [Prov. *tamborin,* dim. of *tambor,* var. of OFr. *tambour,* tambour.]
tam·bou·rine (tăm′bə-rēn′) *n.* A musical instrument consisting of a small drumhead with jingling disks fitted into the rim that is carried and shaken with one hand and struck with the other. [OFr. *tambourin,* dim. of *tambour,* tambour.]
tam·bu·ra (tŭm-bo͝or′ə) *n.* Variant of **tamboura.**
tame (tām) *adj.* **tam·er, tam·est. 1.** Brought from wildness into a domesticated or tractable state. **2.** Naturally gentle or unafraid; not timid: *"The sea otter is gentle and relatively tame"* (Peter Matthiessen). **3.** Submissive; docile; fawning: *a tame child.* **4.** Insipid; flat: *a tame Christmas party.* **5.** Sluggish; languid; inactive: *a tame river.* *—tr.v.* **tamed, tam·ing, tames. 1.** To make tractable; domesticate. **2.** To subdue or curb. **3.** To tone down; soften. [ME < OE *tam.*] **—tam′a·ble, tame′a·ble** *adj.*
Tam·il (tăm′əl, tŭm′-) *n.* **1.** A member of a Dravidian race of southern India and Sri Lanka. **2.** The Dravidian language of the Tamil. *—adj.* Of or pertaining to the Tamils. [Tamil.]
Tam·muz also **Tham·muz** (tä′mo͞oz′) *n.* The tenth month in the Hebrew calendar. See table at **calendar.** [Heb. *Tammūz* < Babylonian *Du'uzu,* the name of a god.]
tam-o'-shan·ter (tăm′ə-shăn′tər) *n.* A tight-fitting Scottish cap or braided bonnet, sometimes having a pompom, tassel, or feather in the center. [After the hero of *Tam o'Shanter,* a poem by Robert Burns (1759–96).]
tamp (tămp) *tr.v.* **tamped, tamp·ing, tamps. 1.** To pack down tightly by a succession of blows or taps. **2.** To pack clay, sand, or dirt into (a drill hole) above an explosive. [Prob. back-formation < TAMPION.]
tam·per[1] (tăm′pər) *v.* **-pered, -per·ing, -pers.** *—intr.* **1.** To interfere in a harmful manner: *tampering with a delicate mechanism.* **2.** To meddle rashly or foolishly: *tamper with another's feelings.* **3.** To bring about an improper situation or condition by clandestine means: *tamper with a jury;*

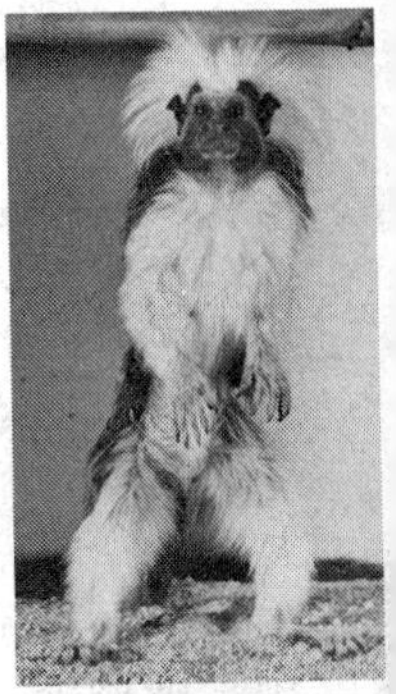
tamarin

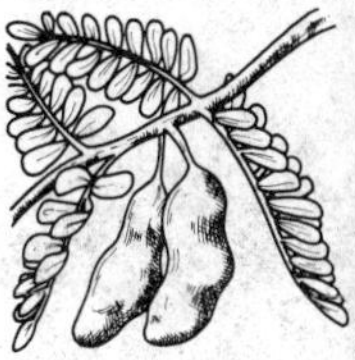
tamarind

tambourine

tam-o'-shanter

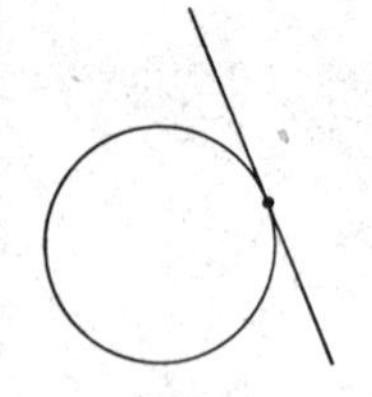

tangent
Tangent to a circle

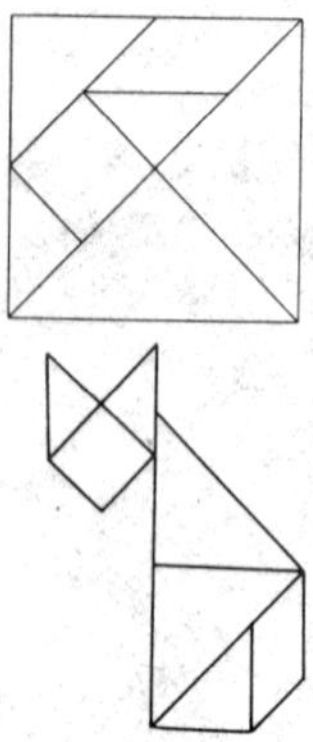

tangram
The square card and an assembly of its pieces representing a cat

tank

tankard

tansy

tamper with a contract. —*tr.* To alter improperly. [Alteration of TEMPER.] —**tam'per·er** *n.*

tamp·er[2] (tămʹpər) *n.* **1.** One that tamps. **2.** A neutron reflector in an atomic bomb that also delays the expansion of the exploding material, making possible a longer-lasting, more energetic, and more efficient explosion.

Tam·pi·co hemp (tăm-pēʹkō) *n.* Pita (sense 1). [After *Tampico,* Mexico.]

tam·pi·on (tămʹpē-ən) also **tom·pi·on** (tŏmʹ-) *n.* A plug or cover for the muzzle of a cannon or gun to keep out dust and moisture. [ME *tampyne,* plug < OFr. *tampon,* of Germanic orig.]

tam·pon (tămʹpŏnʹ) *n.* A plug of absorbent material inserted into a bodily cavity or wound to check a flow of blood or absorb secretions. —*tr.v.* **-poned, -pon·ing, -pons.** To plug or stop with a tampon. [Fr. < OFr., of Germanic orig.]

tam-tam (tŭmʹtŭmʹ, tămʹtămʹ) *n.* **1.** One of a set of tuned gongs used in a gamelan orchestra. **2.** A tom-tom. [Hindi *ṭamṭam.*]

tan (tăn) *v.* **tanned, tan·ning, tans.** —*tr.* **1.** To convert (hide) into leather, as by treating with tannin. **2.** To make brown by exposure to the sun. **3.** *Informal.* To thrash; beat. —*intr.* To become brown or tawny from exposure to sun. —*n.* **1.** A light or moderate yellowish brown to brownish orange. **2.** The brown color sun rays impart to the skin. **3.** Tanbark. **4.** Tannin or a solution derived from it. —*adj.* **tan·ner, tan·nest. 1.** Of the color tan. **2.** Having a sun tan. **3.** Used in or relating to tanning. [ME *tannen* < OFr. *tanner* < Med. Lat. *tannare* < *tannum,* tanbark, prob. of Celt. orig.]

Tan (tăn) *n., pl.* **Tan** or **Tans.** The Tanka.

tan·a·ger (tănʹĭ-jər) *n.* Any of various small New World birds of the family Thraupidae, often having brightly colored plumage in the males. [NLat. *tanagra* < Port. *tangará* < Tupi.]

tan·bark (tănʹbärkʹ) *n.* **1.** The bark of various trees, used as a source of tannin. **2.** Shredded bark from which the tannin has been extracted, used to cover circus arenas, racetracks, and the like.

tan·dem (tănʹdəm) *n.* **1.** A two-wheeled carriage drawn by horses harnessed one before the other. **2.** A team of carriage horses harnessed in single file. **3.** A tandem bicycle. **4.** An arrangement of two or more persons or objects placed one behind the other. —*adv.* One behind the other: *driving horses in tandem.* [< Lat., at last, at length.] —**tanʹdem** *adj.*

tandem bicycle *n.* A bicycle built for two or more persons sitting one behind the other.

tang[1] (tăng) *n.* **1.** A sharp, distinctive taste, flavor, or odor, as that of orange juice. **2.** A distinctive quality that adds piquancy. **3.** A trace, hint, or smattering. **4. a.** A sharp point, shank, tongue, or prong. **b.** A projection by which a tool, such as a chisel or knife, is attached to its handle or stock. —*tr.v.* **tanged, tang·ing, tangs.** To furnish with a tang. [ME *tonge,* of Scand. orig.] —**tangʹy** *adj.*

tang[2] (tăng) *n.* A loud ringing sound; twang. —*intr. & tr.v.* **tanged, tang·ing, tangs.** To twang or cause to twang; ring. [Imit.]

tan·ge·lo (tănʹjə-lōʹ) *n., pl.* **-los. 1.** A hybrid citrus tree that is a cross between certain varieties of grapefruit and tangerine. **2.** The fruit of the tangelo, having an acid orange pulp. [Blend of TANGERINE and POMELO.]

tan·gen·cy (tănʹjən-sē) also **tan·gence** (-jəns) *n.* The condition of being tangent.

tan·gent (tănʹjənt) *adj.* **1.** Making contact at a single point or along a line; touching but not intersecting. **2.** Irrelevant. —*n.* **1.** A line, curve, or surface touching but not intersecting another line, curve, or surface. **2.** The trigonometric function of an acute angle in a right triangle that is the ratio of the length of the side opposite the angle to the length of the side adjacent to the angle. **3.** A sudden digression or change of course: *go off on a tangent.* [Lat. *tangens, tangent-,* pr.part. of *tangere,* to touch.]

tan·gen·tial (tăn-jĕnʹshəl) also **tan·gen·tal** (-jĕnʹtl) *adj.* **1.** Of, pertaining to, or moving along or in the direction of a tangent. **2.** Merely touching or slightly connected. **3.** Only superficially relevant; divergent: *a tangential remark.* —**tan·genʹti·alʹi·ty** (-shē-ălʹĭ-tē) *n.* —**tan·genʹtial·ly** *adv.*

tangent plane *n.* The plane containing all the lines tangent to a specified point on a surface.

tan·ger·ine (tănʹjə-rēnʹ, tănʹjə-rēnʹ) *n.* **1.** A widely cultivated citrus tree, *Citrus nobilis deliciosa,* bearing edible fruit having an easily peeled deep-orange skin and sweet, juicy pulp. **2.** The fruit of the tangerine. **3.** A strong reddish orange to strong or vivid orange. [< Fr. *Tanger,* Tangier, Morocco.] —**tanʹger·ineʹ** *adj.*

tan·gi·ble (tănʹjə-bəl) *adj.* **1. a.** Discernible by the touch; capable of being touched; palpable. **b.** Capable of being treated as fact; real; concrete: *tangible evidence.* **2.** Capable of being understood or realized: *a tangible benefit.* **3.** *Law.* Capable of being valued monetarily, as land or securities: *tangible property.* —*n.* **1.** Something palpable or concrete. **2. tangibles.** Material assets. [LLat. *tangibilis* < Lat. *tangere,* to touch.] —**tanʹgi·bilʹi·ty, tanʹgi·ble·ness** *n.* —**tanʹgi·bly** *adv.*

tan·gle[1] (tăngʹgəl) *v.* **-gled, -gling, -gles.** —*tr.* **1.** To mix together or intertwine in a confused mass; snarl. **2.** To involve in hampering or awkward complications; entangle. **3.** To trap; ensnare. —*intr.* To be or become entangled. —*n.* **1.** A confused, intertwined mass. **2.** A jumbled or confused state or condition. **3.** A state of bewilderment. **4.** *Informal.* An argument; altercation. —***idiom.* tangle with.** *Informal.* To come to grips or blows with. [ME *tangilen,* to involve in embarrassment.] —**tanʹgly** *adj.*

tan·gle[2] (tăngʹgəl) *n.* A large seaweed of the genus *Laminaria.* [Of Scand. orig.]

tan·gled (tăngʹgəld) *adj.* Complicated in a random way.

tan·go (tăngʹgō) *n., pl.* **-gos. 1.** A Latin-American ballroom dance in 2/4 or 4/4 time. **2.** The music for the tango. —*intr.v.* **-goed, -go·ing, -gos.** To dance the tango. [Am. Sp., poss. of African orig.]

tang·o·re·cep·tor (tăngʹgō-rĭ-sĕpʹtər) *n.* A cutaneous receptor that responds to touch and pressure. [Lat. *tangere,* to touch + RECEPTOR.]

tan·gram (tăngʹgrəm) *n.* A Chinese puzzle consisting of a square cut into five triangles, a square, and a rhomboid, to be reassembled into different figures. [Perh. Chin. *tang²,* a Chinese dynasty + -GRAM.]

tan·ist (tănʹĭst, thôʹnĭst) *n.* The heir apparent to an ancient Celtic chief, elected during the chief's lifetime. [Ir. Gael. *tānaiste* < OIr. *tānaise.*]

tan·ist·ry (tănʹĭ-strē, thôʹnĭ-) *n.* The system of electing a tanist.

tank (tăngk) *n.* **1.** A large container for holding or storing fluids or gases. **2.** The amount a tank holds: *buy a tank of gas.* **3.** A pool, pond, reservoir, or cistern, esp. one for drinking water or irrigation. **4.** An enclosed, heavily armored combat vehicle that is mounted with cannon and guns and moves on caterpillar treads. **5.** *Slang.* A jail or jail cell. —*tr.v.* **tanked, tank·ing, tanks.** To place, store, or process in a tank. —***phrasal verb.* tank up.** *Slang.* **1.** To drink alcoholic beverages to excess. **2.** To be or become drunk. [Port. *tanque,* pond < Lat. *stagnum.*]

tan·ka[1] (tängʹkə) *n.* A Japanese verse form in five lines, the first and third composed of five syllables and the rest of seven. [J.]

tan·ka[2] (tängʹkə) *n.* A Tibetan religious painting, usually mounted on fabric. [Tibetan *taṅka.*]

Tan·ka (tängʹkä) *n., pl.* **Tanka** or **-kas.** A people in southern China and Hong Kong who live on small boats, clustered in colonies. [Cantonese.]

tank·age (tăngʹkĭj) *n.* **1. a.** The capacity or contents of a tank or tanks. **b.** The act or process of putting or storing in a tank. **c.** The fee for such storage. **2.** Animal residues left after rendering fat in a slaughterhouse and used for fertilizer or feed.

tank·ard (tăngʹkərd) *n.* A large drinking cup having a single handle and often a hinged cover, esp. a tall pewter or silver mug. [ME.]

tank destroyer *n.* A high-speed armored vehicle equipped with antitank guns.

tanked (tăngkt) *adj. Slang.* Drunk.

tank·er (tăngʹkər) *n.* **1.** A ship, plane, or truck constructed to transport oil or other liquids in bulk. **2.** A member of a tank crew.

tank suit *n.* A simply designed one-piece swimsuit with shoulder straps.

tank top *n.* A casual sleeveless shirt with usually wide shoulder straps and no front opening. [From its resemblance to a TANK SUIT.]

tank town *n.* A small or unimportant town. [So called because trains would stop there only to replenish water.]

tank trailer *n.* A truck trailer equipped as a tanker.

tan·nage (tănʹĭj) *n.* **1.** The act, process, or skill of tanning. **2.** Something tanned.

tan·nate (tănʹātʹ) *n.* A salt or ester of tannic acid. [TANN(IN) + -ATE.]

tan·ner[1] (tănʹər) *n.* A person who tans hides.

tan·ner[2] (tănʹər) *n. Chiefly Brit. Slang.* A sixpence. [Orig. unknown.]

tan·ner·y (tănʹə-rē) *n., pl.* **-ies.** A place where hides are tanned.

tan·nic (tănʹĭk) *adj.* Pertaining to or obtained from tannin. [TANN(IN) + IC.]

tannic acid *n.* A lustrous yellowish to light-brown amorphous, powdered, flaked, or spongy mass having the approximate composition $C_{76}H_{52}O_{46}$, derived from the bark and fruit of many plants and used in tanning, as a mordant, to clarify wine and beer, and as an astringent and styptic.

tan·nif·er·ous (tăn-ĭfʹər-əs) *adj.* Containing or yielding tannin.

tan·nin (tănʹĭn) *n.* **1.** Tannic acid. **2.** Any of various chemically different substances capable of promoting tanning. [Fr. < *tanner,* to tan < OFr.]

tan·ning (tănʹĭng) *n.* **1.** The art or process of making leather from rawhides. **2.** The browning of the skin by exposure to sun and weather. **3.** *Informal.* A beating; a whipping.

Ta·no·an (täʹnō-ən) *n.* An American Indian language family of New Mexico and northeastern Arizona. [< *Tano,* an American Indian people.] —**Taʹno·an** *adj.*

tan·rec (tănʹrĕkʹ) *n.* Variant of **tenrec.**

tan rot *n.* A disease of the strawberry plant caused by the fungus *Pezizella lythri* and marked by the formation of tan indentations on the surface of the fruit.

tan·sy (tănʹzē) *n., pl.* **-sies.** Any of several plants of the genus

Tanacetum, esp. *T. vulgare,* native to the Old World, having clusters of buttonlike yellow flowers and pungent, aromatic juice sometimes used medicinally and as a flavoring. [ME < OFr. *tanesie* < Med. Lat. *athanasia* < Gk., immortality : *a-*, without + *thanatos,* death.]

tan·tal·ic (tăn-tăl′ĭk) *adj.* Of, pertaining to, or containing tantalum.

tan·ta·lite (tăn′tə-līt′) *n.* A black to red-brown mineral, essentially $(Fe,Mn)(Ta,Nb)_2O_6$, distinguished from columbite by the predominance of tantalum over niobium and used as an ore of both elements. [Swed. *tantalit* < *tantalum,* tantalum.]

tan·ta·lize (tăn′tə-līz′) *tr.v.* **-lized, -liz·ing, -liz·es.** To excite (another) by exposing something desirable while keeping it out of reach. [After *Tantalus.*] **—tan′ta·li·za′tion** *n.* **—tan′ta·liz′er** *n.* **—tan′ta·liz′ing·ly** *adv.*

tan·ta·lum (tăn′tə-ləm) *n. Symbol* **Ta** A very hard, heavy gray metallic element that is exceptionally resistant to chemical attack below 150°C. It is used to make electric-light-bulb filaments, electrolytic capacitors, lightning arresters, nuclear reactor parts, and some surgical instruments. Atomic number 73; atomic weight 180.948; melting point 2,996°C; boiling point 5,425°C; specific gravity 16.6; valences 2, 3, 4, 5. [After *Tantalus,* from its nonabsorbent quality.]

Tan·ta·lus (tăn′tə-ləs) *n.* **1.** *Gk. Myth.* A king who for his crimes was condemned in Hades to stand in water that receded when he tried to drink, and with fruit hanging above him that receded when he reached for it. **2. tantalus.** A locked-up stand in which decanters are displayed. [Lat. < Gk. *Tantalos.*]

tan·ta·mount (tăn′tə-mount′) *adj.* Equivalent in effect or value: *a request tantamount to a demand.* [< obs. *tantamount,* an equivalent < AN *tant amunter,* to amount to as much.]

tan·ta·ra (tăn-tăr′ə, -tär′ə) *n.* **1. a.** A trumpet or horn fanfare. **b.** A sound resembling such a fanfare. **2.** A hunting cry. [Imit.]

tan·tiv·y (tăn-tĭv′ē) *adv.* At full gallop; at top speed. *—n., pl.* **-ies. 1.** A hunting cry. **2.** A fast and furious gallop; top speed. [Orig. unknown.]

tan·tra (tŭn′trə) *n.* One of a class of Hindu or Buddhist religious writings concerned with mysticism and magic. [Skt. *tantram* < *tanoti,* he weaves.] **—tan′tric** (-trĭk) *adj.*

tan·trum (tăn′trəm) *n.* A fit of bad temper. [Orig. unknown.]

tan·yard (tăn′yärd′) *n.* The section in a tannery where the tanning vats are located.

tan·zan·ite (tăn′zə-nīt′) *n.* A hydrated calcium aluminum silicate mineral, exhibiting blue, violet, or greenish coloration depending on the polarization of incident light, and used as a gem. [After *Tanzania.*]

Tao·ism (tou′ĭz′əm, dou′-) *n.* A principal philosophy and system of religion of China based upon the teachings of Lao-tse in the 6th century B.C. [< Chin. (Mandarin) *dao*[4], way.] **—Tao′ist** *n.* **—Tao·is′tic** *adj.*

tap[1] (tăp) *v.* **tapped, tap·ping, taps.** *—tr.* **1.** To strike gently with a light blow or blows: *tap him on the shoulder.* **2.** To give a light rap with: *tap a pencil.* **3.** To produce with a succession of light blows: *tap out a rhythm.* **4. a.** To repair (shoe heels or toes) by applying a tap. **b.** To attach metal taps to. *—intr.* **1.** To deliver a gentle, light blow or blows. **2.** To walk making light clicks. *—n.* **1. a.** A gentle blow. **b.** The sound made by such a blow. **2. a.** A thin layer of leather or a substitute applied to a worn-down shoe heel or toe. **b.** A metal plate attached to the toe or heel of a shoe, as for tap-dancing. [ME *tappen,* poss. < OFr. *taper.*]

tap[2] (tăp) *n.* **1.** A valve and spout used to regulate delivery of a fluid at the end of a pipe. **2.** A plug for a bunghole; spigot. **3. a.** Liquor drawn from a tap. **b.** Liquor of a particular brew, cask, or quality. **4.** *Med.* The removal of bodily fluid: *a spinal tap.* **5.** A tool for cutting an internal screw thread. **6.** A makeshift terminal in an electric circuit. *—tr.v.* **tapped, tap·ping, taps. 1.** To furnish with a spigot or tap. **2.** To pierce in order to draw off liquid: *tap a maple tree.* **3.** To draw (liquid) from a vessel or container. **4.** *Med.* To withdraw fluid from (a bodily cavity). **5.** To make a connection with or open outlets from: *tap a water main.* **6. a.** To wiretap (a telephone). **b.** To establish an electric connection in (a power line), as to divert current secretly. **7.** To cut screw threads in (a collar, socket, or other fitting). **8.** *Informal.* To ask (a person) for money. **—*idiom.* on tap. 1.** Ready to be drawn; in a tapped cask: *beer on tap.* **2.** Available for immediate use; ready: *extra personnel on tap.* [ME < OE *tæppa.*]

ta·pa (tä′pə, tăp′ə) *n.* **1.** The inner bark of the paper mulberry. **2.** A paperlike cloth made in the Pacific islands by pounding tapa or similar bark. [Marquesan and Tahitian.]

tap dance *n.* A dance in which the rhythm is sounded out by the clicking heels and toes of a dancer's shoes. **—tap dancer** *n.*

tap-dance (tăp′dăns′) *intr.v.* **-danced, -danc·ing, -danc·es.** To perform a tap dance.

tape (tāp) *n.* **1.** A narrow strip of strong woven fabric, such as that used in sewing or bookbinding. **2.** Any continuous narrow, flexible strip of cloth, metal, paper, or plastic, esp.: **a.** Adhesive tape. **b.** Magnetic tape. **c.** A tape measure. **3.** A string stretched across the finish line of a racetrack to be broken by the winner. **4.** A tape recording. *—v.* **taped, tap·ing, tapes.** *—tr.* **1. a.** To fasten, secure, strengthen, or wrap with a tape. **b.** To bind together (the sections of a book) by applying strips of tape to. **2.** To measure with a tape measure. **3.** To record on magnetic tape. *—intr.* To measure. [ME < OE *tæppe.*]

tape cartridge *n.* **1.** A cartridge containing an endless loop of magnetic tape and designed for automatic use on insertion into a tape recorder or player designed to receive it. **2.** Cassette (sense 2.a.).

tape deck *n.* A tape recorder and player having no built-in amplifiers or speakers, used as a component in a high-fidelity sound system.

tape grass *n.* An aquatic plant, *Vallisneria spiralis,* having long, grasslike, submerged leaves.

tape·line (tāp′līn′) *n.* Tape measure.

tape measure *n.* A tape of cloth, paper, or steel marked off in a linear scale, as inches or centimeters, for taking measurements.

tape player *n.* A self-contained machine for playing back recorded magnetic tapes.

ta·per (tā′pər) *n.* **1.** A small or very slender candle. **2.** A long wax-coated wick used to light candles or gas lamps. **3.** Something that gives off a feeble light. **4.** A gradual decrease in thickness or width of an elongated object. *—v.* **-pered, -per·ing, -pers.** *—intr.* **1.** To become gradually narrower or thinner toward one end. **2.** To become gradually smaller or less; slacken and finally stop: *The storm finally tapered off.* *—tr.* **1.** To make thinner or narrower at one end. **2.** To diminish or make smaller gradually. *—adj.* Gradually decreasing in size toward a point. [ME < OE *tapor,* poss. < Lat. *papyrus,* papyrus.] **—ta′per·ing·ly** *adv.*

tape-re·cord (tāp′rĭ-kôrd′) *tr.v.* **-cord·ed, -cord·ing, -cords.** To record on magnetic tape.

tape recorder *n.* An apparatus used to record sound on magnetic tape and, usually, to play back sound so recorded.

tape recording *n.* **1. a.** Magnetized tape on which sound has been recorded. **b.** The sound recorded on a magnetic tape. **2.** The act of recording on magnetic tape.

tap·es·try (tăp′ĭ-strē) *n., pl.* **-tries. 1.** A heavy cloth woven with rich, often varicolored designs or scenes, usually hung on walls for decoration and sometimes used to cover furniture. **2.** Something resembling a tapestry, as in complexity. *—tr.v.* **-tried, -try·ing, -tries. 1.** To hang or decorate with tapestry. **2.** To make, weave, or depict in a tapestry. [ME *tapstery* < OFr. *tapisserie* < *tappisser,* to cover with carpet < *tapis,* carpet < Gk. *tapēs.*]

ta·pe·tum (tə-pē′təm) *n., pl.* **-ta** (-tə). **1.** *Bot.* A layer of nutritive cells within the sporangium of ferns and related plants or within the anther of seed plants. **2.** *Anat.* A membranous layer or region, esp. in the choroid coat or retina. **3.** A stratum of fibers of the corpus callosum. [NLat. < Lat. *tapete,* carpet < Gk. *tapēs.*]

tape·worm (tāp′wûrm′) *n.* Any of various ribbonlike, often very long flatworms of the class Cestoda, that are parasitic in the intestines of vertebrates, including man.

tap house *n.* A tavern; bar.

tap·i·o·ca (tăp′ē-ō′kə) *n.* A beady starch obtained from the root of the cassava, used for puddings and as a thickening agent in cooking. [Port. and Sp., both < Guarani *tipiog.*]

ta·pir (tā′pər, tə-pîr′) *n.* Any of several ungulate mammals of the genus *Tapirus,* of tropical America or southern Asia, having a heavy body, short legs, and a fleshy proboscis. [NLat. *Tapirus,* genus name < Tupi *tapira,* tapir.]

tap·per (tăp′ər) *n.* One that taps.

tap·pet (tăp′ĭt) *n.* A lever or projecting arm that moves or is moved by contact with another part, usually to communicate a certain motion, as between a driving mechanism and a valve. [< TAP[1].]

tap·ping (tăp′ĭng) *n.* **1.** The act of one that taps. **2.** Something that is taken or drawn by tapping.

tap·pit-hen (tăp′ĭt-hĕn′) *n. Scot.* **1.** A crested hen. **2.** A large mug with a knobbed lid. [Sc. *tappit,* crested + HEN.]

tap·room (tăp′ro͞om′, -ro͝om′) *n.* A bar or barroom.

tap·root (tăp′ro͞ot′, -ro͝ot′) *n.* The main root of a plant, usually stouter than the lateral roots and growing straight downward from the stem.

taps (tăps) *pl.n. (used with a sing. verb).* A military bugle call or a drum signal sounded at night as an order to put out lights, and also sounded at military funerals and memorial services. [Perh. alteration of obs. *taptoo,* tattoo. —see TATTOO (signal).]

tap·ster (tăp′stər) *n.* A person who draws and serves liquor for customers; tavernkeeper or bartender.

Ta·pu·ya (tä-po͞o′yə) *n., pl.* **Tapuya** or **-yas.** A Tapuyan Indian. [Tupi *Tapua.*]

Ta·pu·yan (tä-po͞o′yən) *n.* A South American Indian linguistic stock of Brazil. **—Tapuyan** *adj.*

tar[1] (tär) *n.* **1.** A dark, oily, viscid mixture, consisting mainly of hydrocarbons, produced by the destructive distillation of organic substances such as wood, coal, or peat. **2.** Coal tar. *—tr.v.* **tarred, tar·ring, tars.** To coat with tar. **—*idiom.* tar and feather. 1.** To punish (a person) by covering with tar and feathers. **2.** *Informal.* To criticize severely and devastatingly; excoriate. [ME *taar* < OE *teru.*]

tar[2] (tär) *n. Informal.* A sailor. [Short for TARPAULIN.]

Tar·a·ca·hi·tian (tăr′ə-kə-hē′shən) *adj.* Of, pertaining to, or

constituting a language family of the Uto-Aztecan group. [Blend of *Tarahumara* and *Cahita,* two peoples of Mexico.]
tar·a·did·dle (tăr′ə-dĭd′l). Variant of **tarradiddle.**
tar·an·tel·la (tăr′ən-tĕl′ə) *n.* **1.** A lively, whirling southern Italian dance once thought to be a remedy for tarantism. **2.** The music for this dance, in 6/8 time. [Ital., after *Taranto,* Italy.]
tar·an·tism (tăr′ən-tĭz′əm) *n.* A malady characterized by an uncontrollable urge to dance, epidemic in southern Italy from the 15th to the 17th century and erroneously believed to result from the bite of the tarantula. [After *Taranto,* Italy.]
ta·ran·tu·la (tə-răn′chə-lə) *n., pl.* **-las** or **-lae** (-lē′). **1.** Any of various large, hairy, chiefly tropical spiders of the family Theraphosidae, capable of inflicting a painful but not seriously poisonous bite. **2.** A similar spider, *Lycosa tarentula,* of southern Europe, once thought to cause tarantism. [Med. Lat. < OItal. *tarantola,* after *Taranto,* Italy.]
tar·boosh also **tar·bush** (tär-bo͞osh′) *n.* A brimless, usually red, felt cap with a silk tassel, worn by Moslem men, either by itself or as the base of a turban. [Ar. *ṭarbūsh.*]
tar camphor *n.* Naphthalene.
tar·di·grade (tär′dĭ-grād′) *n.* Any of various minute, slow-moving arthropods of the class Tardigrada, having eight legs and living in water or damp moss. —*adj.* **1.** Of or belonging to the Tardigrada. **2.** Slow in action; slow-moving. [NLat. *Tardigrada,* class name < Lat. *tardigradus,* slow-moving : *tardus,* slow + *gradi,* to go.]

tarboosh

tar·dy (tär′dē) *adj.* **-di·er, -di·est. 1.** Occurring, arriving, or acting later than expected or scheduled; delayed; late. **2.** Moving slowly; sluggish. [ME *tardyve,* slow < OFr. *tardif* < Lat. *tardus.*] —**tar′di·ly** *adv.* —**tar′di·ness** *n.*
Synonyms: *tardy, late, overdue, dilatory, lagging.* These adjectives mean not arriving, occurring, or acting within a prescribed time. *Tardy* refers principally to persons who arrive after an appointed time, whereas *late* can apply also to the arrival or occurrence of things after a due or usual time. *Overdue,* applicable to persons and things, implies a marked violation of a scheduled time. *Dilatory* describes the habits or actions of persons who delay doing what should be done promptly. *Lagging* refers principally to persons or their actions or development and implies failure to maintain a schedule or standard of achievement.

tarot

tare[1] (târ) *n.* **1.** The common vetch, *Vicia sativa.* **2.** Any of several weedy plants that grow in grain fields. **3. tares.** An undesirable element. [ME.]
tare[2] (târ) *n.* **1.** The weight of a container or wrapper that is deducted from the gross weight to obtain net weight. **2.** A deduction from gross weight made to allow for the weight of a container. **3.** *Chem.* A counterbalance, esp. an empty vessel used to counterbalance the weight of a similar container. —*tr.v.* **tared, tar·ing, tares.** To determine, allow for, or indicate the tare. [ME < OFr. < OSp. *tara* < Ar. *ṭarḥah,* that which is thrown away < *ṭaraḥa,* to reject.]
targe (tärj) *n. Archaic.* A light shield or buckler. [ME < OFr. —see TARGET.]
tar·get (tär′gĭt) *n.* **1.** An object, as a padded disc, with a marked surface, that is shot at to test accuracy in rifle or archery practice. **2.** Anything aimed or fired at. **3. a.** An object of criticism or attack. **b.** Something considered as an object to be acted on with a view to transforming it. **4.** A desired goal. **5.** A railroad signal that indicates the position of a switch by its color, position, and shape. **6.** The sliding sight on a surveyor's leveling rod. **7.** A small, round shield. **8. a.** A structure in a camera tube with a storage surface that is scanned by an electron beam to generate a signal output current similar to the charge-density pattern stored on the surface. **b.** A usually metal part in an x-ray tube on which a beam of electrons is focused and from which x-rays are emitted. —*tr.v.* **-get·ed, -get·ing, -gets. 1.** To make a target of. **2.** To aim at or for. **3.** To establish as a target or goal. [ME, small targe < OFr. *targette,* dim. of *targe,* light shield, of Germanic orig.]
target date *n.* A date established as a target or goal, as for the completion of a project.
Tar·gum (tär′go͝om′, -go͞om′) *n.* Any of several Aramaic translations or paraphrasings of the Old Testament. [Heb. *targūm,* interpretation < *targēm,* to interpret.]
Tar Heel or **Tar·heel** (tär′hēl′) *n.* A native or resident of North Carolina.
tar·iff (tăr′ĭf) *n.* **1.** A list or system of duties imposed by a government on imported or exported goods. **2.** A duty or duties imposed by a government on imported or exported goods. **3.** Any schedule of prices or fees. —*tr.v.* **-iffed, -iff·ing, -iffs.** To fix a duty or price on. [Ital. *tariffa* < Ar. *ta'rīf,* notification < *'arafa,* to make known.]
tar·la·tan also **tar·le·tan** (tär′lə-tən) *n.* A thin, stiffly starched open-weave muslin. [Fr. *tarlatane.*]
tar·mac (tär′măk′) *n.* **1.** A bituminous substance used as a binder in paving. **2.** A tarmacadam road or pavement. [Orig. a trademark.]
tar·mac·ad·am (tär′mə-kăd′əm) *n.* A pavement consisting of layers of crushed stone with a tar binder pressed to a smooth surface.
tarn (tärn) *n.* A small mountain lake. [ME *tarne,* of Scand. orig.]

tartan[1]

tar·nal (tär′nəl) *adj. & adv. Regional.* Damned. [Alteration of ETERNAL.] —**tar′nal·ly** *adv.*
tar·na·tion (tär-nā′shən) *n. & interj. Regional.* Damnation.
tar·nish (tär′nĭsh) *v.* **-nished, -nish·ing, -nish·es.** —*tr.* **1.** To dull the luster of; discolor, esp. by exposure to air or dirt. **2.** To detract from or spoil; taint: *tarnished her reputation.* —*intr.* **1.** To lose luster; become discolored. **2.** To diminish or become tainted. —*n.* **1.** The condition of being tarnished. **2.** A changed or discolored luster. **3.** The condition of being spoiled or tainted; besmirchment. [OFr. *ternir, terniss-,* to dull.] —**tar′nish·a·ble** *adj.*
ta·ro (tär′ō, tăr′ō) *n., pl.* **-ros. 1.** A widely cultivated tropical plant, *Colocasia esculenta,* having broad leaves and a large, starchy, edible rootstock. **2.** The rootstock of the taro. [Of Polynesian orig.]
tar·ok also **tar·oc** (tăr′ək) *n.* A card game developed in Italy in the 14th century, played with a 78-card pack consisting of four suits plus the 22 tarot cards as trumps. [Ital. *tarrochi,* pl. of *tarocco,* tarot.]
tar·ot (tăr′ō) *n.* **1.** Any of a set of 22 playing cards consisting of a joker plus 21 cards depicting vices, virtues, and elemental forces, used in fortunetelling and as trump in tarok games. **2. tarots.** Tarok. [OFr. < OItal. *tarocco.*]
tarp (tärp) *n.* A tarpaulin. [Short for TARPAULIN.]
tar·pa·per (tär′pā′pər) *n.* Heavy paper impregnated or coated with tar, used as a waterproof protective material in building.
tar·pau·lin (tär-pô′lĭn, tär′pə-lĭn) *n.* **1.** Waterproof material, as canvas, used to cover and protect things from moisture. **2.** A sheet of tarpaulin. [Obs. *tarpawling* : TAR[1] + PALL[1].]
tar·pon (tär′pən) *n., pl.* **tarpon** or **-pons.** Any of several fishes of the family Elopidae or Megalopidae, esp. a large, silvery game fish, *Megalops atlantica,* of Atlantic coastal waters. [Orig. unknown.]
tar·ra·did·dle also **tar·a·did·dle** (tăr′ə-dĭd′l) *n. Informal.* A petty falsehood; fib. [Orig. unknown.]
tar·ra·gon (tăr′ə-gŏn′, -gən) *n.* **1.** An aromatic herb, *Artemisia dracunculus,* native to Eurasia. **2.** The leaves of the tarragon, used as seasoning. [Med. Lat. *tragonia* < Med. Gk. *tarkhōn,* prob. < Ar. *ṭarkhūn.*]
tar·ri·ance (tăr′ē-əns) *n. Archaic.* **1.** The act of tarrying. **2.** A temporary stay; sojourn.
tar·ry[1] (tăr′ē) *v.* **-ried, -ry·ing, -ries.** —*intr.* **1.** To delay or be late in going or coming; linger. **2.** To wait. **3.** To remain or stay temporarily, as in a place; sojourn. —*tr. Archaic.* To await. —*n.* A temporary stay; a sojourn. [ME *tarien.*] —**tar′ri·er** *n.*
tar·ry[2] (tär′ē) *adj.* **-ri·er, -ri·est.** Of, like, or covered with tar.
tar·sal (tär′səl) *adj.* **1.** Of, pertaining to, or situated near the tarsus of the foot. **2.** Of or pertaining to the tarsus of the eyelid. [NLat. *tarsalis* < Gk. *tarsos,* ankle.]
tarsal gland *n.* Any of the branched sebaceous glands located in the tarsus of the eyelid.
tarsal plate *n.* Tarsus (sense 2).
tar·si (tär′sī′) *n.* Plural of **tarsus.**
tar·si·er (tär′sē-ər, -sē-ā′) *n.* Any of several small nocturnal primates of the genus *Tarsius,* of the East Indies, having large, round eyes and a long tail. [Fr. < *tarse,* tarsus < NLat. *tarsus.*]
tar·so·met·a·tar·sus (tär′sō-mĕt′ə-tär′səs) *n., pl.* **-si** (-sī′). A compound bone between the tibia and the toes of a bird's leg, formed by fusion of the tarsal and metatarsal bones.
tar·sus (tär′səs) *n., pl.* **-si** (-sī′). **1. a.** The section of the vertebrate foot between the leg and the metatarsus. **b.** The seven bones making up this section. **2.** A fibrous plate that supports and shapes the edge of the eyelid. **3.** *Zool.* **a.** The tarsometatarsus. **b.** The distal segmented structure on the leg of an insect or an arachnid. [NLat. < Gk. *tarsos,* ankle.]
tart[1] (tärt) *adj.* **-er, -est. 1.** Having a sharp, pungent taste; sour. **2.** Sharp or bitter in tone or meaning; cutting. [ME < OE *teart,* severe.] —**tart′ly** *adv.* —**tart′ness** *n.*
tart[2] (tärt) *n.* **1.** A small open pie with a sweet filling. **2.** A loose woman; prostitute. —***phrasal verb.* tart up.** *Chiefly Brit.* To dress up or make fancy in a tawdry, garish way. [ME *tarte* < OFr.]
tar·tan[1] (tär′tn) *n.* **1. a.** Any of numerous textile patterns consisting of stripes of varying widths and colors crossed at right angles against a solid background, each forming a distinctive design worn by the members of a Scottish clan. **b.** A twilled wool fabric or garment having such a pattern. **2.** Any plaid fabric. [Poss. < OFr. *tertaine,* linsey-woolsey.] —**tar′tan** *adj.*
tar·tan[2] (tär′tn, tär-tăn′) *n.* A small, single-masted Mediterranean ship with a large lateen sail. [Fr. *tartane* < OItal. *tatana.*]
tar·tar (tär′tər) *n.* **1.** A reddish acid compound, chiefly potassium bitartrate, found in the juice of grapes and deposited on the sides of casks during wine-making. **2.** A hard, yellowish deposit on the teeth, consisting of organic secretions and food particles deposited in various salts, such as calcium carbonate. [ME *tartre* < OFr. < Med. Lat. *tartarum* < Med. Gk. *tartaron.*]
Tar·tar (tär′tər) also **Ta·tar** (tä′tər) *n.* **1.** A member of any of the Mongolian peoples of central Asia who invaded western Asia and eastern Europe in the 13th century. **2.** A descendant of these Mongolian peoples. **3.** Often **tartar** or **tatar.** A

ferocious or violent person. **4.** Any of the Turkic languages of the Tartars. ***—idiom.* catch a Tartar.** To grapple with an unexpectedly formidable opponent. [ME *Tartre* < OFr. *Tartare* < Med. Lat. *Tartarus,* alteration of Pers. *Tātār,* of Turkic orig.]
tartar emetic *n.* A poisonous crystalline compound, $KSbOC_4H_4O_6 \cdot 1/2H_2O$, used in the medical treatment of amoebiasis.
tar·tar·e·ous (tär-târ′ē-əs) *adj.* Consisting of or similar to tartar.
tar·tare steak (tär′tər) *n.* Steak tartare.
tar·tar·ic (tär-tăr′ĭk) *adj.* Of, relating to, or derived from tartar or tartaric acid.
tartaric acid *n.* Any of four isomeric crystalline organic compounds, $C_4H_6O_6$, used to make cream of tartar, as a sequestrant, in tanning, and in effervescent beverages, baking powders, and photographic chemicals.
tar·tar·ize (tär′tə-rīz′) *tr.v.* **-ized, -iz·ing, -iz·es.** To treat, impregnate, or combine with tartar, tartar emetic, or cream of tartar. **—tar′tar·i·za′tion** *n.*
tar·tar·ous (tär′tər-əs) *adj.* Consisting of, derived from, or containing tartar.
tar·tar sauce also **tar·tare sauce** (tär′tər) *n.* Mayonnaise mixed with chopped onion, olives, pickles, and capers and served as a sauce with fish.
Tar·ta·rus (tär′tər-əs) *n.* **1.** *Gk. Myth.* The abysmal regions below Hades where the Titans were confined. **2.** An infernal region; hell. [Lat. < Gk. *Tartaros.*] **—Tar·tar′e·an** (-târ′ē-ən) *adj.*
tar·trate (tär′trāt′) *n.* A salt or ester of tartaric acid.
tar·trat·ed (tär′trā′tĭd) *adj.* Containing, combined with, or derived from tartaric acid.
tar·tuffe also **tar·tufe** (tär-to͝of′, -to͞of′) *n.* A hypocrite, esp. one who affects religious piety. [After the protagonist of *Tartuffe,* a play by Molière (1622–1673).]
tar·weed (tär′wēd′) *n.* **1.** Any of several strong-smelling, resinous western American plants of the genus *Madia,* having yellow, rayed flowers. **2.** Any of several plants similar to or related to the tarweed.
task (tăsk) *n.* **1.** A piece of work assigned or done as part of one's duties. **2.** A difficult or tedious undertaking. **3.** A function to be performed; objective. *—tr.v.* **tasked, task·ing, tasks. 1.** To assign a task to or impose a task upon. **2.** To overburden with labor; tax. ***—idiom.* take to task.** To reprimand or censure. [ME *taske,* imposed work < ONFr. *tasque* < Med. Lat. *tasca* < *taxare,* to tax.]

Synonyms: *task, job, chore, stint, assignment.* These nouns refer to work considered as a specific individual undertaking. *Task* applies to a well-defined piece of work that is often imposed, of short duration, and burdensome. *Job* can refer to virtually any work, including one's regular full-time employment; in this comparison it suggests a specific short-term undertaking. *Chore* generally denotes a small, routine, or odd job; sometimes the word is applied to a specific arduous task. *Stint* usually refers to temporary work, either voluntary or one's prescribed share in a larger enterprise. *Assignment* generally denotes clearly defined short-term work given to one person or persons by another who is in authority.

task force *n.* A temporary grouping of forces and resources, esp. of military units, for the accomplishment of a specific objective.
task·mas·ter (tăsk′măs′tər) *n.* One who imposes work, esp. heavy work.
Tas·ma·ni·an devil (tăz-mā′nē-ən, -mān′yən) *n.* A burrowing carnivorous marsupial, *Sarcophilus harrisii,* of Tasmania, having a predominantly blackish coat and a long, almost hairless tail.
Tasmanian wolf *n.* The thylacine.
tasse (tăs) also **tas·set** (tăs′ĭt) *n.* One of a series of jointed overlapping metal splints hanging from the corselet, used as armor for the lower trunk and thighs. [Poss. < OFr., pouch.]
tas·sel (tăs′əl) *n.* **1.** A bunch of loose threads or cords bound at one end and hanging free at the other, used as an ornament, as on curtains or clothing. **2.** Something (such as the pollen-bearing inflorescence of a corn plant) that resembles a tassel. *—v.* **-seled, -sel·ing, -sels** or **-selled, -sel·ling, -sels.** *—tr.* To fringe or decorate with tassels. *—intr.* To put forth a tassellike inflorescence. Used esp. of corn. [ME < OFr. < VLat. **tascellus* < Lat. *taxillus,* small die.]
tas·set (tăs′ĭt) *n.* Variant of **tasse.**
taste (tāst) *v.* **tast·ed, tast·ing, tastes.** *—tr.* **1.** To distinguish the flavor of by taking into the mouth. **2.** To eat or drink a small quantity of. **3.** To experience or partake of, esp. for the first time: *finally tasted real success.* **4.** *Archaic.* To appreciate; enjoy. *—intr.* **1.** To distinguish flavors in the mouth. **2.** To have a distinct flavor: *The stew tastes salty.* **3.** To eat or drink a small amount. **4.** To have an experience; partake. *—n.* **1. a.** The sense that distinguishes the sweet, sour, salty, and bitter qualities of dissolved substances in contact with the taste buds on the tongue. **b.** This sense in combination with the senses of smell and touch, which together receive a sensation of a substance in the mouth. **2. a.** The sensation of sweet, sour, salty, or bitter qualities produced by or as if by a substance placed in the mouth. **b.** The unified sensation produced by any of these qualities plus a distinct smell and texture; flavor. **3.** The act of tasting. **4.** A small quantity eaten or tasted. **5.** A limited or first experience; sample: *"Thousands entered the war, got just a taste of it, and then stepped out"* (Mark Twain). **6.** A personal preference or liking for something: *a taste for adventure.* **7. a.** The faculty of discerning what is aesthetically excellent or appropriate. **b.** A manner indicative of the quality of such discernment: *furnished with superb taste.* **8. a.** The sense of what is proper, seemly, or least likely to give offense in a given social situation. **b.** A manner indicative of the quality of this sense. **9.** *Obs.* The act of testing; trial. [ME *tasten* < OFr. *taster* < VLat. **taxitare,* freq. of Lat. *taxare,* to touch.] **—tast′a·ble** *adj.*
taste bud *n.* Any of numerous spherical or ovoid nests of cells that are distributed over the tongue and embedded in the epithelium, consisting of gustatory cells and supporting cells and constituting the end organs of the sense of taste.
taste·ful (tāst′fəl) *adj.* **1.** Exhibiting good taste. **2.** Tasty. **—taste′ful·ly** *adv.* **—taste′ful·ness** *n.*
taste·less (tāst′lĭs) *adj.* **1.** Lacking flavor; insipid. **2.** Exhibiting poor taste. **—taste′less·ly** *adv.* **—taste′less·ness** *n.*
tast·er (tā′stər) *n.* **1.** One who tastes, esp. a person who samples a food or beverage for quality. **2.** Any of several devices or implements used in tasting.
tast·y (tā′stē) *adj.* **-i·er, -i·est. 1.** Having a pleasing flavor; savory. **2.** Having good taste; tasteful. **—tast′i·ly** *adv.* **—tast′i·ness** *n.*
tat (tăt) *intr. & tr.v.* **tat·ted, tat·ting, tats.** To make or produce by tatting. [Prob. back-formation < TATTING.] **—tat′ter** *n.*
ta·ta·mi (tä-tä′mē, tə-) *n.* Straw matting used as a covering for the floor esp. in Japan. [J.]
Ta·tar (tä′tər) *n.* Variant of **Tartar.**
ta·ter (tā′tər) *n. Regional.* A potato. [Shortening and alteration of POTATO.]
tat·ter (tăt′ər) *n.* **1.** A torn and hanging piece of cloth; shred. **2. tatters.** Torn and ragged clothing; rags. *—tr. & intr.v.* **-tered, -ter·ing, -ters.** To make or become ragged. [ME *tater,* of Scand. orig.]
tat·ter·de·mal·ion (tăt′ər-dĭ-māl′yən, -mā′lē-ən) *n.* A person wearing ragged or tattered clothing; ragamuffin. *—adj.* Ragged; tattered. [Orig. unknown.]
tat·tered (tăt′ərd) *adj.* **1.** Torn into shreds or tatters; ragged. **2.** Having ragged clothes; dressed in tatters.
tat·ter·sall also **Tat·ter·sall** (tăt′ər-sôl′, -səl). *—adj.* Having a pattern of dark lines forming squares on a solid, generally light background. *—n.* **1.** A pattern of dark lines forming squares on a light background. **2.** Cloth woven with this pattern. [After *Tattersall's* horse market, London, England.]
tat·ting (tăt′ĭng) *n.* **1.** Handmade lace fashioned by looping and knotting a single strand of heavy-duty thread on a small hand shuttle. **2.** The act or art of making tatting. [Orig. unknown.]
tat·tle (tăt′l) *v.* **-tled, -tling, -tles.** *—intr.* **1.** To reveal the plans or activities of another; gossip. **2.** To chatter aimlessly; prate. *—tr.* To reveal through gossiping. *—n.* **1.** Aimless chatter; prattle. **2.** Gossip; talebearing. **3.** A tattletale. [ME *tattlen,* to stammer, of Flem. orig.] **—tat′tling·ly** *adv.*
tat·tler (tăt′lər) *n.* **1.** A person who tattles. **2.** Any of several shore birds related to and resembling the sandpipers, esp. one of the genus *Heteroscelus,* of coastal areas of the Pacific.
tat·tle·tale (tăt′l-tāl′) *n.* A person who tattles on others; informer; talebearer. *—adj.* Revealing; telltale.
tat·too[1] (tă-to͞o′) *n., pl.* **-toos. 1.** A signal sounded on a drum or bugle to summon soldiers or sailors to their quarters at night. **2.** A display of military exercises offered as evening entertainment. **3.** A continuous even drumming or rapping. *—v.* **-tooed, -too·ing, -toos.** *—intr.* To beat out an even rhythm, as with the fingers. *—tr.* To beat or tap rhythmically on; rap or drum on. [Obs. *taptoo* < Du. *taptoe* : *tap,* spigot, tap + *toe,* to shut.] **—tat·too′er** *n.*
tat·too[2] (tă-to͞o′) *n., pl.* **-toos.** A permanent mark or design made on the skin by a process of pricking and ingraining an indelible pigment or by raising scars. *—tr.v.* **-tooed, -too·ing, -toos. 1.** To mark (the skin) with a tattoo. **2.** To form (a tattoo) on the skin. [Of Polynesian orig.] **—tat·too′er** *n.*
tat·ty (tăt′ē) *adj.* **-ti·er, -ti·est.** Shabby; frayed. [Orig. unknown.]
tau (tou, tô) *n.* The 19th letter of the Greek alphabet. See table at **alphabet.** [Gk., of Phoenician orig.; akin to Heb. *tāw,* tav.]
tau cross *n.* A cross in the form of a T.
taught (tôt) *v.* Past tense and past participle of **teach.**
taunt[1] (tônt) *tr.v.* **taunt·ed, taunt·ing, taunts. 1.** To deride or reproach with contempt; mock; jeer at. **2.** To drive or incite (a person) by taunting. *—n.* A scornful remark or tirade; jeer. [Prob. < OFr. *tant pour tant,* so much for so much.] **—taunt′er** *n.* **—taunt′ing·ly** *adv.*
taunt[2] (tônt) *adj.* Unusually tall. Used of masts. [Orig. unknown.]
taupe (tōp) *n.* Brownish gray to dark yellowish brown. [Fr., mole < Lat. *talpa.*] **—taupe** *adj.*
tau·rine[1] (tôr′īn′) *adj.* Of or relating to a bull. [Lat. *taurinus* < *taurus,* bull < Gk. *tauros.*]
tau·rine[2] (tôr′ēn′) *n.* A crystalline amino acid, $C_2H_7NO_3S$, found in bile. [Gk. *tauros,* bull (from having been obtained first from ox bile) + -INE.]

tassel

tatting
Tatting with two colors requiring two shuttles

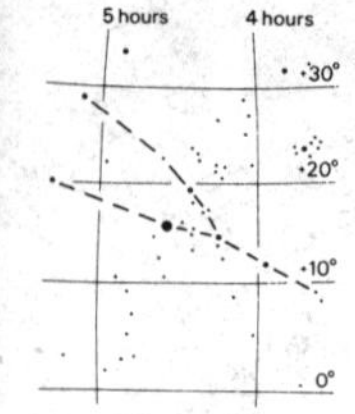

Taurus

tau·ro·cho·lic acid (tôr′ō-kō′lĭk, -kŏl′ĭk) *n.* A crystalline acid, $C_{26}H_{45}NO_7S$, occurring as a constituent of bile. [Gk. *tauros,* bull (from having been obtained first from ox bile) + CHOLIC ACID.]

Tau·rus (tôr′əs) *n.* **1.** A constellation in the Northern Hemisphere near Orion and Aries. **2.** The second sign of the zodiac. [ME < Lat., bull < Gk. *tauros.*]

taut (tôt) *adj.* **-er, -est. 1.** Pulled or drawn tight; not slack. **2.** Strained; tense. **3.** Kept in trim shape; neat; tidy. [ME *toght,* distended.] **—taut′ly** *adv.* **—taut′ness** *n.*

Usage: In nautical usage *taut* and *tight* are used interchangeably to describe a ship on which strict discipline is maintained.

taut– *pref.* Variant of **tauto-.**

taut·en (tôt′n) *tr. & intr.v.* **-ened, -en·ing, -ens.** To make or become taut.

tauto– or **taut–** *pref.* Same; identical: *tautomerism.* [< Gk. *tauto,* the same, contraction of *to auto.*]

tau·tog also **tau·taug** (tô′tôg′, -tŏg′, tô-tôg′, -tŏg′) *n.* A dark-colored, edible marine fish, *Tautoga onitis,* of the North American Atlantic coast. [Narraganset *tautauog,* plural of *taut.*]

tau·tol·o·gize (tô-tŏl′ə-jīz′) *intr.v.* **-gized, -giz·ing, -giz·es.** To use tautology. **—tau·tol′o·gist** *n.*

tau·tol·o·gy (tô-tŏl′ə-jē) *n., pl.* **-gies. 1. a.** Needless repetition of the same sense in different words; redundancy. **b.** An instance of such repetition. **2.** *Logic.* A statement composed of simpler statements in a fashion that makes it true whether the simpler statements are true or false; for example, *Either it will rain tomorrow or it will not rain tomorrow.* [LLat. *tautologia* < Gk. < *tautologos,* redundant : *tauto,* the same + *logos,* saying.] **—tau′to·log′i·cal** (tô′tə-lŏj′ĭ-kəl), **tau′to·log′ic** *adj.* **—tau′to·log′i·cal·ly** *adv.*

tau·tom·er·ism (tô-tŏm′ə-rĭz′əm) *n.* Chemical isomerism characterized by relatively easy interconversion of isomeric forms in equilibrium. [TAUTO- + (ISO)MERISM.] **—tau′to·mer** (tô′tə-mər) *n.* **—tau′to·mer′ic** (tô′tə-mĕr′ĭk) *adj.*

tau·to·nym (tô′tə-nĭm′) *n.* A taxonomic designation, such as *Gorilla gorilla,* commonly used in zoology but no longer in botany, in which the genus and species names are the same. **—tau′to·nym′ic, tau·ton′y·mous** (tô-tŏn′ə-məs) *adj.* **—tau·ton′y·my** *n.*

tav also **taw** (täf, tôf) *n.* The 23rd letter of the Hebrew alphabet. See table at **alphabet.** [Heb. *tāw.*]

tav·ern (tăv′ərn) *n.* **1.** An establishment licensed to sell liquor and beer to be drunk on the premises. **2.** An inn for travelers. [ME *taverne* < OFr. < Lat. *taberna.*]

taw¹ (tô) *tr.v.* **tawed, taw·ing, taws.** To convert (skin) into white leather by mineral tanning, as with alum and salt. [ME *tawen* < OE *tawian.*] **—taw′er** *n.*

taw² (tô) *Games.* *—n.* **1.** A large, fancy marble used for shooting. **2.** The line from which a player shoots in marbles. **3.** A game of marbles. *—intr.v.* **tawed, taw·ing, taws.** To shoot a marble. [Orig. unknown.]

taw³ (tô) *n.* Variant of **tav.**

taw·dry (tô′drē) *adj.* **-dri·er, -dri·est.** Gaudy and cheap in nature or appearance. *—n.* Vulgarly ornamental finery. [< *tawdry lace,* lace necktie, after *St. Audrey* (d. 679).] **—taw′dri·ly** *adv.* **—taw′dri·ness** *n.*

taw·ny (tô′nē) *n.* Light brown to brownish orange. [ME < AN *tauné* < OFr. *tane* < *tan,* tan < Med. Lat. *tannum,* tanbark, prob. of Celt. orig.] **—taw′ny** *adj.*

tax (tăks) *n.* **1.** A contribution for the support of a government required of persons, groups, or businesses within the domain of that government. **2.** A fee or due levied on the members of an organization to meet its expenses. **3.** A burdensome or excessive demand; strain. *—tr.v.* **taxed, tax·ing, tax·es. 1.** To place a tax on (income, property, or goods). **2.** To exact a tax from. **3.** *Law.* To assess (court costs, for example). **4.** To make difficult or excessive demands upon. **5.** To make a charge against; accuse: *He was taxed with failure to appear on the day appointed.* [< ME *taxen,* to tax < OFr. *taxer* < Med. Lat. *taxare* < Lat., to handle, freq. of *tangere,* to touch.] **—tax′a·bil′i·ty, tax′a·ble·ness** *n.* **—tax′a·ble** *adj.* **—tax′er** *n.*

tax– *pref.* Variant of **taxo-.**

ta·xa (tăk′sə) *n.* Plural of **taxon.**

tax·a·tion (tăk-sā′shən) *n.* **1. a.** The act or practice of imposing taxes. **b.** The fact of being taxed. **2.** An assessed amount of tax.

tax-de·duct·i·ble (tăks′dĭ-dŭk′tə-bəl) *adj.* Exempt from inclusion in one's taxable income.

tax·eme (tăk′sēm′) *n.* A minimal linguistic feature, as the order or stress of words in a compound or phonemes in a word. [TAX- + (PHON)EME.]

tax evasion *n.* Intentional avoidance of tax payment usually by inaccurately declaring taxable income.

tax-ex·empt (tăks′ĭg-zĕmpt′) *adj.* Not subject to taxation, as the capital or income of a philanthropic organization.

tax·i (tăk′sē) *n., pl.* **-is** or **-ies.** A taxicab. *—v.* **tax·ied, taxi·ing** or **taxy·ing, tax·ies** or **tax·is.** *—intr.* **1.** To be transported by taxi. **2.** To move slowly on the ground or on the surface of the water before takeoff or after landing. *—tr.* To cause (an airplane) to taxi. [Short for TAXICAB.]

teapot

taxi– *pref.* Variant of **taxo-.**

tax·i·cab (tăk′sē-kăb′) *n.* An automobile that carries passengers for a fare, usually calculated by a taximeter. [TAXI(METER) + CAB.]

taxi dancer *n.* A girl employed, as by a dance hall or nightclub, to dance with the patrons for a fee.

tax·i·der·my (tăk′sĭ-dûr′mē) *n.* The art or operation of preparing, stuffing, and mounting the skins of dead animals for exhibition in a lifelike state. **—tax′i·der′mal, tax′i·der′mic** *adj.* **—tax′i·der′mist** *n.*

tax·i·me·ter (tăk′sē-mē′tər) *n.* An instrument installed in a taxicab to measure distance traveled and waiting time and to compute and indicate the fare. [Fr. *taximètre* : *taxe,* charge (< OFr. *taxer,* to tax) + *-metre,* -meter.]

tax·ing (tăk′sĭng) *adj.* Burdensome; wearing.

tax·is (tăk′sĭs) *n., pl.* **tax·es** (tăk′sēz′). **1.** *Biol.* The responsive movement of an organism toward or away from an external stimulus. **2.** The moving of an organ, as in a dislocation or hernia protrusion, into normal position by manipulation. [Gk., arrangement < *tattein,* to arrange.]

–taxis *suff.* **1.** Order; arrangement: *homotaxis.* **2.** Taxis; responsive movement: *chemotaxis.* [< Gk. *taxis,* arrangement < *tattein,* to arrange.]

taxi stand *n.* A reserved area where taxicabs park while waiting to be hired.

taxo– or **taxi–** or **tax–** *pref.* Order; arrangement: *taxidermy.* [< Gk. *taxis,* arrangement < *tattein,* to arrange.]

tax·on (tăk′sŏn′) *n., pl.* **ta·xa** (tăk′sə). *Biol.* A group of organisms constituting one of the categories or formal units in taxonomic classification, such as a phylum, order, family, genus, or species, and characterized by common characteristics in varying degrees of distinction. [NLat., back-formation < TAXONOMY.]

tax·on·o·my (tăk-sŏn′ə-mē) *n.* **1.** The science, laws, or principles of classification. **2.** *Biol.* The theory, principles, and process of classifying organisms in established categories. [Fr. *taxonomie* : Gk. *taxis,* arrangement + *-nomie,* -nomy.] **—tax′o·nom′ic** (tăk′sə-nŏm′ĭk), **tax′o·nom′i·cal** *adj.* **—tax′o·nom′i·cal·ly** *adv.* **—tax·on′o·mist** *n.*

tax·pay·er (tăks′pā′ər) *n.* One that pays taxes.

tax shelter *n.* A financial operation, such as the use of special depletion allowances, that reduces taxes on current earnings. **—tax′-shel′tered** *adj.*

–taxy *suff.* -taxis: *anthotaxy.* [Gk. *-taxia* < *tattein,* to arrange.]

Ta·yg·e·ta (tā-ĭj′ĭ-tə) *n.* **1.** *Gk. Myth.* One of the Pleiades, the seven daughters of Atlas. **2.** One of the six visible stars in the Pleiades cluster. [Lat. *Taygete* < Gk. *Taugetē.*]

Tay-Sachs disease (tā′săks′) *n.* A hereditary disease in which the absence of a specific enzyme causes the accumulation of certain lipids in nerve and brain cells resulting in mental retardation, convulsions, blindness, and, ultimately, death. [After Warren *Tay* (1843–1927) and Bernard *Sachs* (1858–1944).]

Tb The symbol for the element terbium.

T-bar lift (tē′bär′) *n.* A ski lift consisting of a bar suspended like an inverted T against which skiers lean while being towed uphill.

T-bone (tē′bōn′) *n.* A thick porterhouse steak taken from the small end of the loin and containing a T-shaped bone.

Tc The symbol for the element technetium.

T cell *n.* A lymphocyte influenced by the thymus that functions in the defense against intracellular pathogens such as viruses and tubercle bacilli.

Te The symbol for the element tellurium.

tea (tē) *n.* **1.** A shrub, *Thea sinensis* or *Camellia sinensis,* of eastern Asia, having fragrant white flowers and evergreen leaves. **2.** The dried leaves of the tea plant, prepared by various processes and in various stages of growth, and used to make a hot beverage. **3.** An aromatic, slightly bitter beverage made by steeping tea leaves in boiling water. **4.** Any of various beverages made, as by steeping the leaves of certain plants or by extracting an infusion esp. from beef. **5.** Any of various plants having leaves used to make a tea-like infusion. **6. a.** *Chiefly Brit.* An afternoon refreshment consisting usually of sandwiches and cakes served with tea. **b.** A social gathering at which tea is taken. **7.** *Chiefly Brit.* High tea. **8.** *Slang.* Marijuana. [Du. *thee* < Malay *teh* < Chin. (Amoy) *te.*]

tea bag *n.* A small porous sack holding sufficient tea leaves to make an individual serving of tea.

tea ball *n.* A small perforated metal ball for holding tea leaves that are to be steeped in hot water.

tea·ber·ry (tē′bĕr′ē) *n., pl.* **-ries.** Wintergreen.

tea biscuit *n.* Any of various plain cookies or biscuits often served with tea.

tea·cart (tē′kärt′) *n.* A tea wagon.

teach (tēch) *v.* **taught** (tôt), **teach·ing, teach·es.** *—tr.* **1.** To impart knowledge or skill to; give instruction to. **2.** To provide knowledge of; instruct in. **3.** To cause to learn by example or experience: *Her rebuff taught him never to ask again.* **4.** To advocate; preach. *—intr.* To give instruction, esp. as an occupation. [ME *techen* < OE *tǣcan.*]

Synonyms: *teach, instruct, educate, tutor, train, school, discipline, drill.* These verbs mean to impart knowledge or skill. *Teach* is the most widely applicable since it can refer to any such act of communicating. *Instruct* usually suggests methodical direction in a specific subject or area. *Educate* is comprehensive and implies a wide area of learning, achieved either by experience or, more often, by formal instruction in many subjects. *Tutor* usually refers to private instruction of one student or a small group. *Train* generally implies concentration on particular skills intended to fit a person, or sometimes an animal, for a desired role. *School* and *discipline* now usually refer to training in modes of behavior. *School* often implies indoctrination, not necessarily in an unfavorable sense, and an arduous learning process. *Discipline* usually refers to teaching of control, especially self-control. *Drill* implies rigorous instruction or training, often by repetition of a routine.

Usage: Some grammarians have objected to the use of *teach* as a transitive verb when its object denotes an institution of learning, as in *Kim teaches grade school.* This usage has wide currency at all levels, however, and is supported by the analogy to phrases like *grade-school teacher.* It should be regarded as entirely correct.

teach·a·ble (tē′chə-bəl) *adj.* **1.** Capable of being taught. **2.** Receptive to learning. **—teach′a·bil′i·ty, teach′a·ble·ness** *n.* **—teach′a·bly** *adv.*

teach·er (tē′chər) *n.* One who teaches, esp. a person hired to teach.

teachers college also **teachers' college** *n.* A college with a special curriculum for training teachers.

teacher's pet *n.* **1.** A student in special favor with a teacher. **2.** One who has gained favor with an authority.

teach-in (tēch′ĭn′) *n.* An extended session, as on a college or university campus, for lectures and discussions on an important and usually controversial issue.

teach·ing (tē′chĭng) *n.* **1.** The work or occupation of teachers. **2.** A precept or doctrine.

teaching fellow *n.* A graduate student in a university or college who is awarded a fellowship that provides him or her with financial aid in exchange for teaching duties. **—teaching fellowship** *n.*

teaching hospital *n.* A hospital that is closely associated with a medical school and that serves as a practical educational setting for medical students, interns, and residents.

teaching machine *n.* Any of various devices designed to teach by presenting the student with a planned sequence of statements and questions and providing an immediate response to his answers.

tea·cup (tē′kŭp′) *n.* A small cup for serving tea.

tea·cup·ful (tē′kŭp′fo͝ol′) *n., pl.* **-fuls.** The amount that a teacup will hold.

tea dance *n.* A late-afternoon dance.

tea garden *n.* A garden open to the public where tea and light refreshments may be consumed.

tea·house (tē′hous′) *n.* A public establishment serving tea and other refreshments.

teak (tēk) *n.* **1. a.** A tall evergreen tree, *Tectona grandis,* of southeastern Asia, having hard, heavy, durable wood. **b.** The yellowish-brown hard wood of this tree, used for furniture and in shipbuilding. **2.** Olive gray or dark olive, to grayish yellowish brown or grayish to moderate brown. [Port. *teca* < Malayalam *tēkka.*] **—teak** *adj.*

tea·ket·tle (tē′kĕt′l) *n.* A kettle, usually with a spout, used for boiling water for tea.

teak·wood (tēk′wo͝od′) *n.* Teak (sense 1.b.).

teal (tēl) *n., pl.* **teal** or **teals. 1.** Any of several small, widely distributed river ducks, esp. those of the genus *Anas,* many of which have brightly marked plumage. **2.** Moderate or dark bluish green to greenish blue. [ME *tele.*] **—teal** *adj.*

team (tēm) *n.* **1. a.** Two or more draft animals used to pull a vehicle or farm implement. **b.** A vehicle along with the animal or animals harnessed to it. **2.** A group of animals exhibited or performing together, as horses at an equestrian show. **3.** A group on the same side, as in a game. **4.** A group organized to work together: *a team of engineers.* **5.** A brood or flock. **6.** *Obs.* Offspring; lineage. *—v.* **teamed, team·ing, teams.** *—tr.* **1.** To harness or join together so as to form a team. **2.** To transport or haul with a draft team. *—intr.* **1.** To form a team. **2.** To drive a team or truck. —See Usage note at **collective noun.** [ME< OE *tēam.*]

team·mate (tēm′māt′) *n.* A fellow member of a team.

team play *n.* **1.** Collective play participated in by team members. **2.** Mutual, cooperative effort. **—team player** *n.*

team·ster (tēm′stər) *n.* **1.** A person who drives a team. **2.** A truck driver.

team teaching *n.* A method of classroom instruction in which several teachers are jointly responsible for teaching a single group of students. **—team-teach** (tēm′tēch′) *v.* **(-taught, -teach·ing, -teach·es).**

team·work (tēm′wûrk′) *n.* Cooperative effort by the members of a group or team to achieve a common goal.

tea·pot (tē′pŏt′) *n.* A covered pot with a spout in which tea is steeped and from which it is served.

tea·poy (tē′poi′) *n.* **1.** A small table for holding a tea service. **2.** A small, decorative three-legged table. [Hindi *tipāī* : *tīn,* three + Pers. *pāī,* foot.]

tear[1] (târ) *v.* **tore** (tôr, tōr), **torn** (tôrn, tōrn), **tear·ing, tears.** *—tr.* **1.** To pull apart or into pieces; rend. **2.** To make (an opening) by ripping. **3.** To lacerate (the skin, for example).

TAXONOMIC CLASSIFICATION

This table includes most of the major taxonomic categories, beginning with the broadest and most inclusive and ending with the narrowest. It is not by any means all inclusive, but consists of a representative, if arbitrary, selection intended to show the relationships between familiar groups and kinds of organisms.

The names shown are widely accepted by taxonomists, and are in general accordance with the taxonomic designations used in this Dictionary. In some instances, especially in the field of botany, there has been considerable change and difference of opinion in recent years, and the terms included in this table reflect an effort to select the most acceptable and authoritative designations.

Kingdom
Animalia* (animals)

*A more recently established third kingdom, Protista, consists of organisms not readily classified as plants or animals and includes among others such unicellular forms as amoeba and paramecium, often placed in the animal kingdom, euglena and various bacteria, often placed in the plant kingdom, as well as the slime molds, sometimes placed in the plant kingdom and sometimes in the animal kingdom.

Phylum
Porifera (sponges)
Coelenterata (coelenterates)
Mollusca (mollusks)
Annelida (segmented worms)
Arthropoda (arthropods)
Echinodermata (echinoderms)
Chordata (chordates)

Subphylum
Vertebrata (vertebrates)

Superclass
Pisces (fishes)

Class
Anthozoa (corals)
Nematoda (roundworms)
Gastropoda (snails, slugs)
Crustacea (crustaceans)
Arachnida (spiders, scorpions, mites)
Insecta (insects)
Osteichthyes (bony fishes)
Amphibia (amphibians)
Reptilia (reptiles)
Aves (birds)
Mammalia (mammals)

Order
Lepidoptera (butterflies, moths)
Chelonia (turtles)
Rodentia (rodents)
Cetacea (whales)
Primates (monkeys, apes, man)

Family
Lumbricidae (earthworms)
Salmonidae (salmon, trout)
Corvidae (crows, jays)
Felidae (cats)

Genus
Strombus (conchs)
Crotalus (rattlesnakes)
Perdix (partridges)
Canis (dogs)

Species
Octopus vulgaris (common octopus)
Rana catesbeiana (bullfrog)
Haliaeetus leucocephalus (bald eagle)
Giraffa camelopardalis (giraffe)

Subspecies
Panthera tigris longipilis
(Siberian tiger)

Kingdom
Plantae* (plants)

Division
Thallophyta** (algae, fungi)
Bryophyta (mosses, liverworts)
Tracheophyta (vascular plants)

**An older designation now sometimes considered a subkingdom.

Class
Basidiomycetes (mushrooms)
Musci (mosses)
Filicinae or Pteridophyta (ferns)
Gymnospermae (gymnosperms)
Angiospermae (flowering plants)

Subclass
Dicotyledonae (dicotyledons)
Monocotyledonae (monocotyledons)

Order
Uredinales (rusts)
Lycopodiales (club mosses)
Coniferales (conifers)
Graminales (grasses)
Rosales (roses, related plants)

Family
Orchidaceae (orchids)
Fagaceae (beeches, oaks)
Cactaceae (cacti)
Compositae (asters, sunflowers)

Genus
Avena (oats)
Morus (mulberries)
Mentha (mints)
Solidago (goldenrods)

Species
Zea mays (corn)
Dianthus caryophyllus (carnation)
Juglans cinerea (butternut)
Taraxacum officinale (common dandelion)

Variety
Lactuca sativa longifolia
(romaine lettuce)

The taxonomic categories in which the Siberian tiger and romaine lettuce are classified are shown below in descending order, beginning with the broadest category.

Kingdom
Animalia (animals)

Phylum
Chordata (chordates)

Subphylum
Vertebrata (vertebrates)

Class
Mammalia (mammals)

Order
Carnivora (carnivores)

Family
Felidae (cats)

Genus
Panthera (lion, tiger, leopard, jaguar)

Species
Panthera tigris (tiger)

Subspecies
Panthera tigris longipilis
(Siberian tiger)

Kingdom
Plantae (plants)

Division
Tracheophyta (vascular plants)

Class
Angiospermae (flowering plants)

Subclass
Dicotyledonae (dicotyledons)

Order
Campanulales or Campanulatae
(bellflowers, lobelias, composites)

Family
Compositae (composites)

Genus
Lactuca (lettuce)

Species
Lactuca sativa (cultivated lettuce)

Variety
Lactuca sativa longifolia
(romaine lettuce)

4. To separate forcefully; wrench. **5.** To divide; disunite: *torn between opposing choices.* —*intr.* **1.** To become torn. **2.** To move with heedless speed; rush headlong. —***phrasal verbs.*** **tear around. 1.** To move about in excited, often angry haste. **2.** To lead a wild life. **tear away.** To remove (as oneself) unwillingly or reluctantly. **tear down. 1.** To demolish: *tear down old tenements.* **2.** To take apart; disassemble: *tear down an engine.* **3.** To vilify; denigrate. **tear into.** To attack with great violence or vigor. **tear off.** To produce hurriedly and casually. **tear up. 1.** To tear to pieces. **2.** To make an opening in: *tore up the sidewalk to add a drain.* —*n.* **1.** An act of tearing. **2.** The result of tearing; a rip or rent. **3.** A great rush; hurry. **4.** *Slang.* A carousal; spree. —See Usage note at **torn.** [ME *teren* < OE *teran.*]

Synonyms: *tear, rip, rend, split, cleave, sever, slit, slash.* These verbs refer to the act of pulling or breaking something apart or to cutting or dividing it, usually forcibly. *Tear* involves either pulling an object apart so as to produce a breach or laceration or a complete separation of parts, or wrenching one object from another to which it has been joined. *Rip* is applicable in the senses specified for *tear* but often implies separation along a seam, joint, or other dividing line. *Rip* also is somewhat stronger in its suggestion of force. *Rend* refers to violent pulling or wrenching apart of a thing's components. *Split* refers either to dividing an object forcibly, by breaking it and thus separating its parts completely, or to producing a fracture in its entire length or breadth. *Cleave* most often refers to splitting by cutting or chopping with a sharp instrument. *Sever* usually means to cut forcibly and decisively, thus removing a part from the whole of something. *Slit* refers to cutting lengthwise and producing a narrow incision, usually methodically rather than violently. *Slash* means to cut with powerful, sweeping strokes.

tear² (tîr) *n.* **1.** A drop of the clear saline liquid that is secreted by the lachrymal gland of the eye and lubricates the surface between the eyeball and the eyelid. **2.** A drop of any liquid or hardened fluid. **3. tears.** The act of weeping: *left her in tears.* —*intr.v.* **teared, tear·ing, tears.** To fill with tears. [ME *tere* < OE *tēar.*]

tear·down (târ'doun') *n.* The act or process of taking apart or demolishing.

tear·drop (tîr'drŏp') *n.* **1.** A single tear. **2.** An object having the shape of a tear.

tear·ful (tîr'fəl) *adj.* **1.** Filled with or accompanied by tears. **2.** So piteous as to excite tears. —**tear'ful·ly** *adv.* —**tear'ful·ness** *n.*

tear gas (tîr) *n.* Any of various agents that on dispersal, usually from grenades or projectiles, irritates the eyes and causes blinding tears.

tear-jerk·er (tîr'jûr'kər) *n. Slang.* A pathetic story, drama, or performance apt to make one weep.

tea·room (tē'ro͞om', -ro͝om') *n.* **1.** A restaurant or shop serving tea and other refreshments. **2.** *Slang.* A men's room used for homosexual activity.

tea rose *n.* **1.** Any of several cultivated roses derived from *Rosa odorata,* having fragrant yellowish or pink flowers. **2.** Pale to strong yellowish pink. —**tea'-rose'** *adj.*

tear sheet (târ) *n.* A page taken from a periodical and used chiefly to provide evidence to an advertiser of the publication of his advertisement.

tease (tēz) *v.* **teased, teas·ing, teas·es.** —*tr.* **1.** To annoy; pester; vex. **2.** To make fun of; playfully mock. **3.** To arouse hope, desire, or curiosity in without affording satisfaction. **4. a.** To coax. **b.** To gain by persistent coaxing. **5.** To cut (tissue, for example) into pieces for examination. **6.** To disentangle and dress the fibers of (wool, for example). **7.** To raise the nap of (cloth) by dressing, as with a fuller's teasel. **8.** To ruffle (the hair) by combing from the ends toward the scalp for an airy, full effect. —*intr.* To annoy or make fun of someone persistently. —*n.* **1.** The act of teasing. **2.** One that teases, as: **a.** One given to playful mocking. **b.** A coquettish woman. **c.** A preliminary remark or action intended to whet the curiosity. [ME *tesen,* to comb apart < OE *tǣsan.*] —**teas'er** *n.* —**teas'ing·ly** *adv.*

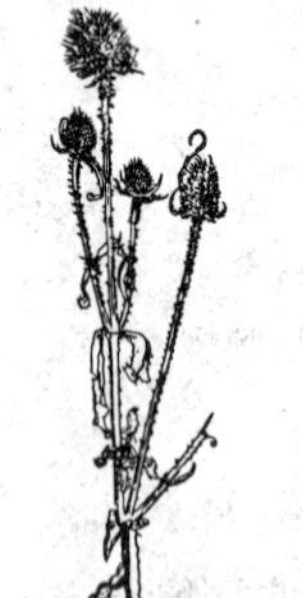

teasel
Fuller's teasel

tea·sel (tē'zəl) *n.* **1.** Any of several plants of the genus *Dipsacus,* native to the Old World, having thistlelike flowers surrounded by prickly bracts. **2. a.** The bristly flower head of *D. fullonum,* used to produce a napped surface on fabrics. **b.** A wire device used for the same purpose. —*tr.v.* **-seled** or **-selled, -sel·ing** or **-sel·ling, -sels.** To produce a napped surface on (a fabric). [ME *tesel* < OE *tǣsel.*]

tea service *n.* The articles, such as matching cups and teapot, used in serving tea.

tea·shop (tē'shŏp') *n.* **1.** A tearoom (sense 1). **2.** *Chiefly Brit.* A lunchroom.

tea·spoon (tē'spo͞on') *n.* **1.** The common small spoon used esp. with tea, coffee, and desserts. **2.** A household cooking measure equal to approximately 5 milliliters or 1/3 tablespoon.

tea·spoon·ful (tē'spo͞on'fo͝ol') *n., pl.* **-fuls.** The amount a teaspoon will hold.

teat (tēt, tĭt) *n.* A mammary gland or nipple; pap. [ME *tete* < OFr., of Germanic orig.] —**teat'ed** *adj.*

tea wagon *n.* A small table on wheels for serving tea or holding dishes.

tech·ne·ti·um (tĕk-nē'shē-əm, -shəm) *n. Symbol* **Tc** A silvery-gray metal, the first synthetically produced element, having 14 isotopes with masses ranging from 92 to 105 and half-lives up to 2.6×10^6 years. It is used as a tracer and to eliminate corrosion in steel. Atomic number 43; melting point 2,200°C; specific gravity 11.50; valences 3, 4, 6, 7. [< Gk. *tekhnētos,* artificial < *teknasthai,* to make by art < *tekhnē* art.]

tech·nic (tĕk'nĭk) *n.* **1. technics.** *(used with a sing. or pl. verb).* The theory, principles, or study of an art or process. **2. technics.** *(used with a sing. or pl. verb).* Technical details, rules, methods, or the like. **3.** Variant of **technique** (sense 2). —*adj.* Technical. [<Gk. *tekhnikos,* of art < *tekhnē,* art.]

tech·ni·cal (tĕk'nĭ-kəl) *adj.* **1.** Of, pertaining to, or derived from technique. **2.** Specialized: *a technical school.* **3. a.** Abstract or theoretical: *a technical analysis.* **b.** Scientific. **4.** According to principle, esp. formal rather than practical: *a technical advantage.* **5.** Industrial and mechanical; technological. **6.** Designating or pertaining to a stock market in which prices are determined or affected by internal manipulation and speculation. [< Gk. *tekhnikos,* of art < *tekhnē,* art.] —**tech'ni·cal·ly** *adv.* —**tech'ni·cal·ness** *n.*

tech·ni·cal·i·ty (tĕk'nĭ-kăl'ĭ-tē) *n., pl.* **-ties. 1.** The condition or quality of being technical. **2.** Something meaningful or relevant only to a specialist: *a legal technicality.*

technical knockout *n. Sports.* A victory in boxing, with immediate termination of the match, awarded by the referee when it appears that one fighter is too badly beaten to continue.

tech·ni·cian (tĕk-nĭsh'ən) *n.* An expert in a technique, as: **a.** A person whose occupation requires training in a specific technical process: *a dental technician.* **b.** One who is known for skill in an intellectual or artistic technique.

Tech·ni·col·or (tĕk'nĭ-kŭl'ər). A trademark for a motion-picture color process.

tech·nique (tĕk-nēk') *n.* **1.** The systematic procedure by which a complex or scientific task is accomplished. **2.** Also **tech·nic** (tĕk'nĭk). The degree of skill or command of fundamentals exhibited in any performance. [Fr. < *technique,* technical < Gk. *tekhnikos.*]

tech·noc·ra·cy (tĕk-nŏk'rə-sē) *n., pl.* **-cies.** A government and social system controlled by scientific technicians. [Gk. *tekhnē,* skill + -CRACY.] —**tech'no·crat'** (-nə-krăt') *n.* —**tech'no·crat'ic** *adj.*

tech·no·log·i·cal (tĕk'nə-lŏj'ĭ-kəl) also **tech·no·log·ic** (-lŏj'ĭk) *adj.* **1.** Pertaining to or involving technology, esp. scientific technology. **2.** Affected by or resulting from scientific and industrial progress. —**tech'no·log'i·cal·ly** *adv.*

tech·nol·o·gize (tĕk-nŏl'ə-jīz') *tr.v.* **-gized, -giz·ing, -giz·es.** To modify or affect by technology; make technological.

tech·nol·o·gy (tĕk-nŏl'ə-jē) *n., pl.* **-gies. 1. a.** The application of science, esp. to industrial or commercial objectives. **b.** The entire body of methods and materials used to achieve such objectives. **2.** *Anthropol.* The body of knowledge available to a civilization that is of use in fashioning implements, practicing manual arts and skills, and extracting or collecting materials. [Gk. *tekhnē,* skill + -LOGY.] —**tech·nol'o·gist** *n.*

tech·no·struc·ture (tĕk'nō-strŭk'chər) *n.* **1.** A large-scale corporate system. **2.** A network of skilled professionals who control a technostructure. [TECHNO(LOGY) + STRUCTURE.]

tech·y (tĕch'ē) *adj.* Variant of **tetchy.**

tec·ton·ic (tĕk-tŏn'ĭk) *adj.* **1.** Pertaining to construction or building. **2.** Architectural. **3.** *Geol.* Pertaining to, causing, or resulting from structural deformation in the earth's crust. [LLat. *tectonicus* < Gk. *tektonikos* < *tektōn,* builder.] —**tec·ton'i·cal·ly** *adv.*

tec·ton·ics (tĕk-tŏn'ĭks) *n. (used with a sing. verb).* **1.** The art or science of construction, esp. of large buildings. **2.** The geology of the earth's structural deformation.

tec·ton·ism (tĕk'tə-nĭz'əm) *n.* Diastrophism. [TECTON(IC) + -ISM.]

tec·trix (tĕk'trĭks) *n., pl.* **-tri·ces** (-trĭ-sēz'). Often **tectrices.** One of the coverts of a bird's wing. [NLat. < fem. of Lat. *tector,* plasterer < *tegere,* to cover.]

tec·tum (tĕk'təm) *n., pl.* **-ta** (-tə). A rooflike body structure, esp. the dorsal part of the midbrain. [NLat. < Lat., roof < neuter p.part. of *tegere,* to cover.] —**tec'tal** *adj.*

ted (tĕd) *tr.v.* **ted·ded, ted·ding, teds.** To strew or spread (newly mown grass, for example) for drying. [ME *tedden.*] —**ted'der** *n.*

ted·dy (tĕd'ē) *n., pl.* **-dies.** A woman's undergarment combining a camisole top and loose-fitting panties. [Orig. unknown.]

teddy bear also **Teddy bear** *n.* A child's toy bear, usually stuffed with soft material and covered with furlike plush. [After *Teddy,* nickname of Theodore Roosevelt (1858–1919), who was depicted in a cartoon sparing the life of a bear cub.]

Teddy boy *n.* A tough British youth wearing a modified style of Edwardian clothes. [< *Teddy,* nickname for *Edward.*]

Te De·um (tā' dā'əm, tē' dē'əm) *n., pl.* **Te De·ums.** A hymn of praise to God sung as part of a liturgy. [< Lat. *Te Deum (laudamus),* You, God, (we praise), the opening words of the hymn.]

te·di·ous (tē'dē-əs) *adj.* **1.** Tiresome or uninteresting due to extreme length or slowness; wearisome: *a tedious lecture.* **2.** *Obs.* Moving or progressing very slowly. [ME < LLat. *taediosus* < Lat. *taedium,* tedium.] **—te'di·ous·ly** *adv.* **—te'di·ous·ness** *n.*

te·di·um (tē'dē-əm) *n.* The quality or condition of being wearisome or tedious. [Lat. *taedium* < *taedēre,* to weary.]

tee¹ (tē) *n.* The letter *t.*

tee² (tē) *n.* **1.** A small peg with a concave top for holding a golf ball for an initial drive. **2.** The designated area from which a player makes his first stroke in golf. *—tr.v.* **teed, tee·ing, tees.** To place (a golf ball) on a tee. ***—phrasal verbs.*** **tee off. 1.** To drive a golf ball from the tee. **2.** *Slang.* To start or begin: *They teed off the fund-raising campaign with a dinner.* **3.** *Slang.* To make or become angry. **tee up.** To place or set up a golf ball for driving. [Orig. unknown.]

tee³ (tē) *n.* A mark aimed at in certain games, as curling or quoits. ***—idiom.*** **to a tee.** Perfectly; exactly: *a suit that fits to a tee.* [Orig. unknown.]

teem¹ (tēm) *v.* **teemed, teem·ing, teems.** *—intr.* **1.** To be full of; abound or swarm: *A drop of water teems with microorganisms.* **2.** *Obs.* To produce young; to bear. *—tr. Archaic.* To give birth to. [ME *temen,* to give birth to < OE *tīeman.*] **—teem'er** *n.*

teem² (tēm) *tr.v.* **teemed, teem·ing, teems.** To pour out or empty: *teemed molten ore into a huge mold.* [ME *temen* < ON *tǿma.*]

teen¹ (tēn) *n.* A teen-ager. *—adj.* Teen-age.

teen² (tēn) *n. Archaic.* Injury; grief. [ME *tene* < OE *tēona.*]

teen-age (tēn'āj') also **teen-aged** (-ājd') *adj.* Of, pertaining to, or descriptive of those aged 13 through 19.

teen-ag·er (tēn'ā'jər) *n.* A person between the ages of 13 and 19 inclusive; adolescent.

teens (tēnz) *pl.n.* **1.** The numbers 13 to 19 inclusive. **2.** The years of one's age between 13 and 19 inclusive.

tee·ny (tē'nē) also **teen·sy** (tēn'sē) *adj.* **-ni·er, -ni·est** also **-si·er, -si·est.** Tiny. [Alteration of TINY.]

teen·y·bop·per (tē'nē-bŏp'ər) *n. Slang.* A teen-ager who follows the latest fad or craze, as in dress or music. [TEEN¹ + -Y¹ + BOP¹ + -ER¹]

tee·pee (tē'pē) *n.* Variant of **tepee.**

tee shirt *n.* Variant of **T-shirt.**

tee·ter (tē'tər) *v.* **-tered, -ter·ing, -ters.** *—intr.* **1.** To walk or move unsteadily or unsurely; totter. **2.** To seesaw; vacillate. *—tr.* To cause to teeter or seesaw. *—n.* **1.** A seesaw. **2.** A teetering or seesaw motion. [ME *titeren,* prob. < ON *titra,* to shake.]

teeter board *n.* A seesaw.

tee·ter-tot·ter (tē'tər-tŏt'ər) *n.* A seesaw.

teeth (tēth) *n.* Plural of **tooth.**

teethe (tē*th*) *intr.v.* **teethed, teeth·ing, teethes.** To grow teeth; cut one's teeth. [ME *tethen* < *teeth,* pl. of *tooth,* tooth. —see TOOTH.]

teething ring *n.* A ring of hard rubber or plastic upon which a teething baby can bite.

tee·to·tal·er or **tee·to·tal·ler** (tē'tōt'l-ər) also **tee·to·tal·ist** (-ĭst) *n.* A person who abstains completely from alcoholic liquors. [TEE¹ (pronunciation of the first letter in *total*) + *total* (*abstinence*) + -ER¹.] **—tee'to'tal** *adj.* **—tee'to'tal·ism** *n.*

tee·to·tum (tē'tō'təm) *n.* A top, usually having four lettered sides, that is used to play various games of chance. [TEE¹ + Lat. *totum,* neuter sing. of *totus,* all (from the inscription of a *T* on the top meaning 'take all').]

Tef·lon (tĕf'lŏn'). A trademark for a waxy, opaque material, polytetrafluoroethylene, used as a coating on cooking utensils and in industrial applications to prevent sticking.

teg·men (tĕg'mən) *n., pl.* **-mi·na** (-mə-nə). *Biol.* A covering or integument, such as the tough, leathery forewing of certain insects or the inner coat of a seed. [NLat. < Lat., covering < *tegere,* to cover.]

teg·men·tum (tĕg-mĕn'təm) *n. Biol.* Tegmen. [NLat. < Lat., covering < *tegere,* to cover.] **—teg·men'tal** *adj.*

te·gua (tā'gwä, tā'wä) *n.* An ankle-high moccasin worn by Mexicans and Indians. [Native word in Mexico.]

teg·u·lar (tĕg'yə-lər) also **teg·u·lat·ed** (-lā'tĭd) *adj.* Pertaining to or resembling a tile. [< Lat. *tegula,* tile < *tegere,* to cover.] **—teg'u·lar·ly** *adv.*

teg·u·ment (tĕg'yə-mənt) *n.* An outer covering; integument. [ME < Lat. *tegumentum* < *tegere,* to cover.] **—teg'u·men'ta·ry** (-mĕn'tə-rē, -mĕn'trē), **teg'u·men'tal** (-mĕn'tl) *adj.*

Te·huel·che (tā-wĕl'chā) *n., pl.* **Tehuelche** or **-ches.** One of a nomadic Indian people of southern Argentina, virtually exterminated by the Spanish colonists. [Of Araucanian orig.] **—Te·huel'che·an** (-chē-ən) *adj.*

teig·lach (tāg'läKH', tĭg'-) *pl.n.* A confection consisting of bits of dough cooked briefly in a mixture of honey, brown sugar, and nuts, then cooled and rolled into balls. [Yiddish *teyglekh* < dim. of *teyg,* dough < MHG *teig* < OHG *teic.*]

tek·tite (tĕk'tīt') *n.* Any of numerous dark brown to green glass objects, generally small and rounded, thought to be of extraterrestrial origin, found chiefly in Czechoslovakia, Australia, Indonesia, the Philippines, Texas and Georgia, and having a largely silica composition with various oxides. [Gk. *tēktos,* molten (< *tēkein,* to melt) + -ITE.] **—tek·tit'ic** *adj.*

tel–¹ *pref.* Variant of **tele-.**

tel–² *pref.* Variant of **telo-.**

tel·aes·the·sia (tĕl'ĭs-thē'zhə) *n.* Variant of **telesthesia.**

tel·a·mon (tĕl'ə-mŏn') *n., pl.* **tel·a·mon·es** (tĕl'ə-mō'nēz). *Archit.* A figure of a man used as a supporting pillar. [Lat. < Gk. *telamōn,* bearer.]

tel·an·gi·ec·ta·sia (tĕl-ăn'jē-ĕk-tā'zhə) also **tel·an·gi·ec·ta·sis** (-ĕk'tə-sĭs) *n.* A chronic dilation of groups of capillaries of the blood vascular system causing dark-red blotches on the skin. [NLat. : TEL(O)- + Gk. *angos,* vessel + Gk. *ektasis,* expansion < *ekteinein,* to stretch out (*ek-,* out + *teinein,* to stretch).] **—tel·an'gi·ec·tat'ic** (-tăt'ĭk) *adj.*

tele– or **tel–** *pref.* **1.** Distance; distant: *telesthesia.* **2. a.** Telegraph: *telegram.* **b.** Television: *telecast.* [< Gk. *tēle,* at a distance.]

tel·e·cast (tĕl'ə-kăst') *v.* **-cast** or **-cast·ed, -cast·ing, -casts.** *—intr.* To broadcast by television. *—tr.* To broadcast (a program) by television. *—n.* A television broadcast. **—tel'e·cast'er** *n.*

tel·e·com·mu·ni·ca·tion (tĕl'ə-kə-myōō'nĭ-kā'shən) *n.* **1.** Often **telecommunications** *(used with a sing. verb).* The science and technology of communication by electronic transmission of impulses, as by telegraphy, cable, telephony, radio, or television. **2.** A message transmitted by means of telecommunications.

tel·e·course (tĕl'ə-kôrs', -kōrs') *n.* A course of televised lectures, as offered by a university.

tel·e·du (tĕl'ə-dōō') *n.* A brownish-black carnivorous mammal, *Mydaus javanensis,* of the East Indies, that, like the skunk, is capable of emitting an offensive odor. [Malay *tĕledu.*]

tel·e·film (tĕl'ə-fĭlm) *n.* A motion picture produced for television broadcasting.

tel·e·gen·ic (tĕl'ə-jĕn'ĭk) *adj.* Presenting a pleasing appearance on television.

te·leg·o·ny (tə-lĕg'ə-nē) *n.* The supposed influence of one sire on offspring sired by subsequent males on the same female. **—tel'e·gon'ic** (tĕl'ə-gŏn'ĭk), **te·leg'o·nous** *adj.*

tel·e·gram (tĕl'ə-grăm') *n.* A communication transmitted by telegraph.

tel·e·graph (tĕl'ə-grăf') *n.* **1.** A communication system that transmits and receives simple unmodulated electric impulses, esp. one in which the transmission and reception stations are directly connected by wires. **2.** A telegram. *—v.* **-graphed, -graph·ing, -graphs.** *—tr.* **1.** To transmit (a message) by telegraph. **2.** To send or convey a message to by telegraph. **3.** To make known in advance or unintentionally. *—intr.* To send or transmit a telegram. **—te·leg'ra·pher** (tə-lĕg'rə-fər), **te·leg'ra·phist** *n.*

tel·e·graph·ic (tĕl'ə-grăf'ĭk) also **tel·e·graph·i·cal** (-ĭ-kəl) *adj.* **1.** Pertaining to or transmitted by telegraph. **2.** Brief or concise like a telegram. **—tel'e·graph'i·cal·ly** *adv.*

telegraph plant *n.* A tropical Asiatic plant, *Desmodium motorium* or *D. gyrans,* having trifoliolate compound leaves, of which the lateral leaflets move or rotate.

te·leg·ra·phy (tə-lĕg'rə-fē) *n.* Communication by means of telegraph.

Tel·e·gu also **Tel·u·gu** (tĕl'ə-gōō') *n., pl.* **Telegu** also **Telugu** or **-gus. 1.** A Dravidian language spoken in Andhra Pradesh, India. **2.** A member of a Dravidian people who speak Telegu. [Native word in India.] **—Telegu** *adj.*

tel·e·ki·ne·sis (tĕl'ə-kĭ-nē'sĭs, -kī-) *n.* The movement of objects by scientifically inexplicable means, as by the exercise of mystical powers. **—tel'e·ki·net'ic** (-nĕt'ĭk) *adj.* **—tel'e·ki·net'i·cal·ly** *adv.*

Te·lem·a·chus (tə-lĕm'ə-kəs) *n. Gk. Myth.* The son of Odysseus and Penelope who helped his father kill Penelope's suitors. [Lat. < Gk. *Tēlemakhos.*]

tel·e·mark also **Tel·e·mark** (tĕl'ə-märk') *n. Sports.* A turn or stop in skiing executed by shifting the weight forward on the ski that will be on the outside of the turn and pulling its tip gradually inward. [Norw., after *Telemark,* a region in Norway.]

tel·e·me·ter (tĕl'ə-mē'tər, tə-lĕm'ĭ-tər) *n.* Any of various measuring devices used in telemetry. *—tr.v.* (tĕl'ə-mē'tər) **-tered, -ter·ing, -ters.** To measure and transmit (data) automatically from a distant source, as from a spacecraft or electric power grid, to a receiving station for recording or display. **—tel'e·met'ric** (tĕl'ə-mĕt'rĭk), **tel'e·met'ri·cal** *adj.* **—tel'e·met'ri·cal·ly** *adv.*

te·lem·e·try (tə-lĕm'ĭ-trē) *n.* The science and technology of automatic measurement and transmission of data by wire, radio, or other means from remote sources, as from space vehicles, to a receiving station for recording and analysis. **—tel'e·met'ric** *adj.* **—tel'e·met'ri·cal·ly** *adv.*

tel·en·ceph·a·lon (tĕl'ĕn-sĕf'ə-lŏn', -lən) *n.* The anterior portion of the forebrain, including the cerebral cortex and related parts. **—tel'en·ce·phal'ic** (-sə-făl'ĭk) *adj.*

tel·e·ol·o·gy (tĕl'ē-ŏl'ə-jē, tē'lē-) *n., pl.* **-gies. 1.** The philosophical study of design or purpose in natural phenomena. **2.** The use of ultimate purpose or design as a means of explaining natural phenomena. **—tel'e·o·log'i·cal** (-ə-lŏj'ĭ-kəl), **tel'e·o·log'ic** *adj.* **—tel'e·o·log'i·cal·ly** *adv.* **—tel'e·ol'o·gist** *n.*

tel·e·ost (tĕl'ē-ŏst', tē'lē-) also **tel·e·os·te·an** (tĕl'ē-ŏs'tē-ən, tē'lē-). *—adj.* Of or belonging to the Teleostei or Teleostomi, a group consisting of numerous fishes having bony skeletons and rayed fins. *—n.* A teleost fish. [< NLat. *Teleostei,* group name (Gk. *teleos,* complete + *osteon,* bone) and

NLat. *Teleostomi,* group name (Gk. *teleos,* complete + *stoma,* mouth).]

te·lep·a·thy (tə-lĕp′ə-thē) *n.* Communication through means other than the senses, as by the exercise of mystical powers. **—tel′e·path′ic** (tĕl′ə-păth′ĭk) *adj.* **—tel′e·path′i·cal·ly** *adv.* **—te·lep′a·thist** *n.*

tel·e·phone (tĕl′ə-fōn′) *n.* An instrument that directly modulates carrier waves with voice or other acoustic source signals to be transmitted to remote locations and that directly reconverts received waves into audible signals, esp. such an instrument connected to others by wire. *—v.* **-phoned, -phon·ing, -phones.** *—tr.* **1.** To communicate with by telephone. **2.** To call (someone) on the telephone. **3.** To transmit by telephone. *—intr.* To communicate by telephone. **—tel′e·phon′er** *n.*

telephone book *n.* A directory of the names of telephone subscribers with corresponding addresses and telephone numbers.

telephone booth *n.* A small enclosure containing a public telephone.

telephone exchange *n.* Any of numerous central systems of switches and other equipment that establish connections between individual telephones.

telephone receiver *n.* The part of a telephone in which incoming electrical impulses are converted into sound.

tel·e·phon·ic (tĕl′ə-fŏn′ĭk) *adj.* **1.** Of or pertaining to a telephone. **2.** Transmitted or conveyed by a telephone. **—tel′e·phon′i·cal·ly** *adv.*

te·leph·o·ny (tə-lĕf′ə-nē) *n.* **1.** The electrical transmission of sound between distant stations, esp. by radio or telephone. **2.** The technology and manufacture of telephone equipment.

tel·e·pho·to (tĕl′ə-fō′tō) *adj.* **1.** Of or pertaining to a photographic lens or lens system used to produce a large image of a distant object. **2.** A telephotograph (sense 1).

tel·e·pho·to·graph (tĕl′ə-fō′tə-grăf′) *n.* **1.** A photograph made with a telephoto lens. **2.** A photograph transmitted and reproduced by telephotography. *—tr.v.* **-graphed, -graph·ing, -graphs. 1.** To photograph with a telephoto lens. **2.** To transmit by telephotography.

tel·e·pho·tog·ra·phy (tĕl′ə-fə-tŏg′rə-fē) *n.* **1.** The process or technique of photographing distant objects, using a telephoto lens on a camera. **2.** The technique or process of transmitting charts, pictures, and photographs over a distance. **—tel′e·pho′to·graph′ic** (-fō′tə-grăf′ĭk) *adj.*

tel·e·play (tĕl′ə-plā′) *n.* A play written or adapted for television.

tel·e·print·er (tĕl′ə-prĭn′tər) *n.* A teletypewriter.

tel·e·proc·ess·ing (tĕl′ə-prŏs′ĕs′ĭng, -prō′sĕs′-) *n.* Computer service by means of terminals remote from the central computer.

Tel·e·Promp·Ter (tĕl′ə-prŏmp′tər). A trademark for a device used in television to show an actor or speaker an enlarged line-by-line reproduction of a script, unseen by the audience.

tel·e·ran (tĕl′ə-răn′) *n.* An air-traffic control system in which the image of a ground-based radar unit is televised to aircraft in the vicinity so that a pilot may see his position in relation to other aircraft. [Orig. a trademark.]

telescope

tel·e·scope (tĕl′ə-skōp′) *n.* An instrument for collecting and examining electromagnetic radiation, esp.: **1.** An arrangement of lenses or mirrors or both that gathers visible light, permitting direct observation or photographic recording of distant objects. **2.** Any of various devices, such as a radio telescope, used to detect and observe distant objects by their emission, transmission, reflection, or other interaction with invisible radiation. *—v.* **-scoped, -scop·ing, -scopes.** *—tr.* **1.** To cause to slide inward or outward in overlapping sections, as the cylindrical sections of a small hand telescope. **2.** To make shorter or more precise; condense. *—intr.* To slide inward or outward in or as if in overlapping cylindrical sections. [NLat. *telescopium* or Ital. *telescopio,* both < Gk. *tēleskopos,* far seeing : *tēle,* at a distance + *skopos,* watcher.]

tel·e·scop·ic (tĕl′ə-skŏp′ĭk) *adj.* **1.** Of or pertaining to a telescope. **2.** Seen or obtained by means of a telescope: *telescopic data.* **3.** Visible only by means of a telescope: *a telescopic binary star.* **4.** Able to discern distant objects: *telescopic vision.* **5.** Extensible or compressible by or as if by the successive sliding of overlapping concentric tubular sections. **—tel′e·scop′i·cal·ly** *adv.*

Tel·e·sco·pi·um (tĕl′ə-skō′pē-əm) *n.* A constellation in the Southern Hemisphere near Pavo and Sagittarius. [NLat. < *telescopium,* telescope.]

te·les·co·py (tə-lĕs′kə-pē) *n.* The art or study of making and operating telescopes. **—te·les′co·pist** *n.*

tel·e·ster·e·o·scope (tĕl′ə-stĕr′ē-ə-skōp′, -stîr′-) *n.* A binocular telescope for stereoscopic viewing of distant objects.

tel·es·the·sia also **tel·aes·the·sia** (tĕl′ĭs-thē′zhə) *n.* Response to or perception of distant stimuli by extrasensory means. **—tel′es·thet′ic** (-thĕt′ĭk) *adj.*

tel·e·text (tĕl′ə-tĕkst′) *n.* An electronic communication system in which printed information is broadcast by television signal to sets equipped with a decoder.

tel·e·ther·mo·scope (tĕl′ə-thûr′mə-skōp′) *n.* An apparatus for indicating or recording the temperatures of distant or inaccessible locations.

tel·e·thon (tĕl′ə-thŏn′) *n.* A long, continuous television program, usually to raise funds for charity. [TELE- + (MARA)THON.]

tel·e·tran·scrip·tion (tĕl′ə-trăn-skrĭp′shən) *n.* The transcription of television programs by means of a kinescope or video tape.

Tel·e·type (tĕl′ə-tīp′). A trademark for a teletypewriter.

tel·e·type·writ·er (tĕl′ə-tīp′rī′tər) *n.* An electromechanical typewriter that either transmits or receives messages coded in electrical signals carried by telegraph or telephone wires.

te·leu·to·spore (tə-lōō′tə-spôr′, -spōr′) *n.* A teliospore. [Gk. *teleutē,* termination (< *telos,* end) + SPORE.] **—te·leu′to·spor′ic** *adj.*

tel·e·vise (tĕl′ə-vīz′) *tr. & intr v.* **-vised, -vis·ing, -vis·es.** To broadcast by television. [Back-formation < TELEVISION.]

tel·e·vi·sion (tĕl′ə-vĭzh′ən) *n.* **1.** The transmission of visual images of moving and stationary objects, generally with accompanying sound, as electromagnetic waves and the reconversion of received waves into visual images. **2. a.** An electronic apparatus that receives electromagnetic waves and displays the reconverted images on a screen. **b.** The integrated audible and visible content of the electromagnetic waves received and converted by such an apparatus. **3.** The industry of broadcasting television programs. [Fr. *télévision* : *télé-,* tele- + *vision,* vision.]

tel·e·vi·sor (tĕl′ə-vī′zər) *n.* A television transmitter.

tel·ex (tĕl′ĕks′) *n.* **1.** A communication system consisting of teletypewriters connected to a telephonic network to send and receive signals. **2.** A message sent or received by such a system. *—tr.v.* **-exed, -ex·ing, -ex·es.** To send (a message) by telex. [TEL(ETYPEWRITER) + EX(CHANGE).]

tel·ic (tĕl′ĭk, tē′lĭk) *adj.* Directed or tending toward a goal or purpose; purposeful. [Gk. *telikos,* final < *telos,* end.]

te·li·o·spore (tē′lē-ə-spôr′, -spōr′) *n.* A thick-walled, blackish resting spore of rusts and smuts, from which the basidium arises. [TELI(UM) + SPORE.] **—te′li·o·spor′ic** *adj.*

te·li·um (tē′lē-əm) *n., pl.* **-li·a** (-lē-ə). A blackish, pustulelike structure formed on the tissue of a plant infected by a rust fungus, and giving rise to teliospores. [NLat. < Gk. *teleios,* complete < *telos,* end.] **—te′li·al** *adj.*

tell (tĕl) *v.* **told** (tōld), **tell·ing, tells.** *—tr.* **1.** To give a detailed account of; narrate. **2.** To communicate by speech or writing; express with words: *"When in doubt tell the truth"* (Mark Twain). **3.** To make known to; notify; inform. **4.** To make known; reveal: *tell fortunes.* **5.** To command; order: *Do what I tell you.* **6.** To assure in an emphatic way: *I tell you, he's an honest man.* **7.** To discover by observation; discern; identify. **8.** To say (a rosary). *—intr.* **1.** To give an account, enumeration, or description. **2.** To give evidence or indication. **3.** To have an effect or impact: *In this game every move tells.* **—phrasal verbs. tell off. 1.** To count and set apart, esp. aloud. **2.** *Informal.* To rebuke severely. **tell on.** *Informal.* To inform against; tattle on. **—idiom. all told.** Including everyone or everything; in all. [ME *tellen* < OE *tellan.*] **—tell′a·ble** *adj.*

tell·er (tĕl′ər) *n.* **1.** One who tells. **2.** A bank employee who receives and pays out money. **3.** A person appointed to count votes in a legislative assembly. **—tell′er·ship′** *n.*

tell·ing (tĕl′ĭng) *adj.* **1.** Having force or effect; striking. **2.** Full of special meaning; revealing: *a telling illustration of his selfishness.* **—tell′ing·ly** *adv.*

tell·tale (tĕl′tāl′) *n.* **1.** One who informs on another person; talebearer. **2.** Something that indicates or reveals information; sign. **3.** Any of various devices that indicate or register information, esp.: **a.** A time clock. **b.** A device indicating the position of a ship's rudder. **c.** A row of strips hung above a railroad track to warn an approaching train of a low clearance ahead. **4.** A metal strip, 2 or 2½ feet high, across the bottom of the front wall of a racquets or squash court above which the ball must be hit.

tellur– *pref.* Variant of **telluro-.**

tel·lu·ri·an (tĕ-lōōr′ē-ən) *adj.* Of, pertaining to, or inhabiting the earth. *—n.* **1.** An inhabitant of the earth; a terrestrial. **2.** Variant of **tellurion.**

tel·lu·ric (tĕ-lōōr′ĭk) *adj.* **1.** Of or relating to the earth; terrestrial. **2.** Derived from or containing tellurium, esp. with valence 6.

telluric acid *n.* A white, crystalline inorganic acid, H_6TeO_4, used as a chemical reagent.

tel·lu·ride (tĕl′yə-rīd′) *n.* A binary compound of tellurium.

tel·lu·ri·on (tĕ-lōōr′ē-ŏn′) also **tel·lu·ri·an** (-ən) *n.* An instrument that shows how the movement of the earth on its axis and around the sun causes day and night and the seasons.

tel·lu·ri·um (tĕ-lōōr′ē-əm) *n. Symbol* **Te** A brittle, silvery-white metallic element, occurring naturally combined with gold and other metals, produced commercially as a by-product of the electrolytic refining of copper, and used to alloy stainless steel and lead, in ceramics, and, in the form of bismuth telluride, in thermoelectric devices. Atomic number 52; atomic weight 127.60; melting point 449.5°C; boiling point 989.8°C; specific gravity 6.24; valences 2, 4, 6.

telluro– or **tellur–** *pref.* **1.** Earth: *tellurian.* **2.** Tellurium: *tellurous.* [< Lat. *tellus, tellur-,* earth.]

tel·lu·rom·e·ter (tĕl′yə-rŏm′ĭ-tər) *n.* A surveying instrument that measures distance by means of microwaves.

tel·lu·rous (tĕl′yər-əs, tĕ-lo͝or′əs) *adj.* Of, relating to, or derived from tellurium, esp. with valence 4.

tel·ly (tĕl′ē) *n., pl.* **-lies.** *Chiefly Brit. Informal.* Television.

telo– or **tel–** *pref.* End: *telophase.* [< Gk. *telos,* end.]

tel·o·cen·tric (tĕl′ə-sĕn′trĭk, tē′lə-) *adj.* Of or pertaining to a chromosome whose centromere is terminally located.

tel·o·lec·i·thal (tĕl′ə-lĕs′ə-thəl, tē′lə-) *adj.* Of or pertaining to an ovum in which the yolk is concentrated at one end.

tel·o·mere (tĕl′ə-mîr′, tē′lə-) *n.* A centromere that is located in a terminal position on a chromosome.

tel·o·phase (tĕl′ə-fāz′, tē′lə-) *n.* The last phase of mitosis, in which the chromosomes of daughter cells are grouped in new nuclei.

tel·pher (tĕl′fər) *n.* **1.** A light transportation car suspended from overhead wire cables, usually driven by electricity. **2.** A transportation system using telphers. *—tr.v.* **-phered, -pher·ing, -phers.** To transport by telpher. [TEL(E)- + Gk. *pherein,* to carry.]

tel·son (tĕl′sən) *n.* A terminal structure of the posterior section of certain arthropods, such as the middle lobe of the tail fin of a lobster or shrimp or the sting of a scorpion. [Gk., limit.]

Tel·star (tĕl′stär′) *n.* One of two privately financed, low-altitude, active communications satellites launched by the U.S. Government in 1962 and 1963, and used commercially to transmit television pictures and telephone messages.

Tel·u·gu (tĕl′ə-go͞o′) *n. & adj.* Variant of **Telegu.**

tem·blor (tĕm′blər, -blôr′) *n.* An earthquake. [Sp. < *temblar,* to shake.]

tem·er·ar·i·ous (tĕm′ə-râr′ē-əs) *adj.* Presumptuously or recklessly daring. [Lat. *temerarius* < *temere,* rashly.] **—tem′er·ar′i·ous·ly** *adv.* **—tem′er·ar′i·ous·ness** *n.*

te·mer·i·ty (tə-mĕr′ĭ-tē) *n.* Foolhardy or heedless disregard of danger. [ME *temeryte* < Lat. *temeritas* < *temere,* rashly.]

Synonyms: *temerity, audacity, impetuosity, effrontery, nerve, cheek, gall.* These nouns are closely related to boldness or aggressiveness in action or speech, often in an unfavorable sense. *Temerity* implies boldness and rashness in the sense of heedlessness of danger, whereas *audacity* suggests heedlessness also of restraints imposed by prudence, propriety, or convention. *Impetuosity* implies haste or vehemence of action or speech that results from obeying impulse rather than reason. The remaining terms are more explicitly derogatory. *Effrontery* is boldness marked by impudence, arrogance, or presumptuousness, whereas *nerve* is an approximately equivalent informal term. *Cheek,* also informal, especially suggests impudence and brashness. *Gall* is a strong informal term that adds to *effrontery* the suggestion of brazenness, insolence, and utter lack of shame.

temp (tĕmp) *n. Informal.* A temporary worker, as in an office. [Short for *temporary worker.*]

tem·peh (tĕm′pā′) *n.* A high-protein food of Indonesian origin made from partially cooked fermented soybeans. [Indonesian *tĕmpe.*]

tem·per (tĕm′pər) *v.* **-pered, -per·ing, -pers.** *—tr.* **1.** To modify by the addition of an agent or quality; moderate: *"temper its doctrinaire logic with a little practical wisdom* (Robert Houghwout Jackson). **2.** To bring to a specified consistency, texture, hardness, or other physical condition by or as if by blending, admixing, or kneading. **3.** To harden, strengthen, or toughen (a metal) by application of heat or by alternate heating and cooling. **4. a.** To attune. **b.** *Mus.* To adjust (the pitch of an instrument) to a temperament. *—intr.* To be or become tempered. *—n.* **1.** A state of mind or emotions; disposition: *an even temper.* **2.** Calmness of mind or emotions; composure: *lose one's temper.* **3. a.** A tendency to become easily angry or irritable: *a quick temper.* **b.** An outburst of rage: *a fit of temper.* **4. a.** The condition of being tempered. **b.** The degree of hardness and elasticity of a metal, chiefly steel, as a result of tempering. **5.** A substance or agent added to something to alter or modify it. **6.** *Obs.* The character or constitution of a human being according to medieval physiology, as determined by the mixture within him of the four humors. **7.** *Archaic.* A middle course; compromise between extremes. [ME *temperen* < OE *temprian* < Lat. *temperare.*] **—tem′per·a·bil′i·ty** *n.* **—tem′per·a·ble** *adj.* **—tem′per·er** *n.*

tem·per·a (tĕm′pər-ə) *n.* **1.** A painting medium in which pigment is mixed with water-soluble glutinous materials such as size or egg yolk. **2.** Painting done with tempera. [Ital. < *temperare,* to mingle < Lat.]

tem·per·a·ment (tĕm′prə-mənt, tĕm′pər-ə-) *n.* **1. a.** The manner of thinking, behaving, or reacting characteristic of a specific individual: *a nervous temperament.* **b.** The distinguishing mental and physical characteristics that established the constitution of a human being according to medieval physiology, caused by the dominance of one of the four humors. **2.** Excessive irritability or sensitiveness. **3.** *Mus.* Equal temperament. [ME < Lat. *temperamentum* < *temperare,* to temper.]

tem·per·a·men·tal (tĕm′prə-mĕn′tl, tĕm′pər-ə-) *adj.* **1.** Pertaining to, caused by, or endowed with temperament or temper. **2. a.** Excessively sensitive or irritable; moody. **b.** Unpredictable in performance: *a temperamental motor.* **—tem′per·a·men′tal·ly** *adv.*

tem·per·ance (tĕm′pər-əns, tĕm′prəns) *n.* **1.** The condition or quality of being temperate; moderation or self-restraint. **2.** Total abstinence from alcoholic liquors.

tem·per·ate (tĕm′pər-ĭt, tĕm′prĭt) *adj.* **1.** Exercising moderation and self-restraint. **2.** Moderate in degree or quality; tempered. **3.** Neither hot nor cold in climate; mild. [ME < Lat. *temperatus* < p.part. of *temperare,* to temper.]

Temperate Zone *n.* Either of two middle latitude zones of the earth, the North Temperate Zone and the South Temperate Zone, lying between $23\frac{1}{2}$ degrees and $66\frac{1}{2}$ degrees north and south.

tem·per·a·ture (tĕm′pər-ə-cho͝or′, tĕm′prə-) *n.* **1. a.** The degree of hotness or coldness of a body or environment. **b.** A specific degree of hotness or coldness as indicated on or referred to a standard scale; a scalar quantity that is independent of the size of the system and that determines the direction of heat flow between any two systems in thermal contact. **2.** An abnormally high temperature caused by illness; fever. [Lat. *temperatura,* composition < *temperare,* to mix.]

temperature gradient *n.* The rate of change of temperature with displacement in a given direction from a given reference point.

tem·pered (tĕm′pərd) *adj.* **1.** Having a specified temper or disposition: *sweet-tempered.* **2.** *Mus.* Tuned to temperament. Used of a scale, interval, semitone, or intonation. **3.** Moderated by the admixture of another substance, quality, or factor: *justice tempered with mercy.* **4.** Having the requisite degree of hardness or elasticity. Used of a metal.

tem·pest (tĕm′pĭst) *n.* **1.** A violent windstorm, frequently accompanied by rain, snow, or hail. **2.** A furious agitation, commotion, or tumult; uproar. *—tr.v.* **-pest·ed, -pest·ing, -pests.** To disturb or agitate violently. [ME < OFr. *tempeste* < Lat. *tempestas* < *tempus,* time.]

tem·pes·tu·ous (tĕm-pĕs′cho͞o-əs) *adj.* **1.** Pertaining to or characteristic of a tempest. **2.** Tumultuous; stormy: *a tempestuous love affair.* [LLat. *tempestuosus* < *tempestas,* tempest.] **—tem·pes′tu·ous·ly** *adv.* **—tem·pes′tu·ous·ness** *n.*

tem·pi (tĕm′pē) *n.* A plural of **tempo.**

Tem·plar (tĕm′plər) *n.* **1.** A knight of a religious military order founded at Jerusalem in the 12th century by the Crusaders. **2. templar.** *Chiefly Brit.* A lawyer or student of law having chambers in the Temple in London. [ME < AN *templer,* var. of OFr. *templier* < Med. Lat. *templarius* < Lat. *templum,* temple.]

tem·plate also **tem·plet** (tĕm′plĭt) *n.* **1.** A pattern or gauge, as a thin metal plate with a cut pattern, used as a guide in making something accurately, as in woodworking. **2.** A piece of stone or timber used to distribute weight or pressure, as over a door frame. **3.** *Biol.* A molecule, such as DNA, that serves as a model for the synthesis of a macromolecule, such as RNA. [Prob. < Fr. *templet,* dim. of OFr. *temple,* temple, device in a loom.]

tem·ple[1] (tĕm′pəl) *n.* **1.** A building or place dedicated to the worship or the presence of a deity. **2. Temple.** Any of three successive buildings in ancient Jerusalem dedicated to the worship of Jehovah. **3.** *Informal.* A synagogue. **4.** *Mormon Ch.* A building in which the sacred ordinances are administered. **5.** Something considered to contain a divine presence. **6.** The headquarters of any of several fraternal orders, esp. of the Knights Templar. **7.** A place or building serving as the focus of a special activity or of something highly valued: *a temple of learning.* **8. Temple.** Either of the two Inns of Court in London housing England's major law societies, and formerly occupied by the Knights Templar. [ME, partly < OE *tempel,* and partly < OFr. *temple,* both < Lat. *templum.*]

temple[1]
Hindu temple in India

tem·ple[2] (tĕm′pəl) *n.* The flat region on either side of the forehead. [ME < OFr. < Lat. *tempora,* pl. of *tempus,* temple of the head.]

tem·ple[3] (tĕm′pəl) *n.* A device in a loom that keeps the cloth stretched to the correct width during weaving. [ME *tempylle* < OFr. *temple,* poss. < Lat. *templum,* small piece of wood.]

tem·plet (tĕm′plĕt) *n.* Variant of **template.**

tem·po (tĕm′pō) *n., pl.* **-pos** or **-pi** (-pē). **1.** *Mus.* The relative speed at which a composition is to be played, as indicated by a descriptive or metronomic direction to the performer. **2.** A characteristic rate or rhythm of activity; pace: *"the tempo and the feeling of modern life"* (Robert L. Heilbroner). [Ital. < Lat. *tempus,* time.]

tem·po·ral[1] (tĕm′pər-əl, tĕm′prəl) *adj.* **1.** Pertaining to, concerned with, or limited by time. **2.** Pertaining to or concerned with worldly affairs. **3.** Enduring for a short time; short-lived: *the temporal dreams of youth.* **4.** Civil, secular, or lay, as distinguished from ecclesiastical. **5.** *Gram.* Expressing time: *a temporal adverb.* [ME < Lat. *temporalis* < *tempus,* time.] **—tem′po·ral·ly** *adv.*

tem·po·ral[2] (tĕm′pər-əl, tĕm′prəl) *adj.* Of, pertaining to, or near the temples of the skull. [LLat. *temporalis* < Lat. *tempora,* pl. of *tempus,* temple.]

temporal bone *n.* Either of two complex, three-part bones forming the sides and base of the skull.

tem·po·ral·i·ty (tĕm′pə-răl′ĭ-tē) *n., pl.* **-ties. 1.** The condition of being temporal or temporary. **2. temporalities.** Temporal possessions, esp. of the church or clergy.

tem·po·rar·y (tĕm'pə-rĕr'ē) *adj.* Lasting, used, or enjoyed for a limited time; impermanent. *—n., pl.* **-ies.** *Informal.* One that serves for a limited time, esp. an office worker. [Lat. *temporarius* < *tempus,* time.] **—tem'po·rar'i·ly** *adv.* **—tem'po·rar'i·ness** *n.*

tem·po·rize (tĕm'pə-rīz') *intr.v.* **-rized, -riz·ing, -riz·es. 1.** To compromise or act evasively in order to gain time, avoid argument, or postpone a decision: *"Colonial officials . . . ordered to enforce unpopular enactments, tended to temporize, to find excuses for evasion"* (J.H. Parry). **2. a.** To behave appropriately under the circumstances. **b.** To yield to current conditions; compromise. [OFr. *temporiser,* to pass one's time < Med. Lat. *temporizare* < Lat. *tempus,* time.] **—tem'po·ri·za'tion** *n.*

tempt (tĕmpt) *tr.v.* **tempt·ed, tempt·ing, tempts. 1.** To entice (someone) to commit an unwise or immoral act, esp. by a promise of reward. **2.** To be inviting or attractive to. **3.** To provoke or to risk provoking: *Don't tempt fate.* **4.** To incline or dispose strongly: *She was tempted to resign.* [ME *tempten* < OFr. *tempter* < Lat. *temptare,* to feel, try.] **—tempt'a·ble** *adj.* **—tempt'er** *n.* **—tempt'ress** (tĕmp'trĭs) *n.*

temp·ta·tion (tĕmp-tā'shən) *n.* **1.** The act of tempting or the condition of being tempted. **2.** Something that tempts or entices.

tempt·ing (tĕmp'tĭng) *adj.* Alluring; seductive. **—tempt'ing·ly** *adv.* **—tempt'ing·ness** *n.*

tem·pu·ra (tĕm'po͝o-rə, tĕm-po͝or'ə) *n.* A Japanese dish of vegetables and shrimp or other seafood dipped in batter and fried in deep fat. [J.]

ten (tĕn) *n.* **1.** The cardinal number that is next after the number 9 and equal to the sum of 9 + 1. **2.** Something having ten parts, units, or members. **3.** A playing card marked with ten spots. **4.** A ten-dollar bill. [ME < OE *tīen;* akin to G. *zehn,* Lat. *decem,* Gk. *deka,* Skt. *daśa.*] **—ten** *adj. & pron.*

ten·a·ble (tĕn'ə-bəl) *adj.* **1.** Capable of being defended or sustained; logical: *a tenable theory.* **2.** Defensible from armed assault: *a tenable outpost.* [Fr. < OFr. < *tenir,* to hold < Lat. *tenēre.*] **—ten'a·bil'i·ty, ten'a·ble·ness** *n.* **—ten'a·bly** *adv.*

ten·ace (tĕn'ās', tĕ-nās', tĕn'ĭs) *n. Games.* A combination of two high cards, as the king and jack, held in a player's hand, esp. in bridge and whist. [Fr. < Sp. *tenaza* < Lat. *tenax,* tenacious.]

te·na·cious (tə-nā'shəs) *adj.* **1.** Holding or tending to hold firmly; persistent: *a man tenacious of his opinions and averse to new ideas.* **2.** Holding together firmly; cohesive. **3.** Clinging to another object or surface; adhesive. **4.** Tending to retain; retentive: *a tenacious memory.* [< Lat. *tenax, tenac-,* holding fast < *tenēre,* to hold.] **—te·na'cious·ly** *adv.* **—te·na'cious·ness** *n.*

te·nac·i·ty (tə-năs'ĭ-tē) *n.* The condition or quality of being tenacious.

te·nac·u·lum (tə-năk'yə-ləm) *n., pl.* **-la** (-lə). A long-handled, slender, hooked instrument for lifting and holding parts, as blood vessels, during surgery. [NLat. < LLat., holder < Lat. *tenēre,* to hold.]

ten·an·cy (tĕn'ən-sē) *n., pl.* **-cies. 1.** The possession or occupancy of lands or tenements by title, under a lease, or on payment of rent. **2.** The period of a tenant's occupancy or possession. **3.** A habitation held or occupied by a tenant. [< TENANT.]

ten·ant (tĕn'ənt) *n.* **1.** One who pays rent to use or occupy land, a building, or other property owned by another. **2.** An occupant, inhabitant, or dweller in a place. **3.** *Law.* One who holds or possesses lands, tenements, and sometimes personal property by any kind of title. *—v.* **-ant·ed, -ant·ing, -ants.** *—tr.* To hold as a tenant; occupy. *—intr.* To be a tenant. [ME < OFr. < pr.part. of *tenir,* to hold < Lat. *tenēre.*]

tenant farmer *n.* One who farms land owned by another and pays rent in cash or in kind.

ten·ant·ry (tĕn'ən-trē) *n., pl.* **-ries. 1.** Tenants collectively. **2.** The state or condition of being a tenant; tenancy.

ten-cent store (tĕn'sĕnt') *n.* A five-and-ten.

tench (tĕnch) *n., pl.* **tench** or **tench·es.** An edible Eurasian freshwater fish, *Tinca tinca,* having small scales and two barbels near the mouth. [ME *tenche* < OFr. < LLat. *tinca.*]

Ten Commandments *pl.n.* The ten injunctions given by God to Moses on Mount Sinai, serving as the basis of Mosaic Law.

tend[1] (tĕnd) *intr.v.* **tend·ed, tend·ing, tends. 1.** To move or extend in a certain direction: *Our course tended toward the north.* **2.** To be likely: *These things tend to work themselves out eventually.* **3.** To be disposed or inclined: *He tends toward laziness.* [ME *tenden* < OFr. *tendre* < Lat. *tendere.*]

tend[2] (tĕnd) *v.* **tend·ed, tend·ing, tends.** *—tr.* **1.** To minister to the needs of; look after: *tend a child.* **2.** To take care of; serve at: *tend bar.* *—intr.* **1.** To serve or wait. **2.** *Informal.* To apply one's attention: *Tend to your own business.* [ME *tenden,* short for *attenden,* to attend. —see ATTEND.]

Usage: *Tend* is an informal variant of *attend* in the phrase *tend to,* meaning "to apply one's attention to": *A special session of the legislature has been called to tend to the problem of redistricting.* In writing that is not expressly informal, this example is unacceptable to a great majority of the Usage Panel.

ten·den·cy (tĕn'dən-sē) *n., pl.* **-cies. 1.** A demonstrated inclination to think, act, or behave in a certain way; propensity: *a tendency to panic.* **2.** The purposeful trend of something that is said or written; purport. [Med. Lat. *tendentia* < Lat. *tendens,* pr.part. of *tendere,* to tend.]

Synonyms: *tendency, trend, current, drift, tenor, inclination.* These nouns are compared as they relate to the direction or course of action or thought. *Tendency* implies a definite proneness or predisposition of a person or thing to behave in a certain way. *Trend* is usually applied to the prevailing direction of thought or practice within a given sphere, such as literature or politics. Like *current* and *drift, trend* specifies a course that reflects the thought or action of relatively large numbers of persons. *Current* suggests a course, as of thought or opinion, closely related to a given time or place. *Drift* often refers to the long-range course of institutions, such as government or law, that exert broad influence or control. *Tenor* implies a continuous course, as of a person's life, and a procedure or practice that is usually unvarying. *Inclination* usually refers to an individual's propensity or bent for behaving in a certain way at a given time. As a motivating force, an *inclination* is not as strong or consistent as a *tendency.*

ten·den·tious also **ten·den·cious** (tĕn-dĕn'shəs) *adj.* Written or said to promote a cause; not impartial. [TENDENCY.] **—ten·den'tious·ly** *adv.* **—ten·den'tious·ness** *n.*

ten·der[1] (tĕn'dər) *adj.* **-er, -est. 1. a.** Easily crushed or bruised; fragile: *a tender petal.* **b.** Easily chewed or cut: *tender beef.* **c.** Having a delicate quality: *a tender song.* **2.** Young and vulnerable: *of tender age.* **3.** Frail; delicate. **4.** Sensitive to frost or severe cold; not hardy: *tender green shoots.* **5. a.** Easily hurt; sensitive: *tender skin.* **b.** Painful; sore: *a tender tooth.* **6. a.** Gentle and solicitous: *a tender mother.* **b.** Expressing gentle emotions; loving: *a tender glance.* **c.** Given to sympathy or sentimentality; soft: *a tender heart.* **7. a.** Considerate and protective: *tender of her reputation.* **b.** Scrupulous; chary: *tender of making false promises.* **8.** Apt to lean under sail; crank. *—tr.v.* **-dered, -der·ing, -ders. 1.** To make tender. **2.** *Archaic.* To treat with tender regard. [ME < OFr. *tendre* < Lat. *tener.*] **—ten'der·ly** *adv.* **—ten'der·ness** *n.*

ten·der[2] (tĕn'dər) *n.* **1.** A formal offer, as: **a.** *Law.* An offer of money or service in payment of an obligation. **b.** A written offer to contract goods or services at a specified cost or rate; a bid. **2.** Something tendered, esp. money: *legal tender.* *—tr.v.* **-dered, -der·ing, -ders.** To offer formally: *tender a letter of resignation.* [< OFr. *tendre,* to offer < Lat. *tendere,* to hold forth.] **—ten'der·er** *n.*

tend·er[3] (tĕn'dər) *n.* **1.** One who tends something: *a lathe tender.* **2.** A vessel attendant on another vessel or vessels, esp. one that ferries supplies between ship and shore. **3.** A railroad car attached to the rear of a locomotive and designed to carry fuel and water.

ten·der·foot (tĕn'dər-fo͝ot') *n., pl.* **-foots** or **-feet. 1.** A newcomer not yet hardened to rough outdoor life; greenhorn. **2.** An inexperienced person; novice. **3.** A beginner in the ranks of the Boy Scouts.

ten·der·heart·ed (tĕn'dər-här'tĭd) *adj.* Easily moved by another's distress; compassionate. **—ten'der·heart'ed·ly** *adv.* **—ten'der·heart'ed·ness** *n.*

ten·der·ize (tĕn'də-rīz') *tr.v.* **-ized, -iz·ing, -iz·es.** To make (meat) tender, as by marinating, pounding, or applying a tenderizer. **—ten'der·i·za'tion** *n.*

ten·der·iz·er (tĕn'də-rī'zər) *n.* A substance, as a plant enzyme, applied to meat to make it tender.

ten·der·loin (tĕn'dər-loin') *n.* **1.** The tenderest part of a loin of beef, pork, or similar cut of meat. **2.** A city district notorious for its vice and graft. [Sense 2, after the *Tenderloin,* an area of New York City (from the easy income it affords a corrupt policeman).]

ten·der-mind·ed (tĕn'dər-mīn'dĭd) *adj.* Resisting harsh facts; idealistic.

ten·di·ni·tis (tĕn'də-nī'tĭs) *n.* Inflammation of a tendon. [NLat. *tendo, tendin-,* tendon (< Med. Lat. *tendo*) + -ITIS.]

ten·di·nous (tĕn'də-nəs) *adj.* **1.** Of, having, or resembling a tendon. **2.** Sinewy. [NLat. *tendinosus* < *tendo, tendin-,* tendon < Med. Lat. *tendo.*]

ten·don (tĕn'dən) *n.* A band of tough, inelastic fibrous tissue that connects a muscle with its bony attachment. [Med. Lat. *tendo, tendon-,* < Lat. *tendere,* to stretch.]

ten·do·ni·tis (tĕn'də-nī'tĭs) *n.* Tendinitis.

tendon of Achilles *n.* The Achilles' tendon.

ten·dril (tĕn'drəl) *n.* **1.** A long, slender, coiling extension, as of a stem, serving as an organ of attachment for certain climbing plants. **2.** Something, such as a ringlet of hair, that is long, slender, and curling. [OFr. *tendrillon* < *tendron,* young shoot < Lat. *tener,* tender.]

Ten·e·brae (tĕn'ə-brā', -brē') *pl.n. (used with a sing. or pl. verb). Rom. Cath. Ch.* The office of matins and lauds sung on the last three days of Holy Week, with a ceremony of candles. [Med. Lat. < Lat. *tenebrae,* darkness.]

ten·e·brif·ic (tĕn'ə-brĭf'ĭk) *adj.* **1.** Serving to obscure or darken. **2.** Gloomy; dark. [Lat. *tenebrae,* darkness + -FIC.]

te·neb·ri·o·nid (tə-nĕb'rē-ə-nĭd', tĕn'ə-brī'-) *n.* Any of several dark-colored herbivorous beetles of the family Tenebrionidae. [< NLat. *Tenebrionidae,* family name < *Tenebrio,* type genus < Lat. *tenebrio,* one who avoids light < *tenebrae,* darkness.] **—te·neb·ri·o·nid'** *adj.*

ten·e·brous (tĕn'ə-brəs) also **te·neb·ri·ous** (tə-nĕb'rē-əs) *adj.* Dark and gloomy. [< Lat. *tenebrae,* darkness.] **—ten'e·bros'i·ty** (-brŏs'ĭ-tē) *n.*

ten·e·ment (tĕn'ə-mənt) *n.* **1.** A building to live in, esp. one intended for rent; residence. **2.** A run-down low-rental apartment building whose facilities and maintenance barely meet minimum standards. **3.** *Chiefly Brit.* An apartment or room leased to a tenant. **4.** *Law.* Property of a permanent nature, as land, rents, or franchises, that may be held by one person for another. [ME, house < OFr. < Med. Lat. *tenementum* < Lat. *tenēre,* to hold.] **—ten'e·men'tal** (-mĕn'tl), **ten'e·men'ta·ry** (-mĕn'tə-rē) *adj.*

te·nes·mus (tə-nĕz'məs) *n.* A painfully urgent but ineffectual attempt to urinate or defecate. [Med. Lat., var. of Lat. *tenesmos* < Gk. *teinesmos* < *teinein,* to strain.]

ten·et (tĕn'ĭt) *n.* An opinion, doctrine, or principle held as being true by a person or esp. by an organization. [< Lat., he holds < *tenēre,* to hold.]

ten·fold (tĕn'fōld') *adj.* **1.** Composed of ten parts or members. **2.** Ten times as great or as many. *—adv.* Ten times in extent or number.

ten-gal·lon hat (tĕn'găl'ən) *n.* A felt hat having an exceptionally tall crown and wide brim.

te·ni·a (tē'nē-ə) *n.* Variant of **taenia.**

te·ni·a·cide also **tae·ni·a·cide** (tē'nē-ə-sīd') *n.* An agent that destroys tapeworms. [TENIA + -CIDE.]

te·ni·a·sis also **tae·ni·a·sis** (tē-nī'ə-sĭs) *n.* Infestation with tapeworms. [TEN(IA) + -IASIS.]

ten·nis (tĕn'ĭs) *n.* **1.** A game played with rackets and a light ball by two players or two pairs of players on a court divided by a net. **2.** Lawn tennis. **3.** Court tennis. [ME *tenetz,* court tennis, prob. < OFr. *tenez,* imper. of *tenir,* to receive.]

tennis shoes *pl.n.* Sneakers (sense 2).

teno– *pref.* Tendon: *tenotomy.* [< Gk. *tenōn,* tendon.]

ten·on (tĕn'ən) *n.* A projection on the end of a piece of wood shaped for insertion into a mortise. *—tr.v.* **-oned, -on·ing, -ons. 1.** To provide with a tenon. **2.** To join with a tenon. [ME < OFr. < *tenir,* to hold < Lat. *tenēre.*]

ten·or (tĕn'ər) *n.* **1. a.** The flow of meaning apparent in something written or spoken. **b.** General sense; purport. **2. a.** *Law.* The exact meaning or actual wording of a document as distinct from its effect. **b.** An exact copy or transcript of a document. **3.** *Mus.* **a.** The highest natural adult male voice. **b.** A part for this voice. **c.** One who sings this part. **—*modifier:*** *a tenor sax.* [ME < OFr. < Lat., uninterrupted course < *tenēre,* to continue.]

te·nor·rha·phy (tĕ-nôr'ə-fē) *n., pl.* **-phies.** The surgical uniting of divided tendons with sutures. [TENO- + Gk. *rhaphē,* suture.]

ten·o·syn·o·vi·tis (tĕn'ō-sĭn'ō-vī'tĭs) *n.* Inflammation of a tendon sheath. [TENO- + SYNOV(IA) + -ITIS.]

te·not·o·my (tĕ-nŏt'ə-mē) *n., pl.* **-mies.** The surgical division of a tendon for the relief of deformities caused by the shortening of a muscle.

ten·pence (tĕn'pəns) *n. Chiefly Brit.* A sum of money equal to ten pennies.

ten·pen·ny (tĕn'pĕn'ē, -pə-nē) *adj. Chiefly Brit.* Valued at or costing tenpence.

tenpenny nail *n.* A nail three inches long. [From its orig. price per hundred.]

ten·pin (tĕn'pĭn') *n.* **1.** A bowling pin used in playing tenpins. **2. tenpins** *(used with a sing. verb).* The game of bowling.

ten·rec (tĕn'rĕk') also **tan·rec** (tăn'-) *n.* Any of various insectivorous, often hedgehoglike mammals of the family Tenrecidae, of Madagascar and adjacent islands. [Fr. < Malagasy *tàndraka.*]

tense¹ (tĕns) *adj.* **tens·er, tens·est. 1.** Tightly stretched; taut; strained: *tense muscles.* **2.** In a state of mental or nervous tension. **3.** Nerve-racking; suspenseful: *a tense situation.* **4.** Enunciated with taut muscles, as the consonant *t.* *—tr. & intr.v.* **tensed, tens·ing, tens·es.** To make or become tense. [Lat. *tensus* < p.part. of *tendere,* to stretch out.]

tense² (tĕns) *n.* **1.** Any one of the inflected forms in the conjugation of a verb that indicates the time (past, present, or future) as well as the continuance (imperfect) or completion (perfect) of the action or state. **2.** A set of tense forms indicating a particular time: *the future tense.* [ME *tens* < OFr., time < Lat. *tempus.*]

ten·sile (tĕn'səl, -sīl') *adj.* **1.** Of or pertaining to tension. **2.** Capable of being stretched or extended; ductile. [NLat. *tensilis* < Lat. *tensus,* stretched out < p.part. of *tendere,* to stretch.] **—ten·sil'i·ty** (tĕn-sĭl'ə-tē) *n.*

tensile strength *n.* The resistance of a material to a force tending to tear it apart.

ten·sim·e·ter (tĕn-sĭm'ĭ-tər) *n.* An apparatus that is used to measure differences in vapor pressure. [TENSI(ON) + -METER.]

ten·si·om·e·ter (tĕn'sē-ŏm'ĭ-tər) *n.* **1.** An instrument for measuring tensile strength. **2.** A torsion-balance apparatus used to measure the surface tension of a liquid. [TENSIO(N) + -METER.] **—ten'si·o·met'ric** *adj.* **—ten'si·om'e·try** *n.*

ten·sion (tĕn'shən) *n.* **1. a.** The act or process of stretching. **b.** The condition of being stretched. **2. a.** A force tending to stretch or elongate something. **b.** The measure of such a force: *a tension of 50 pounds.* **3. a.** Mental, emotional, or nervous strain. **b.** A strained relation or barely controlled hostility between persons or groups. **c.** Uneasy suspense. **4.** A device for regulating tautness, esp. a device regulating the tautness of thread on a sewing machine. **5.** *Elect.* Voltage or potential; electromotive force. *—tr.v.* **-sioned, -sion·ing, -sions.** To subject to tension; make taut. [OFr. < LLat. *tensio* < Lat. *tendere,* to stretch.] **—ten'sion·al** *adj.*

ten·si·ty (tĕn'sĭ-tē) *n.* The state of being tense; tenseness.

ten·sive (tĕn'sĭv) *adj.* Of, pertaining to, or causing tension.

ten·sor (tĕn'sər, -sôr') *n.* **1.** *Anat.* A muscle that tenses a part, making it firm. **2.** *Math.* An element of an abstract system used to denote position determined within the context of more than one coordinate system, a special case of which is a vector that is determined in a single coordinate system. **—ten·so'ri·al** (-sôr'ē-əl, -sōr'-) *adj.*

Ten·sor lamp (tĕn'sər, -sôr'). A trademark for a high-intensity electric lamp.

ten-strike (tĕn'strīk') *n.* **1.** A strike in tenpins. **2.** *Informal.* A remarkably successful stroke or action.

tent¹ (tĕnt) *n.* **1.** A portable shelter of canvas, plastic, or skins stretched over a supporting framework of poles with ropes and pegs. **2.** Something resembling a tent in construction or outline. *—v.* **tent·ed, tent·ing, tents.** *—intr.* To encamp in a tent. *—tr.* **1.** To form a tent over. **2.** To put up in tents. [ME < OFr. *tente* < VLat. **tenta* < fem. p.part. of Lat. *tendere,* stretch out.]

tent² (tĕnt) *n.* A small roll or plug, usually of lint or gauze, for placing in a wound or orifice to keep it open or for probing. *—tr.v.* **tent·ed, tent·ing, tents.** To keep (a wound or cut) open with a tent. [ME *tente* < OFr. < *tenter,* to probe < Lat. *tentare,* to feel.]

tent³ (tĕnt) *tr.v.* **tent·ed, tent·ing, tents.** *Scot.* **1.** To pay heed to. **2.** To attend; wait upon. [ME *tenten* < *tent,* attention, short for *attent* < OFr. *attente* < *attendre,* to attend < Lat. *attendere.* —see ATTEND.]

ten·ta·cle (tĕn'tə-kəl) *n.* **1.** *Zool.* An elongated, flexible, unsegmented protrusion, as one of those surrounding the mouth or oral cavity of the squid. **2.** *Bot.* One of the hairs on the leaves of insectivorous plants, as the sundew. **3.** Something resembling a tentacle, esp. in ability to grasp or hold. [NLat. *tentaculum* < Lat. *tentare,* to touch.] **—ten·tac'u·lar** (-tăk'yə-lər) *adj.*

tent·age (tĕn'tĭj) *n.* **1.** Tents collectively. **2.** A supply of tents available for accommodation. **3.** Tent equipment.

ten·ta·tive (tĕn'tə-tĭv) *adj.* **1.** Of an experimental nature; provisional. **2.** Uncertain: *a tentative smile.* *—n.* An experiment. [Med. Lat. *tentativus* < Lat. *tentare,* to try.] **—ten'ta·tive·ly** *adv.* **—ten'ta·tive·ness** *n.*

tent caterpillar *n.* Any of several destructive caterpillars, esp. the hairy larva of a North American moth, *Malacosoma americanum,* that live in colonies in tentlike webs constructed in deciduous trees.

tent·ed (tĕn'tĭd) *adj.* **1.** Covered with tents. **2.** Sheltered in tents. **3.** Resembling a tent.

ten·ter (tĕn'tər) *n.* **1.** A framework upon which milled cloth is stretched for drying without shrinkage. **2.** *Obs.* A tenterhook. *—tr.v.* **-tered, -ter·ing, -ters.** To stretch (cloth) on a tenter. [ME *teyntur.*]

ten·ter·hook (tĕn'tər-ho͝ok') *n.* A hooked nail for securing cloth on a tenter. **—*idiom.* on tenterhooks.** In a state of uneasiness, suspense, or anxiety.

tenth (tĕnth) *n.* **1.** The ordinal number that matches the number ten in a series. **2.** One of ten equal parts. [ME *tenthe* (< *ten,* ten), alteration of *tethe* < OE *teoða.*] **—tenth** *adj. & adv.*

tent stitch *n.* A short diagonal embroidery stitch that forms close, even, parallel rows to fill in a pattern or a background.

ten·u·is (tĕn'yo͞o-ĭs) *n., pl.* **-u·es** (-yo͞o-ēz'). A voiceless stop in Greek. [NLat. (transl. of Gk. *psilos*) < Lat., thin.]

te·nu·i·ty (tĕ-no͞o'ĭ-tē, -nyo͞o'-) *n.* **1.** Lack of firmness or mettle. **2.** Fragility. [Lat. *tenuitas,* thinness < *tenuis,* thin.]

ten·u·ous (tĕn'yo͞o-əs) *adj.* **1.** Having a thin or slender form. **2.** Having a thin consistency; dilute. **3.** Having little substance; flimsy: *a tenuous argument.* [Lat. *tenuis.*] **—ten'u·ous·ly** *adv.* **—ten'u·ous·ness** *n.*

ten·ure (tĕn'yər, -yo͝or') *n.* **1.** The fact or condition of holding something, as real estate or an office; occupation. **2.** The terms under which something is held. **3. a.** The period of holding something. **b.** Permanence of position, often granted an employee after a specified number of years: *academic tenure.* [ME < OFr. < *tenir,* to hold, < Lat. *tenēre.*] **—ten'ured** *adj.* **—ten·u'ri·al** (tĕn-yo͝or'ē-əl) *adj.* **—ten·u'ri·al·ly** *adv.*

ten·ured (tĕn'yərd, -yo͝ord') *adj.* Having academic tenure.

te·nu·to (tā-no͞o'tō) *adv. & adj. Mus.* So as to be held for the full time value; sustained. [Ital. < p.part. of *tenere,* to hold < Lat. *tenēre.*]

te·o·cal·li (tē'ə-kăl'ē) *n., pl.* **-lis. 1.** A temple of ancient Mexico and Central America, usually built upon a mound of a truncated pyramidal shape. **2.** The mound upon which a teocalli is built. [Nahuatl : *teotl,* sacred + *calli,* house.]

tenrec

tentacle
Of an octopus

tepee

te·o·sin·te (tē′ə-sĭn′tē, tā′ō-) *n.* A tall Central American grass, *Euchlaena mexicana,* related to corn and cultivated for fodder. [Mex. Sp. < Nahuatl *teocentli* : *teotl,* sacred + *centli,* dried ear of corn.]

te·pal (tē′pəl, tĕp′əl) *n. Bot.* A division of the perianth of a flower having petals and sepals that are virtually indistinguishable. [Fr. *tépale.*]

tep·a·ry bean (tĕp′ə-rē) *n.* **1.** A vine, *Phaseolus acutifolius latifolius,* of the southwestern United States and adjacent Mexico, bearing edible beans. **2.** The bean borne by the tepary bean. [Orig. unknown.]

te·pee also **tee·pee** or **ti·pi** (tē′pē) *n.* A cone-shaped tent of skins or bark used by North American Indians, esp. the Plains Indians. [Dakota *tipi.*]

tep·e·fy (tĕp′ə-fī′) *tr. & intr.v.* **-fied, -fy·ing, -fies.** To make or become tepid. [Lat. *tepefacere* : *tepēre,* to be tepid + *facere,* to make.] **—tep′e·fac′tion** (-făk′shən) *n.*

tep·id (tĕp′ĭd) *adj.* Moderately warm; lukewarm. [Lat. *tepidus* < *tepēre,* to be lukewarm.] **—te·pid′i·ty** (tĕ-pĭd′ĭ-tē), **tep′id·ness** *n.* **—tep′id·ly** *adv.*

te·qui·la (tə-kē′lə) *n.* An alcoholic liquor distilled from a Central American century plant, *Agave tequilana.* [Mex. Sp., after *Tequila,* Mexico.]

tera– *pref.* One trillion (10^{12}): *terahertz.* [< Gk. *teras,* monster.]

ter·a·hertz (tĕr′ə-hûrts′) *n.* One trillion (10^{12}) hertz.

ter·a·ohm (tĕr′ə-ōm′) *n.* One trillion (10^{12}) ohms.

ter·aph (tĕr′əf) *n., pl.* **ter·a·phim** (tĕr′ə-fĭm). An image of a Semitic household idol. [< Heb. *tĕrāphīm,* idols.]

ter·a·to·car·ci·no·ma (tĕr′ə-tō-kär′sə-nō′mə) *n.* A teratoma that is carcinomatous in nature. [Gk. *teras, terat-,* monster + CARCINOMA.]

te·rat·o·gen (tə-răt′ə-jən, tĕr′ə-tə-) *n.* A teratogenic agent. [Gk. *teras, terat-,* monster + -GEN.]

ter·a·to·gen·ic (tĕr′ə-tə-jĕn′ĭk) *adj.* Causing fetal malformations or monstrosities. **—ter′a·to·ge·nic′i·ty** (-jə-nĭs′ĭ-tē) *n.*

ter·a·toid (tĕr′ə-toid′) *adj.* Like a monster; monstrous. [Gk. *teras, terat-,* monster + -OID.]

ter·a·tol·o·gy (tĕr′ə-tŏl′ə-jē) *n.* The biological study of the production, development, anatomy, and classification of monsters. [Gk. *teras, terat-,* monster + -LOGY.] **—ter′a·to·log′i·cal** (-tə-lŏj′ĭ-kəl) *adj.*

ter·a·to·ma (tĕr′ə-tō′mə) *n., pl.* **-mas** or **-ma·ta** (-mə-tə). A tumor consisting of different types of tissue, caused by the development of independent germ cells. [Gk. *teras, terat-,* monster + -OMA.] **—ter′a·to′ma·tous** (-tō′mə-təs) *adj.*

ter·bi·um (tûr′bē-əm) *n. Symbol* **Tb** A soft, silvery-gray metallic rare-earth element, used as a solid-state dopant and as a laser material. Atomic number 65; atomic weight 158.924; melting point 1,356°C; boiling point 2,800°C; specific gravity 8.272; valences 3, 4. [After *Ytterby,* Sweden.]

terbium metal *n.* Any of several rare-earth metals separable from other metals as a group and including europium, terbium, and gadolinium.

terce (tûrs) *n.* Variant of **tierce.**

ter·cel (tûr′səl) also **tier·cel** (tîr′səl) *n.* A male hawk used in falconry. [ME < OFr. < VLat. **tertiolus,* dim. of Lat. *tertius,* third.]

ter·cen·ten·a·ry (tûr′sĕn-tĕn′ə-rē, tər-sĕn′tə-nĕr′ē) *n., pl.* **-ries.** A 300th anniversary or its celebration. *—adj.* Of or pertaining to a span of 300 years or to a 300th anniversary. [Lat. *ter,* thrice + CENTENARY.]

ter·cen·ten·ni·al (tûr′sĕn-tĕn′ē-əl) *n. & adj.* Tercentenary.

ter·cet (tûr′sĭt) *n.* **1.** A poetic triplet of lines that rhyme together or that are connected with adjacent rhymes. **2.** *Mus.* A triplet (sense 4). [Ital. *terzetto,* dim. of *terzo,* third < Lat. *tertius.*]

ter·e·bene (tĕr′ə-bēn′) *n.* A mixture of terpenes prepared from oil of turpentine, used as an expectorant and antiseptic. [Fr. *térébène* < *térébinthe,* terebinth < OFr. *terebinte.*]

te·reb·ic acid (tə-rĕb′ĭk, -rē′bĭk) *n.* A white crystalline compound, $C_7H_{10}O_4$, resulting from the action of nitric acid on turpentine. [TEREB(INTH) + -IC + ACID.]

ter·e·binth (tĕr′ə-bĭnth′) *n.* A small tree, *Pistachia terebinthus,* of the Mediterranean region that yields a resinous liquid. [ME *terebinthe* < OFr. *terebinte* < Lat. *terebinthus* < Gk. *terebinthos.*]

ter·e·bin·thine (tĕr′ə-bĭn′thĭn, -thīn′) also **ter·e·bin·thic** (-thĭk) *adj.* **1.** Of or pertaining to the terebinth. **2.** Pertaining to, consisting of, or resembling turpentine.

te·re·do (tə-rē′dō, -rā′dō) *n., pl.* **-dos.** A shipworm. [NLat. *Teredo,* mollusk genus < Lat. *teredo,* a kind of worm < Gk. *terēdōn.*]

te·rete (tĕ-rēt′) *adj.* Cylindrical but usually slightly tapering at both ends, circular in cross section, and smooth-surfaced. [Lat. *teres, teret-,* rounded.]

Te·reus (tē′ro͞os′, tîr′ē-əs) *n. Gk. Myth.* A king of Thrace who raped Philomela and who was changed into a hoopoe. [Lat. < Gk. *Tēreus.*]

ter·ga (tûr′gə) *n.* Plural of **tergum.**

ter·gal (tûr′gəl) *adj.* Of or pertaining to the tergum; dorsal.

ter·giv·er·sate (tər-jĭv′ər-săt′, tûr′jĭ-vər-) *intr.v.* **-sat·ed, -sat·ing, -sates. 1.** To use evasions or ambiguities; equivocate. **2.** To change sides; apostatize. [Lat. *tergiversari, tergiversat-* : *tergum,* a back + *versare,* to whirl.] **—ter·giv′er·sa′tion** *n.* **—ter′gi·ver·sa′tor** (-sā′tər) *n.*

ter·gum (tûr′gəm) *n., pl.* **-ga** (-gə). *Zool.* The upper or dorsal surface, esp. of a body segment of an insect or other arthropod. [NLat. < Lat., back.]

ter·i·ya·ki (tĕr′ē-yä′kē) *n.* A Japanese dish consisting of skewered and broiled slices of marinated meat or shellfish. [J. : *teri,* sunshine, flame + *yaki,* to broil.]

term (tûrm) *n.* **1. a.** A limited period of time during which something lasts. **b.** The time during which a court is in session. **c.** A period of a school year during which instruction is given. **2. a.** A point of time beginning or ending a period. **b.** A deadline, as for making a payment. **c.** The end of a normal gestation period. **3.** *Law.* **a.** A fixed period of time during which an estate may be held. **b.** The estate to be granted. **c.** A period of time allowed a debtor to meet an obligation. **4. a.** A word having a precise meaning, esp. one that is peculiar to a particular group or activity: *a medical term.* **b. terms.** Language or a manner of expression employed: *He spoke in no uncertain terms.* **5. a.** A condition or stipulation that defines the nature and limits of an agreement: *peace terms.* **b. terms.** The relation between two persons or groups; footing: *on speaking terms.* **6.** *Math.* **a.** Each of the quantities composing a ratio or a fraction or forming a series. **b.** Each of the quantities connected by addition or subtraction signs in an equation; member. **7.** *Logic.* Each of the two concepts being compared or related in a proposition. **8.** A stone or post marking a boundary, esp. a square and tapering pillar adorned with a head and upper torso. *—tr.v.* **termed, term·ing, terms.** To designate; call. ***—idioms.* come to terms.** To reach an agreement. **in terms of.** With regard to; respecting. [ME *terme* < OFr. < Lat. *terminus,* boundary.] **—term′ly** *adv.*

ter·ma·gant (tûr′mə-gənt) *n.* A quarrelsome, scolding woman; shrew. *—adj.* Abusive; shrewish. [ME *Termagaunt,* imaginary Moslem deity portrayed as a violent and overbearing character in medieval mystery plays.]

term·er (tûr′mər) *n.* A person serving a specified term, esp. in prison: *a second termer.*

ter·mi·na·ble (tûr′mə-nə-bəl) *adj.* **1.** Capable of being terminated. **2.** Terminating after a designated date: *a terminable annuity.* **—ter′mi·na·bil′i·ty, ter′mi·na·ble·ness** *n.* **—ter′mi·na·bly** *adv.*

ter·mi·nal (tûr′mə-nəl) *adj.* **1.** Of, pertaining to, situated at, or forming an end or boundary. **2.** *Biol.* Growing or appearing at the end of a stem, branch, stalk, or similar part. **3.** Pertaining to or occurring at the end of a section or series; final. **4.** Pertaining to or occurring in a term or each term; appearing regularly or periodically. **5.** Ending in death; fatal. *—n.* **1.** A terminating point, limit, or part. **2.** An ornamental figure or object, as a finial of a lamp, that is situated at the end of another object. **3.** *Elect.* **a.** A position in an electric circuit or device at which an electric connection is normally established or broken. **b.** A passive conductor at such a position used to facilitate the connection. **4. a.** Either end of a railroad or other transportation line; terminus. **b.** A station at such a point or at a major junction on such a line. **c.** A town at the end of a carrier line. **5.** *Computer Sci.* An instrument through which data or information can enter or leave a computer. [Lat. *terminalis* < *terminus,* boundary.] **—ter′mi·nal·ly** *adv.*

terminal leave *n.* Final leave equal to accumulated unused leave granted to a member of the armed forces immediately prior to separation or discharge from service.

ter·mi·nate (tûr′mə-nāt′) *v.* **-nat·ed, -nat·ing, -nates.** *—tr.* **1.** To bring to an end or halt: *terminate a project for lack of funding.* **2.** To occur at or form the end of; conclude. **3.** To discontinue the employment of: *terminated 300 workers.* *—intr.* **1.** To come to an end: *Negotiations terminated yesterday.* **2.** To have as an end or result: *"the Peloponnesian war . . . terminated in the ruin of the Athenian commonwealth"* (Alexander Hamilton). [Lat. *terminare, terminat-* < *terminus,* end.]

ter·mi·na·tion (tûr′mə-nā′shən) *n.* **1.** The act of terminating or the condition of being terminated. **2.** The spatial or temporal end of something. **3.** A result or outcome of something. **4.** The end of a word, as an inflectional ending, suffix, or final morpheme. **—ter′mi·na′tion·al** *adj.*

ter·mi·na·tive (tûr′mə-nā′tĭv) *adj.* Serving, designed, or tending to terminate; conclusive. **—ter′mi·na′tive·ly** *adv.*

ter·mi·na·tor (tûr′mə-nā′tər) *n.* **1.** One that terminates. **2.** The dividing line between the bright and shaded regions of the disk of the moon or an inner planet.

ter·mi·ni (tûr′mə-nī′) *n.* A plural of **terminus.**

ter·mi·nol·o·gy (tûr′mə-nŏl′ə-jē) *n., pl.* **-gies. 1.** The vocabulary of technical terms and usages appropriate to a particular field, subject, science, or art; nomenclature. **2.** The study of nomenclature. [Med. Lat. *terminus,* expression (< Lat., limit) + -LOGY.] **—ter′mi·no·log′i·cal** (-nə-lŏj′ĭ-kəl) *adj.* **—ter′mi·no·log′i·cal·ly** *adv.* **—ter′mi·nol′o·gist** *n.*

term insurance *n.* Insurance for a specifically stated period providing coverage for losses to the insured during that period but becoming void upon its expiration.

ter·mi·nus (tûr′mə-nəs) *n., pl.* **-nus·es** or **-ni** (-nī′). **1.** The end of something; the final point. **2.** A terminal on a transportation line or the town in which it is located. **3. a.** A boundary or border. **b.** A stone or post marking such a border. [Lat.]

ter·mi·tar·i·um (tûr′mĭ-târ′ē-əm) *n., pl.* **-i·a.** A nest of termites.

ter·mite (tûr′mīt′) *n.* Any of numerous superficially antlike social insects of the order Isoptera, many species of which feed on wood and are highly destructive to living trees and wooden structures. [Lat. *termes, termit-,* a wood-eating worm.]

term·less (tûrm′lĭs) *adj.* **1.** Having no bounds or limits; unending. **2.** Unconditional.

term paper *n.* A lengthy report or essay required of a student on a topic drawn from the subject matter of a course of study.

tern[1] (tûrn) *n.* Any of various sea birds of the genus *Sterna* and related genera, related to and resembling the gulls but characteristically smaller and having a forked tail. [Of Scand. orig.]

tern[2] (tûrn) *n.* **1.** A set of three, esp. a combination of three numbers that wins a lottery prize. **2.** A three-masted schooner. [Lat. *terni,* three each < *ter,* thrice.]

ter·na·ry (tûr′nə-rē) *adj.* **1.** Composed of three or arranged in threes. **2.** *Math.* **a.** Having the base three. **b.** Involving three variables. —*n., pl.* **-ries.** A set or group of three. [ME < Lat. *ternarius* < *terni,* three each < *ter,* thrice.]

ter·nate (tûr′nāt′, -nĭt) *adj.* Arranged in or consisting of sets or groups of three, as a compound leaf with three leaflets. [NLat. *ternatus* < Med. Lat., p.part. of *ternare,* to multiply by three < Lat. *terni,* three each < *ter,* thrice.] —**ter′nate′ly** *adv.*

terne (tûrn) *n.* Terneplate.

terne·plate (tûrn′plāt′) *n.* Sheet iron or steel plated with an alloy of three or four parts of lead to one part of tin, used as a roofing material. [Prob. Fr. *terne,* dull (< OFr. < *ternir,* to tarnish) + PLATE.]

ter·pene (tûr′pēn′) *n.* Any of various unsaturated hydrocarbons, $C_{10}H_{16}$, found in essential oils and oleoresins of plants such as conifers and used in organic syntheses. [Obs. *terpentin,* turpentine + -ENE.] —**ter·pen′ic** *adj.* —**ter′pe·noid′** *adj. & n.*

ter·pin·e·ol (tər-pĭn′ē-ôl′, -ōl′) *n.* Any of three isomeric alcohols, $C_{10}H_{17}OH$, occurring naturally in the essential oils of certain plants and used as a solvent, in perfumes, soaps, and medicine. [TERP(ENE) + -INE + -OL.]

ter·pol·y·mer (tər-pŏl′ə-mər) *n.* A polymer that consists of three distinct monomers. [Lat. *ter,* three times + POLYMER.]

Terp·sich·o·re (tûrp-sĭk′ə-rē) *n. Gk. Myth.* The Muse of dancing and choral singing. [Gk. *Terpsikhorē* : *terpein,* to delight + *khoros,* dance.]

terp·si·cho·re·an (tûrp′sĭk-ə-rē′ən, tûrp′sĭ-kôr′ē-ən, -kōr′-) Of or pertaining to dancing. —*n.* A dancer. [< TERPSICHORE.]

ter·ra al·ba (tĕr′ə ăl′bə, ôl′bə) *n.* **1.** Finely pulverized gypsum used in making paper, paints, and plastics. **2.** Kaolin. [NLat. < Lat., white earth.]

ter·race (tĕr′ĭs) *n.* **1. a.** An open colonnaded platform, as a porch or promenade. **b.** A platform extending outdoors from a floor of a house or apartment building. **2.** An open, often paved area adjacent to a house serving as an outdoor living area; patio. **3.** A raised bank of earth having vertical or sloping sides and a flat top: *descending terraces on the lawn.* **4.** A flat, narrow stretch of ground, often having a steep slope facing a river or sea. **5. a.** A row of buildings erected on raised ground or on a sloping site. **b.** A section of row houses. **6. a.** A narrow strip of landscaped earth in the middle of a street. **b.** A street, esp. one having such a terrace. —*tr.v.* **-raced, -rac·ing, -rac·es.** To make into or supply with a terrace. [OFr. < Lat. *terra,* earth.]

ter·ra cot·ta (tĕr′ə kŏt′ə) *n.* **1. a.** A hard, semifired, waterproof ceramic clay used in pottery and building construction. **b.** Ceramic wares made of this material. **2.** A brownish orange color. [Ital. : *terra,* earth + *cotta,* baked.] —**ter′ra-cot′ta** *adj.*

ter·ra fir·ma (tĕr′ə fûr′mə) *n.* Solid ground; dry land. [Lat.]

ter·rain (tə-rān′, tĕ-) *n.* **1.** A tract of land; ground. **2.** The character of land; topography. **3.** A particular geographic area; region. **4.** Variant of **terrane.** [Fr. < OFr. < Lat. *terrenus,* terrene.]

Ter·ra·my·cin (tĕr′ə-mī′sĭn). A trademark for oxytetracycline.

Ter·ran (tĕr′ən) *n.* An earthman. [< Lat. *terra,* earth.]

ter·rane also **ter·rain** (tə-rān′, tĕ-) *n.* **1.** A series of related rock formations. **2.** An area having a preponderance of a particular rock or rock groups. [Alteration of TERRAIN.]

ter·ra·pin (tĕr′ə-pĭn) *n.* **1.** Any of various aquatic North American turtles of the genus *Malaclemys* and related genera. **2.** *Chiefly Brit.* A partly terrestrial freshwater turtle. [Of Algonquian orig.]

ter·ra·que·ous (tĕr-ā′kwē-əs, -ăk′wē-) *adj.* Composed of both land and water. [Lat. *terra,* earth + AQUEOUS.]

ter·rar·i·um (tə-râr′ē-əm) *n., pl.* **-i·ums** or **-i·a** (-ē-ə). A small enclosure or closed container in which small plants are grown or small animals, as turtles or lizards, are kept. [Lat. *terra,* earth + -ARIUM.]

ter·raz·zo (tə-răt′sō, -răz′ō) *n.* A flooring material of marble or other stone chips set in mortar and polished when dry. [Ital.]

ter·rene (tĕ-rēn′, tĕr′ēn′) *adj.* Of or pertaining to the earth; earthly. [ME < Lat. *terrenus* < *terra,* earth.]

ter·re·plein (tĕr′ə-plān′) *n.* A horizontal platform behind a parapet where heavy guns are mounted. [OFr. *terreplein* < OItal. *terrapieno* < *terrapienare,* to fill with earth : *terra,* earth (< Lat.) + *pieno,* full (< Lat. *plenus*).]

ter·res·tri·al (tə-rĕs′trē-əl) *adj.* **1.** Of or pertaining to the earth or its inhabitants. **2.** Having a worldly, mundane character or quality. **3.** Of, pertaining to, or composed of land as distinct from water or air. **4.** *Biol.* Living or growing on land; not aquatic. —*n.* An inhabitant of the earth. [ME < Lat. *terrestris* < *terra,* earth.] —**ter·res′tri·al·ly** *adv.* —**ter·res′tri·al·ness** *n.*

ter·ret (tĕr′ĭt) *n.* **1.** One of the metal rings on a harness through which the reins pass. **2.** A ring on an animal's collar, used for attaching a leash. [ME *teret* < OFr. *toret,* dim. of *tor,* a round.]

terre-verte (tĕr′vĕrt′) *n.* An olive-green pigment used by artists and commonly made from glauconite. [Fr. : *terre,* earth + *verte,* green.]

ter·ri·ble (tĕr′ə-bəl) *adj.* **1.** Causing fear or alarm; dreadful. **2.** Extremely formidable: *terrible responsibilities.* **3.** Extreme in extent or degree: *"the life for which he had paid so terrible a price"* (Leslie Fiedler). **4. a.** Unpleasant; disagreeable: *a terrible time at the party.* **b.** Markedly unattractive or objectionable: *terrible hypocrisy.* [ME < OFr. < Lat. *terribilis* < *terrēre,* to frighten.] —**ter′ri·ble·ness** *n.* —**ter′ri·bly** *adv.*

Usage: *Terrible* in the meaning of "causing terror" has now largely been replaced by *terrifying,* though this word lacks the sense of "eliciting awe." *Terrible* is now most frequently used in general speech in the sense "extremely poor or severe" (*a terrible movie; a terrible cold*), and the adverb *terribly* has a similar intensive use (*terribly hot; terribly friendly*). Both these uses, though they have long been established in general speech, are considered imprecise by careful writers and unacceptable in formal style.

ter·ric·o·lous (tĕ-rĭk′ə-ləs) *adj. Biol.* Living on or in the ground. [< Lat. *terricola,* earth-dweller : *terra,* earth + *colere,* to dwell.]

ter·ri·er (tĕr′ē-ər) *n.* Any of various usually small, active dogs originally bred for hunting animals that live in burrows. [Fr. terrier, burrow < *terre,* earth < Lat. *terra.*]

ter·rif·ic (tə-rĭf′ĭk) *adj.* **1.** Causing terror or great fear; terrifying: *a terrific wail.* **2.** Very bad or unpleasant; frightful: *a terrific headache.* **3.** Very good or fine; splendid: *a terrific chef.* **4.** Awesome; astounding: *a terrific speed.* [Lat. *terrificus* : *terrēre,* to frighten + *facere,* to make.] —**ter·rif′i·cal·ly** *adv.*

ter·ri·fy (tĕr′ə-fī′) *tr.v.* **-fied, -fy·ing, -fies. 1.** To fill with terror; alarm. **2.** To menace or threaten; intimidate. [Lat. *terrificare* < *terrificus,* terrific.]

ter·rig·e·nous (tĕ-rĭj′ə-nəs) *adj.* Derived from the land, esp. by erosive action. Used primarily of sediments. [Lat. *terrigena,* earth-born : *terra,* earth + *gignere,* to bring forth.]

ter·ri·to·ri·al (tĕr′ĭ-tôr′ē-əl, -tōr′-) *adj.* **1.** Of or pertaining to a territory or to its powers of jurisdiction. **2.** Pertaining or restricted to a particular territory; regional. **3. Territorial.** Organized for national or home defense: *the British Territorial Army.* —*n.* **Territorial.** A member of a territorial army. —**ter′ri·to′ri·al·ly** *adv.*

ter·ri·to·ri·al·ism (tĕr′ĭ-tôr′ē-ə-lĭz′əm, -tōr′-) *n.* **1.** A social system that gives authority and influence in a state to the landowners. **2.** A system of church government based on primacy of civil power. —**ter′ri·to′ri·al·ist** *n.*

ter·ri·to·ri·al·i·ty (tĕr′ĭ-tôr′ē-ăl′ĭ-tē, -tōr′-) *n., pl.* **-ties. 1.** The status of a territory. **2.** A behavior pattern in animals consisting of the occupation and defense of a territory.

ter·ri·to·ri·al·ize (tĕr′ĭ-tôr′ē-ə-līz′, -tōr′-) *tr.v.* **-ized, -iz·ing, -iz·es. 1.** To add to by the acquisition of territory. **2.** To reduce to the status of a territory. **3.** To distribute among particular territories. —**ter′ri·to′ri·al·i·za′tion** *n.*

territorial waters *pl.n.* Inland and coastal waters under the jurisdiction of a state, esp. the ocean waters within three miles of the shoreline.

ter·ri·to·ry (tĕr′ĭ-tôr′ē, -tōr′ē) *n., pl.* **-ries. 1.** An area of land; region. **2.** The land and waters under the jurisdiction of a state, nation, or sovereign. **3. Territory. a.** A part of the United States that is not admitted as a state, that is administered by a governor, and that has its own legislature. **b.** A semi-autonomous geographic region, as a colonial possession, that is dependent on an external government. **4.** The area for which a person is responsible as representative or agent: *a salesman's territory.* **5.** *Sports.* The area of a field defended by a team. **6.** *Biol.* An area inhabited by an individual animal or a mating pair or group of animals, and often vigorously defended against intruders. **7.** A sphere of action or interest; province. [ME < Lat. *territorium* < *terra,* land.]

ter·ror (tĕr′ər) *n.* **1.** Intense, overpowering fear. **2.** Something, as a terrifying object or occurrence, that instills intense fear. **3.** The ability to instill intense fear: *the terror of the haunted house.* **4.** Violence promoted by a group to achieve or maintain supremacy. **5.** *Informal.* An annoying or intolerable pest; nuisance: *a holy terror.* [ME *terrour* < OFr. < Lat. *terror* < *terrēre,* to frighten.]

ter·ror·ism (tĕr′ə-rĭz′əm) *n.* The systematic use of terror, vio-

Terpsichore

lence, and intimidation to achieve an end. **—ter′ror·ist** *n.* **—ter′ror·is′tic** *adj.*

ter·ror·ize (tĕr′ə-rīz′) *tr.v.* **-ized, -iz·ing, -iz·es. 1.** To fill or overpower with terror; terrify. **2.** To coerce by intimidation or fear. **—ter′ror·i·za′tion** *n.* **—ter′ror·iz′er** *n.*

ter·ry (tĕr′ē) *n., pl.* **-ries. 1.** Any of the uncut loops that form the pile of a fabric. **2.** Also **terry cloth.** A pile fabric, usually woven of cotton, with uncut loops on both sides, used for such articles as bath towels and robes. [Orig. unknown.]

terse (tûrs) *adj.* **ters·er, ters·est.** Effectively concise; free of superfluity. [Lat. *tersus,* p.part. of *tergēre,* to cleanse.] **—terse′ly** *adv.* **—terse′ness** *n.*

ter·tian (tûr′shən) *adj.* Recurring every other day or, when considered inclusively, every third day. *—n. Pathol.* Tertian fever. [ME, tertian fever < Lat. *tertianus,* of the third < *tertius,* third.]

tertian fever *n.* A form of malaria caused by the invasion of *Plasmodium vivax* into new red blood cells, characterized by a 48-hour life cycle in the human body with a recurrence of fever paroxysms at the end of each such period.

ter·ti·ar·y (tûr′shē-ĕr′ē) *adj.* **1.** Third in place, order, degree, or rank. **2.** Of, pertaining to, or designating the short flight feathers nearest the body on the inner edge of a bird's wing. **3.** *Chem.* **a.** Of or pertaining to salts of acids containing three replaceable hydrogen atoms. **b.** Of or pertaining to organic compounds in which a group, as an alcohol or amine, is bound to three nonelementary radicals. **4.** *Eccles.* Of or pertaining to the third order of a monastic system. **5. Tertiary.** Of, belonging to, or designating the geologic time, system of rocks, and sedimentary deposits of the first period of the Cenozoic era, extending from the Cretaceous period of the Mesozoic era to the Quaternary period of the Cenozoic era, characterized by the appearance of modern flora and of apes and other large mammals. *—n., pl.* **-ies. 1.** A tertiary feather. **2.** *Eccles.* A member of a tertiary order. **3. Tertiary.** The Tertiary period or system of deposits. [Lat. *tertiarius* < *tertius,* third.]

tertiary color *n.* A color resulting from the mixture of two secondary colors.

ter·ti·um quid (tûr′shē-əm kwĭd′) *n.* Something that cannot be classified into either of two groups considered to be exhaustive; an intermediate thing or factor. [LLat.]

ter·va·lent (tər-vā′lənt, tûr′vā′-) *adj.* Variant of **trivalent.**

ter·za ri·ma (tĕr′tsə rē′mə) *n., pl.* **ter·ze ri·me** (tĕr′tsā rē′mā). A verse form consisting of a series of triplets having 10-syllable or 11-syllable lines of which the middle line of one triplet rhymes with the first and third lines of the following triplet. [Ital : *terza,* third + *rima,* rhyme.]

tes·la (tĕs′lə) *n.* The unit of magnetic flux density in the International System, equal to one weber per square meter. [After Nikola *Tesla* (1857–1943).]

tesla coil *n.* A transformer with an air-core primary and a capacitor-tuned secondary, used as a source of high-frequency power, as for x-ray tubes.

tes·sel·late (tĕs′ə-lāt′) *tr.v.* **-lat·ed, -lat·ing, -lates.** To form into a mosaic pattern, as by using small squares of stone or glass. [Lat. *tessellatus,* of small square stones < *tessella,* small cube, dim. of *tessera,* a square.] **—tes′sel·la′tion** *n.*

tes·ser·a (tĕs′ər-ə) *n., pl.* **tes·ser·ae** (tĕs′ə-rē′). One of the small squares of stone or glass used in making mosaic patterns. [Lat., a square < Gk. *tesseres,* four.]

testudo
Detail from Trajan's Column in Rome

test¹ (tĕst) *n.* **1.** A means of examination, trial, or proof. **2.** A series of questions or problems designed to determine knowledge or intelligence. **3.** A criterion; standard. **4.** *Chem.* **a.** A physical or chemical reaction by which a substance may be detected or its properties ascertained. **b.** The reagent used in such determination. **c.** A positive result obtained. **5.** A cupel. *—v.* **test·ed, test·ing, tests.** *—tr.* **1.** To subject to a test; examine. **2. a.** To determine the presence or properties of (a substance). **b.** To assay (metal) in a cupel. *—intr.* **1.** To undergo a test. **2.** To achieve as a score or rating through testing. **3.** To exhibit certain properties under test conditions. **4.** To administer a test in order to diagnose: *test for acid content.* [ME, cupel < OFr., pot < Lat. *testum.*]

test² (tĕst) *n.* A hard external covering, as that of certain insects and other invertebrates. [Lat. *testa,* shell.]

tes·ta (tĕs′tə) *n., pl.* **-tae** (-tē′). The often thick or hard outer coat of a seed. [Lat., shell.]

tes·ta·cean (tĕs-tā′shən) *n.* Any of various rhizopods of the order Testacea that contain a shell. [< NLat. *Testacea,* order name < Lat. *testaceus,* covered with a shell < *testa,* brick, tile.] **—tes·ta′cean** *adj.*

tes·ta·ceous (tĕs-tā′shəs) *adj.* **1.** *Biol.* Of, pertaining to, or having a shell or shell-like outer covering. **2.** Having the characteristic reddish-brown or brownish-yellow color of bricks. [Lat. *testaceus* < *testa,* shell.]

tes·ta·cy (tĕs′tə-sē) *n. Law.* The condition of being testate.

tes·tae (tĕs′tē′) *n.* Plural of **testa.**

tes·ta·ment (tĕs′tə-mənt) *n.* **1.** *Law.* **a.** A written document providing for the disposition of one's personal property after death. **b.** A will: *last will and testament.* **2. a.** A tangible proof or tribute that testifies to or serves as evidence. **b.** A statement of belief or conviction; credo. **3. a.** *Archaic.* A covenant between man and God. **b. Testament.** Either of the two main divisions of the Bible. [ME < Lat. *testamentum* < *testari,* to make a will < *testis,* witness.] **—tes′ta·men′ta·ry** (-mĕn′tə-rē, -mĕn′trē) *adj.*

tes·tate (tĕs′tāt′) *adj.* Having made a legally valid will before death. [ME < Lat. *testatus,* p.part. of *testari,* to make one's will.]

tes·ta·tor (tĕs′tā′tər, tĕs-tā′tər) *n.* A person who has made a legally valid will before death. [ME *testatour* < AN < Lat. *testator* < *testari,* to make one's will.]

tes·ta·trix (tĕs-tā′trĭks) *n.* A woman who has made a legally valid will before death. [Lat., fem. of *testator,* testator.]

test case *n.* A legal action whose outcome is likely to set a precedent or test the constitutionality of a statute.

test·cross (tĕst′krôs′, -krŏs′) *n.* A genetic cross between an individual having a dominant trait with a homozygous recessive individual to determine if the genotype of the dominant individual is homozygous or heterozygous. *—tr.v.* **-crossed, -cross·ing, -cross·es.** To subject to a testcross.

test-drive (tĕst′drīv′) *tr.v.* **-drove** (-drōv), **-driv·en** (-drĭv′ən), **-driv·ing, -drives.** To drive, as a new automobile, to evaluate performance.

tes·ter¹ (tĕs′tər) *n.* A canopy over a bed. [ME < Med. Lat. *testerium* < LLat. *testa,* skull < Lat., shell.]

tes·ter² (tĕs′tər) *n.* A teston (sense 2). [Alteration of TESTON.]

test·er³ (tĕs′tər) *n.* One that tests.

tes·tes (tĕs′tēz′) *n.* Plural of **testis.**

tes·ti·cle (tĕs′tĭ-kəl) *n.* A testis. [ME *testicule* < Lat. *testiculus,* dim. of *testis,* testis.]

tes·tic·u·late (tĕs-tĭk′yə-lĭt) also **tes·tic·u·lar** (-lər) *adj.* Having the shape of a testicle; ovoid.

tes·ti·fy (tĕs′tə-fī′) *v.* **-fied, -fy·ing, -fies.** *—intr.* **1.** To make a declaration of truth or fact under oath. **2.** To make a serious or solemn statement in support of an argument, position, or asserted fact. **3.** *Law.* To bear witness; submit testimony. **4.** To serve as witness or evidence. *—tr.* **1.** To bear witness to; provide evidence for. **2.** To state or affirm under oath. **3.** To declare publicly; make known. [ME *testifien* < Lat. *testificari* : *testis,* witness + *facere,* to make.] **—tes′ti·fi·ca′tion** *n.* **—tes′ti·fi′er** *n.*

tes·ti·mo·ni·al (tĕs′tə-mō′nē-əl) *n.* **1.** A formal or written statement testifying to a particular truth or fact. **2.** A written affirmation of another's character or worth. **3.** Something given as a tribute for a person's service or achievement. *—adj.* Relating to or constituting a testimony or testimonial. [ME < OFr. < LLat. *testimonialis,* of evidence < Lat. *testimonium,* testimony.]

tes·ti·mo·ny (tĕs′tə-mō′nē) *n., pl.* **-nies. 1.** A declaration or affirmation of fact or truth, as that given before a court. **2.** Evidence in support of a fact or assertion; proof. **3.** The collective written and spoken testimony offered in a legal case. **4.** A public declaration regarding a religious experience. **5.** Often **Testimony. a.** The law of Moses, inscribed on the tablets of stone. **b.** The ark containing these tablets. [ME < Lat. *testimonium* < *testari,* to testify.]

tes·tis (tĕs′tĭs) *n., pl.* **-tes** (-tēz′). The male reproductive gland, the source of spermatozoa and of the androgens, normally occurring paired in an external scrotum in man and certain other mammals. [Lat.]

tes·ton (tĕs′tŏn′) also **tes·toon** (tĕs-to͞on′) *n.* Any of various coins with the image of a head on one side, esp.: **1.** A 16th-century silver coin of France. **2.** An English coin stamped with the head of Henry VIII. [OFr. < OItal. *testone,* dim. of *testa,* head < LLat., skull < Lat., shell.]

tes·tos·ter·one (tĕs-tŏs′tə-rōn′) *n.* A male sex hormone, $C_{19}H_{28}O_2$, produced in the testes and functioning to control secondary sex characteristics. [TEST(IS) + STER(OL) + -ONE.]

test paper *n.* **1.** A paper saturated with a reagent, as litmus, used in making chemical tests. **2.** A paper or booklet bearing a student's work for an examination.

test pilot *n.* A pilot who flies aircraft of new or experimental design to test them for conformity to planned standards.

test stand *n.* A facility for static test firing of rocket engines to determine performance characteristics.

test tube *n.* A cylindrical clear glass tube usually open at one end and rounded at the other, used in laboratory experimentation.

test-tube baby (tĕst′to͞ob′) *n.* A baby that has been conceived outside the womb through fertilization of an egg removed from the mother.

tes·tu·di·nate (tĕs-to͞od′n-ĭt, -āt′, -tyo͞od′-) *adj.* Of or pertaining to a turtle or tortoise. *—n.* A turtle or tortoise. [< NLat. *Testudinata,* order name < Lat. *testudo,* tortoise. —see TESTUDO.]

tes·tu·do (tĕs-to͞o′dō, -tyo͞o′-) *n., pl.* **-dos.** A Roman siege device consisting of a movable screen protecting the besiegers' approach to a wall. [Lat. < *testa,* shell.]

tes·ty (tĕs′tē) *adj.* **-ti·er, -ti·est. 1.** Irritable; peevish. **2.** Characterized by irritability, impatience, or exasperation: *a testy remark.* [ME *testif,* headstrong < AN < OFr. *teste,* head.] **—tes′ti·ly** *adv.* **—tes′ti·ness** *n.*

Tet (tĕt) *n.* The lunar New Year as celebrated in Southeast Asia. [Vietnamese *tết,* of Chin. orig.]

te·tan·ic (tĕ-tăn′ĭk) *adj.* **1.** Of or pertaining to tetanus. **2.** Of or pertaining to tetany. **—te·tan′i·cal·ly** *adv.*

tet·a·nize (tĕt′n-īz′) *tr.v.* **-nized, -niz·ing, -niz·es.** To affect with tetanic convulsions; produce or induce tetanus in. **—tet'a·ni·za'tion** *n.*

tet·a·nus (tĕt'n-əs) *n.* **1.** An acute, often fatal infectious disease caused by a bacillus, *Clostridium tetani,* that generally enters the body through wounds, characterized by rigidity and spasmodic contraction of the voluntary muscles. **2.** A state of continuous muscular contraction caused by reaction to rapidly repeated stimuli. [ME *tetane* < Lat. *tetanus* < Gk. *tetanos* < *teinein,* to stretch.] **—tet'a·nal** (tĕt'n-əl) *adj.*

tet·a·ny (tĕt'n-ē) *n.* An abnormal condition, occurring chiefly in children and young adults, characterized by periodic painful muscular spasms caused by faulty calcium metabolism. [< TETANUS.]

tetch·y also **tech·y** (tĕch'ē) *adj.* **-i·er, -i·est.** Peevish; testy. [Orig. unknown.] **—tetch'i·ly** *adv.* **—tetch'i·ness** *n.*

tête-à-tête (tāt'ə-tāt') *adv.* Together without the intrusion of a third person; in intimate privacy: *talk tête-à-tête.* —*n.* **1.** A private conversation between two people. **2.** A sofa for two, esp. an S-shaped one allowing the occupants to face each other. [Fr : *tête,* head + *à,* to + *tête,* head.]

tête-bêche (tĕt'bĕsh') *adj.* Of, pertaining to, or characteristic of postage stamps printed upside-down in relation to one another. [Fr., head to foot : *tête,* head + OFr. *bechevet,* head to foot.]

teth (tĕt, tĕs) *n.* The 9th letter in the Hebrew alphabet. See table at **alphabet.** [Heb. *ṭēth.*]

teth·er (tĕ*th*'ər) *n.* **1.** A rope, chain, or halter for an animal, allowing it a short radius in which to move about. **2.** The range or scope of one's resources or abilities. —*tr.v.* **-ered, -er·ing, -ers.** To restrict or bind with or as with a tether. —*idiom.* **at the end of (one's) tether.** At the extreme limit of one's endurance or powers. [ME *tethir* < ON *tjōðr.*]

teth·er·ball (tĕ*th*'ər-bôl') *n.* A game played by two people with paddles and a ball hung by a cord from an upright post, the objective being to wind the cord around the post.

Te·thys (tē'thĭs) *n. Gk. Myth.* A Titaness and sea goddess who was both sister and wife of Oceanus. [Gk. *Tēthus.*]

tetr– *pref.* Variant of **tetra-.**

tet·ra (tĕt'rə) *n.* Any of various small, colorful tropical freshwater fishes of the family Characidae, popular in home aquariums. [Short for NLat. *Tetragonopterus,* former genus name : LLat. *tetragonum,* tetragon + Gk. *pteron,* wing.]

tetra– or **tetr–** *pref.* **1.** Four: *tetrode.* **2.** Containing four of a specified kind of atom, radical, or group: *tetrachloride.* [Gk.]

tet·ra·ba·sic (tĕt'rə-bā'sĭk) *adj.* **1.** Containing four replaceable hydrogen atoms in a molecule. Used of acids. **2.** Containing four univalent basic atoms or radicals. Used of bases or salts. **—tet'ra·ba·sic'i·ty** (-sĭs'ĭ-tē) *n.*

tet·ra·caine hydrochloride (tĕt'rə-kān') *n.* A crystalline compound, $C_{15}H_{24}N_2O_2 \cdot HCl$, used medically as a local anesthetic.

tet·ra·chlo·ride (tĕt'rə-klôr'īd', -klōr'-) *n.* A chemical compound containing four chlorine atoms per molecule.

tet·ra·chord (tĕt'rə-kôrd') *n. Mus.* A series of four diatonic tones encompassing the interval of a perfect fourth. [Gk. *tetrakhordon* < *tetrakhordos,* four-stringed : *tetra-,* four + *khordē,* string.] **—tet'ra·chor'dal** *adj.*

te·trac·id (tĕ-trăs'ĭd) *adj.* **1.** Capable of reacting with four molecules of a monobasic acid. Used of a base. **2.** Containing four replaceable hydrogen atoms. Used of an acid or acid salt. —*n.* An acid containing four replaceable hydrogen atoms.

tet·ra·cy·cline (tĕt'rə-sī'klēn') *n.* A yellow crystalline compound, $C_{22}H_{24}N_2O_8$, synthesized or derived from certain microorganisms of the genus *Streptomyces* and used as an antibiotic. [TETRA- + CYCL(IC) + -INE.]

tet·rad (tĕt'răd') *n.* **1.** A group or set of four. **2.** A tetravalent atom, radical, or element. **3.** *Biol.* **a.** A group of four chromatids formed at meiosis by synapsis of two chromatids from each of a pair of homologous chromosomes. **b.** A body formed of four cells, as pollen grains from one mother cell. [Gk. *tetras, tetrad-,* group of four < *tetra-,* four.]

te·trad·y·mite (tĕ-trăd'ə-mīt') *n.* A steel-gray bismuth ore, chiefly Bi_2Te_2S. [G. *Tetradymit* < LGk. *tetradumos* : Gk. *tetra-,* four + *didumos,* double.]

tet·ra·dy·na·mous (tĕt'rə-dī'nə-məs) *adj. Bot.* Having six stamens, of which two are shorter than the others. [TETRA- + Gk. *dynamis,* strength + -OUS.]

tet·ra·eth·yl lead (tĕt'rə-ĕth'əl) also **tet·ra·eth·yl·lead** (-lĕd') *n.* A colorless, poisonous, oily liquid, $Pb(C_2H_5)_4$, used in gasoline for internal-combustion engines as an antiknock agent.

tet·ra·gon (tĕt'rə-gŏn') *n.* A four-sided polygon; quadrilateral. [LLat. < Gk. *tetragonon* : *tetra-,* four + *-gonon,* -gon.] **—te·trag'o·nal** (tĕ-trăg'ə-nəl) *adj.* **—te·trag'o·nal·ly** *adv.*

Tet·ra·gram·ma·ton (tĕt'rə-grăm'ə-tŏn') *n.* The four Hebrew letters usually transliterated as YHWH or JHVH (Yahweh or Jehovah) and used as a biblical proper name for God. [ME *Tetragramaton* < Gk. *tetragrammaton,* four-letter word : *tetra-,* four + *gramma,* letter.]

tet·ra·he·dra (tĕt'rə-hē'drə) *n.* A plural of **tetrahedron.**

tet·ra·he·dral (tĕt'rə-hē'drəl) *adj.* **1.** Pertaining to a tetrahedron. **2.** Having four faces. **—tet'ra·he'dral·ly** *adv.*

tet·ra·he·drite (tĕt'rə-hē'drīt') *n.* A grayish-black copper ore, essentially $(CuFe)_{12}Sb_4S_{13}$, often containing other elements and sometimes used as an ore of silver. [G. *Tetraëdrit* < Gk. *tetraedros,* four-faced. —see TETRAHEDRON.]

tet·ra·he·dron (tĕt'rə-hē'drən) *n., pl.* **-drons** or **-dra** (-drə). A polyhedron with four faces. [Gk. *tetraedron* < *tetraedros,* four-faced : *tetra-,* four + *hedra,* face.]

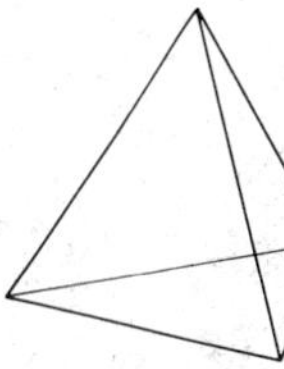

tetrahedron

tet·ra·hy·dro·can·nab·i·nol (tĕt'rə-hī'drə-kə-năb'ə-nôl', -nōl') *n.* A compound found in cannabis or made synthetically that is the primary intoxicant in marijuana.

tet·ra·hy·drox·y (tĕt'rə-hī-drŏk'sē) *adj.* Having four hydroxyl groups in a molecule.

te·tral·o·gy (tĕ-trăl'ə-jē, -trŏl'-) *n., pl.* **-gies. 1.** In ancient Athens, a series of four dramas, three tragic, one satiric, performed at the festivals dedicated to Dionysus. **2.** A series of four related dramatic, operatic, or literary works. **3.** *Med.* A complex of four symptoms. [Gk. *tetralogia* : *tetra-,* four + *-logia,* -logy.]

tetralogy of Fallot *n.* Fallot's tetralogy.

tet·ra·mer (tĕt'rə-mər) *n.* A polymer that consists of four identical monomers. **—tet'ra·mer'ic** (-mĕr'ĭk) *adj.*

te·tram·er·ous (tĕ-trăm'ər-əs) *adj.* **1.** Having or consisting of four similar parts. **2.** *Bot.* Having flower parts, as sepals, petals, and stamens, in sets of four. [NLat. *tetramerus* < Gk. *tetramerēs* : *tetra-,* four + *meros,* part.] **—te·tram'er·ism** *n.*

te·tram·e·ter (tĕ-trăm'ĭ-tər) *n.* **1.** A line of verse consisting of four metrical feet. **2.** A verse composed of tetrameters. [LLat. *tetrametrus* < Gk. *tetrametros* (adj.) : *tetra-,* tetra- + *-metron,* measure.] **—te·tram'e·ter** *adj.*

tet·ra·ploid (tĕt'rə-ploid') *Genetics.* —*adj.* Having four haploid sets of chromosomes. —*n.* A tetraploid individual.

tet·ra·pod (tĕt'rə-pŏd') *adj.* Having four feet, legs, or leglike appendages. [NLat. *tetrapodus* < Gk. *tetrapous,* four-footed : *tetra-,* four + *pous,* foot.] **—tet'ra·pod'** *n.*

te·trap·ter·ous (tĕ-trăp'tər-əs) *adj.* Having four wings, as certain insects. [Gk. *tetrapteros* : *tetra-,* four + *pteron,* wing.]

tet·rarch (tĕt'rärk', tē'trärk') *n.* **1.** A governor of one of the four divisions of a country or province, esp. under the ancient Roman Empire. **2. a.** A subordinate ruler. **b.** One of four joint rulers. **3.** The commander of a subdivision of a phalanx in ancient Greece. [ME < LLat. *tetrarcha* < Lat. *tetrarches* < Gk. *tetrarkhēs* : *tetra-,* four + *arkein,* to rule.] **—te·trar'chic** (tĕ-trär'kĭk, tē-) *adj.*

tet·rar·chy (tĕt'rär'kē, tē'trär'-) also **tet·rar·chate** (-kāt', -kĭt) *n., pl.* **-chies** also **-chates. 1.** The area or jurisdiction of a tetrarch. **2. a.** Rule by four governors jointly. **b.** The four governors ruling jointly.

tet·ra·spore (tĕt'rə-spôr', -spōr') *n.* One of four spores produced in a group from a sporangium, as in red algae. **—tet'ra·spor'ic** *adj.*

te·tras·ti·chous (tĕ-trăs'tĭ-kəs) *adj.* Arranged in four vertical rows, as leaves or flowers on a stalk. [NLat. *tetrastichus* < Gk. *tetrastikhos,* having four rows : *tetra-,* four + *stikhos,* row.]

tet·ra·tom·ic (tĕt'rə-tŏm'ĭk) *adj.* **1.** Having four atoms per molecule. **2.** Having four replaceable univalent atoms or radicals.

tet·ra·va·lent (tĕt'rə-vā'lənt) *adj. Chem.* Having valence 4.

Tet·raz·zi·ni (tĕt'rə-zē'nē) *adj.* Made with noodles, mushrooms, and almonds in a cream sauce topped with cheese: *turkey Tetrazzini.* [After Luisa *Tetrazzini* (1871–1940).]

tet·rode (tĕt'rōd') *n.* A four-element electron tube containing a cathode, a control grid, a screen grid, and an anode. [TETR(A)- + -ODE.]

te·trox·ide (tĕ-trŏk'sīd') *n.* A chemical compound containing four oxygen atoms per molecule.

tet·ryl (tĕt'rəl) *n.* A yellow crystalline explosive, $C_7H_5N_5O_8$, used chiefly as a primer or detonator.

tet·ter (tĕt'ər) *n.* Any of various skin diseases, as psoriasis, herpes, and esp. eczema, characterized by eruptions and itching. [ME *teter* < OE.]

Teu·ton (to͞ot'n, tyo͞ot'n) *n.* **1. Teutons.** An ancient people, probably of Germanic or Celtic origin, who lived in Jutland until about 100 B.C. **2.** One of the peoples speaking a Germanic language, esp. a German. [Lat. *Teutoni.*]

Teu·ton·ic (to͞o-tŏn'ĭk, tyo͞o-) *adj.* **1.** Of or relating to the Teutons. **2.** Of or relating to the Germanic languages. —*n.* Germanic. [Lat. *Teutonicus* < *Teutoni,* Teutons.]

Teu·ton·ism (to͞ot'n-ĭz'əm, tyo͞ot'-) also **Teu·ton·i·cism** (to͞o-tŏn'ĭ-sĭz'əm, tyo͞o-) *n.* **1.** A German practice or idiom. **2.** German character or civilization. **—Teu'ton·ist** *n.*

Teu·ton·ize (to͞ot'n-īz', tyo͞ot'-) *tr.v.* **-ized, -iz·ing, -iz·es.** To make German; Germanize. **—Teu'ton·i·za'tion** *n.*

Te·vet also **Te·bet** or **Te·beth** (tā'vəs, tā-vāt') *n.* The fourth month of the Hebrew year. [Heb. *tēbhēth* < Akkadian *ṭebētu.*]

Te·wa (tā'wə, tē'wə) *n., pl.* **Tewa** or **-was. 1.** A Tanoan-speaking North American Indian tribe of New Mexico and northeastern Arizona. **2.** A member of the Tewa. **3.** The Tanoan language of the Tewa.

tex·as (tĕk'səs) *n.* The structure on a river steamboat containing the pilothouse and the officers' quarters. [After *Texas.*]

Tex·as fever *n.* An infectious disease of cattle and related animals, caused by a parasitic microorganism, *Babesia bigemina,* and transmitted by ticks.

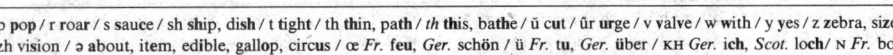

Texas leaguer *n. Baseball.* A fly ball that drops between the infielder and the outfielder for a hit. [After *Texas League,* a baseball minor league.]

Texas Ranger *n.* **1.** A member of the Texas mounted police force. **2.** A member of a band of men originally organized in Texas to fight Indians and maintain order.

Texas tower *n.* A radar tower built offshore. [After *Texas.*]

text (tĕkst) *n.* **1. a.** The wording or words of something written or printed. **b.** The words of a speech appearing in print. **2.** The body of a printed work as distinct from a preface, footnote, or appendix; the formal content. **3.** The exact wording and word sequence of an author as opposed to a translation, revision, or condensation. **4.** A theme; topic. **5.** A reference used as the starting point of a discussion. **6.** A textbook. [ME *texte* < OFr. < Med. Lat. *textus* < Lat. < *texere,* to construct.]

text·book (tĕkst′bo͝ok′) *n.* A book used as a standard work for the formal study of a particular subject.

text edition *n.* An edition of a book designed esp. for use in schools.

tex·tile (tĕks′tīl′, -təl) *n.* **1.** Fabric, esp. one that is woven or knitted. **2.** Fiber or yarn for weaving or knitting into fabric. [Lat. < *textilis,* woven < *textus,* p.part. of *texere,* to weave.]

tex·tu·al (tĕks′cho͞o-əl) *adj.* **1.** Of, pertaining to, or contained in a text. **2.** Based on or conforming to a text. **3.** Word for word; literal. **—tex′tu·al·ly** *adv.*

textual criticism *n.* **1.** A study of a written work that seeks to establish the original text. **2.** Literary criticism stressing scholarly study and analysis of the text.

tex·tu·al·ism (tĕks′cho͞o-ə-lĭz′əm) *n.* **1.** Strict adherence to a text, esp. of the Scriptures. **2.** Textual criticism, esp. of the Scriptures. **—tex′tu·al·ist** *n.*

tex·tu·ar·y (tĕks′cho͞o-ĕr′ē) *adj.* Of, pertaining to, or contained in a text; textual. *—n., pl.* **-ies.** A specialist in the study of the Scriptures.

tex·ture (tĕks′chər) *n.* **1. a.** The appearance of a fabric resulting from the woven arrangement of its yarns or fibers. **b.** A surface appearance suggesting the weave of a fabric: *the rough texture of plowed fields.* **2.** A grainy, fibrous, woven, or dimensional quality as opposed to a uniformly flat, smooth aspect: *Brick walls give a room texture.* **3.** The representation of the structure of a surface as distinct from color or form. **4.** The composition or structure of a substance; grain: *the smooth texture of ivory.* **5.** Distinctive or identifying character: *the texture of suburban life.* [Lat. *textura* < *textum,* that which is woven < *tegere,* to weave.] **—tex′tur·al** *adj.* **—tex′tur·al·ly** *adv.*

tex·tured (tĕks′chərd) *adj.* **1.** Having a particular kind of texture: *a rough-textured tweed.* **2.** Having marked texture: *a textured wall of stucco.*

tex·tus re·cep·tus (tĕks′təs rĭ-sĕp′təs) *n.* Received text, esp. the received text of the Greek New Testament. [Lat.]

T-group (tē′gro͞op′) *n.* A group of individuals, as in a corporation, who seek to improve awareness and sensitivity in interpersonal relations during sessions with a trained leader. [T(RAINING) GROUP.]

Th The symbol for the element thorium.

-th¹ *suff.* Variant of **-eth¹**.

-th² *suff.* **1.** Act; process: *spilth.* **2.** State; quality: *dearth.* [ME < OE *-ðu,* n. suffix.]

-th³ *suff.* Used to form ordinal numbers: *millionth.* [ME *-the* < OE *-ða, -ðe.*]

Thai (tī) *n., pl.* **Thai. 1. a.** A native or citizen of Thailand. **b.** A member of the predominant ethnic group of Thailand, a people with both Mongoloid and Indonesian characteristics. **2.** The Tai language that is the official language of Thailand. *—adj.* Also **Tai.** Of or pertaining to Thailand, its people, or its language.

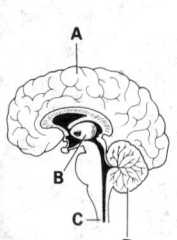

thalamus
A. Cerebrum
B. Thalamus
C. Spinal cord
D. Cerebellum

thal·a·men·ceph·a·lon (thăl′ə-mĕn-sĕf′ə-lŏn′) *n. Anat.* The diencephalon. [THALAM(US) + ENCEPHALON.]

thal·a·mus (thăl′ə-məs) *n., pl.* **-mi** (-mī′). **1.** *Anat.* A large ovoid mass of gray matter that relays sensory stimuli to the cerebral cortex and acts in integrative and nonspecific functions. **2.** *Bot.* The receptacle of a flower. [NLat. < Gk. *thalamos,* inner chamber.] **—tha·lam′ic** (thə-lăm′ĭk) *adj.* **—tha·lam′i·cal·ly** *adv.*

thal·as·se·mi·a (thăl′ə-sē′mē-ə) *n.* An inherited form of anemia that results from a faulty synthesis of hemoglobin. [Gk. *thalassa,* sea + -EMIA.] **—thal′as·se′mic** *adj.*

tha·las·sic (thə-lăs′ĭk) *adj.* **1.** Of or pertaining to deep seas or oceans. **2.** Of, pertaining to, or situated about inland seas. [Fr. *thalassique* < Gk. *thalassa,* sea.]

thal·as·soc·ra·cy (thăl′ə-sŏk′rə-sē) *n., pl.* **-cies.** Supremacy on the seas. [Gk. *thalassokratia* : *thalassa,* sea + *-kratia,* -cracy.] **—tha·las′so·crat′** (thə-lăs′ə-krăt′) *n.*

tha·ler (tä′lər) *n.* Variant of **taler.**

Tha·li·a (thə-lī′ə, thā′lē-ə) *n. Gk. Myth.* **1.** The Muse of comedy and pastoral poetry. **2.** One of the three Graces. [Gk. *Thaleia* < *thallein,* to bloom.]

tha·lid·o·mide (thə-lĭd′ə-mīd′) *n.* A sedative and hypnotic drug, $C_{13}H_{10}N_2O_4$, withdrawn from sale because of association with fetal abnormalities. [(PH)THAL(IC ACID) + (IM)ID(E) + (I)MIDE.]

thall- *pref.* Variant of **thallo-.**

thal·li (thăl′ī′) *n.* A plural of **thallus.**

thal·lic (thăl′ĭk) *adj.* Of, pertaining to, or containing thallium, esp. with valence 3.

thal·li·um (thăl′ē-əm) *n. Symbol* **Tl** A soft, malleable, highly toxic metallic element, used in rodent and ant poisons, in photocells, infrared detectors, and low-melting glass. Atomic number 81; atomic weight 204.37; melting point 303.5°C; boiling point 1,457°C; specific gravity 11.85; valences 1, 3. [THALL(O)- (from its green spectral line) + -IUM.]

thallo- or **thall-** *pref.* **1. a.** Young green shoot: *thallium.* **b.** Thallus: *thalloid.* **2.** Thallium: *thallous.* [< Gk. *thallos,* young green shoot.]

thal·loid (thăl′oid′) also **thal·loi·dal** (thə-loid′l) *adj.* Of, resembling, or constituting a thallus.

thal·lo·phyte (thăl′ə-fīt′) *n.* A plant or plantlike organism of the division or subkingdom Thallophyta, which includes the algae, fungi, and bacteria. **—thal′lo·phyt′ic** (-fĭt′ĭk) *adj.*

thal·lous (thăl′əs) *adj.* Of, pertaining to, or containing thallium, esp. with valence 1.

thal·lus (thăl′əs) *n., pl.* **thal·li** (thăl′ī′) or **-lus·es.** The undifferentiated stemless, rootless, leafless plant body characteristic of thallophytes. [NLat. < Lat., green stalk < Gk. *thallos* < *thallein,* to sprout.]

Tham·muz (tä′mo͞oz′) *n.* Variant of **Tammuz.**

than (*th*ăn, *th*ən) *conj.* **1.** Used to introduce the second element or clause of an unequal comparison: *She is a better athlete than I.* **2.** Used to introduce the rejected alternative in statements of preference: *I would rather dance than eat.* *—prep.* In comparison with: *disliked no one more than her.* [ME < OE *ðanne.*]

Usage: In comparisons, a pronoun following *than* or *as* may be taken as either the subject or the object of a "missing" verb whose sense is understood. Thus, in a sentence such as *John is taller than I,* the nominative *I* is traditionally required on the grounds that the sentence is equivalent to *John is taller than I am.* In *it does not surprise me as much as him,* the use of the objective *him* is justified by analogy to the sentence *it does not surprise me as much as it surprises him.* • On the other hand, pronouns introduced by *but* or *except* should properly be regarded as objective, demonstrated by the following sentence whose subject is a complex phrase of which a pronoun is a part: *Everybody but us* (not *we*) *has* (and not, of course, *have*) *left.* Since the verb in such a sentence always agrees in person and number with the element preceding *but,* logic similarly favors *No one except them* (not *they*) *has* (not *have*) *seen the report.* Some grammarians nonetheless illogically insist on the nominative in sentences like these and require *no one but they, everyone but he,* and so forth. When the phrase with *but* or *except* is moved to the end of the sentence, however, the objective form of the pronoun is universally acceptable: *Everyone left but me. No one left except us.* See also Usage note at **as.**

than·age (thā′nĭj) *n.* **1.** The rank, jurisdiction, or office of a thane; thaneship. **2.** The land held by a thane.

than·a·top·sis (thăn′ə-tŏp′sĭs) *n.* A meditation upon death. [Gk. *thanatos,* death + -OPSIS.]

Than·a·tos (thăn′ə-tŏs′) *n.* **1.** Death as a personification or as a philosophical notion. **2. thanatos.** An alleged instinct to self-destruction; death wish. [Gk.] **—than′a·tot′ic** (-tŏt′ĭk) *adj.*

thane (thān) *n.* **1.** In Anglo-Saxon England: **a.** A freeman granted land by the king in return for military service. **b.** A man ranking above an ordinary freeman and below a nobleman. **2.** A feudal lord or baron in Scotland. [ME < OE *ðegn.*]

thane·ship (thān′shĭp′) *n.* The position or office of a thane, esp. in Scotland.

thank (thăngk) *tr.v.* **thanked, thank·ing, thanks. 1.** To express gratitude to; give thanks to. **2.** To hold responsible; credit. [ME *thanken* < OE *ðancian.*]

thank·ful (thăngk′fəl) *adj.* **1.** Grateful. **2.** Expressive of thanks. **—thank′ful·ly** *adv.* **—thank′ful·ness** *n.*

thank·less (thăngk′lĭs) *adj.* **1.** Not feeling or showing gratitude; ungrateful. **2.** Not apt to be appreciated: *a thankless job.* **—thank′less·ly** *adv.* **—thank′less·ness** *n.*

thanks (thăngks) *pl.n.* **1.** An acknowledgment of a favor, gift, or benefit; gratitude. **2.** An expression of gratitude: *to give thanks.* *—interj.* Used to express thanks. ***—idioms.*** **no thanks to.** Without the benefit of help from: *He finally passed the test, no thanks to you.* **thanks to. 1.** Thanks be given to. **2.** On account of; because of: *We were an hour late, thanks to the storm.*

thanks·giv·ing (thăngks-gĭv′ĭng) *n.* **1.** An act of giving thanks; an expression of gratitude, esp. to God. **2. Thanksgiving.** Thanksgiving Day.

Thanksgiving Day *n.* A national holiday set apart for giving thanks to God, celebrated in the United States on the fourth Thursday of November and in Canada on the second Monday of October.

thank·wor·thy (thăngk′wûr′*th*ē) *adj.* **-thi·er, -thi·est.** Worthy of thanks.

thank-you (thăngk′yo͞o′) *n.* An expression of gratitude.

thank-you-ma'am (thăngk′yo͞o-măm′) *n.* A bump or depression in a road.

that (*th*ăt, *th*ət) *adj., pl.* **those** (*th*ōz) **1.** Being the one singled out, implied, or understood: *that place; those things.* **2.** Being the one further removed or less obvious: *That route is shorter than this one.* **3.** *Archaic.* Such: *"I heard a humming,*

/*And that a strange one too*" (Shakespeare). —*pron., pl.* **those. 1. a.** The one designated, implied, mentioned, or understood: *What kind of soup is that?* **b.** The one, thing, or type specified as follows: *The relics found were those of an earlier time.* **c.** The event, action, or time just mentioned: *After that, he became a recluse.* **2.** The further or less immediate one: *That is for sale; this is not.* **3.** Used to emphasize the idea of a previously expressed word or phrase: *He was fed up, and that to a great degree.* **4. a.** The one, kind, or thing; something: *He followed the calling of that he loved. What's that you say?* **b. those.** Some persons: *those who refused to join.* **5.** Used as a relative pronoun to introduce a clause, esp. a restrictive clause: *the car that has the flat tire.* **6. a.** In, on, by, or with which: *each summer that the concerts are performed.* **b.** In accordance with: *He never knew her, that I know of.* Used after a negative. —*adv.* **1.** To such an extent or degree: *Is your problem that complicated?* **2.** To a high degree: *didn't take what he said that seriously.* —*conj.* **1.** Used to introduce a noun clause that is chiefly the subject or object of a verb or a predicate nominative: *said that he was poor.* **2.** Used to introduce a subordinate clause stating a fact, wish, reason, or cause: *We thought that they were lost. She hoped that he would arrive on time. He was saddened that she felt so little for him.* **3. a.** Used to introduce an anticipated subordinate clause following the expletive *it* occurring as subject of the verb: *It is unlikely that she will accept the apology.* **b.** Used to introduce a subordinate clause modifying an adverb or adverbial expression: *will go anywhere that they are welcome.* **c.** Used to introduce a subordinate clause that is joined to an adjective or noun as a complement: *He was sure that he was right.* **4.** Used to introduce an elliptical exclamation of desire: *Oh, that I were rich!* —***idioms.* all that. 1.** All of the kind specified: *intelligence, beauty, and all that.* **2. a.** More of the same type: *a store selling nails, hammers, saws, and all that.* **b.** To the degree indicated: *It is really not as bad as all that.* **at that. 1.** In addition; besides: *merchandise of good quality and inexpensive at that.* **2.** Regardless of what has been said or implied. [ME < OE *ðæt.*]

Usage: The standard rule is that *that* should be used only to introduce a restrictive (or "defining") relative clause, which serves to identify the entity being talked about; in this use it should never be preceded by a comma. Thus, we say *the house that Jack built has been torn down,* where the clause *that Jack built* tells which house was torn down, or *I am looking for a book that is easy to read,* where *that is easy to read* tells what kind of book is desired. Only *which* is to be used with nonrestrictive (or "nondefining") clauses, which give additional information about an entity that has already been identified in the context; in this use, *which* is always preceded by a comma. Thus, we say *The students in Chemistry 10 have been complaining about the textbook, which* (not *that*) *is hard to follow.* The clause *which is hard to follow* does not indicate which text is being complained about; even if it were omitted, we would know that the phrase *the textbook* refers to "the text in chemistry 10." Similarly we say *The boys wanted to go to The Godfather, which* (not *that*) *I had already seen.* The title *The Godfather* is by itself sufficient to identify the film that the boys wanted to see; the clause *which I had already seen* merely gives further information about the film. The use of *that* in nonrestrictive clauses like these last, while once common in writing and still frequent in speech, is now generally held to be an error that should be avoided in written prose. • Some grammarians have argued that symmetry requires that *which* should be used only in nonrestrictive clauses, as *that* is to be used only in restrictive clauses. Thus, they suggest that we should avoid sentences like *I need a book which will tell me all about city gardening,* where the clause *which will tell me all about city gardening* indicates which sort of book is needed. But the use of *which* in such clauses is widely supported by general usage and is in no sense incorrect. It is particularly useful where two or more relative clauses are joined by *and* or *or,* as in *It is a philosopy in which the common man may find solace and which many have found reason to praise. Which* is also preferred to introduce a restrictive relative clause when the preceding phrase itself contains a *that,* as in *I can only give you that which I don't need* (not *that that I don't need*) or *We want to assign only that book which will be most helpful* (preferred to *that book that will be most helpful*). *That* may be omitted in a relative clause when the subject of the clause is different from the referent of the phrase preceding the clause. Thus, we may say either *the book that I was reading* or *the book I was reading,* where the subject of the clause *(I)* is not the referent of the phrase *the book.* The omission of *that* in these cases is entirely acceptable at any level. See also Usage notes at **this** and **who.**

thatch (thăch) *n.* **1.** Plant stalks or foliage, as reeds or palm fronds, used for roofing. **2.** Something resembling thatch, as a thick growth of hair on the head. —*tr.v.* **thatched, thatch·ing, thatch·es.** To cover with or as if with thatch. [ME *thacche* < *thacchen,* to thatch < OE *ðeccan,* to cover.] —**thatch'er** *n.* —**thatch'y** *adj.*

thau·ma·tol·o·gy (thô'mə-tŏl'ə-jē) *n., pl.* **-gies.** The study of or a discourse on miracles. [Gk. *thauma, thaumat-,* wonder + -LOGY.]

thau·ma·turge (thô'mə-tûrj') also **thau·ma·tur·gist** (-tûr'jĭst) *n.* A performer of miracles or magic feats. [Med. Lat. *thaumaturgus* < Gk. *thaumatourgos* : *thauma,* wonder + *-ergos,* working < *ergon,* work.]

thau·ma·tur·gy (thô'mə-tûr'jē) *n.* The working of miracles or wonders. —**thau'ma·tur'gic, thau'ma·tur'gi·cal** *adj.*

thaw (thô) *v.* **thawed, thaw·ing, thaws.** —*intr.* **1.** To change from a frozen solid to a liquid by gradual warming. **2.** To lose stiffness, numbness, or impermeability by being warmed. **3.** To become warm enough for snow and ice to melt. **4.** To become less reserved; relax. —*tr.* To melt (a frozen solid) by gradual warming. —*n.* **1.** The process of thawing. **2.** A period of warm weather during which ice and snow melt. **3.** A relaxation of reserve, restraints, or tensions. [ME *thawen* < OE *ðawian.*]

THC *n.* Tetrahydrocannabinol.

the[1] (*thē before a vowel; thə before a consonant*) *def.art.* **1. a.** Used before singular or plural nouns and noun phrases that denote particular, specified persons or things: *read the newspaper.* **b.** Used before a noun, and generally stressed, emphasizing one of a group or type as the most outstanding or prominent: *the social event of 1981.* **c.** Used before a title or rank or office designating its holder: *The Prince of Wales; The President of the United States; the Reverend John Doe.* **d.** Used before nouns that designate natural phenomena or points of the compass: *The weather looks bad. A wind is coming from the north.* **e.** Used as the equivalent of a possessive adjective before names of some parts of the body: *grab him by the neck; an infection of the hand.* **f.** Used before a noun specifying a particular human endeavor: *the law; the film industry; the stage.* **g.** Used before a proper name, as of a monument or ship: *the Alamo; the Titanic.* **h.** Used before the plural form of a numeral denoting a specific decade or period in one's life: *rural life in the thirties.* **2.** Used before a singular noun indicating that the noun is generic: *The wolf is an endangered species.* **3. a.** Used before an adjective extending it to signify a class and giving it the function of a noun: *"The rich were dull and they drank too much"* (Ernest Hemingway). **b.** Used before an absolute adjective: *the best we can offer.* **4.** Used before a present participle, signifying the action in the abstract: *the weaving of rugs.* **5.** Used before a noun with the force of *per: ten dollars the box.* [ME < OE *ðe,* alteration of *se,* masc. nominative sing. demonstrative adj.]

the[2] (*thē before a vowel; thə before a consonant*) *adv.* **1.** To that extent; by that much: *the sooner the better.* **2.** Beyond any other: *enjoyed reading the most.* [ME < OE *ðȳ,* instrumental case of *the* and *that.*]

the– *pref.* Variant of **theo-.**

the·an·throp·ic (thē'ăn-thrŏp'ĭk) also **the·an·throp·i·cal** (-ĭ-kəl) *adj.* Both divine and human in nature or quality. [< LGk. *theanthrōpos,* god-man : Gk. *theos,* god + Gk. *anthrōpos,* man.]

the·an·thro·pism (thē-ăn'thrə-pĭz'əm) *n.* **1.** The attribution of human traits to God; anthropomorphism. **2.** *Theol.* The doctrine of the union of human and divine natures in Christ. —**the·an'thro·pist** *n.*

the·ar·chy (thē'är'kē) *n., pl.* **-chies. 1.** Government or rule by a god; theocracy. **2.** A hierarchy or order of gods. [LGk. *thearkhia* : Gk. *theos,* god + Gk. *-arkhia,* -archy.]

the·a·ter also **the·a·tre** (thē'ə-tər) *n.* **1.** A building, room, or outdoor structure for the presentation of plays, motion pictures, or other dramatic performances. **2.** A room with tiers of seats used for lectures or demonstrations; auditorium. **3. a.** Dramatic literature or its performance: *the theater of Shakespeare and Marlowe.* **b.** The milieu of actors and playwrights. **c.** The quality or effectiveness of a theatrical production: *This play is good theater.* **4.** The audience assembled for a dramatic performance. **5. a.** A place that is the setting for dramatic events. **b.** A large geographic area in which military operations are coordinated. [ME *theatre* < OFr. < Lat. *theatrum* < Gk. *theatron* < *theasthai,* to watch.]

the·a·ter·go·er (thē'ə-tər-gō'ər) *n.* A person who often attends the theater.

the·a·ter-in-the-round (thē'ə-tər-ĭn-*th*ə-round') *n., pl.* **theaters-in-the-round.** An arena theater.

theater of the absurd *n.* Dramatic literature dealing with the absurd.

the·a·tre (thē'ə-tər) *n.* Variant of **theater.**

the·at·ri·cal (thē-ăt'rĭ-kəl) also **the·at·ric** (-ăt'rĭk) *adj.* **1.** Of, relating to, or suitable for the theater or dramatic performance. **2.** Marked by exaggerated self-display and unnatural behavior; affectedly dramatic. —*n.* Often **theatricals.** Stage performances, esp. by amateurs. —**the·at'ri·cal'i·ty, the·at'ri·cal·ness** *n.* —**the·at'ri·cal·ly** *adv.*

the·at·ri·cal·ism (thē-ăt'rĭ-kə-lĭz'əm) *n.* Theatrical manner or style; showiness.

the·at·ri·cal·ize (thē-ăt'rĭ-kə-līz') *tr.v.* **-ized, -iz·ing, -iz·es. 1.** To make theatrical; dramatize. **2.** To display in a showy or flashy manner. —**the·at'ri·cal'i·za'tion** *n.*

the·at·rics (thē-ăt'rĭks) *n.* **1.** *(used with a sing. verb).* The art of the theater. **2.** *(used with a pl. verb).* Theatrical effects or mannerisms; histrionics.

the·ba·ine (thē'bə-ēn', thĭ-bā'ĭn) *n.* A poisonous alkaloid,

thatch

$C_{19}H_{21}NO_3$, obtained from opium. [Gk. *Thēbai,* Thebes + -INE.]

the·ca (thē′kə) *n., pl.* **-cae** (-sē′, -kē′). A case, covering, or sheath, as the spore case of a moss capsule or the outer covering of the pupa of certain insects. [NLat. < Lat., case < Gk. *thēkē.*] **—the′cal** (-kəl) *adj.*

the·cate (thē′kāt′) *adj.* Having a theca; encased or sheathed.

thee (*th*ē) *pron. Archaic.* The objective case of **thou. 1.** Used: **a.** As the direct object of a verb. **b.** As the indirect object of a verb. **c.** As the object of a preposition. **2.** Used in the nominative as well as the objective case, esp. by members of the Society of Friends.

thee·lin (thē′lĭn) *n.* Estrone. [Gk. *thēlus,* female + -IN.]

thee·lol (thē′lôl′, -lōl′) *n.* Estriol. [THEEL(IN) + -OL.]

theft (thĕft) *n.* **1.** The act or an instance of stealing; larceny. **2.** *Obs.* That which is stolen. [ME < OE *þiefþ.*]

their (*th*âr) *pron.* The possessive form of **they. 1.** Used attributively to indicate possession or the agent or recipient of an action: *their house; pursuing their tasks; suffered their first defeat.* **2.** *Informal.* His, hers, or its: *Does everyone have their books?* —See Usage note at **everyone.** [ME < ON *þeira.*]

theirs (*th*ârz) *pron. (used with a sing. or pl. verb).* **1.** That or those belonging to them: *The choice ought to be theirs. Mine is here, and theirs are on the table.* **2.** *Informal.* His or hers: *brought his skis and expected everybody else to bring theirs.* [ME < *their,* their.]

the·ism (thē′ĭz′əm) *n.* Belief in the existence of a god or gods, esp. belief in a personal God as creator and ruler of the world. **—the′ist** *n.* **—the·is′tic, the·is′ti·cal** *adj.* **—the·is′ti·cal·ly** *adv.*

them (*th*ĕm, *th*əm) *pron.* The objective case of **they.** Used: **a.** As the direct object of a verb: *She accompanied them.* **b.** As the indirect object of a verb: *He offered them a new contract.* **c.** As the object of a preposition: *It was ruined by them.* —See Usage notes at **be, everyone,** and **I.** [ME, partly < ON *þeim,* and partly < OE *þem.*]

the·mat·ic (thĭ-măt′ĭk) *adj.* **1.** Of, constituting, or relating to a theme. **2.** *Ling.* Constituting the theme or stem of a word. [Gk. *thematikos* < *thema, themat-,* theme.] **—the·mat′i·cal·ly** *adv.*

theme (thēm) *n.* **1.** A topic of discourse or discussion. **2.** An idea, point of view, or perception embodied and expanded upon in a work of art; an underlying or essential subject of artistic representation. **3.** A short composition assigned to a student as a writing exercise. **4.** *Mus.* A principal melody in a musical composition. **5.** *Ling.* A stem. [ME < Lat. *thema* < Gk., proposition < *tithenai,* to place.]

theme song *n.* **1.** A melody or song played throughout a dramatic performance and often intended to convey a mood. **2.** A song that is identified with a performer, group, or radio or television program; signature.

them·selves (*th*ĕm-sĕlvz′, *th*əm-) *pron.* **1.** Those ones identical with them. Used: **a.** Reflexively as the direct or indirect object of a verb or the object of a preposition: *prepared themselves for battle; gave themselves plenty of time; were left by themselves.* **b.** For emphasis: *they themselves were affected.* **2.** Their normal or healthy condition or state: *The members of the cast were themselves again after the crisis passed.* —See Usage note at **myself.**

then (*th*ĕn) *adv.* **1.** At that time in the past: *I was younger then.* **2.** Next in time, space, or order; immediately afterward: *I watched the late movie and then went to bed.* **3.** Used after *but* to make noticeable or to balance a preceding statement: *lost the election, but then never really expected to win.* **4.** In that case; accordingly: *If you're late, then you'd better go now.* **5.** In addition; moreover; besides: *then there's the excise tax to pay.* **6.** As it appears: *The case, then, is closed.* **7.** Consequently: *If x equals 3 and y equals 2, then x plus y equals 5.* —*n.* A particular time or moment: *Until then let's remain here.* —*adj.* Being so at that time: *the then headmistress.* **—idiom. and then some.** With considerably more in addition: *It'll take all his skill and then some.* [ME < OE *þenne.*]

the·nar (thē′năr′) *n.* The fleshy mass on the palm of the hand at the base of the thumb. —*adj.* Of, pertaining to, or related to the thenar. [Gk.]

thence (*th*ĕns, thĕns) *adv.* **1.** From that place; from there. **2.** From that time; thenceforth. **3.** From that circumstance or source; therefrom. [ME *thannes* < *thanne,* from there < OE *þanon.*]

thence·forth (*th*ĕns-fôrth′, -fōrth′, thĕns-) *adv.* From that time forward; thereafter.

thence·for·ward (*th*ĕns-fôr′wərd, thĕns-) also **thence·for·wards** (-wərdz) *adv.* **1.** Thenceforth. **2.** From that time or place onward.

theo- or **the-** *pref.* God: *theomorphism.* [Gk. *theos,* god.]

the·o·bro·mine (thē′ō-brō′mēn′) *n.* A bitter, colorless alkaloid, $C_7H_8N_4O_2$, that occurs in chocolate products, is derived principally from the cacao bean, and is used as a diuretic and a nerve stimulant. [NLat. *Theobroma,* genus of trees (Gk. *theos,* god + *brōma,* food) + -INE.]

the·o·cen·tric (thē′ō-sĕn′trĭk) *adj.* Centering on God as the prime concern: *a theocentric cosmology.*

the·oc·ra·cy (thē-ŏk′rə-sē) *n., pl.* **-cies. 1.** Government by a god regarded as the ruling power or by priests or officials claiming divine sanction. **2.** A state governed by a theocracy. [Gk. *theokratia* : *theos,* god + *-kratia,* -cracy.]

the·o·crat (thē′ə-krăt′) *n.* **1.** A ruler of a theocracy. **2.** A believer in theocracy. **—the′o·crat′ic, the′o·crat′i·cal** *adj.* **—the′o·crat′i·cal·ly** *adv.*

the·od·i·cy (thē-ŏd′ĭ-sē) *n., pl.* **-cies.** A vindication of divine justice in the face of the existence of evil. [After *Théodicée,* a work by Gottfried Wilhelm von Leibnitz (1646–1716) : Gk. *theos,* god + Gk. *dikē,* order, right.]

the·od·o·lite (thē-ŏd′ə-līt′) *n.* A surveying instrument used to measure horizontal and vertical angles with a small telescope that can move in horizontal and vertical planes. [Orig. unknown.] **—the·od′o·lit′ic** *adj.*

the·og·o·ny (thē-ŏg′ə-nē) *n., pl.* **-nies.** A recitation of the origin and genealogy of the gods, esp. as in ancient epic poetry. [Gk. *theogonia* : *theos,* god + *-gonia,* -gony.] **—the′o·gon′ic** (-ə-gŏn′ĭk) *adj.* **—the·og′o·nist** *n.*

the·o·lo·gi·an (thē′ə-lō′jən) *n.* A specialist in theology.

the·o·log·i·cal (thē′ə-lŏj′ĭ-kəl) also **the·o·log·ic** (-lŏj′ĭk) *adj.* Of or pertaining to a theology or religious philosophy. **—the′o·log′i·cal·ly** *adv.*

the·ol·o·gize (thē-ŏl′ə-jīz′) *v.* **-gized, -giz·ing, -giz·es.** —*tr.* To make theological in form or significance. —*intr.* To speculate about theology. **—the·ol′o·giz′er** *n.*

the·ol·o·gy (thē-ŏl′ə-jē) *n., pl.* **-gies. 1.** The study of the nature of God and religious truth; rational inquiry into religious questions, esp. those posed by an organized religious community. **2.** An organized, often formalized body of opinions concerning God and man's relationship to God. **3.** A course of specialized religious study usually at a college or seminary. [ME *theologie* < OFr. < Lat. *theologia* < Gk. : *theos,* god + *-logia,* -logy.]

the·om·a·chy (thē-ŏm′ə-kē) *n., pl.* **-chies.** Strife or battle among gods, as in the Homeric poems. [Gk. *theomakhia* : *theos,* god + *makhia,* fighting < *makhē,* battle.]

the·o·mor·phism (thē′ō-môr′fĭz′əm) *n.* The depiction or conception of man as having the form of a god. **—the′o·mor′phic** *adj.*

the·oph·a·ny (thē-ŏf′ə-nē) *n., pl.* **-nies.** An appearance of a god to a man; divine manifestation. [Med. Lat. *theophania* < LGk. *theophaneia* : Gk. *theos,* god + Gk. *phainein,* to show.]

the·oph·yl·line (thē-ŏf′ə-lĭn, thē′ō-fĭl′ēn′) *n.* A colorless crystalline alkaloid, $C_7H_8N_4O_2.H_2O$, derived from tea leaves and also made synthetically, used as a diuretic and cardiac stimulant. [THEO(BROMINE) + PHYLL(O)- + -INE.]

the·or·bo (thē-ôr′bō) *n., pl.* **-bos.** A 17th-century lute having two sets of strings and an S-shaped neck with two sets of pegs, one set above and somewhat to the side of the other. [Ital. *tiorba.*]

the·o·rem (thē′ər-əm, thîr′əm) *n.* **1.** An idea that is demonstrably true or is assumed to be so. **2.** *Math.* **a.** A proposition that is provable on the basis of explicit assumptions. **b.** A proven proposition. [LLat. *theorema* < Gk. *theōrēma* < *theōrein,* to look at < *theōros,* spectator. —see THEORY.]

the·o·ret·i·cal (thē′ə-rĕt′ĭ-kəl) also **the·o·ret·ic** (-rĕt′ĭk) *adj.* **1.** Of, pertaining to, or based on theory. **2.** Restricted to theory; lacking verification or practical application: *theoretical physics.* **3.** Given to theorizing; speculative. [LLat. *theoreticus* < Gk. *theōrētikos,* contemplative < *theōrētos,* observable < *theōrein,* to look at. —see THEOREM.] **—the′o·ret′i·cal·ly** *adv.*

the·o·re·ti·cian (thē′ər-ə-tĭsh′ən) *n.* A person who formulates, studies, or is expert in the theory of a science or art.

the·o·ret·ics (thē′ə-rĕt′ĭks) *n. (used with a sing. verb).* The theoretical part of a science or art; principles.

the·o·rist (thē′ər-ĭst) *n.* A theoretician.

the·o·rize (thē′ə-rīz′) *intr.v.* **-rized, -riz·ing, -riz·es. 1.** To formulate or analyze theories. **2.** To analyze by means of theory. **3.** To speculate. **—the′o·ri·za′tion** *n.* **—the′o·riz′er** *n.*

the·o·ry (thē′ə-rē, thîr′ē) *n., pl.* **-ries. 1. a.** Systematically organized knowledge applicable in a relatively wide variety of circumstances, esp. a system of assumptions, accepted principles, and rules of procedure devised to analyze, predict, or otherwise explain the nature or behavior of a specified set of phenomena. **b.** Such knowledge or such a system distinguished from experiment or practice. **2.** Abstract reasoning; speculation. **3.** An assumption or guess based on limited information or knowledge. [LLat. *theoria* < Gk. *theōria* < *theōros,* spectator < *theasthai,* to observe.]

theory of games *n.* Game theory.

the·os·o·phy (thē-ŏs′ə-fē) *n., pl.* **-phies. 1.** Religious philosophy or speculation based on mystical insight into the nature of God and divine teachings. **2.** Often **Theosophy.** The doctrines and beliefs of a modern religious sect, the Theosophical Society, incorporating aspects of Buddhism and Brahmanism. [Med. Lat. *theosophia* < LGk. : Gk. *theos,* god + Gk. *sophia,* wisdom.] **—the′o·soph′ic** (-ə-sŏf′ĭk), **the′o·soph′i·cal** *adj.* **—the′o·soph′i·cal·ly** *adv.* **—the·os′o·phist** *n.*

ther·a·peu·tic (thĕr′ə-pyōō′tĭk) also **ther·a·peu·ti·cal** (-tĭ-kəl) *adj.* **1.** Having healing or curative powers. **2.** Of or pertaining to therapeutics. [Gk. *therapeutikos* < *therapeutēs,* one who administers < *therapeuein* < *theraps,* attendant. —see THERAPY.] **—ther′a·peu′ti·cal·ly** *adv.*

ther·a·peu·tics (thĕr′ə-pyōō′tĭks) *n. (used with a sing. verb).* The medical treatment of disease. **—ther′a·peu′tist** *n.*

ther·a·pist (thĕr′ə-pĭst) *n.* A specialist in conducting therapy.

the·rap·sid (thə-răp′sĭd) *n.* Any of various reptiles of the order Therapsida of the Permian and Triassic periods that are considered to be direct ancestors of mammals. [< NLat. *Therapsida,* order name < Gk. *theraps,* attendant.] **—the·rap′sid** *adj.*

ther·a·py (thĕr′ə-pē) *n., pl.* **-pies. 1.** The treatment of illness or disability. **2.** Healing power or quality. **3.** Psychotherapy. [NLat. *therapia* < Gk. *therapeia* < *therapeuein,* to treat medically < *theraps,* attendant.]

Ther·a·va·da (thĕr′ə-vä′də) *n.* Hinayana. [Pali *theravāda* : *thera,* elder (< Skt. *sthavira-,* old) + *vāda,* doctrine (< Skt. *vādah,* speech, doctrine).]

there (*th*âr) *adv.* **1.** At or in that place: *sit over there.* **2.** To, into, or toward that place: *wouldn't go there again.* **3.** At a point of action or time: *Stop there before you make any more mistakes.* **4.** In that matter: *I can't agree with you there.* *—pron.* **1.** Used to introduce a clause or sentence: *There are numerous items to choose from.* **2.** Used in place of a name: *Hello there.* *—adj.* **1.** Used as an intensive: *That man there ought to know.* **2.** Present: *He was still there when I left.* *—n.* That place or point: *stopped and went on from there.* *—interj.* Used to express emotion, as relief, satisfaction, or consolation: *There, now I can have some peace!* [ME < OE *ðǣr.*]

Usage: *There* frequently precedes a linking verb such as *be, seem,* or *appear* in beginning a sentence or clause: *There has been a great deal of uncertainty as to the exact meaning of the law.* The number of the verb is governed by the subject, which in such constructions follows the verb: *There is a garage across the street. There seem to be many good candidates.* But a singular verb is also possible before a compound subject whose parts are joined by a conjunction or conjunctions, especially when the parts are singular: *There is* (or *are*) *much pain and toil involved. There appears* (or *appear*) *to be a man and a wagon in the distance.* When the first element of such a subject is singular, a singular verb is also possible even though the other element is plural: *There were* (or *was*) *a man and two children in the car.* But: *there were two children and a man.* • *There* (adverb) meaning "in that place" comes after the noun in constructions introduced by the demonstrative *that: That boy there is to blame.* While some dialects allow *there* before the noun, as in *that there boy,* this use is inappropriate in formal English.

there·a·bout (*th*âr′ə-bout′) also **there·a·bouts** (-bouts′) *adv.* **1.** Near that number or degree: *She was 21, or thereabouts.* **2.** Near that place or time.

there·af·ter (*th*âr-ăf′tər) *adv.* From a specified time onward; from then on: *an apprentice for three years, an assistant thereafter.*

there·a·gainst (*th*âr′ə-gĕnst′) *adv.* Against or in opposition to; contrary to.

there·at (*th*âr-ăt′) *adv.* **1.** At a specified place; there. **2.** At such time; on that occasion.

there·by (*th*âr-bī′) *adv.* **1.** Through or with the agency of. **2.** In a specified connection or relation wherein.

there·for (*th*âr-fôr′) *adv. Archaic.* For that, this, or it.

there·fore (*th*âr′fôr′, -fōr′) *adv.* For that reason; hence: *Your information is inaccurate and your conclusion therefore wrong.*

there·from (*th*âr-frŭm′, -frŏm′) *adv.* From that, this, or it; coming from that time, location, or thing.

there·in (*th*âr-ĭn′) *adv.* **1.** In that place. **2.** In that circumstance or respect: *Therein lies the fault.*

there·in·af·ter (*th*âr′ĭn-ăf′tər) *adv.* In a later or subsequent portion, as of a speech or book.

ther·e·min (thĕr′ə-mĭn) *n.* An electronic consolelike musical instrument often used for high tremolo effects. [After Leo *Theremin* (b. 1896), its inventor.]

there·of (*th*âr-ŭv′, -ŏv′) *adv.* **1.** Of or concerning this, that, or it. **2.** From or because of a stated cause or origin; therefrom.

there·on (*th*âr-ŏn′, -ôn′) *adv.* **1.** On or upon this, that, or it. **2.** Following that immediately; thereupon.

there·to (*th*âr-tōō′) *adv.* **1.** To that, this, or it; thereunto: *affixed his seal thereto.* **2.** *Archaic.* In addition to that; furthermore.

there·to·fore (*th*âr′tə-fôr′, -fōr′) *adv.* Until or prior to a specified time; before that: *a theretofore little known politician.*

there·un·der (*th*âr-ŭn′dər) *adv.* Under this, that, or it.

there·un·to (*th*âr′ŭn-tōō′) *adv.* To that, this, or it.

there·up·on (*th*âr′ə-pŏn′, -pôn′) *adv.* **1.** Upon this, that, or it; concerning a specified subject or object. **2.** Directly following that. **3.** In consequence of that; therefore.

there·with (*th*âr-wĭ*th*′, -wĭth′) *adv.* **1.** With that, this, or it. **2.** In addition to that. **3.** Immediately thereafter.

there·with·al (*th*âr′wĭ*th*-ôl′, -wĭth-) *adv.* **1.** With all that, this, or it; besides. **2.** *Obs.* Therewith; with that, this, or it.

the·ri·o·mor·phic (thĭr′ē-ə-môr′fĭk) also **the·ri·o·mor·phous** (-fəs) *adj.* Having the form of a beast. [Gk. *thērion,* beast, dim. of *thēr,* beast + -MORPHIC.]

therm (thûrm) *n.* A unit of heat equal to: **a.** One hundred thousand British thermal units. **b.** One thousand large calories. **c.** The large calorie. **d.** The small calorie. [Gk. *thermē,* heat.]

therm– *pref.* Variant of **thermo–.**

–therm *suff.* An animal having a specified kind of body temperature: *poikilotherm.* [< Gk. *thermē,* heat.]

ther·mal (thûr′məl) also **ther·mic** (-mĭk) *adj.* **1.** Of, pertaining to, using, producing, or caused by heat. **2.** Designed to help retain body heat: *thermal underwear.* *—n.* A rising current of warm air. [< Gk. *thermē,* heat.] **—ther′mal·ly** *adv.*

thermal neutron *n.* A slow neutron.

therm·i·on (thûr′mī′ən) *n.* An electrically charged particle or ion emitted by a conducting material at high temperatures. **—therm′i·on′ic** (-mī-ŏn′ĭk) *adj.*

thermionic current *n.* A flow of thermions.

thermionic emission *n.* The emission of thermions from a conducting material at high temperatures.

therm·i·on·ics (thûr′mī-ŏn′ĭks) *n. (used with a sing. verb).* The physics of thermionic phenomena.

thermionic tube *n.* An electron tube in which the source of electrons is a heated electrode.

therm·is·tor (thûr′mĭs′tər) *n.* A resistor made of semiconductors having resistance that varies rapidly and predictably with temperature. [THERM(AL) + (RES)ISTOR.]

Ther·mit (thûr′mĭt, -mīt′). A trademark for a welding and incendiary mixture of fine aluminum powder with a metallic oxide, as of iron or chromium, which when ignited yields an intense heat.

thermo– or **therm–** *pref.* **1.** Heat: *thermochemistry.* **2.** Thermoelectric: *thermojunction.* [< Gk. *thermē,* heat.]

ther·mo·chem·is·try (thûr′mō-kĕm′ĭ-strē) *n.* The chemistry of heat and heat-associated chemical phenomena. **—ther′mo·chem′i·cal** (-kĕm′ĭ-kəl) *adj.* **—ther′mo·chem′ist** *n.*

ther·mo·cline (thûr′mə-klīn′) *n.* The region in a thermally stratified body of water, as a lake, in which the temperature decrease with depth is greater than that of the water above and below it.

ther·mo·co·ag·u·la·tion (thûr′mō-kō-ăg′yə-lā′shən) *n.* The use of heat produced by high frequency currents to bring about the localized destruction of tissues.

ther·mo·cou·ple (thûr′mə-kŭp′əl) *n.* A thermoelectric device used to measure temperatures accurately, esp. one consisting of two dissimilar metals joined so that a potential difference generated between the points of contact is a measure of the temperature difference between the points.

ther·mo·dur·ic (thûr′mō-dŏŏr′ĭk, -dyŏŏr′-) *adj.* Of or pertaining to microorganisms that are able to survive high temperatures. [THERMO- + Lat. *durare,* to last + -IC.]

ther·mo·dy·nam·ics (thûr′mō-dī-năm′ĭks) *n. (used with a sing. verb).* The physics of the relationships between heat and other forms of energy. **—ther′mo·dy·nam′ic** *adj.* **—ther′mo·dy·nam′i·cal·ly** *adv.*

ther·mo·e·lec·tric (thûr′mō-ĭ-lĕk′trĭk) also **ther·mo·e·lec·tri·cal** (-trĭ-kəl) *adj.* Characteristic of or resulting from electrical phenomena occurring in conjunction with a flow of heat. **—ther′mo·e·lec′tri·cal·ly** *adv.*

ther·mo·e·lec·tric·i·ty (thûr′mō-ĭ-lĕk-trĭs′ĭ-tē) *n.* Electricity generated by a flow of heat, as in a thermocouple.

ther·mo·e·lec·tron (thûr′mō-ĭ-lĕk′trŏn′) *n.* An electron emitted by a material at high temperatures.

ther·mo·gram (thûr′mə-grăm′) *n.* A record made by a thermograph.

ther·mo·graph (thûr′mə-grăf′) *n.* A thermometer that records the temperature it indicates.

ther·mog·ra·phy (thər-mŏg′rə-fē) *n.* **1.** A process for producing raised lettering, as on stationery or calling cards, by transferring the inked lines on a plate to the paper by pressure and suction. **2.** A diagnostic technique for measuring blood flow by determining the variations in heat emitted from the body. **—ther′mo·graph′ic** *adj.* **—ther′mo·graph′i·cal·ly** *adv.*

ther·mo·junc·tion (thûr′mō-jŭngk′shən) *n.* A point of contact between two dissimilar metals at which a thermoelectric current is produced.

ther·mo·la·bile (thûr′mō-lā′bĭl′, -bəl) *adj.* Subject to destruction, to decomposition, or to great change by moderate heating. Used esp. of certain biochemicals. **—ther′mo·la·bil′i·ty** *n.*

ther·mo·lu·mi·nes·cence (thûr′mō-lōō′mə-nĕs′əns) *n.* A phenomenon in which certain minerals release previously absorbed radiation upon being moderately heated. **—ther′mo·lu′mi·nes′cent** *adj.*

ther·mol·y·sis (thər-mŏl′ĭ-sĭs) *n.* **1.** *Physiol.* The loss of heat from the body. **2.** *Chem.* The dissociation or decomposition of compounds by heat. **—ther·mo·lyt′ic** *adj.*

ther·mom·e·ter (thər-mŏm′ĭ-tər) *n.* An instrument for measuring temperature, esp. one having a graduated glass tube with a bulb containing a liquid, typically mercury, that expands and rises in the tube as the temperature increases.

ther·mom·e·try (thər-mŏm′ĭ-trē) *n.* **1.** The measurement of temperature. **2.** The technology of temperature measurement. **—ther′mo·met′ric** (thûr′mō-mĕt′rĭk) *adj.*

ther·mo·mo·tor (thûr′mō-mō′tər) *n.* An engine operated by heat, esp. by the expansion of heated air.

ther·mo·nu·cle·ar (thûr′mō-nōō′klē-ər, -nyōō′-) *adj.* **1.** Of, pertaining to, or derived from the fusion of atomic nuclei at high temperatures. **2.** Of or pertaining to atomic weapons based on fusion, esp. as distinguished from those based on fission.

ther·mo·pe·ri·od·ism (thûr′mō-pîr′ē-ə-dĭz′əm) also **ther·**

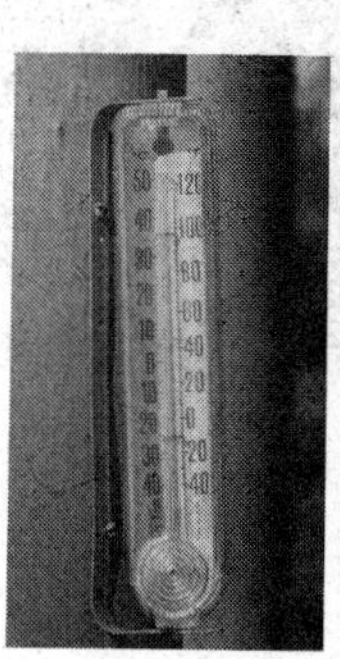

thermometer

mo·pe·ri·o·dic·i·ty (-dĭs′ĭ-tē) *n.* The effect of the rhythmic fluctuation of temperature upon an organism, including responses corresponding to thermal changes due to alternation of day and night.

ther·mo·phil·ic (thûr′mə-fĭl′ĭk) *adj. Biol.* Requiring high temperatures for normal development, as certain bacteria. **—ther′mo·phile′** (-fīl′) *n.*

ther·mo·pile (thûr′mə-pīl′) *n.* A device to measure temperature, consisting of a number of thermocouples connected in series. [THERMO- + PILE[1].]

ther·mo·plas·tic (thûr′mə-plăs′tĭk) *adj.* Becoming soft when heated and hard when cooled. *—n.* A thermoplastic resin, such as polystyrene or polyethylene. **—ther′mo·plas·tic′i·ty** (-plă-stĭs′ĭ-tē) *n.*

Theseus

ther·mo·re·cep·tor (thûr′mō-rĭ-sĕp′tər) *n.* A sensory receptor that responds to heat and cold.

ther·mo·reg·u·la·tion (thûr′mō-rĕg′yə-lā′shən) *n.* The maintenance of a constant internal body temperature regardless of the environmental temperature. **—ther′mo·reg′u·la·to′ry** (-rĕg′yə-lə-tôr′ē, -tōr′ē) *adj.*

Ther·mos bottle (thûr′məs). A trademark for a vacuum flask.

ther·mo·set·ting (thûr′mō-sĕt′ĭng) *adj.* Permanently hardening or solidifying on being heated. Used of certain synthetic resins.

ther·mo·sphere (thûr′mə-sfîr′) *n.* The outermost shell of the atmosphere, between the mesosphere and outer space, where temperatures increase steadily with altitude. **—ther′mo·spher′ic** *adj.*

ther·mo·sta·ble (thûr′mō-stā′bəl) also **ther·mo·sta·bile** (-bəl, -bīl′) *adj.* Unaffected by relatively high temperatures. **—ther′mo·sta·bil′i·ty** (-stə-bĭl′ĭ-tē) *n.*

ther·mo·stat (thûr′mə-stăt′) *n.* A device that automatically responds to temperature changes and activates switches controlling equipment such as furnaces, refrigerators, and air conditioners. **—ther′mo·stat′ic** *adj.*

ther·mo·tax·is (thûr′mə-tăk′sĭs) *n.* **1.** The movement of a living organism in response to heat. **2.** The normal regulation or adjustment of body temperature. **—ther′mo·tac′tic** (-tăk′tĭk) *adj.*

ther·mo·ther·a·py (thûr′mō-thĕr′ə-pē) *n.* Therapy by application of heat.

ther·mot·ro·pism (thər-mŏt′rə-pĭz′əm) *n. Biol.* Growth or movement of plants or other organisms in response to heat. **—ther′mo·trop′ic** (thûr′mə-trŏp′ĭk) *adj.*

-thermy *suff.* Heat: *diathermy.* [NLat. *-thermia* < Gk. *thermē,* heat.]

the·ro·pod (thîr′ə-pŏd′) *n.* Any of various carnivorous dinosaurs of the suborder Theropoda, of the Jurassic and Cretaceous periods, characteristically having small forelimbs. [NLat. *Theropoda,* suborder name : Gk. *thēr,* beast + Gk. *pous,* foot.] **—the·rop′o·dan** (thĭ-rŏp′ə-dən) *adj. & n.*

Thetis
Thetis with dolphins

the·sau·rus (thĭ-sôr′əs) *n., pl.* **-sau·ri** (-sôr′ī′) or **-sau·rus·es.** **1.** A book of selected words or concepts, as a specialized vocabulary of a particular field, as medicine or music. **2.** A book of synonyms. [Lat., collection < Gk. *thēsauros,* treasure.]

these (thēz) *pron.* Plural of **this.**

The·se·us (thē′sē-əs, -syo͞os′) *n. Gk. Myth.* A hero and king of Athens who slew the Minotaur and conquered the Amazons and married Phaedra, their queen. **—The·se′an** (thĭ-sē′ən) *adj.*

the·sis (thē′sĭs) *n., pl.* **-ses** (-sēz′). **1.** A proposition, as one advanced by a candidate for an academic degree, that is maintained by argument. **2.** A dissertation advancing an original point of view as a result of research, esp. as a requirement for an academic degree. **3.** A hypothetical proposition, esp. one put forth for the sake of argument or one to be accepted without proof. **4.** The first stage of dialectic. **5.** The unstressed part of a foot in prosody. **6.** *Mus.* The accented section of a measure. [Lat. < Gk. < *tithenai,* to place.]

Thes·pi·an (thĕs′pē-ən) *adj.* **1.** Of or pertaining to Thespis. **2.** Often **thespian.** Of or pertaining to drama; dramatic. *—n.* Also **thes·pi·an.** An actor or actress.

Thes·sa·lo·ni·ans (thĕs′ə-lō′nē-ənz) *pl.n. (used with a sing. verb).* See table at **Bible.**

the·ta (thā′tə, thē′-) *n.* The 8th letter in the Greek alphabet. See table at **alphabet.** [Gk. *thēta,* of Phoenician orig.; akin to Heb. *ṭēth,* teth.]

thet·ic (thĕt′ĭk, thē′tĭk) also **thet·i·cal** (thĕt′ĭ-kəl, thē′tĭ-) *adj.* **1.** In prosody, beginning with, constituting, or relating to the thesis. **2.** Presented dogmatically; arbitrarily prescribed. [Gk. *thetikos,* fit for placing < *thetos,* placed < *tithenai,* to place.] **—thet′i·cal·ly** *adv.*

The·tis (thē′tĭs) *n. Gk. Myth.* One of the Nereids, the wife of Peleus and mother of Achilles. [Gk.]

the·ur·gy (thē′ûr-jē) *n., pl.* **-gies. 1.** Divine or supernatural intervention in the affairs of man. **2.** The performance of miracles with supernatural assistance. **3.** Magic performed supposedly with aid of beneficent spirits, as practiced by Neo-Platonists. [LLat. *theurgia* < Gk. *theourgia,* sorcery : *theos,* god + *-ergos,* working.] **—the·ur′gic** (thē-ûr′jĭk), **the·ur′gi·cal** *adj.* **—the·ur′gi·cal·ly** *adv.* **—the′ur·gist** *n.*

thew (thyo͞o) *n.* **1.** A well-developed sinew or muscle. **2. thews.** Muscular power or strength. [ME, good quality < OE *ðēaw,* a characteristic.] **—thew′y** *adj.*

they (*th*ā) *pron.* **1.** Those ones: *We had a dog and cat, but they fought all the time.* **2.** People in general: *They said it couldn't be done. He's as tough as they come.* **3.** *Informal.* He or she: *Every person has rights under the law, but they don't always know them.* —See Usage notes at **be, everyone,** and **I.** [ME < ON *ðeir,* masc. pl. demonstrative and personal pronoun.]

they'd (*th*ād). **1.** They had. **2.** They would.

they'll (*th*āl). They will.

they're (*th*âr). They are.

they've (*th*āv). They have.

thi- *pref.* Variant of **thio-.**

thi·a·ben·da·zole (thī′ə-bĕn′də-zōl′) *n.* A white compound, $C_{10}H_7N_3S$, used medically as an antifungal agent and as a drug to control parasitic roundworms. [THIA(ZOLE) + BENZ(O)- + (IMI)D(E) + AZOLE.]

thi·a·mine (thī′ə-mĭn, -mēn′) also **thi·a·min** (-mĭn) *n.* A B-complex vitamin, $C_{12}H_{17}ClN_4OS$, produced synthetically and occurring naturally in the bran coat of grains, in yeast, and in meat, that is necessary for carbohydrate metabolism, maintenance of normal neural activity, and the prevention of beriberi. [Alteration of *thiamin* : THI(O)- + (VIT)AMIN.]

thi·a·zine (thī′ə-zēn′) *n.* Any of a class of organic chemical compounds containing a ring composed of one sulfur atom, one nitrogen atom, and four carbon atoms.

thi·a·zole (thī′ə-zōl′) *n.* **1.** A colorless or pale-yellow liquid, C_3H_3NS, containing a five-member ring composed of a nitrogen atom, a sulfur atom, and three carbon atoms, used in making dyes and fungicides. **2.** Any of various thiazole derivatives.

thick (thĭk) *adj.* **-er, -est. 1. a.** Relatively great in depth or in extent from one surface to the opposite: *a thick board.* **b.** Measuring in this dimension: *two inches thick.* **2.** Heavy in build or stature; thickset: *a thick neck.* **3.** Having component parts in a close, compact arrangement; dense: *a thick forest.* **4.** Having a heavy or viscous consistency: *thick tomato sauce.* **5.** Marked by the lack of fresh air; sultry. **6.** Having a great number of; abounding: *a room thick with flies.* **7.** Impenetrable by the eyes: *a thick fog.* **8.** Not easy to hear or understand; indistinctly articulated: *the thick speech of a drunkard.* **9.** Pronounced; heavy: *a thick brogue.* **10.** *Informal.* Lacking mental agility; stupid. **11.** *Informal.* Very friendly; intimate: *thick friends.* **12.** *Informal.* Going beyond what is tolerable; excessive. *—adv.* So as to be thick; thickly: *Slice it thick.* *—n.* **1.** The thickest part of something. **2.** The most active or intense part: *in the thick of the fighting.* **—*idiom.* through thick and thin.** Through both good and bad times. [ME *thicke* < OE *ðicce.*] **—thick′ly** *adv.*

thick·en (thĭk′ən) *v.* **-ened, -en·ing, -ens.** *—tr.* **1.** To make thick or thicker. **2.** To make more intense, intricate, or complex. *—intr.* To become thickened. **—thick′en·er** *n.*

thick·en·ing (thĭk′ə-nĭng) *n.* **1.** The act or process of making or becoming thick. **2.** Material used to thicken liquid: *stir in a thickening of flour and water.* **3.** A thickened part.

thick·et (thĭk′ĭt) *n.* **1.** A dense growth of shrubs or underbrush; copse. **2.** Something suggestive of a thicket in impenetrability or thickness: *"the thicket of unreality which stands between us and the facts of life"* (Daniel J. Boorstin). [ME **thikket* < OE *ðiccet* < *ðicce,* thick.]

thick·head (thĭk′hĕd′) *n.* A stupid person; blockhead. **—thick′head′ed** *adj.*

thick·ness (thĭk′nĭs) *n.* **1.** The quality or condition of being thick. **2.** The dimension between two of an object's surfaces, usually the dimension of smallest measure. **3.** A layer, sheet, stratum, or ply: *a single thickness.*

thick·set (thĭk′sĕt′) *adj.* **1.** Having a solid, stocky body; stout. **2.** Positioned or placed closely together.

thick-skinned (thĭk′skĭnd′) *adj.* **1.** Having a thick skin. **2.** Not easily offended; insensitive.

thick-wit·ted (thĭk′wĭt′ĭd) *adj.* Stupid; dull.

thief (thēf) *n., pl.* **thieves** (thēvz). A person who steals. [ME *theef* < OE *ðēof.*]

thieve (thēv) *v.* **thieved, thiev·ing, thieves.** *—tr.* To take by theft; steal. *—intr.* To commit theft. [< THIEF.]

thiev·er·y (thē′və-rē) *n., pl.* **-ies.** The act or practice of thieving.

thieves (thēvz) *n.* Plural of **thief.**

thiev·ish (thē′vĭsh) *adj.* **1.** Given to thieving or stealing. **2.** Of, similar to, or characteristic of a thief; furtive.

thigh (thī) *n.* **1. a.** The portion of the human leg between the hip and the knee. **b.** A homologous structure in animals. **2.** The femur of an insect's leg. [ME < OE *ðēoh.*]

thigh·bone (thī′bōn′) *n.* The femur (sense 1.a.).

thig·mo·tax·is (thĭg′mə-tăk′sĭs) *n.* Movement of an organism in response to a direct tactile stimulus. [Gk. *thigma,* touch (< *thinganein,* to touch) + -TAXIS.] **—thig′mo·tac′tic** (-tăk′tĭk) *adj.* **—thig′mo·tac′ti·cal·ly** *adv.*

thig·mot·ro·pism (thĭg-mŏt′rə-pĭz′əm) *n.* The response or motion of an organism to direct contact with a surface or object. [Gk. *thigma,* touch (< *thinganein,* to touch) + -TROPISM.]

thill (thĭl) *n.* Either of the two long shafts between which an animal is fastened when pulling a wagon. [ME *thille.*]

thim·ble (thĭm′bəl) *n.* **1.** A small metal, ceramic, or plastic cup worn to protect the finger that pushes the needle in

thimble

sewing. **2.** Any of various tubular sockets or sleeves in machinery. **3.** *Naut.* **a.** A metal ring fitted in an eye of a sail to prevent chafing. **b.** A metal ring around which a rope splice is passed. [ME *thymbyl,* leather sheath for fingers < OE *ðymel* < *ðūma,* thumb.]

thim·ble·ber·ry (thĭm′bəl-bĕr′ē) *n., pl.* **-ries.** Any of several raspberries or related plants having thimble-shaped fruit, esp. *Rubus parviflora,* of western and central North America.

thim·ble·ful (thĭm′bəl-fo͝ol′) *n.* A very small quantity.

thim·ble·rig (thĭm′bəl-rĭg′) *n.* **1.** A gambling game, usually a swindle, in which the operator shuffles three inverted shells or thimbles, under one of which he or she has placed a marker, and spectators bet on the location of the marker. **2.** A person who operates a thimblerig. *—tr.v.* **-rigged, -rig·ging, -rigs.** To swindle with or as if with a thimblerig. **—thim′ble·rig′ger** *n.*

thim·ble·weed (thĭm′bəl-wēd′) *n.* **1.** Any of several North American plants of the genus *Anemone,* having cylindrical, thimblelike fruiting heads. **2.** Any of several coneflowers.

thi·mer·o·sal (thī-mĕr′ə-săl′) *n.* A crystalline powder, $C_9H_9HgNaO_2S$, used as an antiseptic for surface tissues. [THI(O)- + MER(CURY) + SAL(ICYLATE).]

thin (thĭn) *adj.* **thin·ner, thin·nest. 1. a.** Having a relatively small distance between opposite sides or surfaces. **b.** Not great in diameter or cross section; fine: *thin wire.* **2.** Lean or slender of figure. **3. a.** Not dense or concentrated; sparse. **b.** More rarefied than normal: *thin air.* **4. a.** Flowing with relative ease; not viscous: *a thin oil.* **b.** Watery: *thin soup.* **5.** Sparsely supplied or provided; scanty: *a thin menu.* **6.** Lacking force or substance; flimsy: *a thin attempt.* **7.** Lacking resonance or fullness; tinny: *the piano had a thin sound.* **8.** Lacking radiance or intensity: *thin light.* **9.** Not having enough photographic density or contrast to make satisfactory prints. *—adv.* So as to be thin. *—tr. & intr.v.* **thinned, thin·ning, thins.** To make or become thin or thinner. [ME *thinn* < OE *ðynne.*] **—thin′ly** *adv.* **—thin′ness** *n.*

thine (*th*īn) *pron. Archaic.* **1.** Belonging to thee. Used predicatively. **2.** The one or ones that belong to thee. Used substantively. **3.** Used instead of *thy* before an initial vowel or *h: thine enemy.* [ME *thin* < OE *ðīn.*]

thing (thĭng) *n.* **1.** An entity, idea, or quality perceived, known, or thought to have a separate existence. **2.** The real or concrete substance of an entity as distinguished from its appearances or from the name, word, or symbol denoting it. **3.** An entity existing in space or time. **4.** An inanimate object as distinguished from a living being. **5. a.** A creature: *the poor little thing.* **b.** An individual: *There wasn't a thing in sight.* **6. a.** That which can be possessed or owned, as distinguished from a person. **b. things.** Possessions; belongings: *packed her things and left.* **7. things.** The equipment needed for an activity or a special purpose: *Where are my fishing things?* **8.** An object or entity that cannot or need not be named specifically: *What's this thing for?* **9. a.** An act, deed, or work: *promised to do great things for the poor.* **b.** The result of work or activity: *is always building things.* **10.** A thought, notion, or utterance: *What a rotten thing to say!* **11.** A piece of information: *wouldn't tell me a thing about the project.* **12.** A means to an end: *just the thing to increase sales.* **13.** A matter of concern: *many things on my mind.* **14.** A turn of events; circumstance: *The accident was a terrible thing.* **15. a. things.** The general state of affairs; conditions: *Things are getting pretty bad.* **b.** A particular state of affairs; situation: *Let's deal with this thing promptly.* **16.** A persistent illogical feeling; obsession: *has a thing about guns.* **17. thing.** The latest fashion; rage: *Jeans are the thing now.* **18.** *Slang.* An activity uniquely suitable and satisfying to one: *Let him do his own thing.* **19. a.** A specified item; detail: *checks every little thing.* **b.** Matter or objects of a specified kind: *told her not to eat so many sweet things.* **—idioms. first thing.** Right away; before anything else. **see (or hear) things.** To have hallucinations. **sure thing.** *Informal.* **1.** A certainty: *His election is a sure thing.* **2.** Of course; certainly: *Sure thing, I'll be there!* [ME < OE *ðing.*]

thing·a·ma·bob (thĭng′ə-mə-bŏb′) *n. Informal.* A thingamajig. [< THING.]

thing·a·ma·jig also **thing·um·a·jig** (thĭng′ə-mə-jĭg′) *n. Informal.* Something difficult to classify or whose name has been forgotten or is not known. [< THING.]

T-hinge (tē′hĭnj′) *n.* A hinge, the two parts of which shape the letter T.

thing-in-itself (thĭng′ĭn-ĭt-sĕlf′) *n., pl.* **things-in-them·selves** (thĭngz′ĭn-*th*ĕm-sĕlvz′). An ultimate metaphysical reality conceived by Kant as beyond the perception of human senses and thought; noumenon. [Transl. of G. *Ding an sich.*]

think (thĭngk) *v.* **thought** (thôt), **think·ing, thinks.** *—tr.* **1.** To have or formulate in the mind. **2. a.** To reason about or reflect on; ponder: *Think how complex language is. Think the matter through.* **b.** To decide by thinking: *thinking what to do.* **3.** To judge or regard; look upon: *I think it only fair.* **4.** To believe; suppose: *always thought he was right.* **5.** To expect; hope: *thought he'd arrive early but couldn't.* **6.** To remember; call to mind: *I can't think what his name was.* **7.** To visualize; imagine: *didn't think so many people would come.* **8.** To devise or evolve; invent: *thought up a plan to get rich quick.* **9.** To bring into a given condition by mental preoccupation: *She thought herself into a terror of going.* **10.** To concentrate one's thoughts on: *does nothing but think profits.* *—intr.* **1.** To exercise the power of reason. **2.** To weigh or consider the idea: *They are thinking of moving.* **3.** To recall a thought or image to mind: *thought of his childhood when he saw the movie.* **4.** To believe; suppose: *thinks of herself as a wit.* **5.** To have care or consideration: *think first of the ones you love.* **6.** To dispose the mind in a given way: *Think rich.* **—idioms. think better of.** To decide against after reconsidering. **think much of.** To consider satisfactory; approve: *didn't think much of her new outfit.* **think nothing of.** To regard as routine or usual. **think twice.** To weigh something carefully. [ME *thenken* < OE *ðencan.*]

think·a·ble (thĭng′kə-bəl) *adj.* Capable of being or fit to be considered; conceivable. **—think′a·bly** *adv.*

think·er (thĭng′kər) *n.* **1.** A person who devotes his time to thought or meditation. **2.** A person who thinks or reasons in a given way: *a careful thinker.*

think·ing (thĭng′kĭng) *n.* **1.** Thought. **2.** A way of reasoning; judgment: *not to my thinking a good idea.* *—adj.* Characterized by thoughtfulness; rational: *Man is a thinking animal.*

thinking cap *n.* A state in which one thinks, esp. carefully: *put on one's thinking cap.*

think piece *n.* A newspaper article consisting of news analysis, background material, and personal opinions.

think tank *n.* A group or institution organized for intensive research and problem-solving, esp. in the area of technology or political strategy.

thin·ner (thĭn′ər) *n.* A liquid, as turpentine, mixed with paint to reduce viscosity for ease in application.

thin-skinned (thĭn′skĭnd′) *adj.* **1.** Having a thin rind or skin. **2.** Oversensitive, esp. to reproach or insult.

thio– or **thi–** *pref.* Containing sulfur: *thiourea.* [Gk. *theio-* < *theion,* sulfur.]

thi·o·car·ba·mide (thī′ō-kär′bə-mīd′) *n.* Thiourea.

thi·o·cy·a·nate (thī′ō-sī′ə-nāt′) *n.* A salt or ester of thiocyanic acid.

thi·o·cy·an·ic acid (thī′ō-sī-ăn′ĭk) *n.* An unstable colorless liquid, HSCN, used in the form of esters as an insecticide.

Thi·o·kol (thī′ə-kôl′, -kōl′). A trademark for any of various polysulfide polymers in the form of liquids, water dispersions, and rubbers used in seals and sealants.

thi·ol (thī′ôl′, -ōl′) *n.* Mercaptan.

thion– *pref.* Sulfur: *thionic.* [< Gk. *theion,* sulfur.]

thi·on·ic (thī-ŏn′ĭk) *adj.* Of, pertaining to, containing, or derived from sulfur.

thi·o·nyl (thī′ə-nĭl′) *n.* Sulfinyl.

thi·o·pen·tal sodium (thī-ō-pĕn′tăl′, -tôl′). *n.* A yellowish-white hygroscopic powder, $C_{11}H_{17}N_2O_2SNa$, injected intravenously as a general anesthetic. [THIO- + PENT(OBARBIT)AL.]

thi·o·phene (thī′ə-fēn′) *n.* A colorless liquid, C_4H_4S, used as a solvent. [THIO- + PH(ENO)- + -ENE.]

thi·o·sul·fate (thī′ō-sŭl′fāt′) *n.* A salt of thiosulfuric acid.

thi·o·sul·fu·ric acid (thī′ō-sŭl-fyo͝or′ĭk) *n.* An acid, $H_2S_2O_3$, formed by the replacement of an oxygen atom by a sulfur atom in sulfuric acid, known only in solution or by its salts and esters.

thi·o·ur·a·cil (thī′ō-yo͝or′ə-sĭl′) *n.* A white crystalline compound, $C_4H_4N_2OS$, used medically to depress the synthesis of thyroxin. [THIO- + UR(O)- + AC(ETIC) + E. *-il,* a substance related to another substance.]

thi·o·u·re·a (thī′ō-yo͞o-rē′ə) *n.* A white, lustrous crystalline compound, $(NH_2)_2CS$, used in photography, photocopying paper, and various organic syntheses.

third (thûrd) *n.* **1.** The ordinal number that matches the number three in a series. **2.** One of three equal parts. **3.** One-sixtieth of a second, as a measure of time or of the arc of an angle. **4.** *Mus.* **a.** An interval of three degrees in a diatonic scale. **b.** A tone separated by three degrees from a given tone, esp. the third tone of a scale. **5.** The third forward gear in an automobile transmission. **6.** *Baseball.* Third base. **7. thirds.** Merchandise whose quality is below the standard set for seconds. [ME *thridd* (adj.) < OE *ðirdda.*] **—third** *adj. & adv.*

third base *n. Baseball.* **1.** The third base to be reached by a runner. **2.** The position played by the third baseman.

third baseman *n. Baseball.* The infielder stationed near third base.

third class *n.* **1.** A class of mail in the U.S. postal system including all printed matter, except newspapers and magazines, that weighs less than 16 ounces and is unsealed. **2.** Accommodations, as on a ship or train, of the third and usually lowest order of luxury and price. **—third′-class′** *adj. & adv.*

third degree *n.* Mental or physical torture to obtain information or a confession from a prisoner.

third-degree burn (thûrd′dĭ-grē′) *n.* A severe burn in which the epidermis is destroyed and sensitive nerve endings are exposed.

third dimension *n.* **1.** The quality of depth or thickness. **2.** The quality of seeming real or lifelike. **—third′di·men′sion·al** (thûrd′dĭ-mĕn′shə-nəl) *adj.*

third·hand (thûrd′hănd′) *adj.* **1.** Acquired from or through two intermediate sources: *a thirdhand report.* **2. a.** Previ-

ously used by two other owners. **b.** Dealing in thirdhand merchandise.
third house *n.* A legislative lobby. [From its role with respect to the two houses of which many legislatures consist.]
third·ly (thûrd′lē) *adv.* In the third place, rank, or order.
Third Order *n.* A confraternity of laymen associated with a religious order of the Roman Catholic Church.
third party *n.* A political party organized as opposition to the existing parties in a two-party system.
third person *n.* **1. a.** A set of grammatical forms used in referring to a person or thing other than the speaker or the one spoken to. **b.** A grammatical form belonging to such a set. **2.** Reference of a grammatical form to a person or thing other than the speaker or the one spoken to.
third rail *n.* The rail through which the current runs to power the train on an electric railway.
third-rate (thûrd′rāt′) *adj.* Of third quality or value, esp. of less value than second-rate.
third-stream (thûrd′strēm′) *adj.* Of, relating to, or being music that blends classical music with jazz improvisation.
Third World also **third world** *n.* **1.** Underdeveloped or developing countries, esp. those not allied with the Communist or non-Communist blocs. **2.** Minority groups as a whole within a larger prevailing culture. **—Third Worlder** *n.*
thirst (thûrst) *n.* **1. a.** A sensation of dryness in the mouth related to a need or desire to drink. **b.** The desire to drink. **2.** An insistent desire; craving. *—intr.v.* **thirst·ed, thirst·ing, thirsts. 1.** To feel a need to drink. **2.** To have a strong craving; yearn. [ME < OE *ðurst.*] **—thirst′er** *n.*
thirst·y (thûr′stē) *adj.* **-i·er, -i·est. 1.** Desiring to drink. **2.** Arid; parched. **3.** Craving something. **—thirst′i·ly** *adv.* **—thirst′i·ness** *n.*
thir·teen (thûr-tēn′) *n.* **1.** The cardinal number that is next after the number 12 and equal to the sum of 12 + 1. **2.** The 13th in a set or sequence. **3.** Something having 13 parts, units, or members. [ME *thrittene* < OE *ðrēotīne.*] **—thir·teen′** *adj. & pron.*
thir·teenth (thûr-tēnth′) *n.* **1.** The ordinal number that matches the number 13 in a series. **2.** One of 13 equal parts. **—thir·teenth′** *adj. & adv.*
thir·ti·eth (thûr′tē-ĭth) *n.* **1.** The ordinal number that matches the number 30 in a series. **2.** One of 30 equal parts. **—thir′ti·eth** *adj. & adv.*
thir·ty (thûr′tē) *n., pl.* **-ties. 1.** The cardinal number equal to 3 × 10. **2.** An indication of the end of a news story, usually written 30. **3.** *Sports.* The second point that is scored by one side in tennis. [ME *thritty* < OE *ðrītig.*] **—thir′ty** *adj. & pron.*
thir·ty-sec·ond note (thûr′tē-sĕk′ənd) *n.* A musical note with a time value equivalent to 1/32 of a whole note.
thir·ty-two·mo (thûr′tē-tōō′mō) *n., pl.* **-mos. 1.** The page size (3½ by 5½ inches) that results when a printers' sheet is folded into 32 equal sections. **2.** A book composed of pages of thirty-twomos.
this (thĭs) *pron., pl.* **these** (thēz). **1. a.** The person or thing present, nearby, or just mentioned: *This is my cat. These are my tools.* **b.** What is about to be said: *Now don't laugh when you hear this.* **c.** The present occasion or time: *said he'd be back before this.* **2.** The one that is nearer than another or the one compared with the other: *This is mine and that's yours.* *—adj., pl.* **these. 1.** Being just mentioned or present in space, time, or thought: *She left early this morning.* **2.** Being nearer than another or compared with another: *this side and that side.* **3.** Being about to be stated or described: *Just wait till you hear this story.* *—adv.* To this extent; so: *never stayed out this late.* [ME < OE *ðis* (nominative and accusative neuter sing.).]
Usage: *This* and *that* are both used as demonstrative pronouns to refer to a thought expressed earlier: *The letter was unopened; that* (or *this*) *in itself casts doubt on the inspector's theory. That* is sometimes prescribed as the better choice in referring to what has gone before (as in the preceding example). When the referent is yet to be mentioned, only *this* is used: *This* (not *that*) *is what bothers me. We have no time to consider late applications.* • *This* is often used in speech as an emphatic variant of the indefinite article *a: This friend of mine came to visit me last night. I have this terrible headache.* This usage should be avoided in writing.

thistle

thorn
Runic letter

this·tle (thĭs′əl) *n.* **1.** Any of numerous weedy plants, chiefly of the genera *Cirsium, Carduus,* or *Onopordum,* having prickly leaves and usually purplish flowers surrounded by prickly bracts. **2.** Any of various plants similar or related to the thistle. [ME *thistel* < OE *ðistel.*]
thistle butterfly *n.* The painted lady.
this·tle·down (thĭs′əl-doun′) *n.* The silky down attached to the seeds of a thistle.
thith·er (thĭ*th*′ər, thĭth′-) *adv.* **1.** To or toward that place; in that direction; there: *running hither and thither.* **2.** *Archaic.* To or toward that end or result. *—adj.* Located or being on the more distant side; farther: *the thither side of the pond.* [ME <OE *ðider.*]
thith·er·to (thĭ*th*′ər-tōō′, thĭth′-) *adv.* Up to that time; until then.
thith·er·ward (thĭ*th*′ər-wərd, thĭth′-) *adv.* In that direction; thither.
thix·ot·ro·py (thĭk-sŏt′rə-pē) *n.* The property exhibited by certain gels of liquefying when stirred or shaken and returning to the hardened state upon standing. [Gk. *thixis,* touch (< *thinganien,* to touch) + -TROPY.] **—thix′o·trop′ic** (thĭk′sə-trŏp′ĭk) *adj.*
tho (thō) *conj. & adv. Informal.* Though.
thole (thōl) *tr.v.* **tholed, thol·ing, tholes.** *Regional.* To endure; to bear. [ME *tholen* < OE *ðolian.*]
thole pin (thōl) *n. Naut.* A wooden peg set in pairs in the gunwale of a boat to serve as an oarlock. [ME *tholle* < OE *ðol.*]
Tho·mism (tō′mĭz′əm) *n.* The theological and philosophical system of Saint Thomas Aquinas, which later became the basis of scholasticism. **—Tho′mist** (tō′mĭst) *n.* **—Tho·mis′tic** (tō-mĭs′tĭk) *adj.*
Thomp·son submachine gun (tŏmp′sən) *n.* A .45-caliber submachine gun. [After John *Thompson* (d. 1940), its co-inventor.]
thong (thông, thŏng) *n.* **1.** A narrow strip of leather or other material used for binding or lashing. **2.** A whiplash of plaited leather or cord. **3.** A sandal held on the foot by a thong that fits between the toes and is connected to a strap usually passing over the top or around the sides of the foot. [ME < OE *ðwong.*]
Thor (thôr) *n. Myth.* The Norse god of thunder. [ON *Þōrr.*]
tho·ra·ces (thôr′ə-sēz′, thōr′-) *n.* A plural of **thorax.**
tho·rac·ic (thə-răs′ĭk) *adj.* Of, relating to, or situated in or near the thorax. **—tho·rac′i·cal·ly** *adv.*
thoracic duct *n.* The main duct of the lymphatic system, ascending along the spinal cord and discharging into the venous system.
tho·ra·cot·o·my (thôr′ə-kŏt′ə-mē, thōr′-) *n., pl.* **-mies.** Surgical incision of the chest wall. [Lat. *thorax, thorac-,* thorax + -TOMY.]
tho·rax (thôr′ăks′, thōr′-) *n., pl.* **tho·rax·es** or **tho·ra·ces** (thôr′ə-sēz′, thōr′-). **1.** *Anat.* The part of the human body between the neck and the diaphragm, partially encased by the ribs; the chest. **2.** A part in animals that corresponds to the thorax. **3.** The second or middle region of the body of an arthropod, in insects bearing the true legs and wings. [ME < Lat. < Gk. *thōrax.*]
tho·ri·a (thôr′ē-ə, thōr′-) *n.* Thorium dioxide. [< THORIUM.]
tho·ric (thôr′ĭk, thŏr′-, thōr′-) *adj.* Of, pertaining to, or containing thorium. [THOR(IUM) + -IC.]
tho·rite (thôr′īt′, thōr′-) *n.* A vitreous brownish-yellow to black thorium ore, essentially $ThSiO_4$. [THOR(IUM) + -ITE[1].]
tho·ri·um (thôr′ē-əm, thōr′-) *n. Symbol* **Th** A silvery-white metallic element with 13 radioactive isotopes only one of which, thorium 232, occurs naturally. It is used in magnesium alloys and isotope 232 is a source of nuclear energy. Atomic number 90; atomic weight 232.038; approximate melting point 1,700°C; approximate boiling point 4,000°C; approximate specific gravity 11.66; valence 4. [After *Thor.*]
thorium dioxide *n.* A heavy white powder, ThO_2, used mainly in ceramics, gas mantles, and nuclear fuels.
thorn (thôrn) *n.* **1.** *Bot.* A modified branch in the form of a sharp, woody spine. **2.** Any of various shrubs, trees, or woody plants bearing thorns. **3.** Any of various sharp, spiny protuberances; prickle. **4.** One that causes sharp pain, irritation, or discomfort: *He is a thorn in my side.* **5.** The runic letter *þ* originally representing either sound of the Modern English *th,* as in *the* and *thin,* used in Old English and Middle English manuscripts. [ME < OE *ðorn.*]
thorn apple *n.* Any of various plants of the genus *Datura,* esp. the jimsonweed.
thorn·back (thôrn′băk′) *n.* Either of two rays, *Raja clavata,* of European waters, or *Platyrhinoidis triseriata,* of Pacific waters, having spines along the back.
thorn·y (thôr′nē) *adj.* **-i·er, -i·est. 1.** Full of or covered with thorns. **2.** Thornlike; spiny. **3.** Painfully controversial; vexatious: *a thorny situation.* **—thorn′i·ness** *n.*
tho·ron (thôr′ŏn′, thōr′-) *n.* A radioactive isotope of radon having a half-life of 54.5 seconds and produced by the disintegration of thorium.
thor·ough (thûr′ō) *adj.* **1.** Exhaustively complete: *a thorough search.* **2.** Painstakingly accurate or careful: *thorough research.* **3.** Completely satisfactory in all respects: *a thorough pleasure.* [ME *thorow,* thorough, through < OE *ðuruh,* through.] **—thor′ough·ly** *adv.* **—thor′ough·ness** *n.*
thor·ough·bass (thûr′ō-bās′, thûr′ə-) *n.* A continuo.
thorough brace *n.* One of several leather bands passed from front to back of a carriage, supporting it and serving as a spring. **—thor′ough-braced′** *adj.*
thor·ough·bred (thûr′ō-brĕd′, thûr′ə-) *n.* **1.** A purebred or pedigreed animal. **2. Thoroughbred.** Any of a breed of horse originating from a cross of Arabian stallions with English mares. **3.** A well-bred person. *—adj.* **1.** Bred of pure stock; purebred. **2. Thoroughbred.** Pertaining or belonging to the Thoroughbred breed of horses. **3.** Thoroughly trained or educated; well-bred.
thor·ough·fare (thûr′ō-fâr′, thûr′ə-) *n.* **1.** A main road or public highway. **2. a.** A place of passage from one location to another. **b.** Right to such passage: *no thoroughfare.* **3.** A heavily traveled passage, as a waterway, strait, or channel. [ME *thurghfare* : *thurgh,* through + *fare,* road.]
thor·ough·go·ing (thûr′ō-gō′ĭng, thûr′ə-) *adj.* **1.** Very thorough; complete. **2.** Unmitigated; unqualified.

thor·ough·paced (thûr′ō-pāst′, thûr′ə-) *adj.* **1.** Trained in all paces or gaits, as a horse. **2.** Thoroughgoing; complete.

thor·ough·pin (thûr′ō-pĭn′, thûr′ə-) *n.* An abnormal swelling on either side of the hock joint of horses and related animals. [THOROUGH, through (obs.) + PIN.]

thor·ough·wort (thûr′ō-wûrt′, -wôrt′, thûr′ə-) *n.* The boneset.

thorp (thôrp) *n. Obs.* A hamlet. [ME < OE *ðorp.*]

those (*th*ōz) *adj. & pron.* Plural of **that.**

thou[1] (*th*ou) *pron.* Used to indicate the one that is spoken to esp. in a literary or ecclesiastical context. [ME < OE *ðū.*]

Usage: Beginning in Middle English, *you,* originally a plural form, came to be used as a mark of polite address to a single person. More and more, the use of *thou* was limited to addressing a person with whom the speaker was familiar or intimate: children, social inferiors, God. This distinction persisted into the 16th century and was used in early Modern English translations of the Bible. Eventually, *you* became the normal singular form, and *thou* was retained only in a few dialects, in some literary styles, and in the religious use.

thou[2] (thou) *n. Slang.* A thousand.

though (*th*ō) *conj.* **1.** Despite the fact that; although: *He still argues, though he knows he's wrong.* **2.** Conceding or supposing that; even if: *Though they may not succeed, they will still try.* —*adv.* However; nevertheless: *We can expect some rain, though not soon.* —See Usage note at **although.** [ME, of Scand. orig.]

thought (thôt) *v.* Past tense and past participle of **think.** —*n.* **1.** The act or process of thinking; cogitation. **2.** A product of thinking; notion. **3.** The intellectual activity or production of a particular time or social class: *ancient Greek thought.* **4.** Consideration; attention: *didn't give much thought to what she said.* **5.** Intention; purpose: *had no thought of committing the crime.* **6.** A trifle; bit: *a thought more considerate.* [ME < OE *geðōht.*]

thought·ful (thôt′fəl) *adj.* **1.** Occupied with thought; contemplative. **2.** Well thought-out; well considered: *a thoughtful essay.* **3.** Showing regard for others; considerate. —**thought′ful·ly** *adv.* —**thought′ful·ness** *n.*

Synonyms: *thoughtful, considerate, indulgent, solicitous.* These adjectives mean showing concern for the well-being of others. *Thoughtful* and *considerate* can often be used interchangeably. *Thoughtful* sometimes implies a tendency to anticipate needs and act accordingly, whereas *considerate* is especially appropriate to situations that stress sensitivity to another's feelings. *Indulgent* suggests willingness to gratify wishes that may be unreasonable and thus to pamper or humor another. *Solicitous,* the strongest of these terms, implies concern for another's welfare that verges on anxiety or expresses itself in extremely close attention to his wishes.

thought·less (thôt′lĭs) *adj.* **1.** Careless; unthinking. **2.** Reckless; rash. **3.** Inconsiderate; inattentive. —**thought′less·ly** *adv.* —**thought′less·ness** *n.*

thought reading *n.* Mind reading (sense 1).

thou·sand (thou′zənd) *n.* The cardinal number equal to 10×100 or 10^3. [ME < OE *ðūsend.*] —**thou′sand** *adj. & pron.*

Thousand Island dressing *n.* A salad dressing made with mayonnaise, chili sauce, and seasonings. [Perh. after the *Thousand Islands,* islands in the St. Lawrence River.]

thou·sandth (thou′zəndth, -zənth) *n.* **1.** The ordinal number that matches the number 1,000 in a series. **2.** One of 1,000 equal parts. —**thou′sandth** *adj. & adv.*

Thra·cian (thrā′shən) *adj.* Of or pertaining to Thrace or its people. —*n.* **1.** A native or inhabitant of Thrace. **2.** The Indo-European language of the ancient Thracians.

thrall (thrôl) *n.* **1. a.** A person, such as a slave or serf, who is held in bondage. **b.** A person who is intellectually or morally enslaved. **2.** Servitude; bondage. —*tr.v.* **thralled, thrall·ing, thralls.** *Archaic.* To make a thrall of; enslave. [ME < OE *ðrǣl* < ON *ðræll.*] —**thrall′dom, thral′dom** (-dəm) *n.*

thrash (thrăsh) *v.* **thrashed, thrash·ing, thrash·es.** —*tr.* **1.** To beat with or as if with a whip or stick; flog. **2.** To swing or strike in a manner suggestive of the action of a flail: *The alligator thrashed its tail.* **3.** To defeat utterly; vanquish. **4.** To thresh. **5.** To sail (a boat) against opposing winds or tides. —*intr.* **1.** To move wildly or violently. **2.** To strike or flail. **3.** To thresh. **4.** To sail against opposing tides or winds. —***phrasal verb.*** **thrash out.** To discuss fully. —*n.* **1.** The act of thrashing. **2.** A swimming kick in the backstroke and crawl. [Alteration of THRESH.] —**thrash′er** *n.*

thrash·er (thrăsh′ər) *n.* Any of various New World songbirds of the genus *Toxostoma,* having a long tail, a long, curved beak, and, in several species, a spotted breast. [Perh. alteration of THRUSH.]

thrash·ing (thrăsh′ĭng) *n.* A severe beating.

thra·son·i·cal (thrā-sŏn′ĭ-kəl, thrə-) *adj.* Boastful. [After *Thraso,* a character in the play *Eunuchus,* by Terence (185–159 B.C.).] —**thra·son′i·cal·ly** *adv.*

thread (thrĕd) *n.* **1. a.** A fine cord of a fibrous material, such as cotton or flax, made of two or more filaments twisted together and used in needlework and the weaving of cloth. **b.** A piece of thread. **2.** A strand, fiber, or filament of natural or manufactured material. **3.** Something suggestive of the fineness or thinness of thread: *a thread of smoke.* **4.** Something suggestive of the continuousness of thread: *lost the thread of his argument.* **5.** A helical or spiral ridge on a screw, nut, or bolt. **6. threads.** *Slang.* Clothes. —*v.* **thread·ed, thread·ing, threads.** —*tr.* **1. a.** To pass one end of a thread through the eye of (a needle or similar device). **b.** To pass (something) through in the manner of a thread: *thread the wire through the opening.* **c.** To pass a tape or film into or through a device: *thread the motion-picture projector.* **2.** To connect by running a thread through; string: *thread beads.* **3.** To make one's way cautiously through: *threading dark alleys.* **4.** To occur throughout; pervade. **5.** To machine a thread on (a screw, nut, or bolt). —*intr.* **1.** To make one's way cautiously. **2.** To proceed by a winding course. **3.** To form a thread when dropped from a spoon, as boiling sugar syrup. [ME < OE *ðrǣd.*] —**thread′er** *n.*

thread·bare (thrĕd′bâr′) *adj.* **1.** Having the nap worn down so that the filling or warp threads show through; frayed or shabby. **2.** Wearing old, shabby clothing. **3.** Hackneyed; trite.

thread·fin (thrĕd′fĭn′) *n.* Any of various chiefly tropical marine fishes of the family Polynemidae, having threadlike rays extending from the lower part of the pectoral fin.

thread mark *n.* A marking made in paper currency by a threading of colored silk fibers to make counterfeiting difficult.

thread·worm (thrĕd′wûrm′) *n.* Any of various threadlike nematode worms, esp. the pinworm.

thread·y (thrĕd′ē) *adj.* **-i·er, -i·est. 1.** Consisting of or resembling thread; filamentous. **2.** Capable of forming or tending to form threads, as a syrupy liquid; viscid. **3.** *Med.* Weak and shallow, as a pulse. **4.** Lacking fullness of tone; thin: *a thready voice.* —**thread′i·ness** *n.*

threat (thrĕt) *n.* **1.** An expression of an intention to inflict pain, injury, evil, or punishment. **2.** An indication of impending danger or harm. **3.** One that is regarded as a possible danger; menace. —*tr.v.* **threat·ed, threat·ing, threats.** *Archaic.* To threaten. [ME < OE *ðrēat.*]

threat·en (thrĕt′n) *v.* **-ened, -en·ing, -ens.** —*tr.* **1.** To express a threat against. **2.** To serve as a threat to; endanger. **3.** To give signs or warning of; portend. **4.** To announce as possible: *threatened to move out of town.* —*intr.* **1.** To express or use threats. **2.** To indicate danger or other harm. —**threat′en·er** *n.* —**threat′en·ing·ly** *adv.*

Synonyms: *threaten, menace, intimidate.* These verbs mean to foretell danger, promise evil or injury, or inspire fear. *Threaten,* the most widely applicable, can refer to verbal promise of harm; to forewarning, as *dark skies threaten rain;* to appearance or overt action calculated or serving to make a person fearful; or to having a character that puts someone or something in danger, as *inflation threatens purchasing power. Menace* is limited principally to the last two of the foregoing senses. *Intimidate* refers to inspiring fear in a person, and often to inhibiting speech or action, by a show or promise of force.

three (thrē) *n.* **1.** The cardinal number that is next after the number 2 and equal to the sum of $2 + 1$. **2.** The third in a set or sequence. **3.** Something having three parts, units, or members. [ME < OE *ðrī;* akin to G. *drei,* Lat. *tres,* Gk. *treis,* Skt. *tri.*] —**three** *adj & pron.*

three-bag·ger (thrē′băg′ər) *n. Baseball.* A three-base hit.

three-base hit (thrē′bās′) *n. Baseball.* A base hit that allows the batter to reach third base without being put out; triple.

three-card mon·te (thrē′kärd mŏn′tē) *n.* A gambling game in which each player is dealt and shown three cards, which are then placed face down on the table, the players betting they can identify a particular card.

three-col·or (thrē′kŭl′ər) *adj.* Designating a color printing or photographic process in which three primary colors are transferred by three different plates or filters to a surface, reproducing all the colors of the subject matter.

three-D or **3-D** (thrē′dē′) *adj.* Three-dimensional. —*n.* A three-dimensional medium, display, or performance, esp. a cinematic or graphic display in three dimensions.

three-decker
U.S.S. *Constitution*

three-deck·er (thrē′dĕk′ər) *n.* **1.** A ship having three decks, esp. one of a class of sail-powered warships with guns on three decks. **2.** Something with three layers, esp. a sandwich having three slices of bread.

three-di·men·sion·al (thrē′dĭ-mĕn′shə-nəl) *adj.* **1.** Of, pertaining to, having, or existing in three dimensions. **2.** Having or appearing to have extension in depth.

three·fold (thrē′fōld′) *adj.* **1.** Having or consisting of three parts. **2.** Three times as many or as much; treble. —**three′fold′** *adv.*

three-gait·ed (thrē′gā′tĭd) *adj.* Trained in the walk, trot, and canter. Used of a horse.

Three Graces *pl.n.* The Graces.

three-leg·ged race (thrē′lĕg′ĭd, -lĕgd′) *n.* A race in which contestants run in pairs with their near legs tied together.

three-mile limit (thrē′mīl′) *n. Law.* The outer limit of the area extending three miles out to sea from the coast of a land that constitutes that land's territorial waters.

three·pence (thrĕp′əns, thrĭp′-, thrŭp′-) *n., pl.* **-pence** or **-penc·es.** *Chiefly Brit.* **1.** A coin worth three pennies. **2.** The sum of three pennies.

three·pen·ny (thrĕp′ə-nē, thrĭp′-, thrŭp′-) *adj. Chiefly Brit.* **1.** Worth or priced at threepence. **2.** Very small; trifling.

three-piece (thrē′pēs′) *adj.* Made in or consisting of three parts or pieces: *a three-piece suit.*
three-ply (thrē′plī′) *adj.* Consisting of three layers or strands.
three-point landing (thrē′point′) *n.* An airplane landing in which the tailskid or tail wheel and the two forward wheels all touch the ground simultaneously.
three-quar·ter (thrē′kwôr′tər) *adj.* Pertaining to, consisting of, or extending to three-fourths of the usual full length of something.
three-quarter binding *n.* A type of bookbinding in which the leather or fabric covering the spine extends onto the covers for one third of their width.
three-ring circus (thrē′rĭng′) *n.* **1.** A circus having simultaneous performances in three separate rings. **2.** A situation characterized by confusing, engrossing, or amusing activity.
three R's *pl.n.* Reading, writing, and arithmetic, considered as the fundamentals of elementary education. [From the phrase *reading, 'riting,* and *'rithmetic,* alteration of *reading, writing,* and *arithmetic.*]
three·score (thrē′skôr′, -skōr′) *adj.* Three times twenty; sixty. **—three′score′** *n.*
three·some (thrē′səm) *adj.* Consisting of or performed by three. *—n.* **1.** A group of three persons. **2.** An activity involving three persons, esp. a golf match in which one player competes against two others who alternate their play.
three-square (thrē′skwâr′) *adj.* Having an equilateral triangular cross section: *a three-square file.*
three wood *n.* A wooden golf club with more loft than a brassie.
threm·ma·tol·o·gy (thrĕm′ə-tŏl′ə-jē) *n.* The scientific breeding of domestic plants and animals. [Gk. *thremma, thremmat-,* nursling + -LOGY.]
thren·o·dy (thrĕn′ə-dē) *n., pl.* **-dies.** A poem or song of lamentation. [Gk. *thrēnōidia* : *thrēnos,* lament + *ōidē,* song.] **—thre·no′di·al** (thrə-nō′dē-əl), **thre·nod′ic** (-nŏd′ĭk) *adj.* **—thren′o·dist** *n.*
thre·o·nine (thrē′ə-nēn′) *n.* A colorless crystalline amino acid, $C_4H_9NO_3$, that is derived from the hydrolysis of protein and is an essential component of human nutrition. [Orig. unknown.]
thresh (thrĕsh) *v.* **threshed, thresh·ing, thresh·es.** *—tr.* **1. a.** To beat the stems and husks of (grain or cereal plants) with a machine or flail to separate the grain or seeds from the straw. **b.** To separate (grain or seed) in this manner. **2.** To discuss or go over (an issue, for example) repeatedly. **3.** To beat severely; thrash. *—intr.* **1.** To thresh grain. **2.** To thrash about; toss. [ME *thresshen* < OE *ðrescan.*]

thresh
Early 19th-century woodcut

thresh·er (thrĕsh′ər) *n.* **1.** One that threshes. **2.** A threshing machine. **3.** Any of various sharks of the genus *Alopias,* having a tail with a long, whiplike upper lobe.
threshing machine *n.* A farm machine used in threshing grain or seed plants.
thresh·old (thrĕsh′ōld′, -hōld′) *n.* **1.** The piece of wood or stone placed beneath a door; doorsill. **2.** An entrance or doorway. **3.** The place or point of beginning; outset. **4.** The intensity below which a mental or physical stimulus cannot be perceived and can produce no response: *a low threshold of pain.* [ME *thresshold* < OE *ðerscold.*]
threw (thro͞o) *v.* Past tense of **throw.**
thrice (thrīs) *adv.* **1.** Three times. **2.** In a threefold quantity or degree. **3.** *Archaic.* Extremely; greatly. [ME *thries,* adv. genitive of *thrie* < OE *ðriga.*]
thrift (thrĭft) *n.* **1.** Wise economy in the management of money and other resources; frugality. **2.** Vigorous growth of living things such as plants. **3.** Any of several densely tufted, chiefly European plants of the genus *Armeria,* esp. *A. maritima,* having rounded clusters of pink flowers. [ME, prosperity < ON *ðrift* < *ðrīfask,* to thrive.]
thrift·less (thrĭft′lĭs) *adj.* **1.** Lacking usefulness or value. **2.** Careless in handling money; wasteful.
thrift shop *n.* A shop that sells used articles and esp. clothing, often to benefit a charitable organization.
thrift·y (thrĭf′tē) *adj.* **-i·er, -i·est.** **1.** Practicing thrift; economical and frugal. **2.** Industrious and thriving; prosperous. **3.** Growing vigorously; thriving, as a plant. **—thrift′i·ly** *adv.* **—thrift′i·ness** *n.*

throne
Of Isabella of Spain

thrill (thrĭl) *v.* **thrilled, thrill·ing, thrills.** *—tr.* **1.** To cause to feel a sudden intense sensation; excite greatly. **2.** To give great pleasure to; delight. **3.** To cause to quiver, tremble, or vibrate. *—intr.* **1.** To feel a sudden quiver of emotion. **2.** To quiver, tremble, or vibrate. *—n.* **1. a.** A quivering or trembling caused by sudden emotion. **b.** Something that produces such excitement. **2.** *Pathol.* A slight vibration that accompanies a cardiac or vascular murmur. [ME *thrillen,* var. of *thirlen,* to pierce < OE *ðyrlian* < *ðyrel,* hole < *ðurh,* through.] **—thrill′ing·ly** *adv.*
thrill·er (thrĭl′ər) *n.* **1.** One that thrills. **2.** *Informal.* A sensational or suspenseful book, story, or motion picture.
thrips (thrĭps) *n., pl.* **thrips.** Any of various small, often wingless insects of the order Thysanoptera, many of which are destructive to plants. [Lat., woodworm < Gk.]
thrive (thrīv) *intr.v.* **throve** (thrōv) or **thrived, thrived** or **thriv·en** (thrĭv′ən), **thriv·ing, thrives.** **1.** To make steady progress; prosper. **2.** To grow vigorously; flourish. [ME *thriven* < ON *ðrīfask,* reflexive of *ðrīfa,* to seize.] **—thriv′er** *n.*
throat (thrōt) *n.* **1.** *Anat.* **a.** The portion of the digestive tract that lies between the rear of the mouth and the esophagus and includes the fauces and the pharynx. **b.** The anterior portion of the neck. **2.** *Bot.* The outer, expanded part of a tubular corolla. **3.** A narrow passage or part suggestive of the human throat: *the throat of a horn.* *—tr.v.* **throat·ed, throat·ing, throats.** To pronounce with a harsh or guttural voice. [ME *throte* < OE *ðrote.*]
throat·latch (thrōt′lăch′) *n.* A strap passing under the neck of a horse for holding a bridle or halter in place.
throat·y (thrō′tē) *adj.* **-i·er, -i·est.** Uttered or sounding as if uttered deep in the throat; guttural, hoarse, or husky. **—throat′i·ly** *adv.* **—throat′i·ness** *n.*
throb (thrŏb) *intr.v.* **throbbed, throb·bing, throbs.** **1.** To beat rapidly or violently; pound. **2.** To vibrate, pulsate, or sound with a steady, pronounced rhythm: *boat engines throbbing.* *—n.* The act of throbbing; a beat, palpitation, or vibration. [ME *throbben.*] **—throb′bing·ly** *adv.*
throe (thrō) *n.* **1.** A severe pang or spasm of pain, as in childbirth. **2. throes.** A condition of agonizing struggle or effort: *a country in the throes of economic collapse.* [ME *throwe* < OE *ðrawe.*]
thromb– *pref.* Variant of **thrombo-.**
throm·bi (thrŏm′bī′) *n.* Plural of **thrombus.**
throm·bin (thrŏm′bĭn) *n.* An enzyme in blood that facilitates blood clotting by reacting with fibrinogen to form fibrin.
thrombo– or **thromb–** *pref.* Blood clot; blood clotting: *thromboplastic.* [< Gk. *thrombos,* clot.]
throm·bo·cyte (thrŏm′bə-sīt′) *n.* A blood platelet. **—throm′bo·cyt′ic** (-sĭt′ĭk) *adj.*
throm·bo·cy·to·pe·ni·a (thrŏm′bə-sī′tə-pē′nē-ə) *n.* A condition characterized by an abnormal decrease in the number of blood platelets. **—throm′bo·cy′to·pe′nic** *adj.*
throm·bo·em·bo·lism (thrŏm′bō-ĕm′bə-lĭz′əm) *n.* The blocking of a blood vessel by a thrombus dislodged from a vein.
throm·bo·phle·bi·tis (thrŏm′bō-flĭ-bī′tĭs) *n.* Inflammation of a vein with the formation of a thrombus.
throm·bo·plas·tic (thrŏm′bō-plăs′tĭk) *adj.* **1.** Causing or promoting blood clotting. **2.** Of or pertaining to thromboplastin. **—throm′bo·plas′ti·cal·ly** *adv.*
throm·bo·plas·tin (thrŏm′bō-plăs′tĭn) *n.* A protein complex essential for thrombin formation and blood clotting.
throm·bo·sis (thrŏm-bō′sĭs) *n., pl.* **-ses** (-sēz′). The formation, presence, or development of a thrombus. [NLat. < Gk. *thrombōsis,* a clotting < *thrombousthai,* to clot < *thrombos,* clot.]
throm·bus (thrŏm′bəs) *n., pl.* **-bi** (-bī′). A blood clot occluding a blood vessel or formed in a heart cavity. [NLat. < Gk. *thrombos,* clot.]
throne (thrōn) *n.* **1.** The chair occupied by an exalted personage such as a sovereign or bishop on state or ceremonial occasions. **2. a.** A personage who occupies a throne. **b.** The power, dignity, or rank of such a personage; sovereignty. **3. thrones.** *Theol.* The third of the nine orders of angels. *—tr. & intr. v.* **throned, thron·ing, thrones.** To enthrone or occupy a throne. [ME *thron* < OFr. *trone* < Lat. *thronus* < Gk. *thronos.*]
throng (thrông, thrŏng) *n.* **1.** A large group of people gathered or crowded closely together; multitude. **2.** A large group of things; host. *—v.* **thronged, throng·ing, throngs.** *—tr.* **1.** To crowd into; fill: *commuters thronging the subway platform.* **2.** To press in on. *—intr.* To gather, press, or move in a throng. [ME < OE *ðrang.*]
thros·tle (thrŏs′əl) *n.* **1.** Any of various Old World thrushes. **2.** A machine formerly used for spinning fibers such as cotton or wool. [ME < OE *ðrostle.*]
throt·tle[1] (thrŏt′l) *n.* **1. a.** A valve in an internal-combustion engine that regulates the amount of vaporized fuel entering the cylinders. **b.** A similar valve in a steam engine regulating the amount of steam. **c.** A lever or pedal controlling either of these valves. **2. a.** The throat. **b.** The windpipe. [Perh. dim. of obs. *throte,* throat < ME.]
throt·tle[2] (thrŏt′l) *tr.v.* **-tled, -tling, -tles.** **1. a.** To regulate the flow of (fuel) in an engine. **b.** To regulate the speed of (an engine) with a throttle. **2.** To strangle; choke. **3.** To suppress: *tried to throttle the press.* [ME *throttlen,* to strangle, perh. < *throte,* throat.] **—throt′tler** *n.*
throt·tle·hold (thrŏt′l-hōld′) *n.* A strangle hold (sense 2).
through (thro͞o) *prep.* **1.** In one side and out the opposite or another side of: *went through the tunnel.* **2.** Among or between; in the midst of: *a walk through the flowers.* **3.** By way of: *climbed in through the window.* **4.** By the means or agency of: *got an antique through a dealer.* **5.** Here and there in; around: *a tour through France.* **6.** From the beginning to the end of: *stayed up through the night.* **7.** At or to the end of; done or finished with, esp. successfully: *We are through the initial testing period.* **8.** Without stopping for: *drove through a red light.* **9.** Because of: *succeeded through hard work.* *—adv.* **1.** From one end or side to another or opposite end or side. **2.** From beginning to end; completely; thoroughly. **3.** To a conclusion or accomplishment: *see the matter through.* **4.** Out into the open. *—adj.* **1.** Passing or extending from one end, side, or surface to another: *a through beam.* **2.** Allowing continuous passage; unobstructed: *a through street.* **3.** Affording transportation to a destination with few

or no stops and no transfers: *a through bus.* **4.** Finished; washed up: *Because of the scandal, he was through politically.* **5.** At completion: *He was through with the project.* ***—idiom.*** **through and through. 1.** In every part of; throughout. **2.** In every aspect; completely. [ME < OE *ðurh.*]

through·ly (thrōō′lē) *adv. Archaic.* Thoroughly.

through·out (thrōō-out′) *prep.* In, to, through, or during every part of; all through. *—adv.* **1.** In or through all parts; everywhere. **2.** During the entire time or extent.

through·put (thrōō′pŏŏt′) *n.* Output or production, as of a computer program, over a period of time.

through street *n.* A street on which traffic is permitted to move without having to stop, as for traffic entering from intersecting streets.

through·way (thrōō′wā′) *n.* Variant of **thruway.**

throve (thrōv) *v.* A past tense of **thrive.**

throw (thrō) *v.* **threw** (thrōō), **thrown** (thrōn), **throw·ing, throws.** *—tr.* **1.** To propel through the air with a swift motion of the arm; hurl: *threw a rock.* **2.** To discharge into the air by any means: *a cannon that throws a shell ten miles.* **3.** To hurl with great force, as in anger: *He threw himself at his opponent.* **4.** To hurl to the ground or floor: *The horse threw its rider.* **5.** To perplex or mislead: *All his excuses couldn't throw her.* **6.** To put on or off hastily or carelessly: *throw on a jacket.* **7.** To put abruptly or forcibly into a specified condition: *threw him into a fit of laughter.* **8.** To form on a potter's wheel: *throw a vase.* **9.** To twist (fibers) into thread. **10. a.** To roll (dice). **b.** To roll (a particular combination) with dice. **c.** To discard or play (a card). **11.** To cast: *The rising sun threw shadows across the lawn.* **12.** To bear (young), as cows or horses. **13.** *Slang.* To arrange or give (a party, for example). **14.** To move (a controlling lever or switch). **15.** *Informal.* To lose (a contest) purposely. **16.** To abandon oneself to: *heard the news and threw a fit.* **17.** To commit (oneself) esp. for leniency or support: *threw himself on the mercy of the court.* **18.** To deliver (a punch), as in boxing: *threw a left hook.* *—intr.* To cast, fling, or hurl something. ***—phrasal verbs.*** **throw away. 1. a.** To get rid of as useless. **b.** To discard: *threw away two aces.* **2. a.** To fail to take advantage of: *threw away a chance to make big money.* **b.** To waste or use in a foolish manner: *threw away the family fortune.* **throw back. 1.** To hinder or check the progress of. **2.** To revert to an earlier type or stage in one's past. **3.** To cause to depend; make reliant. **throw in. 1.** To engage (a clutch, for example). **2.** To add (an extra amount) with no additional charge. **3.** To insert or introduce into a course of something: *threw in a few snide comments.* **throw off. 1.** To cast out; reject. **2.** To give off; emit: *exhaust pipes throwing off fumes.* **3.** To rid oneself of: *threw off all unpleasant memories.* **throw out. 1.** To give off; emit: *searchlights throwing out powerful beams.* **2.** To reject or discard: *The committee threw out her proposal.* **3.** To get rid of as useless: *threw out the garbage.* **4.** To offer, as a suggestion or plan. **5.** To disengage (a clutch or gears). **6.** *Baseball.* To put out (a base runner) by throwing the ball to the player guarding the base to which he is running. **7.** To eject from a place, esp. in an abrupt or unexpected manner: *The drunk was thrown out of the restaurant.* **throw over. 1.** To overturn. **2.** To abandon. **throw up. 1.** To abandon; relinquish. **2.** To vomit. **3.** To construct hurriedly. **4.** To refer to something repeatedly and often reproachfully: *She threw up his past to him whenever they argued.* *—n.* **1.** The act of throwing; cast. **2.** The distance, height, or direction of something thrown: *a low throw.* **3. a.** A roll or cast of dice. **b.** The combination of numbers so obtained. **4.** A chance; venture. **5.** The technique used to throw an opponent in wrestling. **6. a.** A light coverlet, such as an afghan. **b.** A scarf or shawl. **7. a.** The length of the radius of a circle described by a crank, cam, or similar machine part. **b.** The maximum displacement of a machine part moved by a crank, cam, or similar machine part. **8.** *Geol.* **a.** The amount of vertical displacement of a fault. **b.** The vertical component of the net slip. ***—idioms.*** **throw in the sponge (**or **towel).** To give up in a contest or undertaking; admit defeat: *finally threw in the sponge after 15 years of teaching.* **throw (one's) weight around.** To use power or authority, esp. in an excessive or heavy-handed way. **throw up (one's) hands.** To give up; admit defeat: *threw up his hands and walked out.* [ME *throwen* < OE *ðrāwan,* to twist.] **—throw′er** *n.*

Synonyms: *throw, cast, hurl, fling, pitch, toss, sling, heave.* These verbs mean to propel an object, usually with a movement of the arm. *Throw* is the general, nonspecific term. Especially in earlier usage, *cast* was often interchangeable with *throw. Cast* now usually refers to propelling with great force or to propelling something light with a quick, skillful movement of the arm that culminates in sudden release. In the latter sense it implies careful aim. *Hurl* and *fling* mean to throw with great force. Both terms, like *pitch,* can imply impetuous or even haphazard action; but *pitch* more often means to propel something with a set aim or purpose in mind. *Toss,* in contrast, usually means to throw a light object in a leisurely or offhand manner. *Sling* stresses force of propulsion. *Heave* generally refers to lifting and throwing a ponderous object.

throw·a·way (thrō′ə-wā′) *n.* A free handbill distributed on the street. *—adj.* **1.** Designed or intended to be discarded after use. **2.** Written or delivered in a low-key or offhand manner: *throwaway lines of dialogue.*

throw·back (thrō′băk′) *n.* **1.** A reversion to a former type or ancestral characteristic. **2.** An atavism (sense 2).

thrown (thrōn) *v.* Past participle of **throw.**

throw rug *n.* A scatter rug.

thru (thrōō) *prep., adv., & adj. Informal.* Through.

thrum[1] (thrŭm) *v.* **thrummed, thrum·ming, thrums.** *—tr.* **1.** To play (a stringed instrument) idly or monotonously. **2.** To repeat or recite in a monotonous tone of voice. *—intr.* **1.** To strum idly on a stringed instrument. **2.** To speak in a monotonous tone of voice; drone. *—n.* A thrumming sound. [Imit.]

thrum[2] (thrŭm) *n.* **1. a.** The fringe of warp threads left on a loom after the cloth has been cut off. **b.** One of these threads. **2.** A loose end, fringe, or tuft of thread. **3. thrums.** *Naut.* Short bits of rope yarn inserted into canvas for the purpose of roughening the surface. *—tr.v.* **thrummed, thrum·ming, thrums. 1.** To cover or trim with thrums; fringe. **2.** *Naut.* To sew thrums in (canvas). [ME < OE *(tunge) ðrum,* ligament (of the tongue).]

thrush[1] (thrŭsh) *n.* **1.** Any of various songbirds of the family Turdidae, characteristically having brownish upper plumage and a spotted breast. **2.** Any of various birds similar or related to the thrush. [ME *thrushe* < OE *ðrȳsce.*]

thrush[2] (thrŭsh) *n.* **1.** An oral infection with a fungus, *Candida albicans,* characterized by white eruptions in the mouth. **2.** A suppurative infection of a horse's foot caused by standing in a wet, unhygienic stall. [Prob. of Scand. orig.]

thrust (thrŭst) *v.* **thrust, thrust·ing, thrusts.** *—tr.* **1. a.** To push or drive quickly and forcibly: *thrust the ax into the tree.* **b.** To stab; pierce: *thrust a dagger into her heart.* **2.** To force (oneself or another) into a specified condition or situation: *thrust himself through the crowd; was thrust into a position of awesome responsibility.* **3.** To put in; interject. *—intr.* **1.** To shove into something; push. **2.** To pierce or stab with or as if with a pointed weapon. **3.** To force one's way. *—n.* **1.** A forceful shove or push; lunge. **2. a.** A driving force or pressure. **b.** The forward-directed force developed in a jet or rocket engine as a reaction to the rearward ejection of fuel gases at high velocities. **3.** A stab. **4.** General direction or tendency: *The whole thrust of the project was to make money.* **5.** *Archit.* Outward or lateral stress in a structure, such as an arch. [ME *thrusten* < ON *ðrȳsta.*] **—thrust′er** *n.*

thrust fault *n. Geol.* A reverse fault having a low angle of inclination in relation to the horizontal plane.

thru·way also **through·way** (thrōō′wā′) *n.* An expressway.

thud (thŭd) *n.* **1.** A dull sound, as that of a heavy object striking a solid surface. **2.** A blow or fall causing a thud. *—intr.v.* **thud·ded, thud·ding, thuds.** To make a thud. [Perh. < ME *thudden,* to strike with a weapon < OE *ðyddan.*]

thug (thŭg) *n.* **1.** A cutthroat or ruffian; hoodlum. **2.** One of a band of professional assassins formerly active in northern India. [Hindi *ṭhag* < Skt. *sthagaḥ,* a cheat < *sthagati,* he conceals.] **—thug′ger·y** *n.* **—thug′gish** *adj.*

thu·ja (thōō′jə, thyōō′-) *n.* Arborvitae (sense 1). [NLat. *Thuja,* arborvitae genus < Med. Lat. *thuja,* cedar < Gk. *thuia.*]

Thu·le (thōō′lē, thyōō′-) *n.* The most northerly region of the ancient habitable world, conceived as an island north of Britain by Ptolemy and other ancient geographers. [Lat. < Gk. *Thoulē.*]

thu·li·um (thōō′lē-əm, thyōō′-) *n. Symbol* **Tm** A bright silvery rare-earth element having 16 known isotopes with mass numbers ranging from 161 to 176. The x-ray emitting isotope Tm 170 is used in small portable medical x-ray units. Atomic number 69; atomic weight 168.934; melting point 1,545°C; boiling point 1,727°C; specific gravity 9.332; valences 2, 3. [< THULE.]

thumb (thŭm) *n.* **1. a.** The short first digit of the human hand, opposable to each of the other four digits. **b.** A corresponding digit in other animals, esp. primates. **c.** The part of a glove or mitten that covers the thumb. **2.** *Archit.* An ovolo. *—v.* **thumbed, thumb·ing, thumbs.** *—tr.* **1.** To disarrange, soil, or wear by careless or frequent handling. **2.** *Informal.* To solicit (a ride) from a passing vehicle by signaling with the thumb. *—intr.* To hitchhike. ***—idioms.*** **all thumbs.** Clumsy; awkward. **thumb (one's) nose.** To express scorn or derision by or as if by placing the thumb on the nose and wiggling the fingers. **thumbs down.** An expression of rejection, refusal, or disapproval. **thumbs up.** An expression of hope or success. **thumb through.** To browse rapidly through (the pages of a publication). [ME < OE *ðūma.*]

thumb·hole (thŭm′hōl′) *n.* The hole on a wind instrument that is opened or closed with the thumb.

thumb index *n.* A series of rounded indentations cut into the front edge of a book, each labeled, as with a letter, to indicate a section of the book.

thumb-in·dex (thŭm′ĭn′dĕks) *tr.v.* **-dexed, -dex·ing, -dex·es.** To furnish with a thumb index.

thumb·nail (thŭm′nāl′) *n.* The nail of the thumb. *—adj.* **1.** Of the size of a thumbnail. **2.** Brief: *a thumbnail sketch.*

thumb·nut (thŭm′nŭt′) *n.* A wing nut.

thumb·print (thŭm′prĭnt′) *n.* A print made by the thumb and esp. by the inside of the first joint of the thumb.

thumb·screw (thŭm′skrōō′) *n.* **1.** A screw so designed that it

thunderbird
Totem pole showing thunderbird at top

tiara
Above: Papal tiara
Below: Jeweled tiara

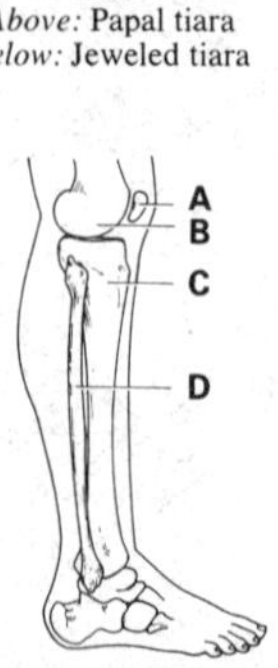

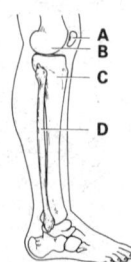

tibia
A. Patella
B. Femur
C. Tibia
D. Fibula

can be turned with the thumb and fingers. **2.** An instrument of torture formerly used to compress the thumb.

thumb·tack (thŭm′tăk′) *n.* A tack with a smooth, rounded head that can be pressed into place with the thumb. —*tr.v.* **-tacked, -tack·ing, -tacks.** To affix with a thumbtack.

thump (thŭmp) *n.* **1.** A blow with a blunt instrument. **2.** The muffled sound produced by or as if by a blow with a blunt instrument; thud. —*v.* **thumped, thump·ing, thumps.** —*tr.* **1.** To beat with or as if with a blunt instrument so as to produce a muffled sound or thud. **2.** To beat soundly or thoroughly; drub. —*intr.* **1.** To hit or fall in such a way as to produce a thump; pound. **2.** To walk with heavy steps; stump. **3.** To throb audibly. [Imit.] **—thump′er** *n.*

thump·ing (thŭm′pĭng) *adj. Informal.* **1.** Large; whopping. **2.** Thoroughly enjoyable. **—thump′ing·ly** *adv.*

thun·der (thŭn′dər) *n.* **1.** The sound emitted by rapidly expanding gases along the path of the electrical discharge of lightning. **2.** A sound similar to thunder. —*v.* **-dered, -der·ing, -ders.** —*intr.* **1.** To produce thunder. **2.** To produce sounds like thunder. **3.** To utter loud, vociferous remarks or threats. —*tr.* To express violently, commandingly, or angrily; roar. [ME < OE *ðunor.*] **—thun′der·er** *n.*

thun·der·bird (thŭn′dər-bûrd′) *n.* Thunder, lightning, and rain personified as a huge bird in the mythology of some North American Indians.

thun·der·bolt (thŭn′dər-bōlt′) *n.* **1.** The discharge of lightning that accompanies thunder. **2.** A flash of lightning imagined as a bolt or dart hurled from the heavens. **3.** One that acts with sudden and destructive fury.

thun·der·clap (thŭn′dər-klăp′) *n.* **1.** A single sharp crash of thunder. **2.** Something similar to a thunderclap in violence, such as a startling or shocking piece of news.

thun·der·cloud (thŭn′dər-kloud′) *n.* **1.** A large, dark cloud charged with electricity and producing thunder and lightning; cumulonimbus. **2.** Something menacing or dreadful: *thunderclouds of impending war.*

thun·der·head (thŭn′dər-hĕd′) *n.* The swollen upper portion of a thundercloud, often associated with the coming of a thunderstorm; cumulonimbus.

thunder lizard *n.* A brontosaur.

thun·der·ous (thŭn′dər-əs) *adj.* **1.** Producing thunder or a similar sound. **2.** Loud and unrestrained: *thunderous applause.* **—thun′der·ous·ly** *adv.*

thun·der·show·er (thŭn′dər-shou′ər) *n.* A brief rainstorm accompanied by thunder and lightning.

thun·der·stone (thŭn′dər-stōn′) *n.* **1.** Any of various mineral concretions, such as a belemnite, formerly supposed to be thunderbolts. **2.** *Archaic.* A flash of lightning conceived as a stone; thunderbolt.

thun·der·storm (thŭn′dər-stôrm′) *n.* An electrical storm accompanied by heavy rain.

thun·der·struck (thŭn′dər-strŭk′) *adj.* Struck with sudden astonishment or amazement.

thu·ri·ble (thŏŏr′ə-bəl) *n.* A censer. [ME *thoryble* < Lat. *thuribulum* < *thus,* incense < Gk. *thuos* < *thuein,* to sacrifice.]

thu·ri·fer (thŏŏr′ə-fər) *n.* An altar boy or acolyte who carries a thurible. [Lat., incense-bearing : *thus,* incense + *-fer,* -fer.]

Thu·rin·gi·an (thŏŏ-rĭn′jē-ən, -jən) *adj.* Of or pertaining to Thuringia or its people. —*n.* **1.** One of an ancient tribe inhabiting central Germany until the 6th century A.D. **2.** A native or inhabitant of Thuringia.

Thurs·day (thûrz′dē, -dā′) *n.* The fifth day of the week. [ME < OE *Ðunresdæg* : *Ðunres,* Thor's + *dæg,* day.]

thus (*th*ŭs) *adv.* **1.** In this manner. **2.** To a stated degree or extent; so: *thus far.* **3.** Therefore; consequently. [ME < OE *ðus.*]

thus·ly (*th*ŭs′lē) *adv.* Thus.

Usage: *Thusly* was formerly widely used and is now occasionally employed humorously for mock-stylish effects. Otherwise, as a variant of *thus* (itself an adverb), *thusly* is termed unacceptable by a great majority of the Usage Panel.

thwack (thwăk) *tr.v.* **thwacked, thwack·ing, thwacks.** To strike or hit with something flat; whack. —*n.* A hard blow with something flat; whack. [Imit.]

thwart (thwôrt) *tr.v.* **thwart·ed, thwart·ing, thwarts.** **1.** To prevent from taking place; frustrate. **2.** To challenge, oppose, or offend; antagonize. —*n.* A seat across a boat on which the oarsman sits. —*adj.* **1.** Extending, lying, or passing across something; transverse. **2.** Perverse; stubborn. —*adv. & prep. Archaic.* Athwart; across. [ME *thwerten* < *thwert,* across < ON *ðvert,* neuter of *ðverr,* transverse.] **—thwart′er** *n.* **—thwart′ly** *adv.*

thy (*th*ī) *pron. Archaic.* Used attributively to indicate possession, agency, or reception of an action by the person or persons spoken to: *"He sees his brood about thy knee"* (Tennyson). [ME < OE *ðīn.*]

thy·la·cine (thī′lə-sīn′) *n.* A wolflike marsupial, *Thylacinus cynocephalus,* of forest areas of Tasmania, having dark transverse bands across its back. [NLat. *Thylacinus,* genus name < Gk. *thulakos,* sack.]

thyme (tīm, thīm) *n.* **1.** Any of several aromatic herbs or low shrubs of the genus *Thymus,* esp. *T. vulgaris,* of southern Europe, having small purplish flowers. **2.** The leaves of the thyme, used as seasoning. [ME < OFr. *thym* < Lat. *thymum* < Gk. *thumon.*]

thy·mec·to·my (thī-mĕk′tə-mē) *n., pl.* **-mies.** Surgical excision of the thymus. [THYM(US) + -ECTOMY.]

-thymia *suff.* State or condition of mind: *schizothymia.* [NLat. < Gk. *thumos,* mind, soul.]

thy·mic¹ (tī′mĭk, thī′-) *adj.* Of or pertaining to thyme.

thy·mic² (thī′mĭk) *adj.* Of or pertaining to the thymus.

thy·mi·dine (thī′mĭ-dēn′) *n.* A nucleoside, $C_{10}H_{14}N_2O_5$, composed of thymine and deoxyribose. [THYM(INE) + -ID(E) + -INE².]

thy·mine (thī′mēn′) *n.* A pyrimidine base, $C_5H_6N_2O_2$, that is an essential constituent of deoxyribonucleic acid. [THYM(US) + -INE².]

thy·mo·cyte (thī′mə-sīt′) *n.* A lymphocyte derived from the thymus. [THYM(US) + -CYTE.]

thy·mol (thī′môl′, -mōl′) *n.* A white, crystalline, aromatic compound, $C_{10}H_{14}O$, derived from thyme oil and other oils and used as an antiseptic, in perfumery, and as a preservative.

thy·mus (thī′məs) *n.* A ductless glandlike structure, situated just behind the top of the sternum, that plays some part in building resistance to disease but is usually vestigial in adults after reaching its maximum development during early childhood. [Gk. *thumos.*]

thyr- *pref.* Variant of **thyro-.**

thyro- or **thyr-** *pref.* Thyroid: *thyroxin.* [< THYROID.]

thy·ro·cal·ci·to·nin (thī′rō-kăl′sĭ-tō′nĭn) *n.* Calcitonin.

thy·roid (thī′roid′) *adj.* Of or relating to the thyroid gland or the thyroid cartilage. —*n.* **1.** The thyroid gland. **2.** The thyroid cartilage. **3.** A dried and powdered preparation of the thyroid gland of certain domestic animals, used in the treatment of hypothyroid conditions. [Gk. *thureoeidēs* : *thureos,* oblong shield + *-eidēs,* -oid.]

thyroid cartilage *n.* The largest cartilage of the larynx, having two broad processes that join anteriorly to form the Adam's apple.

thy·roid·ec·to·my (thī′roi-dĕk′tə-mē) *n., pl.* **-mies.** Surgical removal of the thyroid gland.

thyroid gland *n.* A two-lobed endocrine gland found in all vertebrates, located in front of and on either side of the trachea in humans, and producing the hormone thyroxin.

thy·roid·i·tis (thī′roi-dī′tĭs) *n.* Inflammation of the thyroid gland.

thyroid stimulating hormone *n.* Thyrotropin.

thy·ro·tox·i·co·sis (thī′rō-tŏk′sĭ-kō′sĭs) *n.* Poisoning from hyperthyroidism.

thy·ro·tro·pin (thī′rə-trō′pĭn) also **thy·ro·tro·phin** (-fĭn) *n.* A hormone of the anterior pituitary that stimulates and regulates the development and secretion of the thyroid gland hormone.

thy·rox·in (thī-rŏk′sĭn) also **thy·rox·ine** (-sēn′, -sĭn) *n.* An iodine-containing hormone, $C_{15}H_{11}I_4NO_4$, that is produced by the thyroid gland to regulate metabolism and made synthetically for treatment of thyroid disorders. [THYR(O)- + OX(Y)- + -IN.]

thyrse (thûrs) *n.* A branched flower cluster, as of the lilac, of which the main axis does not terminate in a flower. [NLat. *thyrsus* < Lat., thyrsus.]

thyr·si (thûr′sī′) *n.* Plural of **thyrsus.**

thyr·soid (thûr′soid′) also **thyr·soid·al** (thûr-soid′l) *adj.* Shaped like or similar to a thyrse.

thyr·sus (thûr′səs) *n., pl.* **-si** (-sī′). **1.** A staff tipped with a pine cone and twined with ivy, represented as carried by Dionysius, Dionysian revelers, or satyrs. **2.** *Bot.* A thyrse. [Lat. < Gk. *thursos.*]

thy·self (*th*ī-sĕlf′) *pron. Archaic.* Yourself. Used as the reflexive or emphatic form of *thee* or *thou.*

ti¹ (tē) *n. Mus.* A syllable representing the seventh tone of the diatonic scale in solmization. [Alteration of SI.]

ti² (tē) *n.* Any of several trees or shrubs of the genus *Cordyline,* of tropical Asia and adjacent Pacific regions, esp. *C. australis,* having a terminal tuft of long, narrow leaves. [Tahitian and Maori.]

Ti The symbol for the element titanium.

ti·ar·a (tē-ăr′ə, -âr′ə, -är′ə) *n.* **1.** The triple crown worn by the pope. **2.** An ornamental crownlike headpiece, often decorated with jewels, worn by women on formal occasions. [Lat., turban < Gk.]

Ti·bet·an (tĭ-bĕt′n) *adj.* Of or pertaining to Tibet, its people, or their language or culture. —*n.* **1.** One of the Mongoloid people of Tibet. **2.** The Tibeto-Burman language of Tibet.

Ti·bet·o-Bur·man (tĭ-bĕt′ō-bûr′mən) *n.* A branch of the Sino-Tibetan language family that includes Tibetan, Burmese, Lolo, and Balti. **—Ti·bet′o-Bur′man** *adj.*

tib·i·a (tĭb′ē-ə) *n., pl.* **-i·ae** (-ē-ē′) or **-i·as.** **1. a.** The inner and larger of the two bones of the lower human leg from the knee to the ankle. **b.** A homologous bone in animals. **2.** The fourth division of an insect's leg, between the femur and the tarsi. **3.** A kind of ancient flute originally made from an animal's leg bone. [Lat.] **—tib′i·al** *adj.*

tic (tĭk) *n.* A habitual spasmodic muscular contraction, usually of the face or extremities. [Fr.]

tic dou·lou·reux (tĭk′ dōō′lōō-rōō′) *n.* Trigeminal neuralgia. [Fr. : *tic,* tic + *douloureux,* painful.]

tick¹ (tĭk) *n.* **1.** The recurring sharp, clicking sound made by a machine, esp. by a clock. **2.** *Chiefly Brit.* A moment. **3.** A light mark used to check off or call attention to an item. —*v.*

ticked, tick·ing, ticks. —*intr.* **1.** To emit recurring sharp, clicking sounds, as a clock. **2.** To function in a characteristic way, as if by means of a motivating mechanism: *What makes him tick?* —*tr.* **1.** To count or record by means of ticks: *The meter ticked off his taxi fare.* **2.** To mark or check off (a listed item) with a tick: *ticked off each word on the list.* ***—phrasal verb.*** **tick off.** *Slang.* To make angry or annoyed: *got really ticked off at her refusal.* [ME *tek.*]

tick[2] (tĭk) *n.* **1.** Any of numerous bloodsucking parasitic arachnids of the family Ixodidae within the order Acarina, many of which transmit infectious diseases. **2.** Any of various usually wingless, louselike insects of the family Hippoboscidae that are parasitic on sheep, goats, and other animals. [ME *teke.*]

tick[3] (tĭk) *n.* **1. a.** The cloth case of a mattress or pillow. **b.** A light mattress without inner springs. **2.** Ticking. [ME *tikke,* prob. < MDu. *tīke* < Lat. *theca,* case < Gk. *thēkē.*]

tick[4] (tĭk) *n. Chiefly Brit.* Credit; trust: *on tick.* [Short for TICKET.]

tick-borne (tĭk'bôrn', -bōrn') *adj.* Transmitted by ticks.

tick·er (tĭk'ər) *n.* **1. a.** A telegraphic instrument that receives and records stock-market quotations on a paper tape. **b.** Any of various devices in current use that record similar information by electronic means rather than paper tape. **2.** *Slang.* A watch. **3.** *Slang.* The heart.

ticker tape *n.* The paper strip on which a telegraphic ticker prints.

tick·et (tĭk'ĭt) *n.* **1.** A paper slip or card indicating that its holder has paid for or is entitled to a specified service, right, or consideration: *a bus ticket.* **2.** A certifying document, esp. a captain's or pilot's license. **3.** An identifying or descriptive tag attached esp. to merchandise; label. **4.** A list of candidates proposed or endorsed by a political party; slate. **5.** A legal summons, esp. for a traffic violation. **6.** *Informal.* The proper thing: *A change of scene would be just the ticket for her.* —*tr.v.* **-et·ed, -et·ing, -ets. 1.** To provide with a ticket for admission or passage. **2.** To attach a tag to; label. **3.** To designate for a specified use or end; destine. **4.** To serve (an offender) with a legal summons. [OFr. *estiquet,* short document < *estiquier,* to stick < MDu. *steken.*]

ticket scalper *n.* A profiteer who buys up desirable admission tickets and resells them at higher prices.

tick fever *n.* Rocky Mountain spotted fever.

tick·ing (tĭk'ĭng) *n.* A strong, tightly woven fabric of cotton or linen used esp. to make pillow and mattress coverings.

tick·le (tĭk'əl) *v.* **-led, -ling, -les.** —*tr.* **1.** To touch (the body) lightly so as to cause laughter or twitching movements. **2. a.** To tease or excite pleasurably; titillate. **b.** To fill with mirth or pleasure; delight. —*intr.* To feel or cause a tingling sensation. —*n.* **1.** The act of tickling. **2.** A tickling sensation. ***—idiom.*** **tickle pink.** *Informal.* To please; delight: *tickled pink by the gift.* [ME *tikelen,* perh. freq. of *ticken,* to touch lightly.]

tick·ler (tĭk'lər) *n.* **1.** One that tickles. **2.** A memorandum book or file to aid the memory.

tick·lish (tĭk'lĭsh) *adj.* **1.** Sensitive to tickling. **2.** Easily offended or upset; touchy. **3.** Requiring skillful or tactful handling; delicate. **—tick'lish·ly** *adv.* **—tick'lish·ness** *n.*

tick·seed (tĭk'sēd') *n.* The coreopsis. [TICK[2] (from its seed's shape) + SEED.]

tick·tack also **tic-tac** (tĭk'tăk') *n.* **1.** A steady ticking sound, as of a clock. **2.** A prankster's device for tapping on a door or window from a distance. [Imit.]

tick·tack·toe also **tick-tack-toe** (tĭk'tăk'tō') *n.* A game played by two persons, each trying to make a line of three X's or three O's in a boxlike figure with nine spaces. [From the sounds of the original game, in which players dropped pencils on a slate.]

tick·tock (tĭk'tŏk') *n.* The ticking sound made by a clock, esp. a pendulum clock. [Imit.]

tick trefoil *n.* Any of various plants of the genus *Desmodium,* having compound leaves with three leaflets, clusters of small purplish or white flowers, and jointed seed pods with easily separable, sticky segments. [< TICK[2] (from the way its pods adhere to animals).]

tick·y-tack·y (tĭk'ē-tăk'ē) *n.* Shoddy material, as for construction. [Coined by Malvina Reynolds (b. 1900).]

tic-tac (tĭk'tăk') *n.* Variant of **ticktack.**

tid·al (tīd'l) *adj.* **1.** Pertaining to, affected by, or having tides: *a tidal river.* **2.** Dependent upon or scheduled by the time of high tide: *a tidal ship.* **—tid'al·ly** *adv.*

tidal wave *n.* **1.** An unusual rise or incursion of water along the seashore, as from a storm or a combination of wind and spring tide. **2.** A tsunami. **3.** An overwhelming manifestation of sentiment, desire, or opinion.

tid·bit (tĭd'bĭt') also **tit·bit** (tĭt'-) *n.* A choice morsel, as of food or gossip. [Perh. dial. *tid,* tender + BIT[1].]

tid·dly·winks (tĭd'lē-wĭngks') also **tid·dle·dy·winks** (tĭd'l-dē-) *n. (used with a sing. verb).* A game in which players try to snap small disks into a cup by pressing them on the edge with a larger disk. [Perh. dial. *tiddly,* little + WINK.]

tide[1] (tīd) *n.* **1. a.** The periodic variation in the surface level of the oceans and of bays, gulfs, inlets, and tidal regions of rivers, caused by the gravitational attraction of the sun and moon, the lunar effect being the more powerful. **b.** A specific occurrence of such a variation. **c.** The waters in such a variation. **2.** Stress exerted on a body or part of a body by the gravitational attraction of another: *atmospheric tide.* **3.** Something that fluctuates like the waters of the tide: *the rising tide of discontent.* **4.** A time or season: *eventide; Christmastide.* **5.** *Archaic.* A favorable occasion; opportunity. —*v.* **tid·ed, tid·ing, tides.** —*intr.* **1.** To rise and fall like the tide. **2.** To drift or ride with the tide. —*tr.* To carry along with or as if with the tide. ***—phrasal verb.*** **tide over.** To support through a difficult period: *loaned him $20 to tide him over till payday.* [ME *tid* < OE *tīd,* season.]

tide[2] (tīd) *intr.v.* **tid·ed, tid·ing, tides.** *Archaic.* To betide; befall. [ME *tiden* < OE *tīdan.*]

tide·land (tīd'lănd') *n.* Coastal land submerged during high tide.

tide·mark (tīd'märk') *n.* A line or artificial indicator marking the high-water or low-water limit of the tides.

tide·rip (tīd'rĭp') *n.* A rip current.

tide·wait·er (tīd'wā'tər) *n.* A customs officer who boards incoming ships at a harbor.

tide·wa·ter (tīd'wô'tər, -wŏt'ər) *n.* **1.** Water that inundates land at flood tide. **2.** Water affected by the tides, esp. tidal streams. **3.** Low coastal land drained by tidal streams.

tide·way (tīd'wā') *n.* A channel in which a tidal current runs.

ti·dings (tī'dĭngz) *pl.n.* Information; news: *tidings of great joy.* [Pl. of obs. *tiding,* event < ME, perh. < ON *tīðendi,* events < *tīðr,* occurring.]

ti·dy (tī'dē) *adj.* **-di·er, -di·est. 1.** Orderly and neat in appearance or procedure. **2.** *Informal.* **a.** Adequate; satisfactory. **b.** Substantial; considerable: *a tidy sum.* —*v.* **-died, -dy·ing, -dies.** —*tr.* To put in order: *tidied up the house.* —*intr.* To make things tidy: *tidied up after dinner.* —*n., pl.* **-dies.** A fancy protective covering for the arms or headrest of a chair. [ME *tidi,* healthy < *tid,* time < OE *tīd.*] **—ti'di·ly** *adv.* **—ti'di·ness** *n.*

ti·dy·tips (tī'dē-tĭps') *n. (used with a sing. or pl. verb).* A plant, *Layia elegans,* of California, having daisylike flowers with yellow, white-tipped rays.

tie (tī) *v.* **tied, ty·ing, ties.** —*tr.* **1.** To fasten or secure with or as if with a cord, rope, or strap. **2.** To fasten by drawing together the parts or sides of and knotting with strings or laces: *tied her shoes.* **3. a.** To make (a knot or bow). **b.** To put a knot or bow in: *tie a necktie.* **4.** To confine or restrict as if with cord: *tied to his job.* **5.** To bring together closely; unite. **6.** To equal (an opponent or his score) in a contest. **7.** *Mus.* To join (notes) by a tie. —*intr.* **1.** To be fastened with strings. **2.** To achieve equal scores in a contest. ***—phrasal verbs.*** **tie in.** To have a connection with; coordinate. **tie up. 1.** To keep occupied: *I was tied up in a meeting all morning. The phone was tied up for an hour.* **2.** To impede the progress of: *The accident tied up traffic.* —*n.* **1.** A means by which something is tied, as a cord or string. **2.** Something that unites; bond: *marital ties.* **3.** A necktie. **4.** A beam or rod that joins parts and gives support. **5.** One of the timbers laid across a railroad bed to support the tracks. **6. a.** An equality of scores, votes, or performance in a contest. **b.** A contest resulting in this; draw. **7.** *Mus.* A curved line above or below two notes of the same pitch, indicating that the tone is to be sustained for their combined duration. ***—idioms.*** **tie one on.** *Slang.* To get drunk. **tie the knot. 1.** To get married. **2.** To perform a marriage ceremony. [ME *tyen* < OE *tīgan.*]

tie·back (tī'băk') *n.* **1.** A decorative loop of fabric, cord, or metal for parting and draping curtains to the sides. **2. tiebacks.** A pair of curtains meant to be tied back at about midlength.

tie beam *n.* A horizontal beam that connects the rafters in a roof.

tie clasp *n.* An ornamental device that holds the ends of a necktie to the shirt front.

tie-dye (tī'dī') *tr.v.* **-dyed, -dye·ing, -dyes.** To dye (fabric) after tying parts of the fabric so that they will not absorb dye, giving the fabric a streaked or mottled look.

tie-in (tī'ĭn') *n.* A connection or relation.

tie line *n.* **1.** A communication link between extensions of a private telephone system. **2.** A connection between major systems, such as electrical power.

tier[1] (tîr) *n.* One of a series of rows placed one above another. —*tr. & intr. v.* **tiered, tier·ing, tiers.** To arrange or rise in tiers. [OFr. *tire,* rank.]

ti·er[2] (tī'ər) *n.* One that ties.

tierce (tîrs) *n.* **1.** Also **terce** (tûrs). **a.** The third of the seven canonical hours. **b.** The time of day set aside for this prayer, usually the third hour after sunrise. **2.** A former measure of liquid capacity, equal to a third of a pipe, or 42 gallons. **3.** A sequence of three cards of the same suit. **4.** The third position from which a parry or thrust can be made in fencing. **5.** *Mus.* An interval of a third. [ME < OFr. < fem. of *tiers,* third < Lat. *tertium.*]

tier·cel (tîr'səl) *n.* Variant of **tercel.**

tier table (tîr) *n.* A table with two or more successive tops.

tie tack *n.* A short pin with a decorative head used to attach a tie to a shirt front by means of a snap or chain.

tie-up (tī'ŭp') *n.* A temporary condition of immobilization, as a traffic jam, work stoppage, or mechanical breakdown.

tiff (tĭf) *n.* **1.** A fit of irritation. **2.** A petty quarrel. —*intr.v.* **tiffed, tiff·ing, tiffs.** To quarrel. [Orig. unknown.]

tide[1]
Above: High tide
Below: Low tide

Tiffany glass
A Tiffany lamp

tiger lily

tile

tiller²

tif·fa·ny (tĭf′ə-nē) *n., pl.* **-nies.** A thin, transparent gauze of silk or cotton muslin. [Prob. < OFr. *tiphanie,* Epiphany < Med. Lat. *theophania,* theophany. —see THEOPHANY.]
Tiffany glass *n.* Stained or iridescent glass of a kind popular in the early 1900's for decorative objects or lamps. [After Louis C. *Tiffany* (1848–1933).]
tif·fin (tĭf′ĭn) *n. Chiefly Brit.* Luncheon. [Short for obs. *tiffing,* gerund. of *tiff,* to sip.]
ti·ger (tī′gər) *n.* **1. a.** A large carnivorous feline mammal, *Panthera tigris,* of Asia, having a tawny coat with transverse black stripes. **b.** Any of various other similar felines. **2.** A fierce, aggressive, or audacious person. [ME *tigre* < OFr. < Lat. *tigris* < Gk.] **—ti′ger·ish** *adj.*
tiger beetle *n.* Any of numerous active, often varicolored beetles of the family Cicindelidae, chiefly of warm, sandy regions.
tiger cat *n.* Any of various small felines resembling the tiger in either appearance or behavior.
ti·ger-eye (tī′gər-ī′) also **ti·ger's-eye** (tī′gərz-) *n.* A yellow-brown, semiprecious chatoyant gemstone made of silicified crocidolite.
tiger lily *n.* A plant, *Lilium tigrinum,* native to Asia, having large, black-spotted reddish-orange flowers with reflexed petals.
tiger moth *n.* Any of numerous, often brightly colored moths of the family Arctiidae, characteristically having wings marked with spots or lines.
tiger salamander *n.* A salamander, *Ambystoma tigrinum,* having distinctive yellowish markings, that is widely distributed over most of North America.
ti·ger's-eye (tī′gərs-ī′) *n.* Variant of **tiger-eye.**
tight (tīt) *adj.* **-er, -est. 1. a.** Of such close construction, texture, or organization as to be impermeable, esp. by water or air. **b.** Closely reasoned or worded. **2.** Fastened, held, or closed securely. **3.** Compressed, leaving few or no intervening spaces; compact. **4.** Drawn out to the fullest extent; taut. **5.** Cramped; constrained. **6.** Snug, often uncomfortably so: *a tight fit.* **7.** Constricted: *a tight feeling in the chest.* **8.** Close-fisted; stingy. **9. a.** Difficult to obtain: *tight money.* **b.** Affected by scarcity: *a tight market.* **10.** Difficult to deal with or get out of: *a tight spot.* **11.** Barely profitable: *a tight bargain.* **12.** Closely contested: *a tight match.* **13.** *Regional.* Neat and trim. **14.** *Slang.* Drunk. **15.** *Slang.* Friendly; compatible. *—adv.* **-er, -est. 1.** Firmly; securely. **2.** Soundly: *sleep tight.* ***—idiom.* sit tight.** To make no move; watch and wait. [ME, var. of *thight,* dense, of Scand. orig.] **—tight′ly** *adv.* **—tight′ness** *n.*
Usage: *Tight* as an adjective appears after the verb when it is used to qualify the process denoted by the verb: *hold on tight; close it tight.* In a few cases this is the only form that may be used: *sit tight; sleep tight.* In most cases the adverb *tightly* may also be used in this position: *close it tightly.* Before a verb only the adverb is used: *The money supply will be tightly* (not *tight*) *controlled.* See also Usage note at **taut.**
tight·en (tīt′n) *tr. & intr.v.* **-ened, -en·ing, -ens.** To make or become tight or tighter. **—tight′en·er** *n.*
tight end *n. Football.* The player at the right end of the offensive team in the modern T-formation that is stationed close to the adjoining tackle.
tight·fist·ed (tīt′fĭs′tĭd) *adj.* Stingy; parsimonious.
tight·lipped (tīt′lĭpt′) *adj.* **1.** Having the lips pressed together. **2.** Reticent.
tight·rope (tīt′rōp′) *n.* **1.** A tightly stretched rope, usually of wire, on which acrobats perform high above the ground. **2.** An extremely precarious situation.
tights (tīts) *pl.n.* A snug stretchable garment covering the body from the waist or neck down, worn by acrobats and dancers and also designed for general wear by women and girls.
tight·wad (tīt′wŏd′) *n. Slang.* One who hates to spend money; miser.
tig·lic acid (tĭg′lĭk) *n.* A thick, syrupy poisonous liquid, $C_5H_8O_2$, derived from croton oil, having a spicy odor and used in making perfumes and flavoring agents. [NLat. *tiglium,* specific epithet of *Croton tiglium* perh. < Gk. *tilos,* liquid feces.]
ti·glon (tī′glən) also **ti·gon** (tī′gən) *n.* The hybrid offspring of a male tiger and a female lion. [Blend of TIGER and LION.]
Ti·gré (tē-grā′) *n.* A Semitic language of northern Ethiopia.
ti·gress (tī′grĭs) *n.* **1.** A female tiger. **2.** A fierce, aggressive, or audacious woman.
Ti·gri·nya (tə-grēn′yə) *n.* A Semitic language of northern Ethiopia.
tike (tīk) *n.* Variant of **tyke.**
ti·ki (tē′kē) *n.* **1. Tiki.** A male figure in Polynesian mythology, sometimes identified as the first man. **2.** A wood or stone image of a Polynesian god. **3.** A Maori figurine representing an ancestor, often intricately carved from greenstone and worn about the neck as a talisman. [Maori.]
til (tĭl) *n.* The sesame plant, esp. as used in India as a source of food and oil. [Hindi < Skt. *tilaḥ.*]
til·bur·y (tĭl′bĕr′ē, -bə-rē) *n., pl.* **-ies.** A light open carriage that has two wheels and seats two persons. [After *Tilbury,* a 19th-cent. London coach builder.]
til·de (tĭl′də) *n.* The diacritical mark (˜) placed over the letter *n* in Spanish to indicate the palatal nasal sound (ny), as in *cañon,* or over a vowel in Portuguese to indicate nasalization, as in *lã, pão.* [Sp. < Lat. *titulus,* superscription.]
tile (tīl) *n.* **1.** A thin, flat, or convex slab of material such as baked clay or plastic, laid in rows to cover walls, floors, and roofs. **2.** A short length of pipe made of clay or concrete, used in sewers and drains. **3.** A hollow fired clay or concrete block used for building walls. **4.** Tiles collectively. **5.** A marked playing piece, as in mahjong. *—tr.v.* **tiled, til·ing, tiles.** To cover or provide with tiles. [ME < OE *tigele* < Lat. *tegula* < *tegere,* to cover.] **—til′er** *n.*
tile·fish (tīl′fĭsh′) *n., pl.* **tilefish** or **-fish·es.** Any of several marine food fishes of the family Branchiostegidae, esp. *Lopholatilus chamaeleonticeps,* of deep Atlantic waters, having varicolored markings. [*Tile-,* short for NLat. *Lopholatilus,* genus name + FISH.]
til·ing (tī′lĭng) *n.* **1.** The laying of tiles. **2.** Tiles collectively. **3.** A tiled surface.
till¹ (tĭl) *tr.v.* **tilled, till·ing, tills.** To prepare (land) for the raising of crops by plowing, harrowing, and fertilizing. [ME *tilien* < OE *tilian,* to labor.] **—till′a·ble** *adj.*
till² (tĭl) *prep.* Until. *—conj.* **1.** Until. **2.** Before or unless. [ME < ON, to.]
till³ (tĭl) *n.* A drawer, small chest, or compartment for money, esp. in a store. [ME *tylle.*]
till⁴ (tĭl) *n.* Glacial drift composed of an unconsolidated, heterogeneous mixture of clay, sand, gravel, and boulders. [Orig. unknown.]
till·age (tĭl′ĭj) *n.* **1.** The cultivation of land. **2.** Land that has been tilled.
til·land·si·a (tĭ-lănd′zē-ə) *n.* Any of various usually epiphytic plants of the genus *Tillandsia,* such as Spanish moss, of tropical and subtropical America. [NLat., genus name, after Elias *Tillands* (1640–1693).]
till·er¹ (tĭl′ər) *n.* One that tills land.
til·ler² (tĭl′ər) *n.* A lever used to turn a rudder and steer a boat. [ME *tiler,* stock of a crossbow < OFr. *telier,* weaver's beam < Med. Lat. *telarium* < Lat. *tela.*]
til·ler³ (tĭl′ər) *n.* A shoot, esp. one that sprouts from the base of a grass. *—intr.v.* **-lered, -ler·ing, -lers.** To send forth tillers. [ME **tiller* < OE *telgor.*]
tilt¹ (tĭlt) *v.* **tilt·ed, tilt·ing, tilts.** *—tr.* **1.** To cause to slope, as by raising one end; incline. **2. a.** To aim or thrust (a lance) in a joust. **b.** To charge (an opponent). **3.** To forge with a tilt hammer. *—intr.* **1.** To slope; incline. **2.** To joust. **3.** To quarrel. *—n.* **1. a.** An inclination from the horizontal or vertical; slant. **b.** A sloping surface, as of the ground. **2.** The act of tilting. **3. a.** A medieval sport in which two mounted knights with lances charged together and attempted to unhorse one another. **b.** A thrust or blow with a lance. **4.** A verbal duel. **5.** A tilt hammer. ***—idiom.* at full tilt.** At full speed. [ME *tylten,* to cause to fall, perh. of Scand. orig.]
tilt² (tĭlt) *n.* A canopy or awning for a boat, wagon, or cart. *—tr.v.* **tilt·ed, tilt·ing, tilts.** To cover with a tilt. [ME *telte,* tent < OE *teld.*]
tilth (tĭlth) *n.* **1.** The cultivation of land; tillage. **2.** Tilled earth. [ME < OE *tilð* < *tilian,* to labor.]
tilt hammer *n.* A heavy forge hammer having a pivoted lever by which it is tilted up and then allowed to drop.
tilt·yard (tĭlt′yärd′) *n.* An enclosed yard for tilting contests.
tim·bal also **tym·bal** (tĭm′bəl) *n.* A kettledrum. [Fr. *timbale,* var. of obs. *tamballe* < OSp. *atabal,* small drum < Ar. *aṭ-ṭabl,* drum.]
tim·bale (tĭm′bəl, tĭm-bäl′, tăm-) *n.* **1.** A bland, custardlike dish of cheese, chicken, fish, or vegetables baked in a drum-shaped pastry mold. **2.** The pastry mold in which a timbale is baked. [Fr., mold, timbal.]
tim·ber (tĭm′bər) *n.* **1.** Trees or wooded land considered as a source of wood. **2. a.** Wood as a building material; lumber. **b.** A dressed piece of wood, esp. a beam in a structure. **c.** A rib in a ship's frame. **3.** Material: *He's executive timber.* *—tr.v.* **-bered, -ber·ing, -bers.** To support or shore up with timbers. *—interj.* Used to warn of a falling tree. [ME < OE.]
tim·bered (tĭm′bərd) *adj.* **1. a.** Constructed of or covered with timber. **b.** Built with exposed timbers. **2.** Wooded.
tim·ber·head (tĭm′bər-hĕd′) *n. Naut.* A timber end that projects above a deck and is used as a bollard.
timber hitch *n. Naut.* A knot used for fastening a rope around a spar or log to be hoisted or towed.
tim·ber·ing (tĭm′bər-ĭng) *n.* Timber or work made of it.
tim·ber·land (tĭm′bər-lănd′) *n.* Forested land considered commercially.
tim·ber·line also **timber line** (tĭm′bər-līn′) *n.* The limit of altitude in mountainous regions beyond which trees do not grow.
timber right *n.* A claim to the trees on property belonging to another.
timber wolf *n.* A grayish or whitish wolf, *Canis lupus,* of forested northern regions.
tim·ber·work (tĭm′bər-wûrk′) *n.* The part of a structure made with timbers, as the framework of a boat or house.
tim·bre (tăm′bər, tĭm′-) *n.* The quality of a sound that distinguishes it from other sounds of the same pitch and volume, esp. the distinctive tone of a musical instrument, a voice, or a voiced speech sound. [Fr. < OFr., timbrel < Med. Gk. *timbanon* < Gk. *tumpanum.*]

tim·brel (tĭm′brəl) *n.* An ancient percussion instrument similar to a tambourine. [ME *timbre* < OFr. —see TIMBRE.]

time (tīm) *n.* **1. a.** A nonspatial continuum in which events occur in apparently irreversible succession from the past through the present to the future. **b.** An interval separating two points on this continuum, measured essentially by selecting a regularly recurring event, such as the sunrise, and counting the number of its occurrences during the interval; duration. **c.** A number, as of years, days, or minutes, representing such an interval. **d.** A similar number representing a specific point, such as the present, as reckoned from an arbitrary past point on the continuum. **e.** A system by which such intervals are measured or such numbers are reckoned: *standard time; solar time.* **2.** Often **times.** An interval, esp. a span of years, marked by similar events, conditions, or phenomena; era: *a time of troubles.* **3.** A suitable or opportune moment or season. **4.** A moment or period designated, as by custom, for a given activity: *harvest time; bedtime.* **5.** An appointed or fated moment, esp. of death: *died before his time.* **6.** One of several instances. **7.** An occasion. **8.** *Informal.* A prison sentence. **9. a.** The customary period of work: *hired for full time.* **b.** The period spent working. **10.** The rate of speed of a measured activity: *marching in double time.* **11.** The characteristic beat of musical rhythm: *three-quarter time.* —*adj.* **1.** Of or relating to time. **2.** Constructed so as to operate at a particular moment: *a time bomb.* **3.** Payable on a future date or dates: *a time loan.* **4.** Of or relating to installment buying. —*tr.v.* **timed, tim·ing, times. 1.** To set the time for (an event or occasion). **2.** To adjust to keep accurate time. **3.** To regulate or adjust for the orderly sequence of movements or events: *timed his leap beautifully.* **4.** To record the speed or duration of. **5.** To set or maintain the tempo, speed, or duration of. —***idioms.*** **against time.** With a quickly approaching time limit. **at one time. 1.** Simultaneously. **2.** At a period or moment in the past. **at the same time.** However; nonetheless. **at times.** On occasion; sometimes. **behind the times.** Out-of-date; old-fashioned. **for the time being.** Temporarily. **from time to time.** Once in a while; at intervals. **gain time.** To run too fast. Used of a timepiece. **high time.** Long overdue. **in good time. 1.** In a reasonable length of time. **2.** When or before due. **3.** Quickly. **in no time.** Almost instantly; immediately. **in time. 1.** Before a time limit expires. **2.** Within an indefinite amount of passing time. **3.** In proper tempo. **keep time. 1.** To indicate the correct time. **2.** To maintain the tempo or rhythm. **lose time. 1.** To run too slowly. Used of a timepiece. **2.** To delay advancement. **on time. 1.** According to schedule; promptly. **2.** By paying in installments. [ME < OE *tīma,* interval between events.]

time and a half *n.* A rate of pay that is one and a half times the regular rate, as for overtime work.

time and motion study *n.* An analysis of the efficiency with which an industrial operation is performed.

time bill *n.* A bill of exchange payable at an indicated future time.

time bomb *n.* A bomb with a detonating mechanism that can be set for a particular time.

time capsule *n.* A sealed container preserving articles and records of contemporary culture for perusal by scientists and scholars of the distant future.

time·card (tīm′kärd′) *n.* A card, either maintained by an employee or stamped by a time clock, recording the employee's arrival and departure time each day.

time clock *n.* A clock that records the arrival and departure times of employees, usually by punching timecards.

time deposit *n.* A bank deposit that cannot be withdrawn before a date specified at the time of deposit.

time dilatation also **time dilation** *n.* The relativistic slowing of a clock that moves with respect to a stationary observer.

time exposure *n.* **1.** A photographic exposure made for a relatively long period of time. **2.** An image made by time exposure.

time-hon·ored (tīm′ŏn′ərd) *adj.* Respected or adhered to because of age or age-old observance.

time immemorial *n.* **1.** Time long past, beyond memory or record. **2.** *Law.* Time antedating legal records.

time·keep·er (tīm′kē′pər) *n.* **1.** A timepiece. **2.** The person who keeps track of time, as in a sports event or in a place of employment. **3.** A railroad dispatcher.

time-lapse (tīm′lăps′) *adj.* Of or using a motion-picture technique for filming a naturally slow process, as the unfolding of a leaf, by photographing it at intervals so that the continuous projection of the frames gives an accelerated view of it.

time·less (tīm′lĭs) *adj.* **1.** Independent of time; unending; eternal. **2.** Unaffected by time; ageless. **3.** *Obs.* Untimely. **—time′less·ly** *adv.* **—time′less·ness** *n.*

time loan *n.* A loan to be paid within or by a specified time.

time lock *n.* A lock set to open at a specific time.

time·ly (tīm′lē) *adj.* **-li·er, -li·est. 1.** Occurring at a suitable or opportune time; well-timed. **2.** *Archaic.* Early; premature. —*adv.* **1.** Opportunely; in time. **2.** *Archaic.* Early; soon. **—time′li·ness** *n.*

time machine *n.* A machine or device that in theory permits travel into the future and the past.

time money *n.* A time loan.

time note *n.* A promissory note or similar instrument specifying a date or dates of payment.

time·ous (tī′məs) *adj. Scot.* Timely. **—time′ous·ly** *adv.*

time-out also **time out** (tīm′out′) *n.* **1.** A brief cessation of play at the request of a sports team for rest or consultation. **2.** A short break from work or play.

time out of mind *n.* Time immemorial (sense 2).

time·piece (tīm′pēs′) *n.* An instrument that measures, registers, or records time.

tim·er (tī′mər) *n.* **1.** A person who keeps track of time; timekeeper. **2.** A timepiece, esp. one used for measuring intervals of time. **3.** A switch or regulator that controls or activates another mechanism at fixed intervals.

time reversal *n.* A mathematical operation representing a transformation from a given physical system undergoing a given sequence of events to a system in which the exact reverse sequence of events is undergone.

times (tīmz) *prep.* Multiplied by: *Five times two is ten.*

time·sav·ing (tīm′sā′vĭng) *adj.* Serving to save time through an efficient method or a shorter route; expeditious. **—time′-sav′er** *n.*

time·serv·er (tīm′sûr′vər) *n.* A person who conforms to the prevailing ways and opinions of his time or condition for personal advantage; opportunist. **—time′serv′ing** *adj. & n.*

time-shar·ing (tīm′shâr′ĭng) *n.* **1.** A technique permitting many users simultaneous access to a central computer through remote terminals. **2.** The joint ownership or lease of vacation property through which the principals occupy the property individually for set periods of time. **—time′-share′** *v.* **(-shared, -shar·ing, -shares).**

time sheet *n.* A sheet that records the number of hours worked by employees during a pay period.

time signature *n. Mus.* A symbol, commonly in the form of a numerical fraction, placed on a staff to indicate the meter.

times sign *n.* The symbol × used to indicate multiplication.

time study *n.* Time and motion study.

time·ta·ble (tīm′tā′bəl) *n.* A schedule listing the times at which certain events, such as arrivals and departures at a transportation station, are expected to take place.

time-test·ed (tīm′tĕs′tĭd) *adj.* Proved effective over a long period of time: *a time-tested recipe.*

time warp *n.* A discontinuity or distortion held to occur in the flow of time.

time·work (tīm′wûrk′) *n.* Work paid for in specified time units, as by the hour. **—time′work′er** *n.*

time·worn (tīm′wôrn′, -wōrn′) *adj.* **1.** Showing the effects of long use or wear. **2.** Used too often; trite.

time zone *n.* Any of the 24 longitudinal divisions of the earth's surface in which a standard time is kept, the primary division being that bisected by the Greenwich meridian. Each zone is 15 degrees of longitude in width, with local variations, and observes a clock time one hour earlier than the zone immediately to the east.

time clock

tim·id (tĭm′ĭd) *adj.* **-er, -est. 1.** Shrinking from dangerous or difficult circumstances; hesitant or fearful. **2.** Shrinking from public attention; shy. [Lat. *timidus* < *timēre,* to fear.] **—ti·mid′i·ty** (tə-mĭd′ĭ-tē), **tim′id·ness** *n.* **—tim′id·ly** *adv.*

tim·ing (tī′mĭng) *n.* The art or operation of regulating occurrence, pace, or coordination to achieve the most desirable effects, as in music, the theater, athletics, or in a machine.

ti·moc·ra·cy (tī-mŏk′rə-sē) *n., pl.* **-cies. 1.** A state described by Plato as being governed on principles of honor and military glory. **2.** An Aristotelian state in which civic honor or political power is proportional to the property one owns. [OFr. *tymocracie* < Med. Lat. *timocratia* < Gk. *timokratia* : *timē,* honor, value + *-kratia,* -cracy.] **—ti′mo·crat′ic** (tī′mə-krăt′ĭk) *adj.*

tim·or·ous (tĭm′ər-əs) *adj.* Full of apprehensiveness; timid. [ME *tymerous* < OFr. *timoureus* < Med. Lat. *timorosus* < Lat. *timor,* fear < *timēre,* to fear.] **—tim′or·ous·ly** *adv.* **—tim′or·ous·ness** *n.*

timothy

tim·o·thy (tĭm′ə-thē) *n.* A grass, *Phleum pratense,* native to Eurasia, having narrow, cylindrical flower spikes and widely cultivated for hay. [Prob. after *Timothy* Hanson, an 18th-cent. American farmer who reportedly took the grass from New York to the Carolinas.]

Tim·o·thy (tĭm′ə-thē) *n.* **1.** A Christian leader and legendary martyr of the 1st century A.D. **2.** See table at **Bible.**

tim·pa·ni also **tym·pa·ni** (tĭm′pə-nē) *pl.n.* A set of kettledrums. [Ital., pl. of *timpano,* kettledrum < Lat. *tympanum,* drum. —see TYMPANUM.] **—tim′pa·nist** *n.*

tim·pa·num (tĭm′pə-nəm) *n.* Variant of **tympanum.**

tin (tĭn) *n.* **1.** *Symbol* **Sn** A malleable, silvery metallic element obtained chiefly from cassiterite. It is used to coat other metals to prevent corrosion, and forms part of numerous alloys, such as soft solder, pewter, type metal, and bronze. Atomic number 50; atomic weight 118.69; melting point 231.89°C; boiling point 2,270°C; specific gravity 7.31; valences 2, 4. **2.** Tin plate. **3.** A tin container or box. **4.** *Chiefly Brit.* A container for preserved foodstuffs; can. —*tr.v.* **tinned, tin·ning, tins. 1.** To plate or coat with tin. **2.** *Chiefly Brit.* To preserve or pack in tins; can. [ME < OE.]

tin·a·mou (tĭn′ə-mōō′) *n.* Any of various chickenlike or quaillike birds of the family Tinamidae, of Central and South America. [Fr. < Galibi *tinamu*.]

George Miksch Sutton

tinamou

tin·cal (tĭng′kəl) *n.* Crude borax. [Malay *tingkal* < Skt. *ṭankanaḥ.*]
tin can *n.* **1.** A container of tin-plated sheet steel used esp. for preserving food. **2.** *Slang.* A destroyer (sense 2).
tinct (tĭngkt) *Archaic.* —*n.* A color or tint. —*adj.* Tinged. [Lat. *tinctus,* a dyeing < p.part. of *tingere,* to dye.]
tinc·to·ri·al (tĭngk-tôr′ē-əl, -tōr′-) *adj.* Pertaining to the processes of dyeing or coloring. [Lat. *tinctorius* < *tingere,* to dye.] **—tinc·to′ri·al·ly** *adv.*
tinc·ture (tĭngk′chər) *n.* **1.** A dyeing substance; pigment. **2.** An imparted color; stain; tint. **3.** A quality that colors, pervades, or distinguishes. **4.** A trace; vestige. **5.** A component of a substance extracted by means of a solvent. **6.** An alcohol solution of a nonvolatile medicine: *tincture of iodine.* **7.** A heraldic metal, color, or fur. —*tr.v.* **-tured, -tur·ing, -tures. 1.** To stain or tint with a color. **2.** To infuse, as with a quality; impregnate. [ME < Lat. *tinctura,* a dyeing < *tingere,* to dye.]
tin·der (tĭn′dər) *n.* Readily combustible material, such as dry twigs, used to kindle fires. [ME < OE *tynder.*]
tin·der·box (tĭn′dər-bŏks′) *n.* **1.** A metal box for holding tinder. **2.** A potentially explosive place or situation.
tine (tīn) *n.* **1.** A branch of a deer's antlers. **2.** A prong on an implement, as a fork or a pitchfork. [ME *tyne* < OE *tind.*]
tin·e·a (tĭn′ē-ə) *n.* Any of several fungous skin diseases, such as ringworm. [Lat., a gnawing worm.] **—tin′e·al** *adj.*
tinea cap·i·tis (kăp′ĭ-tĭs) *n.* A fungous infection of the scalp. [NLat., worm of the head.]
tin ear *n.* **1.** A cauliflower ear. **2.** An insensitive ear: *has a tin ear for music.*
tin·foil also **tin foil** (tĭn′foil′) *n.* A thin, pliable sheet of aluminum or of tin-lead alloy, used as a protective wrapping.
ting (tĭng) *n.* A single light metallic sound, as of a small bell. —*intr.v.* **tinged** (tĭngd), **ting·ing, tings.** To give forth a light metallic sound. [ME *tyngen,* to cause to ring.]
tinge (tĭnj) *tr.v.* **tinged** (tĭnjd), **tinge·ing** or **ting·ing, ting·es. 1.** To apply a trace of color to; tint. **2.** To affect slightly, as with a contrasting quality: *comedy tinged with tragedy.* —*n.* **1.** A faint trace of a color incorporated or added. **2.** A slight admixture. [ME *tyngen* < Lat. *tingere.*]
tin·gle (tĭng′gəl) *v.* **-gled, -gling, -gles.** —*intr.* **1.** To have a prickling, stinging sensation, as from cold, a sharp slap, or excitement: *tingle all over with joy.* **2.** To cause a prickling, stinging sensation or feeling. —*tr.* To cause to tingle. —*n.* A prickly or stinging sensation. [ME *tinglen.*] **—tin′gler** *n.* **—tin′gly** *adj.*
tin·horn (tĭn′hôrn′) *n. Slang.* A petty braggart, esp. a gambler, who pretends to be wealthier than he is.
tin·ker (tĭng′kər) *n.* **1.** A traveling mender of metal household utensils. **2.** A person who enjoys repairing and experimenting with machine parts. **3.** A person who is clumsy at his work; bungler. —*v.* **-kered, -ker·ing, -kers.** —*intr.* **1.** To work as a tinker. **2.** To play with machine parts experimentally. —*tr.* To mend as a tinker. [ME *tinkere.*]
tinker's damn also **tinker's dam** *n. Slang.* Something of the smallest value: *not worth a tinker's damn.* [Prob. from the cursing attributed to tinkers.]
Tin·ker·toy (tĭng′kər-toi′). A trademark for a construction toy consisting of pieces that fit together.
tin·kle (tĭng′kəl) *v.* **-kled, -kling, -kles.** —*intr.* To make light metallic sounds, such as those of a small bell. —*tr.* **1.** To cause to tinkle. **2.** To signal or call by tinkling. —*n.* **1.** A light, clear metallic sound or a sound suggestive of it. **2.** The act of tinkling. [ME *tynclen,* freq. of *tynken,* to emit a brief metallic sound.] **—tin′kly** *adj.*
tin lizzie (lĭz′ē) *n. Slang.* A dilapidated or cheap car. [< *Lizzie,* a nickname for Elizabeth.]
tin·ner (tĭn′ər) *n.* **1.** A tin miner. **2.** A person who makes or deals in tinware; tinsmith.
tin·ni·tus (tĭn′ĭ-təs) *n.* A sound in the ears, such as buzzing, ringing, or whistling, caused by a defect in the auditory nerve. [Lat. < p.part. of *tinnire,* to ring.]
tin·ny (tĭn′ē) *adj.* **-ni·er, -ni·est. 1.** Of, containing, or yielding tin. **2.** Shiny and attractive but cheap. **3.** Having a thin metallic sound. **4.** Tasting or smelling of tin, as food from a tin can. **—tin′ni·ly** *adv.* **—tin′ni·ness** *n.*
Tin Pan Alley also **tin-pan alley** (tĭn′păn′) *n.* **1.** A district associated with musicians, composers, and publishers of popular music. **2.** The publishers and composers of popular music as a group. [From the use of *tin pans* for drums.]
tin plate *n.* Thin sheet iron or steel coated with tin.
tin-plate (tĭn′plāt′) *tr.v.* **-plat·ed, -plat·ing, -plates.** To coat with tin. **—tin′-plat′er** *n.*
tin pyrites *n.* Stannite.
tin·sel (tĭn′səl) *n.* **1.** Very thin sheets, strips, or threads of a glittering material used as a decoration. **2.** Something superficially sparkling or showy but basically valueless. —*adj.* **1.** Made of or decorated with tinsel. **2.** Gaudy and showy but basically valueless. —*tr.v.* **-seled, -sel·ing, -sels** or **-selled, -sel·ling, -sels. 1.** To decorate with or as if with tinsel. **2.** To give a false sparkle to. [< OFr. *estincele,* adorned with metallic thread < *estinceler,* to sparkle < *estencele,* spark. —see STENCIL.]
tin·smith (tĭn′smĭth′) *n.* One who makes and repairs things made of light metal, such as tin.
tin·stone (tĭn′stōn′) *n.* Cassiterite.

tippet

tint (tĭnt) *n.* **1.** A shade of a color, esp. a pale or delicate variation; tinge. **2.** A gradation of a color made by adding white to it to lessen its saturation. **3.** A slight coloration; hue. **4.** A barely detectable degree; trace. **5.** In engraving, a shaded effect produced by hatching. **6.** *Printing.* A panel of color on which matter in another color, as an illustration, may be printed. **7.** A dye for the hair. —*v.* **tint·ed, tint·ing, tints.** —*tr.* To give a tint to; color. —*intr.* To take on a tint. [Alteration of TINCT.]
tin·tin·nab·u·la (tĭn′tĭ-năb′yə-lə) *n.* Plural of **tintinnabulum.**
tin·tin·nab·u·lar (tĭn′tĭ-năb′yə-lər) also **tin·tin·nab·u·lar·y** (-lĕr′ē) or **tin·tin·nab·u·lous** (-ləs) *adj.* Of or relating to bells or the ringing of bells. [< TINTINNABULUM.]
tin·tin·nab·u·la·tion (tĭn′tĭ-năb′yə-lā′shən) *n.* The ringing or sounding of bells. [< TINTINNABULUM.]
tin·tin·nab·u·lum (tĭn′tĭ-năb′yə-ləm) *n., pl.* **-la** (-lə). A small, tinkling bell. [Lat. < *tintinnare,* to jingle, redup. of *tinnire,* to ring.]
tin·type (tĭn′tīp′) *n.* A ferrotype (sense 1).
tin·work (tĭn′wûrk′) *n.* **1.** Work in tin. **2. tinworks** *(used with a sing. or pl. verb).* A place where tin is smelted and rolled.
ti·ny (tī′nē) *adj.* **-ni·er, -ni·est.** Extremely small; minute. [Alteration of ME *tine.*] **—ti′ni·ness** *n.*
-tion *suff.* Action; process: *adsorption.* [ME *-cioun* < OFr. *-tion* < Lat. *-tio.*]
tip¹ (tĭp) *n.* **1.** The end or extremity of something, esp. of something pointed or projecting. **2.** A piece or attachment, as a cap or ferrule, meant to be fitted to the end of something. —*tr.v.* **tipped, tip·ping, tips. 1.** To furnish with a tip. **2.** To cover, decorate, or remove the tip of. **3.** To attach (an insert) in a book by gluing along the binding edge. **4.** To dye strands or ends of hair, as of furs, in order to blend or improve appearance. **—*idiom.* tip of the iceberg.** The most obvious or superficial manifestation or evidence. [ME.]
tip² (tĭp) *v.* **tipped, tip·ping, tips.** —*tr.* **1.** To knock over or upset; topple. **2.** To move to a slanting position; tilt. **3.** To touch or raise (one's hat) in greeting. —*intr.* **1.** To topple over; overturn. **2.** To become tilted; slant. **3.** *Chiefly Brit.* To empty by overturning; dump. —*n.* **1.** A tilt or slant; an incline. **2.** *Chiefly Brit.* An area or place for dumping something, as rubbish or refuse from a mine. [ME *tipen.*]
tip³ (tĭp) *tr.v.* **tipped, tip·ping, tips. 1.** To strike gently; tap. **2.** *Baseball.* To hit (the ball) with the side of the bat so that it glances off. —*n.* A light blow; tap. [ME *tippen.*]
tip⁴ (tĭp) *n.* **1.** A small sum of money given as an acknowledgment of services rendered; gratuity. **2. a.** Advance or inside information given as a guide to action. **b.** A helpful hint. —*v.* **tipped, tip·ping, tips.** —*tr.* **1.** To give a tip or gratuity to. **2.** To provide advance or inside information to. —*intr.* To give a tip or tips. **—*idiom.* tip (one's) hand.** To reveal one's resources or intentions. [< slang *tip,* to give.] **—tip′per** *n.*
tip·cart (tĭp′kärt′) *n.* A cart having a body that can be tilted to facilitate unloading.
ti·pi (tē′pē) *n.* Variant of **tepee.**
tip-off (tĭp′ôf′, -ŏf′) *n. Informal.* **1.** An item of advance or inside information; a hint or warning. **2.** The act or practice of beginning a basketball game or overtime period with a jump ball.
tip·pet (tĭp′ĭt) *n.* **1.** A covering for the shoulders, as of fur, with long ends that hang in front. **2.** A long stole worn by members of the Anglican clergy. **3.** A long hanging part, as of a sleeve, hood, or cape. [ME *tipet.*]
tip·ple¹ (tĭp′əl) *v.* **-pled, -pling, -ples.** —*intr.* To drink alcoholic liquor, esp. habitually or to excess. —*tr.* To drink (alcoholic liquor), esp. habitually. —*n.* Alcoholic liquor. [Back-formation < obs. *tippler,* drunkard < ME *tipeler,* bartender.] **—tip′pler** *n.*
tip·ple² (tĭp′əl) *n.* An apparatus for unloading freight cars by tipping them, or the place where this is done. [< dial. *tipple,* to overturn, freq. of TIP².]
tip·staff (tĭp′stăf′) *n., pl.* **-staves** (-stāvz′, -stăvz′) or **-staffs. 1.** A staff with a metal tip, carried as a sign of office. **2.** An officer who carries a tipstaff, as a bailiff or constable. [Alteration of *tipped staff.*]
tip·ster (tĭp′stər) *n. Informal.* A person who sells tips or information, as to bettors or speculators.
tip·sy (tĭp′sē) *adj.* **-si·er, -si·est. 1.** Slightly drunk. **2.** Likely to tip over; unsteady; crooked. [< TIP².] **—tip′si·ly** *adv.* **—tip′si·ness** *n.*
tip·toe (tĭp′tō′) *intr.v.* **-toed, -toe·ing, -toes.** To walk or move on or as if on the tips of one's toes; walk stealthily or quietly. —*n.* The tip of a toe. —*adj.* **1.** Standing or walking on or as if on the tips of one's toes. **2.** Stealthy; wary. —*adv.* On or as if on tiptoe. **—*idiom.* on tiptoe.** Full of anticipation; eager.
tip·top (tĭp′tŏp′) *n.* **1.** The highest point or summit. **2.** The highest degree of quality or excellence. —*adj.* Excellent; first-rate. —*adv.* At the highest point of excellence.
ti·rade (tī′răd′, tĭ-răd′) *n.* A long angry or violent speech, usually of a censorious or denunciatory nature; diatribe. [Fr. < OItal. *tirata,* volley < p.part. of *tirare,* to draw.]
tire¹ (tīr) *v.* **tired, tir·ing, tires.** —*intr.* **1.** To grow weary or fatigued. **2.** To grow bored or impatient; lose interest: *He tired of reading.* —*tr.* **1.** To make weary; fatigue. **2.** To ex-

haust the interest or patience of; bore. ***—phrasal verb.*** **tire out.** To fatigue or exhaust. [ME *tyren* < OE *tyrian.*]

tire[2] (tīr) *n.* **1.** A covering for a wheel, usually made of rubber reinforced with cords of nylon, fiber glass, or other material, and filled with compressed air. **2.** A hoop of metal or rubber fitted around a wheel. [ME *tyre,* curved metal plates for wheels, prob. < *tyr,* attire.]

tire[3] (tīr) *Archaic.* —*tr.v.* **tired, tir·ing, tires.** To adorn or attire. —*n.* **1.** Attire. **2.** A headband or headdress. [ME *tiren,* short for *attiren,* to attire. —see ATTIRE.]

tired (tīrd) *adj.* **1. a.** Worn-out; fatigued. **b.** Impatient; bored. **2.** Overused; hackneyed: *a tired joke..* **—tired'ly** *adv.* **—tired'ness** *n.*

Synonyms: *tired, weary, exhausted, fatigued, jaded, bushed.* These adjectives apply to conditions in which physical strength or strength of spirit is depleted, usually as the result of exertion or tribulation. *Tired* is the general, nonspecific term. *Weary,* like *tired,* is applicable to deficiency of strength or spirit, but often carries a stronger implication of discontent resulting from what is burdensome, irksome, boring, or the like. *Exhausted* and *fatigued* are much stronger terms. *Exhausted* specifies complete or nearly complete expenditure of physical strength. *Fatigued* implies great, though not necessarily complete, expenditure of physical or mental power. *Jaded* refers largely to dullness of spirit, often resulting from overindulgence. *Bushed* informally suggests temporary deficiency of strength resulting usually from physical exertion.

tire·less (tīr'lĭs) *adj.* Untiring; indefatigable. **—tire'less·ly** *adv.* **—tire'less·ness** *n.*

tire·some (tīr'səm) *adj.* Causing fatigue or boredom; wearisome; tedious. **—tire'some·ly** *adv.* **—tire'some·ness** *n.*

tire·wom·an (tīr'wo͝om'ən) *n.* **1.** A dressing assistant, as in a theater. **2.** *Archaic.* A lady's maid.

ti·ro (tī'rō) *n.* Variant of **tyro.**

'tis (tĭz). *Archaic.* It is.

ti·sane (tĭ-zăn', -zän') *n.* A herbal infusion or similar preparation drunk as a beverage or for its mildly medicinal effect. [ME *tysan* < OFr. *tisane* < Lat. *ptisana.* —see PTISAN.]

Tish·ri (tĭsh'rē) *n.* The first month of the civil year in the Hebrew calendar. See table at **calendar.** [Heb. *Tishrī* < Akkadian *Tashrītu* < *shurru,* to begin.]

Ti·siph·o·ne (tĭ-sĭf'ə-nē) *n. Gk. Myth.* One of the three Furies. [Lat. < Gk. *Tisiphonē.*]

tis·sue (tĭsh'o͞o) *n.* **1.** *Biol.* **a.** An aggregation of morphologically and functionally similar cells. **b.** Cellular matter regarded as a collective entity. **2.** A soft, absorbent piece of paper, generally made up of two thin layers and used as a disposable handkerchief or towel. **3.** Also **tissue paper.** Thin, translucent paper used for packing, wrapping, or protecting delicate articles. **4.** A fine sheer cloth, such as gauze. **5.** An interwoven or interrelated number of things; web; network: *"The text is a tissue of mocking echoes"* (Richard Kain). [ME *tyssu,* a rich kind of cloth < OFr. *tissu* < p.part. of *tistre,* to weave < Lat. *texere.*] **—tis'su·lar** *adj.*

tissue culture *n.* The in vitro preparation and growth of tissue cells in culture media.

tit[1] (tĭt) *n.* **1.** Any of various small Old World birds of the family Paridae, related to and resembling the New World chickadees. **2.** Any of various birds, similar or related to the tit. [Short for TITMOUSE.]

tit[2] (tĭt) *n.* **1.** A teat. **2.** *Vulgar.* A breast. [ME *titte* < OE *tit.*]

Ti·tan (tĭt'n) *n.* **1.** *Gk. Myth.* One of a family of giants, the children of Uranus and Gaea, who sought to rule heaven and were overthrown and supplanted by the family of Zeus. **2. titan.** A person of colossal size, strength, or achievement: *a titan of American industry.* **3.** *Astron.* The largest satellite of Saturn. [Gk.]

ti·tan·ate (tĭt'n-āt') *n.* A salt of titanic acid.

Ti·tan·ess (tĭt'n-ĭs) *n. Gk. Myth.* A female Titan.

Ti·ta·ni·a (tĭ-tā'nē-ə, -tān'yə, tī-) *n.* In medieval folklore, the queen of the fairies and wife of Oberon.

ti·tan·ic[1] (tī-tăn'ĭk) *adj.* **1. a.** Having great stature or enormous strength; huge; colossal. **b.** Of enormous scope, power, or influence. **2. Titanic.** Of or pertaining to the Titans. **—ti·tan'i·cal·ly** *adv.*

ti·tan·ic[2] (tī-tăn'ĭk, -tā'nĭk, tĭ-) *adj.* Pertaining to or containing titanium, esp. with valence 4.

titanic acid *n.* **1.** A white, powdered inorganic acid, H_2TiO_3, derived from an acid solution of titanates and used as a mordant. **2.** Titanium dioxide.

ti·tan·if·er·ous (tĭt'n-ĭf'ər-əs) *adj.* Containing or yielding titanium.

Ti·tan·ism (tĭt'n-ĭz'əm) *n.* The spirit of rebellion; defiance of and revolt against the established order or authority.

ti·tan·ite (tĭt'n-īt') *n. Mineral.* Sphene. [G. *Titanit.*]

ti·ta·ni·um (tī-tā'nē-əm, tĭ-) *n. Symbol* **Ti** A strong, low-density, highly corrosion-resistant, lustrous white metallic element that occurs widely in igneous rocks and is used to alloy aircraft metals for low weight, strength, and high-temperature stability. Atomic number 22; atomic weight 47.90; melting point 1,675°C; boiling point 3,260°C; specific gravity 4.54; valences 2, 3, 4. [NLat. < Gk. *Titan,* Titan.]

titanium dioxide *n.* A white powder, TiO_2, used as an exceptionally opaque white pigment.

titanium white *n.* Titanium dioxide used as a paint pigment with great covering power and durability.

ti·tan·o·there (tī-tăn'ə-thîr') *n.* Any of various extinct herbivorous mammals of the genus *Brontotherium* and related genera, of the Eocene and Oligocene epochs, resembling the rhinoceros. [NLat. *Titanotherium* : Gk. *Titan,* Titan + Gk. *thērion,* little beast < *thēr,* beast.]

ti·tan·ous (tī-tăn'əs, -tā'nəs, tĭ-, tĭt'n-) *adj.* Pertaining to or containing titanium, esp. with valence 3.

tit·bit (tĭt'bĭt') *n.* Variant of **tidbit.**

ti·ter also **ti·tre** (tī'tər) *n.* **1.** The concentration of a substance in solution or the strength of such a substance determined by titration. **2.** The minimum volume needed to cause a particular result in titration. [Fr. < OFr., title.]

tit for tat *n.* Repayment in kind, as for an injury; retaliation. [Alteration of *tip for tap.*]

tithe (tīth) *n.* **1.** A tenth part of one's annual income, either in kind or money, contributed voluntarily for charitable purposes or due as a tax for the support of the clergy or church. **2.** A tax or assessment of one tenth. **3. a.** The tenth part of something. **b.** A very small part. —*v.* **tithed, tith·ing, tithes.** —*tr.* **1.** To contribute or pay a tenth part of (one's annual income). **2.** To levy a tithe upon. —*intr.* To pay a tithe. [ME < OE *tēoða.*] **—tith'a·ble** (tī'thə-bəl) *adj.* **—tith'er** (tī'thər) *n.*

tith·ing (tī'thĭng) *n.* **1.** The act of levying or paying tithes. **2.** A tithe. **3.** An administrative division consisting of ten householders in the old English system of frankpledge.

ti·ti[1] (tī'tī', tē'tē') *n.* Any of several New World shrubs of the genus *Cyrilla* and related genera, esp. *C. racemiflora,* of warm, swampy areas, having leathery leaves, clusters of white flowers, and yellow fruit. [Orig. unknown.]

ti·ti[2] (tē-tē') *n.* Any of various small, long-tailed South American monkeys of the genus *Callicebus.* [Sp., perh. of Tupian orig.]

ti·tian (tĭsh'ən) *n.* A brownish orange. [After *Titian* (1477–1576), from his frequent use of the color in his paintings.] **—ti'tian** *adj.*

tit·il·late (tĭt'l-āt') *tr.v.* **-lat·ed, -lat·ing, -lates. 1.** To stimulate by tickling or touching lightly. **2.** To excite agreeably. [Lat. *titillare, titillat-,* to tickle.] **—tit'il·lat'ing·ly** *adv.* **—tit'il·la'tion** *n.* **—tit'il·la'tive** *adj.*

tit·i·vate (tĭt'ə-vāt') *tr.v.* **-vat·ed, -vat·ing, -vates.** To make decorative additions to; spruce up. [Perh. TIDY + (CULTI)VATE.] **—tit'i·va'tion** *n.*

tit·lark (tĭt'lärk') *n.* The pipit. [TIT(MOUSE) + LARK.]

ti·tle (tīt'l) *n.* **1.** An identifying name given to a book, play, motion picture, musical composition, or work of art. **2.** A general or descriptive heading, as of a book chapter. **3. a.** Written matter included in a motion picture or television show to give credits. **b.** The subtitle in a motion picture. **4. a.** The heading that names a legal document or statute. **b.** The heading or caption of a legal document in a court proceeding. **5.** A division of a law book, declaration, or bill, generally larger than a section or article. **6.** *Law.* **a.** The coincidence of all the elements that constitute the fullest legal right to control and dispose of property or a claim. **b.** The aggregate evidence that gives rise to a legal right of possession or control. **c.** The evidence of such means. **d.** The instrument constituting this evidence, such as a deed. **7.** Anything that provides ground for or justifies a claim. **8.** A formal appellation attached to a person or family by virtue of office, rank, hereditary privilege, noble birth, attainment, or as a mark of respect. **9.** A descriptive appellation; epithet. **10.** *Sports.* A championship. **11.** *Eccles.* **a.** A source of income or area of work required of a candidate for ordination in the Church of England. **b.** A Roman Catholic church in or near Rome having a cardinal for its nominal head. —*tr.v.* **-tled, -tling, -tles.** To give a title to; confer a name upon. [ME < OFr. < Lat. *titulus.*]

George Miksch Sutton

tit[1]

ti·tled (tīt'ld) *adj.* Having a title, esp. of nobility.

ti·tle·hold·er (tīt'l-hōl'dər) *n.* One that holds a title, esp. for a championship.

title page *n.* A page at the front of a book giving the complete title, the names of the author and publisher, and the place of publication.

tit·mouse (tĭt'mous') *n., pl.* **-mice** (-mīs'). **1.** Any of several small North American birds of the genus *Parus,* having grayish plumage and a pointed crest. **2.** A tit[1] (sense 1). [By folk ety < ME *titmose* : *tit- (of Scand. orig.) + *mose,* titmouse < OE *māse,* a kind of bird.]

Ti·to·ism (tē'tō-ĭz'əm) *n.* The Communist policies and practices associated with the late Marshal Tito of Yugoslavia, esp. the assertion by a Communist state of its national interests independently of and often in opposition to Soviet policy.

ti·trant (tī'trənt) *n.* A substance, such as a solution, of known concentration used in titration.

ti·trate (tī'trāt') *v.* **-trat·ed, -trat·ing, -trates.** —*tr.* To determine the concentration of (a solution) by titration. —*intr.* To perform the operation of titration. [Fr. *titrer* < *titre,* titer.] **—ti'trat'a·ble** *adj.* **—ti'tra'tor** *n.*

ti·tra·tion (tī-trā'shən) *n.* The process or method of determining the concentration of a substance in solution by adding to it a standard reagent of known concentration in carefully measured amounts until a reaction of definite and known proportion is completed, as shown by a color change or by electrical measurement, and then calculating the unknown concentration.

ti·tre (tī′tər) *n.* Variant of **titer.**

ti·tri·met·ric (tī′trə-mĕt′rĭk) *adj.* Utilizing the process of titration. [TITR(ATION) + -METRIC.] **—ti′tri·met′ri·cal·ly** *adv.*

tit·ter (tĭt′ər) *intr.v.* **-tered, -ter·ing, -ters.** To utter a restrained, nervous giggle. *—n.* A nervous giggle. [Imit.] **—tit′ter·er** *n.* **—tit′ter·ing·ly** *adv.*

tit·tle (tĭt′l) *n.* **1.** A small diacritical mark, such as an accent, vowel mark, or dot over an *i.* **2.** The tiniest bit; iota. [ME *titel* < Med. Lat. *titulus* < Lat., title.]

tit·tle-tat·tle (tĭt′l-tăt′l) *n.* Petty gossip; trivial talk. *—intr.v.* **-tled, -tling, -tles.** To talk idly or foolishly; gossip. [Redup. of TATTLE.]

tit·tup (tĭt′əp) *intr.v.* **-tuped, -tup·ing, -tups** or **-tupped, -tup·ping, -tups.** To move in a lively, capering manner; prance. *—n.* A lively, capering manner of moving or walking; prance. [Imit. of the sound of a horse's hoofs.]

tit·u·ba·tion (tĭch′ə-bā′shən) *n.* A staggering or stumbling gait characteristic of certain nervous disorders. [Lat. *titubatio,* a staggering < *titubare,* to stagger.]

tit·u·lar (tĭch′ə-lər) *adj.* **1.** Pertaining to, having the nature of, or constituting a title. **2.** Existing as such in name only; nominal: *the titular head of the company.* **3. a.** Bearing a title. **b.** Related to or arising from a title, as honors. **4.** Derived from a title: *the titular role in a play.* **5.** Of or designating one of the ancient churches in or near Rome from which a cardinal takes his title. *—n.* Also **tit·u·lar·y** (tĭch′ə-lĕr′ē) *pl.* **-ies.** A person who holds a title. [< Lat. *titulus,* title.] **—tit′u·lar·ly** *adv.*

Ti·tus (tī′təs) *n.* **1.** An early Christian missionary and disciple of Paul. **2.** See table at **Bible.**

Ti·u (tē′o͞o) *n. Myth.* The Germanic god of war and the sky, identified with the Norse god Tyr. [OE *Tīw.*]

tiz·zy (tĭz′ē) *n., pl.* **-zies.** *Slang.* A state of nervous confusion; a dither. [Orig. unknown.]

Tl The symbol for the element thallium.

Tlin·git (tlĭng′gĭt, tlĭng′ĭt) *n., pl.* **Tlingit** or **-gits. 1.** A group of North American Indian seafaring tribes inhabiting the coastal areas of southern Alaska and northern British Columbia. **2.** A member of any of the Tlingit tribes. **3.** A language family of the Na-dene phylum consisting only of the language of the Tlingit.

T lymphocyte *n.* T cell.

Tm The symbol for the element thulium.

tme·sis (tmē′sĭs, mē′-) *n.* The separation of the parts of a compound word by one or more intervening words; for example, *where I go ever* instead of *wherever I go.* [LLat. < Gk. *tmēsis,* a cutting < *temnein,* to cut.]

TNT (tē′ĕn-tē′) *n.* Trinitrotoluene. [T(RI)N(ITRO)T(OLUENE).]

to (to͞o; tə *when unstressed*) *prep.* **1.** In a direction toward: *went to the city; turned to me and spoke; going back to our original plan.* **2. a.** Reaching as far as: *cut to the bone; rotten to the core.* **b.** To the extent or degree of: *starved to death; defended the city to the last man.* **c.** With the resultant condition of: *torn to shreds.* **3.** Toward a given state: *the Nazi rise to power.* **4.** In contact with; against: *their faces pressed to the windows.* **5.** In front of: *stood face to face.* **6.** Used to indicate possession: *Do you have the belt to this dress?* **7.** Concerning; regarding: *deaf to my pleas.* **8.** In a particular relationship with: *parallel to the road.* **9.** As an accompaniment or complement of: *danced to the tune; played Romeo to her Juliet.* **10.** In respect of: *the secret to her success.* **11.** Composing; constituting: *two cups to a pint.* **12.** In accord with: *not to his liking; to the best of my recollection.* **13.** As compared with: *a score of two to one; a book superior to his others.* **14. a.** Before: *The time is ten to five.* **b.** Until; up till: *worked from nine to five.* **15. a.** For the purpose of: *came to my aid; went out to lunch.* **b.** In honor of: *a toast to the queen.* **16.** Used before a verb to indicate the infinitive: *I'd like to go.* Also used alone when the infinitive is understood: *Go if you want to.* **17. a.** Used to indicate the relationship of a verb with its complement: *refer to a dictionary; refer me to a dictionary.* **b.** Used with a reflexive pronoun to indicate exclusivity or separateness: *had the plane all to ourselves.* *—adv.* **1.** In a direction toward: *ran to and fro.* **2.** Into a shut or closed position: *pushed the door to.* **3.** Into a state of consciousness: *The nurses brought the patient to.* **4.** Into a state of action or attentiveness: *sat down for lunch and fell to.* **5.** *Naut.* Into the wind. Used of a sailing vessel. [ME < OE *tō.*]

toad

toby
Toby mug

toad (tōd) *n.* **1.** Any of numerous tailless amphibians chiefly of the family Bufonidae, related to and resembling the frogs but characteristically more terrestrial and having rougher, drier skin. **2.** The horned toad. **3.** A repulsive person. [ME *tode* < OE *tādige.*]

toad·eat·er (tōd′ē′tər) *n.* A toady.

toad·fish (tōd′fĭsh′) *n., pl.* **toadfish** or **-fish·es.** Any of various bottom-dwelling, chiefly marine fishes of the family Batrachoididae, having a broad, flattened head and a wide mouth.

toad·flax (tōd′flăks′) *n.* Any of various plants of the genus *Linaria,* having narrow leaves and spurred, two-lipped flowers, esp. the common wildflower butter-and-eggs.

toad·stone (tōd′stōn′) *n.* A stone formerly believed to be formed in the body of a toad and worn as a charm.

toad·stool (tōd′sto͞ol′) *n.* An inedible fungus with an umbrella-shaped fruiting body, as distinguished from an edible mushroom. [ME *tadestole.*]

toad·y (tō′dē) *n., pl.* **-ies.** A person who obsequiously flatters or defers to others for the sake of personal gain; sycophant. *—v.* **-ied, -y·ing, -ies.** *—tr.* To be a toady to. *—intr.* To be or behave like a toady. [< TOADEATER.]

to and fro *adv.* Back and forth. **—to′-and-fro′** (to͞o′ən-frō′) *adj. & n.*

toast¹ (tōst) *v.* **toast·ed, toast·ing, toasts.** *—tr.* **1.** To heat and brown (bread, for example) by placing close to a fire or in a toaster. **2.** To warm thoroughly, as before a fire: *toast one's feet.* *—intr.* To become toasted. *—n.* Sliced bread heated and browned. [ME *tosten* < OFr. *toster* < Lat. *torrēre,* to bake.]

toast² (tōst) *n.* **1.** The act of drinking in honor of or to the health of a person or thing. **2.** The person or thing honored by a toast. **3.** A person receiving much attention or acclaim: *the toast of Broadway.* *—v.* **toast·ed, toast·ing, toasts.** *—tr.* To drink to the health or honor of. *—intr.* To propose or drink a toast. [< TOAST¹ (from the use of spiced toast to flavor drinks).]

toast·er (tō′stər) *n.* A device used to toast bread, esp. by exposure to electrically heated wire coils.

toast·mas·ter (tōst′măs′tər) *n.* One who proposes the toasts and introduces the speakers at a banquet.

toast·mis·tress (tōst′mĭs′trĭs) *n.* A woman who serves as a toastmaster.

toast·y (tō′stē) *adj.* **-i·er, -i·est.** Pleasantly warm: *her feet all toasty in fur slippers.*

to·bac·co (tə-băk′ō) *n., pl.* **-cos** or **-coes. 1.** Any of various plants of the genus *Nicotiana,* esp. *N. tabacum,* native to tropical America, and widely cultivated for its leaves, which are used primarily for smoking. **2.** The leaves of cultivated tobacco, dried and processed chiefly for use in cigarettes, snuff, or cigars or for smoking in pipes. **3.** Products made from tobacco. **4.** The habit of smoking tobacco: *I gave up tobacco.* **5.** A crop of tobacco. [Sp. *tabaco,* of Caribbean orig.]

tobacco mosaic *n.* Any of several viral diseases of tobacco and nightshade characterized by mottled leaves.

to·bac·co·nist (tə-băk′ə-nĭst) *n.* A dealer in tobacco.

to-be (to͞o-bē′) *adj.* That is to be; future: *a graduate-to-be.*

To·bit (tō′bĭt) *n.* **1.** A Hebrew captive in Nineveh. **2.** See table at **Bible.** [Gk. *Tōbit* < Heb. *Tobhiyyāh* : *ṭōbh,* good + *yāh,* God.]

to·bog·gan (tə-bŏg′ən) *n.* A long, narrow, runnerless sled constructed of thin boards curled upward at the front. *—intr.v.* **-ganed, -gan·ing, -gans. 1.** To coast, ride, or travel on a toboggan. **2.** To decline or fall rapidly: *His good fortune tobogganed.* [Canadian Fr. *tobagan* < Micmac *tobākan.*] **—to·bog′gan·er, to·bog′gan·ist** *n.*

to·by also **To·by** (tō′bē) *n., pl.* **-bies.** A drinking mug usually in the shape of a stout man wearing a large three-cornered hat. [After *Toby,* a nickname for *Tobias.*]

toc·ca·ta (tə-kä′tə) *n.* A musical composition, usually for the organ or another keyboard instrument, in free style with elaborate runs and harmonies. [Ital. < fem. p.part. of *toccare,* to touch.]

To·char·i·an also **To·khar·i·an** (tō-kâr′ē-ən, -kär′-, -kăr′-) *n.* **1.** A member of a people of possible European origin, with an advanced culture, living in Asia until about the 10th century **2.** An Indo-European language of central Asia attested in documents of the 7th century. [Lat. *Tochari* < Gk. *Tokharoi.*]

to·col·o·gy also **to·kol·o·gy** (tō-kŏl′ə-jē) *n.* The practice of obstetrics or midwifery. [Gk. *tokos,* childbirth (< *tiktein,* to beget) + -LOGY.]

to·coph·er·ol (tō-kŏf′ə-rôl′, -rōl′) *n.* Any of a group of four chemically related compounds, differing slightly in structure, that together constitute vitamin E. [Gk. *tokos,* offspring (< *tiktein,* to beget) + Gk. *pherein,* to carry + -OL.]

toc·sin (tŏk′sĭn) *n.* **1.** An alarm sounded on a bell. **2.** A warning; omen. [OFr. *toquassen* < OProv. *tocasenh* : *tocar,* to strike + *senh,* bell < Lat. *signum,* sign.]

tod (tŏd) *n. Chiefly Brit.* **1.** A unit of weight used esp. for wool, equivalent to about 28 pounds. **2.** A bushy clump, as of ivy. [ME.]

to·day also **to-day** (tə-dā′) *—adv.* **1.** During or on the present day. **2.** During or at the present time. *—n.* The present day, time, or age. ***—modifier:*** *the today generation.* [ME < OE *tō dæg.*]

tod·dle (tŏd′l) *intr.v.* **-dled, -dling, -dles.** To walk with short, unsteady steps, as a small child. *—n.* A slow, unsteady gait. [Orig. unknown.]

tod·dler (tŏd′lər) *n.* **1.** A child who has learned to walk but not yet perfectly. **2.** A size of clothing for children between the ages of about one and three years.

tod·dy (tŏd′ē) *n., pl.* **-dies. 1.** A drink consisting of brandy or other liquor mixed with hot water, sugar, and spices. **2. a.** The sweet sap of several tropical Asian palm trees, esp. *Caryota urens,* used as a beverage. **b.** A liquor fermented from this sap. [Hindi *tāṛī,* sap of palm < *tāṛ,* palm < Skt. *tālaḥ.*]

to-do (tə-do͞o′) *n., pl.* **-dos** (-do͞oz′). *Informal.* Commotion or bustle; stir; fuss.

to·dy (tō′dē) *n., pl.* **-dies.** Any of various small, colorful birds of the family Todidae, of the West Indies. [Fr. *todier* < Lat. *todus,* a kind of small bird.]

toe (tō) *n.* **1.** One of the digits of the foot, esp. of a vertebrate animal. **2.** The part of a sock, shoe, or boot that covers the toes. **3. a.** The base or lower tip of something, as the end of the head on a golf club. **b.** Anything that resembles a toe in form, function, or location. —*v.* **toed, toe·ing, toes.** —*tr.* **1.** To touch, kick, or reach with the toe. **2.** To drive (a golf ball) with the toe of the club. **3. a.** To drive (a nail or spike) at an oblique angle. **b.** To fasten or secure with nails or spikes driven obliquely. —*intr.* To walk or move with the toes pointed in a specified direction: *He toes out.* —***idioms.*** **on (one's) toes.** Ready to act; alert. **step on (someone's) toes.** To hurt, offend, or encroach upon the feelings, actions, or province of (another). **toe the mark (**or **line). 1.** To touch a mark or line with the toe or hands in readiness for the start of a race or competition. **2.** To obey rules conscientiously; conform. [ME < OE *tā.*]

toe·a (toi′ə) *n., pl.* **toea.** See table at **currency.** [Prob. Pidgin English < E. DOLLAR.]

toe·cap (tō′kăp′) *n.* A reinforced covering of leather or metal for the toe of a shoe or boot.

toed (tōd) *adj.* **1.** Having a specified number or kind of toes: *a two-toed sloth.* **2. a.** Driven obliquely: *a toed nail.* **b.** Secured by obliquely driven nails: *a toed beam.*

toe dance *n.* A dance that is performed on the toes. —**toe dancer** *n.*

toe·hold (tō′hōld′) *n.* **1.** A small indentation or ledge on which the toe can find support in climbing. **2.** A slight or initial advantage useful for future progress: *Family connections gave him a toehold in politics.* **3.** A wrestling hold in which one competitor wrenches the other's foot.

toe·nail (tō′nāl′) *n.* **1.** The nail on a toe. **2.** A nail driven obliquely, as to join vertical and horizontal beams. —*tr.v.* **-nailed, -nail·ing, -nails.** To secure (beams) with obliquely driven nails.

toff (tŏf) *n. Chief Brit.* A dandy. [Prob. var. of TUFT, a gold tassel worn by titled students at Oxford and Cambridge.]

tof·fee (tŏf′ē, tô′fē) *n.* A hard or chewy candy of brown sugar and butter. [Alteration of TAFFY.]

toft (tôft, tŏft) *n. Chiefly Brit.* **1.** A homestead. **2.** A hillock. [ME < OE < ON *topt.*]

to·fu (tō′fo͞o) *n.* Bean curd. [J. *tōfu.*]

tog (tŏg, tôg) *Informal.* —*n.* **1.** A coat or cloak. **2. togs.** Clothes: *gardening togs.* —*tr.v.* **togged, tog·ging, togs.** To dress or clothe: *togged himself out in cowboy boots.* [Obs. *togeman* < Fr. *toge,* cloak < Lat. *toga,* garment.]

to·ga (tō′gə) *n.* **1.** A loose one-piece outer garment worn in public by citizens of ancient Rome. **2.** A loose robe or gown characteristic of a profession. [Lat. < *tegere,* to cover.] —**to′gaed** (tō′gəd) *adj.*

toga vi·ri·lis (və-rē′lĭs, -rĭl′ĭs) *n.* A white toga symbolizing manhood that boys of ancient Rome were allowed to wear at age 15. [Lat., toga of a man.]

to·geth·er (tə-gĕth′ər) *adv.* **1.** In or into a single group, mass, or place: *We gather together.* **2.** Against or in relationship to one another; mutually or reciprocally: *getting along together.* **3.** Regarded collectively; in total: *She is worth more than all of us together.* **4.** Simultaneously: *The bells rang out together.* **5.** In harmony or accord: *We stand together on this issue.* **6.** *Informal.* In an effective, coherent condition: *Get yourself together.* —*adj. Slang.* **1.** In tune with what is going on; hip. **2.** Unified and performing effectively. —***idiom.*** **get (**or **put) it (all) together.** *Slang.* To unify and harmonize one's resources so as to perform with top effectiveness. [ME < OE *tōgædere.*] —**to·geth′er·ness** *n.*

Usage: *Together with,* like *in addition to,* is often employed following the subject of a sentence or clause to introduce an addition. The addition, however, does not alter the number of the verb, which is governed by the subject: *The king* (singular), *together with two aides, is expected in an hour.* The same is true of *along with, as well as, besides, in addition to,* and *like: Common sense as well as training is a requisite for a good job.* See also Usage note at **altogether.**

tog·ger·y (tŏg′ə-rē, tô′gə-) *n., pl.* **-ies.** *Informal.* **1.** Clothing; togs. **2.** A clothing store.

tog·gle (tŏg′əl) *n.* **1.** A pin, rod, or crosspiece fitted or inserted into a loop in a rope, chain, or strap to prevent slipping, to tighten, or to hold an attached object. **2.** An ornamental crosspiece or button of wood, bone, or other material inserted into a loop of rope or other material as a closure or fastening, as on sports clothes. **3.** A device or apparatus with a toggle joint. —*tr.v.* **-gled, -gling, -gles.** To furnish or fasten with a toggle. [Orig. unknown.]

toggle bolt *n.* A fastener consisting of a threaded bolt and a mated toggle.

toggle joint *n.* An elbowlike joint consisting of two arms pivoted together so that force applied to the pivot point to straighten the joint produces a corresponding outward force at the ends of each arm.

toggle switch *n.* A switch in which a projecting lever employing a toggle joint with a spring is used to open or close an electric circuit.

togue (tōg) *n.* The lake trout. [Canadian Fr.]

toil¹ (toil) *intr.v.* **toiled, toil·ing, toils. 1.** To labor continuously and untiringly. **2.** To proceed with difficulty: *toiling over the mountains.* —*n.* **1.** Exhausting labor or effort. **2.** *Obs.* Strife; contention. [ME *toilen* < AN *toiler,* to strive < OFr. *toillier,* to stir up < Lat. *tudiclare,* to stir about < *tudicula,* a machine for bruising olives < *tudes,* hammer.]

toil² (toil) *n.* **1.** Often **toils.** Something that binds, snares, or entangles one; entrapment: *in the toils of despair.* **2.** A net for trapping game. [OFr. *toile,* web < Lat. *tela.*]

toile (twäl) *n.* **1.** A sheer linen fabric. **2.** Fine cretonne printed in a single color. [Fr. < OFr., cloth. —see TOIL².]

toi·let (toi′lĭt) *n.* **1. a.** A disposal apparatus consisting of a porcelain bowl that is fitted with a hinged seat and a flushing device, used for urination and defecation. **b.** A room or booth containing such an apparatus. **2.** Toilette. **3.** *Archaic.* A dressing table. **4.** Dress; attire; costume. [Fr. *toilette* < OFr., cloth cover for a dressing table, dim. of *toile,* cloth. —see TOIL².]

toilet paper *n.* Thin, absorbent paper, usually in rolls, used after defecation or urination.

toi·let·ry (toi′lĭ-trē) *n., pl.* **-ries.** An article or cosmetic used in dressing or grooming.

toi·lette (twä-lĕt′) *n.* **1.** The act or process of dressing or grooming oneself; toilet. **2.** A person's dress or style of dress. **3.** A gown or costume. [Fr. —see TOILET.]

toilet training *n.* The process of training a child to use the toilet for defecation and urination.

toilet water *n.* A scented liquid weaker than perfume and stronger than cologne.

toil·some (toil′səm) *adj.* Characterized by or requiring toil; done with difficulty. —**toil′some·ly** *adv.* —**toil′some·ness** *n.*

to-ing and fro-ing (to͞o′ĭng ən frō′ĭng) *n., pl.* **to-ings and fro-ings.** A moving or passing back and forth: *much to-ing and fro-ing in the hotel lobby.*

to·ka·mak (tô′kə-măk′, tŏk′ə-) *n.* A small doughnut-shaped nuclear reactor in which a plasma is heated and confined by electric and magnetic fields. [R.]

To·kay (tō-kā′) *n.* **1.** A variety of grape originally grown near Tokay, Hungary. **2.** A wine made from Tokay grapes.

toke (tōk) *n. Slang.* A puff on a marijuana cigarette. [Orig. unknown.]

to·ken (tō′kən) *n.* **1.** Something that serves as an indication or representation of a fact, event, or emotion; sign; symbol: "*Tears are queer tokens of happiness*" (O'Neill). **2.** Something that signifies or evidences authority, validity, or identity: *The scepter is a token of kingship.* **3.** A keepsake or souvenir. **4.** A piece of stamped metal used as a substitute for currency. —*tr.v.* **-kened, -ken·ing, -kens.** To betoken or symbolize; portend. —*adj.* **1.** Done as an indication or pledge: *a token payment.* **2. a.** Perfunctory: *a token gesture of reconciliation.* **b.** Merely symbolic: *a token woman on the board of directors.* —***idioms.*** **by the same token.** In like manner; similarly. **in token of.** As an indication of. [ME < OE *tācen.*]

to·ken·ism (tō′kə-nĭz′əm) *n.* The policy of making only a perfunctory effort or symbolic gesture toward the accomplishment of a goal, such as racial integration.

To·khar·i·an (tō-kâr′ē-ən, -kär′-, -kăr′-) *n.* Variant of **Tocharian.**

to·kol·o·gy (tō-kŏl′ə-jē) *n.* Variant of **tocology.**

to·la (tō′lə, tō-lä′) *n.* A unit of weight used in India, equal to the weight of one silver rupee, 11.7 grams, or 180 troy grains. [Hindi *tolā* < Skt. *tulā,* weight.]

tol·booth also **toll·booth** (tōl′bo͞oth′) *n. Scot.* A prison; jail. [ME (Scotland) *tolbothe,* town hall containing customs offices and prison cells : *tol,* toll + *bothe,* booth.]

tol·bu·ta·mide (tŏl-byo͞o′tə-mīd′) *n.* A white powder, $C_{12}H_{18}N_2O_3S$, used in the treatment of diabetes. [TOL(U) + BUT + AMIDE.]

told (tōld) *v.* Past tense and past participle of **tell.**

tole also **tôle** (tōl) *n.* Lacquered or enameled metalware, usually gilded and elaborately painted. [Fr. *tôle,* sheet metal < Lat. *tabula,* board.]

To·le·do also **to·le·do** (tə-lē′dō) *n., pl.* **-dos.** A fine-tempered sword or steel sword blade made in Toledo, Spain.

tol·er·a·ble (tŏl′ər-ə-bəl) *adj.* **1.** Able to be tolerated; endurable. **2.** Allowable; permissible. **3.** Fair or adequate; passable. —**tol′er·a·bil′i·ty, tol′er·a·ble·ness** *n.* —**tol′er·a·bly** *adv.*

tol·er·ance (tŏl′ər-əns) *n.* **1.** The capacity for or practice of recognizing and respecting the opinions, practices, or behavior of others. **2. a.** Leeway for variation from a standard. **b.** The permissible deviation from a specified value of a structural dimension. **3.** The capacity to endure hardship or pain. **4. a.** Physiological resistance to poison. **b.** The capacity to absorb a drug continuously or in large doses without adverse effect.

tol·er·ant (tŏl′ər-ənt) *adj.* **1.** Inclined to tolerate the beliefs, practices, or traits of others; forbearing. **2.** Able to withstand or endure an adverse environmental condition: *plants tolerant of extreme heat.* [Lat. *tolerans, tolerant-,* pr.part. of *tolerare,* to tolerate.] —**tol′er·ant·ly** *adv.*

tol·er·ate (tŏl′ə-rāt′) *tr.v.* **-at·ed, -at·ing, -ates. 1.** To allow without prohibiting or opposing; permit. **2.** To recognize and respect (the rights, opinions, or practices of others). **3.** To put up with; endure. **4.** *Med.* To have tolerance for (a drug or poison). [Lat. *tolerare, tolerat-,* to bear.] —**tol′er·a′tive** *adj.* —**tol′er·a′tor** *n.*

George Miksch Sutton

tody

toga

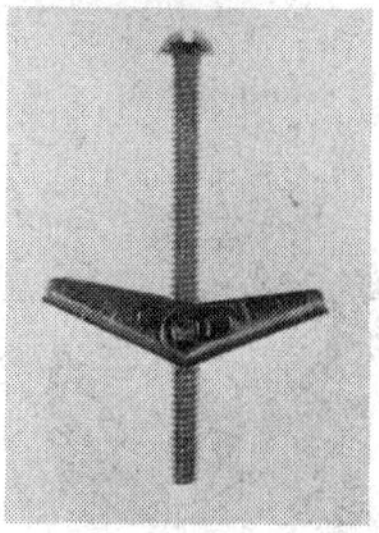

toggle bolt

tol·er·a·tion (tŏl′ə-rā′shən) *n.* **1.** Tolerance. **2.** Official recognition of the rights of individuals and groups to hold dissenting opinions, esp. on religion.

tol·i·dine (tŏl′ĭ-dēn′) *n.* Any of several isomeric bases, $C_{14}H_{16}N_2$, derived from toluene, one of which is used as a reagent for gold and for chlorine in water. [TOL(UENE) + -ID(E) + -INE.]

toll[1] (tōl) *n.* **1.** A fixed charge or tax for a privilege, esp. for passage across a bridge or along a road. **2.** A charge for a service, such as a long-distance telephone call. **3.** The amount or extent of loss or destruction, as of life, health, or property, caused by a disaster. —*tr.v.* **tolled, toll·ing, tolls.** To exact as a toll. [ME *tol* < OE *toll* < Med. Lat. *toloneum* < LLat. *teloneum,* tollbooth < Gk. *telōnion* < *telōnēs,* tax collector < *telos,* tax.]

toll[2] (tōl) *v.* **tolled, toll·ing, tolls.** —*tr.* **1.** To sound (a large bell) slowly at regular intervals. **2.** To announce or summon by tolling. —*intr.* To sound in slowly repeated single tones. —*n.* **1.** The act of tolling. **2.** The sound of a tolling bell. [ME *tollen,* to ring an alarm, perh. < *tollen,* to pull.]

toll·booth[1] (tōl′bo͞oth′) *n.* A booth at a tollgate where a toll is collected.

toll·booth[2] (tōl′bo͞oth′) *n. Scot.* Variant of **tolbooth.**

toll call *n.* A telephone call for which a higher rate is charged than that standard for a local call.

toll collector *n.* One employed to receive toll payments.

toll·er (tō′lər) *n.* **1.** One who tolls a bell. **2.** A bell used for tolling.

toll·gate (tōl′gāt′) *n.* A gate barring passage to a road, tunnel, or bridge until a toll is collected.

toll·house (tōl′hous′) *n.* **1.** A house occupied by the toll collector adjoining a tollgate. **2.** A tollbooth.

toll line *n.* A long-distance telephone line or circuit.

Tol·tec (tŏl′tĕk′, tōl′-) *n.* One of an ancient Nahuatl people of central and southern Mexico whose culture flourished in about 1000 A.D. —*adj.* Also **Tol·tec·an** (tōl-tĕk′ən, tŏl-). Of or pertaining to the Toltecs or their culture. [Sp. *Tolteca* < Nahuatl *tolecatl,* artisan.]

to·lu (tə-lo͞o′) *n.* The balsam of Tolu. [Sp. *tolú,* after Santiago de *Tolú,* Colombia.]

tol·u·ate (tŏl′yo͞o-āt′) *n.* A salt or ester of toluic acid. [TOLU(IC ACID) + -ATE.]

tol·u·ene (tŏl′yo͞o-ēn′) *n.* A colorless flammable liquid, $CH_3C_6H_5$, obtained from coal tar or petroleum and used in aviation and other high-octane fuels, in dyestuffs, explosives, and as a solvent for gums and lacquers. [TOLU (from which it was originally obtained) + -ENE.]

to·lu·ic acid (tə-lo͞o′ĭk) *n.* Any of four isomeric acids, $C_8H_8O_2$, derived from toluene. [TOLU(ENE) + -IC.]

to·lu·i·dine (tə-lo͞o′ĭ-dēn′) *n.* Any of three isomeric compounds, C_7H_9N, used to make dyes. [TOLU(ENE) + -ID(E) + -INE.]

tol·u·ol (tŏl′yo͞o-ôl′, -ōl′) *n.* Commercial-grade toluene.

tol·yl (tŏl′əl) *n.* The univalent organic radical $CH_3C_6H_4$. [TOL(U) + -YL.]

tom (tŏm) *n.* The male of various animals, esp. a male cat or turkey. [*Tom,* nickname for *Thomas.*]

Tom (tŏm) *n. Slang.* An Uncle Tom.

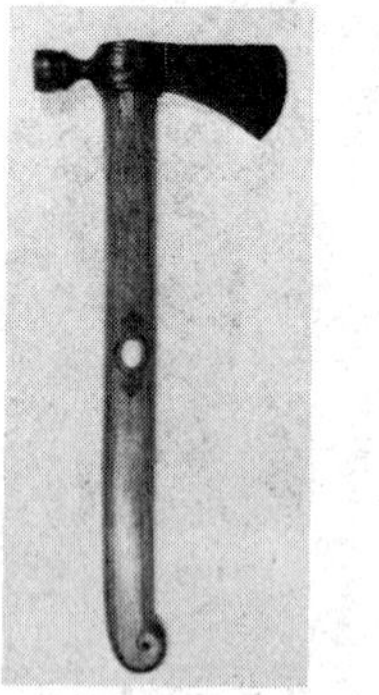

tomahawk

tom·a·hawk (tŏm′ə-hôk′) *n.* **1.** A light ax formerly used as a tool or weapon by North American Indians. **2.** An implement or weapon similar to a tomahawk. —*tr.v.* **-hawked, -hawk·ing, -hawks.** To strike with a tomahawk. [Algonquian (Virginia) *tamahaac.*]

to·mal·ley (tə-măl′ē, tŏm′ăl′ē) *n., pl.* **-leys.** The liver of a lobster, esteemed as a culinary delicacy. [Of Cariban orig.]

Tom and Jer·ry (tŏm′ ən jĕr′ē) *n.* A hot drink consisting of rum, a beaten egg, milk or water, sugar, and spices. [After Corinthian *Tom* and *Jerry* Hawthorn, characters in the novel *Life in London* by Pierce Egan (1772–1849).]

tomato

to·ma·to (tə-mā′tō, -mä′-) *n., pl.* **-toes. 1. a.** A plant, *Lycopersicon esculentum,* native to South America, widely cultivated for its edible, fleshy, usually red fruit. **b.** The fruit of this plant. **2.** *Slang.* An attractive girl. [Alteration of Sp. *tomate* < Nahuatl *tomatl.*]

tomb (to͞om) *n.* **1.** A vault or chamber for the burial of the dead. **2.** A grave or place of burial. **3.** A monument commemorating the dead. [ME < OFr. *tombe* < Lat. *tumba* < Gk. *tumbos.*]

tom·bac also **tam·bac** or **tom·back** or **tam·bak** (tŏm′băk′) *n.* Any one of several alloys of copper and zinc, used in making inexpensive jewelry. [Fr. < Du. *tombak* < Malay *tĕmbaga.*]

tom·boy (tŏm′boi′) *n.* A young girl who behaves like a boy. **—tom′boy′ish** *adj.*

tomb·stone (to͞om′stōn′) *n.* A gravestone.

tom·cat (tŏm′kăt′) *n.* A male cat.

tom·cod (tŏm′kŏd′) *n., pl.* **tomcod** or **-cods.** Either of two edible marine fishes, *Microgadus tomcod,* of North American Atlantic waters, or *M. proximus,* of northern Pacific waters, related to and resembling the cod.

Tom Col·lins (tŏm′ kŏl′ĭnz) *n.* A beverage consisting of gin, lemon or lime juice, carbonated water, and sugar. [*Tom,* a kind of gin + *Collins,* a name.]

Tom, Dick, and Har·ry (tŏm′ dĭk′ ən hăr′ē) *n.* Anybody at all; everyone: *Every Tom, Dick, and Harry came to the party.*

tome (tōm) *n.* **1.** One of the books in a work of several volumes. **2.** A book, esp. a large or scholarly book. [OFr. < Lat. *tomus* < Gk. *tomos* < *temnein,* to cut.]

-tome *suff.* **1.** Part; area; segment: *dermatome.* **2.** Cutting instrument: *microtome.* [NLat. *-tomus* < Gk. *-tomos,* a cutting < *temnein,* to cut.]

to·men·tose (tō-mĕn′tōs′, tō′mən-tōs′) *adj. Biol.* Covered with dense, short, matted hairs. [NLat. *tomentosus* < Lat. *tomentum,* cushion stuffing.]

to·men·tum (tō-mĕn′təm) *n., pl.* **-ta** (-tə). **1.** *Anat.* A network of extremely small blood vessels passing between the pia mater and cerebral cortex. **2.** *Biol.* A covering of closely matted woolly hairs. [NLat. < Lat., cushion stuffing.]

tom·fool (tŏm′fo͞ol′) *n.* A stupid or foolish person; blockhead. —*adj.* Extremely foolish or stupid. [ME *Thome Fole.*]

tom·fool·er·y (tŏm-fo͞o′lə-rē) *n., pl.* **-ies. 1.** Foolish behavior. **2.** Something trivial or foolish; nonsense.

tom·my (tŏm′ē) *n., pl.* **-mies.** *Chiefly Brit. Informal.* **1.** A loaf or piece of bread. **2.** Food; victuals; provisions. **3.** Often **Tommy.** A Tommy Atkins. [*Tommy,* nickname for *Thomas.*]

Tommy At·kins (ăt′kĭnz) *n.* A British soldier. [From the use of the name on sample forms.]

Tommy gun *n. Informal.* A Thompson submachine gun.

tom·my·rot (tŏm′ē-rŏt′) *n. Informal.* Utter foolishness; nonsense. [Dial. *tommy,* fool + ROT.]

to·mog·ra·phy (tō-mŏg′rə-fē) *n.* Any of several techniques for making x-ray pictures of a predetermined plane section of a solid object by blurring out the images of other planes. [Gk. *tomos,* section (< *temnein,* to cut) + -GRAPHY.] **—to′mo·gram′** (tō′mə-grăm′) *n.* **—to′mo·graph′** (-grăf′) *n.*

to·mor·row also **to-mor·row** (tə-môr′ō, -mŏr′ō) —*n.* **1.** The day following today. **2.** The near future. —*adv.* On or for the day following today. [ME *to morow* < OE *tō morgenne,* in the morning.]

tom·pi·on (tŏm′pē-ən) *n.* Variant of **tampion.**

Tom Thumb *n.* **1.** A diminutive hero of English folklore. **2.** A tiny person; midget.

tom·tit (tŏm′tĭt′) *n.* A small bird, as a tit.

tom-tom

tom-tom (tŏm′tŏm′) *n.* **1.** Any of various small-headed drums, usually long and narrow, that are beaten with the hands. **2.** A gong having a metal disk struck with a felt-covered hammer or stick. **3.** A monotonous rhythmical drumbeat or similar sound. [Hindi *ṭamṭam.*]

-tomy *suff.* Act of cutting; incision: *gastrotomy.* [NLat. *-tomia* < Gk. < *tomos,* cutting, sharp < *temnein,* to cut.]

ton (tŭn) *n.* **1. a.** A unit of weight equal to 1.016 metric ton, 2,240 pounds, or 1016.06 kilograms. **b.** A unit of weight equal to .907 metric ton, 2,000 pounds, or 907.20 kilograms. **c.** A metric ton. **2.** A unit of capacity for cargo in maritime shipping, normally estimated at 40 cubic feet. **3.** A unit of inside capacity of a ship equal to 100 cubic feet. **4.** *Informal.* A very large quantity. [ME *toun,* a measure of weight < OE *tunne,* large cask.]

to·nal (tō′nəl) *adj.* Of or pertaining to a tone, tones, or tonality. **—to′nal·ly** *adv.*

to·nal·i·ty (tō-năl′ĭ-tē) *n., pl.* **-ties. 1.** *Mus.* **a.** A system or arrangement of seven tones built on a tonic key. **b.** The arrangement of all the tones and chords of a musical composition in relation to a tonic. **2.** The scheme or interrelation of the tones in a painting.

tone (tōn) *n.* **1. a.** A sound of distinct pitch, quality, or duration; musical note. **b.** The quality or character of sound: *sweet, clear tones of a lute.* **2.** *Mus.* **a.** The interval of a major second; whole step. **b.** The characteristic quality or timbre of a particular instrument or voice. **3.** The pitch of a word used to determine its meaning or to distinguish differences in meaning. **4.** The particular or relative pitch of a word, phrase, or sentence. **5.** Manner of expression in speech or writing: *an angry tone of voice.* **6.** A general quality, effect, or atmosphere: *an elegant tone to the room; a debate with an antagonistic tone.* **7. a.** A color or shade of color. **b.** Quality of color. **8.** *Physiol.* **a.** The tension in resting muscles. **b.** Normal firmness of tissue. —*v.* **toned, ton·ing, tones.** —*tr.* **1.** To give a particular tone or inflection to. **2.** To soften or change the color of (a painting or photographic negative, for example). **3.** To sound monotonously; intone. —*intr.* **1.** To assume a particular color quality. **2.** To harmonize in color. ***—phrasal verbs.*** **tone down.** To make less vivid, harsh, or violent; moderate. **tone up.** To make or become brighter or more vigorous. [ME < Lat. *tonus* < Gk. *tonos.*]

tone arm *n.* The pivoted arm of a record player that holds the cartridge and stylus.

tone color *n.* The timbre of a singing voice or instrument.

tone language *n.* A language that distinguishes meanings among words of similar form by variations in pitch and tone.

tone·less (tōn′lĭs) *adj.* **1.** Lacking tone. **2.** Lacking vitality; listless. **—tone′less·ly** *adv.* **—tone′less·ness** *n.*

tone poem *n.* A symphonic poem.

tong[1] (tông, tŏng) *tr.v.* **tonged, tong·ing, tongs.** To seize, hold, or manipulate with tongs. [Back-formation < TONGS.]

tong[2] (tông, tŏng) *n.* **1.** A Chinese association, clan, or fraternity. **2.** A secret society of Chinese in the United States, at one time believed to control criminal activity among Chinese Americans. [Cantonese, assembly hall.]

Ton·gan (tŏng′gən, tŏng′ən) *n.* A Polynesian language spoken in Tonga.

tongs (tôngz, tŏngz) *pl.n.* *(used with a sing. or pl. verb).* A grasping device consisting of two arms joined at one end by a pivot or hinge. [ME < OE *tong.*]

tongue (tŭng) *n.* **1. a.** The fleshy muscular organ, attached in most vertebrates to the floor of the mouth, that is the principal organ of taste, an important organ of speech, and moves to aid chewing and swallowing. **b.** A homologous invertebrate structure, as in insects or certain mollusks. **2.** The tongue of an animal, such as a cow, used as food. **3.** A spoken language or dialect. **4.** Style or quality of utterance: *her sharp tongue.* **5.** The flap of material under the laces or buckles of a shoe. **6.** A spit of land; promontory. **7.** Something resembling the shape of a tongue, as a flame. **8.** A bell clapper. **9.** The harnessing pole attached to the front axle of a horse-drawn vehicle. **10.** A protruding strip along the edge of a board that fits into a matching groove on the edge of another board. *—v.* **tongued, tongu·ing, tongues.** *—tr.* **1.** To separate or articulate (musical notes played on a wind instrument) by shutting off the stream of air with the tongue. **2.** To touch or lick with the tongue. **3. a.** To provide (a board) with a tongue. **b.** To join by means of a tongue and groove. **4.** *Archaic.* To scold. *—intr.* **1.** To articulate notes on a wind instrument. **2.** To project, as a promontory. *—**idioms.*** **hold (one's) tongue.** To be or keep silent. **on the tip of (one's) tongue.** On the verge of being recalled or expressed. [ME < OE *tunge.*]

tongue and groove *n.* A joint made by fitting a tongue on the edge of a board into a matching groove on another board.

tongue·fish (tŭng′fĭsh′) *n., pl.* **tonguefish** or **-fish·es.** Any of various marine flatfishes of the family Cynoglossidae, having the posterior part of the body tapering to a point. [From its tongue-shaped body.]

tongue-in-cheek (tŭng′ĭn-chēk′) *adj.* Meant or expressed ironically or facetiously.

tongue-lash·ing (tŭng′lăsh′ĭng) *n.* *Informal.* A scolding.

tongue-tie (tŭng′tī′) *n.* Restricted mobility of the tongue resulting from abnormal shortness of the frenum. *—tr.v.* **-tied, -ty·ing, -ties.** To make tongue-tied.

tongue-tied (tŭng′tīd′) *adj.* **1.** Speechless or confused in expression, as from shyness, embarrassment, or astonishment. **2.** Affected with tongue-tie.

tongue twister *n.* **1.** A word or words difficult to articulate rapidly, usually because of a succession of similar consonantal sounds, as: *Shall she sell seashells?* **2.** Anything difficult to pronounce.

tongu·ing (tŭng′ĭng) *n.* *Mus.* Interruption of the wind stream through an instrument by movement of the tongue in order to articulate notes.

-tonia *suff.* Degree or state of tonicity: *myotonia.* [NLat. < *tonus.* —see TONE.]

ton·ic (tŏn′ĭk) *n.* **1.** Something that invigorates, refreshes, or restores. **2.** A medicine or other agent that restores or increases bodily tone. **3.** *Mus.* The first note of a diatonic scale; keynote. **4. a.** Quinine water. **b.** *Regional.* A flavored carbonated beverage. **5.** *Ling.* **a.** A tonic accent. **b.** *Obs.* A voiced sound. *—adj.* **1.** Producing or stimulating physical, mental, or emotional vigor. **2.** *Mus.* Of or based on the tonic. **3.** *Ling.* **a.** Stressed, as a syllable; accented. **b.** *Obs.* Voiced. **4.** *Physiol.* Of or pertaining to tissue or muscular tension. [< Gk. *tonikos,* capable of extension < *tonos,* tone.] **—ton′i·cal·ly** *adv.*

tonic accent *n.* A stress produced by rising pitch as distinguished from increased volume.

to·nic·i·ty (tō-nĭs′ĭ-tē) *n.* **1.** Normal functional readiness in bodily tissues. **2.** Active resistance to stretching in muscles.

tonic sol-fa *n.* *Mus.* A system of notation that is based on key relationships and that replaces usual staff notation with solmization syllables or their abbreviations.

to·night also **to-night** (tə-nīt′) *—adv.* On or during the present or coming night. *—n.* This night or the night of this day. [ME *to night* < OE *tō niht,* at night.]

ton·ka bean (tŏng′kə) *n.* **1.** Any of several South American trees of the genus *Dipteryx,* esp. *D. odorata,* having seeds that yield the fragrant compound coumarin. **2.** The seed of the tonka bean tree. [Perh. < Galibi *tonka.*]

ton·nage (tŭn′ĭj) *n.* **1.** The number of tons of water a ship displaces afloat. **2.** The capacity of a merchant ship in units of 100 cubic feet. **3.** A duty or charge per ton on cargo, as at a port or canal. **4.** The total shipping of a country or port, figured in tons, with reference to carrying capacity. **5.** Weight measured in tons.

ton·neau (tə-nō′, tŏn′ō′) *n.* The rear seating compartment of an early type of automobile. [Fr. < OFr. *tonnel,* cask. —see TUNNEL.]

to·nom·e·ter (tō-nŏm′ĭ-tər) *n.* **1.** Any of various instruments for measuring fluid or vapor pressure. **2.** *Mus.* An instrument or device, such as a graduated set of tuning forks, used to determine the pitch or vibration rate of tones. **3.** An instrument for measuring hydrostatic pressure within the eyeball. [Gk. *tonos,* tension + -METER.] **—to′no·met′ric** (tō′nə-mĕt′rĭk) *adj.* **—to·nom′e·try** *n.*

to·no·plast (tō′nə-plăst′) *n.* The cytoplasmic membrane that surrounds a vacuole of a plant cell. [Gk. *tonos,* tension + -PLAST.]

ton·sil (tŏn′səl) *n.* A mass of lymphoid tissue, esp. either of two such masses, embedded in the lateral walls of the aperture between the mouth and the pharynx. [Lat. *tonsillae,* tonsils.] **—ton′sil·lar** (tŏn′sə-lər) *adj.*

tonsill- *pref.* Variant of **tonsillo-.**

ton·sil·lec·to·my (tŏn′sə-lĕk′tə-mē) *n., pl.* **-mies.** The surgical removal of a tonsil.

ton·sil·li·tis (tŏn′sə-lī′tĭs) *n.* Inflammation of the tonsils. **—ton′sil·lit′ic** (-lĭt′ĭk) *adj.*

tonsillo- or **tonsill-** *pref.* Tonsil: *tonsillectomy.* [< Lat. *tonsillae,* tonsils.]

ton·sil·lot·o·my (tŏn′sə-lŏt′ə-mē) *n., pl.* **-mies.** The surgical incision of a tonsil.

ton·so·ri·al (tŏn-sôr′ē-əl, -sōr′-) *adj.* Of or pertaining to a barber or to barbering. [Lat. *tonsorius* < *tonsor,* barber < *tondēre,* to shear.]

ton·sure (tŏn′shər) *n.* **1.** The act of shaving the crown of the head, esp. as a preliminary to becoming a priest or a member of a monastic order. **2.** The part of a monk's or priest's head that has been shaved. *—tr.v.* **-sured, -sur·ing, -sures.** To shave the head of. [ME < Med. Lat. *tonsura* < Lat. *tondēre,* to shear.]

ton·tine (tŏn′tēn′, tŏn-tēn′) *n.* **1.** An annuity or insurance plan whereby a group of participants hold shares in a common fund with right of survivorship, each participant's share being increased as one of the other dies, the final survivor receiving the whole. **2.** Each member's share of a tontine. **3.** The subscribers to a tontine collectively. [Fr., after Lorenzo *Tonti* (1635–1690).]

to·nus (tō′nəs) *n.* Tonicity. [Lat., tone.]

ton·y (tō′nē) *adj.* **-i·er, -i·est.** Marked by an elegant or exclusive manner or quality: *a tony country club.*

To·ny (tō′nē) *n.* An annual award for outstanding achievement in the theater. [After *Tony,* nickname of *Antoinette* Perry (1888–1946).]

too (to͞o) *adv.* **1.** Also; as well: *He's coming too.* **2.** More than enough; excessively: *He studied too much.* **3.** Very; extremely; immensely: *He's only too willing to be of service.* **4.** *Informal.* Indeed; so: *You will too do it!* [ME *to* < OE *tō.*]

Usage: *Too* preceded by *not* or another form of negative is frequently employed as a form of understatement to convey humor or sarcasm: *He was not too pleased when she ignored him. He is not too bright.* When used for effect, it is employed on all levels. *Not too,* when used to mean approximately "not very," is generally considered informal: *Passage of the bill is not now considered too likely* (unacceptable in written usage to a large majority of the Usage Panel). *Too* can often be eliminated from such sentences without loss, but if such deletion gives undue stress to the negative sense, the writer may find *not very* or *none too* preferable choices. *Too* is often used in writing in place of *moreover* or *in addition* to introduce a sentence, as in *There has been a cutback in oil production. Too, rates have been increasing.* This usage is not sufficiently well established to be entirely acceptable.

took (to͝ok) *v.* Past tense of **take.**

tool (to͞ol) *n.* **1.** Any hand-held implement, as a hammer, saw, or drill, used to accomplish work. **2. a.** A machine, such as a lathe, used to cut and shape mechanical parts or other objects. **b.** The cutting part of such a machine. **3.** Anything used in the performance of an operation; instrument: *"modern democracies have the fiscal and monetary tools . . . to end chronic slumps and galloping inflations"* (Paul A. Samuelson). **4.** Anything regarded as necessary to the carrying out of one's occupation or profession: *Words are the tools of his trade.* **5.** A person utilized to carry out the designs of another; dupe. **6. a.** A bookbinder's hand stamp. **b.** A design impressed on a book cover by this means. **7.** One that is manipulated or used by another; cat's-paw. *—v.* **tooled, tool·ing, tools.** *—tr.* **1.** To form, work, or decorate with a tool. **2.** To ornament (a book cover) with a bookbinder's tool. **3.** *Informal.* To drive (a vehicle). *—intr.* **1.** To work with a tool. **2.** *Informal.* To travel in a vehicle. *—**idiom.*** **tool up.** To prepare an industry or a factory for production by providing machinery and tools suitable for a particular job. [ME < OE *tōl.*]

Synonyms: *tool, instrument, implement, utensil, appliance, gadget.* These nouns refer to devices or aids for performing work. *Tool* can apply broadly to any device for doing or facilitating work. Specifically, it refers to a small manually operated device of the kind employed by carpenters and plumbers, to a power-driven machine tool such as a lathe, or to the part of a machine that cuts or shapes. *Instrument* refers to any of the relatively small precision tools used by specially trained professionals such as doctors, technicians, and drafters. *Implement* is the preferred term for tools used in agriculture and certain building trades, or it can mean any device essential for performing work. *Utensil* usually refers to a device for household work, such as a pot, pan, or vessel. *Appliance* denotes a power-driven machine or tool, such as a device for household cleaning. *Gadget* refers informally to a small contrivance, or accessory of a machine, that performs a specific function.

tool·box (to͞ol′bŏks′) *n.* A case for carrying or storing hand tools.

tool·ing (to͞o′lĭng) *n.* **1.** Work or ornamentation done with tools, esp. stamped or gilded designs on leather. **2.** The

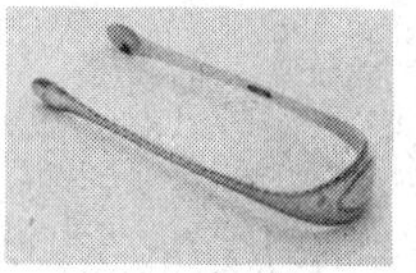
tongs

tongue and groove

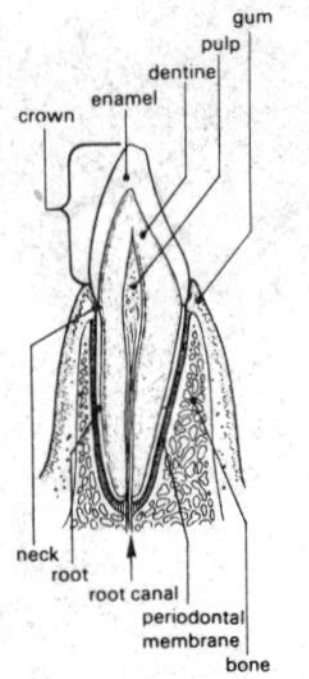

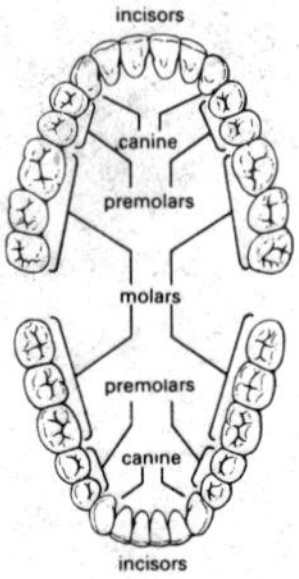

tooth
Above: Cross section of a human incisor
Below: The upper and lower teeth of an adult human

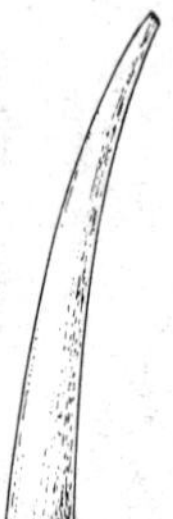

tooth shell

top hat

process of providing a factory with machinery in preparation for production.

tool·ma·ker (to͞ol′mā′kər) *n.* A master machinist skilled in making tools and parts.

toon (to͞on) *n.* **1.** A tall tree, *Cedrela toona* (or *Toona ciliata*), of tropical Asia and Australia, having reddish, aromatic wood. **2.** The wood of the toon. [Hindi *tūn* < Skt.]

toot (to͞ot) *v.* **toot·ed, toot·ing, toots.** —*intr.* **1.** To sound a horn or whistle in short blasts. **2.** To make the sound of a horn or whistle blown in short blasts or a sound resembling this. —*tr.* **1.** To blow or sound (a horn or whistle). **2.** To sound (a blast or series of blasts) on a horn or whistle. —*n.* The act or sound of tooting. [Prob. imit.] **—toot′er** *n.*

tooth (to͞oth) *n., pl.* **teeth** (tēth). **1. a.** In most vertebrates, one of a set of hard, bonelike structures rooted in sockets in the jaws, typically composed of a core of soft pulp surrounded by a layer of hard dentine that is coated with cement or enamel at the crown, used to seize, hold, or masticate. **b.** A similar structure in invertebrates, such as one of the pointed denticles or ridges on the exoskeleton of an arthropod or the shell of a mollusk. **2.** A projecting part resembling a tooth in shape or function, as on a comb, gear, or saw. **3.** A small, notched projection along a margin, esp. of a leaf. **4. teeth. a.** Something that injures or destroys with force: *the teeth of the blizzard.* **b.** Effective means of enforcing something; muscle: *a law with teeth to it.* **5.** Taste or appetite for something: *She always had a sweet tooth.* —*v.* (to͞oth, to͞o*th*) **toothed, tooth·ing, tooths.** —*tr.* **1.** To furnish (a tool, for example) with teeth. **2.** To make a jagged edge on. —*intr.* To become interlocked; mesh. —***idioms.* get (one's) teeth into.** To be actively involved in; get a firm grasp of. **in the teeth of. 1.** Directly and forcefully against. **2.** In defiance of. **put teeth into.** To make (a law, for example) effective or forceful. **show (one's) teeth.** To express a readiness to fight; threaten defiantly. **to the teeth.** Lacking nothing; completely: *armed to the teeth; dressed to the teeth.* [ME < OE *tōð.*]

tooth·ache (to͞oth′āk′) *n.* An aching pain in or near a tooth.

toothache tree *n.* The prickly ash.

tooth and nail *adv.* With great ferocity; as hard as possible.

tooth·brush (to͞oth′brŭsh′) *n.* A brush used for cleaning teeth.

toothed (to͞otht, to͞o*th*d) *adj.* **1.** Having teeth. **2.** Having a certain number or type of teeth: *saw-toothed.*

toothed whale *n.* Any of various whales of the suborder Odontoceti with numerous conical teeth.

tooth·less (to͞oth′lĭs) *adj.* **1.** Lacking teeth. **2.** Lacking force; ineffectual. **—tooth′less·ly** *adv.* **—tooth′less·ness** *n.*

tooth·paste (to͞oth′pāst′) *n.* A paste for cleaning teeth.

tooth·pick (to͞oth′pĭk′) *n.* A small piece of wood or other material for removing food particles from between the teeth.

tooth·pow·der (to͞oth′pou′dər) *n.* A powder for cleaning teeth.

tooth shell *n.* Any of various burrowing marine mollusks of the class Scaphopoda, having a long, tapering, slightly curved tubular shell.

tooth·some (to͞oth′səm) *adj.* **1.** Delicious; luscious: *a toothsome morsel of pie.* **2.** Pleasant; attractive: *a toothsome offer.* **3.** Sexually attractive or exciting. **—tooth′some·ly** *adv.* **—tooth′some·ness** *n.*

tooth·wort (to͞oth′wûrt′, -wôrt′) *n.* **1.** Any of several plants of the genus *Dentaria,* such as the crinkleroot. **2.** A parasitic European plant, *Lathraea squamaria,* having scaly cream-colored or pink stems and pinkish flowers.

tooth·y (to͞o′thē) *adj.* **-i·er, -i·est.** Having or showing prominent teeth. **—tooth′i·ly** *adv.*

too·tle (to͞ot′l) *intr.v.* **-tled, -tling, -tles.** To toot softly and repeatedly, as on a flute. —*n.* The act or sound of tootling. [Freq. of TOOT.]

toots (to͞ots) *n. Slang.* Dear; sweetheart. [Orig. unknown.]

toot·sy also **toot·sie** (to͞ot′sē) *n., pl.* **-sies.** A person's foot. [Alteration of *footsy* < FOOT.]

top¹ (tŏp) *n.* **1.** The uppermost part, point, surface, or end. **2.** The crown of the head. **3.** The part of a plant, such as a rutabaga, that is above the ground. **4.** Something, as a lid or cap, that covers or forms the uppermost part. **5.** *Naut.* A platform enclosing the head of each mast of a sailing ship, to which the topmast rigging is attached. **6.** *Sports.* **a.** A stroke that lands above the center of a ball, as in golf or tennis, giving it forward spin. **b.** A forward spin on a ball resulting from such a stroke. **7.** The highest degree, pitch, or point; peak; acme; zenith. **8. a.** The highest position or rank: *at the top of her profession.* **b.** A person in this position. **9.** *Games.* The highest card or cards in a suit or a hand. **10.** The best part; pick; cream. **11.** The earliest part or beginning: *the top of the first inning.* —***modifier:*** *at top speed; the top shelf; the top singing group in England.* —*v.* **topped, top·ping, tops.** —*tr.* **1.** To form, furnish with, or serve as a top. **2.** To reach the top of. **3.** To go over the top of. **4.** To exceed or surpass. **5.** To be at the head of: *He topped his class.* **6.** To remove the top or uppermost part from; crop: *topped all the fruit trees.* **7.** *Sports.* **a.** To strike the upper part of (a ball), giving it forward spin. **b.** To make (a stroke) in this way. —*intr.* To make a finish, end, or conclusion. —***phrasal verbs.* top off.** To finish up. **top out. 1.** To put the framework for the top story on (a building). **2.** *Informal.* To give up one's career just as one becomes highly successful. —***idioms.* blow (one's) top.** *Slang.* **1.** To lose one's temper. **2.** To lose one's mind; become insane. **off the top of (one's) head.** In an impromptu way: *recited the sales figures off the top of his head.* **on top. 1.** At the highest point or peak. **2.** In a dominant, controlling, or successful position. **on top of. 1.** On or at the uppermost part or side of. **2.** *Informal.* **a.** In control of. **b.** Fully informed about. **3.** In addition to; besides. **4.** Following closely upon; coming immediately after. **on top of the world.** In a position of great happiness or success. **over the top. 1.** Over the breastwork, as an attack in trench warfare. **2.** Surpassing a goal or quota. [ME < OE.]

top² (tŏp) *n.* A toy consisting of a symmetrical rigid body spun on a pointed end about the axis of symmetry. [ME *topp* < OE *top.*]

top– *pref.* Variant of **topo-.**

Top 40 *n.* The 40 most popular records during a designated period of time.

to·paz (tō′păz′) *n.* **1.** A colorless, blue, yellow, brown, or pink aluminum silicate mineral, often found in association with granitic rocks and valued as a gemstone, esp. in the brown and pink varieties. **2.** Any of various yellow gemstones, esp. a yellow variety of sapphire or corundum. **3.** A light-yellow variety of quartz. **4.** Either of two colorful South American hummingbirds, *Topaza pyra* or *T. pella.* [ME *topace* < OFr. < Lat. *topazus* < Gk. *topazos.*]

top banana *n. Informal.* **1.** The main comedian in a burlesque show. **2.** The head person, as of a group or project. [So called from the presentation of a banana to the comedian who has the punch line in a three-man burlesque routine.]

top boot *n.* A high boot usually having its upper part trimmed with a contrasting color or texture of leather.

top·coat (tŏp′kōt′) *n.* A lightweight overcoat.

top dog *n. Informal.* One considered to have the highest authority, esp. as a result of a competitive victory; kingpin. **—top′-dog′** *adj.*

top-drawer (tŏp′drôr′) *adj. Informal.* Of the highest importance, rank, privilege, or merit.

top-dress (tŏp′drĕs′) *tr.v.* **-dressed, -dress·ing, -dress·es.** To cover (land or a road surface) with loose material that is not worked in, esp. to cover (farmland) with fertilizer.

top dressing *n.* **1.** A covering of manure or other fertilizer spread on soil without being plowed under. **2.** A covering of loose gravel on a road.

tope¹ (tōp) *v.* **toped, top·ing, topes.** —*tr.* To drink (alcoholic liquors) habitually and excessively. —*intr.* To drink to excess habitually. [Prob. < obs. *tope,* interjection used in proposing a toast.]

tope² (tōp) *n.* Any of several small sharks, esp. one of the genus *Galeorhinus.* [Orig. unknown.]

tope³ (tōp) *n.* A dome-shaped Buddhist shrine with a cupola on top. [Hindi *tōp.*]

to·pee (tō-pē′, tō′pē) *n.* Variant of **topi.**

top·er (tō′pər) *n.* A chronic drinker; drunkard.

top·flight (tŏp′flīt′) *adj.* First-rate; superior.

top·full also **top·ful** (tŏp′fo͝ol′) *adj.* Full to the brim.

top·gal·lant (tə-găl′ənt, tŏp-) *adj. Naut.* Designating the mast above the topmast, its sails, or its rigging.

top-ham·per also **top hamper** (tŏp′hăm′pər) *n.* **1.** *Naut.* Rigging, cables, spars, or other materials or weight not immediately necessary and stored either aloft or on the upper decks. **2.** Cumbersome and unnecessary or meaningless matter.

top hat *n.* A man's hat having a narrow brim and a tall cylindrical crown, usually made of silk.

top-heav·y (tŏp′hĕv′ē) *adj.* **-i·er, -i·est. 1.** Likely to topple because overloaded at the top. **2.** Overcapitalized. **—top′-heav′i·ness** *n.*

To·phet (tō′fĕt′, -fĭt) *n.* **1.** A shrine near Gehenna where human sacrifices were made. **2. a.** Hell. **b.** A hellish place. [ME < Heb. *tōpheth.*]

top-hole (tŏp′hōl′) *adj. Chiefly Brit.* First-rate; excellent.

to·phus (tō′fəs) *n., pl.* **-phi** (-fī′). **1.** *Pathol.* A urate deposit found in tissue, such as cartilage, around the joints. **2.** A concretion of mineral salts and organic matter deposited on the surface of the teeth. [Lat., tufa.]

to·pi also **to·pee** (tō-pē′, tō′pē) *n., pl.* **-pis** also **-pees.** A pith helmet worn for protection against sun and heat. [Hindi *topī,* hat.]

to·pi·ar·y (tō′pē-ĕr′ē) *adj.* Of or characterized by the clipping or trimming of live shrubs or trees into decorative shapes, as those of animals or birds. —*n., pl.* **-ies. 1.** Topiary work or art. **2.** A topiary garden. [Lat. *topiarius* < *topia,* ornamental gardening < Gk. *topia,* pl. of *topion,* field, dim. of *topos,* place.]

top·ic (tŏp′ĭk) *n.* **1.** A subject treated in a speech, essay, thesis, or portion of a discourse; theme. **2.** A subject of discussion or conversation. **3.** A subdivision of a theme, thesis, or outline. [Obs. *topic,* rhetorical argument < *Topics,* a work by Aristotle < Lat. *Topica* < Gk. *Topika,* neuter pl. of *topikos,* of a place < *topos,* place.]

top·i·cal (tŏp′ĭ-kəl) *adj.* **1.** Of or belonging to a particular location or place; local. **2.** Currently of interest; contemporary. **3.** *Med.* Of or applied to an isolated part of the body.

4. Of or pertaining to a particular topic or topics. [Gk. *topikos* < *topos,* place.] **—top′i·cal′i·ty** (-kăl′ĭ-tē) *n.* **—top′i·cal·ly** *adv.*
topic sentence *n.* The sentence within a paragraph that states the main thought, often placed at the beginning.
top kick *n. Slang.* A first sergeant.
top·knot (tŏp′nŏt′) *n.* **1.** A crest or knot of hair or feathers on the crown of the head. **2.** A decorative ribbon or bow worn as a headdress.
top·less (tŏp′lĭs) *adj.* **1.** Having no top: *a collection of topless jars; a topless bathing suit.* **2.** Wearing a topless garment: *a topless waitress.* **3.** So high as to appear to extend out of sight: *the topless Alps.*
top·loft·y (tŏp′lôf′tē, -lŏf′tē) *adj.* **-i·er, -i·est.** *Informal.* Haughty; pretentious. **—top′loft′i·ness** *n.*
top·mast (tŏp′məst, -măst′) *n. Naut.* The mast that is below the topgallant mast in a square-rigged ship and next above the lower mast in a fore-and-aft-rigged ship.
top·min·now (tŏp′mĭn′ō) *n.* **1.** Any of several small New World freshwater fishes of the genus *Fundulus,* related to the killifishes. **2.** Any of various small, viviparous New World fishes of the family Poeciliidae, of fresh or brackish waters. [So called because it swims near the surface of water.]
top·most (tŏp′mōst′) *adj.* Highest; uppermost.
top·notch (tŏp′nŏch′) *adj. Informal.* First-rate; excellent.
topo– or **top–** *pref.* Place; region: *toponymy.* [< Gk. *topos,* place.]
to·pog·ra·pher (tə-pŏg′rə-fər, tō-) *n.* **1.** A person skilled in topography. **2.** A person who describes and maps the surface features of geographical regions.
to·pog·ra·phy (tə-pŏg′rə-fē, tō-) *n., pl.* **-phies. 1.** Detailed and precise description of a place or region. **2.** The technique of graphically representing the exact physical features of a place or region on a map. **3.** The physical features of a place or region. **4.** The surveying of the features of a region or place. [ME *topographie* < LLat. *topographia* < Gk. < *topographein,* to describe a place : *topos,* place + *graphein,* to write.] **—top′o·graph′** (tŏp′ə-grăf′) *n.* **—top′o·graph′ic** (tŏp′-ə-grăf′ĭk), **top′o·graph′i·cal** *adj.* **—top′o·graph′i·cal·ly** *adv.*
to·pol·o·gy (tə-pŏl′ə-jē, tō-) *n., pl.* **-gies. 1.** The topographical study of a given place in relation to its history. **2.** The anatomy of specific areas of the body. **3.** *Math.* The study of the properties of geometric configurations invariant under transformation by continuous mappings. **—top′o·log′ic** (tŏp′ə-lŏj′ĭk), **top′o·log′i·cal** *adj.* **—top′o·log′i·cal·ly** *adv.* **—to·pol′o·gist** *n.*
top·o·nym (tŏp′ə-nĭm′) *n.* Any name derived from a place or region. [Back-formation < TOPONYMY.] **—top′o·nym′ic, top′-o·nym′i·cal** *adj.*
to·pon·y·my (tə-pŏn′ə-mē, tō-) *n., pl.* **-mies. 1.** *Anat.* Nomenclature with respect to a region of the body rather than to organs or structures. **2.** The study of place names.
top·o·type (tŏp′ə-tīp′) *n. Biol.* A specimen of an organism taken from the area typical for that species.
top·per (tŏp′ər) *n.* **1.** One that removes tops: *a carrot topper.* **2.** A short, lightweight topcoat for a woman. **3.** *Slang.* A top hat. **4.** *Slang.* One that outdoes or climaxes what has gone before, esp. a bantering remark. **5.** One that is at or on the top.
top·ping (tŏp′ĭng) *n.* **1.** A sauce, frosting, or garnish for food. **2.** A part or layer that forms the top of something. **3. toppings.** The cropped parts of plants or trees after pruning. *—adj.* **1.** Held in very high opinion; outstanding. **2.** *Chiefly Brit.* First-rate; excellent.
top·ple (tŏp′əl) *v.* **-pled, -pling, -ples.** *—tr.* To push over; overturn. *—intr.* **1.** To totter and fall. **2.** To lean over as if about to fall. [Freq. of TOP[1].]
top round *n.* A cut of meat, as steak or a roast, taken from the inner section of a round of beef.
tops (tŏps) *adj. Slang.* First-rate; excellent; topmost: *She is tops in her field.*
top·sail (tŏp′səl, -sāl′) *n. Naut.* **1.** A square sail set above the lowest sail on the mast of a square-rigged ship. **2.** A triangular or square sail set above the gaff of a lower sail on a fore-and-aft-rigged ship.
topsail schooner *n.* A schooner carrying two or more square topsails on her foremast.
top-se·cret (tŏp′sē′krĭt) *adj.* Designating materials or information of the highest level of security classification.
top sergeant *n. Informal.* A first sergeant.
top·side (tŏp′sīd′) *n.* **1.** Often **topsides.** The upper parts of a ship that are above the main deck. **2.** The highest position of authority. *—adv. & adj.* **1.** On or to the upper parts of a ship; on deck. **2.** In a position of authority.
top·sid·er (tŏp′sī′der) *n.* One who is at the highest level of authority.
Top-Sid·er (tŏp′sī′der). A trademark for a soft leather or canvas shoe with a rubber sole.
top·soil (tŏp′soil′) *n.* The surface layer of soil. *—tr.v.* **-soiled, -soil·ing, -soils.** To remove the surface layer of soil from (land).
top·stitch (tŏp′stĭch′) *tr.v.* **-stitched, -stitch·ing, -stitch·es.** To sew a line of stitching close to the seam or edge of (a garment) on the right side of the fabric.
top·sy-tur·vy (tŏp′sē-tûr′vē) *adv.* **1.** With the top downward and the bottom up; upside-down. **2.** In a state of utter disorder or confusion. *—adj.* Being in a confused or disordered condition. *—n.* Confusion; chaos. [Prob. TOP[1] + obs. *terve,* to overturn.] **—top′sy-tur′vi·ly** *adv.* **—top′sy-tur′vi·ness** *n.*
toque (tōk) *n.* **1.** A small brimless, close-fitting woman's hat. **2.** A plumed velvet cap with a full crown and small rolled brim, worn by men and women in 16th-century France. [Fr. < Sp. *toca.*]
tor (tôr) *n.* A high rock or pile of rocks on the top of a hill. [ME < OE *torr.*]
to·rah also **To·rah** (tôr′ə, tōr′ə) *n.* **1.** The entire body of Jewish religious law and learning including both sacred literature and oral tradition. **2.** A scroll or scrolls of parchment containing the Pentateuch, used in a synagogue during services. [Heb. *tōrāh* < *hārāh,* he taught.]
tor·bern·ite (tôr′bər-nīt′) *n.* An emerald- or grass-green hydrous crystalline phosphate of uranium and copper. [G. *Torbernit,* after *Torbern* O. Bergman (1735–1784).]
torch (tôrch) *n.* **1.** A portable light produced by the flame of a flammable material wound about the end of a stick of wood and ignited; flambeau. **2.** A portable apparatus that produces a very hot flame by the combustion of gases, used in welding and construction. **3.** Anything that serves to illuminate, enlighten, or guide. **4.** *Chiefly Brit.* A flashlight. *—tr.v.* **torched, torch·ing, torch·es.** *Slang.* To cause to burn or undergo combustion. **—*idiom.* carry a (or the) torch for.** To love (someone) who does not reciprocate. [ME *torche* < OFr. < Lat. *torquēre,* to twist.]
torch·bear·er (tôrch′bâr′ər) *n.* **1.** A person who carries a torch. **2.** A person who imparts knowledge, truth, or inspiration to others, as the leader of a movement.
tor·chon lace (tôr′shŏn′) *n.* A lace made of coarse linen or cotton thread twisted in simple geometric patterns. [Fr. *torchon,* duster < OFr., twisted straw < *torche,* torch.]
torch song *n.* A sentimental popular song, typically one in which the singer laments a lost love. **—torch singer** *n.*
torch·wood (tôrch′wo͝od′) *n.* **1.** Any of several tropical American trees of the genus *Amyris,* esp. *A. balsamifera,* having resinous wood that burns with a torchlike flame. **2.** The wood of the torchwood.
tore[1] (tôr, tōr) *v.* Past tense of **tear[1]**. —See Usage note at **torn.**
tore[2] (tôr, tōr) *n.* A torus (sense 4). [Fr. < Lat. *torus.*]
tor·e·a·dor (tôr′ē-ə-dôr′) *n.* A bullfighter. [Sp. < *toreado,* p.part. of *torear,* to fight bulls < *toro,* bull < Lat. *taurus.*]
to·re·ro (tə-râr′ō) *n., pl.* **-ros.** A matador or one of his team. [Sp. < LLat. *taurarius* < Lat. *taurus,* bull.]
to·reu·tics (tə-ro͞o′tĭks) *n. (used with a sing. verb).* The art of working metal or other materials by the use of embossing and chasing to form minute detailed reliefs. [< Gk. *toreutikos,* of metal work < *toreuein,* to work in relief < *toreus,* a boring tool.] **—to·reu′tic** *adj.*
to·ri (tôr′ī′, tōr′ī′) *n.* Plural of **torus.**
tor·ic (tôr′ĭk, tōr′-) *adj.* Of, pertaining to, or shaped like a torus or a part of a torus.
to·ri·i (tôr′ē-ē′, tōr′-) *n., pl.* **torii.** The gateway of a Shinto temple, consisting of two uprights with a straight crosspiece at the top and a concave lintel above the crosspiece. [J. : *tori,* bird + *iru-,* to dwell.]
tor·ment (tôr′mĕnt′) *n.* **1.** Great physical pain or mental anguish. **2.** A source of harassment, annoyance, or pain. **3.** The torture inflicted on prisoners being interrogated. *—tr.v.* (tôr-mĕnt′, tôr′mĕnt′) **-ment·ed, -ment·ing, -ments. 1.** To cause to undergo great physical pain or mental anguish. **2.** To agitate or upset greatly. **3.** To annoy, pester, or harass. [ME < OFr. < Lat. *tormentum* < *torquēre,* to twist.] **—tor·ment′ing·ly** *adv.*
tor·men·til (tôr′mən-tĭl′) *n.* A Eurasian plant, *Potentilla tormentilla* or *P. erecta,* having yellow flowers and astringent roots. [ME *tormentille* < Med. Lat. *tormentilla.*]
tor·men·tor also **tor·ment·er** (tôr-mĕn′tər, tôr′mĕn′tər) *n.* **1.** One that torments. **2.** A hanging at each side of a stage directly behind the proscenium to block the wing area and sidelights from the audience. **3.** A sound-absorbent screen used on a motion-picture set to prevent echo.
torn (tôrn, tōrn) *v.* Past participle of **tear[1]**.
Usage: *Torn,* never *tore,* is the standard past participle of the verb *tear.*
tor·na·do (tôr-nā′dō) *n., pl.* **-does** or **-dos. 1.** A rotating column of air usually accompanied by a funnel-shaped downward extension of a cumulonimbus cloud and having a vortex several hundred yards in diameter whirling destructively at speeds of up to 300 miles per hour. **2.** A violent thunderstorm in West Africa and nearby Atlantic waters. **3.** A whirlwind or hurricane. [Alteration of Sp. *tronada,* thunderstorm < *tronar,* to thunder < Lat. *tonare.*] **—tor·na′dic** (-nā′dĭk, -năd′ĭk) *adj.*
to·roid (tôr′oid′, tōr′-) *n.* **1.** *Math.* **a.** A surface generated by a closed curve rotating about, but not intersecting or containing, an axis in its own plane. **b.** A solid having such a surface. **2.** An object having the shape of a toroid. [TOR(US) + -OID.] **—to·roi′dal** (tô-roid′l) *adj.*
to·rose (tôr′ōs′, tōr′-) *adj.* Cylindrical and having ridges or swellings. [Lat. *torosus,* knotty < *torus,* knot.]
tor·pe·do (tôr-pē′dō) *n., pl.* **-does. 1.** A cigar-shaped, self-propelled underwater projectile launched from a plane, ship, or submarine, and designed to detonate on contact

topiary

torah
17th-century Spanish torah scroll

torii

with or in the vicinity of a target. **2.** Any of various submarine explosive devices, esp. a submarine mine. **3.** A small explosive placed on a railroad track that is fired by the weight of the train to sound a warning of an approaching hazard. **4.** An explosive fired in an oil or gas well to begin or increase the flow. **5.** A small firework consisting of some gravel wrapped in tissue paper with a percussion cap that explodes when thrown against a hard surface. **6.** Any of several cartilaginous fishes of the genus *Torpedo,* related to the skates and rays. **7.** A professional assassin or thug. **8.** A hero (sense 6). *—tr.v.* **-doed, -do·ing, -does.** To attack, explode, or destroy with or as if with a torpedo. [NLat. *Torpedo,* genus of fish that give electric shocks < Lat. *torpedo,* electric ray < *torpēre,* to be astounded.]

torpedo boat *n.* A fast, thinly plated boat equipped with heavy machine guns and torpedo tubes.

tor·pe·do-boat destroyer (tôr-pē'dō-bōt') *n.* A fast vessel, larger and more heavily armed than a torpedo boat, designed to destroy the latter, but often serving the same purpose.

torpedo tube *n.* The torpedo-launching tube in the hull of certain naval vessels such as submarines.

tor·pid (tôr'pĭd) *adj.* **1.** Deprived of the power of motion or feeling; benumbed. **2.** Dormant; hibernating. **3.** Lethargic; apathetic. [Lat. *torpidus* < *torpēre,* to be sluggish.] **—tor·pid'i·ty** (-pĭd'ĭ-tē) *n.* **—tor'pid·ly** *adv.*

tor·por (tôr'pər) *n.* **1.** A condition of mental or physical inactivity or insensibility. **2.** Lethargy; apathy. [Lat. < *torpēre,* to be numb.] **—tor'po·rif'ic** (-pə-rĭf'ĭk) *adj.*

tor·quate (tôr'kwāt') *adj. Zool.* Having a ringlike or collarlike band or marking about the neck. [Lat. *torquatus,* having a collar < *torques,* collar. —see TORQUE[2].]

torque[1] (tôrk) *n.* **1.** The moment of a force, a measure of its tendency to produce torsion and rotation about an axis, equal to the vector product of the radius vector from the axis of rotation to the point of application of the force by the force applied. **2.** A turning or twisting force. *—tr.v.* **torqued, torqu·ing, torques.** To impart torque to. [< Lat. *torquēre,* to twist.] **—torqu'er** *n.*

torque[2] (tôrk) *n.* A collar, necklace, or armband made of a strip of twisted metal, worn by the ancient Gauls, Germans, and Britons. [Fr. < Lat. *torques* < *torquēre,* to twist.]

torque converter *n.* A mechanical or hydraulic device for changing the ratio of torque to speed between the input and output shafts of a mechanism.

tor·ques (tôr'kwēz') *n. Zool.* A band of feathers, hair, or coloration around the neck. [Lat., collar. —see TORQUE[2].]

torr (tôr) *n., pl.* **torr.** A unit of pressure that is equal to 1.316×10^{-3} atmosphere. [After Evangelista *Torricelli* (1608–1647).]

tor·rent (tôr'ənt, tŏr'-) *n.* **1.** A turbulent, swift-flowing stream. **2.** A raging flood; deluge. **3.** Any turbulent or overwhelming flow: *a torrent of insults; torrents of mail.* [Fr. < Ital. *torrente* < Lat. *torrens* < pr.part. of *torrēre,* to burn.]

tor·ren·tial (tô-rĕn'shəl, tə-) *adj.* **1.** Of or pertaining to a torrent. **2.** Resembling a torrent; turbulent; wild: *torrential applause.* **3.** Resulting from the action of a torrent or torrents: *torrential erosion.* **—tor·ren'tial·ly** *adv.*

tor·rid (tôr'ĭd, tŏr'-) *adj.* **1.** Parched with the heat of the sun. **2.** Scorching; burning. **3.** Passionate; ardent. [Lat. *torridus* < *torrēre,* to parch.] **—tor·rid'i·ty** (tô-rĭd'ĭ-tē), **tor'rid·ness** *n.* **—tor'rid·ly** *adv.*

Torrid Zone *n.* The region of the earth's surface between the tropics of Cancer and Capricorn.

tor·sade (tôr-säd', -sād') *n.* A decorative trimming for hats of twisted ribbon or cord. [Fr. < obs. *tors,* twisted < LLat. *torsus* < p.part. of Lat. *torquēre,* to twist.]

tor·si (tôr'sē') *n.* A plural of **torso.**

tor·sion (tôr'shən) *n.* **1. a.** The act of twisting or turning. **b.** The condition of being twisted or turned. **2.** The stress caused when one end of an object is twisted in one direction and the other end is held motionless or twisted in the opposite direction. [LLat. *torsio* < *torsus,* twisted. —see TORSADE.] **—tor'sion·al** *adj.* **—tor'sion·al·ly** *adv.*

torsion balance *n.* An instrument with which small forces, as of electricity or magnetism, are measured by means of the torsion they produce in a wire or slender rod.

torsion bar *n.* A part of an automobile suspension consisting of a bar that twists to maintain stability.

tor·so (tôr'sō) *n., pl.* **-sos** or **-si** (-sē'). **1.** The trunk of the human body. **2.** A statue of the trunk of the human body, esp. with the head and limbs truncated. **3.** A truncated or unfinished thing. [Ital., trunk of a statue < Lat. *thyrsus,* stalk. —see THYRSUS.]

tort (tôrt) *n. Law.* A wrongful act, damage, or injury done willfully, negligently, or in circumstances involving strict liability, but not involving breach of contract, for which a civil suit can be brought. [ME, injury < OFr. < Med. Lat. *tortum* < Lat., neuter p.part. of *torquēre,* to twist.]

torte (tôrt, tôr'tə) *n., pl.* **tortes** or **tor·ten** (tôr'tn). A kind of rich cake made with many eggs and little flour and usually containing chopped nuts. [G., perh. < Ital. *torta,* cake < LLat. *torta,* a kind of bread.]

tor·tel·li·ni (tôr'tl-ē'nē) *n.* Small stuffed pasta dumplings. [Ital., dim. of *tortelli,* a kind of pasta < LLat. *torta,* a kind of bread.]

tor·ti·col·lis (tôr'tĭ-kŏl'ĭs) *n.* A contracted state of the neck muscles producing an unnatural position of the head. [Lat. *tortus,* twisted (< *torquēre,* to twist) + *collum,* neck.] **—tor'ti·col'lar** (-kŏl'ər) *adj.*

tor·ti·lla (tôr-tē'yə) *n.* A thin, round unleavened bread, usually made from cornmeal and served hot with various toppings of ground meat or cheese. [Mex. Sp. < Sp., omelet < Sp. *torta,* cake < LLat. *torta,* a kind of bread.]

tor·toise (tôr'tĭs) *n.* **1. a.** Any of various terrestrial turtles, esp. one of the family Testudinidae, characteristically having thick, scaly limbs and a high, rounded carapace. **b.** *Chiefly Brit.* A terrestrial or freshwater chelonian. **2.** One that moves slowly. [ME *tortuce* < OFr. *tortue.*]

tor·toise·shell also **tor·toise-shell** or **tortoise shell** (tôr'tĭs-shĕl') *n.* **1.** The mottled, horny, translucent brownish covering of the carapace of certain of the sea turtles, esp. the hawksbill, used to make combs, jewelry, and other articles. **2.** A domestic cat having fur with brown, black, and yellowish markings. **3.** Any of several butterflies, chiefly of the genus *Nymphalis,* having wings with orange, black, and brown markings. **—tor'toise·shell'** *adj.*

tor·tu·os·i·ty (tôr'cho͞o-ŏs'ĭ-tē) *n., pl.* **-ties. 1.** The state of being tortuous; twistedness; crookedness. **2.** A bent or twisted part, passage, or thing; twist; turn.

tor·tu·ous (tôr'cho͞o-əs) *adj.* **1.** Having or marked by repeated turns or bends; winding; twisting: *a tortuous trail through the jungle.* **2.** Not straightforward; deceitful; devious: *a tortuous plot.* **3.** Highly involved; circuitous; complex: *tortuous legal procedures.* [ME < OFr. < Lat. *tortuosus* < *tortus,* a twisting < p.part of *torquēre,* to twist.] **—tor'tu·ous·ly** *adv.* **—tor'tu·ous·ness** *n.*

Usage: Although *tortuous* and *torturous* have a common root, their primary meanings are distinct. *Tortuous* means "twisting" (*a tortuous road*) or by extension "extremely strained or devious" (*tortuous reasoning*). *Torturous* refers primarily to the pain of torture. However, *torturous* can also be used in the sense of "twisted" or "strained," and *tortured* is an even stronger synonym: *tortured reasoning.*

tor·ture (tôr'chər) *n.* **1. a.** The infliction of severe physical pain as a means of punishment or coercion. **b.** The experience of this. **2.** Mental anguish. **3.** Something causing pain or anguish. *—tr.v.* **-tured, -tur·ing, -tures. 1.** To subject (a person or animal) to torture. **2.** To afflict with great physical or mental pain. **3.** To twist or turn abnormally; distort. [OFr. < LLat. *tortura* < Lat. *torquēre,* to twist.] **—tor'tur·er** *n.* **—tor'tur·ous** *adj.* **—tor'tur·ous·ly** *adv.*

to·rus (tôr'əs, tōr'-) *n., pl.* **to·ri** (tôr'ī', tōr'ī'). **1.** *Archit.* A large convex molding, semicircular in cross section, located at the base of a classical column. **2.** *Anat.* A bulging or rounded projection or swelling. **3.** *Biol.* A moundlike or rounded structure, as the receptacle of a flower. **4.** *Math.* A toroid generated by a circle; a surface having the shape of a doughnut. [Lat., bulge.]

To·ry (tôr'ē, tōr'ē) *n., pl.* **-ries. 1.** A member of a British political party, founded in 1689, that was the opposition party to the Whigs and has been known as the Conservative Party since about 1832. **2.** An American who during the period of the American Revolution favored the English side. **3.** Often **tory.** A member of a Conservative Party, as in Canada. [Ir. Gael. *tōraidhe,* robber < OIr. *tōir,* pursuit.] **—To'ry** *adj.* **—To'ry·ism** *n.*

toss (tôs, tŏs) *v.* **tossed, toss·ing, toss·es.** *—tr.* **1.** To throw, fling, or heave continuously about; pitch to and fro. **2.** To throw lightly with or as if with the hand or hands; pitch gently or with a sudden slight jerk. **3.** *Informal.* To discuss informally; bandy about. **4.** To move or lift (the head) with a sudden motion. **5.** To disturb or agitate; upset. **6.** To throw to the ground. **7. a.** To flip (coins) in order to decide something. **b.** To flip coins with. **8.** To mix (a salad) lightly so as to cover with dressing. *—intr.* **1.** To be thrown here and there; be flung to and fro. **2.** To move oneself about vigorously; throw oneself from side to side: *toss in one's sleep.* **3.** To flip a coin. ***—phrasal verbs.* toss down.** To drink in one draft by suddenly tilting: *He tossed down one glass of beer after another.* **toss off. 1.** To drink up in one draft. **2.** To do, finish, accomplish, or perform in a casual, easy manner: *He tossed off a few appropriate jokes.* *—n.* **1.** The act of tossing or the condition of being tossed. **2.** The distance something can be tossed. **3.** A rapid movement or lift, as of the head. **4.** An even chance. [Poss. of Scand. orig.] **—toss'er** *n.*

toss·pot (tôs'pŏt', tŏs'-) *n.* A drunkard.

toss·up (tôs'ŭp', tŏs'-) *n. Informal.* **1.** The flipping of a coin to decide an issue. **2.** An even chance or choice.

tot[1] (tŏt) *n.* **1.** A small child. **2.** A small amount, as of liquor. [Orig. unknown.]

tot[2] (tŏt) *tr.v.* **tot·ted, tot·ting, tots.** To total: *totted up the bill.*

to·tal (tōt'l) *n.* **1.** The amount or quantity obtained by addition; sum. **2.** A whole quantity; entirety. *—adj.* **1.** Constituting or pertaining to the whole; entire. **2.** Complete; utter; absolute: *a total effort.* *—v.* **-taled, -tal·ing, -tals** or **-talled, -tal·ling, -tals.** *—tr.* **1.** To determine the sum or total of. **2.** To equal a total of; amount to. **3.** *Slang.* To demolish (a vehicle) completely. *—intr.* To add up; to amount: *It totals to three dollars.* [ME, whole < OFr. < Med. Lat. *totalis* < Lat. *totus.*]

total eclipse *n.* An eclipse in which the entire surface of a celestial body is obscured by another.

to·tal·i·tar·i·an (tō-tăl′ĭ-târ′ē-ən) *adj.* Designating a form of government in which one person or party exercises absolute control over all spheres of human life and opposing parties are not permitted to exist. [TOTAL + (AUTHOR)ITARIAN.] **—to·tal′i·tar′i·an·ism** *n.*

to·tal·i·ty (tō-tăl′ĭ-tē) *n., pl.* **-ties. 1.** The state or condition of being total. **2.** An aggregate amount; sum. **3.** The state of an eclipse when it is total.

to·tal·i·za·tor (tōt′l-ĭ-zā′tər) *n.* A machine for computing and showing totals, esp. a pari-mutuel machine showing the total number and amounts of bets at a racetrack.

to·tal·ize (tōt′l-īz′) *tr.v.* **-ized, -iz·ing, -iz·es.** To make or combine into a total. **—to′tal·i·za′tion** *n.*

to·tal·iz·er (tōt′l-ī′zər) *n.* **1.** A pari-mutuel machine. **2.** An adding machine.

to·tal·ly (tōt′l-ē) *adv.* Entirely; wholly; completely.

to·ta·quine (tō′tə-kwīn′, -kwēn′, -kwĭn) *n.* A powdered yellowish, bitter mixture of quinine and alkaloids from cinchona bark, used as an antimalarial. [TOTA(L) + Sp. *quina,* cinchona bark.]

tote[1] (tōt) *Informal.* *—tr.v.* **tot·ed, tot·ing, totes. 1.** To haul; lug. **2.** To have on one's person; pack: *toting guns.* *—n.* **1.** A load; burden. **2.** A tote bag. [Orig. unknown.] **—tot′er** *n.*

tote[2] (tōt) *n. Informal.* A pari-mutuel machine. [Short for TOTALIZATOR.]

tote bag *n. Informal.* A large handbag or shopping bag.

to·tem (tō′təm) *n.* **1. a.** An animal, plant, or natural object serving among certain primitive peoples as the emblem of a clan or family by virtue of an asserted ancestral relationship. **b.** A representation of this being. **2.** A social group having a common totemic affiliation. **3.** Any venerated emblem or symbol. [Ojibwa *nintōtēm.*] **—to·tem′ic** (-tĕm′ĭk) *adj.*

to·tem·ism (tō′tə-mĭz′əm) *n.* **1.** The belief in kinship through common totemic affiliation or the identification of an individual or group with a totem. **2.** The primitive kinship system of which totemism is a reflection. **—to′tem·ist** *n.* **—to′tem·is′tic** *adj.*

totem pole *n.* **1.** A post carved and painted with a series of totemic symbols and erected before a dwelling, as among certain Indian peoples of the northwestern coast of North America. **2.** *Slang.* A hierarchy: *low man on the totem pole.*

toth·er or **t'oth·er** (tŭ*th*′ər) *pron. & adj. Informal.* The other. [ME < *thet other,* that other.]

to·ti·pal·mate (tō′tĭ-păl′māt′) *adj.* Having webbing that connects each of the four anterior toes, as in water birds such as pelicans and gannets. [Lat. *totus,* whole + PALMATE.]

to·tip·o·ten·cy (tō-tĭp′ə-tən-sē, tō′tĭ-pōt′n-sē) also **to·tip·o·tence** (tō-tĭp′ə-təns, tō′tĭ-pōt′ns) *n.* The ability of a cell, such as an egg, to give rise to unlike cells and thus to form a new individual or part. [Lat. *totus,* whole + POTENCY.] **—to·tip′o·tent** *adj.*

tot·ter (tŏt′ər) *intr.v.* **-tered, -ter·ing, -ters. 1. a.** To sway as if about to fall. **b.** To appear about to collapse: *a tottering empire.* **2.** To walk unsteadily or feebly. **3.** To waver; vacillate: *"His extreme oddness still tottered this side of lunacy"* (Evelyn Waugh). *—n.* The act or condition of tottering. [ME *toteren* < MDu. *touter,* to swing.] **—tot′ter·er** *n.* **—tot′ter·y** *adj.*

tou·can (to͞o′kăn′, -kän′, to͞o-kăn′, -kän′) *n.* Any of various tropical American birds of the family Ramphastidae, having brightly colored plumage and a very large bill. [Fr. < Port. *tucano* < Tupi *tucana.*]

touch (tŭch) *v.* **touched, touch·ing, touch·es.** *—tr.* **1.** To cause or permit a part of the body, esp. the hand or fingers, to come in contact with so as to feel. **2. a.** To bring something into contact with: *touch the contact with a wire.* **b.** To bring (one thing) into contact with something else: *touch a wire to the contact.* **3.** To cause (one thing) to be in contact with something else: *He touched the control and the plane leveled off.* **4.** To tap or nudge very lightly. **5.** To strike or lay hands on in violence: *I never touched him!* **6.** To eat or drink; taste: *She didn't touch her food.* **7.** To disturb or move by handling: *Just don't touch anything in my room!* **8. a.** To meet; adjoin; border. **b.** *Math.* To be tangent to. **9.** To come up to; equal: *His work couldn't touch his master's.* **10.** To deal with as a subject; treat of. **11.** To be pertinent to; concern: *a problem that touches many people.* **12.** To have an effect upon; move emotionally: *Her crying touched him deeply.* **13.** To injure or spoil slightly. **14.** To color slightly; tinge. **15.** To draw with light strokes. **16.** To change or improve by adding fine lines or strokes. **17.** To strike or pluck the keys or strings of (a musical instrument). **18.** To play (a musical piece). **19.** To stamp (tested metal). **20.** *Slang.* To wheedle a loan from. *—intr.* **1.** To touch someone or something. **2.** To be or come into contact. ***—phrasal verbs.*** **touch down.** To land or make contact with a landing surface, as an airplane or spacecraft. **touch off. 1.** To cause to explode; fire. **2.** To initiate (a chain of events, for example); trigger. **touch on** (or **upon**). **1.** To deal with (a topic) in passing. **2.** To pertain to; concern. **3.** To approach being; verge on. **touch up.** To improve by making minor changes or additions. *—n.* **1.** The act or an instance of touching. **2.** The physiological sense by which external objects or forces are perceived through contact with the body. **3.** A sensation experienced in touching something with a characteristic texture. **4.** A mild tap or shove. **5.** A discernible mark or effect left by contact with something. **6.** A subtle effect wrought by a small change or addition: *Candlelight provided just the right touch.* **7.** A suggestion; hint; tinge: *a touch of jealousy.* **8.** A mild attack: *a touch of the flu.* **9.** A small amount; trace; dash: *a touch of paprika.* **10. a.** A manner or technique of striking the keys of a keyboard instrument, as a piano or typewriter. **b.** The resistance to being struck by the fingers characteristic of a keyboard. **11.** A characteristic way or style of doing things. **12.** A facility; knack: *lose one's touch.* **13.** The state of being in contact or communication: *Let's keep in touch.* **14.** The official stamp indicating the quality of a metal product. **15.** *Slang.* **a.** The act of approaching someone to wheedle a loan. **b.** A sum of money borrowed. **c.** A person liable to be the victim of an approach for a loan: *a soft touch; an easy touch.* **16.** *Sports.* The area just outside the sidelines in Rugby football and soccer. [ME *touchen* < OFr. *tochier.*] **—touch′a·ble** *adj.* **—touch′a·ble·ness** *n.* **—touch′er** *n.*

touch-and-go (tŭch′ən-gō′) *adj.* **1.** Of insecure future; uncertain. **2.** Of or performed without attention; casual.

touch·back (tŭch′băk′) *n. Football.* A play in which a player recovers and touches the ball to the ground behind his own goal line after it has been propelled into or beyond the end zone by a player on the opposing team.

touch·down (tŭch′doun′) *n.* **1.** *Football.* A play worth six points, accomplished by being in possession of the ball when it is declared dead on or behind the opponent's goal line. **2.** The contact, or moment of contact, of a landing aircraft or spacecraft with the landing surface.

tou·ché (to͞o-shā′) *interj.* Used to express concession to an opponent for a point well made, as in an argument. [Fr. < p.part. of *toucher,* to touch (from a fencing term indicating the success of an opponent's attack).]

touched (tŭcht) *adj.* **1.** Emotionally affected or moved. **2.** Somewhat demented or mentally unbalanced.

touch football *n.* A variety of football for playing on an improvised field and without protective equipment, involving the substitution of touching for tackling.

touch·hole (tŭch′hōl′) *n.* The opening in early firearms and cannons through which the powder was ignited.

touch·ing (tŭch′ĭng) *adj.* Eliciting a tender reaction. *—prep. Archaic.* Concerning; about. **—touch′ing·ly** *adv.* **—touch′ing·ness** *n.*

touch·line (tŭch′līn′) *n.* Either of the sidelines bordering the playing field in Rugby.

touch-me-not (tŭch′mē-nŏt′) *n.* Any of several plants of the genus *Impatiens,* esp. the jewelweed. [From the bursting of ripe seed pods when touched.]

touch paper *n.* A type of paper impregnated with saltpeter so that it burns slowly and without a flame. [From its use to ignite gunpowder.]

touch·stone (tŭch′stōn′) *n.* **1.** A hard black stone, as jasper or basalt, formerly used to test the quality of gold or silver by comparing the streak left on the stone by one of these metals with that of a standard alloy. **2.** A criterion; standard: *"The touchstone of an art is its precision"* (Ezra Pound).

touch-type (tŭch′tīp′) *intr.v.* **-typed, -typ·ing, -types.** To type without having to look at the keyboard, the fingers having been trained to locate the keys by position.

touch·up (tŭch′ŭp′) *n.* The act or process of finishing or improving by small alterations and additions.

touch·wood (tŭch′wo͝od′) *n.* Decayed wood or similar material used as tinder; punk. [From its being easy to ignite.]

touch·y (tŭch′ē) *adj.* **-i·er, -i·est. 1.** Tending to take offense with very slight cause; oversensitive. **2.** Requiring tact or skill: *a touchy situation.* **3.** Sensitive to touch. Used of a bodily part. **4.** Easily ignited; flammable. **—touch′i·ly** *adv.* **—touch′i·ness** *n.*

tough (tŭf) *adj.* **-er, -est. 1.** Strong and resilient; able to withstand great strain without tearing or breaking. **2.** Hard to cut or chew. **3.** Physically hardy; rugged. **4.** Severe; harsh: *a tough winter.* **5.** Aggressive; pugnacious. **6.** Demanding or troubling; difficult. **7.** Strong-minded; resolute. **8.** Vicious; rough. **9.** *Informal.* Unfortunate; too bad. **10.** *Slang.* Fine; great. *—n.* A hoodlum; thug. ***—idiom.*** **tough it out.** *Slang.* To remain unyielding in adverse circumstances. [ME < OE *tōh.*] **—tough′ly** *adv.* **—tough′ness** *n.*

tough·en (tŭf′ən) *v.* **-ened, -en·ing, -ens.** *—tr.* To make tough. *—intr.* To become tough. **—tough′en·er** *n.*

tough·ie (tŭf′ē) *n. Informal.* **1.** A tough. **2.** A difficult problem.

tough-mind·ed (tŭf′mīn′dĭd) *adj.* Not sentimental or timorous. **—tough′-mind′ed·ly** *adv.* **—tough′-mind′ed·ness** *n.*

tou·pee (to͞o-pā′) *n.* **1.** A partial wig or hair piece worn to cover a bald spot. **2.** A curl or lock of hair worn during the 18th century as a topknot on a periwig. [Fr. *toupet,* tuft of hair < OFr. *toup.*]

tour (to͝or) *n.* **1.** A comprehensive trip with visits to places of established interest. **2.** A group organized for a comprehensive trip or for a shorter sightseeing excursion. **3.** A brief trip to or through a place for the purpose of seeing it: *a tour of the house.* **4.** A journey to fulfill a round of engagements in several places: *a concert tour.* **5.** A shift, as in a factory.

totem pole

totipalmate
Totipalmate foot of a pelican

toucan

George Miksch Sutton
touraco

tower
Eiffel Tower, Paris

6. A period of duty at a single place or job. —*v.* **toured, tour·ing, tours.** —*intr.* To go on a tour. —*tr.* **1.** To make a tour of. **2.** To present (a theatrical performance) on a tour. [ME, one's turn < OFr., turn < Lat. *tornus,* lathe. —see TURN.]

tou·ra·co also **tu·ra·co** (to͝or'ə-kō') *n., pl.* **-cos.** Any of various African birds of the family Musophagidae, many of which have brightly colored plumage. [Fr.]

tour·bil·lion (to͝or-bĭl'yən) *n.* **1. a.** A whirlwind. **b.** A vortex, as of a whirlwind or whirlpool. **2.** A skyrocket that has a spiral flight. [ME *turbilloun* < OFr. *torbeillon* < Lat. *turbo.*]

tour de force (to͝or' də fôrs', fōrs') *n.* A feat of strength or virtuosity. [Fr.]

tour·ing (to͝or'ĭng) *n.* **1.** Participation in a tour. **2.** Ski touring.

touring car *n.* A large open automobile for five or more persons, popular in the 1920's.

tour·ism (to͝or'ĭz'əm) *n.* **1.** The practice of traveling for pleasure. **2.** The business of providing tours and services for tourists.

tour·ist (to͝or'ĭst) *n.* A person who is traveling for pleasure. **—tour·is'tic** (to͞o-rĭs'tĭk) *adj.*

tourist class *n.* A grade of travel accommodations less luxurious than first class or cabin class.

tourist trap *n.* A place, as a shop or resort area, that offers goods and services to tourists at a high price.

tour·ma·line also **tur·ma·line** (to͝or'mə-lĭn, -lēn') *n.* A complex crystalline silicate containing aluminum, boron, and other elements, used in electronic instrumentation and, esp. in its green, clear, and blue varieties, as a gemstone. [Singhalese *toramalli,* carnelian.]

tour·na·ment (to͝or'nə-mənt, tûr'-) *n.* **1.** A contest involving a number of contestants who compete in a series of elimination games or trials. **2.** A medieval martial sport in which two groups of mounted and armored contestants fought against each other with blunted lances or swords. [ME *tournement,* a medieval sport < OFr. *torneiement* < *torneier,* to tourney.]

tour·ne·dos (to͝or'nə-dō') *n., pl.* **tour·ne·dos** (-dō', -dōz'). A fillet of beef cut from the tenderloin, often bound in bacon or suet for cooking. [Fr. : *tourner,* to turn + *dos,* back < Lat. *dorsum.*]

tour·ney (to͝or'nē, tûr'-) *intr.v.* **-neyed, -ney·ing, -neys.** To compete in a tournament. —*n., pl.* **-neys.** A tournament. [ME *torneyen* < OFr. *torneier* < Lat. *tornus,* lathe. —see TURN.]

tour·ni·quet (to͝or'nĭ-kĭt, tûr'-) *n.* A device used to stop temporarily the flow of blood through a large artery in a limb, esp. a cloth band tightened around a limb, often over a pad placed to focus pressure on the artery. [Fr. < *tourner,* to turn < OFr. —see TURN.]

tou·sle also **tou·zle** (tou'zəl) —*tr.v.* **-sled, -sling, -sles** also **-zled, -zling, -zles.** To disarrange or rumple; dishevel. —*n.* A disheveled mass, as of hair. [ME *touselen,* freq. of *tousen,* to pull roughly.]

tout (tout) *Informal.* —*v.* **tout·ed, tout·ing, touts.** —*intr.* **1.** To solicit customers, votes, or patronage, esp. in a brazen way. **2.** To obtain and deal in horseracing information. —*tr.* **1.** To solicit or importune. **2.** To obtain or sell information on (a racing horse or stable) for the guidance of bettors. **3.** To publicize as being of great worth: *a rookie highly touted by the press.* —*n.* **1.** A person who obtains information on racehorses and their prospects and sells it to bettors. **2.** A person who solicits customers persistently or brazenly. [ME *tuten,* to peer.] **—tout'er** *n.*

to·va·rish or **to·va·rich** (tə-vär'ĭsh, -ĭch) *n.* A comrade. [R.]

tow[1] (tō) *tr.v.* **towed, tow·ing, tows.** To draw or pull along behind by a chain or line. —*n.* **1. a.** An act of towing. **b.** The condition of being towed. **2.** Something, as a barge or car, that is towed. **3.** Something, as a tugboat, that tows. **4.** A rope or cable used in towing. ***—idiom.*** **in tow.** Under one's sway or control. [ME *towen* < OE *togian.*]

tow[2] (tō) *n.* Coarse broken flax or hemp fiber prepared for spinning. [ME, poss. < OE *tow-,* spinning.]

tow·age (tō'ĭj) *n.* **1.** The act or service of towing. **2.** A charge for towing.

to·ward (tôrd, tōrd, tə-wôrd') also **to·wards** (tôrdz, tōrdz, tə-wôrdz') *prep.* **1.** In the direction of: *driving toward home.* **2.** In a position facing: *had his back toward me.* **3.** Somewhat before in time: *It began to rain toward morning.* **4.** With regard to; in relation to: *She didn't like his attitude toward her.* **5.** In furtherance or partial fulfillment of: *gave him five dollars toward the bill.* **6.** By way of achieving; with a view to: *efforts toward peace.* —*adj.* **toward** (tôrd, tōrd). **1.** Favorable. **2.** In progress or imminent. **3.** Tractable; docile. [ME < OE *tōweard* : *tō,* to + *-weard,* -ward.]

to·ward·ly (tôrd'lē, tōrd'-) *adj. Archaic.* **1.** Promising. **2.** Advantageous; favorable. **—to'ward·li·ness** *n.*

tow-a·way zone (tō'ə-wā') *n.* A no-parking zone from which cars may be towed away.

tow·boat (tō'bōt') *n.* A tugboat.

tow·el (tou'əl) *n.* A piece of absorbent cloth or paper used for wiping or drying. —*v.* **-eled, -el·ing, -els** or **-elled, -el·ling, -els.** —*tr.* To wipe or rub dry with a towel. —*intr.* To dry oneself with a towel. [ME < OFr. *toaille,* of Germanic orig.]

tow·el·ette (tou'ə-lĕt') *n.* A small, usually moist piece of material used for cleansing, as of the hands or face.

tow·el·ing (tou'ə-lĭng) *n.* Any of various fabrics of cotton or linen used for making towels.

tow·er (tou'ər) *n.* **1. a.** An exceptionally tall building. **b.** An exceptionally tall part of a building. **2.** A tall framework or structure used for observation, signaling, or pumping. —*intr.v.* **-ered, -er·ing, -ers. 1.** To rise to a conspicuous height; loom: *"There he stood, grown suddenly tall, towering above them"* (J.R.R. Tolkien). **2.** To fly directly upward before swooping or falling. Used of certain birds. [ME *tour* < OE *torr* and OFr. *tor,* both < Lat. *turris* < Gk. *tursis.*]

tow·er·ing (tou'ər-ĭng) *adj.* **1.** Of imposing height. **2.** Outstanding; pre-eminent. **3.** Awesomely intense: *a towering rage.*

tow·head (tō'hĕd') *n.* **1.** A head of white-blond hair resembling tow. **2.** One with a towhead. **—tow'head'ed** *adj.*

tow·hee (tō'hē, tō-hē') *n.* Any of several North American birds of the genera *Pipilo* or *Chlorura,* esp. *P. erythrophthalmus,* having black, white, and rust-colored plumage in the male. [Imit. of the song of some of these birds.]

tow·line (tō'līn') *n.* A line, cable, or chain used in towing a vessel or vehicle.

town (toun) *n.* **1.** A population center, often incorporated, larger than a village and smaller than a city. **2.** *Informal.* A city. **3.** *Chiefly Brit.* A rural village that has a market or fair periodically. **4.** The commercial district or center of an area: *I'm going into town.* **5.** The residents of a town. ***—idioms.*** **go to town.** *Slang.* To go all out. **on the town.** *Slang.* On a spree. [ME < OE *tūn,* hamlet.]

town clerk *n.* A public official in charge of keeping the records of a town.

town crier *n.* A person formerly employed by a town to walk the streets proclaiming announcements.

town hall *n.* The building that contains the offices of the public officials of a town and houses the town council and courts.

town house *n.* **1.** A house or other residence in the city as distinguished from one in the country. **2.** One of a row of houses connected by common side walls.

town·ie also **town·y** (tou'nē) *n., pl.* **-ies.** *Informal.* **1.** A townsman. **2.** A resident of a college town as opposed to a student.

town manager *n.* A town official having the same status and duties as a city manager.

town meeting *n.* A legislative assembly of townspeople.

towns·folk (tounz'fōk') *n.* Townspeople.

town·ship (toun'shĭp') *n.* **1.** A subdivision of a county in most northeastern and midwestern states, having the status of a unit of local government with varying governmental powers. **2.** A public land surveying unit of 36 sections, or 36 square miles. **3.** An ancient administrative division of a large parish in England.

towns·man (tounz'mən) *n.* **1.** A resident of a town. **2.** A fellow resident of one's town.

towns·peo·ple (tounz'pē'pəl) *pl.n.* The inhabitants or citizens of a town or city.

towns·wom·an (tounz'wo͝om'ən) *n.* **1.** A female resident of a town. **2.** A female resident of one's town.

town·y (tou'nē) *n.* Variant of **townie.**

tow·path (tō'păth', -päth') *n.* A path along a canal or river used by animals towing boats.

tox- *pref.* Variant of **toxi-.**

tox·al·bu·min (tŏk'săl-byo͞o'mĭn) *n.* Any of various toxic proteins.

tox·a·phene (tŏk'sə-fēn') *n.* A toxic solid compound, $C_{10}H_{10}Cl_8$, used as an insecticide. [Blend of TOXI- and CAMPHENE.]

tox·e·mi·a (tŏk-sē'mē-ə) *n.* A condition in which toxins produced by body cells at a local source of infection or derived from the growth of microorganisms are contained in the blood. **—tox·e'mic** *adj.*

toxi- or **toxo-** or **tox-** *pref.* Poison; poisonous: *toxalbumin.* [< Lat. *toxicum.* —see TOXIC.]

tox·ic (tŏk'sĭk) *adj.* **1.** Of or pertaining to a toxin. **2.** Harmful, destructive, or deadly. [LLat. *toxicus* < Lat. *toxicum,* poison < Gk. *toxikon,* poison for arrows < *toxikos,* of a bow < *toxon,* bow.] **—tox'i·cal·ly** *adv.*

toxic- *pref.* Variant of **toxico-.**

tox·i·cant (tŏk'sĭ-kənt) *n.* A poison or poisonous agent. —*adj.* Poisonous; toxic. [Med. Lat. *toxicans, toxicant-,* pr.part. of *toxicare,* to poison < Lat. *toxicum,* poison. —see TOXIC.]

tox·ic·i·ty (tŏk-sĭs'ĭ-tē) *n., pl.* **-ties. 1.** The quality or condition of being toxic. **2.** The degree to which a poison is toxic.

toxico- or **toxic-** *pref.* Poison: *toxicosis.* [Lat. *toxicum.* —see TOXIC.]

tox·i·co·gen·ic (tŏk'sĭ-kō-jĕn'ĭk) *adj.* **1.** Producing poison or toxic substances. **2.** Derived from toxic matter.

tox·i·col·o·gy (tŏk'sĭ-kŏl'ə-jē) *n.* The study of the nature, effects, and detection of poisons and the treatment of poisoning. **—tox'i·co·log'i·cal** (-kə-lŏj'ĭ-kəl) *adj.* **—tox'i·co·log'i·cal·ly** *adv.* **—tox'i·col'o·gist** *n.*

tox·i·co·sis (tŏk'sĭ-kō'sĭs) *n., pl.* **-ses** (-sēz'). A pathological condition resulting from poisoning.

tox·i·gen·ic (tŏk′sə-jĕn′ĭk) *adj.* Producing toxins. **—tox′i·ge·nic′i·ty** (-jə-nĭs′ĭ-tē) *n.*
tox·in (tŏk′sĭn) *n.* A poisonous substance, having a protein structure, that is secreted by certain organisms and is capable of causing toxicosis when introduced into the body tissues but is also capable of inducing a counteragent or an antitoxin.
tox·in-an·ti·tox·in (tŏk′sĭn-ăn′tĭ-tŏk′sĭn) *n.* A mixture of a toxin and its antitoxin with a slight excess of toxin, formerly used as a vaccine.
toxo– *pref.* Variant of **toxi-.**
tox·oid (tŏk′soid′) *n.* A toxin that has lost toxicity but has retained the capacity to stimulate the production of or combine with antitoxins, used in immunization.
tox·o·plas·ma (tŏk′sə-plăz′mə) *n.* Any of various microorganisms of the genus *Toxoplasma,* including some vertebrate pathogens. [< NLat. *Toxoplasma,* genus name : TOXO- + Lat. *plasma,* plasma.]
tox·o·plas·mo·sis (tŏk′sō-plăz-mō′sĭs) *n.* A disease caused by infection with a microorganism, *Toxoplasma gondii,* and characterized by lesions, esp. in the case of infants, in the brain and eye. [TOXOPLASMA + -OSIS.]
toy (toi) *n.* **1.** An object for children to play with. **2.** Something of little importance; trifle. **3.** A small ornament; bauble. **4.** A diminutive thing or person. **5.** A dog of a very small breed or one much smaller than is characteristic of its breed. **6.** *Scot.* A loose covering for the head, formerly worn by women. *—intr.v.* **toyed, toy·ing, toys.** To amuse oneself idly; trifle: *a cat toying with a mouse.* [ME *toye,* amorous play.]
toy·on (toi′ŏn′) *n.* An evergreen shrub, *Heteromeles arbutifolia* or *Photinia arbutifolia,* of the Pacific coast of southern North America, having clusters of fragrant white flowers and red, berrylike fruit. [Am. Sp.]
tra·be·at·ed (trā′bē-ā′tĭd) also **tra·be·ate** (-bē-ĭt, -āt′) *adj.* *Archit.* Having horizontal beams or lintels rather than arches. [< Lat. *trabs,* beam.] **—tra′be·a′tion** *n.*
tra·bec·u·la (trə-bĕk′yə-lə) *n., pl.* **-lae** (-lē′). **1.** A small supporting beam or bar. **2.** *Anat.* Any of the supporting strands of connective tissue projecting into an organ and constituting part of the framework of that organ. **3.** *Bot.* A transverse rodlike or platelike structure, often extending across a cavity. [Lat., dim. of *trabs,* beam.] **—tra·bec′u·lar** *adj.*
trace¹ (trās) *n.* **1.** A visible mark or sign of the former presence or passage of a person, thing, or event. **2.** A barely perceivable indication of something; touch. **3. a.** An extremely small amount. **b.** A constituent, as a chemical compound or element, present in quantities less than a standard limit. **4.** A path or trail through a wilderness that has been beaten out by the passage of animals or people. **5.** *Archaic.* A way or route followed. **6.** A line drawn by a recording instrument, as a cardiograph. **7.** *Math.* **a.** The point at which a line, or the curve in which a surface, intersects a coordinate plane. **b.** The sum of the elements of the principal diagonal of a matrix. *—v.* **traced, trac·ing, trac·es.** *—tr.* **1.** To follow the course or trail of. **2.** To ascertain the successive stages in the development or progress of. **3.** To locate or discover (a cause, for example) by searching or researching evidence. **4.** To delineate or sketch (a figure). **5.** To imprint (a design) on something. **6.** To form (letters) with special concentration or care. **7.** To copy by following lines seen through a sheet of transparent paper. **8.** To make a design or series of markings on (a surface). **9.** To record (a variable), as on a graph. *—intr.* **1.** To make one's way; follow a path. **2.** To have origins; be traceable. [ME, track < OFr. < *tracier,* to make one's way < Lat. *tractus,* a drawing < p.part. of *trahere,* to draw.] **—trace′a·bil′i·ty, trace′a·ble·ness** *n.* **—trace′a·ble** *adj.* **—trace′a·bly** *adv.*
Synonyms: *trace, vestige, track, trail, spoor.* These nouns refer to indications of something that has gone before. *Trace* applies broadly to any such evidence, such as a footprint, a fragment, or a slight indication of something intangible. *Vestige* refers to a perceptible mark of what is past or no longer existent or to an existing biological form of something that was once more fully developed. *Track* usually denotes a single mark or, more often, a succession of marks left by something that has passed through. *Trail* can refer to such a succession of marks or to the scent of a person or animal. *Spoor* is applied most often to sensible evidence of the passage of a wild animal.
trace² (trās) *n.* **1.** One of two side straps or chains connecting a harnessed draft animal to the vehicle it is pulling. **2.** A bar or rod, hinged at either end to another part, that transfers movement from one part of a machine to another. [ME *trais* (pl.) < OFr., pl. of *trait,* strap < Lat. *tractus,* a hauling < p.part. of *trahere,* to haul.]
trace element *n.* A chemical element that occurs in minute quantities in a substance.
trac·er (trā′sər) *n.* **1.** A person employed to locate missing goods or persons. **2.** An investigation or inquiry organized to trace missing goods or persons. **3.** Any of several instruments used in making tracings or other drawings. **4.** A tracer bullet. **5.** An identifiable substance, as a dye or radioactive isotope, that can be followed through the course of a mechanical or biological process, providing information on the pattern of events in the process or on the redistribution of the parts or elements involved.
tracer bullet *n.* A bullet that leaves a luminous or smoky trail.
trac·er·y (trā′sə-rē) *n., pl.* **-ies.** Ornamental work of interlaced and ramified lines, esp. the lacy openwork in a Gothic window. [< TRACE¹.]
trache– *pref.* Variant of **tracheo-.**
tra·che·a (trā′kē-ə) *n., pl.* **-che·ae** (-kē-ē′) or **-che·as.** **1.** *Anat.* A thin-walled tube of cartilaginous and membranous tissue descending from the larynx to the bronchi and carrying air to the lungs. **2.** *Zool.* One of the internal respiratory tubes of insects and some other terrestrial arthropods. **3.** *Bot.* One of the tubular conductive vessels in the xylem of plants. [ME *trache* < Med. Lat. *trachea* < LLat. *trachia* < Gk. (*artēria*) *trakheia,* rough (artery) < fem. of *trakhus,* rough.] **—tra′che·al** *adj.*
tra·che·id (trā′kē-ĭd, -kēd′) *n.* One of the elongated tapering supporting and conductive cells in woody tissue. **—tra·che′i·dal** (trā-kē′ĭ-dl, -kēd′l) *adj.*
tra·che·i·tis (trā′kē-ī′tĭs) *n.* Inflammation of the trachea.
tracheo– or **trache–** *pref.* Trachea: *tracheid.* [NLat. < Med. Lat. *trachea.* —see TRACHEA.]
tra·che·o·e·soph·a·ge·al (trā′kē-ō′ĭ-sŏf′ə-jē′əl) *adj.* Pertaining to the trachea and the esophagus.
tra·che·o·phyte (trā′kē-ə-fīt′) *n.* Any of various plants of the division Tracheophyta that includes all vascular plants characterized by their specialized conducting system of xylem and phloem. [< NLat. *Tracheophyta,* division name : TRACHEO- + Gk. *phuta,* pl. of *phuton,* plant.]
tra·che·ot·o·my (trā′kē-ŏt′ə-mē) *n., pl.* **-mies.** The act or procedure of cutting into the trachea through the neck.
tra·cho·ma (trə-kō′mə) *n.* A contagious viral disease of the conjunctiva of the eye characterized by inflammation, hypertrophy, and granules of adenoid tissue. [Gk. *trakhōma* < *trakhus,* rough.] **—tra·cho′ma·tous** (-kō′mə-təs) *adj.*
tra·chyte (trā′kīt′, trăk′īt′) *n.* A light-colored igneous rock consisting essentially of alkalic feldspar. [Fr. < Gk. *trakhus,* rough.] **—tra·chyt′ic** (trə-kĭt′ĭk) *adj.*
trac·ing (trā′sĭng) *n.* **1.** A reproduction made by superimposing a transparent sheet and tracing the original upon it. **2.** A graphic record made by a recording instrument, as a cardiograph.
track (trăk) *n.* **1. a.** A mark left by the passage of a person, animal, or thing. **b.** The path, route, or course indicated by such marks: *an old wagon track through the mountains.* **2.** A course of action; method of proceeding. **3. a.** *Sports.* A road or course laid out for running or racing. **b.** Athletic competition on such a course; track events. **c.** Track and field. **4.** A rail or set of parallel rails upon which a train or trolley runs. **5.** One of several courses of study to which students are assigned in tracking. *—v.* **tracked, track·ing, tracks.** *—tr.* **1.** To follow the footprints or traces of; trail. **2.** To pursue successfully: *"When, like a running grave, time tracks you down"* (Dylan Thomas). **3.** To move over or along; traverse. **4.** To carry on the shoes and deposit as footprints: *tracked mud on her new rug.* **5. a.** To observe or monitor the course of (aircraft, for example), as by radar. **b.** *Informal.* To observe (something) carefully: *tracking that company's performance on a daily basis.* **6.** To equip with a track. **7.** To assign to a curricular track. *—intr.* **1.** To keep a constant distance apart. Used of a pair of wheels. **2.** To be,in alignment. **3.** To pursue a track. ***—idiom.* in (one's) tracks.** Exactly where one is standing: *stopped him right in his tracks.* [ME *trak* < OFr. *trac,* perh. of Germanic orig.] **—track′a·ble** *adj.* **—track′er** *n.*
track·age (trăk′ĭj) *n.* **1.** Railway tracks. **2. a.** The right of one railroad company to use the track system of another. **b.** The charge for this.
track and field *n.* *Sports.* Athletic events performed on a running track and the field associated with it.
track events *pl.n.* The running events at a track meet as distinguished from the field events.
track·ing (trăk′ĭng) *n.* The homogeneous grouping of students in any of several courses of study according to intelligence or level of ability.
tracking station *n.* An observing station for maintaining contact by means of radar or radio with an object in the atmosphere or in space.
track·less (trăk′lĭs) *adj.* **1.** Not running on tracks or rails. **2.** Unmarked by trails or paths.
trackless trolley *n.* A trolley bus.
track·man (trăk′mən) *n.* A workman employed to maintain or inspect railroad tracks.
track meet *n.* *Sports.* A track and field competition.
track record *n.* A record of performance or accomplishment: *the company's excellent track record.*
track·side (trăk′sīd′) *adj.* Of, relating to, or located in the area near a track.
track·suit (trăk′so͞ot′) *n.* A loose-fitting outfit usually consisting of a jacket and pants worn while exercising or running.
track·walk·er (trăk′wô′kər) *n.* A worker employed to inspect a section of track.
tract¹ (trăkt) *n.* **1.** An expanse of land. **2.** *Anat.* **a.** A system of organs and tissues that together perform one specialized

tracery

track and field
Above: Athlete sprinting
Below: Athlete jumping hurdles

function: *the alimentary tract.* **b.** A bundle of nerve fibers having a common origin, termination, and function. **3.** *Archaic.* A stretch or lapse of time. [Lat. *tractus* < p.part. of *trahere,* to draw.]

tract[2] (trăkt) *n.* A distributed paper or pamphlet containing a declaration or appeal, esp. one put out by a religious or political group. [ME *tracte* < Lat. *tractatus* < p.part. of *tractare,* to discuss < *trahere,* to draw.]

tract[3] (trăkt) *n.* The verses from Scripture sung during Lent or on Ember days after the gradual in the Roman Catholic Mass. [ME *tracte* < Med. Lat. *tractus* < Lat., a drawing out (from singing without a break in one's voice). —see TRACT[1].]

trac·ta·ble (trăk'tə-bəl) *adj.* **1.** Easily managed or controlled; governable. **2.** Easily handled or worked; malleable. [Lat. *tractabilis* < *tractare,* to manage, freq. of *trahere,* to draw.] **—trac'ta·bil'i·ty, trac'ta·ble·ness** *n.* **—trac'ta·bly** *adv.*

Trac·tar·i·an·ism (trăk-târ'ē-ə-nĭz'əm) *n.* The religious opinions and principles of the founders of the Oxford movement, put forth in a series of 90 pamphlets entitled *Tracts for the Times,* published at Oxford, England (1833–41). **—Trac·tar'i·an** *adj. & n.*

trac·tate (trăk'tāt') *n.* A treatise; essay. [Lat. *tractatus,* tract.]

tract house *n.* One of numerous houses of similar or complementary design constructed on a tract of land. **—tract housing** *n.*

trac·tile (trăk'təl, -tīl') *adj.* Capable of being drawn out in length, as certain metals; ductile. [LLat. *tractilis* < Lat. *trahere,* to draw.] **—trac·til'i·ty** (-tĭl'ĭ-tē) *n.*

trac·tion (trăk'shən) *n.* **1.** The act of drawing or pulling, as a load over a surface by motor power. **2.** The condition of being drawn or pulled. **3.** Adhesive friction, as of a wheel on a track. **4.** The pulling power of a railroad engine. [Med. Lat. *tractio* < Lat. *trahere,* to pull.] **—trac'tion·al** *adj.*

trac·tive (trăk'tĭv) *adj.* Serving to pull or draw; exerting traction. [< Lat. *trahere, tract-,* to draw.]

tractor

trac·tor (trăk'tər) *n.* **1.** A small vehicle, powered by a gasoline or diesel motor, having large, heavily treaded tires, and used in farming for pulling machinery. **2.** A truck having a cab and no body, used for pulling large vehicles such as vans or trailers. **3.** An airplane having a propeller mounted in front of the supporting surfaces. [< Lat. *trahere, tract-,* to draw.]

trade (trād) *n.* **1.** An occupation, esp. one requiring skilled labor; craft. **2.** The business of buying and selling commodities; commerce. **3.** The persons working in or associated with a specified business or industry. **4.** The customers, collectively, of a specified business or industry. **5.** An instance of buying or selling; transaction. **6.** An exchange of one thing for another. **7. trades.** The trade winds. *—v.* **trad·ed, trad·ing, trades.** *—intr.* **1.** To engage in buying and selling for profit. **2.** To make an exchange of one thing for another. **3.** To shop or buy regularly at a given store. *—tr.* **1.** To give in exchange for something else. **2.** To buy and sell (stock, for example). **3.** To pass back and forth: *We traded jokes.* ***—phrasal verbs.* trade in.** To give (an old or used item) as partial payment on a new purchase. **trade on.** To put to advantage; utilize. **trade up.** To trade an item in, as one less valuable for one more valuable. [ME *trad,* habit < MLG *trade,* track.] **—trad'a·ble** *adj.*

trade acceptance *n.* A bill of exchange for the amount of a purchase drawn by the seller on the purchaser, bearing the purchaser's signature and specifying time and place of payment.

trade book *n.* A book published for distribution to the general public through booksellers, as distinguished from a textbook or a limited edition.

trade discount *n.* A discount on the list price granted by a manufacturer or wholesaler to buyers in the same trade.

trade edition *n.* A trade book or a trade version of a book.

trade-in (trād'ĭn') *n.* **1.** A piece of merchandise accepted as partial payment for a new purchase. **2.** A transaction involving a trade-in.

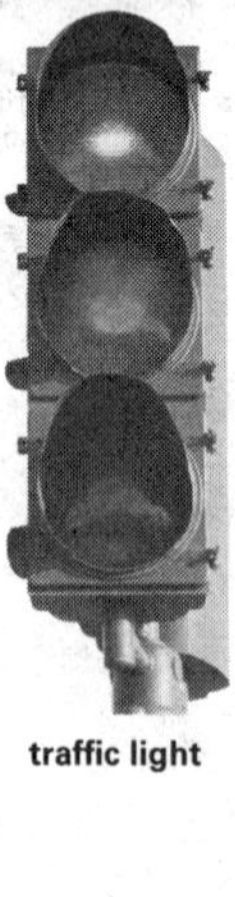

traffic light

trade language *n.* A language, as pidgin, common to peoples of diverse speech that is used esp. for communication in commercial trade.

trade-last (trād'lăst') *n. Informal.* A favorable remark that one has overheard about another person and offers to repeat to that person when he can come forward with a similar compliment overheard.

trade magazine *n.* A magazine published regularly by a particular business or industry to give pertinent news and developments.

trade·mark (trād'märk') *n.* **1.** A name, symbol, or other device identifying a product, officially registered and legally restricted to the use of the owner or manufacturer. **2.** A distinctive sign by which a person or thing comes to be known. *—tr.v.* **-marked, -mark·ing, -marks. 1.** To label (a product) with a trademark. **2.** To register as a trademark.

trade name *n.* **1.** The name by which a commodity, service, or process is known to the trade. **2.** The name under which a business firm operates.

trade·off also **trade-off** (trād'ôf', -ŏf') *n.* An exchange of one thing in return for another, esp. a giving up of something desirable, as a benefit or advantage, for another regarded as more desirable. **—trade'off'** *adj.*

trad·er (trā'dər) *n.* **1.** One that trades; dealer. **2.** A ship employed in foreign trade. **3.** A member of a stock exchange who trades for himself and not as a broker for customers.

trade rat *n.* The pack rat (sense 1).

trade route *n.* A sea lane used by trading ships.

trade school *n.* A secondary school that offers instruction in skilled trades; vocational school.

trade secret *n.* A secret formula, method, or device that gives one an advantage over competitors.

trades·man (trādz'mən) *n.* **1.** A man engaged in the retail trade, esp. a shopkeeper; dealer. **2.** A skilled worker; craftsman.

trade union *n.* A labor union, esp. one limited in membership to people in the same trade, as distinguished from people in the same company or industry. **—trade unionism** *n.* **—trade unionist** *n.*

trade wind *n.* An extremely consistent system of winds occupying most of the tropics, constituting the major component of the general circulation of the atmosphere, blowing northeasterly in the Northern Hemisphere and southeasterly in the Southern Hemisphere.

trading cards *n.* Picture cards or playing cards with designs on the backs, collected and traded esp. by children.

trading post *n.* A station or store in a sparsely settled area established by traders to barter supplies for local products.

trading stamp *n.* A stamp given by a retailer to a buyer for a purchase of a specified amount and intended to be redeemed in quantity for merchandise.

tra·di·tion (trə-dĭsh'ən) *n.* **1.** The passing down of elements of a culture from generation to generation, esp. by oral communication. **2. a.** A mode of thought or behavior followed by a people continuously from generation to generation; custom or usage. **b.** A set of such customs and usages viewed as a coherent body of precedents influencing the present. **3.** A body of unwritten religious precepts. **4.** A time-honored practice or a set of such practices. **5.** *Law.* The transfer of property to another. [ME *tradicion* < OFr. < Lat. *traditio* < *tradere,* to hand down : *trans,* over + *dare,* to give.]

tra·di·tion·al (trə-dĭsh'ə-nəl) *adj.* Of, pertaining to, or in accord with tradition. **—tra·di'tion·al·ly** *adv.*

tra·di·tion·al·ism (trə-dĭsh'ə-nə-lĭz'əm) *n.* **1.** Adherence to tradition, esp. strict reverence for religious tradition. **2.** A philosophical system holding that all knowledge is derived from original divine revelation and is transmitted by tradition. **—tra·di'tion·al·ist** *n.* **—tra·di'tion·al·is'tic** *adj.*

tra·di·tion·al·ize (trə-dĭsh'ə-nə-līz') *tr.v.* **-ized, -iz·ing, -iz·es.** To make traditional.

trad·i·tor (trăd'ĭ-tər) *n., pl.* **-to·res** (trăd'ĭ-tôr'ēz, -tōr'-). One of the early Christians who betrayed fellow Christians during the Roman persecutions. [ME *traditour* < Lat. *traditor,* betrayer < *tradere,* to betray. —see TRADITION.]

tra·duce (trə-do͞os', -dyo͞os') *tr.v.* **-duced, -duc·ing, -duc·es.** To speak falsely or maliciously of. [Lat. *traducere,* to dishonor : *trans,* across + *ducere,* to lead.] **—tra·duce'ment** *n.* **—tra·duc'er** *n.* **—tra·duc'i·ble** *adj.* **—tra·duc'ing·ly** *adv.*

tra·du·cian·ism (trə-do͞o'shə-nĭz'əm, -dyo͞o'-) *n. Theol.* The belief that the soul is inherited from the parents along with the body. [Med. Lat. *traducianus,* believer in traducianism < *tradux,* inheritance < Lat., shoot for propagation < *traducere,* to lead across. —see TRADUCE.] **—tra·du'cian·ist** *n.* **—tra·du'cian·is'tic** *adj.*

traf·fic (trăf'ĭk) *n.* **1. a.** The commercial exchange of goods; trade. **b.** Illegal or improper commercial activity: *drug traffic from South America.* **2. a.** The business of moving passengers and cargo through a transportation system. **b.** The amount of cargo or number of passengers conveyed. **3. a.** The passage of persons, vehicles, or messages through transportation routes. **b.** The amount, as of vehicles, in transit: *heavy traffic on the turnpike.* **4.** Dealings or communication between groups or individuals. *—intr.v.* **-ficked, -fick·ing, -fics. 1.** To carry on trade. **2.** To utilize something: *a candidate who will not traffic in sloganeering.* [OFr. *trafique* < OItal. *traffico* < *trafficare,* to trade.] **—traf'fick·er** *n.*

traffic circle *n.* A circular one-way road at a junction of thoroughfares, facilitating uninterrupted traffic.

traffic island *n.* A raised area over which cars may not pass, placed at a junction of thoroughfares or between opposing traffic lanes.

traffic light *n.* A road signal that flashes a red, green, or amber warning light to direct traffic to stop, proceed, or proceed with caution.

trag·a·canth (trăg'ə-kănth', trăj'-) *n.* **1.** Any of various thorny shrubs of the genus *Astragalus,* esp. *A. gummifer,* of southwestern Asia, yielding a gum used in pharmacy, adhesives, and textile printing. **2.** The gum of the tragacanth. [Lat. *tragacantha* < Gk. *tragakantha* : *tragos,* goat + *akantha,* thorn.]

tra·ge·di·an (trə-jē'dē-ən) *n.* **1.** A writer of tragedies. **2.** An actor of tragic roles. [ME *tragedyen,* prob. < OFr. *tragediane* < *tragedie,* tragedy.]

tra·ge·di·enne (trə-jē'dē-ĕn') *n.* An actress of tragic roles. [Fr., fem. of *tragédien,* tragedian < OFr. *tragediane.*]

trag·e·dy (trăj'ĭ-dē) *n., pl.* **-dies. 1.** A dramatic or literary work depicting a protagonist engaged in a morally significant struggle ending in ruin or profound disappointment, specifically: **a.** A classical verse drama in which a noble protagonist is brought to ruin essentially as a consequence of an extreme quality that is both his greatness and his downfall. **b.** A Renaissance or modern drama like the classical model in representing terrible struggle and calamity but freer in style and choice of protagonist. **c.** A play or narrative that seriously treats of calamitous events and has an unhappy but meaningful ending. **d.** The literary genre of tragic dramatic works. **2.** A dramatic, disastrous event, esp. one of moral significance. **3.** A tragic aspect or element. [ME *tragedie* < OFr. < Lat. *tragoedia* < Gk. *tragōidia* : *tragos,* goat + *ōidē,* song.]

tra·gi (trā'gī', -jī') *n.* Plural of **tragus.**

trag·ic (trăj'ĭk) also **trag·i·cal** (trăj'ĭ-kəl) *adj.* **1.** Pertaining to, in the style of, or having the character of tragedy. **2.** Writing or performing in tragedy: *a tragic poet.* **3.** Having the elements of tragedy; disastrous: *a tragic accident.* [OFr. *tragique* < Lat. *tragicus* < Gk. *tragikos* < *tragōidia,* tragedy.] **—trag'i·cal·ly** *adv.* **—trag'i·cal·ness** *n.*

tragic flaw *n.* A flaw in the character of the protagonist of a tragedy that causes his ruin.

tragic irony *n.* Irony (sense 6).

trag·i·com·e·dy (trăj'ĭ-kŏm'ĭ-dē) *n., pl.* **-dies.** A drama combining elements of both tragedy and comedy. [OFr. *tragicomédie* < LLat. *tragicōmoedia* < Lat. *tragicocomoedia* : *tragicus,* tragic + *comoedia,* comedy. —see COMEDY.] **—trag'i·com'ic, trag'i·com'i·cal** *adj.* **—trag'i·com'i·cal·ly** *adv.*

trag·o·pan (trăg'ə-păn') *n.* Any of several Asian pheasants of the genus *Tragopan,* of which the male has brightly colored plumage and two hornlike appendages on the head. [NLat. *Tragopan,* genus name < Lat. *tragopan,* a fabulous bird < Gk. : *tragos,* goat + *Pan,* Pan.]

tra·gus (trā'gəs) *n., pl.* **-gi** (-gī', -jī'). **1.** The projection of skin-covered cartilage in front of the meatus of the external ear. **2.** Any of the hairs growing at the entrance to the meatus of the external ear. [NLat. < Gk. *tragos,* a part of the ear.]

trail (trāl) *v.* **trailed, trail·ing, trails.** *—tr.* **1.** To allow to drag or stream behind, as along the ground. **2.** To drag (the body, for example) wearily or heavily. **3. a.** To follow the traces or scent of, as in hunting; track. **b.** To follow in the footsteps of (another). **4. a.** To follow slowly. **b.** To lag behind (an opponent). *—intr.* **1.** To drag or be dragged along, brushing the ground. **2.** To extend, grow, or droop over a surface, as a vine or plant. **3.** To drift in a tenuous stream, as smoke from a cigarette. **4.** To become gradually fainter; dwindle: *Her voice trailed off in confusion.* **5. a.** To walk with dragging steps; trudge. **b.** To fall behind in competition; lag. *—n.* **1.** Something that hangs loose and long: *trails of ticker tape.* **2.** Something that is drawn along or follows behind; train. **3.** The part of a gun carriage that rests or slides on the ground. **4. a.** A mark, trace, course, or path left by a moving body: *jet trails.* **b.** Scent; track: *the trail of a fox.* **c.** A blazed path or beaten track, as through woods or wilderness. **d.** A chain of consequences: *a trail of bitter recriminations.* **5.** The act or action of trailing. [ME *trailen,* prob. < ONFr. *trailler,* to tow < VLat. **tragulare,* to drag < Lat. *tragula,* dragnet < *trahere,* to pull.]

trail bike *n.* A small motorcycle not designed for highway use but for cross-country, off-road riding.

trail·blaz·er (trāl'blā'zər) *n.* **1.** One that blazes a trail. **2.** A leader in a field; pioneer.

trail boss *n.* The person in charge of a cattle drive in the West.

trail·break·er (trāl'brā'kər) *n.* A trailblazer.

trail·er (trā'lər) *n.* **1.** One that trails. **2.** A large transport vehicle designed to be hauled by a truck or tractor. **3.** A furnished van drawn by a truck or automobile and used as a house or office. **4. a.** A short filmed advertisement for a motion picture. **b.** A short, blank strip of film at the end of a reel. *—tr. & intr.v.* **-ered, -er·ing, -ers.** To transport or be transported by a trailer: *trailered the boat to the beach.* **—trail'er·a·ble** *adj.*

trailer camp *n.* A campsite for house trailers.

trailing arbutus *n.* A low-growing plant, *Epigaea repens,* of eastern North America, having evergreen leaves and clusters of fragrant pink or white flowers.

trailing edge *n.* The rearmost edge of a structure, esp. of an airfoil.

train (trān) *n.* **1.** A part of a gown that trails behind the wearer. **2.** A staff of persons following behind in attendance; retinue: *persons in the king's train.* **3.** A service unit of men, vehicles, and equipment following and attending an army. **4.** A long line of moving persons, animals, or vehicles. **5.** A string of connected railroad cars. **6.** An orderly succession of related events or thoughts; sequence. **7.** A set of linked mechanical parts: *a train of gears.* **8.** A string of gunpowder that acts as a fuse for exploding a charge. *—v.* **trained, train·ing, trains.** *—tr.* **1.** To coach in or accustom to a mode of behavior or performance. **2.** To make proficient with specialized instruction and practice. **3.** To prepare physically, as with a regimen: *train a long-distance runner.* **4.** To cause (a plant or one's hair) to take a desired course or shape, as by manipulating. **5.** To focus or direct; aim: *Train your sights on the hilltop.* **6.** To draw, drag, or trail. *—intr.* To give or undergo a course of training. [ME *trayne* < OFr. *train* < *trainer,* to drag < Lat. *trahere.*] **—train'a·ble** *adj.*

train·band (trān'bănd') *n.* A militia trained as a supplement to the army in England from the 16th to the 18th century. [Contraction of *trained band.*]

train·bear·er (trān'bâr'ər) *n.* An attendant who holds up the train of a robe or gown, as in a procession.

train·ee (trā-nē') *n.* A person who is being trained.

train·ee·ship (trā-nē'shĭp') *n.* The status or position of a trainee, esp. one involving advanced scientific or medical training and carrying a stipend and expense allowances.

train·er (trā'nər) *n.* **1.** One who trains, esp. one who coaches athletes, racehorses, or show animals. **2.** A contrivance or apparatus used in training. **3.** The member of a naval gun crew who trains the cannon horizontally.

train·ing (trā'nĭng) *n.* **1.** The act, process, or routine of one who trains. **2.** The state of being trained.

training school *n.* **1.** A school that gives practical vocational and technical instruction. **2.** A detention house for juvenile delinquents that offers vocational training.

training table *n.* A table, as in a mess hall, providing carefully planned meals for athletes in training.

train·load (trān'lōd') *n.* The full capacity of a freight or passenger train.

train·man (trān'mən) *n.* A member of the operating crew on a railroad train, esp. the brakeman.

train·mas·ter (trān'măs'tər) *n.* A railroad official who supervises a division of a rail line.

train oil *n.* Oil obtained from the blubber of a whale or other marine animal. [ME *trane,* train oil < MLG *trān.*]

traipse (trāps) *intr.v.* **traipsed, traips·ing, traips·es.** *Informal.* To walk about idly or intrusively. [Orig. unknown.]

trait (trāt) *n.* **1.** A distinguishing feature, as of the character. **2. a.** A stroke with or as if with a pencil. **b.** A touch; trace. [Fr. < OFr., stroke < Lat. *tractus,* a drawing. —see TRACT[1].]

trai·tor (trā'tər) *n.* A person who betrays his country, a cause, or a trust, esp. one who commits treason. [ME < OFr. *traitre* < Lat. *traditor* < *tradere,* to betray. —see TRADITION.]

trai·tor·ous (trā'tər-əs) *adj.* **1.** Having the character of a traitor; disloyal. **2.** Constituting treason: *a traitorous act.* **—trai'tor·ous·ly** *adv.* **—trai'tor·ous·ness** *n.*

trai·tress (trā'trĭs) or **trai·tor·ess** (trā'tər-ĭs) *n.* A woman who betrays her country, a cause, or a trust, esp. one who commits treason.

tra·ject (trə-jĕkt') *tr.v.* **-ject·ed, -ject·ing, -jects.** To transmit. [Lat. *trajicere, traject-,* to throw across : *trans,* across + *jacere,* to throw.] **—tra·jec'tion** *n.*

tra·jec·to·ry (trə-jĕk'tə-rē) *n., pl.* **-ries. 1.** The path of a moving particle or body, esp. such a path in three dimensions. **2.** *Math.* A curve that cuts all of a given family of curves or surfaces at the same angle. [Med. Lat. *trajectorius* < Lat. *trajicere,* to throw across. —see TRAJECT.]

tram[1] (trăm) *n.* **1.** *Chiefly Brit.* **a.** A streetcar. **b.** A tramway. **c.** A cable car. **2.** A four-wheeled, open box-shaped wagon or iron car run on tracks in a coal mine. *—tr.v.* **trammed, tram·ming, trams.** To move or convey in a tram. [Dial., shaft of a barrow, prob. < MLG *trame,* beam.]

tram[2] (trăm) *n.* **1.** A trammel (sense 5). **2.** Accurate mechanical adjustment: *The device is in tram.* *—tr.v.* **trammed, tram·ming, trams.** To adjust or align (mechanical parts) with a trammel. [Short for TRAMMEL.]

tram[3] (trăm) *n.* A heavy silk thread used for the weft, or cross threads, in fine velvet or silk. [ME *tramm* < OFr. *traime* < Lat. *trama.*]

tram·car (trăm'kär') *n.* **1.** *Chiefly Brit.* A streetcar. **2.** A coal car in a mine.

tram·line (trăm'līn') *n.* *Chiefly Brit.* A streetcar line.

tram·mel (trăm'əl) *n.* **1.** A shackle used to teach a horse to amble. **2.** Often **trammels.** Something that restricts activity or free movement. **3.** A vertically set fishing net of three layers, consisting of a finely meshed net between two nets of coarse mesh. **4. a.** An instrument for describing ellipses. **b.** The pivoted beam of a beam compass. **5.** An instrument for gauging and adjusting parts of a machine. **6.** An arrangement of links and a hook in a fireplace for raising or lowering a kettle. *—tr.v.* **-meled, -mel·ing, -mels** or **-melled, -mel·ling, -mels. 1.** To confine or hinder. **2.** To entrap. [ME *tramale,* a kind of net < OFr. *tramail* < LLat. *tremaculum* : Lat. *tres,* three + Lat. *macula,* mesh.] **—tram'mel·er** *n.*

tra·mon·tane (trə-mŏn'tān', trăm'ən-tān') *adj.* **1. a.** Dwelling beyond or coming from the far side of the mountains, esp. the Alps as viewed from Italy. **b.** Foreign. **c.** Barbarous. **2.** Sweeping down from the mountains. Used of a wind. *—n.* **1.** A person who lives beyond the mountains; outsider. **2.** In Italy, a north or cold wind. [Ital. *tramontano* < Lat. *transmontanus* : *trans,* beyond + *montanus,* mountainous.]

tramp (trămp) *v.* **tramped, tramp·ing, tramps.** *—intr.* **1.** To walk with a firm, heavy step; trudge. **2. a.** To go on foot; hike. **b.** To wander about aimlessly. *—tr.* **1.** To traverse on foot: *tramp the fields.* **2.** To tread down; trample: *tramp down snow.* *—n.* **1. a.** A heavy footfall. **b.** The sound produced by heavy walking or marching: *the tramp of soldiers' boots.* **2.** A walking trip; hike. **3.** A person who travels aimlessly about on foot, doing odd jobs or begging for a living; vagrant. **4. a.** A prostitute. **b.** A promiscuous person. **5.** A

tragopan
A male of the species *Tragopan satyra*

trailing arbutus

train

cargo vessel that has no regular schedule but takes on freight wherever it may be found and discharges it wherever required. **6.** A metal plate attached to the sole of a shoe for protection, as when spading ground. [ME *trampen.*] **—tramp'er** *n.*

trampoline

tram·ple (trăm'pəl) *v.* **-pled, -pling, -ples.** *—tr.* **1.** To beat down with the feet so as to crush, bruise, or destroy; tramp upon. **2.** To treat harshly or ruthlessly. *—intr.* To tread heavily or contemptuously. *—n.* The action or sound of treading underfoot. [ME *tramplen,* freq. of *trampen,* to tramp.] **—tram'pler** *n.*

tram·po·line (trăm'pə-lēn', -lĭn) *n.* A sheet of strong, taut canvas attached with springs to a metal frame and used for acrobatic tumbling. [Sp. *trampolín* < Ital. *trampolino* < *trampoli,* stilts, of Germanic orig.] **—tram'po·lin'er, tram'po·lin'ist** *n.*

tram·way (trăm'wā') *n. Chiefly Brit.* **1. a.** A street track or railway for trams. **b.** A streetcar line. **2.** A cable or system of cables for a cablecar.

trance (trăns) *n.* **1.** A hypnotic, cataleptic, or ecstatic state. **2.** A state of detachment from one's physical surroundings, as in contemplation or daydreaming. **3.** A dazed state, as between sleeping and waking; stupor. *—tr.v.* **tranced, tranc·ing, tranc·es.** To put into a trance. [ME *traunce* < OFr. *transe* < *transir,* to depart < Lat. *transire,* to go across. —see TRANSIENT.]

tran·quil (trăng'kwəl, trăn'-) *adj.* **1.** Free from agitation or other disturbance; serene: *a tranquil rural life.* **2.** Steady; even: *a tranquil flame.* [Lat. *tranquillus.*] **—tran'quil·ly** *adv.* **—tran'quil·ness** *n.*

tran·quil·ize also **tran·quil·lize** (trăng'kwə-līz', trăn'-) *tr. & intr.v.* **-ized, -iz·ing, -iz·es** also **-lized, -liz·ing, -liz·es.** To make or become tranquil. **—tran'quil·i·za'tion** *n.*

tran·quil·iz·er (trăng'kwə-līz'ər, trăn'-) *n.* **1.** Something, as music or liquor, that tranquilizes. **2.** A drug used to calm or pacify.

tran·quil·li·ty or **tran·quil·i·ty** (trăn-kwĭl'ĭ-tē, trăng-) *n.* The state or quality of being tranquil; serenity.

tran·quil·lize (trăng'kwə-līz', trăn'-) *v.* Variant of **tranquilize.**

trans- *pref.* **1.** Across; on the other side; beyond: *transpolar.* **2.** Through: *transcutaneous.* **3.** Change; transfer: *transliterate.* [< Lat. *trans,* beyond, through.]

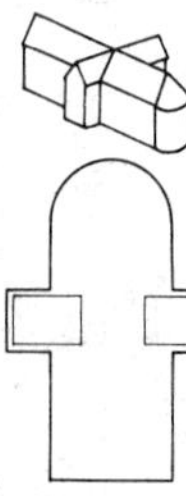
transept

trans·act (trăn-săkt', -zăkt') *v.* **-act·ed, -act·ing, -acts.** *—tr.* To do, carry out, perform, manage, or conduct (business, for example). *—intr.* To do business. [Lat. *transigere, transact-,* to carry through : *trans,* through + *agere,* to drive.] **—trans·ac'tor** *n.*

trans·ac·tion (trăn-săk'shən, -zăk'-) *n.* **1.** The act of transacting or the fact of being transacted. **2.** Something transacted, esp. a piece of business. **3. transactions.** The proceedings, as of a convention. **—trans·ac'tion·al** *adj.*

transactional analysis *n.* A system of psychotherapy that seeks to analyze intrapsychic conflict and interpersonal interactions in order to afford insight and facilitate constructive communication.

trans·al·pine (trăns-ăl'pīn', trănz-) *adj.* Pertaining to, living on, or coming from the northern side of the Alps.

trans·am·i·nase (trăns-ăm'ə-nās', -nāz', trănz-) *n.* Any of a group of enzymes that catalyze transamination.

trans·am·i·na·tion (trăns-ăm'ə-nā'shən, trănz-) *n.* **1.** The transfer of an amino group from one chemical compound to another. **2.** The transposition of an amino group within a chemical compound.

trans·at·lan·tic (trăns'ət-lăn'tĭk, trănz'-) *adj.* **1.** On the other side of the Atlantic. **2.** Spanning or crossing the Atlantic.

trans·ceiv·er (trăn-sē'vər) *n.* A module consisting of a radio receiver and transmitter. [TRANS(MITTER) + (RE)CEIVER.]

tran·scend (trăn-sĕnd') *v.* **-scend·ed, -scend·ing, -scends.** *—tr.* **1. a.** To pass beyond (a human limit): *an emotion that transcends understanding.* **b.** To exist above and independent of (material experience or the universe). **2.** To rise above or across: *"He not only transcends himself in various ways, he also transcends his culture"* (Abraham H. Maslow). *—intr.* To surpass. [ME *transcenden* < OFr. *transcendre* < Lat. *transcendere* : *trans,* over + *scandere,* to climb.]

tran·scen·dent (trăn-sĕn'dənt) *adj.* **1.** Surpassing others of the same kind; pre-eminent. **2. a.** *Philos.* Transcending the Aristotelian categories. **b.** In Kant's theory of knowledge, designating knowledge that is beyond the limits of experience. **3.** Above and independent of the material universe. Used of the Deity. **—tran·scen'dence, tran·scen'den·cy** *n.* **—tran·scen'dent·ly** *adv.*

tran·scen·den·tal (trăn'sĕn-dĕn'tl) *adj.* **1.** *Philos.* **a.** Concerned with the a priori basis of knowledge; minimizing the importance or denying the reality of sense experience. **b.** Asserting a fundamental irrationality or supernatural element in experience. **2.** Rising above common thought or ideas; mystical. **3.** *Math.* **a.** Not capable of being determined by any combination of a finite number of equations with rational integral coefficients. **b.** Not expressible as an integer or quotient of integers. Used of numbers, esp. nonrepeating infinite decimals. **—tran'scen·den'tal·ly** *adv.*

tran·scen·den·tal·ism (trăn'sĕn-dĕn'tl-ĭz'əm) *n.* **1.** *Philos.* **a.** The belief that knowledge of reality is derived from intuitive sources rather than from objective experience. **b.** A doctrine based on this belief, as the philosophy of Kant. **2.** The quality or condition of being transcendental. **—tran'scen·den'tal·ist** *n.*

transcendental meditation *n.* A technique of meditation in which deep mental and physical relaxation is achieved esp. through the use of a mantra.

trans·con·ti·nen·tal (trăns'kŏn-tə-nĕn'tl) *adj.* Spanning or crossing a continent.

tran·scribe (trăn-skrīb') *tr.v.* **-scribed, -scrib·ing, -scribes.** **1. a.** To write or type a copy of; write out fully, as from shorthand notes or from an electronic recording medium: *transcribe a letter.* **b.** To transfer (information) from one recording and storing system to another. **2.** To adapt or arrange (a musical composition) for a voice or instrument other than the original. **3.** To record, usually on tape, for broadcasting at a later date. **4.** To represent (speech sounds) by phonetic symbols. **5.** *Genetics.* To cause (DNA) to undergo transcription. [Lat. *transcribere* : *trans,* across + *scribere,* to write.] **—tran·scrib'a·ble** *adj.* **—tran·scrib'er** *n.*

tran·script (trăn'skrĭpt') *n.* **1.** Something transcribed, esp. a written, typewritten, or printed copy, as of a legal record or a student's school record. **2.** *Genetics.* The RNA sequence produced by transcription. [ME < OFr. *transcrit* < Lat. *transcriptum* < neuter p.part. of *transcribere,* to transcribe.]

tran·scrip·tion (trăn-skrĭp'shən) *n.* **1.** The act or process of transcribing. **2.** Something that has been transcribed, esp.: **a.** An adaptation of a musical composition. **b.** A recorded radio or television program. **3.** *Genetics.* The process by which a messenger RNA molecule is synthesized from a DNA molecule template that results in the transfer of genetic information from the DNA to the messenger RNA. **—tran·scrip'tion·al** *adj.* **—tran·scrip'tion·al·ly** *adv.*

trans·cul·tu·ra·tion (trăns'kŭl-chə-rā'shən) *n.* Cultural change induced by the introduction of elements of a foreign culture.

trans·cur·rent (trăns-kûr'ənt, -kŭr'-) *adj.* Extending, passing, or running transversely.

trans·duc·er (trăns-dōō'sər, -dyōō'-, trănz-) *n.* Any of various substances or devices, as a piezoelectric crystal or a photoelectric cell, that convert input energy of one form into output energy of another. [< Lat. *transducere,* to transfer : *trans,* across + *ducere,* to lead.] **—trans·duce'** *v.* **(-duced, -duc·ing, -duc·es).**

trans·duc·tion (trăns-dŭk'shən, trănz-) *n.* The transfer of genetic material from one bacterial cell to another by a bacteriophage. [Lat. *transductio,* transfer < *transducere,* to transfer. —see TRANSDUCER.]

tran·sect (trăn-sĕkt') *tr.v.* **-sect·ed, -sect·ing, -sects.** To divide by cutting transversely. **—tran·sec'tion** *n.*

tran·sept (trăn'sĕpt') *n. Archit.* Either of the two lateral arms of a cruciform church. [TRANS- + Lat. *saeptum,* partition. —see SEPTUM.]

tran·se·unt (trăn'sē-ənt) *adj. Philos.* Productive of effects outside of the mind. [Lat. *transiens, transeunt-,* pr.part. of *transire,* to go over. —see TRANSIENT.]

trans·fec·tion (trăns-fĕk'shən) *n.* The infection of a cell with purified viral nucleic acid with subsequent replication of the virus in the cell. [TRANS- + (IN)FECTION.] **—trans·fect'** *v.* **(-fect·ed, -fect·ing, -fects).**

trans·fer (trăns-fûr', trăns'fər) *v.* **-ferred, -fer·ring, -fers.** *—tr.* **1.** To convey or shift from one person or place to another. **2.** To make over the possession or legal title of to another. **3.** To convey (a design, for example) from one surface to another. *—intr.* **1.** To move oneself from one location, job, or school to another. **2.** To change from one motor carrier to another. *—n.* (trăns'fər). **1.** Also **trans·fer·al** (trăns-fûr'əl). The conveyance or removal of something from one person or place to another. **2. a.** Also **transferal.** One that has or has been transferred, as a student enrolled in a new school. **b.** A design conveyed or to be conveyed from one surface to another. **3. a.** A ticket entitling a passenger to change from one motor carrier to another. **b.** A place where such changes are permitted or required. **4.** Also **transferal.** *Law.* **a.** The conveyance of title or property from one person to another. **b.** The document effecting such conveyance. [ME *transferren* < OFr. *transferer* < Lat. *transferre* : *trans,* across + *ferre,* to carry.] **—trans·fer'a·bil'i·ty** *n.* **—trans·fer'a·ble** *adj.* **—trans·fer'rer** *n.*

trans·fer·al also **trans·fer·ral** (trăns-fûr'əl) *n.* **1.** A transfer. **2.** *Psychoanal.* Transference.

trans·fer·ase (trăns'fə-rās', -rāz') *n.* Any of various enzymes that catalyze the transfer of atoms or groups of atoms from one molecule to another.

trans·fer·ee (trăns'fə-rē') *n.* **1.** *Law.* One to whom a transfer of title or property is made. **2.** One who is transferred.

trans·fer·ence (trăns-fûr'əns, trăns'fər-əns) *n.* **1. a.** An act or process of transferring. **b.** The condition of being transferred. **2.** *Psychoanal.* The process in and by which an individual's feelings, thoughts, and wishes shift from one person to another, esp. this process in psychoanalysis with the analyst made the object of the shift. **—trans'fer·en'tial** (trăns'fə-rĕn'shəl) *adj.*

trans·fer·or (trăns'fə-rôr') *n. Law.* A person who makes a transfer of title or property.

trans·fer·rin (trăns-fĕr'ĭn) *n.* A blood globulin that can combine reversibly with and transport iron ions in the body.

transfer RNA *n.* A ribonucleic acid that acts as a carrier in the transport of a specific amino acid to the ribosomal site where a protein molecule is being synthesized.

trans·fig·u·ra·tion (trăns-fĭg′yə-rā′shən) *n.* **1.** A radical transformation of figure or appearance; metamorphosis. **2. Transfiguration. a.** The sudden emanation of radiance from Jesus' person that occurred on the mountain. **b.** The Christian commemoration of this, observed on August 6.

trans·fig·ure (trăns-fĭg′yər) *tr.v.* **-ured, -ur·ing, -ures. 1.** To transform the figure or appearance of; alter radically. **2.** To exalt; glorify. [ME *transfiguren* < Lat. *transfigurare* : *trans,* beyond + *figura,* figure.] **—trans·fig′ure·ment** *n.*

trans·fi·nite (trăns-fī′nīt′) *adj.* Beyond the finite.

transfinite number *n.* A cardinal or ordinal number that is not an integer.

trans·fix (trăns-fĭks′) *tr.v.* **-fixed, -fix·ing, -fix·es. 1.** To pierce through with or as if with a pointed weapon. **2.** To fix fast; impale. **3.** To render motionless, as with terror, amazement, or awe. [Lat. *transfigere, transfix-* : *trans,* through + *figere,* to pierce.] **—trans·fix′ion** (-fĭk′shən) *n.*

trans·form (trăns-fôrm′) *v.* **-formed, -form·ing, -forms.** *—tr.* **1.** To change markedly the form or appearance of. **2.** To change the nature, function, or condition of; convert. **3.** To subject to a mathematical transformation. **4.** To subject to a linguistic transformation. **5.** *Elect.* To subject to the action of a transformer. *—intr.* To undergo a transformation. *—n.* (trăns′fôrm′). The result, esp. a mathematical quantity, of a transformation. [ME *transformen* < Lat. *transformare* : *trans,* across + *forma,* shape.] **—trans·form′a·ble** *adj.*

trans·for·ma·tion (trăns′fər-mā′shən, -fôr-) *n.* **1. a.** An act or an instance of transforming. **b.** The state of being transformed. **c.** Something that has been transformed. **2.** *Math.* **a.** The replacement of the variables in an algebraic expression by their values in terms of another set of variables. **b.** A mapping of one space onto another or onto itself. **3.** *Ling.* **a.** The process of converting a syntactic construction into a semantically equivalent construction according to the rules shown to generate the syntax of the language. **b.** A construction derived by such transformation; transform. **—trans·for′ma·tive** (-fôr′mə-tĭv) *adj.*

trans·for·ma·tion·al grammar (trăns′fər-mā′shə-nəl, -fôr-) *n.* A grammar that accounts for the constructions of a language by linguistic transformations and phrase structures, esp. generative transformational grammar.

trans·form·er (trăns-fôr′mər) *n.* **1.** One that transforms. **2.** A device used to transfer electric energy, usually that of an alternating current, from one circuit to another, esp. a pair of multiply wound, inductively coupled wire coils that effect such a transfer with a change in voltage, current, phase, or other electric characteristic.

trans·fuse (trăns-fyōōz′) *tr.v.* **-fused, -fus·ing, -fus·es. 1.** To transfer (liquid) by pouring from one vessel into another. **2.** To permeate; instill. **3.** *Med.* To administer a transfusion of or to. [ME *transfusen,* to transmit < Lat. *transfundere,* to pour out : *trans,* across + *fundere,* to pour.] **—trans·fus′er** *n.* **—trans·fus′i·ble** *adj.* **—trans·fu′sive** (-fyōō′sĭv, -zĭv) *adj.*

trans·fu·sion (trăns-fyōō′zhən) *n.* **1.** The act or process of transfusing. **2.** *Med.* The direct injection of whole blood, plasma, or another solution into the blood stream. **—trans·fu′sion·al** *adj.*

trans·gress (trăns-grĕs′, trănz-) *v.* **-gressed, -gress·ing, -gress·es.** *—tr.* **1.** To go beyond or over (a limit or boundary). **2.** To act in violation of (the law, for example). *—intr.* To trespass; sin. [Lat. *transgredi, transgress-,* to step across : *trans,* across + *gradi,* to step.] **—trans·gress′i·ble** *adj.* **—trans·gres′sive** *adj.* **—trans·gres′sive·ly** *adv.* **—trans·gres′sor** *n.*

trans·gres·sion (trăns-grĕsh′ən, trănz-) *n.* **1.** The violation of a law, command, or duty. **2.** The exceeding of due bounds or limits.

tran·ship (trăn-shĭp′, trăns-) *v.* Variant of **transship.**

trans·hu·mance (trăns-hyōō′məns, trănz-) *n.* The movement of livestock and herders to different grazing grounds with the changing of the seasons. [Fr. < *transhumer,* to move livestock seasonally < Sp. *transhumar* : Lat. *trans,* across + Lat. *humus,* ground.] **—trans·hu′mant** *adj. & n.*

tran·sience (trăn′shəns, -zhəns, -zē-əns) also **tran·sien·cy** (-shən-sē, -zhən-sē, -zē-ən-sē) *n.* The state or quality of being transient.

tran·sient (trăn′shənt, -zhənt, -zē-ənt) *adj.* **1.** Passing away with time; transitory. **2.** Passing through from one place to another: *transient laborers.* **3.** *Physics.* Decaying with time, esp. as a simple exponential function of time. *—n.* **1.** One that is transient, esp. a person staying a single night at a hotel. **2.** *Physics.* A transient phenomenon or property, esp. a transient electric current. [Lat. *transiens, transeunt-,* pr.part. of *transire,* to go over : *trans,* over + *ire,* to go.] **—tran′sient·ly** *adv.*

Synonyms: *transient, transitory, ephemeral, fleeting, fugitive, momentary, evanescent, temporary, provisional.* These adjectives mean being present or having existence for a short or limited time. In modern usage *transient* usually refers to what literally remains only a short time, such as a guest at a hotel. It can also mean inherently short-lived or impermanent, but the latter sense is more often expressed by *transitory. Ephemeral, fleeting, fugitive, momentary,* and *evanescent* all underscore the idea of very brief existence. *Ephemeral* often implies lack of enduring quality or appeal. *Fleeting,* in contrast, is often applied to what passes more swiftly than one would wish. *Fugitive* especially suggests what passes but leaves a distinct impression. *Momentary* stresses mere brevity, and *evanescent* suggests that which has the substance and lasting power of a vapor. *Temporary* usually describes what is meant to last for a limited period pending establishment of something intended as long-range. *Provisional* refers to what is adapted to a present necessity and consequently may be a stopgap.

trans·il·lu·mi·na·tion (trăns′ĭ-lōō′mə-nā′shən, trănz′-) *n.* *Med.* The examination of a bodily part or organ by passing a light through its walls. **—trans′il·lu′mi·nate′** (-lōō′mə-nāt′) *v.* **(-nat·ed, -nat·ing, -nates). —trans′il·lu′mi·na′tor** *n.*

tran·sis·tor (trăn-zĭs′tər, -sĭs′-) *n.* **1.** A three-terminal semiconductor device used for amplification, switching, and detection, typically containing two rectifying junctions and characteristically operating so that the current between one pair of terminals controls the current between the other pair, one terminal being common to input and output. **2.** A radio equipped with transistors. [TRANS(FER) + (RES)ISTOR.]

tran·sis·tor·ize (trăn-zĭs′tə-rīz′, -sĭs′-) *tr.v.* **-ized, -iz·ing, -iz·es.** To equip (an electronic circuit or device) with transistors.

transistor radio *n.* A transistor (sense 2).

tran·sit (trăn′sĭt, -zĭt) *n.* **1. a.** The act of passing over, across, or through; passage. **b.** The conveyance of persons or goods from one place to another, esp. on a local public transportation system. **2.** A transition or change, esp. from one life to another at death. **3.** *Astron.* **a.** The passage of a celestial body across the observer's meridian. **b.** The passage of a smaller celestial body across the disk of a larger celestial body. **4.** A surveying instrument similar to a theodolite that measures horizontal and vertical angles. *—v.* **-sit·ed, -sit·ing, -sits.** *—tr.* **1.** To pass over, across, or through. **2.** To revolve (the telescope of a surveying transit) about its horizontal transverse axis in order to reverse its direction. *—intr. Astron.* To make a transit. [Lat. *transitus* < p.part. of *transire,* to go across. —see TRANSIENT.]

transit
Surveying instrument

tran·si·tion (trăn-zĭsh′ən, -sĭsh′-) *n.* **1.** The process or an instance of changing from one form, state, activity, or place to another. **2.** Passage from one subject to another, as in discourse. **3.** *Mus.* **a.** A modulation, esp. a brief one. **b.** A passage connecting two themes. **—tran·si′tion·al, tran·si′tion·ar′y** (-ə-nĕr′ē) *adj.* **—tran·si′tion·al·ly** *adv.*

transition element *n.* **1.** Any of the elements that serve as transitional links between the most and the least electropositive in a series of elements, and that are characterized by high melting points, densities, magnetic moments, multiple valences, and the ability to form stable complex ions. **2.** Any of the elements in which an inner electron shell rather than an outer shell is only partially filled, generally taken to include elements 21–29, 38–46, and 71–78.

transition metal *n.* A transition element.

tran·si·tive (trăn′sĭ-tĭv, -zĭ-) *adj.* **1.** *Gram.* Expressing an action that is carried from the subject to the object; requiring a direct object to complete meaning. Used of a verb or verb construction. **2.** Characterized by or effecting transition. *—n. Gram.* A transitive verb. [LLat. *transitivus* < *transitio,* transition < *transire,* to go over. —see TRANSIENT.] **—tran′si·tive·ly** *adv.* **—tran′si·tive·ness, tran′si·tiv′i·ty** (-tĭv′ĭ-tē) *n.*

tran·si·to·ry (trăn′sĭ-tôr′ē, -tōr′ē, trăn′zĭ-) *adj.* Existing only briefly; short-lived. [ME *transitorie* < AN < LLat. *transitorius* < Lat., having a passageway < *transitus,* transit. —see TRANSIT.] **—tran′si·to′ri·ly** *adv.* **—tran′si·to′ri·ness** *n.*

trans·late (trăns-lāt′, trănz-, trăns′lāt′, trănz′-) *v.* **-lat·ed, -lat·ing, -lates.** *—tr.* **1.** To express in another language, systematically retaining the original sense. **2.** To put in simpler terms; explain. **3.** To convey from one form or style to another; convert: *translate ideas into reality.* **4.** To transfer (a bishop) to another see. **5.** To forward or retransmit (a telegraphic message). **6.** *Theol.* To convey to heaven without natural death. **7.** *Physics.* To subject (a body) to translation. **8.** *Archaic.* To transport; enrapture. **9.** *Genetics.* To subject (a genetic code) to translation during protein synthesis. *—intr.* **1. a.** To make a translation. **b.** To work as a translator. **2.** To admit of translation. **3.** *Aerospace.* To move from one place to another in space by means of reaction power. [ME *translaten* < Lat. *transferre, translat-* : *trans,* across + *ferre,* to carry.] **—trans·lat′a·bil′i·ty, trans·lat′a·ble·ness** *n.* **—trans·lat′a·ble** *adj.*

trans·la·tion (trăns-lā′shən, trănz-) *n.* **1. a.** The act or process of translating, esp. from one language to another. **b.** The condition of being translated. **2.** A translated version of a text. **3.** *Physics.* Motion of a body in which every point of the body moves parallel to and the same distance as every other point of the body; nonrotational displacement. **4.** *Genetics.* The process by which the genetic information in a messenger RNA molecule directs the linear sequence of amino acids in a protein molecule during protein synthesis at a ribosomal site. **—trans·la′tion·al** *adj.*

trans·la·tor (trăns-lā′tər, trănz-, trăns′lā′tər, trănz′-) *n.* **1.** One who translates, esp. one professionally employed to

transom

translate written works. **2.** An interpreter. **—trans'la·to'ri·al** (trăns'lə-tôr'ē-əl, -tōr'-, trănz'-) *adj.*
trans·lit·er·ate (trăns-lĭt'ə-rāt', trănz-) *tr.v.* **-at·ed, -at·ing, -ates.** To represent (letters or words) in the corresponding characters of another alphabet. [TRANS- + Lat. *littera,* letter + -ATE[1].] **—trans·lit'er·a'tion** *n.*
trans·lo·cate (trăns'lō-kāt', trănz'-) *tr.v.* **-cat·ed, -cat·ing, -cates.** To cause to change from one position to another; displace.
trans·lo·ca·tion (trăns'lō-kā'shən, trănz'-) *n.* **1.** A change in location. **2.** *Genetics.* A chromosomal aberration in which different nonhomologous genes are interchanged.
trans·lu·cent (trăns-lo͞o'sənt, trănz-) *adj.* Transmitting light but causing sufficient diffusion to eliminate perception of distinct images. [Lat. *translucens, translucent-,* pr.part. of *translucēre,* to shine through : *trans,* through + *lucēre,* to shine.] **—trans·lu'cence, trans·lu'cen·cy** *n.* **—trans·lu'cent·ly** *adv.*
trans·ma·rine (trăns'mə-rēn', trănz'-) *adj.* **1.** Crossing the sea. **2.** Being beyond or coming from across the sea. [Lat. *transmarinus* : *trans,* across + *mare,* sea.]
trans·mem·brane (trăns-mĕm'brān', trănz-) *adj.* Passing across a membrane.
trans·mi·grant (trăns-mī'grənt, trănz-) *n.* **1.** One who transmigrates. **2.** An immigrant in transit through a country on his way to the country in which he intends to settle.
trans·mi·grate (trăns-mī'grāt', trănz-) *intr.v.* **-grat·ed, -grat·ing, -grates.** **1.** To migrate. **2.** To pass into another body after death. Used of the soul. [Lat. *transmigrare, transmigrat-* : *trans,* across + *migrare,* to migrate.] **—trans·mi'gra'tor** *n.* **—trans·mi'gra·to'ry** (-mī'grə-tôr'ē, -tōr'ē) *adj.*
trans·mi·gra·tion (trăns'mī-grā'shən, trănz'-) *n.* **1.** The act or process of transmigrating. **2.** The passing of a soul into another body after death; metempsychosis. **—trans'mi·gra'tion·ism** *n.*
trans·mis·si·ble (trăns-mĭs'ə-bəl, trănz-) *adj.* Capable of being transmitted. **—trans·mis'si·bil'i·ty** *n.*
trans·mis·sion (trăns-mĭsh'ən, trănz-) *n.* **1. a.** The act or process of transmitting. **b.** The state of being transmitted. **2.** Something transmitted, as a voice or message. **3. a.** An automotive assembly of gears and associated parts by which power is transmitted from the engine to a driving axle. **b.** A system of gears. **4.** The sending of modulated carrier waves from a transmitter. [Lat. *transmissio,* a sending across < *transmittere,* to transmit.] **—trans·mis'sive** (-mĭs'ĭv) *adj.*
trans·mis·som·e·ter (trăns'mĭ-sŏm'ĭ-tər, trănz'-) *n.* A device used to measure the transmission of light through a medium. [TRANSMISS(ION) + -METER.] **—trans'mis·som'e·try** *n.*
trans·mit (trăns-mĭt', trănz-) *v.* **-mit·ted, -mit·ting, -mits.** *—tr.* **1.** To send from one person, thing, or place to another; convey. **2.** To cause to spread; pass on: *transmit an infection.* **3.** To impart or convey to others by heredity; hand down. **4.** *Electronics.* To send (a signal), as by wire or radio. **5.** *Physics.* To cause (a disturbance) to propagate through a medium. **6.** To convey (force or energy) from one part of a mechanism to another. *—intr.* To send out a signal. [ME *transmitten* < Lat. *transmittere* : *trans,* across + *mittere,* to send.] **—trans·mit'ta·ble** *adj.*
trans·mit·tal (trăns-mĭt'l, trănz-) *n.* The act or process of transmitting; transmission.
trans·mit·tance (trăns-mĭt'ns, trănz-) *n.* **1.** A transmission. **2.** *Physics.* The ratio of the radiant energy transmitted to the total radiant energy incident on a given body.
trans·mit·ter (trăns-mĭt'ər, trănz-) *n.* **1.** One that transmits. **2.** A telegraphic sending instrument. **3.** The portion of a telephone that converts the incident sounds into electrical impulses that are conveyed to a remote receiver. **4.** Electronic equipment that generates and amplifies a carrier wave, modulates it with a meaningful signal, as derived from speech or other sources, and radiates the resulting signal from an antenna.
trans·mog·ri·fy (trăns-mŏg'rə-fī', trănz-) *tr.v.* **-fied, -fy·ing, -fies.** To change into a different shape or form, esp. one that is fantastic or bizarre. [Orig. unknown.] **—trans·mog'ri·fi·ca'tion** *n.*
trans·mon·tane (trăns-mŏn'tān', trănz-, trăns'mŏn-tān', trănz'-) *adj.* Located beyond a mountain or mountain range; tramontane. [Lat. *transmontanus.* —see TRAMONTANE.]
trans·mu·ta·tion (trăns'myo͞o-tā'shən, trănz'-) *n.* **1.** The act of transmuting. **2.** The state of being transmuted. **3.** In alchemy, the alleged conversion of base metals into gold or silver. **4.** *Physics.* The transformation of one element into another by one or a series of nuclear reactions. **—trans'mu·ta'tion·al, trans·mut'a·tive** (-myo͞o'tə-tĭv) *adj.*
trans·mute (trăns-myo͞ot', trănz-) *tr.v.* **-mut·ed, -mut·ing, -mutes.** To change from one form, nature, substance, or state into another; transform. [ME *transmuten* < Lat. *transmutare* : *trans,* across + *mutare,* to change.] **—trans·mut'a·bil'i·ty, trans·mut'a·ble·ness** *n.* **—trans·mut'a·ble** *adj.* **—trans·mut'a·bly** *adv.* **—trans·mut'er** *n.*
trans·na·tion·al (trăns-năsh'ə-nəl, trănz-) *adj.* Transcending or reaching beyond national boundaries.
trans·o·ce·an·ic (trăns'ō-shē-ăn'ĭk, trănz'-) *adj.* **1.** Situated beyond or on the other side of the ocean. **2.** Spanning or crossing the ocean.
tran·som (trăn'səm) *n.* **1. a.** A small hinged window above a door or another window. **b.** The horizontal crosspiece to which such a window is hinged. **2.** A horizontal dividing piece of wood or stone in a window. **3.** *Naut.* **a.** A transverse beam affixed to the sternpost of a wooden ship and forming part of the stern. **b.** In steel ships, the aftermost transverse structural member including the floor, frame, and beam assembly at the sternpost. **c.** The stern of a square-sterned boat when it is a structural member. **4.** The horizontal beam on a cross or gallows. [ME *traunson,* prob. < Lat. *transtrum* < *trans,* across.] **—tran'somed** *adj.*
tran·son·ic (trăn-sŏn'ĭk) *adj.* Of or pertaining to aerodynamic flow or flight conditions at speeds close to the speed of sound. [TRANS- + (SUPER)SONIC.]
trans·pa·cif·ic (trăns'pə-sĭf'ĭk) *adj.* **1.** Crossing the Pacific Ocean. **2.** Situated across or beyond the Pacific Ocean.
trans·par·en·cy (trăns-pâr'ən-sē, -păr'-) *n., pl.* **-cies.** **1.** Also **trans·par·ence** (-pâr'əns, -păr'-). The quality or state of being transparent. **2.** A transparent object, esp. a photographic slide.
trans·par·ent (trăns-pâr'ənt, -păr'-) *adj.* **1.** Capable of transmitting light so that objects or images can be seen as if there were no intervening material. **2.** Permeable to electromagnetic radiation of specified frequencies, as to visible light or radio waves. **3.** Of such fine or open texture that objects may be easily seen on the other side; diaphanous. **4.** Easily understood or detected; obvious: *transparent lies.* **5.** Guileless; candid. **6.** *Obs.* Shining through; luminous. [ME < OFr. < Med. Lat. *transparens,* pr.part. of *transparēre,* to be seen through : Lat. *trans,* through + Lat. *parēre,* to show.] **—trans·par'ent·ly** *adv.* **—trans·par'ent·ness** *n.*
trans·per·son·al (trăns-pûr'sə-nəl) *adj.* Transcending or reaching beyond the personal or individual.
tran·spi·ra·tion (trăn'spə-rā'shən) *n.* The act or process of transpiring, esp. through the stomata of plant tissue or the pores of the skin.
tran·spire (trăn-spīr') *v.* **-spired, -spir·ing, -spires.** *—tr.* To give off (vapor containing waste products) through the pores of the skin or the stomata of plant tissue. *—intr.* **1.** To give off vapor containing waste products through animal or plant pores. **2.** To become known; come to light. **3.** To happen; occur. [Fr. *transpirer* : Lat. *trans,* across + Lat. *spirare,* to breathe.]

Usage: *Transpire* has long been used in the sense of "to become known": *It soon transpired that he had known the secret all along.* The meaning "to happen" or "to take place" has come into use more recently: *He wondered what would transpire next.* This use, though widespread, is unacceptable to a majority of the Usage Panel.
trans·pla·cen·tal (trăns'plə-sĕn'tl) *adj.* Passing through the placenta. **—trans'pla·cen'tal·ly** *adv.*
trans·plant (trăns-plănt') *v.* **-plant·ed, -plant·ing, -plants.** *—tr.* **1.** To uproot and replant (a growing plant). **2.** To transfer from one place or residence to another; resettle; relocate. **3.** *Med.* To transfer (tissue or an organ) from one body, or body part, to another. *—intr.* **1.** To engage in transplanting. **2.** To withstand transplanting. *—n.* (trăns'plănt'). **1.** The act or process of transplanting. **2.** Something transplanted. [ME *transplaunten* < LLat. *transplantare* : Lat. *trans,* across + Lat. *plantare,* to plant.] **—trans'plan·ta'tion** *n.* **—trans·plant'er** *n.*
trans·po·lar (trăns-pō'lər) *adj.* Extending across or crossing over either of the geographic polar regions.
tran·spond·er (trăn-spŏn'dər) *n.* A radio or radar receiver-transmitter activated for transmission by reception of a predetermined signal. [TRAN(SMITTER) + (RE)SPONDER.]
trans·pon·tine (trăns-pŏn'tīn') *adj.* **1.** Situated across or beyond a bridge. **2.** Similar to or characteristic of melodramas formerly popular in London theaters located south of the Thames River.
trans·port (trăns-pôrt', -pōrt') *tr.v.* **-port·ed, -port·ing, -ports.** **1.** To carry from one place to another; convey. **2.** To move to strong emotion; enrapture. **3.** To send abroad to a penal colony. *—n.* (trăns'pôrt', -pōrt'). **1.** The act of transporting; conveyance. **2.** The state of being transported by emotion; rapture. **3.** A ship or aircraft used to transport troops or military equipment. **4.** A vehicle, as an aircraft, used to transport passengers, mail, or freight. [ME *transporten* < OFr. *transporter* < Lat. *transportare* : *trans,* across + *portare,* to carry.] **—trans·port'a·bil'i·ty** *n.* **—trans·port'a·ble** *adj.* **—trans·port'er** *n.* **—trans·por'tive** *adj.*
trans·por·ta·tion (trăns'pər-tā'shən) *n.* **1.** The act of transporting. **2.** The state of being transported. **3. a.** A means of transport; conveyance. **b.** The business of transporting passengers, goods, or materials. **4.** A charge for transporting; fare. **5.** Deportation to a penal colony.
trans·pose (trăns-pōz') *v.* **-posed, -pos·ing, -pos·es.** *—tr.* **1.** To reverse or transfer the order or place of; interchange. **2.** To put into a different place or order. **3.** *Math.* To move (a term) from one side of an algebraic equation to the other side, reversing its sign to maintain equality. **4.** *Mus.* To write or perform (a composition) in a key other than the original or given key. **5.** To alter in form or nature; transform. *—intr.* **1.** *Mus.* To write or perform music in a differ-

ent key. **2.** To admit of being transposed. [ME *transposen,* to transform < OFr. *transposer* < Lat. *transponere* : *trans,* across + *ponere,* to place.] **—trans·pos'a·ble** *adj.*

trans·po·si·tion (trăns'pə-zĭsh'ən) *n.* **1.** The act of transposing. **2.** The state of being transposed. **3.** Something that has been transposed. **—trans'po·si'tion·al** *adj.*

trans·sex·u·al (trăns-sĕk'shōō-əl) *n.* **1.** A person with an overwhelming desire to become a member of the other sex. **2.** A person whose sex has been changed externally through surgery. **—trans·sex'u·al** *adj.* **—trans·sex'u·al·ism, trans·sex'u·al'i·ty** (-ăl'ĭ-tē) *n.*

trans·ship (trăns-shĭp') also **tran·ship** (trăn-shĭp', trăns-) *v.* **-shipped, -ship·ping, -ships.** *—tr.* To transfer from one vessel or vehicle to another for reshipment. *—intr.* To transfer cargo from one vessel or conveyance to another. **—trans·ship'ment** *n.*

trans·tho·rac·ic (trăns'thə-răs'ĭk) *adj.* Across the thoracic cavity. **—trans'tho·rac'i·cal·ly** *adv.*

tran·sub·stan·ti·ate (trăn'səb-stăn'shē-āt') *tr.v.* **-at·ed, -at·ing, -ates. 1.** To change (one substance) into another; transmute. **2.** *Theol.* To change the substance of (the Eucharistic bread and wine) into the true presence of Christ. [Med. Lat. *transubstantiare, transubstantiat-* : Lat. *trans,* beyond + Lat. *substantia,* substance.]

tran·sub·stan·ti·a·tion (trăn'səb-stăn'shē-ā'shən) *n.* **1.** *Theol.* The doctrine that the bread and wine of the Eucharist are transformed into the true presence of Christ, although their appearance remains the same. **2.** The conversion of one substance into another; transformation. **—tran'sub·stan'ti·a'tion·al·ist** *n.*

tran·su·date (trăn-sōō'dāt', -syōō'-, trăn'sōō-dāt', -syōō-) also **tran·su·da·tion** (trăn'sōō-dā'shən, -syōō-) *n.* **1.** A substance that transudes. **2.** The act of transuding.

tran·sude (trăn-sōōd', -syōōd', -zōōd', -zyōōd') *intr.v.* **-sud·ed, -sud·ing, -sudes.** To exude or pass through pores or interstices, in the manner of perspiration. [Lat. *trans,* across + *sudare,* to sweat.] **—tran·su'da·to'ry** (trăn-sōō'də-tôr'ē, -tōr'ē, -syōō'-) *adj.*

trans·u·ran·ic (trăns'yōō-răn'ĭk, -rā'nĭk, trănz'-) also **trans·u·ra·ni·um** (-rā'nē-əm) *adj.* Having an atomic number greater than 92. [TRANS- + URAN(IUM) + -IC.]

trans·val·ue (trăns-văl'yōō, trănz-) *tr.v.* **-ued, -u·ing, -ues.** To evaluate by a new standard or principle, esp. by one that varies from conventional standards. **—trans·val'u·a'tion** *n.*

trans·ver·sal (trăns-vûr'səl, trănz-) *adj.* Transverse. *—n.* A line that intersects a system of lines.

trans·verse (trăns-vûrs', trănz-, trăns'vûrs', trănz'-) *adj.* Situated or lying across; crosswise. *—n.* Something, as a part or beam, that is transverse. [Lat. *transversus* < p.part. of *transvertere,* to direct across : *trans,* across + *vertere,* to turn.] **—trans·verse'ly** *adv.* **—trans·verse'ness** *n.*

transverse colon *n.* The part of the colon that lies across the upper part of the abdominal cavity.

transverse process *n.* A lateral projection from the side of a vertebra.

trans·ves·tite (trăns-vĕs'tīt') *n.* A person, esp. a male, who dresses in the clothing of the opposite sex for psychological reasons. **—trans·ves'tism** *n.*

trap[1] (trăp) *n.* **1.** A device for catching and holding animals, as a net, or a clamplike apparatus that springs shut suddenly. **2.** A stratagem or device employed in betraying, tricking, or exposing an unsuspecting victim. **3. a.** A receptacle for collecting waste or other materials, as a grease trap. **b.** A device for sealing a passage against the escape of gases, esp. a U-shaped or S-shaped bend in a drainpipe that prevents the return flow of sewer gas. **4.** A device that hurls clay pigeons, balls, or disks into the air to be shot at. **5.** A land hazard or bunker on a golf course. **6.** A light two-wheeled carriage with springs. **7.** A trap door. **8. traps.** Percussion instruments, as snare drums, cymbals, or bells. **9.** *Slang.* The mouth. **10. traps.** A measured length of roadway over which electronic timers register the speed of a racing vehicle. *—v.* **trapped, trap·ping, traps.** *—tr.* **1.** To catch in or as if in a trap; ensnare. **2.** To place in a confining or embarrassing position. **3.** To seal off (gases) by a trap. **4.** To furnish (a drain) with a trap. *—intr.* **1.** To set traps. **2.** To trap fur-bearing animals, esp. as a business. [ME < OE *træppe.*]

trap[2] (trăp) *n.* Often **traps.** *Informal.* Personal belongings or household goods. *—tr.v.* **trapped, trap·ping, traps.** To furnish with trappings. [ME *trap,* trapping < OFr. *drap,* cloth.]

trap[3] (trăp) *n.* Any of several dark, fine-grained igneous rocks often used in making roads. [Swed. *trapp* < *trappa,* step < MLG *trappe.*]

tra·pan (trə-păn') *v.* Variant of **trepan[2]**.

trap door *n.* A hinged or sliding door in a floor, roof, or ceiling.

trap-door spider (trăp'dôr', -dōr') *n.* Any of various spiders of the family Ctenizidae that construct a silk-lined burrow concealed by a hinged lid.

tra·peze (tră-pēz', trə-) *n.* A short horizontal bar suspended from the ends of two parallel ropes, used for exercises or for acrobatic stunts. [Fr. *trapèze* < LLat. *trapezium,* trapezium. —see TRAPEZIUM.]

trapeze artist *n.* A person who performs, usually professionally, on the trapeze.

tra·pe·zi·um (trə-pē'zē-əm) *n., pl.* **-zi·ums** or **-zi·a** (-zē-ə). **1. a.** A quadrilateral having no parallel sides. **b.** *Chiefly Brit.* A trapezoid (sense 1). **2.** A bone in the wrist at the base of the thumb. [LLat. < Gk. *trapezion,* dim. of *trapeza,* table : *tra-,* four + *peza,* foot.]

tra·pe·zi·us (trə-pē'zē-əs) *n.* Either of two large, flat muscles running from the base of the occiput to the middle of the back that support and make it possible to raise the head and shoulders. [NLat. < LLat. *trapezium,* trapezium (from the shape of the muscles paired).]

tra·pe·zo·he·dron (trə-pē'zō-hē'drən, trăp'ə-zō-) *n., pl.* **-drons** or **-dra** (-drə). Any of several forms of crystal with trapeziums as faces. [TRAPEZ(IUM) + -HEDRON.]

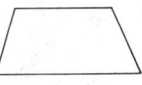

trap·e·zoid (trăp'ĭ-zoid') *n.* **1.** A quadrilateral having two parallel sides. **2.** A small bone in the wrist, situated near the base of the index finger. [NLat. *trapezoides* < Gk. *trapezoeidēs,* trapezium-shaped: *trapeza,* table + *-eidēs,* -oid.] **—trap'e·zoid', trap'e·zoi'dal** (-zoid'l) *adj.*

trap gun *n.* A shotgun designed for trapshooting.

trap house *n.* The enclosure housing the spring traps that hurl into the air the clay pigeons, balls, or disks used in trapshooting and skeet.

trap·light (trăp'līt') *n.* Any of various devices using a light to trap insects.

trap·per (trăp'ər) *n.* One whose occupation is trapping animals for their furs.

trap·ping (trăp'ĭng) *n.* **1.** Often **trappings.** An ornamental covering or harness for a horse; caparison. **2. trappings. a.** Articles of dress or adornment. **b.** Outward signs or indications: *has all the trappings of self-righteousness.*

Trap·pist (trăp'ĭst) *n.* A member of a branch of the Cistercian order of monks, characterized by austerity and a vow of absolute silence, established in 1664 in La Trappe, Normandy. *—adj.* Of or pertaining to the Trappists.

trap·shoot·ing (trăp'shōō'tĭng) *n.* The sport of shooting at clay pigeons hurled into the air from spring traps. **—trap'shoot'er** *n.*

tra·pun·to (trə-pōōn'tō) *n., pl.* **-tos.** Quilting having a raised effect made by outlining the design with running stitches and then filling it with cotton. [Ital. < *trapungere,* to embroider : Lat. *trans,* across + Lat. *pungere,* to prick.]

trash (trăsh) *n.* **1.** Worthless or discarded material or objects; refuse. **2. a.** Cheap or empty expressions or ideas. **b.** Worthless literary or artistic material. **3.** Something broken off or removed to be discarded, esp. plant trimmings. **4.** A person or group regarded as ignorant or contemptible. *—tr.v.* **trashed, trash·ing, trash·es. 1.** To cut off leaves or branches from, esp. to lop off the outer leaves from (growing sugar cane). **2.** To throw away; discard. **3.** *Slang.* **a.** To vandalize: *a school trashed by vandals.* **b.** To smash: *trash car windows.* **c.** To criticize harshly: *trashed his latest film.* [Orig. unknown.]

trash·y (trăsh'ē) *adj.* **-i·er, -i·est.** Resembling or of the nature of trash; inferior. **—trash'i·ly** *adv.* **—trash'i·ness** *n.*

trass (trăs) *n.* A light-colored tuff used in hydraulic cement. [Du. *tras.*]

trau·ma (trou'mə, trô'-) *n., pl.* **-mas** or **-ma·ta** (-mə-tə). **1.** *Pathol.* A wound, esp. one produced by sudden physical injury. **2.** *Psychiat.* An emotional shock that creates substantial and lasting damage to the psychological development of the individual, generally leading to neurosis. [Gk.] **—trau·mat'ic** (-măt'ĭk) *adj.* **—trau·mat'i·cal·ly** *adv.*

trau·ma·tism (trou'mə-tĭz'əm, trô'-) *n.* **1.** An injury. **2.** A wound produced by injury; trauma.

trau·ma·tize (trou'mə-tīz', trô'-) *tr.v.* **-tized, -tiz·ing, -tiz·es. 1.** To wound or injure. **2.** To damage the psychological development of (an individual).

tra·vail (trə-vāl', trăv'āl') *n.* **1.** Strenuous mental or physical exertion. **2.** Tribulation or agony; anguish. **3.** The labor of childbirth. *—intr.v.* **-vailed, -vail·ing, -vails. 1.** To labor strenuously; toil. **2.** To be in the labor of childbirth. [ME < OFr. < *travailler,* to work hard < LLat. *tripalium,* instrument of torture < Lat. *tripalis,* having three stakes : *ter,* three + *palus,* stake.]

trave (trāv) *n.* *Archit.* **1.** A crossbeam. **2.** A section, as of a ceiling, formed by crossbeams. [ME < OFr. < Lat. *trabs.*]

trav·el (trăv'əl) *v.* **-eled, -el·ing, -els** or **-elled, -el·ling, -els.** *—intr.* **1.** To go from one place to another; journey. **2.** To journey from one place to another as a traveling salesman. **3.** To be transmitted, as light. **4.** To keep or be in company; associate: *travel in wealthy circles.* **5.** To admit of being transported: *Some wines travel poorly.* **6.** *Informal.* To move swiftly. **7.** *Basketball.* To walk or run illegally while holding the ball. *—tr.* To pass or journey over or through: *travel the roads of Europe.* *—n.* **1.** The act or process of traveling. **2. travels. a.** A series of journeys. **b.** A written account of these journeys. **3.** Activity or traffic along a route or through a given point. [ME *travelen* < OFr. *travailler,* to travail. —see TRAVAIL.]

travel agency *n.* A business that arranges for itineraries, transportation tickets, and accommodations for travelers. **—travel agent** *n.*

travel bureau *n.* A travel agency.

trav·eled also **trav·elled** (trăv'əld) *adj.* **1.** Having journeyed widely. **2.** Much frequented by travelers: *a heavily traveled road.*

trapeze

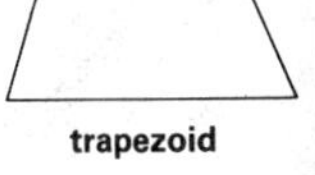

trapezoid

p **pop** / r **roar** / s **sauce** / sh **ship, dish** / t **tight** / th **thin, path** / *th* **this, bathe** / ŭ **cut** / ûr **urge** / v **valve** / w **with** / y **yes** / z **zebra, size** / zh **vision** / ə **about, item, edible, gallop, circus** / œ *Fr.* **feu,** *Ger.* **schön** / ü *Fr.* **tu,** *Ger.* **über** / KH *Ger.* **ich,** *Scot.* **loch** / N *Fr.* **bon.**

trav·el·er also **trav·el·ler** (trăv′əl-ər, trăv′lər) *n.* **1.** A person who travels. **2.** *Chiefly Brit.* A traveling salesman. **3.** *Naut.* **a.** A metal ring that moves freely back and forth on a rope, rod, or spar. **b.** The rope, rod, or spar on which such a ring moves.

traveler's check *n.* An internationally redeemable draft purchasable from a bank, express company, or travel agency, in various denominations, valid only with the holder's own endorsement against his original signature.

trav·el·er's-joy (trăv′əl-ərz-joi′, trăv′lərz-) *n.* Any of several climbing vines of the genus *Clematis,* esp. *C. vitalba,* of the Old World, having clusters of white flowers.

traveling salesman *n.* A salesman who solicits business orders or sells merchandise through personal dealings with potential customers within a given territory.

trav·e·logue also **trav·e·log** (trăv′ə-lôg′, -lŏg′) *n.* **1.** A lecture illustrated by travel slides or films. **2.** A narrated motion picture about travels.

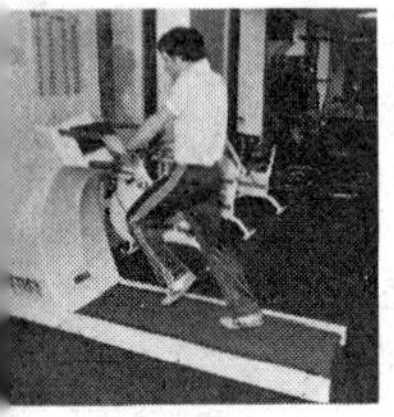

treadmill
Exercise treadmill

tra·verse (trə-vûrs′, trăv′ərs) *v.* **-versed, -vers·ing, -vers·es.** *—tr.* **1.** To travel across, over, or through. **2.** To move forward and backward over; cross and recross. **3. a.** To go up, down, or across (a hill, for example) at an angle. **b.** To ski across rather than down (a hill). **4.** To move (a gun, for example) laterally; cause to swivel. **5.** To extend across; cross. **6.** To look over carefully; examine. **7.** To go counter to; thwart. **8.** *Law.* **a.** To deny formally (an allegation of fact by the opposition) in a suit. **b.** To join issue upon (an indictment). **9.** To make a traverse survey of. **10.** *Naut.* To brace (a yard) fore and aft. *—intr.* **1.** To move or go along, across, or back and forth. **2.** To turn laterally; swivel. **3.** To descend a slope in a zigzag manner, as in skiing. **4.** In fencing, to glide or pressure one's blade toward the hilt of the opponent's weapon. *—n.* (trăv′ərs, trə-vûrs′). **1. a.** The act of traversing. **b.** A route or path across. **2.** Something lying across something else, esp.: **a.** A transversal. **b.** *Archit.* A structural crosspiece; transom. **c.** A gallery, deck, or loft crossing from one side of a building to the other. **d.** A railing, curtain, or screen. **e.** A defensive barrier across a rampart or trench, as a bank of earth thrown up for protection from enfilade fire. **3.** Something that obstructs and thwarts; obstacle. **4. a.** *Naut.* The zigzag route of a vessel forced by contrary winds to sail on different courses. **b.** The zigzag course made by a skier on a steep slope. **5.** The horizontal swivel of a mounted gun. **6. a.** A lateral movement, as of a lathe tool across a piece of work. **b.** A part of a mechanism that moves in this manner. **7.** A line established by sighting in surveying a tract of land. **8.** *Law.* The formal denial of an allegation of fact in a suit. *—adj.* **trav·erse** (trăv′ərs, trə-vûrs′). **1.** Lying or extending across; transverse. **2.** Relating to the installation or operation of draperies that can be drawn: *a traverse rod.* [ME *traversen* < OFr. *traverser* < LLat. *traversare* < Lat. *transvertere,* to direct across. —see TRANSVERSE.] **—tra·vers′a·ble** *adj.* **—tra·vers′al** (trə-vûr′səl) *n.* **—tra·vers′er** *n.*

trav·er·tine (trăv′ər-tēn′, -tĭn) *n.* **1.** A light-colored, porous calcite, $CaCO_3$, deposited from solution in ground or surface waters and forming, among other deposits, the stalactites and stalagmites of caverns. **2.** A compact type of creamy-colored calcium carbonate, used as a facing material in construction. [Ital. *travertino* < Lat. *(lapis) tiburtinus,* (stone) of Tibur, an ancient Italian city.]

treasury note
One-dollar note issued in 1862

trav·es·ty (trăv′ĭ-stē) *n., pl.* **-ties. 1.** An exaggerated or grotesque imitation with intent to ridicule. **2.** A broad and grotesque parody on a lofty work or theme. **3.** A grotesque, debased, highly inferior imitation: *a travesty of the Christian rites.* *—tr.v.* **-tied, -ty·ing, -ties.** To make a travesty on or of; ridicule. [Fr. *travesti,* p.part. of *travestir,* to take on someone's habits < OItal. *travestire,* to disguise : *tra-,* trans- + *vestire,* to dress < Lat. < *vestis,* garment.]

tra·vois (trə-voi′, trăv′oi′) or **tra·voise** (trə-voiz′, trăv′oiz′) *n., pl.* **tra·vois** (trə-voiz′, trăv′oiz′) or **tra·vois·es** (trə-voi′zĭz, trăv′oi′zĭz). A primitive sledge formerly used by Plains Indians and consisting of a platform or netting supported by two long trailing poles, the forward ends of which are fastened to a dog or horse. [Canadian Fr.]

trawl (trôl) *n.* **1.** A large, tapered fishing net of flattened conical shape, towed along the sea bottom. **2.** A setline. *—v.* **trawled, trawl·ing, trawls.** *—tr.* To catch (fish) by means of a trawl. *—intr.* **1.** To fish with a trawl net or line. **2.** To troll. [ME *trawelle,* perh. < MDu. *tragel,* dragnet.]

trawl·er (trô′lər) *n.* **1.** A boat used for trawling. **2.** One who trawls.

tray (trā) *n.* A flat, shallow receptacle with a raised edge or rim, used for carrying, holding, or displaying articles. [ME < OE *trēg.*]

treach·er·ous (trĕch′ər-əs) *adj.* **1.** Betraying a trust; traitorous. **2. a.** Unreliable; undependable. **b.** Not to be trusted; dangerous: *treacherous waters.* **—treach′er·ous·ly** *adv.* **—treach′er·ous·ness** *n.*

treach·er·y (trĕch′ə-rē) *n., pl.* **-ies. 1.** Willful betrayal of fidelity, confidence, or trust; perfidy. **2.** An act or instance of treachery. [ME *trecherie* < OFr. *trecherie* < *trichier,* to trick.]

trea·cle (trē′kəl) *n.* **1.** Cloying speech or sentiment. **2.** *Chiefly Brit.* Molasses. **3.** A medicinal compound formerly used as an antidote for poison. [ME, antidote for poison < OFr. *triacle* < Lat. *theriaca* < Gk. *thēriakē* < *thērion,* poisonous beast, dim. of *thēr,* beast.] **—trea′cly** (-klē) *adj.*

tread (trĕd) *v.* **trod** (trŏd), **trod·den** (trŏd′n) or **trod, tread·ing, treads.** *—tr.* **1.** To walk on, over, or along. **2.** To press beneath the foot; trample. **3.** To treat or put down harshly or cruelly; crush. **4.** To make by walking or trampling, as a path. **5.** To execute by walking or dancing: *tread a measure.* **6.** To copulate with. Used of male birds. *—intr.* **1.** To go on foot. **2.** To trample so as to press, crush, or injure. **3.** To copulate. Used of birds. *—n.* **1. a.** The act, manner, or sound of treading. **b.** An instance of treading; step. **2.** The horizontal part of a step in a staircase. **3.** The part of a wheel that makes contact with the ground or rails. **4.** The grooved face of a tire. **5.** The part of a shoe sole that touches the ground. *—**idiom.*** **tread water.** To keep one's head above water while in an upright position by moving the feet up and down as if walking. [ME *treden* < OE *tredan.*] **—tread′less** *adj.*

tread·le (trĕd′l) *n.* A pedal or lever operated by the foot for circular drive, as in a potter's wheel or sewing machine. *—intr.v.* **-led, -ling, -les.** To work a treadle. [ME *tredel* < OE, step of a stair < *tredan,* to tread.] **—tread′ler** (trĕd′lər) *n.*

tread·mill (trĕd′mĭl′) *n.* **1. a.** A mechanism operated by one or more persons walking on the moving steps of a wheel, or treading an endless sloping belt. **b.** A similar device operated by an animal. **2.** A monotonous task or routine.

trea·son (trē′zən) *n.* **1.** Violation of allegiance toward one's country or sovereign, esp. the betrayal of one's own country by waging war against it or by consciously and purposely acting to aid its enemies. **2.** A betrayal of trust or confidence. [ME < AN *treson* < Lat. *traditio,* surrender. —see TRADITION.]

trea·son·a·ble (trē′zə-nə-bəl) *adj.* Pertaining to or involving treason. **—trea′son·a·ble·ness** *n.* **—trea′son·a·bly** *adv.*

trea·son·ous (trē′zə-nəs) *adj.* Treasonable; treacherous. **—trea′son·ous·ly** *adv.*

treas·ure (trĕzh′ər) *n.* **1.** Accumulated, stored, or cached wealth in the form of valuables, as money or jewels. **2.** A person or thing considered esp. precious or valuable. *—tr.v.* **-ured, -ur·ing, -ures. 1.** To accumulate and save for future use. **2.** To value highly. [ME *tresure* < OFr. *tresor* < Lat. *thesaurus* < Gk. *thēsauros.*] **—treas′ur·a·ble** *adj.*

treas·ur·er (trĕzh′ər-ər) *n.* A person having charge of funds or revenues, esp. a financial officer or recorder for a government, corporation, or society. [ME *tresurer* < AN *tresorer* < OFr. *tresor,* treasure.] **—treas′ur·er·ship′** *n.*

treas·ure-trove (trĕzh′ər-trōv′) *n.* **1. a.** Treasure found hidden and not claimed by its owner. **b.** *Law.* Silver or gold, as in the form of bullion, plate, or money, that is found hidden and the ownership of which is unknown. **2.** A discovery of great value. [AN *tresor trove.*]

treas·ur·y (trĕzh′ə-rē) *n., pl.* **-ies. 1.** A place where treasure is kept or stored. **2.** A place where private or public funds are received, kept, managed, and disbursed. **3.** Public funds or revenues. **4.** A collection of valuables or things considered as valuable. **5. Treasury.** The executive department of a government in charge of the collection, management, and expenditure of the public revenue. [ME *tresory* < OFr. *tresorie* < *tresor,* treasure.]

treasury note *n.* A note or bill issued by the U.S. Treasury as legal tender for all debts.

treat (trēt) *v.* **treat·ed, treat·ing, treats.** *—tr.* **1.** To act or behave in a specified manner toward. **2.** To regard or consider in a certain way: *treated her as a sister.* **3.** To deal with in writing or speech; expound: *an article that treats all aspects of nuclear power.* **4.** To deal with or represent in a specified manner or style, as in art or literature: *treat a subject poetically.* **5.** To entertain at one's own expense: *treat her to the theater.* **6.** To subject to a process, action, or change, esp.: **a.** To give medical aid to. **b.** To subject to a chemical or physical process or application. *—intr.* **1.** To deal with a subject or topic in writing, speaking, or thought: *The essay treats of courtly love.* **2.** To pay for another's entertainment, food, or the like. **3.** To negotiate; bargain. *—n.* **1.** Something, as food or entertainment, generously paid for by someone else. **2.** The act of providing a treat, esp. in return. **3.** Something considered a special delight or pleasure. [ME *treten* < AN *treter* < Lat. *tractare,* freq. of *trahere,* to draw.] **—treat′a·ble** *adj.* **—treat′er** *n.*

trea·tise (trē′tĭs) *n.* **1.** A formal account in writing treating systematically of some subject. **2.** *Obs.* A tale; narrative. [ME *treatis* < AN *tretis* < *treter,* to treat.]

treat·ment (trēt′mənt) *n.* **1.** The act or manner of treating; handling. **2.** The application of remedies with the object of effecting a cure; therapy.

trea·ty (trē′tē) *n., pl.* **-ties. 1. a.** A formal agreement between two or more states. **b.** A document in which such an agreement is set down. **2.** A contract or agreement. **3.** *Obs.* Negotiation for the purpose of reaching an agreement. **4.** *Obs.* An entreaty. [ME *tretee* < AN *trete* < Lat. *tractus,* discussion < *tractare,* to handle. —see TREAT.]

treaty port *n.* A port once kept open for foreign trade according to the terms of a treaty, esp. in China, Korea, and Japan.

treb·le (trĕb′əl) *adj.* **1.** Triple; threefold. **2.** *Mus.* Of, having, or performing the highest part, voice, or range. **3.** High-pitched; shrill. *—n.* **1.** *Mus.* **a.** The highest part, voice, instrument, or range; soprano. **b.** A singer or player that performs this part. **2.** A high, shrill sound or voice. *—tr. & intr.v.* **-led, -ling, -les.** To make or become triple. [ME < OFr. < Lat. *triplus.*] **—treb'le·ness** *n.* **—treb'ly** (trĕb'lē) *adv.*

treble clef *n. Mus.* A symbol centered on the second line of the staff to indicate the position of G above middle C.

treb·u·chet (trĕb'yə-shĕt') also **treb·uc·ket** (trĕb'ə-kĕt') *n.* A medieval catapult for throwing heavy stones. [ME < OFr. < *trebucher,* to overthrow : *tre-,* trans- + *buc,* trunk of the body.]

tre·cen·to (trā-chĕn'tō) *n.* The 14th century, with reference esp. to Italian art and literature. [Ital., short for *milletrecento,* one thousand three hundred.]

tree (trē) *n.* **1.** A usually tall, woody plant, distinguished from a shrub by having comparatively greater height and, characteristically, a single trunk rather than several stems. **2.** A plant or shrub resembling a tree in form or size. **3.** A wooden beam, post, stake, or bar used as a part of a framework or structure. **4.** *Archaic.* A gallows; gibbet. **5.** Often **Tree.** *Archaic.* The cross on which Jesus was crucified. **6.** A saddletree. **7.** Something suggestive of a tree: *a clothes tree.* **8.** A diagram showing a family lineage. *—tr.v.* **treed, tree·ing, trees. 1.** To force to climb a tree in evasion of pursuit. **2.** *Informal.* To force into a difficult position; corner. **3.** To stretch (shoes) on a shoetree. ***—idiom.* up a tree.** *Informal.* In a situation of confusion or embarrassment from which there is no retreat. [ME < OE *treow.*]

tree farm *n.* An area of forest land on which trees are grown for commercial use.

tree fern *n.* Any of various treelike tropical ferns, esp. of the family Cyatheaceae, having a woody, trunklike stem and a terminal crown of large, divided fronds.

tree frog *n.* Any of various small, arboreal frogs of the genus *Hyla* and related genera, having long toes terminating in adhesive disks.

tree house *n.* A structure built by or for children among the limbs of a tree.

tree line *n.* **1.** The limit of northern or southern latitude beyond which trees do not grow except as stunted forms. **2.** A timberline.

tree·nail or **tre·nail** (trē'nāl', trĕn'əl, trŭn'əl) also **trun·nel** (trŭn'əl) *n.* A wooden peg that swells when wet, used to fasten timbers, esp. in shipbuilding.

tree of heaven *n.* The ailanthus.

tree of knowledge *n.* The tree in the Garden of Eden whose forbidden fruit Adam and Eve ate, causing loss of innocence.

tree of life *n.* **1.** The arborvitae (sense 1). **2.** A tree in the Garden of Eden whose fruit, if eaten, gave man immortality.

tree poppy *n.* A shrub, *Dendromecon rigidum,* of southern California, having evergreen foliage and showy, golden-yellow flowers.

tree surgery *n.* The treatment of diseased or damaged trees by filling cavities, pruning, and bracing branches. **—tree surgeon** *n.*

tree toad *n.* A tree frog.

tree·top (trē'tŏp') *n.* The uppermost part of a tree.

tref (trāf) *adj.* Unclean and unfit for consumption according to Jewish dietary law. [Yiddish *treyf* < Heb. *tĕrēphāh* < *tāraph,* he tore.]

tre·foil (trē'foil', trĕf'oil') *n.* **1.** Any of various plants of the genera *Trifolium, Lotus,* and related genera, having compound leaves with three leaflets. **2.** An ornament, symbol, or architectural form having the appearance of a trifoliate leaf. [ME < AN *trifoil* < Lat. *trifolium* : *ter,* three + *folium,* leaf.]

tre·ha·la (trĭ-hä'lə) *n.* A sugarlike, edible substance obtained from the pupal case of an Old World beetle, *Larinus maculatus.* [Turk. *tīqāla* < Pers. *tīghāl.*]

tre·ha·lase (trĭ-hä'lās') *n.* An enzyme that catalyzes the hydrolysis of trehalose.

tre·ha·lose (trĭ-hä'lōs', -lōz') *n.* A sweet-tasting, crystalline disaccharide, $C_{12}H_{22}O_{11}\cdot 2H_2O$, found in trehala and in many fungi that store it instead of starch.

treil·lage (trĕ-yäzh', trā'lĭj) *n.* Latticework, esp. a trellis for vines. [Fr. < OFr. *treille,* bower supported by trelliswork < Lat. *trichila,* bower.]

trek (trĕk) *intr.v.* **trekked, trek·king, treks. 1.** To make a slow or arduous journey. **2.** To travel by ox wagon in South Africa. *—n.* **1.** A journey or leg of a journey, esp. when slow or difficult. **2.** A migration. **3.** A journey by ox wagon in South Africa. [Afr., to travel by ox wagon < Du. *trekken,* to travel.] **—trek'ker** *n.*

trel·lis (trĕl'ĭs) *n.* **1.** A frame supporting open latticework, used for training vines and other creeping plants. **2.** An arbor or arch made with a trellis. *—tr.v.* **-lised, -lis·ing, -lis·es. 1.** To provide with a trellis, esp. to train (a plant) on a trellis. **2.** To make in the form of a trellis. [ME *trelis* < OFr. < Lat. *trilix,* woven with three threads: *ter,* three + *licium,* thread.]

trel·lis·work (trĕl'ĭs-wûrk') *n.* Latticework.

trem·a·tode (trĕm'ə-tōd') *n.* Any of numerous parasitic flatworms of the class Trematoda, having a thick outer cuticle, and one or more suckers for attaching to host tissue. *—adj.* Of or belonging to the Trematoda. [NLat. *Trematoda,* class name < Gk. *trēmatōdēs,* having holes < *trēma,* hole.]

trem·a·to·di·a·sis (trĕm'ə-tō-dī'ə-sĭs) *n.* Infestation with trematodes.

trem·ble (trĕm'bəl) *intr.v.* **-bled, -bling, -bles. 1.** To shake involuntarily, as from fear, cold, or sickness. **2.** To feel or express fear or anxiety: *I tremble to think of it.* **3.** To vibrate; quiver: *The leaves trembled in the wind.* *—n.* **1.** The act or state of trembling. **2.** Often **trembles.** A convulsive fit of trembling. **3. trembles** *(used with a sing. verb). Med.* **a.** A viral encephalomyelitis of sheep. **b.** Poisoning of domestic animals, esp. cattle and sheep, caused by eating white snakeroot. [ME *tremblen* < OFr. *trembler* < Lat. *tremulus,* tremulous < *tremere,* to tremble.] **—trem'bler** *n.* **—trem'bling·ly** *adv.* **—trem'bly** *adj.*

trebuchet

tre·men·dous (trĭ-mĕn'dəs) *adj.* **1.** Capable of making one tremble; terrible: *the tremendous tragedy of war.* **2. a.** Extremely large in amount, extent, or degree; enormous: *a tremendous task.* **b.** *Informal.* Marvelous; wonderful. [Lat. *tremendus,* gerund. of *tremere,* to tremble.] **—tre·men'dous·ly** *adv.* **—tre·men'dous·ness** *n.*

trem·o·lite (trĕm'ə-līt') *n.* A white to dark-gray calcium magnesium amphibole, $Ca_2Mg_5Si_8O_{22}(OH)_2$, usually occurring in aggregates, used as a substitute for asbestos and in paints and ceramics. [Fr. *trémolite,* after *Tremola,* valley in Switzerland.]

trem·o·lo (trĕm'ə-lō') *n., pl.* **-los.** *Mus.* **1. a.** A tremulous effect produced by the rapid repetition of a single tone. **b.** A similar effect produced by the rapid alternation of two tones. **2.** A device on an organ for producing a tremolo. **3.** A vibrato in singing, used for emotional effect or resulting from poor vocal control. [Ital. < Lat. *tremulus,* tremulous.]

trem·or (trĕm'ər) *n.* **1.** A quick shaking or vibrating movement: *an earth tremor.* **2.** An involuntary trembling motion of the body. **3.** A nervous quiver; thrill. **4.** A state of nervous agitation or tension: *all in a tremor.* **5. a.** An uncertain, insecure feeling. **b.** A cause of uncertainty or insecurity. **6.** A tremulous sound; quaver. [ME, a trembling < OFr. *tremour* < Lat. *tremor* < *tremere,* to tremble.]

trem·u·lous (trĕm'yə-ləs) *adj.* **1.** Vibrating or quivering; trembling. **2.** Timid; timorous. [Lat. *tremulus* < *tremere,* to tremble.] **—trem'u·lous·ly** *adv.* **—trem'u·lous·ness** *n.*

tre·nail (trē'nāl', trĕn'əl, trŭn'əl) *n.* Variant of **treenail.**

trench (trĕnch) *n.* **1.** A deep furrow. **2.** A ditch. **3.** A long, narrow, crooked ditch embanked with its own soil and used for concealment and protection in warfare. *—v.* **trenched, trench·ing, trench·es.** *—tr.* **1.** To cut or dig a trench in. **2.** To fortify with a trench. **3.** To put into a trench. **4.** To cut. **5.** To slash, sever, slice, or gash by cutting. *—intr.* **1.** To dig a trench or ditch. **2.** To cut, carve, or slash. **3.** To verge or encroach. [ME *trenche* < OFr. < *trenchier,* to cut < Lat. *truncare* < *truncus,* trunk.]

trench·ant (trĕn'chənt) *adj.* **1.** Forceful and effective; vigorous: *a trenchant argument.* **2. a.** Extremely perceptive; incisive. **b.** Caustic; cutting. **3.** Distinct; clear-cut. [ME < OFr., cutting < *trenchier,* to cut. —see TRENCH.] **—trench'an·cy** *n.* **—trench'ant·ly** *adv.*

trench coat *n.* A loose-fitting, belted raincoat having many pockets and flaps, suggesting a military style.

trefoil

trench·er[1] (trĕn'chər) *n.* **1.** A wooden board or plate on which food is cut or served. **2.** One that carves meat. [ME *trenchur* < AN *trenchour* < OFr. *trenchier,* to cut. —see TRENCH.]

trench·er[2] (trĕn'chər) *n.* One that digs trenches.

trench·er·man (trĕn'chər-mən) *n.* **1.** A hearty eater. **2.** *Archaic.* One who frequents another's table; hanger-on.

trench fever *n.* An acute infectious relapsing fever caused by a microorganism, *Rickettsia quintana,* and transmitted by a louse, *Pediculus humanus.*

trellis

trench foot *n.* A condition of the foot resembling frostbite, often afflicting soldiers obliged to stand in cold water over long periods of time.

trench knife *n.* A knife, used in warfare, having a short, double-edged blade.

trench mouth *n.* A form of gingivitis characterized by pain, foul odor, and the formation of a gray film over the diseased area.

trend (trĕnd) *n.* **1.** A direction of movement; course: *the trend of a line.* **2.** A general inclination or tendency: *a trend to more fuel-efficient automobiles.* *—intr.v.* **trend·ed, trend·ing, trends. 1.** To extend, bend, turn, or move in a specified direction: *The prevailing wind trends east-northeast.* **2.** To have a general tendency; tend. [ME *trenden,* to roll < OE *trendan.*]

trend·set·ter (trĕnd'sĕt'ər) *n.* One that sets a trend.

trend·y (trĕn'dē) *adj.* **-i·er, -i·est.** *Informal.* Of or in accordance with the latest fad or fashion: *trendy clothes.* **—trend'i·ly** *adv.* **—trend'i·ness** *n.*

trente et qua·rante (träNT' ā' kä-räNT') *n.* Rouge et noir. [Fr. : *trente,* thirty + *et,* and + *quarante,* forty.]

tre·pan[1] (trĭ-păn') *n.* **1.** A rock-boring tool used for sinking shafts in mining. **2.** A trephine. *—tr.v.* **-panned, -pan·ning, -pans. 1.** To bore (a shaft) with a trepan. **2.** *Med.* To trephine. [ME *trepane,* surgical crown saw < Med. Lat. *tre-*

trestle

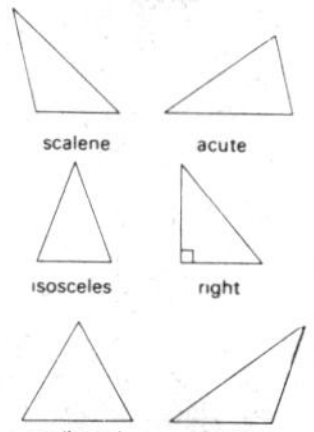

triangle
Above: Geometric figures
Below: Percussion instrument

panum < Gk. *trupanon,* borer < *trupan,* to pierce < *trupē,* hole.] **—trep'a·na'tion** (trĕp'ə-nā'shən) *n.*

tre·pan² (trĭ-păn') also **tra·pan** (trə-păn') *Archaic.* *—tr.v.* **-panned, -pan·ning, -pans.** To trap; ensnare. *—n.* **1.** A prankster; trickster. **2.** A trick; stratagem. [Orig. unknown.]

tre·pang (trĭ-păng') *n.* **1.** Any of several sea cucumbers of the genus *Holothuria,* of the southern Pacific and Indian oceans. **2.** The eviscerated, dried, or smoked body of the trepang, used as food in the Orient. [Malay *tĕripang.*]

tre·phine (trĭ-fīn') *n.* A surgical instrument having circular, sawlike edges, used to cut out disks of bone, usually from the skull. *—tr.v.* **-phined, -phin·ing, -phines.** To operate on with a trephine. [< Lat. *tres fines,* three ends.] **—treph'i·na'tion** (trĕf'ə-nā'shən) *n.*

trep·id (trĕp'ĭd) *adj.* Timid; timorous. [Lat. *trepidus,* anxious.]

trep·i·da·tion (trĕp'ĭ-dā'shən) *n.* **1.** A state of alarm or dread; apprehension. **2.** A quivering movement. [Lat. *trepidatio* < *trepidare,* to be in a state of confusion < *trepidus,* anxious.]

trep·o·ne·ma (trĕp'ə-nē'mə) *n., pl.* **-ma·ta** (-mə-tə) or **-mas.** A treponeme. [NLat. *Treponema, Treponemat-,* treponeme genus.] **—trep'o·ne'mal, trep'o·nem'a·tous** (-nĕm'ə-təs) *adj.*

trep·o·neme (trĕp'ə-nēm') *n.* Any of a group of spirochetes of the genus *Treponema,* including those that cause syphilis and yaws. [NLat. *Treponema,* genus name : Gk. *trepein,* to turn + Gk. *nēma,* thread.]

tres·pass (trĕs'pəs, -păs') *intr.v.* **-passed, -pass·ing, -pass·es. 1.** To commit an offense or sin; transgress. **2.** To infringe upon the privacy, time, or attention of another: *shouldn't trespass on their patience.* **3.** *Law.* To invade the property, rights, or person of another without his consent and with the actual or implied commission of violence, esp. to enter onto another's land illegally. *—n.* (trĕs'păs', -pəs). **1.** The transgression of a law, code, or duty. **2.** A transgression against another. **3.** *Law.* **a.** The act of trespassing. **b.** A legal suit brought for this. [ME *trespassen* < OFr. *trespasser* < Med. Lat. *transpassare* : Lat. *trans,* across + Med. Lat. *passare,* to pass < Lat. *passus,* step.] **—tres'pass·er** *n.*

tress (trĕs) *n.* **1.** A lock of hair, esp. a long lock of a woman's hair. **2.** A plait or braid of hair. **3. tresses.** A woman's long hair, esp. when unbound. [ME *tresse* < OFr.]

tres·tle (trĕs'əl) *n.* **1.** A horizontal beam or bar held up by two pairs of divergent legs and used as a support. **2.** A framework consisting of vertical, slanted supports and horizontal crosspieces supporting a bridge. [ME *trestel* < OFr. < Lat. *transtrum,* beam.]

tres·tle·tree (trĕs'əl-trē') *n. Naut.* One of a pair of horizontal beams set into a masthead to support the crosstrees.

tres·tle·work (trĕs'əl-wûrk') *n.* A trestle or system of trestles, as that supporting a bridge.

trews (trōōz) *pl.n. (used with a sing. verb).* Close-fitting trousers, usually of tartan. [Sc. Gael. *triubhas.*]

trey (trā) *n.* A card, die, or domino with three pips; three. [ME *treye* < OFr. *treie* < Lat. *tres,* three.]

tri– *pref.* **1.** Three: *trilobate.* **2. a.** Occurring at intervals of three: *trimonthly.* **b.** Occurring three times during: *triweekly.* [ME < Lat. (< *tres,* three) and Gk. (< *treis,* three).]

tri·a·ble (trī'ə-bəl) *adj.* **1.** Capable of being tried or tested. **2.** *Law.* Subject to judicial examination. **—tri'a·ble·ness** *n.*

tri·ac·id (trī-ăs'ĭd) *adj.* **1.** Capable of reacting with three molecules of a monobasic acid. Used of a base. **2.** Containing three replaceable hydrogen atoms. Used of an acid or an acid salt. *—n.* An acid containing three replaceable hydrogen atoms.

tri·ad (trī'ăd', -əd) *n.* **1.** A group of three persons or things. **2.** *Mus.* A chord of three tones, esp. one built on a given root tone plus a major or minor third and a perfect fifth. [LLat. *trias, triad-* < Gk. < *treis,* three.] **—tri·ad'ic** (trī-ăd'ĭk) *adj.*

tri·age (trē-äzh') *n.* **1.** A system designed to produce the greatest benefit from limited treatment facilities for battlefield casualties by giving full treatment to those who may survive and not to those who have no chance of survival and those who will survive without it. **2.** A system used to allocate a scarce commodity, such as food, only to those capable of deriving the greatest benefit from it. [Fr. < *trier,* to sort < OFr.]

tri·al (trī'əl, trīl) *n.* **1.** *Law.* The examination of evidence and applicable law by a competent tribunal to determine the issue of specified charges or claims. **2. a.** The act or process of testing, trying, or putting to the proof by actual or simulated use and experience: *a trial of one's faith.* **b.** A single complete instance of such testing, esp. as part of an experimental series. **3.** An effort or attempt. **4.** A state of pain or anguish caused by a difficult situation or condition: *"The fiery trial through which we pass"* (Lincoln). **5.** A test of patience or endurance: *He was a trial to his parents.* *—adj.* **1.** Of or pertaining to a trial. **2.** Made, done, used, or performed during the course of a trial or trials: *a trial run at Daytona.* [AN < OFr. *trier,* to try.]

trial and error *n.* An empirical method of establishing a satisfactory solution to a problem for which there is no existing or conveniently applicable theory, consisting of repeating experimental trials of various hypotheses until error is sufficiently reduced or eliminated.

trial balance *n.* A bookkeeping statement of all the open debit and credit items in a double-entry ledger made to test their equality.

trial balloon *n.* A preliminary statement or campaign released on a small scale to test public reaction. [From the use of balloons to test weather conditions.]

trial jury *n.* A petit jury.

trial run *n.* An experimental test.

tri·am·cin·o·lone (trī'ăm-sĭn'ə-lōn') *n.* A white crystalline compound, $C_{21}H_{27}FO_6$, used in photographic developing and in the medical treatment of respiratory disorders. [TRI- + AM(YL) + E. *cinene,* a turpene + E. *prednisolone,* a corticoid.]

tri·an·gle (trī'ăng'gəl) *n.* **1.** The plane figure formed by connecting three points not in a straight line by straight line segments; a three-sided polygon. **2.** Something having the shape of a triangle. **3.** Any of various flat, three-sided drawing and drafting guides, used esp. to draw straight lines at specified angles. **4.** *Mus.* A percussion instrument consisting of a piece of metal in the shape of a triangle open at one angle. **5.** A relationship among three persons, two of whom are in love with the third. [ME < OFr. or < Lat. *triangulum* < *triangulus,* three-angled : *tri-* tri- + *angulus,* angle.]

tri·an·gu·lar (trī-ăng'gyə-lər) *adj.* **1.** Of, pertaining to, or shaped like a triangle. **2.** Having a triangle for a base. **3.** Pertaining to, involving, or consisting of three interrelated entities, as three persons, objects, or ideas. **—tri·an'gu·lar'i·ty** (-lăr'ĭ-tē) *n.* **—tri·an'gu·lar·ly** *adv.*

tri·an·gu·late (trī-ăng'gyə-lāt') *tr.v.* **-lat·ed, -lat·ing, -lates. 1.** To divide into triangles. **2.** To survey by the method of triangulation. **3.** To make triangular. **4.** To measure by using trigonometry. *—adj.* (trī-ăng'gyə-lĭt). **1.** Of or pertaining to triangles; triangular. **2.** Made up of or marked with triangles.

tri·an·gu·la·tion (trī-ăng'gyə-lā'shən) *n.* **1. a.** A surveying technique in which a region is divided into a series of triangular elements based on a line of known length so that accurate measurements of distances and directions may be made by the application of trigonometry. **b.** The network of triangles so laid out. **2.** The location of an unknown point, as in navigation, by forming a triangle having the unknown point and two known points as the vertices.

Tri·an·gu·lum (trī-ăng'gyə-ləm) *n.* A constellation in the northern sky near Aries and Andromeda. [< Lat. *triangulum,* triangle.]

Triangulum Aus·tra·le (ô-strā'lē) *n.* A constellation in the polar region of the southern sky near Apus and Norma. [NLat.]

tri·ar·chy (trī'är'kē) *n., pl.* **-chies. 1.** Government by three persons; triumvirate. **2.** A country governed by three rulers. [Gk. *triarkhia* : *tri-,* tri- + *-arkhia,* -archy.]

Tri·as·sic (trī-ăs'ĭk) *adj.* Of, belonging to, or designating the geologic time, system of rocks, and sedimentary deposits of the first period of the Mesozoic era, after the Permian period of the Paleozoic era and before the Jurassic period of the Mesozoic era. *—n.* The Triassic period or system of deposits. [< LLat. *trias,* triad (from the subdivision of this period into three parts).]

tri·ath·lon (trī-ăth'lən, -lŏn') *n.* An athletic competition consisting of a race with three parts, cross-country running, long-distance swimming, and long-distance bicycling. [Gk. *tri-,* three + *athlon,* contest.]

tri·a·tom·ic (trī'ə-tŏm'ĭk) *adj.* **1.** Containing three atoms per molecule. **2.** Containing three replaceable atoms or radicals.

tri·ax·i·al (trī-ăk'sē-əl) *adj.* Having three axes. **—tri·ax'i·al'i·ty** (-ăl'ĭ-tē) *n.*

tri·a·zine (trī'ə-zēn', trī-ăz'ēn') *n.* **1.** Any of three isomeric compounds, $C_3H_3N_3$, each having three carbon and three nitrogen atoms in a six-membered ring. **2.** A compound derived from triazine.

tri·a·zole (trī'ə-zōl', trī-ăz'ōl') *n.* Any of several compounds with composition $C_2H_3N_3$ having a five-membered ring of two carbon atoms and three nitrogen atoms.

trib·al (trī'bəl) *adj.* Pertaining to or of the nature of a tribe. **—trib'al·ly** *adv.*

trib·al·ism (trī'bə-lĭz'əm) *n.* **1.** The organization, culture, or beliefs of a tribe. **2.** The sense of entity of a tribe.

tri·ba·sic (trī-bā'sĭk) *adj.* **1.** Containing three replaceable hydrogen atoms per molecule. Used of acids. **2.** Containing three univalent basic atoms or radicals per molecule. Used of bases or salts.

tribe (trīb) *n.* **1.** Any of various systems of social organization comprising several local villages, bands, districts, lineages, or other groups and sharing a common ancestry, language, culture, and name. **2.** A political, ethnic, or ancestral division of ancient states and cultures, specifically: **a.** Any of the three divisions of the ancient Romans, the Latin, Sabine, and Etruscan. **b.** Any of the 12 divisions of ancient Israel. **c.** A phyle of ancient Greece. **3.** A group of persons with a common occupation, interest, or habit: *a tribe of beggars.* **4.** *Informal.* A large family. **5.** *Biol.* A taxonomic category sometimes placed between a family and a genus. [ME < OFr. *tribu* or < Lat. *tribus.*]

tribes·man (trībz'mən) *n.* A member of a tribe.

tri·bo·e·lec·tric·i·ty (trī'bō-ĭ-lĕk-trĭs'ĭ-tē, -ē'lĕk-, trĭb'ō-) *n.* An electrical charge produced by friction between two objects. [Gk. *tribein,* to rub + ELECTRICITY.] **—tri'bo·e·lec'tric** *adj.*

tri·bol·o·gy (trī-bŏl'ə-jē, trĭb-ŏl'-) *n.* The science of the mechanisms of friction, lubrication, and wear of interacting surfaces that are in relative motion. [Gk. *tribein,* to rub + -LOGY.] **—tri'bo·log'i·cal** (trī'bə-lŏj'ĭ-kəl, trĭb'ə-) *adj.* **—tri·bol'o·gist** *n.*

tri·brach (trī'brăk') *n.* In prosody, a foot of three short or unstressed syllables. [Lat. *tribrachys* < Gk. *tribrakhus* : *tri-,* tri- + *brakhus,* short.]

tri·bro·mo·eth·a·nol (trī-brō'mō-ĕth'ə-nôl', -nōl') *n.* A white crystalline compound, CBr_3CH_2OH, having a slight aromatic odor and taste, and used as a basal anesthetic.

trib·u·la·tion (trĭb'yə-lā'shən) *n.* **1.** Great affliction, trial, or distress; suffering: *the tribulations of the persecuted.* **2.** An experience or condition that causes tribulation. [ME *tribulacioun* < OFr. < LLat. *tribulatio* < *tribulare,* to oppress < Lat. *tribulum,* threshing-sledge.]

tri·bu·nal (trī-byōō'nəl, trĭ-) *n.* **1.** A seat or court of justice. **2.** The platform or seat upon which a judge or other presiding officer sits in court. **3.** One that has the power of determining or judging: *the tribunal of public opinion.* [Lat. < *tribunus,* tribune.]

trib·u·nate (trĭb'yə-nāt', trĭ-byōō'nĭt) *n.* The rank, office, dignity, or authority of a tribune.

trib·une[1] (trĭb'yōōn', trĭ-byōōn') *n.* **1.** An official of ancient Rome chosen by the plebs to protect their rights against the patricians. **2.** A protector or champion of the people. [ME < Lat. *tribunus* < *tribus,* tribe.] **—trib'u·nar'y** (trĭb'yə-nĕr'ē) *adj.*

trib·une[2] (trĭb'yōōn', trĭ-byōōn') *n.* A raised platform or dais from which a speaker addresses an assembly. [Fr. < OItal. *tribuna* < Med. Lat. *tribuna,* var. of Lat. *tribunal.*]

trib·u·tar·y (trĭb'yə-tĕr'ē) *adj.* **1.** Making additions or offering supplies; contributory. **2.** Having the nature of tribute: *a tributary payment.* **3.** Paying tribute: *a tributary colony.* —*n., pl.* **-ies. 1.** A stream or river flowing into a larger stream or river. **2.** One that pays tribute. [ME *tributarye,* of paying tribute < Lat. *tributarius* < *tributum,* tribute. —see TRIBUTE.]

trib·ute (trĭb'yōōt) *n.* **1.** A gift, payment, declaration, or other acknowledgment of gratitude, respect, or admiration. **2. a.** A sum of money or other valuables paid by one ruler or nation to another as acknowledgment of submission or as the price for protection by that nation. **b.** A payment made for protection. **3. a.** A payment or tax given by a feudal vassal to his overlord. **b.** The obligation involved in such a payment. [ME *tribut* < Lat. *tributum* < neuter p.part. of *tribuere,* to assign < *tribus,* tribe.]

tri·car·box·yl·ic (trī'kär-bŏk-sĭl'ĭk) *adj.* Having three carboxyl groups.

tricarboxylic acid cycle *n.* The Krebs cycle.

trice (trīs) *n.* A very short period of time. —*tr.v.* **triced, tric·ing, tric·es.** To hoist and secure (a sail, for example); lash. [ME *tryse* < *trisen,* to hoist < MDu.]

tri·cen·ten·ni·al (trī'sĕn-tĕn'ē-əl) *adj.* Tercentenary. —*n.* A tercentenary event or celebration.

tri·ceps (trī'sĕps') *n.* A large three-headed muscle running along the back of the upper arm and serving to extend the forearm. [< Lat., three-headed : *tri-,* tri- + *caput,* head.]

tri·cer·a·tops (trī-sĕr'ə-tŏps') *n.* A horned herbivorous dinosaur of the genus *Triceratops,* of the Cretaceous period, having a bony plate covering the neck. [NLat. *Triceratops,* genus name : *tri-,* tri- + Gk. *keras,* horn + *ops,* face.]

trich– *pref.* Variant of **tricho-.**

tri·chi·a·sis (trĭ-kī'ə-sĭs) *n.* A condition of ingrowing hairs about an orifice, esp. ingrowing eyelashes. [LLat. < Gk. *trikhiasis* < *trikhian,* to be hairy.]

tri·chi·na (trĭ-kī'nə) *n., pl.* **-nae** (-nē) or **-nas.** A parasitic nematode worm, *Trichinella spiralis,* infesting the intestines of various mammals, and having larvae that move through the blood vessels and become encysted in the muscles. [NLat. < Gk. *trikhinos,* hairy < *thrix,* hair.]

trich·i·nize (trĭk'ə-nīz') *tr.v.* **-nized, -niz·ing, -niz·es.** To infect with trichinae. **—trich'i·ni·za'tion** *n.*

trich·i·no·sis (trĭk'ə-nō'sĭs) *n.* A disease caused by eating inadequately cooked pork containing trichinae, and characterized by intestinal disorders, fever, muscular swelling, pain, and insomnia.

tri·chi·nous (trĭ-kī'nəs, trĭk'ə-nəs) *adj.* **1.** Containing trichinae: *trichinous pork.* **2.** Of or relating to trichinae or trichinosis: *a trichinous infection.*

trich·ite (trĭk'īt') *n.* A small needle-shaped filament or crystal. [G. *Trichit* < Gk. *thrix,* hair.] **—tri·chit'ic** (trĭ-kĭt'ĭk) *adj.*

tri·chlor·fon (trī-klôr'fŏn', -klōr'-) *n.* A colorless crystalline compound, $C_4H_8Cl_3O_4P$, used as an agricultural insecticide. [TRI- + CHLOR(O)- + *-fon* (< PHOSPHONATE).]

tri·chlo·ride (trī-klôr'īd', -klōr'-) also **tri·chlo·rid** (-klôr'ĭd, -klōr'-) *n.* A compound containing three chlorine atoms per molecule.

tri·chlo·ro·a·ce·tic acid (trī-klôr'ō-ə-sē'tĭk, -klōr'-) *n.* A colorless, deliquescent, corrosive, crystalline compound, CCl_3COOH, used as a herbicide and topically as an astringent and antiseptic.

tri·chlo·ro·eth·yl·ene (trī-klôr'ō-ĕth'ə-lēn', -klōr'-) also **tri·chlor·eth·yl·ene** (trī'klôr-ĕth'ə-lēn', -klōr-) *n.* A heavy, colorless, toxic liquid, $CHCl{:}CCl_2$, used to degrease metals, as an extraction solvent for oils and waxes, as a refrigerant, in dry cleaning, and as a fumigant.

tricho– or **trich–** *pref.* Hair; thread; filament: *trichocyst.* [Gk. *trikho-* < *thrix,* hair.]

trich·o·cyst (trĭk'ə-sĭst') *n.* One of the minute capsulelike bodies in the outer cytoplasm of certain protozoans, capable of ejecting a threadlike or bristlelike extension. **—trich'o·cys'tic** *adj.*

trich·o·gyne (trĭk'ə-jīn', -gīn') *n.* A receptive filament of the female reproductive structure of certain fungi or algae.

trich·oid (trĭk'oid', trī'koid') *adj.* Resembling hair; hairlike. [Gk. *trikhoeidēs* : *trikho-,* tricho- + *-oeidēs,* -oid.]

trich·ome (trĭk'ōm', trī'kōm') *n.* A hairlike or bristlelike outgrowth, as from the epidermis of a plant. [G. *Trichom* < Gk. *trikhoma,* growth of hair < *trikhoun,* to cover with hair < *thrix,* hair.] **—tri·chom'ic** (trĭ-kŏm'ĭk, -kō'mĭk, trī-) *adj.*

trich·o·mo·nad (trĭk'ə-mō'năd') *n.* Any of various flagellate protozoans of the genus *Trichomonas,* occurring in the digestive and urogenital tracts of vertebrates. [NLat. *Trichomonas, Trichomonad-,* genus name : TRICHO- + LLat. *monas,* unit. —see MONAD.] **—trich'o·mo·nad'al, trich'o·mon'al** *adj.*

trich·o·mo·ni·a·sis (trĭk'ə-mə-nī'ə-sĭs) *n., pl.* **-ses** (-sēz'). **1.** A vaginal infection caused by a protozoan, *Trichomonas vaginalis,* and resulting in inflammation and discomfort. **2.** An infection caused by trichomonads.

tri·chop·ter·an (trĭ-kŏp'tər-ən) *n.* An insect of the order Trichoptera, which includes the caddis flies. [NLat. *Trichoptera,* order name.]

tri·cho·sis (trĭ-kō'sĭs) *n.* Disease of the hair. [NLat. < Gk. *trikhōsis,* growth of hair < *trikhoun,* to cover with hair. —see TRICHOME.]

tri·chot·o·my (trī-kŏt'ə-mē) *n., pl.* **-mies.** Division into three parts, esp. the theological division of man into body, soul, and spirit. [Gk. *trikha,* in three parts + -TOMY.] **—tri·chot'o·mous** *adj.* **—tri·chot'o·mous·ly** *adv.*

–trichous *suff.* Having a specified kind of hair or hairlike part: *peritrichous.* [Gk. *-trikhos* < *thrix,* hair.]

tri·chro·ism (trī'krō-ĭz'əm) *n.* The property possessed by certain minerals of exhibiting three different colors when illuminated by white light and viewed from three different directions. [Gk. *trikhroos,* three-colored : *tri-,* three + *khrōs,* color.] **—tri·chro'ic** *adj.*

tri·chro·mat·ic (trī'krō-măt'ĭk) also **tri·chrome** (trī'krōm') or **tri·chro·mic** (trī-krō'mĭk) *adj.* **1.** Of, relating to, or having three colors, as in photography or printing. **2.** Having visual perception of the three primary colors, as in normal vision. **—tri·chro'ma·tism** (trī-krō'mə-tĭz'əm) *n.*

trich·u·ri·a·sis (trĭk'yə-rī'ə-sĭs) *n., pl.* **-ses.** Infestation of the large intestine with whipworms of the genus *Trichuris.* [NLat. *Trichuris,* genus name (TRICH(O)- + Gk. *oura,* tail) + -IASIS.]

trick (trĭk) *n.* **1.** A device or action designed to achieve an end by deceptive or fraudulent means. **2.** A mischievous action; prank. **3.** A stupid, disgraceful, or childish act or performance. **4.** A peculiar trait or characteristic; mannerism: *"Mimicry is the trick by which a moth or other defenseless insect comes to look like a wasp"* (Marston Bates). **5.** A special skill; knack: *Is there a trick to getting this window to stay up?* **6.** A feat of magic or legerdemain. **7.** A difficult, dexterous, or clever act designed to amuse. **8.** All the cards played in a single round. **9.** A period or turn of duty. **10.** *Slang.* A prostitute's customer. —*v.* **tricked, trick·ing, tricks.** —*tr.* **1.** To cheat or deceive. **2.** To ornament or adorn. —*intr.* To practice deception or trickery. —*adj.* Weak, defective, or liable to fail: *a trick knee.* **—idiom. do (or turn) the trick.** To bring about the desired result. [ME *trik* < ONFr. *trique* < *trikier,* to deceive.] **—trick'er** *n.*

triceratops
Skeleton and reconstruction

trick·er·y (trĭk'ə-rē) *n., pl.* **-ies.** The practice or use of tricks; deception by stratagem.

trick·ish (trĭk'ĭsh) *adj.* Characterized by or tending to use tricks or trickery. **—trick'ish·ly** *adv.* **—trick'ish·ness** *n.*

trick·le (trĭk'əl) *v.* **-led, -ling, -les.** —*intr.* **1.** To flow or fall in drops or in a thin stream. **2.** To move or proceed slowly or bit by bit: *The audience trickled in.* —*tr.* To cause to trickle. —*n.* **1.** The act or condition of trickling. **2.** A slow, small, or irregular quantity that moves, proceeds, or occurs intermittently. [ME *triklen.*]

trick·le-down (trĭk'əl-doun') *adj.* Of or pertaining to the trickle-down theory.

trickle-down theory *n.* A theory in economics that financial benefits accorded to big business enterprises will in turn pass down to smaller businesses and consumers.

trick·ster (trĭk'stər) *n.* One that swindles or plays tricks.

trick·y (trĭk'ē) *adj.* **-i·er, -i·est. 1.** Given to or characterized by deception or trickery; wily. **2.** Requiring caution or skill: *a tricky recipe.* **—trick'i·ly** *adv.* **—trick'i·ness** *n.*

tri·clin·ic (trī-klĭn'ĭk) *adj.* Having three unequal axes intersecting at oblique angles. Used of certain crystals.

tri·clin·i·um (trī-klĭn'ē-əm) *n., pl.* **-i·a** (-ē-ə). **1.** A couch surrounding three sides of a table, used by the ancient Romans for reclining at meals. **2.** A room containing a triclinium. [Lat. < Gk. *triklinion,* dim. of *triklinos,* room with three couches : *tri-,* tri- + *klinē,* couch.]

tricorn

tricycle

triforium

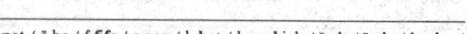

tri·col·or (trī'kŭl'ər) *n.* **1.** A flag having three colors. **2. Tricolor.** The French flag. **—tri'col'ored** *—adj.*
tri·corn also **tri·corne** (trī'kôrn') *n.* A hat having the brim turned up on three sides. [Fr. *tricorne* or < Lat. *tricornis,* three-horned : *tri-,* tri + *cornu,* horn.]
tri·cor·nered (trī'kôr'nərd) *adj.* Having three corners.
tri·cos·tate (trī-kŏs'tāt') *adj.* Having three costae or riblike ridges.
tri·cot (trē'kō) *n.* **1.** A plain, warp-knitted cloth of any of various yarns. **2.** A soft, ribbed cloth of wool or a wool blend, usually used for dresses. [Fr. < *tricoter,* to knit.]
tric·o·tine (trĭk'ə-tēn', trē'kə-) *n.* A sturdy, worsted fabric with a double twill, used for dresses and suits. [Fr. < *tricot,* tricot.]
tri·cot·y·le·do·nous (trī'kŏ-tə-lēd'n-əs) *adj.* Having three cotyledons.
tri·crot·ic (trī-krŏt'ĭk) *adj. Med.* Having three waves or elevations to one beat of the pulse. [Gk. *trikrotos,* having a triple beat : *tri-,* tri- + *krotein,* to beat.] **—tri'cro·tism** (trī'krə-tĭz'-əm) *n.*
tri·cus·pid (trī-kŭs'pĭd) also **tri·cus·pi·dal** (-pĭ-dəl) *adj.* **1.** Having three points or cusps, as a molar tooth. **2.** Of or pertaining to the tricuspid valve of the heart. *—n.* A tricuspid organ or part, esp. a tooth. [Lat. *tricuspis, tricuspid-,* having three points : *tri-,* tri- + *cuspis,* point.]
tricuspid valve *n.* The three-segmented valve of the heart that keeps the blood from flowing back from the right ventricle into the right atrium.
tri·cy·cle (trī'sĭk'əl, -sĭ-kəl) *n.* A vehicle with three wheels usually propelled by pedals.
tri·dac·tyl (trī-dăk'təl) also **tri·dac·ty·lous** (-tə-ləs) *adj.* Having three toes, claws, or similar parts. [Gk. *tridaktulos,* three-fingered : *tri-,* tri- + *daktulos,* finger.]
tri·dent (trīd'nt) *n.* A long, three-pronged fork or weapon, esp. the three-pronged spear carried by the classical god of the sea, Neptune or Poseidon. [Lat. *tridens, trident-* : *tri-,* tri- + *dens,* tooth.] **—tri·den'tate'** (trī-dĕn'tāt') *—adj.*
Tri·den·tine (trī-dĕn'tīn', -tēn') *adj.* Of or relating to a council held by the Roman Catholic Church in Trent, Italy from 1545 to 1563. [Med. Lat. *Tridentinus* < *Tridentum,* Trent, a city in Italy.]
tri·di·men·sion·al (trī'dĭ-mĕn'shə-nəl) *adj.* Of, relating to, or having three dimensions.
tri·e·cious (trī-ē'shəs) *adj.* Variant of **trioecious.**
tried (trīd) *adj.* **1.** Thoroughly tested and proved to be good or trustworthy. **2.** Made to undergo trials or distress: *a much-tried teacher.* *—v.* Past tense and part participle of **try.**
tried and true *adj.* Tried (sense 1).
tri·en·ni·al (trī-ĕn'ē-əl) *adj.* **1.** Occurring every third year. **2.** Lasting three years. *—n.* **1.** A third anniversary. **2.** A celebration or other ceremony occurring every three years. [Lat. *triennis* < *triennium,* triennium.] **—tri·en'ni·al·ly** *adv.*
tri·en·ni·um (trī-ĕn'ē-əm) *n., pl.* **-ni·ums** or **-ni·a** (-ē-ə). A period of three years. [Lat. : *tri-,* tri- + *annus,* year.]
tri·er·arch (trī'ə-rärk') *n.* **1.** The captain of a Greek trireme. **2.** An Athenian who outfitted and maintained a trireme as a part of his civic duties. [Lat. *trierarchus* < Gk. *triērarkhos* : *triērēs,* trireme + *-arkhos,* -arch.]
tri·er·ar·chy (trī'ə-rär'kē) *n., pl.* **-chies. 1.** The authority or office of the commander of a trierarch. **2.** The ancient Athenian system whereby individual citizens furnished and maintained triremes as a part of their public duty.
tries (trīz) *v.* Third person singular present tense of **try.** *—n.* Plural of **try.**
tri·fa·cial (trī-fā'shəl) *adj.* Trigeminal.
tri·fec·ta (trī-fĕk'tə) *n.* A system of betting in which the bettor must pick the first three winners in the correct sequence. [TRI- + (PER)FECTA.]
tri·fid (trī'fĭd') *adj.* Divided or cleft into three narrow parts or lobes. [Lat. *trifidus,* split into three : *tri-,* tri- + *findere,* to split.]
tri·fle (trī'fəl) *n.* **1.** Something of slight importance or very little value. **2.** A small amount; jot. **3.** A dessert consisting of sponge cake spread with jam, soaked in wine, sprinkled with crushed macaroons, and topped with custard and whipped cream. **4. a.** A moderately hard variety of pewter. **b. trifles.** Utensils made from this. *—v.* **-fled, -fling, -fles.** *—intr.* **1.** To deal with something as if it were of little significance or value. **2.** To act, perform, or speak with little seriousness or purpose; jest. **3.** To play or toy with something: *She trifled with my affections.* *—tr.* To waste (time, for example). **—idiom. a trifle.** Very little; somewhat: *a trifle stingy.* [ME < OFr. *trufle,* trickery.] **—tri'fler** (trī'flər) *n.*
tri·fling (trī'flĭng) *adj.* **1.** Of slight importance; insignificant. **2.** Characterized by frivolity or idleness. **—tri'fling·ly** *adv.*
tri·flu·ra·lin (trī-flo͝or'ə-lĭn) *n.* A crystalline compound, $C_{13}H_{16}F_3N_3O_4$, used as a herbicide. [TRI- + FLU(O)R(O)- + A(NI)LIN(E).]
tri·fo·cal (trī-fō'kəl) *adj.* Having three focal lengths. *—pl.n.* **trifocals.** Eyeglasses having trifocal lenses.
tri·fold (trī'fōld') *adj.* Having three parts; triple.
tri·fo·li·ate (trī-fō'lē-ĭt) also **tri·fo·li·at·ed** (-ā'tĭd) *adj.* Having three leaves, leaflets, or leaflike parts.
tri·fo·li·o·late (trī-fō'lē-ə-lāt') *adj.* Having three leaflets.
tri·fo·ri·um (trī-fôr'ē-əm, -fōr') *n., pl.* **-fo·ri·a** (-fôr'ē-ə, -fôr'-) *Archit.* A gallery of arches above the side-aisle vaulting in the nave of a church. [Orig. unknown.]
tri·formed (trī'fôrmd') also **tri·form** (-fôrm') *adj.* Having three different forms or parts.
tri·fur·cate (trī-fûr'kĭt, -kāt', trī'fər-kāt') also **tri·fur·cat·ed** (trī'fər-kā'tĭd) *adj.* Having three forks or branches. **—tri'fur·ca'tion** *n.*
trig¹ (trĭg) *adj.* **1.** Trim; neat. **2.** In good condition. *—tr.v.* **trigged, trig·ging, trigs.** To make trim or neat, esp. in dress. [ME, true < ON *tryggr.*] **—trig'ly** *adv.* **—trig'ness** *n.*
trig² (trĭg) *tr.v.* **trigged, trig·ging, trigs. 1.** To stop (a wheel) from rolling, as with a wedge. **2.** To prop up; support. *—n.* A wedge or other braking device. [Perh. of Scand. orig.]
tri·gem·i·nal (trī-jĕm'ə-nəl) *adj.* Pertaining to the trigeminus.
trigeminal neuralgia *n.* An intensely painful inflammation of the facial area around the trigeminal nerve.
tri·gem·i·nus (trī-jĕm'ə-nəs) *n., pl.* **-ni** (-nī'). The chief facial sensory nerve and the motor nerve of the masticatory muscles. [NLat. < Lat. three fold : *tri-,* tri- + *geminus,* twin.]
trig·ger (trĭg'ər) *n.* **1.** The lever pressed by the finger to discharge a firearm. **2.** A device similar to a trigger used to release or activate a mechanism. **3.** An event that precipitates others. *—tr.v.* **-gered, -ger·ing, -gers.** To initiate; set off. [Du. *trekker* < MDu. *trecker* < *trecken,* to pull.]
trig·ger·fish (trĭg'ər-fĭsh') *n., pl.* **triggerfish** or **-fish·es.** Any of various brightly colored fishes of the family Balistidae, of warm coastal seas, characteristically having a sharp, erectile dorsal spine.
trig·ger-hap·py (trĭg'ər-hăp'ē) *adj. Slang.* Inclined to react violently at the slightest provocation.
trig·ger·man (trĭg'ər-mən) *n.* An underworld gunman who shoots the victim in a planned murder.
tri·glyc·er·ide (trī-glĭs'ə-rīd') *n.* An ester of three fatty acids and glycerol.
tri·glyph (trī'glĭf') *adj. Archit.* An ornament in a Doric frieze, consisting of a projecting block having three parallel vertical channels on its face. [Lat. *triglyphus* < Gk. *trigluphos* : *tri-,* tri- + *gluphē,* carving < *gluphein,* to carve.] **—tri·glyph'ic** *adj.*
tri·gon (trī'gŏn') *n.* **1.** A triangular lyre or harp of Roman and Greek antiquity. **2.** Triplicity (sense 3). **3.** *Obs.* A triangle. [Lat. *trigonum* < Gk. *trigōnon* < *trigōnos,* triangular.]
trigonometric function *n.* A function of an angle expressed as the ratio of two of the sides of a right triangle that contains the angle; in general, for any angle formed in a coordinate plane by the intersection of the abscissal axis with the radius vector from the origin to a point in the plane, the ratio of any two of the values abscissa, ordinate, and radius vector of that point.
trig·o·nom·e·try (trĭg'ə-nŏm'ĭ-trē) *n.* The study of the properties and applications of trigonometric functions. [Gk. *trigōnon,* triangle + Gk. *-metria,* -metry.] **—trig'o·no·met'ric** (-nə-mĕt'rĭk), **trig'o·no·met'ri·cal** *adj.* **—trig'o·no·met'ri·cal·ly** *adv.*
tri·he·dral (trī-hē'drəl) *adj.* Formed by the plane surfaces of a trihedron. *—n.* A trihedron.
tri·he·dron (trī-hē'drən) *n., pl.* **-drons** or **-dra** (-drə). A figure formed by the intersection of three noncoplanar lines.
tri·hy·brid (trī-hī'brĭd) *n. Genetics.* An individual that is heterozygous for three pairs of genes.
tri·lat·er·al (trī-lăt'ər-əl) *adj.* Having three sides. [Lat. *trilaterus* : *tri-,* tri- + *latus* side.] **—tri·lat'er·al·ly** *adv.*
tril·by (trĭl'bē) *n. Chiefly Brit.* A soft felt hat with a deeply creased crown. [So called because such a hat was worn in the original London stage production of the novel *Trilby* by George du Maurier (1834–1896).]
tri·lin·e·ar (trī-lĭn'ē-ər) *adj.* Relating to, having, or bounded by three lines.
tri·lin·gual (trī-lĭng'gwəl) *adj.* Having or expressed in three languages.
tri·lit·er·al (trī-lĭt'ər-əl) *adj.* Consisting of three letters. Used chiefly of consonantal roots in Semitic languages. *—n.* A three-letter word or word element.
trill (trĭl) *n.* **1.** A fluttering or tremulous sound, as that made by certain birds; warble. **2.** *Mus.* **a.** The rapid alternation of two tones either a whole or a half tone apart. **b.** A vibrato. **3. a.** A rapid vibration of one speech organ against another, as of the tongue against the alveolar ridge in Spanish *rr.* **b.** A speech sound pronounced with such a vibration. *—v.* **trilled, trill·ing, trills.** *—tr.* **1.** To sound, sing, or play with a trill. **2.** To articulate (a sound) with a trill. *—intr.* To produce or give forth a trill. [Ital. *trillo* < *trillare,* to trill.]
tril·lion (trĭl'yən) *n.* **1.** The cardinal number that is equal to 10^{12}. **2.** *Chiefly Brit.* The cardinal number that is equal to 10^{18}. [Fr. : *tri-,* third power + *(m)illion,* million.] **—tril'lion** *adj.*
tril·lionth (trĭl'yənth) *n.* **1.** The ordinal number that matches the number one trillion in a series. **2.** One of a trillion equal parts. **—tril'lionth** *adj. & adv.*
tril·li·um (trĭl'ē-əm) *n.* Any of various plants of the genus *Trillium,* of North America and eastern Asia, usually having a single whorl of three leaves, and a variously colored, three-petaled flower. [NLat. *Trillium,* genus name < Swed. *trilling,* triplet (from its three leaves).]
tri·lo·bate (trī-lō'bāt') or **tri·lo·bat·ed** (-lō'bā'tĭd) also **tri·**

lobed (trī'lōbd') *adj.* Having three lobes, as certain leaves.

tri·lo·bite (trī'lə-bīt') *n.* Any of numerous extinct marine arthropods of the class Trilobita, of the Paleozoic era, having a segmented exoskeleton divided by grooves or furrows into three longitudinal lobes. [NLat. *Trilobites,* division name < Gk. *trilobos,* three-lobed : *tri-,* tri- + *lobos,* lobe.] **—tri'lo·bit'ic** (-bĭt'ĭk) *adj.*

tri·loc·u·lar (trī-lŏk'yə-lər) *adj.* Having three chamberlike divisions or cavities.

tril·o·gy (trĭl'ə-jē) *n., pl.* **-gies.** A group of three dramatic or literary works related in subject or theme. [Gk. *trilogia* : *tri,* tri- + *-logia,* -logy.]

trim (trĭm) *v.* **trimmed, trim·ming, trims.** *—tr.* **1.** To make neat or tidy by clipping, smoothing, or pruning. **2.** To remove (excess) by cutting: *trim a budget.* **3.** To ornament; decorate. **4.** *Informal.* **a.** To thrash. **b.** To defeat soundly. **c.** To cheat. **5.** *Naut.* **a.** To adjust (the sails and yards) so that they receive the wind properly. **b.** To balance (a ship) by shifting its cargo or contents. **6.** To balance (an airplane) in flight by regulating the control surfaces and tabs. **7.** To furnish or equip. *—intr.* **1.** *Naut.* **a.** To be in or retain equilibrium. **b.** To make sails and yards ready for sailing. **2. a.** To affect cautious neutrality. **b.** To fashion one's views for momentary popularity or advantage. *—n.* **1.** State of order, arrangement, or appearance; condition. **2. a.** Exterior ornamentation, as moldings or framework. **b.** Ornamentation, as for clothing. **3.** Material used in commercial window displays. **4.** Excised or rejected material. **5.** Personal quality; character. **6.** *Naut.* **a.** The readiness of a vessel for sailing with regard to ballast, sails, and yards. **b.** The balance of a ship. **c.** The difference between the draft at the bow and at the stern. **7.** The position of an aircraft relative to its horizontal axis. *—adj.* **trim·mer, trim·mest. 1.** Being in good or neat order. **2.** Having lines, edges, or forms of neat and pleasing simplicity. *—adv.* In a trim manner. [Perh. < ME **trimmen* < OE *trymman,* to arrange.] **—trim'ly** *adv.* **—trim'ness** *n.*

tri·ma·ran (trī'mə-răn') *n.* A fast sailboat with three parallel hulls. [TRI- + (CATA)MARAN.]

tri·mer (trī'mər) *n.* A polymeric compound consisting of three identical monomeric molecules. [TRI- + Gk. *meros,* part.] **—tri·mer'ic** (-mĕr'ĭk) *adj.*

trim·er·ous (trĭm'ər-əs) *adj.* **1.** Having three similar segments or parts. **2.** *Bot.* Having flower parts, as petals, sepals, and stamens, in sets of three. [NLat. *trimerus* < Gk. *trimerēs* : *tri-,* tri- + *meros,* part.] **—trim'er·ism** *n.*

tri·mes·ter (trī-mĕs'tər, trī'mĕs'tər) *n.* **1.** A period or term of three months. **2.** One of three equal academic terms in some universities. [Fr. *trimestre* < Lat. *trimestris,* of three months : *tri-,* tri- + *mensis,* month.] **—tri·mes·tral** (-trəl), **tri·mes·tri·al** (-trē-əl) *adj.*

trim·e·ter (trĭm'ĭ-tər) *n.* A verse line of three metrical feet or three prosodic units. [Lat. *trimetrus* < Gk. *trimetros* : *tri-,* tri- + *metros,* meter.] **—tri·met'ric** (trī-mĕt'rĭk), **tri·met'ri·cal** (-rĭ-kəl) *adj.*

tri·meth·a·di·one (trī-mĕth'ə-dī'ōn') *n.* A granular, crystalline substance, $C_6H_9NO_3$, used in treating epilepsy. [TRI- + METH(YL) + DI- + -ONE.]

tri·met·ro·gon (trī-mĕt'rə-gŏn') *n.* A system of aerial photography in which one vertical and two oblique photographs are simultaneously taken for use in topographic mapping. [TRI- + Gk. *metron,* measure + -GON.]

trim·mer (trĭm'ər) *n.* **1. a.** One that trims. **b.** A device such as a lumber trimmer, that is used for trimming. **2.** A person who changes his opinions to suit the needs of the moment.

trim·ming (trĭm'ĭng) *n.* **1.** Something added as decoration or ornament. **2. trimmings.** Accessories; extras: *roast turkey with all the trimmings.* **3. trimmings.** Scraps or material removed when something is trimmed. **4.** *Informal.* A sound defeat, beating, or punishment.

tri·mo·lec·u·lar (trī'mə-lĕk'yə-lər) *adj.* Pertaining to or formed from three molecules.

tri·month·ly (trī-mŭnth'lē) *adj.* Done, occurring, or appearing every three months. **—tri·month'ly** *adv.*

tri·morph (trī'môrf') *n.* **1.** A substance that occurs in three distinct forms. **2.** One of the forms in which a trimorphic substance occurs. [Back-formation < TRIMORPHIC.]

tri·mor·phic (trī-môr'fĭk) also **tri·mor·phous** (-fəs) *adj.* **1.** *Biol.* Having or occurring in three differing forms. **2.** *Chem.* Crystallizing in three distinct forms. [Gk. *trimorphos,* having three forms : *tri-,* tri- + *morphē,* shape.] **—tri·mor'phi·cal·ly** *adv.* **—tri·mor'phism** *n.*

Tri·mur·ti (trĭ-mŏŏr'tē) *n. Hindu Myth.* The triad of Hindu gods consisting of Brahma, Vishnu, and Shiva. [Skt. *trimūrtiḥ* : *tri-,* three + *murtiḥ,* form.]

tri·nal (trī'nəl) *adj.* Having three parts; threefold. [Lat. *trinalis* < Lat. *trinus,* trine.]

tri·na·ry (trī'nə-rē) *adj.* Consisting of three parts or proceeding by threes; ternary. [LLat. *trinarius* < Lat. *trinus,* trine.]

trine (trīn) *adj.* **1.** Threefold; triple. **2. a.** In astrology, situated in trine. **b.** Of or relating to a favorable positioning of two planets. *—n.* **1.** A group of three. **2.** In astrology, the aspect of two planets when 120 degrees apart. [ME < OFr. < Lat. *trinus* < *tres,* three.]

Trine (trīn) *n.* The Trinity. [< TRINE.]

Tri·nil man (trē'nĭl') *n.* Pithecanthropus. [After *Trinil,* Indonesia.]

Trin·i·tar·i·an (trĭn'ĭ-târ'ē-ən) *adj.* **1.** Describing or relating to the Trinity. **2.** Believing or professing belief in the Trinity or the doctrine of the Trinity. **3. trinitarian.** Having three members, parts, or facets. *—n.* **1.** A person who believes in the doctrine of the Trinity. **2.** A member of a religious teaching and nursing order founded for men in 1198. **—Trin'i·tar'i·an·ism** *n.*

tri·ni·tro·ben·zene (trī-nī'trō-bĕn'zēn', -bĕn-zēn') *n.* A yellow crystalline compound, $C_6H_3N_3O_6$, derived from trinitrotoluene and used as an explosive.

tri·ni·tro·cre·sol (trī-nī'trō-krē'sôl', -sōl') *n.* A yellow crystalline compound, $C_7H_5N_3O_7$, used in high explosives.

tri·ni·tro·glyc·er·in (trī-nī'trō-glĭs'ər-ĭn) *n. Chem.* Nitroglycerin.

tri·ni·tro·phe·nol (trī-nī'trō-fē'nōl', -nôl') *n. Chem.* Picric acid.

tri·ni·tro·tol·u·ene (trī-nī'trō-tŏl'yōō-ēn') *n.* A yellow crystalline compound, $C_7H_5N_3O_6$, used mainly as a high explosive.

tri·ni·tro·tol·u·ol (trī-nī'trō-tŏl'yōō-ôl', -ōl') *n.* Trinitrotoluene.

trin·i·ty (trĭn'ĭ-tē) *n., pl.* **-ties. 1.** A group consisting of three closely related members. **2. Trinity.** The union of three divine figures, the Father, Son, and Holy Ghost, in one Godhead. **3. Trinity.** Trinity Sunday. [ME *trinite* < OFr. < Lat. *trinitas* < *trinus,* trine.]

Trinity Sunday *n.* The first Sunday after Pentecost, or Whitsunday, dedicated to the Trinity.

trin·ket (trĭng'kĭt) *n.* **1.** A small ornament, such as a piece of jewelry. **2.** A trivial thing; trifle. [Orig. unknown.]

tri·no·mi·al (trī-nō'mē-əl) *adj.* **1.** Consisting of three names or terms, as a taxonomic designation. **2.** *Math.* Having three algebraic terms connected by plus or minus signs. *—n.* **1.** *Math.* A trinomial algebraic expression. **2.** A three-part taxonomic designation indicating genus, species, and subspecies or variety, such as *Brassica oleracea botrytis,* the cauliflower. [TRI- + (BI)NOMIAL.]

tri·nu·cle·o·tide (trī-nōō'klē-ə-tīd', -nyōō'-) *n.* A triplet of nucleotides; codon.

tri·o (trē'ō) *n., pl.* **-os. 1.** A group of three people or things joined or associated. **2.** *Mus.* **a.** A composition for three performers. **b.** The group performing a trio. **c.** The middle section of a minuet or scherzo, a march, or of various dance forms. [Fr., composition for three voices < Ital. < *tre,* three < Lat. *tres.*]

tri·ode (trī'ōd') *n.* A highly evacuated electron tube containing an anode, a cathode, and a control grid.

tri·oe·cious also **tri·e·cious** (trī-ē'shəs) *adj.* Having male, female, and bisexual flowers borne on separate plants. [< NLat. *Trioecia,* former order name : TRI- + Gk. *oikia,* dwelling < *oikos,* house.] **—tri·oe'cious·ly** *adv.*

tri·ol (trī'ôl', -ōl') *n.* A chemical compound containing three hydroxyl groups.

tri·o·let (trē'ə-lĭt, trī'-, trē'ə-lā') *n.* A poem or stanza of eight lines with a rhyme scheme *ABaAabAB* in which the fourth and seventh lines are the same as the first, and the eighth line is the same as the second. [Fr., dim. of *trio,* trio. —see TRIO.]

tri·ose (trī'ōs') *n.* One of a group of monosaccharides that contain three carbon atoms.

tri·ox·ide (trī-ŏk'sīd') also **tri·ox·id** (-ŏk'sĭd) *n.* A chemical compound containing three oxygen atoms per molecule.

trip (trĭp) *n.* **1.** A going from one place to another; journey. **2.** *Slang.* **a.** A hallucinatory experience induced by a psychedelic drug. **b.** An intense, stimulating, or exciting experience. **3.** *Slang.* **a.** A usually temporary but absorbing interest: *on a health food trip.* **b.** A certain lifestyle or situation: *did the whole money-making trip.* **4.** A light or nimble tread. **5.** A stumble or fall. **6.** A maneuver causing someone to stumble or fall. **7.** A mistake. **8. a.** A device, such as a pawl, for triggering a mechanism. **b.** The action of such a device. *—v.* **tripped, trip·ping, trips.** *—intr.* **1.** To stumble. **2.** To move nimbly with light, rapid steps; skip. **3.** To make a mistake. **4.** To be released, as a tooth on an escapement wheel in a watch. **5.** To make a trip. **6.** *Slang.* To have a drug-induced hallucination. *—tr.* **1.** To cause to stumble or fall. **2.** To trap or catch in an error or inconsistency. **3.** *Archaic.* To perform (a dance) nimbly. **4.** To release a catch, trigger, or switch, setting something in operation. **5.** *Naut.* **a.** To raise (an anchor) from the bottom. **b.** To tip or turn (a yardarm) into a position for lowering. **c.** To lift (an upper mast) in order to remove the fid before lowering. *—idiom.* **trip the light fantastic.** To dance. [ME, maneuver to cause someone to fall < *trippen,* to move nimbly < OFr. *tripper* < MDu. *trippen,* to hop.] **—trip'per** *n.*

tri·pal·mi·tin (trī-păl'mĭ-tĭn) *n.* Palmitin.

tri·par·tite (trī-pär'tīt') *adj.* **1.** Composed of or divided into three parts. **2.** Relating to or executed by three parties.

tri·par·ti·tion (trī'pär-tĭsh'ən) *n.* Division into three parts or among three parties: *the tripartition of a defeated nation.*

tripe (trīp) *n.* **1.** The light-colored, rubbery lining of the stomach of cattle or other ruminants, used as food. **2.** *Informal.* Something of no value; rubbish. [ME < OFr.]

triplane

tripod

triptych
16th-century Rhenish

triskelion

triton[1]
Late 17th-century sculpture of Triton

tri·ped·al (trī-pĕd′l) *adj.* Having three feet or legs; tripodal. [Lat. *tripedalis* : *tri-*, three + *pes, ped-*, foot.]

tri·pep·tide (trī-pĕp′tīd′) *n.* A peptide containing three amino acids.

tri·pet·al·ous (trī-pĕt′l-əs) *adj.* Having three petals.

trip hammer also **trip·ham·mer** or **trip-ham·mer** (trĭp′-hăm′ər) *n.* A heavy, power-operated hammer that is lifted by a cam or lever and then dropped.

tri·phen·yl·meth·ane (trī-′fĕn′əl-mĕth′ān′, -fē′nəl-) *n.* A colorless, crystalline hydrocarbon, $(C_6H_5)_3CH$, from which a large number of synthetic dyes are derived by substitution.

tri·phib·i·an (trī-fĭb′ē-ən) *adj.* Designed to operate on land, water, or in air. —*n.* A triphibian aircraft. [TRI- + (AM)-PHIBIAN.]

tri·phos·phate (trī-fŏs′fāt′) *n.* A salt or ester containing three phosphate groups.

triph·thong (trĭf′thông′, -thŏng′, trĭp′-) *n.* A compound vowel sound resulting from the succession of three simple ones and functioning as a unit. [TRI- + (DI)PHTHONG.] **—triph·thon′gal** (trĭf-thông′əl, -thŏng′əl, trĭp-) *adj.*

triph·y·lite (trĭf′ə-līt′) also **triph·y·line** (-lēn′) *n.* Any of a vitreous, bluish-gray mineral series of lithium, iron, and manganese phosphates. [TRI- + Gk. *phulon*, tribe + -ITE.]

tri·pin·nate (trī-pĭn′āt′) *adj.* Divided into leaflets that are subdivided into smaller, further subdivided leaflets or lobes. **—tri·pin′nate′ly** *adv.*

tri·plane (trī′plān′) *n.* An airplane with wings placed above each other in three levels.

tri·ple (trĭp′əl) *adj.* **1.** Consisting of three parts; threefold. **2.** Three times as many or as much. **3.** Repeated three times. **4.** *Mus.* Characterized by three beats in a measure. —*n.* **1.** A number or quantity three times as great as another. **2.** A group or set of three; triad. **3.** *Baseball.* A three-base hit. **4.** A trifecta. —*v.* **-pled, -pling, -ples.** —*tr.* To make three times as great in number or amount. —*intr.* **1.** To be or become three times as great in number or amount. **2.** *Baseball.* To make a three-base hit. [OFr. < Lat. *triplus* < Gk. *triplous*.]

Triple Crown *n.* **1.** An unofficial championship title attained by a horse that wins the three traditional races for a specified category. **2.** *Baseball.* An unofficial championship title achieved by a player who is at the head of his league in batting average, home runs, and runs batted in.

tri·ple-head·er (trĭp′əl-hĕd′ər) *n.* A sports contest consisting of three contests in a row.

triple measure *n.* Triple time.

triple play *n. Baseball.* A defensive play in which three putouts, on two base runners and the batter, are executed during one turn at bat, thereby ending suddenly the offensive threat and the inning.

trip·let (trĭp′lĭt) *n.* **1.** A group or set of three of one kind. **2.** One of three children born at one birth. **3.** A group of three lines of verse. **4.** *Mus.* A group of three notes having the time value of two notes of the same kind. **5.** *Physics.* A multiplet with three components. [TRIPL(E) + (DOUBL)ET.]

tri·ple·tail (trĭp′əl-tāl′) *n.* Any of several chiefly marine fishes of the family Lobotidae, esp. *Lobotes surinamensis*, having prominent dorsal and anal fins that resemble extra tails.

triple time *n.* A musical time or rhythm having three beats to the measure, with the accent on the first beat.

tri·plex (trĭp′lĕks′, trī′plĕks′) *adj.* Composed of three parts; threefold; triple. —*n.* Something triplex. [Lat.]

trip·li·cate (trĭp′lĭ-kĭt) *n.* One of a set of three identical objects or copies. —*tr.v.* (trĭp′lĭ-kāt′) **-cat·ed, -cat·ing, -cates.** **1.** To make threefold; triple. **2.** To make three identical copies of. [ME < Lat. *triplicatus*, p.part. of *triplicare*, to triple < *triplex*, threefold.] **—trip′li·cate·ly** *adv.* **—trip′li·ca′tion** *n.*

tri·plic·i·ty (trĭ-plĭs′ĭ-tē, trī-) *n., pl.* **-ties.** **1.** The condition or quality of being triple. **2.** A group or set of three. **3.** One of four groups of the zodiac, each consisting of three astrological signs. [ME, three signs of zodiac < LLat. *triplicitas*, triplicity < *triplex*, triplex.]

trip·lo·blas·tic (trĭp′lō-blăs′tĭk) *adj.* Having three germ layers. [Lat. *triplus*, triple + -BLASTIC.]

trip·loid (trĭp′loid′) *adj.* Having three haploid sets of chromosomes in each nucleus. [TRIPL(E) + (HAPL)OID.] **—trip′-loid** *n.*

tri·pod (trī′pŏd′) *n.* **1.** A three-legged object, such as a caldron, stool, or table. **2.** An adjustable three-legged stand, as for supporting a transit or camera. [Lat. *tripus, tripod-*, tripod < Gk. *tripous*, three-footed : *tri-*, tri- + *pous*, foot.] **—trip′o·dal** (trĭp′ə-dəl, trī′pŏd′l) *adj.*

trip·o·li (trĭp′ə-lē) *n.* A porous, lightweight, siliceous rock of various colors, derived from weathering of chert and siliceous limestone. [After *Tripoli*, Libya.]

tri·pos (trī′pŏs′) *n.* Any of the examinations for the B.A. degree with honors at Cambridge University in England. [Alteration of Lat. *tripus*, tripod (from the stool upon which a candidate sat to dispute humorously with other candidates).]

trip·pet (trĭp′ĭt) *n.* A cam or projection in a mechanism designed to strike another part at regular intervals. [ME *tripet*, piece of wood used in a game < *trippen*, to trip. —see TRIP.]

trip·ping·ly (trĭp′ĭng-lē) *adv.* Lightly and easily; fluently.

trip·tane (trĭp′tān′) *n.* A colorless liquid antiknock additive, C_7H_{16}, used in aviation fuels. [Short for *trimethylbutane*.]

trip·tych (trĭp′tĭk) *n.* **1.** A hinged writing tablet consisting of three leaves, used in ancient Rome. **2.** A work of art consisting of three hinged or folding panels, esp. one with a religious theme, used as an altarpiece. [< Gk. *triptukhos*, threefold : *tri-*, tri- + *ptukhē*, fold < *ptussein*, to fold.]

tri·reme (trī′rēm′) *n.* An ancient Greek or Roman galley or warship, having three tiers of oars on each side. [Lat. *triremis* : *tri-*, tri- + *remus*, oar.]

tri·sac·cha·ride (trī-săk′ə-rīd′, -rĭd) *n.* A carbohydrate that upon hydrolysis yields three monosaccharides.

tri·sect (trī′sĕkt′, trī-sĕkt′) *tr.v.* **-sect·ed, -sect·ing, -sects.** To divide into three equal parts. **—tri′sec′tion** (trī′sĕk′shən, trī-sĕk′-) *n.* **—tri′sec′tor** (trī′sĕk′tər, trī-sĕk′-) *n.*

tri·sep·al·ous (trī-sĕp′ə-ləs) *adj.* Having three sepals.

tri·skel·i·on (trī-skĕl′ē-ən, trĭs-kĕl′-) also **tri·skele** (trī′skēl′, trĭs′kēl′) *n., pl.* **tri·skel·i·a** (trī-skĕl′ē-ə, trĭs-kĕl′-) also **tri·skeles.** A figure consisting of three curved lines or branches, or three stylized human arms or legs, radiating from a common center. [NLat. < Gk. *triskelēs*, three-legged : *tri-*, tri-, + *skelos*, leg.]

tris·mus (trĭz′məs) *n.* Lockjaw. [NLat. < Gk. *trismos*, a grinding.] **—tris′mic** *adj.*

tris·oc·ta·he·dron (trĭs-ŏk′tə-hē′drən) *n., pl.* **-drons** or **-dra** (-drə) *Math.* **1.** A solid figure having 24 congruent triangular faces and an octahedron as a base. **2.** A trapezohedron. [Gk. *tris*, thrice + OCTAHEDRON.] **—tris·oc′ta·he′dral** *adj.*

tri·so·di·um (trī-sō′dē-əm) *adj.* Containing three sodium atoms.

tri·so·mic (trī-sō′mĭk) *adj.* Having at least one triploid chromosome in an otherwise diploid set. [TRI- + (CHROMO)-SOM(E) + -IC.] **—tri′some′** (trī′sōm′) *n.* **—tri·so′my** *n.*

Tris·tan (trĭs′tən, -tän′, -tăn′) *n.* A prince who, according to Arthurian legend, fell in love with the Irish princess Iseult and died with her.

triste (trēst) *adj.* Sad; wistful. [ME < OFr. < Lat. *tristis*.]

tri·ste·a·rin (trī-stē′ə-rĭn, -stîr′ĭn) *n.* Stearin.

trist·ful (trĭst′fəl) *adj. Archaic.* Sorrowful; gloomy. [ME *trist*, sad (< OFr. *triste* < Lat. *tristis*) + -FUL.] **—trist′ful·ly** *adv.*

tris·tich (trĭs′tĭk) *n.* A stanza or strophic unit of three lines. [TRI- + (DI)STICH.]

Tris·tram (trĭs′trəm) *n.* Tristan.

tri·sul·fide (trī-sŭl′fīd′) also **tri·sul·phide** or **tri·sul·fid** or **tri·sul·phid** (-fĭd) *n.* A sulfide containing three sulfur atoms per molecule.

tri·syl·la·ble (trī′sĭl′ə-bəl) *n.* A three-syllable word. **—tri′syl·lab′ic** (-sĭ-lăb′ĭk), **tri′syl·lab′i·cal** *adj.* **—tri′syl·lab′i·cal·ly** *adv.*

tri·tan·o·pi·a (trī′tə-nō′pē-ə) *n.* A rare visual defect involving an inability to distinguish the color blue. [Gk. *tritos*, a third + Gk. *anopia*, blindness.]

trite (trīt) *adj.* **trit·er, trit·est.** Overused and commonplace; hackneyed. [Lat. *tritus* < *terere*, to wear out.] **—trite′ly** *adv.* **—trite′ness** *n.*

Synonyms: *trite, hackneyed, shopworn, stereotyped, commonplace, threadbare, stale, banal.* These adjectives describe writing and speech that is without freshness of expression and consequently without appeal. *Trite, hackneyed,* and *shopworn* all imply overfamiliarity resulting from overuse of combinations of words or overworking of a theme; *hackneyed* is strongest in suggesting reduction of a once forceful expression or idea to an empty verbal formula or cliché. *Stereotyped* can refer to a theme or treatment of theme so lacking in originality or creative force that it seems a mechanical reproduction of timeworn generalizations or clichés. *Commonplace* applies to speech or writing that is pedestrian through its stress on what is obvious, conventional, or platitudinous. *Threadbare* describes a theme or topic or an individual expression that has been overworked to the point where its further employment with profit is extremely unlikely. *Stale* can imply loss of taste or appeal through overuse or through mere age. *Banal* often adds to lack of freshness the implication of inanity or of lack of good taste.

tri·the·ism (trī′thē-ĭz′əm) *n.* The belief that the Father, Son, and Holy Ghost are three separate and distinct gods. **—tri′-the·ist** *n.* **—tri′the·is′tic, tri′the·is′ti·cal** *adj.*

trit·i·um (trĭt′ē-əm, trĭsh′ē-) *n.* A rare radioactive hydrogen isotope with atomic mass 3 and half-life 12.5 years, prepared artificially for use as a tracer and as a constituent of hydrogen bombs. [NLat. < Gk. *tritos*, third.]

tri·ton[1] (trīt′n) *n.* **1. Triton.** *Gk. Myth.* A god of the sea, son of Poseidon and Amphitrite, portrayed as having the head and trunk of a man and the tail of a fish. **2.** Any of various chiefly tropical marine gastropod mollusks of the genus *Cymatium* and related genera, having a pointed, spirally twisted, often colorfully marked shell. [Lat. < Gk. *Tritōn*.]

tri·ton[2] (trī′tŏn′) *n.* The nucleus of a tritium atom consisting of two neutrons and one proton. [TRIT(IUM) + -ON[2].]

tri·tone (trī′tōn′) *n. Mus.* An interval composed of three whole tones. [Med. Lat. *tritonus* < Gk. *tritonos*, having three tones : *tri-*, tri- + *tonos*, tone.]

trit·u·rate (trĭch′ə-rāt′) *tr.v.* **-rat·ed, -rat·ing, -rates.** To rub, crush, grind, or pound into fine particles or a powder; pulverize. —*n.* (trĭch′ər-ĭt) A triturated substance, esp. a powdered drug. [LLat. *triturare, triturat-*, to thresh < Lat. *tritura*, a threshing < *tritor,* grinder < *terere,* to rub.] **—trit'u·ra·ble** (trĭch'ər-ə-bəl) *adj.* **—trit'u·ra'tor** *n.*

trit·u·ra·tion (trĭch'ə-rā'shən) *n.* **1.** The act or process of triturating. **2.** The composing of a dental amalgam by mortar and pestle.

tri·umph (trī'əmf) *intr.v.* **-umphed, -umph·ing, -umphs. 1.** To be victorious or successful; win. **2.** To rejoice over a success or victory; exult. **3.** To receive honors upon return from a victory in ancient Rome. *—n.* **1.** The instance or fact of being victorious; success. **2.** Exultation or merriment derived from victory. **3.** A public celebration in ancient Rome to welcome a returning victorious commander and his army. **4.** *Obs.* A public celebration or spectacular pageant. [Lat. *triumphare* < *triumphus,* triumph.] **—tri'umph·er** *n.*

tri·um·phal (trī-ŭm'fəl) *adj.* **1.** Pertaining to or having the nature of a triumph. **2.** Celebrating or commemorating a victory or triumph.

tri·um·phant (trī-ŭm'fənt) *adj.* **1.** Exulting in success or victory. **2.** Victorious; conquering. **3.** *Archaic.* Triumphal. **4.** *Obs.* Magnificent; splendid. **—tri·um'phant·ly** *adv.*

tri·um·vir (trī-ŭm'vər) *n., pl.* **-virs** or **-vi·ri** (-və-rī'). One of three men sharing public administration or civil authority, as in ancient Rome. [Lat., back-formation < *triumviri,* board of three : *tres,* three + *vir,* man.] **—tri·um'vi·ral** *adj.*

tri·um·vi·rate (trī-ŭm'vər-ĭt) *n.* **1.** Government by triumvirs. **2.** The office or term of a triumvir. **3.** A body or group of triumvirs. **4.** An association or group of three. [Lat. *triumviratus* < *triumviri,* board of three. —see TRIUMVIR.]

tri·une (trī'yo͞on') *adj.* Being three in one. Used esp. of the Trinity. *—n.* A trinity. [TRI- + Lat. *unus,* one.]

tri·u·ni·ty (trī-yo͞o'nĭ-tē) *n., pl.* **-ties.** A trinity (sense 1).

tri·va·lent (trī-vā'lənt) also **ter·va·lent** (tər-vā'lənt, tûr'vā'-lənt) *adj.* Having valence 3. **—tri·va'lence, tri·va'len·cy** *n.*

tri·valve (trī'vălv') *adj.* Having three valves.

triv·et (trĭv'ĭt) *n.* **1.** A three-legged stand. **2.** A metal stand with short feet, used under a hot dish on a table. [ME *trevet,* prob. < OE **trefet* < Lat. *tripes,* three-footed : *tri-,* tri- + *pes,* foot.]

triv·i·a[1] (trĭv'ē-ə) *pl.n. (used with a sing. or pl. verb).* Insignificant or inessential matters; trifles. [NLat., back-formation < Lat. *trivialis,* trivial.]

triv·i·a[2] (trĭv'ē-ə) *n.* Plural of **trivium.**

triv·i·al (trĭv'ē-əl) *adj.* **1.** Of little importance or significance. **2.** Ordinary; commonplace. **3.** Concerned with or involving trivia. [Lat. *trivialis,* ordinary < *trivium,* public square. —see TRIVIUM.] **—triv'i·al·ly** *adv.*

Synonyms: *trivial, trifling, paltry, petty, picayune.* These adjectives all apply to what is small or unimportant, but they are not always interchangeable. *Trivial* refers principally to things that have little importance or significance in themselves or that require no intellectual depth on the part of persons concerned with them. *Trifling* describes things so unimportant or so small in size or value as to be scarcely worth notice. *Paltry* describes things, especially sums of money, whose size or value arouses contempt; thus the term implies marked insufficiency in relation to what is required or desired. *Petty* can refer to insignificant things or to persons who have subordinate rank or who are small-minded or mean. *Picayune* describes things of little significance or value, in the sense of paltriness; or it can apply figuratively to persons totally lacking in stature, capacity, breadth of outlook, or fineness of temperament.

triv·i·al·i·ty (trĭv'ē-ăl'ĭ-tē) *n., pl.* **-ties. 1.** The condition or quality of being trivial. **2.** Something that is trivial.

triv·i·al·ize (trĭv'ē-ə-līz') *tr.v.* **-ized, -iz·ing, -iz·es.** To reduce to triviality. **—triv'i·al·i·za'tion** *n.*

trivial name *n.* **1.** In taxonomic nomenclature, the term following the genus name and designating the species, as *troglodytes* in *Pan troglodytes,* the chimpanzee. **2.** A common or vernacular name as distinguished from a taxonomic designation.

triv·i·um (trĭv'ē-əm) *n., pl.* **-i·a** (-ē-ə). The lower division of the seven liberal arts in medieval schools, consisting of grammar, logic, and rhetoric. [Med. Lat. < Lat., public square : *tri-,* tri- + *via,* road.]

tri·week·ly (trī-wēk'lē) *adj.* **1.** Happening, done, or appearing three times a week. **2.** Happening, done, or appearing every three weeks. *—adv.* **1.** Three times a week. **2.** Every three weeks. *—n., pl.* **-lies.** A periodical published triweekly.

-trix *suff.* **1.** A female that is connected with a specified thing: *aviatrix.* **2.** A geometric point, line, or surface: *directrix.* [ME < Lat., fem. of *-tor,* n. suffix.]

tRNA (tē'är-ĕn'ā') *n.* Transfer RNA.

tro·car (trō'kär') *n.* A sharp-pointed surgical instrument, used with a cannula to puncture a body cavity for fluid aspiration. [Fr. *trocart* : *trois,* three + *carre,* side of an instrument.]

tro·cha·ic (trō-kā'ĭk) *adj.* Of, pertaining to, or consisting of trochees. [Fr. *trochaïque* or < Lat. *trochaicus* < Gk. *trokhaikos* < *trokhaios,* trochee.] **—tro·cha'ic** *n.*

tro·chal (trō'kəl) *adj.* Shaped like a wheel. [< Gk. *trokhos,* wheel.]

tro·chan·ter (trō-kăn'tər) *n.* **1.** Any of several bony processes on the upper part of the femur of many vertebrates. **2.** The second proximal segment of the leg of an insect. [Gk. *trokhantēr* < *trekhein,* to run.] **—tro·chan'ter·al, tro·chan'ter·ic** *adj.*

tro·che (trō'kē) *n.* A small, circular medicinal lozenge; pastille. [ME *trocis* < LLat. *trochiscus* < Gk. *trokhiskos,* dim. of *trokhos,* wheel < *trekhein,* to run.]

tro·chee (trō'kē) *n.* A metrical foot in prosody consisting of one long or stressed syllable followed by one short or unstressed syllable. [Fr. *trochée* < Lat. *trochaeus* < Gk. *trokhaios* < *trokhos,* a running < *trekhein,* to run.]

troch·le·a (trŏk'lē-ə) *n., pl.* **-le·ae** (-lē-ē'). An anatomical structure that resembles a pulley, esp. the part of the distal end of the humerus that articulates with the ulna. [Lat., system of pulleys < Gk. *trokhalia.*]

troch·le·ar (trŏk'lē-ər) *adj.* **1.** Of, resembling, or situated near a trochlea. **2.** Of or pertaining to the trochlear, or fourth, cranial nerve. **3.** *Bot.* Shaped like a pulley.

tro·choid (trō'koid', trŏk'oid') also **tro·choi·dal** (trō-koid'l, trŏk-oid'l) *adj.* Capable of or exhibiting rotation about a central axis. *—n.* The plane locus of a point on the radius or on an extension of the radius of a circle, as the circle rolls along a fixed straight line. [Gk. *trokhoeidēs,* wheellike : *trokhos,* wheel + *-eidēs,* -oid.] **—tro·choi'dal·ly** *adv.*

troch·o·phore (trŏk'ə-fôr', -fōr') *n.* The small aquatic larva of various invertebrates, including certain mollusks and annelids. [Gk. *trokhos,* wheel (< *trekhein,* to run) + -PHORE.]

trod (trŏd) *v.* Past tense and a past participle of **tread.**

trod·den (trŏd'n) *v.* A past participle of **tread.**

trof·fer (trŏf'ər, trô'fər) *n.* An inverted trough suspended from a ceiling as a fixture for fluorescent lighting tubes. [Alteration of TROUGH.]

trog·lo·dyte (trŏg'lə-dīt') *n.* **1.** A prehistoric cave dweller. **2.** A person considered to be like a cave man, as in reclusiveness or brutishness. [< Lat. *Troglodytae,* cave dwellers < Gk. *Troglodutai* : *troglos,* cave + *duein,* to enter.] **—trog'lo·dyt'ic** (-dĭt'ĭk), **trog'lo·dyt'i·cal** *adj.*

tro·gon (trō'gŏn') *n.* Any of various colorful tropical birds of the family Trogonidae, which includes the quetzal. [NLat. *Trogonidae,* family name < Gk. *trōgōn,* pr.part. of *trogein,* to gnaw.]

troi·ka (troi'kə) *n.* **1.** A Russian carriage drawn by a team of three horses abreast. **2.** A triumvirate. [R. *troyka* < *troje,* three.]

Troi·lus (troi'ləs, trō'ə-ləs) *n.* A son of Priam of Troy, depicted as Cressida's lover in medieval romance.

Tro·jan (trō'jən) *n.* **1.** A native or inhabitant of ancient Troy. **2.** A person of courageous determination or energy. [ME *Troyan* < Lat. *Troianus* < *Troia,* Troy < Gk. *Trōias,* the plain of Troy < *Trōs,* the mythical founder of Troy.] **—Tro'jan** *adj.*

Trojan horse *n.* **1.** The hollow wooden horse in which, according to legend, Greeks hid and gained entrance to Troy, later opening the gates to their army. **2.** A subversive group or device placed within enemy ranks.

Trojan War *n.* The prehistoric ten-year war waged against Troy by the confederated Greeks, caused by the abduction of the Spartan queen, Helen, by Paris, a Trojan prince, and resulting in the burning and destruction of Troy.

troll[1] (trōl) *v.* **trolled, troll·ing, trolls.** *—tr.* **1.** To fish for by trailing a baited line from behind a slowly moving boat. **2.** To trail (a baited line) in fishing. **3.** To sing in succession the parts of (a round, for example). **4.** To sing heartily: *troll a carol.* **5.** To roll or revolve. *—intr.* **1.** To fish by trailing a line, as from a moving boat. **2.** To sing heartily or gaily. **3.** To roll or spin around. **4.** To wander about; ramble. *—n.* **1.** A vocal composition in successive parts; round. **2.** The act of trolling for fish. **3.** A lure that is used for trolling, as a spoon or spinner. [ME *trollen,* to wander about.] **—troll'er** *n.*

troll[2] (trōl) *n.* A supernatural creature of Scandinavian folklore variously portrayed as a friendly or mischievous dwarf or as a giant, that lives in caves, in the hills, or under bridges. [Norw. < ON.]

trol·ley also **trol·ly** (trŏl'ē) *—n., pl.* **-leys** also **-lies. 1.** A streetcar. **2.** A wheeled carriage, cage, or basket that is suspended from and travels on an overhead track. **3.** A device that collects electric current from an underground conductor, an overhead wire, or a third rail, and transmits it to the motor of an electric vehicle. **4.** A small truck or car operating on a track and used in a mine, quarry, or factory for conveying materials. **5.** *Chiefly Brit.* A cart. *—v.* **-leyed, -ley·ing, -leys** also **-lied, -ly·ing, -lies.** *—tr.* To convey by trolley. *—intr.* To travel by trolley. [Prob. < TROLL[1].]

trolley bus *n.* An electric bus that does not run on tracks and is powered by electricity from an overhead wire.

trolley car *n.* A streetcar.

trol·lop (trŏl'əp) *n.* **1.** A slovenly, untidy woman; slattern. **2.** A loose woman; strumpet. [Perh. < TROLL[1].]

trom·bic·u·li·a·sis (trŏm-bĭk'yə-lī'ə-sĭs) also **trom·bic·u·lo·sis** (-lō'sĭs) or **trom·bi·di·a·sis** (trŏm'bĭ-dī'ə-sĭs) *n.* Infestation with chiggers. [NLat. *Trombicula,* genus of mites + -IASIS.]

trom·bone (trŏm-bōn', trəm-, trŏm'bōn') *n.* A brass musical instrument consisting of a long cylindrical tube bent upon itself twice and ending in a bell-shaped mouth. [Ital., aug. of *tromba,* trumpet, of Germanic orig.] **—trom·bon'ist** *n.*

trom·mel (trŏm'əl) *n.* A revolving cylindrical sieve used for

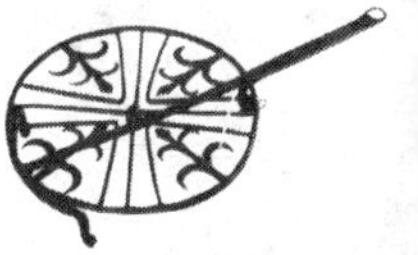

trivet

Trojan horse

trolley

trombone

screening or sizing rock and ore. [G., drum < MHG *trummel* < *trumme*.]

tromp (trŏmp) *v.* **tromped, tromp·ing, tromps.** *Informal.* —*intr.* To walk heavily and noisily; tramp. —*tr.* **1.** To trample underfoot. **2.** To defeat soundly; trounce. [Alteration of TRAMP.]

trompe (trŏmp) *n.* An apparatus in which water falling through a perforated pipe entrains air into and down the pipe to produce an air blast for a furnace or forge. [Fr.]

trompe l'oeil (trômp'loi') *n.* **1.** A style of painting that gives an illusion of photographic reality. **2.** A trompe l'oeil painting or effect. [Fr. : *tromper,* to deceive + *le,* the + *oeil,* eye.]

-tron *suff.* **1.** Vacuum tube: *dynatron.* **2.** Device for manipulating subatomic particles: *betatron.* [Gk., n. suffix.]

tro·na (trō'nə) *n.* A natural vitreous gray or white mineral, $Na_2CO_3{\cdot}NaHCO_3{\cdot}2H_2O$, used as a source of sodium compounds. [Swed.]

troop (tro͞op) *n.* **1.** A group or company of people, animals, or things. **2.** A group of soldiers. **3. troops.** Military units; soldiers. **4.** A unit of at least five Boy Scouts or Girl Scouts under the guidance of an adult leader. **5.** A great many; a lot. —*intr.v.* **trooped, troop·ing, troops. 1.** To move or go as a throng. **2.** To assemble or move in crowds. **3.** To consort; associate. [OFr. *trope,* prob. of Germanic orig.]

troop·er (tro͞o'pər) *n.* **1. a.** A cavalryman. **b.** A cavalry horse. **2.** A mounted police officer. **3.** A state police officer.

troop·ship (tro͞op'shĭp') *n.* A transport ship designed for carrying troops.

troost·ite (tro͞o'stīt') *n.* A reddish crystalline mineral, a variety of willemite, in which the zinc is partly replaced by manganese. [After Gerald *Troost* (1776–1850).]

trop- *pref.* Variant of **tropo-.**

trope (trōp) *n.* **1.** The figurative use of a word or expression; figure of speech. **2.** A word or phrase interpolated as an embellishment in the sung parts of certain medieval liturgies. [Lat. *tropus* < Gk. *tropos,* manner.] **—trop·i·cal** *adj.*

troph- *pref.* Variant of **tropho-.**

troph·al·lax·is (trŏf'ə-lăk'sĭs, trō'fə-) *n.* The exchange of food substances between organisms, esp. among social insects. [TROPH(O)- + Gk. *allaxis,* exchange < *allassein,* to exchange < *allos,* other.]

-trophic *suff.* Of, pertaining to, or characterized by a specified kind of nutrition: *polytrophic.* [< -TROPHY.]

trophic level *n. Ecol.* A feeding stratum in a food chain of an ecosystem characterized by organisms that occupy a similar functional position in the ecosystem.

tropho- or **troph-** *pref.* Nutrition; nutritive: *trophoblast.* [< Gk. *trophē,* food < *trephein,* to nourish.]

tro·pho·blast (trō'fə-blăst') *n.* The outermost layer of cells of the morula that attaches the fertilized ovum to the uterine wall and acts as a nutritive pathway. **—tro'pho·blas'tic** *adj.*

tro·pho·derm (trō'fə-dûrm') *n.* Trophoblast.

tro·pho·zo·ite (trō'fə-zō'īt') *n.* A protozoan of the class Sporozoa in the active stage.

tro·phy (trō'fē) *n., pl.* **-phies. 1.** Something won or received as a symbol of victory or achievement, often mounted or preserved as a memento. **2.** A monument customarily erected in classical antiquity to commemorate an enemy's defeat. **3.** *Archit.* An ornament depicting a group of weapons or armor. [OFr. < Lat. *trophaeum,* monument to victory < Gk. *tropaion* < *tropē,* a putting to flight.]

trophy
Tennis trophy

-trophy *suff.* Nutrition; growth: *hypertrophy.* [NLat. *-trophia* < Gk. < *trophē,* food.]

trop·ic (trŏp'ĭk) *n.* **1.** *Astron.* Either of two circles on the celestial sphere parallel to and at an angular distance of 23 degrees 27 minutes from the equator that are the limits of the apparent northern and southern passages of the sun. **2. a.** Either of the two corresponding parallels of latitude on the earth that constitute the boundaries of the Torrid Zone. **b. Tropics.** The region of the earth's surface lying between these latitudes. —*adj.* Of or relating to the Tropics; tropical. [ME *tropik,* solstice < LLat. *tropicus* < Gk. *tropikos* < *tropē,* turn.]

-tropic *suff.* **1.** Turning in response to a specified stimulus: *heliotropic.* **2.** Acting upon something specified: *gonadotropic.* [< Gk. *tropos,* turn.]

trop·i·cal (trŏp'ĭ-kəl) *adj.* **1.** Of, occurring in, or characteristic of the Tropics. **2.** Hot and humid; torrid. **—trop'i·cal·ly** *adv.*

tropical cyclone *n.* A very low pressure area 80 to 160 kilometers or 50 to 100 miles in radius that originates in tropical regions and is frequently marked by winds of hurricane strength circulating around a calm eye in the center.

tropical fish *n.* Any of various small or brightly colored fishes native to tropical waters and often kept in home aquariums.

tropical storm *n.* A tropical cyclone having winds ranging from approximately 48 to 121 kilometers or 30 to 75 miles per hour.

tropical year *n.* The time interval between two successive passages of the sun through the vernal equinox; the calendar year, or 365.2422 mean solar days.

trop·ic·bird (trŏp'ĭk-bûrd') *n.* Any of several predominantly white sea birds of the genus *Phaethon,* of warm regions, having a pair of long, slender, projecting tail feathers.

tropic of Cancer *n.* The parallel of latitude 23 degrees 27 minutes north of the equator, the northern boundary of the Torrid Zone, and the most northerly latitude at which the sun reaches an altitude of 90 degrees.

tropic of Capricorn *n.* The parallel of latitude 23 degrees 27 minutes south of the equator, the southern boundary of the Torrid Zone, and the most southerly latitude at which the sun reaches an altitude of 90 degrees.

tro·pine (trō'pēn', -pĭn) also **tro·pin** (-pĭn) *n.* A white, crystalline, poisonous alkaloid, $C_8H_{15}NO$, having a tobacco odor and used as a medicine. [< ATROPINE.]

tro·pism (trō'pĭz'əm) *n.* The responsive growth of movement of an organism toward or away from an external stimulus. [< -TROPISM.] **—tro'pic** *adj.*

-tropism *suff.* Tropism: *phototropism.* [< Gk. *tropos,* turn.]

tropo- or **trop-** *pref.* **1.** Turning; change: *troposphere.* **2.** Tropism: *tropotaxis.* [< Gk. *tropos,* turn.]

tro·pol·o·gy (trō-pŏl'ə-jē) *n., pl.* **-gies.** A mode of biblical interpretation insisting on the morally edifying sense of tropes in Scripture. [LLat. *tropologia* < LGk. : Gk. *tropos,* trope + Gk. *-logia,* -logy.] **—tro'po·log'ic** (trō'pə-lŏj'ĭk, trŏp'ə-), **tro'po·log'i·cal** *adj.* **—tro'po·log'i·cal·ly** *adv.*

tro·po·pause (trō'pə-pôz', trŏp'ə-) *n.* The boundary between the upper troposphere and the lower stratosphere that varies in altitude from approximately 8 kilometers or 5 miles at the poles to approximately 18 kilometers or 11 miles at the equator.

tro·po·phyte (trō'pə-fīt', trŏp'ə-) *n.* A plant adapted to climatic conditions in which periods of heavy rainfall alternate with periods of drought. **—tro'po·phyt'ic** (-fĭt'ĭk) *adj.*

tro·po·sphere (trō'pə-sfîr', trŏp'ə-) *n.* The lowest region of the atmosphere between the earth's surface and the tropopause, characterized by decreasing temperature with increasing altitude. **—tro'po·spher'ic** *adj.*

-tropous *suff.* Turning in a specified way or from a specified stimulus: *amphitropous.* [Gk. *-tropos,* of turning < *trepein,* to turn.]

-tropy *suff.* The state of turning in a specified way or from a specified stimulus: *thixotropy.* [Gk. *-tropia* < *-tropos,* -tropous.]

trot (trŏt) *n.* **1.** A gait of a four-footed animal, between a walk and a run in speed, in which diagonal pairs of legs move forward together. **2.** A gait of a person, faster than a walk; jog. **3.** A race for trotters. **4.** *Informal.* A literal translation, made of a foreign text. **5.** A toddler. **6.** An old woman; crone. —*v.* **trot·ted, trot·ting, trots.** —*intr.* **1.** To go or move at a trot. **2.** To proceed rapidly; hurry. —*tr.* To cause to move at a trot. ***—phrasal verb.* trot out.** *Informal.* To bring out and show for inspection or admiration. [ME < OFr. < *troter,* to trot, of Germanic orig.]

troth (trôth, trŏth, trōth) *n.* **1.** Good faith; fidelity. **2. a.** One's pledged fidelity. **b.** Betrothal. —*tr.v.* **trothed, troth·ing, troths.** To pledge or betroth. [ME *trothe* < OE *trēowð,* truth.]

troth·plight (trôth'plīt', trŏth'-, trōth'-) *Archaic.* —*n.* A betrothal. —*tr.v.* **-plight·ed, -plight·ing, -plights.** To betroth.

trot·line (trŏt'līn') *n.* A setline. [Perh. < TROT.]

Trots·ky·ism (trŏt'skē-ĭz'əm) *n.* The theories of Communism advocated by Leon Trotsky and his followers, who argued for worldwide revolution and bitterly opposed the leadership of Stalin. **—Trots'ky·ist, Trots'ky·ite'** *n.*

trot·ter (trŏt'ər) *n.* **1.** A horse that trots, esp. one trained for harness racing. **2.** *Informal.* A foot, esp. the foot of a pig or sheep prepared as food.

trou·ba·dour (tro͞o'bə-dôr', -dōr', -do͝or') *n.* **1.** One of a class of 12th- and 13th-century lyric poets attached to the courts of Provence and northern Italy, who composed songs in complex metrical forms. **2.** A strolling minstrel. [Fr. < OProv. *trobador* < *trobar,* to compose, perh. < VLat. **tropare* < Lat. *tropus,* trope.]

trou·ble (trŭb'əl) *n.* **1.** A state of distress, affliction, danger, or need: *in trouble with the police.* **2.** A cause or source of distress, disturbance, or difficulty: *One trouble after another delayed the job.* **3.** Exertion; effort; pains. **4.** A condition of pain, disease, or malfunction: *heart trouble.* —*v.* **-led, -ling, -les.** —*tr.* **1.** To agitate; stir up. **2.** To afflict with pain or discomfort. **3.** To cause distress or confusion in; perturb. **4.** To inconvenience; bother: *May I trouble you to close the window.* —*intr.* To take pains: *They trouble over every detail.* [ME < OFr. < *troubler,* to trouble < Lat. *turbidare* < *turbidus,* confused < *turba,* turmoil.] **—trou'bler** *n.* **—trou'bling·ly** *adv.*

trou·ble·mak·er (trŭb'əl-mā'kər) *n.* One that stirs up trouble or strife.

trou·ble-shoot·er (trŭb'əl-sho͞o'tər) *n.* **1.** A worker whose job is to locate and eliminate sources of trouble, as in mechanical operations. **2.** A mediator skilled in settling disputes esp. of a diplomatic or political nature. **—trou'ble-shoot'** *v.* **(-shot, -shoot·ing, -shoots).**

trou·ble·some (trŭb'əl-səm) *adj.* **1.** Causing trouble or anxiety; worrisome. **2.** Difficult; trying. **—trou'ble·some·ly** *adv.* **—trou'ble·some·ness** *n.*

trou·blous (trŭb'ləs) *adj.* **1. a.** Full of trouble. **b.** Uneasy; troubled. **2.** Causing trouble; troublesome.

trou-de-loup (tro͞o'də-lo͞o') *n., pl.* **trous-de-loup** (tro͞o'də-lo͞o'). Any of a series of conical pits having pointed stakes set upright in their centers, once used as an obstacle to enemy cavalry. [Fr. : *trou,* hole + *de,* of + *loup,* wolf.]

trough (trôf, trŏf) *n.* **1.** A long, narrow, generally shallow receptacle, esp. one for holding water or feed for animals. **2.** A gutter under the eaves of a roof. **3.** A long, narrow depression, as between waves or ridges. **4.** A low point in a business cycle or on a statistical graph. **5.** *Meteorol.* An elongated region of low atmospheric pressure, often associated with a front. [ME < OE *trog.*]

trounce (trouns) *tr.v.* **trounced, trounc·ing, trounc·es. 1.** To thrash; beat. **2.** To defeat decisively. [Orig. unknown.]

troupe (tro͞op) *n.* A company or group, esp. of theatrical or dramatic performers. —*intr.v.* **trouped, troup·ing, troupes.** To tour with a theatrical company. [Fr., troop.]

troup·er (tro͞o'pər) *n.* **1.** A member of a theatrical company. **2.** A veteran actor or performer.

trou·pi·al (tro͞o'pē-əl) *n.* Any of several tropical American birds of the genus *Icterus,* related to the orioles and New World blackbirds, esp. *I. icterus,* having orange and black plumage. [Fr. *troupiale* < *troupe,* flock. —see TROOP.]

trou·ser (trou'zər) *adj.* Of, for, or on trousers: *trouser cuffs.* [Back-formation < TROUSERS.]

trou·sers also **trow·sers** (trou'zərz) *pl.n.* An outer garment for covering the body from the waist to the ankles, divided into sections to fit each leg separately, worn esp. by men and boys. [< obs. *trouse* < Sc. Gael. *triubhas.*]

trous·seau (tro͞o'sō, tro͞o-sō') *n., pl.* **-seaux** (-sōz, -sōz') or **-seaus.** The possessions, such as clothing and linens, that a bride assembles for her marriage. [Fr. < OFr., dim. of *trousse,* bundle. —see TRUSS.]

trout (trout) *n., pl.* **trout** or **trouts. 1. a.** Any of various freshwater or anadromous food and game fishes of the genera *Salvelinus* and *Salmo,* usually having a speckled body. **b.** Any of various similar fishes. **2.** *Chiefly Brit.* A silly old woman. [ME *troute* < OE *trūht* < LLat. *tructa* < Gk. *trōktēs,* a kind of seafish with sharp teeth < *trōgein,* to gnaw.]

trout lily *n.* The dogtooth violet. [From its spotted leaves.]

trou·vère (tro͞o-vâr') also **trou·veur** (-vûr') *n.* Any of a school of poets flourishing in northern France in the 12th and 13th centuries, who composed chiefly narrative works, such as the chansons de geste. [Fr. < OFr. *trovere* < *trover,* to compose, perh. < VLat. **tropare* < Lat. *tropus,* trope.]

trove (trōv) *n.* Something of value discovered or found; find. [(TREASURE-)TROVE.]

tro·ver (trō'vər) *n. Law.* A common-law action to recover damages for property illegally withheld or wrongfully converted to use by another. [< OFr., to find. —see TROUVÈRE.]

trow (trō) *intr.v.* **trowed, trow·ing, trows.** *Archaic.* To think; suppose. [ME *trowen* < OE *trēowian.*]

trow·el (trou'əl) *n.* **1.** A flat-bladed hand tool for leveling, spreading, or shaping substances such as cement or mortar. **2.** A small implement with a pointed, scoop-shaped blade used for digging, as in setting plants. —*tr.v.* **-eled, -el·ing, -els** or **-elled, -el·ling, -els.** To spread, smooth, form, or scoop with a trowel. [ME *trowell* < OFr. *truelle* < LLat. *truella* < Lat. *trulla,* dim. of *trua,* ladle.] —**trow'el·er** *n.*

trow·sers (trou'zərz) *n.* Variant of **trousers.**

troy (troi) *adj.* Of or expressed in troy weight. [ME, after *Troyes,* France.]

troy weight *n.* A system of units of weight in which the grain is the same as in the avoirdupois system and the pound contains 12 ounces, 240 pennyweights, or 5,760 grains.

tru·an·cy (tro͞o'ən-sē) also **tru·ant·ry** (-ən-trē) *n., pl.* **-cies** also **-ries. 1.** An act of being truant. **2.** The condition of being truant.

tru·ant (tro͞o'ənt) *n.* **1.** A person who is absent without permission, esp. from school. **2.** A person who shirks his work or duty. —*adj.* **1.** Absent without permission, esp. from school. **2.** Idle, lazy, or neglectful. —*intr.v.* **-ant·ed, -ant·ing, -ants.** To be truant. [ME, beggar < OFr., of Celt. orig.]

truant officer *n.* An official who investigates unauthorized absences from school.

truce (tro͞os) *n.* **1.** A temporary cessation or suspension of hostilities by agreement of the opposing sides; armistice. **2.** A respite from a disagreeable state of affairs. [ME *trewes,* pl. of *trewe,* truce < OE *trēow,* pledge.] —**truce** *v.* **(truced, truc·ing, truc·es).**

truck¹ (trŭk) *n.* **1.** Any of various heavy automotive vehicles designed for transporting loads. **2.** A two-wheeled barrow for moving heavy objects by hand. **3.** A wheeled platform, sometimes equipped with a motor, for conveying loads in a warehouse or freight yard. **4.** *Chiefly Brit.* A railroad freight car without a top. **5.** One of the swiveling frames of wheels under each end of a railroad car, trolley car, or the like. —*v.* **trucked, truck·ing, trucks.** —*tr.* To transport by truck. —*intr.* **1.** To carry goods by truck. **2.** To drive a truck. [Prob. short for TRUCKLE.]

truck² (trŭk) *v.* **trucked, truck·ing, trucks.** —*tr.* **1.** To exchange; barter. **2.** To peddle. —*intr.* To have dealings or commerce; traffic. —*n.* **1.** Trade goods; articles of commerce. **2.** Garden produce raised for the market. **3.** *Informal.* Worthless articles; rubbish. **4.** Barter; exchange. **5.** *Informal.* Dealings; business. [ME *trukken* < OFr. *troquer.*]

truck·age (trŭk'ĭj) *n.* **1.** Transportation of goods by truck. **2.** A charge for transportation by truck.

truck·er (trŭk'ər) *n.* **1.** A truck driver. **2.** A person or company engaged in trucking goods.

truck farm *n.* A farm producing vegetables for the market. —**truck farmer** *n.* —**truck farming** *n.*

truck·le (trŭk'əl) *n.* **1.** A small wheel or roller; caster. **2.** A trundle bed. —*intr.v.* **-led, -ling, -les.** To be servile or submissive. [ME *trocle,* pulley < AN < Lat. *trochlea,* system of pulleys. —see TROCHLEA.] —**truck'ler** *n.*

truck·load (trŭk'lōd') *n.* The quantity or weight that a truck carries.

truck·man (trŭk'mən) *n.* **1.** A truck driver. **2.** A member of the crew of a hook-and-ladder fire truck.

truck system *n.* The practice of paying wages in goods instead of money.

truc·u·lence (trŭk'yə-ləns) also **truc·u·len·cy** (-lən-sē) *n.* **1.** Savagery. **2.** Pugnacity; belligerence.

truc·u·lent (trŭk'yə-lənt) *adj.* **1.** Savage and cruel; fierce. **2.** Vitriolic; scathing. **3.** Disposed to fight; pugnacious. [Lat. *truculentus* < *trux,* fierce.] —**truc'u·lent·ly** *adv.*

trudge (trŭj) *intr.v.* **trudged, trudg·ing, trudg·es.** To walk in a laborious, heavy-footed way; plod. —*n.* A long, tedious walk. [Orig. unknown.] —**trudg'er** *n.*

trudg·en also **trudg·eon** (trŭj'ən) *n.* A swimming stroke in which a double overarm movement is combined with a scissors kick. [After John *Trudgen* (1852–1902).]

true (tro͞o) *adj.* **tru·er, tru·est. 1.** Consistent with fact or reality; not false or erroneous. **2.** Exactly conforming to a rule, standard, or pattern. **3.** Reliable; accurate: *a true prophecy.* **4.** Real; genuine. **5.** Faithful, as to a friend, vow, or cause; loyal. **6.** *Archaic.* Honorable; upright. **7.** Sincerely felt or expressed; unfeigned. **8.** Fundamental; essential: *his true motive.* **9.** Rightful; legitimate: *the true heir.* **10.** Accurately shaped or fitted. **11.** Accurately placed, delivered, or thrown. **12.** Quick and exact in sensing and responding. **13.** Determined with reference to the earth's axis, not the magnetic poles: *true north.* **14.** Conforming to the definitive criteria of a natural group: *The horseshoe crab is not a true crab.* —*adv.* **1.** Rightly; truthfully. **2.** Unswervingly; exactly: *He aimed true.* **3.** So as to conform to a type, standard, or pattern. —*tr.v.* **trued, tru·ing** or **true·ing, trues.** To adjust or fit so as to conform with a standard. —*n.* **1.** Truth. **2.** Proper alignment or adjustment: *out of true.* [ME < OE *trēowe,* loyal.] —**true'ness** *n.*

true bill *n. Law.* A bill of indictment endorsed by a grand jury.

true-blue also **true blue** (tro͞o'blo͞o') *n.* A person of unswerving loyalty. [From an association of blue with constancy.] —**true'-blue'** *adj.*

true·born (tro͞o'bôrn') *adj.* Being authentically or genuinely such by birth.

true-false test (tro͞o'fôls') *n.* A test in which statements are to be marked either true or false.

true-life (tro͞o'līf') *adj.* True to life: *a true-life romance.*

true·love (tro͞o'lŭv') *n.* One's beloved; sweetheart.

true lovers' knot *n.* A stylized knot, generally a form of bowknot, used as an emblem of love.

true·pen·ny (tro͞o'pĕn'ē) *n., pl.* **-nies.** An honest or trustworthy person. [From an association with a genuine coin.]

true rhyme *n.* Perfect rhyme.

true rib *n.* Any of the ribs, esp. in man any of the upper seven, that are attached to the sternum by a costal cartilage.

truf·fle (trŭf'əl) *n.* Any of various edible, fleshy, subterranean fungi, chiefly of the genus *Tuber.* [OFr. *truffe* < OProv. *trufa* < VLat. **tufera* < Lat. *tuber.*]

tru·ism (tro͞o'ĭz'əm) *n.* A self-evident or obvious truth. —**tru·is'tic** (tro͞o-ĭs'tĭk) *adj.*

trull (trŭl) *n.* A prostitute; harlot. [Perh. < G. *Trulle.*]

tru·ly (tro͞o'lē) *adv.* **1.** Sincerely; genuinely. **2.** Truthfully; accurately. **3.** Indeed: *truly ugly.* **4.** Properly.

trump¹ (trŭmp) *n.* **1. a.** Often **trumps.** A suit in card games which outranks all other suits for the duration of a hand. **b.** A card of such a suit. **2.** A key resource to be used at the opportune moment. **3.** *Informal.* A reliable or admirable person. —*v.* **trumped, trump·ing, trumps.** —*tr.* To take (a card or trick) with a trump. —*intr.* To play a trump card. —***phrasal verb.* trump up.** To devise fraudulently. [Alteration of TRIUMPH.]

trump² (trŭmp) *n.* A trumpet. [ME *trompe* < OFr.]

trump·er·y (trŭm'pə-rē) *n., pl.* **-ies. 1.** Showy but worthless finery; bric-a-brac. **2.** Nonsense; rubbish. **3.** Deception; trickery; fraud. [ME *trompery,* deceit < OFr. *tromperie* < *tromper,* to deceive.]

trum·pet (trŭm'pĭt) *n.* **1.** A soprano brass wind instrument consisting of a long metal tube looped once and ending in a flared bell, the modern type being equipped with three valves for producing variations in pitch. **2.** Something shaped like or sounding like a trumpet. **3.** An organ stop that produces a tone like that of the trumpet. **4.** A resounding call, as that of the elephant. —*v.* **-pet·ed, -pet·ing, -pets.** —*intr.* **1.** To play a trumpet. **2.** To give forth a resounding call. —*tr.* To sound or proclaim loudly. [ME *trumpette* < OFr. *trompette,* dim. of *tromp,* trumpet.]

trumpet creeper *n.* A woody vine, *Campsis radicans,* of the eastern United States, having compound leaves and trumpet-shaped reddish-orange flowers.

trum·pet·er (trŭm'pĭt-ər) *n.* **1.** A trumpet player. **2.** A per-

trough

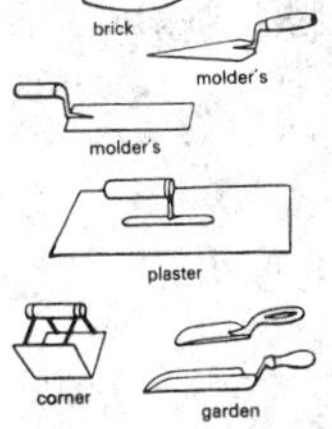

trowel
Above: Stonemason using a trowel
Below: Different types of trowels

trumpet

son who announces something, as on a trumpet; herald. **3.** Any of several large birds of the genus *Psophia,* of tropical South America, having a loud, resonant call. **4.** The trumpeter swan.

trumpeter swan *n.* A large white swan, *Olor buccinator,* of western North America, having a loud, buglelike call.

trumpet honeysuckle *n.* A vine, *Lonicera sempervirens,* of the eastern United States, having tubular reddish flowers.

trumpet vine *n.* Trumpet creeper.

trun·cate (trŭng'kāt') *tr.v.* **-cat·ed, -cat·ing, -cates. 1.** To shorten by or as if by cutting off. **2.** To replace (the edge of a crystal) with a plane face. *—adj.* **1.** Appearing to terminate abruptly, as a leaf or a coiled gastropod shell that lacks a spire. **2.** Truncated. [Lat. *truncare, truncat-* < *truncus,* trunk.] **—trun'cate'ly** *adv.* **—trun·ca'tion** *n.*

trun·ca·ted (trŭng'kā'tĭd) *adj.* **1.** Having the apex cut off and replaced by a plane, esp. one parallel to the base. Used of a cone or pyramid. **2.** Truncate.

trun·cheon (trŭn'chən) *n.* **1.** A staff carried as a symbol of office or authority; baton. **2.** A short stick carried by policemen; billy. **3.** *Obs.* A heavy club; cudgel. **4.** *Obs.* A thick cutting from a plant, as for grafting. *—tr.v.* **-cheoned, -cheon·ing, -cheons.** *Archaic.* To beat with a club; bludgeon. [ME *tronchon,* club < OFr. < *truncus,* trunk.]

trun·dle (trŭn'dl) *n.* **1.** A small wheel or roller. **2.** The motion or noise of rolling. **3.** A trundle bed. **4.** A low-wheeled cart; dolly. *—v.* **-dled, -dling, -dles.** *—tr.* **1.** To push or propel on wheels or rollers. **2.** To spin; twirl. *—intr.* To move along by or as if by rolling. [Var. of dial. *trendle,* wheel < ME *trendel* < OE, circle.] **—trun'dler** *n.*

trundle bed *n.* A low bed on casters that can be rolled under another bed when not in use.

trunk (trŭngk) *n.* **1.** The main woody axis of a tree. **2. a.** The human body excluding the head and limbs; torso. **b.** An analogous part of an organism, as the thorax of an insect. **3.** A main body, apart from tributaries or appendages. **4.** A trunk line. **5.** A large packing case or box that clasps shut, used as luggage or for storage. **6.** A covered compartment for luggage and storage, generally at the rear of an automobile. **7.** A proboscis, esp. the long, prehensile proboscis of an elephant. **8.** A chute or conduit. **9.** *Naut.* A shaft connecting two or more decks. **10.** The housing for the centerboard of a vessel. **11.** *Naut.* Any of certain structures projecting above part of a main deck, as: **a.** A covering over a ship's hatches. **b.** An expansion chamber on a tanker. **c.** A cabin on a small boat. **12.** *Archit.* The shaft of a column. **13. trunks.** Men's shorts worn for swimming or other athletics. [ME *troncke* < OFr. *tronc* < Lat. *truncus.*]

trunk

trunk·fish (trŭngk'fĭsh') *n., pl.* **trunkfish** or **-fish·es.** Any of various tropical marine fishes of the family Ostraciidae, having boxlike armor enclosing the body.

trunk hose *pl.n.* Short, ballooning breeches, extending from the waist to midthigh, worn by men in the 16th and 17th centuries. [Perh. < obs. *trunk,* to truncate.]

trunk line *n.* **1.** A direct line between two telephone switchboards. **2.** The main line of a communication or transportation system.

trun·nel (trŭn'əl) *n.* Variant of **treenail.**

trun·nion (trŭn'yən) *n.* A pin or gudgeon, esp. either of two small cylindrical projections on a cannon forming an axis on which it pivots. [Fr. *trognon,* stump.]

truss (trŭs) *n.* **1.** *Med.* A supportive device worn to prevent enlargement of a hernia or the return of a reduced hernia. **2.** A rigid framework, as of wooden beams or metal bars, designed to support a structure. **3.** *Archit.* A bracket. **4.** Something gathered into a bundle; pack. **5.** *Naut.* An iron fitting by which a lower yard is secured to a mast. **6.** A compact cluster of flowers at the end of a stalk. *—tr.v.* **trussed, truss·ing, truss·es. 1.** To tie up or bind tightly. **2.** To bind or skewer the wings or legs of (a fowl) before cooking. **3.** To support or brace with a truss. [ME *trusse,* bundle < OFr. *trousse* < *trousser,* to truss.]

truss bridge

truss bridge *n.* A bridge supported by trusses.

truss·ing (trŭs'ĭng) *n.* **1.** The parts forming a truss. **2.** A system of trusses supporting a structure.

trust (trŭst) *n.* **1.** Confidence in the integrity, ability, character, and truth of a person or thing. **2.** One in which confidence is placed. **3.** Custody; care. **4.** Something committed into the care of another; charge. **5.** The condition and resulting obligation of having confidence placed in one: *violated his public trust.* **6.** Reliance on something in the future; hope. **7.** Reliance on the intention and ability of a purchaser to pay in the future; credit. **8.** *Law.* **a.** A legal title to property held by one party for the benefit of another. **b.** The confidence reposed in a trustee in giving him legal title to property to administer for another, and his obligation with respect to the property and the beneficiary. **c.** The property so held. **9.** A combination of firms or corporations for the purpose of reducing competition and controlling prices throughout a business or industry. *—v.* **trust·ed, trust·ing, trusts.** *—intr.* **1.** To rely; depend. **2.** To be confident; hope. **3.** To sell on credit. *—tr.* **1.** To have confidence in; feel sure of. **2.** To expect with assurance; assume: *I trust you will be on time.* **3.** To believe: *I trust what you say.* **4.** To place in the care of another; entrust. **5.** To grant discretion to confidently: *Shall I trust him with the boat?* **6.** To extend credit to. *—**idiom.*** **in trust.** In the possession or care of a trustee. [ME *truste,* perh. < ON *traust,* confidence.] **—trust'er** *n.*

Synonyms: *trust, faith, confidence, reliance, dependence.* These nouns refer to a feeling that a person or thing will not fail in performance. *Trust* implies depth and assurance of such feeling, which may not always be supported by proof. When acceptance of someone or something is unquestioning and emotionally charged, *faith* is the more appropriate term. *Confidence* suggests less intensity of feeling but, frequently, good evidence for being sure. *Reliance* implies a decision to commit oneself to another and to accept the consequences in case of failure; with *dependence* the commitment is not a free choice.

trust·bust·er (trŭst'bŭs'tər) *n. Informal.* One who seeks to prosecute or dissolve business trusts.

trust company *n.* A commercial bank or other corporation that manages trusts.

trus·tee (trŭs-tē') *n.* **1.** A person or agent, such as a bank, holding legal title to property in order to administer it for a beneficiary. **2.** A member of a board elected or appointed to direct the funds and policy of an institution. **3.** A country having the responsibility of supervising a trust territory. *—v.* **-teed, -tee·ing, -tees.** *—tr.* To place (property) in the care of a trustee. *—intr.* To function or serve as a trustee.

trus·tee·ship (trŭs-tē'shĭp') *n.* **1.** The position or function of a trustee. **2. a.** The administration of a territory by a country or countries so commissioned by the United Nations. **b.** A trust territory.

trust·ful (trŭst'fəl) *adj.* Inclined to believe or confide readily; full of trust. **—trust'ful·ly** *adv.* **—trust'ful·ness** *n.*

trust fund *n.* Property, esp. money and securities, held or settled in trust.

trust territory *n.* A colony or territory placed under the administration of a country or countries by commission of the United Nations.

trust·wor·thy (trŭst'wûr'*thē*) *adj.* **-thi·er, -thi·est.** Warranting trust; reliable. **—trust'wor'thi·ly** *adv.* **—trust'wor'thi·ness** *n.*

trust·y (trŭs'tē) *adj.* **-i·er, -i·est.** Dependable; faithful; reliable. *—n., pl.* **-ies. 1.** A trusted person. **2.** A convict held to be worthy of trust and granted special privileges. **—trust'i·ly** *adv.* **—trust'i·ness** *n.*

truth (tro͞oth) *n., pl.* **truths** (tro͞o*thz,* tro͞oths). **1.** Conformity to fact or actuality. **2.** Fidelity to an original or standard. **3.** Reality; actuality. **4.** A statement proven to be or accepted as true. **5.** Sincerity; integrity. **6. Truth.** God. [ME *trewthe,* fidelity < OE *trēowð.*]

Synonyms: *truth, veracity, verity, verisimilitude, candor, frankness.* These nouns name qualities of being in accordance with reality. *Truth* is most commonly used to mean correspondence with facts or with what actually occurred. *Veracity* implies factual accuracy and honesty, principally with respect to spoken or written expression. *Verity* applies principally to an enduring or repeatedly demonstrated truth. *Verisimilitude,* the quality of having the appearance of truth or reality, is often applied to effective artistic representation. *Candor* and *frankness* both refer to forthrightness, openness, and outspokenness.

truth·ful (tro͞oth'fəl) *adj.* **1.** Consistently telling the truth; honest. **2.** Corresponding to reality; true. **—truth'ful·ly** *adv.* **—truth'ful·ness** *n.*

truth serum *n.* Any of various hypnotic drugs that are assumed to cause a subject under questioning to talk without inhibition.

truth-val·ue (tro͞oth'văl'yo͞o) *n. Logic.* The truth or the falsity of a proposition.

try (trī) *v.* **tried, try·ing, tries.** *—tr.* **1.** To taste, sample, or otherwise test in order to determine strength, effect, worth, or desirability. **2. a.** To examine or hear (evidence or a case) by judicial process. **b.** To put (an accused person) on trial. **3.** To subject to great strain or hardship; tax: *The last steep ascent tried his every muscle.* **4.** To melt (lard, for example) to separate out impurities; render. **5.** To make an effort to do or accomplish (something); attempt: *tried to ski.* **6.** To smooth, fit, or align accurately. *—intr.* To make an effort; strive. *—**phrasal verbs.*** **try on. 1.** To don (a garment) to test its fit. **2.** To test or use experimentally. **try out.** To undergo a competitive qualifying test, as for a job. *—n., pl.* **tries.** An attempt; effort. *—**idioms.*** **try conclusions.** To test one's strength or skill against an opponent. **try one's hand.** To attempt to do something for the first time: *tried his hand at skiing.* [ME *trien* < OFr. *trier,* to pick out.]

Usage: *Try and* is common in speech for *try to,* especially in such established combinations as *try and stop me* and *try and get some rest.* In most contexts, however, it is usually not interchangeable with *try to* unless the level is clearly informal. As an example in writing, the following is unacceptable to a large majority of the Usage Panel: *It is a mistake to try and force compliance with a regulation that is so unpopular* (preferably *try to force*).

try·ing (trī'ĭng) *adj.* Causing severe strain, hardship, or distress.

try·ma (trī'mə) *n., pl.* **-ma·ta** (-mə-tə). A nut, such as a pecan or walnut, having an outer husk or rind that separates from the shell of the tryma. [NLat. < Gk. *truma,* hole < *truein,* to wear out.]

try·out (trī'out') *n.* A test to ascertain the qualifications of

ă **pat** / ā **pay** / âr **care** / ä **father** / b **bib** / ch **church** / d **deed** / ĕ **pet** / ē **be** / f **fife** / g **gag** / h **hat** / hw **which** / ĭ **pit** / ī **pie** / îr **pier** / j **judge** / k **kick** / l **lid, needle** / m **mum** / n **no, sudden** / ng **thing** / ŏ **pot** / ō **toe** / ô **paw, for** / oi **noise** / ou **out** / o͝o **took** / o͞o **boot** /

applicants, as for an athletic team or for a theatrical role.
try·pan·o·some (trĭ-păn′ə-sōm′) *n.* Any of various parasitic protozoans of the genus *Trypanosoma,* transmitted to the vertebrate blood stream by certain insects, and often causing diseases such as sleeping sickness. [NLat. *Trypanosoma,* genus name : Gk. *trupanon,* auger + Gk. *sōma,* body.]
try·pan·o·so·mi·a·sis (trĭ-păn′ə-sō-mī′ə-sĭs) *n., pl.* **-ses** (-sēz′). A disease caused by a trypanosome.
try·pars·a·mide (trĭ-pär′sə-mīd′) *n.* A white crystalline powder, $C_8H_{10}AsN_2O_4Na \cdot {}^1/_2H_2O$, used in the treatment of spirochetal and trypanosomic diseases. [TRYP(ARSAMIDE) + ARS(ENIC) + AMIDE.]
tryp·sin (trĭp′sĭn) *n.* One of the proteolytic enzymes of the pancreatic juice, important in the digestive processes. [Perh. Gk. *tripsis,* a rubbing (from its having been first obtained by rubbing a pancreas with glycerin) + -IN.] **—tryp′tic** (-tĭk) *adj.*
tryp·sin·o·gen (trĭp-sĭn′ə-jən) *n.* The substance produced by the pancreas that is converted into trypsin when acted upon by certain enzymes.
tryp·to·phan (trĭp′tə-făn′) also **tryp·to·phane** (-fān′) *n.* An amino acid, $C_{11}H_{12}N_2O_2$, that is produced in the digestive process and is essential in human nutrition. [TRYPT(IC) + -PHAN(E).]
try·sail (trī′səl, -sāl′) *n. Naut.* A small fore-and-aft sail hoisted abaft the foremast and mainmast in a storm to keep a ship's bow to the wind. [TRY, to lie to in a storm (obs.) + SAIL.]
try square *n.* A carpenter's tool consisting of a ruled metal straightedge set at right angles to a wooden straight piece, used for measuring and marking square work.
tryst (trĭst) *n.* **1.** An agreement, as between lovers, to meet at a certain time and place. **2.** A meeting or meeting place that has been agreed on. *—intr.v.* **tryst·ed, tryst·ing, trysts.** To keep a tryst. [ME *trist* < OFr. *triste,* an appointed station in hunting.] **—tryst′er** *n.*
tsa·de (tsä′də, -dē) *n.* Variant of **sade.**
tsar (tsär) *n.* Variant of **czar.**
tset·se disease (tsĕt′sē, tsē′sē) *n.* Nagana.
tset·se fly also **tzet·ze fly** (tsĕt′sē, tsē′sē) *n.* Any of several bloodsucking African flies of the genus *Glossina,* often carrying and transmitting pathogenic trypanosomes to human beings and livestock. [Tswana *tsetse.*]
Tshi (chwē, chē) *n.* Variant of **Twi.**
T-shirt also **tee shirt** (tē′shûrt′) *n.* **1.** A short-sleeved, collarless undershirt worn by men and boys. **2.** An outer shirt of a design similar to the T-shirt and worn by men and women. [From its being shaped like the letter *T.*]
tsim·mes also **tzim·mes** (tsĭm′ĭs) *n.* **1.** A stew of vegetables or fruits cooked slowly over very low heat. **2.** *Informal.* A state of confusion. [Yiddish *tsimes.*]
T-square (tē′skwâr′) *n.* A rule having a short, sometimes sliding, perpendicular crosspiece at one end, used by drafters for establishing and drawing parallel lines.
tsu·na·mi (tso͞o-nä′mē) *n.* A very large ocean wave caused by an underwater earthquake or volcanic eruption. [J. : *tsu,* port + *nami,* wave.]
tsu·ris also **tzu·ris** (tso͝or′ĭs, tsôr′-) *n. Informal.* Trouble; aggravation. [Yiddish *tsores.*]
tsu·tsu·ga·mu·shi disease (tso͞o′tso͞o-gə-mo͞o′shē) *n.* Scrub typhus. [J. *tsutsugamushi* : *tsutsuga,* illness + *mushi,* tick.]
Tswa·na (tswä′nə, sä′-) *n.* **1.** A Bantu people of southern Africa, living mainly in Botswana. **2.** The Sotho language of the Tswanas.
Tuan (twän) *n.* Used in Malay as a form of respectful address, equivalent to the English "Sir" or "Mister." [Malay.]
Tua·reg (twä′rĕg′) *n., pl.* **Tuareg** or **-regs.** A member of one of the tall, nomadic, Hamitic-speaking peoples who occupy western and central Sahara and an area along the Niger and who have adopted the Moslem religion. [Ar. *Tawāriq.*]
tu·a·ta·ra (to͞o′ə-tär′ə) *n.* A lizardlike reptile, *Sphenodon punctatus,* of New Zealand, the only surviving representative of the order Rhynchocephalia that flourished during the Mesozoic era. [Maori *tuatàra.*]
tub (tŭb) *n.* **1. a.** A round, open, flat-bottomed vessel, usually wider than it is tall, and used for packing, storing, or washing. **b.** The amount held by such a vessel. **c.** The contents of such a vessel. **2. a.** A bathtub. **b.** *Informal.* A bath taken in a bathtub. **3.** *Informal.* A wide, clumsy, slow-moving boat. **4. a.** A bucket used for conveying ore or coal up a mine shaft. **b.** A coal car used in a mine. *—v.* **tubbed, tub·bing, tubs.** *—tr.* **1.** To pack or store in a tub. **2.** To wash or bathe in a tub. *—intr.* To take a bath. [ME *tubbe* < MDu.] **—tub′ba·ble** *adj.* **—tub′ber** *n.*
tu·ba (to͞o′bə, tyo͞o′-) *n.* **1.** A large, valved, brass musical wind instrument with a bass pitch. **2.** A reed stop in an organ, having eight-foot pitch. [Ital. < Lat., trumpet.]
tu·bal (to͞o′bəl, tyo͞o′-) *adj.* Of, pertaining to, or occurring in a tube, esp. the Fallopian tube.
tu·bate (to͞o′bāt′, tyo͞o′-) *adj.* Forming or having a tube.
tub·by (tŭb′ē) *adj.* **-bi·er, -bi·est.** **1.** Short and fat. **2.** Having a dull sound; lacking resonance. **—tub′bi·ness** *n.*
tube (to͞ob, tyo͞ob) *n.* **1. a.** A hollow cylinder, esp. one that conveys a fluid or functions as a passage. **b.** An organic structure so shaped or so functioning; duct. **2.** A small, flexible cylindrical container sealed at one end and having a screw cap at the other, for pigments, toothpaste, or other pastelike substances. **3.** The cylindrical part of a wind instrument. **4. a.** An electron tube. **b.** A vacuum tube. **5.** *Bot.* The lower, joined part of a gamopetalous corolla or a gamosepalous calyx. **6.** *Chiefly Brit.* The subway (sense 1). **7.** A tunnel. **8.** A flexible, airtight cylinder that is usually made of rubber and inserted into the casing of a pneumatic tire for holding air under pressure. **9.** *Informal.* **a.** Television. **b.** A television set. *—tr.v.* **tubed, tub·ing, tubes.** **1.** To provide with a tube; insert a tube in. **2.** To place in or enclose in a tube. ***—idiom.* down the tubes** (or **tube**). *Slang.* Into a state of failure or ruin: *saw all her dreams go down the tubes.* [Fr. or < Lat. *tubus.*]
tube foot *n.* One of the numerous external, fluid-filled muscular tubes of echinoderms, such as the starfish, serving primarily as organs of locomotion.
tube·less tire (to͞ob′lĭs, tyo͞ob′-) *n.* A pneumatic vehicular tire in which the air is held in the assembly of casing and rim without an inner tube.
tu·ber (to͞o′bər, tyo͞o′-) *n.* **1.** *Bot.* A swollen, usually underground stem, such as the potato, bearing buds from which new plant shoots arise. **2.** *Anat.* A swelling; tubercle. [Lat., lump.]
tu·ber·cle (to͞o′bər-kəl, tyo͞o′-) *n.* **1.** A small, rounded prominence or process, such as a wartlike excrescence on the roots of some leguminous plants or a knoblike process in the skin or on a bone. **2.** *Pathol.* **a.** A nodule or swelling. **b.** The characteristic lesion of tuberculosis. [Lat. *tuberculum,* dim. of *tuber,* lump.]
tubercle bacillus *n.* A rod-shaped bacterium, *Mycobacterium tuberculosis,* that causes tuberculosis.
tu·ber·cu·lar (to͞o-bûr′kyə-lər, tyo͞o-) *adj.* **1.** Of, relating to, or covered with tubercles; tuberculate. **2.** Of, relating to, or afflicted with tuberculosis. *—n.* A person having tuberculosis.
tu·ber·cu·late (to͞o-bûr′kyə-lĭt, tyo͞o-) also **tu·ber·cu·la·ted** (-lā′tĭd) *adj.* **1.** Having tubercles. **2.** Tubercular. **—tu·ber′cu·late·ly** *adv.* **—tu·ber′cu·la′tion** *n.*
tu·ber·cu·lin (to͞o-bûr′kyə-lĭn, tyo͞o-) *n.* A substance derived from cultures of tubercle bacilli and used in the diagnosis and treatment of tuberculosis. [Lat. *tuberculum,* tubercle + -IN.]
tuberculin test *n.* Any of various tests used to determine past or present infection with the tubercle bacillus and based on hypersensitivity to tuberculin.
tu·ber·cu·loid (to͞o-bûr′kyə-loid′, tyo͞o-) *adj.* **1.** Resembling tuberculosis. **2.** Resembling a tubercle.
tu·ber·cu·lo·sis (to͞o-bûr′kyə-lō′sĭs, tyo͞o-) *n.* **1.** A communicable disease of man and animals caused by a microorganism, *Mycobacterium tuberculosis,* and manifesting itself in lesions of the lung, bone, and other parts of the body. **2.** Tuberculosis of the lungs. [Lat. *tuberculum,* tubercle + -OSIS.]
tu·ber·cu·lous (to͞o-bûr′kyə-ləs, tyo͞o-) *adj.* **1.** Of, relating to, or having tuberculosis. **2.** Of, affected with, or caused by tubercles. [NLat. *tuberculosus* < Lat. *tuberculum,* tubercle.] **—tu·ber′cu·lous·ly** *adv.*
tube·rose[1] (to͞ob′rōz′, tyo͞ob′-, to͞o′bə-rōz′, -rōs′, tyo͞o′-) *n.* A tuberous plant, *Polianthes tuberosa,* native to Mexico, cultivated for its fragrant white flowers. [NLat. *tuberosa,* specific epithet < fem. of Lat. *tuberosus,* full of lumps.]
tu·ber·ose[2] (to͞o′bə-rōs′, tyo͞o′-) *adj.* Variant of **tuberous.**
tu·ber·os·i·ty (to͞o′bə-rŏs′ĭ-tē, tyo͞o′-) *n., pl.* **-ties.** A projection or protuberance, esp. one at the end of a bone for the attachment of a muscle or tendon.
tu·ber·ous (to͞o′bər-əs, tyo͞o′-) also **tu·ber·ose** (-bə-rōs′) *adj. Bot.* **1.** Producing or bearing tubers. **2.** Resembling a tuber: *a tuberous root.* [Lat. *tuberosus,* full of lumps < *tuber,* lump.]
tu·bi·fex (to͞o′bə-fĕks′, tyo͞o′-) *n., pl.* **tubifex** or **-fex·es.** Any of various small, slender, reddish freshwater worms of the genus *Tubifex,* often used as food for tropical aquarium fish. [NLat. *Tubifex,* genus name : Lat. *tubus,* tube + Lat. *facere,* to make.]
tub·ing (to͞o′bĭng, tyo͞o′-) *n.* **1.** Tubes collectively. **2.** A system of tubes. **3.** A piece or length of tube. **4.** Tubular fabric, such as that used for making pillowcases.
tu·bu·lar (to͞o′byə-lər, tyo͞o′-) *adj.* **1.** Of or pertaining to a tube. **2.** Having the form of a tube. **3.** Constituting or consisting of tubes. **—tu′bu·lar′i·ty** (-lăr′ĭ-tē) *n.* **—tu′bu·lar·ly** *adv.*
tu·bu·late (to͞o′byə-lĭt, -lāt′, tyo͞o′-) also **tu·bu·lat·ed** (-lā′tĭd) *adj.* **1.** Formed into or resembling a tube; tubular. **2.** Having a tube. [Lat. *tubulatus* < *tubulus,* dim. of *tubus,* tube.] **—tu′bu·la′tion** *n.* **—tu′bu·la′tor** *n.*
tu·bule (to͞o′byo͞ol, tyo͞o′-) *n.* A very small tube or tubular structure. [Lat. *tubulus,* dim. of *tubus,* tube.]
tu·bu·lif·er·ous (to͞o′byə-lĭf′ər-əs, tyo͞o′-) *adj.* Having or consisting of tubules.
tu·bu·li·flo·rous (to͞o′byə-lə-flôr′əs, -flōr′-, tyo͞o′-) *adj.* Having flowers or florets with tubular corollas.
tu·bu·lous (to͞o′byə-ləs, tyo͞o′-) *adj.* **1.** Tubular. **2. a.** Composed of tubes. **b.** Having tubular parts. [< Lat. *tubulus,* dim. of *tubus,* tube.] **—tu′bu·lous·ly** *adv.*
Tu·ca·na (to͞o-kā′nə, -kä′-, tyo͞o-) *n.* A constellation in the polar region of the Southern Hemisphere near Indus and Hydrus, containing the smaller Magellanic cloud. [Tupi *tucana,* toucan.]

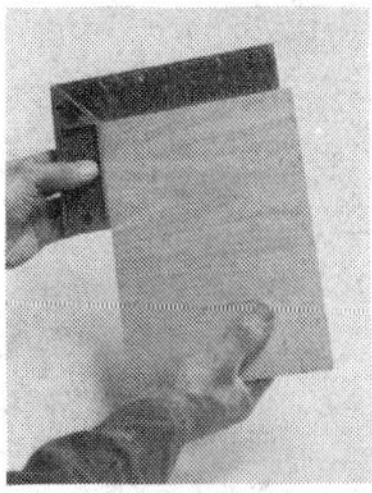

try square

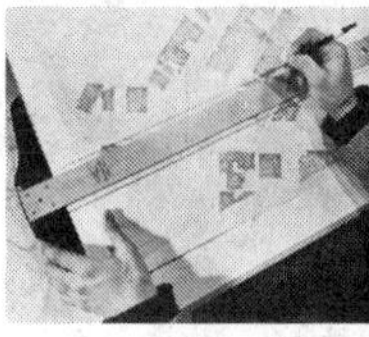

T-square

tuba

tu·chun (dōō'jün', -jōōn') *n., pl.* **-chuns** or **tuchun.** A Chinese military governor of a province. [Chin. (Mandarin) *du[1] jun[1]* : *du[1]*, to supervise + *jun[1]*, army.]

tuck[1] (tŭk) *v.* **tucked, tuck·ing, tucks.** —*tr.* **1.** To make one or more folds in. **2.** To gather up and fold, thrust, or turn in in order to secure or confine: *tuck a scarf into a shirt.* **3. a.** To put in a snug spot. **b.** To put in an out-of-the-way and snug place: *a cabin tucked among the pines.* **c.** To store in a safe spot; save: *tuck away a bit of lace; tuck away millions.* **4.** To draw in; contract. —*intr.* To make tucks. —***phrasal verb.*** **tuck in** (or **away**). *Informal.* To consume (food) heartily. —*n.* **1.** A flattened pleat or fold, esp. a very narrow one stitched in place. **2.** The act of tucking. **3.** *Naut.* The part of a ship's hull under the stern where the ends of the bottom planks come together. **4.** *Chiefly Brit. Slang.* Food, esp. sweets and pastry. **5. a.** A bodily position used in some sports, as diving, in which the knees are bent, the thighs are drawn close to the chest, and the hands are clasped around the shins. **b.** A position in skiing in which the skier squats while holding the poles parallel to the ground and under the arms. [ME *tukken* < OE *tūcian,* to torment.]

tulip

tuck[2] (tŭk) *n.* A beat or tap, esp. on a drum. [< ME *tukken,* to beat a drum < ONFr. *toquer,* to strike.]

tuck[3] (tŭk) *n. Archaic.* A slender sword; rapier. [Dial. Fr. *étoc* < OFr. *estoc,* of Germanic orig.]

tuck[4] (tŭk) *n.* Energy; vigor. [Orig. unknown.]

tuck·a·hoe (tŭk'ə-hō') *n.* Any of various plants or plant parts used by American Indians as food, esp. the edible root of certain arums or the sclerotium of certain fungi. [Algonquian *taccaho.*]

tuck·er[1] (tŭk'ər) *n.* **1.** One that tucks, esp. a sewing-machine attachment that makes tucks. **2.** A piece of linen or frill of lace formerly worn by women around the neck and shoulders.

tuck·er[2] (tŭk'ər) *tr.v.* **-ered, -er·ing, -ers.** *Informal.* To weary; exhaust. [< TUCK[1].]

tuck·er-bag (tŭk'ər-băg') *n. Austral. Informal.* A bag for carrying food, used by a traveler in the bush or by a swagman.

tuck·et (tŭk'ĭt) *n.* A trumpet fanfare. [ME *tuk* < *tukken,* to beat a drum. —see TUCK[2].]

tuck pointing *n.* The pointing of grooved mortar joints with a thin ridge of fine lime mortar or putty.

tuck-shop (tŭk'shŏp') *n. Chiefly Brit.* A confectionery.

-tude *suff.* A condition, state, or quality: *exactitude.* [OFr. < Lat. *-tudo.*]

Tu·dor (tōō'dər, tyōō'-) *adj.* **1.** Of or pertaining to the royal house that ruled England from 1485 through 1603. **2. a.** Of, pertaining to, or characteristic of the Tudor period, esp. in architecture. **b.** Of, pertaining to, or characteristic of an architectural style derived from the Tudor period, having exposed beams as a typical feature.

Tues·day (tōōz'dē, -dā', tyōōz'-) *n.* The third day of the week, following Monday and preceding Wednesday. [ME *Tuesdai* < OE *Tīwesdæg,* Tiu's day.]

tu·fa (tōō'fə, tyōō'-) *n.* **1.** The calcareous and siliceous rock deposits of springs, lakes, or ground water. **2.** Tuff. [Obs. Ital. < Lat. *tofus.*] —**tu·fa'ceous** (-fā'shəs) *adj.*

tuff (tŭf) *n.* A rock composed of compacted volcanic ash varying in size from fine sand to coarse gravel. [OFr. *tuf* < OItal. *tufo,* tufa.] —**tuff·a'ceous** (tŭ-fā'shəs) *adj.*

tuf·fet (tŭf'ĭt) *n.* **1.** A clump or tuft of grass. **2.** A low seat such as a stool. [Alteration of TUFT.]

tu·fo·li (tōō-fō'lē, tyōō-) *n.* A large macaroni shell suitable for stuffing. [Sicilian, pl. of *tufolo,* duct < LLat. *tubulus,* dim. of Lat. *tubus,* tube.]

tuft (tŭft) *n.* **1.** A short cluster of elongated strands, as of yarn, hair, or grass, attached at the base or growing close together. **2.** A dense clump, esp. of trees or bushes. **3.** A goatee. —*v.* **tuft·ed, tuft·ing, tufts.** —*tr.* **1.** To furnish or ornament with a tuft. **2.** To pass threads through the layers of (a quilt, mattress, or upholstery), securing the thread ends with a knot or button in the depressions created. —*intr.* **1.** To separate or form into tufts. **2.** To grow in a tuft. [ME, prob. < OFr. *tofe.*] —**tuft'er** *n.* —**tuft'y** *adj.*

tug (tŭg) *v.* **tugged, tug·ging, tugs.** —*tr.* **1.** To pull at vigorously; strain at. **2.** To move by pulling with great effort or exertion; drag. **3.** To tow by tugboat. —*intr.* **1.** To pull hard: *tugged at her boots.* **2.** To toil or struggle; strain. **3.** To vie; contend. —*n.* **1.** A strong pull or pulling force: *the tug of the sea.* **2.** A contest; struggle: *a tug between loyalty and desire.* **3.** A tugboat. **4.** A rope, chain, or strap used in hauling, esp. a harness trace. [ME *tuggen.*] —**tug'ger** *n.*

tug·boat (tŭg'bōt') *n.* A powerful small boat designed for towing larger vessels.

tug of war *n.* **1.** A contest of strength in which two teams tug on opposite ends of a rope, each trying to pull the other across a dividing line. **2.** A struggle for supremacy.

tu·grik (tōō'grĭk) *n.* See table at **currency.** [Mongolian *dughurik.*]

tuille (twēl) *n.* A steel plate used in medieval armor for protecting the thigh. [ME *toile* < OFr. *tieule* < Lat. *tugula,* tile < *tegere,* to cover.]

tu·i·tion (tōō-ĭsh'ən, tyōō-) *n.* **1.** A fee for instruction, esp. at a formal institution of learning. **2.** Instruction; teaching. **3.** *Archaic.* Guardianship. [ME *tuicion,* protection < OFr. < Lat. *tuitio* < *tueri,* to protect.] —**tu·i'tion·al, tu·i'tion·ar'y** (-ə-nĕr'ē) *adj.*

tu·la·re·mi·a (tōō'lə-rē'mē-ə, tyōō'-) *n.* An infectious disease caused by the bacterium *Pasteurella tularensis,* transmitted from infected rodents to man by insect vectors or by handling infected animals and characterized by fever and swelling of the lymph nodes. [NLat., after *Tulare* county, California.] —**tu'la·re'mic** *adj.*

tu·le (tōō'lē) *n.* Any of several bulrushes of the genus *Scirpus,* growing in marshy lowlands of the southwestern United States. [Sp. < Nahuatl *tollin,* reed.]

tu·lip (tōō'lĭp, tyōō'-) *n.* **1.** Any of several bulbous plants of the genus *Tulipa,* native to Asia, widely cultivated for their showy, variously colored flowers. **2.** The flower of the tulip. [NLat. *Tulipa,* genus name < Turk. *tülibend,* turban < Pers. *dulband.*]

tulip poplar *n.* The tulip tree.

tulip tree *n.* A tall deciduous tree, *Liriodendron tulipifera,* having large, tuliplike green and orange flowers and yellowish, easily worked wood.

tu·lip·wood (tōō'lĭp-wŏŏd', tyōō'-) *n.* **1.** The wood of the tulip tree. **2.** The irregularly striped, ornamental wood of any of several trees related or similar to the tulipwood, esp. that of *Dalbergia variabilis,* of tropical South America.

tulle (tōōl) *n.* A fine, often starched net of silk, rayon, or nylon, used esp. for veils, tutus, or gowns. [Fr., after *Tulle,* France.]

tum·ble (tŭm'bəl) *v.* **-bled, -bling, -bles.** —*intr.* **1.** To perform acrobatic feats such as somersaults, rolls, or twists. **2. a.** To fall or roll end over end: *The kittens tumbled over each other.* **b.** To spill or roll out in confusion or disorder: *Schoolchildren tumbled out of the bus.* **c.** To pitch headlong; fall: *tumbled on the ice.* **d.** To proceed haphazardly: *tumble into clothes.* **3. a.** To topple, as from power or high position; fall. **b.** To collapse: *and the walls came tumbling down.* **c.** To drop: *Prices tumbled.* **4.** To come upon accidentally; happen on: *tumbled on a first-rate restaurant.* **5.** *Slang.* To come to a sudden understanding; catch on. —*tr.* **1.** To cause to fall; bring down. **2.** To put, spill, or toss haphazardly. **3.** To toss or whirl in a drum, tumbler, or tumbling box. —*n.* **1.** An act of tumbling; fall. **2.** A condition of confusion or disorder. [ME *tumblen,* freq. of *tumben,* to dance < OE *tumbian.*]

tum·ble·bug (tŭm'bəl-bŭg') *n.* Any of various beetles of the family Scarabaeidae that roll up balls of dung to protect their eggs and serve as food for the newly hatched larvae.

tum·ble-down (tŭm'bəl-doun') *adj.* Dilapidated; rickety.

tum·ble-home (tŭm'bəl-hōm') *n.* The inward curve of a ship's topsides. [< TUMBLE, to slope inward (obs.).]

tum·bler (tŭm'blər) *n.* **1.** One that tumbles, esp. an acrobat or gymnast. **2. a.** A drinking glass, originally with a rounded bottom. **b.** A flat-bottomed glass having no handle, foot, or stem. **c.** The contents of a drinking glass. **3.** A toy made with a weighted, rounded base so that it can rock over and then right itself. **4.** One of a breed of domestic pigeons characteristically tumbling or somersaulting in flight. **5.** A piece in a gunlock that forces the hammer forward by action of the mainspring. **6.** The part in a lock that releases the bolt when moved by a key. **7. a.** The drum of a clothes dryer. **b.** A tumbling box. **8. a.** A projecting piece on a revolving or rocking part in a mechanism that transmits motion to the part it engages. **b.** The rocking frame that moves a gear into place in a selective transmission, as in an automobile.

tum·ble·weed (tŭm'bəl-wēd') *n.* Any of various densely branched New World plants, chiefly of the genus *Amaranthus,* that when withered break off and are rolled about by the wind, esp. *A. albus,* of western prairies.

tum·bling (tŭm'blĭng) *n.* The skill or sport of gymnastic falling, rolling, or somersaulting.

tumbling box *n.* A revolving drum in which objects are dried, reduced in size, polished, or cleaned.

tum·brel or **tum·bril** (tŭm'brəl) *n.* **1.** A two-wheeled cart, esp. a farmer's cart that can be tilted to dump a load. **2.** A crude cart used to carry condemned prisoners to their place of execution, as during the French Revolution. [ME *tumberell* < OFr. *tomberel* < *tomber,* to let fall, of Germanic orig.]

tu·me·fa·cient (tōō'mə-fā'shənt, tyōō'-) *adj.* Producing or tending to produce swelling or tumefaction. [Lat. *tumefaciens, tumefacient-,* pr.part. of *tumefacere,* to tumefy : *tumēre,* to swell + *facere,* to make.]

tu·me·fac·tion (tōō'mə-făk'shən, tyōō'-) *n.* **1. a.** The action or process of puffing or swelling. **b.** A swollen condition. **2.** A puffy or swollen part. [OFr. < Lat. *tumefacere,* to tumefy. —see TUMEFACIENT.] —**tu'me·fac'tive** *adj.*

tu·me·fy (tōō'mə-fī', tyōō'-) *intr & tr.v.* **-fied, -fy·ing, -fies.** To swell or cause to swell. [OFr. *tumefier* < Lat. *tumēre.*]

tu·mes·cence (tōō-mĕs'əns, tyōō-) *n.* **1. a.** A swelling or enlarging. **b.** A swollen condition. **2.** A swollen part or organ.

tu·mes·cent (tōō-mĕs'ənt, tyōō-) *adj.* Somewhat tumid. [Lat. *tumescens, tumescent-,* pr.part. of *tumescere,* to begin to swell < *tumēre,* to swell.]

tu·mid (tōō'mĭd, tyōō'-) *adj.* **1.** Swollen; distended. Used of a bodily part or organ. **2.** Of a bulging shape; protuberant. **3.** Overblown; bombastic: *tumid political prose.* [Lat. *tumi-*

dus < *tumēre,* to swell.] **—tu·mid′i·ty** (-mĭd′ĭ-tē), **tu′mid·ness** *n.* **—tu′mid·ly** *adv.*

tumm·ler (to͝om′lər) *n.* **1.** One, as a social director or an entertainer, who encourages guest or audience participation. **2.** One who incites others to action. [Yiddish < G. *tummeln,* to move about.]

tum·my (tŭm′ē) *n., pl.* **-mies.** *Informal.* The stomach. [Alteration of STOMACH.]

tu·mor (to͞o′mər, tyo͞o′-) *n.* **1.** A circumscribed, noninflammatory growth arising from existing tissue but growing independently of the normal rate or structural development of such tissue and serving no physiological function. **2.** A swollen part. [Lat. *tumor* < *tumēre,* to swell.] **—tu′mor·al, tu′mor·ous** *adj.*

tu·mor·i·gen·e·sis (to͞o′mər-ə-jĕn′ĭ-sĭs, tyo͞o′-) *n.* The formation of tumors.

tu·mor·i·gen·ic (to͞o′mər-ə-jĕn′ĭk, tyo͞o′-) *adj.* Causing the formation of tumors. **—tu′mor·i·ge·nic′i·ty** (-jə-nĭs′ĭ-tē) *n.*

tump·line (tŭmp′līn′) *n.* A strap slung across the forehead or the chest to support a load carried on the back. [*Tump,* tumpline (perh. of Algonquian orig.) + LINE.]

tu·mu·lar (to͞o′myə-lər, tyo͞o′-) *adj.* Pertaining to or having the shape of a tumulus.

tu·mu·li (to͞o′myə-lī′, tyo͞o′-) *n.* Plural of **tumulus.**

tu·mu·lose (to͞o′myə-lōs′, tyo͞o′-) also **tu·mu·lous** (-ləs) *adj.* Having many mounds or small hills. [Lat. *tumulosus* < *tumulus,* mound.] **—tu′mu·los′i·ty** (-lŏs′ĭ-tē) *n.*

tu·mult (to͞o′mŭlt′, tyo͞o′-) *n.* **1.** The din and commotion of a great crowd. **2. a.** A disorderly commotion or disturbance. **b.** A tempestuous uprising; riot. **3.** Agitation of the mind or emotions. [ME *tumulte* < Lat. *tumultus.*]

tu·mul·tu·ar·y (to͞o-mŭl′cho͞o-ĕr′ē, tyo͞o-) *adj.* Marked by haste, confusion, disorder, and irregularity. [Lat. *tumultuarius* < *tumultus,* commotion.]

tu·mul·tu·ous (to͞o-mŭl′cho͞o-əs, tyo͞o-) *adj.* **1.** Characterized by tumult; noisy and disorderly. **2.** Tending to cause tumult. **3.** Confusedly or violently agitated. **—tu·mul′tu·ous·ly** *adv.* **—tu·mul′tu·ous·ness** *n.*

tu·mu·lus (to͞o′myə-ləs, tyo͞o′-) *n., pl.* **-li** (-lī′). An ancient grave mound; barrow. [Lat.]

tun (tŭn) *n.* **1.** A large cask for liquids, esp. wine. **2.** A measure of liquid capacity, esp. one equivalent to approximately 954 liters, or 252 gallons. [ME < OE *tunne,* poss. of Celt. orig.]

tu·na[1] (to͞o′nə, tyo͞o′-) *n., pl.* **tuna** or **-nas. 1. a.** Any of various often large marine food fishes of the genus *Thunnus* and related genera, many of which, including *T. thynnus* and the albacore, are commercially important sources of canned fish. **b.** Any of several related fishes, such as the bonito. **2.** The edible flesh of tuna, often canned or processed. [Ult. < Lat. *thunnus.* —see TUNNY.]

tu·na[2] (to͞o′nə, tyo͞o′-) *n.* **1.** Any of several tropical American cacti of the genus *Opuntia,* which includes the prickly pears, esp. *O. tuna,* bearing edible red fruit. **2.** The edible fruit of the tuna. [Sp. < Taino.]

tun·a·ble also **tune·a·ble** (to͞o′nə-bəl, tyo͞o′-) *adj.* **1.** Capable of being tuned. **2.** *Archaic.* Tuneful. **—tun′a·ble·ness** *n.* **—tun′a·bly** *adv.*

tuna fish *n.* Tuna[1] (sense 2).

tun·dra (tŭn′drə) *n.* A treeless area between the ice cap and the tree line of arctic regions, having a permanently frozen subsoil and supporting low-growing vegetation such as lichens, mosses, and stunted shrubs. [R. < Lapp.]

tune (to͞on, tyo͞on) *n.* **1.** A melody, esp. of simple and easily remembered character. **2. a.** Correct musical pitch. **b.** The state of being properly adjusted for pitch: *a piano out of tune.* **3. a.** Agreement in pitch: *play in tune with the piano.* **b.** Concord or agreement; harmony: *in tune with the times.* **c.** *Archaic.* Frame of mind; disposition. **4.** *Electronics.* Adjustment of a receiver or circuit for maximum response to a given signal or frequency. **5.** *Obs.* A musical tone. *—v.* **tuned, tun·ing, tunes.** *—tr.* **1.** To put in proper musical pitch. **2. a.** To adjust in order to bring into harmony. **b.** To adapt; adjust: *tune oneself to life in the tropics.* **3.** To adjust (an engine, for example) for maximum performance. **4.** *Archaic.* To utter musically; sing. *—intr.* To become attuned. ***—phrasal verbs.*** **tune in. 1.** To adjust a radio or television receiver to receive signals at a particular frequency. **2.** *Slang.* To make or become aware or responsive. **tune out. 1.** To adjust a radio receiver so as not to receive a particular signal. **2.** *Slang.* To disassociate oneself from one's environment. **3.** *Slang.* To become unresponsive to; ignore: *tuned out the children's screaming.* **tune up. 1.** To adjust a musical instrument to a desired pitch or key. **2.** To adjust a machine so as to put it into proper condition. **3.** To prepare oneself for a specified activity. ***—idioms.*** **change (one's) tune.** To change one's approach or attitude. **to the tune of.** To the sum or extent of. [ME, var. of *tone,* tone. —see TONE.]

tune·a·ble (to͞o′nə-bəl, tyo͞o′-) *adj.* Variant of **tunable.**

tuned-in (to͞ond′ĭn′, tyo͞ond′-) *adj. Slang.* Quite excited; turned-on.

tune·ful (to͞on′fəl, tyo͞on′-) *adj.* **1.** Full of tune; melodious; musical. **2.** Producing musical sounds. **—tune′ful·ly** *adv.* **—tune′ful·ness** *n.*

tune·less (to͞on′lĭs, tyo͞on′-) *adj.* **1.** Deficient in melody; not tuneful. **2.** Producing no music; silent. **—tune′less·ly** *adv.* **—tune′less·ness** *n.*

tun·er (to͞o′nər, tyo͞o′-) *n.* **1.** One that tunes: *a piano tuner.* **2.** A device for tuning, esp. an electronic circuit or device used to select signals at a specific radio frequency for amplification and conversion to sound.

tune-up (to͞on′ŭp′, tyo͞on′-) *n.* **1.** An adjustment of a motor or engine to put it in efficient working order. **2.** An engine warm-up.

tung oil (tŭng) *n.* A yellow or brownish oil extracted from the seeds of the tung tree and used as a drying agent in varnishes and paints and for waterproofing.

tung-oil tree (tŭng′oil′) *n.* A tung tree.

tung·state (tŭng′stāt′) *n.* A chemical compound derived from tungstic acid and containing tungsten with valence 6. [TUNG(STEN) + -ATE.]

tung·sten (tŭng′stən) *n. Symbol* **W** A hard, brittle, corrosion-resistant, gray to white metallic element extracted from wolframite, scheelite, and other minerals, having the highest melting point and lowest vapor pressure of any metal. Tungsten and its alloys are used in high-temperature structural materials, electrical elements, notably lamp filaments, and instruments requiring thermally compatible glass-to-metal seals. Atomic number 74; atomic weight 183.85; melting point 3,410°C; boiling point 5,927°C; specific gravity 19.3 (20°C); valences 2, 3, 4, 5, 6. [Swed. : *tung,* heavy (< ON *þungr*) + *sten,* stone (< ON *steinn*).] **—tung·sten′ic** (-stĕn′ĭk) *adj.*

tungsten carbide *n.* An extremely hard, fine gray powder whose composition is WC, used in tools, dies, wear-resistant machine parts, and abrasives.

tungsten lamp *n.* An incandescent electric lamp with a tungsten filament.

tungsten steel *n.* A very hard, heat-resistant steel containing tungsten.

tung·stic (tŭng′stĭk) *adj.* Of, pertaining to, or containing tungsten, esp. with valence 6.

tungstic acid *n.* A yellow powder, H_2WO_4, used in textiles and plastics.

tung·stite (tŭng′stīt′) *n.* A yellow or yellowish-green mineral, essentially WO_3, often occurring with tungsten ores.

tung tree (tŭng) *n.* Any of several Asian trees of the genus *Aleurites,* esp. *A. fordii,* cultivated for its seeds that yield a commercially valuable drying oil. [Chin. (Mandarin) *tong*[2], tung tree + TREE.]

Tun·gus (to͝ong-go͞oz′, tŭn-) *n., pl.* **Tungus** or **-gus·es. 1.** A Mongoloid people inhabiting eastern Siberia. **2.** The Tungusic language of the Tungus. [R.]

Tun·gus·ic (to͝ong-go͞o′zĭk, tŭn-) *n.* A subfamily of the Altaic language family spoken in eastern Siberia and northern Manchuria that includes Tungus and Manchu. *—adj.* Of or pertaining to the Tungus peoples or to Tungusic.

tu·nic (to͞o′nĭk, tyo͞o′-) *n.* **1. a.** A loose-fitting garment, sleeved or sleeveless, extending to the knees and worn by men and women esp. in ancient Greece and Rome. **b.** A medieval surcoat. **2. a.** A long plain close-fitting military jacket, usually with a high stiff collar. **b.** A long plain sleeved or sleeveless blouse worn over a skirt by women. **c.** A short pleated and belted dress worn by women for some sports. **3.** *Anat.* A coat or layer enveloping an organ or part. **4.** *Bot.* A membranous outer covering, as of a seed. **5.** A tunicle. [Lat. *tunica,* of Semitic orig.]

tu·ni·ca (to͞o′nĭ-kə, tyo͞o′-) *n., pl.* **-cae** (-kē′, -sē′). An enclosing membrane or layer of tissue. [NLat. < Lat., tunic.]

tu·ni·cate (to͞o′nĭ-kĭt, -kāt′, tyo͞o′-) *n.* Any of various chordate marine animals of the subphylum Urochordata or Tunicata, having a cylindrical or globular body enclosed in a tough outer covering, or tunic, and including the sea squirts and salps. *—adj.* **1.** Of or pertaining to the tunicates. **2.** *Anat.* Having a tunic. **3.** *Bot.* Having concentric layers, as the bulb of an onion. [< Lat. *tunicare, tunicat-,* to clothe with a tunic < *tunica,* tunic.]

tu·ni·cle (to͞o′nĭ-kəl, tyo͞o′-) *n.* A short vestment worn over the alb by a subdeacon or with the dalmatic by a bishop or cardinal. [ME < Lat. *tunicula,* dim. of *tunica,* tunic.]

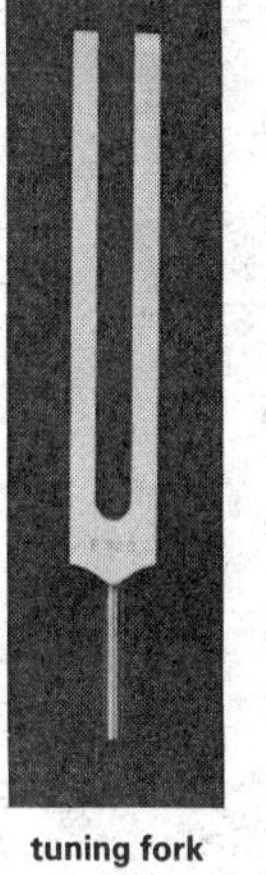

tuning fork

tuning fork *n.* A small two-pronged metal device that when struck produces a sound of fixed pitch that is used as a reference, as in tuning musical instruments.

Tu·ni·sian (to͞o-nē′zhən, -nĭzh′ən, tyo͞o-) *adj.* Of or pertaining to Tunisia, Tunis, or their inhabitants. *—n.* A native or inhabitant of Tunisia or Tunis.

tun·nel (tŭn′əl) *n.* **1.** An underground or underwater passage. **2.** A passage through or under a barrier. **3.** *Obs.* The main flue on a chimney. *—v.* **-neled, -nel·ing, -nels** or **-nelled, -nel·ling, -nels.** *—tr.* **1.** To make a tunnel through or under. **2.** To shape or dig in the form of a tunnel: *tunnel a passage.* *—intr.* To make a tunnel. [ME *tonel,* tubular net < OFr. < *ton,* tun.] **—tun′nel·er, tun′nel·ler** *n.*

tunnel vision *n.* **1.** A constricted visual field in which peripheral perception is eliminated. **2.** An extremely narrow point of view; narrow-mindedness.

tun·ny (tŭn′ē) *n., pl.* **tun·nies** or **tunny.** Tuna[1] (sense 1.a.). [OItal. *tonno* < OProv. *ton* < Lat. *thynnus* < Gk. *thunnos.*]

tup (tŭp) *n.* **1.** *Chiefly Brit.* A male sheep; ram. **2.** A heavy metal body, esp. the head of a power hammer. *—v.* **tupped,**

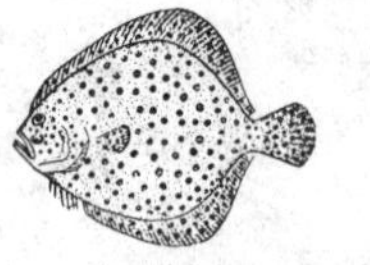

turbot

tureen

tup·ping, tups. —*tr.* To copulate with (a ewe). Used of a ram. —*intr.* To copulate with a ewe. [ME *tup.*]

tu·pe·lo (to͞o'pə-lō', tyo͞o'-) *n., pl.* **-los. 1.** Any of several trees of the genus *Nyssa,* esp. *N. aquatica,* of the southeastern United States, having soft, light wood. **2.** The wood of a tupelo. [Creek *ito opila* : *ito,* tree + *opilwa,* swamp.]

Tu·pi (to͞o'pē, to͞o-pē') *n., pl.* **Tupi** or **-pis. 1.** A member of any of a group of peoples living along the coast of Brazil, in the Amazon River valley, and in Paraguay. **2.** The Tupian language of the Tupi.

Tu·pi·an (to͞o'pē-ən, to͞o-pē'-) *adj.* Of or pertaining to the Tupi. —*n.* A subdivision of Tupi-Guarani that includes Tupi.

Tu·pi-Gua·ra·ni (to͞o-pē'gwär-ə-nē', to͞o'pē-) *n.* A language family widely spread throughout the Amazon River valley, coastal Brazil, and northeastern South America. **—Tu·pi'-Gua·ra·ni', Tu·pi'-Gua·ra·ni'an** *adj.*

tup·pence (tŭp'əns) *n. Chiefly Brit.* Variant of **twopence.**

tup·pen·ny (tŭp'nē) *n. Chiefly Brit.* Variant of **twopenny.**

tuque (to͝ok, tyo͝ok) *n.* A knitted woolen cap in the form of a cylindrical bag with tapered ends that is worn with one end tucked into the other. [Canadian Fr. < Fr. *toque,* toque < Sp. *toca.*]

tu quo·que (to͞o kwō'kwē, kō'-, tyo͞o) *n.* A retort accusing an accuser of a similar offense or similar behavior. [< Lat., you also.]

tu·ra·co (to͝or'ə-kō') *n.* Variant of **touraco.**

Tu·ra·ni·an (to͞o-rā'nē-ən, -rä'-, tyo͞o-) *adj.* Of or pertaining to the Ural-Altaic languages or to the peoples who speak them. —*n.* **1.** Ural-Altaic. **2.** A member of any of the peoples who speak languages of the Ural-Altaic group. [< Pers. *Tūrān,* a region of central Asia.]

tur·ban (tûr'bən) *n.* **1.** A headdress of Moslem origin, consisting of a cap attached to a long scarf of linen, cotton, or silk that is wound around the head. **2.** A woman's hat that resembles a turban. [OFr. *turbant* < OItal. *turbante* < Turk. *tülibend* < Pers. *dulband.*]

tur·ba·ry (tûr'bə-rē) *n., pl.* **-ries. 1.** A place where peat can be dug; peat bog. **2.** *Law.* The right to dig peat or turf on someone else's ground in Great Britain. [ME *turbarye* < AN *turberie* < Med. Lat. *turbaria* < *turb,* peat, of Germanic orig.]

tur·bel·lar·i·an (tûr'bə-lâr'ē-ən) *n.* Any of various chiefly aquatic ciliate flatworms of the class Turbellaria. —*adj.* Of or belonging to the Turbellaria. [NLat. *Turbellaria,* class name < Lat. *turbella,* bustle < *turba,* turmoil.]

tur·bid (tûr'bĭd) *adj.* **1.** Having sediment or foreign particles stirred up or suspended; muddy: *turbid water.* **2.** Heavy, dark, or dense, as smoke or fog. **3.** In turmoil; muddled: *turbid feelings.* [Lat. *turbidus,* disordered < *turba,* turmoil.] **—tur'bid·ly** *adv.* **—tur'bid·ness, tur·bid'i·ty** (-bĭd'ĭ-tē) *n.*

tur·bi·dim·e·ter (tûr'bĭ-dĭm'ĭ-tər) *n.* An instrument used to measure the scattering of a light beam through a solution that contains suspended particulate matter. **—tur'bi·di·met'ric** (-də-mĕt'rĭk) *adj.* **—tur'bi·di·met'ri·cal·ly** *adv.* **—tur'bi·dim'e·try** *n.*

tur·bi·nal (tûr'bə-nəl) *adj.* Having the shape of a cone resting on its apex. —*n. Anat.* A turbinate bone. [Lat. *turbo, turbin-,* spinning top.]

tur·bi·nate (tûr'bə-nĭt, -nāt') also **tur·bi·nat·ed** (-nā'tĭd) *adj.* **1.** Shaped like a top. **2.** Spinning like a top. **3.** *Zool.* Spiral and decreasing sharply in diameter from base to apex. Used of shells. **4.** *Anat.* Designating a small curved bone that extends horizontally along the lateral wall of the nasal passage. [Lat. *turbinatus* < *turbo,* spinning top.]

tur·bi·na·tion (tûr'bə-nā'shən) *n.* A turbinate formation.

tur·bine (tûr'bĭn, -bīn') *n.* Any of various machines in which the kinetic energy of a moving fluid is converted to mechanical power by the impulse or reaction of the fluid with a series of buckets, paddles, or blades arrayed about the circumference of a wheel or cylinder. [Fr. < Lat. *turbo,* spinning top.]

tur·bit (tûr'bĭt) *n.* One of a breed of domestic pigeons having a small crested head and a ruffled breast. [Orig. unknown.]

turbo– *pref.* **1.** Turbine: *turbocharger.* **2.** Driven by a turbine: *turbojet.* [< TURBINE.]

tur·bo·charg·er (tûr'bō-chär'jər) *n.* A device that uses the exhaust gas of an internal-combustion engine to drive a turbine that in turn drives a supercharger attached to the engine.

tur·bo·fan (tûr'bō-făn') *n.* **1.** A turbojet engine in which a fan supplements the total thrust by forcing air diverted from the main engine directly into the hot turbine exhaust. **2.** An aircraft in which a turbofan is used.

tur·bo·jet (tûr'bō-jĕt') *n.* **1.** A jet engine having a turbine-driven compressor and developing thrust from the exhaust of hot gases. **2.** An aircraft in which a turbojet is used.

tur·bo·prop (tûr'bō-prŏp') *n.* **1.** A turbojet engine used to drive an external propeller. **2.** An aircraft in which a turboprop is used. [Short for *turbopropeller.*]

tur·bo·ram·jet (tûr'bō-răm'jĕt') *n.* **1.** A turbojet engine that at high speeds compresses air taken in as a ramjet and increases exhaust velocities with an afterburner. **2.** An aircraft in which a turboramjet is used.

tur·bo·su·per·charg·er (tûr'bō-so͞o'pər-chär'jər) *n.* A supercharger that uses an exhaust-driven turbine to maintain air-intake pressure in high-altitude aircraft.

tur·bot (tûr'bət) *n., pl.* **turbot** or **-bots. 1.** A European flatfish, *Psetta maxima* or *Scophthalmus maximus,* esteemed as food. **2.** Any of various flatfishes similar or related to the turbot. [ME < OFr. *torbout.*]

tur·bu·la·tor (tûr'byə-lā'tər) *n.* A device designed to cause turbulence in fluids. [< TURBULENT.]

tur·bu·lence (tûr'byə-ləns) *n.* **1.** The state or quality of being turbulent. **2.** Turbulent flow.

tur·bu·lent (tûr'byə-lənt) *adj.* **1.** Violently agitated or disturbed; tumultuous: *turbulent rapids.* **2.** Having a chaotic or restless character or tendency: *a turbulent period of history.* **3.** Causing unrest or disturbance; unruly. [Lat. *turbulentus* < *turba,* turmoil.] **—tur'bu·lent·ly** *adv.*

turbulent flow *n.* The motion of a fluid having local velocities and pressures that fluctuate randomly.

Tur·co·man (tûr'kə-mən) *adj. & n.* Variant of **Turkoman.**

turd (tûrd) *n.* **1.** *Vulgar.* A piece of dung. **2.** *Vulgar Slang.* A worthless or contemptible person. [ME < OE *tord.*]

tu·reen (to͞o-rēn', tyo͞o-) *n.* A broad, deep dish, usually with a cover, used for serving foods, as soups or stews. [Fr. *terrine* < OFr. < *terrin,* earthen < Lat. *terra,* earth.]

turf (tûrf) *n.,* **1.** A surface layer of earth containing a dense growth of grass and its matted roots; sod. **2.** A piece cut from a layer of earth or sod. **3.** A piece of peat that is burned for use as fuel. **4.** *Slang.* **a.** The area claimed by a juvenile gang as its personal territory **b.** An indefinite geographical area; territory. **5 a.** A racetrack. **b.** The sport or business of racing horses. [ME < OE.] **—turf'y** *adj.*

tur·ges·cence (tûr-jĕs'əns)). *n.* **1 a.** The process of swelling. **b.** The condition of being swollen. **2.** Pomposity; self-importance. [< Lat. *turgescens,* pr.part. of *turgescere,* to begin to swell < *turgēre,* to be swollen.] **—tur·ges'cent** *adj.*

tur·gid (tûr'jĭd) *adj.* **1.** Swollen or distended, as from a fluid; bloated: *turgid legs.* **2.** Excessively ornate in style or language; grandiloquent: *turgid prose.* [Lat. *turgidus* < *turgēre,* to be swollen.] **—tur·gid'i·ty** (tûr-jĭd'ĭ-tē), **tur'gid·ness** *n.* **—tur'gid·ly** *adv.*

tur·gor (tûr'gər, -gôr') *n.* **1.** The state of being turgid. **2.** *Biol.* The normal fullness or tension produced by the fluid content of blood vessels, capillaries, and plant or animal cells. [LLat. < Lat. *turgēre,* to be swollen.]

Turk (tûrk) *n.* **1.** A native or inhabitant of Turkey. **2.** A person speaking a Turkic language. **3.** A Moslem. **4.** A brutal or tyrannical person. [ME < OFr. *Turc* < Med. Lat. *Turcus* < Turk. *Türk.*]

tur·key (tûr'kē) *n., pl.* **-keys. 1. a.** A large North American bird, *Meleagris gallopavo,* that has brownish plumage and a bare, wattled head and neck and is widely domesticated for food. **b.** A related bird, *Agriocharis ocellata,* of Mexico and Central America. **2.** *Slang.* Something, esp. a theatrical production, that is a failure. **3.** *Slang.* A person regarded as being inept or undesirable. [After *Turkey,* from a confusion with the guinea fowl imported from Turkish territory.]

turkey buzzard *n.* A New World vulture, *Cathartes aura,* having dark plumage and a bare red head and neck similar to that of the turkey.

turkey cock *n.* **1.** A male turkey. **2.** A strutting, conceited person.

Turkey red *n.* A moderate red.

turkey trot *n.* A ragtime dance characterized by a springy walk with the feet well apart and a swinging up-and-down movement of the shoulders.

turkey vulture *n.* A turkey buzzard.

Tur·ki (tûr'kē) *adj.* **1.** Of or pertaining to Turkic. **2.** Of or pertaining to the Turks, esp. those speaking an Eastern Turkic language. —*n.* **1.** Any of the Turkic languages. **2.** A member of a people speaking a Turkic language. [Pers. *turkī* < *Turk,* Turk < Turk. *Türk.*]

Turk·ic (tûr'kĭk) *n.* A subfamily of the Altaic language family that includes Turkish. —*adj.* **1.** Of or pertaining to the Turks. **2.** Of or pertaining to Turkic.

Turk·ish (tûr'kĭsh) *adj.* **1.** Of or relating to Turkey or the Turks. **2.** Of or relating to the Turkic language of Turkey. —*n.* The Turkic language of Turkey.

Turkish bath *n.* **1.** A steam bath that induces heavy perspiration in the bather and is followed by a shower and massage. **2.** An establishment where facilities are available for Turkish baths.

Turkish coffee *n.* A sweetened brew of pulverized coffee.

Turkish delight *n.* A candy usually consisting of jellylike cubes covered with powdered sugar.

Turkish towel *n.* A thick towel with a nap of uncut pile.

Turk·ism (tûr'kĭz'əm) *n.* The cultural, religious, or social system of the Turks.

Tur·ko·man also **Tur·co·man** (tûr'kə-mən) *n., pl.* **-mans. 1.** Any of a formerly nomadic people inhabiting the Turkmen, Uzbek, Kazakh, and Kara-Kalpak republics of the U.S.S.R. **2.** The Turkic language of the Turkomans. —*adj.* **1.** Of or pertaining to Turkoman. **2.** Of or pertaining to the Turkomans. [Med. Lat. *Turcomannus* < Pers. *Turkuman* < *Turkmān,* like a Turk < *Turk,* Turk < Turk. *Türk.*]

Turk's-cap lily (tûrks'kăp') *n.* **1.** A North American lily,

Lilium superbum, having orange-red, spotted flowers with reflexed petals. **2.** The martagon.
Turk's-head (tûrks'hĕd') *n. Naut.* A turban-shaped knot made by winding a smaller rope around a larger one.
tur·ma·line (to͝or'mə-lĭn, -lēn') *n.* Variant of **tourmaline.**
tur·mer·ic (tûr'mər-ĭk) *n.* **1.** A plant, *Curcuma longa,* of India, having yellow flowers and an aromatic rootstock. **2.** The powdered rootstock of the turmeric, used as a condiment and as a yellow dye. **3.** Any of several plants having roots similar to those of the turmeric. [OFr. *terre mérite* < Med. Lat. *terra merita* : Lat. *terra,* earth + Lat. *merita,* deserved.]
turmeric paper *n.* Paper saturated with turmeric and used as an indicator for the presence of alkalis, which turn the paper brown, or for boric acid, which turns it red-brown.
tur·moil (tûr'moil') *n.* Utter confusion; extreme agitation; commotion; tumult: *a country in turmoil over labor strikes.*
turn (tûrn) *v.* **turned, turn·ing, turns.** *—tr.* **1.** To cause to move around a central or focal point; rotate or revolve: *turn a knob.* **2.** To cause to move around in order to achieve a desired result; change the position of by rotating: *turn a window plant frequently so that it keeps its shape.* **3.** To alter or control the functioning of (a mechanical device, for example) by the use of a rotating or similar movement: *turn the dial to the right on the stereo.* **4.** To perform or accomplish by rotating or revolving: *turn a somersault.* **5. a.** To change the position of so that the underside becomes the upperside: *turn the steak; turn a page.* **b.** To spade or plow (soil) to bring the undersoil to the surface. **c.** To reverse and resew the material of (a collar, for example). **6. a.** To produce a rounded shape in (wood, for example) by applying a cutting tool. **b.** To produce a rounded form in by any means: *turn a heel in knitting a sock.* **c.** To shape or form: *turn a vase on a potter's wheel.* **d.** To give distinctive, artistic, or graceful form to: *turn a phrase.* **7. a.** To change the position of by traversing an arc of a circle; pivot: *turned his chair toward the speaker.* **b.** To change the position of by folding, twisting, or bending: *turn the blankets down.* **c.** To injure by twisting: *turn an ankle.* **d.** To upset or make nauseated: *That turns my stomach.* **8.** To change the direction or course of: *turn the car to the left.* **9. a.** To divert or deflect: *turn a stampede.* **b.** To reverse the course of; cause to retreat. **10.** To make a course around or about: *turn the corner.* **11.** To change the purpose, intention, or content of by persuasion or influence: *His speech turned my thinking.* **12.** To change the order or disposition of; unsettle: *"Sudden prosperity had turned Garrick's head."* (Macaulay). **13.** To set in a specified way or direction; point. **14.** To aim or focus; train: *turn one's gaze to the sky.* **15.** To devote or apply (oneself, for example) to something: *He turned himself to music.* **16.** To become, reach, or surpass (a certain age, time, or amount): *The price had turned ten dollars by the next bid.* **17.** To cause to act or go against; make antagonistic: *She turned his sister against him.* **18.** To cause to go in any direction; direct: *They turned their way back.* **19.** To send, drive, or let go: *turn the braggart out of the bar.* **20.** To pour, let fall, or otherwise release (contents) from a receptacle: *turn the dough onto a floured board.* **21.** To make sour; ferment: *Lack of refrigeration turned the milk.* **22.** To affect or change the color of: *Autumn turns the foliage.* **23.** To change; transform: *turn a run-down house into a showplace.* **24.** To exchange; convert: *turns her singing talent into extra money.* **25.** To cause to take on a specified character, nature, or appearance. **26. a.** To fold, bend, or curve (something). **b.** To make a bend or curve in: *He could turn a bar of steel.* **c.** To blunt or dull (the edge of a cutting instrument). **27.** To keep in circulation; sell and restock: *We turned a great deal of merchandise during the holidays.* **28.** To get by buying and selling: *turn a fair profit.* *—intr.* **1.** To move around an axis or center; rotate or revolve: *wheels turning at a rapid rate.* **2.** To have a sensation of revolving or whirling, esp. as a result of dizziness or giddiness. **3.** To roll from side to side or back and forth: *I tossed and turned all night.* **4. a.** To operate a lathe. **b.** To be formed on a lathe. **5.** To direct one's way or course. **6.** To change or reverse one's way, course, or direction. **7.** To have a specific reaction or effect, esp. when adverse. **8.** To change one's actions or attitudes adversely; become hostile or antagonistic: *All the world has turned against him.* **9.** To attack suddenly and violently with no apparent motive: *The animal turned on the children.* **10.** To channel one's attention, interest, or thought toward or away from something. **11.** To convert from one religion to another. **12.** To switch one's loyalty from one side or party to another. **13.** To have recourse to a person or thing for help, support, or information. **14.** To devote or apply oneself to something, as to a field of study. **15.** To depend upon something for success or failure; rely: *The game turned on the play of the quarterback.* **16.** To change; become transformed. **17.** To change color: *The leaves have turned.* **18.** To be stocked and easily sold: *This merchandise will turn easily.* **19.** To become dull or blunt after bending back. Used of the edge of a cutting instrument. ***—phrasal verbs.*** **turn away. 1.** To send away; dismiss: *turned the salesman away.* **2.** To avert; deflect: *turned away all criticism.* **3.** To begin to leave. **turn back. 1. a.** To cease to go forward. **b.** To move in a reverse direction. **2.** To drive back and away: *stopped on the road and had to turn back to town.* **3.** To halt the advance of: *turned the invaders back.* **4.** To fold back. **turn down. 1.** To diminish the speed, volume, intensity, or flow of. **2.** *Informal.* To reject or refuse, as a person, advice, or a suggestion. **3.** To fold or be capable of folding down: *turn a collar down; a collar that turns down.* **turn in. 1.** To hand in; give over: *turn in an income-tax return.* **2.** To inform on (another); betray. **3.** To produce: *turns in good work.* **4.** To bend inward. **5.** *Informal.* To go to bed. **turn off. 1.** To stop the operation, activity, or flow of; shut off. **2.** To dismiss (an employee). **3.** *Slang.* **a.** To affect with dislike, displeasure, or revulsion: *Her behavior turns me off.* **b.** To affect with boredom: *a play that turned the audience off.* **c.** To lose or cause to lose interest; withdraw: *kids turning off to school.* **4.** To divert; deflect. **5.** To leave a path or road at one point and enter another: *turned off at the first exit.* **turn on. 1.** To cause to begin the operation, activity, or flow of: *turn on the light bulb; turn on the charm.* **2.** *Slang.* **a.** To smoke or ingest a drug for the purpose of experiencing a heightened sensual response. **b.** To be or cause to become interested or pleasurably excited or stimulated: *Surfing turns her on.* **c.** To excite or become excited sexually. **turn out. 1.** To shut off, as a light. **2.** To arrive or assemble, as for a public event or entertainment. **3.** To produce by a given process; make: *an assembly line turning out cars.* **4.** To be found to be, as after experience or trial: *The machine turned out to be in perfect repair.* **5.** To end up; result: *The cake turned out beautifully.* **6.** To equip; outfit. **7.** *Informal.* To get out of bed. **8.** To evict; expel: *turned his tenants out.* **turn over. 1.** To bring the bottom to the top or vice versa; reverse in position. **2.** To shift the position of, as by rolling from one side to the other. **3.** To rotate: *The engine won't turn over in cold weather.* **4.** To think about; consider. **5. a.** To transfer to another; give over. **b.** To give up. **6.** To do business to the extent or amount of: *turn over a million dollars a year.* **7.** To seem to lurch or heave convulsively: *My stomach turned over at the carnage.* **turn to. 1.** To begin work on. **2.** To refer to, as for information or support. **turn up. 1. a.** To find: *He turned up the missing papers under his blotter.* **b.** To be found: *The papers will turn up sooner or later.* **2.** To make an appearance; arrive. **3.** To happen unexpectedly: *Something turned up and I was unable to go.* **4.** To be evident: *His name turns up in gossip columns.* *—n.* **1.** The act of turning or the condition of being turned; rotation; revolution. **2.** A change of direction, motion, or position: *a right turn.* **3.** A departure or deviation, as in a trend: *a turn of events.* **4.** A point of change in time: *at the turn of the century.* **5. a.** A chance or opportunity to do something. **b.** One of a series of such opportunities accorded individuals in succession or in scheduled order: *waiting his turn at bat.* **6.** A period of participation in something: *a turn at creative writing.* **7.** A characteristic mood, style, or habit; natural inclination: *a curious and speculative turn of mind.* **8.** A propensity or adeptness: *a turn for carpentry.* **9.** A movement or development in a particular direction: *a turn for the worse.* **10.** A deed or action having a specified effect on another: *"He thought some friend had done him an ill turn"* (Stephen Crane). **11.** Advantage or purpose: *It served his turn.* **12.** A short tour or excursion: *a turn in the park.* **13.** A twist or other distortion in shape. **14.** The condition of being twisted or wound. **15. a.** A winding of one thing about another. **b.** A single wind or convolution, as of wire upon a spool. **16.** *Mus.* A figure or ornament consisting of four or more notes in rapid succession and including in addition to the principal note the one that is a degree above and the one that is a degree below it. **17.** An attack of illness or severe nervousness; spell. **18.** *Informal.* A momentary shock or scare: *I had quite a turn when I first heard the news.* **19.** A variation of kind or type: *"his muse occasionally takes a humorous and satirical turn"* (Albert C. Baugh). **20. a.** A brief theatrical act: *the turns of a vaudeville show.* **b.** A performer in such an act. **c.** A histrionic or overdramatic performance. **21. a.** A transaction on the stock market involving both a sale and a purchase. **b.** A similar commercial transaction. ***—idioms.*** **at every turn.** In every place; at every moment. **by turns.** One after another; alternately. **in turn.** In the proper order or sequence. **out of turn. 1.** Not in the proper order or sequence. **2.** At an inappropriate time or in an inappropriate manner. **take turns.** To take part or do in order, one after another. **to a turn.** To a precise degree; perfectly: *The roast was done to a turn.* **turn a blind eye.** To refuse to see: *turned a blind eye to government corruption.* **turn a deaf ear.** To refuse to listen to or hear: *turned a deaf ear to her protests.* **turn a hair.** To become afraid or upset: *didn't turn a hair during the holdup.* **turn loose. 1.** To set free; release. **2.** To fire off; discharge: *turned loose the heavy guns.* **turn (one's) back on. 1.** To deny; reject. **2.** To abandon; forsake. **turn (one's) hand.** To apply oneself to a task. **turn (one's) head. 1.** To become infatuated. **2.** To be egotistical and conceited: *Success has turned his head.* **turn over a new leaf.** To change for the better. **turn tail.** To run away. **turn the other cheek.** To respond to insult or injury with patience and eschew retaliation. **turn the scales.** To tip the scales in another direction: *a decisive battle that turned*

Turk's-head

the scales in our favor. **turn the tables.** To reverse the fortunes of two contending parties. **turn the trick.** To accomplish a desired goal or end. **turn up (one's) nose.** To regard with disdain or scorn: *turned up her nose at the food.* [ME *turnen* < OE *tyrnan* and OFr. *tourner, torner,* both < Lat. *tornare,* to turn in a lathe < *tornus,* lathe < Gk. *tornos.*]

Synonyms: *turn, rotate, revolve, gyrate, spin, whirl, circle, eddy, swirl, swivel, roll.* These verbs all refer to movement in a pattern that is circular or approximately so. *Turn* can mean to move around an axis or pivot or to travel around a relatively fixed object in the way that planets move around the sun. In either case a complete or partial circular course is indicated. *Rotate* and *revolve,* which generally imply repeated movement in a complete course, are narrower. *Rotate* involves movement around an object's own axis or center: *The earth rotates. A wheel rotates on its axle. Revolve* primarily involves the other sense of turning, that of orbital movement, as of the earth around the sun; less often the term applies to rotation. *Gyrate* can refer to either revolving or rotating movement on a spiral course. *Spin* refers to rapid, continuous rotating movement, usually within a narrow compass: *A top spins. Automobile wheels spin on ice. Whirl* applies to continuous revolving or rotating movement at high speed. *Circle* can refer to any circular movement, including that which encompasses something. *Eddy* usually refers to rapid movement of water or air in a circular course contrary to the main current; a whirlpool is a product of such action. *Swirl* is interchangeable with either *whirl* or *eddy,* depending on the context involved. *Swivel* usually refers to circular movement in a horizontal plane from a fixed position or pivot. *Roll,* in this comparison, specifies movement of a curved object, such as a wheel, over a surface with which the object's circumference is in continuous contact.

turnbuckle

turnip

turn·a·bout (tûrn′ə-bout′) *n.* **1.** The act of turning about and facing or moving in the opposite direction. **2.** A shift or change in opinion, loyalty, or allegiance. **3.** *Regional.* A dance or party to which girls invite boys.

turn·a·round (tûrn′ə-round′) *n.* **1.** A space, as in a driveway, permitting the turning around of a vehicle. **2.** The time needed to load, unload, and service a vehicle, as a ship or airplane. **3.** An act or instance of turning about and facing or moving in the opposite direction.

turn·buck·le (tûrn′bŭk′əl) *n.* A metal coupling device, used for tightening a rod or wire rope, consisting of an oblong piece internally threaded at both ends into which a threaded rod is screwed.

turn·coat (tûrn′kōt′) *n.* One who traitorously switches allegiance.

turn·down (tûrn′doun′) *n.* **1.** A rejection. **2.** Something that is turned down. **3.** A downturn.

turned-on (tûrnd′ŏn′,-ôn′) *adj. Slang.* **1.** Highly aware of and responsive to what is fashionable and up-to-date. **2 a.** Pleasantly excited or stimulated. **b.** Sexually aroused.

turn·er¹ (tûr′nər) *n.* One that turns, esp. a person who works a lathe.

tur·ner² (tûr′nər) *n.* A tumbler or gymnast, esp. a member of a turnverein. [G. < *turnen,* to do gymnastics < OHG *turnēn,* to turn < Lat. *tornare,* to turn in a lathe. —see TURN.]

turnpike

turn·er·y (tûr′nə-rē) *n., pl.* **-ies.** The work or workshop of a lathe operator.

turn·ing (tûr′nĭng) *n.* **1.** A deviation from a straight course; turn. **2.** The shaping of metal or wood on a lathe.

turning point *n.* **1.** A point at which a very significant change occurs; decisive moment. **2.** *Math.* A maximum or minimum point on a curve.

tur·nip (tûr′nĭp) *n.* **1.** A widely cultivated plant, *Brassica rapa,* native to the Old World, having a large, edible yellow or white root. **2.** The root of the turnip, eaten as a vegetable. **3.** Any of several plants similar or related to the turnip. **4.** A large, rounded pocket watch. [Perh. TURN (from its rounded shape) + dial. *nepe,* turnip < ME < OE *nǣp* < Lat. *napus.*]

turnip cabbage *n.* Kohlrabi.

turtle¹
Snapping turtle

turn·key (tûrn′kē′) *n., pl.* **-keys.** The keeper of the keys in a prison; jailer.

turn·off (tûrn′ôf′, -ŏf′) *n.* **1.** A branch of a road or path leading from a main thoroughfare, esp. an exit on a highway. **2.** An act or instance of turning off. **3.** *Slang.* **a.** One that is distasteful: *an evening that was a real turnoff.* **b.** Something that causes loss of interest.

turn-on (tûrn′ŏn′, -ôn′) *n. Slang.* Something that causes pleasure or excitement.

turn·out (tûrn′out′) *n.* **1.** The act of turning out. **2.** The number of people at a gathering; attendance. **3.** A number of things produced; output. **4.** *Chiefly Brit.* **a.** A labor strike. **b.** A laborer on strike. **5.** An array of equipment; outfit. **6.** An outfit of a carriage with its horse or horses; equipage. **7.** A railroad siding. **8.** A widening in a highway to allow vehicles to pass.

turn·o·ver (tûrn′ō′vər) *n.* **1.** The act of turning over; an upset or overthrow. **2.** An abrupt change; reversal. **3.** A small pastry made by covering one half of a piece of dough with fruit, preserves, or other filling and turning the other half over on top. **4.** The number of times a particular stock of goods is sold and restocked during a given period of time. **5.** The amount of business transacted during a given period of time. **6.** The number of shares of stock sold on the market during a given period of time. **7.** The amount of capital loaned on call during a given period of time. **8. a.** The number of workers hired by a given establishment to replace those who have left. **b.** The ratio of this number to the number of employed workers. *—adj.* Capable of being turned or folded down or over, as a collar.

turn·pike (tûrn′pīk′) *n.* **1.** A road, esp. a wide, modern highway with tollgates. **2.** A tollgate. [ME *turnepike,* spiked barrier : *turnen,* to turn + *pike,* pike.]

turn·sole (tûrn′sōl′) *n.* Any of various plants, as the heliotrope, that move or are believed to move in response to the sun. [ME *turnesole,* purple dye obtained from the plant < OFr. *tournesol* < OItal. *tornasole,* heliotrope : *tornare,* to turn (< Lat. *tornare*) + *sole,* sun (< Lat. *sol*).]

turn·spit (tûrn′spĭt′) *n.* **1.** A person who turns a roasting spit. **2.** A dog formerly used in a treadmill to turn a roasting spit.

turn·stile (tûrn′stīl′) *n.* **1.** A mechanical device used to control passage from one public area to another, typically consisting of several horizontal arms supported by and radially projecting from a central vertical post. **2.** A structure similar to a turnstile that permits the passage of persons but not of horses or cattle.

turn·stone (tûrn′stōn′) *n.* Either of two wading birds, *Arenaria interpres,* having predominantly reddish and white plumage, or *A. melanocephala,* having black and white plumage. [From its method of finding food.]

turn·ta·ble (tûrn′tā′bəl) *n.* **1.** A circular, usually horizontal rotating platform equipped with a railway track, used for turning locomotives, as in a roundhouse. **2. a.** The circular horizontal rotating platform of a phonograph on which the record is placed. **b.** A phonograph exclusive of amplifying circuitry and speakers. **3.** A rotating platform or disk, as on a microscope.

turn·up (tûrn′ŭp′) *n.* Something that is turned up or turns up, as the cuffs on trousers. *—adj.* Turned up or capable of being turned up.

turn·ver·ein (tûrn′və-rīn′, to͝orn′-) *n.* A club of turners or gymnasts. [G. : *turnen,* to do gymnastics + *Verein,* club < *vereinen,* to unite.]

tur·pen·tine (tûr′pən-tīn′) *n.* **1.** A thin volatile essential oil, $C_{10}H_{16}$, obtained by steam distillation or other means from the wood or the exudate of certain pine trees and used as a paint thinner, solvent, and medicinally as a liniment. **2.** The sticky mixture of resin and volatile oil from which turpentine is distilled. **3.** A brownish-yellow resinous liquid obtained from the terebinth. *—tr.v.* **-tined, -tin·ing, -tines. 1.** To apply turpentine to or mix turpentine with. **2.** To extract turpentine from (a tree). [ME *terpentin,* resin of the terebinth < OFr. *terbentine* < Lat. *terebinthina* < *terebinthus,* terebinth.] **—tur′pen·tin′ic,** (-tĭn′ĭk), **tur′pen·tin′ous** (-tĭn′əs) *adj.*

tur·peth (tûr′pĭth) *n.* **1.** A vine, *Ipomoea turpethum* or *Operculina turpethum,* of tropical Asia and Australia, having roots that yield a resinous substance used medicinally as a purgative. **2.** The root of the turpeth. [ME, *turbit,* purgative < OFr. < Med. Lat. *turbitum* < Ar. *turbid.*]

tur·pi·tude (tûr′pĭ-to͞od′, -tyo͞od′) *n.* **1.** Baseness; depravity. **2.** A base act. [Lat. *turpitudo* < *turpis,* shameful.]

turps (tûrps) *pl.n. (used with a sing. verb). Informal.* Turpentine. [Shortening and alteration of TURPENTINE.]

tur·quoise (tûr′kwoiz′, -koiz′) *n.* **1.** A blue to blue-green mineral of aluminum and copper, mainly $CuAl_6(PO_4)_4(OH)_8 \cdot 4H_2O$, esteemed as a gemstone in its polished blue form. **2.** A light to brilliant bluish green. [ME *turkeis* < OFr. *turqueise* < *turqueis,* Turkish < *Turc,* Turk.] **—tur′quoise′** *adj.*

tur·ret (tûr′ĭt) *n.* **1.** A small ornamented tower or tower-shaped projection on a building. **2. a.** A low, heavily armored structure, usually rotating horizontally, containing mounted guns and their gunners or crew, as on a warship or tank. **b.** A domelike gunner's enclosure projecting from the fuselage of a military aircraft. **3.** A tall wooden structure mounted on wheels and used in ancient warfare by besiegers to scale the walls of an enemy fortress. **4.** An attachment for a lathe consisting of a rotating, cylindrical block holding various cutting tools. [ME *turet* < OFr. *tourete,* dim. of *tour,* tower < Lat. *turris* < Gk. *tursis.*]

tur·ret·ed (tûr′ĭ-tĭd) *adj.* **1.** Furnished with a turret or turrets. **2.** Having the shape or form of a turret, as certain long-spired gastropod shells.

tur·tle¹ (tûr′tl) *n.* **1.** Any of various reptiles of the order Chelonia, having horny, toothless jaws and the body enclosed in a bony or leathery shell into which the head, limbs, and tail can be withdrawn in most species. **2.** *Chiefly Brit.* A marine chelonian. *—intr.v.* **-tled, -tling, -tles.** To hunt for turtles, esp. as an occupation. [Perh. < Fr. *tortue.*]

tur·tle² (tûr′tl) *n. Archaic.* A turtledove. [ME < OE < Lat. *turtur.*]

tur·tle³ (tûr′tl) *n.* A turtleneck.

tur·tle·dove (tûr′tl-dŭv′) *n.* **1.** A slender European dove, *Streptopelia turtur,* having a white-edged tail and a soft, purring voice. **2.** The mourning dove.

tur·tle·head (tûr′tl-hĕd′) *n.* Any of several plants of the ge-

nus *Chelone*, esp. *C. glabra*, of eastern North America, having white or pink flowers.
tur·tle·neck (tûr'tl-nĕk') *n.* **1.** A high, turned-down collar that fits closely about the neck. **2.** A sweater or other garment having a turtleneck.
turves (tûrvz) *n. Archaic.* Plural of **turf**.
Tus·can (tŭs'kən) *adj.* **1.** Of or pertaining to Tuscany or to its people. **2.** *Archit.* Of or pertaining to the Tuscan order. —*n.* **1.** A native or inhabitant of Tuscany. **2. a.** Any of the dialects of Italian spoken in Tuscany. **b.** The standard literary form of Italian. [Lat. *Tuscanus* < *Tuscus*, Etruscan.]
Tuscan order *n. Archit.* A classical order similar to Roman Doric, but having an unfluted shaft with a simplified base, capital, and entablature.
Tus·ca·ro·ra (tŭs'kə-rôr'ə, -rōr'ə) *n., pl.* **Tuscarora** or **-ras.** **1.** A tribe of North American Indians formerly inhabiting North Carolina and now living in New York and Ontario. **2.** A member of the Tuscarora tribe. **3.** The Iroquoian language of the Tuscarora. [Tuscarora *Skărūeⁿ*.]
tu·sche (to͝osh'ə) *n.* A black substance used for drawing in lithography and as a resist in etching and silk-screen work. [G., back-formation < *tuschen*, to lay on colors < Fr. *toucher* < OFr. *tochier*, to touch.]
tush[1] (tŭsh) *interj.* Used to express mild reproof, disapproval, or admonition: *Tush, tush, my dear, it's nothing.* [ME *tussch.*]
tush[2] (tŭsh) *n.* A tusk. —*tr.v.* **tushed, tush·ing, tush·es.** To tusk. [ME *tusche* < OE *tūsc.*]
tush[3] (to͝osh) *n. Slang.* The buttocks. [Yiddish *toches.*]
tush·y also **tush·ie** (to͝osh'ē) *n., pl.* **-ies.** *Slang.* Tush[3].
tusk (tŭsk) *n.* **1.** An elongated, pointed tooth, usually one of a pair, extending outside of the mouth in certain animals such as the walrus, elephant, or wild boar. **2.** A long, projecting tooth or toothlike part. —*tr.v.* **tusked, tusk·ing, tusks.** To dig or gore with the tusks or a tusk. [ME < OE *tūsc.*]
tusk·er (tŭs'kər) *n.* An animal bearing tusks, such as a wild boar.
tusk shell *n.* A tooth shell.
tus·sah (tŭs'ə, tŭs'ô') also **tus·sore** (tŭs'ôr', -ōr') *n.* **1.** An undomesticated Asian silkworm, *Antheraea paphia*, that produces a coarse brownish or yellowish silk. **2.** The silk produced by the tussah or a fabric woven from it. [Hindi *tasar* < Skt. *tasaram*, shuttle.]
tus·sis (tŭs'ĭs) *n.* A cough. [Lat.] —**tus'sal** (tŭs'əl), **tus'sive** (tŭs'ĭv) *adj.*
tus·sle (tŭs'əl) *intr.v.* **-sled, -sling, -sles.** To struggle; scuffle. —*n.* A rough-and-tumble struggle; scuffle. [ME *tussillen*, freq. of *tousen*, to pull roughly.]
tus·sock (tŭs'ək) *n.* **1.** A clump or tuft of growing grass or a similar plant. **2.** A tuft of hair or feathers. [Orig. unknown.] —**tus'sock·y** *adj.*
tussock moth *n.* Any of various moths of the family Lymantriidae, having hairy caterpillars that are often destructive to deciduous trees.
tut (tŭt) *interj.* Used to express annoyance, impatience, or mild reproof.
tu·tee (to͞o-tē', tyo͞o-) *n.* One who is being tutored. [TUT(OR) + -EE[1].]
tu·te·lage (to͞ot'l-ĭj, tyo͞ot'-) *n.* **1.** The function or capacity of a guardian; guardianship. **2.** The act or capacity of a tutor; instruction; teaching. **3.** The state of being under a guardian or tutor. [Lat. *tutela* < *tueri*, to guard.]
tu·te·lar·y (to͞ot'l-ĕr'ē, tyo͞ot'-) also **tu·te·lar** (to͞ot'l-ər, -är', tyo͞ot'-). —*adj.* **1.** Being or serving as a guardian or protector: *tutelary gods.* **2.** Of or relating to a guardian or guardianship. —*n., pl.* **-lar·ies** also **-lars.** One that has tutelary powers. [< Lat. *tutelarius*, guardianship < *tutelaris*, tutelar < *tutela*, tutelage < *tueri*, to guard.]
tu·tor (to͞o'tər, tyo͞o'-) *n.* **1. a.** A private instructor. **b.** One who gives additional, special, or remedial instruction. **2.** A teacher or teaching assistant in some universities and colleges having a rank lower than that of an instructor. **3.** A graduate responsible for the special supervision of an undergraduate at some British universities. **4.** *Law.* The guardian of a minor and of his property. —*v.* **-tored, -tor·ing, -tors.** —*tr.* **1.** To act as a tutor to; instruct or teach privately. **2.** To have the guardianship, tutelage, or care of. —*intr.* **1.** To function as a tutor or private instructor. **2.** To be instructed by or study under a tutor. [ME *tutour* < OFr. < Lat. *tutor* < *tueri*, to guard.] —**tu·to'ri·al** (to͞o-tôr'ē-əl, -tōr'-, tyo͞o-) *adj.* —**tu'tor·ship'** —*n.*
tutorial system *n.* An instructional system in which college or university tutors are responsible for the special supervision of students individually or in small groups.
tut·ti (to͞o'tē) *Mus.* —*adj. & adv.* All. Used as a direction to indicate that all performers are to take part. —*n., pl.* **tut·tis.** A passage of ensemble music intended to be executed by all the performers simultaneously. [Ital., pl. of *tutto*, all < Lat. *totus.*]
tut·ti-frut·ti (to͞o'tē-fro͞o'tē) *n.* **1.** A confection, esp. ice cream, containing a variety of chopped candied fruits. **2.** A flavoring simulating the flavor of many fruits. —*adj.* Having a combination of fruit flavors. [Ital. : *tutti*, all + *frutti*, fruits.]
tut·ty (tŭt'ē) *n.* An impure zinc oxide obtained as a sublimate from the flues of zinc-smelting furnaces and used as a polishing powder. [ME < OFr. < Ar. *tūtiyā.*]
tu·tu (to͞o'to͞o) *n.* A very short ballet skirt consisting of many layers of gathered sheer fabric. [Fr.]
tux·e·do (tŭk-sē'dō) *n., pl.* **-dos** or **-does.** **1.** A man's usually dark jacket with satin or grosgrain lapels worn for formal or semiformal occasions. **2.** A complete outfit including a tuxedo jacket, black trousers with a stripe down the side, and a black bow tie. [After *Tuxedo* Park, New York.]
tu·yère (twē-yâr') *n.* The pipe, nozzle, or other opening through which air is forced into a blast furnace or forge to facilitate combustion. [Fr. < OFr. *tuyere* < *tuyau*, pipe.]
TV (tē'vē') *n, pl.* **TVs** or **TV's.** Television.
TV Dinner. A trademark for a packaged frozen meal that only needs to be heated before serving.
twad·dle (twŏd'l) *intr.v.* **-dled, -dling, -dles.** To talk foolishly; prate. —*n.* **1.** Foolish, trivial, or idle talk or chatter. **2.** Silly pretentious speech or writing. [Prob. var. of dial. *twattle.*] —**twad'dler** *n.*
twain (twān) *adj. Archaic.* Two. —*n.* **1.** A set of two: *"Oh, East is East, and West is West, and never the twain shall meet"* (Kipling). **2.** The two-fathom mark on a sounding line used on riverboats. [ME *twayne* < OE *twēgen.*]
twang (twăng) *v.* **twanged, twang·ing, twangs.** —*intr.* **1.** To emit a sharp, vibrating sound, as the string of a musical instrument when plucked: *guitars twanging in the night.* **2.** To resound with a sharp, vibrating sound. —*tr.* **1.** To cause to make a sharp, vibrating sound. **2.** To utter with an excessively nasal tone of voice. —*n.* **1.** A sharp, vibrating sound, as that of a plucked string. **2.** An excessively nasal tone of voice, esp. as a peculiarity of certain regional dialects. [Imit.] —**twang'y** *adj.*
tway·blade (twā'blād') *n.* Any of various small terrestrial orchids of the genera *Liparis* and *Listera*, having two basal leaves and a terminal cluster of greenish or purplish flowers. [Obs. *tway*, two + BLADE.]
tweak (twēk) *tr.v.* **tweaked, tweak·ing, tweaks.** To pinch, pluck, or twist sharply. —*n.* A sharp, twisting pinch. [Prob. var. of dial. *twick* < ME *twikken* < OE *twiccian.*] —**tweak'y** *adj.*
tweed (twēd) *n.* **1.** A coarse, rugged, often nubby woolen fabric made in any of various twill weaves and used chiefly for casual suits and coats. **2. tweeds.** Clothing made of tweed: *wear tweeds to the races.* [Alteration of Sc. *tweel*, twill < ME *twyl.*]
twee·dle·dum and twee·dle·dee (twēd'l-dŭm' ən twēd'-l-dē') *n.* Two persons or groups resembling each other so closely that they are practically indistinguishable. [After *Tweedledum* and *Tweedledee*, proverbial rival fiddlers, imit. of low and high musical notes.]
tweed·y (twē'dē) *adj.* **-i·er, -i·est.** **1.** Made of or similar to tweed. **2. a.** Wearing tweeds. **b.** *Informal.* Suggestive of casual, informal taste, habits, and lifestyle: *a tweedy, preppy look.* —**tweed'i·ness** *n.*
'tween (twēn) *prep.* Between.
tweet (twēt) *intr.v.* **tweet·ed, tweet·ing, tweets.** To utter a weak, chirping sound, as a young or small bird. —*n.* A weak, chirping sound. [Imit.]
tweet·er (twē'tər) *n.* A loudspeaker designed to reproduce high-pitched sounds in a high-fidelity audio system.
tweeze (twēz) *tr.v.* **tweezed, tweez·ing, tweez·es.** To handle or extract with tweezers. [Back-formation < TWEEZERS.]
tweez·ers (twē'zərz) *pl.n.* A small, usually metal, pincerlike tool used for plucking or handling small objects. [< obs. *tweeze*, a case of small instruments < Fr. *étui*, étui. —see ÉTUI.]
twelfth (twĕlfth) *n.* **1.** The ordinal number that matches the number 12 in a series. **2.** One of 12 equal parts. **3.** *Mus.* **a.** A 12-degree interval in a diatonic scale. **b.** A tone 12 degrees below or above a given tone. [ME *twelfthe* < OE *twelfta.*] —**twelfth** *adj. & adv.*
Twelfth-day (twĕlfth'dā') *n.* The day of Epiphany, January 6, 12 days after Christmas.
Twelfth-night (twĕlfth'nīt') *n.* The evening of January 5, before Twelfth-day.
Twelfth·tide (twĕlfth'tīd') *n.* The season of Epiphany.
twelve (twĕlv) *n.* **1.** The cardinal number that is next after the number 11 and equal to the sum of 11 + 1. **2.** The twelfth in a series. [ME < OE *twelf.*] —**twelve** *adj. & pron.*
twelve·mo (twĕlv'mō') *n., pl.* **-mos.** Duodecimo (sense 2).
twelve·month (twĕlv'mŭnth') *n.* A year.
twelve-tone (twĕlv'tōn') *adj. Mus.* Relating to, consisting of, or based on an atonal arrangement of the traditional 12 chromatic tones.
twen·ti·eth (twĕn'tē-ĭth) *n.* **1.** The ordinal number that matches the number 20 in a series. **2.** One of 20 equal parts. —**twen'ti·eth** *adj. & adv.*
twen·ty (twĕn'tē) *n.* The cardinal number equal to 2 × 10. [ME < OE *twēntig.*] —**twen'ty** *adj. & pron.*
twen·ty-one (twĕn'tē-wŭn') *n. Games.* Blackjack[1] (sense 3).
twen·ty-twen·ty or **20/20** (twĕn'tē-twĕn'tē) *adj.* Having normal visual acuity. [From a method of testing vision by reading charts at a distance of 20 feet.]
twerp also **twirp** (twûrp) *n. Slang.* A silly, contemptible person. [Orig. unknown.]

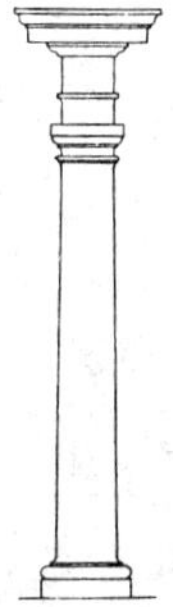

Tuscan order

tutu

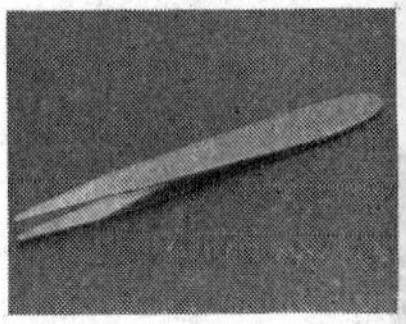

tweezers

Twi also **Tshi** (chwē, chē) *n.* A language of western Africa spoken esp. by the Ashanti.

twi·bil also **twi·bill** (twī′bĭl′) *n.* **1.** A battle-ax with two cutting edges. **2.** A mattock with one arm like an ax and the other like an adz. [ME < OE : *twi-,* two + *bil,* billhook.]

twice (twīs) *adv.* **1.** In two cases or on two occasions; two times. **2.** In doubled degree or amount: *twice as many.* [ME < OE *twiga*]

twice-laid (twīs′lād′) *adj.* Made from strands of old or used rope.

twice-told twīs′tōld′) *adj.* Very familiar due to repeated telling: *twice-told tales.*

twid·dle (twĭd′l) *v.* **-dled, -dling, -dles.** —*tr.* To turn over or around idly or lightly; fiddle with. —*intr.* **1.** To trifle with something. **2.** To be busy about trifles. **3.** To twirl or rotate without purpose. —*n.* The act of twiddling; an idle, twirling motion. —***idiom.*** **twiddle one's thumbs. 1.** To twirl one's thumbs idly around each other. **2.** To do little or nothing; be idle. [Poss. a blend of TWIRL and FIDDLE.] —**twid′dler** *n.*

twig[1] (twĭg) *n.* A small branch or slender shoot, as of a tree or shrub. [ME < OE *twigge.*]

twig[2] (twĭg) *v.* **twigged, twig·ging, twigs.** *Chiefly Brit.* —*tr.* **1.** To observe or watch; notice. **2.** To understand. —*intr.* To be aware of the situation; understand. [Ir. Gael. *tuigim,* I understand.]

twig[3] twĭg) *n. Chiefly Brit.* The current style; fashion. [Orig. unknown.]

twig·gen (twĭg′ən) *adj.* Constructed of twigs; wicker.

twig·gy (twĭg′ē) *adj.* **-gi·er, -gi·est. 1.** Resembling a twig or twigs; slender; fragile. **2.** Abounding in twigs.

twi·light (twī′līt′) *n.* **1. a.** The time interval during which the sun is below the horizon at an angle less than any of several standard angular distances. **b.** The state of illumination of the atmosphere during this interval, esp. after a sunset. **2.** Any dim or faint illumination. **3.** Any period or condition of decline following growth, glory, or success: *in the twilight of his life.* —*adj.* Pertaining to or characteristic of twilight. [ME *twylyghte.*]

twilight sleep *n.* An amnesic condition characterized by the absence of sensibility to pain without loss of consciousness that is induced by an injection of morphine and scopolamine administered during labor in childbirth.

twill (twĭl) *n.* **1.** A fabric with diagonal parallel ribs. **2.** The weave used to produce twill. —*tr.v.* **twilled, twill·ing, twills.** To weave (cloth) so as to produce the pattern of twill. [ME *twyl* < OE *twilic.*]

twilled (twĭld) *adj.* Woven so as to have diagonal parallel ribs.

twin (twĭn) *n.* **1.** One of two offspring born at the same birth. **2.** One of two identical or similar persons, animals, or things; counterpart. **3. Twins.** Gemini. **4. twins.** Two interwoven crystals in which unlike faces are parallel. —*adj.* **1.** Being two or one of two offspring born at the same birth. **2.** Being one of two identical or similar persons, animals, or things: *a twin bed.* **3.** Consisting of two identical or similar related or connected parts. —*v.* **twinned, twin·ning, twins.** —*intr.* **1.** To give birth to twins. **2.** *Archaic.* To be one of twin offspring. **3.** To be paired or coupled. —*tr.* **1.** To pair or couple. **2.** To provide a match or counterpart to. [ME < OE *twinn,* twofold.]

twin·ber·ry (twĭn′bĕr′ē) *n.* The partridgeberry.

twine (twīn) *v.* **twined, twin·ing, twines.** —*tr.* **1.** To twist together; intertwine, as threads. **2.** To form by twisting, intertwining, or interlacing. **3.** To encircle or coil about: *A vine twined the fencepost.* **4.** To wind, coil, or wrap around something. —*intr.* **1.** To become twisted, interlaced, or interwoven. **2.** To go in a winding course; twist about: *a stream twining through the forest.* —*n.* **1.** A strong string or cord formed of two or more threads twisted together. **2.** Something formed by twining: *a twine of bread dough.* **3.** A tangle; knot. [ME *twinen* < *twin,* strong string < OE *twīn.*] —**twin′er** *n.*

twinflower

twin·flow·er (twĭn′flou′ər) *n.* A creeping evergreen plant, *Linnaea borealis,* of northern regions, having roundish, evergreen leaves and paired, bell-shaped, pinkish flowers.

twinge (twĭnj) *n.* **1.** A sharp, sudden physical pain. **2.** A mental or emotional pain: *a twinge of conscience.* —*v.* **twinged, twing·ing, twing·es.** —*tr.* **1.** To cause to feel a sharp pain. **2.** *Obs.* To tweak; pinch. —*intr.* To feel a twinge or twinges. [ME *twengen,* to pinch < OE *twengan.*]

twi·night (twī′nīt′) *adj. Baseball.* Designating a doubleheader in which the first game begins in late afternoon. [TWI(LIGHT) + NIGHT.]

twin·kle (twĭng′kəl) *intr.v.* **-kled, -kling, -kles. 1.** To shine with slight, intermittent gleams, as distant lights or stars; flicker; glimmer. **2.** To be bright or sparkling: *eyes that twinkled with delight.* **3.** To blink or wink. —*n.* **1.** A slight, intermittent gleam of light; glimmer; a sparkling flash. **2.** A sparkle of merriment or delight in the eye. **3.** A brief interval; twinkling. [ME *twynklen* < OE *twinclian.*] —**twin′kler** *n.*

twin·kling (twĭng′klĭng) *n.* **1.** An act of blinking. **2.** A blink or twinkle. **3.** The time it takes to blink once; an instant.

twin-leaf

twin-leaf (twĭn′lēf′) *n., pl.* **-leaves** (-lēvz′). A woodland plant, *Jeffersonia diphylla,* of eastern North America, having leaves deeply cleft into two lobes, and a solitary white flower.

twinned (twĭnd) *adj.* **1.** Born at a single birth. **2.** Paired or coupled with something identical or similar. **3.** Formed of crystals by the process of twinning.

twin·ning (twĭn′ĭng) *n.* **1.** The bearing of twins. **2.** A pairing or union of two similar or identical objects. **3.** The formation of twin crystals.

twin-screw (twĭn′skrōō′) *adj. Naut.* Having two propellers, one on either side of the keel, that usually revolve in opposite directions.

twin-size (twĭn′sīz′) *adj.* Relating to or being a bed that is 39 inches by 75 inches in dimension.

twirl (twûrl) *v.* **twirled, twirl·ing, twirls.** —*tr.* **1.** To rotate or revolve briskly; swing in a circle; spin. **2.** To twist or wind around: *twirl thread on a spindle.* **3.** *Baseball.* To pitch. —*intr.* **1.** To move or spin around rapidly, suddenly, or repeatedly. **2.** To whirl or turn suddenly; make an about-face. —*n.* **1.** A twirling or being twirled; a quick spinning or twisting. **2.** Something twirled; twist: *a twirl of cotton candy.* [Orig. unknown.] —**twirl′er** *n.*

twirp (twûrp) *n.* Variant of **twerp.**

twist (twĭst) *v.* **twist·ed, twist·ing, twists.** —*tr.* **1. a.** To entwine (two or more threads) so as to produce a single strand. **b.** To form in this manner: *twist a length of rope.* **2.** To wind or coil (vines or rope, for example) about something. **3.** To interlock or interlace: *twist flowers in one's hair.* **4.** To impart a coiling or spiral shape to. **5. a.** To turn or open by turning. **b.** To pull, break, or snap by turning: *twist off a dead branch.* **6.** To wrench or sprain: *twist one's wrist.* **7.** To alter the normal aspect of; contort: *twist one's mouth into a wry smile.* **8.** To alter or distort the intended meaning of: *a cross-examiner who twisted the witness' words.* —*intr.* **1.** To be or become twisted. **2.** To move or progress in a winding course; meander. **3.** To squirm; writhe: *twist with pain.* **4.** To rotate or revolve. **5.** To dance the twist. **6.** To move so as to face in another direction. —*n.* **1.** Something twisted or formed by winding, esp.: **a.** A length of yarn, cord, or thread, esp. a strong silk thread used mainly to bind the edges of buttonholes. **b.** Tobacco leaves processed into the form of a rope or roll. **c.** Bread or other bakery products for which the dough was twisted before baking. **d.** A sliver of citrus peel twisted over or dropped into a beverage to impart flavor. **2.** The act of twisting or the condition of being twisted; a spin or twirl; rotation. **3.** A spinning motion given to a ball when thrown or struck in a specific way. **4. a.** The state of being twisted into a spiral; torsional stress or strain. **b.** The degree or angle of such stress. **5.** A sprain or wrench, as of a muscle. **6.** An unexpected change in a process or a departure from a pattern, often producing a distortion or perversion: *a twist of fate; story with a quirky twist.* **7.** A contortion or distortion, as of the face. **8.** A personal inclination or eccentricity; penchant or flaw: *a twist to his character.* **9.** A dance characterized by vigorous arm and hip motions. [ME *twisten.*] —**twist′a·bil′i·ty** *n.* —**twist′a·ble** *adj.* —**twist′ing·ly** *adv.*

twist drill *n.* A drill having deep helical grooves along the shank from the point.

twist·er (twĭs′tər) *n.* **1.** One that twists. **2.** A ball thrown or batted with a twist. **3.** *Informal.* **a.** A cyclone. **b.** A tornado.

twit (twĭt) *tr.v.* **twit·ted, twit·ting, twits.** To taunt, ridicule, or tease, esp. for embarrassing mistakes or faults. —*n.* **1.** The act of twitting. **2.** A reproach, gibe, or taunt. **3.** *Chiefly Brit. Slang.* An idiot. [ME *atwiten* < OE *ætwītan* : *æt,* at + *wītan,* to reproach.]

twitch (twĭch) *v.* **twitched, twitch·ing, twitch·es.** —*tr.* To draw, pull, or move suddenly and sharply; jerk: *The fisherman twitched his line.* —*intr.* **1.** To move jerkily or spasmodically. **2.** To ache sharply from time to time; twinge. —*n.* **1.** A sudden involuntary or spasmodic muscular movement: *a twitch in the eye.* **2.** A sudden pulling; tug. **3.** *Western U.S.* A looped cord used to restrain a horse by tightening it around the animal's upper lip. [ME *twicchen.*] —**twitch′ing·ly** *adv.*

twitch grass *n.* Couch grass.

twit·ter[1] (twĭt′ər) *v.* **-tered, -ter·ing, -ters.** —*intr.* **1.** To utter a succession of light chirping or tremulous sounds, as a bird; chirrup. **2.** To titter. **3.** To tremble with nervous agitation or excitement. —*tr.* To utter or say with a twitter: *She twittered her greeting.* —*n.* **1.** The light chirping sounds made by certain birds. **2.** Light, tremulous speech or laughter. **3.** A state of agitation or excitement; flutter. [ME *twiteren.*] —**twit′ter·er** *n.* —**twit′ter·y** *adj.*

twit·ter[2] (twĭt′ər) *n.* One who twits.

twixt also **'twixt** (twĭkst) *prep.* Betwixt.

two (tōō) *n.* **1.** The cardinal number that is next after the number 1 and equal to the sum of 1 + 1. **2.** The second in a set or sequence. **3.** Something having two parts, units, or members, esp. a playing card, die, or domino with two pips. [ME < OE *twā* : akin to G. *zwei,* Lat. *duo,* Gk. *duo,* Skt. *dva.*] —**two** *adj. & pron.*

two-base hit (tōō′bās′) *n. Baseball.* A hit enabling the batter to reach second base; double.

two-bit (tōō′bĭt′) *adj. Slang.* Worth very little; cheap; insignificant.

two bits *pl.n. Informal.* **1.** Twenty-five cents. **2.** A petty sum.

two-by-four (tōō′bī-fôr′, -fōr′, tōō′bə-) *adj.* **1.** Measuring two by four inches, or in the same ratio in other units. **2.** *Informal.* Small in size; boxed-in; cramped: *a two-by-four apartment.* —*n.* A length of lumber measuring $1\frac{5}{8}$ inches in thickness and $3\frac{3}{8}$ inches in width.

two cents worth *n.* An opinion: *got in his two cents worth about the new policy.*

two-di·men·sion·al (to͞o′dĭ-mĕn′shə-nəl) *adj.* **1.** Having only two dimensions, esp. length and width; planar; flat. **2.** Lacking dimension or completion; limited in range or depth.

two-edged (to͞o′ĕjd′) *adj.* **1.** Having a keen edge on both sides, as a razor or sword blade. **2.** Having two contrasting effects, meanings, or interpretations.

two-faced (to͞o′fāst′) *adj.* **1.** Having two faces or surfaces. **2.** Hypocritical or double-dealing; deceitful. **—two′-fac′ed·ly** (to͞o′fā′sĭd-lē, -fāst′lē) *adv.* **—two′-fac′ed·ness** *n.*

two-fer also **two·fer** (to͞o′fər) *n. Informal.* **1.** A special offer of two tickets, as for a play or show, for the price of one. **2.** Any cheap, discounted item. [Shortening and alteration of *two for the price of one.*]

two-fisted (to͞o′fĭs′tĭd) *adj. Informal.* Aggressive; virile; vigorous: *a two-fisted drinker.*

two·fold (to͞o′fōld′, -fōld′) *adj.* **1.** Having two components. **2.** Having twice as much or twice as many; double. —*adv.* Two times as much or as many; doubly.

two-hand·ed (to͞o′hăn′dĭd) *adj.* **1.** Requiring the use of two hands at once: *a two-handed sledgehammer.* **2.** Made to be operated by two people. **3.** Able to use both hands with equal facility; ambidextrous. **4.** Having two hands.

two iron *n. Sports.* A midiron.

two-mast·er (to͞o′măs′tər) *n.* A sailing vessel rigged with two masts.

two-name (to͞o′nām′) *adj.* Pertaining to or designating a commercial paper bearing the signatures of two persons liable to the obligation.

two·pence (tŭp′əns) *n., pl.* **twopence** or **-penc·es.** *Chiefly Brit.* **1.** Two pennies regarded as a monetary unit. **2. a.** A silver coin worth two pennies, since 1662 minted only for distribution on Maundy Thursday. **b.** A copper coin of this value minted during the reign of George III. **3.** A very small amount; whit: *He didn't care twopence about politics.*

two·pen·ny (tŭp′ə-nē, to͞o′pĕn′ē) *adj.* **1.** Worth or costing twopence: *twopenny candy.* **2.** Cheap; worthless.

two-phase (to͞o′fāz′) *adj.* Pertaining to two alternating electrical currents with phases at 90 degrees.

two-piece (to͞o′pēs′) *adj.* Made in or consisting of two parts or pieces, as a clothing ensemble. —*n.* A garment, as a swimsuit, that is two-piece.

two-ply (to͞o′plī′) *adj.* **1.** Made of two interwoven layers. **2.** Consisting of two thicknesses or strands: *two-ply yarn.*

two·some (to͞o′səm) *n.* **1.** Two persons or things together; pair; couple; duo. **2.** A game played by two people, as a round of golf.

two-spot (to͞o′spŏt′) *n.* **1.** A playing card bearing two spots or pips; deuce. **2.** *Slang.* **a.** A two-dollar bill. **b.** Two dollars.

two-step (to͞o′stĕp′) *n.* **1.** A ballroom dance in $\frac{2}{4}$ time and characterized by long, sliding steps. **2.** The music to which a two-step is danced.

two-time (to͞o′tīm′) *tr.v.* **-timed, -tim·ing, -times.** *Slang.* To be unfaithful or deceitful to (a loved one). **—two′-tim′er** *n.*

two-tone (to͞o′tōn′) or **two-toned** (-tōnd′) *adj.* Consisting of two colors or two shades of a single color.

two-way (to͞o′wā′) *adj.* **1.** Affording passage to vehicular traffic in two directions: *a two-way street.* **2.** Permitting communication in two directions, as a telephone connection. **3. a.** Expressive of or involving mutual action, relationship, or responsibility. **b.** Involving two participants, as a treaty. **4.** Permitting the flow in either of two directions: *a two-way valve.*

-ty *suff.* Condition; quality: *realty.* [ME *-te* < OFr. < Lat. *-tas.*]

ty·coon (tī-ko͞on′) *n.* **1.** A wealthy and powerful businessman or industrialist; magnate. **2.** A title formerly applied to the Japanese shogun. [J. *taikun,* title of a shogun, of Chin. orig.]

tyke also **tike** (tīk) *n* **1.** *Informal.* A small child, esp. a mischievous one. **2.** A mongrel or cur. **3.** *Scot.* A mean or uncouth fellow; boor. [ME, mongrel < ON *tīk,* bitch.]

ty·lo·sin (tī′lə-sĭn′) *n.* An antibiotic, $C_{45}H_{77}NO_{17}$, obtained from the actinomycete *Streptomyces fradiae* and used as an antibacterial drug in veterinary medicine. [Orig. unknown.]

tym·bal (tĭm′bəl) *n.* Variant of **timbal.**

tym·pan (tĭm′pən) *n.* **1.** *Printing.* A padding of paper or cloth placed over the platen of a printing press to provide support for the sheet being printed. **2.** *Archit.* A tympanum. **3.** A tightly stretched sheet or membrane, as on the head of a drum. [ME *timpan,* drum < OE *timpana* < Lat. *tympanum* < Gk. *tumpanon.*]

tym·pa·na (tĭm′pə-nə) *n.* A plural of **tympanum.**

tym·pa·ni (tĭm′pə-nē) *n.* Variant of **timpani.**

tym·pan·ic (tĭm-păn′ĭk) *adj.* **1.** Pertaining to or resembling a drum. **2.** Also **tym·pa·nal** (tĭm′pə-nəl) *Anat.* Of or pertaining to the tympanum. [< TYMPANUM.]

tympanic bone *n.* The part of the temporal bone of the skull that partially encloses the auditory canal and supports the tympanic membrane.

tympanic membrane *n.* The thin, semitransparent, oval-shaped membrane separating the middle ear from the external ear.

tym·pa·nist (tĭm′pə-nĭst) *n.* The member of an orchestra who plays the kettledrums and other percussion instruments. [Lat. *tympanista* < Gk. *tumpanistēs* < *tumpanizein,* to beat a drum < *tumpanon,* drum.]

tym·pa·ni·tes (tĭm′pə-nī′tēz) *n.* A distention of the abdomen resulting from the accumulation of gas or air in the intestine or peritoneal cavity. [ME < LLat. *tympanites* < Gk. *tumpanitēs* < *tumpanon,* drum.] **—tym′pa·nit′ic** *adj.*

tym·pa·num also **tim·pa·num** (tĭm′pə-nəm) *n., pl.* **-na** (-nə) or **-nums. 1. a.** The middle ear. **b.** The eardrum. **2.** *Zool.* A membranous external auditory structure, as in certain insects. **3.** *Archit.* **a.** The recessed, ornamental space or panel enclosed by the cornices of a triangular pediment. **b.** A similar space between an arch and the lintel of a portal. **4.** The diaphragm of a telephone. [Med. Lat. < Lat., drum < Gk. *tumpanon.*]

tym·pa·ny (tĭm′pə-nē) *n., pl.* **-nies. 1.** Inflated manner or style; bombast. **2.** A low-pitched resonance obtained by percussion. [Med. Lat. *tympanias,* tympanites < Gk. *tumpanias* < *tumpanon,* drum.]

typ·al (tī′pəl) *adj.* Pertaining to or serving as a type; typical.

type (tīp) *n.* **1.** A group of persons or things sharing common traits or characteristics that distinguish them as an identifiable group or class; kind; category. **2.** A person or thing having the features of a group or class. **3.** An example or model; embodiment: *"He was the perfect type of a military dandy"* (Joyce Cary). **4.** *Informal.* A person regarded as exemplifying a particular profession, rank, or social group: *a group of executive types.* **5.** A figure, representation, or symbol of something to come, as an event in the Old Testament that foreshadows another in the New Testament. **6. a.** A taxonomic designation, such as the name of a species or genus, used as the basis of ascription to or characterization of the next highest taxonomic category. **b.** A specimen or sample used as the basis of description of a species. **7.** *Printing.* **a.** A small block of metal or wood bearing a raised letter or character on the upper end, that, when inked and pressed upon paper, leaves a printed impression. **b.** Such pieces collectively. **8.** Printed or typewritten characters; print. **9.** A pattern, design, or image impressed or stamped upon the face of a coin: *Morgan type.* —*v.* **typed, typ·ing, types.** —*tr.* **1.** To write (something) with a typewriter; typewrite. **2.** To determine the type of (a blood sample). **3.** To classify according to a particular type: *typed him a hero.* **4.** To represent or typify. **5.** To prefigure. —*intr.* To write with a typewriter; typewrite. —See Usage note at **kind**[2]. [LLat. < Lat., figure < Gk. *tupos,* impression.]

Synonyms: *type, kind, sort, nature, character, ilk.* These nouns refer to groups of persons or things whose members show resemblance and consequently are regarded as constituting a class. In precise usage, *type* implies such close resemblance that the distinction between the group in question and other groups is clear-cut. Less formally, *type* can refer to a group whose members' resemblance is not so marked; in this sense it does not imply such rigid classification. *Kind* can refer to a natural class in which the resemblance of members is innate, or to a group of less precisely related members. *Sort* is generally applied when the resemblance or relationship is not precisely definable; when a close relationship is implied, the term generally refers to persons, often disparagingly: *men of his sort. Nature,* in this context, is approximately equivalent to essence; hence close resemblance and distinctness of class are indicated. *Character* implies resemblance based on qualities peculiar to members of the group. *Ilk* refers to persons considered as a particular class or breed; often the reference is disparaging.

Usage: *Type* is followed by *of* in constructions like *that type of leather.* The variant form omitting *of,* as in *that type leather,* is considered unacceptable to a large majority of the Usage Panel, though it is common in many varieties of American English. As the accompanying synonymy indicates, *type* is most appropriate when reference is being made to a well-defined or sharply distinct category, as in *that type of chassis, this type of aspirin.* When the categorization is vaguer or less well accepted, *kind* or *sort* is preferable: *He is not the sort of person one can trust. It is the kind of book that keeps you up all night.*

type·cast (tīp′kăst′) *tr.v.* **-cast, -cast·ing, -casts. 1.** To cast in an acting role akin or natural to one's own personality or fitted to one's physical appearance. **2.** To assign (an actor or actress) repeatedly to the same kind of part.

type·face (tīp′fās′) *n. Printing.* **1 a.** The surface of a body of type that makes the impression. **b.** The impression itself. **2.** The size or style of the letter or character on the type. **3.** The full range of type of the same design.

type foundry *n.* A factory where type metal is cast. **—type founder** *n.*

type genus *n.* The name of a taxonomic genus that is designated as representative of the family to which it belongs. For example, the genus *Canis,* which includes dogs and wolves, is the type genus of the family Canidae.

tympanum

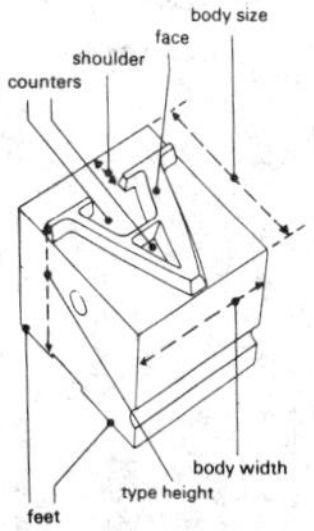

type
Above: The letter *A*
Below: Wooden type in tray

p **pop** / r **roar** / s **sauce** / sh **ship, dish** / t **tight** / th **thin, path** / *th* **this, bathe** / ŭ **cut** / ûr **urge** / v **valve** / w **with** / y **yes** / z **zebra, size** / zh **vision** / ə **about, item, edible, gallop, circus** / œ *Fr.* **feu,** *Ger.* **schön** / ü *Fr.* **tu,** *Ger.* **über** / KH *Ger.* **ich,** *Scot.* **loch** / N *Fr.* **bon.**

type-high (tīp′hī′) *adj. Printing.* As high as the standard height of type, 0.9186 of an inch.
type metal *n. Printing.* An alloy used for making metal types, consisting mainly of tin, lead, and antimony.
type·script (tīp′skrĭpt′) *n.* **1.** A typewritten copy, as of a book. **2.** Typewritten matter.
type·set·ter (tīp′sĕt′ər) *n.* One that sets type; compositor. **—type′set′ting** *n.*
type-site (tīp′sīt′) *n.* An archaeological site regarded as definitively characteristic of a particular culture and often supplying the culture with its name.
type species *n.* The name of a taxonomic species that is designated as representative of the genus to which it belongs. For example, *Panthera pardus,* the leopard, is the type species of the genus *Panthera.*
type specimen *n.* The individual specimen used as a basis for determining the characteristics of a species.
type·write (tīp′rīt′) *v.* **-wrote** (-rōt′), **-writ·ten** (-rĭt′n), **-writ·ing, -writes.** *—tr.* To write (something) with a typewriter; to type. *—intr.* To write with a typewriter; to type. [Back-formation < TYPEWRITER.]

typewriter

type·writ·er (tīp′rī′tər) *n.* **1.** A keyboard machine that prints characters and numerals esp. by means of a set of metal hammers bearing raised, inked type that strike the paper when actuated by manually pressed keys. **2.** *Archaic.* A typist. **3.** *Printing.* A type style like that of typewritten copy.
type·writ·ing (tīp′rī′tĭng) *n.* **1.** The act, process, or skill of using a typewriter. **2.** Copy produced by typewriting; typescript.
typh·lo·sole (tĭf′lə-sōl′) *n. Zool.* A longitudinal fold of the dorsal intestinal wall in some invertebrates that serves to increase the absorptive and digestive surface of the intestine. [Gk. *tuphlos,* blind + Gk. *sōlēn,* pipe.]
ty·pho·gen·ic (tī′fə-jĕn′ĭk) *adj.* Causing typhus.
ty·phoid (tī′foid′) *n.* Typhoid fever. *—adj.* Also **ty·phoi·dal** (tī-foid′l). Of, relating to, or resembling typhoid fever.

tyrannosaur

typhoid fever *n.* An acute, highly infectious disease caused by the typhoid bacillus, *Salmonella typhosa,* transmitted by contaminated food or water and characterized by red rashes, high fever, bronchitis, and intestinal hemorrhaging.
Typhoid Mary *n.* A person from whom something undesirable or deadly spreads to those around him or her. [After *Mary* Mallon (d. 1938), a carrier of typhoid.]
Ty·phon (tī′fŏn′) *n. Gk. Myth.* A monster called by Hesiod the son of Typhoeus. [Gk. *Tuphōn.*]
ty·phoon (tī-fo͞on′) *n.* A severe tropical hurricane occurring in the western Pacific or the China Sea. [Cantonese *tai fung.*]
ty·phus (tī′fəs) *n.* Any of several forms of an infectious disease caused by microorganisms of the genus *Rickettsia,* esp. when flea-borne as in endemic typhus, louse-borne as in epidemic typhus, or mite-borne as in scrub typhus, and characterized generally by severe headache, sustained high fever, depression, delirium, and red rashes. [NLat. < Gk. *tuphos,* stupor arising from a fever < *tuphein,* to make smoke.] **—ty′phous** (-fəs) *adj.*
typhus fever *n.* Typhus.
typ·i·cal (tĭp′ĭ-kəl) also **typ·ic** (-ĭk) *adj.* **1.** Exhibiting the traits or characteristics peculiar to its kind, class, or group; representative of a whole group: *a typical suburban community.* **2.** Of or pertaining to a representative specimen; characteristic; distinctive. **3.** Conforming to a type, as a species. **4.** Of the nature of, constituting, or serving as a type; emblematic. [LLat. *typicalis* < *typicus* < Gk. *tupikos,* impressionable < *tupos,* impression.] **—typ′i·cal·ly** *adv.* **—typ′i·cal·ness, typ′i·cal′i·ty** *n.*
typ·i·fy (tĭp′ə-fī′) *tr.v.* **-fied, -fy·ing, -fies. 1.** To serve as a typical example of; embody the essential characteristics of. **2.** To represent by an image, form, or model; symbolize; prefigure. [TYP(E) + -FY.] **—typ′i·fi·ca′tion** *n.* **—typ′i·fi′er** *n.*
typ·ist (tī′pĭst) *n.* One who operates a typewriter.
ty·po (tī′pō) *n., pl.* **-os.** *Informal.* A typographical error.
ty·pog·ra·pher (tī-pŏg′rə-fər) *n.* A printer or compositor.
typographical error *n.* A mistake in printing, typing, or writing.
ty·pog·ra·phy (tī-pŏg′rə-fē) *n., pl.* **-phies. 1. a.** The composition of printed material from movable type. **b.** The art and technique of this. **2.** The arrangement and appearance of printed matter. [Med. Lat. *typographia* : Gk. *tupos,* impression + *-graphia,* -graphy.] **—ty′po·graph′i·cal** (tī′pə-grăf′ĭ-kəl), **ty′po·graph′ic** *adj.* **—ty′po·graph′i·cal·ly** *adv.*
ty·pol·o·gy (tī-pŏl′ə-jē) *n., pl.* **-gies. 1.** The study of types, as in a systematic classification. **2.** A theory or doctrine of types, as in scriptural studies. **—ty′po·log′i·cal** (tī′pə-lŏj′ĭ-kəl) *adj.* **—ty′po·log′i·cal·ly** *adv.* **—ty·pol′o·gist** *n.*
Tyr (tîr) *n. Myth.* A Norse god of war, son of Odin. [ON *Tȳr.*]
ty·ra·mine (tī′rə-mēn′) *n.* A colorless, crystalline amine, $C_8H_{11}NO$, found in mistletoe, putrefied animal tissue, certain cheeses, and ergot and also produced synthetically, used in medicine. [TYR(OSINE) + AMINE.]
ty·ran·ni·cal (tĭ-răn′ĭ-kəl, tī-) also **ty·ran·nic** (-răn′ĭk) *adj.* Of, pertaining to, or characteristic of a tyrant; despotic; arbitrary; oppressive. **—ty·ran′ni·cal·ly** *adv.* **—ty·ran′ni·cal·ness** *n.*
tyr·an·nize (tĭr′ə-nīz′) *v.* **-nized, -niz·ing, -niz·es.** *—intr.* **1.** To exercise absolute power, esp. arbitrarily: *"So it is the nature of such persons to insult and tyrannize over little people"* (Fielding). **2.** To rule as a tyrant. *—tr.* To treat tyrannically; crush; oppress. [OFr. *tyranniser* < *tyran,* tyrant.] **—tyr′an·niz′er** *n.* **—tyr′an·niz′ing·ly** *adv.*
ty·ran·no·saur (tĭ-răn′ə-sôr′, tī-) also **ty·ran·no·saur·us** (tĭ-răn′ə-sôr′əs, tī-) *n.* A large carnivorous dinosaur of the genus *Tyrannosaurus,* of the Cretaceous period, having small forelimbs and a large head. [NLat. *Tyrannasaurus,* genus name : Gk. *turannos,* tyrant + Gk. *sauros,* lizard.]
tyr·an·nous (tĭr′ə-nəs) *adj.* Characterized by tyranny; despotic; tyrannical. **—tyr′an·nous·ly** *adv.*
tyr·an·ny (tĭr′ə-nē) *n., pl.* **-nies. 1.** A government in which a single ruler is vested with absolute power. **2.** The office, authority, or jurisdiction of an absolute ruler. **3.** Absolute power, esp. when exercised unjustly or cruelly: *"I have sworn eternal hostility to every form of tyranny over the mind of man"* (Jefferson). **4. a.** The arbitrary use of absolute power. **b.** A tyrannical act. **5.** Extreme harshness or severity; rigor. [ME < OFr. *tyrannie* < LLat. *tyrannia* < Gk. *turannia* < *turannos,* tyrant.]
ty·rant (tī′rənt) *n.* **1.** An absolute ruler who governs arbitrarily without constitutional or other restrictions, esp. one in ancient Greece. **2.** A ruler who exercises power in a harsh, cruel manner; oppressor. **3.** A tyrannical or despotic person. [ME < OFr. < Lat. *tyrannus* < Gk. *turannos.*]
tyre (tīr) *n. Chiefly Brit.* Variant of **tire**[2].
Tyr·i·an purple (tĭr′ē-ən) *n.* A reddish dyestuff obtained from the bodies of certain mollusks of the genus *Murex* and highly prized in ancient times. [After *Tyre,* ancient capital of Phoenicia, famous for its purple dyes.]
ty·ro also **ti·ro** (tī′rō) *n., pl.* **-ros.** An inexperienced person; a beginner; neophyte. [Med. Lat., squire < Lat. *tiro,* recruit.]
ty·ro·ci·dine (tī′rə-sīd′n) *n.* A polypeptide antibiotic produced by the soil microorganism *Bacillus brevis.* [TYRO-(THRICIN) + (GRAMI)CID(IN) + -INE[2].]
Ty·ro·le·an (tĭ-rō′lē-ən, tī-) *n. & adj.* Tyrolese.
Tyr·o·lese (tĭr′ə-lēz′, -lēs′, tī′rə-) *n., pl.* **Tyrolese.** A native or inhabitant of Tyrol. *—adj.* Of or pertaining to Tyrol or the Tyrolese.
ty·ros·i·nase (tī-rŏs′ə-nās′, -nāz′) *n.* A copper-containing enzyme of plant and animal tissues that catalyzes the production of melanin from tyrosine, as in the blackening of a potato exposed to air.
ty·ro·sine (tī′rə-sēn′) *n.* A white crystalline amino acid, $C_9H_{11}NO_3$, derived from the hydrolysis of protein, used as a growth factor in nutrition and as a dietary supplement. [Gk. *turos,* cheese + -INE[2].]
ty·ro·thri·cin (tī′rō-thrī′sĭn) *n.* A grayish to brown mixture of antibiotics obtained from cultures of soil bacteria, esp. *Bacillus brevis,* used topically in treating infections caused by Gram-positive bacteria. [< NLat. *Tyrothrix, Tyrothric-,* former bacteria genus name : Gk. *turos,* cheese + Gk. *thrix,* hair.]
tzar (tsär) *n.* Variant of **czar.**
tzet·ze fly (tsĕt′sē, tsēt′sē) *n.* Variant of **tsetse fly.**
tzim·mes (tsĭm′ĭs) *n.* Variant of **tsimmes.**
tzu·ris (tso͝or′ĭs, tsôr′-) *n.* Variant of **tsuris.**

U

Around 1000 B.C. the Phoenicians and other Semitic peoples began to use graphic signs to represent individual speech sounds instead of syllables or words. They used a symbol (1,2) which is the ancestor of the letters F, V, W, and Y as well as U to represent the sound of the semivowel "w" and called it *wāw,* their word for "hook." The Greeks, adapting the Phoenician alphabet, varied the shape of *wāw* slightly (3,4,5,6) and altered its name to *upsilon.* They used *upsilon* to represent the sound of the vowel "u." The Romans borrowed the alphabet from the Greeks via the Etruscans, who used a tailless variant of *upsilon.* The Romans used *upsilon* to represent both the vowel "u" and the semivowel "w," which later developed into the consonant "v," and adapted the shape for monumental inscriptions (8). Medieval scribes adapted the Roman capitals to being quickly written on paper, parchment, and vellum. Like the Roman letter V, medieval U was still used to represent the vowel "u" and the consonant "v." Medieval uncial and cursive minuscules (9,10) are the prototypes of modern lower-case letters, both written and printed (14,13). Until the 17th century, U and V were distinguished, not by phonetic value, but by position within a word: V was used word-initially and U elsewhere. During the 17th century, U and V were assigned their modern phonetic values and the rounded shape of capital U (11,12) was developed, but it was not until the early 19th century that their position in the alphabet was fixed.

u

p pop / **r** roar / **s** sauce / **sh** ship, dish / **t** tight / **th** thin, path / ***th*** this, bathe / **ŭ** cut / **ûr** urge / **v** valve / **w** with / **y** yes / **z** zebra, size / **zh** vision / **ə** about, item, edible, gallop, circus / **œ** *Fr.* feu, *Ger.* schön / **ü** *Fr.* tu, *Ger.* über / **KH** *Ger.* ich, *Scot.* loch/ **N** *Fr.* bon.

u or **U** (yo͞o) *n., pl.* **u's** or **U's. 1.** The 21st letter of the modern English alphabet. **2.** Any of the speech sounds represented by the letter *u.* **3.** Something shaped like the letter U. **4.** The 21st in a series.

U[1] The symbol for the element uranium.

U[2] (yo͞o) *adj. Informal.* Of or appropriate to the upper class, esp. in language usage. [U(PPER CLASS).]

u·biq·ui·tous (yo͞o-bĭk'wĭ-təs) *adj.* Being or seeming to be everywhere at the same time; omnipresent: *"plodded through the shadows fruitlessly like an ubiquitous spook"* (Joseph Heller). **—u·biq'ui·tous·ly** *adv.* **—u·biq'ui·tous·ness** *n.*

u·biq·ui·ty (yo͞o-bĭk'wĭ-tē) *n.* Existence everywhere at the same time; omnipresence. [NLat. *ubiquitas* < Lat. *ubique,* everywhere : *ubi,* where + *-que,* generalizing particle.]

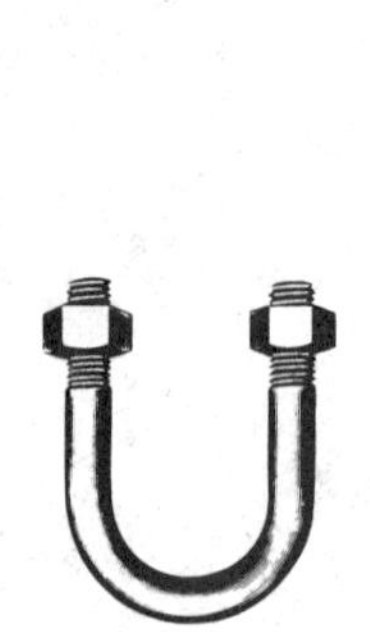

U-bolt

U-boat (yo͞o'bōt') *n.* A German submarine. [Transl. of G. *U-boot,* short for *Unterseeboot* : *unter,* under + *See,* sea + *Boot,* boat.]

U-bolt (yo͞o'bōlt') *n.* A bolt shaped like the letter U, fitted with threads and a nut at each end.

UBV photometry (yo͞o'bē-vē') *n.* A system of photometry used to obtain stellar magnitudes by comparing observed magnitudes to a standard sequence of stars. [U(LTRAVIOLET) + B(LUE) + V(ISUAL).]

ud·der (ŭd'ər) *n.* The baglike mammary organ characteristic of cows, sheep, and goats, having two or more teats. [ME < OE *ūder.*]

u·do (o͞o'dō) *n.* A Japanese plant, *Aralia cordata,* of which the young shoots are cooked and eaten as a vegetable. [J.]

UFO (yo͞o'ĕf-ō') *n., pl.* **UFOs** or **UFO's.** An unidentified flying object.

u·fol·o·gy (yo͞o-fŏl'ə-jē) *n.* The study of unidentified flying objects. [UFO + -LOGY.] **—u·fol'o·gist** (yo͞o-fŏl'ə-jĭst) *n.*

U·ga·rit·ic (o͞o'gə-rĭt'ĭk, yo͞o'-) *n.* The Semitic language of the ancient city of Ugarit. **—U'ga·rit'ic** *adj.*

ugh (ŭg, ŭk) *interj.* Used to express horror, disgust, or repugnance.

ug·li (ŭg'lē) *n., pl.* **-lis** or **-lies.** A citrus fruit indigenous to Jamaica, produced by a cross between a grapefruit and a tangerine and having a loose, wrinkled yellowish rind. [Poss. < UGLY, from the appearance of its wrinkled skin.]

ukulele

ug·li·fy (ŭg'lə-fī') *tr.v.* **-fied, -fy·ing, -fies.** To make ugly; disfigure. **—ug'li·fi·ca'tion** *n.*

ug·ly (ŭg'lē) *adj.* **-li·er, -li·est. 1.** Displeasing to the eye; unsightly. **2.** Repulsive or offensive in any way; objectionable; unpleasant. **3.** Morally reprehensible; bad. **4.** Threatening or ominous: *ugly weather.* **5.** *Informal.* Cross or disagreeable: *an ugly temper.* [ME, frightful < ON *uggligr* < *uggr,* fear.] **—ug'li·ness** *n.*

ugly duckling *n.* One considered ugly or unpromising at first but having the potential of becoming beautiful or admirable. [< *The Ugly Duckling,* story by Hans Christian Andersen (1805–1875).]

U·gri·an (o͞o'grē-ən, yo͞o'-) *n.* **1.** A member of a group of Finno-Ugric peoples of western Siberia and Hungary, including the Magyars. **2.** Ugric. [OR *Ugrin',* of Turkic orig.] **—U'gri·an** *adj.*

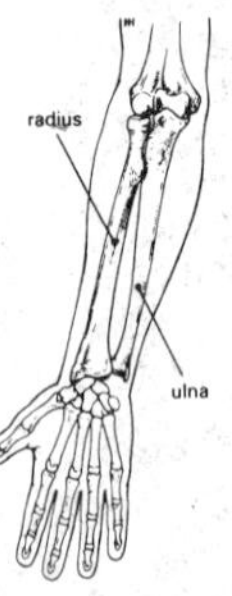

ulna

U·gric (o͞o'grĭk, yo͞o'-) *n.* The branch of the Finno-Ugric subfamily of languages that includes Hungarian. **—U'gric** *adj.*

ug·some (ŭg'səm) *adj. Archaic.* Disgusting; loathsome. [ME : *uggen,* to fear (< ON *ugga*) + *-some,* -some.]

uh (ŭ) *interj.* Used to express hesitation or uncertainty.

uh-huh (ə-hŭ') *interj. Informal.* Yes.

uh·lan also **u·lan** (o͞o'län', yo͞o'lən) *n.* One of a body of cavalry armed with lances that formed part of the former Polish and, later, German armies. [G. < Pol. < Turk. *uğlan,* youth.]

Ui·gur also **Ui·ghur** (wē'go͝or) *n.* **1.** One of a Turkic people dominant in Mongolia and eastern Turkestan from the 8th to the 12th century, now inhabiting northwestern China. **2.** The Turkic language of the Uigurs. [Uigur.] **—Ui·gu'ri·an, Ui·gu'ric** *adj.*

u·in·ta·ite (yo͞o-ĭn'tə-īt') *n.* Gilsonite. [After the *Uinta,* mountains in Utah.]

uit·land·er (oit'lăn'dər, īt'-) *n.* **1.** In South Africa, an outlander; foreigner. **2. Uitlander.** A native of Great Britain residing in the former republics of the Orange Free State or Transvaal. [Afr. < MDu. *utelander* < *utelant,* foreign land : *ute,* out + *land,* land.]

u·kase (yo͞o-kās', -kāz', yo͞o'kās', -kāz') *n.* **1.** A proclamation of the czar having the force of law in imperial Russia. **2.** An authoritative order or decree; edict. [Fr. < R. *ukaz,* decree < *ukazat',* to order.]

U·krain·i·an (yo͞o-krā'nē-ən) *n.* **1.** An inhabitant or native of the Ukraine. **2.** The Slavic language of the Ukrainians, which is closely related to Russian. [Ukrainian *Ukrayina* < OR *Ukraina.*] **—U·krain'i·an** *adj.*

u·ku·le·le (yo͞o'kə-lā'lē, o͞o'kə-) *n.* A small four-stringed guitar popularized in Hawaii. [Hawaiian *'ukulele* : *'uku,* flea + *lele,* jumping.]

u·lan (o͞o'län', yo͞o'lən) *n.* Variant of **uhlan.**

-ular *suff.* Of, relating to, or resembling: *tubular.* [Lat. *-ularis* < *-ulus,* -ule.]

ul·cer (ŭl'sər) *n.* **1. a.** An inflammatory, often suppurating lesion on the skin or an internal mucous surface of the body, resulting in necrosis of the tissue. **b.** A necrotic lesion of the stomach and duodenum. **2.** A corrupting condition or influence. [ME < OFr. *ulcere* < Lat. *ulcus.*]

ul·cer·ate (ŭl'sə-rāt') *v.* **-at·ed, -at·ing, -ates.** *—intr.* To become affected with or as if with an ulcer. *—tr.* To affect with ulcers. **—ul'cer·a'tive** (-rā'tĭv, -sər-ə-tĭv) *adj.*

ul·cer·a·tion (ŭl'sə-rā'shən) *n.* **1.** The development of an ulcer. **2.** An ulcer or ulcerous condition.

ul·cer·o·gen·ic (ŭl'sə-rō-jĕn'ĭk) *adj.* Tending to cause the formation of ulcers.

ul·cer·ous (ŭl'sər-əs) *adj.* Pertaining to or exhibiting ulcers.

-ule *suff.* Small one: *valvule.* [Fr. < Lat. *-ulus,* dim. suffix.]

u·le·ma (o͞o'lə-mä') *n.* **1.** *pl.* **ulema.** *(used with a sing. verb).* The scholars or priests trained in traditional Moslem religion and law. **2.** *pl.* **-mas.** A Moslem scholar or religious leader. [Turk. *'ulemā* < Ar. *'ulamā,* pl. of *'alim,* wise < *'alimā,* to know.]

u·lex·ite (yo͞o'lĭk-sīt', yo͞o-lĕk'-) *n.* A white mineral, $NaCaB_5O_9 \cdot 8H_2O$, that forms rounded masses of very fine acicular crystals. [After George L. *Ulex* (d. 1883).]

ul·lage (ŭl'ĭj) *n.* The amount of liquid within a container that is lost during shipment or storage. [ME *oylage* < OFr. *ouillage* < *ouiller,* to fill up a cask < *oeil,* eye, bunghole < Lat. *oculus,* eye.]

ul·na (ŭl'nə) *n., pl.* **-nae** (-nē) or **-nas.** *Anat.* **1.** The bone extending from the elbow to the wrist on the side opposite to the thumb. **2.** A bone homologous to the ulna in the vertebrate forelimb. [NLat. < Lat., elbow.] **—ul'nar** *adj.*

u·lot·ri·chous (yo͞o-lŏt'rĭ-kəs) *adj.* Having wiry or woolly hair. [< Gk. *oulothrix, oulotrikh-* : *oulos,* woolly + *thrix,* hair.] **—u·lot'ri·chy** (-kē) *n.*

ul·ster (ŭl'stər) *n.* A loose, long overcoat made of heavy, rugged fabric. [After *Ulster,* Ireland.]

ul·te·ri·or (ŭl-tîr'ē-ər) *adj.* **1.** Lying beyond or outside the area of immediate interest. **2.** Lying beyond what is evident or avowed, esp. concealed intentionally so as to deceive: *an ulterior motive.* **3.** Occurring later; subsequent. [Lat., farther, comp. of *ulter,* on the other side.]

ul·ti·ma (ŭl'tə-mə) *n.* The last syllable of a word. [Lat., fem. of *ultimus,* last. —see ULTIMATE.]

ul·ti·ma·ta (ŭl'tə-mā'tə, -mä'tə) *n.* A plural of **ultimatum.**

ul·ti·mate (ŭl'tə-mĭt) *adj.* **1.** Representing the farthest possible extent of analysis or division into parts: *an ultimate particle.* **2.** Fundamental; elemental. **3.** Of the greatest possible size or significance; maximum. **4. a.** Most remote in time or space: farthest. **b.** Last, as in a series or a progression: *Our ultimate destination is Moscow.* **c.** Eventual: *hoped for ultimate victory.* **d.** Utmost; extreme: *the ultimate insult.* *—n.* **1.** The basic or fundamental fact. **2.** The final point; conclusion. **3.** The maximum; greatest extreme: *His actions represented the ultimate in political expediency.* [Med. Lat. *ultimatus,* p.part. of *ultimare,* to come to an end < Lat. *ultimus,* last, superl. of *ulter,* on the other side.] **—ul'ti·mate·ly** *adv.* **—ul'ti·mate·ness** *n.*

ultima Thu·le (tho͞o'lē) *n.* **1.** The northernmost region of the habitable world as thought of by ancient geographers. **2.** A remote goal or ideal. [Lat., farthest Thule.]

ul·ti·ma·tum (ŭl'tə-mā'təm, -mä'təm) *n., pl.* **-tums** or **-ta** (-tə). **1.** A final statement of terms made by one party to another. **2.** A statement, esp. in diplomatic negotiations, that expresses or implies the threat of serious penalties if the terms are not accepted. [NLat. < Med. Lat., neuter of *ultimatus,* last. —see ULTIMATE.]

ul·ti·mo (ŭl'tə-mō') *adv.* In or of the month before the present one. [Lat. *ultimo (mense),* in the last (month) < *ultimus,* last. —see ULTIMATE.]

ul·tra (ŭl'trə) *adj.* Immoderately adhering to a belief, fashion, or course of action; extreme. *—n.* An extremist. [< ULTRA-.]

ultra- *pref.* **1.** Beyond; on the other side of: *ultraviolet.* **2.** Beyond the range, scope, or limit of: *ultrasonic.* **3.** Beyond the normal or proper degree; excessively: *ultraconservative.* [Lat. < *ultra,* beyond < *ulter,* on the other side < *uls,* beyond.]

ul·tra·cen·tri·fuge (ŭl'trə-sĕn'trə-fyo͞oj') *n.* A convection-free high-velocity centrifuge that is used in the separation of colloidal or submicroscopic particles. **—ul'tra·cen·trif'u·gal** (-trĭf'yə-gəl, -trĭf'ə-gəl) *adj.* **—ul'tra·cen'tri·fu·ga'tion** (-fyo͞o-gā'shən) *n.*

ul·tra·con·ser·va·tive (ŭl'trə-kən-sûr'və-tĭv) *adj.* Conservative to an extreme, particularly in political beliefs; reactionary. *—n.* One who is extremely conservative.

ul·tra·fiche (ŭl'trə-fēsh') *n.* A microfiche upon which material is reduced by a factor of 100 or more.

ul·tra·fil·tra·tion (ŭl'trə-fĭl-trā'shən) *n.* The filtration of a collodial substance through a semipermeable medium that allows only the passage of small molecules.

ul·tra·high (ŭl'trə-hī') *adj.* Exceedingly high: *an ultrahigh vacuum.*

ultrahigh frequency *n.* A band of radio frequencies from 300 to 3,000 megacycles per second.

ul·tra·ism (ŭl'trə-ĭz'əm) *n.* Extremism, esp. in politics or government; radicalism. **—ul'tra·ist** *n.*

ul·tra·lib·er·al (ŭl'trə-lĭb'ər-əl, -lĭb'rəl) *adj.* Liberal to an extreme, esp. in political beliefs; radical. *—n.* One who is extremely liberal.

ul·tra·ma·rine (ŭl'trə-mə-rēn') *n.* **1. a.** A blue pigment made from powdered lapis lazuli. **b.** A similar pigment made from other substances. **2.** A vivid or strong blue to purplish blue. *—adj.* **1.** Having a deep-blue purplish color. **2.** Of or from some place beyond the sea. [< Med. Lat. *ultramarinus,* from beyond the sea : Lat. *ultra,* beyond + Lat. *marinus,* of the sea < *mare,* sea.]

ul·tra·mi·cro·fiche (ŭl'trə-mī'krō-fēsh) *n.* Ultrafiche.

ul·tra·mi·crom·e·ter (ŭl'trə-mī-krŏm'ĭ-tər) *n.* An extremely accurate micrometer.

ul·tra·mi·cro·scope (ŭl'trə-mī'krə-skōp') *n.* A microscope with high-intensity illumination used to study very minute objects, such as colloidal particles, by means of their diffraction system that appears as a bright spot against a black background.

ul·tra·mi·cro·scop·ic (ŭl'trə-mī'krə-skŏp'ĭk) *adj.* **1.** Too small to be seen with an ordinary microscope. **2.** Of or relating to an ultramicroscope.

ul·tra·mi·cro·tome (ŭl'trə-mī'krə-tōm') *n.* A microtome for cutting very thin sections of material for use in electron microscopy. **—ul'tra·mi·crot'o·my** (-mī-krŏt'ə-mē) *n.*

ul·tra·mil·i·tant (ŭl'trə-mĭl'ĭ-tnt) *adj.* Militant to an extreme. *—n.* One who is extremely militant.

ul·tra·min·i·a·ture (ŭl'trə-mĭn'ē-ə-chŏŏr', -mĭn'ə-, -chər) *adj.* Subminiature. **—ul'tra·min'i·a·tur·i·za'tion** *n.*

ul·tra·mod·ern (ŭl'trə-mŏd'ərn) *adj.* Extremely modern in ideas or style. **—ul'tra·mod'ern·ism** *n.* **—ul'tra·mod'ern·ist** *n.* **—ul'tra·mod'ern·is'tic** *adj.*

ul·tra·mon·tane (ŭl'trə-mŏn'tān', -mŏn-tān') *adj.* **1.** Of or pertaining to peoples or regions lying beyond the mountains, esp. the Alps. **2.** Supporting the authority of the papal court over national or diocesan authority in the Roman Catholic Church. **3.** Pertaining to or supporting the doctrine of papal supremacy. *—n.* **1.** A person living beyond the mountains, esp. south of the Alps. **2.** Often **Ultramontane.** A Roman Catholic who advocates support of papal policy in ecclesiastical and political matters. [Med. Lat. *ultramontanus* : Lat. *ultra,* beyond + Lat. *montanus,* of mountains < *mons,* mountain.]

ul·tra·mon·ta·nism (ŭl'trə-mŏn'tə-nĭz'əm) *n.* Often **Ultramontanism.** The policy that absolute authority in the Roman Catholic Church should be vested in the pope.

ul·tra·mun·dane (ŭl'trə-mŭn'dān', -mŭn-dān') *adj.* Extending or being beyond the world or the limits of the universe. [LLat. *ultramundanus* : Lat. *ultra,* beyond + Lat. *mundanus,* of the world < *mundus,* world.]

ul·tra·na·tion·al·ism (ŭl'trə-năsh'ə-nə-lĭz'əm) *n.* Extreme nationalism, esp. when opposed to international cooperation. **—ul'tra·na'tion·al** *adj.* **—ul'tra·na'tion·al·ist** *n.* **—ul'tra·na'tion·al·is'tic** *adj.*

ul·tra·pure (ŭl'trə-pyŏŏr') *adj.* Of exceeding purity.

ul·tra·son·ic (ŭl'trə-sŏn'ĭk) *adj.* Pertaining to acoustic frequencies above the range audible to the human ear, or above approximately 20,000 cycles per second.

ul·tra·son·ics (ŭl'trə-sŏn'ĭks) *n.* *(used with a sing. verb).* **1.** The acoustics of ultrasonic sound. **2.** A technology using ultrasonic sound, as for medical therapy.

ul·tra·so·nog·ra·phy (ŭl'trə-sə-nŏg'rə-fē) *n.* The diagnostic use of ultrasonic waves to visualize internal bodily structures and organs. [ULTRASON(IC) + -GRAPHY.] **—ul'tra·son'o·graph'ic** (-sŏn'ə-grăf'ĭk, -sō'nə-) *adj.*

ul·tra·so·phis·ti·cat·ed (ŭl'trə-sə-fĭs'tĭ-kā'tĭd) *adj.* Very sophisticated.

ul·tra·sound (ŭl'trə-sound') *n.* Ultrasonic sound.

ul·tra·thin (ŭl'trə-thĭn') *adj.* Very thin.

ul·tra·vi·o·let (ŭl'trə-vī'ə-lĭt) *adj.* Of or pertaining to the range of radiation wavelengths from about 4,000 angstroms, just beyond the violet in the visible spectrum, to about 40 angstroms, on the border of the x-ray region. *—n.* Ultraviolet light or the ultraviolet part of the spectrum.

ultraviolet lamp *n.* A mercury-vapor lamp that produces ultraviolet light.

ul·tra·vi·rus (ŭl'trə-vī'rəs) *n.* A virus small enough to pass through the finest bacterial filter.

ul·u·late (ŭl'yə-lāt') *intr.v.* **-lat·ed, -lat·ing, -lates.** To howl, wail, or lament loudly. [Lat. *ululare, ululat-.*] **—ul'u·la'tion** *n.*

U·lys·ses (yŏŏ-lĭs'ēz') *n.* Odysseus. [Lat., alteration of *Ulixes.*]

u·man·gite (ōō-măn'gīt', -măng'-) *n.* A dark red mineral, Cu_3Se_2, consisting of copper selenide. [After Sierra de *Umango,* a province in Argentina.]

um·bel (ŭm'bəl) *n. Bot.* A flat-topped or rounded flower cluster in which the individual flower stalks arise from about the same point as in the carrot and related plants. [NLat. *umbella* < Lat., umbrella < dim. of *umbra,* shadow.]

um·bel·late (ŭm'bə-lāt', ŭm-bĕl'ĭt) *adj.* Having, forming, or of the nature of an umbel.

um·bel·lif·er·ous (ŭm'bə-lĭf'ər-əs) *adj.* Bearing umbels. [< NLat. *umbellifer* : *umbella,* umbel + Lat. *ferre,* to bear.]

um·bel·lule (ŭm'bəl-yōōl', ŭm-bĕl'yōōl') *n. Bot.* One of the smaller secondary umbels forming a compound umbel. [NLat. *umbellula,* dim. of *umbella,* umbel.]

um·ber (ŭm'bər) *n.* **1.** A natural brown earth composed of ferric oxide, silica, alumina, lime, and manganese oxides and used as pigment. **2.** Any of the shades of brown produced by umber in its various states. *—adj.* **1.** Of or related to umber. **2.** Having a brownish hue. *—tr.v.* **-bered, -ber·ing, -bers.** To darken with or as if with umber. [Prob. < obs. *umber,* shade < ME < OFr. *umbre* < Lat. *umbra.*]

um·bil·i·cal (ŭm-bĭl'ĭ-kəl) *adj.* **1.** Of, pertaining to, or resembling an umbilicus. **2.** Pertaining to or located near the central area of the abdomen. *—n. Aerospace.* An umbilical cord.

umbilical cord *n.* **1.** *Anat.* The flexible, cordlike structure connecting the fetus at the navel with the placenta and containing two umbilical arteries and one vein that nourish the fetus and remove its wastes. **2.** *Aerospace.* **a.** Any of various external electrical lines or fluid tubes supplying a rocket before launch. **b.** The line that supplies an astronaut with oxygen and in some cases with communications while outside the spacecraft.

um·bil·i·cate (ŭm-bĭl'ĭ-kĭt) also **um·bil·i·cat·ed** (-kā'tĭd) *adj.* **1.** Having a central mark or depression resembling a navel. **2.** Having an umbilicus. **—um'bil'i·ca'tion** *n.*

um·bil·i·cus (ŭm-bĭl'ĭ-kəs, ŭm'bə-lī'kəs) *n., pl.* **-ci** (-sī'). **1.** The navel. **2.** *Biol.* A small opening or depression similar to a navel, such as the hollow at the base of the shell of some gastropod mollusks or one of the openings in the shaft of a feather. [Lat.]

um·bo (ŭm'bō) *n., pl.* **um·bo·nes** (ŭm-bō'nēz) or **um·bos.** **1.** The boss or knob at the center of a shield. **2.** *Biol.* A knoblike protuberance similar to an umbo, such as a prominence near the hinge of a bivalve shell. **3.** *Anat.* A small projection at the center of the outer surface of the tympanic membrane of the ear. [Lat.] **—um'bo·nal** (ŭm'bə-nəl, ŭm-bō'nəl), **um·bon'ic** (ŭm-bŏn'ĭk) *adj.*

um·bo·nate (ŭm'bə-nāt', ŭm-bō'nĭt) *adj.* Having or resembling a knob or knoblike protuberance.

um·bra (ŭm'brə) *n., pl.* **-brae** (-brē). **1.** A dark area, esp. the blackest part of a shadow from which all light is cut off. **2.** *Astron.* **a.** The shadow region over an area of the earth where a solar eclipse is total. **b.** The darkest region of a sunspot. [Lat., shadow.]

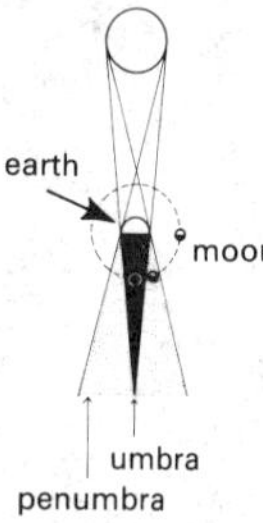

umbra

um·brage (ŭm'brĭj) *n.* **1.** Offense; resentment: *took umbrage at their rudeness.* **2.** *Archaic.* **a.** Something that affords shade. **b.** Shadow or shade. **3.** A vague or indistinct indication; hint. [ME, shade < OFr. < Lat. *umbraticum,* neuter of *umbraticus,* of shade < Lat. *umbra,* shadow.]

um·bra·geous (ŭm-brā'jəs) *adj.* **1.** Affording or forming shade; shady. **2.** Easily offended; irritable. **—um·bra'geous·ly** *adv.* **—um·bra'geous·ness** *n.*

um·brel·la (ŭm-brĕl'ə) *n.* **1.** A device for protection from the weather consisting of a collapsible canopy mounted on a central rod. **2.** Something that covers or protects. **3.** An air cover. **4.** Something that encompasses or covers many different elements or groups. **5.** *Zool.* The contractile gelatinous, rounded mass constituting the major part of the body of most jellyfishes. [Ital. *ombrella,* dim. of *ombra,* shade < Lat. *umbra.*]

umbrella bird *n.* Any of several tropical American birds of the genus *Cephalopterus,* esp. *C. ornatus,* having a retractile black crest and a long, feathered wattle.

George Miksch Sutton
umbrella bird

umbrella leaf *n.* A plant, *Diphylleia cymosa,* of the southeastern United States, having a broad, rounded basal leaf and a terminal cluster of white flowers.

umbrella palm *n.* A palm tree, *Hedyscepe canterburyana,* of the South Pacific, cultivated for its feathery, drooping foliage.

umbrella tree *n.* **1.** Any of several trees of the genus *Magnolia,* of the southeastern United States, esp. *M. tripetala,* having large leaves clustered in an umbrellalike form at the ends of the branches. **2.** A tree, *Schefflera actinophylla,* native to Australia, having compound leaves and widely cultivated in its smaller forms as a house plant.

umbrella tree

Um·bri·an (ŭm'brē-ən) *adj.* Of or pertaining to Umbria or its people. *—n.* **1.** An inhabitant or native of ancient or modern Umbria. **2.** The Italic language of ancient Umbria.

u·mi·ak (ōō'mē-ăk') *n.* A large open Eskimo boat made of skins stretched on a wooden frame, usually propelled by paddles. [Eskimo.]

um·laut (ŏŏm'lout') *Ling. —n.* **1. a.** A change in a vowel sound caused by partial assimilation to a vowel or semivowel occurring in the following syllable. **b.** A vowel sound changed in this manner. **2.** The diacritical mark (¨) placed over a vowel to indicate an umlaut, esp. in German. *—tr.v.* **-laut·ed, -laut·ing, -lauts.** **1.** To modify by umlaut. **2.** To write or print (a vowel) with an umlaut. [G. : *um-,* around (< MHG *umb-* < OHG *umbi-*) + *Laut,* sound (< MHG *lut* < OHG *hlūt*).]

ump (ŭmp) *n.* An umpire (sense 1). *—intr.v.* **umped, ump·ing, umps.** To serve as an umpire.

um·pir·age (ŭm'pīr'ĭj) *n.* **1.** The position, function, or authority of an umpire. **2.** A ruling or decision of an umpire.

um·pire (ŭm'pīr') *n.* **1.** *Sports.* A person appointed to rule on plays, esp. in baseball. **2.** A person selected or empowered to settle a dispute between persons or groups. **3.** A judge. *—v.* **-pired, -pir·ing, -pires.** *—tr.* To act as umpire for. *—intr.* To be or act as an umpire. [ME *(an) oumpere,* alteration of *(a) noumpere,* mediator < OFr. *nomper* : *non,* not (< Lat.) + *per,* equal < Lat. *par.*]

ump·teen (ŭmp'tēn', ŭm') *adj. Informal.* Large but indefinite in number: *umpteen reasons; umpteen guests.* [Slang *umpty,* dash in Morse code + *-teen,* as in *thirteen.*] **—ump'teenth'** *adj.*

un–[1] *pref.* **1.** Not: *unhappy.* **2.** Opposite of; contrary to: *unrest.* [ME < OE.]

Usage: Many compounds other than those entered here may be formed with *un-*. In forming compounds, *un-* is normally joined with the following element without space or a hyphen: *unnamed.* However, if the second element begins with a capital letter, it is separated with a hyphen: *un-American.*

un–[2] *pref.* **1.** To reverse or undo a specified action: *unbind.* **2. a.** To deprive of or remove a specified thing: *unfrock.* **b.** To release, free, or remove from: *unyoke.* **3.** Used as an intensive: *unloose.* [ME < OE *on-*, alteration of *ond-, and-,* against.]

Usage: Strictly speaking, the prefix *un-* is not necessary in *unloose,* which has the same meaning as *loose,* but the acceptability of *unloose* is well established. With other verbs, however, *un-* is sometimes prefixed incorrectly. One *peels* (not *unpeels*) *an orange,* and something *thaws* (not *unthaws*) when it has been frozen.

un·a·bashed (ŭn′ə-băsht′) *adj.* **1.** Not disconcerted or embarrassed; poised. **2.** Not disguised: *unabashed disgust.* **—un′a·bash′ed·ly** (-băsh′ĭd-lē) *adv.*

un·a·bat·ed (ŭn′ə-bā′tĭd) *adj.* At original full force; as strong as before: *They fought with unabated violence.* **—un′a·bat′ed·ly** *adv.*

un·a·ble (ŭn-ā′bəl) *adj.* **1.** Lacking the necessary power, authority, or means; not able. **2.** Lacking mental capability or efficiency; incompetent.

un·a·bridged (ŭn′ə-brĭjd′) *adj.* Having the original content; not condensed. Used of books and other documents.

un·ac·cent·ed (ŭn-ăk′sĕn-tĭd) *adj.* **1.** Having no diacritical mark. Used of a word, syllable, or letter. **2.** Having weak or no stress.

un·ac·cept·a·ble (ŭn′ăk-sĕp′tə-bəl) *adj.* Not acceptable, esp. not satisfactory or pleasing. **—un′ac·cept′a·bil′i·ty** *n.* **—un′ac·cept′a·bly** *adv.*

un·ac·com·mo·dat·ed (ŭn′ə-kŏm′ə-dā′tĭd) *adj.* **1.** Not adapted or accommodated. **2.** Lacking accommodations; unprovided.

un·ac·com·pa·nied (ŭn′ə-kŭm′pə-nēd) *adj.* **1.** Going or acting without a companion. **2.** *Mus.* Performed or scored without accompaniment.

un·ac·com·plished (ŭn′ə-kŏm′plĭsht) *adj.* **1.** Not completed or done; unfinished. **2.** Lacking special skills or abilities; unpolished, as in the social graces.

un·ac·count·a·ble (ŭn′ə-koun′tə-bəl) *adj.* **1.** Not able to be accounted for; inexplicable. **2.** Free from being held to account; not responsible. **—un′ac·count′a·bil′i·ty, un′ac·count′a·ble·ness** *n.* **—un′ac·count′a·bly** *adv.*

un·ac·cus·tomed (ŭn′ə-kŭs′təmd) *adj.* **1.** Not used to; not accustomed. **2.** Unfamiliar: *unaccustomed surroundings.*

u·na cor·da (o͞o′nə kôr′də) *adj. & adv. Mus.* With the soft pedal of the piano depressed. Used as a direction. [Ital., one string.]

un·a·dorned (ŭn′ə-dôrnd′) *adj.* Without adornment; simple; plain.

un·a·dul·ter·at·ed (ŭn′ə-dŭl′tə-rā′tĭd) *adj.* Not mingled or diluted with extraneous matter; pure.

un·ad·vised (ŭn′əd-vīzd′) *adj.* **1.** Having received no advice; not informed. **2.** Ill-advised; imprudent. **—un′ad·vis′ed·ly** (-vī′zĭd-lē) *adv.* **—un′ad·vis′ed·ness** *n.*

un·af·fect·ed (ŭn′ə-fĕk′tĭd) *adj.* **1.** Not changed, modified, or affected. **2.** Natural; genuine. **—un′af·fect′ed·ly** *adv.* **—un′af·fect′ed·ness** *n.*

un·a·fraid (ŭn′ə-frād′) *adj.* Not feeling, showing, or expressing fear.

u·nai (yo͞o′nô, o͞o′nou) *n.* Variant of **unau.** [Fr. *unau* < Tupi *unáu.*]

un·al·ien·a·ble (ŭn-āl′yə-nə-bəl, -ā′lē-ə-) *adj.* Not to be separated; inalienable: *unalienable rights.*

un·a·ligned (ŭn′ə-līnd′) *adj.* Nonaligned.

un·al·loyed (ŭn′ə-loid′) *adj.* **1.** Not in mixture with other metals; pure. **2.** Complete; unqualified: *an unalloyed success.*

un·al·ter·a·ble (ŭn-ôl′tər-ə-bəl) *adj.* Not capable of being altered. **—un·al′ter·a·bil′i·ty, un·al′tera·ble·ness** *n.* **—un·al′ter·a·bly** *adv.*

un·am·big·u·ous (ŭn′ăm-bĭg′yo͞o-əs) *adj.* Not ambiguous or uncertain; clear **—un′am·big′u·ous·ly** *adv.*

un-A·mer·i·can (ŭn′ə-mĕr′ĭ-kən) *adj.* Considered contrary to the institutions or principles of the United States.

un·a·neled (ŭn′ə-nēld′) *adj. Archaic.* Not having received extreme unction.

u·na·nim·i·ty (yo͞o′nə-nĭm′ĭ-tē) *n.* The condition of being unanimous.

u·nan·i·mous (yo͞o-năn′ə-məs) *adj.* **1.** Sharing the same opinions or views; being in complete harmony or accord. **2.** Based on or characterized by complete assent or agreement. [Lat. *unanimus* : *unus,* one + *animus,* mind.] **—u·nan′i·mous·ly** *adv.* **—u·nan′i·mous·ness** *n.*

un·an·swer·a·ble (ŭn-ăn′sər-ə-bəl) *adj.* Impossible to answer; or refute; incontrovertible. **—un·an′swer·a·bil′i·ty** *n.* **—un·an′swer·a·bly** *adv.*

un·an·tic·i·pat·ed (ŭn′ăn-tĭs′ə-pā′tĭd) *adj.* Not anticipated or expected. **—un′an·tic′i·pat′ed·ly** *adv.*

un·ap·peal·a·ble (ŭn′ə-pē′lə-bəl) *adj.* Not subject to appeal.

un·ap·pe·tiz·ing (ŭn-ăp′ĭ-tī′zĭng) *adj.* Not appetizing in appearance or aroma. **—un·ap′pe·tiz′ing·ly** *adv.*

un·ap·proach·a·ble (ŭn′ə-prō′chə-bəl) *adj.* **1.** Not friendly; aloof; distant. **2.** Not accessible; inapproachable. **—un′ap·proach′a·bil′i·ty, un′ap·proach′a·ble·ness** *n.* **—un′ap·proach′a·bly** *adv.*

un·ap·pro·pri·at·ed (ŭn′ə-prō′prē-ā′tĭd) *adj.* **1.** Not designated for a specific use. **2.** Not possessed by or formally assigned to a particular person or organization.

un·arm (ŭn-ärm′) *tr.v.* **-armed, -arm·ing, -arms.** To divest of armor or arms; disarm.

un·armed (ŭn-ärmd′) *adj.* **1.** Lacking weapons or armor; defenseless. **2.** *Biol.* Having no thorns or spines.

un·ar·tic·u·lat·ed (ŭn′är-tĭk′yə-lā′tĭd) *adj.* Not articulated, esp. not carefully or thoroughly thought out.

un·asked (ŭn-ăskt′, -äskt′) *adj.* **1.** Not asked. **2.** Not invited: *unasked company.* **3.** Not requested: *unasked suggestions.*

un·as·sail·a·ble (ŭn′ə-sā′lə-bəl) *adj.* **1.** Not capable of being disputed or disproven; undeniable. **2.** Not capable of being attacked or seized successfully; impregnable. **—un′as·sail′a·bil′i·ty, un′as·sail′a·ble·ness** *n.* **—un′as·sail′a·bly** *adv.*

un·as·ser·tive (ŭn′ə-sûr′tĭv) *adj.* Not assertive; reserved.

un·as·sist·ed (ŭn′ə-sĭs′tĭd) *adj.* **1.** Not assisted; unaided. **2.** *Baseball.* Designating a play handled by only one fielder.

un·as·sum·ing (ŭn′ə-so͞o′mĭng) *adj.* Not pretentious, boastful, or ostentatious; modest. **—un′as·sum′ing·ly** *adv.* **—un′as·sum′ing·ness** *n.*

un·at·tached (ŭn′ə-tăcht′) *adj.* **1.** Not attached or joined, esp. to surrounding tissue. **2. a.** Not committed to or dependent upon a person, group, or organization. **b.** Not engaged or married. **3.** *Law.* Not possessed or seized as security.

un·at·test·ed (ŭn′ə-tĕs′tĭd) *adj.* Not attested.

u·nau also **u·nai** (yo͞o′nô, o͞o′nou) *n.* A two-toed sloth of the genus *Choloepus.* [Fr. < Tupi *unáu.*]

un·a·vail·ing (ŭn′ə-vā′lĭng) *adj.* Useless; unsuccessful. **—un′a·vail′ing·ly** *adv.* **—un′a·vail′ing·ness** *n.*

u·na vo·ce (yo͞o′nə vō′sē) *adj. & adv.* With one voice; unanimously.

un·a·void·a·ble (ŭn′ə-voi′də-bəl) *adj.* Not able to be avoided; inevitable. **—un′a·void′a·bil′i·ty, un′a·void′a·ble·ness** *n.* **—un′a·void′a·bly** *adv.*

un·a·ware (ŭn′ə-wâr′) *adj.* Not aware or cognizant. *—adv.* Unawares.

un·a·wares (ŭn′ə-wârz′) *adv.* **1.** By surprise; unexpectedly: "*Sorrow comes to all, and to the young it comes with bittered agony because it takes them unawares*" (Lincoln). **2.** Without forethought or plan.

un·backed (ŭn-băkt′) *adj.* **1.** Lacking backing or support. **2.** Not having a back. **3.** Never ridden, as a horse.

un·bal·ance (ŭn-băl′əns) *tr.v.* **-anced, -anc·ing, -anc·es.** **1.** To upset the balance, stability, or equilibrium of. **2.** To derange (the mind). *—n.* The condition of being unbalanced.

un·bal·anced (ŭn-băl′ənst) *adj.* **1.** Not in balance or in proper balance. **2. a.** Mentally deranged. **b.** Not of sound judgment; irrational. **3.** In bookkeeping, not adjusted so that debit and credit correspond.

un·bal·last·ed (ŭn-băl′ə-stĭd) *adj.* **1.** Not stabilized or properly stabilized by ballast. **2.** Unsteady; wavering.

un·bar (ŭn-bär′) *v.* **-barred, -bar·ring, -bars.** *—tr.* To remove the bars from. *—intr.* To become unbarred; open.

un·bat·ed (ŭn-bā′tĭd) *adj.* **1.** Unabated. **2.** *Archaic.* Not blunted by a guard on the tip.

un·bear·a·ble (ŭn-bâr′ə-bəl) *adj.* Not endurable; intolerable. **—un·bear′a·bly** *adv.*

un·beat·a·ble (ŭn-bē′tə-bəl) *adj.* Impossible to surpass or defeat. **—un·beat′a·bly** *adv.*

un·beat·en (ŭn-bēt′n) *adj.* **1.** Not defeated. **2.** Untrod. **3.** Not beaten or pounded.

un·be·com·ing (ŭn′bĭ-kŭm′ĭng) *adj.* **1.** Not appropriate, attractive, or flattering: *an unbecoming dress.* **2.** Not seemly; improper: *unbecoming behavior.* **—un′be·com′ing·ly** *adv.*

un·be·got·ten (ŭn′bĭ-gŏt′n) *adj.* **1.** Not yet begotten. **2.** Self-existent; eternal.

un·be·known (ŭn′bĭ-nōn′) *adj.* Occurring or existing without the knowledge of; unknown. [UN-[1] + obs. *beknown,* known < ME *beknowen,* p.part. of *beknowen,* to get to know < OE *becnawan.*]

un·be·knownst (ŭn′bĭ-nōnst′) *adj.* Unbeknown. *—adv.* Without the knowledge of: *She had been ill for years, unbeknownst to her family.* [UNBEKNOWN + *-st,* as in *amongst.*]

un·be·lief (ŭn′bĭ-lēf′) *n.* Lack of belief or faith, esp. in religious matters. **—un′be·liev′er** *n.*

un·be·liev·a·ble (ŭn′bĭ-lē′və-bəl) *adj.* Not to be believed; incredible. **—un′be·liev′a·bly** *adv.*

un·be·liev·ing (ŭn′bĭ-lē′vĭng) *adj.* Not believing; doubting: *The incident occurred right before our unbelieving eyes.*

un·bend (ŭn-bĕnd′) *v.* **-bent** (-bĕnt′), **-bend·ing, -bends.** *—tr.* **1.** To unwind, as from mental tension; relax. **2.** To release (a bow, for example) from flexure or tension. **3.** *Naut.* To untie or loosen (a rope or sail). **4.** To straighten (something crooked or bent). *—intr.* **1.** To become less tense; relax. **2.** To become less strict. **3.** To become straight.

Usage: In the sense of "to straighten," *unbend* means the opposite of *bend.* But in the sense of "to relax, become less rigid," it is curiously close to *bend* in meaning. *Unbending,* on the other hand, preserves the sense of rigidity.

un·bend·ing (ŭn-bĕn′dĭng) *adj.* **1.** Inflexible; unyielding: *an* *unbending will to dominate.* **2.** Aloof and often antisocial; extremely reserved.

un·bi·ased also **un·bi·assed** (ŭn-bī′əst) *adj.* Without bias or prejudice; impartial. **—un·bi′ased·ly** *adv.* **—un·bi′ased·ness** *n.*

un·bid·den (ŭn-bĭd′n) also **un·bid** (-bĭd′) *adj.* Not invited; unasked.

un·bind (ŭn-bīnd′) *tr.v.* **-bound** (-bound′), **-bind·ing, -binds. 1.** To untie or unfasten, as wrappings or bindings. **2.** To release from restraints or bonds; free.

un·blenched (ŭn-blĕncht′) *adj.* Undaunted.

un·blessed also **un·blest** (ŭn-blĕst′) *adj.* **1.** Deprived of a blessing. **2.** Unholy; evil.

un·blink·ing (ŭn-blĭng′kĭng) *adj.* **1.** Without blinking. **2.** Without visible emotion. **3.** Fearless in facing reality: *His self-analysis was unblinking.* **—un·blink′ing·ly** *adv.*

un·blush·ing (ŭn-blŭsh′ĭng) *adj.* **1.** Without shame or remorse. **2.** Not blushing. **—un·blush′ing·ly** *adv.*

un·bod·ied (ŭn-bŏd′ēd) *adj.* **1.** Without body or form; incorporeal. **2.** Disembodied.

un·bolt (ŭn-bōlt′) *tr.v.* **-bolt·ed, -bolt·ing, -bolts.** To release the bolts of (a door, for example); unlock.

un·bolt·ed (ŭn-bōl′tĭd) *adj.* Not sifted, as flour.

un·born (ŭn-bôrn′) *adj.* **1.** Not yet born: *an unborn child.* **2.** Having not yet appeared; future.

un·bos·om (ŭn-bo͝oz′əm, -bo͞o′zəm) *v.* **-omed, -om·ing, -oms.** *—tr.* **1.** To confide (one's thoughts or feelings). **2.** To relieve (oneself) of troublesome thoughts or feelings. *—intr.* To reveal one's thoughts or feelings. **—un·bos′om·er** *n.*

un·bound (ŭn-bound′) *adj.* **1.** Not bound, as a book. **2.** Freed from bonds or shackles; released.

un·bound·ed (ŭn-boun′dĭd) *adj.* **1.** Having no boundaries or limits. **2.** Not kept within bounds; unrestrained: *unbounded enthusiasm.* **—un·bound′ed·ly** *adv.* **—un·bound′ed·ness** *n.*

un·bowed (ŭn-boud′) *adj.* **1.** Not bowed; unbent. **2.** Not subdued; unyielding: *"My head is bloody but unbowed"* (W.E. Henley).

un·brace (ŭn-brās′) *tr.v.* **-braced, -brac·ing, -brac·es. 1.** To set free by removing bands or braces. **2.** To release from tension; relax. **3.** To weaken; make slack.

un·breath·a·ble (ŭn-brē′*th*ə-bəl) *adj.* Not fit or suitable for breathing.

un·bred (ŭn-brĕd′) *adj.* **1.** *Obs.* Ill-bred; impolite. **2.** Not taught or instructed; untaught. **3.** Not bred.

un·bri·dle (ŭn-brīd′l) *tr.v.* **-dled, -dling, -dles. 1.** To free from a bridle. **2.** To free from restriction or restraint.

un·bri·dled (ŭn-brīd′ld) *adj.* **1.** Not wearing or fitted with a bridle. **2.** Unrestrained; uncontrolled: *unbridled passions.* **—un·bri′dled·ly** *adv.*

un·bro·ken (ŭn-brō′kən) also **un·broke** (-brōk′) *adj.* **1.** Not broken or tampered with; intact. **2.** Not violated or breached. **3.** Uninterrupted; continuous. **4.** Not tamed or broken to harness. **5.** Not disordered or disorganized. **—un·bro′ken·ly** *adv.* **—un·bro′ken·ness** *n.*

un·buck·le (ŭn-bŭk′əl) *v.* **-led, -ling, -les.** *—tr.* To loosen or undo the buckle or buckles of. *—intr.* **1.** To undo buckles. **2.** *Informal.* To relax.

un·bun·dling (ŭn-bŭn′dlĭng) *n.* The separate pricing of goods and services.

un·bur·den (ŭn′bûr′dn) *tr.v.* **-dened, -den·ing, -dens.** To free or relieve from a burden or trouble.

un·but·ton (ŭn-bŭt′n) *v.* **-toned, -ton·ing, -tons.** *—tr.* **1.** To unfasten the buttons of. **2.** To free or remove (a button) from a buttonhole. **3.** To open as if by unbuttoning: *unbutton the hatches.* *—intr.* To undo buttons.

un·caged (ŭn-kājd′) *adj.* **1.** Not confined in or as if in a cage. **2.** Released from a cage.

un·cal·cu·lat·ed (ŭn-kăl′kyə-lā′tĭd) *adj.* Not thought out in advance.

un·cal·cu·lat·ing (ŭn-kăl′kyə-lā′tĭng) *adj.* Not using or involving calculation.

un·called-for (ŭn-kôld′fôr′) *adj.* **1.** Not required or requested. **2.** Out of place; unnecessary.

un·can·ny (ŭn-kăn′ē) *adj.* **-ni·er, -ni·est. 1.** Exciting wonder and fear; inexplicable. **2.** So keen and perceptive as to seem preternatural. **—un·can′ni·ly** *adv.* **—un·can′ni·ness** *n.*

un·cap (ŭn-kăp′) *tr. v.* **-capped, -cap·ping, -caps.** To remove the cap or covering of.

un·caused (ŭn-kôzd′) *adj.* Existing without having been caused; spontaneous.

un·ceas·ing (ŭn-sē′sĭng) *adj.* Not ceasing or letting up; continuous. **—un·ceas′ing·ly** *adv.*

un·cel·e·brat·ed (ŭn-sĕl′ə-brā′tĭd) *adj.* **1.** Not formally or officially honored. **2.** Not famous or well-known; obscure.

un·cer·e·mo·ni·ous (ŭn-sĕr′ə-mō′nē-əs) *adj.* **1.** Not ceremonious; informal. **2.** Without the due formalities; abrupt. **—un·cer′e·mo′ni·ous·ly** *adv.* **—un·cer′e·mo′ni·ous·ness** *n.*

un·cer·tain (ŭn-sûr′tn) *adj.* **1.** Not known or established; doubtful: *an uncertain outcome.* **2.** Not determined; undecided: *uncertain plans.* **3.** Not having sure knowledge. **4.** Subject to change; variable: *uncertain weather.* **5.** Unsteady; fitful: *uncertain light.* **—un·cer′tain·ly** *adv.* **—un·cer′tain·ness** *n.*

un·cer·tain·ty (ŭn-sûr′tn-tē) *n., pl.* **-ties. 1.** The condition of being in doubt; lack of certainty. **2.** Something that is uncertain.

Synonyms: *uncertainty, doubt, dubiety, skepticism, suspicion, mistrust.* These nouns all involve the condition of being unsure about something or someone. *Uncertainty, doubt,* and *dubiety* are interchangeable in this sense in many contexts. Usually they imply a questioning state of mind that causes a person to hesitate in accepting some premise or in making a decision. *Skepticism* generally suggests a habitual tendency to question and demand proof of truth, merit, or the like before committing oneself. More than the preceding terms, *suspicion* and *mistrust* imply rather intense resistance to belief or acceptance, arising more from a specific lack of trust than from mere tentativeness of feeling. *Mistrust,* the stronger of the two terms, especially suggests a feeling that the person or thing in question is wrong, evil, or otherwise unworthy of confidence.

uncertainty principle *n.* A principle in quantum mechanics that increasing the accuracy of measurement of one observable quantity increases the uncertainty with which other quantities may be known.

un·chain (ŭn-chān′) *tr.v.* **-chained, -chain·ing, -chains.** To release from or as if from a chain or bond; set free.

un·change·a·ble (ŭn-chān′jə-bəl) *adj.* Not capable of being altered; immutable. **—un·change′a·bil′i·ty, un·change′a·ble·ness** *n.* **—un·change′a·bly** *adv.*

un·charged (ŭn-chärjd′) *adj.* **1.** Not loaded. Used of weapons. **2.** *Law.* Not formally accused. **3.** Lacking electric charge.

un·char·i·ta·ble (ŭn-chăr′ĭ-tə-bəl) *adj.* Not charitable or generous; unkind. **—un·char′i·ta·ble·ness** *n.* **—un′char′i·ta·bly** *adv.*

un·chart·ed (ŭn-chär′tĭd) *adj.* Not charted or recorded on a map or plan; unknown.

un·chaste (ŭn-chāst′) *adj.* Not chaste or modest. **—un·chaste′ly** *adv.* **—un·chaste′ness, un·chas′ti·ty** (-chăs′tĭ-tē) *n.*

un·chris·tian (ŭn-krĭs′chən) *adj.* **1.** Not Christian. **2.** Not in accordance with the Christian spirit. **3.** Uncivilized; barbaric.

un·church (ŭn-chûrch′) *tr.v.* **-churched, -church·ing, -church·es. 1.** To expel from a church or from church membership. **2.** To deprive (a congregation or sect) of the status of a church.

un·ci (ŭn′sī′) *n.* Plural of **uncus.**

un·cial also **Un·cial** (ŭn′shəl, -sē-əl) *—adj.* Of or pertaining to a style of writing characterized by somewhat rounded capital letters and found esp. in Greek and Latin manuscripts of the 4th to the 8th centuries A.D. *—n.* **1.** The uncial style or hand. **2.** An uncial letter. [LLat. *uncialis,* inch-high < Lat. *uncia,* a twelfth part, ounce, inch.]

un·ci·form (ŭn′sə-fôrm′) *adj.* Hook-shaped. [NLat. *unciformis* : Lat. *uncus,* hook + Lat. *forma,* shape.]

un·ci·nar·i·a (ŭn′sə-nâr′ē-ə) *n.* Hookworm. [NLat. *Uncinaria,* hookworm genus < Lat. *uncinus,* barb < *uncus,* hook.]

un·ci·nate (ŭn′sə-nāt′, -nĭt) *adj.* Hooked at the tip. [Lat. *uncinatus* < *uncinus,* barb < *uncus,* hook.]

un·ci·nus (ŭn-sī′nəs) *n., pl.* **-ni** (-nī′). A small hooklike structure, such as one of the setae of certain annelid worms. [NLat. < Lat., barb < *uncus,* hook.]

un·cir·cum·cised (ŭn-sûr′kəm-sīzd′) *adj.* **1.** Not circumcised. **2.** Not Jewish; Gentile. **3.** Heathen. **—un·cir′cum·ci′sion** (-sĭzh′ən) *n.*

un·civ·il (ŭn-sĭv′əl) *adj.* **1.** Discourteous; rude. **2.** Uncivilized; barbarous. **—un·civ′il·ly** *adv.*

un·civ·i·lized (ŭn-sĭv′ə-līzd′) *adj.* Not civilized; barbarous.

un·clad (ŭn-klăd′) *adj.* Not wearing clothes; naked.

un·clasp (ŭn-klăsp′) *v.* **-clasped, -clasp·ing, -clasps.** *—tr.* **1.** To release or loosen the clasp of. **2.** To release or loosen from a clasp or embrace. *—intr.* **1.** To become unfastened. **2.** To release or relax a clasp or grasp; let go.

un·clas·si·fied (ŭn-klăs′ə-fīd′) *adj.* Not placed or included in a class or category.

un·cle (ŭng′kəl) *n.* **1. a.** The brother of one's mother or father. **b.** The husband of one's aunt. **2.** A form of respectful address to an older man, used esp. by children. **3.** One who counsels. **4.** *Slang.* A pawnbroker. **5. Uncle.** Uncle Sam. *—interj. Slang.* Used to express surrender: *They beat him until he cried uncle.* [ME < OFr. *oncle* < Lat. *avunculus,* maternal uncle.]

un·clean (ŭn-klēn′) *adj.* **-er, -est. 1.** Not clean; foul. **2.** Morally defiled; unchaste. **3.** Ceremonially impure. **—un·clean′ly** *adv.*

un·clean·ly (ŭn-klĕn′lē) *adj.* **-li·er, -li·est.** Unclean. **—un·clean′li·ness** *n.*

un·clear (ŭn-klîr′) *adj.* **-er, -est.** Not clearly defined; not explicit.

un·clench (ŭn-klĕnch′) *v.* **-clenched, -clench·ing, -clench·es.** *—tr.* To loosen from a clenched position; relax: *unclench one's fists.* *—intr.* To become unclenched.

Uncle Sam (săm) *n.* **1.** The U.S. Government, often personified by a representation of a tall, thin man with a white beard and a blue swallow-tailed coat, red-and-white-striped trousers, and a tall hat with a band of stars. **2.** The American nation or its people. [< *U.S.,* abbr. of *United States.*]

Uncle Sam

Uncle Tom (tŏm) *n.* A black who is held to be humiliatingly subservient or deferential to whites. [After *Uncle Tom,* a slave in *Uncle Tom's Cabin,* a novel by Harriet Beecher Stowe (1811–1896).]

Uncle Tom·ism (tŏm'ĭz'əm) *n.* Behavior and attitudes held to be characteristic of an Uncle Tom.

un·cloak (ŭn-klōk') *tr.v.* **-cloaked, -cloak·ing, -cloaks. 1.** To remove a cloak or cover from. **2.** To expose; reveal.

un·close (ŭn-klōz') *v.* **-closed, -clos·ing, -clos·es.** —*tr.* To open or disclose. —*intr.* To become opened or disclosed.

un·clothe (ŭn-klōth') *tr.v.* **-clothed, -cloth·ing, -clothes.** To remove the clothing or cover from; strip.

un·co (ŭng'kō) *Scot.* —*adj.* So unusual as to be surprising; uncanny. —*n., pl.* **-cos. 1.** An unusual or amazing person. **2.** A stranger. **3. uncos.** News. —*adv.* To an excessive degree; remarkably. [ME *unkow,* var. of *uncouth,* strange. — see UNCOUTH.]

un·coil (ŭn-koil') *v.* **-coiled, -coil·ing, -coils.** —*tr.* To unwind; untwist. —*intr.* To become unwound or untwisted.

un·coined (ŭn-koind') *adj.* **1.** Not minted. **2.** Not artificial or counterfeit.

un·com·fort·a·ble (ŭn-kŭm'fər-tə-bəl, -kŭmf'tə-bəl) *adj.* **1.** Experiencing discomfort; uneasy. **2.** Causing discomfort; disquieting. **—un·com'fort·a·ble·ness** *n.* **—un·com'fort·a·bly** *adv.*

un·com·mer·cial (ŭn'kə-mûr'shəl) *adj.* **1.** Not engaged in or involving trade or commerce. **2.** Not in accordance with the spirit or methods of commerce.

un·com·mit·ted (ŭn'kə-mĭt'ĭd) *adj.* Not pledged to a specific cause or course of action.

un·com·mon (ŭn-kŏm'ən) *adj.* **-er, -est. 1.** Not common; rare. **2.** Wonderful; remarkable. **—un·com'mon·ly** *adv.* **—un·com'mon·ness** *n.*

un·com·mu·ni·ca·tive (ŭn'kə-myōō'nĭ-kā'tĭv, -kə-tĭv) *adj.* Not disposed to be communicative; taciturn. **—un'com·mu'ni·ca'tive·ly** *adv.* **—un'com·mu'ni·ca'tive·ness** *n.*

un·com·plain·ing (ŭn'kəm-plā'nĭng) *adj.* Not complaining; showing patience. **—un'com·plain'ing·ly** *adv.*

un·com·pli·cat·ed (ŭn-kŏm'plĭ-kā'tĭd) *adj.* **1.** Not complex or involved; simple. **2.** Not complicated by something extraneous, esp. not involving medical complications.

un·com·pli·men·ta·ry (ŭn'kŏm-plə-mĕn'tə-rē, -mĕn'trē) *adj.* Not complimentary; derogatory.

un·com·pro·mis·ing (ŭn-kŏm'prə-mī'zĭng) *adj.* Not granting concessions; inflexible. **—un·com'pro·mis'ing·ly** *adv.*

un·con·ceiv·a·ble (ŭn'kən-sē'və-bəl) *adj.* Inconceivable.

un·con·cern (ŭn'kən-sûrn') *n.* **1.** Lack of interest; indifference. **2.** Lack of worry or apprehensiveness.

un·con·cerned (ŭn'kən-sûrnd') *adj.* **1.** Not interested; indifferent. **2.** Not anxious or apprehensive; unworried. **—un'con·cern'ed·ly** (-sûr'nĭd-lē) *adv.* **—un'con·cern'ed·ness** (-sûr'nĭd-nĭs) *n.*

un·con·di·tion·al (ŭn'kən-dĭsh'ə-nəl) *adj.* Without conditions or limitations; absolute. **—un'con·di'tion·al·ly** *adv.*

un·con·di·tioned (ŭn'kən-dĭsh'ənd) *adj.* **1.** Unconditional; unrestricted. **2.** *Psychol.* Not the result of conditioning.

unconditioned response *n.* A response evoked by a stimulus before the initiation of a learning or conditioning process.

unconditioned stimulus *n.* A stimulus that evokes a certain response before the initiation of a conditioning process.

un·con·form·a·ble (ŭn'kən-fôr'mə-bəl) *adj.* **1.** Not conforming or capable of conforming. **2.** *Geol.* Showing unconformity. **—un'con·form'a·bil'i·ty, un'con·form'a·ble·ness** *n.* **—un'con·form'a·bly** *adv.*

un·con·for·mi·ty (ŭn'kən-fôr'mĭ-tē) *n., pl.* **-ties. 1.** Lack of conformity; nonconformity. **2.** *Geol.* **a.** An eroded space. **b.** A space caused by lack of deposit that separates younger strata from older rocks.

un·con·gen·ial (ŭn'kən-jēn'yəl) *adj.* **1.** Not compatible. **2. a.** Not suitable or appropriate. **b.** Not agreeable or pleasing. **—un'con·ge'ni·al'ity** (-jē'nē-ăl'ĭ-tē) *n.*

un·con·nect·ed (ŭn'kə-nĕk'tĭd) *adj.* **1.** Not joined or connected. **2.** Not coherent; disconnected. **—un'con·nect'ed·ly** *adv.* **—un'con·nect'ed·ness** *n.*

un·con·quer·a·ble (ŭn-kŏng'kər-ə-bəl) *adj.* Incapable of being overcome or defeated. **—un·con'quer·a·bly** *adv.*

un·con·scion·a·ble (ŭn-kŏn'shə-nə-bəl) *adj.* **1.** Not restrained by conscience; unscrupulous. **2.** Beyond prudence or reason; excessive. **—un·con'scion·a·ble·ness** *n.* **—un·con'scion·a·bly** *adv.*

un·con·scious (ŭn-kŏn'shəs) *adj.* **1.** Without conscious awareness, esp. without psychological rather than physiological awareness, and hence not capable of being consciously scrutinized: *unconscious resentment; unconscious fears.* **2. a.** Having lost, esp. temporarily, the capacity for sensory perception. **b.** Temporarily lacking full awareness. **3.** Without conscious control; involuntary. —*n.* The division of the psyche not subject to direct conscious observation but inferred from its effects on conscious processes and behavior. **—un·con'scious·ly** *adv.* **—un·con'scious·ness** *n.*

un·con·sid·ered (ŭn'kən-sĭd'ərd) *adj.* Not reasoned or considered; rash: *an unconsidered remark.*

un·con·sti·tu·tion·al (ŭn'kŏn-stĭ-tōō'shə-nəl, -tyōō'-) *adj.* Not in accord with the principles set forth in the constitution of a nation or state. **—un'con·sti·tu'tion·al'i·ty** *n.* **—un'con·sti·tu'tion·al·ly** *adv.*

un·con·trol·la·ble (ŭn'kən-trō'lə-bəl) *adj.* Not able to be controlled or governed. **—un'con·trol'la·bil'i·ty, un'con·trol'la·ble·ness** *n.* **—un'con·trol'la·bly** *adv.*

un·con·trolled (ŭn'kən-trōld') *adj.* Not under control or governance. **—un'con·trolled'ness** *n.*

un·con·ven·tion·al (ŭn'kən-vĕn'shə-nəl) *adj.* Not adhering to convention; out of the ordinary. **—un'con·ven'tion·al'i·ty** *n.* **—un'con·ven'tion·al·ly** *adv.*

un·cool (ŭn-kōōl') *adj. Slang.* **1.** Devoid of assurance, self-control, or sophistication. **2.** Not in accord with the standards or mores of a specified group.

un·cork (ŭn-kôrk') *tr.v.* **-corked, -cork·ing, -corks. 1.** To draw the cork from. **2.** To free from a sealed or constrained state.

un·count·ed (ŭn-koun'tĭd) *adj.* **1.** Not counted. **2.** Unable to be counted; innumerable.

un·cou·ple (ŭn-kŭp'əl) *v.* **-led, -ling, -les.** —*tr.* **1.** To disconnect: *uncouple railroad cars.* **2.** To set loose or release from a couple. —*intr.* To come or break loose.

un·couth (ŭn-kōōth') *adj.* **1.** Crude; unrefined. **2.** Awkward or clumsy; ungraceful. **3.** *Archaic.* Foreign; unfamiliar. [ME, unknown, strange < OE *uncūð* : *un-,* not + *cūð,* known.] **—un·couth'ly** *adv.* **—un·couth'ness** *n.*

un·cov·e·nant·ed (ŭn-kŭv'ə-nən-tĭd) *adj.* **1.** Not bound by a covenant. **2.** Not promised or guaranteed by a covenant.

un·cov·er (ŭn-kŭv'ər) *v.* **-ered, -er·ing, -ers.** —*tr.* **1.** To remove the cover from. **2.** To manifest or disclose; reveal. **3.** To remove the hat from, as in respect or reverence. —*intr.* **1.** To remove a cover. **2.** To bare the head in respect or reverence.

un·cov·ered (ŭn-kŭv'ərd) *adj.* **1.** Having no cover or protection. **2.** Lacking the protection of insurance or collateral security. **3.** Bareheaded.

un·cre·at·ed (ŭn'krē-ā'tĭd) *adj.* **1.** Not created; not yet existing. **2.** Existing of itself; uncaused.

un·crit·i·cal (ŭn-krĭt'ĭ-kəl) *adj.* **1.** Not discriminating. **2.** Not using critical standards or methods, as in evaluating something.

un·cross (ŭn-krôs', -krŏs') *tr.v.* **-crossed, -cross·ing, -cross·es.** To move (one's legs, for example) from a crossed position.

unc·tion (ŭngk'shən) *n.* **1.** The act of anointing as part of a religious, ceremonial, or healing ritual. **2.** An ointment or oil; salve. **3.** Something that serves to soothe; balm. **4.** Affected or exaggerated earnestness, esp. in language. [ME < Lat. *unctio* < *unguere,* to anoint.]

unc·tu·ous (ŭngk'chōō-əs) *adj.* **1.** Having the quality or characteristics of oil or ointment; greasy. **2.** Containing or composed of oil or fat. **3.** Abundant in organic materials: *unctuous soil.* **4.** Characterized by affected, exaggerated, or insincere earnestness: *unctuous flattery.* [ME < Med. Lat. *unctuosus* < Lat. *unctum,* ointment < *unguere,* to anoint.] **—unc'tu·ous·ly** *adv.* **—unc'tu·ous·ness, unc'tu·os'i·ty** (-ŏs'ĭ-tē) *n.*

un·cus (ŭng'kəs) *n., pl.* **un·ci** (ŭn'sī'). *Biol.* A hook-shaped part or process. [NLat. < Lat., hook.]

un·cut (ŭn-kŭt') *adj.* **1.** Not cut. **2.** Having the book page edge not slit or trimmed. **3.** Not cut to a specific shape. Used of a gemstone. **4.** Not shortened; unabridged.

un·damped (ŭn'dămpt') *adj.* **1.** Not tending toward a state of rest; not damped. Used of oscillations. **2.** Not stifled or discouraged; unchecked: *His ardor was undamped.*

un·daunt·a·ble (ŭn-dôn'tə-bəl, -dän'-) *adj.* Not capable of being discouraged or disheartened.

un·daunt·ed (ŭn-dôn'tĭd, -dän'-) *adj.* Not discouraged or disheartened; resolute. **—un·daunt'ed·ly** *adv.* **—un·daunt'ed·ness** *n.*

un·de·ceive (ŭn'dĭ-sēv') *tr.v.* **-ceived, -ceiv·ing, -ceives.** To free from illusion or deception.

un·de·cid·ed (ŭn'dĭ-sī'dĭd) *adj.* **1.** Not yet determined or settled; open. **2.** Not having reached a decision; uncommitted. **—un'de·cid'ed·ly** *adv.* **—un'de·cid'ed·ness** *n.*

un·decked[1] (ŭn-dĕkt') *adj.* Not decorated; unornamented.

un·decked[2] (ŭn-dĕkt') *adj.* Having no deck. Used of a ship.

un·de·mon·stra·tive (ŭn'dĭ-mŏn'strə-tĭv) *adj.* Not disposed to expressions of feeling; reserved. **—un'de·mon'stra·tive·ly** *adv.* **—un'de·mon'stra·tive·ness** *n.*

un·de·ni·a·ble (ŭn'dĭ-nī'ə-bəl) *adj.* **1.** Not able to be denied; irrefutable. **2.** Unquestionably good; outstanding. **—un'de·ni'a·bly** *adv.* **—un'de·ni'a·ble·ness** *n.*

un·der (ŭn'dər) *prep.* **1.** In a lower position or place than: *a signature under a painting.* **2.** Beneath the surface of: *under the ground.* **3.** Beneath the assumed surface or guise of: *under a false name.* **4.** Less than; smaller than. **5.** Less than the required amount or degree of: *under voting age.* **6.** Inferior to in status or rank. **7.** Subject to the authority, rule, or control of: *under a dictatorship.* **8.** Subject to the supervision, instruction, or influence of: *under parental guidance.* **9.** Undergoing or receiving the effects of: *under intensive care.* **10.** Subject to the restraint or obligation of: *under contract.* **11.** Within the group or classification of: *listed under biology.* **12.** In the process of: *under discussion.* **13.** In view of; because of: *under these conditions.* **14.** With the authorization of: *under the king's seal.* **15.** Sowed or planted with: *an acre under oats.* —*adv.* **1.** In or into a place below or beneath. **2.** In or into a subordinate or inferior condition or position. **3.** So as to be covered or enveloped by. **4.** So as to be less than the required amount or degree. —*adj.* **1.** Located or situated on a lower level or beneath something else: *the under parts of a machine.* **2.** Lower in rank, power, or authority; subordinate. **3.** Less than is required or customary: *an under dose of medication.* [ME < OE.]

under– *pref.* **1.** Beneath or below in position: *underground.* **2.** Inferior or subordinate in rank or importance: *undersecretary.* **3.** Less in degree, rate, or quantity than normal or proper: *undersized.* [ME < OE < *under,* under.]

Usage: Many compounds other than those entered here may be formed with *under-.* In forming compounds, *under-* is joined with the following element without space or a hyphen: *underrate; undergrow.* Note, however, that the adjective *under* may combine with other words as a unit modifier. In such cases the words are joined by hyphens: *an under-the-table deal.*

un·der·a·chieve (ŭn′dər-ə-chēv′) *intr.v.* **-chieved, -chiev·ing, -chieves.** To perform below an expected level as indicated by tests of intelligence, aptitude, or ability, esp. in schoolwork. **—un′der·a·chieve′ment** *n.* **—un′der·a·chiev′er** *n.*

un·der·act (ŭn′dər-ăkt′) *v.* **-act·ed, -act·ing, -acts.** —*tr.* **1.** To perform (a role) weakly. **2.** To understate (a role) intentionally. —*intr.* To perform in an understated way.

un·der·age (ŭn′dər-āj′) *adj.* Below the customary or legal age, as for drinking or voting.

un·der·arm (ŭn′dər-ärm′) *adj.* **1.** Located, placed, or used under the arm. **2.** *Sports.* Executed with the hand kept below the level of the shoulder. —*adv.* With an underarm motion or delivery. —*n.* The armpit.

un·der·bel·ly (ŭn′dər-bĕl′ē) *n., pl.* **-lies. 1.** The lowest part of an animal's body. **2.** The vulnerable or weak part: *"the soft underbelly of Europe"* (Winston Churchill).

un·der·bid (ŭn′dər-bĭd′) *v.* **-bid, -bid·ding, -bids.** —*tr.* **1.** To bid lower than (a competitor). **2.** To bid less than the full value of (one's hand) in bridge. —*intr.* To make an unnecessarily low bid. **—un′der·bid′der** *n.*

un·der·bod·y (ŭn′dər-bŏd′ē) *n.* **1.** The underbelly (sense 1). **2.** The under parts of the body of a motor vehicle.

un·der·bred (ŭn′dər-brĕd′) *adj.* **1.** Badly brought up; ill-bred. **2.** Not thoroughbred; of mixed breed.

un·der·brush (ŭn′dər-brŭsh′) *n.* Small trees, shrubs, or similar plants growing beneath the taller trees in a forest.

un·der·car·riage (ŭn′dər-kăr′ĭj) *n.* **1.** A supporting framework or structure, as for the body of an automobile. **2.** The landing gear of an aircraft.

un·der·charge (ŭn′dər-chärj′) *tr.v.* **-charged, -charg·ing, -charg·es. 1.** To charge (someone) less than is customary or required. **2.** To load (a firearm) with an insufficient charge. —*n.* (ŭn′dər-chärj′). An insufficient or improper charge.

un·der·class (ŭn′dər-klăs′) *n.* The lowest societal stratum, usually composed of the disadvantaged.

un·der·class·man (ŭn′dər-klăs′mən) *n.* A student in the freshman or sophomore class at a secondary school or college.

un·der·clothes (ŭn′dər-klōz′, -klō*thz*′) *pl.n.* Clothes worn next to the skin, beneath one's outer clothing; underwear.

un·der·cloth·ing (ŭn′der-klō′*th*ĭng) *n.* Underclothes.

un·der·coat (ŭn′dər-kōt′) *n.* **1.** A coat worn beneath another coat. **2.** A covering of short hairs or fur concealed by the longer outer hairs of an animal's coat. **3.** Also **un·der·coat·ing** (-kō′tĭng). **a.** A coat of sealing material applied to a surface before the topcoat is applied. **b.** A tarlike substance sprayed on the underside of an automobile to prevent rusting. —*tr.v.* **-coat·ed, -coat·ing, -coats.** To apply an undercoat to.

un·der·cool (ŭn′dər-ko͞ol′) *tr.v.* **-cooled, -cool·ing, -cools.** To supercool.

un·der·cov·er (ŭn′dər-kŭv′ər) *adj.* **1.** Performed or occurring in secret: *an undercover investigation.* **2.** Engaged or employed in spying or secret investigation: *undercover FBI agents.*

un·der·croft (ŭn′dər-krôft′, -krŏft′) *n.* A crypt. [ME *under croft* : *under,* under + *croft,* crypt < Med. Lat. *crupta* < Lat. *crypta.* —see CRYPT.]

un·der·cur·rent (ŭn′dər-kûr′ənt) *n.* **1.** A current, as of air or water, below another current or beneath a surface. **2.** An underlying tendency, force, or influence often contrary to what is superficially evident; intimation.

un·der·cut (ŭn′dər-kŭt′) *v.* **-cut, -cut·ting, -cuts.** —*tr.* **1.** To make a cut under or below. **2.** To create an overhang by cutting material away from, as in carving. **3.** To sell at a lower price than or to work for lower wages or fees than (a competitor). **4.** To diminish or destroy the province or effectiveness of; undermine. **5.** *Sports.* **a.** To impart backspin to (a ball) by striking downward as well as forward, as in golf and baseball. **b.** To cut or slice (a ball) with an underarm stroke, as in tennis. —*intr.* To undercut someone or something. —*n.* (ŭn′dər-kŭt′) **1. a.** A cut made in the under part to remove material. **b.** The material so removed. **2.** A notch cut in a tree to direct its fall and insure a clean break. **3.** *Chiefly Brit.* The tenderloin of beef; fillet. **4.** *Sports.* **a.** A spin given to a ball opposite to its direction of flight; backspin. **b.** A cut or slice made with an underarm motion.

un·der·de·vel·oped (ŭn′dər-dĭ-vĕl′əpt) *adj.* **1.** Not adequately or normally developed. **2.** Left in a photographic developing solution for too short a time to produce a normal degree of contrast. **3.** Industrially or economically backward: *underdeveloped countries.*

un·der·do (ŭn′dər-do͞o′) *tr.v.* **-did** (-dĭd′), **-done** (-dŭn′), **do·ing, -does** (-dŭz′). To do to an insufficient degree.

un·der·dog (ŭn′dər-dôg′, -dŏg′) *n.* **1.** One who is expected to lose a contest or struggle, as in sports or politics. **2.** One who is at a disadvantage.

un·der·done (ŭn′dər-dŭn′) *adj.* Not sufficiently cooked: *an underdone turkey.*

un·der·draw·ers (ŭn′dər-drôrz′) *pl.n.* Shorts or briefs worn as undergarments, esp. those for a man; underpants.

un·der·dress (ŭn′dər-drĕs′) *n.* **1.** Apparel worn beneath outer garments; underclothing. **2.** An outer garment worn as part of a costume or suit, such as a dress beneath a tunic or coat.

un·der·dressed (ŭn′dər-drĕst′) *adj.* Too informally dressed.

un·der·drive (ŭn′dər-drīv′) *n.* A gearing device causing the output drive shaft to rotate at a slower rate than the engine input shaft.

un·der·ed·u·cat·ed (ŭn′dər-ĕj′o͞o-kā′tĭd) *adj.* Poorly or insufficiently educated.

un·der·em·pha·size (ŭn′dər-ĕm′fə-sīz′) *tr.v.* **-sized, -siz·ing, -siz·es.** To fail to give enough emphasis to. **—un′der·em′pha·sis** (-sĭs) *n.*

un·der·em·ployed (ŭn′dər-ĕm-ploid′) *adj.* Being partially or inadequately employed, esp. being employed at a low-paying job that requires less skill or training than one possesses. **—un′der·em·ploy′ment** *n.*

un·der·es·ti·mate (ŭn′dər-ĕs′tə-māt′) *tr.v.* **-mat·ed, -mat·ing, -mates.** To make too low an estimate of the quantity, degree, or worth of. —*n.* (ŭn′dər-ĕs′tə-mĭt). An estimate that is or proves to be too low. **—un′der·es′ti·ma′tion** *n.*

un·der·ex·pose (ŭn′dər-ĭk-spōz′) *tr.v.* **-posed, -pos·ing, -pos·es.** To expose (film) to light for too short a time to produce normal image contrast. **—un′der·ex·po′sure** (-ĭk-spō′zhər) *n.*

un·der·feed (ŭn′dər-fēd′) *tr.v.* **-fed** (-fĕd′), **-feed·ing, -feeds. 1.** To feed insufficiently. **2.** To supply (an engine) with or channel fuel from below.

un·der·flow (ŭn′dər-flō′) *n.* A data processing error arising when a computed quantity is a smaller number than the device is capable of displaying.

un·der·foot (ŭn′dər-fo͝ot′) *adv.* **1.** Below or under the foot or feet; directly below. **2.** In the way.

un·der·fund (ŭn′dər-fŭnd′) *tr.v.* **-fund·ed, -fund·ing, -funds.** To provide insufficient funding for.

un·der·fur (ŭn′dər-fûr′) *n.* The dense, soft, fine fur beneath the coarse outer hairs of certain mammals.

un·der·gar·ment (ŭn′dər-gär′mənt) *n.* A garment that is worn under outer garments, esp. one worn next to the skin.

un·der·gird (ŭn′dər-gûrd′) *tr.v.* **-gird·ed** or **-girt** (-gûrt′), **-gird·ing, -girds.** To gird, support, or strengthen from beneath.

un·der·glaze (ŭn′dər-glāz′) *n.* Coloring applied to pottery before it is glazed.

un·der·go (ŭn′dər-gō′) *tr.v.* **-went** (-wĕnt′), **-gone** (-gôn′, -gŏn′), **-go·ing, -goes** (-gōz′). **1.** To experience; be subjected to. **2.** To endure; suffer. [ME *undergon* : *under,* under + *gon,* go.]

un·der·grad·u·ate (ŭn′dər-grăj′o͞o-ĭt) *n.* A college or university student who has not yet received a degree. —*adj.* **1.** Of, pertaining to, or characteristic of undergraduates. **2.** Having undergraduate standing.

un·der·ground (ŭn′dər-ground′) *adj.* **1.** Situated, occurring, or operating below the surface of the earth: *underground caverns; underground nuclear testing.* **2.** Hidden or concealed; clandestine: *underground resistance to the tyrant.* **3.** Of or pertaining to an organization involved in secret or illegal activity: *underground black markets.* **4.** Of, pertaining to, or describing an avant-garde movement or its films, publications, and art, usually privately produced and of special appeal and often concerned with social or artistic experiment. —*n.* **1.** A clandestine, often nationalist, organization fostering or planning hostile activities against, or the overthrow of, a government in power, such as an occupying military government. **2.** *Chiefly Brit.* A subway system. **3.** An avant-garde movement or publication. —*adv.* (ŭn′dər-ground′). **1.** Below the surface of the earth. **2.** In secret; stealthily. —*tr.v.* **-ground·ed, -ground·ing, -grounds.** To situate under the ground: *workers undergrounding telephone lines.*

Underground Railroad *n.* Before 1861 in the United States, a secret network of cooperation aiding fugitive slaves in reaching sanctuary in the free states or Canada.

un·der·grown (ŭn′dər-grōn′) *adj.* Not fully grown; puny.

un·der·growth (ŭn′dər-grōth′) *n.* **1. a.** Low-growing plants, saplings, and shrubs beneath trees in a forest. **b.** Something resembling this, as a growth of short, fine hairs beneath longer ones. **2.** The condition of being undergrown.

un·der·hand (ŭn′dər-hănd′) *adj.* **1.** Done in a treacherous or deceitful manner; sneaky. **2.** *Sports.* Underarm (sense 2). —*adv.* **1.** With an underhand movement. **2.** Slyly; secretly.

un·der·hand·ed (ŭn′dər-hăn′dĭd) *adj.* **1.** Underhand. **2.** Lacking the required number of workers or players; short-handed. **—un′der·hand′ed·ly** *adv.* **—un′der·hand′ed·ness** *n.*

un·der·hung (ŭn′dər-hŭng′) *adj.* **1. a.** Protruding from beneath. **b.** Supported by or lying over something that projects. **2.** Resting on or mounted along a supporting track, as a sliding door on rollers. **3.** Underslung, as a machine.

un·der·kill (ŭn′dər-kĭl′) *n.* Insufficient force to defeat an enemy.

un·der·laid (ŭn′dər-lād′) *adj.* **1.** Placed or laid underneath. **2.** Supported or raised by something from beneath; having an underlay.

un·der·lay (ŭn′dər-lā′) *tr.v.* **-laid, -lay·ing, -lays. 1.** To put (one thing) under another. **2.** To provide with a base or sublining. **3.** *Printing.* To raise or support (the level of a printing bed) by inserting a piece of paper or other material under the type. —*n.* (ŭn′dər-lā′). **1.** Something underlaid, as felt under a carpet. **2.** *Printing.* Paper or other material used to underlay.

un·der·let (ŭn′dər-lĕt′) *tr.v.* **-let, -let·ting, -lets. 1.** To lease for less than the proper value. **2.** To sublet.

un·der·lie (ŭn′dər-lī′) *tr.v.* **-lay** (-lā′), **-lain** (-lān′), **-ly·ing, -lies. 1.** To be located under or below. **2.** To be the support or basis of; account for: *Many factors underlie my decision.* **3.** To comprise a prior financial claim over: *Dividends for preferred stock underlie those of common stock.*

un·der·line (ŭn′dər-līn′, ŭn′dər-līn′) *tr.v.* **-lined, -lin·ing, -lines. 1.** To draw a line under; underscore, esp. to emphasize or cause to stand out. **2.** To emphasize or stress. —*n.* (ŭn′dər-līn′). A line under something, such as a symbol, word, or phrase to indicate emphasis or italic type.

un·der·ling (ŭn′dər-lĭng) *n.* A subordinate; inferior.

un·der·lin·ing (ŭn′dər-lī′nĭng) *n.* **1.** The act of drawing a line under; underscoring. **2.** Emphasis or stress, as in instruction or argument.

un·der·lip (ŭn′dər-lĭp′) *n.* The lower lip.

un·der·ly·ing (ŭn′dər-lī′ĭng) *adj.* **1.** Lying under or beneath something: *underlying strata.* **2.** Basic; fundamental. **3.** Implicit; hidden: *an underlying meaning.* **4.** Taking precedence; prior: *an underlying financial claim.*

un·der·mine (ŭn′dər-mīn′) *tr.v.* **-mined, -min·ing, -mines. 1.** To dig a mine or tunnel beneath. **2.** To weaken by wearing away a base or foundation: *Water undermined the stone foundations.* **3.** To weaken, injure, or impair, often by degrees or imperceptibly; sap: *Late hours undermine one's health.*

un·der·mod·u·late (ŭn′dər-mŏj′ə-lāt′) *tr.v.* **-lat·ed, -lat·ing, -lates.** To utilize less of a sound reproduction or transmission device than is optimally possible. —**un′der·mod′u·la′tion** *n.*

un·der·most (ŭn′dər-mōst′) *adj.* Lowest in position, rank, or place; bottom. —*adv.* Lowest.

un·der·neath (ŭn′dər-nēth′) *adv.* **1.** In a place beneath; below. **2.** On the lower face or underside. —*prep.* **1.** Under; below; beneath. **2.** Under the power or control of. —*adj.* Lower; under. —*n.* The part or side below or under. [ME *undernethe* < OE *underneoðan* : *under,* under + *neoðan,* below.]

un·der·nour·ish (ŭn′dər-nûr′ĭsh) *tr.v.* **-ished, -ish·ing, -ish·es.** To provide with insufficient quantity or quality of nourishment to sustain proper health and growth. —**un′der·nour′ish·ment** *n.*

un·der·nu·tri·tion (ŭn′dər-no͞o-trĭsh′ən, -nyo͞o-) *n.* Inadequate nutrition due to undernourishment or poor assimilation of food.

un·der·pants (ŭn′dər-pănts′) *pl.n.* Pants, shorts, or drawers worn as underwear.

un·der·pass (ŭn′dər-păs′) *n.* A passage underneath something, esp. a section of road that passes under another road or railroad.

underpass

un·der·pay (ŭn′dər-pā′) *tr.v.* **-paid, -pay·ing, -pays.** To pay insufficiently or less than deserved.

un·der·pin (ŭn′dər-pĭn′) *tr.v.* **-pinned, -pin·ning, -pins. 1.** To support from below, as with props, girders, or masonry. **2.** To corroborate or substantiate.

un·der·pin·ning (ŭn′dər-pĭn′ĭng) *n.* **1.** Material or masonry used to support a structure, such as a wall. **2.** Often **underpinnings.** Something serving as a support or foundation. **3.** Often **underpinnings.** *Informal.* The legs.

un·der·play (ŭn′dər-plā′, ŭn′dər-plā′) *v.* **-played, -play·ing, -plays.** —*tr.* To act (a role) subtly or with restraint. —*intr.* To act a role subtly or with restraint.

un·der·pop·u·lat·ed (ŭn′dər-pŏp′yə-lā′tĭd) *adj.* Lacking the normal or required population density. —**un′der·pop·u·la′tion** *n.*

un·der·price (ŭn′dər-prīs′) *tr.v.* **-priced, -pric·ing, -pric·es. 1.** To price lower than the real value. **2.** To undercut in price: *underprice a competitor.*

un·der·priv·i·leged (ŭn′dər-prĭv′ə-lĭjd) *adj.* Not having opportunities or advantages enjoyed by other members of one's community; deprived.

un·der·pro·duc·tion (ŭn′dər-prə-dŭk′shən) *n.* **1.** Production below full capacity. **2.** Production below demand.

un·der·proof (ŭn′dər-pro͞of′) *adj.* Having a smaller proportion of alcohol than proof spirit.

un·der·prop (ŭn′dər-prŏp′) *tr.v.* **-propped, -prop·ping, -props.** To prop (something) from below.

un·der·quote (ŭn′dər-kwōt′) *tr.v.* **-quot·ed, -quot·ing, -quotes. 1.** To sell (goods) at a price lower than the official list or market price; undersell. **2.** To quote a lower price than (another).

un·der·rate (ŭn′dər-rāt′) *tr.v.* **-rat·ed, -rat·ing, -rates.** To rate too low; underestimate.

un·der·re·port (ŭn′dər-rĭ-pôrt′, -pōrt′) *tr.v.* **-port·ed, -port·ing, -ports.** To report (income, for example) to be less than is actually so.

un·der·run (ŭn′dər-rŭn′) *tr.v.* **-ran** (-răn′), **-run, -run·ning, -runs. 1.** To run, pass, or go beneath. **2.** *Naut.* To haul (a line or cable) up to a boat and examine or repair it.

un·der·score (ŭn′dər-skôr′, -skōr′) *tr.v.* **-scored, -scor·ing, -scores. 1.** To underline. **2.** To emphasize or stress. —*n.* A line drawn under writing to indicate emphasis or italic type.

un·der·sea (ŭn′dər-sē′) *adj.* Pertaining to, existing, or created for use beneath the surface of the sea. —*adv.* (ŭn′dər-sē′) also **un·der·seas** (-sēz′). Beneath the surface of the sea.

un·der·sec·re·tar·y (ŭn′dər-sĕk′rə-tĕr′ē) *n., pl.* **-ies.** An official directly subordinate to a Cabinet member.

un·der·sell (ŭn′dər-sĕl′) *tr.v.* **-sold** (-sōld′), **-sell·ing, -sells. 1.** To sell goods for a lower price than: *undersell the competition.* **2.** To sell at a price less than the actual value.

un·der·set (ŭn′dər-sĕt′) *n.* An ocean undercurrent.

un·der·sexed (ŭn′dər-sĕkst′) *adj.* Having less sexual potency or desire than normal.

un·der·shirt (ŭn′dər-shûrt′) *n.* An upper undergarment, usually having short sleeves, worn next to the skin under a shirt.

un·der·shoot (ŭn′dər-sho͞ot′) *v.* **-shot** (-shŏt′), **-shoot·ing, -shoots.** —*tr.* **1.** To shoot a missile short of (a target). **2. a.** To start the approach of one's aircraft to (a landing area) too low or too soon. **b.** To land an aircraft short of (a landing area). —*intr.* To shoot or to land short of a target or a landing area.

un·der·shorts (ŭn′dər-shôrts′) *pl.n.* Underdrawers.

un·der·shot (ŭn′dər-shŏt′) *adj.* **1.** Driven by water passing from below, as a water wheel. **2.** Projecting from below.

un·der·shrub (ŭn′dər-shrŭb′) *n.* A low-growing shrub.

un·der·side (ŭn′dər-sīd′) *n.* The side or surface that is underneath; bottom side.

un·der·sign (ŭn′dər-sīn′) *tr.v.* **-signed, -sign·ing, -signs.** To sign one's name at the bottom of (a letter or document).

un·der·signed (ŭn′dər-sīnd′) *n., pl.* **undersigned.** A signer whose name appears at the bottom of a document.

un·der·sized (ŭn′dər-sīzd′) also **un·der·size** (-sīz′) *adj.* Being of subnormal or insufficient size.

un·der·skirt (ŭn′dər-skûrt′) *n.* **1.** A skirt worn under another. **2.** One skirt of a layered gown over which outer skirts are formed and draped.

un·der·sleeve (ŭn′dər-slēv′) *n.* **1.** A sleeve worn under another. **2.** An ornamental sleeve worn under another, designed to extend below or show through slashes in the outer sleeve.

un·der·slung (ŭn′dər-slŭng′) *adj.* Having springs attached to the axles from below. Used of a vehicle.

un·der·soil (ŭn′dər-soil′) *n.* Soil below the ground surface.

un·der·spin (ŭn′dər-spĭn′) *n.* A backspin.

un·der·staffed (ŭn′dər-stăft′) *adj.* Having insufficient personnel: *an understaffed hospital.*

un·der·stand (ŭn′dər-stănd′) *v.* **-stood** (-sto͝od′), **-stand·ing, -stands.** —*tr.* **1.** To perceive and comprehend the nature and significance of; know: *"I don't pretend to understand the Universe—it's a great deal bigger than I am"* (Carlyle). **2.** To know thoroughly by close contact with or long experience of: *That teacher understands children.* **3. a.** To grasp or comprehend the meaning intended or expressed by (another). **b.** To comprehend the language, sounds, form, or symbols of (a kind of expression): *understands Spanish.* **4.** To know and be tolerant or sympathetic toward: *I can understand his point of view even though I disagree with it.* **5.** To learn indirectly, as by hearsay; gather; assume. **6.** To conclude; infer: *Am I to understand that you are staying the night?* **7.** To accept as an agreed fact: *It is understood that the fee will be five dollars.* —*intr.* **1.** To have understanding, knowledge, or comprehension. **2.** To learn indirectly or at secondhand; gather: *They were just married, or so I understand.* [ME *understanden* < OE *understandan* : *under,* under + *standan,* to stand.] —**un′der·stand′a·bil′i·ty** *n.* —**un′der·stand′a·ble** *adj.* —**un′der·stand′a·bly** *adv.*

un·der·stand·ing (ŭn′dər-stăn′dĭng) *n.* **1.** The quality or condition of one who understands; comprehension. **2.** The faculty by which one understands; intelligence. **3.** Individual or specified judgment or outlook in a matter; opinion. **4. a.** A compact implicit between two or more persons or groups. **b.** The matter implicit in such a compact. **5.** A reconciliation of differences; agreement: *They finally reached an understanding.* —*adj.* **1.** Having or characterized by comprehension, good sense, or discernment. **2.** Compassionate and sympathetic. —**un′der·stand′ing·ly** *adv.*

un·der·state (ŭn′dər-stāt′) *v.* **-stat·ed, -stat·ing, -states.** —*tr.* **1.** To state with less completeness or truth than seems warranted by the facts. **2.** To express with restraint or lack of emphasis, esp. ironically or for dramatic impact. **3.** To state (a quantity, for example) that is too low: *understate one's age.* —*intr.* To give an understatement.

un·der·state·ment (ŭn′dər-stāt′mənt) *n.* **1.** A disclosure or statement that is less than complete. **2.** Intentional lack of emphasis in expression, as in irony.

un·der·stood (ŭn′dər-sto͝od′) *adj.* **1.** Agreed upon; assumed. **2.** Not expressed in writing; implied.

un·der·stra·tum (ŭn′dər-strā′təm, -străt′əm) *n., pl.* **-stra·ta** (-strā′tə, -străt′ə) or **-stra·tums.** A substratum.

un·der·stud·y (ŭn′dər-stŭd′ē) *v.* **-ied, -y·ing, -ies.** —*tr.* **1.** To study or know (a role) so as to be able to replace the regular performer when required. **2.** To act as an understudy to. —*intr.* To be engaged in studying a role so as to be able to replace the regular performer when required. —*n., pl.* **-ies. 1.** An actor or actress who understudies. **2.** A person trained to do the work of another.

un·der·sur·face (ŭn′dər-sûr′fəs) *n.* An underside.

un·der·take (ŭn′dər-tāk′) *v.* **-took** (-to͝ok′), **-tak·en, -tak·ing, -takes.** —*tr.* **1.** To take upon oneself; decide or agree to do: *undertake a task.* **2.** To pledge or commit oneself to. **3.** *Obs.* To accept combat with; take on. —*intr. Archaic.* To make oneself responsible. Used with *for.* [ME *undertaken* : *under,* under + *taken,* to take.]

un·der·tak·er (ŭn′dər-tā′kər) *n.* **1.** One who undertakes a task or job, esp. an entrepreneur. **2.** (ŭn′dər-tā′kər). One whose business it is to arrange for the burial or cremation of the dead and to assist at funeral rites; mortician.

un·der·tak·ing (ŭn′dər-tā′kĭng) *n.* **1.** A task or assignment undertaken; venture. **2.** A guaranty, engagement, or promise. **3.** The profession or duties of an undertaker.

un·der-the-count·er (ŭn′dər-*th*ə-koun′tər) *adj.* Transacted, given, or sold illicitly.

un·der-the-ta·ble (ŭn′dər-*th*ə-tā′bəl) *adj.* Under-the-counter.

un·der·tint (ŭn′dər-tĭnt′) *n.* A slight or subtle tint.

un·der·tone (ŭn′dər-tōn′) *n.* **1.** A tone of low pitch or volume, esp. of spoken sound. **2. a.** A pale or subdued color. **b.** A color applied under or seen through another color. **3.** An underlying or implied tendency or meaning; undercurrent.

un·der·tow (ŭn′dər-tō′) *n.* The seaward pull of receding waves breaking on a shore.

un·der·trick (ŭn′dər-trĭk′) *n.* A card trick, esp. in bridge, the loss of which prevents a declarer from making his contract.

un·der·trump (ŭn′dər-trŭmp′) *intr.v.* **-trumped, -trump·ing, -trumps.** To play a trump lower than another card player's trump when trump has not been led.

un·der·val·ue (ŭn′dər-văl′yo͞o) *tr.v.* **-ued, -u·ing, -ues. 1.** To assign too low a value to; underestimate. **2.** To have too little regard or esteem for. —**un′der·val′u·a′tion** *n.*

un·der·vest (ŭn′dər-vĕst′) *n. Chiefly Brit.* An undershirt.

un·der·wa·ter (ŭn′dər-wô′tər, -wŏt′ər) *adj.* Pertaining to, occurring, used, or performed beneath the surface of water. —**un′der·wa′ter** *adv.*

under way *adv.* **1.** Being put in motion or operation; started. **2.** Already commenced or initiated; afoot. **3.** *Naut.* In motion; not anchored and not moored to a fixed object.

un·der·wear (ŭn′dər-wâr′) *n.* Clothing worn under the outer clothes and next to the skin; underclothes.

un·der·weight (ŭn′dər-wāt′) *adj.* Weighing less than is normal, healthy, or required. —*n.* Insufficiency of weight.

un·der·whelm (ŭn′dər-hwĕlm′, -wĕlm′) *tr.v.* **-whelmed, -whelm·ing, -whelms.** *Informal.* To fail to excite, stimulate, or impress.

un·der·wing (ŭn′dər-wĭng′) *n.* **1.** One of a pair of hind wings partially or wholly covered by the forewings, as in certain moths. **2.** Any of various moths of the genus *Calocala,* having brightly colored underwings.

un·der·wood (ŭn′dər-wo͝od′) *n.* Shrubs and small trees growing beneath taller trees; underbrush.

un·der·world (ŭn′dər-wûrld′) *n.* **1.** A region, realm, or dwelling place conceived to be below the surface of the earth. **2.** The opposite side of the earth; antipodes. **3.** *Gk. & Rom. Myth.* The world of the dead, said to be below the world of the living; Hades. **4.** The part of society that is engaged in and organized for the purpose of crime and vice. **5.** *Archaic.* The world beneath the heavens; earth.

un·der·write (ŭn′dər-rīt′) *v.* **-wrote** (-rōt′), **-writ·ten** (-rĭt′n), **-writ·ing, -writes.** —*tr.* **1. a.** To write under or at the end of something. **b.** To subscribe, esp. to sign or endorse (a document). **2.** To assume financial responsibility for: *underwrite a theatrical production.* **3. a.** To sign (an insurance policy) so as to assume liability in case of specified losses. **b.** To insure. **c.** To insure against losses totaling (a given amount). **4.** To agree to buy (stock not yet sold publicly) at a fixed time and price. —*intr.* To act as an underwriter, esp. to issue an insurance policy.

un·der·writ·er (ŭn′dər-rī′tər) *n.* **1. a.** A person or firm engaged in an insurance business. **b.** An insurance agent who assesses the risk of enrolling an applicant for coverage or a policy. **2.** A person or company that guarantees the purchase of a full issue of stocks or bonds.

undescended testicle *n.* A testicle that has remained within the inguinal canal and has not descended to the scrotum.

un·de·serv·ed·ly (ŭn′dĭ-zûr′vĭd-lē) *adv.* Unfairly or unjustifiably.

un·de·sign·ing (ŭn′dĭ-zī′nĭng) *adj.* Without ulterior motives; straightforward.

un·de·sir·a·ble (ŭn′dĭ-zīr′ə-bəl) *adj.* Not desirable; objectionable. —*n.* An undesirable person. —**un′de·sir′a·bil′i·ty** *n.* —**un′de·sir′a·bly** *adv.*

un·de·ter·mined (ŭn′dĭ-tûr′mĭnd) *adj.* **1.** Not yet determined; undecided. **2.** Not specifically known or ascertained.

un·dies (ŭn′dēz) *pl.n. Informal.* Underwear, esp. women's underwear.

un·dig·ni·fied (ŭn-dĭg′nə-fīd′) *adj.* Not dignified; lacking in or damaging to dignity.

un·dine (ŭn-dēn′, ŭn′dēn′) *n.* In folklore, a female water spirit who could earn a soul by marrying a mortal and bearing his child. [NLat. *undina* < Lat. *unda,* wave.]

un·dip·lo·mat·ic (ŭn-dĭp′lə-măt′ĭk) *adj.* Not diplomatic or tactful. —**un·dip′lo·mat′i·cal·ly** *adv.*

un·di·rect·ed (ŭn′dĭ-rĕk′tĭd, -dī-) *adj.* Not guided; without object or purpose.

un·dis·crim·i·nat·ing (ŭn′dĭs-krĭm′ə-nā′tĭng) *adj.* **1.** Indiscriminate. **2.** Lacking sensitivity, taste, or judgment.

un·dis·posed (ŭn′dĭs-pōzd′) *adj.* **1.** Not settled, removed, or resolved. **2.** Disinclined; unwilling.

un·dis·tin·guished (ŭn′dĭ-stĭng′gwĭsht) *adj.* Not distinguished; ordinary.

un·dis·turbed (ŭn′dĭ-stûrbd′) *adj.* Not disturbed; calm.

un·do (ŭn-do͞o′) *v.* **-did** (-dĭd′), **-done** (-dŭn′), **-do·ing, -does** (-dŭz′). —*tr.* **1.** To reverse or erase; annul: *no way to undo the suffering caused by the war.* **2.** To untie, disassemble, or loosen: *undo a shoelace.* **3.** To open (a parcel, for example); unwrap. **4.** *Obs.* To solve or interpret; unravel. **5. a.** To cause the ruin or downfall of; destroy. **b.** To throw into confusion; unsettle. —*intr.* To come open or undone. [ME *undon* < OE *undōn* : *un-,* un- + *don,* to do.] —**un·do′er** *n.*

un·dock (ŭn-dŏk′) *tr.v.* **-docked, -dock·ing, -docks.** To uncouple.

un·do·ing (ŭn-do͞o′ĭng) *n.* **1.** The act of reversing or annulling something accomplished; cancellation. **2.** The act of unfastening or loosening. **3. a.** The act of bringing to ruin. **b.** The cause or source of ruin; downfall.

un·doubt·ed (ŭn-dou′tĭd) *adj.* Accepted as beyond question; undisputed. —**un·doubt′ed·ly** *adv.*

un·draw (ŭn-drô′) *tr.v.* **-drew** (-dro͞o′), **-drawn** (-drôn′), **-draw·ing, -draws.** To draw to one side, as a curtain.

un·dress (ŭn-drĕs′) *v.* **-dressed, -dress·ing, -dress·es.** —*tr.* **1.** To remove the clothing of; disrobe. **2.** To remove the bandages from (a wound, for example). —*intr.* To take off one's clothing. —*n.* **1.** Informal attire as distinguished from formal attire. **2.** Nakedness.

un·dressed (ŭn-drĕst′) *adj.* **1. a.** Naked. **b.** Not fully dressed. **2.** Not specially treated or processed: *undressed leather.*

un·due (ŭn-do͞o′, -dyo͞o′) *adj.* **1.** Exceeding what is appropriate or normal; excessive. **2.** Not just, proper, or legal: *undue use of power.* **3.** Not yet payable or due.

un·du·lant (ŭn′jə-lənt, ŭn′dyə-, ŭn′də-) *adj.* Resembling waves in occurrence, appearance, or motion.

undulant fever *n.* A persistent and recurrent fever caused by bacteria of the genus *Brucella,* transmitted by contact with infected animals or by consuming infected meat or milk and marked by weakness and painful joints.

un·du·late (ŭn′jə-lāt′, ŭn′dyə-, ŭn′də-) *v.* **-lat·ed, -lat·ing, -lates.** —*tr.* **1.** To cause to move in a smooth wavelike motion. **2.** To give a wavelike appearance or form to. —*intr.* **1.** To move in waves or with a wavelike or sinuous motion; ripple. **2.** To have a wavelike appearance or form. —*adj.* (ŭn′jə-lĭt, -lāt′, ŭn′dyə-, ŭn′də-) also **un·du·lat·ed** (-lā′tĭd). Having a wavy outline or appearance: *leaves with undulate margins.* [< Lat. *undulatus,* having wave-like markings < *unda,* wave.]

un·du·la·tion (ŭn′jə-lā′shən, ŭn′dyə-, ŭn′də-) *n.* **1.** A regular rising and falling or movement to alternating sides; movement in waves. **2.** A wavelike form, outline, or appearance. **3.** One of a series of waves or wavelike segments. —**un′du·la·to′ry** (-lə-tôr′ē, -tōr′ē) *adj.*

un·du·ly (ŭn-do͞o′lē, -dyo͞o′-) *adv.* Excessively; immoderately.

un·du·ti·ful (ŭn-do͞o′tĭ-fəl, -dyo͞o′-) *adj.* Lacking a sense of duty. —**un·du′ti·ful·ly** *adv.* —**un·du′ti·ful·ness** *n.*

un·dy·ing (ŭn-dī′ĭng) *adj.* Endless; everlasting; immortal.

un·earned (ŭn-ûrnd′) *adj.* **1.** Not gained by work or service. **2.** Not deserved. **3.** Not yet earned: *unearned interest.*

unearned increment *n.* The increase in property value resulting from factors independent of the owner, such as a general rise in demand for land, as opposed to increase of value earned directly by the efforts of the owner.

un·earth (ŭn-ûrth′) *tr.v.* **-earthed, -earth·ing, -earths. 1.** To bring up out of the earth; dig up. **2.** To bring to public notice; uncover.

un·earth·ly (ŭn-ûrth′lē) *adj.* **-li·er, -li·est. 1.** Not of the earth; supernatural. **2.** Frighteningly weird and unaccountable; unnatural: *an unearthly shriek.* **3.** Ridiculously unreasonable or uncustomary; absurd: *out of bed at an unearthly hour.* —**un·earth′li·ness** *n.*

un·eas·y (ŭn-ē′zē) *adj.* **-i·er, -i·est. 1.** Lacking ease, comfort, or a sense of security: *The farmers were uneasy until the crop was in.* **2.** Affording no ease or reassurance: *an uneasy calm.* **3.** Awkward or unsure in manner; constrained: *uneasy with strangers.* —**un·eas′i·ly** *adv.* —**un·ease′, un·eas′i·ness** *n.*

un·ed·it·ed (ŭn-ĕd′ĭ-tĭd) *adj.* **1. a.** Not edited or revised. **b.** Not adapted for a special audience or purpose. **2.** Still to be but not yet edited.
un·ed·u·cat·ed (ŭn-ĕj′ə-kā′tĭd) *adj.* Not educated.
un·e·mo·tion·al (ŭn′ĭ-mō′shə-nəl) *adj.* **1.** Not easily stirred or moved. **2.** Involving little or no emotion; rational. **—un′e·mo′tion·al·ly** *adv.*
un·em·ploy·a·ble (ŭn′ĭm-ploi′ə-bəl) *adj.* Not able to find or hold a job. **—un′em·ploy′a·ble** *n.*
un·em·ployed (ŭn′ĭm-ploid′) *adj.* **1.** Out of work; jobless. **2.** Not being used; idle. *—n.* A person who does not have a job. **—un′em·ploy′ment** *n.*
unemployment compensation *n.* Financial compensation for unemployed workers provided by the social security system.
un-Eng·lish (ŭn-ĭng′glĭsh) *adj.* **1.** Not having the characteristics of English. **2.** Not in agreement with standard English usage.
un·e·qual (ŭn-ē′kwəl) *adj.* **1.** Not the same in any measurable aspect, as extent or quantity. **2.** Not the same as another in rank or social position. **3.** Consisting of ill-matched opponents: *an unequal race.* **4.** Having unbalanced sides or parts; asymmetric. **5.** Not even or consistent; variable. **6.** Not having the required abilities; inadequate: *His talents were unequal to his aspirations.* **7.** Not fair. *—n.* One that is not the equal of another. **—un·e′qual·ly** *adv.*
un·e·qualed (ŭn-ē′kwəld) also **un·e·qualled** *adj.* Not matched or paralleled by others of its kind; unrivaled.
un·e·quiv·o·cal (ŭn′ĭ-kwĭv′ə-kəl) *adj.* Admitting of no doubt or misunderstanding; clear. **—un′e·quiv′o·cal·ly** *adv.*
un·err·ing (ŭn-ûr′ĭng, -ĕr′ĭng) *adj.* Committing no mistakes; consistently accurate. **—un·err′ing·ly** *adv.*
un·es·sen·tial (ŭn′ĭ-sĕn′shəl) *adj.* Not necessary or important; dispensable. *—n.* A nonessential.
un·e·ven (ŭn′ē′vən) *adj.* **-er, -est. 1.** Not equal, as in size, length, or quality. **2.** Not consistent or uniform: *an uneven color.* **3.** Not smooth or level: *the uneven surface of a cobblestone road.* **4.** Not straight or parallel: *uneven margins.* **5.** Not fair or equitable. **6.** Designating an odd number. **—un·e′ven·ly** *adv.* **—un·e′ven·ness** *n.*
un·e·vent·ful (ŭn′ĭ-vĕnt′fəl) *adj.* Lacking in significant events; without incident. **—un′e·vent′ful·ly** *adv.* **—un′e·vent′ful·ness** *n.*
un·ex·am·pled (ŭn′ĭg-zăm′pəld) *adj.* Without precedent; unparalleled.
un·ex·cep·tion·a·ble (ŭn′ĭk-sĕp′shə-nə-bəl) *adj.* Beyond the least reasonable objection; irreproachable. —See Usage note at **unexceptional. —un′ex·cep′tion·a·ble·ness** *n.* **—un′ex·cep′tion·a·bly** *adv.*
un·ex·cep·tion·al (ŭn′ĭk-sĕp′shə-nəl) *adj.* **1.** Not varying from a norm; usual. **2.** Not subject to exceptions; absolute. **—un′ex·cep′tion·al·ly** *adv.*

Usage: *Unexceptional* is often confused with *unexceptionable.* When the desired meaning is "not open to objection" or "above reproach," the term is *unexceptionable. Unexceptional* is not acceptable in that sense according to a large majority of the Usage Panel.

un·ex·pect·ed (ŭn′ĭk-spĕk′tĭd) *adj.* Coming without warning; unforeseen. **—un′ex·pect′ed·ly** *adv.* **—un′ex·pect′ed·ness** *n.*
un·ex·ploit·ed (ŭn′ĕk-sploi′tĭd) *adj.* **1.** Not exploited. **2.** Not developed: *unexploited farmland.*
un·ex·pres·sive (ŭn′ĭk-sprĕs′ĭv) *adj.* **1.** Not conveying the meaning intended or the emotion felt. **2.** *Obs.* Inexpressible. **—un′ex·pres′sive·ly** *adv.* **—un′ex·pres′sive·ness** *n.*
un·fad·ing (ŭn-fā′dĭng) *adj.* **1.** Retaining color or freshness. **2.** Retaining value or usefulness. **—un·fad′ing·ly** *adv.*
un·fail·ing (ŭn-fā′lĭng) *adj.* **1.** Inexhaustible. **2.** Constant; unflagging. **3.** Incapable of error; infallible. **—un·fail′ing·ly** *adv.* **—un·fail′ing·ness** *n.*
un·fair (ŭn′fâr′) *adj.* **-er, -est. 1.** Not just or evenhanded; biased. **2.** Contrary to laws or conventions, esp. in commerce; unethical. **—un′fair′ly** *adv.* **—un′fair′ness** *n.*
un·faith (ŭn-fāth′) *n.* An absence of faith; disbelief.
un·faith·ful (ŭn-fāth′fəl) *adj.* **1.** Not adhering to a pledge or contract; disloyal. **2.** Not true or constant to a sexual partner, esp. guilty of adultery. **3.** Not justly representing or reflecting the original; inaccurate. **4.** *Obs.* Without or deficient in religious faith; unbelieving. **—un·faith′ful·ly** *adv.* **—un·faith′ful·ness** *n.*
un·fa·mil·iar (ŭn′fə-mĭl′yər) *adj.* **1.** Not within one's knowledge; strange. **2.** Not being acquainted; not conversant: *unfamiliar with the roads here.* **—un′fa·mil·iar′i·ty** (-mĭl-yăr′ĭ-tē, -mĭl′ē-ăr′ĭ-tē) *n.* **—un′fa·mil′iar·ly** *adv.*
un·fash·ion·a·ble (ŭn-făsh′ə-nə-bəl) *adj.* **1.** Not currently fashionable. **2.** Not socially approved: *an unfashionable part of town.* **—un·fash′ion·a·bly** *adv.*
un·fas·ten (ŭn-făs′ən) *v.* **-tened, -ten·ing, -tens.** *—tr.* To separate the connected parts of. *—intr.* To become loosened or separated.
un·fa·thered (ŭn-fä′*th*ərd) *adj.* **1.** Having no known father. **2.** Of uncertain origin or authenticity.
un·fath·om·a·ble (ŭn-fă*th*′ə-mə-bəl) *adj.* **1.** Incapable of being understood. **2.** Incapable of being measured.
un·fa·vor·a·ble (ŭn-fā′vər-ə-bəl, -fāv′rə-bəl) *adj.* **1.** Not propitious. **2.** Negative; adverse. **3.** Undesirable; disadvantageous. **4.** Not pleasing. **—un′fa′vor·a·ble·ness** *n.* **—un·fa′vor·a·bly** *adv.*
un·feel·ing (ŭn′fē′lĭng) *adj.* **1.** Having no feeling or sensation; insentient. **2.** Not sympathetic; callous. **—un·feel′ing·ly** *adv.* **—un·feel′ing·ness** *n.*
un·feigned (ŭn′fānd′) *adj.* Not simulated; genuine. **—un·feign′ed·ly** (ŭn-fā′nĭd-lē) *adv.*
un·fet·ter (ŭn-fĕt′ər) *tr.v.* **-tered, -ter·ing, -ters. 1.** To free from fetters. **2.** To liberate.
un·fin·ished (ŭn-fĭn′ĭsht) *adj.* **1.** Not brought to an end; incomplete: *unfinished business.* **2.** Not having received special processing; natural: *unfinished wood.*
un·fit (ŭn′fĭt′) *adj.* **1.** Not meant or adapted for a given purpose; inappropriate. **2.** Below the required standard; unqualified. **3.** Not in good physical or mental health. *—tr.v.* **-fit·ted, -fit·ting, -fits.** To cause to be unsuited or unqualified; disqualify. **—un′fit′ly** *adv.* **—un′fit′ness** *n.*
un·fix (ŭn-fĭks′) *tr.v.* **-fixed, -fix·ing, -fix·es. 1.** To detach from what secures; unfasten. **2.** To unsettle; disturb.
un·flap·pa·ble (ŭn-flăp′ə-bəl) *adj.* Not easily upset or excited. **—un·flap′pa·bil′i·ty** *n.* **—un·flap′pa·bly** *adv.*
un·flat·ter·ing (ŭn-flăt′ər-ĭng) *adj.* Not flattering; unfavorable: *gave the film an unflattering review.* **—un·flat′ter·ing·ly** *adv.*
un·fledged (ŭn-flĕjd′) *adj.* **1.** Not yet having the flight feathers necessary to fly. **2.** Inexperienced, immature, or untried.
un·flinch·ing (ŭn-flĭn′chĭng) *adj.* Not betraying fear or indecision; resolute. **—un·flinch′ing·ly** *adv.* **—un·flinch′ing·ness** *n.*
un·fo·cused also **un·fo·cussed** (ŭn-fō′kəst) *adj.* **1.** Not brought into focus. **2.** Not centered on something specific.
un·fold (ŭn-fōld′) *v.* **-fold·ed, -fold·ing, -folds.** *—tr.* **1.** To open and spread out (something folded); extend. **2.** To remove the coverings from; disclose to view. **3.** To reveal gradually by written or spoken explanation; make known. *—intr.* **1.** To become spread out; open out. **2.** To be revealed gradually to the understanding. **—un·fold′ment** *n.*
un·fore·seen (ŭn′fər-sēn′) *adj.* Not anticipated in advance; unexpected: *unforeseen difficulties.*
un·for·get·ta·ble (ŭn′fər-gĕt′ə-bəl) *adj.* Earning a permanent place in the memory; memorable. **—un′for·get′ta·bly** *adv.* **—un′for·get′ta·bil′i·ty, un′for·get′ta·ble·ness** *n.*
un·for·mat·ted (ŭn-fôr′măt′ĭd) *adj.* *Computer Sci.* Of or relating to computer input or output data that have not been edited before display.
un·formed (ŭn-fôrmd′) *adj.* **1.** Having no definite shape or structure; unorganized. **2.** Not yet developed to maturity. **3.** Not yet given a physical existence; uncreated.
un·for·tu·nate (ŭn-fôr′chə-nĭt) *adj.* **1.** Characterized by undeserved lack of good fortune; unlucky. **2.** Causing misfortune; disastrous. **3.** Regrettable; deplorable: *an unfortunate lack of good manners.* *—n.* A victim of bad luck. **—un·for′tu·nate·ly** *adv.* **—un·for′tu·nate·ness** *n.*
un·found·ed (ŭn-foun′dĭd) *adj.* **1.** Not yet established. **2.** Not based on fact or sound observation; groundless. **—un·found′ed·ly** *adv.* **—un·found′ed·ness** *n.*
un·fre·quent·ed (ŭn′frē-kwĕn′tĭd, ŭn-frē′kwən-tĭd) *adj.* Receiving few or no visitors; unpatronized.
un·friend·ed (ŭn-frĕn′dĭd) *adj.* Having no friends.
un·friend·ly (ŭn-frĕnd′lē) *adj.* **-li·er, -li·est. 1.** Not disposed to friendship. **2.** Indicating a bad prospect; unfavorable. **—un·friend′li·ness** *n.*
un·frock (ŭn-frŏk′) *tr.v.* **-frocked, -frock·ing, -frocks. 1.** To strip of priestly privileges and functions. **2.** To deprive of the right to practice a profession.
un·fruit·ful (ŭn-fro͞ot′fəl) *adj.* **1.** Not bearing fruit or offspring; barren. **2.** Not productive of good or valuable results. **—un·fruit′ful·ly** *adv.* **—un′fruit′ful·ness** *n.*
un·fund·ed (ŭn-fŭn′dĭd) *adj.* **1.** Not funded, as a floating debt. **2.** Not furnished with funds: *an unfunded project.*
un·furl (ŭn-fûrl′) *v.* **-furled, -furl·ing, -furls.** *—tr.* To spread or open out; unroll. *—intr.* To become spread or opened out.
un·fuss·y (ŭn-fŭs′ē) *adj.* **1.** Not particular or concerned, as with details. **2.** Not cluttered or complicated, as with extraneous matters or details.
un·gain·ly (ŭn-gān′lē) *adj.* **-li·er, -li·est. 1.** Without grace or ease of movement; clumsy. **2.** Difficult to move or use; unwieldy. **—un·gain′li·ness** *n.*
un·gen·er·os·i·ty (ŭn-jen′ə-rŏs′ĭ-tē) *n.* The quality or condition of being ungenerous; stinginess.
un·gen·er·ous (ŭn-jĕn′ər-əs) *adj.* **1.** Not generous; stingy. **2.** Harsh in judgment; unkind. **—un·gen′er·ous·ly** *adv.*
un·girt (ŭn-gûrt′) *adj.* **1.** Having the belt or girdle removed or loosened. **2.** Loose or free; slack.
un·glue (ŭn-glo͞o′) *tr.v.* **-glued, -glu·ing, -glues.** To separate by or as if by dissolving a glue or other adhesive.
un·glued (ŭn-glo͞od′) *adj.* **1.** Loosened or separated; unfastened. **2.** *Slang.* Upset; dicombobulated.
un·god·ly (ŭn-gŏd′lē) *adj.* **-li·er, -li·est. 1.** Not revering God; impious. **2.** Sinful; wicked. **3.** Outrageous: *He called at an ungodly hour.* **—un·god′li·ness** *n.*
un·gov·ern·a·ble (ŭn-gŭv′ər-nə-bəl) *adj.* Not capable of being governed; not controllable. **—un·gov′ern·a·ble·ness** *n.* **—un·gov′ern·a·bly** *adv.*
un·gra·cious (ŭn-grā′shəs) *adj.* **1.** Lacking social grace or graciousness; rude. **2.** Not welcome or acceptable; unattrac-

tive. **3.** *Archaic.* Evil; wicked. **—un·gra′cious·ly** *adv.* **—un·gra′cious·ness** *n.*

un·gram·mat·i·cal (ŭn′grə-măt′ĭ-kəl) *adj.* Not in accord with grammar.

un·grate·ful (ŭn-grāt′fəl) *adj.* **1.** Not feeling or exhibiting gratitude, thanks, or appreciation. **2.** Not agreeable or pleasant; repellent: *"I will not perform the ungrateful task of comparing cases of failure"* (Lincoln). **—un·grate′ful·ly** *adv.* **—un·grate′ful·ness** *n.*

un·gual (ŭng′gwəl) *adj. Zool.* Of, resembling, or bearing a hoof, nail, or claw. [< Lat. *unguis,* nail.]

un·guard·ed (ŭn-gär′dĭd) *adj.* **1.** Without guard or protection; vulnerable. **2.** Without discretion; incautious. **—un·guard′ed·ly** *adv.* **—un·guard′ed·ness** *n.*

un·guent (ŭng′gwənt) *n.* A salve for soothing or healing; ointment. [ME < Lat. *unguentum* < *unguere,* to anoint.]

un·guic·u·late (ŭng-gwĭk′yə-lĭt, -lāt′) *adj.* **1.** *Zool.* Having nails or claws. **2.** *Bot.* Having a claw-shaped base, as a petal. *—n.* A mammal having nails or claws. [NLat. *unguiculatus* < Lat. *unguiculus,* fingernail, dim. of *unguis,* nail.]

un·guis (ŭng′gwĭs) *n., pl.* **-gues** (-gwēz). A nail, claw, hoof, or clawlike structure. [Lat., nail.]

un·gu·late (ŭng′gyə-lĭt, -lāt′) *adj.* **1.** Having hoofs. **2.** Of or belonging to the former order Ungulata, now divided into the orders Perissodactyla and Artiodactyla, and including hoofed mammals such as horses, cattle, deer, swine, and elephants. *—n.* An ungulate mammal. [LLat. *ungulatus* < *ungula,* hoof, dim. of *unguis,* nail.]

un·hal·low (ŭn-hăl′ō) *tr.v.* **-lowed, -low·ing, -lows.** *Archaic.* To profane; desecrate.

un·hal·lowed (ŭn-hăl′ōd) *adj.* **1.** Not hallowed or consecrated. **2. a.** Impious; irreligious. **b.** Not conforming to accepted moral standards; immoral.

un·hand (ŭn-hănd′) *tr.v.* **-hand·ed, -hand·ing, -hands.** To remove one's hand from; let go.

un·hand·some (ŭn′hăn′səm) *adj.* **1.** Not attractive or beautiful; homely. **2.** Not courteous or in good taste; ungracious. **—un·hand′some·ly** *adv.* **—un·hand′some·ness** *n.*

un·hand·y (ŭn-hăn′dē) *adj.* **-i·er, -i·est. 1.** Difficult to handle or manage; unwieldy. **2.** Lacking manual skill or dexterity. **—un·hand′i·ly** *adv.* **—un·hand′i·ness** *n.*

un·hap·py (ŭn-hăp′ē) *adj.* **-pi·er, -pi·est. 1.** Not happy or joyful; sad. **2.** Not bringing good fortune; unlucky: *an unhappy accident.* **3.** Not suitable; inappropriate: *an unhappy choice of words.* **—un·hap′pi·ly** *adv.* **—un·hap′pi·ness** *n.*

un·har·ness (ŭn′här′nĭs) *tr.v.* **-nessed, -ness·ing, -ness·es. 1.** To remove the harness from. **2.** To release or liberate.

un·health·y (ŭn-hĕl′thē) *adj.* **-i·er, -i·est. 1.** In a state of ill health; sick. **2.** Characterizing or symptomatic of ill health: *an unhealthy pallor.* **3.** Causing or conducive to poor health; unwholesome. **4.** Harmful to character or moral health; corruptive. **5.** Of a risky nature; dangerous. **—un′health′i·ly** *adv.* **—un·health′i·ness** *n.*

un·heard (ŭn-hûrd′) *adj.* **1.** Not heard. **2.** Not given a hearing; not listened to. **3.** *Archaic.* Not heard of; obscure.

un·heard-of (ŭn-hûrd′ŭv′, -ŏv′) *adj.* Not previously known.

un·hes·i·tat·ing (ŭn-hĕz′ĭ-tā′tĭng) *adj.* **1.** Prompt; ready. **2.** Unfaltering; steadfast. **—un·hes′i·tat′ing·ly** *adv.*

un·hinge (ŭn-hĭnj′) *tr.v.* **-hinged, -hing·ing, -hing·es. 1.** To remove from hinges. **2.** To remove the hinges from. **3.** To confuse; disrupt.

un·hip (ŭn-hĭp′) *adj. Slang.* Not aware or informed of the latest fashions or developments.

un·hitch (ŭn-hĭch′) *tr.v.* **-hitched, -hitch·ing, -hitch·es.** To release from or as if from a hitch; unfasten.

un·ho·ly (ŭn′hō′lē) *adj.* **-li·er, -li·est. 1.** Not hallowed or consecrated. **2.** Wicked; immoral. **3.** *Informal.* Outrageous: *took unholy risks to win the downhill race.* **—un·ho′li·ly** *adv.* **—un·ho′li·ness** *n.*

un·hook (ŭn-ho͝ok′) *tr.v.* **-hooked, -hook·ing, -hooks. 1.** To release or remove from a hook. **2.** To unfasten the hooks of.

un·hoped (ŭn-hōpt′) *adj. Archaic.* Not hoped or looked for.

un·hoped-for (ŭn-hōpt′fôr′) *adj.* Not expected or hoped for.

un·horse (ŭn-hôrs′) *tr.v.* **-horsed, -hors·ing, -hors·es. 1.** To cause to fall from a horse. **2.** To overthrow or dislodge; upset.

un·hou·seled (ŭn′hou′zəld) *adj. Archaic.* Not having received the Eucharist.

uni– *pref.* Single; one: *unicycle.* [Lat. < *unus,* one.]

U·ni·at also **U·ni·ate** (yo͞o′nē-ăt′) *n.* A member of a Uniat Church. *—adj.* Of or pertaining to the Uniat Church or its members, practices, or doctrines. [R. *uniyat* < Pol. *uniat* < *unja,* union < LLat. *unio* < *unus,* one.]

Uniat Church also **Uniate Church** *n.* An Eastern Christian church that acknowledges the supremacy of the pope but retains its own distinctive liturgy.

u·ni·ax·i·al (yo͞o′nē-ăk′sē-əl) *adj.* **1.** Having only one axis. **2.** Of or along a single axis.

u·ni·cam·er·al (yo͞o′nĭ-kăm′ər-əl) *adj.* Having or consisting of a single legislative chamber. **—u′ni·cam′er·al·ly** *adv.*

UNICEF (yo͞o′nĭ-sĕf′) *n.* United Nations International Children's Emergency Fund.

u·ni·cel·lu·lar (yo͞o′nĭ-sĕl′yə-lər) *adj.* Consisting of one cell; one-celled: *unicellular organisms.*

u·ni·col·or (yo͞o′nĭ-kŭl′ər) *adj.* Monochromatic.

u·ni·corn (yo͞o′nĭ-kôrn′) *n.* **1.** A fabled creature usually represented as a horse with a single spiraled horn projecting from its forehead and often with a goat's beard and a lion's tail. **2. Unicorn.** *Astron.* The constellation Monoceros. [ME < OFr. < Lat. *unicornis,* having one horn : *unus,* one + *cornu,* horn.]

unicorn plant *n.* A plant, *Proboscidea louisiana,* of the southern United States, having yellowish-purple flowers and a beaked, woody pod.

u·ni·cos·tate (yo͞o′nĭ-kŏs′tāt′) *adj.* Having a single main costa, rib, or riblike part.

u·ni·cy·cle (yo͞o′nĭ-sī′kəl) *n.* A vehicle consisting of a frame mounted over a single wheel and usually propelled by pedals. **—u′ni·cy′clist** *n.*

unidentified flying object *n.* **1.** A flying or apparently flying object of an unknown nature. **2.** A flying saucer.

u·ni·di·rec·tion·al (yo͞o′nĭ-dĭ-rĕk′shən-əl, -dī-rĕk′shən-əl) *adj.* Having, operating, or moving in one direction only.

u·ni·fi·a·ble (yo͞o′nə-fī′ə-bəl) *adj.* Capable of unification.

unified field theory *n.* A physical theory that combines the treatment of two or more types of fields in order to deduce previously unrecognized interrelationships, esp. such a theory unifying the theories of nuclear, electromagnetic, and gravitational forces.

u·ni·fi·lar (yo͞o′nə-fī′lər) *adj.* Having or utilizing only one filament, such as a thread or wire.

u·ni·fo·li·ate (yo͞o′nə-fō′lē-ĭt, -āt′) *adj.* Having a single leaf.

u·ni·fo·li·o·late (yo͞o′nĭ-fō′lē-ə-lāt′) *adj.* Compound in structure, but having a single leaflet and often a winglike extension along the leafstalk.

u·ni·form (yo͞o′nə-fôrm′) *adj.* **1. a.** Always the same; unvarying: *a uniform gait.* **b.** Without fluctuation or variation; consistent. **2.** Being the same as another or others; identical: *"Language was not uniform throughout the country but fell into dialects"* (Kemp Malone). **3.** Consistent in appearance; having an unvaried texture, color, or design. *—n.* **1.** A distinctive outfit intended to identify those who wear it as members of a specific group. **2.** A single outfit of a uniform. *—tr.v.* **-formed, -form·ing, -forms. 1.** To make uniform. **2.** To provide or dress with a uniform. [OFr. *uniforme* < Lat. *uniformis* : *unus,* one + *forma,* shape.] **—u′ni·for′mi·ty** (-fôr′mĭ-te), **u′ni·form′ness** *n.* **—u′ni·form′ly** *adv.*

u·ni·for·mi·tar·i·an·ism (yo͞o′nə-fôr′mĭ-târ′ē-ə-nĭz′əm) *n.* The theory that all geological phenomena may be explained as the result of existing forces having operated uniformly from the origin of the earth to the present time. **—u′ni·for′mi·tar′i·an** *adj. & n.*

u·ni·fy (yo͞o′nə-fī′) *v.* **-fied, -fy·ing, -fies.** *—tr.* To make into a unit; consolidate. *—intr.* To become unified. [OFr. *unifier* < LLat. *unificare* : Lat. *unus,* one + Lat. *facere,* to make.] **—u′ni·fi·ca′tion** *n.* **—u′ni·fi′er** *n.*

u·ni·lat·er·al (yo͞o′nə-lăt′ər-əl) *adj.* **1.** Of, on, pertaining to, involving, or affecting only one side. **2.** Obligating only one of two or more parties, nations, or persons, as a contract or agreement. **3.** Emphasizing or recognizing only one side of a subject. **4.** Having only one side. **5.** Tracing the lineage of one parent only: *a unilateral genealogy.* **—u′ni·lat′er·al·ly** *adv.*

u·ni·lin·e·ar (yo͞o′nĭ-lĭn′ē-ər) *adj.* Of or developing in a progressive sequence usually from the primitive to the advanced.

u·ni·lin·gual (yo͞o′nĭ-lĭng′gwəl) *adj.* Written in or making use of one language only.

u·ni·loc·u·lar (yo͞o′nə-lŏk′yə-lər) *adj. Bot.* Having a single compartment or chamber.

un·im·pas·sioned (ŭn′ĭm-păsh′ənd) *adj.* Not impassioned, esp. marked by a reasonable approach totally devoid of emotional influence or appeal: *answered the charges with an unimpassioned defense.*

un·im·peach·a·ble (ŭn′ĭm-pē′chə-bəl) *adj.* Beyond doubt or reproach; unquestionable. **—un′im·peach′a·bly** *adv.*

un·im·por·tant (ŭn′ĭm-pôr′tnt) *adj.* Not important; petty. **—un′im·por′tance** *n.*

un·im·proved (ŭn′ĭm-pro͞ovd′) *adj.* **1.** Not improved; not bettered. **2.** Not made use of or put to advantage. **3.** Not built upon or cultivated so as to increase in value. Used of land.

un·in·form·a·tive (ŭn′ĭn-fôr′mə-tĭv) *adj.* Not informative. **—un′in·form′a·tive·ly** *adv.*

un·in·hab·it·ed (ŭn′ĭn-hăb′ĭ-tĭd) *adj.* Not inhabited; having no residents.

un·in·hib·it·ed (ŭn′ĭn-hĭb′ĭ-tĭd) *adj.* **1.** Not inhibited; open: *uninhibited laughter.* **2.** Free from the expected social or moral constraints. **—un′in·hib′it·ed·ly** *adv.* **—un′in·hib′it·ed·ness** *n.*

un·in·i·ti·ate (ŭn′ĭ-nĭsh′ē-ĭt) *adj.* Not experienced.

un·in·spired (ŭn′ĭn-spīrd′) *adj.* Having no intellectual, emotional or spiritual excitement; dull.

un·in·tel·li·gent (ŭn′ĭn-tĕl′ə-jənt) *adj.* Lacking intelligence; ignorant. **—un′in·tel′li·gent·ly** *adv.*

un·in·ter·est·ed (ŭn-ĭn′trĭs-tĭd, -ĭn′tə-rĕs′tĭd) *adj.* **1. a.** Without an interest: *uninterested parties.* **b.** Not having a financial interest. **2.** Not paying attention; indifferent: *was totally uninterested in the proceedings.* —See Usage note at **disinterested.**

u·ni·nu·cle·ate (yo͞o′nĭ-no͞o′klē-ĭt, -nyo͞o′) *adj.* Having one nucleus.

unicorn

unicycle

un·ion (yo͞on′yən) *n.* **1. a.** The act of uniting or the state of being united. **b.** A combination so formed, esp. an alliance or confederation of persons, parties, or political entities for mutual interest or benefit: *"I projected and drew a plan for the union of all the colonies under one government"* (B. Franklin). **2.** *Symbol* **∪** *Math.* A set, every member of which is an element of one or another of two or more given sets. **3.** Agreement resulting from an alliance; concord. **4. a.** The state of matrimony; marriage. **b.** Sexual intercourse. **5. a.** A combination of parishes for joint administration of relief for the poor in Britain. **b.** A workhouse maintained by such a union. **6.** A labor union. **7.** A coupling device for connecting parts, such as pipes or rods. **8.** A device on a flag or ensign, occupying the upper inner corner or the entire field, that signifies the union of two or more sovereignties. **9. Union. a.** An organization at a college or university that provides facilities for recreation. **b.** A building housing such facilities. **10. Union.** The United States of America, esp. during the Civil War. **—*modifier:*** *the union movement.* [ME < OFr. < LLat. *unio* < Lat. *unus,* one.]

union catalog *n.* A library catalog combining in alphabetical sequence the contents of a number of catalogs or the contents of more than one library.

un·ion·ism (yo͞on′yə-nĭz′əm) *n.* **1.** The principle or theory of forming a union. **2.** The principles, theory, or system of a union, esp. a trade union. **3. Unionism.** Loyalty to the Federal Government during the Civil War. **—un′ion·ist** *n.*

un·ion·ize (yo͞on′yə-nīz′) *v.* **-ized, -iz·ing, -iz·es.** *—tr.* **1.** To organize into a labor union. **2.** To cause to join a labor union. *—intr.* To organize or join a labor union. **—un′ion·i·za′tion** *n.*

union jack
The Union Jack flag of the United Kingdom

union jack *n.* **1.** A flag consisting entirely of a union. **2. Union Jack.** The flag of the United Kingdom.

union label *n.* An identifying mark attached to a product indicating it has been produced by members of a trade union.

union shop *n.* A business or industrial establishment whose employees are required to be union members or to agree to join the union within a specified time after being hired.

union suit *n.* Undershirt and underpants combined in a single garment.

u·nip·a·rous (yo͞o-nĭp′ər-əs) *adj.* **1.** Producing only one offspring at a time. **2.** Having produced only one offspring. **3.** *Bot.* Forming a single axis at each branching, as certain flower clusters.

u·ni·per·son·al (yo͞o′nĭ-pûr′sə-nəl) *adj.* Being manifested as or existent in the form of only one person: *a unipersonal spirit.*

u·ni·pla·nar (yo͞o′nĭ-plā′nər, -när′) *adj.* Situated or occurring in one plane.

u·ni·po·lar (yo͞o′nĭ-pō′lər) *adj.* Having, acting by means of, or produced by a single pole.

u·nique (yo͞o-nēk′) *adj.* **1.** Being the only one of its kind; sole. **2.** Being without an equal or equivalent; unparalleled. [Fr. < Lat. *unicus,* sole < *unus,* one.] **—u·nique′ly** *adv.* **—u·nique′ness** *n.*

Usage: Traditional grammarians are uncompromising in the insistence that *unique* is an "absolute" term—either something is unique or it isn't—so that it does not allow qualification of degree. The vast majority of the Usage Panel finds unacceptable such uses as are found in the advertising claim *"Omaha's most unique restaurant is now even more unique,"* whose author might have avoided the scorn of the grammarians if he had used instead a word like *unusual* or *remarkable.* Like other absolute words such as *chief* and *unanimous,* however, *unique* can be modified by words like *almost* and *nearly.*

u·ni·sex (yo͞o′nĭ-sĕks′) *n.* The elimination or absence of sexual distinctions, esp. in dress. *—adj.* **1.** Not distinguished or distinguishable on the basis of sex: *unisex hair styles.* **2.** Designed for or suitable to both males and females: *unisex clothing.*

u·ni·sex·u·al (yo͞o′nĭ-sĕk′sho͞o-əl) *adj.* **1.** Of only one sex. **2.** Having only one type of sexual organ. **3.** *Bot.* Having either stamens or pistils but not both. **4.** Unisex. **—u′ni·sex′u·al′i·ty** *n.* **—u′ni·sex′u·al·ly** *adv.*

u·ni·son (yo͞o′nĭ-sən, -zən) *n.* **1. a.** Identity of musical pitch; the interval of a perfect prime. **b.** The combination of musical parts at the same pitch or in octaves. **2.** The act or an instance of speaking of the same words simultaneously by two or more speakers. **3.** An instance of agreement; concord. **—*idiom.* in unison.** In complete agreement; harmonizing exactly. [OFr. < Med. Lat. *unisonus,* in unison : Lat. *unus,* one + Lat. *sonus,* sound.]

u·nit (yo͞o′nĭt) *n.* **1.** An individual, group, structure, or other entity regarded as an elementary structural or functional constituent of a whole. **2.** A group regarded as a distinct entity within a larger group. **3. a.** A mechanical part or module. **b.** An entire apparatus or the equipment that performs a specific function. **4.** A precisely specified quantity in terms of which the magnitudes of other quantities of the same kind can be stated. **5.** A fixed amount of scholastic study used as a basis for calculating academic credits, usually measured in hours of classroom instruction or laboratory work. **6.** The number immediately to the left of the decimal point in the Arabic numeral system. [Back-formation from UNITY.]

U·ni·tar·i·an (yo͞o′nĭ-târ′ē-ən) *n.* **1.** A monotheist who rejects the doctrine of the Trinity. **2.** A member of a Christian denomination that rejects the doctrine of the Trinity and emphasizes freedom and tolerance in religious belief and the autonomy of each congregation. *—adj.* Of, pertaining to, or supporting the Unitarians or their beliefs. [< NLat. *unitarius* < Lat. *unitas,* unity < *unus,* one.] **—U′ni·tar′i·an·ism** *n.*

u·ni·tar·y (yo͞o′nĭ-tĕr′ē) *adj.* **1.** Of or pertaining to a unit. **2.** Having the nature of a unit; whole. **3.** Based on or characterized by one or more units.

u·nite (yo͞o-nīt′) *v.* **-nit·ed, -nit·ing, -nites.** *—tr.* **1.** To bring together so as to form a whole. **2.** To combine (people) in interest, attitude, or action: *"The ancient schools of philosophy were bodies of men united by a common spirit"* (W.D. Ross). **3.** To join (a couple) in marriage. **4.** To cause to adhere. **5.** To have or demonstrate in combination: *He unites common sense with vision.* *—intr.* **1.** To become or seem to become joined, formed, or combined into a unit. **2.** To join and act together in a common purpose or endeavor. **3.** To be or become bound together by adhesion. [ME *uniten* < LLat. *unire* < Lat. *unus,* one.]

United Church of Christ *n.* A Protestant denomination founded in 1957 by a merger of the Congregational Christian Church and the Evangelical and Reformed Church.

United Methodist Church *n.* A Protestant church formed in 1968 by the union of the Methodist Church and the Evangelical United Brethren.

United Nations *pl.n. (used with a sing. or pl. verb).* An international organization comprising most of the countries of the world, formed in 1945 to promote peace, security, and economic development.

United Nations Trust Territory *n.* A trust territory.

United States *pl.n. (used with a sing. or pl. verb).* A federation of states, esp. one forming a nation within a definitely specified territory: *politicians who proposed a United States of Africa.*

u·ni·tive (yo͞o′nĭ-tĭv, yo͞o-nī′-) *adj.* Tending to promote unity or serving to unite.

u·nit·ize (yo͞o′nĭ-tīz′) *tr.v.* **-ized, -iz·ing, -iz·es.** To separate, classify, or package in discrete units.

unit pricing *n.* The pricing of goods on the basis of cost per unit of measure.

unit rule *n.* In a Democratic Party national convention, a rule that a state's entire vote must go to the candidate preferred by the majority of that state's delegates.

u·ni·ty (yo͞o′nĭ-tē) *n., pl.* **-ties. 1.** The state of being one; singleness. **2.** The state, quality, or condition of accord or agreement; concord. **3. a.** The combination or arrangement of parts into a whole; unification. **b.** A combination or union thus formed. **4. a.** An ordering of all elements in a work of art or literature so that each contributes to a unified aesthetic effect. **b.** The effect thus produced. **5.** Singleness or constancy of purpose or action; continuity. **6.** *Math.* **a.** The number l. **b.** An element I in a groupoid satisfying $x \cdot I = x = I \cdot x$ for each x in the groupoid. **7.** One of three principles of dramatic composition derived from Aristotle's *Poetics,* based upon unity of time, action, and place, and stating that a drama should have but one plot, the action of which should be contained within one day and confined to one locality. [ME *unite* < OFr. <Lat. *unitas* < *unus,* one.]

Synonyms: *unity, union, solidarity, homogeneity.* These nouns refer to the condition of oneness in some sense; they are not always interchangeable, however. *Unity* is the fact or condition of being one; in most contexts it implies fundamental agreement of interdependent and usually varied components, which in turn produces harmony, as of thought, purpose, or artistic quality. *Union* is interchangeable with the preceding term when both refer to harmony or concord; but *union* more often refers to the act of joining persons or things and to the product that results, such as an organization of persons, a political body, or a marriage. In its most common application, *solidarity* is an intensification of *unity,* for it refers to the identity or likeness of interests, objectives, and responsibilities that enables a group of persons to think and act as one. *Homogeneity* involves oneness in the sense of uniformity of overall structure or character, resulting from likeness or compatibility of components.

U·ni·vac (yo͞o′nə-văk′). A trademark for a general-purpose digital computer.

u·ni·va·lent (yo͞o′nĭ-vā′lənt) *adj. Chem.* **1.** Having valence 1. **2.** Having only one valence. *—n. Genetics.* An unpaired chromosome.

u·ni·valve (yo͞o′nĭ-vălv′) *n.* **1.** A mollusk, esp. a gastropod, having a single shell. **2.** The shell of a univalve mollusk. *—adj.* Pertaining to or having a univalve shell.

u·ni·ver·sal (yo͞o′nə-vûr′səl) *adj.* **1.** Of, pertaining to, extending to, or affecting the entire world or all within the world; worldwide. **2.** Including, pertaining to, or affecting all members of the class or group under consideration: *the universal skepticism of philosophers.* **3.** Applicable or common to all purposes, conditions, or situations. **4.** Of or pertaining to the universe or cosmos; cosmic. **5.** Comprising all or many subjects; comprehensively broad. **6.** Adapted or adjustable to many sizes or mechanical uses. **7.** *Logic.* Predicable of all the members of a class or genus denoted by the subject. Used of a proposition. —*n.* **1.** *Logic.* **a.** A universal proposition. **b.** A general or abstract concept or term considered absolute or axiomatic. **2.** A general or widely held principle, concept, or notion. **3.** A trait or pattern of behavior characteristic of all the members of a particular culture or of all human beings. **—u'ni·ver'sal·ly** *adv.* **—u'ni·ver'sal·ness** *n.*

universal coupling *n.* A universal joint.

universal donor *n.* A person of blood type O.

u·ni·ver·sal·ism (yōō'nə-vûr'sə-lĭz'əm) *n.* **1. Universalism.** *Theol.* The doctrine of universal salvation. **2.** Universality.

U·ni·ver·sal·ist (yōō'nə-vûr'sə-lĭst) *n.* One who believes that salvation is extended to all mankind, esp. a member of a Christian denomination that adheres to this doctrine. —*adj.* Of or pertaining to Universalism or Universalists.

u·ni·ver·sal·i·ty (yōō'nə-vər-săl'ĭ-tē) *n., pl.* **-ties. 1.** The quality, fact, or condition of being universal. **2.** Great or unbounded versatility of the mind.

u·ni·ver·sal·ize (yōō'nə-vûr'sə-līz') *tr.v.* **-ized, -iz·ing, -iz·es.** To make universal; generalize. **—u'ni·ver'sal·i·za'tion** *n.*

universal joint *n.* A joint or coupling that allows parts of a machine not collinear with each other limited freedom of movement in any direction while transmitting rotary motion.

universal set *n.* A mathematical set containing all elements of the variety under consideration.

universal time *n.* Greenwich mean time.

u·ni·verse (yōō'nə-vûrs') *n.* **1.** All existing things, including the earth, the heavens, the galaxies, and all therein, regarded as a whole. **2. a.** The earth together with all its inhabitants and created things. **b.** All mankind. **3.** The sphere or realm in which something exists or takes place. **4.** *Logic.* The universe of discourse. [ME < OFr. *univers* < Lat. *Universum,* neuter of *universus,* whole : *unus,* one + *versus,* p.part. of *vertere,* to turn.]

universe of discourse *n.* *Logic.* A class containing all the entities referred to in a discourse or argument.

u·ni·ver·si·ty (yōō'nə-vûr'sĭ-tē) *n., pl.* **-ties. 1.** An institution for higher learning with teaching and research facilities comprising a graduate school and professional schools that award master's degrees and doctorates and an undergraduate division that awards bachelor's degrees. **2.** The buildings and grounds of a university. **3.** The students and faculty of a university regarded as a body. [ME *universite* < OFr. < Med. Lat. *universitas* < LLat., a society < Lat., the whole < *universus,* whole. —see UNIVERSE.]

u·niv·o·cal (yōō-nĭv'ə-kəl) *adj.* Having only one meaning. —*n.* A word or term having only one meaning. [LLat. *univocus* : Lat. *unus,* one + Lat. *vox,* voice.] **—u·niv'o·cal·ly** *adv.*

un·just (ŭn-jŭst') *adj.* **1.** Violating principles of justice or fairness. **2.** *Archaic.* Faithless; dishonest. **—un·just'ly** *adv.* **—un·just'ness** *n.*

un·kempt (ŭn-kĕmpt') *adj.* **1. a.** Uncombed: *unkempt hair.* **b.** Lacking neatness of appearance; messy: *an unkempt lawn.* **2.** *Archaic.* Unpolished; rude. [UN- + *kempt,* p.part. of dial. *kemb,* to comb < ME *kemben* < OE *cemban.*]

un·ken·nel (ŭn-kĕn'əl) *tr.v.* **-neled, -nel·ing, -nels** or **-nelled, -nel·ling, -nels. 1. a.** To drive from a lair or den. **b.** To loose from a kennel. **2.** To uncover; disclose.

un·kind (ŭn-kīnd') *adj.* **-er, -est.** Lacking kindness; unsympathetic or harsh. **—un·kind'ly** *adv.* **—un·kind'ness** *n.*

un·kind·ly (ŭn-kīnd'lē) *adj.* **-li·er, -li·est.** Unkind. **—un·kind'li·ness** *n.*

un·kink (ŭn-kĭngk')v. **-kinked, -kink·ing, -kinks.** —*tr.* To free from kinks; make straight. —*intr.* To become relaxed.

un·knit (ŭn-nĭt') *v.* **-knit** or **-knit·ted, -knit·ting, -knits.** —*tr.* To unravel or undo (something knit or tied). —*intr.* To become unknit or undone.

un·know·a·ble (ŭn-nō'ə-bəl) *adj.* Impossible to know; beyond the range of human experience or understanding. **—un·know'a·ble** *n.* **—un·know'a·ble·ness** *n.* **—un·know'a·bly** *adv.*

un·know·ing (ŭn-nō'ĭng) *adj.* Not knowing; unaware. **—un·know'ing·ly** *adv.*

un·known (ŭn-nōn') *adj.* **1.** Not known; unfamiliar. **2. a.** Not identified or ascertained. **b.** Not established or verified. —*n.* **1.** One that is unknown. **2.** *Math.* **a.** A quantity of unknown numerical value. **b.** The symbol for this quantity.

un·la·bored (ŭn-lā'bərd) *adj.* **1.** Done with or requiring little effort; effortless. **2.** Not tilled; uncultivated.

un·lace (ŭn-lās') *tr.v.* **-laced, -lac·ing, -lac·es. 1. a.** To loosen or undo the lace or laces of. **b.** To remove or loosen the clothing of. **2.** *Obs.* To disgrace.

un·lade (ŭn-lād') *v.* **-lad·ed, -lad·ing, -lades.** —*tr.* **1.** To unload (a cargo) from a ship. **2.** To unload (a ship). —*intr.* To discharge a cargo.

un·lash (ŭn-lăsh') *tr.v.* **-lashed, -lash·ing, -lash·es.** To untie the lashing of; loose.

un·latch (ŭn-lăch') *v.* **-latched, -latch·ing, -latch·es.** —*tr.* To unfasten or open by releasing the latch. —*intr.* To become unfastened or opened.

un·law·ful (ŭn-lô'fəl) *adj.* **1.** Not lawful; illegal. **2.** Illegitimate. Used of offspring. **—un·law'ful·ly** *adv.* **—un·law'ful·ness** *n.*

un·lay (ŭn-lā') *v.* **-laid** (-lād'), **-lay·ing, -lays.** *Naut.* —*tr.* To untwist the strands of (a rope). —*intr.* To untwist.

un·lead (ŭn-lĕd') *tr.v.* **-lead·ed, -lead·ing, -leads. 1.** To remove the lead from. **2.** *Printing.* To extricate the leads from between (lines of type).

un·lead·ed (ŭn-lĕd'ĭd) *adj.* **1.** Not containing lead: *unleaded gasoline.* **2.** *Printing.* Not spaced or separated with lead, as lines of type.

un·learn (ŭn-lûrn') *tr.v.* **-learned, -learn·ing, -learns. 1.** To put (something learned) out of the mind; forget. **2.** To undo the effect of (something): *tried to unlearn smoking.*

un·learn·ed (ŭn-lûr'nĭd) *adj.* **1.** Not educated; ignorant or illiterate. **2.** Not skilled or versed in a specified discipline. **3.** (ŭn-lûrnd'). Not acquired by training or studying: *an unlearned response.* **—un·learn'ed·ly** (-lûr'nĭd-lē) *adv.*

un·leash (ŭn-lēsh') *tr.v.* **-leashed, -leash·ing, -leash·es.** To release or loose from or as if from a leash: *"The malignant death instinct can unleash those hydrogen bombs"* (Norman O. Brown).

un·leav·ened (ŭn-lĕv'ənd) *adj.* Made without leavening.

un·less (ŭn-lĕs') *conj.* Except on the condition that; except under the circumstances that. —*prep.* Except; except for. [ME *unlesse,* alteration of *onlesse* : *on,* on + *lesse,* less.]

un·let·tered (ŭn-lĕt'ərd) *adj.* **1. a.** Not educated. **b.** Illiterate. **2.** Devoid of lettering.

un·li·censed (ŭn-lī'sənst) *adj.* **1.** Having no license. **2.** Unauthorized. **3.** Unrestrained.

un·licked (ŭn-lĭkt') *adj.* *Archaic.* **1.** Not licked clean. **2.** Not having proper shape or form.

un·like (ŭn'līk') *adj.* **1.** Not alike; different; dissimilar. **2.** Not equal, as in strength. —*prep.* **1.** Different from; not like. **2.** Not typical of. **—un·like'ness** *n.*

un·like·li·hood (ŭn-līk'lē-hŏŏd') *n.* The state of being unlikely or improbable; improbability.

un·like·ly (ŭn-līk'lē) *adj.* **-li·er, -li·est. 1.** Not likely; improbable. **2.** Likely to fail. **—un·like'li·ness** *n.*

un·lim·ber (ŭn-lĭm'bər) *v.* **-bered, -ber·ing, -bers.** —*tr.* **1.** To detach (a gun or caisson) from its limber. **2.** To make ready for action. —*intr.* To prepare for action.

un·lim·it·ed (ŭn-lĭm'ĭ-tĭd) *adj.* Having no limits, bounds, or qualifications. **—un·lim'it·ed·ly** *adv.* **—un·lim'it·ed·ness** *n.*

un·link (ŭn-lĭngk') *tr.v.* **-linked, -link·ing, -links.** To disconnect the links of; unfasten.

un·list·ed (ŭn-lĭs'tĭd) *adj.* **1.** Not appearing on a list. **2.** Designating stock or securities not listed on a stock exchange.

un·live (ŭn-lĭv') *tr.v.* **-lived, -liv·ing, -lives.** To live in such a manner as to undo the effects of.

un·load (ŭn-lōd') *v.* **-load·ed, -load·ing, -loads.** —*tr.* **1. a.** To remove the load or cargo from. **b.** To discharge (a cargo or load). **2. a.** To relieve of something oppressive; unburden. **b.** To pour forth. **3.** To remove the charge from (a firearm). **4.** To dispose of, esp. by selling in great quantity; dump. —*intr.* To discharge a cargo or some other burden. **—un·load'er** *n.*

un·lock (ŭn-lŏk') *v.* **-locked, -lock·ing, -locks.** —*tr.* **1. a.** To undo (a lock) by turning a key or a corresponding part. **b.** To undo the lock of. **2.** To cause to open; give access to: *unlocked her heart.* **3.** To set free; release. **4.** To provide a key to: *unlock a mystery.* —*intr.* To become unfastened, loosened, or freed from.

un·looked-for (ŭn-lŏŏkt'fôr') *adj.* Not looked for or expected; unforeseen.

un·loose (ŭn-lōōs') *tr.v.* **-loosed, -loos·ing, -loos·es. 1.** To let loose or unfasten; release. **2.** To relax, as a hold upon something. [ME *unloosen* : *un-,* un- + *loosen,* to loosen < *loos,* loose.]

un·loos·en (ŭn-lōō'sən) *tr.v.* **-ened, -en·ing, -ens.** To unloose.

un·love·ly (ŭn-lŭv'lē) *adj.* **-li·er, -li·est.** Not pleasant; disagreeable.

un·luck·y (ŭn-lŭk'ē) *adj.* **-i·er, -i·est. 1.** Subjected to or marked by misfortune. **2.** Forecasting bad luck; inauspicious. **3.** Not producing the desired outcome; disappointing. **—un·luck'i·ly** *adv.* **—un·luck'i·ness** *n.*

un·make (ŭn-māk') *tr.v.* **-made** (-mād'), **-mak·ing, -makes. 1.** To deprive of position, rank, or authority; depose. **2.** To ruin; destroy. **3.** To alter the characteristics of.

un·man (ŭn-măn') *tr.v.* **-manned, -man·ning, -mans. 1.** To cause to lose courage. **2.** To deprive of virility; emasculate.

un·man·ly (ŭn-măn'lē) *adj.* **-li·er, -li·est. 1. a.** Dishonorable; degrading. **b.** Cowardly. **2.** Effeminate. **—un·man'li·ness** *n.*

un·manned (ŭn-mănd') *adj.* **1.** Without crew: *an unmanned ship.* **2.** *Obs.* Untrained. Used of a hawk.

un·man·nered (ŭn-măn'ərd) *adj.* Without manners; rude.

un·man·ner·ly (ŭn-măn'ər-lē) *adj.* Rude; ill-mannered. **—un·man'ner·li·ness** *n.*

un·marked (ŭn-märkt') *adj.* **1.** Not bearing a mark. **2.** Not observed or noticed.

un·mar·ried (ŭn-măr'ēd) *adj.* Not married.

un·mask (ŭn-măsk', -mäsk') *v.* **-masked, -mask·ing, -masks.** —*tr.* **1.** To remove a mask from. **2.** To disclose the true character of; expose. —*intr.* To remove one's mask.

un·mean·ing (ŭn-mē'nĭng) *adj.* **1.** Meaningless; senseless. **2.** Expressionless; vacant. **—un·mean'ing·ly** *adv.*

un·meant (ŭn-mĕnt') *adj.* Not meant or intentional.

un·meet (ŭn-mēt') *adj.* Improper; unseemly.

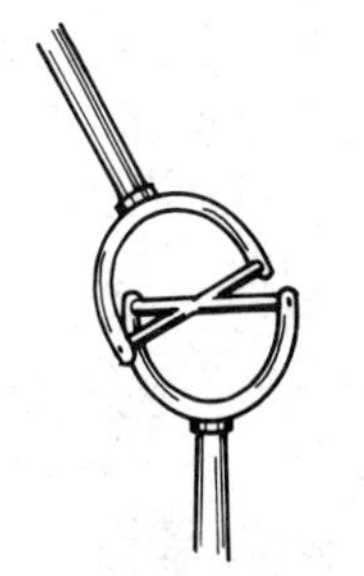

universal joint

un·men·tion·a·ble (ŭn-mĕn′shə-nə-bəl) *adj.* **1.** Not fit to be mentioned. **2.** Unspeakable. —*n.* **1.** One that is not to be or is not fit to be mentioned. **2. unmentionables.** Underwear. —**un·men′tion·a·ble·ness** *n.* —**un·men′tion·a·bly** *adv.*

un·mer·ci·ful (ŭn-mûr′sĭ-fəl) *adj.* **1.** Having no mercy; merciless. **2.** Excessive: *unmerciful heat.* —**un·mer′ci·ful·ly** *adv.* —**un·mer′ci·ful·ness** *n.*

un·mind·ful (ŭn-mīnd′fəl) *adj.* Inattentive or oblivious: *unmindful of the passage of time.* —**un·mind′ful·ly** *adv.* —**un·mind′ful·ness** *n.*

un·mis·tak·a·ble (ŭn′mĭ-stā′kə-bəl) *adj.* Obvious; evident. —**un′mis·tak′a·bly** *adv.*

un·mit·i·gat·ed (ŭn-mĭt′ĭ-gā′tĭd) *adj.* **1.** Not diminished or moderated in intensity or severity; unrelieved. **2.** Absolute; unconscionable: *an unmitigated lie.* —**un·mit′i·gat′ed·ly** *adv.*

un·mod·u·lat·ed (ŭn-mŏj′ə-lā′tĭd) *adj.* Not modulated.

un·moor (ŭn-mo͝or′) *v.* **-moored, -moor·ing, -moors.** —*tr.* **1.** To release from or as if from moorings. **2.** To release (a ship) from all but one anchor. —*intr.* To cast off moorings.

un·mor·al (ŭn-môr′əl, -mŏr′əl) *adj.* Having no moral quality; amoral. —**un·mor′al·ly** *adv.*

un·mor·tise (ŭn-môr′tĭs) *tr.v.* **-tised, -tis·ing, -tis·es. 1.** To loosen a mortised joint of. **2.** To separate.

un·muf·fle (ŭn-mŭf′əl) *v.* **-fled, -fling, -fles.** —*tr.* To free from a garment or device that muffles. —*intr.* To remove or cast off something that muffles.

un·my·e·lin·at·ed (ŭn-mī′ə-lĭ-nā′tĭd) *adj.* Lacking a myelin sheath.

un·nat·u·ral (ŭn-năch′ər-əl) *adj.* **1.** Violating natural law. **2.** Inconsistent with an individual pattern or custom. **3.** Deviating from a behavioral, ethical, or social norm: *an unnatural attachment.* **4.** Contrived or constrained; artificial: *an unnatural manner.* **5.** Outrageously violating natural feelings; inhuman. —**un·nat′u·ral·ly** *adv.* —**un·nat′u·ral·ness** *n.*

un·nec·es·sar·y (ŭn-nĕs′ĭ-sĕr′ē) *adj.* Not necessary; needless. —**un·nec′es·sar′i·ly** (-sâr′ə-lē) *adv.*

un·nerve (ŭn-nûrv′) *tr.v.* **-nerved, -nerv·ing, -nerves.** To deprive of composure, energy, or firmness.

un·no·tice·a·ble (ŭn-nō′tĭ-sə-bal) *adj.* Not readily noticeable.

un·num·bered (ŭn-nŭm′bərd) *adj.* **1.** Innumerable; countless. **2.** Not marked with an identifying number.

un·ob·tru·sive (ŭn′əb-tro͞o′sĭv) *adj.* Not readily noticeable. —**un′ob·tru′sive·ly** *adv.* —**un′ob·tru′sive·ness** *n.*

un·oc·cu·pied (ŭn-ŏk′yə-pīd′) *adj.* **1.** Not occupied; vacant. **2.** Unemployed; idle.

un·of·fi·cial (ŭn′ə-fĭsh′əl) *adj.* **1.** Not official. **2.** Not acting officially. —**un′of·fi′cial·ly** *adv.*

un·or·gan·ized (ŭn-ôr′gə-nīzd′) *adj.* **1.** Lacking order, system, or unity. **2.** Having no organic qualities; inorganic. **3.** Not unionized.

un·o·rig·i·nal (ŭn′ə-rĭj′ə-nəl) *adj.* Lacking originality; trite.

un·or·tho·dox (ŭn-ôr′thə-dŏks′) *adj.* Not orthodox; breaking with convention or tradition. —**un·or′tho·dox′ly** *adv.* —**un·or′tho·dox′y** *n.*

un·pack (ŭn-păk′) *v.* **-packed, -pack·ing, -packs.** —*tr.* **1.** To remove the contents of (a suitcase, for example). **2.** To remove from a container or from packaging. **3.** To remove a pack from (a pack animal). —*intr.* To unpack objects from a container.

un·paged (ŭn-pājd′) *adj.* Having no page numbers.

un·paid (ŭn-pād′) *adj.* **1.** Not yet paid: *an unpaid bill.* **2.** Serving without pay; unsalaried.

un·pal·at·a·ble (ŭn-păl′ə-tə-bəl) *adj.* **1.** Not pleasing to the taste. **2.** Not pleasant or agreeable: *unpalatable truths.* —**un′pal·at·a·bil′i·ty** *n.*

un·par·al·leled (ŭn-păr′ə-lĕld′) *adj.* Without parallel; unequaled.

un·par·lia·men·ta·ry (ŭn′pär-lə-mĕn′tə-rē, -mĕn′trē) *adj.* Not in accordance with parliamentary procedure.

un·peg (ŭn-pĕg′) *tr.v.* **-pegged, -peg·ging, -pegs. 1.** To remove a peg from. **2.** To unfasten.

un·peo·ple (ŭn-pē′pəl) *tr.v.* **-pled, -pling, -ples.** To depopulate (an area).

un·peo·pled (ŭn-pē′pəld) *adj.* Uninhabited.

un·per·fo·rat·ed (ŭn-pûr′fə-rā′tĭd) *adj.* **1.** Lacking perforations. **2.** Imperforate. Used of a postage stamp.

un·per·son (ŭn′pûr′sən) *n.* A nonperson.

un·pick (ŭn-pĭk′) *tr.v.* **-picked, -pick·ing, -picks.** To undo (sewing) by removing stitches: *unpick a seam.*

un·pin (ŭn-pĭn′) *tr.v.* **-pinned, -pin·ning, -pins. 1.** To remove a pin from. **2. a.** To open or unfasten by removing pins. **b.** To free.

un·pleas·ant (ŭn-plĕz′ənt) *adj.* Not pleasing; disagreeable. —**un·pleas′ant·ly** *adv.*

un·pleas·ant·ness (ŭn-plĕz′ənt-nĭs) *n.* **1.** The condition or quality of being unpleasant. **2.** An unpleasant experience or situation.

un·plug (ŭn-plŭg′) *tr.v.* **-plugged, -plug·ging, -plugs. 1.** To remove a plug, stopper, or obstruction from. **2. a.** To remove (an electric plug). **b.** To disconnect (an electric appliance) by removing a plug from an outlet.

un·plumbed (ŭn-plŭmd′) *adj.* Not explored as to depth or signification.

un·po·lit·i·cal (ŭn′pə-lĭt′ĭ-kəl) *adj.* Not political.

un·polled (ŭn-pōld′) *adj.* **1.** Not interviewed in a poll. **2.** Not registered at the polls.

un·pop·u·lar (ŭn-pŏp′yə-lər) *adj.* Lacking general approval or acceptance. —**un′pop·u·lar′i·ty** (-lăr′ĭ-tē) *n.*

un·prac·ticed (ŭn-prăk′tĭst) *adj.* **1.** Not yet tested or tried. **2.** Without benefit of experience; unskilled.

un·prec·e·dent·ed (ŭn′prĕs′ĭ-dĕn′tĭd) *adj.* Without precedent. —**un·prec′e·dent′ed·ly** *adv.*

un·pre·dict·a·ble (ŭn′prĭ-dĭk′tə-bəl) *adj.* Not predictable. —**un′pre·dict′a·bly** *adv.*

un·prej·u·diced (ŭn-prĕj′ə-dĭst) *adj.* Free from prejudice; impartial.

un·pre·med·i·tat·ed (ŭn′prĭ-mĕd′ĭ-tā′tĭd) *adj.* Not premeditated; not planned. —**un′pre·med′i·tat′ed·ly** *adv.*

un·pre·pared (ŭn-prĭ-pârd′) *adj.* **1.** Having made no preparations. **2.** Not equipped to meet a contingency. **3.** Impromptu; off-the-cuff. —**un′pre·par′ed·ly** (-pâr′ĭd-lē) *adv.* —**un′pre·par′ed·ness** (-pâr′ĭd-nĭs, -pârd′nĭs) *n.*

un·pre·pos·sess·ing (ŭn′prē-pə-zĕs′ĭng) *adj.* Failing to impress favorably; nondescript. —**un′pre·pos·sess′ing·ly** *adv.*

un·pre·tend·ing (ŭn′prĭ-tĕn′dĭng) *adj.* Unpretentious.

un·pre·ten·tious (ŭn′prĭ-tĕn′shəs) *adj.* Lacking pretention or affectation; modest. —**un′pre·ten′tious·ly** *adv.* —**un′pre·ten′tious·ness** *n.*

un·priced (ŭn-prīst′) *adj.* Having no price assigned.

un·prin·ci·pled (ŭn-prĭn′sə-pəld) *adj.* Lacking principles or moral scruples; unscrupulous: *unprincipled behavior.*

un·print·a·ble (ŭn-prĭn′tə-bəl) *adj.* Not proper for publication for legal or social reasons.

un·pro·duc·tive (ŭn′prə-dŭk′tĭv) *adj.* **1.** Not productive. **2.** *Econ.* Adding nothing to exchangeable value. —**un′pro·duc′tive·ly** *adv.* —**un′pro·duc′tive·ness** *n.*

un·pro·fes·sion·al (ŭn′prə-fĕsh′ə-nəl) *adj.* **1. a.** Not in a profession. **b.** Not a qualified member of a professional group. **2.** Not conforming to the standards of a profession. **3.** Amateurish. —**un′pro·fes′sion·al·ly** *adv.*

un·prof·it·a·ble (ŭn-prŏf′ĭ-tə-bəl) *adj.* Not profitable; serving no purpose.

un·pro·nounce·a·ble (ŭn′prə-noun′sə-bəl) *adj.* **1.** Difficult to pronounce correctly. **2.** Not fit to be mentioned.

un·pro·vid·ed (ŭn′prə-vī′dĭd) *adj.* Not supplied, furnished, or equipped. —**un′pro·vid′ed·ly** *adv.*

un·pro·voked (ŭn′prə-vōkt′) *adj.* Not provoked or prompted: *an unprovoked attack.*

un·qual·i·fied (ŭn-kwŏl′ə-fīd′) *adj.* **1.** Lacking the proper or required qualifications. **2.** Without reservations; unconditioned: *an unqualified refusal.*

un·ques·tion·a·ble (ŭn-kwĕs′chə-nə-bəl) *adj.* Beyond question or doubt; certain. —**un·ques′tion·a·bil′i·ty, un′ques′tion·a·ble·ness** *n.* —**un·ques′tion·a·bly** *adv.*

un·ques·tioned (ŭn-kwĕs′chənd) *adj.* **1.** Not subjected to questioning; not interrogated. **2.** Not able to be questioned or doubted; indisputable. **3.** Not called into question or examination; not doubted.

un·qui·et (ŭn-kwī′ĭt) *adj.* **-er, -est. 1.** Emotionally or mentally uneasy. **2.** Characterized by unrest or disorder; turbulent. —**un·qui′et·ly** *adv.* —**un·qui′et·ness** *n.*

un·quote (ŭn-kwōt′) *v.* **-quot·ed, -quot·ing, -quotes.** —*tr.* To close (a quotation). —*intr.* To close a quotation. Used by a speaker to indicate the end of a quotation.

un·rav·el (ŭn-răv′əl) *v.* **-eled, -el·ing, -els** or **-elled, -el·ling, -els.** —*tr.* **1. a.** To undo or ravel the knitted fabric of. **b.** To separate (entangled threads). **2.** To separate and clarify the elements of (something mysterious or baffling); solve. —*intr.* To become unraveled.

un·read (ŭn-rĕd′) *adj.* **1.** Not read, studied, or perused. **2.** Having read little; ignorant.

un·read·a·ble (ŭn-rē′də-bəl) *adj.* **1.** Illegible. **2.** Not interesting; dull. **3.** Incomprehensible; obscure. **4.** Unsuitable for or not worth reading. —**un·read′a·bil′i·ty** *n.*

un·read·y (ŭn-rĕd′ē) *adj.* **-i·er, -i·est. 1.** Not ready or prepared. **2.** Slow to see or respond; not prompt. —**un·read′i·ly** *adv.* —**un·read′i·ness** *n.*

un·re·al (ŭn-rē′əl, -rēl′) *adj.* **1.** Not real or substantial; illusory. **2.** *Slang.* Excellent; fantastic.

un·re·al·i·ty (ŭn′rē-ăl′ĭ-tē) *n.* **1.** The quality or state of being unreal. **2.** Something unreal, insubstantial, or imaginary. **3.** A lack of ability to deal with reality.

un·rea·son (ŭn-rē′zən) *n.* **1.** Absence or lack of reason; irrationality. **2.** Nonsense; absurdity.

un·rea·son·a·ble (ŭn-rē′zə-nə-bəl) *adj.* **1.** Not governed by reason. **2.** Exceeding reasonable limits; immoderate. —**un·rea′son·a·ble·ness** *n.* —**un·rea′son·a·bly** *adv.*

un·rea·son·ing (ŭn-rē′zə-nĭng) *adj.* Not governed by reason; unchecked by reason. —**un·rea′son·ing·ly** *adv.*

un·reck·on·a·ble (ŭn-rĕk′ə-nə-bəl) *adj.* Incalculable.

un·re·con·struct·ed (ŭn′rē-kən-strŭk′tĭd) *adj.* Unreconciled to social and economic change.

un·reel (ŭn-rēl′) *v.* **-reeled, -reel·ing, -reels.** —*tr.* To unwind from or as if from a reel. —*intr.* To unwind.

un·reeve (ŭn-rēv′) *v.* **-reeved** or **-rove** (-rōv′), **-reeved** or **-ro·ven** (-rō′vən), **-reev·ing, -reeves.** *Naut.* —*tr.* To withdraw (a rope, for example) from an opening such as a block or thimble. —*intr.* **1.** To become unreeved. **2.** To unreeve a rope.

un·re·flec·tive (ŭn′rĭ-flĕk′tĭv) *adj.* Not reflective. —**un′re·flec′tive·ly** *adv.*

un·re·gen·er·ate (ŭn′rĭ-jĕn′ər-ĭt) *adj.* **1.** Not regenerated; unrepentant. **2.** Unreconstructed. **—un′re·gen′er·a·cy** (-ə-sē) *n.* **—un′re·gen′er·ate·ly** *adv.*
un·re·hearsed (ŭn′rĭ-hûrst′) *adj.* Not rehearsed.
un·re·lent·ing (ŭn′rĭ-lĕn′tĭng) *adj.* **1.** Inexorable. **2.** Not diminishing in intensity, speed, or effort.
un·re·li·a·ble (ŭn′rĭ-lī′ə-bəl) *adj.* Not reliable. **—un′re·li′a·bil′i·ty, un′re·li′a·ble·ness** *n.* **—un′re·li′a·bly** *adv.*
un·re·li·gious (ŭn′rĭ-lĭj′əs) *adj.* **1.** Irreligious. **2.** Having no connection with religion.
un·re·mark·a·ble (ŭn′rĭ-mär′kə-bəl) *adj.* Lacking distinction; ordinary. **—un′re·mark′a·bly** *adv.*
un·re·marked (ŭn′rĭ-märkt′) *adj.* Not noticed.
un·re·mit·ting (ŭn′rĭ-mĭt′ĭng) *adj.* Never slackening; persistent. **—un′re·mit′ting·ly** *adv.* **—un′re·mit′ting·ness** *n.*
un·re·proved (ŭn′rĭ-pro͞ovd′) *adj.* Not reproved; uncensured.
un·re·serve (ŭn′rĭ-zûrv′) *n.* Frankness of manner; candor.
un·re·served (ŭn′rĭ-zûrvd′) *adj.* **1.** Not reserved for a particular person: *an unreserved seat.* **2.** Given without reservation; unqualified: *unreserved praise.* **3.** Not reserved in manner; candid. **—un′re·serv′ed·ly** (-zûr′vĭd-lē) *adv.*
un·re·spon·sive (ŭn′rĭ-spŏn′sĭv) *adj.* Not responsive. **—un′re·spon′sive·ly** *adv.* **—un′re·spon′sive·ness** *n.*
un·rest (ŭn-rĕst′) *n.* Uneasiness; disquiet: *social unrest.*
un·re·strained (ŭn′rĭ-strānd′) *adj.* **1. a.** Unchecked. **b.** Not given to restraint. **2.** Not constrained; natural. **—un′re·strain′ed·ly** (-strā′nĭd-lē) *adv.*
un·rid·dle (ŭn-rĭd′l) *tr.v.* **-dled, -dling, -dles.** To solve or explain (a riddle or mystery).
un·ri·fled (ŭn-rī′fəld) *adj.* Having a smooth bore, as a gun.
un·rig (ŭn-rĭg′) *tr.v.* **-rigged, -rig·ging, -rigs.** *Naut.* To strip (a vessel) of rigging.
un·right·eous (ŭn-rī′chəs) *adj.* **1.** Not righteous; wicked: *an unrighteous man.* **2.** Not right or fair; unjust. **—un·right′eous·ly** *adv.* **—un·right′eous·ness** *n.*
un·rip (ŭn-rĭp′) *tr.v.* **-ripped, -rip·ping, -rips.** To rip open; separate or detach by ripping.
un·ripe (ŭn-rīp′) *adj.* **-rip·er, -rip·est. 1.** Not matured; immature. **2.** Not ready. **—un·ripe′ness** *n.*
un·ri·valed (ŭn-rī′vəld) *adj.* Unequaled; peerless; supreme.
un·roll (ŭn-rōl′) *v.* **-rolled, -roll·ing, -rolls.** *—tr.* **1.** To unwind and open out (something rolled up). **2.** To unfold; reveal. *—intr.* To become unrolled.
un·root (ŭn-ro͞ot′, -ro͝ot′) *tr.v.* **-root·ed, -root·ing, -roots.** To uproot.
un·round (ŭn-round′) *tr.v.* **-round·ed, -round·ing, -rounds.** To pronounce (a sound) with the lips in a flattened or neutral position.
un·ruf·fled (ŭn-rŭf′əld) *adj.* Not ruffled or agitated; calm.
un·ru·ly (ŭn-ro͞o′lē) *adj.* **-li·er, -li·est.** Difficult or impossible to govern. [ME *unreuly* : *un-*, un- + *reuly,* easy to govern < *reule,* rule.]
Synonyms: *unruly, ungovernable, intractable, refractory, recalcitrant, willful, headstrong, wayward.* These adjectives all mean difficult to control. *Unruly* usually refers to disorderly human conduct. *Ungovernable,* which is stronger, applies to what defies handling or restraint, to things made insuperable by sheer size, nature, or complexity, and to persons and their attributes that are beyond discipline. *Intractable* implies unyieldingness in persons who resist authority or guidance and in things that resist human efforts to control, adapt, or manipulate them. *Refractory* applies to things in this same sense; more often it and *recalcitrant,* which is stronger, describe persons who not only resist authority but rebel openly against it. *Willful* and *headstrong* describe the attitude and behavior of persons bent on having their own way, regardless of counsel to the contrary. *Wayward* implies insistence on taking a course in violation of established authority or of a sense of responsibility or virtue.
un·sad·dle (ŭn-săd′l) *v.* **-dled, -dling, -dles.** *—tr.* **1.** To remove the saddle from. **2.** To throw from the saddle; unhorse. *—intr.* To remove the saddle from a horse.
un·safe (ŭn-sāf′) *adj.* Not safe; dangerous.
un·san·i·tar·y (ŭn-săn′ĭ-tĕr′ē) *adj.* Not sanitary.
un·sat·is·fac·to·ry (ŭn-săt′ĭs-făk′tə-rē) *adj.* Not satisfactory; inadequate.
un·sat·u·rate (ŭn-săch′ə-rĭt) *n.* An unsaturated compound.
un·sat·u·rat·ed (ŭn-săch′ə-rā′tĭd) *adj.* **1.** Of or pertaining to a compound, esp. of carbon, containing atoms that share more than one valence bond. **2.** Capable of dissolving more of a solute at a given temperature.
un·saved (ŭn-sāvd′) *adj.* Not saved, esp. not redeemed from sin.
un·sa·vor·y (ŭn-sā′və-rē) *adj.* **1.** Not savory; tasteless; insipid. **2.** Distasteful or disagreeable. **3.** Morally offensive: *an unsavory scandal.* **—un·sa′vor·i·ly** *adv.* **—un·sa′vor·i·ness** *n.*
un·say (ŭn-sā′) *tr.v.* **-said** (-sĕd′), **-say·ing, -says.** To retract (something said).
un·scathed (ŭn-skā*th*d′) *adj.* Unharmed; uninjured.
un·schooled (ŭn-sko͞old′) *adj.* **1.** Not schooled; uninstructed. **2.** Not the result of training; natural.
un·sci·en·tif·ic (ŭn′sī-ən-tĭf′ĭk) *adj.* **1.** Not in accord with the principles of science. **2.** Not knowledgeable about science or scientific method. **—un′sci·en·tif′i·cal·ly** *adv.*
un·scram·ble (ŭn-skrăm′bəl) *tr.v.* **-bled, -bling, -bles. 1.** To disentangle; straighten out. **2.** To restore (a scrambled message) to intelligible form. **—un·scram′bler** *n.*
un·screw (ŭn-skro͞o′) *v.* **-screwed, -screw·ing, -screws.** *—tr.* **1.** To take out the screw or screws from. **2.** To loosen, adjust, or detach by rotating. *—intr.* To become or allow to become unscrewed.
un·scru·pu·lous (ŭn-skro͞o′pyə-ləs) *adj.* Devoid of scruples; contemptuous of what is right or honorable. **—un·scru′pu·lous·ly** *adv.* **—un·scru′pu·lous·ness** *n.*
un·seal (ŭn-sēl′) *tr.v.* **-sealed, -seal·ing, -seals.** To break or remove the seal of; open.
un·seam (ŭn-sēm′) *tr.v.* **-seamed, -seam·ing, -seams.** To undo the seam of.
un·search·a·ble (ŭn-sûr′chə-bəl) *adj.* Beyond search or investigation; inscrutable; imponderable.
un·sea·son·a·ble (ŭn-sē′zə-nə-bəl) *adj.* **1.** Not suitable to or appropriate for the season. **2.** Not characteristic of the time of year: *unseasonable weather.* **3.** Poorly timed; inopportune. **—un·sea′son·a·ble·ness** *n.* **—un·sea′son·a·bly** *adv.*
un·sea·soned (ŭn-sē′zənd) *adj.* **1.** Not made savory with seasoning. **2.** Inadequately aged or seasoned; not ripe or mature: *unseasoned wood.* **3.** Inexperienced.
un·seat (ŭn-sēt′) *tr.v.* **-seat·ed, -seat·ing, -seats. 1.** To remove from a seat, esp. from a saddle. **2.** To dislodge from a position or office.
un·seem·ly (ŭn-sēm′lē) *adj.* **-li·er, -li·est.** Not in good taste; indecorous. *—adv.* In an unseemly manner. **—un·seem′li·ness** *n.*
un·seen (ŭn-sēn′) *adj.* Not directly evident; invisible.
un·seg·re·gat·ed (ŭn-sĕg′rĭ-gā′tĭd) *adj.* Not segregated, esp. not racially segregated.
un·se·lect·ed (ŭn′sĭ-lĕk′tĭd) *adj.* **1.** Not selected. **2.** Chosen arbitrarily.
un·se·lec·tive (ŭn′sĭ-lĕk′tĭv) *adj.* **1.** Not selective; indiscriminate. **2.** Marked by random selection.
un·self·ish (ŭn-sĕl′fĭsh) *adj.* Not selfish; generous. **—un·self′ish·ly** *adv.* **—un·self′ish·ness** *n.*
un·set (ŭn′sĕt′) *adj.* **1.** Not yet firm, stiff, or solidified. **2.** Unmounted in a setting.
un·set·tle (ŭn-sĕt′l) *v.* **-tled, -tling, -tles.** *—tr.* **1.** To displace from a settled condition; disrupt. **2.** To make uneasy; disturb. *—intr.* To become unsettled. **—un·set′tle·ment** *n.*
un·set·tled (ŭn-sĕt′ld) *adj.* **1.** Disordered; disturbed: *unsettled times.* **2.** Variable; uncertain: *unsettled weather.* **3.** Not determined or resolved: *an unsettled issue.* **4.** Not paid or adjusted: *an unsettled bill.* **5.** Unpopulated. **6.** Not fixed or established. **—un·set′tled·ness** *n.*
un·sex (ŭn-sĕks′) *tr.v.* **-sexed, -sex·ing, -sex·es. 1.** To deprive of sexual capacity or sexual attributes. **2.** To castrate.
un·shack·le (ŭn-shăk′əl) *tr.v.* **-led, -ling, -les.** To free from or as if from shackles.
un·shak·a·ble (ŭn-shā′kə-bəl) *adj.* Not capable of being shaken; firm. **—un·shak′a·bly** *adv.*
un·shaped (ŭn-shāpt′) *adj.* **1.** Not shaped or formed. **2.** Imperfectly shaped or formed.
un·shap·en (ŭn-shā′pən) *adj.* Unshaped.
un·sheathe (ŭn-shē*th*′) *tr.v.* **-sheathed, -sheath·ing, -sheathes.** To draw from or as if from a sheath or scabbard.
un·shell (ŭn-shĕl′) *tr.v.* **-shelled, -shell·ing, -shells.** To remove from a shell.
un·ship (ŭn-shĭp′) *v.* **-shipped, -ship·ping, -ships.** *—tr.* **1.** To unload from a ship; discharge. **2.** To remove (a piece of nautical gear) from its proper place. *—intr.* To be removable or detachable.
un·shod (ŭn-shŏd′) *adj.* Not having or wearing shoes.
un·sight·ed (ŭn-sī′tĭd) *adj.* **1.** Not sighted or examined. **2.** Not equipped with or assisted by a sight for aiming.
un·sight·ly (ŭn-sīt′lē) *adj.* **-li·er, -li·est.** Unpleasant or offensive to look at; unattractive. **—un·sight′li·ness** *n.*
un·skilled (ŭn-skĭld′) *adj.* **1.** Lacking skill or technical training: *unskilled labor.* **2.** Requiring no training or skill. **3.** Showing no skill; crude.
un·skill·ful (ŭn-skĭl′fəl) *adj.* **1.** Without skill or proficiency; inexpert. **2.** *Obs.* Ignorant. **—un·skill′ful·ly** *adv.* **—un′skill′ful·ness** *n.*
un·sling (ŭn-slĭng′) *tr.v.* **-slung** (-slŭng′), **-sling·ing, -slings. 1.** To remove from a sling or a slung position. **2.** *Naut.* To remove the slings of (a yard, for example).
un·snap (ŭn-snăp′) *tr.v.* **-snapped, -snap·ping, -snaps.** To undo the snaps of; unfasten.
un·snarl (ŭn-snärl′) *tr.v.* **-snarled, -snarl·ing, -snarls.** To free of snarls; disentangle.
un·so·cia·ble (ŭn′sō′shə-bəl) *adj.* **1.** Not disposed to seek the company of others; reserved. **2.** Not congenial; incompatible. **3.** Not conducive to social exchange: *an unsociable atmosphere.* **—un·so′cia·bil′i·ty, un·so′cia·ble·ness** *n.* **—un′so′cia·bly** *adv.*
un·so·cial (ŭn-sō′shəl) *adj.* Unsociable. **—un·so′cial·ly** *adv.*
un·so·phis·ti·cat·ed (ŭn′sə-fĭs′tĭ-kā′tĭd) *adj.* Not sophisticated. **—un′so·phis′ti·cat′ed·ly** *adv.* **—un′so·phis′ti·cat′ed·ness** *n.* **—un′so·phis′ti·ca′tion** *n.*
un·sought (ŭn-sôt′, ŭn′sôt′) *adj.* Not looked for or requested: *unsought advice.*
un·sound (ŭn-sound′) *adj.* **-er, -est. 1.** Not dependably strong or solid. **2.** Not physically healthy; diseased. **3.** Not

true or logically valid; fallacious. **—un·sound'ly** *adv.* **—un·sound'ness** *n.*
un·spar·ing (ŭn-spâr'ĭng) *adj.* **1.** Not frugal. **2.** Unmerciful; severe. **—un·spar'ing·ly** *adv.* **—un·spar'ing·ness** *n.*
un·speak (ŭn-spēk') *tr.v.* **-spoke** (-spōk'), **-spo·ken** (-spō'kən), **-speak·ing, -speaks.** *Obs.* To retract; unsay.
un·speak·a·ble (ŭn-spē'kə-bəl) *adj.* **1.** Beyond description; inexpressible: *unspeakable happiness.* **2.** Inexpressibly bad or objectionable. **3.** Not to be spoken: *an unspeakable word.* **—un·speak'a·ble·ness** *n.* **—un·speak'a·bly** *adv.*
un·spe·cial·ized (ŭn-spĕsh'ə-līzd') *adj.* Having no special function; without specialty or specialization.
un·sphere (ŭn-sfîr') *tr.v.* **-sphered, -spher·ing, -spheres.** To remove from a sphere or position in the heavens.
un·spot·ted (ŭn-spŏt'ĭd) *adj.* **1.** Not spotted. **2.** Morally unblemished. **—un·spot'ted·ness** *n.*
un·sta·ble (ŭn-stā'bəl) *adj.* **-bler, -blest. 1. a.** Tending strongly to change. **b.** Not constant; fluctuating. **2. a.** Of fickle temperament; flighty. **b.** Psychologically maladjusted. **3.** Not firmly placed; unsteady. **4.** *Chem.* **a.** Decomposing readily. **b.** Highly or violently reactive. **5.** *Physics.* **a.** Decaying with relatively short lifetime. Used of subatomic particles. **b.** Radioactive. **—un·sta'ble·ness** *n.* **—un·sta'bly** *adv.*
un·stead·y (ŭn-stĕd'ē) *adj.* **-i·er, -i·est. 1.** Not securely in place; unstable. **2.** Fluctuating; inconstant. **3.** Wavering; uneven: *an unsteady voice.* *—tr.v.* **-ied, -y·ing, -ies.** To cause to become unsteady. **—un·stead'i·ly** *adv.* **—un·stead'i·ness** *n.*
un·steel (ŭn-stēl') *tr.v.* **-steeled, -steel·ing, -steels.** To make soft; disarm.
un·step (ŭn-stĕp') *tr.v.* **-stepped, -step·ping, -steps.** *Naut.* To remove (a mast) from a step.
un·stick (ŭn-stĭk') *tr.v.* **-stuck** (-stŭk'), **-stick·ing, -sticks.** To free from being stuck.
un·stop (ŭn-stŏp') *tr.v.* **-stopped, -stop·ping, -stops. 1.** To remove a stopper or stop from. **2.** To remove an obstruction from; open.
un·stop·pa·ble (ŭn-stŏp'ə-bəl) *adj.* Not capable of being stopped. **—un·stop'pa·bly** *adv.*
un·stopped (ŭn-stŏpt') *adj.* **1.** Not stopped. **2.** Capable of being prolonged, as the consonants *z* and *l.*
un·strap (ŭn-străp') *tr.v.* **-strapped, -strap·ping, -straps.** To remove or loosen a strap of.
un·strat·i·fied (ŭn-străt'ə-fīd') *adj.* Lacking definite layers.
un·stressed (ŭn-strĕst') *adj.* **1.** Not stressed or having the weakest stress. **2.** Not emphasized.
un·stri·at·ed (ŭn-strī'ā'tĭd) *adj.* Lacking striations; smooth-textured.
un·string (ŭn-strĭng') *tr.v.* **-strung** (-strŭng'), **-string·ing, -strings. 1.** To remove from a string. **2.** To unfasten or loosen the strings of. **3.** To weaken the nerves of; unnerve.
un·struc·tured (ŭn-strŭk'chərd) *adj.* **1.** Lacking structure. **2.** *Psychol.* **a.** Having no intrinsic or objective meaning; meaningful by subjective interpretation only: *unstructured inkblot tests.* **b.** Not regulated or regimented: *an unstructured environment.*
un·strung (ŭn-strŭng') *adj.* **1.** Having a string or strings loosened or removed. **2.** Emotionally upset; unnerved.
un·stud·ied (ŭn-stŭd'ēd) *adj.* **1.** Not contrived for effect; natural. **2.** Not gained by instruction.
un·sub·stan·tial (ŭn'səb-stăn'shəl) *adj.* **1.** Lacking material substance; insubstantial. **2.** Lacking firmness or strength; flimsy. **3.** Lacking basis in fact. **—un'sub·stan'ti·al'i·ty** *n.* **—un'sub·stan'tial·ly** *adv.*
un·suc·cess·ful (ŭn'sək-sĕs'fəl) *adj.* Not succeeding; without success. **—un'suc·cess'ful·ly** *adv.* **—un'suc·cess'ful·ness** *n.*
un·suit·a·ble (ŭn-so͞o'tə-bəl) *adj.* Not suitable; unfitting. **—un·suit'a·bil'i·ty, un·suit'a·ble·ness** *n.* **—un·suit'a·bly** *adv.*
un·sung (ŭn-sŭng') *adj.* **1.** Not sung. **2.** Not honored or praised; uncelebrated: *unsung heroes of battle.*
un·sus·pect·ed (ŭn'sə-spĕk'tĭd) *adj.* **1.** Not under suspicion. **2.** Not known to exist. **—un'sus·pect'ed·ly** *adv.*
un·sus·pect·ing (ŭn'sə-spĕk'tĭng) *adj.* Not suspicious; trusting. **—un'sus·pect'ing·ly** *adv.*
un·swathe (ŭn-swŏ*th*', -swô*th*', -swā*th*') *tr.v.* **-swathed, -swath·ing, -swathes.** To remove the swathes or bindings from.
un·swear (ŭn-swâr') *v.* **-swore** (-swôr', -swōr'), **-sworn** (-swôrn', -swōrn'), **-swear·ing, -swears.** *Archaic.* *—tr.* To retract (an oath), often by swearing another oath. *—intr.* To recant or retract something sworn.
un·sym·met·ri·cal (ŭn'sĭ-mĕt'rĭ-kəl) *adj.* Asymmetric. **—un'sym·met'ri·cal·ly** *adv.*
un·tan·gle (ŭn-tăng'gəl) *tr.v.* **-gled, -gling, -gles. 1.** To free from a tangle; disentangle. **2.** To clarify; resolve.
un·tapped (ŭn-tăpt') *adj.* **1.** Not having been tapped: *an untapped cask of wine.* **2.** Not utilized: *untapped resources.*
un·taught (ŭn-tôt') *adj.* **1.** Not instructed; ignorant. **2.** Not acquired by instruction; natural.
un·teach (ŭn'tēch') *tr.v.* **-taught** (-tôt'), **-teach·ing, -teach·es. 1.** To cause to forget or unlearn something. **2.** To negate (what has been taught) with contradictory information.
un·ten·a·ble (ŭn-tĕn'ə-bəl) *adj.* **1.** Not capable of being defended or maintained. **2.** Not capable of being occupied. **—un·ten'a·bil'i·ty, un·ten'a·ble·ness** *n.* **—un·ten'a·bly** *adv.*
un·thank·ful (ŭn-thăngk'fəl) *adj.* **1.** Not thankful; ungrateful. **2.** Not drawing thanks; unwelcome. **—un·thank'ful·ly** *adv.* **—un·thank'ful·ness** *n.*
un·think (ŭn-thĭngk') *tr.v.* **-thought** (-thôt'), **-think·ing, -thinks.** To dismiss from the mind; disregard.
un·think·a·ble (ŭn-thĭng'kə-bəl) *adj.* **1.** Impossible to imagine; inconceivable. **2.** Not to be thought of or considered; out of the question. **3.** Contrary to what is reasonable or probable. **—un·think'a·bly** *adv.*
un·think·ing (ŭn'thĭng'kĭng) *adj.* **1.** Not mindful or considerate; thoughtless. **2.** Not deliberate; inadvertent. **3.** Incapable of the power of thought. **—un·think'ing·ly** *adv.* **—un·think'ing·ness** *n.*
un·thread (ŭn-thrĕd') *tr.v.* **-thread·ed, -thread·ing, -threads. 1.** To draw out the thread from. **2.** To find one's way out of (a labyrinth, for example).
un·throne (ŭn-thrōn') *tr.v.* **-throned, -thron·ing, -thrones.** To depose from or as if from a throne.
un·ti·dy (ŭn-tī'dē) *adj.* **-di·er, -di·est. 1.** Not neat and tidy; sloppy. **2.** Lacking orderliness or organization. **—un·ti'di·ly** *adv.* **—un·ti'di·ness** *n.*
un·tie (ŭn-tī') *v.* **-tied, -ty·ing, -ties.** *—tr.* **1.** To undo or loosen (a knot or something knotted). **2.** To free from something that binds or restrains. **3.** To straighten out (difficulties, for example); resolve. *—intr.* To become untied.
un·til (ŭn-tĭl') *prep.* **1.** Up to the time of: *We danced until dawn.* **2.** Before a specified time: *We can't leave until Friday.* **3.** *Chiefly Scot.* Unto; to. *—conj.* **1.** Up to the time that: *We played until it was dark.* **2.** Before: *You can't leave until your work is finished.* **3.** To the point or extent that: *He talked until he was hoarse.* [ME : *un-*, till + *til,* till.]
un·time·ly (ŭn-tīm'lē) *adj.* **-li·er, -li·est. 1.** Occurring or done at an inappropriate time; inopportune. **2.** Occurring too soon; premature. *—adv.* **1.** Inopportunely. **2.** Prematurely. **—un·time'li·ness** *n.*
un·tir·ing (ŭn-tīr'ĭng) *adj.* **1.** Not tiring. **2.** Not ceasing despite fatigue or frustration; indefatigable: *untiring efforts in his friend's behalf.* **—un·tir'ing·ly** *adv.*
un·ti·tled (ŭn-tīt'ld) *adj.* **1.** Having no right or claim. **2.** Having no title: *an untitled novel; untitled nobility.*
un·to (ŭn'to͞o) *prep.* To. [ME : *un-*, till + *to,* to.]
un·told (ŭn-tōld') *adj.* **1.** Not told or revealed: *untold secrets.* **2.** Beyond description or enumeration: *untold suffering.*
un·touch·a·ble (ŭn-tŭch'ə-bəl) *adj.* **1.** Not to be touched. **2.** Out of reach; unobtainable. **3.** Beyond the reach of criticism, impeachment, or attack. **4.** Loathsome or unpleasant to the touch. *—n.* Often **Untouchable.** A member of the lowest Hindu caste, who was considered unclean and with whom physical contact was considered defiling by Hindus of higher castes. **—un·touch'a·bil'i·ty** *n.*
un·to·ward (ŭn-tôrd', -tōrd') *adj.* **1.** Unfavorable; unpropitious. **2.** Hard to guide or control; refractory. **3.** *Archaic.* **a.** Awkward. **b.** Improper. **—un·to'ward·ly** *adv.* **—un·to'ward·ness** *n.*
un·trav·eled (ŭn-trăv'əld) *adj.* **1.** Not traversed, as a road. **2. a.** Not having traveled. **b.** Provincial; narrow-minded.
un·tread (ŭn-trĕd') *tr.v.* *Archaic.* **-trod** (-trŏd'), **-trod·den** (-trŏd'n) or **-trod, -tread·ing, -treads.** To retrace (one's course).
un·tried (ŭn-trīd') *adj.* **1.** Not attempted, tested, or proved. **2.** Not tried in a court of law.
un·true (ŭn-tro͞o') *adj.* **-tru·er, -tru·est. 1.** Contrary to fact; false. **2.** Deviating from a standard; not straight, even, level, or exact. **3.** Disloyal; unfaithful. **—un·tru'ly** *adv.*
un·truss (ŭn-trŭs') *v.* **-trussed, -truss·ing, -truss·es.** *Archaic.* *—tr.* **1.** To unfasten; undo. **2.** To undress. *—intr.* To remove one's clothes, esp. one's breeches.
un·truth (ŭn-tro͞oth') *n.* **1.** Something untrue; a lie. **2.** The condition of being false; lack of truth. **3.** *Archaic.* Unfaithfulness.
un·truth·ful (ŭn-tro͞oth'fəl) *adj.* **1.** Contrary to truth. **2.** Given to falsehood; mendacious. **—un·truth'ful·ly** *adv.* **—un·truth'ful·ness** *n.*
un·tu·tored (ŭn-to͞o'tərd, -tyo͞o'-) *adj.* **1.** Having had no formal education or instruction: *an untutored genius.* **2.** Unsophisticated; unrefined.
un·twine (ŭn-twīn') *v.* **-twined, -twin·ing, -twines.** *—tr.* **1.** To loosen or separate, as strands of twisted fiber. **2.** To disentangle. *—intr.* To become untwined.
un·twist (ŭn-twĭst') *v.* **-twist·ed, -twist·ing, -twists.** *—tr.* To loosen or separate (that which is twisted together) by turning in the opposite direction; unwind. *—intr.* To become untwisted.
un·used (ŭn-yo͞ozd', ŭn-yo͞ost') *adj.* **1.** Not in use or put to use. **2.** Never having been used. **3.** Not accustomed: *unused to city traffic.*
un·u·su·al (ŭn-yo͞o'zho͞o-əl) *adj.* Not usual, common, or ordinary. **—un·u'su·al·ly** *adv.* **—un·u'su·al·ness** *n.*
un·ut·ter·a·ble (ŭn-ŭt'ər-ə-bəl) *adj.* **1.** Not capable of being uttered or expressed; defying expression: *"I burned in the unutterable beauty of being alive"* (John Peale Bishop). **2.** Not capable of being pronounced. **—un·ut'ter·a·ble·ness** *n.* **—un·ut'ter·a·bly** *adv.*
un·val·ued (ŭn-văl'yo͞od) *adj.* **1.** Not prized or valued; unappreciated. **2.** Not appraised or assayed: *an unvalued gemstone.* **3.** *Obs.* Inestimable; invaluable.

un·var·nished (ŭn'vär'nĭsht) *adj.* **1.** Not varnished. **2.** Stated or otherwise presented without any effort to soften or disguise: *the unvarnished truth.*

un·veil (ŭn-vāl') *v.* **-veiled, -veil·ing, -veils.** *—tr.* **1.** To remove a veil or covering from. **2.** To disclose; reveal. *—intr.* To take off one's veil; reveal oneself.

un·voice (ŭn-vois') *tr.v.* **-voiced, -voic·ing, -voic·es.** To utter (a sometimes or formerly voiced sound) without vibrating the vocal cords; devoice.

un·voiced (ŭn'voist') *adj.* **1.** Not expressed or uttered. **2.** Uttered without vibrating the vocal cords; voiceless.

un·war·rant·a·ble (ŭn-wôr'ən-tə-bəl, -wŏr'-) *adj.* Not justifiable; inexcusable. **—un'war'rant·a·bly** *adv.*

un·war·rant·ed (ŭn-wôr'ən-tĭd, -wŏr'-) *adj.* Having no justification; groundless: *"A judgment is unwarranted whenever it lacks basis in fact"* (Gordon W. Allport).

un·war·y (ŭn-wâr'ē) *adj.* **-i·er, -i·est.** Not alert to danger or deception; unguarded. **—un·war'i·ly** *adv.* **—un·war'i·ness** *n.*

un·washed (ŭn-wŏsht', -wôsht') *adj.* **1.** Not washed; unclean. **2.** Plebeian: *the unwashed masses.*

un·wea·ried (ŭn'wîr'ēd) *adj.* **1.** Not tired; fresh. **2.** Never wearying; tireless. **—un·wea'ried·ly** *adv.*

un·well (ŭn-wĕl') *adj.* **1.** Not well; ill. **2.** Menstruating.

un·wept (ŭn-wĕpt') *adj.* **1.** Not mourned or wept for: *the unwept dead.* **2.** Not shed: *unwept tears.*

un·whole·some (ŭn-hōl'səm) *adj.* **1.** Injurious to physical, mental, or moral health. **2.** Suggestive of disease or degeneracy. **3.** Offensive or loathsome. **—un·whole'some·ly** *adv.* **—un·whole'some·ness** *n.*

un·wield·y (ŭn-wēl'dē) *adj.* **-i·er, -i·est.** **1.** Difficult to carry or manage because of bulk or shape. **2.** Clumsy; ungainly.

un·willed (ŭn-wĭld') *adj.* Involuntary; spontaneous.

un·will·ing (ŭn-wĭl'ĭng) *adj.* **1.** Hesitant; loath. **2.** Done, given, or said reluctantly: *unwilling consent.* **—un·will'ing·ly** *adv.* **—un·will'ing·ness** *n.*

un·wind (ŭn-wīnd') *v.* **-wound** (-wound'), **-wind·ing, -winds.** *—tr.* **1.** To reverse the winding or twisting direction of. **2.** To separate the tangled parts of; disentangle. **3.** To free from tension. *—intr.* **1.** To become unwound. **2.** To relax.

un·wise (ŭn-wīz') *adj.* **-wis·er, -wis·est.** Lacking wisdom; foolish or imprudent: *an unwise decision.* **—un·wise'ly** *adv.*

un·wish (ŭn-wĭsh') *tr.v.* **-wished, -wish·ing, -wish·es.** **1.** To retract a wish for. **2.** *Obs.* To wish out of existence.

un·wit·ting (ŭn-wĭt'ĭng) *adj.* **1.** Not knowing; unaware: *an unwitting victim of fraud.* **2.** Not intended; unintentional. [ME : *un-*, un- + *witting,* p.part. of *witten,* to know < OE *witan.*] **—un·wit'ting·ly** *adv.*

un·wont·ed (ŭn-wôn'tĭd, -wōn'-, -wŭn'-) *adj.* **1.** Not habitual or ordinary; unusual. **2.** *Archaic.* Not accustomed; unused to. **—un·wont'ed·ly** *adv.* **—un·wont'ed·ness** *n.*

un·world·ly (ŭn-wûrld'lē) *adj.* **-li·er, -li·est.** **1.** Not of this world; spiritual. **2.** Concerned with matters of the spirit or soul. **3.** Not worldly-wise; naive. **—un·world'li·ness** *n.*

un·worn (ŭn-wôrn', -wōrn') *adj.* **1.** Not worn out or worn away. **2.** Not worn before; new. **3.** Not stale or overused.

un·wor·thy (ŭn-wûr'*th*ē) *adj.* **-thi·er, -thi·est.** **1.** Insufficient in worth; undeserving: *a silly plan unworthy of consideration.* **2.** Not suiting or befitting: *"The acquaintances she had already formed were unworthy of her"* (Jane Austen). **3.** Lacking value or merit; worthless. **4.** Vile; despicable. **—un·wor'thi·ly** *adv.* **—un·wor'thi·ness** *n.*

un·wrap (ŭn-răp') *v.* **-wrapped, -wrap·ping, -wraps.** *—tr.* To remove the wrappings from; open. *—intr.* To become unwrapped.

un·writ·ten (ŭn-rĭt'n) *adj.* **1.** Not written or recorded. **2.** Forceful or effective through custom; traditional. **3.** Not written upon; blank.

unwritten law *n.* A code, rule, or law of morality, conduct or procedure whose authority lies in custom, tradition, or general usage rather than in a specific enactment.

un·yield·ing (ŭn-yēl'dĭng) *adj.* **1.** Not bending; inflexible. **2.** Obdurate. **—un·yield'ing·ly** *adv.* **—un·yield'ing·ness** *n.*

un·yoke (ŭn-yōk') *v.* **-yoked, -yok·ing, -yokes.** *—tr.* **1.** To release from or as if from a yoke. **2.** To separate or disjoin. *—intr.* **1.** To remove a yoke. **2.** *Archaic.* To stop working.

un·zip (ŭn-zĭp') *v.* **-zipped, -zip·ping, -zips.** *—tr.* To open or unfasten (a zipper or something held by a zipper). *—intr.* To become unzipped.

up (ŭp) *adv.* **1.** From a lower to a higher position. **2.** In or toward a higher position: *looking up.* **3.** From a reclining to an upright position: *sat up in bed.* **4. a.** Above a surface: *coming up for air.* **b.** Above the horizon. **5.** Into view, existence, or consideration: *bring a matter up for discussion.* **6.** In or toward a position conventionally regarded as higher, as on a scale, chart, or map. **7.** To or at a higher price. **8.** So as to advance, increase, or improve. **9.** With or to a greater intensity, pitch, or volume. **10.** Into a state of excitement or turbulence. **11.** So as to detach or unearth: *pulling up weeds.* **12.** Used as an intensifier of the action of a verb: *typed up a list.* **13.** Apart; into pieces: *tore it up.* **14.** *Naut.* To windward. **15.** Each; apiece. **16.** Completely; entirely: *fastened up his coat.* *—adj.* **1.** High or relatively high. **2. a.** Standing; erect. **b.** Out of bed. **3.** Moving or directed upward: *an up elevator.* **4. a.** Actively functioning; healthy: *up and around.* **b.** *Slang.* Happily excited; euphoric. **5.** Rising toward the flood level. **6.** Marked by agitation or acceleration: *The winds are up.* **7.** *Informal.* Taking place; going on: *What's up?* **8.** Being considered; under study: *a contract that is up for renewal.* **9.** Running as a candidate. **10.** Charged; on trial. **11.** Finished; over: *His time was up.* **12.** *Informal.* Well-informed: *I am not up on sports.* **13.** Being ahead of the opponent: *up two holes in a golf match.* **14.** *Baseball.* At bat. **15.** As a bet; at stake. **16.** *Naut.* Bound for a specified place. *—prep.* **1.** From a lower to or toward a higher point on. **2.** Toward or at a point farther along: *up the road.* **3.** In a direction toward the source of: *up the Hudson.* **4.** Against: *up the wind.* *—n.* **1.** An upward slope; rise or ascent. **2.** An upward movement or trend. **3.** *Slang.* A feeling of excitement or euphoria. *—v.* **upped, up·ping, ups.** *—tr.* **1.** To increase or improve. **2.** To raise to a higher level, esp. to promote to a higher position. *—intr.* **1.** To get up; rise. **2.** *Informal.* To act suddenly or unexpectedly: *"She upped and perjured her immortal soul"* (Margery Allingham). ***—idioms.*** **on the up and up.** *Slang.* Open and honest. **up against.** Confronted with; facing. **up to. 1.** Occupied with, esp. devising and scheming: *He's up to no good.* **2.** Primed and prepared for. **3.** Dependent upon: *the success of this project is up to us.* [ME *up,* upward and *uppe,* on high, both < OE.]

up– *pref.* **1.** Up; upward: *upheave.* **2.** Upper: *upland.* [ME < OE.]

up-and-com·ing (ŭp'ən-kŭm'ĭng) *adj.* Marked for future success; promising.

up-and-down (ŭp'ən-doun') *adj.* **1.** Consisting of alternating upward and downward movement. **2.** Vertical.

U·pan·i·shad (o͞o-păn'ə-shăd') *n.* Any of a group of philosophical treatises contributing to the theology of ancient Hinduism, elaborating upon the earlier Vedas. [Skt. *upaniṣad.*] **—U·pan'i·shad'ic** *adj.*

u·pas (yo͞o'pəs) *n.* **1.** A tree, *Antiaris toxicaria,* of tropical Asia, that yields a juice used as an arrow poison. **2.** The poison obtained from the upas or similar trees or plants. [Malay *(pōhun) upas,* poison (tree).]

up·beat (ŭp'bēt') *n.* *Mus.* An unaccented beat, esp. the last beat of a measure. *—adj.* *Informal.* **1.** Optimistic. **2.** Happy; cheerful.

up-bow (ŭp'bō') *n.* *Mus.* A stroke performed on a stringed instrument in which the bow is moved across the strings from its tip to its heel.

up·braid (ŭp-brād') *tr.v.* **-braid·ed, -braid·ing, -braids.** To reprove sharply; reproach. [ME *upbreyden* < OE *ūpbrēdan* : *up,* up + *bregdan,* to throw.] **—up·braid'er** *n.* **—up·braid'ing·ly** *adv.*

up·bring·ing (ŭp'brĭng'ĭng) *n.* The rearing and training received during childhood.

up·build (ŭp-bĭld') *tr.v.* **-built** (-bĭlt'), **-build·ing, -builds.** To build up; enlarge or enhance. **—up·build'er** *n.*

up·cast (ŭp'kăst') *adj.* Directed or thrown upward. *—n.* **1.** Something cast upward. **2.** A ventilating shaft, as in a mine.

up·chuck (ŭp'chŭk') *v.* **-chucked, -chuck·ing, -chucks.** *Slang.* *—intr.* To vomit. *—tr.* To vomit (stomach contents).

up·com·ing (ŭp'kŭm'ĭng) *adj.* Anticipated; forthcoming.

up·coun·try (ŭp'kŭn'trē) *n.* The interior region of a country. *—adj.* (ŭp'kŭn'trē). Of, located in, or coming from the upcountry. *—adv.* (ŭp-kŭn'trē). In, to, or toward the upcountry.

up·date (ŭp-dāt') *tr.v.* **-dat·ed, -dat·ing, -dates.** To bring up to date: *update a textbook.* *—n.* (ŭp'dāt'). **1.** Information that updates. **2.** The act or an instance of updating.

up·draft (ŭp'drăft') *n.* An upward current of air.

up·end (ŭp-ĕnd') *v.* **-end·ed, -end·ing, -ends.** *—tr.* **1.** To stand, set, or turn on one end. **2.** To overturn or overthrow. *—intr.* To be upended.

up-front (ŭp'frŭnt') *adj.* **1.** Straightforward; frank: *up-front about his personal finances.* **2.** Required in advance: *up-front cash.*

up·grade (ŭp'grād') *tr.v.* **-grad·ed, -grad·ing, -grades.** **1.** To raise to a higher grade or standard. **2.** To improve the quality of (livestock) by selective breeding for desired characteristics. *—n.* An upward incline. *—adj.* Uphill. *—adv.* Up along an incline. ***—idiom.*** **on the upgrade.** Improving or progressing.

up·growth (ŭp'grōth') *n.* **1.** The process of growing upward. **2.** Upward growth or development.

up·heav·al (ŭp-hē'vəl) *n.* **1.** The process or an instance of being heaved upward. **2.** A sudden and violent disruption or upset: *"The psychic upheaval caused by war"* (Wallace Fowlie). **3.** *Geol.* A lifting up of the earth's crust by the movement of stratified or other rocks.

up·heave (ŭp-hēv') *v.* **-heaved, -heav·ing, -heaves.** *—tr.* To heave upward; lift forcefully from beneath. *—intr.* To be lifted or thrust upward.

up·hill (ŭp'hĭl') *adj.* **1.** Going up a hill or slope. **2.** Prolonged, difficult, and laborious. *—n.* (ŭp'hĭl'). An upward slope or incline. *—adv.* (ŭp'hĭl'). **1.** To or toward higher ground; upward. **2.** Against adversity; with difficulty.

up·hold (ŭp-hōld') *tr.v.* **-held** (-hĕld'), **-hold·ing, -holds.** **1.** To hold aloft; raise. **2.** To prevent from falling or sinking; support. **3.** To maintain or affirm in the face of a challenge: *"The Declaration of Right upheld the principle of*

upholstery

uproot

hereditary monarchy" (Edmund Burke). [ME *upholden* : *up,* up + *holden,* to hold.] **—up·hold'er** *n.*

up·hol·ster (ŭp-hōl'stər) *tr.v.* **-stered, -ster·ing, -sters.** To supply (furniture) with stuffing, springs, cushions, and covering fabric. [Back-formation from UPHOLSTERER.]

up·hol·ster·er (ŭp-hōl'stər-ər) *n.* One that upholsters furniture. [< obs. *upholster* < ME *upholdester* < *upholden,* to repair.]

up·hol·ster·y (ŭp-hōl'stə-rē, -strē) *n., pl.* **-ies. 1.** The fabrics and other materials used in upholstering. **2.** The craft or business of upholstering.

up·keep (ŭp'kēp') *n.* **1.** Maintenance in proper operation, condition, and repair. **2.** The cost of upkeep.

up·land (ŭp'lənd, -lănd') *n.* **1.** The higher parts of a region or tract of land. **2.** Inland country; upcountry. *—adj.* Of, pertaining to, or located in an upland.

upland cotton *n.* A plant, *Gossypium hirsutum,* native to tropical America and widely cultivated for its fiber.

upland plover *n.* A brownish, long-necked New World bird, *Bartramia longicauda,* of fields and prairies.

up·lift (ŭp-lĭft') *tr.v.* **-lift·ed, -lift·ing, -lifts. 1.** To raise up or aloft; elevate. **2.** To raise to a higher social, intellectual, or moral level or condition. **3.** To raise to spiritual or emotional heights; exalt. *—adj.* (ŭp'lĭft'). Uplifted. *—n.* (ŭp'lĭft'). **1.** The act, process, or result of raising or lifting up. **2.** A movement to improve social, moral, or intellectual standards. **3.** An agent or influence causing upward movement or lifting. **4.** *Geol.* An upheaval.

up·man·ship (ŭp'mən-shĭp) *n.* One-upmanship.

up·most (ŭp'mōst') *adj.* Uppermost.

up·on (ə-pŏn', ə-pôn') *prep.* On. [ME : *up,* up + *on,* on.]

up·per (ŭp'ər) *adj.* **1.** Higher in place, position, or rank. **2. a.** Situated on higher ground. **b.** Lying farther inland. **c.** Northern. **3. Upper.** *Geol. & Archaeol.* Being a later division of the period named. *—n.* **1.** That part of a shoe or boot above the sole. **2.** *Informal.* An upper berth. **3. uppers.** *Informal.* The upper teeth or a set of upper dentures. **4.** *Slang.* **a.** A drug used as a stimulant, esp. an amphetamine. **b.** Something that brings about a feeling of well-being or euphoria: *the whole experience was an upper.* ***—idiom.* on one's uppers.** *Informal.* Impoverished; destitute.

upper atmosphere *n.* The atmosphere that extends above the troposphere.

upper bound *n. Math.* A number that is not exceeded by any number in a given set.

Upper Carboniferous *adj. & n. Geol.* Pennsylvanian.

upper case *n.* The case of printing type containing the capital letters and special characters.

up·per-case (ŭp'ər-kās') *adj.* Pertaining to or printed in capital letters; capital. *—tr.v.* **-cased, -cas·ing, -cas·es.** To print in upper-case letters.

up·per-class (ŭp'ər-klăs') *adj.* **1.** Of or belonging to an upper social class. **2.** Of or belonging to the junior and senior classes in a school or college.

up·per·class·man (ŭp'ər-klăs'mən) *n.* A student in the junior or senior class of a secondary school or college.

upper crust *n. Informal.* The highest social class or group.

up·per·cut (ŭp'ər-kŭt') *n.* In boxing, a short swinging blow directed upward, as to the opponent's chin. **—up'per·cut'** *v.* **(-cut, -cut·ting, -cuts).**

upper hand *n.* A position of control or advantage.

Upper House or **upper house** *n.* The branch of a bicameral legislature that is smaller and less broadly representative of the population, such as the U.S. Senate.

up·per·most (ŭp'ər-mōst') *adj.* Highest in position, place, rank, or influence. *—adv.* In the first or highest rank, position, or place; first.

up·pish (ŭp'ĭsh) *adj.* Uppity. **—up'pish·ly** *adv.* **—up'pish·ness** *n.*

up·pi·ty (ŭp'ĭ-tē) *adj. Informal.* Snobbish or arrogant. [< UP.]

up·raise (ŭp-rāz') *tr.v.* **-raised, -rais·ing, -rais·es.** To raise or lift up; elevate.

up·rear (ŭp-rîr') *v.* **-reared, -rear·ing, -rears.** *—tr.* To raise or lift up. *—intr.* To be raised up; rise.

up·right (ŭp'rīt') *adj.* **1. a.** In a vertical position, direction, or stance. **b.** Erect in posture or carriage: *"She sat with grim determination, upright as a darning needle stuck in a board"* (Harriet Beecher Stowe). **2.** Morally respectable; honorable. *—adv.* Vertically: *walk upright.* *—n.* **1.** A perpendicular position; verticality. **2.** Something standing upright, as a beam. **3.** An upright piano. [ME < OE *upriht* : *up,* up + *riht,* right.] **—up'right'ly** *adv.* **—up'right'ness** *n.*

upright piano *n.* A piano having the strings mounted vertically in a rectangular case with the keyboard at a right angle to the case.

up·rise (ŭp-rīz') *intr.v.* **-rose** (-rōz'), **-ris·en** (-rĭz'ən), **-ris·ing, -ris·es. 1.** To get up or stand up; rise. **2.** To go, move, or incline upward; ascend. **3.** To rise into view, esp. from below the horizon. **4.** To increase in size; swell. *—n.* (ŭp'rīz'). **1.** The act or process of rising up. **2.** An upward slope; ascent.

up·ris·ing (ŭp'rī'zĭng) *n.* **1.** A revolt; insurrection. **2.** An act of rising or rising up. **3.** An ascent; upward slope.

up·riv·er (ŭp'rĭv'ər) *adj.* Toward or near the source of a river; in the direction opposite to that of the flow of water. *—n.* A region lying upriver. **—up'riv'er** *adv.*

up·roar (ŭp'rôr', -rōr') *n.* **1.** A condition of noisy excitement and confusion; tumult. **2.** A heated controversy. [By folk ety. < Du. *oproer* < MDu. : *op,* up + *roer,* motion.]

up·roar·i·ous (ŭp-rôr'ē-əs, -rōr'-) *adj.* **1.** Causing or accompanied by an uproar. **2.** Loud and full; boisterous. **3.** Causing hearty laughter; hilarious. **—up·roar'i·ous·ly** *adv.* **—up·roar'i·ous·ness** *n.*

up·root (ŭp-ro͞ot', -ro͝ot') *tr.v.* **-root·ed, -root·ing, -roots. 1.** To tear or remove (a plant and its roots) from the ground. **2.** To destroy or remove completely; eradicate. **3.** To force to leave an accustomed or native location. **—up·root'er** *n.*

ups and downs *pl.n.* Alternating periods of good and bad fortune or spirits.

up·set (ŭp-sĕt') *v.* **-set, -set·ting, -sets.** *—tr.* **1.** To overturn or capsize; tip over. **2.** To disturb in usual or normal functioning, order, or course. **3.** To distress or perturb mentally or emotionally. **4.** To defeat unexpectedly. **5.** To make shorter and thicker by hammering on the end. *—intr.* **1.** To become overturned; capsize. **2.** To become disturbed. *—n.* (ŭp'sĕt'). **1. a.** An act of upsetting. **b.** The condition of being upset. **2.** A disturbance, disorder, or agitation. **3.** A game or contest in which the favorite is defeated. **4. a.** A tool used for upsetting; swage. **b.** An upset part or piece. *—adj.* (ŭp-sĕt'). **1.** Overturned; capsized. **2.** Disordered; disturbed. **3.** Distressed; distraught. [ME *upsetten,* to set up : *up,* up + *setten,* to set.] **—up·set'ter** *n.*

upset price *n.* The lowest price at which merchandise or property will be auctioned or sold at public sale.

up·shot (ŭp'shŏt') *n.* The final result; outcome. [Obs. *upshot,* the last shot in an archery contest.]

up·side-down (ŭp'sīd-doun') *adj.* **1.** Overturned completely so that the upper side is down. **2.** In great disorder or confusion; topsy-turvy. *—adv.* Also **upside down.** Topsy-turvy. [Alteration of ME *up so down,* up as if down.]

upside-down cake *n.* A single-layer cake baked with sliced fruit at the bottom, then served with the fruit side up.

up·si·lon (ŭp'sə-lŏn', yo͞op'sə-lŏn') *n.* The 20th letter of the Greek alphabet. See table at **alphabet.** [Med. Gk., *u psilon,* simple u.]

up·spring (ŭp-sprĭng') *intr. v.* **-sprang** (-sprăng') or **-sprung** (-sprŭng'), **-sprung, -spring·ing, -springs. 1.** To spring up, as from the soil. **2.** To come into being; arise.

up·stage (ŭp'stāj') *adj.* **1.** Pertaining to, involving, or located at the rear of a stage. **2.** *Informal.* Haughty; aloof. *—adv.* Toward, to, on, or at the rear of the stage. *—tr.v.* (ŭp-stāj') **-staged, -stag·ing, -stag·es. 1.** To distract attention from (another actor) by moving upstage and forcing him to perform with his back to the audience. **2.** *Informal.* To steal the show from; force out of the spotlight. **3.** *Informal.* To treat haughtily.

up·stairs (ŭp'stârz') *adv.* **1.** In, on, or to an upper floor or story. **2.** To or at a higher level: *promoted upstairs to management.* *—adj.* (ŭp'stârz'). Of or to an upper floor or floors: *an upstairs maid.* *—n.* (ŭp'stârz'). *(used with a sing. or pl. verb).* A floor or story above ground level. ***—idiom.* kick upstairs.** *Informal.* To dispose of by promotion to a higher but less effectual position.

up·stand·ing (ŭp-stăn'dĭng, ŭp'stand'ĭng) *adj.* **1.** Standing erect or upright. **2.** Morally upright; honest.

up·start (ŭp'stärt') *n.* **1.** A person of humble origin who attains sudden wealth, power, or prestige, esp. one who assumes an arrogant attitude; parvenu. **2.** A person having an exaggerated sense of his own importance or ability. *—adj.* **1.** Suddenly raised to a position of consequence. **2.** Self-important; presumptuous. *—intr.v.* (ŭp-stärt') **-start·ed, -start·ing, -starts.** To spring or start up suddenly.

up·state (ŭp'stāt') *adj. & adv.* Of, at, in, or toward that part of a state lying inland or farther north of a large city. *—n.* An upstate region. **—up'stat'er** *n.*

up·stream (ŭp'strēm') *adv.* In, at, or toward the source of a stream or current.

up·stroke (ŭp'strōk') *n.* An upward stroke, as of a brush.

up·surge (ŭp-sûrj') *intr.v.* **-surged, -surg·ing, -surg·es.** To surge up. *—n.* (ŭp'sûrj'). A rapid upward swell or rise.

up·sweep (ŭp'swēp') *n.* **1.** A curve or sweep upward. **2.** A hairdo that is smoothed upward in the back and piled on top of the head. *—tr.v.* **-swept** (-swĕpt'), **-sweep·ing, -sweeps.** To brush, curve, or sweep upward.

up·swing (ŭp'swĭng') *n.* **1.** An upward swing or trend. **2.** An increase, as in movement or activity: *an upswing of the stock market.*

up·take (ŭp'tāk') *n.* **1.** A passage for drawing up smoke or air. **2.** Understanding; comprehension: *very quick on the uptake.*

up-tem·po (ŭp'tĕm'pō) *n.* A fast-paced tempo, as in jazz. **—up-tem'po** *adj.*

up·throw (ŭp'thrō') *n.* **1.** A throwing upward. **2.** *Geol.* An upward displacement of rock on one side of a fault.

up·tick (ŭp'tĭk') *n.* A transaction in a stock market security above the price of the previous transaction.

up·tight also **up tight** (ŭp'tīt') *adj. Slang.* **1.** Tense; nervous. **2.** Financially pressed; destitute. **3.** Outraged; angry. **4.** Conforming rigidly to convention.

up·time (ŭp′tīm′) *n.* The time during which a device, as a computer, is functioning or available for use.
up-to-date (ŭp′tə-dāt′) *adj.* Informed of or reflecting the latest improvements, facts, or style; modern. **—up′-to-date′-ness** *n.*
up-to-the-min·ute (ŭp′tə-thə-mĭn′ĭt) *adj.* Marked by or including the most up-to-date information; current: *an up-to-the-minute newsbreak.*
up·town (ŭp′toun′) *adv.* In or toward the upper part of a town or city. *—n.* The upper part of a town or city. **—up′-town′** *adj.*
up·turn (ŭp′tûrn′, ŭp-tûrn′) *v.* **-turned, -turn·ing, -turns.** *—tr.* **1.** To turn up or over, as soil. **2.** To upset; overturn. **3.** To direct upward. *—intr.* To turn over or up. *—n.* (ŭp′tûrn′). An upward movement, curve, or trend.
up·ward (ŭp′wərd) also **up·wards** (-wərdz) *adv.* **1.** In, to, or toward a higher place, level, or position. **2.** To or toward the source, origin, or interior. **3.** Toward the head or upper parts. **4.** Toward a higher amount, degree, or rank: *Prices soared upward.* **5.** Toward a later time or age. **6.** Toward something greater or better. *—adj.* **upward.** Directed toward a higher place or position: *upward mobility in business.* *—idiom.* **upward (or upwards) of.** More than; in excess of: *"the onslaught of upwards of seventy divisions"* (Winston Churchill). [ME < OE *ūpweard, up,* up + *-weard,* -ward.] **—up′ward·ly** *adv.*
up·wind (ŭp′wĭnd′) *adv.* In or toward the direction from which the wind blows. **—up′wind′** *adj.*
ur–¹ *pref.* Variant of **uro-¹**.
ur–² *pref.* Variant of **uro-²**.
u·ra·cil (yo͝or′ə-sĭl) *n.* A pyrimidine, $C_4H_4N_2O_2$, a constituent of ribonucleic acids. [UR(EA) + AC(ETIC) + -IL(E).]
u·rae·mi·a (yo͞o-rē′mē-ə) *n.* Variant of **uremia.**
u·rae·us (yo͞o-rē′əs) *n.* The figure of the sacred serpent, depicted on the headdress of ancient Egyptian rulers and deities as an emblem of sovereignty. [NLat. < LGk. *ouraios,* cobra, of Egyptian orig.]
U·ral-Al·ta·ic (yo͝or′əl-ăl-tā′ĭk) *n.* A hypothetical language group that comprises the Uralic and Altaic language families. **—Ural-Altaic** *adj.*
U·ral·ic (yo͞o-răl′ĭk) also **U·ra·li·an** (yo͞o-rā′lē-ən) *n.* A language family that comprises the Finno-Ugric and Samoyedic subfamilies. **—U·ral′ic, U·ra′li·an** *adj.*
uran– *pref.* Variant of **urano-.**
u·ra·ni·a (yo͞o-rā′nē-ə, -rān′yə) *n.* Uranium dioxide. [NLat. < URANIUM.]
U·ra·ni·a (yo͞o-rā′nē-ə, -rān′yə) *n.* *Gk. Myth.* The Muse of astronomy. [Lat. < Gk. *Ourania* < *ouranos,* heaven.]
u·ran·ic (yo͞o-răn′ĭk, -rā′nĭk) *adj.* **1.** Of or relating to the heavens; celestial. **2.** *Chem.* Of, pertaining to, or derived from uranium, esp. with valence higher than in comparable uranous compounds. [Sense 1 : < Gk. *ouranos,* heaven. Sense 2 : < URANIUM.]
u·ra·ni·nite (yo͞o-rā′nə-nīt′) *n.* A complex brownish-black mineral, chiefly UO_2 partially oxidized to UO_3, containing variable amounts of radium, lead, thorium, rare-earth metals, helium, argon, and nitrogen. [G. *Uranin,* uraninite (< NLat. *uranium,* uranium) + -ITE¹.]
u·ra·ni·um (yo͞o-rā′nē-əm) *n.* *Symbol* **U** A heavy silvery-white metallic element, radioactive, easily oxidized, and having 14 known isotopes of which U 238 is the most abundant in nature. The element occurs in several minerals, including pitchblende and carnotite, from which it is extracted and processed for use in research, nuclear fuels, and nuclear weapons. Atomic number 92; atomic weight 238.03; melting point 1,132°C; boiling point 3,818°C; specific gravity 18.95; valences 3, 4, 5, 6. [After URANUS.]
uranium 235 *n.* The uranium isotope with mass number 235 and half-life 7.13×10^8 years, fissionable with slow neutrons and capable in a critical mass of sustaining a chain reaction that can proceed explosively with appropriate mechanical arrangements.
uranium 238 *n.* The most common isotope of uranium, having mass number 238 and half-life 4.51×10^9 years, nonfissionable but irradiated with neutrons to produce fissionable plutonium 239.
uranium dioxide *n.* A black, highly toxic crystalline powder, UO_2, once used in ceramic glazes and gas mantles, now used primarily to pack nuclear fuel rods.
uranium enrichment *n.* A chemical process performed on natural uranium to increase the ratio of uranium 235 to uranium 238, used in fission technology.
uranium trioxide *n.* A radioactive orange powder, UO_3, used for uranium refining and as a coloring agent in ceramics.
urano– or **uran–** *pref.* Uranium: *uranyl.* [< URANIUM.]
u·ra·nous (yo͞o-rā′nəs, yo͝or′ə-nəs) *adj.* *Chem.* Of or pertaining to uranium, esp. with valence lower than in comparable uranic compounds.
U·ra·nus (yo͝or′ə-nəs, yo͞o-rā′nəs) *n.* **1.** *Gk. Myth.* The earliest supreme god, a personification of the sky, who was the son and consort of Gaea and the father of the Cyclopes and Titans. **2.** The seventh planet from the sun, revolving about it every 84.02 years at a distance of approximately 1,790,000,000 miles. It has an equatorial diameter of 30,000 miles, a mass 14.6 times that of Earth, and five satellites. [Lat. < Gk. *Ouranos* < *ouranos,* heaven.]
u·ra·nyl (yo͝or′ə-nĭl, yo͞o-rā′nəl) *n.* The divalent radical UO_2.
u·rase (yo͝or′ās′, -āz′) *n.* Variant of **urease.**
u·rate (yo͝or′āt′) *n.* A salt of uric acid. [UR(IC ACID) + -ATE².]
ur·ban (ûr′bən) *adj.* **1.** Of or located in a city. **2.** Characteristic of the city or city life. [Lat. *urbanus* < *urbs,* city.]
urban district *n.* An administrative district of England, Wales, and Northern Ireland, usually composed of several densely populated communities, resembling a borough but lacking a borough charter.
ur·bane (ûr-bān′) *adj.* Having or showing the refined manners of polite society; elegant: *"Urbane and pliant . . . he was at ease even in the drawing rooms of Paris"* (R.R. Palmer). [Fr. *urbain* < Lat. *urbanus,* of a city < *urbs,* city.] **—ur·bane′-ly** *adv.*
ur·ban·ism (ûr′bə-nĭz′əm) *n.* **1.** The culture or life style of city dwellers. **2.** Urbanization.
ur·ban·ite (ûr′bə-nīt′) *n.* A city dweller.
ur·ban·i·ty (ûr-băn′ĭ-tē) *n., pl.* **-ties. 1.** Refinement and elegance of manner; polished courtesy. **2. urbanities.** Courtesies; civilities.
ur·ban·ize (ûr′bə-nīz′) *tr.v.* **-ized, -iz·ing, -iz·es.** To make urban in nature or character. **—ur′ban·i·za′tion** *n.*
ur·ban·ol·o·gist (ûr′bə-nŏl′ə-jĭst) *n.* One who is a specialist in urban problems. **—ur′ban·ol′o·gy** *n.*
urban renewal *n.* The state-sponsored destruction of slum neighborhoods with a view to the construction of new housing.
urban sprawl *n.* The gradual spreading of urban dwellings, businesses, and industry to the relatively unexploited land adjoining the urban area.
ur·ce·o·late (ûr-sē′ə-lĭt, ûr′sē-ə-lāt′) *adj.* Urn-shaped: *an urceolate corolla.* [NLat. *urceolatus* < Lat. *urceolus,* dim. of *urceus,* jug.]
ur·chin (ûr′chĭn) *n.* **1.** A small, mischievous boy; a scamp: *"Those urchins who pencil mustaches on the faces of girls in advertisements"* (W.H. Auden). **2.** A sea urchin. **3.** *Archaic.* A hedgehog. [ME *urchone,* hedgehog < OFr. *herichon* < Lat. *ericius* < *er.*]
Ur·du (o͝or′do͞o, ûr′-) *n.* An Indic language that is the official literary language of Pakistan and is widely used esp. by Moslems in India. [Hindi, short for *zabān-i-urdū,* language of the camp.]
–ure *suff.* **1.** Act; process: *erasure.* **2. a.** Function; office: *judicature.* **b.** Body performing a function: *legislature.* [ME < OFr. < Lat. *-ura.*]
u·re·a (yo͞o-rē′ə) *n.* A white crystalline or powdery compound, $CO(NH_2)_2$, found in mammalian urine and other body fluids, synthesized from ammonia and carbon dioxide, and used as fertilizer, in animal feed, and in resins. [NLat. < Fr. *urée* < *urine,* urine < OFr. < Lat. *urina.*]
u·re·a-for·mal·de·hyde resin (yo͞o-rē′ə-fôr-măl′də-hīd′) *n.* Any of various thermosetting resins made by combining urea and formaldehyde and widely used to make molded household and mechanical objects.
u·re·ase (yo͝or′ē-ās′, -āz′) also **u·rase** (yo͝or′ās′, -āz′) *n.* An enzyme occurring in urine, jack beans, soy beans, and as a secretion of certain microorganisms, used to determine the urea content of blood and urine. [URE(A) + -ASE.]
u·re·da·stage (yo͞o-rē′də-stāj′) *n.* The stage of a rust fungus in which uredinia are produced. [URED(INIA) + STAGE.]
u·re·din·i·o·spore (yo͝or′ə-dĭn′ē-ə-spôr′, -spōr′) *n.* Variant of **uredospore.** [UREDINI(UM) + SPORE.]
u·re·din·i·um (yo͝or′ə-dĭn′ē-əm) also **u·re·di·um** (yo͞o-rē′dē-əm) *n., pl.* **-din·i·a** (-dĭn′ē-ə) also **-di·a** (-dē-ə). A reddish, pustulelike structure formed on the tissue of a plant infected by a rust fungus, and having hyphae that produce uredospores. [NLat. < Lat. *uredo,* blight < *urere,* to burn.]
u·re·do (yo͞o-rē′dō) *n.* *Pathol.* Urticaria. [Lat., burning itch < *urere,* to burn.]
u·re·do·spore (yo͞o-rē′də-spôr′, -spōr′) also **u·re·din·i·o·spore** (yo͝or′ə-dĭn′ē-ə-spôr′, -spōr′) *n.* A reddish spore that is produced in the uredinium of a rust fungus and that spreads to and infects other plants. [URED(INIUM) + SPORE.]
u·re·ide (yo͝or′ē-īd′) *n.* *Chem.* Any of various derivatives of urea. [URE(A) + -IDE.]
u·re·mi·a (yo͞o-rē′mē-ə) also **u·rae·mi·a** *n.* **1.** An excess of urea in the blood. **2.** A condition usually accompanying kidney disease and characterized by headache, nausea, vomiting, and coma.
u·re·o·tel·ic (yo͞o-rē′ə-tĕl′ĭk, yo͝or′ē-ō-) *adj.* Eliminating unneeded nitrogen in the form of urea. **—u·re′o·tel′ism** (-tĕl′ĭz′əm, yo͝or′ē-ŏt′l-ĭz′əm) *n.*
u·re·ter (yo͞o′rə-tər) *n.* The long, narrow duct that conveys urine from the kidney to the urinary bladder. [Gk. *ourētēr* < *ourein,* to urinate < *ouron,* urine.]
u·re·thane (yo͝or′ə-thān′) *n.* **1.** A colorless crystalline or white granular compound, $C_3H_7NO_2$, used in palliative treatment for leukemia and as a solvent. **2.** Any of several esters, other than the ethyl ester, of carbamic acid. [UR(O)-¹ + ETH(YL) + -ANE.]
u·re·thra (yo͞o-rē′thrə) *n., pl.* **-thras** or **-thrae** (-thrē). The canal through which urine is discharged in most mammals and which serves as the male genital duct. [LLat. *urethra* < Gk. *ourethra* < *ourein,* to urinate < *ouron,* urine.] **—u·re′thral** *adj.*

Urania
Shown holding an armillary sphere in a woodcut by Albrecht Dürer

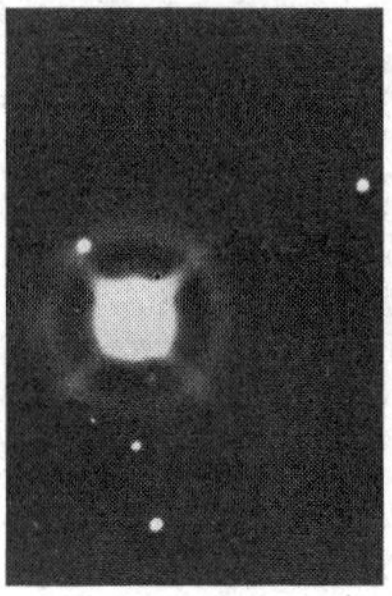
Uranus

urn
Silver coffee urn

u·re·thri·tis (yŏŏr′ĭ-thrī′tĭs) *n.* Inflammation of the urethra.
u·re·thro·scope (yŏŏ-rē′thrə-skōp′) *n.* An instrument for examining the interior of the urethra.
u·ret·ic (yŏŏ-rĕt′ĭk) *adj.* Of or relating to urine; urinary. [LLat. *ureticus* < Gk. *ourētikos* < *ourein,* to urinate < *ouron,* urine.]
urge (ûrj) *v.* **urged, urg·ing, urg·es.** —*tr.* **1.** To drive forward or onward forcefully; impel. **2.** To entreat earnestly and repeatedly; exhort: *The board was urged to approve the budget.* **3.** To advocate persistently the doing, consideration, or approval of; press emphatically: *urge passage of the bill.* **4.** To stimulate; excite: *"It urged him to an intensity like madness"* (D.H. Lawrence). **5.** To persuade, force, or otherwise move to some course of action. —*intr.* **1.** To present a forceful argument, claim, or case. **2.** To exert an impelling force; push vigorously. —*n.* **1.** The act or process of urging. **2.** An irresistible or impelling force, influence, or instinct: *"There is a human urge to clarify, rationalize, justify"* (Leonard Bernstein). [Lat. *urgere.*]
Synonyms: *urge, press, exhort, plead, coax.* These verbs mean to request or pressure a person to do something that one advocates. *Urge* suggests making an earnest appeal for such action. *Press* implies a somewhat more forceful act of urging or soliciting or repeated acts of this sort. *Exhort* suggests a stirring, eloquent appeal; *plead,* a humble but fervent one; and *coax,* an attempt to persuade through persistent application of courtesy, flattery, or blandishment.
ur·gen·cy (ûr′jən-sē) *n., pl.* **-cies. 1.** The condition of being urgent; pressing importance: *"His work has the urgency of personal creation"* (John R. Taylor). **2.** A pressing necessity.
ur·gent (ûr′jənt) *adj.* **1.** Compelling immediate action; imperative: *a crisis of an urgent nature.* **2.** Insistent or importunate; earnest: *urgent pleas.* **3.** Conveying a sense of pressing importance: *an urgent message.* [ME < OFr. < Lat. *urgens,* pr.part. of *urgere,* to urge.]
Synonyms: *urgent, pressing, imperative.* These adjectives are compared as they refer to degrees of importance or order of priority. *Urgent* and *pressing* are applied to what requires or demands immediate attention. The terms are often interchangeable, though *urgent* sometimes conveys a stronger sense of need. *Imperative,* which is stronger than either, specifies a need or demand that cannot be deferred or evaded and from which, in most instances, no appeal is possible.
-urgy *suff.* Technique or process for working with: *zymurgy.* [NLat. *-urgia* < Gk. *-ourgos,* worker < *ergon,* work.]
-uria *suff.* **1.** The condition of having a specified substance in the urine: *aciduria.* **2.** The condition of having a specified kind of urine: *polyuria.* [NLat. < Gk. *-ouria* < *ouron,* urine.]
U·ri·ah (yŏŏ-rī′ə) *n.* In the Old Testament, the husband of Bathsheba and a Hittite officer in the Israelite army, whose death was contrived by David in order that he might marry Bathsheba. [Heb. *ūriyāh.*]
u·ric (yŏŏr′ĭk) *adj.* Pertaining to, contained in, or obtained from urine.
uric acid *n.* A white crystalline compound, $C_5H_4N_4O_3$, the end product of purine metabolism in man and other primates, birds, terrestrial reptiles, and most insects.
u·ri·co·sur·ic (yŏŏr′ĭ-kə-sŏŏr′ĭk) *adj.* Promoting the excretion of uric acid in the urine. [URIC + -O- + *-s-* (connective element) + URIC.]
u·ri·co·tel·ic (yŏŏr′ĭ-kō-tĕl′ĭk) *adj.* Eliminating unneeded nitrogen primarily in the form of uric acid. **—u′ri·co·tel′ism** (-tĕl′ĭz′əm, -kŏt′l-) *n.*
u·ri·dine (yŏŏr′ĭ-dēn′) *n.* A white, odorless powder, $C_9H_{12}N_2O_6$, that is the nucleoside of uracil, important in carbohydrate metabolism and used in biochemical experiments.
U·ri·el (yŏŏr′ē-əl) *n.* One of the archangels. [Heb. *ūrī′ēl.*]
U·rim and Thum·mim (yŏŏr′ĭm ən thŭm′ĭm) *pl.n.* Objects carried inside the breastplate of the chief priests of ancient Israel and used as oracular media to divine the will of God.
urin- *pref.* Variant of **urino-.**
u·ri·nal (yŏŏr′ə-nəl) *n.* **1. a.** An upright wall fixture used by men for urinating. **b.** A room or other place containing such a fixture. **2.** A receptacle for urine used by a bedridden patient. [ME, chamber pot < OFr. < LLat. < *urina,* urine.]
u·ri·nal·y·sis (yŏŏr′ə-năl′ĭ-sĭs) *n.* The chemical analysis of urine. [URIN(O)- + (AN)ALYSIS.]
u·ri·nar·y (yŏŏr′ə-nĕr′ē) *adj.* Of or relating to urine, its production, function, or excretion. —*n., pl.* **-ies.** A reservoir for keeping animal urine for use as fertilizer.
urinary bladder *n.* A muscular membrane-lined sac situated in the anterior part of the pelvic cavity and used as a urine reservoir prior to excretion.
urinary calculus *n.* A solid concretion of mineral and organic substances in the urinary system.
u·ri·nate (yŏŏr′ə-nāt′) *intr.v.* **-nat·ed, -nat·ing, -nates.** To excrete urine. [Med. Lat. *urinare, urinat-* < Lat. *urina,* urine.]
u·rine (yŏŏr′ĭn) *n.* The fluid and dissolved substances secreted by the kidneys, stored in the bladder, and excreted from the body through the urethra. [ME < OFr. < Lat. *urina.*]
u·ri·nif·er·ous (yŏŏr′ə-nĭf′ər-əs) *adj.* Conveying urine.
urino- or **urin-** *pref.* Urine: *urinalysis.* [< Lat. *urina,* urine.]
u·ri·no·gen·i·tal (yŏŏr′ə-nō-jĕn′ĭ-təl) *n.* Variant of **urogenital.**
u·ri·nous (yŏŏr′ə-nəs) also **u·ri·nose** (-nōs′) *adj.* Of, resembling, or containing urine.
urn (ûrn) *n.* **1.** A vase of varying size and shape, usually having a footed base or pedestal. **2.** A closed metal vessel having a spigot and used for warming or serving tea or coffee. **3.** *Bot.* The spore-bearing part of a moss capsule. [ME *urne* < Lat. *urna.*]
uro-¹ or **ur-** *pref.* **1.** Urine: *uric.* **2.** Urinary tract: *urology.* **3.** Urea: *urethane.* [NLat. < Gk. *ouro-* < *ouron,* urine.]
uro-² or **ur-** *pref.* Tail: *urochord.* [NLat. < Gk. *oura,* tail.]
u·ro·chord (yŏŏr′ə-kôrd′) *n. Zool.* A notochord limited to the caudal region, as in tunicates. [URO-² + CHORD.]
u·ro·chrome (yŏŏr′ə-krōm′) *n.* The pigment responsible for the normal yellow color of urine.
u·ro·gen·i·tal (yŏŏr′ō-jĕn′ĭ-təl) also **u·ri·no·gen·i·tal** (yŏŏr′-ə-nō-) *adj.* Of, pertaining to, or involving both the urinary and genital functions.
u·ro·ki·nase (yŏŏr′ō-kī′nās) *n.* An enzyme found in human urine that is used for dissolving intravascular blood clots.
u·ro·lith (yŏŏr′ə-lĭth′) *n. Pathol.* A urinary calculus. **—u′ro·lith′ic** *adj.*
u·ro·lith·i·a·sis (yŏŏr′ə-lĭ-thī′ə-sĭs) *n.* The formation or presence of urinary calculi.
u·rol·o·gy (yŏŏ-rŏl′ə-jē) *n.* The medical study of the physiology and pathology of the urogenital tract.
-uronic *suff.* Connected with urine: *hyaluronic.* [< Gk. *ouron,* urine.]
u·ro·pod (yŏŏr′ə-pŏd′) *n.* One of a pair of posterior abdominal appendages of certain crustaceans, such as the lobster or shrimp. [URO-² + -POD.]
u·ro·py·gi·al gland (yŏŏr′ə-pī′jē-əl, -pĭj′ē-) *n.* An oil-secreting gland at the base of a bird's tail.
u·ro·py·gi·um (yŏŏr′ə-pī′jē-əm, -pĭj′ē-) *n.* The posterior part of a bird's body, from which the tail feathers grow. [NLat. < Gk. *ouropygion* : *oura,* tail + *pugē,* rump.] **—u′ro·py′gi·al** *adj.*
u·ros·co·py (yŏŏ-rŏs′kə-pē) *n., pl.* **-pies.** The examination of urine with a microscope.
-urous *suff.* Having a specified kind of tail: *anurous.* [NLat. *-urus* < Gk. *-ouros* < *oura,* tail.]
Ur·sa Major (ûr′sə) *n.* A constellation in the region of the north celestial pole, near Draco and Leo, containing the seven stars that form the Big Dipper. [Lat., the greater bear.]
Ursa Minor *n.* A constellation having the shape of a ladle with Polaris at the tip of its handle. [Lat., the lesser bear.]
ur·sine (ûr′sīn′) *adj.* Of or characteristic of a bear. [Lat. *ursinus* < *ursus,* bear.]
Ur·spra·che (ŏŏr′shprä′KHə) *n.* A parent language reconstructed from the evidence of later languages. [G. : *ur-,* original (< OHG *ur,* out of) + *Sprache,* language < OHG *sprāhha,* speech.]
Ur·su·line (ûr′sə-lĭn, -līn′, -lēn′, ûr′syə-) *n.* A member of an order of nuns of the Roman Catholic Church, founded in the early 16th century and devoted to the education of girls. —*adj.* Of or belonging to the Ursuline. [After St. *Ursula.*]
ur·ti·cant (ûr′tĭ-kənt) *adj.* Causing itching or stinging. —*n.* A substance that causes itching or stinging.
ur·ti·car·i·a (ûr′tĭ-kâr′ē-ə) *n.* A skin condition characterized by intensely itching welts and caused by allergic reactions to internal or external agents, by foci of infection, or by psychic stimuli. [NLat. < Lat. *urtica,* nettle.]
ur·ti·cate (ûr′tĭ-kāt′) *intr.v.* **-cat·ed, -cat·ing, -cates.** To sting or whip with or as with nettles. —*adj.* (ûr′tĭ-kĭt, -kāt′). Characterized by the presence of itching or stinging wheals. [Med. Lat. *urticare, urticat-* < Lat. *urtica,* nettle.]
ur·ti·ca·tion (ûr′tĭ-kā′shən) *n.* **1.** A lashing with nettles formerly used to treat a paralyzed part of the body. **2.** The sensation of having been stung by nettles. **3.** Urticaria.
u·rus (yŏŏr′əs) *n.* An extinct bovine mammal, *Bos primigenius,* of northern Africa, Europe, and western Asia, believed to be the forerunner of domestic cattle. [Lat., of Germanic orig.]
u·ru·shi·ol (ŏŏ-rŏŏ′shē-ôl′, -ōl′) *n.* A toxic substance that is present in the resin of plants of the genus *Rhus,* which includes poison ivy and the lacquer tree, *R. verniciflua,* from which a black Japanese lacquer is obtained. [J. *urushi,* lacquer + -OL.]
us (ŭs) *pron.* The objective case of **we.** Used: **a.** As the direct object of a verb: *The movie impressed us.* **b.** As the indirect object of a verb: *His father gave us money.* **c.** As the object of a preposition: *His father gave money to us.* —See Usage notes at **be** and **I.** [ME < OE *ūs.*]
us·a·ble also **use·a·ble** (yŏŏ′zə-bəl) *adj.* **1.** Capable of being used. **2.** In a fit condition for use; intact or operative. **—us′a·bil′i·ty, us′a·ble·ness** *n.* **—us′a·bly** *adv.*
us·age (yŏŏ′sĭj, -zĭj) *n.* **1.** The act or manner of using or treating; use or employment. **2.** Customary practice; accepted manner of procedure. **3.** The actual or expressed way in which a language or its elements are used, interrelated, or pronounced in expression: *contemporary English usage.* **4.** A particular expression in speech or writing: *a nonce usage.* [ME < OFr. < *user,* to use. —see USE.]
Usage: *Usage* has a more specialized sense than *use,*

usually denoting a customary social practice, particularly with respect to language. Thus, we might say *the term* settee *no longer has wide usage,* but we refer to *the increased use of drugs* or *the use of synthetic materials in modern dress,* where only the sense of "employment" is intended.

us·ance (yo͞o′zəns) *n.* **1.** The length of time, established by custom and varying between countries, that is allowed for payment of a foreign bill of exchange. **2.** *Obs.* Use. **3.** *Obs.* Usage; custom. **4.** *Obs.* Interest paid on money. [ME, usage < OFr. < VLat **usantia* < **usare,* to use. —see USE.]

Us·beg (o͝os′bĕg′, ŭs′-) or **Us·bek** (-bĕk′) *n.* Variants of **Uzbek.**

use (yo͞oz) *v.* **used, us·ing, us·es.** —*tr.* **1.** To bring or put into service; employ: *use soap for washing.* **2.** To make a practice of; make a habit of employing. **3.** To conduct oneself toward in treating or handling: *"the peace-offering of a man who once used you unkindly"* (Lawrence Sterne). **4.** *Informal.* To exploit for one's own advantage or gain: *He gave nothing to his friends; he merely used them.* **5.** To take or partake of, as tobacco, alcohol, or drugs. —*intr.* (yo͞os, yo͞ost). Used in the past tense with *to* in order to indicate a former state, habitual practice, or custom: *used to go to Florida every winter.* **—phrasal verb. use up.** To consume completely: *used up all her money.* —*n.* (yo͞os) **1. a.** The act of using; the application or employment of something for some purpose: *the use of a pencil for writing.* **b.** The condition or fact of being used. **2.** The manner of using; usage: *the proper use of power tools.* **3. a.** The permission, privilege, or benefit of using something: *have use of the car.* **b.** The power or ability to use something: *lose the use of one arm.* **4.** The need or occasion to use or employ: *Do you still have any use for this book?* **5.** The quality of being suitable or adaptable to an end; usefulness. **6.** The goal, object, or purpose for which something is used. **7.** Accustomed or usual procedure; habitual practice. **8.** *Law.* **a.** The enjoyment of property, as by occupying or exercising it. **b.** The benefit or profit of lands and tenements of which the legal title and possession are vested in another who holds them in trust for the beneficiary. **c.** The arrangement establishing the equitable right to such benefits and profits. **9.** The special or distinctive form of ritual, ceremony, or public worship practiced in a particular church, ecclesiastical district, or community. **10.** *Obs.* Usual occurrence or experience. —See Usage note at **usage.** [ME *usen* < OFr. *user* < VLat. **usare* < Lat. *uti.*]

Synonyms: *use, employ, utilize.* These verbs mean to avail oneself of something or to turn it to one's service. *Use* can apply to any such act, taking as its object either a person or thing. In a related but narrower sense, *use* refers to taking advantage of another person as a means of achieving an end: *He used his glamorous sister to advance his political career. Employ* is generally interchangeable with *use* in a broad sense; moreover, *employ* applies to the hiring of persons. *Utilize* is especially appropriate in the narrower sense of making useful or productive what has been otherwise or of expanding productivity by finding new uses for the thing or person involved.

use·a·ble (yo͞o′zə-bəl) *adj.* Variant of **usable.**

used (yo͞ozd) *adj.* Not new; secondhand: *a used car.*

use·ful (yo͞os′fəl) *adj.* Capable of being used advantageously; serviceable. **—use′ful·ly** *adv.* **—use′ful·ness** *n.*

use·less (yo͞os′lĭs) *adj.* **1.** Having no beneficial purpose or use. **2.** Futile; to no avail. **—use′less·ly** *adv.* **—use′less·ness** *n.*

us·er (yo͞o′zər) *n.* **1.** One that uses. **2.** *Law.* The exercise or enjoyment of a right or property. **3.** *Slang.* A drug addict.

ush·er (ŭsh′ər) *n.* **1.** One who serves as official doorkeeper, as in a courtroom or legislative chamber. **2.** A person employed to escort people to their seats, as in a theater, church, or stadium. **3.** A male attendant at a wedding. **4.** An official whose duty is to make introductions between unacquainted persons or to precede persons of rank in a procession. **5.** *Archaic.* An assistant teacher in a school. —*tr.v.* **-ered, -er·ing, -ers. 1.** To serve as an usher to; escort. **2.** To lead or conduct; cause to enter. **3.** To precede and introduce; serve as the beginning of: *a celebration to usher in the new century.* [ME < AN *usser* < OFr. *ussier* < Med. Lat. *ustiarius* < Lat. *ostiarius* < *ostium,* entrance.]

ush·er·ette (ŭsh′ə-rĕt′) *n.* A woman employed to escort people to their seats.

us·ne·a (ŭs′nē-ə, ŭz′-) *n.* Any of various widely distributed lichens of the genus *Usnea* characterized by a gray pendulous thallus. [< NLat. *Usnea,* genus name < Ar. *ushnah,* moss.]

us·que·baugh (ŭs′kwĭ-bô′, -bä′) *n. Ir. & Scot.* Whiskey. [Sc. Gaelic and Ir. Gaelic *uisge beatha,* water of life.]

u·su·al (yo͞o′zho͞o-əl) *adj.* **1.** Such as is commonly or frequently encountered, experienced, observed, or used. **2.** Habitual or customary; particular. [ME < OFr. < LLat. *usualis* < Lat. *usus,* use < p.part. of *uti,* to use.] **—u′su·al·ly** *adv.* **—u′su·al·ness** *n.*

Synonyms: *usual, typical, habitual, customary, accustomed.* These adjectives apply to what is frequent in occurrence and consequently considered regular or expected. *Usual* refers to what accords with normal or ordinary practice or procedure and is therefore common and familiar. It is closely related to, but somewhat broader than *typical,* which implies conformity and a well-established, clearly defined pattern. *Habitual* implies almost unfailing repetition of practice and suggests force of habit or addiction. *Customary* can refer to conformity with prevailing custom or convention or with an individual's own established practice. *Accustomed* applies principally to what an individual is familiar with, or used to, through regular experience, or to something considered as a distinguishing quality: *her accustomed optimism.* In the latter sense, *accustomed* is interchangeable with *customary.*

u·su·fruct (yo͞o′zə-frŭkt′, -sə-) *n. Law.* The right to utilize and enjoy the profits and advantages of something belonging to another so long as the property is not damaged or altered in any way. [Lat. *ususfructus* : *usus,* use (< p.part. of *uti,* to use) + *fructus,* enjoyment < *frui,* to enjoy.]

u·su·fruc·tu·ar·y (yo͞o′zə-frŭk′cho͞o-ĕr′ē, -sə-) *n., pl.* **-ies.** A person who holds property by usufruct. —*adj.* Of or of the nature of a usufruct.

u·su·rer (yo͞o′zhər-ər) *n.* A person who lends money at an exorbitant or unlawful rate of interest. [ME < AN < Med. Lat. *usuarius* < Lat. *usura,* usury. —see USURY.]

u·su·ri·ous (yo͞o-zho͝or′ē-əs) *adj.* **1.** Practicing usury. **2.** Of or constituting usury: *a usurious rate of interest.* **—u·su′ri·ous·ly** *adv.* **—u·su′ri·ous·ness** *n.*

u·surp (yo͞o-sûrp′, -zûrp′) *v.* **-surped, -surp·ing, -surps.** —*tr.* **1.** To seize and hold, such as the power, position, or rights of another, by force and without legal right or authority. **2.** To take over or occupy physically, such as territory or possessions. —*intr.* To seize another's power, rights, or possession illegally. [ME *usurpen* < OFr. *usurper* < Lat. *usurpare,* to make use of.] **—u·surp′er** *n.* **—u·surp′ing·ly** *adv.*

u·sur·pa·tion (yo͞o′sər-pā′shən, -zər-) *n.* **1.** The act of usurping, esp. the illegal seizure of royal sovereignty. **2.** *Law.* The illegal encroachment upon or exercise of authority or privilege belonging to another: *"in our own day, gross usurpations upon the liberty of private life"* (John Stuart Mill).

u·su·ry (yo͞o′zhə-rē) *n., pl.* **-ries. 1. a.** The act or practice of lending money at an exorbitant or illegal rate of interest. **b.** Such an excessive rate of interest. **2.** The act or practice of lending money at any rate of interest. **3.** *Archaic.* Interest charged or paid on a loan. [ME < AN **usurie* < Med. Lat. *usuria* < Lat. *usura* < *usus,* use. —see USUAL.]

ut (ŭt, o͞ot) *n. Mus.* A syllable representing the tone *C,* otherwise represented by *do,* in the French system of solmization. [Med. Lat. —see GAMUT.]

Ute (yo͞ot) *n., pl.* **Ute** or **Utes. 1.** A tribe of Uto-Aztecan-speaking North American Indians formerly inhabiting Utah, Colorado, and New Mexico and now living on reservations in Utah and Colorado. **2.** A member of the Ute. **3.** The Uto-Aztecan language of the Ute. [Ute *Yuta.*]

u·ten·sil (yo͞o-tĕn′səl) *n.* An instrument or container, esp. one used domestically, as in a kitchen or on a farm. [ME *utensele* < OFr. *utensile* < Lat. *utensilia,* utensils, neuter pl. of *utensilis,* fit for use < *uti,* to use.]

utensil
Cooking utensils

u·ter·ine (yo͞o′tər-ĭn, -tə-rīn′) *adj.* **1.** Of or concerning the uterus. **2.** Having the same mother but different fathers. [LLat. *uterinus* < *uterus,* uterus.]

u·ter·us (yo͞o′tər-əs) *n.* **1.** A pear-shaped muscular organ of gestation that is located in the pelvic cavity of female mammals and receives and holds the fertilized ovum during the development of the fetus and is the principal agent in its expulsion at birth. **2.** A part of the female reproductive tract in many invertebrates that is similar to the uterus, serving as a repository for the storage or development of eggs or embryos. [Lat.]

U·ther (yo͞o′thər) or **Uther Pen·drag·on** (pĕn-drăg′ən) *n.* A legendary king of Britain and father of Arthur.

u·tile (yo͞ot′l, yo͞o′tīl′) *adj.* Useful. [ME < OFr. < Lat. *utilis* < *uti,* to use.]

u·til·i·tar·i·an (yo͞o-tĭl′ĭ-târ′ē-ən) *adj.* **1.** Pertaining to or associated with utility. **2.** Stressing the value of practical over aesthetic qualities. **3.** Intended or made for the purposes of utility. **4.** Believing in or advocating utility. —*n.* An advocate or adherent of utilitarianism. [UTILIT(Y) + -ARIAN.]

u·til·i·tar·i·an·ism (yo͞o-tĭl′ĭ-târ′ē-ə-nĭz′əm) *n.* **1.** The philosophical doctrine that considers utility as the criterion of action and the useful as good or worthwhile. **2.** The ethical theory proposed by Jeremy Bentham and John Stuart Mill that all moral, social, or political action should be directed toward achieving the greatest good for the greatest number of people.

u·til·i·ty (yo͞o-tĭl′ĭ-tē) *n., pl.* **-ties. 1.** The condition or quality of being useful; usefulness: *"I have always doubted the utility of these conferences on disarmament"* (Winston Churchill). **2.** A useful article or device. **3.** A public service, such as gas, electricity, water, or transportation. —*adj.* Of the lowest U.S. Government grade of meat. [ME *utilite* < OFr. < Lat. *utilitas* < *utilis,* useful < *uti,* to use.]

utility man *n.* **1.** A member of a theatrical cast who must be prepared to play any of the smaller roles on short notice. **2.** *Sports.* A reserve player capable of playing several positions. **3.** A worker expected to serve in several capacities.

u·til·ize (yo͞ot′l-īz′) *tr.v.* **-ized, -iz·ing, -iz·es.** To put to use for a certain purpose. [Fr. *utiliser* < Ital. *utilizzare* < *utile,* useful < Lat. *utilis* < *uti,* to use.] **—u′til·iz′a·ble** *adj.* **—u′til·i·za′tion** *n.* **—u′til·iz′er** *n.*

ut·most (ŭt′mōst′) *adj.* **1.** Being or situated at the farthest limit or point; most extreme. **2.** Of the highest or greatest degree, amount, or intensity: *a matter of the utmost secrecy.* —*n.* The greatest possible amount, degree, or extent; maximum. [ME < OE *ūtmest* : *ūt,* out + *-mest,* -most.]

U·to-Az·tec·an (yo͞o′tō-ăz′tĕk′ən) *n.* **1.** A language phylum of North and Central America that includes Ute, Hopi, Nahuatl, and Shoshone. **2. a.** A tribe speaking a Uto-Aztecan language. **b.** A member of such a tribe. —*adj.* Of or pertaining to the Uto-Aztecans or to the languages spoken by them. [UTE + AZTEC.]

u·to·pi·a (yo͞o-tō′pē-ə) *n.* **1. Utopia.** An ideally perfect place, esp. in its socio-political aspects. **2.** An impractical, idealistic concept for social and political reform. [NLat. : Gk. *ou,* not + Gk. *topos,* place.]

u·to·pi·an (yo͞o-tō′pē-ən) *adj.* **1. Utopian.** Of, pertaining to, or having the characteristics of Utopia. **2.** Excellent or ideal but existing only in visionary or impractical thought or theory. —*n.* A zealous but impractical reformer of human society.

u·to·pi·an·ism (yo͞o-tō′pē-ə-nĭz′əm) *n.* The ideals or principles of a utopian; idealistic and impractical social theory.

u·tri·cle (yo͞o′trĭ-kəl) also **u·tric·u·lus** (yo͞o-trĭk′yə-ləs) *n., pl.* **u·tri·cles** also **u·tric·u·li** (-lī′). **1.** A small, delicate membranous sac connecting with the semicircular canals of the inner ear and functioning in the maintenance of bodily equilibrium and coordination. **2.** *Bot.* A small, bladderlike one-seeded fruit. [Fr. < Lat. *utriculus,* dim. of *uter,* leather bottle.]

u·tric·u·lar (yo͞o-trĭk′yə-lər) *adj.* **1.** Of, pertaining to, or resembling a utricle. **2.** Having one or more utricles. **3.** Pertaining to the uterus.

u·tric·u·lus (yo͞o-trĭk′yə-ləs) *n.* Variant of **utricle.**

ut·ter[1] (ŭt′ər) *tr.v.* **-tered, -ter·ing, -ters. 1.** To express audibly. **2.** To express by means of speech; pronounce. **3. a.** To put (counterfeit money or a forgery) into circulation. **b.** To deliver (something counterfeit) to another. **4.** To publish (a book, for example). **5.** *Obs.* To sell or deliver (merchandise) in trading. [ME *utteren* < MDu. *ūteren.*] **—ut′ter·a·ble** *adj.* **—ut′ter·er** *n.*

ut·ter[2] (ŭt′ər) *adj.* Complete; absolute; entire: *utter nonsense; utter darkness.* [ME < OE *ūtera,* outer < *ūt,* out.]

ut·ter·ance[1] (ŭt′ər-əns) *n.* **1. a.** The act of uttering or expressing vocally. **b.** The power of speaking. **2.** Something that is uttered or expressed.

ut·ter·ance[2] (ŭt′ər-əns) *n.* The uttermost end or extremity; bitter end: *fight to the utterance.* [ME < OFr. *outrance* < *outrer,* to go beyond limits < VLat. **ultrare* < Lat. *ultra,* beyond.]

ut·ter·ly (ŭt′ər-lē) *adv.* Completely; absolutely; entirely.

ut·ter·most (ŭt′ər-mōst′) *adj.* **1.** Utmost. **2.** Outermost. —*n.* Utmost. [ME : *utter,* outer + *-most,* -most.]

U-turn (yo͞o′tûrn′) *n.* A turn, as by a vehicle, completely reversing the direction of travel.

u·va·rov·ite (yo͞o-vär′ə-vīt′, o͞o-) *n.* An emerald-green garnet, $Ca_3Cr_2(SiO_4)_3$, found in chromium deposits. [G. *Uvarovit,* after Count Sergei S. *Uvarov* (1785–1855).]

u·ve·a (yo͞o′vē-ə) *n.* The pigmented vascular layer of the eye including the iris, ciliary body, and choroid. [Med. Lat. < Lat. *uva,* grape.] **—u′ve·al** *adj.*

u·ve·i·tis (yo͞o′vē-ī′tĭs) *n.* Inflammation of the uvea. [UVE(A) + -ITIS.]

u·vu·la (yo͞o′vyə-lə) *n.* The small, conical, fleshy mass of tissue suspended from the center of the soft palate above the back of the tongue. [LLat., dim. of Lat. *uva,* grape.]

u·vu·lar (yo͞o′vyə-lər) *adj.* **1.** Pertaining to or associated with the uvula. **2.** Articulated by vibration of the uvula or with the back of the tongue near or touching the uvula.

u·vu·li·tis (yo͞o′vyə-lī′tĭs) *n.* Inflammation of the uvula. [UVUL(A) + -ITIS.]

ux·o·ri·al (ŭk-sôr′ē-əl, -sōr′-, ŭg-zôr′-, -zōr′-) *adj.* Of or befitting a wife. [< Lat. *uxorius* < *uxor,* wife.]

ux·o·ri·cide (ŭk-sôr′ĭ-sīd′, -sōr′-, ŭg-zôr′-, ŭg-zōr′-) *n.* **1.** The killing of a wife by her husband. **2.** A man who kills his wife. [Med. Lat. *uxoricidium* : Lat. *uxor,* wife + Lat. *-cidium,* killing < *caedere,* to kill.]

ux·o·ri·ous (ŭk-sôr′ē-əs, -sōr′-, ŭg-zôr′-, -zōr′-) *adj.* Excessively or irrationally submissive or devoted to one's wife. [Lat. *uxorius* < *uxor,* wife.] **—ux·o′ri·ous·ly** *adv.* **—ux·o′ri·ous·ness** *n.*

Uz·bek (o͝oz′bĕk′, ŭz′-) also **Uz·beg** (-bĕg′) or **Us·bek** (o͝os′-bĕk′, ŭs′-), or **Us·beg** (-bĕg′). **1.** A member of a group of Turkic people inhabiting the Uzbek S.S.R. **2.** The Turkic language of the Uzbeks.

V

1 2 Phoenician — 3 4 5 6 Greek — 7 8 Roman — 9 10 Medieval — 11 12 13 14 Modern

---

Around 1000 B.C. the Phoenicians and other Semitic peoples began to use graphic signs to represent individual speech sounds instead of syllables or words. They used a symbol (1,2) which is the ancestor of the letters F, U, W, and Y as well as V to represent the sound of the semivowel "w" and called it *wāw,* their word for "hook." The Greeks, adapting the Phoenician alphabet, varied the shape of *wāw* slightly (3,4,5,6) and altered its name to *upsilon.* They used *upsilon* to represent the sound of the vowel "u." The Romans borrowed the alphabet from the Greeks via the Etruscans, who used a tailless variant of *upsilon.* The Romans used *upsilon* to represent both the vowel "u" and the semivowel "w," which later developed into the consonantal sound "v," and adapted the shape for monumental inscriptions. Monumental script (8) is the prototype of modern capital letters (11,12). Medieval scribes adapted the Roman capitals to being quickly written on paper, parchment, and vellum. The cursive alphabet had both tailless and tailed variants of V which were distinguished not by phonetic value but by position within a word, V being used initially and U elsewhere. During the 17th century U and V were assigned their modern phonetic values and fully distinguished, but it was not until the early 19th century that their position in the alphabet was fixed.

---

v

v or **V** (vē) *n., pl.* **v's** or **V's. 1.** The 22nd letter of the modern English alphabet. **2.** Any of the speech sounds represented by the letter *v.* **3.** Something shaped like the letter V. **4.** The 22nd in a series. **5.** The Roman numeral for five.
V The symbol for the element vanadium.
V-1 (vē′wŭn′) *n.* A robot bomb (sense 1). [G. *Vergeltungswaffe eins,* retaliation weapon (number) one.]
V-2 (vē′to͞o′) *n.* A long-range liquid-fuel rocket used by the Germans as a ballistic missile in World War II. [G. *Vergeltungswaffe zwei,* retaliation weapon (number) two.]
va·can·cy (vā′kən-sē) *n., pl.* **-cies. 1.** The state or condition of being vacant or unoccupied; emptiness. **2.** An empty or unoccupied space; gap. **3.** A position, office, or accommodation that is unfilled or unoccupied. **4.** Emptiness of mind; inanity. **5.** *Archaic.* A period of leisure; idleness.
va·cant (vā′kənt) *adj.* **1.** Containing nothing; empty. **2.** Without an incumbent or occupant: *a vacant position.* **3.** Not occupied or put to use: *a vacant lot.* **4.** *Law.* Not claimed, as by an heir: *a vacant estate.* **5. a.** Lacking intelligence or knowledge. **b.** Expressionless; blank: *a vacant stare.* **6.** Not filled with activity: *vacant hours.* [ME < OFr. < Lat. *vacans,* pr.part. of *vacare,* to be empty.] **—va′cant·ly** *adv.* **—va′cant·ness** *n.*

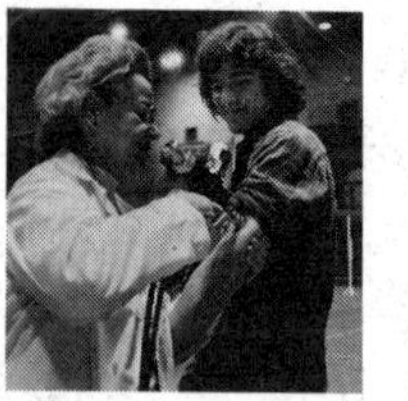
vaccination

va·cate (vā′kāt′, vā-kāt′) *v.* **-cat·ed, -cat·ing, -cates.** *—tr.* **1. a.** To cease to occupy or hold; give up. **b.** To empty of occupants or incumbents. **2.** *Law.* To make void; annul. *—intr.* To leave a job, office, or lodging. [Lat. *vacare, vacat-,* to be empty.]
va·ca·tion (vā-kā′shən, və-) *n.* **1.** A period of time devoted to pleasure, rest, or relaxation, esp. one with pay granted to an employee. **2. a.** A holiday. **b.** A fixed period of holidays, esp. one during which a school, court, or business suspends activities; recess. **3.** *Archaic.* An act or instance of vacating. *—intr.v.* **-tioned, -tion·ing, -tions.** To take or spend a vacation. [ME *vacacioun* < OFr. *vacation* < Lat. *vacatio,* freedom from occupation < *vacare,* to be at leisure.] **—va·ca′tion·er** *n.*
va·ca·tion·ist (vā-kā′shə-nĭst, və-) *n.* A person on vacation.
va·ca·tion·land (vā-kā′shən-lănd′) *n.* A place with special attractions for vacationists.
vac·ci·nal (văk′sə-nəl, văk-sē′-) *adj.* Of or relating to vaccine or vaccination.
vac·ci·nate (văk′sə-nāt′) *v.* **-nat·ed, -nat·ing, -nates.** *—tr.* To inoculate with a vaccine in order to produce immunity to a disease, such as smallpox. *—intr.* To perform a vaccination. [< VACCINE.] **—vac′ci·na′tor** *n.*
vac·ci·na·tion (văk′sə-nā′shən) *n.* **1.** Inoculation with a vaccine in order to protect against a given disease. **2.** A scar left on the skin by vaccinating.
vac·cine (văk-sēn′, văk′sēn′) *n.* **1.** A suspension of attenuated or killed microorganisms, as of viruses or bacteria, incapable of inducing severe infection but capable when inoculated of counteracting the unmodified species. **2.** A vaccine prepared from the cowpox virus and inoculated against smallpox. [< Lat. *vaccinus,* of cows < *vacca,* cow.]
vac·cin·i·a (văk-sĭn′ē-ə) *n.* Cowpox. [NLat. < Lat. *vaccinus,* of cows.] **—vac·cin′i·al** *adj.*
vac·il·lant (văs′ə-lənt) *adj.* Vacillating.
vac·il·late (văs′ə-lāt′) *intr.v.* **-lat·ed, -lat·ing, -lates. 1.** To sway from one side to the other; oscillate. **2.** To swing indecisively from one course of action or opinion to another; waver. [Lat. *vacillare, vacillat-,* to waver.] **—vac′il·lat′ing·ly** *adv.* **—vac′il·la′tion** *n.* **—vac′il·la′tor** *n.*
vac·il·la·to·ry (văs′ə-lə-tôr′ē, -tōr′ē) *adj.* Inclined to waver; irresolute.

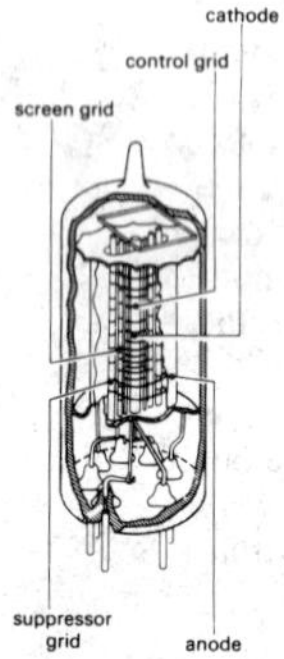

vacuum tube

vac·u·a (văk′yo͞o-ə) *n.* A plural of **vacuum.**
va·cu·i·ty (vă-kyo͞o′ĭ-tē, və-) *n., pl.* **-ties. 1.** Total absence of matter; emptiness. **2.** An empty space; vacuum. **3.** Total lack of ideas; emptiness of mind. **4.** Absence of meaningful occupation; idleness. **5.** The quality or fact of being devoid of something specified: *a vacuity of taste.* **6.** Something, esp. a remark, that is pointless or inane. [OFr. *vacuite* < Lat. *vacuitas* < *vacuus,* empty. —see VACUUM.]
vac·u·o·lat·ed (văk′yo͞o-ō-lā′tĭd) also **vac·u·o·late** (-lāt′, -lĭt) *adj.* Containing a vacuole or vacuoles.
vac·u·ole (văk′yo͞o-ōl′) *n.* A small cavity in the protoplasm of a cell. [Fr. < Lat. *vacuum,* vacuum. —see VACUUM.] **—vac′u·o′lar** (-ō′lər, -lär′) *adj.* **—vac′u·o·la′tion** *n.*
vac·u·ous (văk′yo͞o-əs) *adj.* **1.** Devoid of matter; empty. **2. a.** Characterized by a lack of intelligence; stupid. **b.** Devoid of substance or meaning; inane: *a vacuous comment.* **3.** Lacking in serious purpose or occupation; idle. [Lat. *vacuus,* empty. —see VACUUM.] **—vac′u·ous·ly** *adv.* **—vac′u·ous·ness** *n.*
vac·u·um (văk′yo͞o-əm, -yo͞om, -yəm) *n., pl.* **-u·ums** or **-u·a** (-yo͞o-ə). **1. a.** The absence of matter. **b.** A space empty of matter. **c.** A space relatively empty of matter. **2.** A state of emptiness; void. **3.** A state of being sealed off from external or environmental influences; isolation. **4.** *pl.* **vacuums.** A vacuum cleaner. *—tr. & intr.v.* **-umed, -um·ing, -ums.** To clean with or use a vacuum cleaner. [Lat., neuter of *vacuus,* empty < *vacare,* to be empty.]
vacuum bottle *n.* A bottle or flask having a vacuum between its inner and outer walls, designed to maintain the desired temperature of the contents.
vacuum casting *n.* The casting of metals under a vacuum.
vacuum cleaner *n.* An electrical appliance that cleans surfaces by suction.
vacuum drying *n.* The removal of liquid material from a solution or mixture under reduced air pressure, resulting in drying at a lower temperature than required at full pressure.
vacuum gauge *n.* A device for determining the pressure in a partial vacuum.
vac·u·um-packed (văk′yo͞o-əm-păkt′, văk′yo͞om-, văk′yəm-) *adj.* Packed in a container with little or no air.
vacuum pump *n.* **1.** A pump used to evacuate an enclosure. **2.** A pulsometer (sense 1).
vacuum tube *n.* An electron tube having an internal vacuum sufficiently high to permit electrons to move with low interaction with any remaining gas molecules.
va·de me·cum (vā′dē mē′kəm, vä′dē mā′-) *n., pl.* **vade me·cums. 1.** A useful thing that a person constantly carries with him. **2.** A book, such as a guidebook, for ready reference. [Lat., go with me.]
va·dose (vā′dōs′) *adj.* Pertaining to or being water that is located in the zone of aeration in the earth's crust above the ground water level. [Lat. *vadosus,* shallow < *vadum,* a shallow, ford.]
vag·a·bond (văg′ə-bŏnd′) *n.* **1.** A person without a permanent home who moves from place to place. **2.** A tramp. *—adj.* **1.** Of, relating to, or characteristic of a wanderer; nomadic. **2.** Aimless; drifting. **3.** Irregular in course or behavior; unpredictable. *—intr.v.* **-bond·ed, -bond·ing, -bonds.** To lead the life of a vagabond; roam about. [ME *vagabonde* < OFr. *vagabond* < Lat. *vagabundus,* wandering < *vagari,* to wander < *vagus,* wandering.] **—vag′a·bond′age** *n.* **—vag′a·bond′ism** *n.*
va·gal (vā′gəl) *adj.* Of or pertaining to the vagus nerve. **—va′gal·ly** *adv.*
va·ga·ry (vā′gə-rē, və-gâr′ē) *n., pl.* **-ries.** An extravagant or erratic notion or action; flight of fancy. [< Lat. *vagari,* to wander < Lat. *vagus,* wandering.]
va·gi (vā′gī′, -jī′) *n.* Plural of **vagus.**
va·gil·i·ty (və-jĭl′ĭ-tē, vă-) *n.* The capacity or tendency of an organism to become widely dispersed. [< obs. *vagile,* free to move about < Lat. *vagus,* wandering.]
va·gi·na (və-jī′nə) *n., pl.* **-nas** or **-nae** (-nē). **1.** *Anat.* **a.** The passage leading from the external genital orifice to the uterus in female mammals. **b.** A similar structure in some invertebrates. **2.** *Biol.* A sheathlike structure or part, such as that formed by the base of a leaf enclosing a stem. [Lat., sheath.]
vag·i·nal (văj′ə-nəl) *adj.* **1.** Of or pertaining to the vagina. **2.** Pertaining to or resembling a sheath. **—vag′i·nal·ly** *adv.*
vag·i·nate (văj′ə-nĭt, -nāt′) also **vag·i·nat·ed** (-nā′tĭd) *adj.* Forming or enclosed in a sheath.
vag·i·nec·to·my (văj′ə-nĕk′tə-mē) *n., pl.* **-mies. 1.** Surgical excision of all or part of the vagina. **2.** Surgical excision of the serous membrane covering the testis and epididymus. [VAGIN(A) + -ECTOMY.]
vag·i·nis·mus (văj′ə-nĭz′məs) *n.* A painful contractional spasm of the vagina. [NLat. : VAGIN(A) + *-ismus,* -ism.]
vag·i·ni·tis (văj′ə-nī′tĭs) *n.* Inflammation of the vagina. [VAGIN(A) + -ITIS.]
va·got·o·my (vā-gŏt′ə-mē) *n., pl.* **-mies.** Surgical division of the lower thoracic or upper abdominal fibers of the vagus nerve, used to diminish acid secretion of the stomach and control a duodenal ulcer. [VAG(US) + -TOMY.]
va·go·to·ni·a (vā′gə-tō′nē-ə) *n.* Pathological overactivity of the vagus nerve. [VAG(US) + -TONIA.] **—va′go·ton′ic** (-tŏn′ĭk) *adj.*
va·go·tro·pic (vā′gə-trō′pĭk) *adj.* Affecting or acting on the vagus nerve. Used chiefly of drugs. [VAG(US) + -TROPIC.]
va·gran·cy (vā′grən-sē) *n., pl.* **-cies. 1.** The state of being a vagrant. **2.** The conduct or mode of existence of a vagrant. **3.** A wandering in mind or thought. **4.** The offense of being a vagrant.
va·grant (vā′grənt) *n.* **1.** A person who wanders from place to place without a permanent home or a means of livelihood. **2.** A wanderer; rover. **3.** A person, such as a drunkard, who lives on the streets and constitutes a public nuisance. *—adj.* **1.** Wandering from place to place and lacking any means of support. **2.** Wayward; unrestrained. **3.** Moving in a random fashion. [ME *vagraunt,* prob. < OFr. *wacrant,* pr.part. of *wacrer,* to wander, of Germanic orig.] **—va′grant·ly** *adv.*
vague (vāg) *adj.* **vagu·er, vagu·est. 1.** Not clearly expressed or outlined: *vague instructions.* **2.** Not thinking or expressing oneself clearly: *She was vague about her future plans.* **3.** Lacking definite shape, form, or character; indistinct: *saw a vague outline of a building through the fog.* **4.** Ambiguous in meaning or application: *vague political promises.* **5.** Indistinctly felt, perceived, understood, or recalled; hazy: *a vague uneasiness.* [OFr. < Lat. *vagus.*] **—vague′ly** *adv.* **—vague′ness** *n.*
va·gus (vā′gəs) *n., pl.* **-gi** (-gī′, -jī′). The tenth and longest of the cranial nerves, passing through the neck and thorax into the abdomen and supplying sensation to part of the ear, the larynx, and the pharynx, motor impulses to the vocal-cord muscles, and motor and secretory impulses to the abdominal and thoracic viscera. [NLat. *vagus (nervus),* wandering (nerve).]

vagus nerve *n.* The vagus.
va·hi·ne (vä-hē′nē, -nā′) *n.* Variant of **wahine.**
vail¹ (vāl) *v.* **vailed, vail·ing, vails.** *Archaic.* —*tr.* **1.** To lower (a banner, for example). **2.** To doff (one's hat) as a token of respect or submission. —*intr.* **1.** To descend; lower. **2.** To doff one's hat. [ME *valen* < *avalen* < OFr. *avaler* < *aval,* downward < Lat. *ad vallem,* to the valley.]
vail² (vāl) *n. Obs.* Variant of **veil.**
vain (vān) *adj.* **-er, -est. 1.** Not yielding the desired outcome; fruitless: *a vain attempt.* **2.** Lacking substance or worth: *vain talk.* **3.** Excessively proud of one's appearance or accomplishments; conceited. **4.** *Archaic.* Foolish. —*idiom.* **in vain. 1.** To no avail; without success: *Our labor was in vain.* **2.** In an irreverent or disrespectful manner: *took the name of the Lord in vain.* [ME < OFr. < Lat. *vanus.*] —**vain′ly** *adv.* —**vain′ness** *n.*
vain·glo·ri·ous (vān-glôr′ē-əs, -glōr′-) *adj.* **1.** Characterized by or expressive of vainglory; boastful. **2.** Proceeding from vainglory. —**vain·glo′ri·ous·ly** *adv.* —**vain·glo′ri·ous·ness** *n.*
vain·glo·ry (vān′glôr′ē, -glōr′ē, vān-glôr′ē, -glōr′ē) *n., pl.* **-ries. 1.** Boastful and unwarranted pride in one's accomplishments or qualities. **2.** Vain and ostentatious display. [ME *veyn glory* < OFr. *vaine glorie* < Lat. *vana gloria,* empty pride.]
vair (vâr) *n.* **1.** A fur, probably squirrel, much used in medieval times to line and trim robes. **2.** A heraldic representation of fur. [ME *vaire* < OFr. *vair* < Lat. *varius,* variegated.]
Vaish·na·va (vīsh′nə-və) *n.* A member of a Hindu sect that worships Vishnu. [Skt. *vaiṣṇava-,* relating to Vishnu < *Viṣṇuḥ,* Vishnu.] —**Vaish′na·vism** (-vĭz′əm) *n.*
Vais·ya (vīs′hə, vīsh′yə) *n.* **1.** A Hindu caste originally composed of farmers and herders but now largely made up of merchants and businessmen. **2.** A member of the Vaisya caste. [Skt. *vaiśyaḥ,* settler < *viś,* house.]
val·ance (văl′əns, vā′ləns) *n.* **1.** An ornamental drapery hung across a top edge, as of a bed, table, or canopy. **2.** A short drapery, decorative board, or metal strip mounted esp. across the top of a window to conceal structural fixtures. —*tr.v.* **-anced, -anc·ing, -anc·es.** To supply with a valance. [ME *valaunce.*]
vale (vāl) *n.* A valley, often coursed by a stream; dale. [ME < OFr. *val* < Lat. *valles.*]
val·e·dic·tion (văl′ĭ-dĭk′shən) *n.* **1.** An act of bidding farewell; leave-taking. **2.** A speech or statement made as a farewell. [< Lat. *valedicere,* to say farewell : *vale,* farewell + *dicere,* to say.]
val·e·dic·to·ri·an (văl′ĭ-dĭk-tôr′ē-ən, -tōr′-) *n.* A student, usually ranking highest in the graduating class, who delivers the farewell oration at commencement.
val·e·dic·to·ry (văl′ĭ-dĭk′tə-rē) *adj.* Pertaining to or by way of a farewell. —*n., pl.* **-ries.** A farewell address, esp. one delivered by a valedictorian.
va·lence (vā′ləns) also **va·len·cy** (-lən-sē) *n., pl.* **-lenc·es** also **-len·cies. 1.** *Chem.* **a.** The capacity of an atom or group of atoms to combine in specific proportions with other atoms or groups of atoms. **b.** An integer, often one of several for any given element, used to represent this capacity in terms of an arbitrary assignment of 1 to an atom or group capable of forming a single bond with chlorine and of −1 to an atom or group capable of forming a single bond with hydrogen. **2.** The capacity of something to unite, react, or interact with something else. [LLat. *valentia,* capacity < Lat. *valens,* pr.part. of *valēre,* to be strong.]
valence bond *n.* A covalent bond.
valence electron *n.* An electron in an outer or next outer shell of an atom that can participate in forming chemical bonds with other atoms.
valence shell *n.* A shell of an atom that contains the valence electrons.
Va·len·ci·ennes (və-lĕn′sē-ĕn′, -ĕnz′, văl′ən-sē-) *n.* A fine lace with a floral pattern originally manufactured at Valenciennes, France.
-valent *suff.* Having a specified valence or valences: *polyvalent.* [< VALENCE.]
val·en·tine (văl′ən-tīn′) *n.* **1. a.** A greeting card of a usually sentimental nature sent to a sweetheart on Saint Valentine's Day. **b.** A greeting or gift sent to one's sweetheart on Saint Valentine's Day. **2.** A person singled out as one's sweetheart on Saint Valentine's Day.
Valentine's Day or **Valentines Day** *n.* Saint Valentine's Day.
va·le·ri·an (və-lîr′ē-ən) *n.* **1.** Any of various plants of the genus *Valeriana,* having dense clusters of small white or pinkish flowers, esp. *V. officinalis,* native to Eurasia and widely cultivated. **2.** The dried roots of a valerian, *V. officinalis,* used medicinally as a sedative. [ME < OFr. *valeriane* < Med. Lat. *valeriana,* prob. < fem. of Lat. *Valerianus,* of Valeria, Roman province where the plant originated.]
va·le·ric acid (və-lîr′ĭk, -lĕr′-) *n.* A colorless liquid, $C_5H_{10}O_2$, used in flavorings, perfumes, plasticizers, and pharmaceuticals. [< VALERIAN, from its occurrence in the plant's root.]
val·et (văl′ĭt, văl′ā′, vă-lā′) *n.* **1.** A man's personal attendant. **2.** A hotel employee who performs personal services for patrons. —*v.* **-et·ed, -et·ing, -ets.** —*tr.* To act as a personal servant to; attend. —*intr.* To work as a valet. [Fr. < OFr. *vaslet,* servant < Med. Lat. **vassellitus,* dim. of *vassus,* vassal, of Celt. orig.]
va·let de cham·bre (vă-lā′ də shäɴ′brə) *n., pl.* **va·lets de cham·bre** (vă-lā′ də shäɴ′brə). A man's valet. [Fr. : *valet,* valet + *de,* of + *chambre,* room.]
val·e·tu·di·nar·i·an (văl′ĭ-to͞od′n-âr′ē-ən, -tyo͞od′-) *n.* A sickly or weak person, esp. one who is constantly and morbidly concerned with his health. [Lat. *valetudinarius* < *valetudo,* state of health < *valēre,* to be well.] —**val′e·tu′di·nar′i·an·ism** *n.*

valance

val·e·tu·di·nar·y (văl′ĭ-to͞od′n-ĕr′ē, -tyo͞od′-) *adj.* Of, relating to, or typical of a valetudinarian. —*n., pl.* **-ies.** A valetudinarian.
val·gus (văl′gəs) *n., pl.* **-gus·es.** *Pathol.* A knock-kneed person. [< Lat., bowlegged.] —**val′goid′** (-goid′) *adj.*
Val·hal·la (văl-hăl′ə) *n. Myth.* The great hall of immortality in which the souls of warriors slain heroically were received by the Norse god Odin and enshrined. [ON *Valhöll* : *valr,* the slain + *höll,* hall.]
val·iant (văl′yənt) *adj.* **1.** Possessing or displaying valor; courageous. **2.** Marked by or done with valor: *valiant feats in battle.* —*n.* A valiant person. [ME *valiaunt* < OFr. *vaillant* < Lat. *valens, valent-,* pr.part. of *valēre,* to be strong.] —**val′ian·cy, val′iance, val′iant·ness** *n.* —**val′iant·ly** *adv.*
val·id (văl′ĭd) *adj.* **1.** Well-grounded; sound: *a valid objection.* **2.** Producing the desired results; efficacious: *valid methods.* **3.** Legally sound and effective; incontestable: *valid title.* **4.** *Logic.* **a.** Containing premises from which the conclusion may logically be derived: *a valid argument.* **b.** Correctly inferred or deduced from a premise: *a valid conclusion.* **5.** *Archaic.* Of sound health; robust. [Fr. *valide* < OFr. < Lat. *validus,* strong < *valēre,* to be strong.] —**va′lid·ly** *adv.* —**va′lid·ness** *n.*

Synonyms: *valid, sound, convincing, telling, conclusive.* These adjectives are applied, not always interchangeably, to such things as statements, arguments, and reasoning; in each case they greatly heighten the effectiveness or force of what they describe. *Valid* and *sound* both refer to qualities that give inner strength and capacity to resist challenge or attack. What is *valid* is justifiable because it is based on truth or fact or has legal force. What is *sound* has a firm basis in truth, right, or wisdom. *Convincing* and *telling* more often refer to assertiveness. *Convincing* implies power to assure, allay doubt, or silence opposition. *Telling* means having a marked effect, sometimes suddenly produced. *Conclusive* means decisive and thus capable of putting an end to doubt or debate.

valentine
19th-century American

val·i·date (văl′ĭ-dāt′) *tr.v.* **-dat·ed, -dat·ing, -dates. 1.** To declare or make legally valid. **2.** To mark with an indication of official sanction. **3.** To substantiate; verify: *Experiments validated his theory.* —**val′i·da′tion** *n.*
va·lid·i·ty (və-lĭd′ĭ-tē) *n.* The state or quality of being valid.
val·ine (văl′ēn′, vā′lēn′) *n.* A crystalline amino acid, $C_5H_{11}NO_2$, essential for normal human growth. [VAL(ERIC ACID) + -INE.]
val·in·o·my·cin (văl′ə-nō-mī′sĭn) *n.* An antibiotic, $C_{54}H_{90}N_6H_{18}$, produced by the bacterium *Streptomyces fulvissimus.* [VALIN(E) + -MYCIN.]
va·lise (və-lēs′) *n.* A small piece of hand luggage. [Fr. < It. *valigia.*]
Val·i·um (văl′ē-əm). A trademark for the tranquilizing drug diazepam.
Val·kyr·ie (văl-kîr′ē, -kī′rē) *n. Myth.* Any of the Norse god Odin's handmaidens who hover over battlefields, choosing the heroes to be slain and then conducting their souls to Valhalla. [ON *Valkyrja,* the chooser of the slain.]

valerian
Left: Flowering plant
Right: Detail of flowers

val·la·tion (vă-lā′shən) *n.* **1.** An earthwork wall used for military defense; rampart. **2.** The art or process of planning or erecting earth fortifications. [LLat. *vallatio* < Lat. *vallare,* to surround with a rampart < *vallum,* rampart < *vallus,* stake.] —**val′la·to′ry** (văl′ə-tôr′ē, -tōr′ē) *adj.*
val·lec·u·la (vă-lĕk′yə-lə, və-) *n., pl.* **-lae** (-lē′). *Biol.* A shallow groove, depression, or furrow. [LLat., dim. of Lat. *valles,* valley.] —**val·lec′u·lar** (-lər), **val·lec′u·late** (-lĭt, -lāt′) *adj.*
val·ley (văl′ē) *n., pl.* **-leys. 1.** An elongated lowland between ranges of mountains, hills, or other uplands, often having a river or stream running along the bottom. **2.** The extensive land area drained or irrigated by a river system. **3.** A depression or hollow resembling or suggesting a valley, such as the point at which the two slopes of a roof meet. [ME *valey* < OFr. *valee* < Lat. *valles.*]
va·lo·ni·a (və-lō′nē-ə, -lōn′yə) *n.* An extract from the dried acorn cups of an oak tree, *Quercus aegilops,* of eastern Europe and Asia Minor, used chiefly in tanning and dyeing. [Ital. *vallonia* < Mod. Gk. *balania,* pl. of *balani,* acorn < Gk. *balanos.*]
val·or (văl′ər) *n.* Courage and boldness, as in battle; bravery. [ME *valour* < OFr. < Med. Lat. *valor* < Lat. *valēre,* to be worth.]
val·or·ize (văl′ə-rīz′) *tr.v.* **-ized, -iz·ing, -iz·es.** To establish and maintain the price of (a commodity) by governmental action. [Port. *valorizar* < *valor,* value < Med. Lat. —see VALOR.] —**val′or·i·za′tion** *n.*
val·or·ous (văl′ər-əs) *adj.* Possessing or marked by personal valor; valiant. —**val′or·ous·ly** *adv.* —**val′or·ous·ness** *n.*

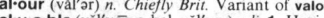

valve
On a trumpet

vampire

val·our (văl′ər) *n. Chiefly Brit.* Variant of **valor.**

val·u·a·ble (văl′yo͞o-ə-bəl, văl′yə-) *adj.* **1.** Having high monetary or material value for use or exchange. **2.** Of great importance, use, or service: *valuable information.* **3.** Having admirable or esteemed qualities or characteristics: *a valuable friend.* —*n.* Often **valuables.** A personal possession, such as a piece of jewelry, having a relatively high monetary value. —**val′u·a·ble·ness** *n.* —**val′u·a·bly** *adv.*

val·u·ate (văl′yo͞o-āt′) *tr.v.* **-at·ed, -at·ing, -ates.** To set a value for; appraise. [Back-formation < VALUATION.]

val·u·a·tion (văl′yo͞o-ā′shən) *n.* **1.** The act or process of assessing the value or price of something; appraisal. **2.** The assessed value or price of something. **3.** An estimation or appreciation of the worth, merit, or character of something. —**val′u·a′tion·al** *adj.*

val·u·a·tor (văl′yo͞o-ā′tər) *n.* A person who estimates values; appraiser.

val·ue (văl′yo͞o) *n.* **1.** An amount considered to be a suitable equivalent for something else; a fair price or return for goods or services. **2.** Monetary or material worth: *the rising value of gold.* **3.** Worth in usefulness or importance to the possessor; utility or merit: *the value of an education.* **4.** A principle, standard, or quality considered worthwhile or desirable: *a background that emphasized traditional values.* **5.** Precise meaning or import, as of a word. **6.** *Math.* An assigned or calculated numerical quantity. **7.** *Mus.* The relative duration of a tone or rest. **8.** The relative darkness or lightness of a color. **9.** The sound quality of a letter or diphthong. **10.** One of a series of specified values: *issued a stamp of new value.* —*tr.v.* **-ued, -u·ing, -ues. 1.** To determine or estimate the worth or value of; appraise. **2.** To regard highly; esteem: *valued her opinion.* **3.** To rate according to relative estimate of worth or desirability; evaluate: *valued health above money.* **4.** To assign a value to (a unit of currency, for example). [ME *valew* < OFr. *value* < *valoir,* to be worth < Lat. *valēre.*] —**val′u·er** *n.*

val·ue-ad·ded tax (văl′yo͞o-ăd′ĭd) *n.* A tax on the estimated market value added to a product or material at each stage of its manufacture or distribution, ultimately passed on to the consumer.

val·ued (văl′yo͞od) *adj.* Highly regarded; much esteemed.

valued policy *n.* An insurance policy requiring the insurer to pay the insured the full face value of the policy in the event of total loss, regardless of the actual value of the lost property.

value judgment *n.* A judgment that assigns a value, as to an object or action.

val·ue·less (văl′yo͞o-lĭs) *adj.* Having no value; worthless.

val·vate (văl′vāt′) *adj.* **1.** Having valvelike parts. **2.** *Bot.* Meeting at the edges without overlapping, as petals.

valve (vălv) *n.* **1.** *Anat.* A membranous structure in a hollow organ or passage, as in an artery or vein, that retards or prevents the return flow of a bodily fluid. **2. a.** Any of various devices that regulate the flow of gases, liquids, or loose materials through structures, such as piping, or through apertures by opening, closing, or obstructing ports or passageways. **b.** The movable control element of such a device. **c.** *Mus.* A device in a brass wind instrument that permits change in pitch by a rapid varying of the air column in a tube. **3.** *Biol.* **a.** One of the paired, hinged shells of many mollusks and of brachiopods. **b.** A similar paired part, as of the cell wall of a diatom. **4.** *Bot.* **a.** One of the sections into which a seed pod or other dehiscent fruit splits. **b.** A lidlike covering of an anther. **5.** *Chiefly Brit.* An electron tube or vacuum tube. **6.** *Archaic.* Either half of a double or folding door. —*tr.v.* **valved, valv·ing, valves. 1.** To provide with a valve. **2.** To control by means of a valve. [ME, leaf of a door < Lat. *valva.*]

valve-in-head engine (vălv′ĭn-hĕd′) *n.* An internal-combustion engine having the inlet and exhaust valves in the cylinder head.

val·vu·la (văl′vyə-lə) *n.* Variant of **valvule.**

val·vu·lar (văl′vyə-lər) *adj.* Pertaining to, having, or operating by means of valves or valvelike parts.

val·vule (văl′vyo͞ol′) also **val·vu·la** (văl′vyə-lə) *n., pl.* **-vules** also **-vu·lae** (-vyə-lē′). A small valve or valvelike structure.

val·vu·li·tis (văl′vyə-lī′tĭs) *n.* Inflammation of a valve, esp. of a cardiac valve.

vam·brace (văm′brās′) *n.* Armor used to protect the forearm. [ME *vambras* < AN *vauntbras* < OFr. *avauntbras* : *avaunt,* before + *bras,* arm.] —**vam′braced′** *adj.*

va·moose (vă-mo͞os′, və-) *intr.v.* **-moosed, -moos·ing, -moos·es.** *Slang.* To leave hurriedly. [< Sp. *vamos,* let's go < Lat. *vadamus,* 1st person pl. subjunctive of *vadere,* to go.]

vamp[1] (vămp) *n.* **1.** The part of a boot or shoe covering the instep and sometimes extending over the toe. **2.** An improvised musical accompaniment. —*v.* **vamped, vamp·ing, vamps.** —*tr.* **1.** To provide (a shoe) with a new vamp. **2.** To patch up (something that is old); refurbish. **3.** *Mus.* To improvise (an accompaniment, for example) for a solo. —*intr. Mus.* To improvise a vamp. [ME *vampe,* sock < OFr. *avantpie* : *avant,* before (< Lat. *abante,* from before) + *pie,* foot (< Lat. *pes*).] —**vamp′er** *n.*

vamp[2] (vămp) *Informal.* —*n.* An unscrupulous woman who seduces or exploits men with her charms. —*v.* **vamped, vamp·ing, vamps.** —*tr.* To seduce or exploit (a man) in the manner of a vamp. —*intr.* To play the part of a vamp. [Short for VAMPIRE.] —**vamp′ish** *adj.*

vam·pire (văm′pīr′) *n.* **1.** A reanimated corpse that is believed to rise from the grave at night to suck the blood of sleeping persons. **2.** A person who preys upon others, as: **a.** An extortionist. **b.** A woman who uses sexual attraction to exploit men. **3. a.** Any of various tropical American bats of the family Desmodontidae that feed on the blood of living mammals. **b.** Any of various other bats, as those of the family Megadermatidae, erroneously believed to feed on blood. [Fr. < G. *Vampir,* of Slav. orig.] —**vam·pir′ic** (văm-pĭr′ĭk) *adj.*

vam·pir·ism (văm′pīr-ĭz′əm) *n.* **1.** Belief in vampires. **2.** The practice or actions of a vampire.

van[1] (văn) *n.* **1.** A covered or enclosed truck or wagon for transporting goods or livestock. **2.** *Chiefly Brit.* A closed railroad car used for carrying baggage or freight. [Short for CARAVAN.]

van[2] (văn) *n.* The vanguard; forefront. [Short for VANGUARD.]

van[3] (văn) *n.* **1.** A wing. **2.** *Archaic.* A winnowing device, as a fan. [ME < OE *fann* and OFr. *van,* both < Lat. *vannus.*]

van·a·date (văn′ə-dāt′) *n.* Any of three anions, VO_3, VO_4, or V_2O_7. [< VANADIUM.]

va·na·dic acid (və-nā′dĭk, -năd′ĭk) *n.* **1.** An acid containing a vanadate group, esp. HVO_3, H_3VO_4, or $H_4V_2O_7$, not existing in a pure state. **2.** Vanadium pentoxide.

va·na·di·nite (və-năd′n-īt′, -năd′-, văn′ə-dē′nīt′) *n.* A deep ruby-red or yellow to brown vanadium and lead ore, essentially $Pb_5(VO_4)_3Cl$. [VANAD(IUM) + -IN + -ITE[1].]

va·na·di·um (və-nā′dē-əm) *n. Symbol* **V** A bright white soft ductile metallic element found in several minerals, notably vanadinite and carnotite, having good structural strength and used in rust-resistant high-speed tools, as a carbon stabilizer in some steels, as a titanium-steel bonding agent, and as a catalyst. Atomic number 23; atomic weight 50.942; melting point 1,890°C; boiling point 3,000°C; specific gravity 6.11; valences 2, 3, 4, 5. [< ON *Vanadīs,* the goddess Freya.]

vanadium pentoxide *n.* A yellow to red crystalline powder, V_2O_5, used as a catalyst in various organic reactions and as a starting material for other vanadium salts.

vanadium steel *n.* Steel alloyed with vanadium for added strength, hardness, and high-temperature stability.

Van Al·len belt (văn ăl′ən) *n.* Either of two zones of high-intensity particulate radiation trapped in the earth's magnetic field and surrounding the planet, beginning at an altitude of approximately 800 kilometers and extending several tens of thousands of kilometers into space. [After James A. *Van Allen* (b. 1914).]

van·co·my·cin (văng′kə-mī′sĭn, văn′kə-) *n.* An antibiotic produced by the bacterium *Streptomyces orientalis* that is effective against staphylococci and spirochetes. [*vanco-* (of unknown orig.) + -MYCIN.]

Van·dal (văn′dl) *n.* **1.** A member of a Germanic people that overran Gaul, Spain, and northern Africa in the 4th and 5th centuries A.D. and sacked Rome in A.D. 455. **2. vandal.** A person who willfully or maliciously defaces or destroys public or private property. [Lat. *Vandalus,* of Germanic orig.] —**Van·dal′ic** (văn-dăl′ĭk) *adj.*

van·dal·ism (văn′dl-ĭz′əm) *n.* The willful or malicious destruction of public or private property. —**van′dal·is′tic** *adj.*

van·dal·ize (văn′dl-īz′) *tr.v.* **-ized, -iz·ing, -iz·es.** To destroy or deface (public or private property) willfully or maliciously. —**van′dal·i·za′tion** *n.*

Van de Graaff generator (văn′ də grăf′) *n.* An electrostatic generator in which an electric charge is either removed from or transferred to a large hollow spherical electrode by a rapidly moving belt, in some configurations producing potentials over a million volts, and used with an acceleration tube as an electron or ion accelerator. [After Robert J. *Van de Graaff* (b.1901).]

van der Waals force (văn′ dər wôlz′) *n.* A force between nonpolar molecules caused by a temporary change in dipole moment arising from a brief shift of orbital electrons to one side of one molecule, creating a similar shift in adjacent molecules, with resulting polarization and attraction. [After Johannes D. *van der Waals* (1837–1923).]

Van·dyke (văn-dīk′) *n.* **1.** A Vandyke beard. **2.** A Vandyke collar. **3. a.** A V-shaped point that is part of a decorative border or edging. **b.** A border made up of such points.

Vandyke beard *n.* A short, pointed beard. [After Sir Anthony *Vandyke* (1599–1641).]

Vandyke brown *n.* A moderate to grayish brown. [After Sir Anthony *Vandyke* (1599–1641), from its frequent use in his paintings.] —**Van·dyke′-brown′** *adj.*

Vandyke collar *n.* A large collar of linen or lace having a deeply indented or scalloped edge. [After Sir Anthony *Vandyke* (1599–1641).]

vane (vān) *n.* **1.** A device that pivots on an elevated object, as a rooftop or spire, to indicate the direction of the wind. **2.** One of several usually relatively thin, rigid, flat, or sometimes curved surfaces radially mounted along an axis that is turned by or used to turn a fluid. **3.** The flattened, weblike part of a feather, consisting of a series of barbs on either side of the shaft. **4. a.** The movable target on a leveling rod.

b. A sight on a quadrant or compass. **5.** One of the metal guidance or stabilizing fins attached to the tail of a bomb or other missile. [ME < OE *fana,* flag.]

vang (văng) *n. Naut.* A guy rope running from the peak of a gaff or derrick to the deck. [Du., a catch < *vangen,* to catch.]

van•guard (văn′gärd′) *n.* **1.** The foremost position in an army or fleet. **2. a.** The foremost or leading position in a trend or movement. **b.** Those occupying a foremost position. [ME *vandgard* < *avaunt garde* < OFr. *avant-garde* : *avant,* before + *garde,* guard < *garder,* to guard.]

va•nil•la (və-nĭl′ə) *n.* **1.** Any of various tropical American orchids of the genus *Vanilla,* esp. *V. planifolia,* cultivated for its long, narrow seed pods from which a flavoring agent is obtained. **2.** The aromatic seed pod of a vanilla. **3.** A flavoring extract prepared from the seed pods of a vanilla or produced synthetically. [Sp. *vainilla,* dim. of *vaina,* sheath < Lat. *vagina* (from the shape of its seed pods).]

vanilla bean *n.* Vanilla (sense 2).

va•nil•lic (və-nĭl′ĭk) *adj.* Of, relating to, or derived from vanilla or vanillin.

va•nil•lin (və-nĭl′ĭn, văn′ə-lĭn) *n.* A white or yellowish crystalline compound, $C_8H_8O_3$, found in vanilla beans and certain balsams and resins and used in perfumes, flavorings, and pharmaceuticals. [VANILL(A) + -IN.]

Va•nir (vä′nîr′) *pl.n. Myth.* An early race of Norse gods who dwelt with the Aesir in Asgard. [ON.]

van•ish (văn′ĭsh) *intr.v.* **-ished, -ish•ing, -ish•es. 1.** To disappear or become invisible, esp. quickly or in an unexplained manner. **2.** To fade or decay to nothing; pass out of existence. **3.** *Math.* To become zero. Used of a function or variable. [ME *vanisshen* < OFr. *esvanir, esvaniss-* < VLat. **exvanire,* alteration of Lat. *evanescere* : *e-,* ex- + *vanescere,* to vanish < *vanus,* empty.] **—van′ish•er** *n.*

vanishing cream *n.* A cosmetic preparation containing less oil than cold cream, used as a powder base and night cream.

vanishing point *n.* **1.** A point in a drawing at which parallel lines drawn in perspective converge or seem to converge. **2.** A point at which a thing disappears or ceases to exist.

van•i•ty (văn′ĭ-tē) *n., pl.* **-ties. 1.** The quality or condition of being vain. **2.** Excessive pride in one's appearance or accomplishments; conceit. **3.** Lack of usefulness, worth, or effect; worthlessness. **4. a.** Something that is vain, futile, or worthless. **b.** Something about which one is vain or conceited. **5.** A vanity case. **6.** A dressing table. [ME *vanite* < OFr. < Lat. *vanitas* < *vanus,* empty.]

vanity case *n.* **1.** A woman's compact. **2.** A small handbag or case used by women for carrying cosmetics or toiletries.

Vanity Fair also **vanity fair** *n.* A place or scene of ostentation or empty, idle amusement and frivolity. [< *Vanity-Fair,* the fair in *Pilgrim's Progress* by John Bunyan (1628–1688).]

vanity plate *n.* An automobile license plate bearing a combination of letters or numbers selected by the purchaser.

vanity press *n.* A publisher that publishes a book at the expense of the author.

vanity publisher *n.* A vanity press.

van•quish (văng′kwĭsh, văn′-) *tr.v.* **-quished, -quish•ing, -quish•es. 1. a.** To defeat or conquer in battle; subjugate. **b.** To defeat in a contest, conflict, or competition. **2.** To overcome or subdue (an emotion, for example); suppress: *His success vanquished his fears.* [ME *vaynquysshen* < OFr. *vainquir, vainquiss-* < Lat. *vincere.*] **—van′quish•a•ble** *adj.* **—van′quish•er** *n.* **—van′quish•ment** *n.*

van•tage (văn′tĭj) *n.* **1.** An advantage in a competition or conflict; superiority. **2.** Something, as a strategic position, that provides superiority or advantage. **3.** *Sports.* An advantage (sense 4). [ME, short for OFr. *avantage,* advantage.]

van•ward (văn′wərd) *adj.* Located in the van or front; advanced. *—adv.* Toward or to the van or front; forward.

vap•id (văp′ĭd, vā′pĭd) *adj.* Lacking liveliness, zest, or interest; flat. [Lat. *vapidus.*] **—va•pid′i•ty** (vă-pĭd′ĭ-tē, vā-, və-), **vap′id•ness** *n.* **—vap′id•ly** *adv.*

va•por (vā′pər) *n.* **1.** Barely visible or cloudy diffused matter, such as mist, fumes, or smoke, suspended in the air. **2. a.** The state of a substance that exists below its critical temperature and that may be liquefied by application of sufficient pressure. **b.** The gaseous state of a substance that is liquid or solid under ordinary conditions. **3. a.** The vaporized form of a substance for use in industrial, military, or medical processes. **b.** A mixture of a vapor and air, as the explosive gasoline-air mixture burned in an internal-combustion engine. **4.** *Archaic.* **a.** Something insubstantial, worthless, or fleeting. **b.** A fantastic or foolish idea. **5. vapors. a.** *Archaic.* Exhalations within a bodily organ, esp. the stomach, supposed to affect the mental or physical condition. **b.** A hysterical or depressed emotional condition. *—v.* **-pored, -por•ing, -pors.** *—tr.* To vaporize. *—intr.* **1.** To give off vapor. **2.** To evaporate. **3.** To engage in boastful talk. [ME *vapour* < OFr. < Lat. *vapor.*] **—va′por•er** *n.*

va•por•es•cence (vā′pə-rĕs′əns) *n.* The formation of vapor.

va•por•if•ic (vā′pə-rĭf′ĭk) *adj.* **1.** Producing or turning to vapor. **2.** Having the nature of vapor; vaporous. [VAPOR + -FIC.]

va•por•ing (vā′pər-ĭng) *n.* Boastful or bombastic talk or behavior: *"all his . . . dreams of fame were the vaporings of a shoddy aesthete without talent"* (Thomas Wolfe).

va•por•ish (vā′pər-ĭsh) *adj.* **1.** Suggestive of or resembling vapor. **2.** *Archaic.* Given to spells of hysteria or low spirits. **—va′por•ish•ness** *n.*

va•por•i•za•tion (vā′pər-ĭ-zā′shən) *n.* **1.** The act or process of vaporizing. **2.** The condition of being vaporized.

va•por•ize (vā′pə-rīz′) *tr. & intr.v.* **-ized, -iz•ing, -iz•es.** To convert or be converted into vapor. **—va′por•iz′a•ble** *adj.*

va•por•iz•er (vā′pə-rī′zər) *n.* One that vaporizes, esp. a device used to vaporize medicine for inhalation.

vapor lock *n.* A pocket of vaporized gasoline in the fuel line of an internal-combustion engine that obstructs normal flow of fuel.

va•por•ous (vā′pər-əs) *adj.* **1.** Pertaining to or resembling vapor. **2. a.** Producing vapors; volatile. **b.** Giving off or full of vapors. **3.** Insubstantial, vague, or ethereal: *"the imponderable mysterious and vaporous illusions of twilight"* (John C. Powys). **4.** Extravagantly fanciful; high-flown: *vaporous conjecture.* **—va′por•os′i•ty** (vā′pə-rŏs′ĭ-tē), **va′por•ous•ness** *n.* **—va′por•ous•ly** *adv.*

vapor pressure *n.* The pressure exerted by a vapor in equilibrium with its solid or liquid phase.

vapor trail *n.* A contrail.

va•por•y (vā′pə-rē) *adj.* Vaporous.

va•pour (vā′pər) *n. & v. Chiefly Brit.* Variant of **vapor**.

va•que•ro (vä-kâr′ō) *n., pl.* **-ros.** *Southwestern U.S.* A cowboy; herdsman. [Sp. < *vaca,* cow < Lat. *vacca.*]

va•ra (vär′ə) *n.* **1.** A Spanish, Portuguese, and Latin American unit of linear measure varying from about 81 to 109 centimeters, or 32 to 43 inches. **2.** A square vara. [Sp. and Port. *vara,* rod, both < Lat. *vara,* forked pole < *varus,* bent.]

va•rac•tor (və-răk′tər, vă-) *n.* A semiconductor device in which the capacitance is sensitive to the applied voltage at the boundary of the semiconductor material and an insulator. [VAR(YING) + (RE)ACTOR.]

vari– *pref.* Variant of **vario-**.

var•i•a (vâr′ē-ə, văr′-) *n.* A miscellany, esp. of literary works. [Lat., neuter pl. of *varius,* various.]

var•i•a•ble (vâr′ē-ə-bəl, văr′-) *adj.* **1. a.** Liable or likely to vary; subject to variation. **b.** Inconstant; fickle. **2.** *Biol.* Tending to deviate from an established type; aberrant. **3.** *Math.* Having no fixed quantitative value. *—n.* **1.** Something that varies or is prone to variation. **2.** *Astron.* A variable star. **3.** *Math.* **a.** A quantity capable of assuming any of a set of values. **b.** A symbol representing such a quantity. **—var′i•a•bil′i•ty, var′i•a•ble•ness** *n.* **—var′i•a•bly** *adv.*

variable cost *n.* A cost that fluctuates directly with output changes.

variable field *n. Computer Sci.* A set of adjacent columns on a punchcard that may be varied in length according to need.

variable logic *n. Computer Sci.* A form of internal machine logic that may be changed to match programming formats.

variable star *n.* A star whose brightness varies because of internal changes or periodic eclipsing of component stars.

var•i•ance (vâr′ē-əns, văr′-) *n.* **1. a.** The act of varying. **b.** The state or quality of being variant or variable; variation. **c.** A difference between what is expected and what actually occurs. **2.** A difference of opinion; dissension. **3.** *Law.* **a.** A discrepancy between two statements or documents in a legal proceeding. **b.** The license to engage in an act contrary to a usual rule: *a zoning variance.* **4.** *Statistics.* The mean of the squares of the variations from the mean of a frequency distribution. **5.** *Chem.* The number of thermodynamic variables required to specify a state of equilibrium of a system, given by the phase rule. ***—idiom.* at variance.** Differing; conflicting.

var•i•ant (vâr′ē-ənt, văr′-) *adj.* **1.** Having or exhibiting variation; differing. **2.** Tending or liable to vary; variable. **3.** Deviating from a standard, usually by only a slight difference. *—n.* Something that differs in form only slightly from something else, as a different spelling or pronunciation of the same word. [ME < OFr. < Lat. *varians, variant-,* pr.part. of *variare,* to vary.]

var•i•ate (vâr′ē-ĭt, -āt′, văr′-) *n.* **1.** Something that varies; variable. **2.** *Statistics.* A random variable with a numerical value that is defined on a given sample space. [< Lat. *variatus,* p.part. of *variare,* to vary.]

var•i•a•tion (vâr′ē-ā′shən, văr′-) *n.* **1. a.** The act, process, or result of varying. **b.** The state or fact of being varied. **2.** The extent or degree to which something varies: *a variation of ten pounds in weight.* **3.** Magnetic declination. **4.** Something that is slightly different from another of the same type. **5.** *Biol.* Marked difference or deviation from characteristic form, function, or structure. **6.** *Math.* A function that relates the values of one variable to those of other variables. **7. a.** A musical form that is an altered version of a given theme, diverging from it by melodic ornamentation and by changes in harmony, rhythm, or key. **b.** One of a series of musical forms based on a single theme. **8.** A solo dance, esp. one forming part of a larger work. **—var′i•a′tion•al** *adj.*

varic– *pref.* Variant of **varico-**.

var•i•cel•la (văr′ĭ-sĕl′ə) *n.* Chicken pox. [NLat. < *variola,* variola.] **—var′i•cel′loid′** (-sĕl′oid′) *adj.*

var•i•ces (văr′ĭ-sēz′) *n.* Plural of **varix**.

varico– or **varic–** *pref.* Varix; varicose vein: *varicosis.* [< Lat. *varix, varic-,* varix.]

var•i•co•cele (văr′ĭ-kō-sēl′) *n.* A varicose condition of veins

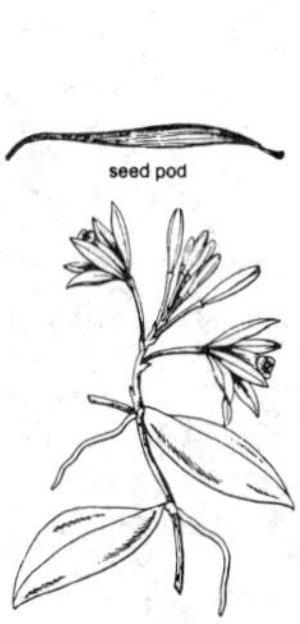

vanilla

of the spermatic cord or the ovaries, forming a soft tumor. [VARICO- + -CELE[1].]

var·i·col·ored (vâr′ĭ-kŭl′ərd, văr′-) *adj.* Having a variety of colors; variegated.

var·i·cose (văr′ĭ-kōs′) *adj.* **1.** Designating blood or lymph vessels that are abnormally dilated, knotted, and tortuous. **2.** Causing unusual swelling. [Lat. *varicosus* < *varix,* swollen vein.]

var·i·co·sis (văr′ĭ-kō′sĭs) *n.* The state of being varicose. [VARIC(O)- + -OSIS.]

var·i·cos·i·ty (văr′ĭ-kŏs′ĭ-tē) *n., pl.* **-ties. 1.** Varicosis. **2. a.** A varicose distention or swelling. **b.** The state of having varicose veins.

var·i·cot·o·my (văr′ĭ-kŏt′ə-mē) *n., pl.* **-mies.** Subcutaneous incision to cure varicose veins. [VARICO- + -TOMY.]

var·ied (vâr′ēd, văr′-) *adj.* **1.** Having various kinds or forms; marked by variety. **2.** Modified or altered. **3.** Varicolored; variegated. **—var′ied·ly** *adv.*

varied thrush *n.* A bird, *Ixoreus naevius,* of western North America, resembling the robin but having a black transverse stripe on the breast.

var·i·e·gate (vâr′ē-ĭ-gāt′, vâr′ĭ-gāt′, văr′-) *tr.v.* **-gat·ed, -gat·ing, -gates. 1.** To change the appearance of, esp. by marking with different colors; streak. **2.** To give variety to; make varied. [Lat. *variegare, variegat-* < Lat. *varius,* various.] **—var′i·e·ga′tor** *n.*

var·i·e·gat·ed (vâr′ē-ĭ-gā′tĭd, vâr′ĭ-gā′-, văr′-) *adj.* **1.** Having streaks, marks, or patches of a different color or colors. **2.** Distinguished or characterized by variety; diversified.

var·i·e·ga·tion (vâr′ē-ĭ-gā′shən, vâr′ĭ-gā′-, văr′-) *n.* The state of being variegated; diversified coloration.

var·i·er (vâr′ē-ər, văr′-) *n.* One that varies.

va·ri·e·tal (və-rī′ĭ-tl) *adj.* Of, indicating, or characterizing a variety, esp. a biological variety. [< VARIETY.] **—va·ri′e·tal·ly** *adv.*

va·ri·e·ty (və-rī′ĭ-tē) *n., pl.* **-ties. 1.** The condition or quality of being various or varied; diversity. **2.** A number or collection of varied things, esp. of a particular group; assortment: *brought home a variety of snacks.* **3.** A group that is distinguished from other groups by a specific characteristic or set of characteristics. **4.** *Biol.* **a.** A taxonomic category forming a subdivision of a species and consisting of naturally occurring or selectively bred individuals having varying characteristics. **b.** An organism, esp. a plant, belonging to such a category. **5.** A variety show. [OFr. *variete* < Lat. *varietas* < *varius,* various.]

variety meat *n.* Meat that has been taken from a part other than skeletal muscles, as liver or sweetbreads, or that has been processed, as sausage.

variety show *n.* A theatrical entertainment consisting of successive unrelated acts, such as songs, dances, and comedy skits.

variety store *n.* A retail store carrying a large variety of merchandise.

var·i·form (vâr′ə-fôrm′, văr′-) *adj.* Having a variety or diversity of forms. [VARI(O)- + -FORM.]

vario– or **vari–** *pref.* Variety; difference; variation: *variometer.* [< Lat. *varius,* speckled.]

va·ri·o·la (və-rī′ə-lə, vâr′ē-ō′lə, văr′-) *n.* Smallpox. [NLat. < Med. Lat., pustule < Lat. *varius,* speckled.]

var·i·o·late (vâr′ē-ə-lāt′, văr′-) *adj.* Having pustules or marks like those of smallpox. *—tr.v.* **-lat·ed, -lat·ing, -lates.** To inoculate with smallpox.

var·i·o·lite (vâr′ē-ə-līt′, văr′-) *n.* A basic rock with a pockmarked appearance due to numerous white, rounded spherules embedded in it.

vase
Crystal vase

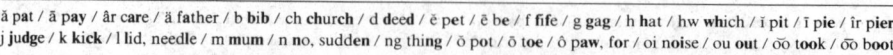

var·i·o·loid (vâr′ē-ə-loid′, văr′-, və-rī′ə-loid′) *n.* A mild form of smallpox in persons who have previously been vaccinated or who have previously had the disease.

va·ri·o·lous (və-rī′ə-ləs, vâr′ē-ō′-, văr′-) *adj.* Of or pertaining to smallpox.

var·i·om·e·ter (vâr′ē-ŏm′ĭ-tər, văr′-) *n.* A variable inductor used to measure variations in terrestrial magnetism.

var·i·o·rum (vâr′ē-ôr′əm, -ōr′-, văr′-) *n.* **1.** An edition of the works of an author, with notes by various scholars or editors. **2.** An edition containing various versions of a text. *—adj.* Designating or pertaining to a variorum edition or text. [< Lat. *(editio cum notis) variorum,* (edition with the notes) of various persons.]

var·i·ous (vâr′ē-əs, văr′-) *adj.* **1. a.** Of diverse kinds: *for various reasons.* **b.** Unlike; different. **2.** More than one; several. **3.** Many-sided; versatile: *people of various skills.* **4.** Having a variegated nature or appearance. **5.** Being an individual or separate member of a class or group: *The various reports all agreed.* **6.** *Archaic.* Changeable; variable. [Lat. *varius.*] **—var′i·ous·ly** *adv.* **—var′i·ous·ness** *n.*

Usage: *Various* sometimes appears as a collective noun followed by *of: He spoke to various of the members.* That usage is unacceptable to a great majority of the Usage Panel.

var·i·sized (vâr′ĭ-sīzd′, văr′-) *adj.* Of different sizes.

Var·i·Typ·er (vâr′ĭ-tī′pər, văr′-). A trademark for a typewriter used to prepare copy in a variety of type styles.

var·ix (văr′ĭks) *n., pl.* **var·i·ces** (văr′ĭ-sēz′). **1.** A vein, artery, or lymph vessel that is abnormally dilated and twisted. **2.** One of the longitudinal ridges marking a resting stage in the development of the lip of a gastropod shell. [Lat., swollen vein.]

var·let (vär′lĭt) *n. Archaic.* **1.** An attendant or servant. **2.** A knight's page. **3.** A rascal; knave. [ME < OFr., var. of *vaslet.* —see VALET.]

var·let·ry (vär′lĭ-trē) *n. Archaic.* A crowd of attendants or menials, esp. when disorderly; rabble.

var·mint (vär′mĭnt) *n. Informal.* **1.** A bird or animal that is considered undesirable or troublesome. **2. a.** An obnoxious or contemptible person. **b.** A person. [Var. of VERMIN.]

var·nish (vär′nĭsh) *n.* **1.** An oil-based paint containing a solvent and an oxidizing or an evaporating binder, used to coat a surface with a hard, glossy, thin film. **2. a.** The smooth coating or gloss resulting from the application of varnish. **b.** Something resembling or like varnish. **3.** A deceptively attractive external appearance; outward show. *—tr.v.* **-nished, -nish·ing, -nish·es. 1.** To cover with varnish. **2.** To give a smooth and glossy finish to. **3.** To give a deceptively attractive appearance to; gloss over. [ME *vernysshe* < OFr. *vernis* < Med. Lat. *veronix,* sandarac resin, prob. < Gk. *Berenikē,* Berenice, a city in Cyrenaica.] **—var′nish·er** *n.*

varnish tree *n.* Any of several trees having milky juice used to make varnish.

var·si·ty (vär′sĭ-tē) *n., pl.* **-ties. 1.** The principal team representing a university, college, or school in sports or other competitions. **2.** *Chiefly Brit.* A university. ***—modifier:*** *varsity sports.* [Alteration of UNIVERSITY.]

Var·u·na (vŭr′ə-nə) *n. Hinduism.* The Vedic god of the skies and seas. [Skt. *Varuṇaḥ.*]

var·us (vâr′əs, văr′-) *n., pl.* **-us·es.** An abnormal position of a bone of the leg or foot. [< Lat., crooked.]

varve (värv) *n.* **1.** A layer of sediment deposited in one year. **2.** A pair of distinct layers of sediment, indicating seasonal deposits. [Swed. *varv,* layer < *varva,* to bend < ON *hverfa.*]

var·y (vâr′ē, văr′ē) *v.* **-ied, -y·ing, -ies.** *—tr.* **1.** To make or cause changes in characteristics or attributes; modify or alter. **2.** To make varied; give variety to: *a program that was varied for all tastes.* **3.** To introduce under new aspects; express in a different manner: *vary the tempo.* *—intr.* **1.** To undergo or show change: *The temperature varied throughout the day.* **2.** To be different; deviate: *vary from established patterns of behavior.* **3.** To undergo successive or alternate changes in attributes or qualities. [ME *varien,* to undergo change < OFr. *varier* < Lat. *variare* < *varius,* various.] **—var′y·ing·ly** *adv.*

varying hare *n.* The snowshoe rabbit.

vas (văs) *n., pl.* **va·sa** (vā′zə). An organic vessel or duct. [NLat. < Lat., vessel.]

vas– *pref.* Variant of **vaso–.**

va·sa (vā′zə) *n.* Plural of **vas.**

vas·cu·la (văs′kyə-lə) *n.* Plural of **vasculum.**

vas·cu·lar (văs′kyə-lər) *adj.* **1.** *Biol.* Of, characterized by, or containing vessels for the transmission or circulation of plant or animal fluids such as blood, lymph, or sap. **2.** Characterized by vigor and ardor; passionate. [< Lat. *vasculum,* dim. of *vas,* vessel.] **—vas′cu·lar′i·ty** (-lăr′ĭ-tē) *n.*

vascular bundle *n.* A strand of supportive and conductive plant tissue consisting essentially of xylem and phloem.

vas·cu·lar·i·za·tion (văs′kyə-lər-ĭ-zā′shən) *n.* The process of new blood-vessel formation.

vascular plant *n.* Any of various plants of the division Tracheophyta, which includes the ferns and seed-bearing plants characterized by a system of specialized conductive and supportive tissue.

vascular tissue *n.* Plant tissue consisting of vascular bundles.

vas·cu·la·ture (văs′kyə-lə-cho͝or′, -chər) *n.* The arrangement of blood vessels in the body or in an organ or part of the body.

vas·cu·lum (văs′kyə-ləm) *n., pl.* **-la** (-lə). A small box or case used for carrying newly collected plant specimens. [Lat., small vessel. —see VASCULAR.]

vas def·er·ens (văs′ dĕf′ər-ənz, -ə-rĕnz′) *n., pl.* **va·sa def·er·en·ti·a** (vā′zə dĕf′ə-rĕn′shē-ə). The vertebrate duct that carries sperm from the epididymal duct to the ejaculatory duct. [NLat., deferent vessel.]

vase (vās, vāz, väz) *n.* An open container, as of glass or porcelain, used for holding flowers or for ornamentation. [Fr. < Lat. *vas,* vessel.]

va·sec·to·my (və-sĕk′tə-mē, vā-zĕk′-) *n., pl.* **-mies.** Surgical excision of a part of the vas deferens, used as a means of sterilization.

Vas·e·line (văs′ə-lēn′). A trademark for a petroleum jelly used primarily as a vehicle for external applications of medicinal agents and as a protective coating for metal surfaces.

vaso– or **vas–** *pref.* **1.** Blood vessel: *vasoconstriction.* **2.** Vas deferens: *vasectomy.* [< Lat. *vas,* vessel.]

va·so·ac·tive (vā′zō-ăk′tĭv) *adj.* Affecting blood vessels. **—va′so·ac·tiv′i·ty** (-tĭv′ĭ-tē) *n.*

va·so·con·stric·tion (vā′zō-kən-strĭk′shən) *n.* Constriction of a blood vessel. **—vas′o·con·stric′tive** *adj.*

va·so·con·stric·tor (vā′zō-kən-strĭk′tər) *n.* An agent, as a nerve or a drug, that causes vasoconstriction.

va·so·dil·a·ta·tion (vā′zō-dĭl′ə-tā′shən, -dī′lə-) also **va·so·di·la·tion** (-dī-lā′shən, -dĭ-) *n.* Dilatation of a blood vessel.

va·so·di·la·tor (vā′zō-dī-lā′tər, -dĭ-) *n.* An agent, as a nerve or drug, that causes vasodilatation.
va·so·mo·tor (vā′zō-mō′tər) *adj.* Causing or regulating vasoconstriction or vasodilatation.
va·so·pres·sin (vā′zō-prĕs′ĭn) *n.* A hormone secreted by the posterior lobe of the pituitary gland that has an antidiuretic and pressor effect. [Orig. a trademark.]
va·so·pres·sor (vā′zō-prĕs′ər) *adj.* Causing a rise in blood pressure. —*n.* An agent that causes a rise in blood pressure.
vas·sal (văs′əl) *n.* **1.** A person who held land from a feudal lord and received protection in return for homage and allegiance. **2.** A subordinate or dependent. **3.** A bondman; slave. [ME < OFr. < Med. Lat. *vassallus* < *vassus,* of Celt. orig.]
vas·sal·age (văs′ə-lĭj) *n.* **1.** The condition of being a vassal. **2.** The service, homage, and fealty required of a vassal. **3.** A position of subordination or subjection; servitude.
vast (văst) *adj.* **-er, -est. 1.** Very great in size, number, amount, or quantity. **2.** Very great in area or extent; immense. **3.** Very great in degree or intensity. —*n. Archaic.* An immense space. [Lat. *vastus.*] **—vast′ly** *adv.* **—vast′ness** *n.*
vas·ti·tude (văs′tĭ-to͞od′, -tyo͞od′) also **vas·ti·ty** (-tē) *n.* Immensity. [Lat. *vastitas* < *vastus,* vast.]
vast·y (văs′tē) *adj.* **-i·er, -i·est.** *Archaic.* Vast.
vat (văt) *n.* A large vessel, such as a tub, cistern, or barrel, used to store or hold liquids. —*tr.v.* **vat·ted, vat·ting, vats.** To put into or treat in a vat. [ME < OE *fæt.*]
vat dye *n.* Any of a series of dyes that produce a fast color by impregnating the fiber with a reduced soluble form that is then oxidized to an insoluble form. **—vat′-dyed′** (văt′dīd′) *adj.*
vat·ic (văt′ĭk) also **vat·i·cal** (-ĭ-kəl) *adj.* Of or characteristic of a prophet; oracular. [< Lat. *vates,* seer.]
Vat·i·can (văt′ĭ-kən) *n.* **1.** The official residence of the pope in Vatican City, Italy. **2.** The papal government; papacy. [Fr. < Lat. *Vaticanus,* the Vatican Hill.]
Vat·i·can·ism (văt′ĭ-kə-nĭz′əm) *n.* The policies and authority of the Vatican.
va·tic·i·nal (vă-tĭs′ə-nəl, və-) *adj.* Prophetic.
va·tic·i·nate (vă-tĭs′ə-nāt′, və-) *v.* **-nat·ed, -nat·ing, -nates.** —*tr.* To prophesy; foretell. —*intr.* To be a prophet. [Lat. *vaticinari, vaticinat-* < *vates,* seer.] **—va·tic′i·na′tor** *n.*
va·tic·i·na·tion (vă-tĭs′ə-nā′shən, və-) *n.* **1.** The act of prophesying. **2.** A prediction or prophecy.
vaude·ville (vôd′vĭl′, vōd′-, vô′də-) *n.* **1. a.** Stage entertainment offering a variety of short acts such as slapstick turns, song-and-dance routines, and juggling performances. **b.** A theatrical performance of this kind; variety show. **2.** A light comic play that often includes songs, pantomime, and dances. **3.** A popular, often satirical song. [Fr. < OFr. *vaudevire,* short for *chanson du Vau de Vire,* song of Vau de Vire, a region in Normandy.]
vaude·vil·lian (vôd-vĭl′yən, vōd-, vô′də-) *n.* A person who works in vaudeville, esp. as a performer. **—vaude·vil′lian** *adj.*
Vau·dois (vō-dwä′) *pl.n.* The Waldenses. [Fr. < Med. Lat. *Waldenses.* —see WALDENSES.]
vault[1] (vôlt) *n.* **1. a.** An arched structure, usually of stone, brick, or concrete, forming a ceiling or roof. **b.** An arched covering, such as the sky, that resembles a vault. **2.** A room or space with arched walls and ceiling, esp. when underground, as a cellar or storeroom. **3.** A room or compartment for the safekeeping of valuables: *a bank vault.* **4.** A burial chamber, esp. when underground. **5.** *Anat.* An arched anatomical part. —*tr.v.* **vault·ed, vault·ing, vaults. 1.** To construct or supply with an arched ceiling; cover with a vault. **2.** To build in the shape of a vault. [ME *vaute* < OFr. < Lat. *voluta,* fem. p.part. of *volvere,* to roll.]
vault[2] (vôlt) *v.* **vault·ed, vault·ing, vaults.** —*tr.* To jump or leap over, esp. with the aid of a support such as the hands or a pole. —*intr.* **1.** To jump or leap, esp. with the use of the hands or a pole. **2.** To accomplish something as if by leaping suddenly or vigorously: *vaulted into a position of wealth.* —*n.* The act of vaulting; jump. [OFr. *volter* < OItal. *voltare* < VLat. **volvitare,* freq. of Lat. *volvere,* to turn.] **—vault′er** *n.*
vault·ing[1] (vôl′tĭng) *n.* Something vaulted or arched.
vault·ing[2] (vôl′tĭng) *adj.* **1.** Leaping upward or over. **2.** Reaching too far; exaggerated: *vaulting ambition.* **3.** Employed in leaping over: *a vaulting pole.*
vaunt (vônt, vŏnt) *v.* **vaunt·ed, vaunt·ing, vaunts.** —*tr.* To describe in boastful terms; brag about. —*intr.* To boast; brag. —*n.* **1.** A boastful remark. **2.** Speech of extravagant self-praise. [ME *vaunten* < OFr. *vanter* < LLat. *vanitare,* to talk frivolously < Lat. *vanus,* empty.] **—vaunt′er** *n.* **—vaunt′ing·ly** *adv.*
vaunt-cour·i·er (vônt′ko͝or′ē-ər, -kûr′-, kŭr′-, vŏnt′-) *n.* **1.** *Obs.* A member of an advance guard of an army. **2.** A person sent in advance, as a herald. [Short for OFr. *avant-courier* : *avant,* in front + *courier,* courier.]
vav (väv, vôv) *n.* The 6th letter of the Hebrew alphabet. See table at **alphabet.** [Heb. *wāw.*]
vav·a·sor also **vav·a·sour** (văv′ə-sôr′, -sōr′, -so͝or′) *n.* A feudal tenant who ranked directly below a baron or peer. [ME *vavasour* < OFr. < Med. Lat. *vavassor,* poss. contraction of *vassus vassorum,* vassal of vassals.]
V-day (vē′dā′) *n.* A day of victory, as at the conclusion of a war. [V(ICTORY) DAY.]
-'ve. Have: *I've been invited.*
Ve·a·dar (vā′ä-där′, vā′ə-) *n.* An extra month of the Hebrew year, having 29 days, added in leap years after the regular month of Adar. [Heb. *va'adhar,* and Adar.]
veal (vēl) *n.* **1.** The meat of a calf. **2.** Also **veal·er** (vē′lər). A calf raised to be slaughtered for food. [ME *veel* < OFr. < Lat. *vitellus,* dim. of *vitulus,* calf.]
vec·tor (vĕk′tər) *n.* **1.** *Math.* **a.** A quantity completely specified by a magnitude and a direction. **b.** A one-dimensional array. **c.** An element of a vector space. **2.** *Pathol.* An organism that carries pathogens from one host to another. **3.** A force or influence. [Lat., carrier < *vehere,* to carry.] **—vec·to′ri·al** (vĕk-tôr′ē-əl, -tōr′-) *adj.*
vector product *n.* A vector, *C,* that has magnitude equal to the product of the magnitudes of two vectors, *A* and *B,* and the sine of the angle between *A* and *B,* and that is perpendicular to the plane of *A* and *B* and in a right-handed coordinate system directed so that a right-handed rotation about *C* carries *A* into *B* through an angle not greater than 180 degrees.
vector space *n.* A set of elements of vectors that are commutative under addition, unchanged after multiplication by a field multiplicative identity, and commutative, closed, and distributive under the multiplicative operation of the field.
Ve·da (vā′də, vē′-) *n.* Any of the oldest sacred writings of Hinduism, including the psalms, incantations, hymns, and formulas of worship incorporated in four collections. [Skt. *vedaḥ,* sacred knowledge, Veda.]
Ve·dan·ta (vā-dän′tə, -dăn′-, və-) *n.* The system of Hindu philosophy that further develops the implications in the Upanishads that all reality is a single principle, Brahman, and teaches that the believer's goal is to transcend the limitations of self-identity and realize his unity with Brahman. [Skt. *vedantaḥ,* essence of the Veda.] **—Ve·dan′tic** *adj.* **—Ve·dan′tism** *n.* **—Ve·dan′tist** *n.*
V-E Day (vē′ē′) *n.* May 8, 1945, the day of victory for the Allied forces in Europe during World War II. [V(ICTORY IN) E(UROPE) DAY.]
Ved·da also **Ved·dah** (vĕd′ə) *n.* One of a small, dark-skinned, wavy-haired aboriginal people of Sri Lanka. [Singhalese, hunter.]
ve·dette also **vi·dette** (vĭ-dĕt′) *n.* **1.** A mounted sentinel stationed in advance of an outpost. **2.** A small scouting boat used to observe and report on an opposing naval force. [Fr. < Ital. *vedetta,* alteration of *veletta* < Sp. *vela,* watch < *velar,* to watch < Lat. *vigilare,* to watch through the night.]
Ve·dic (vā′dĭk, vē′-) *adj.* Of or pertaining to the Veda or Vedas, the language in which they are written, or the Hindu culture that produced them.
vee (vē) *n.* The letter *v.*
vee·na (vē′nə) *n.* Variant of **vina.**
veep (vēp) *n. Slang.* **1.** A vice president. **2. Veep.** The Vice President of the United States. [Pronunciation of *V.P.,* abbr. of *vice president.*]
veer[1] (vîr) *v.* **veered, veer·ing, veers.** —*intr.* **1.** To turn aside from a course, direction, or purpose; swerve. **2.** To shift in direction by a clockwise motion. Used of the wind. **3.** *Naut.* To change the direction of a ship by turning away from the direction of the wind. —*tr.* **1.** To alter the direction of; turn. **2.** *Naut.* To change the course of (a ship) by turning away from the direction of the wind. —*n.* A change in direction; swerve. [OFr. *virer,* poss. of Celt. orig.]
veer[2] (vîr) *tr.v.* **veered, veer·ing, veers.** *Naut.* To let out or release (an anchor chain, for example). [ME *veren* < MDu. *vieren.*]
vee·ry (vîr′ē) *n., pl.* **-ries.** A thrush, *Hylocichla fuscescens,* of the New World, having a reddish-brown back and an indistinctly spotted breast. [Poss. imit. of its song.]
Ve·ga (vē′gə, vā′-) *n.* The brightest star in the constellation Lyra. [Med. Lat. < Ar. *(al nasr) al wāqi',* the falling (vulture).]
veg·an·ism (vĕj′ə-nĭz′əm) *n.* An extreme form of vegetarianism in which no animal food or dairy products are consumed and no products derived from animals, as leather or soap, are used. [Alteration of VEGETARIANISM.] **—veg′an** (vĕj′ən, -ăn′) *n.*
veg·e·ta·ble (vĕj′tə-bəl, vĕj′ĭ-tə-) *n.* **1. a.** A plant, such as the beet or spinach, cultivated for an edible part, such as the root, stem, leaf, or flower. **b.** The edible part of such a plant. **2.** An organism classified as a plant; a member of the vegetable kingdom. **3.** A person who leads a monotonous, passive, or merely physical existence. —*adj.* **1.** Of, pertaining to, or derived from a plant or plants. **2. a.** Suggesting or resembling a vegetable, as in passivity or dullness of existence; inactive. **b.** Boundlessly growing or multiplying. [< ME, vegetative < Med Lat. *vegetabilis* < LLat., enlivening < Lat. *vegetare,* to enliven < *vegetus,* lively < *vegēre,* to be lively.]
vegetable ivory *n.* A hard, ivorylike material obtained from the ivory nut and used in making small objects such as buttons.
vegetable kingdom *n.* The category of living organisms that includes all plants.
vegetable marrow *n. Chiefly Brit.* An edible squash having very large, elongated greenish fruit.

vat

barrel vault

intersecting vault

vault[1]
Above: Architectural structures
Below: Bank vault

veil
Veiled Arab woman

velocipede

vegetable oil *n.* Any of various oils obtained from plants, used in food products and industrially.
vegetable oyster *n.* Salsify (sense 2).
vegetable silk *n.* Any of several silky fibers from the seed pods of certain plants.
vegetable sponge *n.* Loofa.
vegetable tallow *n.* Any of various waxy fats obtained from certain plants, such as the bayberry, and used in making soap and candles.
vegetable wax *n.* A waxy substance of plant origin, as that obtained from certain palm trees.
veg·e·tal (vĕj′ĭ-tl) *adj.* **1.** Of, pertaining to, or characteristic of a plant or plants. **2.** Pertaining to growth rather than to sexual reproduction; vegetative. [Fr. < Med. Lat. *vegetalis* < Lat. *vegetare,* to enliven. —see VEGETABLE.]
veg·e·tar·i·an (vĕj′ĭ-târ′ē-ən) *n.* **1.** A person who practices or advocates vegetarianism. **2.** A herbivore. —*adj.* **1.** Of, pertaining to, practicing, or advocating vegetarianism. **2.** Consisting primarily of vegetables and vegetable products; containing little or no animal food: *a vegetarian diet.* [VEGET(ABLE) + -ARIAN.]
veg·e·tar·i·an·ism (vĕj′ĭ-târ′ē-ə-nĭz′əm) *n.* The practice of or belief in eating a diet consisting primarily of vegetables, grains, fruits, nuts, seeds, and sometimes dairy products, such as milk or cheese.
veg·e·tate (vĕj′ĭ-tāt′) *intr.v.* **-tat·ed, -tat·ing, -tates. 1.** To grow or sprout as a plant does. **2.** *Pathol.* To grow or spread abnormally. **3.** To lead a monotonous, passive, or merely physical existence. [Lat. *vegetare,* to enliven. —see VEGETABLE.]
veg·e·ta·tion (vĕj′ĭ-tā′shən) *n.* **1.** The act or process of vegetating. **2.** The plants of an area or region; plant life collectively. **3.** *Pathol.* An abnormal growth on the body. **—veg′e·ta′tion·al** *adj.*
veg·e·ta·tive (vĕj′ĭ-tā′tĭv) also **veg·e·tive** (vĕj′ĭ-tĭv) *adj.* **1.** Of, pertaining to, or characteristic of plants or plant growth. **2.** *Biol.* **a.** Of, pertaining to, or capable of growth. **b.** Of, pertaining to, or functioning in processes such as growth or nutrition rather than sexual reproduction. **c.** Of or pertaining to asexual reproduction, as fission or budding.
veg·gies or **veg·ies** (vĕj′ēz) *pl.n. Informal.* Vegetables.
ve·he·ment (vē′ə-mənt) *adj.* **1.** Characterized by forcefulness of expression or intensity of emotion, passion, or conviction; fervid: *a vehement denial.* **2.** Marked by or full of vigor or energy; strong. [OFr. < Lat. *vehemens.*] **—ve′he·mence, ve′he·men·cy** *n.* **—ve′he·ment·ly** *adv.*
ve·hi·cle (vē′ĭ-kəl) *n.* **1.** A device, such as a car or sled, for carrying passengers, goods, or equipment; conveyance. **2.** A medium through which something is conveyed, transmitted, expressed, or achieved. **3.** A play, role, or piece of music used to display the special talents of one performer or company. **4.** A substance of no therapeutic value used as the medium in which active medicines are administered. **5.** A substance, as oil, in which paint pigments are mixed for application. [Fr. *véhicule* < Lat. *vehiculum* < *vehere,* to carry.] **—ve·hic′u·lar** (vē-hĭk′yə-lər) *adj.*
veil (vāl) *n.* **1. a.** A piece of cloth, often wide-meshed and transparent, worn by women over the head, shoulders, and often part of the face for concealment or protection or as a token of modesty. **b.** A length of netting attached to a woman's hat or headdress for decoration, hanging before all or part of the face. **2. a.** The part of a nun's headdress that frames the face and falls over the shoulders. **b.** The vows or life of a nun: *took the veil.* **3. a.** A piece of light fabric hung to separate or conceal what is behind it; curtain. **b.** Something that conceals, separates, or screens like a curtain: *a veil of secrecy.* **4.** *Biol.* A membranous covering, such as that partially or completely enveloping the developing fruiting body of certain mushrooms; velum. —*tr.v.* **veiled, veil·ing, veils.** To cover, conceal, mask, or disguise with or as if with a veil: *"veiling cruelty under apparent harmony"* (Johan Huizinga). [ME *veile* < Norman Fr. < Lat. *vela,* pl. of *velum.*]
veil·ing (vā′lĭng) *n.* **1.** A veil. **2.** Gauzy material used for veils.
vein (vān) *n.* **1. a.** *Anat.* A vessel that transports blood toward the heart. **b.** Any blood vessel. **2.** *Bot.* One of the vascular bundles that form the branching framework and support of a leaf. **3.** *Zool.* One of the chitinous, usually longitudinal ribs that stiffen and support the wing of an insect. **4.** *Geol.* A regularly shaped and lengthy occurrence of an ore; lode. **5.** A long, wavy strip of color, as in wood or marble. **6.** A fissure, crack, or cleft. **7.** A pervading character or quality; streak: *"all through the interminable narrative there ran a vein of impressive earnestness"* (Mark Twain). **8.** A transient or temporary attitude or mood: *a talk in a serious vein.* —*tr.v.* **veined, vein·ing, veins. 1.** To supply or fill with veins. **2.** To mark or decorate with veins. [ME *veine* < OFr. < Lat. *vena.*] **—vein′al** *adj.*
veined (vānd) *adj.* Exhibiting veins or veinlike markings.
vein·ing (vā′nĭng) *n.* Venation.
vein·let (vān′lĭt) *n.* A small or secondary vein, as of an insect's wing.
vein·stone (vān′stōn′) *n.* Mineral matter in a vein exclusive of the ore; gangue.
vein·y (vā′nē) *adj.* **-i·er, -i·est. 1.** Having, showing, or full of veins. **2.** Veined.
ve·la (vē′lə) *n.* Plural of **velum.**
ve·la·men (və-lā′mən) *n., pl.* **ve·lam·i·na** (və-lăm′ə-nə). **1.** *Anat.* A membranous covering or integument; velum. **2.** *Bot.* The spongy outer covering of the aerial roots of epiphytic orchids and certain other plants, capable of absorbing atmospheric moisture. [Lat., covering < *velare,* to cover < *velum,* a covering.] **—vel′a·men′tous** (vĕl′ə-mĕn′təs) *adj.*
ve·lar (vē′lər) *adj.* **1. a.** Of or pertaining to a velum. **b.** Concerning or using the soft palate. **2.** Formed with the back of the tongue on or near the soft palate, as (g) in *good* and (k) in *cup.* —*n.* A velar sound. [Lat. *velaris,* of a curtain < *velum,* curtain.]
ve·lar·ize (vē′lə-rīz′) *tr.v.* **-ized, -iz·ing, -iz·es.** To articulate (a sound) by retracting the back of the tongue toward the soft palate. **—ve′lar·i·za′tion** *n.*
ve·late (vē′lāt′, -lĭt) *adj. Biol.* Having or covered by a velum or veil. [Lat. *velatus,* p.part. of *velare,* to cover < *velum,* a covering.]
Vel·cro (vĕl′krō′). A trademark for a fastening tape used esp. for cloth products.
veldt also **veld** (vĕlt, fĕlt) *n.* Any of the open grazing areas of southern Africa. [Afrikaans *veld* < MDu., field.]
ve·li·ger (vē′lə-jər, vĕl′ə-) *n.* A larval stage of a mollusk characterized by the presence of the ciliated velum. [NLat. : VELUM + Lat. *gerere,* to bear.]
vel·le·i·ty (vĕ-lē′ĭ-tē, və-) *n., pl.* **-ties. 1.** The lowest level of volition. **2.** A mere wish not accompanied by action or effort to obtain it. [NLat. *velleitas* < Lat. *velle,* to want.]
vel·lum (vĕl′əm) *n.* **1.** A fine parchment made from the skins of calf, lamb, or kid and used for the pages and binding of fine books. **2.** A work written or printed on vellum. **3.** A heavy off-white fine-quality paper resembling vellum. [ME *velim* < OFr. *velin,* pertaining to a calf < *veel,* calf.]
ve·lo·ce (vā-lō′chā) *adv. Mus.* Rapidly. Used as a direction. [Ital. < Lat. *velox,* swift.]
ve·lo·cim·e·ter (vē′lō-sĭm′ĭ-tər, vĕl′ō-) *n.* A device for measuring the speed of sound in water. [VELOCI(TY) + -METER.]
ve·loc·i·pede (və-lŏs′ə-pēd′) *n.* **1.** An early bicycle propelled by pushing the feet along the ground while straddling the vehicle. **2.** Any of several early bicycles having pedals attached to the front wheel. **3.** A tricycle. [Fr. *vélocipède* : *véloci-,* swift (< Lat. *velox, veloci-*) + *-pède,* -ped.]
ve·loc·i·ty (və-lŏs′ĭ-tē) *n., pl.* **-ties. 1.** Rapidity or speed. **2.** *Physics.* A vector quantity the magnitude of which is a body's speed and the direction of which is the body's direction of motion. **3.** The rate of rapidity or action. [Fr. *vélocité* < Lat. *velocitas* < *velox,* swift.]
ve·lour or **ve·lours** (və-lo͝or′) *n., pl.* **-lours** (-lo͝orz′). **1.** A closely napped, velvetlike fabric, used chiefly for clothing and upholstery. **2.** A felt resembling velvet, used in making hats. [Fr. *velours,* velvet < OFr. *velous* < Lat. *villosus,* hairy < *villus,* shaggy hair.]
ve·lou·té (və-lo͞o-tā′) *n.* A white sauce made with flour, butter, and chicken or veal stock. [Fr. < *velouter,* to give the appearance of velvet < *velours,* velvet. —see VELOUR.]
ve·lum (vē′ləm) *n., pl.* **-la** (-lə). **1.** *Biol.* A covering or partition of thin membranous tissue, such as the veil of a mushroom. **2.** *Anat.* The soft palate. **3.** *Zool.* A ciliated swimming organ that develops in certain larval stages of many marine gastropod mollusks. [NLat. < Lat., veil.]
ve·lure (vĕ-lo͝or′, vĕl′yər) *n. Obs.* **1.** Velvet. **2.** A velvetlike fabric. [Fr. *velours.* —see VELOUR.]
ve·lu·ti·nous (və-lo͞ot′n-əs) *adj.* Covered with dense, soft, silky hairs; velvety. [NLat. *velutinus* < Med. Lat. *velutum,* velvet < *villutus,* shaggy. —see VELVET.]
vel·vet (vĕl′vĭt) *n.* **1. a.** A fabric made usually of silk or a synthetic fiber such as rayon or nylon and having a smooth, dense pile and a plain back. **b.** Something suggesting or resembling velvet. **2.** Smoothness; softness. **3.** The soft covering on the newly developing antlers of deer and related animals. [ME *veluet* < OFr. *velute* < *velu,* shaggy < Med. Lat. *villutus* < Lat. *villus,* shaggy hair.] **—vel′vet·y** *adj.*
velvet ant *n.* Any of various wasps of the family Mutillidae, having a dense, hairy, often brightly colored covering.
vel·vet·een (vĕl′vĭ-tēn′) *n.* A velvetlike cotton fabric. [< VELVET.]
velvet plant *n.* Mullein (sense 1).
ven– *pref.* Variant of **veno-.**
ve·na (vē′nə) *n., pl.* **ve·nae** (vē′nē). *Anat.* A vein. [Lat.]
ve·na ca·va (vē′nə kā′və) *n., pl.* **ve·nae ca·vae** (vē′nē kā′vē). Either of the two large veins in air-breathing vertebrates that enter into and return blood to the right atrium of the heart. [Lat., hollow vein.]
ve·nae (vē′nē) *n.* Plural of **vena.**
ve·nal (vē′nəl) *adj.* **1. a.** Open or susceptible to bribery. **b.** Capable of betraying one's honor, duty, or scruples for a price; corruptible. **2.** Marked by corrupt or unscrupulous dealings: *a venal administration.* **3.** Obtainable by purchase or bribery rather than by merit. [Lat. *venalis,* for sale < *venum,* sale.] **—ve′nal·ly** *adv.*
ve·nal·i·ty (vē-năl′ĭ-tē) *n., pl.* **-ties. 1.** The quality of being open to bribery or corruption. **2.** The use of a position of trust for dishonest gain.
ve·nat·ic (vē-năt′ĭk) also **ve·nat·i·cal** (-ĭ-kəl) *adj.* **1.** Pertaining to or used in hunting. **2.** Given to hunting for sport or livelihood. [Lat. *venaticus* < *venari,* to hunt.]

ve·na·tion (vē-nā′shən, vĕ-) *n.* The distribution or arrangement of veins. **—ve·na′tion·al** *adj.*

vend (vĕnd) *v.* **vend·ed, vend·ing, vends.** *—tr.* **1.** To sell. **2.** To offer (an idea, for example) for public consideration. *—intr.* **1. a.** To sell goods. **b.** To sell by means of a vending machine. **2.** To have a market. [Fr. *vendre* < OFr. < Lat. *vendere* : *venum,* sale + *dare,* to give.]

vend·a·ble (vĕn′də-bəl) *adj.* Variant of **vendible.**

vend·ee (vĕn-dē′) *n.* A buyer.

vend·er also **ven·dor** (vĕn′dər) *n.* **1. a.** One that sells or vends. **b.** A peddler or salesman. **2.** A vending machine.

ven·det·ta (vĕn-dĕt′ə) *n.* **1.** A bitter blood feud between two families motivated by the desire for revenge. **2.** An act or attitude motivated by vengeance. [Ital., revenge < Lat. *vindicta* < *vindicare,* to avenge.]

vend·i·ble also **vend·a·ble** (vĕn′də-bəl) *adj.* **1.** Capable of being sold or suitable for sale. **2.** Venal. *—n.* Something that can be sold.

vending machine *n.* A coin-operated machine that dispenses merchandise.

ven·dor (vĕn′dər) *n.* Variant of **vender.**

ven·due (vĕn′do͞o′, -dyo͞o′, vän′-, vĕn-do͞o′, -dyo͞o′, vän-) *n.* A public sale; auction. [Du. *vendu* < OFr. *vendue* < *vendre,* to sell. —see VEND.]

ve·neer (və-nîr′) *n.* **1.** A thin layer of material, as wood or plastic, bonded to and used to cover a usually inferior material. **2.** Any of the thin layers glued together in making plywood. **3.** A deceptive or superficial outward show or pretense: *a veneer of friendliness.* *—tr.v.* **-neered, -neer·ing, -neers. 1.** To overlay (a surface) with a thin layer of material. **2.** To glue together (layers of wood) in making plywood. **3.** To conceal (something common or crude) with an attractive but superficial appearance; gloss over. [G. *Furnier* < *furnieren,* to veneer < OFr. *fournir,* to furnish.] **—ve·neer′er** *n.*

ve·neer·ing (və-nîr′ĭng) *n.* **1.** Material used as a veneer. **2.** A surface of veneer.

ven·er·a·ble (vĕn′ər-ə-bəl) *adj.* **1.** Worthy of reverence or respect by virtue of dignity, character, position, or age: *a venerable judge.* **2.** Commanding respect or reverence esp. by religious or historical association: *venerable relics.* **3.** *Eccles.* Honored above others. Used in titles of respect given to an Anglican archdeacon or to a Roman Catholic who has attained the first degree of sanctity. [ME < OFr. < Lat. *venerabilis* < *venerari,* to venerate.] **—ven′er·a·ble·ness, ven′er·a·bil′i·ty** *n.* **—ven′er·a·bly** *adv.*

ven·er·ate (vĕn′ə-rāt′) *tr.v.* **-at·ed, -at·ing, -ates.** To regard with respect, reverence, or deference. [Lat. *venerari, venerat-,* to venerate.] **—ven′er·a′tor** *n.*

ven·er·a·tion (vĕn′ə-rā′shən) *n.* **1.** The act of venerating. **2.** Profound respect or reverence. **3.** The condition or status of one who is venerated.

ve·ne·re·al (və-nîr′ē-əl) *adj.* **1.** Of or pertaining to sexual intercourse. **2. a.** Transmitted by sexual intercourse. **b.** Of or pertaining to venereal disease. **3.** Of or pertaining to the genitals. [ME *venerealle* < Lat. *venereus* < *Venus,* Venus, love.]

venereal disease *n.* Any of several contagious diseases, such as syphilis and gonorrhea, contracted through sexual intercourse.

ve·ne·re·ol·o·gy (və-nîr′ē-ŏl′ə-jē) *n.* The study of venereal disease. [VENERE(AL) + -LOGY.] **—ve·ne′re·o·log′i·cal** (-ə-lŏj′ĭ-kəl) *adj.* **—ve·ne′re·ol′o·gist** *n.*

ven·er·y[1] (vĕn′ə-rē) *n. Archaic.* **1.** Indulgence in or the pursuit of sexual activity. **2.** Sexual intercourse. [ME *venerie* < Med. Lat. *veneria* < Lat. *Venus,* Venus, love.]

ven·er·y[2] (vĕn′ə-rē) *n. Archaic.* The act, art, or sport of hunting. [ME < OFr. *venerie* < *vener,* to hunt < Lat. *venari.*]

ven·e·sec·tion (vĕn′ĭ-sĕk′shən, vē′nĭ-) *n.* Phlebotomy. [Med. Lat. *venae sectio,* cutting of a vein.]

Ve·ne·tian blind also **ve·ne·tian blind** (və-nē′shən) *n.* A window blind consisting of thin horizontal slats that may be raised and lowered and set at a desired angle to regulate the amount of light admitted.

venetian blue *n.* A strong blue to greenish blue.

venetian red *n.* A deep to strong reddish brown.

venge (vĕnj) *tr.v.* **venged, veng·ing, veng·es.** *Archaic.* To avenge. [ME *vengen* < OFr. *vengier.* —see VENGEANCE.]

ven·geance (vĕn′jəns) *n.* The act or motive of punishing another in payment for a wrong or injury he has committed; retribution. **—*idiom.* with a vengeance. 1.** With great violence or fury. **2.** Excessively. [ME < OFr. < *vengier,* to avenge < Lat. *vindicare.*]

venge·ful (vĕnj′fəl) *adj.* **1.** Desiring vengeance; vindictive. **2.** Indicating or proceeding from a desire for revenge. **3.** Inflicting or serving to inflict vengeance. **—venge′ful·ly** *adv.* **—venge′ful·ness** *n.*

V-en·gine (vē′ĕn′jən) *n.* An internal-combustion engine having cylinders arranged so that pairs form V shapes.

veni– *pref.* Variant of **veno–.**

ve·ni·al (vē′nē-əl, vēn′yəl) *adj.* **1.** Easily excused or forgiven; pardonable: *a venial offense.* **2.** *Rom. Cath. Ch.* Minor in nature and warranting only temporal punishment: *a venial sin.* [ME < OFr. < LLat. *venialis* < Lat. *venia,* forgiveness.] **—ve′ni·al′i·ty** (vē′nē-ăl′ĭ-tē, vēn-yăl′-), **ve′ni·al·ness** *n.* **—ve′ni·al·ly** *adv.*

ve·ni·punc·ture (vē′nĭ-pŭngk′chər, vĕn′ĭ-) *n.* Puncture of a vein, as for drawing blood, intravenous feeding, or administration of medicine.

ve·ni·re (və-nī′rē) *n. Law.* **1.** Also **ve·ni·re fa·ci·as** (və-nī′rē fā′shē-əs). A writ issued by a judge to a sheriff, ordering him to summon prospective jurors. **2.** The panel of prospective jurors from which a jury is selected. [Med. Lat. *venire (facias),* (you should cause) to come, a phrase used in the writ.]

ve·ni·re·man (və-nī′rē-mən, -nîr′ē-) *n.* A person summoned to jury duty under a venire.

ven·i·son (vĕn′ĭ-sən, -zən) *n.* **1.** The flesh of a deer, used for food. **2.** *Archaic.* The flesh of a game animal used for food. [ME *veneson* < OFr. < Lat. *venatio,* hunting < *venari,* to hunt.]

Venn diagram (vĕn) *n.* A pictorial representation using circles and squares so positioned as to represent an operation in set theory. [After John *Venn* (1824–1923).]

veno– or **veni–** or **ven–** *pref.* Vein: *venipuncture.* [< Lat. *vena.*]

ve·no·gram (vē′nə-grăm′) *n.* A roentgenogram of a vein or veins.

ve·nog·ra·phy (vĭ-nŏg′rə-fē) *n.* Roentgenography of a vein or veins following the injection of a radiopaque substance.

ven·om (vĕn′əm) *n.* **1.** A poisonous secretion of an animal, such as a snake, spider, or scorpion, usually transmitted by a bite or sting. **2.** A poison. **3.** Malice; spite. [ME *venim* < OFr. < VLat. *venimen < Lat. *venenum,* poison.]

ven·om·ous (vĕn′ə-məs) *adj.* **1.** Secreting and transmitting venom: *a venomous snake.* **2.** Full of or containing venom. **3.** Malicious; spiteful: *a venomous remark.* **—ven′om·ous·ly** *adv.* **—ven′om·ous·ness** *n.*

ve·nose (vē′nōs′) *adj.* **1.** Having noticeable veins or veinlike markings. **2.** Venous. [Lat. *venosus,* venous < *vena,* vein.]

ve·nos·i·ty (vē-nŏs′ĭ-tē) *n.* The condition or quality of being venous or venose.

ve·nous (vē′nəs) *adj.* **1.** Of or pertaining to a vein or veins. **2.** *Physiol.* Returning to the heart through the great veins. [Lat. *venosus* < *vena,* vein.] **—ve′nous·ly** *adv.* **—ve′nous·ness** *n.*

vent (vĕnt) *n.* **1.** A means of escaping or leaving a confined space; exit. **2.** An opening permitting the passage or escape of a liquid, gas, or vapor: *a vent above the kitchen stove.* **3.** The small hole at the breech of a gun through which the charge is ignited. **4.** *Zool.* The cloacal or anal excretory opening in animals such as birds, reptiles, amphibians, and fish. *—tr.v.* **vent·ed, vent·ing, vents. 1.** To give forceful expression or utterance to; express: *vented his complaint to the officials.* **2.** To relieve by venting: *a device to vent tank pressure.* **3.** To discharge through a vent. **4.** To provide with a vent. **—*idiom.* give vent to.** To give utterance or expression to. [ME *vente,* a slit in a garment < ME *venten,* to provide with an outlet < OFr. *esventer,* to let out air : *es-,* ex- + *vent,* wind (< Lat. *ventus*).] **—vent′er** *n.*

Synonyms: *vent, express, utter, voice, air, broach.* These verbs mean to give an outlet to thought or emotion. *Vent* is applied to speech, writing, or other action by which a person unburdens himself of a strong, hitherto pent-up emotion such as anger or grief. *Express,* a more comprehensive word, can refer to communication by any means, including the nonverbal. *Utter* involves vocal expression, either words or inarticulate sounds; with reference to speech it often implies forthright or even bold public statement. *Voice* generally refers to the public expression, in speech or writing, of ideas, opinions, or beliefs. *Air* especially suggests public discussion of such ideas or opinions. *Broach* refers to introducing a subject, usually after careful thought, as a topic of discussion or written discourse.

vent·age (vĕn′tĭj) *n.* A small opening; vent. [< VENT.]

ven·tail (vĕn′tāl′) *n.* The lower front part of a medieval helmet, fitting over the neck. [ME < OFr. *vantail* < *vent,* wind < Lat. *ventus.*]

ven·ter (vĕn′tər) *n.* **1. a.** *Anat.* The abdomen or belly. **b.** The uterus. **c.** The wide swelling portion of a muscle. **2.** *Biol.* A swollen structure or part similar to a venter. **3.** *Law.* The womb as the source of offspring. [Norman Fr. < Lat.]

ven·ti·late (vĕn′tl-āt′) *tr.v.* **-lat·ed, -lat·ing, -lates. 1.** To admit fresh air into in order to replace stale air. **2.** To circulate air within in order to freshen: *ventilate a mine shaft.* **3.** To provide with a vent or a similar means of airing. **4.** To expose (a substance) to the circulation of fresh air for the purpose of retarding spoilage. **5.** To expose to public discussion or examination. **6.** To aerate or oxygenate (blood). [ME *ventilaten* < Lat. *ventilare,* to fan < *ventus,* wind.] **—ven′ti·la′tion** *n.*

ven·ti·la·tor (vĕn′tl-ā′tər) *n.* One that ventilates, esp. a device, such as an exhaust fan, that expels stale air and circulates fresh air. **—ven′ti·la·to′ry** (vĕn′tl-ə-tôr′ē, -tōr′ē) *adj.*

ven·tral (vĕn′trəl) *adj.* **1.** *Anat.* **a.** Pertaining to or situated on or close to the belly; abdominal. **b.** Pertaining to the anterior aspect of the human body or the lower surface of the body of an animal. **2.** *Bot.* Of or on the lower or inner surface of an organ. [Fr. < Lat. *ventralis* < *venter,* belly.] **—ven′tral·ly** *adv.*

ventral fin *n. Zool.* A pelvic fin.

ven·tri·cle (vĕn′trĭ-kəl) *n.* A small anatomical cavity or chamber, as of the brain or heart, esp.: **a.** The chamber on

vender
Parisian street vender

Venetian blind

the left side of the heart that receives arterial blood from the left atrium and contracts to drive it into the aorta. **b.** The chamber on the right side of the heart that receives venous blood from the right atrium and drives it into the pulmonary artery. [ME < OFr. < Lat. *ventriculus,* dim. of *venter,* belly.] **—ven·tric′u·lar** (-trĭk′yə-lər) *adj.*

ven·tri·cose (vĕn′trĭ-kōs′) also **ven·tri·cous** (-kəs) *adj.* Inflated, swollen, or distended. [NLat. *ventricosus* < Lat. *venter,* belly.] **—ven′tri·cos′i·ty** (-kŏs′ĭ-tē) *n.*

ven·tric·u·lus (vĕn-trĭk′yə-ləs) *n., pl.* **-li** (-lī′). A hollow digestive organ, esp. the stomach of an insect or the gizzard of a bird. [Lat., dim. of *venter,* belly.]

ven·tri·lo·qui·al (vĕn′trə-lō′kwē-əl) *adj.* Of, pertaining to, or practicing ventriloquism. **—ven′tri·lo′qui·al·ly** *adv.*

ven·tril·o·quism (vĕn-trĭl′ə-kwĭz′əm) also **ven·tril·o·quy** (-kwē) *n.* A method of producing vocal sounds so that they seem to originate in a source other than the speaker, as from a mechanical dummy. [< LLat. *ventriloquus,* speaking from the belly : Lat. *venter,* belly + *loqui,* to speak.] **—ven·tril′o·quist** (-kwĭst) *n.* **—ven·tril′o·quis′tic** *adj.*

ven·tril·o·quize (vĕn-trĭl′ə-kwīz′) *intr.v.* **-quized, -quiz·ing, -quiz·es.** To practice ventriloquism.

ven·tril·o·quy (vĕn-trĭl′ə-kwē) *n.* Variant of **ventriloquism.**

ven·ture (vĕn′chər) *n.* **1.** An undertaking that is dangerous, daring, or of doubtful outcome. **2.** Something at hazard in a venture; stake. *—v.* **-tured, -tur·ing, -tures.** *—tr.* **1.** To expose to danger or risk. **2.** To brave the dangers of: *ventured the high seas in a light boat.* **3.** To express at the risk of denial, criticism, or censure; dare: *ventured his opinion.* *—intr.* To take a risk or dare; make a venture. ***—idiom.* at a venture.** By mere chance or fortune; at random. [ME, chance < *aventure,* adventure.—see ADVENTURE.] **—ven′tur·er** *n.*

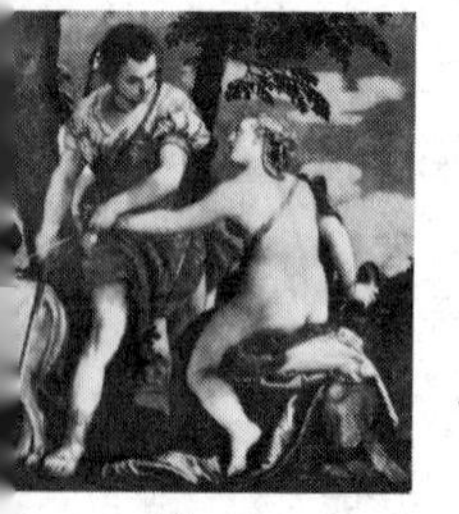

Venus
"Venus and Adonis" by Veronese

ven·ture·some (vĕn′chər-səm) *adj.* **1.** Disposed to venture or to take risks; bold: *a venturesome daredevil.* **2.** Involving risk or danger; hazardous: *a venturesome climb in the mountains.* **—ven′ture·some·ly** *adv.* **—ven′ture·some·ness** *n.*

ven·tu·ri (vĕn-to͝or′ē) *n.* **1.** A short tube with a constricted throat that is used to determine fluid pressures and velocities by measurement of differential pressures generated at the throat as a fluid traverses the tube. **2.** A constricted throat in the air passage of a carburetor, causing a reduction in pressure by means of which fuel vapor is drawn out of the carburetor bowl. [After G. B. *Venturi* (1742–1822).]

ven·tur·ous (vĕn′chər-əs) *adj.* **1.** Courageous and daring; adventurous. **2.** Hazardous, dangerous, or risky. **—ven′tur·ous·ly** *adv.* **—ven′tur·ous·ness** *n.*

ven·ue (vĕn′yo͞o) *n.* **1.** *Law.* **a.** The locality where an alleged crime or other cause of legal action occurs. **b.** The locality or political division from which a jury must be called and in which a trial must be held. **c.** The clause within a declaration naming the locality in which the trial is occurring or will occur. **d.** The clause in an affidavit naming the locality where it was made and sworn to. **2.** The locality of a gathering, as for a convention. [ME, arrival < OFr. < *venir,* to come < Lat. *venire.*]

ven·ule (vĕn′yo͞ol, vēn′-) *n.* A minute vein, as one joining with a capillary or branching from a vein in an insect's wing. [Lat. *venula,* dim. of *vena,* vein.] **—ven′u·lar** (-yə-lər) *adj.*

Venus's-flytrap

Ve·nus (vē′nəs) *n.* **1.** *Rom. Myth.* The goddess of love and beauty. **2.** The second planet from the sun, having an average radius of 6,114 kilometers, or 3,800 miles, a mass 0.816 times that of the earth, and a sidereal period of revolution about the sun of 224.7 days at a mean distance of approximately 108.1 million kilometers, or 67.2 million miles. [ME < OE < Lat. < *venus,* love.]

Ve·nu·sian (vĭ-no͞o′zhən, -nyo͞o′-) *adj.* Pertaining to or characteristic of the planet Venus. *—n.* A hypothetical inhabitant of the planet Venus.

Venus's flower basket *n.* A sponge of the genus *Euplectella,* of deep marine waters, having a cylindrical skeleton of glassy, intricately interlaced latticework.

Ve·nus's-fly·trap (vē′nəs-flī′trăp′, vē′nə-sĭz-) *n.* An insectivorous plant, *Dionaea muscipula,* of boggy areas of the southeastern United States, having marginally spined, hinged leaf blades that close and entrap insects.

Venus's girdle *n.* A ribbon-shaped marine animal, *Cestum veneris,* having a jellylike bluish-green iridescent body.

Venus's-hair (vē′nə-sĭz-hâr′) *n.* A maidenhair fern, *Adiantum capillus-veneris,* of moist warm regions, having slender blackish stalks.

Ve·nus's-look·ing-glass (vē′nə-sĭz-lo͝ok′ĭng-glăs′) *n.* Any of several plants of the genus *Specularia,* esp. *S. speculum-veneris,* native to Europe, and *S. perfoliata,* of North America, having small blue or white star-shaped flowers.

ve·ra·cious (və-rā′shəs) *adj.* **1.** Honest; truthful. **2.** Accurate; precise. [< Lat. *verax, verac-.*] **—ve·ra′cious·ly** *adv.* **—ve·ra′cious·ness** *n.*

ve·rac·i·ty (və-răs′ĭ-tē) *n., pl.* **-ties. 1.** Adherence to the truth; truthfulness. **2.** Conformity to truth or fact; accuracy: *"There was no question about the veracity of these doctrines"* (Fritz Kahn). **3.** Something that is true. [Med. Lat. *veracitas* < Lat. *verax,* true.]

ve·ran·dah or **ve·ran·da** (və-răn′də) *n.* A porch or balcony, usually roofed and often partly enclosed, extending along the outside of a building. [Hindi.]

ve·rat·ri·dine (və-răt′rĭ-dēn′) *n.* A yellowish-white, amorphous powdered alkaloid, $C_{36}H_{51}NO_{11}$, obtained from sabadilla seeds and from the rhizome of a species of hellebore, *Veratrum album.* [VERATR(INE) + -ID + -INE².]

ver·a·trine (vĕr′ə-trēn′, -trĭn) *n.* A poisonous mixture of colorless crystalline alkaloids extracted from sabadilla seeds and formerly used medicinally as a counterirritant. [Fr. *vératrine* < NLat. *Veratrum,* genus name of a hellebore < Lat. *veratrum,* hellebore.]

verb (vûrb) *n.* **1. a.** The part of speech that expresses existence, action, or occurrence in most language. **b.** Any of the words within this part of speech, as *be, run,* or *conceive.* **2.** A phrase or other construction used as a verb. ***—modifier:*** *a verb phrase.* [ME *verbe* < OFr. < Lat. *verbum,* word.]

ver·bal (vûr′bəl) *adj.* **1.** Of, pertaining to, or associated with words: *verbal instructions.* **2. a.** Concerned with words rather than with the facts or ideas they represent. **b.** Using or consisting of words alone without action: *a verbal confrontation.* **3.** Expressed or transmitted in speech; unwritten: *a verbal contract.* **4.** Word for word; literal: *a verbal translation.* **5.** *Gram.* **a.** Pertaining to, having the nature or function of, or derived from a verb. **b.** Used to form verbs: *a verbal suffix.* **6.** Of or relating to proficiency in the use and understanding of words: *a verbal aptitude test.* *—n. Gram.* A verbal noun, adjective, or other word derived from a verb and preserving some of the verb's characteristics. [OFr. < LLat. *verbalis* < Lat. *verbum,* word.] **—ver′bal·ly** *adv.*

Usage: In the sense "by word of mouth" *verbal* is synonymous with *oral.* In other senses *verbal* has to do with words, whether written or spoken: *verbal communication* (as opposed, say, to gestures). *Verbal,* when applied to such terms as *agreement, promise, commitment,* or *understanding,* is well established in the sense of *oral.* But anyone who fears misunderstanding may use *oral* instead.

ver·bal·ism (vûr′bə-lĭz′əm) *n.* **1.** An expression in words; word or phrase. **2.** A meaningless phrase or sentence. **3.** An expression, sentence, or other construction emphasizing words over content or idea.

ver·bal·ist (vûr′bə-lĭst) *n.* **1.** One skilled in the employment of words. **2.** One who favors words over ideas or facts. **—ver′bal·is′tic** *adj.*

ver·bal·ize (vûr′bə-līz′) *v.* **-ized, -iz·ing, -iz·es.** *—tr.* **1.** To express in words: *tried to verbalize her feelings.* **2.** To convert (a noun, for example) to verbal use. *—intr.* **1.** To express oneself in words. **2.** To be verbose. **—ver′bal·i·za′tion** *n.* **—ver′bal·iz′er** *n.*

verbal noun *n.* A noun that is derived from a verb and that in some uses preserves the verb's characteristics and sense.

ver·ba·tim (vər-bā′tĭm) *adj.* Using exactly the same words; word for word. *—adv.* In exactly the same words. [ME < Med. Lat. < Lat. *verbum,* word.]

ver·be·na (vər-bē′nə) *n.* **1.** Any of various New World plants of the genus *Verbena,* esp. one of several species cultivated for their showy clusters of variously colored flowers. **2.** Any of several plants, such as the lemon verbena, similar to or related to the verbena. [NLat. *Verbena,* genus name < Lat. *verbena,* sing. of *verbenae,* sacred boughs.]

ver·bi·age (vûr′bē-ĭj, -bĭj) *n.* **1.** Words in excess of those needed for clarity or precision; wordiness. **2.** The manner in which one expresses oneself in words; diction. [Fr. < OFr. *verbier,* to chatter < *verbe,* word < Lat. *verbum.*]

verb·i·fy (vûr′bə-fī′) *tr.v.* **-fied, -fy·ing, -fies.** To use (a noun, for example) as a verb; make into a verb.

ver·bose (vər-bōs′) *adj.* Using or containing an excessive number of words; wordy. [Lat. *verbosus* < *verbum,* word.] **—ver·bose′ly** *adv.* **—ver·bose′ness, ver·bos′i·ty** (-bŏs′ĭ-tē) *n.*

ver·bo·ten (fər-bōt′n, vər-) *adj.* Strictly forbidden. [G. < OHG *farboten,* p.part. of *farbiotan,* to forbid.]

ver·dant (vûr′dnt) *adj.* **1. a.** Green with vegetation. **b.** Covered with a green growth. **2.** Green in color. **3.** Inexperienced or unsophisticated. [OFr. *verdoyant,* pr.part. of *verdoyer,* to become green < *verd,* green < Lat. *viridis* < *virēre,* to be green.] **—ver′dan·cy** *n.* **—ver′dant·ly** *adv.*

verd antique also **verde antique** (vûrd) *n.* **1.** A dull-green mottled or veined serpentine marble used in interior decoration. **2.** Verdigris. [Obs. Fr., antique green.]

ver·der·er also **ver·der·or** (vûr′dər-ər) *n.* The official in charge of the royal forests of England. [AN < OFr. *verdier,* an official in charge of forests < *verd,* green. —see VERDANT.]

ver·dict (vûr′dĭkt) *n.* **1.** The decision reached by a jury at the conclusion of a trial. **2.** An expressed conclusion; judgment. [ME *verdit* < AN, var. of OFr. *veirdit* : *veir,* true (< Lat. *verus*) + *dit,* speech (< Lat. *dictum* < neuter p.part. of *dicere,* to speak).]

ver·di·gris (vûr′dĭ-grēs′, -grĭs′, -grē′) *n.* **1.** A blue or green basic copper acetate used as a paint pigment, fungicide, and insecticide. **2.** A green patina or crust of copper sulfate or copper chloride formed on copper, brass, and bronze exposed to air or sea water for long periods of time. [ME *vertegres* < OFr. *vertegrez,* alteration of *vert-de-Grice,* green of Greece.]

ver·din (vûr′dn) *n.* A small grayish bird, *Auriparus flaviceps,* of the southwestern United States and adjacent Mexico,

having a yellowish head and throat. [Fr., yellowhammer.]
ver·di·ter (vûr′dĭ-tər) *n.* Either of two basic carbonates of copper, used as a blue or green pigment. [Alteration of OFr. *verd de terre,* green of earth.]
ver·dure (vûr′jər) *n.* **1. a.** The fresh, vibrant greenness of flourishing vegetation. **b.** Such vegetation itself. **2.** A fresh or flourishing condition: *the verdure of childhood.* [ME < OFr. < *verd,* green. —see VERDANT.] **—ver′dur·ous** *adj.* **—ver′dur·ous·ness** *n.*
verge[1] (vûrj) *n.* **1.** The extreme edge, rim, or margin of something; brink: *the verge of a stream.* **2. a.** An enclosing boundary. **b.** The space enclosed by such a boundary. **3.** The point beyond which an action, state, or condition is likely to begin or occur: *on the verge of tears.* **4.** *Archit.* The edge of the tiling that projects over a roof gable. **5.** A rod, wand, or staff carried as an emblem of authority or office. **6.** *Obs.* The rod held by a feudal tenant swearing fealty to his lord. **7.** The spindle of a balance wheel in a clock or watch, esp. such a spindle in a clock with vertical escapement. **8.** The male organ of an invertebrate. *—intr.v.* **verged, verg·ing, verg·es. 1.** To approach the verge or limit; come near: *enthusiasm verging on fanaticism.* **2.** To constitute the verge or limit; border: *tracks that verge on the slum area.* [ME < OFr. < Lat. *virga,* rod.]
verge[2] (vûrj) *intr.v.* **verged, verg·ing, verg·es. 1.** To slope or incline. **2.** To be in the process of becoming something else: *dusk verging into night.* [Lat. *vergere.*]
verg·er (vûr′jər) *n.* **1.** A person who carries the verge before a scholastic, legal, or religious dignitary in a procession. **2.** *Chiefly Brit.* A person who has charge of the interior of a church.
ve·rid·i·cal (və-rĭd′ĭ-kəl) also **ve·rid·ic** (-rĭd′ĭk) *adj.* Expressing the truth; veracious. [Lat. *veridicus* : *verus,* true + *dicere,* to say.] **—ve·rid′i·cal′i·ty** (-kăl′ĭ-tē) *n.* **—ve·rid′i·cal·ly** *adv.*
ver·i·fi·ca·tion (vĕr′ə-fĭ-kā′shən) *n.* **1.** The act of verifying or condition of being verified. **2. a.** A confirmation of the truth of a theory or fact. **b.** A formal statement of such a confirmation. **3.** *Law.* A short formulaic oath concluding a pleading and affirming that the pleader is ready to prove his allegations. **—ver′i·fi·ca′tive** *adj.*
ver·i·fy (vĕr′ə-fī′) *tr.v.* **-fied, -fy·ing, -fies. 1.** To prove the truth of by the presentation of evidence or testimony; substantiate: *Two neighbors verified his story.* **2.** To determine or test the truth or accuracy of, as by comparison, investigation, or reference: *conduct experiments to verify a hypothesis.* **3.** *Law.* **a.** To affirm formally or under oath. **b.** To append a verification to (a pleading); conclude with a verification. [ME *verifien* < OFr. *verifier* < Med. Lat. *verificare* : Lat. *verus,* true + Lat. *facere,* to make.] **—ver′i·fi′a·ble** *adj.* **—ver′i·fi′er** *n.*
ver·i·ly (vĕr′ə-lē) *adv.* **1.** In truth; in fact. **2.** With confidence; assuredly. [ME *verraily* < *verray,* true. —see VERY.]
ver·i·sim·i·lar (vĕr′ə-sĭm′ə-lər) *adj.* Appearing to be true or real; probable. [Lat. *verisimilis* : *veri,* genitive of *verum,* truth < *verus,* true + *similis,* similar.] **—ver′i·sim′i·lar·ly** *adv.*
ver·i·si·mil·i·tude (vĕr′ə-sĭ-mĭl′ĭ-to͞od′, -tyo͞od′) *n.* **1.** The quality of appearing to be true or real; likelihood. **2.** Something that has the appearance of being true or real. [Lat. *verisimilitudo* < *verisimilis,* verisimilar.] **—ver′i·si·mil′i·tu′di·nous** (-to͞od′n-əs, -tyo͞od′-) *adj.*
ver·ism (vĕr′ĭz′əm) *n.* Realism in art and literature. [Ital. *verismo* : *vero,* true (< Lat. *verus*) + *-ismo,* -ism.] **—ver′ist** *n.* **—ve·ris′tic** (və-rĭs′tĭk) *adj.*
ver·i·ta·ble (vĕr′ĭ-tə-bəl) *adj.* Unquestionable; true: *The house was a veritable pigpen.* [ME < OFr. < *verite,* truth. —see VERITY.] **—ver′i·ta·ble·ness** *n.* **—ver′i·ta·bly** *adv.*
ver·i·ty (vĕr′ĭ-tē) *n., pl.* **-ties. 1.** The condition or quality of being real, accurate, or correct. **2.** A statement, principle, or belief considered to be established and permanent truth: *religious verities.* [ME *verite* < OFr. < Lat. *veritas,* truth < *verus,* true.]
ver·juice (vûr′jo͞os′) *n.* The acidic juice of sour or unripe fruit such as grapes or crab apples. [ME *verjus* < OFr. *vertjus* : *vert,* green, vert + *jus,* juice.]
ver·meil (vûr′məl, -māl′) *n.* **1.** Vermilion or a similar bright-red color. **2.** (vĕr-mā′). Gilded metal such as silver, bronze, or copper. *—adj.* Bright red in color. [ME *vermayl* < OFr. *vermeil* < LLat. *vermiculus,* a kind of red worm, dim. of *vermis,* worm.]
vermi– *pref.* Worm: *vermicide.* [< Lat. *vermis,* worm.]
ver·mi·cel·li (vûr′mə-chĕl′ē, -sĕl′ē) *n.* Pasta made into long threads thinner than spaghetti. [Ital., pl. of *vermicello,* dim. of *verme,* worm < Lat. *vermis.*]
ver·mi·cide (vûr′mĭ-sīd′) *n.* An agent used to kill worms. **—ver′mi·cid′al** (-sīd′l) *adj.*
ver·mic·u·lar (vər-mĭk′yə-lər) *adj.* **1.** Having the shape or motion of a worm. **2.** Having wormlike markings; vermiculate. **3.** Caused by or relating to worms. [Med. Lat. *vermicularis* < Lat. *vermiculus,* dim. of *vermis,* worm.] **—ver·mic′u·lar·ly** *adv.*
ver·mic·u·late (vər-mĭk′yə-lāt′) *tr.v.* **-lat·ed, -lat·ing, -lates.** To adorn or decorate with wavy or winding lines. *—adj.* (-lĭt, -lāt′). **1.** Bearing wormlike wavy lines. **2.** Having a wormlike motion; twisting or wriggling. **3.** Sinuous; tortuous. **4.** Infested with worms; worm-eaten. [Lat. *vermiculari, vermiculat-* < *vermiculus,* dim. of *vermis,* worm.]
ver·mic·u·la·tion (vər-mĭk′yə-lā′shən) *n.* **1.** Motion resembling that of a worm, esp. the wavelike contractions of the intestine; peristalsis. **2.** Wormlike marks or carvings, as in mosaic or masonry. **3.** The condition of being worm-eaten.
ver·mic·u·lite (vər-mĭk′yə-līt′) *n.* Any of a group of micaceous hydrated silicates of varying composition, related to the chlorites and used as heat insulation and for starting plant seeds and cuttings. [Lat. *vermiculus,* dim. of *vermis,* worm + -ITE[1].]
ver·mi·form (vûr′mə-fôrm′) *adj.* Resembling or having the shape of a worm.
vermiform appendix *n.* The narrow blind vestigial process of the cecum found in some mammals, including man.
vermiform process *n.* The vermiform appendix.
ver·mi·fuge (vûr′mə-fyo͞oj′) *n.* An agent that expels or destroys intestinal worms.
ver·mil·ion also **ver·mil·lion** (vər-mĭl′yən) *—n.* **1.** A bright red mercuric sulfide used as a pigment. **2.** A vivid red to reddish orange. *—adj.* Of a vivid red to reddish orange. *—tr.v.* **-ioned, -ion·ing, -ions** also **-lioned, -lion·ing, -lions.** To color or dye vermilion. [ME *vermelyon* < OFr. *vermeillon* < *vermeil.* —see VERMEIL.]

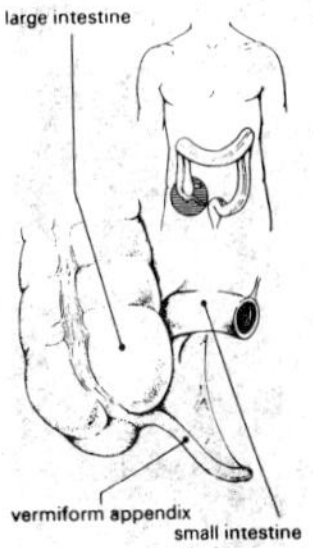

vermiform appendix

ver·min (vûr′mĭn) *n., pl.* **vermin. 1.** Any of various small animals or insects that are destructive, annoying, or injurious to health, as cockroaches or rats. **2.** Any of various animals that prey on game, as the fox or weasel. **3. a.** A contemptible or offensive person. **b.** Contemptible or offensive persons collectively: *"the most pernicious race of little odious vermin that nature ever suffered to crawl upon the surface of the earth"* (Swift). [ME < OFr. < VLat. **verminum* < Lat. *vermis,* worm.]
ver·mi·na·tion (vûr′mə-nā′shən) *n.* **1.** The condition of being infested with vermin or worms. **2.** The breeding of worms, larvae, or vermin.
ver·min·o·sis (vûr′mĭ-nō′sĭs) *n., pl.* **-ses** (-sēz′). Infestation with parasitic worms.
ver·min·ous (vûr′mə-nəs) *adj.* **1.** Of, pertaining to, or infested with vermin. **2.** Of the nature of vermin; noxious. **—ver′min·ous·ly** *adv.*
ver·miv·o·rous (vər-mĭv′ər-əs) *adj.* Feeding on worms.
ver·mouth (vər-mo͞oth′) *n.* A sweet or dry white wine flavored with aromatic herbs and spices and used chiefly as an ingredient in cocktails. [Fr. *vermout* < G. *Wermut* < MHG *wermuot,* wormwood < OHG *wermuota.*]
ver·nac·u·lar (vər-năk′yə-lər) *n.* **1.** The native language of a country or region, esp. as distinct from literary language. **2.** The nonstandard or substandard everyday speech of a country or region. **3.** The idiom of a particular trade or profession: *in the legal vernacular.* **4.** An idiomatic word, phrase, or expression. **5.** The commonly used name of a plant or animal as distinguished from the taxonomic designation. *—adj.* **1.** Native to or commonly spoken by the members of a particular country or region. **2.** Using the native language of a region, esp. as distinct from literary language: *a vernacular poet.* **3.** Pertaining to, spoken in, or written in the native language or dialect. **4.** Pertaining to the style of architecture and decoration peculiar to a specific culture. **5.** Occurring or existing in a particular locality; endemic: *a vernacular disease.* **6.** Designating or pertaining to the commonly used nonscientific name of a plant or animal. [< Lat. *vernaculus,* native < *verna,* native slave.] **—ver·nac′u·lar·ly** *adv.*
ver·nac·u·lar·ism (vər-năk′yə-lə-rĭz′əm) *n.* A vernacular word, phrase, or expression.
ver·nal (vûr′nəl) *adj.* **1.** Of, pertaining to, or occurring in the spring. **2.** Characteristic of or resembling spring. **3.** Fresh and young; youthful. [Lat. *vernalis* < *vernus* < *ver,* spring.] **—ver′nal·ly** *adv.*

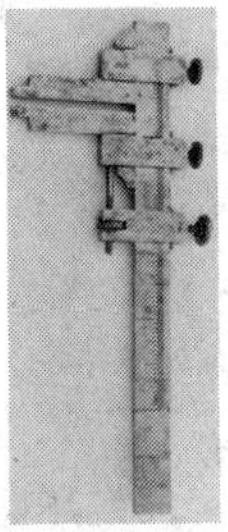
vernier caliper

vernal equinox *n.* **1.** The point at which the ecliptic intersects the celestial equator, the sun having a northerly motion. **2.** The moment at which the sun passes through the vernal equinox, about March 21, marking the beginning of spring.
ver·nal·i·za·tion (vûr′nə-lĭ-zā′shən) *n.* The subjection of seeds or seedlings to low temperature in order to hasten plant development.
ver·na·tion (vər-nā′shən) *n.* The arrangement of the folded leaves in a bud. [NLat. *vernatio, vernation-* < *vernare,* to flourish.]
Ver·ner's Law (vûr′nərz, vĕr′-) *n. Ling.* A law stating essentially that Proto-Germanic noninitial voiceless fricatives in voiced environments became voiced when the previous syllable was unstressed in Proto-Indo-European. [After Karl Adolph *Verner* (1846–1896), its formulator.]
ver·ni·er (vûr′nē-ər) *n.* **1.** A small, movable auxiliary graduated scale attached parallel to a main graduated scale, calibrated to indicate fractional parts of the subdivisions of the larger scale, and used on certain precision instruments to increase accuracy in measurement. **2.** An auxiliary device designed to facilitate fine adjustments or measurements on precision instruments. *—adj.* Of a vernier. [After Pierre *Vernier* (1580–1637), its inventor.]
vernier caliper *n.* A measuring instrument consisting of an L-shaped frame with a linear scale along its longer arm and

an L-shaped sliding attachment with a vernier scale, used to read directly the dimension of an object represented by the separation between the inner or outer edges of the two shorter arms.

vernier rocket *n.* A small rocket engine used primarily to make fine adjustments in velocity and trajectory.

vernier scale *n.* A vernier (sense 2).

ver·o·nal (vĕr′ə-nôl′, -nəl) *n.* A type of barbital. [Orig. a trademark.]

veronica[2]

ve·ron·i·ca[1] (və-rŏn′ĭ-kə) *n.* Any of various plants of the genus *Veronica,* which includes the speedwells. [NLat. *Veronica,* genus name.]

ve·ron·i·ca[2] (və-rŏn′ĭ-kə) *n.* **1. a.** The representation or image of the face of Jesus, which, according to legend, was impressed upon the handkerchief offered to him by Saint Veronica on the road to Calvary. **b.** The handkerchief itself. **2.** A representation of Jesus' face on a textile fabric similar to the legendary veronica.

ve·ron·i·ca[3] (və-rŏn′ĭ-kə) *n.* A maneuver in bullfighting in which the matador stands immobile and passes the cape slowly before the charging bull. [Sp.]

ver·ru·ca (və-ro͞o′kə) *n., pl.* **-cae** (-kē). **1.** *Med.* A wart. **2.** *Biol.* A wartlike projection, as on the back of a toad or on some leaves. [Lat.]

ver·ru·cose (və-ro͞o′kōs′) also **ver·ru·cous** (-kəs) *adj.* Covered with warts or wartlike projections. [Lat. *varrucosus* < *verruca,* wart.]

ver·sant (vûr′sənt) *n.* **1.** The slope of one side of a mountain or mountain range. **2.** The general slope of a region. [Fr. < OFr. < Lat. *versans,* pr.part. of *versare,* to turn frequently. —see VERSATILE.]

ver·sa·tile (vûr′sə-təl, -tīl′) *adj.* **1.** Capable of doing many things competently. **2.** Having varied uses or serving many functions: *"The most versatile of vegetables is the tomato"* (Craig Claiborne). **3.** Inconstant or variable; changeable. **4.** *Biol.* Capable of moving freely in all directions, as the antenna of an insect or the loosely attached anther of a flower. [Fr. < Lat. *versatilis* < *versare,* freq. of *vertere,* to turn.] **—ver′sa·tile·ly** *adv.* **—ver′sa·til′i·ty** (-tĭl′ĭ-tē), **ver′sa·tile·ness** *n.*

verse[1] (vûrs) *n.* **1.** Writing arranged according to a metrical pattern; poetry. **2. a.** One line of poetry. **b.** A section or subdivision of a metrical composition, as a stanza. **3.** Light, often whimsical poetry as distinct from serious poetry. **4.** A specific type of metrical composition, such as blank verse or free verse. **5.** One of the numbered subdivisions of a chapter in the Bible. *—v.* **versed, vers·ing, vers·es.** *—tr.* To versify (something). *—intr.* To write poetry; versify. [ME *vers,* a line of poetry < OE *fers* and OFr. *vers,* both < Lat. *versus* < p.part. of *vertere,* to turn.]

verse[2] (vûrs) *tr.v.* **versed, vers·ing, vers·es.** To make familiar, knowledgeable, or skilled; school: *versed himself in political science.* [Back-formation < *versed,* experienced < Lat. *versatus,* p.part. of *versari,* to occupy oneself.]

versed cosine (vûrst) *n.* A trigonometric function of an angle equal to one minus the sine of that angle. [VERSED (SINE) + COSINE.]

versed sine *n.* A trigonometric function of an angle equal to one minus the cosine of that angle. [Transl. of NLat. *sinus versus.*]

ver·si·cle (vûr′sĭ-kəl) *n.* **1.** A short verse. **2.** A short sentence spoken or chanted by a priest and followed by a response from the congregation. [ME < OFr. *versicule* < Lat. *versiculus,* dim. of *versus,* verse.]

ver·si·col·or (vûr′sĭ-kŭl′ər) also **ver·si·col·ored** (-kŭl′ərd) *adj.* **1.** Having a variety of colors; variegated. **2.** Changing in color; iridescent. [Lat. : *versus,* p.part. of *vertere,* to turn + *color,* color.]

ver·si·fi·er (vûr′sə-fī′ər) *n.* One who versifies.

ver·si·fy (vûr′sə-fī′) *v.* **-fied, -fy·ing, -fies.** *—tr.* **1.** To change from prose into metrical form. **2.** To treat or tell in verse; write a poem about: *"Narrative poets liked to versify Bible stories"* (George Sherburn). *—intr.* To write verses. [ME *versifien* < OFr. *versifier* < Lat. *versificare* : *versus,* verse + *facere,* to make.] **—ver′si·fi·ca′tion** *n.*

ver·sine (vûr′sīn′) *n.* A versed sine. [Contraction of VERSED SINE.]

ver·sion (vûr′zhən, -shən) *n.* **1.** A description, narration, or account related from a specific point of view: *Her version of the accident differed from his.* **2. a.** A translation from another language. **b.** Often **Version.** A translation of the entire Bible or a part of it: *the King James Version.* **3.** A form or variation of an earlier or original model: *his customized version of the Ford Model T.* **4.** An adaptation of a work of art or literature into another medium or style: *the motion-picture version of the novel.* **5.** *Med.* **a.** Manipulation of a fetus in the uterus to bring it into a favorable position for delivery. **b.** A deflection of an organ, such as the uterus, from its normal position. [OFr. < Med. Lat. *versio,* act of turning < Lat. *vertere,* to turn.] **—ver′sion·al** *adj.*

vers li·bre (vĕr lē′brə) *n.* Free verse. [Fr.]

ver·so (vûr′sō) *n., pl.* **-sos.** **1.** *Printing.* The left-hand page of a book or the reverse side of a leaf as opposed to the recto. **2.** The back of a coin or medal. [NLat. *verso (folio),* (with the page) turned.]

verst (vûrst) *n.* A Russian measure of linear distance equivalent to about two thirds of a mile. [Fr. *verste* < R. *versta.*]

ver·sus (vûr′səs) *prep.* **1.** Against: *the plaintiff versus the defendant.* **2.** As an alternative to or in contrast with: *death versus dishonor.* [Med. Lat. < Lat., toward < p.part. of *vertere,* to turn.]

vert (vûrt) *n.* **1. a.** In English forest law, a green vegetation that can serve as cover for deer. **b.** The right to cut such vegetation. **2.** The color green, esp. in heraldry. [ME *verte* < AN < OFr. *vert, verd,* green. —see VERDANT.]

ver·te·bra (vûr′tə-brə) *n., pl.* **-brae** (-brē) or **-bras.** Any of the bones or cartilaginous segments forming the spinal column. [Lat. < *vertere,* to turn.]

ver·te·bral (vûr′tə-brəl, vər-tē′brəl) *adj.* **1.** Of, relating to, or of the nature of a vertebra. **2.** Having or consisting of vertebrae. **—ver′te·bral·ly** *adv.*

vertebral canal *n.* The spinal canal.

vertebral column *n.* The spinal column.

ver·te·brate (vûr′tə-brĭt, -brāt′) *adj.* **1.** Having a backbone or spinal column. **2.** Of or characteristic of a vertebrate or vertebrates. *—n.* A member of the subphylum Vertebrata, a primary division of the phylum Chordata that includes the fishes, amphibians, reptiles, birds, and mammals, all of which are characterized by a segmented bony or cartilaginous spinal column. [Lat. *vertebratus* < *vertebra,* vertebra.]

ver·tex (vûr′tĕks′) *n., pl.* **-tex·es** or **-ti·ces** (-tĭ-sēz′). **1.** The highest point of something; apex. **2.** *Anat.* **a.** The highest point of the skull. **b.** The top of the head. **3.** *Astron.* The highest point reached in the apparent motion of a celestial body. **4. a.** The point at which the sides of an angle intersect. **b.** The point on a triangle opposite to and farthest away from its base. **c.** A point on a polyhedron common to three or more sides. **d.** The fixed point that is one of the three generating characteristics of a conic section. [Lat. < *vertere,* to turn.]

ver·ti·cal (vûr′tĭ-kəl) *adj.* **1.** At right angles to the horizon; extending perpendicularly from a plane; upright. **2.** Pertaining to or situated at the vertex or highest point; directly overhead. **3.** *Anat.* Of or pertaining to the vertex of the head. **4.** *Econ.* Pertaining to, composed of, or controlling all the grades or levels in the manufacture and sale of a product. *—n.* **1.** A vertical line, plane, or circle. **2.** A vertical position. [Fr. or LLat. *verticalis,* both < Lat. *vertex,* highest point.] **—ver′ti·cal′i·ty** (-kăl′ĭ-tē), **ver′ti·cal·ness** *n.* **—ver′ti·cal·ly** *adv.*

Synonyms: *vertical, upright, perpendicular, plumb.* These adjectives are compared as they mean at right angles, or approximately so, to the plane of the horizon or to the plane of a supporting surface. *Vertical* and especially *upright* are often used to signify contradistinction to what is horizontal or situated crosswise. In such a general sense they do not always imply a strict right angle but an approximation instead. *Perpendicular* and *plumb* are generally used with precision and thus specify an angle of 90 degrees.

vertical circle *n.* A great circle on the celestial sphere that passes through the zenith and the nadir and thus is perpendicular to the horizon.

vertical file *n.* A collection of articles such as pamphlets, sheets of paper, and mounted photographs that have been collected and arranged for ready reference, as in a library.

vertical union *n.* A labor union in which workers are organized according to the industry for which they work instead of by their particular skill or craft.

ver·ti·ces (vûr′tĭ-sēz′) *n.* A plural of **vertex.**

ver·ti·cil (vûr′tĭ-sĭl′) *n.* A circular arrangement, as of flowers or leaves, about a point on an axis; whorl. [Lat. *verticillus,* the whorl of a spindle, dim. of *vertex,* highest point.]

ver·ti·cil·las·ter (vûr′tĭ-sə-lăs′tər) *n.* An inflorescence resembling a whorl but actually arising in the axils of opposite leaves. [NLat. < Lat. *verticillus.* —see VERTICIL.] **—ver′ti·cil·las′trate′** (-trāt′) *adj.*

ver·ti·cil·late (vûr′tĭ-sĭl′ĭt, -āt′) also **ver·ti·cil·lat·ed** (-sĭl′ā′tĭd) *adj.* Arranged in or forming a whorl or whorls. **—ver′ti·cil′late·ly** *adv.* **—ver′ti·cil·la′tion** *n.*

ver·tig·i·nous (vər-tĭj′ə-nəs) *adj.* **1.** Turning about an axis; revolving. **2.** Affected by vertigo; dizzy. **3.** Tending to produce vertigo: *vertiginous speed.* **4.** Liable to quick change; unstable. [Lat. *vertiginosus* < *vertigo,* a whirling < *vertere,* to turn.] **—ver·tig′i·nous·ly** *adv.* **—ver·tig′i·nous·ness** *n.*

ver·ti·go (vûr′tĭ-gō′) *n., pl.* **-goes** or **-gos.** **1.** The sensation of dizziness and the feeling that oneself or one's environment is whirling about. **2.** A confused, disoriented state of mind. [Lat. < *vertere,* to turn.]

ver·tu (vər-to͞o′) *n.* Variant of **virtu.**

ver·vain (vûr′vān′) *n.* Any of several plants of the genus *Verbena,* having slender spikes of small blue, purplish, or white flowers. [ME *verveine* < OFr. < Lat. *verbena.* —see VERBENA.]

verve (vûrv) *n.* **1.** Energy and enthusiasm in the expression of ideas and esp. in artistic performance or composition: *The play lacks verve.* **2.** Vitality; liveliness. **3.** *Archaic.* Aptitude; talent. [Fr. < OFr., fanciful expression < Lat. *verba,* pl. of *verbum,* word.]

ver·vet (vûr′vĭt) *n.* A small, long-tailed African monkey, *Cercopithecus pygerythrus,* having a yellowish-brown or greenish coat. [Fr.]

ver·y (vĕr′ē) *adv.* **1.** In a high degree; extremely: *very happy.*

2. Truly; absolutely: *the very best money can buy.* **3.** Precisely: *the very same one.* —*adj.* **-i·er, -i·est. 1.** Complete; absolute: *at the very end of his career.* **2.** Identical; selfsame: *the very questions she asked me yesterday.* **3.** Used as an intensive to emphasize the importance of the thing described: *The very mountains shook.* **4. a.** Being particularly suitable or appropriate: *the very item needed to increase sales.* **b.** Being precisely as stated: *the very center of town.* **5.** Mere: *The very mention of the name was frightening.* **6.** Actual: *caught in the very act.* **7.** *Archaic.* Genuine; real: *"Like very sanctity she did approach"* (Shakespeare). [ME *verray* < OFr. *verai,* true < Lat. *verus.*]

Usage: There is often uncertainty whether to write, for instance, *very encouraged* or *very much encouraged.* The reason for uncertainty is that a word such as *encouraged* can function either as a past participle or as an adjective. When a word is fully accepted as an adjective, *very* is used alone: *very tired; very pleased; very interested.* When a term functions as a past participle, the appropriate modifiers are *much, very much, greatly,* and the like: *has been much praised by the critics; was greatly enlightened by your explanation.* There are many borderline cases, however, where either form may be used: *very* (or *very much*) *distressed; very* (or *much*) *mistaken; very* (or *greatly*) *concerned.*

very high frequency *n.* A band of radio frequencies falling between 30 and 300 megahertz.

very low frequency *n.* A band of radio frequencies falling between 3 and 30 kilohertz.

Ver·y pistol (vĕr′ē, vîr′ē) *n.* A pistol used for firing colored signal flares. [After Edward W. *Very* (d. 1910), its inventor.]

ve·si·ca (və-sī′kə, -sē′-) *n., pl.* **-cae** (-kē, -sē). A bladder, esp. the urinary bladder or the gallbladder. [Lat.] —**ves′i·cal** (vĕs′ĭ-kəl) *adj.*

ves·i·cant (vĕs′ĭ-kənt) *n.* A blistering agent, esp. an agent, as mustard gas, used in chemical warfare. —*adj.* Causing blisters.

ves·i·cate (vĕs′ĭ-kāt′) *tr. & intr.v.* **-cat·ed, -cat·ing, -cates.** To blister or become blistered. [LLat. *vesicare, vesicat-* < Lat. *vesica,* bladder.] —**ves′i·ca′tion** *n.*

ves·i·ca·to·ry (vĕs′ĭ-kə-tôr′ē, -tōr′ē) *adj.* Vesicant. —*n., pl.* **-ries.** A vesicant.

ves·i·cle (vĕs′ĭ-kəl) *n.* **1.** A small bladderlike cell or cavity. **2.** *Anat.* A small bladder or sac, esp. one containing fluid. **3.** *Pathol.* A serum-filled blister formed in or beneath the skin. **4.** *Geol.* A small air pocket or cavity formed in volcanic rock during solidification. [Fr. *vésicule* < Lat. *vesicula,* dim. of *vesica,* bladder.]

ve·sic·u·lar (vĕ-sĭk′yə-lər, və-) *adj.* **1.** Of or pertaining to vesicles. **2.** Composed of or containing vesicles. **3.** Having the form of a vesicle. —**ve·sic′u·lar·ly** *adv.*

ve·sic·u·late (vĕ-sĭk′yə-lāt′, və-) *tr. & intr.v.* **-lat·ed, -lat·ing, -lates.** To make or become vesicular. —*adj.* (-lĭt, -lāt′). Full of or bearing vesicles; vesicular. —**ve·sic′u·la′tion** *n.*

ves·per (vĕs′pər) *n.* **1.** A bell used to summon persons to vespers. **2. Vesper.** The evening star. **3.** *Archaic.* Evening. [Lat., evening star, evening.]

ves·per·al (vĕs′pər-əl) *n.* **1.** A book containing the words and hymns to be used at vespers. **2.** A covering used to protect an altar cloth between services. —*adj.* Of or pertaining to vesper or vespers.

ves·pers also **Ves·pers** (vĕs′pərz) *pl.n.* **1. a.** The sixth of the seven canonical hours. **b.** The time of day set aside for this prayer, in the late afternoon or evening. **2.** A worship service held in the late afternoon or evening. **3.** Evening Prayer. **4.** *Rom. Cath. Ch.* A service held on Sundays or holy days that includes the office of vespers. [OFr. *vespres* < Lat. *vesperas,* acc. pl. of *vespera,* evening < *vesper.*]

vesper sparrow *n.* A North American sparrow, *Pooecetes gramineus,* having white markings on its outer tail feathers. [From its singing in the evening.]

ves·per·til·i·o·nid (vĕs′pər-tĭl′ē-ə-nĭd) *n.* Any of various widely distributed insectivorous bats of the family Vespertilionidae, characterized by a long tail. [< NLat. *Vespertilionidae,* family name < *Vespertilio,* bat genus < Lat. *vespertilio,* bat < *vesper,* evening.]

ves·per·tine (vĕs′pər-tīn′) also **ves·per·ti·nal** (vĕs′pər-tī′nəl) *adj.* **1.** Pertaining to or appearing in the evening. **2.** *Bot.* Opening or blooming in the evening. **3.** *Zool.* Becoming active in the evening; crepuscular. [Lat. *vespertinus* < *vesper,* evening.]

ves·pi·ar·y (vĕs′pē-ĕr′ē) *n., pl.* **-ies.** A nest or colony of wasps or hornets. [Lat. *vespa,* wasp + (AP)IARY.]

ves·pid (vĕs′pĭd) *n.* Any of various insects of the family Vespidae, which includes certain wasps, hornets, and yellow jackets. —*adj.* Of or belonging to the Vespidae. [NLat. *Vespidae,* family name < Lat. *vespa,* wasp.]

ves·pine (vĕs′pīn′) *adj.* Of, pertaining to, or resembling a wasp. [< Lat. *vespa,* wasp.]

ves·sel (vĕs′əl) *n.* **1. a.** A hollow utensil used as a container, esp. for liquids. **b.** A person considered as a receptacle or agent of some quality: *a vessel of mercy.* **2.** A craft, esp. one larger than a rowboat, designed to navigate on water. **3.** An airship. **4.** *Anat.* A duct, canal, or other tube for containing or circulating a bodily fluid: *a blood vessel.* **5.** *Bot.* One of the tubular conductive structures of woody tissue, consisting of cylindrical, often dead cells that are attached end to end. [ME < OFr. *vaissel* < LLat. *vascellum,* dim. of *vas,* vessel.]

vest (vĕst) *n.* **1.** A short sleeveless collarless garment, either open or fastening in front, worn over a shirt or blouse and often under a suit coat or jacket. **2.** A fabric trimming or decoration worn by women to fill in the neckline of a garment such as a coat. **3.** *Chiefly Brit.* An undershirt. **4.** *Archaic.* Clothing; raiment. **5.** *Obs.* An ecclesiastical vestment. —*v.* **vest·ed, vest·ing, vests.** —*tr.* **1.** To clothe or dress with or as if with ecclesiastical vestments. **2.** To place (ownership, for example) in the possession of: *He vested his entire estate in his daughter.* **3.** To place (authority, for example) in the control of: *vesting the President with enormous power.* —*intr.* **1.** To dress oneself, esp. in ecclesiastical vestments. **2.** To be or become legally vested. [Fr. *veste* < Ital. < Lat. *vestis,* garment.]

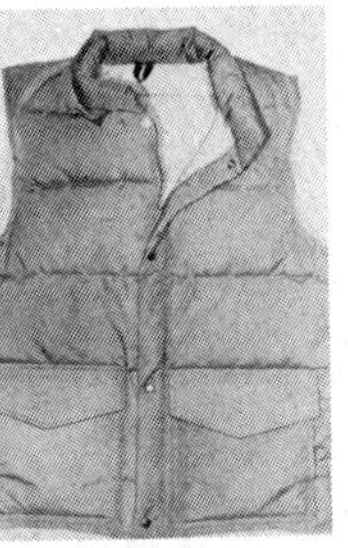

vest

Ves·ta (vĕs′tə) *n.* **1.** *Rom. Myth.* The goddess of the hearth, identified with the Greek goddess Hestia and worshiped in a temple containing the sacred fire tended by the vestal virgins. **2.** The third-largest asteroid in the solar system, having a diameter of approximately 386 kilometers, or 240 miles. **3. vesta.** A short friction match made of wax or wood. [Lat.]

ves·tal (vĕs′təl) *adj.* **1.** Pertaining to or sacred to Vesta. **2.** Pertaining to or characteristic of the vestal virgins. **3.** Chaste; pure. —*n.* **1.** A vestal virgin. **2.** A woman who is a virgin. **3.** A nun.

vestal virgin *n.* One of the six virgin priestesses who tended the sacred fire in the temple of Vesta in ancient Rome.

vest·ed (vĕs′tĭd) *adj.* **1.** *Law.* Settled, complete, or absolute; without contingency. **2.** Dressed or clothed, esp. in ecclesiastical vestments.

vested interest *n.* **1.** *Law.* A right or title that can be conveyed to another. **2.** A strong concern for something, such as an institution, from which one expects private benefit. **3.** A group that has a vested interest.

vest·ee (vĕ-stē′) *n.* A decorative garment worn by women to cover the bosom. [< VEST.]

ves·ti·ar·y (vĕs′tē-ĕr′ē, -chē-) *adj.* Of or pertaining to clothes. —*n., pl.* **-ies.** A dressing room, cloakroom, or vestry. [< ME *vestiarie,* vestry < OFr. < Med. Lat. *vestiarium* < Lat., wardrobe < *vestiarius,* of clothes < *vestis,* garment.]

ves·tib·u·lar (vĕ-stĭb′yə-lər) *adj.* Of, pertaining to, or serving as a vestibule.

vestibular nerve *n.* A division of the acoustic nerve.

ves·ti·bule (vĕs′tə-byo͞ol′) *n.* **1.** A small entrance hall or lobby. **2.** An enclosed area at the end of a passenger car on a railroad train. **3.** *Anat.* A cavity, chamber, or channel that serves as an approach or entrance to another cavity. —*tr.v.* **-buled, -bul·ing, -bules.** To furnish with a vestibule. [Fr. < Lat. *vestibulum.*]

ves·tige (vĕs′tĭj) *n.* **1.** A visible trace, evidence, or sign of something that has once existed but exists or appears no more. **2.** *Biol.* A small, degenerate, or rudimentary organ or part existing in an organism as a usually nonfunctioning remnant of an organ or part fully developed and functional in a preceding generation or earlier developmental stage. [Fr. < Lat. *vestigium,* footprint.]

ves·tig·i·al (vĕ-stĭj′ē-əl, -stĭj′əl) *adj.* **1.** Of, pertaining to, or constituting a vestige. **2.** *Biol.* Occurring or persisting as a rudimentary or degenerate structure. —**ves·tig′i·al·ly** *adv.*

vestigial sideband *n.* The reduction in bandwidth of a transmitted signal occurring when frequencies to either side of the signal frequency are filtered out.

vest·ment (vĕst′mənt) *n.* **1.** A garment, esp. a robe or gown worn as an indication of office or state. **2.** *Eccles.* Any of the ritual robes worn by members of the clergy, altar boys, or other assistants at services or rites, esp. a garment worn at the celebration of the Eucharist. [ME *vestiment* < OFr. < Lat. *vestimentum* < *vestire,* to clothe < *vestis,* garment.] —**vest·ment′al** (-mĕn′tl) *adj.*

vest-pock·et (vĕst′pŏk′ĭt) *adj.* **1.** Designed to fit into a vest pocket: *a vest-pocket book.* **2.** Relatively small; diminutive.

ves·try (vĕs′trē) *n., pl.* **-tries. 1.** A room in a church where the clergy put on their vestments and where these robes and other sacred objects are stored; sacristy. **2.** A meeting room in a church. **3. a.** In the Anglican and Episcopal churches, a committee of members of the parish or congregation that administers the affairs of the parish or congregation. **b.** A meeting of this group or of the entire congregation. **c.** The place in which such a meeting is held. [ME *vestrie,* var. of *vestiarie,* vestiary.]

ves·try·man (vĕs′trē-mən) *n.* A member of a vestry.

ves·ture (vĕs′chər) *n.* **1.** Clothing; apparel. **2.** Something that covers or cloaks: *hills in a vesture of mist.* —*tr.v.* **-tured, -tur·ing, -tures.** To cover with vesture; clothe. [ME, clothes < OFr. < *vestir* < Lat. *vestire,* to clothe < *vestis,* garment.]

ve·su·vi·an (və-so͞o′vē-ən) *n.* **1.** Idocrase. **2.** A match used esp. for lighting cigars; fusee. —*adj.* Marked by or given to sudden, often violent flare-ups or outbursts. [< *Vesuvius,* a volcano in southwestern Italy.]

ve·su·vi·an·ite (və-so͞o′vē-ə-nīt′) *n.* Idocrase.

vet (vĕt) *Informal.* —*n.* **1.** A veterinarian. **2.** A veteran. —*v.* **vet·ted, vet·ting, vets.** —*tr.* **1.** To practice veterinary medicine upon. **2.** To examine or appraise expertly: *vet a manuscript.* —*intr.* To be or become a veterinarian.

vetch

viaduct
Part of a 1st-century B.C. Roman aqueduct in Nîmes, France

vibraphone

viburnum

vetch (vĕch) *n.* Any of various climbing or twining plants of the genus *Vicia,* having pinnate leaves and small, usually purplish flowers. [ME *fecche* < OFr. *veche* < Lat. *vicia.*]

vetch·ling (vĕch′lĭng) *n.* Any of several plants of the genus *Lathyrus,* having pinnate leaves, slender tendrils, and small, variously colored flowers.

vet·er·an (vĕt′ər-ən, vĕt′rən) *n.* **1.** One who has a long record of service in a given activity or capacity. **2.** One who has been a member of the armed forces. ***—modifier:*** *a veteran actor; veteran benefits.* [Fr. *vétéran* < Lat. *veteranus* < *vetus,* old.]

Veterans Day *n.* November 11, a holiday celebrated in memory of the armistice ending World War I in 1918 and in honor of veterans of the armed services.

vet·er·i·nar·i·an (vĕt′ər-ə-nâr′ē-ən, vĕt′rə-) *n.* A person trained and authorized to treat animals medically.

vet·er·i·nar·y (vĕt′ər-ə-nĕr′ē, vĕt′rə-) *adj.* Of, pertaining to, or being the science of the diagnosis and treatment of diseases and injuries of animals, esp. domestic animals. *—n., pl.* **-ies.** A veterinarian. [Lat. *veterinarius,* pertaining to beasts of burden < *veterinus* < *veterinae,* beasts of burden.]

veterinary medicine *n.* The medical science of the diagnosis and treatment of animal diseases and injuries.

veterinary surgeon *n.* A veterinarian.

vet·i·ver (vĕt′ə-vər) *n.* **1.** A grass, *Vetiveria zizanioides,* of tropical Asia, cultivated for its aromatic roots that yield an oil used in perfumery. **2.** The roots of the vetiver. [Fr. < Tamil *veṭṭivēru.*]

vet·i·vert (vĕt′ə-vûrt′) *n.* The essential oil of the vetiver. [Alteration of VETIVER.]

ve·to (vē′tō) *n., pl.* **-toes. 1. a.** The vested power or constitutional right of one branch or department of government, esp. the right of a chief executive, to reject a bill passed by a legislative body and thus prevent or delay its enactment into law. **b.** The exercise of this right. **c.** The official document communicating the rejection and the reasons for it. **2.** An authoritative prohibition or rejection of a proposed or intended act. *—tr.v.* **-toed, -to·ing, -toes. 1.** To prevent (a legislative bill) from becoming law by exercising the power of veto. **2.** To forbid or prevent authoritatively; prohibit. [Lat., I forbid.] **—ve′to·er** *n.*

vex (vĕks) *tr.v.* **vexed, vex·ing, vex·es. 1. a.** To irritate or annoy; bother: *vexed by his daughter's constant talking.* **b.** To bring physical discomfort to: *His sprained ankle vexed him all night.* **2.** To baffle; puzzle. **3.** To talk about or debate at length: *a vexed question.* **4.** To toss about or shake up. [ME *vexen* < OFr. *vexer* < Lat. *vexare.*] **—vex′ed·ly** (vĕk′sĭd-lē) *adv.* **—vex′er** *n.* **—vex′ing·ly** *adv.*

vex·a·tion (vĕk-sā′shən) *n.* **1.** The act of vexing. **2.** The state or condition of being vexed; annoyance. **3.** A source of irritation or annoyance.

vex·a·tious (vĕk-sā′shəs) *adj.* **1.** Causing or creating vexation; annoying. **2.** Full of vexation; annoyed. **3.** Intended to vex or annoy. **—vex·a′tious·ly** *adv.* **—vex·a′tious·ness** *n.*

vex·il·la (vĕk-sĭl′ə) *n.* Plural of **vexillum.**

vex·il·lar·y (vĕk′sə-lĕr′ē) *n., pl.* **-ies. 1.** A member of the oldest class of army veterans who served under a special standard in ancient Rome. **2.** A standard-bearer. [Lat. *vexillarius* < *vexillum,* flag, dim. of *velum,* a covering.]

vex·il·late (vĕk′sə-lĭt, -lāt′) *adj.* Having a vexillum.

vex·il·lum (vĕk-sĭl′əm) *n., pl.* **-il·la** (-sĭl′ə). **1.** *Bot.* A usually enlarged upper petal of certain flowers; standard. **2.** *Zool.* The weblike part of a feather; vane. [Lat., flag, dim. of *velum,* a covering.]

V format *n. Computer Sci.* A method of presenting data-processor output in such a way as to begin each record with an indication of its length.

vi·a (vī′ə, vē′ə) *prep.* **1.** By way of: *went to Pittsburgh via Philadelphia.* **2.** By means of: *sent the letter via airmail.* [Lat., ablative of *via,* road.]

vi·a·ble (vī′ə-bəl) *adj.* **1.** Capable of living, as a newborn infant or fetus reaching a stage of development that will permit it to survive and develop under normal conditions. **2.** Capable of living, developing, or germinating under favorable conditions. **3.** Capable of success or continuing effectiveness; practicable: *a viable national economy.* [Fr. < OFr. < *vie,* life < Lat. *vita.*] **—vi′a·bil′i·ty** *n.* **—vi′a·bly** *adv.*

Vi·a Do·lo·ro·sa (vī′ə dō′lə-rō′sə, vē′ə) *n.* **1.** Jesus' route from Pilate's judgment hall to Golgotha. **2.** A difficult course or experience. [Lat., road of sorrow.]

vi·a·duct (vī′ə-dŭkt′) *n.* A series of spans or arches used to carry a road or railroad over a wide valley or over other roads or railroads. [Lat. *via,* road + (AQUA)DUCT.]

vi·al (vī′əl) *n.* A small container, usually with a closure, used esp. for liquids. *—tr.v.* **-aled, -al·ing, -als** or **-alled, -al·ling, -als.** To put or keep in or as if in a vial. [ME *viole,* var. of *fiol.* —see PHIAL.]

vi·a me·di·a (vī′ə mē′dē-ə, mĕd′ē-ə, mā′dē-ə, vē′ə) *n.* A middle course or way. [Lat.]

vi·and (vī′ənd) *n.* **1. a.** An article of food. **b.** A very choice or delicious dish. **2. viands.** Provisions; victuals. [ME *viaunde* < OFr. *viande* < VLat. **vivanda,* var. of Lat. *vivenda,* neuter pl. gerund. of *vivere,* to live.]

vi·at·ic (vī-ăt′ĭk) also **vi·at·i·cal** (-ĭ-kəl) *adj.* Of or pertaining to traveling, a road, or a way. [Lat. *viaticus* < *via,* road.]

vi·at·i·cum (vī-ăt′ĭ-kəm, vē-) *n., pl.* **-ca** (-kə) or **-cums. 1.** *Eccles.* The Eucharist given to a dying person or one in danger of death. **2.** Supplies for a journey. [Lat., traveling provisions < *viaticus,* viatic.]

vibes (vībz) *pl.n.* **1.** *Informal.* A vibraphone. **2.** *Slang.* A distinctive emotional reaction; vibrations. [Shortened var. of VIBRAPHONE.]

vi·brac·u·lum (vī-brăk′yə-ləm) *n., pl.* **-la** (-lə). One of the long, whiplike filaments on the surface of certain bryozoan colonies. [NLat. < Lat. *vibrare,* to shake.] **—vi·brac′u·lar** *adj.* **—vi·brac′u·loid′** *adj.*

vi·bra·harp (vī′brə-härp′) *n.* A vibraphone.

vi·brant (vī′brənt) *adj.* **1.** Exhibiting, characterized by, or resulting from vibration; vibrating. **2.** Pulsing or throbbing with energy or activity: *a vibrant personality.* **—vi′bran·cy** *n.* **—vi′brant·ly** *adv.*

vi·bra·phone (vī′brə-fōn′) *n.* A musical instrument similar to a marimba but having metal bars and rotating disks in the resonators to produce a vibrato. [VIBRA(TE) + -PHONE.] **—vi′bra·phon′ist** *n.*

vi·brate (vī′brāt′) *v.* **-brat·ed, -brat·ing, -brates.** *—intr.* **1.** To move back and forth rapidly. **2.** To produce a sound; resonate. **3.** To be moved emotionally; thrill: *vibrate with excitement.* **4.** To fluctuate or waver in making choices; vacillate. *—tr.* **1.** To cause to tremble or quiver. **2.** To cause to move back and forth rapidly. **3.** To produce (sound) by vibration. [Lat. *vibrare, vibrat-.*]

vi·bra·tile (vī′brə-tl, -tīl′) *adj.* **1.** Characterized by vibration. **2.** Capable of or adapted to vibratory motion. [Fr. < Lat. *vibrare,* to vibrate.] **—vi′bra·til′i·ty** (-tĭl′ĭ-tē) *n.*

vi·bra·tion (vī-brā′shən) *n.* **1.** The act of vibrating. **2.** The condition of being vibrated. **3.** *Physics.* **a.** A rapid linear motion of a particle or of an elastic solid about an equilibrium position. **b.** A periodic process. **4.** A single complete vibrating motion; quiver. **5. vibrations.** *Slang.* A distinctive emotional aura or atmosphere capable of being instinctively sensed or experienced; vibes. **—vi·bra′tion·al** *adj.*

vi·bra·tive (vī′brə-tĭv) *adj.* Vibratory.

vi·bra·to (və-brä′tō, vē-) *n., pl.* **-tos.** *Mus.* A tremulous or pulsating effect produced in an instrumental or vocal tone by barely perceptible minute and rapid variations in pitch. [Ital. < Lat. *vibratus,* p.part. of *vibrare,* to vibrate.]

vi·bra·tor (vī′brā′tər) *n.* **1.** Something that vibrates. **2.** An electrically operated device used for massage. **3.** An electrical device consisting basically of a vibrating conductor interrupting a current.

vi·bra·to·ry (vī′brə-tôr′ē, -tōr′ē) *adj.* **1.** Of, characterized by, or consisting of vibration. **2.** Causing vibration. **3.** Vibrating or capable of vibration.

vib·ri·o (vĭb′rē-ō′) *n., pl.* **-os.** Any of various S-shaped or comma-shaped microorganisms of the genus *Vibrio,* esp. *V. comma,* which causes cholera. [NLat. *Vibrio,* genus name < *vibrare,* to vibrate (from their vibratory motion).] **—vib′ri·oid′** (-oid′) *adj.*

vib·ri·o·sis (vĭb′rē-ō′sĭs) *n., pl.* **-ses** (-sēz′) A disease caused by vibrios.

vi·bris·sa (vī-brĭs′ə, və-) *n., pl.* **-bris·sae** (-brĭs′ē). A stiff hair or hairlike projection, as a nostril hair, one of the whiskers of a cat, or one of the modified feathers near the beak of an insectivorous bird. [Lat. *vibrissae* (pl.) < *vibrare,* to vibrate.]

vi·bron·ic (vī-brŏn′ĭk) *adj.* Of or pertaining to changes in molecular energy states resulting from vibrational energy. [VIBR(ATION) + (ELECTR)ONIC.]

vi·bur·num (vī-bûr′nəm) *n.* Any of various shrubs or trees of the genus *Viburnum,* characteristically having clusters of small white flowers and berrylike red or black fruit. [NLat. *Viburnum,* genus name < Lat. *viburnum,* the wayfaring tree.]

vic·ar (vĭk′ər) *n.* **1.** In the Church of England, the priest of a parish who receives a stipend or salary but does not receive the tithes of a parish. **2.** In the Episcopal Church of the United States, a clergyman in charge of a chapel. **3.** In the Anglican Communion generally, a clergyman acting in the place of a rector or bishop. **4.** *Rom. Cath. Ch.* A clergyman who acts for or represents another, often higher-ranking member of the clergy. [ME < OFr. *vicaire* < Lat. *vicarius,* a substitute < *vicarius,* vicarious < *vicis,* change.]

vic·ar·age (vĭk′ər-ĭj) *n.* **1.** The residence of a vicar. **2.** The benefice of a vicar. **3.** The duties or office of a vicar.

vicar apostolic *n., pl.* **vicars apostolic.** *Rom. Cath. Ch.* **1.** A titular bishop who administers a region that is not yet a diocese as a representative of the Holy See. **2.** A titular bishop appointed to administer to a vacant see in which the succession of bishops has been interrupted. **3.** A bishop or archbishop formerly delegated by the pope to act in his stead in a particular region.

vic·ar·ate (vĭk′ər-ĭt, -ə-rāt′) *n.* A vicariate.

vicar fo·rane (fô-rān′, fō-) *n., pl.* **vicars forane.** *Rom. Cath. Ch.* A priest who by a bishop's appointment exercises limited jurisdiction over the clergy in a district of a diocese. [Med. Lat. *foranus,* foreign < Lat. *foras,* outside.]

vicar general *n., pl.* **vicars general. 1.** *Rom. Cath. Ch.* **a.** A priest acting as deputy to a bishop to assist him in the administration of his diocese. **b.** The head of a religious order. **2.** An ecclesiastical official in the Church of England, usually a layman, who assists an archbishop or bishop in administrative and judicial duties.

vi·car·i·al (vī-kâr′ē-əl, -kăr′-, vĭ-) *adj.* **1.** Of or relating to a vicar. **2.** Acting as or having the position of a vicar. **3.** Serving in the place of someone or something else.

vi·car·i·ate (vī-kâr′ē-ĭt, -āt′, -kăr′-, vĭ-) *n.* **1.** The office or authority of a vicar. **2.** The district under a vicar's jurisdiction. [Med. Lat. *vicariatus* < Lat. *vicarius,* a substitute. —see VICAR.]

vi·car·i·ous (vī-kâr′ē-əs, -kăr′-, vĭ-) *adj.* **1.** Endured or done by one person substituting for another: *vicarious punishment.* **2.** Acting in place of someone or something else. **3.** Felt or undergone as if one were taking part in the experience or feelings of another: *read about mountain climbing and experienced vicarious thrills.* **4.** *Physiol.* Occurring in or performed by a part of the body not normally associated with a certain function. [Lat. *vicarius.* —see VICAR.] **—vi·car′i·ous·ly** *adv.* **—vi·car′i·ous·ness** *n.*

Vicar of Christ *n. Rom. Cath. Ch.* The pope.

vic·ar·ship (vĭk′ər-shĭp′) *n.* The office or tenure of a vicar.

vice¹ (vīs) *n.* **1. a.** An evil, degrading, or immoral practice or habit. **b.** A serious moral failing. **2.** Wicked or evil conduct or habits; corruption. **3.** Sexual immorality, esp. prostitution. **4.** A slight personal failing; foible: *the vice of untidiness.* **5.** A flaw or imperfection; defect. **6.** A physical defect or weakness. **7.** Abnormal behavior in a domestic animal. **8. Vice. a.** A character representing generalized or particular vice in English morality plays. **b.** A jester; buffoon. [ME < OFr. < Lat. *vitium.*]

vice² (vīs) *n. & v.* Variant of **vise.**

vice³ (vīs) *n.* One who acts in the place of another; deputy: *the vice-chairman.* —*prep.* **vi·ce** (vī′sē). In place of; replacing. [< Lat. *vice,* ablative of *vicis,* change.]

vice admiral *n.* An officer in the Navy or Coast Guard ranking next below an admiral.

vice-ad·mir·al·ty (vīs-ăd′mər-əl-tē) *n., pl.* **-ties.** The office, rank, or command of a vice admiral.

vice chancellor *n.* **1.** *Law.* A judge in equity courts ranking below a chancellor. **2.** A deputy or assistant chancellor in a university. **3.** A deputy or substitute for a head of state or official bearing the title chancellor. **—vice-chan′cel·lor·ship′** (vīs-chăn′sə-lər-shĭp′, -chăns′lər-) *n.*

vice consul *n.* A consular officer who is subordinate to and a deputy of a consul or consul general. **—vice-con′su·lar** (vīs-kŏn′sə-lər) *adj.* **—vice-con′su·late** (-sə-lĭt) *n.* **—vice-con′sul·ship′** (-səl-shĭp′) *n.*

vice·ge·ren·cy (vīs-jîr′ən-sē) *n., pl.* **-cies. 1.** The position, function, or authority of a vicegerent. **2.** A district under a vicegerent's jurisdiction.

vice·ge·rent (vīs-jîr′ənt) *n.* A person appointed by a ruler or head of state to act as an administrative deputy. [Med. Lat. *vicegerens* : Lat. *vice,* ablative of *vicis,* change + Lat. *gerens,* governing. —see GERENT.] **—vice·ge′ral** (vīs-jîr′əl) *adj.*

vic·e·nar·y (vĭs′ə-nĕr′ē) *adj.* **1.** Consisting of or pertaining to 20. **2.** Designating a notation system based on 20. [Lat. *vicenarius* < *viceni,* twenty each < *viginti,* twenty.]

vi·cen·ni·al (vī-sĕn′ē-əl) *adj.* **1.** Happening once every 20 years. **2.** Existing or lasting for 20 years. [< LLat. *vicennium,* period of twenty years : Lat. *viciens,* twenty times + Lat. *annus,* year.]

vice president *n.* **1.** An officer ranking next below a president, usually empowered to assume the president's duties under such conditions as absence, illness, or death. **2.** A deputy of a president, esp. in a corporation, in charge of a separate department or location: *vice president of sales.* **—vice-pres′i·den·cy** (vīs-prĕz′ĭ-dən-sē, -dĕn′-) *n.* **—vice-pres′i·den′tial** (-dĕn′shəl) *adj.*

vice·re·gal (vīs-rē′gəl) *adj.* Of or pertaining to a viceroy. **—vice·re′gal·ly** *adv.*

vice regent *n.* One who acts as a regent's deputy. **—vice-re′gen·cy** (vīs-rē′jən-sē) *n.*

vice·reine (vīs′rān′) *n.* **1.** The wife of a viceroy. **2.** A woman who functions as a viceroy. [Fr. : *vice-,* vice + *reine,* queen < Lat. *regina,* fem. of *rex,* king.]

vice·roy (vīs′roi′) *n.* **1.** A governor of a country, province, or colony, ruling as the representative of a sovereign. **2.** An orange and black North American butterfly, *Limenitis archippus,* resembling but somewhat smaller than the monarch. [Fr. : *vice,* vice + *roi,* king < Lat. *rex* < *regere,* to rule.]

vice·roy·al·ty (vīs′roi′əl-tē, vīs-roi′-) *n., pl.* **-ties. 1.** The office, authority, or term of service of a viceroy. **2.** A district or province governed by a viceroy.

vice·roy·ship (vīs′roi′shĭp′) *n.* Viceroyalty.

vice squad *n.* A police division charged with the control of vice.

vi·ce ver·sa (vī′sə vûr′sə, vīs′) *adv.* With the order or meaning reversed; conversely. [Lat., the position being reversed.]

vi·chys·soise (vĭsh′ē-swäz′, vē′shē-) *n.* A thick, creamy potato soup flavored with leeks, onions, and chicken stock that is usually served cold. [Fr. < fem. of *vichyssois,* of Vichy, a town in France.]

Vi·chy water (vĭsh′ē, vē′shē) *n.* **1.** A naturally effervescent mineral water from the springs at Vichy, France. **2.** A sparkling mineral water resembling Vichy water.

vic·i·nage (vĭs′ə-nĭj) *n.* **1. a.** A limited region around a particular area; vicinity. **b.** A number of places situated near each other and considered collectively. **2.** The residents of a particular neighborhood. **3.** The state of living in a neighborhood; proximity. [ME *vesinage* < OFr. *visenage* < Lat. *vicinus,* neighboring. —see VICINITY.]

vic·i·nal (vĭs′ə-nəl) *adj.* **1.** Of, belonging to, or restricted to a limited area or neighborhood; local. **2.** Designating a local road as opposed to a highway. **3.** Approximating, resembling, or taking the place of a fundamental crystalline form or face. **4.** *Chem.* Designating the consecutive positions of substituted elements or radicals on a benzene ring. [Lat. *vicinalis* < *vicinus,* neighboring. —see VICINITY.]

vi·cin·i·ty (vĭ-sĭn′ĭ-tē) *n., pl.* **-ties. 1.** The state of being near in space or relationship; proximity: *two restaurants in close vicinity.* **2.** A nearby, surrounding, or adjoining region; neighborhood. **3.** An approximate degree or amount: *houses priced in the vicinity of $200,000.* [Lat. *vicinitas* < *vicinus,* neighboring < *vicus,* village.]

vi·cious (vĭsh′əs) *adj.* **1.** Having the nature of vice, evil, or immorality; depraved. **2.** Addicted to vice, immorality, or depravity; evil. **3.** Characterized by spite or malice: *vicious gossip.* **4.** Failing to meet a standard or criterion; having a fault, flaw, or defect. **5.** Impure; foul. **6.** Characterized by violence or ferocity: *a vicious storm.* **7.** Savagely aggressive; dangerous: *a vicious shark.* [ME < OFr. *vitiosus* < *vitium,* vice.] **—vi′cious·ly** *adv.* **—vi′cious·ness** *n.*

vicious circle *n.* **1.** A situation in which the solution of one problem in a chain of circumstances creates a new problem and increases the difficulty of solving the original problem. **2.** A condition in which a disorder or disease gives rise to another that subsequently affects the first. **3.** *Logic.* A circle (sense 10).

vi·cis·si·tude (vĭ-sĭs′ĭ-to͞od′, -tyo͞od′) *n.* **1.** Often **vicissitudes. a.** A change or variation. **b.** The quality of being changeable; mutability. **2.** One of the sudden or unexpected changes or shifts often encountered in one's life, activities, or surroundings. [OFr. < Lat. *vicissitudo* < *vicissim,* in turn < *vicis,* change.]

vi·cis·si·tu·di·nar·y (vĭ-sĭs′ĭ-to͞od′n-ĕr′ē, -tyo͞od′-) also **vi·cis·si·tu·di·nous** (-to͞od′n-əs, -tyo͞od′-) *adj.* Characterized by, full of, or subject to vicissitudes.

vic·tim (vĭk′tĭm) *n.* **1.** Someone who is harmed or killed by another: *the muggers and their elderly victims.* **2.** A living creature slain and offered as a sacrifice to a deity or as part of a religious rite. **3.** One who is harmed by or made to suffer from an act, circumstance, agency, or condition: *victims of war.* **4.** A person who suffers injury, loss, or death as a result of a voluntary undertaking: *a victim of his own scheming.* **5.** A person who is tricked, swindled, or taken advantage of: *the victim of a cruel hoax.* [Lat. *victima.*]

vic·tim·ize (vĭk′tə-mīz′) *tr.v.* **-ized, -iz·ing, -iz·es. 1.** To subject to swindle or fraud. **2.** To make a victim of. **—vic′tim·i·za′tion** *n.* **—vic′tim·iz′er** *n.*

vic·tim·less (vĭk′tĭm-lĭs) *adj.* Having or involving no victim: *a victimless crime.*

vic·tim·ol·o·gy (vĭk′tə-mŏl′ə-jē) *n.* The study of the roles played by victims in the crimes committed against them. **—vic′tim·ol′o·gist** *n.*

vic·tor (vĭk′tər) *n.* One who defeats or vanquishes an adversary; the winner in a fight, battle, contest, or struggle. [ME < Lat. < *vincere,* to conquer.]

vic·to·ri·a (vĭk-tôr′ē-ə, -tōr′-) *n.* **1.** A low, light four-wheeled carriage for two with a folding top and an elevated driver's seat in front. **2.** A touring car with a folding top usually covering only the rear seat. [After Queen *Victoria* of England (1819-1901).]

Victoria Cross *n.* A bronze Maltese cross, Britain's highest military award for conspicuous valor.

Vic·to·ri·an (vĭk-tôr′ē-ən, -tōr′-) *adj.* **1.** Of, pertaining to, or belonging to the period of the reign of Queen Victoria of England: *a Victorian novel.* **2.** Exhibiting qualities, as moral severity or hypocrisy, middle-class stuffiness, and pompous conservatism, that are usually associated with the time of Queen Victoria. **3.** Being in the highly ornamented, massive style of architecture, decor, and furnishings popular in 19th-century England. —*n.* A person belonging to or exhibiting characteristics typical of the Victorian period.

Vic·to·ri·an·a (vĭk-tôr′ē-ăn′ə, -ä′nə, -tōr′-) *n.* Material or a collection of materials of, relating to, or characteristic of the Victorian era.

Vic·to·ri·an·ism (vĭk-tôr′ē-ə-nĭz′əm, -tōr′-) *n.* **1.** The state or quality of being Victorian, as in attitude, style, or taste. **2.** Something exhibiting Victorian characteristics.

Vic·to·ri·an·ize (vĭk-tôr′ē-ə-nīz′, -tōr′-) *tr.v.* **-ized, -iz·ing, -iz·es.** To make Victorian, as in character or style. **—Vic·to′ri·an·i·za′tion** *n.*

vic·to·ri·ous (vĭk-tôr′ē-əs, -tōr′-) *adj.* **1.** Being the winner in a contest or struggle: *the victorious team.* **2.** Characteristic of or expressing a sense of victory or fulfillment: *a victorious cheer.* [ME < Lat. *victoriosus* < *victoria,* victory.] **—vic·to′ri·ous·ly** *adv.* **—vic·to′ri·ous·ness** *n.*

vic·to·ry (vĭk′tə-rē) *n., pl.* **-ries. 1.** Final and complete defeat of the enemy in a military engagement. **2.** A successful struggle against an opponent or obstacle. **3.** The state of having triumphed. [ME < OFr. *victorie* < Lat. *victoria* < *victor,* victor.]

Synonyms: *victory, conquest, triumph.* These nouns refer to the fact of winning, as in war or in a competition. *Victory,* the general term, is broadly interchangeable with

video terminal
Video display terminal

vignette

Viking
Detail from "The Discovery of America by Leif Ericson" by Clyde O. De Land

the others but lacks their overtones. *Conquest* connotes physically subjugating or harnessing something, such as an enemy nation or a rampaging river, or it can refer to surmounting a physical barrier, as a mountain peak, or overcoming barriers to knowledge, understanding, and control: *the conquest of yellow fewer. Triumph* refers to a victory or success that is especially noteworthy because it is decisive, significant, or spectacular.

vic·tress (vĭk′trĭs) *n.* A woman who is a victor.

vict·ual (vĭt′l) *n.* **1.** Food fit for human consumption. **2. victuals.** Food supplies; provisions. —*v.* **-ualled, -ual·ling, -uals** or **-ualed, -ual·ing, -uals.** —*tr.* To provide with food. —*intr.* **1.** To lay in food supplies. **2.** To eat. [ME *vitaille* < OFr. < LLat. *victualia,* provisions, pl. of *victualis,* of nourishment < *victus,* nourishment < *vivere,* to live.]

vict·ual·er also **vict·ual·ler** (vĭt′l-ər) *n.* **1.** A supplier of victuals; sutler. **2.** A supply ship. **3.** *Chiefly Brit.* An innkeeper.

vi·cu·ña also **vi·cu·na** (vĭ-ko͞on′yə, -ko͞o′nə, -kyo͞o′nə, vī-) *n.* **1.** A llamalike ruminant mammal, *Vicugna vicugna,* of the central Andes, having fine, silky fleece. **2. a.** The fleece of the vicuña. **b.** Fabric made from this fleece. [Sp. < Quechua *wikuña.*]

vi·de (vī′dē, vē′dā′). See. Used to direct a reader's attention: *Vide page 64.* [Lat., imper. of *vidēre,* to see.]

vi·del·i·cet (vĭ-dĕl′ĭ-sĕt′, vī-). That is; namely. Used to introduce examples, lists, or items. [Lat., clearly : *vidēre,* to see + *licet,* it is permitted.]

vid·e·o (vĭd′ē-ō′) *adj.* Of or pertaining to television, esp. to televised images. —*n.* **1.** The visual portion of a televised broadcast as distinguished from audio. **2.** Television: *a star of stage, screen, and video.* [< Lat. *vidēre,* to see.]

vid·e·o·cas·sette (vĭd′ē-ō-kə-sĕt′, -kă-) *n.* A recording on videotape contained in a cassette.

vid·e·o·disc also **vid·e·o·disk** (vĭd′ē-ō-dĭsk′) *n.* A disc recording of sounds and images, as of a motion-picture production, that may be played back on a home television receiver. [Orig. a G. trademark.]

video game *n.* An electronic or computerized game played by manipulating images on a television or other display screen.

vid·e·o·gen·ic (vĭd′ē-ō-jĕn′ĭk) *adj.* Appearing to advantage on television; telegenic. [VIDEO + (PHOTO)GENIC.]

Vid·e·o·phone (vĭd′ē-ō-fōn′). A trademark for a telephone equipped for both audio and video transmission.

Vid·e·o·scan (vĭd′ē-ō-skăn′). A trademark for a method for machine character recognition in which a video camera records the shapes of the characters to be recognized and then matches the shapes to data held in machine storage.

vid·e·o·tape (vĭd′ē-ō-tāp′) *n.* **1.** A relatively wide magnetic tape used to record television images, usually together with the associated sound, for subsequent playback and broadcasting. **2.** A recording made on videotape. —*tr.v.* **-taped, -tap·ing, -tapes.** To make a videotape recording of.

videotape recorder *n.* A device for making a videotape recording.

video terminal *n.* A computer input-output device utilizing a cathode-ray tube to display data on a screen.

vi·dette (vĭ-dĕt′) *n.* Variant of **vedette.**

vid·i·con (vĭd′ĭ-kŏn′) *n.* A small television camera tube that forms a charge-density image on a photoconductive surface for subsequent electron-beam scanning. [VID(EO) + ICON(OSCOPE).]

vie (vī) *v.* **vied, vy·ing, vies.** —*intr.* To strive for victory or superiority; contend: *The contestants vied for first place.* —*tr.* **1.** To offer in competition; match. **2.** To wager; bet. [ME *envien* < OFr., to challenge < Lat. *invitare,* to invite.]

Vi·en·na sausage (vē-ĕn′ə) *n.* A small sausage resembling a frankfurter, often served as an hors d'oeuvre. [After *Vienna,* Austria.]

Viet·cong also **Viet Cong** (vē-ĕt′kŏng′, -kông′, vyĕt-) *n., pl.* **Vietcong** also **Viet Cong.** A Vietnamese belonging to or supporting the National Liberation Front of the former nation of South Vietnam. —*adj.* Of or pertaining to the Vietcong. [Vietnamese, contraction of *Viet Nam Cong Sam,* Vietnamese Communist.]

Viet·minh also **Viet Minh** (vē-ĕt′mĭn′, vyĕt-) *n., pl.* **Vietminh** also **Viet Minh.** A member of the Vietnamese army that defeated the Japanese and the French between 1941 and 1954. —*adj.* Of or pertaining to the Vietminh. [Vietnamese, contraction of *Viet Nam Doc Lap Dong Minh Hoi,* Vietnam Federation of Independence.]

Viet·nam·ese (vē-ĕt′nə-mēz′, -mēs′, vyĕt′-) *n.* **1.** A native or inhabitant of Vietnam. **2.** The language of the largest ethnic group in Vietnam and the official language of the nation. —**Viet′nam·ese′** *adj.*

Viet·nam·ize (vē-ĕt′nə-mīz′, vyĕt′-) *tr.v.* **-ized, -iz·ing, -iz·es.** To turn over responsibility for (military operations, for example) to the Vietnamese: *"A policy of Vietnamizing the actual fighting"* (C.L. Sulzberger). —**Viet′nam·i·za′tion** *n.*

view (vyo͞o) *n.* **1.** An examination or inspection: *used a magnifying glass for a closer view.* **2.** A systematic survey; coverage: *a view of Romantic poetry.* **3.** Often **views.** A specific perception, observation, or interpretation; opinion: *her views on education.* **4.** The field of vision: *The airplane disappeared from view.* **5.** A scene; vista: *the view from the tower.* **6.** A picture of a landscape. **7.** A way of showing or seeing something, as from a particular position or angle: *a side view of the house.* **8.** An aim; intention. **9.** Expectation; chance: *The measure has no view of success.* —*tr.v.* **viewed, view·ing, views. 1. a.** To see; behold. **b.** To be present at a showing of. **2. a.** To examine; inspect. **b.** To survey or study mentally; consider. —***idioms.*** **in view of.** Taking into account; in consideration of. **on view.** Being exhibited; placed so as to be seen. [ME *vewe* < OFr. *veue* < *veoir,* to see < Lat. *vidēre.*]

view·er (vyo͞o′ər) *n.* **1.** One that views, esp. an onlooker or spectator. **2.** Any of various optical devices used to facilitate the viewing of photographic transparencies by illuminating or magnifying them.

view finder *n.* A finder (sense 2).

view hal·loo (vyo͞o′ hə-lo͞o′) *n.* A strident call given during a fox hunt by a servant or a follower to inform the huntsman that a fox has been viewed.

view·less (vyo͞o′lĭs) *adj.* **1.** Providing no view. **2.** Not having or expressing opinions or views.

view·point (vyo͞o′point′) *n.* A point of view.

view·y (vyo͞o′ē) *adj.* **-i·er, -i·est. 1.** Exhibiting extravagant or visionary opinions. **2.** Conspicuous or striking in appearance; showy.

vi·ges·i·mal (vī-jĕs′ə-məl) *adj.* **1.** Twentieth. **2.** Proceeding or occurring in intervals of 20. **3.** Based on or pertaining to 20. [< Lat. *vicesimus,* twentieth < *viginti,* twenty.]

vig·il (vĭj′əl) *n.* **1. a.** A watch kept during normal sleeping hours. **b.** A period or act of observing; surveillance. **2.** The eve of a religious festival as observed by devotional watching. **3.** Often **vigils.** Ritual devotions observed on the eve of a holy day. [ME *vigile* < OFr. < Lat. *vigilia* < *vigil,* awake.]

vig·i·lance (vĭj′ə-ləns) *n.* Alert watchfulness.

vigilance committee *n.* A volunteer group of citizens that without authority takes on itself powers such as pursuing and punishing those suspected of being criminals or offenders.

vig·i·lant (vĭj′ə-lənt) *adj.* On the alert; watchful. [ME < OFr. < Lat. *vigilans.* —see VIGILANTE.] —**vig′i·lant·ly** *adv.*

vig·i·lan·te (vĭj′ə-lăn′tē) *n.* A person belonging to a vigilance committee. [Sp. < Lat. *vigilans,* pr.part. of *vigilare,* to be watchful < *vigil,* on the watch.]

vigil light *n.* **1.** A small candle kept burning in the chancel of Christian churches to symbolize the presence of the Holy Sacrament; altar light. **2.** A candle lighted by a worshiper for a special devotional purpose. **3.** A light or candle kept burning at a shrine.

vi·gnette (vĭn-yĕt′) *n.* **1.** A decorative design placed at the beginning or end of a book or a chapter of a book or along the border of a page. **2.** An unbordered portrait that shades off into the surrounding color at the edges. **3. a.** A short, usually descriptive literary sketch. **b.** A short scene or incident, as from a movie. —*tr.v.* **-gnett·ed, -gnett·ing, -gnettes. 1.** To soften the edges of (a picture) in vignette style. **2.** To describe in a brief way. [Fr. < OFr., dim. of *vigne,* vine.]

vi·gnett·er (vĭn-yĕt′ər) *n.* **1.** A device used to print borderless illustrations and photographs. **2.** Also **vi·gnett·ist** (-ĭst). A person who makes or specializes in vignettes.

vig·or (vĭg′ər) *n.* **1.** Physical energy or strength: *full of health and vigor.* **2.** The capacity for natural growth and survival, as of plants or animals. **3.** Strong feeling; enthusiasm or intensity. **4.** Legal effectiveness or validity. [ME *vigour* < OFr. < Lat. *vigor* < *vigēre,* to be lively.]

vig·o·ro·so (vĭg′ə-rō′sō, -zō, vē′gə-) *adj. & adv. Mus.* With emphasis and spirit. Used as a direction. [Ital. < Med. Lat. *vigorosus* < Lat. *vigor,* vigor.]

vig·or·ous (vĭg′ər-əs) *adj.* **1.** Robust; hardy. **2.** Energetic; lively. —**vig′or·ous·ly** *adv.* —**vig′or·ous·ness** *n.*

vig·our (vĭg′ər) *n. Chiefly Brit.* Variant of **vigor.**

Vi·king (vī′kĭng) *n.* One of a seafaring Scandinavian people who plundered the coasts of northern and western Europe from the 8th through the 10th century. [ON *víkingr.*]

vi·la·yet (vē′lä-yĕt′) *n.* An administrative division of Turkey. [Turk. *vilāyet* < Ar. *wilāyat,* province < *wāli,* governor.]

vile (vīl) *adj.* **vil·er, vil·est. 1.** Loathsome; disgusting: *vile language.* **2.** Unpleasant or objectionable: *vile weather.* **3.** Having an abominable taste; unpalatable: *vile food.* **4.** Miserably poor; wretched: *a vile existence in a labor camp.* **5.** Depraved; ignoble. [ME < OFr. *vil* < Lat. *vilis.*] —**vile′ly** *adv.* —**vile′ness** *n.*

vil·i·fy (vĭl′ə-fī′) *tr.v.* **-fied, -fy·ing, -fies.** To defame; denigrate. [ME *vilifien* < LLat. *vilificare* : Lat. *vilis,* worthless + Lat. *facere,* to make.] —**vil′i·fi·ca′tion** *n.* —**vil′i·fi′er** *n.*

vil·i·pend (vĭl′ə-pĕnd′) *tr.v.* **-pend·ed, -pend·ing, -pends. 1.** To view or treat with contempt; despise. **2.** To disparage or abuse. [ME *vilipenden* < OFr. *vilipender* < Lat. *vilipendere* : *vilis,* worthless + *pendere,* to consider.]

vil·la (vĭl′ə) *n.* **1.** A sometimes large and luxurious country house. **2.** A Roman country estate with a substantial house. **3.** *Chiefly Brit.* A middle-class house in the suburbs. [Ital. < Lat.]

vil·lage (vĭl′ĭj) *n.* **1.** A small group of dwellings in a rural area, usually ranking in size between a hamlet and a town. **2.** In some U.S. states, an incorporated community smaller in population than a town. **3.** The inhabitants of a village; villagers. —***modifier:*** *a village square.* [ME < OFr. < *ville* < Lat. *villa,* country estate.]

ă **pat** / ā **pay** / âr **care** / ä **father** / b **bib** / ch **church** / d **deed** / ĕ **pet** / ē **be** / f **fife** / g **gag** / h **hat** / hw **which** / ĭ **pit** / ī **pie** / îr **pier** / j **judge** / k **kick** / l **lid, needle** / m **mum** / n **no, sudden** / ng **thing** / ŏ **pot** / ō **toe** / ô **paw, for** / oi **noise** / ou **out** / o͝o **took** / o͞o **boot** /

vil·lag·er (vĭl′ə-jər) *n.* An inhabitant of a village.

vil·lain (vĭl′ən) *n.* **1.** A wicked or evil person; scoundrel. **2.** A dramatic or fictional character who is typically at odds with the hero. **3.** *Obs.* A vile, brutish peasant. **4.** (*also* vĭl′ān′, vĭ-lān′). Variant of **villein. 5.** Something said to be the cause of a particular trouble or evil: *poverty, the villain in the rise in crime.* [ME *vilain* < OFr., feudal serf < Med. Lat. *villanus* < Lat. *villa,* country estate.]

vil·lain·age (vĭl′ə-nĭj) *n.* Variant of **villeinage.**

vil·lain·ess (vĭl′ə-nĭs) *n.* A woman who is a villain.

vil·lain·ous (vĭl′ə-nəs) *adj.* **1.** Viciously wicked or criminal. **2.** Obnoxious. **—vil′lain·ous·ly** *adv.* **—vil′lain·ous·ness** *n.*

vil·lain·y (vĭl′ə-nē) *n., pl.* **-ies. 1.** Viciousness of conduct or action. **2.** Baseness of mind or character. **3.** A treacherous or vicious act.

vil·la·nelle (vĭl′ə-nĕl′) *n.* A 19-line poem of fixed form consisting of five tercets and a final quatrain on two rhymes, with the first and third lines of the first tercet repeated alternately as a refrain closing the succeeding stanzas and joined as the final couplet of the quatrain. [Fr. < Ital. *villanella* < *villanello,* rustic < *villano,* peasant < Med. Lat. *villanus* < Lat. *villa,* country estate.]

vil·lat·ic (vĭ-lăt′ĭk) *adj.* Rustic; rural. [Lat. *villaticus,* of a country estate < *villa,* country estate.]

vil·lein also **vil·lain** (vĭl′ən, -ān′, vĭ-lān′) *n.* One of a class of feudal serfs who held the legal status of freemen in their dealings with all persons except their lord. [ME *vilein,* var. of *vilain,* villain.]

vil·lein·age also **vil·lain·age** (vĭl′ə-nĭj) *n.* **1.** The legal status or condition of a villein. **2.** The legal tenure by which a villein held his land.

vil·li (vĭl′ī′) *n.* Plural of **villus.**

vil·li·form (vĭl′ə-fôrm′) *adj.* Having the form of a villus or the appearance of villi.

vil·lose (vĭl′ōs′) *adj.* Variant of **villous.**

vil·los·i·ty (vĭ-lŏs′ĭ-tē) *n., pl.* **-ties. 1.** The condition of being villous. **2.** A villous surface or coating. **3.** A villus.

vil·lous (vĭl′əs) also **vil·lose** (-ōs′) *adj.* **1.** Of, pertaining to, resembling, or covered with villi. **2.** *Bot.* Covered with fine, unmatted hairs. [ME < Lat. *villosus,* hairy < *villus,* shaggy hair.] **—vil′lous·ly** *adv.*

vil·lus (vĭl′əs) *n., pl.* **vil·li** (vĭl′ī′). **1.** *Anat.* A minute projection arising from a mucous membrane. **2.** *Bot.* A fine, hairlike epidermal outgrowth. [Lat., shaggy hair.]

vim (vĭm) *n.* Ebullient vitality and energy. [Lat., accusative of *vis,* force.]

vin– *pref.* Variant of **vini-.**

vi·na also **vee·na** (vē′nə) *n.* A stringed musical instrument of India that has a long, fretted fingerboard with resonating gourds at each end. [Hindi *vīṇā* < Skt. *vīṇā.*]

vi·na·ceous (vī-nā′shəs, vĭ-) *adj.* Having the color of red wine; wine-colored. [Lat. *vinaceus,* of wine < *vinum,* wine.]

vin·ai·grette (vĭn′ĭ-grĕt′) *n.* **1.** A small decorative bottle or container with a perforated top, used for holding an aromatic preparation such as smelling salts. **2.** Vinaigrette sauce. [Fr. < OFr. *vinaigre,* vinegar.]

vinaigrette sauce *n.* A cold sauce or dressing made of vinegar or lemon juice and oil flavored with finely chopped onions, herbs, and other seasonings.

vi·nasse (vĭ-năs′, vī-) *n.* The residue left in a still after the process of distillation. [Fr. < Lat. *vinacea,* fem. of *vinaceus,* of wine.]

vin·blas·tine (vĭn-blăs′tēn′) *n.* An alkaloid, $C_{46}H_{58}N_4O_9$, obtained from the Madagascar periwinkle plant, that is used as an antineoplastic drug. [NLat. *Vinca,* periwinkle genus + E. *leuroblast,* a developing leukocyte + -INE.]

Vin·cent's angina (vĭn′sənts) *n.* Trench mouth. [After Jean Hyacinthe *Vincent* (1862–1950), its discoverer.]

vin·ci·ble (vĭn′sə-bəl) *adj.* Capable of being overcome or defeated. [Lat. *vincibilis* < *vincere,* to conquer.] **—vin′ci·bil′i·ty** *n.* **—vin′ci·bly** *adv.*

vin·cris·tine (vĭn-krĭs′tēn′) *n.* An alkaloid, $C_{46}H_{56}N_4O_{10}$, obtained from the Madagascar periwinkle plant, that is used as an antineoplastic drug, esp. in the treatment of leukemia. [NLat. *Vinca,* periwinkle genus + Lat. *crista,* crest + -INE.]

vin·cu·lum (vĭng′kyə-ləm) *n., pl.* **-lums** or **-la** (-lə). **1.** *Math.* A bar drawn over two or more algebraic terms to indicate that they are to be treated as a single term. **2.** *Anat.* A ligament that limits the movement of an organ or part. **3.** A bond or tie. [Lat., cord < *vincire,* to tie.]

vin·di·ca·ble (vĭn′dĭ-kə-bəl) *adj.* Able to be vindicated.

vin·di·cate (vĭn′dĭ-kāt′) *tr.v.* **-cat·ed, -cat·ing, -cates. 1.** To clear of accusation, blame, suspicion, or doubt with supporting arguments or proof. **2.** To justify or support: *vindicate one's claim.* **3.** To justify or prove the worth of, esp. in light of later developments. [Lat. *vindicare, vindicat-,* to lay claim to < *vindex,* avenger.] **—vin′di·ca′tor** *n.*

vin·di·ca·tion (vĭn′dĭ-kā′shən) *n.* **1.** The act of vindicating or condition of being vindicated. **2.** The defense, as evidence or argument, that serves to justify a claim or deed.

vin·di·ca·to·ry (vĭn′dĭ-kə-tôr′ē, -tōr′ē) *adj.* **1.** Vindicating; justifying. **2.** Exacting retribution; punitive.

vin·dic·tive (vĭn-dĭk′tĭv) *adj.* **1.** Disposed to seek revenge; revengeful. **2.** Intended to cause pain or harm; spiteful. [< Lat. *vindicta,* vengeance < *vindicare,* to avenge.] **—vin·dic′tive·ly** *adv.* **—vin·dic′tive·ness** *n.*

Synonyms: *vindictive, spiteful, vengeful, revengeful.* These adjectives describe the attitudes and, in some cases, the actions of persons filled with ill will, usually as a result of the infliction on them of a real or imagined wrong. *Vindictive* and *spiteful* both imply abundance of rancor and resentment and disposition to do harm, but *vindictive* is more specific in its suggestion of desire for revenge. *Vengeful* and *revengeful* can refer both to the attitude of one seeking to pay back another and to an act that implements such a desire.

vine (vīn) *n.* **1. a.** A plant having a flexible stem supported by climbing, twining, or creeping along a surface. **b.** The stem of such a plant. **2. a.** A grapevine. **b.** Grapevines collectively: *products of the vine.* [ME < OFr. < Lat. *vinea* < fem. of *vineus,* of wine < *vinum,* wine.]

vine·dress·er (vīn′drĕs′ər) *n.* A person who cultivates and prunes grapevines.

vin·e·gar (vĭn′ĭ-gər) *n.* An impure dilute solution of acetic acid obtained by fermentation beyond the alcohol stage and used as a condiment and preservative. [ME *vinegre* < OFr. *vinaigre* : *vin,* wine (< Lat. *vinum*) + *aigre,* sour < Lat. *acer.*]

vinegar eel *n.* A small nematode worm, *Anguillula aceti,* that feeds on the organisms that cause fermentation in vinegar.

vin·e·gar·roon (vĭn′ĭ-gə-ro͞on′) also **vin·e·ga·rone** (-rōn′) *n.* A large, nonvenomous scorpionlike arachnid, *Mastigoproctus giganteus,* of the southern United States and Mexico, that emits a strong odor of vinegar when disturbed. [Mex. Sp. *vinagrón,* aug. of Sp. *vinagre,* vinegar < OFr. *vinaigre.*]

vin·e·gar·y (vĭn′ĭ-gə-rē, -grē) also **vin·e·gar·ish** (-gər-ĭsh, -grĭsh) *adj.* **1.** Having the nature of vinegar; sour: *a vinegary taste.* **2.** Unpleasant and irascible in disposition or speech.

vin·er·y (vī′nə-rē) *n., pl.* **-ies.** An area or greenhouse for growing vines.

vine·yard (vĭn′yərd) *n.* **1.** Ground planted with cultivated grapevines. **2.** A sphere of spiritual, mental, or physical endeavor.

vini– or **vino–** or **vin–** *pref.* Wine: *vinic.* [< Lat. *vinum,* wine.]

vi·nic (vī′nĭk) *adj.* Of, contained in, or derived from wine.

vin·i·cul·ture (vĭn′ĭ-kŭl′chər, vī′nĭ-) *n.* The cultivation of grapes; viticulture. **—vin′i·cul′tur·al** *adj.* **—vin′i·cul′tur·ist** *n.*

vi·no (vē′nō) *n., pl.* **-nos.** Wine. [Ital. and Sp., both < Lat. *vinum.*]

vino– *pref.* Variant of **vini-.**

vi·nom·e·ter (vĭ-nŏm′ĭ-tər, vī-) *n.* A hydrometer used to determine the percentage of alcohol in a wine.

vin or·di·naire (văɴ′ ôr-dē-nâr′) *n., pl.* **vins or·di·naires** (văɴ′ ôr-dē-nâr′). An inexpensive red table wine. [Fr., ordinary wine.]

vi·nous (vī′nəs) *adj.* **1.** Of, pertaining to, or made with wine. **2.** Affected or caused by the consumption of wine. **3.** Having the color of wine. [Lat. *vinosus* < *vinum,* wine.] **—vi·nos′i·ty** (vī-nŏs′ĭ-tē) *n.* **—vi′nous·ly** *adv.*

vin·tage (vĭn′tĭj) *n.* **1.** The yield of wine or grapes from a particular vineyard or district during one season. **2.** Wine, usually of high quality, identified as to year and vineyard or district of origin. **3.** The year or place in which a particular wine is bottled. **4. a.** The harvesting of a grape crop. **b.** The initial stages of winemaking. **5.** *Informal.* **a.** A group or collection of persons or things sharing certain characteristics. **b.** A year or period of origin: *a car of 1942 vintage.* **c.** Length of existence; age. *—adj.* **1.** Of or relating to a vintage. **2.** Characterized by excellence, maturity, and enduring appeal; classic. **3.** Old or outmoded. **4.** Of the best or most distinctive: *agreed that the play was vintage O'Neill.* [ME *vyntage,* alteration of *vendage* < OFr. *vendange* < Lat. *vindemia* : *vinum,* grapes + *demere,* to take off.]

vin·tag·er (vĭn′tə-jər) *n.* A producer or harvester of wine grapes.

vintage year *n.* **1.** The year in which a vintage wine is produced. **2.** A year of outstanding achievement or success.

vint·ner (vĭnt′nər) *n.* **1.** A wine merchant. **2.** One who makes wine. [ME *vineter* < OFr. *vinetier* < Med. Lat. *vinetarius* < Lat. *vinetum,* vineyard < *vinum,* wine.]

vin·y (vī′nē) *adj.* **-i·er, -i·est. 1.** Of, pertaining to, or of the nature of vines. **2.** Overgrown with or abounding in vines.

vi·nyl (vī′nəl) *n.* **1.** The univalent chemical radical CH_2CH, derived from ethylene. **2.** Any of various compounds containing the vinyl radical, typically highly reactive, easily polymerized, and used as basic materials for plastics. **3.** Any of various plastics, typically tough, flexible, and shiny, often used for coverings and clothing. [VIN(I)- + -YL.] **—vi·nyl′ic** (-nĭl′ĭk) *adj.*

vinyl chloride *n.* A flammable gas, $CH_2{:}CHCl$, used as a monomer for polyvinyl chloride.

vi·ol (vī′əl) *n.* **1.** Any of a family of stringed instruments, chiefly of the 16th and 17th centuries, having a fretted fingerboard, usually six strings, and a flat back and played with a curved bow. **2.** A viola da gamba (sense 1). [OFr. *viole* < OProv. *viola.*]

vi·o·la[1] (vē-ō′lə) *n.* **1.** A stringed musical instrument of the violin family, slightly larger than a violin, tuned a fifth lower, and having a deeper, more sonorous tone. **2.** An organ stop usually of eight-foot or four-foot pitch yielding stringlike tones. [Ital. < OProv., viol.] **—vi·o′list** *n.*

violet

vi·o·la[2] (vī-ō'lə, vē-, vī'ə-lə) *n.* A plant of the genus *Viola,* which includes the violets and pansies, esp. a variety having flowers resembling violets in size and shape and pansies in coloration. [NLat. *Viola,* genus name < Lat. *viola,* the violet.]

vi·o·la·ble (vī'ə-lə-bəl) *adj.* Capable of being violated. —**vi'o·la·bil'i·ty, vi'o·la·ble·ness** *n.* —**vi'o·la·bly** *adv.*

vi·o·la·ceous (vī'ə-lā'shəs) *adj.* **1.** Of or belonging to the family Violaceae, which includes the violets. **2.** Of the color violet. [NLat. *Violaceae,* family name < Lat. *violaceus,* violet-colored < *viola,* the violet.]

vi·o·la da brac·cio (vē-ō'lə də brä'chō) *n.* A stringed instrument of the viol family with approximately the range of the viola. [Ital., viol of the arm.]

vi·o·la da gam·ba (vē-ō'lə də gäm'bə, găm'-) *n.* **1.** A stringed instrument, the bass of the viol family, with approximately the range of the cello. **2.** An organ stop of eight-foot pitch yielding tones similar to those of the viola da gamba. [Ital., viol of the leg.]

violin

vi·o·la d'a·mo·re (vē-ō'lə dä-môr'ē, -mōr'ē) *n.* A stringed instrument, the tenor of the viol family, having six or seven stopped strings and an equal number of sympathetic strings that produce a characteristic silvery tone. [Ital., viol of love.]

vi·o·late (vī'ə-lāt') *tr.v.* **-lat·ed, -lat·ing, -lates. 1.** To break (a law, for example) intentionally or unintentionally; disregard: *violate a promise.* **2.** To injure the person or property of, esp. to rape. **3.** To do harm to (property or qualities considered sacred); desecrate. **4.** To disturb rudely or improperly; interrupt: *violated our privacy.* [ME *violaten* < Lat. *violare, violat-* < *vis,* force.] —**vi'o·la'tive** *adj.* —**vi'o·la'tor** *n.*

vi·o·la·tion (vī'ə-lā'shən) *n.* **1. a.** The act of violating. **b.** The condition of being violated: *the violation of a peace treaty.* **2.** An instance of violating: *a traffic violation.*

George Miksch Sutton

vireo

vi·o·lence (vī'ə-ləns) *n.* **1.** Physical force exerted for the purpose of violating, damaging, or abusing: *crimes of violence.* **2.** An act or instance of violent action or behavior. **3.** Intensity or severity, as in natural phenomena; untamed force: *the violence of a hurricane.* **4.** The abusive or unjust exercise of power. **5.** Abuse or injury to meaning, content, or intent: *do violence to a text.* **6.** Vehemence of feeling or expression; fervor.

vi·o·lent (vī'ə-lənt) *adj.* **1.** Marked by or resulting from great physical force or rough action: *a violent attack.* **2.** Showing or having great emotional force: *a violent outburst of anger.* **3.** Severe; intense: *violent pain; a violent storm.* **4.** Caused by unexpected force or injury rather than by natural causes: *a violent death.* **5.** Tending to distort or injure meaning, phrasing, or intent. [ME < OFr. < Lat. *violentus* < *vis,* force.] —**vi'o·lent·ly** *adv.*

Virginia creeper

vi·o·let (vī'ə-lĭt) *n.* **1. a.** Any of various low-growing plants of the genus *Viola,* having spurred, irregular flowers that are characteristically purplish-blue but sometimes yellow or white. **b.** Any of several similar plants, such as the African violet. **2.** Any of a group of colors, reddish blue in hue, that may vary in lightness and saturation; the hue of that portion of the spectrum that may be evoked in the normal observer by radiant energy of wavelengths approximately 420 nanometers. [ME < OFr. *violete,* dim. of *viole* < Lat. *viola.*]

vi·o·lin (vī'ə-lĭn') *n.* A stringed instrument played with a bow, having four strings tuned at intervals of a fifth, an unfretted fingerboard, and a shallower body than the viol and capable of great flexibility in range, tone, and dynamics. [Ital. *violino,* dim. of *viola,* viola.] —**vi'o·lin'ist** *n.*

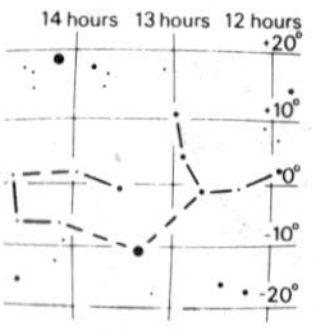

Virgo

vi·o·lon·cel·lo (vē'ə-lən-chĕl'ō, vī'ə-) *n., pl.* **-los.** A cello. [Ital., dim. of *violone,* violone.] —**vi'o·lon·cel'list** *n.*

vi·o·lo·ne (vē'ə-lō'nā) *n.* **1.** A 16-foot organ stop yielding stringlike tones similar to those of a cello. **2.** A double bass. [Ital., aug. of *viola,* viola.]

vi·o·my·cin (vī'ə-mī'sĭn) *n.* An antibiotic, $C_{23}H_{36}N_{12}O_8$, produced by the bacterium *Streptomyces puniceus,* that is used in the form of its sulfate in the treatment of tuberculosis. [VIO(LET) + -MYCIN.]

vi·os·ter·ol (vī-ŏs'tə-rôl', -rōl') *n.* Ultraviolet irradiated ergosterol; vitamin D_2. [(ULTRA)VIO(LET) + STEROL.]

VIP (vē'ī-pē') *n., pl.* **VIPs.** *Informal.* A very important person.

vi·per (vī'pər) *n.* **1.** Any of various venomous Old World snakes of the family Viperidae, esp. a common Eurasian species, *Vipera berus.* **2.** A pit viper. **3.** A venomous or supposedly venomous snake. **4.** A treacherous or malicious person. [OFr. *vipere* < Lat. *vipera,* snake.]

vi·per·ine (vī'pə-rīn') *adj.* Of, resembling, or characteristic of a viper.

vi·per·ous (vī'pər-əs) *adj.* **1.** Suggestive of a viper or venomous snake. **2.** Venomous; malicious. —**vi'per·ous·ly** *adv.*

viper's bugloss *n.* A bristly plant, *Echium vulgare,* native to Eurasia, having bright blue flowers.

vir·a·gin·i·ty (vîr'ə-jĭn'ĭ-tē) *n.* Masculine mentality and psychology in a woman. [< Lat. *virago, viragin-,* virago.]

vi·ra·go (və-rä'gō, -rā'-, vîr'ə-gō') *n., pl.* **-goes** or **-gos. 1.** A noisy, domineering woman; scold. **2.** A large, strong, and courageous woman. [Lat. < *vir,* man.] —**vi·rag'i·nous** (və-răj'ə-nəs) *adj.*

vi·ral (vī'rəl) *adj.* Of, pertaining to, or caused by a virus. —**vi'ral·ly** *adv.*

vir·e·lay (vîr'ə-lā') *n.* Any of several medieval French verse and song forms, esp. one in which each stanza has two rhymes, the end rhyme recurring as the first rhyme of the following stanza. [ME *virelai* < OFr.]

vi·re·mi·a (vī-rē'mē-ə) *n.* The presence of viral particles in the blood. [VIR(US) + -EMIA.] —**vi·re'mic** (-mĭk) *adj.*

vir·e·o (vîr'ē-ō') *n., pl.* **-os.** Any of various small New World birds of the genus *Vireo,* having grayish or greenish plumage. [NLat. *Vireo,* genus name < Lat. *vireo,* a kind of bird < *virēre,* to be green.]

vi·res·cence (və-rĕs'əns, vī-) *n.* The state or process of becoming green, esp. the abnormal development of green coloration in plant parts normally not green.

vi·res·cent (və-rĕs'ənt, vī-) *adj.* **1.** Becoming green. **2.** Greenish. [Lat. *virescens,* p.part. of *virescere,* to become green < *virēre,* to be green.]

vi·res ma·jo·res (vī'rēz mə-jôr'ēz', -jōr'-) *n.* Plural of **vis major.**

vir·ga (vûr'gə) *n.* Wisps of precipitation streaming from a cloud but evaporating before reaching the earth. [Lat., twig, virga.]

vir·gate[1] (vûr'gāt') *adj.* Shaped like a wand or rod; straight, long, and slender. [Lat. *virgatus,* made of twigs < *virga,* twig.]

vir·gate[2] (vûr'gĭt) *n.* An early English measure of land area of varying value, often equivalent to about 30 acres. [Med. Lat. *virgata* < *virga,* rod.]

vir·gin (vûr'jĭn) *n.* **1.** A person who has not experienced sexual intercourse. **2.** A chaste or unmarried woman; maiden. **3.** An unmarried woman who has taken religious vows of chastity. **4. Virgin.** The Virgin Mary. **5.** A female animal that has not mated. **6. Virgin.** Virgo. —*adj.* **1.** Characteristic of or appropriate to a virgin; chaste. **2.** In a pure or natural state; unsullied: *virgin snow.* **3.** Unused, uncultivated, or unexplored: *virgin territory.* **4.** Existing in native or raw form; not processed or refined. **5.** Happening for the first time; initial. **6.** Obtained directly from the first pressing. Used of vegetable oils. [ME < OFr. *virgine* < Lat. *virgo.*]

vir·gin·al[1] (vûr'jə-nəl) *adj.* **1.** Pertaining to, characteristic of, or befitting a virgin; chaste. **2.** Remaining in a state of virginity. **3.** Untouched or unsullied; fresh. —**vir'gin·al·ly** *adv.*

vir·gin·al[2] (vûr'jə-nəl) *n.* Often **virginals.** A small, legless rectangular harpsichord popular in the 16th and 17th centuries: *a pair of virginals.* [< VIRGIN, from its being played by young girls.]

virgin birth *n. Theol.* The doctrine that Jesus was miraculously begotten by God and born of Mary, who was a virgin.

Vir·gin·ia cowslip (vər-jĭn'yə, -jĭn'ē-ə) *n.* A plant, *Mertensia virginica,* of eastern North America, having clusters of nodding blue flowers.

Virginia creeper *n.* A North American climbing vine, *Parthenocissus quinquefolia,* having compound leaves with five leaflets and bluish-black, berrylike fruit.

Virginia deer *n.* The white-tailed deer.

Virginia fence *n.* A worm fence.

Virginia ham *n.* A lean hickory-smoked ham with dark red meat.

Virginia reel *n.* An American country dance in which couples perform various steps together to the instructions of a caller.

vir·gin·i·ty (vər-jĭn'ĭ-tē) *n., pl.* **-ties. 1.** The condition of being a virgin; chastity. **2.** The state of being pure, unsullied, or untouched.

Virgin Mary *n.* The mother of Jesus.

vir·gin's-bow·er (vûr'jĭnz-bou'ər) *n.* Any of several plants of the genus *Clematis,* esp. *C. virginiana,* of eastern North America, having clusters of white flowers and plumed seeds.

virgin wool *n.* Wool that has not previously been used in manufacture.

Vir·go (vûr'gō, vîr'-) *n.* **1.** A constellation in the region of the celestial equator near Leo and Libra. **2.** The sixth sign of the zodiac. [Lat. < *virgo,* virgin.]

vir·gu·late (vûr'gyə-lĭt, -lāt') *adj.* Shaped like a small rod. [< Lat. *virgula,* small rod < *virga,* rod.]

vir·gule (vûr'gyōōl) *n. Printing.* A diagonal mark (/) used esp. to separate alternatives, as in *and/or,* to represent the word *per,* as in *miles/hour,* and to indicate the ends of verse lines printed continuously, as in *Candy/Is dandy.* [Fr., comma < Lat. *virgula,* small rod < *virga,* rod.]

vi·ri·cide (vī'rĭ-sīd') *n.* An agent that destroys or inhibits viruses. [VIR(US) + -CIDE.] —**vi'ri·cid'al** (-sīd'l) *adj.*

vir·id (vîr'ĭd) *adj.* Bright green with or as if with vegetation; verdant. [Lat. *viridis* < *virēre,* to be green.]

vir·i·des·cent (vîr'ĭ-dĕs'ənt) *adj.* Green or slightly green. [< Lat. *viridescere,* to become green.] —**vir'i·des'cence** *n.*

vi·rid·i·an (və-rĭd'ē-ən) *n.* A durable bluish-green pigment. [< Lat. *viridis,* green.]

vi·rid·i·ty (və-rĭd'ĭ-tē) *n.* Greenness; verdancy.

vir·ile (vîr'əl, -īl') *adj.* **1.** Of or having the characteristics of a man; masculine. **2.** Having energy, vigor, or force: *virile prose.* **3.** Capable of performing sexually as a male; potent. [OFr. *viril* < Lat. *virilis* < *vir,* man.]

vir·il·ism (vîr'ə-lĭz'əm) *n.* The development of male secondary sexual characteristics in a woman.

vi·ril·i·ty (və-rĭl'ĭ-tē) *n.* **1.** The quality or state of being virile. **2.** Masculine vigor; potency.

vi·ri·on (vī′rē-ŏn′, vîr′ē-) *n.* A complete virus particle. [VIR(US) + -ON[1].]
vi·rol·o·gy (vī-rŏl′ə-jē) *n.* The study of viruses and viral diseases. **—vi′ro·log′i·cal** (-rə-lŏj′ĭ-kəl), **vi′ro·log′ic** (-ĭk) *adj.* **—vi·rol′o·gist** *n.*
vir·tu (vər-tōō′, vîr-) also **ver·tu** (vər-tōō′) *n.* **1.** A knowledge of, love for, or taste for fine objects of art. **2.** Objects of art, esp. fine antique objets d'art. [Ital. *virtù* < Lat. *virtus,* excellence. —see VIRTUE.]
vir·tu·al (vûr′chōō-əl) *adj.* Existing or resulting in essence or effect though not in actual fact, form, or name: *the virtual extinction of the buffalo.* [ME *virtuall,* effective < Med. Lat. *virtualis* < Lat. *virtus,* excellence. —see VIRTUE.] **—vir′tu·al′i·ty** (-ăl′ĭ-tē) *n.*
virtual focus *n.* The point from which divergent rays of reflected or refracted light seem to have emanated, as from the image of a point in a plane mirror.
virtual image *n.* An image from which rays of reflected or refracted light appear to diverge, as from an image seen in a plane mirror.
vir·tu·al·ly (vûr′chōō-ə-lē) *adv.* In fact or to all purposes; practically: *The mountain lion is now virtually extinct in the eastern United States.*
virtual machine *n.* A computer designed to replicate copies of its entire hardware-software interface in order to develop new software.
virtual memory *n.* Computer memory, separate from a specific machine, that can be used as an extension of the machine's own memory.
vir·tue (vûr′chōō) *n.* **1. a.** Moral excellence and righteousness; goodness. **b.** An example or kind of moral excellence: *the virtue of patience.* **2.** Chastity, esp. of a girl or woman. **3.** A particularly efficacious, good, or beneficial quality; advantage: *a plan with the virtue of being practical.* **4.** Effective force or power: *believed in the virtue of prayer.* **5.** *Obs.* Manly courage; valor. **6. virtues.** *Theol.* One of the orders of angels. **—*idiom.* by** (or **in**) **virtue of.** On the grounds or basis of; by reason of: *By virtue of the authority vested in me I pronounce you man and wife.* [ME *virtu* < OFr. *vertu* < Lat. *virtus,* manliness, goodness < *vir,* man.]
vir·tu·o·sa (vûr′chōō-ō′sə, -zə) *n.* A woman who is a virtuoso. [Ital., fem. of *virtuoso,* virtuoso.]
vir·tu·o·si (vûr′chōō-ō′sē) *n.* A plural of **virtuoso.**
vir·tu·os·i·ty (vûr′chōō-ŏs′ĭ-tē) *n.* The technical skill, fluency, or style exhibited by a virtuoso.
vir·tu·o·so (vûr′chōō-ō′sō, -zō) *n., pl.* **-sos** or **-si** (-sē). **1.** A musician with masterly ability, technique, or personal style. **2.** A person with masterly skill or technique in the arts. **3.** A person who experiments or investigates in the arts and sciences; savant. [Ital. < LLat. *virtuosus,* good < Lat. *virtus,* excellence. —see VIRTUE.] **—vir′tu·o′sic** (-ō′sĭk, -zĭk) *adj.*
vir·tu·ous (vûr′chōō-əs) *adj.* **1.** Exhibiting virtue; righteous: *virtuous conduct.* **2.** Possessing or characterized by chastity; pure: *a virtuous woman.* **—vir′tu·ous·ly** *adv.* **—vir′tu·ous·ness** *n.*
vi·ru·cide (vī′rə-sīd′) *n.* A viricide. [VIRU(S) + -CIDE.] **—vi′ru·cid′al** (-sīd′l) *adj.*
vir·u·lent (vîr′yə-lənt, vîr′ə-) *adj.* **1.** Extremely poisonous or pathogenic. Used of a disease, toxin, or microorganism. **2.** Bitterly hostile or antagonistic; hateful: *virulent criticism.* **3.** Intensely irritating, obnoxious, or harsh. [ME < Lat. *virulentus* < *virus,* poison.] **—vir′u·lence** *n.* **—vir′u·lent·ly** *adv.*
vi·rus (vī′rəs) *n., pl.* **-rus·es. 1.** Any of various submicroscopic pathogens consisting essentially of a core of a single nucleic acid surrounded by a protein coat, having the ability to replicate only inside a living cell. **2.** A specific pathogen. **3.** Something that poisons one's soul or mind: *the pernicious virus of racism.* [Lat., poison.]
vi·sa (vē′zə) *n.* An official authorization appended to a passport, permitting entry into and travel within a particular country or region. *—tr.v.* **-saed, -sa·ing, -sas. 1.** To endorse or ratify (a passport). **2.** To give a visa to. [Fr. < Lat., neuter pl. of *visus,* p.part. of *vidēre,* to see.]
vis·age (vĭz′ĭj) *n.* **1.** The face or facial expression of a person; countenance. **2.** Appearance; aspect: *the visage of winter.* [ME < OFr. < *vis,* face < *visus,* appearance < p.part. of *vidēre,* to see.]
vis·ard (vĭz′ərd, -ärd′) *n.* Variant of **vizard.**
vis-à-vis (vē′zə-vē′) *n., pl.* **vis-à-vis** (-vēz′, -vē′). One of two persons or things opposite or corresponding to the other; counterpart. *—adv.* Face to face. *—prep.* **1.** Opposite to. **2.** Compared with. **3.** In relation to. [Fr., face to face.] **—vis′-à-vis′** *adj.*
Vi·sa·yan (və-sī′ən) *n.* **1.** A member of the largest native group of the Philippines, found in the Visayan Islands. **2.** The Malay language of the Visayans. **—Vi·sa′yan** *adj.*
vis·ca·cha (vĭ-skä′chə) *n.* Any of several gregarious, burrowing South American rodents of the genera *Lagostomus* and *Lagidium,* related to and resembling the chinchilla. [Sp. *vizcacha* < Quechua *wiscacha.*]
vis·cer·a (vĭs′ər-ə) *pl.n.* **1.** The internal organs of the body, esp. those contained within the abdominal and thoracic cavities. **2.** The intestines. [Lat., pl. of *viscus,* flesh.]
vis·cer·al (vĭs′ər-əl) *adj.* **1.** Pertaining to, situated in, or affecting the viscera. **2.** Perceived in or as if in the viscera; profound: *"The scientific approach to life is not really appropriate to states of visceral anguish"* (Anthony Burgess). **3.** Instinctive: *visceral needs.* **—vis′cer·al·ly** *adv.*
vis·cer·o·mo·tor (vĭs′ər-ə-mō′tər) *adj.* Producing or related to movements of the viscera. [VISCER(A) + MOTOR.]
vis·cid (vĭs′ĭd) *adj.* **1.** Thick and adhesive. Used of a fluid. **2.** Covered with a sticky or clammy coating. [LLat. *visadus* < Lat. *viscum,* mistletoe, birdlime made from mistletoe berries.] **—vis·cid′i·ty** (vĭ-sĭd′ĭ-tē), **vis′cid·ness** *n.* **—vis′cid·ly** *adv.*
vis·com·e·ter (vĭ-skŏm′ĭ-tər) *n.* An instrument used to measure viscosity. **—vis′co·met′ric** (vĭs′kə-mĕt′rĭk) *adj.* **—vis·com′e·try** *n.*
vis·cose (vĭs′kōs′) *n.* **1.** A thick, golden-brown viscous solution of cellulose xanthate, used in the manufacture of rayon and cellophane. **2.** Viscose rayon. *—adj.* **1.** Viscous. **2.** Of, relating to, or made from viscose. [ME, viscid < LLat. *viscosus* < *viscum,* mistletoe, birdlime made from mistletoe berries.]
viscose rayon *n.* A rayon made by reconverting cellulose from a soluble xanthate form to tough fibers by washing in acid.
vis·co·sim·e·ter (vĭs′kə-sĭm′ĭ-tər) *n.* A viscometer. **—vis·cos′i·met′ric** (vĭ-skŏs′ə-mĕt′rĭk) *adj.*
vis·cos·i·ty (vĭ-skŏs′ĭ-tē) *n., pl.* **-ties. 1.** The condition or property of being viscous. **2.** *Physics.* The degree to which a fluid resists flow under an applied force.
vis·count (vī′kount′) *n.* A peer ranking below an earl and above a baron. [ME < OFr. *visconte* < Med. Lat. *vicecomes, vicecomit-* : *vice-,* vice + *comes,* count.]
vis·count·cy (vī′kount′sē) *n., pl.* **-cies.** The rank, title, or dignity of a viscount.
vis·count·ess (vī′koun′tĭs) *n.* The wife of a viscount.
vis·cous (vĭs′kəs) *adj.* **1.** Having relatively high resistance to flow. **2.** Viscid. [ME *viscouse* < LLat. *viscosus* < Lat. *viscum,* mistletoe, birdlime made from mistletoe berries.] **—vis′cous·ly** *adv.* **—vis′cous·ness** *n.*
vis·cus (vĭs′kəs) *n.* Singular of **viscera.**
vise also **vice** (vīs) *—n.* A clamping device of metal or wood, usually consisting of two jaws closed or opened by a screw or lever, used in carpentry or metalworking to hold a piece in position. *—tr.v.* **vised, vis·ing, vis·es** also **viced, vic·ing, vic·es.** To hold in or as if in a vise. [ME *vice,* spiral staircase < OFr. *vis* < Lat. *vitis,* vine.]

vise

Vish·nu (vĭsh′nōō) *n.* *Hinduism.* The chief deity worshiped by the Vaishnava and the second member of the trinity including also Brahma and Shiva. [Skt. *Viṣṇuḥ.*]
vis·i·bil·i·ty (vĭz′ə-bĭl′ĭ-tē) *n., pl.* **-ties. 1.** The fact, state, or degree of being visible. **2.** The greatest distance under given weather conditions to which it is possible to see without instrumental assistance.
vis·i·ble (vĭz′ə-bəl) *adj.* **1.** Capable of being seen; perceptible to the eye: *a visible object.* **2.** Obvious to the eye: *a visible change of expression.* **3.** Manifest; apparent: *no visible solution.* **4.** Available; on hand: *a visible supply.* **5.** Constructed or designed to keep important parts in easily accessible view: *a visible file.* **6.** Represented visually, as by symbols. [ME < OFr. < Lat. *visibilis* < *vidēre,* to see.] **—vis′i·ble·ness** *n.* **—vis′i·bly** *adv.*
visible speech *n.* A system of phonetic notation used as an aid for teaching speech to the deaf and consisting of diagrams of the organs of speech in the various positions required to articulate sounds.
Vis·i·goth (vĭz′ĭ-gŏth′) *n.* A member of the western Goths that invaded the Roman Empire in the fourth century A.D. and settled in France and Spain, establishing a monarchy that lasted until the early eighth century A.D. [LLat. *Visigothi,* the Visigoths.] **—Vis′i·goth′ic** *adj.*
vi·sion (vĭzh′ən) *n.* **1. a.** The faculty of sight: *poor vision.* **b.** Something that is or has been seen. **2.** Unusual competence in discernment or perception; intelligent foresight: *a man of vision.* **3.** The manner in which one sees or conceives of something. **4.** A mental image produced by the imagination. **5.** The mystical experience of seeing as if with the eyes the supernatural or a supernatural being. **6.** A person or thing of extraordinary beauty. *—tr.v.* **-sioned, -sion·ing, -sions.** To see in or as if in a vision. [ME < OFr. < Lat. *visio* < *vidēre,* to see.] **—vi′sion·al** *adj.* **—vi′sion·al·ly** *adv.*
vi·sion·ar·y (vĭzh′ə-nĕr′ē) *adj.* **1.** Characterized by vision or foresight. **2.** Having the nature of fantasies or dreams. **3.** Characterized by or given to apparitions, prophecies, or revelations. **4.** Not practicable; utopian. *—n., pl.* **-ies. 1.** One who has visions; seer. **2.** One who is given to impractical or speculative ideas; dreamer.
vis·it (vĭz′ĭt) *v.* **-it·ed, -it·ing, -its.** *—tr.* **1.** To go or come to see (a person); call on: *visit Aunt Martha.* **2.** To go or come to see (a place), as on a tour: *visit a museum.* **3.** To stay with as a guest. **4.** To go or come to see in an official or professional capacity. **5.** To go or come to: *visits the bank on Fridays.* **6.** To go or come to in order to aid: *visit the wounded.* **7.** To afflict; assail: *A plague visited the village.* **8.** To inflict punishment upon or for; avenge: *The sins of the fathers were visited on their sons.* *—intr.* **1.** To make a visit. **2.** *Informal.* To converse or chat: *Stay and visit with me for a while.* *—n.* **1.** An act or instance of visiting a person, place, or thing. **2.** A stay or sojourn as a guest. **3.** An act of visiting in a professional capacity. **4.** An act of visiting in an official ca-

pacity, as an inspection or examination. [ME *visiten* < OFr. *visiter* < Lat. *visitare,* to go to see, freq. of *visere,* to view, freq. of *vidēre,* to see.]

vis·it·a·ble (vĭz'ĭ-tə-bəl) *adj.* **1.** Capable of or suitable for a visit. **2.** Subject to or allowing official visits, as for inspection.

vis·i·tant (vĭz'ĭ-tənt) *n.* **1.** A visitor; guest. **2.** A supernatural being; ghost or specter. **3.** A migratory animal or bird that stops in a particular place for a limited period of time. *—adj.* Visiting. [Lat. *visitans, visitant-,* pr.part. of *visitare,* to go to see.]

vis·i·ta·tion (vĭz'ĭ-tā'shən) *n.* **1.** The act of visiting or an instance of being visited; visit. **2.** A visit for the purpose of making an official inspection or examination, as of a bishop to his diocese. **3.** The right of a parent to visit a child as specified in a divorce or separation order. **4. a.** A visit of punishment or affliction or of comfort and blessing regarded as being ordained by God. **b.** A calamitous event or experience; grave misfortune. **5.** The appearance or arrival of a supernatural being. **6. Visitation. a.** The visit of the Virgin Mary to her cousin Elizabeth. **b.** The Roman Catholic Church festival held July 2 in commemoration of this visit. **—vis'i·ta'tion·al** *adj.*

vis·i·ta·to·ri·al (vĭz'ĭ-tə-tôr'ē-əl, -tōr'-) *adj.* **1.** Of or pertaining to an official visitor or visit. **2.** Having the right or power of visitation.

visiting card *n.* A calling card.

visiting fireman *n. Informal.* **1.** An influential visitor who is entertained impressively. **2.** A visitor who is welcomed because he is thought to be a free spender.

visiting nurse *n.* A registered nurse employed by a public health agency or hospital to promote community health and esp. to visit sick persons in their homes.

visiting professor *n.* A professor on leave invited to serve as a member of the faculty of another college or university for a limited period of time, often an academic year.

visiting teacher *n.* **1.** A school social worker who works individually with students having special problems in adjusting to school or in functioning well in school. **2.** In some states, a teacher who visits and instructs sick or physically impaired students who are unable to attend school.

vis·i·tor (vĭz'ĭ-tər) *n.* One who visits.

vis ma·jor (vĭs mā'jər) *n., pl.* **vi·res ma·jo·res** (vī'rēz mə-jôr'ēz', -jōr'-). *Law.* An overwhelming force of nature having unavoidable consequences that under certain circumstances can exempt one from the obligations of a contract. [Lat., greater force.]

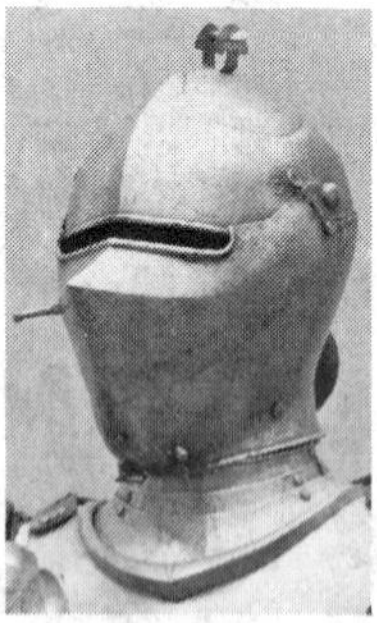

visor
Visor on 15th-century Spanish armor

vi·sor also **vi·zor** (vī'zər) *—n.* **1.** A piece projecting from the front of a cap to shade the eyes or protect against wind or rain. **2.** A fixed or movable shield against glare above the windshield of an automobile. **3.** The front piece of the helmet of a suit of armor, capable of being raised and lowered and designed to protect the eyes, nose, and forehead. **4.** A means of concealment or disguise, esp. a mask. *—tr.v.* **-sored, -sor·ing, -sors** also **-zored, -zor·ing, -zors.** To mask or protect with a visor. [ME *viser* < AN < OFr. *vis,* face < Lat. *visus,* appearance < *vidēre,* to see.] **—vi'sored** (vī'zərd) *adj.*

vis·ta (vĭs'tə) *n.* **1. a.** A distant view seen through an opening, as between buildings; prospect. **b.** The passage framing the approach to such a scene; avenue. **2.** A comprehensive awareness of a series of remembered, present, or anticipated events. [Ital. < *visto,* p.part. of *vedere,* to see < Lat. *vidēre.*]

VISTA (vĭs'tə) *n.* An organization, sponsored by the U.S. Office of Economic Opportunity, composed of volunteer members devoted to educating and teaching skills to the poor. [V(OLUNTEERS) I(N) S(ERVICE) T(O) A(MERICA).]

vi·su·al (vĭzh'o͞o-əl) *adj.* **1.** Serving, resulting from, or pertaining to the sense of sight. **2.** Capable of being seen by the eye; visible. **3.** Optical. **4.** Done, maintained, or executed by sight only: *visual navigation.* **5.** Having the nature of or producing an image in the mind. **6.** Of or relating to a method of instruction involving sight. [ME < LLat. *visualis* < Lat. *visus,* sight < *vidēre,* to see.] **—vi'su·al·ly** *adv.*

visual aid *n.* Graphic material used in education to impart instruction by visual means.

visual field *n.* The entire area visible to the immobile eyes at a given moment; field of vision.

vi·su·al·ize (vizh'o͞o-ə-līz') *v.* **-ized, -iz·ing, -iz·es** *—tr.* To form a mental image or vision of; envisage. *—intr.* To form a mental image. **—vi'su·al·i·za'tion** *n.* **—vi'su·al·iz'er** *n.*

visual purple *n.* A red-light-sensitive pigment of the retina, esp. rhodopsin.

vi·tal (vīt'l) *adj.* **1.** Of or characteristic of life: *vital processes.* **2.** Necessary to the continuation of life; life-sustaining: *vital functions.* **3.** Full of life; animated. **4.** Imparting life or animation; invigorating. **5.** Having immediate importance; essential: *"Irrigation was vital to early civilization"* (William H. McNeill). **6.** Concerned with or recording data pertinent to lives. **7.** Destructive to life; fatal. [ME < OFr. < Lat. *vitalis* < *vita,* life.] **—vi'tal·ly** *adv.* **—vi'tal·ness** *n.*

vital capacity *n.* The amount of air that can be forcibly expelled from the lungs following a full inspiration.

vi·tal·ism (vīt'l-ĭz'əm) *n.* The philosophical doctrine that life processes possess a unique character radically different from physiochemical phenomena. **—vi'tal·ist** *n.* **—vi'tal·is'tic** *adj.*

vi·tal·i·ty (vī-tăl'ĭ-tē) *n., pl.* **-ties. 1.** The characteristic that distinguishes the living from the nonliving. **2.** The capacity to live, grow, or develop. **3.** Physical or intellectual vigor; energy. **4.** The power to survive.

vi·tal·ize (vīt'l-īz') *tr.v.* **-ized, -iz·ing, -iz·es. 1.** To endow with life. **2.** To invigorate or animate. **—vi'tal·i·za'tion** *n.* **—vi'tal·iz'er** *n.*

vi·tals (vīt'lz) *pl.n.* **1.** Bodily parts or organs regarded as the center or source of life. **2.** Those elements essential to continued functioning, as of a system.

vital signs *pl.n. Med.* The pulse rate, temperature, and respiratory rate of an individual.

vital statistics *pl.n.* Data that record significant events and dates in human life, as births, deaths, and marriages.

vi·ta·mer (vī'tə-mər) *n.* One of two or more similar chemical compounds capable of fulfilling a specific vitamin function. [VITA(MIN) + (ISO)MER.] **—vi'ta·mer'ic** (-mĕr'ĭk) *adj.*

vi·ta·min (vī'tə-mĭn) *n.* Any of various relatively complex organic substances occurring naturally in plant and animal tissue and essential in small amounts for the control of metabolic processes. [G. *Vitamine* : Lat. *vita,* life + *-amine,* amine.] **—vi'ta·min'ic** *adj.*

vitamin A *n.* A vitamin or a mixture of vitamins, esp. vitamin A_1 or a mixture of vitamins A_1 and A_2, occurring principally in fish-liver oils and some yellow and dark-green vegetables, functioning in normal cell growth and development, and responsible in deficiency for hardening and roughening of the skin, night blindness, and degeneration of mucous membranes.

vitamin A_1 *n.* A yellow crystalline compound, $C_{20}H_{30}O$, extracted from fish-liver oils.

vitamin A_2 *n.* A golden-yellow oil, $C_{20}H_{28}O$, occurring in pike-liver oils and having approximately 40 per cent of the biological activity of vitamin A_1.

vitamin B *n.* **1.** Vitamin B complex. **2.** A member of the vitamin B complex, esp. thiamine.

vitamin B_c *n.* Folic acid.

vitamin B_1 *n.* Thiamine.

vitamin B_2 *n.* Riboflavin.

vitamin B_6 *n.* Pyridoxine.

vitamin B_{12} *n.* A complex, cobalt-containing coordination compound produced in the normal growth of certain microorganisms, found in liver, and widely used to treat pernicious anemia.

vitamin B complex *n.* A group of vitamins originally thought to be a single substance, generally regarded as including thiamine, riboflavin, niacin, pantothenic acid, biotin, pyridoxine, folic acid, inositol, and vitamin B_{12}, and occurring chiefly in yeast, liver, eggs, and some vegetables.

vitamin C *n.* Ascorbic acid.

vitamin D *n.* Any of several chemically similar activated sterols, esp. vitamin D_2 or vitamin D_3, produced in general by ultraviolet irradiation of sterols, obtained from milk, fish, and eggs, required for normal bone growth, and used to treat rickets in children and osteomalacia in adults.

vitamin D_2 *n.* A white crystalline compound, $C_{28}H_{44}O$, produced by ultraviolet irradiation of ergosterol.

vitamin D_3 *n.* A colorless crystalline compound, $C_{27}H_{44}O$, with essentially the same biological activity as vitamin D_2 but significantly more potent in poultry.

vitamin E *n.* Any of several chemically related viscous oils, esp. $C_{29}H_{50}O_2$, found chiefly in grains and vegetable oils and used to treat sterility and various abnormalities of the muscles, red blood cells, liver, and brain.

vitamin G *n.* Riboflavin.

vitamin H *n.* Biotin.

vitamin K *n.* Any of several natural and synthetic substances essential for the promotion of blood clotting and prevention of hemorrhage, occurring naturally in leafy green vegetables, tomatoes, and vegetable oils.

vitamin P *n.* A crystalline fraction of citrus juices used to treat certain conditions involving hemorrhage into the skin.

vi·tel·lin (vĭ-tĕl'ĭn, vī-) *n.* A protein found in egg yolk. [VITELL(US) + -IN.]

vi·tel·line (vĭ-tĕl'ĭn, -ēn', vī-) *adj.* **1.** Of, pertaining to, or associated with the yolk of an egg: *the vitelline membrane.* **2.** Having the yellow color of an egg yolk; dull-yellow. *—n.* The yolk of an egg. [VITELL(US) + -INE.]

vi·tel·lus (vĭ-tĕl'əs, vī-) *n.* The yolk of an egg. [Lat., dim. of *vitulus,* calf.]

vi·ti·ate (vĭsh'ē-āt') *tr.v.* **-at·ed, -at·ing, -ates. 1.** To impair the value or quality of. **2.** To corrupt morally; debase. **3.** To make ineffective; invalidate. [Lat. *vitiare, vitiat-* < *vitium,* fault.] **—vi'ti·a·ble** (vĭsh'ē-ə-bəl) *adj.* **—vi'ti·a'tion** *n.* **—vi'ti·a'tor** *n.*

vit·i·cul·ture (vĭt'ĭ-kŭl'chər, vī'tĭ-) *n.* The cultivation of grapes. [Lat. *vitis,* vine + CULTURE.] **—vit'i·cul'tur·al** *adj.* **—vit'i·cul'tur·ist** *n.*

vit·i·li·go (vĭt'l-ī'gō, -ē'gō) *n.* A skin disorder characterized by the occurrence of whitish nonpigmented areas surrounded by hyperpigmented borders. [NLat. < Lat., tetter.]

vit·rec·to·my (vĭ-trĕk'tə-mē) *n., pl.* **-mies.** The surgical removal of the vitreous humor from the eyeball. [VITR(EOUS HUMOR) + -ECTOMY.]

vit·re·ous (vĭt′rē-əs) *adj.* **1.** Pertaining to, resembling, or having the nature of glass; glassy. **2.** Obtained or made from glass. **3.** Of or pertaining to the vitreous humor. [Lat. *vitreus* < *vitrum,* glass.] **—vit′re·os′i·ty** (-ŏs′ĭ-tē), **vit′re·ous·ness** *n.*

vitreous enamel *n.* Porcelain enamel.

vitreous humor *n.* Clear gelatinous matter that fills the part of the eyeball between the retina and the lens.

vi·tres·cent (vĭ-trĕs′ənt) *adj.* **1. a.** Tending to turn into glass. **b.** Similar to glass. **2.** Capable of being turned into glass. [Lat. *vitrum,* glass + -ESCENT.] **—vi·tres′cence** *n.*

vit·ri·fy (vĭt′rə-fī′) *v.* **-fied, -fy·ing, -fies.** *—tr.* To change or make into glass or a similar substance, esp. through heat fusion. *—intr.* To become vitreous. [Fr. *vitrifier* < Med. Lat. **vitrificare* : Lat. *vitrum,* glass + Lat. *facere,* to make.] **—vit′ri·fi′a·bil′i·ty** *n.* **—vit′ri·fi′a·ble** *adj.* **—vit′ri·fi·ca′tion** *n.*

vit·ri·ol (vĭt′rē-ōl′, -əl) *n.* **1.** *Chem.* **a.** Sulfuric acid. **b.** Any of various sulfates of metals, such as ferrous sulfate (green vitriol), zinc sulfate (white vitriol), or copper sulfate (blue vitriol). **2.** Vituperative feeling or expression. *—tr.v.* **-oled, -ol·ing, -ols** or **-olled, -ol·ling, -ols.** To expose or subject to vitriol. [ME < Med. Lat. *vitriolum* < LLat. *vitreolum,* neuter of *vitreolus,* of glass < Lat. *vitrum,* glass.]

vit·ri·ol·ic (vĭt′rē-ŏl′ĭk) *adj.* **1.** Of, similar to, or derived from a vitriol. **2.** Bitterly scathing; caustic: *vitriolic criticism.*

vit·ta (vĭt′ə) *n., pl.* **vit·tae** (vĭt′ē). **1.** *Biol.* A streak or band of color. **2.** *Bot.* An oil tube in the fruit of certain plants, as the carrot or parsley. [Lat., ribbon.] **—vit′tate′** (vĭt′āt′) *adj.*

vit·tle (vĭt′l) *n. & v. Nonstandard.* Variant of **victual.**

vi·tu·per·ate (vī-to͞o′pə-rāt′, -tyo͞o′-, vĭ-) *tr.v.* **-at·ed, -at·ing, -ates.** To rail against severely or abusively; berate. [Lat. *vituperare, vituperat-.*] **—vi·tu′per·a′tor** *n.*

vi·tu·per·a·tion (vī-to͞o′pə-rā′shən, -tyo͞o′-, vĭ-) *n.* **1.** Censure; blame. **2.** Invective; railing.

vi·tu·per·a·tive (vī-to͞o′pər-ə-tĭv, -tyo͞o′-, -pə-rā′-, vĭ-) *adj.* Harshly abusive; acrimonious. **—vi·tu′per·a·tive·ly** *adv.*

vi·va (vē′və, -vä′) *interj.* Used to express acclamation, salute, or applause. [Ital., long live < *vivere,* to live < Lat.]

vi·va·ce (vē-vä′chā) *adv. & adj. Mus.* In a lively or vivacious manner. Used as a direction. [Ital. < Lat. *vivax,* vivacious < *vivere,* to live.]

vi·va·cious (vĭ-vā′shəs, vī-) *adj.* Full of animation and spirit; lively. [< Lat. *vivax* < *vivere,* to live.] **—vi·va′cious·ly** *adv.* **—vi·va′cious·ness** *n.*

vi·vac·i·ty (vĭ-văs′ĭ-tē, vī-) *n.* The condition or quality of being vivacious; liveliness.

vi·van·dière (vē′väɴ-dyâr′) *n.* A woman who accompanies troops to sell them food, supplies, and liquor. [Fr., fem. of *vivandier* < OFr. < *viande,* food. —see VIAND.]

vi·var·i·um (vī-vâr′ē-əm) *n., pl.* **-i·ums** or **-i·a** (-ē-ə). A place or enclosure for keeping and raising living animals for observation or research. [Lat. < neuter of *vivarius,* of living creatures < *vivus,* alive < *vivere,* to live.]

vi·va vo·ce (vī′və vō′sē) *adv. & adj.* By word of mouth; oral. [Med. Lat., with the living voice.]

vi·ver·rine (vī-vĕr′īn, -ĭn′) *adj.* Of or belonging to the family Viverridae, which includes carnivorous mammals such as the civets and mongooses. *—n.* A member of the Viverridae. [< Lat. *viverra,* ferret.]

viv·id (vĭv′ĭd) *adj.* **1.** Perceived as bright and distinct; brilliant: *a vivid star.* **2. a.** Having intensely bright colors: *a vivid tapestry.* **b.** Very strong: *a vivid purple.* **3.** Full of the vigor and freshness of immediate experience. **4. a.** Evoking lifelike images within the mind; heard, seen, or felt as if real: *a vivid description.* **b.** Active in forming lifelike images: *a vivid imagination.* [Lat. *vividus* < *vivere,* to live.] **—viv′id·ly** *adv.* **—viv′id·ness** *n.*

viv·i·fy (vĭv′ə-fī′) *tr.v.* **-fied, -fy·ing, -fies. 1.** To give or bring life to; animate. **2.** To make more lively, intense, or striking; enliven. [OFr. *vivifier* < LLat. *vivificare* : Lat. *vivus,* alive + Lat. *facere,* to make.] **—viv′i·fi·ca′tion** *n.* **—viv′i·fi′er** *n.*

vi·vip·a·rous (vī-vĭp′ər-əs, vĭ-) *adj.* **1.** *Zool.* Giving birth to living offspring that develop within the mother's body. **2.** *Bot.* **a.** Germinating or producing seeds that germinate before becoming detached from the parent plant. **b.** Producing bulbils or new plants rather than seed. [Lat. *viviparus* : *vivus,* alive + *parere,* to give birth.] **—vi′vi·par′i·ty** (vī′və-păr′ĭ-tē, vĭv′ə-) *n.* **—vi·vip′a·rous·ly** *adv.*

viv·i·sect (vĭv′ĭ-sĕkt′) *v.* **-sect·ed, -sect·ing, -sects.** *—tr.* To perform vivisection on (a living animal). *—intr.* To practice vivisection. [Back-formation < VIVISECTION.] **—viv′i·sec′tor** *n.*

viv·i·sec·tion (vĭv′ĭ-sĕk′shən, vĭv′ĭ-sĕk′-) *n.* The act of cutting into or dissecting the body of a living animal, esp. for the purpose of scientific research. [Lat. *vivus,* alive + -SECTION.] **—viv′i·sec′tion·al** *adj.* **—viv′i·sec′tion·al·ly** *adv.* **—viv′i·sec′tion·ist** *n.*

vix·en (vĭk′sən) *n.* **1.** A female fox. **2.** A quarrelsome, shrewish, or malicious woman. [ME *fixen.*] **—vix′en·ish** *adj.* **—vix′en·ish·ly** *adv.* **—vix′en·ish·ness** *n.*

viz·ard also **vis·ard** (vĭz′ərd, -ärd′) *n.* **1.** A visor. **2.** A mask. [Alteration of obs. *vizar* < ME *viser.* —see VISOR.]

vi·zier also **vi·zir** (vĭ-zîr′) *n.* A high officer in a Moslem government, esp. in the old Turkish Empire. [Fr. *vizir* < Turk. *vezīr* < Ar. *wazīr.*] **—vi·zier′ate** (-ĭt, -āt′) *n.* **—vi·zier′i·al** *adj.*

vi·zor (vī′zər) *n. & v.* Variant of **visor.**

V-J Day (vē′jā′) *n.* The day of victory for the Allied forces over Japan in World War II; officially, September 2, 1945. [V(ICTORY IN) J(APAN) DAY.]

V-mail (vē′māl′) *n.* A postal service used during World War II in which letters were reduced photographically, transmitted overseas, and there enlarged and delivered. [< V(ICTORY).]

V-neck (vē′nĕk′) *n.* A V-shaped neckline, as of a sweater.

vo·ca·ble (vō′kə-bəl) *n.* A word considered only as a sequence of sounds or letters rather than as a unit of meaning. *—adj.* Capable of being voiced or spoken. [OFr. < Lat. *vocabulum,* name < *vocare,* to call.]

vo·cab·u·lar·y (vō-kăb′yə-lĕr′ē) *n., pl.* **-ies. 1.** A list of words and often phrases, usually arranged alphabetically and defined or translated; lexicon or glossary. **2.** All the words of a language. **3.** The sum of words used by, understood by, or at the command of a particular person or group. **4.** A command or reserve of techniques; repertoire: *a dancer's vocabulary of movement.* [Med. Lat. *vocabularium* < neuter of *vocabularius,* of words < Lat. *vocabulum,* name < *vocare,* to call.]

vo·cal (vō′kəl) *adj.* **1.** Of or pertaining to the voice. **2.** Uttered or produced by the voice. **3.** Having a voice and capable of emitting sound or speech. **4.** Full of voices; resounding. **5.** Quick to speak or criticize; outspoken. **6. a.** Vocalic. **b.** Voiced. *—n.* **1.** A vocal sound. **2.** A popular piece of music for a singer, often with instrumental accompaniment. [ME < Lat. *vocalis* < *vox,* voice.] **—vo′cal·ly** *adv.* **—vo′cal·ness** *n.*

vocal cords *pl.n.* The lower of two pairs of bands or folds in the larynx that vibrate when pulled together and when air is passed up from the lungs, thereby producing vocal sounds.

vo·cal·ic (vō-kăl′ĭk) *adj.* **1.** Containing, marked by, or consisting of vowels. **2.** Of, pertaining to, or having the nature of a vowel. **—vo·cal′i·cal·ly** *adv.*

vo·cal·ism (vō′kə-lĭz′əm) *n.* **1.** The use of the voice in speaking or singing. **2.** The act, technique, or art of singing. **3.** A vowel or vocalic sound. **4.** A system of vowels, as within a specific language.

vo·cal·ist (vō′kə-lĭst) *n.* A singer.

vo·cal·ize (vō′kə-līz′) *v.* **-ized, -iz·ing, -iz·es.** *—tr.* **1.** To produce with the voice. **2.** To give voice to; articulate. **3.** To mark (a vowelless Hebrew text, for example) with diacritical vowel points. **4. a.** To change (a consonant) into a vowel during articulation. **b.** To voice. *—intr.* **1. a.** To use the voice. **b.** To sing. **2.** To be changed into a vowel. **—vo′cal·i·za′tion** *n.* **—vo′cal·iz′er** *n.*

vo·ca·tion (vō-kā′shən) *n.* **1.** A regular occupation or profession, esp. one for which a person is specially suited or qualified. **2.** An urge or predisposition to undertake a certain kind of work, esp. a religious career; calling. [ME *vocacioun,* divine call to a religious life < Lat. *vocatio,* a calling < *vocare,* to call.]

vo·ca·tion·al (vō-kā′shə-nəl) *adj.* **1.** Of or pertaining to a vocation. **2.** Pertaining to, providing, or undergoing training in a special skill to be pursued as a trade. **—vo·ca′tion·al·ly** *adv.*

vo·ca·tion·al·ism (vō-kā′shə-nə-lĭz′əm) *n.* The stressing of vocational training in education. **—vo·ca′tion·al·ist** *n.*

vocational school *n.* A school, esp. one on a secondary level, that trains persons with special aptitudes for qualification in specific trades or occupations, as mechanics.

voc·a·tive (vŏk′ə-tĭv) *adj.* **1.** Pertaining to, characteristic of, or used in calling. **2.** Pertaining to or designating a grammatical case used in Latin and certain other languages to indicate the person or thing being addressed. *—n.* **1.** The vocative case. **2.** A word in the vocative case. [ME *vocatif* < OFr. < Lat. *vocativus* < *vocare,* to call.] **—voc′a·tive·ly** *adv.*

vo·cif·er·ant (vō-sĭf′ər-ənt) *adj.* Vociferous.

vo·cif·er·ate (vō-sĭf′ə-rāt′) *intr. & tr.v.* **-at·ed, -at·ing, -ates.** To cry out or utter vehemently, esp. in protest; clamor. [Lat. *vociferari, vociferat-* : *vox,* voice + *ferre,* to bear.] **—vo·cif′er·a′tion** *n.* **—vo·cif′er·a′tor** *n.*

vo·cif·er·ous (vō-sĭf′ər-əs) *adj.* **1.** Making an outcry; clamorous. **2.** Characterized by loudness and vehemence. **—vo·cif′er·ous·ly** *adv.* **—vo·cif′er·ous·ness** *n.*

Synonyms: *vociferous, blatant, boisterous, strident, clamorous.* These adjectives describe what is conspicuously loud, usually offensively so. *Vociferous* suggests the noise of an outcry, as of vehement demanding or protesting. *Blatant* suggests noise associated with coarseness, vulgarity, or obtrusive behavior. *Boisterous* is even stronger in implying a combination of noise and rowdy behavior, caused usually by unruliness or high spirits. *Strident* describes noise that is offensively harsh, shrill, or discordant. *Clamorous* adds to *vociferous* the idea of long duration; the term can also refer to any combination of loud, distracting sounds.

vod·ka (vŏd′kə) *n.* An alcoholic liquor originally distilled from fermented wheat mash but now also made from a mash of rye, corn, or potatoes. [R., dim of *voda,* water.]

vogue (vōg) *n.* **1.** The prevailing fashion, practice, or style: *Hoop skirts were once in vogue.* **2.** Popular acceptance or favor; popularity. [Fr. < OItal. *voga* < *vogare,* to row.]

vogu·ish (vō′gĭsh) *adj.* **1.** Chic; fashionable. **2.** In vogue for a temporary period of time. **—vogu′ish·ness** *n.*

voice (vois) *n.* **1. a.** The sound produced by the vocal organs

voided
Voided lozenges

volant
A martlet volant

volcanic
Volcanic ash covering a house in Iceland

volcano
Mount St. Helens in the Cascade Range of Washington erupting in May 1980

of a vertebrate, esp. by those of a human being. **b.** The ability to produce such sounds. **2.** A sound resembling or reminiscent of vocal utterance. **3.** The specified quality, condition, or timbre of vocal sound: *a hoarse voice.* **4. a.** A medium or agency of expression: *give voice to one's anger.* **b.** The right or opportunity to express a choice or opinion. **5.** *Gram.* A verb form indicating the relation between the subject and the action expressed by the verb. **6.** The expiration of air through vibrating vocal cords, used in the production of the vowels and voiced consonants. **7. a.** Musical tone produced by the vibration of vocal cords and resonated within the throat and head cavities. **b.** The quality or condition of a person's singing: *a baritone in excellent voice.* **c.** A singer: *a choir of excellent voices.* **8.** Any of the melodic parts for a musical composition. —*tr.v.* **voiced, voic·ing, voic·es. 1.** To give voice to; utter. **2.** To pronounce with vibration of the vocal cords. **3.** *Mus.* To regulate the tone of (the pipes of an organ, for example). —*idiom.* **with one voice.** In unison; unanimously. [ME < OFr. *vois* < Lat. *vox.*]

voice box *n.* The larynx.

voiced (voist) *adj.* **1.** Having a voice or a specified kind of voice: *harsh-voiced.* **2.** Uttered with vibration of the vocal cords, as the consonants *d* and *b.* —**voiced'ness** (voist'nĭs, voi'sĭd-) *n.*

voice·ful (vois'fəl) *adj.* Having a voice, esp. a loud voice; resounding. —**voice'ful·ness** *n.*

voice·less (vois'lĭs) *adj.* **1.** Having no voice; mute. **2.** Uttered without vibration of the vocal cords, as the consonants *t* and *p.* —**voice'less·ly** *adv.* —**voice'less·ness** *n.*

voice-o·ver (vois'ō'vər) *n.* In motion pictures and television, the voice of a narrator who does not appear on camera.

voice part *n. Mus.* A voice (sense 8).

voice·print (vois'prĭnt') *n.* An electronically recorded graphic representation of voice, typically with time plotted on the horizontal axis, frequency on the vertical, and amplitude exhibited in a series of contour lines, the configuration being characteristic of an individual speaker's articulation of a given word.

voic·er (voi'sər) *n.* One that voices organ pipes.

void (void) *adj.* **1.** Containing no matter; empty. **2.** Unoccupied, as a position; vacant. **3.** Devoid; lacking: *void of understanding.* **4.** Ineffective; useless. **5.** Having no legal force or validity; null. —*n.* **1. a.** An empty space. **b.** A vacuum. **2.** An open space or break in continuity; gap. **3.** A feeling or state of emptiness, loneliness, or loss. —*v.* **void·ed, void·ing, voids.** —*tr.* **1.** To make void or of no effect; invalidate. **2. a.** To take out (the contents of something); empty. **b.** To evacuate (body wastes). **3.** To leave; vacate. —*intr.* To evacuate body wastes. [ME < OFr. *voide* < VLat. **vocitus,* alteration of Lat. *vacuus* < *vacare,* to be empty.] —**void'er** *n.*

void·a·ble (voi'də-bəl) *adj.* Capable of being voided, esp. capable of being annulled. —**void'a·ble·ness** *n.*

void·ance (void'ns) *n.* **1.** The act of voiding, emptying, or evacuating. **2.** The condition of being vacant; emptiness.

void·ed (voi'dĭd) *adj. Heraldry.* Having the central area cut out or left vacant, leaving a narrow border or outline.

voile (voil) *n.* A sheer fabric of cotton, rayon, silk, or wool used esp. for making dresses and curtains. [Fr. < Lat. *vela,* neuter pl. of *velum,* covering.]

voir dire (vwär dîr') *n. Law.* A preliminary examination concerning the competence of a prospective witness or juror. [OFr., to speak the truth.]

voix cé·leste (vwä' sā-lĕst') *n.* An organ stop that produces a gentle tremolo effect. [Fr., celestial voice.]

Vo·lans (vō'lănz') *n.* A constellation in the polar region of the Southern Hemisphere near Carina and Dorado. [Lat. *volans,* pr.part. of *volare,* to fly.]

vo·lant (vō'lənt) *adj.* **1.** Flying or capable of flying. **2.** Moving quickly or nimbly; agile. **3.** *Heraldry.* Depicted with the wings extended as in flying. [Lat. *volans, volant-,* pr.part. of *volare,* to fly.]

Vo·la·pük (vō'lə-po͝ok', vŏl'ə-) *n.* An artificial international language based on English. [Volapük, world's speech : *vol,* world (< E. WORLD) + *pük,* speech (< E. SPEECH).]

vo·lar (vō'lər) *adj.* Of or pertaining to the sole of the foot or the palm of the hand. [< Lat. *vola,* sole.]

vol·a·tile (vŏl'ə-tl, -tīl') *adj.* **1.** Evaporating readily at normal temperatures and pressures. **2.** Capable of being readily vaporized. **3.** Changeable, esp.: **a.** Inconstant; fickle. **b.** Tending to violence; explosive. **c.** Lighthearted; flighty. **d.** Ephemeral; fleeting. **4.** Flying or capable of flying; volant. [Fr. < Lat. *volatilis,* flying < *volare,* to fly.] —**vol'a·tile·ness** *n.*

volatile oil *n.* A rapidly evaporating oil, esp. an essential oil, that does not leave a stain.

vol·a·til·i·ty (vŏl'ə-tĭl'ĭ-tē) *n.* The quality or state of being volatile.

vol·a·til·ize (vŏl'ə-tl-īz') *intr. & tr.v.* **-ized, -iz·ing, -iz·es. 1.** To become or make volatile. **2.** To evaporate or cause to evaporate. —**vol'a·til·iz'a·ble** *adj.* —**vol'a·til·i·za'tion** *n.* —**vol'a·til·iz'er** *n.*

vol-au-vent (vô'lō-väN') *n.* A light pastry shell filled with a ragout of meat or fish. [Fr. : *vol,* flight + *au,* with the + *vent,* wind.]

vol·can·ic (vŏl-kăn'ĭk, vôl-) *adj.* **1.** Of or resembling an erupting volcano. **2.** Produced by or discharged from a volcano. **3.** Powerfully explosive: *a volcanic temper.* —**vol·can'i·cal·ly** *adv.*

volcanic glass *n.* A volcanic igneous rock of vitreous or glassy texture, as obsidian or pitchstone.

vol·ca·nism (vŏl'kə-nĭz'əm, vôl'-) also **vul·ca·nism** (vŭl'-) *n.* Volcanic force or activity.

vol·ca·nize (vŏl'kə-nīz', vôl'-) *tr.v.* **-nized, -niz·ing, -niz·es.** To subject to or change by the effects of volcanic heat. —**vol'ca·ni·za'tion** *n.*

vol·ca·no (vŏl-kā'nō, vôl-) *n., pl.* **-noes** or **-nos. 1.** A vent in the earth's crust through which molten lava and gases are ejected. **2.** A mountain formed by the materials ejected from a volcano. [Ital. < Lat. *Volcanus,* Vulcan.]

vol·ca·no·gen·ic (vŏl'kə-nə-jĕn'ĭk, vôl'-) *adj.* Of volcanic origin.

vol·ca·nol·o·gy (vŏl'kə-nŏl'ə-jē, vôl'-) also **vul·ca·nol·o·gy** (vŭl'-) *n.* The science concerned with volcanic phenomena. —**vol'ca·no·log'i·cal** (-nə-lŏj'ĭ-kəl) *adj.* —**vol'ca·nol'o·gist** *n.*

vole[1] (vōl) *n.* Any of various rodents of the genus *Microtus* and related genera, resembling rats or mice but having a relatively short tail. [Short for obs. *volemouse* < Norw. **vollmus* : ON *vǫllr,* field + ON *mūs,* mouse.]

vole[2] (vōl) *n.* A grand slam. [Fr. < *voler,* to fly < OFr. < Lat. *volare,* to fly.]

vol·i·tant (vŏl'ĭ-tnt) *adj.* **1.** Flying or capable of flying. **2.** Moving about rapidly. [Lat. *volitans, volitant-,* pr.part. of *volitare,* to fly to and fro, freq. of *volare,* to fly.]

vol·i·ta·tion (vŏl'ĭ-tā'shən) *n.* **1.** The act of flying; flight. **2.** The ability to fly. —**vol'i·ta'tion·al** *adj.*

vo·li·tion (və-lĭsh'ən) *n.* **1.** An act of willing, choosing, or deciding. **2.** A conscious choice; decision. **3.** The power or capability of choosing; will. [Fr. < Med. Lat. *volitio* < Lat. *velle,* to wish.] —**vo·li'tion·al** *adj.* —**vo·li'tion·al·ly** *adv.*

vol·i·tive (vŏl'ĭ-tĭv) *adj.* **1.** Of, pertaining to, or originating in the will. **2.** Expressing a wish or permission.

volks·lied (fōk'slēt', fôlk'-) *n., pl.* **-lie·der** (-slē'dər). A folk song. [G. : *Volk,* people + *Lied,* song.]

vol·ley (vŏl'ē) *n., pl.* **-leys. 1. a.** The simultaneous discharge of a number of missiles. **b.** The missiles thus discharged. **2.** A bursting forth: *a volley of oaths.* **3.** *Sports.* A shot, esp. in tennis, made by striking the ball before it touches the ground. —*v.* **-leyed, -ley·ing, -leys.** —*tr.* **1.** To discharge in or as if in a volley. **2.** *Sports.* To strike (a tennis ball, for example) before it touches the ground. —*intr.* To be discharged in or as if in a volley. [OFr. *volee* < *voler,* to fly < Lat. *volare.*] —**vol'ley·er** *n.*

vol·ley·ball (vŏl'ē-bôl') *n.* **1.** A court game in which one team attempts to score by grounding a ball on the opposing team's side of a high net. **2.** The large inflated ball used in volleyball.

vol·plane (vŏl'plān', vôl'-) *intr.v.* **-planed, -plan·ing, -planes.** To glide toward the earth with the engine cut off. Used of an airplane or winged missile. —*n.* The glide of an airplane or winged missile. [Fr. *vol plané,* gliding flight.]

Vol·sci (vôl'skē', vŏl'sī') *pl.n.* A people of ancient Italy whose territory was conquered by the Romans in the fourth century B.C.

Vol·scian (vŏl'shən, vôl'skē-ən) *adj.* Of or pertaining to the Volsci or their language. —*n.* The Italic language of the Volsci.

volt[1] (vōlt) *n.* **1.** The International System unit of electric potential and electromotive force, equal to the difference of electric potential between two points on a conducting wire carrying a constant current of one ampere when the power dissipated between the points is one watt. **2.** A unit of electric potential and electromotive force equal to 1.00034 times the International System unit. [After Count Alessandro *Volta* (1745–1827).]

volt[2] also **volte** (vōlt, vôlt) *n.* **1.** A circular movement executed by a horse in manège. **2.** A sudden movement made in avoiding a thrust in fencing. [Fr. *volte* < OItal. *volta,* turn < *voltare,* to turn, leap. —see VAULT[2].]

volt·age (vōl'tĭj) *n.* Electromotive force or potential difference, usually expressed in volts.

voltage divider *n.* A number of resistors in series provided with taps at certain points to make available a fixed or variable fraction of the applied voltage.

vol·ta·ic (vŏl-tā'ĭk, vōl-, vôl-) *adj.* **1.** Pertaining to or denoting electricity or electric current produced by chemical action; galvanic. **2.** Producing electricity by chemical action. [< VOLT.]

voltaic battery *n.* An electric battery composed of a primary cell or cells.

voltaic cell *n.* A primary cell.

voltaic couple *n.* Two dissimilar conductors in contact or in the same electrolytic solution, resulting in a difference of potential between them.

voltaic pile *n.* A source of electricity consisting of a number of alternating disks of two different metals separated by acid-moistened pads, forming primary cells connected in series.

vol·ta·ism (vŏl'tə-ĭz'əm, vōl'-, vôl'-) *n.* Galvanism. [VOLTA(IC) + -ISM.]

volt·am·me·ter (vōlt'ăm'mē'tər) *n.* An instrument designed to measure current or potential. [VOLT-AM(PERE) + -METER.]

volt-am·pere (vōlt'ăm'pîr') *n.* A unit of electric power equal to the product of one volt and one ampere, equivalent to one watt.

volte (vōlt, vôlt) *n.* Variant of **volt²**.

volte-face (vôlt-fäs′, vôl′tə-) *n.* A reversal, as in policy; about-face.

volt·me·ter (vōlt′mē′tər) *n.* An instrument, such as a galvanometer, for measuring potential differences in volts.

vol·u·ble (vŏl′yə-bəl) *adj.* **1.** Characterized by a ready flow of words in speaking; fluent. **2.** Turning easily on an axis; rotating. **3.** Twining or twisting, as a plant. [OFr. < Lat. *volubilis* < *volvere,* to roll.] **—vol′u·bil′i·ty, vol′u·ble·ness** *n.* **—vol′u·bly** *adv.*

vol·ume (vŏl′yo͞om, -yəm) *n.* **1.** A collection of written or printed sheets bound together; book. **2.** One of the books within a complete set. **3.** Written material in a library that has been assembled and catalogued as an individual unit. **4.** A roll of parchment; scroll. **5. a.** The size or extent of a three-dimensional object or region of space. **b.** The capacity of such a region or of a specified container. **6.** A large amount: *volumes of praise.* **7. a.** The amplitude or loudness of a sound. **b.** A control, as on a radio, for adjusting loudness. [ME < OFr. < Lat. *volumen,* roll of writing < *volvere,* to roll.] **—vol′umed** *adj.*

vol·u·me·ter (vŏl′yo͞o-mē′tər) *n.* Any of several instruments for measuring the volume of liquids, solids, and gases. [VOLU(ME) + -METER.]

vol·u·met·ric (vŏl′yo͞o-mĕt′rĭk) *adj.* Of or pertaining to measurement of volume. [VOLU(ME) + -METRIC.] **—vol′u·met′ri·cal·ly** *adv.*

volumetric analysis *n.* **1.** Quantitative analysis using accurately measured, esp. titrated volumes of standard chemical solutions. **2.** The analysis of a gas by volume.

vo·lu·mi·nous (və-lo͞o′mə-nəs) *adj.* **1.** Having great volume, fullness, size, or number. **2. a.** Filling or capable of filling volumes. **b.** Prolific in speech or writing. **3.** Having many coils; winding: *the voluminous labyrinth.* [LLat. *voluminosus,* having many folds < Lat. *volumen,* roll of writing < *volvere,* to roll.] **—vo·lu′mi·nos′i·ty** (-nŏs′ĭ-tē), **vo·lu′mi·nous·ness** *n.* **—vo·lu′mi·nous·ly** *adv.*

vol·un·ta·rism (vŏl′ən-tə-rĭz′əm) *n.* Belief in the primacy of will. **—vol′un·ta·rist** *n.* **—vol′un·ta·ris′tic** *adj.*

vol·un·tar·y (vŏl′ən-tĕr′ē) *adj.* **1. a.** Arising from one's own free will. **b.** Acting on one's own initiative. **2.** Acting or serving in a specified capacity willingly and without constraint or guarantee of reward. **3.** Normally controlled by or subject to individual volition. **4.** Capable of exercising will; volitional. **5.** Proceeding from impulse; spontaneous. **6.** *Law.* **a.** Acting or performed without external persuasion or compulsion. **b.** Without legal obligation, payment, or valuable consideration: *a voluntary conveyance.* **c.** Not accidental; intentional: *voluntary manslaughter.* *—n., pl.* **-ies. 1.** *Mus.* Solo organ music, occasionally improvised, that is played usually before and sometimes during or after a church service. **2.** A volunteer. [ME < Lat. *voluntarius* < *voluntas,* choice < *velle,* to wish.] **—vol′un·tar′i·ly** (-târ′ə-lē) *adv.* **—vol′un·tar′i·ness** *n.*

Synonyms: *voluntary, intentional, deliberate, willful, willing, spontaneous.* These adjectives mean unforced. *Voluntary* is applied in several related senses to what is done by choice, to physical movement subject to regulation by the will, and less often to action that is not only of one's choice but premeditated. The last-named sense is more basic to *intentional* and *deliberate;* in addition, *deliberate* stresses the idea of action taken with full awareness of the consequences. *Willful* can mean merely in accordance with one's will but often implies headstrong persistence in a self-determined course of action. *Willing* suggests acceding to a course proposed by another, without reluctance or even eagerly. *Spontaneous* refers to behavior that seems wholly unpremeditated, a natural response and a true reflection of one's feelings.

vol·un·tar·y·ism (vŏl′ən-tĕr′ē-ĭz′əm) *n.* The principle of reliance on voluntary contributions rather than government funds, as for churches or schools. **—vol′un·tar′y·ist** *n.*

voluntary muscle *n.* Muscle normally controlled by individual volition.

vol·un·teer (vŏl′ən-tîr′) *n.* **1.** A person who performs or gives his services of his own free will. **2.** *Law.* **a.** A person who renders aid, performs a service, or assumes an obligation voluntarily. **b.** A person who holds property under a deed made without valuable consideration. **3.** A cultivated plant growing from self-sown or accidentally dropped seed. *—adj.* **1.** Pertaining to or consisting of volunteers: *a volunteer militia.* **2.** Enlisted or serving as a volunteer. **3.** Growing from self-sown or accidentally dropped seed. Used of a cultivated plant or crop that has reseeded itself. *—v.* **-teered, -teer·ing, -teers.** *—tr.* To give or offer to give on one's own initiative. *—intr.* To enter into or offer to enter into an undertaking of one's own free will. [Obs. Fr. *voluntaire* < Lat. *voluntarius,* voluntary.]

vol·un·teer·ism (vŏl′ən-tîr′ĭz′əm) *n.* The theory, act, or practice of being a volunteer or of using volunteers in community service work.

vo·lup·tu·ar·y (və-lŭp′cho͞o-ĕr′ē) *n., pl.* **-ies.** A person whose life is given over to luxury and sensual pleasures; sensualist. [LLat. *voluptuarius* < Lat. *voluptarius* < *voluptas,* pleasure.] **—vo·lup′tu·ar′y** *adj.*

vo·lup·tu·ous (və-lŭp′cho͞o-əs) *adj.* **1.** Consisting of or characterized by strong visual and tactile delights: *voluptuous sculpture.* **2.** Devoted to or frequently indulging in sensual gratifications. **3. a.** Full and appealing in form: *a voluptuous mouth.* **b.** Directed toward or anticipating sensuous gratification: *voluptuous thoughts.* **c.** Arising from the satisfying of luxurious or sensual desires. [ME < Lat. *voluptuosus,* full of pleasure < *voluptas,* pleasure.] **—vo·lup′tu·ous·ly** *adv.* **—vo·lup′tu·ous·ness** *n.*

vo·lute (və-lo͞ot′) *n.* **1.** A spiral, scroll-like ornament such as that used on an Ionic capital. **2.** A twisted or spiral formation, such as one of the whorls of a gastropod shell. **3.** Any of various marine gastropod mollusks of the family Volutidae, having a spiral, often colorfully marked shell. [Lat. *voluta* < fem. p.part. of *volvere,* to turn.] **—vo·lut′ed** (-lo͞o′tĭd) *adj.*

volute
On an Ionic capital

vol·u·tin (vŏl′yə-tĭn, və-lo͞ot′n) *n.* A basophilic granular substance found in many microorganisms that is thought to be nucleic acid. [G. < NLat. *volutans,* specific epithet of *Spirillum volutans,* a bacterium in which it was first found < Lat., pr.part. of *volutare,* to roll around, freq. of *volvere,* to roll.]

vo·lu·tion (və-lo͞o′shən) *n.* **1.** A turn or twist about a center; spiral. **2.** *Zool.* One of the whorls of a spiral shell. [< Lat. *volvere, volut-,* to turn.]

vol·va (vŏl′və, vôl′-) *n.* A cuplike structure around the base of the stalk of certain fungi. [Lat., a covering.] **—vol′vate′** (-vāt′) *adj.*

vol·vox (vŏl′vŏks′, vôl′-) *n.* Any of various flagellate protozoans of the genus *Volvox* that form hollow, spherical multicellular colonies. [NLat. *Volvox,* genus name < Lat. *volvere,* to turn.]

vol·vu·lus (vŏl′vyə-ləs, vôl′-) *n.* An obstruction in the intestine caused by abnormal twisting. [NLat. < Lat. *volvere,* to turn.]

vo·mer (vō′mər) *n.* The flat bone forming the inferior and posterior part of the nasal septum. [Lat., plowshare.] **—vo′mer·ine′** (-mə-rīn′) *adj.*

vom·i·ca (vŏm′ĭ-kə) *n., pl.* **-cae** (-sē′). **1.** The profuse expectoration of putrid matter. **2. a.** An abnormal pus-containing cavity in a lung, caused by the deterioration of tissue. **b.** The purulent matter contained in such a cavity. [Lat., ulcer < *vomere,* to vomit.]

vom·it (vŏm′ĭt) *v.* **-it·ed, -it·ing, -its.** *—intr.* **1.** To eject part or all of the contents of the stomach through the mouth, usually in a series of involuntary spasmic movements. **2.** To be discharged forcefully and abundantly; spew forth. *—tr.* **1.** To eject from the stomach through the mouth. **2.** To eject or discharge in a gush; spew out. *—n.* **1.** The act of ejecting matter from the stomach. **2.** Matter that is ejected from the stomach. **3.** An emetic. [ME *vomiten* < Lat. *vomere.*] **—vom′it·er** *n.*

vom·i·tive (vŏm′ĭ-tĭv) *adj.* Pertaining to or causing vomiting. *—n.* An emetic.

vom·i·to·ry (vŏm′ĭ-tôr′ē, -tōr′ē) *adj.* Inducing vomiting; vomitive. *—n., pl.* **-ries. 1.** Something that induces vomiting. **2.** An aperture through which matter is discharged. **3.** One of the passageways of a Roman amphitheater leading from the outside wall to the foot of the banked seats.

vom·i·tu·ri·tion (vŏm′ĭ-chə-rĭsh′ən, -ĭ-to͞o-) *n.* Forceful but ineffectual attempts at vomiting; retching. [VOMIT + (MICT)URITION.]

vom·i·tus (vŏm′ĭ-təs) *n.* Vomited matter. [Lat., p.part of *vomere,* to vomit.]

voo·doo (vo͞o′do͞o) *n., pl.* **-doos. 1.** A religious cult characterized by a belief in sorcery, fetishes, and rituals in which participants communicate by trance with ancestors, saints, or animistic deities. **2.** A charm, fetish, spell, or curse believed by adherents of voodoo to hold magic power. **3.** One who performs rites at a meeting of adherents of voodoo. *—tr.v.* **-dooed, -doo·ing, -doos.** To place under the influence of a voodoo spell; hex. [Louisiana Fr. *voudou* < Ewe *vòdú.*]

voo·doo·ism (vo͞o′do͞o-ĭz′əm) *n.* **1.** The view of life and death embodied in the voodoo cult. **2.** The practice of voodoo. **—voo′doo·ist** *n.* **—voo′doo·is′tic** *adj.*

vo·ra·cious (vô-rā′shəs, və-) *adj.* **1.** Consuming or eager to consume great amounts of food; ravenous. **2.** Having an insatiable appetite for an activity or pursuit; greedy: *a voracious reader.* [< Lat. *vorax, vorac-* < *vorare,* to devour.] **—vo·ra′cious·ly** *adv.* **—vo·rac′i·ty** (-răs′ĭ-tē), **vo·ra′cious·ness** *n.*

vor·la·ge (fôr′lä′gə, fōr′-) *n.* A posture assumed in skiing in which the skier leans forward from the ankles, usually without lifting the heels. [G. : *vor,* before + *Lage,* stance.]

-vorous *suff.* Eating; feeding on: *vermivorous.* [Lat. *-vorus* < *vorare,* to devour.]

vor·tex (vôr′tĕks′) *n., pl.* **-tex·es** or **-ti·ces** (-tĭ-sēz′). **1.** Fluid flow involving rotation about an axis, esp. a whirlpool. **2.** A situation regarded as drawing into its center all that surrounds it: *"As happened with so many theater actors, he was swept up in the vortex of Hollywood."* (New York Times). [Lat. *vortex, vortic-* < *vertere,* to turn.]

vor·ti·cal (vôr′tĭ-kəl) *adj.* Of, pertaining to, or resembling a vortex; whirling. **—vor′ti·cal·ly** *adv.*

vor·ti·cel·la (vôr′tĭ-sĕl′ə) *n., pl.* **-cel·lae** (-sĕl′ē) or **-cel·las.**

votary
Votary of Diana

voting machine

Any of various bell-shaped, ciliated, stalked protozoans of the genus *Vorticella.* [NLat. *Vorticella,* genus name < Lat. *vortex,* vortex.]

vor·ti·ces (vôr′tĭ-sēz′) *n.* A plural of **vortex.**

vor·ti·cose (vôr′tĭ-kōs′) *adj.* Vortical.

vor·tig·i·nous (vôr-tĭj′ə-nəs) *adj.* Vortical. [< Lat. *vertigo, vertigin-,* a whirling < *vertere,* to turn.]

vo·ta·ry (vō′tə-rē) *n., pl.* **-ries. 1.** A person bound by vows to live a life of religious worship or service; monk or nun. **2.** A person fervently devoted to a religion, activity, leader, or ideal. [< Lat. *votum,* vow < *vovēre,* to vow.]

Synonyms: *votary, devotee, habitué, fan.* These nouns mean an adherent of a person, cause, or activity. *Votary* and *devotee* imply strong personal commitment to the service of a person or thing, usually in a favorable sense. Both can refer to religious dedication or, by extension, to attachment to a branch of learning, a hobby, or a cultural pursuit. *Habitué* refers to one in regular attendance at a place offering a certain kind of activity. *Fan* is an informal term for an ardent enthusiast or admirer.

vote (vōt) *n.* **1. a.** A formal expression of preference for a candidate for office or for a proposed resolution of an issue. **b.** The way by which such a preference is made known, as by a raised hand or a ballot. **2.** The number of votes cast in an election or to resolve an issue: *a heavy vote in his favor.* **3.** A group of voters: *the labor vote.* **4.** The result of an election or referendum. **5.** The right to participate as a voter; suffrage. *—v.* **vot·ed, vot·ing, votes.** *—intr.* To express one's preference by a vote; cast one's vote. *—tr.* **1.** To express one's preference for; endorse by a vote. **2.** To bring into existence or make available by vote: *vote new funds for a program.* **3.** To declare or pronounce by general consent: *voted the play a success.* ***—phrasal verbs.* vote down.** To defeat by casting a negative vote. **vote in.** To elect. **vote out.** To remove from elective office by supporting the opposition. [Lat. *votum,* vow < *vovēre,* to vow.] **—vot′a·ble, vote′a·ble** *adj.* **—vot′er** *n.*

vote getter *n.* **1.** A candidate with abilities and qualities that attract votes in his favor. **2.** A means of drawing votes.

vote·less (vōt′lĭs) *adj.* Having no vote, esp. denied a political vote.

voting machine *n.* An apparatus for use in polling places that mechanically records and counts votes.

vo·tive (vō′tĭv) *adj.* **1.** Given or dedicated in fulfillment of a vow or pledge: *a votive offering.* **2.** Expressing a wish, desire, or vow: *a votive prayer.* [Lat. *votivus* < *votum,* vow.] **—vo′tive·ly** *adv.*

votive Mass *n. Rom. Cath. Ch.* A Mass differing from one prescribed for a certain day in that it is celebrated at the direction of authority, because of special circumstances, or at the decision of the priest.

vouch (vouch) *v.* **vouched, vouch·ing, vouch·es.** *—tr.* **1.** To substantiate by supplying evidence; verify. **2.** *Law.* To summon as a witness to give warranty of title. **3.** *Archaic.* To cite (an authority, for example) as supporting evidence for one's statements, opinions, or actions. **4.** *Archaic.* To assert; declare. *—intr.* **1.** To furnish a guarantee; give personal assurance. **2.** To function or serve as a guarantee; furnish supporting evidence. *—n. Obs.* A declaration of opinion; assertion. [ME *vouchen,* to summon to court < OFr. *voucher* < Lat. *vocare,* to call.]

vouch·er (vou′chər) *n.* **1.** A person who vouches. **2.** A document that serves as proof that the terms of a transaction have been met.

vouch·safe (vouch-sāf′, vouch′sāf′) *tr.v.* **-safed, -saf·ing, -safes.** To condescend to grant or bestow (a privilege, for example); deign. [ME *vouchen sauf,* to warrant as safe.] **—vouch·safe′ment** *n.*

vous·soir (vōō-swär′) *n.* Any of the wedge-shaped stones that form the curved parts of an arch or vaulted ceiling. [Fr. < OFr. *vossoir* < VLat. **volsorium* < **volsus,* var. of Lat. *volutus,* p.part. of *volvere,* to turn.]

vow (vou) *n.* **1.** An earnest promise or pledge that binds one to perform a specified act or behave in a certain manner, esp. a solemn promise to live and act in accordance with the prescriptions of a religious body: *a nun's vows.* **2.** A formal declaration or assertion. *—v.* **vowed, vow·ing, vows.** *—tr.* **1.** To promise or pledge solemnly. **2.** To make a pledge or threat to undertake: *vowing revenge on their persecutors.* **3.** To declare or assert formally. *—intr.* To express a promise or pledge; make a vow. ***—idiom.* take vows.** To enter a religious order. [ME *vowe* < OFr. < Lat. *votum* < *vovēre,* to vow.] **—vow′er** *n.*

vow·el (vou′əl) *n.* **1.** A speech sound created by the relatively free passage of breath through the larynx and oral cavity, usually forming the most prominent and central sound of a syllable. **2.** A letter that represents a vowel, as *a, e, i, o, u,* and sometimes *y* in the English alphabet. [ME *vowelle* < OFr. *vouel* < Lat. *vocalis,* sounding < *vox,* voice.]

vowel fracture *n. Ling.* Breaking.

vow·el·ize (vou′ə-līz′) *tr.v.* **-ized, -iz·ing, -iz·es.** To provide with vowel points. **—vow′el·i·za′tion** *n.*

vowel point *n.* Any of a number of diacritical marks written above or below consonants to indicate a preceding or following vowel in languages such as Hebrew and Arabic that are usually written without vowel letters.

vox an·gel·i·ca (vŏks′ ăn-jĕl′ĭ-kə) *n.* Voix céleste. [NLat., angelic voice.]

vox hu·ma·na (vŏks′ hyōō-mā′nə, -mä′-) *n.* An organ reed stop that produces tones imitative of the human voice. [Lat., human voice.]

vox pop·u·li (vŏks′ pŏp′yə-lī′, -lē) *n.* Popular opinion or sentiment. [Lat., voice of the people.]

voy·age (voi′ĭj) *n.* **1.** A long journey, usually to a foreign or distant land, esp. a journey across an open sea or ocean. **2.** A record or account of a journey of exploration or discovery. *—v.* **-aged, -ag·ing, -ag·es.** *—intr.* To make a voyage. *—tr.* To sail across; traverse. [ME < OFr. *veyage* < Lat. *viaticum,* provisions for a journey < *viaticus,* of a journey < *via,* road.] **—voy′ag·er** *n.*

voy·a·geur (voi′ə-zhûr′, vwä′yä-) *n., pl.* **-geurs** (-zhûr′). A woodsman, boatman, or guide, esp. one employed by fur companies to transport furs and supplies between remote stations in the U.S. and Canadian northwest. [Fr., traveler < *voyage,* journey < OFr. *veyage.* —see VOYAGE.]

vo·yeur (voi-yûr′) *n.* A person who derives sexual gratification from observing the sex organs or sexual acts of others, esp. from a secret vantage point. [Fr. < OFr., one who sees < *voir,* to see < Lat. *vidēre,* to see.] **—vo·yeur′ism** *n.* **—vo′yeur·is′tic** (voi′yə-rĭs′tĭk) *adj.* **—vo′yeur·is′ti·cal·ly** *adv.*

V-par·ti·cle (vē′pär′tĭ-kəl) *n.* Any of several subatomic particles with half-lives in the range of 10^{-10} to 10^{-6} second. [From the shape of the track left by its decay product in a cloud chamber.]

vrouw or **vrow** (frou, frō) *n.* A Dutch woman. [Du., woman < MDu. *vrouwe.*]

V-shaped (vē′shăpt′) *adj.* Having the shape of the letter V.

V sign *n.* A symbol of victory formed by holding the raised index and middle fingers in the shape of a V.

VT fuze (vē′tē′) *n.* A proximity fuze. [V(ARIABLE) T(IME) FUZE.]

Vul·can (vŭl′kən) *n. Rom. Myth.* The god of fire and craftsmanship, esp. metalworking, identified with the Greek god Hephaestus. [Lat. *Vulcanus, Volcanus.*]

vul·ca·ni·an (vŭl-kā′nē-ən) *adj.* **1.** *Geol.* Of, pertaining to, or from a volcano or volcanic eruption. **2. Vulcanian. a.** Of or pertaining to the god Vulcan. **b.** Of or pertaining to craftsmanship or metalworking.

vul·ca·nism (vŭl′kə-nĭz′əm) *n.* Variant of **volcanism.**

vul·ca·nite (vŭl′kə-nīt′) *n.* A hard rubber produced by vulcanization.

vul·ca·nize (vŭl′kə-nīz′) *tr.v.* **-nized, -niz·ing, -niz·es.** To improve the strength, resiliency, and freedom from stickiness and odor of (rubber, for example) by combining with sulfur or other additives in the presence of heat and pressure. [< VULCAN.] **—vul′ca·niz′a·ble** *adj.* **—vul′ca·ni·za′tion** *n.* **—vul′ca·niz′er** *n.*

vul·ca·nol·o·gy (vŭl′kə-nŏl′ə-jē) *n.* Variant of **volcanology.**

vul·gar (vŭl′gər) *adj.* **1.** Of or associated with the great masses of people as distinguished from the educated or cultivated classes; common. **2.** Spoken by or expressed in language spoken by the common people; vernacular. **3. a.** Deficient in taste, delicacy, or refinement. **b.** Ill-bred; boorish. **c.** Ostentatious in appearance or quality; pretentious: *a vulgar display of wealth.* **4.** Obscene or indecent; lewd: *a vulgar joke.* [ME < Lat. *vulgaris* < *vulgus,* the common people.] **—vul′gar·ly** *adv.* **—vul′gar·ness** *n.*

vul·gar·i·an (vŭl-gâr′ē-ən) *n.* A vulgar person, esp. one who makes a conspicuous display of his money.

vul·gar·ism (vŭl′gə-rĭz′əm) *n.* **1.** Vulgarity. **2. a.** A vulgar word or phrase. **b.** A word, phrase, or manner of expression used mainly by uncultivated people.

vul·gar·i·ty (vŭl-găr′ĭ-tē) *n., pl.* **-ties. 1.** The condition or quality of being vulgar. **2.** Something, as an act or expression, that offends good taste or propriety.

vul·gar·ize (vŭl′gə-rīz′) *tr.v.* **-ized, -iz·ing, -iz·es. 1.** To make vulgar; debase. **2.** To popularize. **—vul′gar·i·za′tion** *n.* **—vul′gar·iz′er** *n.*

Vulgar Latin *n.* The common speech of the ancient Romans, which is distinguished from standard literary Latin and is the ancestor of the Romance languages.

vul·gate (vŭl′gāt′, -gĭt) *n.* **1.** The common speech of a people; vernacular. **2.** A widely accepted text or version of a work. **3. Vulgate.** The Latin translation of the Bible made by Saint Jerome at the end of the 4th century A.D., now used in a revised form as the Roman Catholic authorized version. [< Lat. *vulgatus,* common < *vulgare,* to make known to all < *vulgus,* the common people.]

vul·ner·a·ble (vŭl′nər-ə-bəl) *adj.* **1.** Susceptible to physical injury. **2.** Susceptible to attack: *"We are vulnerable both by water and land, without either fleet or army"* (Alexander Hamilton). **3. a.** Liable to censure or criticism; assailable. **b.** Liable to succumb to persuasion or temptation. **4.** In a position to receive greater penalties or bonuses in the game of bridge. Used of the partners of a team that has won one game of a rubber. [LLat. *vulnerabilis* < Lat. *vulnerare,* to wound < *vulnus,* wound.] **—vul′ner·a·bil′i·ty, vul′ner·a·ble·ness** *n.* **—vul′ner·a·bly** *adv.*

vul·ner·ar·y (vŭl′nə-rĕr′ē) *adj.* Used in the healing or treating of wounds. *—n., pl.* **-ies.** A remedy used in healing or treating wounds. [Lat. *vulnerarius* < *vulnus,* wound.]

Vul·pec·u·la (vŭl-pĕk′yə-lə) *n.* A constellation in the North-

ern Hemisphere near Cygnus and Sagitta. [Lat. *vulpecula,* small fox, dim. of *vulpes,* fox.]
vul·pine (vŭl′pīn′) *adj.* **1.** Of, resembling, or characteristic of a fox. **2.** Cunning; foxy. [Lat. *vulpinus* < *vulpes,* fox.]
vul·ture (vŭl′chər) *n.* **1.** Any of various large birds of the family Cathartidae, of the New World, or the family Accipitridae, of the Old World, characteristically having dark plumage and a naked head and neck and feeding on carrion. **2.** A person of a rapacious or predatory nature. [ME < OFr. *voltour* < Lat. *vultur.*]
vul·tur·ine (vŭl′chə-rīn′) also **vul·tur·ous** (-chər-əs) *adj.* **1.** Of, pertaining to, or characteristic of a vulture. **2.** Suggestive of a vulture; predatory.
vul·va (vŭl′və) *n., pl.* **-vae** (-vē′). The external female genitalia, including the labia majora, labia minora, clitoris, and vestibule of the vagina. [Lat., womb, covering.] **—vul′val, vul′var** (-vər, -vär′) *adj.* **—vul′vate′** (-vāt′, -vĭt) *adj.* **—vul′vi·form′** (-və-fôrm′) *adj.*
vul·vi·tis (vŭl-vī′tĭs) *n.* Inflammation of the vulva.
vul·vo·vag·i·ni·tis (vŭl′vō-văj′ə-nī′tĭs) *n.* Simultaneous inflammation of the vulva and vagina.
vy·ing (vī′ĭng) *v.* Present participle of **vie.**

vulture

W

Around 1000 B.C. the Phoenicians and other Semitic peoples began to use graphic signs to represent individual speech sounds instead of syllables or words. They used a symbol (1,2) which is the ancestor of the letters F, U, V, and Y as well as W to represent the sound of the semivowel "w" and called it *wāw,* their word for "hook." The Greeks, adapting the Phoenician alphabet, varied the shape of *wāw* slightly (3,4,5,6) and altered its name to *upsilon.* They used *upsilon* to represent the sound of the vowel "u." The Romans borrowed the alphabet from the Greeks via the Etruscans who used a tailless variant of *upsilon.* The Romans used *upsilon* to represent both the vowel "u" and the semivowel "w," which later developed into the consonantal sound "v." The symbol W was developed in England during the 7th century to represent the semivowel "w" which, though lost in Latin, was an important sound in Old English. It was called "double-u" because it was formed by writing two cursive U's joined by a ligature, but later it was written as one character (10). Since the invention of printing about 500 years ago the shape of W, based on the medieval letter, has become standardized. Although both the modern upper- and lower-case printed letters are based on the letter V, the original name has persisted in English.

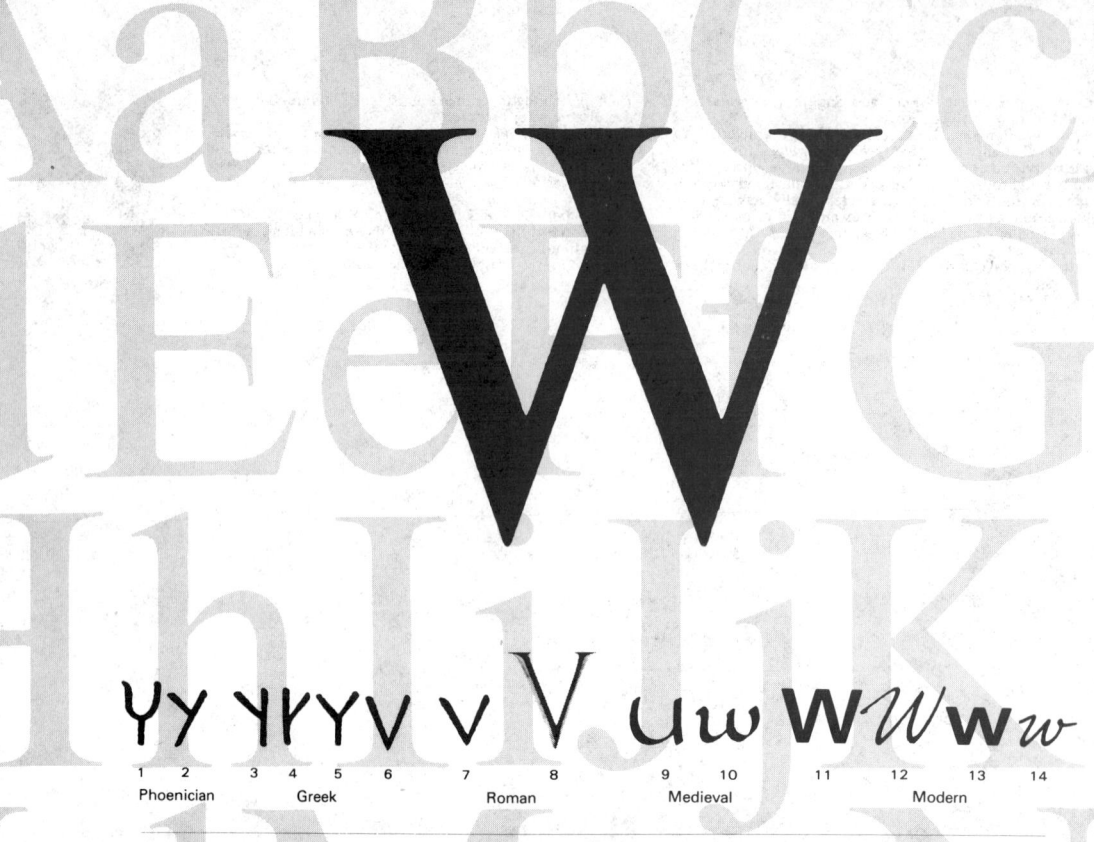

w

w or **W** (dŭb′əl-yo͞o, -yo͞o) *n., pl.* **w's** or **W's.** **1.** The 23rd letter of the modern English alphabet. **2.** Any of the speech sounds represented by the letter *w.* **3.** Something shaped like the letter W. **4.** The 23rd in a series.
W The symbol for the element tungsten. [G. *Wolfram.*]
wab·ble (wŏb′əl) *v. & n.* Variant of **wobble.**
Wac (wăk) *n.* A member of the Women's Army Corps of the U.S. Army, organized during World War II. [Abbr. of *Women's Army Corps.*]
wack·y (wăk′ē) also **whack·y** (hwăk′ē, wăk′ē) *adj.* **-i·er, -i·est.** *Slang.* **1.** Highly irrational or erratic: *a wacky person.* **2.** Crazy; silly: *a wacky idea.* [Orig. unknown.] **—wack′i·ly** *adv.* **—wack′i·ness** *n.*
wad (wŏd) *n.* **1.** A small mass of soft material, often folded or rolled, used for padding, stuffing, or packing. **2.** A compressed ball, roll, or lump of something, such as tobacco. **3. a.** A plug, as of cloth or paper, used to hold in a powder charge in a muzzleloading gun or cannon. **b.** A disk, as of felt or paper, used to keep the powder and shot in place in a shotgun cartridge. **4.** *Informal.* A large amount. **5.** *Informal.* **a.** A sizable roll of paper money. **b.** A considerable amount of money. *—v.* **wad·ded, wad·ding, wads.** *—tr.* **1.** To compress into a wad. **2.** To pad, pack, line, or plug with wadding. **3. a.** To hold (shot or powder) in place with a wad. **b.** To insert a wad in (a gun). *—intr.* To form into a wad. [Orig. unknown.]
wad·die (wŏd′ē) *n.* Variant of **waddy**[2].
wad·ding (wŏd′ĭng) *n.* **1. a.** A wad. **b.** Wads collectively. **2.** A soft layer of fibrous cotton or wool used for padding or stuffing. **3.** Material for gun wads.
wad·dle (wŏd′l) *intr.v.* **-dled, -dling, -dles. 1.** To walk with short steps that tilt the body from side to side. **2.** To walk heavily and clumsily with a pronounced sway. *—n.* A waddling gait. [Freq. of WADE.] **—wad′dler** *n.*
wad·dy[1] (wŏd′ē) *Austral. —n., pl.* **-dies.** A heavy straight stick or club thrown as a weapon by Australian aborigines. *—tr.v.* **-died, -dy·ing, -dies.** To strike with a waddy. [Native word in Australia.]
wad·dy[2] also **wad·die** (wŏd′ē) *n., pl.* **-dies.** *Western U.S.* **1.** A cowboy. **2.** A cattle rustler. [Orig. unknown.]
wade (wād) *v.* **wad·ed, wad·ing, wades.** *—intr.* **1.** To walk in or through water or other medium that similarly impedes normal movement. **2.** To make one's way arduously: *waded through the thick crowd.* *—tr.* To cross or pass through by wading: *wade a creek.* **—*phrasal verb.* wade in** (or **into**). To plunge into, begin, or attack resolutely and energetically: *waded into the task.* *—n.* The act of wading. [ME *waden* < OE *wadan.*]
wad·er (wā′dər) *n.* **1.** One that wades. **2.** A long-legged bird that frequents shallow water. **3. waders.** Waterproof hip boots or trousers worn esp. by fishermen or hunters.
wa·di also **wa·dy** (wä′dē) *n., pl.* **-dis** also **-dies. 1. a.** A valley, gully, or riverbed in northern Africa and southwestern Asia that remains dry except during the rainy season. **b.** A stream that flows through such a channel. **2.** An oasis. [Ar. *wādī.*]
wading bird *n.* A wader (sense 2).
Waf (wăf) *n.* A member of the Women in the Air Force, organized after World War II. [Abbr. of *Women in the Air Force.*]
wa·fer (wā′fər) *n.* **1.** A small, thin, crisp cake, biscuit, or candy. **2.** *Eccles.* A small, thin disk of unleavened bread used in the sacrament of the Eucharist. **3.** A flat tablet of dried flour paste encasing a powdered drug. **4.** A small disk of adhesive material used as a seal for papers. **5.** *Electronics.* A small thin flat circular disk of a semiconducting material, such as pure silicon, that is masked, oxide-coated, doped, and otherwise processed for ultimate separation into numerous individual electronic devices or for packaging as an integrated circuit. *—tr.v.* **-fered, -fer·ing, -fers. 1.** To seal or fasten together with a wafer. **2.** To prepare in the form of wafers. **3.** *Electronics.* To divide into wafers. [ME *wafre* < ONFr. *waufre,* of Germanic orig.]
waff (wăf, wäf) *Scot. —v.* **waffed, waff·ing, waffs.** *—intr.* To wave; flutter. *—tr.* To cause to wave or flutter. *—n.* **1.** A waving motion. **2.** A gust of air; waft. [ME *waffen,* to wave.]
waf·fle[1] (wŏf′əl) *n.* A light, crisp batter cake baked in a waffle iron. [Du. *wafel.*]
waf·fle[2] (wŏf′əl) *Informal. —intr.v.* **-fled, -fling, -fles.** To speak or write evasively; willfully mislead. *—n.* Evasive, vague, or misleading speech or writing. [Prob. freq. of obs. *waff,* to yelp.]
waffle iron *n.* An appliance having hinged, indented plates that impress a grid pattern into waffle batter as it bakes.
waft (wäft, wăft) *v.* **waft·ed, waft·ing, wafts.** *—tr.* **1.** To cause to go gently and smoothly through the air or over water. **2.** To convey or send floating through the air or over water. *—intr.* To float easily and gently, as on the air; drift. *—n.* **1.** Something, as an odor, carried through the air. **2.** A light breeze; rush of air. **3.** The act of wafting or waving. **4.** *Naut.* **a.** A flag used for signaling or indicating wind direction. **b.** A signal with a flag. [ME **waughten,* to convoy < MDu. or MLG *wachten,* to guard.]
waft·age (wăf′tĭj, wäf′-) *n.* The act or state of being wafted.
waf·ture (wăf′chər, wäf′-) *n.* **1.** The act or action of waving. **2.** The action of wafting.
wag[1] (wăg) *v.* **wagged, wag·ging, wags.** *—intr.* **1. a.** To move briskly and repeatedly from side to side, to and fro, or up and down. **b.** To be incessantly active. **2.** To walk with a clumsy sway; waddle. **3.** *Archaic.* To be on one's way; depart. *—tr.* To wag (a part of the body) as in playfulness, agreement, admonition, or chatter. *—n.* The act or motion of wagging. [ME *waggen.*] **—wag′ger** *n.*
wag[2] (wăg) *n.* A mischievous person. [Orig. unknown.]
wage (wāj) *n.* **1.** Payment for services to a worker, esp. remuneration on an hourly, daily, or weekly basis or by the piece. **2. wages.** *Econ.* The portion of the national product that represents the aggregate paid for all contributing labor and services as distinguished from the portion retained by management or reinvested in capital goods. **3.** Often **wages** *(used with a sing. or pl. verb).* A fitting return; recompense: *the wages of sin.* *—tr.v.* **waged, wag·ing, wag·es.** To engage in (a war or campaign). [ME < ONFr., of Germanic orig.]
wage earner *n.* **1.** A person who works for wages. **2.** One whose earnings support a household.
wa·ger (wā′jər) *n.* **1.** An agreement under which each bettor pledges a certain amount to the other depending upon the outcome of an unsettled matter. **2.** The matter bet on; gamble. **3.** Something staked on an uncertain outcome; bet. **4.** *Archaic.* A pledge of personal combat to resolve an issue or case. *—v.* **-gered, -ger·ing, -gers.** *—tr.* To risk or stake (an amount or possession) on an uncertain outcome; bet. *—intr.* To make a wager. [ME < AN *wageure* < ONFr. *wagier,* to pledge.] **—wa′ger·er** *n.*
wage scale *n.* The scale of wages paid to employees for the various jobs within an industry, factory, or company.
wage·work·er (wāj′wûr′kər) *n.* A wage earner.
wag·ger·y (wăg′ə-rē) *n., pl.* **-ies. 1.** Waggish behavior or spirit; drollery. **2.** A droll remark or act.
wag·gish (wăg′ĭsh) *adj.* Characteristic of a wag; playfully humorous. **—wag′gish·ly** *adv.* **—wag′gish·ness** *n.*
wag·gle (wăg′əl) *v.* **-gled, -gling, -gles.** *—tr.* To move (an attached part, for example) with short, quick motions: *waggled her foot impatiently.* *—intr.* To move shakily; wobble. *—n.* A waggling motion. [Freq. of WAG[1].] **—wag′gly** *adj.*
Wag·ner·i·an (väg-nîr′ē-ən) *adj.* Of, pertaining to, or characteristic of Richard Wagner, his music dramas, or his theories. *—n.* **1.** An admirer or disciple of Richard Wagner. **2.** A performer of Wagner's music, esp. a vocalist or conductor.
wag·on (wăg′ən) *n.* **1.** A four-wheeled, usually horse-drawn vehicle having a large rectangular body for transporting loads and often a detachable cover. **2. a.** A light automotive transport or delivery vehicle. **b.** A station wagon. **c.** A police patrol wagon. **3.** A child's low, four-wheeled cart hauled by a long handle that governs the direction of the front wheels. **4.** A small table or tray on wheels for serving drinks or food: *a dessert wagon.* **5.** *Chiefly Brit.* An open railway freight car. **6. Wagon.** The Big Dipper. *—v.* **-oned, -on·ing, -ons.** *—tr.* To transport by wagon. *—intr.* To travel or transport goods by wagon. **—*idioms.* off the wagon.** *Slang.* No longer abstaining from liquor. **on the wagon.** *Slang.* Abstaining from liquor. [Du. *wagen* < MDu.]
wag·on·er (wăg′ə-nər) *n.* **1.** A wagon driver. **2. Wagoner.** The constellation Auriga.
wag·on·ette (wăg′ə-nĕt′) *n.* A light horse-drawn wagon with two seats facing lengthwise placed behind the driver's seat.
wa·gon-lit (vä′gôN-lē′) *n., pl.* **wa·gons-lits** or **wa·gon-lits** (vä′gôN-lē′). A railroad sleeping car. [Fr. : *wagon,* railroad car (< E.) + *lit,* bed (< Lat. *lectus).*]
wag·on·load (wăg′ən-lōd′) *n.* The load held by one wagon.
wagon train *n.* A line or train of wagons traveling cross-country.
wag·tail (wăg′tāl′) *n.* Any of various birds of the genus *Motacilla* and related genera, having a long, constantly wagging tail.
Wah·ha·bi or **Wa·ha·bi** (wä-hä′bē) *n.* A member of a Moslem sect founded by Abdul Wahhab in the 18th century, known for its strict observance of the Koran and flourishing mainly in Arabia. **—Wah·ha′bism** (-bĭz′əm) *n.*
wa·hi·ne (wä-hē′nē, -nā′) *n.* **1.** A Polynesian woman. **2.** A female surfer. [Hawaiian and Maori.]
wa·hoo[1] (wä-ho͞o′, wä′ho͞o) *n., pl.* **-hoos.** A shrub or small tree, *Euonymus atropurpureus,* of eastern North America, having small purplish flowers and red fruit. [Dakota *wāhu.*]
wa·hoo[2] (wä-ho͞o′, wä′ho͞o) *n., pl.* **-hoos. 1.** An elm, *Ulmus alata,* of the southeastern United States, having twigs with winged, corky edges. **2.** Any of several trees similar to the wahoo. [Creek *ûhawhu.*]
wa·hoo[3] (wä-ho͞o′, wä′ho͞o) *n., pl.* **wahoo** or **-hoos.** A tropical marine game fish, *Acanthocybium solanderi.* [Orig. unknown.]
wa·hoo[4] (wä′ho͞o′) *interj. Chiefly Western U.S.* Used to express exuberance.
waif[1] (wāf) *n.* **1. a.** A stray homeless person, esp. a forsaken or orphaned child. **b.** A young animal that has been abandoned. **2.** Something found and unclaimed, such as an object cast up by the sea. [ME *waife,* ownerless property < AN *waif,* of Scand. orig.]
waif[2] (wāf) *n.* A small flag for signaling; waft. [Prob. of Scand. orig.]
wail (wāl) *v.* **wailed, wail·ing, wails.** *—intr.* **1.** To grieve or protest audibly; lament. **2.** To make a prolonged, high-

wader
Waders

waffle iron

George Miksch Sutton
wagtail

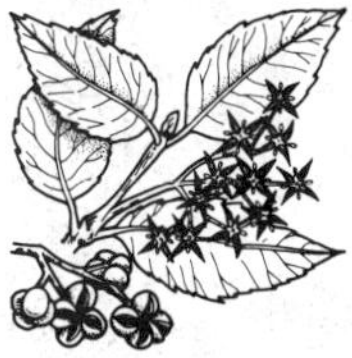

wahoo[1]

pitched sound suggestive of a cry: *The wind wailed through the trees.* —*tr. Archaic.* To lament over; bewail. —*n.* **1.** A long, loud, high-pitched cry, as of grief or pain. **2.** A long, loud, high-pitched sound. [ME *wailen,* of Scand. orig.] —**wail'er** *n.* —**wail'ing·ly** *adv.*

wail·ful (wāl'fəl) *adj.* **1.** Resembling a wail; mournful. **2.** Issuing a sound like a wail. —**wail'ful·ly** *adv.*

Wailing Wall *n.* A wall in the old city of Jerusalem believed to be a remnant of the temple of Solomon and revered by Jews as a place of pilgrimage, lamentation, and prayer.

wain (wān) *n.* **1.** A large open farm wagon. **2. Wain.** The Big Dipper. [ME < OE *wægn.*]

wain·scot (wān'skət, -skŏt', -skōt') *n.* **1.** A facing or paneling, usually of wood, applied to the walls of a room. **2.** The lower part of an interior wall when finished in a material different from that of the upper part. —*tr.v.* **-scot·ed, -scot·ing, -scots** or **-scot·ted, -scot·ting, -scots.** To line or panel (a room or wall) with wainscot. [ME *waynscot* < MDu. *wagenschot.*]

wain·scot·ing also **wain·scot·ting** (wān'skə-tĭng, -skŏt'ĭng, -skō'tĭng) *n.* **1.** A wainscoted wall or walls; paneling. **2.** Wood or other material for wainscoting.

wain·wright (wān'rīt') *n.* One who builds and repairs wagons.

waist (wāst) *n.* **1.** The part of the human trunk between the bottom of the rib cage and the pelvis. **2. a.** The part of a garment that encircles the waist of the body. **b.** The upper part of a garment, extending from the shoulders to the waistline, esp. the bodice of a woman's dress. **c.** A blouse. **d.** A child's undershirt. **3.** The middle section or part of an object, esp. when narrower than the rest. **4.** *Naut.* The middle part of the deck of a ship between the forecastle and the quarter-deck. [ME *wast.*]

waist·band (wāst'bănd') *n.* **1.** A garment band encircling and fitting the waist, as on trousers or a skirt. **2.** A sash.

waist·cloth (wāst'klôth', -klŏth') *n.* A loincloth.

waist·coat (wĕs'kĭt, wāst'kōt') *n.* **1.** *Chiefly Brit.* A vest (sense 1). **2.** A garment formerly worn by men under a doublet. —**waist'coat'ed** *adj.*

waist·line (wāst'līn') *n.* **1. a.** The natural indentation of the body at the waist. **b.** The measurement of this circumference. **2.** The point or line at which the skirt and bodice of a dress join.

wait (wāt) *v.* **wait·ed, wait·ing, waits.** —*intr.* **1. a.** To remain inactive or stay in one spot until something anticipated occurs. **b.** To tarry until another catches up. **2.** To remain or be in readiness or expectation. **3.** To remain temporarily neglected, unattended to, or postponed: *The trip will have to wait.* **4.** To work as a waiter or waitress. —*tr.* **1.** To remain or stay in expectation of; await: *wait one's turn.* **2.** *Informal.* To delay (a meal or event); postpone: *They waited lunch.* **3.** To be a waiter or waitress at: *wait table.* —***phrasal verbs.*** **wait on (or upon). 1.** To serve the needs of; be in attendance upon. **2.** To make a formal call upon; visit. **3.** To follow as a result; depend upon. **wait out.** To delay until the termination of: *wait out a war.* **wait up. 1.** To postpone going to bed in anticipation of something or someone. **2.** *Informal.* To stop or pause so that another can catch up. —*n.* **1.** The act of waiting or the time spent waiting. **2.** *Chiefly Brit.* **a.** One of a group of musicians employed, usually by a city, to play in parades or public ceremonies. **b.** One of a group of musicians or carolers who perform in the streets at Christmastime. —***idiom.*** **lie in wait.** To be on the watch for; await a chance to ambush. [ME *waiten* < ONFr. *waitier,* to watch, of Germanic orig.]

Usage: *Wait on* is correctly used in the senses given above. Though some dialects use *wait on* as an equivalent of *wait for,* in general usage this variation has not yet become established: *They will wait for* (not *on*) *you if you hurry.*

wait-a-bit (wāt'ə-bĭt') *n.* Any of several plants having sharp, often hooked thorns. [Transl. of Afr. *wacht-en-bitje.*]

wait·er (wā'tər) *n.* **1.** A man who waits on table. **2.** A tray or salver.

wait·ing (wā'tĭng) *n.* **1.** The act of one that waits. **2.** The period of time spent waiting. —***idiom.*** **in waiting.** In attendance.

waiting game *n.* The stratagem of deferring action and allowing the passage of time to work in one's favor.

waiting list *n.* A list of persons waiting, as for an appointment.

waiting room *n.* A room, as in a railroad station or doctor's office, for the use of persons waiting.

wait·ress (wā'trĭs) *n.* A woman who waits on table.

waive (wāv) *tr.v.* **waived, waiv·ing, waives. 1.** To relinquish or give up (a claim or right) voluntarily. **2.** To refrain from insisting upon or enforcing; dispense with: *"The original ban on private trading had long since been waived"* (William L. Schurz). **3.** To put aside or off for the time. [ME *weiven,* to abandon < AN *weyver* < *waif,* ownerless property. —see WAIF[1].]

waiv·er (wā'vər) *n.* **1.** The intentional relinquishment of a right, claim, or privilege. **2.** The document that evidences a waiver. [AN *weyver* < *weyver,* to abandon. —see WAIVE.]

Wa·kash·an (wô'kə-shăn', wä-kăsh'ən) *n.* A family of North American Indian languages spoken by the Nootka and other tribes of Washington and British Columbia. [< Wakashan *waukash,* good.] —**Wa'kash·an** *adj.*

wake[1] (wāk) *v.* **woke** (wōk) or **waked** (wākt), **waked** or **wok·en** (wō'kən), **wak·ing, wakes.** —*intr.* **1. a.** To cease to sleep: *woke up late.* **b.** To be brought into a state of awareness or alertness. **2.** To keep watch or guard, esp. over a corpse. **3.** To be or remain awake. —*tr.* **1.** To rouse from sleep; awaken. **2.** To stir, as from a dormant or inactive condition; rouse: *wake old animosities.* **3.** To make aware of; alert: *It waked him to the facts.* **4. a.** To keep a vigil over. **b.** To hold a wake over. —*n.* **1. a.** A watch; vigil. **b.** A watch over the body of a deceased person before burial, sometimes accompanied by festivity. **2. wakes** *(used with a sing. or pl. verb). Chiefly Brit.* A parish festival held annually, often in honor of the patron saint. **3. wakes** *(used with a sing. or pl. verb). Chiefly Brit.* An annual vacation. [ME *waken* < OE *wacian.*]

wake[2] (wāk) *n.* **1.** The visible track of turbulence left by something moving through water: *the wake of a ship.* **2.** The track or course left behind something that has passed: *The war left famine in its wake.* —***idiom.*** **in the wake of. 1.** Following directly upon. **2.** In the aftermath of; as a consequence of. [Poss. < MLG < ON *vök,* hole in the ice.]

wake·ful (wāk'fəl) *adj.* **1. a.** Not sleeping or able to sleep. **b.** Without sleep; sleepless. **2.** Watchful; alert. —**wake'ful·ly** *adv.* —**wake'ful·ness** *n.*

wake·less (wāk'lĭs) *adj.* Unbroken. Used of sleep.

wak·en (wā'kən) *v.* **-ened, -en·ing, -ens.** —*tr.* **1.** To rouse from sleep; awake. **2.** To rouse from a quiescent or inactive state; stir. —*intr.* To become awake; wake up. [ME *wakenen* < OE *wæcnan.*] —**wak'en·er** *n.*

wake-rob·in (wāk'rŏb'ĭn) *n.* **1.** The trillium. **2.** Any of several plants that bloom early in the spring.

Wal·den·ses (wŏl-dĕn'sēz) *pl.n.* A Christian sect of dissenters that originated in southern France in the late 12th century and adopted Calvinist doctrines in the 16th century. [Med. Lat. < Peter *Waldo,* their leader.] —**Wal·den'sian** (-chən) *adj. & n.*

Wal·dorf salad (wôl'dôrf') *n.* A salad of diced raw apples, celery, and walnuts mixed with mayonnaise. [After the *Waldorf*-Astoria Hotel, New York City, where it was first served.]

wale (wāl) *n.* **1.** A welt (sense 3.a.). **2. a.** One of the parallel ribs or ridges in the surface of a fabric such as corduroy. **b.** The texture or weave of such a fabric: *a wide wale.* **3.** *Naut.* **a.** The gunwale. **b.** One of the heavy planks or strakes extending along the sides of a wooden ship. —*tr.v.* **waled, wal·ing, wales.** To mark (the skin) with wales. [ME < OE *walu.*]

Wal·hal·la *n.* Variant of **Valhalla.**

walk (wôk) *v.* **walked, walk·ing, walks.** —*intr.* **1.** To move over a surface by taking steps with the feet at a pace slower than a run. **2.** To go or travel on foot. **3.** To go on foot for pleasure or exercise; stroll. **4.** To move in a manner suggestive of walking. **5.** To conduct oneself or behave in a particular manner; live: *He walks in peace and joy among his parishioners.* **6.** To roam about in a visible form, as a ghost; appear: *The specter walks at midnight.* **7. a.** *Baseball.* To go to first base after the pitcher has thrown four balls. **b.** To travel (sense 7). **8.** *Obs.* To be in constant motion. —*tr.* **1.** To go or pass over, on, or through by walking: *walk the streets.* **2.** To bring to a specified condition by walking: *walked him to exhaustion.* **3.** To cause to walk or proceed at a walk: *walk a horse uphill.* **4.** To accompany in walking; escort on foot: *walk her home.* **5.** To traverse on foot in order to survey or measure; pace off: *walked the bounds of his property.* **6.** To move (a heavy or cumbersome object) in a manner suggestive of walking: *walk a bureau into a hall.* **7.** *Baseball.* To allow (a batter) to go to first base by pitching four balls. —***phrasal verbs.*** **walk out. 1.** To go on strike. **2.** To leave suddenly, often as a signal of disapproval. **walk over. 1.** *Informal.* To treat badly or contemptuously. **2.** To gain an easy or uncontested victory. **walk through.** To perform (a play, for example) in a perfunctory fashion, as at a first rehearsal. —*n.* **1. a.** The act or an instance of walking, esp. a stroll for pleasure or exercise. **b.** The gait of a human being or other biped in which the feet are lifted alternately with one part of a foot always on the ground. **c.** The gait of a quadruped in which at least two feet are always touching the ground, esp. the gait of a horse in which the feet touch the ground in the four-beat sequence of near hind foot, near forefoot, off hind foot, off forefoot. **d.** The self-controlled movement in space of an astronaut. **2. a.** The rate at which one walks; pace. **b.** The characteristic way in which one walks. **3.** The distance covered or to be covered in walking. **4.** A place, as a sidewalk or promenade, on which one may walk. **5. a.** *Baseball.* The act or instance of taking first base after four balls have been pitched to the batter. **b.** The act or an instance of traveling with the basketball. **c.** *Sports.* A track event in which contestants compete in walking a specified distance: *the 1,000-meter walk.* **6.** An enclosed area designated for the exercise or pasture of livestock. **7.** An arrangement of or space between trees or shrubs planted in widely spaced rows. —***idioms.*** **walk away from. 1.** To outdo, outrun, or defeat with little difficulty. **2.** To survive (an accident) with very little injury. **walk off with. 1.** To win easily or unexpectedly. **2.** To steal. **walk of life.**

Social class or occupation. **walk out on.** *Informal.* To desert; abandon. **walk the plank.** To be executed at sea by walking the length of a plank and falling into the water. [ME *walken* < OE *wealcan,* to roll.]

walk·a·bout (wôk'ə-bout') *n.* **1.** A brief retreat to the roaming life of the Australian bush occasionally taken by an aborigine as a respite from regular work. **2.** A walking trip.

walk·a·way (wôk'ə-wā') *n.* A contest or victory easily won.

walk·er (wô'kər) *n.* **1.** One that walks, esp. a contestant in a footrace. **2.** A frame device used to support an infant learning to walk or a handicapped or convalescent person learning to walk again. **3.** A shoe specially designed for walking comfortably.

walk·ie-talk·ie also **walk·y-talk·y** (wô'kē-tô'kē) *n., pl.* **-ies.** A battery-powered portable sending and receiving radio set.

walk-in (wôk'ĭn') *adj.* **1.** Large enough to admit entrance, as a closet. **2.** Located so as to be entered directly from the street, as an apartment. *—n.* **1.** A room large enough to admit entrance. **2.** An easily won victory, esp. in an election. **3.** A person who walks in without having an appointment.

walking bass *n. Mus.* A repetitive bass figure composed of nonsyncopated eighth notes, used in jazz.

walking catfish *n.* A catfish, *Clarius batrachus,* able to travel short distances on land between bodies of water.

walking delegate *n.* A trade-union official appointed to inspect and confer with the local unions or to serve as a representative of the union in dealings with an employer.

walking fern *n.* A North American fern, *Camptosorus rhizophyllus,* having leaflike fronds with slender tips that often take root.

walking leaf *n.* **1.** A walking fern. **2.** A leaf insect.

walking papers *pl.n. Informal.* Notice of discharge or dismissal.

walking stick *n.* **1.** A cane or staff used as an aid in walking. **2.** Any of various insects of the family Phasmidae, having the appearance of twigs or sticks.

walk-on (wôk'ŏn', -ôn') *n.* **1.** A minor role in a theatrical production, usually having no speaking lines. **2.** An actor playing a walk-on role.

walk·out (wôk'out') *n.* **1.** A labor strike. **2.** The act of leaving or quitting a meeting, company, or organization, esp. as a sign of protest.

walk·o·ver (wôk'ō'vər) *n.* **1.** A horse race with only one horse entered, won by the mere formality of walking the length of the track. **2.** A walkaway.

walk-through (wôk'thro͞o') *n.* **1.** A brief rehearsal, as of a play or a role, performed usually in an early stage of production. **2.** A television rehearsal during which no cameras are used.

walk·up also **walk-up** (wôk'ŭp') *n.* **1.** An apartment house or office building with no elevator. **2.** An apartment or office in a walkup.

walk·way (wôk'wā') *n.* A passage for walking.

Wal·kyr·ie (văl-kîr'ē, -kī'rē, văl'kîr'ē, -kī'rē) *n. Myth.* Variant of **Valkyrie.**

walk·y-talk·y (wô'ke-tô'kē) *n.* Variant of **walkie-talkie.**

wall (wôl) *n.* **1.** An upright structure of masonry, wood, plaster, or other building material serving to enclose, divide, or protect an area, esp. a vertical construction forming an inner partition or exterior siding of a building. **2.** Often **walls.** A continuous structure of masonry or other material forming a rampart and built for defensive purposes. **3.** A structure of stonework, cement, or other material built to retain a flow of water. **4.** Something resembling a wall in appearance, function, or construction, as the exterior surface of a bodily organ or part: *the abdominal wall.* **5.** The vertical surface of an ocean wave in surfing. **6.** Something resembling a wall in impenetrability or strength: *a wall of silence; a wall of fog.* **7.** An extreme or desperate condition or position, such as defeat or ruin: *pushed us to the wall.* *—tr.v.* **walled, wall·ing, walls. 1.** To enclose, surround, or fortify with or as if with a wall: *wall up an old window.* **2.** To divide or separate with or as if with a wall: *wall off half a room.* **3.** To enclose within a wall; immure. **4.** To block or close (an opening or passage, for example) with or as if with a wall. ***—idiom.*** **up the wall.** *Informal.* Into a state of extreme frustration or distress: *tensions that are driving me up the wall.* [ME < OE *weall* < Lat. *vallum,* palisade < *vallus,* stake.]

wal·la·by (wŏl'ə-bē) *n., pl.* **-bies.** Any of various marsupials of the genus *Wallabia* and related genera, of Australia and adjacent islands, related to and resembling the kangaroos but generally smaller. [Native word in Australia.]

wal·lah also **wal·la** (wä'lä) *n.* One employed in a particular occupation or activity: *a kitchen wallah.* [< Hindi *-wālā,* pertaining to, connected with.]

wal·la·roo (wŏl'ə-ro͞o') *n., pl.* **-roos.** A kangaroo, *Macropus robustus* or *Osphranter robustus,* of hilly regions of Australia. [Native word in Australia.]

wall·board (wôl'bôrd', -bōrd') *n.* Any of several structural boards or sheets of various materials, such as gypsum plaster encased in paper or compressed wood fibers and chips, used in construction as a substitute for plaster or wood panels.

wall creeper *n.* A long-billed crimson and grayish bird, *Tichodroma muraria,* of alpine regions of the Old World, characteristically seeking food on rocky cliffs or walls.

wal·let (wŏl'ĭt) *n.* A flat pocket-size folding case, usually made of leather, for holding paper money, cards, or photographs; billfold. [ME *walet,* knapsack.]

wall·eye (wôl'ī') *n.* **1.** An eye in which the cornea is white or opaque. **2.** *Pathol.* **a.** Leukoma of the cornea. **b.** A divergent strabismus. **3.** A freshwater food and game fish, *Stizostedium vitreum,* of North America, having large, conspicuous eyes. [Back-formation from WALLEYED.]

wall·eyed (wôl'īd') *adj.* **1.** Having a whitish or grayish eye or eyes. **2. a.** Having leukoma of the cornea. **b.** Having divergent strabismus. **3. a.** Having large bulging or staring eyes. **b.** *Slang.* Having eyes with greatly distended pupils. **4.** *Slang.* Drunk. [ME *wawileyed* < ON *vagleygr* : *vagl,* beam + *auga,* eye.]

walleyed pike *n.* Walleye (sense 3).

wall fern *n.* Any of various small low-growing ferns of the genus *Polypodium* characterized by creeping stems that form dense mats.

wall·flow·er (wôl'flou'ər) *n.* **1. a.** A widely cultivated plant, *Cheiranthus cheiri,* native to Europe, having fragrant yellow, orange, or brownish flowers. **b.** A similar, related plant, *Erysimum asperum,* of the western United States. **2.** A person who does not participate in the activity at a social event because of shyness or unpopularity.

wall hanging *n.* A decorative tapestry hung against a wall.

Wal·loon (wŏ-lo͞on') *n.* **1.** One of a French-speaking people of Celtic descent inhabiting southern and southeastern Belgium and adjacent regions of France. **2.** The dialect of French spoken by the Walloons. *—adj.* Of or pertaining to the Walloons or their language. [OFr. *Wallon* < Med. Lat. *Wallo,* of Germanic orig.]

wal·lop (wŏl'əp) *Informal. —v.* **-loped, -lop·ing, -lops.** *—tr.* **1.** To beat soundly; thrash. **2.** To strike with a hard blow. **3.** To defeat thoroughly. *—intr.* **1.** To move in a rolling, clumsy manner; waddle. **2.** To boil noisily. Used of a liquid. *—n.* **1.** A hard or severe blow. **2. a.** The ability to strike a wallop: *a punch that packs a wallop.* **b.** The capacity to create a forceful effect; impact. [ME *walopen,* to gallop < ONFr. *waloper.*] **—wal'lop·er** *n.*

wal·lop·ing (wŏl'ə-pĭng) *Informal. —adj.* **1.** Very large; huge: *a walloping fish.* **2.** Very fine; truly smashing. *—adv.* To an exaggerated degree: *a walloping huge lie.* *—n.* A sound thrashing or defeat.

wal·low (wŏl'ō) *intr.v.* **-lowed, -low·ing, -lows. 1.** To roll the body about indolently or clumsily in water, snow, or mud. **2.** To luxuriate; revel: *wallow in self-righteousness.* **3.** To be abundantly supplied with something: *wallowing in money.* **4.** To move with difficulty in a clumsy or rolling manner; flounder. **5.** To swell or surge forth; billow. *—n.* **1.** An act of wallowing. **2.** A pool of water or mud where animals go to wallow. **3.** The depression, pool, or pit produced by wallowing animals. **4.** A condition of degradation or baseness. [ME *walowen* < OE *wealwian.*] **—wal'low·er** *n.*

wall·pa·per (wôl'pā'pər) *n.* Paper printed with designs or colors, used as a decorative wall covering. *—v.* **-pered, -per·ing, -pers.** *—tr.* To cover with wallpaper. *—intr.* To decorate a wall or room with wallpaper.

wall plate *n.* **1.** A horizontal timber situated along the top of a wall at the level of the eaves for bearing the ends of joists or rafters. **2.** A plate used to attach a bracket or similar device to a wall.

wall plug *n.* An electric socket, usually located in a wall, that is connected to and used as a source of electric power.

wall rock *n.* The rock that forms the walls of a vein or lode.

wall rue *n.* A small, delicate fern, *Asplenium ruta-muraria,* growing on rocks or in rocky crevices.

Wall Street *n.* The controlling financial interests of the United States. [After *Wall Street,* New York City, the main street of the financial district.] **—Wall'Street·er** *n.*

wall-to-wall (wôl'tə-wôl') *adj.* **1.** Covering a floor completely: *wall-to-wall carpeting.* **2. a.** Present or spreading throughout an entire area: *wall-to-wall people at the convention.* **b.** Found everywhere or including everything: *wall-to-wall luxury.* *—n.* A wall-to-wall carpet.

wal·nut (wôl'nŭt', -nət) *n.* **1. a.** Any of several trees of the genus *Juglans,* having round, sticky fruit enclosing an edible nut. **b.** The ridged or corrugated nut of such a tree. **2.** The hard, dark-brown wood of the walnut, used for gunstocks and in cabinetwork. [ME *walnot* < OE *wealhhnutu* : *wealh,* Celt, foreigner + *hnutu,* nut.]

Wal·pur·gis Night (väl-po͝or'gĭs) *n.* **1.** The eve of May Day, believed in medieval Europe to be the occasion of a witches' Sabbath. **2.** An episode or situation having the quality of nightmarish wildness associated with Walpurgis Night. [Partial transl. of G. *Walpurgisnacht* : *Walpurgis,* St. Walpurga + *nacht,* night.]

wal·rus (wôl'rəs, wŏl'-) *n., pl.* **walrus** or **-rus·es.** A large marine mammal, *Odobenus rosmarus,* of Arctic regions, having tough, wrinkled skin and large tusks. [Du., of Scand orig.]

walrus mustache *n.* A bushy, drooping mustache.

waltz (wôlts) *n.* **1.** A dance in triple time with a strong accent on the first beat. **2.** The music for a waltz. *—v.* **waltzed, waltz·ing, waltz·es.** *—intr.* **1.** To dance the waltz. **2.** To move unhesitantly and briskly; flounce. **3.** To accomplish a

walkie-talkie

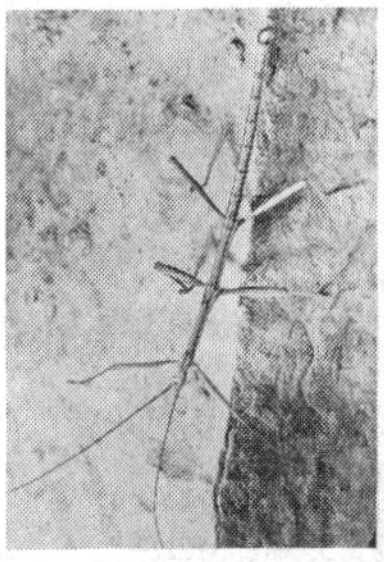

walking stick

wallaby

walnut

task, chore, or assignment with little effort: *waltzed through her exams.* —*tr.* **1.** To dance the waltz with. **2.** To lead or force to move briskly and purposefully; march: *waltzed him into the principal's office.* [G. *Walzer* < MHG *walzen,* to dance < OHG *walzan,* to roll.] **—waltz'er** *n.*

wam·ble (wŏm'bəl, wăm'-) *intr.v.* **-bled, -bling, -bles. 1.** To move in a weaving, wobbling, or rolling manner. **2.** To turn or roll. Used of the stomach. —*n.* **1.** A wobble or roll. **2.** A stomach upset. [ME *wamelen,* to feel nausea.] **—wam'bling·ly** *adv.* **—wam'bly** *adj.*

Wam·pa·no·ag (wăm'pə-nō'ăg') *n., pl.* **Wampanoag** or **-ags. 1. a.** A tribe of North American Indians, formerly inhabiting eastern Rhode Island and adjacent parts of Massachusetts. **b.** A member of this tribe. **2.** The Algonquian language of the Wampanoag. [Natick *Wampan-okhe,* (people of the) eastern land.] **—Wam'pa·no'ag** *adj.*

wam·pum (wŏm'pəm, wôm'-) *n.* **1.** Small cylindrical beads made from polished shells, formerly used by North American Indians as currency and jewelry. **2.** *Informal.* Money. [Short for WAMPUMPEAG.]

wam·pum·peag (wŏm'pəm-pēg', wôm'-) *n.* White shell beads used by the North American Indians as wampum. [Algonquian *wampumpeage,* white strings.]

wan (wŏn) *adj.* **wan·ner, wan·nest. 1.** Unnaturally pale, as from physical or emotional distress. **2.** Suggestive of or indicating weariness, illness, or unhappiness; melancholy: *a wan expression.* —*intr.v.* **wanned, wan·ning, wans.** To become pale. [ME, pale, gloomy < OE *wann,* gloomy, dark.] **—wan'ly** *adv.* **—wan'ness** *n.*

wand (wŏnd) *n.* **1.** A thin supple twig or stick. **2.** A slender rod carried as a symbol of office in a procession; scepter. **3.** A musician's baton. **4.** A stick, baton, or rod used by a magician, diviner, or conjurer. **5.** A six foot by two foot slat used as an archery target. [ME < ON *vöndr.*]

wan·der (wŏn'dər) *v.* **-dered, -der·ing, -ders.** —*intr.* **1.** To move about with no destination or purpose; roam aimlessly. **2.** To go by an indirect route or at no set pace; amble: *wander toward town.* **3.** To proceed in an irregular course or action; meander. **4.** To go astray: *wander from the path of righteousness.* **5.** To think or express oneself unclearly or incoherently. —*tr.* To wander across or through: *wander the forests and fields.* —*n.* The act of wandering; stroll. [ME *wanderen* < OE *wandrian.*] **—wan'der·er** *n.* **—wan'der·ing·ly** *adv.*

Synonyms: *wander, ramble, roam, rove, range, meander, stray, gallivant, gad.* These verbs all mean to move or travel about freely. *Wander* and *ramble* stress the absence of a fixed course or goal; figuratively they apply to writers or speakers who digress freely. *Roam* and *rove* emphasize freedom of movement over a wide area but do not necessarily imply aimlessness. *Range* also suggests a wide radius and does not rule out the possibility of a clear purpose; especially in figurative usage, the term can stress inclusiveness of coverage: *the speech ranged over a broad area of social problems. Meander* suggests leisurely and sometimes aimless progression over a course as irregular as that of a winding river. *Stray* refers to movement, physical or figurative, away from a direct course; figuratively it can also apply to deviation from proper behavior. *Gallivant* refers to traveling about in search of pleasure, and *gad,* to thoughtless idle travel.

Wandering Jew
Tradescantia fluminensis

Wandering Jew *n.* **1.** In medieval legend, a Jew condemned to wander until the Day of Judgment for having mocked Christ on the day of Crucifixion. **2. wandering Jew.** Either of two trailing plants, *Tradescantia fluminensis* or *Zebrina pendula,* native to tropical America, having usually variegated foliage and popular as house plants.

wan·der·lust (wŏn'dər-lŭst') *n.* A strong or irresistible impulse to travel. [G. : *wandern,* to wander + *Lust,* desire.]

wan·der·oo (wŏn'də-rōō') *n., pl.* **-oos.** A monkey, *Macaca silenus,* of south-central Asia, having a glossy black coat and a ruff of gray hair about the face. [Singhalese *vandaru,* pl. of *vandurā,* monkey < Skt. *vānaraḥ,* forest dweller < *vanam,* forest.]

wane (wān) *intr.v.* **waned, wan·ing, wanes. 1.** To decrease gradually in size, amount, intensity, or degree; decline. **2.** To show decreasing illuminated area from full moon to new moon. **3.** To approach an end. —*n.* **1.** The act or process of waning; a gradual declining or diminishing. **2.** A period or phase of waning; specifically, the period of the decrease of the moon's illuminated visible surface. **3.** A defective edge of a board caused by remaining bark or a beveled end. **—*idiom.* on the wane.** In a period of decline; waning: *"The tide was near the turn and already the day was on the wane"* (Joyce). [ME *wanen* < OE *wanian.*]

wan·gle (wăng'gəl) *Informal.* —*v.* **-gled, -gling, -gles.** —*tr.* **1.** To make, achieve, or get by contrivance: *wangled a job for which she had no training.* **2.** To manipulate or juggle, esp. fraudulently. **3.** To extricate (oneself) from difficulty. —*intr.* **1.** To use indirect, tricky, or fraudulent methods. **2.** To extricate oneself by subtle or indirect means, as from difficulty; wriggle. —*n.* An act of wangling. [Orig. unknown.] **—wang'ler** *n.*

wan·i·gan also **wan·ni·gan** (wŏn'ə-gən) *n.* **1.** A supply chest used in a logging camp. **2.** A shack on wheels or a movable platform, used in a logging camp for shelter or by workmen. [Ojibwa *wanikkan,* man-made hole.]

Wan·kel engine (väng'kəl, wăng'-) *n.* A rotary internal-combustion engine in which a triangular rotor turning in a specially shaped housing performs the functions allotted to the pistons of a conventional engine, thereby allowing great savings in weight and moving parts. [After Felix *Wankel* (b. 1902).]

want (wŏnt, wônt) *v.* **want·ed, want·ing, wants.** —*tr.* **1.** To desire greatly; wish for: *He wants to leave.* **2.** To fail to have; be without; lack: *A house that wants cheer is melancholy.* **3.** To need or require. **4. a.** To request the presence of. **b.** To seek with intent to capture: *The fugitive is wanted by the police.* **5. a.** To have a desire for. **b.** To have an inclination toward; like: *Say what you want, but he is still incompetent.* —*intr.* **1.** To have need. **2.** To be destitute or needy. **3.** To be disposed; wish: *Call her if you want.* **—*phrasal verbs.* want in.** *Informal.* **1.** To desire greatly to come. **2.** To wish to join a project, business, or other undertaking. **want out.** *Informal.* **1.** To desire greatly to go. **2.** To wish to leave a project, business, or other undertaking. —*n.* **1.** The condition or quality of lacking a usual or necessary amount. **2.** Pressing need; destitution: *live in want.* **3.** Something needed or desired; need: *moderate wants.* **4.** A defect of character; fault. [ME *wanten,* to be lacking < ON *vanta.*]

Usage: When *want* is followed immediately by an infinitive construction, it does not take *for: I want you to go* (not *want for you*). When *want* and the infinitive are separated in the sentence, however, *for* is used: *What I want is for you to go, I want very much for you to go.*

want ad *n. Informal.* A classified advertisement.

want·ing (wŏn'tĭng, wôn'-) *adj.* **1.** Absent; lacking. **2.** Not up to standards or expectations. —*prep.* **1.** Without. **2.** Minus; less: *an hour wanting 15 minutes.*

wan·ton (wŏn'tən) *adj.* **1.** Immoral or unchaste; lewd. **2. a.** Maliciously cruel; merciless. **b.** Characterized by malicious cruelty; unjust. **3.** Freely extravagant; excessive: *wanton spending.* **4.** Luxuriant; overabundant: *wanton tresses.* **5.** Frolicsome; playful. **6.** *Obs.* Rebellious; refractory. —*v.* **-toned, -ton·ing, -tons.** —*intr.* To act, grow, or move in a wanton manner; be wanton. —*tr.* To waste or squander wantonly. —*n.* **1.** An immoral, lewd, or licentious person, esp. a woman. **2.** One that is playful or frolicsome. **3.** One that is undisciplined or spoiled. [ME *wantowen* : *wan-,* mis- + *towen,* p.part. of *teen,* to bring up < OE *tēon.*] **—wan'ton·ly** *adv.* **—wan'ton·ness** *n.*

wap·en·take (wŏp'ən-tāk', wăp'-) *n.* A historical subdivision of some northern counties in England, corresponding roughly to the hundred. [ME < OE *wæpengetæc* < ON *vāpnatak,* act of taking weapons: *vāpn,* weapons + *tak,* act of taking < *taka,* to take.]

wap·i·ti (wŏp'ĭ-tē) *n., pl.* **wapiti** or **-tis.** A large North American deer, *Cervus canadensis.* [Shawnee, white rump.]

war (wôr) *n.* **1. a.** A state of open, armed, often prolonged, conflict carried on between nations, states, or parties. **b.** The period of such conflict. **2.** A condition of active antagonism or contention: *a war of words.* **3.** The techniques or procedures of war; military science. —*intr.v.* **warred, war·ring, wars. 1.** To wage or carry on war. **2.** To be in a state of hostility; contend. **—*idioms.* at war.** In an active state of conflict or contention. **declare war on. 1.** To state formally the intention to carry on hostilities against. **2.** To state one's intent to suppress or eradicate: *declared war on poor grammar.* [ME *warre* < ONFr. *werre,* of Germanic orig.]

war baby *n.* A child born during wartime, esp. during World War I or World War II.

war·ble¹ (wôr'bəl) *v.* **-bled, -bling, -bles.** —*tr.* To sing (a note or song, for example) with trills, runs, or other melodic embellishments. —*intr.* **1.** To sing with trills, runs, or quavers. **2.** To be sounded in a trilling or quavering manner. —*n.* **1.** The act of warbling. **2.** A song, esp. one that is warbled. [ONFr. *werbler* < *werble,* a warbling, of Germanic orig.]

war·ble² (wôr'bəl) *n.* **1.** An abscessed swelling under the hide of the back of cattle or other animals, caused by the larva of a warble fly. **2.** The warble fly, esp. in its larval stage. [Prob. of Scand. orig.] **—war'bled** *adj.*

warble fly *n.* Any of several flies of the family Oestridae, whose larvae form warbles within the bodies of cattle and other animals.

war·bler (wôr'blər) *n.* **1.** Any of various small New World birds of the family Parulidae, many of which have yellowish plumage or markings. **2.** Any of various small, brownish or grayish Old World birds of the subfamily Silviinae.

war bonnet *n.* A ceremonial headdress used by some North American Plains Indians consisting of a cap or band and a trailing extension decorated with erect feathers.

war chest *n.* **1.** An accumulation of funds to finance a war effort. **2.** A fund reserved for a particular purpose such as a political campaign.

war club *n.* A weapon consisting of a weight of iron or stone fixed to a handle, widely used by American Indians.

war correspondent *n.* A journalist, reporter, or commentator assigned to report directly from a combat zone.

war crime *n.* Any of various crimes, as mistreatment of prisoners of war or genocide, committed during a war and considered to be in violation of the customs of warfare. **—war criminal** *n.*

war cry *n.* **1.** A cry uttered by combatants as they attack;

battle cry. **2.** A phrase or slogan used to rally people to a cause.

ward (wôrd) *n.* **1.** A division of a city or town for administrative and representative purposes. **2.** A district of some English and Scottish counties corresponding roughly to the hundred or wapentake. **3. a.** A room in a hospital usually holding six or more patients. **b.** A division in a hospital for the care of a particular group of patients: *maternity ward.* **4.** One of the divisions of a penal institution, as a jail. **5.** An open court or area of a castle or fortification enclosed by walls. **6. a.** *Law.* A minor or incompetent person placed under the care or protection of a guardian or court. **b.** A person under the protection or care of another. **7.** The state of being under guard; custody. **8.** The act of guarding or protecting someone; guardianship. **9.** A means of protection; defense. **10.** A defensive movement or attitude, esp. in fencing; a guard. **11. a.** The projecting ridge of a lock or keyhole that prevents the turning of a key other than the proper one. **b.** The notch cut into a key that corresponds to such a ridge. —*tr.v.* **ward·ed, ward·ing, wards.** To guard; protect. ***—phrasal verb.*** **ward off. 1.** To turn aside; parry: *ward off an opponent's blows.* **2.** To avert: *took vitamins to ward off headcolds.* [ME, action of guarding < OE *weard.*]

-ward or **-wards** *suff.* **1. a.** In a specified direction in time or space: *downward.* **b.** Toward a specified place or position: *skywards.* **2. a.** Occurring or situated in a specified direction: *leftward.* **b.** Having a direction toward a specified place or position: *landward.* [ME < OE *-weard.*]

Usage: Since the suffix *-ward* or *-wards* indicates direction, there is no need to use *to the* with it: *The ship is sailing westward* (or *to the west* but not *to the westward*).

war dance *n.* A tribal dance performed before a battle or as a celebration after a victory.

ward·ed (wôr′dĭd) *adj.* Having notches or wards. Used of keys.

war·den (wôrd′n) *n.* **1.** The chief administrative official of a prison. **2.** An official, as an air-raid warden, charged with the enforcement of certain laws and regulations. **3.** *Chiefly Brit.* **a.** The chief executive official in charge of a port or market. **b.** Any of various crown officers having administrative duties. **4.** The chief executive of a borough in certain states. **5.** *Chiefly Brit.* One of the governing officials of certain colleges, schools, guilds, or hospitals; trustee. **6.** A churchwarden. [ME *wardein* < ONFr. < *warder,* to guard, of Germanic orig.]

war·den·ry (wôrd′n-rē) *n., pl.* **-ries.** The office, duties, or jurisdiction of a warden.

ward·er[1] (wôr′dər) *n.* **1.** A guard, porter, or watchman of a gate or tower. **2.** *Chiefly Brit.* A prison guard. [ME < AN *wardere* < ONFr. *warder,* to guard, of Germanic orig.] **—war′der·ship′** *n.*

ward·er[2] (wôr′dər) *n.* A baton formerly used by a ruler or commander to signal orders. [ME, poss. < *warden,* to ward < OE *weardian.*]

ward heel·er (hē′lər) *n. Slang.* A worker for the ward organization of a political machine.

ward·ress (wôr′drĭs) *n.* A prison matron.

ward·robe (wôr′drōb′) *n.* **1.** A tall cabinet, closet, or small room designed to hold clothes. **2.** Garments collectively, esp. all the articles of clothing belonging to one person. **3. a.** The costumes belonging to a theater or theatrical troupe. **b.** The place in which theatrical costumes are kept. **4.** The department in charge of wearing apparel, jewelry, and accessories in a royal or noble household. [ME *warderobe* < ONFr. : *warder,* to keep + *robe,* garment.]

ward·room (wôrd′ro͞om′, -ro͝om′) *n.* **1.** The common recreation area and dining room for the commissioned officers on a warship. **2.** The commissioned officers on a warship.

-wards *suff.* Variant of **-ward**.

ward·ship (wôrd′shĭp′) *n.* **1.** The state of being a ward or in the charge of a guardian. **2.** Guardianship; custody.

ware[1] (wâr) *n.* **1.** Articles of the same general kind: *silverware; glassware.* **2.** Pottery or ceramics or a special kind of pottery: *earthenware.* **3. wares. a.** Articles of commerce; goods. **b.** An incorporeal asset or benefit, as a service or personal accomplishment, that is regarded as an article of commerce. [ME < OE *waru.*]

ware[2] (wâr) *tr.v.* **wared, war·ing, wares.** To beware of. —*adj. Archaic.* Watchful; wary. [ME *waren* < OE *warian.*]

ware·house (wâr′hous′) *n.* **1.** A place in which goods or merchandise are stored; storehouse. **2.** *Chiefly Brit.* A large, usually wholesale shop. —*tr.v.* **-housed, -hous·ing, -hous·es.** To place or store in a warehouse, esp. in a bonded or government warehouse.

ware·room (wâr′ro͞om′, -ro͝om′) *n.* A room used for the storage or display of goods or wares.

war·fare (wôr′fâr′) *n.* **1.** The waging of war; armed conflict. **2.** Conflict of any kind; struggle. [ME : *war,* war + *fare,* journey < OE *faru.*]

war·fa·rin (wôr′fər-ən) *n.* A colorless crystalline compound, $C_{19}H_{16}O_4$, used to kill rodents and medicinally as an anticoagulant. [After the *W(isconsin) A(lumni) R(esearch) F(oundation)* + (COUM)ARIN.]

war game *n.* A simulated battle in military training maneuvers.

war hawk *n.* **1.** A member of the Twelfth U.S. Congress (1811–1813) who advocated war with Great Britain. **2.** A person who advocates war.

war·head (wôr′hĕd′) *n.* A part of the armament system in the forward part of a projectile, such as a guided missile, torpedo, or bomb, containing the explosive charge.

war-horse also **war horse** (wôr′hôrs′) *n.* **1.** A horse used in combat; charger. **2.** *Informal.* A person who has been through many battles, struggles, or fights. **3.** *Informal.* A musical or dramatic work that has become hackneyed.

war·like (wôr′līk′) *adj.* **1.** Belligerent; hostile. **2.** Of or pertaining to war; martial. **3.** Threatening or indicative of war.

war·lock (wôr′lŏk′) *n.* A male witch, sorcerer, wizard, or demon. [ME *warloghe* < OE *wǣrloga,* oath-breaker : *wǣr,* pledge + *-loga,* liar, < *lēogan,* to lie.]

war·lord (wôr′lôrd′) *n.* A military commander exercising civil power in a given region, whether in nominal allegiance to the national government or in defiance of it.

warm (wôrm) *adj.* **-er, -est. 1.** Somewhat hotter than temperate; moderately hot: *a warm climate.* **2.** Having the natural heat of living beings. **3.** Preserving or imparting heat: *a warm overcoat.* **4.** Having a sensation of unusually high bodily heat, as from exercise or hard work; overheated. **5.** Marked by enthusiasm; ardent: *warm support.* **6.** Characterized by liveliness, excitement, or disagreement: *a warm debate.* **7.** Marked by or revealing friendliness or sincerity; cordial: *warm greetings.* **8.** Loving; passionate: *a warm embrace.* **9.** Quick to be aroused; fiery: *a warm temper.* **10.** Predominantly red or yellow in color: *a warm sunset.* **11.** Recently made; fresh: *a warm trail.* **12.** Close to discovering, guessing, or finding something, as in certain games. **13.** *Informal.* Uncomfortable because of danger or annoyance: *Things are getting warm for the bookies.* —*v.* **warmed, warm·ing, warms.** —*tr.* **1.** To raise slightly in temperature; make warm: *warm some rolls.* **2.** To make zealous or ardent; enliven. **3.** To fill with pleasant emotions. —*intr.* **1.** To become warm. **2.** To become ardent, enthusiastic, or animated: *warming to his subject.* **3.** To become kindly disposed or friendly. ***—phrasal verb.*** **warm up. 1.** To make or become warm or warmer. **2.** To prepare for an athletic event by exercising or practicing. **3.** To make or become ready for an event or operation. **4.** To approach a state of confrontation or violence. —*n. Informal.* A warming or heating. [ME < OE *wearm.*] **—warm′er** *n.* **—warm′ish** *adj.* **—warm′ly** *adv.* **—warm′ness** *n.*

Usage: *Warmly* when used with *feel toward* is an exception to the rule that adverbs do not follow linking verbs. It is acceptable to say either *I feel warm toward her* or *I feel warmly toward her.*

warm-blood·ed (wôrm′blŭd′ĭd) *adj.* **1.** *Zool.* Maintaining a relatively constant and warm body temperature independent of environmental temperature; homoiothermous. **2.** Ardent; passionate. **—warm′-blood′ed·ness** *n.*

warmed-o·ver (wôrmd′ō′vər) *adj. Informal.* **1.** Reheated: *warmed-over tidbits.* **2.** Not new, fresh, or spontaneous.

warm front *n.* A front along which an advancing mass of warm air rises over a mass of cold air.

warm-heart·ed (wôrm′här′tĭd) *adj.* Characterized by kindness, affection, and generosity. **—warm′heart′ed·ly** *adv.* **—warm′heart′ed·ness** *n.*

warming pan *n.* A metal pan with a cover and a long handle, designed to hold hot liquids or coals and used to warm a bed.

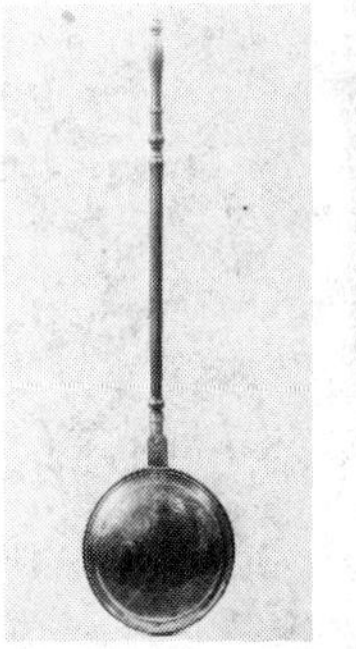

warming pan
18th-century American

war·mon·ger (wôr′mŭng′gər, -mŏng′-) *n.* One who advocates or attempts to stir up war. **—war′mon′ger·ing** *adj. & n.*

warmth (wôrmth) *n.* **1.** The state, sensation, or quality of producing or having a moderate degree of heat. **2. a.** Kindness and affection; love: *human warmth.* **b.** Excitement or intensity, as of love or passion; ardor. **3.** The glowing effect produced by using predominantly red or yellow colors. [ME.]

warm-up (wôrm′ŭp′) *n.* An act, procedure, or period of warming up.

warn (wôrn) *v.* **warned, warn·ing, warns.** —*tr.* **1.** To make aware of potential or probable harm, danger, or evil; caution. **2.** To admonish as to action or manners. **3.** To notify (a person) to go or stay away: *warned him off.* **4.** To notify or apprise in advance. —*intr.* To give a warning. [ME *warnen* < OE *warnian.*] **—warn′er** *n.*

Synonyms: *warn, admonish, caution, forewarn.* These verbs mean to give a person advance notice of actual danger or of the possibility of danger, risk, or error. *Warn,* the most comprehensive, can refer either to giving specific word of impending danger or to counseling about something, such as a fault, trait, or circumstance, that could have dangerous or unpleasant consequences. The latter sense is basic to *admonish* and *caution.* However, *caution* is the stronger of these two in implying the act of alerting to danger or risk; *admonish* primarily suggests reproving for a shortcoming. *Forewarn* intensifies the sense of notice in advance and usually implies the presence of, or strong probability of, real danger.

warn·ing (wôr′nĭng) *n.* **1.** An intimation, threat, or sign of impending danger or evil. **2. a.** Advice to beware, as of a person or thing. **b.** Counsel to desist from a specified undesirable course of action. **3.** A cautionary or deterrent example. —*adj.* Acting or serving as a warning. **—warn'ing·ly** *adv.*

war of nerves *n.* A conflict marked by psychological tactics, such as intimidation and threats, that is intended primarily to confuse one's enemy and erode his morale.

warp (wôrp) *v.* **warped, warp·ing, warps.** —*tr.* **1.** To turn or twist out of shape. **2.** To turn from a correct, healthy, or true course; pervert. **3.** In weaving, to arrange (strands of yarn or thread) so that they run lengthwise. **4.** *Naut.* To move (a vessel) by hauling on a line that is fastened to or around a piling, anchor, or pier. —*intr.* **1.** To become bent or twisted out of shape, as wood. **2.** To turn aside from a true, correct, or natural course; go astray; deviate. **3.** *Naut.* To move a vessel by hauling on a line that is fastened to or around a piling, anchor, or pier. —*n.* **1.** The state of being twisted or bent out of shape. **2.** A distortion or twist, esp. in a piece of wood. **3.** A mental or moral twist, aberration, or deviation. **4.** The threads that run lengthwise in a fabric, crossed at right angles by the woof. **5.** *Naut.* A towline used in warping a vessel. [ME *werpen* < OE *weorpan,* to throw.] **—warp'er** *n.*

war paint *n.* **1.** Pigments applied to the face or body by certain tribes, as the Indians of North America, preparatory to going to war. **2.** *Informal.* Cosmetics such as lipstick, rouge, or mascara. **3.** *Informal.* Official dress; regalia.

warp and woof *n.* The underlying structure upon which something is built; base.

war party *n.* **1.** A band of North American Indians on the warpath. **2.** A usually blatantly patriotic political party supporting a war.

war·path (wôr'păth', -päth') *n.* **1.** The route taken by a party of North American Indians on the attack. **2.** A hostile course or mood: *He's on the warpath today.*

war·plane (wôr'plān') *n.* A combat aircraft.

war·rant (wôr'ənt, wŏr'-) *n.* **1.** Authorization or certification; sanction, as given by a superior. **2.** Justification for an action; grounds. **3.** Something that assures, attests to, or guarantees some event or result; proof. **4.** An order that serves as authorization for something, esp.: **a.** A voucher authorizing payment or receipt of money. **b.** *Law.* A judicial writ authorizing an officer to make a search, seizure, or arrest or to execute a judgment. **c.** A certificate of appointment given to warrant officers. —*tr.v.* **-rant·ed, -rant·ing, -rants. 1.** To guarantee or attest to the quality, accuracy, or condition of. **2.** To guarantee or attest to the character or reliability of; vouch for. **3. a.** To guarantee (a product). **b.** To guarantee (a purchaser) indemnification against damage or loss. **4.** To guarantee the immunity or security of. **5.** To justify or call for; deserve. **6.** To grant authorization or sanction to (someone); authorize or empower. **7.** *Law.* To guarantee clear title to (real property). [ME < ONFr. *warant,* of Germanic orig.] **—war'rant·a·ble** *adj.* **—war'rant·a·ble·ness** *n.* **—war'rant·a·bly** *adv.* **—war'rant·er** *n.*

war·ran·tee (wôr'ən-tē', wŏr'-) *n. Law.* A person to whom a warranty is made.

warrant officer *n.* A military officer, usually a skilled technician, intermediate in rank between a noncommissioned officer and a commissioned officer, having authority by virtue of a warrant.

war·ran·tor (wôr'ən-tər, -tôr', wŏr'-) *n. Law.* A person who makes a warrant or gives a warranty to another.

war·ran·ty (wôr'ən-tē, wŏr'-) *n., pl.* **-ties. 1.** Official authorization, sanction, or warrant. **2.** Justification or valid grounds for an act or course of action. **3.** *Law.* **a.** An assurance by the seller of property that the goods or property are as represented or will be as promised. **b.** The insured's guarantee that the facts are as stated in reference to an insurance risk or that specified conditions will be fulfilled to keep the contract effective. **c.** A covenant by which the seller of land binds himself and his heirs to defend the security of the estate conveyed. **d.** A judicial writ; warrant. [ME *warantie* < ONFr. < *warantir,* to guarantee.]

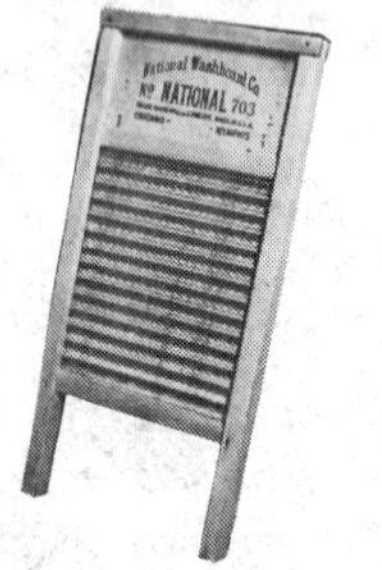

washboard

war·ren (wôr'ən, wŏr'-) *n.* **1. a.** An area where rabbits live in burrows. **b.** A colony of rabbits. **2.** An enclosure for small game animals. **3.** An overcrowded place of habitation. [ME *warenne* < ONFr.]

war·ren·er (wôr'ə-nər, wŏr'-) *n.* **1.** One who keeps a rabbit warren. **2.** A gamekeeper.

war·ri·or (wôr'ē-ər, wŏr'-) *n.* One engaged or experienced in battle. [ME *werreour* < ONFr. *werreieur* < *werreier,* to make war < *werre,* war.]

war·saw (wôr'sô) *n.* A large grouper, *Epinephelus nigritus,* of warm Atlantic waters. [Alteration of Sp. *guasa.*]

war·ship (wôr'shĭp') *n.* A combat ship.

wart (wôrt) *n.* **1. a.** A circumscribed hypertrophy of the outer region of the corium, caused by a virus, covered with a keratinous layer, and occurring typically on the hands or feet. **b.** A similar protuberance, as on a plant. **2.** One resembling or suggestive of a wart, esp. in unattractiveness or smallness. [ME < OE *wearte.*] **—wart'ed, wart'y** *adj.*

wart hog *n.* A wild African hog, *Phacochoerus aethiopicus,* having tusks and wartlike protuberances on the face.

war·time (wôr'tīm') *n.* A period or time of war.

war whoop *n.* A war cry, esp. of North American Indians.

war·y (wâr'ē) *adj.* **-i·er, -i·est. 1.** On one's guard; watchful. **2.** Characterized by caution: *a wary glance.* [ME *ware* < OE *wær.*] **—war'i·ly** *adv.* **—war'i·ness** *n.*

was (wŏz, wŭz; wəz *when unstressed*). First and third person singular past tense of **be.** [ME < OE *wæs.*]

wash (wŏsh, wôsh) *v.* **washed, wash·ing, washes.** —*tr.* **1.** To cleanse, using water or other liquid, usually with soap, detergent, or bleach, by immersing, dipping, rubbing, or scrubbing: *wash windows; wash one's hands.* **2.** To soak, rinse out, and remove (dirt or stain) with or as if with water: *wash grease out of overalls.* **3.** To make moist or wet; drench: *Tears washed her cheeks.* **4.** To flow over, against, or past: *waves washing the sandy shores.* **5.** To carry, erode, remove, or destroy by the action of moving water: *Heavy rains washed the topsoil away.* **6.** To rid of corruption or guilt; cleanse or purify: *wash sins away.* **7.** To cover or coat with a watery layer of paint or other coloring substance. **8.** *Chem.* **a.** To purify (a gas) by passing through or over a liquid, as to remove soluble matter. **b.** To pass a solvent, such as distilled water, through (a precipitate). **9.** To remove particulate constituents from (an ore) by immersion in or agitation with water. **10.** To cause to undergo a swirling action: *She washed the tea around in her cup.* —*intr.* **1.** To wash something in or by means of water or other liquid. **2.** To undergo washing without fading or other damage: *This fabric will wash.* **3.** To be carried away, removed, or drawn by the action of water: *washed out to sea; washed away from the river bank.* **4.** To flow, sweep, or beat with a characteristic lapping sound: *The waves washed over the pilings.* **5.** *Informal.* To hold up under examination; be convincing: *Your excuse just won't wash.* **—phrasal verbs. wash down. 1.** To clean by washing with water from top to bottom, as a wall or car. **2.** To follow the ingestion of (food, for example) with the ingestion of a liquid: *washed the cake down with coffee.* **wash out. 1.** To remove or be removed by washing. **2.** To carry or wear away or be carried or worn away by the action of moving water: *The river rose and washed out the dam. The road washed out.* **3. a.** To cause to fade by laundering: *color washed out by bleach.* **b.** To deplete or become depleted of vitality: *feel washed out by evening.* **c.** To eliminate or be eliminated as unsatisfactory: *a football player who was washed out.* **d.** To cause (an event) to be rained out. **wash up. 1.** To wash one's hands. **2.** *Chiefly Brit.* To wash dishes after a meal. **3.** To exhaust; burn out: *I'm all washed up as an editor.* —*n.* **1.** The act or process of washing or cleansing. **2.** A quantity of articles washed or intended for washing. **3.** Waste liquid; swill. **4.** Fermented liquid from which liquor is distilled. **5.** A preparation or product used in washing or coating. **6.** A cosmetic or medicinal liquid, such as a mouthwash. **7. a.** A thin layer of water color or India ink spread on a drawing. **b.** A light tint or hue: *"When old Godolphin awoke it was to a wash of red sunset through the window"* (Thomas Pynchon). **8. a.** A rush or surge of water or waves. **b.** The sound of this rush or surge. **9. a.** The removal or erosion of soil by the action of moving water. **b.** A deposit of recently eroded debris. **10. a.** Low or marshy ground washed by tidal waters. **b.** A stretch of shallow water. **11.** *Western U.S.* The dry bed of a stream. **12.** A turbulence in air or water caused by the motion or action of an oar, propeller, jet, or airfoil. —*adj.* **1.** Used for washing. **2.** Capable of being washed; washable. **—*idiom.* wash one's hands of. 1.** To refuse to accept responsibility for. **2.** To abandon or renounce. [ME *washen* < OE *wacsan.*]

wash·a·ble (wŏsh'ə-bəl, wôsh'-) *adj.* Capable of being washed without fading or other injury.

wash-and-wear (wŏsh'ən-wâr', wôsh'-) *adj.* Treated so as to be easily or quickly washed or rinsed clean and to require little or no ironing: *a wash-and-wear shirt.*

wash·ba·sin (wŏsh'bā'sən, wôsh'-) *n.* A washbowl.

wash·board (wŏsh'bôrd', -bōrd', wôsh'-) *n.* **1. a.** A board having a corrugated surface upon which clothes can be rubbed in the process of laundering. **b.** A similar board used as a percussion instrument. **2.** A board fastened to a wall at the floor; baseboard. **3.** *Naut.* A thin plank fastened to the side of a boat or to the sill of a port to keep out the sea and the spray.

wash·bowl (wŏsh'bōl', wôsh'-) *n.* A basin that can be filled with water for use in washing oneself.

wash·cloth (wŏsh'klôth', -klŏth', wôsh'-) *n.* A small, usually square cloth of absorbent material used for washing the face or body.

wash·day (wŏsh'dā', wôsh'-) *n.* A day, often the same day of every week, set aside for doing the household washing.

washed-out (wŏsht'out', wôsht'-) *adj.* **1.** Lacking color or intensity; faded. **2.** Exhausted; tired-looking.

washed-up (wŏsht'ŭp', wôsht'-) *adj.* **1.** No longer successful or needed; finished. **2.** Ready to give up in disgust.

wash·er (wŏsh'ər, wôsh'-) *n.* **1.** One that washes. **2.** A small perforated disk, as of metal, rubber, leather, or plastic, placed beneath a nut or at an axle bearing or joint to relieve friction, prevent leakage, or distribute pressure. **3.** A machine or apparatus for washing, esp. one for washing clothes or dishes.

wash·er·wom·an (wŏsh'ər-wo͝om'ən, wô'shər-) also **wash·wom·an** (wŏsh'wo͝om'ən, wôsh'-) *n.* A woman who washes clothes as a means of livelihood; laundress.

wash·ing (wŏsh′ĭng, wô′shĭng) *n.* **1.** The act or process of one that washes. **2.** A quantity of articles washed or intended to be washed at one time: *the week's washing.* **3.** The residue after an ore or other material has been washed. **4.** Often **washings.** The liquid that is used to wash something.

washing machine *n.* A usually automatic machine for washing clothes and linens.

washing soda *n.* A hydrated sodium carbonate, used as a general cleanser.

Wash·ing·ton's Birthday (wŏsh′ĭng-tən) *n.* February 22, officially observed on the third Monday in February as a legal holiday in most U.S. states in honor of the birthday of George Washington.

wash·out (wŏsh′out′, wôsh′-) *n.* **1. a.** The erosion of a relatively soft surface, such as a roadbed, by a transient stream of water. **b.** A channel produced by washout. **2. a.** A total failure or disappointment. **b.** One who fails to measure up to a given standard, esp. one who fails a course of training or study.

wash·rag (wŏsh′răg′, wôsh′-) *n.* A washcloth.

wash·room (wŏsh′ro͞om′, -ro͝om′, wôsh′-) *n.* A bathroom, rest room, or lavatory, esp. in a public place.

wash sale *n.* The illegal buying of stock by a seller's agents to give the impression of an active market.

wash·stand (wŏsh′stănd′, wôsh′-) *n.* **1.** A stand designed to hold a basin and pitcher of water for washing. **2.** A stationary bathroom sink.

wash·tub (wŏsh′tŭb′, wôsh′-) *n.* A tub used for washing clothes.

wash·wom·an (wŏsh′wo͝om′ən, wôsh′-) *n.* Variant of **washerwoman.**

wash·y (wŏsh′ē, wô′shē) *adj.* **-i·er, -i·est. 1.** Watery; diluted: *washy tea.* **2.** Lacking intensity or strength. **—wash′i·ness** *n.*

was·n't (wŏz′ənt, wŭz′-). Was not.

wasp (wŏsp, wôsp) *n.* Any of numerous social or solitary insects, chiefly of the superfamilies Vespoidea and Sphecoidea, having a slender body with a constricted abdomen, membranous wings, and in the females an ovipositor often modified as a sting. [ME *waspe* < OE *wæps.*] **—wasp′like′** *adj.*

Wasp or **WASP** *n.* A white Protestant of Anglo-Saxon ancestry. [W(HITE) + A(NGLO)-S(AXON) + P(ROTESTANT).] **—Wasp′ish** *adj.* **—Wasp′y** *adj.*

wasp·ish (wŏs′pĭsh, wô′spĭsh) *adj.* **1.** Pertaining to or suggestive of a wasp. **2.** Easily irritated or annoyed; snappish. **—wasp′ish·ly** *adv.* **—wasp′ish·ness** *n.*

wasp waist *n.* A very slender or tightly corseted waist. **—wasp′-waist′ed** (wŏsp′wās′tĭd, wôsp′-) *adj.*

wasp·y (wŏs′pē, wô′spē) *adj.* **-i·er, -i·est.** Characteristic of a wasp; wasplike.

was·sail (wŏs′əl, wŏ-sāl′) *n.* **1. a.** A salutation or toast formerly given in drinking someone's health or as an expression of good will at a festivity. **b.** The drink used in such toasting, commonly ale or wine spiced with roasted apples and sugar. **2.** A festivity characterized by much drinking. *—v.* **-sailed, -sail·ing, -sails.** *—tr.* To drink to the health of; toast. *—intr.* To engage in or drink a wassail. [ME *wassayl,* contraction of *wæs hæil,* be healthy < ON *ves heill* : *ves,* imper. sing. of *vera,* to be + *heill,* healthy.] **—was′sail·er** *n.*

Was·ser·mann reaction (wä′sər-mən) *n.* A complement-fixing reaction to the Wassermann test.

Wassermann test *n.* A diagnostic test for syphilis involving the fixation or inactivation of a complement by an antibody in a blood serum sample. [After August von *Wassermann* (1866–1925), its inventor.]

wast (wăst, wŭst) *v. Archaic.* Second person singular past tense of **be.** [WAS + -(E)ST².]

wast·age (wā′stĭj) *n.* **1.** Loss by deterioration, wear, or destruction: *"Disease and desertion still caused much greater wastage than battle"* (Theodore Ropp). **2.** The gradual process of wasting. **3.** Something wasted or lost by wear.

waste (wāst) *v.* **wast·ed, wast·ing, wastes.** *—tr.* **1.** To use, consume, or expend thoughtlessly or carelessly; squander. **2.** To cause to lose energy, strength, or vigor; exhaust, tire, or enfeeble: *Disease wasted his body.* **3.** To fail to take advantage of or use for profit; lose: *waste an opportunity.* **4. a.** To destroy completely. **b.** *Slang.* To kill; murder: *soldiers who wasted hundreds of civilians.* *—intr.* **1.** To lose energy, strength, or vigor; become weak or enfeebled. **2.** To pass without being put to use: *Time is wasting.* ***—phrasal verb.*** **waste away.** To grow gradually weaker, thinner, or more feeble. *—n.* **1.** The act of wasting or the condition of being wasted. **2.** A place, region, or land that is uninhabited or uncultivated; desert or wilderness. **3.** A devastated or destroyed region, town, or building; ruin. **4. a.** A useless or worthless by-product. **b.** Something, as steam, that escapes without being used. **5.** Garbage; trash. **6.** The undigested residue of food eliminated from the body. *—adj.* **1.** Regarded or discarded as worthless or useless: *waste paper.* **2.** Used as a conveyance or container for refuse: *a waste can.* **3.** Excreted from the body as useless. ***—idioms.*** **lay waste.** To destroy; ravage. **waste one's breath.** To gain nothing by speaking. [ME *wasten* < ONFr. *waster* < Lat. *vastare,* to make empty.]

waste·bas·ket (wāst′băs′kĭt) *n.* An open-topped container for rubbish.

wast·ed (wā′stĭd) *adj.* **1.** Not profitably used or maintained. **2.** Needless or superfluous: *wasted words.* **3.** Deteriorated; ravaged. **4.** Physically haggard, as from disease: *the wasted bodies of the prisoners.* **5.** *Slang.* Stoned (sense 2). **6.** *Archaic.* Elapsed.

waste·ful (wāst′fəl) *adj.* Characterized by or given to waste; extravagant. **—waste′ful·ly** *adv.* **—waste′ful·ness** *n.*

waste·land (wāst′lănd′) *n.* **1.** Uncultivated or desolate country. **2.** A place, era, or aspect of life considered humanistically, spiritually, or culturally barren.

waste·pa·per (wāst′pā′pər) *n.* Discarded paper.

wast·er (wā′stər) *n.* **1. a.** One that wastes: *Many bureaucratic procedures are wasters of time.* **b.** A spendthrift; wastrel. **2.** One that lays waste; destroyer.

wast·ing (wā′stĭng) *adj.* **1.** Gradually deteriorating; declining. **2.** Sapping the strength, energy, or substance of the body; emaciating: *a wasting disease.* **—wast′ing·ly** *adv.*

wast·rel (wā′strəl) *n.* **1.** A person who wastes, esp. one who wastes money. **2.** An idler or loafer; good-for-nothing. [< WASTE.]

wa·tap (wă-tăp′, wä-) also **wa·ta·pe** (-tä′pē) *n.* A stringy thread made from the roots of various conifers and used by American Indians in sewing and weaving. [Cree *watapiy.*]

watch (wŏch) *v.* **watched, watch·ing, watch·es.** *—intr.* **1.** To look or observe attentively or carefully; be closely observant. **2.** To look and wait expectantly or in anticipation: *watch for an opportunity.* **3.** To act as a spectator; look on. **4.** To stay awake at night while serving as a guard, sentinel, or watchman. **5.** To stay alert as a devotional or religious exercise; keep vigil. *—tr.* **1.** To look at steadily; observe carefully or continuously: *watch a parade.* **2.** To keep a watchful eye on; guard: *watched the prisoner all day.* **3.** To observe the course of mentally; keep up on or informed about: *watch the election returns.* **4.** To tend (a flock, for example). ***—phrasal verbs.*** **watch out.** To be careful or on the alert; take care. **watch over.** To superintend; be in charge of. *—n.* **1.** The act or process of keeping awake or mentally alert, as for the purpose of guarding. **2.** Any of the periods into which the night is divided; a part of the night. **3.** A period of close observation, often in order to discover something: *a watch during the child's illness.* **4.** A person or group of persons serving, esp. at night, to guard or protect. **5.** The post or period of duty of a guard, sentinel, or watchman. **6.** A small, portable timepiece, esp. one worn on the wrist or carried in the pocket. **7. a.** A period of wakefulness, esp. one observed as a religious vigil. **b.** A wake. **8.** *Naut.* **a.** Any of the periods of time into which the day aboard ship is divided and during which a part of the crew is assigned to duty. **b.** The members of a ship's crew on duty during a specific watch. **c.** A chronometer on a ship. **9.** A flock of nightingales. ***—idioms.*** **watch it.** To be careful: *Watch it when you step on the ice.* **watch (one's) step.** To act or proceed with caution. [ME *wachen* < OE *wæccan,* to watch, be awake.]

watch cap *n.* A small woolen cap of dark blue worn for cold-weather duty by naval enlisted personnel.

watch·case (wŏch′kās′) *n.* The casing for the mechanism of a watch.

watch·dog (wŏch′dôg′, -dŏg′) *n.* **1.** A dog trained to guard property. **2.** A person who serves as a guardian or protector against waste, loss, or illegal practices.

watch·er (wŏch′ər) *n.* **1.** One that watches. **2.** A person keeping vigil, as at a sick person's bedside.

watch·eye (wŏch′ī′) *n.* A walleye, esp. of a dog.

watch fire *n.* A fire kept burning at night, as for a signal or for the use of a watchman.

watch·ful (wŏch′fəl) *adj.* **1.** Closely observant or alert; vigilant. **2.** *Archaic.* Not sleeping; awake. **—watch′ful·ly** *adv.* **—watch′ful·ness** *n.*

watch glass *n.* A shallow glass dish used as a beaker cover or evaporating surface.

watch·mak·er (wŏch′mā′kər) *n.* One whose occupation is making or repairing watches. **—watch′mak′ing** *n.*

watch·man (wŏch′mən) *n.* A man employed to stand guard or keep watch.

watch night *n.* **1.** New Year's Eve. **2.** A religious service held on New Year's Eve.

watch·tow·er (wŏch′tou′ər) *n.* An observation tower upon which a guard or lookout is stationed to keep watch, as for forest fires or over prisoners.

watch·word (wŏch′wûrd′) *n.* **1.** A prearranged reply to a challenge, as from a guard or sentry; password. **2.** A rallying cry: *Let our watchword be freedom.*

wa·ter (wô′tər, wŏt′ər) *n.* **1.** A clear, colorless, nearly odorless and tasteless liquid, H_2O, essential for most plant and animal life and the most widely used of all solvents. Melting point 0°C (32°F); boiling point 100°C (212°F); specific gravity (4°C) 1.0000; weight per gallon (15°C) 8.337 pounds. **2.** Any of various forms of water, such as rain. **3.** A body of water such as a sea, lake, river, or stream. **4.** Any of the liquids passed out of the body, as urine, perspiration, or tears. **5.** The fluid surrounding the fetus in the uterus; amniotic fluid. **6.** An aqueous solution of a substance, esp. a gas: *ammonia water.* **7.** A wavy finish or sheen, as of a fabric.

wasp

wasp waist

watch
Pocket watch

water buffalo

waterfall

water hyacinth

water lily

water-ski

8. a. The valuation of the assets of a business firm beyond their real value. **b.** Stock issued in excess of paid-in capital. **9. a.** Clarity and luster of a gem. **b.** Degree or quality: *of the first water.* —*v.* **-tered, -ter·ing, -ters.** —*tr.* **1.** To pour water upon; make wet. **2. a.** To give drinking water to. **b.** To lead (an animal) to drinking water. **3.** To give a sheen to the surface of (silk, linen, or metal). **4.** To increase (the number of shares of stock) without increasing the value of the assets represented. **5.** To irrigate (land). —*intr.* **1.** To produce or discharge fluid, as from the eyes. **2.** To salivate in anticipation of food. **3.** To take on a supply of water, as a ship. **4.** To drink water, as an animal. ***—phrasal verb.* water down.** To reduce or dilute the strength or effectiveness of. ***—idioms.* above water.** Out of trouble. **hold water.** To be logical or consistent: *His story doesn't hold water.* **in deep water.** In great difficulty. **make (one's) mouth water.** To cause to anticipate with relish. [ME < OE *wæter.*] **—wa'ter·er** *n.*

Usage: The plural *waters* was once common but now has limited use. It survives in a few phrases, such as *take the waters* (at a spa), and in references to a body of water (*northern waters*).

wa·ter·age (wô'tər-ĭj, wŏt'ər-) *n. Chiefly Brit.* **1.** The movement of goods or merchandise by water. **2.** The fee paid for waterage.

water ballet *n.* The art of dancelike movement in water; synchronized swimming.

Water Bearer *n.* Aquarius.

water bed *n.* A bed with a mattress made of a tough plastic that is filled with water.

water beetle *n.* Any of various aquatic beetles, esp. of the family Dytiscidae, characteristically having a smooth, oval body and flattened hind legs adapted for swimming.

water bird *n.* A swimming or wading bird.

water biscuit *n.* A biscuit made of flour and water.

water blister *n.* A blister having a nonpurulent watery content.

water bloom *n.* A growth of algae at or near the surface of a body of water, as a pond.

water boatman *n.* Any of various aquatic insects of the family Corixidae, having long, oarlike hind legs adapted for swimming.

wa·ter·borne (wô'tər-bôrn', -bōrn', wŏt'ər-) *adj.* **1.** Floating on or supported by water; afloat. **2.** Transported by water, as freight. **3.** Transmitted in water, as a disease germ.

water boy *n.* One who keeps a group, as a football team, supplied with drinking water.

water brash *n.* Regurgitation of watery acid from the stomach.

wa·ter·buck (wô'tər-bŭk', wŏt'ər-) *n.* Any of several African antelopes of the genus *Kobus,* having curved, ridged horns and frequenting swamps or bodies of water.

water buffalo *n.* A large buffalo, *Bubalus bubalis,* of Asia and Africa, having large, spreading horns and often domesticated, esp. as a draft animal.

water bug *n.* Any of various insects of wet places, esp. a large aquatic insect of the family Belostomatidae.

water cal·trop (kăl'trəp) *n.* Water chestnut (sense 1).

water chestnut *n.* **1.** A floating aquatic plant, *Trapa natans,* native to Asia, bearing four-pronged, nutlike fruit. **2. a.** A Chinese sedge, *Eleocharis tuberosa,* having an edible corm. **b.** The succulent corm of this plant, used in Oriental cookery.

water chinquapin *n.* A North American aquatic plant, *Nelumbo lutea,* related to the lotus and the water lilies and having large, cup-shaped leaves, large, pale-yellow flowers, and edible, nutlike seeds.

water clock *n.* Any of various time-keeping or time-measuring devices based on the motion of running water.

water closet *n.* A room or booth containing a toilet and often a washbowl.

water color also **wa·ter-col·or** or **wa·ter·col·or** (wô'tər-kŭl'ər, wŏt'ər-) *n.* **1.** A paint composed of a water-soluble pigment. **2.** A work that is done in water colors. **3.** The art of using water colors. **—wa'ter-col'or** *adj.* **—water colorist** *n.*

wa·ter-cool (wô'tər-ko͞ol', wŏt'ər-) *tr.v.* **-cooled, -cool·ing, -cools.** To cool (an engine) with water, esp. with circulating water.

water cooler *n.* A vessel, device, or apparatus for cooling, storing, and dispensing drinking water.

wa·ter·course (wô'tər-kôrs', -kōrs', wŏt'ər-) *n.* **1.** A waterway. **2.** The bed or channel of a waterway.

wa·ter·craft (wô'tər-krăft', wŏt'ər-) *n.* **1.** Skill in water-related activities such as managing boats or swimming. **2.** Water vehicles used esp. for cargo transport.

wa·ter·cress (wô'tər-krĕs', wŏt'ər-) *n.* **1.** A plant, *Nasturtium officinale,* native to Eurasia, growing in freshwater ponds and streams and having pungent leaves used in salads and as a garnish. **2.** Any of several plants similar or related to the watercress.

water cure *n. Med.* Hydropathy or hydrotherapy.

water dog *n.* **1.** A dog that is at home in water, esp. one trained for hunting waterfowl. **2.** A person who is at home in or on the water. **3.** A mud puppy.

water elm *n.* The planer tree.

wa·ter·fall (wô'tər-fôl', wŏt'ər-) *n.* A steep descent of water from a height; cascade.

wa·ter·find·er (wô'tər-fīn'dər, wŏt'ər-) *n.* A dowser.

water flea *n.* Any of various small aquatic crustaceans of the order Cladocera, characteristically swimming with jerking, flealike motions.

wa·ter·fowl (wô'tər-foul', wŏt'ər-) *n., pl.* **waterfowl** or **-fowls.** **1.** A swimming bird, as a duck or goose, usually frequenting freshwater areas. **2.** Swimming game birds collectively.

wa·ter·front (wô'tər-frŭnt', wŏt'ər-) *n.* **1.** Land abutting on a body of water, such as a lake or harbor. **2.** The district of a town or city that borders the water, esp. a wharf district where ships dock.

water gap *n.* A transverse cleft in a mountain ridge through which a stream flows.

water gas *n.* A fuel gas containing about 50 per cent carbon monoxide, 40 per cent hydrogen, and small amounts of carbon dioxide and nitrogen, made by passing steam over heated coke.

water gate *n.* A floodgate (sense 1).

Wa·ter·gate (wô'tĕr-gāt', wŏt'ər-) *n. Informal.* A scandal that involves officials violating public or corporate trust through perjury, bribery, and other acts of abuse of power in order to keep their elective or appointive positions. [After *Watergate,* a building complex in Washington, D.C., the site of illegal activities that gave rise to such a scandal.]

water gauge also **water gage** *n.* An instrument indicating the level of water, as in a boiler, tank, reservoir, or stream.

water glass *n.* **1.** A drinking glass or goblet. **2.** A tube or similar structure having a glass bottom for making observations below the surface of the water. **3.** Sodium silicate. **4.** A water gauge made of glass. **5.** A clepsydra.

water gum *n.* A gum tree, *Nyssa biflora,* that grows on swampy land.

water gun *n.* A squirt gun.

water hammer *n.* **1.** A banging noise heard in a water pipe following an abrupt alteration of the flow with resulting pressure surges. **2.** A banging noise in steam pipes, caused by steam bubbles entering a cold pipe partially filled with water.

water hemlock *n.* Any of several poisonous plants of the genus *Cicuta,* esp. *C. maculata,* of marshy areas, having clusters of small white flowers.

water hen *n.* Any of various chickenlike birds of marshy areas, as a rail or coot.

water hole *n.* A small natural depression in which water collects, esp. a pool used by animals as a watering place.

water hyacinth *n.* A floating aquatic plant, *Eichhornia crassipes,* native to tropical America, having bluish-purple flowers and often forming dense masses in ponds and streams.

water ice *n.* A dessert made from sweetened, flavored, finely crushed ice.

watering can *n.* A watering pot.

watering hole *n.* A watering place.

watering place *n.* **1.** A place where animals find water. **2.** A health resort featuring water activities or mineral springs; spa. **3.** A place, as a nightclub or bar, where drink is served.

watering pot *n.* A vessel, often with a spout and a perforated nozzle, used to water plants.

wa·ter·ish (wô'tər-ĭsh, wŏt'ər-) *adj.* Watery.

wa·ter-jack·et (wô'tər-jăk'ĭt, wŏt'ər-) *tr.v.* **-et·ed, -et·ing, -ets.** To encase in or provide with a water jacket.

water jacket *n.* A casing containing water circulated by a pump, used around a part to be cooled, esp. in water-cooled internal-combustion engines.

wa·ter·leaf (wô'tər-lēf', wŏt'ər-) *n., pl.* **-leafs.** Any of various North American plants of the genus *Hydrophyllum,* having clusters of white or purplish flowers.

wa·ter·less (wô'tər-lĭs, wŏt'ər-) *adj.* **1.** Without water; dry. **2.** Not requiring water, as a cooling system.

water level *n.* **1.** The level of the surface of a body of water. **2.** *Geol.* A water table (sense 2). **3.** The water line of a ship.

water lily *n.* **1.** Any of various aquatic plants of the genus *Nymphaea,* having floating leaves and showy, variously colored flowers, esp. *N. odorata,* having fragrant, many-petaled white or pinkish flowers. **2.** Any of various plants similar or related to the water lily.

water line *n.* **1.** *Naut.* **a.** The line on the hull of a ship to which the water surface rises. **b.** Any of several lines parallel to this marked on the hull of a ship, indicating the depth to which the ship sinks under various loads. **2.** A line or stain, as that left on a sea wall, indicating the height to which water has risen or may rise; watermark.

wa·ter·log (wô'tər-lôg', wŏt'ər-lŏg') *tr.v.* **-logged, -log·ging, -logs.** To soak or saturate with water, causing to lose buoyancy. [WATER + *log,* to lie or cause to lie like a log.]

wa·ter-logged (wô'tər-lôgd', wŏt'ər-lŏgd') *adj.* **1.** Heavy and sluggish in the water because of flooding in the hold. Used of a ship. **2.** Soaked or saturated with water: *waterlogged fields.*

wa·ter·loo (wô'tər-lo͞o', wŏt'ər-) *n., pl.* **-loos.** A disastrous or crushing defeat: *finally met his waterloo.* [After *Waterloo,* Belgium, the town where Napoleon was defeated in 1815.]

water main *n.* A principal pipe in a system of pipes for conveying water, esp. one installed underground.

wa·ter·man (wô′tər-mən, wŏt′ər-) *n.* A boatman. —**wa′ter·man·ship′** *n.*

wa·ter·mark (wô′tər-märk′, wŏt′ər-) *n.* **1.** A mark showing the height to which water has risen, esp. a line indicating the heights of high and low tide. **2. a.** A translucent design impressed on paper during manufacture and visible when the finished paper is held to the light. **b.** The metal pattern that produces this design. —*tr.v.* **-marked, -mark·ing, -marks. 1.** To mark (paper) with a watermark. **2.** To impress (a pattern or design) as a watermark.

wa·ter·mel·on (wô′tər-mĕl′ən, wŏt′ər-) *n.* **1.** A vine, *Citrullus vulgaris,* native to Africa, cultivated for its large, edible fruit. **2.** The fruit of the watermelon, having a hard green rind and sweet, watery pink or reddish flesh.

water meter *n.* An instrument that records the quantity of water passing through a pipe.

water milfoil *n.* Any of various aquatic plants of the genus *Myriophyllum,* having feathery, finely dissected leaves.

water mill *n.* A mill with water-driven machinery.

water moccasin *n.* A venomous snake, *Agkistrodon piscivorus* or *Ancistrodon piscivorus,* of lowlands and swampy regions of the southern United States.

water oak *n.* Any of various oak trees that grow in wet land.

water of crystallization *n.* Water in chemical combination with a crystal and necessary for the maintenance of crystalline properties but capable of being removed by sufficient heat.

water of hydration *n.* Water chemically combined with a substance so that it can be removed, as by heating, without substantially changing the chemical composition of the substance.

water ouzel *n.* Any of several small birds of the genus *Cinclus* that dive into swift-moving streams and feed along the bottom.

water parting *n.* A watershed (sense 1).

water pepper *n.* A marsh plant, *Polygonum hydropiper* or *Persicaria hydropiper,* having reddish stems, clusters of small, greenish flowers, and acrid-tasting leaves.

water pipe *n.* **1.** A water conduit. **2.** A hookah.

water pistol *n.* A squirt gun.

water plantain *n.* Any of various aquatic plants of the genus *Alisma,* having branching clusters of small white or pinkish flowers.

water polo *n.* A water sport with two teams each of which tries to pass a ball into the other's goal.

wa·ter·pow·er (wô′tər-pou′ər, wŏt′ər-) *n.* **1. a.** The energy of running or falling water as used for driving machinery, esp. for generating electricity. **b.** A source of such power, as a waterfall. **2.** A water right owned by a mill.

wa·ter·proof (wô′tər-pro͞of′, wŏt′ər-) *adj.* **1.** Impenetrable to or unaffected by water. **2.** Made of or treated with rubber, plastic, or a sealing agent to resist water penetration. —*n.* **1.** A waterproof material or fabric. **2.** *Chiefly Brit.* A waterproof garment, such as a raincoat. —*tr.v.* **-proofed, -proof·ing, -proofs.** To make waterproof.

water purslane *n.* **1.** An aquatic plant, *Didiplis diandra,* having small greenish flowers. **2.** A marsh plant, *Ludwigia palustris,* having reddish stems and small reddish flowers.

water rat *n.* **1.** Any of various semiaquatic rodents, as one of the genus *Hydromis,* of Australia and adjacent islands, or *Neofiber alleni,* of Florida and southern Georgia, resembling the muskrat. **2.** *Slang.* A waterfront thief, ruffian, or habitué.

wa·ter-re·pel·lent (wô′tər-rĭ-pĕl′ənt, wŏt′ər-) *adj.* Resistant to water but not entirely waterproof.

wa·ter-re·sis·tant (wô′tər-rĭ-zĭs′tənt, wŏt′ər-) *adj.* Water-repellent.

water right *n.* **1.** The right to draw water from a particular source, such as a lake, irrigation canal, or stream. **2.** The right to navigate on particular waters.

water sapphire *n.* A deep-blue cordierite often used as a gemstone.

wa·ter·scape (wô′tər-skāp′, wŏt′ər-) *n.* A seascape.

water scorpion *n.* Any of various aquatic insects of the family Nepidae, having a respiratory tube projecting from the posterior part of the abdomen and inflicting a painful sting.

wa·ter·shed (wô′tər-shĕd′, wŏt′ər-) *n.* **1.** A ridge of high land dividing two areas that are drained by different river systems. **2.** The region draining into a river, river system, or body of water. **3.** A critical point that serves as a dividing line: *reached a watershed in the peace negotiations.* [Prob. transl. of G. *Wasserscheide.*]

water shield *n.* **1.** An aquatic plant, *Brasenia schreberi,* having floating oval leaves and purplish flowers. **2.** Any of several related plants of the genus *Cabomba.*

wa·ter-sick (wô′tər-sĭk′, wŏt′ər-) *adj.* Not productive owing to the results of excessive irrigation. Used of land.

wa·ter·side (wô′tər-sīd′, wŏt′ər-) *n.* Land bordering a body of water; shore. —*adj.* **1.** Of, pertaining to, or situated at the waterside. **2.** Living or working along the waterside.

water skater *n.* A water strider.

wa·ter-ski (wô′tər-skē′, wŏt′ər-) *intr.v.* **-skied, -ski·ing, -skis.** To ski on water while being towed by a motorboat. —*n.* Also **water ski.** *pl.* **skis** or **ski.** A broad ski used in water-skiing. —**wa′ter-ski′er** *n.*

water snake *n.* **1.** Any of various nonvenomous snakes of the genus *Natrix,* frequenting freshwater streams and ponds. **2.** Any of various aquatic or semiaquatic snakes.

wa·ter-soak (wô′tər-sōk′, wŏt′ər-) *tr.v.* **-soaked, -soak·ing, -soaks.** To soak or saturate with water.

water spaniel *n.* A spaniel of a breed characterized by a curly, water-resistant coat, often used for retrieving waterfowl.

wa·ter·spout (wô′tər-spout′, wŏt′ər-) *n.* **1.** A tornado or lesser whirlwind occurring over water and resulting in a whirling column of spray and mist. **2.** A hole or pipe from which water is discharged.

water sprite *n.* A sprite or nymph living in or near the water.

water strider *n.* Any of various insects of the family Gerridae, having long, slender legs with which they support themselves on the surface of water.

water supply *n.* **1.** The water available for a community or region. **2.** The sources and delivery system of a water supply.

water system *n.* **1.** A river and all its tributaries. **2.** A water supply.

water table *n.* **1.** A projecting ledge, molding, or stringcourse along the side of a building, designed to throw off rainwater. **2.** The depth or level below which the ground is saturated with water.

water thrush *n.* Either of two brownish New World birds, *Seiurus noveboracensis* or *S. motacilla,* characteristically walking along the edges of streams or ponds.

water tiger *n.* The predacious larva of a diving beetle.

wa·ter·tight (wô′tər-tīt′, wŏt′ər-) *adj.* **1.** Assembled or constructed so that water cannot enter or escape; waterproof. **2.** Having no flaws or loopholes: *a watertight alibi.*

water tower *n.* **1.** A standpipe or elevated tank used as a reservoir or for maintaining equal pressure in a water system. **2.** A towerlike fire-fighting apparatus for lifting hoses to the upper levels of a tall structure.

water turkey *n.* A blackish New World bird, *Anhinga anhinga,* of swampy regions, having a long, slender, flexible neck.

water vapor *n.* Water diffused as a vapor in the atmosphere, esp. at a temperature below the boiling point.

wa·ter·way (wô′tər-wā′, wŏt′ər-) *n.* A navigable body of water, such as a river, channel, or canal.

wa·ter·weed (wô′tər-wēd′, wŏt′ər-) *n.* Any of various aquatic plants, esp. one of the genus *Anacharis* or *Elodea,* having submerged stems with densely crowded, narrow leaves.

water wheel *n.* **1.** A wheel propelled by falling or running water used to power machinery. **2.** A wheel with buckets attached to its rim used for raising water.

water wings *pl.n.* An inflatable device used to support the body in learning to swim.

water witch *n.* A person who professes the ability to find underground water esp. by means of a divining rod.

wa·ter·works (wô′tər-wûrks′, wŏt′ər-) *pl.n.* *(used with a sing. or pl. verb).* **1. a.** The water system, including reservoirs, tanks, buildings, pumps, and pipes, of a city or town. **b.** A single unit, as a pumping station, within such a system. **2.** An exhibition of moving water, as artificial fountains or waterfalls. **3.** *Slang.* Tears.

wa·ter·y (wô′tə-rē, wŏt′ə-) *adj.* **-i·er, -i·est. 1.** Filled with, consisting of, or containing water; moist: *watery soil.* **2.** Resembling or suggestive of water; liquid. **3.** Diluted: *watery soup.* **4.** Without force; insipid: *watery prose.* **5.** Secreting or discharging water, esp. as a symptom of disease. —**wa′ter·i·ness** *n.*

Wat·son-Crick (wät′sən-krĭk′) *adj.* Of or pertaining to the Watson-Crick model of DNA.

Watson-Crick model *n.* A structural model of DNA in which the molecule is represented as a two-stranded helix with each strand composed of alternating links of phosphate and deoxyribose and with the strands connected in a ladderlike fashion by pairs of purine and pyrimidine bases, these in turn connected by hydrogen bonds. [After James D. *Watson* (b. 1928) and Francis H. C. *Crick* (b. 1916), its devisers.]

watt (wŏt) *n.* A unit of power in the International System equal to one joule per second. [After James *Watt* (1736–1819).]

watt·age (wŏt′ĭj) *n.* **1.** An amount of power, esp. electric power, expressed in watts. **2.** The electric power required by an appliance or device.

watt-hour (wŏt′our′) *n.* A unit of energy, esp. electrical energy, equal to the energy of one watt acting for one hour and equivalent to 3,600 joules.

wat·tle (wŏt′l) *n.* **1. a.** Poles intertwined with twigs, reeds, or branches for use in construction, as of walls or fences. **b.** Materials thus used. **2.** A fleshy, often brightly colored fold of skin hanging from the neck or throat, characteristic of certain birds and some lizards. **3.** Any of various Australian trees or shrubs of the genus *Acacia.* —*tr.v.* **-tled, -tling, -tles. 1.** To construct from wattle. **2.** To weave into wattle. [ME *wattel* < OE *watel.*] —**wat′tled** *adj.*

wattle and daub *n.* An interweaving of rods and twigs overlaid with clay that is used in building construction.

water ouzel

water spaniel

water wheel

wattle

wat·tle·bird (wŏt′l-bûrd′) *n.* Any of several birds of the genus *Anthochaera,* of Australia and adjacent regions, having pendent wattles on each side of the head.
watt·me·ter (wŏt′mē′tər) *n.* An instrument for measuring in watts the power flowing in a circuit.
Wa·tu·si (wä-tōō′sē) *n., pl.* **Watusi** or **-sis. 1.** A member of a pastoral people of Rwanda and Burundi in central equatorial Africa, distinguished by their tall stature. **2.** A dance supposedly imitative of Watusi tribal dances. *—intr.v.* **-sied, -si·ing, -sis.** To dance the Watusi.
wave (wāv) *v.* **waved, wav·ing, waves.** *—intr.* **1.** To move back and forth or up and down in the air; flutter: *branches waving in the wind.* **2.** To make a signal with an up-and-down or back-and-forth movement of the hand or of an object in the hand: *He waved in salute.* **3.** To curve or curl; undulate: *Her hair waves.* *—tr.* **1.** To move back and forth or up and down; cause to flutter: *She waved her fan.* **2. a.** To move or swing as in giving a signal: *wave one's hand.* **b.** To signal or express by such a movement: *He waved good-by.* **3.** To arrange into curves, curls, or undulations: *wave one's hair.* *—n.* **1. a.** A ridge or swell moving along the surface of a large body of water and generated by the action of gravity or the wind. **b.** A small ridge or swell moving across the interface of two fluids and dependent on the surface tension. **2.** Often **waves.** The sea. **3.** A moving curve or succession of curves in or on a surface; undulation: *waves of wheat in the wind.* **4. a.** A curve or succession of curves, as in the hair. **b.** A curved shape, outline, or pattern. **5.** A movement up and down or back and forth: *a wave of the hand.* **6. a.** A sweeping, surging sensation; surge: *a wave of indignation.* **b.** A movement that sweeps large numbers along with it; contagion: *waves of tax protests throughout the country.* **c.** A peak of activity: *a wave of investing.* **7.** A widespread, persistent meteorological condition, esp. of temperature: *a heat wave.* **8.** *Physics.* **a.** A disturbance or oscillation propagated from point to point in a medium or in space and described, in general, by mathematical specification of its amplitude, velocity, frequency, and phase. **b.** A graphic representation of the variation of such a disturbance with time. **c.** A single cycle of such a disturbance. **9. a.** A surging movement of large numbers of individuals: *a wave of pioneers moving westward.* **b.** A sudden and rapid increase in population density. [ME *waven* < OE *wafian.*] **—wav′er** *n.*
Wave (wāv) *n.* A member of the women's reserve of the U.S. Navy, organized during World War II. [Abbr. of *Women Accepted for Volunteer Emergency Service.*]
wave·band (wāv′bănd′) *n.* A range of frequencies, esp. of radio frequencies such as those assigned to communication transmissions.
wave equation *n.* **1.** A partial differential equation in one, two, or three dimensions whose solution represents the propagation of a wave with constant velocity. **2.** The fundamental equation of wave mechanics.
wave·form (wāv′fôrm′) *n.* The mathematical representation of a wave, esp. a graph of deviation at a fixed point versus time.
wave front *n.* A surface of a propagating wave that is the locus of all points having identical phase, the surface being usually but not always perpendicular to the direction of propagation.
wave function *n.* A mathematical function used in wave mechanics to describe a specified state of a quantum system, the square of the amplitude of the function at a given point being representative of the probability of the system in that state being found at that point.
wave-guide (wāv′gīd′) *n.* A system of material boundaries in the form of a solid dielectric rod or dielectric-filled tubular conductor capable of guiding high-frequency electromagnetic waves.
wave·length (wāv′lĕngth′) *n.* **1.** In a periodic wave, the distance between two points of corresponding phase in consecutive cycles. **2.** *Informal.* A spontaneous understanding of another person's situation, thoughts, or motivations: *We are on the same wavelength.*
wave·let (wāv′lĭt) *n.* A small wave or ripple.
wave mechanics *n. (used with a sing. or pl. verb).* The formulation of quantum mechanics, based on a partial differential equation whose solutions specify the possible dynamic states of an atomic system.
wave number *n.* A frequency of a wave divided by its velocity of propagation; the reciprocal of the wavelength.
wave-par·ti·cle duality (wāv′pär′tĭ-kəl) *n. Physics.* The exhibition of both wavelike and particlelike properties by a single entity, as of both diffraction and linear propagation by light.
wa·ver (wā′vər) *intr.v.* **-vered, -ver·ing, -vers. 1.** To swing or move back and forth; sway. **2.** To show irresolution or indecision; vacillate: *wavered over buying the new car.* **3.** To falter or yield: *His resolve began to waver.* **4.** To tremble or flicker, as sound or light. *—n.* An act or instance of wavering. [ME *waveren,* to wander.] **—wa′ver·ing·ly** *adv.*
wave train *n. Physics.* A succession of similar wave pulses.
wave trap *n.* An electronic filtering device designed to exclude unwanted signals or interference from a receiver.
wav·y (wā′vē) *adj.* **-i·er, -i·est. 1.** Abounding in, having, or rising in waves: *a wavy sea.* **2.** Proceeding in a wavelike form or motion; sinuous. **3.** Having curls, curves, or undulations: *wavy hair.* **4.** Characteristic of, resembling, or suggestive of waves. **5.** Wavering; unstable. **—wav′i·ly** *adv.* **—wav′i·ness** *n.*
waw (väv, vôv) *n.* Variant of **vav.**
wax[1] (wăks) *n.* **1. a.** Any of various natural unctuous, viscous or solid heat-sensitive substances, consisting essentially of high molecular weight hydrocarbons or esters of fatty acids, characteristically insoluble in water but soluble in most organic solvents. **b.** A substance secreted by bees; beeswax. **c.** A waxy substance found in the ears; cerumen. **2.** A solid plastic or pliable liquid substance of mineral origin, primarily petroleum, such as ozocerite or paraffin, used in paper coating, as insulation, in crayons, and often in medicinal preparations. **3.** A resinous mixture used by shoemakers to wax their thread. **4.** A waxlike substance that is readily molded and impressionable. **5.** A recording for a phonograph. **6.** A preparation containing wax used for polishing surfaces, as of floors. *—tr.v.* **waxed, wax·ing, wax·es.** To coat or treat with wax. [ME < OE *weax.*]
wax[2] (wăks) *intr.v.* **waxed, wax·ing, wax·es. 1.** To become gradually larger, more numerous, stronger, or more intense: *Economic discontent waxed among the people.* **2.** To show a progressively larger light surface, as the moon does in passing from new to full. **3.** To grow or become as specified: *The seas wax calm.* [ME *waxen* < OE *weaxan.*]
wax bean *n.* A variety of string bean having yellow pods.
wax·ber·ry (wăks′bĕr′ē) *n.* The waxy fruit of the wax myrtle or the snowberry.
wax·bill (wăks′bĭl′) *n.* Any of various tropical Old World birds of the genus *Estrilda* and related genera, having a short, often brightly colored waxy beak.
waxed paper (wăkst) *n.* Wax paper.
wax·en (wăk′sən) *adj.* **1.** Made of or covered with wax. **2.** Like wax, as in being pale or smooth: *waxen skin.*
wax insect *n.* Any of various scale insects of the family Coccidae that secrete a waxy substance.
wax moth *n.* A bee moth.
wax museum *n.* A collection of wax figures, usually representing famous individuals, on permanent exhibit.
wax myrtle *n.* A shrub, *Myrica cerifera,* of the southeastern United States, having evergreen leaves and small, berrylike fruit with a waxy coating.
wax palm *n.* Any of several palm trees that yield wax, as *Copernica cerifera,* the source of carnauba wax, or *Ceroxylon andicola,* of South America.
wax paper *n.* Paper that has been made moistureproof by treatment with wax.
wax plant *n.* A tropical Old World vine, *Hoya carnosa,* having waxy white or pinkish flowers.
wax·wing (wăks′wĭng′) *n.* Any of several birds of the genus *Bombycilla,* having crested heads, predominantly brown plumage, and waxy red tips on the secondary wing feathers.
wax·work (wăks′wûrk′) *n.* **1.** A figure made of wax, esp. a life-size wax representation of a famous person. **2. waxworks** *(used with a sing. or pl. verb).* An exhibition of waxwork in a museum. **—wax′work′er** *n.*
wax·y (wăk′sē) *adj.* **-i·er, -i·est. 1.** Resembling wax, as: **a.** Pale. **b.** Smooth and lustrous. **c.** Pliable or impressionable. **2.** Consisting of, abounding in, or covered with wax. **3.** *Pathol.* Containing white, insoluble deposits of a waxlike protein in certain portions of the body; amyloid.
way (wā) *n.* **1. a.** A road, path, or highway affording passage from one place to another. **b.** An opening affording passage: *This door is the only way into the attic.* **2.** Room or space to proceed with an action or course of action: *clear the way for a parade.* **3.** A course that is or may be used in going from one place to another: *Show me the way through the mountains.* **4.** Progress or travel along a certain route or in a specific direction: *on my way north.* **5.** A course of conduct or action: *always tried to take the easy way out.* **6.** A manner of doing something: *several ways of solving this problem.* **7.** A usual or habitual manner or mode of being, living, or acting: *the American way of life.* **8.** An individual or personal manner of behaving, acting, or doing: *Have it your own way.* **9.** Also **ways.** Distance: *a good way off.* **10. a.** A specific direction: *He glanced my way.* **b.** A participant: *a three-way conversation.* **11.** An aspect, particular, or feature: *resembles his father in many ways.* **12.** Freedom to do as one prefers; wish or will: *if I had my way.* **13.** Talent; facility: *has a way with words.* **14.** *Informal.* A state or condition: *in a bad way financially.* **15.** *Informal.* A district, neighborhood, or area: *Drop in our way soon.* **16.** Often **ways.** A longitudinal strip on a surface that serves to guide a moving machine part. **17. ways** *(used with a sing. or pl. verb). Naut.* The timbered structure upon which a ship is built and from which it slides when launched. *—adv.* Also **'way.** *Regional.* **1.** At a great distance; far: *way off yonder.* **2.** Away: *go 'way.* **—idioms. by the way.** Incidentally. **by way of. 1.** Through; via. **2.** As a means of: *made no comment by way of apology.* **go out of one's (or the) way.** To inconvenience oneself in doing something beyond what is required. **in a way. 1.** Within bounds or with reservations: *I like the new styles, in a way.* **2.** From one point of view: *In a way, you're right.* **in the way. 1.** In a position to obstruct,

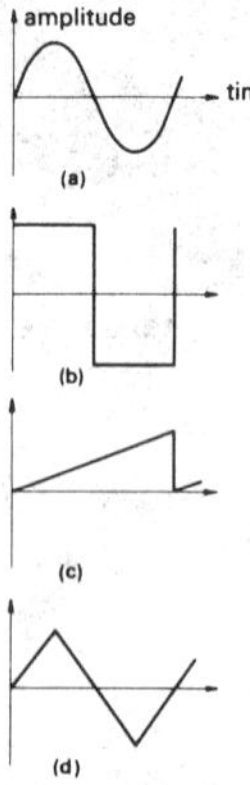

waveform
Single period of common electrical waveforms: (a) sine wave; (b) square wave; (c) saw-tooth wave; (d) triangular wave

George Miksch Sutton
waxwing

hinder, or interfere. **2.** In a position to be come upon: *A number of opportunities were put in the way.* **on one's (**or **the) way. 1.** In the process of coming, going, or traveling: *Winter is on the way.* **2.** On the route of one's journey. **out of the way. 1.** In such a position as not to obstruct, interfere, or hinder. **2.** In a remote location. **3.** Of an unusual character; remarkable. **4.** Improper; wrong. [ME < OE *weg.*]

Synonyms: *way, path, route, course, passage, pass, artery, trail.* These nouns refer in various ways to movement or travel. *Way, path, route, course,* and *passage* are all used in the general sense of direction followed: *the way home; the path of a missile; the route of a voyage; the course of a satellite; the passage to the Northwest Territory. Passage* also denotes the act or condition of going: *grant them safe passage.* In a narrower sense *route* frequently refers to a planned, well-established, or regularly traveled way or course, and *passage,* to a water route. Some of the terms also specify that over which or through which a person or thing travels. *Path* refers to a footway, especially to one worn by frequent travel, and *passage,* to a corridor of a building or similar enclosed area that connects buildings. *Pass* denotes a narrow opening between mountains; *artery,* a main route, such as a highway; and *trail,* a track or path worn by travel or marked for guidance through a wilderness.

Usage: *Way,* not *ways,* is the generally accepted form in writing when the term refers to distance: *a long way to go.* The phrase *under way* (meaning "in motion" or "in progress") is written thus in all contexts, including the nautical (not as *under weigh*). Confusion sometimes arises because an anchor is *weighed* and, when off the bottom, is *aweigh.*

way·bill (wā'bĭl') *n.* A document containing a list of goods and shipping instructions relative to a shipment.

way·far·er (wā'fâr'ər) *n.* A person who travels, esp. one who travels on foot. [ME *weyfarere* : *wey,* way + *faren,* to go.]

way·far·ing (wā'fâr'ĭng) *n.* Traveling, esp. on foot. [ME *wayfaringe* < OE *wegfarende* : *weg,* way + *farende,* p.part. of *faran,* to go.] **—way'far'ing** *adj.*

wayfaring tree *n.* A shrub, *Viburnum lantana,* having clusters of white flowers and berries that turn from red to black.

way·lay (wā'lā') *tr.v.* **-laid** (-lād'), **-lay·ing, -lays. 1.** To lie in wait for and attack from ambush. **2.** To accost unexpectedly. **3.** To intercept or delay the progress or movement of. **—way'lay'er** *n.*

way-out (wā'out') *adj. Slang.* Far-out.

ways (wāz) *n. (used with a sing. verb). Regional.* Way (sense 9). —See Usage note at **way.**

-ways *suff.* In a specified way, manner, direction, or position: *sideways.* [ME < *weyes,* in such a way < OE *weges,* genitive of *weg,* way.]

ways and means *pl.n.* Means or methods of increasing the financial resources available to a person or group in order to accomplish a specific end.

way·side (wā'sīd') *n.* The side or edge of a road. **—*modifier:*** *a wayside inn.* **—*idiom.* go (**or **let go) by the wayside.** To postpone or be postponed because of a more worthy or urgent consideration.

way station *n.* A station between major stops on a route.

way·ward (wā'wərd) *adj.* **1.** Stubborn or disobedient; willful: *a wayward boy.* **2.** Swayed by caprice; unpredictable. [ME *awayward,* turned away.] **—way'ward·ly** *adv.* **—way'ward·ness** *n.*

way·worn (wā'wôrn', -wōrn') *adj.* Wearied from traveling.

we (wē) *pron.* **1.** Used to refer to the speaker and another or others. **2.** Used instead of *I,* esp. by a sovereign or by a writer wishing to maintain an impersonal tone. **3.** Often used to refer to people in general, including the speaker or writer: *We cannot see beyond the grave.* —See Usage notes at **be** and **I.** [ME < OE *wē.*]

weak (wēk) *adj.* **-er, -est. 1.** Lacking physical strength, energy, or vigor; feeble. **2.** Likely to fail under pressure, stress, or strain: *a weak timber in a bridge.* **3.** Lacking effectiveness, firmness, or force of will: *a weak leader.* **4.** Lacking the usual, proper, or full strength of a component or an ingredient: *weak coffee.* **5.** Lacking the capacity to function well or in a normal manner; unsound: *a weak heart.* **6.** Lacking capacity, capability, or skill: *a weak student.* **7.** Resulting from a lack of persuasiveness; unconvincing: *a weak argument.* **8.** Lacking authority, influence, or power to rule: *a weak monarchy.* **9.** Lacking power or intensity; faint: *a weak voice; weak light.* **10.** Lacking or deficient in a specified quality or component: *was weak in math.* **11.** *Ling.* Designating those verbs in Germanic languages that form a past tense by means of a dental suffix, as *start, started; have, had; bring, brought.* **12.** Unstressed or unaccented, as a syllable. **13.** Being a verse ending in which the stress falls on a word or syllable that is normally unstressed, as a preposition. **14.** Tending downward in price. Used of the stock market. [ME *weike* < ON *veikr.*] **—weak'ly** *adv.* **—weak'ness** *n.*

Synonyms: *weak, feeble, frail, infirm, decrepit, debilitated.* These adjectives mean deficient in strength. *Weak,* the most widely applicable, can refer to things or persons; with respect to persons it may imply lack of physical, mental, or moral strength, deficiency of will or purpose, or general ineptitude. Applied to things, it indicates relative lack of force or effect. *Feeble,* said of persons, suggests either marked physical weakness or mental incompetence; with respect to things it usually means hopelessly inadequate to a specified requirement. *Frail* primarily suggests slightness of physique or structure. *Infirm* generally implies lack of physical or mental soundness in persons, caused by advanced age or illness; or it can imply lack of firm will or purpose. *Decrepit* describes things or persons worn out or broken down by age. *Debilitated* suggests more gradual impairment of strength, as through strenuous use.

weak·en (wē'kən) *tr. & intr.v.* **-ened, -en·ing, -ens.** To make or become weak or weaker. **—weak'en·er** *n.*

weak·fish (wēk'fĭsh') *n., pl.* **weakfish** or **-fish·es.** Any of several marine food and game fishes of the genus *Cynoscion,* esp. *C. regalis,* of North American Atlantic waters. [Obs. Du. *weekvis* : *week,* soft + *vis,* fish.]

weak force *n.* Weak interaction.

weak interaction *n.* A fundamental interaction between elementary particles that is several orders of magnitude weaker than the electromagnetic interaction and is responsible for some particle decay, for nuclear beta decay, and for neutrino absorption and emission.

weak-kneed (wēk'nēd') *adj.* Irresolute; timid.

weak·ling (wēk'lĭng) *n.* A person of weak constitution or character.

weak·ly (wēk'lē) *adj.* **-li·er, -li·est.** Sickly; delicate. **—weak'li·ness** *n.*

weak-mind·ed (wēk'mīn'dĭd) *adj.* **1. a.** Irresolute; indecisive. **b.** Foolish; silly. **2.** Feeble-minded. **—weak'-mind'ed·ness** *n.*

weak·ness (wēk'nĭs) *n.* **1. a.** The state or quality of being weak. **b.** An instance or display of being weak. **2.** A personal defect or failing. **3.** A special fondness or liking: *a weakness for chocolate.*

weak sister *n. Slang.* A member of a group who is considered a weakling or an incompetent.

weal¹ (wēl) *n.* **1.** Prosperity or happiness. **2.** The welfare of the community; the general good. [ME *wele* < OE *wela.*]

weal² (wēl) *n.* A ridge on the flesh raised by a blow; welt. [Var. of WALE.]

weald (wēld) *n. Chiefly Brit.* **1.** A woodland. **2.** An area of open rolling upland. [< *Weald,* a once-forested area in southeastern England < OE *weald,* forest.]

wealth (wĕlth) *n.* **1.** An abundance of valuable material possessions or resources; riches. **2.** The state of being rich; affluence. **3.** A profusion or abundance. **4.** *Econ.* All goods and resources having economic value. [ME *welthe* < *wele* < OE *wela.*]

wealth·y (wĕl'thē) *adj.* **-i·er, -i·est. 1.** Having wealth; affluent. **2.** Richly supplied; abundant. **—wealth'i·ly** *adv.* **—wealth'i·ness** *n.*

wean (wēn) *tr.v.* **weaned, wean·ing, weans. 1.** To withhold mother's milk from (the young of a mammal) and substitute other nourishment. **2.** To cause to give up a habit or interest: *was weaned from cigarettes.* [ME *wenen* < OE *wenian.*]

wean·ling (wēn'lĭng) *n.* A recently weaned child or animal.

weap·on (wĕp'ən) *n.* **1. a.** An instrument used in offensive or defensive combat. **b.** A part of the body, such as an animal's horns or claws, that is used in attack or defense. **2.** A means employed to disarm, persuade, or get the better of another. *—tr.v.* **-oned, -on·ing, -ons.** To supply with a weapon; arm. [ME *wepen* < OE *wæpen.*]

weap·on·eer (wĕp'ən-îr') *n.* **1.** An individual who arms and otherwise prepares a nuclear weapon for release onto a target. **2.** An individual who designs or devises nuclear weapons.

weap·on·ry (wĕp'ən-rē) *n.* Weapons collectively.

wear¹ (wâr) *v.* **wore** (wôr, wōr), **worn** (wôrn, wōrn), **wear·ing, wears.** *—tr.* **1.** To have on or put on (clothes, for example): *wear a dress.* **2.** To have or carry habitually on one's person: *wear a gun.* **3.** To exhibit: *wear a smile.* **4.** To bear, carry, or maintain in a particular manner: *wears her hair long.* **5.** To fly or display (colors), as a ship. **6.** To damage, diminish, erode, or use up by long or hard use, as constant rubbing or exposure: *wore the elbows of his jacket.* **7. a.** To produce by constant use, rubbing, or exposure: *eventually wore hollows in the steps.* **b.** To bring to a specific state by use or exposure: *wore her clothes to rags.* **8.** To fatigue, weary, or exhaust: *His incessant criticism wore her patience.* *—intr.* **1.** To withstand continual or hard use; last: *fabric that wears well.* **2.** To break down or diminish through use: *The rear tires began to wear.* **3.** To become by use or attrition: *The gold band wore thin.* **4.** To pass gradually or tediously: *The hours wore on endlessly.* **—*phrasal verbs.* wear down.** To break down the resistance of by relentless pressure. **wear off. 1.** To diminish gradually and vanish: *The headache wore off.* **2.** To become removed from: *The paint soon wore off the fence.* **wear out. 1.** To make or become unusable through heavy use. **2.** To use up; consume: *wore out his welcome.* **3.** To exhaust; tire: *was worn out after work.* **4.** To last through; outlast: *wore out the bitter cold.* *—n.* **1. a.** The act of wearing. **b.** The state of being worn; use: *The coat has had heavy wear.* **2.** Clothing, esp. of a particular kind or for a particular use: *men's wear; evening wear.* **3.** Gradual damage or diminution resulting from use or age: *The rug is showing signs of wear.* **4.** The capacity to withstand use; durability: *The engine has plenty of wear left.* **—*idioms.* wear stripes.** To do time in prison. **wear the pants (**or **trousers).** To exercise controlling authority in a household. [ME *weren* < OE *werian.*] **—wear'er** *n.*

wear² (wâr) *v.* **wore** (wôr, wōr), **worn** (wôrn, wōrn), **wear·ing, wears.** *Naut. —tr.* To make (a sailing ship) come about with the wind aft. *—intr.* To come about with the stern to windward. [Orig. unknown.]

wear·a·ble (wâr'ə-bəl) *adj.* **1.** Suitable for wear. **2.** Capable of being worn. *—pl.n.* **wearables.** Garments. **—wear'a·bil'i·ty** *n.*

wear and tear *n.* Loss, damage, or depreciation resulting from ordinary use or exposure.

wea·ri·ful (wîr'ĕ-fəl) *adj.* Wearisome; tedious. **—wea'ri·ful·ly** *adv.* **—wea'ri·ful·ness** *n.*

wea·ri·less (wîr'ē-lĭs) *adj.* Tireless. **—wea'ri·less·ly** *adv.*

wear·ing (wâr'ĭng) *adj.* **1.** Designating articles of clothing: *wearing apparel.* **2.** Causing fatigue or wear; tiring; exhausting: *a wearing experience.* **—wear'ing·ly** *adv.*

wea·ri·some (wîr'ē-səm) *adj.* Causing mental or physical fatigue. **—wea'ri·some·ly** *adv.* **—wea'ri·some·ness** *n.*

wea·ry (wîr'ē) *adj.* **-ri·er, -ri·est. 1.** Tired; fatigued. **2.** Exhausted of tolerance; impatient: *weary of constant complaints.* **3.** Causing fatigue; wearisome: *a weary task.* *—v.* **-ried, -ry·ing, -ries.** *—tr.* To make weary; fatigue. *—intr.* To become weary; grow tired. [ME *wery* < OE *wērig.*] **—wear'i·ly** *adv.* **—wear'i·ness** *n.*

weasel

wea·sand (wē'zənd) *n.* The gullet or throat. [ME *wesand.*]

wea·sel (wē'zəl) *n.* **1.** Any of various carnivorous mammals of the genus *Mustela,* having a long, slender body, a long tail, and brownish fur that in many species turns white in winter. **2.** A treacherous or sneaky person. *—intr.v.* **-seled, -sel·ing, -sels** also **-selled, -sel·ling, -sels.** To be evasive; equivocate. ***—phrasal verb.* weasel out.** *Informal.* To back out of a situation or commitment in a sneaky or cowardly manner. [ME *wesele* < OE *wesle.*]

weasel word *n.* A word of an equivocal nature used to deprive a statement of its force or to evade a direct commitment. [From the weasel's habit of sucking the contents out of an egg without breaking the shell.]

weather vane

weath·er (wĕth'ər) *n.* **1.** The state of the atmosphere at a given time and place, described by specification of variables such as temperature, moisture, wind velocity, and barometric pressure. **2. a.** Unpleasant or destructive atmospheric conditions: *The house must be protected from the weather.* **b.** Violent conditions such as high winds and heavy rain on the seas and in the air: *We flew into weather over the Azores.* *—v.* **-ered, -er·ing, -ers.** *—tr.* **1.** To expose to the action of the weather, as for drying, seasoning, or coloring. **2.** To discolor, disintegrate, wear, or otherwise affect adversely by exposure. **3.** To pass through safely; survive; outride: *weather a storm.* **4.** To slope (a roof, for example) so as to shed water. **5.** *Naut.* To pass to windward of, despite bad weather. *—intr.* **1.** To show the effects of exposure to the weather, as by discoloration or disintegration: *The barn walls had weathered and mellowed.* **2.** To resist or withstand the effects of weather or adverse conditions: *Some house paints weather better than others.* *—adj. Naut.* Of or pertaining to the windward side of a ship. ***—idioms.* make heavy weather of.** To exaggerate the difficulty of something to be done. **under the weather.** *Informal.* Slightly indisposed; unwell. [ME *weder* < OE.]

weather balloon *n.* A balloon used to carry instruments aloft to gather meteorological data in the atmosphere.

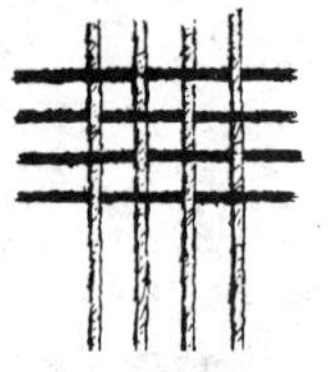

weave
Diagram of plain-weave fabric showing warp (vertical strands) and woof (horizontal strands)

weath·er-beat·en (wĕth'ər-bēt'n) *adj.* **1.** Worn by exposure to the weather. **2.** Tanned and leathery from being outdoors.

weath·er·board (wĕth'ər-bôrd', -bōrd') *n.* Clapboard; siding.

weath·er·board·ing (wĕth'ər-bôr'dĭng, -bōr'dĭng) *n.* Weatherboards collectively; siding.

weath·er-bound (wĕth'ər-bound') *adj.* Delayed, halted, or kept indoors by bad weather.

Weather Bureau *n.* A bureau of the U.S. Department of Commerce responsible for the gathering of meteorological data for weather forecasts and weather study.

weath·er·cast (wĕth'ər-kăst') *n.* A broadcast of weather conditions. **—weath'er·cast'er** *n.*

weath·er·cock (wĕth'ər-kŏk') *n.* **1.** A weather vane, esp. one in the form of a rooster. **2.** Someone or something that is very changeable or fickle. *—intr.v.* **-cocked, -cock·ing, -cocks.** To have a tendency to veer in the direction of the wind. Used of an aircraft or a missile.

weath·ered (wĕth'ərd) *adj.* **1.** Worn, stained, or warped by or as by exposure to weather; seasoned. **2.** *Archit.* Sloped to allow water to run off: *a weathered masonry joint.* ***—idiom.* weathered in.** Having weather conditions that prevent flying.

weather eye *n.* An eye trained to recognize indications of weather changes.

weath·er·glass (wĕth'ər-glăs') *n.* A barometer.

weath·er·ing (wĕth'ər-ĭng) *n.* Any of the chemical or mechanical processes by which rocks exposed to the weather decay to soil.

weath·er·ize (wĕth'ə-rīz') *tr.v.* **-ized, -iz·ing, -iz·es.** To make repairs and improvements on as a protective measure against cold weather.

weath·er·ly (wĕth'ər-lē) *adj. Naut.* Capable of sailing close to the wind with little drift to leeward. **—weath'er·li·ness** *n.*

weath·er·man (wĕth'ər-măn') *n.* A person who reports weather conditions.

weather map *n.* A map or chart depicting the meteorological conditions over a specific geographic area at a specific time.

weath·er·proof (wĕth'ər-pro͞of') *adj.* Able to withstand exposure to weather without damage. *—tr.v.* **-proofed, -proof·ing, -proofs.** To render weatherproof.

weather ship *n.* An oceangoing vessel equipped to make meteorological observations.

weather station *n.* A station at which meteorological data are gathered, recorded, and released.

weath·er-strip (wĕth'ər-strĭp') *tr.v.* **-stripped, -strip·ping, -strips.** To fit or equip with weather stripping.

weather stripping *n.* **1.** A narrow piece of material, such as rubber, felt, or metal, installed around doors and windows to protect an interior from external extremes of temperature. **2.** Weather stripping collectively.

weather vane *n.* A vane for indicating wind direction.

weath·er-wise (wĕth'ər-wīz') *adj.* Experienced or expert in predicting shifts, as in the weather or public opinion.

weath·er·worn (wĕth'ər-wôrn', -wōrn') *adj.* Weather-beaten.

weave (wēv) *v.* **wove** (wōv), **wo·ven** (wō'vən), **weav·ing, weaves.** *—tr.* **1. a.** To make (cloth) by interlacing the threads of the woof and the warp on a loom. **b.** To interlace (yarns) into cloth. **2.** To construct by interlacing or interweaving the materials or components of: *weave a basket.* **3.** To interweave or combine (elements) into a whole: *He wove the incidents into a story.* **4.** To run (something) in and out through some material or composition. **5.** To spin, as a web. **6.** *past tense* **weaved.** To make (a course, for example) by winding in and out or shuttling from side to side: *weave one's way through traffic.* *—intr.* **1. a.** To engage in weaving an article. **b.** To work at a loom. **2.** *past tense* **weaved.** To sway or move from side to side. *—n.* The pattern, method of weaving, or construction of a fabric: *a twill weave; a loose weave.* [ME *weven* < OE *wefan.*]

weav·er (wē'vər) *n.* **1.** A person who weaves. **2.** A weaverbird.

weav·er·bird (wē'vər-bûrd') *n.* Any of various chiefly tropical Old World birds of the family Ploceidae, many of which build complex communal nests of intricately woven vegetation.

weaver's hitch *n. Naut.* A sheet bend.

weaver's knot *n. Naut.* A weaver's hitch.

web (wĕb) *n.* **1. a.** A textile fabric, esp. one being woven on a loom or in the process of being removed from it. **b.** The structural part of cloth as distinguished from its pile or pattern. **2.** A latticed or woven structure; an interlacing of materials: *A web of palm branches formed the roof of the hut.* **3.** A structure of threadlike filaments characteristically spun by spiders or certain insect larvae. **4.** Something intricately constructed, esp. something that ensnares or entangles: *a web of lies.* **5.** A complex network: *a web of telephone and electrical wires.* **6.** A fold of skin or membranous tissue, esp. the membrane connecting the toes of certain water birds. **7.** The vane of a feather. **8.** *Archit.* The surface between the ribs of a ribbed vault. **9.** A metal sheet or plate connecting the heavier sections, ribs, or flanges of any structural element. **10.** A thin metal plate or strip, as the bit of a key or the blade of a saw. **11.** A large continuous roll of paper, such as newsprint, either in the process of manufacture or as it is fed into a rotary printing press. *—tr.v.* **webbed, web·bing, webs. 1.** To provide with a web. **2.** To cover or envelop with a web. **3.** To ensnare in a web. [ME < OE.]

webbed (wĕbd) *adj.* Having or connected by a web.

web·bing (wĕb'ĭng) *n.* **1.** A strong, generally narrow, closely woven fabric used esp. for seat belts, harnesses, or upholstery. **2.** Anything forming a web.

web·by (wĕb'ē) *adj.* **-bi·er, -bi·est.** Having, resembling, or consisting of a web.

we·ber (wĕb'ər) *n.* The International System unit of magnetic flux equal to the magnetic flux that in linking a circuit of one turn produces in it an electromotive force of one volt as it is uniformly reduced to zero within one second. [After Wilhelm E. *Weber* (1804–1891).]

web-foot·ed (wĕb'fo͝ot'ĭd) *adj.* Having feet with webbed toes. **—web'foot'** *n.*

web member *n.* One of the structural elements connecting the top and bottom flanges of a lattice girder or the outside members of a truss.

web press *n.* A printing press that prints on a continuous roll of paper.

web·ster (wĕb'stər) *n. Obs.* A weaver (sense 1). [ME < OE *webbestre,* fem. of *webba,* weaver < *webb,* web.]

web·worm (wĕb'wûrm') *n.* Any of various usually destructive caterpillars that construct webs.

wed (wĕd) *v.* **wed·ded, wed** or **wed·ded, wed·ding, weds.** *—tr.* **1.** To take as husband or wife; marry. **2.** To perform the marriage ceremony for; join in matrimony. **3.** To bind or join; unite. *—intr.* To take a husband or wife; marry. [ME *wedden* < OE *weddian.*]

we'd (wēd). **1.** We had. **2.** We should. **3.** We would.

wed·ding (wĕd'ĭng) *n.* **1.** The act of marrying; the ceremony or celebration of a marriage. **2.** The anniversary of a marriage: *a silver wedding.* **3.** A close association or union: *a wedding of ideas.* ***—modifier:*** *a wedding vow; a wedding dress.*

wedding ring *n.* **1.** A ring, usually a plain gold or platinum band, given by the groom to the bride during the wedding ceremony. **2.** A ring sometimes given by the bride to the groom.

we·del (vād′l) *intr.v.* **-deled, -del·ing, -dels.** To ski by executing wedelns. [G. < *wedeln,* to fan < *wedel,* fan < OHG *wadal.*]

we·deln (vād′ln) *n.* A skiing style in which the skier executes a series of short quick parallel turns by moving the back of the skis from side to side at a constant speed.

wedge (wĕj) *n.* **1.** A piece of metal or wood tapered for insertion in a narrow crevice and used for splitting, tightening, securing, or levering. **2.** Anything that has the triangular shape of a wedge: *a wedge of pie.* **3.** A wedge-shaped formation, as in football or ground warfare. **4.** Any tactic, event, policy, or idea that tends to divide or split associations of people: *His nomination drove a wedge into the party.* **5.** *Meteorol.* An elongated, V-shaped region of relatively high atmospheric pressure. **6.** *Sports.* An iron in golf with a very slanted face, used to lift the ball, as from sand. **7.** One of the triangular characters of cuneiform writing. *—v.* **wedged, wedg·ing, wedg·es.** *—tr.* **1.** To split or force apart with or as with a wedge. **2.** To fix in place with a wedge. **3.** To crowd, push, or force into a limited space. *—intr.* To become lodged like a wedge. [ME *wegge* < OE *wecg.*]

wedg·ies (wĕj′ēz) *pl.n.* Shoes having a wedge-shaped heel joined to a half-sole so as to form a continuous undersurface. [Orig. a trademark.]

Wedg·wood (wĕj′wo͝od′). A trademark for a type of pottery made by Josiah Wedgwood and his successors.

wed·lock (wĕd′lŏk′) *n.* The state of being married; matrimony. ***—idiom.* out of wedlock.** Born of parents not married to one another. [ME *wedlocke* < OE *wedlāc* < *wedd,* pledge.]

Wednes·day (wĕnz′dē, -dā′) *n.* The fourth day of the week, occurring after Tuesday and before Thursday. [ME < OE *Wōdnesdæg,* Woden's day.]

wee (wē) *adj.* **we·er, we·est. 1.** Very small; tiny. **2.** Very early: *the wee hours.* *—n. Scot.* A short time; a little bit: *bide a wee.* [ME < *we,* a small amount < OE *wæge,* weight.]

weed[1] (wēd) *n.* **1. a.** A plant considered undesirable, unattractive, or troublesome, esp. one growing where it is not wanted, as in a garden. **b.** A rank growth of such plants. **2.** A waterplant, esp. seaweed. **3.** The leaves or stems of a plant as distinguished from the seeds: *dill weed.* **4.** *Informal.* **a.** Tobacco. **b.** A cigarette. **5.** *Slang.* Marijuana. **6.** Something useless, detrimental, or worthless, esp. an animal unfit for breeding. *—v.* **weed·ed, weed·ing, weeds.** *—tr.* To remove weeds from; clear of weeds: *weed a flower bed.* *—intr.* To remove weeds from a plot. ***—phrasal verb.* weed out.** To remove or get rid of as unsuitable or unwanted: *weed out unqualified applicants.* [ME < OE *wēod.*]

weed[2] (wēd) *n.* **1.** A sign of mourning, as a black band worn usually on the sleeve. **2. weeds.** A widow's mourning clothes. **3.** Often **weeds.** Any garment. [ME *wede,* garment < OE *wæd.*]

weed·er (wē′dər) *n.* One that removes weeds.

weed·y (wē′dē) *adj.* **-i·er, -i·est. 1.** Full of or consisting of weeds. **2.** Resembling or characteristic of a weed. **3.** Of a scrawny build; spindly; gawky. **—weed′i·ly** *adv.* **—weed′i·ness** *n.*

week (wēk) *n.* **1. a.** A period of seven days: *a week of rain.* **b.** A seven-day calendar period, esp. one starting with Sunday and continuing through Saturday. **2. a.** A week designated by an event or holiday occurring within it: *commencement week.* **b.** A week set aside for the honoring of a cause or institution: *Home Safety Week.* **3.** The part of a calendar week devoted to work, school, or business. **4. a.** One week from a specified day: *I'll see you Friday week.* **b.** One week ago from a specified day: *It was Friday week that we last met.* [ME *weke* < OE *wicu.*]

week·day (wēk′dā′) *n.* **1.** Any day of the week except Sunday. **2.** Any day exclusive of the days of the weekend.

week·end (wēk′ĕnd′) *n.* The end of the week, esp. the period from Friday evening through Sunday evening. ***—modifier:*** *weekend activities.* *—intr.v.* **-end·ed, -end·ing, -ends.** To spend the weekend.

week·end·er (wēk′ĕn′dər) *n.* **1.** A person who vacations or visits, esp. habitually, on weekends. **2.** A small suitcase or bag for carrying clothing and toiletries for a weekend.

week·ly (wēk′lē) *adv.* **1.** Once a week. **2.** Every week. **3.** By the week. *—adj.* **1.** Of or pertaining to a week. **2.** Occurring once a week or each week. **3.** Computed by the week. *—n., pl.* **-lies.** A publication issued once a week.

week·night (wēk′nīt′) *n.* A night of the week exclusive of Saturday and Sunday.

ween (wēn) *v.* **weened, ween·ing, weens.** *Archaic.* *—tr.* To think; suppose. *—intr.* To think it possible. [ME *wenen* < OE *wenan.*]

ween·ie (wē′nē) *n. Informal.* A wienerwurst.

wee·ny (wē′nē) *adj.* **-ni·er, -ni·est.** *Informal.* Very small; tiny; wee. [Blend of WEE and TINY.]

weep (wēp) *v.* **wept** (wĕpt), **weep·ing, weeps.** *—tr.* **1.** To mourn; lament; bewail. **2.** To shed (tears) as an expression of emotion. **3.** To bring to a specified condition by weeping: *She wept herself into a state of exhaustion.* **4.** To ooze, exude, or let fall drops of liquid. *—intr.* **1.** To express emotion by shedding tears; shed tears. **2.** To mourn or grieve: *wept for the families of the dead.* **3.** To emit or run with drops of moisture. *—n.* Often **weeps.** A period or fit of weeping. [ME *wepen* < OE *wēpan.*]

weep·er (wē′pər) *n.* **1.** One that weeps. **2.** A hired mourner. **3.** A badge of mourning formerly worn by men. **4.** A hole or pipe in a wall to allow water to run off.

weep·ing (wē′pĭng) *adj.* **1.** Tearful. **2.** Dropping rain: *weeping clouds.* **3.** Having slender, drooping branches.

weeping willow *n.* A widely cultivated tree, *Salix babylonica,* native to China, having long, slender, drooping branches and narrow leaves.

weep·y (wē′pē) *adj.* **-i·er, -i·est.** Lachrymose; tearful.

wee·ver (wē′vər) *n.* Any of several marine fishes of the family Trachinidae, having venomous spines. [ONFr. *wivre,* snake < Lat. *vipera.*]

wee·vil (wē′vəl) *n.* Any of numerous beetles, chiefly of the family Curculionidae, characteristically having a downward-curving snout and destructive to plants and stored plant products. [ME *wevel* < OE *wifel.*] **—wee′vil·y, wee′vil·ly** *adj.*

weft (wĕft) *n.* **1. a.** The horizontal threads interlaced through the warp in a woven fabric; filling; woof. **b.** Yarn to be used for the weft. **2.** Woven fabric. [ME < OE *wefta.*]

wei·ge·la (wī-gē′lə, -jē′lə, wī′jə-lə) *n.* Any of various shrubs of the genus *Weigela,* esp. *W. florida,* widely cultivated for its pink, white, or red flowers. [NLat., genus name, after Christian E. *Weigel* (1748–1831).]

weigh[1] (wā) *v.* **weighed, weigh·ing, weighs.** *—tr.* **1.** To determine the weight of by or as if by using a scale or similar instrument. **2.** To measure off an amount equal in weight to: *weigh out a pound of nuts.* **3.** To balance in one's mind to determine the worth of; ponder; evaluate: *weighed all the alternatives.* **4.** *Naut.* To raise (anchor). *—intr.* **1.** To have or be of a specific weight. **2.** To carry weight; be considered important; have influence: *The decision weighed heavily against her.* **3.** To be a burden on; oppress: *The crime weighed on him like lead.* **4.** *Naut.* **a.** To raise anchor. **b.** To sail out of port. ***—phrasal verbs.* weigh down. 1.** To overburden or bend down. **2.** To burden or oppress. **weigh in. 1.** To weigh or be weighed before entering a sports contest. **2.** To have one's baggage weighed. **3.** To enter as a participant: *She weighed in with some caustic comments.* ***—idiom.* weigh (one's) words.** To choose one's words with great care; express oneself with deliberation. [ME *weyen* < OE *wegan.*] **—weigh′er** *n.*

weigh[2] (wā) *n. Naut.* Way. Used only in the phrase *under weigh.* [Variant of WAY.]

weight (wāt) *n.* **1.** A measure of the heaviness or mass of an object. **2.** The gravitational force exerted by the earth or another celestial body on an object, equal to the product of the object's mass and the local value of gravitational acceleration. **3. a.** A unit measure of gravitational force: *a table of weights and measures.* **b.** A system of such measures: *avoirdupois weight; troy weight.* **4.** The measured heaviness of a specific object: *put a two-pound weight on the scale.* **5.** Any object used principally to exert a force by virtue of its gravitational attraction to the earth, esp.: **a.** A metallic solid used as a standard of comparison in weighing. **b.** An object used to hold something down. **c.** A counterbalance in a machine. **d.** A heavy object, as a dumbbell, used for exercise or in athletic competition. **6.** *Math.* One of a set of numbers assigned as multipliers to quantities to be averaged to indicate the relative importance of each quantity's contribution to the average. **7.** Burden; oppressiveness: *the weight of responsibilities.* **8.** The greatest part or stress; preponderance: *the weight of evidence.* **9. a.** Influence; importance; authority: *His approval carried a lot of weight.* **b.** Ponderous quality: *the weight of his words.* **10.** A classification according to comparative lightness or heaviness. *—tr.v.* **weight·ed, weight·ing, weights. 1.** To add heaviness or weight to; make heavy or heavier. **2.** To load down; burden. **3.** To treat (fabric) with chemical substances in order to give it body or extra weight. **4.** *Math.* To assign a weight or weights to. ***—idioms.* by weight.** According to weight rather than volume or other measure. **pull (one's) weight.** To do one's job or share. **throw (one's) weight around.** To make a show of one's importance. [ME *wight* < OE *wiht.*]

weight·less (wāt′lĭs) *adj.* **1.** Having little or no weight. **2.** Experiencing little or no gravitational force. **—weight′less·ly** *adv.* **—weight′less·ness** *n.*

weight lifter *n.* A person who lifts heavy weights for exercise or in an athletic competition.

weight·lift·ing (wāt′lĭf′tĭng) *n.* The lifting of heavy weights in a prescribed manner as an exercise or in athletic competition.

weight·y (wā′tē) *adj.* **-i·er, -i·est. 1.** Heavy; ponderous. **2.** Burdensome; oppressive. **3.** Of great consequence; momentous: *the weighty matters before the peace delegates.* **4.** Carrying weight; efficacious: *a weighty argument.* **5.** Solemn; serious. **6.** Fat. **—weight′i·ly** *adv.* **—weight′i·ness** *n.*

Wedgwood

weeping willow

weevil
Boll weevil

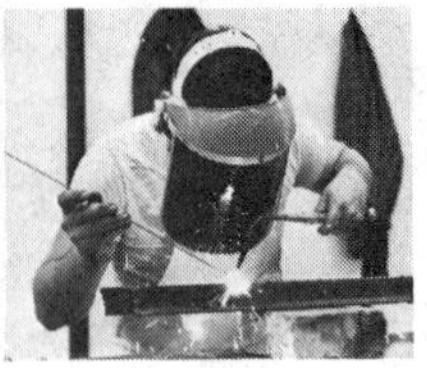

weld[1]

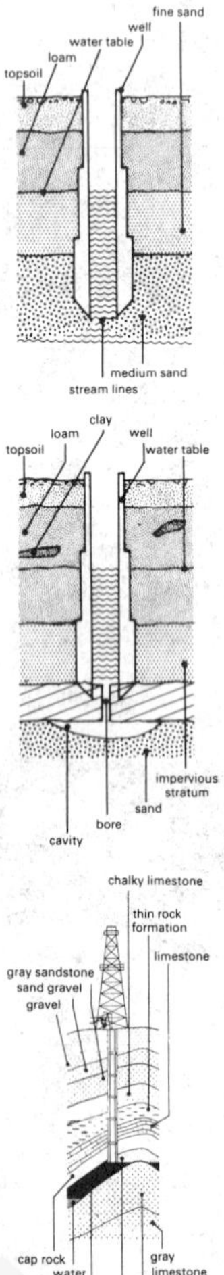

well[1]
Above: Shallow well
Center: Deep well
Below: Oil well

Wei·mar·an·er (vī′mä-rä′nər, wī′-) *n.* A large dog of a breed originating in Germany, having a smooth grayish coat. [G. < *Weimar,* Weimar, Germany.]

weir (wîr) *n.* **1.** A fence or wattle placed in a stream to catch or retain fish. **2.** A dam placed across a river or canal to raise or divert the water, as for a millrace or to regulate the flow. [ME *wer* < OE.]

weird (wîrd) *adj.* **-er, -est. 1.** Suggestive of or concerned with the supernatural; unearthly; eerie. **2.** Of an odd and inexplicable character; strange; fantastic. **3.** Of or pertaining to fate or the Fates. *—n.* **1. a.** Fate; destiny. **b.** One's assigned lot or fortune; kismet. **2.** Often **Weird.** One of the Fates. [ME *werde,* having power to control fate < OE *wyrd,* fate.] **—weird′ly** *adv.* **—weird′ness** *n.*

Synonyms: *weird, eerie, uncanny, unearthly.* These adjectives refer to what is inexplicably strange and, sometimes, frightening. *Weird* can mean mysterious in the sense of occult, but is also applied to what is bizarre, grotesque, eccentric, or markedly unconventional. *Eerie* describes what inspires fear, uneasiness, or wonder that cannot be explained rationally and therefore may suggest the preternatural or a sinister influence. *Uncanny* refers to what is extremely puzzling as a source of wonder or fascination, such as a talent or knack. *Unearthly* literally means so strange as to suggest what is not of this world; in popular usage it is sometimes applied, like *weird,* to what is merely very odd or far-fetched.

weird·ie also **weird·y** (wîr′dē) *n., pl.* **-ies.** *Slang.* An unusually strange person, thing, or event.

weird·o (wîr′dō) *n., pl.* **-oes.** *Slang.* A weirdie.

weis·en·hei·mer (wī′zən-hī′mər) *n.* Variant of **wisenheimer.**

we·ka (wē′kə, wā′-) *n.* A flightless bird, *Gallirallus australis,* of New Zealand, having brown, mottled plumage. [Maori.]

welch (wĕlch) *v.* Variant of **welsh.**

wel·come (wĕl′kəm) *adj.* **1.** Received with pleasure and hospitality into one's company or home: *a welcome guest.* **2.** Gratifying: *a welcome respite.* **3.** Cordially permitted or invited, as to do or enjoy. **4.** Freely granted one's courtesy. Used to acknowledge an expression of gratitude, usually in the exchange "Thank you!" "You're welcome!" *—n.* **1.** A cordial greeting to or reception of an arriving person. **2.** The state of being welcome; hospitable reception. **3.** The act of welcoming; willing or glad acceptance. *—tr.v.* **-comed, -com·ing, -comes. 1.** To greet, receive, or entertain cordially or hospitably. **2.** To receive or accept gladly: *welcome a little privacy.* *—interj.* Used to greet cordially a visitor or recent arrival. [ME < OE *wilcuma,* welcome guest.] **—wel′come·ly** *adv.* **—wel′come·ness** *n.* **—wel′com·er** *n.*

weld[1] (wĕld) *v.* **weld·ed, weld·ing, welds.** *—tr.* **1.** To join (metals) by applying heat, sometimes with pressure and sometimes with an intermediate or filler metal having a high melting point. **2.** To bring into close association; bring together as a unit. *—intr.* To be capable of being welded. *—n.* **1.** The union of two metal parts by welding. **2.** The joint formed by welding. [Alteration of WELL, to weld (obs.).]

weld[2] (wĕld) also **wold** (wōld) *n.* **1.** The dyer's rocket. **2.** The yellow dye obtained from the weld. [ME *welde.*]

weld·ment (wĕld′mənt) *n.* A unit composed of an assemblage of pieces welded together.

wel·fare (wĕl′fâr′) *n.* **1. a.** Health, happiness, and general well-being. **b.** Prosperity. **2.** Welfare work. **3.** The provision of economic or social benefits to a certain group of people, esp. aid furnished by the government or by private agencies to the needy or disabled. *—idiom.* **on welfare.** Receiving assistance from the government because of need or poverty. [ME < *wel faren,* to fare well.]

welfare state *n.* **1.** A social system whereby the state assumes primary responsibility for the welfare of citizens. **2.** A nation characterized by its adoption of the welfare system.

welfare work *n.* Organized efforts by a community or an organization for the betterment of the poor.

wel·far·ism (wĕl′fâr-ĭz′əm) *n.* The set of policies, practices, and social attitudes associated with a welfare state.

wel·kin (wĕl′kĭn) *n.* **1.** The vault of heaven; sky. **2.** The upper air. [ME *welken* < OE *wolcen.*]

well[1] (wĕl) *n.* **1.** A deep hole or shaft dug or drilled to obtain water, oil, gas, or brine. **2.** A container or reservoir, as an inkwell, used to hold a liquid. **3.** A vertical opening that passes through the floors of a building, as for stairs or ventilation. **4.** An enclosure in a ship's hold for the pumps. **5.** A cistern with a perforated bottom in the hold of a fishing vessel for keeping fish alive. **6.** *Chiefly Brit.* The space in a law court where the counsel or solicitor sits. **7.** A spring; fountain. **8.** A source to be drawn upon: *a well of information.* *—v.* **welled, well·ing, wells.** *—intr.* **1.** To rise to the surface, ready to flow: *Tears welled in her eyes.* **2.** To rise or surge from an inner source: *anger welling up in him.* *—tr.* To pour forth. [ME < OE *wælla.*]

well[2] (wĕl) *adv.* **better** (bĕt′ər), **best** (bĕst). **1.** In a good or proper manner: *behaved well.* **2.** Skillfully or proficiently: *She dances well.* **3.** Satisfactorily or sufficiently: *slept well.* **4.** Successfully or effectively: *got along well with people.* **5.** In a comfortable or affluent manner: *lived well.* **6.** Advantageously: *married well.* **7.** Suitably; appropriately. **8.** With reason or propriety; reasonably: *I can't very well say no.* **9.** Prudently: *You would do well to say nothing.* **10.** On close or familiar terms: *knew him well.* **11.** Favorably: *spoke well of her.* **12.** Thoroughly; completely: *well cooked.* **13.** Perfectly; clearly: *well understood her meaning.* **14.** Widely; generally: *He is known well.* **15.** To a considerable or suitable extent or degree: *I am well pleased.* **16.** With close and careful attention: *listen well.* **17.** Entirely; fully: *well worth seeing.* **18.** Far: *well after sunset.* **19.** In all likelihood: *His alibi may well be true.* *—adj.* **1.** In a satisfactory state or circumstances; right; proper: *All is well.* **2. a.** In good health; not ailing or diseased. **b.** Cured or healed, as a wound. **3. a.** Advisable; prudent: *It would be well not to ask.* **b.** Fortunate; good: *It is well that you stayed.* *—interj.* **1.** Used to express surprise. **2.** Used to introduce a remark or as a filler in a pause during conversation. ***—idioms.*** **as well. 1.** In addition; also. **2.** With equal or better effect: *I might as well go.* **as well as. 1.** In addition to; moreover. **2.** As satisfactorily as: *He did as well as you.* **3.** As much as: *He would like to go as well as you.* **in well with.** *Informal.* In a position to have the ear of; in favor with: *He's in well with management.* [ME < OE *wel.*]

Usage: *As well as* in the sense of "in addition to" does not have the conjunctive force of *and.* Consequently, in the following examples the singular subjects remain singular and govern singular verbs: *The parent company, as well as its affiliate, was named in the indictment. Harris, as well as Lewis, has announced his candidacy. As well as* is held to be redundant in combination with *both.* Therefore, the following example should be avoided: *Both in theory as well as in practice, the idea is unsound.* Acceptable alternatives are: *both in theory and in practice; in theory, as well as in practice.* See also Usage note at **bad.**

we'll (wēl). **1.** We will. **2.** We shall.

well-ap·point·ed (wĕl′ə-poin′tĭd) *adj.* Having a full array of suitable equipment or furnishings: *a well-appointed kitchen.*

well·a·way (wĕl′ə-wā′) also **well·a·day** (-dā′) *Archaic.* *—interj.* Alas! Woe is me! *—n., pl.* **-ways** also **-days.** A lamentation. [ME < OE *wei lā wei.*]

well-bal·anced (wĕl′băl′ənst) *adj.* **1.** Evenly proportioned, balanced, or regulated. **2.** Mentally stable; sensible; sound.

well-be·ing (wĕl′bē′ĭng) *n.* The state of being healthy, happy, or prosperous; welfare.

well-born (wĕl′bôrn′) *adj.* Of good lineage or stock.

well-bred (wĕl′brĕd′) *adj.* **1.** Of good upbringing; well-mannered; refined. **2.** Of good breed. Used of animals.

well-de·fined (wĕl′dĭ-fīnd′) *adj.* **1.** Having definite and distinct lines or features: *well-defined hills.* **2.** Accurately and unambiguously stated or described: *a well-defined argument.*

well-dis·posed (wĕl′dĭs-pōzd′) *adj.* Disposed to be kindly, friendly, or sympathetic.

well-done (wĕl′dŭn′) *adj.* **1.** Cooked all the way through: *a well-done steak.* **2.** Satisfactorily or properly accomplished.

well-fa·vored (wĕl′fā′vərd) *adj.* Attractive; comely; handsome.

well-fed (wĕl′fĕd′) *adj.* **1.** Adequately or properly nourished. **2.** Overfed; fat.

well-fixed (wĕl′fĭkst′) *adj. Informal.* Financially secure; well-to-do.

well-found (wĕl′found′) *adj.* Properly furnished or equipped.

well-found·ed (wĕl′foun′dĭd) *adj.* Based on sound judgment, reasoning, or evidence; substantiated well.

well-groomed (wĕl′grōōmd′) *adj.* **1.** Attentive to details of dress; meticulously neat. **2.** Carefully tended or curried: *a well-groomed horse.* **3.** Trim and tidy: *a well-groomed lawn.*

well-ground·ed (wĕl′groun′dĭd) *adj.* **1.** Adequately versed in a subject. **2.** Having a sound basis; well-founded.

well-han·dled (wĕl′hăn′dəld) *adj.* **1.** Managed well. **2.** Showing the signs of much handling.

well·head (wĕl′hĕd′) *n.* **1.** The source of a well or stream. **2.** A principal source or fountainhead. **3.** The top of a structure built over a well.

well-heeled (wĕl′hēld′) *adj. Slang.* Well-to-do.

Wel·ling·ton boot (wĕl′ĭng-tən) *n.* A boot extending to the top of the knee in front but cut low in back. [After Arthur Wellesley (1769–1852), 1st Duke of *Wellington.*]

well-in·ten·tioned (wĕl′ĭn-tĕn′shənd) *adj.* Having or marked by good intentions: *well-intentioned criticism.*

well-knit (wĕl′nĭt′) *adj.* Strongly knit, esp. strongly and firmly constructed: *a well-knit body; a well-knit production.*

well-known (wĕl′nōn′) *adj.* **1.** Widely known; familiar or famous. **2.** Fully known.

well-man·nered (wĕl′măn′ərd) *adj.* Polite; courteous.

well-mean·ing (wĕl′mē′nĭng) *adj.* Well-intentioned.

well-meant (wĕl′mĕnt′) *adj.* Kindly or honestly intended.

well-nigh (wĕl′nī′) *adv.* Nearly; almost.

well-off (wĕl′ôf′, -ŏf′) *adj.* **1.** In fortunate circumstances. **2.** Well-to-do.

well-read (wĕl′rĕd′) *adj.* Knowledgeable through having read extensively.

well-round·ed (wĕl′roun′dĭd) *adj.* **1.** Comprehensively developed: *a well-rounded scholar.* **2.** Having a shapely figure.

well-spo·ken (wĕl′spō′kən) *adj.* **1.** Chosen or expressed with aptness or propriety. **2.** Courteous in speech.

well·spring (wĕl′sprĭng′) *n.* **1.** The source of a stream or spring; fountainhead. **2.** A source of supply: *a wellspring of ideas.*

well-thought-of (wĕl-thôt′ŭv′, -ŏv′) *adj.* Respected; esteemed.

well-tim·bered (wĕl′tĭm′bərd) *adj.* **1.** Having a good framework or structure. **2.** Covered with a good growth of timber.

well-timed (wĕl′tīmd′) *adj.* Occurring or done at an opportune time: *a well-timed remark.*

well-to-do (wĕl′tə-dōō′) *adj.* Prosperous; affluent; well-off. [From the phrase *to do well.*]

well-turned (wĕl′tûrnd′) *adj.* **1.** Expertly turned: *a well-turned tower.* **2.** Shapely: *a well-turned ankle.* **3.** Concisely or aptly expressed: *a well-turned phrase.*

well-wish·er (wĕl′wĭsh′ər) *n.* One who wishes another well; one who extends good wishes. **—well′-wish′ing** *adj. & n.*

well-worn (wĕl′wôrn′, -wōrn′) *adj.* **1.** Showing signs of much wear or use. **2.** Repeated too often; trite; hackneyed. **3.** Carried or worn in a becoming manner: *well-worn fame.*

Wels·bach burner (wĕlz′băk′, -bäk′). A trademark for a gauze mantle impregnated with cerium and thorium compounds and used with a gas burner that becomes incandescent when heated, producing light.

welsh (wĕlsh, wĕlch) also **welch** (wĕlch) *intr.v.* **welshed, welsh·ing, welsh·es** also **welched, welch·ing, welch·es.** *Slang.* **1.** To swindle a person by not paying a debt or wager. **2.** To fail to fulfill an obligation. [Orig. unknown.] **—welsh′er** *n.*

Welsh (wĕlsh) *adj.* Of or pertaining to Wales, its people, its language, or its culture. *—n.* **1.** The natives or inhabitants of Wales. **2.** The Celtic language of Wales. [ME *Walische* < OE *Wælisc* < *Wealh,* Welshman.]

Welsh cor·gi (kôr′gē) *n.* A dog of a breed originating in Wales, having a long body, short legs, and a foxlike head.

Welsh·man (wĕlsh′mən) *n.* A native of Wales.

Welsh rabbit *n.* A dish made of melted cheese, milk or cream, seasonings, and sometimes ale, served hot over toast or crackers.

Welsh rare·bit (râr′bĭt) *n.* Welsh rabbit.

Welsh terrier *n.* A terrier of a breed originating in Wales, having a wiry black-and-tan coat and resembling a small Airedale.

welt (wĕlt) *n.* **1.** A strip of leather or other material stitched into a shoe between the sole and the upper. **2.** A tape or covered cord sewn into a seam as reinforcement or trimming; welting. **3. a.** A ridge or bump raised on the skin by a lash or blow or sometimes by an allergic disorder. **b.** A lash or blow producing such a mark. *—tr.v.* **welt·ed, welt·ing, welts. 1.** To reinforce or trim with a welt or welting. **2.** To beat severely; flog. **3.** To raise a welt or welts on. [ME *welte.*]

Welt·an·schau·ung (vĕlt′än′shou′ōōng) *n., pl.* **-ungs** or **-ung·en** (-ōōng-ən). A comprehensive world view, esp. from a specified standpoint. [G.]

wel·ter (wĕl′tər) *intr.v.* **-tered, -ter·ing, -ters. 1.** To wallow, roll, or toss about, as in mud or high seas. **2.** To lie soaked in a liquid. **3.** To roll and surge, as the sea. *—n.* **1.** Confusion; turmoil. **2.** A confused mass; a jumble: *a welter of papers and magazines.* [ME *welteren.*]

wel·ter·weight (wĕl′tər-wāt′) *n.* A boxer or wrestler who weighs between 136 and 147 pounds or approximately 62 and 67 kilograms. [Perh. < WELT.]

welt·ing (wĕl′tĭng) *n.* A cord or strip used to welt a seam.

Welt·schmerz (vĕlt′shmĕrts′) *n.* Sadness over the evils of the world, esp. as an expression of romantic pessimism. [G.]

wen[1] (wĕn) *n.* A cyst containing sebaceous matter. [ME < OE.]

wen[2] (wĕn) *n.* An Old English runic letter represented by the Modern English *w.* [OE.]

wench (wĕnch) *n.* **1.** A young woman or girl, esp. a peasant girl. **2.** A female servant. **3.** A wanton woman; prostitute. *—intr.v.* **wenched, wench·ing, wench·es.** To consort with prostitutes. [ME *wench* < *wenchel* < OE *wencel,* child, girl.] **—wench′er** *n.*

wend (wĕnd) *v.* **wend·ed, wend·ing, wends.** *—tr.* To proceed on or along; go: *wend one's way home.* *—intr.* To go one's way; proceed. [ME *wenden* < OE *wendan,* to turn.]

Wend (wĕnd) *n.* One of a Slavic people inhabiting Saxony and Brandenburg. [G. *Wende* < OHG *Winidia.*] **—Wend** *adj.*

Wend·ish (wĕn′dĭsh) *adj.* Of or pertaining to the Wends or their language. *—n.* The Slavic language of the Wends.

went[1] (wĕnt) *v.* Past tense of **go**[1]. [ME < OE *wende,* p.t. of *wendan,* to go.]

went[2] (wĕnt) *v. Archaic.* A past tense and past participle of **wend.**

wen·tle·trap (wĕnt′l-trăp′) *n.* Any of various marine snails of the family Epitoniidae, having a tapering spiral shell with numerous raised longitudinal ridges. [Du. *wendeltrappe* : *wendel,* winding < *wenden,* to wind + *trappe,* stairs.]

wept (wĕpt) *v.* Past tense and past participle of **weep.**

were (wûr) *v.* **1.** Second person singular past tense of **be. 2.** First, second, and third person plural past tense of **be. 3.** Past subjunctive of **be.** [ME < OE *wæron.*]

we're (wîr). We are.

were·n't (wûrnt, wûr′ənt). Were not.

were·wolf also **wer·wolf** (wîr′wŏŏlf′, wûr′-, wâr′-) *n.* A person transformed into a wolf or capable of assuming the form of a wolf at will; lycanthrope. [ME < OE *werewulf* : *wer,* man + *wulf,* wolf.]

wer·geld (wûr′gĕld′) also **wer·gild** or **were·gild** (-gĭld′) *n.* In Anglo-Saxon and Germanic law, a price set upon a man's life on the basis of his rank and paid as compensation by the family of a slayer to the kindred or lord of a slain man to free the culprit of further punishment or obligation. [ME *wargeld* < OE *wergeld* : *wer,* man + *geld,* payment.]

wer·ner·ite (wûr′nə-rīt′) *n. Mineral.* Scapolite. [Fr., after A. G. *Werner* (1750–1817).]

wert (wûrt) *v. Archaic.* Second person singular past indicative and past subjunctive of **be.** [WERE + *t* as in *shalt.*]

wer·wolf (wîr′wŏŏlf′, wûr′-, wâr′-) *n.* Variant of **werewolf.**

wes·kit (wĕs′kĭt) *n.* A waistcoat; vest. [Var. of WAISTCOAT.]

Wes·ley·an (wĕs′lē-ən, wĕz′-) *adj.* Of or pertaining to John or Charles Wesley or to Methodism. *—n.* A Methodist. **—Wes′ley·an·ism** *n.*

west (wĕst) *n.* **1. a.** The direction opposite to the direction in which the earth rotates on its axis; the general direction of the sunset. **b.** One of the four cardinal points on the mariner's compass 90° left of north and 180° from east. **2.** Often **West.** Any area or region lying in this direction. **3. the West. a.** The part of the earth west of Asia and Asia Minor, esp. Europe and the Western Hemisphere; the Occident. **b.** The western part of the United States, esp. the region west of the Mississippi River. **c.** The noncommunist countries of Europe and the Americas. *—adj.* **1.** To, toward, of, facing, or in the west. **2.** Coming from or originating in the west, as a wind. **3. West.** Officially designating the western part of a country, continent, or other geographic area: *West Germany.* *—adv.* In, from, or toward the west. [ME < OE.]

Welsh corgi

Welsh terrier

west·bound (wĕst′bound′) *adj.* Going toward the west.

west by north *n.* The direction or point on the mariner's compass halfway between due west and west-northwest. It is 78 degrees 45 minutes west of due north. *—adv. & adj.* Toward or from west by north.

west by south *n.* The direction or point on the mariner's compass halfway between due west and west-southwest. It is 101 degrees 15 minutes west of due north. *—adv. & adj.* Toward or from west by south.

west·er (wĕs′tər) *intr.v.* **-ered, -er·ing, -ers. 1.** To move westward. Used of the sun, moon, or a star. **2.** To shift to the west. Used of the wind. *—n.* A storm or wind coming from the west. [ME *westeren* < *west,* west.]

west·er·ly (wĕs′tər-lē) *adj.* **1.** Situated toward the west. **2.** From the west. Used of wind. *—n., pl.* **-lies.** A storm or wind from the west. [< obs. *wester,* western < ME < OE *westra* < *west,* west.] **—west′er·ly** *adv.*

west·ern (wĕs′tərn) *adj.* **1.** Situated toward, in, or facing the west. **2.** Coming from the west. Used of wind. **3.** Growing in the west. **4.** Often **Western.** Of, pertaining to, or characteristic of western regions or the West. **5. Western.** Of, pertaining to, or characteristic of Europe and the Western Hemisphere; Occidental: *Western technology.* **6.** Often **Western.** Of, pertaining to, or characteristic of the American West. **7. Western.** Of or pertaining to the Roman Catholic Church as distinguished from the Eastern Orthodox Church. *—n.* **1.** A westerner. **2.** Often **Western.** A novel, motion picture, or television or radio program about cowboys or frontier life in the American West. [ME *westeren* < OE *westerne.*]

west·ern·er (wĕs′tər-nər) *n.* **1.** A native or inhabitant of the west. **2.** Often **Westerner.** A native or inhabitant of the western United States.

Western Hemisphere *n.* The half of the earth that includes all of North and South America, the surrounding waters, and all neighboring islands.

west·ern·ize (wĕs′tər-nīz′) *tr.v.* **-ized, -iz·ing, -iz·es.** To convert to the customs of Western civilization. **—west′ern·i·za′tion** *n.*

west·ern·most (wĕs′tərn-mōst′) *adj.* Farthest west.

western omelet *n.* An omelet cooked with diced ham, chopped green pepper, and onion.

western sandwich *n.* A sandwich having a western omelet as a filling.

West Germanic *n.* A subdivision of the Germanic languages that includes High German, Low German, Yiddish, Dutch, Afrikaans, Flemish, Frisian, and English.

west·ing (wĕs′tĭng) *n.* **1.** *Naut.* **a.** The distance sailed by a ship on a westerly course. **b.** The longitudinal distance from a given meridian on a westward course. **2.** A westward direction or movement. [< WEST.]

west-north·west (wĕst′nôrth′wĕst′; *Naut.* -nôr′wĕst′) *n.* The direction or point on the mariner's compass halfway between west and northwest; 67 degrees 30 minutes west of due north. *—adj.* Situated toward, facing, or in this direction. *—adv.* In, from, or toward this direction.

West Saxon *n.* **1.** The dialect of Old English used in southern England that was the chief literary dialect of England before the Norman Conquest. **2.** One of the Saxons inhabiting Wessex during the centuries before the Norman Conquest.

west-south·west (wĕst′south′wĕst′; *Naut.* -sou-wĕst′) *n.* The direction or point on the mariner's compass halfway between west and southwest; 112 degrees 30 minutes west of due north. —*adj.* Situated toward, facing, or in this direction. —*adv.* In, from, or toward this direction.

west·ward (wĕst'wərd) *adj. & adv.* At or toward the west. —*n.* **1.** A direction or point toward the west. **2.** A region situated in or toward the west. **—west'ward·ly** *adj. & adv.* **—west'wards** *adv.*

wet (wĕt) *adj.* **wet·ter, wet·test. 1.** Covered or saturated with a liquid, esp. water; moistened. **2.** Not yet dry or firm: *wet paint.* **3.** Stored or preserved in liquid. **4.** Used or prepared with water or other liquids. **5. a.** Rainy, humid, or foggy: *wet weather.* **b.** Characterized by frequent or heavy rainfall or snowfall: *a wet climate.* **6.** *Informal.* Allowing the sale of alcoholic beverages. —*n.* **1.** Something that wets; moisture. **2.** Rainy or snowy weather: *go out into the wet.* **3.** *Informal.* One who supports the legality of the production and sale of alcoholic beverages. —*v.* **wet** or **wet·ted, wet·ting, wets.** —*tr.* **1.** To make wet; dampen: *wet a sponge.* **2.** To make (a bed or one's clothes) wet by urinating. —*intr.* To become wet. **—*idioms.* all wet.** *Slang.* Entirely mistaken. **wet behind the ears.** Inexperienced; green. **wet one's whistle.** To take a drink. [ME < OE *wǣt.*]

Synonyms: *wet, damp, moist, dank, humid.* These adjectives refer to the presence of a liquid, usually water. *Wet* generally describes what is soaked or saturated or has a surface covered with liquid, as *a wet sidewalk,* or what is not yet dry, as *wet paint. Damp* and *moist* both mean slightly wet, but *damp* often implies an unpleasant sensation. *Dank* suggests the odorous and perhaps injurious atmosphere of marshes or enclosed spaces. *Humid* refers to moisture in the atmosphere; when used without qualification, it implies unpleasantly high saturation.

wet·back (wĕt'băk') *n. Offensive Slang.* A Mexican, esp. a laborer who crosses the U.S. border illegally. [From the fact that many enter the United States by crossing the Rio Grande.]

wet blanket *n. Informal.* One that discourages enjoyment or enthusiasm.

wet cell *n.* A primary cell having an electrolyte in the form of a liquid bath.

wet dream *n.* An erotic dream accompanied by sexual climax.

weth·er (wĕ*th*'ər) *n.* A gelded male sheep. [ME < OE.]

wet·land (wĕt'lănd') *n.* Often **wetlands.** A lowland area, such as a marsh or swamp, that is saturated with moisture, esp. when thought of as the natural habitat of wildlife.

wet monsoon *n. Meteorol.* A monsoon.

wet nurse *n.* **1.** A woman who suckles another woman's child. **2.** A person who treats another with excessive care or solicitude.

wet-nurse (wĕt'nûrs') *tr.v.* **-nursed, -nurs·ing, -nurs·es. 1.** To serve as wet nurse for. **2.** To treat with excessive care.

wet pack *n.* A therapeutic pack made of a material, as gauze, that has been moistened in hot or cold water and then wrung out.

wet suit *n.* A tight-fitting permeable suit worn by a skin diver in order to retain body heat.

wetting agent *n.* A compound that causes a liquid to spread more easily across or penetrate into the surface of a solid by reducing the surface tension of the liquid.

we've (wēv). We have.

whack (hwăk, wăk) *v.* **whacked, whack·ing, whacks.** —*tr.* To strike with a sharp blow; slap. —*intr.* To deal a sharp, resounding blow. —*n.* **1.** A sharp, swift blow. **2.** The sound made by a sharp, swift blow. **—*idioms.* have** (or **take**) **a whack at.** *Informal.* To attempt; try out. **out of whack.** *Informal.* Improperly ordered or balanced; not functioning correctly. **whacked out.** *Slang.* Crazy; insane. [Prob. imit.]

whack·ing (hwăk'ĭng) *Chiefly Brit. Informal.* —*adj.* Superlative. —*adv.* Superlatively.

whack·y (hwăk'ē, wăk'ē) *adj.* Variant of **wacky.**

whale[1] (hwāl, wāl) *n.* **1.** Any of various marine mammals of the order Cetacea, having a generally fishlike form with forelimbs modified to form flippers and a tail with horizontal flukes, esp. one of the very large species as distinguished from the smaller dolphins, porpoises, and others. **2.** *Informal.* An impressive example of something specified: *a whale of a story.* —*intr.v.* **whaled, whal·ing, whales.** To engage in the hunting of whales. [ME < OE *hwæl.*]

whale[2] (hwāl, wāl) *v.* **whaled, whal·ing, whales.** —*tr.* To strike or hit repeatedly and forcefully; thrash. —*intr.* To attack vehemently: *The poet whaled away at his critics.* [Orig. unknown.]

whale·back (hwāl'băk', wāl'-) *n.* A steamship with the bow and upper deck rounded so as to shed water.

whale·boat (hwāl'bōt', wāl'-) *n.* **1.** A long rowboat, pointed at both ends and designed to move and turn swiftly, formerly used in the pursuit and harpooning of whales. **2.** A boat similar to a whaleboat in size and shape.

whale·bone (hwāl'bōn', wāl'-) *n.* **1.** The durable, elastic, hornlike material forming plates or strips in the upper jaw of whalebone whales. **2.** An object made of whalebone, as a corset stay.

whalebone whale *n.* The mysticete.

whale oil *n.* A yellowish oil obtained from whale blubber, used in making soap and candles and as a lubricating oil.

whale[1]
Performing whale

whaleboat

wharf

wheat

whal·er (hwā'lər, wā'-) *n.* **1.** One who hunts or processes whales. **2.** A whaling ship. **3.** A whaleboat.

whale shark *n.* A large shark, *Rhincodon typus,* of warm marine waters, having a spotted body and feeding chiefly on plankton.

whal·ing (hwā'lĭng, wāl-) *n.* The business or practice of hunting, killing, and processing whales.

wham (hwăm, wăm) *n.* **1.** A forceful, resounding blow. **2.** The sound of a forceful, resounding blow; thud. —*v.* **whammed, wham·ming, whams.** —*tr.* To strike or smash into with resounding impact. —*intr.* To smash with great force. [Imit.]

wham·my (hwăm'ē, wăm'ē) *n., pl.* **-mies.** *Slang.* A supernatural spell capable of subduing an adversary; hex: *put the whammy on someone.* [Perh. < WHAM.]

whang[1] (hwăng, wăng) *n. Informal.* **1.** A thong or whip of hide or leather. **2. a.** A lashing blow, as of a whip. **b.** The sound of such a blow. —*tr.v.* **whanged, whang·ing, whangs.** *Informal.* **1.** To beat or whip with a thong. **2.** To beat with a sharp blow or blows. [Var. of ME *thwang,* thong.]

whang[2] (hwăng, wăng) *Informal.* —*v.* **whanged, whang·ing, whangs.** —*tr.* To strike so as to produce a loud, reverberant noise. —*intr.* To produce a loud, reverberant noise. —*n.* A loud, reverberant noise. [Imit.]

whang·ee (hwăng-gē', wăng'-) *n.* **1.** Any of several bamboo-like Asian grasses of the genus *Phyllostachys.* **2.** A walking stick made from the woody stem of a whangee. [Chin. (Mandarin) *huang*[2] *li*[2] : *huang*[2], yellow + *li*[2], a kind of bramble.]

wharf (hwôrf, wôrf) *n., pl.* **wharves** (hwôrvz, wôrvz) or **wharfs. 1.** A landing place or pier where ships may tie up and load or unload. **2.** *Obs.* A shore or riverbank. —*v.* **wharfed, wharf·ing, wharfs.** —*tr.* **1.** To moor (a vessel) at a wharf. **2.** To take to or store (cargo) on a wharf. **3.** To furnish, equip, or protect with a wharf or wharves. —*intr.* To berth at a wharf. [ME *wharfe* < OE *hwearf.*]

wharf·age (hwôr'fĭj, wôr'fĭj) *n.* **1. a.** The use of a wharf or wharves. **b.** The charges for this. **2.** Wharves collectively.

wharf·in·ger (hwôr'fĭn-jər, wôr'-) *n.* The owner or manager of a wharf. [Alteration of WHARFAGE + -ER.]

wharf rat *n.* **1.** A rat that infests wharves and shipping. **2.** *Slang.* An undesirable person who frequents wharves.

wharves (hwôrvz, wôrvz) *n.* A plural of **wharf.**

what (hwŏt, hwŭt, wŏt, wŭt; hwət, wət *when unstressed*) *pron.* **1. a.** Which thing or which particular one of many: *What are you having for dinner? What did he say?* **b.** Which kind, character, or designation: *What are these objects?* **c.** One of how much value or significance: *What are possessions to a dying man?* **2. a.** That which; the thing that: *Listen to what I tell you.* **b.** Whatever thing that: *come what may.* **3. a.** *Nonstandard.* Which, who, or that: *It's the poor what gets the blame.* **b.** *Informal.* Something: *I'll tell you what.* —*adj.* **1.** Which one or ones of several or many: *What college are you attending? You should know what musical that song is from.* **2.** Whatever: *They soon repaired what damage had been done.* **3.** *Archaic.* How much; which degree of. **4.** How great; how astonishing: *What a fool!* —*adv.* **1.** How much; in what respect; how: *What does it matter?* **2.** Why; which reason: *What are you hurrying for?* —*conj. Nonstandard.* That: *I don't know but what I'll go.* —*interj.* **1.** Used to express surprise, incredulity, or other strong and sudden excitement. **2.** *Chiefly Brit.* Used to express agreement: *A fine evening, what?* **—*idioms.* and what not.** And other less prominent or unspecified things: *nails, bolts, screws, and what not.* **what for.** A scolding or strong reprimand: *I really got what for when I came in late.* **what have you.** What remains and need not be mentioned: *chairs, lamps, radios, and what have you.* **what if. 1.** What would occur if; suppose that. **2.** What does it matter. **what it takes.** The necessary expertise or qualities needed for success. **what's what.** *Informal.* The fundamentals and details of a situation or process; the true state or condition. **what with.** *Informal.* Taking into consideration; because of: *What with the humidity, we really suffered.* [ME < OE *hwæt.*]

Usage: When *what* is the subject of a clause, it may be construed either as singular or as plural, depending on the sense. It is singular when it is taken as equivalent to *that which* or *the thing which: What seems to be a dead tree is blocking the road.* It may be plural when it is equivalent to *those which* or *the things which: What were intended as friendly gestures were misconstrued by the enemy.* But when a *what* clause is the subject of a sentence, it will not in general take a plural main verb unless it is the subject of a plural verb in its own clause. Thus, we say *what most surprise me are the remarks at the end of the article,* where the main verb *are* is plural because the verb *surprise* is plural in the subordinate clause. But we say *what she was holding in her lap was* (not *were*) *four kittens,* because *what* is not the subject of a plural verb in its own clause. In the same way, we say *what were called predicates by traditional grammarians are called verb phrases by modern linguists,* but *what I am most interested in is* (not *are*) *German stamps.*

what·ev·er (hwŏt-ĕv'ər, hwŭt-wŏt-, wŭt-) *pron.* **1.** Everything or anything that: *Do whatever you please.* **2.** What amount that; the whole of what: *Whatever is left over is yours.* **3.** No matter what: *Whatever happens, we'll meet here* *tonight.* **4.** *Informal.* What; which thing or things: *Whatever does he mean?* —*adj.* **1.** Of any number or kind; any: *Whatever requests you make will be granted.* **2.** All of; the whole of: *He applied whatever strength he had left to the task.* **3.** Of any kind at all: *No campers whatever may use the lake before noon.*

Usage: *Whatever* (pronoun) and *what ever* are used in questions and statements: *Whatever* (or *what ever*) *made her say that?* Both forms are used, although some meticulous writers prefer the two-word form. The same is true of *whoever, whenever, wherever,* and *however,* when used in corresponding senses. For the adjective, only the one-word form is used: *Take whatever books you need.* • When a clause beginning with *whatever* is the subject of its sentence, no comma should be used: *Whatever you do is right.* Otherwise, a comma may be used: *Whatever you do, don't burn the toast.* • When the phrase preceding a restrictive clause is introduced by *whichever* or *whatever, that* should not be used in formal writing. It is held to be incorrect to write *whatever book that you want to look at;* one should write instead *whatever book you want to look at will be sent to your office* or *whichever book costs less* (not *that costs less*) *is fine with us.* See also Usage note at **that.**

what·not (hwŏt′nŏt′, hwŭt′-, wŏt′-, wŭt′-) *n.* **1.** A minor or unspecified object or article. **2.** A set of light, open shelves for ornaments.

what·so·ev·er (hwŏt′sō-ĕv′ər, hwŭt′-, wŏt′-, wŭt′-) *pron.* Whatever. —*adj.* Whatever: *no power whatsoever.*

wheal (hwēl, wēl) *n.* A small acute swelling on the skin. [Var. of WALE.]

wheat (hwēt, wēt) *n.* **1.** Any of various cereal grasses of the genus *Triticum,* esp. *T. aestivum,* widely cultivated in many varieties for its commercially important edible grain. **2.** The grain of a wheat plant, ground to produce flour used in breadstuffs and pasta products such as spaghetti and macaroni. [ME *whete* < OE *hwǣte.*]

wheat bread *n.* A bread made from a mixture of white and whole-wheat flours.

wheat·ear (hwēt′îr′, wēt′-) *n.* A brown, black, and white bird, *Oenanthe oenanthe,* indigenous to northern regions. [Back-formation from obs. *wheatears,* wheatear, prob. by folk ety. < WHITE + ARSE.]

wheat·en (hwēt′n, wēt′n) *adj.* Of, pertaining to, or derived from wheat.

wheat germ *n.* The vitamin-rich embryo of the wheat kernel that is separated before milling for use as a cereal or food supplement.

wheat rust *n.* **1.** A destructive disease of wheat. **2.** A fungus, such as *Puccinia gyraminis,* that causes wheat rust.

Wheat·stone bridge (hwēt′stōn′, wēt′-) also **Wheat·stone's bridge** (-stōnz′) *n.* An instrument or circuit consisting of four resistors, or their equivalent, in series, with a galvanometer linking the junction between one pair and the other, used to determine the value of an unknown resistance when the other three resistances are known. [After Sir Charles *Wheatstone* (1802–1875).]

wheat·worm (hwēt′wûrm′, wēt′-) *n.* A nematode worm, *Anguina tritici,* that is parasitic on and destructive to wheat.

whee (hwē, wē) *interj.* Used to express extreme pleasure or enthusiasm.

whee·dle (hwēd′l, wēd′l) *v.* **-dled, -dling, -dles.** —*tr.* **1.** To persuade or attempt to persuade by flattery or guile; cajole. **2.** To obtain through the use of flattery or guile: *a con artist who wheedled her entire savings out of her.* —*intr.* To use flattery or cajolery to achieve one's ends. [Orig. unknown.] **—whee′dler** *n.* **—whee′dling·ly** *adv.*

wheel (hwēl, wēl) *n.* **1.** A solid disk or a rigid circular ring connected by spokes to a hub, designed to turn around an axle passed through the center. **2.** Anything resembling a wheel in appearance or movement or having a wheel as its principal part or characteristic, as: **a.** In the Middle Ages, an instrument to which a victim was bound for torture. **b.** A type of firework that rotates while burning. **c.** The steering device on a vehicle. **d.** *Informal.* A bicycle. **e.** A spinning wheel. **f.** A water wheel. **g.** A potter's wheel. **h.** A device used in roulette and other games of chance. **3. wheels.** Forces that provide energy, movement, or direction: *the wheels of commerce.* **4.** The act or process of turning; revolution or rotation. **5.** A military maneuver to change the direction of movement of a formation, as of troops or ships, in which the formation is maintained while the outer unit describes an arc and the inner unit remains stationary as a pivot. **6. wheels.** *Slang.* An automobile or access thereto. **7.** *Slang.* A person with a great deal of power or influence: *thinks he's a wheel because he works for the town.* —*v.* **wheeled, wheel·ing, wheels.** —*tr.* **1.** To roll, move, or transport on a wheel or wheels. **2.** To cause to turn around or as if around a central axis; revolve or rotate. **3.** To provide with a wheel or wheels. —*intr.* **1.** To turn around or as if around a central axis; revolve or rotate. **2.** To roll or move on or as if on a wheel or wheels. **3.** To fly in a curving or circular course: *A flock of birds wheeled just above the house.* **4.** To turn or whirl around in place; pivot: *"the boy wheeled and the fried eggs leaped from his tray"* (Ivan Gold). **5.** To reverse one's opinion or practice: *can never tell when he'll wheel about on that subject.* **—*idioms.* at** (or **behind**) **the wheel. 1.** Operating the steering mechanism of a vehicle; driving. **2.** In charge; directing or controlling. **wheel and deal.** *Informal.* To engage in the advancement of one's own interests. [ME < OE *hwēol.*]

wheel and axle *n.* A mechanical device, analogous to the lever, consisting of two coaxial wheels of different diameters conjoined so that the effort applied by a cord to the larger wheel in the form of a torque is transmitted as an action by a cord around the circumference of the smaller, yielding a mechanical advantage equal to the ratio of the diameters of the wheels.

wheel animalcule *n.* A rotifer.

wheel·bar·row (hwēl′băr′ō, wēl′-) *n.* A one- or two-wheeled vehicle with handles, used to convey small heavy loads by hand.

wheel·base (hwēl′bās′, wēl′-) *n.* The distance from front to rear axle in a motor vehicle, usually expressed in inches.

wheel bug *n.* A large predatory insect, *Arilus cristatus,* having a notched, wheellike projection on the thorax.

wheel·chair also **wheel chair** (hwēl′châr′, wēl′-) *n.* A chair mounted on large wheels for the use of the sick or disabled.

wheeled (hwēld, wēld) *adj.* Having a wheel or wheels: *a three-wheeled bike.*

wheel·er (hwē′lər, wē′-) *n.* **1.** One that wheels. **2.** A thing that moves on or is equipped with a wheel or wheels: *a three-wheeler.* **3.** A wheel horse.

wheel·er-deal·er (hwē′lər-dē′lər, wē′-) *n. Informal.* A person who wheels and deals; sharp operator.

wheel horse *n.* **1.** In a team, the horse that follows the leader and is harnessed nearest to the front wheels. **2.** A diligent, dependable worker, esp. in a political organization.

wheel house *n.* A pilothouse.

wheel lock *n.* A firing mechanism in certain obsolete small arms, in which a small wheel produces sparks by revolving against a flint.

wheel·man (hwēl′mən, wēl′-) *n.* **1.** One who steers a ship; helmsman. **2.** A bicyclist.

wheels·man (hwēlz′mən, wēlz′-) *n.* A wheelman.

wheel·work (hwēl′wûrk′, wēl′-) *n.* An arrangement of gears or wheels in a mechanical device.

wheel·wright (hwēl′rīt′, wēl′-) *n.* One whose trade is the building and repairing of wheels.

wheeze (hwēz, wēz) *v.* **wheezed, wheez·ing, wheez·es.** —*intr.* **1.** To breathe with difficulty, producing a hoarse whistling sound. **2.** To make a sound suggestive of laborious breathing. —*tr.* To produce or utter with a hoarse whistling sound: *The old locomotive wheezed steam.* —*n.* **1.** A wheezing sound. **2.** *Informal.* An old joke. [ME *whesen,* prob. < ON *hvæsa,* to hiss.] **—wheez′er** *n.* **—wheez′ing·ly** *adv.*

wheez·y (hwē′zē, wē′-) *adj.* **-i·er, -i·est. 1.** Given to wheezing. **2.** Producing a wheezing sound. **—wheez′i·ly** *adv.* **—wheez′i·ness** *n.*

whelk[1] (hwĕlk, wĕlk) *n.* Any of various large, sometimes edible marine snails of the family Buccinidae, having pointed, turreted shells. [ME *whelke* < OE *weoloc.*]

whelk[2] (hwĕlk, wĕlk) *n. Pathol.* A swelling, protuberance, or pustule; wheal. [ME *whelke* < OE *hwylca* < *hwelian,* to suppurate.] **—whelk′y** *adj.*

whelm (hwĕlm, wĕlm) *tr.v.* **whelmed, whelm·ing, whelms. 1.** To cover with water; submerge. **2.** To overwhelm. [ME *whelmen,* to turn over.]

whelp (hwĕlp, wĕlp) *n.* **1.** A young offspring of a mammal, such as a dog or wolf. **2. a.** A child; youth. **b.** An impudent young fellow. **3. a.** A tooth of a sprocket wheel. **b.** Any of the ridges on the barrel of a windlass or capstan. —*v.* **whelped, whelp·ing, whelps.** —*intr.* To give birth to a whelp or whelps. —*tr.* To give birth to (a whelp or whelps). [ME *whelpe* < OE *hwelp.*]

when (hwĕn, wĕn) *adv.* **1.** At what time: *When will we leave?* **2.** At which time: *I know when to leave.* —*conj.* **1.** At the time that: *in the spring, when the snow melts.* **2.** As soon as: *I'll call you when I get there.* **3.** Whenever: *When the wind blows, all the doors rattle.* **4.** During the time at which; while: *when I was younger.* **5.** Whereas; although: *He stopped short when he might have reached his goal.* **6.** Considering that; if: *How can he succeed when he won't work?* —*pron.* What or which time: *Since when has this been going on?* —*n.* The time or date: *Have they decided the where and when?* [ME < OE *hwenne.*]

Usage: In informal style *when* is often used to mean "a situation or event in which," as in *A dilemma is when you don't know which way to turn.* This usage is best avoided in formal writing.

when·as (hwĕn-ăz′, wĕn-) *conj. Archaic.* **1.** When. **2.** Whereas.

whence (hwĕns, wĕns) *adv.* **1.** From where; from what place: *Whence came this man?* **2.** From what origin or source: *Whence comes this splendid feast?* —*conj.* **1.** Out of which place; from or out of which. **2.** By reason of which; from which: *The dog was coal black from nose to tail, whence the name Shadow.* [ME *whennes* < *whenne,* whence < OE *hwanon.*]

Usage: Historically, *whence* contains the sense of *from.* Therefore the construction *from whence,* although it can be found in the works of good writers, is often held to be redundant. Examples such as *Tell us the place from whence he*

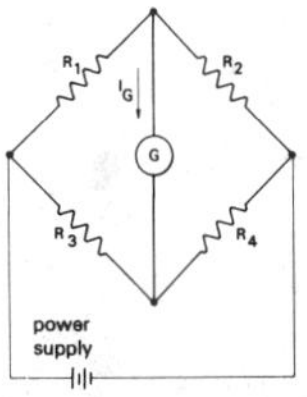

Wheatstone bridge
The current I_G, measured by detector G, is zero when $R_1 \times R_4 = R_2 \times R_3$

wheelbarrow

wheel bug

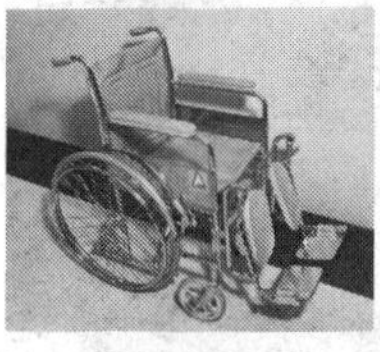

wheelchair

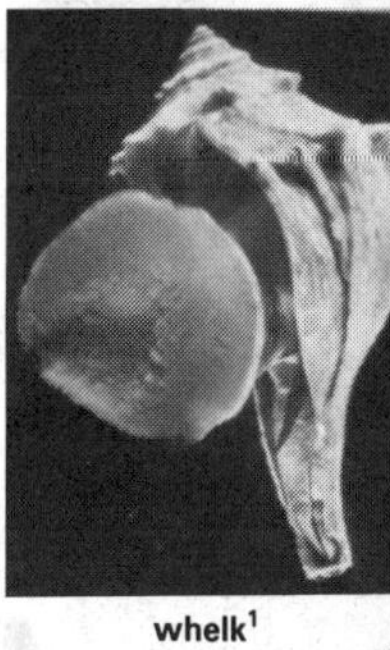

whelk[1]

came are unacceptable to a large majority of the Usage Panel. As an adverb *whence* is regarded by many as most appropriate to a formal or literary style, though as a conjunction it is still in general use.

whence·so·ev·er (hwĕns′sō-ĕv′ər, wĕns′-) *adv.* From whatever place or source. —*conj.* From any place or source that.

when·ev·er (hwĕn-ĕv′ər, wĕn-) *adv.* **1.** At whatever time. **2.** Also **when ever.** When. —*conj.* **1.** At whatever time that: *We can leave whenever you're ready.* **2.** Every time that: *He smiles whenever he sees her.*

when·so·ev·er (hwĕn′sō-ĕv′ər, wĕn) *adv.* At whatever time at all; whenever. —*conj.* Whenever.

where (hwâr, wâr) *adv.* **1.** At or in what place: *Where is the telephone?* **2.** In what situation or position: *Where would we be without your help?* **3.** From what place or source: *Where did you get this idea?* **4.** To what place; toward what end: *Where is this argument leading?* —*conj.* **1.** At what or which place: *He moved to the city, where jobs are available.* **2. a.** In a place in which: *He lives where the climate is mild.* **b.** In any place or situation in which; wherever: *Where there's smoke, there's fire.* **3. a.** To a place in which: *We should go where it is quieter.* **b.** To a place or situation in which: *He will go where he is happy.* —*n.* **1.** The place or occasion: *We know the when but not the where of it.* **2.** What place, source, or cause: *Where are you from?* [ME < OE *hwær.*]

Usage: When *where* refers to "the place from which," it requires the preposition *from: Where did you come from?* When it refers to "the place to which," it requires no preposition: *Where did he go* (better than *where did he go to?*). When *where* refers to "the place at which," it also requires no preposition: *Where are they* (not *where are they at?*). See also Usage note at **see.**

where·a·bouts (hwâr′ə-bouts′, wâr′-) *adv.* About where; in, at, or near what location: *Whereabouts do you live?* —*n.* *(used with a sing. or pl. verb).* The approximate location of someone or something: *I don't know his whereabouts right now.*

where·as (hwâr-ăz′, wâr-) *conj.* **1.** It being the fact that; inasmuch as. **2.** While at the same time. **3.** While on the contrary. —*n.* **1.** An introductory statement to a formal document; preamble. **2.** A conditional statement.

wherry

where·at (hwâr-ăt′, wâr-) *conj.* **1.** Toward or at which. **2.** As a result or consequence of; whereupon.

where·by (hwâr-bī′, wâr-) *conj.* In accordance with which; by or through which.

where·fore (hwâr′fôr′, -fōr′, wâr′-) *adv.* **1.** For what purpose or reason; why. **2.** Therefore. —*n.* A purpose or cause: *wanted to know all the whys and wherefores.* [ME *wherfor* : *wher,* where + *fore,* for.]

where·from (hwâr′frŏm′, -frŭm′, wâr′-) *conj.* From which.

where·in (hwâr-ĭn′, wâr-) *adv.* In what way; how: *Wherein have we sinned?* —*conj.* **1.** In which location; where: *the country wherein those people live.* **2.** During which. **3.** In what way; how: *showed them wherein they were wrong.*

where·in·to (hwâr-ĭn′to͞o, wâr-) *conj.* Into which.

whetstone

where·of (hwâr-ŏv′, -ŭv′, wâr-) *conj.* **1.** Of what: *I know whereof I speak.* **2. a.** Of which: *ancient pottery whereof many examples are lost.* **b.** Of whom. —*adv. Archaic.* Of what.

where·on (hwâr-ŏn′, -ôn′, wâr-) *adv. Archaic.* On which or what.

where·so·ev·er (hwâr′sō-ĕv′ər, wâr′-) *conj. Archaic.* In, to, or from whatever place at all; wherever.

where·through (hwâr′thro͞o′, wâr′-) *conj.* Through, because of, or during which.

where·to (hwâr′to͞o′, wâr′-) *adv.* To what place; toward what end. —*conj.* To which.

where·un·to (hwâr-ŭn′to͞o, wâr-) *adv. & conj.* Whereto.

where·up·on (hwâr′ə-pŏn′, -pôn′) *conj.* **1.** On which. **2.** In close consequence of which: *The instructor entered the room, whereupon we got to our feet.*

wher·ev·er (hwâr-ĕv′ər, wâr-) *adv.* **1.** In or to whatever place: *used red pencil wherever needed.* **2.** Also **where ever.** Where: *Where ever have you been so long?* —*conj.* In or to whichever place or situation: *makes enemies wherever he goes.* [ME : *wher,* where + *ever,* ever.]

where·with (hwâr′wĭth′, -wĭ*th*′, wâr′-) *adv.* With what or which. —*pron.* The thing or things with which. —*conj.* By means of which.

where·with·al (hwâr′wĭ*th*-ôl′, -wĭth-, wâr′-) *conj.* Wherewith. —*pron.* Wherewith. —*n.* The necessary means, esp. financial means: *didn't have the wherewithal to survive a recession.*

wher·ry (hwĕr′ē, wĕr′ē) *n., pl.* **-ries. 1.** A light, swift rowboat built for one person and often used in racing. **2.** A sailing barge used in East Anglia. [ME *whery.*]

whet (hwĕt, wĕt) *tr.v.* **whet·ted, whet·ting, whets. 1.** To sharpen (a knife or other tool); hone. **2.** To make more keen; stimulate: *The frying bacon whetted his appetite.* —*n.* **1.** The act of whetting. **2.** Something that whets. **3.** *Informal.* An appetizer. [ME *whetten* < OE *hwettan.*]

wheth·er (hwĕ*th*′ər, wĕ*th*′-) *conj.* **1.** Used in indirect questions to introduce one alternative: *We should find out whether the museum is open.* **2.** Used to introduce alternative possibilities: *Whether he wins or (whether he) loses, this is his last fight.* **3.** Either: *He passed the test, whether by skill or luck.* —*pron. Obs.* Which. —***idiom.*** **whether or no.** Regardless of circumstances. —See Usage note at **if.** [ME < OE *hweðer.*]

whet·stone (hwĕt′stōn′, wĕt′-) *n.* A stone for honing tools.

whew (hwo͞o, hwyo͞o) *interj.* Used to express strong emotion such as relief or amazement.

whey (hwā, wā) *n.* The watery part of milk that separates from the curds, as in the process of making cheese. [ME < OE *hwaeg.*] —**whey′ey** *adj.*

whey-face (hwā′fās′, wā′-) *n.* A person with a pallid face.

which (hwĭch, wĭch) *pron.* **1.** What particular one or ones: *Which of these is yours?* **2.** The particular one or ones: *Take those which are yours.* **3.** The one or ones previously designated or implied, specifically: **a.** Used as a relative pronoun in a clause that provides additional information about the antecedent: *my house, which is small and old.* **b.** Used as a relative pronoun preceded by *that* or a preposition in a clause that defines or restricts the antecedent: *that which he needed; the subject on which he spoke.* **c.** Used instead of *that* as a relative pronoun in a clause that defines or restricts the antecedent: *The movie which was shown later was better.* **4.** *Archaic.* The person designated or implied. **5.** Any of the things, events, or persons designated or implied; whichever: *Choose which you like best.* **6.** A thing or circumstance that: *He left early, which was wise.* —*adj.* **1.** What particular one or ones of a number of things or persons: *Which part of town?* **2.** Any one or any number of; whichever: *Use which door you please.* **3.** Being the one or ones previously designated: *It started to rain, at which point we ran.* [ME < OE *hwilc.*]

Usage: *Which* sometimes refers back to an entire preceding statement rather than to a single word: *She ignored him, which proved unwise.* In this example, acceptable to a large majority of the Usage Panel, the reference is clear. But when *which* follows a noun, the antecedent may be in doubt and ambiguity may result: *We learned that Edna had made the complaint, which came as a shock.* If *which* is intended to refer to the entire first clause rather than to *complaint,* the desired sense would be expressed more clearly by this construction: *We learned that Edna had made the complaint, and the discovery came as a shock.* See also Usage note at **that.**

which·ev·er (hwĭch-ĕv′ər, wĭch-) *pron.* Whatever one or ones. —*adj.* Being any one or any number of a group: *Read whichever books you please. It's a long trip whichever road you take.* —See Usage notes at **everyone** and **whatever.**

which·so·ev·er (hwĭch′sō-ĕv′ər, wĭch′-) *pron. & adj.* Whichever.

whick·er (hwĭk′ər, wĭk′-) *intr.v.* **-ered, -er·ing, -ers.** To whinny. —*n.* A whinny. [Imit.]

whid·ah (hwĭd′ə, wĭd′ə) *n.* Variant of **whydah.**

whiff (hwĭf, wĭf) *n.* **1.** A slight, gentle gust of air; waft: *a whiff of cool air.* **2.** A brief, passing odor carried in the air: *a whiff of her perfume.* **3.** An inhalation, as of air or smoke: *Take a whiff of this pipe.* —*v.* **whiffed, whiff·ing, whiffs.** —*intr.* To be carried in brief gusts; waft: *puffs of smoke whiffing from the chimney.* —*tr.* **1.** To blow or convey in whiffs. **2.** To inhale through the nose; sniff: *a dog whiffing the air.* [ME *weffe,* offensive smell.] —**whiff′er** *n.*

whif·fle (hwĭf′əl, wĭf′-) *v.* **-fled, -fling, -fles.** —*intr.* **1.** To move or think erratically; vacillate. **2.** To blow in fitful gusts; puff: *The wind whiffled through the trees.* **3.** To whistle lightly. —*tr.* To blow, displace, or scatter with gusts of air. [< WHIFF.]

whif·fle·tree (hwĭf′əl-trē, wĭf′-) *n.* The pivoted horizontal crossbar to which the harness traces of a draft animal are attached and which is in turn attached to a vehicle or an implement. [Var. of WHIPPLETREE.]

Whig (hwĭg, wĭg) *n.* **1.** A member of an 18th- and 19th-century English political party that was opposed to the Tories. **2.** A supporter of the war against England during the American Revolution. **3.** A 19th-century American political party formed to oppose the Democratic Party, and favoring high tariffs and a loose interpretation of the Constitution. [Prob. short for *Whiggamore,* a member of a body of 17th-cent. Scottish insurgents.] —**Whig′ger·y** *n.* —**Whig′gish** *adj.* —**Whig′gism** *n.*

while (hwīl, wīl) *n.* **1.** A period of time: *stay for a while; sang (all) the while.* **2.** The time, effort, or trouble taken in doing something: *wasn't worth my while.* —*conj.* **1.** As long as; during the time that: *It was lovely while it lasted.* **2.** Although; at the same time that: *While he loves his children, he is strict with them.* **3.** Whereas; and: *The soles are leather, while the uppers are canvas.* —*tr.v.* **whiled, whil·ing, whiles.** To spend (time) idly or pleasantly: *while the hours away.* —See Usage note at **awhile.** [ME < OE *hwīl.*]

whiles (hwīlz, wīlz) *conj. Archaic.* While. [ME, genitive of *while,* while.]

whi·lom (hwī′ləm, wī′-) *adj.* Former; having once been: *She is the whilom Miss Smith.* —*adv. Archaic.* Formerly. [ME < OE *hwīlum.*]

whilst (hwīlst, wīlst) *conj. Chiefly Brit.* While. [ME *whylst* < *whiles,* whiles.]

whim (hwĭm, wĭm) *n.* **1.** A sudden or capricious idea; a passing fancy. **2.** Arbitrary thought or impulse: *governed by whim.* **3.** A vertical horse-powered drum used as a hoist in a mine. [Short for obs. *whim-wham.*]

whim·brel (hwĭm′brəl, wĭm′-) *n.* A grayish-brown wading

bird, *Numenius phaeopus,* having long legs and a long, downward-curving bill. [Orig. unknown.]
whim·per (hwĭm′pər, wĭm′-) *v.* **-pered, -per·ing, -pers.** —*intr.* **1.** To cry or sob with soft intermittent sounds; whine. **2.** To complain. —*tr.* To utter in a whimper. —*n.* A low, broken, sobbing sound; whine. [Imit.] **—whim′per·er** *n.* **—whim′per·ing·ly** *adv.*
whim·si·cal (hwĭm′zĭ-kəl, wĭm′-) *adj.* **1.** Capricious, playful, or fanciful: *a whimsical prank.* **2.** Characterized by erratic behavior or unpredictability: *a whimsical personality.* [< WHIMSY.] **—whim′si·cal·ly** *adv.*
whim·si·cal·i·ty (hwĭm′zĭ-kăl′ə-tē, wĭm′-) *n., pl.* **-ties. 1.** The quality of being whimsical. **2.** A whimsical idea or its expression; caprice.
whim·sy also **whim·sey** (hwĭm′zē, wĭm′-) *n., pl.* **-sies** also **-seys. 1.** An odd or capricious idea; idle fancy. **2.** Something quaint, fanciful, or odd. [< WHIM.]
whin[1] (hwĭn, wĭn) *n.* Gorse. [ME *whynne.*]
whin[2] (hwĭn, wĭn) *n.* Whinstone. [ME *quin.*]
whin·chat (hwĭn′chăt′, wĭn′-) *n.* A brownish Old World bird, *Saxicola rubetra,* frequenting open country.
whine (hwīn, wīn) *v.* **whined, whin·ing, whines.** —*intr.* **1.** To utter a plaintive, high-pitched, protracted sound, as in pain, fear, supplication, or complaint. **2.** To complain or protest in a childish, annoying fashion. **3.** To produce a sustained noise of relatively high pitch: *jet engines whining.* —*tr.* To utter with a whine. —*n.* **1.** A whining sound. **2.** The act of whining. **3.** A complaint uttered in a plaintive tone. [ME *whinen* < OE *hwīnan,* to make a whizzing sound.] **—whin′er** *n.* **—whin′ing·ly** *adv.* **—whin′y** *adj.*
whin·ny (hwĭn′ē, wĭn′ē) *v.* **-nied, -ny·ing, -nies.** —*intr.* To neigh, as a horse, esp. in a gentle tone. —*tr.* To express in a whinny. —*n., pl.* **-nies.** The sound made in whinnying; neigh. [Prob. imit.]
whin·stone (hwĭn′stōn′, wĭn′-) *n.* Any of various hard, dark-colored rocks, esp. basalt and chert.
whip (hwĭp, wĭp) *v.* **whipped** or **whipt** (hwĭpt, wĭpt), **whip·ping, whips.** —*tr.* **1.** To strike with repeated strokes, as of a strap or rod; lash. **2. a.** To punish or chastise by repeated striking with a strap or rod; flog. **b.** To afflict, castigate, or reprove severely: *"For nonconformity the world whips you with its displeasure"* (Emerson). **3.** To drive, force, or compel by flogging, lashing, or other means of coercion: *His demands whipped her into running away.* **4.** To strike or affect in a manner similar to whipping or lashing: *Icy winds whipped his face.* **5.** To beat (cream or eggs, for example) into a froth or foam. **6.** To snatch, pull, or remove in a sudden manner: *He whipped off his cap.* **7.** To sew with a loose overcast or overhand stitch. **8.** To wrap or bind (a rope, for example) with twine to prevent unraveling or fraying. **9.** *Naut.* To hoist by means of a rope passing through an overhead pulley. **10.** *Informal.* To defeat; outdo: *Our team can whip your team.* —*intr.* **1.** To move in a sudden, quick manner; dart. **2.** To move in a manner similar to a whip; thrash or snap about: *Branches whipped against the windows.* **—*phrasal verbs.* whip in.** To keep together, as members of a political party or hounds in a pack. **whip up. 1.** To arouse; excite: *whip up the mob; whip up enthusiasm.* **2.** *Informal.* To prepare quickly: *whip up a light lunch.* —*n.* **1.** An instrument, either a flexible rod or a flexible thong or lash attached to a handle, used for driving animals or administering corporal punishment. **2.** A whipping or lashing motion or stroke; whiplash. **3.** A blow, wound, or cut made by or as if by whipping. **4.** Something, as an automobile radio antenna, that is similar to a whip in form or flexibility. **5.** Flexibility, as in the shaft of a golf club. **6.** A whipper-in (sense 1). **7. a.** A member of a legislative body, such as the U.S. Congress or the British Parliament, charged by his party with enforcing party discipline and insuring attendance. **b.** A call issued to party members in a lawmaking body to insure attendance at a particular time. **8.** A dessert made of sugar and stiffly beaten egg whites or cream, often with fruit or fruit flavoring: *prune whip.* **9.** A windmill arm. **10.** *Naut.* A hoist consisting of a single rope passing through an overhead pulley. **11.** A ride in an amusement park, consisting of small cars that move in a rapid, whipping motion. **—*idiom.* whip into shape.** To bring to a specified state or condition, often forcefully. [ME *wippen.*] **—whip′per** *n.*
whip·cord (hwĭp′kôrd′, wĭp′-) *n.* **1.** A worsted fabric with a distinct diagonal rib. **2.** A strong twisted or braided cord sometimes used in making whiplashes. **3.** Catgut.
whip hand *n.* **1.** The hand in which the whip is held. **2.** A dominating position; advantage.
whip·lash (hwĭp′lăsh′, wĭp′-) *n.* **1.** The lash of a whip. **2.** An injury to the cervical spine caused by an abrupt jerking motion of the head, either backward or forward.
whip·per-in (hwĭp′ər-ĭn′, wĭp′-) *n., pl.* **whip·pers-in. 1.** In foxhunting, a person who assists the huntsman in handling a pack of hounds. **2.** A whip (sense 7.a.).
whip·per·snap·per (hwĭp′ər-snăp′ər, wĭp′-) *n.* An insignificant and pretentious person. [Alteration of dial. *snippersnapper.*]
whip·pet (hwĭp′ĭt, wĭp′-) *n.* A short-haired, swift-running dog of a breed developed in England, resembling the greyhound but smaller. [Prob. < WHIP.]
whip·ping (hwĭp′ĭng, wĭp′-) *n.* **1.** The act of one that whips. **2.** A thrashing administered esp. as punishment. **3.** Material, as cord or thread, used to lash or bind parts.
whipping boy *n.* **1.** A scapegoat. **2.** A boy formerly raised with a prince or other young nobleman and whipped for the latter's misdeeds.
whip·ple·tree (hwĭp′əl-trē, wĭp′-) *n.* A whiffletree. [Alteration of WHIP + TREE.]
whip·poor·will also **whip-poor-will** (hwĭp′ər-wĭl′, wĭp′-, hwĭp′ər-wĭl′, wĭp′-) *n.* A brownish nocturnal North American bird, *Caprimulgus vociferus.* [Imit. of its call.]
whip·saw (hwĭp′sô′, wĭp′-) *n.* A narrow two-man crosscut saw. —*tr.v.* **-sawed** or **-sawn** (-sôn′), **-saw·ing, -saws. 1.** To cut with a whipsaw. **2.** To win two bets from (a person) at one time, as in faro. **3.** To defeat or best in two ways at once.
whip scorpion *n.* Any of various nonvenomous scorpionlike arachnids of the order Pedipalpi, such as the vinegarroon.
whip snake *n.* **1.** Any of several slender nonvenomous snakes of the genus *Masticophis,* of the New World. **2.** Any of several snakes similar or related to the whip snake.
whip·stall (hwĭp′stôl′, wĭp′-) *n.* A usually intentional stall in which a small aircraft enters a vertical climb, pauses, slips backward momentarily, then drops nose downward.
whip·stitch (hwĭp′stĭch′, wĭp′-) *tr.v.* **-stitched, -stitch·ing, -stitch·es.** To sew with overcast stitches, as in finishing a fabric edge or binding two pieces of fabric together. —*n.* A stitch made in this manner.
whipt (hwĭpt, wĭpt) *v.* A past tense and past participle of **whip.**
whip·tail (hwĭp′tāl′) *n.* Any of various New World lizards of the genus *Cnemidophorus,* having a long, slender tail.
whip·worm (hwĭp′wûrm′, wĭp′-) *n.* A slender, whiplike parasitic roundworm, *Trichuris trichiura,* that infests the large intestine in man.
whir (hwûr, wûr) *v.* **whirred, whir·ring, whirs.** —*intr.* To move so as to produce a vibrating or buzzing sound. —*tr.* To cause to make a vibratory sound. —*n.* **1.** A sound of buzzing or vibration: *the whir of turning wheels.* **2.** An excited and noisy activity; bustle: *the whir of busy shoppers.* [ME *whirren,* of Scand. orig.]
whirl (hwûrl, wûrl) *v.* **whirled, whirl·ing, whirls.** —*intr.* **1.** To revolve rapidly about a center or axis. **2.** To rotate or spin rapidly: *The dancer whirled across the stage.* **3.** To turn rapidly, changing direction; wheel: *She whirled around to face him.* **4.** To have the sensation of spinning; reel. **5.** To move circularly and rapidly in varied, random directions: *The wind whirled across the steppes.* —*tr.* **1.** To cause to rotate or turn rapidly: *whirl a baton.* **2.** To move or drive in a circular or curving course. **3.** To drive at high speed. **4.** *Obs.* To hurl. —*n.* **1.** The act of rotating or revolving rapidly. **2.** Something, as a cloud of dust, that whirls or is whirled. **3.** A state of confusion; tumult. **4.** A swift succession or round of events: *the social whirl.* **5.** A state of mental confusion or giddiness; dizziness: *My head is in a whirl.* **6.** *Informal.* A short trip or ride. **7.** *Informal.* A brief try: *Let's give it a whirl.* [ME *whirlen* < ON *hvirfla.*] **—whirl′er** *n.*
whirl·i·gig (hwûr′lĭ-gĭg′, wûr′-) *n.* **1.** Any of various spinning toys. **2.** A carousel or merry-go-round. **3.** Something that continuously whirls. **4.** The whirligig beetle. [ME *whirlegigge* : *whirlen,* whirl + *-gigg,* something that rotates.]
whirligig beetle *n.* Any of various beetles of the family Gyrinidae that circle about rapidly on the surface of quiet water.
whirl·pool (hwûrl′po͞ol′, wûrl′-) *n.* **1.** Water in rapid rotating movement, as from the converging of two tides; vortex. **2. a.** Turmoil; whirl. **b.** A magnetic, impelling force into which one may be pulled.
whirl·wind (hwûrl′wĭnd′, wûrl′-) *n.* **1. a.** A column of air centered on an area of low atmospheric pressure, rotating violently around a more or less vertical axis and moving forward; tornado. **b.** A small, momentary current of such whirling air over dusty flat land; a dust devil. **2. a.** A tumultuous, confused rush. **b.** A destructive force or thing. —*adj.* Hard-driving: *a whirlwind campaign.*
whirl·y·bird (hwûr′lē-bûrd′, wûr′-) *n. Slang.* A helicopter.
whirr (hwûr, wûr) *v.* & *n. Chiefly Brit.* Variant of **whir.**
whisk (hwĭsk, wĭsk) *v.* **whisked, whisk·ing, whisks.** —*tr.* **1.** To move or cause to move with quick light sweeping motions: *whisked the children away; whisked crumbs off the table.* **2.** To whip (eggs or cream). —*intr.* To move lightly, nimbly, and rapidly. —*n.* **1.** A quick light sweeping motion. **2.** A whiskbroom. **3.** A small bunch, as of twigs or hair, attached to a handle and used in brushing. **4.** A kitchen utensil for whipping foodstuffs. [ME, of Scand. orig.]
whisk·broom (hwĭsk′bro͞om′, -bro͝om′, wĭsk′-) *n.* A small short-handled broom used esp. to brush clothes.
whisk·er (hwĭs′kər, wĭs′-) *n.* **1. a. whiskers.** The unshaven hair on a man's face that forms the beard and mustache. **b.** A single hair of the beard or mustache. **2.** One of the long stiff bristles or hairs growing near the mouth of certain animals. **3.** *Informal.* A narrow margin; hairsbreadth: *He lost by a whisker.* **4.** *Naut.* One of two spars or booms projecting from the side of a bowsprit for spreading the jib or flying-jib guys. **5.** *Chem.* An extremely fine filamentary crystal that

whip
Drawing by
Charles M. Russell

whippet

whippoorwill

whirligig

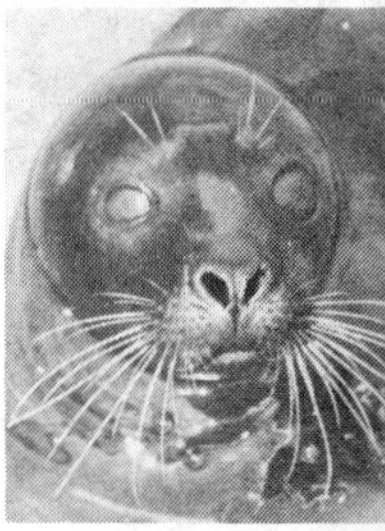

whisker
Of a seal

can be grown from supersaturated solutions of certain minerals and metals and that possesses extraordinary shear strength and unusual electrical or surface properties. [< WHISK.] **—whisk'ered, whisk'er·y** *adj.*

whis·key (hwĭs'kē, wĭs'-) *n., pl.* **-keys. 1.** An alcoholic liquor distilled from grain, such as corn, rye, or barley, and containing approximately 40 to 50 per cent ethyl alcohol by volume. **2.** A drink of whiskey. [Sc. *whiskybae* < Sc. Gael. *uisge beatha,* water of life.]

whiskey jack *n.* The Canada jay. [< obs. *whiskyjohn,* by folk ety. < Cree *wiskačan.*]

whiskey sour *n.* A cocktail made with whiskey, lemon juice, and sugar.

whis·ky (hwĭs'kē, wĭs'-) *n. Scot.* Variant of **whiskey.**

whis·per (hwĭs'pər, wĭs'-) *n.* **1.** Soft speech produced without full voice. **2.** Something uttered very softly. **3.** A secretly or surreptitiously expressed belief, rumor, or hint: *not a whisper of scandal.* **4.** A low rustling sound: *the whisper of wind in the pines.* *—v.* **-pered, -per·ing, -pers.** *—intr.* **1.** To speak softly, without full voice. **2.** To speak quietly, as by way of gossip, slander, or intrigue. **3.** To make a soft rustling sound. *—tr.* **1.** To utter very softly. **2.** To say or tell privately or secretly. [ME *whisperen* < OE *hwisprian.*] **—whis'per·er** *n.*

whist (hwĭst, wĭst) *n.* A game of cards played with 52 cards by two teams of two players each. [Orig. unknown.]

whistle

whis·tle (hwĭs'əl, wĭs'-) *v.* **-tled, -tling, -tles.** *—intr.* **1.** To produce a clear musical sound by forcing air through the teeth or through an aperture formed by pursing the lips. **2.** To produce a clear, shrill, sharp musical sound by blowing on or through a device. **3.** To produce a high-pitched sound when moving swiftly through the air: *The book whistled past his head.* **4.** To emit a shrill, sharp, high-pitched cry, as some birds and animals. **5.** To summon by whistling. *—tr.* **1.** To produce by whistling: *whistle a tune.* **2.** To summon, signal, or direct by whistling. **3.** To cause to move with a whistling noise. *—n.* **1. a.** A small wind instrument for making whistling sounds by means of the breath. **b.** A device for making whistling sounds by means of forced air or steam: *a factory whistle.* **2.** A sound produced by a device or by whistling through the lips. **3.** A whistling sound, as of an animal or projectile. **4.** The act of whistling. **5.** A whistling sound used to summon or command. ***—idiom.* whistle in the dark.** To attempt to keep one's courage up. [ME *whistlen* < OE *hwistlian.*]

whis·tler (hwĭs'lər, wĭs'-) *n.* **1.** One that whistles. **2.** A marmot, *Marmota caligata,* of the mountains of northwestern North America, having a grayish coat and a shrill, whistling cry. **3.** Any of various birds that produce a whistling sound. **4.** *Physics.* An electromagnetic wave of audio frequency produced by atmospheric disturbances such as lightning, having a characteristically decreasing frequency responsible for a whistling sound of descending pitch in detection equipment. **5.** A horse having a respiratory disease characterized by wheezing.

George Miksch Sutton

white-eye

whistle stop *n.* **1.** A town at which a train stops only if signaled. **2.** A brief appearance of a political candidate in a small town, traditionally on the observation platform of a train.

whis·tle-stop (hwĭs'əl-stŏp', wĭs'-) *intr.v.* **-stopped, -stop·ping, -stops.** To conduct a political campaign by making brief appearances or speeches in a series of small towns.

whistling swan *n.* A North American swan, *Olor columbianus,* having a black beak marked with yellow at the base.

whit (hwĭt, wĭt) *n.* The least bit; iota: *not a whit afraid.* [Alteration of WIGHT.]

white (hwīt, wīt) *n.* **1.** An achromatic color of maximum lightness, the complement or antagonist of black, the other extreme of the neutral gray series. Although typically a response to maximum stimulation, white appears always to depend upon contrast. **2.** The white or nearly white part of something, as: **a.** The albumen of an egg. **b.** The white part of an eyeball. **c.** A blank unprinted area, as of an advertisement. **3.** One that is white or nearly white, as: **a. whites.** White trousers or a white outfit of a special nature: *tennis whites.* **b.** A white wine. **c.** A white pigment. **d.** A white breed of animal. **e.** A Caucasoid. **f.** Often **whites.** Products of a white color, as flour, salt, and sugar. **4.** *Games.* **a.** The white or light-colored pieces in chess and checkers. **b.** The player using these pieces. **5. a.** The outermost ring of an archery target. **b.** A hit in this ring. **6. whites.** *Pathol.* Leukorrhea. **7.** A politically ultraconservative or reactionary person. *—adj.* **whit·er, whit·est. 1.** Being of the color white; devoid of hue, as new snow. **2.** Approaching the color white, as: **a.** Pale; weakly colored; almost colorless: *white wine.* **b.** Pale gray; silvery and lustrous: *white hair.* **c.** Bloodless; blanched. **3.** Light or whitish in color or having light or whitish parts. Used with animal and plant names. **4. a.** Having the comparatively pale complexion typical of Caucasoids. **b.** Of, pertaining to, characteristic of, or dominated by Caucasians. **c.** *Slang.* Fair or generous; decent: *That was very white of you!* **5.** Not written or printed upon; blank. **6.** Unsullied; pure. **7.** Habited in white: *white nuns.* **8.** Accompanied by or mantled with snow: *a white Christmas.* **9. a.** Incandescent: *white flames.* **b.** Intensely heated; impassioned: *white with fury.* **10.** Ultraconservative or reactionary. **11.** *Chiefly Brit.* With milk added. Used of tea or coffee. *—tr.v.* **whit·ed, whit·ing, whites. 1.** *Printing.* To create or leave blank spaces in (printed or illustrated matter): *white out a line.* **2.** *Archaic.* **a.** To whiten; whitewash. **b.** To blanch. [ME < OE *hwīt.*] **—white'ness** *n.*

white ant *n.* A termite.

white·bait (hwīt'bāt', wīt'-) *n.* **1.** The young of various fishes, such as the herring, considered a delicacy when fried. **2.** Any of various small edible fishes similar or related to the whitebait.

white birch *n.* Any of several birch trees having white bark, such as *Betula pendula,* of Europe, or the paper birch.

white blood cell *n.* A leukocyte.

white book *n.* An official publication of a national government. [From its formerly being bound in white.]

white bryony *n.* A climbing European vine, *Bryonia dioica,* having lobed leaves, greenish-white flowers, and scarlet berries.

white·cap (hwīt'kăp', wīt') *n.* A wave with a crest of foam.

white cedar *n.* Any of several North American evergreen trees, chiefly of the genus *Chamaecyparis,* having light-colored wood.

white cell *n.* A leukocyte.

white chip *n.* **1.** A white poker chip of minimal value. **2.** Something of minimal value or worth.

white cloud *n.* A small, brightly colored freshwater fish, *Tanichthys albonubes,* native to China and popular in home aquariums.

white clover *n.* A common clover, *Trifolium repens,* native to Eurasia, having rounded white flower heads.

white-col·lar (hwīt'kŏl'ər, wīt'-) *adj.* Of or pertaining to workers, salaried or professional, whose work usually does not involve manual labor and who are expected to dress with some degree of formality.

white corpuscle *n.* A leukocyte.

white crappie *n.* A silvery, edible North American sunfish, *Pomoxis annularis.*

white daisy *n.* Daisy (sense 1).

whited sepulcher *n.* An evil person who pretends to be holy or good; hypocrite. [From the simile applied by Jesus Christ to the scribes and Pharisees in the Gospel according to St. Matthew.]

white dwarf *n.* A faint, very dense star that has a radius approximately the same as that of the earth.

white elephant *n.* **1.** A rare whitish or light-gray form of the Asian elephant, often regarded with special veneration in regions of southeastern Asia. **2. a.** A rare and expensive possession that is financially a burden to maintain. **b.** Something of dubious or limited value. **3.** An article, ornament, or household utensil no longer wanted by its owner. **4.** An endeavor or venture that proves to be a conspicuous failure.

white-eye (hwīt'ī', wīt'ī') *n.* Any of various small greenish birds of the genus *Zosterops,* of Africa, southern Asia, and the Pacific islands, having a narrow ring of white feathers around each eye.

white-faced (hwīt'fāst', wīt'-) *adj.* **1.** Having a pale face; pallid. **2.** Having a white patch extending from the muzzle to the forehead.

white feather *n.* A sign of cowardice. ***—idiom.* show the white feather.** To act like a coward. [From the belief that a gamecock with a white feather in its plumage was a poor fighter.]

white·fish (hwīt'fĭsh', wīt'-) *n., pl.* **whitefish** or **-fish·es. 1.** Any of various chiefly North American freshwater food fishes of the genus *Coregonus,* having a generally silvery color. **2.** Any of various fishes similar or related to the whitefish.

white flag *n.* A white cloth or flag signaling surrender or truce.

white·fly (hwīt'flī', wīt'-) *n.* Any of various small whitish insects of the family Aleyrodidae, often injurious to plants.

white-foot·ed mouse (hwīt'fo͝ot'ĭd, wīt'-) *n.* The deer mouse.

white fox *n.* The arctic fox in its winter color phase.

White Friar *n.* A Carmelite. [From the color of the habit.]

white frost *n.* Hoarfrost.

white gasoline *n.* Gasoline that contains no tetraethyl lead.

white gold *n.* An alloy of gold and nickel, and sometimes palladium or zinc, having a platinumlike color.

White·hall (hwīt'hôl', wīt'-) *n.* The British civil-service administration as distinct from the party government. [After *Whitehall,* a street in London where most of the departments of government are located.]

white-head·ed (hwīt'hĕd'ĭd, wīt'-) *adj.* **1.** Having white hair or plumage on the head, as a bird or animal. **2. a.** White-haired, as from old age. **b.** Flaxen-haired. **3.** *Ir.* Favorite; darling: *the white-headed boy.*

white heat *n.* **1. a.** The temperature of a white-hot substance. **b.** The physical condition of a white-hot substance. **2.** A state of intense emotion or excitement.

white horse *n.* A wave capped with foam; whitecap.

white-hot (hwīt'hŏt', wīt'-) *adj.* **1.** So hot as to glow with a bright white light. **2.** Zealous; fervid.

White House *n.* **1.** The executive mansion of the President of the United States. **2.** The executive branch of the United States Government.

white iron pyrites *n.* Marcasite.

white lead *n.* A heavy white poisonous compound of basic lead carbonate, lead silicate, or lead sulfate, used in paint pigments.

white leather also **whit·leath·er** (hwīt′lĕth′ər, wīt′-) *n.* A leather specially treated with salt and alum.

white lie *n.* A diplomatic or well-intentioned untruth.

white list *n.* A list of persons or organizations considered worthy of approval or acceptance. [WHITE + (BLACK)LIST.] —**white′-list′ed** (hwīt′lĭst′ĭd, wīt′-) *adj.*

white-liv·ered (hwīt′lĭv′ərd, wīt′-) *adj.* Cowardly; lily-livered.

white magic *n.* Magic or incantation that is practiced for good purposes or as a counter to evil.

white mahogany *n.* Primavera (sense 2).

white man's burden *n.* The supposed responsibility of the white peoples to govern the nonwhite peoples of the world. [From *The White Man's Burden,* a poem by Rudyard Kipling (1865–1936).]

white matter *n.* White brain and spinal-cord tissue, consisting mostly of myelinated nerve fibers.

white meat *n.* Light-colored meat, esp. of poultry.

white metal *n.* Any of various whitish alloys, such as pewter, that contain high percentages of tin or lead.

white mica *n.* Muscovite.

white mulberry *n.* A tree, *Morus alba,* native to China, having whitish or purplish fruit.

whit·en (hwīt′n, wīt′n) *tr. & intr.v.* **-ened, -en·ing, -ens.** —*tr.* To make or become white, esp. by bleaching. —**whit′en·er** *n.*

white noise *n.* Acoustical or electrical noise in which the intensity is the same at all frequencies within a given band.

white oak *n.* **1.** A large oak, *Quercus alba,* of eastern North America, having heavy, hard, light-colored wood. **2.** The roble (sense 1).

white·out (hwīt′out′, wīt′-) *n.* A polar weather condition caused by a heavy cloud cover over the snow, in which the light coming from above is approximately equal to the light reflected from below, and which is characterized by the absence of shadow, the invisibility of the horizon, and the discernibility of only very dark objects.

white paper *n.* **1.** A paper published by a government on a topic. **2.** An investigative television news program on one major issue.

white pepper *n.* Peppercorns that have had their outer black layer removed before grinding.

white perch *n.* A small food fish, *Roccus americanus,* of the Atlantic coast and freshwater ponds of North America.

white pine *n.* **1.** A timber tree, *Pinus strobus,* of eastern North America, having needles in clusters of five and durable, easily worked wood. **2.** Any of several other pines having needles in clusters of five. **3.** The wood of the white pine.

white plague *n.* Tuberculosis of the lungs.

white poplar *n.* A tree, *Populus alba,* native to Eurasia, having leaves with whitish undersides.

white potato *n.* Potato (sense 2).

white·print (hwīt′prĭnt′, wīt′-) *n.* A photomechanical copy, usually of line drawings, in which black or colored lines appear on a white background.

white room *n.* A clean room.

white sauce *n.* A sauce made with butter, flour, and milk, cream, or stock, used as a base for other sauces.

white slave *n.* A woman held unwillingly for purposes of prostitution.

white slaver *n.* A procurer of white slaves.

white slavery *n.* Imposed prostitution.

white snakeroot *n.* A poisonous North American plant, *Eupatorium rugosum,* having heart-shaped leaves and flat-topped clusters of small white flowers.

white squall *n.* A sudden squall occurring in tropical or subtropical waters, characterized by the absence of a dark cloud and the presence of white-capped waves or broken water.

white·tail (hwīt′tāl′, wīt′-) *n.* White-tailed deer.

white-tailed deer (hwīt′tāld′, wīt′-) *n.* A North American deer, *Odocoileus virginianus,* having a grayish coat that turns reddish brown in summer and a tail that is white on the underside.

white·throat (hwīt′thrōt′, wīt′-) *n.* Either of two Old World songbirds, *Sylvia communis* or *S. curruca,* having brownish plumage and a white throat.

white-throat·ed sparrow (hwīt′thrō′tĭd, wīt′-) *n.* A North American sparrow, *Zonotrichia albicollis,* having a white throat and a distinctive song.

white tie *n.* **1.** A white bow tie worn as a part of men's formal evening dress. **2.** Men's formal evening dress. —**white′-tie′** (hwīt′tī′, wīt′-) *adj.*

white trash *n.* *Offensive Slang.* A poor white or poor whites as a class.

white vitriol *n.* Zinc sulfate.

white·wall tire also **white·wall** (hwīt′wôl′, wīt′-) *n.* A vehicular tire having a white band on the visible side.

white walnut *n.* The butternut.

white·wash (hwīt′wŏsh′, -wôsh′, wīt′-) *n.* **1.** A mixture of lime and water, often with whiting, size, or glue added, that is used to whiten structures, as exterior walls or fences, made of wood, stone, or concrete. **2.** A cosmetic application for whitening the skin. **3.** A concealing or glossing over of flaws or failures. **4.** *Informal.* A defeat in a game in which the loser scores no points. —*tr.v.* **-washed, -wash·ing, -wash·es. 1.** To paint or coat with or as if with whitewash. **2.** To conceal or gloss over (a flaw, for example). —**white′-wash′er** *n.*

white water *n.* Turbulent or frothy water, as in rapids. —**white′-wa′ter** (hwīt′wô′tər, -wŏt′ər, wīt′-) *adj.*

white whale *n.* A small whale, *Delphinapterus leucas,* chiefly of northern waters, that is white when full-grown.

white·wood (hwīt′wo͝od′, wīt′-) *n.* The soft, light-colored wood of any of various trees such as the tulip tree, basswood, or cottonwood.

whit·ey (hwī′tē, wī′-) *n., pl.* **-eys. 1.** *Slang.* A blond man or boy. **2.** *Offensive Slang.* A white person.

whith·er (hwĭth′ər, wĭth′-) *adv.* **1.** To what place, result, or condition: *Whither are we wandering?* **2.** To which specified place or position: *landed on the shores whither the storm had tossed them.* **3.** To whatever place, result, or condition: "*Whither thou goest, I will go*" (Ruth 1:16). [ME < OE *hwider.*]

whith·er·so·ev·er (hwĭth′ər-sō-ĕv′ər, wĭth′-) *adv.* To whatever place; to any place whatsoever.

whit·ing[1] (hwī′tĭng, wī′-) *n.* A pure white grade of chalk that has been ground and washed for use in paints, ink, and putty. [ME *whityng* < *whiten,* to whiten < *white,* white.]

whit·ing[2] (hwī′tĭng, wī′-) *n.* **1.** A food fish, *Gadus merlangus,* of European Atlantic waters, related to the cod. **2.** Any of several marine fishes of the genera *Menticirrhus* and *Merluccius,* of North American coastal waters. [ME *whitynge* < MDu. *wijting.*]

whit·ish (hwī′tĭsh, wī′-) *adj.* Somewhat white.

whit·leath·er (hwīt′lĕth′ər, wīt′-) *n.* Variant of **white leather.**

whit·low (hwĭt′lō, wĭt′-) *n.* An inflammation of the area of a finger or toe around the nail. [ME *whitflawe* : *white,* white + *flawe,* flaw.]

Whit·mon·day also **Whit-Mon·day** (hwĭt′mŭn′dē, -dā′, wĭt′-) or **Whit·sun-Mon·day** (hwĭt′sən-, wĭt′sən-) *n.* The Monday following Whitsunday.

Whit·sun (hwĭt′sən, wĭt′-) *adj.* Of, pertaining to, or observed on Whitsunday or at Whitsuntide. [ME *whitsone* < *whitsonday,* Whitsunday.]

Whit·sun·day (hwĭt′sən-dē, -dā′, wĭt′-) *n.* Pentecost (sense 1). [ME *whitsonday* < OE *hwita sunnandæg,* White Sunday.]

Whit·sun·tide also **Whit·sun Tide** (hwĭt′sən-tīd′, wĭt′-) *n.* The week beginning with Whitsunday or Pentecost, esp. the first three days of this week.

whit·tle (hwĭt′l, wĭt′l) *v.* **-tled, -tling, -tles.** —*tr.* **1. a.** To cut small bits or pare shavings from (a piece of wood). **b.** To fashion or shape in this way. **2.** To reduce or eliminate gradually by or as if by whittling with a knife: *He whittled down his expenditures by $60.* —*intr.* **1.** To cut or shape wood with a knife. **2.** To wear oneself or another out by fretting and carping. [ME *whyttel,* knife, var. of *thwitel* < *thwiten,* to whittle < OE *ðwitan.*] —**whit′tler** *n.*

whit·tling (hwĭt′lĭng, wĭt′-) *n.* A shaving from a piece of wood being whittled.

whiz also **whizz** (hwĭz, wĭz) *v.* **whizzed, whiz·zing, whiz·zes.** —*intr.* **1.** To make a whirring, buzzing, or hissing sound, as of something rushing through air. **2.** To rush past. —*tr.* To cause to whiz: *The pitcher whizzed the ball to first.* —*n., pl.* **whiz·zes. 1.** The sound or passage of something that whizzes. **2.** A quick trip. **3.** *Slang.* One who has remarkable skill: *a whiz at tennis.* [Imit.]

whiz kid *n.* A young person who is exceptionally intelligent, innovatively clever, and successful.

whizz-bang (hwĭz′băng′, wĭz′-) *n.* One that is extremely conspicuous due to noise, speed, or startling effect. [< *whizz-bang,* a shell used in World War I that was heard only an instant before landing and exploding: WHIZZ + BANG.]

who (ho͞o) *pron.* **1.** What or which person or persons: *Who left?* **2.** That. Used as a relative pronoun to introduce a clause when the antecedent is a human or is understood to be a human: *The boy who came yesterday; informed sources who denied the story.* **3.** The person or persons that; whoever. [ME < OE *hwā.*]

Usage: The traditional rules that determine the use of *who* and *whom* are relatively simple: *who* is used for a grammatical subject, where a nominative pronoun like *I* or *he* would be appropriate, and *whom* is used elsewhere. Thus, we write *the actor who played Hamlet was there,* since *who* stands for the subject of *played Hamlet;* and *who do you think is the best candidate,* where *who* stands for the subject of *is the best candidate.* But we write *to whom did you give the letter,* since *whom* is the object of the preposition *to;* and *the man whom the papers criticized did not show up,* since *whom* is the object of the verb *criticized.* •It requires considerable effort and attention to apply the rules correctly in complicated sentences, however. To produce correctly a sentence like *I met the man whom the government had tried to get France to extradite,* we must anticipate when we write *whom* that it will function as the object of the verb *extradite,* several clauses distant from it. In consequence, few writers and

white oak

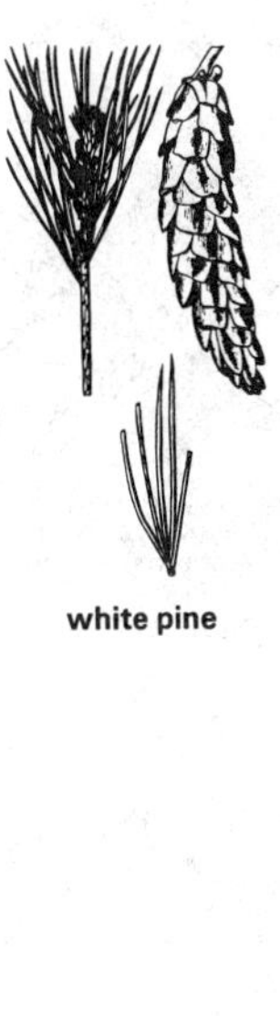

white pine

speakers succeed in getting *who* and *whom* right all of the time, and a slavish adherence to the rules, especially in informal contexts, may be taken as a sign of pedantry. • When the relative stands for the object of a preposition left at the end of a sentence, *whom* is technically the correct form: The strict grammarian will insist on *Whom* (not *who*) *did you give it to?* But grammarians since Noah Webster have argued that the excessive formality of *whom* in these cases is at odds with the relative informality associated with the practice of stranding the preposition and that the use of *who* in these cases should be regarded as entirely acceptable. The grammatical rules governing the use of *who* and *whom* apply equally to *whoever* and *whomever.* • The relative pronoun *who* may be used both in restrictive relative clauses, in which case it is not preceded by a comma, or in nonrestrictive clauses, in which case a comma is required. Thus, we may say either *the scientist who discovers a cure for cancer will be immortalized,* where the clause *who discovers a cure for cancer* indicates which scientist will be immortalized; or *the mathematician over there, who solved the four-color theorem, is widely known,* where the clause *who solved the four-color theorem* adds information about a person already identified by the phrase *the mathematician over there.* Some grammarians have argued that only *who,* and not *that,* should be used to introduce a restrictive relative clause that identifies a person. But this restriction has no basis either in logic or in the usage of the best writers; it is entirely acceptable to write either *the man that wanted to talk to you* or *the man who wanted to talk to you.* See also Usage note at **that**.

whooping crane

whoa (hwō, wō) *interj.* Used to command a horse to stop. [ME *whoo,* var. of *ho,* halt!]

who'd (ho͞od). **1.** Who would. **2.** Who had.

who·dun·it (ho͞o-dŭn′ĭt) *n. Informal.* A mystery story. [WHO + DONE + IT.]

who·ev·er (ho͞o-ĕv′ər) *pron.* **1.** No matter who: *Whoever comes will be welcomed.* **2.** Who: *Whoever could have dreamed of such a thing?* —See Usage note at **everyone** and **who**.

whole (hōl) *adj.* **1.** Containing all component parts; complete: *a whole formal wardrobe.* **2.** Not divided or disjoined; in one unit: *a whole acre.* **3. a.** Sound; healthy: *a whole organism.* **b.** Restored; healed: *a whole man again.* **4.** Constituting the full amount, extent, or duration: *He cried the whole trip home.* **5.** Having the same parents: *a whole sister.* **6.** *Math.* Integral; not fractional. —*n.* **1.** All of the component parts or elements of a thing. **2.** A complete entity or system. —*adv. Informal.* Entirely; wholly: *a whole new idea.* —***idioms.* as a whole.** Altogether; all things considered. **on the whole.** Considering everything; as a rule. [ME *hole,* unharmed < OE *hāl.*] —**whole′ness** *n.*

whorl
Whorled leaves and flower parts of *Lilium philadelphicum*

whole blood *n.* **1.** Blood drawn directly from a living human being and prepared for use in transfusion. **2.** Blood from which no constituent has been removed.

whole gale *n.* A wind with a speed from 88.5 to 103.4 kilometers per hour, or 55 to 63 miles per hour.

whole·heart·ed (hōl′här′tĭd) *adj.* Marked by sincerity and energy. —**whole′heart′ed·ly** *adv.* —**whole′heart′ed·ness** *n.*

whole hog *n. Slang.* The whole way; the fullest extent.

whole life insurance *n.* A type of insurance that provides death protection for the insured's entire lifetime.

whole milk *n.* Milk from which no constituent has been removed.

whole note *n. Mus.* A note having, in common time, the value of four beats.

whole number *n.* An integer.

whole·sale (hōl′sāl′) *n.* The sale of goods in large quantities, as for resale by a retailer. —*adj.* **1.** Pertaining to or engaged in the sale of goods at wholesale. **2.** Sold in large bulk or quantity, usually at a lower cost. **3.** Made or accomplished extensively and indiscriminately; blanket: *the wholesale elimination of life by nuclear weapons.* —*adv.* **1.** In large bulk or quantity; on wholesale terms. **2.** Extensively and indiscriminately. —*v.* **-saled, -sal·ing, -sales.** —*tr.* To sell at wholesale. —*intr.* **1.** To engage in wholesale selling. **2.** To be sold wholesale. [ME *holesale* : *hole,* whole + *sale,* sale.] —**whole′sal′er** *n.*

whole·some (hōl′səm) *adj.* **1.** Conducive to sound health or well-being; salutary. **2.** Morally or socially salubrious. **3.** Healthy. [ME *holsom.*] —**whole′some·ly** *adv.* —**whole′some·ness** *n.*

whole-wheat (hōl′hwēt′) *adj.* **1.** Made from the entire grain of wheat, including the bran: *whole-wheat flour.* **2.** Made with whole-wheat flour, as bread.

who'll (ho͞ol). **1.** Who will. **2.** Who shall.

whol·ly (hō′lē, hōl′lē) *adv.* **1.** Entirely: *"The old American purposes are still wholly relevant"* (John F. Kennedy). **2.** Exclusively.

whom (ho͞om) *pron.* The objective case of **who**.

whom·ev·er (ho͞om-ĕv′ər) *pron.* The objective case of **whoever**. —See Usage note at **who**.

whom·so·ev·er (ho͞om′sō-ĕv′ər) *pron.* The objective case of **whosoever**.

whydah

whoop (ho͞op, hwo͞op, wo͞op) *n.* **1. a.** A cry of exultation or excitement. **b.** A battle cry or hunter's halloo. **2.** A hooting cry, as of a bird. **3.** The paroxysmal gasp characteristic of whooping cough. —*v.* **whooped, whoop·ing, whoops.** —*intr.* **1.** To utter a loud shout or cry. **2.** To utter a hooting cry. **3.** To make the paroxysmal gasp characteristic of whooping cough. —*tr.* **1.** To utter with a whoop. **2.** To chase, call, urge on, or drive with a whoop: *whooping the horses on down the road.* —***idiom.* whoop it up.** *Slang.* **1.** To have a jolly time. **2.** To arouse interest or enthusiasm. [ME *whopen* < OFr. *houpper.*]

whoop·ee (hwo͝o′pē, wo͝o′-, hwo͞o′-, wo͞o′-) *interj. Slang.* Used to express jubilance. —***idiom.* make whoopee. 1.** To celebrate noisily. **2.** To make love. [< WHOOP.]

whoop·er (ho͞o′pər, hwo͞o′-, wo͞o′-) *n.* **1.** One that whoops. **2.** An Old World swan, *Cygnus cygnus* or *Olor cygnus,* having a loud cry.

whooping cough *n.* An infectious disease involving catarrh of the respiratory passages and characterized by spasms of coughing interspersed with deep, noisy inspiration.

whooping crane *n.* A large, long-legged North American bird, *Grus americana,* now very rare, having black and white plumage and a shrill, trumpeting cry.

whoops (hwo͝ops, wo͝ops, hwo͞ops, wo͞ops) *interj.* Used to express mild surprise or apology.

whoosh (hwo͞osh, wo͞osh, hwo͝osh, wo͝osh) *intr.v.* **whooshed, whoosh·ing, whoosh·es. 1.** To hurtle or gush rapidly. **2.** To make a gushing or rushing sound. —*n.* A whooshing sound. [Imit.]

whop (hwŏp, wŏp) *tr.v.* **whopped, whop·ping, whops.** To thrash; defeat. —*n.* A sharp thud. —*adv.* With a sudden thud. [ME *whappen,* var. of *wappen,* to throw violently.]

whop·per (hwŏp′ər, wŏp′-) *n.* **1.** Something exceptionally big or remarkable. **2.** A gross untruth.

whop·ping (hwŏp′ĭng, wŏp′-) *adj. & adv.* Used as an intensive: *a whopping lie; a whopping good joke.*

whore (hôr, hōr) *n.* A prostitute. —*intr.v.* **whored, whor·ing, whores. 1.** To consort or have sexual intercourse with whores. **2.** To be or behave like a whore. [ME *hore* < OE *hōre.*]

whore·dom (hôr′dəm, hōr′-) *n.* **1.** Fornication; harlotry. **2.** In Biblical use, idolatry. [ME *hordom* < ON *hōrdōmr.*]

whore·house (hôr′hous′, hōr′-) *n.* A brothel.

whore·mas·ter (hôr′măs′tər, hōr′-) *n.* One who consorts with whores; fornicator.

whore·mong·er (hôr′mŭng′gər, -mŏng′gər, hōr′-) *n. Archaic.* A whoremaster.

whore·son (hôr′sən, hōr′-) *n.* A bastard. —*adj.* Abominable; bastardly.

whor·ish (hôr′ĭsh, hōr′-) *adj.* Characteristic of a whore; lewd. —**whor′ish·ly** *adv.* —**whor′ish·ness** *n.*

whorl (hwôrl, wôrl, hwûrl, wûrl) *n.* **1.** A small flywheel that regulates the speed of a spinning wheel. **2.** *Bot.* An arrangement of three or more parts, as leaves or petals, radiating from a single organ or node. **3.** *Zool.* A single turn or volution of a spiral shell. **4.** One of the circular ridges or convolutions of a fingerprint. **5.** *Archit.* An ornamental device consisting of stylized vine leaves and tendrils. **6.** A coil, curl, or convolution: *spread icing in whorls and peaks.* [ME *whorle,* prob. var. of *whirle,* whirl < *whirlen,* to whirl < ON *hvirfla.*]

whorled (hwôrld, wôrld, hwûrld, wûrld) *adj.* **1.** Having or forming a whorl. **2.** Having convolutions, as of vine leaves: *"halls, giddy with plush and whorled designs in gold"* (Djuna Barnes).

whort (hwûrt, wûrt) also **whor·tle** (hwûrt′l, wûrt′l) *n.* The whortleberry or its fruit. [Var. of dial. *hurt.*]

whor·tle·ber·ry (hwûrt′l-bĕr′ē, wûrt′-) *n.* **1.** A small European shrub, *Vaccinium myrtillus,* having edible blackish berries. **2.** The fruit of the whortleberry. [Var. of dial. *hurtleberry.*]

who's (ho͞oz). **1.** Who is. **2.** Who has.

whose (ho͞oz) *pron.* **1.** The possessive form of **who**: *Did you see the patient whose arm is broken?* **2.** The possessive form of **which**: *an old oak in whose branches I sat.* [ME *whos* < OE *hwæs.*]

Usage: *Whose,* as the possessive form of a relative pronoun, can refer to both persons and things. Thus, it functions as the possessive of both *who* and *which.* The following example, in which *whose* refers to an inanimate object, is acceptable on all levels to a large majority of the Usage Panel: *The play, whose style is rigidly formal, is typical of the period.* The alternative possessive form *of which* is also used in referring to things but is sometimes cumbersome in application.

who·so·ev·er (ho͞o′sō-ĕv′ər) *pron.* Whoever.

who's who or **Who's Who** *n.* A compilation of short biographical sketches of well-known personages: *a who's who of musicians.*

why (hwī, wī) *adv.* For what purpose, reason, or cause; with what intention, justification, or motive: *Why did you have to leave?* —*conj.* **1.** The reason, cause, or purpose for which: *I know why you left.* **2.** On account of which; for which: *"The reason why they are called regular is that we can predict what all the other three forms are"* (Randolph Quirk). —*n., pl.* **whys. 1.** The cause or intention underlying a given action or situation: *the whys and wherefores.* **2.** A difficult problem or question. —*interj.* Used to express mild indignation, surprise, or impatience. [ME < OE *hwȳ.*]

Usage: *Why* is sometimes held to be redundant in *the* *reason why.* Although the expression is frequently used, it is found unacceptable by a majority of the Usage Panel in this example: *The reason why he opposed the nomination is not clear.* Alternative phrasings include: *Why he opposed the nomination is not clear. His reason for opposing the nomination is not clear.*

whyd·ah also **whid·ah** (hwĭd′ə, wĭd′ə) *n.* Any of several African birds of the genus *Vidua,* the breeding plumage of the male being predominantly black with long tail feathers. [Prob. alteration of WIDOW (BIRD).]

Wic·ca (wĭk′ə) *n.* The cult of witchcraft. [OE *wicca,* wizard.] **—Wic′can** *adj. & n.*

Wich·i·ta (wĭch′ə-tô′) *n., pl.* **Wichita** or **-tas. 1.** A confederacy of North American Indians, formerly living between the Arkansas River and central Texas. **2.** A member of the Wichita. **3.** The Caddoan language of the Wichita.

wick (wĭk) *n.* **1.** A cord or strand of loosely woven, twisted, or braided fibers, as on a candle or oil lamp, that draws up fuel to the flame by capillary action. **2.** A device similar to a wick that conveys liquid by capillary action. [ME *wike* < OE *wēoce.*]

wick·ed (wĭk′ĭd) *adj.* **-er, -est. 1.** Vicious; depraved: *wicked habits.* **2.** Mischievous or playfully malicious: *a wicked joke.* **3.** Harmful; pernicious: *a wicked cough.* **4.** Obnoxious; offensive: *a wicked stench.* **5.** Formidable; excellent: *a wicked tennis player.* [ME, alteration of *wicke,* wicked.] **—wick′ed·ly** *adv.* **—wick′ed·ness** *n.*

wick·er (wĭk′ər) *n.* **1.** A flexible shoot, as of a willow, used in weaving baskets or certain articles of furniture. **2.** Wickerwork. *—adj.* Constructed, consisting of, or covered with wicker. [ME *wiker,* of Scand. orig.]

wick·er·work (wĭk′ər-wûrk′) *n.* Woven wicker.

wick·et (wĭk′ĭt) *n.* **1.** A small door or gate, esp. one built into or near a larger one. **2.** A small window or opening, often fitted with glass or a grating. **3.** A sluice gate for regulating the amount of water in a millrace or a canal or for emptying a lock. **4.** In cricket: **a.** Either of the two sets of three stumps, topped by bails, that forms the target of the bowler and is defended by the batsman. **b.** A batsman's innings, which may be terminated by the ball knocking the bails off the stumps. **c.** The termination of a batsman's innings. **d.** The period during which two batsmen are in together. **e.** The pitch, esp. with respect to wetness or other conditions. **5.** *Games.* Any of the small croquet arches, usually made of wire, through which one tries to direct the ball. [ME < ONFr. *wiket,* prob. of Germanic orig.]

wick·et·keep·er (wĭk′ĭt-kē′pər) *n. Sports.* The cricket player positioned immediately behind the wicket in play.

wick·i·up also **wik·i·up** (wĭk′ē-ŭp′) *n.* A frame hut covered with matting, such as of bark or brush, used by the nomadic Indians of North America. [Fox *wikiyapi,* dwelling.]

wic·o·py (wĭk′ə-pē) *n., pl.* **-pies.** The leatherwood (sense 1). [Cree *wikopiy,* willow bark.]

Wi·dal test (vē-däl′) *n.* A serological test that uses an agglutination reaction to diagnose typhoid fever. [After Fernand *Widal* (1862–1929).]

wid·der·shins (wĭd′ər-shĭnz′) *adv.* Variant of **withershins.**

wide (wīd) *adj.* **wid·er, wid·est. 1.** Extending over a large area from side to side; broad. **2.** Having a specified extent from side to side; in width: *a ribbon two inches wide.* **3.** Having great range or scope: *a wide selection.* **4.** Full or ample, as clothing: *The legs on these jeans are too wide.* **5.** Fully open or extended: *look with wide eyes.* **6.** Far, apart, or away from the desired goal or point: *wide of the mark; wide of the truth.* **7.** Lax (sense 4). *—adv.* **1.** Over a large area; extensively: *journey far and wide.* **2.** To the full extent; completely: *the door was open wide.* **3.** So as to miss the target; astray. *—n. Sports.* A ball bowled outside of the batsman's reach, counting as a run for the batting team in cricket. [ME < OE *wīd.*] **—wide′ly** *adv.* **—wide′ness** *n.*

-wide *suff.* **1.** Extending over a specified area or region: *citywide.* **2.** Throughout a specified area or region: *statewide.* [< WIDE.]

wide-an·gle lens (wīd′ăng′gəl) *n.* A lens that has a relatively short focal length and permits an angle of view wider than approximately 70 degrees.

wide-a·wake (wīd′ə-wāk′) *adj.* **1.** Completely awake. **2.** Alert; watchful. **—wide′a·wake′ness** *n.*

wide-eyed (wīd′īd′) *adj.* **1.** With the eyes completely opened, as in wonder. **2.** Innocent; credulous.

wide-mouthed (wīd′mouthd′, -moutht′) *adj.* **1.** Having a wide mouth: *a wide-mouthed jug.* **2.** With the mouth completely open, as in surprise.

wid·en (wīd′n) *tr. & intr.v.* **-ened, -en·ing, -ens.** To make or become wide or wider. **—wid′en·er** *n.*

wide-o·pen (wīd′ō′pən) *adj.* **1.** Opened completely: *a wide-open door.* **2.** Without laws or law enforcement: *a wide-open town.*

wide receiver *n. Football.* A receiver who usually lines up several yards to the side of an offensive formation.

wide·spread also **wide-spread** (wīd′sprĕd′) or **wide-spreading** (-sprĕd′ĭng) *adj.* **1.** Spread or scattered over a considerable extent. **2.** Occurring or accepted widely.

wid·geon (wĭj′ən) *n., pl.* **widgeon** or **-geons.** Either of two ducks, *Mareca americana,* of North America, or *M. penelope,* of Europe, having brownish plumage. [Orig. unknown.]

widg·et (wĭj′ĭt) *n. Informal.* **1.** A small mechanical device or part; gadget. **2.** An unknown or unspecified item representing a manufacturer's output. [Alteration of GADGET.]

wid·ow (wĭd′ō) *n.* **1.** A woman whose husband has died and who has not remarried. **2.** *Games.* An additional hand of cards dealt to the table. **3.** *Printing.* **a.** An incomplete usually short line of type, as one ending a paragraph, carried over to the top of the next page or column. **b.** A short line at the bottom of a page or column. *—tr.v.* **-owed, -ow·ing, -ows.** To make a widow of: *She was widowed during the war.* [ME *widewe* < OE *widuwe.*]

widow bird *n.* The whydah. [From its black plumage.]

wid·ow·er (wĭd′ō-ər) *n.* A man whose wife has died and who has not remarried. [ME *widewer* < *widewe,* widow.]

wid·ow·er·hood (wĭd′ō-ər-ho͝od′) *n.* The condition or period of being a widower.

wid·ow·hood (wĭd′ō-ho͝od′) *n.* The condition or period of being a widow.

widow's mite (wĭd′ōz) *n.* A small contribution made by one who has little. [From the widow who gave two small coins to the Temple treasury in the Gospel according to St. Mark.]

widow's peak *n.* A V-shaped point formed by the hair at the middle of the forehead. [From the superstition that it is a sign of early widowhood.]

widow's walk *n.* A railed, rooftop gallery on a dwelling, designed to observe vessels at sea.

width (wĭdth, wĭth) *n.* **1.** The state, quality, or fact of being wide. **2.** The measurement of the extent of something from side to side. **3.** Something that has a specified width, esp. a piece of fabric measured from selvage to selvage in sewing: *a skirt having four widths.* [< WIDE.]

wield (wēld) *tr.v.* **wield·ed, wield·ing, wields. 1.** To handle (a weapon, for example). **2.** To exercise or exert (power or influence). [ME *welden* < OE *wieldan.*] **—wield′a·ble** *adj.* **—wield′er** *n.*

wield·y (wēl′dē) *adj.* **-i·er, -i·est.** Easily wielded or managed.

wie·ner (wē′nər) *n.* A wienerwurst. [G., short for *Wienerwurst,* wienerwurst.]

Wie·ner schnit·zel (vē′nər shnĭt′səl) *n.* A breaded veal cutlet. [G., Vienna cutlet.]

wie·ner·wurst (wē′nər-wûrst′, -wo͝orst′) *n.* A smoked pork or beef sausage, similar to a frankfurter. [G. : *Wien,* Vienna + *Wurst,* sausage.]

wife (wīf) *n., pl.* **wives** (wīvz). **1.** A woman married to a man. **2.** *Archaic.* A woman. [ME < OE *wīf.*] **—wife′hood′, wife′dom** *n.* **—wife′ly** *adj.*

wig (wĭg) *n.* A headpiece of artificial or human hair worn as personal adornment, part of a costume, or to conceal baldness. *—tr.v.* **wigged, wig·ging, wigs.** To scold or censure. [Short for PERIWIG.]

wig·an (wĭg′ən) *n.* A stiff fabric used for stiffening. [After *Wigan,* a textile-manufacturing town in England.]

wi·geon (wĭj′ən) *n. Chiefly Brit.* Variant of **widgeon.**

wig·gle (wĭg′əl) *intr. & tr.v.* **-gled, -gling, -gles.** To move or cause to move with short irregular twisting motions from side to side. *—n.* A wiggling movement or course. ***—idiom.*** **get a wiggle on.** *Slang.* To hurry or hurry up. [ME *wiglen,* prob. < MLG *wiggelen,* to totter.] **—wig′gly** *adj.*

wig·gler (wĭg′lər) *n.* **1.** One that wiggles. **2.** The larva or pupa of a mosquito.

wight¹ (wīt) *n.* A human being; creature. [ME < OE *wiht.*]

wight² (wīt) *adj. Archaic.* Valorous; brave. [ME < ON *vīgt,* neuter of *vīgr,* able to fight.]

wig·wag (wĭg′wăg′) *v.* **-wagged, -wag·ging, -wags.** *—tr.* **1.** To move back and forth. **2.** To signal by moving (the hand, for example) back and forth. *—intr.* **1.** To move back and forth; wag. **2.** To wave the hand or a device in signaling. *—n.* **1.** The act or practice of giving signals by wigwagging. **2.** A message relayed by wigwagging. [Dial. *wig,* to move + WAG.] **—wig′wag′ger** *n.*

wig·wam (wĭg′wŏm′) *n.* A North American Indian dwelling, commonly having an arched or conical framework overlaid with bark, hides, or mats. [Abnaki *wikəwam.*]

wik·i·up (wĭk′ē-ŭp) *n.* Variant of **wickiup.**

wild (wīld) *adj.* **-er, -est. 1.** Occurring, growing, or living in a natural state; not domesticated, cultivated, or tamed. **2.** Not inhabited; desolate. **3.** Uncivilized or barbarous; savage. **4.** Lacking discipline, restraint, or control; unruly: *wild children.* **5.** Disorderly; disarranged. **6.** Incoherent or chaotic; frenzied: *wild talk.* **7.** Full of intense, ungovernable emotion: *wild with jealousy.* **8. a.** Notoriously odd or amusing: *a wild character.* **b.** Extravagant; fantastic: *a wild idea.* **9.** Furiously disturbed or turbulent; stormy: *wild seas.* **10.** Reckless; risky. **11.** Random or spontaneous; whimsical: *make a wild guess.* **12.** Deviating widely; erratic: *a wild bullet.* **13.** *Games.* Having an arbitrary equivalence or value determined by the card holder's needs or choice: *playing poker with deuces wild.* *—adv.* In a wild manner. *—n.* An uninhabited or uncultivated region. [ME *wilde* < OE.] **—wild′ly** *adv.* **—wild′ness** *n.*

wild bergamot *n.* An aromatic plant, *Monarda fistulosa,* of eastern North America, having clusters of lilac-purple flowers.

wild boar *n.* The boar (sense 2).

wicker
Wicker baskets

widow's walk

wig
British judges wearing traditional robes and wigs

wigwam
Above: Drawing showing structural details
Below: Birch-bark wigwam in Micmac, Nova Scotia

wild carrot *n.* Queen Anne's lace.
wild·cat (wīld′kăt′) *n.* **1.** Any of various wild felines of small to medium size, esp. one of the genus *Lynx.* **2.** A quick-tempered or fierce person. **3.** An oil well drilled in an area not known to yield oil. —*adj.* **1. a.** Risky or unsound, esp. financially. **b.** Issued by a financially irresponsible bank: *wildcat currency.* **c.** Operating or accomplished outside the boundaries of standard, ethical business procedures: *wildcat life insurance schemes.* **2.** Accomplished or operating without official sanction or authority: *a wildcat strike; a wildcat work stoppage.* —*v.* **-cat·ted, -cat·ting, -cats.** —*tr.* To prospect for (oil, for example) in an area supposed to be unproductive. —*intr.* To prospect in an untapped or questionable area.
wild·cat·ter (wīld′kăt′ər) *n.* **1.** A person engaged in mining or oil-drilling in untapped or doubtful areas. **2.** A promoter of speculative or fraudulent enterprises. **3.** A worker who participates in a wildcat strike or work stoppage.
wild celery *n.* The tape grass.
wil·de·beest (wĭl′də-bēst′, vĭl′-) *n.* The gnu. [Obs. Afr. : Du. *wild,* wild + Du. *beest,* beast.]
wil·der (wĭl′dər) *v.* **-dered, -der·ing, -ders.** *Archaic.* —*tr.* **1.** To lead astray; mislead. **2.** To bewilder; perplex. —*intr.* **1.** To lose one's way. **2.** To become bewildered. [Orig. unknown.] **—wil′der·ment** *n.*
wil·der·ness (wĭl′dər-nĭs) *n.* **1.** An unsettled, uncultivated region left in its natural condition, esp.: **a.** A large wild tract of land covered with dense vegetation or forests. **b.** An extensive area, as a desert or ocean, that is barren or empty; waste. **c.** A piece of land set aside to grow wild. **2.** Something likened to a wild region in bewildering vastness, perilousness, or unchecked profusion: *a wilderness of voices.* [ME < *wilddēornes* < *wilddēor,* wild beast.]
wild-eyed (wīld′īd′) *adj.* **1.** Marked by a wild expression in the eyes. **2.** Advocating or consisting of extreme social or political measures: *wild-eyed conservatives.*
wild·fire (wīld′fīr′) *n.* **1.** A highly flammable material formerly used in warfare. **2.** A raging fire that travels and spreads rapidly. **3.** Lightning occurring without thunder being heard. **4.** A luminosity that appears at night hovering over swamps or marshes; ignis fatuus. **5.** Something that acts very quickly and intensely: *Revolution spread through the country like wildfire.*
wild·flow·er also **wild flower** (wīld′flou′ər) *n.* **1.** A flowering plant that grows in a natural, uncultivated state. **2.** The flower of a wildflower.
wild·fowl (wīld′foul′) *n., pl.* **wildfowl** or **-fowls.** A wild bird, such as a duck, goose, or quail, hunted as game.
wild geranium *n.* A North American woodland plant, *Geranium maculatum,* having rose-purple flowers.
wild ginger *n.* A North American plant, *Asarum canadense,* having broad leaves, a solitary brownish flower, and an aromatic root.

wild ginger

wild-goose chase (wīld′go͞os′) *n.* A hopeless pursuit of an unattainable or imaginary object.
wild hyacinth *n.* A plant, *Camassia scilloides,* of the central United States, having narrow leaves and a cluster of pale-blue or white flowers.
wild indigo *n.* Any of several North American plants of the genus *Baptisia,* esp. *B. tinctoria,* having compound leaves with three leaflets and yellow flowers.
wild·ing (wīl′dĭng) *n.* **1.** A plant that grows wild or has escaped from cultivation, esp. a wild apple tree or its fruit. **2.** A wild animal. —*adj.* **1.** Growing wild; not cultivated. **2.** Undomesticated. [< WILD.]
wild·life (wīld′līf′) *n.* Wild animals and vegetation, esp. animals living in a natural, undomesticated state.
wild lily of the valley *n.* A woodland plant, *Maianthemum canadense,* of eastern North America, having a terminal cluster of small white flowers.
wild·ling (wīld′lĭng) *n.* A wild plant or animal, esp. a wild plant transplanted to a cultivated spot.
wild marjoram *n.* Marjoram (sense 2).
wild mustard *n.* Charlock.
wild oat *n.* **1.** Often **wild oats.** A grass, *Avena fatua,* native to Eurasia, related to the cultivated oat. **2. wild oats.** The excesses of youth: *sow one's wild oats.*
wild olive *n.* Any of various trees resembling the olive.

willow

wild pansy *n.* The heartsease.
wild pink *n.* Any of several North American plants of the genus *Silene,* esp. *S. caroliniana,* having pink or white flowers.
wild pitch *n.* *Baseball.* An erratic pitch that the catcher cannot be expected to catch and that enables a runner to advance.
wild rice *n.* **1.** A tall aquatic grass, *Zizania aquatica,* of northern North America, bearing edible grain. **2.** The grain of the wild rice.
wild rye *n.* Any of various grasses of the genus *Elymus.*
wild type *n.* The typical form of an organism as it occurs in nature, as distinguished from mutant specimens that may result from selective breeding.
wild vanilla *n.* A plant, *Trilisa odoratissima,* of the southeastern United States, having vanilla-scented leaves.
Wild West *n.* The western United States during the period of its settlement, esp. with reference to its lawlessness.
wild·wood (wīld′wo͝od′) *n.* A forest or wooded area in its natural state.
wile (wīl) *n.* **1.** A deceitful stratagem or trick. **2.** A disarming or seductive manner, device, or procedure. **3.** Trickery; cunning. —*tr.v.* **wiled, wil·ing, wiles. 1.** To influence or lead by means of wiles; entice. **2.** To pass (time) agreeably: *wile away a Sunday afternoon.* [ME *wil.*]
wil·ful (wĭl′fəl) *adj.* Variant of **willful.**
will[1] (wĭl) *n.* **1.** The mental faculty by which one deliberately chooses or decides upon a course of action; volition. **2.** An instance of the exercising of will; choice. **3.** Something desired or decided upon by a person of authority or supremacy: *It is the king's will that the prisoner be spared.* **4.** Deliberate intention or wish: *against his will.* **5.** Free discretion; inclination: *wandered about at will.* **6.** Bearing or attitude toward others; disposition: *full of good will.* **7. a.** The power to arrive at one's own decision and to act upon it independently in spite of opposition: *A woman of strong will and purpose.* **b.** The collective desire of a given group: *the will of the people.* **8. a.** Determination; diligent purposefulness: *the will to win.* **b.** Self-control; self-discipline. **9. a.** A legal declaration of how a person wishes his possessions to be disposed of after his death. **b.** The document containing this declaration. —*v.* **willed, will·ing, wills.** —*tr.* **1.** To decide upon; choose. **2.** To desire; yearn for: *"She makes you will your own destruction"* (G.B. Shaw). **3.** To decree; dictate; order. **4.** To resolve with a forceful will; determine. **5.** To influence or induce by sheer force of will or by supernatural power: *We willed the sun to come out.* **6.** To bequeath; grant in a legal will. —*intr.* **1.** To exercise the will. **2.** To decree or make a firm choice. **—*idiom.* at will.** Just as one wishes. [ME < OE *willa.*]
will[2] (wĭl) *aux.v.* past tense **would** (wo͝od). Used to indicate: **1.** Simple futurity: *They will appear later.* **2.** Likelihood or certainty: *You will regret this.* **3.** Willingness: *Will you help me with this package?* **4.** Requirement or command: *You will report to me afterward.* **5.** Intention: *I will too if I feel like it.* **6.** Customary or habitual action: *She would spend hours in the kitchen.* **7.** Capacity or ability: *This metal will not crack under heavy pressure.* **8.** *Informal.* Probability or expectation: *That will be the postman ringing.* —*tr. & intr.v.* To wish; desire: *Do what you will. Sit here if you will.* —See Usage notes at **if, shall,** and **should.** [ME *willen,* to intend to < OE *willan.*]
willed (wĭld) *adj.* Having a will of a specified kind: *weak-willed.*
wil·lem·ite (wĭl′ə-mīt′) *n.* A colorless vitreous to resinous silicate of zinc, Zn_2SiO_4, often fluorescent, and a minor ore of zinc. [Du. *Willemit,* after *Willem,* William I (1772–1843), king of the Netherlands.]
wil·let (wĭl′ĭt) *n.* A long-billed New World shore bird, *Catoptrophorus semipalmatus.* [Imit. of its song.]
will·ful also **wil·ful** (wĭl′fəl) *adj.* **1.** Being in accordance with one's will; deliberate. **2.** Inclined to impose one's will; unreasoningly obstinate. **—will′ful·ly** *adv.* **—will′ful·ness** *n.*
wil·lies (wĭl′ēz) *pl.n.* *Slang.* Feelings of uneasiness: *This place gives me the willies.* [Orig. unknown.]
will·ing (wĭl′ĭng) *adj.* **1.** Of or resulting from the process of choosing; volitional. **2.** Disposed to accept or tolerate; acquiescent. **3.** Acting or ready to act gladly; eagerly compliant: *"the spirit indeed is willing, but the flesh is weak"* (Matthew 26:41). **4.** Done, given, accepted, or offered freely and heartily. **—will′ing·ly** *adv.* **—will′ing·ness** *n.*
wil·li·waw (wĭl′ē-wô′) *n.* **1.** A violent gust of cold wind blowing seaward from a mountainous coast. **2.** A sudden gust of wind; squall. [Orig. unknown.]
will-o'-the-wisp (wĭl′ə-*th*ə-wĭsp′) *n.* **1.** Ignis fatuus. **2.** A delusive or misleading goal. [*Will* (nickname for *William*) + OF + THE + WISP.]
wil·low (wĭl′ō) *n.* **1. a.** Any of various deciduous trees or shrubs of the genus *Salix,* having usually narrow leaves, flowers borne in catkins, and strong, lightweight wood. **b.** The wood of any of these trees. **2.** Something, as a cricket bat, that is made from willow. **3.** A textile machine consisting of a spiked drum revolving inside a chamber fitted internally with spikes, used to open and clean unprocessed cotton or wool. —*tr.v.* **-lowed, -low·ing, -lows.** To open and clean (textile fibers) with a willow. [ME *wilowe* < OE *welig.*]
willow herb *n.* Any of various plants of the genus *Epilobium,* having narrow leaves and terminal clusters of pink, purplish, or white flowers.
willow oak *n.* A timber tree, *Quercus phellos,* of the southern and central United States, having narrow, willowlike leaves.
wil·low·ware (wĭl′ō-wâr′) *n.* Household china decorated with a blue-on-white design depicting a willow tree and often a river.
wil·low·y (wĭl′ō-ē) *adj.* **-i·er, -i·est. 1.** Planted with or abounding in willows. **2.** Resembling or suggestive of a willow tree, esp.: **a.** Flexible; pliant. **b.** Slender and graceful.
will power *n.* The ability to carry out one's decisions, wishes, or plans; strength of mind.
wil·ly-nil·ly (wĭl′ē-nĭl′ē) *adv.* Whether desired or not. —*adj.* Being or occurring whether desired or not. [Alteration of *will ye, nill ye,* be you willing, be you unwilling. —see NILL.]
Wil·son's disease (wĭl′sənz) *n.* A hereditary disease in which the serum level of a glycoprotein needed to metabo-

lize copper is diminished, thus causing the accumulation of copper in various organs of the body such as the brain, liver, and kidneys. [After Samuel A.K. *Wilson* (1877–1937).]

wilt[1] (wĭlt) *v.* **wilt·ed, wilt·ing, wilts.** —*intr.* **1.** To become limp or flaccid; droop. **2.** To become less active or energetic; weaken: *"his brain wilted from hitherto unprecedented weariness"* (Vladimir Nabokov). —*tr.* **1.** To cause to droop or lose freshness. **2.** To deprive of energy or courage; enervate. —*n.* **1.** The act of wilting or the state of being wilted. **2.** Any of various plant diseases characterized by slow or rapid collapse of terminal shoots, branches, or entire plants. [Poss. alteration of dial. *welk* < ME *welken.*]

wilt[2] (wĭlt) *aux.v. Archaic.* Second person singular present tense of **will**[2].

Wil·ton (wĭl'tən) *n.* A carpet woven on a Jacquard loom and having a velvety surface formed by the cut loops of a pile. [After *Wilton,* England.]

Wilt·shire (wĭlt'shîr, -shər) *n.* A sheep of a breed originating in England, characterized by a long head and pure white fleece.

wi·ly (wī'lē) *adj.* **-li·er, -li·est.** Full of wiles; sly. **—wil'i·ly** *adv.* **—wil'i·ness** *n.*

wim·ble (wĭm'bəl) *n.* Any of numerous hand tools for boring holes. —*tr.v.* **-bled, -bling, -bles.** To bore with a wimble. [ME < AN, prob. < MDu. *wimmel.*]

wimp (wĭmp) *n. Slang.* A person who is weak or ineffectual. [Orig. unknown.]

wim·ple (wĭm'pəl) *n.* **1.** A cloth wound around the head, framing the face, and drawn into folds beneath the chin, worn by women in medieval times and as part of the habit of certain orders of nuns. **2. a.** A fold or pleat in cloth. **b.** A ripple, as on the surface of water. **c.** A curve or bend. —*v.* **-pled, -pling, -ples.** —*tr.* **1.** To cover or furnish with a wimple. **2.** To cause to form folds, pleats, or ripples. —*intr.* **1.** To form or lie in folds. **2.** To ripple. [ME *wimpel* < OE.]

Wims·hurst machine (wĭmz'hûrst') *n.* An electrostatic generator having oppositely rotating mica or glass disks with metal carriers on which charges are produced by induction, used chiefly as a demonstration apparatus. [After James *Wimshurst* (1832–1903).]

win (wĭn) *v.* **won** (wŭn), **win·ning, wins.** —*intr.* **1.** To achieve victory over others in a competition. **2.** To achieve success in an effort or venture. —*tr.* **1.** To achieve victory in. **2.** To receive as a prize or reward for performance. **3.** To achieve by effort; earn: *win fame.* **4.** To reach with difficulty: *The ship won a safe port.* **5.** To take in battle; capture: *won the city after a long siege.* **6.** To succeed in gaining the favor or support of; prevail upon: *His eloquence won his audience.* **7. a.** To gain the affection or loyalty of. **b.** To appeal successfully to (someone's sympathy, for example). **c.** To persuade (someone) to marry one. **8.** To make (one's way) with effort. **9. a.** To discover and open (a vein or deposit) in mining. **b.** To extract from a mine. ***—phrasal verbs.*** **win out.** To succeed or prevail. **win through.** To overcome difficulties and attain a desired goal or end. —*n.* **1.** A victory, esp. in a competition. **2.** An amount won or earned. ***—idiom.*** **win the day.** To be successful. [ME *winnen* < OE *winnan,* to strive.]

Usage: *Win* used as a noun in the sense of "victory" or "success" is frequently used in sports reporting and other informal contexts. Some object to its use in writing on a more formal level, as in *An impressive win in the primary would strengthen his position greatly.*

wince (wĭns) *intr.v.* **winced, winc·ing, winc·es.** To shrink or start involuntarily, as in pain or distress; flinch. —*n.* A wincing movement or gesture. [ME *wincen,* to kick.] **—winc'er** *n.*

winch (wĭnch) *n.* **1.** A stationary motor-driven or hand-powered hoisting machine having a drum around which a rope or chain winds as the load is lifted. **2.** The crank used to give motion to a grindstone or similar device. —*tr.v.* **winched, winch·ing, winch·es.** To move with or as if with a winch. [ME *winche,* pulley < OE *wince.*] **—winch'er** *n.*

Win·ches·ter (wĭn'chĕs'tər, -chə-stər). A trademark for a shoulder firearm.

wind[1] (wĭnd) *n.* **1. a.** Moving air, esp. a natural and perceptible movement of air parallel to or along the ground. **b.** Moving air where artificially produced, as by a fan. **2.** A movement or current of air blowing from one of the four cardinal points of the compass: *the four winds.* **3. a.** Something that disrupts or destroys. **b.** Often **winds.** A tendency; trend: *the winds of change.* **4.** *Naut.* The direction from which the wind is blowing. **5.** Moving air carrying an odor, scent, or sound. **6. winds. a.** The wind instruments in an orchestra or band. **b.** Players of wind instruments. **7.** Gas produced in the body during digestion; flatulence. **8.** Respiration; breath, esp. normal or adequate breathing. **9. a.** Utterance empty of meaning; verbiage. **b.** Futile or idle labor or thought. —*tr.v.* **wind·ed, wind·ing, winds. 1.** To expose to the free movement of air; ventilate or dry. **2. a.** To catch a scent or trace of. **b.** To pursue by following a scent. **3.** To cause to be out of or short of breath. **4.** To afford a recovery of breath. ***—idioms.*** **before the wind.** In the same direction as the wind. **break wind.** To eject intestinal gas. **close to the wind.** As close as possible to the main force of the wind. **get wind of.** To receive hints or intimations of. **have the wind of.** To hold an advantage over (an opponent). **in the wind.** Likely to occur; in the offing. **near the wind. 1.** Close to the wind. **2.** Close to danger. **off the wind.** In a direction away from the wind. **on (or into or down) the wind.** In the same or nearly the same direction as the wind. **under the wind. 1.** To the leeward. **2.** In a location protected from the wind. **up the wind.** In a direction opposite or nearly opposite to the wind. [ME < OE.]

wind[2] (wīnd) *v.* **wound** (wound), **wind·ing, winds.** —*tr.* **1.** To wrap (something) around an object or center once or repeatedly. **2.** To wrap or encircle (an object) in a series of coils; entwine: *She wound her waist with ribbons.* **3.** To set on a curving or twisting course. **4.** To proceed on (one's way) with a curving or twisting course. **5.** To present or introduce in a disguised or devious manner: *He wound a plea for money into his letter.* **6.** To turn (a crank, for example) in a series of circular motions. **7.** To coil the spring of (a mechanism) by turning a stem, cord, or similar device: *wind a watch.* **8.** To lift or haul by means of a windlass or winch: *Wind the pail to the top of the well.* —*intr.* **1.** To move in or as if in a bending or coiling course: *a river winding through a valley.* **2. a.** To move in or have a spiral or circular course: *a column of smoke winding into the sky.* **b.** To be coiled or spiraled about something. **3.** To be twisted or whorled into curved forms. **4.** To proceed misleadingly or insidiously in discourse or conduct. **5.** To become wound: *a clock that winds with difficulty.* — ***phrasal verbs.*** **wind down. 1.** To decrease or diminish in energy, intensity, or scope, esp. so as to stop gradually. **2.** *Informal.* To relax; unwind. **wind up. 1.** *Informal.* To come or bring to a finish; end: *wind up a project.* **2.** To put in order: *wound up his affairs before leaving the country.* **3.** *Informal.* To arrive in a place or situation as a result of a given course of action: *wound up in New York; wound up in debt.* **4.** *Baseball.* To swing back the arm and raise the foot in preparation for pitching the ball. —*n.* **1.** The act of winding. **2.** A single turn, twist, or curve. [ME *winden* < OE *windan.*]

wimple

wind[3] (wīnd, wĭnd) *tr.v.* **wind·ed** (wīn'dĭd, wĭn'-) or **wound** (wound), **wind·ing, winds. 1.** To blow (a wind instrument). **2.** To sound by blowing. [< WIND[1].] **—wind'er** *n.*

wind·age (wĭn'dĭj) *n.* **1. a.** The effect of wind on the course of a projectile. **b.** The point or degree at which the wind gauge or sight of a rifle or gun must be set to compensate for the effect of the wind. **2.** The difference in a given firearm between the diameter of the projectile fired and the diameter of the bore of the firearm. **3.** The disturbance of air caused by the passage of a fast-moving object, such as a railway train or missile. **4.** *Naut.* The part of the surface of a ship that is left exposed to the wind.

wind·bag (wĭnd'băg') *n. Slang.* A talkative person who communicates nothing of substance or interest.

wind·blast (wĭnd'blăst') *n.* **1.** An exceedingly strong gust of wind. **2.** The damaging effect of air friction on a pilot ejected from a high-speed aircraft.

wind-blown (wĭnd'blōn') *adj.* **1.** Blown or dispersed by the wind. **2.** Growing or shaped in a manner governed by the prevailing winds. **3.** Cut short and curled or combed toward the front of the head: *a wind-blown hair style.*

wind-borne (wĭnd'bôrn', -bōrn') *adj.* Carried by the wind.

wind·break (wĭnd'brāk') *n.* A hedge, fence, or row of trees serving to lessen or break the force of the wind.

Wind·break·er (wĭnd'brā'kər). A trademark for a warm outer jacket having close-fitting, often elastic, cuffs and waistband.

wind-bro·ken (wĭnd'brō'kən) *adj.* Suffering from the heaves or other impairment of respiration. Used of horses.

wind·burn (wĭnd'bûrn') *n.* A reddened irritation of the skin caused by exposure to wind. **—wind'burned'** *adj.*

wind-chill factor (wĭnd'chĭl') *n.* The temperature of windless air that would have the same effect on the exposed human skin as a given combination of wind speed and air temperature.

wind cone (wĭnd) *n.* A windsock.

wind·ed (wĭn'dĭd) *adj.* **1.** Having breath or respiratory power: *short-winded.* **2.** Out of breath.

wind·er (wīn'dər) *n.* **1.** One that winds, esp. a person who winds cloth or materials in a textile factory. **2.** A spool, barrel, or other object around which material is wound. **3.** A device, such as a key, for winding up a spring-driven mechanism. **4.** One of the steps of a winding staircase.

wind·fall (wĭnd'fôl') *n.* **1.** Something, as a ripened fruit, that has been blown down by the wind. **2.** A sudden and unexpected piece of good fortune or personal gain.

wind·flaw (wĭnd'flô') *n.* A sudden gust or blast of wind.

wind·flow·er (wĭnd'flou'ər) *n.* An anemone (sense 1).

wind gap (wĭnd) *n.* A shallow notch or ravine on the side of a deep mountain ridge.

wind harp (wĭnd) *n.* An Aeolian harp.

wind·ing (wīn'dĭng) *n.* **1. a.** The act of one that winds. **b.** One complete turn of something wound. **2.** Something wound; spiral. **3.** A curve or bend, as of a road. **4.** *Elect.* **a.** Wire wound into a coil. **b.** The manner in which such a coil is wound. **c.** A single loop of such a coil. —*adj.* **1.** Twisting or turning; sinuous. **2.** Spiral. **—wind'ing·ly** *adv.*

winding-sheet (wīn'dĭng) *n.* A sheet for wrapping a dead body; shroud.

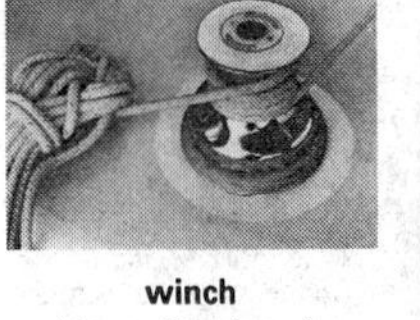

winch
Above: Drawing of a hand winch
Below: Hand winch on a boat

windlass

windmill
Two types of windmills

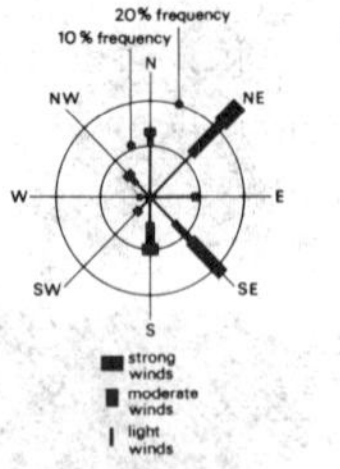

wind rose
Strength of winds indicated by thickness of radial segment; frequency of winds in a given direction indicated by length of segment

wind instrument (wĭnd) *n.* A musical instrument, as a clarinet, trumpet, or harmonica, that is sounded by wind, esp. by the breath.
wind·jam·mer (wĭnd′jăm′ər) *n.* **1.** A large sailing ship. **2.** A crew member of a sailing ship.
wind·lass (wĭnd′ləs) *n.* Any of numerous hauling or lifting machines consisting essentially of a drum or cylinder wound with rope and turned by a crank. *—tr.v.* **-lassed, -lass·ing, -lass·es.** To raise with a windlass. [ME *wyndlas,* var. of *windas* < ON *vindāss* : *vinda,* to wind + *āss,* pole.]
win·dle·straw (wĭn′dəl-strô′) *n. Chiefly Brit.* A thin, dried grass stalk. [OE *windelstrēaw* : *windel,* basket (< *windan,* to wind) + *strēaw,* straw.]
wind·mill (wĭnd′mĭl′) *n.* **1.** A mill or other machine that runs on the energy generated by a wheel of adjustable blades or slats rotated by the wind. **2.** Something, as a toy pinwheel, that is similar to a windmill in appearance or operation. **3.** One that is imagined to be threatening or evil: *tilting at windmills.*
win·dow (wĭn′dō) *n.* **1.** An opening constructed in a wall or roof and functioning to admit light or air to an enclosure, usually framed and spanned with glass mounted to permit opening and closing. **2. a.** A framework enclosing a pane of glass; sash. **b.** A pane of glass, clear plastic, or similar material enclosed in such a framework. **3.** Something felt to resemble a window in function or appearance: *St. Petersburg was Peter the Great's window onto the Baltic.* **4.** Chaff[1] (sense 4). **5.** A range of electromagnetic frequencies that pass unobstructed through a planetary atmosphere. **6.** A period of time or a physical space within which an activity must take place to ensure successful completion. [ME < ON *vindauga* : *vindr,* wind, air + *auga,* eye.]
window box *n.* **1.** A usually long and narrow box for growing plants, placed on a windowsill or ledge. **2.** One of the vertical grooves on the inner sides of a window frame for the weights that counterbalance the sash.
win·dow-dress·ing also **window dressing** (wĭn′dō-drĕs′ĭng) *n.* **1. a.** The decorative exhibition of retail merchandise in store windows. **b.** Goods and trimmings used in such displays. **2.** Something used to improve appearances or create a false favorable impression. **—win′dow-dress′er** *n.*
window envelope *n.* An envelope with a transparent panel through which the address on the enclosure is visible.
win·dow·pane (wĭn′dō-pān′) *n.* A plate of glass in a window.
window shade *n.* An opaque fabric mounted to cover or expose a window.
win·dow-shop (wĭn′dō-shŏp′) *intr.v.* **-shopped, -shop·ping, -shops.** To look at merchandise in store windows or showcases without making purchases. **—win′dow-shop′per** *n.*
win·dow·sill (wĭn′dō-sĭl′) *n.* The horizontal ledge at the base of a window opening.
wind·pipe (wĭnd′pīp′) *n. Anat.* The trachea (sense 1).
wind rose (wĭnd) *n.* Any of a class of meteorological diagrams depicting the distribution of wind direction over a period of time. [G. *Windrose,* compass card : *Wind,* wind, air + *Rose,* rose.]
wind·row (wĭnd′rō′) *n.* **1.** A row, as of leaves or snow, heaped up by the wind. **2.** A long row of cut hay or grain left to dry in a field before being bundled. *—tr.v.* **-rowed, -row·ing, -rows.** To shape or arrange into a windrow. **—wind′row′er** *n.*
wind·shake (wĭnd′shāk′) *n.* A crack or separation between growth rings in timber, attributed to the straining of tree trunks in high winds.
wind·shield (wĭnd′shēld′) *n.* **1.** A framed pane of usually curved glass or other transparent shielding located in front of the occupants of a vehicle to protect them from the wind. **2.** A shield placed to protect an object from the wind.
wind sleeve *n.* A windsock.
wind·sock (wĭnd′sŏk′) *n.* A tapered, open-ended sleeve pivotally attached to a standard that indicates the direction of the wind blowing through it.
Wind·sor chair *n.* A wooden chair having a high spoked back, outward-slanting legs connected by a crossbar, and a saddle seat. [After *Windsor,* England.]
Windsor tie *n.* A wide silk necktie tied in a loose bow.
wind sprint (wĭnd) *n.* A sprint run to develop the breath.
wind·storm (wĭnd′stôrm′) *n.* A storm with high winds or violent gusts but little or no rain.
wind·suck·er (wĭnd′sŭk′ər) *n.* A horse given to swallowing quantities of air.
wind·swept (wĭnd′swĕpt′) *adj.* Exposed to or moved by the force of wind.
wind tee (wĭnd) *n.* A large weather vane with a horizontal T-shaped wind indicator, commonly found at airfields.
wind tunnel (wĭnd) *n.* A chamber through which air is forced at controllable velocities in order to study the aerodynamic flow around and effects on airfoils, scale models, or other objects mounted within.
wind-up (wĭnd′ŭp′) *n.* **1. a.** The act of bringing something to a conclusion. **b.** The concluding part of something, such as an action, presentation, or speech. **2.** *Baseball.* The coordinated movements of a pitcher's arm, body, and legs preparatory to pitching the ball. *—adj.* Having a spring that is wound up by hand for use or operation: *a wind-up toy.*
wind·ward (wĭnd′wərd) *n.* The direction from which the wind blows. *—adj.* **1.** Of or moving toward the quarter from which the wind blows. **2.** Of or on the side exposed to the wind or to prevailing winds. *—adv.* In a direction from which the wind blows; against the wind.
wind·y (wĭn′dē) *adj.* **-i·er, -i·est.** **1.** Characterized by or abounding in wind. **2.** Open to the wind; unsheltered. **3.** Resembling wind in swiftness, force, or variability. **4. a.** Characterized by lack of substance; empty: *windy talk.* **b.** Characterized by or given to prolonged talk: *a windy speaker.* **5.** Flatulent. **—wind′i·ly** *adv.* **—wind′i·ness** *n.*
wine (wīn) *n.* **1. a.** The fermented juice of any of various kinds of grapes, usually containing from 10 to 15 per cent alcohol by volume. **b.** The fermented juice of any of various other fruits or plants. **2.** Something that intoxicates or exhilarates. **3.** The color of red wine. *—v.* **wined, win·ing, wines.** *—tr.* To provide or entertain with drink: *The guests were wined and dined.* *—intr.* To drink wine. [ME < OE *wīn,* ult. < Lat. *vinum.*]
wine·bib·bing (wīn′bĭb′ĭng) *adj.* Given to much drinking of wine. *—n.* The habitual drinking of wine. **—wine′bib′ber** *n.*
wine cellar *n.* **1.** A place for storing wine. **2.** A stock of wines.
wine·glass (wīn′glăs′) *n.* A glass, usually with a stem, from which wine is drunk.
wine·grow·er (wīn′grō′ər) *n.* One who owns a vineyard and produces wine.
wine palm *n.* Any of various palm trees having sap or juice from which wine is prepared.
wine·press (wīn′prĕs′) also **wine presser** *n.* A vat in which the juice is pressed from grapes.
win·er·y (wī′nə-rē) *n., pl.* **-ies.** A wine-making establishment.
Wine·sap (wīn′săp′) *n.* A variety of apple having fruit with dark-red skin.
wine·skin (wīn′skĭn′) *n.* A bag for holding and dispensing wine, made from the skin of a goat or another animal.
wing (wĭng) *n.* **1.** One of a pair of specialized organs of flight, as: **a.** The feather-covered modified forelimb of a bird. **b.** The membranous tissue supported by the elongated digits of the forelimb of a bat. **c.** A reticulated, membranous structure extending from the thorax of an insect. **d.** The enlarged pectoral fin of a flying fish. **2.** Any organ or structure homologous to or resembling a wing. **3.** *Bot.* **a.** A thin or membranous extension, as of the fruit of the maple or ash. **b.** One of the lateral petals of the flower of a pea or related plant. **4.** *Informal.* An arm of a human being. **5.** An airfoil whose principal function is providing lift, esp. either of two such airfoils symmetrically positioned on each side of the fuselage. **6.** Something that resembles a wing in appearance, function, or position relative to a main body. **7.** A means of flight or of rapid ascent. **8.** Something that is moved by or moves against the air, as a weather vane. **9.** *Chiefly Brit.* The fender of an automobile. **10.** A folding section, as of a double door or of a movable partition. **11.** Either of the two side projections on the back of a wing chair. **12. a.** A flat of theatrical scenery projecting onto the stage from the side. **b. wings.** The unseen backstage area on either side of the stage of a proscenium theater. **13.** A structure attached to the side of a building. **14.** A section of a large building devoted to a specific purpose: *the children's wing of the hospital.* **15.** A group affiliated with or subordinate to an older or larger organization. **16.** A section of a party, legislature, or community holding distinct, esp. dissenting, political views: *the conservative wing.* **17.** Either the left or right flank of an army or a naval fleet. **18.** *Sports.* Either of the forward positions played near the sideline, esp. in hockey. **19.** An air force unit larger than a group but smaller than a division or command. **20. wings.** An outspread pair of stylized bird's wings that is the insignia worn by qualified pilots. *—v.* **winged, wing·ing, wings.** *—intr.* To move on or as if on wings; fly. *—tr.* **1.** To furnish with wings. **2.** To feather (an arrow). **3.** To carry or transport by or as if by flying; speed along. **4.** To wound superficially, as in the arm. **5.** To furnish with side or subordinate extensions, as a building or altarpiece. ***—idioms.* in the wings.** In the background; close by: *a presidential candidate waiting in the wings, ready to take over.* **on the wing.** In flight; flying. **take wing.** To fly off; soar away. **under one's wing.** Under one's protection; in one's care. **wing it.** *Informal.* To improvise or ad-lib. [ME *wenge,* of Scand. orig.]
wing and wing *adv. Naut.* With sails extended on both sides.
wing·back (wĭng′băk′) *n. Football.* **1.** A back positioned on offense behind or outside of an end. **2.** The position of wingback.
wing·bow (wĭng′bō′) *n.* A mark of color on the bend of the wing in a domestic fowl.
wing chair *n.* An armchair with a high back from which project large, enclosing side pieces.
wing·ding (wĭng′dĭng′) *n.* A lavish or lively party or celebration. [Orig. unknown.]
winged (wĭngd, wĭng′ĭd) *adj.* **1.** Having wings or winglike appendages. **2.** Moving on or as if on wings; flying. **3.** Soaring; elevated; sublime. **4.** Swift; fleet.
wing-foot·ed (wĭng′fo͝ot′ĭd) *adj.* Swift; fleet.

ă pat / ā pay / âr care / ä father / b bib / ch church / d deed / ĕ pet / ē be / f fife / g gag / h hat / hw which / ĭ pit / ī pie / îr pier / j judge / k kick / l lid, needle / m mum / n no, sudden / ng thing / ŏ pot / ō toe / ô paw, for / oi noise / ou out / o͝o took / o͞o boot /

wing·less (wĭng′lĭs) *adj.* Having no wings or rudimentary wings.
wing·let (wĭng′lĭt) *n.* A small or rudimentary wing.
wing loading *n.* The gross weight of an airplane divided by the wing area. Used in stress analysis.
wing nut *n.* A nut with winglike projections for thumb and forefinger leverage in turning.
wing·o·ver (wĭng′ō′vər) *n.* A flight maneuver or stunt in which a plane enters a climbing turn until almost stalled and is allowed to fall while the turn is continued until normal flight is attained in a direction opposite the original heading.
wing·span (wĭng′spăn′) *n.* **1.** The linear distance between the extremities of an airfoil. **2.** Wingspread.
wing·spread (wĭng′sprĕd′) *n.* The distance between the tips of the wings when fully extended, as of an airplane, bird, or insect.
wing tip *n.* **1.** A shoe part, often perforated, that covers the toe and extends backward along the sides of the shoe from a point at the center. **2.** A style of shoe having a wingtip.
wink (wĭngk) *v.* **winked, wink·ing, winks.** —*intr.* **1.** To close and open the eyelid of one eye deliberately, as to convey a message, signal, or suggestion. **2.** To close and open the eyelids of both eyes; blink. **3.** To shine fitfully; twinkle: *harbor lights winking in the distance.* —*tr.* **1.** To close and open (an eye or the eyes) rapidly. **2.** To signal or express by winking. —*n.* **1.** The act of winking. **2.** The time required for a wink. **3.** A signal or hint conveyed by winking. **4.** A gleam; twinkle. **5.** *Informal.* A brief moment of sleep. ***—phrasal verbs.*** **wink at.** To pretend not to see: *winked at corruption in his ministry.* **wink out. 1.** To come to a close; end. **2.** To cease shining. [ME *winken,* to close one's eyes < OE *wincian.*]
win·kle (wĭng′kəl) *n.* The periwinkle (sense 2).
win·na·ble (wĭn′ə-bəl) *adj.* Capable of being won or achieved.
Win·ne·ba·go (wĭn′ə-bā′gō) *n., pl.* **Winnebago** or **-gos** or **-goes. 1.** A tribe of North American Indians, inhabiting eastern Wisconsin. **2.** A member of the Winnebago. **3.** The Siouan language of the Winnebago.
win·ner (wĭn′ər) *n.* **1.** One that wins, esp. a successful person or a victor in sports. **2.** *Slang.* One of exceptionally poor quality or character: *That guy's a real winner.*
winner's circle *n.* An enclosed area at a racetrack where the winning horse and jockey are brought for awards and publicity.
win·ning (wĭn′ĭng) *adj.* **1.** Successful; victorious. **2.** Charming: *a winning personality.* —*n.* **1.** The act of one that wins; victory. **2.** Often **winnings.** Something won, esp. money. **3.** A section of a mine that has been recently prepared or opened for working. **—win′ning·ly** *adv.* **—win′ning·ness** *n.*
winning gallery *n.* In court tennis, an opening below the side penthouse.
winning post *n.* The post at the end of a racecourse.
win·now (wĭn′ō) *v.* **-nowed, -now·ing, -nows.** —*tr.* **1.** To separate the chaff from (grain) by means of a current of air. **2.** To blow (chaff) off or away. **3.** To blow away; scatter. **4.** To blow upon; cause to flutter or fly. **5.** To examine closely in order to separate the good from the bad; sift. **6.** To separate (a desirable or undesirable part). —*intr.* **1.** To separate grain from chaff. **2.** To separate the good from the bad. —*n.* **1.** A device for winnowing grain. **2.** An act of winnowing. [ME *wynewer* < OE *windwian* < *wind,* wind.] **—win′now·er** *n.*
win·o (wī′nō) *n., pl.* **-os.** *Slang.* One who is habitually drunk on wine.
win·some (wĭn′səm) *adj.* Winning; charming. [ME *winsum* < OE *wynsum* < *wynn,* joy.] **—win′some·ly** *adv.* **—win′some·ness** *n.*
win·ter (wĭn′tər) *n.* **1.** The usually coldest season of the year, occurring between autumn and spring, extending in the Northern Hemisphere from the winter solstice to the vernal equinox, and popularly considered to comprise December, January, and February. **2.** A year as expressed through the recurrence of the winter season. **3.** A period of time characterized by coldness, misery, barrenness, or death. ***—modifier:*** *winter grains; a winter crop; winter clothing.* —*v.* **-tered, -ter·ing, -ters.** —*intr.* To spend the winter. —*tr.* To lodge, keep, or care for during the winter: *wintering the sheep in the stable.* [ME < OE.]
winter aconite *n.* A frequently cultivated European plant, *Eranthis hyemalis,* having a solitary yellow flower that blooms in winter or early spring.
win·ter·ber·ry (wĭn′tər-bĕr′ē) *n.* Any of several North American shrubs of the genus *Ilex,* having showy red berries.
winter cherry *n.* A frequently cultivated Eurasian plant, *Physalis alkekengi,* having red berries enclosed in inflated papery, orange-red seed cases.
win·ter-feed (wĭn′tər-fēd′) *tr.v.* **-fed** (-fĕd′), **-feed·ing, -feeds.** To feed (livestock) when grazing is not possible.
win·ter·green (wĭn′tər-grēn′) *n.* **1. a.** A low-growing plant, *Gaultheria procumbens,* of eastern North America, having white or pinkish flowers, aromatic evergreen leaves, and spicy, edible red berries. **b.** An oil or flavoring obtained from the wintergreen. **2.** Any of several plants similar or related to the wintergreen, such as the pipsissewa. [Transl. of Du. *wintergroen.*]
win·ter·ize (wĭn′tə-rīz′) *tr.v.* **-ized, -iz·ing, -iz·es.** To prepare or equip (an automobile, for example) for winter weather. **—win′ter·i·za′tion** *n.*
win·ter·kill (wĭn′tər-kĭl′) *v.* **-killed, -kill·ing, -kills.** —*tr.* To kill (plants, for example) by exposing to extremely cold winter weather. —*intr.* To die from exposure to cold winter weather. Used esp. of plants. —*n.* Death, as of plants, resulting from exposure to winter weather.
winter melon *n.* A variety of melon, *Cucumis melo inodorus,* having fruit with sweet, usually light-colored flesh. [Transl. of Chin. *dong[1] gua[1].*]
winter purslane *n.* A plant, *Montia perfoliata,* of western North America, having small white flowers and leaves sometimes eaten in salads.
winter savory *n.* Savory[2] (sense 1).
winter solstice *n.* *Astron.* A solstice (sense 1).
winter squash *n.* Any of several thick-rinded varieties of squash, such as the acorn squash, that can be stored for long periods.
win·ter·time (wĭn′tər-tīm′) *n.* The winter season.
winter wheat *n.* Wheat planted in the autumn and harvested the following spring or early summer.
win·try (wĭn′trē) also **win·ter·y** (wĭn′tə-rē) *adj.* **-tri·er, -tri·est** also **-i·er, -i·est. 1.** Belonging to or characteristic of winter; cold. **2.** Suggestive of winter; cheerless: *a wintry smile.* **—win′tri·ly** *adv.* **—win′tri·ness** *n.*
win·y (wī′nē) *adj.* **-i·er, -i·est.** Having the qualities or taste of wine; intoxicating; heady.
winze (wĭnz) *n.* In mining, an inclined or vertical shaft or passage between levels. [Orig. unknown.]
wipe (wīp) *tr.v.* **wiped, wip·ing, wipes. 1.** To subject to light rubbing or friction, as of a cloth or paper, in order to clean or dry. **2.** To remove by rubbing: *wipe off dirt; wipe away grease.* **3.** To rub, move, or pass over something. **4.** *Slang.* To defeat decisively esp. in a sports event. **5.** To form (a joint) in plumbing by spreading solder with a piece of cloth or leather. ***—phrasal verbs.*** **wipe out. 1.** To destroy; annihilate. **2.** *Informal.* To murder. **3.** In surfing, to lose balance and fall or jump off a surfboard. **wipe up.** To destroy; annihilate. —*n.* **1.** The act of wiping. **2.** A wiper. **3.** A blow; swipe. **4.** *Informal.* A jeer; gibe. [ME *wipen* < OE *wīpian.*]
wipe·out (wīp′out′) *n.* **1. a.** An act or an instance of wiping out. **b.** Complete destruction. **2.** In surfing, a fall from the board, as from being knocked off by a wave.
wip·er (wī′pər) *n.* **1.** One that wipes. **2.** A device designed for wiping, as for a windshield. **3.** A cam that projects from a rotating horizontal shaft to activate another machine part. **4.** *Elect.* A movable electrical contact, as in a rheostat.
wire (wīr) *n.* **1.** A usually pliable metallic strand or rod made in many lengths and diameters, sometimes clad and often electrically insulated, used chiefly for structural support or to conduct electricity. **2.** A group of wire strands bundled or twisted together as a functional unit; cable. **3.** Something resembling a wire, as in slenderness or stiffness. **4.** The telegraph service. **5.** A telegram. **6.** An open telephone connection. **7.** The screen on which sheets of paper are formed in a papermaking machine. **8.** The finish line of a racetrack. **9. wires. a.** The system of wires employed in manipulating puppets in a show. **b.** Hidden controlling influences affecting a person or a group. **10.** *Slang.* A pickpocket. —*v.* **wired, wir·ing, wires.** —*tr.* **1.** To bind, connect, or attach with a wire or wires. **2.** To string (beads, for example) on wire. **3.** To equip with a system of electrical wires. **4.** To send by telegraph: *wire congratulations.* **5.** To send a telegram to. —*intr.* To send a telegram. ***—idioms.*** **get (in) under the wire.** To arrive somewhere or finish something just in the nick of time. **pull wires.** To use secret, often underhand, means to accomplish something; manipulate. [ME, slender metal rod < OE.]
wire cloth *n.* A mesh woven of fine wire.
wired (wīrd) *adj.* *Slang.* **1.** In a fever of excitement; hyper. **2.** Equipped with or wearing an electronic eavesdropping device: *a wired hotel room.*
wire-draw (wīr′drô′) *tr.v.* **-drew** (-drōō′), **-drawn** (-drôn′), **-draw·ing, -draws. 1.** To draw (metal) into wire. **2.** To treat (a subject, for example) with great length, excessive detail, or overrefinement; spin out. **—wire′draw′er** *n.*
wire gauge *n.* **1.** A gauge for measuring the diameter of wire, usually in the form of a disk having variously sized slots in its periphery or a long graduated plate with similar slots along its edge. **2.** A standardized system of wire sizes.
wire gauze *n.* A material woven of very fine wires.
wire glass *n.* Sheet glass reinforced with wire netting.
wire·grass (wīr′grăs′) *n.* Any of various grasses having tough, wiry roots or rootstocks, such as Bermuda grass.
wire-haired (wīr′hârd′) *adj.* Having a coat of stiff, wiry hair. Used of breeds of dogs.
wire·less (wīr′lĭs) *adj.* Without wires. —*n.* **1.** A radio telegraph or telephone system. **2.** A message transmitted by wireless telegraph or telephone. **3.** *Chiefly Brit.* Radio. —*v.* **-lessed, -less·ing, -less·es.** —*tr.* To communicate with by wireless. —*intr.* To communicate by wireless.
wireless telegraphy *n.* Telegraphy by radio rather than by long-distance transmission lines.

Windsor chair

wine cellar

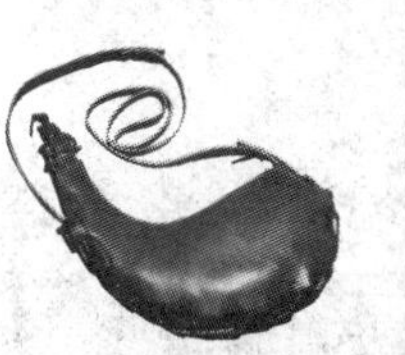

wineskin

wing chair

wintergreen

wisteria

witchcraft
17th-century witchcraft trial in Salem, Massachusetts

witches' Sabbath

wireless telephone *n.* A radiotelephone.
wire·man (wīr'mən) *n.* One who works with electric wiring; lineman.
wire netting *n.* Netting made of woven wire, as for fences.
Wire·pho·to (wīr'fō'tō). A trademark for a photograph electrically transmitted over telephone wires.
wire·pull·er (wīr'po͝ol'ər) *n.* **1.** One who pulls wires or strings, as of puppets. **2.** One who uses subterfuge, private influence, or underhand means in order to reach a goal.
wir·er (wīr'ər) *n.* **1.** A trapper who uses wire traps to snare game. **2.** One that wires.
wire recorder *n.* A forerunner of the tape recorder that recorded sound on a spool of wire rather than on magnetic tape.
wire rope *n.* A rope composed of twisted strands of wire.
wire·tap (wīr'tăp') *n.* **1.** A concealed listening or recording device connected to a communications circuit. **2.** The act of installing a wiretap. —*v.* **-tapped, -tap·ping, -taps.** —*tr.* **1.** To connect a wiretap to. **2.** To monitor (a telephone line) by means of a wiretap. —*intr.* To install or monitor by a wiretap. **—wire'tap'per** *n.*
wire·work (wīr'wûrk') *n.* **1.** Wire fabric. **2.** Articles made of wire or wire fabric.
wire·worm (wīr'wûrm') *n.* **1.** The wirelike larva of various click beetles, causing severe damage by boring into the roots of many kinds of plants. **2.** Any of various millipedes.
wire-wove (wīr'wōv') *adj.* **1.** Denoting a high grade of writing paper with a smooth finish. **2.** Made of woven wire.
wir·ing (wīr'ĭng) *n.* **1.** The act of attaching, connecting, or installing electric wires. **2.** A system of electric wires.
wir·ra (wĭr'ə) *interj. Ir.* Used to express sorrow. [< Ir. Gael. *a Muire,* O Mary.]
wir·y (wīr'ē) *adj.* **-i·er, -i·est. 1.** Of or relating to wire. **2.** Wirelike; kinky: *wiry hair.* **3.** Sinewy and lean; slender but tough: *a wiry farm hand.* **—wir'i·ly** *adv.* **—wir'i·ness** *n.*
wis·dom (wĭz'dəm) *n.* **1.** Understanding of what is true, right, or lasting. **2.** Common sense; good judgment: *"It is a characteristic of wisdom not to do desperate things"* (Thoreau). **3.** Learning; erudition. [ME < OE *wīsdōm* < *wīs,* wise.]
Wisdom of Jesus, the Son of Si·rach (sī'răk') *n.* See table at **Bible.**
Wisdom of So·lo·mon (sŏl'ə-mən) *n.* See table at **Bible.**
wisdom tooth *n.* One of four molars, the last on each side of both jaws, usually erupting much later than the others. [< NLat. *dentes sapientiae,* teeth of wisdom, from their usu. being cut around the age of 20.]
wise¹ (wīz) *adj.* **wis·er, wis·est. 1.** Having wisdom or discernment for what is true, right, or lasting; judicious: *a wise leader.* **2. a.** Exhibiting common sense; prudent: *a wise decision.* **b.** Shrewd; crafty. **3.** Having great learning; erudite: *a wise man.* **4.** Having knowledge or information; informed: *was wise to his opponent's intentions.* **5.** *Slang.* Offensively self-assured; arrogant: *a wise child who talked back.* **—*phrasal verb.* wise up.** *Slang.* To become or make aware or sophisticated. **—*idiom.* get wise.** *Slang.* **1.** To learn the facts or become aware: *Get wise and stop fighting the system.* **2.** To become provocatively insolent: *a student who got wise with the teacher.* [ME < OE *wīs.*] **—wise'ly** *adv.*
wise² (wīz) *n.* Method or manner of doing; fashion; way: *in no wise; in this wise; in any wise.* [ME < OE *wīse.*]
-wise *suff.* **1.** In a specified manner, direction, or position: *clockwise.* **2.** With reference to; in regard to: *dollarwise.* [ME < OE *-wīsan* < *-wīse,* manner.]
Usage: The suffix *-wise* has a long history of use in the sense "in the manner or direction of": *clockwise, likewise, otherwise, slantwise.* In recent times, *-wise* has been in vogue as a suffix meaning "with relation to" and attachable to any noun: *saleswise, inflationwise.* But indiscriminate use of these coinages can lead to confusion, as the exact nature of the relation the writer intends is not always clear from the context. Most new or temporary coinages of this sort are thus unacceptable in writing, and are considered by many to be inappropriate in speech. The following typical examples are unacceptable in general speech to a large majority of the Usage Panel: *The report is not encouraging saleswise. Taxwise, it is an unattractive arrangement.*
wise·a·cre (wīz'ā'kər) *n. Informal.* An offensively self-assured person. [MDu. *wijsseggher,* soothsayer, alteration of OHG *wīssago,* seer.]
wise·crack (wīz'krăk') *Slang.* —*n.* A flippant, commonly sardonic remark or retort. —*intr.v.* **-cracked, -crack·ing, -cracks.** To make or utter a wisecrack. **—wise'crack'er** *n.*
wise guy *n. Slang.* An offensively self-assured person.
wis·en·heim·er also **weis·en·heim·er** (wīz'ən-hī'mər) *n. Informal.* An offensively self-assured person. [< WISE + G. *-enheimer* (as in G. surnames such as *Oppenheimer*).]
wi·sent (vē'zĕnt') *n.* The European bison, *Bison bonasus.* [G. < OHG *wisunt.*]
wish (wĭsh) *n.* **1.** A desire, longing, or strong inclination for a specific thing. **2.** An expression or confession of a desire, longing, or strong inclination; petition. **3.** Something desired or longed for. —*v.* **wished, wish·ing, wish·es.** —*tr.* **1.** To desire or long for; want. **2.** To entertain or express wishes for; bid: *He wished her good night.* **3.** To call or invoke upon: *I wish him luck.* **4.** To order or entreat: *I wish you to go.* **5.** To impose or force; foist: *They wished a hard job on him.* —*intr.* **1.** To have or feel a desire: *wish for the moon.* **2.** To express a wish. [ME *wisshen* < OE *wȳscan.*] **—wish'er** *n.*
wish·bone (wĭsh'bōn') *n.* The forked bone, or furcula, anterior to the breastbone of most birds, formed by the fusion of the clavicles. [From the superstition that when two people pull it apart a wish will be fulfilled for the person who retains the longer piece.]
wish·ful (wĭsh'fəl) *adj.* Having or expressing a wish or longing. **—wish'ful·ly** *adv.* **—wish'ful·ness** *n.*
wish fulfillment *n.* **1.** The gratification of a desire. **2.** *Psychoanal.* The satisfaction of a desire or the release of tension by the exercise of imagination.
wishful thinking *n.* Erroneous identification of one's own wishes with reality.
wish-wash (wĭsh'wŏsh', -wôsh') *n. Informal.* A thin, watery drink; slops. [Redup. of WASH.]
wish·y-wash·y (wĭsh'ē-wŏsh'ē, -wô'shē) *adj.* **-i·er, -i·est.** *Informal.* **1.** Watery; thin. **2.** Lacking in strength or purpose; feeble. [Redup. of *washy* < WASH.]
wisp (wĭsp) *n.* **1.** A small bunch or bundle, as of straw, hair, or grass. **2. a.** One that is thin, frail, or slight. **b.** A thin or faint streak or fragment, as of smoke or clouds. **3.** A fleeting trace or indication; hint: *a wisp of a smile.* **4.** A flock of birds, esp. of snipe. **5.** Ignis fatuus. —*v.* **wisped, wisp·ing, wisps.** —*tr.* To twist into a wisp. —*intr.* To drift in wisps: *smoke wisping from chimneys.* [ME.] **—wisp'y** *adj.*
wist (wĭst) *v. Archaic.* Past tense and past participle of **wit².**
wis·ter·i·a (wĭ-stîr'ē-ə) also **wis·tar·i·a** (wĭ-stâr'ē-ə) *n.* Any of several climbing woody vines of the genus *Wisteria,* having compound leaves and drooping clusters of showy purplish or white flowers. [NLat. *Wisteria,* genus name, after Caspar *Wistar* (1761–1818).]
wist·ful (wĭst'fəl) *adj.* Full of a melancholy yearning; longing pensively; wishful. [< obs. *wistly,* intently.] **—wist'ful·ly** *adv.* **—wist'ful·ness** *n.*
wit¹ (wĭt) *n.* **1.** The natural ability to perceive or know; intelligence. **2. wits. a.** Keenness of perception or discernment; ingenuity: *using one's wits.* **b.** Sound mental faculties; sanity: *scared out of one's wits.* **3. a.** The ability to perceive and express in an ingeniously humorous manner the relationship or similarity between seemingly incongruous or disparate things. **b.** One noted for this ability, esp. one skilled in repartee. **—*idioms.* at one's wits' end.** At the limit of one's mental resources; utterly at a loss. **have (or keep) one's wits about one.** To remain alert or calm, esp. in a crisis. [ME < OE.]
Synonyms: *wit, humor, repartee, sarcasm, irony.* These nouns, related but not always interchangeable, are compared as they denote forms of expression. *Wit* especially implies mental keenness, ability to discern those elements of a situation or condition that relate to what is comic, and talent for making an effective comment on them. *Humor,* closely related, suggests the ability to recognize the incongruity and absurdity inherent in life and to use them as the basis of expression in some medium. Both *wit* and *humor* are associated with amusement or laughter, but *wit* often implies brilliant, pointed, or cutting statement, whereas *humor* is also applicable to what is kindly or broadly funny. *Repartee,* or the exchange of wit, generally in conversation, implies facility in answering quickly and cleverly. *Sarcasm* is usually a form of wit intended to taunt, wound, or subject another to ridicule or contempt. Often it involves *irony,* a form of statement whose witty intent is contrary to, and sometimes the opposite of, the literal meaning of the words employed. In this sense *irony* is often employed to point up mockingly the discrepancies between reality, with its shortcomings, and a more desirable state.
wit² (wĭt) *v.* **wist** (wĭst), **wit·ting,** first and third persons present **wot** (wŏt). *Archaic.* —*tr.* To be or become aware of; learn. —*intr.* To know. **—*idiom.* to wit.** That is to say; namely. [ME < OE *witan.*]
wit·an (wĭt'ăn) *pl.n.* **1.** The members of the witenagemot in Anglo-Saxon England. **2.** The witenagemot. [OE, pl. of *wita,* councilor.]
witch (wĭch) *n.* **1.** A woman who practices sorcery or is believed to have dealings with the devil. **2.** An ugly, vicious old woman; hag. **3.** *Informal.* A bewitching young woman or girl. —*tr.v.* **witched, witch·ing, witch·es. 1.** To work or cast a spell upon; bewitch. **2.** To cause, bring, or effect by witchcraft. [ME *wicche* < OE *wicce,* witch and < OE *wicca,* wizard.]
witch·craft (wĭch'krăft') *n.* **1.** Black magic; sorcery. **2.** A magical or irresistible influence, attraction, or charm.
witch doctor *n.* A medicine man or shaman among primitive peoples.
witch elm *n.* Variant of **wych elm.**
witch·er·y (wĭch'ə-rē) *n., pl.* **-ies. 1.** Sorcery; witchcraft. **2.** Power to charm or fascinate.
witch·es-broom (wĭch'ĭz-bro͞om', -bro͝om') *n.* An abnormal, brushlike growth of weak, closely clustered shoots or branches on a tree or woody plant, caused by fungi or viruses.
witches' Sabbath *n.* An orgy of demons, witches, and sorcerers.

witch grass *n.* **1.** A North American grass, *Panicum capillare,* having branching, purplish panicles. **2.** Couch grass.
witch hazel *n.* **1.** Any of several shrubs of the genus *Hamamelis,* esp. *H. virginiana,* of eastern North America, having yellow flowers that bloom in late autumn or winter. **2.** An alcoholic solution containing an extract of the bark and leaves of the witch hazel, applied externally as a mild astringent. [From Middle English *wyche,* WYCH (ELM) + HAZEL.]
witch-hunt (wĭch′hŭnt′) *n.* A political campaign launched on the pretext of investigating activities subversive to the state. **—witch′-hunt′** *v.* **(-hunt·ed, -hunt·ing, -hunts). —witch′-hunt′er** *n.*
witch·ing (wĭch′ĭng) *adj.* **1.** Pertaining to or appropriate for witchcraft: *the witching hour.* **2.** Having power to charm or enchant; bewitching: *a witching young woman.* —*n.* Witchcraft. **—witch′ing·ly** *adv.*
witch moth *n.* Any of several large moths of the genus *Erebus,* of the southern United States and tropical America. [From its nocturnal habits.]
witch of Ag·ne·si (än-yā′zē) *n.* A planar cubic curve that is symmetric about the *y*-axis and that approaches the *x*-axis as an asymptote. [After Maria Gaetana *Agnesi* (1718–1799).]
wite (wīt) *n. Chiefly Scot.* Blame; fault. [ME < OE *wīte,* punishment.]
wit·e·na·ge·mot (wĭt′n-ə-gə-mōt′) *n.* An Anglo-Saxon advisory council to the king, composed of about 100 nobles, prelates, and other officials, convened at intervals to discuss administrative and judicial affairs. [OE *witena gemōt,* meeting of councilors.]
with (wĭ*th,* wĭth) *prep.* **1.** As a companion of; accompanying: *Who went with him?* **2.** Next to: *Stand with him.* **3.** Having as a possession, attribute, or characteristic: *a man with a moustache.* **4. a.** In a manner characterized by: *perform with skill.* **b.** In the performance, use, or operation of: *had trouble with the car.* **5.** In the charge or keeping of: *She left the letter with the doorman.* **6.** In the opinion or estimation of: *if it's all right with you.* **7.** In support of; on the side of: *Are you with me or against me?* **8.** Of the same opinion or belief as: *He is with us on that.* **9.** In the same group or mixture as; among: *Mix the roses with the fern.* **10.** In the membership or employment of: *He is with a publishing company.* **11.** By the means or agency of: *eat with a fork.* **12.** In spite of: *With all his talent, he could not get a job.* **13.** In the same direction as: *bend with the wind.* **14.** At the same time as: *rise with the sun.* **15.** In regard to: *I am pleased with her.* **16.** In comparison or contrast to: *a dress identical with the one she has just bought.* **17.** Having received: *With her permission, he left.* **18.** And; plus; added to. **19.** In opposition to; against: *wrestling with an opponent.* **20.** As a result or consequence of; under the influence of: *trembling with fear.* **21.** To; onto: *Couple the first car with the second.* **22.** So as to be free of or separated from: *part with a friend.* **23.** In the course of: *We grow older with the hours.* **24.** In proportion to: *wines that improve with age.* **25.** In relationship to: *at ease with his peers.* **26.** As well as; in favorable comparison to: *She sings with the best of them.* **27.** According to the experience or practice of: *With me, it is a question of priorities.* **28.** Used as a function word to indicate close association: *With the advent of the V-1, the Space Age began.* **—idiom. in with.** In league or association with: *He is in with the wrong crowd.* [ME, with, against, from < OE *wið.*]
Usage: *With* does not have the conjunctive force of *and.* Consequently, in the following example the verb is governed by the singular subject and remains singular: *The governor, with his aides, is expected at the fair on Monday.*
with·al (wĭ*th*-ôl′, wĭth-) *adv.* **1.** Besides; in addition: *"And, withal, a wider publicity was given to thought-provoking ideas"* (Holbrook Jackson). **2.** Despite that; nevertheless. **3.** *Archaic.* Therewith. —*prep. Archaic.* With. [ME : *with,* with + *al,* all.]
with·draw (wĭ*th*-drô′, wĭth-) *v.* **-drew** (-dro͞o′), **-drawn** (-drôn′), **-draw·ing, -draws.** —*tr.* **1.** To take back or away; remove. **2.** To recall; retract. —*intr.* **1.** To move or draw back; retire. **2.** To remove oneself from activity or a social or emotional environment. [ME *withdrawen* : *with,* away from + *drawen,* to pull.]
with·draw·al (wĭ*th*-drô′əl, wĭth-) *n.* **1.** The act or process of withdrawing, as: **a.** A retreat or retirement. **b.** A detachment, as from emotional involvement. **c.** A removal from a place or position of something that has been deposited. **2. a.** Termination of the administration of a habit-forming substance. **b.** The physiological readjustment that takes place upon such discontinuation.
with·drawn (wĭ*th*-drôn′, wĭth-) *adj.* **1.** Not readily approached; remote. **2.** Socially retiring; modest; shy. **3.** Emotionally unresponsive.
withe (wĭth, wĭ*th,* wī*th*) *n.* A tough, supple twig, esp. a willow twig, used for binding things together; withy. [ME < OE *wiððe.*]
with·er (wĭ*th*′ər) *v.* **-ered, -er·ing, -ers.** —*intr.* **1.** To dry up or shrivel from or as if from loss of moisture. **2.** To lose freshness; droop. —*tr.* **1.** To cause to shrivel or fade. **2.** To render speechless or incapable of action; stun: *withered her with a glance.* [ME *widderen.*]
with·er·ite (wĭ*th*′ə-rīt′) *n.* A white, yellow, or gray vitreous mineral, chiefly $BaCO_3$. [G. *Witherit,* after William *Withering* (1741–1799).]
withe rod *n.* A shrub, *Viburnum cassinoides,* of eastern North America, having clusters of small white flowers and bluish-black fruit.
with·ers (wĭ*th*′ərz) *pl.n.* The high point of the back of a horse or of a similar animal, located at the base of the neck and between the shoulder blades. [Prob. < obs. *wither-,* against < ME < OE *wiðer-,* from the strain exerted on them when a horse draws a load.]
with·er·shins (wĭ*th*′ər-shĭnz′) also **wid·der·shins** (wĭd′-) *adv.* In the opposite direction; in reverse; counterclockwise. [Alteration of *widdershins* < MLG *weddersinnes* < MHG *widersinnes* < *widersinnen,* to go back : *wider,* back (< OHG *widar*) + *sinnen,* to go (< OHG *sinnan*).]
with·hold (wĭth-hōld′, wĭ*th*-) *v.* **-held** (-hĕld′), **-hold·ing, -holds.** —*tr.* **1.** To keep in check; restrain. **2.** To refrain from giving, granting, or permitting. **3.** To deduct (withholding tax) from an employee's salary. —*intr.* To refrain; forbear. [ME *witholden*: *with,* away from + *holden,* to hold.] **—with·hold′er** *n.*
withholding tax *n.* A portion of an employee's wages or salary withheld by the employer as partial payment of the employee's income tax.
with·in (wĭ*th*-ĭn′, wĭth-) *adv.* **1.** In or into the inner part; inside. **2.** Inside the body, mind, heart, or soul; inwardly. —*prep.* **1.** In the inner part or parts of; inside: *resentment within him.* **2.** Inside the limits or extent of in time, degree, or distance: *within ten miles of home.* **3.** Inside the fixed limits of; not beyond: *lived within her income; acted within the laws of the land.* **4.** In the scope or sphere of: *within the medical profession.* —*n.* An inner position, place, or area: *a revolution from within.* [ME *withinne* < OE *wiðinnan* : *wið,* with + *innan,* into < *in,* in.]
with·in·doors (wĭ*th*-ĭn′dôrz′, -dōrz′, wĭth-) *adv.* Indoors.
with-it (wĭ*th*′ĭt′) *adj. Informal.* Up-to-date; hip.
with·out (wĭ*th*-out′, wĭth-) *adv.* **1.** On the outside: *a sturdy structure within and without.* **2.** With something absent or lacking: *had to do without.* —*prep.* **1.** Not having; lacking: *a family without a car; without doubt.* **2.** At, on, to, or toward the outside or exterior of: *standing without the door.* —*conj. Regional.* Unless: *"You don't know about me without you have read a book by the name of* The Adventures of Tom Sawyer" (Mark Twain). [ME *withouten* < OE *wiðūtan* : *wið,* with + *ūtan,* outside of < *ūt,* out.]
with·out·doors (wĭ*th*-out′dôrz′, -dōrz′, wĭth-) *adv.* Outside of a house or shelter; outdoors.
with·stand (wĭth-stănd′, wĭ*th*-) *v.* **-stood** (-sto͝od′), **-stand·ing, -stands.** —*tr.* To oppose (something) with force; resist. —*intr.* To resist or endure successfully. [ME *withstanden, withstonden* < OE *wiðstandan* : *wið,* against + *standan,* to stand.] **—with·stand′er** *n.*
with·y (wĭ*th*′ē, wĭth′ē) *adj.* **1.** Made of or as flexible as withes; tough. **2.** Wiry and agile. —*n., pl.* **-ies. 1.** A rope or band made of withes. **2. a.** A long, flexible twig, as that of an osier. **b.** A tree or shrub having such twigs. [ME *withye,* flexible twig < OE *wiðig.*]
wit·less (wĭt′lĭs) *adj.* Lacking intelligence or wit; stupid. **—wit′less·ly** *adv.* **—wit′less·ness** *n.*
wit·ling (wĭt′lĭng) *n.* One who has little wit.
wit·loof (wĭt′lōf′) *n.* The endive (sense 2). [Du. : *wit,* white + *loof,* leaf.]
wit·ness (wĭt′nĭs) *n.* **1. a.** One who has seen or heard something. **b.** One who furnishes evidence. **2.** Anything that serves as evidence; sign. **3.** *Law.* **a.** One who is called upon to testify before a court. **b.** One who is called upon to be present at a transaction in order to attest to what takes place. **c.** One who signs his name to a document for the purpose of attesting to its authenticity. **4.** An attestation to a fact, statement, or event. —*v.* **-nessed, -ness·ing, -ness·es.** —*tr.* **1.** To be present at or have personal knowledge of. **2.** To provide or serve as evidence of. **3.** To testify to; bear witness. **4.** To be the setting or site of: *This auditorium witnesses many ceremonies.* **5.** To attest to the legality or authenticity of by signing one's name. —*intr.* To furnish or serve as evidence; testify. [ME < OE < *wit,* knowledge.] **—wit′ness·er** *n.*
witness box *n. Chiefly Brit.* Witness stand.
witness stand *n.* The place in a courtroom from which a witness presents testimony.
wit·ti·cism (wĭt′ĭ-sĭz′əm) *n.* A witty remark or saying. [< WITTY.]
wit·ting (wĭt′ĭng). *Archaic.* Present participle of **wit**[2]. —*adj.* **1.** Aware or conscious. **2.** Done intentionally or with premeditation; deliberate. —*n. Regional.* **1.** Knowledge or awareness; cognizance. **2.** Information obtained and passed on; news. **—wit′ting·ly** *adv.*
wit·tol (wĭt′l) *n. Archaic.* A man who tolerates his wife's infidelity. [ME *wetewold* : *weten,* to know (< OE *witan*) + *(coke)wold,* cuckold. —see CUCKOLD.]
wit·ty (wĭt′ē) *adj.* **-ti·er, -ti·est. 1.** Possessing or demonstrating wit in speech or writing; very clever and humorous. **2.** Characterized by or having the nature of wit: *a witty saying.* **3.** Quick to discern and express amusing insights. **—wit′ti·ly** *adv.* **—wit′ti·ness** *n.*
wive (wīv) *v.* **wived, wiv·ing, wives.** —*tr.* **1.** To marry (a

witch hazel

woman); take as a wife. **2.** To provide a wife for. —*intr.* To marry a woman. [ME *wiven* < OE *wīfian* < *wīf,* wife.]
wi·vern (wī′vərn) *n.* Variant of **wyvern.**
wives[1] (wīvz) *n.* Plural of **wife.**
wives[2] (wīvz) *v.* Third person singular present tense of **wive.**
wiz (wĭz) *n. Informal.* A person considered exceptionally gifted or skilled. [Short for WIZARD.]
wiz·ard (wĭz′ərd) *n.* **1.** A sorcerer or magician. **2.** A skillful or clever person: *a wizard at math.* **3.** *Archaic.* A wise man or sage. —*adj.* **1.** Of or pertaining to wizards or wizardry. **2.** *Chiefly Brit.* Excellent. [ME *wysard* < *wys,* wise < OE *wīs.*]
wiz·ard·ry (wĭz′ər-drē) *n.* The art, skill, or practice of a wizard; witchcraft; sorcery.

wizard

wiz·en (wĭz′ən) *v.* **-ened, -en·ing, -ens.** —*intr.* To wither or sear; dry up; shrivel. —*tr.* To cause to wither or dry up. —*adj.* Shriveled or dried up; withered: *"There would be a day when his face would be wrinkled and wizen"* (Oscar Wilde). [ME *wisenen* < OE *wisnian.*]
wiz·ened (wĭz′ənd) *adj.* Shriveled; wizen.
wo (wō) *n. Archaic.* Variant of **woe.**
woad (wōd) *n.* **1.** An Old World plant, *Isatis tinctoria,* formerly cultivated for its leaves that yield a blue dye. **2.** The dye obtained from the woad. [ME *wode* < OE *wād.*]
woad·wax·en (wōd′wăk′sən) *n.* Dyer's greenweed. [Alteration of WOODWAXEN.]
wob·ble also **wab·ble** (wŏb′əl) *v.* **-bled, -bling, -bles.** —*intr.* **1.** To move erratically from side to side. **2.** To tremble or quaver; shake, as a voice. **3.** To waver or vacillate in one's opinions or feelings. —*tr.* To cause to wobble. —*n.* **1.** The act or an instance of wobbling; unsteady motion. **2.** A tremulous and uncertain tone or sound: *a vocal wobble.* [Prob. < LG *wabbeln.*] **—wob′bler** *n.*
wob·bly (wŏb′lē) *adj.* **-bli·er, -bli·est.** Tending to wobble; unsteady; shaky.
Wob·bly (wŏb′lē) *n., pl.* **-blies.** *Slang.* A member of the Industrial Workers of the World. [Orig. unknown.]
Wo·den also **Wo·dan** (wōd′n) *n. Myth.* The chief Teutonic god, often identified with the Norse god Odin. [OE *Wōden.*]
woe (wō) *n.* **1.** Deep sorrow; grief. **2.** Misfortune; calamity: *economic and political woes.* —*interj.* Used to express sorrow or dismay. [ME < OE *wā,* woe!]
woe·be·gone (wō′bĭ-gôn′, -gŏn′) *adj.* **1.** Mournful or sorrowful in appearance. **2.** Being in a sorry state: *a run-down, woebegone old shack.* [ME *wo begon,* beset with woe.]
woe·ful also **wo·ful** (wō′fəl) *adj.* **1.** Afflicted with woe; mournful. **2.** Causing woe. **3.** Pitiful or deplorable.
wok (wŏk) *n.* A metal pan having a convex bottom and used esp. for frying and steaming in Oriental cooking. [Cantonese.]

wolf

woke (wōk) *v.* A past tense of **wake**[1].
wok·en (wō′kən) *v.* A past participle of **wake**[1].
wold[1] (wōld) *n.* An unforested rolling plain; moor. [ME < OE *weald,* forest.]
wold[2] (wōld) *n.* Variant of **weld**[2].
wolf (wo͝olf) *n., pl.* **wolves** (wo͝olvz). **1. a.** Either of two carnivorous mammals, *Canis lupus,* of northern regions, or *C. rufus* or *C. niger,* of southwestern North America, related to and resembling the dogs. **b.** The fur of such an animal. **2.** Any of various mammals similar or related to the wolf. **3.** The destructive larva of any of various moths, beetles, or flies. **4. a.** One that is rapacious, predatory, and fierce. **b.** *Slang.* A man given to avid amatory pursuit of women. **5.** *Mus.* **a.** A harshness in some tones of a bowed stringed instrument produced by defective vibration. **b.** Dissonance in some intervals of a keyboard instrument tuned to a system of unequal temperament. —*tr.v.* **wolfed, wolf·ing, wolfs.** To eat voraciously: *"The town's big shots were . . . wolfing down the buffet"* (Ralph Ellison). **—*idiom.* cry wolf.** To raise a false alarm. [ME < OE *wulf.*] **—wolf′ish** *adj.* **—wolf′ish·ly** *adv.*

wolverine

wolf·ber·ry (wo͝olf′bĕr′ē) *n.* A shrub, *Symphoricarpos occidentalis,* of western North America, having white berries.
Wolf Cub *n. Chiefly Brit.* A Cub Scout.
wolf dog *n.* **1.** A dog trained to hunt wolves. **2.** The offspring of a dog and a wolf.
Wolff·i·an body (wo͝ol′fē-ən) *n. Biol.* The mesonephros. [After Kasper Friedrich *Wolff* (1733–1794).]
wolf fish *n.* Any of several northern marine fishes of the genus *Anarhichas,* having sharp, powerful teeth.
wolf·hound (wo͝olf′hound′) *n.* Any of various large dogs trained to hunt wolves or other large game.
wolf pack *n.* A group of submarines that attack a single vessel or a convoy.
wolf·ram (wo͝ol′frəm) *n.* Tungsten. [G.]
wolf·ram·ite (wo͝ol′frə-mīt′) *n.* Any of several red-brown to black minerals with the general formula $(Fe,Mn)WO_4$, a major source of tungsten.
wolfs·bane (wo͝olfs′bān′) *n.* The monkshood.
wol·las·ton·ite (wo͝ol′ə-stə-nīt′) *n.* A mineral, essentially $CaSiO_3$, found in metamorphic rocks and used in various ceramics, paints, plastics, and cements. [After William H. *Wollaston* (1766–1828).]
Wo·lof (wō′lŏf′) *n.* A Niger-Congo language of Senegal.
wol·ver·ine (wo͝ol′və-rēn′) *n.* **1.** A carnivorous mammal, *Gulo gulo* or *G. luscus,* of northern regions, having dark fur and a bushy tail. **2. Wolverine.** A native or inhabitant of Michigan. [< WOLF.]

wooden Indian

wolves (wo͝olvz) *n.* Plural of **wolf.**
wom·an (wo͝om′ən) *n., pl.* **wom·en** (wĭm′ĭn). **1.** An adult female human being. **2.** Women collectively; womankind: *Woman is wise.* **3.** Feminine quality or aspect; womanliness: *brought out the woman in me.* **4.** A maidservant. **5.** A mistress; paramour. **6.** *Informal.* A wife. **—*modifier:* *a woman athlete.*** [ME *wumman* < OE *wīfman* : *wīf,* wife + *man,* person.]
wom·an·hood (wo͝om′ən-ho͝od′) *n.* **1.** The state of being a woman. **2.** Woman's nature. **3.** Womankind.
wom·an·ish (wo͝om′ə-nĭsh) *adj.* **1.** Characteristic of a woman; womanlike. **2.** Effeminate and weak: *a womanish old man.* **—wom′an·ish·ly** *adv.* **—wom′an·ish·ness** *n.*
wom·an·ize (wo͝om′ə-nīz′) *v.* **-ized, -iz·ing, -iz·es.** —*tr.* To give feminine characteristics to. —*intr.* To pursue women illicitly or excessively. **—wom′an·iz′er** *n.*
wom·an·kind (wo͝om′ən-kīnd′) *n.* Female human beings collectively; women.
wom·an·ly (wo͝om′ən-lē) *adj.* **-li·er, -li·est.** Having the becoming qualities of a woman. **—wom′an·li·ness** *n.*
wom·an·pow·er (wo͝om′ən-pou′ər) *n.* Power in terms of the women available to a particular group, or required for a particular task.
woman suffrage *n.* The right of women to vote; exercise of the franchise by women. **—wom′an-suf′fra·gist** *n.*
womb (wo͞om) *n.* **1.** *Anat.* The uterus (sense 1). **2. a.** A place where something is generated. **b.** A protective and confining organ, receptacle, or area. **3.** *Obs.* The belly. [ME < OE *wamb.*]
wom·bat (wŏm′băt′) *n.* Either of two Australian marsupials, *Phascolomis ursinus* or *Lasiorhinus latifrons,* somewhat resembling a small bear. [Native word in Australia.]
wom·en (wĭm′ĭn) *n.* Plural of **woman.**
wom·en·folk (wĭm′ĭn-fōk′) also **wom·en·folks** (-fōks′) *pl.n.* **1.** Women collectively. **2.** The female members of a community or family.
women's rights *pl.n.* **1.** Economic, political, legal, and social rights for women equal to those granted men. **2.** A movement in support of women's rights.
women's room *n.* A restroom for women.
won[1] (wŭn) *intr.v.* **wonned, won·ning, wons.** *Archaic.* To dwell; abide. [ME *wonen* < OE *wunian.*]
won[2] (wôn) *n., pl.* **won.** See table at **currency.** [Korean.]
won[3] (wŭn) *v.* Past tense and past participle of **win.**
won·der (wŭn′dər) *n.* **1. a.** Something that arouses awe, astonishment, surprise, or admiration; marvel: *"The decision of one age or country is a wonder to another"* (John Stuart Mill). **b.** The emotion thus aroused. **2.** A feeling of puzzlement or doubt. **3.** Often **Wonder.** A monumental human creation regarded with awe, esp. one of seven monuments of the ancient world that appeared on various lists of late antiquity. —*v.* **-dered, -der·ing, -ders.** —*intr.* **1.** To have a feeling of awe or admiration; marvel. **2.** To be filled with curiosity or doubt. —*tr.* To have doubts or curiosity about. ***idiom.* for a wonder.** Surprisingly. [ME < OE *wundor.*] **—won′der·er** *n.*
won·der·ful (wŭn′dər-fəl) *adj.* **1.** Capable of exciting wonder; astonishing: *"The Greenland whale is one of the most wonderful animals in the world"* (Darwin). **2.** Admirable; excellent. **—won′der·ful·ly** *adv.* **—won′der·ful·ness** *n.*
won·der·land (wŭn′dər-lănd′) *n.* **1.** A marvelous imaginary realm. **2.** A marvelous real place or scene.
won·der·ment (wŭn′dər-mənt) *n.* **1.** Astonishment, awe, or surprise. **2.** Something that produces wonder; marvel. **3.** Puzzlement or curiosity.
won·der·work (wŭn′dər-wûrk′) *n.* A miracle or marvel. **—won′der·work′er** *n.* **—won′der·work′ing** *adj.*
won·drous (wŭn′drəs) *adj.* Wonderful. —*adv. Archaic.* To a wonderful or remarkable extent. **—won′drous·ly** *adv.* **—won′drous·ness** *n.*
won·ky (wŏng′kē) *adj.* **-ki·er, -ki·est.** *Chiefly Brit.* **1.** Shaky; feeble. **2.** Wrong; awry. [Prob. alteration of dial. *wankle* < ME *wankel* < OE *wancol.*]
wont (wônt, wōnt, wŭnt) *adj.* **1.** Accustomed or used to: *"The poor man is wont to complain that this is a cold world"* (Thoreau). **2.** Apt or likely: *He is wont to arrive early.* —*n.* Usage or custom: *It is not my wont to look back to the past.* —*v.* **wont, wont** or **wont·ed, wont·ing, wonts.** —*tr.* To make (someone) accustomed to. —*intr.* To be in the habit of. [ME < p.part. of *wonen,* to be used to, dwell. —see WON[1].]
won't (wōnt). Will not.
wont·ed (wôn′tĭd, wōn′-, wŭn′-) *adj.* Accustomed; usual: *answered with his wonted rapidity.*
won ton (wŏn′ tŏn′) *n., pl.* **won tons. 1.** In Chinese cookery, a noodle-dough dumpling filled with spiced minced pork, usually served in soup. **2.** Soup containing won tons. [Cantonese *wan tan.*]
woo (wo͞o) *v.* **wooed, woo·ing, woos.** —*tr.* **1.** To seek the affection of with intent to marry. **2. a.** To seek to achieve; try to gain. **b.** To tempt or invite. **3.** To entreat, solicit, or importune. —*intr.* To court a woman. [ME *wowen* < OE *wōgian.*] **—woo′er** *n.*
wood (wo͝od) *n.* **1. a.** The tough, fibrous cellular substance constituting the xylem of trees and shrubs, lying beneath the

bark and consisting largely of cellulose and lignin. **b.** This substance, often cut and dried, used for building material, as fuel, and for many other purposes. **2.** Often **woods.** A dense growth of trees; forest. **3.** An object made of wood, esp.: **a.** A woodwind. **b.** A golf club having a wooden head. ***—modifier:*** *a wood box; a wood screw.* *—v.* **wood·ed, wood·ing, woods.** *—tr.* **1.** To fuel with wood. **2.** To cover with trees; forest. *—intr.* To gather or be supplied with wood. [ME *wode* < OE *wudu.*]

wood alcohol *n.* Methyl alcohol.

wood anemone *n.* Either of two plants, *Anemone quinquefolia,* of eastern North America, or *A. nemorosa,* of Europe, having deeply divided leaves and a solitary white flower.

wood betony *n.* The lousewort.

wood·bin (wo͝od′bĭn′) *n.* A box for holding firewood.

wood·bine (wo͝od′bīn′) *n.* Any of various climbing vines, esp.: **a.** An Old World honeysuckle, *Lonicera periclymenum,* having yellowish flowers. **b.** The Virginia creeper. [ME wodebinde < OE *wudubinde* : *wudu,* wood + *bindan,* to bind.]

wood·block (wo͝od′blŏk′) *n.* **1.** A woodcut. **2.** Also **wood block.** *Mus.* A hollow block of wood struck with a drumstick to produce percussive effects in an orchestra.

wood·bor·er (wo͝od′bôr′ər, -bōr′ər) *n.* Any of various insects, insect larvae, or mollusks that bore into wood.

wood·carv·ing (wo͝od′kär′vĭng) *n.* **1.** The art of carving in wood. **2.** An object carved from wood. **—wood′carv′er** *n.*

wood·chat (wo͝od′chăt′) *n.* An Old World bird, *Lanius senator,* having black and white plumage with a reddish crown.

wood·chuck (wo͝od′chŭk′) *n.* A common rodent, *Marmota monax,* of northern and eastern North America, having a short-legged, heavy-set body and grizzled brownish fur. [By folk ety. < Cree *oček.*]

wood coal *n.* **1.** Charcoal. **2.** Lignite.

wood·cock (wo͝od′kŏk′) *n., pl.* **woodcock** or **-cocks.** Either of two related game birds, *Scolopax rusticola,* of the Old World, or *Philohela minor,* of North America, having brownish plumage, short legs, and a long bill. [ME *wodecok* < OE *wuducocc* : *wudu,* wood + *cocc,* cock.]

wood·craft (wo͝od′krăft′) *n.* **1.** Skill and experience in matters pertaining to the woods, as hunting, fishing, or camping. **2.** The act, process, or art of working with wood.

wood·cut (wo͝od′kŭt′) *n.* **1.** A piece of wood upon which a design for printing is engraved, esp. in the plane of the grain. **2.** A print made from a woodcut.

wood·cut·ter (wo͝od′kŭt′ər) *n.* One that cuts wood or trees. **—wood′cut′ting** *n.*

wood duck *n.* A brightly colored American duck, *Aix sponsa,* that nests in trees.

wood·ed (wo͝od′ĭd) *adj.* Having trees or woods.

wood·en (wo͝od′n) *adj.* **1.** Made or consisting of wood. **2.** Stiff and unnatural; without spirit: *a wooden performance; a wooden smile.* **3.** Clumsy and awkward; ungainly. **—wood′en·ly** *adv.* **—wood′en·ness** *n.*

wood engraving *n.* **1. a.** A piece of wood upon which a design for printing is engraved, usually on the end grain. **b.** A print made from such a piece of wood. **2.** The art or process of making wood engravings.

wood·en·head (wo͝od′n-hĕd′) *n.* A blockhead. **—wood′en·head′ed** *adj.*

wooden Indian *n.* A wooden effigy of an American Indian brave holding a cluster of cigars and used formerly as the emblem of a tobacconist.

wood ibis *n.* Any of several large wading birds of the subfamily Mycteriinae, related to and resembling the storks, esp. *Mycteria americana,* of the New World.

wood·ie (wo͝od′ē) *n.* Variant of **woody.**

wood·land (wo͝od′lənd, -lănd′) *n.* Land having a cover of trees and shrubs. ***—modifier:*** *woodland flowers.* **—wood′land·er** (-lən-dər) *n.*

wood·lark (wo͝od′lärk′) *n.* An Old World songbird, *Lullula arborea,* resembling but smaller than the skylark.

wood lot *n.* An area restricted to the growing of forest trees.

wood louse *n.* The sow bug.

wood·man (wo͝od′mən) *n.* A woodsman.

wood·note (wo͝od′nōt′) *n.* A song or call of or characteristic of a woodland bird.

wood nymph *n.* **1.** A nymph of the forest. **2.** Any of several tropical hummingbirds of the genera *Thalurania* and *Cyanophaia.* **3.** Any of various butterflies of the family Satyridae, esp. *Cercyonis pegala,* having brownish wings with dark eyespots.

wood·peck·er (wo͝od′pĕk′ər) *n.* Any of various birds of the family Picidae, having strong claws and a stiff tail adapted for clinging to and climbing trees, and a chisellike bill for drilling through bark and wood.

wood pigeon *n.* A large Eurasian pigeon, *Columba palumbus,* having a white band on each wing.

wood·pile (wo͝od′pīl′) *n.* A pile of wood, esp. when stacked for use as fuel.

wood·print (wo͝od′prĭnt′) *n.* A woodcut.

wood pulp *n.* Any of various cellulose pulps ground from wood, chemically processed, and used esp. to make paper.

wood pussy *n. Informal.* A skunk.

wood rat *n.* Pack rat (sense 1).

wood·ruff (wo͝od′rəf, -rŭf′) *n.* Any of several plants of the genus *Asperula,* esp. *A. odorata,* native to Eurasia, having small white flowers and narrow, fragrant leaves used as flavoring and in sachets. [ME *woderofe* < OE *wudurofe.*]

wood·shed (wo͝od′shĕd′) *n.* A shed in which firewood is stored.

woods·man (wo͝odz′mən) *n.* One who works or lives in the woods or is versed in woodcraft; forester.

wood sorrel *n.* Any of various plants of the genus *Oxalis,* having compound leaves with three leaflets and yellow, white, or pinkish flowers.

wood spirits *n.* Methyl alcohol.

wood sugar *n.* Xylose.

woods·y (wo͝od′zē) *adj.* **-i·er, -i·est.** Of, relating to, characteristic of, or suggestive of the woods.

wood tar *n.* A black, syruplike viscous fluid that is a by-product of the destructive distillation of wood and is used in pitch, preservatives, and medicines.

wood thrush *n.* A North American thrush, *Hylocichla mustelina,* having a melodious song.

wood tick *n.* Any of various ticks of the genus *Dermacentor* that transmit the microorganism that causes Rocky Mountain spotted fever and tularemia in humans.

wood·turn·ing (wo͝od′tûr′nĭng) *n.* The art or process of shaping wood into forms on a lathe. **—wood′turn′er** *n.*

wood vinegar *n.* Pyroligneous acid.

wood·wax·en (wo͝od′wăk′sən) *n.* The dyer's greenweed. [ME *wodewaxen* < OE *wudu weaxe* : *wudu,* wood + *weaxan,* to grow.]

wood·wind (wo͝od′wĭnd′) *n.* **1.** Any of a group of musical wind instruments that includes the bassoons, clarinets, flutes, oboes, and sometimes the saxophones. **2. woodwinds.** The section of an orchestra or band composed of woodwind instruments.

wood·work (wo͝od′wûrk′) *n.* Objects made of or work done in wood, esp. wooden interior fittings in a house, such as moldings, doors, staircases, or windowsills.

wood·worm (wo͝od′wûrm′) *n.* A worm or insect larva that bores into wood.

wood·y (wo͝od′ē) *adj.* **-i·er, -i·est. 1.** Forming or consisting of wood; ligneous: *woody tissue.* **2.** Characterized by the presence of wood or xylem: *woody plants.* **3.** Characteristic or suggestive of wood: *a woody smell.* **4.** Abounding in trees; wooded. *—n.* Also **wood·ie** *pl.* **-ies.** A station wagon with exterior wood paneling.

woof[1] (wo͝of, wo͞of) *n.* **1.** The threads that run crosswise in a woven fabric, at right angles to the warp threads. **2.** The texture of a fabric. **3.** A basically essential element. [Alteration of ME *oof* < OE *ōwef* : *ō-,* on + *wefan,* to weave.]

woof[2] (wo͝of) *n.* **1.** The deep, gruff bark of a dog. **2.** A sound similar to a woof. [Imit.]

woof·er (wo͝of′ər) *n.* A loudspeaker designed to reproduce bass frequencies. [< WOOF[2].]

wool (wo͝ol) *n.* **1.** The dense, soft, often curly hair forming the coat of sheep and certain other mammals, valued as a textile fabric. **2.** A material or garment made of wool. **3.** Any filamentous or fibrous covering or substance suggestive of the texture of wool. ***—modifier:*** *wool socks.* [ME *wolle* < OE *wull.*]

wool-clip (wo͝ol′klĭp′) *n.* The annual yield of wool.

wool·en also **wool·len** (wo͝ol′ən). *—adj.* Of, pertaining to, or consisting of wool. *—n.* Often **woolens.** Fabric or clothing made from wool.

wool fat *n.* Lanolin.

wool·gath·er·ing (wo͝ol′găth′ər-ĭng) *n.* Absent-minded indulgence in fanciful daydreams. *—adj.* Indulging in fancies; absent-minded. **—wool′gath′er·er** *n.*

wool·grow·er (wo͝ol′grō′ər) *n.* One that raises sheep or other animals for the production of wool. **—wool′grow′ing** *n.*

wool·len (wo͝ol′ən) *adj. & n.* Variant of **woolen.**

wool·ly also **wool·y** (wo͝ol′ē) *—adj.* **-li·er, -li·est** also **-i·er, -i·est. 1. a.** Pertaining to, consisting of, or covered with wool. **b.** Resembling wool. **2.** Lacking sharp detail or clarity; blurry; fuzzy: *woolly thinking.* **3.** Having the characteristics of the rough, generally lawless atmosphere of frontier America: *wild and woolly.* *—n., pl.* **-lies** also **-ies. 1.** A garment made of wool, esp. an undergarment. **2.** *Western U.S. & Austral.* A sheep. **—wool′li·ness** *n.*

woolly bear *n.* The hairy caterpillar of any of various tiger moths, esp. that of *Isia isabella.*

wool·pack (wo͝ol′păk′) *n.* **1.** A bag used for packing a bale of wool for shipment. **2.** A cumulus cloud.

wool·sack (wo͝ol′săk′) *n.* **1.** A sack for wool. **2.** The official seat of the Lord Chancellor in the House of Lords.

wool shed *n.* A building or complex of buildings in which sheep are sheared and wool is prepared for shipment to market.

wool·skin (wo͝ol′skĭn′) *n.* A sheepskin with the wool still on it.

wool-sort·er's disease (wo͝ol′sôr′tərz) *n.* A pulmonary form of anthrax that results from the inhalation of *Bacillus anthracis* spores in contaminated sheep's wool.

wool·sta·pler (wo͝ol′stā′plər) *n.* **1.** A dealer in wool. **2.** A person who sorts wool by the quality of the staple or fiber. **—wool′-sta′pling** *adj. & n.*

wool·work (wo͝ol′wûrk′) *n.* Needlework.

wool·y (wo͝ol′ē) *adj. & n.* Variant of **woolly.**

George Miksch Sutton

woodpecker

wood sorrel

woofer

woolly bear

Worcester
Covered Worcester porcelain vase made about 1775

word processing

C R A B
R A R E
A R T S
B E S T

B R A T
R A C E
A C R E
T E E M

word square

workbench

wooz·y (wŏŏ′zē, wŏŏz′ē) *adj.* **-i·er, -i·est. 1.** Dazed; stunned; confused. **2.** Dizzy or queasy. [Poss. alteration of OOZY.] **—wooz′i·ly** *adv.* **—wooz′i·ness** *n.*

wop (wŏp) *n. Offensive Slang.* An Italian. [Ital. dial. *guappo,* thug.]

Worces·ter (wŏŏs′tər). A trademark for a fine porcelain made in Worcester, England.

Worces·ter·shire (wŏŏs′tər-shîr, -shər). A trademark for a piquant sauce of soy, vinegar, and spices.

word (wûrd) *n.* **1.** A sound or a combination of sounds, or its representation in writing or printing, that symbolizes and communicates a meaning and may consist of a single morpheme or of a combination of morphemes. **2.** Something that is said; an utterance, remark, or comment: *May I say a word about that?* **3.** *Computer Sci.* A set of bits comprising the smallest unit of addressable computer memory. **4. words.** A discourse or talk; speech. **5. words.** The text of a vocal musical composition; lyrics. **6.** An assurance or promise; sworn intention: *kept his word.* **7. a.** A command or direction; an order: *executed at the general's word.* **b.** A verbal signal; a password or watchword. **8. a.** News: *the latest word.* **b.** Rumor: *Word has it she's married.* **9. words.** Hostile or angry remarks made back and forth; quarrel. **10. Word. a.** The Logos. **b.** The Scriptures or Gospel: *the Word of God.* *—tr.v.* **word·ed, word·ing, words.** To express in words. **—*idioms.* at a word.** In immediate response. **by word of mouth.** Orally; by speech. **good word. 1.** A favorable utterance or word: *She put in a good word for me.* **2.** Favorable news. **have no words for.** To be unable to describe or talk about. **in a word.** In short: *You are, in a word, a fool.* **in so many words.** Precisely as stated; exactly. **of few words.** Not conversational or loquacious; laconic: *a man of few words.* **of (one's) word.** That can be depended on to keep one's promise: *a man of his word.* **take (one) at (one's) word.** To be convinced of another's sincerity and act in accordance with his statement. **upon my word.** Indeed; assuredly: *Upon my word, I've never heard of such a thing.* **word for word.** In the same words. [ME < OE.]

word·age (wûr′dĭj) *n.* **1.** Words collectively. **2.** The use of an excessive number of words; verbiage. **3.** The number of words used, as in a novel. **4.** Wording.

word blindness *n.* Alexia. **—word′-blind′** (wûrd′blīnd′) *adj.*

word·book (wûrd′bŏŏk′) *n.* A lexicon, vocabulary, or dictionary.

word deafness *n.* One form of aphasia in which information in the form of speech is incomprehensible.

word·ing (wûr′dĭng) *n.* The act or style of expressing in words; phraseology; diction.

word·less (wûrd′lĭs) *adj.* **1.** Without words; unspoken. **2.** Inarticulate. **—word′less·ly** *adv.* **—word′less·ness** *n.*

word·mon·ger (wûrd′mŭng′gər, -mŏng′-) *n.* A writer or speaker who uses language pretentiously or carelessly.

word order *n.* The syntactic arrangement of words in a sentence, clause, or phrase.

word play *n.* **1.** A witty or clever exchange of words; repartee. **2.** A play on words; pun.

word processing *n.* A system of producing typewritten documents, such as business letters, by use of automated typewriters and electronic text-editing equipment. **—word processor** *n.*

word square *n.* A group of words arranged in a square that read the same vertically and horizontally.

word·y (wûr′dē) *adj.* **-i·er, -i·est. 1.** Pertaining to, consisting of, or having the nature of words; verbal. **2.** Expressed in or using more words than are necessary to convey meaning. **—word′i·ly** *adv.* **—word′i·ness** *n.*

wore[1] (wôr, wōr) *v.* Past tense of **wear**[1].

wore[2] (wôr, wōr) *v.* Past tense of **wear**[2].

work (wûrk) *n.* **1.** Physical or mental effort or activity directed toward the production or accomplishment of something; toil; labor. **2.** Employment; job: *look for work.* **3.** The means by which one earns one's livelihood; a trade, craft, business, or profession. **4. a.** Something that one is doing, making, or performing, esp. as a part of one's occupation; a duty or task: *begin the day's work.* **b.** The amount of this done or required. **5.** Something that has been done, made, or performed as a result of one's occupation, effort, or activity, esp.: **a. works.** The output of an artist or artisan considered or collected as a whole: *the works of Verdi.* **b. works.** Engineering structures, such as bridges or dams. **c.** A piece of needlework or embroidery. **6.** Any material or piece being processed in a machine during manufacture. **7.** The area, office, or place where one pursues an occupation: *He called her at work.* **8. works** *(used with a sing. verb).* A factory, plant, or similar building or system of buildings where a specific type of business or industry is carried on. **9. works.** Mechanism: *the works of a watch.* **10.** The manner or style of working or the quality of treatment; workmanship: *good work.* **11.** A froth produced during the process of fermentation, as on vinegar or cider. **12.** *Physics.* The transfer of energy from one physical system to another, esp. the transfer of energy to a body by the application of force, calculated as the line integral between any two points of the scalar product of the force and the body's displacement along the path over which the integral is taken. **13. works.** *Theol.* Moral or righteous acts or deeds: *salvation by faith rather than works.* **14. the works.** *Slang.* The whole of a set; everything: *He had the works, from appetizer to dessert.* *—v.* **worked** or **wrought** (rôt), **work·ing, works.** *—intr.* **1.** To exert one's efforts for the purpose of doing or making something; labor; toil. **2.** To be employed; have a job. **3.** To perform a function or act; operate: *The machine doesn't work.* **4.** To operate effectively or successfully; prove successful: *The combination seemed to work.* **5.** To be changed into a specified state, esp. gradually or by repeated movement: *The stitches worked loose.* **6.** To force a passage or way: *They worked through the snow to the street.* **7.** To move or contort from emotion or pain: *Her mouth worked with fear.* **8.** To be handled or processed: *Not all metals work easily.* **9.** To ferment. **10.** *Naut.* To be under strain in heavy seas so that seams loosen and fastenings become slack. **11.** To undergo small motions that result in friction and wear: *The gears work against each other.* *—tr.* **1.** To cause or effect; bring about: *I can't work miracles.* **2.** To cause to operate or function; handle or use: *work a power mower.* **3.** To form or shape; mold; forge: *They work glass. The metal sculpture was finely wrought.* **4.** To make or decorate by using a needle. **5.** To solve (a problem) by calculation and reasoning. **6.** To handle or manipulate for the purpose of preparing: *work the butter and sugar before adding eggs.* **7.** To achieve (a specified condition) by gradual or repeated effort: *They worked their way out of the wood.* **8.** To arrange; contrive: *He worked it so that all his weekends were free.* **9.** To make productive; cultivate: *work a farm.* **10.** To make or force to work or to do work: *He works his laborers hard.* **11.** To excite, rouse, or provoke: *He worked the children into a frenzy.* **12.** To influence or persuade, esp. by somewhat underhand means; woo or induce: *Work him to do your bidding.* **13.** *Informal.* To use or employ for one's own ends or purposes: *work one's contacts.* **14.** *Informal.* To practice trickery or deception on; cheat. **15.** To function or operate in; cover: *This mailman works our street.* **16.** To ferment (liquors). **—*phrasal verbs.* work in. 1.** To put in or introduce; insert: *work a few jokes in during a speech.* **2.** To cause to be inserted by repeated, continuous effort. **work off.** To get rid of; eliminate; dissipate: *work off extra pounds.* **work on** (or **upon**). **1.** To affect: *worked on our sympathies.* **2.** To attempt to persuade or influence. **work out. 1.** To exhaust (a mine or soil, for example). **2.** To accomplish by work or effort. **3.** To find a solution for; solve. **4.** To formulate; develop: *work out a plan.* **5.** To prove successful, effective, or satisfactory: *Did your new job work out?* **6.** To perform a series of exercises: *I work out at a gym every day.* **work over. 1.** To do for a second time; rework. **2.** *Slang.* To inflict severe physical damage upon; beat up. **work up. 1.** To arouse the emotions of; excite. **2.** To develop or formulate by mental or physical effort: *worked up a patient profile; worked up a variety show.* [ME *worke* < OE *weorc.*]

Synonyms: *work, labor, toil, drudgery, travail.* These nouns refer to the exertion of physical or mental faculties in order to accomplish something, contrasted with play or recreation. *Work* is the most widely applicable; it alone can refer not only to the effort of persons but also to the activity of machines and of the forces of nature. *Labor* is largely restricted to human effort, especially physical and manual. *Toil* is principally applicable to strenuous and fatiguing labor; *drudgery,* to dull, wearisome, monotonous, and sometimes demeaning labor; and *travail,* to work involving great effort and pain or suffering.

work·a·ble (wûr′kə-bəl) *adj.* **1.** Capable of being worked, dealt with, or handled. **2.** Capable of being worked conveniently; feasible. **—work′a·bil′i·ty, work′a·ble·ness** *n.*

work·a·day (wûr′kə-dā′) *adj.* **1.** Pertaining or appropriate to working days; everyday. **2.** Mundane; commonplace: *"the practical, workaday world, of . . . ordinary undistinguished things"* (Lionel Trilling). [< ME *werkeday,* workday.]

work·a·hol·ic (wûr′kə-hô′lĭk, -hŏl′ĭk) *n.* A person who works compulsively. [WORK + (ALC)OHOLIC.] **—work′a·hol′ism** *n.*

work·bag (wûrk′băg′) *n.* A bag to hold material on which one is working or implements needed for work such as needlework.

work·bench (wûrk′bĕnch′) *n.* A sturdy table or bench at which manual work is done, as by a machinist, carpenter, or jeweler.

work·book (wûrk′bŏŏk′) *n.* **1.** A booklet containing problems and exercises in which a student may directly write or calculate. **2.** A manual containing operating instructions, as for an appliance or a machine. **3.** A book in which a record is kept of work proposed or accomplished.

work·box (wûrk′bŏks′) *n.* A box for implements or materials used in sewing or other work.

work·day (wûrk′dā′) *n.* **1.** A day on which work is done. **2.** The part of the day during which one works: *an eight-hour workday.* *—adj.* Workaday.

work·er (wûr′kər) *n.* **1.** One that works. **2. a.** One who does manual or industrial labor. **b.** One who belongs to the working class. **3.** One of the sterile females of certain social insects, as the ant or bee, that performs specialized work.

workers' compensation *n.* Payments required by law to be made to an employee who is injured in the course of work.

work ethic *n.* The belief that work is morally good.

work·fare (wûrk′fâr′) *n.* A form of welfare in which the recipients of aid are required to perform public service work.

work·folk (wûrk′fōk′) also **work·folks** (-fōks′) *pl.n.* Laborers, esp. farm laborers.

work force *n.* **1.** Those workers employed in a specific project; staff. **2.** All workers potentially available, as to a nation, project, or industry.

work function *n.* The amount of work required to remove an electron from a solid, esp. the work exerted against coulomb forces in removing an electron from just inside to just outside the surface of a metal.

work hardening *n.* The increase in strength that sometimes accompanies plastic deformation of a solid.

work·horse (wûrk′hôrs′) *n.* **1.** A horse that is used for labor rather than for racing or riding. **2.** *Informal.* A person who works tirelessly, esp. at difficult tasks.

work·house (wûrk′hous′) *n.* **1.** A prison in which limited sentences, under one year in most systems, are served at manual labor. **2.** *Chiefly Brit.* A poorhouse.

work·ing (wûr′kĭng) *adj.* **1.** Pertaining to or designating one that works; employed: *the working wife; the working population.* **2.** Pertaining to, used for, or spent in working: *a working uniform.* **3.** Sufficient or large enough for using or being worked: *a working knowledge of Spanish.* **4.** Capable of being used as the basis of further work: *a working mode.* **5.** In the process of fermentation. Used of alcoholic liquors. **6. a.** Functioning, esp. on a reduced scale: *a working model.* **b.** Used as a guide: *a working drawing.*

working capital *n.* **1.** The assets of a business enterprise that can be applied to its operation. **2.** The current assets of an individual or business enterprise as opposed to the current liabilities.

working class *n.* The part of society whose income is from wages; proletariat. **—work′ing-class′** *adj.*

working fluid *n.* A working substance.

work·ing·man (wûr′kĭng-măn′) *n.* A man who works for wages, esp. at manual labor.

working papers *pl.n.* Legal documents certifying the right of an individual to employment.

working storage *n.* *Computer Sci.* The section of a data storage disk reserved for data to be temporarily stored during the running of a program.

working substance *n.* A substance, such as a coolant, used to effect a thermodynamic change in a system.

work·less (wûrk′lĭs) *adj.* Unemployed.

work·load (wûrk′lōd′) *n.* **1.** The amount of work assigned to or done by a worker or unit of workers in a given time period. **2.** The capacity of a machine for work in a given time period.

work·man (wûrk′mən) *n.* **1.** A man who performs some form of labor. **2.** A person who works in a specified way: *a creative workman.*

work·man·like (wûrk′mən-līk′) also **work·man·ly** (-lē) *adj.* Characteristic of or befitting a skilled workman or craftsman: *workmanlike pottery.*

work·man·ship (wûrk′mən-shĭp′) *n.* **1. a.** The art, skill, or technique of a workman. **b.** The quality of such art, skill, or technique: *silver of poor workmanship.* **2.** Something that is produced by a workman. **3.** The product of effort or endeavor.

workmen's compensation *n.* Workers' compensation.

work of art *n.* A piece of superior work.

work·out (wûrk′out′) *n.* **1.** A period of exercise or practice, esp. in athletics. **2.** An exhausting task.

work·peo·ple (wûrk′pē′pəl) *pl.n.* *Chiefly Brit.* Those who work for wages.

work release *n.* A corrections program in which prisoners are released from confinement every day to work full-time.

work·room (wûrk′rōōm′, -rŏŏm′) *n.* A room where work is done.

work·shop (wûrk′shŏp′) *n.* **1.** An area, room, or establishment in which manual or industrial work is done. **2.** A group of people who meet regularly for a seminar in a specialized field: *a creative-writing workshop.*

work stoppage *n.* A protest measure by a group of workers that is marked by cessation of work and is usually less serious than a formal strike.

work·ta·ble (wûrk′tā′bəl) *n.* A table designed for a specific task or activity, such as needlework or graphic arts.

work·up (wûrk′ŭp′) *n.* A thorough medical study for diagnostic purposes.

work·week (wûrk′wēk′) *n.* The number of hours worked or required to be worked in one week.

world (wûrld) *n.* **1.** The earth. **2.** The universe. **3.** The earth and its inhabitants collectively. **4.** The human race: *All the world applauds a true hero.* **5.** Man considered as a social creature; the public: *the world's response to Lindbergh's flight.* **6.** Often **World.** A particular part of the earth: *the Western World.* **7.** A particular period in history, including its people, culture, and social order: *the Victorian world.* **8.** A sphere, realm, or domain including all things pertaining to or associated with it: *the animal world; a child's world.* **9.** A field or sphere of human endeavor: *the world of the arts.* **10.** A specified way of life or state of being: *the world of the rich; the world of the deaf.* **11.** Secular life and its concerns as distinguished from religious life: *a man of the world; forsook the world for a hermit's life.* **12.** Often **worlds.** A large amount; much: *I have worlds of time.* **13.** A planet or other celestial body: *the possibility of life on another world.* **—idioms. for all the world. 1.** For anything or for any reason: *I wouldn't go for all the world.* **2.** Precisely; exactly: *He looked for all the world like a movie star.* **out of this world.** *Informal.* Excellent; very fine: *a dinner that was out of this world.* [ME < OE *weorold.*]

World Court *n.* The Permanent Court of International Justice, established by the League of Nations (1920).

world line *n.* The path in space-time traveled by an elementary particle for the time and distance it retains its identity.

world·ling (wûrld′lĭng) *n.* A person absorbed in or devoted to this world; a worldly person.

world·ly (wûrld′lē) *adj.* **-li·er, -li·est. 1.** Of, pertaining to, or devoted to the temporal world; not spiritual or religious; secular. **2.** Sophisticated or cosmopolitan; worldly-wise: *"an experienced and worldly man who had been almost everywhere"* (Willa Cather). *—adv.* In a worldly manner. **—world′li·ness** *n.*

world·ly-wise (wûrld′lē-wīz′) *adj.* Experienced in the ways of the world; sophisticated.

world power *n.* A political entity whose actions influence or change the course of international events.

World Series *n.* The series of professional baseball games played each fall between the championship teams of the American League and the National League.

world's fair *n.* An exposition featuring international exhibits and participation.

world-shak·ing (wûrld′shā′kĭng) *adj.* Of great significance.

world soul *n.* A spiritual principle relating to the world as the human soul relates to a human being.

world view *n.* A Weltanschauung.

World War I *n.* A war fought from 1914 to 1918, in which Great Britain, France, Russia, Belgium, Italy, Japan, the United States, and other allies defeated Germany, Austria-Hungary, Turkey, and Bulgaria.

World War II *n.* A war fought from 1939 to 1945, in which Great Britain, France, the Soviet Union, the United States, and other allies defeated Germany, Italy, and Japan.

world-wea·ry (wûrld′wîr′ē) *adj.* **-ri·er, -ri·est.** Tired of the world and its pleasures. **—world′-wea′ri·ness** *n.*

world·wide (wûrld′wīd′) *adj.* Reaching or extending throughout the world; universal. **—world′wide′** *adv.*

worm (wûrm) *n.* **1.** Any of various invertebrates, as those of the phyla Annelida, Nematoda, or Platyhelminthes, having a long, flexible rounded or flattened body, often without obvious appendages. **2.** Any of various insect larvae having a soft, elongated body. **3.** Any of various unrelated animals resembling a worm in habit or appearance, as the shipworm or the slowworm. **4.** Something, as a threaded screw, that is like a worm in appearance or movement. **5.** An insidiously tormenting or devouring force: *the worm of guilt.* **6.** A pitiable, contemptible, or weak-willed person. **7. worms.** *Pathol.* Intestinal infestation with worms or wormlike parasites. *—v.* **wormed, worm·ing, worms.** *—tr.* **1.** To make (one's way) with or as if with the sinuous crawling motion of a worm. **2.** To elicit by artful or devious means: *wormed a confession out of her.* **3.** To cure of intestinal worms. **4.** *Naut.* To wrap yarn or twine around (rope). *—intr.* **1.** To move in a sinuous manner suggestive of a worm. **2.** To make one's way by artful or devious means: *He can't worm out of this situation.* [ME < OE *wyrm.*]

worm-eat·en (wûrm′ēt′n) *adj.* **1.** Bored through or gnawed by worms. **2.** Decayed; rotten. **3.** Antiquated; decrepit.

worm fence

worm fence *n.* A fence of crossed rails supporting one another and forming a zigzag pattern.

worm gear *n.* **1.** A gear consisting of a threaded shaft and a wheel with teeth that mesh into it. **2.** A worm wheel.

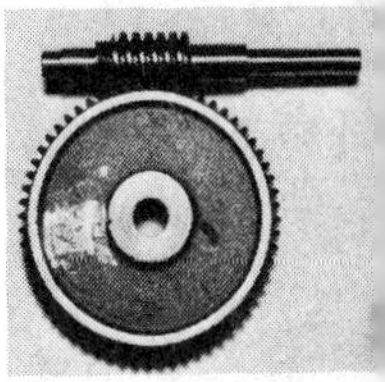

worm gear

worm·grass (wûrm′grăs′) *n.* The pinkroot. [From its use as a vermifuge.]

worm·hole (wûrm′hōl′) *n.* A hole made by a burrowing worm.

worm screw *n.* The threaded shaft of a worm gear.

worm·seed (wûrm′sēd′) *n.* **1.** A tropical American plant, *Chenopodium ambrosioides,* yielding an oil used as an anthelmintic. **2.** Any of several other plants used as an anthelmintic.

worm's-eye view (wûrmz′ī′) *n.* **1.** A close-up view. **2.** A view from a low or inferior position.

worm wheel *n.* The toothed wheel of a worm gear.

worm·wood (wûrm′wŏŏd′) *n.* **1.** Any of several aromatic plants of the genus *Artemisia,* esp. *A. absinthium,* native to Europe, yielding a bitter extract used in making absinthe and in flavoring certain wines. **2.** Something harsh or embittering. [ME *wormwode,* alteration of *wermode* < OE *wermōd.*]

worm·y (wûr′mē) *adj.* **-i·er, -i·est. 1.** Infested with or damaged by worms. **2.** Suggestive of a worm. **—worm′i·ness** *n.*

worn[1] (wôrn, wōrn) *v.* Past participle of **wear**[1]. *—adj.* **1.** Affected by wear or use. **2.** Impaired or damaged by wear or use: *worn pockets on a jacket.* **3. a.** Exhausted; spent. **b.** Showing exhaustion; drawn. **4.** Trite; hackneyed. [ME, p.part. of *weren,* to wear.]

worn[2] (wôrn, wōrn) *v.* Past participle of **wear**[2].

worn-out (wôrn′out′, wōrn′-) *adj.* **1.** Worn or used until no longer usable: *a worn-out suit.* **2.** Thoroughly exhausted; spent.

wor·ri·ment (wûr'ē-mənt, wŭr'-) *n.* The act or a cause of worrying; worry.

wor·ri·some (wûr'ē-səm, wŭr'-) *adj.* **1.** Causing worry or anxiety. **2.** Tending to worry; anxious. **—wor'ri·some·ly** *adv.*

wor·ry (wûr'ē, wŭr'ē) *v.* **-ried, -ry·ing, -ries.** *—intr.* **1.** To feel uneasy about; be troubled. **2.** To pull, bite, or tear at something. **3.** To work under difficulty or hardship; struggle: *worried away at a problem.* *—tr.* **1.** To cause to feel anxious, distressed, or troubled. **2.** To bother; annoy: *Don't worry me with your complaints.* **3. a.** To grasp and tug at repeatedly: *a dog worrying a bone.* **b.** To touch, press, or handle idly; toy with: *worrying the sore tooth with his tongue.* *—n., pl.* **-ries. 1.** The act of worrying or the condition of being worried; mental uneasiness or anxiety. **2.** A source of nagging concern or uneasiness. [ME *worien,* to strangle < OE *wyrgan.*] **—wor'ri·er** *n.*

worry beads *pl.n.* A string of beads that a person fingers to keep the hands occupied.

wor·ry·wart (wûr'ē-wôrt', wŭr'-) *n.* One who tends to worry excessively and needlessly.

worse (wûrs). **1.** Comparative of **bad. 2.** Comparative of **ill.** *—adj.* **1.** More inferior, as in quality, condition, or effect. **2.** More severe or unfavorable. **3.** Further from a standard; less desirable or satisfactory. *—n.* Something that is worse. *—adv.* In a worse way. [ME < OE *wyrsa.*]

wors·en (wûr'sən) *tr. & intr.v.* **-ened, -en·ing, -ens.** To make or become worse.

wors·er (wûr'sər) *adj. & adv. Archaic.* Variant of **worse.**

wor·ship (wûr'shĭp) *n.* **1. a.** The reverent love and allegiance accorded a deity, idol, or sacred object. **b.** A set of ceremonies, prayers, or other religious forms by which this love is expressed. **2. a.** Ardent, humble devotion. **b.** The object of such devotion. **3.** Often **Worship.** *Chiefly Brit.* A title of honor used in addressing magistrates, mayors, and certain other dignitaries: *Your Worship.* *—v.* **-shiped, -ship·ing, -ships** or **-shipped, -ship·ping, -ships.** *—tr.* **1.** To honor and love as a deity; venerate. **2.** To love or pursue devotedly. *—intr.* **1.** To participate in religious rites of worship. **2.** To perform an act of worship. [ME < OE *weorðscipe,* honor : *weorð,* worth + *-scipe,* -ship.] **—wor'ship·er** *n.*

wor·ship·ful (wûr'shĭp-fəl) *adj.* **1.** Given to or expressive of worship; reverent or adoring. **2.** *Chiefly Brit.* Honorable by virtue of position or rank. Used in titles of respect. **—wor'ship·ful·ly** *adv.* **—wor'ship·ful·ness** *n.*

worst (wûrst). **1.** Superlative of **bad. 2.** Superlative of **ill.** *—adj.* **1.** Most inferior, as in quality, condition, or effect. **2.** Most severe or unfavorable. **3.** Furthest from an ideal or standard; least desirable or satisfactory. *—adv.* In the worst manner or degree. *—tr.v.* **worst·ed, worst·ing, worsts.** To gain the advantage over; defeat. *—n.* Something that is worst. **—*idioms.* at worst.** Under the most negative foreseeable circumstances. **get the worst of it.** To suffer a defeat or disadvantage. **if (the) worst comes to (the) worst.** At the very worst. **in the worst way.** *Informal.* Very much; a great deal: *wanted in the worst way to see the movie.* [ME < OE *wyrsta.*]

wor·sted (wŏŏs'tĭd, wûr'stĭd) *n.* **1.** Firm-textured, compactly twisted woolen yarn made from long-staple fibers. **2.** Fabric made from worsted. *—adj.* Consisting of or made from worsted. [ME *worthstede,* after *Worthstede,* a village in Norfolk, England.]

wort (wûrt, wôrt) *n.* **1.** A plant: *liverwort; milkwort.* **2.** An infusion of malt fermented to make beer. [ME < OE *wyrt,* plant.]

worth[1] (wûrth) *n.* **1.** The quality of something that renders it desirable, useful, or valuable: *the worth of higher education.* **2.** The material or market value of something: *stocks having a worth of ten million dollars.* **3.** The number or quantity of something that may be purchased for a specific sum: *ten dollars' worth of gasoline.* **4.** Wealth; riches. **5.** The quality within a person that renders him deserving of respect: *the worth of the individual.* *—adj.* **1.** Equal in value to something specified: *worth its weight in gold.* **2.** Deserving of; meriting: *a proposal worth consideration.* **3.** Having wealth or riches amounting to: *a man not worth three cents.* **—*idiom.* for all one is worth.** To the utmost of one's powers or ability. [ME < OE *weorð.*]

worth[2] (wûrth) *intr.v.* **worthed, worth·ing, worths.** *Archaic.* To befall; betide: *"Howl ye, Woe worth the day!"* (Ezekiel 30:2). [ME *worthen* < OE *weorðan.*]

worth·less (wûrth'lĭs) *adj.* **1.** Devoid of worth, use, or value. **2.** Lacking dignity or honor; low and despicable. **—worth'less·ly** *adv.* **—worth'less·ness** *n.*

worth·while (wûrth'hwīl', -wīl') *adj.* Sufficiently valuable or important to justify the expenditure of time or effort. **—worth'while'ness** *n.*

wor·thy (wûr'thē) *adj.* **-thi·er, -thi·est. 1.** Having worth, merit, or value; useful or valuable. **2.** Honorable; admirable: *a worthy fellow.* **3.** Having sufficient worth; deserving: *worthy to be revered; worthy of acclaim.* *—n., pl.* **-thies. 1.** A person esteemed for his worth, dignity, or importance. **2.** A figure locally renowned or respected. **—wor'thi·ly** *adv.* **—wor'thi·ness** *n.*

-worthy *suff.* **1.** Of sufficient worth for: *creditworthy.* **2.** Suitable or safe for: *crashworthy.* [< WORTHY.]

wot (wŏt) *v. Archaic.* First and third person singular present tense of **wit**[2].

Wo·tan (vō'tän') *n. Myth.* A Teutonic god identified with Woden. [G.]

would (wŏŏd) *v.* Past tense of **will**[2].

would-be (wŏŏd'bē') *adj.* Desiring or pretending to be.

would·n't (wŏŏd'nt). Would not.

wouldst (wŏŏdst) or **would·est** (wŏŏd'ĭst) *v. Archaic.* Second person singular past tense of **will**[2].

wound[1] (wŏŏnd) *n.* **1.** An injury, esp. one in which the skin or other external organic surface is torn, pierced, cut, or otherwise broken. **2.** An injury to the feelings. *—v.* **wound·ed, wound·ing, wounds.** *—tr.* To inflict a wound upon. *—intr.* To inflict a wound. [ME < OE *wund.*]

wound[2] (wound) *v.* Past tense and past participle of **wind**[2].

wound[3] (wound) *v.* A past tense and past participle of **wind**[3].

wound·wort (wŏŏnd'wûrt', -wôrt') *n.* **1.** Any of several plants of the genus *Stachys,* having downy leaves formerly used to treat wounds. **2.** Any of several plants used similarly to woundwort.

wove (wōv) *v.* Past tense and past participle of **weave.**

wo·ven (wō'vən) *v.* Past participle of **weave.**

wove paper *n.* Paper made on a closely woven wire roller or mold and having a faint mesh pattern.

wow[1] (wou) *Informal.* *—interj.* Used in expressing wonder or amazement. *—n.* An outstanding success. *—tr.v.* **wowed, wow·ing, wows.** To have a strong and usually pleasurable impact on: *a performance that wowed the audience.*

wow[2] (wou) *n.* A slow variation in the pitch of sound reproduced by a phonograph or tape recorder, usually the result of irregular movement of a mechanical part. [Imit.]

W particle *n.* A large elementary particle hypothesized to be responsible for weak interaction.

wrack[1] (răk) *n.* Severe damage or wreckage: *bring to wrack and ruin.* [ME < OE *wræc,* punishment.]

wrack[2] (răk) *n.* **1. a.** Wreckage, esp. of a ship cast ashore. **b.** *Regional.* Violent destruction of a building or vehicle. **2.** Dried seaweed. **3.** Marine vegetation, esp. kelp. *—v.* **wracked, wrack·ing, wracks.** *—tr.* To cause the ruin of; wreck. *—intr.* To be wrecked. [ME *wrak* < MDu.]

wrack[3] (răk) *v.* Variant of **rack**[2].

wraith (rāth) *n.* **1.** An apparition of a living person. **2.** The ghost of a dead person. [Orig. unknown.]

wran·gle (răng'gəl) *v.* **-gled, -gling, -gles.** *—intr.* To dispute noisily or angrily; quarrel; bicker. *—tr.* **1.** To win or obtain by argument. **2.** To herd (horses or other livestock). *—n.* **1.** An angry, noisy argument or dispute. **2.** The act of wrangling. [ME *wranglen,* prob. of LG orig.]

wran·gler (răng'glər) *n.* **1.** One who wrangles. **2.** A cowboy, esp. one who tends saddle horses.

wrap (răp) *v.* **wrapped** or **wrapt** (răpt), **wrap·ping, wraps.** *—tr.* **1.** To arrange or fold about in order to cover or protect something: *wrapped her coat about her.* **2.** To cover, envelop, or encase. **3.** To package, as with paper. **4.** To clasp, fold, or coil about something: *She wrapped her arms about his neck.* **5.** To envelop and obscure, often with the effect of concealing or disguising the nature of: *Fog wrapped the countryside.* **6. a.** To suffuse with a particular aura: *a plan wrapped in secrecy.* **b.** To engross: *wrapped in thought.* *—intr.* **1.** To coil, wind, or twist about or around something: *The flag wrapped around the pole.* **2.** To put on warm clothing; bundle up. **—*phrasal verb.* wrap up. 1.** To work out and complete the details of: *wrap up a business deal.* **2.** To encompass in a few words; summarize. *—n.* **1.** A garment to be wrapped or folded about a person, esp. a robe, cloak, shawl, or coat. **2.** A blanket. **3.** A wrapping or wrapper. **4.** *Computer Sci.* A single turn of metallic magnetic tape in a tape-wound magnetic core. **—*idiom.* keep under wraps.** To keep secret or concealed. [ME *wrappen.*]

wrap·a·round (răp'ə-round') *n.* **1.** A garment, such as a dress or skirt, that is open to the hem and that is wrapped around the body before being fastened. **2.** Something that curves and laps over something else. **—wrap'a·round'** *adj.*

wrap·per (răp'ər) *n.* **1.** One that wraps. **2.** The paper or other material in which something is wrapped: *a candy wrapper.* **3.** The paper encircling a mailed magazine or newspaper. **4.** A book jacket. **5.** The tobacco leaf covering a cigar. **6.** A loose robe or negligee.

wrap·ping (răp'ĭng) also **wrap·pings** (-ĭngz) *n.* The material in which something is wrapped.

wrapt (răpt) *v.* A past tense of **wrap.**

wrap-up (răp'ŭp') *n.* A brief summary, as of the news.

wrasse (răs) *n.* Any of numerous chiefly tropical, often brightly colored marine fishes of the family Labridae. [Cornish and Welsh *gwrach.*]

wrath (răth, räth) *n.* **1.** Violent, resentful anger; rage; fury: *hot with wrath.* **2. a.** A manifestation of anger. **b.** Divine retribution for sin. *—adj. Archaic.* Wrathful. [ME < OE *wrǣððð* < *wrāð,* angry.]

wrath·ful (răth'fəl, räth'-) *adj.* **1.** Full of wrath; very angry. **2.** Proceeding from or expressing wrath: *wrathful vengeance.* **—wrath'ful·ly** *adv.* **—wrath'ful·ness** *n.*

wreak (rēk) *tr.v.* **wreaked, wreak·ing, wreaks. 1.** To inflict (vengeance or punishment) upon a person. **2.** To express or gratify (anger, malevolence, or resentment); vent. **3.** *Archaic.* To take vengeance for; avenge. [ME *wreken* < OE *wrecan.*]

Usage: *Wreak* is sometimes confused with *wreck,* perhaps because the wreaking of damage may leave a wreck: *The storm wreaked* (not *wrecked*) *havoc along the coast.* The past tense and past participle of *wreak* is *wreaked,* not *wrought,* which is an alternate past tense and past participle of *work.* Thus, the Bible says *God wreaked punishment on sinners,* but Samuel F. B. Morse properly asked, "*What hath God wrought?*"

wreath (rēth) *n., pl.* **wreaths** (rēthz). **1. a.** A ring or circlet of flowers or leaves worn on the head, placed as a memorial, or used as a decoration. **b.** A representation of this, as in woodwork. **2.** A ring or similar curling form: *a wreath of smoke.* [ME *wrethe* < OE *wriða.*] **—wreath'y** *adj.*

wreathe (rē*th*) *v.* **wreathed, wreath·ing, wreathes.** *—tr.* **1.** To twist or entwine into a wreath. **2.** To twist or curl into a wreathlike shape or contour. **3.** To crown or decorate with or as with a wreath. **4.** To coil or curl. **5.** To form a wreath around. *—intr.* **1.** To assume the form of a wreath. **2.** To curl, writhe, or spiral. [< WREATH.]

wreck (rĕk) *n.* **1. a.** The action of wrecking or the condition of being wrecked; destruction. **b.** The accidental destruction of a ship; shipwreck. **2.** The stranded hulk of a ship that has been gravely damaged, as by being driven on rocks. **3.** The remains of something that has been wrecked or ruined, as by collision. **4.** Fragments of a ship or goods cast ashore by the sea after a shipwreck; wreckage. **5.** One that is in a shattered, broken-down, or worn-out state: *This hat is a wreck. She is a wreck from overwork.* *—v.* **wrecked, wreck·ing, wrecks.** *—tr.* **1.** To destroy accidentally, as by collision. **2.** To tear down or dismantle. **3.** To bring to a state of ruin; disable or destroy; undermine. *—intr.* **1.** To suffer destruction, ruin, or shipwreck. **2.** To engage in wrecking or tearing down. [ME *wrek* < AN *wrec,* of Scand. orig.]

wreck·age (rĕk'ĭj) *n.* **1.** The act of wrecking or the condition of being wrecked. **2.** The debris of anything wrecked.

wreck·er (rĕk'ər) *n.* **1. a.** One who wrecks or causes a wreck. **b.** A member of a wrecking or demolition crew. **c.** One who destroys or ruins: *a wrecker of dreams.* **2. a.** One that is used in recovering or removing a wreck, esp. a truck with a hoist and towing apparatus used in towing disabled or wrecked vehicles. **b.** One that salvages wrecked cargo or parts. **3. a.** One that lures a vessel to destruction, as on a rocky coastline, in order to plunder. **b.** A plunderer.

wrecking bar *n.* A small crowbar with a claw at one end and a slight curve at the other end.

wren (rĕn) *n.* **1.** Any of various small, brownish birds of the family Troglodytidae. **2.** Any of various birds similar to the wren. [ME *wrenne* < OE *wrenna.*]

Wren (rĕn) *n. Chiefly Brit. Informal.* A member of the Women's Royal Naval Service.

wrench (rĕnch) *n.* **1.** A sudden sharp, forcible twist or turn. **2.** An injury produced by twisting or straining. **3.** A sudden tug at one's emotions; a surge of compassion, sorrow, anguish, or the like. **4. a.** A break or parting that causes emotional distress. **b.** The pain associated with this: *felt a wrench when she was parted from her children.* **5.** A distortion in the original form of a speech or the like, or a twisted interpretation. **6.** Any of various hand or power tools with fixed or adjustable jaws for gripping, turning, or twisting an object such as a nut, bolt, or pipe. *—v.* **wrenched, wrench·ing, wrench·es.** *—tr.* **1. a.** To twist or turn suddenly and forcibly. **b.** To twist and sprain: *wrenched my knee.* **2. a.** To force free by pulling at; yank; wrest. **b.** To pull with a wrench. **3.** To pull at the feelings or emotions of; give pain to: *It wrenched her to say good-by.* **4.** To distort or twist the original character or import of. *—intr.* To give a wrench, twist, or turn. **—wrench'ing·ly** *adv.* [< ME *wrenchen,* to twist < OE *wrencan.*]

wrest (rĕst) *tr.v.* **wrest·ed, wrest·ing, wrests.** **1.** To obtain by or as by pulling with violent twisting movements: *wrest a book out of another's hands.* **2.** To usurp forcefully: *wrest power.* **3.** To extract by force, guile, or persistent effort; wring: *wrest the meaning from an obscure poem.* **4. a.** To distort or twist the nature or meaning of. **b.** To divert to an improper use; misapply. *—n.* **1.** The action of wresting. **2.** A small tuning key for the pins of a harp or piano. [ME *wresten* < OE *wrǣstan.*] **—wrest'er** *n.*

wres·tle (rĕs'əl) *v.* **-tled, -tling, -tles.** *—intr.* **1.** To contend by grappling and attempting to throw one's opponent, esp. under certain contest rules. **2. a.** To contend; to struggle: *city planners wrestling with budget cuts.* **b.** To strive in an effort to master: *wrestle with one's conscience.* *—tr.* **1. a.** To take part in (a wrestling match). **b.** To wrestle with. **2.** To throw (a calf or other animal) for branding. *—n.* **1.** An act of wrestling, esp. a wrestling match. **2.** A struggle. [ME *wrestlen* < OE *wrǣstlian.*] **—wres'tler** *n.*

wres·tling (rĕs'lĭng) *n.* A gymnastic exercise or contest between two competitors who attempt to throw each other by grappling.

wrest pin *n.* One of the pins to which the strings, esp. of a keyboard stringed instrument, are attached and tuned.

wretch (rĕch) *n.* **1.** A miserable, unfortunate, or unhappy person. **2.** A base, mean, or despicable person: *"A stony adversary, an inhuman wretch"* (Shakespeare). [ME *wrecche* < OE *wrecca.*]

wretch·ed (rĕch'ĭd) *adj.* **-er, -est.** **1.** Living in degradation and misery; miserable: *"The wretched prisoners huddling in the stinking cages"* (George Orwell). **2.** Attended by misery and woes: *a wretched life.* **3.** Of a poor or mean character; dismal: *a wretched building.* **4.** Contemptible; despicable: *wretched treatment of prisoners.* **5.** Inferior in performance or quality: *wretched prose.* **6.** Very unpleasant; deplorable: *a wretched thing to say.* [ME *wrecched* < *wrecche,* wretch.] **—wretch'ed·ly** *adv.* **—wretch'ed·ness** *n.*

wrig·gle (rĭg'əl) *v.* **-gled, -gling, -gles.** *—intr.* **1.** To turn or twist the body with sinuous writhing motions; squirm. **2.** To proceed with writhing motions. **3.** To worm one's way into or out of a situation; insinuate or extricate oneself by sly or subtle means. *—tr.* **1.** To move with a wriggling motion: *wriggle a toe.* **2.** To make (one's way, for example) by wriggling: *He wriggled his way into favor.* *—n.* The action or movement of wriggling. [ME *wrigglen* < MLG *wriggeln.*] **—wrig'gly** *adj.*

wrig·gler (rĭg'lər) *n.* **1.** One that wriggles. **2.** The larva of a mosquito.

wright (rīt) *n.* A person who constructs something: *playwright; shipwright.* [ME < OE *wryhta.*]

wring (rĭng) *v.* **wrung** (rŭng), **wring·ing, wrings.** *—tr.* **1.** To twist and squeeze; compress, as between the rollers of a machine, esp. to extract liquid. **2.** To extract (liquid) by twisting or compressing. **3.** To wrench or twist forcibly or painfully: *wring someone's neck.* **4.** To clasp and twist or squeeze, as in distress: *wring one's hands.* **5.** To cause distress to; affect with painful emotion: *wring one's heart.* **6.** To obtain by applying force or pressure to: *wring the truth out of a person.* *—intr.* To writhe or squirm, as in pain. *—n.* The act of wringing; squeeze or twist. [ME *wringen* < OE *wringan.*]

wring·er (rĭng'ər) *n.* One that wrings, esp. a device in which laundry is pressed or spun to extract water.

wrin·kle (rĭng'kəl) *n.* **1.** A small furrow, ridge, or crease on a normally smooth surface, caused by crumpling, folding, or shrinking. **2.** A line or crease in the skin, as from age. **3.** *Informal.* An ingenious new trick or method; clever innovation. *—v.* **-kled, -kling, -kles.** *—tr.* **1.** To make a wrinkle or wrinkles in. **2.** To draw up; pucker: *wrinkle one's nose in disdain.* *—intr.* To form wrinkles. [ME, back-formation from *wrinkled,* wrinkled, prob. < OE *gewrinclod,* p.part. of *gewrinclian,* to wind.] **—wrin'kly** *adj.*

wrist (rĭst) *n.* **1. a.** The junction between the hand and forearm. **b.** *Anat.* The system of bones forming this junction. **2.** The part of a sleeve or glove that encircles the wrist. [ME < OE.]

wrist·band (rĭst'bănd') *n.* A band, as on a long sleeve or on a wrist watch, that encircles the wrist.

wrist·let (rĭst'lĭt) *n.* **1.** A band of material worn round the wrist for warmth or additional strength. **2.** A bracelet.

wrist·lock (rĭst'lŏk') *n.* A wrestling hold in which an opponent's wrist is gripped and twisted to immobilize him.

wrist pin *n.* A pin that joins a piston to its connecting rod.

wrist watch *n.* A watch worn on a band that fastens about the wrist.

writ[1] (rĭt) *n.* **1.** *Law.* A written order issued by a court, commanding the party to whom it is addressed to perform or cease performing some specified act. **2.** Writings: *Holy Writ.* [ME < OE.]

writ[2] (rĭt) *v. Archaic.* A past tense and past participle of **write.**

write (rīt) *v.* **wrote** (rōt), **writ·ten** (rĭt'n), **writ·ing, writes.** *—tr.* **1.** To form (letters, for example) on a surface with a tool such as a pen or pencil. **2.** To form (a word, for example) by inscribing letters or symbols on a surface: *write one's name.* **3.** To compose and set down, esp. in literary or musical form. **4.** To draw up; draft: *write a will.* **5.** To fill in or cover with writing: *write a check; write a page.* **6.** To express: *write one's thoughts.* **7.** To communicate, as by correspondence: *write the news from home; write your aunt a note; write a letter to your lawyer.* **8.** To underwrite, as an insurance policy. **9.** To mark with the signs of (a quality, for example): *"Utter dejection was written on every face"* (Winston Churchill). **10.** To ordain by fate or prophecy. **11.** *Computer Sci.* To record (data) either transiently or permanently in a computer storage device or on an external medium. *—intr.* **1.** To trace or form letters, words, or symbols on paper or another surface. **2.** To produce written material, such as articles or books. **3. a.** To compose and send a letter or letters. **b.** To maintain a correspondence. ***—phrasal verbs.*** **write down.** **1.** To reduce in rank, value, or price. **2.** To disparage in writing. **3.** To write in a conspicuously simplified or condescending style: *had to write down to his students.* **write in.** **1.** To cast a vote by inserting (a name not listed on a ballot). **2.** To insert in a text or document. **write off.** **1.** To reduce the entered value of (an asset); depreciate. **2.** To cancel from business accounts as a loss: *wrote off the cost overruns.* **3.** To consider as a loss or failure. **write up.** **1.** To write a report or description of, as for publication. **2.** To bring (a journal, for example) up to date. **3.** To overstate the value of (assets). **4.** *Informal.* To write a summons for: *wrote me up*

wrecker

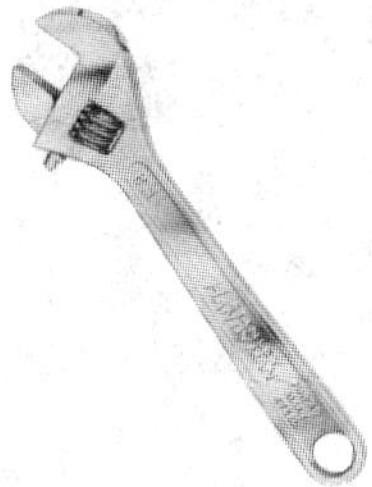
wrench

wrestling

for speeding. **—*idiom.* write (one's) own ticket.** To set one's own terms or choose a course that meets one's own desires and requirements. [ME *writen* < *OE wrītan.*]

write-down (rīt′doun′) *n.* A reduction of the entered value of an asset.

write-in (rīt′ĭn′) *n.* A vote cast by writing in the name of a candidate not on the ballot.

write-off (rīt′ôf′, -ŏf′) *n.* **1. a.** A cancellation in account books. **b.** An amount canceled or lost. **2.** A reduction or depreciation of the entered value of an item.

writ·er (rī′tər) *n.* One who writes, esp. as an occupation or profession; author.

writer's cramp *n.* A cramp chiefly affecting the muscles of the thumb and two adjacent fingers after prolonged writing.

write-up (rīt′ŭp′) *n.* **1.** A published account, review, or notice, esp. a favorable one. **2.** An intentional overevaluation of a corporation's assets.

writhe (rī*th*) *v.* **writhed, writh·ing, writhes.** *—intr.* **1.** To twist or squirm, as in pain, struggle, or embarrassment. **2.** To move with a twisting or contorted motion. **3.** To suffer acutely. *—tr.* To cause to twist or squirm; contort. *—n.* An act or instance of writhing; contortion. [ME *writhen* < OE *wrīðan.*] **—writhe** *n.* **—writh′er** *n.*

writ·ing (rī′tĭng) *n.* **1.** Written form: *Put it in writing.* **2.** Language symbols or characters written or imprinted on a surface; readable matter. **3.** A written work, esp. a literary composition. **4.** The activity, art, or occupation of a writer. **5. Writings.** Hagiographa. **—*idiom.* writing** (or **handwriting**) **on the wall.** A usually ominous indication of future events: *saw the writing on the wall and realized he would be jobless soon.*

writing paper *n.* Paper for writing on, esp. in ink.

writ of election *n.* A writ ordering that an election be held, esp. a special election to fill a vacancy in an elective office.

writ of error *n. Law.* A writ commissioning an appellate court to review the proceedings of another court and correct the judgment given if deemed necessary.

writ of prohibition *n. Law.* An order issued by a higher court commanding a lower court to cease from proceeding in some matter not within its jurisdiction.

writ of summons *n. Law.* A writ directing a person to appear in court to answer a complaint.

writ·ten (rĭt′n) *v.* Past participle of **write.**

wrong (rông, rŏng) *adj.* **1.** Not in conformity with fact or truth; incorrect. **2. a.** Contrary to conscience, morality, or law; immoral. **b.** Unfair or unjust. **3.** Not required, intended, or wanted: *took the wrong turn.* **4.** Not fitting or suitable; inappropriate: *the wrong moment.* **5.** Not in accordance with an established usage, method, or procedure. **6.** Not functioning properly. **7.** Unacceptable or undesirable according to social convention. **8.** Of, relating to, or being the side of something that is less finished or that is opposite to the right, principal, or more prominent side: *socks worn wrong side out.* *—adv.* **1.** In a wrong manner; mistakenly or erroneously. **2.** Immorally or unjustly: *behave wrong.* *—n.* **1. a.** An unjust or injurious act. **b.** Something that is contrary to ethics or morality. **2. a.** An invasion or violation of another's legal rights. **b.** *Law.* A tort. **3.** The condition of being in error or at fault: *in the wrong.* *—tr.v.* **wronged, wrong·ing, wrongs. 1.** To treat unjustly, injuriously, or dishonorably. **2.** To discredit unjustly; malign. **—*idioms.* do (someone) wrong.** *Informal.* To be unfaithful. **go wrong. 1.** To take a wrong turn or course. **2.** To go astray morally. **3.** To happen or turn out badly; go amiss. [ME, of Scand. orig.] **—wrong′er** *n.* **—wrong′ly** *adv.*

George Miksch Sutton
wryneck

wrong·do·er (rông′do͞o′ər, rŏng′-) *n.* One who does wrong. **—wrong′do′ing** *n.*

wrong·ful (rông′fəl, rŏng′-) *adj.* **1.** Wrong; unjust. **2.** Unlawful. **—wrong′ful·ly** *adv.* **—wrong′ful·ness** *n.*

wrong-head·ed (rông′hĕd′ĭd, rŏng′-) *adj.* Persistently wrong in stubborn defiance of the evidence. **—wrong′-head′ed·ly** *adv.* **—wrong′-head′ed·ness** *n.*

wrote (rōt) *v.* Past tense of **write.**

wroth (rôth) *adj.* Wrathful; angry. [ME < OE *wrāð.*]

wrought (rôt) *v.* A past tense and past participle of **work.** *—adj.* **1.** Put together: *carefully wrought.* **2.** Shaped by hammering with tools. Used chiefly of metals or metalwork. **3.** Made delicately or elaborately. **—*idiom.* wrought up.** Agitated; excited.

wrought iron *n.* An easily welded or forged iron containing approximately 0.2 per cent carbon and total impurities less than approximately 0.5 per cent.

wrung (rŭng) *v.* Past tense and past participle of **wring.**

wry (rī) *adj.* **wri·er, wri·est** also **wry·er, wry·est. 1.** Abnormally twisted or bent to one side; crooked: *a wry neck.* **2.** Temporarily twisted in an expression of distaste or displeasure. **3.** At variance with what is right or proper. **4.** Drily humorous, often with a touch of irony. [< ME *wrien,* to turn aside < OE *wrigian,* to move.] **—wry′ly** *adv.* **—wry′ness** *n.*

wry·neck (rī′nĕk′) *n.* **1.** Either of two Old World birds, *Jynx torquilla* or *J. ruficollia,* that are capable of twisting the neck into unusual contortions. **2.** *Pathol.* Torticollis.

wul·fen·ite (wo͝ol′fə-nīt′) *n.* A yellow to orange-red mineral, $PbMoO_4$, used as a molybdenum ore. [G. *Wulfenit,* after Franz X. von *Wulfen* (1728–1805).]

wurst (wûrst, wo͝orst) *n.* Sausage. [G. < OHG.]

wu shu (wo͞o′ sho͞o′) *n.* The Chinese martial arts. [Chin. (Mandarin) wu^3 shu^4.]

Wy·an·dot also **Wy·an·dotte** (wī′ən-dŏt′) *n., pl.* **Wyandot** or **-dots** also **Wyandotte** or **-dottes. 1.** A North American Indian of a tribe in the Huron confederacy. **2.** The Iroquoian language of the Wyandot. [Wyandot *wâdát,* tribal name.]

Wy·an·dotte (wī′ən-dŏt′) *n.* **1.** A domestic fowl of a breed developed in North America. **2.** Variant of **Wyandot.**

wych elm also **witch elm** (wĭch) *n.* An Old World elm, *Ulmus glabra,* often planted as a shade tree. [< ME *wyche* < OE *wice.*]

wye (wī) *n.* **1.** The letter *y.* **2.** A Y-shaped object.

wy·vern also **wi·vern** (wī′vərn) *n. Heraldry.* A two-legged dragon having wings and a barbed and knotted tail. [ME *wyvere,* viper < ONFr. *wivre* < Lat. *vipera.*]

X

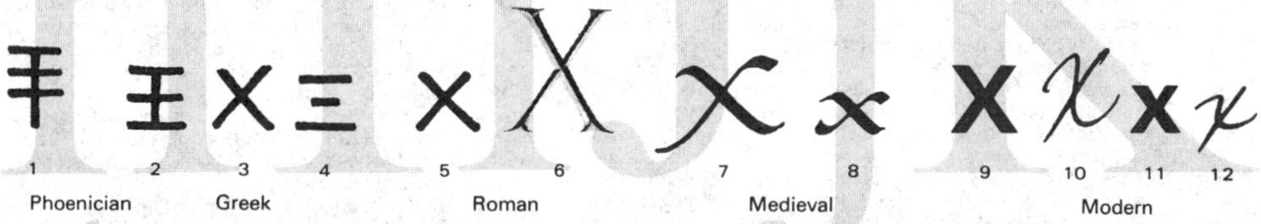

Around 1000 B.C. the Phoenicians and other Semitic peoples began to use graphic signs to represent individual speech sounds instead of syllables or words. They used this symbol (1) to represent the sound of the consonant "s" and called it *sāmekh,* their word for "fish." The Greeks, adapting the Phoenician alphabet, simplified the shape of *sāmekh* and changed its orientation (2,3,4). Some dialects of Greek used *sāmekh* to represent the sound "kh" and called it *chi,* but others used it to represent the sound "ks" and called it *xi.* The Romans borrowed the alphabet from the Greeks via the Etruscans, who used X to represent "ks." They also adapted the alphabet for monumental inscriptions. Monumental script (6) is the prototype of modern capital letters (9,10). Medieval scribes adapted the Roman capitals to being quickly written on paper, parchment, and vellum. These uncial and cursive minuscules (7,8) are the prototypes of modern lower-case letters, both written and printed (12,11).

x

p **pop** / r **roar** / s **sauce** / sh **ship, dish** / t **tight** / th **thin, path** / *th* **this, bathe** / ŭ **cut** / ûr **urge** / v **valve** / w **with** / y **yes** / z **zebra, size** / zh **vision** / ə **about, item, edible, gallop, circus** / œ *Fr.* **feu,** *Ger.* **schön** / ü *Fr.* **tu,** *Ger.* **über** / KH *Ger.* **ich,** *Scot.* **loch**/ N *Fr.* **bon.**

x or **X** (ĕks) *n., pl.* **x's** or **X's. 1.** The 24th letter of the modern English alphabet. **2.** Any of the speech sounds represented by the letter *x*. **3.** Something shaped like the letter X. **4.** The mark (X) inscribed to represent the signature of an illiterate person. **5.** An unknown or unnamed factor, thing, or person. **6.** The 24th in a series. —*tr.v.* **x'd, x'ing, x's. 1.** To mark or sign with an X. **2.** To delete, cancel, or obliterate with a series of x's.

X (ĕks) *adj.* Indicating a motion-picture rating of such nature that no one under the age of 17 is to be admitted.

Xan·a·du (zăn'ə-dōō', -dyōō') *n.* An idyllic, beautiful place. [After *Xanadu,* a place in *Kubla Khan,* a poem by Samuel T. Coleridge (1772–1834).]

xanth– *pref.* Variant of **xantho-.**

xan·than gum (zăn'thən) *n.* A natural gum of high molecular weight produced by culture fermentation of glucose and used as a stabilizer in commercial food preparation.

xan·thate (zăn'thāt') *n.* A salt of a xanthic acid, esp. a simple xanthic acid salt, as of sodium or potassium, used as a flotation collector for copper, silver, and gold.

xan·thene (zăn'thēn') *n.* A yellow crystalline organic compound, $CH_2(C_6H_4)_2O$, that is soluble in ether and used as a fungicide and in organic synthesis.

xan·thic acid (zăn'thĭk) *n.* Any of various unstable acids of the form ROC(S)SH, in which R is usually an alkyl radical. [So called from the yellow color of its salts. —see XANTHO-.]

xan·thine (zăn'thēn', -thĭn) *n.* A yellowish-white purine base, $C_5H_4N_4O_2$, found in blood, urine, and some plants.

xantho– or **xanth–** *pref.* **1.** Yellow: *xanthine.* **2.** Xanthic acid: *xanthate.* [NLat. < Gk. *xanthos,* yellow.]

xan·tho·chroid (zăn'thə-kroid') *adj.* Having a light complexion and light hair. —*n.* A xanthochroid individual. [< NLat. *xanthochroi,* yellow-haired, fair-skinned people : XANTH(O)- + Gk. *ōkhros,* pale.]

xan·tho·ma (zăn-thō'mə) *n.* A skin disease characterized by nodular yellowish-orange patches, esp. on the eyelids.

xan·tho·phyll (zăn'thə-fĭl') *n.* A yellow carotenoid pigment, $C_{40}H_{56}O_2$, found with chlorophyll in green plants and in egg yolk. [Fr. *xanthophylle* : *xantho-,* xantho- + *-phylle,* -phyll.]

xan·thous (zăn'thəs) *adj.* **1.** Yellow. **2.** Having light-brown or yellowish skin.

x-ax·is (ĕks'ăk'sĭs) *n., pl.* **x-ax·es** (-sēz). **1.** The horizontal axis of a two-dimensional Cartesian coordinate system. **2.** One of three axes in a three-dimensional Cartesian coordinate system.

X-chro·mo·some (ĕks'krō'mə-sōm') *n.* The sex chromosome associated with female characteristics, occurring paired in the female and single in the male sex-chromosome pair.

Xe The symbol for the element xenon.

xebec

xe·bec (zē'bĕk') *n.* A small three-masted Mediterranean vessel with both square and triangular sails. [Fr. *chebec* < Ar. *shabbāk.*]

xen– *pref.* Variant of **xeno-.**

xe·ni·a (zē'nē-ə) *n. Bot.* The effect on a hybrid plant produced by the transfer of pollen from one strain to the seed of a different strain. [NLat. < Gk., hospitality < *xenos,* guest, stranger.]

xeno– or **xen–** *pref.* **1.** Stranger; foreigner: *xenophobia.* **2.** Strange; foreign; different: *xenolith.* [NLat. < Gk. *xenos,* stranger.]

xen·o·blast (zĕn'ə-blăst', zē'nə-) *n.* A mineral deposit that has developed during metamorphism without developing crystalline faces.

xen·o·cryst (zĕn'ə-krĭst') *n.* A crystal foreign to the igneous rock in which it occurs. [XENO- + CRYST(AL).]

xen·o·cur·ren·cy (zĕn'ō-kûr'ən-sē, -kŭr'-, zē'nō-) *n.* A currency that is in circulation outside its own country.

xe·nog·a·my (zĭ-nŏg'ə-mē) *n. Bot.* The transfer of pollen from one plant to another; cross-pollination. —**xe·nog'a·mous** *adj.*

xen·o·gen·e·sis (zĕn'ə-jĕn'ə-sĭs) *n.* The supposed production of offspring markedly different from and showing no relationship to either of its parents. —**xen'o·ge·net'ic** (-jə-nĕt'ĭk), **xen'o·gen'ic** (-jĕn'ĭk) *adj.*

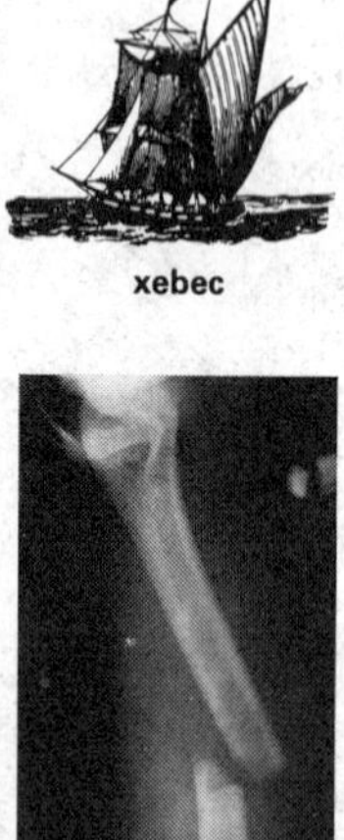
x-ray
Showing a fractured humerus

xen·o·lith (zĕn'ə-lĭth') *n.* A rock fragment foreign to the igneous mass in which it occurs.

xe·non (zē'nŏn') *n. Symbol* **Xe** A colorless, odorless, highly unreactive gaseous element found in minute quantities in the atmosphere, extracted commercially from liquefied air, and used in stroboscopic, bactericidal, and laser-pumping lamps. Atomic number 54; atomic weight 131.30; melting point −111.9°C; boiling point −107.1°C; density 5.887 grams per liter; specific gravity (liquid) 3.52 (−109°C). [< Gk., neuter of *xenos,* stranger.]

xenon hex·a·flu·o·ride (hĕk'sə-flōō'ə-rīd', -flōōr'īd', -flôr'-, -flōr'-) *n.* A highly reactive, colorless, crystalline compound, XeF_6.

xenon tet·ra·flu·o·ride (tĕt'rə-flōō'ə-rīd, -flōōr'īd', -flôr'-, -flōr'-) *n.* A colorless crystalline compound, XeF_4, derived from fluorine and xenon by heating under pressure and characterized by its ease of sublimation in air.

xen·o·phobe (zĕn'ə-fōb') *n.* A person unduly fearful or contemptuous of strangers or foreigners. —**xen'o·pho'bi·a** *n.* —**xen'o·pho'bic** *adj.*

xer– *pref.* Variant of **xero-.**

xer·ic (zĕr'ĭk, zîr'-) *adj.* Of, characterized by, or adapted to an extremely dry habitat. —**xer'i·cal·ly** *adv.*

xero– or **xer–** *pref.* Dry; dryness: *xeroderma.* [NLat. < Gk. *xēros,* dry.]

xer·o·der·ma (zîr'ō-dûr'mə) also **xe·ro·der·mi·a** (-mē-ə) *n.* Abnormal dryness of the skin.

xe·rog·ra·phy (zĭ-rŏg'rə-fē) *n.* A dry photographic or photocopying process in which a negative image formed by a resinous powder on an electrically charged plate is electrically transferred to and thermally fixed as positive on a paper or other copying surface. —**xe·rog'raph·er** *n.* —**xer'o·graph'ic** (zîr'ə-grăf'ĭk) *adj.* —**xer'o·graph'i·cal·ly** *adv.*

xe·roph·i·lous (zĭ-rŏf'ə-ləs) *adj.* Flourishing in or able to withstand a dry, hot environment. —**xe·roph'i·ly** *adv.*

xer·oph·thal·mi·a (zîr'əf-thăl'mē-ə) *n.* Extreme dryness of the conjunctiva, thought to result from vitamin A deficiency. [LLat. < Gk. *xērophthalmia* : *xēros,* dry + *ophthalmia,* ophthalmia < *ophthalmos,* eye.]

xer·o·phyte (zîr'ə-fīt') *n.* A plant that grows in and is adapted to an environment deficient in moisture. —**xer'o·phyt'ic** (-fĭt'ĭk) *adj.* —**xer'o·phyt'i·cal·ly** *adv.*

xe·ro·sere (zîr'ə-sîr') *n.* A sequence of ecological communities beginning in a dry area.

xe·ro·sis (zĭ-rō'sĭs) *n.* **1.** Abnormal dryness, esp. of the skin, conjunctiva, or mucous membranes. **2.** The normal evolutionary sclerosis of aging tissue.

Xer·ox (zîr'ŏks). **1.** A trademark for a photocopying process or machine using xerography. **2.** A copy made on a Xerox machine. —*tr.v.* **-oxed, -ox·ing, -ox·es.** To reproduce or print by means of a Xerox machine.

x-height (ĕks'hīt') *n. Printing.* The height of a lower-case *x.*

Xho·sa also **Xo·sa** (kō'sä) *n., pl.* **Xhosa** or **-sas** also **Xosa** or **-sas. 1.** One of a Bantu people of Cape of Good Hope Province, South Africa. **2.** The Bantu language of the Xhosa.

xi (zī, sī) *n.* **1.** The 14th letter of the Greek alphabet. See table at **alphabet. 2.** Also **xi particle.** *Physics.* Either of two unstable subatomic particles in the baryon family that have masses 2,572 and 2,585 times that of an electron. [Gk. *xei.*]

xiph·i·ster·num (zĭf'ĭ-stûr'nəm) *n., pl.* **-na** (-nə). The posterior and smallest of the three divisions of the sternum. [Gk. *xiphos,* sword + STERNUM.]

xiph·oid (zĭf'oid') *adj.* **1.** Having the shape of a sword. **2.** Of or pertaining to the xiphisternum. —*n.* The xiphisternum. [Gk. *xiphoeidēs* : *xiphos,* sword + *eidos,* shape.]

xiph·o·su·ran (zĭf'ə-sŏŏr'ən) *n.* An arthropod of the order Xiphosura, which includes the horseshoe crab and many extinct forms. —*adj.* Of or belonging to the order Xiphosura. [<NLat. *Xiphosura,* order name : Gk. *xiphos,* sword + Gk. *oura,* tail.]

X·mas (krĭs'məs, ĕks'məs) *n. Informal.* Christmas. [< *X,* the Greek letter chi, abbr. of *Khristos,* Christ.]

Usage: The abbreviation *Xmas* has been used for hundreds of years. In modern use it is considered informal and appropriate only in such commercial contexts as advertisements and signs.

Xo·sa (kō'sä) *n.* Variant of **Xhosa.**

x-ra·di·a·tion (ĕks'rā'dē-ā'shən) *n.* **1.** Treatment with or exposure to x-rays. **2.** Radiation composed of x-rays.

X-rat·ed (ĕks'rā'tĭd) *adj.* **1.** Having the rating X. **2.** Explicit in the treatment of sex: *an X-rated movie.*

X rating *n. Informal.* A classification assigned to a motion picture featuring explicit sex.

x-ray also **X-ray** (ĕks'rā') —*n.* Also **x ray** or **X ray. 1. a.** A relatively high-energy photon with wavelength in the approximate range from 0.05 angstroms to 100 angstroms. **b.** Often **x-rays.** A stream of such photons, used for their penetrating power in radiography, radiology, radiotherapy, and research. **2.** A photograph taken with x-rays. —*tr.v.* **x-rayed, x-ray·ing, x-rays** also **X-rayed, X-ray·ing, X-rays. 1.** To irradiate with x-rays. **2.** To photograph with x-rays. [Transl. of G. *X Strahl.*]

x-ray astronomy *n.* The branch of astronomy that deals with the properties of celestial bodies as indicated by the x-rays they emit.

x-ray burster *n.* Any of several celestial phenomena characterized by the emission of very powerful bursts of x-radiation in cycles lasting from a few seconds to a few minutes.

x-ray crystallography *n.* The study of crystal structure by means of x-ray diffraction.

x-ray diffraction *n.* The scattering of x-rays by crystal atoms, producing a diffraction pattern that yields information about the structure of the crystal.

x-ray microscope *n.* An instrument used to render a highly magnified image of the atomic structure of a crystalline system by means of the contrasts arising from the differences in such a structure's absorption or emission of x-rays.

x-ray star *n.* A celestial object resembling a star but emitting a major portion of its radiation in x-rays.

x-ray therapy *n.* Radiotherapy with x-rays.

x-ray tube *n.* A vacuum tube containing electrodes that accelerate electrons and direct them to a metal anode, where their impacts produce x-rays.

Xu·thus (zōō'thəs) *n. Gk. Myth.* The ancestor of the Ionian Greeks. [Lat. < Gk. *Xouthos.*]

xyl– *pref.* Variant of **xylo-**.
xy·lan (zī′lən) *n.* A yellow, gummy pentosan found in plant cell walls and yielding xylose upon hydrolysis.
xy·lem (zī′ləm) *n.* The supporting and water-conducting tissue of vascular plants, consisting primarily of tracheids and vessels; woody tissue. [G. < Gk. *xulon,* wood.]
xy·lene (zī-lēn′, zī′lēn′) *n.* **1.** Any of three flammable isomeric hydrocarbons, $C_6H_4(CH_3)_2$, obtained from wood and coal tar. **2.** A mixture of xylene isomers used as a solvent in making lacquers and rubber cement and as an aviation fuel.
xy·li·dine (zī′lĭ-dēn′, -dĭn, zĭl′-) *n.* **1.** Any of six toxic isomers, $(CH_3)_2C_6H_3NH_2$, derived from xylene, used chiefly as dye intermediates. **2.** Any of various mixtures of xylidine isomers.
xylo– or **xyl–** *pref.* **1.** Wood: *xylograph.* **2.** Xylene: *xylidine.* [< Gk. *xulon,* wood.]
xy·lo·graph (zī′lə-grăf′) *n.* **1.** An engraving on wood. **2.** An impression from a wood block. —*tr.v.* **-graphed, -graph·ing, -graphs.** To print from a wood engraving. **—xy·log′ra·pher** (-lŏg′rə-fər) *n.*
xy·log·ra·phy (zī-lŏg′rə-fē) *n.* **1.** Wood engraving, esp. of an early period. **2.** The art of printing texts or illustrations, sometimes with color, from wood blocks, as distinct from typography. **—xy′lo·graph′ic** (-lə-grăf′ĭk), **xy′lo·graph′i·cal** (-ĭ-kəl) *adj.* **—xy′lo·graph′i·cal·ly** *adv.*
xy·loid (zī′loid′) *adj.* Of or similar to wood.
xy·lol (zī′lôl′, -lōl′) *n.* Xylene (sense 1).
xy·loph·a·gous (zī-lŏf′ə-gəs) *adj.* Feeding on wood, as certain insects.
xy·lo·phone (zī′lə-fōn′) *n.* A musical percussion instrument consisting of a mounted row of wooden bars graduated in length to sound a chromatic scale, played with two small mallets. **—xy′lo·phon′ist** *n.*
xy·lose (zī′lōs′) *n.* A white crystalline aldose sugar, $C_5H_{10}O_5$, used in dyeing, tanning, and in diabetic diets.
xy·lot·o·my (zī-lŏt′ə-mē) *n.* The preparation of sections of wood for microscopic study.
XY recorder (eks′wī′) *n.* An output device that sketches the relationship between two variables onto a grid of plane rectangular coordinates.
xys·ter (zĭs′tər) *n.* A surgical instrument for scraping bones. [Gk. *xustēr,* scraper < *xuein,* to scrape.]

xylophone

Y

Around 1000 B.C. the Phoenicians and other Semitic peoples began to use graphic signs to represent individual speech sounds instead of syllables or words. They used a symbol (1,2) which is the ancestor of the letters F, U, V, and W as well as Y to represent the sound of the semivowel "w" and called it *wāw,* their word for "hook." The Greeks, adapting the Phoenician alphabet, varied the shape of *wāw* slightly (3,4,5) and altered its name to *upsilon.* They used *upsilon* to represent the sound of the vowel "u." The Romans borrowed the alphabet from the Greeks via the Etruscans, who used a tailless variant of *upsilon* that ultimately developed into the letter V. After the Romans became acquainted with Greek learning and literature they re-borrowed *upsilon* in a different form (5) in order to transliterate Greek words. Monumental script (7) became the basis for modern capital letters. Medieval scribes adapted the Roman capitals to being quickly written on parchment, paper, and vellum (8,9). The phonetic value of Y, originally the same as *upsilon,* gradually became that of I, and the two letters were used interchangeably for both the vowel "i" and the semivowel "y." Medieval uncial and cursive minuscules are the prototypes of modern lower-case letters. In the modern period Y came to be used exclusively for the semivowel and I for the vowel.

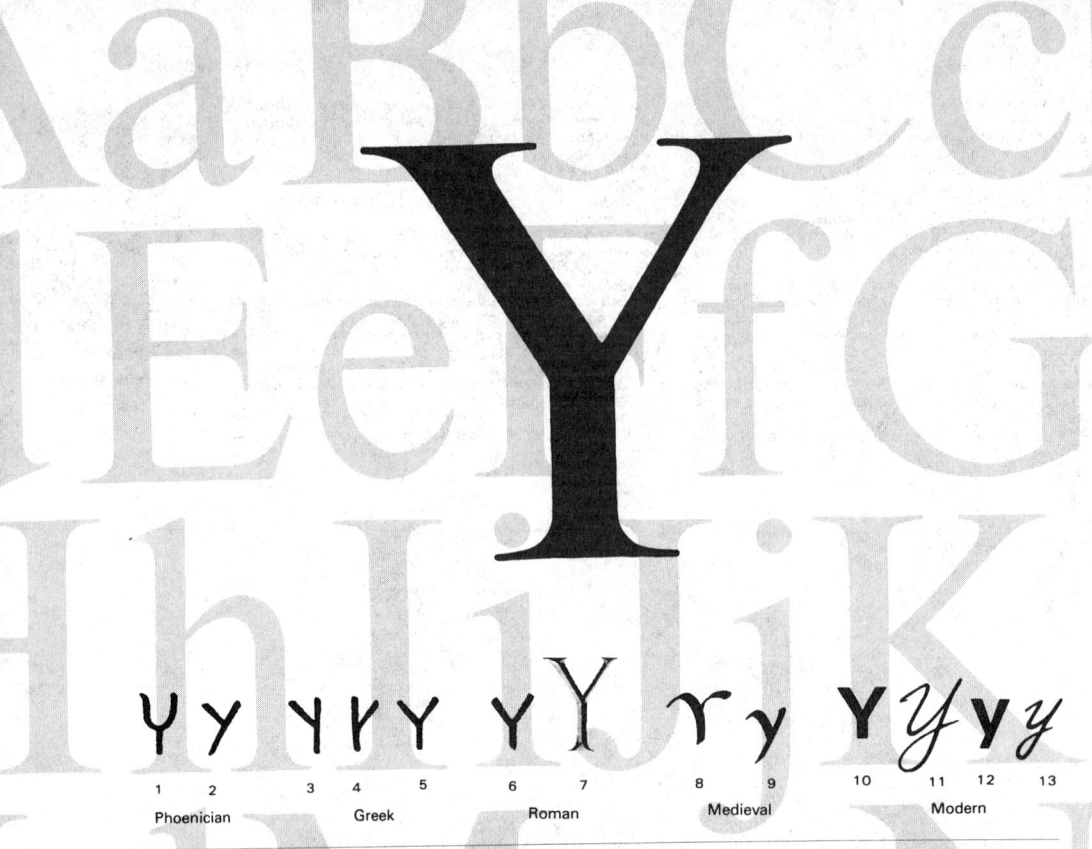

y

y or **Y** (wī) *n., pl.* **y's** or **Y's.** **1.** The 25th letter of the modern English alphabet. **2.** Any of the speech sounds represented by the letter *y.* **3.** Something shaped like the letter Y. **4.** The 25th in a series.
Y The symbol for the element yttrium.
-y[1] *suff.* **1.** Characterized by; consisting of: *clayey.* **2. a.** Like: *summery.* **b.** To some degree; somewhat; rather: *chilly.* **3.** Tending toward; inclined toward: *sleepy.* [ME *-ie, -ey* < OE *-ig.*]
-y[2] *suff.* **1.** Condition; state; quality: *jealousy.* **2. a.** Activity: *cookery.* **b.** Instance of a specified action: *entreaty.* **3. a.** Place for an activity: *cannery.* **b.** Result or product of an activity: *laundry.* **4.** Collection; body; group: *soldiery.* [ME *-ie* < OFr. < Lat. *-ia* and Gk. *-ia,* n. suffixes.]
-y[3] *suff.* **1.** Small one: *doggy.* **2.** Dear one: *sweetie.* **3.** One having to do with or characterized by: *towny.* [ME.]
yab·ber (yăb′ər) *Austral.* —*n.* Jabber. —*intr. & tr.v.* **-bered, -ber·ing, -bers.** To jabber. [Alteration of JABBER.]
yacht (yät) *n.* Any of various relatively small sailing or mechanically propelled vessels, generally with smart, graceful lines, used for pleasure cruises or racing. —*intr.v.* **yacht·ed, yacht·ing, yachts.** To race, sail, or cruise in a yacht. [Obs. Du. *jaghte,* short for *jaghtschip* : *jagen,* to chase + *schip,* ship.]
yacht club *n.* A club that promotes and supports yachting and boating.
yacht·ing (yät′ĭng) *n.* The sport of sailing in yachts.
yachts·man (yäts′mən) *n.* A person who owns or sails a yacht. —**yachts′man·ship′** *n.*
yack (yăk) *v. & n.* Variant of **yak**[2].
yack·e·ty-yak (yăk′ĭ-tē-yăk′) *n. Slang.* Yap (sense 2). [Imit.]
YAG (yăg) *n.* A hard synthetic yttrium aluminum garnet used in laser technology and as a gemstone. [Y(TTRIUM) + A(LUMINUM) + G(ARNET).]
ya·gi (yä′gē, yăg′ē) *n.* A directional radio and television antenna consisting of a horizontal conductor with several insulated dipoles parallel to and in the plane of the conductor. [After Hidetsugu *Yagi* (b. 1888), its inventor.]
yah (yä) *adv. Informal.* Yes. [Var. of YEA.]
ya·hoo (yä′hōō, yā′-) *n., pl.* **-hoos.** A crude or brutish person. [< *Yahoo,* member of a savage race in *Gulliver's Travels* by Jonathan Swift (1667–1745).] —**ya′hoo·ism** *n.*
Yah·weh (yä′wā) also **Yah·veh** (-vā) *n.* A name for God assumed by modern scholars to be a rendering of the pronunciation of the Tetragrammaton. [Heb.]
Yah·wist (yä′wĭst) also **Yah·vist** (-vĭst) *n.* The author of the earliest sources of the Hexateuch, in which God is called Yahweh. —**Yah·wis′tic** *adj.*
yak[1] (yăk) *n.* A long-haired bovine mammal, *Bos grunniens,* of the mountains of central Asia, where it is often domesticated. [Tibetan *gyag.*]
yak[2] also **yack** (yăk) *Slang.* —*intr.v.* **yakked, yak·king, yaks** also **yacked, yack·ing, yacks.** To talk or chatter persistently and meaninglessly. —*n.* Continuous, meaningless chatter. [Imit.]
ya·ki·to·ri (yä′kĭ-tôr′ē) *n.* A dish consisting of bite-sized marinated chicken pieces that are grilled on small skewers. [J. : *yaki,* roasting + *tori,* bird.]
Ya·kut (yä-kōōt′) *n.* **1.** One of a people living in the Yakut region of northeastern Russia. **2.** The Turkic language of the Yakuts.
y'all (yôl) *pron.* Variant of **you-all.**
yam (yăm) *n.* **1.** Any of various chiefly tropical vines of the genus *Dioscorea,* many of which have edible tuberous roots. **2.** The starchy root of the yam, used in the tropics as food. **3.** A sweet potato having reddish flesh. [Port. *inhame,* poss. < Bantu *nyama,* meat, or Bambara *nyana,* wild yam.]
ya·men (yä′mən) *n.* The office or residence of an official in the Chinese Empire. [Chin. (Mandarin) *ya*[2] *men*[2] : *ya*[2], magistracy (< *ya*[2], tooth, flag with a serrated edge) + *men*[2], gate.]
yam·mer (yăm′ər) *Informal.* —*v.* **-mered, -mer·ing, -mers.** —*intr.* **1.** To complain peevishly or whimperingly; whine. **2.** To talk volubly and loudly. —*tr.* To utter or say in a complaining or clamorous tone. —*n.* An act or instance of yammering. [Alteration of ME *yomeren,* to lament < OE *gēomrian.*] —**yam′mer·er** *n.*
yang also **Yang** (yăng) *n.* The active, masculine cosmic principle in Chinese dualistic philosophy. [Chin. (Mandarin) *yang*[2], sun, light, masculine element.]
yank (yăngk) *v.* **yanked, yank·ing, yanks.** *Informal.* —*tr.* To pull or extract suddenly; jerk. —*intr.* To pull on something suddenly; jerk. —*n.* A sudden vigorous pull; jerk. [Orig. unknown.]
Yank (yăngk) *n. Informal.* Yankee. [Short for YANKEE.]
Yan·kee (yăng′kē) *n.* **1.** A native or inhabitant of New England. **2.** A native or inhabitant of a Northern state, esp. a Union soldier during the Civil War. **3.** A native or inhabitant of the United States. [Orig. unknown.]
Yan·kee·dom (yăng′kē-dəm) *n.* **1.** The Northern states or New England. **2.** The United States. **3.** Yankees collectively.
Yankee Doo·dle (dōōd′l) *n.* A Yankee. [From the title of a song popular during the Revolutionary War.]
Yan·kee·ism (yăng′kē-ĭz′əm) *n.* **1.** A Yankee custom or characteristic. **2.** A Yankee peculiarity, as of language or pronunciation.
yap (yăp) *v.* **yapped, yap·ping, yaps.** —*intr.* **1.** To bark sharply or shrilly; yelp. **2.** *Slang.* To talk noisily or stupidly; jabber. **3.** *Slang.* To talk abusively; scold. —*tr.* To utter by yapping. —*n.* **1.** A sharp, shrill bark; yelp. **2.** *Slang.* Noisy, stupid talk; jabber. **3.** *Slang.* A crude, loud, stupid person. **4.** *Slang.* The mouth. [Imit.] —**yap′per** *n.*
ya·pok (yə-pŏk′) *n.* An aquatic marsupial mammal, *Chironectes minimus,* of tropical America, having dense fur, webbed hind feet, and a long tail. [After the *Oyapock,* a river in South America.]
Ya·qui (yä′kē) *n., pl.* **Yaqui** or **-quis.** **1. a.** A tribe of North American Indians now living in Sonora, Mexico. **b.** A member of this tribe. **2.** The Uto-Aztecan language of the Yaqui.
Yar·bor·ough (yär′bər-ō, -bər-ə) *n.* A bridge or whist hand containing no card higher than a nine. [After Charles Anderson Worsley (1809–1897), 2nd Earl of *Yarborough,* said to have bet 1,000 to 1 that such a hand would not occur.]
yard[1] (yärd) *n.* **1.** The fundamental unit of length in both the U.S. Customary System and the British Imperial System, equal to 0.9144 meter. **2.** *Naut.* A long tapering spar slung at right angles to a mast to support and spread the head of a square sail, lugsail, or lateen. [ME *yerde,* measuring rod < OE *gerd,* stick.]
yard[2] (yärd) *n.* **1.** A tract of ground adjacent to, surrounding, or surrounded by a building or group of buildings. **2.** A tract of ground, often enclosed, used for a specific work, business, or other activity. **3.** An area provided with a system of tracks where railroad trains are made up and cars are switched, stored, or serviced. **4.** A winter pasture for deer or other grazing animals. **5.** An enclosed tract of ground in which animals, such as chickens or pigs, are kept. —*v.* **yarded, yard·ing, yards.** —*tr.* To enclose, collect, or put in or as if in a yard. —*intr.* To gather in or as if in a yard. [ME < OE *geard,* enclosed area.]
yard·age[1] (yär′dĭj) *n.* **1.** The amount or length of something measured in yards. **2.** Cloth sold by the yard.
yard·age[2] (yär′dĭj) *n.* **1.** The use of a livestock yard at a station in the process of transporting cattle by railroad. **2.** The fee paid for yardage.
yard·arm (yärd′ärm′) *n. Naut.* Either end of a yard of a square sail.
yard bird *n. Slang.* **1. a.** A low-ranking enlisted man who is untrained. **b.** An enlisted man who is confined to base and is assigned menial tasks as punishment. **2.** A convict; prisoner.
yard goods *pl.n.* Piece goods.
yard grass *n.* Any of several weedy grasses of the genus *Eleusine.*
yard·man (yärd′mən) *n.* A man employed in a yard, esp. a railroad yard.
yard·mas·ter (yärd′măs′tər) *n.* A railroad employee in charge of a yard.
yard of ale *n.* **1.** A slender glass shaped like a horn that is about three feet tall and that holds about three pints. **2.** The amount of liquid that a yard of ale contains.
yard sale *n.* A sale of used household belongings on the front or back lawn of a house.
yard·stick (yärd′stĭk′) *n.* **1.** A graduated measuring stick one yard in length. **2.** A test or standard used in measurement, comparison, or judgment.
yare (yâr) *Archaic.* —*adj.* **1.** Responding easily; maneuverable. Used of a vessel. **2.** Bright; lively. **3.** Ready; prepared. —*adv.* Soon; quickly. [ME < OE *gearo,* ready.] —**yare′ly** *adv.*
yar·mul·ke also **yar·mel·ke** (yär′məl-kə, yä′məl-) *n.* A skullcap worn by male Jews, esp. those adhering to Orthodox or Conservative tradition. [Yiddish < Pol. and Ukranian *yarmulka,* poss. < Turk. *yağmurluk,* raincoat < *yağmur,* rain.]
yarn (yärn) *n.* **1.** A continuous strand of twisted threads of natural or synthetic material, such as wool or nylon, used in weaving or knitting. **2.** *Informal.* A long, complicated story or a tale of real or fictitious adventures, often elaborated upon by the teller during the telling. —*intr.v.* **yarned, yarn·ing, yarns.** *Informal.* To tell a long, complicated story. [ME < OE *gearn.*]
yarn-dyed (yärn′dīd′) *adj.* Made of yarn that has been dyed before weaving.
yar·row (yăr′ō) *n.* Any of several plants of the genus *Achillea,* esp. *A. millefolium,* native to Eurasia, having finely dissected foliage and flat clusters of usually white flowers. [ME *yarow* < OE *gearwe.*]
yash·mak also **yash·mac** (yäsh-mäk′, yăsh′măk) *n.* A veil worn by Moslem women to cover the face in public. [Ar.]
yat·a·ghan also **yat·a·gan** (yăt′ə-găn′, -gən) *n.* A Turkish sword or scimitar having a double-curved blade, an eared pommel, and lacking a handle guard. [Turk. *yatağan.*]
yaup (yôp) *v. & n.* Variant of **yawp.**
yau·pon (yô′pən) *n.* A holly, *Ilex vomitoria,* of the southeastern United States, having scarlet fruit and evergreen leaves, once used medicinally. [Catawba *yopun,* dim. of *yop,* tree.]
yaw (yô) *v.* **yawed, yaw·ing, yaws.** —*intr.* **1.** To deviate from the intended course. Used of a ship. **2.** To move unsteadily; weave. **3.** To turn about the vertical axis. Used of an aircraft or projectile. —*tr.* To cause to yaw. —*n.* **1.** The action of

yam

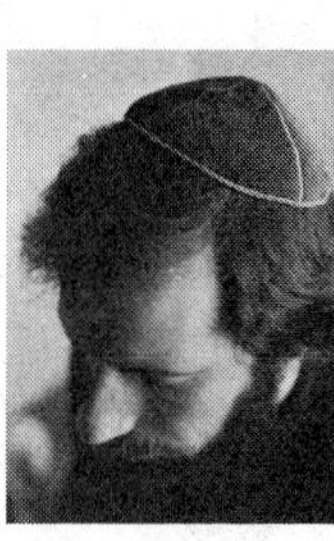

yarmulke

yarrow

yawing. **2.** The extent of the yawing, measured in degrees. [Orig. unknown.]

yawl (yôl) *n.* **1.** A two-masted fore-and-aft-rigged sailing vessel similar to the ketch but having a smaller jigger mast stepped abaft the rudder. **2.** A ship's small boat, manned by oarsmen. [MLG *jolle.*]

yawn (yôn) *v.* **yawned, yawn·ing, yawns.** *—intr.* **1.** To open the mouth wide with a deep inspiration, usually involuntarily, from drowsiness, fatigue, or boredom. **2.** To open wide; gape: *The chasm yawned at our feet.* *—tr.* To utter wearily, as if in yawning. *—n.* An act or instance of yawning. [ME *yanen* < OE *gēonian.*] **—yawn'er** *n.*

yawn·ing (yôn'ĭng) *adj.* Gaping open; cavernous. **—yawn'ing·ly** *adv.*

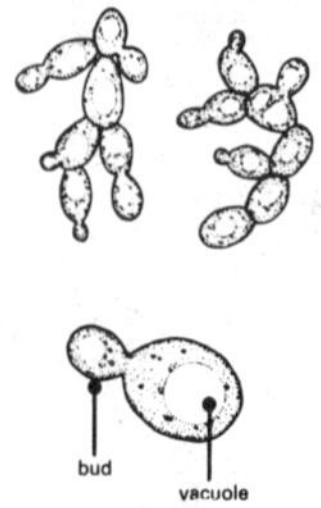

yeast
Yeast cells and buds

yawp also **yaup** (yôp) *—intr.v.* **yawped, yawp·ing, yawps** also **yauped, yaup·ing, yaups. 1.** To utter a sharp cry; yelp. **2.** *Slang.* To talk loudly and stupidly. *—n.* **1.** A bark; yelp. **2.** *Slang.* Loud, stupid talk. [ME *yolpen,* poss. var. of *yelpen,* to cry aloud. —see YELP.] **—yawp'er** *n.*

yaws (yôz) *n.* *(used with a sing. or pl. verb).* An infectious tropical skin disease, caused by a spirochete, *Treponema pertenue,* and characterized by multiple red pimples. [Carib.]

y-ax·is (wī'ăk'sĭs) *n., pl.* **y-ax·es** (-sēz). **1.** The vertical axis of a two-dimensional Cartesian coordinate system. **2.** One of three axes in a three-dimensional Cartesian coordinate system.

Yb The symbol for the element ytterbium.

Y-chro·mo·some (wī'krō'mə-sōm') *n.* The sex chromosome associated with male characteristics, occurring with one X-chromosome in the male sex-chromosome pair.

y·clept also **y·cleped** (ĭ-klĕpt', ĭ-klēpt') *v.* Past participle of **clepe.** [ME *ycleped* < OE *geclepod,* p.part. of *cleopian,* to call.]

ye[1] (*thē*) *adj. Archaic.* The. [Alteration of OE *þē,* from the use of *y* for *þ* (thorn) by the early printers.]

ye[2] (yē) *pron.* **1.** *Archaic.* You (plural). **2.** *Regional.* You (singular). [ME < OE *gē.*]

yea (yā) *adv.* **1.** Yes; aye. **2.** Indeed; truly: *They have spoken, yea, shouted their reply.* *—n.* **1.** An affirmative statement or vote. **2.** One who votes affirmatively. [ME < OE *gēa.*]

yeah also **yeh** (yĕ'ə, yă'ə, yā'ə) *adv. Informal.* Yes. [Var. of YEA.]

yean (yēn) *v.* **yeaned, yean·ing, yeans.** *—intr.* To bear young. Used of sheep and goats. *—tr.* To give birth to; bear. [ME *yenen* < OE **geēanian* : *ge-,* verb prefix + *ēanian,* to bear young.]

yean·ling (yēn'lĭng) *n.* The young of a sheep or goat; a lamb or kid. *—adj.* Newly born; infant.

year (yîr) *n.* **1. a.** The period of time as measured by the Gregorian calendar in which the earth completes a single revolution around the sun, consisting of 365 days, 5 hours, 49 minutes, and 12 seconds of mean solar time divided into 12 months, 52 weeks, and 365 or 366 days, and beginning on January 1 and ending on December 31. **b.** A period approximately equal to a year in other calendars. **2.** Sidereal year. **3.** Tropical year. **4.** A period of approximately the duration of a calendar year: *We were married a year ago.* **5.** A period equal to the calendar year but beginning on a different date: *a fiscal year.* **6.** A specific period of time, usually shorter than 12 months, devoted to a special activity: *the academic year.* **7. years.** Age, esp. old age: *feeling his years.* **8. years.** An indefinitely long period of time: *It's been years since we saw him.* [ME *yere* < OE *gēar.*]

year·book (yîr'bo͝ok') *n.* **1.** A documentary, memorial, or historical book published every year, containing information about the previous year. **2.** A yearly record or book published by the graduating class of a high school or college.

year-end also **year·end** (yîr'ĕnd') *n.* The end of a fiscal year.

year·ling (yîr'lĭng) *n.* **1.** An animal that is one year old or has not completed its second year. **2.** A thoroughbred racehorse one year old dating from January 1 of the year that it was foaled. *—adj.* Being one year old.

year·long (yîr'lông', -lŏng') *adj.* Lasting through one year.

year·ly (yîr'lē) *adj.* Occurring once a year or every year; annual. *—adv.* Once a year; annually. *—n., pl.* **-lies.** A publication issued once a year.

yearn (yûrn) *intr.v.* **yearned, yearn·ing, yearns. 1.** To have a strong or deep desire; be filled with longing. **2.** To feel deep pity, sympathy, or tenderness. [ME *yernen* < OE *gyrnan.*]

Synonyms: *yearn, long, pine, hanker, hunger, thirst.* These verbs mean to have a strong desire. *Yearn* and *long* both stress protracted and insistent desire or craving. Sometimes *yearn* is applied to a wish for the return of something lost, and *long* to desire for the attainment of something unfulfilled. *Pine* implies lingering desire that saps strength or spirit. *Hanker* often refers to a fleeting desire, but it can also apply to an urge to satisfy a physical appetite or to a craving for fame, power, or wealth. *Hunger* and *thirst* are applied figuratively to compelling desire for the attainment or possession of something.

year-round (yîr'round') *adj.* Existing, active, or continuous throughout the year; during all seasons.

yea-say·er (yā'sā'ər) *n.* **1.** One who is confidently affirmative in attitude. **2.** One who uncritically agrees.

yeast (yēst) *n.* **1.** Any of various unicellular fungi of the genus *Saccharomyces* and related genera, reproducing by budding and capable of fermenting carbohydrates. **2.** Froth consisting of yeast cells together with the carbon dioxide they produce in the process of fermentation, present in or added to fruit juices and other substances in the production of alcoholic beverages. **3.** A commercial preparation, either in powdered or compressed form, containing yeast cells and inert material such as meal, and used esp. as a leavening agent or as a dietary supplement. **4.** Foam; froth. **5.** An agent of ferment or activity. *—intr.v.* **yeast·ed, yeast·ing, yeasts. 1.** To ferment. **2.** To froth or foam. [ME *yeest* < OE *gist.*]

yeast·y (yē'stē) *adj.* **-i·er, -i·est. 1.** Of, similar to, or containing yeast. **2.** Causing or characterized by a ferment. **3.** Restless; turbulent. **4.** Frothy; frivolous. **—yeast'i·ly** *adv.* **—yeast'i·ness** *n.*

yecch also **yech** (yĕKH, yŭKH, yĕk, yŭk) *Slang. —interj.* Used to express strong disgust or contempt. *—n.* Something disgusting. *—adj.* Disgusting; sickening. **—yech'y** *adj.*

yegg (yĕg) *n. Slang.* A thief, esp. a burglar or safecracker. [Orig. unknown.]

yeh (yĕ'ə, yă'ə, yā'ə) *adv.* Variant of **yeah.**

yell (yĕl) *v.* **yelled, yell·ing, yells.** *—intr.* To cry out loudly, as in pain, fright, surprise, or enthusiasm. *—tr.* To utter loudly; shout. *—n.* **1.** A loud cry; shout. **2.** A rhythmic cheer uttered or chanted in unison by a group: *a college yell.* [ME *yellen* < OE *giellan.*] **—yell'er** *n.*

yel·low (yĕl'ō) *n.* **1. a.** Any of a group of colors of a hue resembling that of ripe lemons and varying in lightness and saturation; the hue of that portion of the spectrum lying between green and orange; one of the psychological primary hues, evoked in the normal observer by radiant energy of wavelength approximately 580 nanometers; also one of the subtractive primaries. **b.** A pigment or dye having this hue. **c.** Something that has this hue. **2.** The yolk of an egg. **3.** A person with yellow or light-brown skin. **4. yellows.** Any of various plant diseases usually caused by fungi of the genus *Fusarium* or viruses of the genus *Chlorogenus* and characterized by yellow or yellowish discoloration. *—adj.* **-er, -est. 1.** Of the color yellow. **2.** Designating a person or people having yellowish skin, esp. Oriental. **3.** *Slang.* Cowardly. *—tr. & intr.v.* **-lowed, -low·ing, -lows.** To make or become yellow. [ME *yelow* < OE *geolu.*] **—yel'low·ness** *n.*

yel·low·bark (yĕl'ō-bärk') *n.* Calisaya.

yel·low-bel·lied (yĕl'ō-bĕl'ēd) *adj.* **1.** Having a belly yellow or yellowish in color, as certain birds. **2.** *Slang.* Cowardly. **—yel'low-bel'ly** *n.*

yellow birch *n.* A North American tree, *Betula lutea,* having yellowish bark and hard, light-colored wood used for furniture and flooring.

yel·low·bird (yĕl'ō-bûrd') *n.* Any of various yellow or predominantly yellow birds, such as the goldfinch or the yellow warbler.

yellow cake *n.* The final precipitate formed in the milling of uranium ore.

yellow card *n. Sports.* A card raised by a referee in soccer, indicating a player's violation.

yellow cypress *n.* The Nootka cypress.

yel·low-dog contract (yĕl'ō-dôg', -dŏg') *n.* An employer-employee contract, no longer legal, by which the employee agrees not to join a union while employed.

yellow fever *n.* An acute infectious disease of subtropical and tropical New World areas, caused by a filterable virus transmitted by a mosquito of the genus *Aedes* and characterized by jaundice and dark-colored vomit resulting from hemorrhages.

yellow flu *n.* The organized absence of students from school in protest of compulsory busing. [So called because school buses are usually yellow.]

yel·low·ham·mer (yĕl'ō-hăm'ər) *n.* **1.** A common North American woodpecker, *Colaptes auratus,* having colorful, distinctive markings. **2.** A Eurasian bird, *Emberiza citrinella,* having brown and yellow plumage. [By folk ety. < obs. *yelambre.*]

yel·low·ish (yĕl'ō-ĭsh) *adj.* Somewhat yellow; tinged with yellow. **—yel'low·ish·ness** *n.*

yellow jack *n.* **1.** Yellow fever. **2.** *Naut.* A yellow flag hoisted to request pratique or to warn of disease on board. **3.** A silvery and yellowish food fish, *Caranx bartholomaei,* of western Atlantic and Caribbean waters.

yellow jacket *n.* Any of several small wasps of the family *Vespidae,* having yellow and black markings and usually nesting in the ground.

yellow journalism *n.* Journalism that exploits, distorts, or exaggerates the news to create sensations and attract readers. [From the use of yellow ink in printing "Yellow Kid," a cartoon strip in the *New York World,* a newspaper noted for sensationalism.]

yel·low·legs (yĕl'ō-lĕgz') *n., pl.* **yellowlegs.** Either of two North American wading birds, *Totanus melanoleucus* or *T. flavipes,* having yellow legs and a long, narrow bill.

yellow ocher *n.* **1.** A yellow pigment, usually containing limonite. **2.** A moderate orange with yellow overtones.

yellow pages or **Yellow Pages** *pl.n.* A section of a telephone directory that lists businesses, services, or products alphabetically according to field. [So called because they are usually printed on yellow paper.]
yellow peril or **Yellow Peril** *n.* The threatened expansion of the Oriental peoples as magnified in the Western imagination.
yellow pine *n.* **1.** Any of several North American evergreen trees having yellowish wood, such as *Pinus echinata,* of the southeastern United States, or the ponderosa pine. **2.** The wood of the yellow pine.
yellow poplar *n.* The tulip tree.
yellow-shafted flicker (yĕl'ō-shăf'tĭd) *n.* The yellowhammer (sense 1).
yellow sheet *n. Slang.* A criminal record; rap sheet.
yellow spot *n.* The macula lutea.
yellow streak *n.* A proneness to cowardice and disloyalty.
yel·low·tail (yĕl'ō-tāl') *n.* **1.** A marine game fish, *Seriola dorsalis,* of coastal waters of southern California and Mexico. **2.** Any of several fishes other than the yellowtail that have a yellowish tail, such as the mademoiselle.
yel·low·throat (yĕl'ō-thrōt') *n.* Any of several small New World birds of the genus *Geothlypis,* esp. *G. trichas,* having a brownish back, a yellow throat, and, in the male, a black facial mask.
yellow warbler *n.* A small New World bird, *Dendroica petechia,* having predominantly yellow plumage.
yel·low·weed (yĕl'ō-wēd') *n.* Any of various plants having yellow flowers, such as the dyer's rocket.
yel·low·wood (yĕl'ō-wŏŏd') *n.* **1.** A tree, *Cladrastis lutea,* of the southeastern United States, having compound leaves, drooping clusters of white flowers, and yellow wood yielding a yellow dye. **2.** Any of various trees having yellow wood. **3.** The wood of the yellowwood.
yel·low·y (yĕl'ō-ē) *adj.* Somewhat yellow; yellowish.
yelp (yĕlp) *v.* **yelped, yelp·ing, yelps.** *—intr.* **1.** To utter a sharp, short bark or cry. **2.** To cry out sharply, as in pain or surprise. *—tr.* To utter by yelping. *—n.* A sharp, short cry or bark. [ME *yelpen,* to cry aloud < OE *gielpan,* to boast.] **—yelp'er** *n.*
yen[1] (yĕn) *Informal.* *—intr.v.* **yenned, yen·ning, yens.** To yearn. *—n.* A yearning; longing. [Cantonese *yan.*]
yen[2] (yĕn) *n., pl.* **yen.** See table at **currency.** [J. *en* < Chin. (Mandarin) *yuan*[2], dollar.]
yen·ta (yĕn'tə) *n. Slang.* A gossipy woman, esp. one who pries into the affairs of others. [Yiddish *yente* < the name *Yente.*]
yeo·man (yō'mən) *n., pl.* **-men. 1.** An independent farmer, esp. a member of a former class of small freeholding farmers in England. **2.** A yeoman of the guard. **3.** An attendant, servant, or lesser official in a royal or noble household. **4.** A petty officer performing chiefly clerical duties in the U.S. Navy. **5.** An assistant or other subordinate, as of a sheriff. **6.** A diligent and dependable worker. *—adj.* Also **yeo·man·ly** (-lē). **1.** Pertaining to or ranking as a yeoman. **2.** Befitting a yeoman; sturdy, staunch, or workmanlike. [ME *yoman,* perh. contraction of *yong man,* young man.]
yeoman of the guard *n.* A member of a ceremonial guard attending the British sovereign and royal family, consisting of 100 yeomen with their officers.
yeo·man·ry (yō'mən-rē) *n.* **1.** The class of yeomen; small farmers. **2.** A British volunteer cavalry force organized in 1761 to serve as a home guard and later incorporated into the Territorial Army.
yep (yĕp) *adv. Slang.* Yes. [Alteration of YES.]
yer·ba ma·té (yâr'bə mä-tā', yûr'bə) *n.* The maté (sense 2). [Am. Sp. : *yerba,* herb (< Lat. *herba*) + *maté,* maté. —see MATÉ.]
Yerk·ish (yûr'kĭsh) *n.* An artificial language using geometric forms to represent words that was created for communication between chimpanzees and humans. [After the *Yerkes* Regional Primate Center in Georgia.]
yes (yĕs) *adv.* It is so; as you say or ask. Used to express affirmation, agreement, positive confirmation, or consent. *—n., pl.* **yes·es. 1.** An affirmative or consenting reply. **2.** An affirmative vote or voter. *—tr.v.* **yessed, yes·sing, yes·es.** To give an affirmative reply to. [ME < OE *gese.*]
ye·shi·va or **ye·shi·vah** (yə-shē'və) *n.* **1.** A Jewish institute of learning where students study the Talmud. **2.** An elementary or secondary school with a curriculum that includes Jewish religion and culture as well as general education. [Heb. *yĕshībhāh* < *yāshábh,* he sat down.]
yes man *n. Informal.* One who slavishly agrees with one's superior; sycophant.
yester– *pref.* Yesterday: *yestermorning.* [ME *yister-* < OE *giestran.*]
yes·ter·day (yĕs'tər-dā', -dē) *n.* **1.** The day before the present day. **2.** Often **yesterdays.** Time in the immediate past. *—adv.* **1.** On the day before the present day. **2.** A short while ago. [ME < OE *giestran dæg* : *giestran,* yesterday + *dæg,* day.]
yes·ter·eve·ning (yĕs'tər-ēv'nĭng) also **yes·ter·eve** (-ēv') or **yes·ter·e·ven** (-ē'vən) *n.* The evening of yesterday. **—yes'ter·eve'ning** *adv.*
yes·ter·morn·ing (yĕs'tər-môr'nĭng) also **yes·ter·morn** (-môrn') *n.* Yesterday morning. **—yes'ter·morn'ing** *adv.*
yes·ter·night (yĕs'tər-nīt') *n.* Last night. **—yes'ter·night'** *adv.*
yes·ter·year (yĕs'tər-yîr') *n.* **1.** The year before this one. **2.** Time past, esp. as thought of nostalgically; yore. **—yes'ter·year'** *adv.*
yes·treen (yĕs-trēn') *n. Scot.* Variant of **yesterevening.**
yet (yĕt) *adv.* **1.** At this time; for the present: *Don't sing yet.* **2.** Up to a specified time; thus far: *The end had not yet come.* **3.** In the time remaining; still: *There is yet a solution to be found.* **4.** Besides; in addition: *Play the tape yet another time.* **5.** Even; still more: *a yet sadder tale.* **6.** Nevertheless: *young yet wise.* **7.** At some future time; eventually: *He may yet see the truth.* *—conj.* Nevertheless; and despite this: *He said he would be late, yet he arrived on time.* **—idiom. as yet.** Up to the present time; up to now. [ME < OE *gīet.*]
ye·ti (yĕt'ē) *n.* The abominable snowman. [Alteration of Tibetan *miti* : *mi,* person + *ti,* a kind of animal.]
yew (yōō) *n.* **1.** Any of several evergreen trees or shrubs of the genus *Taxus,* of which the flat, dark-green needles and often the scarlet berries are poisonous. **2.** The wood of a yew, esp. the durable, fine-grained wood of an Old World species, *T. baccata,* used in cabinetmaking and for archery bows. [ME *ew* < OE *īw.*]

yew

yé-yé (yā'yā') *adj. Slang.* Of, pertaining to, or featuring French rock 'n' roll. [Fr. < E. *yeah, yeah,* a phrase used in rock 'n' roll music.]
Ygg·dra·sil also **Yg·dra·sil** (ĭg'drə-sĭl, üg'-) *n. Myth.* The great ash tree that holds together earth, heaven, and hell by its roots and branches in Norse mythology. [ON.]
YHWH (yä'wā) also **YHVH** (yä'vā) *n.* The Hebrew Tetragrammaton representing the name of God.
yid (yĭd) *n. Offensive Slang.* A Jew. [Back-formation from YIDDISH.]
Yid·dish (yĭd'ĭsh) *n.* A High German language with many words borrowed from Hebrew and Slavic that is written in Hebrew characters and spoken chiefly as a vernacular in eastern European Jewish communities and by emigrants from these communities throughout the world. [Yiddish *Yidish* < MHG *jüdisch (diutsch),* Jewish (German) < *Jüde,* Jew < OHG *judo* < Lat. *Judaeus.* —see JEW.] **—Yid'dish** *adj.* **—Yid'dish·ism** *n.*
yield (yēld) *v.* **yield·ed, yield·ing, yields.** *—tr.* **1.** To give forth by or as if by a natural process, esp. by cultivation: *a field that yields many bushels.* **2.** To furnish or give in return; be productive of: *an investment that yields six per cent.* **3.** To surrender (something) in deference or defeat; relinquish: *yielded the field to a rival.* **4.** To grant or concede: *yield the right of way.* *—intr.* **1.** To furnish or give a return; be productive. **2.** To give up; submit. **3.** To give way to pressure, force, or persuasion. **4.** To give way to what is stronger or better; be overcome: *"Wrong opinions and practices gradually yield to fact and argument"* (John Stuart Mill). *—n.* **1.** The amount yielded or produced; product. **2.** The profit obtained from investment; return. **3.** The energy released by an explosion, esp. by a nuclear explosion, expressed in units of weight of TNT required to produce an equivalent release: *a 100-megaton yield.* [ME *yielden* < OE *gieldan,* to pay.] **—yield'er** *n.*

Synonyms: *yield, relent, bow, defer, submit, capitulate.* These verbs all have a sense of abandoning or retreating from a position or stand. *Yield* has the widest application. It can refer to giving way for reasons ranging from recognition that one is overmatched to acknowledgment that an adversary's position is the more correct one. *Relent* refers to moderating a stand one has taken with respect to another and thus showing him clemency. *Bow* involves giving way either out of necessity or out of respect for or courtesy to another. *Defer* can mean either giving way to authority or changing one's stand as an act of courtesy, respect, or recognition of another's superior knowledge, judgment, or the like. *Submit* implies giving way out of necessity after opposing unsuccessfully. *Capitulate,* in this sense, also implies surrender but not necessarily after active opposition.

yield·ing (yēl'dĭng) *adj.* Inclined to yield; docile. **—yield'ing·ly** *adv.* **—yield'ing·ness** *n.*
yin (yĭn) *n.* The passive, female cosmic principle in Chinese dualistic philosophy. [Chin. (Mandarin) *yin*[1], moon, shade, femininity.]
yip (yĭp) *n.* A sharp, high-pitched bark; yelp. *—intr.v.* **yipped, yip·ping, yips.** To emit sharp, high-pitched barks; yelp. [Imit.]
yipe (yīp) also **yipes** (yīps) *interj.* Used to express surprise, fear, or dismay.
yip·pee (yĭp'ē) *interj.* Used to express joy or elation.
-yl *suff.* A chemical radical: *carbonyl.* [Fr. *-yle* < Gk. *hulē,* wood, matter.]
y·lang-y·lang (ē'läng-ē'läng) *n.* **1.** A tropical Asian tree, *Cananga odorata* (or *Canangium odoratum*), having fragrant greenish-yellow flowers that yield an oil used in perfumery. **2.** An oil or perfume obtained from the flowers of the ylang-ylang. [Tagalog *ilang-ilang.*]
y·lem (ī'ləm) *n.* A form of matter hypothesized by proponents of the big bang theory to have existed before the formation of the chemical elements. [ME, universal matter < OFr. *ilem* < Med. Lat. *hylem,* accusative of *hyle,* matter < Gk. *hulē.*]
yock (yŏk, yŭk) *Slang.* *—intr.v.* **yocked, yock·ing, yocks.** To

laugh or joke, esp. in a rowdy manner. *—n.* A joke; laugh: *"it contains a few yocks, but the humor . . . never emerges"* (Variety). [Imit.]

yod also **yodh** (yōd, yo͝od) *n.* The 10th letter of the Hebrew alphabet. See table at **alphabet**. [Heb *yōdh* < *yādh,* hand.]

yo·del (yōd'l) *v.* **-deled, -del·ing, -dels** or **-delled, -del·ling, -dels.** *—intr.* To sing so that the voice fluctuates between the normal chest voice and a falsetto. *—tr.* To sing (a song) in a yodeling fashion. *—n.* A song or cry that is yodeled. [G. *jodeln.*] **—yo'del·er** *n.*

yodh (yōd, yo͝od) *n.* Variant of **yod**.

yo·ga (yō'gə) *n.* **1.** Often **Yoga.** A Hindu discipline aimed at training the consciousness for a state of perfect spiritual insight and tranquillity. **2.** A system of exercises practiced as part of the discipline of yoga to promote control of the body and mind. [Skt. *yogaḥ,* union, yoking.]

ȝ

yogh

yogh (yōKH) *n.* The Middle English letter ȝ representing a velar or palatal fricative or the sound of *w* between vowels. [ME, poss. < *yok,* yoke < OE *geoc* (from its shape).]

yo·ghurt or **yo·ghourt** (yō'gərt) *n.* Variants of **yogurt**.

yo·gi (yō'gē) *n., pl.* **-gis.** One who practices yoga. [Hindi < Skt. *yogī.*] **—yo'gic** *adj.*

yo·gurt also **yo·ghurt** or **yo·ghourt** (yō'gərt) *n.* A food of a custardlike consistency, prepared from milk curdled by bacteria, esp. *Lactobacillus bulgaricus* and *Streptococcus thermophilus,* and often sweetened or flavored with fruit. [Turk. *yoğurt.*]

yo·him·bine (yō-hĭm'bēn') *n.* A poisonous alkaloid, $C_{21}H_{26}N_2O_3$, derived from the bark of a tree, *Corynanthe yohimbe,* and formerly used as an aphrodisiac, local anesthetic, and mydriatic. [NLat. *yohimbe,* specific epithet of *Corynanthe yohimbe,* species of tree from which it is derived, of Bantu orig.]

yoicks (yoiks) *interj. Archaic.* Used as a hunting cry to urge the hounds after the fox.

yoke (yōk) *n.* **1.** A crossbar with two U-shaped pieces that encircle the necks of a pair of oxen, mules, or other draft animals working in a team. **2.** *pl.* **yoke** or **yokes.** A pair of draft animals joined by a yoke or trained to work together. **3.** A frame or crossbar designed to be carried across a person's shoulders with equal loads suspended from each end. **4.** A bar used with a double harness to connect the collar of each horse to the tongue of a wagon or coach. **5.** *Naut.* A crossbar on a ship's rudder to which the steering cables are connected. **6.** A clamp or vise that holds a machine part in place or controls its movement or that holds two such parts together. **7.** A piece of a garment that is closely fitted, either around the neck and shoulders or at the hips, and from which an unfitted or gathered part of the garment is hung. **8.** Something that connects or joins together; bond. **9.** *Electronics.* A series of two or more magnetic recording heads fastened securely together for playing or recording on more than one track simultaneously. **10.** A structure made of two upright spears with a third laid across them, under which conquered enemies of ancient Rome were forced to march in subjection. **11.** A form or symbol of subjugation or bondage. *—v.* **yoked, yok·ing, yokes.** *—tr.* **1.** To fit or join with a yoke. **2. a.** To harness a draft animal to. **b.** To harness (a draft animal) to something. **3.** To connect, join, or bind together. **4.** To force into bondage or servitude. *—intr.* To become connected, joined, or bound together. [ME *yok* < OE *geoc.*]

yoke

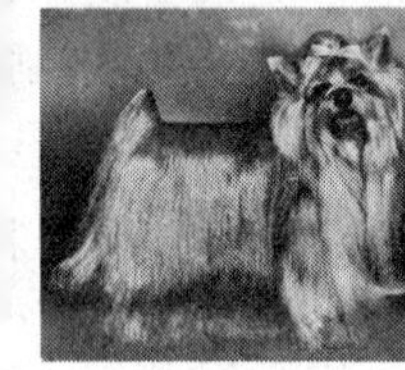

Yorkshire terrier

yoke·fel·low (yōk'fĕl'ō) *n.* A work companion; comrade.

yo·kel (yō'kəl) *n.* A naive or gullible rustic. [Orig. unknown.]

yoke·mate (yōk'māt') *n.* A yokefellow.

yo·ko·zu·na (yō'kō-zo͞o-nä') *n.* A champion sumo wrestler. [J.]

yolk (yōk) *n.* **1.** The nutritive material of an ovum, consisting primarily of protein and fat, esp. the yellow, usually spheroidal mass of the egg of a bird or reptile, surrounded by the albumen. **2.** A greasy substance found in unprocessed sheep's wool. [ME *yolke* < OE *geolca* < *geolu,* yellow.] **—yolk'y** *adj.*

yolk sac *n.* A membranous sac attached to the embryo and providing early nourishment in the form of yolk in bony fishes, sharks, reptiles, birds, and primitive mammals, and functioning as the circulatory system of the human embryo prior to the initiation of internal circulation by the pumping of the heart.

Yom Kip·pur (yōm' kĭp'ər, yōm' kĭ-po͝or') *n.* The holiest Jewish holiday, celebrated on the tenth day of Tishri, on which fasting and prayer for the atonement of sins are prescribed. [Heb. *yōm kippūr,* day of atonement.]

yon (yŏn) *adj. & adv.* Yonder. *—pron. Regional.* That one or those yonder. [ME < OE *geon.*]

yond (yŏnd) *adj. & adv. Archaic.* Yonder. [ME < OE *geond.*]

yon·der (yŏn'dər) *adj.* Being at an indicated distance, usually within sight. *—adv.* In or at that indicated place; over there. *—pron.* One that is at an indicated place, usually within sight. [ME < *yond,* yond.]

yo·ni (yō'nē) *n.* A symbol for the vulva in Indian and Tibetan religion. [Skt. *yoniḥ,* womb, abode, source.]

yoo-hoo (yo͞o'ho͞o) *interj.* Used to hail persons or to attract attention.

yore (yôr, yōr) *n.* Time long past: *days of yore.* [ME < OE *gēara,* long ago < *gēar,* year.]

York·ist (yôr'kĭst) *n.* A supporter of the House of York in its contention with the House of Lancaster during the Wars of the Roses.

York·shire pudding (yôrk'shîr', -shər) *n.* A pudding of popover batter made of eggs, flour, and milk and baked in the drippings of roast beef.

Yorkshire terrier *n.* A toy terrier of a breed developed in Yorkshire, England, having a long, bluish-gray coat.

Yo·ru·ba (yō'ro͞o-bä) *n., pl.* **Yoruba** or **-bas. 1.** A member of a West African Negro people living chiefly in southwestern Nigeria. **2.** The Kwa language of the Yoruba. **—Yo'ru·ban** *adj.*

you (yo͞o) *pron.* **1.** The one or ones being addressed by the speaker. Used in all grammatical relations except that of the possessive: *You ought to work harder. Did he give you his opinion? I'll call you next week.* **2.** Used to indicate an individual of an indefinitely specified group: *You can't win them all.* [ME < OE *ēow,* dative and accusative of *gē,* ye.]

you-all (yo͞o'ôl') also **y'all** (yôl) *pron. Southeastern U.S.* You. Used in addressing two or more persons or referring to two or more persons, one of whom is addressed.

you'd (yo͞od). **1.** You had. **2.** You would.

you'll (yo͞ol, yo͞o'əl, yo͝ol). **1.** You will. **2.** You shall.

young (yŭng) *adj.* **-er, -est. 1.** Being in the early or undeveloped period of life or growth; not old. **2.** Newly begun or formed; not advanced: *The evening is young.* **3.** Pertaining to or suggestive of youth or early life: *young for her age.* **4.** Vigorous or fresh; youthful. **5.** Lacking experience; immature. **6.** Being the junior of two people having the same name: *The young Richard Roe.* **7.** *Geol.* Being of an early stage in a geologic cycle. Used of bodies of water and land formations. *—n.* **1.** Young persons collectively; youth. **2.** Offspring; brood: *a lioness with her young.* ***—idiom.*** **with young.** Pregnant. [ME *yong* < OE *geong.*] **—young'ness** *n.*

Synonyms: *young, youth, juvenile, adolescent, teen-ager.* These nouns refer to persons in the age group between childhood and maturity. *Young* and *youth* denote persons in that span considered collectively, and *youth* also is applied in the singular to any male of that age. Both are essentially neutral, categorizing terms, whereas *juvenile* and *adolescent* usually stress immaturity. *Adolescent* in particular suggests the difficulties of physical and emotional maturation. *Teen-ager* refers to a person between thirteen and nineteen, often considered with respect to the tastes and interests of that age group.

young·ber·ry (yŭng'bĕr'ē) *n.* **1.** A trailing, prickly hybrid between a blackberry and a dewberry, cultivated in the western United States. **2.** The edible, dark-red berry of the youngberry. [After B. M. *Young,* 20th-cent. American fruit grower.]

young·ish (yŭng'ĭsh) *adj.* Somewhat young.

young·ling (yŭng'lĭng) *n.* **1.** A young person. **2.** A young animal. **3.** A young plant. [ME *yongling* < OE *geongling* < *geong,* young.]

young·ster (yŭng'stər) *n.* **1.** A young person; a child or youth. **2.** A young animal. **3.** A midshipman of the second-year class in the U.S. Naval Academy.

Young Turk *n.* A progressive or insurgent member of a political party or other collective enterprise. [After the *Young Turks,* a 20th-cent. revolutionary party in Turkey.]

youn·ker (yŭng'kər) *n.* **1.** A young man. **2.** A child. [Du. *jonker* < MDu. *jonckher,* young nobleman : *jonc,* young + *here,* lord.]

your (yo͝or, yôr, yōr; yər *when unstressed) adj.* The possessive form of **you**. **1.** Used to indicate that the person addressed is the possessor or the agent or recipient of an action: *your pencil; your comments; your comprehension.* **2.** Of or relating to one or oneself: *The light switch is on your right.* **3.** *Informal.* Used with little or no sense of possession but suggesting mutual knowledge or experience: *He is not one of your two-bit philosophers.* [ME < OE *ēower,* genitive of *gē,* ye.]

you're (yo͝or; yər *when unstressed).* You are.

yours (yo͝orz, yôrz, yōrz) *pron. (used with a sing. or pl. verb).* **1.** That or those belonging to you: *I can't find my scarf, so I'll borrow yours. My books are here and yours are on the table.* **2.** Often used with an adverbial modifier in the complimentary close of a letter: *Yours truly.* [ME *youres,* genitive of *your,* your.]

your·self (yo͝or-sĕlf', yôr'-, yōr-, yər-) *pron.* **1.** That one identical with you. Used: **a.** Reflexively as the direct or indirect object of a verb or the object of a preposition: *Don't hurt yourself. Give yourself plenty of time. Are you talking to yourself?* **b.** For emphasis: *You yourself must insist upon his compliance.* **c.** In an absolute construction: *Yourself a victim of fraud, you can certainly understand how they feel.* **2.** Your normal or healthy condition or state. **3.** Oneself. —See Usage note at **myself**.

your·selves (yo͝or-selvz', yōr-, yər-) *pron.* **1.** Those that are identical with you. Used: **a.** Reflexively as the direct or indirect object of a verb or the object of a preposition: *Help yourselves. Have yourselves a good time. You should all watch out for yourselves.* **b.** For emphasis: *You should take care of the matter yourselves.* **c.** In an absolute construction. **2.** Your normal or healthy condition or state. —See Usage note at **myself**.

youth (yo͞oth) *n., pl.* **youths** (yo͞oths, yo͞o*th*z). **1.** The condition or quality of being young. **2.** An early period of development or existence. **3. a.** The time of life between childhood and maturity. **b.** Young people collectively. **c.** A young person, esp. a young man. [ME < OE *geoguð*.]
youth·ful (yo͞oth′fəl) *adj.* **1.** Possessing youth; still young. **2.** Characteristic of youth; fresh. **3.** Of or belonging to youth. **4.** In an early stage of development; new. **5.** *Geol.* Young. **—youth′ful·ly** *adv.* **—youth′ful·ness** *n.*
youth hostel *n.* A hostel.
you've (yo͞ov). You have.
yow (you) *interj.* Used to express alarm, pain, or surprise.
yowl (youl) *v.* **yowled, yowl·ing, yowls.** *—intr.* To utter a loud, long, mournful cry; wail. *—tr.* To say or utter with a yowl. *—n.* A loud, mournful cry; wail. [ME *yowlen*.]
yo-yo (yō′yō′) *n., pl.* **-yos. 1.** A toy consisting of a flattened spool wound with string that is spun down from and reeled up to the hand by unwinding and winding the string. **2.** *Informal.* One that vacillates. **3.** *Slang.* A dope; jerk. *—intr.v.* **-yoed, -yo·ing, -yos.** *Informal.* To move repeatedly from one position to another; vacillate. [Orig. a trademark.]
Y·quem (ē-kĕm′) *n.* A variety of sauterne wine. [After Chateau d'*Yquem*, an estate in southwestern France where it is made.]
yt·ter·bi·a (ĭ-tûr′bē-ə) *n.* Ytterbium oxide. [NLat. < YTTERBIUM.]
yt·ter·bi·um (ĭ-tûr′bē-əm) *n. Symbol* **Yb** A soft bright silvery rare-earth element occurring in two allotropic forms and used as an x-ray source for portable irradiation devices, in some laser materials, and in some special alloys. Atomic number 70; atomic weight 173.04; melting point 824°C; boiling point 1,427°C; specific gravity 6.977 or 6.54 depending on allotropic form; valences 2, 3. [After *Ytterby*, town in Sweden where it was discovered.] **—yt·ter′bic** (-bĭk) *adj.*
ytterbium oxide *n.* A colorless hygroscopic compound, Yb_2O_3, used in certain alloys.
yt·tri·a (ĭt′rē-ə) *n.* Yttrium oxide. [NLat., after *Ytterby*. —see YTTERBIUM.]
yt·tri·um (ĭt′rē-əm) *n. Symbol* **Y** A silvery metallic element, not a rare earth but occurring in nearly all rare-earth minerals, used in various metallurgical applications, notably to increase the strength of magnesium and aluminum alloys. Atomic number 39; atomic weight 88.905; melting point 1,495°C; boiling point 2,927°C; specific gravity 4.45; valence 3. [< YTTRIA.] **—yt′tric** (ĭt′rĭk) *adj.*
yttrium oxide *n.* A yellowish powder, Y_2O_3, used in optical glasses, ceramics, and color-television tubes.
yu·an (yü′än′) *n., pl.* **yuan** or **yuans.** See table at **currency.** [Chin. (Mandarin) *yuan*[2], dollar.]
Yuc·a·tec (yo͞o′kə-tĕk′) *n., pl.* **Yucatec** or **-tecs. 1.** A member of an Indian people inhabiting the Yucatán Peninsula, Mexico. **2.** The Mayan language of the Yucatec.
yuc·ca (yŭk′ə) *n.* Any of various chiefly tropical New World plants of the genus *Yucca*, often tall and stout-stemmed, and having a terminal cluster of white flowers. [Sp. *yuca*, of American Indian orig.]

yucca

Yu·ga (yo͝og′ə) also **Yug** (yo͝og) *n. Hinduism.* One of the four ages constituting the cycle of history. [Skt. *yugam*, yoke, pair, era.]
Yukon Time *n.* Time at the 135th meridian west of Greenwich, England, and in the ninth time zone based on it in North America. It is nine hours earlier than Greenwich time.
yu·lan (yo͞o′lăn, yü′län′) *n.* A tree, *Magnolia denudata*, native to China and often cultivated for its large, cup-shaped, fragrant white flowers. [Chin. (Mandarin) *yu*[4] *lan*[2] : *yu*[4], jade + *lan*[2], orchid.]
Yule (yo͞ol) *n.* Christmas or the season or feast celebrating Christmas. [ME *yole* < OE *gēol*.]
yule log *n.* A large log traditionally burned in the fireplace at Christmas.
Yule·tide (yo͞ol′tīd′) *n.* The Christmas season.
Yu·ma (yo͞o′mə) *n., pl.* **Yuma** or **-mas. 1.** A tribe of North American Indians of southwestern Arizona and the adjacent parts of California and Mexico. **2.** A member of the Yuma. **3.** The Yuman language of the Yuma. [Sp.]
Yu·man (yo͞o′mən) *n.* A language family comprising the languages of the Yuma and Mohave Indians and other Indian languages of southwestern Arizona and the adjacent parts of California and Mexico. **—Yu′man** *adj.*
yum·my (yŭm′ē) *adj.* **-mi·er, -mi·est.** *Slang.* Delightful; delicious. [< *yum*, the sound of smacking the lips.]
yurt (yûrt) *n.* A circular, domed portable tent used by the nomadic Mongols of Siberia. [R. *yurta*, of Turkic orig.]
y·wis (ĭ-wĭs′) *adv. Archaic.* Variant of **iwis.**

Z

1 2 3 4 5 6 7 8 9 10 11 12 13

Phoenician Greek Roman Medieval Modern

Around 1000 B.C. the Phoenicians and other Semitic peoples began to use graphic signs to represent individual speech sounds instead of syllables or words. They used a symbol in the forms (1,2,3) to represent the sound of the consonant "z" and called it *zayin.* The Greeks, adapting the Phoenician alphabet, retained the phonetic value and shape of *zayin* (4,5) but altered its name to *zēta.* The Romans borrowed the alphabet from the Greeks via the Etruscans. Since Latin had no "z" sound, the Romans at first omitted Z from their alphabet, but after they had become acquainted with Greek learning and literature they borrowed Z directly from Greek in order to transliterate Greek words. The Romans also adapted the alphabet for monumental inscriptions, and their monumental script (7) is the prototype of modern capital letters (10,11). Medieval scribes adapted the Roman capitals to being quickly written on paper, parchment, and vellum. These uncial and cursive minuscules (8,9) are the prototypes of modern lower-case letters, both written and printed (13,12).

z

z or **Z** (zē) *n., pl.* **z's** or **Z's. 1.** The 26th letter of the modern English alphabet. **2.** Any of the speech sounds represented by the letter *z.* **3.** The 26th in a series.

za·ba·glio·ne (zä'bəl-yō'nē) *n.* A dessert consisting of egg yolks, sugar, and wine beaten until thick and served hot or cold. [Ital.]

Zach·a·ri·as (zăk'ə-rī'əs) also **Zech·a·ri·ah** (zĕk'ə-rī'ə) *n.* In the New Testament, the husband of Elizabeth and father of John the Baptist. [LLat. < Gk. *Zakharias* < Heb. *Zĕkhar'yah* : *zĕkhar',* remembrance + *Yāh,* God.]

zaf·fer also **zaf·fre** (zăf'ər) *n.* An impure oxide of cobalt, used to produce a blue color in enamel and in the making of smalt. [Ital. *zaffera* < OFr. *safre* < Ar. *ṣufr,* yellow copper.]

zaf·tig or **zof·tig** (zäf'tĭk, -tĭg) *adj. Slang.* **1.** Full-bosomed. **2.** Having a comfortably ample figure. [Yiddish, juicy < G. *saftig* < *Saft,* juice.]

Za·greus (zā'grōōs, -grē-əs) *n. Gk. Myth.* The son of Zeus and Persephone who was slain by the Titans and reborn as Dionysus. [Gk.]

zai·bat·su (zī'bät-sōō') *n., pl.* **zaibatsu.** A powerful family-controlled commercial combine of Japan. [J. : *zai,* wealth (< Chin. *cai*[2]) + *batsu,* powerful person or family (< Chin. *fa*[2]).]

zai·kai (zī'kī') *n.* The commercial and financial community of Japan. [J. : *zai,* money + *-kai,* community.]

zaire (zīr, zä-îr') *n.* See table at **currency.** [Port. < Kongo *nzadi,* large river.]

za·mi·a (zā'mē-ə) *n.* Any of various chiefly tropical American cycads of the genus *Zamia,* having a thick, usually underground trunk and palmlike terminal leaves. [NLat. *Zamia,* genus name, prob. < Gk. *azein,* to dry.]

zam·in·dar also **zem·in·dar** (zăm'ən-där', zĕm'-, zə-mēn-där') *n.* **1.** An official in precolonial India assigned to collect the land taxes of his district. **2.** A native landholder in British colonial India responsible for collecting and paying to the government the taxes on the land under his jurisdiction. [Hindi *zamīndār* < Pers. : *zamīn,* earth + *-dār,* holder.]

zam·in·dar·i also **zem·in·dar·y** (zăm'ən-där'ē, zĕm'-, zə-mēn-) *n., pl.* **-is** also **-ies. 1.** The system of tax collection by zamindars. **2.** The area administered by a zamindar. [Hindi *zamīndārī* < Pers. *zamīndār,* zamindar.]

za·na·na (zə-nä'nə) *n.* Variant of **zenana.**

za·ny (zā'nē) *n., pl.* **-nies. 1.** A ludicrous, buffoonish character in old comedies who attempts feebly to mimic the tricks of the clown. **2.** A comical person given to extravagant or outlandish behavior. *—adj.* **-ni·er, -ni·est. 1.** Ludicrously comical; clownish. **2.** Comical because of incongruity or strangeness; bizarre. [Ital. *zani,* buffoon, < *Zanni,* dial. var. of *Gianni,* nickname for *Giovanni,* John, the name of servants who act as clowns in commedia dell'arte.] **—za'ni·ly** *adv.* **—za'ni·ness** *n.*

zap (zăp) *Slang. —v.* **zapped, zap·ping, zaps.** *—tr.* **1. a.** To destroy or kill with a burst of gunfire, flame, or electric current. **b.** To kill or destroy as if by shooting. **c.** To strike suddenly and forcefully as if with a projectile or weapon: *"His . . . narrative runs marvelously on and on, zapping the reader with often surprising and . . . painful glimpses"* (Publishers Weekly). **2.** To attack (an enemy in warfare) with heavy firepower; strafe or bombard. *—intr.* To move swiftly; zoom. *—n.* Something that imparts excitement or great interest. *—interj.* **1.** Used to imitate a sound made by a gun when fired. **2.** Used to indicate a sudden occurrence. [Imit.]

Za·pa·ta mustache (sä-pä'tä, zə-pä'tə) *n.* A mustache that curves downward on each side. [After Emiliano *Zapata* (1880?–1919).]

za·pa·te·a·do (zä'pä-tā-ä'dō) *n., pl.* **-dos. 1.** The rhythmic stamping of the heels characteristic of Spanish flamenco dances. **2.** A Spanish flamenco dance in which the performer stamps rhythmically with his heels. [Sp. < *zapatear,* to tap with the shoe < *zapato,* shoe.]

Za·po·tec (zä'pə-tĕk', sä'-) *n.* Any of a group of related languages spoken in southern Mexico. [Sp. *Zapoteca* < Nahuatl *Tzapoteca.*] **—Za'po·tec'** *adj.*

zap·per (zăp'ər) *n.* **1.** A device used for aiming radiation at a target, esp. insects, weeds, and other pests. **2.** *Slang.* Forceful, pointed criticism.

zap·py (zăp'ē) *adj.* **-pi·er, -pi·est.** *Slang.* Zippy: *a zappy advertisement.*

za·re·ba also **za·ree·ba** (zə-rē'bə) *n.* **1.** An enclosure of bushes or stakes protecting a campsite or village in northeastern Africa. **2.** A campsite or village protected by a zareba. [Ar. *zarībah,* pen for cattle, < *zarb,* sheepfold.]

zarf (zärf) *n.* A chalicelike holder for a hot coffee cup, typically made of ornamented metal, used in the Middle East. [Ar. *ẓarf,* container.]

zas·tru·ga (zə-strōō'gə) *n.* Variant of **sastruga.**

zax (zăks) *n.* A hatchetlike tool for cutting and dressing roofing slates. [Alteration of ME *sax,* knife < OE *seax.*]

z-ax·is (zē'ăk'sĭs) *n., pl.* **z-ax·es** (-sēz'). One of three axes in a three-dimensional Cartesian coordinate system.

za·yin (zä'yĭn, zī-) *n.* The 7th letter of the Hebrew alphabet. See table at **alphabet.** [Heb. < Aram.]

za·zen (zä'zĕn') *n.* Meditation as practiced in Zen Buddhism. [J. : *za,* to sit down + *zen,* silent meditation. —see ZEN BUDDHISM.]

zeal (zēl) *n.* Enthusiastic and diligent devotion in pursuit of a cause, ideal, or goal; fervor. [ME *zele* < LLat. *zelus* < Gk. *zēlos.*]

Zeal·ot (zĕl'ət) *n.* **1.** A member of a Jewish sect that resisted Roman rule in Palestine during the first century A.D. **2. zealot. a.** A person who is zealous, esp. excessively so. **b.** A fanatically committed person. [LLat. *zelotes* < Gk. *zēlōtēs* < *zēlos,* zeal.]

zeal·ot·ry (zĕl'ə-trē) *n.* Excessive zeal; fanaticism.

zeal·ous (zĕl'əs) *adj.* Filled with or motivated by zeal; fervent. **—zeal'ous·ly** *adv.* **—zeal'ous·ness** *n.*

ze·bec or **ze·beck** (zē'bĕk') *n.* Variants of **xebec.**

ze·bra (zē'brə) *n.* **1.** Any of several horselike African mammals of the genus *Equus,* having characteristic overall markings of conspicuous dark and whitish stripes. **2.** *Slang.* A referee or other official in a football game. [Port. < OSp. *cebro, ecebro,* wild ass, poss. < Lat. *equiferus,* wild horse : *equus,* horse + *ferus,* wild.]

zebra

zebra crossing *n.* A pedestrian crosswalk. [So called because it is marked with white stripes.]

zebra finch *n.* A small Australian bird, *Poephila castanotis,* having black and white striped markings and popular as a cage bird.

zebra fish *n.* A small freshwater tropical fish, *Brachydanio rerio,* of India, having horizontal dark-blue and silvery stripes and popular in home aquariums.

ze·bra·wood (zē'brə-wŏŏd') *n.* **1.** Any of several African or tropical American trees having striped wood. **2.** The wood of the zebrawood, used in cabinetmaking.

ze·bu (zē'bōō, -byōō) *n.* A domesticated bovine mammal, *Bos indicus,* of Asia and Africa, having a prominent hump on the back and a large dewlap. [Fr. *zébu.*]

zebu

Zeb·u·lon also **Zeb·u·lun** (zĕb'yə-lən) *n.* **1.** In the Old Testament, a son of Jacob and Leah. **2.** A tribe of Israel descended from Zebulon. [Heb. *Zĕbhūlōn* < *zĕbhūl,* dwelling < *zābhal,* he dwelled.]

zec·chi·no (zĕ-kē'nō) also **zec·chin** or **zech·in** (zĕk'ĭn) *n., pl.* **-ni** (-nē) or **-nos** also **-chins** or **-ins.** A sequin (sense 2). [Ital. —see SEQUIN.]

Zech·a·ri·ah (zĕk'ə-rī'ə) *n.* **1.** Variant of **Zacharias. 2.** A Hebrew prophet of the 6th century B.C. **3.** See table at **Bible.** [Heb. *Zĕkhar'yah.* —see ZACHARIAS.]

zed (zĕd) *n. Chiefly Brit.* The letter *z.* [ME < OFr. *zede* < LLat. *zeta,* zeta < Gk. *zēta.* —see ZETA.]

Zed·e·ki·ah (zĕd'ĭ-kī'ə) *n.* In the Old Testament, the last king of Judah (597–586 B.C.), who died in captivity at Babylon. [Heb. *Ṣidqīyāh.*]

zed·o·ar·y (zĕd'ō-ĕr'ē) *n., pl.* **-ies.** The dried rhizome of a tropical Asian plant, *Curcuma zedoaria,* used as a stimulant and condiment. [ME *zeodoarye* < Med. Lat. *zeodoaria* < Ar. *zadwār* < Pers.]

zee (zē) *n.* The letter *z.*

Zee·man effect (zā'män') *n.* The splitting of single spectral lines of an emission spectrum into three or more polarized components when the radiation source is in a magnetic field. [After Pieter *Zeeman* (1865–1943).]

ze·in (zē'ĭn) *n.* A prolamine protein derived from corn and used in the manufacture of various plastics, coatings, and lacquers. [< NLat. *Zea,* corn genus < Gk. *zeia,* wheat.]

Zeit·geist (tsīt'gīst') *n.* The taste and outlook characteristic of a period or generation. [G. : *Zeit,* time + *Geist,* spirit.]

zek (zĕk) *n.* An inmate of a Soviet labor camp. [R. < *zaklyuchenny,* prisoner.]

zem·in·dar (zăm'ən-där', zĕm'-, zə-mēn-där') *n.* Variant of **zamindar.**

zem·in·dar·y (zăm'ən-där'ē, zĕm'-, zə-mēn-) *n.* Variant of **zamindari.**

zemst·vo (zĕmst'vō) *n., pl.* **-vos.** An elective council responsible for the local administration of a provincial district in czarist Russia. [R. < *zemlya,* land.]

Zen (zĕn) *n.* Zen Buddhism.

ze·na·na also **za·na·na** (zə-nä'nə) *n.* The part of a house in India and Pakistan reserved for the women of the household. [Hindi *zenāna* < Pers. < *zan,* woman.]

Zen Buddhism *n.* A Chinese and Japanese school of Mahayana Buddhism that asserts that enlightenment can be attained through meditation, self-contemplation, and intuition rather than through the scriptures. [J. *zen* < Chin. (Mandarin) *chan*[2], short for *chan*[2] *na*[4], meditation < Pali *jhānaṃ* < Skt. *dhyānam* < *dhyāti,* he meditates.] **—Zen Buddhist.** *n.*

Zend (zĕnd) *n.* The Zend-Avesta.

Zend-A·ves·ta (zĕn'də-vĕs'tə) *n.* The entire body of sacred writings of the Zoroastrian religion. [Pers. *zandavastā* < *Avesta-va-zend,* Avesta with an interpretation.] **—Zend'-A·ves·ta'ic** (-vĕ-stā'ĭk) *adj.*

ze·ner diode or **Ze·ner diode** (zē'nər) *n.* A silicon semiconductor device used as a voltage regulator because of its ability to conduct heavy currents under reverse bias. [After Clarence M. *Zener* (b. 1905).]

ze·nith (zē'nĭth) *n.* **1.** The point on the celestial sphere that is directly above the observer. **2. a.** The upper region of the sky. **b.** The highest point above the observer's horizon attained by a celestial body. **3.** The highest or culminating point; peak: *the zenith of her career.* [ME *senith* < OFr. *cenith* < OSp. *zenit* < Ar. *samt (arra's),* path (over the head).]

zeppelin

Zeus

zinnia

ze·o·lite (zē′ə-līt′) *n.* Any of a group of approximately 30 hydrous aluminum silicate minerals or their corresponding synthetic compounds, used chiefly as molecular filters and ion-exchange agents. [Swed. *zeolit* < Gk. *zeein,* to boil (from its swelling and boiling under the blowpipe).]

Zeph·a·ni·ah (zĕf′ə-nī′ə) *n.* **1.** A Hebrew prophet of the 7th century B.C. **2.** See table at **Bible.** [Heb. *Sĕphanyāh.*]

zeph·yr (zĕf′ər) *n.* **1. a.** The west wind. **b.** A gentle breeze. **2.** Any of various light, soft fabrics, yarns, or garments. **3.** Something that is airy, insubstantial, or passing. [ME *Zephirus,* Zephyrus < Lat. *Zephyrus.*]

zephyr lily *n.* Any of several plants of the genus *Zephyranthes,* native to tropical America, having grasslike leaves and variously colored flowers.

Zeph·y·rus (zĕf′ər-əs) *n. Gk. Myth.* A god personifying the gentle west wind. [Lat. < Gk. *Zephuros.*]

zep·pe·lin also **Zep·pe·lin** (zĕp′ə-lĭn) *n.* A rigid airship having a long, cylindrical body supported by internal gas cells. [After Count Ferdinand von *Zeppelin* (1838–1917), its inventor.]

ze·ro (zîr′ō, zē′rō) *n., pl.* **-ros** or **-roes. 1.** The numerical symbol "0"; a cipher. **2.** *Math.* **a.** An element of a set that when added to any other element in the set produces a sum identical with the element to which it is added. **b.** A cardinal number indicating the absence of any or all units under consideration. **c.** An ordinal number indicating an initial point or origin. **d.** An argument at which the value of a function vanishes. **3.** The temperature indicated by the numeral 0 on a thermometer. **4.** A sight setting that enables a firearm to shoot on target. **5.** One having no influence or importance; nonentity. **6.** The lowest point: *His prospects were set at zero.* **7.** Nothing; nil: *Today we accomplished zero.* —*adj.* **1.** Of, pertaining to, or being zero. **2. a.** Having no measurable or otherwise determinable value. **b.** Absent, inoperative, or irrelevant in specified circumstances: *zero gravity.* **3. a.** Limited by cloud cover to little or no vertical visibility. **b.** Permitting little or no horizontal visibility. —*tr.v.* **-roed, -ro·ing, -roes.** To adjust (an instrument or device) to zero value. —***phrasal verb.* zero in. 1.** To aim or concentrate firepower on an exact target location. **2.** To adjust the aim or sight of by repeated firings. **3.** To converge intently; close in: *The children zeroed in on the toy display.* [Ital. < Arab. *ṣifr,* cipher.]

ze·ro-base (zîr′ō-bās′, zē′rō-) or **ze·ro-based** (-bāst′) *adj. Econ.* Having each expenditure or item justified as to need or cost: *"zero-base budgeting requires its practitioners to justify every dollar they spend"* (Wall Street Journal).

ze·ro-de·fect (zîr′ō-dē′fĕkt′, -dĭ-fĕkt′, zē′rō-) *adj.* Without flaw or error: *a zero-defect political campaign.*

zero economic growth *n. Econ.* A condition characterized by negligible increase in a nation's per capita income.

zero gravity *n.* The condition of apparent weightlessness occurring when the centrifugal force on a body exactly counterbalances the gravitational attraction upon it.

ze·ro-growth (zîr′ō-grōth′, zē′rō-) *n.* **1.** *Econ.* A policy that inhibits or prevents economic development and expansion. **2.** *Econ.* Zero economic growth. **3.** Zero population growth.

zero hour *n.* The scheduled time for the start of an operation or action, esp. a concerted military attack.

ze·ro-point energy (zîr′ō-point′, zē′rō-) *n.* The irreducible minimum energy possessed by a substance at absolute zero temperature.

zero population growth *n.* The limiting of population increase to the number of live births needed to replace the existing population, estimated at 2.11 children per family.

ze·ro-rate (zîr′ō-rāt′, zē′rō-) *tr.v.* **-rat·ed, -rat·ing, -rates.** *Chiefly Brit.* To exempt from paying a value-added tax.

zest (zĕst) *n.* **1.** Flavor or interest; piquancy. **2.** Spirited enjoyment; gusto: *"At fifty-three he retains all the heady zest of adolescence"* (Kenneth Tynan). **3.** The outermost part of the rind of an orange or lemon, used as flavoring. —*tr.v.* **zest·ed, zest·ing, zests.** To give zest, charm, or spirit to. [Obs. Fr., orange or lemon peel.] —**zest′ful** *adj.* —**zest′ful·ly** *adv.* —**zest′ful·ness** *n.*

ze·ta (zā′tə, zē′-) *n.* The 6th letter of the Greek alphabet. See table at **alphabet.** [Gk. *zēta,* of Phoenician orig.; akin to Heb. *zayin.*]

Ze·thus also **Ze·thos** (zē′thəs) *n. Gk. Myth.* The twin brother of Amphion. [Lat. < Gk. *Zēthos.*]

zeug·ma (zo͞og′mə) *n.* A construction in which a word is used to modify or govern two or more words, often so that its use is grammatically or logically correct with only one. [Lat. < Gk., a joining < *zeugnunai,* to yoke.]

Zeus (zo͞os) *n. Gk. Myth.* The principal god of the Greek pantheon, ruler of the heavens, and father of other gods and mortal heroes. [Gk.]

zib·e·line or **zib·el·line** (zĭb′ə-lēn′, -līn′) *n.* **1.** A thick, lustrous, soft fabric of wool and other animal hair, such as mohair, having a silky nap. **2.** The sable or its fur. [OFr., sable < OItal. *zibellino,* of Slav. orig.]

zib·et also **zib·eth** (zĭb′ĭt) *n.* A civet cat, *Viverra zibetha,* of southeastern Asia. [Med. Lat. *zibethum* < Ar. *zabād,* civet.]

zig·gu·rat (zĭg′ə-răt′) *n.* A temple tower of the ancient Assyrians and Babylonians, having the form of a terraced pyramid of successively receding stories. [Assyrian *ziqquratu,* summit.]

zig·zag (zĭg′zăg′) *n.* **1. a.** A line or course that proceeds by sharp turns in alternating directions. **b.** One of a series of such sharp turns. **2.** Something, such as a road or design, that exhibits one or a series of sharp turns. —*adj.* Having or moving in a zigzag. —*adv.* In a zigzag manner or pattern. —*v.* **-zagged, -zag·ging, -zags.** —*intr.* To move in or form a zigzag. —*tr.* To cause to move in or form a zigzag. [Fr., prob. < G. *Zickzack.*]

zig·zag·ger (zĭg′zăg′ər) *n.* **1.** One that zigzags. **2.** A sewing-machine attachment for sewing zigzag stitches.

zilch (zĭlch) *Slang.* —*n.* **1.** Zero; nothing. **2.** An insignificant person; nonentity. —*adj.* Amounting to nothing; nil: *"business was zilch"* (New York Magazine). [Orig. unknown.]

zill (zĭl) *n.* One of a pair of round metal cymbals attached to the fingers and struck together for rhythm and percussion in belly-dancing. [Perh. < Turk. *zil,* cymbals.]

zil·lion (zĭl′yən) *n. Informal.* An extremely large indefinite number. [Alteration of MILLION.]

Zil·pah (zĭl′pə) *n.* The servant of Leah who bore Jacob two sons, Gad and Asher. [Heb. *Zilpāh.*]

zinc (zĭngk) *n. Symbol* **Zn** A bluish-white, lustrous metallic element that is brittle at room temperatures but malleable with heating. It is used to form a wide variety of alloys including brass, bronze, German silver, various solders, and nickel silver, in galvanizing iron and other metals, for electric fuses, anodes, and meter cases, and in roofing, gutters, and various household objects. Atomic number 30; atomic weight 65.37; melting point 419.4°C; boiling point 907°C; specific gravity 7.133 (25°C); valence 2. —*tr.v.* **zinced, zinc·ing, zincs** or **zincked, zinck·ing, zincs.** To coat or treat with zinc; galvanize. [G. *Zink,* poss. < *Zinke,* spike < OHG *zinko.*]

zinc·ate (zĭng′kāt′) *n.* Any of several chemical compounds derived from the reaction of zinc or zinc oxide with certain alkali solutions.

zinc blende *n.* Sphalerite.

zinc·ite (zĭng′kīt′) *n.* A red to yellow-orange zinc ore, essentially ZnO.

zinck·en·ite (zĭng′kə-nīt′) *n.* Variant of **zinkenite.**

zinc·o·graph (zĭng′kə-grăf′) *n.* **1.** A prepared zinc plate used in zincography. **2.** A print or picture obtained from a zincograph.

zinc·og·ra·phy (zĭng-kŏg′rə-fē) *n.* The process of engraving zinc printing plates. —**zinc·og′ra·pher** *n.* —**zinc′o·graph′ic** (zĭng′kə-grăf′ĭk), **zinc′o·graph′i·cal** *adj.*

zinc ointment *n.* A salve consisting of about 20 per cent zinc oxide with beeswax or paraffin and petrolatum, used in the treatment of skin diseases.

zinc oxide *n.* An amorphous white or yellowish powder, ZnO, used as a pigment, in compounding rubber, in the manufacture of plastics, and in pharmaceuticals and cosmetics.

zinc sulfate *n.* A colorless crystalline compound, $ZnSO_4 \cdot 7H_2O$, used medicinally as an emetic and astringent, as a fungicide, and in wood and skin preservatives.

zinc white *n.* Zinc oxide.

zin·fan·del also **Zin·fan·del** (zĭn′fən-dĕl′) *n.* A dry red table wine from California. [Orig. unknown.]

zing (zĭng) *n.* A brief high-pitched humming or buzzing sound, such as that made by a swiftly passing object or a taut vibrating string. —*v.* **zinged, zing·ing, zings.** —*intr.* **1.** *Informal.* To make a zing. **2.** *Informal.* To move swiftly with or as if with a zing: *an arrow zinging toward its target.* **3.** To be vivacious or lively: *a conversation zinging along.* —*tr. Informal.* **1.** To attack verbally; criticize sharply: *zing an opponent in a debate.* **2.** To zap (sense 1.c.). [Imit.]

zing·er (zĭng′ər) *n. Informal.* **1.** A witty, often caustic remark. **2.** A sudden, striking surprise, shock, revelation, or turn of events.

zing·y (zĭng′ē) *adj.* **-i·er, -i·est.** *Informal.* **1.** Pleasantly stimulating: *"The times are good. The living is easy. The vibes are zingy"* (Saturday Review). **2.** Exceptionally attractive or appealing: *a zingy gown.*

zink·en·ite also **zinck·en·ite** (zĭng′kə-nīt′) *n.* A steel-gray mineral, essentially $Pb_6Sb_{14}S_{27}$. [G. *Zinkenit,* after J. K. L. *Zinken* (1790–1862).]

zin·ni·a (zĭn′ē-ə) *n.* Any of various plants of the genus *Zinnia,* native to tropical America, esp. *Z. elegans,* widely cultivated for its showy, variously colored flowers. [NLat. *Zinnia,* genus name, after Johann Gottfried *Zinn* (1727–1759).]

Zi·on (zī′ən) *n.* **1. a.** The Jewish people; Israel. **b.** The Jewish homeland as a symbol of Judaism. **2.** A place or religious community regarded as sacredly devoted to God. **3.** An idealized harmonious community; utopia. [ME *Sion* < OE < LLat. < Gk. *Seiōn* < Heb. *Ṣīyōn.*]

Zi·on·ism (zī′ə-nĭz′əm) *n.* **1.** A plan or movement of the Jewish people to return from the Diaspora to Palestine. **2.** A movement originally aimed at the re-establishment of a Jewish national homeland and state in Palestine and now concerned with the development of Israel. —**Zi′on·ist** *n.* —**Zi′on·is′tic** *adj.*

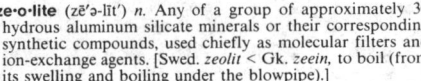

zip (zĭp) *n.* **1.** A brief, sharp, hissing sound. **2.** Energy; vim. **3.** *Slang.* Zero (sense 7). —*v.* **zipped, zip·ping, zips.** —*intr.* **1. a.** To move with a sharp, hissing sound. **b.** To move or act with a speed that suggests such a sound: *The cars zipped* *by endlessly.* **2.** To act or proceed swiftly and energetically: *zipped through her homework.* **3.** To become fastened or unfastened by a zipper. *—tr.* **1.** To give speed and force to. **2.** To impart life or zest to. **3.** To fasten or unfasten with a zipper. [Imit.]

Zip Code also **zip code** or **ZIP Code.** A trademark for a system designed to expedite the sorting and delivery of mail by assigning a series of numbers to each delivery area in the United States.

zip gun *n.* A crude homemade pistol.

zip·per (zĭp′ər) *n.* A fastening device consisting of parallel rows of metal or nylon teeth on adjacent edges of an opening that are interlocked by a sliding tab. [< ZIP.]

zip·py (zĭp′ē) *adj.* **-pi·er -pi·est.** Full of energy; lively.

zir·ca·loy (zûr′kə-loi′) *n.* Any of several stable, corrosion-resistant zirconium alloys. [Blend of ZIRCONIUM and ALLOY.]

zir·con (zûr′kŏn′) *n.* A brown to colorless mineral, essentially $ZrSiO_4$, which is heated, cut, and polished to form a brilliant blue-white gem. [G. *Zirkon* < Fr. *jargon,* a variety of zircon < Ital. *giargone.*]

zir·con·ate (zûr′kə-nāt′) *n.* Any of several chemical compounds formed by heating zirconium oxide with a metal carbonate or oxide in the presence of an acid.

zir·co·ni·a (zûr-kō′nē-ə) *n.* Zirconium oxide. [NLat. < ZIRCON.]

zir·co·ni·um (zûr-kō′nē-əm) *n. Symbol* **Zr** A lustrous, grayish-white, strong, ductile metallic element obtained primarily from zircon and used chiefly in ceramic and refractory compounds, as an alloying agent, and in nuclear reactors. Atomic number 40; atomic weight 91.22; melting point 1,852°C; boiling point 3,578°C; specific gravity 6.53 (calculated); principal valence 4.

zirconium oxide *n.* A hard white amorphous powder, ZrO_2, derived from zirconium and also found naturally, used chiefly in pigments, refractories, and ceramics and as an abrasive.

zit (zĭt) *n. Slang.* A pimple. [Orig. unknown.]

zith·er (zĭth′ər, zĭ*th*′-) also **zith·ern** (-ərn) *n.* A musical instrument constructed of a flat sounding box with about 30 to 40 strings stretched over it and played horizontally with the fingertips or a plectrum. [G. < OHG *zithera* < Lat. *cithara,* cithara < Gk. *kithara.*] **—zith′er·ist** *n.*

zi·ti (zē′tē) *n., pl.* **ziti.** Medium-sized tubular pasta. [Ital. < pl. of *zito,* boy.]

zi·zith (tsēt-sēt′, tsĭt′sĭs) *pl.n.* The tassels or fringes of thread on the four corners of prayer shawls worn by Jewish males. [Heb. *ṣīṣīth.*]

zlo·ty (zlô′tē) *n., pl.* **zloty** or **-tys.** See table at **currency.** [Pol. *złoty.*]

Zn The symbol for the element zinc.

zo– *pref.* Variant of **zoo-.**

zo·a (zō′ə) *n.* A plural of **zoon.**

zo·di·ac (zō′dē-ăk′) *n.* **1. a.** *Astron.* A band of the celestial sphere extending about eight degrees to either side of the ecliptic that represents the path of the principal planets, the moon, and the sun. **b.** In astrology, this band divided into 12 equal parts called signs, each 30 degrees wide, bearing the name of a constellation for which it was originally named but with which it no longer coincides owing to the precession of the equinoxes. **c.** A diagram or figure representing the zodiac. **2.** A complete circuit; circle. [ME < OFr. *zodiaque* < Lat. *zodiacus* < Gk. *zōdiakos (kuklos),* (circle) of the zodiac < *zōidion,* small represented figure, dim. of *zōion,* living being.] **—zo·di′a·cal** (-dī′ə-kəl) *adj.*

zodiacal light *n.* A faint, hazy cone of light, often visible in the west just after sunset or in the east just before sunrise, apparently caused by the reflection of sunlight from meteoric particles surrounding the sun.

zof·tig (zăf′tĭk, -tĭg) *adj.* Variant of **zaftig.**

-zoic *suff.* **1.** Relating to a specified manner of animal existence: *holozoic.* **2.** Of or relating to a specified geologic era: *Archeozoic.* [< Gk. *zōikos,* of animals < *zōion,* living being.]

zoi·site (zoi′sīt′) *n.* A gray, brown, or pink mineral, essentially $Ca_2Al_3(SiO_4)_3(OH)$, used in ornamental stonework. [G. *Zoisit,* after Baron Sigismund *Zois* von Edelstein (1747–1819), its discoverer.]

zom·bie also **zom·bi** (zŏm′bē) *n.* **1.** A snake god of voodoo cults in West Africa, Haiti, and the southern United States. **2. a.** A supernatural power or spell that according to voodoo belief can enter into and reanimate a corpse. **b.** A corpse revived in this way. **3.** One who looks or behaves like an automaton. **4.** A tall drink made of various rums, liqueur, and fruit juice. [Poss. < Kongo *zumbi,* fetish.]

zo·nal (zō′nəl) also **zo·na·ry** (-nə-rē) *adj.* **1.** Of or associated with a zone. **2.** Divided into zones. **—zo′nal·ly** *adv.*

zo·nate (zō′nāt′) also **zo·nat·ed** (-nā′tĭd) *adj.* Having zones; belted, striped, or ringed.

zo·na·tion (zō-nā′shən) *n.* **1.** Arrangement or formation in zones; zonate structure. **2.** *Ecol.* The distribution of organisms in biogeographic zones.

zone (zōn) *n.* **1.** An area, region, or division distinguished from adjacent parts by some distinctive feature or character. **2. a.** Any of the five regions of the surface of the earth that are loosely divided according to prevailing climate and latitude, including the Torrid Zone, the North and South Temperate Zones, and the North and South Frigid Zones. **b.** A similar division on any planet. **c.** *Math.* A portion of a sphere bounded by the intersections of two parallel planes with the sphere. **3.** *Ecol.* An area characterized by distinct physical conditions and populated by communities of certain kinds of organisms. **4.** *Geol.* A region or stratum distinguished by composition or content. **5.** A section or division of an area or territory established to distinguish it from other similar areas for a specific purpose: *a war zone; a residential zone.* **6.** The total number of railroad stations located in a given radius from a particular shipping point. **7.** *Archaic.* A belt or girdle. **8.** *Computer Sci.* A region on a punch card or on a magnetic tape in which nondigital information is recorded. *—tr.v.* **zoned, zon·ing, zones. 1.** To divide into zones. **2.** To designate or mark off into zones. **3.** To surround or encircle with or as if with a belt or girdle. [Lat. *zona,* girdle < Gk. *zōnē.*]

zone melting *n.* A purification technique for crystalline substances in which a heating system passes slowly over a bar of the material to be refined, creating a molten region that carries impurities with it across the bar.

zone refining *n.* Zone melting.

zone·time (zōn′tīm′) *n.* Standard time used at sea according to the time zone in which a ship is located.

zonk (zôngk, zŏngk) *v.* **zonked, zonk·ing, zonks.** *Slang. —tr.* **1.** To stupefy; stun. **2.** To intoxicate with drugs or alcohol: *"zonk their patients with tranquilizers"* (Psychology Today). *—intr.* To be intoxicated with drugs or alcohol. [Orig. unknown.]

zoo (zo͞o) *n., pl.* **zoos. 1.** A public park or institution in which living animals are kept and exhibited to the public. **2.** A place or situation marked by rampant confusion or disorder. [Short for ZOOLOGICAL GARDEN.]

zoo– or **zo–** *pref.* **1.** Animal; animal kingdom: *zoography.* **2.** Motile: *zoospore.* [Gk. *zōio-* < *zōion,* living being.]

zo·o·chore (zō′ə-kôr′, -kōr′) *n.* A plant dispersed by animals.

zo·o·ge·o·graph·ic region (zō′ə-jē′ə-grăf′ĭk) *n.* An ecological region characterized by the dominance of certain kinds of animal life.

zo·o·ge·og·ra·phy (zō′ə-jē-ŏg′rə-fē) *n.* The biological study of the geographic distribution of animals. **—zo′o·ge·og′ra·pher** *n.* **—zo′o·ge′o·graph′ic** (-ə-grăf′ĭk), **zo′o·ge′o·graph′i·cal** (-ĭ-kəl) *adj.* **—zo′o·ge′o·graph′i·cal·ly** *adv.*

zo·o·gle·a (zō′ə-glē′ə) *n., pl.* **-gle·ae** (-glē′ē′) or **-gle·as.** Any of various bacteria of the genus *Zoogloea,* forming colonies in a jellylike secretion. [NLat. *Zoogloea,* genus name : ZOO- + Med. Gk. *glia,* gum < Gk. *gloios.*]

zo·og·ra·phy (zō-ŏg′rə-fē) *n.* The biological description of animals. **—zo′o·graph′ic** (-ə-grăf′ĭk), **zo′o·graph′ic·al** (-ĭ-kəl) *adj.*

zo·oid (zō′oid′) *n.* **1.** *Biol.* An organic cell or organized body that has independent movement within a living organism, esp. a motile gamete such as a spermatozoon. **2.** *Zool.* One of the usually microscopic animals forming an aggregate or colony, as of bryozoans. **—zo·oid′al** (-oid′l) *adj.*

zo·ol·a·try (zō-ŏl′ə-trē) *n.* The worship of animals. **—zo·ol′a·ter** *n.* **—zo·ol′a·trous** *adj.*

zo·o·log·i·cal (zō′ə-lŏj′ĭ-kəl) also **zo·o·log·ic** (-lŏj′ĭk) *adj.* **1.** Of or pertaining to animals or animal life. **2.** Of or pertaining to the science of zoology. **—zo′o·log′i·cal·ly** *adv.*

zoological garden *n.* A zoo (sense 1).

zo·ol·o·gy (zō-ŏl′ə-jē) *n., pl.* **-gies. 1.** The biological science of animals. **2.** The animal life of a particular area. **3.** The characteristics of an animal group or category: *the zoology of mammals.* **4.** A book or scholarly work on zoology. **—zo·ol′o·gist** *n.*

zoom (zo͞om) *v.* **zoomed, zoom·ing, zooms.** *—intr.* **1. a.** To make a continuous low-pitched buzzing or humming sound. **b.** To move while making such a sound. **2.** To climb suddenly and sharply in an airplane. **3.** To move about rapidly; swoop. **4. a.** To move rapidly toward or away from a photographic subject. **b.** To simulate such a movement, as by means of a zoom lens. *—tr.* To cause to zoom. *—n.* The act or sound of zooming. [Imit.]

zo·om·e·try (zō-ŏm′ĭ-trē) *n.* Measurement and comparison of the sizes of animals or animal parts, esp. the measurement of bulk. **—zo′o·met′ric** (-ə-mĕt′rĭk), **zo′o·met′ri·cal** (-rĭ-kəl) *adj.* **—zo′o·met′ri·cal·ly** *adv.*

zoom lens *n.* A camera lens whose focal length can be rapidly changed, allowing rapid change in the size of an image.

zo·o·mor·phism (zō′ə-môr′fĭz′əm) *n.* **1.** The attribution of animal characteristics or qualities to a god. **2.** The use of animal forms in symbolism, literature, or graphic representation. **—zo′o·mor′phic** *adj.*

zo·on (zō′ŏn′) *n., pl.* **zo·ons** or **zo·a** (zō′ə). An animal developed from a fertilized egg. [NLat. < Gk. *zōion,* living being.]

-zoon *suff.* Animal; independently moving organic unit: *spermatozoon.* [NLat. < Gk. *zōion,* living being.]

zo·on·o·sis (zō-ŏn′ə-sĭs) *n., pl.* **-ses** (-sēz′). A disease such as rabies or malaria that can be transmitted from animals to man. [NLat. : ZOO- + Gk. *nosos,* disease.]

zo·oph·a·gous (zō-ŏf′ə-gəs) *adj.* Feeding on animal matter.

zo·o·phile (zō′ə-fīl′) *n.* A lover of animals, esp. one opposed to vivisection.

zither

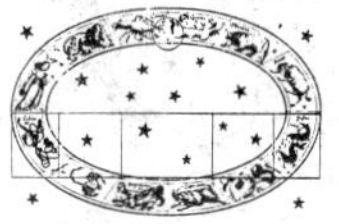

zodiac

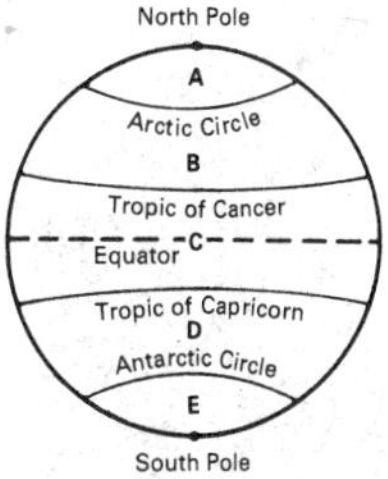

zone
Geographic Zones
A. North Frigid Zone
B. North Temperate Zone
C. Torrid Zone
D. South Temperate Zone
E. South Frigid Zone

zo·oph·i·lous (zō-ŏf′ə-ləs) *adj. Bot.* Pollinated by animals.

zo·o·pho·bi·a (zō′ə-fō′bē-ə) *n.* An irrational fear of animals. **—zo′o·phobe′** *n.*

zo·o·phyte (zō′ə-fīt′) *n.* An invertebrate animal such as a sea anemone or sponge that remains attached to a surface and superficially resembles a plant. [Gk. *zōophuton* : *zōion,* animal + *phuton,* plant.] **—zo′o·phyt′ic** (-fĭt′ĭk), **zo′o·phyt′i·cal** *adj.*

zo·o·plank·ton (zō′ə-plăngk′tən) *n.* Floating, often microscopic aquatic animals.

zo·o·plas·ty (zō′ə-plăs′tē) *n.* Surgical transfer of tissue from a lower animal to man. **—zo′o·plas′tic** *adj.*

zo·o·sperm (zō′ə-spûrm′) *n.* A spermatozoon.

zo·o·spo·ran·gi·um (zō′ə-spə-răn′jē-əm) *n., pl.* **-gi·a** (-jē-ə). A sporangium in which zoospores develop.

zo·o·spore (zō′ə-spôr′, -spōr′) *n.* A motile, flagellated asexual spore, as of certain algae and fungi. **—zo′o·spor′ic, zo′o·spor′ous** *adj.*

zo·os·ter·ol (zō-ŏs′tə-rôl′, -rōl′) *n.* Any of several animal sterols, such as cholesterol.

zo·o·tech·nics (zō′ə-tĕk′nĭks) *n. (used with a sing. or pl. verb).* Zootechny.

zo·o·tech·ny (zō′ə-tĕk′nē) *n.* The domestication, breeding, and improvement of animals; the technology of animal husbandry. [zoo- + Gk. *tekhnē,* art.] **—zo′o·tech′ni·cal** *adj.* **—zo′o·tech·ni′cian** (-nĭsh′ən) *n.*

zo·ot·o·my (zō-ŏt′ə-mē) *n.* **1.** Dissection of animals other than man. **2.** Comparative anatomy.

zoot suit (zo͞ot) *n. Slang.* A man's suit popular during the early 1940's, characterized by full-legged, tight-cuffed trousers and a long coat with wide lapels and wide, heavily padded shoulders. [Orig. unknown.] **—zoot′-suit′er** *n.*

zo·ri (zôr′ē, zōr′ē) *n., pl.* **zori.** A flat sandal with thongs, usually made of straw or leather. [J. *zōri* : *zo,* grass, straw + *-ri,* footwear.]

zor·ille also **zor·il** (zôr′ĭl, zŏr′-)*n.* An African mammal, *Ictonyx striatus,* resembling the skunk in appearance and defensive action. [Fr. < Sp. *zorillo,* skunk, dim. of *zorro,* fox.]

Zo·ro·as·tri·an·ism (zôr′ō-ăs′trē-ə-nĭz′əm) *n.* The religious system founded in Persia by Zoroaster and set forth in the Zend-Avesta, teaching the worship of Ormazd in the context of a universal struggle between the forces of light and of darkness. **—Zo′ro·as′tri·an** *adj. & n.*

zucchini

zos·ter (zŏs′tər) *n.* **1.** A belt or girdle worn by men in ancient Greece. **2.** Herpes zoster. [Gk. *zōstēr,* girdle.]

Zou·ave (zo͞o-äv′) *n.* **1.** A member of a French infantry unit, formerly composed of Algerian recruits, characterized by colorful oriental uniforms and precision drilling. **2.** A member of a group patterned after the French Zouaves, esp. a member of such a unit of the Union Army in the Civil War. [Fr. < Berber *Zwāwa,* an Algerian tribe.]

zounds (zoundz) *interj.* Used to express anger, surprise, or indignation. [Shortening and alteration of *by God's wounds.*]

zoy·sia (zoi′shə, -zhə, -sē-ə, -zē-ə) *n.* Any of several creeping grasses of the genus *Zoysia,* native to Asia and Australia and widely cultivated as a lawn grass. [NLat. *Zoysia,* genus name, after Karl von *Zois* (1756–1800).]

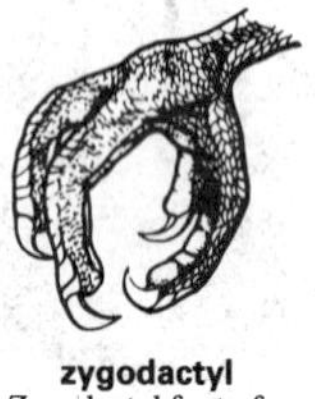

zygodactyl
Zygodactyl foot of a parrot

Zr The symbol for the element zirconium.

Z score *n.* A statistical measure of the distance, in standard deviations, of a sample from the mean.

Z-ther·a·py (zē′thĕr′ə-pē) *n.* A form of psychotherapy in which the patient is forced by a group of people into a cathartic release of pent-up emotions. [After Robert W. *Zaslow,* its developer.]

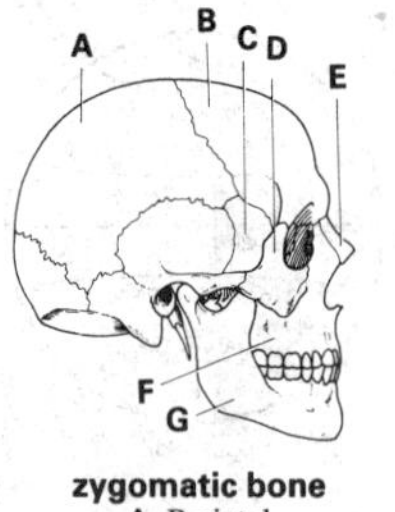

zygomatic bone
A. Parietal
B. Frontal
C. Sphenoid
D. Zygomatic
E. Nasal
F. Maxilla
G. Mandible

zuc·chet·to (zo͞o-kĕt′ō, tso͞o-) *n., pl.* **-tos.** *Rom. Cath. Ch.* A skullcap worn by clergymen, varying in color with the rank of the wearer. [Ital., dim. of *zucca,* gourd, head < LLat. *cucutia,* gourd.]

zuc·chi·ni (zo͞o-kē′nē) *n., pl.* **zucchini.** A variety of squash having an elongated shape and a smooth, thin, dark-green rind. [Ital., pl. of *zucchino,* dim. of *zucca,* gourd < LLat. *cucutia.*]

Zu·lu (zo͞o′lo͞o) *n., pl.* **Zulu** or **-lus. 1.** A member of a large Bantu nation of southeastern Africa between Natal and Lourenço Marques. **2.** The Bantu language of the Zulu. **—Zu′lu** *adj.*

Zu·ñi (zo͞o′nyē, -nē) *n., pl.* **Zuñi** or **-ñis. 1.** A member of a pueblo-dwelling tribe of North American Indians of western New Mexico. **2.** The language of the Zuñi.

Zu·ñi·an (zo͞on′yē-ən) *n.* A language family consisting only of Zuñi. **—Zu′ñi·an** *adj.*

zwie·back (swē′băk′, -bäk′, swī′-, zwē′-, zwī′-) *n.* A usually sweetened bread baked first as a loaf and later cut into slices and toasted. [G. : *zwie-,* twice + *backen,* to bake.]

Zwing·li·an (zwĭng′lē-ən, swĭng′-, tsfĭng′-) *adj.* Of or pertaining to Ulrich Zwingli or to his theological system, esp. his doctrine that the physical body of Christ is not present in the Eucharist and that the ceremony is merely a symbolic commemoration of Christ's death. *—n.* A follower of Zwingli. **—Zwing′li·an·ism** *n.*

zwit·ter·i·on (zwĭt′ər-ī′ən, swĭt′-) *n. Physics.* An ion carrying both a positive and a negative charge, thus forming an electrically neutral molecule. [G. : *Zwitter,* hybrid (< OHG *zwitarn* < *zwi-,* twice) + *ion,* ion < Gk., something that goes, neuter pr.part of *ienai,* to go.] **—zwit′ter·i·on′ic** (-ī-ŏn′ĭk) *adj.*

zy·de·co (zī′dĭ-kō′) *n.* Popular music of southern Louisiana that combines French dance melodies, elements of Caribbean music, and the blues, played by small groups featuring the guitar, the accordion, and a washboard. [Prob. of Fr. orig.]

zyg– *pref.* Variant of **zygo-.**

zyg·a·poph·y·sis (zĭg′ə-pŏf′ĭ-sĭs, zī′gə-) *n., pl.* **-ses** (-sēz′) One of two usually paired processes of a vertebra that articulate with corresponding parts of adjacent vertebrae.

zygo– or **zyg–** *pref.* **1.** Yoke; pair: *zygodactyl.* **2.** Union: *zygospore.* [NLat. < Gk. *zugon,* yoke.]

zy·go·dac·tyl (zī′gə-dăk′təl) *adj.* Having two toes projecting forward and two projecting backward, as certain birds. *—n.* A zygodactyl bird.

zy·go·ma (zī-gō′mə) *n., pl.* **-ma·ta** (-mə-tə) or **-mas. 1.** The zygomatic bone. **2.** The zygomatic arch. **3.** The zygomatic process. [NLat. < Gk. *zugōma,* bolt < *zugoun,* to join.]

zy·go·mat·ic (zī′gə-măt′ĭk) *adj.* Of, pertaining to, or located in the area of the zygoma.

zygomatic arch *n.* The bony arch in vertebrates that extends along the side or front of the skull beneath the orbit.

zygomatic bone *n.* A small quadrangular bone in vertebrates on the side of the face below the eye, forming, in mammals, part of the orbit and part of the zygomatic arch.

zygomatic process *n.* Any of the three processes that articulate to make up the zygomatic arch.

zy·go·mor·phic (zī′gə-môr′fĭk) also **zy·go·mor·phous** (-fəs) *adj.* Bilaterally symmetrical so as to be capable of being symmetrically divided only along a single longitudinal plane. Used of organisms or parts. **—zy′go·mor′phism** *n.*

zy·go·sis (zī-gō′sĭs) *n., pl.* **-ses** (-sēz′). The union of gametes to form a zygote; conjugation.

zy·go·spore (zī′gə-spôr′, -spōr′) *n.* A thick-walled resting spore formed by conjugation of similar gametes, as in algae or fungi.

zy·gote (zī′gōt′) *n.* **1.** The cell formed by the union of two gametes. **2.** The organism that develops from a zygote as characterized by its genetic constitution and subsequent development. [< Gk. *zugōtos,* yoked < *zugoun,* to yoke.] **—zy·got′ic** (-gŏt′ĭk) *adj.* **—zy·got′i·cal·ly** *adv.*

–zygous *suff.* Having a zygotic constitution of a specified kind: *heterozygous.* [Gk. *-zugos,* yoked < *zugon,* yoke.]

zym– *pref.* Variant of **zymo-.**

zy·mase (zī′mās′, -māz′) *n.* The enzyme complex found in yeasts, bacteria, and higher plants and animals that acts in glycolysis.

–zyme *suff.* Enzyme: *lysozyme.* [< Gk. *zumē,* leaven.]

zymo– or **zym–** *pref.* **1.** Fermentation: *zymurgy.* **2.** Enzyme: *zymoplastic.* [NLat. < Gk. *zumē,* leaven.]

zy·mo·gen (zī′mə-jən) *n.* The inactive protein precursor of an enzyme.

zy·mo·gen·ic (zī′mə-jĕn′ĭk) also **zy·mog·e·nous** (zī-mŏj′ə-nəs) *adj.* **1.** Of or pertaining to a zymogen. **2.** Capable of causing fermentation. **3.** Enzyme-producing.

zy·mol·o·gy (zī-mŏl′ə-jē) *n.* The chemistry of fermentation. **—zy′mo·log′ic** (-mə-lŏj′ĭk), **zy′mo·log′ic·al** *adj.* **—zy·mol′o·gist** *n.*

zy·mol·y·sis (zī-mŏl′ĭ-sĭs) *n.* Fermentation. **—zy′mo·lyt′ic** (-mə-lĭt′ĭk) *adj.*

zy·mo·plas·tic (zī′mə-plăs′tĭk) *adj.* Participating in enzyme production.

zy·mo·scope (zī′mə-skōp′) *n.* An instrument used to determine fermentation efficiency by measurement of carbon dioxide produced.

zy·mo·sis (zī-mō′sĭs) *n.* **1.** Fermentation. **2.** *Med.* The process of infection. [Gk. *zymōsis* < *zumoun,* to leaven < *zumē,* leaven.] **—zy·mot′ic** (-mŏt′ĭk) *adj.* **—zy·mot′i·cal·ly** *adv.*

zy·mur·gy (zī′mûr′jē) *n.* The manufacturing chemistry of fermentation processes in brewing.

zyz·zy·va (zĭz′ə-və) *n.* Any of various tropical American weevils of the genus *Zyzzyva,* often destructive to plants. [NLat. *Zyzzyva,* genus name.]

BIOGRAPHICAL ENTRIES

Biographical entries are listed in alphabetical order. Persons having the same name or last name are combined in one entry and listed chronologically by date of birth.

A

Aal·to (äl′tô), **Alvar.** 1898–1976. Finnish architect and industrial designer.
Aar·on (âr′ən, ăr′-). **1.** Hebrew high priest and brother of Moses. **2. Henry Louis ("Hank").** b. 1934. Amer. baseball player; holds home-run record. **—Aar·on′ic** (â-rŏn′ĭk, ăr-ŏn′-), **Aar·on′i·cal** *adj.*

Hank Aaron

Ab·bas·side (ăb′ə-sīd′, ə-băs′īd′) also **Ab·bas·sid** (ăb′ə-sĭd, ə-băs′ĭd). Dynasty of Moslem caliphs (750–1258).
Ab·be (ăb′ē), **Cleveland.** "Father of the Weather Bureau." 1838–1916. Amer. meteorologist.
Ab·bey (ăb′ē), **Edwin Austin.** 1852–1911. Amer. painter and illustrator.
Ab·bot (ăb′ət), **Charles Greeley.** 1872–1973. Amer. astrophysicist.
Ab·bott (ăb′ət). **1.** Sir **John Joseph Caldwell.** 1821–93. Canadian prime minister (1891–92). **2. Lyman.** 1835–1922. Amer. clergyman, author, and editor. **3. Robert Sengstacke.** 1868–1940. Amer. publisher and civil-rights worker. **4. Grace.** 1878–1939. Amer. social reformer. **5. William ("Bud").** 1898–1974. Amer. comedian.
Abd-el-Ka·der also **Abd-al-Ka·dir** (ăb′dəl-kä′dər, -kä-dîr′). 1807?–83. Arab emir and scholar.
Abd-er-Rah·man Khan (ăb′-dər-rä-män′ kän′, KHän′). 1844–1901. Afghanistan emir (1880–1901).
Abd·ul-A·ziz (ăb′dəl-ə-zēz′, ăb′-do͝ol-ä-). 1830–76. Turkish sultan (1861–76); deposed.
Abd·ul Ba·ha (ăb′do͝ol bä-hä′, ăb-do͝ol′). Abbas Effendi. 1844–1921. Persian leader of Bahai sect.
Abdul Ha·mid (hä-mēd′, hä-mĭt′). Name of 2 Turkish sultans, esp. **II,** 1842–1918, ruled 1876–1909; abdicated.
Abd·ul-Jab·bar (ăb-do͝ol′jə-bär′), **Kareem.** b. 1947. Amer. basketball player.
Abd·ul·lah ibn-Hu·sein (ăb′do͝o′lä′ ĭb′n-ho͞o-sān′). 1882–1951. Emir (1921–46) and king (1946–51) of Jordan; assassinated.
Abd·ul-Me·djid I also **Abd·ul-Me·jid I** (ăb′do͝ol-mĕ-jēd′, -jĭt′). 1823–61. Turkish sultan (1839–61).
A·bel (ā′bəl). **1.** Son of Adam and Eve, killed by his brother Cain. **2.** Sir **Frederick Augustus.** 1827–1902. English chemist.
Ab·e·lard (ăb′ə-lärd′) also **A·bé·lard** (ä-bā-lär′), **Peter** or **Pierre.** 1079–1142. French theologian and philosopher; condemned for heresy.
A·bell (ā′bəl), **Arunah Sheperdson.** 1806–88. Amer. newspaper publisher.
Ab·er·crom·by or **Ab·er·crom·bie** (ăb′ər-krŏm′bē, -krŭm′-), **James.** 1706–81. Scottish-born British army officer.
Ab·er·nath·y (ăb′ər-năth′ē), **Ralph David.** b. 1926. Amer. clergyman and civil-rights leader.
Ab·ing·ton (ăb′ĭng-tən), **Frances Barton.** 1737–1815. English actress.
A·bra·ham (ā′brə-hăm′). Hebrew patriarch.
A·brams (ā′brəmz), **Creighton W., Jr.** 1914–74. Amer. general.
A·bra·va·nel (ä-brä′vä-nĕl′), **Isaac.** 1437–1508. Jewish theologian and scholar.
A·bruz·zi (ä-bro͞ot′tsē), Duke of. Prince Luigi Amedeo of Savoy-Aosta. 1873–1933. Italian explorer, mountaineer, and naval officer.
A·bu-Bakr (ä′bo͞o-bä′kər) also **A·bu Bekr** (bĕk′ər). 573–634. 1st Moslem caliph (632–34).
A·bul Ka·sim (ä′bo͝ol kä′sĭm, kä-sĭm′). d. 1013? Arab surgeon and writer.
Ab·zug (ăb′zo͝og′, -zŭg′), **Bella.** b. 1920. Amer. politician.

Bella Abzug

Ach·e·son (ăch′ĭ-sən), **Dean Gooderham.** 1893–1971. Amer. public official.
A·ço·ka (ä-shō′kä). Variant of **Asoka.**
Ac·ton (ăk′tən), 1st Baron. John Emerich Edward Dalberg-Acton. 1834–1902. English historian.
Ad·am (ăd′əm). **1.** In the Bible, the 1st man. **2. Robert** (1728–92) and **James** (1730–94). English architects and designers.
Ad·ams (ăd′əmz). **1. Samuel.** 1722–1803. Amer. Revolutionary leader. **2. John.** 1735–1826. 2nd U.S. President (1797–1801), diplomat, and political philosopher. **3. Abigail Smith.** 1744–1818. Amer. letter writer and wife of John Adams. **4. Hannah.** 1755–1831. Amer. author and compiler. **5. John Quincy.** 1767–1848. 6th U.S. President (1825–29), diplomat, and legislator. **6. Charles Francis.** 1807–86. Amer. diplomat and public official. **7. William Taylor.** "Oliver Optic." 1822–97. Amer. author. **8. Charles Francis, Jr.** 1835–1915. Amer. historian and railroad authority. **9. Henry Brooks.** 1838–1918. Amer. historian and philosopher. **10. Brooks.** 1848–1927. Amer. historian. **11. Herbert Baxter.** 1850–1901. Amer. historian. **12. Samuel Hopkins.** 1871–1958. Amer. author. **13. Maude Kiskadden.** 1872–1953. Amer. actress. **14. James Truslow.** 1878–1949. Amer. historian. **15. Franklin Pierce.** "F.P.A." 1881–1960. Amer. journalist and humorist. **16. Ansel.** 1902–84. Amer. photographer. **—Ad′am·so′ni·an** *adj.*

John Adams

Abigail Adams

Ad·am·son (ăd′əm-sən), **Joy.** 1910–80. Austrian-born naturalist and conservationist in Africa.
Ad·dams (ăd′əmz). **1. Jane.** 1860–1935. Amer. social reformer and pacifist (Nobel, 1931). **2. Charles Samuel.** b. 1912. Amer. cartoonist.
Ad·di·son (ăd′ĭ-sən), **Joseph.** 1672–1719. English essayist. **—Ad′di·so′ni·an** *adj.*
Ade (ād), **George.** 1866–1944. Amer. journalist and humorist.
Ad·en·au·er (ăd′n-ou′ər, äd′-), **Konrad.** 1876–1967. West German chancellor (1949–63).
Ad·ler (ăd′lər). **1.** (*also* äd′lər), **Felix.** 1851–1933. German-born Amer. educator and reformer. **2. Cyrus.** 1863–1940. Amer. religious leader and educator. **3.** (ăd′lər, äd′-), **Alfred.** 1870–1937. Austrian psychiatrist. **4. Mortimer Jerome.** b. 1902. Amer. philosopher and educator. **5. Luther** (1903–84) and **Stella** (b. 1902). Amer. drama educators.
A·dri·an (ā′drē-ən). **1.** Name of 6 popes, esp. **IV,** 1100?–59, only English-born pope, reigned 1154–59. **2. Edgar Douglas.** 1889–1977. English physiologist (Nobel, 1932).
A·dy (ô′dē), **Endre.** 1877–1919. Hungarian symbolist poet and critic.
Ael·fric (ăl′frĭk). "Grammaticus." 955?–1020? English abbot and author.
Aes·chy·lus (ĕs′kə-ləs, ēs′-). 525–456 B.C. Greek dramatist. **—Aes′chy·le′an** (-lē′ən) *adj.*
Ae·sop (ē′səp, -sŏp′). 6th cent. B.C. Greek fabulist. **—Ae·so′pi·an** (ē-sō′pē-ən), **Ae·sop′ic** (ē-sŏp′ĭk) *adj.*
Aeth·el·red (ĕth′əl-rĕd′). Variant of **Ethelred.**
A·ga Khan (ä′gä kän′). Title of the head of the Ismaili Moslems, esp. **III** (1877–1957) and **IV** (b. 1936).
Ag·as·siz (ăg′ə-sē). **1. (Jean) Louis (Rodolphe).** 1807–73. Swiss-born Amer. naturalist and educator. **2. Elizabeth Cabot Cary.** 1822–1907. Amer. educator; a founder of Radcliffe. **3. Alexander.** 1835–1910. Swiss-born Amer. zoologist and oceanographer.
A·gath·o·cles (ə-găth′ə-klēz′). 361–289 B.C. Sicilian despot and tyrant of Syracuse (317–289).
A·gee (ā′jē), **James.** 1909–55. Amer. author and critic.
A·ges·i·la·us II (ə-jĕs′ə-lā′əs). 444?–360? B.C. Spartan king (399?–60?).
Ag·nes (ăg′nĭs), Saint. d. 304? Christian martyr.
Ag·new (ăg′no͞o′, -nyo͞o′). **1. David Hayes.** 1818–92. Amer. surgeon and educator. **2. Spiro Theodore.** b. 1918. U.S. Vice President (1969–73); resigned.
Ag·non (äg-nôn′), **Shmuel Yosef.** 1888–1970. Polish-born Israeli author (Nobel, 1966).
A·gric·o·la (ə-grĭk′ə-lə, -ô′lə), **Gnaeus Julius.** A.D. 37–93. Roman soldier and politician.
A·grip·pa (ə-grĭp′ə), **Marcus Vipsanius.** 63–12 B.C. Roman soldier and statesman.
Ag·rip·pi·na (ăg′rə-pī′nə, -pē′-). **1.** "the Elder." 13 B.C.?–A.D. 33. Roman matron; mother of Caligula. **2.** "the Younger." A.D. 15?–59. Roman empress; mother of Nero.
A·gui·nal·do (ä′gē-näl′dô), **Emilio.** 1869–1964. Philippine revolutionary leader.
Ah·med (ä′mĕd, ä′mĕt). Name of 3 Turkish sultans, esp. **III,** 1673–1736, ruled 1703–30; deposed.
Ai·ken (ā′kən), **Conrad Potter.** 1889–1973. Amer. author.
Ai·ley (ā′lē, ī′lē), **Alvin, Jr.** b. 1931. Amer. choreographer.
Ains·worth (ānz′wûrth), **William Harrison.** 1805–82. English author.
A·i·sha also **A·ye·sha** (ä′ē-shə). 611–78. Chief wife of Mohammed.
Ak·bar (ăk′bär, äk′-). "the Great." 1542–1605. Mogul emperor (1556–1605).
Ake·ley (āk′lē), **Carl Ethan.** 1864–1926. Amer. naturalist and sculptor.
a Kem·pis (ə kĕm′pĭs, ä), **Thomas.** See **Thomas a Kempis.**
A·khe·na·ton or **A·khe·na·ten** (ä′kə-nä′tn, äk′nä′-) also **Ikh·na·ton** (ĭk′nä′tn). Egyptian pharaoh (1375–58 B.C.) and religious reformer.
A·ki·ba ben Jo·seph (ä-kē′bä bĕn jō′zəf, -səf). A.D. 50?–132. Jewish religious leader.
A·lar·cón (ä′lär-kôn′), **Pedro Antonio de.** 1833–91. Spanish politician and author.
Al·ar·ic (ăl′ər-ĭk). **1.** 370?–410. Visigoth king and conqueror of Rome (410). **2. II.** d. 507. Visigoth king.
Al·ba (ăl′bə), Duke of. See **Alva.**
Al·bee (ôl′bē, ŏl′-, ăl′-), **Edward Franklin.** b. 1928. Amer. playwright.
Al·be·marle (ăl′bə-märl), Duke of. George Monck.
Al·bé·niz (äl-bā′nēs′, äl-), **Isaac.** 1860–1909. Spanish composer and pianist.
Al·bers (ăl′bərz, ŏl′-), **Josef.** 1888–1976. German-born Amer. painter.
Al·bert (ăl′bərt). **1.** Prince. 1819–61. Consort of Queen Victoria of England. **2. I.** 1875–1934. Belgian king (1909–34). **3. Carl Bert.** b. 1908. Amer. legislator.
Al·ber·tus Mag·nus (ăl-bûr′təs măg′nəs), Saint. 1206?–80. German religious philosopher.
Al·bright (ôl′brīt, ŏl′-). **1. William Foxwell.** 1891–1971. Amer. archaeologist and educator. **2. Ivan Le Lorraine.** b. 1897. Amer. painter.
Al·bu·quer·que (ăl′bə-kûr′kē, äl′-bə-kûr′-, ôl′bo͞o-kĕr′kə), **Affonso de.**

1453-1515. Portuguese admiral and colonial administrator.

Al·cae·us (ăl-sē'əs). fl. 611?–580 B.C. Greek poet.

Al·ci·bi·a·des (ăl'sə-bī'ə-dēz'). 450?–404 B.C. Athenian politician and general.

Al·cott (ôl'kət,-kŏt, ŏl'-). **1. Amos Bronson.** 1799–1888. Amer. educator and philosopher. **2. Louisa May.** 1832–88. Amer. author and reformer.

Louisa May Alcott

Al·cuin (ăl'kwĭn). 735–804. English prelate and scholar.

Al·da (ăl'də, ăl'-), **Frances (Davis).** 1883–1952. New Zealand-born soprano.

Al·den (ôl'dən, ŏl'-). **1. John** (1599?–1687) and **Priscilla Mullins** (b. 1602?). Pilgrim colonists. **2. Isabella Macdonald.** 1841–1930. Amer. author.

Al·der (ăl'dər), **Kurt.** 1902–58. German chemist (Nobel, 1950).

Al·ding·ton (ôl'dĭng-tən, ŏl'-), **Richard.** 1892–1962. English Imagist poet.

Al·drich (ôl'drĭch, ŏl'-). **1. Thomas Bailey.** 1836–1907. Amer. author and editor. **2. Nelson Wilmarth.** 1841–1915. Amer. financier and legislator.

Al·dridge (ôl'drĭj, ŏl'-), **Ira Frederick.** 1804?–67. Amer. actor.

Al·drin (ôl'drĭn, ŏl'-), **Edwin Eugene ("Buzz"), Jr.** b. 1930. Amer. astronaut.

Al·dus Ma·nu·tius (ôl'dəs mə-no͞o'shəs, -shē'əs, -nyo͞o'-, ŏl'-). See **Manutius.**

A·lei·chem (ä-lā'kĕm, -KHĕm), **Sholem** or **Shalom.** 1859–1916. Russian-born Amer. Yiddish humorist.

A·leix·an·dre (ä'lā-ksän'drĕ), **Vicente.** b. 1898. Spanish poet (Nobel, 1977).

A·le·mán (ä'lĕ-män'), **Mateo.** 1547–1610? Spanish-born Mexican author.

Alemán Val·dés (väl-dĕs'), **Miguel.** b. 1902. Mexican statesman.

A·lem·bert (ăl'əm-bâr', ä-läN-bĕr'), **Jean Le Rond d'.** 1717–83. French mathematician, scientist, philosopher, and Encyclopedist.

Al·ex·an·der (ăl'ĭg-zăn'dər, -zän'-). **1. III.** "the Great." 356–23 B.C. Macedonian king (336–23) and conqueror of Greece, Persia, and Egypt. **2.** Name of 8 popes, esp.: **a. III.** d. 1181. Reigned 1159–81. **b. VI.** 1431?–1503. Reigned 1492–1503. **3.** Name of 3 Russian czars: **a. I.** 1777–1825. Ruled 1801–25. **b. II.** 1818–81. Ruled 1855–81; emancipated serfs (1861). **c. III.** 1845–94. Ruled 1881–94. **4. I.** Also **Alexander O·bre·no·vić** (ô-brĕn'ô-vĭch'). 1876-1903. Serbian king (1889–1903); assassinated. **5. I.** 1888–1934. Yugoslavian king (1921–34); assassinated. **6. of Tu·nis** (to͞o'nĭs, tyo͞o'-), 1st Earl. Harold Rupert Leofric George Alexander. 1891–1969. British field marshal. **—Al'ex·an'dri·an** *adj.*

Alexander Nev·ski (nĕv'skē, nĕf'-, nyĕf'-). 1220?–63. Russian saint and national hero.

Alexander Se·ve·rus (sə-vîr'əs), **Marcus Aurelius.** 203?–35. Roman emperor (222–35).

Al·ex·an·der·son (ăl'ĭg-zăn'dər-sən), **Ernst Frederick Werner.** 1878–1973. Swedish-born Amer. electrical engineer.

A·lex·is I Mi·khai·lo·vich (ä-lĕk'sĭs mĭk-ī'lə-vĭch, mĭ-KHī'-). 1629–76. Russian czar (1645–76) and reformer.

Alexis Pe·tro·vich (pĕ-trô'vĭch). 1690–1718. Russian czarevitch; condemned for treason.

A·lex·i·us Com·ne·nus (ə-lĕk'sē-əs kŏm'nē'nəs). Name of 5 Eastern Roman emperors, esp. **I,** 1048–1118, ruled 1081–1118.

Al·fie·ri (ăl-fē-âr'ē, äl-fyâ'rē), Conte **Vittorio.** 1749–1803. Italian dramatist.

Al·fon·so (ăl-fŏn'sō, -zō, äl-fôn'sô). **1.** Name of 6 kings of Portugal, esp.: **a. I.** 1112–85. Ruled 1139–85. **b. V.** 1432–81. Ruled 1438–81. **2. XIII.** 1886–1941. Spanish king (1886–1931, ruled 1902–31); abdicated.

Al·fred (ăl'frĭd). "the Great." 849–99. West Saxon king (871–99), scholar, and lawmaker.

Alf·vén (äl-vān', -vĕn', älf-, äl-), **Hannes Olof Gösta.** b. 1908. Swedish physicist (Nobel, 1970).

Al·ger (ăl'jər). **1. Cyrus.** 1781–1856. Amer. inventor and industrialist. **2. Horatio.** 1832–99. Amer. author.

A·li (ä-lē'). **1.** 600?–61. Moslem caliph (656–61); assassinated. **2.** Or **Ali Pa·sha** (pä'shä). 1741–1822. Turkish colonial governor; assassinated. **3. Muhammad.** b. 1942. Amer. prizefighter.

Muhammad Ali

Al·len (ăl'ən). **1. William.** 1532–94. English cardinal. **2. Ethan.** 1738-89. Amer. Revolutionary soldier. **3. Richard.** 1760–1831. Amer. religious leader. **4. John.** 1810–92. Amer. dentistry pioneer. **5. Henry Watkins.** 1820–66. Amer. Confederate soldier and public official. **6. Florence Ellinwood.** 1884–1966. Amer. jurist. **7. Frederick Lewis.** 1890–1954. Amer. editor and historian. **8. Fred.** 1894–1956. Amer. humorist. **9. Grace Ethel Cecile Rosalie ("Gracie").** 1906–64. Amer. comedienne. **10. Melvin Israel ("Mel").** b. 1913. Amer. sportscaster. **11. Steve.** b. 1921. Amer. entertainer. **12. Woody.** b. 1935. Amer. actor, writer, and filmmaker.

Al·len·by (ăl'ən-bē), 1st Viscount. Edmund Henry Hynman. 1861–1936. British field marshal.

Al·len·de Gos·sens (ä-yĕn'dĕ gô'sĕns), **Salvador.** 1908–73. Chilean president (1970–73); died in coup.

Al·leyn (ăl'ən, -ĕn'), **Edward.** 1566–1626. English actor.

Al·lou·ez (ä-lo͞o-ā'), **Claude Jean.** 1622–89. French Jesuit missionary.

All·ston (ôl'stən, ŏl'-). **1. Washington.** 1779–1843. Amer. painter. **2. Robert Francis Withers.** 1801–64. Amer. agriculturist and politician.

Al·ma-Tad·e·ma (ăl'mə-tăd'ə-mə), Sir **Lawrence.** 1836–1912. Dutch-born English painter.

Al·mei·da (ăl-mā'də), **Francisco de.** 1450?–1510. Portuguese colonial administrator.

A·lon·so (ə-lŏn'zō, ä-lôn'sō), **Alicia.** b. 1921? Cuban ballerina and choreographer.

Al·sop (ôl'səp, ŏl'-), **Joseph W., Jr.** (b. 1910) and **Stewart** (1914–74). Amer. journalists.

Al·ter (ôl'tər, ŏl'-), **David.** 1807–81. Amer. physicist, physician, and inventor.

Alt·geld (ôlt'gĕld, ŏlt'-), **John Peter.** 1847–1902. German-born Amer. politician.

Alt·man (ôlt'mən), **Benjamin.** 1840–1913. Amer. merchant and art patron.

Al·va (ăl'və, äl'vä) also **Al·ba** (ăl'bə), Duke of. Fernando Álvarez de Toledo. 1508–82. Spanish general and colonial administrator in the Netherlands.

Al·va·ra·do (ăl'və-rä'dō, äl'vä-rä'*th*ô), **Alonso de** (1490?–1554) and **Pedro de** (1486–1541). Spanish soldiers and adventurers in the New World.

Al·va·rez (ăl'və-rĕz), **Luis Walter.** b. 1911. Amer. physicist (Nobel, 1968).

Al·ve·ar (äl'vē-är'), **Carlos María de.** 1789–1853. Argentine revolutionary soldier and politician.

A·ma·do (ə-mä'do͞o), **Jorge.** b. 1912. Brazilian author.

A·ma·ti (ä-mä'tē). Family of Italian violin makers, esp. **Nicolò** or **Nicola** (1596–1684).

Am·bler (ăm'blər), **Eric.** b. 1909. English author.

Am·brose (ăm'brōz'), Saint. 340?–97. Author, composer, and bishop of Milan (374–97). **—Am·bro'sian** *adj.*

A·men·ho·tep (ä'mĕn-hō'tĕp, ăm'ən-) also **Am·e·no·phis** (ăm'ə-nō'fəs). Name of 4 Egyptian pharaohs, esp.: **1. III.** Reigned 1411?–1375 B.C. **2. IV.** Akhenaton.

Ames (āmz), **Fisher.** 1758–1808. Amer. political leader and author.

A·min Da·da (ä-mēn' dä-dä'), **Idi.** b. 1925? Ugandan dictator (1971–79); deposed.

A·mis (ā'mĭs), **Kingsley.** b. 1922. English author.

A·mo·ry (ā'mə-rē), **Cleveland.** b. 1917. Amer. author and conservationist.

A·mos (ā'məs). 8th cent. B.C. Hebrew prophet.

Am·père (ăm'pîr, äN-pĕr'), **André Marie.** 1775–1836. French physicist and mathematician.

A·mund·sen (ä'mənd-sən, ä'mo͝on-), **Roald.** 1872–1928. Norwegian polar explorer.

A·nac·re·on (ə-năk'rē-ən). 572?–488? B.C. Greek poet.

An·ax·ag·o·ras (ăn'ăk-săg'ər-əs). 500?–428 B.C. Greek philosopher.

A·nax·i·man·der (ə-năk'sə-măn'dər). 611–547 B.C. Greek philosopher and mathematician.

An·der·sen (ăn'dər-sən), **Hans Christian.** 1805–75. Danish author.

An·der·son (ăn'dər-sən). **1. Joseph Reid.** 1813–92. Amer. manufacturer and Confederate general. **2. Mary Antoinette.** 1859–1940. Amer. actress. **3. Sherwood.** 1876–1941. Amer. author. **4. Sir John.** Viscount Waverley. 1882–1958. British politician and public official **5. Maxwell.** 1888–1959. Amer. playwright. **6. Margaret Caroline.** 1893?–1973. Amer. editor. **7.** Dame **Judith.** b. 1898. Australian-born actress. **8. Marian.** b. 1902. Amer. contralto. **9. Carl David.** b. 1905. Amer. physicist (Nobel, 1936). **10. Robert Woodruff.** b. 1917. Amer. dramatist. **11. Philip Warren.** b. 1923. Amer. physicist (Nobel, 1977).

Marian Anderson

An·dra·da e Sil·va (äN-drä'də ē sĕl'və), **José Bonifácio de.** 1763?–1838. Brazilian statesman, scientist, and poet.

An·drás·sy (ăn-drăs'ē, ôn'drä-shē), Counts **Gyula** (1823–90) and **Gyula** (1860–1929). Hungarian politicians.

An·dré (ăn'drā, ăn'drē), **John.** 1751–80. English soldier; hanged as Revolutionary spy.

An·dre·a del Sar·to (ăn-drā'ä dĕl' sär'tō). 1486–1531. Italian painter.

An·dre·ev (ăn-drā'yəf), **Leonid Nikolaevich.** 1871–1919. Russian author.

An·drew (ăn'dro͞o). **1.** Saint. One of the 12 Apostles. **2. John Albion.** 1818–67. Amer. antislavery leader.

An·drews (ăn'dro͞oz). **1. Stephen Pearl.** 1812–86. Amer. abolitionist and reformer. **2. Thomas.** 1813–85. Irish physicist and chemist. **3. Charles McLean.** 1863–1943. Amer. historian. **4. Fannie Fern Phillips.** 1867–1950. Canadian-born Amer. reformer. **5. Roy Chapman.** 1884–1960. Amer. naturalist.

An·dríc (ăn'drĭch), **Ivo.** 1892–1975. Yugoslavian author (Nobel, 1961).

An·dros (ăn'drŏs, -drəs), Sir **Edmund.** 1637–1714. English colonial administrator.

Edmund Andros

An·fin·sen (ăn'fən-sən), **Christian Boehmer.** b. 1916. Amer. biochemist (Nobel, 1972).

An·gel·a Me·ri·ci (ăn'jə-lə mə-rē'chē, ăn'jä-lä mā-rē'chē), Saint. 1474–1540. Italian founder of the Ursuline order.

An·gel·i·co (ăn-jĕl'ĭ-kō', ăn-jä'lē-kō), Fra. Giovanni da Fiesole. 1387–1455. Italian painter.

An·gell (ān'jəl). **1. James Burrill.** 1829–1916. Amer. educator and diplomat. **2.** Sir **Norman.** 1872–1967. English economist and author (Nobel, 1933).

Ång·ström (ăng'strəm, ông'strœm), **Anders Jonas.** 1814–74. Swedish physicist and astronomer.

An·na I·va·nov·na (ä'nə ē-vä'nəv-nə). 1693–1740. Russian empress (1730–40).

Anne (ăn). **1. of Cleves** (klēvz). 1515–57. English queen as 4th wife of Henry VIII. **2. of Aus·tri·a** (ô'strē-ə). 1601–66. Wife of Louis XIII of France and regent (1643–61). **3.** 1665–1714. Queen of Great Britain and Ireland (1702–14).

A·nou·ilh (ä-no͞o'ē), **Jean.** b. 1910. French dramatist.

An·selm (ăn'sĕlm), Saint. 1033–1109. Italian-born English prelate and philosopher.

An·theil (ăn'tīl), **George.** 1900–59. Amer. pianist and composer.

An·tho·ny (ăn'thə-nē). **1.** Saint. c. 250–350. Egyptian ascetic monk. **2. of Pad·u·a** (păj'o͞o-ə, păd'yo͞o-ə), Saint. 1195–1231. Italian theologian. **3. Susan Brownell.** 1820–1906. Amer. reformer.

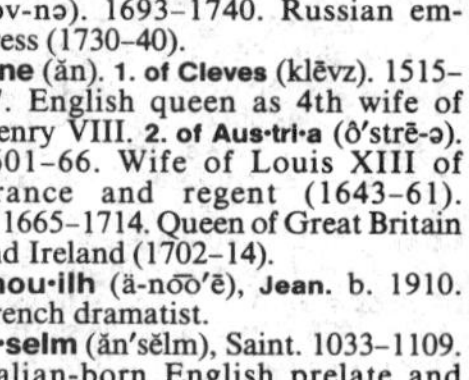

Susan B. Anthony

An·tig·o·nus (ăn-tĭg'ə-nəs). Name of 3 kings of Macedonia, esp. **I,** 382–301 B.C., one of Alexander II's generals.

An·ti·o·chus (ăn-tī'ə-kəs). Name of 13 Seleucid kings of Syria, esp.: **1. III.** "the Great." c. 241–187 B.C. Ruled 223–187. **2. IV.** Antiochus Epiphanes. d. 163 B.C. Ruled 175–163.

An·tip·a·ter (ăn-tĭp'ə-tər) . 398?–19 B.C. Macedonian general and diplomat.

An·tis·the·nes (ăn-tĭs'thə-nēz'). 444?–371? B.C. Greek philosopher.

An·toine (äN-twän'), Père. 1748–1829. Spanish priest in Louisiana.

An·to·nel·lo da Mes·si·na (än-tō-nĕl'ō dä mĕs-sē'nä). 1430?–79. Italian painter.

An·to·ne·scu (ăn'tə-nĕs'ko͞o), **Ion.** 1882–1946. Rumanian general and dictator.

An·to·ni·nus Pi·us (ăn'tə-nī'nəs pī'əs). 86–161 A.D. Roman emperor (138–61).

An·to·ni·on·i (ăn-tō'nē-ō'nē, än-), **Michelangelo.** b. 1912. Italian filmmaker.

An·to·ni·us (ăn-tō'nē-əs), **Marcus.** Mark Antony.

An·za (än'sä), **Juan Bautista de.** 1735–88? Spanish colonial administrator and explorer.

A·pel·les (ə-pĕl'ēz). 4th cent. B.C. Greek painter.

Ap·gar (ăp'gär), **Virginia.** 1909–74. Amer. physician.

A·pol·li·naire (ä-pô'lē-nĕr'), **Guillaume.** 1880–1918. Polish-born French poet.

A·pol·lo·dor·us (ə-pŏl'ō-dôr'əs). "Skiagraphos." 5th cent. B.C. Greek painter.

Ap·ol·lo·ni·us of Rhodes (ăp'ə-lō'nē-əs; rōdz). 3rd–2nd cent. B.C. Greek poet.

Ap·ple·by (ăp'əl-bē), **John Francis.** 1840–1917. Amer. inventor.

Ap·ple·gate (ăp'əl-gāt'), **Jesse.** 1811–88. Amer. Western pioneer, surveyor, and legislator.

Ap·ple·seed (ăp'əl-sēd'), **Johnny.** John Chapman.

Ap·ple·ton (ăp'əl-tən), Sir **Edward Victor.** 1892–1965. English physicist (Nobel, 1947).

A·pra·ksin also **A·prax·in** (ə-prăk'sən, ä-prä'ksĭn), **Fëdor Matveevich.** 1671–1728. Russian admiral.

Ap·u·lei·us (ăp'yə-lē'əs), **Lucius.** 2nd cent. A.D. Roman philosopher and satirist.

A·qui·nas (ə-kwī'nəs), Saint **Thomas.** 1225?–74. Italian theologian and philosopher.

Ar·a·fat (ä-rä-făt'), **Yasir.** b. 1929. Palestinian leader.

Ar·am (âr'əm, âr'-), **Eugene.** 1704–59. English philologist; executed for murder.

Ar·ber (är'bər). **1. Edward.** 1836–1912. English scholar and editor. **2. Werner.** b. 1929. Swiss microbiologist (Nobel, 1978).

Ar·buth·not (är-bŭth'nət, är'bəth-nŏt'), **John.** 1667–1735. Scottish physician and author.

Ar·car·o (är-kâr'ō), **George Edward ("Eddie").** b. 1916. Amer. jockey.

Ar·cher (är'chər), **William.** 1856–1924. Scottish critic, dramatist, and translator.

Ar·chi·me·des (är'kə-mē'dēz). 287?–12 B.C. Greek mathematician, engineer, and physicist. —**Ar'chi·me'de·an** *adj.*

Ar·chi·pen·ko (är'kə-pĕng'kō, -KHē-pĕng'kə), **Alexander Porfirievich.** 1887–1964. Russian-born Amer. sculptor.

Ar·den (är'dən), **Elizabeth.** 1891–1966. Canadian-born Amer. businesswoman.

Ar·drey (är'drē), **Robert.** 1908–80. Amer. anthropologist.

A·rendt (âr'ənt, är'-), **Hannah.** 1906–75. German-born Amer. historian.

A·re·ti·no (ä'rä-tē'nō), **Pietro.** 1492–1556. Italian author.

Ar·gall (är'gôl, -gəl), Sir **Samuel.** 1572?–1626. English colonial adventurer and administrator.

Ar·gyll (är-gīl', är'gīl'), 9th Duke of. John Douglas Sutherland Campbell. 1845–1914. English author, politician, and colonial administrator.

A·ri·os·to (är'ē-ŏs'tō, -ō'stō, är'-, ä'rē-ôs'tô), **Lodovico.** 1474–1533. Italian poet.

Ar·is·tar·chus (ăr'ĭ-stär'kəs). **1. of Sa·mos** (sä'mäs'). 3rd cent. B.C. Greek astronomer. **2.** 220?–150 B.C. Greek grammarian and critic.

Ar·is·ti·des also **Ar·is·tei·des** (ăr'ĭ-stī'dēz). "the Just." 530?–468? B.C. Athenian statesman and general.

Ar·is·tip·pus (ăr'ĭ-stĭp'əs). 5th–4th cent. B.C. Greek philosopher.

Ar·is·toph·a·nes (ăr'ĭ-stŏf'ə-nēz). **1. of By·zan·ti·um** (bĭ-zăn'shē-əm, -tē-əm). 257?–180? B.C. Greek philologist. **2.** 448?–380? B.C. Athenian dramatist.

Ar·is·tot·le (ăr'ĭ-stŏt'l). 384–22 B.C. Greek philosopher. —**Ar'is·to·te'li·an** (ə-rĭ'stə-tē'lē-ən) *adj. & n.*

A·ri·us (ə-rī'əs, ăr'ē-, âr'-). 256?–336. Greek theologian; condemned as a heretic. —**A'ri·an** *adj. & n.*

Ark·wright (ärk'rīt'), Sir **Richard.** 1732–92. English inventor (spinning frame) and manufacturer.

Ar·len (är'lən), **Michael.** 1895–1956. Armenian-born English author.

Ar·min·i·us (är-mĭn'ē-əs). **1.** Also **Ar·min** (är'mĭn). 17 B.C.?–A.D. 21. German hero. **2. Jacobus.** 1560–1609. Dutch theologian.

Ar·mour (är'mər), **Philip Danforth.** 1832–1901. Amer. industrialist.

Arm·strong (ärm'strông'). **1. John.** 1758–1843. Amer. general, politician, and diplomat. **2. William George.** 1810–1900. Baron Armstrong of Cragside. English inventor and industrialist. **3. Samuel Chapman.** 1839–93. Amer. educator. **4. Edwin Howard.** 1890–1954. Amer. engineer and inventor. **5. Hamilton Fish.** 1893–1973. Amer. editor and author. **6. Louis ("Satchmo").** 1900–71. Amer. jazz musician. **7. Neil Alden.** b. 1930. Amer. astronaut; 1st to walk on the moon.

Louis Armstrong

Arne (ärn), **Thomas Augustine.** 1710–78. English composer.

Ar·no (är'nō), **Peter.** 1904–68. Amer. cartoonist.

Ar·nold (är'nəld). **1. Benedict.** 1741–1801. Amer. Revolutionary general and traitor. **2. Thomas.** 1795–1842. English educator and historian. **3. Matthew.** 1822–88. English poet and critic. **4. Henry Harley ("Hap").** 1886–1950. Amer. air-force officer. **5. Thurman Wesley.** 1891–1969. Amer. jurist.

Ar·nold·son (är'nəld-sən, är'no͝old-sôn'), **Klas Pontus.** 1844–1916. Swedish politician and pacifist (Nobel, 1908).

Arp (ärp), **Jean** or **Hans.** 1887–1966. French artist.

Ar·pád (är'päd). d. 907. Hungarian national hero.

Ar·rhe·ni·us (ä-rā'nē-o͝os'), **Svante August.** 1859–1927. Swedish physicist and chemist (Nobel, 1903).

Ar·row (ăr'ō), **Kenneth Joseph.** b. 1921. Amer. economist (Nobel, 1972).

Ar·son·val (där-sôN-väl'), **Jacques Arsène d'.** 1851–1940. French physicist.

Ar·ta·xer·xes (är'tə-zûrk'sēz). Name of 3 Persian kings: **1. I.** d. 424 B.C. Ruled 464–24. **2. II** d. 359 B.C. Ruled 404–359. **3. III** d. 338 B.C. Ruled 359–38.

Ar·te·vel·de (är'tə-vĕl'də), **Jacob van.** "Brewer of Ghent." 1290?–1345. Flemish political leader.

Ar·thur (är'thər). **1. Timothy Shay.** 1809–85. Amer. journalist and temperance advocate. **2. Chester Alan.** 1829–86. 21st U.S. President (1881–85).

As·bur·y (ăz'bûr'ē, -bə-rē), **Francis.** 1745–1816. English-born Amer. religious leader.

Asch (ăsh), **Sholem** or **Shalom.** 1880–1957. Polish-born Amer. Yiddish author.

As·cham (ăs'kəm), **Roger.** 1515–68. English scholar and author.

Ash·burn·er (ăsh'bûr'nər), **Charles Albert.** 1854–89. Amer. geologist.

Ashe (ăsh), **Arthur Robert, Jr.** b. 1943. Amer. tennis player.

Ash·ley (ăsh'lē), **William Henry.** 1778?–1838. Amer. fur trader and politician.

Ash·mun (ăsh'mŭn), **Jehudi.** 1794–1828. Amer. colonial agent in Africa.

Ash·ton (ăsh'tən), Sir **Frederick.** b. 1906. English choreographer.

A·shur·ba·ni·pal (ä'sho͝or-bä'nē-päl') also **As·sur·ba·ni·pal** (ä'so͝or-). Assyrian king (669–26 B.C.).

As·i·mov (ăz'ĭ-mŏf), **Isaac.** b. 1920. Russian-born Amer. author.

A·so·ka (ə-sō'kə) also **A·ço·ka** (ä-shō'kä). "the Great." d. 232 B.C. Buddhist king of Magadha (273–32).

As·pa·sia (ă-spā'zhə). fl. c. 440 B.C. Greek courtesan.

As·quith (ăs'kwĭth), **Herbert Henry.** 1st Earl of Oxford and Asquith. 1852–1928. British prime minister (1908–16).

As·sad (ä-säd'), **Hafez al-.** b. 1928. Syrian statesman.

As·ser (ä'sər), **Tobias Michael Carel.** 1838–1913. Dutch statesman and jurist (Nobel, 1911).

A·staire (ə-stâr'), **Fred.** b. 1899. Amer. dancer and actor.

As·ton (ăs'tən), **Francis William.** 1877–1945. English chemist and physicist (Nobel, 1922).

As·tor (ăs'tər). **1. John Jacob.** 1763–1848. German-born Amer. fur trader and capitalist. **2. Caroline Webster Schermerhorn.** 1830–1908. Amer. socialite. **3. William Waldorf.** 1st Viscount Astor of Hever Castle. 1848–1919. Amer.-born British capitalist. **4. Nancy Witcher Langhorne,** Viscountess. 1879–1964. Amer.-born British politician.

As·tu·ri·as (ä-sto͝or'ē-əs, ä-sto͝or'yäs), **Miguel Angel.** 1899–1974. Guatemalan author (Nobel, 1966).

A·ta·hual·pa (ä'tä-wäl'pä) also **A·ta·ba·li·pa** (ä'tä-bä'lē-pä'). 1502?–33. Incan emperor (1525–33); executed.

At·a·türk (ăt'ə-tûrk', ä-tä-tûrk'), **Kemal.** See **Kemal Atatürk.**

Ath·a·na·sius (ăth'ə-nā'shəs), Saint. 293–373. Greek patriarch of Alexandria. —**Ath'a·na'sian** *adj. & n.*

Ath·el·stan (ăth'əl-stăn'). 895–940. English king (924–40).

Ath·er·ton (ăth'ər-tən), **Gertrude Franklin Horn.** 1857–1948. Amer. author.

At·kin·son (ăt'kĭn-sən). **1. Henry.** 1782–1842. Amer. soldier and explorer. **2. Edward.** 1827–1905. Amer. industrialist. **3. (Justin) Brooks.** 1894–1984. Amer. critic.

At·las (ăt'ləs), **Charles.** 1894–1972. Italian-born Amer. physical culturist.

At·tar (ă'tär'). 1119–1229? Persian poet and mystic.

At·ti·la (ăt'l-ə, ə-tĭl'ə). "Scourge of the Gods." 406?–53. King of the Huns (433?–53).

Att·lee (ăt'lē), **Clement Richard.** 1883–1967. British prime minister (1945–51).

At·tucks (ăt'əks), **Crispus.** 1723?–70. Killed in the Boston Massacre.

At·wat·er (ăt'wô'tər, -wŏt'ər), **Wilbur Olin.** 1844–1907. Amer. pioneer in agricultural chemistry.

Au·ber (ō-bĕr'), **Daniel François Esprit.** 1782–1871. French composer.

Chester A. Arthur

Au·brey (ô'brē), **John.** 1626–97. English antiquarian.

Au·chin·closs (ô'kĭn-klôs, -klŏs), **Louis Stanton.** b. 1917. Amer. author.

Au·den (ôd'n), **Wystan Hugh.** 1907–73. English-born Amer. author.

Au·du·bon (ô'də-bŏn', -bən), **John James.** 1785–1851. Haitian-born Amer. ornithologist and artist.

Au·gus·tine (ô'gə-stēn', ô-gŭs'tĭn). **1.** Saint. 354–430. Church father and philosopher. **2.** Also **Aus·tin** (ô'stən). "Apostle of the English." d. 604? Missionary and prelate. —**Au'gus·tin'i·an** (ô'gə-stĭn'ē-ən) *adj. & n.*

Au·gus·tus (ô-gŭs'təs). "Octavian." 63 B.C.–A.D. 14. 1st Roman emperor (27 B.C.–A.D. 14). —**Au·gus'tan** *adj. & n.*

Au·rang·zeb also **Au·rung·zeb** or **Au·rung·zebe** (ôr'əng-zĕb'). 1618–1707. Hindustani emperor (1658–1707).

Au·re·lian (ô-rē'lē-ən, ô-rēl'yən). 212?–75. Roman emperor (270–75).

Au·ri·ol (ôr'ē-ōl', ō-ryôl'), **Vincent.** 1884–1966. French statesman.

Aus·ten (ô'stən), **Jane.** 1775–1817. English author.

Aus·tin (ô'stən). **1.** Variant of **Augustine** (sense 2). **2. John.** 1790–1859. English jurist. **3. Stephen Fuller.** 1793–1836. Amer. colonizer and Texas political leader. **4. Alfred** 1835–1913. English author. **5. Mary Hunter.** 1868–1934. Amer. author and feminist.

Stephen Austin

Au·try (ô'trē), **Gene.** b. 1907. Amer. singer and actor.

Av·en·zo·ar (ăv'ən-zō'ər). 1090?–1162. Spanish-Arab physician and author.

A·ver·ro·ës or **A·ver·rho·ës** (ə-vĕr'ō-ēz'). 1126–1198. Spanish-Arab physician and philosopher.

Av·i·cen·na (ăv'ĭ-sĕn'ə). 980–1037. Arab physician and philosopher.

A·viz also **A·vis** (ä'vĭsh). Dynasty of Portuguese rulers (1385–1850).

A·vo·ga·dro (ä'və-gä'drō, ä'vō-), **Amedeo.** 1776–1856. Italian physicist.

A·von (ā'vŏn, ăv'ən), Earl of. Anthony Eden.

Ax·el·rod (ăk'səl-räd'), **Julius.** b. 1912. Amer. biochemist (Nobel, 1970).

Ay·de·lotte (ăd'l-ŏt'), **Frank.** 1880–1956. Amer. educator.

Ay·er (âr), **Francis Wayland.** 1848–1923. Amer. advertising executive.

A·ye·sha (ä'ē-shä'). Variant of **Aisha.**

Ay·res (ârz), **Anne.** 1816–96. English-born Amer. religious leader.

Ayr·ton (âr'tn), **William Edward.** 1847–1908. English physicist, electrical engineer, and inventor.

A·za·ña y Dí·ez (ä-sä'nyä ē dē'ĕs), **Manuel.** 1880–1940. Spanish statesman.

A·ze·glio (ä-zĕ'lyô), Marchese d'. Massimo Taparelli. 1798–1866. Italian politician and author.

A·zue·la (ä-swā'lä, ä-swĕ'lä), **Mariano.** 1873–1952. Mexican author.

B

Baa·de (bä'də), **Walter.** 1893–1960. German-born Amer. astronomer.

Baal Shem Tov (bäl' shĕm' tōv', shäm') also **Baal Shem Tob** (tōb'). 1700?–60. Jewish religious leader.

Bab (bäb, băb), **the.** Ali Mohammed of Shiraz. 1819–50. Persian founder of Babism.

Bab·bitt (băb′ĭt), **Irving.** 1865–1933. Amer. scholar and humanist.

Bab·cock (băb′kŏk′), **Stephen Moulton.** 1843–1931. Amer. agricultural chemist.

Ba·ben·berg (bä′bən-bĕrкн′). Franconian dynasty ruling margraviate (976–1156) and duchy (1156–1246) of Austria.

Ba·ber also **Ba·bar** or **Ba·bur** (bä′bər). 1483–1530. Mongol conqueror of India.

Ba·beuf or **Ba·boeuf** (bä-bœf′), **François Noël** or **Émile.** 1760–97. French revolutionary.

Bab·ing·ton (băb′ĭng-tən), **Anthony.** 1561–86. English Catholic conspirator; executed for treason.

Bab·son (băb′sən), **Roger Ward.** 1875–1967. Amer. financial statistician.

Bach (bäкн, bäk). Family of German composers and musicians, including **Johann Sebastian** (1685–1750) and his sons **Wilhelm Friedemann** (1710–84), **Karl Philip Emanuel** (1714–88), **Johann Christoph Friedrich** (1732–95), and **Johann Christian** (1735–82).

Johann Sebastian Bach

Bache (bāch). **1. Benjamin Franklin.** 1769–98. Amer. journalist. **2. Alexander Dallas.** 1806–67. Amer. physicist and educator.

Back·us (băk′əs), **Isaac.** 1724–1806. Amer. Separatist leader and historian.

Ba·con (bā′kən). **1. Roger.** "the Admirable Doctor." 1214?–94. English friar, scientist, and philosopher. **2. Francis.** Baron Verulam, Viscount St. Albans. 1561–1626. English philosopher, essayist, courtier, jurist, and statesman. **3. Nathaniel.** 1647–76. English-born colonist; led Bacon's Rebellion (1676). **4. Delia Salter.** 1811–59. Amer. author; disputed authorship of Shakespeare's plays. **5. Francis** b. 1910. Irish-born British painter. —**Ba·co′ni·an** *adj. & n.*

Ba·den-Pow·ell (băd′n-pō′əl, băd′n-pou′əl), Sir **Robert Stephenson Smyth.** 1857–1941. English soldier; founder of the Boy Scouts.

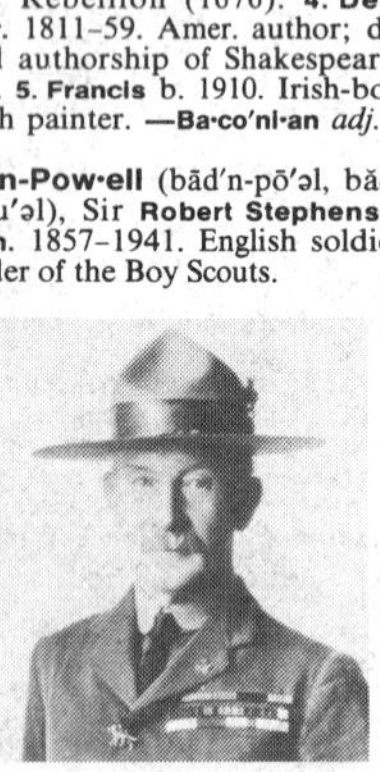

Robert Baden-Powell

Ba·do·glio (bä-dô′lyō), **Pietro.** 1871–1956. Italian general and politician.

Bae·da (bē′də). Variant of **Bede.**

Bae·de·ker (bā′dĭ-kər), **Karl.** 1801–59. German guidebook publisher.

Baeke·land (bāk′lănd′), **Leo Hendrik.** 1863–1944. Belgian-born Amer. chemist.

Baer (bâr). **1. Karl Ernst von.** 1792–1876. Estonian naturalist and pioneer embryologist. **2. George Frederick.** 1842–1914. Amer. lawyer and railroad magnate. **3. Arthur** ("**Bugs**"). 1886–1969. Amer. journalist.

Bae·yer (bā′ər, bĕ′yər), **(Johann Friedrich Wilhelm) Adolf von.** 1835–1917. German organic chemist (Nobel, 1905).

Ba·ez (bī′ĕz′, bī-ĕz′), **Joan.** b. 1941. Amer. folk singer.

Baf·fin (băf′ĭn), **William.** 1584–1622. English explorer.

Bage·hot (băj′ət), **Walter.** 1826–77. English economist, social scientist, and journalist.

Bag·ley (băg′lē), **William Chandler.** 1874–1946. Amer. psychologist and educator.

Bag·nold (băg′nəld), **Enid.** 1889–1981. English author.

Ba·gra·tion (bä-grä′tē-ôn′), Prince **Pëtr Ivanovich.** 1765–1812. Russian general.

Ba·ha·ul·lah (bä-hä′o͞o-lä′). 1817–92. Persian founder of Bahai sect.

Bai·ley (bā′lē). **1. Nathan** or **Nathaniel.** d. 1742. English lexicographer. **2. Ann.** "White Squaw of the Kanawha." 1742–1825. English-born Amer. frontier heroine. **3. Anna Warner.** "Mother Bailey." 1758–1851. Amer. Revolutionary heroine. **4. Gamaliel.** 1807–59. Amer. physician, journalist, and antislavery advocate. **5. Liberty Hyde.** 1858–1954. Amer. botanist, horticulturist, and educator. **6. Florence Augusta Merriam.** 1863–1948. Amer. ornithologist. **7. Pearl Mae.** b. 1918. Amer. entertainer. **8. F(rancis) Lee.** b. 1933. Amer. lawyer.

Bail·lie (bā′lē), **Joanna.** 1762–1851. Scottish dramatist.

Bain (bān), **Alexander.** 1818–1903. Scottish psychologist and author.

Bain·bridge (bān′brĭj′), **William.** 1774–1833. Amer. naval officer.

Baird (bârd). **1. Spencer Fullerton.** 1823–87. Amer. zoologist, naturalist, and ornithologist. **2. John Logie.** "Father of Television." 1888–1946. Scottish inventor.

Bairns·fa·ther (bârnz′fä′*th*ər), **Bruce.** 1888–1959. English cartoonist and journalist.

Ba·jer (bī′ər), **Fredrik.** 1837–1922. Danish pacifist (Nobel, 1908).

Ba·ker (bā′kər). **1. Sir Samuel White.** 1821–93. English explorer. **2. George Fisher.** 1840–1931. Amer. financier and philanthropist. **3. George Pierce.** 1866–1935. Amer. drama professor. **4. Ray Stannard.** 1870–1946. Amer. author and muckraking journalist. **5. Newton Diehl.** 1871–1937. Amer. politician and public official. **6. Sara Josephine.** 1873–1945. Amer. pediatrician and public-health pioneer. **7. George.** "Father Divine." 1877–1965. Amer. religious leader. **8. Josephine.** 1906–75. Amer.-born French entertainer. **9. George.** 1915–75. Amer. cartoonist ("Sad Sack").

Bakst (bäkst), **Léon Nikolaevich.** 1867–1924. Russian painter and scenic designer.

Ba·ku·nin (bä-ko͝o′nĭn, -nyĭn), **Mikhail Aleksandrovich.** 1814–76. Russian anarchist.

Ba·la·ki·rev (bä′lä-kē′rĕf, bä-lä′kĭ-ryĭf), **Mili Alekseevich.** 1837–1910. Russian composer.

Bal·an·chine (băl′ən-chēn′, băl′ən-chēn′), **George.** 1904–83. Russian-born Amer. choreographer.

Bal·bo (băl′bō). **1. Count Cesar.** 1789–1853. Italian statesman and author. **2. Italo.** 1896–1940. Italian aviator and politician.

Bal·bo·a (băl-bō′ə, bäl-bô′ä), **Vasco Núñez de.** 1475–1517. Spanish explorer; discovered the Pacific.

Bal·bue·na (bäl-bwā′nə, -bwĕ′nä), **Bernardo de.** 1562?–1627. Mexican poet.

Balch (bôlch), **Emily Greene.** 1867–1961. Amer. economist and sociologist (Nobel, 1946).

Bald·win (bôld′wĭn). **1.** Name of 5 kings of Jerusalem, esp. **I,** 1058–1118, ruled 1108–18. **2. Loammi** (1740–1807) and **Loammi** (1780–1838). Amer. engineers. **3. Henry.** 1780–1844. Amer. legislator and jurist. **4. Matthias William.** 1795–1866. Amer. locomotive manufacturer. **5. Maria Louise.** 1856–1922. Amer. educator. **6. James Mark.** 1861–1934. Amer. psychologist and editor. **7. Stanley.** 1st Earl Baldwin of Bewdley. 1867–1947. British prime minister (1923–24, 1924–29, 1935–37). **8. Faith.** 1893–1978. Amer. author. **9. James Arthur.** b. 1924. Amer. author.

Ba·len·ci·a·ga (bə-lĕn′sē-ä′gə, bä′lĕn-thyä′gä), **Cristobal.** 1895–1972. Spanish fashion designer.

Balfe (bălf), **Michael William.** 1808–70. Irish composer and singer.

Bal·four (băl′fo͝or′, -fôr′, -fōr′), **Arthur James.** 1st Earl of Balfour. 1848–1930. British prime minister (1902–5) and diplomat.

Bal·iol (băl′yəl, bā′lē-əl), **John de.** 1249–1315. Scottish king (1292–96).

Ball (bôl). **1. John.** "the Mad Priest." d. 1381. English priest and social agitator; executed. **2. Lucille.** b. 1911. Amer. comedienne.

Bal·lan·tyne (băl′ən-tīn′), **James.** 1792–1833. Scottish printer.

Bal·lou (bə-lo͞o′), **1. Hosea.** 1771–1852. Amer. clergyman and editor. **2. Adin.** 1803–90. Amer. religious leader and Utopian reformer.

Bal·main (băl-măɴ′), **Pierre.** 1914–82. French fashion designer.

Bal·ti·more (bôl′tə-môr′, -mōr′). **1.** Barons. See **Calvert. 2. David.** b. 1938. Amer. microbiologist (Nobel, 1975).

Bal·zac (bôl′zăk′, băl′-, bäl-zäk′), **Honoré de.** 1799–1850. French author. —**Bal·zac′i·an** *adj.*

Ban·croft (băn′krôft′). **1. George.** 1800–91. Amer. historian and diplomat. **2. Hubert Howe.** 1832–1918. Amer. publisher and historian.

Ban·de·lier (băn′də-lîr′), **Adolph Francis Alphonse.** 1840–1914. Swiss-born Amer. historian, explorer, archaeologist, and anthropologist.

Ban·del·lo (bän-dĕl′lō), **Matteo.** 1480–1562? Italian prelate and author.

Bangs (băngz), **John Kendrick.** 1862–1922. Amer. humorist and editor.

Bank·head (băngk′hĕd′). **1. William Brockman.** 1874–1940. Amer. legislator. **2. Tallulah Brockman.** 1903–68. Amer. actress.

Banks (băngks). **1. Sir Joseph.** 1743–1820. English botanist. **2. Nathaniel Prentiss.** 1816–94. Amer. politician and general.

Ban·ne·ker (băn′ĭ-kər), **Benjamin.** 1731–1806. Amer. mathematician and astronomer.

Ban·nis·ter (băn′ĭ-stər), **Roger.** b. 1929. English physician and runner (1st 4-minute mile).

Ban·ting (băn′tĭng), Sir **Frederick Grant.** 1891–1941. Canadian physiologist (Nobel, 1923); a discoverer of insulin.

Bar·a (băr′ə), **Theda.** 1890?–1955. Amer. actress.

Ba·rab·bas (bə-răb′əs). Condemned thief whose release was demanded instead of that of Jesus.

Ba·ra·ka (bə-rä′kə), **Imamu Amiri.** b. 1934. Amer. poet and playwright.

Ba·ra·nov (băr′ə-nŏf′, bä-rä′nəf), **Aleksandr Andreevich.** 1746–1819. Russian fur trader and colonial administrator.

Bá·rá·ny (bä′rän′yə), **Robert.** 1876–1936. Austrian otologist (Nobel, 1914).

Bar·ba·ros·sa (bär′bə-rŏs′ə, -rôs′-). **1.** Holy Roman Emperor Frederick I. **2. Khair el-Din** (1466?–1546) and **Koruk** (1474–1518). Greek-born Moslem corsairs.

Bar·ber (bär′bər), **Samuel.** 1910–81. Amer. composer.

Bar·bour (bär′bər), **Philip Pendleton.** 1783–1841. Amer. legislator and jurist.

Bar·busse (bär-büs′), **Henri.** 1873–1935. French author and editor.

Bar·clay (bär′klē), **Robert.** 1648–90. Scottish Quaker author.

Bar·clay de Tol·ly (bär-klī′ dĭ tôl′yə), Prince **Mikhail.** 1761–1818. Scottish-born Russian field marshal.

Bard (bärd). **1. John.** 1716–99. Amer. physician; pioneer in dissection. **2. Samuel.** 1742–1821. Amer. physician and educator. **3. William.** 1778–1853. Amer. life-insurance company organizer.

Bar·deen (bär-dēn′), **John.** b. 1908. Amer. physicist (Nobel, 1956, 1972).

Bar·dot (bär-dō′), **Brigitte.** b. 1935? French actress.

Bar·en·boim (băr′ĭn-boim′), **Daniel.** b. 1942. Israeli concert pianist.

Bar·ents (băr′ənts), **Willem.** 1550?–97. Dutch Arctic explorer.

Bar·ing (bâr′ĭng). **1. Alexander.** 1st Baron Ashburton. 1774–1848. English financier and statesman. **2. Evelyn.** 1st Earl of Cromer. 1841–1917. English financier and diplomat.

Bark·la (bärk′lə), **Charles Glover.** 1877–1944. English physicist (Nobel, 1917).

Bar·kley (bär′klē), **Alben William.** 1877–1956. U.S. Vice President (1949–53).

Bar·low (bär′lō′), **Joel.** 1754–1812. Amer. poet and diplomat.

Bar·na·bas (bär′nə-bəs), **Joses** or **Joseph.** 1st cent. Christian convert and missionary.

Bar·nard (bär′nərd). **1. Frederick Augustus Porter.** 1809–89. Amer. college president and advocate of equal education for women. **2. Henry.** 1811–1900. Amer. advocate of free public education. **3. Edward Emerson.** 1857–1923. Amer. astronomer; pioneer in photography. **4. George Grey.** 1863–1938. Amer. sculptor and art collector. **5. Kate.** 1875–1930. Amer. political reformer. **6.** (*also* bär-närd′), **Christian Neethling.** b. 1923. South African surgeon (1st successful human heart transplant).

Barnes (bärnz). **1. Albert Coombs.** 1873–1951. Amer. physician and art collector. **2. Harry Elmer.** 1889–1968. Amer. sociologist, educator, and author.

Bar·ne·veldt or **Bar·ne·veld** (bär′nə-vĕlt′), **Jan van Olden.** 1547–1619. Dutch statesman; beheaded.

Bar·num (bär′nəm), **Phineas Taylor** ("**P.T.**"). 1810–91. Amer. showman.

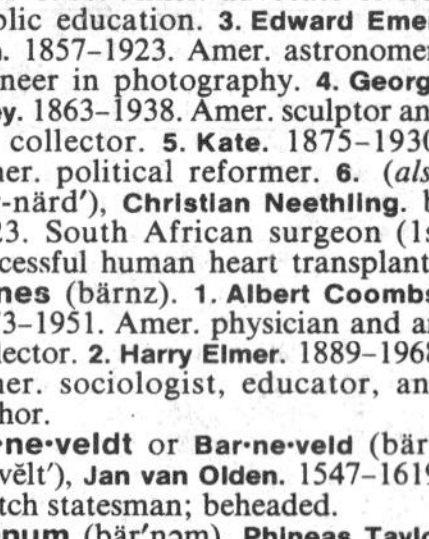

Phineas T. Barnum

Ba·ro·ja y Nes·si (bä-rô′hä ē nĕs′ē), **Pío.** 1872–1956. Spanish author

Bar·res (bä-rĕs′), **Auguste Maurice.** 1862–1923. French author and politician.

Bar·rett (băr′ĭt). **1. Kate Harwood Waller.** 1857–1925. Amer. social worker. **2. Janie Porter.** 1865–1948. Amer. welfare worker.

Bar·rie (băr′ē), Sir **James Matthew.** 1860–1937. Scottish author.

Bar·ron (băr′ən) **Clarence Walker.** 1855–1923? Amer. financial editor.

Bar·ros (bär′o͞osh′), **João de.** 1496–1570. Portuguese historian.

Bar·row (băr′ō), **Isaac.** 1630–77. English theologian, scholar, and mathematician.

Bar·ry (băr′ē). **1. John.** 1745–1803. Amer. naval commander.

Bar·ry·more (băr′ĭ-môr′, -mōr′). Family of Amer. actors, including **Maurice Herbert Blythe** (English-born, 1847–1905), **Georgiana Emma Drew** (1854–93), **Lionel Blythe** (1878–1954), **Ethel** (1879–1959), **John Blythe** (1882–1942), **Diana** (1921–60), and **John Drew** (b. 1932).

Bart (bär) or **Barth** (bärt), **Jean.** 1651?–1702. French naval hero.

Barth (bärth). **1.** (*also* bärt), **Karl.** 1886–1968. Swiss Protestant theologian. **2. John Simmons.** b. 1930. Amer. novelist.

Barthes (bärt), **Roland.** 1915–80. French critic.

Bar·thol·di (bär-thŏl′dē, -tôl-dē′), **Frédéric Auguste.** 1834–1904. French sculptor.

Bar·thol·o·mew (bär-thŏl'ə-myōō'), Saint. One of the 12 Apostles.

Bart·lett (bärt'lĭt). **1. John Russell.** 1805–86. Amer. historian and antiquarian. **2. John.** 1820–1905. Amer. publisher and editor. **3. Robert Abram ("Captain Bob").** 1875–1946. Amer. Arctic explorer.

Bar·tók (bär'tŏk', -tôk'), **Béla.** 1881–1945. Hungarian pianist and composer.

Bar·to·lom·me·o (bär-tŏl'ə-mā'ō, bär'tô-lôm-mĕ'ô), Fra. 1475?–1517. Italian painter.

Bar·ton (bar'tn). **1. Clara.** 1821–1912. Amer. nurse and founder of the Amer. Red Cross. **2. Bruce.** 1886–1967. Amer. advertising executive, author, and politician. **3.** Sir **Derek Harold Richard.** b. 1918. English chemist (Nobel, 1969).

Clara Barton

Bar·tram (bär'trəm), **John** (1699–1777) and **William** (1739–1823). Amer. botanists.

Ba·ruch (bə-rōōk'), **Bernard Mannes.** 1870–1965. Amer. stock broker, political adviser, and public official.

Ba·rysh·ni·kov (bə-rĭsh'nĭ-kôf'), **Mikhail Nikolayavich.** b. 1948. Latvian-born ballet dancer and choreographer.

Bar·zun (bär'zŭn), **Jacques Martin.** b. 1907. French-born Amer. educator, author, and historian.

Bas·com (băs'kəm), **Florence.** 1862–1945. Amer. geologist.

Ba·sho (bä'shō, bä-shō'), **Matsuo.** 1644–94. Japanese poet.

Ba·sie (bā'sē), **William ("Count").** b. 1904–84. Amer. jazz composer and band leader.

Bas·il (băz'əl, băs'-, bā'zəl, -səl), Saint. "the Great." 330?–379? Greek Christian leader.

Bas·ker·ville (băs'kər-vĭl'), **John.** 1706–75. English printer and type designer.

Bas·kin (băs'kĭn), **Leonard.** b. 1922. Amer. artist.

Ba·sov (bä'səf, -sôf'), **Nikolai Gennadievich.** b. 1922. Russian physicist (Nobel, 1964).

Bass (băs), **Sam.** 1851–78. Amer. desperado.

Bas·sa·no (bä-sä'nō), **Jacapo.** 1510–92. Venetian genre painter.

Bate·man (bāt'mən), **Hezekiah Linthicum.** 1812–75. Amer. actor and theatrical manager.

Bates (bāts). **1. Edward.** 1793–1869. Amer. politician and public official. **2. Katherine Lee.** 1859–1929. Amer. educator and poet. **3. Blanche.** 1873–1941. Amer. actress. **4. Herbert Ernest ("H.E.").** 1905–74. English author.

Bath·she·ba (băth-shē'bə, băth'shə-). In the Bible, 2nd wife of David and mother of Solomon.

Ba·tis·ta y Zal·di'var (bä-tēs'tä ē zäl-dē'vär'), **Fulgenico.** 1901–73. Cuban military and political leader; deposed and exiled (1959).

Bat·ta·ni (bä-tä'nē), **al-.** 850?–929. Arab astronomer.

Baude·laire (bōd-lâr', -lĕr'), **Charles Pierre.** 1821–67. French poet and critic.

Bau·douin (bō-dwăN'), b. 1930. Belgian king (since 1951).

Baugh (bô), **Samuel Adrian ("Slinging Sammy").** b. 1914. Amer. football player.

Baum. 1. (bôm, bäm), **Lyman Frank.** 1856–1919. Amer. author (*Oz* stories). **2.** (boum), **Vicki.** 1896–1960. Austrian-born Amer. author.

Bau·mé (bō-mā', bō'mā), **Antoine.** 1728–1804. French chemist.

Bax·ter (băk'stər), **Richard.** 1615–91. English nonconformist chaplin and scholar.

Bay·ard (bā'ərd) **1.** (*also* bī'ərd, bä-yär'), Chevalier de. Pierre Terrail. 1473–1524. French battle hero. **2. James Asheton** (1767–1815) and **Thomas Francis** (1828–98). Amer. politicians and diplomats.

Bayes (bāz), **Nora.** 1880–1928. Amer. vaudeville entertainer.

Bayle (bāl, bĕl), **Pierre.** 1647–1706. French philosopher and critic.

Bay·ley (bā'lē), **Richard.** 1745–1801. Amer. physician.

Bay·lor (bā'lər), **Robert Emmet Bledsoe.** 1793–1873. Amer. politician, lawyer, and clergyman.

Beach (bēch). **1. Moses Yale** (1800–68) and **Moses Sperry** (1822–92). Amer. publishers and inventors. **2. Alfred Ely.** 1826–96. Amer. inventor and editor. **3. Frederick Converse.** 1848–1918. Amer. publisher and photographer. **4. Amy Marcey Cheney.** 1867–1944. Amer. pianist and composer. **5. Sylvia Woodbridge.** 1887–1962. Amer. bookseller and publisher in Paris.

Bea·cons·field (bē'kənz-fēld'), 1st Earl of. Benjamin Disraeli.

Bea·dle (bēd'l). **1. Erastus Flavel.** 1821–94. Amer. publisher. **2. George Wells.** b. 1903. Amer. biologist (Nobel, 1958).

Bean (bēn), **Roy.** 1825?–1903. Amer. frontiersman.

Beard (bîrd). **1. Charles Austin.** 1874–1948. Amer. historian and educator. **2. Mary Ritter.** 1876–1958. Amer. historian and feminist. **3. Daniel Carter ("Dan").** 1850–1941. Amer. author, illustrator, and founder of the Amer. Boy Scouts.

Beards·ley (bîrdz'lē), **Aubrey Vincent.** 1872–98. English illustrator.

Beat·les (bēt'lz), **the.** Former group of English composers and musicians, including John Lennon, Ringo Starr, Paul McCartney, and George Harrison.

Bea·ton (bēt'n), **Cecil Walter Hardy.** 1904–80. English photographer, author and theatrical designer.

Be·a·trix (bā'ə-trĭks'), b. 1938. Queen of the Netherlands (since 1980).

Beat·tie (bā'tē, bē'-), **James.** 1735–1803. Scottish author and philosopher.

Beau·fort (bō'fərt) **1. Henry.** 1377?–1447. English prelate and statesman. **2. Margaret.** Countess of Richmond and Derby. 1441–1509. English Lancastrian and patron of education.

Beau·har·nais (bō-är-nā', -nĕ'). **1. Alexandre de.** 1760–94. French politician and military leader. **2. Joséphine de.** 1763–1814. 1st wife of Napoleon I; divorced (1809). **3. Eugène de.** 1781–1824. French soldier and statesman. **4. Hortense.** 1783–1837. Mother of Napoleon III.

Beau·mar·chais (bō-mär-shā', -shĕ'), **Pierre Augustin Caron de.** 1732–99. French author.

Beau·mont (bō'mŏnt'). **1.** (*also* -mənt), **Francis.** 1584–1616. English poet and dramatist. **2. William.** 1785–1853. Amer. pioneer surgeon.

Beau·re·gard (bō'rĭ-gärd'), **Pierre Gustave Toutant.** 1818–93. Amer. Confederate general.

Beau·voir (bō-vwär'), **Simone de.** 1908–86. French author.

Beaux (bō), **Cecelia.** 1863–1942. Amer. painter.

Bea·ver·brook (bē'vər-brōōk'), 1st Baron. William Maxwell Aitken. 1879–1964. Canadian-born British newspaper publisher and politician.

Be·bel (bā'bəl), **(Ferdinand) August.** 1840–1913. German socialist leader.

Beck·er (bĕk'ər). **1. George Ferdinand.** 1847–1919. Amer. geologist and physicist. **2. Carl Lotus.** 1873–1945. Amer. historian.

Beck·et (bĕk'ĭt), Saint **Thomas à.** 1118?–70. English Roman Catholic martyr.

Beck·ett (bĕk'ĭt), **Samuel.** b. 1906. Irish author (Nobel, 1969).

Beck·ford (bĕk'fərd), **William.** 1759?–1844. English author and collector.

Beck·man (bĕk'män), **Max.** 1884–1950. German artist.

Beck·nell (bĕk'nəl), **William.** 1790?–1832. Amer. frontier explorer.

Bec·que·rel (bĕk'ə-rĕl', bĕk-rĕl'). Family of French physicists, including **Antoine César** (1788–1878), **Alexandre Edmond** (1820–91), and **Antoine Henri** (1852–1908; Nobel, 1903).

Bed·does (bĕd'ōz), **Thomas Lovell.** 1803–49. English poet and physician.

Bede (bēd) also **Bae·da** or **Be·da** (bē'də). "Venerable Bede" c. 673–735. English theologian, historian, and scientist.

Bed·ford (bĕd'fərd), Duke of. John of Lancaster.

Bee·be (bē'bē). **1. (Charles) William.** 1877–1962. Amer. naturalist and explorer. **2. Lucius Morris.** 1902–66. Amer. journalist.

Bee·cham (bē'chəm), Sir **Thomas.** 1879–1961. English conductor.

Bee·cher (bē'chər). **1. Lyman.** 1775–1863. Amer. theologian. **2. Catharine Esther.** 1800–78. Amer. educator, reformer, and antisuffragist. **3. Edward.** 1803–95. Amer. clergyman and theologian. **4. Henry Ward.** 1813–87. Amer. clergyman, editor, and abolitionist.

Beer (bār), **Wilhelm.** 1797–1850. German banker and astronomer.

Beer·bohm (bîr'bōm'), Sir **Max.** 1872–1956. English caricaturist, critic, and author.

Beer·naert (bâr'närt, bĕr-närt'), **Auguste Marie François.** 1829–1912. Belgian statesman (Nobel, 1909).

Beers (bîrz), **Clifford Whittingham.** 1876–1943. Amer. mental-health pioneer.

Beer·y (bîr'ē), **Wallace.** 1886?–1949. Amer. actor.

Bee·tho·ven (bā'tō-vən, bāt'hō-fən), **Ludwig van.** 1770–1827. German composer.

Be·gin (bā'gĭn, bə-gēn'), **Menachem.** b. 1913. Russian-born Israeli statesman (Nobel, 1978).

Be·han (bē'ən), **Brendan Francis.** 1923–64. Irish author.

Beh·ring (bâr'ĭng, bĕr'-, bā'rĭng). **1. Vitus.** See **Bering. 2. Emil von.** 1854–1917. German physiologist (Nobel, 1901).

Behr·man (bâr'mən), **Samuel Nathaniel.** 1893–1973. Amer. playwright.

Bei·der·becke (bī'dər-bĕk'), **Leon Bismark ("Bix").** 1903–31. Amer. jazz composer and cornetist.

Beis·sel (bī'səl), **Johann Konrad.** 1690–1768. German religious leader and hymn writer.

Be·ke·sy (bā'kā-shē), **Georg von.** 1899–1972. Hungarian-born Amer. physiologist (Nobel, 1961).

Be·las·co (bə-lăs'kō), **David.** 1853?–1931. Amer. playwright and theatrical producer.

Bel·cher (bĕl'chər), **Jonathan.** 1682–1757. Amer. merchant and colonial governor.

Bel·i·sar·i·us (bĕl'ĭ-sâr'ē-əs). 505?–65. Byzantine general.

Bell (bĕl). **1. John.** 1797?–1869. Amer. politician. **2. Alexander Graham.** 1847–1922. Scottish-born Amer. inventor (telephone). **3. (Arthur) Clive (Howard).** 1881–1964. English critic.

Bel·la·my (bĕl'ə-mē), **Edward.** 1850–98. Amer. author and utopian socialist.

Bel·lay (bĕ-lā'), **Joachim du.** 1524–60. French poet.

Bel·lings·hau·sen (bĕl'ĭngz-hou'zən), **Fabian Gottlieb von.** 1778–1852. Russian naval officer and explorer.

Bel·li·ni (bə-lē'nē, bĕ-lē'-). **1.** Family of Venetian painters, including **Jacopo** (1400?–70?), **Gentile** (1429?–1507), and **Giovanni** (1430?–1516). **2. Vincenzo.** 1801–35. Italian operatic composer.

Bel·loc (bĕl'ŏk',-ək), **Hilaire.** 1870–1953. French-born English author.

Bel·low (bĕl'ō), **Saul.** b. 1915. Canadian-born Amer. novelist (Nobel, 1976).

Bel·lows (bĕl'ōz). **1. Albert Fitch.** 1829–83. Amer. painter. **2. George Wesley.** 1882–1925. Amer. artist.

Bel·mont (bĕl'mŏnt'). **1. August.** 1816–90. German-born Amer. banker, public official, and art collector. **2. Alva Ertskin Smith Vanderbilt.** 1853–1933. Amer. socialite and suffragist.

Bel·mon·te (bĕl-môn'tā, -tĕ), **Juan.** 1893–1962. Spanish bullfighter.

Bel·shaz·zar (bĕl-shăz'ər). In the Bible, the son of Nebuchadnezzar II and last king of Babylon.

Be·ly (bĕ'lē, byĕ'-), **Andrei.** Boris Nikolaevich Bugaev. 1880–1934. Russian author.

Bel·zo·ni (bĕl-tsō'nē), **Giovanni Battista.** 1778–1823. Italian explorer and Egyptologist.

Be·mel·mans (bĕ'məl-mənz, bĕm'əl-), **Ludwig.** 1898–1962. Austrian-born Amer. illustrator and author.

Be·mis (bē'mĭs), **Samuel Flagg.** 1891–1973. Amer. historian and educator.

Ben·a·cer·raf (bĕ-nä-sĕ-räf'), **Baruj.** b. 1920. Venezuelan-born Amer. pathologist (Nobel, 1980).

Be·na·ven·te y Mar·ti'nez (bĕ'nä-vĕn'tĕ ē mär-tē'nĕs), **Jacinto.** 1866–1954. Spanish playwright (Nobel, 1922).

Be·na·vi·des (bĕ'nä-vē'*th*ĕs), **Alonzo de.** b. 1580? Spanish missionary in New Mexico.

Ben Bel·la (bĕn'bĕl'ə), **Ahmed.** b. 1919. Algerian revolutionary statesman; deposed.

Bench·ley (bĕnch'lē), **Robert Charles.** 1889–1945. Amer. humorist, critic, and actor.

Ben·dix (bĕn'dĭks), **Vincent.** 1882?–1945. Amer. inventor and industrialist.

Ben·e·dict (bĕn'ĭ-dĭkt'). **1. of Nur·si·a** (nûr'shē-ə, -shə), Saint. 480?–543. Italian founder of Benedictine order. **2.** Name of 15 popes, esp.: **a. XIV.** 1675–1758. Reigned 1740–58. **b. XV.** 1854–1922. Reigned 1914–22. **3. Ruth Fulton.** 1887–1948. Amer. anthropologist. **—Ben'e·dic'tine** *adj. & n.*

Be·neš (bĕ'nĕsh), **Eduard.** 1884–1948. Czechoslovakian statesman.

Be·nét (bĭ-nā'), **William Rose** (1886–1950) and **Stephen Vincent** (1898–1943). Amer. authors.

Ben Gur·i·on (bĕn'gōōr'ē-ən, -gōōr-yôn'), **David.** 1886–1973. Polish-born Israeli statesman.

Ben·ja·min (bĕn'jə-mən). **1.** In the Bible, the youngest son of Rachel and Jacob. **2. Asher.** 1773–1845. Amer. architect. **3. Judah Philip.** 1811–84. British-born Amer. Confederate statesman.

Ben·nett (bĕn'ĭt). **1. James Gordon** (1795–1872) and **James Gordon** (1841–1918). Amer. journalists and publishers. **2. (Enoch) Arnold.** 1867–1931. English author. **3. Richard Bedford.** Viscount Bennett. 1870–1947. Canadian prime minister (1930–35). **4. Edward Herbert.** 1874–1954. English-born Amer. architect. **5. Floyd.** 1890–1928. Amer. aviator and Arctic explorer.

Ben·ny (bĕn'ē), **Jack.** 1894–1974. Amer. comedian.

Jack Benny

Be·noît de Sainte-Maure (bə-nwä' dĭ sănt-môr'), 12th cent. French trouvère.

Ben·son (bĕn'sən). **1. Edward White.** 1829–96. English prelate. **2. Arthur Christopher.** 1862–1925. English educator and author. **3. Stella.** 1892–1933. English author.

Bent (bĕnt). **Charles** (1799–1847) and

p pop / r roar / s sauce / sh ship, dish / t tight / th thin, path / *th* this, bathe / ŭ cut / ûr urge / v valve / w with / y yes / z zebra, size / zh vision / ə about, item, edible, gallop, circus / œ *Fr.* feu, *Ger.* schön / ü *Fr.* tu, *Ger.* über / KH *Ger.* ich, *Scot.* loch / N *Fr.* bon.

William (1809–69). American pioneers.
Ben·tham (bĕn'thəm, -təm), **Jeremy.** 1748–1832. English reformer, author, and philosopher. **—Ben'tham·ite'** *n.*
Ben·tinck (bĕn'tĭngk). **1. William Henry Cavendish.** 1738–1809. British prime minister (1783, 1807–9). **2.** Lord **William Cavendish.** 3rd Duke of Portland. 1774–1839. English general and colonial administrator.
Bent·ley (bĕnt'lē), **Richard.** 1662–1742. English cleric, scholar, and critic.
Ben·ton (bĕn'tən). **1. Thomas Hart.** "Old Bullion." 1782–1858. Amer. legislator. **2. Thomas Hart.** 1889–1975. Amer. artist and writer. **3. William.** 1900–73. Amer. advertising executive, publisher, and public official.
Benz (bĕnts), **Karl Friedrich.** 1844–1929. German automobile pioneer.
Bé·ran·ger (bā-räN-zhā'), **Pierre Jean de.** 1780–1857. French poet.
Ber·dya·ev (bĕr-dyä'yəf), **Nikolai Aleksandrovich.** 1874–1948. Russian philosopher.
Ber·en·gar·i·a (bĕr'ən-gâr'ē-ə), d. 1230? Castilian-born English queen as wife of Richard I.
Ber·en·son (bĕr'ĭn-sən), **Bernard** also **Bernhard.** 1865–1959. Lithuanian-born Amer. art critic and historian.
Berg (bûrg). **1.** (bĕrg, bĕrk), **Alban.** 1885–1935. Austrian composer. **2. Gertrude.** 1899–1966. Amer. actress and radio, television, and screen writer. **3. Patricia Jane.** b. 1918. Amer. golfer. **4. Paul.** b. 1926. Amer. chemist (Nobel, 1980).
Ber·gen (bûr'gən), **Edgar John.** 1903–78. Amer. ventriloquist and comedian.
Ber·ger. 1. (bûr'gər), **Victor Louis.** 1860–1929. Transylvanian-born Amer. politician and editor. **2.** (bĕr'-), **Hans.** 1873–1941. German psychiatrist.
Bergh (bûrg), **Henry.** 1811–88. Amer. founder of the Amer. Society for the Prevention of Cruelty to Animals.
Ber·gi·us (bĕr'gē-o͝os'), **Friedrich.** 1884–1949. German chemist (Nobel, 1931).
Berg·man (bûrg'mən). **1. Ingrid.** 1915–82. Swedish actress. **2. Ingmar.** b. 1918. Swedish film director.
Berg·son (bûrg'sən, bĕrg'-, bĕrg-sôN'), **Henri Louis.** 1859–1941. French philosopher and author (Nobel, 1927).
Ber·i·a (bĕr'ē-ə), **Lavrenti Pavlovich.** 1899–1953. Soviet secret police chief.
Ber·ing also **Beh·ring** (bâr'ĭng, bĕr'-, bā'rĭng), **Vitus.** 1680–1741. Danish navigator and explorer.
Berke·ley (bûrk'lē). **1.** (*also* bärk'-), Sir **William.** 1606–77. English colonial administrator. **2.** (*also* bärk'-), **George.** 1685–1753. English-born Irish prelate and philosopher. **3. Busby.** 1895–1976. Amer. choreographer and film director.
Berle (bûrl), **Milton.** b. 1908. Amer. entertainer.
Ber·le (bûr'lē), **Adolf Augustus, Jr.** 1895–1971. Amer. educator and diplomat.
Ber·lich·ing·en (bĕr'lĭKH-ĭng'ən), **Götz** or **Gottfried von.** 1480?–1562. German peasant revolutionary leader.
Ber·lin (bər-lĭn'), **Irving.** b. 1888. Russian-born Amer. songwriter.
Ber·lin·er (bûr'l-nər), **Emile.** 1851–1929. German-born Amer. inventor (gramophone).
Ber·li·oz (bĕr'lē-ōz', -ŏs', bĕr-lyōz'), **(Louis) Hector.** 1803–69. French composer.
Ber·na·dette of Lourdes (bûr'-nə-dĕt'; lo͝ord), Saint. 1844–79. French peasant girl whose visions led to the establishment of the shrine at Lourdes, France.
Ber·na·dotte (bûr'nə-dŏt', bĕr-nä-dôt'). **1.** Dynasty of Swedish kings (since 1818). **2.** Count **Folke.** 1895–1948. Swedish statesman, diplomat, and Red Cross official; assassinated.
Ber·na·nos (bĕr-nä-nôs'), **Georges.** 1888–1948. French author.
Ber·nard. 1. of Clair·vaux (bər-närd'; klâr-vō'), Saint. 1090–1153. French monastic reformer and political figure. **2.** (bĕr-när'), **Claude.** 1813–78. French physiologist.
Ber·nar·din de Saint-Pierre (bĕr-när-dăN' də săN-pyĕr'), **Jacques Henri.** 1737–1814. French author.
Bern·hardt (bûrn'härt', bĕrn'-, bĕr-när'), **Sarah.** "the Divine Sarah." 1844–1923. French actress.

Sarah Bernhardt

Ber·ni·ni (bər-nē'nē, bĕr-), **Giovanni Lorenzo.** 1598–1680. Italian sculptor, painter, and architect.
Ber·noul·li (bər-no͞o'lē, bĕr-). Family of Swiss mathematicians and scientists, including **Jakob** or **Jacques** (1654–1705), **Johann** or **Jean** (1667–1748), and **Daniel** (1700–82).
Bern·stein (bûrn'stīn', -stēn'), **Leonard.** b. 1918. Amer. conductor and composer.

Leonard Bernstein

Bern·storff (bĕrn'shtôrf), Count **Johann Heinrich von.** 1862–1939. German diplomat.
Ber·ra (bĕr'ə), **Lawrence Peter ("Yogi").** b. 1925. Amer. baseball player.
Ber·ry (bĕr'ē). **1. Martha McChesney.** 1866–1942. Amer. educator. **2. Charles Edward Anderson ("Chuck").** b. 1926. Amer. musician and singer.
Ber·ry·man (bĕr'ē-mən), **John.** 1914–72. Amer. poet.
Ber·the·lot (bĕr-tə-lō'), **Pierre Eugène Marcelin.** 1827–1907. French chemist and public official.
Ber·thier (bĕr-tyā'), **Louis Alexandre.** Duc de Valangin, Prince de Neuchâtel and de Wagram. 1753–1815. French marshal.
Ber·til·lon (bûr'tə-lŏn, bĕr-tē-yôN'), **Alphonse.** 1853–1914. French anthropologist and criminologist.
Ber·ze·li·us (bər-zē'le-əs, -zā'-, bĕr-sā'lē-o͝os'), Baron **Jöns Jakob.** 1779–1848. Swedish chemist.
Bes·ant (bĕs'ənt, bĕz'-), **Annie Wood.** 1847–1933. English theosophist, philosopher, and political figure in India.
Bes·sel (bĕs'əl), **Friedrich Wilhelm.** 1784–1846. Prussian astronomer.
Bes·se·mer (bĕs'ə-mər), Sir **Henry.** 1813–98. British inventor and metallurgist.
Best (bĕst), **Charles Herbert.** 1899–1978. Amer.-born Canadian physiologist; a discoverer of insulin.
Be·tan·court (bĕ-tän-ko͝or'), **Romulo.** 1908–81. Venezuelan statesman.
Be·the (bā'tə), **Hans Albrecht.** b. 1906. German-born Amer. physicist (Nobel, 1967).
Beth·mann-Holl·weg (bāt'män-hôl'väk'), **Theobald von.** 1856–1921. German statesman.
Be·thune (bə-tho͞on', -thyo͞on'). **1. Louise Blanchard.** 1856–1913. Amer. architect. **2. Mary McLeod.** 1875–1955. Amer. educator.

Mary McLeod Bethune

Bet·je·man (bĕch'ə-mən), Sir **John.** 1906–84. English poet.
Bet·ter·ton (bĕt'ər-tən), **Thomas.** 1635?–1710. English actor.
Bev·an (bĕv'ən), **Aneurin.** 1897–1960. English politician.
Bev·er·idge (bĕv'ər-ĭj, bĕv'rĭj). **1. Albert Jeremiah.** 1862–1927. Amer. politician and historian. **2.** Sir **William Henry.** 1st Baron Tuggal. 1879–1963. British economist.
Bev·er·ley (bĕv'ər-lē), **Robert.** 1673?–1722. Amer. colonial official and historian.
Bev·i·er (bĕv'ē-ā'), **Isabel.** 1860–1942. Amer. home-economics educator.
Bev·in (bĕv'ĭn), **Ernest.** 1884–1951. English labor leader and politician.
Bhu·mi·bol A·dul·ya·dej (po͞o-mē-pôn' ä-do͞ol-yä'dĕ). b. 1927. Thai king (since 1946).
Bhut·to (bo͞o'tō), **Zulfikar Ali.** 1928–79. Pakistani statesman; executed.
Bi·chat (bē-shä'), **Marie François Xavier.** 1771–1802. French pioneer anatomist and histologist.
Bick·er·dyke (bĭk'ər-dīk'), **Mary Ann Ball.** 1817–1901. Amer. Civil War nurse.
Bid·dle (bĭd'l). **1. John.** 1615–62. English Unitarian theologian. **2. James.** 1783–1848. Amer. naval officer and diplomat. **3. Nicholas.** 1786–1844. Amer. financier and scholar. **4. George.** 1885–1973. Amer. artist. **5. Francis.** 1886–1968. French-born Amer. jurist and public official.
Bid·well (bĭd'wĕl), **John.** 1819–1900. Amer. California pioneer and politician.
Bien·ville (byĕn'vĭl', byăN-vēl'), Sieur **Jean Baptiste Lemoyne de.** 1680–1768. French colonial administrator.
Bierce (bîrs), **Ambrose Gwinett.** 1842–1914? Amer. author.
Bier·stadt (bîr'stăt', -shtät'), **Albert.** 1830–1902. German-born Amer. painter.
Big·e·low (bĭg'ə-lō). **1. Jacob.** 1787–1879. Amer. botanist and physician. **2. Erastus Brigham.** 1814–79. Amer. inventor and manufacturer. **3. John.** 1817–1911. Amer. author and diplomat. **4. Poultney.** 1855–1954. Amer. author.
Bi·kel (bĭ-kĕl'), **Theodore.** b. 1924. Austrian-born actor and folk singer.
Bil·bo (bĭl'bō), **Theodore Gilmore.** 1877–1947. Amer. politician.
Bil·lings (bĭl'ĭngz). **1. William.** 1746–1800. Amer. composer. **2. Josh.** Henry Wheeler Shaw. **3. Frederick.** 1823–90. Amer. businessman and philanthropist. **4. John Shaw.** 1838–1913. Amer. physician and librarian.
Bil·ly the Kid (bĭl'ē; kĭd). William H. Bonney.
Bing (bĭng), Sir **Rudolf.** b. 1902. Austrian-born opera manager.
Bing·ham (bĭng'əm). **1. Anne Willing.** 1764–1801. Amer. socialite. **2. George Caleb.** 1811–79. Amer. genre painter.
Bin·ney (bĭn'ē), **Horace.** 1780–1875. Amer. lawyer.
Birds·eye (bûrd'zī'), **Clarence.** 1886–1956. Amer. inventor (quick freezing).
Birk·beck (bûrk'bĕk'), **George.** 1776–1841. English physician and reformer.
Bir·ken·head (bûr'kən-hĕd'), 1st Earl of. Frederick Edwin Smith. 1872–1930. English statesman.
Birk·hoff (bûr'kôf), **George David.** 1884–1944. Amer. mathematician.
Bir·ney (bûr'nē), **James Gillespie.** 1792–1857. Amer. politician and abolitionist.
Bi·ron (bē'rôn'), **Ernst Johann.** 1690–1772. Russian statesman and regent.
Bish·op (bĭsh'əp). **1. Hazel Gladys.** b. 1906. Amer. chemist and businesswoman. **2. Elizabeth.** 1911–79. Amer. poet.
Bis·marck (bĭz'märk', bĭs'-), Prince **Otto Eduard Leopold von.** "the Iron Chancellor." 1815–98. Creator and 1st chancellor of the German Empire (1871–90). **—Bis·marck'i·an** *adj.*
Bis·sell (bĭs'əl) **George Henry.** 1821–84. Amer. pioneer oilman.
Bit·ter (bĭt'ər), **Karl Theodore Francis.** 1867–1915. Austrian-born Amer. sculptor.
Bi·zet (bē-zā'), **(Alexandre César Léopold) Georges.** 1838–75. French composer.
Björn·son (byûrn'sŏn, byœrn'-), **Björnstjerne.** 1832–1910. Norwegian author (Nobel, 1903).
Black (blăk). **1. Joseph.** 1728–99. Scottish chemist. **2. Jeremiah Sullivan.** 1810–83. Amer. jurist and public official. **3. Greene Vardiman.** 1836–1915. Amer. pioneer dentist. **4. Hugo La Fayette.** 1886–1971. Amer. jurist. **5. Shirley Temple.** b.1927? Amer. actress and public official.
Black·beard (blăk'bîrd'). Edward Teach.
Black·ett (blăk'ĕt, -ĭt), **Patrick Maynard Stuart.** Baron Blackett. 1897–1974. English physicist (Nobel, 1948).
Black Hawk (blăk'hôk'). 1767–1838. Amer. Indian leader.

Black Hawk

Black·more (blăk'môr', -mōr'), **Richard Doddridge.** 1825–1900. English author.
Black·mun (blăk'mən), **Harry Andrew.** b. 1908. Amer. jurist.
Black·stone (blăk'stōn', -stən), Sir **William.** 1723–80. English jurist, educator, and author.
Black·well (blăck'wĕl', -wəl). **1. Elizabeth** (1821–1910) and **Emily** (1826–1910). English-born Amer. physicians and pioneer hospital administrators. **2. Antoinette Louisa Brown.** 1825–1921. Amer. social reformer. **3. Alice Stone.** 1857–1950. Amer. suffragist and reformer.

Alice Stone Blackwell

ă pat / ā pay / âr care / ä father / b bib / ch church / d deed / ĕ pet / ē be / f fife / g gag / h hat / hw which / ĭ pit / ī pie / îr pier / j judge / k kick / l lid, needle / m mum / n no, sudden / ng thing / ŏ pot / ō toe / ô paw, for / oi noise / ou out / o͝o took / o͞o boot /

Black·wood (blăk'wo͝od'), **William.** 1776–1834. Scottish publisher and editor.

Blaine (blān), **James Gillespie.** 1830–93. Amer. politician.

Blair (blâr). **1. James.** 1655–1743. Scottish-born Amer. clergyman, educator, and colonial official. **2. John.** 1732–1800. Amer. jurist. **3. Francis Preston** (1791–1876) and **Francis Preston** (1821–75). Amer. politicians. **4. Montgomery.** 1813–83. Amer. lawyer and public official.

Blake (blāk). **1. Robert.** 1599–1657. English admiral. **2. William.** 1757–1827. English mystic, poet, and artist. **3. Lillie Devereux.** 1833–1913. Amer. author and suffragist.

Blake·lock (blāk'lŏk'), **Ralph Albert.** 1847–1919. Amer. landscape painter.

Blanc. **1.** (bläN), **Louis.** 1811–82. French socialist. **2.** (blăngk), **Melvin Jerome ("Mel").** b. 1908. Amer. actor and voice specialist.

Blan·chard (blăn'chərd), **Thomas.** 1788–1864. Amer. inventor.

Bland (blănd), **James A.** 1854–1911. Amer. composer.

Blan·ding (blăn'dĭng), **Sarah Gibson.** 1898–1985. Amer. educator and college administrator.

Blas·co I·bá·ñez (bläs'kō ē-bä'nyĕs), **Vincente.** 1867–1928. Spanish author.

Blass (blăs), **Bill.** b. 1922. Amer. fashion designer.

Blatch (blăch), **Harriot Eaton Stanton.** 1856–1940. Amer. suffragist.

Blatch·ford (blăch'fərd), **Samuel.** 1820–93. Amer. jurist.

Bla·vat·sky (blə-văt'skē, -vät'-), Madame **Helena** or **Elena Petrovna Hahn.** 1831–91. Russian-born theosophist.

Blé·riot (blē-ryō'), **Louis.** 1872–1936. French inventor and aviator.

Bligh (blī), **William.** 1754–1817. English naval officer (H.M.S. *Bounty*).

Bliss (blĭs), **Tasker Howard.** 1853–1930. Amer. army officer and diplomat.

Blitz·stein (blĭts'stīn'), **Marc.** 1905–64. Amer. composer.

Blix·en (blĭk'sən, blĕk'-), **Karen.** Isak Dinesen.

Bloch (blŏk) **1.** (*also* blôk, blôKH), **Ernest.** 1880–1959. Swiss-born Amer. composer. **2. Felix.** b. 1905. Swiss-born Amer. physicist (Nobel, 1952). **3.** (*also* blôKH), **Konrad.** b. 1912. German-born Amer. biochemist (Nobel, 1964).

Block (blŏk), **Herbert Lawrence.** "Herblock." b. 1909. Amer. editorial cartoonist.

Bloem·ber·gen (blo͞om'bûr-gən), **Nicolaas.** b. 1920. Dutch-born Amer. physicist (Nobel, 1981).

Blok (blôk), **Aleksandr Aleksandrovich.** 1880–1921. Russian symbolist poet.

Bloom·er (blo͞o'mər), **Amelia Jenks.** 1818–94. Amer. social reformer.

Bloom·field (blo͞om'fēld'), **Leonard.** 1887–1949. Amer. linguist.

Bloor (blo͝or), **Ella Reeve.** 1862–1951. Amer. labor organizer and political radical.

Blount (blŭnt), **William.** 1749–1800. Amer. politician.

Blow (blō), **Susan Elizabeth.** 1843–1916. Amer. pioneer in children's education.

Blü·cher (blo͞o'kər, -chər, blü'KHər), **Gebhard Leberecht von.** Prince of Wahlstatt. 1742–1819. Prussian field marshal.

Blum (blo͞om), **Léon.** 1872–1950. French author and socialist leader.

Blum·berg (blŭm'bərg, blo͞om'-), **Baruch Samuel.** b. 1925. Amer. virologist (Nobel, 1976).

Blu·men·bach (blo͞o'mən-bäKH'), **Johann Friedrich.** 1752–1840. German pioneer zoologist and anthropologist.

Blun·den (blŭn'dən), **Edmund Charles.** 1896–1974. English poet.

Bluntsch·li (blo͝onch'lē), **Johann Kaspar.** 1808–81. Swiss legal scholar and politician.

Bly (blī), **Nellie.** Elizabeth Cochrane Seaman.

Bo·ab·dil (bō'əb-dēl, bô'-, bō'əb-dēl'). d. 1533? Last Moorish king of Granada (1482–83, 1486–92).

Bo·ad·i·ce·a (bō'ăd-ĭ-sē'ə) also **Bou·dic·ca** (bo͞o-dĭk'ə). d. 62 A.D. Queen of ancient Britain.

Bo·as (bō'ăz), **Franz.** 1858–1942. German-born Amer. anthropologist.

Bo·az (bō'ăz). In the Old Testament, the husband of Ruth.

Bo·ba·di·lla (bō-bä-dē'lyä, -yä), **Francisco de.** d. 1502. Spanish colonial administrator.

Boc·cac·cio (bō-kä'chē-ō', -chō', bə-, bŏk-kät'chō), **Giovanni.** 1313–75. Italian poet.

Bod·en·heim (bŏd'n-hīm'), **Maxwell.** 1893?–1954. Amer. author.

Bod·ley (bŏd'lē). Sir Thomas. 1545–1613. English diplomat and library founder.

Bo·do·ni (bō-dō'nē), **Gianbattista.** 1740–1813. Italian printer and type designer.

Bo·e·thi·us (bō-ē'thē-əs), **Anicius Manlius Severinus.** 480?–524? Roman Christian philosopher.

Bo·gan (bō'gən), **Louise.** 1897–1970. Amer. poet.

Bo·gart (bō'gärt), **Humphrey DeForest.** 1899–1957. Amer. actor.

Boh·len (bō'lĭn), **Charles Eustis.** 1904–74. Amer. diplomat.

Böh·me also **Boeh·me** (bœ'mə) or **Boehm** (bœm), **Jakob.** 1575–1624. German theosophist and mystic.

Bohr (bôr, bōr). **1. Niels Henrik David.** 1885–1962. Danish physicist (Nobel, 1922). **2. Aage Niels.** b. 1922. Danish physicist (Nobel, 1975).

Bo·iar·do (boi-är'dō, bô-yär'dō), **Matteo Maria.** 1434?–94. Italian lyric poet.

Boi·leau-Des·pré·aux (bwä-lō'dā-prā-ō'), **Nicolas.** 1636–1711. French critic and poet.

Bo·i·to (bō'ē-tō'), **Arrigo.** 1842–1918. Italian composer and librettist.

Bok (bŏk), **Edward William.** 1863–1930. Dutch-born Amer. journalist, editor, and pacifist.

Bol·eyn (bo͝ol'ĭn, bo͝o-lĭn', bō-), **Anne.** 1507–36. English queen as 2nd wife of Henry VIII; beheaded.

Bol·ger (bōl'jər), **Ray.** 1904–1981. Amer. dancer and actor.

Bol·ing·broke (bŏl'ĭng-bro͝ok', bo͝ol', bō'lĭng-), 1st Viscount. Henry St. John. 1678–1751. English statesman and orator.

Bo·lí·var (bō'lə-vär', bŏl'ə-, bô-lē'vär), **Simón.** "the Liberator". 1783–1830. Venezuelan soldier and South American liberator.

Böll (bœl), **Heinrich.** 1917–85. German author (Nobel, 1972).

Boltz·mann (bōlts'män), **Ludwig.** 1844–1906. Austrian physicist.

Bom·beck (bŏm'bĕk), **Erma.** b. 1927. Amer. humorist.

Bo·na·parte (bō'nə-pärt', bō-nä-pärt'). Corsican family, including: **1. Joseph.** 1768–1844. King of Naples (1806–8) and Spain (1808–13). **2.** Napoleon I. **3. Lucien.** Prince of Canino. 1775–1840. Politician and diplomat. **4. Louis.** 1778–1846. King of Holland (1806–10); abdicated. **5. Jérôme.** 1784–1860. King of Westphalia (1807).

Bon·a·ven·ture (bŏn'ə-vĕn'chər) also **Bon·a·ven·tu·ra** (bŏn'ə-vĕn-cho͝or'ə, bô'nä-vĕn-to͞o'rä), Saint. 1221–74. Italian theologian and philosopher.

Bond (bŏnd). **1. Thomas.** 1712–84. Amer. physician and hospital founder. **2. William Cranch** (1789–1859) and **George Phillips** (1825–65). Amer. astronomers. **3. Carrie Jacobs.** 1862–1946. Amer. songwriter and author. **4. Julian.** b. 1940. Amer. politician and civil-rights leader.

Bone (bōn), Sir **Muirhead.** 1876–1953. Scottish artist.

Bon·fils (bŏn-tēs'), **Frederick Gilmer.** 1860–1933. Amer. publisher.

Bon·heur (bō-nûr', bô-nœr'), **Rosa.** 1822–99. French painter.

Bon·i·face (bŏn'ə-fəs, -făs'). **1.** Saint. 680?–755? English missionary. **2.** Name of 9 popes, esp.: **a. I,** Saint. d. 422. Reigned 418–22. **b. VIII.** 1235?–1303. Reigned 1294–1303. **c. IX.** d. 1404. Reigned 1389–1404.

Bon·nard (bô-när'), **Pierre.** 1867–1947. French painter.

Bon·ner (bŏn'ər). **1. Edmund.** 1500?–69. English prelate. **2. Robert.** 1824–99. Irish-born Amer. publisher.

Bon·net (bô-nĕ'), **Georges.** 1889–1973. French politician and diplomat.

Bon·ne·ville (bŏn'ə-vĭl'), **Benjamin Louis Eulalie de.** 1796–1878. French-born Amer. soldier and explorer.

Bon·ney (bŏn'ē). **1. Mary Lucinda.** 1816–1900. Amer. educator and reformer. **2. William H.** "Billy the Kid." 1859–81. Amer. outlaw. **3. Thérèse.** 1894?–1978. Amer. photographer.

Bo·non·ci·ni (bō'nôn-chē'nē) also **Buo·non·ci·ni** (bwō). Family of Italian composers, including **Giovanni Maria** (1640–78), **Giovanni Battista** (1670?–1750), and **Marcantonio** (1675?–1726).

Bon·stelle (bŏn'stĕl), **Jessie.** 1871–1932. Amer. actress and producer.

Bon·temps (bôN-täN'), **Arna Wendell.** 1902–73. Amer. author.

Boole (bo͞ol), **George.** 1815–64. English mathematician and logician.

Boone (bo͞on), **Daniel.** 1734–1820. Amer. frontiersman.

Booth (bo͞oth). **1.** Family of English and Amer. actors, including **Junius Brutus** (1796–1852); **Edwin Thomas** (1833–93); and **John Wilkes** (1838–65), assassinated Abraham Lincoln, died of gunshot wound. **2.** Family of English and Amer. reformers, including **William** ("General Booth," 1829–1912), founder of the Salvation Army; **William Bramwell** (1856–1929); **Ballington** (1859–1940), founder of Volunteers of America; **Maud Ballington** (1865–1948); and **Evangeline Cory** (1865–1950). **3. Mary Louise.** 1831–89. Amer. historian and editor.

John Wilkes Booth

Bo·rah (bôr'ə, bōr'ə), **William Edgar.** 1865–1940. Amer. legislator.

Bor·den (bôr'dn). **1. Gail.** 1801–74. Amer. surveyor and inventor (condensed milk). **2. Lizzie Andrew.** 1860–1927. Amer. accused murderess; acquitted. **3.** Sir **Robert.** 1854–1937. Canadian prime minister (1911–20).

Bor·det (bôr-dā', -dĕ'), **Jules Jean Baptiste Vincent.** 1870–1961. Belgian bacteriologist (Nobel, 1919).

Bo·rel·li (bō-rĕl'ē), **Giovanni Alfonso.** 1608–79. Italian mathematician, astronomer, and physiologist.

Borg (bôrg), **Bjorn.** b. 1956. Swedish tennis player.

Bor·ge (bôr'gə), **Victor.** b. 1909. Danish pianist and comedian.

Bor·ges (bôr'hĕs), **Jorge Luis.** 1899–1986. Argentinian author.

Bor·gia (bôr'jə, -jä, -zhə). Influential Italian family, including: **1. Alfonso.** Pope Calixtus III. **2. Cesare.** 1475?–1507. Cardinal, diplomat, and soldier. **3. Lucrezia.** Duchess of Ferrara. 1480–1519. Patron of learning and the arts. **4. Rodrigo.** Pope Alexander VI.

Bor·glum (bôr'gləm), **Gutzon.** 1867–1941. Amer. sculptor.

Bo·ri (bôr'ē, bō'rē), **Lucrezia.** 1887–1960. Spanish-born Amer. lyric soprano.

Bor·ing (bôr'ĭng, bō'rĭng), **Edwin Garrigues.** 1886–1968. Amer. psychologist.

Bor·laug (bôr'lôg), **Norman Ernest.** b. 1914. Amer. agronomist (Nobel, 1970).

Bor·mann (bôr'män'), **Martin Ludwig.** b. 1900. German politician; reported dead in 1945.

Born (bôrn), **Max.** 1882–1970. German-born physicist (Nobel, 1954).

Bo·ro·din (bôr'ə-dēn', bär'-, bôr'ə-dēn'), **Aleksandr Porfirevich.** 1834–87. Russian composer and chemist.

Bor·ro·mi·ni (bôr'rō-mē'nē), **Francesco.** 1599–1667. Italian artist.

Bor·row (bŏr'ō), **George.** 1803–81. English philologist, traveler, and author.

Bosch. **1.** (bôs, bŏs, bŏsh, bôsh), **Hieronymous.** 1450?–1516. Dutch painter. **2.** (bôsh), **Carl.** 1874–1940. German chemist (Nobel, 1931).

Bos·suet (bô-swĕ'), **Jacques Bénigne.** 1627–1704. French prelate and historian.

Bos·well (bŏz'wĕl, -wəl), **James.** 1740–95. Scottish diarist and biographer.

Bo·tha (bō'tə, -tä'). **1. Louis.** 1862–1919. South African general and statesman. **2. Pieter Willem.** b. 1916. South African statesman.

Bo·the (bō'tə), **Walther Wilhelm.** 1891–1957. German physicist (Nobel, 1954).

Both·well (bŏth'wĕl', -wəl, bŏ*th*-), 4th Earl of. James Hepburn. 1536?–78. Scottish Protestant nobleman and husband of Mary Queen of Scots.

Bot·ti·cel·li (bŏt'ĭ-chĕl'ē, bōt'tē-chĕl'lē), **Sandro.** 1444?–1510. Italian painter.

Bou·cher (bo͞o-shā'), **François.** 1703–70. French artist.

Bou·ci·cault (bo͞o'sē-kō', -kôlt'), **Dion.** 1820?–90. Irish-born Amer. actor and playwright.

Bou·dic·ca (bo͞o-dĭk'ə). Boadicea.

Bou·gain·ville (bo͞o'gən-vĭl', bo͞o-gäN-vēl'), **Louis Antoine de.** 1729–1811. French explorer.

Bou·lan·ger (bo͞o'-läN-zhā'). **1. Georges Ernest Jean Marie.** 1837–91. French military and political leader. **2. Nadia Juliette.** 1885?–1979. French music teacher.

Bou·lez (bo͞o-lĕz'), **Pierre.** b. 1925. French conductor and composer.

Bour·bon (bo͝or'bən, bo͞or-bôN'). **1.** French royal family ruling in France (1589–1793), Spain (1700–1868, 1874–1931), and Naples and the Two Sicilies (1735–1861). **2.** Duc **Charles de.** 1490–1527. French general.

Bour·geois (bo͝or-zhwä', bo͝or-), **Léon Victor Auguste.** 1851–1925. French statesman (Nobel, 1920).

Bour·get (bo͝or-zhā', bo͝or-zhĕ'), **Paul.** 1852–1935. French author.

Bourke-White (bûrk'hwīt', -wīt'), **Margaret.** 1906–71. Amer. photographer.

Bourne (bo͝orn, bôrn, bōrn), **Randolph Silliman.** 1886–1918. Amer. critic and pacifist.

Bout·well (bout'wĕl'), **George Sewall.** 1818–1905. Amer. politician.

Bo·vet (bō-vā', -vĕt'), **Daniel.** b. 1907. Swiss-born Italian physiologist (Nobel, 1957).

Bow (bō), **Clara.** 1905–65. Amer. actress.

Bow·ditch (bou'dĭch'), **Nathaniel.** 1773–1838. Amer. mathematician and astronomer.

Bow·doin (bōd'n), **James.** 1726–90. Amer. merchant and Revolutionary leader.

Bow·ell (bō'əl), Sir **Mackenzie.** 1823–1917. English-born Canadian prime minister (1894–96).

Bow·en (bō'ən). **1. Catherine Drinker.** 1897–1973. Amer. author. **2. Elizabeth Dorothea Cole.** 1899–1973. Irish-born English author.

Bow·ers (bou'ərz), **Claude Gernade.** 1878–1958. Amer. journalist, diplomat, and historian.

Bow·ie (bō'ē, bo͞o'ē), **James.** 1799–1836. Amer.-born Mexican colonist; died at the Alamo.

Bow·ker (bou'kər), **Richard Rogers.** 1848–1933. Amer. author, publisher, and editor.

Bowles (bōlz). **1. Samuel.** 1797–1851. Amer. newspaper publisher. **2. Samuel.** 1826–78. Amer. newspaper editor and author. **3. Chester Bliss.** b. 1901. Amer. diplomat and author.

Bow·man (bō'mən), **Isaiah.** 1878–1950. Canadian-born Amer. geographer.

Boyd (boid), **Belle.** 1844?–1900. Amer. Confederate spy.

Boy·den (boid'n). **1. Seth.** 1788–1870. Amer. inventor and manufacturer.

2. Uriah Atherton. 1804–79. Amer. engineer and inventor.

Boyd Orr (boid' ôr', ōr'), Lord **John.** 1880–1971. English nutritionist (Nobel, 1949).

Bo·ye (bô'yə), **Karin.** 1900–41. Swedish author.

Boy·er (boi-ā'), **Charles.** 1899–1978. French actor.

Boyle (boil). **1. Robert.** 1627–91. British physicist and chemist. **2. Kay.** b. 1903. Amer. author.

Boyl·ston (boil'stən), **Zabdiel.** 1679–1766. Amer. physician (1st smallpox inoculation).

Boze·man (bōz'mən), **John M.** 1835–67. Amer. explorer.

Brace (brās), **Charles Loring.** 1826–90. Amer. social reformer.

Brack·en·ridge (brăk'ĭn-rĭj'), **Hugh Henry.** 1748–1816. Scottish-born Amer. author, politician, and judge.

Brad·bur·y (brăd'bĕr'ē, -bə-rē), **Ray Douglas.** b. 1920. Amer. science-fiction author.

Brad·dock (brăd'ək), **Edward.** 1695–1755. Scottish-born English general in America.

Brad·ford (brăd'fərd). **1. William.** 1590–1657. English Puritan colonist in America. **2. William.** 1663–1752. English-born Quaker colonist and pioneer printer. **3. Roark.** 1896–1948. Amer. author.

Brad·ley (brăd'lē). **1. James.** 1693–1762. English astronomer and educator. **2. Joseph P.** 1813–92. Amer. jurist. **3. Lydia Moss.** 1816–1908. Amer. businesswoman and philanthropist. **4. Milton.** 1836–1911. Amer. game manufacturer and publisher. **5. Henry.** 1845–1923. English lexicographer and historian. **6. Francis Herbert.** 1846–1924. English philosopher. **7. Omar Nelson.** 1893–1981. Amer. military leader. **8. Thomas.** b. 1917. Amer. policeman and politician. **9. William Warren ("Bill").** b. 1943. Amer. basketball player and politician.

Brad·street (brăd'strēt'). **1. Simon.** 1603–97. English colonial administrator. **2. Anne Dudley.** 1612–72. English-born colonial poet.

Brad·well (brăd'wĕl), **Myra Colby.** 1831–94. Amer. lawyer, editor, and feminist.

Bra·dy (brā'dē). **1. Mathew B.** 1823–96. Amer. pioneer photographer. **2. James Buchanan ("Diamond Jim").** 1856–1917. Amer. financier and philanthropist. **3. William Aloysius.** 1863–1950. Amer. actor and theatrical manager.

Bra·gan·za (brə-găn'zə). Dynasty of Portuguese rulers (1640–1910).

Bragg (brăg). **1. Braxton.** 1817–76. Amer. Confederate soldier. **2.** Sir **William Henry** (1862–1942) and Sir **William Lawrence** (1890–1971). English physicists (shared Nobel, 1915).

Bra·he (brä, brä'hē, brä'ə), **Tycho.** 1546–1601. Danish astronomer.

Brahms (brämz), **Johannes.** 1833–97. German composer. **—Brahms'i·an** *adj.*

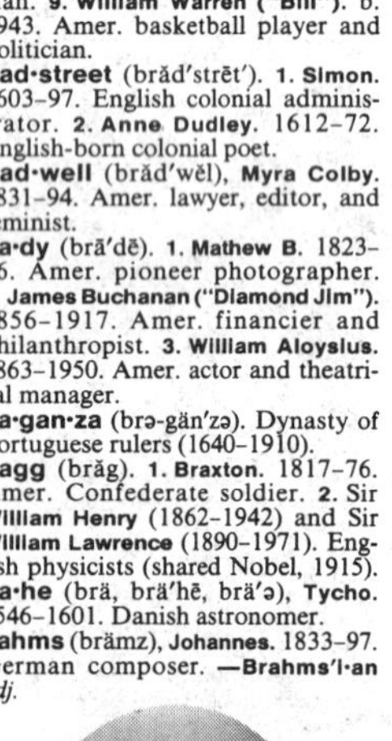

Johannes Brahms

Braille (brāl, brī), **Louis.** 1809?–52. French musician, educator, and inventor of writing and printing systems for the blind.

Bra·man·te (brä-män'tā). 1444?–1514. Italian architect.

Bran·cu·si (brăng-kōō'zē, brăng-kōōsh'-), **Constantin.** 1876–1957. Rumanian-born sculptor.

Bran·deis (brăn'dīs, -dīz), **Louis Dembitz.** 1856–1941. Amer. jurist.

Bran·do (brăn'dō), **Marlon.** b. 1924. Amer. actor.

Brandt (brănt, bränt), **Willy.** b. 1913. West German statesman (Nobel, 1971).

Bran·nan (brăn'ən), **Samuel.** 1819–89. Amer. California pioneer and publisher.

Brant (brănt), **Joseph.** 1742–1807. Amer. Indian leader.

Bran·ting (brăn'tĭng, brän'-), **(Karl) Hjalmar.** 1860–1925. Swedish statesman and journalist (Nobel, 1921).

Braque (bräk, brăk), **Georges.** 1882–1963. French painter.

Brat·tain (brăt'n), **Walter Houser.** b. 1902. Amer. physicist (Nobel, 1956).

Braun (broun). **1. Karl Ferdinand.** 1850–1918. German physicist (Nobel, 1909). **2.** (*also* brôn), **Eva.** 1910?–45. German mistress of Adolf Hitler. **3.** (*also* brôn), **Wernher Magnus Maximilian von.** 1912–77. German-born Amer. rocket engineer.

Breas·ted (brĕs'tĭd), **James Henry.** 1865–1935. Amer. archaeologist and historian.

Brecht (brĕkt, brĕKHt), **Bertolt.** 1898–1956. German poet and playwright.

Breck·in·ridge (brĕk'ĭn-rĭj'). **1. John Cabell.** 1821–75. U.S. Vice President (1857–61). **2. Sophonisba Preston.** 1866–1948. Amer. social worker, author, and educator.

Brel (brĕl), **Jacques.** 1929–78. Belgian singer and composer.

Bren·nan (brĕn'ən), **William Joseph, Jr.** b. 1906. Amer. jurist.

Brent (brĕnt), **Margaret.** 1600?–71? English-born colonist and feminist.

Bresh·kov·sky (brĕsh-kôf'skē), **Catherine.** 1844–1934. Russian revolutionary and social reformer.

Bre·ton (brĭ-tôN'), **André.** 1896–1966. French author and critic.

Bre·ton·neau (brĭ-tô-nō'), **Pierre.** 1778–1862. French surgeon.

Breu·er (broi'ər), **Marcel Lajos.** 1902–81. Hungarian-born Amer. architect and designer.

Breu·ghel (broi'gəl, brōō'-, brœ'-). Variant of **Brueghel.**

Brew·er (brōō'ər), **David Josiah.** 1837–1910. Amer. jurist.

Brew·ster (brōō'stər). **1. William.** 1567–1644. English Pilgrim colonist. **2. Kingman, Jr.** b. 1919. Amer. educator.

Brezh·nev (brĕzh'nĕf, -nyĕf), **Leonid Ilyich.** b. 1906–82. Soviet statesman.

Bri·an Bo·ru (brī'ən bô-rōō', -rō', bō-, brēn'). 941–1014. Irish king (1002–14).

Bri·and (brē-änd', -äN'), **Aristide.** 1862–1932. French statesman (Nobel, 1926).

Brice (brīs), **Fannie.** 1891–1951. Amer. entertainer.

Bri·co (brē'kō), **Antonia.** b. 1902. Dutch-born Amer. conductor and pianist.

Bridg·er (brĭj'ər), **James.** 1804–81. Amer. frontiersman and fur trader.

Bridg·es (brĭj'ĭz). **1. Robert Seymour.** 1844–1930. English author. **2. Harry.** b. 1900. Amer. labor leader.

Bridg·man (brĭj'mən). **1. Laura Dewey.** 1829–89. Amer. educator; first blind deaf-mute to be systematically educated. **2. Percy Williams.** 1882–1961. Amer. physicist (Nobel, 1946).

Bri·eux (brē-œ'), **Eugène.** 1858–1932. French playwright.

Briggs (brĭgz). **1. Henry.** 1561–1630? English mathematician. **2. Emily Pomona Edson.** 1830–1910. Amer. journalist. **3. Lyman James.** 1874–1963. Amer. physicist.

Bright (brīt), **John.** 1811–89. English politician and orator.

Brill (brĭl), **Abraham Arden.** 1874–1948. Austrian-born Amer. psychiatrist.

Bril·lat-Sa·va·rin (brē-yä'sä-vä-răN'), **Anthelme.** 1755–1826. French politician and gourmet.

Brink·ley (brĭngk'lē), **David.** b. 1920. Amer. broadcast journalist.

Brin·ton (brĭn'tən), **Daniel Garrison.** 1837–99. Amer. anthropologist and physician.

Bris·bane (brĭz'băn, -bən). **1. Albert.** 1809–90. Amer. social reformer. **2. Arthur.** 1864–1936. Amer. newspaper editor.

Bris·tow (brĭs'tō), **Benjamin Helm.** 1832–96. Amer. lawyer and public official.

Brit·ten (brĭt'n), **(Edward) Benjamin.** 1913–76. English composer.

Bro·gan (brō'gən), Sir **Denis William.** 1900–74. English political scientist.

Bro·glie (brô-glē', broi-), **Louis Victor de.** b. 1892. French physicist (Nobel, 1929).

Brom·field (brŏm'fēld'), **Louis.** 1896–1956. Amer. author.

Bron·të (brŏn'tē). Family of English novelists, including **Charlotte** (1816–55), **Emily Jane** (1818–48), and **Anne** (1820–49).

Charlotte Brontë

Brook (brŏŏk). **1.** Sir **Alan Francis.** 1st Viscount Alanbrooke. 1883–1963. British field marshal. **2. Rupert.** 1887–1915. English poet.

Brook·ings (brŏŏk'ĭngz), **Robert Somers.** 1850–1932. Amer. businessman and philanthropist.

Brooks (brŏŏks). **1. Maria Gowen.** 1794?–1845. Amer. poet. **2. Phillips.** 1835–93. Amer. prelate and author. **3. Van Wyck.** 1886–1963. Amer. literary historian and critic. **4. Gwendolyn Elizabeth.** b. 1917. Amer. author.

Broun (brōōn), **(Matthew) Heywood (Campbell).** 1888–1939. Amer. journalist.

Brow·der (brou'dər), **Earl Russell.** 1891–1973. Amer. socialist leader.

Brown (broun). **1. Moses.** 1738–1836. Amer. manufacturer and social reformer. **2. Charles Brockden.** 1771–1810. Amer. author and editor. **3. Robert.** 1773–1858. Scottish botanist. **4. Jacob Jennings.** 1775–1828. Amer. military leader. **5. John.** 1800–59. Amer. abolitionist; executed. **6. William Wells.** 1815–84. Amer. author and social reformer. **7. Ford Madox.** 1821–93. English historical painter. **8. Benjamin Gratz.** 1826–85. Amer. politician. **9. Olympia.** 1835–1926. Amer. clergywoman and suffragist. **10. Henry Billings.** 1836–1913. Amer. jurist. **11. Martha McClellan.** 1838–1916. Amer. temperance leader. **12. Hallie Quinn.** 1850–1945? Amer. educator and lecturer. **13. Alice.** 1856?–1948. Amer. author. **14. John Mason.** 1900–69. Amer. drama critic. **15. Herbert Charles.** b. 1912. English-born Amer. chemist (Nobel, 1979). **16. Helen Gurley.** b. 1922. Amer. editor and author.

Browne (broun). **1.** Sir **Thomas.** 1605–82. English physician and author. **2. Charles Farrar.** "Artemus Ward." 1834–67. Amer. humorist.

Brown·ing (brou'nĭng). **1. Elizabeth Barrett** (1806–61) and **Robert** (1812–89). English poets. **2. John Moses.** 1855–1926. Amer. firearms inventor.

Robert Browning

Brown·son (broun'sən), **Orestes Augustus.** 1803–76. Amer. clergyman, author, and editor.

Broz (brōz, brôz), **Josip.** See **Tito.**

Bru·beck (brōō'bĕk), **David Warren.** b. 1920. Amer. pianist and composer.

Bruce (brōōs). **1. Robert the.** Robert I of Scotland. **2. Blanche Kelso.** 1841–98. Amer. politician and public official. **3.** Sir **David.** 1855–1931. Australian physician and bacteriologist. **4.** Viscount **Stanley Melbourne.** 1883–1967. Australian statesman. **5. David Kirkpatrick Este.** 1898–1977. Amer. diplomat. **6. Lenny.** 1926–66. Amer. comedian.

Bruck·ner (brŭk'nər, brŏŏk'-), **Anton.** 1824–96. Austrian composer.

Brue·ghel also **Brue·gel, Breu·ghel** (broi'gəl, brōō'-, brœ'-). Flemish family of painters, including **Pieter** "the Elder" (1525?–69), **Pieter** "the Younger" (1564?–1637), and **Jan** (1568–1625).

Bruhn (brōōn), **Erik.** 1928–86. Danish-born ballet dancer.

Bru·lé (brü-lā'), **Étienne.** 1592?–1632. French explorer.

Brum·mell (brŭm'əl), **George Bryan ("Beau").** 1778–1840. English fashionable gentleman.

Brun·dage (brŭn'dĭj), **Avery.** 1887–1975. Amer. businessman and sports figure.

Bru·nel·le·schi (brōō'nə-lĕs'kē, -nĕl-lĕs'-), **Filippo.** 1377?–1446. Italian architect.

Bru·ne·tière (brōō'nə-tyĕr', brü'-), **Vincent de Paul Marie Ferdinand.** 1849?–1906. French critic and editor.

Brü·ning also **Brue·ning** (brōō'nĭng, brü'-), **Heinrich.** 1885–1970. German statesman.

Bru·no (brōō'nō). **1. of Co·logne** (kə-lōn'), Saint. 1030?–1101. German religious writer and founder of Carthusian order. **2. Giordano.** 1548?–1600. Italian philosopher.

Bru·tus (brōō'təs), **Marcus Junius.** 85?–42 B.C. Roman politician, general, and chief assassin of Julius Caesar.

Bry·an (brī'ən), **William Jennings.** 1860–1925. Amer. lawyer and political leader.

Bry·ant (brī'ənt), **William Cullen.** 1794–1878. Amer. poet and editor.

Bryce (brīs), **James.** Viscount Bryce of Dechmont. 1838–1922. English statesman, diplomat, and historian.

Brze·zin·ski (brĭ-zhĭn'skē, brĕ-), **Zbigniew.** b. 1928. Polish-born Amer. political adviser.

Bu·ber (bōō'bər), **Martin.** 1878–1965. Austrian-born Judaic scholar and philosopher.

Buch·an (bŭk'ən, bŭKH'-), Sir **John.** 1st Baron Tweedsmuir. 1875–1940. Scottish historian and government official.

Bu·chan·an (byōō-kăn'ən, bə-). **1. James.** 1791–1868. 15th U.S. President (1857–61). **2. Franklin.** 1800–74. Amer. Confederate naval officer.

James Buchanan

Buch·man (bŏŏk'mən, bŭk'-), **Frank Nathan Daniel.** 1878–1961. Amer. evangelist.

Buch·ner (bŏŏk'nər, bōōKH'-), **Eduard.** 1860–1917. German chemist (Nobel, 1907).

Buck (bŭk), **Pearl Sydenstricker.**

1892–1973. Amer. author (Nobel, 1938).
Buck·ing·ham (bŭk′ĭng-əm, -hăm′), 1st Duke. George Villiers. 1592–1628. English political adviser; assassinated.
Buck·ley (bŭk′lē), **William Frank, Jr.** b. 1925. Amer. editor and author.
Buck·ner (bŭk′nər), **Simon Bolivar.** 1823–1914. Amer. Confederate general and politician.
Bud·dha (bo͞od′ə, bo͞o′də), 563?–483? B.C. Indian philosopher and founder of Buddhism. **—Bud′dhist** *adj. & n.*
Budge (bŭj), **John Donald ("Don").** b. 1915. Amer. tennis player.
Bu·ell (byo͞o′əl). **1. Abel.** 1742–1822. Amer. silversmith, type designer, and engraver. **2. Don Carlos.** 1818–98. Amer. army officer.
Buf·fa·lo Bill (bŭf′ə-lō bĭl′). William Frederick Cody.
Buf·fet (bü-fĕ′), **Bernard.** b. 1928. French painter.
Buf·fon (bü-fôɴ′), Comte **Georges Louis Leclerc de.** 1707–88. French naturalist.
Buis·son (bwē-sôɴ′), **Ferdinand.** 1841–1932. French educator (Nobel, 1927).
Bu·kha·rin (bo͞o-ᴋʜä′rĭn), **Nikolai Ivanovich.** 1888–1938. Bolshevik theoretician and revolutionary; executed.
Bul·finch (bo͝ol′fĭnch′). **1. Charles.** 1763–1844. Amer. architect. **2. Thomas.** 1796–1867. Amer. author.
Bul·ga·nin (bo͝ol-gä′nĭn, -nyĭn, -găn′ĭn), **Nikolai Aleksandrovich.** 1895–1975. Russian military and political leader.
Bull (bo͝ol, bo͞ol), **Ole Bornemann.** 1810–80. Norwegian violinist.
Bul·litt (bo͝ol′ĭt, bŭl′-), **William Christian.** 1891–1967. Amer. diplomat.
Bü·low (bü′lō, byo͞o′-), Prince **Bernhard von.** 1849–1929. German statesman and diplomat.
Bul·wer (bo͝ol′wər), **William Henry Lytton Earle.** Baron Dalling and Bulwer. 1801–72. English author, politician, and diplomat.
Bum·bry (bŭm′brē), **Grace.** b. 1937. Amer. opera singer.
Bunche (bŭnch), **Ralph Johnson.** 1904–71. Amer. diplomat (Nobel, 1950).
Bun·dy (bŭn′dē), **McGeorge.** b. 1919. Amer. educator and political adviser.
Bu·nin (bo͞o′nĭn, -nyĭn), **Ivan Alekseevich.** 1870–1953. Russian author (Nobel, 1933).
Bun·ker (bŭng′kər), **Ellsworth.** b. 1894. Amer. diplomat.
Bun·sen (bŭn′sən, bo͝on′zən), **Robert Wilhelm.** 1811–99. German chemist.
Bunt·line (bŭnt′lĭn′, -lĭn′), **Ned.** Edward Zane Carroll Judson.
Bu·ñu·el (bo͞o-nyo͞o-ĕl), **Luis.** 1900–83. Spanish-born film director.
Bun·yan (bŭn′yən), **John.** 1628–88. English preacher and author.
Buo·non·ci·ni (bwō′nôn-chē′nē). Variant of **Bononcini.**
Bur·bage (bûr′bĭj), **Richard.** 1567?–1619. English actor and theater manager.
Bur·bank (bûr′băngk′), **Luther.** 1849–1926. Amer. horticulturist and pioneer plant breeder.

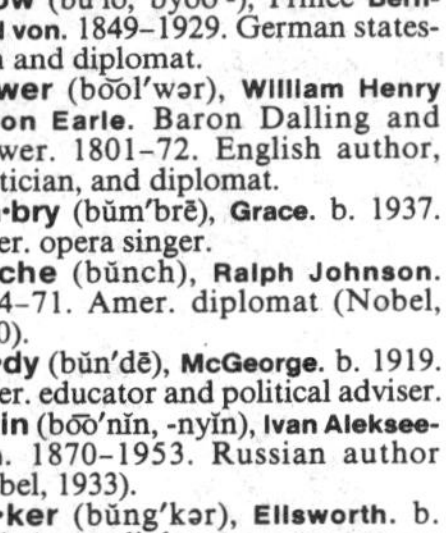

Luther Burbank

Burch·field (bûrch′fēld′), **Charles Ephraim.** 1893–1967. Amer. painter.
Burck·hard (bo͝ork′härt), **Jakob.** Swiss art historian.
Bur·ger (bûr′gər), **Warren Earl.** b. 1907. Amer. jurist.
Bür·ger (bo͞or′gər, bĭr′-, bür′-), **Gottfried August.** 1747?–94. German poet.
Bur·gess (bûr′jĭs). **1. (Frank) Gelett.** 1866–1951. Amer. author and illustrator. **2. Anthony.** b. 1917. English author.
Burgh·ley or **Bur·leigh** (bûr′lē), 1st Baron. William Cecil.
Bur·goyne (bər-goin′), **John.** 1722–92. English general and playwright.
Bur·gun·dy (bûr′gən-dē). Dynasty of Portuguese rulers (1139–1383).
Burke (bûrk). **1. Edmund.** 1729–97. British politician, orator, and author. **2.** Also **Burk, Martha Jane.** "Calamity Jane." 1852?–1903. Amer. frontier heroine. **3. Billie.** 1886–1970. Amer. actress.
Bur·leigh (bûr′lē), **Harry Thatcher.** 1866–1949. Amer. composer.
Bur·lin (bûr′lĭn), **Natalie Curtis.** 1875–1921. Amer. musicologist.
Bur·lin·game (bûr′lĭn-găm′, -lĭng-), **Anson.** 1820–70. Amer. diplomat.
Burne-Jones (bûrn′jōnz′), Sir **Edward Coley.** 1833–98. English pre-Raphaelite painter.
Bur·net (bər-nĕt′, bûr′nĭt), Sir **Frank Macfarlane.** 1899–1985. Australian medical scientist (Nobel, 1960).
Bur·nett (bər-nĕt′). **1.** (*also* bûr′nĭt), **Frances Eliza Hodgson.** 1849–1924. English-born Amer. writer. **2. Carol.** b. 1936. Amer. comedienne.
Bur·ney (bûr′nē), **Frances ("Fanny").** 1752–1840. English author.
Burn·ham (bûr′nəm), **Daniel Hudson.** 1846–1912. Amer. architect and city planner.
Burns (bûrnz). **1. Robert.** 1759–96. Scottish poet. **2. George.** b. 1896. Amer. comedian. **3. Arthur Frank.** b. 1904. Austrian-born Amer. economist. **—Burns′i·an** *adj.*
Burn·side (bûrn′sīd′), **Ambrose Everett.** 1824–81. Amer. politician and general.
Bur·pee (bûr′pē), **David.** 1893–1980. Amer. horticulturist.
Burr (bûr), **Aaron.** 1756–1836. U.S. Vice President (1801–5), soldier, and adventurer; killed Alexander Hamilton in a duel.

Aaron Burr

Bur·ritt (bûr′ĭt, bŭr′-), **Elihu.** 1810–79. Amer. social reformer.
Bur·roughs (bûr′ōz, bŭr′-). **1. John.** 1837–1921. Amer. naturalist and author. **2. William Seward.** 1855–98. Amer. inventor (adding machine). **3. Edgar Rice.** 1875–1950. Amer. author (Tarzan series).
Bur·rows (bûr′ōz, bŭr′-), **Abe.** 1910–85. Amer. playwright.
Burt (bûrt), **William Austin.** 1792–1858. Amer. surveyor and inventor.
Bur·ton (bûr′tn). **1. Robert.** 1577–1640. English clergyman and author. **2.** Sir **Richard Francis.** 1821–90. English explorer and Orientalist. **3. Harold Hitz.** 1888–1964. Amer. jurist.
Busch (bo͝osh), **Adolphus.** 1839–1913. German-born Amer. brewer, businessman, and philanthropist.
Bush (bo͝osh). **1. Vannevar.** 1890–1974. Amer. electrical engineer. **2. George Herbert Walker.** b. 1924. U.S. Vice President (since 1981).
Bush·man (bo͝osh′mən), **Francis Xavier.** 1883–1966. Amer. actor.
Bush·nell (bo͝osh′nəl). **1. David.** 1742?–1824. Amer. inventor. **2. Horace.** 1802–76. Amer. theologian.
Bu·so·ni (byo͞o-sō′nē, bo͞o-zō′-), **Ferruccio Benvenuto.** 1866–1924. Italian pianist and composer.
Bu·te·nandt (bo͞ot′n-änt′), **Adolf Friedrich.** b. 1903. German chemist (Nobel, 1939).
But·ler (bŭt′lər). **1. Samuel.** 1612–80. English poet. **2. Joseph.** 1692–1752. English prelate and theologian. **3. Benjamin Franklin.** 1818–93. Amer. political and military leader. **4. Samuel.** 1835–1902. English novelist. **5. Nicholas Murray.** 1862–1947. Amer. educator (Nobel, 1931). **6. Pierce.** 1866–1939. Amer. jurist.
But·ter·field (bŭt′ər-fēld′), **John.** 1801–69. Amer. expressman and financier.
But·ton (bŭt′n), **Richard Totten ("Dick").** b. 1929. Amer. figure skater and television producer.
Bux·te·hu·de (bo͞oks′tə-ho͞o′də), **Dietrich.** 1637–1707. German composer.
Byng (bĭng). **1. George.** 1663–1733. English admiral. **2. Julian Hedworth George.** 1862–1935. English military and law-enforcement leader.
Byrd (bûrd). **1. William.** 1674–1744. Amer. planter, author, and colonial official. **2. Richard Evelyn.** 1888–1957. Amer. naval officer and polar explorer.

Richard E. Byrd

Byrne (bûrn), **Jane Margaret.** b. 1934. Amer. public official.
Byrnes (bûrnz), **James Francis.** 1879–1972. Amer. politician and jurist.
By·ron (bī′rən), **George Gordon.** 6th Baron Byron of Rochdale. 1788–1824. English poet. **—By·ron′ic** *adj.*

C

Cab·ell (kăb′əl), **James Branch.** 1879–1958. Amer. author.
Ca·be·za de Va·ca (kä-bĕ′sä dĕ vä′kä), **Álvar Núñez.** 1490?–1577? Spanish explorer and colonial administrator.
Ca·ble (kā′bəl), **George Washington.** 1844–1925. Amer. author.
Cab·ot (kăb′ət). **1. John.** 1450–98. Italian-born explorer. **2. Sebastian.** 1476?–1557. Italian-born explorer and cartographer.

Sebastian Cabot

Ca·bral (kə-bräl′), **Pedro Alvares.** 1460?–1526? Portuguese explorer.
Ca·bri·llo (kä-brē′lyô), **Juan Rodríguez.** d. 1543. Portuguese-born explorer.
Ca·bri·ni (kə-brē′nē), Saint **Frances Xavier.** "Mother Cabrini." 1850–1917. Italian-born Amer. religious leader.
Cade (kād), **John ("Jack").** d. 1450. English rebel.
Cad·il·lac (kăd′l-ăk′, kä-dē-yäk′), Sieur **Antoine de la Mothe.** 1656?–1730. French explorer and colonial administrator.
Caed·mon (kăd′mən). fl. c. 670. English poet.
Cae·sar (sē′zər), **Gaius Julius.** 100–44 B.C. Roman general, statesman, and historian. **—Cae·sar′e·an, Cae·sar′i·an** (sĭ-zâr′ē-ən) *adj.*
Cage (kāj), **John Milton, Jr.** b. 1912. Amer. composer.
Ca·glio·stro (kăl-yō′strō, kä-lyô′-), Count **Alessandro di.** 1743–95. Italian adventurer.
Cag·ney (kăg′nē), **James.** 1899–1986. Amer. actor.
Ca·han (kän), **Abraham.** 1860–1951. Lithuanian-born Amer. Yiddish editor and author.
Cai·a·phas (kā′ə-fəs, kī′-), **Joseph.** Jewish high priest (A.D. 18?–36).
Cain (kān). Son of Adam and Eve and murderer of Abel.
Ca·ius (kā′əs). Variant of **Gaius.**
Ca·lam·i·ty Jane (kə-lăm′ĭ-tē jān′). Martha Jane Burke.
Cal·der (kôl′der, kŏl′-), **Alexander.** 1898–1976. Amer. sculptor.
Cal·de·rón de la Bar·ca (käl′-*th*ĕ-rôn′ dĕ lä bär′kä), **Pedro.** 1600–81. Spanish author.
Cald·well (kôl′dwĕl′, -dwəl, kŏl′-). **1. (Janet) Taylor.** 1900–85. English-born Amer. author. **2. Erskine Preston.** b. 1903. Amer. author. **3. Sarah.** b. 1928. Amer. conductor and opera producer.
Cal·houn (kăl-ho͞on′), **John Caldwell.** 1782–1850. U.S. Vice President (1824–32) and political philosopher.
Ca·lig·u·la (kə-lĭg′yə-lə). A.D. 12–41. Roman emperor (37–41).
Ca·lix·tus (kə-lĭk′stəs). Name of 3 popes and 1 antipope, esp. **III,** 1378–1458, reigned 1455–58.
Cal·kins (kô′kĭnz), **Mary Whiton.** 1863–1930. Amer. psychologist, philosopher, and educator.
Cal·la·ghan (kăl′ə-hən, -hăn′). **1. Morley Edward.** b. 1903. Canadian author. **2. James.** b. 1912. British prime minister (1976–79).
Cal·las (kăl′əs, kä′ləs), **Maria Meneghini.** 1923–77. Amer. soprano.
Ca·lles (kī′ās, kä′yĕs), **Plutarco Elías.** 1877–1945. Mexican general and statesman.
Cal·lim·a·chus (kə-lĭm′ə-kəs). **1.** 5th cent. B.C. Greek sculptor. **2.** 3rd cent. B.C. Greek author and scholar.
Cal·lis·the·nes (kə-lĭs′thə-nēz′). 360?–28? B.C. Greek philosopher.
Cal·lo·way (kăl′ə-wā′), **Cabell ("Cab").** b. 1907. Amer. musician.
Cal·vert (kăl′vərt). Family of English colonists and administrators, including **George,** 1st Baron Baltimore (1580?–1632); **Cecilius,** 2nd Baron Baltimore (1605–75); **Leonard** (1606–47); and **Charles,** 3rd Baron Baltimore (1637–1715).
Cal·vin (kăl′vĭn). **1. John.** 1509–64. French-born Swiss Protestant theologian. **2. Melvin.** b. 1911. Amer. chemist (Nobel, 1961).
Ca·ma·cho (kä-mä′chô), **Manuel Avila.** 1897–1955. Mexican general and statesman.
Cam·ba·cé·rès (käɴ-bä-sā-rĕs′), Duc de. Jean Jacques Régis. 1753–1824. French statesman and jurist.
Cam·by·ses (kăm-bī′sēz). d. 522 B.C. Persian king (529–22).
Cam·den (kăm′dən), **William.** 1551–1623. English historian.
Cam·er·on (kăm′ər-ən). **1. of Loch·iel** (lŏk-ēl′, lŏᴋʜ-), **Donald.** 1695?–1748. Scottish chieftain and soldier. **2. Simon.** 1799–1889. Amer. politician and diplomat.
Ca·mo·ëns (kăm′ō-ənz, kə-mō′-) also **Ca·mões** (kə-moiɴsh′), **Luiz Vaz de.** 1524–80. Portuguese author.
Camp (kămp), **Walter Chauncey.** 1859–1925. Amer. football coach and promoter.
Camp·bell (kăm′bəl). **1. John.** 4th Earl of Loudoun. 1705–82. English general in North America. **2. Thomas**

p pop / r roar / s sauce / sh ship, dish / t tight / th thin, path / *th* this, bathe / ŭ cut / ûr urge / v valve / w with / y yes / z zebra, size / zh vision / ə about, item, edible, gallop, circus / œ *Fr.* feu, *Ger.* schön / ü *Fr.* tu, *Ger.* über / ᴋʜ *Ger.* ich, *Scot.* loch / ɴ *Fr.* bon.

(1763–1854) and **Alexander** (1788–1866). Irish-born Amer. religious leaders. **3. Thomas.** 1777–1844. British author. **4.** Sir **Colin.** Baron Clyde. 1792–1863. British field marshal. **5. John Archibald.** 1811–89. Amer. jurist and Confederate official. **6. William Wallace.** 1862–1938. Amer. astronomer. **7.** Mrs. **Patrick.** Beatrice Stella Tanner. 1867–1940. English actress. **8.** Sir **Malcolm** (1885–1945) and **Donald Malcolm** (1921–67). English automobile and speedboat racers.

Camp·bell-Ban·ner·man (kăm′bəl-băn′ər-mən, kăm′əl-), Sir **Henry.** 1836–1908. British prime minister (1905–8).

Cam·pi (kăm′pē). Family of Italian painters, including **Galeazzo** (1475?–1536), **Giulio** (1500?–72), **Antonio** (1530?–91), and **Vincenzo** (1532?–91).

Cam·pi·on (kăm′pē-ən), **Thomas.** 1567–1620. English poet and songwriter.

Ca·mus (kä-mü′), **Albert.** 1913–60. French author (Nobel, 1957).

Ca·na·let·to (kăn′ə-lĕt′ō, kä-nä-lāt′tō), **Antonio.** 1697–1768. Italian painter.

Can·by (kăn′bē), **Henry Seidel.** 1878–1961. Amer. author and editor.

Cand·ler (kănd′lər), **Asa Griggs.** 1851–1929. Amer. manufacturer and philanthropist.

Can·dolle (käN-dôl′), **Augustin Pyrame de.** 1778–1841. Swiss botanist.

Ca·net·ti (kä-nĕt′ē), **Elias.** b. 1905. Bulgarian-born German-language author (Nobel, 1981).

Can·ning (kăn′ĭng). **1. George.** 1770–1827. British prime minister (1827). **2.** Sir **Stratford.** 1st Viscount Stratford de Redcliffe. 1786–1880. English diplomat. **3.** Earl **Charles John.** 1812–62. English colonial administrator.

Can·non (kăn′ən). **1. Joseph Gurney ("Uncle Joe").** 1836–1926. Amer. legislator. **2. Annie Jump.** 1863–1941. Amer. astronomer.

Ca·no·va (kə-nō′və, kä-nō′vä), **Antonio.** 1757–1822. Italian sculptor.

Can·tor (kăn′tər), **Eddie.** 1892–1964. Amer. comedian.

Ca·nute also **Cnut** or **Knut** (kə-no͞ot′, -nyo͞ot′). **1.** "the Great." 994?–1035. King of England (1016–35), Denmark (1018–35), and Norway (1028–35). **2. II.** See **Hardecanute.**

Ča·pek (chä′pĕk′), **Karel.** 1890–1938. Czech author.

Ca·pet (kā′pĭt, kăp′ĭt, kä-pā′, kä-pĕ′). Dynasty of French kings (987–1328), including **Hugh Capet** (940?–96), ruled 987–96. —**Ca·pe′tian** (kə-pē′shən) *adj. & n.*

Ca·pone (kə-pōn′), **Alphonse ("Al").** "Scarface." 1899–1947. Italian-born Amer. gangster.

Ca·po·te (kə-pō′tē), **Truman.** 1924–84. Amer. author.

Capp (kăp), **Al.** 1909–79. Amer. cartoonist.

Cap·ra (kăp′rə), **Frank.** b. 1897. Amer. filmmaker.

Car·a·cal·la (kăr′ə-kăl′ə). 188–217. Roman emperor (211–17); assassinated.

Ca·ra·vag·gio (kăr′ə-vä′jō, kär′rä-väd′jō), **Michelangelo Amerighi** or **Merisa da.** 1565?–1609? Italian painter.

Car·a·way (kăr′ə-wā′), **Hattie Ophelia Wyatt.** 1878–1950. Amer. legislator.

Cár·de·nas (kär′*thĕ*-näs), **Lázaro.** 1895–1970. Mexican soldier and statesman.

Car·din (kär-dăN′), **Pierre.** b. 1922. Italian-born French fashion designer.

Car·do·zo (kär-dō′zō), **Benjamin Nathan.** 1870–1938. Amer. jurist.

Car·duc·ci (kär-do͞ot′chē), **Giosuè.** 1835–1907. Italian poet (Nobel, 1906).

Ca·rew (kə-ro͞o′), **Thomas.** 1595?–1639? English poet.

Ca·rey (kâr′ē), **Matthew** (1760–1839) and **Henry Charles** (1793–1879). Amer. publishers and economic theorists.

Carl XVI Gus·tav (kärl′gŭs′täv, -täf, go͞os′-). b. 1946. Swedish king (since 1973).

Carle·ton (kärl′tən), Sir **Guy.** 1st Baron Dorchester. British soldier and colonial administrator.

Car·los (kär′ləs, -lôs). **1. de Aus·tri·a** (dĭ ou′strē-ä), Don. 1545–68. Heir to Spanish throne; died mysteriously. **2.** Don. "Count of Molino." 1788–1855. Spanish pretender to the throne. —**Carl′ist** (kär′lĭst) *adj. & n.*

Car·lo·ta (kär-lô′tä). 1840–1927. Belgian-born empress of Mexico as wife of Archduke Maximilian of Austria.

Carl·son (kärl′sən), **Chester Floyd.** 1906–68. Amer. inventor (xerography).

Car·lyle (kär-līl′, kär′līl), **Thomas.** 1795–1881. Scottish historian.

Car·man (kär′mən), **(William) Bliss.** 1861–1929. Canadian author.

Car·mi·chael (kär′mī-kəl), **Hoagland Howard ("Hoagy" or "Hoagie").** 1899–1981. Amer. songwriter.

Car·mo·na (kär-mô′nə), **Antônio Oscar de Fragoso.** 1869–1951. Portuguese general and statesman.

Car·ne·gie (kär′nə-gē). **1.** (*also* kär-nā′gē, -nĕg′ē), **Andrew.** 1835–1919. Scottish-born Amer. industrialist and philanthropist. **2. Dale.** 1888–1955. Amer. author and educator.

Car·not (kär-nō′). **1. Lazare Nicolas Marguerite.** 1753–1823. French statesman and military strategist. **2. Nicolas Léonard Sadi.** 1796–1832. French physicist. **3. (Marie François) Sadi.** 1837–94. French statesman.

Car·ol (kăr′əl). Name of 2 kings of Rumania, esp. **II,** 1893–1953, ruled 1930–40; abdicated.

Car·o·lin·gi·an (kăr′ə-lĭn′jē-ən) also **Car·lo·vin·gi·an** (kär′lə-vĭn′-). Dynasty of rulers in France (751–987), Germany (752–911), and Italy (774–961).

Ca·roth·ers (kə-rŭ*th*′ərz), **Wallace Hume.** 1896–1937. Amer. chemist and inventor (nylon).

Car·pac·cio (kär-pät′chō), **Vittore.** 1460?–1525? Venetian painter.

Car·ran·za (kə-răn′zə, -rän′-, kär-rän′sä), **Venustiano.** 1859–1920. Mexican revolutionary statesman.

Car·rel (kə-rĕl′, kăr′əl), **Alexis.** 1873–1944. French-born Amer. surgeon and biologist (Nobel, 1912).

Car·rère (kə-râr′), **John Merven.** 1858–1911. Amer. architect.

Car·roll (kăr′əl). **1. John.** 1735–1815. Amer. religious leader. **2. Charles.** "Carroll of Carrollton." 1737–1832. Amer. Revolutionary leader and legislator. **3. Anna Ella.** 1815–93. Amer. political pamphleteer and adviser. **4. Lewis.** Charles Lutwidge Dodgson.

Car·son (kär′sən). **1. Christopher ("Kit").** 1809–68. Amer. frontiersman, fur trapper, and Indian agent. **2. Rachel Louise.** 1907–64. Amer. environmentalist and author.

Carte (kärt), **Richard D'Oyly.** 1844–1901. English operetta impresario.

Car·ter (kär′tər). **1. Samuel Powhatan.** 1819–91. Amer. army and navy officer. **2. Howard.** 1873–1939. English Egyptologist. **3. James Earl ("Jimmy"), Jr.** b. 1924. 39th U.S. President (1977–81).

Jimmy Carter

Car·ter·et (kär′tər-ət), **John.** Earl Granville. 1690–1763. English statesman and diplomat.

Jacques Cartier

Car·tier (kär-tyā′, kär′tē-ā′). **1. Jacques.** 1491–1557. French explorer. **2.** Sir **George Étienne.** 1814–73. Canadian statesman and prime minister (1858–62).

Car·tier-Bres·son (kär-tyā′brĕ-sôN′), **Henri.** b. 1908. French photographer.

Cart·wright (kärt′rīt′), **Edmund.** 1743–1823. English clergyman and inventor.

Car·ty (kär′tē), **John Joseph.** 1861–1932. Amer. electrical engineer and telephone pioneer.

Ca·ru·so (kə-ro͞o′sō, -zō), **Enrico.** 1873–1921. Italian-born operatic tenor.

Enrico Caruso

Car·ver (kär′vər). **1. John.** 1576?–1621. English-born Pilgrim colonist. **2. Jonathan.** 1710–80. Amer. soldier and explorer. **3. George Washington.** 1864?–1943. Amer. botanist, agricultural chemist, and educator.

George Washington Carver

Car·y (kâr′ē). **1. Henry Francis.** 1772–1844. Anglo-Irish poet and translator. **2. Alice** (1820–71) and **Phoebe** (1824–71). Amer. authors. **3. Elisabeth Luther.** 1867–1936. Amer. critic. **4. (Arthur) Joyce (Lunel).** 1888–1957. Irish-born author.

Ca·sa·bian·ca (kä-zä-byäN-kä′), **Louis de.** 1752?–98. French naval officer.

Ca·sals (kə-sälz′, -sălz′, kä-säls′), **Pablo.** 1876–1973. Spanish-born cellist.

Ca·sa·no·va de Sein·galt (kăz′ə-nō′və dē săN-gält′, kăs′-, kä′sä-nô′vä), **Giovanni Jacopo.** 1725–98. Italian adventurer and author.

Case·ment (kās′mənt), Sir **Roger David.** 1864–1916. British diplomat and Irish rebel; executed for treason.

Ca·si·mir-Pé·rier (kä-zē-mîr′pā-ryā′), **Jean Paul Pierre.** 1847–1907. French statesman.

Cas·lon (kăz′lən), **William.** 1692–1766. English type designer and founder.

Cass (kăs), **Lewis.** 1782–1866. Amer. soldier, politician, and diplomat.

Cas·satt (kə-săt′), **Mary Stevenson.** 1845–1926. Amer. painter.

Mary Cassatt

Cas·sin (kä-săN′), **René.** 1887–1976. French statesman (Nobel, 1968).

Cas·si·ni (kə-sē′nē, kä-). **1. Giovanni Domenico** or **Jean Dominique.** 1625–1712. Italian-born French astronomer. **2. Oleg.** b. 1913. French-born Amer. fashion designer.

Cas·si·o·dor·us (kăs′ē-ə-dôr′əs, -dōr′-), **Flavius Magnus Aurelius.** 6th cent. A.D. Roman statesman and historian.

Cas·sir·er (kä-sîr′ər, kə-), **Ernst.** 1874–1945. German philosopher.

Cas·sius Lon·gi·nus (kăsh′əs lŏn-jī′nəs), **Gaius.** d. 42 B.C. Roman general and politician.

Cas·ta·gno (kä-stä′nyō), **Andrea del.** 1423–57. Florentine painter.

Cas·ti·glio·ne (kä-stē-lyō′nā), Count **Baldassare.** 1478–1529. Italian courtier, diplomat, and author.

Cas·ti·lho (kəsh-tē′lyo͞o), **Antonio Feliciano de.** 1800–75. Portuguese author and translator.

Cas·tle (kăs′əl), **Vernon Blythe** (1887–1918) and **Irene Foote** (1893–1969). English-born dancers.

Cas·tle·reagh (kăs′əl-rā′, kă′səl-), Viscount. Robert Stewart, Marquis of Londonderry. 1769–1822. British statesman.

Cas·tro (kăs′trō, kä′strô). **1. Cipriano.** 1858?–1924. Venezuelan soldier and politician. **2. Fidel.** b. 1927. Cuban revolutionary premier (since 1959).

Fidel Castro

Cates·by (kāts′bē). **1. Robert.** 1573–1605. English conspirator. **2. Mark.** 1679?–1749. English naturalist.

Cath·er (kăth′ər, kă*th*′-), **Willa Sibert.** 1873–1947. Amer. author.

Cath·e·rine (kăth′ər-ĭn, kăth′rĭn). **1. of Si·en·a** (syĕ′nä), Saint. 1347–80. Italian religious leader. **2. of Ar·a·gon** (ăr′ə-gən, -gŏn′). 1485–1536. Queen of England as 1st wife of Henry VIII. **3. de Mé·di·cis** (kä-tə-rēn′ də mā-dē-sēs′). 1519–89. Queen of France as wife of Henry II and regent (1560–63). **4. of Bra·gan·za** (brə-găn′zə). 1638–1705. Wife of Charles II of England. **5.** Name of 2 empresses of Russia: **a. I.** 1684?–1727. Wife and successor of Peter the Great; ruled 1725–27. **b. II.** "the Great." 1729–96. Ruled 1762–96.

Cat·i·line (kăt′l-īn′). 108?–62 B.C. Roman politician and conspirator.

Cat·lin (kăt′lĭn), **George.** 1796–1872. Amer. artist.

Ca·to (kā′tō), **Marcus Porcius. 1.** "the Elder," "the Censor." 234–149 B.C. Roman statesman and general. **2.** "the Younger." 95–46 B.C. Roman statesman and philosopher.

Cat·ron (kăt′rən), **John.** 1786?–1865. Amer. jurist.

Catt (kăt), **Carrie (Clinton Lane) Chapman.** 1859–1947. Amer. suffragist.

Carrie Chapman Catt

Cat·ton (kăt′n), **(Charles) Bruce.** 1899–1978. Amer. historian, author, and editor.

Ca·tul·lus (kə-tŭl′əs), **Gaius Valerius.** 84?–54? B.C. Roman poet.

Cav·ell (kăv′əl, kə-vĕl′), **Edith Louisa.** 1865–1915. English nurse; executed.

Cav·en·dish (kăv′ən-dĭsh). **1.** Sir **William.** 1505?–57. English politician. **2. Thomas.** 1555?–92. English navigator. **3. Henry.** 1731–1810. English chemist and physicist. **4. Spencer Compton.** Marquis of Compton, 8th Duke of Devonshire. 1833–1908. English statesman.

Ca·vour (kə-vo͝or′, kä-vo͝or′), Conte **Camillo Benso di.** 1810–61. Italian political leader.

Ca·xi·as (kə-shē′əs), Duque de. Luiz Alves de Lima e Silva. 1803–80. Brazilian general and statesman.

Cax·ton (kăk′stən), **William.** 1422?–91. 1st English printer.

Ceau·ses·cu (chou-shĕs′ko͞o), **Nicolae.** b. 1918. Rumanian statesman.

Cec·il (sĕs′əl). **1. William.** 1st Baron Burghley or Burleigh. 1520–98. English statesman. **2. Robert.** 1st Earl of Salisbury, 1st Viscount Cranborne. 1563?–1612. English statesman. **3. Robert Arthur Talbot Gascoyne.** 3rd Marquis of Salisbury. 1830–1903. British prime minister (1885–92, 1895–1902). **4. (Edgar Algernon) Robert.** 1st Viscount Cecil of Chelwood. 1864–1958. English statesman (Nobel, 1937).

Ce·cil·ia (sĭ-sēl′yə), Saint. 3rd cent. Christian martyr.

Cel·li·ni (chə-lē′nē, chĕl′lē-nē), **Benvenuto.** 1500–71. Italian artist.

Cel·si·us (sĕl′sē-əs, -shē-, -shəs), **Anders.** 1701–44. Swedish astronomer.

Cen·ci (chĕn′chē), **Beatrice.** 1577–99. Italian noblewoman; hanged for patricide.

Cerf (sûrf), **Bennett Alfred.** 1898–1971. Amer. editor and publisher.

Cer·van·tes Saa·ve·dra (sər-văn′tēz sə-vä′drə, sĕr-vän′tĕs sä-vĕ′*th*rä), **Miguel de.** 1547–1616. Spanish author (*Don Quixote*).

Cé·zanne (sā-zän′), **Paul.** 1839–1906. French artist.

Chad·wick (chăd′wĭk). **1. Henry.** 1824–1908. English-born Amer. sportswriter. **2.** Sir **James.** 1891–1974. English physicist (Nobel, 1935).

Cha·fee (chā′fē), **Zechariah.** 1885–1957. Amer. lawyer and civil libertarian.

Cha·gall (shə-gäl′, -găl′, shä-), **Marc.** 1887–1985. Russian-born artist.

Cha·ga·ti (chăg′ə-tī′). Jagatai.

Chain (chān), **Ernst Boris.** 1906–79. German-born British biochemist (Nobel, 1945).

Cha·lia·pin (shä-lyä′pĭn), **Feodor Ivanovich.** 1873–1938. Russian-born French operatic basso.

Cham·ber·lain (chām′bər-lĭn). **1.** Family of English statesmen, including **Joseph** (1836–1914), Sir **(Joseph) Austen** (1863–1937; Nobel, 1925), and **(Arthur) Neville** (1869–1940; prime minister 1937–40). **2. Owen.** b. 1920. Amer. physicist (Nobel, 1959).

Cham·ber·lin (chām′bər-lĭn), **Thomas Chrowder.** 1843–1928. Amer. geologist.

Cham·bers (chām′bərz). **1. Robert.** 1802–71. Scottish publisher and author. **2. (Jay David) Whittaker.** 1901–61. Amer. journalist and recanted Communist agent.

Cham·bord (shäN-bôr′), Comte de. **Henri Charles Ferdinand Marie Dieudonné d'Artois.** Duc de Bordeaux. 1820–83. Bourbon claimant to the French throne.

Cham·pi·on (chămp′yən), **Gower.** 1921–80. Amer. dancer and choreographer.

Cham·plain (shăm-plān′, shäN-plăN′), **Samuel de.** 1567?–1635. French explorer.

Cham·pol·lion (shäN-pô-lyôN′), **Jean François.** 1790–1832. French pioneer Egyptologist.

Chand·ler (chănd′lər, chänd′-). **1. Charles Frederick.** 1836–1925. Amer. chemist and public-health pioneer. **2. Raymond Thornton.** 1888–1959. Amer. author.

Chan·dra·gup·ta (chŭn′drə-go͞op′tə). **1.** d. 286? B.C. Indian king (322?–298). **2. I.** Indian king (320–30?). **3. II.** Indian king (383?–413).

Cha·nel (shə-nĕl′, shä-, shăn-ĕl′), **Gabrielle Bonheur ("Coco").** 1883–1971. French fashion designer.

Cha·ney (chā′nē), **Lon.** 1883–1930. Amer. actor.

Chan·ning (chăn′ĭng). **1. William Ellery.** 1780–1842. Amer. religious leader. **2. Edward.** 1856–1931. Amer. historian.

Cha·nute (shə-no͞ot′), **Octave.** 1832–1910. French-born Amer. engineer and aviation pioneer.

Chao K'uang-yin (jou′ kwäng′yĭn′). Zhao Kuangyin.

Chap·lin (chăp′lĭn), Sir **Charles Spencer ("Charlie").** 1889–1977. British-born actor, director, and producer.

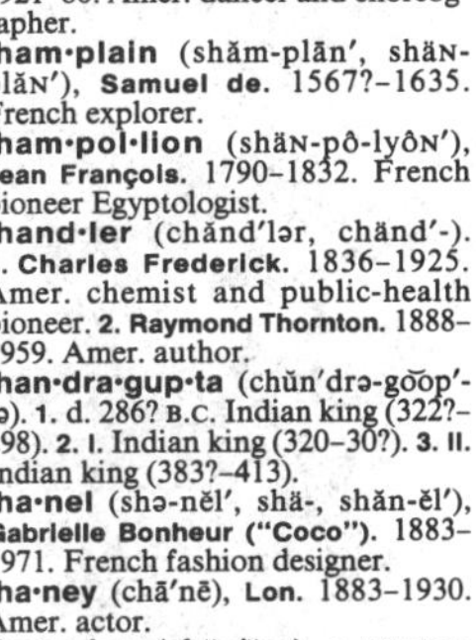

Charlie Chaplin

Chap·man (chăp′mən). **1. George.** 1559?–1634. English author, dramatist, and translator. **2. John.** "Johnny Appleseed." 1775?–1845. Amer. pioneer. **3. John Jay.** 1862–1933. Amer. author. **4. Frank Michler.** 1864–1945. Amer. ornithologist.

Char·cot (shär-kō′). **1. Jean Martin.** 1825–93. French neurologist. **2. Jean Baptiste Étienne Auguste.** 1867–1936. French physician and Antarctic explorer.

Char·le·magne (shär′lə-mān′, shär-lə-mä′nyə). "Charles I," "Charles the Great." 742–814. King of the Franks (768–814) and emperor of the West (800–14).

Charles (chärlz). **1.** Name of 7 Holy Roman Emperors, esp.: **a. I.** "the Great." Charlemagne. **b. II.** "the Bald." 823–77. Ruled 875–77; king of France as **Charles I** (840–77). **c. V.** 1500–58. Ruled 1519; king of Spain as **Charles I** (1516–56). **2.** Name of 10 kings of France, esp.: **a. IV.** "the Fair." 1294–1328. Ruled 1322–28. **b. V.** "the Wise." 1337–80. Ruled 1364–80. **c. VI.** "the Well Beloved." 1368–1422. Ruled 1380–1422. **d. VII.** 1403–61. Ruled 1422–61. **e. IX.** 1550–74. Ruled 1560–74. **f. X.** 1757–1836. Ruled 1824–30. **3.** Name of 2 kings of England: **a. I.** 1600–49. Ruled 1625–49; beheaded. **b. II.** 1630–85. Ruled 1649–85. **4.** Name of 15 kings of Sweden, esp.: **a. XII.** 1682–1718. Ruled 1697–1718. **b. XIV.** Jean Baptiste Jules Bernadotte. 1763–1844. Ruled 1818–44. **5. Jacques Alexandre César.** 1746–1823. French physicist. **6. I.** 1887–1922. Austrian emperor (1916–18); deposed. **7. Ray.** b. 1930. Amer. singer and composer. **8.** Prince of Wales. b. 1948. English heir apparent.

Charles Ed·ward Stu·art (ĕd′wərd sto͞o′ərt, styo͞o′-). See **Stuart.**

Charles Lou·is (lo͞o′ē). 1771–1847. Austrian archduke and military leader.

Charles Mar·tel (mär-tĕl′). 689–741. Frankish ruler of Austrasia (715–41).

Chase (chās). **1. Samuel.** 1741–1811. Amer. jurist and Revolutionary War leader. **2. Philander.** 1775–1852. Amer. religious leader. **3. Salmon Portland.** 1808–73. Amer. jurist and politician. **4. Mary Ellen.** 1887–1973. Amer. author and educator. **5. Stuart.** b. 1888. Amer. economist.

Châ·teau·bri·and (shä-tō′brē-äN′, shăt-ō′-), Vicomte **François René de.** 1768–1848. French political leader, diplomat, and author.

Chat·ham (chăt′əm), 1st Earl of. William Pitt.

Chat·ter·ton (chăt′ər-tn), **Thomas.** 1752–70. English poet.

Chau·cer (chô′sər), **Geoffrey.** 1340?–1400. English poet (*Canterbury Tales*). **—Chau·cer′i·an** *adj. & n.*

Chaun·cy (chôn′sē, chŏn′-), **Charles.** 1706?–87. Amer. religious leader.

Chau·temps (shō-täN′), **Camille.** 1885–1963. French statesman.

Cha·vannes (shä-văn′), **Pierre Puvis de.** See **Puvis de Chavannes.**

Chá·vez (chä′vĕz′, -vĕs′). **1. Carlos.** 1899–1978. Mexican conductor and composer. **2. Cesar Estrada.** b. 1927. Amer. labor organizer.

Cesar Chávez

Cha·yef·sky (chī-ĕf′skē, chä-), **Paddy.** 1923–81. Amer. playwright and screenwriter.

Chee·ver (chē′vər), **John.** 1912–82. Amer. author.

Che·khov also **Che·kov** or **Tche·khov** (chĕk′ôf, -ŏf, -ŏv, chĕ′KHôf), **Anton Pavlovich.** 1860–1904. Russian author. **—Che·kho′vi·an** *adj.*

Chen also **Ch'ên** (chŭn). Chinese dynasty (557–89).

Ché·nier (shā-nyā′), **André Marie de.** 1762–94. French poet; guillotined.

Chen·nault (shə-nôlt′), **Claire Lee.** 1890–1958. Amer. air-force officer.

Che·ops (kē′ŏps). Egyptian king (2900–1877 B.C.).

Che·ren·kov (chə-rĕng′kôf, -kəf), **Pavel Alekseevich.** b. 1904. Soviet physicist (Nobel, 1958).

Che·ru·bi·ni (kĕr′o͞o-bē′nē, kā′ro͞o-), **(Maria) Luigi Carlo Zenobio Salvatore.** 1760–1842. Italian composer.

Ches·nutt (chĕs′nŭt′), **Charles Waddell.** 1858–1932. Amer. lawyer and author.

Ches·ter·field (chĕs′tər-fēld′), 4th Earl of. Philip Dormer Stanhope. 1694–1773. English statesman and author.

Ches·ter·ton (chĕs′tər-tən), **Gilbert Keith.** 1874–1936. English author.

Che·va·lier (shə-văl′yā, -väl′-, shə-vä-lyā′), **Maurice.** 1888–1972. French actor and singer.

Ch'i (chyē). Qi.

Chiang Kai-shek (chăng′ kī′shĕk′, chyäng′, jē-äng′, jyäng′). 1887–1975. Chinese military and political leader; exiled in Taiwan (1949–75).

Ch'ien-lung (chyĕn′lo͞ong′, chē-ĕn′-). Qianlong.

Chif·ley (chĭf′lē), **Joseph Benedict.** 1885–1951. Australian statesman.

Chi·ka·ma·tsu Mon·za·e·mon (chē′kä-mät′so͞o môn′zä-ĕ-môn′). 1653?–1724. Japanese playwright.

Child (chīld). **1. Lydia Maria Francis.** 1802–80. Amer. author and abolitionist. **2. Francis James.** 1825–96. Amer. philologist and educator. **3. Julia.** b. 1912. Amer. cookery expert.

Chil·ders (chĭl′dərz), **Erskine Hamilton.** 1905–74. Irish statesman.

Chin (jĭn). Jin.

Ch'in (chĭn). Qin.

Ch'ing (chĭng). Qing.

Chip·pen·dale (chĭp′ən-dāl′), **Thomas.** 1718?–1779. English cabinetmaker.

Chi·ri·co (kĭr′ĭ-kō′, kē′rē-kô), **Giorgio de.** 1888–1978. Italian painter.

Chis·holm (chĭz′əm), **Shirley Anita St. Hill.** b. 1924. Amer. politician.

Shirley Chisholm

Chi·sum (chĭz′əm), **John Simpson.** 1824–84. Amer. cattleman.

Choate (chōt). **1. Rufus.** 1799–1859. Amer. politician. **2. Joseph Hodges.** 1832–1917. Amer. lawyer and diplomat.

Choi·seul (shwä-zœl′), Duc **Étienne François de.** 1719–85. French diplomat and statesman.

Chom·sky (chŏm′skē), **Noam.** b. 1928. Amer. linguist.

Cho·pin (shō′păn′, -păN′, shô-păN′). **1. Frédéric François.** 1810–49. Polish-born French composer. **2. Kate O'Flaherty.** 1851–1904. Amer. author.

Chou or **Chow** (jō). Zhou.

Chou En-lai (jō′ ĕn′lī′). Zhou Enlai.

Chou·teau (sho͞o-tō′). Amer. family of pioneers and fur traders, including **René Auguste** (1749–1829), **Jean Pierre** (1758–1849), **Auguste Pierre** (1786–1838), and **Pierre** (1789–1865).

Chré·tien also **Chré·tien de Troyes** (krā-tyăN dĭ trwä). 12th cent. French trouvère.

Christ (krīst). Jesus.

Chris·tian X (krĭs′chən). 1870–1947. Danish king (1912–47).

Chris·tie (krĭs′tē), Dame **Agatha.** 1891–1976. English mystery writer and playwright.

Chris·ti·na (krĭ-stē′nə). 1626–89. Swedish queen (1632–54); abdicated.

Chris·tophe (krē-stôf′), **Henri.** 1767–1820. Haitian king (1811–20).

Chris·to·pher (krĭs′tə-fər), Saint. fl. 3rd cent. Christian martyr.

Chris·ty (krĭs′tē). **1. Edwin P.** 1815–62. Amer. minstrel-show producer. **2. Howard Chandler.** 1873–1952. Amer. artist.

Chrys·ler (krīs'lər), **Walter Percy.** 1875–1940. Amer. automobile manufacturer.

Chry·sos·tom (krĭs'əs-təm, krĭ-sŏs'-), Saint **John.** 345?–407. Antioch-born Greek church father.

Church (chûrch). **1. Benjamin.** 1734–78? Amer. physician, soldier, and spy. **2. Frederick Edwin.** 1826–1900. Amer. painter.

Chur·chill (chûr'chĭl', chûrch'hĭl'). **1. John.** 1st Duke of Marlborough. 1650–1722. English general and statesman. **2. Randolph Henry Spencer.** 1849–95. English politician. **3. Jennie Jerome.** 1854–1921. Amer. socialite. **4. Winston.** 1871–1947. Amer. author. **5.** Sir **Winston Leonard Spencer.** 1874–1965. English prime minister (1940–45 and 1951–55; Nobel, 1953).

Winston Churchill

Chu Teh (jo͞o' dŭ'). Zhu De.

Cia·no (chä'nō), Conte **Galeazzo.** 1903–44. Italian Fascist statesman; executed.

Ciar·di (chär'dē), **John Anthony.** 1916–86. Amer. poet and author.

Cib·ber (sĭb'ər), **Colley.** 1671–1757. English author, playwright, and theatrical manager.

Cic·e·ro (sĭs'ə-rō'), **Marcus Tullius.** 106–43 B.C. Roman statesman, orator, and philosopher. **—Cic'e·ro'ni·an** *adj.*

Cid (sĭd, sēd), **the.** Rodrigo or Ruy Díaz de Bivar. 1040?–99. Spanish soldier and national hero.

Ci·ma·bu·e (chē'mä-bo͞o'ā), **Giovanni.** Late 13th cent. Italian painter.

Ci·mon (sī'mən, -mŏn'). 507?–449 B.C. Athenian military and political leader.

Cin·ci·na·tus (sĭn'sə-nā'təs, -năt'əs), **Lucius Quinctius.** 519?–439 B.C. Roman general.

Clair (klâr, klĕr), **René.** 1898–1981. French film director.

Clar·en·don (klăr'ən-dən), 1st Earl of. Edward Hyde. 1609–74. English statesman and historian.

Clare of As·si·si (klâr; ə-sē'zē, -sē) or **Clar·a** (klâr'ə, klăr'ə), Saint. 1194–1253. Italian nun and religious leader.

Clark (klärk). **1. George Rogers.** 1752–1818. Amer. military leader and frontiersman. **2. William.** 1770–1838. Amer. Western explorer, military officer, and public official. **3. Alvan.** 1804–87. Amer. astronomer and lens manufacturer. **4. John Bates.** 1847–1938. Amer. economist. **5. James Beauchamp ("Champ").** 1850–1921. Amer. legislator. **6. Mark Wayne.** 1896–1984. Amer. army officer. **7. Tom Campbell.** 1899–1977. Amer. jurist. **8. Kenneth Bancroft.** b. 1914. Panamanian-born Amer. psychologist and author. **9. Charles Joseph ("Joe").** b. 1939. Canadian prime minister (1979–80).

Clarke (klärk). **1. Charles Cowden** (1787–1877) and **Mary Victoria Cowden** (1809–98). English Shakespearean scholars. **2. James Freeman.** 1810–88. Amer. religious leader, Transcendentalist, and reformer. **3. John Hessin.** 1857–1945. Amer. jurist. **4. Helen Archibald.** 1860–1926. Amer. editor and critic.

Claude (klōd), **Albert.** 1898–1983. Luxembourg-born biologist (Nobel, 1974).

Clau·del (klō-dĕl'), **Paul Louis Charles.** 1868–1955. French author.

Clau·di·us (klô'dē-əs). **1. Appius.** "Crassus." 471–451 B.C. Roman consul. **2. Appius.** "Caecus." 312–307? B.C. Roman statesman. **3.** Name of 2 Roman emperors: **a. I.** 10 B.C.–A.D. 54. Ruled 41–54. **b. II.** "Gothicus." 214–70. Ruled 268–70.

Clau·se·witz (klou'zə-vĭts), **Karl von.** 1780–1831. Prussian army officer and military theorist.

Clay (klā). **1. Henry.** 1777–1852. Amer. statesman. **2. Cassius Marcellus.** 1810–1903. Amer. political figure and abolitionist. **3. Lucius DuBignon.** 1897–1978. Amer. army officer and engineer. **4. Cassius Marcellus.** See Muhammad **Ali.**

Clay·ton (klāt'n), **John Middleton.** 1796–1856. Amer. politician and diplomat.

Cle·an·thes (klē-ăn'thēz'). 331?–232? B.C. Greek philosopher.

Cle·ar·chus (klē-är'kəs). d. 401 B.C. Greek military leader.

Cleis·the·nes (klīs'thə-nēz') or **Clis·the·nes** (klĭs'-). 6th cent. B.C. Greek tyrant.

Cle·men·ceau (klĕm'ən-sō', klĕ-mäN-sō'), **Georges.** 1841–1929. French statesman.

Clem·ens (klĕm'ənz), **Samuel Langhorne.** "Mark Twain." 1835–1910. Amer. author and humorist.

Clem·ent (klĕm'ənt). **1.** Name of 14 popes, esp.: **a. I.** Saint. "Clement of Rome." 1st cent. A.D. Reigned A.D. 88–97. **b. V.** 1264–1314. Reigned 1305–14. **c. VII.** 1478–1534. Reigned 1523–1534. **2. of Al·ex·an·dri·a** (ăl'ĭg-zăn'drē-ə). 150?–220? Greek Christian theologian.

Cle·on (klē'ŏn). d. 422 B.C. Athenian political and military leader.

Cle·o·pat·ra (klē'ə-păt'rə, -pä'trə, -pā'-). 69–30 B.C. Egyptian queen.

Cleve·land (klēv'lənd), **(Stephen) Grover.** 1837–1908. 22nd and 24th U.S. President (1885–89 and 1893–97).

Grover Cleveland

Cli·burn (klī'bərn), **Van.** b. 1934. Amer. pianist.

Clif·ford (klĭf'ərd). **1. Nathan.** 1803–81. Amer. jurist. **2. Clark McAdams.** b. 1906. Amer. lawyer and public official.

Clift (klĭft), **Montgomery.** 1920–66. Amer. actor.

Clin·ton (klĭn'tən). **1. George.** 1686?–1761. English admiral and colonial administrator. **2. James.** 1733–1812. Amer. military leader. **3.** Sir **Henry.** 1738–95. English general in America. **4. George.** 1739–1812. U.S. Vice President (1805–12). **5. DeWitt.** 1769–1828. Amer. politician.

Clis·the·nes (klĭs'thə-nēz'). Variant of **Cleisthenes.**

Clive (klīv), **Robert.** Baron Clive of Plassey. 1725–74. English colonial administrator in India.

Clough (klŭf), **Arthur Hugh.** 1819–61. English poet.

Clo·vis I (klō'vĭs, klô-vēs'). 466?–511. Frankish king (481–511).

Clur·man (klûr'mən), **Harold.** 1901–80. Amer. theatrical director and critic.

Cnut (kə-no͞ot', -nyo͞ot'). Variant of **Canute.**

Cobb (kŏb). **1. Irwin Shrewsbury.** 1876–1944. Amer. humorist and author. **2. Tyrus Raymond ("Ty").** 1886–1961. Amer. baseball player and manager.

Cob·bett (kŏb'ĭt), **William.** 1763?–1835. English journalist and social reformer.

Cob·den (kŏb'dən), **Richard.** 1804–65. English statesman and reformer.

Co·ca (kō'kə), **Imogene.** b. 1914? Amer. comedienne.

Co·chise (kō-chēs', chēz'). 1812?–74. Amer. Apache chief.

Coch·ran (kŏk'rən), **Jacqueline.** 1910–80. Amer. aviator and businesswoman.

Cock·croft (kŏk'krôft', -krŏft'), Sir **John Douglas.** 1897–1967. English physicist (Nobel, 1951).

Coc·teau (kŏk-tō', kôk-), **Jean.** 1891?–1963. French modernist author.

Co·dy (kō'dē), **William Frederick.** "Buffalo Bill." 1846–1917. Amer. frontier scout and showman.

William F. Cody
"Buffalo Bill"

Coeur de Lion (kûr' de lē'ən, kœr də lyôN'). Richard I of England.

Cof·fin (kô'fĭn, kŏf'ĭn). **1. Levi.** 1789–1877. Amer. abolitionist. **2. Robert Peter Tristam.** 1892–1955. Amer. author.

Co·han (kō'hăn', kō-hăn'), **George Michael.** 1878–1942. Amer. singer, songwriter, and playwright.

Co·hen (kō'ən), **Morris Raphael.** 1880–1947. Russian-born Amer. educator and philosopher.

Cohn (kōn), **Ferdinand Julius.** 1828–98. German botanist and bacteriologist.

Coke (ko͝ok, kōk), Sir **Edward.** 1552–1634. English jurist.

Col·bert (kôl-bĕr', kōl-), **Jean Baptiste.** 1619–83. French statesman.

Col·den (kōl'dən), **Cadwallader.** 1688–1776. Irish-born Loyalist official, scientist, and philosopher.

Cole (kōl). **1. Thomas.** 1801–48. Amer. painter. **2. Nat ("King").** 1919–65. Amer. singer and pianist.

Cole·ridge (kōl'rĭj, kō'lə-rĭj), **Samuel Taylor.** 1772–1834. English poet, critic, and theologian.

Col·et (kŏl'ət), **John.** 1467?–1519. English scholar and theologian.

Co·lette (kō-lĕt', kô-), **(Sidonie Gabrielle Claudine).** 1873–1954. French novelist.

Col·fax (kōl'făks), **Schuyler.** 1823–85. U.S. Vice President (1869–73).

Col·gate (kōl'gāt'), **William.** 1783–1857. Amer. manufacturer and philanthropist.

Co·li·gny or **Co·li·gni** (kô-lē-nyē'), **Gaspard de.** 1519–72. French general and Huguenot leader.

Col·lier (kŏl'yər, -ē-ər). **1. Jeremy.** 1650–1726. English clergyman. **2. John Payne.** 1789–1883. English lawyer and critic. **3. John.** 1884–1968. Amer. sociologist and public official.

Col·lins (kŏl'ĭnz). **1. William.** 1721–59. English poet. **2. (William) Wilkie.** 1824–89. English novelist. **3. Michael.** 1890–1922. Irish Sinn Fein leader.

Col·man (kōl'mən). **1. George.** "Colman the Elder." 1732–94. English author and theater manager. **2. Ronald.** 1891–1958. English actor.

Colt (kōlt), **Samuel.** 1814–62. Amer. inventor and firearms manufacturer.

Col·um. 1. (kŭl'əm). *Irish.* St. Columba. **2.** (kŏl'əm), **Padraic** (1881–1972 and **Mary Maguire Gunning** (1887?–1957). Irish-born poets and playwrights.

Co·lum·ba (kə-lŭm'bə), Saint. 521–597. Irish missionary.

Co·lum·bus (kə-lŭm'bəs), **Christopher.** 1451?–1506. Italian navigator in service of Spain; traditional discoverer of America. **—Co·lum'bi·an** *adj.*

Christopher Columbus

Com·a·ne·ci (kō-mə-nĕch'), **Nadia.** b. 1961. Rumanian gymnast.

Co·me·ni·us (kə-mē'nē-əs), **John Amos.** 1592–1670. Czech educational reformer, scholar, and theologian.

Co·mines also **Com·mines** or **Com·mynes** or **Co·mynes** (kô-mēn'), **Philipe de.** 1447?–1511. French diplomat, political adviser, and historian.

Com·ma·ger (kŏm'ə-jər), **Henry Steele.** b. 1902. Amer. historian.

Com·mo·dus (kŏm'ə-dəs), **Lucius Aelius Aurelius.** 161–192. Roman emperor (180–92).

Com·mons (kŏm'ənz), **John Rogers.** 1862–1945. Amer. political economist.

Comp·ton (kŏmp'tən), **Karl Taylor** (1887–1954) and **Arthur Holly** (1892–1962; Nobel, 1927). Amer. physicists.

Comp·ton–Bur·nett (kŏmp'-tən-bər-nĕt'), **Ivy.** 1892–1969. English author.

Com·stock (kŭm'stŏk', kŏm'-). **1. Elizabeth Leslie Rous.** 1815–91. English-born Amer. Quaker leader. **2. Anthony.** 1844–1915. Amer. social reformer. **3. Anna Botsford.** 1854–1930. Amer. author, wood engraver, and naturalist.

Comte (kōnt, kônt), **(Isidore) Auguste (Marie François).** 1798–1857. French philosopher and mathematician.

Co·nant (kō'nənt), **James Bryant.** 1893–1978. Amer. educator and diplomat.

Con·boy (kŏn'boi), **Sara Agnes McLaughlin.** 1870–1928. Amer. labor leader.

Con·dé (kôN-dā'), Prince de. Louis II de Bourbon. "the Great Condé." 1621–87. French general.

Con·don (kŏn'dən), **Edward Uhler.** 1902–74. Amer. physicist.

Con·dor·cet (kôn-dôr-sĕ'), Marquis de. Marie Jean Antoine Nicolas Caritat. 1743–94. French revolutionary, philosopher, and mathematician.

Con·fu·cius (kən-fyo͞o'shəs). 551–479 B.C. Chinese philosopher and educator. **—Con·fu'cian** *adj. & n.*

Confucius

Con·greve (kŏn′grēv′, kŏng′-), **William.** 1670–1729. English playwright.
Conk·ling (kŏngk′lĭng), **Roscoe.** 1829–88. Amer. politician.
Con·nal·ly (kŏn′ə-lē, kŏn′lē), **John Bowden.** b. 1917. Amer. politician.
Con·nel·ly (kŏn′ə-lē), **Marcus Cook ("Marc").** 1890–1980. Amer. playwright, producer, and director.
Con·nol·ly (kŏn′ə-lē), **Maureen Catherine ("Little Mo").** 1934–69. Amer. tennis player.
Con·nors (kŏn′ərz), **James Scott ("Jimmy").** b. 1952. Amer. tennis player.
Con·rad (kŏn′răd′), **Joseph.** 1857–1924. Polish-born English novelist.
Con·sta·ble (kŭn′stə-bəl, kŏn′-), **John.** 1776–1837. English landscape painter.
Con·stant de Re·becque (kôN-stäN′ də rə-bĕk′), **Benjamin.** 1767–1830. French author and politician.
Con·stan·tine (kŏn′stən-tēn′, -tīn′). **1.** Name of 2 Roman emperors, esp. **I,** "the Great," 280?–337, ruled 306–37. **2. XI.** 1404?–53. Last Byzantine emperor (1448–53). **3.** Name of 2 Greek kings: **a. I.** 1868–1923. Ruled 1913–17, 1920–22; abdicated. **b. II.** b. 1940. Ruled 1964–73.
Con·ti (kŏn′tē), **Niccolò de′.** 15th cent. Italian merchant, traveler, and author.
Con·way (kŏn′wā), **Thomas.** 1735–1800? Irish-born Amer. Revolutionary general.
Con·well (kŏn′wĕl′, -wəl), **Russell Herman.** 1843–1925. Amer. clergyman and educator.
Cook (ko͝ok) **1. James.** "Captain Cook." 1728–79. English navigator and explorer; murdered in Sandwich Is. **2. Frederick Albert.** 1865–1940. Amer. physician and Arctic explorer.
Cooke (ko͝ok), **1. Jay.** 1821–1905. Amer. financier. **2. (Alfred) Alistair.** b. 1908. British-born Amer. broadcaster and author.
Coo·ley (ko͞o′lē). **1. Thomas McIntyre.** 1824–98. Amer. jurist. **2. Charles Horton.** 1864–1929. Amer. sociologist.
Coo·lidge (ko͞o′lĭj). **1. (John) Calvin.** 1872–1933. 30th U.S. President (1923–29). **2. Julian Lowell.** 1873–1954. Amer. mathematician and educator.

Calvin Coolidge

Coo·ney (ko͞o′nē), **Joan Ganz.** b. 1929. Amer. television producer.
Coo·per (ko͞o′pər, ko͝op′ər). **1. Thomas.** 1759–1839. English-born Amer. chemist and educator. **2. James Fenimore.** 1789–1851. Amer. novelist ("Leather-Stocking Tales"). **3. Peter.** 1791–1883. Amer. manufacturer, inventor, and philanthropist. **4. Gary.** 1906–61. Amer. actor. **5. Leon N.** b. 1930. Amer. physicist (Nobel, 1972).
Co·per·ni·cus (kō-pûr′nə-kəs, kə-), **Nicolaus.** 1473–1543. Polish astronomer. **—Co·per′ni·can** *adj.*
Cop·land (kŏp′lənd), **Aaron.** b. 1900. Amer. composer.
Cop·ley (kŏp′lē), **John Singleton.** 1738–1815. Amer. portrait painter.
Cop·pin (kŏp′ĭn), **Fanny Marion Jackson.** 1837–1913. Amer. educator and missionary.
Cor·bett (kôr′bət), **James John ("Gentleman Jim").** 1866–1933. Amer. boxer.
Cor·bin (kôr′bĭn), **Margaret Cochran.** 1751–1800. Amer. Revolutionary heroine.
Cor·co·ran (kôr′kə-rən). **1. William Wilson.** 1798–1888. Amer. banker, art collector, and philanthropist. **2. Thomas Gardiner.** 1900–81. Amer. public official.
Cor·day (kôr-dā′, kôr′dā), **Charlotte.** 1768–93. French revolutionary heroine; guillotined.
Co·rel·li (kə-rĕl′ē, kō-rĕl′lē), **Arcangelo.** 1653–1713. Italian violinist and composer.
Co·ri (kôr′ē, kŏr′ē), **Carl Ferdinand** (b. Czechoslovakia, 1896–1984) and **Gerty Theresa Radnitz** (1896–1957). Amer. biochemists (Nobel, 1947).
Cor·liss (kôr′lĭs), **George Henry.** 1817–88. Amer. inventor and manufacturer.
Cor·mack (kôr′mək), **Allan MacLeod.** b. 1924. South African-born Amer. physicist (Nobel, 1979).
Cor·neille (kôr-nā′), **Pierre.** 1606–84. French dramatist.
Cor·ne·lia (kôr-nēl′yə, -nē-lē-ə), 2nd cent. B.C. Roman matron.
Cor·ne·lius (kôr-nēl′yəs, -näl′-, -nā′-lē-o͞os′), **Peter von.** 1783–1867. German painter.
Cor·nell (kôr-nĕl′). **1. Ezra.** 1807–74. Amer. businessman and university benefactor. **2. Katherine.** 1898–1974. Amer. actress.
Corn·forth (kôrn′fərth, -fôrth′, -fōrth′), **John Warcup.** b. 1917. Australian-born British chemist (Nobel, 1975).
Corn·wal·lis (kôrn-wŏl′ĭs, -wô′lĭs), **Charles.** 1st Marquis and 2nd Earl Cornwallis. 1738–1805. English military and political leader.
Co·ro·na·do (kôr′ə-nä′dō, kôr′, kô′-rô-nä′*th*ô), **Francisco Vásquez de.** 1510–54. Spanish explorer and colonial administrator.
Co·rot (kô-rō′, kə-), **Jean Baptiste Camille.** 1796–1875. French painter.
Cor·reg·gio (kə-rĕj′ō, -ē-ō′, kô-rĕd′-jō), **Antonio Allegri da.** 1494–1534. Italian painter.
Cor·ri·gan (kôr′ĭ-gən), **Mairead.** b. 1944. Irish peace advocate (Nobel, 1976).
Cor·tel·you (kôr′tl-yo͞o′), **George Bruce.** 1862–1940. Amer. public official.
Cor·tés also **Cor·tez** (kôr-tĕz′, -tĕs′), **Hernando** or **Fernando.** 1485–1547. Spanish explorer and conquistador.
Cor·win (kôr′wĭn), **Edward Samuel.** 1878–1963. Amer. political scientist and educator.
Cos·by (kŏz′bē), **Bill.** b. 1937. Amer. comedian and actor.
Co·sell (kō-sĕl′), **Howard.** b. 1920. Amer. sportscaster.
Cos·grave (kŏz′grāv′), **William Thomas.** 1880–1965. Irish Sinn Fein leader.
Cos·ta Ca·bral (kôs′tə kə-bräl′, kôsh′-), **Antônio Bernardo da.** 1803–89. Portuguese statesman.
Cos·tel·lo (kŏs -tĕl′ō). **1. John Aloysius.** 1891–1976. Irish political leader. **2. Lou.** 1908–59. Amer. comedian.
Cot·ton (kŏt′n). **1. John.** 1584–1652. English-born Amer. clergyman. **2. Charles.** 1630–87. English poet and translator.
Co·ty (kō-tē′, kô-), **René.** 1882–1962. French statesman.
Cou·é (ko͞o-ā′, kwā), **Émile.** 1857–1926. French psychotherapist.
Coues (kouz), **Elliott.** 1842–99. Amer. ornithologist, biologist, and editor.
Cough·lin (kŏg′lĭn), **Charles Edward.** 1891–1979. Canadian-born Amer. priest and political activist.
Cou·lomb (ko͞o′lŏm′, -lōm′, ko͞o-lŏm′, -lôN′), **Charles Augustin de.** 1736–1806. French physicist.
Cou·pe·rin (ko͞op-răN′, ko͞o-pə-), **François.** 1668–1733. French composer and organist.
Cou·pe·rus (ko͞o-pä′ro͞os, -pĕr′əs), **Louis.** 1863–1923. Dutch novelist.
Cour·bet (ko͞or-bā′, -bĕ′), **Gustave.** 1819–77. French painter.
Cour·nand (ko͞or′nănd, -nənd, ko͞or-näN′), **André Frédéric.** b. 1895. French-born Amer. physiologist (Nobel, 1956).
Cour·règes (ko͞o-rĕzh′), **André.** b. 1923. French fashion designer.
Cous·ins (kŭz′ənz), **Norman.** b. 1915. Amer. editor and writer.
Cous·teau (ko͞o-stō′), **Jacques Yves.** b. 1910. French underwater explorer, film producer, and author.
Cou·sy (ko͞o′zē), **Robert Joseph ("Bob").** b. 1928. Amer. basketball player, coach, and sportscaster.
Co·var·ru·bias (kō′və-ro͞o′bē-əs, kô′vä-ro͞o′byäs), **Miguel.** 1904–57. Mexican artist and author.
Cov·er·dale (kŭv′ər-dāl′), **Miles.** 1488–1568. English clergyman and Bible translator.
Cow·ard (kou′ərd), Sir **Noel Pierce.** 1899–1973. English actor, author, and composer.
Cowl (koul), **Jane.** 1884?–1950. Amer. actress.
Cowles (koulz). **1. Henry Chandler.** 1869–1939. Amer. botanist and pioneer ecologist. **2. Gardner.** 1903–85. Amer. publisher.
Cow·ley (kou′lē). **1. Abraham.** 1618–67. English author. **2. Malcolm.** b. 1898. Amer. author, editor, and critic.
Cow·per (ko͞o′pər, kou′-, ko͝op′ər), **William.** 1731–1800. English poet.
Coxe (kŏks), **Tench.** 1755–1824. Amer. political economist.
Cox·ey (kŏk′sē), **Jacob Sechler.** 1854–1951. Amer. businessman and politician.
Coz·zens (kŭz′ənz), **James Gould.** 1903–78. Amer. author.
Crabbe (krăb), **George.** 1754–1832. English poet.
Craig (crāg), **(Edward) Gordon.** 1872–1966. English theatrical producer, director, and designer.
Craig·av·on (krā-găv′ən, -gā′vən), 1st Viscount. James Craig. 1871–1940. Northern Ireland statesman.
Crai·gie (krā′gē), Sir **William Alexander.** 1876–1957. English lexicographer and philologist.
Cram (krăm), **Ralph Adams.** 1863–1942. Amer. architect.
Cra·nach (krä′näKH), **Lucas.** 1472–1553. German artist.
Cran·dall (krăn′dəl) **Prudence.** 1803–90. Amer. educator and reformer.
Crane (krān). **1. Walter.** 1845–1915. English artist. **2. Winthrop Murray.** 1853–1920. Amer. manufacturer and legislator. **3. Stephen.** 1871–1900. Amer. author. **4. (Harold) Hart.** 1899–1932. Amer. poet.
Cran·mer (krăn′mər), **Thomas.** 1489–1556. English prelate and religious reformer.
Crap·sey (krăp′sē), **Adelaide.** 1878–1914. Amer. poet.
Crash·aw (krăsh′ô), **Richard.** 1613–49. English poet.
Cras·sus (krăs′əs), **Marcus Licinius.** 115?–53? B.C. Roman politician and general.
Cra·ter (krā′tər), **Joseph Force.** "Judge Crater." 1889–1937? Amer. jurist; disappeared.
Craw·ford (krô′fərd), **1. William Harris.** 1772–1834. Amer. public official. **2. Thomas.** 1814–57. Amer. sculptor. **3. Francis Marion.** 1854–1909. Amer. author. **4. Joan.** 1908–77. Amer. actress.
Cra·zy Horse (krā′zē hôrs′). 1849?–77. Amer. Indian leader.
Cré·bil·lon (krā-bē-yôN′), **Prosper Jolyot de.** 1674–1762. French poet.
Cre·mer (krē′mər), Sir **William Randal.** 1838–1908. English pacifist (Nobel, 1903).
Crève·coeur (krĕv-kœr′), **Michel Guillaume Jean de.** 1731?–1813. French agriculturalist, author, and diplomat.
Crich·ton (krīt′n), **James.** "the Admirable Crichton." 1560?–82. Scottish adventurer, linguist, and scholar.
Crick (krĭk), **Francis Henry Compton.** b. 1916. British biologist (Nobel, 1962).
Crile (krīl), **George Washington.** 1864–1943. Amer. surgeon.
Cripps (krĭps), Sir **(Richard) Stafford.** 1889–1952. English statesman.
Cris·pi (krĭs′pē, krē′spē), **Francesco.** 1819–1901. Italian statesman.
Cris·pin (krĭs′pĭn), Saint. 3rd cent. Christian martyr.
Crit·ten·den (krĭt′n-dən), **John Jordan.** 1787–1863. Amer. politician.
Cro·ce (krō′chā), **Benedetto.** 1866–1952. Italian philosopher, historian, and critic.
Crock·er (krŏk′ər), **Charles.** 1822–88. Amer. railroad financier.
Crock·ett (krŏk′ĭt), **David ("Davy").** 1786–1836. Amer. politician and frontiersman; died at the Alamo.

Davy Crockett

Croe·sus (krē′səs). d. 546 B.C. Lydian king (560–46).
Cro·ghan (krō′gən), **George.** 1720?–82. Irish-born Amer. Indian agent and land speculator.
Cro·ly (krō′lē). **1. Jane Cunningham.** 1829–1901. Amer. author, editor, and feminist. **2. Herbert David.** 1869–1930. Amer. author and editor.
Cromp·ton (krŏmp′tən), **Samuel.** 1753–1927. English inventor.
Crom·well (krŏm′wĕl′, -wəl, krŭm′-). **1. Thomas.** Earl of Essex. 1485?–1540. English statesman; executed. **2. Oliver** (1599–1658) and **Richard** (1626–1712). English military, political, and religious leaders. **—Crom·well′i·an** *adj.*

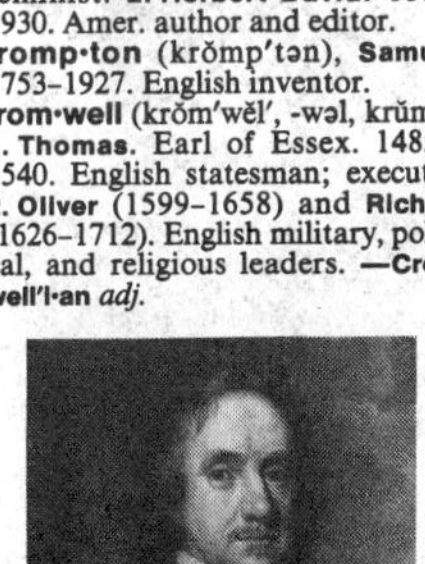

Oliver Cromwell

Cro·nin (krō′nĭn). **1. Archibald Joseph ("A. J.").** 1896–1981. English physician and novelist. **2. James W.** b. 1931. Amer. educator and physicist (Nobel, 1980).
Cron·je (krôn′yā), **Piet Arnoldus.** 1840?–1911. Boer general.
Cron·kite (krŏn′kīt, krŏng′-), **Walter Leland, Jr.** b. 1916. Amer. broadcast journalist.
Crook (kro͝ok), **George.** 1829–90. Amer. general and Indian fighter.
Crookes (kro͝oks), Sir **William.** 1832–1919. English chemist and physicist.
Cros·by (krôz′bē, krŏz′-). **1. Frances Jane ("Fanny").** 1820–1915. Amer. hymn writer and poet. **2. Harry Lillis ("Bing").** 1903–77. Amer. singer and actor.
Cross (krôs, krŏs). **1. Wilbur Lucius.** 1862–1948. Amer. politician and educator. **2. Milton.** 1897–1975. Amer. opera commentator.
Croth·ers (krŭ*th*′ərz), **Rachel.** 1878–1958. Amer. playwright, director, and producer.
Crouse (krous), **Russel.** 1893–1966. Amer. author.
Cruik·shank (kro͝ok′shăngk′), **George.** 1792–1878. English artist.
Cu·kor (kyo͞o′kər, -kôr, ko͞o′-). **George.** 1899–1983. Amer. filmmaker.
Cul·bert·son (kŭl′bərt-sən), **Ely.**

1891–1955. Amer. contract bridge authority.
Cul·len (kŭl′ən), **Countée.** 1903–46. Amer. poet.
Cul·pep·er (kŭl′pĕp′ər), Lord **Thomas.** 1635–89. English colonial administrator.
Cum·mings (kŭm′ĭngz), **Edward Estlin.** "e. e. cummings." 1894–1962. Amer. poet.
Cun·ha (ko͞o′nyə), **Tristão da.** 1460?–1540. Portuguese navigator and explorer.
Cun·ning·ham (kŭn′ĭng-hăm′, -əm). **1. Allen.** 1784–1842. Scottish author. **2. Kate Richards O'Hare.** 1877–1948. Amer. socialist and reformer. **3. Merce.** b. 1922? Amer. dancer and choreographer.
Cu·rie (kyo͝o-rē′, kü-, kyo͝or′ē). **1. Pierre** (1859–1906) and **Marie** (b. Poland, 1867–1934). French chemists and physicists (shared Nobel, 1903). **2.** Also **Cu·rie-Jo·liot** (-zhô-lyō′), **Irene.** See **Joliot-Curie. 3. Eve Denise.** b. 1904. French pianist, author, and editor.

Marie Curie

Cur·ley (kûr′lē), **James Michael.** 1874–1958. Amer. politician.
Cur·ri·er (kûr′ē-ər, kŭr′), **Nathaniel.** 1813–88. Amer. lithographer.
Cur·ry (kûr′ē, kŭr′ē), **John Steuart.** 1897–1946. Amer. painter.
Cur·tin (kûr′tn), **John.** 1885–1945. Australian statesman.
Cur·tis (kûr′tĭs). **1. Benjamin Robbins.** 1809–74. Amer. jurist. **2. George Ticknor.** 1812–94. Amer. lawyer, politician, and author. **3. George William.** 1824–92. Amer. journalist and reformer. **4. Cyrus Hermann Kotzschmar.** 1850–1933. Amer. publisher. **5. Charles.** 1860–1936. U.S. Vice President (1929–33).
Cur·tiss (kûr′tĭs), **Glenn Hammond.** 1878–1930. Amer. aviation pioneer.
Cur·wen (kûr′wən), **John.** 1816–80. English music educator and publisher.
Cur·zon (kûr′zən), **George Nathaniel.** 1859–1925. English colonial administrator.
Cush·ing (ko͝osh′ĭng). **1. William.** 1732–1810. Amer. jurist. **2. Caleb.** 1800–79. Amer. politician and diplomat. **3. William Barker.** 1842–74. Amer. Civil War naval hero. **4. Harvey Williams.** 1869–1939. Amer. brain surgeon.
Cush·man (ko͝osh′mən), **Charlotte Saunders.** 1816–76. Amer. actress.
Cus·ter (kŭs′tər). **George Armstrong.** 1839–76. Amer. general; killed at Little Bighorn.

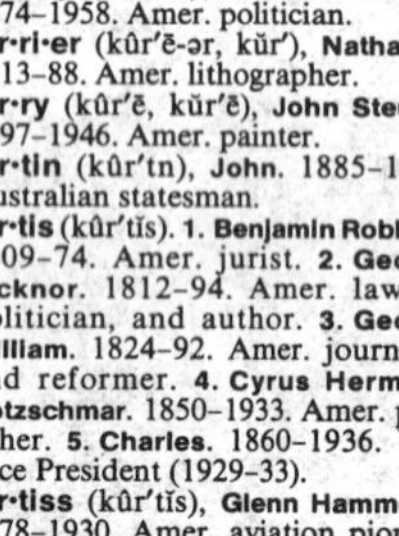

George Armstrong Custer

Cut·ler (kŭt′lər), **Manasseh.** 1742–1823. Amer. clergyman and botanist.
Cu·vier (kyo͞o′vē-ā′, ko͞ov-yā′, kü-vyā′), Baron **Georges Léopold Chrétien Frédéric.** 1769–1832. French naturalist.
Cyn·e·wulf or **Kyn·e·wulf** (kĭn′ə-wo͝olf′) or **Cyn·wulf** (kĭn′wo͝olf′). Late 8th cent. Anglo-Saxon poet.
Cyp·ri·an (sĭp′rē-ən), Saint. d. 258. Christian prelate and martyr.
Cy·ra·no de Ber·ge·rac (sîr′ə-nō də bûr′jə-răk′, -zhə-, bâr-, sē-rä-nô′ də bĕr-zhə-räk′), **Savinien de.** 1619?–55. French satirist and duelist.
Cyr·il (sîr′əl), Saint. 827–69. Christian missionary and theologian.
Cy·rus (sī′rəs). 600?–529 B.C. "the Great." Persian king (550–529) and founder of Persian empire.
Czer·ny (chĕr′nē), **Karl.** 1791–1857. Austrian pianist and composer.

D

Daft (dăft), **Leo.** 1843–1922. English-born Amer. engineer and inventor.
Da·guerre (də-gâr′, dä-gĕr′), **Louis Jacques Mandé.** 1787?–1851. French artist and inventor.
Dahl·gren (dăl′grən), **John Adolphus Bernard.** 1809–70. Amer. naval officer and inventor.
Daim·ler (dīm′lər), **Gottlieb.** 1834–1900. German engineer and inventor.
Da·kin (dā′kĭn), **Henry Drysdale.** 1880–1952. English biochemist.
Da·la·dier (dä-lä-dyā′), **Édouard.** 1884–1970. French statesman.
Da·lai La·ma (dä′lī lä′mə). b. 1934. Tibetan spiritual leader.
Dale (dāl). **1.** Sir **Thomas.** d. 1619. English-born colonial administrator. **2.** Sir **Henry Hallett.** 1875–1968. English physiologist (Nobel, 1936).
Da·lén (də-lān′, dă-), **Nils Gustaf.** 1869–1937. Swedish inventor (Nobel, 1912).
Da·ley (dā′lē), **Richard Joseph.** 1902–76. Amer. public official.
Dal·hou·sie (dăl-ho͞o′zē, -hou′-), 10th Earl and 1st Marquis of. James Andrew Broun Ramsay. 1812–60. English colonial administrator.
Da·lí (dä′lē), **Salvador.** b. 1904. Spanish artist.
Dall (dôl), **Caroline Wells Healey.** 1822–1912. Amer. author and reformer.
Dal·las (dăl′əs). **1. Alexander James.** 1759–1817. West Indian-born Amer. statesman. **2. George Mifflin.** 1792–1864. U.S. Vice President (1845–49).
Dal·rym·ple (dăl-rĭm′pəl, dăl′rĭm-). **1.** Sir **James.** 1st Viscount Stair. 1619–95. Scottish jurist. **2.** Sir **John.** 2nd Earl of Stair. 1673–1747. Scottish general and diplomat.
Dal·ton (dôl′tən). **1. John.** 1766–1844. English chemist and philosopher. **2. Robert Hugh.** 1887–1962. English politician.
Da·ly (dā′lē). **1. (John) Augustin.** 1839–99. Amer. playwright and theatrical manager. **2. Marcus.** 1841–1900. Amer. mining financier.
Dam (dăm, däm), **(Carl Peter) Henrik.** 1895–1976. Danish biochemist (Nobel, 1943).
d'Am·boise (däN-bwäz′), **Jacques.** b. 1934. Amer. ballet dancer.
Da·mien de Veus·ter (dā′mē-ən də vyo͞os′tər, dä-myăN′ də vœ-stĕr′), **Joseph.** "Father Damien." 1840–88. Belgian Roman Catholic missionary.
Dam·pi·er (dăm′pē-ər), **William.** 1652–1715. English explorer.
Dam·rosch (dăm′rŏsh), **Leopold** (1832–85) and **Walter Johannes** (1862–1950). German-born Amer. musicians and composers.
Da·na (dā′nə). **1. James Dwight.** 1813–95. Amer. geologist and mineralogist. **2. Richard Henry.** 1815–82. Amer. author. **3. Charles Anderson.** 1819–97. Amer. newspaper editor.
Dan·dridge (dăn′drĭj), **Dorothy.** 1923?–65. Amer. actress.
Dan·iel (dăn′yəl). **1.** Hebrew prophet. **2. Samuel.** 1562?–1619. English author. **3. Peter Vivian.** 1784–1860. Amer. jurist.
Dan·iels (dăn′yəlz), **Josephus.** 1862–1948. Amer. journalist.
Da·ni·lo·va (də-nē′lə-və, -lô-, dä-nē′lô-vä), **Alexandra.** b. 1906. Russian-born Amer. ballerina.
Dan·nay (dăn′ā), **Frederic.** With Manfred B. Lee, "Ellery Queen." 1905–82. Amer. author.
D'An·nun·zio (dän-no͞on′tsyō), **Gabriele.** 1863–1938. Italian author.
Dan·te A·li·ghie·ri (dän′tā ä-lē-gyā′rē, dăn′tē). 1265–1321. Italian poet (*Divine Comedy*). —**Dan′te·an** *adj.* & *n.* —**Dan·tesque′** (dăn-tĕsk′) *adj.*
Dan·ton (dăn′tən, däN-tôN′), **Georges Jacques.** 1759–94. French revolutionary leader.
Dare (dâr), **Virginia.** 1587–1587? 1st child of English parents born in Amer.
Da·ri·us (də-rī′əs). Name of 3 kings of Persia, esp.: **1. I.** "the Great." 558?–486? B.C. Ruled 521–486 B.C. **2. III.** 380?–30 B.C. Ruled 336–30 B.C.
Dar·lan (där-läN′), **Jean Louis Xavier François.** 1881–1942. French admiral.
Darn·ley (därn′lē), Lord. Henry Stuart or Stewart. 1545–67. Scottish nobleman; 2nd husband of Mary Queen of Scots.
Dar·row (dăr′ō), **Clarence Seward.** 1857–1938. Amer. lawyer.

Clarence Darrow

Dar·win (där′wĭn). **1. Erasmus.** 1731–1802. English physician, scientist, reformer, and poet. **2. Charles Robert.** 1809–82. English naturalist (theory of evolution). —**Dar·win′i·an** *adj.* & *n.*
Dau·bi·gny (dō-bē-nyē′), **Charles François.** 1817–78. French landscape painter.
Dau·det (dō-dā′, -dĕ′). **1. Alphonse.** 1840–97. French author. **2. Léon.** 1867–1942. French journalist.
Daugh·er·ty (dô′ər-tē), **Henry Micajah.** 1860–1941. Amer. politician.
Dau·mier (dō-myā′), **Honoré.** 1808–79. French artist.
Dau·sett (dō-sĕt′), **Jean.** b. 1915. French physiologist (Nobel, 1980).
Dav·e·nant or **D'Av·e·nant** (dăv′ə-nənt), Sir **William.** 1606–68. English dramatist.
Dav·en·port (dăv′ən-pôrt′, -pōrt′). **1. John.** 1597–1670. English Puritan clergyman and colonist. **2. Thomas.** 1802–51. Amer. inventor.
Da·vid (dā′vĭd). **1.** 1010?–970? B.C. 2nd king of Judah and Israel. **2.** Name of 2 kings of Scotland, esp. **I,** 1084–1153, ruled 1124–53. **3.** (dä′vət), **Gerard.** 1450?–1523. Flemish painter. **4.** (dä-vēd′), **Jacques Louis.** 1748–1825. French painter.
Da·vid·son (dā′vĭd-sən), **Jo.** 1883–1952. Amer. sculptor.
Da·vies (dā′vēz). **1. Arthur Bowen.** 1862–1928. Amer. painter. **2. Marion.** 1898?–1961. Amer. actress.
Dá·vi·la y Pa·di·lla (dä-vē′lä ē pä-*thē*′yä), **Agustín.** 1562–1604. Mexican prelate and historian.
Da·vis (dā′vĭs). **1. Jefferson.** 1808–89. Amer. soldier and Confederate statesman. **2. Paulina Kellogg Wright.** 1813–76. Amer. editor and suffragist. **3. David.** 1815–86. Amer. politician and jurist. **4. Rebecca Blaine Harding.** 1831–1910. Amer. author. **5. William Morris.** 1850–1934. Amer. geologist and geographer. **6. Katherine Bement.** 1860–1935. Amer. penologist and social worker. **7. Richard Harding.** 1864–1916. Amer. journalist. **8. John William.** 1873–1955. Amer. politician and diplomat. **9. Benjamin Oliver.** 1877–1970. Amer. cavalry officer. **10. Dwight Filley.** 1879–1945. Amer. public official and tennis player. **11. Stuart.** 1894–1964. Amer. artist. **12. Ruth Elizabeth ("Bette").** b. 1908. Amer. actress. **13. Sammy, Jr.** b. 1925. Amer. entertainer. **14. Miles Dewey, Jr.** b. 1926. Amer. musician. **15. Angela.** b. 1944. Amer. political activist.
Da·vis·son (dā′vĭ-sən), **Clinton Joseph.** 1881–1958. Amer. physicist (Nobel, 1937).
Da·vout (dä-vo͞o′), **Louis Nicolas.** 1770–1823. French marshal.
Da·vy (dā′vē), Sir **Humphrey.** 1778–1829. English chemist.
Da·vys (dā′vĭs), **John.** 1550?–1605. English navigator.
Dawes (dôz). **1. Henry Laurens.** 1816–1903. Amer. politician. **2. Charles Gates.** 1865–1951. U.S. Vice President (1925–29; Nobel, 1925).
Day (dā). **1. Thomas.** 1748–89. English author and philanthropist. **2. Benjamin Henry.** 1810–89. Amer. printer and journalist. **3. William Rufus.** 1849–1923. Amer. jurist. **4. Clarence Shepard, Jr.** 1874–1935. Amer. author. **5. Dorothy.** 1897–1981. Amer. journalist and reformer.
Da·yan (dī-än′, dä-yän′), **Moshe.** 1915–81. Israeli political leader.

Moshe Dayan

Dean (dēn). **1. Jay Hanna** or **Jerome Herman ("Dizzy").** 1911–74. Amer. baseball player and sportscaster. **2. James.** 1931–55. Amer. actor.
Deane (dēn), **Silas.** 1737–89. Amer. diplomat.
Dear·born (dîr′bôrn′, -bərn), **Henry.** 1751–1829. Amer. soldier and politician.
De Ba·key (də bā′kē), **Michael Ellis.** b. 1908. Amer. heart surgeon.
De·bierne (də-byĕrn′), **André Louis.** 1874–1949. French chemist.
De Bow (dē bō′), **James Dunwoody Brownson.** 1820–67. Amer. statistician and editor.
Debs (dĕbz), **Eugene Victor.** 1855–1926. Amer. labor organizer and socialist leader.

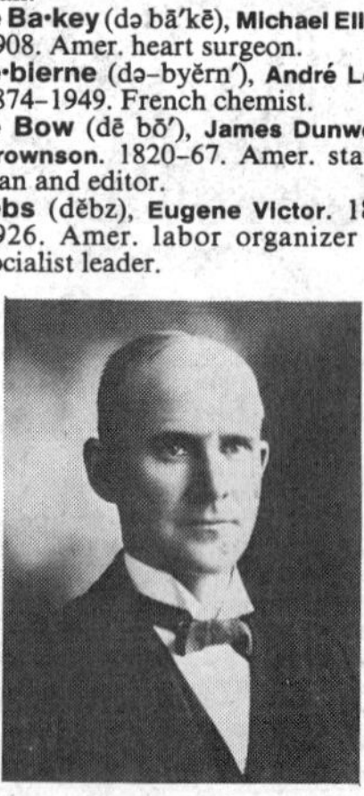

Eugene V. Debs

De·bus·sy (dĕb′yo͞o-sē′, də-byo͞o′sē, də-bü-sē′), **Claude Achille.** 1862–1918. French composer.
De·bye (də-bī′), **Peter Joseph Wilhelm.** 1884–1966. Dutch-born Amer.

physicist (Nobel, 1936).

De·ca·tur (dĭ-kā'tər), **Stephen.** 1779–1820. Amer. naval officer.

De·cius (dē'shəs, dĕsh'əs). 201–51. Roman emperor (249–51).

Deck·er (dĕk'ər). Variant of **Dekker.**

De·de·kind (dā'dĭ-kĭnt'), **Julius Wilhelm Richard.** 1831–1916. German mathematician.

Dee (dē), **Ruby.** b. 1924? Amer. actress.

Dee·ping (dē'pĭng), **(George) Warwick.** 1877–1950. English novelist.

Deere (dîr), **John.** 1804–1886. Amer. manufacturer and inventor.

Def·fand (dĭ-fäN'), Marquise du. Marie de Vichy-Chamrond. 1697–1780. French literary patron.

De·foe (dĭ-fō'), **Daniel.** 1660–1731. English author.

De For·est (dĭ fôr'ĭst, fŏr'-), **Lee.** "the Father of Radio." 1873–1961. Amer. inventor.

De·gas (də-gä'), **(Hilaire Germain) Edgar.** 1834–1917. French painter.

De Gaulle (də gōl', gôl'), **Charles André Joseph Marie.** 1890–1970. French general and statesman.

Dek·ker or **Deck·er** (dĕk'ər), **Thomas.** 1572–1632. English dramatist.

de Koo·ning (dĭ kōō'nĭng), **Willem.** b. 1904. Dutch-born Amer. painter.

De·la·croix (də-lä-krwä'), **(Ferdinand Victor) Eugène.** 1798–1863. French painter.

de la Mare (də lə mâr', dĕl'ə mâr'), **Walter John.** 1873–1956. English author.

De·la·mat·er (də-lăm'ə-tər), **Cornelius Henry.** 1821–1889. Amer. mechanical engineer.

De Lan·cey (də lăn'sē), **James.** 1703–60. Amer. colonial judge and official.

De·land (də-lănd'), **Margaret.** 1857–1945. Amer. author.

Del·a·no (dĕl'ə-nō), **Jane Arminda.** 1862–1919. Amer. nurse.

De·lan·y (də-lā'nē), **Martin Robinson.** 1812–85. Amer. physician and social reformer.

de la Ren·ta (dā lə rĕn'tə), **Oscar.** b. 1934? Dominican-born Amer. fashion designer.

De La Rey (də lə rī', -rā', dĕl'ə rī'), **Jacobus Hercules.** 1847–1914. Boer general and statesman.

De·la·roche (də-lä-rôsh'), **Hippolyte Paul.** 1797–1856. French painter.

de la Roche (də lä rôsh'), **Mazo.** 1885–1961. Canadian novelist (*Jalna* series).

De Lau·ren·tis (dē lô-rĕn'təs), **Dino.** b. 1919. Italian filmmaker.

De·la·vigne (də-lä-vēn'yə), **(Jean François) Casimir.** 1793–1843. French author.

De La Warr (dĕl'ə wâr', wər), Baron. Thomas West. 1577–1618. English-born Amer. colonial administrator.

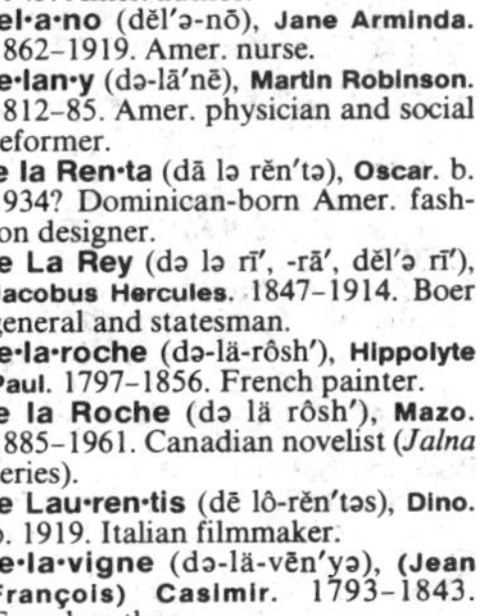

Baron De La Warr

Del·brück (dĕl'brük', -brŏŏk'), **Max.** 1906–81. German-born Amer. biologist (Nobel, 1969).

De·led·da (dā-lād'dä), **Grazia.** 1875–1936. Italian novelist (Nobel, 1926).

de Les·seps (də lĕs'ĕps, lē-sĕps'), Vicomte **Ferdinand Marie.** 1805–94. French diplomat.

De·libes (də-lēb'), **(Clément Philibert) Léo.** 1836–91. French composer.

De·lius (dē'lē-əs, dēl'yəs), **Frederick.** 1862–1934. English composer.

Dell (dĕl), **Floyd.** 1887–1969. Amer. author.

del·la Rob·bia (dĕl'ə rō'bē-ə, dĕl'lä rôb'byä). Family of Italian sculptors, including **Luca** (1400?–82), **Andrea** (1437–1528) and **Giovanni** (1469–1529?).

Del·mon·i·co (dĕl-mŏn'ĭ-kō), **Lorenzo.** 1813–81. Amer. restaurateur.

De Long (də lông'), **George Washington.** 1844–81. Amer. Arctic explorer.

De·lorme or **de l'Orme** (də-lôrm'), **Philibert.** 1515?–70. French architect.

De Mille (də mĭl'). **1. Cecil Blount.** 1881–1959. Amer. movie producer. **2. Agnes George.** b. 1905. Amer. choreographer.

De·moc·ri·tus (dĭ-mŏk'rĭ-təs). 460?–357 B.C. Greek philosopher.

Dem·o·rest (dĕm'ə-rĕst'), **Ellen Louis Curtis.** 1824–98. Amer. businesswoman.

De Mor·gan (dĭ môr'gən), **William Frend.** 1836–1917. English artist, author, and inventor.

De·mos·the·nes (dĭ-mŏs'thə-nēz'). 385?–22 B.C. Greek orator.

Demp·sey (dĕmp'sē). **1.** Sister **(Julia) Mary Joseph.** 1856–1939. Amer. hospital administrator. **2. William Harrison ("Jack").** 1895–1983. Amer. heavyweight boxer.

De·muth (dĭ-mōōth'), **Charles.** 1883–1935. Amer. painter.

Deng Xi·ao·ping (dŭng' ksē-ou-pĭng'). b. 1904. Chinese Communist leader.

De·ni·ker (dĕ-nē-kĕr'), **Joseph.** 1852–1918. French anthropologist.

De·nis or **De·nys** (dĕn'ĭs, də-nē'), Saint. 3rd cent. martyred apostle to the Gauls.

Den·nett (dĕn'ĭt), **Mary Coffin Ware.** 1872–1947. Amer. social reformer.

Den·nie (dĕn'ē), **Joseph.** 1768–1812. Amer. editor and author.

Dent (dĕnt), **Joseph Malaby ("J.M.").** 1849–1926. English publisher.

De·pew (dĭ-pyōō), **Chauncey Mitchell.** 1834–1928. Amer. lawyer, railroad executive, and politician.

De Quin·cey (dĭ kwĭn'sē, -zē), **Thomas.** 1785–1859. English essayist.

De·rain (də-răN'), **André.** 1880–1954. French artist.

Der·zha·vin (dĭr-zhä'vĭn), **Gavriil Romanovish.** 1743–1816. Russian poet.

De·saix de Vey·goux (dĕ-zĕ' də vā-gōō'), **Louis Charles Antoine.** 1768–1800. French general.

De·sargues (dā-zärg'), **Gérard.** 1593–1662. French army officer and mathematician.

Des·cartes (dā-kärt'), **René.** 1596–1650. French mathematician and philospher.

Des·cha·nel (dā'shə-nĕl'), **Paul Eugène Louis.** 1856–1922. French statesman and author.

de Se·ver·sky (də sə-vĕr'skē), **Alexander Procofieff.** 1894–1974. Russian-born Amer. aeronautical engineer.

De Si·ca (də sē'kə, dā sē'kä), **Vittorio.** 1901–74. Italian filmmaker.

De Smet (də smĕt'), **Pierre Jean.** 1801–73. Belgian-born missionary in America.

Des·mou·lins (dā-mōō-lăN'), **(Lucie Simplice) Camille (Benoît).** 1760–94. French revolutionary; guillotined.

de So·to (dĭ sō'tō, dĕ sô'tō), **Hernando.** 1496?–1542. Spanish explorer.

Des·saix (dĭ-sā', dā-sĕ'), Comte **Joseph Marie.** 1764–1834. French general.

Des·sa·lines (dā-sä-lēn'), **Jean Jacques.** 1758–1806. Haitian emperor (1804–06); assassinated.

De·taille (dĭ-tī'), **(Jean Baptiste) Édouard.** 1848–1912. French painter.

De·us Ra·mos (dĕ'ōōsh rä'mōōsh), **João de.** 1830–1896. Portuguese poet.

De Va·le·ra (dĕv'ə-lĕr'ə, -lĭr'ə, dĕ vä-lĕ'rä), **Eamon.** 1882–1975. Amer.-born Irish statesman.

De Ve·ga (də vā'gə, dĕ bĕ'gä), **Lope.** See **Vega.**

de Vere (də vĭr'), **Aubrey Thomas.** 1814–1902. Irish author.

Dev·er·eux (dĕv'ə-rōō'), **Robert.** 2nd Earl of Essex. 1566–1601. English nobleman and favorite of Elizabeth I.

De Vin·ne (də vĭn'ē), **Theodore Low.** 1828–1914. Amer. printer.

De Vo·to (də vō'tō), **Bernard Augustine.** 1897–1955. Amer. author and editor.

De Vries (də vrēs', vrĕs'), **1. Hugo.** 1848–1935. Dutch botanist. **2. Peter.** b. 1910. Amer. author.

Dew·ar (dōō'ər, dyōō'-), Sir **James.** 1842–1923. Scottish-born chemist and physicist.

De Wet (də wĕt'), **Christiaan Rudolph.** 1854–1922. Boer general.

Dew·ey (dōō'ē, dyōō'-). **1. George.** 1837–1917. Amer. naval officer. **2. John.** 1859–1952. Amer. philosopher and educator. **3. Melvil.** 1851–1931. Amer. librarian and founder of decimal system of classification. **4. Thomas Edmund.** 1902–71. Amer. politician.

De Witt (də wĭt'), **Jan.** 1625–72. Dutch statesman; murdered.

De Wolfe (də wŏŏlf'), **Elsie.** 1865–1950. Amer. actress and decorator.

Dia·ghi·lev (dyä'gĭ-lĭf), **Sergei Pavlovich.** 1872–1929. Russian ballet producer (Ballet Russe).

Di·an·a (dī-ăn'ə). Princess of Wales. Lady Diana Spencer. b. 1961. British crown princess.

Di·as or **Dí·az** (dē'əs, -əsh), **Bartholomeu.** 1450?–1500. Portuguese navigator; discovered Cape of Good Hope.

Dí·az. **1.** (dē'äs), **(José de la Cruz) Porfirio.** 1830–1915. Mexican general and statesman. **2.** (dē'äts), **Armando.** 1861–1929. Italian general and statesman.

Dí·az de Bi·var (dē'äs dĭ bē-vär'), **Rodrigo** or **Ruy.** The Cid.

Dí·az Or·daz (dē'äs ŏr'däs), **Gustavo.** 1911–79. Mexican statesman.

Dick (dĭk), **George Frederick** (1881–1967) and **Gladys Henry.** (1881–1963). Amer. physicians.

Dick·ens (dĭk'ĭnz), **Charles John Huffam.** "Boz." 1812–70. English author. **—Dick·en'si·an** *adj.*

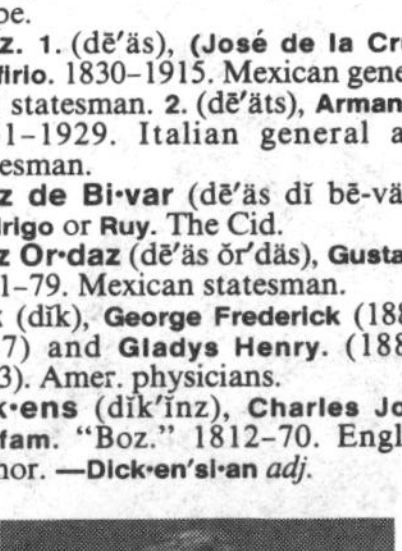

Charles Dickens

Dick·ey (dĭk'ē), **James.** b. 1923. Amer. author.

Dick·in·son (dĭk'ĭn-sən). **1. John.** 1732–1808. Amer. statesman. **2. Emily Elizabeth.** 1830–86. Amer. poet. **3. Anna Elizabeth.** 1842–1932. Amer. reformer and lecturer.

Emily Dickinson

Di·de·rot (dē'də-rō', dē-drō'), **Denis.** 1713–1784. French philosopher, author, and Encyclopedist.

Did·rik·son (dĭd'rĭk-sən), **Mildred Ella ("Babe").** 1914–56. Amer. athlete.

Die·fen·ba·ker (dē'fən-bā'kər), **John George.** 1895–1979. Canadian prime minister (1957–63).

Diels (dēlz, dēls), **Otto Paul Hermann.** 1876–1954. German chemist (Nobel, 1950).

Di·em (dē-ĕm', dyĕm), **Ngo Dinh.** 1901–63. Vietnamese political leader; assassinated.

Dies (dīz), **Martin.** 1901–72. Amer. legislator.

Die·sel (dē'zəl), **Rudolf.** 1858–1913. German engineer and inventor.

Die·trich (dē'trĭk, -trĭKH), **Marlene.** b. 1901? German-born Amer. actress.

Diez (dēts), **Friedrich Christian.** 1794–1876. German philologist.

Dig·by (dĭg'bē), Sir **Kenelm.** 1603–65. English naval officer, diplomat, and philosopher.

Diggs (dĭgz), **Annie LePorte.** 1848–1916. English-born Amer. reformer and politician.

Dill (dĭl), Sir **John Greer.** 1881–1944. Irish-born British army officer.

Dil·lin·ger (dĭl'ĭn-jər), **John.** 1902–34. Amer. bank robber.

Dil·lon (dĭl'ən), **John.** 1851–1927. Irish nationalist political leader.

Di Mag·gio (də-mä'jē-ō', -măj'ē-ō), **Joseph Paul.** b. 1914. Amer. baseball player.

Dim·net (dēm-nĕ'), **Ernest.** 1866–1954. French abbé and author.

Di·ne·sen (dē'nə-sən, dĭn'ĭ-), **Isak.** Baroness Karen Blixen. 1885–1962. Danish author.

Din·wid·die (dĭn-wĭd'ē, dĭn'wĭd-ē), **Robert.** 1693–1770. Scottish-born British colonial administrator.

Di·o·cle·tian (dī'ə-klē'shən). 245–313. Roman emperor (284–305).

Di·og·e·nes (dī-ŏj'ə-nēz'). 412?–323 B.C. Greek philosopher.

Di·o·ny·si·us (dī-ə-nĭsh'ē-əs, -nĭs-). **1.** "the Elder" (430?–367 B.C.) and "the Younger" (395?–43? B.C.). Greek tyrants. **2. of Hal·i·car·nas·sus** (hăl'ə-kär-năs'əs). 1st cent. B.C. Greek historian. **3. of Al·ex·an·dri·a** (ăl-ĭg-zăn'drē-ə), Saint. 190?–264? Christian theologian.

Dionysius Ex·ig·u·us (ĕg-zĭg'yō-əs, ek-sĭg'-). 6th cent. monk and scholar.

Di·or (dē-ôr'), **Christian.** 1905–57. French fashion designer.

Di·rac (dĭ-răk'), **Paul Adrien Maurice.** 1902–84. English mathematician and physicist (Nobel, 1933).

Dirk·sen (dûrk'sən), **Everett McKinley.** 1896–1969. Amer. legislator.

Dis·ney (dĭz'nē), **Walter Elias ("Walt").** 1901–66. Amer. cartoonist, showman, and film producer.

Walt Disney

Dis·rae·li (dĭz-rā'lē), **Benjamin.** 1st Earl of Beaconsfield. "Dizzy." 1804–81. British prime minister (1868 and 1874–80), author, and diplomat.

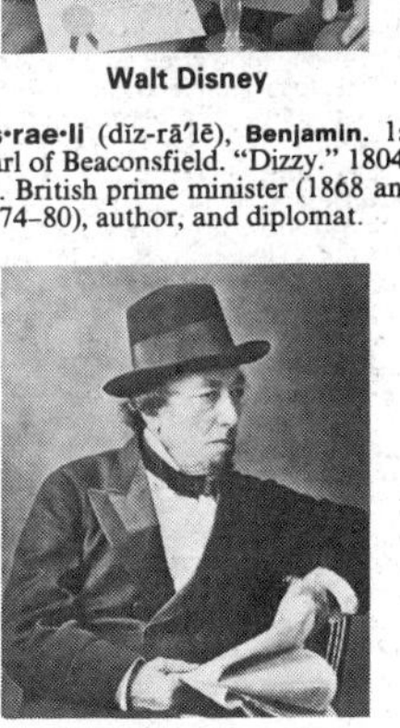

Benjamin Disraeli

Dit·mars (dĭt′märz), **Raymond Lee.** 1876–1942. Amer. naturalist and author.

Dix (dĭks). **1. John Adams.** 1798–1879. Amer. politician and diplomat. **2. Dorothea Lynde.** 1802–87. Amer. philanthropist, reformer, author, and educator. **3. Dorothy.** Elizabeth Meriwether Gilmer.

Dix·on (dĭk′sən), **Jeremiah.** fl. 1763–67. English-born surveyor (Mason-Dixon line).

Dji·las (jĭl′äs), **Milovan.** b. 1911. Yugoslavian author and political leader.

Dmow·ski (dmôf′skē), **Roman.** 1864–1939. Polish nationalist political leader.

Do·bie (dō′bē), **James Frank.** 1888–1964. Amer. historian, folklorist, and author.

Do·brée (dō′brē), **Bonamy.** 1891–1974. English literary historian.

Do·bry·nin (dō-brē′nĭn), **Anatoly F.** b. 1919. Soviet diplomat.

Dob·son (dŏb′sən), **(Henry) Austin.** 1840–1921. English author.

Dodge (dŏj). **1. Grenville Mellen.** 1831–1916. Amer. civil engineer and politician. **2. Mary Elizabeth Mapes.** 1831–1905. Amer. author and editor. **3. Grace Hoadley.** 1856–1914. Amer. philanthropist and social worker. **4. Josephine Marshall Jewell.** 1855–1928. Amer. antisuffragist and daycare advocate.

Dodg·son (dŏj′sən), **Charles Lutwidge.** "Lewis Carroll." 1832–98. English mathematician and author.

Dods·ley (dŏdz′lē), **Robert.** 1703–64. English author, editor, and bookseller.

Doe·nitz also **Dö·nitz** (dœ′nĭts), **Karl.** 1891–1980. German admiral.

Do·her·ty (dō′ər-tē, dŏr′ə-), **Henry Latham.** 1870–1939. Amer. engineer and utilities magnate.

Doi·sy (doi′zē), **Edward Adelbert.** b. 1893. Amer. biochemist (Nobel, 1943).

Dole (dōl), **Sanford Ballard.** 1844–1926. Amer. jurist and administrator in Hawaii.

Doll·fuss (dôl′fo͞os), **Engelbert.** 1892–1934. Austrian statesman; assassinated.

Do·magk (dō′mäk′), **Gerhard.** 1895–1964. German biochemist (Nobel, 1939).

Do·me·ni·chi·no (dō-mā′nē-kē′nō). 1581–1641. Italian painter.

Do·min·go (də-mĕng′gō, dô-mêng′gô), **Placido.** b. 1941. Spanish-born opera singer.

Dom·i·nic (dŏm′ə-nĭk), Saint. 1170–1221. Spanish-born founder of Dominican order.

Do·mi·tian (də-mĭsh′ən, -ē-ən), A.D. 51–96. Roman emperor (81–96).

Don·a·tel·lo (dŏn′ə-tĕl′ō, dō′nä-tĕl′lō). 1386?–1466. Italian sculptor.

Don·i·phan (dŏn′ĭ-fən), **Alexander William.** 1808–87. Amer. army officer and frontiersman.

Dö·nitz (dœ′nĭts). Variant of **Doenitz.**

Don·i·zet·ti (dŏn′ĭ-zĕt′ē, dō-nē-dzĕt′tē), **Gaetano.** 1797–1848. Italian composer.

Donne (dŭn), **John.** 1572?–1631. English poet.

Don·nel·ly (dŏn′ə-lē), **Ignatius.** 1831–1901. Amer. politician and reformer.

Don·o·van (dŏn′ə-vən), **William Joseph ("Wild Bill").** 1883–1959. Amer. army officer.

Doo·lit·tle (do͞o′lĭt′l). **1. Hilda.** "H.D." 1886–1961. Amer. poet. **2. James Harold ("Jimmy").** b. 1896. Amer. army officer and aviator.

Dopp·ler (dŏp′lər), **Christian Johann.** 1803–53. Austrian physicist and mathematician.

Do·ra·ti (dō-rä′tē, dô-), **Antal.** b. 1906. Hungarian-born Amer. conductor and composer.

Do·ré (dō-rā′), **(Paul) Gustave.** 1833–83. French artist.

Do·re·mus (dō-rē′mŭs), **Sarah Platt Haines.** 1802–77. Amer. social worker and philanthropist.

Dor·nier (dôr-nēr′, -nyā′), **Claude.** 1884–1969. German aircraft designer.

Dorr (dôr), **Thomas Wilson.** 1805–54. Amer. politician and reformer.

Dor·set (dôr′sĭt), Earl of. Thomas Sackville.

Dos Pas·sos (dōs păs′ōs), **John Roderigo.** 1896–1970. Amer. novelist.

Dos·to·ev·ski or **Dos·to·yev·sky** (dŏs′tə-yef′skē, -toi-, dŭs-, də-stō-yĕf′skĭ), **Feodor Mikhailovich.** 1821–81. Russian author. —**Dos′to·ev′ski·an** *adj.*

Dou or **Dow** or **Douw** (dou), **Gerard.** 1613–1675. Dutch genre painter.

Dou·ble·day (dŭb′əl-dā′). **1. Abner.** 1819–93. Amer. army officer and reputed inventor of baseball. **2. Frank Nelson.** 1862–1934. Amer. publisher.

Dough·ty (dou′tē), **Charles Monagu.** 1843–1926. English author and traveler.

Doug·las (dŭg′ləs). **1. Stephen Arnold.** "the Little Giant." 1813–61. Amer. legislator. **2.** Sir **John Sholto.** 8th Marquis of Queensberry. 1844–1900. English nobleman and boxing promoter. **3. Lloyd Cassel.** 1877–1951. Amer. clergyman and author. **4. William Orville.** 1898–1980. Amer. jurist. **5. Helen Mary Gahagan.** 1900–80. Amer. actress and politician. **6. Melvyn.** 1901–81. Amer. actor.

Stephen A. Douglas

Douglas-Home (dŭg′ləs-hyo͞om′), Sir **Alexander Frederick.** b. 1903. British prime minister (1963–64).

Doug·lass (dŭg′ləs), **Frederick.** 1817?–95. Amer. abolitionist and journalist.

Dou·mer (do͞o-mĕr′), **Paul.** 1857–1932. French statesman; assassinated.

Dou·mergue (do͞o-mĕrg′), **Gaston.** 1863–1937. French statesman.

Dou·vil·lier (do͞o-vēl-yā), **Suzanne Théodore Vaillande.** 1778–1826. French-born Amer. dancer and choreographer.

Douw (dou). Variant of **Dou.**

Dow (dou). **1.** Variant of **Dou. 2. Neal.** 1804–97. Amer. temperance leader. **3. Charles Henry.** 1851–1902. Amer. economist and publisher. **4. Herbert Henry.** 1866–1930. Amer. chemist and manufacturer.

Dow·den (doud′n), **Edward.** 1843–1913. Irish editor, author, and educator.

Downes (dounz), **(Edwin) Olin.** 1886–1955. Amer. music critic.

Down·ing (dou′nĭng), **Andrew Jackson.** 1815–52. Amer. landscape architect and horticulturist.

Dow·son (dou′sən), **Ernest Christopher.** 1867–1900. English author and translator.

Doyle (doil), Sir **Arthur Conan.** 1859–1930. English author (Sherlock Holmes stories).

D'Oy·ly Carte (doi′lē kärt′), **Richard.** See **Carte.**

Drach·mann (dräk′mən, dräĸʜ′-män), **Holger Henrik Herholdt.** 1846–1908. Danish author.

Dra·co (drā′kō). 7th cent. B.C. Athenian lawgiver. —**Dra·co′ni·an** *adj.*

Drake (drāk). **1.** Sir **Francis.** 1540?–96. English naval hero and explorer. **2. Daniel.** 1785–1852. Amer. physician and pioneer medical educator. **3. Edwin Laurentine.** 1819–80. Amer. oil-industry leader.

Dra·per (drā′pər). **1. John William.** 1811–82. English-born Amer. chemist and historian. **2. Henry.** 1837–82. Amer. pioneer astronomer and photographer. **3. Ruth.** 1884–1956. Amer. monologuist.

Dray·ton (drāt′n). **1. Michael.** 1563–1631. English poet. **2. William Henry.** 1742–79. Amer. Revolutionary leader.

Drei·ser (drī′sər, -zər), **Theodore (Herman Albert).** 1871–1945. Amer. author and editor.

Dress·ler (drĕs′lər), **Marie.** 1871?–1934. Canadian-born Amer. comedienne.

Drew (dro͞o). **1. Daniel.** 1797–1879. Amer. financier. **2.** Amer. family of actors, including **Louisa Lane** (1820–97), **John** (1826–62), and **John** (1853–1927).

Drey·fus (drā′fəs, drī-, drā-füs′), **Alfred.** 1859–1935. French army officer; central figure in the Dreyfus Affair (1894 ff.).

Driesch (drēsh), **Hans Adolf Eduard.** 1867–1941. German biologist and philosopher.

Drink·wa·ter (drĭngk′wô′tər, -wŏt′-ər), **John.** 1882–1937. English author.

Drum·mond (drŭm′ənd). **1. William.** 1585–1649. Scottish poet. **2. Henry.** 1851–97. Scottish clergyman and author. **3. William Henry.** 1854–1907. Irish-born Canadian poet and physician.

Dru·sus (dro͞o′səs), **Nero Claudius.** 38–9 B.C. Roman general.

Dry·den (drīd′n), **John.** 1631–1700. English author.

Duane (do͞o-ān′, dwān), **William.** 1760–1835. Amer. journalist and politician.

Du Bar·ry (do͞o băr′ē, dyo͞o-, dü bä-rē′), Comtesse. Marie Jeanne Bécu. 1746?–93. Mistress of Louis XIV; guillotined.

Dub·ček (do͝ob′chĕk), **Alexander.** b. 1921. Czech political leader.

du Bel·lay (do͞o bə-lā′, dü bĕ-lā′), **Joachim.** See **Bellay.**

Du·bin·sky (do͞o-bĭn′skē), **David.** b. 1892. Russian-born Amer. labor leader.

Du·bois (dü-bwä′). **1. Paul.** 1829–1905. French artist. **2. Théodore.** 1837–1924. French composer and educator. **3. Eugène.** 1858–1940. Dutch paleontologist.

Du Bois (do͞o bois′), **William Edward Burghardt.** 1868–1963. Amer. sociologist, educator, and author; a founder of the NAACP.

W. E. B. Du Bois

Du·bos (dü-bôs′, -bō′), **René Jules.** 1901–82. French-born Amer. bacteriologist.

Du·buf·fet (dü-bü-fĕ′), **Jean.** 1901–85. French artist.

Du Cange (dü käɴzh), Sieur. Charles du Fresne. 1610–88. French philologist and historian.

Duc·cio di Buo·nin·se·gna (do͞ot′chō dē bwô′nēn-sā′nyä). 13th–14th cent. Italian painter.

Du Chail·lu (do͞o shī′yo͞o, -shäl′-, dyo͞o, dü shä-yü′), **Paul Belloni.** 1831–1903. French-born African explorer.

Du·champ (dü-shäɴ′), **Marcel.** 1887–1968. French-born modernist painter.

Du·chesne (dü-shĕn′), **Rose Philippine.** 1769–1852. French-born religious leader in America.

Du·com·mun (dü-kô-mœɴ′), **Élie.** 1833–1906. Swiss journalist (Nobel, 1902).

Dud·ley (dŭd′lē). **1. Robert.** 1st Earl of Leicester. 1532–88. English courtier, politician, and favorite of Elizabeth I. **2. Thomas** (1576–1653) and **Joseph** (1647–1720). English colonial administrators in America.

Du·fay (dü-fā′), **Guillaume.** 1400?–74. Flemish composer.

Duf·fer·in and A·va (dŭf′ər-ĭn; ä′və), 1st Marquis of. Frederick Temple Hamilton-Temple Blackwood. 1826-1902. English diplomat.

Duff-Gor·don (dŭf′gôr′dn), Lady **Lucie** or **Lucy.** 1821–69. English writer and translator.

Duf·fy (dŭf′ē), Sir **Charles Gavan.** 1816–1903. Irish-born writer and political leader in Ireland and Australia.

Du·fy (dü-fē′), **Raoul.** 1877–1953. French artist.

Du Gues·clin (dü gĕ-klăɴ′), **Bertrand.** 1320?–80. French military commander.

Du·ha·mel (do͞o′ə-mĕl′, dyo͞o′-, dü-ä-), **Georges.** 1844–1966. French author and physician.

Duke (do͞ok, dyo͞ok), **Benjamin Newton** (1855–1929) and **James Buchanan** (1856–1925). Amer. tobacco-industry leaders.

Du·la·ny (do͞o-lā′nē, də-), **Daniel.** 1722–97. Amer. politician.

Dul·bec·co (dəl-bĕk′ō), **Renato.** b.1914. Italian-born Amer. virologist (Nobel, 1975).

Dul·les (dŭl′ĭs). **1. John Foster.** 1888–1959. Amer. diplomat and statesman. **2. Allen Welsh.** 1893–1969. Amer. public official.

Du·mas (do͞o′mä, do͞o-mä′, dü-mä′), **Alexandre** ("Dumas père"; 1802–70) and **Alexandre** ("Dumas fils"; 1824–95). French authors.

du Mau·ri·er (do͞o môr′ē-ā′, dyo͞o, dü mō-ryā′) **1. George Louis Palmella Busson.** 1834–96. English illustrator and author. **2.** Sir **Gerald.** 1873–1934. English actor and theatrical manager. **3.** Dame **Daphne.** b. 1907. English author.

Du·mou·riez (dü-mo͞o′ryā), **Charles François.** 1739–1823. French general.

Du·nant (dü-näɴ′), **Jean Henri.** 1828–1910. Swiss philanthropist and founder of the Red Cross (Nobel, 1901).

Dun·bar. 1. (dŭn-bär′), **William.** 1460?–1520. Scottish poet. **2.** (dŭn′bär), **Paul Laurence.** 1872–1906. Amer. author.

Dun·can (dŭng′kən), **Isadora.** 1878–1927. Amer. dancer.

Dun·das (dŭn-dăs′), **Henry.** 1st Viscount Melville, Baron Dunira. 1742–1811. English statesman.

Dun·i·way (dŭn′ə-wā), **Abigail Jane Scott.** 1834–1915. Amer. Western pioneer and suffragist.

Dun·lap (dŭn′lăp), **William.** 1766–1839. Amer. playwright, theatrical manager, painter, and historian.

Dun·lop (dŭn-lŏp′, dŭn′lŏp), **John Boyd.** 1840–1921. Scottish inventor (pneumatic tire).

Dun·more (dŭn-môr′, -mōr′), 4th Earl of. John Murray. 1732–1809. English colonial administrator.

Dunne (dŭn), **Finley Peter.** 1867–1936. Amer. humorist and journalist.

Du·nois (dü-nwä′), Comte **Jean de.** 1403?–68. French battle hero and companion of Joan of Arc.

Dun·sa·ny (dŭn-sā′nē), 18th Baron. Edward John Moreton Drax Plunkett. 1878–1957. Irish author.

Duns Sco·tus (dŭnz skō′təs), **John.** "Doctor Subtilis." 1265?–1308. Scottish Scholastic theologian.

Dun·stan (dŭn′stən), Saint. 925?–88. English prelate.

Dun·ster (dŭn′stər), **Henry.** 1609–59. English-born Amer. clergyman and educator.

Du·pleix (dü-plĕks′), Marquis **Joseph-François.** 1697–1763. French colonial administrator.

Du·ples·sis-Mor·nay (dü-plĕ-sē′ môr-nā′). See Philippe de **Mornay.**

Du Pont (do͞o-pŏnt′, dyo͞o-, do͞o′pŏnt, dyo͞o′-). **1. Eleuthère Irénée.** 1771–1834. French-born Amer. industrialist. **2. Samuel Francis.** 1803–65. Amer. naval leader.

Du Pont de Nemours (do͞o pŏnt′ də nə-mo͝or′, dü pôɴ′), **Pierre Samuel.** 1739–1817. French-born economist and politician.

Du·quesne (do͞o-kān′, dyo͞o-, dü-kĕn′), Marquis **Abraham.** 1610–88. French naval commander.
Du·rand (do͞o-rănd′), **Asher Brown.** 1796–1886. Amer. artist.
Du·rant (də-rănt′). **1. Thomas Clark.** 1820–85. Amer. railroad financier. **2. William Crapo.** 1861–1947. Amer. automobile industrialist. **3. Will(iam James)** (1885–1981) and **Ariel** (1898–1981). Amer. authors.
Du·rante (də-răn′tē), **Jimmy.** 1893–1980. Amer. comedian.
Dü·rer (do͝or′ər, dyo͝or′-, dü′rər), **Albrecht.** 1471–1528. German artist.
Durk·heim (dûrk′hīm, dür-kĕm′), **Émile.** 1858–1917. French sociologist and philosopher.
Du·roc (do͝or′ŏk, dyo͝or′-), **Géraud Christophe Michel.** Duc de Friuli. 1772–1813. French general and diplomat.
Du·ro·cher (do͞o-rō′chər, -shər), **Leo Ernest.** b. 1906. Amer. baseball player and manager.
Dur·rell (dûr′əl), **Lawrence George.** b. 1912. English author.
Du·ruy (dü-rü-ē′), **(Jean) Victor.** 1811–94. French historian and statesman.
Dur·yea (do͝or′yā, -ē-ā′). **Charles Edgar** (1861–1938) and **James Frank** (1869–1967). Amer. automobile manufacturers.
Du·se (do͞o′zā), **Eleonora.** 1849–1924. Italian actress.
Dus·tin (dŭs′tĭn), **Hannah.** 1657–1736? Amer. colonial heroine.
Du·tra (do͞o′trə), **Eurico Gaspar.** 1885–1974. Brazilian military and political leader.
Du·va·lier (do͞o′väl-yā′, dü-vä-lyā′), **François** ("Papa Doc"; 1907–71) and **Jean-Claude** ("Baby Doc"; b. 1951). Haitian political leaders.
Du·vall (do͞o-väl′), **Gabriel.** 1752–1844. Amer. jurist and public official.
Du·ve (dü′və), **Christian Marie René Joseph de.** b. 1917. English-born Belgian physiologist (Nobel, 1974).
Du·ve·neck (do͞o′və-nĕk′), **Frank.** 1848–1919. Amer. artist and educator.
du Vi·gneaud (do͞o-vēn′yō, dyo͞o-), **Vincent.** 1901–78. Amer. biochemist.
Dvoř·ák (dvôr′zhäk, -zhăk, dvô′rzhäk), **Anton** or **Antonín.** 1841–1904. Czech composer.
Dwig·gins (dwĭg′ĭnz), **William Addison.** 1880–1956. Amer. type and book designer.
Dwight (dwīt). **1. Timothy.** 1752–1817. Amer. clergyman, author, and educator. **2. John Sullivan.** 1813–93. Amer. music editor and critic. **3. Timothy.** 1828–1916. Amer. clergyman and scholar.
Dyce (dīs), **Alexander.** 1798–1869. Scottish-born critic and Shakespearean scholar.
Dy·er (dī′ər). **1. Mary.** d. 1660. English-born Amer. Quaker martyr. **2. John.** 1700?–58. Welsh-born English poet.
Dy·lan (dĭl′ən), **Bob.** b. 1941. Amer. musician.
Dy·ott (dī′ət), **Thomas W.** 1771–1861. English-born Amer. patent-medicine manufacturer and social reformer.

E

Eads (ēdz), **James Buchanan.** 1820–87. Amer. engineer and inventor.
Ead·wine or **Ead·win** (ĕd′wĭn′). Variants of **Edwin.**
Ea·gels (ē′gəlz), **Jeanne.** 1890–29. Amer. actress.
Ea·ker (ā′kər), **Ira Clarence.** b. 1896. Amer. aviator.
Ea·kins (ā′kĭnz), **Thomas.** 1844–1916. Amer. artist and educator.
Eames (ēmz), **Charles.** 1907–78. Amer. designer.
Ear·hart (âr′härt′), **Amelia.** 1897–1937? Amer. aviator; lost on flight over the Pacific.
Earle (ûrl). **1. Ralph.** 1751–1801. Amer. painter. **2. Alice Morse.** 1851–1911. Amer. antiquarian.
Ear·ly (ûr′lē), **Jubal Anderson.** 1816–94. Amer. Confederate soldier.

Amelia Earhart

Earp (ûrp), **Wyatt.** 1848–1929. Amer. frontier law officer.
East·man (ēst′mən). **1. George.** 1854–1932. Amer. inventor (photographic materials), industrialist, and philanthropist. **2. Charles Alexander.** 1858–1939. Amer. physician and author. **3. Max Forrester.** 1883–1969. Amer. editor, author, and translator.
Ea·ton (ēt′n). **1. Theophilus.** 1590–1658. English-born Amer. merchant and colonizer. **2. William.** 1764–1811. Amer. army officer and diplomat. **3. Margaret O'Neale** or **O'Neill** ("**Peggy**"). 1796–1879. American socialite. **4. Cyrus Stephen.** 1883–1979. Amer. industrialist and financier.
E·ban (ē′bən), **Abba.** b.1915. Israeli political leader.
E·bert (ā′bərt), **Friedrich.** 1871–1925. German statesman.
E·berth (ā′bərt), **Karl Joseph.** 1835–1926. German bacteriologist and pathologist.
Ec·cles (ĕk′əlz). **1. Marriner Stoddard.** 1890–1977. Amer. economist and public official. **2.** Sir **John Carew.** b. 1903. Australian-born Amer. physiologist (Nobel, 1963).
E·che·ga·ray y Ei·za·guir·re (ĕ′chĕ-gä-rī′ ē ā′sə-gwĭr′ā), **José.** 1832–1916. Spanish mathematician, statesman, and dramatist (Nobel, 1904).
E·che·ver·rí·a Al·va·rez (ĕ′chĕ-vĕr-rē′ä äl′vä-rĕs′), **Luis.** b. 1922. Mexican statesman.
Eck (ĕk), **Johann.** 1486–1543. German theologian.
Eck·hart also **Eck·art** or **Eck·ardt** (ĕk′härt′), **Johannes.** 1260?–1327? German mystic and theologian.
Ed·ding·ton (ĕd′ĭng-tən), Sir **Arthur Stanley.** 1882–1944. English mathematician, astronomer, and physicist.
Ed·dy (ĕd′ē). **1. Mary Morse Baker.** 1821–1910. Amer. founder of Christian Science. **2. Nelson.** 1901–67. Amer. singer and actor.
Ed·el·man (ĕd′l-mən), **Gerald Maurice.** b. 1929. Amer. biochemist (Nobel, 1972).
E·den (ēd′n), Sir **(Robert) Anthony.** Earl of Avon. 1897–1977. British prime minister (1955–57).
E·der·le (ā′dər-lē), **Gertrude Caroline.** b. 1906. Amer. channel swimmer.
Edge·worth (ĕj′wûrth′), **Maria.** 1767–1849. English gothic novelist.
Ed·in·burgh (ĕd′n-bûr′ə, -bûrg′), Duke of. See Prince **Philip.**
Ed·i·son (ĕd′ĭ-sən), **Thomas Alva.** 1847–1931. Amer. inventor (phonograph, incandescent lamp, etc.).
Ed·mund or **Ead·mund II** (ĕd′mŭnd, -mənd). 980?–1016. West Saxon king (1016).
Ed·munds (ĕd′məndz), **George Franklin.** 1828–1919. Amer. legislator.
Ed·son (ĕd′sən), **Katherine Phillips.** 1870–1933. Amer. reformer and public official.
Ed·ward (ĕd′wərd). **1.** "the Confessor." 1002–66. West Saxon king (1042–66). **2.** Prince of Wales. "the Black Prince." 1330–76. English soldier. **3.** Name of 8 English kings: **a. I.** 1239–1307. Ruled 1272–1307. **b. II.** 1284–1327. Ruled 1307–27; murdered. **c. III.** 1312–77. Ruled 1327–77. **d. IV.** 1442–83. Ruled 1461–83. **e. V.** 1470–83. Ruled 1483; murdered in the Tower of London. **f. VI.** 1537–53. Ruled 1547–53. **g. VII.** 1841–1910. Ruled 1901–10; also Emperor of India. **h. VIII.** Later Duke of Windsor. 1894–1972. Ruled 1936; abdicated. —**Ed·ward′i·an** *adj.* & *n.*

Edward VIII

Ed·wards (ĕd′wərdz), **Jonathan.** 1703–58. Amer. theologian and philosopher.
Ed·win or **Ead·wine** or **Ead·win** (ĕd′wĭn′). 585?–633. Northumbrian king (617–33).
E·gas Mo·niz (ĕ-gäs′ mô-nēsh′), **Antonio de.** 1874–1955. Portuguese neurologist (Nobel, 1949).
Eg·bert (ĕg′bərt). 775?–839. West Saxon king (802–39); 1st overlord of all the English (829).
Eg·gle·ston (ĕg′əl-stən), **Edward.** 1837–1902. Amer. author.
Eg·mont (ĕg′mŏnt, ĕKH′mônt), Comte **Lamoral d'.** 1522–68. Flemish general and statesman.
Eh·ren·burg (ā′rən-bo͝org′, -bo͝ork′), **Ilya Grigorievich.** 1891–1967. Russian author.
Ehr·lich (âr′lĭKH), **Paul.** 1853–1915. German bacteriologist (Nobel, 1908).
Eif·fel (ī′fəl, ĭ-fĕl′), **Alexandre Gustave.** 1832–1923. French engineer.
Ei·gen (ī′gən), **Manfred.** b. 1927. German chemist (Nobel, 1967).
Eijk·man (īk′män, āk′-), **Christiaan.** 1858–1930. Dutch hygienist and pathologist (Nobel, 1929).
Ein·stein (īn′stīn′), **Albert.** 1879–1955. German-born Amer. theoretical physicist (Nobel, 1921).

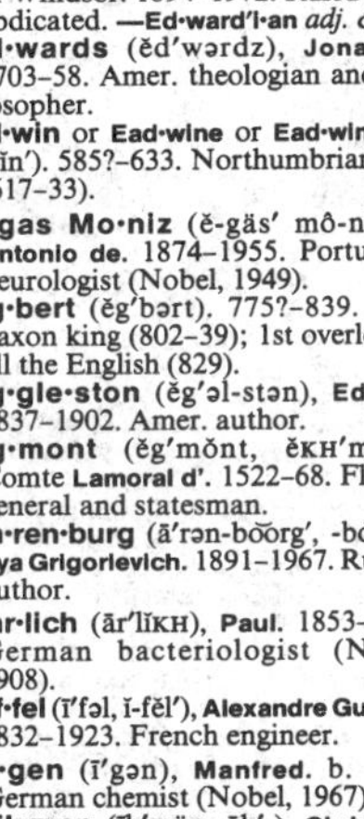

Albert Einstein

Eint·ho·ven (īnt′hō′vən), **Willem.** 1860–1927. Dutch physiologist (Nobel, 1924).
Ei·sen·how·er (ī′zən-hou′ər), **Dwight David.** 1890–1969. 34th U.S. President (1953–61) and World War II commander.
Ei·sen·stein (ī′zən-stīn′, ī′zĕn-shtān′), **Sergei Mikhailovich.** 1898–1948. Soviet filmmaker.
El Cor·do·bes (ĕl kôr-dô′bĕs). b. 1936? Spanish matador.
El·don (ĕl′dən), 1st Earl of. **John Scott.** 1751–1838. English jurist.
El·ea·nor (ĕl′ə-nər, -nôr′). **1. of Aq·ui·taine** (ăk′wĭ-tān′). 1122?–1204. Queen of France and England. **2. of Cas·tile** (kă-stēl′). d. 1290. Queen of England as wife of Edward I. **3. of Pro·vence** (prô-väNs′). d. 1291. Queen of England as wife of Henry III.

El·gar (ĕl′gär, -gər), Sir **Edward.** 1857–1934. English composer.
El Grec·o (ĕl grĕk′ō). See **Greco.**
E·li·jah (ĭ-lī′jə). 9th cent. B.C. Hebrew prophet.
El·i·ot (ĕl′ē-ət). **1.** Sir **John.** 1592–1632. English statesman. **2. John.** 1604–90. English missionary in America. **3. George.** Mary Ann Evans. 1819–80. English novelist. **4. Charles William.** 1834–1926. Amer. educator and editor. **5. Thomas Stearns** ("**T.S.**"). 1888–1965. Amer.-born English critic and author (Nobel, 1948).
E·li·sha (ĭ-lī′shə). 9th cent. B.C. Hebrew prophet.
E·liz·a·beth (ĭ-lĭz′ə-bəth). **1.** In the Bible, mother of John the Baptist. **2.** "Queen of Hearts." 1596–1662. Queen of Bohemia. **3.** 1843–1916. Author and queen of Rumania (1881–1916). **4.** Name of 5 English queens, esp.: **a. I.** "the Virgin Queen," 1533–1603. Ruled 1558–1603. **b.** b. 1900. Wife of George VI. **c. II.** b. 1926. Ruled since 1952. —**E·liz′a·be′than** *adj.* & *n.*

Elizabeth II

Elizabeth Pe·trov·na (pə-trôv′nə). 1709–62. Russian empress (1741–62).
El·let (ĕl′ĭt, -ĕt′). **1. Charles.** 1810–62. Amer. engineer. **2. Elizabeth Fries Lummis.** 1812?–77. Amer. author, critic, and translator.
El·ling·ton (ĕl′ĭng-tən), **Edward Kennedy ("Duke").** 1899–1974. Amer. jazz composer, pianist, and bandleader.
El·li·ott (ĕl′ē-ət). **1. Sara Barnwell.** 1848–1928. Amer. author and suffragist. **2. Maxine.** 1871–1940. Amer. actress.
El·lis (ĕl′ĭs). **1. Alexander John.** 1814–90. English philologist and mathematician. **2. (Henry) Havelock.** 1859–1939. English psychologist and author.
El·li·son (ĕl′ĭ-sən), **Ralph Waldo.** b. 1914. Amer. author.
Ells·worth (ĕlz′wûrth′). **1. Oliver.** 1745–1807. Amer. Revolutionary leader and jurist. **2. Lincoln.** 1880–1951. Amer. engineer and explorer.
El·man (ĕl′mən), **Mischa.** 1891–1967. Russian-born Amer. violinist.
El·phin·stone (ĕl′fĭn-stōn′, -stən), **Mountstuart.** 1779–1859. English colonial administrator in India.
E·ly (ē′lē), **Richard Theodore.** 1854–1943. Amer. economist.

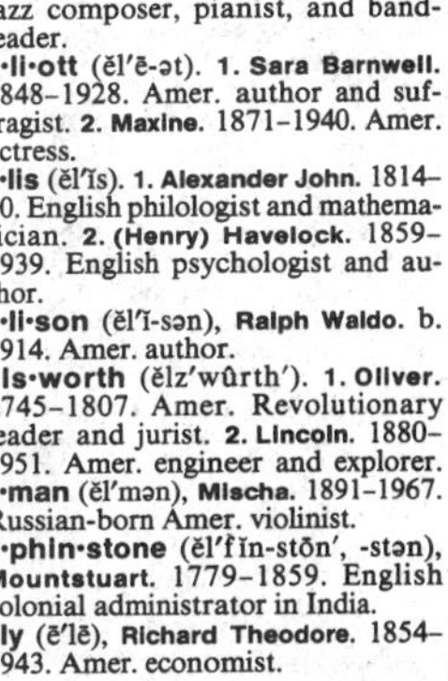

Dwight D. Eisenhower

El·yot (ĕl'yət, ĕl'ē-ət), Sir **Thomas.** 1490?–1546. English scholar and diplomat.
El·y·tis (ĕl'ē-tēs'), **Odysseus.** b. 1911. Greek poet (Nobel, 1979).
Em·er·son (ĕm'ər-sən), **Ralph Waldo.** 1803–82. Amer. author. —**Em'er·so'ni·an** *adj.*
Em·met (ĕm'ĭt), **Robert.** 1778–1803. Irish patriot.
Em·ped·o·cles (ĕm-pĕd'ə-klēz'). 5th cent. B.C. Greek philosopher.
En·de·cott also **En·di·cott** (ĕn'dĭ-kət, -kŏt'), **John.** 1589–1665. English-born Amer. colonial governor.

John Endecott

En·ders (ĕn'dərz), **John Franklin.** 1897–1985. Amer. bacteriologist (Nobel, 1954).
E·nes·co (ĕ-nĕs'kō), **Georges.** 1881–1955. Rumanian composer.
En·gels (ĕng'əlz, -əls), **Friedrich.** 1820–95. German socialist theorist and author.
En·ver Pa·sha (ĕn'vĕr' pä'shä). 1881?–1922. Turkish soldier and politician.
E·pam·i·non·das (ĭ-păm'ə-năn'dəs). 418?–362 B.C. General and statesman of Thebes.
Ep·ic·te·tus (ĕp'ĭk-tē'təs). 1st–2nd cent. A.D. Greek Stoic philosopher.
Ep·i·cu·rus (ĕp'ĭ-kyŏŏr'əs). 342–270 B.C. Greek philosopher. —**Ep'i·cu·re'an** *adj. & n.*
Ep·stein (ĕp'stīn'), Sir **Jacob.** 1880–1959. Amer.-born sculptor.
E·ras·mus (ĭ-răz'məs), **Desiderius.** 1466?–1536. Dutch Renaissance scholar and theologian.
E·ras·tus (ĭ-răs'təs), **Thomas.** 1524–83. German-Swiss theologian and philosopher.
E·ra·tos·the·nes (ĕr-ə-tŏs'thə-nēz'). 3rd cent. B.C. Greek mathematician, astronomer, and geographer.
Er·hard (ĕr'härt'), **Ludwig.** 1897–1977. German statesman.
Er·ic (ĕr'ĭk). "the Red." 10th cent. Norwegian navigator; discovered and colonized Greenland.
Er·ic·son also **Er·ics·son** (ĕr'ĭk-sən), **Leif.** fl. c. 1000. Norwegian navigator; discovered Vinland.
Er·ics·son (ĕr'ĭk-sən), **John.** 1803–89. Amer. engineer and inventor; designed the ironclad ship *Monitor.*
E·rig·e·na (ĭ-rĭj'ə-nə), **John Scotus.** 815?–77? Irish-born theologian and philosopher.
Er·lang·er (ûr'lăng'ər), **Joseph.** 1874–1965. Amer. physiologist (Nobel, 1944).
Ernst (ĕrnst), **Max.** 1891–1976. German-born Amer. surrealist artist.
Er·skine (ûr'skĭn'), **John.** 1509–91. Scottish religious reformer.
Er·vin (ûr'vĭn), **Samuel James, Jr.** 1896–1985. Amer. legislator.
Er·vine (ûr'vĭn), **St. John Greer.** 1833–1971. Irish author, theatrical manager, and educator.
Erz·ber·ger (ĕrts'bĕr'gər), **Matthias.** 1875–1921. German statesman; assassinated.
Es·a·ki (ə-sä'kē), **Leo.** b. 1925. Japanese-born physicist (Nobel, 1973).
E·sar·had·don (ē-sär-hăd'n). Assyrian king (681–69 B.C.).
Es·cof·fier (ĕs-kô-fyā'), **Auguste.** 1847–1935. French chef and author of cookery books.
E·se·nin (yĭs-ān'yən), **Sergei Alexsandrovich.** 1895–1925. Russian poet.
Esh·kol (ĕsh'kôl, ĕsh-kôl'), **Levi.** 1895–1969. Russian-born Israeli statesman.
Es·par·te·ro (ĕs-pär-tĕ'rô), **Baldomero.** 1792–1879. Spanish general and statesman.
Es·po·si·to (ĕs'pə-zē'tō), **Philip Anthony ("Phil").** b. 1942. Amer. hockey player.
Es·py (ĕs'pē), **James Pollard.** 1785–1860. Amer. pioneer meterologist.
Es·qui·vel (ĕs'kē-vĕl'), **Adolfo Perez.** b. 1932. Argentine civil-rights activist (Nobel, 1980).
Es·sex (ĕs'ĭks), Earl of. Robert Devereux.
Es·taing (ĕs-tăN'), Comte **Charles Hector d'.** 1729–94. French naval commander; guillotined.
Es·te (ĕs'tā). Italian princely family (996–1803), including **Isabella d'** (1474–1539), diplomat and patron of the arts.
Es·ter·ha·zy (ĕs'tər-hä'zē, ĕ-stĕr-ä-zē'), **(Marie Charles) Ferdinand Walsin.** 1847–1923. French army officer and forger; involved in the Dreyfus Affair.
Es·ther (ĕs'tər). In the Old Testament, Persian queen who saved the Jews from massacre.
Es·tienne (ĕs-tyĕn') or **É·tienne** (ē-tyĕn'). French family of printers, including **Henri** (1460?–1520), **Robert** (1503–59), and **Henri** (1528?–98).
Es·tour·nelles de Con·stant (ĕ-stŏŏr-nĕl' də kôn-stäN'), Baron **Constant de Rebecque d'.** Paul Henri Benjamin Balluat. 1852–1924. French diplomat and pacifist (Nobel, 1909).
Es·trith (ĕs'trəth). Danish ruling dynasty (1047–1375).
Eth·el·bert (ĕth'əl-bûrt'). 552?–616. Anglo-Saxon king, lawgiver, and Christian convert.
Eth·el·red also **Aeth·el·red II** (ĕth'əl-rĕd'). "the Unready." 968?–1016. English king (978–1016).
Eth·er·ege (ĕth'ər-ĭj, ĕth'rĭj), Sir **George.** 1635?–91. English dramatist.
Euck·en (oi'kən), **Rudolf Christoph.** 1846–1926. German philosopher (Nobel, 1908).
Eu·clid (yōō'klĭd). 3rd cent. B.C. Greek mathematician and physicist. —**Eu·clid'e·an, Eu·clid'i·an** *adj.*
Eu·gene (yōō-jēn', yōō'jēn', œ-zhĕn'). Prince of Savoy. 1663–1736. Austrian general.
Eu·gé·nie (yōō-jē'nē, œ-zhā-nē'). 1826–1920. French empress as wife of Napoleon III.
Eu·ler (oi'lər). **1. Leonhard.** 1707–83. Swiss mathematician. **2. Ulf Svante von.** b. 1905. Swedish physiologist (Nobel, 1970).
Eu·ler-Chel·pin (oi'lər-kĕl'pĭn), **Hans August Simon von.** 1873–1964. German-born Swedish chemist (Nobel, 1929).
Eu·rip·i·des (yōō-rĭp'ĭ-dēz'). 480?–406 B.C. Greek dramatist. —**Eu·rip'i·de'an** *adj.*
Eu·se·bi·us of Caes·a·re·a (yōō-sē'bē-əs; sĕs'ə-rē'ə, sĕz'-). 260?–340? Theologian and church historian.
Eu·sta·chi·o (ā'ōō-stä'kyō), **Bartolommeo.** 1524?–74. Italian anatomist.
Eu·stis (yōō'stĭs), **Dorothy Leib Harrison Wood.** 1886–1946. Amer. philanthropist; organized The Seeing Eye.
E·vald (ā'vält). Variant of **Ewald.**
Ev·ans (ĕv'ənz). **1. Oliver.** 1755–1819. Amer. inventor and steam-engine manufacturer. **2. George Henry.** 1805–56. Amer. labor and agrarian reformer. **3. John.** 1814–97. Amer. physician, businessman, and philanthropist. **4. Mary Ann.** George Eliot. **5.** Sir **Arthur John.** 1851–1941. English archaeologist. **6. Elizabeth Glendower.** 1856–1937. Amer. reformer and suffragist. **7. Herbert McLean.** 1881–1971. Amer. anatomist and embryologist. **8.** Dame **Edith.** 1888–1976. English-born actress. **9. Maurice.** b. 1901. English-born actor. **10. Walker.** 1903–1975. Amer. photographer. **11. Bergen.** 1904–78. Amer. author.
Ev·arts (ĕv'ərts), **William Maxwell.** 1818–1901. Amer. legislator and public official.
Eve (ēv). In the Old Testament, Adam's wife.
Eve·lyn (ēv'lĭn, ĕv'-), **John.** 1620–1706. English diarist.
Ev·er·ett (ĕv'ər-ĭt, ĕv'rĭt), **Edward.** 1794–1865. Amer. clergyman, orator, educator, and diplomat.
Ev·ers (ĕv'ərz), **Charles** (b. 1923) and **Medgar Wiley** (1925–63; assassinated). Amer. civil-rights leaders.
Ev·ert Lloyd (ĕv'ərt loid), **Christine Marie.** b. 1954. Amer. tennis player.
E·wald or **E·vald** (ā'vält), **Johannes.** 1743–81. Danish lyric poet.
Ew·ell (yōō'əl), **Richard Stoddert.** 1817–72. Amer. Confederate general.
Eyck (īk). See **van Eyck.**
Ez·e·ki·as (ĕz'ĭ-kī'əs). Hezekiah.
E·ze·ki·el (ĭ-zē'kē-əl). **1.** 6th cent. B.C. Hebrew prophet. **2. Moses Jacob.** 1844–1917. Amer. artist and musician.
Ez·ra (ĕz'rə). 5th cent. B.C. Hebrew scribe and priest.

F

Fa·ber (fā'bər, fä'-), **John Eberhard.** 1822–79. German-born Amer. manufacturer.
Fa·ber·gé (făb'ər-zhā'), **Peter Carl.** 1846–1920. Russian designer and jeweler.
Fa·bi·o·la (făb-ē-ō'lə, fəb-yō'). b. 1928. Belgian queen as wife of Baudouin I.
Fa·bi·us Max·i·mus Ver·ru·co·sus (fā'bē-əs măk'sə-məs vĕr-yōō-kō'səs, -ōō-), **Quintus.** d. 203 B.C. Roman general. —**Fa'bi·an** *adj. & n.*
Fa·bre (fä'bər, fä'brə), **Jean Henri.** 1823–1915. French entomologist.
Fad·den (făd'n), Sir **Arthur William.** 1895–1973. Australian statesman.
Fad·i·man (făd'ə-mən), **Clifton Paul.** b. 1904. Amer. author and editor.
Fahd (fäd), **Fahn ibn Abdel Aziz al-Saud al-.** b. 1922. King of Saudi Arabia (since 1982).
Fah·ren·heit (făr'ən-hīt', fär'-), **Gabriel Daniel.** 1686–1736. German-born physicist.
Fair·banks (fâr'băngks'). **1. Charles Warren.** 1852–1918. U.S. Vice President (1905–9). **2. Douglas** (1883–1939) and **Douglas Elton, Jr.** (b. 1909). Amer. actors.

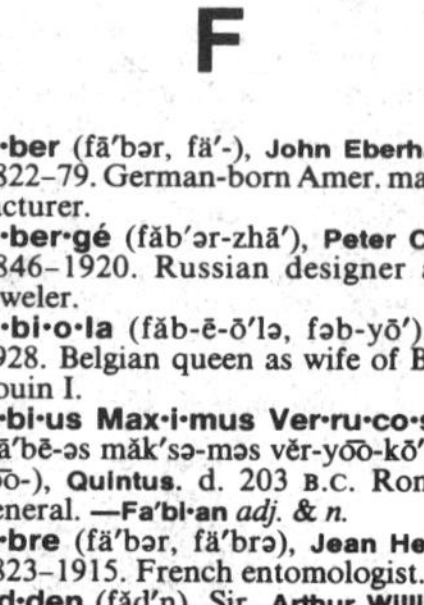

Douglas Fairbanks

Fair·child (fâr'chīld'), **Mary Salome Cutler.** 1855–1921. Amer. pioneer librarian.
Fair·fax (fâr'făks). **1. Thomas.** 3rd Baron Fairfax of Cameron. 1612–71. English Civil War soldier. **2. Thomas.** 6th Baron Fairfax. 1692–1782. English colonist in America.
Fai·sal also **Fei·sal** or **Fei·sul** (fī'səl). **1.** Name of 2 kings of Iraq: **a. I.** 1885–1933. Ruled 1921–33. **b. II.** 1935–58. Ruled 1939–58; assassinated. **2. Faisal ibn Abdel Aziz al-Saud.** 1906?–75. Saudi Arabian king (1964–75); assassinated.
Fa·lie·ri (fä-lyĕ'rē) also **Fa·lie·ro** (-rō) or **Fa·lier** (fä-lyĕr'), **Marino.** 1278?–1355. Venetian doge; executed for treason.
Falk·ner (fôk'nər). Variant of **Faulkner.**
Fall (fôl), **Albert Bacon.** 1861–1944. Amer. politician.
Fal·la (fä'yə, -lyä), **Manuel de.** 1876–1946. Spanish composer.
Fal·lières (fä-lyĕr'), **(Clément) Armand.** 1841–1931. French statesman.
Fan·euil (făn'l, făn'yəl), **Peter.** 1700–43. Amer. merchant.
Far·a·day (făr'ə-dā', -dē), **Michael.** 1791–1867. English physicist and chemist.
Far·go (fär'gō), **William George.** 1818–81. Amer. transportation pioneer.
Far·ley (fär'lē). **1. Harriet.** 1817–1907. Amer. author and editor. **2. James Aloysius.** 1888–1976. Amer. businessman and politician.
Far·man (fär'mən, fär-mäN'), **Henri** (1873–1934) and **Maurice** (1877–1964). French-born aviation pioneers.
Far·mer (fär'mər). **1. Moses Gerrish.** 1820–93. Amer. inventor and electrical pioneer. **2. Fannie Merritt.** 1857–1915. Amer. cookbook author. **3. James Leonard.** b. 1920. Amer. civil-rights leader.
Far·ne·se (fär-nā'zā), **Alessandro.** 1545–92. Italian general and diplomat.
Farns·worth (färnz'wûrth'), **Philo Taylor.** 1906–71. Amer. radio and television pioneer.
Fa·rouk I also **Fa·ruk I** (fä-rōōk'). 1920–65. Egyptian king (1936–52); abdicated.
Far·quhar (fär'kwər, -kər, -kwär), **George.** 1678–1707. Irish-born playwright.
Far·ra·gut (făr'ə-gət), **David Glasgow.** 1801–70. Amer. naval officer.

David G. Farragut

Far·rar (fär'ər). **1. Frederic William.** 1831–1903. English theologian and author. **2.** (fə-rär'), **Geraldine.** 1882–1967. Amer. soprano. **3. Margaret Petherbridge.** 1897–1984. Amer. crossword-puzzle editor.
Far·rell (făr'əl). **1. James Thomas.** 1904–79. Amer. author. **2. Eileen.** b. 1920. Amer. soprano. **3. Suzanne.** b. 1945. Amer. ballerina.
Fa·ruk (fä-rōōk'). Variant of **Farouk.**
Fat·i·ma (făt'ə-mə, fä'tē-mä'). 606–32. Daughter of Mohammed.
Fat·i·mid (făt'ə-mĭd) also **Fat·i·mite** (-mīt'). Moslem dynasty of North Africa and Egypt (909–1171).
Fau·chard (fō-shär'), **Pierre.** 1678–1761. French dentistry pioneer.
Faulk·ner also **Falk·ner** (fôk'nər), **William.** 1897–1962. Amer. author (Nobel, 1949).
Faure (fôr, fōr), **François Félix.** 1841–99. French statesman.
Fau·ré (fō-rā'), **Gabriel Urbain.** 1845–1924. French composer.
Faust (foust). Variant of **Fust.**
Faus·ta (fôs'tə, fous'-), **Flavia Maximiana.** 289–326. Roman empress as wife of Constantine I.
Fawkes (fôks), **Guy.** 1570–1606. English conspirator.
Fech·ner (fĕk'nər, fĕKH'-), **Gustav Theodor.** 1801–87. German psychologist and physicist.
Feif·fer (fī'fər), **Jules.** b. 1929. Amer. cartoonist.
Fei·ning·er (fī'nĭng-ər), **Lyonel Charles Adrian.** 1871–1956. Amer.-born artist.
Fei·sal or **Fei·sul** (fī'səl). Variants of **Faisal.**
Feke (fēk), **Robert.** 1705?–50? Amer. portrait painter.
Fel·li·ni (fə-lē'nē, fĕl-), **Federico.** b. 1920. Italian filmmaker.
Fell·tham also **Fel·tham** (fĕl'thəm), **Owen.** 1602?–68. English author.

Fel·ton (fĕl′tən), **Rebecca Ann Latimer.** 1835–1930. Amer. author, reformer, and legislator.
Fé·ne·lon (fā-nə-lôɴ′, făn-lôɴ′), **François de Salignac de la Mothe.** 1651–1715. French prelate and author.
Feng Yu·xiang or **Yu-hsiang** (fŭng′ yü′shyäng′). 1880–1948. Chinese military leader.
Fer·ber (fûr′bər), **Edna.** 1887–1968. Amer. author.
Fer·di·nand (fûr′dn-ănd′). **1.** Name of 5 kings of Castile and León, esp.: **a. I.** "the Great." d. 1065. Ruled 1037–65. **b. II.** "the Saint." 1199–1252. Ruled 1230–52. **c. V.** "the Catholic." 1452–1516. Ruled 1474–1504 with Isabella; also ruled Aragon (1479–1516) as **Ferdinand II** and Naples (1504–16) as **Ferdinand III.** **2.** Name of 3 Holy Roman Emperors: **a. I.** 1503–64. Ruled 1556–64; also king of Bohemia and Hungary (1526–64). **b. II.** 1578–1637. Ruled 1619–37; also king of Bohemia (1617–19, 1620–37) and Hungary (1618–37). **c. III.** 1608–57. Ruled 1637–57; also king of Hungary (1625–57). **3.** Name of 2 Bourbon kings of Spain: **a. VI.** "the Wise." 1712–59. Ruled 1746–59. **b. VII.** 1784–1833. Ruled 1808 and 1814–33. **4. I.** 1861–1948. Bulgarian king (1908–18).
Fer·mat (fĕr-mä′), **Pierre de.** 1601–65. French mathematician.
Fer·mi (fĕr′mē, fûr′-), **Enrico.** 1901–54. Italian-born Amer. physicist (Nobel, 1938).
Fer·nán·dez (fər-năn′dĕz′, fĕr-, fĕr-nän′dĕs), **Juan.** 1536?–1602? Spanish navigator.
Fer·now (fûr′nō), **Bernhard Edward.** 1851–1923. Prussian-born Amer. forestry pioneer.
Fer·ris (fĕr′ĭs), **George Washington Gale.** 1859–96. Amer. engineer and inventor.
Fes·sen·den (fĕs′ən-dən). **1. William Pitt.** 1806–69. Amer. politician and financier. **2. Reginald Aubrey.** 1866–1932. Canadian-born inventor and radio pioneer.
Fes·tus (fĕs′təs), **Porcius.** fl. c. 60 A.D. Roman procurator of Judea.
Feucht·wang·er (foiKHt′văng′ər), **Lion.** 1884–1958. German-born author.
Feu·er·bach (foi′ər-bäKH′), **Ludwig Andreas von.** 1804–72. German philosopher.
Feuil·let (fœ-yā′), **Octave.** 1821–90. French author.
Fewkes (fyo͞oks), **Jesse Walter.** 1850–1930. Amer. ethnologist and zoologist.
Feyn·man (fīn′mən), **Richard Phillips.** b. 1918. Amer. physicist (Nobel, 1965).
Fi·bi·ger (fē′bĭ-gər, -bē-), **Johannes Andreas Grib.** 1867–1928. Danish pathologist (Nobel, 1926).
Fich·te (fĭk′tə, fĭKH′-), **Johann Gottlieb.** 1762–1814. German philosopher.
Fied·ler (fēd′lər), **Arthur.** 1894–1979. Amer. musical conductor.
Field (fēld). **1. David Dudley.** 1805–94. Amer. jurist. **2. Stephen Johnson.** 1816–99. Amer. jurist. **3. Cyrus West.** 1819–92. Amer. merchant and financier. **4. Marshall.** 1834–1906. Amer. merchant and philanthropist. **5. Eugene.** 1850–95. Amer. author.
Field·ing (fēl′dĭng), **Henry.** 1707–54. English author.
Fields (fēldz). **1. W. C.** 1880–1946. Amer. entertainer. **2. Gracie.** 1898–1979. English comedienne.
Fie·so·le (fyĕ′zō-lā), **Giovanni Angelica da.** See Fra **Angelica.**
Fi·lene (fĭ-lēn′, fī-), **Edward Albert.** 1860–1937. Amer. merchant.
Fill·more (fĭl′môr′, -mōr′), **Millard.** 1800–74. 13th U.S. President (1850–53).
Fil·son (fĭl′sən), **John.** 1747–88. Amer. explorer and historian.
Fink (fĭngk). **1. Mike.** 1770?–1822. Amer. frontiersman. **2. Albert.** 1827–97. German-born Amer. railroad engineer.
Fin·lay (fĭn′lā, fĭn-lī′), **Carlos Juan.** 1833–1915. Cuban-born Amer. physician.
Fin·ney (fĭn′ē), **Charles Grandison.** 1792–1876. Amer. religious leader and educator.
Fin·sen (fĭn′sən), **Niels Ryberg.** 1860–1904. Danish physician (Nobel, 1903).
Fir·bank (fûr′băngk′), **Ronald.** 1886–1926. English author.
Fir·dau·si (fîr-dou′sē) also **Fir·du·si** (fər-do͞o′-). Abul Kasim, or Qasim, Mansur. 940?–1020? Persian epic poet.
Fire·stone (fīr′stōn′), **Harvey Samuel.** 1868–1938. Amer. industrialist.
Fi·scher (fĭsh′ər). **1. Emil.** 1852–1919. German chemist (Nobel, 1902). **2. Hans.** 1881–1945. German chemist (Nobel, 1930). **3. Ernst Otto.** b. 1918. German chemist (Nobel, 1973). **4. Robert James ("Bobby").** b. 1943. Amer. chess player.
Fish (fĭsh), **Hamilton.** 1808–93. Amer. politician and public official.
Fish·bein (fĭsh′bīn), **Morris.** 1889–1976. Amer. physician, author, and editor.
Fish·er (fĭsh′ər). **1. Clara.** 1811–98. English-born Amer. actress. **2. John Arbuthnot.** 1st Baron Fisher of Kilverstone. 1841–1920. British naval officer. **3. Andrew.** 1862–1928. Scottish-born Australian statesman. **4. Herbert Albert Laurens.** 1865–1940. English historian, educator, and public official. **5. Irving.** 1867–1947. Amer. economist. **6. Dorothy Canfield.** 1879–1958. Amer. author.
Fisk (fĭsk), **James.** 1834–72. Amer. railroad financier and speculator.
Fiske (fĭsk). **1. John.** 1842–1901. Amer. historian and philosopher. **2. Haley.** 1852–1929. Amer. insurance executive and innovator. **3. Minnie Maddern.** 1865–1932. Amer. actress.
Fitch (fĭch). **1. John.** 1743–98. Amer. inventor and steamboat pioneer. **2. Asa.** 1809–79. Amer. entomologist. **3. (William) Clyde.** 1865–1909. Amer. playwright. **4. Val L.** b. 1923. Amer. physicist (Nobel, 1980).
Fitz (fĭts), **Reginald Heber.** 1843–1913. Amer. pathology pioneer.
Fitz·ger·ald (fĭts-jĕr′əld). **1. F(rancis) Scott (Key).** 1896–1940. Amer. author. **2. Ella.** b. 1918. Amer. singer.
Fitz·Ger·ald (fĭts-jĕr′əld). **1. Edward.** 1809–83. English poet and translator. **2. George Francis.** 1851–1901. Irish physicist.
Fitz·gib·bon (fĭts-gĭb′ən), Sister **Irene.** 1823–96. English-born Amer. hospital pioneer.
Fitz·her·bert (fĭts-hûr′bərt), **Marie Anne Smythe.** 1756–1837. 1st wife of George IV of England; marriage declared invalid.
Fitz·hugh (fĭts-hyo͞o′), **George.** 1806–81. Lawyer and pro-slavery advocate.
Fitz·pat·rick (fĭts-păt′rĭk), **Thomas.** 1799?–1854. Irish-born Amer. trapper, guide, and Indian agent.
Fitz·sim·mons (fĭt-sĭm′ənz), **Robert Prometheus.** 1862–1917. English-born, New Zealand-raised Amer. prizefighter.
Flagg (flăg), **James Montgomery.** 1877–1960. Amer. artist and writer.
Flag·ler (flăg′lər), **Henry Morrison.** 1830–1913. Amer. capitalist and promoter.
Flag·stad (flăg′stăd′, flăg′stä′), **Kirsten Marie.** 1895–1962. Norwegian-born operatic soprano.
Fla·her·ty (flă′ər-tē, flä′-), **Robert Joseph.** 1884–1951. Amer. explorer, author, and filmmaker.

Millard Fillmore

Fla·min·i·us (flə-mĭn′ē-əs), **Gaius.** d. 217. Roman general and politician.
Flam·ma·rion (flä-mä-ryôɴ′), **Camille.** French astronomer and author.
Flan·a·gan (flăn′ə-gən), **Edward Joseph.** 1886–1948. Amer. clergyman and founder of Boys Town.
Flan·ner (flăn′ər), **Janet.** "Genêt." 1892–1978. Amer. journalist in Paris.
Flau·bert (flō-bâr′, -bĕr′), **Gustave.** 1821–80. French author. —**Flau·ber′ti·an** *adj.*
Flax·man (flăks′mən), **John.** 1755–1826. English sculptor.
Flem·ing (flĕm′ĭng). **1.** Sir **John Ambrose.** 1849–1945. English electrical engineer and inventor. **2. Williamina Paton Stevens.** 1857–1911. Scottish-born Amer. astronomer. **3.** Sir **Alexander.** 1881–1955. British bacteriologist (Nobel, 1945). **4. Ian Lancaster.** 1908–64. English author. **5. Peggy Gale.** b. 1948. Amer. figure skater.
Fletch·er (flĕch′ər). **1. John.** 1579–1625. English dramatist. **2. Alice Cunningham.** 1838–1923. Cuban-born Amer. ethnologist.
Fleu·ry (flœ-rē′), **André Hercule de.** 1653–1743. French prelate and statesman.
Flex·ner (flĕks′nər), **Abraham.** 1866–1959. Amer. educator.
Flin·ders (flĭn′dərz), Sir **Matthew.** 1774–1814. English explorer.
Flint (flĭnt). **1. Timothy.** 1780–1840. Amer. missionary and author. **2. Austin** (1812–86) and **Austin** (1836–1915). Amer. physicians.
Flo·res (flô′rĕs), **Juan José.** 1800–64. Ecuadorian general and statesman.
Flo·rey (flôr′ē, flōr′ē), Sir **Howard Walter.** 1898–1968. Australian-born English pathologist (Nobel, 1945).
Flo·ri·o (flôr′ē-ō′, flōr′-), **John.** 1553?–1625. English lexicographer.
Flo·ry (flôr′ē, flōr′ē), **Paul John.** 1910–85. Amer. chemist (Nobel, 1974).
Flynn (flĭn). **1. Elizabeth Gurley.** 1890–1964. Amer. political radical. **2. Errol.** 1909–59. Amer. actor.
Foch (fŏsh, fôsh), **Ferdinand.** 1851–1929. French army commander.
Fock·e (fôk′ə), **Heinrich.** 1890–1980. German aircraft designer and manufacturer.
Fo·gar·ty (fō′gər-tē), **Anne.** 1920?–80. Amer. fashion designer.
Fo·kine (fō-kēn′, fō′kĭn), **Michel.** 1880–1942. Russian-born Amer. choreographer.
Fok·ker (fŏk′ər, fō′kər), **Anthony Herman Gerard.** 1890–1939. Dutch aircraft designer and manufacturer.
Fo·ley (fō′lē), **John Henry.** 1818–74. Irish sculptor.
Fol·ger (fōl′jər), **Henry Clay.** 1857–1930. Amer. capitalist and bibliophile.
Fol·kung (fôl′ko͝ong′). Swedish ruling dynasty (1250–1523).
Fol·lett (fŏl′ət), **Mary Parker.** 1868–1933. Amer. author and counselor.
Fon·da (fŏn′də), **Henry.** 1905–82. Amer. actor.
Fon·tanne (fŏn-tăn′), **Lynn.** 1887?–1983. English-born Amer. actress.
Fon·teyn (fŏn-tān′), Dame **Margot.** b. 1919. English ballerina.
Foote (fo͝ot). **1. Samuel.** 1720–77. English actor and dramatist. **2. Andrew Hull.** 1806–63. Amer. naval officer. **3. Mary Hallock.** 1847–1938. Amer. author and illustrator.
Forbes (fôrbz), **Malcolm Stevenson.** b. 1919. Amer. publisher and sportsman.
Forbes-Rob·ert·son (fôrbz-rŏb′ərt-sən), Sir **Johnston.** 1853–1937. English actor.
Force (fôrs), **Peter.** 1790–1868. Amer. historian and printer.
Ford (fôrd, fōrd). **1. John.** 1586–1639. English dramatist. **2. Henry** (1863–1947) and **Henry, Jr.** (b. 1917). Amer. automobile manufacturers. **3. Paul Leicester.** 1865–1902. Amer. author and historian. **4. Ford Madox.** 1873–1939. English author. **5. John.** 1895–1973. Amer. filmmaker. **6. Gerald Rudolph.** b. 1913. 38th U.S. President (1974–77). **7. Edward ("Whitey").** b. 1928. Amer. baseball player.
For·es·ter (fôr′ĭ-stər, fŏr′-), **Cecil Scott ("C. S.").** 1899–1966. English author.
For·rest (fôr′ĭst, fŏr′). **1. Edwin.** 1806–72. Amer. actor. **2. Nathan Bedford.** 1821–77. Amer. Confederate general.
For·res·tal (fôr′ĭ-stəl, -stôl′, fŏr′-), **James Vincent.** 1892–1949. Amer. banker and public official.
Forss·mann (fôrs′män′, -mən, fŏrs′-), **Werner Theodor Otto.** 1904–79. German physician (Nobel, 1956).
For·ster (fôr′stər), **Edward Morgan ("E.M.").** 1879–1970. English author.
For·syth (fôr-sīth′, fər-, fôr′sĭth), **John.** 1780–1841. Amer. politician and diplomat.
For·tas (fôr′təs), **Abraham ("Abe").** 1910–82. Amer. jurist; resigned from Supreme Court.
For·ten (fôr′tn), **James.** 1766–1842. Amer. businessman and reformer.
For·tes·cue (fôr′tĭs-kyo͞o′), Sir **John.** 1394?–1476? English jurist.
Fos·dick (fŏz′dĭk), **Harry Emerson.** 1878–1969. Amer. religious leader.
Fos·se (fŏs′ē), **Robert Louis ("Bob").** b. 1927. Amer. choreographer and director.
Fos·ter (fô′stər, fŏs′tər). **1. Hannah Webster.** 1759–1840. Amer. author. **2. Abigail Kelley ("Abby").** 1810–87. Amer. abolitionist and suffragist. **3. Stephen Collins.** 1826–64. Amer. songwriter. **4. John Watson.** 1836–1917. Amer. diplomat. **5. William Zebulon.** 1881–1961. Amer. labor leader and radical politician.

Stephen Foster

Fou·cault (fo͞o-kō′), **Jean Bernard Léon.** 1819–68. French physicist.
Fou·quet also **Fouc·quet** (fo͞o-kĕ′). **1. Jean.** 1415?–80. French artist. **2. Nicolas.** Marquis de Belle-Isle. 1615–80. French financier and public official.
Four·dri·nier (fo͝or-drĭn′ē-ər, fôr-, fōr-), **Henry** (1766–1854) and **Sealy** (d. 1847). English papermakers and inventors.
Fou·rier (fo͝or′ē-ā′, -ē-ər, fo͞o-ryā′). **1.** Baron **Jean Baptiste Joseph.** 1768–1830. French mathematician and physicist. **2. François Marie Charles.** 1772–1837. French socialist author.
Fow·ler (fou′lər), **Henry Watson.** 1858–1933. English lexicographer.
Fox (fŏks). **1. George.** 1624–91. English Quaker religious leader. **2. Henry.** 1st Baron Holland. 1705–74. English statesman. **3. Charles James.** 1749–1806. English politician and orator. **4. Gustavus Vasa.** 1821–83. Amer. naval officer. **5. Margaret.** 1833–93.

Gerald R. Ford

Amer. spiritualist medium. **6. Richard Kyle.** 1846–1922. Irish-born Amer. journalist. **7. John William, Jr.** 1863–1919. Amer. author. **8. Dixon Ryan.** 1887–1945. Amer. historian.

Foxe (fŏks). **1.** Or **Fox, Richard.** 1448?–1528. English prelate. **2. John.** 1516–87. English martyrologist.

Foy (foi), **Eddie.** 1856–1928. Amer. entertainer.

Frac·ci (frät'chē), **Carla.** b. 1936. Italian-born ballerina.

Fra·go·nard (frăg'ə-när', frä-gô-), **Jean Honoré.** 1732–1806. French artist.

France (frăns, fräns, fräɴs), **Anatole.** 1844–1924. French author (Nobel, 1921).

Fran·ce·sca (frăn-chĕs'kə, frän-, frän-chĕ'skä), **Piero della.** 1420?–92. Italian painter.

Francesca da Ri·mi·ni (də rĭm'ĭ-nē, rē'mə-, dä rē'mē-nē). d. 1285? Italian noblewoman.

Fran·cis (frăn'sĭs). **1. of As·si·si** (ə-sē'-zē, -sē, ə-sĭs'ē), Saint. 1182?–1226. Italian monk and founder of the Franciscan order. **2.** Name of 2 French kings, esp. **I,** 1494–1547, ruled 1515–47. **3. of Sales** (sālz, säl), Saint. 1567–1622. French ecclesiastic. **4.** Name of 2 Holy Roman Emperors, esp. **II,** 1768–1835, ruled 1792–1806; also Austrian emperor (1804–35) as **Francis I.**

Francis Fer·di·nand (fûr'dn-ănd'). 1863–1914. Austrian archduke; assassinated.

Francis Jo·seph I (jō'zəf, -səf). 1830–1916. Austrian emperor (1848–1916).

Francis Xa·vi·er (zā'vē-ər, -vyər, ĭg-zā'-, zăv'ē-ər), Saint. See **Xavier.**

Franck (frängk). **1.** (*also* fräɴk), **César Auguste.** 1822–90. French composer. **2. James.** 1882–1964. German-born Amer. physicist (Nobel, 1925).

Franck·e (fräng'kə), **Kuno.** 1855–1930. German-born Amer. historian and educator.

Fran·co (frăng'kō, fräng'kô), **Francisco.** "El Caudillo." 1892–1975. Spanish soldier and dictator (1939–75).

Frank (frăngk). **1. Glenn.** 1887–1940. Amer. editor and educator. **2.** (frängk), **Ilya Mikhailovich.** b. 1908. Russian physicist (Nobel, 1958). **3.** (*also* frängk), **Anne.** 1929–45. Dutch Jewish diarist.

Frank·en·thal·er (frăng'kən-thô'lər, -thŏl'-), **Helen.** b. 1928. Amer. artist.

Frank·furt·er (frăngk'fər-tər), **Felix.** 1882–1965. Austrian-born Amer. jurist.

Frank·lin (frăngk'lĭn). **1. Benjamin.** 1706–90. Amer. statesman, diplomat, author, scientist, and printer. **2. Sir John.** 1786–1847. English Arctic explorer. **3. John Hope.** b. 1915. Amer. historian. **4. Aretha.** b. 1942. Amer. singer.

Benjamin Franklin

Franks (frăngks), Baron **Oliver Shewell.** b. 1905. English educator and diplomat.

Franz Jo·sef I (fränts jō'səf, yō'zəf). *German.* Francis Joseph I.

Fra·ser (frā'zər). **1. Simon.** 12th Baron Lovat. 1667?–1747. Scottish Jacobite; beheaded. **2. Simon.** 1776?–1862. Amer.-born Canadian explorer and fur trader. **3. James Earle.** 1876–1953. Amer. sculptor. **4. Peter.** 1884–1950. Scottish-born New Zealand statesman. **5. (John) Malcolm.** b. 1930. Australian statesman.

Fra·zer (frā'zər), Sir **James George.** 1854–1941. Scottish anthropologist (*The Golden Bough*).

Fra·zier (frā'zhər). **1. Edward Franklin.** 1894–1962. Amer. sociologist. **2. Joe.** b. 1944. Amer. prizefighter. **3. Walt.** b. 1945. Amer. basketball player.

Fred·er·ick (frĕd'rĭk, -ər-ĭk). **1.** Name of 3 Holy Roman Emperors: **a. I.** "Frederick Barbarossa." 1123?–90. Ruled 1152–90 (crowned 1155); also king of Germany (1152–90) and Italy (1155–90). **b. II.** 1194–1250. Ruled 1215–50 (crowned 1220); also king of Sicily (1198–1250) as **Frederick I. c. III.** 1415–93. Ruled 1440–93 (crowned 1452); also king of Germany as **Frederick IV. 2.** Name of 3 Prussian kings: **a. I.** 1657–1713. Ruled 1701–13; also elector of Brandenburg (1688–1701) as **Frederick III. b. II.** "the Great." 1712–86. Ruled 1740–86. **c. III.** 1831–88. Ruled 1888. **3.** Name of 6 kings of Denmark and Norway, esp.: **a. II.** 1534–88. Ruled 1559–88. **b. III.** 1609–70. Ruled 1648–70. **c. IV.** 1671–1730. Ruled 1699–1730. **d. V.** 1723–66. Ruled 1746–66. **4.** Name of 9 Danish kings, esp. **IX,** 1899–1972, ruled 1947–72.

Frederick Wil·liam (wĭl'yəm). **1.** "the Great Elector." 1620–88. Elector of Brandenburg (1640–88). **2.** Name of 4 Prussian kings: **a. I.** 1688–1740. Ruled 1713–40. **b. II.** 1744–97. Ruled 1786–97. **c. III.** 1770–1840. Ruled 1797–1840. **d. IV.** 1795–1861. Ruled 1840–61.

Free·man (frē'mən). **1. Mary Eleanor Wilkins.** 1852–1930. Amer. author. **2. Douglas Southall.** 1886–1953. Amer. historian and editor.

Fre·ling·huy·sen (frē'lĭng-hī'zən), **Frederick Theodore.** 1817–85. Amer. legislator and public official.

Fré·mont (frē'mŏnt'), **John Charles.** 1813–90. Amer. soldier, explorer, and politician.

French (frĕnch), **Daniel Chester.** 1850–1931. Amer. sculptor.

Fre·neau (frĭ-nō'), **Philip Morin.** 1752–1832. Amer. author.

Fres·co·bal·di (frĕs'kō-bäl'dē), **Girolamo.** 1583–1643. Italian composer.

Fres·nel (frā-nĕl', frə-), **Augustin Jean.** 1788–1827. French physicist.

Freud (froid), **Sigmund.** 1856–1939. Austrian physician and pioneer psychoanalyst. —**Freud'i·an** *adj. & n.*

Frey·berg (frī'bûrg'), 1st Baron. Bernard Cyril Freyberg. 1890–1963. English-born New Zealand soldier and statesman.

Frey·tag (frī'täk', -täg'), **Gustav.** 1816–95. German author.

Frick (frĭk), **Henry Clay.** 1849–1919. Amer. industrialist and art patron.

Fried (frēd, frēt), **Alfred Herman.** 1864–1921. Austrian pacifist (Nobel, 1911).

Frie·dan (frī-dăn'), **Betty Naomi Goldstein.** b. 1921. Amer. feminist.

Fried·man (frēd'mən). **1. Milton.** b. 1912. Amer. economist (Nobel, 1976). **2. Esther Pauline** ("Ann Landers") and **Pauline Esther** ("Abigail Van Buren," "Dear Abby"). b. 1918. Amer. advice columnists.

Friet·chie (frĭch'ē), **Barbara Hauer.** 1766–1862. Amer. Civil War heroine.

Friml (frĭm'əl), **(Charles) Rudolf.** 1879–1972. Amer. pianist and composer.

Frisch (frĭsh). **1. Karl von.** 1886–1982. Austrian-German zoologist (Nobel, 1973). **2. Ragnar.** 1895–1973. Norwegian economist (Nobel, 1969).

Fro·bish·er (frō'bĭ-shər, frŏb'ĭ-), Sir **Martin.** 1535?–94. English navigator.

Froe·bel also **Frö·bel** (frœ'bəl), **Friedrich Wilhelm August.** 1782–1852. German educator; founder of kindergarten system.

Froh·man (frō'mən), **Charles.** 1860–1915. Amer. theatrical manager.

Frois·sart (froi'särt', frwä-sär'), **Jean.** 1333?–1400. French historian.

Fromm (frŏm, frōm), **Erich.** 1900–80. German-born Amer. psychoanalyst.

Fron·te·nac (frŏn'tə-năk', frôɴt-näk'), Comte **Louis de Buade de.** 1622–98. French colonial administrator.

Frost (frôst, frŏst), **Robert Lee.** 1874–1963. Amer. poet.

Froth·ing·ham (frŏth'ĭng-hăm', -əm), **Octavius Brooks.** 1822–95. Amer. clergyman and author.

Froude (frōōd), **James Anthony.** 1818–94. English historian.

Fry (frī), **Roger Eliot.** 1866–1934. English artist and critic.

Fu·ad I (fōō-äd'). 1868–1936. Egyptian king (1922–36).

Fu·en·tes (fōō-ĕn'tās', fwĕn'tĕs), **Carlos.** b. 1928. Mexican author.

Fuer·tes (fyōōr'tēz, -tĕs, fyōō'ər-), **Louis Agassiz.** 1874–1927. Amer. naturalist and artist.

Fug·ger (fōōg'ər). Family of German bankers, including **Johannes** (1348–1409), **Andreas** (d. 1457), **Jakob I** (d. 1469), **Ulrich** (1441–1510), **Georg** (1453–1506), **Jakob II** ("the Rich"; 1459–1525), **Raymund** (1489–1535), **Anton** (1493–1560), **Hans Jakob** (1516–79), **Ulrich** (1526–84), and **Georg** (d. 1569).

Fu·ku·i (fōō'kōō-ē'), **Kenichi.** b. 1918. Japanese chemist (Nobel, 1981).

Ful·bright (fōōl'brīt'), **J(ames) William.** b. 1905. Amer. legislator.

Ful·da (fōōl'də, -dä), **Ludwig.** 1862–1939. German playwright.

Ful·ler (fōōl'ər). **1. Thomas.** 1608–61. English clergyman. **2. (Sara) Margaret.** 1810–50. Amer. author, critic, and reformer. **3. George.** 1822–84. Amer. painter. **4. Melville Weston.** 1833–1910. Amer. jurist. **5. Sarah.** 1836–1927. Amer. educator. **6. Loie.** 1862–1928. Amer. dancer. **7. Alfred Carl.** 1885–1973. Amer. businessman. **8. (Richard) Buckminster.** 1895–1983. Amer. inventor.

Ful·ton (fōōl'tən), **Robert.** 1765–1815. Amer. artist, engineer, and inventor.

Funk (fŭngk). **1. Isaac Kauffman.** 1839–1912. Amer. clergyman, editor, and publisher. **2.** (*also* fōōngk), **Casimir.** 1884–1967. Polish-born Amer. biochemist.

Fun·ston (fŭn'stən), **Frederick.** 1865–1917. Amer. botanist, explorer, and soldier.

Fur·ness. 1. (fûr'nĭs), **Horace Howard** (1833–1912) and **Horace Howard** (1865–1930). Amer. Shakespearean scholars. **2.** (fər-nĕs'), **Elizabeth ("Betty").** b. 1916. Amer. consumer advocate.

Fur·ni·vall (fûr'nə-vəl), **Frederick James.** 1825–1910. English scholar and editor.

Furt·wäng·ler (fōōrt'vĕng'lər), **Wilhelm.** 1886–1954. German conductor.

Fu·sel·i (fyōō'zə-lē'), **Henry.** 1741–1825. Swiss-born English artist.

Fust (fōōst) also **Faust** (foust), **Johann.** 1400?–66? German printer.

G

Ga·ble (gā'bəl), **(William) Clark.** 1901–60. Amer. actor.

Ga·bo (gä'bə, -bō), **Naum.** 1890–1977. Russian-born Amer. constructivist sculptor and designer.

Ga·bor (gä'bôr, gə-bôr'), **Dennis.** 1900–79. Hungarian-born British physicist (Nobel, 1971).

Ga·bo·riau (gä-bô-ryō'), **Émile.** 1835–73. French detective novelist.

Gad·da·fi (gə-dä'fē), **Muammar.** See **Qaddafi.**

Gads·den (gădz'dən), **James.** 1788–1858. Amer. diplomat, politician and railroad promoter.

Gad·ski (gät'skē), **Johanna.** 1872–1932. German operatic soprano.

Gág (gäg), **Wanda Hazel.** 1893–1946. Amer. author and illustrator.

Ga·ga·rin (gä-gär'ĭn, gə-), **Yuri Alekseyevich.** 1934–68. Soviet cosmonaut; 1st man in space.

Gage (gāj). **1. Thomas.** 1721–87. British general and colonial administrator. **2. Matilda Joslyn.** 1826–98. Amer. feminist.

Gail·lard (gĭl-yärd'), **David Du Bose.** 1859–1913. Amer. army engineer.

Gaines (gānz), **Edmund Pendleton.** 1777–1849. Amer. army officer.

Gains·bor·ough (gānz'bûr'ō, -bər-ə), **Thomas.** 1727–88. English portrait and landscape painter.

Gai·ser·ic (gī'zə-rĭk'). Variant of **Genseric.**

Gait·skell (gāt'skəl), **Hugh Todd Naylor.** 1906–63. British politician.

Ga·ius (gā'əs, gī'-) or **Ca·ius** (kā'-, kī'-). 2nd cent. A.D. Roman jurist.

Gaj·du·sek (gī'də-shĕk'), **D(aniel) Carleton.** b. 1923. Amer. virologist (Nobel, 1976).

Gal·ba (găl'bə, gôl'-), **Servius Sulpicius.** 5 B.C.?–A.D. 69. Roman emperor (68–69).

Gal·braith (găl'brāth', -brəth), **John Kenneth.** b. 1908. Canadian-born Amer. economist, diplomat, and author.

Gale (gāl), **Zona.** 1874–1938. Amer. novelist and playwright.

Ga·len (gā'lən). 130?–201? Greek anatomist, physician, and author.

Ga·le·ri·us (gə-lîr'ē-əs). d. 311. Roman emperor (305–11).

Ga·li·le·o Ga·li·lei (găl'ə-lē'ō găl'-ə-lā'ē, -lā'ō, gä'lē-lĕ'ō gä'lē-lĕ'ē). 1564–1642. Italian astronomer and physicist.

Gal·la·tin (găl'ə-tĭn, -tn), **(Abraham Alfonso) Albert.** 1761–1849. Swiss-born Amer. financier and politician.

Gal·lau·det (găl'ə-dĕt'), **Thomas Hopkins.** 1787–1851. Amer. educator.

Ga·lle·gos Fre·ire (gä-yĕ'gôs frĕ'rĕ), **Rómulo.** 1884–1969. Venezuelan author.

Gal·li·co (găl'ĭ-kō'), **Paul.** 1897–1976. Amer. author.

Gal·li-Cur·ci (găl'ĭ-kûr'chē, gä'-lē-kōōr'-), **Amelita.** 1899–1963. Italian operatic soprano.

Gal·lié·ni (gä-lyā-nē'), **Joseph Simon.** 1849–1916. French army officer and colonial administrator.

Gal·li·e·nus (găl'ē-ē'nəs, -ā'nəs), **Publius Licinius Valerianus.** d. 268. Roman emperor (253–68).

Gal·lo·way (găl'ə-wā'), **Joseph.** 1731?–1803. English Loyalist in America.

Gal·lup (găl'əp), **George Horace.** 1901–84. Amer. public-opinion analyst.

Ga·lois (gä-lwä'), **Evariste.** 1811–32. French mathematician.

Gals·wor·thy (gôlz'wûr'thē), **John.** 1867–1933. English author (Nobel, 1932).

Gal·ton (gôlt'n), Sir **Francis.** 1822–1911. English scientist; founder of science of eugenics.

Gal·va·ni (găl-vä'nē, găl'-), **Luigi** or **Aloisio.** 1737–98. Italian physicist and physician.

Gál·vez (găl'vĕs'), **José de.** 1729–87. Spanish colonial administrator.

Gal·way (gôl'wā), **James.** b. 1939. Irish-born British flutist.

Ga·ma (găm'ə, gä'mə), **Vasco da.** 1469?–1524. Portuguese explorer and colonial administrator.

Ga·mar·ra (gä-mär'rä), **Agustín.** 1785–1841. Peruvian general and statesman.

Gam·bet·ta (găm-bĕt'ə, gäɴ-bĕ-tä'), **Léon.** 1838–82. French political leader.

Ga·me·lin (gäm-lăɴ'), **Maurice Gustave.** 1872–1958. French army officer.

Ga·mow (gă'mŏv, -mou), **George.** 1904–68. Russian-born Amer. physicist.

Gan·dhi (gän'dē, găn'-). **1. Mohandas Karamchand ("Mahatma").** 1869–

Mohandas Gandhi

1948. Indian nationalist and spiritual leader; assassinated. **2. Indira Nehru.** 1917–84. Indian political leader; assassinated.
Gan·nett (găn′ĭt), **Henry.** 1846–1914. Amer. geographer and statistician.
Gar·a·mond (găr′ə-mŏnd, gä-rä-mô**N**′), **Claude.** d. 1561. French type designer.
Ga·rand (gə-rănd′, găr′ənd), **John Cantius.** 1888–1974. Canadian-born Amer. firearms designer.
Gar·bo (gär′bō), **Greta.** b. 1905. Swedish-born Amer. actress.
Gar·cí·a Gu·tiér·rez (gär-sē′ä gōō-tyĕr′rĕs), **Antonio.** 1813–84. Spanish author.
García Lor·ca (lôr′kä), **Federico.** 1899–1936. Spanish author.
García Mo·re·no (mô-rĕ′nô), **Gabriel.** 1821–75. Ecuadorian political leader; assassinated.
García y Íñi·guez (ē ē′nyē-gĕs′), **Calixto.** 1836?–98. Cuban military and political leader.
Gar·ci·la·so de la Ve·ga (gär-sē-lä′-sô de lä vĕ′gä). "El Inca." 1539?–1616. Peruvian soldier, historian, and translator.
Gar·den (gär′dn). **1. Alexander.** 1730?–91. Scottish-born naturalist and physician. **2. Mary.** 1874?–1967. Scottish-born operatic soprano.
Gar·den·er (gär′dn-ər, gärd′nər), **Helen Hamilton.** 1853–1925. Amer. suffragist.
Gar·di·ner (gärd′nər, gär′dn-ər). **1. Stephen.** 1483?–1555. English religious and political leader. **2. Samuel Rawson.** 1829–1902. English historian, educator, and editor.
Gard·ner (gärd′nər). **1. Isabella Stewart.** 1840–1924. Amer. socialite and art collector. **2. Erle Stanley.** 1889–1970. Amer. lawyer and detective novelist.
Gar·field (gär′fēld′). **1. James Abram.** 1831–81. 20th U.S. President (1881); assassinated. **2. John.** 1913–52. Amer. actor.

James A. Garfield

Gar·i·bal·di (găr′ə-bôl′dē, gä-rē-bäl′-dē), **Giuseppe.** 1807–82. Italian general and nationalist leader.
Gar·land (gär′lənd). **1. (Hannibal) Hamlin.** 1860–1940. Amer. author. **2. Judy.** 1922–69. Amer. actress and singer.
Gar·ner (gär′nər), **John Nance.** 1868–1967. U.S. Vice President (1933–41).
Gar·nett (gär′nĭt), **Constance Black.** 1862–1946. English translator.
Gar·rick (găr′ĭk), **David.** 1717–79. English actor and theatrical manager.
Gar·ri·son (găr′ĭ-sən). **1. William Lloyd.** 1805–79. Amer. abolitionist, journalist, and lecturer. **2. Mabel.** 1886–1963. Amer. operatic soprano.
Gar·vey (gär′vē), **Marcus (Moziah) Aurelius.** 1887–1940. Jamaican black nationalist active in America; deported.
Gar·y (gâr′ē, găr′ē), **Elbert Henry.** 1846–1927. Amer. lawyer and financier.
Gas·coigne (găs′koin′), **George.** 1535?–77. English author.
Gas·kell (găs′kəl), **Elizabeth Cleghorn Stevenson.** 1810–65. English novelist.
Gas·ser (găs′ər), **Herbert Spencer.** 1888–1963. Amer. physiologist (Nobel, 1944).
Gates (gāts). **1. Horatio.** 1727?–1806. Amer. Revolutionary general. **2. Frederick Taylor.** 1853–1929. Amer. clergyman and philanthropist. **3. John Warne ("Bet-you-a-million").** 1855–1911. Amer. speculator and promoter.
Gat·ling (găt′lĭng), **Richard Jordan.** 1818–1903. Amer. firearms inventor.
Gau·dí (gou′dē, gou-dē′), **Antonio.** 1852–1926. Spanish architect.
Gau·guin (gō-gă**N**′), **(Eugène Henri) Paul.** 1848–1903. French painter.
Gauss (gous), **Karl Friedrich.** 1777–1855. German mathematician and astronomer.
Gau·tier (gō-tyā′), **Théophile.** 1811–72. French author.
Gay (gā), **John.** 1685–1732. English poet.
Gay-Lus·sac (gā′lə-săk′, -lü-säk′), **Joseph Louis.** 1778–1850. French chemist and physicist.
Gay·nor (gā′nər), **Janet.** 1906–84. Amer. actress.
Gea·ry (gîr′ē), **John White.** 1819–73. Amer. general and politician.
Ge·ber (jē′bər, gā′-) also **Ja·bir** (jä′bîr, jā′bər). 721–66. Arab scholar and alchemist.
Ged·des (gĕd′ēz), **Norman Bel.** 1893–1958. Amer. architect and theatrical and industrial designer.
Geh·rig (gĕr′ĭg), **Henry Louis ("Lou").** 1903–42. Amer. baseball player.
Gei·kie (gē′kē), Sir **Archibald.** 1835–1924. Scottish geologist.
Gei·sel (gī′zəl), **Theodor Seuss.** "Dr. Seuss." b. 1904. Amer. author and illustrator.
Gell-Mann (gĕl′măn′), **Murray.** b. 1929. Amer. physicist (Nobel, 1969).
Ge·net (zhə-nā′, -nĕ′), **Jean.** 1910–86. French author.
Ge·nêt (zhə-nā′, -nĕ′). **1. Edmond Charles Edouard.** 1763–1834. French diplomat. **2.** Janet Flanner.
Gen·ghis Khan (jĕng′gĭs kän′, gĕng′-). 1162?–1227. Mongol conqueror.
Gen·ser·ic (jĕn′sə-rĭk′, gĕn′-) also **Gai·ser·ic** (gī′zə-). d. 477. Vandal king (428–77).
Gen·ti·le da Fa·bri·a·no (jĕn-tē′lä dä fä-brē-ä′nō). 1370?–1427? Italian painter.
Geof·frey of Mon·mouth (jĕf′rē; mŏn′məth). 1100?–54? English prelate and chronicler.
George (jôrj). **1.** Saint. d. c.303. Christian martyr. **2.** Name of 6 kings of Great Britain: **a. I.** 1660–1727. Ruled 1714–27. **b. II.** 1683–1760. Ruled 1727–60. **c. III.** 1738–1820. Ruled 1760–1820. **d. IV.** 1762–1830. Ruled 1820–30. **e. V.** 1865–1936. Ruled 1910–36. **f. VI.** 1895–1952. Ruled 1936–1952. **3. Henry.** 1839–97. Amer. journalist and reformer. **4.** Name of 2 kings of Greece: **a. I.** 1845–1913. Ruled 1863–1913; assassinated. **b. II.** 1890–1947. Ruled 1922–23 and 1935–47. **5. Stefan.** 1868–1933. German lyric symbolist poet.

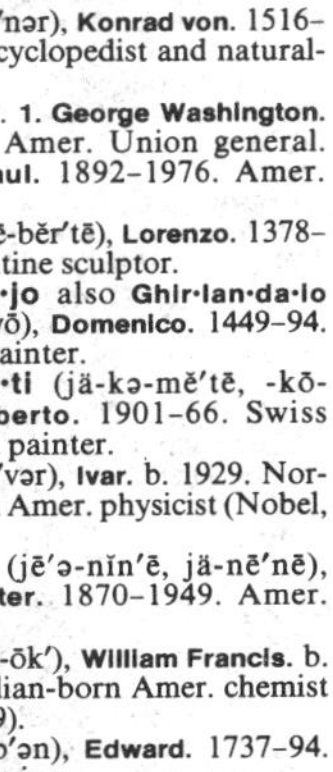

George III

Ge·rard (jə-rärd′). **1.** (*also* jĕr′ärd′), **Charles.** 1st Baron Gerard of Brandon, 1st Earl of Macclesfield. 1618?–94. English Royalist commander. **2. James Watson.** 1867–1951. Amer. diplomat.
Gé·ri·cault (zhā-rē-kō′), **Jean Louis André Théodore.** 1791–1824. French painter.
Ger·man·i·cus Cae·sar (jər-măn′-ĭ-kəs sē′zər). 15 B.C.–A.D. 19. Roman general.
Gé·rôme (zhā-rōm′), **Jean Léon.** 1824–1904. French painter.
Ge·ron·i·mo (jə-rŏn′ə-mō′). 1829–1909. Amer. Apache leader.

Geronimo

Ger·ould (jĕr′əld), **Katherine Elizabeth Fullerton.** 1879–1944. Amer. author.
Ger·ry (gĕr′ē), **Elbridge.** 1744–1814. U.S. Vice President (1813–14); died in office.

Elbridge Gerry

Gersh·win (gûrsh′wĭn). **1. Ira.** 1896–1983. Amer. lyricist. **2. George.** 1898–1937. Amer. composer.
Ge·sell (gĭ-zĕl′), **Arnold Lucius.** 1880–1961. Amer. physiologist and pediatrician.
Ges·ner (gĕs′nər), **Konrad von.** 1516–65. Swiss encyclopedist and naturalist.
Get·ty (gĕt′ē). **1. George Washington.** 1819–1901. Amer. Union general. **2. J(ean) Paul.** 1892–1976. Amer. oilman.
Ghi·ber·ti (gē-bĕr′tē), **Lorenzo.** 1378–1455. Florentine sculptor.
Ghir·lan·da·jo also **Ghir·lan·da·io** (gēr-län-dä′yō), **Domenico.** 1449–94. Florentine painter.
Gia·co·met·ti (jä-kə-mĕ′tē, -kō-mĕt′tē), **Alberto.** 1901–66. Swiss sculptor and painter.
Giae·ver (yā′vər), **Ivar.** b. 1929. Norwegian-born Amer. physicist (Nobel, 1973).
Gi·an·nin·i (jē′ə-nĭn′ē, jä-nē′nē), **Amadeo Peter.** 1870–1949. Amer. banker.
Gi·auque (jē-ōk′), **William Francis.** b. 1895. Canadian-born Amer. chemist (Nobel, 1949).
Gib·bon (gĭb′ən), **Edward.** 1737–94. English historian.
Gib·bons (gĭb′ənz), **Abigail Hopper.** 1801–93. Amer. social reformer and philanthropist.
Gibbs (gĭbz). **1. Oliver Wolcott.** 1822–1908. Amer. chemist. **2. Josiah Willard.** 1839–1903. Amer. mathematician and physicist. **3.** Sir **Philip.** 1877–1962. English author and editor.
Gib·ran (jĭ-brän′), **(Gibran) Kahlil.** 1883–1931. Syrian-born Amer. mystic poet (*The Prophet*) and painter.
Gib·son (gĭb′sən). **1. Charles Dana.** 1867–1944. Amer. illustrator. **2. Althea.** b. 1927. Amer. tennis player.
Gid·dings (gĭd′ĭngz), **Joshua Reed.** 1795–1864. Amer. abolitionist and politician.
Gide (zhēd), **André.** 1869–1951. French author (Nobel, 1947).
Gid·e·on (gĭd′ē-ən). Hebrew judge and hero in the Old Testament.
Giel·gud (gĭl′gōōd′, gēl′-), Sir **(Arthur) John.** b. 1904. English actor and director.
Gil·bert (gĭl′bərt). **1.** Sir **Humphrey.** 1539?–83. English navigator and soldier; drowned at sea. **2. William.** 1540–1603. English court physician. **3. Anne Jane Hartley.** 1821–1904. English-born Amer. actress. **4.** Sir **William Schwenck.** 1836–1911. English playwright and lyricist. **5. Grove Karl.** 1843–1918. Amer. geologist and surveyor. **6. Cass.** 1859–1934. Amer. architect. **7. Henry Franklin Belknap.** 1868–1928. Amer. composer. **8. John.** 1897–1936. Amer. actor. **9. Walter.** b. 1932. Amer. biologist (Nobel, 1980).
Gil·der (gĭl′dər), **Richard Watson** (1844–1909) and **Jeannette Leonard** (1849–1916). Amer. authors and editors.
Gil·der·sleeve (gĭl′dər-slēv′), **Basil Lanneau.** 1831–1924. Amer. philologist.
Gill (gĭl), **Theodore Nicholas.** 1837–1914. Amer. zoologist.
Gil·lett (jə-lĕt′), **Frederick Huntington.** 1851–1935. Amer. legislator.
Gil·lette (jə-lĕt′). **1. William Hooker.** 1855?–1937. Amer. actor and playwright. **2. King Camp.** 1855–1932. Amer. inventor (safety razor) and manufacturer.
Gil·liss (gĭl′ĭs), **James Melville.** 1811–65. Amer. naval officer and astronomer.
Gil·man (gĭl′mən). **1. Caroline Howard.** 1794–1888. Amer. author. **2. Daniel Coit.** 1831–1908. Amer. educator. **3. Arthur.** 1837–1909. Amer. educator. **4. Charlotte Anna Perkins Stetson.** 1860–1935. Amer. reformer and author.
Gil·mer (gĭl′mər), **Elizabeth Meriwether.** "Dorothy Dix." 1870–1951. Amer. journalist.
Gil·pin (gĭl′pĭn), **Charles Sidney.** 1878–1930. Amer. actor.
Gins·berg (gĭnz′bərg), **Allen.** b. 1926. Amer. poet.
Gior·gio·ne (jôr-jō′nā, -nē), **II.** 1478?–1511. Venetian painter.
Giot·to (jŏt′ō, jôt′tō). 1266?–1337. Florentine painter, architect, and sculptor.
Gi·rard. **1.** (jə-rärd′), **Stephen.** 1750–1831. French-born Amer. financier and philanthropist. **2.** (zhē-rär′), **Jean Baptiste.** 1765?–1850. Swiss educator.
Gi·raud (zhē-rō′), **Henri Honoré.** 1879–1949. French military officer and politician.
Gi·rau·doux (zhē-rō-dōō′), **Jean.** 1882–1944. French author.
Gir·tin (gûr′tn), **Thomas.** 1775–1802. English landscape painter.
Gis·card d'Es·taing (zhē-skär′ dĕs-tă**N**′), **Valéry.** b. 1926. French political leader.
Gish (gĭsh), **Lillian Diana** (b. 1896) and **Dorothy** (1898–1968). Amer. actresses.
Gis·sing (gĭs′ĭng), **George Robert.** 1857–1903. English novelist and critic.
Gist (gĭst), **Christopher.** 1706?–59. Amer. frontier explorer.
Gi·ven·chy (gə-vĭn′chē, zhē-vä**N**-shē′), **Hubert.** b. 1927. French fashion designer.
Gjel·le·rup (gĕl′ə-rōōp), **Karl.** 1857–1919. Danish author (Nobel, 1917).
Glack·ens (glăk′ənz), **William James.** 1870–1938. Amer. artist.
Glad·den (glăd′n), **Washington.** 1836–1918. Amer. clergyman and author.
Glad·stone (glăd′stōn′), **William Ewart.** 1809–98. British prime minister (4 times between 1868 and 1894).
Gla·ser (glā′zər), **Donald Arthur.** b. 1926. Amer. physicist (Nobel, 1960).
Glas·gow (glăs′kō′, -gō′, glăz′-), **Ellen Anderson Gholson.** 1874–1945. Amer. novelist.
Glash·ow (glăsh′ō), **Sheldon Lee.** b.

1932. Amer. physicist (Nobel, 1979).

Glas·pell (glăs'pĕl'), **Susan Keating.** 1882–1948. Amer. author.

Glass (glăs). **1. Hugh.** d. 1833. Amer. frontiersman. **2. Carter.** 1858–1946. Amer. legislator.

Gla·zu·nov (glăz'ə-nôf', -nôv', glä-zo͞o-nôf'), **Aleksandr Konstantinovich.** 1865–1936. Russian composer.

Glea·son (glē'sən), **Herbert John ("Jackie").** b. 1916. Amer. entertainer.

Glen·dow·er (glĕn'dou'ər, glĕn-dou'-), **Owen.** 1359?–1416? Welsh rebel.

Glenn (glĕn), **John Herschel, Jr.** b. 1921. Amer. astronaut and legislator; 1st Amer. to orbit in space.

Glid·den (glĭd'n). **1. Joseph Farwell.** 1813–1906. Amer. farmer, inventor (barbed wire), and manufacturer. **2. Charles Jasper.** 1857–1927. Amer. telephone-industry pioneer and sportsman.

Glin·ka (glĭng'kə, glĕn'kə), **Mikhail Ivanovich.** 1803–57. Russian composer.

Glov·er (glŭv'ər). **1. John.** 1732–97. Amer. Revolutionary general. **2. Sarah Ann.** 1785–1867. English music teacher.

Gluck (glo͝ok). **1. Christoph Willibald.** 1714–87. German composer. **2. Alma.** 1884?–1938. Rumanian-born Amer. operatic soprano.

Glyn (glĭn), **Elinor (Sutherland).** 1864?–1943. English novelist.

Go·bat (gô-bä'), **Charles Albert.** 1843–1914. Swiss statesman (Nobel, 1902).

Go·dard (gô-där'), **Jean Luc.** b. 1930. French filmmaker.

God·dard (gŏd'ərd). **1. Mary Katherine.** 1738–1816. Amer. printer and publisher. **2. Robert Hutchings.** 1882–1945. Amer. physicist and rocket pioneer.

Go·dey (gō'dē), **Louis Antoine.** 1804–78. Amer. publisher.

God·frey (gŏd'frē). **1. of Bouil·lon** (bo͞o-yôN'). 1061?–1100. French Crusade leader. **2. Thomas.** 1704–49. Amer. inventor and mathematician. **3. Thomas.** 1736–63. Amer. author. **4. Arthur Michael.** b. 1903. Amer. entertainer.

God·kin (gŏd'kĭn), **Edwin Lawrence.** 1831–1902. Irish-born Amer. journalist.

Go·dol·phin (gə-dŏl'fĭn), **Sidney.** 1st Earl of Godolphin. 1645–1712. English statesman and financier.

Go·doy (gô-*th*oi'), **Manuel de.** 1767–1851. Spanish statesman.

Go·du·nov (gŏd'n-ôf', go͝od'-, gŏd'-, gə-do͞o-nôf'), **Boris Fëdorovich.** 1552–1605. Russian czar (1598–1605).

God·win (gŏd'wĭn), **William.** 1756–1836. English author and political philosopher.

God·win-Aus·ten (gŏd'wĭn-ô'stən), **Henry Haversham.** 1834–1923. English geologist, explorer, and author.

Goeb·bels (gœ'bəls), **Joseph Paul.** 1897–1945. German Nazi propaganda minister.

Goe·ring (gœ'rĭng, gĕr'ĭng). Variant of **Göring.**

Goes (go͞os), **Hugo van der.** 1440?–82? Flemish painter.

Goe·thals (gō'thəlz), **George Washington.** 1858–1928. Amer. army engineer and public official; supervised construction of Panama Canal.

Goe·the (gœ'tə), **Johann Wolfgang von.** 1749–1832. German author.

Gogh (gō, gôKH, KHôKH), **Vincent van.** See **van Gogh.**

Go·gol (gô'gəl, gō'gôl), **Nikolai Vasilievich.** 1809–52. Russian author.

Gold·berg (gōld'bərg). **1. Reuben Lucius ("Rube").** 1883–1970. Amer. cartoonist. **2. Arthur Joseph.** b. 1908. Amer. jurist and diplomat.

Gold·berg·er (gōld'bər-gər), **Joseph.** 1874–1929. Austrian-born Amer. physician.

Gol·den (gōl'dən), **Harry Lewis.** 1902–81. Amer. journalist.

Gol·den·wei·ser (gōl'dən-vī'zər, -wī'-), **Alexander.** 1880–1940. Russian-born Amer. educator, anthropologist, and sociologist.

Gold·ing (gōl'dĭng), **William Gerald.** b. 1911. English novelist. (Nobel, 1983).

Emma Goldman

Gold·man (gōld'mən), **Emma.** 1869–1940. Russian-born Amer. anarchist.

Gold·mark (gōld'märk'), **Josephine Clara.** 1877–1950. Amer. investigator of social conditions.

Gol·do·ni (gōl-dō'nē), **Carlo.** 1707–93. Italian dramatist.

Gold·smith (gōld'smĭth'), **Oliver.** 1728–74. Irish author.

Gold·wa·ter (gōld'wô'tər, -wŏt'ər), **Barry Morris.** b. 1909. Amer. politician.

Gold·wyn (gōld'wĭn), **Samuel.** 1882–1974. Polish-born Amer. film producer.

Gol·gi (gôl'jē), **Camillo.** 1844–1926. Italian histologist (Nobel, 1906).

Go·li·ath (gə-lī'əth). In the Bible, Philistine giant slain by David.

Gó·mez (gō'mĕs), **Juan Vicente.** 1857?–1935. Venezuelan general and political leader.

Gom·pers (gŏm'pərz), **Samuel.** 1850–1924. English-born Amer. labor leader.

Gon·çal·ves Di·as (go͞oN-säl'vəs dē'əs), **Antônio.** 1823–64. Brazilian lyric poet.

Gon·court (gôN-ko͞or'), **Edmond Louis Antoine de** (1822–96) and **Jules Alfred Huot** (1830–70). French authors.

Gon·do·mar (gôn'dô-mär'), Count of. Diego Sarmiento de Acuña. 1567–1626. Spanish diplomat.

Gon·za·ga (gən-zä'gə, gän-, gôn-tsä'-gä), Saint **Aloysius.** 1568–91. Italian Jesuit priest.

Gon·za·les (gən-zä'lĭs), **Richard Alonzo ("Pancho").** b. 1928. Amer. tennis player.

Gon·zá·lez (gôn-sä'lĕs), **Manuel.** 1833–93. Mexican statesman.

Gon·za·lo de Cór·do·ba (gôn-sä'lô dĕ kôr'*th*ō-bä), **Hernández.** 1453–1515. Spanish general.

Good·hue (go͝od'hyo͞o'), **Bertram Grosvenor.** 1869–1924. Amer. architect.

Good·man (go͝od'mən). **1. Benjamin David ("Benny").** 1909–86. Amer. musician and conductor. **2. Paul.** 1911–72. Amer. author.

Good·night (go͝od'nīt'), **Charles.** 1836–1929. Amer. cattleman.

Good·rich (go͝od'rĭch'), **Samuel Griswold.** "Peter Parley." 1793–1860. Amer. author and publisher.

Good·ridge (go͝od'rĭj'), **Sarah.** 1788–1853. Amer. miniature painter.

Good·year (go͝od'yîr'), **Charles.** 1800–60. Amer. inventor (vulcanized rubber) and manufacturer.

Goo·la·gong Caw·ley (go͞o'lə-gông kô'lē), **Evonne.** b. 1951. Australian-born tennis player.

Gor·cha·kov (gŏr-chä-kôf', -kôv', gôr-), Prince **Aleksandr Mikhailovich.** 1798–1883. Russian diplomat.

Gor·din (gôr'dĭn, gŏr'-), **Jacob.** 1853–1909. Russian-born Amer. Yiddish playwright.

Gor·don (gôr'dn). **1.** Lord **George.** 1751–93. English rebel. **2. Charles George.** "Chinese Gordon." 1833–85. English army officer and colonial administrator. **3. Laura de Force.** 1838–1907. Amer. lawyer and suffragist. **4. Charles William.** 1860–1937. Canadian clergyman, missionary, and author.

Go·ren (gôr'ən), **Charles Henry.** b. 1901. Amer. contract bridge expert.

Gor·gas (gôr'gəs). **1. Josiah.** 1818–83. Amer. Confederate soldier and educator. **2. William Crawford.** 1854–1920. Amer. army surgeon.

Gor·ham (gôr'əm), **Nathaniel.** 1738–96. Amer. Revolutionary politician and businessman.

Gö·ring also **Goe·ring** (gœ'rĭng, gĕr'-ĭng), **Hermann Wilhelm.** 1893–1946. German Nazi politician.

Gor·ki also **Gor·ky** (gôr'kē), **Maksim** also **Maxim.** 1868–1936. Russian author.

Gor·ky (gôr'kē), **Arshile.** 1905?–48. Armenian-born Amer. painter.

Gor·rie (gôr'ē), **John.** 1803–55. Amer. physician and inventor.

Gor·ton (gôr'tn), **John Grey.** b. 1911. Australian political leader.

Gos·nold (gŏz'nōld'), **Bartholomew.** d. 1607. English navigator and Jamestown colonist.

Gosse (gŏs), Sir **Edmund William.** 1848–1928. English poet and critic.

Gott·schalk (gŏt'shôk'), **Louis Moreau.** 1829–69. Amer. composer and pianist.

Gou·dy (gou'dē), **Frederic William.** 1865–1947. Amer. printer and type designer.

Gouin (go͞o-ăN', gwăN), **Félix.** 1884–1977. French statesman.

Gould (go͞old). **1. Jay.** 1836–92. Amer. financier and speculator. **2. Chester.** 1900–85. Amer. cartoonist ("Dick Tracy").

Gou·nod (go͞o'nō, go͞o-nō'), **Charles François.** 1818–93. French composer.

Gour·mont (go͞or-môN'), **Remy de.** 1858–1915. French novelist and critic.

Gow·er (gou'ər, gōr', gôr'), **John.** 1325?–1408. English poet.

Go·ya y Lu·cien·tes (goi'ə ē lo͞o-syĕn'tĕs, gô'yä), **Francisco José de.** 1746–1828. Spanish painter.

Goya

Grac·chus (grăk'əs), **Tiberius Sempronius** (163–133 B.C.) and **Gaius Sempronius** (153–121 B.C.). "The Gracchi." Roman statesmen.

Grace (grās). **1. William Russell.** 1832–1904. Irish-born Amer. financier, industrialist, and shipping magnate. **2.** Princess. Grace Patricia Kelly. 1929–82. Amer. actress and princess of Monaco as wife of Rainier III (1956–82).

Gra·dy (grā'dē), **Henry Woodfin.** 1850–89. Amer. journalist and orator.

Gra·ham (grā'əm). **1. John.** 1st Viscount Dundee. 1649?–89. Scottish Jacobite leader. **2. Sylvester.** 1794–1851. Amer. nutritionist and reformer. **3. Thomas.** 1805–69. Scottish chemist. **4. Martha.** b. 1894. Amer. choreographer and dancer. **5. Katharine Meyer.** b. 1917. Amer. newspaper publisher. **6. William Franklin ("Billy").** b. 1918. Amer. evangelist.

Gra·hame (grā'əm), **Kenneth.** 1859–1932. English author.

Gram·mat·i·cus (grə-măt'ĭ-kəs). Aelfric.

Gramme (grăm), **Zénobe Théophile.** 1826–1901. Belgian inventor.

Gra·na·dos (grä-nä'*th*ôs), **Enrique.** 1867–1916. Spanish pianist and composer.

Gran·di (grän'dē), Count **(di Mordano) Dino.** b. 1895. Italian Fascist politician.

Grand·ma Mo·ses (grănd'mä mō'zĭz, -zĭs). See Anna Mary Robertson **Moses.**

Grange (grānj), **Harold Edward ("Red").** b. 1903. Amer. football player.

Gra·nit (grä-nēt'), **Ragnar Arthur.** b. 1900. Finnish-born Swedish physiologist (Nobel, 1967).

Grant (grănt). **1. Ulysses Simpson.** 1822–85. 18th U.S. President (1869–77) and Civil War general. **2. Heber Jedediah.** 1856–1945. Amer. Mormon leader. **3. Cary.** b. 1904. English-born Amer. actor.

Ulysses S. Grant

Gran·ville-Bar·ker (grăn'vĭl-bär'-kər), **Harley Granville.** 1877–1946. English actor, playwright, and theater manager.

Grass (gräs), **Günter Wilhelm.** b. 1927. German writer.

Grasse (gräs), Comte **François Joseph Paul de.** Marquis de Grasse-Tilly. 1722?–88. French naval officer.

Gras·so (grăs'ō, grä'sō), **Ella.** 1919–81. Amer. public official.

Ella Grasso

Gra·tian (grā'shē-ən, -shən). 359–83. Roman emperor (367–83).

Grat·tan (grăt'n), **Henry.** 1746–1820. Irish politician and orator.

Grau (grou), **Shirley Ann.** b. 1929. Amer. author.

Graup·ner (group'nər), **Johann Christian Gottlieb.** 1767–1836. German-born Amer. musician and composer.

Graves (grāvz). **1. Robert Ranke.** 1895–1985. English-born Amer. author and critic. **2. Morris Cole.** b. 1910. Amer. painter.

Gray (grā). **1. Thomas.** 1716–71. English poet. **2. Robert.** 1755–1806. Amer. trader and explorer. **3. Asa.** 1810–88. Amer. botanist. **4. Horace.** 1828–1902. Amer. jurist. **5. Elisha.** 1835–1910. Amer. inventor. **6. Hanna Holborn.** b. 1930. German-born Amer. educator and university administrator.

Gra·zia·ni (grä-tsyä'nē), **Rodolpho.** 1882–1955. Italian politician and colonial administrator.

Gre·co (grĕk'ō), **El.** 1541?–1614? Greek-born Spanish artist, architect, and scholar.

Gree·ley (grē'lē), **Horace.** 1811–72. Amer. journalist and politician.

Gree·ly (grē'lē), **Adolphus Washington.** 1844–1935. Amer. army officer and Arctic explorer.

Green (grēn). **1. Duff.** 1791–1875. Amer. journalist and politician. **2. Henrietta Howland ("Hetty").** 1834–1916. Amer. financier. **3. John Richard.** 1837–83. English historian.

4. Anna Katherine. 1846–1935. Amer. detective author. **5. William.** 1873–1952. Amer. labor leader. **6. Paul Eliot.** 1894–1981. Amer. author and educator.
Gree·na·way (grē'nə-wā'), **Catherine ("Kate").** 1846–1901. English artist and author.
Greene (grēn). **1. Robert.** 1558?–92. English author. **2. Nathanael.** 1742–86. Amer. Revolutionary general. **3. Bella Da Costa.** 1883–1950. Amer. librarian and bibliographer. **4. Graham.** b. 1904. English novelist.
Green·how (grē'nou), **Rose O'Neal.** 1815?–1864. Amer. Confederate spy.
Gree·nough (grē'nō'), **Horatio.** 1805–52. Amer. sculptor.
Gregg (grĕg). **1. William.** 1800–67. Amer. cotton manufacturer. **2. Josiah.** 1806–50. Amer. frontiersman and author.
Greg·o·ry (grĕg'ə-rē). **1. of Nys·sa** (nĭs'ə), Saint. 331?–96? Eastern church father. **2. of Tours** (to͝or, to͞or), Saint. 538–94? Frankish prelate. **3.** Name of 16 popes, esp.: **a. I.** Saint. "the Great." 540?–604. Reigned 590–604. **b. VII.** Saint. 1020?–85. Reigned 1073–85. **c. XIII.** 1502–85. Reigned 1572–85. **4.** Lady **(Isabella) Augusta Persse.** 1852–1932. Irish author. **5. Cynthia.** b. 1946. Amer. ballerina.
Gren·fell (grĕn'fĕl', -fəl), Sir **Wilfred Thomason.** 1865–1940. English missionary and physician.
Gren·ville (grĕn'vĭl'). **1.** Or **Greyn·ville** (grān'vĭl, grĕn'-), Sir **Richard.** 1542?–91. English naval officer. **2.** (*also* -vəl), **George.** 1712–70. English statesman.
Gresh·am (grĕsh'əm), Sir **Thomas.** 1519?–79. English financier.
Greuze (grœz), **Jean Baptiste.** 1725–1805. French painter.
Gré·vy (grā-vē'), **(François Paul) Jules.** 1807–91. French statesman.
Grew (gro͞o), **Joseph Clark.** 1880–1965. Amer. diplomat.
Grey (grā). **1.** Lady **Jane.** 1537–54. English queen (1553); executed for treason. **2. Charles.** 2nd Earl Grey. 1764–1845. British prime minister (1830–34) and parliamentary reformer. **3.** Sir **Edward.** 1862–1933. English statesman. **4. Zane.** 1875–1939. Amer. author of Western adventures.
Grieg (grēg, grĭg), **Edvard Hagerup.** 1843–1907. Norwegian composer.
Grier (grîr), **Robert Cooper.** 1794–1870. Amer. jurist.
Grier·son (grîr'sən), Sir **Herbert John Clifford.** 1866–1960. Scottish literary scholar.
Grieve (grēv), **Christopher Murray.** Hugh MacDiarmid.
Grif·fin (grĭf'ĭn), **Walter Burley.** 1876–1937. Amer. architect.
Grif·fith (grĭf'ĭth). **1. Arthur.** 1872–1922. Irish journalist and Sinn Fein leader. **2. David Lewelyn Wark ("D.W.").** 1875–1948. Amer. filmmaker.

D.W. Griffith

Grif·fiths (grĭf'ĭths), **John Willis.** 1809–82. Amer. naval architect.
Gri·gnard (grēn-yärd', grē-nyär'), **François Auguste Victor.** 1871–1934. French chemist (Nobel, 1912).
Grill·par·zer (grĭl'pär'tsər), **Franz.** 1791–1872. Austrian author.
Grim·ké (grĭm'kē), **Sarah Moore** (1792–1873) and **Angeline Emily** (1805–79). Amer. feminists and abolitionists.
Grimm (grĭm), **Jakob Ludwig Karl** (1785–1863) and **Wilhelm Karl** (1786–1859). German philologists and folklorists.
Grin·nell (grĭ-nĕl'), **George Bird.** 1849–1938. Amer. naturalist and conservationist.
Gris (grēs), **Juan.** 1887–1927. Spanish artist.
Gris·wold (grĭz'wôld', -wōld', -wəld), **Rufus Wilmot.** 1815?–57. Amer. editor and critic.
Gro·lier de Ser·vières (grô-lyā' də sĕr-vyĕr'), **Jean.** Viscomte d'Aquisy. 1479–1565. French bibliophile.
Gro·my·ko (grō-mē'kō, grə-, grŏ-), **Andrei Andreevich.** b. 1909. Soviet diplomat.
Gron·lund (grŏn'lŭnd', -lənd), **Laurence.** 1846–99. Danish-born Amer. lawyer and socialist.
Groot (grōt, KHrōt), **Gerhard.** 1340–84. Dutch religious reformer.
Gro·pi·us (grō'pē-əs), **Walter Adolph.** 1883–1969. German-born Amer. architect.
Grop·per (grŏp'ər), **William.** 1897–1977. Amer. artist.
Gross (grōs), **Samuel David.** 1805–84. Amer. surgeon and educator.
Gros·ve·nor (grōv'nər), **Gilbert Hovey.** 1875–1966. Amer. editor and geographer.
Grosz (grōs), **George.** 1893–1959. German-born Amer. artist.
Grote (grōt), **George.** 1794–1871. English historian.
Gro·ti·us (grō'shē-əs), **Hugo.** 1583–1645. Dutch jurist, statesman, and theologian; founder of science of international law.
Grou·chy (gro͞o-shē'), Marquis **Emmanuel de.** 1766–1847. French marshal.
Grove (grōv), Sir **George.** 1820–1900. English engineer and musicologist.
Groves (grōvz), **Leslie Richard.** 1896–1970. Amer. army officer; directed Manhattan Project.
Grü·ne·wald (grü'nə-vält'), **Matthias.** 1480?–1530? German painter.
Gryph·i·us (grĭf'ē-əs, grē'fē-), **Andreas.** 1616–64. German author.
Guar·nie·ri (gwär-nyĕ'rē) or **Guar·ne·ri** (-nĕ'rē). Family of Italian violin makers, including **Andrea** (1626–98), **Pietro** (1655–1728), **Giuseppe** (1666–1739), and **Giuseppe Antonio** (1687–1745?).
Gue·dal·la (gwĭ-dăl'ə), **Philip.** 1889–1944. English biographer, historian, and essayist.
Gue·rick·e (gā'rĭ-kə, gâr'ə-kē, -kə, gwâr'-), **Otto von.** 1602–86. German physicist and inventor.
Gue·rin (gĕr'ĭn), **Jules.** 1866–1946. Amer. painter.
Guesde (gĕd), **Jules.** 1845–1922. French journalist and socialist.
Guest (gĕst), **Edgar Albert.** 1881–1959. English-born Amer. journalist.
Gue·va·ra (gē-vä'rä), **Ernesto ("Che").** 1928–67. Argentine-born revolutionary in Latin America.
Gug·gen·heim (go͞o'gən-hīm', go͝og'-ən-). **1. Meyer.** 1828–1905. Swiss-born Amer. financier and industrialist. **2. Daniel.** 1856–1930. Amer. industrialist and philanthropist.
Gui·do d'A·rez·zo (gwē'dō dä-rāt'-tsō) or **A·re·ti·no** (ä-rā-tē'nō). 995?–1050? Benedictine monk and music theorist.
Guil·laume (gē-ōm'), **Charles Édouard.** 1861–1938. French physicist (Nobel, 1920).
Guille·min (gē-măN'), **Roger Charles Louis.** b. 1924. French-born Amer. physicist (Nobel, 1977).
Guin·an (gwĭn'ən), **Mary Louise Cecilia ("Tex").** 1884–1933. Amer. actress and hostess.
Gui·ney (gī'nē), **Louise Imogen.** 1861–1920. Amer. author.
Guin·ness (gĭn'ĭs), Sir **Alec.** b. 1914. English actor.
Guis·card (gē-skär'), **Robert.** 1015?–85. Norman leader.
Guise (gēz). **1.** 2nd Duc. François de Lorraine. 1519–63. French general and statesman. **2.** 3rd Duc. Henri de Lorraine. 1550–88. French military leader; assassinated.
Gui·te·ras y Ge·ner (gē-tĕ'räs ē hĕ-nĕr'), **Juan.** 1852–1925. Cuban pathologist and physician.
Gui·zot (gē-zō'), **François Pierre Guillaume.** 1787–1874. French historian and diplomat.
Gull·strand (gŭl'strănd'), **Allvar.** 1862–1930. Swedish ophthalmologist (Nobel, 1911).
Gun·nars·son (gün'närs-sôn), **Gunnar.** b. 1889. Icelandic author.
Gun·ter (gŭn'tər), **Edmund.** 1581–1626. English astronomer, mathematician, and inventor.
Gun·ther (gŭn'thər), **John.** 1901–70. Amer. journalist, broadcaster, and author.
Gus·ta·vus (gŭs-tā'vəs, -tä'-). Name of 6 kings of Sweden: **1. I.** 1496–1560. Ruled 1523–60. **2. II.** 1594–1632. Ruled 1611–32. **3. III.** 1746–92. Ruled 1771–92. **4. IV.** 1778–1837. Ruled 1792–1809. **5. V.** 1858–1950. Ruled 1907–50. **6. VI.** 1882–1973. Ruled 1950–73.
Gu·ten·berg (go͞ot'n-bûrg'), **Johann** or **Johannes.** 1400?–68? German printer; invented movable type.

Johann Gutenberg

Guth·rie (gŭth'rē). **1. Woodrow Wilson ("Woody").** 1912–67. Amer. folk singer and composer. **2. Janet.** b. 1938. Amer. automobile racer.

Woody Guthrie

Gutz·kow (go͞ots'kō), **Karl.** 1811–78. German author.
Guz·mán Blan·co (go͞os-män' blăng'kō), **Antonio.** 1828?–99. Venezuelan statesman.
Gwin·net (gwə-nĕt'), **Button.** 1735–77. Amer. Revolutionary patriot.
Gwyn or **Gwynne** (gwĭn), **Eleanor ("Nell").** 1650?–87. English actress and mistress of Charles II.

H

Haa·kon (hô'kən, -ko͞on). Name of 7 kings of Norway, esp. **VII,** 1872–1957, ruled 1905–57.
Ha·bak·kuk (hə-băk'ək, hăb'ə-kŭk'). Late 7th cent. B.C. Hebrew prophet.
Ha·ber (hä'bər), **Fritz.** 1868–1934. German chemist (Nobel, 1918).
Habs·burg (hăps'bûrg', häps'bo͝ork'). Variant of **Hapsburg.**
Had·ley (hăd'lē). **1. Arthur Twining.** 1856–1930. Amer. educator and economist. **2. Henry Kimball.** 1871–1937. Amer. composer and conductor.
Had·ow (hăd'ō), Sir **(William) Henry.** 1859–1937. English educator and author.
Ha·dri·an (hā'drē-ən). A.D. 76–138. Roman emperor (117–38).
Haeck·el (hĕk'əl), **Ernst Heinrich.** 1834–1919. German philosopher and naturalist.
Ha·fiz (hä-fĭz', -fēz'). 14th cent. Persian poet, philosopher, and grammarian.
Ha·gar (hā'gər, -gär). In the Old Testament, Egyptian concubine of Abraham.
Ha·gen (hā'gən), **Walter Charles.** 1892–1969. Amer. golfer.
Hag·er·ty (hăg'ər-tē), **James C.** 1909–81. Amer. journalist and public official.
Hag·ga·i (hăg'ē-ī', hăg'ī). 6th cent. B.C. Hebrew prophet.
Hag·gard (hăg'ərd), Sir **(Henry) Rider.** 1856–1925. English novelist.
Hahn (hän), **Otto.** 1879–1968. German chemist (Nobel, 1944).
Hah·ne·mann (hä'nə-mən, -män'), **(Christian Friedrich) Samuel.** 1755–1843. German physician; founder of homeopathy.
Haig (hāg). **1. Douglas.** 1st Earl Haig. Scottish-born British field marshal. **2. Alexander Meigs, Jr.** b. 1924. Amer. general and public official.
Hai·le Se·las·sie (hī'lē sə-lăs'ē, -lä'-sē). Ras Taffari Makonnen. 1891–1975. Ethiopian emperor (1930–74); exiled (1936–41); deposed.
Hak·luyt (hăk'lo͞ot'), **Richard.** 1552–1616. English geographer.
Hal·as (hăl'əs), **George Stanley.** 1895–1983. Amer. football player and coach.
Hal·dane (hôl'dān', -dən). **1. Richard Burdon.** 1856–1928. Scottish-born British philosopher and statesman. **2. John Scott.** 1860–1936. Scottish-born British scientist. **3. John Burdon Sanderson.** 1892–1964. English geneticist.
Hale (hāl). **1.** Sir **Matthew.** 1609–76. English jurist. **2. Nathan.** 1755–76. Amer. Revolutionary; hanged by the British as a spy. **3. Sarah Josepha Buell.** 1788–1879. Amer. editor and author. **4. John Parker.** 1806–73. Amer. politician and diplomat. **5. Lucretia Peabody.** 1820–1900. Amer. author. **6. Edward Everett.** 1822–1909. Amer. clergyman and author ("Man Without a Country"). **7. George Ellery.** 1868–1938. Amer. astrophysicist and inventor.
Hales (hālz), **Stephen.** 1677–1761. English physiologist and inventor.
Ha·lé·vy (ä-lā-vē'). **1. Jacques Fromental Élie Lévy.** 1799–1862. French composer. **2. Ludovic.** 1834–1908. French author.
Ha·ley (hā'lē). **1. Margaret Angela.** 1861–1939. Amer. educator and labor organizer. **2. Alex.** b. 1921. Amer. author.
Hal·i·fax (hăl'ə-făks'), 1st Earl of. Edward Frederick Lindley Wood. 1881–1959. English statesman.
Hall (hôl). **1.** Sir **James.** 1761–1832. Scottish-born British geologist and chemist. **2. James.** 1793–1868. Amer. author, jurist, and banker. **3. James.** 1811–1898. Amer. geologist and paleontologist. **4. Charles Francis.** 1821–71. Amer. Arctic explorer. **5. Abraham Oakey ("O.K.").** 1826–98. Amer. politician and journalist. **6. Asaph.** 1829–1907. Amer. astronomer. **7. Granville Stanley.** 1844–1924. Amer. psychologist and educator. **8. Charles Martin.** 1863–1914. Amer. chemist and pioneer aluminum manufacturer. **9. James Norman.** 1887–1951. Amer. author.
Hal·lam (hăl'əm). **1. Lewis.** 1740–1808. English-born Amer. actor and theatrical manager. **2. Henry.** 1777–1859. English historian.
Hal·leck (hăl'ĭk, -ək). **1. Fitz-Greene.** 1790–1867. Amer. poet. **2. Henry Wager.** 1815–72. Amer. Union general.

p pop / r roar / s sauce / sh ship, dish / t tight / th thin, path / *th* this, bathe / ŭ cut / ûr urge / v valve / w with / y yes / z zebra, size / zh vision / ə about, item, edible, gallop, circus / œ *Fr.* feu, *Ger.* schön / ü *Fr.* tu, *Ger.* über / KH *Ger.* ich, *Scot.* loch / N *Fr.* bon.

Hal·ley (hăl'ē, hā'lē), **Edmund.** 1656–1742. English astronomer.

Hals (hälz, häls), **Frans.** 1580–1666. Dutch painter.

Hal·sey (hôl'zē, hŏl'-), **William Frederick.** 1882–1959. Amer. naval officer.

Hal·sted (hôl'stəd, -stĕd', hŏl'-), **William Stewart.** 1852–1922. Amer. surgeon.

Ham (hăm). In the Old Testament, Noah's son.

Ha·mil·car Bar·ca (hə-mĭl'kär' bär'-kə, hăm'əl-). 270?–28 B.C. Carthaginian general.

Ham·ill (hăm'əl), **Dorothy.** b. 1956. Amer. figure skater.

Ham·il·ton (hăm'əl-tən). **1. Alexander.** 1755?–1804. Amer. statesman and political and economic theorist; killed by Aaron Burr in a duel. **2.** Lady **Emma Lyon.** 1765–1815. English socialite and mistress of Lord Nelson. **3. Edith.** 1867–1963. German-born Amer. classicist. **—Ham'il·to'ni·an** *adj.*

Alexander Hamilton

Ham·lin (hăm'lĭn), **Hannibal.** 1809–91. U.S. Vice President (1861–65).

Ham·mar·skjöld (hä'mər-shōld', -shoold', -shŭld', -shĕld', hăm'ər-, hăm'är-shœld'), **Dag Hjalmar Agné Carl.** 1905–61. Swedish statesman and UN official (Nobel, 1961).

Ham·mer·stein (hăm'ər-stīn', -stēn'). **1. Oscar.** 1847?–1919. German-born Amer. operatic manager. **2. Oscar, II.** 1895–1960. Amer. lyricist.

Ham·mett (hăm'ĭt), **Dashiell.** 1894–1961. Amer. author.

Ham·mond (hăm'ənd). Family of Amer. engineers and inventors, including **John Hays** (1855–1936), **John Hays** (1888–1965), and **Laurens** (1895–1973).

Ham·mu·ra·bi (hä'moo-rä'bē, hăm'-ə-). c. 20th or 18th cent. B.C. Babylonian king and lawgiver.

Hamp·den (hămp'dən, hăm'-), **John.** 1594–1643. English statesman.

Hamp·ton (hămp'tən). **1. Wade** (1752?–1835) and **Wade** (1818–1902). Amer. generals and politicians. **2. Lionel.** b. 1914. Amer. musician.

Ham·sun (häm'soon, -sən), **Knut.** 1859–1952. Norwegian author (Nobel, 1920).

Han (hän). Name of 3 Chinese dynasties: **Western Han,** 206 B.C.–A.D. 24; **Eastern Han,** A.D. 25–220; and **Later Han,** 947–50.

Han·cock (hăn'kŏk'). **1. John.** 1737–93. Amer. merchant, politician, and Revolutionary leader. **2. Winfield Scott.** 1824–86. Amer. Civil War general.

Hand (hănd), **(Billings) Learned.** 1872–1961. Amer. jurist.

Han·del (hăn'dl), **George Frederick.** 1685–1759. German-born English composer.

Hand·lin (hănd'lĭn), **Oscar.** b. 1915. Amer. historian and educator.

Han·dy (hăn'dē), **William Christopher ("W.C.").** 1873–1958. Amer. musician and composer.

Han·na (hăn'ə), **Marcus Alonzo ("Mark").** 1837–1904. Amer. financier and politician.

Han·nay (hăn'ā, hăn'ē), **James Owen.** 1865–1950. Irish clergyman and novelist.

Han·ni·bal (hăn'ə-bəl). 247?–183 B.C. Carthaginian general.

Han·no (hăn'ō). "the Great." fl. 3rd cent. B.C. Carthaginian political leader.

Ha·no·taux (ä-nô-tō'), **(Albert Auguste) Gabriel.** 1853–1944. French historian and statesman.

Han·o·ver (hăn'ō'vər). English ruling family (1714–1901).

Han·sard (hăn'sərd, -särd'), **Luke.** 1752–1828. English parliamentary printer.

Hans·ber·ry (hănz'bĕr-ē), **Lorraine.** 1930–65. Amer. playwright.

Han·sen (hăn'sən), **Marcus Lee.** 1892–1938. Amer. historian.

Han·son (hăn'sən). **1. John.** 1721–83. Amer. Revolutionary leader. **2. Howard Harold.** 1896–1981. Amer. composer and teacher.

Hans·son (hän'sôn), **Per Albin.** 1885–1946. Swedish statesman and journalist.

Hap·good (hăp'good'), **Isabel Florence.** 1850–1928. Amer. translator and author.

Haps·burg also **Habs·burg** (hăps'-bûrg', häps'boork'). Royal German family ruling Austria (1276–1740) and Spain (1516–1700).

Har·bach (här'băk'), **Otto Abels.** 1873–1963. Amer. playwright and librettist.

Har·de·ca·nute or **Har·di·ca·nute** (här'dĭ-kə-noot', -nyoot'). 1019?–42. King of England (1040–42) and of Denmark as **Canute II** (1035–42).

Har·den (här'dn). **1. Maximilian.** 1861–1927. German journalist and critic. **2.** Sir **Arthur.** 1865–1940. English biochemist (Nobel, 1929).

Har·den·berg (här'dn-bûrg', -bĕrk'), Prince **Karl August von.** 1750–1822. Prussian statesman.

Har·ding (här'dĭng). **1. Chester.** 1792–1866. Amer. portrait painter. **2. Warren Gamaliel.** 1865–1923. 29th U.S. President (1921–23); died in office.

Warren G. Harding

Hard·wicke (härd'wĭk'), Sir **Cedric Webster.** 1893–1964. English actor.

Har·dy (här'dē). **1. Thomas.** 1840–1928. English author. **2. Oliver.** 1892–1957. Amer. comedian.

Har·greaves (här'grēvz'), **James.** d. 1778. English inventor (spinning jenny).

Har·ing·ton or **Har·ring·ton** (hăr'-ĭng-tən), Sir **John.** 1561–1612. English poet and translator.

Ha·ri·ri (hä-rē'rē, -rĭr'ē, hä-), **al-.** 1054–1122. Arabian poet and scholar.

Hark·ness (härk'nĭs, -nĕs'), **Anna M. Richardson** (1837–1926) and **Edward Stephen** (1874–1940). Amer. philanthropists.

Har·lan (här'lən), **John Marshall** (1833–1911) and **John Marshall** (1899–1971). Amer. jurists.

Har·ley (här'lē), **Robert.** 1st Earl of Oxford. 1661–1724. English statesman and bibliophile.

Har·low (här'lō'), **Jean.** 1911–37. Amer. actress.

Harms·worth (härmz'wûrth'), **Alfred Charles William** (Viscount Northcliffe; Irish-born, 1865–1922) and **Harold Sidney** (1st Viscount Rothermere; 1868–1940). English newspaper publishers.

Har·old (hăr'əld). **1.** Name of 2 kings of England: **a. I.** d. 1040. Ruled 1035–40. **b. II.** 1022–66. Ruled 1066; killed at the Battle of Hastings. **2.** Name of 3 kings of Norway, esp. **III,** 1015–66, ruled 1046–66.

Ha·roun al-Ra·schid (hä-roon' äl-rä-shēd'). Variant of **Harun al-Rashid.**

Har·per (här'pər). **1. Robert Goodloe.** 1765–1825. Amer. Federalist politician. **2.** Family of Amer. printers and publishers, including **James** (1795–1869), **John** (1797–1875), **Joseph Wesley** (1801–70), and **Fletcher** (1806–77). **3. Frances Ellen Watkins.** 1825–1911. Amer. author and reformer. **4. Ida Husted.** 1851–1931. Amer. suffragist and journalist. **5. William Rainey.** 1856–1906. Amer. educator and scholar.

Har·ri·man (hăr'ə-mən). **1. Edward Henry.** 1848–1909. Amer. railway magnate. **2. Florence Jaffray.** 1870–1967. Amer. diplomat. **3. (William) Averell.** 1891–1986. Amer. financier and diplomat.

Har·ring·ton (hăr'ĭng-tən). **1.** Variant of **Harington. 2. (Edward) Michael.** b. 1928. Amer. author and reformer.

Har·ris (hăr'ĭs). **1. Benjamin.** fl. 1673–1713. English publisher and author. **2. Townsend.** 1804–78. Amer. diplomat. **3. Chapin Aaron.** 1806–60. Amer. pioneer dentist. **4. William Torrey.** 1835–1909. Amer. philosopher and educator. **5. Joel Chandler.** 1848–1908. Amer. author and journalist. **6. Frank.** 1854–1931. Irish-born Amer. author. **7. Roy Ellsworth.** 1898–1979. Amer. composer. **8. Louis ("Lou").** b. 1921. Amer. public-opinion analyst. **9. Patricia Roberts.** b. 1924. Amer. ambassador and educator. **10. Julie.** b. 1925. Amer. actress.

Har·ri·son (hăr'ĭ-sən). **1. Peter.** 1717–75. English-born Amer. architect and merchant. **2. Benjamin.** 1726–91. Amer. Revolutionary statesman. **3. William Henry.** 1773–1841. 9th U.S. President (1841); died in office. **4. Frederic.** 1831–1923. English author and positivist philosopher. **5. Benjamin.** 1833–1901. 23rd U.S. President (1889–93). **6. Elizabeth.** 1849–1927. Amer. pioneer educator. **7. Reginald Carey ("Rex").** b. 1908. English actor. **8. George.** b. 1943. English singer and songwriter.

William Henry Harrison

Benjamin Harrison

Hart (härt). **1.** Sir **Robert.** 1835–1911. English diplomat. **2. Albert Bushnell.** 1854–1943. Amer. historian and editor. **3. William Surrey.** 1870–1946. Amer. actor. **4. Lorenz.** 1895–1943. Amer. lyricist. **5. Moss.** 1904–61. Amer. playwright, librettist, and director.

Harte (härt), **(Francis) Bret.** 1836–1902. Amer. author.

Hart·line (härt'līn'), **Haldan Keffer.** b. 1903. Amer. biophysicist (Nobel, 1967).

Ha·run al-Ra·shid or **Ha·roun al-Ra·schid** (hä-roon' äl-rä-shēd') also **Harun ar-Ra·shid** (är'rä-shēd'). 764?–809. Caliph of Baghdad (786–809).

Har·vard (här'vərd), **John.** 1607–38. Amer. clergyman and philanthropist.

Har·vey (här'vē). **1. William.** 1578–1657. English physician, anatomist, and physiologist. **2. Frederick Henry.** 1835–1901. English-born Amer. restaurateur. **3. William Hope ("Coin").** 1851–1936. Amer. economist and publicist. **4. George Brinton McClellan.** 1864–1928. Amer. journalist and diplomat.

Has·brouck (hăz'brook'), **Lydia Sayer.** 1827–1910. Amer. editor and reformer.

Has·dru·bal (hăz'droo'bəl, hăz-droo'-). d. 207 B.C. Carthaginian general.

Has·sam (hăs'əm), **(Frederick) Childe.** 1859–1935. Amer. painter.

Has·sel (hä'səl), **Odd.** b. 1897. Norwegian chemist (Nobel, 1969).

Hass·ler (hăs'lər), **Ferdinand Rudolf.** 1770–1843. Amer. scientist and coastal surveyor.

Has·tie (hā'stē), **William Henry.** 1904–76. Amer. jurist.

Ha·stings (hā'stĭngz). **1. Warren.** 1732–1818. English colonial administrator in India. **2.** 1st Marquis of. Francis Rawdon-Hastings. 1754–1826. English general in the Amer. Revolution. **3. Thomas.** 1860–1929. Amer. architect.

Hatch (hăch), **William Henry.** 1833–96. Amer. legislator.

Hath·a·way (hăth'ə-wā'), **Anne.** 1557?–1623. Wife of William Shakespeare.

Hat·shep·sut (hăt-shĕp'soot') also **Hat·shep·set** (-sĕt'). Egyptian queen.

Hauk or **Hauck** (houk), **Minnie.** 1851?–1929. Amer. soprano.

Haupt·mann (houpt'män'), **Gerhart.** 1862–1946. German author (Nobel, 1912).

Haus·ho·fer (hous'hō-fər), **Karl.** 1869–1946. German geopolitician.

Hauss·mann (hous'mən, ōs-män'), Baron **Georges Eugène.** 1809–91. French public official; directed civic improvements and rebuilding of Paris.

Have·lock (hăv'lŏk', -lək), Sir **Henry.** 1795–1857. English general in India.

Ha·ven (hā'vən), **Emily Bradley Neal.** 1827–63. Amer. author and editor.

Hawes (hôz), **Harriet Ann Boyd.** 1871–1945. Amer. archaeologist.

Haw·kins (hô'kĭnz). **1.** Or **Haw·kyns,** Sir **John.** 1532–95. English naval hero. **2.** Sir **Anthony Hope.** 1863–1933. English author.

Hawks (hôks), **Howard Winchester.** 1896–1977. Amer. filmmaker.

Haworth (härth, hou'ərth), Sir **(Walter) Norman.** 1883–1950. English biochemist (Nobel, 1937).

Haw·thorne (hô'thôrn', hŏth'ôrn'), **Nathaniel.** 1804–64. Amer. novelist.

Nathaniel Hawthorne

Hay (hā), **John Milton.** 1838–1905. Amer. diplomat, public official, and author.

Ha·ya·ka·wa (hī'ə-kou'ə), **Samuel Ichiye ("S.I.")**. b. 1906. Canadian-born Amer. philologist, educator, and legislator.
Hay·den (hād'n). **1. Ferdinand Vandeveer.** 1829–87. Amer. geologist and Western explorer and surveyor. **2. Carl Trumbull.** 1877–1972. Amer. legislator. **3. Melissa.** b. 1923. Canadian-born Amer. ballerina.
Haydn (hīd'n), **(Franz) Joseph ("Papa").** 1732–1809. Austrian composer.
Hay·ek (hī'ĕk), **Friedrich August von.** b. 1899. Austrian-born English economist (Nobel, 1974).
Hayes (hāz). **1. Rutherford Birchard.** 1822–93. 19th U.S. President (1877–81). **2. Isaac Israel.** 1832–81. Amer. physician and Arctic explorer. **3. Carlton Joseph Huntley.** 1882–1964. Amer. historian and diplomat. **4. Roland.** 1887–1977. Amer. tenor. **5. Helen.** b. 1900. Amer. actress.

Rutherford B. Hayes

Hayne (hān), **Robert Young.** 1791–1839. Amer. politician and railroad executive; debated Webster (1830).
Haynes (hānz), **Elwood.** 1857–1925. Amer. inventor (horseless carriage).
Hays (hāz). **1. John Coffee ("Jack").** 1817–83. Amer. frontiersman and soldier. **2. William Harrison ("Will").** 1879–1954. Amer. politician and motion-picture executive. **3. Arthur Garfield.** 1881–1954. Amer. libertarian lawyer.
Hay·wood (hā'wo͝od'), **William Dudley ("Big Bill").** 1869–1928. Amer. labor leader; founded I.W.W.
Ha·zard (ä-zär'), **Paul Gustave Marie Camille.** 1878–1944. French literary historian.
Haz·litt (hăz'lĭt), **William.** 1778–1830. English critic and essayist.
Head (hĕd), **Edith.** 1898?–1981. Amer. motion-picture costume and fashion designer.
Hea·ly (hē'lē), **Timothy Michael.** 1855–1931. Irish nationalist politician.
Hearn (hûrn), **Lafcadio.** 1850–1904. Greek-born Amer.-Japanese author.
Hearst (hûrst). **1. George.** 1820–91. Amer. mine owner, publisher, and politician. **2. Phoebe Apperson.** 1842–1919. Amer. philanthropist. **3. William Randolph.** 1863–1951. Amer. newspaper publisher.
Heath (hēth), **Edward Richard George.** b. 1916. British prime minister (1969–74).
Heat·ter (hē'tər), **Gabriel.** 1890–1972. Amer. journalist and radio commentator.
Heav·i·side (hĕv'ē-sīd'), **Oliver.** 1850–1925. English physicist and electrical theorist.
Heb·bel (hĕb'əl), **Friedrich.** 1813–63. German dramatist.
Hé·bert (ā-bĕr'), **Jacques René.** 1755–94. French revolutionary and journalist; guillotined.
Hecht (hĕkt), **Ben.** 1894–1964. Amer. author.
Heck·er (hĕk'ər), **Isaac Thomas.** 1819–88. Amer. priest; founder of Paulist order.
He·din (hĕ-dēn'), **Sven Anders von.** 1865–1952. Swedish explorer and scientist.
Hef·ner (hĕf'nər), **Hugh Marston.** b. 1926. Amer. editor and publisher.
He·gel (hā'gəl), **Georg Wilhelm Friedrich.** 1770–1831. German philosopher. —**He·ge'li·an** (hā-gā'lē-ən) *adj. & n.*
Hei·deg·ger (hī'dĕg'ər, -dĭg'-), **Martin.** 1889–1976. German philosopher.
Hei·den·stam (hād'n-stăm', -stàm'), **Verner von.** 1859–1940. Swedish author (Nobel, 1916).
Hei·fetz (hī'fĭts), **Jascha.** b. 1901. Russian-born Amer. violinist.

Jascha Heifetz

Hei·ne (hī'nə), **Heinrich.** 1797–1856. German lyric poet and critic.
Hein·lein (hīn'līn), **Robert Anson.** b. 1907. Amer. science-fiction author.
Heinz (hīnz), **Henry John.** 1844–1919. Amer. manufacturer of prepared foods.
Hei·sen·berg (hī'zən-bûrg', -bĕrk'), **Werner.** 1901–76. German physicist (Nobel, 1932).
Hei·ser (hī'zər), **Victor George.** 1873–1972. Amer. physician and public-health pioneer.
Held (hĕld). **1. Anna.** 1865?–1918. French-born Amer. entertainer. **2. John, Jr.** 1889–1958. Amer. illustrator and author.
He·li·o·gab·a·lus (hē'lē-ə-găb'ə-ləs, -lē-ō-). 204–22. Roman emperor (218–22).
Hel·ler (hĕl'ər), **Joseph.** b. 1923. Amer. author.
Hell·man (hĕl'mən), **Lillian.** 1905–84. Amer. playwright.
Helm·holtz (hĕlm'hōlts'), **Hermann Ludwig Ferdinand von.** 1821–94. German physiologist and physicist.
Hé·lo·ïse (ĕl'ō-ēz', ā-lô-ēz'). 1101?–64? Abelard's beloved.
Hel·per (hĕl'pər), **Hinton Rowan.** 1829–1909. Amer. author, promoter, and antislavery advocate.
Hel·vé·tius (hĕl-vē'shəs, -shē-əs, -vā'-, ĕl-vā-syüs'), **Claude Adrien.** 1715–71. French philosopher and author.
He·mans (hĕm'ənz, hē'mənz), **Felicia Dorothea.** 1793–1835. English poet.
Hem·en·way (hĕm'ən-wā'), **Mary Porter Tileston.** 1820–94. Amer. philanthropist.
Hem·ing or **Hem·minge** (hĕm'ĭng), **John.** 1556?–1630. English actor and editor of 1st folio of Shakespeare's plays.
Hem·ing·way (hĕm'ĭng-wā'), **Ernest Miller.** 1899?–1961. Amer. author (Nobel, 1954).

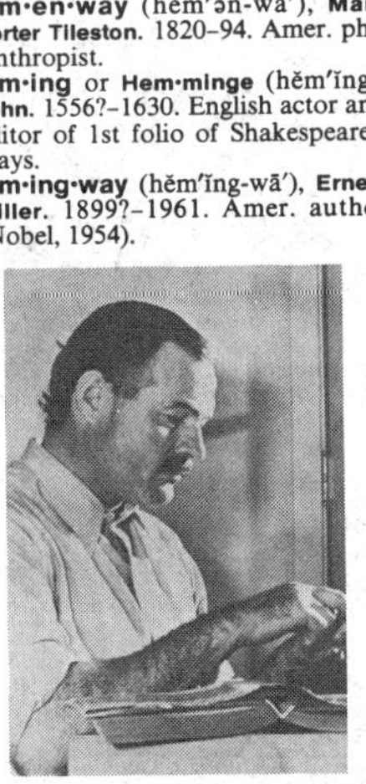
Ernest Hemingway

Hench (hĕnch), **Philip Showalter.** 1896–1965. Amer. physician (Nobel, 1950).
Hen·der·son (hĕn'dər-sən). **1. Richard.** 1735–85. Amer. frontier land developer. **2. Arthur.** 1863–1935. Scottish-born British labor leader and statesman (Nobel, 1934). **3. Sir Nevile Meyrick.** 1882–1942. English diplomat.
Hen·dricks (hĕn'drĭks), **Thomas Andrews.** 1819–85. U.S. Vice President (1885); died in office.
Hen·ie (hĕn'ē), **Sonja.** 1912–69. Norwegian-born figure skater.
Hen·ley (hĕn'lē), **William Ernest.** 1849–1903. English editor and author.
Hen·ne·pin (hĕn'ə-pĭn, ĕn-ə-păN'), **Louis.** 1640?–1701?. French-born missionary and explorer in America.
Hen·ri (hĕn'rē), **Robert.** 1865–1929. Amer. painter and educator.
Hen·ry (hĕn'rē). **1.** Name of 4 kings of France: **a. I.** 1008?–1060. Ruled 1031–60. **b. II.** 1519–59. Ruled 1547–59. **c. III.** 1551–89. Ruled 1574–89. **d. IV.** "Henry of Navarre." 1553–1610. Ruled 1589–1610. **2. IV.** 1050–1106. King of Germany (1056–1106). **3.** Name of 8 kings of England: **a. I.** 1068–1135. Ruled 1100–35. **b. II.** 1133–1189. Ruled 1154–89. **c. III.** 1207–72. Ruled 1216–72. **d. IV.** 1367–1413. Ruled 1399–1413. **e. V.** 1387–1422. Ruled 1413–22. **f. VI.** 1421–71. Ruled 1422–61 and 1470–71. **g. VII.** 1457–1509. Ruled 1485–1509. **h. VIII.** 1491–1547. Ruled 1509–47. **4.** "the Navigator." 1394–1460. Portuguese prince. **5. Patrick.** 1736–99. Amer. Revolutionary leader and orator. **6. Andrew.** 1775?–1833. Amer. frontier explorer and fur trader. **7. Joseph.** 1797–1878. Amer. physicist.

Henry VIII

Hens·lowe (hĕnz'lō), **Philip.** d. 1616. English theatrical manager.
Hep·burn (hĕp'bûrn', -bərn). **1. Katharine.** b. 1909. Amer. actress. **2. Audrey.** b. 1929. Belgian-born actress.
Hep·ple·white (hĕp'əl-hwīt', -wīt'), **George.** d. 1786. English cabinetmaker.
Her·a·cli·tus (hĕr'ə-klī'təs). 6th–5th cent. B.C. Greek philosopher. —**Her'a·cli'te·an** *adj.*
Her·a·cli·us (hĕr'ə-klī'əs, hĭ-răk'lē-). 575?–641. Byzantine emperor.
Her·bart (hĕr'bärt'), **Johann Friedrich.** 1776–1841. German psychologist, philosopher, and educator.
Her·bert (hûr'bərt). **1. William.** 3rd Earl of Pembroke. 1580–1630. English statesman and poetry patron; identified by some as Shakespeare's "Mr. W.H." **2. George.** 1593–1633. Welsh-born English metaphysical poet. **3. Victor.** 1859–1924. Amer. musician, composer, and conductor.
Her·block (hûr'blŏk). Herbert Lawrence Block.
Her·der (hĕr'dər), **Johann Gottfried von.** 1744–1803. German philosopher and author.
He·re·dia (ā-rā-dyä', -rā'dē-ə, hā-, ĕ-rē'*th*yä), **José Maria de.** 1842–1905. Cuban-born French poet and translator.
Her·ford (hûr'fərd), **Oliver Brooke.** 1863–1935. English author and illustrator.
Her·ges·hei·mer (hûr'gəs-hī'mər), **Joseph.** 1880–1954. Amer. novelist.
Her·ki·mer (hûr'kə-mər), **Nicholas.** 1728–77. Amer. Revolutionary general.
Hern·don (hûrn'dən), **William Henry.** 1818–91. Amer. lawyer and author.
Herne (hûrn), **James A.** 1839–1901. Amer. actor and playwright.
He·ro (hē'rō, hîr'ō) or **He·ron** (hē'rŏn). 2nd or 3rd cent. A.D. Alexandrian scientist.
Her·od (hĕr'əd). "the Great." 73?–4 B.C. King of Judea (40–4).
Herod An·ti·pas (ăn'tĭ-păs', -pəs). 4 B.C.–A.D. 40. Ruler of Judea and tetrarch in Galilee.
He·rod·o·tus (hĭ-rŏd'ə-təs). "the Father of History." 5th cent. B.C. Greek historian.
Her·rick (hĕr'ĭk). **1. Robert.** 1591–1674. English lyric poet. **2. Myron Timothy.** 1854–1929. Amer. diplomat, businessman, and politician.
Her·ri·ot (ĕ-rē-ō', ĕ-ryō'), **Édouard.** 1872–1957. French statesman.
Her·schel (hûr'shəl). Family of English astronomers, including Sir **William** (German-born; 1738–1822), **Caroline Lucretia** (1750–1848), and Sir **John Frederick William** (1792–1871).
Her·sey (hûr'sē). **John Richard.** b. 1914. Amer. author.
Her·shey (hûr'shē). **1. Milton Snavely.** 1857–1945. Amer. industrialist and philanthropist. **2. Lewis Blaine.** 1893–1977. Amer. general. **3. Alfred Day.** b. 1908. Amer. biologist (Nobel, 1969).
Her·sko·vits (hûr'skə-vĭts'), **Melville Jean.** 1895–1963. Amer. anthropologist.
Her·ter (hûr'tər), **Christian Archibald.** 1895–1966. Amer. diplomat.
Hertz (hûrts, hĕrts). **1. Heinrich Rudolf.** 1857–94. German physicist. **2. Gustav Ludwig.** 1887–1975. German physicist (Nobel, 1925).
Hert·zog (hûrt'sŏg, -sôg', hĕrt'-, hĕr'tsôKH), **James Barry Munnik.** 1866–1942. South African statesman.
Herz·berg (hûrts'bûrg'), **Gerhard.** b. 1904. German-born Canadian physicist (Nobel, 1971).
Her·zl (hĕr'tsəl), **Theodor.** 1860–1904. Hungarian-born Austrian founder of Zionism.
He·si·od (hē'sē-əd, hĕs'ē-). 8th cent. B.C. Greek poet.
Hess (hĕs). **1. Walter Rudolf.** 1881–1973. Swiss physiologist (Nobel, 1949). **2. Victor Franz.** 1883–1964. Austrian-born Amer. physicist (Nobel, 1936). **3.** Dame **Myra.** 1890–1965. English pianist. **4. (Walter Richard) Rudolf.** b. 1894. German Nazi leader.
Hes·se (hĕs'ə), **Hermann.** 1877–1962. German-born Swiss author (Nobel, 1946).
He·ve·sy (hĕ'vĕ-shē), **George von.** 1885–1966. Hungarian chemist (Nobel, 1943).
Hew·ish (hyo͞o'ĭsh), **Antony.** b. 1924. English astronomer (Nobel, 1974).
Hew·itt (hyo͞o'ĭt), **Abram Stevens.** 1822–1903. Amer. industrialist, politician, and reformer.
Hey·er·dahl (hā'ər-däl', hī'-), **Thor.** b. 1914. Norwegian ethnologist and explorer.
Hey·mans (hī'mäns, ā-mäNs'), **Corneille.** 1892–1968. Belgian physiologist (Nobel, 1938).
Hey·rov·sky (hā-rôf'skē), **Jaroslav.** 1890–1967. Czechoslovakian chemist (Nobel, 1959).
Hey·se (hī'zə), **Paul von.** 1830–1914. German author (Nobel, 1910).
Hey·ward (hā'wərd), **DuBose** 1885–1940. Amer. author.
Hey·wood (hā'wo͝od). **1. John.** 1497?–1580? English author. **2. Thomas.** 1574?–1641. English playwright.
Hez·e·ki·ah (hĕz'ə-kī'ə). 740?–692? B.C. King of Judah.
Hich·ens (hĭch'ənz), **Robert Smythe.** 1864–1950. English novelist.
Hick·ok (hĭk'ŏk'), **James Butler ("Wild Bill").** 1837–76. Amer. frontier scout and marshal.
Hicks (hĭks). **1. Edward.** 1780–1849. Amer. primitive painter. **2.** Sir **John Richard.** b. 1904. English economist (Nobel, 1972).

Hi·e·ro I (hī'ə-rō') or **Hi·e·ron** (-rŏn'). d. 466 B.C. Tyrant of Sicily (478–66 B.C.).

Hig·gin·son (hĭg'ĭn-sən), **Thomas Wentworth Storrow.** 1823–1911. Amer. clergyman, author, and Union soldier.

High·et (hī'ĭt), **Gilbert.** 1906–78. Scottish-born Amer. classicist.

Hil·de·brand (hĭl'də-brănd'). Pope Gregory VII.

Hill (hĭl). **1.** Sir **Rowland.** 1795–1879. English postal reformer. **2. Ambrose Powell.** 1825–65. Amer. Confederate soldier. **3. James Jerome.** 1838–1916. Amer. financier and railway promoter. **4. Joe.** 1872?–1915. Swedish-born Amer. labor organizer and lyricist. **5. George Washington.** 1884–1946. Amer. tobacco executive. **6. Archibald Vivian.** 1886–1977. English physiologist (Nobel, 1922).

Hil·la·ry (hĭl'ə-rē), Sir **Edmund Percival.** b. 1919. New Zealand mountaineer, explorer, and author; 1st Westerner to scale Mt. Everest.

Hil·lel (hĭl'ĕl). fl. 30 B.C.–A.D. 9. Palestinian rabbi.

Hil·liard (hĭl'yərd), **Nicholas.** 1537–1619. English painter.

Hill·man (hĭl'mən), **Sidney.** 1887–1946. Amer. labor leader.

Hill·quit (hĭl'kwĭt'), **Morris.** 1869–1933. Amer. socialist leader.

Hil·ton (hĭl'tən). **1. Conrad Nicholson.** 1887–1979. Amer. hotel-chain organizer. **2. James.** 1900–54. English novelist.

Himm·ler (hĭm'lər), **Heinrich.** 1900–45. German Nazi SS official.

Hin·de·mith (hĭn'də-mĭth, -mĭt), **Paul.** 1895–1963. German violinist and composer.

Hin·den·burg (hĭn'dən-bûrg', -bo͝ork'), **Paul von.** 1847–1934. German general and statesman.

Hine (hīn), **Lewis Wickes.** 1874–1940. Amer. pioneer photographer.

Hines (hīnz). **1. Duncan.** 1880–1959. Amer. publisher and author of restaurant guides. **2. Earl ("Fatha").** b. 1905. Amer. musician.

Hin·kle (hĭng'kəl), **Beatrice Moses Van Geisen.** 1874–1953. Amer. psychiatrist and public-health official.

Hin·shel·wood (hĭn'shəl-wo͝od', -chəl-), Sir **Cyril Norman.** 1897–1967. English chemist (Nobel, 1956).

Hip·par·chus (hĭ-pär'kəs). **1.** d. 6th cent. B.C. Athenian tyrant (527–14). **2.** fl. 130 B.C. Greek astronomer.

Hip·pi·as (hĭp'ē-əs). 6th cent. B.C. Athenian ruler.

Hip·poc·ra·tes (hĭ-pŏk'rə-tēz'). "the Father of Medicine." 460?–377? B.C. Greek physician. **—Hip'po·crat'ic** (hĭp'ə-krăt'ĭk) *adj.*

Hires (hīrz), **Charles Elmer.** 1851–1937. Amer. soft-drink manufacturer.

Hi·ro·hi·to (hîr'ō-hē'tō, hē'rô-hē'tô). b. 1901. Japanese emperor (since 1926).

Hi·ro·shi·ge (hîr'ō-shē'gā, hē'rô-shē'gĕ), **Ando.** 1797–1858. Japanese painter.

Hirsch·horn (hûrsh'hôrn), **Joseph Herman.** 1899–1981. Amer. financier and arts patron.

Hiss (hĭs), **Alger.** b. 1904. Amer. public official.

Hitch·cock (hĭch'kŏk'). **1. Edward.** 1793–1864. Amer. geologist and educator. **2. Ethan Allen.** 1835–1909. Amer. manufacturer, diplomat, and public official. **3. Alfred Joseph.** 1899–1980. British filmmaker.

Hit·ler (hĭt'lər), **Adolf.** 1889–1945. Austrian-born German Nazi dictator.

Hit·torf (hĭt'ôrf'), **Johann Wilhelm.** 1824–1914. German physicist.

Hoar (hôr, hōr). **1. Ebenezer Rockwood.** 1816–95. Amer. jurist. **2. George Frisbie.** 1826–1904. Amer. legislator.

Hoard (hôrd, hōrd), **William Dempster.** 1836–1918. Amer. editor, agricultural pioneer, and politician.

Hoare (hôr, hōr), Sir **Samuel John Gurney.** 1st Viscount Templewood. 1880–1959. English diplomat and public official.

Ho·ban (hō'bən), **James.** 1762?–1831. Irish-born Amer. architect.

Ho·bart (hō'bərt, -bärt'), **Garret Augustus.** 1844–99. U.S. Vice President (1897–99).

Hob·be·ma (hŏb'ə-mə, hô'bə-mä), **Meindert.** 1638–1709. Dutch landscape painter.

Hobbes (hŏbz), **Thomas.** 1588–1679. English philosopher. **—Hobbes'i·an** *adj. & n.*

Hob·by (hŏb'ē), **Oveta Culp.** b. 1905. Amer. public official.

Hob·son (hŏb'sən), **Richmond Pearson.** 1870–1937. Amer. naval officer, politician, and reformer.

Hoc·cleve (hŏk'lēv'), **Thomas.** 1370?–1450? English poet.

Ho Chi Minh (hō' chē' mĭn'). 1890–1969. Vietnamese Communist leader.

Hock·ing (hŏk'ĭng), **William Ernest.** 1873–1966. Amer. philosopher.

Hodg·es (hŏj'ĭz), **Gil.** 1924–72. Amer. baseball player and manager.

Hodg·kin (hŏj'kĭn). **1. Dorothy Mary Crowfoot.** b. 1910. Egyptian-born British chemist (Nobel, 1964). **2.** Sir **Alan Lloyd.** b. 1914. British physiologist (Nobel, 1963).

Hoe (hō). **1. Robert.** 1784–1833. Amer. manufacturer. **2. Richard March.** 1812–86. Amer. inventor (printing equipment) and manufacturer.

Ho·fer (hō'fər), **Andreas.** 1767–1810. Tyrolese patriot; executed.

Hof·fa (hŏf'ə), **James Riddle ("Jimmy").** 1913–75? Amer. labor leader; presumed murdered.

Hoff·man (hŏf'mən). **1. Malvina.** 1887–1966. Amer. artist and author. **2. Roald.** b. 1937. Polish-born Amer. chemist (Nobel, 1981).

Hoff·mann (hŏf'mən, hôf'män'). **1. Ernst Theodor Amadeus (Wilhelm).** 1776–1822. German author, critic, and composer. **2. August Heinrich.** "Hoffmann von Fallersleben." German author, philologist, and literary historian.

Hof·mann (hŏf'mən, hôf'män'). **1. August Wilhelm von.** 1818–92. German chemist. **2. Josef Casimir.** 1876–1957. Polish-born pianist and composer. **3. Hans.** 1880–1966. German-born Amer. artist.

Hof·manns·thal (hôf'mäns-täl', hōf'-), **Hugo von.** 1874–1929. Austrian author.

Hof·stadt·er (hŏf'stăt'ər). **1. Robert.** b. 1915. Amer. physicist (Nobel, 1961). **2. Richard.** 1916–70. Amer. historian.

Ho·gan (hō'gən), **William Benjamin ("Ben").** b. 1912. Amer. golfer.

Ho·garth (hō'gärth'), **William.** 1697–1764. English artist.

Hogg (hŏg, hôg), **James.** 1770–1835. Scottish poet.

Ho·hen·lo·he (hō'ən-lō'ə). German princely family (12th–19th cent.).

Ho·hen·stau·fen (hō'ən-shtou'fən). German princely family, ruling in Germany and Sicily (12th–13th cent.).

Ho·hen·zol·lern (hō'ən-zŏl'ərn, hō'ən-zôl'ərn, -tsôl'-). German royal family, ruling Brandenburg (1415–1918), Prussia (1701–1918), and Germany (1871–1918).

Ho·kin·son (hō'kĭn-sən), **Helen Elna.** 1893–1949. Amer. cartoonist.

Ho·ku·sai (hō'ko͞o-sī', hō'ko͞o-sī', hô'ko͞o-). 1760–1849. Japanese artist.

Adolf Hitler

Hol·bein (hōl'bīn, hôl'-), **Hans. 1.** "the Elder." 1465?–1524. German painter. **2.** "the Younger." 1497?–1543. German-born artist in Switzerland and England.

Hol·berg (hōl'bĕrg'), **Ludvig.** 1684–1754. Danish dramatist.

Hol·brook (hōl'bro͝ok'), **Josiah.** 1788–1854. Amer. educational reformer; founder of lyceum movement.

Hol·i·day (hŏl'ĭ-dā'), **Eleanora ("Billie").** "Lady Day." 1915–59. Amer. singer.

Hol·in·shed (hŏl'ĭn-shĕd', -ĭnz-hĕd') also **Hol·lings·head** (-ĭngz-hĕd'), **Raphael.** b. 1580? English chronicler.

Hol·la·day (hŏl'ə-dā'), **Ben.** 1819–87. Amer. businessman and financier.

Hol·land (hŏl'ənd). **1. Josiah Gilbert.** "Timothy Titcomb." 1819–81. Amer. author and editor. **2. John Philip.** 1840–1914. Irish-born Amer. inventor and submarine pioneer. **3. Sidney George.** 1893–1961. New Zealand statesman.

Hol·ler·ith (hŏl'ə-rĭth'), **Herman.** 1860–1929. Amer. inventor (tabulating machine).

Hol·ley (hŏl'ē). **1. Alexander Lyman.** 1832–82. Amer. metallurgist, engineer, and author. **2. Marietta.** 1836–1926. Amer. author and feminist. **3. Robert William.** b. 1922. Amer. biochemist (Nobel, 1968).

Hol·li·day (hŏl'ĭ-dā'), **Judith Tuvim ("Judy").** 1922–65. Amer. comedienne.

Holmes (hōmz, hōlmz). **1. Oliver Wendell.** 1809–94. Amer. physician and author. **2. Oliver Wendell, Jr.** 1841–1935. Amer. jurist. **3. John Haynes.** 1879–1964. Amer. clergyman and libertarian. **—Holmes'i·an** *adj.*

Hol·stein-Got·torp (hōl'stīn-gôt'-tôrp, -tōrp, -shtīn-). Swedish ruling dynasty (1751–1818).

Holt (hōlt). **1. Luther Emmett.** 1855–1924. Australian pioneer pediatrician. **2. Winifred.** 1870–1945. Amer. sculptor and philanthropist. **3. Harold Edward.** 1908–67. Australian statesman.

Hol·yoake (hōl'yōk', hō'lē-ōk'), **Keith Jacka.** b. 1904. New Zealand statesman.

Ho·mer (hō'mər). **1.** fl. 850? B.C. Greek epic poet (*Iliad* and *Odyssey*). **2. Winslow.** 1836–1910. Amer. painter. **3. Louise Dilworth Beatty.** 1871–1947. Amer. opera singer. **—Ho·mer'ic** (hō-mĕr'ĭk) *adj.*

Hone (hōn), **Philip.** 1780–1851. Amer. diarist and public official.

Hon·eg·ger (hŏn'ə-gər, hŭn'-, hō'-nĕg'ər, ô-nĕ-gĕr'), **Arthur.** 1892–1955. French-born Swiss composer.

Ho·no·ri·us (hō-nôr'ē-əs, -nōr'-, hə-), **Flavius.** 384–423. Western Roman emperor (395–23).

Hood (ho͝od). **1. Samuel.** 1724–1816. English admiral. **2. Thomas.** 1799–1845. English poet and editor. **3. John Bell.** 1831–79. Amer. Confederate soldier.

Hook (ho͝ok), **Sidney.** b. 1902. Amer. philosopher.

Hooke (ho͝ok), **Robert.** 1635–1703. English philosopher, inventor, and mathematician.

Hook·er (ho͝ok'ər). **1. Richard.** 1554?–1600. English author and theologian. **2. Thomas.** 1586?–1647. English-born Amer. colonizer and clergyman. **3. Joseph.** 1814–79. Amer. Union army officer. **4.** Sir **Joseph Dalton.** 1817–1911. English botanist and explorer. **5. Isabella Beecher.** 1822–1907. Amer. philanthropist and feminist.

Hoo·ton (ho͞ot'n), **Earnest Albert.** 1887–1954. Amer. anthropologist.

Hoo·ver (ho͞o'vər). **1. Herbert Clark.** 1874–1964. 31st U.S. President (1929–33), relief administrator, and statesman. **2. J(ohn) Edgar.** 1895–1972. Amer. director of FBI (1924–72).

Hope (hōp). **1. John.** 1868–1936. Amer. educator. **2. Leslie Towne ("Bob").** English-born Amer. entertainer.

Hop·kins (hŏp'kĭnz). **1. Esek.** 1718–1802. Amer. Revolutionary naval officer. **2. Samuel.** 1721–1803. Amer. theologian. **3. Johns.** 1795–1873. Amer. financier and philanthropist. **4. Mark.** 1802–87. Amer. educator and theologian. **5. Gerard Manley.** 1844–89. English priest, poet, and artist. **6.** Sir **Frederick Gowland.** 1861–1947. English biochemist (Nobel, 1929).

Hop·kin·son (hŏp'kĭn-sən), **Francis.** 1737–91. Amer. Revolutionary leader and author.

Hop·pe (hŏp'ē), **William Frederick.** 1887–1959. Amer. billiards player.

Hop·per (hŏp'ər). **1. Edward.** 1882–1967. Amer. painter. **2. (William) DeWolf.** 1858–1935. Amer. musical-comedy actor. **3. Hedda.** 1890–1966. Amer. actress and columnist.

Hor·ace (hôr'əs, hŏr'-). 65–8 B.C. Roman poet. **—Ho·ra'tian** (hə-rā'-shən) *adj.*

Hor·na·day (hôr'nə-dā'), **William Temple.** 1854–1937. Amer. zoologist.

Horne (hôrn). **1. Lena.** b. 1917. Amer. singer. **2. Marilyn.** b. 1934. Amer. operatic soprano.

Hor·ney (hôr'nī), **Karen Danielsen.** 1885–1952. German-born Amer. psychoanalyst.

Horns·by (hôrnz'bē), **Rogers.** 1896–1963. Amer. baseball player and manager.

Ho·ro·witz (hôr'ə-wĭts, hŏr'-), **Vladimir.** b. 1904. Russian-born Amer. pianist.

Hor·thy (hôr'tē, hŏr'-), **Miklós von Nagybánya.** 1868–1957. Hungarian admiral and statesman.

Hor·ton (hôr'tn), **Edward Everett.** 1887–1970. Amer. actor.

Hor·wich (hôr'wĭch), **Frances Rappaport.** b. 1908. Amer. educator and pioneer in children's television programming.

Ho·se·a (hō-zā'ə, -zē'-ə). 8th cent. B.C. Hebrew prophet.

Hos·mer (hŏz'mər), **Harriet Goodhue.** 1830–1908. Amer. sculptor.

Hou·di·ni (ho͞o-dē'nē), **Harry.** 1874–1926. Amer. magician.

Hou·don (o͞o-dôɴ'), **Jean Antoine.** 1741–1828. French sculptor.

Hou·dry (ho͞o'drē, ho͞o-drē'), **Eugene Jules.** 1892–1962. French-born Amer. engineer and manufacturer.

Hough (hŭf), **Emerson.** 1857–1923. Amer. author.

Houns·field (hounz'fēld'), **Godfrey Newbold.** b. 1919. English engineer and inventor (Nobel, 1979).

House (hous), **Edward Mandell ("Colonel").** 1858–1938. Amer. diplomat and Presidential adviser.

House·man (hous'mən), **John.** b. 1902. Amer. producer, director, and actor.

Hous·man (hous'mən). **1. Alfred Edward.** 1859–1936. English poet and scholar. **2. Laurence.** 1865–1959. English author and illustrator.

Hous·say (o͞o-sī'), **Bernardo Alberto.** 1887–1971. Argentine physiologist (Nobel, 1947).

Hous·ton (hyo͞o'stən), **Samuel.** 1793–1863. Amer. general and politician.

Hov·ey (hŭv'ē), **Richard.** 1864–1900. Amer. poet.

How·ard (hou'ərd). **1. Henry.** "Earl of Surrey." 1517?–47. English poet and soldier; beheaded for treason. **2. Catherine.** 1520?–42. Queen of

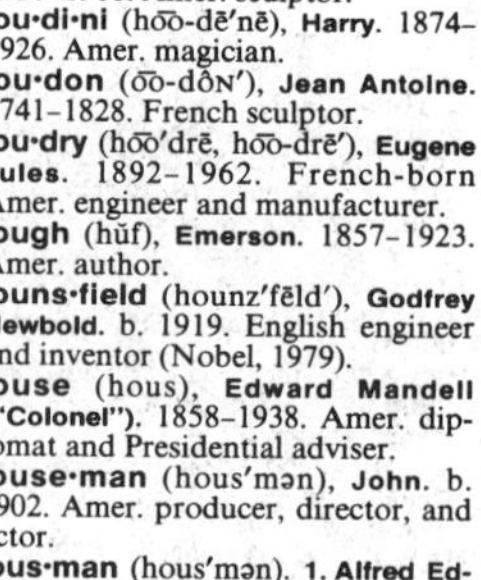

Herbert Hoover

England as 5th wife of Henry VIII (1540–42); executed for adultery. **3. Ada Lydia.** 1829–1907. Amer. educator and college administrator. **4. Oliver Otis.** 1830–1909. Amer. Union general. **5. Roy Wilson.** 1883–1964. Amer. journalist and publisher. **6. Sidney Coe.** 1891–1939. Amer. playwright.

Howe (hou). **1. Richard.** Earl Howe. 1726–99. English admiral. **2.** Sir **William.** 5th Viscount Howe. 1729–1814. English general in America. **3. Samuel Gridley.** 1801–76. Amer. humanitarian and reformer. **4. Elias.** 1819–67. Amer. inventor (sewing machine) and manufacturer. **5. Julia Ward.** 1819–1910. Amer. author, feminist, and philanthropist. **6. Irving.** b. 1920. Amer. critic.

How·ells (hou'əlz), **William Dean.** 1837–1920. Amer. author and editor.

How·land (hou'lənd), **Emily.** 1827–1929. Amer. educator, philanthropist, and reformer.

Hr·dlič·ka (hûrd'lĭch-kə), **Aleš.** 1869–1943. Bohemian-born Amer. anthropologist.

Hrolf (hrŏlf, rŏlf). Rollo.

Hsia (shyä). Xia.

Hua Guo·feng also **Kuo·feng** (hwä' gwō'fŭng'). b. 1920. Chinese Communist leader.

Huás·car (wäs'kär). 1495?–1533. Incan chief.

Hub·bard (hŭb'ərd). **1. Gardiner Greene.** 1822–97. Amer. lawyer and geographer. **2. Elbert Green.** 1856–1915. Amer. author and publisher.

Hub·ble (hŭb'əl), **Edwin Powell.** 1889–1953. Amer. astronomer.

Hu·bel (hyōō'bəl), **David.** b. 1926. Amer. neurobiologist (Nobel, 1981).

Hud·son (hŭd'sən). **1. Henry.** d. 1611. English navigator and Arctic explorer. **2. William Henry.** 1841–1922. English naturalist and author. **3. Manley Ottmer.** 1886–1960. Amer. jurist and educator.

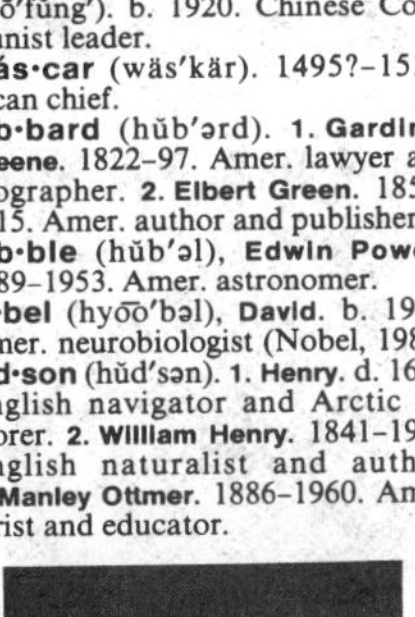

Henry Hudson

Huer·ta (wĕr'tə, -tä), **Victoriano.** 1854–1916. Mexican statesman.

Hug·gins (hŭg'ĭnz). **1.** Sir **William.** 1824–1910. English astronomer. **2. Charles Brenton.** b. 1901. Canadian-born Amer. surgeon (Nobel, 1966).

Hugh Ca·pet (hyōō' kā'pĭt, kăp'ĭt, kä-pā', kä-pĕ'). See **Capet.**

Hughes (hyōōz). **1. Thomas.** 1822–96. English reformer and author. **2. Charles Evans.** 1862–1948. Amer. jurist and statesman. **3. William Morris.** 1864–1952. Australian statesman. **4. Rupert.** 1872–1956. Amer. author. **5. (James) Langston.** 1902–67. Amer. author. **6. Howard Robard.** 1905–76. Amer. manufacturer, film producer, and recluse.

Langston Hughes

Hu·go (hyōō'gō, ü-gō'), **Victor Marie.** 1802–85. French author.

Hui·zing·a (hoi'zĭng-ə, -zĭng-ä, hī'-), **Johan.** 1872–1945. Dutch historian.

Hu·la·gu (hōō-lä'gōō). 1217–65. Mongol ruler.

Hull (hŭl). **1. William.** 1753–1825. Amer. general. **2. Isaac.** 1773–1843. Amer. naval officer. **3. Cordell.** 1871–1955. Amer. statesman (Nobel, 1945).

Hum·boldt (hŭm'bōlt', hōōm'bôlt'). **1.** Baron **(Friedrich) Wilhelm (Christian Karl Ferdinand) von.** 1767–1835. German philologist and diplomat. **2.** Baron **(Friedrich Heinrich) Alexander von.** 1769–1859. German naturalist, author, and statesman.

Hume (hyōōm), **David.** 1711–76. Scottish philosopher and historian.

Hum·per·dinck (hōōm'pər-dĭngk', hŭm'-), **Engelbert.** 1854–1921. German composer.

Hum·phrey (hŭm'frē). **1.** Duke of Gloucester and Earl of Pembroke. 1391–1447. English statesman and collector. **2. Doris.** 1895–1958. Amer. dancer and choreographer. **3. Hubert Horatio.** 1911–78. U.S. Vice President (1965–69) and legislator.

Hum·phreys (hŭm'frēz), **Joshua.** 1751–1838. Amer. naval architect.

Hun·e·ker (hŭn'ĭ-kər), **James Gibbons.** 1860–1921. Amer. critic.

Hun·sa·ker (hŭn'sā'kər), **Jerome Clarke.** 1886–1984. Amer. aeronautical engineer.

Hunt (hŭnt). **1. (James Henry) Leigh.** 1784–1859. English author. **2. Harriot Kezia.** 1805–75. Amer. pioneer physician and reformer. **3. Ward.** 1810–86. Amer. jurist. **4. William Morris.** 1824–79. Amer. painter. **5. Richard Morris.** 1827–95. Amer. architect. **6. (William) Holman.** 1827–1910. English pre-Raphaelite painter. **7. Mary Hannah Hanchett.** 1830–1906. Amer. temperance reformer. **8. Haroldson Lafayette ("H.L.").** 1889–1974. Amer. businessman.

Hun·ter (hŭn'tər). **1. John.** 1728–93. English anatomist. **2. Robert Mercer Taliaferro.** 1809–87. Amer. politician and Confederate statesman.

Hun·ting·ton (hŭn'tĭng-tən). **1. Samuel.** 1731–96. Amer. Revolutionary leader. **2. Collis Potter.** 1821–1900. Amer. transportation executive. **3. Henry Edwards.** 1850–1927. Amer. railroad executive, art collector, and philanthropist. **4. Ellsworth.** 1876–1947. Amer. geographer and explorer.

Hunt·ley (hŭnt'lē), **Chet.** 1911–74. Amer. broadcast journalist.

Hu·nya·di or **Hu·nya·dy** (hōō'nyô-dē), **János.** 1387?–1456. Hungarian general.

Hur·ley (hûr'lē), **Patrick Jay.** 1883–1963. Amer. public official and diplomat.

Hur·ok (hyōōr'ŏk'), **Solomon ("Sol").** 1888–1974. Russian-born Amer. impresario.

Hurst (hûrst). **1.** Sir **Cecil James Barrington.** 1870–1963. English jurist. **2. Fannie.** 1889–1968. Amer. author.

Hur·ston (hûr'stən), **Zora Neale.** 1901?–60. Amer. author.

Hu·sein ibn-A·li (hōō-sān' ĭb'-ən-ä-lē'). 1856–1931. King of Hejaz (1916–24) and Arabia (1917–24); abdicated.

Hu Shi also **Shih** (hōō' shœ'). 1891–1962. Chinese philosopher and diplomat.

Huss or **Hus** (hŭs, hōōs), **John** or **Jan.** 1374–1415. Bohemian religious reformer.

Hus·sein or **Hu·sain** or **Hu·sayn ibn Ta·lal** (hōō-sān' ĭb'ən tä-läl'). b. 1935. King of Jordan (since 1953).

Hus·sey (hŭs'ē), **Obed.** 1792–1860. Amer. inventor (reaper) and manufacturer.

Hus·ted (hyōō'stĭd'), **Marjorie Child.** "Betty Crocker." b. 1892? Amer. home-economics executive.

Hus·ton (hyōō'stən). **1. Walter.** 1884–1950. Amer. actor. **2. John.** b. 1906. Amer. filmmaker.

Hu·szár (hōō'sär), **Károly.** 1882–1941. Hungarian journalist and politician.

Hutch·ins (hŭch'ĭnz). **1. Thomas.** 1730–89. Amer. cartographer and engineer. **2. Robert Maynard.** 1899–1977. Amer. educator.

Hutch·in·son (hŭch'ĭn-sən). **1. Anne.** 1591–1643. English-born Amer. colonist and religious leader. **2. Thomas.** 1711–80. Amer. colonial official.

Hut·ten (hōōt'n), **Ulrich von.** 1488–1523. German author and humanist.

Hut·ton (hŭt'n), **Barbara.** 1912–79. Amer. socialite.

Hux·ley (hŭks'lē). **1. Thomas Henry.** 1825–95. English biologist. **2.** Sir **Julian Sorell.** 1887–1975. English biologist and author. **3. Aldous Leonard.** 1894–1963. English author. **4. Andrew Fielding.** b. 1917. English physiologist (Nobel, 1963).

Aldous Huxley

Hu Yao·bang also **Yao-pang** (hōō' you'bäng'). b. 1915. Chinese politician.

Huy·gens or **Huy·ghens** (hī'gənz), **Christian.** 1629–95. Dutch physicist and astronomer.

Huys·mans (wēs-mäns'). **1. Joris Karl.** 1848–1907. French novelist. **2. Camille.** 1871–1968. Belgian politician and journalist.

Hy·att (hī'ət). **1. John Wesley.** 1837–1920. Amer. inventor. **2. Alpheus.** 1838–1902. Amer. naturalist. **3. Anna Vaugh.** 1876–1973. Amer. sculptor.

Hyde (hīd). **1. Edward.** 1st Earl of Clarendon. 1609–74. English statesman and historian. **2. Douglas.** 1860–1949. Irish nationalist and author.

Hy·mans (hī'mäns', ē-mäns'), **Paul.** 1865–1941. Belgian diplomat and statesman.

I

I·ber·ville (dē-bĕr-vēl'), Sieur d'. Pierre Le Moyne. 1661–1706. Canadian-born French explorer.

ibn-Khal·dun (ĭb'ən-κhäl-dōōn'). 1332–1406. Arab historian.

ibn-Sa·ud (ĭb'ən-sä-ōōd'), **Abdul Aziz.** 1880–1953. Saudi Arabian king (1932–53).

Ib·ra·him Pa·sha (ĭb'rä-hēm' pä'-shä). 1789–1849. Egyptian general and viceroy.

Ib·sen (ĭb'sən, ĭp'-), **Henrik.** 1828–1906. Norwegian dramatist. **—Ib·sen'i·an** *adj.*

Ick·es (ĭk'ēz, -əs), **Harold LeClair.** 1874–1952. Amer. politician and author.

Ic·ti·nus (ĭk-tī'nəs). 5th cent. B.C. Greek architect.

Ig·na·tius (ĭg-nā'shəs). **1.** Saint. 2nd cent. A.D. Martyred bishop of Antioch. **2. of Loy·o·la** (loi-ō'lə), Saint. 1491–1556. Spanish ecclesiastic; founder of the Society of Jesus.

Ikh·na·ton (ĭk-nät'n). Variant of **Akhenaton.**

In·di·an·a (ĭn'dē-ăn'ə), **Robert.** b. 1928. Amer. artist.

In·dy (ăn-dē'), **(Paul Marie Théodore) Vincent d'.** 1851–1931. French composer.

Inge. **1.** (ĭng), **William Ralph.** 1860–1954. English clergyman and author. **2.** (ĭnj), **William.** 1913–73. Amer. playwright.

In·ger·soll (ĭng'gər-sôl', -sŏl', -səl), **Robert Green.** 1833–99. Amer. politician and lecturer.

In·gra·ham (ĭng'grə-hăm', ĭng'grəm), **Prentiss.** 1843–1904. Amer. author and adventurer.

In·gram (ĭng'grəm), **Arthur Foley Winnington.** 1858–1946. English prelate and reformer.

In·gres (ăn'grə), **Jean Auguste Dominique.** 1780–1867. French painter.

In·man (ĭn'mən), **Henry.** 1801–46. Amer. portrait painter.

In·ness (ĭn'ĭs), **George.** 1825–94. Amer. landscape painter.

In·no·cent (ĭn'ə-sənt). Name of 13 popes, esp.: **1. II.** d. 1143. Reigned 1130–43. **2. III.** 1161–1216. Reigned 1198–1216. **3. IV.** d. 1254. **4. XI.** 1611–89. Reigned 1676–89.

I·nö·nü (ĭ-nœ-nü'), **Ismet.** 1884–1973. Turkish statesman.

In·sull (ĭn'səl), **Samuel.** 1859–1938. English-born Amer. utilities mogul.

Io·nes·co (yə-nĕs'kō, ē'-ə-nĕs'-), **Eugène.** b. 1912. Rumanian-born French dramatist.

I·pa·tieff (ē-pä'tyĭf), **Vladimir Nikolaevich.** 1867–1952. Russian-born Amer. chemist.

Ire·dell (ĭr'dĕl'), **James.** 1751–99. Amer. jurist.

Ire·ton (ĭr'tn), **Henry.** 1611–51. English Civil War general.

I·ri·go·yen (ĭr'ĭ-gō'yĕn', ē-rē-), **Hipólito.** 1852–1933. Argentine statesman.

Ir·ving (ûr'vĭng). **1. Washington.** 1783–1859. Amer. writer. **2.** Sir **Henry.** 1838–1905. English actor.

Ir·win (ûr'wĭn). **1. May.** 1862–1938. Amer. comedienne. **2. William Henry ("Will").** 1873–1948. Amer. author. **3. Wallace.** 1875–1959. Amer. humorist and author.

I·saac (ī'zək). Hebrew patriarch.

I·saacs (ī'zəks), Sir **Isaac Alfred.** 1855–1948. Australian jurist and statesman.

Is·a·bel·la I (ĭz'ə-bĕl'ə). "the Catholic." 1451–1504. Queen of Castile and Aragon; sponsored Christopher Columbus.

Isabella I

I·sa·iah (ī-zā'ə). 8th cent. B.C. Hebrew prophet.

Ish·er·wood (ĭsh'ər-wŏŏd'), **Christopher William Bradshaw.** 1904–86. British-born Amer. writer.

I·shi·i (ē'shē-ē), Viscount **Kikujiro.** 1866–1945. Japanese diplomat.

Is·i·dore of Se·ville (ĭz'ĭ-dôr', -dōr'-, sə-vĭl'), Saint. 560?–636. Spanish scholar and ecclesiastic.

Is·ma·il Pa·sha (ĭs-mä'ēl pä'shä). 1830–95. Egyptian viceroy (1863–79).

I·soc·ra·tes (ī-sŏk'rə-tēz). 436–338 B.C. Athenian orator and rhetorician.

I·to (ē'tô'). **1.** Prince **Hirobumi.** 1841–1909. Japanese statesman; assassinated. **2.** Count **Yuko.** 1843–1914. Japanese admiral.

I·tur·bi (ĭ-tûr'bē, ē-tōōr'-), **José.** 1895–1980. Spanish-born pianist and conductor.

I·tur·bi·de (ē'tōōr-bē'*thĕ*), **Agustín de.** 1783–1824. Mexican revolutionary.

I·van III Va·sil·ie·vich (ē-vän', ī'vən; və-sĭl'yə-vĭch'). "the Great." 1440–

1505. Grand Duke of Muscovy (1462–1505).

Ivan IV Vasilievich. "the Terrible." 1530–1584. Grand Duke of Muscovy (1533–84) and czar of Russia (1547–84).

Ives (īvz). **1. James Merritt.** 1824–95. Amer. lithographer. **2. Frederick Eugene.** 1856–1937. Amer. inventor. **3. Charles Edward.** 1874–1954. Amer. composer.

Iz·ard (ĭz'ərd), **Ralph.** 1742–1804. Amer. Revolutionary leader and diplomat.

J

Ja·bir (jä'bîr, jā'bər). Variant of **Geber.**

Jack·son (jăk'sən). **1. Andrew.** "Old Hickory." 1767–1845. Soldier and 7th U.S. President (1829–37).

Andrew Jackson

2. Charles Thomas. 1805–80. Amer. physician, chemist, and geologist. **3. Thomas Jonathan ("Stonewall").** 1824–63. Amer. Confederate general. **4. Helen (Maria Fiske) Hunt.** 1830–85. Amer. author. **5. Howell Edmunds.** 1832–95. Amer. jurist. **6. Robert Houghwout.** 1892–1954. Amer. jurist. **7. Mahalia.** 1911–72. Amer. singer. **8. Jesse Louis.** b. 1941. Amer. civil-rights leader. **—Jack·son'i·an** *adj. & n.*

Ja·cob. 1. (jā'kəb). Hebrew patriarch. **2.** (zhä-kôb'), **François.** b. 1920. French geneticist (Nobel, 1965).

Ja·co·bi (jə-kō'bē), **Abraham** (German-born; 1830–1919) and **Mary Corinna Putnam** (English-born; 1842–1906). Amer. physicians.

Jac·quard (jăk'ärd, zhä-kär'), **Joseph Marie.** 1752–1834. French inventor (mechanical loom).

Jag·a·tai (jăg'ə-tī'). d. 1242. Mongol ruler.

Jag·ger (jăg'ər), **Michael Phillip ("Mick").** b. 1943. English musician.

Mick Jagger

Ja·han·gir (jə-hän-gēr'). 1569–1627. Mongol emperor (1605–27).

James (jāmz). **1.** Saint. "the Less." Traditionally regarded as the brother of Jesus. **2.** Saint. "the Greater." d. A.D. 44. One of the 12 Apostles; martyred. **3.** Saint. One of the 12 Apostles. **4.** Name of 6 kings of Scotland and Great Britain, esp.: **a. I.** 1566–1625. Ruled 1603–25 in England and 1567–1625 in Scotland as **James VI. b. II.** 1633–1701. Ruled 1685–88; succeeded by his Protestant son-in-law, William of Orange. **5. William.** 1842–1910. Amer. psychologist and philosopher. **6. Henry.** 1843–1916. Amer. novelist and critic. **7. Jesse Woodson.** 1847–82. Amer. outlaw. **—James'i·an** *adj. & n.*

Jame·son (jām'sən), Sir **Leander Starr.** 1853–1917. Scottish physician and colonial administrator.

Ja·me·son (jā'mə-sən), **John Franklin.** 1859–1937. Amer. historian and educator.

Ja·mi (jä'mē). 1414–92. Persian poet and mystic.

Ja·mi·son (jā'mĭ-sən), **Cecilia Viets Dakin Hamilton.** 1837–1909. Canadian-born Amer. author and painter.

Ja·ná·ček (yä'nä-chĕk'), **Leoš.** 1854–1928. Czechoslovakian composer.

Jan·sen (jăn'sən, yän'-), **Cornelius.** 1585–1638. Dutch theologian. **—Jan'sen·ist** *adj. & n.* **—Jan'sen·is'tic** *adj.*

Ja·pheth (jā'fĭth', jăf'ĭth). In the Bible, Noah's son.

Jaques-Dal·croze (zhäk'däl-krōz'), **Emile.** 1865–1950. Swiss composer and educator.

Jar·rell (jə-rĕl'), **Randall.** 1914–65. Amer. poet.

Jar·ves (jär'vəs), **James Jackson.** 1818–88. Amer. critic and art collector.

Jas·pers (yäs'pərs), **Karl.** 1883–1969. German psychiatrist and existentialist philosopher.

Jau·rès (zhô-rĕs'), **Jean Léon.** 1859–1914. French journalist and socialist leader; assassinated.

Jay (jā), **John.** 1745–1829. Amer. diplomat and jurist.

Jeanne d'Arc (zhäɴ därk'). *French.* Joan of Arc.

Jeans (jēnz), Sir **James Hopwood.** 1877–1946. English astronomer, physicist, and mathematician.

Jef·fers (jĕf'ərz), **Robinson.** 1887–1962. Amer. poet.

Jef·fer·son (jĕf'ər-sən). **1. Thomas.** 1743–1826. 3rd U.S. President (1801–9), author, scientist, architect, educator, and diplomat. **2. Joseph.** 1829–1905. Amer. actor. **—Jef'fer·so'ni·an** *adj. & n.*

Thomas Jefferson

Jef·frey (jĕf'rē), **Francis.** Lord Jeffrey. 1773–1850. Scottish critic and jurist.

Jef·fries (jef'rēz), **John.** 1745–1819. Amer. physician and balloonist.

Je·hosh·a·phat (jə-hŏsh'ə-făt', -hŏs'-). 9th cent. B.C. king of Judah.

Je·hu (jē'hyo͞o). 9th cent. B.C. Israeli king.

Jel·li·coe (jĕl'ĭ-kō), **John Rushworth.** 1st Earl Jellicoe. 1859–1935. English naval officer.

Jen·ghis also **Jen·ghiz Khan** (jĕn'gĭz kän', -gĭs, jĕng'-). Genghis Khan.

Jen·ner (jĕn'ər), **Edward.** 1749–1823. English physician; discovered vaccination.

Jen·ney (jĕn'ē). **William Le Baron.** 1832–1907. Amer. inventor and architect (1st skyscraper).

Jen·sen. 1. (yĕn'sən), **Johannes Vilhelm.** 1873–1950. Danish author (Nobel, 1944). **2.** (yĕn'zən), **(Johannes) Hans Daniel.** 1906–73. German physicist (Nobel, 1963).

Jer·e·mi·ah (jĕr'ə-mī'ə). 7th and 6th cent. B.C. Hebrew prophet.

Je·ri·tza (yĕ'rē-tsä', yĕr'ĭt-sə), **Maria.** b. 1887. Austrian-born operatic soprano.

Je·rome (jə-rōm'), Saint. 340?–420. Latin scholar.

Jer·vis (jûr'vĭs), **John.** Earl of St. Vincent. 1735–1823. English naval officer.

Jes·per·sen (yĕs'pər-sən), **(Jens) Otto (Harry).** 1860–1943. Danish philologist.

Jes·se (jĕs'ē). In the Old Testament, King David's father.

Jes·sel (jĕs'əl), **George Albert ("Georgie").** 1898–1981. Amer. actor, film producer, and toastmaster.

Je·sus (jē'zŭs) also **Jesus Christ** (krīst). 4? B.C.–A.D. 29? Founder of Christianity.

Jev·ons (jĕv'ənz), **William Stanley.** 1835–82. English economist and logician.

Jew·ett (jo͞o'ĭt), **Sarah Orne.** 1849–1909. Amer. author.

Jez·e·bel (jĕz'ə-bĕl). 9th cent. B.C. queen of Israel.

Ji·mé·nez (hē-mĕ'nĕs), **Juan Ramón.** 1881–1958. Spanish poet (Nobel, 1956).

Jiménez de Cis·ne·ros (dĕ sēs-nĕ'rôs), **Francisco.** 1436–1517. Spanish prelate and statesman.

Jin (jyĭn). Name of 4 Chinese dynasties: **Western Jin,** 265–316; **Eastern Jin,** 317–420; **Later Jin,** 936–46; and **Jin,** 1115–1234.

Jin·nah (jĭn'ə), **Mohammed Ali.** 1876–1948. Indian nationalist Moslem leader.

Jo·a·chim (yō'ä-ᴋʜĭm, yō-ä'-), **Joseph.** 1831–1907. Hungarian violinist and composer.

Joan of Arc (jōn; ärk). 1412–31. French military leader and heroine.

Job (jōb). Hebrew patriarch.

Jo·el (jō'əl). Hebrew prophet.

Jof·fre (zhôf'rə), **Joseph Jacques Césaire.** 1852–1931. French field marshal.

John (jŏn). **1.** Saint. "the Evangelist." One of the 12 Apostles. **2.** Saint. "the Baptist." 5 B.C.–A.D. 30. Baptizer of Jesus. **3. of Da·mas·cus** (də-măs'kəs). 700–54? Greek theologian. **4. of Salis·bur·y** (sôlz'bĕr'ē, -brē). d. 1180. English bishop and author. **5. of Lack·land** (lăk'lənd). 1167?–1216. English king (1199–1216). **6.** Name of 6 kings of Portugal, esp. **I,** 1357–1433, ruled 1385–1433. **7. of Gaunt** (gônt, gänt). Duke of Lancaster. 1340–99. English nobleman and soldier. **8. of Lan·cas·ter** (lăng'kə-stər). Duke of Bedford. 1389–1435. Regent of England and France. **9. of Lei·den** (līd'n). 1509–36. Dutch Anabaptist fanatic. **10. of Aus·tri·a** (ôs'trē-ə). 1547–78. Spanish general. **11. Augustus Edwin.** 1878–1961. English artist. **12.** Name of 21 popes, esp. **XXIII,** 1881–1963, reigned 1958–63.

John·ny Ap·ple·seed (jŏn'ē ăp'əl-sēd'). John Chapman.

John Paul (jŏn pôl, pōl). Name of 2 popes: **1. I.** 1912–78. Reigned 1978. **2. II.** b. 1920. Reigned since 1978.

John III So·bies·ki (sô-byĕs'kē). 1629–96. Polish king (1674–96).

Johns (jŏnz), **Jasper.** b. 1930. Amer. artist.

John·son (jŏn'sən). **1. Samuel.** "Dr. Johnson." 1709–84. English author and lexicographer. **2.** Sir **William.** 1715–74. Amer. pioneer and superintendent of Indian affairs. **3. William Samuel.** 1727–1819. Amer. Revolutionary leader, jurist, and college administrator. **4. Thomas.** 1732–1819. Amer. jurist. **5. William.** 1771–1834. Amer. jurist. **6. Richard Mentor.** 1780–1850. U.S. Vice President (1837–41) and soldier. **7. Reverdy.** 1796–1876. Amer. lawyer, politician, and diplomat. **8. Andrew.** 1808–75. 17th U.S. President (1865–69); impeached and acquitted. **9. Eastman.** 1824–1906. Amer. genre painter. **10. Tom Loftin.** 1854–1911. Amer. inventor and municipal administrator. **11. Hiram Warren.** 1866–1945. Amer. legislator. **12. James Weldon.** 1871–1938. Amer. author and educator. **13. John Arthur ("Jack").** 1878–1946. Amer. prizefighter. **14. Hugh Samuel.** 1882–1942. Amer. public official. **15. Osa Helen Leighty.** 1894–1953. Amer. explorer and filmmaker. **16. Howard Deering.** 1896?–1972. Amer. restaurateur. **17.** (yōn'sôn), **Eyvind.** 1904–76. Swedish author (Nobel, 1974). **18. Philip Cortelyou.** b. 1906. Amer. architect. **19. Lyndon Baines.** 1908–73. 36th U.S. President (1963–69). **20. John Harold.** b. 1918. Amer. publisher. **—John·so'ni·an** *adj. & n.*

Andrew Johnson

Lyndon B. Johnson

John·ston (jŏn'stən). **1. Henrietta.** d. 1729. Irish-born Amer. portrait painter. **2. Albert Sidney.** 1803–62. Amer. Confederate general. **3. Joseph Eggleston.** 1807–91. Amer. Confederate general. **4. Annie Fellows.** 1863–1931. Amer. author.

Join·ville (zhwăɴ-vēl'), **Jean de.** 1224?–1317. French chronicler.

Jó·kai (yô'koi), **Maurus** or **Mór.** 1825–1904. Hungarian author and politician.

Jo·li·et also **Jol·li·et** (jō'lē-ĕt', jō'lē-ĕt', zhô-lyĕ'), **Louis.** 1645–1700. French-Canadian explorer of America.

Jo·li·ot-Cu·rie (zhô-lyō' kü-rē'), **Irène** (1897–1956) and **Frédéric** (1900–58). French physicists (Nobel, 1935).

Jol·son (jōl'sən), **Al.** 1886–1950. Amer. entertainer.

Jo·nah (jō'nə). Hebrew prophet.

Jones (jōnz). **1. Inigo.** 1573–1652. English architect. **2. John Paul.** 1747–92. Scottish-born Amer. naval officer. **3. Sybil.** 1808–73. Amer. Quaker preacher. **4. Mary Harris.** "Mother Jones." 1830–1930. Irish-born Amer. labor leader. **5. Samuel Milton.** 1846–1904. Amer. manufacturer, politician, and reformer. **6. Henry Arthur.** 1851–1929. English dramatist. **7. Rufus Matthew.** 1863–1948. Amer. Quaker philosopher. **8. John Luther ("Casey").** 1864–1900. Amer. locomotive engineer. **9. Jesse Holman.** 1874–1956. Amer. financier and public official. **10. Howard Mumford.** 1892–1980. Amer. educator and author. **11. Thomas Hudson.** 1892–1969. Amer. sculptor. **12. Robert Tyre ("Bobby").** 1902–71. Amer. golfer. **13. LeRoi.** See Imamu Amiri **Baraka.**

Jon·son (jŏn'sən), **Benjamin ("Ben").** 1573–1637. English actor and author.

Jop·lin (jŏp'lĭn), **Scott.** 1868–1917.

Amer. pianist and composer.
Jor·dan (jôr′dn), **David Starr.** 1851–1931. Amer. biologist and educator.
Jo·seph (jō′zəf, -səf). **1.** Father of Jesus. **2. of Ar·i·ma·the·a** (ăr′-ə-mə-thē′ə). Israelite who buried Jesus. **3.** Name of 2 Holy Roman emperors, esp. **II,** 1741–90, ruled 1765–90. **4.** Chief. 1840?–1904. Nez Percé leader.

Joseph

Jo·sé·phine de Beau·har·nais (zhō-zā-fēn′ də bō-är-nĕ′). See **Beauharnais.**
Jo·seph·son (jō′zəf-sən, -səf-), **Brian David.** b. 1940. English physicist (Nobel, 1973).
Jo·se·phus (jō-sē′fəs), **Flavius.** A.D. 37–100? Jewish general and historian.
Josh·u·a (jŏsh′ōō-ə). Old Testament Hebrew leader.
Jo·si·ah (jō-sī′ə, -zī′ə). King of Judah (638?–607? B.C.).
Jou·bert (you′bərt), **Petrus Jacobus.** 1834–1900. Boer general and statesman.
Jou·haux (zhōō-ō′), **Léon.** 1879–1954. French politician and labor leader (Nobel, 1951).
Joule (joul, jōōl), **James Prescott.** 1818–89. English physicist.
Jour·dan (zhōōr-dăɴ′), Comte **Jean Baptiste.** 1762–1833. French marshal.
Jo·vi·an (jō′vē-ən). 331?–64. Roman emperor (363–64).
Jow·ett (jou′ĭt), **Benjamin.** 1817–93. English classical scholar.
Joyce (jois), **James.** 1882–1941. Irish author (*Ulysses*). **—Joyc′e·an** (joi′-sē-ən) *adj.*
Juan Car·los (wän kär′lôs, hwän). b. 1938. Spanish king (since 1975).
Juan Ma·nuel (män-wĕl′), Don. 1282–1349. Spanish soldier and author.
Juá·rez (wär′ĕz, hwä′rĕs), **Benito Pablo.** 1806–72. Mexican statesman.
Ju·dah (jōō′də). Hebrew patriarch.
Ju·das Is·car·i·ot (jōō′dəs ĭs-kăr′-ē-ət). Betrayer of Jesus.
Jude (jōōd), Saint. One of the 12 Apostles.
Ju·dith (jōō′dĭth). Jewish biblical heroine.
Jud·son (jŭd′sən). **1. Adoniram.** 1788–1850. Amer. Baptist missionary. **2. Edward Zane Carroll.** "Ned Buntline." 1823–86. Amer. author.
Jul·ian (jōōl′yən). 331–63. Roman emperor (361–63).
Ju·li·an·a (jōō′lē-ăn′ə, yü′lē-ä′nä). b. 1909. Queen of the Netherlands (1948–80); abdicated.
Ju·li·us (jōōl′yəs). Name of 3 popes, esp. **II,** 1443–1513, reigned 1503–13.
Ju·neau (jōō′nō, jōō-nō′, zhü-), **Solomon Laurent.** 1793–1856. Canadian-born Amer. fur trader and settler.
Jung (yŏŏng), **Carl Gustav.** 1875–1961. Swiss psychologist and psychiatrist.
Jun·kers (yŏŏng′kərs), **Hugo.** 1859–1935. German aircraft designer.
Jusse·rand (zhüs-räɴ′), **Jean Jules.** 1855–1932. French scholar and diplomat.
Jus·tin (jŭs′tĭn), Saint. A.D. 100?–65. Greek church father.
Jus·tin·i·an (jŭ-stĭn′ē-ən). Name of 2 Byzantine emperors, esp. **I,** "the Great." 483–565, ruled 527–65; lawgiver.
Ju·ve·nal (jōō′və-nəl). A.D. 60?–140? Roman satirist.

K

Ka·a·hu·ma·nu (kä′ä-hōō-mä′hōō). d. 1832 Hawaiian queen regent (1824–32).
Ká·dar (kä′där), **János.** b. 1912. Hungarian statesman.
Kael (kāl), **Pauline.** b. 1919. Amer. critic.
Kaf·ka (käf′kä, -kə), **Franz.** 1883-1924. Austrian author.
Kahn (kän). **1. Otto Herman.** 1867–1934. Amer. banker and philanthropist. **2. Louis I.** 1901–74. Estonian-born Amer. architect.
Kai·ser (kī′zər), **Henry John.** 1882-1967. Amer. industrialist.
Kalb (kălb, kälp), **Johann.** "Baron de Kalb." 1721-80. German general in the Amer. Revolution.
Ka·li·nin (kä-lē′nĭn, -nyĭn), **Mikhail Ivanovich.** 1875–1946. Russian Communist leader.
Kal·ten·born (kôl′tən-bôrn′, kăl′-), **Hans von.** 1878-1965. Amer. news commentator.
Ka·me·ha·me·ha (kä-mā′hä-mā′hä, kə-mā′ə-mā′ə). Name of 5 kings of Hawaii, esp. **I,** "the Great," 1753?–1819, ruled 1795–1819.
Ka·me·nev (kä′mĭ-nĕf, -nyĭf), **Lev Borisovich.** 1883-1936. Russian Communist leader.
Ka·mer·lingh On·nes (kä′mər-lĭng ô′nəs), **Heike.** 1853–1926. Dutch physicist (Nobel, 1913).
Kan·din·ski (kăn-dĭn′skē, kän-dēn′-, -dyēn′-), **Vasili.** 1866–1944. Russian artist.
Kane (kān), **Elisha Kent.** 1820–57. Amer. physician and Arctic explorer.
Ka·nin (kā′nĭn), **Garson.** b. 1912. Amer. author.
Kant (kănt, känt), **Immanuel.** 1724–1804. German philosopher. **—Kant′i·an** *adj.*
Kan·tor (kăn′tər), **MacKinlay.** 1904-77. Amer. author.
Kan·to·ro·vich (kăn′tə-rō′vĭch, -tô′-rə-vĭch), **Leonid Vitalevich.** b. 1912. Russian economist (Nobel, 1975).
Ka·pi·tsa (kä′pē-tsə, kä′pyĭ-), **Pëtr Leonidovich.** 1894–1984. Russian physicist (Nobel, 1978).
Kap·lan (kăp′lən), **Mordecai Menahem.** 1881–1983. Amer. Jewish educator.
Kar·a·george (kăr-ə-jôrj′). 1776?–1817. Serbian nationalist leader.
Ka·ra·jan (kär′ə-yän′, kăr′ə-yən), **Herbert von.** b. 1908. Austrian conductor.
Karl·feldt (kärl′fĕlt′), **Erik Axel.** 1864-1931. Swedish poet (Nobel, 1931).
Kar·loff (kär′lôf′, -lŏf′), **Boris.** 1887–1969. English-born Amer. actor.
Karl Lud·wig (kärl′ lōōt′vĭk). *German.* Charles Louis.
Kár·mán (kär′män), **Theodor von.** 1881–1963. Hungarian-born Amer. physicist and aeronautical engineer.
Ká·ro·lyi (kär′əl-yē, kär′-, kä′rō-yē), Count **Mihály.** 1875–1955. Hungarian statesman.
Kar·rer (kär′ər), **Paul.** 1889–1971. Russian-born Swiss chemist (Nobel, 1937).
Kar·sa·vi·na (kär-sä′vē-nə, -və-), **Tamara.** 1885–1978. Russian ballerina.
Kast·ler (kăst′lər), **Alfred.** 1902–84. French physicist (Nobel, 1966).
Katz (kăts), Sir **Bernard.** b. 1911. German-born English physicist (Nobel, 1970).
Kauf·man (kôf′mən), **George Simon.** 1889–1961. Amer. playwright.
Kau·nitz (kou′nĭts), Prince **Wenzel Anton von.** Count of Rietberg. 1711–94. Austrian statesman.
Kaut·sky (kout′skē), **Karl Johann.** 1854–1938. German socialist leader.
Ka·wa·ba·ta (kä′wä-bä′tä, kä-wä′-bä-tä′), **Yasunari.** 1899–1972. Japanese author (Nobel, 1968).
Kaye (kā), **Danny.** b. 1913. Amer. entertainer.
Kaye-Smith (kā′smĭth′), **Sheila.** 1887–1956. English novelist.
Ka·zan (kə-zăn′, -zän′), **Elia.** b. 1909. Turkish-born Amer. filmmaker.
Ka·zan·tza·kis (kä-zän-dzä′kēs), **Nikos.** 1885–1957. Greek author.
Kean (kēn), **Edmund.** 1787–1833. English actor.
Kear·ny (kär′nē). **1. Stephen Watts.** 1794–1848. Amer. army officer. **2. Philip.** 1814–62. Amer. general.
Kea·ton (kēt′n), **Buster.** 1895–1966. Amer. actor.
Keats (kēts), **John.** 1795–1821. English poet. **—Keats′i·an** *adj.*
Ke·ble (kē′bəl), **John.** 1792–1866. English clergyman and poet.
Kee·ler (kē′lər), **Ruby.** b. 1910. Canadian-born dancer and actress.
Kee·ley (kē′lē), **Leslie Enraught.** 1834–1900. Amer. physician.
Keene (kēn), **Laura.** 1826?–73. English-born actress and theatrical producer.
Kee·shan (kē′shən), **Robert James.** "Captain Kangaroo." b. 1927. Amer. television personality.
Ke·fau·ver (kē′fô′vər), **(Carey) Estes.** 1903-63. Amer. legislator.
Ke·hew (kē′hyōō′), **Mary Morton Kimball.** 1859-1918. Amer. reformer.
Kei·tel (kīt′l), **Wilhelm.** 1882–1946. German general; executed.
Kek·ko·nen (kĕ′kô-nĕn′, -nən), **Urho Kaleva.** b. 1900. Finnish statesman.
Kel·land (kĕl′ənd), **Clarence Budington.** 1881–1964. Amer. author.
Kel·ler (kĕl′ər), **Helen Adams.** 1880–1968. Amer. author and lecturer.

Helen Keller

Kel·ley (kĕl′ē). **1. Oliver Hudson.** 1826–1913. Amer. farm organizer; founder of the Grange movement. **2. Florence.** 1859–1932. Amer. social worker.
Kel·logg (kĕl′ôg′, -ŏg′, -əg). **1. Clara Louise.** 1842–1916. Amer. operatic soprano. **2. Frank Billings.** 1856–1937. Amer. statesman (Nobel, 1929). **3. Will Keith.** 1860–1951. Amer. cereal manufacturer and philanthropist. **4. Louise Phelps.** 1862–1942. Amer. historian.
Kel·ly (kĕl′ē). **1. William.** 1811–88. Amer. inventor and steel manufacturer. **2. Ellsworth.** b. 1923. Amer. artist. **3. Emmett.** 1898–1979. Amer. circus clown. **4. Walter Crawford ("Walt").** 1913–73. Amer. cartoonist and illustrator. **5. Grace Patricia.** See Princess **Grace.**
Kel·vin (kĕl′vĭn), 1st Baron. William Thompson. 1824–1907. Irish-born British mathematician and physicist.
Ke·mal At·a·türk (kĕ-mäl′ ăt′ə-tûrk′, ä-tä-tûrk′). 1881–1938. Turkish soldier and statesman.
Kem·ble (kĕm′bəl). **1. John Philip.** 1757–1823. English actor and theatrical manager. **2. Frances Anne ("Fanny").** English-born Amer. actress.
Kem·pis (kĕm′pĭs), **Thomas a.** See **Thomas a Kempis.**
Ken or **Kenn** (kĕn), **Thomas.** 1637–1711. English prelate and hymn writer.
Ken·dall (kĕn′dl). **1. Amos.** 1789–1869. Amer. journalist and public official. **2. (William) Sergeant.** 1869–1938. Amer. artist. **3. Edward Calvin.** 1886–1972. Amer. biochemist (Nobel, 1962).
Ken·drew (kĕn′drōō′), Sir **John Cowdery.** b. 1917. English biologist (Nobel, 1962).
Ken·nan (kĕn′ən), **George Frost.** b. 1904. Amer. diplomat, historian, and author.
Ken·ne·dy (kĕn′ĭ-dē), **Joseph Patrick.** 1888–1969. Amer. businessman and diplomat, with his wife **Rose Fitzgerald** (b. 1890) parents of: **1. John Fitzgerald ("Jack").** 1917–63. 35th U.S. President (1961–63); assassinated. **2. Robert Francis ("Bobby").** 1925–68. Legislator and public official; assassinated. **3. Edward Moore ("Ted").** b. 1932. Legislator.

John F. Kennedy

Ken·nel·ly (kĕn′ə-lē), **Arthur Edwin.** 1861-1939. Amer. electrical engineer.
Ken·ny (kĕn′ē), **Elizabeth.** 1886–1952. Australian-born nursing pioneer.
Kent (kĕnt). **1. James.** 1763–1847. Amer. jurist. **2. Rockwell.** 1882–1971. Amer. artist.
Ken·yat·ta (kĕn-yä′tə), **Jomo.** 1893?–1978. Kenyan statesman.
Ken·yon (kĕn′yən), **John Samuel.** 1874–1959. Amer. educator and phonetician.
Ke·o·kuk (kē′ə-kŭk′). 1790?–1848. Amer. Sauk chief.
Kep·ler (kĕp′lər), **Johannes.** 1571–1630. German astronomer and mathematician.
Kep·pel (kĕp′əl), **Augustus.** 1st Viscount Keppel. 1725–86. English naval officer.
Ke·ren·ski or **Ke·ren·sky** (kə-rĕn′skē, kĕr′ən-), **Aleksandr Feodorovich.** 1881–1970. Russian revolutionary leader.
Kern (kûrn), **Jerome David.** 1885–1945. Amer. composer.
Ker·ou·ac (kĕr′ōō-ăk′, kîr′-), **Jean-Louis ("Jack").** 1922–69. Canadian-born Amer. author.
Kerr (kär, kûr), **Jean Collins.** b. 1923. Amer. author.
Kes·sel·ring (kĕs′əl-rĭng), **Albert** 1887–1960. German general.
Ket·ter·ing (kĕt′ə-rĭng), **Charles Franklin.** 1876–1958. Amer. electrical engineer and manufacturer.
Key (kē), **Francis Scott.** 1779–1843. Amer. lawyer and poet ("The Star-Spangled Banner").
Keyes (kēz), **Francis Parkinson.** 1885–1970. Amer. author.
Keynes (kānz), **John Maynard.** 1st Baron of Tilton. 1883–1943. English economist. **—Keynes′i·an** *adj. & n.*
Key·ser·ling (kī′zər-lĭng), Count **Hermann Alexander von.** 1880–1946. Estonian-born German scientist, philosopher, and author.
Kha·cha·tu·ri·an (kä′chä-tōōr′ē-ən, kăch′ə-, KHä′chä-tōō-ryän′), **Aram Ilich.** 1903-78. Russian composer.
Kha·da·fy (kə-dä′fē), **Moammar.** See **Qaddafi.**
Kha·lid (kä-lĕd′, KHä-), **Khalid Abdul Aziz al-Saud al-.** 1913–82. Saudi Arabian king (1975–82).
Khay·yám (kī-yäm′, -yăm′), **Omar.** See **Omar Khayyam.**
Khe·ra·skov (kə-räs′kəf, KHĭ-), **Mikhail Mateevich.** 1733–1806. Russian epic poet.
Kho·mei·ni (kō-mā′nē, KHō-, hō-),

Ayatollah **Ruholla.** b. 1900. Iranian leader.

Kho·ra·na (kō-rä′nə), **Har Gobind.** b. 1922. Indian-born Amer. biochemist (Nobel, 1968).

Khru·shchev (kro͝osh′chĕf, -chôf, -chôv, -chĕv, kro͝osh′-, kro͝osh-chĕf′, -chôf′, -chôv′, -chĕv′), **Nikita Sergeevich.** 1894–1971. Soviet statesman.

Nikita Khrushchev

Khu·fu (ko͞o′fo͞o). Cheops.

Khwa·riz·mi (kwär′ĭz-mē, KHo͞o-ĕr-ĭz′-), **al-.** 780–850? Arab mathematician.

Kid (kĭd). Variant of **Kyd.**

Kidd (kĭd). **1. William.** "Captain Kidd." 1645?–1701. Scottish-born English pirate. **2. Michael.** b. 1917. Amer. choreographer.

Kie·ran (kîr′ən), **John Francis.** 1892–1981. Amer. naturalist and journalist.

Kier·ke·gaard (kîr′kĭ-gärd′, -gôr′), **Sören Aaby.** 1813–55. Danish philosopher and theologian.

Kie·sing·er (kē′zĭng-ər, -sĭng-), **Kurt Georg.** b. 1904. West German statesman.

Kil·mer (kĭl′mər), **(Alfred) Joyce.** 1886–1918. Amer. author.

Kim Il Sung (kĭm′ ĭl′ so͝ong′, sŭng′). b. 1912? Korean soldier and statesman.

Kim·mel (kĭm′əl), **Husband Edward.** 1882–1968. Amer. naval officer.

King (kĭng). **1. Rufus.** 1755–1827. Amer. politician and diplomat. **2. William Rufus DeVane.** 1786–1853 U.S. Vice President (1853). **3. Richard.** 1825–85. Amer. steamboat captain and rancher. **4. Clarence.** 1842–1901. Amer. geologist and mining engineer. **5. William Lyon Mackenzie.** 1874–1950. Canadian prime minister (1921–26, 1926–30, 1935–48). **6. Ernest Joseph** 1878–1968. Amer. naval officer. **7. Coretta Scott.** b. 1927. Amer. civil-rights leader. **8. Martin Luther, Jr.** 1929–68. Amer. clergyman and civil-rights leader (Nobel, 1964); assassinated. **9. Billie Jean Moffitt.** b. 1943. Amer. tennis player.

Martin Luther King, Jr.

King·lake (kĭng′lāk′), **Alexander William.** 1809–91. English historian.

Kings·ley (kĭngz′lē), **Charles.** 1819–75. English clergyman and author.

Kin·kaid (kĭn-kād′), **Thomas Cassin.** 1888–1972. Amer. naval officer.

Ki·no (kē′nō), **Eusebio Francisco.** 1645?–1711. Italian-born Jesuit missionary in America.

Kin·sey (kĭn′zē), **Alfred Charles.** 1894–1956. Amer. sociologist and biologist.

Kip·ling (kĭp′lĭng), **(Joseph) Rudyard.** 1865–1936. English author (Nobel, 1907).

Kir·by-Smith (kûr′bē-smĭth′), **Edmund.** 1824–93. Amer. Confederate soldier and educator.

Kirch·hoff (kîr′kôf′, kîrKH′hôf), **Gustav Robert.** 1824–87. German physicist.

Kirch·ner (kîrk′nər, kîrKH′-), **Ernst Ludwig.** 1880–1938. German expressionist artist.

Kirch·wey (kûrch′wā′), **Freda.** 1893–1976. Amer. editor and publisher.

Kirk (kûrk), **Norman.** 1923–74. New Zealand statesman.

Kirk·land (kûrk′lənd). **1. Caroline Matilda Stansbury.** 1801–64. Amer. author. **2. Gelsey.** b. 1952. Amer. ballerina.

Kirk·us (kûr′kəs), **Virginia.** 1893–1980. Amer. author and critic.

Ki·rov (kē′rôf, -rŏf, -rəf), **Sergei Mironovich.** 1888–1934. Russian revolutionary.

Kir·sten (kîr′stən), **Dorothy.** b. 1917. Amer. soprano.

Kis·sin·ger (kĭs′ĭn-jər), **Henry Alfred.** b. 1923. German-born American scholar and diplomat (Nobel, 1973).

Kitche·ner (kĭch′nər), **Horatio Herbert.** 1st Earl Kitchener of Khartoum and of Broome. 1850–1916. Irish-born British soldier and colonial administrator.

Kit·tredge (kĭt′rĭj), **George Lyman.** 1860–1941. Amer. educator.

Klee (klā), **Paul.** 1879–1940. Swiss artist.

Klein (klīn). **1. Lawrence R.** b. 1920. Amer. economist (Nobel, 1980). **2. Calvin.** b. 1942. Amer. fashion designer.

Kleist (klīst), **Heinrich Bernt Wilhelm von.** 1777–1811. German dramatist.

Klem·per·er (klĕm′pər-ər), **Otto.** 1885–1973. German composer and conductor.

Kline (klīn), **Franz Joseph.** 1919–62. Amer. painter.

Klop·stock (klôp′shtôk′, klŏp′stŏk′), **Friedrich Gottlieb.** 1724–1803. German poet.

Knel·ler (nĕl′ər), Sir **Godfrey.** 1646–1723. German-born English painter.

Knie·vel (knē′vəl), **Evel.** b. 1938. Amer. daredevil motorcyclist.

Knight (nīt). **1. Sarah Kemble.** 1666–1727. Amer. educator and diarist. **2. John S.** 1894–1981. Amer. publisher.

Knopf (knŏpf), **Alfred Abraham.** 1892–1984. Amer. publisher.

Knox (nŏks). **1. John.** 1505?–72. Scottish religious reformer. **2. Henry.** 1750–1806. Amer. Revolutionary soldier and public official. **3. Philander Chase.** 1853–1921. Amer. public official and legislator. **4. Rose Markward.** 1857–1950. Amer. businesswoman. **5. William Franklin ("Frank").** 1874–1944. Amer. soldier, publisher, and public official.

Knud·sen (no͞od′sən, kə-no͞od′sən, -no͞o′-), **William Signius.** 1879–1948. Danish-born Amer. industrialist and public official.

Knut (kə-no͞ot′, -nyo͞ot′). Variant of **Canute.**

Koch (kôk, kôKH), **Robert.** 1843–1910. German physician and bacteriologist (Nobel, 1905).

Ko·cher (kō′kər, -KHər), **Emil Theodor.** 1841–1917. Swiss surgeon (Nobel, 1909).

Kock (kôk), **Charles Paul de.** 1794–1871. French author.

Ko·dál·y (kō′dī′, -dä′yə, kō-dī′, -dä′ē), **Zoltán.** 1882–1967. Hungarian composer.

Koest·ler (kĕst′lər, kœst′-), **Arthur.** 1905–83. Hungarian-born author.

Koi·so (koi′sō′, kō′ē-sō′), **Kuniaki.** 1880–1950. Japanese general and public official.

Ko·kosch·ka (kō-kôsh′kä), **Oskar.** 1886–1980. Austrian-born artist and author.

Kol·chak (kŏl-chäk′, kôl-), **Aleksandr Vasilievich.** 1875–1920. Russian admiral and counterrevolutionary; executed.

Kol·lon·tai (kō-lŏn-tī′), **Aleksandra Mikhailovna.** 1872–1952. Russian revolutionary and author.

Koll·witz (kôl′vĭts′, kōl′wĭts′), **Käthe** or **Kaethe Schmidt.** 1867–1945. German artist.

Kol·tsov (kōl-tsôf′, kōl-), **Aleksei Vasilievich.** 1809–42. Russian lyric poet.

Ko·mu·ra (kô′mo͞o-rä′, kô-mo͞o′rä), Marquis **Jutaro.** 1855–1911. Japanese diplomat.

Kon·dy·les or **Kon·dy·lis** (kôn-thē′lĕs, -dē′-), **Georgios.** 1879–1936. Greek general and statesman.

Ko·nev (kô′nyĕf, -nyəf), **Ivan Stepanovich.** 1897–1973. Russian field marshal and revolutionary.

Ko·no·ye (kô′nô-yē′, kô-nô′yē), Prince **Fumimaro.** 1891–1945. Japanese statesman.

Koo (ko͞o), **Vi Kyuin Wellington.** 1887–1985. Chinese diplomat.

Koop·mans (ko͞op′mənz), **Tjalling Charles.** 1910–1985. Dutch-born Amer. economist (Nobel, 1975).

Ko·per·nik (kô-pĕr′nĕk) also **Kop·per·nigk** (kŏp′ər-nĭk′), **Mikolaj** also **Niklas.** *Polish.* Nicolaus Copernicus.

Korn·berg (kôrn′bûrg′), **Arthur.** b. 1918. Amer. biochemist (Nobel, 1959).

Korn·gold (kôrn′gōld′, -gōlt′), **Erich Wolfgang.** 1897–1957. Austrian-born Amer. composer and pianist.

Kor·ni·lov (kôr-nē′ləf, kŏr-nyē′-), **Lavr Georgievich.** 1870–1918. Russian general.

Ko·ro·len·ko (kŏr′ə-lĕng′kō, kôr′-), **Vladimir Galaktionovich.** 1853–1921. Russian author.

Kor·zyb·ski (kôr-zĭb′skē, -zĭp′-, kô-zhĭp′-), **Alfred Habdank Skarbek.** 1879–1950. Polish-born Amer. author and scientist.

Kos·ci·us·ko (kŏs′ē-ŭs′kō, kôsh-cho͞osh′kô), **Thaddeus.** 1746–1817. Polish general and patriot.

Kos·sel (kôs′əl), **Albrecht.** 1853–1927. German biochemist (Nobel, 1910).

Kos·suth (kŏs′o͞oth′, kô′sho͝ot′). **1. Lajos.** 1802–94. Hungarian revolutionary patriot and statesman. **2. Ferenc.** 1841–1914. Hungarian politician.

Ko·sy·gin (kō-sē′gĭn, kə-, kō-), **Aleksei Nikolaevich.** 1904–80. Russian statesman.

Kot·ze·bue (kŏt′sə-bo͞o′, kŏt′-), **August Friedrich Ferdinand von.** 1761–1819. German dramatist.

Kou·fax (kō′făks′), **Sanford ("Sandy").** b. 1935. Amer. baseball player.

Koun·dou·ri·o·tes (ko͞on-do͝or′ē-ō′tēs, -do͞o-ryô′tēs), **Pavlos.** 1855–1935. Greek admiral and statesman.

Kous·se·vitz·ky (ko͞o′sə-vĭt′skē), **Sergei Aleksandrovich ("Serge").** 1874–1951. Russian-born Amer. conductor.

Ko·vacs (kō′văks′), **Ernie.** 1919–62. Amer. comedian.

Krafft-E·bing (krăft′ĕb′ĭng, kräft′ā′-bĭng), Baron **Richard von.** 1840–1902. German physician and neurologist.

Kra·mer (krā′mər), **Stanley E.** b. 1913. Amer. filmmaker.

Kraus-Boel·té (krous′bōl′tē, -bœl′-tə), **Maria.** 1836–1918. German-born Amer. educator.

Krebs (krĕbz, krĕps), Sir **Hans Adolf.** 1900–81. German-born British biochemist (Nobel, 1953).

Kreh·biel (krā′bēl′), **Henry Edward.** 1854–1923. Amer. critic.

Krei·sler (krī′slər), **Fritz.** 1875–1962. Austrian-born Amer. violinist.

Kreps (krĕps), **Juanita Morris.** b. 1921. Amer. economist and public official.

Kress (krĕs), **Samuel Henry.** 1863–1955. Amer. merchant and art patron.

Krock (krŏk), **Arthur.** 1886–1974. Amer. journalist.

Kroe·ber (krō′bər), **Alfred Louis.** 1876–1960. Amer. anthropologist.

Krogh (krôg, krôKH), **(Schack) August Steenberg.** 1874–1946. Danish physiologist (Nobel, 1920).

Kroll (krōl), **Leon.** 1884–1974. Amer. artist.

Kro·pot·kin (krə-pŏt′kĭn, krō-), Prince **Pëtr Alekseevich.** 1842–1921. Russian scientist and revolutionary.

Kru·ger (kro͞o′gər, krü′gər), **Stephanus Johannes Paulus.** "Oom Paul." 1825–1904. South African statesman.

Kru·pa (kro͞o′pə), **Gene.** 1909–73. Amer. musician.

Krupp (krŭp, kro͞op). Family of German steel manufacturers, including **Friedrich** (1787–1826), **Alfred** (1812–87), **Friedrich Alfred** (1854–1902), and **Bertha** (1886–1957) and her husband **Gustav** (1870–1950) and son **Alfred-Felix** (1907–67), both surnamed **Krupp von Boh·len und Hal·bach** (kro͞op fən bō′lən o͝ont häl′bäKH).

Krup·ska·ya (kro͞op′skä-yä, -skə-yə), **Nadezhda Konstantinovna.** 1869–1939. Russian revolutionary.

Krutch (krŭch), **Joseph Wood.** 1893–1970. Amer. educator, critic, and naturalist.

Ku·bi·tschek (ko͞o′bə-chĕk′), **Juscelino.** 1901–76. Brazilian statesman.

Ku·blai Khan (ko͞o′blī kän′) also **Ku·bla Khan** (-blə). 1216–94. Mongol emperor.

Ku·brick (ko͞o′brĭk′, kyo͞o′-), **Stanley.** b. 1928. Amer. filmmaker.

Kuhn (ko͞on), **Richard.** 1900–67. Austrian chemist (Nobel, 1938; ordered by Nazis to decline).

Kui·by·shev (kwē′bĭ-shĕf, ko͞o′ĭ-), **Valerian Vladimirovich.** 1888–1935. Russian Communist leader.

Kun (ko͞on), **Béla.** 1885–1937. Hungarian Communist leader.

Kung (ko͝ong, go͝ong). **1. Prince.** 1833–98. Chinese statesman. **2. H. H.** K'ung Hsiang-hsi. 1881–1967. Chinese Nationalist financier.

Ku·ro·pat·kin (ko͞o′rō-pät′kĭn), **Aleksei Nikolaevich.** 1848–1925. Russian general.

Ku·ru·su (ko͞o-ro͞o′so͞o, ko͞o′ro͞o-so͞o′), **Saburo.** 1888?–1954. Japanese diplomat.

Kusch (ko͝osh), **Polykarp.** b. 1911. German-born Amer. physicist (Nobel, 1955).

Ku·tu·zov (ko͞o-to͞o′zôf, -zəf), **Mikhail Ilarionovich.** Prince of Smolensk. 1745–1813. Russian field marshal.

Kuz·nets (ko͞oz′nĕts′, kŭz′nəts), **Simon.** 1901–85. Russian-born Amer. economist (Nobel, 1971).

Ky (kē), **Nguyen Cao.** b. 1930. Vietnamese statesman.

Kyd or **Kid** (kĭd), **Thomas.** 1558–94. English dramatist.

Kyn·e·wulf (kĭn′ə-wo͝olf′). Variant of **Cynewulf.**

L

La Bru·yère (lä bro͞o-yĕr′, brē-, brü-), **Jean de.** 1645–96. French moralist.

La·chaise (lə-shāz′, lä-shĕz′), **Gaston.** 1882–1935. French-born Amer. sculptor.

Ladd-Franklin (lăd-frăngk′lĭn), **Christine.** 1847–1930. Amer. psychologist and logician.

Laemm·le (lĕm′lē), **Carl.** 1867–1939. German-born Amer. film producer.

La·ën·nec (lā-nĕk′), **René.** 1781–1826. French physician; invented stethoscope.

La Farge (lə färzh′, färj′). **1. John.** 1835–1910. Amer. artist. **2. Oliver Hazard Perry.** 1901–63. Amer. novelist.

La·fa·yette (lä′fē-ĕt′, -fā-, lăf′ē-, lä-fä-yĕt′), Marquis de. Marie Joseph Paul Yves Roch Gilbert du Motier de Lafayette. 1757–1834. French military, political, and revolutionary leader.

Marquis de Lafayette

Laf·fite or **La·fitte** (lä-fēt′), **Jean.** 1780?–1826? French pirate.
La Flesche (lä flĕsh′, lə), **Susette.** "Bright Eyes." 1854–1903. Amer. Indian leader.
La Fol·lette (lə fŏl′ət), **Robert Marion.** 1855–1925. Amer. politician and reformer.
La·fon·taine (lä-fŏn-tān′, -fôN-tĕn′), **Henri.** 1854–1943. Belgian politician and peace advocate (Nobel, 1913).
La Fon·taine (lä fŏn-tān′, fôN-tĕn′), **Jean de.** 1621–95. French poet and fabulist.
La·ger·kvist (lä′gər-kvĭst′, -yər-), **Pär Fabian.** 1891–1974. Swedish author (Nobel, 1951).
La·ger·löf (lä′yər-ləv), **Selma Ottiliana Lovisa.** 1858–1940. Swedish novelist (Nobel, 1909).
La·grange (lə-gränzh′, -gränj′), Comte **Joseph Louis.** 1736–1813. French mathematician.
La Guar·di·a (lə gwär′dē-ə), **Fiorello Henry.** 1882–1947. Amer. politician.
Lahr (lär), **Bert.** 1895–1967. Amer. entertainer.
Lake (lāk), **Simon.** 1866–1945. Amer. naval architect.
La·mar (lə-mär′). **1. Mirabeau Buonaparte.** 1798–1859. Amer. politician and diplomat. **2. Lucius Quintus Cincinnatus.** 1825–93. Amer. jurist and politician. **3. Joseph Rucker.** 1857–1916. Amer. jurist.
La·marck (lə-märk′, lä-), Chevalier de. Jean Baptiste Pierre Antoine de Monet. 1744–1829. French naturalist.
La·mar·tine (lä-mär-tēn′), **Alphonse Marie Louis de Prat de.** 1790–1869. French poet and politician.
Lamb (lăm). **1. Charles.** "Elia." 1775–1834. English critic and essayist. **2. William.** 2nd Viscount Melbourne. 1779–1848. British prime minister (1834, 1835–41). **3. Martha Joanna Reade Nash.** 1826–93. Amer. historian. **4. Willis Eugene, Jr.** b. 1913. Amer. physicist (Nobel, 1955).
Lam·bert (lăm′bərt), **John.** 1619–83. English Civil War general.
Lam·masch (lăm′ăsh), **Heinrich.** 1853–1920. Austrian jurist and diplomat.
La Motte-Fou·qué (lä môt′fōō-kā′), Baron **Friedrich Heinrich Karl.** 1777–1843. German author.
Lan·cas·ter (lăng′kə-stər). English royal house (1399–1461); vied against the Plantagenets in the War of the Roses. —**Lan·cas′tri·an** *adj.* & *n.*
Land (lănd), **Edwin Herbert.** b. 1909. Amer. inventor (polarized lenses, cameras).
Lan·dau (län-dou′), **Lev Davidovich.** 1908–68. Soviet physicist (Nobel, 1962).
Lan·ders (lăn′dərz), **Ann.** Esther Pauline Friedman.
Lan·dis (lăn′dĭs), **Kenesaw Mountain.** 1866–1944. Amer. jurist and baseball commissioner.
Lan·don (lăn′dən), **Alfred Mossman.** b. 1887. Amer. politician.
Lan·dor (lăn′dôr, -dər), **Walter Savage.** 1775–1864. English author.
Lan·dow·ska (lăn-dôf′skə, län-dôf′skä), **Wanda.** 1877–1959. Polish-born musician.
Land·seer (lănd′sîr′, -syər), Sir **Edwin Henry.** 1802–73. English animal painter.
Land·stei·ner (lănd′stī′nər, länt′shtī′-), **Karl.** 1868–1943. Austrian-born Amer. pathologist (Nobel, 1930).
Lane (lān). **1. Edward William.** 1801–76. English Egyptologist and Orientalist. **2. James Henry.** 1814–66. Amer. politician and soldier.
La·ney (lā′nē), **Lucy Craft.** 1854–1933. Amer. educator.
Lan·franc (lăn′frăngk′). 1005?–89. Italian-born English prelate and political adviser.
Lang (lăng). **1. Andrew.** 1844–1912. Scottish author. **2. Cosmo Gordon.** 1st Baron Lang of Lambeth. 1864–1945. English prelate and reformer. **3. Fritz.** 1890–1976. Austrian filmmaker.
Lang·dell (lăng′dəl), **Christopher Columbus.** 1826–1906. Amer. legal educator.
Lange (lăng), **Dorothea.** 1895–1965. Amer. photographer.
Lang·e (läng′ə), **Christian Louis.** 1869–1938. Norwegian pacifist and historian (Nobel, 1921).
Lang·er (lăng′ər). **1. Susanne Knauth.** 1895–1985. Amer. educator and philosopher. **2. William Leonard.** 1896–1977. Amer. historian.
Lang·ford (lăng′fərd), **Nathaniel Pitt.** 1832–1911. Amer. public official, conservationist, and explorer.
Lang·ley (lăng′lē), **Samuel Pierpoint.** 1834–1906. Amer. astronomer, aviation pioneer, and administrator.
Lang·muir (lăng′myo͝or′), **Irving.** 1881–1957. Amer. chemist (Nobel, 1932).
Lang·ston (lăng′stən), **John Mercer.** 1829–97. Amer. diplomat, politician, and educator.
Lang·ton (lăng′tən), **Stephen.** d. 1228? English prelate and author.
Lang·try (lăng′trē), **Lillie** or **Lily.** "the Jersey Lily." 1852–1929. English actress and beauty.
La·nier (lə-nîr′), **Sidney.** 1842–81. Amer. author and musician.
Lan·sing (lăn′sĭng), **Robert.** 1864–1928. Amer. public official.
Lan·za (lăn′zə, -zä), **Mario.** 1925–59. Amer. singer and actor.
Lao-tse also **Lao-tzu** or **Lao-tsze** (lou′dzŭ′). 604?–531? B.C. Chinese philosopher.
La Pé·rouse (lä pā-ro͞oz′), Comte de. Jean François de Galaup. 1741–88. French explorer.
La·place (lə-pläs′, lä-), Marquis **Pierre Simon de.** 1749–1827. French mathematician and astronomer.
Lar·com (lär′kəm), **Lucy.** 1824–93. Amer. poet.
Lard·ner (lärd′nər), **Ringgold Wilmer ("Ring").** 1885–1933. Amer. journalist and author.
Lar·go Ca·ba·lle·ro (lär′gô kä′-bä-yĕ′rô), **Francisco.** 1869–1946. Spanish socialist and labor leader.
La Roche·fou·cauld (lä rôsh-fo͞o-kō′, -rōsh-), Duc **François de.** 1613–80. French author.
La·rousse (lä-ro͞os′, lə-), **Pierre Athanase.** 1817–75. French grammarian, lexicographer, and encyclopedist.
Lar·tet (lär-tā′), **Édouard Armand Isidore Hippolyte.** 1801–71. French archaeologist and pioneer paleontologist.
La Salle (lə săl′, lä säl′), Sieur de. Robert Cavelier. 1643–87. French explorer in America.
Las Ca·sas (läs kä′säs), **Bartolomé de.** "Apostle of the Indies." 1474–1566. Spanish missionary and historian.
Las·ker (lăs′kər), **Albert Davis.** 1880–1952. Amer. advertising executive, philanthropist, and public official.
Las·ki (lăs′kē), **Harold Joseph.** 1893–1950. English political scientist.
Las·ky (lăs′kē), **Jesse Louis.** 1880–1958. Amer. film producer.
Las·salle (lə-săl′, lä-säl′), **Ferdinand.** 1825–64. German socialist.
La·throp (lā′thrəp), **Julia Clifford.** 1858–1932. Amer. social reformer.
Lat·i·mer (lăt′ə-mər), **Hugh.** 1485–1555. English prelate and religious reformer; executed.
La Tour (lä to͝or′, -to͝or′), **Georges de.** 1593–1652. French painter.
La·trobe (lə-trōb′), **Benjamin Henry.** 1764–1820. English-born Amer. engineer and architect; rebuilt Capitol.
Lat·ti·more (lăt′ə-môr′, -mōr′), **Owen.** b. 1900. Amer. Asian scholar and author.
Laud (lôd), **William.** 1573–1645. English prelate; executed for treason.
Lau·der (lô′dər), Sir **Harry.** 1870–1950. Scottish singer and songwriter.
Lau·e (lou′ə), **Max Theodor Felix von.** 1879–1960. German physicist (Nobel, 1914).
Laugh·ton (lôt′n), **Charles.** 1899–1962. English actor.
Lau·rel (lôr′əl, lŏr′-), **Arthur Stanley Jefferson ("Stan").** 1890–1965. English-born Amer. comedian.
Lau·ren·cin (lô-räN-săN′), **Marie.** 1885–1956. French artist.
Lau·rens. 1. (lôr′ənz, lŏr′-), **Henry.** 1724–92. Amer. Revolutionary statesman and diplomat. **2.** (lô-räNs′), **Henri.** 1885–1954. French cubist artist.
Lau·ri·er (lôr′ē-ā′, lŏr′-, lô-ryā′), Sir **Wilfrid.** 1841–1919. Canadian prime minister (1896–1911).
La·val (lä-väl′), **Pierre.** 1883–1945. French politician; executed for treason.
La Val·lière (lä vä-lyĕr′), Duchesse de. Françoise Louise de la Baume Le Blanc. 1644–1710. French mistress of Louis XIV.
La·ve·ran (läv-räN′), **Charles Louis Alphonse.** 1845–1922. French pathologist (Nobel, 1907).
La Vé·ren·drye (lä vā-räN-drē′), Sieur de. Pierre Gaultier de Varennes. 1685–1749. French-Canadian explorer.
La·ver·y (lā′və-rē, lăv′ə-), Sir **John.** 1856–1941. English painter.
La·voi·sier (lä-vwä-zyā′), **Antoine Laurent.** 1743–94. French pioneer chemist; guillotined.

Antoine Lavoisier

Law (lô, lŏ). **1. John.** 1671–1729. Scottish financier and speculator ("Mississippi Bubble"). **2. William.** 1686–1761. English theological author. **3. Sallie Chapman Gordon.** 1805–94. Amer. Confederate hospital administrator. **4. (Andrew) Bonar.** 1858–1923. Canadian-born British prime minister (1922–23).
Lawes (lôz, lŏz), **Henry.** 1595?–1662. English composer.
Law·rence (lôr′əns, lŏr′-). **1.** Sir **Thomas.** 1769–1830. English portrait painter. **2. James.** 1781–1813. Amer. naval officer. **3. Abbott.** 1792–1855. Amer. merchant and politician. **4. Amos Adams.** 1814–86. Amer. businessman and philanthropist. **5. David Herbert ("D.H.").** 1885–1930. English novelist. **6. David.** 1888–1973. Amer. journalist. **7. Thomas Edward ("T.E.").** "Lawrence of Arabia." 1888–1935. Welsh-born British soldier, archaeologist, adventurer, and author. **8. Ernest Orlando.** 1901–58. Amer. physicist and inventor of cyclotron (Nobel, 1939). **9. Gertrude.** 1901–52. English actress.
Law·rie (lôr′ē, lŏr′ē), **Lee.** 1877–1963. German-born Amer. sculptor.
Laws (lôz, lŏz), **Samuel Spahr.** 1824–1921. Amer. clergyman and inventor (stock-market ticker).
Lax·ness (läks′nĕs′), **Halldór Kiljan.** b. 1902. Icelandic novelist (Nobel, 1955).
Lay·a·mon (lā′ə-mən, lī′-, lä′yə-). 13th cent. English priest and poet.
Lay·ard (lā′ərd, -ärd), Sir **Austen Henry.** 1817–94. English archaeologist and diplomat.
Laz·a·rus (lăz′ər-əs). **1.** In the Bible, the brother of Mary and Martha, believed to have been raised from the dead. **2. Emma.** 1849–87. Amer. poet and philanthropist.
Lea·cock (lē′kŏk′), **Stephen Butler.** 1869–1944. Canadian economist and author.
Leaf (lēf), **Walter.** 1852–1927. English banker and classical scholar.
Lea·hy (lā′hē), **William Daniel.** 1875–1959. Amer. naval officer and diplomat.
Lea·key (lē′kē), **Louis Seymour Bazett.** 1903–72. English anthropologist.
Lean (lēn), **David.** b. 1908. English-born filmmaker.
Lear (lîr). **1. Edward.** 1812–88. English artist and author of nonsense verse. **2. William Powell.** 1902–78. Amer. engineer and manufacturer.
Leav·en·worth (lĕv′ən-wərth), **Henry.** 1783–1834. Amer. frontier military officer.
Leav·itt (lĕv′ĭt). **1. Mary Greenleaf Clement.** 1830–1912. Amer. educator and temperance reformer. **2. Henrietta Swan.** 1868–1921. Amer. astronomer.
Le·brun (lə-brœN′). **1. Charles.** 1619–90. French historical painter. **2. Albert.** 1871–1950. French statesman.
le Car·ré (lə kă-rā′), **John.** David John Moore Cornwell. b. 1931. English author.
Leck·y (lĕk′ē), **William Edward Hartpole.** 1838–1903. Irish historian.
Le·conte de Lisle (lə kôNt′ də lēl′), **Charles Marie.** 1818–94. French poet.
Le Cor·bu·sier (lə kôr-bü-zyā′). Charles Édouard Jenneret. 1887–1965. Swiss-born architect.
Led·bet·ter (lĕd′bĕt′ər), **Huddie ("Leadbelly").** 1888–1949. Amer. musician.

Huddie Ledbetter

Led·er·berg (lĕd′ər-bûrg′, lā′dər-), **Joshua.** b. 1925. Amer. geneticist (Nobel, 1958).
Le Duc Tho (lā′ dŭk′ tō′). b. 1911. Vietnamese political leader; declined 1973 Nobel.
Led·yard (lĕd′yərd), **John.** 1751–89. Amer. adventurer and traveler.
Lee (lē). **1. Charles.** 1731–82. British-born Amer. Revolutionary general. **2. Richard Henry.** 1732–94. Amer. Revolutionary leader. **3. Ann.** "Mother Ann." 1736–84. English religious leader in America; founder of Shaker sect. **4. Arthur.** 1740–92. Amer. diplomat and essayist. **5. Henry ("Lighthorse Harry").** 1756–1818. Amer. Revolutionary statesman and commander. **6. Jason.** 1803–45. Amer. missionary and Western pioneer. **7. Robert Edward.** 1807–70. Amer. Confederate general; surrendered to Grant (1865).

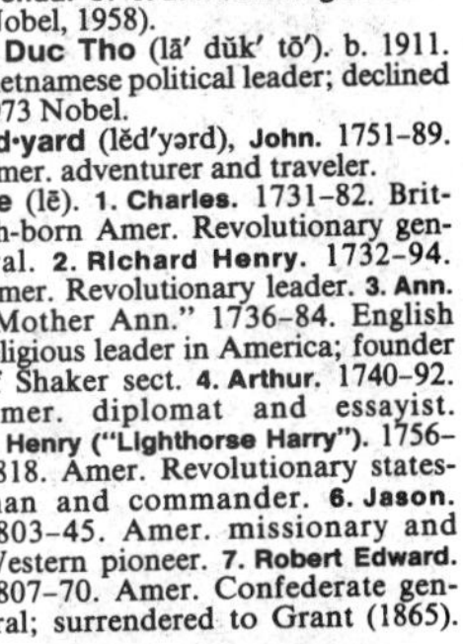

Robert E. Lee

8. Fitzhugh. 1835–1905. Amer. Confederate general and politician. **9.** Sir **Sidney.** 1859–1926. English biographer and editor. **10. Ivy Ledbetter.** 1877–1934. Amer. public-relations expert. **11. Manfred Bennington.** With Frederic Dannay, "Ellery Queen."

1905–71. Amer. author. **12. Gypsy Rose.** 1914–70. Amer. entertainer and author. **13. Tsung Dao.** b. 1926. Chinese-born Amer. physicist (Nobel, 1957).

Leech (lēch), **Margaret Kernochan.** 1893–1974. Amer. historian.

Leeu·wen·hoek or **Leu·wen·hoek** (lā'wən-ho͝ok', -vən-), **Anton van.** 1632–1723. Dutch microscopy pioneer and naturalist.

Le Gal·lienne (lə găl'yən, găl-yĕn'). **1. Richard.** 1866–1947. English author. **2. Eva.** b. 1899. English-born Amer. actress.

Le·gen·dre (lə-zhän'dər, -zhänd', -zhän'drə), **Adrien Marie.** 1752?–1833. French mathematician.

Lé·ger (lā-zhā'). **1. Fernand.** 1881–1955. French painter. **2. Alexis Saint-Léger.** "Saint-John Perse." 1887–1975. French poet and diplomat (Nobel, 1960).

Le·guía y Sal·ce·do (lĕ-gē'ä ē' säl-sĕ'thō), **Augusto Bernadino.** 1863–1932. Peruvian statesman.

Le·hár (lā'här), **Franz.** 1870–1948. Hungarian composer.

Leh·man (lē'mən, lā'-), **Herbert Henry.** 1878–1963. Amer. banker, politician, and philanthropist.

Leib·nitz or **Leib·niz** (līb'nĭts, lĭp'-), Baron **Gottfried Wilhelm von.** 1646–1716. German philosopher and mathematician.

Leices·ter (lĕs'tər), 1st Earl of. Robert Dudley.

Lei·dy (lī'dē), **Joseph.** 1823–91. Amer. naturalist and anatomist.

Leigh (lē), **Vivien.** 1913–67. English actress.

Leigh·ton (lāt'n), **Frederick.** Baron Leighton of Stretton. 1830–96. English portrait painter and historian.

Leins·dorf (līnz'dôrf', līns'-), **Erich.** b. 1912. Austrian-born Amer. conductor.

Leis·ler (lī'slər), **Jacob.** 1640–91. German-born Amer. patriot, merchant, and insurrectionist; executed.

Leith-Ross (lēth'rôs', -rŏs'), Sir **Frederick William.** 1887–1968. English economist and public official.

Le·land (lē'lənd) or **Ley·land** (lā'-), **John.** 1506?–52. English antiquarian.

Le·loir (lĕ-lwär'), **Luis Federico.** b. 1906. French-born Argentine biochemist (Nobel, 1970).

Le·ly (lē'lē, lā'-), Sir **Peter.** 1618–80. Dutch painter in England.

Le·maî·tre (lə-mĕ'trə), Abbé **Georges Edouard.** 1894–1966. Belgian astrophysicist.

Le May (lə-mā'), **Curtis Emerson.** b. 1906. Amer. air-force officer.

Le·nard (lā'närt), **Philipp.** 1862–1947. German physicist (Nobel, 1905).

Len·clos or **L'En·clos** (läɴ-klō'), **Anne.** 1620–1705. French courtesan.

L'En·fant (läɴ-fäɴ'), **Pierre Charles.** 1754–1825. French-born engineer; planned Washington, D.C.

Le·nin (lĕn'ĭn, -ĕn), **Vladimir Ilich.** 1870–1924. Russian revolutionary leader. —**Len'in·ist'** *adj. & n.*

Len·non (lĕn'ən), **John.** 1940–80. English musician and composer; murdered.

John Lennon

Len·ya (lān'yə), **Lotte.** 1898–1981. Austrian singer and actress.

Leo (lē'ō). Name of 13 popes, esp.: **1. I.** Saint. "the Great." 390?–461. Reigned 440–61. **2. III.** Saint. 750?–816. Reigned 795–816. **3. X.** 1475–1521. Reigned 1513–21. **4. XIII.** 1810–1903. Reigned 1878–1903.

Leon·ard (lĕn'ərd), **William Ellery.** 1876–1944. Amer. poet and educator.

Le·o·nar·do da Vin·ci (lē'ə-när'dō də vĭn'chē). 1452–1519. Florentine artist, engineer, musician, and scientist.

Leonardo da Vinci

Le·on·ca·val·lo (lā'ōn-kä-vä'lō), **Ruggiero.** 1858–1919. Italian composer.

Le·on·i·das I (lē-ŏn'ĭ-dəs). d. 480 B.C. Spartan king (490–80).

Le·on·tief (lē-ŏn'tyĕf, -ŏn'-), **Wassily.** b. 1906. Russian-born Amer. economist (Nobel, 1973).

Le·o·par·di (lā'ō-pär'dē), Conte **Giacomo.** 1798–1837. Italian poet and philologist.

Le·o·pold (lē'ə-pōld'). **1.** Name of 2 Holy Roman Emperors: **a. I.** 1640–1705. Ruled 1658–1705. **b. II.** 1747–92. Ruled 1790–92. **2.** Name of 3 kings of Belgium: **a. I.** 1790–1865. Ruled 1831–65. **b. II.** 1835–1909. Ruled 1865–1909. **c. III.** 1901–83. Ruled 1934–51; abdicated.

Lep·i·dus (lĕp'ĭ-dəs), **Marcus Aemilius.** b. 13 B.C. Roman triumvir (43–36).

Ler·mon·tov (lĕr'mən-tôf), **Mikhail Yurievich.** 1814–41. Russian author.

Ler·ner (lûr'nər), **Alan Jay.** 1918–86. Amer. playwright and lyricist.

Le·sage (lə-säzh'), **Alain René.** 1668–1747. French author.

Le·sche·titz·ky (lĕ'shĕ-tĭt'skē), **Theodor.** 1830–1915. Polish pianist, composer, and educator.

Les·lie (lĕs'lē, lĕz'-). **1. Frank.** 1821–80. Amer. publisher. **2. Miriam Florence Folline.** 1836–1914. Amer. editor and author.

Les·seps (lĕs'əps, lĕ-sĕps'), Vicomte **Ferdinand Marie de.** See **de Lesseps.**

Les·sing (lĕs'ĭng). **1. Gotthold Ephraim.** 1729–81. German playwright and critic. **2. Doris.** b. 1919. English author.

L'Es·trange (lə-strānj', lĕ-), Sir **Roger.** 1616–1704. English Royalist pamphleteer.

Leu·wen·hoek (lā'wən-ho͝ok', -vən-). Variant of **Leeuwenhoek.**

Leut·ze (loit'sə), **Emanuel Gottlieb.** 1816–68. German historical painter.

Le·vas·seur (lə-vä-sœr'), **Pierre Émile.** 1828–1911. French economist.

Le·ven·son (lĕv'ən-sən), **Sam.** 1911–80. Amer. author and humorist.

Le·ver (lē'vər), **Charles James.** 1806–72. Irish novelist.

Lé·vesque (lə-vĕk'), **René.** b. 1922. Canadian political leader.

Le·vi. 1. (lē'vī'). In the Bible, son of Jacob and Leah. **2.** (lā'vē), **Carlo.** 1902–75. Italian author.

Le·vine (lə-vēn'), **Jack.** b. 1915. Amer. painter.

Le·vy (lē'vē), **Uriah Phillips.** 1792–1862. Amer. naval officer.

Lew·es (lo͞o'ĭs), **George Henry.** 1817–78. English philosopher and critic.

Lew·is (lo͞o'ĭs). **1. Meriwether.** 1774–1809. Amer. Northwest explorer and soldier. **2. Matthew Gregory ("Monk").** 1775–1818. English gothic author. **3. Isaac Newton.** 1858–1931. Amer. firearms inventor. **4. John Llewellyn.** 1880–1969. Amer. labor leader. **5. (Percy) Wyndham.** 1884–1957. English artist. **6. (Harry) Sinclair.** 1885–1951. Amer. novelist (Nobel, 1930). **7. Clive Staples ("C.S.").** 1898–1963. English novelist. **8. Cecil Day.** 1904–72. English author. **9.** Sir **Arthur.** b. 1915. West-Indies-born British economist (Nobel, 1979).

Lew·i·sohn (lo͞o'ĭ-sən, -zən, -sōn'). **1. Ludwig.** 1883–1955. German-born Amer. author. **2. Irene.** 1892–1944. Amer. social worker and theatrical patron.

Ley·land (lā'lənd). Variant of **Leland.**

Ley·poldt (lī'pōlt'), **Frederick.** 1835–84. German-born Amer. editor and publisher.

Liang (lyäng). Name of 2 Chinese dynasties (502–57, 907–23).

Liao (lyou). Chinese dynasty (916–1125).

Lib·by (lĭb'ē), **Willard Frank.** 1908–80. Amer. chemist (Nobel, 1960).

Lib·er·a·ce (lĭb'ə-rä'chē), **(Wladziu).** b. 1919. Amer. pianist and entertainer.

Lich·ten·stein (lĭk'tĭn-stīn', -stēn'), **Roy.** b. 1923. Amer. painter.

Li·cin·i·us (lī-sĭn'ē-əs), 270?–324. Roman emperor (308–24).

Lid·dell Hart (lĭd'l härt'), **Basil Henry.** 1895–1970. English military authority.

Lie (lē). **1. Jonas.** 1833–1909. Norwegian author. **2. Jonas.** 1880–1940. Norwegian-born Amer. landscape painter. **3. Trygve Halvden.** 1896–1968. Norwegian statesman and United Nations secretary-general.

Lie·ber (lē'bər), **Francis.** 1800–72. German-born Amer. historian and political economist.

Lie·big (lē'bĭg, -bĭk), Baron **Justus von.** 1803–73. German chemist.

Lieb·knecht (lēp'knĕkt', -knĕKHt'), **Karl.** 1871–1919. German Communist leader; assassinated.

Li·far (lē-fär', lē'fär), **Serge.** b. 1905. Russian dancer and choreographer.

Li Hong·zhang also **Hung-chang** (lē ho͝ong'jäng'). 1823–1901. Chinese statesman.

Lil·ien·thal. 1. (lē'lyən-täl'), **Otto.** 1848–96. German aeronautical pioneer. **2.** (lĭl'yən-thôl'), **David Eli.** 1899–1981. Amer. public official.

Li·li·u·o·ka·la·ni (lē-lē'o͞o-ō-kä-lä'-nē). Lydia Kamekeha Paki. 1838–1917. Hawaiian queen (1891–93); deposed.

Liliuokalani

Lil·lie (lĭl'ē), **Beatrice.** Lady Peel. b. 1898. Canadian-born comedienne.

Lil·lo (lĭl'ō), **George.** 1693?–1739. English playwright.

Li·món (lĭ-mōn', lē-môn'), **José Arcadio.** 1908–72. Mexican-born Amer. dancer and choreographer.

Lin·a·cre (lĭn'ĭ-kər), **Thomas.** 1460?–1524. English physician and scholar.

Lin Biao (lĭn' byou'). 1907–71. Chinese political leader.

Lin·coln (lĭng'kən). **1. Benjamin.** 1733–1810. Amer. general. **2. Abraham.** 1809–65. 16th U.S. President (1861–65); assassinated. **3. Mary Todd.** 1818–82. Wife of Abraham Lincoln.

Lind (lĭnd), **Jenny.** "Swedish Nightingale." 1820–87. Swedish singer.

Lind·bergh (lĭnd'bûrg', lĭn'-). **1. Charles Augustus.** "Lucky Lindy." 1902–74. Amer. aviator; (1st solo transatlantic flight). **2. Anne Spencer Morrow.** b. 1906. Amer. aviator and author.

Lind·ley (lĭnd'lē, lĭn'-), **John.** 1799–1865. English botanist and horticulturist.

Lind·say (lĭn'zē, lĭnd'-). **1. (Nicholas) Vachel.** 1879–1931. Amer. poet. **2. Howard.** 1889–1968. Amer. playwright and producer. **3. John Vliet.** b. 1921. Amer. politician.

Lind·sey (lĭnd'zē, lĭn'-), **Benjamin Barr ("Ben").** 1869–1943. Amer. jurist and social reformer.

Link·la·ter (lĭngk'lā'tər, -lə-), **Eric.** 1899–1974. English author.

Link·let·ter (lĭngk'lĕt'ər), **Art.** b. 1912. Canadian-born entertainer.

Lin·nae·us (lĭ-nē'əs, -nā'-), **Carolus.** 1707–78. Swedish botanist; founder of binomial taxonomic classification. —**Lin·nae'an** *adj.*

Lin Piao (lĭn' byou'). Lin Biao.

Lin Sen (lĭn' sĕn'). 1867?–1943. Chinese statesman.

Lin·ton (lĭn'tən), **Ralph.** 1893–1953. Amer. anthropologist.

Lin Yu·tang (lĭn' yo͞o'täng'). 1895–1976. Chinese-born Amer. philologist.

Lip·mann (lĭp'mən), **Fritz Albert.** 1899–1986. German-born Amer. biochemist (Nobel, 1953).

Li Po (lē' pō', bō') or **Bo** (bō'). d. 762? Chinese poet.

Lip·pi (lĭp'ē, lēp'pē), Fra **Filippo** or **Lippo** (1406?–69) and **Filippo** or **Filippino** (1457?–1504). Florentine painters.

Lip·pin·cott (lĭp'ĭn-kŏt', -kət), **Sara Jane Clarke.** 1823–1904. Amer. author.

Lipp·mann. 1. (lĕp-män'), **Gabriel.** 1845–1921. French physicist (Nobel, 1908). **2.** (lĭp'mən), **Walter.** 1889–1974. Amer. journalist.

Lip·scomb (lĭp'skəm), **William Nunn, Jr.** b. 1919. Amer. chemist (Nobel, 1976).

Lip·ton (lĭp'tən), Sir **Thomas Johnstone.** 1850–1931. Scottish-born businessman, philanthropist, and sportsman.

Li·sa (lē'sə, -sä'), **Manuel.** 1772–1820. Amer. explorer and fur trader.

Lis·ter (lĭs'tər), **Joseph.** 1st Baron Lister. 1827–1912. English founder of antiseptic surgery.

Liszt (lĭst), **Franz.** 1811–86. Hungarian pianist and composer.

Lit·tle·ton (lĭt'l-tən), Sir **Thomas.** 1407?–81. English jurist.

Lit·tré (lĭ-trā', lē-), **Maximilien Paul Émile.** 1801–81. French philosopher and lexicographer.

Lit·vi·nov (lĭt-vē'nəf, -nôf'), **Maxim Maximovich.** 1876–1951. Russian diplomat.

Liu Shao-qi also **Shao-chi** (lyo͞o' shou'chē'). 1898?–1973. Chinese political leader.

Liv·er·more (lĭv'ər-môr', -mōr'), **Mary Ashton Rice.** 1820–1905. Amer. suffragist, reformer, and lecturer.

Liv·ing·ston (lĭv'ĭng-stən). **1. Robert.** 1654–1728. Scottish-born Amer. colonist and public official. **2. William.** 1723–90. Amer. politician. **3. Robert R.** 1746–1813. Amer. Revolutionary leader and diplomat. **4. Henry Brockholst.** 1757–1823. Amer. jurist. **5. Edward.** 1764–1836. Amer. politician and diplomat.

Liv·ing·stone (lĭv'ĭng-stən), **David.** 1813–73. Scottish missionary and African explorer.

Abraham Lincoln

Liv·y (lĭv′ē), 59 B.C.–A.D. 17. Roman historian.

Llew·el·lyn (lo͞o-ĕl′ĭn), **Richard.** 1906–83. Welsh-born British author.

Lloyd (loid). **1. Henry Demarest.** 1847–1903. Amer. reformer. **2. Harold Clayton.** 1894–1971. Amer. actor.

Lloyd George (jôrj′), **David.** 1st Earl of Dwyfor. 1863–1945. British prime minister (1916–22).

Lo·ba·chev·ski (lō′bə-chĕf′skē, lə-bä-), **Nikolai Ivanovich.** 1793–1856. Russian mathematician.

Locke (lŏk). **1. John.** 1632–1704. English philosopher. **2. David Ross.** "Petroleum V. Nasby." 1833–88. Amer. satirist. **3. Alain LeRoy.** 1886–1954. Amer. educator and author.

Lock·hart (lŏk′ərt, -härt′), **John Gibson.** 1794–1854. Scottish author and editor.

Lock·wood (lŏk′wo͝od′), **Belva Ann Bennett.** 1830–1917. Amer. lawyer and suffragist.

Lock·yer (lŏk′yər), Sir **Joseph Norman.** 1836–1920. English astronomer.

Lodge (lŏj). **1. Thomas.** 1558?–1625. English author. **2. Henry Cabot.** 1850–1924. Amer. politician and author. **3.** Sir **Oliver Joseph.** 1851–1940. English physicist. **4. Henry Cabot, Jr.** 1902–85. Amer. politician and diplomat.

Loeb (lōb). **1. Jacques.** 1859–1924. German-born Amer. physiologist. **2. James Morris.** 1867–1933. German-born Amer. banker and philanthropist. **3. Sophie Irene Simon.** 1876–1929. Russian-born Amer. journalist and social-welfare advocate.

Loes·ser (lĕs′ər), **Frank Henry.** 1910–69. Amer. composer.

Loewe (lō), **Frederick.** b. 1904. Austrian-born Amer. composer.

Loe·wi (lō′ē), **Otto.** 1873–1961. German-born Amer. pharmacologist (Nobel, 1936).

Loe·wy (lō′ē), **Raymond Fernand.** 1893–1986. French-born Amer. industrial designer.

Löff·ler (lœf′lər, lĕf′-), **Friedrich August Johannes.** 1852–1915. German bacteriologist.

Lo·gan (lō′gən). **1. James.** 1674–1751. Irish-born Amer. colonial politician. **2. James** or **John.** 1725–80. Amer. Indian leader. **3. John Alexander.** 1826–86. Amer. soldier and politician. **4. Joshua.** b. 1908. Amer. producer and director.

Lo·max (lō′măks′), **John Avery.** 1867–1948. Amer. folklorist and musicologist.

Lom·bard (lŏm′bärd′). **1.** (*also* -bərd, lŭm′-), **Peter.** 1100?–60? Italian theologian. **2. Carole.** 1908–42. Amer. actress.

Lom·bar·di (lŏm-bär′dē, lŭm-), **Vincent Thomas ("Vince").** 1913–70. Amer. football coach.

Lom·bar·do (lŏm-bär′dō, lŭm-), **Guy Albert.** 1902–77. Canadian-born Amer. bandleader.

Lom·bro·so (lŏm-brō′sō, lŏm′-), **Cesare.** 1836–1909. Italian criminologist.

Lon·don (lŭn′dən). **1. Meyer.** 1871–1926. Amer. labor leader and politician. **2. John Griffith ("Jack").** 1876–1916. Amer. author.

Long (lông, lŏng). **1. Stephen Harriman.** 1784–1864. Amer. railroad engineer and explorer. **2. Crawford Williamson.** 1815–78. Amer. surgeon and pioneer anesthetist. **3. Huey Pierce.** 1893–1935. Amer. politician; assassinated.

Long·fel·low (lông′fĕl′ō, lŏng′-), **Henry Wadsworth.** 1807–82. Amer. poet.

Lon·gi·nus (lŏn-jī′nəs), **Dionysius Cassius.** 210?–73. Greek philosopher.

Long·street (lông′strēt′, lŏng′-). **1. Augustus Baldwin.** 1790–1870. Amer. clergyman, educator, and author. **2. James.** 1821–1904. Amer. Confederate general.

Long·worth (lông′wûrth′, lŏng′-). **1. Nicholas.** 1869–1931. Amer. politician. **2. Alice Roosevelt.** 1884–1980. Amer. socialite and wit.

Lönn·rot (lĕn′rŏt, -ro͞ot, lœn′rôt), **Elias.** 1802–84. Finnish scholar and anthologist.

Lons·dale (lŏnz′dāl′), **Frederick.** 1881–1954. English playwright.

Loos (lo͞os), **Anita.** 1893?–1981. Amer. author.

Ló·pez (lō′pĕz, lô′pĕs), **Carlos Antonio** (1790–1862) and **Francisco Solano** (1827–70). Paraguayan political leaders.

López Ma·te·os (mä-tē′ōs), **Adolfo.** 1910–69. Mexican statesman.

López Por·ti·llo (pôr-tē′yō), **José.** b. 1920. Mexican statesman.

Lor·ca (lôr′kə, -kä), **Federico García.** See **García Lorca.**

Lord (lôrd), **Walter.** b. 1917. Amer. author.

Lo·renz (lō′rĕnts′), **Konrad Zacharias.** b. 1903. Austrian psychologist (Nobel, 1973).

Lor·en·zet·ti (lôr′ən-zĕt′ē, lō′-rĕn-dzĕt′tē), **Ambrogio.** d. 1348? Sienese painter.

Lor·i·mer (lôr′ə-mər, lŏr′-), **George Horace.** 1867–1937. Amer. editor.

Lor·rain (lō-rān′, lô-răN′) or **Lor·raine** (lô-rĕn′), **Claude.** 1600–82. French landscape painter.

Lor·re (lôr′ē), **Peter.** 1904–64. Czechoslovakian-born Amer. actor.

Lot (lŏt). In the Bible, Abraham's nephew, whose wife was turned into a pillar of salt when she looked back as they fled Sodom.

Lo·thair (lō-thâr′, -târ′). Name of 2 Holy Roman Emperors: **1. I.** 795?–855. Ruled 840–55. **2. II.** 1070?–1137. Ruled 1125–37.

Lo·throp (lō′thrəp). **1. Harriet Mulford Stone.** "Margaret Sidney." 1844–1924. Amer. author. **2. Alice Louise Higgins.** 1870–1920. Amer. social worker.

Lo·ti (lô-tē′), **Pierre.** 1850–1923. French novelist.

Lou·bet (lo͞o-bĕ′), **Émile.** 1838–1929. French statesman.

Lou·is (lo͞o′ē, lo͞o′ĭs). **1.** Name of 2 Holy Roman Emperors: **a. I.** 778–840. Ruled 814–40. **b. IV.** 1287?–1347. Ruled 1314–47. **2.** Name of 18 kings of France, esp.: **a. V.** 966?–87. Ruled 986–87. **b. IX.** "Saint Louis." 1214–70. Ruled 1226–70. **c. XI.** 1423–83. Ruled 1461–83. **d. XII.** 1462–1515. Ruled 1498–1515. **e. XIII.** 1601–43. Ruled 1610–43. **f. XIV.** "the Sun King." 1638–1715. Ruled 1643–1715. **g. XV.** 1710–74. Ruled 1715–74. **h. XVI.** 1754–93. Ruled 1774–92. **i. XVII.** 1785–95. Titular king, 1793–95. **j. XVIII.** 1755–1824. Ruled 1814–24. **3.** (lo͞o′ĭs), **Joseph ("Joe").** 1914–81. Amer. prizefighter.

Lou·is Na·po·le·on (lo͞o′ē nə-pō′lē-ən). Napoleon III.

Louis Phi·lippe (fĭ-lēp′, fē-), "the Citizen King." 1773–1850. French king (1830–48).

Louns·bury (lounz′bĕr′ē, -bə-rē), **Thomas Raynesford.** 1838–1915. Amer. educator and philologist.

Lou·ÿs (lo͞o-ē′, lwē), **Pierre.** 1870–1925. French author.

Love·joy (lŭv′joi′), **Elijah Parish.** 1802–37. Amer. clergyman, abolitionist, and journalist.

Love·lace (lŭv′lās′), **Richard.** 1618–58. English Cavalier poet.

Lov·ell (lŭv′əl), Sir **(Alfred Charles) Bernard.** b. 1913. English astronomer.

Lov·er (lŭv′ər), **Samuel.** 1797–1868. Irish author and songwriter.

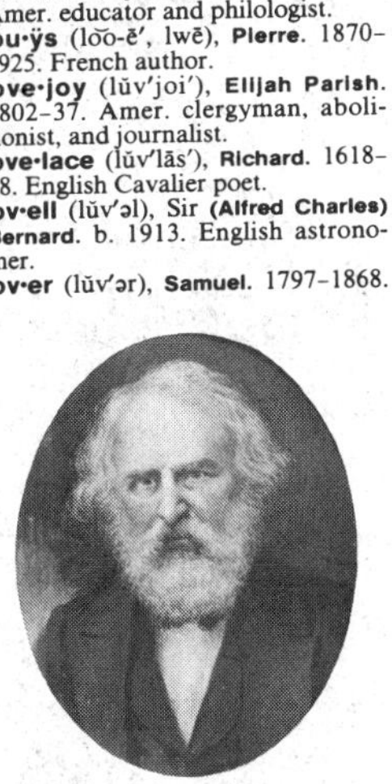

Henry Wadsworth Longfellow

Low (lō). **1. Seth.** 1850–1916. Amer. educator, reformer, and public official. **2. Juliette Magill Kinzie Gordon.** 1860–1927. Amer. founder of Girl Scouts. **3.** Sir **David Alexander Cecil.** 1891–1963. English political cartoonist.

Lowe (lō), **Thaddeus Sobieski Coulincourt.** 1832–1913. Amer. inventor and aeronaut.

Low·ell (lō′əl). **1. James Russell.** 1819–91. Amer. editor, poet, and diplomat. **2. Josephine Shaw.** 1843–1905. Amer. philanthropist and reformer. **3. Percival.** 1855–1916. Amer. astronomer. **4. Abbott Lawrence.** 1856–1943. Amer. educator. **5. Amy.** 1874–1925. Amer. poet. **6. Robert Traill Spence, Jr.** 1917–77. Amer. poet.

Lowes (lōz), **John Livingston.** 1867–1945. Amer. educator and literary critic.

Lo·wie (lō′ē), **Robert Harry.** 1883–1957. Austrian-born Amer. anthropologist.

Lowndes (loundz), **William Thomas.** 1798–1843. English bibliographer and bookseller.

Loy·o·la (loi-ō′lə), Saint **Ignatius.** See **Ignatius.**

Lo·zi·er (lō′zē-ər), **Clemence Sophia Harned.** 1813–88. Amer. physician and feminist.

Lub·bock (lŭb′ək). **1.** Sir **John William.** 1803–65. English astronomer and mathematician. **2.** Sir **John.** 1st Baron Avebury. 1834–1913. English banker, politician, and naturalist.

Lu·bitsch (lo͞o′bĭch), **Ernst.** 1892–1947. German filmmaker.

Lu·can (lo͞o′kən). A.D. 39–65. Roman poet.

Luce (lo͞os). **1. Henry Robinson.** 1898–1967. Amer. editor and publisher. **2. Clare Boothe.** b. 1903. Amer. editor, politician, diplomat, and playwright.

Lu·cian (lo͞o′shən). 2nd cent. A.D. Greek satirist.

Lu·cre·tius (lo͞o-krē′shəs, -shē-əs). 96?–55 B.C. Roman philosopher and poet. —**Lu·cre′tian** *adj.*

Lu·cul·lus (lo͞o-kŭl′əs), **Lucius Licinius.** 110?–57? B.C. Roman general, consul, and patron of the arts. —**Lu·cul′lan** *adj.*

Lu·den·dorff (lo͞od′n-dôrf′), **Erich Friedrich Wilhelm von.** 1865–1937. German general and political leader.

Lud·wick (lŭd′wĭk), **Christopher.** 1720–1801. Amer. Revolutionary patriot, baker, and philanthropist.

Lu·go·si (lo͞o-gō′sē, lə-), **Bela.** 1884–1956. Hungarian-born Amer. actor.

Lu·han (lo͞o′hän′), **Mabel Ganson Dodge.** 1879–1962. Amer. author.

Luke (lo͝ok), Saint. Companion of St. Paul.

Luks (lŭks), **George.** 1867–1933. Amer. painter.

Lul·ly 1. (lo͞o-lē′, lü-) or **Lul·li** (lo͞o′lē), **Jean Baptiste.** 1632–87. Italian-born French composer. **2.** (lŭl′ē), **Raymond.** 1235?–1315. Spanish missionary and scholar.

Lu·met (lo͞o-mĕt′), **Sidney.** b. 1924. Amer. filmmaker.

Lu·mière (lü-myĕr′). **Auguste Marie Louis Nicolas** (1862–1954) and **Louis Jean** (1864–1948). French chemists, inventors, and cinematography pioneers.

Lu·mum·ba (lo͞o-mo͝om′bə), **Patrice Emergy.** 1925–61. Congolese (Zaire) statesman; murdered.

Lun·dy (lŭn′dē), **Benjamin.** 1789–1839. Amer. abolitionist and editor.

Lunt (lŭnt), **Alfred.** 1893–1977. Amer. actor.

Lu·ri·a (lo͝or′ē-ə), **Salvador Edward.** b. 1912. Italian-born Amer. biologist (Nobel, 1969).

Lur·ton (lûr′tn), **Horace Harmon.** 1844–1914. Amer. jurist.

Lu·ther (lo͞o′thər), **Martin.** 1483–1546. German monk and Protestant religious reformer. —**Lu′ther·an** *adj.* & *n.*

Lu·thu·li (lo͞o-to͞o′lē, -tyo͞o′-), **Albert John.** 1898–1967. Zulu chieftain and reformer (Nobel, 1960).

Lux·em·burg (lŭk′səm-bûrg′, lo͝ok′-səm-bo͝ork′), **Rosa.** "Red Rosa." 1870–1919. German socialist leader; assassinated.

Lwoff (lwôf, lə-wôf′), **André Michel.** b. 1902. French microbiologist (Nobel, 1965).

Ly·cur·gus (lī-kûr′gəs). 9th cent. B.C. Spartan lawmaker.

Lyd·gate (lĭd′gāt′, -gət), **John.** 1370?–1451? English poet.

Ly·ell (lī′əl), Sir **Charles.** 1797–1875. English geologist.

Lyl·y (lĭl′ē), **John.** 1554?–1606. English novelist and playwright.

Lynch (lĭnch). **1. Charles.** 1736–96. Amer. judge and planter. **2. John Mary.** b. 1917. Irish political leader.

Lynd (lĭnd), **Robert Staughton** (1892–1970) and **Helen** (1897–1982). Amer. sociologists.

Ly·nen (lē′nən, lü′-), **Feodor.** 1911–79. German biochemist (Nobel, 1964).

Lynn (lĭn), **Janet.** b. 1953. Amer. figure skater.

Ly·on (lī′ən), **Mary Mason.** 1797–1849. Amer. educator.

Mary Lyon

Ly·ons (lī′ənz), **Joseph Aloysius.** 1879–1939. Australian statesman.

Ly·san·der (lī-săn′dər). d. 395 B.C. Spartan military leader.

Ly·sen·ko (lĭ-sĕng′kō), **Trofim Denisovich.** 1898–1976. Soviet biologist and agronomist.

Ly·sim·a·chus (lī-sĭm′ə-kəs). 361?–281 B.C. Macedonian general.

Ly·sip·pus (lī-sĭp′əs). 4th cent. B.C. Greek sculptor.

Lyt·ton (lĭt′n). **1.** 1st Baron. Edward George Earle Lytton-Bulwer. 1803–73. English author. **2.** 1st Earl of. Edward Robert Lytton Bulwer-Lytton. 1831–91. English politician and diplomat. **3.** 2nd Earl of. Victor Alexander George Robert Lytton. 1876–1947. English colonial administrator and diplomat.

M

Mac·Ar·thur (mək-är′thər). **1. Arthur.** 1845–1912. Amer. general. **2. Douglas.** 1880–1964. Amer. general. **3. Charles.** 1895–1956. Amer. dramatist and screenwriter.

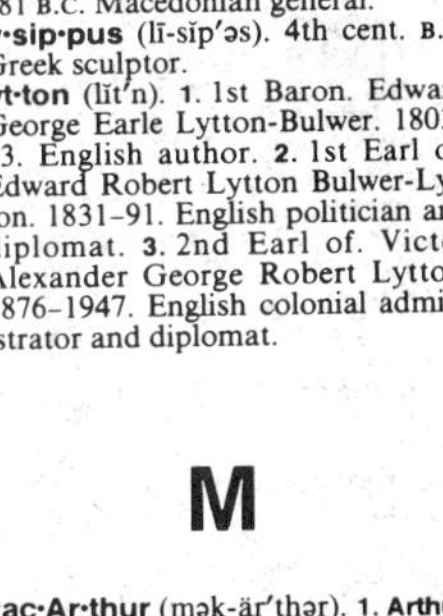

Douglas MacArthur

Ma·cau·lay (mə-kô′lē). **1. Thomas Babington.** 1800–59. English historian and statesman. **2.** Dame **Rose.**

1881–1958. English author.
Mac·beth (mək-bĕth′). d. 1057. King of Scotland (1040–57).
Mac·Bride (mək-brīd′), **Sean.** b. 1904. Irish statesman (Nobel, 1974).
Mac·ca·bees (măk′ə-bēz′). Family of Jewish patriots of 2nd and 1st cent. B.C., including **Judas** or **Judah Mac·ca·be·us** (-bē′əs), d. 160 B.C.
Mac·Crack·en (mə-krăk′ən), **Henry Noble.** 1880–1970. Amer. educator.
Mac·Diar·mid (mək-dûr′mĭd), **Hugh.** 1892–1978. Scottish poet.
Mac·don·ald (mək-dŏn′əld). **1.** Sir **John Alexander.** 1815–91. Canadian prime minister (1867–73, 1878–91). **2. George.** 1824–1905. Scottish author. **3. Dwight.** b. 1906. Amer. author and editor.
Mac·Don·ald (mək-dŏn′əld), **(James) Ramsay.** 1866–1937. British prime minister (1924, 1929–35).
Mac·don·ough (mək-dŏn′ə), **Thomas.** 1783–1825. Amer. naval officer.
Mac·Dow·ell (mək-dou′əl), **Edward Alexander.** 1861–1908. Amer. composer.
Mac·Fad·den (mək-făd′n), **Bernarr.** 1868–1955. Amer. physical-culture advocate and publisher.
Mach (mäk, măk, mäkн), **Ernst.** 1838–1916. Austrian physicist and philosopher.
Ma·cha·do y Mo·ra·les (mä-chä′*th*ô ē mô-rä′lĕs), **Gerardo.** 1871–1939. Cuban politician.
Ma·chen (mā′chən), **John Gresham.** 1881–1937. Amer. theologian.
Mach·i·a·vel·li (măk′ē-ə-vĕl′ē, mä′-kyä-vĕl′lē), **Niccolò.** 1469–1527. Italian statesman and political theorist. —**Mach′i·a·vel′li·an** *adj. & n.*
Mac·In·nes (mə-kĭn′ĭs), **Helen Clark.** 1907–85. Scottish-born Amer. author.
Mac·I·ver (mə-kī′vər), **Robert Morrison.** 1882–1970. Scottish-born Amer. sociologist.
Mack (măk), **Connie.** 1862–1956. Amer. baseball player and manager.
Mack·ay (măk′ē), **Clarence Hungerford.** 1874–1938. Amer. financier and philanthropist.
Mac·Kaye (mə-kī′). **1. (James Morrison) Steele.** 1842–94. Amer. actor, playwright, and producer. **2. Percy.** 1875–1956. Amer. poet and playwright. **3. Benton.** 1879–1975. Amer. forester and regional planner.
Mac·ken·zie (mə-kĕn′zē). **1.** Sir **Alexander.** 1764–1820. Scottish explorer. **2. William Lyon.** 1795–1861. Scottish-born Canadian insurgent. **3. Alexander.** 1822–92. Scottish-born Canadian prime minister (1873–78). **4.** Sir **Compton.** 1883–1972. English author.
Mac·kin·der (mə-kĭn′dər), Sir **Halford John.** 1861–1947. English geographer.
Mack·in·tosh (măk′ĭn-tŏsh′), Sir **James.** 1765–1832. Scottish historian and philosopher.
Mac·Leish (mə-klēsh′), **Archibald.** 1892–1982. Amer. poet and dramatist.
Mac·Len·nan (mə-klĕn′ən), **Hugh.** b. 1907. Canadian author.
Mac·leod (mə-kloud′), **John James Rickard.** 1876–1935. Scottish physiologist (Nobel, 1923).
Mac·mil·lan (mək-mĭl′ən), **(Maurice) Harold.** b. 1894. British prime minister (1957–63).
Mac·Mil·lan (mək-mĭl′ən), **Donald Baxter.** 1874–1970. Amer. Arctic explorer.
Mac·Mon·nies (mək-mŏn′ĭz), **Frederick William.** 1863–1937. Amer. sculptor.
Mac·Neice (mək-nēs′), **Louis.** 1907–63. Irish-born British poet and scholar.
Mac·Neil (mək-nēl′), **Hermon Atkins.** 1866–1947. Amer. sculptor.
Ma·con (mā′kən), **Nathaniel.** 1758–1837. Amer. legislator.
Mac·pher·son (mək-fûr′sən), **James.** 1736–96. Scottish poet.
Mac·rea·dy (mə-krē′dē), **William Charles.** 1793–1873. English actor.
Ma·da·ria·ga y Ro·jo (mä′*th*ä-ryä′gä ē rô′hô), **Salvador de.** 1886–1978. Spanish diplomat.
Ma·de·ro (mä-*th*ĕ′rô), **Francisco Indalecio.** 1873–1913. Mexican revolutionary.
Mad·i·son (măd′ĭ-sən). **1. James.** 1751–1836. 4th U.S. President (1809–17) and political theorist. **2. Dolley Payne Todd.** 1768–1849. Amer. hostess. —**Mad′i·so′ni·an** *adj.*

James Madison

Dolley Madison

Mae·ce·nas (mē-sē′nəs, mī-), **Gaius.** 70?–8 B.C. Roman statesman and literature patron.
Mae·ter·linck (mā′tər-lĭngk′, mĕt′-, mä′-), Count **Maurice.** 1862–1949. Belgian poet, dramatist, and naturalist (Nobel, 1911).
Ma·gel·lan (mə-jĕl′ən), **Ferdinand.** 1480?–1521. Portuguese navigator; killed while circumnavigating the globe.
Ma·gi·not (măzh′ə-nō′, măj′-, mä-zhē-nō′), **André.** 1877–1932. French politician.
Mag·nes (măg′nĭs), **Judah Leon.** 1877–1948. Amer. religious leader and educator.
Ma·gritte (mä-grēt′), **René.** 1898–1967. Belgian painter.
Mag·say·say (mäg-sī′sī′), **Ramón.** 1907–57. Philippine statesman.
Ma·han (mə-hăn′), **Alfred Thayer.** 1840–1914. Amer. naval officer and author.
Mah·ler (mä′lər), **Gustav.** 1860–1911. Austrian composer and conductor.
Mah·mud II (mä-mŏŏd′). 1785–1839. Turkish sultan (1803–39).
Mail·er (mā′lər), **Norman.** b. 1923. Amer. author.
Mail·lol (mä-yôl′), **Aristide.** 1861–1944. French sculptor.
Mai·mon·i·des (mī-mŏn′ĭ-dēz′), **Moses.** 1135–1204. Spanish-born Jewish philosopher.
Maine (mān), Sir **Henry James Sumner.** 1822–88. English jurist.
Main·te·non (măɴt-nôɴ′), **Marquise de.** Françoise d'Aubigné. 1635–1719. French consort of Louis XIV.
Mait·land (măt′lənd), **Frederic William.** 1850–1906. English jurist and historian.
Ma·kar·i·os III (mə-kăr′ē-əs, -ōs′, mä-kä′rē-ôs). 1913–77. Cypriot prelate and statesman.
Ma·ki·no (mä-kē′nô), Count **Nobuaki.** 1861–1949. Japanese statesman.
Mal·a·chi (măl′ĭ-kī′). 5th cent. B.C. Hebrew prophet.
Mal·a·mud (măl′ə-məd), **Bernard.** 1914–86. Amer. author.
Ma·lan (mə-län′, mä-), **Daniel François.** 1874–1959. South African journalist and statesman.
Mal·bone (môl′bōn′), **Edward Greene.** 1777–1807. Amer. painter.
Mal·colm X (măl′kəm ĕks). 1925–65. Amer. civil-rights leader; assassinated.
Male·branche (mäl-bräɴsh′), **Nicolas de.** 1638–1715. French philosopher.
Ma·len·kov (măl′ĭn-kôf′, mä′lĕn-), **Georgi Maximilianovich.** b. 1902. Soviet statesman.
Mal·herbe (mä-lĕrb′), **François de.** 1555–1628. French poet.
Mal·i·now·ski (măl′ə-nôf′skē, mä′lĭ-), **Bronislaw Kasper.** 1884–1942. Polish-born English anthropologist.
Mal·lar·mé (mä-lär-mā′), **Stéphane.** 1842–98. French poet.
Mal·lon (măl′ən), **Mary.** "Typhoid Mary." 1870?–1938. Amer. cook and disease carrier.
Ma·lone (mə-lōn′), **Edmund** or **Edmond.** 1741–1812. Irish scholar and critic.
Mal·o·ry (măl′ə-rē), Sir **Thomas.** fl. 1470. English author.
Mal·pi·ghi (mäl-pē′gē), **Marcello.** 1628–94. Italian anatomist.
Mal·raux (mäl-rō′), **André.** 1901–76. French author and politician.
Mal·thus (măl′thəs), **Thomas Robert.** 1766–1834. English economist. —**Mal·thu′sian** *adj. & n.*
Ma·nas·seh (mə-năs′ə). 7th cent. B.C. king of Judah.
Man·de·ville (măn′də-vĭl′). **1.** Sir **John.** d.1372. Pseudonym of unknown compiler of travel books. **2. Bernard.** 1670?–1733. Dutch-born English physician and satirist.
Ma·nes (mā′nēz). 216?–76? Persian prophet.
Ma·net (mə-nā′, mä-nĕ′), **Edouard.** 1832–83. French painter.
Ma·nil·i·us (mə-nĭl′ē-əs), **Gaius.** 1st cent. B.C. Roman politician.
Mann (măn). **1. Horace.** 1796–1859. Amer. educator. **2.** (*also* män), **Thomas.** 1875–1955. German-born Amer. author (Nobel, 1929).

Horace Mann

Man·ner·heim (mä′nər-hām′, măn′-ər-, -hīm′), Baron **Carl Gustaf Emil von.** 1867–1951. Finnish soldier and statesman.
Man·nes (măn′ĭs). **1. Clara Damrosch.** 1869–1948. Polish-born Amer. musician. **2. Marya.** b. 1904. Amer. author.
Man·ning (măn′ĭng), **Henry Edward.** 1808–92. English religious leader.
Ma·no·le·te (mä′nô-lĕ′tĕ). 1917–47. Spanish bullfighter.
Mans·field (măns′fēld′). **1. Richard.** 1854?–1907. English-born Amer. actor. **2. Katherine.** 1888–1923. New Zealand-born British author.
Man·son (măn′sən), Sir **Patrick.** 1844–1922. British parasitologist.
Man·sur (măn-sŏŏr′), **al-.** 712?–75. Arab caliph (754–75).
Man·te·gna (män-tā′nyä), **Andrea.** 1431–1506. Italian painter.
Man·tle (măn′tl). **1. (Robert) Burns.** 1873–1948. Amer. journalist. **2. Mickey Charles.** b. 1931. Amer. baseball player.
Ma·nu·ti·us (mə-nōō′shəs, -shē-əs, -nyōō′-), **Aldus.** 1450–1515. Italian scholar and printer.
Man·zo·ni (män-dzō′nē), **Alessandro.** 1785–1873. Italian author.
Mao Ze·dong (mou′ dzŭ′dŏŏng′) also **Tse-tung** (tsə-tŏŏng′). 1893–1976. Chinese Communist leader.
Ma·rat (mä-rä′), **Jean Paul.** 1743–93. Swiss-born French revolutionary; assassinated.
Mar·cel·lus (mär-sĕl′əs), **Marcus Claudius.** 268?–208 B.C. Roman general.
March (märch), **Francis Andrew.** 1825–1911. Amer. philologist and lexicographer.
Mar·ci·a·no (mär′sē-ä′nō), **Rocco Francis ("Rocky").** 1924–69. Amer. boxer.
Mar·co·ni (mär-cō′nē), Marchese **Guglielmo.** 1874–1937. Italian engineer and inventor (wireless telegraphy; Nobel, 1909).

Guglielmo Marconi

Mar·co Po·lo (mär′kō pō′lō). See **Polo.**
Mar·cos (mär′kōs). **1. Ferdinand Edralin.** b. 1917. Philippine president (1965–86). **2. Imelda.** b. 1930. Wife of Ferdinand Marcos.
Mar·cus Au·re·li·us An·to·ni·nus (mär′kəs ô-rē′lē-əs ăn′tə-nī′nəs). 121–80. Roman emperor and philosopher.
Mar·cu·se (mär-kōō′zə), **Herbert.** 1898–1979. German-born Amer. philosopher.
Mar·gar·et (mär′gə-rət). **1. of An·jou** (äɴ-zhōō′). 1430–82. Queen of Henry IV of England. **2. of Na·varre** (nə-vär′). 1492–1549. Author and queen of Navarre (1544–49). **3. of Va·lois** (väl-wä′). 1553–1615. Author and queen of Navarre.
Margaret Rose (rōz). b. 1930. Princess of Great Britain.
Mar·gre·the II (mär-grā′tə). b. 1940. Queen of Denmark (since 1972).
Ma·ri·a The·re·sa (mə-rē′ə tə-rē′sə, -zə). 1717–80. Queen of Hungary and Bohemia.
Ma·rie (mə-rē′). 1875–1938. Queen of Rumania (1914–27); queen dowager (1927–38).
Marie An·toi·nette (ăn′twə-nĕt′). 1755–93. Queen of France (1774–93) as wife of Louis XVI; executed.
Marie Lou·ise (lōō-ēz′). 1791–1847. 2nd wife of Napoleon I.
Mar·in (mär′ĭn), **John.** 1872–1953. Amer. painter.
Ma·ri·net·ti (mär′ə-nĕt′ē, mä′rē-nĕt′-tē), **Emilio Filippo Tommaso.** 1876–1944. Italian poet.
Ma·ri·ni (mä-rē′nē, mä-) or **Ma·ri·no** (-nō), **Giambattista.** 1569–1625. Italian poet.
Mar·i·on (măr′ē-ən, mâr′-), **Francis.** "The Swamp Fox." 1732?–95. Amer. Revolutionary soldier.
Ma·ri·tain (mä-rē-tăɴ′), **Jacques.** 1882–1973. French philosopher and critic.
Mar·i·us (mâr′ē-əs), **Gaius.** 155?–86 B.C. Roman general.
Ma·ri·vaux (mä-rē-vō′), **Pierre Carlet de Chamblain de.** 1688–1763. French author.
Mark (märk), Saint. Author of the 2nd Gospel.
Mark An·to·ny (ăn′tə-nē) or **An·tho·ny** (ăn′thə-nē). 83?–30 B.C. Roman orator, politician, and soldier.
Mark·ham (mär′kəm), **(Charles) Edwin.** 1852–1940. Amer. poet.
Mar·ko·va (mär′kə-və), Dame **Alicia.** b. 1910. British ballerina.
Marl·bor·ough (märl′bər-ə, môl′-), 1st Duke of. **John Churchill.** 1650–1722. English general and statesman.
Mar·lowe (mär′lō). **1. Christopher.** 1564–93. English dramatist and poet.

2. Julia. 1866–1950. English-born Amer. actress.
Mar·mon·tel (mär-môɴ-tĕl′), **Jean François.** 1723–99. French author.
Ma·rot (mä-rō′), **Clément.** 1495?–1544. French poet.
Mar·quand (mär-kwŏnd′), **John Phillips.** 1893–1960. Amer. author.
Mar·quette (mär-kĕt′), Père **Jacques.** 1637–75. French missionary and explorer.
Mar·quis (mär′kwĭs), **Donald Robert Perry.** 1878–1937. Amer. journalist.
Mar·ry·at (măr′ē-ĭt), **Frederick.** 1792–1848. English naval officer and author.
Marsh (märsh). **1. George Perkins.** 1801–82. Amer. diplomat and linguist. **2. Othniel Charles.** 1831–99. Amer. paleontologist. **3. Reginald.** 1898–1954. Amer. painter. **4. Ngaio.** 1899–1982. New Zealand author.
Mar·shall (mär′shəl). **1. John.** 1755–1835. Amer. jurist and statesman.

John Marshall

2. James Wilson. 1810–85. Amer. Western pioneer. **3. Clara.** 1847–1931. Amer. physician and educator. **4. Thomas Riley.** 1854–1925. U.S. Vice President (1913–21). **5. Louis.** 1856–1929. Amer. lawyer and religious leader. **6. George Catlett.** 1880–1959. Amer. soldier, diplomat, and statesman (Nobel, 1953). **7. Thurgood.** b. 1908. Amer. jurist.
Mar·sil·i·us of Pad·u·a (mär-sĭl′ē-əs; păd′yo͞o-ə). 1290?–1343. Italian philosopher.
Mar·ston (mär′stən), **John.** 1575?–1634. English dramatist.
Mar·tel (mär-tĕl′), **Charles.** See **Charles Martel.**
Mar·tens (mär′tnz), **Fedor Fedorovich.** 1845–1909. Russian jurist.
Mar·tha (mär′thə). Biblical sister of Lazarus and Mary.
Mar·tí (mär-tē′), **José Julian.** 1853–95. Cuban revolutionary leader.
Mar·tial (mär′shəl). 1st cent. A.D. Roman epigrammist.
Mar·tin (mär′tn). **1. of Tours** (to͞or), Saint. 315?–99? Patron of France. **2.** Name of 5 popes, esp.: **a. I,** Saint. d. 655. Reigned 649–55. **b. V.** 1368–1431. Reigned 1417–31; ended Western Schism. **3. Luther.** 1748?–1826. Amer. Revolutionary leader. **4. Homer Dodge.** 1836–97. Amer. painter. **5. Lillien Jane.** 1851–1943. Amer. psychologist. **6. Joseph William, Jr.** 1884–1968. Amer. publisher and politician. **7. Glenn Luther.** 1886–1955. Amer. airplane manufacturer. **8. Archer John Porter.** b. 1910. British chemist (Nobel, 1952). **9. Mary.** b. 1913. Amer. actress.
Martin Du Gard (dü gär′), **Roger.** 1881–1958. French author (Nobel, 1937).
Mar·ti·neau (mär′tə-nō). **1. Harriet.** 1802–76. English author. **2. James.** 1805–1900. English theologian and philosopher.
Mar·ti·ni (mär-tē′nē), **Simone.** 1283?–1344. Italian painter.
Mar·tin·son (mär′tn-sôn′, -tēn-), **Harry Edmund.** 1904–78. Swedish author (Nobel, 1974).
Mar·vell (mär-vĕl′), **Andrew.** 1621–78. English poet and satirist.
Marx (märks). **1. Karl.** 1818–83. German political philosopher and economist. **2.** Family of Amer. comedians, including: **Leonard ("Chico"),** 1891–1961; **Adolph Arthur ("Harpo"),** 1893–1964; **Julius ("Groucho"),** 1895–1977. —**Marx′i·an** *adj.* & *n.* —**Marx′ist** *n.*
Mar·y (mâr′e). **1.** Mother of Jesus. **2.** Name of 2 English queens: **a. I.** Also **Mary Tu·dor** (to͞o′dər). "Bloody Mary." 1516–58. Ruled 1553–58. **b. II.** 1662–94. Ruled jointly with William III (1689–94). **3.** Also **Mary of Teck** (tĕk). 1867–1953. Queen of George V of England.
Mary Mag·da·lene (măg′də-lĕn′, -lēn′). Biblical figure cured of evil spirits; also identified with the prostitute who kissed Jesus' feet.
Mary Queen of Scots also **Mary Stu·art** (sto͞o′ərt). 1542–87. Queen of Scotland (1542–67); beheaded.
Ma·sac·cio (mə-sä′chē-ō′, mä-sät′-chō). 1401–28. Italian painter.
Mas·a·ryk (măs′ə-rĭk, mä′sä-). **1. Tomáš Garrigue.** 1850–1937. Czech statesman. **2. Jan Garrigue.** 1886–1948. Czech statesman and diplomat.
Mas·ca·gni (mäs-kä′nyē), **Pietro.** 1863–1945. Italian composer.
Mase·field (măs′fēld′), **John.** 1878–1967. English author.
Ma·son (mā′sən). **1. George.** 1725–92. Amer. Revolutionary statesman. **2. Charles.** 1730?–87. English surveyor and astronomer. **3. Lowell.** 1792–1872. Amer. musician and composer. **4. James Murray.** 1798–1871. Amer. lawyer and Confederate diplomat.
Mas·sa·soit (măs′ə-soit′). 1580?–1661. New England Indian leader.
Mas·se·net (măs′ə-nā′, mäs-nĕ′), **Jules Émile Frédéric.** 1842–1912. French composer.
Mas·sey (măs′ē). **1. William Ferguson.** 1856–1925. New Zealand statesman. **2. Vincent.** 1887–1967. Canadian statesman. **3. Raymond.** 1896–1983. Canadian actor.
Mas·sine (mä-sēn′), **Léonide.** 1894–1979. Russian-born Amer. choreographer.
Mas·sin·ger (măs′ĭn-jər), **Philip.** 1583–1640. English dramatist.
Mas·son (măs′ən), **David.** 1822–1907. Scottish author and editor.
Mas·ters (măs′tərz), **Edgar Lee.** 1869–1950. Amer. poet.
Mas·ter·son (măs′tər-sən), **William Barclay ("Bat").** 1853–1921. Amer. journalist and frontier marshal.
Ma·ta Ha·ri (mä′tə här′ē, măt′ə hăr′ē). 1867–1917. German dancer and spy.
Math·er (măth′ər). **1. Richard.** 1596–1669. English-born Amer. clergyman. **2. Increase** (1639–1723) and **Cotton** (1663–1728). Amer. clergymen and authors. **3. Stephen Tyng.** 1867–1930. Amer. conservationist.
Math·ew·son (măth′yo͞o-sən), **Christopher ("Christy").** 1880–1925. Amer. baseball player.
Ma·thi·as (mə-thī′əs), **Robert Bruce ("Bob").** b. 1930. Amer. Olympic decathlon champion.
Ma·tisse (mä-tēs′), **Henri.** 1869–1954. French painter and sculptor.
Ma·tsu·o·ka (mä′tso͞o-ō′kä), **Yosuke.** 1880–1946. Japanese statesman.
Mat·te·ot·ti (mät′tā-ôt′tē), **Giacomo.** 1885–1924. Italian socialist politician.
Mat·thew (măth′yo͞o), Saint. Apostle and author of the 1st Gospel.
Mat·thews (măth′yo͞oz). **1. Stanley.** 1824–89. Amer. jurist. **2. (James) Brander.** 1852–1929. Amer. educator and author.
Mat·ting·ly (măt′ĭng-lē), **Garrett.** 1900–62. Amer. historian.
Maugham (môm), **William Somerset.** 1874–1965. English author.
Maul·din (môl′dĭn), **William Henry ("Bill").** 1921–81. Amer. cartoonist.
Mau·pas·sant (mō′pə-sänt′, mō-pä-säɴ′), **(Henri René Albert) Guy de.** 1850–93. French author.
Mau·per·tuis (mō-pĕr-twē′), **Pierre Louis Moreau de.** 1698–1759. French scientist.
Mau·riac (mô-ryäk′), **François.** 1885–1970. French author (Nobel, 1952).
Mau·rice (môr′ĭs, mŏr′-, mô-rēs′). **1.** 1521–53. Duke (1541–53) and elector (1547–53) of Saxony. **2. of Nas·sau** (năs′ô). Prince of Orange. 1567–1625. Dutch general and statesman.
Mau·rois (mô-rwä′), **André.** 1885–1967. French author and historian.
Mau·ry (môr′ē), **Matthew Fontaine.** 1806–73. Amer. naval officer, meteorologist, and oceanographer.
Mau·ser (mou′zər), **Peter Paul** (1838–1914) and **Wilhelm** (1834–82). German inventors.
Mav·er·ick (măv′ər-ĭk, măv′rĭk), **Samuel Augustus.** 1803–70. Amer. pioneer and cattle rancher.
Maw·son (mô′sən), Sir **Douglas.** 1882–1958. English explorer and geologist.
Max·im (măk′sĭm). **1.** Sir **Hiram Stevens.** 1840–1916. Amer.-born British inventor. **2. Hudson.** 1853–1927. Amer. inventor.
Max·i·mil·ian (măk′sə-mĭl′yən). **1.** Name of 2 Holy Roman Emperors: **a. I.** 1459–1519. Ruled 1493–1519. **b. II.** 1527–76. Ruled 1564–76. **2.** 1832–67. Austrian archduke and emperor of Mexico (1864–67); executed.

Maximilian

Max·well (măks′wĕl′, -wəl). **1. James Clerk.** 1831–79. Scottish physicist. **2. Elsa.** 1883–1963. Amer. columnist and hostess.
May (mā). **1.** Sir **Thomas Erskine.** 1st Baron Farnborough. 1815–86. English jurist. **2. Geraldine Pratt.** b. 1895. Amer. air-force officer.
Ma·ya·kov·ski (mä′yä-kôf′skē), **Vladimir Vladimirovich.** 1893–1930. Russian poet.
May·er. 1. (mī′ər), **Julius Robert von.** 1814–78. German physicist and physician. **2.** (mā′ər), **Louis Burt.** 1885–1957. Russian-born Amer. motion-picture producer. **3.** (mī′ər), **Marie Goeppert.** 1906–72. German-born Amer. physicist (Nobel, 1963).
May·o (mā′ō). **1. Henry Thomas.** 1856–1937. Amer. naval officer. **2. William James** (1861–1939) and **Charles Horace** (1865–1939). Amer. surgeons and founders of the Mayo Clinic.
Mays (māz), **Willie Howard, Jr.** b. 1931. Amer. baseball player.
Maz·a·rin (măz′ə-rĭn′, mä-zä-răɴ′), **Jules.** 1602–61. Italian-born French cardinal and statesman.
Maz·ze·i (mät-tsā′ē), **Philip.** 1730–1816. Italian-born Amer. physician and merchant.
Maz·zi·ni (mät-tsē′nē, mäd-dzē′-), **Giuseppe.** 1805–72. Italian revolutionary patriot.
Mc·A·doo (măk′ə-do͞o′), **William Gibbs.** 1863–1941. Amer. lawyer and politician.
Mc·Al·lis·ter (mə-kăl′ĭ-stər), **(Samuel) Ward.** 1827–95. Amer. lawyer and socialite.
M′Car·thy (mə-kär′thē). **1. Justin.** 1830–1912. Irish writer and politician. **2. Justin Huntly.** 1861–1936. Irish author.
Mc·Au·liffe (mə-kô′lĭf), **Anthony Clement.** 1898–1975. Amer. soldier.
Mc·Bride (mək-brīd′), **Mary Margaret.** 1899–1976. Amer. broadcast journalist.
Mc·Bur·ney (mək-bûr′nē), **Charles.** 1845–1913. Amer. surgeon.
Mc·Car·thy (mə-kär′thē). **1. Joseph Raymond.** 1908–57. Amer. politician. **2. Mary Therese.** b. 1912. Amer. author. **3. Eugene Joseph.** b. 1916. Amer. politician and poet.
Mc·Cart·ney (mə-kärt′nē), **(James) Paul.** b. 1942. English musician and composer.
Mc·Cau·ley (mə-kô′lē), **Mary Ludwig Hays.** "Molly Pitcher." 1754–1832. Amer. Revolutionary heroine.
Mc·Clel·lan (mə-klĕl′ən), **George Brinton.** 1826–85. Amer. general and politician.
Mc·Clos·key (mə-klôs′kē), **John.** 1810–85. Amer. religious leader.
Mc·Cloy (mə-kloi′), **John Jay.** b. 1895. Amer. banker and public official.
Mc·Clure (mə-klo͝or′), **Samuel Sidney.** 1857–1949. Irish-born Amer. editor and publisher.
Mc·Cor·mack (mə-kôr′mək). **1. John.** 1884–1945. Amer. opera singer. **2. John William.** 1891–1981. Amer. politician.
Mc·Cor·mick (mə-kôr′mĭk). **1. Cyrus Hall.** 1809–84. Amer. inventor (reaper) and manufacturer. **2. Joseph Medill** (1877–1925) and **Robert Rutherford** (1880–1955). Amer. newspaper publishers. **3. Anne Elizabeth O'Hare.** 1882–1954. English-born Amer. journalist.
Mc·Coy (mə-koi′), **Joseph Geating.** 1837–1915. Amer. cattleman.
Mc·Crae (mə-krā′), **John.** 1872–1918. Canadian physician and poet.
Mc·Cul·lers (mə-kŭl′ərz), **Carson Smith.** 1917–67. Amer. author.
Mc·Cutch·eon (mə-kŭch′ən), **John Tinney.** 1870–1949. Amer. cartoonist.
Mc·Dou·gall (mək-do͞o′gəl), **William.** 1871–1938. English-born Amer. psychologist.
Mc·Dow·ell (mək-dou′əl). **1. Ephraim.** 1771–1830. Amer. surgeon. **2. Irvin.** 1818–85. Amer. general.
Mc·Duf·fie (mək-dŭf′ē), **George.** 1790?–1851. Amer. legislator.
Mc·Fee (mək-fē′), **William.** 1881–1966. English author.
Mc·Gill (mə-gĭl′), **James.** 1774–1813. Scottish-born Canadian philanthropist.
Mc·Gil·li·vray (mə-gĭl′ə-vrā), **Alexander.** 1759?–93. Amer. Indian leader.
Mc·Gov·ern (mə-gŭv′ərn), **George Stanley.** b. 1922. Amer. politician.
Mc·Graw (mə-grô′), **John Joseph.** 1873–1934. Amer. baseball player and manager.
Mc·Guf·fey (mə-gŭf′ē), **William Holmes.** 1800–73. Amer. educator.
Mc·In·tire (măk′ĭn-tīr′), **Samuel.** 1757–1811. Amer. architect and craftsman.
Mc·Kay (mə-kā′). **1. Donald.** 1810–80. Amer. shipbuilder. **2. Claude.** 1889–1948. Amer. poet.
Mc·Kean (mə-kēn′), **Thomas.** 1734–1817. Amer. Revolutionary statesman.
Mc·Ken·na (mə-kĕn′ə). **1. Joseph.** 1843–1926. Amer. jurist. **2. Siobhan.** b. 1923. Irish actress.
Mc·Kim (mə-kĭm′), **Charles Follen.** 1847–1909. Amer. architect.
Mc·Kin·ley (mə-kĭn′lē). **1. John.** 1780–1852. Amer. jurist. **2. William.** 1843–1901. 25th U.S. President (1897–1901); assassinated.

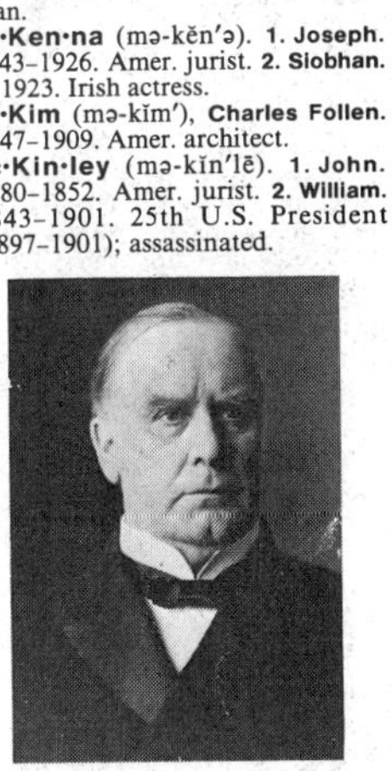

William McKinley

Mc·Lean (mə-klēn′). **1. John.** 1785–1861. Amer. jurist. **2. Evalyn Walsh.** 1886–1947. Amer. socialite. **3. Alice Throckmorton.** 1886–1968. Amer. volunteer-service organizer.
Mc·Lough·lin (mək-lôf′lĭn), **John.** 1784–1857. Canadian-born Amer. fur trader.

Mc·Lu·han (mə-klo͞o′ən), **(Herbert) Marshall.** 1911–81. Canadian educator.

Mc·Ma·hon (mək-mä′ən, mək-măn′), **William.** b. 1908. Australian statesman.

Mc·Mas·ter (mək-măs′tər), **John Bach.** 1852–1932. Amer. historian.

Mc·Mein (mək-măn′), **Neysa.** 1888–1949. Amer. artist.

Mc·Mil·lan (mək-mĭl′ən), **Edwin Mattison.** b. 1907. Amer. physicist and chemist (Nobel, 1951).

Mc·Na·mar·a (măk′nə-măr′ə), **Robert Strange.** b. 1916. Amer. public official.

Mc·Naugh·ton (mək-nôt′n), **Andrew George Latta.** 1887–1966. Canadian general and statesman.

Mc·Nutt (mək-nŭt′), **Paul Vories.** 1891–1955. Amer. lawyer and politician.

Mc·Pher·son (mək-fûr′sən), **Aimee Semple.** 1890–1944. Canadian-born Amer. evangelist.

Mc·Rey·nolds (mək-rĕn′əldz), **James Clark.** 1862–1946. Amer. jurist.

Mead (mēd). **1. George Herbert.** 1863–1931. Amer. social behaviorist. **2. Margaret.** 1901–78. Amer. anthropologist.

Meade (mēd). **1. George Gordon.** 1815–72. Amer. Union general. **2. James Edward.** b. 1907. English economist (Nobel, 1977).

Means (mēnz), **Gaston Bullock.** 1879–1938. Amer. espionage agent and detective.

Mea·ny (mē′nē), **George.** 1894–1980. Amer. labor leader.

Mears (mērz), **Helen Farnsworth.** 1872–1916. Amer. sculptor.

Med·a·war (mĕd′ə-wər), Sir **Peter Brian.** b. 1915. Brazilian-born British biologist (Nobel, 1960).

Med·i·ci (mĕd′ə-chē′, mä′dē-, mĕ′-). Italian Renaissance family, including: **1. Cosimo de.** 1389–1464. Banker, art patron, and statesman. **2. Giovanni de.** Pope Leo X. **3. Giulio de.** Pope Clement VII. **4. Lorenzo de.** "Lorenzo the Magnificent." 1449–92. Art patron and statesman. **5. Cosimo I de.** "Cosimo the Great." 1519–74. Statesman.

Me·dill (mə-dĭl′), **Joseph.** 1823–99. Amer. editor and publisher.

Me·di·na-Si·do·nia (mĕ-*thē*′nä-sē-*thô*′nyä), 7th Duke of. Alonso Pérez de Guzman. 1550–1615. Spanish naval officer.

Me·he·met A·li (mĭ-hĕm′ĕt ä-lē′, mä′mĕt) also **Mo·ham·med Ali** (mō-hăm′ĭd). 1769–1849. Viceroy of Egypt (1805–48).

Meiggs (mĕgz), **Henry.** 1811–77. Amer. railroad builder.

Meigh·en (mē′ən), **Arthur.** 1874–1960. Canadian prime minister (1920–21, 1926).

Mei·kle·john (mĭk′əl-jŏn′), **Alexander.** 1872–1964. Amer. educator.

Me·ir (mĭ′ər, mä-ēr′), **Golda.** 1898–1978. Russian-born Amer.-Israeli prime minister (1969–74).

Golda Meir

Meis·so·nier (mā′sô-nyā′), **Jean Louis Ernest.** 1815–91. French painter.

Meit·ner (mĭt′nər), **Lise.** 1878–1968. Austrian-born Swedish physicist.

Me·lanch·thon (mə-lăngk′thən, mā-länkʜ′tôn), **Philipp.** 1497–1560. German theologian.

Mel·ba (mĕl′bə), Dame **Nellie.** 1861–1931. Australian singer.

Mel·bourne (mĕl′bərn), 2nd Viscount. William Lamb. 1779–1848. British prime minister (1834, 1835–41).

Mel·chers (mĕl′chərz), **Gari.** 1860–1932. Amer. painter.

Mel·chi·or (mĕl′kē-ôr′), **Lauritz Lebrecht Hommel.** 1890–1973. Danish-born Amer. opera singer.

Mel·lon (mĕl′ən), **Andrew William.** 1855–1937. Amer. financier and public official.

Me·lo·ney (mə-lō′nē), **Marie Mattingly.** 1878–1943. Amer. journalist.

Mel·ville (mĕl′vĭl). **1. Herman.** 1819–91. Amer. author. **2. George Wallace.** 1841–1912. Amer. naval officer and explorer.

Mem·ling (mĕm′lĭng) also **Mem·linc** (-lĭngk), **Hans.** 1430?–95. Flemish painter.

Me·nan·der (mə-năn′dər). 4th cent. B.C. Greek dramatist.

Men·ci·us (mĕn′shē-əs). 4th cent. B.C. Chinese philosopher.

Menck·en (mĕng′kən), **Henry Louis.** 1880–1956. Amer. editor and critic.

H.L. Mencken

Men·del (mĕn′dl), **Gregor Johann.** 1822–84. Austrian botanist. —**Men·de′li·an** *adj.*

Men·de·le·ev (mĕn′də-lā′əf, -lĕ′yəf), **Dmitri Ivanovich.** 1834–1907. Russian chemist.

Men·dels·sohn (mĕn′dl-sən). **1. Moses.** 1729–86. German philosopher. **2. (Jakob Ludwig) Felix.** 1809–47. German composer, pianist, and conductor.

Men·dès-France (mäɴ-dĕs-fräɴs′), **Pierre.** 1907–82. French statesman.

Men·do·za (mĕn′dō-zə, -dô′sä, -thä), **Antonio de.** 1485–1552. Spanish colonial administrator.

Men·e·lik II (mĕn′ə-lĭk). 1844–1913. Ethiopian emperor (1889–1913).

Me·nen·dez de A·vi·les (mĕ-nĕn′dĕth dĕ ä′vē-lĕs′), **Pedro.** 1519–74. Spanish New World colonizer.

Me·nes (mē′nēz). fl. 3000 B.C. Egyptian king.

Men·ken (mĕng′kən), **Adah Isaacs.** 1835–68. Amer. actress and poet.

Men·ning·er (mĕn′ĭn-jər), **Karl Augustus.** 1893–1983. Amer. psychiatrist.

Me·not·ti (mə-nŏt′ē, mā-nôt′tē), **Gian Carlo.** b. 1911. Italian-born Amer. composer.

Men·u·hin (mĕn′yə-wĭn), **Yehudi.** b. 1916. Amer. violinist.

Men·zies (mĕn′zēz), Sir **Robert Gordon.** 1894–1978. Australian statesman.

Mer·ca·tor (mər-kā′tər, mĕr-kä′tôr), **Gerhardus.** 1512–94. Flemish geographer.

Mer·cier (mĕr-syā′), **Désiré Joseph.** 1851–1956. Belgian religious leader.

Mer·e·dith (mĕr′ĭ-dĭth). **1. George.** 1828–1909. English author. **2. James Howard.** b. 1933. Amer. civil-rights leader.

Mer·gen·thal·er (mûr′gən-thô′lər, mĕr′gən-tä-), **Ottmar.** 1854–99. German-born Amer. inventor (Linotype typesetter).

Mé·ri·mée (mā-rē-mā′), **Prosper.** 1803–70. French author.

Mer·man (mûr′mən), **Ethel.** 1908–84. Amer. musical-comedy actress.

Mer·o·vin·gi·an (mĕr′ə-vĭn′jē-ən, -jən). French ruling dynasty (428–751).

Mer·rick (mĕr′ĭk), **David.** b. 1912. Amer. theatrical producer.

Mer·ritt (mĕr′ĭt), **Anna Lea.** 1844–1930. Amer. artist.

Mer·ton (mûr′tn). **1. Robert King.** b. 1910. Amer. sociologist. **2. Thomas.** 1915–1968. Amer. clergyman and author.

Mes·mer (mĕz′mər, mĕs′-), **Franz** also **Friedrich Anton.** 1734–1815. Austrian physician.

Mes·sa·la Cor·vi·nus (mə-săl′ə kôr-vī′nəs, mĕ-sä′lə), **Marcus Valerius.** 1st cent. B.C. Roman general and statesman.

Mes·sa·li·na (mĕs′ə-lī′nə), **Valeria.** d. 48 A.D. Roman empress as 3rd wife of Claudius.

Mes·ser·schmitt (mĕs′ər-shmĭt′), **Willy.** 1898–1978. German aircraft manufacturer.

Mes·sier (mā-syā′), **Charles.** 1730–1817. French astronomer.

Mes·ta (mĕs′tə), **Perle.** 1889–1975. Amer. socialite and diplomat.

Meš·tro·vić (mĕsh′trə-vĭch′, -trō-), **Ivan.** 1883–1962. Yugoslavian-born Amer. sculptor.

Me·tax·as (mə-tăk′səs, -täk-säs′), **Joannes.** 1871–1941. Greek dictator (1936–40).

Metch·ni·kov (mĕch′nĭ-kôf), **Elie.** 1845–1916. Russian zoologist (Nobel, 1908).

Met·ter·nich (mĕt′ər-nĭk, -nĭkʜ), Prince **Klemens Wenzel Nepomuk Lothar von.** 1773–1859. Austrian statesman.

Klemens von Metternich

Metz (mĕts), **Christian.** 1794–1867. Prussian-born Amer. religious leader.

Mey·er (mĭ′ər), **Annie Florance Nathan.** 1867–1951. Amer. educator and author.

Mey·er·beer (mĭ′ər-bîr′, -bâr′), **Giacomo.** 1791–1864. German opera composer.

Mey·er·hof (mĭ′ər-hôf′), **Otto.** 1884–1951. German-born Amer. physiologist (Nobel, 1922).

Mi·cah (mĭ′kə). 8th cent. B.C. Hebrew prophet.

Mi·chael (mĭ′kəl). b. 1921. King of Rumania (1927–30, 1940–47); abdicated.

Mi·chel·an·ge·lo Buo·nar·ro·ti (mĭ′kəl-ăn′jə-lō′ bwôn′ə-rô′tē, mĭk′əl-, mē′kĕl-än′jĕ-lô). 1475–1564. Italian sculptor, painter, architect, and poet.

Mi·che·let (mēsh-lā′), **Jules.** 1798–1874. French historian.

Mi·chel·son (mĭ′kəl-sən), **Albert Abraham.** 1852–1931. German-born Amer. physicist (Nobel, 1907).

Miche·ner (mĭsh′nər), **Daniel Roland.** b. 1900. Canadian statesman.

Mich·e·ner (mĭch′ə-nər, mĭch′nər), **James Albert.** b. 1907. Amer. author.

Mic·kie·wicz (mĕts-kyĕ′vĕch), **Adam.** 1798–1855. Polish poet.

Mid·dle·ton (mĭd′l-tən), **Thomas.** 1570?–1627. English dramatist.

Mies Van Der Ro·he (mēz′ văn dər rō′ə, fän, mēs′), **Ludwig.** 1886–1969. German-born Amer. architect.

Mif·flin (mĭf′lĭn), **Thomas.** 1744–1800. Amer. Revolutionary soldier and politician.

Mi·koy·an (mē′kō-yän′), **Anastas Ivanovich.** 1895–1978. Soviet statesman.

Miles (mīlz), **Nelson Appleton.** 1839–1925. Amer. general.

Mil·haud (mē-yō′), **Darius.** 1892–1974. French composer.

Mill (mĭl). **1. James.** 1773–1836. Scottish historian and economist. **2. John Stuart.** 1806–73. English philosopher and economist.

Mil·lais (mĭ-lā′), Sir **John Everett.** 1829–96. English painter.

Mil·lay (mĭ-lā′), **Edna St. Vincent.** 1892–1950. Amer. poet.

Edna St. Vincent Millay

Mil·ler (mĭl′ər). **1. William.** 1782–1849. Amer. religious leader. **2. Samuel Freeman.** 1816–90. Amer. jurist. **3. Harriet Mann.** "Olive Thorne Miller." 1831–1918. Amer. author. **4. Cincinnatus Hiner ("Joaquin").** 1837–1913. Amer. poet. **5. Henry John.** 1860–1926. English-born Amer. actor, director, and producer. **6. Alice Duer.** 1874–1942. Amer. author. **7. Henry Valentine.** 1891–1980. Amer. author. **8. Perry Gilbert Eddy.** 1905–63. Amer. historian and critic. **9. Glenn.** 1909–44. Amer. bandleader. **10. Arthur.** b. 1915. Amer. dramatist.

Mil·le·rand (mēl-räɴ′), **Alexandre.** 1859–1943. French statesman.

Mil·les (mĭl′əs), **Carl.** 1875–1955. Swedish sculptor.

Mil·let (mĭ-lā′, mē-lĕ′), **Jean François.** 1814–75. French painter.

Mil·li·kan (mĭl′ĭ-kən), **Robert Andrews.** 1868–1953. Amer. physicist (Nobel, 1923).

Mills (mĭlz), **Robert.** 1781–1855. Amer. architect and engineer.

Mil·man (mĭl′mən), **Henry Hart.** 1791–1868. English historian and poet.

Milne (mĭln). **1. John.** 1850–1913. British mining engineer and seismologist. **2. Alan Alexander ("A.A.").** 1882–1956. English author.

Mil·ti·a·des (mĭl-tī′ə-dēz′). 540?–489 B.C. Athenian general.

Mil·ton (mĭl′tən), **John.** 1608–74. English poet.

Mil·yu·kov (mĭ-lyo͞o-kôf′), **Pavel Nikolaevich.** 1859–1943. Russian historian and politician.

Ming (mĭng). Chinese dynasty (1368–1644).

Min·ne·wit (mĭn′ə-wĭt), **Peter.** Peter Minuit.

Mi·not (mĭ′nət), **George Richards.** 1885–1950. Amer. physician (Nobel, 1934).

Min·ton (mĭn′tən), **Sherman.** 1890–1965. Amer. jurist.

Min·u·it (mĭn′yo͞o-wĭt) also **Min·ne·wit** (mĭn′ə-wĭt), **Peter.** 1580–1638. Dutch colonial administrator.

Mi·ra·beau (mĭr′ə-bō′, mē-rä-bō′), Comte de. Honoré Gabriel Victor Riqueti. 1749–91. French revolutionist.

Mi·ró (mē-rō′), **Joan.** 1893–1983. Spanish artist.

Mis·tral. **1.** (mē-sträl′), **Frédéric.** 1830–1914. French Provençal poet (Nobel, 1904). **2.** (mēs-träl′), **Gabriela.** 1889–1957. Chilean educator and poet (Nobel, 1945).

Mitch·ell (mĭch′əl). **1. John.** d. 1768. Amer. physician, botanist, and cartographer. **2. Maria.** 1818–89. Amer. astronomer. **3. Silas Weir.** 1829–1914. Amer. physician and author. **4. Margaret Julia ("Maggie").** 1832–1918.

Amer. actress. **5. Lucy Myers Wright.** 1845–88. Persian-born Amer. archaeologist. **6. John.** 1870–1919. Amer. labor leader. **7. Wesley Clair.** 1874–1948. Amer. economist. **8. William ("Billy").** 1879–1936. Amer. soldier and aviation pioneer. **9. Margaret Munnerlyn.** 1900–49. Amer. author. **10. Peter Dennis.** b. 1920. British biochemist (Nobel, 1978).

Mit·ford (mĭt′fərd). **1. William.** 1744–1827. English historian. **2. Mary Russell.** 1787–1855. English author.

Mith·ri·da·tes VI (mĭth′rĭ-dā′tēz). "The Great." 132?–63 B.C. King of Pontus (120–63).

Mi·tro·pou·los (mĭ-trŏp′ə-ləs, mē-trô′pōō-lôs), **Dimitri.** 1896–1960. Greek-born Amer. conductor.

Mit·ter·and (mē′tə-räN′, -ränd′), **François Maurice.** b. 1916. French president (since 1981).

Mix (mĭks), **Thomas Edwin ("Tom").** 1880–1940. Amer. actor.

Miz·ner (mĭz′nər), **Addison.** 1872–1933. Amer. architect and real-estate developer.

Moc·te·zu·ma (môk′tā-sōō′mä). Montezuma II.

Mo Di (mō′ dē′). 5th–4th cent. B.C. Chinese philosopher.

Mo·di·glia·ni (mō-dē′lē-ä′nē, -lyä′-nē), **Amedeo.** 1884–1920. Italian artist.

Mo·djes·ka (mə-jĕs′kə), **Helena.** 1840–1909. Polish-born Amer. actress.

Mo·ham·med (mō-hăm′ĭd) also **Mu·ham·mad** (mōō-). **1.** 570?–632. Arab prophet and founder of Islam. **2.** 1429?–81. Sultan of Turkey (1451–81).

Mohammed A·li (ä-lē′). Mehemet Ali.

Mo·holy-Nag·y (mō′hoi-nŏd′yə), **Laszlo** or **Ladislaus.** 1895–1946. Hungarian-born Amer. artist and educator.

Mois·san (mwä-säN′), **(Ferdinand Frédéric) Henri.** 1852–1907. French chemist (Nobel, 1906).

Mo·ley (mō′lē), **Raymond Charles.** 1886–1975. Amer. journalist.

Mo·lière (mōl-yâr′). **Jean Baptiste Poquelin.** 1622–73. French actor and playwright.

Mol·nár (mōl′när′, môl′-), **Ferenc.** 1878–1952. Hungarian author.

Mo·lo·tov (mŏl′ə-tôf′, -tŏf′, môl′-, mō′lə-), **Vyacheslav Mikhailovich.** b. 1890. Russian statesman.

Molt·ke (môlt′kə), Count **Helmuth von.** 1800–91. Prussian soldier.

Momm·sen (mŏm′sən, môm′zən), **Theodor.** 1817–1903. German historian (Nobel, 1902).

Monck or **Monk** (mŭngk), **George.** 1st Duke of Albemarle. 1608–70. English general.

Mon·dale (mŏn′dāl′), **Walter Frederick.** b. 1928. U.S. Vice President (1977–81).

Mon·dri·an (môn′drē-än′, mŏn′-), **Piet.** 1872–1944. Dutch painter.

Mo·net (mō-nā′, mô-nĕ′), **Claude.** 1840–1926. French painter.

Claude Monet

Mo·ne·ta (mō-nā′tə), **Ernesto Teodoro.** 1833–1918. Italian journalist and pacifist (Nobel, 1907).

Mo·niz (mô-nēsh′), **Antonio Caetano de Abreu Freire Egas.** 1874–1955. Portuguese neurologist.

Monk (mŭngk). **1.** Variant of **Monck. 2. Marie.** 1816–49. Canadian-born Amer. author. **3. Thelonious Sphere.** 1917–82. Amer. jazz pianist and composer.

Mon·mouth (mŏn′məth), Duke of. James Scott. 1649–85. English pretender to the throne; beheaded.

Mon·net (mō-nā′, mô-nĕ′), **Jean.** 1888–1979. French economist and statesman.

Mo·nod (mô-nō′), **Jacques Lucien.** 1910–76. French biochemist (Nobel, 1965).

Mon·roe (mən-rō′). **1. James.** 1758–1831. 5th U.S. President (1817–25) and diplomat. **2. Harriet.** 1860–1936. Amer. editor and poet. **3. Marilyn.** 1926–62. Amer. actress.

James Monroe

Mon·ta·gna (mōn-tä′nyä), **Bartolommeo.** 1450?–1523. Italian painter.

Mon·ta·gu (mŏn′tə-gyōō′). **1.** Lady **Mary Wortley.** 1689–1762. English author. **2. Ashley.** b. 1905. English-born Amer. anthropologist.

Mon·taigne (mŏn-tān′, môn-tĕn′yə), **Michel Eyquem de.** 1533–92. French essayist.

Mon·ta·le (mōn-tä′lā), **Eugenio.** b. 1896. Italian poet (Nobel, 1975).

Mont·calm de Saint-Ve·ran (mŏnt-käm′ də săN′vā-räN′, môn-kälm′), Marquis **Louis Joseph de.** 1712–59. French commander in Canada.

Mon·tes·quieu (mŏn′tə-skyōō′, môn-tĕs-kyœ′), Baron de la Brede et de. Charles de Secondat. 1689–1755. French political philosopher and jurist.

Mon·tes·so·ri (mŏn′tĭ-sôr′ē, -sōr′ē, môn′tĕs-sô′rē), **Maria.** 1870–1952. Italian physician and pioneer educator.

Mon·teux (môN-tû′), **Pierre.** 1875–1964. French-born Amer. conductor.

Mon·te·ver·di (mŏn′tə-vâr′dē, mōn′-tā-vĕr′-), **Claudio.** 1567–1643. Italian composer.

Mon·tez (mŏn-tĕz′), **Lola.** 1818–61. Irish-born Amer. dancer.

Mon·te·zu·ma II (mŏn′tə-zōō′mə). 1480?–1520. Last Aztec emperor in Mexico.

Mont·fort (mŏnt′fərt, môN-fôr′), **Simon de.** Earl of Leicester. 1208?–65. English soldier and statesman.

Montfort l'A·mau·ry (lä′mə-rē), **Simon IV de.** Earl of Leicester and Comte de Toulouse. 1160?–1218. French crusader.

Mont·gol·fi·er (mŏnt-gŏl′fē-ər, môN-gôl-fyā′), **Joseph Michel** (1740–1810) and **Jacques Etienne** (1745–89). French aeronautic inventors and aeronautic pioneers.

Mont·gom·er·y (mənt-gŭm′rē, mŏnt-gŭm′ə-rē), Sir **Bernard Law.** 1st Viscount Montgomery of Alamein. 1887–1976. Irish-born British army officer.

Mont·mo·ren·cy (mŏnt′mə-rĕn′sē, môN-mô-räN-), Duc **Anne de.** 1493–1567. French marshal.

Mon·trose (mŏn-trōz′), 1st Marquis of. James Graham. 1612–50. Scottish Covenanter.

Moo·dy (mōō′dē). **1. Dwight Lyman.** 1837–99. Amer. evangelist. **2. William Henry.** 1853–1917. Amer. jurist. **3. William Vaughn.** 1869–1910. Amer. poet and playwright. **4. Helen Wills.** See Helen Newington **Wills.**

Moon (mōōn), **Sun Myung.** b. 1920. South Korean evangelist.

Moo·ney (mōō′nē), **James.** 1861–1921. Amer. ethnologist.

Moore (mŏŏr). **1. Alfred.** 1755–1810. Amer. jurist. **2. Thomas.** 1779–1852. Irish poet. **3. Clement Clarke.** 1779–1863. Amer. scholar and poet. **4. William Henry.** (1848–1923) and **James Hobart** (1852–1916). Amer. financiers. **5. George.** 1852–1933. Irish author. **6. John Bassett.** 1860–1947. Amer. jurist. **7. George Edward.** 1873–1958. English philosopher. **8. Marianne Craig.** 1887–1972. Amer. poet. **9. Grace.** 1898–1947. Amer. singer. **10. Henry.** b. 1898. English sculptor. **11. Stanford.** b. 1913. Amer. biochemist (Nobel, 1972).

Mo·ra·vi·a (mō-rä′vē-ə, -rā′-, mō-rä′-vyä), **Alberto.** b. 1907. Italian author.

More (môr, mōr). **1.** Saint (Sir) **Thomas.** 1478–1535. English statesman and author; beheaded for treason. **2. Henry.** 1614–87. English philosopher. **3. Hannah.** 1745–1833. English writer and social reformer. **4. Paul Elmer.** 1864–1937. Amer. philosopher and critic.

Mor·gan (môr′gən). **1.** Sir **Henry.** 1635?–88. Welsh buccaneer. **2. John.** 1735–89. Amer. physician. **3. Daniel.** 1736–1802. Amer. Revolutionary soldier. **4. William.** 1774?–1826. Amer. Freemason; disappeared. **5. Lewis Henry.** 1818–81. Amer. anthropologist. **6. John Hunt.** 1825–64. Amer. Confederate soldier. **7. John Pierpont.** 1837–1913. Amer. financier. **8. Mary Kimball.** 1861–1948. Amer. educator. **9. Thomas Hunt.** 1866–1945. Amer. biologist (Nobel, 1933). **10. John Pierpont, Jr.** 1867–1943. Amer. financier. **11. Anne Tracy.** 1873–1952. Amer. philanthropist. **12. Helen.** 1900–41. Amer. singer.

Mor·gen·thau (môr′gən-thou′). **1. Henry.** 1856–1946. German-born Amer. public official and diplomat. **2. Henry, Jr.** 1891–1967. Amer. public official.

Mor·i·son (môr′ĭ-sən), **Samuel Eliot.** 1887–1976. Amer. historian.

Mo·ri·sot (mô-rē-zō′), **Berthe.** 1841–95. French painter.

Mor·ley (môr′lē). **1. Edward Williams.** 1838–1923. Amer. chemist and physicist. **2. John.** Viscount Morley of Blackburn. 1838–1923. English statesman and author. **3. Christopher Darlington.** 1890–1957. Amer. author.

Mor·nay (môr-nā′), **Philippe de.** "Duplessis-Mornay." 1549–1623. French Huguenot leader.

Mor·phy (môr′fē), **Paul Charles.** 1837–84. Amer. chess master.

Mor·rill (môr′əl), **Justin Smith.** 1810–98. Amer. politician.

Mor·ris (môr′ĭs, mŏr′-). **1. Robert.** 1734–1806. Amer. Revolutionary statesman and financier. **2. Gouverneur.** 1752–1816. Amer. diplomat and political leader. **3. Esther Hobart McQuigg Slack.** 1814–1902. Amer. suffragist. **4. William.** 1834–96. English poet, artist, and craftsman. **5. Clara.** 1847–1925. Canadian-born Amer. actress.

Mor·ri·son (môr′ĭ-sən, mŏr′-). **1. Robert.** 1782–1834. Scottish missionary in China. **2.** Baron **Herbert Stanley.** 1888–1965. British labor leader and politician.

Bernard L. Montgomery

Mor·row (môr′ō, mŏr′ō), **Dwight Whitney.** 1873–1931. Amer. lawyer, banker, and diplomat.

Morse (môrs). **1. Jedidiah.** 1761–1826. Amer. religious leader and geographer. **2. Samuel Finley Breese.** 1791–1872. Amer. painter and inventor (telegraphy code and instruments). **3. Charles Wyman.** 1856–1933. Amer. speculator and promoter.

Samuel F. B. Morse

Mor·ti·mer (môr′tə-mər), **Roger IV de.** 1st Earl of March. 1287–1330. Welsh rebel.

Mor·ton (môr′tn). **1. Thomas.** d. 1647. English-born Amer. Colonial leader. **2. Sarah Wentworth Apthorp.** 1759–1846. Amer. poet. **3. William Thomas Green.** 1819–68. Amer. dentist and pioneer anesthetist. **4. Oliver Perry.** 1823–77. Amer. legislator. **5. Levi Parsons.** 1824–1920. U.S. Vice President (1889–93). **6. Julius Sterling.** 1832–1902. Amer. agriculturalist and public official. **7. Ferdinand Joseph La Menthe ("Jelly Roll").** 1885–1941. Amer. jazz musician and composer. **8. Rogers Clark Ballard.** 1914–79. Amer. public official.

Mos·by (mōz′bē), **John Singleton.** 1833–1916. Amer. Confederate soldier.

Mós·cic·ki (môsh-chĕt′skē), **Ignacy.** 1867–1946. Polish chemist and statesman.

Mose·ley (mōz′lē), **Henry Gwyn-Jeffreys.** 1887–1915. English physicist.

Mos·es (mō′zĭz, -zĭs). **1.** Hebrew prophet and lawgiver. **2. Anna Mary Robertson.** "Grandma Moses." 1860–1961. Amer. painter. **3. Robert.** 1888–1981. Amer. public official.

Grandma Moses

Mo·sher (mō′zhər), **Eliza Maria.** 1846–1928. Amer. physician and educator.

Mos·ley (mōz′lē), Sir **Oswald Ernald.** 1896–1980. English politician.

Moss·bau·er (mœs′bou′ər, mŏs′-), **Rudolf Ludwig.** b. 1929. German physicist (Nobel, 1961).

Moth·er·well (mŭth′ər-wĕl′), **Robert.** b. 1915. Amer. artist.

Mo Ti (mō′ dē′). Mo Di.

Mot·ley (mŏt′lē), **John Lothrop.** 1814–77. Amer. historian and diplomat.

Mo·ton (mōt′n), **Robert Russa.** 1867–1940. Amer. educator.

Mott (mŏt). **1. Lucretia Coffin.** 1793–1880. Amer. social reformer. **2. John Raleigh.** 1865–1955. Amer. YMCA leader (Nobel, 1946). **3.** Sir **Neville Francis.** b. 1905. British physicist (Nobel, 1977).

Mot·tel·son (mŏt'l-sən, -sôn), **Ben Roy.** b. 1926. Amer.-born Danish physicist (Nobel, 1975).
Mot·teux (mô-tô'), **Peter Anthony.** 1663?–1718. French-born English dramatist and translator.
Moul·ton (mōl'tən). **1. Ellen Louise Chandler.** 1835–1908. Amer. author. **2. Forest Ray.** 1872–1952. Amer. astronomer.
Moul·trie (mo͞ol'trē), **William.** 1730–1805. Amer. Revolutionary soldier.
Mount (mount), **William Sidney.** 1807–68. Amer. painter.
Mount·bat·ten (mount-băt'n), **Louis.** 1st Earl Mountbatten of Burma. 1900–79. English naval officer and colonial administrator; assassinated.
Mous·sorg·sky (mə-zôrg'skē, mo͞o-sôrg'skĭ). Variant of **Mussorgsky.**
Mow·att (mou'ət), **Anna Cora Ogden.** 1819–70. French-born Amer. author and actress.
Mo·zart (mōt'särt'), **Wolfgang Amadeus.** 1756–91. Austrian composer.
Mo·ze (mō'dzŭ'). Mo Di.
Mu·bar·ak (mo͞o-bär'ək), **Hosni.** b. 1928. Egyptian statesman; president (since 1981).
Mu·ga·be (mo͞o-gä'bē), **Robert Gabriel.** b. 1925. Zimbabwean statesman.
Mu·ham·mad (mo͞o-hăm'ĭd). **1.** Variant of **Mohammed. 2. Elijah.** 1897–1975. Amer. religious leader.
Muhl·en·berg (myo͞o'lən-bûrg'). **1. John Peter Gabriel.** 1746–1807. Amer. religious leader, soldier, and public official. **2. Frederick Augustus.** 1750–1801. Amer. religious leader and public official.
Mühl·en·berg (myo͞o'lən-bûrg'), **Henry Melchior.** 1711–87. German-born Amer. religious leader.
Muir (myo͝or), **John.** 1838–1914. Scottish-born Amer. naturalist.
Mul·doon (mŭl-do͞on'), **Robert David.** b. 1922. New Zealand statesman.
Mul·ler (mŭl'ər), **Hermann Joseph.** 1890–1967. Amer. geneticist (Nobel, 1946).
Mül·ler (mŭl'ər, mü'lər). **1. Johann.** "Regiomontanus." 1436–76. German mathematician and astronomer. **2. Friedrich Max.** 1823–1900. German-born English philologist. **3. Paul Hermann.** 1899–1965. Swiss chemist (Nobel, 1948).
Mul·li·kan (mŭl'ĭ-kən), **Robert Sanderson.** b. 1896. Amer. chemist and physicist (Nobel, 1966).
Mum·ford (mŭm'fərd), **Lewis.** b. 1895. Amer. author and critic.
Munch (mo͞ongk), **Edvard.** 1863–1944. Norwegian artist.
Munch·hau·sen also **Mun·chau·sen** (münkʜ'hou'zən, mŭn'chou'zən, mŭnch'hou'-), Baron **Karl Friedrich Hieronymus von.** 1720–97. German soldier and anecdote teller.
Mu·ñoz Ma·rin (mo͞o-nyōs' mä-rēn'), **Luis.** 1898–1980. Puerto Rican journalist and statesman.
Mun·ro (mən-rō'), **Hector Hugh.** "Saki." 1870–1916. British author.
Mun·sey (mŭn'sē), **Frank Andrew.** 1854–1925. Amer. publisher.
Mun·ster·berg (mo͞on'stər-bûrg', mün'stər-bĕrkʜ'), **Hugo.** 1863–1916. Prussian-born Amer. psychologist.
Mu·ra·sa·ki (mo͞o'rä-sä'kē), Baroness. 11th cent. Japanese author.
Mu·rat (mü-rä'), **Joachim.** 1767?–1815. French marshal.
Mur·doch (mûr'dŏk'), **(Jean) Iris.** b. 1919. Irish-born British author.
Mur·dock (mûr'dŏk'), **William.** 1754–1839. Scottish-born British engineer and inventor.
Mu·rel (mə-rĕl'). Variant of **Murrell.**
Mur·free (mûr'frē), **Mary Noailles.** 1850–1922. Amer. author.
Mu·ril·lo (myo͞o-rĭl'ō, mo͞o-rē'lyô), **Bartolomé Esteban.** 1617–82. Spanish painter.
Mur·phy (mûr'fē). **1. Michael Charles.** 1861–1913. Amer. athletic coach. **2. Frank.** 1890–1949. Amer. jurist. **3. William Parry.** b. 1892. Amer. physician (Nobel, 1934). **4. Robert Daniel.** 1894–1978. Amer. diplomat. **5. Audie.** 1924–71. Amer. soldier and actor.
Mur·ray (mûr'ē, mŭr'ē). **1. Lindley.** 1745–1826. Amer. grammarian. **2.** Sir **James Augustus Henry.** 1837–1915. Scottish-born British philologist and lexicographer. **3. (George) Gilbert (Aimé).** 1866–1957. Australian-born British classical scholar. **4. Philip.** 1886–1952. Scottish-born Amer. labor leader. **5. John Courtney.** 1904–67. Amer. theologian.
Mur·rell or **Mur·rel** or **Mu·rel** (mə-rĕl'), **John A.** 1804?–50? Amer. outlaw.
Mur·row (mûr'ō), **Edward Roscoe.** 1908–65. Amer. broadcast journalist.
Mu·si·al (myo͞o'zē-əl), **Stanley Frank ("Stan").** b. 1920 Amer. baseball player.
Mus·kie (mŭs'kē), **Edmund Sixtus.** b. 1914. Amer. politician.
Mus·set (mü-sā'), **(Louis Charles) Alfred de.** 1810–57. French poet.
Mus·so·li·ni (mo͞os'ə-lē'nē, mo͞o'sə-, mo͞os'sô-), **Benito.** "Il Duce." 1883–1945. Italian Fascist dictator (1922–45); assassinated.

Benito Mussolini

Mus·sorg·sky also **Mous·sorg·sky** (mə-zôrg'skē, mo͞o-sôrg'skĭ), **Modest Petrovich.** 1835–81. Russian composer.
Mu·tsu·hi·to (mo͞o'tso͞o-hē'tô). "Meiji." 1852–1912. Japanese emperor (1867–1912).
Muy·bridge (mī'brĭj), **Eadweard.** 1830–1904. British-born Amer. motion-picture pioneer.
Mu·zo·re·wa (mo͞oz'ə-rā'wə), **Abel Tendekayi.** b. 1925. Zimbabwean statesman.
Muz·zey (mŭz'ē), **David Saville.** 1870–1965. Amer. historian.
Myr·dal (mür'däl'), **(Karl) Gunnar.** b. 1898. Swedish economist (Nobel, 1974).
My·ron (mī'rən). 5th cent. B.C. Greek sculptor.

N

Na·bo·kov (nä'bô-kôf', nä-bô'kôf'), **Vladimir Vladimirovich.** 1899–1977. Russian-born Amer. author.
Na·der (nā'dər), **Ralph.** b. 1934. Amer. consumer advocate.
Na·hum (nā'həm, -əm). 7th cent. B.C. Hebrew prophet.
Nai·du (nī'do͞o), **Sarojini.** 1879–1949. Hindu poet and reformer.
Nai·smith (nā'smĭth'), **James.** 1861–1939. Canadian-born Amer. sports educator; invented basketball.
Na·math (nā'məth), **Joseph Williams ("Joe").** b. 1943. Amer. football player.
Na·nak (nä'nək). 1469–1538. Hindu Sikh religious leader.
Nan·sen (năn'sən, nän'-), **Fridtjof.** 1861–1930. Norwegian Arctic explorer, zoologist, and statesman (Nobel, 1922).
Na·o·mi (nā-ō'mē). In the Bible, Ruth's mother-in-law.
Naph·ta·li (năf'tə-lī'). Hebrew patriarch.
Na·pi·er (nā'pē-ər, nə-pîr'). **1. John.** Laird of Merchiston. 1550–1617. Scottish mathematician. **2.** Sir **Charles James.** 1782–1853. English general. **3. Robert Cornelius.** 1st Baron Napier of Magdala. 1810–90. English general and colonial administrator.
Na·po·le·on (nə-pō'lē-ən, -pōl'yən). **1. I.** Napoleon Bonaparte. French emperor (1804–14); exiled. **2. II.** François Charles Joseph Bonaparte. 1811–32. Titular king of Rome and French emperor. **3. III.** Charles Louis Napoleon Bonaparte. 1808–73. French emperor (1852–70). —**Na·po'le·on'ic** (nə-pō'lē-ŏn'ĭk) *adj.*

Napoleon I

Nar·vá·ez (när-vä'ĕs), **Pánfilo de.** 1478?–1528. Spanish conquistador.
Nas·by (năz'bē), **Petroleum V.** David Ross Locke.
Nash (năsh). **1.** Or **Nashe, Thomas.** 1567–1601. English author. **2. Walter.** 1882–1968. English-born New Zealand statesman. **3. Ogden.** 1902–71. Amer. humorous poet.
Na·smyth (nā'smĭth', năz'mĭth', năs'-), **Alexander.** 1758–1840. Scottish portrait painter.
Nas·ser (nä'sər, năs'ər), **Gamal Abdel.** 1918–70. Egyptian soldier and statesman.
Nast (năst), **Thomas.** 1840–1902. German-born Amer. editorial cartoonist.
Na·than (nā'thən). **1.** Old Testament prophet. **2. Maud.** 1862–1946. Amer. reformer. **3. George Jean.** 1882–1958. Amer. author, editor, and critic.
Na·than·ael (nə-thăn'yəl). Bartholomew.
Na·thans (nā'thənz), **Daniel.** b. 1928. Amer. microbiologist (Nobel, 1978).
Na·tion (nā'shən), **Carry** or **Carrie Amelia Moore.** 1846–1911. Amer. temperance reformer.
Nat·ta (nä'tä), **Giulio.** 1903–79. Italian chemist (Nobel, 1963).
Naz·i·mo·va (nə-zĭm'ə-və, -zē'mə-, nä-), **Alla.** 1879–1945. Russian-born actress.
Neb·u·chad·nez·zar II (nĕb'-ə-kəd-nĕz'ər, nĕb'yo͞o-). King of Babylonia (605–562 B.C.).
Neck·er (nĕk'ər, nĕ-kĕr'), **Jacques.** 1732–1804. French financier and statesman.
Né·el (nā-ĕl'), **Louis Eugène Félix.** b. 1904. French physicist (Nobel, 1970).
Nef·er·ti·ti (nĕf'ər-tē'tē). 14th cent. B.C. Egyptian queen as wife of Akhenaton.

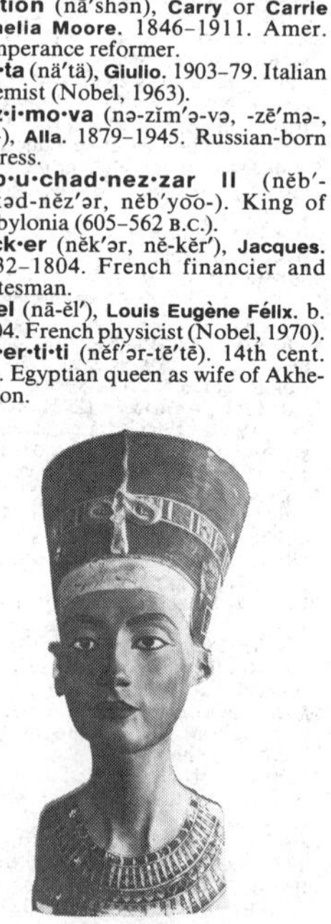
Nefertiti

Ne·he·mi·ah (nē'hə-mī'ə, nē'ə-). 5th cent. B.C. Hebrew leader.
Neh·ru (nā'ro͞o), Pandits **Motilal** (1861–1931) and **Jawaharlal** (1889–1964). Indian nationalist leaders and statesmen.
Neil·son (nēl'sən), **William Allan.** 1869–1946. Scottish-born Amer. educator, author, and lexicographer.
Nel·son (nĕl'sən). **1. Horatio.** Viscount Nelson. 1758–1805. English admiral. **2. Samuel.** 1792–1873. Amer. jurist.

Horatio Nelson

Ne·pos (nē'pŏs, nĕp'ŏs), **Cornelius.** 1st cent. B.C. Roman historian.
Ne·ri (nā'rē), San **Filippo de'** or Saint **Philip.** 1515–95. Italian ecclesiastic.
Nernst (nĕrnst), **Walther Hermann.** 1864–1941. German physicist and chemist (Nobel, 1920).
Ne·ro (nîr'ō, nē'rō). A.D. 37–68. Roman emperor (54–68). —**Ne·ro'ni·an** (nĭ-rō'nē-ən) *adj.*
Ne·ru·da (nĕ-ro͞o'də, *-thä*), **Pablo.** 1904–73. Chilean poet and diplomat (Nobel, 1971).
Ner·va (nûr'və), **Marcus Cocceius.** A.D. 30?–98. Roman emperor (96–98).
Ner·vi (nĕr'vē), **Pier Luigi.** 1891–1979. Italian architect.
Nes·to·ri·us (nĕ-stôr'ē-əs, -stōr'-). d. 451. Syrian-born patriarch of Constantinople.
Neu·mann (noi'män'), **John von.** 1903–57. Hungarian-born Amer. mathematician.
Neu·rath (noi'rät'), Baron **Konstantin von.** 1873–1956. German diplomat.
Ne·va·da (nə-vä'də), **Emma.** 1862–1940. Amer. operatic soprano.
Nev·el·son (nĕv'əl-sən), **Louise.** b. 1900. Russian-born Amer. sculptor.
Nev·ins (nĕv'ĭnz), **Allan.** 1890–1971. Amer. historian.
New·bolt (no͞o'bōlt', nyo͞o'-), Sir **Henry John.** 1862–1938. English author and editor.
New·comb (no͞o'kəm, nyo͞o'-). **1. Josephine Louise Le Monnier.** 1816–1901. Amer. philanthropist. **2. Simon.** 1835–1909. Amer. pioneer astronomer.
New·house (no͞o'hous', nyo͞o'-), **Samuel I.** 1895–1979. Amer. publisher.
New·man (no͞o'mən, nyo͞o'-), **John Henry.** 1801–90. English prelate and theologian.
New·ton (no͞ot'n, nyo͞ot'n), Sir **Isaac.** 1642–1727. English mathematician, scientist, and philosopher. —**New·to'ni·an** *adj.*

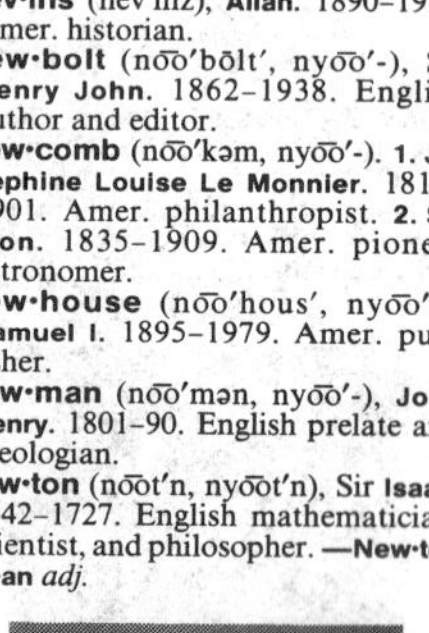
Isaac Newton

Ney. 1. (nā), **Michel.** Duc d'Elchingen, Prince de la Moskowa. 1769–1815. French marshal. 2. (nī), **Elisabet.** 1833–1907. German-born Amer. sculptor.

Nich·o·las (nĭk'ə-ləs). 1. Saint. 4th cent. prelate. 2. **of Cu·sa** (kyo͞o'zə, -sə). 1401?–64. German prelate and philosopher. 3. Name of 2 czars of Russia: **a. I.** 1796–1855. Ruled 1825–55. **b. II.** 1868–1918. Ruled 1894–1918; abdicated and was executed.

Nich·olls (nĭk'əlz), **Rhoda Holmes.** 1854–1930. English-born Amer. water-color painter.

Nich·ols (nĭk'əlz). 1. **Anne.** 1891–1966. Amer. playwright. 2. **Mike.** b. 1931. German-born Amer. comedian and director.

Nich·ol·son (nĭk'əl-sən). 1. Sir **Francis.** 1655–1728. English colonial administrator. 2. **Eliza Jane Poitevent Holbrook.** 1849–96. Amer. author and publisher.

Ni·ci·as (nĭsh'ē-əs, nĭs'-). d. 413 B.C. Athenian general and politician; executed.

Nick·laus (nĭk'lous', -ləs), **Jack William.** b. 1940. Amer. golfer.

Nic·o·lay (nĭk'ə-lā'), **John George.** 1832–1901. Amer. author and editor.

Nic·o·let (nĭk'ə-lā', nē-kô-lĕ'), **Jean.** 1598–1642. French explorer.

Ni·colle (nē-kôl'), **Charles Jean Henri.** 1866–1936. French physician and bacteriologist (Nobel, 1928).

Ni·col·let (nē-kô-lĕ'), **Joseph Nicolas.** 1786–1843. French-born mathematician and explorer.

Nic·ol·son (nĭk'əl-sən), Sir **Harold George.** 1886–1968. English diplomat, author, and critic.

Nie·buhr (nē'bo͝or', -bər). 1. (*also* nē'bo͝or), **Barthold George.** 1776–1831. German historian, philologist, and diplomat. 2. **Reinhold.** 1892–1971. Amer. theologian.

Niel·sen (nēl'sən). 1. **Carl August.** 1865–1931. Danish composer. 2. **Alice.** 1870–1943. Amer. operatic soprano.

Niem·ce·wicz (nyĕm-tsĕ'vĕch, nĕm-sā'vĭch), **Julian Ursyn.** 1758–1841. Polish author and revolutionary; exiled.

Nie·mey·er Soa·res Fil·ho (nē'mī'ər swä'rĕsh fēl'yo͞o), **Oscar.** b. 1907. Brazilian architect.

Nie·tzsche (nē'chə, -chē), **Friedrich Wilhelm.** 1844–1900. German philologist and philosopher. —**Nie'tzsche·an** *adj. & n.*

Night·in·gale (nīt'n-gāl', nī'tĭng-), **Florence.** "the Lady with the Lamp." 1820–1910. English nursing pioneer.

Ni·jin·sky (nĭ-zhĭn'skē, -jĭn'-), **Vaslav** or **Waslaw.** 1890–1950. Russian-born dancer and choreographer.

Niles (nīlz), **Hezekiah.** 1777–1839. Amer. journalist.

Nils·son (nĭl'sən), **Birgit.** b. 1918. Swedish operatic soprano.

Nim·itz (nĭm'ĭts), **Chester Williams.** 1885–1966. Amer. naval officer.

Nin (nēn, nĭn), **Anaïs.** 1903–77. French-born Amer. author and diarist.

Nir·en·berg (nîr'ĭn-bûrg'), **Marshall Warren.** b. 1927. Amer. biochemist (Nobel, 1968).

Nit·ti (nĕt'tē), **Francesco Saverio.** 1868–1953. Italian economist and politician.

Nix·on (nĭk'sən), **Richard Milhous.** b. 1913. 37th U.S. President (1969–74); resigned.

Richard M. Nixon

Ni·zer (nī'zər), **Louis.** b. 1902. English-born Amer. lawyer and author.

Nkru·mah (əng-kro͞o'mə, ən-), **Kwame.** 1909–72. Ghanaian statesman.

No·ah (nō'ə). Hebrew patriarch.

No·bel (nō-bĕl'), **Alfred Bernhard.** 1833–96. Swedish chemist, engineer, inventor, and philanthropist (Nobel prizes).

Alfred Nobel

No·bi·le (nô'bē-lā), **Umberto.** 1885–1978. Italian soldier, aeronautical engineer, and Arctic explorer.

No·el-Ba·ker (nō'əl-bā'kər), **Philip John.** 1889–1982. English statesman and author (Nobel, 1959).

No·gu·chi (nō-go͞o'chē, nô-). 1. **Hideyo.** 1876–1928. Japanese-born Amer. pioneer bacteriologist. 2. **Isamu.** b. 1904. Amer. sculptor.

No·mu·ra (nô-mo͞o'rä), **Kichisaburo.** 1887–1964. Japanese naval officer and diplomat.

Nor·dau (nôr'dou'), **Max Simon.** 1849–1923. Hungarian-born German author and Zionist leader.

Nor·den·skjöld (no͞or'dən-shœld', -shəld, -sho͞old', -shĕld'), Baron **Nils Adolf Erik.** 1832–1901. Swedish Arctic explorer and geologist.

Nor·di·ca (nôr'dĭ-kə), **Lillian.** 1859–1914. Amer. operatic soprano.

No·rell (nô-rĕl'), **Norman.** 1900–72. Amer. fashion designer.

Nor·ris (nôr'ĭs, nŏr'-). 1. **George William.** 1861–1944. Amer. legislator. 2. Family of Amer. authors, including **Benjamin Franklin, Jr. ("Frank")** (1870–1902), **Kathleen Thompson** (1880–1966), and **Charles Gilman** (1881–1945).

Nor·rish (nôr'ĭsh), **Ronald George Wreyford.** 1897–1978. English chemist (Nobel, 1967).

North (nôrth). 1. Sir **Thomas.** 1535?–1601. English translator. 2. **Frederick.** 2nd Earl of Guilford, "Lord North." 1732–92. English prime minister (1770–82). 3. **Frank Joshua.** 1840–85. Amer. frontiersman and soldier.

North·cliffe (nôrth'klĭf'), Viscount. Alfred Charles William Harmsworth.

Nor·throp (nôr'thrəp), **John Howard.** b. 1891. Amer. biochemist (Nobel, 1946).

Nor·ton (nôr'tn). 1. **Thomas.** 1532–84. English lawyer, author, and translator. 2. **Charles Eliot.** 1827–1908. Amer. author, editor, and educator.

Nos·tra·da·mus (nŏs'trə-dā'məs, -dä'-, nŏs'-). 1503–66. French physician and astrologer.

Noyes (noiz). 1. **John Humphrey.** 1811–86. Amer. social reformer. 2. **Arthur Amos.** 1866–1936. Amer. chemist and educator. 3. **Clara Dutton.** 1869–1936. Amer. nurse and educator. 4. **Alfred.** 1880–1958. English poet.

Nu·re·yev (no͝or'ĭ-yĕv, no͞o-rā'yəf, -ĕf, -ĕv), **Rudolf.** b. 1938. Russian-born Austrian ballet dancer and choreographer.

Nut·tall (nŭt'ôl), **Zelia Maria Magdelena.** 1858–1933. Amer. archaeologist.

Nut·ting (nŭt'ĭng), **Wallace.** 1861–1941. Amer. clergyman, antiquarian, and painter.

Nye (nī), **Edgar Wilson ("Bill").** 1850–96. Amer. humorist.

O

Oak·ley (ōk'lē), **Annie.** 1860–1926. Amer. markswoman.

Oates (ōts). 1. **Titus.** 1649–1705. English conspirator. 2. **Joyce Carol.** b. 1938. Amer. author.

O·ba·di·ah (ō'bə-dī'ə). 6th cent. B.C. Hebrew prophet.

O·bre·gón (ō'brē-gôn'), **Alvaro.** 1880–1928. Mexican soldier and statesman.

O'Ca·sey (ō-kā'sē), **Sean.** 1880–1964. Irish playwright.

Oc·cleve (ŏk'lēv'), **Thomas.** See **Hoccleve.**

O·cho·a (ō-chō'ə), **Severo.** b. 1905. Spanish-born Amer. biochemist (Nobel, 1959).

Ochs (ŏks), **Adolph Simon.** 1858–1935. Amer. newspaper publisher.

Ock·ham also **Oc·cam** (ŏk'əm), **William of.** 1300?–49. English scholastic philosopher.

O'Con·nor (ō-kŏn'ər). 1. **Thomas Power.** "Tay Pay." 1845–1929. Irish journalist and politician. 2. **Flannery.** 1925–64. Amer. author.

Oc·ta·vi·an (ŏk-tā'vē-ən). Augustus.

O·dets (ō-dĕts'), **Clifford.** 1906–63. Amer. playwright.

O·do·a·cer (ō'dō-ā'sər) also **O·do·va·car** or **O·do·va·kar** (-vä'-). 434?–93. Germanic tribal leader.

Oeh·len·schlä·ger (œ'lən-shlā-gər), **Adam Gottlob.** 1779–1850. Danish romantic author.

O'Fao·láin (ō-fāl'ən, ō-fā'lən), **Seán.** b. 1900. Irish author.

Of·fen·bach (ô'fən-bäk', ŏf'ən-), **Jacques.** 1819–80. French composer.

O'Fla·her·ty (ō-flă'hər-tē), **Liam.** 1896–1984. Irish author.

Og·den (ŏg'dən, ôg'-). 1. **William Butler.** 1805–77. Amer. railroad executive. 2. **Charles Kay.** 1889–1957. English psychologist and educator; inventor of Basic English, a simplified form of English.

O·gle·thorpe (ō'gəl-thôrp'), **James Edward.** 1696–1785. English soldier, philanthropist, and colonizer.

O'Hair (ō-hâr'), **Madalyn Murray.** b. 1919. Amer. reformer.

O'Ha·ra (ō-hâr'ə, ō-hăr'ə), **John Henry.** 1905–70. Amer. author.

O. Hen·ry (ō hĕn'rē). William Sidney Porter.

O'Hig·gins (ō-hĭg'ĭnz, ô-ē'gēns), **Bernardo.** 1778–1842. Chilean general and statesman.

Oh·lin (ō'lĭn, ō'lēn), **Bertil Gottard.** 1899–1979. Swedish economist (Nobel, 1977).

Ohm (ōm), **Georg Simon.** 1787–1854. German physicist.

Ois·trakh (oi'sträk, -strək), **David Feodorovich.** 1908–74. Russian violinist.

O'Keeffe (ō-kēf'), **Georgia.** 1887–1986. Amer. painter.

O'Kel·ly (ō-kĕl'ē), **Seán Thomas.** 1883–1966. Irish political leader.

O·laf (ō'läf, ō'ləf) or **O·lav** (ō'läv, ō'ləv). Name of 5 Norwegian kings, esp.: 1. I. "Olaf Tryggvesson." 969?–1000. Ruled 995?–1000. 2. II. "Olaf Haraldsson," "Saint Olaf." 995?–1030. Ruled 1015–28. 3. V. b. 1903. Ruled since 1957.

Old·cas·tle (ōld'kăs'əl, -kä'səl), Sir **John.** "Lord Cobham." d. 1417. English Lollard conspirator; burned for heresy.

Ol·den·burg (ōl'dən-bûrg'). 1. Danish ruling house (1448–1523). 2. **Claes Thure.** b. 1929. Swedish-born Amer. sculptor.

Old·field (ōld'fēld'), **Berna Eli ("Barney").** 1878–1946. Amer. automobile racer.

Olds (ōldz), **Ransom Eli.** 1864–1950. Amer. automobile inventor and manufacturer.

Ol·i·ver (ŏl'ə-vər), **Joseph ("King").** 1885?–1938. Amer. jazz musician and composer.

O·liv·i·er (ō-lĭv'ē-ā'), Sir **Laurence Kerr.** Baron Olivier of Brighton. b. 1907. English actor and director.

Olm·sted (ōm'stĕd', -stĭd, ŏm'-), **Frederick Law.** 1822–1903. Amer. landscape architect.

Ol·ney (ōl'nē), **Richard.** 1835–1917. Amer. public official.

O·mar Khay·yám (ō'mär kī-yäm', -ăm', ō'mər). 1050–1123. Persian poet, mathematician, and astronomer.

Om·mi·ad also **O·may·yad** (ō-mī'ăd). Dynasty of Arab caliphs (661–750).

O·nas·sis (ō-năs'ĭs, -nä'sĭs). 1. **Aristotle.** 1906–75. Turkish-born Greek financier and shipping magnate. 2. **Jacqueline Lee Bouvier Kennedy.** b. 1929. Amer. socialite and editor.

O·ña·te (ô-nyä'tē), **Juan de.** 1549–1624? Spanish explorer and conquistador.

O'Neill (ō-nēl'). 1. **Rose Cecil.** 1874–1944. Amer. artist and author. 2. **Eugene Gladstone.** 1888–1953. Amer. playwright (Nobel, 1936). 3. **Thomas Philip, Jr. ("Tip").** b. 1912. Amer. legislator.

Eugene O'Neill

On·ions (ŭn'yənz), **Charles Talbut.** 1873–1965. English philologist and lexicographer.

On·sa·ger (ôn'sä'gər), **Lars.** 1903–76. Norwegian-born Amer. chemist (Nobel, 1968).

Op·pen·heim (ŏp'ən-hīm'), **E(dward) Phillips.** 1866–1946. English author.

Op·pen·hei·mer (ŏp'ən-hī'mər), **J(ulius) Robert.** 1904–67. Amer. physicist.

Or·ange (ôr'ĭnj). Dutch ruling family (since 1815).

Or·cag·na (ôr-kä'nyä), **Andrea.** 1308–68? Florentine artist and architect.

Or·czy (ôr'tsē), Baroness **Emmuska.** 1865–1947. Hungarian-born English author.

O'Reil·ly (ō-rī'lē), **John Boyle.** 1844–90. Irish-American journalist and poet.

Orff (ôrf), **Carl.** 1895–1982. German composer.

Or·i·gen (ôr'ĭ-jĕn', -jən, ŏr'-). 185?–254? Greek church father.

Or·lan·do (ôr-lăn'dō, -län'-), **Vittorio Emanuele.** 1860–1952. Italian statesman.

Or·man·dy (ôr'mən-dē), **Eugene.** 1899–1985. Hungarian-born Amer. conductor.

Orms·by-Gore (ôrmz'bē-gôr', -gōr'), **David.** 5th Baron Harlech. b. 1918. English diplomat.

O·roz·co (ô-rôs'kô), **José Clemente.** 1883–1949. Mexican fresco painter.

Orr (ôr). 1. **James Lawrence.** 1822–73. Amer. legislator and diplomat. 2. **Robert ("Bobby").** b. 1948. Canadian-born hockey player.

Or·te·ga y Gas·set (ôr-tĕ'gä ē gä-sĕt'), **José.** 1883–1955. Spanish philosopher, author, and politician.

Or·tiz Ru·bio (ôr-tēs' ro͞o'byô), **Pascual.** 1877–1963. Mexican statesman.

Or·well (ôr'wĕl', -wəl), **George.** Eric Blair. 1903–50. English author.

Os·born (ŏz'bərn, -bôrn'). 1. **Henry Fairfield.** 1857–1935. Amer. paleontologist. 2. **(Henry) Fairfield.** 1887–1969. Amer. conservationist.

Os·borne (ŏz'bərn, -bôrn', -bōrn'). 1. Sir **Thomas.** 1st Earl of Danby, Marquis of Carmarthen, Duke of Leeds. 1631–1712. English politician. 2. **Thomas Mott.** 1859–1926. Amer. prison reformer. 3. **John James.** b. 1929. English playwright, producer, and actor.

Os·car (ŏs'kər) also **Os·kar** (ŏs'kär). Name of 2 kings of Norway and Sweden, esp. II, 1829–1907, ruled

Sweden 1872–1907 and Norway 1872–1905.

Os·ce·o·la (ŏs′ē-ō′lə, ō′sē-). 1804?–38. Amer. Seminole leader.

Os·ler (ōs′lər, ōz′-), Sir **William.** 1849–1919. Canadian-born British physician and educator.

Os·man (ŏz′mən, ŏs′-, ŏs-män′, ōs-) also **Oth·man** (ŏth′mən, ŏth-män′, ōth-, o͞oth-). Name of 3 Ottoman rulers, esp. **I,** 1259–1326, emir 1299–1326 and founder of dynasty.

Os·me·ña (ôs-mĕ′nyä), **Sergio.** 1878–1961. Philippine statesman.

Os·si·etz·ky (ŏ′sē-ĕts′kē, ŏ′syĕt′skē), **Carl von.** 1887–1938. German journalist and pacifist (Nobel, 1935).

Ost·wald (ôst′vält), **Wilhelm.** 1853–1932. German chemist and educator (Nobel, 1909).

O'Sul·li·van (ō-sŭl′ə-vən), **Timothy.** 1840–82. Amer. photographer.

Os·wald (ŏz′wôld′), **Lee Harvey.** 1939–63. Amer. alleged Presidential assassin; assassinated.

O·tis (ō′tĭs). **1. James** 1725–83. Amer. Revolutionary politician and publicist. **2. Harrison Gray.** 1765–1848. Amer. legislator. **3. Elisha Graves.** 1811–61. Amer. inventor (steam and safety elevators) and manufacturer. **4. Harrison Gray.** 1837–1917. Amer. soldier, journalist, and politician.

Ot·ter·bein (ŏt′ər-bīn′), **Philip William.** 1726–1813. German-born Amer. religious leader.

Ot·to (ŏt′ō, ôt′ō) also **O·tho** (ō′thō, ō′tō). Name of 4 Holy Roman Emperors, esp. **I,** "the Great," 912–73, ruled 962–73.

Ot·way (ŏt′wā), **Thomas.** 1652–85. English classical poet.

Oui·da (wē′də). Marie Louise de la Ramée.

Out·cault (out′kôlt), **Richard Felton.** 1863–1925. Amer. cartoonist ("Yellow Kid").

Ov·id (ŏv′ĭd). 43 B.C.–A.D. 18. Roman poet.

Ow·en (ō′ĭn). **1. Robert.** 1771–1858. Welsh-born British manufacturer, educator, and socialist. **2. Robert Dale.** 1801–77. Scottish-born Amer. social reformer, politician, diplomat, and author. **3. Sir Richard.** 1804–92. English anatomist and paleontologist. **4. Wilfred.** 1893–1918. English poet.

Ow·ens (ō′ĭnz), **Jesse.** 1913–80. Amer. athlete.

Jesse Owens

Ox·en·stier·na also **Ox·en·stjer·na** (o͝ok′sən-shĕr′nä, ŏk′-) or **Ox·en·stiern** (ŏk′sən-stîrn′, o͝ok′sən-shĕrn), Count **Axel Gustafsson.** 1583–1654. Swedish statesman.

O·za·wa (ō-zä′wä), **Seiji.** b. 1935. Japanese-born conductor.

P

Paa·si·ki·vi (pä′sĭ-kĭ-vĭ, -kē′vē), **Juho K.** 1870–1956. Finnish statesman.

Pack·ard (păk′ərd). **1. Sophia.** 1824–91. Amer. educator. **2. Vance.** b. 1914. Amer. author.

Pa·de·rew·ski (păd′ə-rĕf′skē, -rĕv′-, pä′də-), **Ignace Jan.** 1860–1941. Polish pianist and statesman.

Pa·ga·ni·ni (păg′ə-nē′nē, pä′gä-nē′-nē), **Nicolò.** 1782–1840. Italian violinist and composer.

Page (pāj). **1. Thomas Nelson.** 1853–1922. Amer. author and diplomat. **2. Walter Hines.** 1855–1918. Amer. journalist and diplomat.

Pag·et (păj′ĭt), Sir **James.** 1814–99. English surgeon and pathologist.

Pah·la·vi (pä-lä-vē′), **Mohammed Reza.** 1919–80. Iranian shah (1941–79); deposed.

Paige (pāj), **Leroy Robert ("Satchel").** 1906–82. Amer. baseball player.

Paine (pān). **1. Robert Treat.** 1731–1814. Amer. Revolutionary leader and jurist. **2. Thomas.** 1737–1809. English-born Amer. author and Revolutionary leader. **3. Robert Treat.** 1773–1811. Amer. poet. **4. Albert Bigelow.** 1861–1937. Amer. author and editor.

Thomas Paine

Pain·le·vé (păN-lə-vā′), **Paul.** 1863–1933. French mathematician and politician.

Pa·la·de (pə-lä′dē), **George Emil.** b. 1912. Russian-born Amer. biologist (Nobel, 1974).

Pa·lat·i·nate (pə-lăt′n-ăt′, nĭt). Swedish ruling dynasty (1654–1751).

Pa·le·stri·na (păl′ĭ-strē′nə, pä′-lā-strē′nä), **Giovanni Pierluigi da.** 1526?–94. Italian composer.

Pa·ley (pā′lē). **1. William.** 1743–1805. English theologian and philosopher. **2. William S.** b. 1901. Amer. broadcasting executive.

Pal·grave (păl′grāv′, pôl′-), **Francis Turner.** 1824–97. English poet.

Pal·la·dio (päl-lä′dyō), **Andrea.** 1508–80. Italian architect. **—Pal·la′di·an** (pə-lā′dē-ən) *adj.*

Pal·ma (päl′mä), **Tomás Estrada.** 1835–1908. Cuban statesman.

Palm·er (pä′mər). **1. Potter.** 1826–1902. Amer. merchant and real-estate promoter. **2. George Herbert.** 1842–1933. Amer. scholar and educator. **3. Daniel David.** 1845–1913. Canadian-born Amer. founder of chiropractic. **4. Alice Elvira Freeman.** 1855–1902. Amer. educator. **5. Alexander Mitchell.** 1872–1936. Amer. lawyer and public official. **6. Arnold.** b. 1929. Amer. golfer.

Palm·er·ston (pä′mər-stən), 3rd Viscount. Henry John Temple. 1784–1865. British prime minister (1855–58, 1859–65).

Pa·lóu (pä-lō′o͞o, pə-lō′), **Francisco.** 1722–1789. Spanish missionary in America.

Pa·ni·ni (pä′nē-nē, -nyē-nē). fl. 350 B.C. Indian Sanskrit grammarian.

Pank·hurst (păngk′hûrst′), **Emmeline Goulden.** 1858–1928. English suffragist.

Pa·nof·sky (pă-nŏf′skē, -nôv-), **Erwin.** 1892–1968. German-born Amer. art historian.

Pa·o·li (pä′ō-lē), **Pasquale di.** 1725–1807. Corsican patriot.

Pa·pa·do·pou·los (pä-pä-dô′-po͞o-lôs), **George.** b. 1919. Greek army officer and statesman.

Pap·an·dre·ou (pä′pən-drā′o͞o, -pän-drĕ′-), **Andreas George.** b. 1919. Greek statesman.

Pa·pen (pä′pən), **Franz von.** 1879–1969. German diplomat.

Papp (păp), **Joseph.** b. 1921. Amer. stage producer and director.

Par·a·cel·sus (păr′ə-sĕl′səs), **Philippus Aureolus.** 1493–1541. German-Swiss alchemist and physician.

Pa·ré (pä-rā′), **Ambroise.** 1517?–90. French pioneer surgeon.

Pares (pârz), Sir **Bernard.** 1876–1949. English Slavonic scholar.

Pa·re·to (pä-rā′tō), **Vilfredo.** 1848–1923. Italian economist and sociologist.

Pa·ris (păr′ĭs), **Matthew.** 1200?–59. English monk and chronicler.

Park (pärk). **1. Mungo.** 1771–1806. Scottish explorer in Africa. **2. Robert Ezra.** 1864–1944. Amer. sociologist. **3. Chung Hee.** 1917–79. South Korean statesman.

Par·ker (pär′kər). **1. Matthew.** 1504–75. English prelate. **2. John.** 1729–75. Amer. Revolutionary soldier. **3. Theodore.** 1810–60. Amer. abolitionist and clergyman. **4. Francis Wayland.** 1837–1902. Amer. pioneer educator. **5.** Sir **(Horatio) Gilbert (George).** 1862–1932. Canadian author. **6. Dorothy Rothschild.** 1893–1967. Amer. author. **7. Charlie.** 1920–55. Amer. musician and composer.

Parkes (pärks), Sir **Henry.** 1815–96. Australian statesman.

Par·kin·son (pär′kĭn-sən), **C(yril) Northcote.** b. 1909. English historian.

Park·man (pärk′mən), **Francis.** 1823–93. Amer. historian.

Parks (pärks), **Rosa.** b. 1913. Amer. civil-rights leader.

Par·men·i·des (pär-mĕn′ĭ-dēz′). 5th cent. B.C. Greek philosopher.

Par·mi·gia·ni·no (pär′mē-jä-nē′nō) or **Par·mi·gia·no** (-jä′nō), **Il.** 1503–40. Italian painter.

Par·nell (pär-nĕl′, pär′nəl), **Charles Stewart.** 1846–91. Irish nationalist leader.

Par·nis (pär′nĭs), **Mollie.** b. 1905. Amer. fashion designer.

Parr (pär), **Catherine.** 1512–48. Queen of England as 6th wife of Henry VIII.

Par·ring·ton (păr′ĭng-tən), **Vernon Louis.** 1871–1929. Amer. literary historian and philosopher.

Par·rish (păr′ĭsh). **1. Anne.** 1760–1800. Amer. philanthropist. **2. Celestia Susannah.** 1853–1918. Amer. educator. **3. Maxfield Frederick.** 1870–1966. Amer. artist.

Par·rott (păr′ət), **Robert Parker.** 1804–77. Amer. ordnance inventor.

Par·ry (păr′ē), Sir **William Edward.** 1790–1855. English navigator and Arctic explorer.

Par·sons (pär′sənz). **1. Theophilus.** 1750–1813. Amer. jurist. **2. Theophilus.** 1797–1882. Amer. legal author. **3. William.** 1800–67. English astronomer. **4. Louella.** 1893–1972. Amer. newspaper columnist. **5. Talcott.** b. 1902. Amer. sociologist.

Par·ton (pär′tn). **1. Sara Payson Willis.** 1811–72. Amer. author. **2. James.** 1822–91. Amer. biographer.

Pas·cal (păs-kăl′, päs′kəl, päs-käl′), **Blaise.** 1623–62. French philosopher and mathematician.

Pa·šić (pä′shĕch, -shĭch), **Nikola.** 1845?–1926. Servian and Yugoslavian statesman.

Pas·sy (pä-sē′, pä-). **1. Frédéric.** 1822–1912. French economist and pacifist (Nobel, 1901). **2. Paul Edouard.** 1859–1940. French philologist.

Pas·ter·nak (păs′tər-năk′, pəs-tyĭr-näk′), **Boris Leonidovich.** 1890–1960. Russian author (Nobel, 1958).

Pas·teur (păs-tûr′, pä-stœr′), **Louis.** 1822–95. French chemist. **—Pas·teur′i·an** *adj.*

Pas·tor (păs′tər), **Antonio ("Tony").** 1837–1908. Amer. actor and theater manager.

Pas·tor·i·us (păs-tôr′ē-əs, -tō′rē-), **Francis Daniel.** 1651–1720? German lawyer and colonist in America.

Patch (păch), **Sam.** 1807?–29. Amer. daredevil.

Pa·ter (pā′tər), **Walter Horatio.** 1839–94. English author.

Pat·er·son (păt′ər-sən), **William.** 1745–1806. Irish-born Amer. Revolutionary leader and jurist.

Pat·more (păt′môr′, -mōr′), **Coventry Kersey Dighton.** 1823–96. English poet.

Pa·ton (păt′n), **Alan Stewart.** b. 1903. South African author.

Pa·tri (pä′trē, păt′rē), **Angelo.** 1877–1965. Italian-born Amer. educator and author.

Pat·rick (păt′rĭk), Saint. 389?–461? Patron saint of Ireland.

Pat·ten (păt′n), **Gilbert.** "Burt L. Standish." 1866–1945. Amer. adventure-story author.

Pat·ter·son (păt′ər-sən). **1. John Henry.** 1844–1922. Amer. salesman and manufacturer. **2.** Family of Amer. newspaper editors and publishers, including **Joseph Medill** (1879–1946), **Eleanor Medill** (1881–1948), and **Alicia** (1906–63). **3. Floyd.** b.1935. Amer. prizefighter.

Pat·ti (păt′ē, pä′tē), **Adelina.** 1843–1919. Spanish-born Amer. singer.

Pat·ti·son (păt′ĭ-sən), **Mark.** 1813–84. English author and educator.

Pat·ton (păt′n), **George Smith, Jr.** 1885–1945. Amer. general.

George S. Patton

Paul (pôl). **1.** Saint. A.D. 5?–67? Apostle to the Gentiles. **2.** Name of 6 popes, esp.: **a. III.** 1468–1549. Reigned 1534–49. **b. V.** 1552–1621. Reigned 1605–21. **c. VI.** 1897–1978. Reigned 1963–78. **3. I.** 1754–1801. Russian czar (1796–1801). **4. Alice.** 1885–1977. Amer. social reformer. **5. I.** 1901–64. Grecian king (1947–64). **—Paul′ine** (-īn) *adj.*

Paul-Bon·cour (pôl-bôN-ko͞or′), **Joseph.** 1873–1972. French statesman and diplomat.

Paul·ding (pôl′dĭng). **1. James Kirke.** 1778–1860. Amer. author and public official. **2. Hiram.** 1797–1878. Amer. admiral.

Pau·li (pou′lē), **Wolfgang.** 1900–58. Austrian-born Amer. physicist (Nobel, 1945).

Pau·ling (pô′lĭng), **Linus Carl.** b. 1901. Amer. chemist (Nobel, 1954 and 1962).

Pau·lus (pô′ləs), **Julius.** 2nd–3rd cent. A.D. Roman jurist.

Pau·sa·ni·as (pô-sā′nē-əs). 2nd cent. A.D. Greek geographer and historian.

Pav·a·rot·ti (păv′ə-rŏt′ē, pä-vä-rôt′-tē), **Luciano.** b. 1935. Italian-born tenor.

Pav·lov (păv′lŏv, -lôv, päv′lôf), **Ivar Petrovich.** 1849–1936. Russian physiologist (Nobel, 1904). **—Pav·lo′vi·an** *adj.*

Pav·lo·va (päv-lō′və, păv-, păv′lə-), **Anna.** 1885–1931. Russian ballerina.

Anna Pavlova

Payne (pān), **John Howard.** 1791–1852. Amer. actor, dramatist, songwriter, and diplomat.

ă pat / ā pay / âr care / ä father / b bib / ch church / d deed / ĕ pet / ē be / f fife / g gag / h hat / hw which / ĭ pit / ī pie / îr pier / j judge / k kick / l lid, needle / m mum / n no, sudden / ng thing / ŏ pot / ō toe / ô paw, for / oi noise / ou out / o͝o took / o͞o boot /

Pea·bod·y (pē′bŏd′ē, -bə-dē). **1. George.** 1795–1869. Amer. merchant and philanthropist. **2. Elizabeth Palmer.** 1804–94. Amer. educator and author. **3. Endicott.** 1857–1944. Amer. educator. **4. Josephine Preston.** 1874–1922. Amer. dramatist.
Pea·cock (pē′kŏk), **Thomas Love.** 1785–1866. English author.
Peale (pēl). **1.** Family of Amer. painters, including **Charles Willson** (1741–1827), **James** (1749–1831), **Raphael** (1774–1825), **Rembrandt** (1778–1860), **Anna Claypoole** (1791–1878), **Titian Ramsay** (1799–1885), and **Sarah Miriam** (1800–85). **2. Norman Vincent.** b. 1898. Amer. clergyman and author.
Pear·son (pîr′sən). **1. Karl.** 1857–1936. English eugenicist and mathematician. **2. Andrew Russell ("Drew").** 1897–1969. Amer. journalist. **3. Lester Bowles.** 1897–1972. Canadian prime minister (1963–68; Nobel, 1957).
Pea·ry (pîr′ē), **Robert Edwin.** 1856–1920. Amer. naval officer and Arctic explorer; discovered North Pole.
Peck (pĕk). **1. Annie Smith.** 1850–1935. Amer. explorer and mountain climber. **2. Gregory.** b. 1916. Amer. actor.
Peck·ham (pĕk′əm), **Rufus Wheeler.** 1838–1909. Amer. jurist.
Pe·cor·a (pĭ-kôr′ə, -kōr′ə), **Ferdinand.** 1882–1971. Amer. jurist.
Pe·dro (pā′drō, -drōō). Name of 2 Brazilian emperors: **1. I.** 1798–1834. Ruled 1822–31; abdicated. **2. II.** 1825–91. Ruled 1831–89 (crowned 1841); forced to abdicate.
Peel (pēl), Sir **Robert.** 1788–1850. British prime minister (1834–35 and 1841–46).
Peele (pēl), **George.** 1556?–96? English author.
Peerce (pîrs), **Jan.** 1904–84. Amer. tenor.
Peg·ler (pĕg′lər), **Westbrook.** 1894–1969. Amer. journalist and author.
Pei (pā), **Ieoh Ming ("I.M.").** b. 1917. Chinese-born Amer. architect.

I.M. Pei

Peirce (pîrs, pûrs). **1. Benjamin.** 1809–80. Amer. mathematician and astronomer. **2. Charles Sanders.** 1839–1914. Amer. pragmatist philosopher, mathematician, and scientist.
Pei·sis·tra·tus (pē-sĭs′trə-təs). Variant of **Pisistratus.**
Pei·xot·to (pā-shō′tō), **Ernest Clifford.** 1869–1940. Amer. artist and educator.
Pe·le (pā′lā). Edson Arantes do Nascimento. b. 1940. Brazilian soccer player.
Pe·lop·i·das (pə-lŏp′ĭ-dəs). d. 364 B.C. Theban general.
Pen·der·gast (pĕn′dər-găst′), **Thomas Joseph.** 1870–1945. Amer. politician.
Pen·dle·ton (pĕn′dl-tən), **Edmund.** 1721–1803. Amer. Revolutionary leader and jurist.
Penn (pĕn). **1.** Sir **William.** 1621–70. English admiral. **2. William.** 1644–1718. English Quaker colonizer in America. **3. Arthur.** b. 1922. Amer. filmmaker.
Pen·nell (pĕn′əl, pə-nĕl′). **1. Elizabeth Robins.** 1855–1936. Amer. author and critic. **2. Joseph.** 1857–1926. Amer. artist.
Pen·ney (pĕn′ē), **James Cash.** 1875–1971. Amer. businessman.
Pen·rose (pĕn′rōz′), **Boies.** 1860–1921. Amer. political boss.
Pen·zi·as (pĕnt′sē-əs), **Arno Allan.** b. 1933. German-born Amer. physicist (Nobel, 1978).
Pep·in (pĕp′ĭn). "the Short." 714?–68. King of the Franks (751–68).
Pep·per (pĕp′ər), **William.** 1843–98. Amer. pioneer physician and educator, author, and hospital benefactor.
Pep·per·rell (pĕp′ər-əl), Sir **William.** 1696–1759. Amer. merchant and colonial official.
Pepys (pēps), **Samuel.** 1633–1701? English diarist. **—Pepys′i·an** *adj.*
Per·cy (pûr′sē). **1.** Sir **Henry.** "Hotspur." 1364–1403. English soldier; killed in battle. **2. Thomas.** 1729–1811. English prelate, antiquary, and poet.
Per·el·man (pĕr′əl-mən), **Sidney Joseph ("S.J.").** 1904–79. Amer. author.
Pé·rez Gal·dós (pĕ′rĕs gäl-dôs′), **Benito.** 1843–1920. Spanish author.
Pérez Ji·me·nez (hē-mĕn′ĕs), **Marcos.** b. 1914. Venezuelan soldier and statesman.
Per·go·le·si (pĕr′gō-lā′zē), **Giovanni Battista.** 1710–36. Italian composer.
Per·i·cles (pĕr′ĭ-klēz′). d. 429 B.C. Athenian statesman and general.
Per·kin (pûr′kĭn), Sir **William Henry.** 1838–1907. English chemist; produced 1st synthetic dye (mauve).
Per·kins (pûr′kĭnz). **1. George Walbridge.** 1862–1920. Amer. financier. **2. Frances.** 1882–1965. Amer. social reformer and public official. **3. Maxwell Evarts.** 1884–1946. Amer. editor. **4. Marlin.** 1905–86. Amer. zoo director.

Frances Perkins

Perl·man (pûrl′mən), **Itzhak.** b. 1945. Israeli-born Amer. violinist.
Pe·rón (pĕ-rôn′). Argentinian popular and political leaders, including **Juan Domingo** (1895–1974), **Maria Eva Duarte de** ("Evita"; 1919–52), and **Isabel** ("Isabelita"; b. 1931).
Per·rault (pĕ-rō′), **Charles.** 1628–1703. French author.
Per·rin (pĕ-răN′), **Jean Baptiste.** 1870–1942. French physicist and chemist (Nobel, 1926).
Per·rot (pĕ-rō′), **Nicolas.** 1644–1717. French explorer and fur trader.
Per·ry (pĕr′ē). **1. Oliver Hazard.** 1785–1819. Amer. naval officer. **2. Matthew Calbraith.** 1794–1858. Amer. naval officer. **3. Bliss.** 1860–1954. Amer. educator, editor, and critic. **4. Ralph Barton.** 1876–1957. Amer. philosopher and educator. **5. Antoinette.** 1888–1946. Amer. actress and director.
Perse (pĕrs, pûrs), **Saint-John.** Alexis Saint-Léger Léger.
Per·shing (pûr′shĭng, -zhĭng), **John Joseph ("Black Jack").** 1860–1948. Amer. army officer.
Per·sius (pûr′shəs, -shē′əs). A.D. 34–62. Roman satirist.
Pe·ru·gi·no (pā-rōō-jē′nō), **II.** 1446–1523? Italian painter.
Per·utz (pĕr′əts, pə-rōōts′), **Max Ferdinand.** b. 1914. Austrian-born English biochemist (Nobel, 1962).
Pe·ruz·zi (pā-rōōt′tsē), **Baldassare.** 1481–1536. Italian architect and painter.
Pes·ta·loz·zi (pĕs′tə-lŏt′sē, pĕs′-tä-lôt′tsē), **Johann Heinrich.** 1746–1827. Swiss educational reformer.
Pé·tain (pā-tăN′), **Henri Philippe.** 1856–1951. French soldier and politician.
Pe·ter (pē′tər). **1.** Saint. d. A.D. 67? One of the 12 Apostles; martyred. **2.** "the Hermit." 1050?–1115? French monk and preacher of the 1st Crusade. **3.** Name of 3 czars of Russia, esp. **I,** "the Great," 1672–1725, ruled 1682–1725. **4. II.** 1923–70. Yugoslavian king (1934–45).
Peter I Ka·ra·geor·ge·vich (kăr′ə-jôr′jə-vĭch′). 1844–1921. Serbian king (1903–21).
Pe·ters. 1. (pā′tərz, -tərs), **Karl.** 1856–1918. German explorer and administrator in Africa. **2.** (pē′tərz), **Roberta.** b. 1930. Amer. soprano.
Pe·ter·son (pē′tər-sən), **Roger Tory.** b. 1908. Amer. ornithologist and artist.
Pe·tö·fi (pĕ′tə-fē, -tœ-), **Sándor.** 1823–49. Hungarian lyric poet and hero.
Pe·trarch (pē′trärk, pĕ′-) or **Pe·trar·ca** (pā-trär′kä), **Francesco.** 1304–74. Italian poet. **—Pe·trarch′an** (pĭ-trär′kən) *adj.*
Pe·trie (pē′trē), Sir **(William Matthew) Flinders.** 1853–1942. English Egyptologist.
Pe·tro·ni·us (pĭ-trō′nē-əs), **Gaius.** 1st cent. A.D. Roman courtier and wit.
Pet·ty (pĕt′ē), Sir **William.** 1623–87. English political economist.
Pevs·ner (pĕvz′nər, pĕfs′-), **Antoine.** 1886–1962. Russian artist.
Phae·drus (fē′drəs). **1.** 5th cent. B.C. Greek philosopher. **2.** 1st cent. A.D. Roman fabulist.
Phid·i·as (fĭd′ē-əs). 5th cent. B.C. Athenian sculptor.
Phil·ip (fĭl′ĭp). **1.** Name of 5 kings of Macedon, esp. **II.** 382–36 B.C. Ruled 359–36. **2.** Saint. One of the 12 Apostles. **3.** Name of 6 kings of France, esp.: **a. II.** or **Philip Au·gus·tus** (ô-gŭs′təs). 1165–1223. Ruled 1180–1223. **b. IV.** "the Fair." 1268–1314. Ruled 1285–1314. **c. VI.** 1293–1350. Ruled 1328–50. **4.** Name of 2 Dukes of Burgundy, esp. "the Good," 1396–1467, ruled 1419–67. **5.** Name of 5 kings of Spain, esp.: **a. I.** "the Handsome." 1478–1506. Ruled 1504–6; died mysteriously. **b. II.** 1527–98. Ruled 1556–98. **c. V.** 1683–1746. Ruled 1700–46 (abdicated briefly in 1724). **6.** d. 1676. Amer. Indian chief. **7.** Prince. Duke of Edinburgh. b. 1921. Consort of Elizabeth II of England.
Phil·ips (fĭl′ĭps), **Ambrose.** 1675?–1749. English author.
Phil·lips (fĭl′ĭps), **Wendell.** 1811–84. Amer. abolitionist.
Phill·potts (fĭl′pŏts), **Eden.** 1862–1960. English novelist.
Phi·lo Ju·dae·us (fī′lō jōō-dē′əs, -dā′-) 30 B.C.–A.D. 45. Alexandrian Jewish philosopher.
Phips (fĭps), Sir **William.** 1651–95. English colonial administrator in America.
Pho·ci·on (fō′sē-ŏn, -shē-ən). 402?–317 B.C. Athenian general and statesman.
Phyfe (fīf), **Duncan.** 1768?–1854. Scottish-born Amer. cabinetmaker.
Pi·af (pē-äf′, pē′äf′), **Edith.** 1916–63. French singer.
Pia·get (pyä-zhā′), **Jean.** 1896–1980. Swiss psychologist.
Piaz·zi (pyät′tsē), **Giuseppi.** 1746–1826. Italian astronomer.
Pi·card (pē-kär′), **Jean.** 1620–82. French cleric and astronomer.
Pi·cas·so (pĭ-kä′sō, pē-kä′sô), **Pablo.** 1881–1973. Spanish artist.

Pablo Picasso

Pic·card (pē-kär′, -kärd′). **1. Auguste.** 1884–1962. Swiss physicist and aeronaut. **2. Jean Felix.** 1884–1963. Swiss-born Amer. chemist and aeronautical engineer.
Pick·er·ing (pĭk′ər-ĭng). **1. Timothy.** 1745–1829. Amer. soldier, Revolutionary leader, and statesman. **2. Edward Charles** (1846–1919) and **William Henry** (1858–1938). Amer. astronomers.
Pick·ett (pĭk′ĭt), **George Edward.** 1825–75. Amer. Confederate general.
Pick·ford (pĭk′fərd), **Mary.** 1893–1979. Canadian-born Amer. actress.

Mary Pickford

Pi·co del·la Mi·ran·do·la (pē′kō dĕl′ə mə-răn′də-lə, dāl-lä mē-rän′-dō-lä), Count **Giovanni.** 1463–94. Italian philosopher.
Pidg·eon (pĭj′ən), **Walter.** 1898–1984. Amer. actor.
Pieck (pēk), **Wilhelm.** 1876–1960. German statesman.
Pierce (pîrs), **Franklin.** 1804–69. 14th U.S. President (1853–57).

Franklin Pierce

Pie·ro di Co·si·mo (pyâr′ō dē kô′-zē-mō, -zə-). 1462–1521. Florentine painter.
Pike (pīk). **1. Zebulon Montgomery.** 1779–1813. Amer. army officer and explorer. **2. Albert.** 1809–91. Amer. soldier and Freemason. **3. Mary Hayden Green.** 1824–1908. Amer. novelist and abolitionist.
Pi·late (pī′lət), **Pontius.** Roman governor of Judea (A.D. 26?–36?).
Pills·bur·y (pĭlz′bĕr′ē, -bə-rē), **Charles Alfred.** 1842–99. Amer. flour manufacturer.
Pil·sud·ski (pĭl-sōōt′skē, pēl-), **Jozef.** 1867–1935. Polish statesman.
Pin·chot (pĭn′shō′), **Gifford.** 1865–1946. Amer. conservationist and politician.
Pinck·ney (pĭngk′nē). Family of

Charles Cotesworth Pinckney

Amer. politicians and diplomats, including **Charles Cotesworth** (1746–1825), **Thomas** (1750–1828), and **Charles** (1757–1824).

Pin·dar (pĭn′dər). 522?–443 B.C. Greek poet. —**Pin·dar′ic** (pĭn-dăr′ĭk) *adj.*

Pi·ne·ro (pə-nîr′ō), Sir **Arthur Wing.** 1855–1934. English playwright.

Pin·ker·ton (pĭng′kər-tən), **Allan.** 1819–84. Scottish-born Amer. detective.

Pink·ham (pĭng′kəm), **Lydia Estes.** 1819–83. Amer. patent-medicine manufacturer.

Pink·ney (pĭngk′nē), **William.** 1764–1822. Amer. politician and diplomat.

Pin·ter (pĭn′tər), **Harold.** b. 1930. English playwright.

Pin·tu·ric·chio (pēn′to͞o-rēk′kyō). 1454–1513. Italian painter.

Pin·za (pĭn′zə, pēn′tsä), **Ezio.** 1895–1957. Italian-born Amer. basso.

Pin·zón (pēn-sôn′), **Martín Alonso** (1440?–93) and **Vicente Yáñez** (1460?–1524). Spanish navigators.

Pioz·zi (pyôt′sē), **Hester Lynch.** "Mrs. Thrale." 1741–1821. English writer.

Pi·ran·del·lo (pîr′ən-dĕl′ō, pē′-rän-dĕl′lō), **Luigi.** 1867–1936. Italian author (Nobel, 1934).

Pi·ra·ne·si (pē′rä-nā′zē), **Giambattista.** 1720–78. Italian architect and artist.

Pire (pîr, pĕr), **Dominique Georges.** 1910–69. Belgian priest (Nobel, 1958).

Pi·sa·no (pē-zä′nō). **1. Nicola** or **Niccolò** (1220–84) and **Giovanni** (1245–1314). Italian sculptors and architects. **2. Andrea.** 1270?–1348. Italian sculptor

Pi·sis·tra·tus (pī-sĭs′trə-təs, pĭ-) or **Pei·sis·tra·tus** (pē-). d. 527 B.C. Athenian tyrant (560–27).

Pis·sar·ro (pĭ-sär′ō, pē-sär-rō′), **Camille.** 1830–1903. French painter.

Pis·ton (pĭs′tən), **Walter Hamor.** 1894–1976. Amer. composer and educator.

Pitch·er (pĭch′ər), **Molly.** Mary McCauley.

Pit·kin (pĭt′kĭn), **Walter Broughton.** 1878–1953. Amer. journalist and educator.

Pit·man (pĭt′mən), Sir **Isaac.** 1813–97. English inventor of shorthand.

Pit·ney (pĭt′nē), **Mahlon.** 1858–1924. Amer. jurist.

Pitt (pĭt). **1. William.** 1st Earl of Chatham. 1708–78. English statesman and orator. **2. William.** 2nd Earl of Chatham. 1759–1806. British prime minister (1783–1801 and 1804–06).

Pi·us (pī′əs). Name of 12 popes, esp.: **1. II.** 1405–64. Reigned 1458–64. **2. V.** 1504–72. Reigned 1566–72. **3. VII.** 1742–1823. Reigned 1800–23. **4. IX.** 1792–1878. Reigned 1846–78. **5. X.** 1835–1914. Reigned 1903–14. **6. XI.** 1857–1939. Reigned 1922–39. **7. XII.** 1876–1958. Reigned 1939–58.

Pi·zar·ro (pĭ-zär′ō, pē-sär′rō), **Francisco.** 1470?–1541. Spanish explorer and conquistador.

Planck (plängk), **Max Karl Ernst Ludwig.** 1858–1947. German physicist (Nobel, 1918).

Plan·tag·e·net (plăn-tăj′ə-nĭt). English ruling dynasty (1154–1485).

Plath (plăth), **Sylvia.** 1932–63. Amer. author.

Pla·to (plā′tō). 427?–347 B.C. Greek philosopher. —**Pla·ton′ic** (plə-tŏn′ĭk) *adj.*

Platt (plăt). **1. Orville Hitchcock.** 1827–1905. Amer. legislator. **2. Thomas Collier.** 1833–1910. Amer. politician.

Plau·tus (plô′təs), **Titus Maccius.** 254?–184 B.C. Roman playwright.

Play·er (plā′ər), **Gary.** b. 1935. South African-born Amer. golfer.

Ple·kha·nov (plĭ-kä′nôf′, -KHä′nəf), **Georgi Valentinovich.** 1857–1918. Russian revolutionary and political philosopher.

Plimp·ton (plĭmp′tən), **George Ames.** b. 1927. Amer. author and editor.

Plim·soll (plĭm′səl, -sôl′), **Samuel.** 1824–98. English politician and philanthropist.

Plin·y (plĭn′ē). **1.** "the Elder." A.D. 23–79. Roman scholar; died observing the eruption of Vesuvius. **2.** "the Younger." A.D. 62–113. Roman consul and author.

Plo·ti·nus (plō-tī′nəs). A.D. 205?–70. Egyptian-born Roman philosopher.

Plu·tarch (plo͞o′tärk′). A.D. 46?–120? Greek biographer and philosopher. —**Plu·tarch′an, Plu·tarch′i·an** *adj.*

Po·ca·hon·tas (pō′kə-hŏn′təs). 1595?–1617. Amer. Indian princess; rescued John Smith.

Pocahontas

Pod·gor·ny (pŏd-gôr′nē), **Nikolai Viktorovich.** 1903–83. Russian statesman.

Poe (pō), **Edgar Allan.** 1809–49. Amer. author.

Edgar Allan Poe

Poin·ca·ré (pwăN-kä-rā′). **1. Jules Henri.** 1854–1912. French mathematician and physicist. **2. Raymond.** 1860–1934. French statesman.

Poin·sett (poin′sĕt′, -sĭt), **Joel Roberts.** 1779–1851. Amer. diplomat.

Poi·tier (pwä′tyā), **Sidney.** b. 1924. Amer. actor and director.

Pole (pōl), **Reginald.** 1500–58. English prelate.

Po·li·tian (pə-lĭsh′ən, pō-). 1454–94. Italian scholar and poet.

Polk (pōk). **1. James Knox.** 1795–1849. 11th U.S. President (1845–49). **2. Leonidas.** 1806–64. Amer. clergyman and Confederate general.

James K. Polk

Pol·lock (pŏl′ək). **1. Oliver.** 1737?–1823. Irish-born Amer. merchant and financier. **2.** Sir **Frederick.** 1845–1937. English jurist and author. **3. Channing.** 1880–1946. Amer. author. **4. Jackson.** 1912–56. Amer. artist.

Po·lo (pō′lō), **Marco.** 1254?–1325? Venetian traveler.

Pol Pot (pŏl pŏt′). b. 1928. Cambodian political leader.

Po·lyb·i·us (pə-lĭb′ē-əs). 205?–125? B.C. Greek historian.

Pol·y·carp (pŏl′ē-kärp′), Saint. A.D. 69?–155? Christian martyr.

Pol·y·cli·tus or **Pol·y·clei·tus** (pŏl′ĭ-klī′təs). 5th cent. B.C. Greek sculptor and architect.

Po·lyc·ra·tes (pə-lĭk′rə-tēz′). 535?–15 B.C. Tyrant of Samos.

Pol·yg·no·tus (pŏl′ĭg-nō′təs). 5th cent. B.C. Greek painter.

Pom·pa·dour (pŏm′pə-dôr′, -dōr′, -do͝or′, pôN-pä-do͝or′), Marquise de. 1721–64. Mistress of Louis XV of France.

Pom·pey (pŏm′pē). "the Great." 106–48 B.C. Roman general and statesman.

Pom·pi·dou (pŏm′pĭ-do͞o′, pôN-pē-do͞o′), **Georges Jean Raymond.** 1911–74. French statesman.

Ponce de Le·ón (pŏns′ də lē′ən, lē-ŏn′, pôn′sĕ dĕ lĕ-ôn′), **Juan.** 1460–1521. Spanish explorer; discovered Florida.

Pon·chi·el·li (pông-kyĕl′lē), **Amilcare.** 1834–86. Italian composer.

Pons (pôNs, pŏnz), **Lily.** 1904–76. French-born Amer. operatic soprano.

Pon·selle (pŏn-sĕl′), **Rosa Melba.** 1897–1981. Amer. operatic soprano.

Pon·ti·ac (pŏn′tē-ăk′). 1720?–69. Amer. Ottawa chief.

Pon·tius Pi·late (pŏn′chəs pī′lət, -shəs, -shē-əs). See **Pilate.**

Pon·top·pi·dan (pŏn-tŏp′ĭ-dän′, -dăn′), **Henrik.** 1857–1943. Danish novelist (Nobel, 1917).

Pool (po͞ol), **Maria Louise.** 1841–98. Amer. author.

Poor (po͝or), **Henry Varnum.** 1812–1905. Amer. historian and economist.

Pope (pōp). **1. Alexander.** 1688–1744. English poet and satirist. **2. John.** 1822–92. Amer. general. **3. Albert Augustus.** 1843–1909. Amer. bicycle manufacturer and popularizer.

Por·son (pôr′sən), **Richard.** 1759–1808. English classical scholar.

Por·ter (pôr′tər). **1. David.** 1780–1843. Amer. naval officer. **2. Noah.** 1811–92. Amer. philosopher and lexicographer. **3. David Dixon.** 1813–91. Amer. naval officer. **4. Sarah.** 1813–1900. Amer. educator. **5. William Sidney.** "O. Henry." 1862–1910. Amer. author. **6. Gene Stratton.** 1863?–1924. Amer. author. **7. Eleanor Hodgman.** 1868–1920. Amer. author ("Pollyanna" stories). **8. Katherine Anne.** 1890–1980. Amer. author. **9. Cole Albert.** 1891?–1964. Amer. composer. **10. Sylvia Field.** b. 1913. Amer. economist and journalist. **11. Rodney Robert.** 1917–85. English biochemist (Nobel, 1972). **12.** Sir **George.** b. 1920. English chemist (Nobel, 1967).

Por·to·lá (pôr-tō-lä′), **Gaspar de.** 1723?–84? Spanish explorer and colonial administrator.

Post (pōst). **1. Christian Frederick.** 1710?–85. German-born Amer. missionary. **2. Charles William.** 1854–1914. Amer. breakfast-food manufacturer. **3. Emily Price.** 1872–1960. Amer. etiquette columnist. **4. Wiley.** 1899–1935. Amer. aviator.

Po·tem·kin (pō-tĕm′kĭn, pə-, pŏ-tyôm′kĭn), **Grigori Aleksandrovich.** 1739–91. Russian army officer and politician.

Po·tok (pō′tŏk′), **Chaim.** b. 1929. Amer. author.

Pot·ter (pŏt′ər). **1. Paul.** 1625–54. Dutch painter. **2. Henry Codman.** 1835–1908. Amer. prelate. **3. Beatrix.** 1866–1943. English author and illustrator.

Pou·lenc (po͞o-läNk′), **Francis.** 1899–1963. French composer.

Pound (pound). **1. Roscoe.** 1870–1964. Amer. botanist and jurist. **2. Ezra Loomis.** 1885–1972. Amer. poet and critic.

Pous·sin (po͞o-săN′), **Nicolas.** 1594–1665. French painter.

Pow·der·ly (pou′dər-lē), **Terence Vincent.** 1849–1924. Amer. labor leader.

Pow·ell (pou′əl). **1. John Wesley.** 1834–1902. Amer. geologist and explorer. **2. Maud.** 1868–1920. Amer. violinist. **3. Cecil Frank.** 1903–69. English physicist (Nobel, 1950). **4. Anthony.** b. 1905. English author. **5. Lewis Franklin, Jr.** b. 1907. Amer. jurist. **6. Adam Clayton, Jr.** 1908–72. Amer. clergyman and politician.

Pow·er (pou′ər), **Tyrone.** 1914–58. Amer. actor.

Pow·ers (pou′ərz), **Hiram.** 1805–73. Amer. sculptor.

Pow·ha·tan (pou′ə-tăn′, pou-hăt′n). 1550?–1618. Amer. Indian chief.

Pow·ys (pō′ĭs, pou′ĭs). Family of English authors, including **John Cowper** (1872–1963), **Theodore Francis** (1875–1953), and **Llewelyn** (1884–1939).

Pra·do Ugar·te·che (prä′*th*ō o͞o′-gär-tĕ′chĕ), **Manuel.** 1889–1967. Peruvian statesman.

Pra·ja·dhi·pok (prə-chä′tĭ-pŏk′, prä-jä′dĭ-pôk′). "Rama VII." 1893–1941. Siamese king (1925–35).

Pratt (prăt). **1. Bela Lyon.** 1867–1917. Amer. sculptor. **2. Edwin John.** 1883–1964. Canadian poet.

Prax·it·e·les (prăk-sĭt′l-ēz′). 400–320 B.C. Greek sculptor.

Preb·le (prĕb′əl), **Edward.** 1761–1807. Amer. naval officer.

Pre·gl (prā′gəl), **Fritz.** 1869–1930. Austrian chemist (Nobel, 1923).

Pre·log (prĕ′lŏg′), **Vladimar.** b. 1906. Yugoslavian-born Swiss chemist (Nobel, 1975).

Prem·in·ger (prĕm′ĭn-jər), **Otto Ludwig.** 1906–86. Austrian-born Amer. producer and director.

Pren·tiss (prĕn′tĭs), **Elizabeth Payson.** 1818–78. Amer. author.

Pres·cott (prĕs′kət, -kŏt′). **1. William.** 1726–95. Amer. Revolutionary commander. **2. Samuel.** 1751–77? Amer. physician and Revolutionary patriot (completed "midnight ride" of Paul Revere). **3. William Hickling.** 1796–1859. Amer. historian.

Pres·ley (prĕs′lē, prĕz′-), **Elvis Aron.** 1935–77. Amer. entertainer.

Pres·ton (prĕs′tən), **Ann.** 1813–72. Amer. pioneer physician and educator.

Pre·to·ri·us (prĭ-tôr′ē-əs, -tōr′-, prä-tō′rē-o͞os′). **1. Andries Wilhelmus Jacobus.** 1799–1853. Dutch South African leader. **2. Marthinus Wessels.** 1819–1901. South African statesman.

Pré·vost d'Ex·iles (prā-vō′ dĕg-zēl′), **Antoine François.** "Abbé Prévost." 1697–1763. French novelist.

Price (prīs). **1. Vincent.** b. 1911. Amer. actor. **2. (Mary) Leontyne.** b. 1927. Amer. operatic soprano.

Pride (prīd), **Thomas.** d. 1658. English Parliamentary commander.

Priest·ley (prēst′lē). **1. Joseph.** 1733–1804. English chemist and clergyman. **2. John Boynton ("J.B.").** 1894–1984. English author.

Pri·go·gine (prĭ-gô′zhən, -gô-zhĕn′), **Ilya.** b. 1917. Russian-born Belgian chemist (Nobel, 1977).

Pri·mo de Ri·ve·ra (prē′mô dĕ rē-vĕ′-rä), **José Antonio.** 1903–36. Spanish fascist politician; executed.

Prince (prĭns), **Harold.** b. 1928. Amer. stage producer.

Pri·or (prī′ər), **Matthew.** 1664–1721. English poet and diplomat.

Pris·cian (prĭsh′ən, -ē-ən). fl. A.D. 500. Latin grammarian.

Pritch·ett (prĭch′ĭt), **Victor Sawdon ("V.S.").** b. 1900. English author and critic.

Pro·clus (prō′kləs, prŏk′ləs). 410?–85. Greek philosopher.

Pro·co·pi·us (prə-kō′pē-əs, prō-). 6th cent. A.D. Byzantine historian.

Pro·kho·rov (prō′KHə-rôf′), **Aleksander Mikailovich.** b. 1916. Russian physicist (Nobel, 1964).

Pro·kof·iev (prə-kôf′yəf, -yĕf′, prō-kō′fē-əf, -ĕf′, prə-), **Sergei Sergeevich.** 1891–1953. Russian composer.

Pro·per·tius (prō-pûr′shəs, -shē-əs), **Sextus.** 50?–15? B.C. Roman elegiac poet.

Pro·tag·o·ras (prō-tăg′ər-əs). 5th cent. B.C. Greek philosopher. —**Pro·tag′o·re′an** *adj.*

Prou·dhon (pro͞o-dôN′), **Pierre Joseph.** 1809–65. French utopian socialist.

Proust (pro͞ost), **Marcel.** 1871–1922. French author. —**Proust′i·an** *adj.*

Prynne (prĭn), **William.** 1600–69. English statesman and pamphleteer.
Przhe·val·ski (pûr'zhĕ-väl'skē, pshə'-väl'-, shə'-), **Nikolai Mikhailovoch.** 1839–88. Russian explorer.
Ptol·e·my (tŏl'ə-mē). **1.** Name of 14 kings of Egypt, esp. **I,** 367?–283 B.C., reigned 305–285 B.C. **2.** 2nd cent. A.D. Greek astronomer and geographer. —**Ptol'e·ma'ic** (tŏl'ə-mā'ĭk) *adj.*
Puc·ci (po͞o'chē), **Emilio.** Marchese di Barsento. b. 1914. Italian fashion designer.
Puc·ci·ni (po͞o-chē'nē), **Giacomo.** 1858–1924. Italian opera composer.
Pu·las·ki (po͞o-lăs'kē, pə-), **Casimir** or **Kazimierz.** 1748?–79. Polish patriot and general in America.
Pu·lit·zer (po͝ol'ĭt-sər, pyo͞o'lĭt-), **Joseph.** 1847–1911. Hungarian-born Amer. journalist and publisher.

Joseph Pulitzer

Pull·man (po͝ol'mən), **George Mortimer.** 1831–97. Amer. industrialist and inventor (railroad sleeping cars).
Pum·pel·ly (pŭm-pĕl'ē) **Raphael.** 1837–1923. Amer. geologist and explorer.
Pu·pin (pyo͞o-pēn', po͞o-, pyo͞o'pĭn), **Michael Idvorsky.** 1858–1935. Yugoslavian-born Amer. physicist and inventor.
Pur·cell. 1. (pûr'səl), **Henry.** 1658?–95. English composer. **2.** (pûr-sĕl'), **Edward Mills.** b. 1912. Amer. physicist (Nobel, 1952).
Pur·chas (pûr'chəs), **Samuel.** 1575?–1626. English clergyman and compiler.
Pur·kin·je (pər-kĭn'jē, po͝or'kən-yā'), **Johannes Evangelista.** 1787?–1869. Czechoslovakian physiologist and poet.
Pu·sey (pyo͞o'zē), **Edward Bouverie.** 1800–82. English theologian.
Push·kin (po͝osh'kĭn, po͞osh'), **Aleksander Sergeevich.** 1799–1837. Russian author.
Put·nam (pŭt'nəm). **1. Israel.** 1718–90. Amer. general. **2. Rufus.** 1738–1824. Amer. Revolutionary officer and Western pioneer.
Pu·vis de Cha·vannes (pü-vē' də shä-vän', -vēs', pyo͞o-), **Pierre.** 1824–98. French artist.
Pye (pī), **Henry James.** 1745–1813. English poet.
Pyle (pīl). **1. Howard.** 1853–1911. Amer. artist and author. **2. Ernest Taylor ("Ernie").** 1900–45. Amer. journalist.
Pym (pĭm), **John.** 1584–1643. English Parliamentary leader.
Py·thag·o·ras (pĭ-thăg'ər-əs). d. 497 B.C. Greek philosopher and mathematician. —**Py·thag'o·re'an** *adj.*

Q

Qad·da·fi (kə-dä'fē), **Muammar.** b. 1943. Libyan political leader.
Qi (chē). Name of 2 Chinese dynasties (479–502, 550–77).
Qiang·long (chyĕn'lo͞ong'). 1711–99. Chinese emperor (1736–96).
Qin (chĭn). Chinese dynasty (221–07 B.C.).
Qing (chĭng). Chinese dynasty (1644–1911).
Qua·dros (kwä'dro͞osh), **Janio de Silva.** b. 1917. Brazilian statesman.
Quan·trill (kwŏn'trĭl'), **William Clarke.** 1837–65. Amer. Confederate guerrilla leader.
Quarles (kwärlz, kwôrlz), **Francis.** 1592–1644. English poet.
Qua·si·mo·do (kwä'zē-mō'dō), **Salvatore.** 1901–68. Italian author (Nobel, 1959).
Quay (kwā), **Matthew Stanley.** 1833–1904. Amer. politician.
Queen (kwēn), **Ellery.** Frederic Dannay and Manfred B. Lee.
Queens·ber·ry (kwēnz'bĕr'ē, -bə-rē), 8th Marquis of. Sir John Sholto Douglas.
Que·ler (kwĕl'ər), **Eve.** b. 1936. Amer. conductor.
Ques·nay (kĕ-nā'), **François.** 1694–1774. French physician and political economist.
Que·zon y Mo·li·na (kĕ-sôn' ē mô-lē'nä), **Manuel Luis.** 1878–1944. Philippine statesman.
Quid·de (kvĭd'ə, kfĭd'ə), **Ludwig.** 1858–1941. German politician and pacifist (Nobel, 1927).
Quil·ler-Couch (kwĭl'ər-ko͞och'), Sir **Arthur Thomas.** 1863–1944. English author, editor, and educator.
Quin·cy (kwĭn'zē, -sē). **1. Josiah.** 1744–75. Amer. Revolutionary patriot. **2. Josiah.** 1772–1864. Amer. politician, educator, and historian.
Quin·te·ro (kēn-tĕ'rô), **Seraffin Alvarez** (1871–1938) and **Joaquin Alvarez** (1873–1944). Spanish dramatists.
Quin·til·ian (kwĭn-tĭl'yən, -ē-ən). A.D. 35?–95? Roman rhetorician.
Qui·ri·no (kē-rē'nô), **Elpidio.** 1890?–1956. Philippine statesman.
Quis·ling (kwĭz'lĭng), **Vidkun Abraham Lauritz.** 1887–1945. Norwegian army officer and political leader; executed for treason.

R

Ra·be·lais (răb'ə-lā', răb'ə-lā', rä-blĕ'), **François.** 1494?–1553. French humanist. —**Rab'e·lai'se·an** (-zē-ən, -zhən) *adj.*
Ra·bi (rä'bē), **Isidor Isaac.** b. 1898. Austrian-born Amer. physicist (Nobel, 1944).
Ra·bin (rä-bēn'), **Itzhak** or **Yitzhak.** b. 1922. Israeli military and political leader.
Ra·chel (rä-shĕl'), **Élisa Félix.** 1820–58. Swiss-born French actress.
Rach·ma·ni·noff (räk-mä'nə-nôf'), **Sergei Vasilievich.** 1873–1943. Russian-born composer and pianist.

Sergei Rachmaninoff

Ra·cine (rä-sēn'), **Jean Baptiste.** 1639–99. French playwright.
Rack·ham (răk'əm), **Arthur.** 1867–1939. English artist.
Rad·cliffe (răd'klĭf'), **Ann Ward.** 1764–1823. English novelist.
Rad·is·son (rä-dē-sôN'), **Pierre Esprit.** 1636?–1710? French explorer.
Rae (rā), **John.** 1813–93. English Arctic explorer.
Rae·burn (rā'bərn), Sir **Henry.** 1756–1823. Scottish portrait painter.
Rae·der (rā'dər), **Erich.** 1876–1960. German admiral.
Rae·mae·kers (rä'mä-kərz, -kərs), **Louis.** 1869–1956. Dutch political cartoonist.
Raf·fles (răf'əlz), Sir **Thomas.** 1781–1826. English colonial administrator.
Ra·fi·nesque (rä-fē-nĕsk') also **Ra·fi·nesque-Schmaltz** (-shmälts), **Constantine Samuel.** 1783–1840. French-Amer. naturalist.
Raft (răft), **George.** 1895–1980. Amer. actor.
Rag·lan (răg'lən), 1st Baron. Fitzroy James Henry Somerset. 1788–1855. English field marshal.
Rai·mon·di (rī-mōn'dē, -mŏn'-), **Marcantonio.** 1475?–1534? Italian engraver.
Rai·ney (rā'nē). **1. Henry Thomas.** 1860–1934. Amer. legislator. **2. Gertrude Malissa Nix Pridgett ("Ma").** 1886–1939. Amer. blues singer.
Rai·nier III (rä-nîr', rĕ-, rə-, rē-nyā'). b. 1923. Prince of Monaco (since 1949).
Rains (rānz), **Claude.** 1899–1967. Amer. actor.
Rain·wat·er (rān'wô'tər, -wŏt'ər), **L(eo) James.** 1917–86. Amer. physicist (Nobel, 1975).
Ra·ja·go·pa·la·cha·ria (rä'jə-gō-pä'-lä-chär'yä), **Chakravarti.** 1879–1972. Indian politician.
Ra·leigh or **Ra·legh** (rô'lē, rŏl'ē), Sir **Walter.** 1552?–1618. English navigator, courtier, writer, and colonizer.

Walter Raleigh

Ra·man (rä'mən), Sir **Chandrasekhara.** 1888–1970. Indian physicist (Nobel, 1930).
Ra·meau (rä-mō'), **Jean Philippe.** 1683–1764. French composer.
Ra·meé (rə-mā'), **Marie Louise de la.** "Ouida." 1839–1908. English author.
Ram·e·ses (răm'ĭ-sēz') or **Ram·ses** (răm'sēz'). Name of 12 kings of Egypt, esp.: **1. II.** Ruled 1292–25 B.C. **2. III.** Ruled 1198–67 B.C.
Ram·say (răm'zē). **1. Allan.** 1686–1758. Scottish poet. **2.** Sir **William.** 1852–1916. British chemist (Nobel, 1904).
Ram·sey (răm'zē), **Arthur Michael.** b. 1904. English prelate.
Rand (rănd). **1. Sally.** 1904–79. Amer. entertainer. **2. Ayn.** 1905–82. Russian-born Amer. author.
Rand·all (răn'dl), **Samuel Jackson.** 1828–90. Amer. legislator.
Ran·dolph (răn'dŏlf'). **1. Edmund Jennings.** 1753–1813. Amer. Revolutionary leader and public official. **2. John.** "Randolph of Roanoke." 1773–1833. Amer. politician and orator.
Ran·jit Singh (rŭn'jĭt sĭng'). "Lion of the Punjab." 1780–1839. Founder of the Sikh kingdom.
Ran·ke (răng'kə), **Leopold von.** 1795–1886. German historian.
Ran·kin (răng'kĭn), **Jeannette.** 1880–1973. Amer. feminist and legislator.
Ran·som (răn'səm), **John Crowe.** 1888–1974. Amer. educator, author, and editor.
Raph·a·el (răf'ē-əl, rā'fē-, rä'-, rä'-fē-ĕl'). 1483–1520. Italian painter and architect.
Rapp (răp, räp), **George.** 1757–1847. German-born Amer. separatist colonizer.
Rask (räsk, răsk), **Rasmus Christian.** 1787–1832. Danish comparative philologist and Orientalist.
Ras·mus·sen (räs'mo͞os-ən), **Knud Johan Victor.** 1879–1933. Danish anthologist and Arctic explorer.
Ras·pu·tin (răs-pyo͞o'tĭn, räs-po͞o'tĭn, -tyĭn), **Grigori Efimovich.** 1871?–1916. Russian monk influential in czarist court; assassinated.

Grigori Rasputin

Rath·bone (răth'bōn'), **Basil.** 1892–1967. South-African-born English actor.
Rath·er (ră*th*'ər), **Dan.** b. 1931. Amer. broadcast journalist.
Rat·ti·gan (răt'ĭ-gən), **Terence.** 1911–78. English playwright.
Rausch·en·berg (rou'shən-bûrg'), **Robert.** b. 1925. Amer. painter.
Rau·schen·busch (rou'shən-bo͝osh'), **Walter.** 1861–1918. Amer. theologian and educator.
Rausch·ning (roush'nĭng), **Hermann.** b. 1887. German-born Amer. author.
Ra·vel (rə-vĕl', rä-), **Maurice Joseph.** 1875–1937. French composer.
Raw·lings (rô'lĭngz), **Marjorie Kinnan.** 1896–1953. Amer. author (*The Yearling*).
Raw·lin·son (rô'lĭn-sən). **1.** Sir **Henry Creswicke.** 1810–95. English diplomat and Assyrian scholar. **2. George.** 1812–1902. English historian and Orientalist.
Ray (rā). **1. John.** 1627?–1705. English pioneer naturalist. **2. Charlotte E.** 1850–1911. Amer. lawyer. **3. Man.** 1890–1976. Amer. surrealist painter and photographer. **4. Dixy Lee.** b. 1914. Amer. public official.
Ray·burn (rā'bûrn'), **Samuel Taliaferro.** 1882–1961. Amer. legislator.
Ray·leigh (rā'lē), 3rd Baron. John William Strutt. 1842–1919. English physicist (Nobel, 1904).
Ray·mond (rā'mənd), **Henry Jarvis.** 1820–69. Amer. journalist and politician.
Read (rēd). **1. George.** 1733–98. Amer. Revolutionary leader, politician, and jurist. **2. Thomas Buchanan.** 1822–72. Amer. poet and painter. **3. Opie.** 1852–1939. Amer. author and editor. **4.** Sir **Herbert Edward.** 1893–1968. English art curator, poet, editor, and critic.
Reade (rēd), **Charles.** 1814–84. English author.
Read·ing (rĕd'ĭng), 1st Marquis of. Rufus Daniel Isaacs. 1860–1935. English politician, diplomat, and colonial administrator.
Rea·gan (rā'gən), **Ronald Wilson.** b. 1911. Actor and 40th U.S. President (since 1980).

Ronald Reagan

Ré·au·mur (rā′ə-myo͝or′, -ō-, rā-ō-mür′), **René Antoine Ferchault de.** 1683–1757. French physicist.

Ré·ca·mi·er (rā-kä-myā′), **Jeanne Françoise Julie Adélaïde Bernard.** 1777–1849. French socialite.

Red Cloud (rĕd′ kloud′), 1822–1909. Amer. Oglala Sioux Indian leader.

Red·grave (rĕd′grāv′). Family of English actors, including Sir **Michael** (1908–85), **Vanessa** (b. 1937), and **Lynn** (b. 1943).

Red Jack·et (jăk′ĭt). 1756?–1830. Amer. Seneca Indian leader.

Red·mond (rĕd′mənd), **John Edward.** 1851?–1918. Irish nationalist leader.

Re·don (rə-dôɴ′), **Odilon.** 1840–1916. French artist.

Reed (rēd). **1. Thomas Brackett.** 1839–1902. Amer. legislator. **2. Walter.** 1851–1902. Amer. physician and army surgeon. **3. Myrtle.** 1874–1911. Amer. novelist. **4. Stanley Forman.** 1884–1980. Amer. jurist. **5. John.** 1887–1920. Amer. journalist; buried in the Kremlin.

Reese (rēs). **1. Lizette Woodworth.** 1856–1935. Amer. lyric poet and educator. **2. Harold ("Pee Wee").** b. 1919. Amer. baseball player.

Reeve (rēv), **Tapping.** 1744–1823. Amer. jurist and educator.

Re·gi·o·mon·ta·nus (rē′jē-ō-mŏn-tā′nəs, -tä′, -tăn-əs, rĕj′ē-). Johann Müller.

Reg·u·lus (rĕg′yə-ləs), **Marcus Atilius.** d. c. 250 B.C. Roman general.

Re·han (rē′ən), **Ada.** 1860–1916. Irish-born Amer. actress.

Rehn·quist (rĕn′kwĭst′), **William Hubbs.** b. 1924. Amer. jurist.

Reich·stein (rīk′stīn′, -shtīn′, rīKH′-shtīn′), **Tadeus.** b. 1897. Polish-born Swiss chemist (Nobel, 1950).

Reid (rēd). **1. Thomas.** 1710–96. Scottish philosopher. **2. Whitelaw.** 1837–1912. Amer. editor and diplomat. **3. Ogden Mills.** 1882–1947. Amer. editor and publisher.

Rei·nach (rĕ-näk′), **Salomon.** 1858–1932. French archaeologist.

Rei·ner (rī′nər), **Fritz.** 1888–1963. Hungarian-born Amer. conductor.

Rein·hardt (rīn′härt′), **Max.** 1873–1943. German theatrical director and manager.

Re·marque (rə-märk′), **Erich Maria.** 1898–1970. German-born Amer. novelist.

Rem·brandt van Rijn or **van Ryn** (rĕm′brănt′ vän rīn′, -bränt′). 1606–69. Dutch painter.

Rembrandt

Rem·ing·ton (rĕm′ĭng-tən). **1. Eliphalet.** 1793–1861. Amer. firearms manufacturer. **2. Frederic.** 1861–1909. Amer. Western painter, sculptor, and author.

Rem·sen (rĕm′sən), **Ira.** 1846–1927. Amer. organic chemist.

Re·nan (rə-näɴ′), **Joseph Ernest.** 1823–92. French philologist, philosopher, and historian.

Re·nault (rə-nō′), **Jean Louis.** 1843–1918. French jurist (Nobel, 1907).

Re·ni (rā′nē), **Guido.** 1575–1642. Italian painter.

Ren·ner (rĕn′ər), **Karl.** 1870–1950. Austrian political leader.

Ren·oir (rĕn′wär′, rə-nwär′). **1. Pierre Auguste.** 1841–1919. French painter. **2. Jean.** 1894–1979. French filmmaker.

Ren·wick (rĕn′wĭk), **James.** 1818–95. Amer. architect.

Rep·plier (rĕp′lîr′), **Agnes.** 1855–1950. Amer. essayist.

Re·spi·ghi (rĕ-spē′gē), **Ottorino.** 1879–1936. Italian composer.

Res·ton (rĕs′tən), **James Barrett ("Scotty").** b. 1909. Scottish-born Amer. journalist.

Retz (rĕts), Cardinal de. Jean François Paul de Gondi. 1614–79. French politician and man of letters.

Reuch·lin (roik′lən, roiKH′lēn, roiKH-lēn′), **Johann.** 1455–1522. German humanist.

Reu·ter (roi′tər), Baron **Paul Julius von.** 1816–99. German-born English news-agency founder.

Reu·ter·dahl (roi′tər-däl′, ro͞o′-), **Henry.** 1871–1925. Swedish-born Amer. marine painter.

Reu·ther (ro͞o′thər), **Walter Philip.** 1907–70. Amer. labor leader.

Re·vere (rĭ-vîr′), **Paul.** 1735–1818. Amer. silversmith, engraver, and Revolutionary patriot.

Paul Revere

Rev·son (rĕv′sən), **Charles.** 1906–75. Amer. cosmetics tycoon.

Rex·roth (rĕks′rôth′), **Kenneth.** 1905–82. Amer. painter and author.

Rey·mont (rā′mônt), **Wladyslaw Stanislaw.** 1867–1925. Polish author (Nobel, 1924).

Rey·naud (rā-nō′), **Paul.** 1878–1966. French statesman.

Reyn·olds (rĕn′əldz), Sir **Joshua.** 1723–92. English portrait painter.

Rhee (rē), **Syngman.** 1875–1965. Korean political leader.

Rhett (rĕt), **Robert Barnwell.** 1800–76. Amer. legislator and secessionist.

Rhine (rīn), **Joseph Banks.** b. 1895. Amer. psychologist.

Rhodes (rōdz). **1. James Ford.** 1848–1927. Amer. historian. **2. Cecil John.** 1853–1902. English financier and colonizer.

Rhond·da (rŏn′də, *-thə*), Viscount. David Alfred Thomas. 1856–1918. Welsh coal magnate and politician.

Rib·ben·trop (rĭb′ən-trŏp, -trŏp, -trôp), **Joachim von.** 1893–1946. German Nazi diplomat; executed.

Ri·be·ra (rē-bĕ′rä), **Jusepe** or **José de.** "Spagnoletta." 1588–1656? Spanish painter.

Ri·car·do (rĭ-kär′dō), **David.** 1772–1823. English economist.

Rice (rīs). **1. Thomas Dartmouth.** 1808–60. Amer. minstrel entertainer. **2. Dan.** 1823–1900. Amer. circus clown. **3. Alice Caldwell Hegan.** 1870–1942. Amer. author. **4. Grantland.** 1880–1954. Amer. journalist. **5. Elmer Leopold.** 1892–1967. Amer. author.

Rich·ard (rĭch′ərd). Name of 3 English kings: **1. I.** "Coeur de Lion" or "the Lion-Hearted." 1157–99. Ruled 1189–99. **2. II.** 1367–1400. Ruled 1377–99. **3. III.** 1452–85. Ruled 1483–85.

Rich·ards (rĭch′ərdz). **1. Ellen Henrietta Swallow.** 1842–1911. Amer. chemist. **2. Laura Elizabeth Howe.** 1850–1943. Amer. author. **3. Theodore William.** 1868–1928. Amer. chemist (Nobel, 1914). **4. Ivor Armstrong ("I.A.").** 1893–1979. English literary critic. **5. Dickinson Woodruff.** 1895–1973. Amer. physician (Nobel, 1956).

Rich·ard·son (rĭch′ərd-sən). **1. Samuel.** 1689–1761. English author. **2. Henry Hobson.** 1838–86. Amer. architect. **3.** Sir **Owen Willans.** 1879–1959. English physicist (Nobel, 1928). **4.** Sir **Ralph David.** 1902–83. English actor.

Ri·che·lieu (rĭsh′ə-lo͞o′, rē-shə-lyœ′), Duc de. Armand Jean du Plessis. 1585–1642. French prelate and political leader.

Ri·chet (rĭ-shā′, rē-shĕ′), **Charles Robert.** 1850–1935. French physiologist (Nobel, 1913).

Rich·ler (rĭch′lər), **Mordecai.** b. 1928. Canadian author.

Rich·mond (rĭch′mənd), **Mary Ellen.** 1861–1928. Amer. pioneer social worker.

Rich·ter (rĭk′tər). **1.** (*also* rĭKH′-), **Jean Paul Friedrich.** 1763–1825. German satirist. **2. Charles Francis.** 1900–85. Amer. seismologist. **3. Burton.** b. 1931. Amer. physicist (Nobel, 1976).

Rick·ard (rĭk′ərd), **George Lewis ("Tex").** 1871–1929. Amer. boxing promoter.

Rick·en·back·er (rĭk′ĭn-băk′ər), **Edward Vernon ("Eddie").** 1890–1973. Amer. aviator, World War I ace, and businessman.

Rick·ert (rĭk′ərt), **Edith.** 1871–1938. Amer. educator and author.

Rick·ey (rĭk′ē), **Branch Wesley.** 1881–1965. Amer. baseball executive.

Rick·o·ver (rĭk′ō′vər), **Hyman George.** 1900–86. Amer. admiral.

Rid·dle (rĭd′l), **Nelson.** b. 1921. Amer. composer, conductor, and arranger.

Ridg·way (rĭj′wā), **Matthew Bunker.** b. 1895. Amer. army officer.

Rid·ley (rĭd′lē), **Nicholas.** 1500?–55. English prelate and martyr.

Ri·el (rē-ĕl′), **Louis.** 1844–85. French-Canadian rebel; executed.

Rie·mann (rē′män′, -mən), **Georg Friedrich Bernhard.** 1826–66. German mathematician and educator.

Ri·en·zi (rē-ĕn′zē) or **Ri·en·zo** (-zō), **Cola di.** 1313?–54. Italian revolutionary leader.

Ries·man (rēs′mən), **David, Jr.** b. 1909. Amer. sociologist.

Riis (rēs), **Jacob August.** 1849–1914. Danish-born Amer. journalist and reformer.

Ri·ley (rī′lē), **James Whitcomb.** 1849–1916. Amer. poet.

Ril·ke (rĭl′kə), **Rainer Maria.** 1875–1926. German-Austrian lyric poet.

Rim·baud (răm-bō′, răɴ-), **Jean Nicholas Arthur.** 1854–91. French poet.

Rim·i·ni (rĭm′ə-nē, rē′mē-), **Francesca da.** See **Francesca da Rimini.**

Rim·mer (rĭm′ər), **William.** 1816–79. English-born Amer. artist.

Rim·ski-Kor·sa·kov or **Rim·sky-Kor·sa·kov** (rĭm′skē-kôr′sə-kôf′), **Nikolai Andreyevich.** 1844–1908. Russian composer.

Rin·cón (rĭng-kôn′), **Antonio del.** 1446–1500. Spanish painter.

Rine·hart (rīn′härt′), **Mary Roberts.** 1876–1958. Amer. author.

Ring·ling (rĭng′lĭng), **Charles.** 1863–1926. Amer. circus owner.

Rip·ley (rĭp′lē). **1. George.** 1802–80. Amer. minister, scholar, and literary critic. **2. Robert LeRoy.** 1893–1949. Amer. cartoonist ("Ripley's Believe It or Not").

Rit·chard (rĭ-chärd′), **Cyril.** 1898–1977. Australian-born actor and director.

Rit·ten·house (rĭt′n-hous′). **1. Davis.** 1732–96. Amer. astronomer, mathematician, and public official. **2. Jessie Belle.** 1869–1948. Amer. poet, anthologist, and critic.

Rit·ter (rĭt′ər), **Woodward Maurice ("Tex").** 1905–73. Amer. singer.

Ri·ve·ra (rē-vĕ′rä), **Diego.** 1886–1957. Mexican artist.

Rivera y Or·ba·ne·ja (ē ôr′bä-nĕ′hä), **Miguel Primo de.** Marqués de Estella. 1870–1930. Spanish military and political leader.

Riv·ers (rĭv′ərz), **Larry.** b. 1923. Amer. artist.

Ri·zal (rē-säl′), **José.** 1861–96. Philippine national leader.

Ri·za Shah Pah·la·vi (rĭ-zä′ shä′ pä-lä-vē′, păl′ə-vē). See **Pahlevi.**

Riz·zio (rĭt′sē-ō′, rĕt′tsē-ō′), **David.** 1533?–66. Italian musician and confidant of Mary Queen of Scots.

Robbe-Gril·let (rôb-grē-yĕ′), **Alain.** b. 1922. French author, filmmaker, and agronomist.

Rob·bins (rŏb′ĭnz). **1. Harold.** b. 1916. Amer. author. **2. Frederick Chapman.** b. 1916. Amer. microbiologist (Nobel, 1954). **3. Jerome.** b. 1918. Amer. dancer and choreographer.

Rob·ert (rŏb′ərt). **1. I.** "the Devil." d. 1035. Duke of Normandy (1028–35). **2. I.** "Robert Bruce" or "the Bruce." 1274–1329. Scottish king (1306–29). **3. Henry Martyn.** 1837–1923. Amer. army officer and parliamentary authority ("Robert's Rules of Order").

Rob·erts (rŏb′ərts). **1.** Sir **Charles George Douglas.** 1860–1943. Canadian author. **2. Owen Josephus.** 1875–1955. Amer. jurist. **3. Kenneth.** 1885–1957. Amer. author. **4. Elizabeth Madox.** 1886–1941. Amer. author. **5. Oral.** b. 1918. Amer. evangelist.

Rob·ert·son (rŏb′ərt-sən), **William.** 1721–93. Scottish historian.

Robe·son (rōb′sən), **Paul Bustill.** 1898–1976. Amer. singer and actor.

Paul Robeson

Robes·pierre (rōbz′pîr, -pē-âr′, rô-bĕs-pyĕr′), **Maximilien François Marie Isidore de.** 1758–94. French revolutionary; guillotined.

Rob·in·son (rŏb′ĭn-sən). **1. Therese Albertine Louise von Jakob.** 1797–1870. German author. **2. George Frederick Samuel.** 1827–1909. English politician and colonial administrator. **3. James Harvey.** 1863–1936. Amer. historian. **4. Edwin Arlington.** 1869–1935. Amer. poet. **5.** Sir **Robert.** 1886–1975. English chemist (Nobel, 1947). **6. (Esmé Stuart) Lennox.** 1886–1958. Irish author and theatrical manager. **7. Edward G.** 1893–1973. Amer. actor. **8. John Roosevelt ("Jackie").** 1919–72. Amer. baseball player. **9. Ray ("Sugar Ray").** b. 1920. Amer. prizefighter.

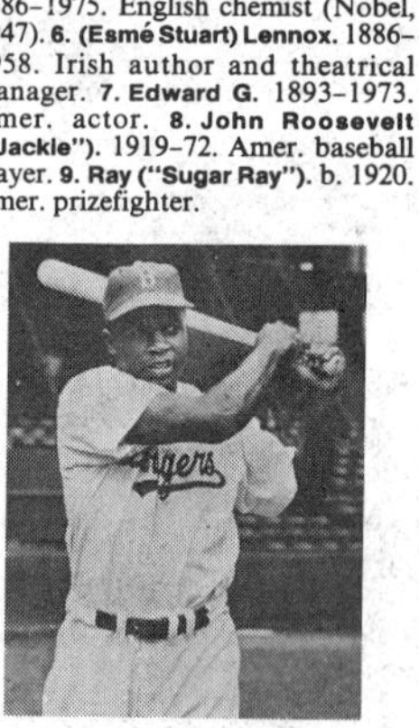

Jackie Robinson

Rob·son (rŏb′sən), **May.** 1858–1942. Amer. actress.

Ro·cham·beau (rō′shăm′bō′, rô-shäɴ-bō′), **Comte de.** Jean Baptiste Donatien de Vimeure. 1725–1807. French army officer.

Rock·e·fel·ler (rŏk′ə-fĕl′ər). Amer. family, including: **1. John Davison.** 1839–1937. Industrialist and philanthropist. **2. John Davison, Jr.** 1874–1960. Philanthropist. **3. Abby Greene Aldrich.** 1874–1948. Philanthropist and art patron. **4. John Davison III.** 1906–78. Philanthropist. **5. Nelson Aldrich.** 1908–79. U.S. Vice President (1974–77). **6. Laurance Spelman.** b. 1910. Conservationist. **7. Winthrop.**

1912–73. Investment manager and politician. **8. David.** b. 1915. Banker.

Rock·hill (rŏk'hĭl'). **William Woodville.** 1854–1914. Amer. author and diplomat.

Rock·ing·ham (rŏk'ĭng-əm), 2nd Marquis of. Charles Watson-Wentworth. 1730–82. English prime minister (1765–66, 1782).

Rock·ne (rŏk'nē), **Knute Kenneth.** 1888–1931. Norwegian-born Amer. football coach.

Rock·well (rŏk'wĕl'), **Norman.** 1894–1978. Amer. illustrator.

Norman Rockwell

Ro·de (rō'*th*ə), **Helge.** 1870–1937. Danish author.

Rod·gers (rŏj'ərz), **1. John.** 1773–1838. Amer. naval officer. **2. Richard.** 1902–79. Amer. composer.

Ro·din (rō-dăn', -dăN'), **François Auguste René.** 1840–1917. French sculptor.

Rod·ney (rŏd'nē), **George Brydges.** 1st Baron Rodney. 1719–92. English naval officer.

Ro·dzin·ski (rō-jĭn'skē, rə-), **Artur.** 1894–1958. Yugoslavian-born Amer. conductor.

Roeb·ling (rō'blĭng), **John Augustus** (German-born, 1806–69) and **Washington Augustus** (1837–1926). Amer. engineers; built Brooklyn Bridge.

Roent·gen (rĕnt'gən, -jən, rŭnt'-, rĕn'chən, rŭn'-) or **Rönt·gen** (rœnt'gən), **Wilhem Konrad.** 1845–1923. German physicist (Nobel, 1901).

Roe·rich (rŭr'ĭk, rœ'rĭKH), **Nicholas Konstantin.** 1874–1947. Russian-born painter and archaeologist.

Roeth·ke (rĕt'kē, rĕth'-), **Theodore.** 1908–63. Amer. poet.

Ro·gers (rŏj'ərz). **1. Robert.** 1731–95. Amer. soldier and frontiersman. **2. Samuel.** 1763–1855. English poet. **3. John.** 1829–1904. Amer. sculptor. **4. Harriet Burbank.** 1834–1919. Amer. educator of the deaf. **5. Henry Huttleston** or **Huddleston.** 1840–1909. Amer. business executive. **6. Bruce.** 1870–1957. Amer. book designer and typographer. **7. William Penn Adair ("Will").** 1879–1935. Amer. author and actor. **8. Ginger.** b. 1911. Amer. actress. **9. Roy.** b. 1912. Amer. singer and actor.

Ro·get (rō-zhā', rō'zhā'), **Peter Mark.** 1779–1869. English physician, scholar, and author (*Roget's Thesaurus*).

Ro·kos·sov·ski (rŏ'kŏ-sôf'skē), **Konstantin.** 1896–1968. Russian-Polish army officer and politician.

Rolfe (rŏlf), **John.** 1585–1622. English colonist in America.

Rol·land (rô-läN'), **Romain.** 1866–1944. French author (Nobel, 1915).

Rol·lo (rŏl'ō) or **Rolf** (rŏlf) or **Hrolf** (rŏlf, hrŏlf). 860?–931? Norse chieftain and 1st duke of Normandy.

Röl·vaag (rŏl'väg'), **Ole Edvart.** 1876–1931. Norwegian-born Amer. author.

Ro·mains (rô-măN'), **Jules.** 1885–1972. French author.

Ro·ma·no (rō-mä'nō), **Giulio.** 1499?–1546. Italian painter.

Ro·ma·noff (rō'mə-nôf), **Michael.** "Prince Mike." 1892?–1971. Lithuanian-born Amer. impostor and businessman.

Ro·ma·nov also **Ro·ma·noff** (rō-măn'əf, rō'mə-nôf', -nŏf'). Russian ruling dynasty (1613–1917).

Rom·bau·er (rŏm'bou'ər), **Irma von Starkloff.** 1877–1962. Amer. cookery expert (*Joy of Cooking*).

Rom·berg (rŏm'bərg), **Sigmund.** 1887–1951. Hungarian-born Amer. composer.

Rome (rōm), **Harold.** b. 1908. Amer. composer.

Rom·mel (rŏm'əl, rŭm'-, rôm'-), **Erwin.** 1891–1944. German general.

Rom·ney (rŏm'nē). **1. George.** 1734–1802. English painter. **2. George Wilcken.** b. 1907. Amer. businessman and public official.

Ro·mu·lo (rŏm'yŏŏ-lō', rō'mŏŏ-lō'), **Carlos Pena.** 1899–1985. Filipino soldier, educator, and diplomat.

Ron·sard (rôN-sär'), **Pierre de.** 1524–85. French poet.

Rönt·gen (rœnt'gən). Variant of **Roentgen.**

Roo·ney (rŏŏ'nē), **Mickey.** b. 1920. Amer. actor.

Roo·se·velt (rō'zə-vĕlt', rōz'vĕlt', -vəlt, rŏŏ'-). **1. Theodore.** 1858–1919. 26th U.S. President (1901–09; Nobel, 1906), soldier, and author. **2. Franklin Delano ("FDR").** 1882–1945. 32nd U.S. President (1933–45). **3. (Anna) Eleanor.** 1884–1962. Amer. diplomat, author, political figure, and wife of Franklin Delano Roosevelt.

Theodore Roosevelt

Franklin D. Roosevelt

Eleanor Roosevelt

Root (rŏŏt). **1. Elihu.** 1845–1937. Amer. lawyer and public official (Nobel, 1912). **2. John Wellborn.** 1850–91. Amer. architect.

Ro·rem (rôr'əm, rōr'-), **Ned.** b. 1923. Amer. composer.

Ro·sa (rō'zə, -zä), **Salvator.** 1615–73. Italian painter.

Rose (rōz), **Billy.** 1899–1966. Amer. showman.

Rose·ber·y (rōz'bĕr'ē, -bə-rē), 5th Earl of. Archibald Philip Primrose. 1847–1929. British prime minister (1894–95).

Rose·crans (rōz'krănz'), **William Starke.** 1819–98. Amer. Union general.

Ro·sen·bach (rō'zĭn-băk'), **Abraham Simon Wolf.** 1876–1952. Amer. scholar and bibliophile.

Ro·sen·berg (rō'zĭn-bûrg', -bĕrg', -bĕrk'). **1. Alfred.** 1893–1946. German politician. **2. Anna Marie.** 1902–83. Amer. public official. **3. Ethel** (1915–53) and **Julius** (1918–53). Amer. spies; executed.

Ro·sen·wald (rō'zĭn-wôld'), **Julius.** 1862–1932. Amer. businessman and philanthropist.

Ross (rôs). **1. Betsy Griscom.** 1752–1836. Amer. patriot and legendary maker of 1st American flag. **2.** Sir **John.** 1777–1856. English naval officer and Arctic explorer. **3. John.** 1790–1866. Amer. Cherokee Indian leader. **4.** Sir **James Clark.** 1800–62. English navigator and polar explorer. **5.** Sir **Ronald.** 1857–1932. English physician (Nobel, 1902). **6. Nellie Tayloe.** 1876?–1977. Amer. politician. **7. Harold Wallace.** 1892–1951. Amer. publisher and editor.

Ros·sel·li·ni (rō'sə-lē'nē, rŏs'ə-, rôs'-sĕl-lē'nē), **Roberto.** 1906–77. Italian filmmaker.

Ros·set·ti (rō-zĕt'ē), **Dante Gabriel** (1828–82) and **Christina Georgina** (1830–94). English pre-Raphaelite poets.

Ros·si (rŏs'ē, rôs'ē, rŏs'sē), **Bruno.** b. 1905. Italian physicist.

Ros·si·ni (rō-sē'nē, rō-, rə-), **Gioacchino Antonio.** 1792–1868. Italian composer.

Ros·tand (rôs-täN'), **Edmond.** 1868–1918. French author.

Ros·tow (rŏs'tou'), **Walt Whitman.** b. 1916. Amer. economist.

Ros·tro·po·vich (rŏs'trə-pō'vĭch), **Mstislav.** b. 1927. Russian-born musician.

Roth (rôth), **Philip Milton.** b. 1933. Amer. novelist.

Roth·ko (rŏth'kō), **Mark.** 1903–70. Russian-born Amer. painter.

Roth·schild (rŏth'chīld, rŏths'-, rôth'-, rōths'-, rōt'shĭlt). Family of German bankers, including **Meyer Amschel** (1743–1812), **Salomon** (1774–1855), and **Nathan Meyer** (1777–1836).

Rou·ault (rŏŏ-ō'), **Georges.** 1871–1958. French artist.

Rou·get de Lisle (rŏŏ-zhā' də lēl'), **Claude Joseph.** 1760–1836. French soldier and songwriter ("Marseillaise").

Rourke (rŏŏrk), **Constance Mayfield.** 1885–1941. Amer. author.

Rous (rous), **Francis Peyton.** 1879–1970. Amer. pathologist (Nobel, 1966).

Rous·seau (rŏŏ-sō'). **1. Jean Jacques.** 1712–78. French author and philosopher. **2. Théodore.** 1812–67. French landscape painter. **3. Henri ("Le Douanier").** 1844–1910. French painter.

Ro·vere (rō-vîr'), **Richard.** b. 1915. Amer. journalist.

Rowe (rō), **Nicholas.** 1674–1718. English author.

Row·land (rō'lənd), **Henry Augustus.** 1848–1901. Amer. physicist.

Row·land·son (rō'lənd-sən), **Thomas.** 1756–1827. English painter and illustrator.

Row·ley (rō'lē), **William.** 1585?–1642? English playwright.

Row·ling (rō'lĭng), **Wallace Edward.** b. 1927. New Zealand statesman.

Row·son (rou'zən), **Susanna Haswell.** 1762?–1824. English author, actress, and educator.

Ro·xas y Acu·ña (rô'häs ē ä-kŏŏ'-nyä), **Manuel.** 1892–1948. Filipino political leader.

Roy·all (roi'əl). **1. Anne Newport.** 1769–1854. Amer. author. **2. Kenneth Claiborne.** 1894–1971. Amer. public official.

Royce (rois), **Josiah.** 1855–1916. Amer. educator and philosopher.

Ro·zelle (rō-zĕl'), **Alvin Ray ("Pete").** b. 1926. Amer. football commissioner.

Ru·bens (rŏŏ'bənz, rü'bəns), **Peter Paul.** 1577–1640. Flemish painter. —**Ru'ben·esque'** *adj.*

Ru·bin·stein (rŏŏ'bĭn-stīn'). **1. Anton Gregor.** 1829–94. Russian pianist, composer,and educator. **2. Arthur** or **Artur.** 1887–1982. Polish-born Amer. pianist. **3. Helena.** 1871–1965. Polish-born Amer. businesswoman.

Ru·dolf (rŏŏ'dŏlf', -dôlf'). **1. I.** 1218–91. Holy Roman Emperor (1273–91) and founder of the Hapsburg dynasty. **2.** 1858–89. Austrian crown prince.

Ru·dolph (rŏŏ'dŏlf'), **Wilma Glodean.** b. 1940. Amer. athlete.

Ruf·fin (rŭf'ĭn), **Edmund.** 1794–1865. Amer. secessionist, farmer, and publisher; fired 1st shot on Ft. Sumter.

Ruis·dael or **Ruys·dael** (rīz'däl', -dāl', rīs'-, rois'-), **Jacob van.** 1628?–82. Dutch painter.

Ruiz Cor·ti·nes (rŏŏ-ēs' kôr-tē'nĕs), **Adolfo.** 1890–1973. Mexican statesman.

Rum·sey (rŭm'zē). **1. James.** 1743–92. Amer. inventor (steamboat, etc.) and engineer. **2. Mary Harriman.** 1881–1934. Amer. public welfare pioneer.

Run·cie (rŭn'sē), **Robert Alexander Kennedy.** b. 1921. English prelate.

Rund·stedt (rŏŏnt'stĕt', -shtĕt'), **Karl Rudolf Gerd von.** 1875–1953. German general.

Ru·ne·berg (rŏŏ'nə-bərg, -bĕr'ē), **Johan Ludvig.** 1804–77. Finnish poet.

Run·yon (rŭn'yən), **Alfred Damon.** 1884?–1946. Amer. journalist and short-story author.

Ru·pert (rŏŏ'pərt), Prince. 1619–82. German-born English military and political leader.

Ru·rik (rŏŏr'ĭk, rŏŏ'rĭk). d. 879. Scandinavian warrior and founder of Russian ruling dynasty (1462–1610).

Rush (rŭsh). **1. Benjamin.** 1745–1813. Amer. physician, politician, author, and educator. **2. William.** 1756–1833. Amer. sculptor and woodcarver. **3. Richard.** 1780–1859. Amer. diplomat and public official.

Rusk (rŭsk), **David Dean.** b. 1909. Amer. public official.

Rus·kin (rŭs'kĭn), **John.** 1819–1900. English author, critic, and philanthropist.

Rus·sell (rŭs'əl). **1.** Lord **John.** Viscount Amberly. 1792–1878. English statesman and political reformer. **2. Mary Baptist (Katherine).** 1829–98. Irish-born Amer. religious leader. **3. Charles Taze.** 1852–1916. Amer. founder of Jehovah's Witnesses. **4. Lillian.** 1861–1922. Amer. entertainer. **5. Annie.** 1864–1936. Amer. actress. **6. George William.** 1867–1935. Irish author. **7.** Lord **Bertrand Arthur William.** 1872–1970. English pacifist, mathematician, philosopher, and author (Nobel, 1950). **8. Henry Norris.** 1877–1957. Amer. astronomer. **9. William Felton ("Bill").** b. 1934. Amer. basketball player, coach, and sportscaster.

Rus·tin (rŭs'tĭn), **Bayard.** b. 1910. Amer. civil-rights leader.

Ruth (rŏŏth), **George Herman**

Babe Ruth

("**Babe**"). 1895–1948. Amer. baseball player.

Ruth·er·ford (rŭth′ər-fərd). 1. **Daniel.** 1749–1819. Scottish chemist and physician. 2. **Ernest.** 1st Baron Rutherford of Nelson. 1871–1937. New Zealand-born British physicist (Nobel, 1908).

Rut·ledge (rŭt′lĭj). 1. **John.** 1739–1800. Amer. jurist and politician. 2. **Wiley Blount, Jr.** 1894–1949. Amer. jurist.

Ruys·dael (rīz′däl′, -dăl′, rīs′-, rois′-). Variant of **Ruisdael.**

Ru·žič·ka (ro͞o′zĭch-kə, -zhĭch-, -tsĭ-kä, -zhĕch-kä, ro͞o-zĭch′-, -zhĭch′-), **Leopold.** 1887–1976. Yugoslavian-born Swiss chemist (Nobel, 1939).

Ry·an (rī′ən), **Thomas Fortune.** 1851–1928. Amer. financier.

Ry·der (rī′dər), **Albert Pinkham.** 1847–1917. Amer. painter.

Ryle (rīl), Sir **Martin.** 1918–84. English astronomer and physicist (Nobel, 1974).

Rys·kind (rĭs′kĭnd), **Morris.** 1895–1985. Amer. playwright.

S

Saa·ri·nen (sär′ĭ-nĕn′, -nən), **Gottlieb Eliel** (1873–1950) and **Eero** (1910–61). Finnish-born Amer. architects.

Saa·ve·dra La·mas (sä′ä-vĕ′thrä lä′mas), **Carlos.** 1880?–1959. Argentinean diplomat (Nobel, 1936).

Sa·ba·tier (sä-bä-tyā′), **Paul.** 1854–1941. French chemist (Nobel, 1912).

Sa·ba·ti·ni (săb′ə-tē′nē, sä′bä-), **Rafael.** 1875–1950. Italian-born English author.

Sa·bin (sā′bĭn). 1. **Florence Rena.** 1871–1953. Amer. pioneer anatomist. 2. **Albert Bruce.** b. 1906. Amer. microbiologist and physician.

Sac·a·ja·we·a (săk′ə-jə-wē′ə). 1788?–1812. Amer. Indian guide and interpreter for the Lewis and Clark expedition.

Sac·co (săk′ō, säk′kō), **Nicola.** 1891–1927. Italian-born Amer. anarchist; convicted and executed for murder.

Sachs (zäks, săks). 1. **Hans.** 1494–1576. German poet. 2. **Nelly.** 1891–1970. German lyric poet (Nobel, 1966).

Sack·ville (săk′vĭl′), **Thomas.** 1st Earl of Dorset, Baron Buckhurst. 1536–1608. English poet and political adviser.

Sack·ville-West (săk′vĭl-wĕst′), **Victoria Mary.** 1892–1962. English author.

Sa·dat (sə-dăt′, -dät′), **Anwar el-.** 1918–81. Egyptian statesman (Nobel, 1978); assassinated.

Sade (säd, săd), Comte **Donatien Alphonse François de.** "Marquis de Sade." 1740–1814. French author and libertine.

Sad·li·er (săd′lē-ər), **Mary Anne Madden.** 1820–1903. Irish-born Amer. author.

Sa·gan. 1. (sā′gən), **Carl.** b. 1934. Amer. astronomer and author. 2. (sä-gäN′), **Françoise.** b. 1935. French author.

Sage (sāj). 1. **Russell.** 1816–1906. Amer. financier. 2. **Margaret Olivia Slocum.** 1828–1918. Amer. philanthropist.

Saint Clair (sānt klâr′, sĭng, sĭn), **Arthur.** 1736–1818. Scottish-born Amer. general.

Saint-Cyr (săN-sēr′), Marquis **Laurent de Gouvion.** 1764–1830. French marshal and war minister.

Saint Denis (sānt dĕn′ĭs), **Ruth.** 1878–1968. Amer. dancer and educator.

Sainte-Beuve (săNt-bœv′), **Charles Augustin.** 1804–69. French poet, critic, and historian.

Saint-Ex·u·pé·ry (săN-tĕg-zü-pā-rē′), **Antoine de.** 1900–44. French author and aviator.

Saint-Gau·dens (sānt-gô′dənz), **Augustus.** 1848–1907. Irish-born Amer. sculptor.

Saint Johns (sānt jŏnz′, sĭnt), **Adela Rogers.** b. 1894. Amer. journalist.

Saint-Just (săN-zhüst′), **Louis Antoine Léon de.** 1767–94. French revolutionary; guillotined.

Saint Lau·rent (săN lô-räN′). 1. **Louis Stephen.** 1882–1973. Canadian prime minister (1948–57). 2. **Yves.** b. 1936. French fashion designer.

Saint-Saëns (săN-säNs′, -säN′), **Charles Camille.** 1835–1921. French composer.

Saints·bur·y (sānts′bĕr′ē, -brē), **George Edward Bateman.** 1845–1933. English critic and historian.

Saint-Si·mon (săN-sē-môN′). 1. Duc de. Louis de Rouvroy. 1675–1755. French diplomat and author. 2. Comte de. Claude Henri de Rouvroy. 1760–1825. French philosopher.

Saint Vrain (săN vrăN′), **Ceran de Hault de Lassus de.** 1802–70. Amer. pioneer, fur trader, and merchant.

Sai·on·ji (sī-ŏn′jē, -ôn′-, sī′ŏn-jē′), Prince **Kimmochi.** 1849–1940. Japanese statesman.

Sa·kha·rov (sä′kə-rôf′, -rôv′), **Andrei Dimitrievich.** b. 1921. Russian physicist and dissident (Nobel, 1975).

Sa·ki (sä′kē). Hector Hugh Munro.

Sal·a·din (săl′ə-dĭn). 1138–93. Sultan of Egypt and Syria.

Sa·lam (sä-läm′), **Abdus.** b. 1926. Pakistani physicist (Nobel, 1979).

Sa·la·zar (săl′ə-zär′, să′lə-), **Antonio de Oliveira.** 1889–1970. Portuguese statesman.

Sal·in·ger (săl′ĭn-jər), **Jerome David ("J.D.").** b. 1919. Amer. author.

Salk (sôlk), **Jonas Edward.** b. 1914. Amer. microbiologist; developed 1st polio vaccine.

Sal·lust (săl′əst). 86?–34? B.C. Roman historian and politician.

Sal·mon (săm′ən, săl′mən), **Lucy Maynard.** 1853–1927. Amer. historian.

Sa·lo·me (sə-lō′mē, săl′ə-mē′). In the Bible, the daughter of Herodias.

Sal·o·mon (săl′ə-mən), **Haym.** 1740?–85. Polish-born Amer. banker and businessman.

Sal·ve·mi·ni (säl-vā′mē-nē), **Gaetano.** 1873–1957. Italian historian.

Sam·o·set (săm′ə-sĕt′, sə-mŏs′ĭt). d. 1653? Amer. Indian chief and friend of Pilgrim colonists at Plymouth.

Samp·son (sămp′sən), **Deborah.** 1760–1827. Amer. Revolutionary soldier.

Sam·u·el (săm′yo͞o-əl). 11th cent. B.C. Hebrew judge and prophet.

Sam·u·el·son (săm′yo͞o-əl-sən, -yo͝ol-sən), **Paul Anthony.** b. 1915. Amer. economist (Nobel, 1970).

San·chez de Bus·ta·man·te y Sir·ven (săn′chĕs dĕ bo͞os′tä-män′tĕ ē sēr-vĕn′), **Antonio.** 1865–1951. Cuban jurist.

Sand (sănd, säNd), **George.** Amadine Aurore Lucie Dupin, Baroness Dudevant. 1804–76. French author.

Sand·burg (sănd′bûrg′, săn′-), **Carl.** 1878–1967. Amer. poet and biographer.

Carl Sandburg

San·ders (săn′dərz), **Harlan ("Colonel").** 1890–1980. Amer. fast-foods businessman.

San·der·son (săn′dər-sən), **Sibyl Swift.** 1865–1903. Amer. operatic soprano.

San·ford (săn′fərd), **Edward Terry.** 1865–1930. Amer. jurist.

San·gal·lo (säng-gäl′lō), **Giuliano da.** 1445–1516. Italian architect, engineer, and sculptor.

Sang·er (săng′ər). 1. **Margaret Higgins.** 1883–1966. Amer. leader of birth-control movement. 2. **Frederick.** b. 1918. English biochemist (Nobel, 1958 and 1980).

Margaret Sanger

Sang·ster (săng′stər), **Margaret Elizabeth Munson.** 1838–1912. Amer. author and editor.

San Mar·tín (săn mär-tēn′, sän), **Jose de.** 1778–1850. Argentine revolutionary leader in South America.

San·ta An·na or **An·a** (săn′tə ăn′ə, sän′tä ä′nä), **Antonio López de.** 1795?–1876. Mexican military and political leader.

Antonio López de Santa Anna

San·tan·der (sän′tän-dĕr′), **Francisco de Paula.** 1792–1840. Colombian statesman.

San·ta·ya·na (săn′tē-ăn′ə, -än′ə, săn′tə-yä′nə, sän′-), **George.** 1863–1952. Spanish-born Amer. educator, philosopher, and poet.

San·tos-Du·mont (săn′təs-do͞o-mŏnt′, -dyoo-, săN′to͞os-do͞o-môNt′), **Alberto.** 1873–1932. Brazilian pioneer aeronaut.

Sa·pir (sə-pîr′), **Edward.** 1884–1939. Amer. linguist and anthropologist.

Sap·pho (săf′ō). 7th cent. B.C. Greek poet.

Sar·a·zen (săr′ə-zən), **Gene.** b. 1901. Amer. golfer.

Sar·da·na·pa·lus (sär′dn-ə-pā′ləs, -ăp′ə-ləs). 9th cent. B.C. Assyrian ruler.

Sar·dou (sär-do͞o′), **Victorien.** 1831–1908. French playwright.

Sar·gent (sär′jənt), **John Singer.** 1856–1925. Amer. painter.

Sar·gon II (sär′gŏn). d. 705 B.C. Assyrian king (722–705).

Sar·noff (sär′nôf′), **David.** 1891–1971. Amer. business executive.

Sa·roy·an (sə-roi′ən), **William.** 1908–81. Amer. author.

Sar·ton (sär′tn), **George Alfred Leon.** 1884–1956. Belgian-born Amer. science historian.

Sar·tre (sär′trə, särt), **Jean Paul.** 1905–80. French philosopher and author (Nobel, 1964).

Sas·soon (sə-so͞on′, să-), **Siegfried Lorraine.** 1886–1967. English poet and biographer.

Sa·tie (sä-tē′), **Erik.** 1866–1925. French composer.

Sa·to (sä′tō). 1. **Naotake.** 1882–1971. Japanese diplomat. 2. **Eisaku.** 1901–75. Japanese statesman (Nobel, 1974).

Sa·ud (sä-o͞od′), **Abdul Aziz Ibn** (1880–1953; reigned 1932–53) and **Abdul Aziz Ibn** (1901?–69; reigned 1953–64). Saudi Arabian kings.

Saul (sôl). 11th cent. B.C. Hebrew king.

Saus·sure (sō-so͞or′, -sûr′, -sür′), **Ferdinand de.** 1857–1913. Swiss pioneer linguist.

Sav·age (săv′ĭj). 1. **Richard.** 4th Earl Rivers. 1697?–1743. English poet. 2. **Michael Joseph.** 1872–1940. Australian-born New Zealand labor leader and politician.

Sa·vo·na·ro·la (săv′ə-nə-rō′lə, sä′-vō-nä-rō′lä), **Girolamo.** 1452–98. Italian reformer; executed.

Sa·voy (sə-voi′). Ruling dynasty of Sardinia and Italy (1720–1946) and of Spain (1870–73).

Saxe (săks, säks), Comte **Hermann Maurice de.** 1696–1750. French military leader.

Saxe-Co·burg (săks-kō′bûrg). English ruling house (1901–10).

Sax·o Gram·mat·i·cus (săk′sō grə-măt′ĭ-kəs). 1150?–1220? Danish historian.

Say (sā), **Thomas.** 1787–1834. Amer. entomologist.

Say·ers (sā′ərz), **Dorothy Leigh.** 1893–1957. English author.

Scal·i·ger (skăl′ə-jər). 1. **Julius Caesar.** 1484–1558. Italian physician. 2. **Joseph Justus.** 1540–1609. French scholar.

Scan·der·beg (skăn′dər-bĕg′). 1403–68. Albanian national hero.

Scar·lat·ti (skär-lät′ē), **Alessandro** (1659–1725) and **(Giuseppe) Domenico** (1685–1767). Italian composers and musicians.

Scar·ron (skä-rôN′), **Paul.** 1610–60. French author.

Schacht (shäkt, shäKHt), **(Horace Greeley) Hjalmar.** 1877–1970. German banker.

Schaff (shäf), **Philip.** 1819–93. Swiss-born Amer. church historian.

Schal·ly (shăl′ē), **Andrew Victor.** b. 1926. Polish-born Amer. physiologist (Nobel, 1977).

Scharn·horst (shärn′hôrst′), **Gerhard Johann David von.** 1755–1813. Prussian general.

Schar·wen·ka (shär-vĕng′kä), **Philipp** (1847–1917) and **Xaver** (1850–1924). German musicians and composers.

Schaw·low (shô′lō), **Arthur Leonard.** b. 1921. Amer. physicist (Nobel, 1981).

Schech·ter (shĕk′tər), **Solomon.** 1847–1915. Rumanian-born Hebrew scholar.

Schee·le (shā′lə), **Karl Wilhelm.** 1742–86. German-born Swedish chemist.

Schel·ling (shĕl′ĭng), **Friedrich Wilhelm Joseph von.** 1775–1854. German philosopher.

Schia·pa·rel·li (skē-ăp′ə-rĕl′ē, skyä′-pä-rĕl′lē). 1. **Giovanni Virginio.** 1835–1910. Italian astronomer. 2. **Elsa.** 1890?–1973. Italian-born fashion designer.

Schick (shĭk), **Béla.** 1877–1967. Hungarian-born Amer. pediatrician.

Schiff (shĭf), **Dorothy.** b. 1903. Amer. newspaper publisher.

Schil·ler (shĭl′ər), **Johann Christoph Friedrich von.** 1759–1805. German poet, playwright, and historian.

Schip·pers (shĭp′ərz), **Thomas.** 1930–77. Amer. conductor.

Schir·mer (shûr′mər, shĭr′-), **Gustav.** 1829–93. German-born Amer. music publisher.

Schle·gel (shlā′gəl). 1. **August Wilhelm von.** 1767–1845. German translator, poet, and critic. 2. **Friedrich.** 1772–1829. German author and philosopher.

Schlei·cher (shlī′kər, -KHər), **Kurt von.** 1882–1934. German military and political leader.

Schlei·er·ma·cher (shlī′ər-mä′kər, -KHər), **Friedrich Ernst Daniel.** 1768–1834. German philosopher.

Schles·in·ger (shlĕs′ĭn-jər), **Arthur Meier** (1888–1965) and **Arthur Meier, Jr.** (b. 1917). Amer. historians and educators.

Schley (slī), **Winfield Scott.** 1839–1911. Amer. naval commander.

Schlie·mann (shlē′män′), **Heinrich.** 1822–90. German archaeologist; discovered site of ancient Troy.

Schmidt (shmĭt), **Helmut.** b. 1918. West German statesman.

Schmuck·er (shmŭk′ər), **Samuel Simon.** 1799–1873. Amer. theologian.

Schna·bel (shnä′bəl), **Artur.** 1882–1951. Austrian pianist and composer.

Schnitz·ler (shnĭts′lər), **Arthur.** 1862–1931. Austrian physician and author.

Scho·field (skō′fēld′), **John McAllister.** 1831–1906. Amer. army officer.

Schön·berg (shœn′bûrg, shərn′-, shœn′bĕrk), **Arnold.** 1874–1951. Austrian modernist composer.

School·craft (sko͞ol′krăft′), **Henry Rowe.** 1793–1864. Amer. geologist, explorer, and ethnologist.

Scho·pen·hau·er (shō′pən-hou′ər), **Arthur.** 1788–1860. German philosopher.

Schrief·fer (shrē′fər), **John Robert.** b. 1931. Amer. physicist (Nobel, 1972).

Schrö·ding·er (shrœ′dĭng-ər), **Erwin.** 1887–1961. Austrian physicist (Nobel, 1933).

Schu·bert (sho͞o′bərt, -bĕrt), **Franz Peter.** 1797–1828. Austrian composer.

Franz Schubert

Schul·ler (sho͞o′lər), **Gunther.** b. 1925. Amer. composer and conductor.

Schultz (sho͞olts), **Theodore.** b. 1902. Amer. economist (Nobel, 1979).

Schulz (sho͞olts), **Charles Monroe.** b. 1922. Amer. cartoonist ("Peanuts").

Schu·man. 1. (sho͞o-män′), **Robert.** 1886–1963. French statesman. **2.** (sho͞o′mən), **William Howard.** b. 1910. Amer. composer.

Schu·mann (sho͞o′män), **Robert.** 1810–56. German composer.

Schu·mann-Heink (sho͞o′mən-hĭngk′), **Ernestine.** 1861–1936. Amer. contralto.

Schum·pe·ter (sho͞om′pā-tər), **Joseph Alois.** 1883–1950. Czechoslovakian-born Amer. economist.

Schur·man (sho͝or′mən, shûr′-), **Jacob Gould.** 1854–1942. Canadian-born Amer. educator and diplomat.

Schurz (sho͝orts, shûrz), **Carl.** 1829–1906. German-born Amer. general, politician, and editor.

Schusch·nigg (sho͝osh′nĭk), **Kurt von.** 1897–1977. Austrian statesman.

Schuy·ler (skī′lər). **1. Philip John.** 1733–1804. Amer. Revolutionary general and politician. **2. Louisa Lee.** 1837–1926. Amer. social worker.

Schwab (shwŏb), **Charles Michael.** 1862–1939. Amer. industrialist.

Schwann (shvän), **Theodor.** 1810–82. German physiologist.

Schweit·zer (shwīt′sər, shvīt′-), **Albert.** 1875–1965. French philosopher, physician, and musician (Nobel, 1952).

Schwing·er (shwĭng′ər), **Julian Seymour.** b. 1918. Amer. physicist (Nobel, 1965).

Scid·more (sĭd′môr′, -mōr′), **Eliza Ruhamah.** 1856–1928. Amer. travel writer.

Scip·io (skĭp′ē-ō′, sĭp′-), **Publius Cornelius. 1.** "the Elder." 237?–183 B.C. Roman military leader. **2.** "the Younger." 185–129 B.C. Roman general and politician.

Scopes (skōps), **John Thomas.** 1901–70. Amer. teacher convicted for teaching evolution.

Scott (skŏt). **1.** Sir **Walter.** 1771–1832. Scottish author. **2. Winfield.** 1786–1866. Amer. general. **3. Dred.** 1795?–1858. Amer. slave; principal in Dred Scott decision (1857). **4.** Sir **George Gilbert.** 1811–78. English architect. **5. James Brown.** 1866–1943. Canadian-born Amer. lawyer. **6. Robert Falcon.** 1868–1912. English Antarctic explorer.

Dred Scott

Scot·to (skŏt′ō, skôt′tō), **Renata.** b. 1936? Italian soprano.

Scri·a·bin (skrē-ä′bĭn), **Alexander Nikolayevich.** 1872–1915. Russian composer.

Scribe (skrēb). **Augustin Eugène.** 1791–1861. French playwright.

Scripps (skrĭps). Amer. family of newspaper publishers, including **James Edmund** (1835–1906), **Ellen Browning** (1836–1932), **Edward Wyllis** (1854–1926), and **Robert Paine** (1895–1938).

Scud·der (skŭd′ər). **1. Horace Elisha.** 1838–1902. Amer. author and editor. **2. Vida Dutton.** 1861–1954. Amer. educator and author. **3. Janet.** 1869–1940. Amer. sculptor and painter.

Scu·dé·ry (skü-dā-rē′), **Madeleine** or **Magdeleine de.** 1607–1701. French author.

Sea·borg (sē′bôrg′), **Glenn Theodore.** b. 1912. Amer. chemist (Nobel, 1951).

Sea·bur·y (sē′bĕr′ē, -bə-rē), **Samuel.** 1729–96. Amer. prelate.

Sea·man (sē′mən), **Elizabeth Cochrane.** "Nellie Bly." 1867–1922. Amer. journalist.

Sears (sîrz). **1. Isaac.** 1730–86. Amer. Revolutionary patriot and businessman. **2. Richard Warren.** 1863–1914. Amer. business executive.

Se·at·tle (sē-ăt′l). 1786?–1866. Amer. Indian leader.

Sedg·wick (sĕj′wĭk). **1. Theodore.** 1746–1813. Amer. politician and judge. **2. Catharine Maria.** 1789–1867. Amer. novelist. **3. Anne Douglas.** 1873–1935. Amer. novelist.

See (sē), **Thomas Jefferson Jackson.** 1866–1962. Amer. astronomer and mathematician.

Seeckt (säkt, zäkt), **Hans von.** 1866–1936. German general.

See·ger (sē′gər). **1. Alan.** 1888–1916. Amer. poet. **2. Peter ("Pete").** b. 1919. Amer. folk singer.

Se·fe·ri·a·des (sĕ-fĕ-rē-ä′dĕs, *-thĕs*), **Giorgos Stylianou.** 1900–71. Greek poet and diplomat (Nobel, 1963).

Se·gal (sē′gəl), **George.** b. 1924. Amer. sculptor.

Se·gar (sē′gär′), **Elzie Crisler.** 1894–1938. Amer. cartoonist ("Popeye").

Se·go·via (sĭ-gō′vē-ə, sĕ-gô′vyä), **Andres.** b. 1894. Spanish guitarist.

Se·grè (sĭ-grā′, sĕ-), **Emilio Gino.** b. 1905. Italian-born Amer. physicist (Nobel, 1959).

Se·ja·nus (sĭ-jā′nəs), **Lucius Aelius.** d. A.D. 31. Roman courtier.

Sel·den (sĕl′dən). **1. John.** 1584–1654. English antiquary and jurist. **2. George Baldwin.** 1846–1922. Amer. inventor and patent lawyer.

Sel·des (sĕl′dĭs), **Gilbert Vivian.** 1893–1970. Amer. author and critic.

Se·leu·cus (sĭ-lo͞o′kəs). Name of 6 Syrian kings, esp. **I,** 358?–280 B.C., ruled 312–280; assassinated. **—Se·leu′cid** (-sĭd) *adj. & n.*

Sel·fridge (sĕl′frĭj), **Harry Gordon.** 1857?–1947. Amer.-born English businessman.

Se·lig·man (sĕl′ĭg-mən). **1. Joseph.** 1819–80. German-born Amer. financier. **2. Edwin Robert Anderson.** 1861–1939. Amer. economist.

Sel·in·court (sĕl′ĭn-kôrt′, -kōrt′), **Hugh de.** 1878–1951. English author.

Sel·kirk (sĕl′kûrk′), **Alexander.** 1676–1721. Scottish seaman; reputed original of Robinson Crusoe.

Selz·nick (sĕlz′nĭk), **David Oliver.** 1902–65. Amer. film producer.

Sem·brich (sĕm′brĭk, zĕm′brĭKH), **Marcella** or **Marcelline.** 1858–1935. Polish-born Amer. operatic soprano.

Se·me·nov (sĭ-myô′nəf), **Nikolai Nikolayevich.** b. 1896. Soviet chemist (Nobel, 1956).

Semmes (sĕmz), **Raphael.** 1809–77. Amer. Confederate naval commander.

Sem·ple (sĕm′pəl), **Ellen Churchill.** 1863–1932. Amer. geographer.

Sen·e·ca (sĕn′ĭ-kə), **Lucius Annaeus.** "the Younger." 4 B.C.–A.D. 65. Roman Stoic philosopher, writer, and politician.

Sen·nach·er·ib (sĭ-năk′ər-ĭb′). d. 681 B.C. Assyrian king (705–681).

Sen·nett (sĕn′ĭt), **Mack.** 1884–1960. Canadian-born Amer. filmmaker.

Se·quoy·a or **Se·quoy·ah** (sĭ-kwoi′ə). 1770?–1843. Amer. Cherokee Indian leader and scholar.

Sequoya

Ser·kin (sûr′kĭn, sĕr′-), **Rudolf.** b. 1903. Czechoslovakian-born pianist.

Ser·ra (sĕr′ə, sĕ′rä), **Junípero.** 1713–84. Spanish missionary in Calif.

Ser·rano Su·ñer (sĕ-rä′nô so͞o-nyĕr′), **Ramón.** b. 1901. Spanish politician.

Ser·to·ri·us (sər-tôr′ē-əs, -tōr′-), **Quintus.** d. 72 B.C. Roman general.

Ser·ve·tus (sər-vē′təs), **Michael.** 1511–53. Spanish-born theologian and physician; executed for heresy.

Ser·vice (sûr′vĭs), **Robert William.** 1874–1958. English-born Canadian author.

Ses·sions (sĕsh′ənz), **Roger Huntington.** 1896–1985. Amer. composer.

Se·ton (sēt′n), Saint **Elizabeth Ann Bayley.** "Mother Seton." 1774–1821. Amer. religious leader.

Elizabeth Seton

Seu·rat (sə-rä′, sœ-), **Georges Pierre.** 1859–91. French pointillist painter.

Seuss (so͞os), Doctor. Theodor Seuss Geisel.

Sev·a·reid (sĕv′ə-rīd′), **Eric.** b. 1912. Amer. broadcast journalist.

Se·ve·rus (sə-vîr′əs), **Lucius Septimus.** 146–211. Roman emperor (193–211).

Se·vier (sĭ-vîr′), **John.** 1745–1815. Amer. pioneer, politician, and Indian fighter.

Sé·vi·gné (sā-vē-nyā′), Marquise de. Marie de Rabutin-Chantal. 1626–96. French author.

Sew·all (so͞o′əl). **1. Samuel.** 1652–1730. English-born Amer. jurist. **2. Mary Eliza Wright.** 1844–1920. Amer. educator and reformer.

Sew·ard (so͞o′ərd), **William Henry.** 1801–72. Amer. statesman.

Sew·ell (so͞o′əl), **Anna.** 1820–78. English author.

Sex·ton (sĕks′tən), **Anne.** 1928–74. Amer. poet.

Sey·mour (sē′môr, -mōr). **1. Jane.** 1509?–37. Queen of England as 3rd wife of Henry VIII. **2. Horatio.** 1810–86. Amer. politician.

Sfor·za (sfôrt′sə, sfôr′tsä), Count **Carlo.** 1873–1952. Italian diplomat and historian.

Shack·le·ton (shăk′əl-tən), Sir **Ernest Henry.** 1874–1922. Irish-born British Antarctic explorer.

Shad·well (shăd′wəl, -wĕl′), **Thomas.** 1640?–92. English author.

Sha·fer (shā′fər), **Helen Almira.** 1839–94. Amer. pioneer educator.

Shaf·ter (shăf′tər), **William Rufus.** 1835–1906. Amer. Union general.

Shaftes·bur·y (shăfts′bĕr′ē, -bə-rē), 1st Earl of. Anthony Ashley Cooper. 1621–83. English statesman.

Shah Je·han or **Ja·han** (shä′ jə-hän′, yə-). 1592?–1666. Mogul emperor (1628–58).

Shahn (shän), **Benjamin ("Ben").** 1898–1969. Russian-born Amer. artist.

Shake·speare or **Shak·spere** (shāk′spîr), **William.** 1564–1616. English playwright and poet. **—Shake·spear′e·an, Shake·spear′i·an** *adj. & n.*

William Shakespeare

Shang (shăng). Chinese dynasty (1766–1122 B.C.).

Shan·kar (shän′kär, shăng-kär′), **Ravi.** b. 1920. Indian-born musician and composer.

Sha·pir·o (shə-pîr′ō), **Karl Jay.** b. 1913. Amer. poet and critic.

Shap·ley (shăp′lē), **Harlow.** 1885–1972. Amer. astronomer.

Shaw (shô). **1. Lemuel.** 1781–1861. Amer. jurist. **2. Henry Wheeler.** "Josh Billings." 1818–85. Amer. humorist. **3. Anna Howard.** 1847–1919. English-born Amer. suffragist. **4. George Bernard.** 1856–1950. Irish-born English playwright (Nobel, 1925). **5. Robert Lawson.** b. 1916. Amer. conductor and chorale director. **—Sha′vi·an** (shā′vē-ən) *adj. & n.*

Shawn (shôn), **Ted.** 1891–1972. Amer. dancer.

Shays (shāz), **Daniel.** 1747?–1825. Amer. Revolutionary soldier and insurrectionist.

Shear·er (shîr′ər), **Moira.** b. 1926. Scottish-born ballerina.

Shee·ler (shē′lər), **Charles.** 1883–1965. Amer. photographer.

Sheen (shēn), **Fulton John.** 1895–1979. Amer. prelate.

Shel·by (shĕl′bē), **Isaac.** 1750–1826. Amer. pioneer and soldier.

Shel·ley (shĕl′ē). **1. Percy Bysshe.** 1792–1822. English poet. **2. Mary Godwin Wollstonecraft.** 1797–1851. English author (*Frankenstein*).

Shen·stone (shĕn′stən, -stōn′), **William.** 1714–63. English poet.

Shep·ard (shĕp′ərd), **Alan Bartlett, Jr.** b. 1923. Amer. astronaut.

Sher·a·ton (shĕr′ə-tn), **Thomas.** 1751–1806. English furniture designer.

Sher·i·dan (shĕr′ĭ-dn). **1. Richard Brinsley.** 1751–1816. English playwright and politician. **2. Philip Henry.** 1831–88. Amer. Union general.

Sher·man (shûr′mən). **1. Roger.** 1721–93. Amer. Revolutionary patriot, politician, and jurist. **2. William Tecumseh.** 1820–91. Amer. Union general. **3. John.** 1823–1900. Amer. politician. **4. James Schoolcraft.** 1855–1912. U.S. Vice President (1909–12). **5. Stuart Pratt.** 1881–1926. Amer. literary critic and educator.

William T. Sherman

Sher·riff (shĕr′ĭf), **Robert Cedric.** 1896–1975. English author.

Sher·ring·ton (shĕr′ĭng-tən), Sir **Charles Scott.** 1861–1952. English physiologist (Nobel, 1932).

Sher·wood (shûr′wo͝od′), **Robert Emmet.** 1896–1955. Amer. playwright.

Shev·chen·ko (shĕf-chĕng′kō), **Taras Grigoryevich.** 1814–61. Ukrainian poet.

Shi·de·ha·ra (shē′dĕ-hä′rä), Baron **Kijuro.** 1872–1951. Japanese statesman.

Shi·ge·mit·su (shē′gĕ-mē′tso͞o), **Mamoru.** 1887–1957. Japanese diplomat.

Shin·well (shĭn′wĕl′, -wəl), **Emanuel.** b. 1884. English labor leader and politician.

Shi·ras (shī′rəs), **George.** 1832–1924. Amer. jurist.

Shir·er (shīr′ər), **William Lawrence.** b. 1904. Amer. journalist.

Shir·ley (shûr′lē). **1. James.** 1596–1666. English playwright. **2. William.** 1694–1771. English colonial administrator.

Shock·ley (shŏk′lē), **William Bradford.** b. 1910. English-born Amer. physicist (Nobel, 1956).

Shoe·ma·ker (sho͞o′mā′kər), **William Lee ("Willie").** b. 1931. Amer. jockey.

Sholes (shōlz), **Christopher Latham.** 1819–90. Amer. journalist and inventor (typewriter).

Sho·lo·khov (shô′lə-kŏf′, -kôf′), **Mikhail Aleksandrovich.** 1905–84. Russian novelist (Nobel, 1965).

Shore (shôr, shōr), **Dinah.** b. 1917? Amer. entertainer.

Shos·ta·ko·vich (shŏs′tə-kō′vĭch, -kô′-, shô′stə-), **Dimitri.** 1906–75. Russian composer.

Shreve (shrēv), **Henry Miller.** 1785–1851. Amer. riverboat captain.

Shu·bert (sho͞o′bərt), **Lee.** 1875–1953. Amer. stage producer and theatrical manager.

Shu Han (sho͞o′ hän′). Chinese dynasty (221–63).

Shute (sho͞ot), **Nevil.** 1899–1960. English novelist and aviation engineer.

Shver·nik (shvĕr′nĭk), **Nikolai Mikhalovich.** 1888–1970. Soviet political leader.

Si·be·li·us (sĭ-bā′lē-əs, -bāl′yəs), **Jean.** 1865–1957. Finnish composer.

Sib·ley (sĭb′lē), **Hiram.** 1807–88. Amer. businessman and philanthropist.

Sick·les (sĭk′əlz), **Daniel Edgar.** 1825–1914. Amer. Union general and politician.

Sid·dons (sĭd′nz), **Sarah.** 1755–1831. English actress.

Sid·ney (sĭd′nē), Sir **Philip.** 1554–86. English poet, soldier, and politician.

Sieg·bahn (sēg′bän′). **1. Karl Manne Georg.** 1886–1978. Swedish physicist (Nobel, 1924). **2. Kai.** b. 1918. Swedish physicist (Nobel, 1981).

Sie·mens (sē′mənz, zē′-), Sir **William.** 1823–83. German-born English engineer and inventor.

Sien·kie·wicz (shĕn-kyā′vĭch, -kyĕ′-), **Henryk.** 1846–1916. Polish author (Nobel, 1905).

Sie·vers (sē′vərz, zē′fərs), **Georg Eduard.** 1850–1932. German philologist.

Sie·yès (syĕ-yĕs′), **Emmanuel Joseph.** "Abbè Sieyès." 1748–1836. French political leader.

Sig·is·mund (sĭg′ĭs-mənd, sĭj′-). 1368–1437. Holy Roman Emperor (1411–37).

Si·gnac (sē-nyäk′), **Paul.** 1863–1935. French neoimpressionist painter.

Si·gno·rel·li (sē-nyō-rĕl′lē), **Luca di Egidio di Ventura de'.** 1441–1523. Italian painter.

Sig·our·ney (sĭg′ər-nē), **Lydia Howard Huntley.** 1791–1865. Amer. author.

Sigs·bee (sĭgz′bē), **Charles Dwight.** 1845–1923. Amer. naval commander.

Si·gurds·son (sĭg′ərd-sən, -ərth-), **Jón.** 1811–79. Icelandic politician and scholar.

Si·ha·nouk (sē′ə-no͝ok′), Prince **Norodom.** b. 1922. Cambodian statesman.

Si·kor·ski (sĭ-kôr′skē), **Wladyslaw.** 1881–1943. Polish general.

Si·kor·sky (sĭ-kôr′skē), **Igor Ivan.** 1889–1972. Russian-born Amer. aviation pioneer.

Sil·lan·pää (sĭl′än-pă′), **Frans Eemil.** 1888–1964. Finnish author (Nobel, 1939).

Sil·li·man (sĭl′ə-mən), **Benjamin** (1779–1864) and **Benjamin, Jr.** (1816–85). Amer. science educators and editors.

Sills (sĭlz), **Beverly.** b. 1929. Amer. operatic soprano.

Si·lo·ne (sĭ-lō′nē, sē-lō′nā), **Ignazio.** 1900–78. Italian novelist.

Sil·ver·man (sĭl′vər-mən). **1. Sime.** 1873–1933. Amer. publisher. **2. Frederick ("Fred").** b. 1937. Amer. broadcasting executive.

Si·me·non (sēm-nôɴ′, sē-mə-), **Georges Joseph Christian.** b. 1903. Belgian-born French author.

Sim·e·on Sty·li·tes (sĭm′ē-ən stī-lī′tēz), Saint. 390?–459. Syrian ascetic.

Sim·kho·vitch (sĭm′kə-vĭch′), **Mary Melinda Kingsbury.** 1867–1951. Amer. settlement worker and reformer.

Simms (sĭmz). **1. William Gilmore.** 1806–70. Amer. author. **2. Ruth Hanna McCormick.** 1880–1944. Amer. politician.

Si·mon (sī′mən). **1.** 1st Viscount. John Allesbrook Simon. 1873–1954. English statesman. **2. Norton.** b. 1907. Amer. businessman. **3. Herbert Alexander.** b. 1916. Amer. economist (Nobel, 1978). **4. Neil.** b. 1927. Amer. playwright. **5. Paul.** b. 1942. Amer. singer and songwriter.

Si·mon·i·des of Ce·os (sī-mŏn′ĭ-dēz; sē′ŏs). 6th–5th cent. B.C. Greek poet.

Si·mo·nov (sē′mə-nŏf, -nôf), **Konstantin Mikhailovich.** b. 1915. Russian author.

Simon Ze·lo·tes (zē-lō′tēz) or **Simon the Ca·naan·ite** (kā′nə-nīt′). 1st cent. A.D. One of the 12 Apostles.

Simp·son (sĭmp′sən). **1.** Sir **James Young.** 1811–70. Scottish physician. **2. Jeremiah ("Sockless Jerry").** 1842–1905. Amer. rancher and politician. **3. George Gaylord.** 1902–84. Amer. paleontologist. **4. Adele.** b. 1903. Amer. fashion designer. **5. Orenthal James ("O.J.").** b. 1947 Amer. football player.

Sims (sĭmz). **1. James Marion.** 1813–83. Amer. pioneer gynecologist. **2. William Sowden.** 1858–1936. Amer. naval commander.

Si·na·tra (sə-nä′trə), **Francis Albert ("Frank").** b. 1915. Amer. entertainer.

Sin·clair (sĭn-klâr′, sĭng-). **1. May.** 1865?–1946. English novelist. **2. Harry Ford.** 1876–1956. Amer. oil executive. **3. Upton Beall.** 1878–1968. Amer. author and reformer.

Sing·er (sĭng′ər). **1. Isaac Merritt.** 1811–75. Amer. inventor (sewing machine) and manufacturer. **2. Isaac Bashevis.** b. 1904. Polish-born Amer. Yiddish author (Nobel, 1978).

Si·quei·ros (sē-kā′rôs), **David Alfaro.** 1898?–1974. Mexican mural painter.

Sis·ley (sĭs′lē, sĭz′-, sēs-lē′, -lā′), **Alfred.** 1840?–99. English-born French painter.

Sis·mon·di (sĭs-mŏn′dē, sēs-môɴ-dē′), **Jean Charles Léonard Simonde.** 1773–1842. Swiss historian and economist.

Sit·ter (sĭt′ər), **Willem de.** 1872–1934. Dutch astronomer.

Sit·ting Bull (sĭt′ĭng bo͝ol′). 1834?–90. Amer. Dakota Indian leader.

Sitting Bull

Sit·well (sĭt′wĕl′, -wəl). English family of poets and critics, including Sir **George Reresby** (1860–1943), Dame **Edith** (1887–1964), Sir **Osbert** (1892–1969), and **Sacheverell** (b. 1897).

Skeat (skēt), **Walter William.** 1835–1912. English philologist.

Skel·ton (skĕl′tən). **1. John.** 1460?–1529. English poet and scholar. **2. Richard ("Red").** b. 1913. Amer. comedian.

Skin·ner (skĭn′ər). **1. Otis.** 1858–1942. Amer. actor. **2. Constance Lindsay.** 1879–1939. Canadian-born Amer. author and historian. **3. Cornelia Otis.** 1901–79. Amer. actress and author. **4. Burrhus Frederick ("B.F.").** b. 1904. Amer. psychologist.

Ško·da (skō′də, shkô′dä), **Emil von.** 1839–1900. Czech engineer and industrialist.

Skou·ras (sko͞or′əs, -äs), **Spyros Panagiotes.** 1893–1971. Greek-born Amer. film executive.

Sla·ter (slā′tər), **Samuel.** 1768–1835. English-born textile pioneer in America.

Sli·dell (slī-dĕl′, slīd′l), **John.** 1793–1871. Amer. politician and Confederate diplomat.

Sli·pher (slī′fər), **Vesto Melvin.** 1875–1969. Amer. astronomer.

Sloan (slōn). **1. John French.** 1871–1951. Amer. painter. **2. Alfred Pritchard.** 1875–1966. Amer. industrialist and philanthropist.

Sloat (slōt), **John Drake.** 1781–1867. Amer. admiral.

Slo·cum (slō′kəm), **Henry Warner.** 1827–94. Amer. military and political leader.

Slo·nim·sky (slō-nĭm′skē), **Nicolas.** b. 1894. Russian-born Amer. composer and musicologist.

Smalls (smôlz), **Robert.** 1839–1915. Amer. Union soldier and politician.

Sme·ta·na (smĕt′n-ə, smĕ′tä-nä), **Bedřich.** 1824–84. Czech composer.

Smi·bert (smī′bərt), **John.** 1688–1751. Scottish-born Amer. painter.

Smig·ly-Rydz (smĭg′lē-rĭts′, -rĭdz′, shmĭg′-), **Edward.** 1886–1941? Polish military leader.

Smith (smĭth). **1. John.** 1580?–1631. English adventurer, colonist, explorer, and author. **2. Adam.** 1723–90. Scottish political economist and philosopher. **3. William.** 1727–1803. Scottish-born Amer. clergyman and educator. **4. Nathan.** 1762–1829. Amer. physician and medical educator. **5. William.** 1769–1839. English geologist. **6. Sydney.** 1771–1845. English clergyman, essayist, and editor. **7. Julia Evelina** (1792–1886) and **Aby Hadassah** (1797–1878). Amer. suffragists. **8. Seba.** "Major Jack Downing." 1792–1868. Amer. journalist and satirist. **9. Sophia.** 1796–1870. Amer. educational philanthropist. **10. Gerritt.** 1797–1874. Amer. reformer and philanthropist. **11. Jedediah Strong.** 1799?–1831. Amer. fur trader and explorer. **12. Joseph.** 1805–44. Amer. Mormon religious leader. **13. Samuel Francis.** 1808–95. Amer. poet and clergyman. **14. Charles Henry.** "Bill Arp." 1826–1903. Amer. author. **15. Hannah Whithall.** 1832–1911. Amer. evangelist, author, and reformer. **16. Francis Marion ("Borax").** 1846–1931. Amer. financier and promoter. **17. Theobold.** 1859–1934. Amer. pathologist. **18. Jessie Wilcox.** 1863–1935. Amer. artist. **19. Alfred Emanuel.** "the Happy Warrior." 1873–1944. Amer. politician. **20. Bessie.** 1894?–1937. Amer. blues singer. **21. Walter Bedell.** 1895–1961. Amer. general. **22. Margaret Chase.** b. 1897. Amer. politician. **23. Walter Wellesley ("Red").** 1905–82. Amer. sportswriter. **24. Kathryn Elizabeth ("Kate").** 1907?–86. Amer. entertainer. **25. Howard Kingsbury.** b. 1914. Amer. broadcast journalist. **26. Ian.** b. 1919. Zimbabwean political leader. **27. Hamilton Othanel.** b. 1931. Amer. microbiologist (Nobel, 1978).

Margaret Chase Smith

Smith·son (smĭth′sən), **James.** 1765–1829. English chemist, mineralogist, and philanthropist (Smithsonian Institution).

Smo·hal·la (smō-hăl′ə). 1815?–1907. Amer. Indian religious prophet.

Smol·lett (smŏl′ĭt), **Tobias George.** 1721–71. English novelist.

Smuts (smŭts, smœts), **Jan Christiaan.** 1870–1950. South African military and political leader.

Smyth (smĭth), **Henry DeWolf.** b. 1898. Amer. physicist.

Snead (snēd), **Samuel Jackson ("Sam").** b. 1912. Amer. golfer.

Snell (snĕl), **George.** b. 1903. Amer. geneticist (Nobel, 1980).

Snor·ri Stur·lu·son (snôr′ē stûr′lə-sən). 1178?–1241. Icelandic historian and statesman; assassinated.

Snow (snō), **Charles Percy ("C.P.").** 1905–80. English novelist.

Soar·es (swär′ĭsh, sə-wär′-), **Mário.** b. 1924. Portuguese statesman.

So·ci·nus (sō-sī′nəs), **Faustus.** 1539–1604. Italian theologian.

Soc·ra·tes (sŏk′rə-tēz′). 470?–399 B.C. Greek philosopher. **—So·crat′ic** (sō-krăt′ĭk) *adj.*

Sod·dy (sŏd′ē), **Frederick.** 1877–1956. English chemist (Nobel, 1921).

Sö·der·blom (sœ′dər-blo͞om′), **Nathan.** 1866–1931. Swedish prelate and historian (Nobel, 1930).

Sol·o·mon (sŏl′ə-mən). 10th cent. B.C. king of Israel.

So·lon (sō′lən). 638?–559 B.C. Athenian statesman and poet.

Sol·ti (sŏl′tē), Sir **Georg.** b. 1912. Hungarian-born English conductor.

Sol·vay (sŏl′vā, sôl-vā′), **Ernest.** 1838–1922. Belgian chemist, industrialist, and philanthropist.

Sol·zhe·ni·tsyn (sōl′zhə-nē′tsĭn), **Aleksandr Isayevich.** b. 1918. Russian author (Nobel, 1970).

Som·er·ville (sŭm′ər-vĭl′), Sir **James Fownes.** 1882–1949. English naval commander.

So·mo·za (sō-mō′sä), **Anastasio Somoza Debayle.** 1925–80. Nicaraguan statesman; assassinated.

Sond·heim (sŏnd′hīm′), **Stephen.** b. 1930. Amer. composer and lyricist.

Song (so͝ong). Name of 3 Chinese

dynasties: Northern (960–1127) and Southern (420–79, 1127–1279).
Son·tag (sŏn′tăg), Susan. b. 1933. Amer. author and critic.
Soong (so͝ong). Prominent Chinese family, including Charles Jones (d. 1927), missionary and merchant; Ai-ling (1888–1973), wife of H.H. Kung; Tse-ven or Tsu-wen (1891?–1971), financier; Ch'ing-ling (b. 1890), wife of Sun Yat-sen; and Mei-ling or Mayling (b. 1898), wife of Chiang Kai-shek.
Soph·o·cles (sŏf′ə-klēz′). 496?–406 B.C. Greek dramatist. —**Soph′o·cle′an** *adj.*
Sor·del·lo (sôr-dĕl′lō). 13th cent. Italian troubadour.
Sor·el (sô-rĕl′), Georges. 1847–1922. French journalist and syndicalist philosopher.
Sor·en·sen. 1. (sûr′ən-sən), Soren Peter Lauritz. 1868–1939. Danish chemist. **2.** (sôr′ĭn-sən), Theodore Chaikin. b. 1928. Amer. author and public official.
Sor·o·kin (sə-rō′kĭn, sô-), Pitirim Alexandrovich. 1889–1968. Russian-born Amer. sociologist.
So·rol·la y Bas·ti·da (sô-rô′lyä ē bäs-tē′*th*ä), Joaquín. 1863–1923. Spanish impressionist painter.
Soth·ern (sŭ*th*′ərn), Edward Hugh. 1859–1933. Amer. actor.
Sou·lé (so͞o-lā′), Pierre. 1801–70. French-born Amer. politician.
Soult (so͞olt), Nicholas Jean de Dieu. 1769–1851. French marshal.
Sou·sa (so͞o′zə, -sə), John Philip. 1854–1932. Amer. bandmaster and composer.
South (south), Robert. 1634–1716. English clergyman.
South·amp·ton (south-hămp′tən, sou-thămp′-), 3rd Earl of. Henry Wriothesley. 1573–1624. English courtier, military leader, and patron of Shakespeare.
Sou·they (sou′*th*ē, sŭ*th*′ē), Robert. 1774–1843. English author.
South·worth (south′wûrth′), Emma Dorothy Eliza Nevitte. 1819–99. Amer. novelist.
Sou·tine (so͞o-tēn′), Chaim. 1894–1943. Lithuanian-born expressionist painter.
Spaak (späk), Paul Henri Charles. 1889–1972. Belgian statesman.
Spaatz (späts, spăts), Carl. 1891–1974. Amer. general.
Spahn (spän, spôn), Warren Edward. b. 1921. Amer. baseball player.
Spal·ding (spôl′dĭng). **1.** Albert Goodwill. 1850–1915. Amer. sports-equipment manufacturer. **2.** Albert. 1888–1953. Amer. violinist and composer.
Spark (spärk), Muriel Sarah. b. 1918. Scottish-born author.
Sparks (spärks), Jared. 1789–1866. Amer. historian.
Spar·ta·cus (spär′tə-kəs). d. 71 B.C. Thracian gladiator.
Speer (shpâr, spîr), Albert. 1905–81. German architect and Nazi politician.
Spell·man (spĕl′mən), Francis Joseph. 1889–1967. Amer. prelate.
Spe·mann (shpā′män′), Hans. 1869–1941. German zoologist and physiologist (Nobel, 1935).
Spen·cer (spĕn′sər). **1.** Platt Rogers. 1800–64. Amer. handwriting expert. **2.** Herbert. 1820–1903. English philosopher. —**Spen·cer′i·an** *adj.*
Spen·der (spĕn′dər), Stephen Harold. b. 1909. English author.
Speng·ler (spĕng′lər, -glər, shpĕng′lər), Oswald. 1880–1936. German philosopher.
Spen·ser (spĕn′sər), Edmund. 1552?–99. English poet. —**Spen·ser′i·an** *adj.*
Sper·ry (spĕr′ē). **1.** Elmer Ambrose. 1860–1930. Amer. engineer and inventor. **2.** Roger. b. 1913. Amer. neurobiologist (Nobel, 1981).
Spiel·berg (spēl′bûrg′), Steven. b. 1947. Amer. film director.
Spil·lane (spə-lān′), Mickey. b. 1918. Amer. author.
Spin·garn (spĭn′gärn′), Joel Elias. 1875–1939. Amer. poet and critic.
Spi·no·za (spĭ-nō′zə), Baruch or Benedict. 1632–77. Dutch philosopher and theologian.
Spit·te·ler (shpĭt′l-ər, shpĭt′lər, spĭt′-), Carl. 1845–1924. Swiss writer and poet (Nobel, 1919).
Spitz (spĭts), Mark. b. 1950. Amer. swimmer.
Spock (spŏk), Benjamin McLane. b. 1903. Amer. pediatrician, educator, and author.

Benjamin Spock

Spode (spōd), Josiah. 1754–1827. English potter.
Spof·ford (spŏf′ərd), Harriet Elizabeth Prescott. 1835–1921. Amer. author.
Spoo·ner (spo͞o′nər), William Archibald. 1844–1930. English clergyman and educator.
Spots·wood (spŏts′wo͝od′), Alexander. 1676–1740. English colonial administrator.
Sprague (sprāg), Frank Julian. 1857–1934. Amer. electrical engineer and inventor.
Spreck·els (sprĕk′əlz), Claus. 1828–1908. German-born Amer. sugar manufacturer.
Spru·ance (spro͞o′əns), Raymond Ames. 1886–1969. Amer. admiral.
Spy·ri (shpē′rē, spîr′ē), Johanna. 1827?–1901. Swiss author (*Heidi*).
Squan·to (skwŏn′tō). d. 1622. Amer. Indian friend of Plymouth colony Pilgrims.
Squibb (skwĭb), Edward Robinson. 1819–1900. Amer. pharmaceutical manufacturer.
Staël (stäl), Madame de. Anne Louise Germaine Neckar. 1766–1817. French novelist, critic, and literary patron.
Stagg (stăg), Amos Alonzo. 1862–1965. Amer. football coach.
Stahl·berg (stôl′bərg, -bĕr′ē, stäl′-), Kaarlo Juho. 1865–1952. Finnish statesman.
Sta·lin (stä′lĭn, stăl′ĭn), Joseph. 1879–1953. Soviet Communist revolutionary leader.

Joseph Stalin

Stan·dish (stăn′dĭsh′), Miles or Myles. 1584?–1656. English Pilgrim colonist in America.
Stan·ford (stăn′fərd), Leland. 1824–93. Amer. financier and politician.
Stan·is·las I Lesz·czyn·ski (stăn′ĭ-slôs, -släs; lĕsh-chĭn′skē). 1677–1766. Polish king (1704–09 and 1733–35).
Stan·i·slav·ski (stăn′ĭ-släv′skē, -släf′-), Konstantin. 1863–1938. Russian actor and director.
Stan·ley (stăn′lē). **1.** Edward George Geoffrey Smith. 14th Earl of Derby. 1799–1869. English political leader. **2.** Sir Henry Morton. 1841–1904. Welsh-born journalist and African explorer. **3.** Francis Edgar (1849–1918) and Freelan (1849–1940). Amer. inventors and automobile manufacturers. **4.** Wendell Meredith. 1904–71. Amer. biochemist (Nobel, 1946).
Stan·ton (stăn′tən). **1.** Edwin McMasters. 1814–69. Amer. jurist and public official. **2.** Elizabeth Cady. 1815–1902. Amer. feminist and social reformer.

Elizabeth Cady Stanton

Stark (stärk). **1.** John. 1728–1822. Amer. Revolutionary general. **2.** (*also* shtärk), Johannes. 1874–1957. German physicist (Nobel, 1919). **3.** Harold Raynsford. 1880–1972. Amer. naval officer.
Starr (stär). **1.** Belle. 1848–89. Amer. outlaw. **2.** Ringo. b. 1940. English musician and composer.
Star·zyn·ski (stär-zĭn′skē, -zhĭn′-), Stefan. 1893–1940? Polish politician and national hero.
Stas·sen (stăs′ən), Harold Edward. b. 1907. Amer. politician.
Sta·tius (stā′shē-əs, -shəs), Publius Papinus. A.D. 45?–96? Roman poet.
Stat·ler (stăt′lər), Ellsworth Milton. 1863–1929. Amer. hotel builder.
Stau·ding·er (shtou′dĭng-ər), Hermann. 1881–1965. German chemist (Nobel, 1953).
Steed (stēd), Henry Wickham. 1871–1956. English journalist.
Steele (stēl), Sir Richard. 1672–1729. English politician and author.
Steen (stān), Jan. 1626–79. Dutch genre painter.
Ste·fáns·son (stĕf′ən-sən), Vilhjálmur. 1879–1962. Canadian Arctic explorer and ethnologist.
Stef·fens (stĕf′ənz), (Joseph) Lincoln. 1866–1936. Amer. journalist.
Stei·chen (stī′kən), Edward Jean. 1879–1973. Amer. photographer and landscape painter.
Stein (stīn). **1.** Gertrude. 1874–1946. Amer. author. **2.** Jules Caesar. 1896–1981. Amer. entertainment executive. **3.** William Howard. 1911–80. Amer. biochemist (Nobel, 1972).
Stein·beck (stīn′bĕk′), John Ernst. 1902–68. Amer. novelist (Nobel, 1962).
Stein·berg (stīn′bûrg′, -bərg), Saul. b. 1914. Rumanian-born Amer. graphic artist and cartoonist.
Stein·em (stī′nəm), Gloria. b. 1935. Amer. feminist, author, and lecturer.

Gloria Steinem

Stein·er (stī′nər, shtī′-), Rudolf. 1861–1925. Austrian social philosopher.
Stein·itz (stī′nĭts, shtī′-), William. 1836–1900. German chess player (1st world champion).
Stein·man (stīn′mən), David Barnard. 1886–1960. Amer. civil engineer and bridge designer.
Stein·metz (stīn′mĕts′), Charles Proteus. 1865–1923. German-born Amer. electrical engineer and inventor.
Stein·way (stīn′wā′), Henry Englehard. 1797–1871. German-born Amer. piano manufacturer.
Stel·la (stĕl′ə), Frank Philip. b. 1936. Amer. painter.
Sten·dhal (stĕn-däl′, stăn-, stän-). Marie Henri Beyle. 1783–1842. French novelist and biographer.
Sten·gel (stĕng′gəl), Charles Dillon ("Casey"). 1891–1975. Amer. baseball player and manager.
Ste·phen (stē′vən). **1.** Saint. 1st cent. Christian martyr. **2. I.** "St. Stephen." 975?–1038. Hungarian king (997–1038). **3.** of Blois (blwä). 1097?–1154. English king (1135–54). **4.** Sir Leslie. 1832–1904. English author and editor.
Ste·phens (stē′vənz). **1.** Alexander Hamilton. 1812–83. Amer. political leader and Confederate Vice President (1861–65). **2.** Uriah Smith. 1821–82. Amer. labor leader. **3.** Alice Barber. 1858–1932. Amer. painter and illustrator. **4.** James. 1882–1950. Irish author.
Ste·phen·son (stē′vən-sən), George (1781–1848) and Robert (1803–59). English railway pioneers.
Stern (stûrn). **1.** Otto. 1888–1969. German-born Amer. physicist (Nobel, 1943). **2.** Gladys Bertha. 1890–1973. English novelist. **3.** Isaac. b. 1920. Russian-born Amer. violinist.
Stern·berg (stûrn′bûrg′), George Miller. 1838–1915. Amer. army physician and bacteriologist.
Sterne (stûrn), Laurence. 1713–68. English satiric novelist.
Stet·son (stĕt′sən). **1.** John Batterson. 1830–1906. Amer. hat manufacturer. **2.** Augusta Emma Simmons. 1842–1928. Amer. Christian Science leader.
Stet·tin·i·us (stĕ-tĭn′ē-əs, -tĭn′yəs), Edward Reilly, Jr. 1900–49. Amer. business executive and public official.
Steu·ben (sto͞o′bən, styo͞o′-, sto͞o-bĕn′, styo͞o-, shtoi′bən), Baron Friedrich Wilhelm Ludolf Gerhard Augustin von. 1730–94. Prussian-born Amer. Revolutionary military leader.
Ste·vens (stē′vənz). **1.** John (1749–1838) and Robert Livingston (1787–1856). Amer. inventors and engineers. **2.** Thaddeus. 1792–1868. Amer. politician. **3.** Edwin Augustus. 1795–1868. Amer. inventor and philanthropist. **4.** Wallace. 1879–1955. Amer. poet. **5.** George. 1905–75. Amer. film director. **6.** Risë. b. 1913. Amer. operatic soprano. **7.** John Paul. b. 1920. Amer. jurist.
Ste·ven·son (stē′vən-sən). **1.** Andrew. 1784–1857. Amer. politician. **2.** Adlai Ewing. 1835–1914. U.S. Vice President (1893–97). **3.** Robert Louis Balfour. 1850–94. Scottish poet and novelist. **4.** Adlai Ewing. 1900–65. Amer. statesman.
Ste·vin (stə-vĭn′, -vĕn′), Simon. 1548–1620. Flemish mathematician.
Stew·art (sto͞o′ərt, styo͞o′-). **1.** Dugald. 1753–1828. Scottish philosopher. **2.** Robert. 2nd Marquis of Londonderry. See Viscount Castlereagh. **3.** Alexander Turney. 1803–76. Irish-born Amer. merchant. **4.** William Morris. 1827–1909. Amer. politician. **5.** James. b. 1908. Amer. actor. **6.** Potter. 1915–85. Amer. jurist.
Steyn (stīn, stān), Martinus Theunis. 1857–1916. South African statesman.
Stie·gel (stē′gəl, shtē′-), Henry William. 1729–85. German-born Amer. iron and glass manufacturer.
Stieg·litz (stēg′lĭts), Alfred. 1864–1946. Amer. pioneer photographer and editor.
Stik·ker (stĭk′ər), Dirk. b. 1897. Dutch industrialist and statesman.

Stiles (stīlz), **Ezra.** 1727–95. Amer. clergyman and educator.
Stil·i·cho (stĭl'ĭ-kō'), **Flavius.** 359?–408. Roman general and statesman; beheaded.
Still (stĭl), **Andrew Taylor.** 1828–1917. Amer. pioneer osteopath.
Stil·well (stĭl'wĕl', -wəl). **Joseph Warren.** 1883–1946. Amer. army officer.
Stim·son (stĭm'sən), **Henry Lewis.** 1867–1950. Amer. public official.
Stin·nes (shtĭn'əs), **Hugo.** 1870–1924. German industrialist.
Stock·mar (stŏk'mär', shtôk'-), Baron **Christian Friedrich von.** 1787–1863. German physician and political adviser to the English crown.
Stock·ton (stŏk'tən). **1. Robert Field.** 1795–1866. Amer. naval commander. **2. Francis Richard ("Frank").** 1834–1902. Amer. author.
Stod·dard (stŏd'ərd). **1. Solomon.** 1643–1729. Amer. clergyman. **2. Richard Henry.** 1825–1903. Amer. poet and critic.
Stod·dert (stŏd'ərt), **Benjamin.** 1751–1813. Amer. public official.
Sto·ker (stō'kər), **Bram.** 1847–1912. English author (*Dracula*).
Stokes (stōks). **1.** Sir **George Gabriel.** 1819–1903. English mathematician and physicist. **2. Olivia Egleston Phelps** (1847–1927) and **Caroline Phelps** (1854–1909). Amer. philanthropists. **3. Rose Harriet Pastor.** 1879–1933. Amer. political activist.
Sto·kow·ski (stə-kou'skē, -kôf'-), **Leopold Antoni Stanislaw.** 1882–1977. English-born Amer. conductor.
Stone (stōn). **1. Lucy.** 1818–93. Amer. feminist. **2. Melville Elijah.** 1848–1929. Amer. journalist. **3. Harlan Fiske.** 1872–1946. Amer. jurist and educator. **4. Edward Durell.** 1902–78. Amer. architect. **5. Irving.** b. 1903. Amer. author. **6. Isidor Feinstein ("I.F.").** b. 1907. Amer. journalist.
Stopes (stōps), **Marie Carmichael.** 1880–1958. British paleontologist and birth-control advocate.
Stor·y (stôr'ē, stōr'ē). **1. Joseph.** 1779–1845. Amer. jurist and legal author. **2. William Wetmore.** 1819–95. Amer. poet and sculptor.
Stout (stout), **Rex.** 1886–1975. Amer. mystery author.
Stow (stō), **John.** 1525?–1605. English historian and antiquarian.
Stowe (stō), **Harriet Elizabeth Beecher.** 1811–96. Amer. novelist and reformer.
Stra·bo (strā'bō'). 63? B.C.–A.D. 24? Greek geographer.
Stra·chey (strā'kē). **1. (Giles) Lytton.** 1880–1932. English historian, biographer, and critic. **2. (Evelyn) St. John Loe.** 1901–63. English statesman and author.
Stra·di·va·ri (străd'ə-vâr'ē, -vär'-, -văr'-), also **Stra·di·var·i·us** (-vâr'ē-əs, -văr'-), **Antonio.** 1644–1737. Italian violinmaker.
Straf·ford (străf'ərd), 1st Earl of. Thomas Wentworth. 1593–1641. English statesman; executed.
Strang (străng), **James Jesse.** 1813–56. Amer. Mormon leader.
Stras·berg (străs'bərg, sträs'-), **Lee.** 1901–82. Austrian-born Amer. theatrical producer, director, and teacher.
Strat·e·mey·er (străt'ə-mī'ər), **Edward.** 1862–1930. Amer. author.
Strath·co·na and Mount Roy·al (străth-kō'nə; mount roi'əl), 1st Baron. Donald Alexander Smith. 1820–1914. English colonial administrator.
Strat·ton (străt'n). **1. Charles Sherwood.** "General Tom Thumb." 1838–83. Amer. circus performer. **2. Samuel Wesley.** 1861–1931. Amer. physicist.
Straus (strous). **1. Isidor** (1845–1912) and **Nathan** (1848–1931). German-born Amer. merchants. **2. Oscar Solomon.** 1850–1926. Amer. politician and diplomat. **3.** (*also* shtrous), **Oscar** or **Oskar.** 1870–1954. Austrian-born French composer.
Strauss (strous). **1.** (*also* shtrous), **Johann** (1804–49), **Johann,** "the Waltz King," (1825–99), and **Josef** (1827–70). Austrian family of composers. **2.** (*also* shtrous), **David Friedrich.** 1808–74. German theologian and biographer. **3. Levi.** 1829?–1902. Amer. clothing manufacturer. **4.** (*also* shtrous), **Richard.** 1864–1949. German composer.
Stra·vin·sky (strə-vĭn'skē), **Igor Fëdorovich.** 1882–1971. Russian-born composer.
Strei·cher (strī'kər shtrī'KHər), **Julius.** 1885–1946. German Nazi leader and editor; executed.
Strei·sand (strī'sănd', -zănd'), **Barbra.** b. 1942. Amer. entertainer.
Stre·se·mann (shtrā'zə-män'), **Gustav.** 1878–1929. German statesman (Nobel, 1926).
Strick·land (strĭk'lənd), **William.** 1787?–1854. Amer. architect, engineer, and graphic artist.
Strind·berg (strĭnd'bûrg, strĭn'-, strĕn'bĕr'ē), **(Johan) August.** 1849–1912. Swedish playwright and novelist. —**Strind·berg'i·an** *adj.*
Stro·heim (strō'hīm'), **Erich von.** 1885–1957. Austrian-born Amer. actor and director.
Strong (strông). **1. William.** 1808–95. Amer. politician and jurist. **2. Josiah.** 1847–1916. Amer. clergyman and author. **3. Anna Louise.** 1885–1970. Amer. author.
Stru·en·see (shtrōō'ən-zā'), Count **Johann Friedrich von.** 1737–72. German-born Danish statesman; executed.
Strutt (strŭt), **Joseph.** 1749–1802. English antiquarian.
Struve (strōō'və), **Otto.** 1897–1963. Russian-born Amer. astronomer.
Stu·art (stōō'ərt, styōō'-). **1.** Ruling house of Scotland (1371–1625) and Great Britain (1603–49, 1660–1714). **2. James Francis Edward.** "the Old Pretender." 1688–1766. Pretender to English throne. **3. Charles Edward.** "the Young Pretender." 1720–88. English prince. **4. Gilbert Charles.** 1755–1828. Amer. painter. **5. James Ewell Brown ("Jeb").** 1833–64. Amer. Confederate general. **6. Ruth McEnery.** 1849–1917. Amer. author.

Jeb Stuart

Stubbs (stŭbz), **William.** 1825–1901. English historian.
Stu·de·ba·ker (stōō'də-bā'kər, styōō'-), **Clement.** 1831–1901. Amer. manufacturer.
Stur·gis (stûr'jĭs), **Russell.** 1836–1909. Amer. architect and author.
Štur·sa (shtōōr'sä) or **Stur·za** (-zä), **Jan.** 1880–1925. Czech. sculptor.
Stutz (stŭts), **Harry Clayton.** 1876–1930. Amer. automobile manufacturer.
Stuy·ve·sant (stī'vĭ-sənt), **Peter** or **Petrus.** 1592?–1672. Dutch colonial administrator in America.

Peter Stuyvesant

Sty·ron (stī'rən), **William.** b. 1925. Amer. novelist.
Suá·rez Gon·zá·lez (swär'əz gən-zäl'əs, swär'ĕs gôn-sä'lĕs), **Adolfo.** b. 1932. Spanish politician.
Suck·ling (sŭk'lĭng), Sir **John.** 1609?–42? English poet.
Sucre (sōō'krē), **Antonio José de.** 1795?–1830. South American revolutionary leader.
Sue (sōō, sü), **Eugène.** 1804–57. French novelist.
Sue·to·ni·us (swī-tō'nē-əs). 2nd cent. A.D. Roman historian.
Su·gi·ya·ma (sōō'gē-yä'mä), **Hajime.** 1880–1945. Japanese army officer.
Su·har·to (sə-här'tō, sōō-), **Raden.** b. 1921. Indonesian military and political leader.
Sui (swā). Chinese dynasty (581–618).
Su·kar·no (sōō-kär'nō). 1901–70. Indonesian statesman.
Su·lei·man I (sōō'lā-män', -lə-, sōō'-lā-män'). 1490?–1566. Turkish sultan (1520–66).
Sul·la (sŭl'ə), **Lucius Cornelius.** 138–78 B.C. Roman general and dictator.
Sul·li·van (sŭl'ə-vən). **1. John.** 1740–95. Amer. Revolutionary general. **2.** Sir **Arthur Seymour.** 1842–1900. English composer of operettas. **3. Louis Henri** or **Henry.** 1856–1924. Amer. architect. **4. John Lawrence.** 1858–1918. Amer. boxer. **5. James Edward.** 1860–1914. Amer. sports promoter. **6. Timothy Daniel ("Big Tim").** 1862–1913. Amer. politician. **7. Anne Mansfield.** 1866–1936. Amer. teacher of Helen Keller. **8. Francis John ("Frank").** 1892–1976. Amer. humorist. **9. John Lawrence.** 1899–1982. Amer. public official. **10. Edward Vincent ("Ed").** 1902–74. Amer. journalist.
Sul·ly (sŭl'ē). **1.** (*also* sü-lē'). Duc de. Maximilien de Béthune. 1560–1641. French statesman and Huguenot leader. **2. Thomas.** 1783–1872. English-born Amer. portrait painter.
Sul·ly-Prud·homme (sü-lē'prü-dôm'), **René François Armand.** 1839–1907. French poet (Nobel, 1901).
Sulz·ber·ger (sŭlz'bûr'gər, sōōlz'-), **Arthur Hays** (1891–1968) and **Arthur Ochs** (b. 1926). Amer. newspaper publishers.
Sum·ner (sŭm'nər). **1. Charles.** 1811–74. Amer. politician. **2. William Graham.** 1840–1910. Amer. economist, sociologist, and author. **3. James Batcheller.** 1887–1955. Amer. biochemist (Nobel, 1946).
Sum·ter (sŭm'tər), **Thomas.** 1734–1832. Amer. Revolutionary general, politician, and diplomat.
Sun·day (sŭn'dē, -dā'), **William Ashley ("Billy").** 1862–1935. Amer. evangelist.
Sung (sōōng). Song.
Sun Yat-sen (sōōn'yät'sĕn'). 1866–1925. Chinese revolutionary leader and statesman.
Sur·ratt (sə-răt'), **Mary Eugenia Jenkins.** 1820?–65. Amer. co-conspirator in Abraham Lincoln's assassination; executed.
Sur·rey (sûr'ē), Earl of. Henry Howard. 1517–47. English soldier and poet.
Sur·tees (sûr'tēz'), **Robert Smith.** 1803–64. English author and editor.
Su·sann (sōō-zăn'), **Jacqueline.** 1921–74. Amer. author.
Suss·kind (sŭs'kĭnd'), **David.** b. 1920. Amer. producer and television host.
Suth·er·land (sŭ*th*'ər-lənd). **1. George.** 1862–1942. English-born Amer. jurist and politician. **2. Earl Wilbur, Jr.** 1915–74. Amer. physiologist (Nobel, 1971). **3. Joan.** b. 1926. Australian operatic soprano.
Su·tro (sōō'trō), **Adolph Heinrich Joseph.** 1830–98. German-born Amer. mining engineer.
Sut·ter (sŭt'ər), **John Augustus.** 1803–80. German-born Amer. pioneer in Calif.; gold found on his land (1848).
Sutt·ner (zōōt'nər, sōōt'-), **Bertha von.** 1843–1914. Austrian writer (Nobel, 1905).
Su·vo·rov (sōō-vô'rəf, -rŏf), Count **Aleksandr Vasilevich.** 1730?–1800. Russian field marshal.
Su·zu·ki (sōō-zōō'kē), **Zenko.** b. 1911. Japanese statesman.
Sved·berg (svĕd'bĕr'ē, -bərg), **The** or **Theodor.** 1884–1971. Swedish chemist (Nobel, 1926).
Sver·drup (svĕr'drəp, -drōōp'), **Otto Neumann.** 1855–1930. Norwegian Arctic explorer.
Swa·dos (swā'dōs), **Elizabeth.** b. 1957. Amer. writer, composer, and director.
Swain (swān), **Clara A.** 1834–1910. Amer. pioneer medical missionary.
Swam·mer·dam (svä'mər-däm'), **Jan.** 1637–80. Dutch naturalist.
Swan·son (swŏn'sən), **Gloria.** 1899–1983. Amer. actress.
Swayne (swān), **Noah Haynes.** 1804–84. Amer. jurist.
Sway·ze (swā'zē), **John Cameron.** b. 1906. Amer. news commentator.
Swe·den·borg (swēd'n-bôrg', svā'-dən-bôr'ē), **Emanuel.** 1688–1772. Swedish scientist and theologian.
Swee·linck or **Swe·linck** (swā'lĭngk, svā'-), **Jan Pieterzoon.** 1562–1621. Dutch composer and organist.
Sweet (swēt), **Henry.** 1845–1912. English phoneticist and philologist.
Swift (swĭft). **1. Jonathan.** "Dean Swift." 1667–1745. English satirist. **2. Gustavus Franklin.** 1839–1903. Amer. meat packer.

Jonathan Swift

Swin·burne (swĭn'bûrn'), **Algernon Charles.** 1837–1909. English poet and critic.
Swin·ner·ton (swĭn'ər-tən), **Frank Arthur.** b. 1884. English author.
Swin·ton (swĭn'tən), 1st Earl of. Philip Cunliffe-Lister. 1884–1972. English statesman.
Swope (swōp). **1. Gerard.** 1872–1957. Amer. business executive and government official. **2. Herbert Bayard.** 1882–1958. Amer. journalist.
Syl·vis (sĭl'vĭs), **William.** 1828–69. Amer. labor leader.
Sy·ming·ton (sī'mĭng-tən), **(William) Stuart.** b. 1901. Amer. politician and public official.
Sym·onds (sĭm'əndz), **John Addington.** 1840–93. English poet, critic, and literary historian.
Sy·mons (sī'mənz), **Arthur.** 1865–1945. English poet and literary critic.
Synge (sĭng). **1. John Millington.** 1871–1909. Irish dramatist. **2. Richard Laurence Millington.** b. 1914. British biochemist (Nobel, 1952).
Szell (sĕl, zĕl), **George.** 1897–1970. Hungarian-born Amer. conductor.
Szent-györ·gyi von Nagy·ra·polt (sĕnt'jûr'jē fən näj'rō'pōlt, sĕnt'-dyœr'dyĭ fən nôd'yĭ-rō'pōlt), **Albert.** b. 1893. Hungarian-born Amer. biochemist.
Szi·ge·ti (sĭg'ĭ-tē, sĭ-gĕt'ē), **Joseph.** 1892–1973. Hungarian-born Amer. violinist.
Szi·lard (sē'lärd', sĭl'ärd', zĭl'-, zə-lärd'), **Leo.** 1898–1964. Hungarian-born Amer. physicist.
Szold (zōld), **Henrietta.** 1860–1945. Amer. Zionist leader.

T

Tabb (tăb), **John Banister.** 1845–1909. Amer. priest and poet.
Tac·i·tus (tăs'ĭ-təs), **Publius Corne-**

lius. A.D. 55?–118? Roman historian and orator.

Taft (tăft). **1. William Howard.** 1857–1930. 27th U.S. President (1909–13) and jurist. **2. Lorado.** 1860–1936. Amer. sculptor. **3. Robert Alphonso.** 1889–1953. Amer. politician.

William Howard Taft

Tag·gard (tăg'ərd), **Genevieve.** 1894–1948. Amer. poet.

Ta·gore (tə-gôr', -gōr'), Sir **Rabindranath.** 1861–1941. Indian poet (Nobel, 1913).

Taine (tān, tĕn), **Hippolyte Adolphe.** 1828–93. French philosopher and historian.

Tal·bot (tôl'bət, tăl'-), **William Henry Fox.** 1800–77. English inventor and antiquarian.

Tall·chief (tôl'chēf'), **Maria.** b. 1925. Amer. dancer.

Tal·ley·rand-Pé·ri·gord (tăl'ə-rănd'-pĕr'ə-gôr', tä-lĕ-räN'pā-rē-gôr'), **Charles Maurice de.** 1754–1838. French statesman and diplomat.

Tam·er·lane (tăm'ər-lān'), or **Tam·bur·laine** (-bər-). 1336?–1405. Mongol conqueror.

Tamm (täm), **Igor Yevgeneevich.** 1895–1971. Russian physicist (Nobel, 1958).

Ta·na·ka (tä-nä'kä), **Kakeui.** b. 1918. Japanese statesman.

Tan·cred (tăng'krĭd). 1078?–1112. Norman Crusade leader.

Ta·ney (tô'nē), **Roger Brooke.** 1777–1864. Amer. jurist; wrote Dred Scott decision.

Tang (täng). Name of 2 Chinese dynasties (618–907 and 923–36).

Tan·guy (täN-gē'), **Yves.** 1900–55. French-born Amer. surrealist painter.

Tan·ner (tăn'ər), **Henry Ossawa.** 1859–1937. Amer. painter in Paris.

Tap·pan (tăp'ən), **Arthur** (1786–1865) and **Lewis** (1788–1873). Amer. merchants, philanthropists and antislavery advocates.

Tar·bell (tär'bĕl', -bəl), **Ida Minerva.** 1857–1944. Amer. muckraking author and editor.

Tar·dieu (tär-dyœ'), **André Pierre Gabriel Amédée.** 1876–1945. French statesman and journalist.

Tar·king·ton (tär'kĭng'tən), **(Newton) Booth.** 1869–1946. Amer. author.

Tas·man (tăz'mən, täs'män'), **Abel Janszoon.** 1603?–59. Dutch navigator and explorer.

Tas·so (tăs'ō, täs'sō), **Torquato.** 1544–95. Italian poet.

Tate (tāt). **1. Nahum.** 1652–1715. English author. **2. Allen.** 1899–1979. Amer. poet, critic, editor, and biographer.

Ta·tum (tā'təm). **1. Edward Lawrie.** 1909–75. Amer. biochemist (Nobel, 1953). **2. Art.** 1910–56. Amer. musician.

Taus·sig (tou'sĭg), **Frank William.** 1859–1940. Amer. political economist.

Taw·ney (tô'nē), **Richard Henry.** 1880–1962. English economist and educator.

Tay·lor (tā'lər). **1. Jeremy.** 1613–67. English bishop and theologian. **2. Edward.** 1645?–1729. English-born Amer. Puritan clergyman and poet. **3. John.** "Taylor of Caroline." 1753–1824. Amer. agriculturalist and political philosopher. **4. Zachary.** "Old Rough and Ready." 1784–1850. 12th U.S. President (1849–50) and army officer. **5. Edward Thompson.** 1793–1871. Amer. religious leader. **6. Tom.** 1817–80. English dramatist. **7. (James) Bayard.** 1825–78. Amer. journalist and novelist. **8. Frederick Winslow.** 1856–1915. Amer. inventor, engineer, and efficiency expert. **9. David Watson.** 1864–1940. Amer. naval officer and architect. **10. Bert Leston.** 1866–1921. Amer. newspaper columnist. **11. Myron Charles.** 1874–1959. Amer. businessman and diplomat. **12. Laurette.** 1884–1946. Amer. actress. **13. (Joseph) Deems.** 1885–1966. Amer. composer and critic. **14. Robert.** 1911–69. Amer. actor. **15. Paul.** b. 1930. Amer. choreographer. **16. Elizabeth.** b. 1932. English-born Amer. actress.

Zachary Taylor

Tchai·kov·sky or **Tschai·kov·sky** (chī-kôf'skē, -kŏf'-), **Peter Ilich.** 1840–93. Russian composer. —**Tchai·kov'sky·an, Tchai·kov'ski·an** *adj.*

Tche·khov (chĕk'ôf, -ŏf). Variant of **Chekhov.**

Teach (tēch), **Edward.** "Blackbeard." d. 1718. English pirate.

Teas·dale (tēz'dāl'), **Sara.** 1884–1933. Amer. poet.

Te·bal·di (tə-bäl'dē, tĕ-), **Renata.** b. 1922. Italian-born operatic soprano.

Te·cum·seh (tĭ-kŭm'sə, -sē) or **Te·cum·tha** (-thə). 1768–1813. Amer. Shawnee chief.

Ted·der (tĕd'ər), Sir **Arthur William.** 1st Baron Tedder of Glenguin. 1890–1967. English air marshal.

Teil·hard de Char·din (tā-yär' də shär-dăN'), **Pierre.** 1881–1955. French priest, paleontologist, and philosopher.

Teisse·renc de Bort (tĕs-räN' də bôr'), **Leon Philippe.** 1855–1913. French meteorologist.

Te Ka·na·wa (tĭ kä'nə-wə, tĕ' kä-nä'-wä), **Kiri.** b. 1946. New Zealand-born operatic soprano.

Te·le·mann (tā'lə-män'), **Georg Philipp.** 1681–1767. German composer.

Tel·ler (tĕl'ər), **Edward.** b. 1908. Hungarian-born Amer. physicist.

Tem·in (tĕm'ĭn), **Howard Martin.** b. 1934. Amer. oncologist (Nobel, 1975).

Tem·ple (tĕm'pəl). **1.** Sir **William.** 1628–99. English author and statesman. **2. Frederick.** 1821–1902. English prelate. **3. Shirley.** See Shirley Temple **Black.**

Teng Hsiao-ping (dŭng' syou'pĭng'). Deng Xiaoping.

Te·niers (tə-nîrz', -nērs', tĕn'yərz, tĕ-nyā'), **David** ("the Elder"; 1582–1649) and **David** ("the Younger"; 1610–90). Flemish painters.

Ten·nent (tĕn'ənt), **William** (1673–1746) and **Gilbert** (1703–64). Irish-born Amer. clergymen.

Ten·niel (tĕn'yəl), Sir **John.** 1820–1914. English cartoonist and artist.

Ten·ny·son (tĕn'ĭ-sən), **Alfred.** 1st Baron Tennyson. "Alfred, Lord Tennyson." 1809–92. English poet. —**Ten'ny·so'ni·an** *adj.*

Ter·borch or **Ter Borch** (tər-bôrk', -bôrKH), **Gerard.** 1617–81. Dutch painter.

Ter·ence (tĕr'əns). 190?–59 B.C. Roman author.

Te·re·sa (tə-rē'sə, -zə, -rā'-). **1.** Saint. Variant of **Theresa. 2.** Mother. b. 1910. Albanian-born Indian nun (Nobel, 1979).

Mother Teresa

Te·resh·ko·va (tĕ-rĕsh-kô'vä, -kō'-), **Valentina Vladmirovna.** b. 1937. Soviet cosmonaut; 1st woman in space.

Ter·hune (tər-hyōōn'), **Mary Virginia Hawes** (1830–1922) and **Albert Payson** (1872–1942). Amer. authors.

Ter·man (tûr'mən), **Lewis Madison.** 1877–1956. Amer. psychologist.

Ter·ry (tĕr'ē). **1. Eli.** 1772–1852. Amer. pioneer clockmaker and inventor. **2. Alfred Howe.** 1827–90. Amer. Union general. **3.** Dame **Ellen Alicia** or **Alice.** 1846–1928. English actress.

Ter·tul·lian (tər-tŭl'ē-ən, -tŭl'yən). 160?–230? Carthaginian church father.

Ter·za·ghi (tər-zä'gē), **Karl.** 1883–1963. Bohemian-born Amer. engineer and soil expert.

Tes·la (tĕs'lə), **Nikola.** 1856–1943. Croatian-born Amer. electrical engineer, physicist, and inventor.

Tet·zel or **Te·zel** (tĕt'səl), **Johann.** 1465?–1519. German monk and preacher of indulgences.

Thack·er·ay (thăk'ə-rē, thăk'rē), **William Makepeace.** 1811–63. Indian-born English novelist and satirist. —**Thack'er·ay·an** *adj.*

Thal·berg (thâl'bûrg'), **Irving Grant.** 1899–1936. Amer. movie executive.

Tha·les (thā'lēz). 640?–546. B.C. Greek philosopher and geometrician. —**Tha·le'sian** *adj.*

Thant (thänt, thănt), **U.** 1909–74. Burmese United Nations secretary-general.

Tharp (thärp), **Twyla.** b. 1941. Amer. dancer and choreographer.

Thatch (thăch), **Edward.** Edward Teach.

Thatch·er (thăch'ər), **Margaret Hilda.** b. 1925. British prime minister (since 1975).

Thax·ter (thăk'stər), **Celia Laighton.** 1835–94. Amer. poet.

Thay·er (thā'ər, thâr). **1. Sylvanus.** 1785–1872. Amer. soldier and educator. **2. William Roscoe.** 1859–1923. Amer. historian and biographer.

Thei·ler (tī'lər, thī'-), **Max.** 1899–1972. South African-born Amer. microbiologist (Nobel, 1951).

The·mis·to·cles (thə-mĭs'tə-klēz'). 527?–460? B.C. Athenian military and political leader.

The·oc·ri·tus (thē-ŏk'rĭ-təs). 3rd cent. B.C. Greek idyllic poet.

The·o·do·ra (thē'ə-dôr'ə, -dōr'-). 508?–48. Byzantine empress as wife of Justinian I.

The·od·o·ric (thē-ŏd'ər-ĭk). 454?–526. King of Ostragoth (474–526).

The·o·do·sius I (thē'ə-dō'shəs, -shē-əs). "the Great." 346?–95. Roman emperor (379–95).

The·o·phras·tus (thē'ə-frăs'təs). 371–287 B.C. Greek philosopher.

The·o·rell (tā'ō-rĕl', tā'ə-rĕl'), **Axel Hugo Theodor.** b. 1903. Swedish biochemist (Nobel, 1955).

The·re·sa or **Te·re·sa** (tə-rē'sə, -zə, -rā'-), Saint. 1515–82. Spanish nun and mystical author.

Thes·pis (thĕs'pĭs). 6th cent. B.C. Greek poet.

Thiers (tyĕr), **Louis Adolphe.** 1797–1877. French statesman and historian.

Tho·burn (thō'bûrn'), **Isabella.** 1840–1901. Amer. missionary in India.

Tho·mas (tô-mä'), **Ambroise.** 1811–96. French composer.

Thom·as (tŏm'əs). **1.** Saint. One of the 12 Apostles. **2. Isaiah.** 1749–1831. Amer. painter and publisher. **3. Seth.** 1785–1859. Amer. clockmaker. **4. George Henry.** 1816–70. Amer. Union general. **5. Theodore.** 1835–1905. German-born Amer. violinist and conductor. **6. Edith Matilda.** 1854–1925. Amer. poet. **7. Augustus.** 1857–1934. Amer. editor and playwright. **8. Martha Carey.** 1857–1935. Amer. educator and feminist. **9. Norman Mattoon.** 1884–1968. Amer. socialist leader. **10. Lowell Jackson.** 1892–1981. Amer. commentator and author. **11. Dylan Marlais.** 1914–53. Welsh poet. **12. Michael Tilson.** b. 1944. Amer. conductor.

Thomas a Kem·pis (ə kĕm'pĭs, ä). 1380–1471. German ecclesiastic and writer.

Thomas A·qui·nas (ə-kwī'nəs), Saint. See **Aquinas.**

Thomas of Er·cel·doune (ûr'-səl-dōōn'). 1220?–97? Scottish seer and poet.

Thomp·son (tŏmp'sən, tŏm'-). **1. Benjamin.** Count Rumford. 1753–1814. Amer. physicist, Loyalist, and philanthropist. **2. Smith.** 1768–1843. Amer. jurist and politician. **3. David.** 1770–1857. Canadian explorer and fur trader. **4.** Sir **John Sparrow David.** 1844–94. Canadian prime minister (1892–94). **5. James Walter.** 1847–1928. Amer. advertising executive. **6. Francis.** 1859–1907. English poet. **7. Dorothy.** 1894–1961. Amer. journalist and author.

Thom·son (tŏm'sən). **1. James.** 1700–48. Scottish-born British poet. **2. James.** "the Poet of Despair." 1834–82. Scottish poet. **3. Elihu.** 1853–1937. English-born Amer. electrical engineer and inventor. **4.** Sir **Joseph John.** 1856–1940. English physicist and mathematician (Nobel, 1906). **5. John Arthur.** 1861–1933. Scottish biologist. **6.** Sir **George Paget.** 1892–1975. English physicist (Nobel, 1937). **7. Virgil Garnett.** b. 1896. Amer. composer and critic.

Tho·reau (thə-rō', thôr'ō), **Henry David.** 1817–62. Amer. essayist and poet. —**Tho·reau'vi·an** *adj.*

Tho·rez (tô-rĕz'), **Maurice.** 1900–64. French Communist leader.

Thor·finn Karl·sef·ni (thôr'fĭn kärl'-sĕv-nē, thôr'-). b. 980? Icelandic navigator and explorer.

Thorn·dike (thôrn'dīk'). **1. Ashley Horace.** 1871–1933. Amer. scholar and educator. **2. Edward Lee.** 1874–1949. Amer. educational psychologist. **3. Lynn.** 1882–1965. Amer. historian. **4.** Dame **Sybil.** 1882–1976. English actress.

Thorn·ton (thôrn'tən), **William.** 1759–1828. Amer. architect, inventor, and public official.

Thorpe (thôrp). **1. Thomas Bangs.** 1815–78. Amer. painter and humorist. **2. Rose Alnora Hartwick.** 1850–1939. Amer. author. **3. James Francis.** 1888–1953. Amer. Indian athlete.

Thor·vald·sen or **Thor·wald·sen** (tōōr'väl'sən, tôr'-), **(Albert) Bertel.** 1768–1844. Danish sculptor.

Thrale (thrāl), Mrs. **Hester Lynch Piozzi.**

Thras·y·bu·lus (thrăs'ə-byōō'ləs). d. 389 B.C. Athenian commander and statesman.

Thu·cyd·i·des (thōō-sĭd'ĭ-dēz'). 471–400 B.C. Greek historian.

Thumb (thŭm). General **Tom.** Charles Sherwood Stratton.

Thur·ber (thûr'bər), **James Grover.** 1894–1961. Amer. author and artist.

Thur·mond (thûr'mənd), **(James) Strom.** b. 1902. Amer. legislator.

Thurs·by (thûrz'bē), **Emma Cecilia.** 1845–1931. Amer. singer and educator.

Thut·mo·se (thōōt-mō'sə, -mōs', tŭt'mōz, thŭt'-) or **Thoth·mes** (thōth'-məs, -mēz, -mĕs, thŏth'-, tōt'-). Name of 4 kings of Egypt, esp. **III,** ruled 1501–1447 B.C.

Thwaites (thwāts), **Reuben Gold.** 1853–1913. Amer. historian, librarian, and editor.

Thys·sen (tĭs′ən), **Fritz.** 1873–1951. German industrialist.

Tib·bett (tĭb′ĭt), **Lawrence Mervil.** 1896–1960. Amer. baritone.

Ti·be·ri·us (tī-bîr′ē-əs). 42 B.C.–A.D. 37. Roman emperor (14–37). —**Ti·be′ri·an** *adj.*

Ti·bul·lus (tə-bŭl′əs), **Albius.** 54?–18? B.C. Roman elegiac poet.

Tick·nor (tĭck′nər, -nôr′), **George.** 1791–1871. Amer. author.

Tieck (tēk), **Ludwig.** 1773–1853. German poet and critic.

Tie·po·lo (tē-ĕp′ə-lō′, tyā′pō-lō), **Giovanni Battista.** 1696–1770. Italian painter.

Tif·fa·ny (tĭf′ə-nē). **1. Charles Lewis.** 1812–1902. Amer. jeweler and merchant. **2. Louis Comfort.** 1848–1933. Amer. painter and decorator.

Tig·lath·pi·le·ser (tĭg′lăth-pə-lē′zər, -pī-). Name of 3 Assyrian kings, esp. **III,** d. 727 B.C., ruled 745?–27.

Til·den (tĭl′dən). **1. Samuel Jones.** 1814–86. Amer. politician and library benefactor. **2. William Tatem, Jr. ("Big Bill").** 1893–1953. Amer. tennis player.

Til·lich (tĭl′ĭk, -ĭKH), **Paul Johannes.** 1886–1965. German-born theologian and philosopher.

Till·man (tĭl′mən), **Benjamin Ryan.** 1847–1918. Amer. farmer and legislator.

Till·strom (tĭl′strəm), **Burr.** 1917–85. Amer. puppeteer.

Til·ly (tĭl′ē), Count of. Johann Tserclass. 1559–1632. Flemish field marshal.

Til·you (tĭl′yo͞o′), **George Cornelius.** 1862–1914. Amer. amusement-park owner and inventor.

Ti·mo·shen·ko (tĭm′ə-shĕng′kō, tē′-mō-shĕn′kə), **Semen Konstantinovich.** 1895–1970. Russian army officer.

Tim·o·thy (tĭm′ə-thē), Saint. 1st cent. A.D. Christian leader.

Ti·mour (tĭ-mo͝or′) or **Ti·mur** (tĭ-mo͝or′) or **Timur Lenk** (lĕngk′). Tamerlane.

Tim·rod (tĭm′rŏd′), **Henry.** 1828–67. Amer. Confederate war poet.

Tin·ber·gen (tĭn′bər-gən, -bĕr′KHən). **1. Jan.** b. 1903. Dutch economist (Nobel, 1969). **2. Nikolaas.** b. 1903. Dutch-born English ethologist (Nobel, 1973).

Tin·dal or **Tin·dale** (tĭn′dl). Variants of **Tyndale.**

Ting (tĭng), **Samuel Chao Chung.** b. 1936. Amer. physicist (Nobel, 1976).

Ting·ley (tĭng′lē), **Katherine Augusta Westcott.** 1847–1929. Amer. theosophist.

Tin·to·ret·to (tĭn′tə-rĕt′ō, tēn′tō-rĕt′-tō), **II.** 1518–94. Italian painter.

Ti·om·kin (tē-ŏmp′kĭn, tyŏm′kĭn), **Dimitri.** b. 1899. Russian-born Amer. musician and composer.

Ti·pu Sa·hib (tē′po͞o sä′ĭb, -ēb, -hĭb) or **Tip·poo Sahib** (tĭp′o͞o). 1751–99. Sultan of Mysore (1782–99).

Tir·pitz (tĭr′pəts), **Alfred von.** 1849–1930. German admiral.

Tir·so de Mo·li·na (tĕr′sô dē mô-lē′-nä). Gabriel Téllez. 1571–1648. Spanish dramatist.

Ti·se·li·us (tē-sā′lē-o͞os, -əs), **Arne Wilhelm Kaurin.** 1902–71. Swedish biochemist (Nobel, 1948).

Titch·e·ner (tĭch′ə-nər), **Edward Bradford.** 1867–1927. English-born psychologist.

Ti·tian (tĭsh′ən). 1477–1576. Italian painter. —**Ti′tian·esque′** *adj.*

Ti·to (tē′tō), Marshal. Josip Broz. 1892–1980. Yugoslavian statesman.

Ti·tus (tī′təs). **1.** A.D. 40?–81. Roman emperor (79–81). **2.** Saint. 1st cent. A.D. Christian leader.

To·bey (tō′bē), **Mark.** 1890–1976. Amer. artist.

To·bin (tō′bĭn, -bən), **James.** b. 1918. Amer. economist (Nobel, 1981).

Tocque·ville (tōk′vĭl, tŏk′-, tôk-vēl′), **Alexis Charles Henri Maurice Clérel de.** 1805–59. French statesman, traveler, and historian.

Todd (tŏd). **1. Thomas.** 1765–1826. Amer. jurist. **2. David.** 1855–1939. Amer. astronomer and inventor. **3. Mabel Loomis.** 1856–1932. Amer. author and editor. **4.** Sir **Alexander Robertus.** b. 1907. English chemist (Nobel, 1957).

Todt (tōt), **Fritz.** 1891–1942. German military engineer.

To·gliat·ti (tô-lyät′tē), **Palmiro.** 1893–1964. Italian editor and Communist leader.

To·go (tō′gō′). **1.** Count **Heihachiro.** 1847–1934. Japanese admiral. **2. Shigenori.** 1882–1950. Japanese diplomat and politician.

To·jo (tō′jō′), **Hideki** or **Eiki.** 1885–1948. Japanese army officer and dictator (1941–44); executed.

To·klas (tō′kləs), **Alice B.** 1877–1967. Amer. author.

Tol·kein (tōl′kēn′), **John Ronald Reuel.** 1892–1973. English author and philologist.

Tol·ler (tō′lər, tŏl′ər), **Ernst.** 1893–1939. German author and politician.

Tol·stoy or **Tol·stoi** (tōl′stoi, tŏl′-, tōl-stoi′, tôl-, tŏl-), Count **Lev** or **Leo Nikolaevich.** 1828–1910. Russian author and philosopher. —**Tol·stoy′an, Tol·stoi′an** *adj.*

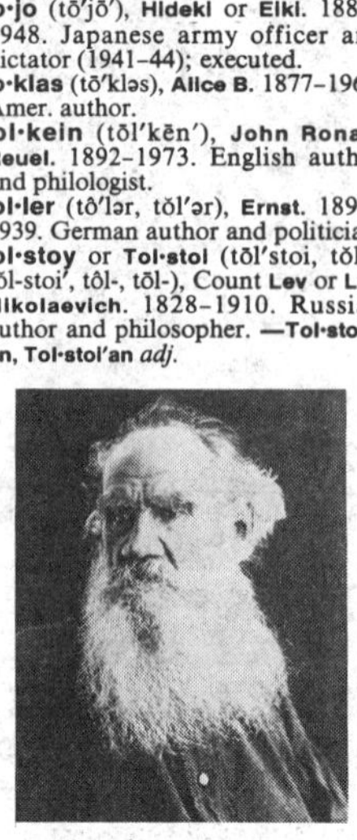

Lev Tolstoy

Tom·baugh (tŏm′bô′), **Clyde William.** b. 1906. Amer. astronomer; discovered Pluto.

Tom·ma·si·ni (tŏm′ə-zē′nē, -sē′-, tōm′mä-zē′nē), **Vicenzo.** 1880–1950. Italian composer.

To·mo·na·ga (tô′mô-nä′gä), **Shinichiro.** 1906–79. Japanese physician (Nobel, 1965).

Tomp·kins (tŏmp′kĭnz, tŏm′-). **1. Daniel D.** 1774–1825. U.S. Vice President (1817–25). **2. Sally Louisa.** 1833–1916. Amer. hospital philanthropist.

Tone (tōn), **(Theobold) Wolfe.** 1763–98. Irish revolutionist.

Ton·ti or **Ton·ty** (tŏn′tē, tōn′-, tôN-tē′), **Henry de.** 1650–1704. Italian explorer and trader in America.

Tooke (to͝ok), **(John) Horne.** 1736–1812. English politician and philologist.

Toombs (to͞omz), **Robert Augustus.** 1810–85. Amer. legislator and Confederate statesman.

Tor·que·ma·da (tôr′kē-mä′*th*ä), **Tomás de.** 1420–98. Spanish grand inquisitor.

Tor·rey (tôr′ē, tŏr′ē), **John.** 1796–1873. Amer. botanist and chemist.

Tor·ri·cel·li (tôr′ə-chĕl′ē, tôr′rē-chĕl′-lē), **Evangelista.** 1608–47. Italian mathematician and physicist.

Tor·ri·jos Her·re·ra (tôr-rē′-hôs ĕr-rĕ′rä), **Omar.** 1929–81. Panamanian general and political leader.

Tos·ca·ni·ni (tŏs′kə-nē′nē, tôs′-kä-nē′nē), **Arturo.** 1867–1957. Italian conductor.

Arturo Toscanini

Tot·le·ben (tôt′lĕ-bĕn, -bən, -lə-), Count **Franz Eduard Ivanovich.** 1818–84. Russian military engineer.

Tou·louse-Lau·trec (to͞o-lo͞oz′ lō-trĕk′), **Henri de.** 1864–1901. French painter and lithographer.

Tour·neur (tûr′nər), **Cyril.** 1575–1626. English dramatist.

Tous·saint L'Ou·ver·ture (to͞o-săN′ lo͞o-vĕr-tür′), **Pierre Dominique.** 1743–1803. Haitian revolutionary and statesman.

Town (toun), **Ithiel.** 1784–1844. Amer. architect.

Townes (tounz), **Charles Hard.** b. 1915. Amer. physicist (Nobel, 1964).

Town·send (toun′zənd), **Francis Everett.** 1867–1960. Amer. physician and social reformer.

Town·shend (toun′zənd), **Charles.** 1725–67. English politician.

Toyn·bee (toin′bē), **Arnold Joseph.** 1889–1975. English historian and educator.

Tra·cy (trā′sē), **Spencer.** 1900–67. Amer. actor.

Tra·jan (trā′jən). A.D. 52?–117. Roman emperor (98–117).

Trask (trăsk), **Kate Nichols ("Katrina").** 1853–1922. Amer. author and philanthropist.

Trau·bel (trou′bəl), **Helen.** 1903–72. Amer. operatic soprano.

Tra·ven (trā′vən), **B. Traven Torsvan.** 1890–1969. Amer. author.

Trav·ers (trăv′ərz), **P(amela) L.** b. 1904. Australian-born English author (*Mary Poppins*) and actress.

Trav·is (trăv′ĭs), **William Barret.** 1809–36. Amer. military leader; killed at the Alamo.

Tree (trē), Sir **Herbert Beerbohm.** 1853–1917. English actor and theatrical producer.

Treitsch·ke (trīch′kə), **Heinrich Gotthard von.** 1834–96. German historian.

Trench (trĕnch), **Richard Chenevix.** 1807–86. English poet and philologist.

Trev·el·lick (trĕv′ə-lĭk′), **Richard F.** 1830–95. English-born Amer. labor leader.

Tre·vel·yan (trə-vĕl′yən, -vĭl′-). **1.** Sir **George Otto.** 1838–1928. English historian and statesman. **2. George McCaulay.** 1876–1962. English historian and biographer.

Tre·vi·no (trə-vē′no), **Lee.** b. 1939. Amer. golfer.

Trev·i·thick (trĕv′ə-thĭk′), **Richard.** 1771–1833. English railroad engineer and inventor.

Tri·gère (trĭ-zhâr′, -jâr′, trē-zhĕr′), **Pauline.** b. 1912. French-born Amer. couturière.

Tril·ling (trĭl′ĭng), **Lionel.** 1905–75. Amer. critic and author.

Trim·ble (trĭm′bəl), **Robert.** 1777–1828. Amer. jurist.

Trippe (trĭp), **Juan.** 1900–81. Amer. aviation pioneer.

Trist (trĭst), **Nicholas Philip.** 1800–74. Amer. diplomat and public official.

Trol·lope (trŏl′əp), **Anthony.** 1815–82. English novelist.

Tromp (trômp, trŏmp), **Maarten** or **Martin Harpertszoon.** 1597–1653. Dutch admiral.

Trot·sky or **Trot·ski** (trŏt′skē, trôt′-), **Leon.** 1879–1940. Russian revolutionary and Soviet statesman; assassinated. —**Trot′sky·ist** or **Trot′sky·ite′** *adj. & n.*

Leon Trotsky

Troy·on (trwä-yôN′), **Constant.** 1813–65. French painter.

Tru·deau (tro͞o-dō′, tro͞o′-dō′), **Pierre Elliott.** b. 1919. Canadian prime minister (1968–79 and since 1980).

Truf·faut (tro͞o-fō′, trü-), **Francois.** 1932–84. French filmmaker.

Tru·ji·llo Mo·li·na (tro͞o-hē′yô mô-lē′nä), **Rafael Leonidas.** 1891–1961. Dominican military and political leader.

Tru·man (tro͞o′mən), **1. Harry S** 1884–1972. 33rd U.S. President (1945–53). **2. Margaret.** b. 1924. Amer. author and singer.

Harry S Truman

Trum·bo (trŭm′bō), **Dalton.** 1905–76. Amer. screenwriter.

Trum·bull (trŭm′bəl). **1. Jonathan** (1710–85) and **Jonathan** (1740–1809). Amer. statesmen. **2. John.** 1750–1831. Amer. lawyer and poet. **3. John.** 1756–1843. Amer. painter.

Truth (tro͞oth), **Sojourner.** 1797–1883. Amer. abolitionist.

Trux·tun (trŭk′stən), **Thomas.** 1755–1822. Amer. naval officer.

Tsal·da·res or **Tsal·da·ris** (tsäl-*thä*′-rēs, -dä′-), **Panages** or **Panagis.** 1868–1936. Greek statesman.

Tschai·kov·sky (chī-kôf′skē, -kŏf′-). Variant of **Tchaikovsky.**

Tub·man (tŭb′mən). **1. Harriet.** 1820–1913. Amer. abolitionist. **2. William Vacanarat Shadrach.** 1895–1971. Liberian statesman.

Harriet Tubman

Tuch·man (tŭck′mən), **Barbara Wertheim.** b. 1912. Amer. historian.

Tuck·er (tŭk′ər). **1. Benjamin Ricketson.** 1854–1939. Amer. anarchist. **2. Sophie.** 1884–1966. Russian-born Amer. entertainer. **3. Richard.** 1914–75. Amer. tenor.

Tu·dor (to͞o′dər, tyo͞o′-). **1.** English ruling family (1485–1603). **2. Antony.** b. 1909. English choreographer.

Tug·well (tŭg′wĕl′, -wəl), **Rexford Guy.** b. 1891. Amer. economist and public official.

Tul·si Das (tŭl′sē däs′, to͞ol′-). 1532–1623. Hindu poet.

Tun·ney (tŭn′ē), **James Joseph ("Gene").** 1898–1978. Amer. prizefighter.

Tup·per (tŭp′ər), Sir **Charles.** 1821–1915. Canadian prime minister (1896).

Tu·renne (tü-rĕn′), Vicomte de. Henri de La Tour d'Auvergne. 1611–75. French military leader.

Tur·ge·nev (to͝or-gā′nyəf, -gĕ′-), **Ivan Sergeevich.** 1818–83. Russian novelist.

Tur·got (to͝or-gō′, tür-), **Anne Robert Jacques.** 1727–81. French statesman and economist.

Tur·ner (tûr′nər). **1. Joseph Mallord**

William. 1775–1851. English painter. **2. Nat.** 1800–31. Amer. slave leader. **3. Frederick Jackson.** 1861–1932. Amer. historian of the West.

Tut·ankh·a·men (to͞ot'ängk-ä'mən) or **Tut·enkh·a·mon** (-ĕngk-). fl. c. 1358 B.C. Egyptian pharaoh.

Tutankhamen

Tut·wi·ler (tŭt'wī'lər), **Julia Strudwick.** 1841–1916. Amer. pioneer educator and reformer.

Twain (twān), **Mark.** Samuel Langhorne Clemens.

Tweed (twēd), **William Marcy.** "Boss Tweed." 1823–78. Amer. politician.

Ty·ler (tī'lər). **1. Walter ("Wat").** d. 1381. English peasant revolutionary. **2. Royall.** 1757–1826. Amer. jurist and playwright. **3. John.** 1790–1862. 10th U.S. President (1841–45). **4. Moses Coit.** 1835–1900. Amer. scholar and educator.

John Tyler

Tyn·dale or **Tin·dal** or **Tin·dale** (tĭn'dl), **William.** 1492–1536. English religious reformer and martyr.

Tyn·dall (tĭn'dl), **John.** 1820–93. Irish-born British physicist.

Tyr·whitt-Wil·son (tĭr'ĭt-wĭl'sən), **Gerald Hugh.** 1883–1950. English composer and painter.

Tzu Hsi (tso͞o' shē'). 1835–1908. Empress dowager of China.

U

Uc·cel·lo (o͞o-chĕl'lō), **Paolo.** 1397–1475? Italian painter.

U·gar·te (o͞o-gär'tē), **Manuel.** 1874?–1951. Argentine author.

Uh·land (o͞o'länt'), **Johann Ludwig.** 1787–1862. German lyric poet.

U·la·no·va (o͞o-lä'nə-və), **Galina.** b. 1910. Russian-born ballerina.

Ul·bricht (o͝ol'brĭkt, -brĭKHt), **Walter.** 1893–1973. German Communist leader.

Ul·pi·an (ŭl'pē-ən). 170?–228. Roman jurist; murdered.

Um·ber·to (o͞om-bĕr'tō). Name of 2 Italian kings: **1. I.** 1844–1900. Ruled 1878–1900. **2. II.** b. 1904. Ruled 1946.

U·na·mu·no y Ju·go (o͞o'nä-mo͞o'nô ē ho͞o'gô), **Miguel de.** 1864–1936. Spanish philosopher.

Un·cas (ŭng'kəs). 1588?–1683? Amer. Mohegan Indian leader.

Un·der·hill (ŭn'dər-hĭl'), **John.** 1597?–1672. English-born Amer. colonist, soldier, and public official.

Un·der·wood (ŭn'dər-wo͝od'), **Oscar Wilder.** 1862–1929. Amer. legislator.

Und·set (o͝on'sĕt'), **Sigrid.** 1882–1949. Danish-born Norwegian novelist (Nobel, 1928).

Un·ter·mey·er (ŭn'tər-mī'ər), **Louis.** 1885–1977. Amer. author and editor.

Un·ter·my·er (ŭn'tər-mī'ər), **Samuel.** 1858–1940. Amer. lawyer and reformer.

Up·dike (ŭp'dīk'), **John Hoyer.** b. 1932. Amer. author.

Up·john (ŭp'jŏn'), **Richard.** 1802–1878. English-born Amer. architect.

Ur·ban (ûr'bən). Name of 8 popes, esp. **II,** 1042?–99, reigned 1088–99.

U·rey (yo͝or'ē), **Harold Clayton.** 1893–1981. Amer. chemist (Nobel, 1934).

Ur·is (yo͝or'ĭs), **Leon Marcus.** b. 1924. Amer. novelist.

Ur·quhart (ûr'kərt, -kärt'), Sir **Thomas.** 1611–1660. Scottish Royalist and author.

Ur·so (ûr'sō), **Camilla.** 1842–1902. French-born Amer. violinist.

Ussh·er (ŭsh'ər), **James.** 1581–1656. Irish-born prelate and theologian.

U Thant (o͞o thänt', thănt). See **Thant.**

U·tril·lo (yo͞o-trĭl'ō, ü-trē-ō'), **Maurice.** 1883–1955. French painter.

V

Vail (vāl). **1. Alfred Lewis.** 1807–59. Amer. telegraph pioneer. **2. Theodore Newton.** 1845–1920. Amer. communications executive.

Val·de·mar (väl'də-mär'). Variant of **Waldemar.**

Val·di·via (väl-dē'vē-ə, väl-dē'vyä), **Pedro de.** 1500?–53. Spanish conqueror of Chile.

Val·do (văl'dō, väl'-). Variant of **Waldo.**

Va·lens (vā'lənz, -lĕnz'), **Flavius.** 328?–78. Eastern Roman emperor.

Val·en·tine (văl'ĭn-tīn'), Saint. 3rd cent. A.D. Christian martyr.

Val·en·tin·ian (văl'ĭn-tĭn'ē-ən, -tĭn'yən). Name of 3 Roman emperors: **1. I.** 321–75. Ruled 364–75. **2. II.** 372?–92. Ruled 383–92; assassinated. **3. III.** 419–55. Ruled 425–55; assassinated.

Val·en·ti·no (văl'ĭn-tē'nō), **Rudolf.** 1895–1926. Italian-born Amer. actor.

Va·le·ra y Al·ca·lá Ga·lia·no (vä-lĕ'rä ē äl-kä-lä' gäl-yä'nô), **Juan.** 1824–1905. Spanish author and diplomat.

Va·le·ri·an (və-lîr'ē-ən). d. 269? Roman emperor (253–60); overthrown and later killed.

Va·lé·ry (vä-lā-rē'), **Paul Ambroise.** 1871–1945. French poet.

Val·lan·dig·ham (və-lăn'dĭ-gəm), **Clement Laird.** 1820–71. Amer. legislator.

Val·lee (văl'ē), **Rudy.** 1901–86. Amer. singer.

Val·le·jo (və-lā'ō, -hō, vä-yĕ'hô), **Mariano Guadalupe.** 1808–90. Mexican-born California pioneer and soldier.

Va·lois (vä-lwä'). French ruling dynasty (1328–1589).

Van Al·len (văn ăl'ən), **James Alfred.** b. 1914. Amer. physicist.

Van·brugh (văn'brə, văn-bro͞o'), Sir **John.** 1664–1726. English dramatist and architect.

Van Bur·en (văn byo͝or'ən). **1. Martin.** 1782–1862. 8th U.S. President (1837–41). **2. Abigail ("Abby").** Pauline Esther Friedman.

Vance (văns). **1. Zebulon Baird.** 1830–94. Amer. politician and soldier. **2. Cyrus Roberts.** b. 1917. Amer. public official.

Van Cort·landt (văn kôrt'lənd, -lənt), **Stephanus.** 1643–1700. Amer. colonial merchant and official.

Van·cou·ver (văn-ko͞o'vər), **George.** 1757–98. English navigator.

Van De·man (văn dē'mən), **Esther Boise.** 1862–1937. Amer. archaeologist.

Van·den·berg (văn'dĭn-bûrg'), **Arthur Hendrick.** 1884–1951. Amer. diplomat and politician.

Van De·poele (văn' də-po͞ol'), **Charles Joseph.** 1846–92. Amer. electrical inventor.

Van·der·bilt (văn'dər-bĭlt'). **1. Cornelius** (1794–1877), **William Henry** (1821–85), and **Cornelius** (1843–99). Amer. railway promoters and financiers. **2. William Kissam.** 1849–1920. Amer. capitalist and sportsman. **3. Harold Stirling.** 1884–1970. Amer. businessman and sportsman. **4. George Washington.** 1862–1914. Amer. capitalist and benefactor. **5. Gloria.** b. 1924. Amer. designer.

Van·der·lyn (văn'dər-lĭn'), **John.** 1775–1852. Amer. artist.

van der Ro·he (văn dər rō'ə, fän). See **Mies van der Rohe.**

Van De·van·ter (văn' də-văn'tər), **Willis.** 1859–1941. Amer. jurist.

van Dong·en (văn dŏng'ən, vän dông'-), **Kees.** 1877–1968. Dutch artist.

Van Dor·en (văn dôr'ən, dōr'-). **1. Carl Clinton.** 1885–1950. Amer. author and critic. **2. Mark Albert.** 1894–1972. Amer. poet and critic.

Van·dyke or **Van Dyck** (văn-dīk', vän-), Sir **Anthony.** 1599–1641. Flemish painter.

Vane (vān), Sir **Henry** or **Harry.** 1613–62. English colonial administrator and statesman; executed for treason.

van Eyck (văn īk'), **Jan.** 1370?–1440? Flemish painter.

van Gogh (văn gō', gôKH', vän KHôKH'), **Vincent.** 1853–90. Dutch postimpressionist painter.

Vincent van Gogh

Van Heu·sen (văn hyo͞o'zən), **James ("Jimmy").** b. 1913. Amer. songwriter.

Van Hise (văn hīs'), **Charles Richard.** 1857–1918. Amer. geologist and educator.

Van Rens·se·laer (văn rĕn'sə-lîr', rĕn'sə-lər). **1.** (*also* văn rĕn'sə-lär), **Killian** or **Kiliaen.** 1595–1644. Dutch merchant. **2. Stephen.** 1764–1839. Amer. military and political leader. **3. Mariana Alley Griswold.** 1851–1934. Amer. art critic.

Van·sit·tart (văn-sĭt'ərt), Sir **Robert Gilbert.** 1st Baron Vansittart of Denham. 1881–1957. English diplomat and author.

Van Swer·in·gen (văn swâr'ĭn-jən), **Oris Paxton** (1879–1936) and **Mantis James** (1881–1935). Amer. real-estate developers and railway executives.

Martin Van Buren

van't Hoff (vänt hôf', hŏf'), **Jacobus Hendricus.** 1852–1911. Dutch chemist (Nobel, 1901).

Van Vech·ten (văn vĕk'tən), **Carl.** 1880–1964. Amer. critic.

Van Vleck (văn vlĕk'), **John Hasbrouck.** b. 1899. Amer. physicist (Nobel, 1977).

Van Zandt (văn zănt'), **Marie.** 1858–1919. Amer. operatic soprano.

Van·zet·ti (văn-zĕt'ē, vän-dzĕt'tē), **Bartolomeo.** 1888–1927. Italian-born Amer. anarchist.

Va·rèse (və-răz', -rĕz', vä-), **Edgard.** 1883–1965. French-born Amer. composer.

Var·gas (vär'gəs), **Getulio Dornelles.** 1883–1954. Brazilian statesman.

Var·num (vär'nəm), **Joseph Bradley.** 1751–1821. Amer. Revolutionary soldier and politician.

Var·ro (văr'ō), **Marcus Terentius.** 116–27 B.C. Roman scholar and encyclopedist.

Va·sa (vä'zə, -sä). Swedish ruling dynasty (1521–1654).

Va·sa·ri (və-zär'ē, -sär'ē, vä-zä'rē), **Giorgio.** 1511–74. Italian artist and architect.

Vas·sar (văs'ər), **Matthew.** 1792–1868. Amer. brewer and philanthropist.

Vau·ban (vō-bäN'), Marquis **Sébastien Le Prestre de.** 1633–1707. French military engineer.

Vaughan (vôn). **1. Henry.** 1622–95. Welsh metaphysical poet. **2. Sarah.** b. 1924. Amer. singer.

Vaughan Wil·liams (wĭl'yəmz), **Ralph.** 1872–1958. English composer.

Vaux (vôks), **Calvert.** 1824–95. English-born Amer. landscape architect.

Veb·len (vĕb'lən). **1. Thorstein Bunde.** 1857–1929. Amer. economist. **2. Oswald.** 1880–1960. Amer. mathematician.

Vega (vā'gə, vĕ'gä), **Lope de.** 1562–1635. Spanish author.

Ve·láz·quez or **Ve·lás·quez** (və-läs'kās, -kəs, -läs'-), **Diego Rodríguez de Silva y.** 1599–1660. Spanish painter.

Ven·dome (väN-dōm'), Duc de. Louis Joseph de Bourbon. 1654–1712. French general.

Ve·ni·ze·los (vĕ'nē-zĕ'lôs), **Eleutherios.** 1864–1936. Greek statesman.

Ven·tur·i (vĕn-to͝or'ē), **Robert Charles.** b. 1925. Amer. architect.

Ver·di (vâr'dē, vĕr'-), **Giuseppe.** 1813–1901. Italian composer.

Ve·re·shcha·gin (vĕ-rĕsh-chä'gĭn, vĕr'ə-shä'-), **Vasili Vasilievich.** 1842–1904. Russian painter.

Ver·gil (vûr'jəl). Variant of **Virgil.**

Ver·laine (vĕr-lĕn'), **Paul.** 1844–1896. French poet.

Ver·meer (vər-mîr', -mâr'), **Jan.** 1632–75. Dutch painter.

Verne (vûrn, vĕrn), **Jules.** 1828–1905. French novelist.

Ver·ner (vûr'nər, vĕr'-), **Karl Adolph.** 1846–1905. Danish philologist.

Ver·nier (vûr'nē-ər, vĕr-nyā'), **Pierre.** 1580–1637. French mathematician.

Ve·ro·ne·se (vā-rō-nā'zā), **Paolo.** 1528–88. Italian painter.

Ver·ra·za·no or **Ver·raz·za·no** (vĕr'ə-zä'nō, vĕr'rä-tsä'nō), **Giovanni da.** 1485?–1528? Italian explorer of Atlantic coast.

Giovanni da Verrazano

Ver·rett (və-rĕt'), **Shirley.** b. 1933. Amer. operatic soprano.

Ver·roc·chio (və-rō'kē-ō, vär-rôk'kyō), **Andrea del.** 1435–88. Florentine artist.

Ve·rus (vîr'əs), **Lucius Aurelius.** 130–69. Roman emperor.

Ver·woerd (fər-vo͝ort), **Hendrik Frensh.** 1901–66. South African statesman; assassinated.

Ver·y (vĕr′ē, vîr′ē), **Jones.** 1813–80. Amer. author.

Ve·sa·li·us (vĭ-sā′lē-əs, -zā′-), **Andreas.** 1514–64. Flemish anatomist.

Ve·sey (vē′zē), **Denmark.** 1767?–1822. Amer. black insurrectionist.

Ves·pa·sian (vĕs-pā′zhən). A.D. 9–79. Roman emperor (69–79).

Ves·puc·ci (vĕs-po͞o′chē, -pyo͞o′-), **Amerigo.** 1454–1512. Italian navigator and explorer.

Vick (vĭk), **James.** 1812–82. English-born Amer. horticulturist.

Vick·ers (vĭk′ərz), **Jon.** b. 1926. Canadian-born tenor.

Vic·tor Em·man·u·el (vĭk′tər ĭ-măn′yo͞o-əl). **1. I.** 1759–1824. Sardinian king (1802–21). **2. II.** 1820–78. Italian king (1861–78). **3. III.** 1869–1947. Italian king (1936–46); abdicated.

Vic·to·ri·a (vĭk-tôr′ē-ə, -tōr′-). 1819–1901. British queen (1837–1901) and Indian empress (1876–1901). —**Vic·to′ri·an** *adj. & n.*

Victoria

Vi·da (vē′dä), **Marco Girolamo.** 1480–1566. Italian prelate and poet.

Vi·dal (vĭ-dăl′), **Gore.** b. 1925. Amer. author.

Vi·dor (vĭ-dôr′, vī′dôr′), **King.** 1894–1982. Amer. filmmaker.

Vi·gée-Le·brun (vē-zhā′lə-brœN′), **Marie Anne Élisabeth.** 1755–1842. French painter.

Vi·gno·la (vē-nyō′lä), **Giacomo da.** 1507–73. Italian architect.

Vi·gny (vē-nyē′), Comte **Alfred Victor de.** 1797–1863. French author.

Vil·la (vē′ə, vē′yä), **Francisco ("Pancho").** 1877?–1923. Mexican revolutionary leader; assassinated.

Vil·la-Lo·bos (vē′lə-lō′bōs, vĭl′ə-, vē′lə-lō′bo͞osh, -bo͞os), **Heitor.** 1881–1959. Brazilian composer.

Vil·lard (vĭ-lär′, -lärd′). **1. Henry.** 1835–1900. German-born Amer. journalist and railway magnate. **2. Oswald Garrison.** 1872–1949. Amer. journalist and editor.

Vil·lars (vē-lär′), Duc **Claude Louis Hector de.** 1653–1734. French marshal.

Vil·lel·la (və-lĕl′ə), **Edward.** b. 1936. Amer. ballet dancer.

Vil·liers (vĭl′ərz, -yərz), **George.** See **Buckingham.**

Vil·lon (vē-yôN′, -lôN′). **1. François.** 1431–1462? French poet. **2. Jacques.** 1875–1963. French cubist artist.

Vin·cent (vĭn′sənt), **John Heyl.** 1832–1920. Amer. clergyman and educator.

Vin·cent de Paul (vĭn′sənt də pôl), Saint. 1581–1660. French ecclesiastic.

Vi·no·gra·doff (vē-nə-grä′dəf, vĭn′ə-grăd′ôf′), Sir **Paul Gavrilovich.** 1854–1925. Russian jurist and historian.

Vin·son (vĭn′sən). **1. Carl** 1884–1981. Amer. legislator. **2. Frederick Moore.** 1890–1953. Amer. jurist.

Viol·let-le-Duc (vē′ə-lā′lə-do͞ok′, -dyo͞ok′, vyô-lĕ′lə-dük′), **Eugène Emmanuel.** 1814–79. French architect.

Vir·chow (fîr′kō, -KHō, vîr′-), **Rudolf.** 1821–1902. German pioneer pathologist.

Vir·gil also **Ver·gil** (vûr′jəl). 70–19 B.C. Roman poet. —**Vir·gil′i·an, Ver·gil′i·an** *adj.*

Vir·ta·nen (vĭr′tä-nĕn), **Artturi Ilmari.** 1895–1973. Finnish biochemist (Nobel, 1945).

Vis·con·ti (vēs-kōn′tē), **Gian Galeazzo.** 1351?–1402. Milanese ruler (1378–1402).

Vi·shin·ski (vĭ-shĭn′skē), **Andrei Yanuarievich.** 1883–1954. Soviet jurist and diplomat.

Vi·tru·vi·us Pol·li·o (vĭ-tro͞o′vē-əs pŏl′ē-ō′), **Marcus.** 1st cent. B.C. Roman architect and engineer.

Vi·val·di (vĭ-väl′dē, -vôl′-, vē-väl′dē), **Antonio.** 1675?–1741. Italian composer.

Viz·ca·í·no (vĭz-kä-ē′nō, vēs-kä-ē′nō), **Sebastián.** 1550?–1615. Spanish explorer.

Vla·minck (vlä-măNk′), **Maurice de.** 1876–1958. French fauve artist.

Vo·gler (fō′glər), **Georg Joseph.** 1749–1814. German organist and composer.

Vol·stead (vŏl′stĕd′, vôl′-, vōl′-), **Andrew John.** 1860–1947. Amer. legislator.

Vol·ta (vōl′tə, vôl′tä), Count **Alessandro.** 1745–1827. Italian physicist.

Vol·taire (vōl-târ′, vŏl-, vôl-tĕr′). François Marie Arouet. 1694–1778. French author.

Von Eu·ler (fôn oi′lər), **Ulf Svante.** b. 1905. Swedish physiologist.

Von·ne·gut (vŏn′ĭ-gət), **Kurt, Jr.** b. 1922. Amer. author.

Von Neu·mann (vŏn noi′män′), **John.** 1903–57. Hungarian-born Amer. mathematician.

Vo·ro·shi·lov (vŏ-rŏ-shē′lôf, -ləf, -lôf), **Kliment Efremovich.** 1881–1969. Soviet military and political leader.

Vor·ster (fôr′stər), **Balthazar Johannes.** 1915–83. South African statesman.

Vought (vôt), **Chance Milton.** 1890–1930. Amer. aircraft designer and manufacturer.

Voz·ne·sen·ski (vŏz-nə-sĕn′skē), **Andrei.** b. 1933. Soviet poet.

Vree·land (vrē′lənd), **Diana Dalziel.** b. 1903. French-born Amer. editor and fashion expert.

Vuil·lard (vwē-yär′), **(Jean) Édouard.** 1868–1940. French painter.

W

Waals (wôlz, väls), **Johannes Diderik van der.** 1837–1923. Dutch physicist (Nobel, 1910).

Wace (wās, wäs). 12th cent. Anglo-Norman poet.

Wad·dell (wŏ-dĕl′), **James Iredell.** 1824–86. Amer. Confederate naval commander.

Wade (wād), **Benjamin Franklin.** 1800–78. Amer. politician.

Wag·ner. 1. (väg′nər), **(Wilhelm) Richard.** 1813–83. German composer. **2.** (wăg′nər), **Robert Ferdinand.** b. 1910. Amer. politician.

Wag·ner von Jau·regg (väg′nər fôn you′rĕk), **Julius.** 1857–1940. Austrian neurologist and psychiatrist (Nobel, 1927).

Wain·wright (wān′rīt′). **1. Richard** (1817–62) and **Richard** (1849–1926). Amer. naval officers. **2. Jonathan Mayhew.** 1883–1953. Amer. general.

Waite (wāt), **Morrison Remick.** 1816–88. Amer. jurist.

Waks·man (wăks′mən), **Selman Abraham.** 1888–1973. Russian-born Amer. microbiologist (Nobel, 1952).

Wal·cott (wôl′kət), **Charles Doolite.** 1850–1927. Amer. geologist and paleontologist.

Wald (wôld). **1. Lillian D.** 1867–1940. Amer. social reformer. **2. George.** b. 1906. Amer. biologist (Nobel, 1967).

Wal·de·mar (wôl′də-mär′, väl′-) or **Val·de·mar** (väl′-). Name of 4 Danish kings, esp. **I,** "the Great," 1132–82, ruled 1157–82.

Wal·der·see (väl′dər-zā′, wôl′-), Count **Alfred von.** 1832–1904. German field marshal.

Wald·heim (vält′hīm), **Kurt.** b. 1918. Austrian diplomat and United Nations secretary-general.

Wal·do (wôl′dō, wäl′-) or **Val·do** (väl′-, väl′-), **Peter.** 12th cent. French heretic.

Wa·le·sa (wä-lĕn′sä), **Lech.** b. 1943? Polish labor leader (Nobel, 1983).

Wal·green (wôl′grēn′), **Charles Rudolph.** 1873–1939. Amer. pharmacist and businessman.

Wal·ker (wô′kər). **1. Thomas.** 1715–94. Amer. physician, explorer, speculator, and politician. **2. David.** 1785–1830. Amer. abolitionist. **3. Joseph Reddeford.** 1798–1876. Amer. frontiersman. **4. Amasa.** 1799–1875. Amer. political economist. **5. Robert John.** 1801–69. Amer. financier and politician. **6. William.** 1824–60. Amer. adventurer and South American revolutionary. **7. Mary Edwards.** 1832–1919. Amer. physician and feminist. **8. Francis Amasa.** 1840–97. Amer. statistician and economist. **9. Sarah Breedlove.** 1867–1919. Amer. businesswoman. **10. James John ("Jimmy").** 1881–1946. Amer. politician.

Wal·lace (wŏl′ĭs). **1.** Sir **William.** 1272?–1305. Scottish national hero; executed for treason. **2. Alfred Russel.** 1823–1913. English naturalist. **3. Lewis ("Lew").** 1827–1905. Amer. general, diplomat, and author. **4. Henry Agard.** 1888–1965. U.S. Vice President (1941–45). **5. De Witt** (1889–1981) and **Lila Bell Acheson** (1899–1984). Amer. publishers. **6. Irving** b. 1916. Amer. novelist. **7. Myron ("Mike").** b. 1918. Amer. broadcast journalist. **8. George Corley.** b. 1919. Amer. politician.

Wal·lach (wäl′ək, väl′äKH), **Otto.** 1847–1931. German chemist (Nobel, 1910).

Wal·lack (wŏl′ək). **1. James William.** 1795?–1864. English-born actor and theatrical manager in America. **2. Lester.** 1820–88. Amer. actor.

Wal·len·stein (wŏl′ən-stīn′, väl′ən-shtīn′), **Albrecht Eusebius Wenzel von.** 1583–1634. Austrian military leader.

Wal·ler (wŏl′ər). **1. Edmund.** 1606–87. English poet. **2. Thomas ("Fats").** 1904–43. Amer. jazz musician.

Wal·lis (wŏl′ĭs). **1. John.** 1616–1703. English mathematician. **2. Hal Brent.** b. 1899. Amer. motion-picture producer.

Wal·pole (wôl′pōl′, wŏl′-). **1.** Sir **Robert.** 1st Earl of Orford. 1676–1745. English statesman. **2. Horace** or **Horatio.** 4th Earl of Orford. 1717–97. English author. **3.** Sir **Hugh Seymour.** 1884–1941. New Zealand-born English novelist and critic.

Walsh (wôlsh), **Thomas James.** 1859–1933. Amer. legislator.

Wal·ter 1. (wôl′tər), **John.** 1739–1812. English newspaper publisher. **2.** (väl′tər), **Bruno.** 1876–1962. German conductor.

Wal·ters (wôl′tərz), **Barbara.** b. 1931. Amer. broadcast journalist.

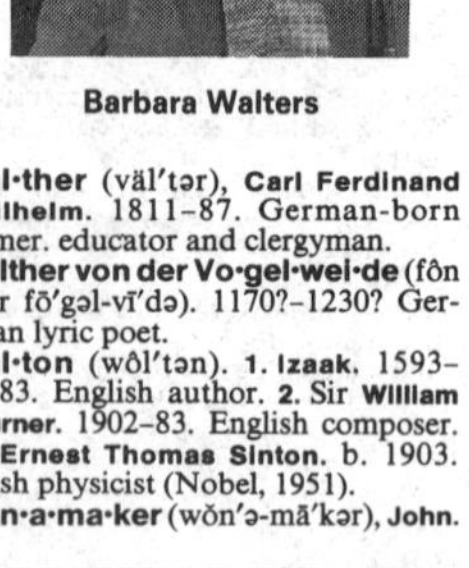

Barbara Walters

Wal·ther (väl′tər), **Carl Ferdinand Wilhelm.** 1811–87. German-born Amer. educator and clergyman.

Walther von der Vo·gel·wei·de (fôn der fō′gəl-vī′də). 1170?–1230? German lyric poet.

Wal·ton (wôl′tən). **1. Izaak.** 1593–1683. English author. **2.** Sir **William Turner.** 1902–83. English composer. **3. Ernest Thomas Sinton.** b. 1903. Irish physicist (Nobel, 1951).

Wan·a·ma·ker (wŏn′ə-mā′kər), **John.** 1838–1922. Amer. merchant and public official.

Wang Jing·wei also **Ching-wei** (wäng′ jyĭng′wā′). 1838–1944. Chinese political leader.

War·beck (wôr′bĕk′), **Perkin.** 1474–99. Flemish or Walloon pretender to English throne; executed.

War·burg (wôr′bərg′, vär′bo͝ork′), **Otto Heinrich.** 1883–1970. German biochemist (Nobel, 1931).

Ward (wôrd). **1. Nathaniel.** 1578?–1652. English-born clergyman and writer in America. **2. Artemus.** 1727–1800. Amer. Revolutionary general. **3. John Quincy Adams.** 1830–1910. Amer. sculptor. **4. Artemus.** Charles Farrar Browne. **5.** Sir **Adolphus William.** 1837–1924. English historian. **6. Lester Frank.** 1841–1913. Amer. botanist, geologist, and sociologist. **7. (Aaron) Montgomery.** 1843–1913. Amer. mail-order merchant. **8. Elizabeth Stuart Phelps.** 1844–1911. Amer. author. **9. Mary Augusta Arnold.** "Mrs. Humphrey Ward." 1851–1920. English novelist. **10.** Sir **Joseph George.** 1856–1930. New Zealand statesman. **11. Barbara.** Baroness Jackson. 1914–81. English economist.

War·hol (wôr′hŏl′, -hôl′), **Andy.** b. 1930? Amer. artist.

War·ing (wâr′ĭng), **Fred.** 1900–84. Amer. conductor.

War·ner (wôr′nər). **1. Susan Bogert** (1819–85) and **Anna Bartlett** (1827–1915). Amer. authors. **2. Charles Dudley.** 1829–1900. Amer. author and editor. **3. Glenn Scobey ("Pop").** 1871–1954. Amer. football coach. **4. Harry Morris** (1881–1958), **Albert** (1884–1967), **Samuel Louis** (1887–1927), and **Jack** (1892–1978). Amer. filmmakers.

War·ren (wô′rən, wŏr′ən). **1. Mercy Otis.** 1728–1814. Amer. author. **2. Joseph** (1741–75), **John** (1753–1815), and **John Collins** (1778–1856). Amer. surgeons and physicians. **3. Gouverneur Kemble.** 1830–82. Amer. army general and engineer. **4. Whitney.** 1864–1943. Amer. architect. **5. Earl.** 1891–1974. Amer. jurist. **6. Robert Penn.** b. 1905. Amer. author.

War·ton (wôr′tn), **Thomas.** 1728–90. English poet, critic, and scholar.

War·wick (wŏr′ĭk), Earl of. Richard Neville. 1428–71. English military and political leader.

Wash·burn (wŏsh′bûrn′, wôsh′-), **Margaret Floy.** 1871–1939. Amer. experimental psychologist.

Wash·ing·ton (wŏsh′ĭng-tən, wôsh′-). **1. Martha Dandridge Custis.** 1731–1802. Wife of George Washington. **2. George.** 1732–99. 1st U.S. President (1789–97) and Revolutionary soldier. **3. Bushrod.** 1762–1829. Amer. jurist. **4. Booker Taliaferro.** 1856–1915. Amer. educator and author. —**Wash′ing·to′ni·an** *adj.*

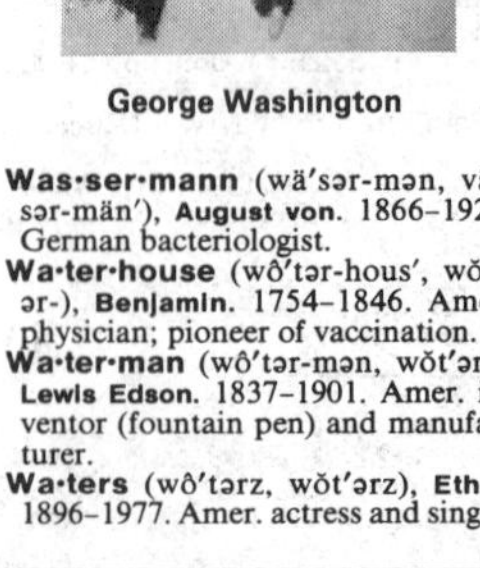

George Washington

Was·ser·mann (wä′sər-mən, vä′sər-män′), **August von.** 1866–1925. German bacteriologist.

Wa·ter·house (wô′tər-hous′, wŏt′ər-), **Benjamin.** 1754–1846. Amer. physician; pioneer of vaccination.

Wa·ter·man (wô′tər-mən, wŏt′ər-), **Lewis Edson.** 1837–1901. Amer. inventor (fountain pen) and manufacturer.

Wa·ters (wô′tərz, wŏt′ərz), **Ethel.** 1896–1977. Amer. actress and singer.

Wat·son (wŏt'sən). **1. Elkanah.** 1758–1842. Amer. banker and agriculturist. **2. Thomas Augustus.** 1854–1934. Amer. telephone pioneer and shipbuilder. **3. Thomas Edward.** 1856–1922. Amer. politician and publisher. **4.** Sir **(John) William.** 1858–1935. English poet. **5. Thomas John.** 1874–1956. Amer. businessman. **6. James Dewey.** b. 1928. Amer. biologist (Nobel, 1962).
Watt (wŏt), **James.** 1736–1819. Scottish-born engineer and inventor (steam engine).
Wat·teau (wŏ-tō', vä-), **Jean Antoine.** 1684–1721. French painter.
Wat·ter·son (wô'tər-sən, wŏt'ər-), **Henry.** "Marse Henry." 1840–1921. Amer. editor and politician.
Watts (wŏts). **1. Isaac.** 1674–1748. English poet, theologian, and hymn writer. **2. George Frederick.** 1817–1904. English painter.
Watts-Dun·ton (wŏts'dŭn'tən), **Walter Theodore.** 1832–1914. English author.
Waugh (wô), **Alec** (1898–1981) and **Evelyn** (1903–66). English authors.
Wa·vell (wā'vəl), 1st Earl of. Archibald Percival Wavell. 1883–1950. English army officer.
Way·land (wā'lənd), **Francis.** 1796–1865. Amer. clergyman.
Wayne (wān). **1. Anthony ("Mad Anthony").** 1745–96. Amer. Revolutionary general. **2. James Moore.** 1790–1867. Amer. jurist. **3. John.** 1907–79. Amer. actor.
Wea·ver (wē'vər). **1. James Baird.** 1833–1912. Amer. Populist leader. **2. Robert Clifton.** b. 1907. Amer. economist.
Webb (wĕb). **1. Beatrice Potter.** 1858–1943. English socialist and author. **2. Sidney James.** 1st Baron Passfield. 1859–1947. English sociologist and economist. **3. Clifton.** 1893–1966. Amer. actor.
We·ber (vā'bər). **1.** Baron **Karl Maria Friedrich Ernst von.** 1786–1826. German composer and conductor. **2. Ernst Heinrich.** 1795–1878. German physiologist and psychologist. **3. Wilhelm Eduard.** 1804–91. German sociologist and economist. **4. Max.** 1864–1920. German sociologist and economist. **5.** (wĕb'ər), **Max.** 1881–1961. Russian-born Amer. painter.
We·bern (vā'bərn), **Anton von.** 1883–1945. Austrian composer.
Web·ster (wĕb'stər). **1. John.** fl. early 17th cent. English dramatist. **2. Noah.** 1758–1843. Amer. lexicographer. **3. Daniel.** 1782–1852. Amer. politician, diplomat, and orator. **4. Alice Jane Chandler ("Jean").** 1876–1916. Amer. author.

Daniel Webster

Wedg·wood (wĕj'wo͝od'), **Josiah.** 1730–95. English potter.
Weed (wēd), **Thurlow.** 1797–1882. Amer. journalist and politician.
Weems (wēmz), **Mason Locke.** 1759–1825. Amer. clergyman and biographer of George Washington.
We·ge·ner (vā'gə-nər), **Alfred Lothar.** 1880–1930. German geophysicist, meteorologist, and explorer.
Wei (wā). Name of several Chinese dynasties (220–65, 386–550, and 535–56).
Weill (wīl, vīl), **Kurt.** 1900–50. German-born composer.
Wein·berg (wīn'bûrg'), **Steven.** b. 1933. Amer. physicist (Nobel, 1979).
Weir (wîr). Family of Amer. painters, including **Robert Walter** (1803–99), **John Ferguson** (1841–1926), and **Julian Alden** (1852–1919).
Weis·man (vīs'män'), **August.** 1834–1914. German biologist.
Weiss·mul·ler (wīs'mŭl'ər, -myo͞o'-lər), **Johnny.** b. 1903. Amer. swimmer and actor.
Weiz·mann (vīts'män', wīts'mən, wīz'-), **Chaim.** 1874–1952. Polish-born Israeli chemist and statesman.
Welch (wĕlch, wĕlsh). **1. William Henry.** 1850–1934. Amer. pathologist and bacteriologist. **2. Joseph Nye.** 1890–1960. Amer. lawyer.
Weld (wĕld), **Theodore Dwight.** 1803–95. Amer. abolitionist.
Welk (wĕlk), **Lawrence.** b. 1903. Amer. musician and bandleader.
Wel·ler (wĕl'ər), **Thomas Huckle.** b. 1915. Amer. microbiologist (Nobel, 1954).
Welles (wĕlz). **1. Gideon.** 1802–78. Amer. editor and public official. **2. Sumner.** 1892–1961. Amer. diplomat and journalist. **3. (George) Orson.** 1915–85. Amer. actor, producer, and director.

Orson Welles

Welles·ley (wĕlz'lē), 1st Marquis. Richard Colley Wellesley. 1760–1842. Irish-born British political leader and colonial administrator.
Wel·ling·ton (wĕl'ĭng-tən). 1st Duke of. Arthur Wellesley. "the Iron Duke." 1769–1852. Irish-born British military leader and statesman.
Well·man (wĕl'mən), **Walter.** 1858–1934. Amer. journalist and Arctic explorer.
Wells (wĕlz). **1. Henry.** 1805–78. Amer. express-company operator. **2. Horace.** 1815–48. Amer. dentist and pioneer anesthetist. **3. David Ames.** 1828–98. Amer. economist. **4. Carolyn.** 1862–1942. Amer. author. **5. Herbert George ("H.G.").** 1866–1946. English author. **6. Mary Georgene.** b. 1928. Amer. businesswoman.
Wel·ty (wĕl'tē), **Eudora.** b. 1909. Amer. author.
Wen·ces·laus (wĕn'sĭs-lôs') or **Wenzel** (vĕn'tsəl). 1361–1419. Holy Roman emperor (1378–1400; deposed) and king of Germany and Bohemia as **Wenceslaus IV** (1378–1419).
Wen·dell (wĕn'dl), **Barrett.** 1855–1921. Amer. educator and author.
Went·worth (wĕnt'wûrth'). **1. William Charles.** 1793?–1872. Australian statesman. **2. Cecile de.** d. 1933. Amer. portrait painter.
Wer·fel (vĕr'fəl), **Franz.** 1890–1945. Austrian author.
Wer·ner (wûr'nər, vĕr'-), **Alfred.** 1866–1919. German-born Swiss chemist (Nobel, 1913).
Wert·mül·ler (vĕrt'myo͞o'lər), **Lina.** b. 1926. Italian filmmaker.
Wes·ley (wĕs'lē, wĕz'-), **John.** 1703–91. British founder of Methodism. **—Wes'ley·an** *adj. & n.*
West (wĕst). **1. Benjamin.** 1738–1820. Amer. painter in England. **2.** Dame **Rebecca.** Cicily Isabel Fairfield. 1892–1983. English novelist and critic. **3. Mae.** 1892–1980. Amer. actress. **4. Jessamyn.** 1902–84. Amer. author. **5. Nathanael.** 1903–40. Amer. author.
West·cott (wĕs'kət, wĕst'-), **Edward Noyes.** 1846–98. Amer. author.
Wes·ter·marck (wĕs'tər-märk',vĕs'-), **Edward Alexander.** 1862–1939. Finnish anthropologist.
West·ing·house (wĕs'tĭng-hous'), **George.** 1846–1914. Amer. engineer and manufacturer.
West·more·land (wĕst-môr'lənd, -mōr'-), **William Childs.** b. 1914. Amer. general.
Wes·ton (wĕs'tən), **Edward.** 1886–1958. Amer. photographer.
Wey·den (wīd'n, vīd'n), **Rogier van der.** 1400?–64. Flemish painter.
Wey·er·haeu·ser (wī'ər-hou'zər), **Frederick.** 1834–1914. German-born Amer. lumberman.
Wey·gand (vā-gäN'), **(Louis) Maxime.** 1867–1965. French army commander.
Whar·ton (hwôr'tn, wôr'-), **Edith Newbold Jones.** 1862–1937. Amer. author.

Edith Wharton

Whate·ly (hwāt'lē, wāt'-), **Richard.** 1787–1863. English theologian and logician.
Wheat·ley (hwēt'lē, wēt'-), **Phillis.** 1753?–84. African-born Amer. poet.
Whea·ton (hwēt'n, wēt'n), **Henry.** 1785–1848. Amer. diplomat and historian.
Wheat·stone (hwēt'stōn', -stən, wēt'-), Sir **Charles.** 1802–75. English physicist and inventor.
Whee·ler (hwē'lər, wē'-). **1. William Almon.** 1819–87. U.S. Vice President (1877–81). **2. Joseph.** 1836–1906. Amer. Confederate general and politician. **3. Wayne Bidwell.** 1869–1927. Amer. lawyer and prohibitionist.
Whee·lock (hwē'lŏk', wē'-), **Eleazar.** 1711–79. Amer. clergyman and educator.
Whip·ple (hwĭp'əl, wĭp'-), **George Hoyt.** 1878–1976. Amer. pathologist (Nobel, 1934).
Whist·ler (hwĭs'lər, wĭs'-), **James Abbott McNeill.** 1834–1903. Amer. artist in London.
Whitch·er (hwĭch'ər, wĭch'-), **Frances Miriam Berry.** "Widow Bedott." 1811–52. Amer. author.
White (hwīt, wīt). **1. John.** d. 1593? English painter and cartographer in America. **2. Gilbert.** 1720–93. English naturalist. **3. William.** 1748–1836. Amer. prelate and author. **4. Canvass.** 1790–1834. Amer. civil engineer. **5. Ellen Gould Harmon.** 1827–1915. Amer. religious leader. **6. Andrew Dickson.** 1832–1918. Amer. editor, historian, and politician. **7. George Leonard.** 1838–95. Amer. choir leader. **8. Edward Douglass.** 1845–1921. Amer. jurist and politician. **9. Stanford.** 1853–1906. Amer. architect. **10. Alma Bridwell.** 1862–1946. Amer. evangelical leader. **11. David.** 1862–1935. Amer. paleobotanist and geologist. **12. William Allen.** 1868–1944. Amer. editor and author. **13. Stewart Edward.** 1873–1946. Amer. novelist. **14. Pearl.** 1889–1938. Amer. actress. **15. Walter Francis.** 1893–1955. Amer. author. **16. Elwyn Brooks ("E.B.").** 1899–1985. Amer. author. **17. Patrick.** b. 1912. Australian author (Nobel, 1973). **18. Theodore Harold ("T.H.").** b. 1915. Amer. political journalist. **19. Byron Raymond.** b. 1917. Amer. jurist and poet.

Mae West

White·field (hwīt'fēld', wīt'-, hwĭt'-, wĭt'-). **George.** 1714–70. English religious leader and orator.
White·head (hwīt'hĕd', wīt'-). **1. William.** 1715–85. English poet. **2. Alfred North.** 1861–1947. English mathematician and philosopher.
White·man (hwīt'mən, wīt'-), **Paul.** 1891–1967. Amer. jazz musician.
Whit·lam (hwĭt'ləm, wĭt'-), **Edward Gough.** b. 1916. Australian statesman.
Whit·lock (hwĭt'lŏk', wĭt'-), **Brand.** 1869–1934. Amer. author and diplomat.
Whit·man (hwĭt'mən, wĭt'-). **1. Marcus.** (1802–47) and **Narcissa Prentice** (1808–47). Amer. pioneers and frontier missionaries. **2. Sarah Helen Power.** 1803–78. Amer. poet and critic. **3. Walter ("Walt").** 1819–92. Amer. poet.

Walt Whitman

Whit·ney (hwĭt'nē, wĭt'-). **1. Eli.** 1765–1825. Amer. inventor (cotton gin) and manufacturer. **2. Asa.** 1791–1874. Amer. inventor and manufacturer. **3. Josiah Dwight.** 1819–96. Amer. geologist. **4. Anne.** 1821–1915. Amer. sculptor and poet. **5. Adeline Dutton Train.** 1824–1906. Amer. author. **6. William Dwight.** 1827–94. Amer. philologist. **7. William Collins.** 1841–1904. Amer. public official. **8. Mary Watson.** 1847–1921. Amer. astronomer. **9. Gertrude Vanderbilt.** 1875–1942. Amer. sculptor. **10. John Hay ("Jock").** 1904–82. Amer. newspaper publisher.
Whit·ta·ker (hwĭt'ə-kər, wĭt'-), **Charles Evans.** 1901–73. Amer. jurist.
Whit·tel·sey (hwĭt'l-sē, -zē, wĭt'-), **Abigail Goodrich.** 1788–1858. Amer. editor.
Whit·ti·er (hwĭt'ē-ər, wĭt'-), **John Greenleaf.** 1807–92. Amer. poet.
Whit·ting·ton (hwĭt'ĭng-tən, wĭt'-), **Richard.** 1358?–1423. English merchant and mayor of London.
Whit·worth (hwĭt'wûrth', wĭt'-), **Kathrynne Ann.** b. 1939. Amer. golfer.
Wick·er·sham (wĭk'ər-shəm), **George Woodward.** 1858–1936. Amer. lawyer.
Wic·lif or **Wick·liffe** (wĭk'lĭf). Variants of **Wycliffe.**
Wi·dor (vē-dôr'), **Charles Marie Jean Albert.** 1845–1937. French organist and composer.
Wie·land (vē'länt). **1. Christoph Martin.** 1733–1813. German author and translator. **2. Heinrich.** 1877–1957.

German chemist (Nobel, 1927).

Wien (vēn), **Wilhelm.** 1864–1928. German physicist (Nobel, 1911).

Wie·ner (wē'nər), **Norbert.** 1894–1964. Amer. mathematician; introduced cybernetics.

Wie·sel (vē'səl), **Torsten N.** b. 1924. Swedish-born Amer. physiologist (Nobel, 1981).

Wig·gin (wĭg'ĭn), **Kate Douglas Smith.** 1856–1923. Amer. author and educator.

Wig·gins (wĭg'ĭnz), **Carleton** (1848–1932) and **Guy Carleton** (1883–1962). Amer. painters.

Wig·gles·worth (wĭg'əlz-wûrth'), **Michael.** 1631–1705. English-born Amer. clergyman and poet.

Wig·more (wĭg'môr', -mōr'), **John Henry.** 1863–1943. Amer. legal educator and author.

Wig·ner (wĭg'nər), **Eugene Paul.** b. 1902. Hungarian-born Amer. physicist (Nobel, 1963).

Wil·ber·force (wĭl'bər-fôrs', -fōrs'), **William.** 1759–1833. English politician, abolitionist, and philanthropist.

Wil·bur (wĭl'bər), **Richard Purdy.** b. 1921. Amer. poet.

Wil·cox (wĭl'kŏks'), **Ella Wheeler.** 1850–1919. Amer. author.

Wilde (wīld), **Oscar Fingal O'Flahertie Wills.** 1854–1900. Irish poet, playwright, and wit.

Oscar Wilde

Wil·der (wĭl'dər). **1. Burt Green.** 1841–1925. Amer. zoologist and anatomist. **2. Laura Ingalls.** 1867–1957. Amer. author. **3. Thornton (Niven).** 1897–1975. Amer. author. **4. Billy.** b. 1906. Austrian-born Amer. filmmaker.

Wi·ley (wī'lē), **Harvey Washington.** 1844–1930. Amer. chemist and pure-food reformer.

Wil·hel·mi·na (wĭl'ə-mē'nə, vĭl'hĕl-mē'nä). 1880–1962. Queen of the Netherlands (1890–1948); abdicated.

Wilkes (wĭlks). **1. John.** 1727–97. English political reformer. **2. Charles.** 1798–1877. Amer. naval officer and explorer.

Wil·kins (wĭl'kĭnz). **1. Sir George Hubert.** 1888–1958. Australian polar explorer and aviator. **2. Roy.** 1901–81. Amer. civil-rights leader. **3. Maurice Hugh Frederick.** b. 1916. British physicist (Nobel, 1962).

Wil·kin·son (wĭl'kĭn-sən). **1. Jemima.** 1752–1819. Amer. religious leader. **2. James.** 1757–1825. Amer. military and political leader. **3. Ellen Cicely.** 1891–1947. English labor leader, politician, and suffragist. **4.** Sir **Geoffrey.** b. 1921. English chemist (Nobel, 1973).

Wil·lard (wĭl'ərd). **1. Emma Hart.** 1787–1870. Amer. poet and educator. **2. Frances Elizabeth Caroline.** 1839–98. Amer. author and temperance leader.

Will·cocks (wĭl'kŏks'), Sir **William.** 1852–1932. British engineer.

Wil·liam (wĭl'yəm). 1. Name of 4 kings of England: **a. I.** 1027–87. Ruled 1066–87. **b. II.** 1056?–1100. Ruled 1087–1100. **c. III.** 1650–1702. Ruled 1689–1702. **d. IV.** 1765–1837. Ruled 1830–37. **2. of Malmes·bur·y** (mämz'bĕr'ē, -bə-rē). 1090?–1143? English monk and historian. **3. I.** Prince of Orange. 1533–84. Dutch stadholder (1579–84). **4.** Name of 2 kings of Prussia: **a. I.** 1797–1888. Ruled 1861–88. **b. II.** 1859–1941. Ruled 1888–1918. **5.** 1882–1951. German crown prince.

Wil·liams (wĭl'yəmz). **1. Roger.** 1603?–83. English clergyman in America and founder of Rhode Island. **2. Eleazar.** 1789?–1858. Amer. missionary **3. Bert.** 1876–1922. Amer. entertainer. **4. William Carlos.** 1883–1963. Amer. physician and poet. **5. Thomas Lanier ("Tennessee").** 1911–83. Amer. playwright. **6. Theodore Samuel ("Ted").** b. 1918. Amer. baseball player. **7. Edward Bennett.** b. 1920. Amer. lawyer. **8. Elizabeth ("Betty").** b. 1943. Irish peace worker (Nobel, 1976).

Wil·lis (wĭl'ĭs), **Nathaniel Parker.** 1806–67. Amer. author.

Will·kie (wĭl'kē), **Wendell Lewis.** 1892–1944. Amer. politician.

Wills (wĭlz), **Helen Newington.** b. 1906. Amer. tennis player.

Will·son (wĭl'sən), **Meredith.** 1902–84. Amer. composer.

Will·stät·ter (vĭl'shtĕt'ər), **Richard.** 1872–1942. German chemist (Nobel, 1915).

Wil·lys (wĭl'ĭs), **John North.** 1873–1935. Amer. automobile manufacturer and diplomat.

Wil·mot (wĭl'mət, -mŏt'), **David.** 1814–68. Amer. politician.

Wil·son (wĭl'sən). **1. James.** 1742–98. Amer. Revolutionary patriot and jurist. **2. Alexander.** 1766–1813. Scottish-born Amer. ornithologist. **3. John.** "Christopher North." 1785–1854. Scottish author. **4. Henry.** 1812–75. U.S. Vice President (1873–75). **5. (Thomas) Woodrow.** 1856–1924. 28th U.S. President (1913–21), educator, and author. **6. William Bauchop.** 1862–1934. Amer. labor leader. **7. Harry Leon.** 1867–1939. Amer. novelist. **8. Charles Thomson Rees.** 1869–1959. British physicist (Nobel, 1927). **9. Charles Erwin.** 1890–1961. Amer. automobile executive. **10. Edmund.** 1895–1972. Amer. literary critic and author. **11. (James) Harold.** b. 1916. British prime minister (1964–70, 1974–79). **12. Robert Woodrow.** b. 1936. Amer. physicist and astronomer (Nobel, 1978).

Woodrow Wilson

Win·chell (wĭn'chəl), **Walter.** 1897–1972. Amer. journalist.

Win·ches·ter (wĭn'chĕs'tər), **Oliver Fisher.** 1810–80. Amer. firearms manufacturer.

Winck·el·mann (vĭng'kəl-män'), **Johann Joachim.** 1717–68. German archaeologist and antiquary.

Win·daus (vĭn'dous), **Adolf.** 1876–1959. German chemist (Nobel, 1928).

Win·dish-Graetz (vĭn'dĭsh-grāts'), Prince **Alfred Candidus Ferdinand zu.** 1787–1862. Austrian field marshal.

Wind·sor (wĭn'zər). **1. Wallis Warfield.** Duchess of Windsor. 1896–1986. Amer. socialite. **2.** Duke of. See **Edward VIII. 3.** British ruling dynasty (since 1917).

Win·gate (wĭn'gāt', -gət), **Orde Charles.** 1903–44. English army officer.

Win·kel·ried (vĭng'kəl-rēt'), **Arnold von.** 14th cent. Swiss national hero.

Win·slow (wĭnz'lō'), **Edward** (English-born; 1595–1655) and **Josiah** (1629?–80). Amer. colonists and administrators.

Win·sor (wĭn'zər), **Justin.** 1831–97. Amer. librarian and historian.

Win·throp (wĭn'thrəp). **1. John** (1588–1649), **John** (1606–76), and **John** (1638–1707). English colonial administrators in America. **2. John.** 1714–79. Amer. astronomer, mathematician, and physicist. **3. Robert Charles.** 1809–94. Amer. legislator and orator.

Win·ton (wĭn'tən), **Alexander.** 1860–1932. Scottish-born Amer. automobile manufacturer.

Wirt (wûrt), **William.** 1772–1834. Amer. public official and author.

Wise (wīz). **1. John.** 1652–1725. Amer. religious reformer. **2. Isaac Mayer.** 1819–1900. Bohemian-born Amer. rabbi and editor. **3. Thomas James.** 1859–1937. English book collector and forger. **4. Stephen Samuel.** 1874–1949. Hungarian-born Amer. religious and civic leader.

Wise·man (wīz'mən), **Nicholas Patrick Stephen.** 1802–65. Spanish-born English prelate and theologian.

Wiss·ler (wĭs'lər), **Clark.** 1870–1947. Amer. anthropologist.

Wis·ter (wĭs'tər), **Owen.** 1860–1938. Amer. author of Westerns.

With·er (wĭ*th*'ər) or **With·ers** (-ərz), **George.** 1588–1667. English poet.

With·er·spoon (wĭ*th*'ər-spo͞on'), **John.** 1723?–94. Scottish-born Amer. clergyman, educator, and Revolutionary patriot.

Wit·te (vĭt'ə), Count **Sergei Yulievich.** 1849–1915. Russian statesman.

Witt·gen·stein (vĭt'gĭn-shtīn', -stīn, -gən-), **Ludwig.** 1889–1951. Austrian-born English philosopher.

Wit·tig (vĭt'ĭKH), **Georg.** b. 1897. German chemist (Nobel, 1979).

Wode·house (wo͝od'hous'), **Pelham George ("P.G.").** 1881–1975. English author and humorist.

Wof·fing·ton (wŏf'ĭng-tən), **Margaret ("Peg").** 1714?–60. Irish actress.

Wöh·ler (wûr'lər, vûr'-, vœ'-), **Friedrich.** 1800–82. German chemist.

Wol·cott (wo͝ol'kət). Amer. family of political leaders, including **Roger** (1679–1767), **Oliver** (1726–97), and **Oliver** (1760–1833).

Wolf (vôlf). **1.** Variant of **Wolff** (sense 1). **2. Friedrich August.** 1759–1824. German classical scholar, founder of scientific philology. **3. Hugo.** 1860–1903. Austrian songwriter.

Wolfe (wo͝olf). **1. James.** 1727–59. English general in Canada. **2. Charles.** 1791–1823. English poet and clergyman. **3. Thomas (Clayton).** 1900–38. Amer. novelist.

Wolff (vôlf). **1.** Or **Wolf** (vôlf), Baron **Christian von.** 1679–1754. German mathematician and philosopher. **2. Kaspar Friedrich.** 1733–94. German pioneer embryologist.

Wol·fram von Esch·en·bach (vôl'främ fôn ĕsh'ən-bäKH'). fl. late 12th cent. German poet.

Wol·las·ton (wo͝ol'ə-stən), **William Hyde.** 1766–1828. English chemist and physicist.

Wolse·ley (wo͝olz'lē), 1st Viscount. Garnet Joseph Wolseley. 1833–1913. Irish-born British general and colonial administrator.

Wol·sey (wo͝ol'zē), **Thomas.** 1475?–1530. English prelate and statesman.

Wood (wo͝od). **1. Fernando.** 1812–81. Amer. politician. **2. James Rushmore.** 1813–82. Amer. surgeon and pioneer hospital administrator. **3. Leonard.** 1860–1927. Amer. colonial administrator and military leader. **4. Robert Elkington.** 1879–1969. Amer. general and business executive. **5. Grant.** 1892–1942. Amer. artist.

Wood·ber·ry (wo͝od'bĕr'ē, -bə-rē), **George Edward.** 1855–1930. Amer. poet, critic, and educator.

Wood·bur·y (wo͝od'bĕr'ē, -bə-rē). **1. Levi.** 1789–1851. Amer. jurist and politician. **2. Helen Laura Sumner.** 1876–1933. Amer. pioneer social economist.

Wood·hull (wo͝od'hŭl'), **Victoria Claflin** (1838–1927) and **Tennessee** (1846–1923). Amer. publishers and feminists.

Woods (wo͝odz), **William Burnham.** 1824–87. Amer. general and jurist.

Wood·ward (wo͝od'wərd). **1. C(omer) Vann.** b. 1908. Amer. historian. **2. Robert Burns.** 1917–79. Amer. chemist (Nobel, 1965).

Woolf (wo͝olf), **(Adeline) Virginia (Stephen).** 1882–1941. English author.

Wooll·cott (wo͝ol'kət, -kŏt'), **Alexander.** 1887–1943. Amer. critic and journalist.

Wool·ley (wo͝ol'ē), **1. Mary Emma.** 1863–1947. Amer. educator and reformer. **2.** Sir **Charles Leonard.** 1880–1960. English archaeologist.

Wool·man (wo͝ol'mən), **John.** 1720–72. Amer. clergyman and abolitionist.

Wool·sey (wo͝ol'sē). **1. Theodore Dwight.** 1801–89. Amer. educator and author. **2. Sarah Chauncey.** 1835–1905. Amer. author.

Wool·son (wo͝ol'sən), **Constance Fenimore.** 1840–94. Amer. novelist.

Wool·ton (wo͝ol'tən), 1st Earl of. Frederick James Marquis. 1883–1964. English banker and public official.

Wool·worth (wo͝ol'wûrth'), **Frank Winfield.** 1852–1919. Amer. merchant.

Worces·ter (wo͝os'tər). **1. Joseph Emerson.** 1784–1865. Amer. lexicographer. **2. Dean Conant.** 1866–1924. Amer. zoologist and colonial administrator.

Worde (wôrd), **Wynkyn de.** d. 1534? English printer.

Words·worth (wûrdz'wûrth'), **William.** 1770–1850. English poet. —**Words·worth'i·an** *adj.*

Work (wûrk), **Henry Clay.** 1832–84. Amer. songwriter.

Work·man (wûrk'mən), **Fanny Bullock.** 1859–1925. Amer. traveler, explorer, and author.

Wot·ton (wŏt'n, wo͝ot'n), Sir **Henry.** 1568–1639. English diplomat and author.

Wouk (wōk), **Herman.** b. 1915. Amer. author.

Wo·vo·ka (wō-vō'kə). Jack Wilson. 1858?–1932. Amer. Indian mystic.

Wran·gel (răng'gəl, vrän'gĭl), Baron **Pëtr Nikolaevich.** 1878–1928. Russian military leader.

Wren (rĕn), Sir **Christopher.** 1632–1723. English architect.

Wright (rīt). **1. Patience Lovell.** 1725–86. Amer. sculptor. **2. Frances ("Fanny").** 1795–1852. Scottish-born Amer. reformer. **3. Elizur.** 1804–85. Amer. abolitionist, journalist, and public official. **4. Chauncey.** 1830–75. Amer. mathematician and philosopher. **5. Henry.** 1835–95. English-born Amer. baseball player and manager. **6. Carroll Davidson.** 1840–1909. Amer. economist and statistician. **7. Joseph.** 1855–1930. English scholar and philologist. **8. Wilbur** (1867–1912) and **Orville** (1871–1948). Amer. aviation pioneers; 1st powered flight. **9. Frank Lloyd.** 1869–1959. Amer. architect. **10. Harold Bell.** 1872–1944. Amer. author. **11. Henry.** 1878–1936. Amer. architect and landscape designer. **12. Willard Huntington.** "S.S. Van Dine." 1888–1939. Amer. novelist and critic. **13. Richard.** 1908–60. Amer. novelist.

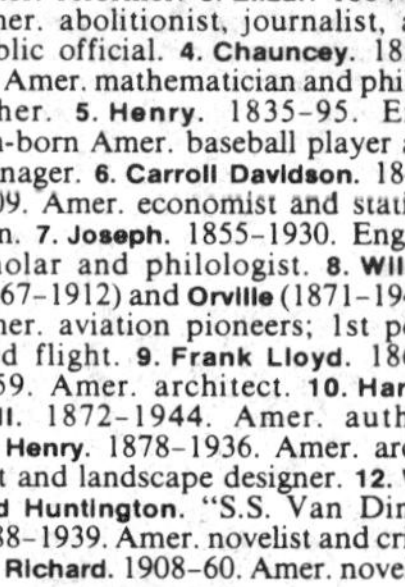

Frank Lloyd Wright

Wrig·ley (rĭg'lē), **William, Jr.** 1861–1932. Amer. chewing-gum manufacturer.

Wu (wo͞o). Chinese dynasty (222–80).

Wundt (vo͝ont), **Wilhelm.** 1832–1920. German psychologist.

Wy·att or **Wy·at** (wī'ət), Sir **Thomas.**

1503–42. English diplomat and poet.
Wych·er·ley (wĭch′ər-lē), **William.** 1640?–1716. English playwright.
Wyc·liffe also **Wick·liffe** or **Wyc·lif** or **Wic·lif** (wĭk′lĭf), **John.** 1320?–84. English religious reformer.
Wy·eth (wī′ĭth), **Newell Convers** (1882–1945) and **Andrew** (b. 1917). Amer. painters.

Andrew Wyeth

Wy·ler (wī′lər), **William.** 1902–81. Amer. filmmaker.
Wy·lie (wī′lē). **1. Elinor Morton Hoyt.** 1885–1928. Amer. poet and novelist. **2. Philip Gordon.** 1902–71. Amer. author.
Wynd·ham (wĭn′dəm). **1.** Sir **Charles.** 1837–1919. English actor. **2. George.** 1863–1913. English public official.
Wynn (wĭn), **Ed.** 1886–1966. Amer. actor.
Wy·szyń·ski (vĭ-shĭn′skē), **Stefan.** 1901–81. Polish prelate.
Wythe (wĭth), **George.** 1726–1806. Amer. Revolutionary patriot and jurist.

X

Xan·thip·pe (zăn-thĭp′ē, -tĭp′ē) or **Xan·tip·pe** (-tĭp′ē). Proverbially shrewish 5th cent. B.C. wife of Socrates.
Xa·vi·er (zā′vē-ər, zā′vyər), Saint **Francis.** 1506–52. Spanish missionary in the Orient.
Xe·noph·a·nes (zə-nŏf′ə-nēz′). 6th cent. B.C. Greek philosopher.
Xen·o·phon (zĕn′ə-fən, -fŏn′). 430?–355? B.C. Greek soldier and historian.
Xer·xes (zûrk′sēz). Name of 2 kings of Persia, esp. **I,** "the Great," 519?–465 B.C., ruled 486–65.
Xia (shyä). 1st Chinese dynasty (2205–1766 B.C.).

Y

Yale (yāl). **1. Elihu.** 1649–1721. Colonial-born English merchant and college benefactor. **2. Linus.** 1821–68. Amer. inventor (locks) and manufacturer. **3. Caroline Ardelia.** 1848–1933. Amer. educator of the deaf.
Yal·ow (yăl′ō), **Rosalyn Sussman.** b. 1921. Amer. physicist (Nobel, 1977).
Ya·ma·ga·ta (yä′mä-gä′tä), Prince **Aritomo.** 1838–1922. Japanese soldier and statesman.
Ya·ma·mo·to (yä′mä-mô′tô), **Isoroku.** 1884–1943. Japanese naval officer and statesman.
Ya·ma·ni (yä-mä′nē), **Ahmed Zaki.** b. 1930. Saudi Arabian oil minister.
Ya·ma·shi·ta (yä′mä-shē′tä), **Tomoyuki.** 1885–1946. Japanese general; executed for war crimes.
Yan·cey (yăn′sē), **William Lowndes.** 1814–63. Amer. legislator and secessionist.
Yang (yäng), **Chen Ning.** b. 1922. Chinese-born Amer. physicist (Nobel, 1957).
Ya·strzem·ski (yə-strĕm′skī), **Carl.** b. 1939. Amer. baseball player.
Yeard·ley (yärd′lē), Sir **George.** 1587–1627. English colonial administrator in Va.
Yeats (yāts), **William Butler.** 1865–1939. Irish author, producer, and politician (Nobel, 1923). **—Yeats′i·an** *adj.*
Yen Hsi-shan (yĕn shyē′shän′). 1882–1960. Chinese general.
Yer·by (yûr′bē), **Frank Garvin.** b. 1916. Amer. novelist.
Yer·kes (yûr′kēz, -kĭs). **1. Charles Tyson.** 1837–1905. Amer. financier. **2. Robert Mearns.** 1876–1956. Amer. psychobiologist.
Yer·sin (yĕr-săN′), **Alexandre Émile John.** 1863–1943. Swiss bacteriologist.
Yev·tu·shen·ko (yĕv′to͞o-shĕng′kō, yĭf-to͞o-shĕng′kə), **Yevgeny Aleksandrovich.** b. 1933. Soviet poet.
Yo·nai (yô′nī′), **Mitsumasa.** 1880–1948. Japanese naval officer and statesman.
York (yôrk). **1.** English ruling house (1461–85). **2. Alvin Cullum.** "Sergeant York." 1887–1964. Amer. World War I hero.
Yo·shi·hi·to (yō′shə-hē′tō, yô′-shē-hē′tô). 1879–1926. Japanese emperor (1912–26).
You·mans (yo͞o′mənz), **Vincent.** 1898–1946. Amer. operetta composer.
Young (yŭng). **1. Edward.** 1683–1765. English poet. **2. Thomas.** 1773–1829. English physician, physicist, and Egyptologist. **3. Brigham.** 1801–77. Amer. Mormon leader. **4. Ella Flagg.** 1845–1918. Amer. educator. **5. Denton True ("Cy").** 1867–1955. Amer. baseball player. **6. Owen D.** 1874–1962. Amer. corporate executive and public official. **7. Francis Brett.** 1884–1954. English novelist. **8. Murat Bernard ("Chic").** 1901–73. Amer. cartoonist ("Blondie"). **9. Whitney Moore.** 1921–71. Amer. civil-rights leader. **10. Andrew Jackson, Jr.** b. 1932. Amer. diplomat and politician.
Young·er (yŭng′gər), **Thomas Coleman ("Cole").** 1844–1916. Amer. desperado.
Young·hus·band (yŭng′hŭz′bənd), Sir **Francis Edward.** 1863–1942. English explorer.
Yu·an (yü′än′). Chinese dynasty (1271–1368).
Yuan Shi·gai also **Shih-kai** (shœ′kī′). 1859–1916. Chinese statesman.
Yu·ka·wa (yo͞o-kä′wä), **Hideki.** b. 1907. Japanese physicist (Nobel, 1949).

Z

Zagh·lul Pa·sha (zăg′lo͞ol pä′shä), **Saad.** 1860?–1927. Egyptian nationalist leader.
Za·har·i·as (zə-hăr′ē-əs), **Mildred Ella Didrikson ("Babe").** See **Didrikson.**
Za·krzew·ska (zä-kshĕv′skä), **Marie Elizabeth.** 1829–1902. Polish-Amer. physician and pioneer hospital administrator.
Za·les·ki (zä-lĕs′kē), **August.** 1883–1972. Polish statesman.
Za·mo·ra y Tor·res (sä-mô′rä ē tôr′rĕs), **Niceto Alcalá.** 1877–1949. Spanish politician.
Zan·gwill (zăng′gwĭl′, -wĭl′), **Israel.** 1864–1926. English author and Zionist.
Zan·uck (zăn′ək), **Darryl Francis.** 1902–79. Amer. motion-picture producer.
Za·pa·ta (sä-pä′tä), **Emiliano.** 1877?–1919. Mexico revolutionary.
Zar·a·thu·stra (zăr′ə-tho͞o′strə). Zoroaster.
Zeb·e·dee (zĕb′ĭ-dē′). In the New Testament, father of James and John.
Zech·a·ri·ah (zĕk′ə-rī′ə). 6th cent. B.C. Hebrew prophet.
Zed·e·ki·ah (zĕd′ĭ-kī′ə). King of Judah (597–86 B.C.).
Zee·man (zā′män′), **Pieter.** 1865–1943. Dutch physicist (Nobel, 1902).
Zef·fi·rel·li (zĕf′ə-rĕl′ē), **Franco.** b. 1923. Italian filmmaker.
Zei·sler (zī′slər), **Fannie Bloomfield.** 1863–1927. Austrian-born Amer. pianist.
Zeng·er (zĕng′ər, -gər), **John Peter.** 1697–1746. German-born colonial printer and journalist.
Ze·no (zē′nō). **1.** 5th cent. B.C. Greek philosopher. **2.** 342?–270? B.C. Greek Stoic philosopher.
Zeph·a·ni·ah (zĕf′ə-nī′ə), 7th cent. B.C. Hebrew prophet.
Zep·pe·lin (tsĕp′ə-lēn′, zĕp′ə-lĭn), Count **Ferdinand von.** 1838–1917. German airship designer and manufacturer.
Zer·ni·ke (zâr′nə-kə, zĕr′nĭ-kē), **Frits.** 1888–1966. Dutch physicist (Nobel, 1953).
Zeux·is (zo͞ok′sĭs). 5th cent. B.C. Greek painter.
Zhao Kuang·yin (jou′ kwäng′yĭn′). Chinese emperor (960–76).
Zhao Zi·yang (tsē-yäng′). b. 1919. Chinese statesman.
Zhda·nov (zhdä′nəf), **Andrei Aleksandrovich.** 1896–1948. Soviet soldier and politician.
Zhou (jō). Name of several Chinese dynasties (1122–221 B.C., 557–81, and 957–60).
Zhou En·lai (ĕn-lī′). 1898–1976. Chinese statesman.
Zhu De (jo͞o′ dŭ′). 1886–1976. Chinese Communist leader.
Zhu·kov (zho͞o′kəf), **Georgi Konstantinovich.** 1896–1974. Russian army officer.
Zieg·feld (zĭg′fĕld′, -fēld′, zĕg′-), **Florenz.** 1869–1932. Amer. theatrical producer.
Zie·gler (zē′glər, tsē′-), **Karl.** 1898–1973. German chemist (Nobel, 1963).
Zim·ba·list (zĭm′bə-lĭst′), **Efrem.** b. 1889. Russian-born Amer. violinist.
Zim·mer·man (zĭm′ər-mən, tsĭm′-ər-män′), **Arthur.** 1864–1940. German diplomat.
Zim·mern (zĭm′ərn), Sir **Alfred.** 1879–1957. English political scientist.
Zi·nov·iev (zi-nôf′yəf), **Grigori Evseevich.** 1883–1936. Soviet politician.
Zins·ser (zĭn′sər), **Hans.** 1878–1940. Amer. bacteriologist and immunologist.
Zin·zen·dorf (tsĭn′tsən-dôrf′), Count **Nikolaus Ludwig von.** 1700–60. German Moravian theologian.
Žiž·ka (zhĭsh′kä), **Jan.** 1360?–1424. Bohemian Hussite leader.
Zog I (zōg). 1895–1961. Albanian king (1928–46); deposed.
Zo·la (zō′lə, zô-lä′), **Emile.** 1840–1902. French author.

Émile Zola

Zor·ach (zō′răk′, -räk′), **William.** 1887–1966. Lithuanian-born Amer. artist.
Zorn (sôrn), **Anders Leonhard.** 1860–1920. Swedish artist.
Zo·ro·as·ter (zōr′ō-ăs′tər, zôr′-). 6th cent. B.C. Persian prophet. **—Zo′ro·as′tri·an** *adj. & n.*
Zor·ri·lla y Mo·ral (sôr-rē′lyä ē mô-räl′), **José.** 1817–93. Spanish author.
Zsig·mon·dy (zhĭg′môn-dē), **Richard.** 1865–1929. German chemist (Nobel, 1926).
Zuk·er·man (zo͞o′kər-mən), **Pinchas.** b. 1948. Israeli violinist.
Zweig (zwīg, swīg, tsvīKH). **1. Stefan.** 1881–1942. Austrian-born English author. **2. Arnold.** 1887–1968. German-born Jewish author.
Zwing·li (zwĭng′lē, swĭng′-, tsvĭng′-), **Ulrich** or **Huldreich.** 1484–1531. Swiss religious reformer.
Zwor·y·kin (zwôr′ĭ-kĭn), **Vladimir Kosma.** 1889–1982. Russian-born Amer. television pioneer.

Geographic Entries

Geographic entries are listed in alphabetical order. Places having the same name are combined in one entry; cities in a combined entry are alphabetized by country and, for U.S. cities, by state.

A

Aa·chen (ä′kən, ä′KHən). City of W West Germany, near the Belgian and Dutch borders. Pop. 242,971.
Aal·borg (ôl′bôrg′). Variant of **Ålborg**.
Aalst (älst). City of W central Belgium, WNW of Brussels. Pop. 79,340.
Aa·re (ä′rə) or **Aar** (är). River of central and N Switzerland, flowing 183 mi (294.5 km) into the Rhine.
Aar·hus (ôr′ho͞os′). Variant of **Århus**.
A·ba (ä′bə). City of SE Nigeria, N of Port Harcourt. Pop. 177,000.
A·ba·co and Cays (ăb′ə-kō′; kēz, kāz). Northernmost islands of the Bahamas.
Ab·a·dan (ăb′ə-dăn′, ä′bä-dän′). City of SW Iran, near the head of the Persian Gulf. Pop. 296,081.
A·ba·jo (ä′bə-hō′). Peak, 11,445 ft (3,490.7 m), of SE Utah, near the Colo. border in the **Abajo Mts.**
A·ba·kan (ä-bä-kän′). **1.** River of central Siberian USSR, flowing 350 mi (563.2 km) to the Yenisei. **2.** City of S central Siberian USSR, on the Yenisei. Pop. 133,000.
A·ba·ya (ä′bä-yä). Lake, 485 sq mi (1,256.2 sq km), of SW Ethiopia.
Abbe·bille (ăb-vēl′, ăb′ē-vĭl). City of N France, on the Somme. Pop. 25,398.
Ab·be·ville (ăb′ē-vĭl′). City of S La., SW of Baton Rouge. Pop. 12,391.
A·be·o·ku·ta (ăb′ē-ō-ko͞o′tə, ä′bā-ō′-ko͞o-tä). City of SW Nigeria, N of Lagos. Pop. 253,000.
Ab·er·dare (ăb′ər-dâr′, ăb′ər-dâr′). Urban district of SW Wales, NW of Cardiff. Pop. 38,030.
Ab·er·deen (ăb′ər-dēn′). **1.** (*also* ăb′ər-dēn′). Burgh of NE Scotland, on the North Sea. Pop. 209,189. **2.** Town of NE Md., ENE of Baltimore. Pop. 11, 533. **3.** City of NE S.Dak., NE of Pierre. Pop. 25,956. **4.** City of W Wash., WSW of Tacoma. Pop. 18,739.
Ab·i·djan (ăb′ĭ-jän′, ä-bē-jäN′). Cap. of Ivory Coast, W Africa, in the S part on the Gulf of Guinea. Pop. 685,800.
Ab·i·lene (ăb′ə-lēn′). City of W central Tex., WSW of Fort Worth. Pop. 98,315.
Ab·ing·ton (ăb′ĭng-tən). Town of E Mass., SSE of Boston. Pop. 13,517.
Ab·i·tib·i (ăb′ĭ-tĭb′ē). Lake of E Ont. and SW Que., Canada, source of the **Abitibi R.**, flowing 230 mi (270 km) to the Moose R.
Ab·kha·zi·a (ăb-kä′zhə, äb-KHä′-). Region of SW European USSR. —**Ab·kha′zi·an** *adj. & n.*
Å·bo (ô′bo͞o, ô′bo͞o). *Swedish.* Turku.
A·bruz·zi (ä-bro͞ot′tsē) also **Abruzzi e Mo·li·se** (ā mō-lē′zä). Region of central Italy, on the Adriatic.
Ab·sa·ro·ka (ăb-sär′ə-kə). Range of the Rocky Mts., in NW Wyo. and S Mont., rising to 13,140 ft (4,007.7 m).
A·bu Dha·bi (ä′bo͞o dä′bē). Sheikdom and cap. of United Arab Emirates, on the Persian Gulf. Pop. 347,000.
A·bu Qir or **A·bu·kir** (ä′bo͞o-kîr′, ə-bo͞o′kər). Village of N Egypt, in the Nile R. delta of the **Bay of Abu Qir** or **Abukir**, site of the Battle of the Nile (1798), Nelson's defeat of a French fleet.
A·bu Sim·bel (ä′bo͞o sĭm′bəl). Village of S Egypt, on the Nile; site of rock temples dating from c. 1250 B.C. that were raised (1964–66) to avoid flooding from Aswan High Dam.
A·by·dos (ə-bī′dŏs). **1.** Ancient town of Asia Minor, on the Hellespont. **2.** Ancient city of S Egypt, NW of Thebes on the Nile.
Ab·ys·sin·i·a (ăb′ĭ-sĭn′ē-ə). Ethiopia. —**Ab′ys·sin′i·an** *adj. & n.*
A·ca·di·a (ə-kā′dē-ə). **1.** Region and former French colony of E Canada, chiefly in N.S. and including N.E., P.E.I., and the coastal area from the St. Lawrence S into Me. **2. National Park.** Scenic area of SE Me., on the Atlantic coast. —**A·ca′di·an** *adj. & n.*
Ac·a·pul·co (ăk′ə-po͞ol′kō, ä′-kä-po͞ol′kô) or **Acapulco de Jua·réz** (dē hwä-rēs′). City of S Mexico, on the Pacific coast. Pop. 421,100.
Ac·ar·na·ni·a (ăk′ər-nā′nē-ə, ä′-kär-nä-nē′ä). Ancient region of W central Greece. —**Ac′ar·na′ni·an** *adj. & n.*
Ac·cad (ăk′ăd′, ä′käd′). Variant of **Akkad**.
Ac·cra (ăk′rə, ə-krä′). Cap. of Ghana, in the S part on the Gulf of Guinea. Pop. 633,800.
Ac·cring·ton (ăk′rĭng-tən). Borough of NW England, N of Manchester. Pop. 79,400.
A·chae·a (ə-kē′ə, ä-kē′ə) also **A·cha·ia** (ə-kā′ə, ə-kī′ə, ä-hī′ä). Ancient region of S Greece, in the N Peloponnesus on the Gulf of Corinth. —**A·chae′an** (ə-kē′ən), **A·cha′ian** (ə-kā′ən, ə-kī′-) *adj. & n.*
Ach·e·lo·us (ăk′ə-lō′əs, ä-khĕ-lô′ôs). River, 137 mi (220.4 km), of NW Greece.
Ach·ill (ăk′ĭl). Island of NW Ireland.
A·ci·re·a·le (ä′chē-rā-ä′lä). City of E Sicily, Italy, near Mt. Etna and the Ionian Sea. Pop. 30,600.
A·co·ma (ä′kō mə). Pueblo of W central N.Mex., W of Albuquerque; regarded as oldest continuously inhabited community in the U.S.
A·con·ca·gua (ä′kông-kä′gwä). Highest mountain (22,835 ft/6,964.7 m) in the Western Hemisphere, in the Andes of W Argentina near the Chilean border.
A·ço·res (ä-sô′rĕsh). *Portuguese.* Azores.
A·cre (ä′krə). **1.** River c. 400 mi (645 km), of W Brazil. **2.** (*also* ä′kər, ā′kər). Akko.
Ac·te (ăk′tē, äk′-). Peninsula of NE Greece, projecting into the Aegean from SE Macedonia.
Ac·ti·um (ăk′tē-əm, -shē-). Promontory and ancient town of W Greece; site of Octavian's victory over Mark Antony and Cleopatra (31 B.C.).
Ac·ton (ăk′tən). Town of NE Mass., WNW of Boston. Pop. 17,544.
A·da (ā′də, ä′də). City of S central Okla., SE of Oklahoma City. Pop. 15,902.
A·dak (ā′dăk′). Island of W Alas., in the Andreanof group of the Aleutians.
A·da·lia (ə-dä′lē-ə, ä-dä′lē-ä). Antalya.
A·da·ma·wa Massif (ä′dä-mä′wä). Plateau of W central Africa, in N central Cameroon and E Nigeria.
Ad·ams (ăd′əmz). **1.** Peak, 5,798 ft (1,768.4 m), in N N.H. in the Presidential Range of the White Mts. **2.** Peak, 12,307 ft (3,753.6 m), in SW Wash., in the Cascade Range. **3.** Town of NW Mass., NNE of Pittsfield. Pop. 10,381.
Ad·am's Bridge (ăd′əmz). Shoals, extending c. 18 mi (30 km) between India and Sri Lanka.
Adam's Peak. Sacred mountain, 7,360 ft (2,244.8 m), in S central Sri Lanka.
A·da·na (ä′dä-nä′). City of S Turkey, on the Seyhan R. Pop. 568,513.
A·da·pa·za·ri (ä′dä-pä′zä-rē′). City of NW Turkey, E of Istanbul. Pop. 131,400.
Ad·dis Ab·a·ba (ăd′ĭs ä′bə-bä, ăd′ĭs ăb′ə-bə). Cap. of Ethiopia, in the center of the country. Pop. 1,125,340.
Ad·di·son (ăd′ĭ-sən). Village of NE Ill., W of Chicago. Pop. 28,836.
Ad·e·laide (ăd′l-ād′). City of S Australia, NW of Melbourne. Metro. area pop. 933,300.
A·dé·lie Coast (ə-dā′lē, ä-dā-lē′). Region of E Antarctica, between George V Coast and Wilkes Land.
A·den (äd′n, ād′n). **1.** Also **Aden Colony.** Former British colony of S Arabia, part of Southern Yemen since 1967. **2.** Former British protectorate of S Arabia, between Yemen and Oman, part of Southern Yemen after 1967. **3.** Cap. of Southern Yemen, on NW shore of the **Gulf of Aden,** W arm of the Arabian Sea. Pop. 264,326.
A·di·ge (ä′dē-jā). River of N Italy, flowing c. 225 mi (360 km) to the Adriatic.
Ad·i·ron·dack Mountains (ăd′-ə-rŏn′dăk′) also **Ad·i·ron·dacks** (-dăks′). Range of NE N.Y., between the St. Lawrence and Mohawk valleys.
Ad·mi·ral·ty (ăd′mər-əl-tē). **1.** Mountains of Antarctica, on the N Coast of Victoria Land. **2.** Island of SE Alas., in the Alexander Archipelago SW of Juneau. **3.** Island group of the SW Pacific, in the Bismarck Archipelago; part of Papua New Guinea.
A·do (ä′dō). City of SW Nigeria, NE of Lagos. Pop. 213,000.
A·dour (ä-do͞or′). River of SW France, flowing 210 mi (337.9 km) to the Bay of Biscay.
A·dri·an (ā′drē-ən). City of SE Mich., SW of Detroit. Pop. 21,186.
A·dri·a·no·ple (ā′drē-ə-nō′pəl). Edirne.
A·dri·at·ic Sea (ā′drē-ăt′ĭk). Arm of the Mediterranean, between Italy and the Balkan Peninsula.
A·du·wa or **A·do·wa** (ä′do͞o-wä, -də-) or **Ad·wa** (äd′wä). Town of N Ethiopia, S of Asmara. Pop. 20,450.
Ad·zhar·i·a (ə-jär′ē-ə, ä-jär′-) or **Ad·zhar·i·stan** (-ĭ-stăn′). Region of SE European USSR, on the Black Sea. —**Ad′zhar** *n.* —**Ad·zhar′i·an** *adj. & n.*
Ae·ga·de·an Isles (ĭ-gā′dē′ən, ē-gā′-) also **Ae·ga·tes** (ĭ-gā′tēz, ē-gā′-). Egadi Is.
Ae·ge·an Sea (ĭ-jē′ən). Arm of the Mediterranean, between Greece and Turkey.
Ae·gi·na (ĭ-jī′nə). **1.** Greek island in the Saronic Gulf near Athens. **2.** Ancient Greek state on this island.
Ae·gos·pot·a·mi (ē′gəs-pŏt′ə-mī′) or **Ae·gos·pot·a·mos** (ē′gəs-pŏt′ə-mŏs′). River and ancient town of S Thrace, in present-day W Turkey.
Ae·o·li·an Islands (ē-ō′lē-ən). Lipari Is.
Ae·o·lis (ē′ə-lĭs) or **Ae·o·li·a** (ē-ō′lē-ə). Ancient region of the W coast of Asia Minor, in present-day Turkey. —**Ae·o′li·an** *adj. & n.*
Ae·to·li·a (ē-tō′lē-ə). Ancient region of Greece, N of the Gulfs of Corinth and Calydon. —**Ae·to′li·an** *adj. & n.*
A·fars and Is·sus (ä′färz; ē-säz′). Djibouti.
Af·ghan·i·stan (ăf-găn′ĭ-stăn′). Country of S central Asia. Cap. Kabul. Pop. 18,294,000. —**Af′ghan′** *adj. & n.*
A·fog·nak (ə-fôg′năk′, -fōg-). Island of Alas., NE of Kodiak and E of the Alaska Peninsula.
Af·ri·ca (ăf′rĭ-kə). 2nd largest continent, c. 11,677,240 sq mi (30,244,050 sq km) including nearby islands, S of Europe and between the Atlantic and Indian oceans. —**Af′ri·can** *adj. & n.*
A·ga·na (ä-gä′nyä). Cap. of Guam, on the W coast. Metro. area pop. 25,000.
Ag·as·siz (ăg′ə-sē′). Glacial lake of the Pleistocene epoch, extending c. 700 mi (1,125 km) over present-day NW Minn., NE N.Dak., S Man., and SW Ont., Canada.
Ag·a·wam (ăg′ə-wŏm′). Town of SW Mass., near Springfield. Pop. 26,271.
A·gen (ä-zhäN′). Town of SW France, on the Garonne R. Pop. 34,039.
Ag·e·nais (äzh′ə-nā′, äzh-nĕ′) or **Ag·e·nois** (äzh′ə-nwä′). Ancient region of SW France.
A·ge·o (ä′gē-ō′). City of central Honshu, Japan, NNW of Tokyo. Pop. 163,985.
A·gin·court (ăj′ĭn-kôrt′, -kōrt′, ä-zhăN-ko͞or′). Village of N France, WNW of Arras; scene of Henry V's victory over the French (1415).
Ag·no (äg′nō). River, 128 mi (206 km), of NW Luzon, Philippines.
A·gra (ä′grə). City of N central India, on the Jumna R. SE of New Delhi. Pop. 591,917.
A·gri·gen·to (ä-grē-jĕn′tō). City of S Sicily, Italy, on the Mediterranean. Pop. 51,725.
A·gua·dil·la (ä′gwä-dē′yä). Town of NW Puerto Rico. Pop. 22,039.
A·gua Fri·a (ä′gwä frē′ä). River, 120 mi (193.1 km), of W Ariz.
A·guas·ca·lien·tes (ä′gwäs-kä-lyĕn′-tĕs). City of central Mexico, NE of Guadalajara. Pop. 247,764.
A·gul·has (ə-gŭl′əs, ä-go͞o′lyəsh), **Cape.** Cliffs in South Africa; southernmost point of Africa.
Ah·ma·da·bad or **Ah·me·da·bad** (ä′-məd-a-băd′). City of NW India, N of Bombay. Pop. 1,585,544.
A·ho·me (ä-ō′mē). City of W Mexico, on the Pacific. Pop. 165,612.
Ah·vaz or **Ah·waz** (ä-wăz′). City of SW Iran, SW of Teheran. Pop. 329,006.
Ah·ven·an·maa (ä′vĕ-nän-mä′). Archipelago in the Baltic Sea at the entrance to the Gulf of Bothnia, between Sweden and Finland.
A·i·e·a (ä′ē-ä′ä). City of Oahu, Hawaii, near Honolulu. Pop. 12,560.
Ai·ken (ā′kən). City of SW S.C., near the Ga. border SW of Columbia. Pop. 14,978.
Ain·tab (īn-tăb′). Gaziantep.
Air·drie (âr′drē). Burgh of S central Scotland, part of Glasgow. Pop. 38,833.
Aisne (ān, ĕn). River of N France, flowing 165 mi (265.5 km) to the Oise.
Aix-en-Pro·vence (āks′ än-prō-väns′, ĕks′-). City of SE France, N of

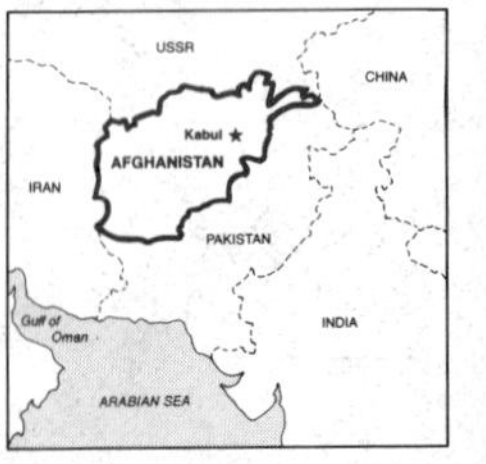

Afghanistan

Marseilles. Pop. 110,659.
Aix-la-Cha·pelle (āks′lä-shä-pĕl′, ĕks′-). Aachen.
Aix-les-Bains (āks′lā-bănz′, ĕks′-lā-băN′). Town of SE France, N of Chambéry. Pop. 22,210.
Ai·yi·na (ā′yē-nä′). *Greek.* Aegina.
Ai·zu Wa·ka·mat·su (ī′zōō wä-kä-mä′tsōō). City of N Honshu, Japan. Pop 113,175.
A·jac·cio (ä-yät′chō). Cap. of Corsica, on the **Gulf of Ajaccio**, an inlet of the Mediterranean. Pop. 50,726.
A·jax (ā′jăks). **1.** Mountain, 10,900 ft (3,324.5 m), in the S Bitterroot Range on the Mont.-Ida. border. **2.** Town of SE Ont., Canada, on Lake Erie NE of Toronto. Pop. 24,380.
Aj·man (ăj′măn). Sheikdom of E Arabia, one of the United Arab Emirates, on the Persian Gulf. Pop. 4,000.
Aj·mer (ăj′mîr). City of NW India, SW of Delhi. Pop. 262,851.
A·jodh·ya (ə-yōd′yə). Pilgrimage village of N India.
A·ka·shi (ä-kä′shē). City of SW Honshu, Japan, near Osaka. Pop. 254,873.
Akh·el·ó·os (ä′KHĕ-lô′ôs). *Greek.* Achelous.
A·ki·ta (ä′kē-tä′). City of NW Honshu, Japan, on the Sea of Japan. Pop. 284,830.
Ak·kad also **Ac·cad** (ăk′ăd′, ä′käd′). **1.** Ancient region of N Babylonia. **2.** Cap. of ancient Babylonia, in central Mesopotamia.
Ak·ko (ä-kō′, ä′kō). City of NW Israel, on the Bay of Haifa. Pop. 37,900.
A·ko·la (ə-kō′lə). Town of W central India, WSW of Amravati. Pop. 168,438.
Ak·ron (ăk′rən). City of NE Ohio, SSE of Cleveland, Pop. 237,177.
Ak·sum or **Ax·um** (äk′sōōm). Town of N Ethiopia; cap. of ancient Ethiopian empire.
Ak·tyu·binsk (äk-tyōō-bĭnsk′). City of S European USSR, WNW of Alma-Ata. Pop. 197,000.
Al·a·bam·a (ăl′ə-băm′ə). **1.** River, 315 mi (506.8 km), of S Ala. **2.** State of S U.S. Cap. Montgomery. Pop. 3,890,061. **—Al′a·ba′man** *adj. & n.*
A·lai or **A·lay** (ä′lī′). Mountain range of S Central Asian USSR, in the W Tian Shan, rising to c. 19,280 ft (5,880 m).
A·lais (ä-lā′). Alès.
Al·a·jue·la (ä-lä-hwĕ′lä). City of central Costa Rica, W of San José. Pop. 35,000.
Al·a·kol (ăl′ə-kôl′). Salt lake of S Central Asian USSR, near the Chinese border.
Al·a·me·da (ăl′ə-mē′də). City of W central Calif., near Oakland. Pop. 63,852.
Al·a·mein (ăl′ə-mān′), **El**, or **Al Al·a·mayn** (ăl′ä-mān′). Village of N Egypt, on the Mediterranean Sea.
Al·a·mo·gor·do (ăl′ə-mə-gôr′dō). City of S central N.Mex., SSE of Albuquerque. Pop. 24,024.
A·land Islands (ä′lənd, ō′länd′). Ahvenanmaa.
A·las·ka (ə-lăs′kə). **1. Gulf of.** N inlet of the Pacific, between the Alaska Peninsula and the Alexander Archipelago. **2.** Mountain range of S central Alas., rising to 20,320 ft (6,197.6 m). **3.** Peninsula of S central Alas., between the Bering Sea and the Pacific. **4.** State of the U.S., in NW North America. Cap. Juneau. Pop. 400,481. **—A·las′kan** *adj. & n.*
A·la-Tau (ä′lä-tou′). Mountain ranges of central Asia, in the Tian Shan.
Al·a·va (ăl′ə-və). Cape of NW Wash., westernmost point of coterminous U.S.
A·lay (ä′lī′). Variant of **Alai**.
Al·ba·ce·te (äl′bä-sĕ′tĕ). City of SE Spain, WSW of Valencia. Pop. 107,725.
Al·ba Iu·li·a (äl′bä yōō′lyä). Town of W central Rumania, on the Mureşul R. Pop. 44,870.
Al·ba Lon·ga (ăl′bə lông′gə). City of ancient Latium, in central Italy SE of Rome.
Al·ba·ni·a (ăl-bā′nē-ə, -bān′yə). **1.** Ancient country of SE Europe, in the E Caucasus W of the Caspian Sea. **2.** Republic of SE Europe, on the Adriatic. Cap. Tiranë. Pop. 2,725,000. **—Al·ba′ni·an** *adj. & n.*
Al·ba·no (äl-bä′nō). Lake of central Italy, SE of Rome, in an extinct volcanic crater.
Al·ba·ny (ôl′bə-nē). **1.** River of W Ont., Canada, flowing 610 mi (981.5 km) to James Bay. **2.** City of W Calif., N of Berkeley. Pop. 15,130. **3.** City of SW Ga., SE of Columbus. Pop. 73,934. **4.** Cap. of N.Y., in the E on the Hudson. Pop. 101,727. **5.** City of NW Ore., S of Salem. Pop. 26,546.
Al·be·marle (ăl′bə-märl′). **1. Sound.** Inland body of generally fresh water in NE N.C. **2.** City of S central N.C., ENE of Charlotte. Pop. 15,110.
Al·ber·ga (äl-bûr′gə). Intermittent river, flowing c. 350 mi (565 km), of S central Australia.
Al·bert (ăl′bərt), **Lake**, or **Albert Ny·an·za** (nī-ăn′zə, nyän′zä). Lake of E central Africa on the Uganda-Zaire border.
Al·ber·ta (ăl-bûr′tə). Province of W Canada. Cap. Edmonton. Pop. 1,838,037. **—Al·ber′tan** *adj. & n.*
Albert Lea (lē). City of S Minn., near the Iowa border S of Minneapolis. Pop. 19,190.
Albert Nile (nīl). Name for part of the upper Nile in NW Uganda.
Al·bert·ville (ăl′bərt-vĭl′). City of NE Ala., NNW of Gadsden. Pop. 12,039.
Al·bi (äl-bē′). Town of S France, NE of Toulouse. Pop. 46,162.
Al·bi·on (ăl′bē-ən). City of S Mich., SW of Detroit. Pop. 11,059.
Al·borg also **Aal·borg** (ôl′bôrg′). City of N Denmark, NNE of Århus. Pop. 153,948.
Al·bu·quer·que (ăl′bə-kûr′kē). City of central N.Mex., SW of Santa Fe. Pop. 331,767.
Al·ca·lá de He·na·res (äl-kä-lä′ dĕ′ ĕ-nä′rĕs). Town of central Spain, ENE of Madrid. Pop. 114,788.
Al·ca·mo (äl′kä-mō′). City of NW Sicily, Italy, SW of Palermo. Pop. 43,593.
Al·ca·traz (ăl′kə-trăz′). Island in San Francisco Bay, W Calif.
Al·co·a (ăl-kō′ə). City of E Tenn., S of Knoxville. Pop.7,739.
Al·coy (äl-koi′). City of SE Spain, N of Alicante. Pop. 65,078.
Al·dan (äl-dän′). River of SE Siberian USSR, flowing c. 1,400 mi (2,255 km) to the Lena.
Al·der·ney (ôl′dər-nē). British island in the English Channel, most northerly of the Channel Is.
Al·der·shot (ôl′dər-shŏt′). Borough of S central England, SW of London. Pop. 81,000.
Al·dridge-Brown·hills (ôl′drĭj-broun′hĭlz). Urban district of central England. Pop. 89,370.
A·lek·san·drov (ä′lĭk-sän′drôf). Zaporozhe.
Al·en·çon (ä-läN-sôN′). Town of NW France, WSW of Paris. Pop. 33,680.
A·lep·po (ə-lĕp′ō) or **A·lep** (ə-lĕp′). City of NW Syria, near the Turkish border. Pop. 878,000.
A·lès (ä-lĕs′). City of S France, NW of Nîmes. Pop. 44,245.
Al·es·san·dri·a (ä′lĕs-sän′drē-ä). City of NW Italy, ESE of Turin. Pop. 101,684.
A·leu·tian (ə-lōō′shən). **1. Range.** Mountain chain of SW Alas., rising to 10,200 ft (3,111 m). **2.** Also **A·leu·tians** (-shənz). Volcanic island chain of SW Alas., curving c. 1,200 mi (1,930 km) W from the Alaska Peninsula. **3. Trench.** Depression, 26,574 ft (8,105.1 m), in floor of the N Pacific, S of the Aleutian Is.

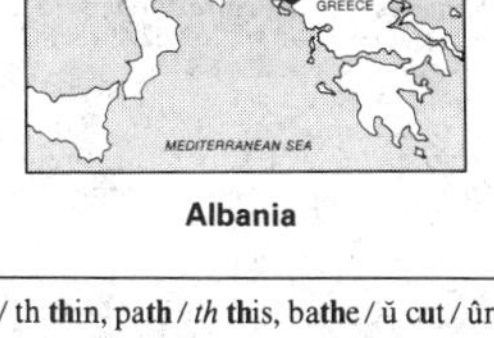

Albania

Alexander I. Island of British Antarctic Territory, off W coast of the Antarctic Peninsula.
Al·ex·an·der Archipelago (ăl′-ĭg-zăn′dər). Group of more than 1,000 islands off SE Alaska.
Alexander City. City of E central Ala., SE of Birmingham. Pop. 13,807.
Al·ex·an·dret·ta (ăl′ĭg-zăn-drĕt′ə, -zän-). Iskenderun.
Al·ex·an·dri·a (ăl′ĭg-zăn′drē-ə). **1.** City of N Egypt, on the Mediterranean. Pop. 2,409,000. **2.** City of central La., NW of Baton Rouge. Pop. 51,565. **3.** Independent city of N Va., near Washington, D.C. Pop. 103,217. **—Al·ex·an′dri·an** *adj. & n.*
Al Fay·yam (äl fā-yōōm′, fī-, ĕl). City of N Egypt, on the Nile SSW of Cairo. Pop. 167,081.
Al·fi·ós (äl-fē-ôs′). *Greek.* Alpheus.
Al·föld (ôl′fĕld). Plain of central Hungary, N Yugoslavia, and W Rumania.
Al·gar·ve (äl-gär′və). Medieval Moorish kingdom, in present-day S coastal Portugal.
Al·ge·ci·ras (ăl′jĭ-sîr′əs, äl′hĕ-sē′räs). City of S Spain, on the **Bay of Algeciras** opposite Gibraltar. Pop. 92,933.
Al·ge·ri·a (ăl-jîr′ē-ə). Republic of NW Africa, on the Mediterranean. Cap. Algiers. Pop. 20,050,000. **—Al·ge′ri·an** *adj. & n.*

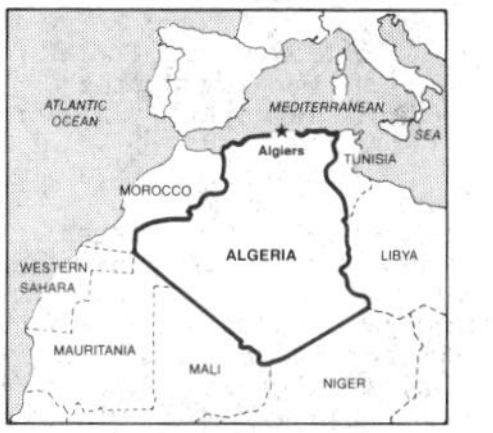

Algeria

Al·giers (ăl-jîrz′). Cap. of Algeria, in the N on the **Bay of Algiers**, an arm of the Mediterranean. Pop. 1,503,720.
Al·ham·bra (ăl-hăm′brə). **1.** (*also* äl-häm′brä). Hill in Granada, S Spain, with Moorish buildings. **2.** City of S Calif., near Los Angeles. Pop. 64,615.
Al Hil·lah (äl hĭl′lä). City of central Iraq, on a branch of the Euphrates. Pop. 128,800.
A·li·ak·mon (ä-lē-äk′môn). River, c. 200 mi (320 km), of N Greece.
Al·i·can·te (ăl′ĭ-kăn′tē, ä′lē-kän′tĕ). City of SE Spain, on the Mediterranean S of Valencia. Pop. 235,868.
Al·ice (ăl′ĭs, -əs). City of S Tex., W of Corpus Christi. Pop. 20,961.
A·li·garh (ä′lē-gôr′). City of N central India, SE of Delhi. Pop. 252,314.
Al·i·quip·pa (ăl′ĭ-kwĭp′ə). Borough of W Pa., on the Ohio NW of Pittsburgh. Pop. 17,094.
Al Ji·zah (ăl jē′zə, ĕl). Giza.
Alk·maar (älk′mär). Town of NW Netherlands, NNW of Amsterdam. Pop. 71,245.
Al Ku·wait (ăl kōō-wāt′). Variant of **Kuwait.**
Al·la·ha·bad (ăl′ə-hə-băd′, ä′-lə-hä-bäd′). City of N central India, at the junction of the Jumna and the Ganges. Pop. 490,622.
Al·le·ghe·ny (ăl′ĭ-gā′nē) **1.** River, 325 mi (523km), of N central Pa., W N.Y., and W Pa., flowing to the Monongahela to form the Ohio R. **2.** Also **Al·le·ghe·nies** (-nēz). W part of the Appalachian Mts., extending from N Pa. to SW Va.
Al·len Park (ăl′ən). City of SE Mich., near Detroit. Pop. 34,196.
Al·len·town (ăl′ən-toun′). City of E Pa., NNW of Philadelphia. Pop. 103,758.
Al·li·ance (ə-lī′əns). City of NE Ohio, SW of Youngstown. Pop. 24,315.
Al·lier (ä-lyā′). River of central France, flowing c. 225 mi (410 km) to the Loire.
Al·ma (ăl′mə). City of S central Que., Canada, on the Saguenay R. Pop. 25,638.
Al·ma-A·ta (äl′mä-ä′tä). City of SE Central Asian USSR, near the Chinese border. Pop. 928,000.
Al Ma·nam·ah (ăl′ mə-năm′ə). Cap. of Bahrain, on the Persian Gulf. Pop. 89,112.
Al·me·lo (äl′mə-lō′). City of E Netherlands. Pop. 63,381.
Al·me·rí·a (äl′mĕ-rē′ä). City of SE Spain, on the Mediterranean. Pop. 136,720.
Al·mi·ran·te Brown (äl-mē-rän′tĕ broun). City of E Argentina, part of Buenos Aires. Pop. 245,017.
Al·or (äl′ôr, ä′lôr). Largest of the **Alor Is.** of Indonesia, in the E Lesser Sundas N of Timor in the S Flores Sea.
A·lost (ä-lôst′). *French.* Aalst.
Al·pe·na (ăl-pē′nə). City of NE Mich., on an arm of Lake Huron NNE of Saginaw. Pop. 12,214.
Al·phe·us (ăl-fē′əs). River of S Greece, in the Peloponnesus, flowing c. 70 mi (112 km) to the Ionian Sea.
Alps (ălps). Mountain system of S central Europe, curving in an arc of c. 500 mi (805 km) from the Riviera on the Mediterranean through N Italy and SE France, Switzerland, S West Germany, and Austria into NW Yugoslavia.
Al·sace (ăl-săs′, -săs′, äl-zäs′). Region and former province of E France, between the Rhine and the Vosges Mts. **—Al·sa′tian** *adj. & n.*
Al·sace-Lor·raine (ăl′săs-lō-rān′, -lô-, -săs-, äl-zäs-lô-rĕn′). Region of NE France comprising Alsace and part of Lorraine.
Al·sek (ăl′sĕk′). River of NW Canada and SE Alas., flowing 260 mi (418.3 km) to the Pacific.
Al·sip (ôl′sĭp). Village of NE Ill., near Chicago. Pop. 17,134.
Al·ta Cal·i·for·nia (äl′tä kä′lē-fôr′-nyä). *Spanish.* Upper California.
Al·tai or **Al·tay** (ăl-tī′, äl-, ăl′tī, äl′-). Mountain system of S Central Asian USSR, W Mongolia, and N China.
Al·ta·ma·ha (ôl′tə-mə-hô′). River of SE Ga., flowing 137 mi (220.4 km) into **Altamaha Sound**, an inlet of the Atlantic.
Al·ta·mi·ra (ăl′tə-mîr′ə, äl′tä-mē′rä). Caves of N Spain, WSW of Santander, containing specimens of Paleolithic art.
Al·ta·monte Springs (ăl′tə-mŏnt). City of E central Fla., N of Orlando. Pop. 22,028.
Al·ta·mu·ra (äl-tä-mōō′rä). City of S Italy, SSW of Bari. Pop. 49,878.
Al·ten·burg (äl′tən-bŏŏrk′). City of S East Germany, S of Leipzig. Pop. 54,281.
Al·ti·pla·no (äl-tē-plä′nô). Plateau in the Andes of W Bolivia and S Peru.
Al·ton (ôl′tən). City of SW Ill., N of St. Louis, Mo. Pop. 34,171.
Al·too·na (ăl-tōō′nə). City of central Pa., E of Pittsburgh. Pop. 57,078.
Al·tus (ăl′təs). City of SW Okla., near the Tex. border SW of Oklahoma City. Pop. 23,101.
Al U·bay·yid (äl ōō-bä-yĭd′). City of central Sudan, SW of Khartoum. Pop. 90,060.
Al·vin (ăl′vĭn). City of SE Tex., S of Houston. Pop. 16,515.
A·ma·ga·sa·ki (ä′mä-gä-sä′kē). City of S Honshu, Japan, on Osaka Bay. Pop. 523,657.
A·mal·fi (ä-mäl′fē). Town of S Italy, on the Gulf of Salerno. Pop. 6,446.
A·ma·mi (ä-mä′mē). Island group of N Ryukyu Is., Japan, NE of Okinawa, between the Philippine Sea and the East China Sea.
Am·a·ril·lo (ăm′ə-rĭl′ō, -rĭl′ə). City of N Tex., in the Panhandle N of Lubbock. Pop. 149,230.
Am·a·zon (ăm′ə-zŏn′, -zən). 2nd longest river in the world, flowing c. 3,900 mi (6,275 km) from N Peru across N Brazil to the Atlantic.
Am·ba·to (äm-bä′tô). City of central Ecuador, S of Quito. Pop. 80,000.
Am·bon (ăm′bôn) also **Am·boi·na** (ăm-boi′nə). Island of E Indonesia, in the Moluccas.
Am·brose Channel (ăm′brōz). Dredged channel in SE N.Y., at the entrance to New York harbor.
Am·chit·ka (ăm-chĭt′kə). Island of W

Alas., in the Rat Is. of the Aleutians.
A·mer·i·ca (ə-mĕr'ĭ-kə). The Western Hemisphere lands of North America, South America, and Central America. —**A·mer'i·can** *adj. & n.*
American Falls. Section (167 ft/51 m high) of Niagara Falls within the U.S.
American Fork (fôrk). City of N central Utah, S of Salt Lake City. Pop. 12,417.
American Sa·mo·a (sə-mō'ə). Unincorporated U.S. territory in the South Pacific, comprising the E half of the Samoa Is. chain. Cap. Pago Pago. Pop. 33,000.

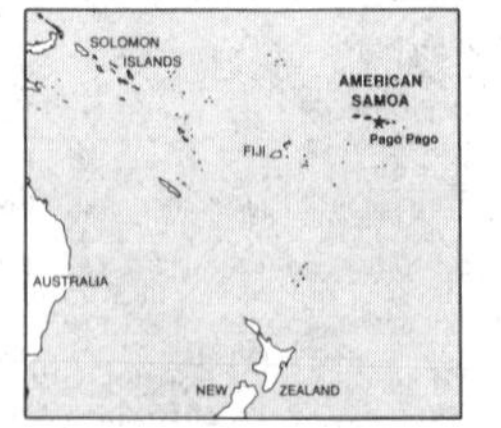

American Samoa

A·mer·i·cus (ə-mĕr'ĭ-kəs). City of central SW Ga., SE of Columbus. Pop. 16,120.
A·mers·foort (ä'mərz-fōrt', -fôrt', -mərs-). City of central Netherlands, NE of Utrecht. Pop. 88,097.
Ames (āmz). City of central Iowa, N of Des Moines. Pop. 45,775.
Ames·bur·y (āmz'bĕr'ē, -bə-rē). Town of NE Mass., NE of Lawrence. Pop. 13,971.
Am·gun (äm-go͞on'). River of SE Far Eastern USSR, flowing 490 mi (788.4 km) to the Amur.
Am·herst (ăm'ərst, -hərst). **1.** Town of N central N.S., Canada, near the N.B. border. Pop. 10,263. **2.** Town of W central Mass., near Northampton. Pop. 33,229. **3.** City of N Ohio, near Lorain. Pop. 10,638.
Am·i·ens (ăm'ē-ənz, ä-myăN'). City of N France, on the Somme N of Paris. Pop. 131,476.
A·min·di·vi (ä'mĭn-dē'vē). Islands of SW India, in the Arabian Sea, part of the Laccadive, Minicoy, and Amindivi Is.
Am·i·rante (ăm'ə-rănt'). British islands of the W Indian Ocean, SW of Seychelles.
Am·i·ty·ville (ăm'ĭ-tē-vĭl'). Village of SE N.Y., on the S shore of Long Is. Pop. 9,076.
Am·man (ä'män). Cap. of Jordan, in the N central part. Pop. 648,587.
Am·ne Ma·chin (ăm'nē mə-jĭn') or **Amne Machin Shan** (shän). Mountains of W central China, rising to 23,490 ft (7,164.5 m).
A·moy (ä-moi'). City of SE China, on the SW shore of **Amoy Is.**, in Formosa Strait W of Taiwan. Pop. 300,000.
Am·ra·va·ti (ŭm'räv'ə-tē, ăm'-). Town of central India, W of Nagpur. Pop. 193, 800.
Am·rit·sar (əm-rĭt'sər). City of NW India, NE of Lahore. Pop. 407,628.
Am·stel·veen (äm'stəl-vān'). Town of W Netherlands, a suburb of Amsterdam. Pop. 69,488.
Am·ster·dam (ăm'stər-dăm') **1.** (*also* äm'stər-däm'). Constitutional cap. of the Netherlands, in the W part on the Ij, an inlet of the Ijsselmeer. Pop. 716,919. **2.** City of E central N.Y., NW of Albany. Pop. 21,872.
A·mu Dar·ya (ä-mo͞o'där'yä). River of central Asia, flowing c. 1,600 mi (2,575 km) along much of the USSR-Afghanistan border to the S Aral Sea.
A·mund·sen (ăm'ŭnd-sən, -ən-sən). **1. Sea.** Arm of the S Pacific, off the coast of Marie Byrd Land, Antarctica. **2. Gulf.** Inlet of the Arctic Ocean, N.W.T., Canada, opening on the Beaufort Sea.
A·mur (ä-mo͝or'). River of NE Asia, flowing c. 1,800 mi (2,895 km) along the USSR-Chinese border.
An·a·con·da (ăn'ə-kŏn'də). City of SW Mont., WNW of Butte. Pop. 12,518.
A·na·dyr (ä-nä-dîr'). River of NE Far Eastern USSR, flowing c. 695 mi (1,120 km) into **Anadyr Bay**, an inlet of the Bering Sea.
An·a·heim (ăn'ə-hīm'). City of S Calif., SE of Los Angeles. Pop. 221,847.
A·ná·huac (ə-nä'wäk'). Plateau of central Mexico.
An·a·pur·na (ăn'ə-po͝or'nə, -pûr'-). Variant of **Annapurna.**
An·a·to·li·a (ăn'ə-tō'lē-ə, -lyə). Asian Turkey, usually synonymous with Asia Minor. —**An'a·to'li·an** *adj. & n.*
An·cas·ter (ăn'kăs'tər). Town of S. Ont., Canada, W of Hamilton. Pop. 14,255.
An·chor·age (ăng'kər-ĭj'). City of S Alas., SSW of Fairbanks. Pop. 173,992.
An·ci·enne-Lor·ette (ăn'sē-ĕn'-lô-rĕt', -lō-, -syĕn'-, äN-syĕn'-). Town of S central Que., Canada, W of Quebec. Pop. 11,694.
An·co·hu·ma (äng'kō-o͞o'mä). Mountain peak, 21,489 ft (6,550 m), of E Bolivia.
An·co·na (än-kō'nä). City of central Italy, on the Adriatic. Pop. 108,371.
An·da·lu·cí·a (än'də-lo͞o'sē'ə). *Spanish.* Andalusia.
An·da·lu·sia (ăn'də-lo͞o'zhə, -shē-ə). **1.** Region of S Spain, on the Mediterranean and the Atlantic. **2.** City of S Ala., S of Montgomery. Pop. 10,415. —**An'da·lu'sian** (-zhən) *adj. & n.*
An·da·man (ăn'də-mən, -măn'). **1. Sea.** Part of the Bay of Bengal, SE Asia. **2.** Islands of India, S of Burma in the Bay of Bengal.
An·der·lecht (än'dər-lĕKHt'). Commune of central Belgium, near Brussels. Pop 95,969.
An·der·son (ăn'dər-sən). **1.** River, c. 465 mi (750 km), of NW N.W.T., Canada. **2.** City of E central Ind., NE of Indianapolis. Pop. 64,695. **3.** City of NW S.C., SW of Greenville. Pop. 27,313.
An·der·son·ville (ăn'dər-sən-vĭl'). Village of SW Ga., site of Civil War Confederate prison.
An·des (ăn'dēz). Mountain system of W South America, extending over 5,000 mi (8,045 km) from Tierra del Fuego to Venezuela and rising at many points to more than 22,000 ft (6,710 m).
An·di·zhan (än'dĭ-zhän'). City of S Central Asian USSR, ESE of Tashkent. Pop. 233,000.
An·dor·ra (ăn dôr'ə, -dŏr-ə, än-dôr'-rä). Country of SW Europe, between France and Spain in the E Pyrenees. Cap. Andorra la Vella. Pop. 32,700. —**An·dor'ran** *adj. & n.*

Andorra

An·do·ver (ăn'dō'vər, -də-). Town of NE Mass., near Lawrence. Pop. 26,370.
An·dre·a·nof (ăn'drē-ăn'ôf, ăn'-drē-ä'nôf). Islands of SW Alas., in the central Aleutians.
An·drews (ăn'dro͞oz). City of W Tex., NW of Midland. Pop. 11,061.
An·dri·a (än'drē-ä). City of S Italy, WNW of Bari. Pop. 83,734.
An·dros (ăn'drəs). **1.** Largest island of the Bahamas, in the W part. **2.** Greek island, one of the Cyclades, in the Aegean.
An·dros·cog·gin (ăn'drə-skŏg'ĭn). River, 157 mi (252.6 km), of NE N.H. and SW Me.
A·ne·to (ä-nā'tō), **Pico de.** See **Pico de Aneto.**
An·ga·ra (än'gä-rä'). River, c. 1,150 mi (1,850 km), of SE Siberian USSR.
An·garsk (än-gärsk'). City of the SE Siberian USSR, on the Angara NW of Irkutsk. Pop. 241,000.
An·gel Fall or **Falls** (ăn'jəl). Highest uninterrupted waterfall in the world (3,212 ft/979.7 m), in SE Venezuela.
Ang·er·ma·näl·ven (ông'ər-mä-nĕl'-vən). River of E central Sweden, flowing c. 280 mi (450 km) to the Gulf of Bothnia.
An·gers (ăn'jərz, äN-zhā'). City of W France, near Nantes. Pop. 137,587.
Ang·kor (ăng'kōr, -kôr). Ruins of Khmer imperial capitals, in NW Cambodia.
An·gle·sey or **An·gle·sea** (ăng'gəl-sē). Island of NW Wales, in the Irish Sea.
An·gle·ton (ăng'gəl-tən). City of SE Tex., S of Houston. Pop. 13,929.
An·gli·a (ăng'glē-ə). **1.** Medieval Latin name for England. **2.** East Anglia. —**An'gli·an** *adj. & n.*
An·go·la (ăng-gō'lə). Country of SW Africa, on the Atlantic. Cap. Luanda. Pop. 7,000,000. —**An·go'lan** *adj. & n.*

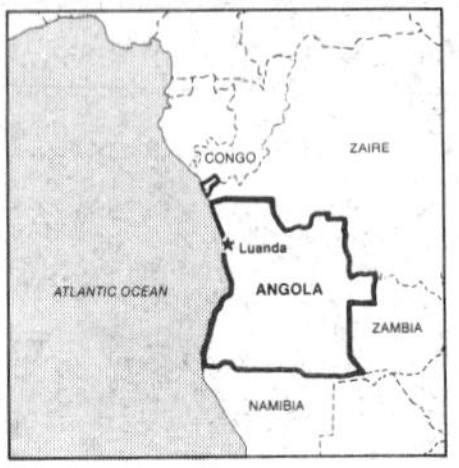

Angola

An·gou·lême (äN-go͞o-lĕm'). City of W France, NE of Bordeaux. Pop. 47,221.
An·gou·mois (äng'go͞om-wä', äN-go͞o-mwä'). Region and former province of W France, in the Charente R. valley.
An·gren (ən-gryĕn'). City of S Central Asian USSR. Pop. 108,000.
An·guil·la (ăng-gwĭl'ə). Island of the British West Indies, in the N Leewards.
An·halt (än'hält). Former state of central Germany, part of East Germany since 1945.
A·ni (ä'nē). Ancient ruined city of Asia Minor, in present-day NE Turkey.
An·i·ak·chak (ăn'ē-ăk'chăk'). Volcano, 4,420 ft (1,384.1 m), of SE Alas., in the Aleutian Range.
An·jo (än'jô). City of S central Honshu, Japan. Pop. 121,178.
An·jou (ăn'jo͞o, äN-zho͞o'). **1.** Region and former province of W France, SE of Brittany in the Loire valley. **2.** Town of S Que., Canada, N of Montreal. Pop. 36,596.
An·ka·ra (ăng'kər-ə, äng'kä-rä'). Cap. of Turkey, in the W central part. Pop. 2,203,729.
An·ke·ny (ăng'kə-nē). City of central Iowa, near Des Moines. Pop. 15,429.
Ann (ăn), **Cape.** Peninsula of NE Mass., N of Massachusetts Bay.
An·na·ba (ə-nä'bə). City of NE Algeria, on the Mediterranean. Pop. 313,174.
An Na·jaf (än nä'jäf). City of S central Iraq, near the Euphrates. Pop. 179,200.
An·nam (ə-năm', ăn'ăm'). Region and former kingdom of central Vietnam, SE Asia, on the South China Sea. —**An'na·mese'** (ăn'ə-mēz', -mēs') *adj. & n.*
An·nap·o·lis (ə-năp'ə-lĭs). **1.** River of W N.S., Canada, flowing c. 75 mi (120 km) to the **Annapolis Basin**, an arm of the Bay of Fundy. **2.** Cap. of Md., SSE of Baltimore. Pop. 31,740.
An·na·pur·na also **An·a·pur·na** (ăn'ə-po͝or'nə, -pûr'-). Massif of the Himalayas in N central Nepal, reaching an elevation of 26,502 ft (8,083.1 m) at **Annapurna I.**
Ann Ar·bor (ăr'bər). City of SE Mich., W of Detroit. Pop. 107,316.
Anne·cy (än-sē'). City of SE France, in the Alps on **Lake Annecy.** Pop. 53,262.
An·nis·ton (ăn'ĭ-stən). City of NE Ala., ENE of Birmingham. Pop. 29,523.
A·no·ka (ə-nō'kə). City of E Minn., NNW of Minneapolis. Pop. 15,634.
An·shan (än'shän'). City of NE China, SSW of Shenyang. Pop. 1,050,000.
An·so·ni·a (ăn-sō'nē-ə, -sōn'yə). Town of SW Conn., WNW of New Haven. Pop. 19,039.
An·ta·kya (än-tä-kyä') or **An·ta·ki·ya** (än'tä-kē'yä). Antioch, Turkey.
An·tal·ya (än'täl-yä'). City of SW Turkey, on the **Gulf of Antalya**, an inlet of the Mediterranean. Pop. 176,446.
An·ta·na·na·ri·vo (än'tə-nä'nə-rē'vō, ăn'-). Cap. of Madagascar, in the E central part. Pop. 484,000.
Ant·arc·tic (ănt-ärk'tĭk, -är'tĭk). **1. Ocean.** Waters surrounding Antarctica, the S extensions of the Atlantic, Pacific, and Indian oceans. **2.** Peninsula of W Antarctica, extending c. 1,200 mi (1,930 km) N toward South America. **3. Archipelago.** Islands of W Antarctica, off the NW coast of the Antarctic peninsula. **4.** Antarctica and surrounding waters.
Ant·arc·ti·ca (ănt-ärk'tĭ-kə, -är'tĭ-). Continent chiefly within the Antarctic Circle and asymmetrically centered on the South Pole.
An·tibes (äN-tēb'). City of SE France, on the Riviera between Nice and Cannes. Pop. 55,960.
An·ti·cos·ti (ăn'tĭ-kô'stē, -kŏs'tē). Island of E Que., Canada, at the head of the Gulf of St. Lawrence.
An·tie·tam (ăn-tē'təm). Creek in W Md., near Sharpsburg; site of Civil War battle (1862).
An·ti·go·nish (ăn'tĭ-gō-nĭsh'). Town of NE N.S., Canada, at the head of **Antigonish Bay**, E of New Glasgow. Pop. 12,131.
An·ti·gua (ăn-tē'gwə, -gə). Associated state of Great Britain, in the N Leewards comprising the large island of **Antigua** and the smaller islands of Barbuda and Redonda. Cap. St. John's. Pop. 74,000. —**An·ti'guan** *adj. & n.*
An·ti-Leb·a·non (ăn'tē-lĕb'ə-nən). Mountain range on the Syria-Lebanon border.
An·til·les (ăn-tĭl'ēz). The West Indies except for the Bahamas, separating the Caribbean Sea from the Atlantic.
An·ti·och (ăn'tē-ŏk'). **1.** Ancient town of Phrygia, in SW Turkey. **2.** City of S Turkey, on the Orontes R. near the Mediterranean. Pop. 91,551. **3.** City of W Calif., ENE of Oakland. Pop. 43,559.
An·tip·o·des (ăn-tĭp'ə-dēz'). Rocky islands of the S Pacific, SE of New Zealand.
An·ti·sa·na (än'tē-sä'nä). Volcano, 18,885 ft (5,760 m), of N central Ecuador, in the Andes SE of Quito.
An·to·fa·gas·ta (än'tō-fə-gä'stə, än'-tō-fä-gäs'tä). City of N Chile, on the Pacific. Pop. 157,000.
An·tung (ăn'to͝ong', än'do͝ong'). Dandong.
Ant·werp (ăn'twərp). City of N Belgium, on the Scheldt R. N of Brussels. Pop. 194,073.
A·nu·ra·dha·pur·a (ə-no͝or'ä-də-po͝or'ə). Town of N central Sri Lanka, NNE of Colombo. Pop. 38,000.
An·vers (äN-vâr'). *French.* Antwerp.
An·yang (än'yäng'). City of E China, NNE of Zhengzhou. Pop. 124,900.
An·zhe·ro-Sud·zhensk (än-zhĕ'-rə-so͞od-zhĕnsk'). City of SW Siberian USSR, NE of Novosibirsk. Pop. 107,000.
An·zi·o (ăn'zē-ō, än'tsyō). Town of central Italy, on the Tyrrhenian Sea. Pop. 27,223.
A·o·mo·ri (ä'ô-mô'rē). City of N Honshu, Japan, on **Aomori Bay.** Pop. 287,609.
Ap·a·lach·ee Bay (ăp'ə-lăch'ē). Inlet of the Gulf of Mexico, in NW Fla.
Ap·a·lach·i·co·la (ăp'ə-lăch'ə-kō'lə). River of NW Fla., flowing 112 mi (180.2 km) to **Apalachicola Bay**, an inlet of the Gulf of Mexico.
Ap·a·po·ris (äp'ə-pōr'ēs, -pôr'-).

River, c. 500 mi (800 km), of S central Colombia.

A·pel·doorn (ä'pəl-dōrn', -dôrn'). City of E central Netherlands, N of Arnhem. Pop. 138,164.

Ap·en·nines (ăp'ə-nīnz'). Mountain system extending from NW Italy S to the Strait of Messina.

A·pi·a (ä-pē'ä, ä'pē-ä'). Cap. of Western Samoa, on N Upolo Is. Pop. 32,099.

A·po (ä'pô). Volcano, 9,692 ft (2,955.6 m), of S Mindanao, Philippines.

Ap·pa·la·chi·a (ăp'ə-lā'chē-ə, -chə, -lăch'ē-ə, -lăch'ə). Region of E U.S. containing the Appalachian Mts.

Ap·pa·la·chi·an (ăp'ə-lā'chē-ən, -chən, -lăch'ē-ən, -lăch'ən). **1. Mountains.** Also **the Ap·pa·la·chi·ans** (-ənz, -chənz). Mountain system of E North America, extending c. 1,600 mi (2,575 km) from S Que., Canada, to central Ala. **2. Trail.** Hiking path of U.S., extending 2,050 mi (3,298.5 km) from Mt. Katahdin in Me. to N Ga.

Ap·pi·an Way (ăp'ē-ən). Ancient Roman road, between Rome and Brindisi.

Ap·ple·ton (ăp'əl-tən). City of E Wis., SW of Green Bay. Pop. 59,032.

Ap·ple Valley (ăp'əl). City of E Minn., S of Minneapolis. Pop. 21,818.

Ap·po·mat·tox Court House National Historical Park (ăp'ə-măt'əks). Site in S central Va., E of Lynchburg, where Robert E. Lee surrendered to Ulysses S. Grant in 1865.

A·pra Harbor (ä'prə). Seaport of W Guam, in the Mariana Is. of the W Pacific.

Ap·she·ron (äp-shĭ-rôn'). Peninsula of SW USSR, extending into the Caspian Sea.

A·pu·li·a (ä-po͝ol'yə). Region of S Italy.

A·pu·re (ä-po͞o'rĕ). River of W central Venezuela, originating in Colombia and flowing c. 500 mi (805 km) to the Orinoco.

A·pu·rí·mac (ä'po͞o-rē'mäk). River of S Peru, flowing c. 550 mi (885 km) to the Urubamba and forming the Ucayali.

A·qa·ba (ä'kä-bä'). Town of SW Jordan, at the head of the **Gulf of Aqaba**, an arm of the Red Sea. Pop. 26,986.

A·quid·neck (ə-kwĭd'nĕk'). Island of SE R.I., in Narragansett Bay.

Aq·ui·taine (ăk'wĭ-tān', ä-kē-tĕn'). Historical region of SW France.

Aq·ui·ta·ni·a (ăk'wĭ-tā'nē-ə). Roman division of SW Gaul S of the Garonne R. —**Aq'ui·ta'ni·an** *adj. & n.*

A·ra·bah or **A·ra·ba** (ă'rə-bə). Depression on the Israel-Jordan border, from the Dead Sea to the Gulf of Aqaba.

A·ra·bi·a (ə-rā'bē-ə). Peninsula of SW Asia, between the Red Sea and the Persian Gulf. —**A·ra'bi·an** *adj. & n.*

Arabian. 1. Sea. NW part of the Indian Ocean, between Arabia and India. **2.** Desert of E Egypt, between the Nile Valley and the Red Sea.

A·ra·ca·ju (ä'rə-kə-zho͞o'). City of E central Brazil, near the Atlantic. Pop. 226,248.

A·rad (ä-räd'). City of W Rumania, on the Mureşul R. Pop. 172,669.

A·ra·fu·ra Sea (ä'rə-fo͞o'rə). Part of the W Pacific, between New Guinea and Australia.

Ar·a·gats (är'ə-gäts, âr'-), **Mount.** Extinct volcano, 13,435 ft (4,097.7 m), of S European USSR, in the Caucasus.

Ar·a·gon (ăr'ə-gŏn, ä'rä-gôn'). Region and former kingdom of NE Spain. —**Ar'a·go·nese'** (ăr'ə-gə-nēz', -nēs') *adj. & n.*

A·ra·guai·a or **A·ra·gua·ya** (ä'rə-gwä'yə). River, c. 1,300 mi (2,090 km), of central Brazil.

A·rak (ä-räk'). City of W central Iran, SW of Teheran. Pop. 114,507.

A·ra·kan (ä'rä-kän', ăr'ə-kăn'). Region of SW Burma, on the Bay of Bengal.

A·raks (ä-räks'). *Russian.* Aras.

Ar·al Sea (ăr'əl). Island sea of Central Asian USSR, E of the Caspian Sea.

Ar·an (ăr'ən). 3 islands of W Ireland, at the entrance to Galway Bay.

A·ran·sas (ə-răn'səs). **1. Bay.** Inlet of the Gulf of Mexico in S Tex. **2. Pass.** Channel of S Tex., between the Gulf of Mexico and the Gulf Intracoastal Waterway near Corpus Christi.

A·rap·a·hoe (ə-răp'ə-hō'). Mountain, 13,506 ft (4,119.3 m), of N central Colo., in the Front Range of the Rockies.

A·ras (ä-räs'). River rising in NE Turkey and flowing c. 600 mi (965 km) along the Turkey-USSR and USSR-Iran borders.

A·rau·ca (ä-rou'kä). River rising in N central Colombia and flowing E c. 500 mi (805 km) to join the Orinoco in central Venezuela.

Ar·au·ca·ni·a (ăr'ô-kā'nē-ə, ä-rou-kä'nyä). Region of central Chile. —**Ar'au·ca'ni·an** *adj. & n.*

A·ra·val·li (ä-rä-vä'lē, ə-rä'və-). Mountain range, c. 300 mi (485 km) long, of NW India.

Ar·be·la (är-bē'lə). Ancient Assyrian town, in present-day N Iraq.

Ar·broath (är-brōth') or **Ab·er·bro·thock** (ăb'ər-brə-thŏk'). Burgh of E central Scotland, on the North Sea. Pop. 23,207.

Ar·buck·le Mountains (är'bŭk'əl). Range of low hills in S Okla., site of a national recreation area.

Ar·ca·di·a (är-kā'dē-ə). **1.** Region of ancient Greece, in the Peloponnesus. **2.** City of S Calif., near Los Angeles. Pop. 45,994.

Ar·ca·ta (är-kā'tə). City of NW Calif., NNE of Eureka. Pop. 12,338.

Arch·an·gel (ärk'ān'jəl). Arkhangelsk.

Ar·ches National Park (är'chĭz). Area of E Utah with many unusual rock formations.

Arc·tic (ärk'tĭk, är'tĭk). **1. Ocean.** Waters surrounding the North Pole, between North America and Eurasia. **2.** Also **the Arctic.** Area between the North Pole and the N timberline. **3. Archipelago.** Islands in the Arctic Ocean between North America and Greenland.

Arctic Red (rĕd). River of W N.W.T., Canada, flowing c. 310 mi (500 km) to the Mackenzie.

Ar·de·bil also **Ar·da·bil** (är'də-bēl'). Town of NW Iran, near the USSR border. Pop. 147,404.

Ar·den (är'dn). District of central England, where the **Forest of Arden** was located.

Ar·dennes (är-dĕn'). Plateau region of N France, SE Belgium, and Luxembourg, E and S of the Meuse R.

Ard·more (ärd'môr, -mōr). City of S Okla., near the Tex. border SSE of Oklahoma City. Pop. 23,689.

A·re·ci·bo (ä'rē-sē'bō). City of N Puerto Rico, on the Atlantic. Pop. 48,779.

A·re·qui·pa (ä'rē-kē'pä). City of S Peru, at the foot of El Misti. Metro. area pop. 304,653.

A·rez·zo (ə-rĕt'sō, ä-rāt'tsō). City of central Italy, on the Arno R. Pop. 92,245.

Ar·gen·teuil (är-zhäN-tœ'yə). City of N France, on the Seine near Paris. Pop. 102,530.

Ar·gen·ti·na (är'jən-tē'nə). Republic of SE South America. Cap. Buenos Aires. Pop. 27,860,000. —**Ar'gen·tine** (-tēn, -tīn) *adj. & n.* —**Ar'gen·tin'e·an** (-tĭn'ē-ən) *adj. & n.*

Ar·ghan·dab (är-găn-dăb'). River, c. 250 mi (400 km), of E and central Afghanistan.

Ar·go·lis (är'gə-lĭs). **1. Gulf of.** Inlet of the Aegean, on the E coast of the Peloponnesus, S Greece. **2.** Ancient region of S Greece, in the NE Peloponnesus.

Ar·gonne (är'gŏn, är-gŏn', är-gôn'). Region of NE France.

Ar·gos (är'gŏs, -gəs). Ancient Greek city in NE Peloponnesus, near the head of the Gulf of Argolis.

Ar·gun (är-go͞on'). River of E central Asia, flowing 950 mi (1,528.6 km) along the USSR-China border.

År·hus also **Aar·hus** (ôr'ho͞os'). City of central Denmark, on **Århus Bay**, an arm of the Kattegat. Pop. 244,839.

A·ri·nos (ə-rē'nōosh). River, c. 400 mi (645 km), of central Brazil.

A·ri·pua·nã (ə-rē'pwä-näN'). River of W central Brazil, flowing c. 400 mi (645 km) to the Madeira.

A·ri·us (âr'ē-əs, ăr'-, ə-rī'əs). Hari Rud.

Ar·i·zo·na (ăr'ĭ-zō'nə). State of the SW U.S., on the Mexican border. Cap. Phoenix. Pop. 2,717,866. —**Ar'i·zo'ni·an** *adj. & n.*

Ar·ka·del·phi·a (är'kə-dĕl'fē-ə). City of SW Ark., S of Hot Springs. Pop. 10,028.

Ar·kan·sas (är'kən-sô, -sō). **1.** (*also* är-kăn'zəs). River of the S central U.S., rising in central Colo. and flowing c. 1,450 mi (2,335 km) to the Mississippi in SE Ark. **2.** State of the S central U.S. Cap. Little Rock. Pop. 2,285,513. —**Ar·kan'san** (är-kăn'zən) *adj. & n.*

Arkansas City. City of S Kans., near the Okla. border SSE of Wichita. Pop. 13,201.

Ark·han·gelsk (är-KHän'gĕlsk). City of NW European USSR, on the Northern Dvina. Pop. 387,000.

Arl·berg (ärl'bûrg, -bĕrk). Alpine pass in W Austria, 5,946 ft (1,813.5 m) high.

Arles (ärlz, ärl). **1.** Medieval kingdom of E and SE France. **2.** City of S central France, on the Rhone R. Pop. 37,340.

Ar·ling·ton (är'lĭng-tən). **1.** Town of E Mass., near Boston. Pop. 48,219. **2.** City of N Tex., E of Fort Worth. Pop. 160,123. **3.** County and unincorporated city of N Va., near Washington, D.C. Pop. 152,599.

Arlington Heights. Village of NE Ill., near Chicago. Pop. 66,116.

Ar·magh (är-mä'). Urban district of S Northern Ireland. Pop. 13,606.

Ar·ma·gnac (är'mən-yăk, är-mä-nyäk'). Region of SW France, in Gascony.

Ar·ma·vir (är'mə-vîr', är-mä-). City of SE European USSR, on the Kuban R. Pop. 163,000.

Ar·me·ni·a (är-mē'nē-ə, -nyə). Region and former kingdom of Asia Minor, in present-day NE Turkey, SE European USSR, and sections of Iranian Azerbaijan. —**Ar·me'ni·an** *adj. & n.*

Ar·me·nia (är-mē'nyä). City of W central Colombia. Pop. 164,000.

Ar·men·tières (är'mən-tîrz', är-mäN-tyĕr'). City of N France, WNW of Lille. Pop. 26,346.

Ar·mor·i·ca (är-môr'ĭ-kə, -mōr'-). Ancient name for NE part of France, especially Brittany.

Arn·hem (ärn'hĕm). City of E Netherlands, on the Rhine. Pop. 127,846.

Arn·hem Land (är'nəm). Region of N Australia, W of the Gulf of Carpentaria.

Ar·no (är'nō). River of central Italy, flowing c. 150 mi (240 km) to the Ligurian Sea.

Ar·nold (är'nəld). City of E Mo., S of St. Louis. Pop. 19,141.

A·roos·took (ə-ro͞os'to͝ok, -tək, -ro͞os'-). River, flowing c. 140 mi (225 km) from N Me. to the St. John R. in N.B., Canada.

Ar·ran (ăr'ən). Island of W Scotland, in the Firth of Clyde.

Ar·ras (ăr'əs, ä-räs'). City of N France, SSW of Lille. Pop. 46,446.

Ar·roy·o Gran·de (ə-roi'ō grăn'dē). City of SW Calif., SSE of San Luis Obispo. Pop. 11,290.

Ar·te·sia (är-tē'zhə). **1.** City of S Calif., near Los Angeles. Pop. 14,301. **2.** City of SE N.Mex., NNW of Carlsbad. Pop. 10,385.

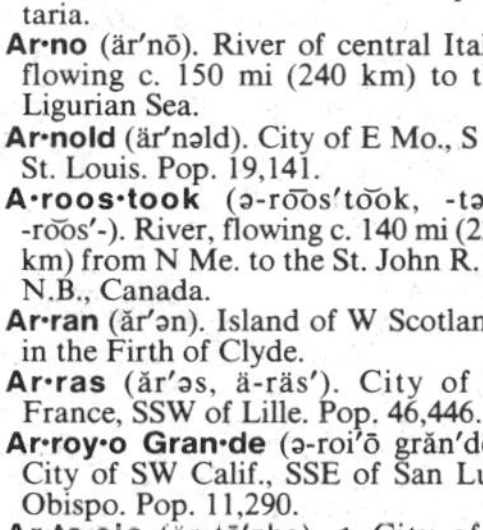

Argentina

Ar·tois (är-twä'). Region of N France, near the English Channel between Picardy and Flanders.

A·ru or **A·roe** or **Ar·roe** (ä'ro͞o). Islands of E Indonesia, part of the Moluccas, in the Arafura Sea SW of New Guinea.

A·ru·ba (ə-ro͞o'bə). Island of the Netherlands Antilles, N of the Venezuela coast.

A·ru·wi·mi (ä'ro͞o-wē'mē). River of N Zaire, flowing c. 800 mi (1,287 km) to the Congo R.

Ar·vad·a (är-văd'ə). City of N central Colo., near Denver. Pop. 84,576.

A·sa·hi·ga·wa (ä'sä-hē-gä'wä) also **A·sa·hi·ka·wa** (-kä'-). City of W central Hokkaido, Japan. Pop. 352,620.

A·sa·ma (ä-sä'mä) or **A·sa·ma·ya·ma** (ä-sä'mä-yä'mä). Active volcano, 8,340 ft (2,543.7 m), of central Honshu, Japan.

A·san·te (ə-sän'tē). Variant of **Ashanti.**

As·bes·tos (ăz-bĕs'təs). Town of SE Que., Canada, N of Sherbrooke. Pop. 9,075.

As·bur·y Park (ăz'bĕr'ē, -bə-rē). City of E N.J., on the Atlantic. Pop. 17,015.

As·ca·lon (ăs'kə-lŏn'). Ashkelon.

As·cen·sion (ə-sĕn'shən). Island in the S Atlantic, NW of St. Helena.

A·schaf·fen·burg (ä-shä'fən-bərg, ä-shäf'ən-bo͝ork'). City of S central West Germany, on the Main R. Pop. 59,054.

A·sco·li Pi·ce·no (ä'skō-lē pē-chā'-nō). City of central Italy, NE of Rome. Pop. 56,200.

As·cot (ăs'kət). Village of S central England, SW of London; site of Ascot racetrack.

As·cu·lum (ăs'kyo͞o-ləm). Ancient Roman town of SE Italy, S of present-day Foggia.

A·shan·ti (ə-shăn'tē, -shän'-) or **A·san·te** (-sän'-). Region and former kingdom of central Ghana, W Africa.

Ash·bur·ton (ăsh'bûr'tn, -bər-). River of NW Australia, flowing c. 400 mi (645 km) to the Indian Ocean.

Ash·dod (ăsh'dŏd, ăsh-dōd'). City of SW Israel, on the Mediterranean, near the site of ancient **Ashdod**, Philistine city-state. Pop. 62,300.

Ashe·bor·o (ăsh'bûr-ō, -bŭr-ō). City of central N.C., S of Greensboro. Pop. 15,252.

Ashe·ville (ăsh'vĭl', -vəl). City of W N.C., WNW of Charlotte. Pop. 53,281.

A·shi·ka·ga (ä'shē-kä'gä). City of central Honshu, Japan, N of Tokyo. Pop. 165,024.

Ash·ke·lon (ăsh'kə-lŏn', ăsh'kə-lôn'). Ancient city of SW Palestine, on the Mediterranean.

Ash·kha·bad (ăsh'kä-băd', -KHä-bät'). City of S Central Asian USSR, near the Iranian border. Pop. 318,000.

Ash·land (ăsh'lənd). **1.** City of E Ky., on the Ohio-W.Va. border. Pop. 27,064. **2.** City of N central Ohio, NE of Mansfield. Pop. 20,326. **3.** City of SW Ore., near Medford and the Calif. border. Pop. 14,943.

Ash·ley (ăsh'lē). River of S S.C., flowing 40 mi (64.3 km) into Charleston harbor.

Ash·ta·bu·la (ăsh'tə-byo͞o'lə). City of NE Ohio, on Lake Erie. Pop. 23,449.

Ash·ton-under-Lyne (ăsh'tən-ŭn-dər-līn'). Borough of NW England, E of Manchester. Pop. 218,500.

Ash·wau·be·non (ăsh-wô'bə-nən, -wŏb'ə-). Village of NE Wis., near Green Bay. Pop. 14,486.

A·sia (ā'zhə, ā'shə). The world's largest continent (17,139,000 sq mi/44,390,010 sq km), occupying the E part of Eurasia and adjacent islands and separated from Europe by the Ural Mts. —**A'sian** *adj. & n.*

Asia Mi·nor (mī'nər). Peninsula of W Asia, between the Black Sea and the Mediterranean.

As·ma·ra (ăs-mä'rä). City of N Ethiopia, near the Red Sea. Pop. 373,827.

As·nières-sur-Seine (ä-nyĕr'-sür-sĕn'). City of N central France, a NW suburb of Paris. Pop. 75,431.

A·so (ä'sō') or **A·so-san** (ä'sō-sän'). Volcanic mountain of central Kyushu, Japan.
As·pen (ăs'pən). City and ski resort of W central Colo., in the Rockies. Pop. 3,678.
As·pern (äs'pərn). Suburb of Vienna, Austria, where Austrians defeated Napoleon in 1809.
As·sa·teague (ăs'ə-tēg'). Island along Md. and Va. coasts, separating Chincoteague Bay and the Atlantic.
As·sen (ä'sən). City of NE Netherlands, S of Groningen. Pop. 45,036.
As·sin·i·boine (ə-sĭn'ə-boin'). **1.** River of S central Canada, flowing 590 mi (949.3 km) from S Sask. to the Red R. at Winnipeg, Man. **2.** Mountain, 11,870 ft (3,620.4 m), in the Canadian Rockies on the B.C.-Alta. line.
As·si·si (ə-sē'zē, -sē, ə-sĭs'ē, äs-sē'zē). Town of central Italy, ESE of Perugia. Pop. 19,400.
As·syr·i·a (ə-sĭr'ē-ə). Ancient empire of W Asia, in the upper valley of the Tigris. —**As·syr'i·an** *adj. & n.*
As·ti (äs'tē). City of NW Italy. Pop. 79,407.
As·to·ri·a (ă-stôr'ē-ə, -stōr'-). City of NW Ore., near the mouth of the Columbia. Pop. 9,998.
As·tra·khan (ăs'trə-kăn', ä'strä-kän', -кнän'yə). City of SE European USSR, on the Volga delta. Pop. 465,000.
As·tu·ri·as (ăs-tŏŏr'ē-əs, -tyŏŏr'-, äs-tōō'ryäs). Region and former kingdom of NW Spain.
A·sun·ción (ä'sōōn-syôn'). Cap. of Paraguay, in the S part. Pop. 462,776.
As·wan or **As·suan** (ăs'wän, ăs-wän', äs-). City of S Egypt, on the Nile near the **Aswan High Dam**, completed in 1970. Pop. 144,377.
As·yut (ä-syōōt', äs-yōōt'). City of E central Egypt, on the Nile. Pop. 213,983.
At·a·ca·ma (ăt'ə-kăm'ə, ä'tä-kä'mä). Desert of N Chile.
A·tas·ca·de·ro (ə-tăs'kə-dâr'ō). City of SW Calif., N of San Luis Obispo. Pop. 15,930.
At·ba·ra (ăt'bä-rä'). River of NE Africa, flowing c. 500 mi (805 km) from NW Ethiopia to the Nile in E Sudan.
A·tchaf·a·lay·a (ə-chăf'ə-lī'ə). River of S central La., flowing c. 170 mi (275 km) into **Atchafalaya Bay**, an inlet of the Gulf of Mexico.
At·chi·son (ăch'ĭ-sən). City of NE Kans., NW of Kansas City. Pop. 11,407.
Ath·a·bas·ca or **Ath·a·bas·ka** (ăth'-ə-băs'kə). **1.** Lake of NE Alta. and NW Sask., Canada. **2.** River of Alta., Canada, flowing 765 mi (1,230.9 km) to Lake Athabasca. **3. Mount.** Peak, 11,452 ft (3,492.9 m), of W Alta., Canada.
Ath·ens (ăth'ĭnz) **1.** Cap. of Greece, in the E central part. Pop. 867,023. **2.** City of N Ala., WNW of Huntsville. Pop. 14,558. **3.** City of NE Ga., ENE of Atlanta. Pop. 42,549. **4.** City of SE Ohio, W of Marietta. Pop. 19,743. **5.** City of E Tenn., NE of Chattanooga. Pop. 12,080. **6.** City of E Tex., SE of Dallas. Pop. 10,197.
Ath·ol (ăth'ôl, -ŏl). Town of N Mass., W of Fitchburg. Pop. 10,634.
Ath·os (ăth'ŏs, ä'thŏs, ä'thôs), **Mount.** Peak, c. 6,670 ft (2,035 m), of NE Greece, in Macedonia; site of virtually independent monastic community of **Mount Athos.**
A·ti·tlán (ä'tē-tlän'). Volcanic lake of SW Guatemala.
At·ka (ăt'kə, ăt'-). Island of SW Alas., in the Andreanof group of the central Aleutians.
At·lan·ta (ăt-lăn'tə). Cap. of Ga., in the NW part. Pop. 425,022.
At·lan·tic (ăt-lăn'tĭk). Ocean, c. 31,800,000 sq mi (82,362,000 sq km), extending from the Arctic to the Antarctic between North and South America on the W and Europe and Africa on the E.
Atlantic City. City of SE N.J., on the Atlantic. Pop. 40,199.
Atlantic Provinces. The E Canadian provinces of N.B., P.E.I., N.S., and Newf.
At·las (ăt'ləs). Mountain system of NW Africa, extending from SW Morocco to N Tunisia between the Sahara and the Mediterranean, and rising to 13,665 ft (4,167.8 m).
At·lin (ăt'lĭn). Lake of NW B.C., Canada.
A·tra·to (ä-trä'tō). River, c. 375 mi (605 km), of W Colombia.
A·trek (ä-trĕk') or **A·trak** (ä-träk'). River of NE Iran, flowing 300 mi (482.7 km), partly along the USSR-Iran border, to the Caspian.
At·su·gi (ä-tsōō'gē). City of E central Honshu, Japan, near Tokyo. Pop. 136,652.
At·ta·wa·pis·kat (ăt'ə-wə-pĭs'kət, -kăt). River, c. 465 mi (750 km), of N Ont., Canada.
At·ti·ca (ăt'ĭ-kə). Ancient region of E central Greece, around Athens.
At·tle·bor·o (ăt'l-bûr'ō, -bŭr'ō). City of SE Mass., NE of Providence, R.I. Pop. 34,196.
At·tu (ăt'tōō'). Island of SW Alas., westernmost of the Aleutians.
A·tu·o·na (ä'tōō-ō'nä) or **A·tu·a·na** (-ä'nä). Town of the Marquesas Is., in the S Pacific in French Polynesia.
At·wa·ter (ăt'wô'tər, -wŏt'ər). City of central Calif., WNW of Merced. Pop. 17,530.
Aube (ōb). River of NE France, flowing 140 mi (225.2 km) to the Seine.
Au·ber·vil·liers (ō'bĕr-vēl-yā', ō-bĕr-vē-yā'). Town of N central France, NE of Paris. Pop. 72,976.
Au·burn (ô'bərn). **1.** City of E Ala., NNE of Tuskegee. Pop. 28,471. **2.** City of SE Me., near Lewiston. Pop. 23,128. **3.** Town of S central Mass., S of Worcester. Pop. 14,845. **4.** City of W central N.Y., WSW of Syracuse. Pop. 32,548. **5.** City of W Wash., ENE of Tacoma. Pop. 26,417.
Auck·land (ôk'lənd, ŏk'-). City of New Zealand, on NW North Is. Metro. area pop. 775,000.
Au·ghra·bies Falls (ô-grä'bēz, -bēs). Waterfall, 480 ft (146.4 m), on the Orange R. in South Africa.
Augs·burg (ôgz'bûrg', ouks'bŏŏrk'). City of S West Germany, WNW of Munich. Pop. 245,940.
Au·gus·ta (ô-gŭs'tə, ə-gŭs'-). **1.** City of E Ga., on the S.C. border NNW of Savannah. Pop. 47,532. **2.** Cap. of Me., in the SW part NNE of Portland. Pop. 21,819.
Au·lis (ô'lĭs). Ancient port of E central Greece, in Boeotia on the Gulf of Euboea.
Au·nis (ō-nēs'). Region and former province of W France, on the Atlantic Ocean.
Au·rang·a·bad (ou-rŭng'gə-bäd', ô-rŭng'-). Town of W India, ENE of Bombay. Pop. 150,483.
Au·ri·gnac (ô-rē-nyäk'). Village of S France, at the foot of the Pyrenees; site of caves with prehistoric relics.
Au·ril·lac (ô-rē-yäk'). Town of S central France, SW of Toulouse. Pop. 30,863.
Au·ro·ra (ô-rôr'ə, -rōr'-, ə-rôr'ə, -rōr'-). **1.** Town of S Ont., Canada, N of Toronto. Pop. 14,249. **2.** City of N central Colo., near Denver. Pop. 158,588. **3.** City of NE Ill., W of Chicago. Pop. 81,293.
Au·sa·ble (ô-sā'bəl, ō-sā'-). River of NE N.Y., flowing 20 mi (32.1 km) through **Ausable Chasm**, a 2 mi (3.2 km) gorge, to Lake Champlain.
Ausch·witz (oush'vĭts). Oświęcim.
Aus·ter·litz (ô'stər-lĭts, ous'tər-). Town of S Czechoslovakia, near site of Napoleon's 1805 defeat of Russian and Austrian armies.
Aus·tin (ô'stən, ŏs'tən). **1.** City of SE Minn., SW of Rochester. Pop. 23,020. **2.** Cap. of Tex., in the S central part. Pop. 345,496.
Aus·tral·a·sia (ô'strə-lā'zhə, -shə). **1.** Islands of Oceania in the S Pacific, including Australia, New Zealand, New Guinea, and associated islands. **2.** Oceania. —**Aus·tral·a'sian** *adj. & n.*
Aus·tra·lia (ô-strāl'yə). **1.** The world's smallest continent, 2,948,366 sq mi (7,636,267.9 sq km), SE of Asia between the Pacific and Indian oceans. **2.** Or **Commonwealth of Australia.** Country comprising the continent of Australia, the island state of Tasmania, two external territories, and several dependencies. Cap. Canberra. Pop. 14,423,500. —**Aus·tra'lian** *adj. & n.*

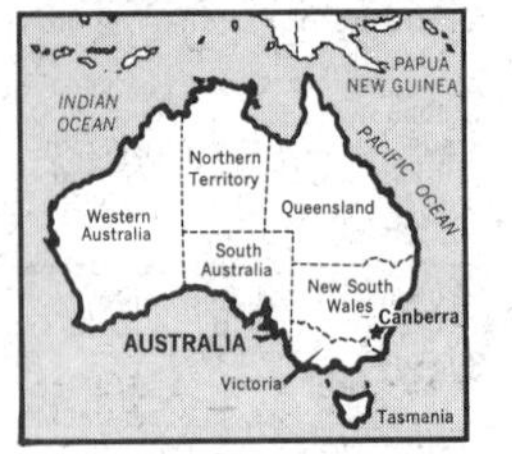

Australia

Australian Alps. Mountain ranges of SE Australia, S part of the Eastern Highlands.
Aus·tra·sia (ô-strā'zhə, -shə). E portion of the Merovingian kingdom of the Franks from the 6th to the 8th cent., consisting of parts of E France, W West Germany, and the Netherlands. —**Aus·tra'sian** *adj. & n.*
Aus·tri·a (ô'strē-ə). Federal republic of central Europe. Cap. Vienna. Pop. 7,456,745. —**Aus'tri·an** *adj. & n.*

Austria

Aus·tri·a-Hun·ga·ry (ô'strē-ə-hŭng'gə-rē). Dual monarchy (1867–1918) of central Europe, consisting of Austria, Hungary, Bohemia, and parts of Poland, Rumania, Yugoslavia and Italy. —**Aus'tro-Hun·gar'i·an** (-gâr'ē-ən) *adj. & n.*
Aus·tro·ne·sia (ô'strō-nē'zhə, -shə). **1.** Islands of the Pacific, including Indonesia, Melanesia, Micronesia, and Polynesia. **2.** Island area of the S hemisphere, extending from Madagascar to Hawaii and Easter Is. —**Aus'tro·ne'sian** *adj. & n.*
Au·vergne (ō-vĕrn', ō-vûrn'). Region and former province of S central France, traversed N to S by the **Auvergne Mts.**, chain of extinct volcanoes.
Av·a·lon (ăv'ə-lŏn'). **1.** Peninsula of SE Newf., Canada. **2.** Or **Isle of Avalon.** District, formerly an island, of SW England.
A·ve·lla·ne·da (ä-vĕ'yä-nĕ'dä, *-thä*). City of E Argentina, near Buenos Aires. Pop. 337,538.
A·venches (ä-vänsh') or **A·ven·ti·cum** (ə-vĕn'tĭ-kəm). Commune and ancient city of W Switzerland.
Av·en·tine (ăv'ən-tīn', -tēn'). One of the 7 hills of ancient Rome.
A·ver·no (ä-vĕr'nō) or **A·ver·nus** (ə-vûr'nəs). Small crater lake of S Italy, W of Naples.
A·vi·gnon (ä-vē-nyôɴ'). City of SE France, on the Rhone. Pop. 90,786.
A·vi·la (ä'vē-lä). Town of central Spain, WNW of Madrid. Pop. 38,105.
A·vi·lés (ä-vē-lĕs'). Town of NW Spain, on the Bay of Biscay. Pop. 90,458.
A·von (ā'vŏn). **1.** (*also* ā'vən, ăv'ən). Also **Bristol** or **Lower Avon.** River of SW England, flowing 75 mi (120.7 km) to the Severn. **2.** Also **East Avon.** River of S England, flowing 48 mi (77.2 km) to the English Channel. **3.** Also **Upper Avon.** River of S central England, flowing 96 mi (154.5 km) to the Severn. **4.** Town of N central Conn., WNW of Hartford. Pop. 11,201.
Avon Lake. City of NE Ohio, on Lake Erie. Pop. 13,222.
A·vranches (ä-vränsh'). Town of NW France, on the English Channel. Pop. 10,136.
A·wa·ji (ä-wä'jē) or **A·wa·ji·shi·ma** (ä-wä'jē-shē'mä). Island of Japan, in the Inland Sea between SW Honshu and Shikoku.
A·wash (ä'wäsh'). Variant of **Hawash.**
Ax·el Hei·berg (ăk'səl hī'bûrg). Island in the Arctic Ocean, N N.W.T., Canada, W of Ellesmere Is.
Ax·um (äk'sōōm). Variant of **Aksum.**
A·ya·cu·cho (ä'yä-kōō'chô). City of S central Peru, S of Buenos Aires. Pop. 34,593.
Ayles·bur·y (ālz'bĕr'ē, -bə-rē). City of central England, NW of London. Pop. 118,800.
Ayl·mer (āl'mər). Town of SW Que., Canada, on the Ottawa R. near Hull. Pop. 25,714.
Ayr (âr). Burgh of SW Scotland, at the mouth of the **Ayr R.** on the Firth of Clyde. Pop. 47,991.
A·yut·thay·a (ä-yōō'tä-yä) or **A·yu·dhya** (ä-yōō'dyä). City of S central Thailand, on the Chao Phraya R. Pop. 46,664.
A·zer·bai·jan (ăz'ər-bī-jän', ä'-zər-bī-jän', -zĕr-) **1.** Region of NW Iran. **2.** Or **A·zer·bai·dzhan.** Region of SE European USSR.
A·zores (ā'zôrz, ā'zōrz, ə-zôrz', ə-zōrz'). Islands in the N Atlantic, c. 900 mi (1,448 km) W of mainland Portugal. —**A·zor'e·an, A·zor'i·an** *adj. & n.*
A·zov (ăs'ôf', -ŏf', ā'zŏf, ä-zôf'), **Sea of.** N arm of the Black Sea, covering an area of c. 14,000 sq mi (36,260 sq km) in S European USSR.
A·zu·sa (ə-zōō'sə). City of S Calif., E of Pasadena. Pop. 29,380.

B

Baal·bek (bäl'bĕk', bā'əl-, bäl'-). Town of Lebanon, NE of Beirut. Pop. 16,000.
Ba·bar (bä'bär'). Islands of E Indonesia, ENE of Timor.
Bab el Man·deb (băb' ĕl măn'dĕb). Strait, 17 mi (27.4 km) wide, between the Red Sea and the Gulf of Aden.
Ba·bel·thu·ap (bä'bĕl-tōō'äp'). Island, 120 sq mi (310.8 sq km), of the Palau group, SW Pacific.
Ba·bia Gó·ra (bä'byä gōō'rä). Highest mountain (5,659 ft/1,725.9 m) of the Beskids, in the West Beskids on the border between Poland and Czechoslovakia.
Ba·bu·yan (bä'bōō-yän'). Main island of the **Babuyan Is.**, in the Philippines N of Luzon.
Bab·y·lon (băb'ə-lən, -lŏn'). **1.** Cap. of ancient Babylonia, in Mesopotamia on the Euphrates R. **2.** Village of SE N.Y., on S Long Is. Pop. 12,388.
Bab·y·lo·ni·a (băb'ə-lō'nē-ə, -nyə). Ancient country of SW Asia, in Mesopotamia in the lower Euphrates valley. —**Bab'y·lo'ni·an** *adj. & n.*
Ba·ca·u (bä-kŭ'ōō). City of E Rumania, NNE of Bucharest. Pop. 135,841.
Back (băk). River, c. 600 mi (965 km), of N.W.T., Canada.
Ba·co·lod (bä-kō'lōd'). City of NW Negros Is., Philippines. Pop. 223,392.
Bac·tra (băk'trə). Balkh.
Bac·tri·a (băk'trē-ə). Ancient country of SW Asia. —**Bac'tri·an** *adj. & n.*
Ba·da·joz (bä'*thä*-hôs'). City of SW Spain, on the Guadiana R. near the Portugal border. Pop. 89,500.
Ba·da·lo·na (bä'*thä*-lō'nä). City of NE Spain, on the Mediterranean near Barcelona. Pop. 216,041.
Ba·den (bäd'n). Region of SW Germany.
Ba·den-Ba·den (bäd'n-bäd'n). City of SW Germany, in the Black Forest. Pop. 49,718.
Bad Go·des·berg (bät' gō'dĭs-bərg, -dĕs-berk'). Godesberg.
Bad Hom·burg vor der Hö·he (hôm'bĕrk' fôr dĕr hœ'ə). City of central West Germany, near Frankfurt. Pop. 51,196.

Bad Kreuz·nach (kroits'näкн'). City of W West Germany. Pop. 42,707.

Bad·lands National Monument (băd'lăndz'). Extensive tract of badlands in SW S.Dak.

Baf·fin Bay (băf'ĭn). Arm of the Atlantic off NE Canada, separating Greenland and **Baffin Is.** (183,810 sq mi/467,068 sq km).

Ba·fing (bə-făng'). River of W Guinea and W Mali, flowing 350 mi (563.2 km) to the Senegal R.

Bagh·dad or **Bag·dad** (băg'dăd', băg-dăd'). Cap. of Iraq, on the Tigris. Pop. 1,300, 000.

Bag·ui·o (băg'ē-ō', bä'gyô'). Summer cap. of the Philippines, in NW Luzon. Pop. 97,449.

Ba·ha·ma Islands (bə-hä'mə, -hā'-) also **Ba·ha·mas** (-məz). Island country in the Atlantic SE of Florida. Cap. Nassau. Pop. 168,812. **—Ba·ha'mi·an** (bə-hā'mē-ən, -hä'-), **Ba·ha'man** (bə-hā'mən) *adj. & n.*

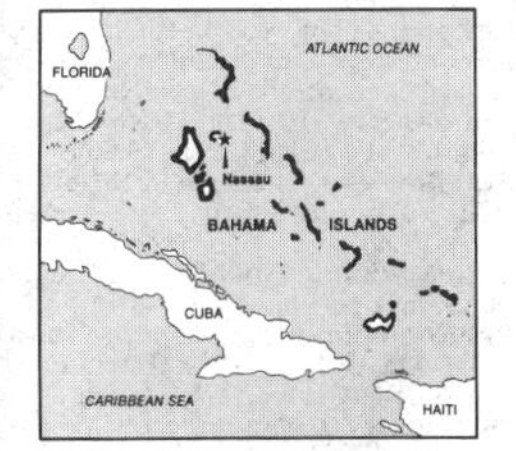

Bahama Islands

Ba·ha·wal·pur (bə-hä'wəl-po͝or', bä'-wəl-, bə-hä'wəl-po͝or'). Region of E central Pakistan, between the Sutlej R. and the Indian border.

Ba·hi·a (bä-ē'ə, bə-). Salvador.

Ba·hí·a Blan·ca (bä-ē'ä bläng'kä). City of SE Argentina, on the **Bahía Blanca**, an inlet of the Atlantic. Pop. 253,000.

Bah·rain or **Bah·rein** (bä-rān', -hrān'). Sheikdom and archipelago in the Persian Gulf between Qatar and Saudi Arabia. Cap. Al Manamah. Pop. 350,000. **—Bah·rain'i** (bä-rā'-nē) *adj. & n.*

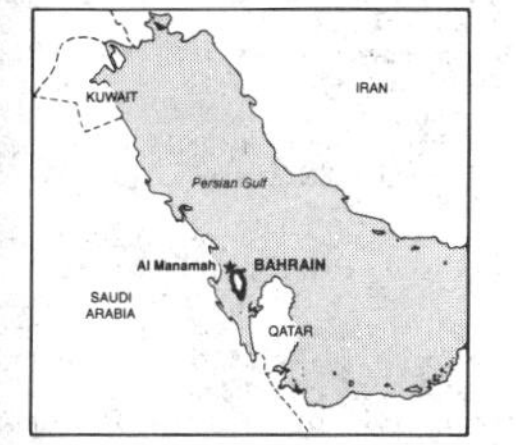

Bahrain

Bahr el Gha·zal (bâr' ĕl' gə-zăl', bär' ĕl' gä-zäl'). River of SW Sudan, flowing c. 500 mi (805 km) E to Lake No, where it joins the Bahr el Jebel.

Bahr el Jeb·el (jĕb'əl). River, 594 mi (955.8 km), of S Sudan, a section of the White Nile.

Bai (bī). River, c. 350 mi (563 km), of NE China.

Baie Co·meau (bā' kō'mō). Town of E Que., Canada, on the St. Lawrence NNE of Rimouski. Pop. 11,911.

Bai·kal or **Bay·kal** (bī-kôl', -kŏl'). Lake, 12,160 sq mi (31,494 sq km), of SE Siberian USSR.

Bain·bridge (băn'brĭj'). City of SW Ga., near the Fla. border SSE of Columbus. Pop. 10,553.

Bai·ri·ki (bī-rē'kē). Cap. of Kiribati, on Tarawa in the W central Pacific. Pop. 17,100.

Ba·ja Cal·i·for·ni·a (bä'hä kä'lē-fôr'-nyä, bä'hə kăl'ə-fôr'nyə). *Spanish.* Lower California.

Bak·er (bā'kər). **1.** Lake, c. 1,000 sq mi (2,590 sq km), in N central N.W.T., Canada. **2.** Peak, 12,460 ft (3,800.3 m), of N Colo. **3.** Peak, 10,778 ft (3,287.3 m) of NW Wash., in the Cascades. **4.** U.S.-owned island in the central Pacific, near the Equator. **5.** City of SE central La., near Baton Rouge. Pop. 12,865.

Ba·kers·field (bā'kərz-fēld'). City of S central Calif., NNW of Los Angeles. Pop. 105,611.

Ba·ku (bä-ko͞o'). City of SW Central Asian USSR, on the Caspian Sea. Pop. 1,030,000.

Bak·wan·ga (bäk-wäng'gä). Mbuji Mayi.

Bal·a·kla·va or **Bal·a·cla·va** (băl'-ə-klä'və, -klăv'ə, bä'lä-klä'vä). Section of Sevastopol, SE European USSR, on the Crimean peninsula; site of the Charge of the Light Brigade (1854).

Bal·a·ton (băl'ə-tŏn', bô'lô-tôn'). Lake, 230 sq mi (595.7 sq km), in W central Hungary, SW of Budapest.

Balch Springs (bôlch). City of NE Tex., near Dallas. Pop. 13,746.

Bald·win (bôld'wĭn). Borough of SW Pa., near Pittsburgh. Pop. 24,598.

Baldwin Park. City of S Calif., near Los Angeles. Pop. 50,554.

Bâle (bäl). *French.* Basel.

Bal·e·ar·ic (băl'ē-ăr'ĭk). Archipelago in the W Mediterranean, E of Spain.

Ba·li (bä'lē). Island, c. 2,220 sq mi (5,700 sq km), of E Indonesia, in the Lesser Sundas E of Java. **—Ba'li·nese'** (bä'lĭ-nēz', -nēs') *adj. & n.*

Bal·kan (bôl'kən). **1.** Mountain range, extending c. 350 mi (565 km) from E Yugoslavia through central Bulgaria to the Black Sea. **2.** Peninsula of SE Europe, bounded by the Black Sea, Sea of Marmara, and the Aegean, Mediterranean, Ionian, and Adriatic seas; occupied by the **Balkan States**: Albania, Bulgaria, continental Greece, SE Rumania, European Turkey, and most of Yugoslavia.

Bal·kar·i·a (bôl-kâr'ē-ə, băl-). Region of S European USSR.

Balkh (bälk, bälкн). Town of N Afghanistan, cap. of ancient Bactria.

Bal·khash (băl-kăsh', băl-kăsh', -кнăsh'). Lake, 6,562 sq mi (16,996 sq km), of SE Central Asian USSR.

Bal·la·rat (băl'ə-răt'). City of SE Australia, WNW of Melbourne. Metro area pop. 38,400.

Ball·win (bôl'wĭn). City of E Mo., near St. Louis. Pop. 12,750.

Bal·sas (bäl'säs). River flowing c. 450 mi (725 km) from E central Mexico to the Pacific.

Bal·tic (bôl'tĭk, bŏl'-). **1. Sea.** Arm of the Atlantic in N Europe. **2. States.** Estonia, Latvia, and Lithuania, on the E coast of the Baltic Sea.

Bal·ti·more (bôl'tə-môr', -mōr', bŏl'-) City of N Md., NE of Washington, D.C. Pop. 786,775.

Ba·lu·chi·stan (bə-lo͞o'chĭ-stăn', -stän'). Desert region of W Pakistan.

Ba·ma·ko (băm'ə-kō', bä-mä-kō'). Cap. of Mali, in the SW on the Niger R. Pop. 404,022.

Bam·berg (băm'bûrg', bäm'bĕrk'). City of S West Germany, W of Bayreuth. Pop. 74,236.

Ba·na·na River (bə-năn'ə). Lagoon in E. Fla., between Cape Canaveral and Merritt Is.

Ba·na·ras (bə-när'ĭs, -ĕz, -nä'rĕz). Varanasi.

Ba·nat (bä-nät', bä'nät'). Region of SE central Europe, extending across W Rumania, NE Yugoslavia, and S Hungary.

Ban·bur·y (băn'bĕr'ē, -bə-rē, băm'-). Borough of central England, SE of Birmingham. Pop. 31,060.

Ban·da (băn'də, băn'dä). **1. Sea.** Arm of the Pacific Ocean, in E Indonesia SE of Sulawesi and N of Timor. **2. Islands.** Archipelago in the Banda Sea, in the Moluccas.

Ban·da O·ri·en·tal (bän'dä ôr'-ē-ĕn-täl', ŏr'-, ō-ryĕn-täl'). Region of S Uruguay.

Ban·dar (bŭn'dər). Masulipatam.

Ban·dar Se·ri Be·ga·wan (bŭn'dər sĕr'ē bə-gä'wən). Cap. of Brunei. Metro. area pop. 37,000.

Ban·dei·ra (băn-dā'rä). Highest peak (9,482 ft/2,892 m) of Brazil, in the SE.

Ban·djar·ma·sin (bän'jär-mä-sĭn'). *Dutch.* Banjarmasin.

Ban·dung (bän'do͝ong'). City of Indonesia, in W Java. Pop. 1,201,730.

Banff (bămf). Resort town of SW Alta., Canada, near Lake Louise in **Banff National Park.** Pop. 3,410.

Ban·ga·lore (băng'gə-lôr', -lōr'). City of S central India, W of Madras. Pop. 1,540,741.

Bang·ka or **Ban·ka** (băng'kə, băng'-kä). Island of W Indonesia, in the Java Sea SE of Sumatra.

Bang·kok (băng'kŏk', băng-kŏk'). Cap. of Thailand, in the SW, on the Chao Phraya R. near the Gulf of Siam. Pop. 4,178,000.

Bang·la·desh (băng'glə-dĕsh', -däsh', băng-). Republic of S Asia, on the Bay of Bengal between India and Burma. Cap. Dacca. Pop. 88,700,000.

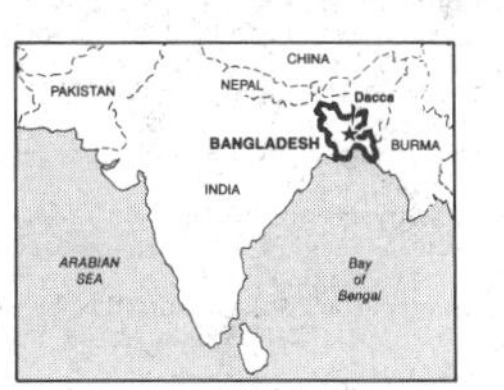

Bangladesh

Ban·gor (băng'gôr, -gər). **1.** Borough of E Northern Ireland, on Belfast Lough. Pop. 35,260. **2.** City of S Me., on the Penobscot. Pop. 31,643.

Ban·gui (bäng-gē', bäɴ-). Cap. of Central African Republic, on the Ubangi R. near the Zaire border. Pop. 187,000.

Bang·we·u·lu (băng'wē-o͞o'lo͞o). Lake and swamps of NE Zambia.

Ba·ni Su·wayf (bă-nē' so͞o-īf') or **Be·ni Su·ef** (bĕ-nē' so͞o-āf'). City of N central Egypt, on the Nile. Pop. 118,148.

Ban·ja Lu·ka (bä'nyä lo͞o'kä). City of W Yugoslavia, in Bosnia NW of Sarajevo. Pop. 89,866.

Ban·jar·ma·sin (bän'jär-mä-sĭn'). City of Indonesia, in S Borneo. Pop. 281,673.

Ban·jul (băn-jo͞ol', băn'jo͞ol'). Cap. of Gambia, on an island in the Gambia R. Pop. 45,600.

Ban·ka (băng'kə, bäng'kä). Variant of **Bangka.**

Banks (băngks). **1.** Island (c. 26,000 sq mi/67,340 sq km) of NW N.W.T., Canada, in the Arctic Archipelago. **2.** Archipelago in the SW Pacific, N of New Hebrides.

Ban·ning (băn'ĭng). City of S Calif., NNE of Santa Ana. Pop. 14,020.

Ban·nock·burn (băn'ək-bûrn', băn'-ək-bûrn'). Town of central Scotland, on the Bannock R.; site of Robert Bruce's defeat of the English (1314).

Ban·ská Bys·tri·ca (bän'skä bē'-strē-tsä). City of E central Czechoslovakia, NE of Bratislava. Pop 66,279.

Ban·try (băn'trē). Inlet of the Atlantic in SW Ireland.

Bao·ding (bou'dĭng'). City of NE China, SSW of Beijing. Pop. 350,000.

Bao·ji (bou'jē). City of central China, W of Xi'an. Pop. 250,000.

Bao·tou (bou'tō'). City of N China, on the Yellow R. W of Hohhot. Pop. 650,000.

Ba·ra·cal·do (bä'rä-käl'dô). City of N Spain, W of Bilbao. Pop. 123,178.

Ba·ra·co·a (bä'rä-kô'ä). City of SE Cuba, on the coast near the E end of the island. Pop. 13,000.

Ba·ra·nof (băr'ə-nôf, -nŏf, bä-rä'nəf). Island off SE Alas., in the Alexander Archipelago.

Ba·ra·no·vi·chi (bä-rä-nô'vē-chē). City of W European USSR, E of Bobruisk. Pop. 135,000.

Bar·a·tar·i·a Bay (băr'ə-tăr'ē-ə, -târ'-, -tĕr'-). Lagoon of SE La., an inlet of the Gulf of Mexico.

Bar·ba·dos (bär-bā'dōz', -dōs', -dŏs'). Island country of E West Indies, E of the Windward Is. Cap. Bridgetown. Pop. 238,141. **—Bar·ba'di·an** *adj. & n.*

Bar·ba·ry (bär'bə-rē, -brē). **1.** Region of N Africa on the **Barbary Coast,** between W border of Egypt and the Atlantic. **2. States.** Formerly, Algeria, Tunisia, Tripoli, and sometimes Morocco.

Bar·ber·ton (bär'bər-tən). City of NE Ohio, near Akron. Pop. 29,751.

Bar·bi·zon (bär'bĭz-ŏn, bär-bē-zôɴ'). Village of N France, SSE of Paris.

Bar·bu·da (bär-bo͞o'də). Island of the West Indies, in the Leeward group N of Antigua.

Bar·ce·lo·na (bär'sə-lō'nə, -sĕ-lô'nä). **1.** City of NE Spain, on the Mediterranean. Pop. 1,902,713. **2.** City of NE Venezuela, near the Caribbean coast. Pop. 78,201.

Ba·reil·ly also **Ba·re·li** (bə-rā'lē). City of N India, ESE of Delhi. Pop. 296,248.

Ba·rents Sea (băr'ənts, bär'-). Arm of the Arctic Ocean, N of Norway and the USSR.

Bar Harbor (bär). Town of SE Me., on Mount Desert Is. Pop. 4,124.

Ba·ri (bä'rē). City of SE Italy, on the Adriatic. Pop. 387,266.

Ba·ri·sal (bŭ-rĭ-säl', băr'ĭ-sôl'). City of S Bangladesh, on the Ganges delta. Pop. 98,127.

Ba·ri·san (bä'rē-sän'). Mountain range of W Sumatra, Indonesia, rising to 12,467 ft (3,802.4 m).

Bar·let·ta (bär-lĕt'ə, bär-lĕt'tä). City of S Italy, on the Adriatic. Pop. 81,414.

Bar·na·ul (bär'nä-o͞ol'). City of SW Siberian USSR, on the Ob R. SSE of Novosibirsk. Pop. 542,000.

Bar·ne·gat Bay (bär'nĭ-găt', -gət'). Inlet of the Atlantic, between E coast of N.J. and offshore islands.

Barns·ley (bärnz'lē). Borough of N England, N of Sheffield. Pop. 221,800.

Barn·sta·ble (bärn'stə-bəl). Town of SE Mass., on central Cape Cod. Pop. 30,898.

Barn·sta·ple (bärn'stə-pəl). Borough of SW England, on **Barnstaple Bay,** inlet of Bristol Channel. Pop. 17,820.

Ba·ro·da (bə-rō'də). City of W central India, SE of Ahmadabad. Pop. 446,696.

Ba·rot·se·land (bə-rŏt'sə-lănd', -sē-). Region of W Zambia.

Bar·qui·si·me·to (bär'kē-sē-mĕ'tô). City of NW Venezuela, WSW of Caracas. Pop. 44,000.

Bar·ran·quil·la (bär'rän-kē'yä). City of N Colombia, on the Magdalena R. near the Caribbean. Pop. 859,000.

Bar·re (băr'ē). City of central Vt., SE of Montpelier. Pop. 9,824.

Barre des É·crins (bär'dā-zā-krăɴ'). Peak, 13,461 ft (4,105.6 m), in SE France, in the Dauphiné Alps.

Bar·ren Grounds or **Lands** (băr'ən). Region of N Canada, NW of Hudson Bay and E of the Mackenzie basin.

Bar·rie (băr'ē). City of S Ont., Canada, NNW of Toronto. Pop. 34,389.

Bar·ring·ton (băr'ĭng-tən). Town of E R.I., near Providence. Pop. 16,174.

Bar·row (băr'ō), **Point.** Northernmost point of Alas., on the Arctic Ocean.

Bar·row-in-Fur·ness (băr'ō-ĭn-fûr'-nĭs). Borough of NW England, NW of Manchester. Pop. 73,400.

Bar·ry (băr'ē). Borough of S Wales, on the Bristol Channel SSW of Cardiff. Pop. 42,780.

Bar·stow (bär'stō'). City of SE Calif., NE of Los Angeles. Pop. 17,690.

Bar·tles·ville (bär'tlz-vĭl'). City of NE Okla., N of Tulsa. Pop. 34,568.

Bart·lett (bärt'lət). **1.** Village of NE Ill., near Chicago. Pop. 13,254. **2.** Town of SW Tenn., near Memphis. Pop. 17,170.

Bar·tow (bär'tō'). City of central Fla., E of Tampa. Pop. 14,780.

Ba·rú (bä-ro͞o'). Volcano, 11,070 ft (3,376.6 m), of W Panama, near the Costa Rican border.

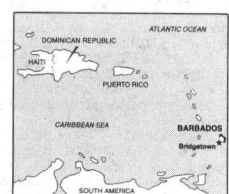

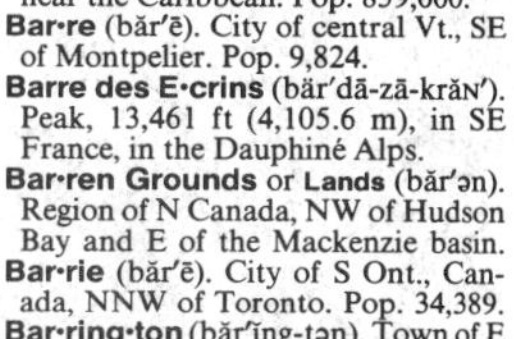

Barbados

Ba·sel (bä′zəl) or **Basle** (bäl). City of N Switzerland, on the Rhine. Metro. area pop. 575,000.
Ba·shan (bā′shən). Ancient region of Palestine, NE of the Sea of Galilee.
Ba·shi (bä′shē). Channel between the northernmost Philippines and S Taiwan.
Bash·kir·i·a (băsh-kîr′ē-ä). Region of E European USSR, in the S Urals.
Ba·si·lan (bä-sē′län′). **1.** Island and islands of the SW Philippines, off SW Mindanao. **2.** City of NW Basilan Is. Pop. 171,266.
Bas·il·don (bā′zəl-dən, băz′əl-). Town of E England, near London. Pop. 148,200.
Ba·si·li·ca·ta (bä-zē′lē-kä′tä). Region of S Italy, forming the instep of the Italian boot.
Ba·sing·stoke (bā′zĭng-stōk′). Borough of S central England, SSW of Reading. Pop. 123,300.
Basque Provinces (băsk). Region of N Spain, on the Bay of Biscay.
Bas·ra (bŭs′rə, bäs′rä). City of SE Iraq, on the Shatt-al-Arab. Pop. 310,950.
Bass (băs). Strait between Tasmania and SE Australia, connecting the Indian Ocean and Tasman Sea.
Bas·sein (băs-ēn′, bä-sān′, -sēn′). Town of S Burma, on the Bassein R. (160 mi/257 km). Pop. 138,000.
Basse·terre (bäs-târ′, băs-). Cap. of St. Kitts-Nevis, on St. Christopher Is. in the Leewards of the West Indies. Pop. 15,930.
Basse-Terre (bäs-târ′, -tĕr′). **1.** Island of the French West Indies in the Leewards; W part of the French department of Guadeloupe. **2.** Cap. of Guadeloupe, at the S end of the island. Pop. 15,457.
Bas·ti·a (bä′stē-ä, bä-stē′ä). City of NE Corsica, France, on the Tyrrhenian Sea. Pop. 50,718.
Bas·trop (băs′trəp). City of NE La., NNE of Monroe. Pop. 15,527.
Ba·su·to·land (bə-sōō′tō-lănd′). Lesotho.
Ba·taan (bə-tăn′, bä-tän′). Peninsula of W Luzon, Philippines, between Manila Bay and the South China Sea.
Ba·tan (bä-tän′). Northernmost island group of the Philippines, separated from Taiwan by the Bashi Channel.
Ba·tan·gas (bä-täng′gäs). City of SW Luzon, Philippines, on **Batangas Bay.** Metro. area pop. 125,363.
Ba·ta·vi·a (bə-tā′vē-ə). **1.** (*also* bä-tä′vē-ä). Djakarta. **2.** City of NE Ill., W of Chicago. Pop. 12,574. **3.** City of W N.Y., WSW of Rochester. Pop. 16,703.
Bath (băth, bäth). **1.** City of SW England, ESE of Bristol. Pop. 83,900. **2.** City of SW Me., on the Kennebec near the Atlantic. Pop. 10,246.
Bath·urst (băth′ərst). **1.** Cape of NW N.W.T., Canada, extending into an inlet of Beaufort Sea. **2.** Island off N Australia, W of Melville Is. **3.** Island in the Arctic Archipelago, N.W.T., Canada; site of the N magnetic pole. **4.** City of N N.B., Canada, on Chaleur Bay NNE of Fredericton. Pop. 16,301. **5.** Banjul.
Bat·ley (băt′lē). Borough of N central England, near Leeds. Pop. 41,630.
Bat·on Rouge (băt′n rōōzh′). City of SE central La., NW of New Orleans. Pop. 219,486.
Bat·ter·y (băt′ə-rē), **The.** Park, 21 acres (8.5 hectares), at S tip of Manhattan Is., New York City.
Bat·tle (băt′l). Rural district of SE England, on site of the Battle of Hastings (1066). Pop. 4,987.
Battle Creek. City of S Mich., E of Kalamazoo. Pop. 35,724.
Ba·tu·mi (bä-tōō′mē) also **Ba·tum** (bä-tōōm′). City of SW Central Asian USSR, on the Black Sea near the Turkish border. Pop. 124,000.
Bat Yam (bät′ yäm′). City of W central Israel, on the Mediterranean near Tel Aviv-Jaffa. Pop. 130,100.
Baut·zen (bout′sən). City of SE East Germany, on the Spree R. ENE of Dresden. Pop. 45,851.
Ba·var·i·a (bə-vâr′ē-ə, -văr′-). Region and former duchy of S Germany. —**Ba·var′i·an** *adj. & n.*
Ba·ya·món (bä′yä-môn′). Town of NE Puerto Rico, near San Juan. Pop. 184,854.
Bay City (bā). **1.** City of E Mich., NNW of Detroit. Pop. 41,593. **2.** City of S Tex., SW of Houston. Pop. 17,837.
Ba·yeux (bī-yōō′, bā-, bä-yœ′). Town of N France, in Normandy near the English Channel. Pop. 13,457.
Bay·kal (bī-kôl′, -kŏl′). Variant of **Baikal.**
Ba·yonne (bā-yōn′, bä-yôn′). Town of SW France, near the Bay of Biscay. Pop. 42,938.
Bay·onne (bā-yōn′). City of NE N.J., S of Jersey City. Pop. 65,047.
Bay·reuth (bī′roit, bī-roit′). City of S West Germany, NE of Nuremberg. Pop. 70,210.
Bay·town (bā′toun′). City of SE Tex., E of Houston. Pop. 56,923.
Bay Village. City of NE Ohio, near Cleveland. Pop 17,846.
Beach·y Head (bē′chē hĕd′). Chalk cliffs, 575 ft (175.4 m) high, on the SE coast of England.
Bea·con (bē′kən). City of SE N.Y., on the Hudson S of Poughkeepsie. Pop. 12,937.
Bea·cons·field (bē′kənz-fēld′). Town of S Que., Canada, on Montreal Is. SW of Montreal. Pop. 20,417.
Bear (bâr). **1.** River of N Utah, SW Wyo., and SE Idaho, flowing 350 mi (563.2 km) to Great Salt Lake. **2.** Mountain, 1,284 ft (391.6 m) of SE N.Y., on the Hudson.
Beard·more (bîrd′môr′, -mōr′). Valley glacier, 260 mi (418.3 km) long, of Antarctica, in the Queen Maud Mts.
Bé·arn (bā-ärn′). Region and former province of SW France, in the Pyrenees.
Be·as (bē′äs′). River, 250 mi (402.3 km), of N India.
Be·at·rice (bē-ăt′rĭs). City of SE Nebr., S of Lincoln. Pop. 12,891.
Beau·fort Sea (bō′fərt). Part of the Arctic Ocean, N of Canada and Alas.
Beau·jo·lais (bō′zhə-lā′, bō-zhô-lĕ′). Region of E central France, W of the Saône.
Beau·mont (bō′mŏnt). City of SE Tex., ENE of Houston. Pop.118,102.
Beau·port (bō′pôrt′, -pōrt′, bō-pôr′). City of S Que., Canada, on the St. Lawrence near Quebec city. Pop. 55,339.
Beau·vais (bō-vā′, -vĕ′). Town of N France, NNW of Paris. Pop. 54,089.
Bea·ver (bē′vər). **1.** River of Alta. and Sask., Canada, flowing 305 mi (490.7 km) to the Churchill. **2.** River, 280 mi (450.5 km), of W Colo. and NW Okla.
Bea·ver·creek (bē′vər-krēk′). Village of SW Ohio, near Dayton. Pop. 31,589.
Beaver Dam. City of S central Wis., NE of Madison. Pop. 14,149.
Beaver Falls. City of W Pa., NW of Pittsburgh. Pop. 12,525.
Bea·ver·head (bē′vər-hĕd′). Mountains on Idaho-Mont. border, in the SE Bitterroot range.
Bea·ver·ton (bē′vər-tn). City of NW Ore., near Portland. Pop. 30,582.
Bech·u·a·na·land (bĕch′ōō-ä′nə-lănd′, bĕk′yōō-). **1.** Former British protectorate of S central Africa. **2.** Botswana.
Beck·ley (bĕk′lē). City of S W.Va., SE of Charleston. Pop. 20,492.
Bed·ford (bĕd′fərd). **1.** Borough of S central England, W of Cambridge. Pop. 74,390. **2.** City of S Ind., S of Bloomington. Pop 14,410. **3.** Town of E Mass., NW of Boston. Pop. 13,067. **4.** City of NE Ohio, near Cleveland. Pop. 15,056. **5.** City of N Tex., NNE of Fort Worth. Pop. 20,821.
Bedford Heights. City of NE Ohio, near Cleveland. Pop. 13,214.
Bed·worth (bĕd′wərth). Urban district of central England, E of Birmingham. Pop. 41,600.
Będ·zin (bĕn′jēn′). Town of SE Poland, near Katowice. Pop. 75,000.
Beech Grove (bēch′grōv′). City of central Ind., near Indianapolis. Pop. 13,196.
Beer·she·ba (bîr-shē′bə, bĕr-, -shĕv′ə). City of S Israel, SW of Jerusalem. Pop. 107,000.
Bee·ville (bē′vĭl′). City of S Tex., NNW of Corpus Christi. Pop. 14,574.
Bei·jing (bā′jyĭng′). Cap. of China, in the NE part. Pop. 5,400,000.
Bei·ra (bā′rə). City of E central Mozambique, on an arm of the Indian Ocean. Metro. area pop. 130,398.
Bei·rut (bā-rōōt′, bā′rōōt′). Cap. of Lebanon, in the W on the Mediterranean. Pop. 474,870.
Be·jaï·a (bĕ-jī′ə). City of N Algeria, on the **Gulf of Bejaïa**, an arm of the Mediterranean. Metro. area pop. 103,996.
Bé·kés·csa·ba (bā′kāsh′chô′bô′). City of SE Hungary, NE of Szeged. Pop. 57,400.
Be·la·ya (bĕl′ə-yə, byĕ′lə-yə). River of E European USSR, flowing c. 880 mi (1,415 km) from the Urals to the Kama R.
Belaya Tser·kov (tsĕr′kəf). City of W central European USSR, in the Ukraine S of Kiev. Pop. 157,000.
Be·lém (bə-lĕm′, -lĕN′). City of N Brazil, on the Pará R. Pop. 899,400.
Bel·fast (bĕl′făst′, bĕl-făst′). Cap. of Northern Ireland, on **Belfast Lough,** an inlet of the North Channel of the Irish Sea. Pop. 357,600.
Bel·fort (bĕl-fôr′). City of E France, commanding the **Belfort Gap** between the Vosges and the Jura Mts. Pop. 54,615.
Bel·gaum (bĕl-goum′). Town of SE India, SSE of Kolhapur. Pop. 192,427.
Bel·gian Con·go (bĕl′jən kŏng′gō, -jē-ən). Zaire.
Belgian East Af·ri·ca (ēst′ ăf′rĭk-ə). Rwanda and Burundi.
Bel·gium (bĕl′jəm). Constitutional kingdom of NW Europe, on the North Sea. Cap. Brussels. Pop. 9,855,110. —**Bel′gian** *adj. & n.*

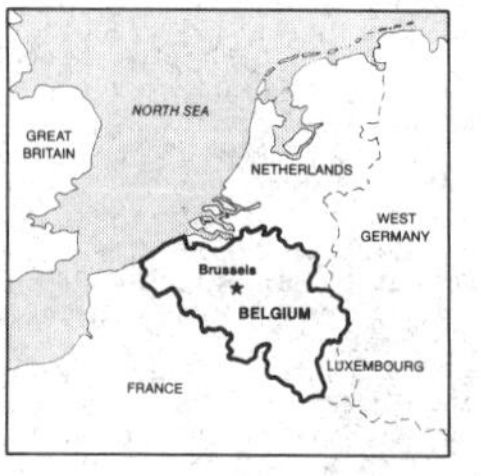

Belgium

Bel·go·rod (bĕl′gə-rŏd′, byĕl′gə-rət). City of S central European USSR, on the Donets R. Pop. 248,000.
Bel·grade (bĕl′grăd′, bĕl-grăd′). Cap. of Yugoslavia, in the E at the confluence of the Danube and Sava rivers. Pop. 770,140.
Bel·gra·vi·a (bĕl-grā′vē-ə). Residential district of SW London, England.
Be·li·tung (bĕ-lē′tōōng). Island of W Indonesia, in the Java Sea between Sumatra and Borneo.
Be·lize (bə-lēz′). **1.** Country of Central America, on the Caribbean. Cap. Belmopan. Pop. 127,200. **2.** City of E Belize, on the Caribbean at the mouth of the **Belize R.** Pop. 41,500.

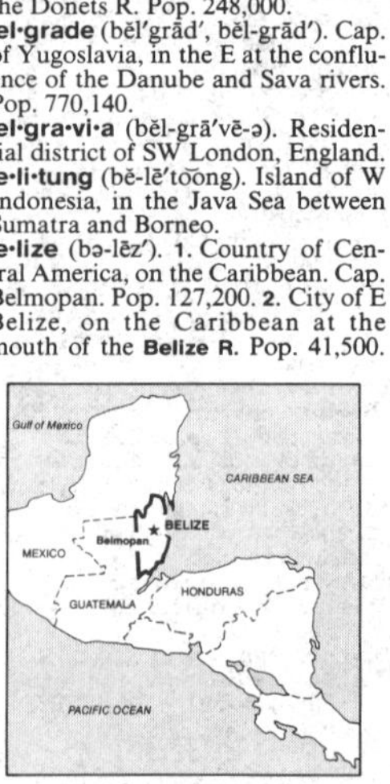

Belize

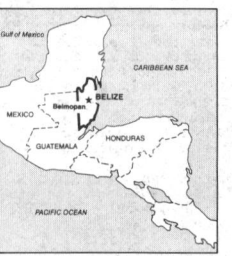

Bell (bĕl). City of S Calif., near Los Angeles. Pop. 25,450.
Bell·aire (bĕl-âr′, bə-lâr′). City of S Tex., near Houston. Pop. 14,950.
Bel·leau Wood (bĕl′ō, bĕ-lō′). Forested area of N France, E of Château-Thierry.
Belle·fon·taine (bĕl-foun′tən, -fŏn′-). City of W central Ohio, N of Springfield. Pop. 11,888.
Bellefontaine Neigh·bors (nā′bərz). City of E Mo., near St. Louis. Pop. 12,082.
Belle Fourche (bĕl′ fōōsh′, fōōrsh′). River, c. 290 mi (466 km), of NE Wyo. and W S.Dak.
Belle Glade (glād). City of SE Fla., on Lake Okeechobee W of West Palm Beach. Pop. 16,535.
Belle Isle (īl), **Strait of.** Channel between SE Labrador and NW Newf., Canada.
Belle·ville (bĕl′vĭl′). **1.** City of SE Ont., Canada, near Lake Ontario ENE of Toronto. Pop. 35,311. **2.** City of SW Ill., SE of East St. Louis. Pop. 42,150. **3.** Town of NE N.J., near Newark. Pop. 35,367.
Belle·vue (bĕl′vyōō′). **1.** City of E Nebr., near Omaha. Pop. 21,813. **2.** Borough of SW Pa., near Pittsburgh. Pop. 10,128. **3.** City of W Wash., near Seattle. Pop. 73,903.
Bell·flow·er (bĕl′flou′ər, bĕl-flou′-). City of S Calif., near Los Angeles. Pop. 53,441.
Bell Gardens. City of S Calif., near Los Angeles. Pop. 34,117.
Bel·ling·ham (bĕl′ĭng-hăm). **1.** Town of S Mass., SE of Worcester. Pop. 14,300. **2.** City of NW Wash., on **Bellingham Bay** near the B.C., Canada, border. Pop. 45,794.
Bel·lings·hau·sen Sea (bĕl′ĭngz-hau′zən). Arm of the S Pacific off the coast of Antarctica, extending from Alexander I Is. to Thurston Is.
Bell·mawr (bĕl′mär′, -môr′). Borough of SW N.J., near Camden. Pop. 13,721.
Bell·wood (bĕl′wōōd′). Village of NE Ill., near Chicago. Pop. 19,811.
Bel·mont (bĕl′mŏnt′) **1.** City of W Calif., SSE of San Francisco. Pop. 24,505. **2.** Town of E Mass., near Boston. Pop. 26,100.
Bel·mo·pan (bĕl′mō-păn′). Cap. of Belize, in the N central part. Pop. 5,000.
Bel·oeil (bĕl-œy′). Town of S Que., Canada, on the Richelieu R. near Montreal. Pop. 15,913.
Be·lo Ho·ri·zon·te (bĕ′lō-rē-zôN′tĭ, -zôNch′). City of E Brazil, N of Rio de Janeiro. Pop. 1,856,800.
Be·loit (bə-loit′). City of S Wis., on the Ill. border SSE of Madison. Pop. 35,207.
Be·lo·rus·sia (bĕl′ō-rŭsh′ə) also **Bye·lo·rus·sia** (byel′-). **1.** Region of E Europe, E of Poland, S of Lithuania and Latvia, and N of the Ukraine. **2.** Region of W central European USSR. —**Be′lo·rus′sian** *adj. & n.*
Be·lo·stok (byĭ-lä-stôk′). *Russian.* Bialystok.
Bel·sen (bĕl′zən). Village of NW West Germany; site of Nazi concentration camp.
Bel·ton (bĕl′tən). **1.** City of W Mo., near Kansas City. Pop. 12,708. **2.** City of central Tex., S of Fort Worth. Pop. 10,660.
Be·lu·kha (bĕ-lōō′kə, byĕ-lōō′KHə). Highest elevation, 15,157 ft (4,662.8 m), of the Altai Mts., in the USSR near Mongolia.
Bel·vi·dere (bĕl-vĭ-dîr′). City of N Ill., E of Rockford. Pop. 15,176.
Be·midj·i (bə-mĭj′ē). City of NW central Minn., WNW of Duluth. Pop. 10,949.
Be·na·res (bə-när′ĭs, -ēz, -nä′rēz). Varanasi.
Ben·brook (bĕn′brōōk′). City of NE Tex., near Fort Worth. Pop. 13,579.
Bend (bĕnd). City of central Ore., E of Eugene. Pop. 17,263.
Ben·de·ry (bĭn-dyĕ′rē). City of SW European USSR, on the Dniester R. Pop. 104,000.
Ben·di·go (bĕn′dĭ-gō′). City of SE Australia, NNW of Melbourne. Metro. area pop. 59,600.
Ben·dzin (bĕn′tsēn). *German.* Będzin.
Be·ne·lux (bĕn′ə-lŭks′). Tripartite

customs union formed in 1947 by Belgium, the Netherlands, and Luxembourg.

Be·ne·ven·to (bĕn'ə-vĕn'tō). City of S Italy, NE of Naples. Pop. 52,800.

Ben·gal (bĕn-gôl', bĕng-). Region of E India and Bangladesh, on the **Bay of Bengal**, arm of the Indian Ocean between Sri Lanka and India on the W and Burma and Thailand on the E. **—Ben'ga·lese'** (bĕn'gə-lēz', -lēs', bĕng'-) *adj. & n.*

Beng·bu (bŭng'bōō'). City of E China, NW of Nanjing. Pop. 400,000.

Ben·gha·zi (bĕn-gä'zē, bĕng-găz'ē). City of NE Libya, on the Mediterranean. Pop. 170,000.

Ben·guel·a (bĕng-gĕl'ə). City of W Angola, on the Atlantic. Pop. 40,996.

Be·ni (bĕ'nē). River of NW and central Bolivia, flowing 994 mi (1,599.3 km) from the Andes to the Mamore.

Be·ni·cia (bə-nē'shə). City of W Calif., NE of Oakland. Pop. 15,376.

Be·nin (bĕ-nēn'). **1.** Former kingdom of W Africa, now part of Nigeria. **2.** Country of W Africa. Cap. Porto-Novo. Pop. 3,469,000. **3.** City of S Nigeria, on the **Benin R.**, flowing c. 100 mi (161 km) into the **Bight of Benin**, an indentation of the Gulf of Guinea. Pop. 136,000.

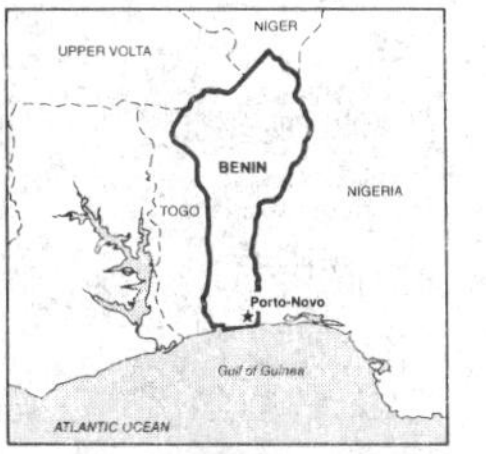

Benin

Be·ni Su·ef (bĕ-nē' sōō-āf'). Variant of **Bani Suwayf.**

Ben Lo·mond (bĕn lō'mənd). Mountain, 3,192 ft (973.5 m), of S central Scotland, on the E shore of Loch Lomond.

Ben Nev·is (nē'vĭs, nĕv'ĭs). Highest elevation, 4,406 ft (1,343.8 m), of Great Britain, in the Grampians of W Scotland.

Ben·ning·ton (bĕn'ĭng-tən). Town of SW Vt., E of Brattleboro. Pop. 15,815.

Be·no·ni (bə-nō'nī, -nē'). Town of NE South Africa, on the Witwatersrand. Pop. 151,294.

Ben·sen·ville (bĕn'sən-vĭl'). Village of NE Ill., WNW of Chicago. Pop. 16,124.

Ben·ton (bĕn'tən). City of central Ark., SW of Little Rock. Pop. 17,676.

Benton Harbor. City of SW Mich., on Lake Michigan SSW of Grand Rapids. Pop. 14,707.

Be·nue (bā'nwā) also **Bin·ue** (bĭn'wā). River of W Africa, flowing c. 670 mi (1,080 km) from Cameroon to the Niger in Nigeria.

Ben·xi (bŭn'shē'). City of NE China, SSE of Shenyang. Pop. 500,000.

Bep·pu (bĕp'pōō'). City of NE Kyushu, Japan, on **Beppu Bay**, an arm of the Inland Sea. Pop. 137,447.

Be·rar (bā-rär'). Region of W central India.

Berch·tes·ga·den (bĕrkʜ'təs-gäd'n). Town of SE West Germany, in the Bavarian Alps. Pop. 8,558.

Ber·dyansk (bĕr-dyänsk'). City of S European USSR, in the Ukraine on the **Berdyansk Gulf** of the Sea of Azov. Pop. 124,000.

Be·re·a (bə-rē'ə). City of NE Ohio, near Cleveland. Pop. 19,567.

Ber·e·ni·ce (bĕr'ə-nī'sē). Ancient Egyptian city, on the Red Sea.

Be·re·zi·na (byə-ryā'zyĭ-nə). River, c. 380 mi (610 km), of E central European USSR.

Be·rez·ni·ki (bĭ-ryĕz-nyĭ-kē'). City of E European USSR, on the Kama R. Pop. 186,000.

Ber·ga·ma (bĕr-gä'mə, bər-, bûr'gə-mə). Town of W Turkey, N of Izmir; site of ancient Pergamum. Pop. 34,386.

Ber·ga·mo (bĕr'gä-mō). City of N Italy, NE of Milan. Pop. 125,544.

Ber·gen (bûr'gən, bĕr'-). City of SW Norway, on inlets of the North Sea. Pop. 209,000.

Ber·gen·field (bûr'gən-fēld'). Borough of NE N.J., near Hackensack. Pop. 25,568.

Ber·gen op Zoom (bĕr'ᴋʜən ôp zōm'). Town of SW Netherlands, on an estuary of the Scheldt. Pop. 43,715.

Ber·gisch-Glad·bach (bĕr'gĭsh-glät'bäᴋʜ). Town of W West Germany, near Cologne. Pop. 101,007.

Be·ring (bîr'ĭng, bĕr'-, bâr'-). Sea, part of the Pacific, between Siberia and Alas., joined to the Arctic Ocean by the **Bering Strait** (c. 55 mi/90 km wide).

Berke·ley (bûrk'lē). **1.** City of W Calif., N of Oakland. Pop. 103,328. **2.** City of E Mo., WNW of St. Louis. Pop. 16,146.

Berk·ley (bûrk'lē). City of SE Mich., near Detroit. Pop. 18,637.

Berk·shire (bûrk'shîr', -shər). Range of hills in W Mass.

Ber·lin. 1. (bĕr-lĭn'). City of NE East Germany, divided since 1945 into **East Berlin**, cap. of East Germany, pop. 1,128,983; and **West Berlin**, part of West Germany, pop. 1,902,250. **2.** (bûr'lĭn). City of N central Conn., near Hartford. Pop. 15,121. **3.** (bûr'lĭn). City of NE N.H., E of Lancaster. Pop. 13,084.

Ber·me·jo (bĕr-mĕ'hô). River of N Argentina, flowing c. 650 mi (1,045 km) to the Paraguay R. at the Paraguay border.

Ber·mu·da (bər-myōō'də). British colony in the Atlantic, SE of Cape Hatteras, an archipelago of c. 350 islands. Cap. Hamilton. Pop. 52,330. **—Ber·mu'di·an** *adj. & n.*

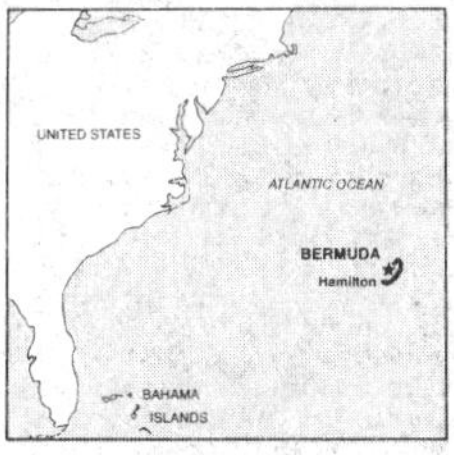

Bermuda

Bern or **Berne** (bûrn, bĕrn). Cap. of Switzerland, in the NW on the Aare. Pop. 141,300.

Bern·burg (bûrn'bərg, bĕrn'bōōrk'). City of central East Germany, on the Saale R. Pop. 43,221.

Ber·nese Alps (bûr'nēz, -nēs, bûr-nēz', -nēs'). Range of the Alps in S central Switzerland, rising to 14,032 ft (4,279.8 m).

Ber·ni·ci·a (bər-nĭsh'ē-ə, -nĭsh'ə). Anglian kingdom of the 6th century A.D., in present-day NE England.

Ber·ni·na (bər-nē'nə, bĕr-nē'nä). Mountain group of SW Switzerland, part of the Rhaetian Alps on the Swiss-Italian border; highest elevation, **Piz Bernina** (13,287 ft/4,052.5 m).

Ber·ry (bĕ-rē'). Former province of central France.

Ber·si·mis (bûr-sē-mē'). Betsiamites.

Ber·wick (bûr'wĭk). Borough of E central Pa., SE of Wilkes-Barre. Pop. 12,189.

Ber·wyn (bûr'wĭn). City of NE Ill., near Chicago. Pop. 46,849.

Be·san·çon (bĭ-zäɴ-sôɴ'). City of E France, E of Dijon. Pop. 120,315.

Bes·kids (bĕs'kĭdz, bĕs-kēdz'). Mountain ranges of the W Carpathians, on the Polish-Czechoslovakian border, divided into the **East Beskids** and the **West Beskids.**

Bes·sa·ra·bi·a (bĕs'ə-rā'bē-ə). Region of SW European USSR. **—Bes'sa·ra'bi·an** *adj. & n.*

Bes·se·mer (bĕs'ə-mər). City of N central Ala., SSW of Birmingham. Pop. 31,729.

Beth·a·ny (bĕth'ə-nē). **1.** Village of biblical Palestine, near Jerusalem. **2.** City of central Okla., near Oklahoma City. Pop. 22,130.

Beth·el (bĕth'əl). **1.** (*also* bĕ-thĕl'). Town of biblical Palestine, N of Jerusalem. **2.** Town of SW Conn., NW of Bridgeport. Pop. 16,004.

Bethel Park. Borough of SW Pa., near Pittsburgh. Pop. 34,755.

Be·thes·da (bə-thĕz'də). City of W central Md., near Washington, D.C. Pop. 78,300.

Beth·le·hem (bĕth'lĭ-hĕm', -lē-əm). **1.** Town of W Jordan, S of Jerusalem. Pop. 25,000. **2.** City of E Pa., NNW of Philadelphia. Pop. 70,419.

Beth·sa·i·da (bĕth-sā'ĭ-də). Town of biblical Palestine, on the NE shore of the Sea of Galilee.

Bet·si·a·mi·tes (bĕt'sē-ə-mē'tēz). River of E Que., Canada, flowing c. 240 mi (385 km) into the St. Lawrence.

Bet·ten·dorf (bĕt'n-dôrf'). City of E Iowa, near Davenport. Pop. 27,381.

Bev·er·ley (bĕv'ər-lē). Borough of NE England, NNW of Hull. Pop. 105,900.

Bev·er·ly (bĕv'ər-lē). City of NE Mass., near Salem. Pop. 37,655.

Beverly Hills. 1. City of S Calif., surrounded by Los Angeles. Pop. 32,367. **2.** Village of SE Mich., near Detroit. Pop. 11,598.

Bex·hill (bĕks'hĭl). Borough of SE England, on the English Channel. Pop. 34,680.

Bex·ley (bĕks'lē). City of central Ohio, surrounded by Columbus. Pop. 13,405.

Bé·ziers (bā-zyā'). City of S France, SW of Montpellier. Pop. 84,029.

Bha·gal·pur (bä'gəl-pōōr'). City of NE India, on the Ganges. Pop. 172,202.

Bhat·pa·ra (bät-pä'rə). City of NE India, on the Hooghly R. N of Calcutta. Pop. 204,750.

Bhav·na·gar (bou-nŭg'ər). City of W India, on the Gulf of Cambay. Pop. 225,358.

Bhi·ma (bē'mə). River, c. 400 mi (645 km), of S India.

Bho·pal (bō-päl'). City of central India, NW of Nagpur. Pop. 298,022.

Bhu·tan (bōō-tăn', -tän'). Kingdom of central Asia, in the E Himalayas. Cap. Thimbu. Pop. 1,232,000. **—Bhu'tan·ese'** (bōō'tn-ēz', -ēs') *adj. & n.*

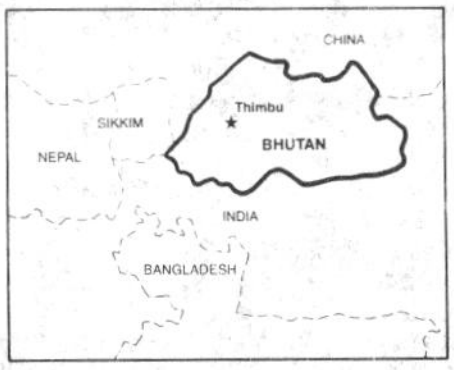

Bhutan

Bi·a·fra (bē-ä'frə, -ăf'rə). Region of E Nigeria, on the **Bight of Biafra**, an inlet of the Gulf of Guinea. **—Bi·a'fran** *adj. & n.*

Bi·ak (bē-yäk'). Largest (948 sq mi/2,455.3 sq km) of the Schouten Is. of Indonesia, off NW New Guinea.

Bia·ly·stok (bē-ä'lĭ-stôk', byä'-wĭ-). City of NE Poland, near the border of Belorussia. Pop. 218,700.

Biar·ritz (bē'ə-rĭts', bē'ə-rĭts', byä-rēts'). City of SW France, on the Bay of Biscay. Pop. 27,595.

Bid·de·ford (bĭd'ə-fərd). City of SW Me., SW of Portland. Pop. 19,638.

Biel (bēl). City of NW Switzerland, at the NE end of the **Lake of Biel** (15 sq mi/39 sq km). Pop. 56,800.

Bie·le·feld (bē'lə-fĕlt'). City of N central West Germany, E of Münster. Pop 312,357.

Biel·la (byĕl'lä). City of NW Italy, WNW of Milan. Pop. 55,857.

Biel·sko-Bia·la (byĕl'skô-byä-lä, -wä). City of S Poland, SW of Kraków. Pop. 160,300.

Bi·enne (bē-ĕn', byĕn). *French.* Biel.

Big Bend (bĭg bĕnd'). **1.** National park of W Tex., in a triangle formed by the Rio Grande. **2.** Portion of the Columbia River, in E central Wash.

Big Black (blăk). River of Miss., flowing c. 330 mi (530 km) to the Mississippi below Vicksburg.

Big Blue (blōō). River of SE Nebr. and NE Kans., flowing c. 300 mi (485 km) to the Kansas R.

Big·horn (bĭg'hôrn'). **1.** River, flowing 461 mi (741.7 km) from W central Wyo. to the Yellowstone R. in S Mont. **2.** Section of the Rocky Mts. of N central Wyo. and S Mont., rising to 13,175 ft (4,018.4 m).

Big Mud·dy (mŭd'ē). River of SW Ill., flowing c. 135 mi (217 km) to the Mississippi.

Big Rap·ids (răp'ĭdz). City of W central Mich., on the Muskegon. Pop. 14,361.

Big Sand·y Creek (săn'dē). River of central and E Colo., flowing c. 200 mi (320 km) to the Arkansas R.

Big Sioux (sōō). River of NE S.Dak., flowing 420 mi (675.8 km) to the Missouri R.

Big Spring (sprĭng). City of W Tex., WSW of Abilene. Pop. 24,804.

Big Sur (sûr). Rugged resort region of central Calif. coast.

Big Thick·et (thĭk'ĭt). Wilderness region of E Tex., NE of Houston.

Bi·ka·ner (bē'kə-nîr', -nâr'). City of NW India, in the Thar Desert near the Pakistan border. Pop. 188,518.

Bi·ki·ni (bĭ-kē'nē). Atoll, c. 2 sq mi (5.2 sq km), of the W central Pacific, in the Marshall Is.

Bi·lauk·taung (bē-louk'toung). Mountain range, extending c. 250 mi (400 km) along the Thailand-Burma border.

Bil·bao (bĭl-bä'ō, -bou', bēl-bä'ô). City of N Spain, near the Bay of Biscay. Pop. 452,921.

Bille·ric·a (bĭl-rĭk'ə). Town of NE Mass., near Lowell. Pop. 36,727.

Bil·lings (bĭl'ĭngz). City of S Mont., ESE of Helena. Pop. 66,798.

Bil·li·ton (bə-lē'tŏn', bē'lē-tŏn'). Belitung.

Bi·lox·i (bə-lŭk'sē, -lŏk'-). City of extreme SE Miss., E of Gulfport. Pop. 49,311.

Bim·i·ni (bĭm'ə-nē). Group of small islands in the Straits of Florida, the NW section of the Bahamas.

Bing·ham·ton (bĭng'əm-tən). City of S N.Y., near the Pa. border SSE of Syracuse. Pop. 55,860.

Bin·tan (bĭn'tän) also **Bin·tang** (-täng). Island of the Riau archipelago, W Indonesia, off the S tip of the Malay peninsula in the South China Sea.

Bin·ue (bĭn'wā). Variant of **Beneu.**

Bi·o-Bi·o (bē'ō-bē'ō). River of central Chile, flowing c. 240 mi (385 km) from the Andes to the Pacific.

Bi·o·ko (bē-ō'kō). Island of Equatorial Guinea, W central Africa, in the Gulf of Guinea.

Bi·qa (bē-kä'), **Al**, also **El Bi·ka** (ĕl' bē-kä'). Valley of Lebanon and Syria, between the Lebanon and Anti-Lebanon ranges.

Bir·ken·head (bûr'kən-hĕd'). Borough of W central England, at the mouth of the Mersey near Liverpool. Pop. 342,300.

Bir·ming·ham (bûr'mĭng-hăm'). **1.** (*also* bûr'mĭng-əm). City of central England, NW of London. Pop. 1,033,900. **2.** City of N central Ala., NE of Tuscaloosa. Pop. 284,413. **3.** City of SE Mich., NW of Detroit. Pop. 21,689.

Bis·cay (bĭs'kā), **Bay of.** Arm of the Atlantic, indenting the W coast of Europe from NW France to NW Spain.

Bis·cayne Bay (bĭs-kān', bĭs'kān'). Inlet of the Atlantic in SE Fla.

Bi·sce·glie (bē-shā'lyā). City of S Italy, on the Adriatic. Pop. 46,962.

Bish·op Auck·land (bĭsh'əp ôk'lənd). Urban district of NE England, S of Newcastle. Pop. 32,940.

Bisk (bĭsk, bĕsk). Biysk.

Bis·marck (bĭz'märk). **1.** Sea in the SW Pacific, NE of New Guinea and NW of New Britain. **2.** Archipelago of some 200 islands and islets in the SW Pacific, NE of New Guinea. **3.** Mountain range of Papua New Guinea, on NE New Guinea, rising to 15,400 ft (4,697 m). **4.** Cap. of N.Dak., in the S central part. Pop. 44,485.

Bis·sau (bĭ-sou'). Cap. of Guinea-Bissau, on an estuary of the Atlantic. Pop. 71,169.

Bi·thyn·i·a (bĭ-thĭn'ē-ə). Ancient country of NW Asia Minor, in present-day Turkey. **—Bi·thyn'i·an** *adj. & n.*

Bi·to·la (bē'tô-lyä). City of S Yugoslavia, near the Greek border. Pop. 65,851.

Bi·ton·to (bē-tōn'tō). City of S Italy, W of Bari. Pop. 48,052.

Bit·ter (bĭt'ər). Two lakes, **Great Bitter** and **Little Bitter**, of NE Egypt, crossed and connected by the Suez Canal.

Bit·ter·root (bĭt'ər-ro͞ot', -ro͝ot'). **1.** River, c. 120 mi (195 km), of SW Mont. **2.** Mountain range of the Rockies, on the Idaho-Mont. border, rising to 10,961 ft (3,343.1 m).

Bi·wa (bē'wä). Lake of S Honshu, Japan, largest (260 sq mi/673.4 sq km) in the country.

Bi·ysk (bē'ĭsk, bēsk). City of S central Siberian USSR, ESE of Barnaul. Pop. 213,000.

Bi·zer·te (bĭ-zûr'tē, -tə, bē-zĕrt'). City of N Tunisia, on the Mediterranean. Pop. 62,856.

Black (blăk). **1.** Sea, c. 159,600 sq mi (413,365 sq km), between Europe and Asia, connected with the Aegean by the Bosporus, the Sea of Marmara, and the Dardanelles. **2.** River of SE Asia, flowing c. 500 mi (805 km) from S China to the Red R. in N Vietnam. **3.** River flowing c. 300 mi (485 km) from SE Mo. to NE Ark. **4.** River of N N.Y., flowing c. 120 mi (195 km) to **Black R. Bay**, an inlet of Lake Ontario. **5.** River of central and W Wis., flowing c. 160 mi (260 km) to the Mississippi. **6.** Range of the Blue Ridge in W N.C. **7.** Canyon of the Colorado R. between Ariz. and Nev. **8.** Canyon of the Gunnison R., a national monument in SW Colo.

Black·burn (blăk'bûrn'). **1. Mount.** Highest peak (16,523 ft/5,039.5 m) of the Wrangell Mts. of S Alas. **2.** City of NW England, NNE of Bolton. Pop. 142,500.

Black·foot (blăk'fo͝ot'). City of SE Idaho, SSW of Idaho Falls. Pop. 10,065.

Black Forest. Mountain range of SW Germany, between the Rhine and the Neckar.

Black·heath (blăk'hēth'). Common, 267 acres (108 hectares), of London, England.

Black Hills. Mountains of SW S.Dak. and NE Wyo.

Black·pool (blăk'po͞ol'). Borough of NW England, on the Irish Sea. Pop. 145,400.

Blacks·burg (blăks'bûrg'). Town of SW Va., W of Roanoke. Pop. 30,638.

Black·town (blăk'toun'). City of SE Australia, near Sydney. Pop. 179,350.

Black Vol·ta (vŏl'tə, vōl'-, vôl'-). River of W Africa, flowing c. 840 mi (1,350 km) from W Upper Volta to the White Volta in Ghana.

Black War·rior (wôr'ē-ər, -yər, wŏr'-). River of central Ala., flowing 178 mi (161 km) to the Tombigbee.

Black·wells Island (blăk'wĕlz', -wəlz). Welfare Is.

Bla·go·vesh·chensk (blä'gə-vyĕsh'chĭnsk). City of Far Eastern USSR, at the confluence of the Amur and Zeya rivers. Pop. 175,000.

Blaine (blān). **1.** City of E Minn., N of St. Paul. Pop. 28,558. **2.** City of NW Wash., on the B.C., Canada, border. Pop. 2,263.

Blanc (blängk, bläɴ). **1.** Cape on the coast of Tunisia; northernmost point of Africa. **2. Mont.** Mont Blanc.

Blan·ca (blăng'kə). Peak, 14,317 ft (4,366.7 m), of S Colo., in the Sierra Blanca of the Sangre de Cristo Mts.

Blan·tyre (blăn-tīr'). City of S Malawi, SE Africa. Pop. 229,000.

Blar·ney (blär'nē). Village of SW Ireland, WNW of Cork.

Blay·don (blād'n). Urban district of NE England, on the Tyne R. Pop. 31,940.

Bli·da (blē'dä). Town of N Algeria, SW of Algiers. Pop. 158,947.

Block (blŏk). Island off S R.I. at the E entrance to Long Is. Sound.

Bloem·fon·tein (blo͞om'fŏn-tān'). City of S South Africa, ESE of Kimberley. Pop. 149,836.

Blois (blwä). Town of central France, on the Loire. Pop. 49,778.

Bloom·field (blo͞om'fēld'). **1.** Town of N central Conn., near Hartford. Pop. 18,608. **2.** Town of NE N.J., near Newark. Pop. 47,792.

Bloo·ming·dale (blo͞o'mĭng-dāl'). Village of NE Ill., WNW of Chicago. Pop. 12,659.

Bloo·ming·ton (blo͞o'mĭng-tən). **1.** City of central Ill., ESE of Peoria. Pop. 44,189. **2.** City of S central Ind., SSW of Indianapolis. Pop. 51,646. **3.** City of SE Minn., near Minneapolis. Pop. 81,831.

Blooms·burg (blo͞omz'bûrg'). Town of E Pa., on the Susquehanna. Pop. 11,717.

Blooms·bur·y (blo͞omz'bĕr'-ē, -bə-rē, -brē). Residential district of N central London, England.

Blue (blo͞o). **1.** Mountain range of SE Australia. **2.** Mountains of E Jamaica, rising to **Blue Mt. Peak**, c. 7,402 ft (2,257 m). **3.** Mountains of NE Ore. and SE Wash.

Blue·field (blo͞o'fēld'). City of S W. Va., SSE of Charleston. Pop. 16,060.

Blue·grass (blo͞o'grăs'). Region of central Ky.

Blue Grot·to (grŏt'ō). Cave on N coast of Capri, S Italy.

Blue Island. City of NE Ill., near Chicago. Pop. 21,855.

Blue Nile (nīl). River of NE Africa, chief headstream of the Nile, flowing c. 1,000 mi (1,610 km) from NW Ethiopia into the Sudan, where it merges with the White Nile to form the Nile at Khartoum.

Blue Ridge (rĭj). Mountain range extending from S Pa. to N Ga., part of the Appalachians.

Blue Springs (sprĭngz). City of W Mo., E of Kansas City. Pop. 25,927.

Blyth (blīth, blīth). Borough of NE England, on the North Sea. Pop. 75,700.

Blythe·ville (blī*th*'vĭl', blī'vəl). City of NE Ark., N of Memphis, Tenn. Pop. 24,326.

Bo·bi·gny (bô-bē-nyē'). City of N central France, near Paris. Pop. 43,125.

Bo·bruisk (bô-bro͞o'ĭsk). City of W central European USSR, SE of Minsk. Pop. 197,000.

Bo·ca Ra·ton (bō'kə rə-tōn'). City of SE Fla., S of Palm Beach. Pop. 49,505.

Bo·chum (bō'ĸʜo͞om). City of W West Germany, in the Ruhr E of Essen. Pop. 402, 988.

Bo·den·see (bōd'n-zā). *German.* Lake of Constance.

Boe·o·tia (bē-ō'shə). Ancient region of Greece, N of Attica and the Gulf of Corinth. **—Boe·o'tian** *adj. & n.*

Boe·roe (bo͞o'ro͞o). Variant of **Buru.**

Bo·ga·lu·sa (bō'gə-lo͞o'sə). City of SE La., NNE of New Orleans. Pop. 16,976.

Bog·nor Re·gis (bŏg'nər rē'jĭs). Urban district of S central England, on the English Channel W of Brighton. Pop. 34,620.

Bo·gor (bō'gôr). City of W Java, Indonesia, S of Djakarta. Pop. 195,882.

Bo·go·tá (bō'gə-tä', bô-gô-tä'). Cap. of Colombia, in the central part. Pop. 4,067,000.

Bo Hai (bō'hī'). Inlet of the Yellow Sea, on the NE coast of China W of the Shandong and Liaodong peninsulas.

Bo·he·mi·a (bō-hē'mē-ə, -hēm'yə). Historical region and former kingdom of W Czechoslovakia. **—Bo·he'mi·an** *adj. & n.*

Bohemian Forest. Mountain range of the N Czechoslovakian-West German border and extending into Austria.

Bo·hol (bō'hôl, bô-hôl'). Island of the central Philippines, SW of Leyte at the N end of the Mindanao Sea.

Bois de Bou·logne (bwä' də bo͞o-lōn', bwäd bo͞o-lôn'yə). Park in Paris, France, bordering the suburb of Neuilly-sur-Seine.

Boi·se (boi'zē, -sē). **1.** River of SW Idaho, flowing c. 160 mi (260 km) to join the Snake at the Ore. border. **2.** Cap. of Idaho, in the SW part near the Ore. border. Pop. 102,451.

Boj·a·dor (bŏj'ə-dôr'), **Cape.** Headland of NW Africa, in the Atlantic on the W central coast of Western Sahara.

Bo·kha·ra (bō-kär'ə, -här'-, -ĸʜä'rə). Variant of **Bukhara.**

Boks·burg (bŏks'bûrg'). City of NE South Africa, E of Johannesburg. Pop. 106,126.

Bo·lan also **Bho·lan** (bō-län'). Mountain pass in W Pakistan, c. 60 mi (95 km) long and located at an altitude of 5,880 ft (1,793.4 m).

Bo·ling·brook (bō'lĭng-bro͝ok'). Village of NE Ill., SW of Chicago. Pop. 37,261.

Bo·liv·i·a (bə-lĭv'ē-ə, bō-). Republic of W South America. Caps. Sucre and La Paz. Pop. 4,804,000.

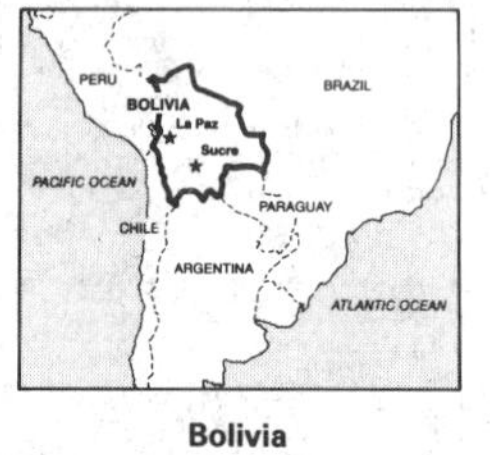

Bolivia

Bo·lo·gna (bə-lōn'yə, bō-lō'nyä). City of N central Italy, NE of Florence. Pop. 471,554. **—Bo·lo'gnan, Bo'lo·gnese'** (bō'lə-nēz', -nēs', -lən-yēz', -yēs') *adj. & n.*

Bol·ton (bōl'tən) also **Bol·ton-le-Moors** (-lə-mo͝orz'). Borough of NW England, part of Greater Manchester. Pop. 260,100.

Bol·za·no (bōl-tsä'nō). City of N Italy, NNW of Venice. Pop. 106,199.

Bom·bay (bŏm-bā'). City of W central India, on coastal **Bombay Is.** and an adjacent island. Pop. 5,970,575.

Bo·mo·seen (bŏ'mə-sēn', bŏm'-ə-zēn'). Lake of W Vt., W of Rutland.

Bo·mu (bō'mo͞o) also **Mbo·mu** (əm-bō'mo͞o). River of central Africa, flowing c. 500 mi (805 km) from SE Central African Republic and along the boundary with Zaire to the Uele, forming the Ubangi.

Bon (bŏn, bôɴ), **Cape.** Peninsula of NE Tunisia.

Bo·na (bō'nə), **Mount.** Peak, 16,420 ft (5,008 m), of S Alas., at the S end of the Wrangell range near the Canadian border.

Bo·naire (bô-nâr'). Island of the Netherlands Antilles, in the Leewards off the N coast of Venezuela.

Bo·nam·pak (bō-näm'päk). Ruined Mayan city, near present-day Tuxtla Gutiérrez in S Mexico.

Bo·nan·za (bə-năn'zə). Creek in W Y.T., Canada, flowing c. 20 mi (30 km) to the Klondike near Dawson.

Bon·a·vis·ta (bŏn-ə-vĭs'tə). Arm of the Atlantic in E Newf.

Bône (bōn). Annaba.

Bo·nin (bō'nĭn). Archipelago of 15 islands in the W Pacific, c. 500 mi (804 km) S of Japan.

Bonn (bŏn, bôn). Cap. of West Germany, on the Rhine. Pop. 286,184.

Bon·ne·ville Salt Flats (bŏn'ə-vĭl' sôlt' flăts). Plain of NW Utah, W of Great Salt Lake, part of the bed of prehistoric **Lake Bonneville.**

Boone (bo͞on). **1.** City of central Iowa, NNW of Des Moines. Pop. 12,602. **2.** Town of NW N.C., NNW of Lenoir. Pop. 10,191.

Boones·bor·o (bo͞onz'bûr'ō). Former settlement of central Ky., on the Kentucky R.

Boo·thi·a (bo͞o'thē-ə), **Gulf of.** Inlet of the Arctic Ocean in NE Canada, E of **Boothia Peninsula**, northernmost tip of the North American mainland.

Boo·tle (bo͞ot'l). Borough of NW England, at the mouth of the Mersey R. Pop. 71,160.

Bo·phu·tha·tswa·na (bō'po͞o-tä-tswä'nä). Autonomous black homeland within South Africa. Cap Mmabatho. Pop. 1,255,000.

Bo·ra Bo·ra (bôr'ə bôr'ə, bōr'ə bōr'ə). Island of French Polynesia, in the Leeward group of the Society Is. in the S Pacific.

Bo·rah (bôr'ə, bōr'ə), **Mount.** Peak 12,662 ft (3,861.9 m), of central Idaho.

Bo·rås (bo͞o-rôs'). City of SW Sweden, E of Göteborg. Pop. 102,914.

Bor·deaux (bôr-dō'). City of SW France, on the Garonne R. Pop 223,131.

Bor·der (bôr'dər) also **Bor·ders** (-dərz). Boundary and adjacent areas between England and Scotland.

Bor·ger (bôr'gər). City of N Tex., in the Panhandle NE of Amarillo. Pop 15,837.

Bor·ger·hout (bôr'gər-hout', -ĸʜər-) City of N Belgium, near Antwerp. Pop. 44,369.

Borgne (bôrn), **Lake.** Inlet of Mississippi Sound, E of New Orleans, La

Bo·ri·sov (bä-rē'səf). City of W European USSR, ENE of Minsk. Pop 115,000.

Bor·ne·o (bôr'nē-ō'). Island, c 287,000 sq mi (743,300 sq km), of the W Pacific, between the Sulu and Java seas SW of the Philippines; divided between Kalimantan and Brunei **—Bor'ne·an** *adj. & n.*

Born·holm (bôrn'hōm', -hōlm', -hôlm'). Island group of E Denmark in the Baltic near Sweden.

Bor·nu (bôr-no͞o', bôr'no͞o). Former Moslem kingdom of W Africa, in present-day NE Nigeria.

Bo·ro·bu·dur (bō'rō-bo͞o-do͝or') Buddhist ruins in central Java.

Bo·ro·di·no (bôr'ə-dē'nō, bə-rə-dyē-nô'). Village of central European USSR, W of Moscow; site of French-Russian battle (1812).

Bos·ni·a (bŏz'nē-ə). Region of W central Yugoslavia. **—Bos'ni·an** *adj. & n.*

Bos·po·rus (bŏs'pər-əs) also **Bos·pho·rus** (-fər-). Strait separating European and Asian Turkey and joining the Black Sea and the Sea of Marmara.

Bos·sier City (bō'zhər). City of NW La., near Shreveport. Pop. 49,969.

Bos·ton (bô'stən, bŏs'tən). **1. Mountains.** Ridge of the Ozarks, in NW Ark. **2.** Borough of E central England, E of Nottingham. Pop. 26,700 **3.** Cap. of Mass., in the E on an arm of Massachusetts Bay. Pop. 562,994 **—Bos·to'ni·an** (bô-stō'nē-ən, bŏs-tō'-) *adj. & n.*

Bos·worth Field (bŏz'wərth). Site of the final battle in the Wars of the Roses (1485), near Leicester in central England.

Bot·a·ny Bay (bŏt'n-ē). Inlet of the Tasman Sea, in SE Australia S of Sydney.

Both·ni·a (bŏth'nē-ə), **Gulf of.** N arm of the Baltic, between Sweden and Finland.

Bot·swa·na (bŏt-swä'nə). Republic of S central Africa. Cap. Gaborone Pop. 661,000.

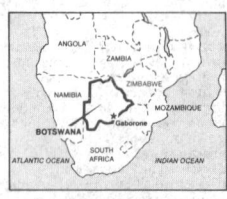

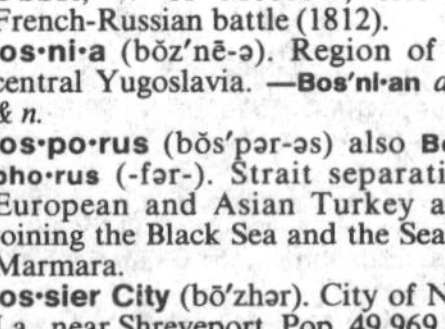

Botswana

Bot·trop (bŏt'rŏp, bôt'rôp). City of W West Germany, in the Ruhr NNW of Essen. Pop. 114,510.

Boua·ké (bwä-kā', bwä'kā). Town of central Ivory Coast. Pop. 230,000.

Bou·cher·ville (bo͞o'shər-vĭl',

bo͞o-shä-vĕl′). Town of S Que., Canada, on the St. Lawrence NE of Montreal. Pop. 29,400.
Bou·gain·ville (bo͞o′gən-vĭl′, bo͞o-gäN-vĕl′). Island, c. 3,880 sq mi (10,050 sq km), of Papua New Guinea, in the Solomon Is. of the SW Pacific.
Bou·gie (bo͞o-zhē′). Bejaïa.
Boul·der (bōl′dər). **1.** Former canyon of the Colorado R. between Ariz. and Nev., now inundated by Lake Mead. **2.** City of N central Colo., NW of Denver. Pop. 76,685.
Bou·logne (bo͞o-lōn′, -loin′, bə-, bo͞o-lôn′yə) or **Boulogne-sur-Mer** (-sür-mĕr′). City of N France, on the English Channel. Pop. 48,400.
Boulogne-Bil·lan·court (bo͞o-lôn′-yə-bē-yäN-ko͞or′). City of N central France, near Paris. Pop. 103,578.
Boun·da·ry (boun′drē, -də-rē). Highest peak, 13,145 ft (4,009.2 m), in Nev., in the SW near the Calif. border.
Boun·ti·ful (boun′tĭ-fəl). City of N Utah, near Salt Lake City. Pop. 32,877.
Bour·bon·nais (bo͝or-bō-nā′, bər-bō′nĭs). Village of NE Ill., near Kankakee. Pop. 13,280.
Bourg-en-Bresse (bo͝or′käN-brĕs′) or **Bourg.** Town of E central France, NNE of Lyons. Pop. 42,181.
Bourges (bo͝orzh). City of central France, SSE of Orléans. Pop. 77,300.
Bourne (bôrn, bo͝orn). Town of SE Mass., on NW Cape Cod. Pop. 13,874.
Bourne·mouth (bôrn′məth, bo͝orn′-, bo͝orn′-). Borough of S central England, on an inlet of the English Channel. Pop. 144,200.
Bou·vet (bo͞o′vā, bo͞o-vā′). Island and Norwegian dependency of the S Atlantic, near the Antarctic Circle SSW of the Cape of Good Hope.
Bow (bō). River, 315 mi (506.8 km), of S Alta., Canada.
Bow·er·y (bou′ə-rē, bou′rē), **the.** Section of Lower Manhattan, New York City.
Bow·ie (bo͞o′ē). City of central Md., ENE of Washington, D.C. Pop. 33,695.
Bowl·ing Green (bō′lĭng grēn′). **1.** City of S Ky., SSE of Louisville. Pop. 40,450. **2.** City of NW Ohio, SSW of Toledo. Pop. 25,728.
Boyne (boin). River of E Ireland, flowing c. 70 mi (115 km) to the Irish Sea.
Boyn·ton Beach (boin′tən). City of SE Fla., N of Boca Raton. Pop. 35,624.
Boz·ca·a·da (bōz′jä-ä-dä′). Island of NW Turkey, in the Aegean.
Boze·man (bōz′mən). City of SW Mont., ESE of Butte. Pop. 21,645.
Bra·bant (brə-bănt′, -bänt′, brä′bənt, -bänt). Former duchy of the Netherlands, now divided between the Netherlands and Belgium.
Brack·nell (brăk′nəl). Town of S England. Pop. 33,953.
Bra·den·ton (brād′n-tən). City of SW Fla., S of Tampa. Pop. 30,170.
Brad·ford (brăd′fərd). **1.** Borough of N central England, WSW of Leeds. Pop. 461,600. **2.** City of N Pa., near the N.Y. border ESE of Erie. Pop. 11,211.
Brad·ley (brăd′lē). Village of NE Ill., near Kankakee. Pop. 11,008.
Bra·ga (brä′gə). City of NW Portugal, NNE of Oporto. Pop. 49,693.
Brah·ma·pu·tra (brä′mə-po͞o′trə). River of S Asia, flowing c. 1,800 mi (2,895 km) from the Himalayas in SW Tibet through NE India and joining with the Ganges to form a delta in central Bangladesh.
Bră·i·la (brə-ē′lä, -lə). City of SE Rumania, on the Danube. Pop. 200,435.
Brai·nerd (brā′nərd). City of central Minn., N of St. Cloud. Pop. 11,489.
Brain·tree (brān′trē′). Town of E Mass., SSE of Boston. Pop. 36,337.
Braintree and Bock·ing (bŏk′ĭng). Urban district of E England, W of Colchester. Pop. 26,300.
Brak·pan (brăk′păn′). City of NE South Africa, S of Johannesburg. Pop. 73,210.
Bramp·ton (brămp′tən). City of S Ont., Canada, near Toronto. Pop. 70,200.
Bran·co (brŭng′ko͞o). River of N Brazil, flowing 350 mi (563 km) to the Rio Negro.
Bran·den·burg (brăn′dən-bûrg′, brän′dən-bo͝ork′). **1.** Former duchy of N central Germany around which the kingdom of Prussia developed. **2.** City of central East Germany, SW of Berlin. Pop. 94,505.
Bran·don (brăn′dən). City of SW Man., Canada, W of Winnipeg. Pop. 34,901.
Bran·dy·wine (brăn′dē-wīn′). Creek of SE Pa. and N Del.
Bran·ford (brăn′fərd). Town of S Conn., on Long Is. Sound E of New Haven. Pop. 23,363.
Brant·ford (brănt′fərd). City of S Ont., Canada, SW of Toronto. Pop. 70,200.
Bras d'Or Lake (brä′dôr′). Arm of the Atlantic, indenting Cape Breton Is. in SE Canada.
Bra·sí·lia (brə-zĭl′yə, brä-sēl′yə). Cap. of Brazil, in the central plateau NW of Rio de Janeiro. Pop. 350,000.
Bra·şov (brä-shôv′). City of central Rumania, NNW of Ploieşti. Pop. 268, 226.
Bra·ti·sla·va (brä′tĭ-slä′və, brăt′ĭ-). City of S Czechoslovakia, on the Danube near the Austrian and Hungarian borders. Pop. 374,860.
Bratsk (brätsk). City of S Siberian USSR, NNE of Irkutsk. Pop. 219,000.
Brat·tle·bor·o (brăt′l-bûr′ō, -bŭr′ō). Town of SE Vt., on the Connecticut R. and N.H. border. Pop. 11, 886.
Braw·ley (brô′lē). City of SE Calif., SE of the Salton Sea. Pop. 14, 946.
Bra·zil (brə-zĭl′). Republic of E South America. Cap. Brasília. Pop. 107,145,200. —**Bra·zil′i·an** *adj. & n.*

Brazil

Braz·os (brăz′əs, brä′zəs). River of E N.Mex. and central Tex., flowing c. 950 mi (1,528 km) to the Gulf of Mexico.
Braz·za·ville (brăz′ə-vĭl′, brä-zä-vēl′). Cap. of Congo, on the Congo R. Pop. 175,000.
Bre·a (brē′ə, brā′ə). City of S Calif., N of Anaheim. Pop. 27,913.
Brèche de Ro·land (brĕsh də rô-läN′). Gorge in the Pyrenees of SW France.
Brecks·ville (brĕks′vĭl′). City of NE Ohio, near Cleveland. Pop. 10,132.
Bre·da (brā-dä′). City of S Netherlands, SSE of Dordrecht. Pop. 117,259.
Breed's Hill (brēdz). Hill in Charlestown, Mass., near Bunker Hill.
Bre·men (brĕm′ən, brā′mən). City of N West Germany, on the Weser R. SW of Hamburg. Pop. 556,128.
Bre·mer·ha·ven (brĕm′ər-hä′vən, -hä′-, brā′mər-hä′fən). City of N West Germany, at the mouth of the Weser near the North Sea. Pop. 138,987.
Brem·er·ton (brĕm′ər-tən). City of W central Wash., on an arm of Puget Sound W of Seattle. Pop. 36,208.
Bren·ham (brĕn′əm). City of S central Tex., WNW of Houston. Pop. 10,966.
Bren·ner Pass (brĕn′ər). Alpine pass, 4,495 ft (1,371 m) high, connecting Innsbruck, Austria, and Bolzano, Italy.
Brent·wood (brĕnt′wo͝od′). **1.** Urban district of SE England, ENE of London. Pop. 58,690. **2.** Borough of SW Pa., near Pittsburgh. Pop. 11,907.
Bre·scia (brĕ′shə, brā′shä). City of N Italy, E of Milan. Pop. 212, 265.
Bres·lau (brĕs′lou). Wroclaw.
Brest (brĕst). **1.** City of NW France, on an inlet of the Atlantic. Pop. 166,826. **2.** Also **Brest Li·tovsk** (lĭ-tôfsk′). City of W European USSR, on the Bug R. near the Polish border. Pop. 186,000.
Bre·ton (brĕt′n, brĭt′n). Cape of E N.S., Canada, on Cape Breton Is.
Brew·er (bro͞o′ər). City of S Me., on the Penobscot R. opposite Bangor. Pop. 9,017.
Bri·ansk (brē-änsk′, bryänsk). Variant of **Bryansk.**
Bri·dal·veil also **Bri·dal Veil** (brīd′-l-vāl′). Waterfall, 620 ft (189.1 m) high, in Yosemite National Park, E central Calif.
Bridge·port (brĭj′pôrt′, -pōrt′). City of SW Conn., on Long Is. Sound. Pop. 142,546.
Bridge·ton (brĭj′tən). **1.** City of E Mo., NW of St. Louis. Pop. 18,445. **2.** City of SW N.J., S of Philadelphia. Pop. 18,795.
Bridge·town (brĭj′toun′). Cap. of Barbados, West Indies. Pop. 8,789.
Bridge·view (brĭj′vyo͞o′). Village of NE Ill., near Chicago. Pop. 14,155.
Bridge·wa·ter (brĭj′wô′tər, -wŏt′ər). Town of E Mass., S of Boston. Pop. 17,202.
Bridg·wa·ter (brĭj′wô′tər, -wŏt′ər). Borough of SE England, NNE of Taunton. Pop. 26,700.
Brid·ling·ton (brĭd′lĭng-tən, bûr′-). Borough of NE England, on **Bridlington Bay,** an inlet of the North Sea. Pop. 26,920.
Brie (brē). Region of N France, E of Paris.
Bri·enz (brē-ĕnts′). Town of central Switzerland, NE of Interlaken at the NE end of the **Lake of Brienz.** Pop. 2,796.
Brig·ham City (brĭg′əm). City of N Utah, N of Ogden. Pop. 15,596.
Brig·house (brĭg′hous′). Borough of N central England, S of Bradford. Pop. 35,320.
Brigh·ton (brĭt′n). **1.** Borough of SE England, on the English Channel S of London. Pop. 152,700. **2.** City of N central Colo., NNE of Denver. Pop. 12,773.
Brin·di·si (brēn′dē-zē). City of S Italy, on the Adriatic. Pop. 89,241.
Bris·bane (brĭz′bən, -bān′). City of SE Australia, on the **Brisbane R.** (215 mi/345.9 km) above its mouth on Moreton Bay. Pop. 702,000.
Bris·tol (brĭs′təl). **1. Bay.** Arm of the Bering Sea in SW Alas., between the mainland and the Alaska Peninsula. **2. Channel.** Inlet of the Atlantic separating Wales from SE England. **3.** City of SW England, W of London. Pop. 408,000. **4.** City of central Conn., SW of Hartford. Pop. 57,370. **5.** Borough of SE Pa., NE of Philadelphia. Pop. 10,867. **6.** Town of E R.I., SE of Providence. Pop. 20,128. **7.** City of NE Tenn. and independent city of SW Va. Pop. 23,986 and 19,042.
Brit·ain (brĭt′n). United Kingdom of Great Britain and Northern Ireland.
Brit·ish A·mer·i·ca (brĭt′ĭsh ə-mĕr′-ĭ-kə) also **British North America** (nôrth). Former British possessions in North America N of the U.S.
British Ant·arc·tic Territory (ănt-ärk′tĭk, -är′tĭk). British island territory of the S Atlantic and Antarctica.
British Cam·e·roons (kăm′ə-ro͞onz′). Former British trust territory of W Africa, divided in 1961 between Nigeria and Cameroon.
British Co·lum·bi·a (kə-lŭm′bē-ə). Province of W Canada. Cap. Victoria. Pop 2,466,608.
British East Af·ri·ca (ēst ăf′rĭ-kə). Former British territories in E Africa, including Kenya, Uganda, Tanganyika, and Zanzibar.
British Gui·a·na (gē-ä′nə, -ăn′ə). Guyana.
British Hon·du·ras (hŏn-do͝or′əs, -dyo͝or′-). Belize.
British Isles. Islands off the NW coast of Europe, comprising Great Britain, Ireland, and adjacent smaller islands.
British Sol·o·mon Islands (sŏl′-ə-mən). Former British protectorate in the Solomon and Santa Cruz Is., SW Pacific.
British So·ma·li·land (sō-mä′-lē-lănd′, sə-). Former British protectorate in E Africa, on the Gulf of Aden.
British To·go·land (tō′gō-lănd′). Former British protectorate of W Africa, part of present-day Ghana since 1957.
British Vir·gin Islands (vûr′jĭn). British colony in the E Caribbean, E of the U.S. Virgin Is. Cap. Road Town, on Tortola Is. Pop. 10,484.
British West In·dies (wĕst ĭn′dēz). Formerly, islands of the West Indies that were under British control.
Brit·ta·ny (brĭt′n-ē). Region and former province of NW France, on a peninsula between the English Channel and the Bay of Biscay.
Br·no (bûr′nō). City of central Czechoslovakia, SE of Prague. Pop. 372,793.
Broad (brôd). River, c. 150 mi (240 km), of N.C. and S.C.
Broads (brôdz), **the.** Lowland region of E England, along coastal Norfolk and Suffolk.
Broad·view Heights (brôd′vyo͞o′). City of NE Ohio, near Cleveland. Pop. 10,920.
Brock·en (brŏk′ən). Peak of W East Germany, highest elevation (3,747 ft/1,142.8 m) of the Harz Mts.
Brock·ton (brŏk′tən). City of E Mass., S of Boston. Pop. 95,172.
Brock·ville (brŏk′vĭl′). City of SE Ont., Canada, on the St. Lawrence S of Ottawa. Pop. 19,967.
Bro·ken Ar·row (brō′kən ăr′ō). City of NE Okla., near Tulsa. Pop. 35,761.
Broms·grove (brŏmz′grōv′). Urban district of central England, SW of Birmingham. Pop. 41,430.
Bronx (brŏngks). **1.** River of SE N.Y., flowing c. 20 mi (32 km) through the Bronx into the East R. **2.** Or **the Bronx.** Borough of New York City, SE N.Y., on the mainland N of Manhattan. Pop. 1,169, 115.
Brook·field (bro͝ok′fēld′). **1.** Town of SW Conn., NNE of Danbury. Pop. 12,872. **2.** Village of NE Ill., near Chicago. Pop. 19,395. **3.** City of SE Wis., near Milwaukee. Pop. 34,035.
Brook·ha·ven (bro͝ok-hā′vən). City of SW Miss., SSW of Jackson. Pop. 10,800.
Brook·ings (bro͝ok′ĭngz). City of E S.Dak., N of Sioux Falls. Pop. 14,951.
Brook·line (bro͝ok′līn′). Town of E Mass., near Boston. Pop. 55,062.
Brook·lyn (bro͝ok′lĭn). **1.** Borough of New York City, SE N.Y., on W Long Is. Pop. 2,230,936. **2.** City of NE Ohio, near Cleveland. Pop. 12,342.
Brooklyn Center. City of E Minn., near Minneapolis. Pop. 31,230.
Brooklyn Park. City of E Minn., near Minneapolis. Pop. 43,332.
Brook Park (bro͝ok). City of NE Ohio, near Cleveland. Pop. 26,195.
Brooks (bro͝oks). Mountain range in Alas., N of the Arctic Circle, rising to 9,239 ft (2,817.8 m).
Broom·field (bro͞om′fēld′). City of N central Colo., near Denver. Pop. 20,730.
Bros·sard (brô-sär′, -särd′). Town of S Que., Canada, on the St. Lawrence near Montreal. Pop. 46,100.
Brown Deer (broun′ dîr′). Village of SE Wis., near Milwaukee. Pop. 12,921.
Brown·field (broun′fēld′). City of NW Tex., SW of Lubbock. Pop. 10,387.
Browns·ville (brounz′vĭl′, -vəl). City of S Tex., on the Rio Grande near the Gulf of Mexico. Pop. 84,997.
Brown·wood (broun′wo͝od′). City of central Tex., W of Waco. Pop. 19,203.
Bruges (bro͞ozh, brüzh). City of NW Belgium, E of Ostend. Pop. 118,243.
Bru·nei (bro͞o-nī′). Sultanate of NW Borneo, on the South China Sea.

Cap. Bandar Seri Bagawan. Pop. 136,256.

Bruns·wick (brŭnz'wĭk). **1.** Former state of central Germany, chiefly in present-day E West Germany. **2.** City of E West Germany, on the Oder R. ESE of Hannover. Pop. 261,669. **3.** City of SE Ga., SSW of Savannah. Pop. 17,605. **4.** Town of SW Me., NE of Portland. Pop. 17,336. **5.** City of NE Ohio, near Cleveland. Pop. 27,689.

Brus·sels (brŭs'əlz). Cap. of Belgium, in the N central part. Pop. 143,957.

Brut·ti·um (brōō't'ē-əm, brŭt'-). Ancient region of S Italy, in the toe of the peninsula.

Bry·an (brī'ən). City of E central Tex., NW of Houston. Pop. 44,337.

Bry·ansk also **Bri·ansk** (brē-änsk', bryänsk). City of central European USSR, SSE of Smolensk. Pop. 401,000.

Bu·bas·tis (byōō-băs'tĭs). Ancient city of NE Egypt, in the Nile delta.

Bu·ca·ra·man·ga (bōō'kä-rä-mäng'-gä). City of N central Colombia. Pop. 402,000.

Bu·cha·rest (bōō'kə-rĕst', byōō'-). Cap. of Rumania, in the SE part. Pop. 1,858,418.

Bu·chen·wald (bōō'kən-wôld', bŏŏk'ən-, bōōKH'ən-vält'). Village of SW East Germany, near Weimar; site of a Nazi concentration camp.

Buck·ing·ham (bŭk'ĭng-əm, -hăm'). City of S Que., Canada, NE of Ottawa. Pop. 14,328.

Bu·co·vi·na (bōō'kə-vē'nə). Variant of **Bukovina**.

Bu·cy·rus (byōō-sī'rəs). City of N central Ohio, WNW of Mansfield. Pop. 13,433.

Bu·da·pest (bōō'də-pĕst', bōō'-də-pĕst', bōō'dô-pĕsht'). Cap. of Hungary, on the Danube in the N central part. Pop. 2,060,000.

Bue·na Park (bwā'nə). City of S Calif., WNW of Alameda. Pop. 64,165.

Bue·na·ven·tu·ra (bwā'nə-vĕn-tŏŏr'ə, -tyŏŏr'ə, bwĕ'nä-vĕn-tōō'rä). City of W Colombia, on the Pacific. Pop. 144,000.

Bue·nos Ai·res (bwā'nəs īr'ĭz, -ēz, âr'-, bō'nəs). **1.** Lake of SE Chile and SW Argentina. **2.** Cap. of Argentina, in the E part on the Río de la Plata. Pop. 2,978,000.

Buf·fa·lo (bŭf'ə-lō'). City of W N.Y., at the E end of Lake Erie at the Canadian border. Pop. 357,870.

Buffalo Grove. Village of NE Ill., NW of Chicago. Pop. 22,230.

Bug (bōōg, bŏŏk). **1.** Or **Western Bug.** River of W European USSR, flowing c. 480 mi (770 km) from the Ukraine to the Vistula near Warsaw, Poland. **2.** Or **Southern Bug.** River of W European USSR, flowing c. 490 mi (790 km) through the Ukraine to the Black Sea.

Bu·gan·da (byōō-găn'də, bōō-). Region and former kingdom of E Africa, in present-day SE Uganda.

Bu·jum·bu·ra (bōō'jəm-bŏŏr'ə, bōō-jŏŏm'bŏŏr'ə). Cap. of Burundi, in the W part on Lake Tanganyika. Pop. 157,000.

Bu·ka (bōō'kə). Island in the SW Pacific, in the N Solomons; part of Papua New Guinea.

Bu·ka·vu (bōō-kä'vōō). City of E Zaire, on Lake Kivu. Pop. 182,000.

Bu·kha·ra (bōō-kär'ə, -här'-, -KHä'rə) also **Bo·kha·ra** (bō-). **1.** Former emirate of central Asia, in the Amu Darya basin. **2.** City of S Central Asian USSR, W of Samarkand. Pop. 188,000.

Bu·ko·vi·na also **Bu·co·vi·na** (bōō'-kə-vē'nə). Historical region of E Europe, in W Ukraine and NE Rumania.

Bu·la·wa·yo (bōō'lə-wā'yō, -wā'ō). City of SW Zimbabwe. Pop. 85,700.

Bul·gar·i·a (bŭl-gâr'ē-ə, bŏŏl'-). Republic of SE Europe, on the Black Sea. Cap. Sofia. Pop. 8,846,417. —**Bul·gar'i·an** *adj. & n.*

Bull Run (bŏŏl'rŭn'). Small stream of NE Va., SW of Washington, D.C., near Manassas; site of 2 Civil War battles (1861, 1862).

Bun·ker Hill (bŭng'kər). Height (107 ft/32.6 m) in Charlestown, Boston, Mass.; near site of 1st major Revolutionary War battle (1775).

Bur·bank (bûr'băngk'). **1.** City of S Calif., near Los Angeles. Pop. 84,625. **2.** City of NE Ill., near Chicago. Pop. 28,462.

Bur·gas (bŏŏr-gäs'). City of SE Bulgaria, on the Black Sea. Pop. 165,994.

Bur·gos (bŏŏr'gôs). City of N Spain, SSW of Bilbao. Pop. 148,487.

Bur·gun·dy (bûr'gən-dē). Region and former province of E France. —**Bur·gun'di·an** (bər-gŭn'dē-ən) *adj. & n.*

Bu·rias (bōō'ryäs). Island of the Philippines, SE of Luzon.

Burk·bur·nett (bûrk'bər-nĕt'). City of N Tex., on the Okla. border N of Wichita Falls. Pop. 10,668.

Bur·le·son (bûr'lə-sən). City of NE Tex., S of Fort Worth. Pop. 11,734.

Bur·lin·game (bûr'lĭng-găm', -lĭn-). City of W Calif., SSE of San Francisco. Pop. 26,173.

Bur·ling·ton (bûr'lĭng-tən). **1.** City of S Ont., Canada, on Lake Ontario near Hamilton. Pop. 111,206. **2.** City of SE Iowa, SSE of Cedar Rapids. Pop. 29,529. **3.** Town of NE Mass., NW of Boston. Pop. 23,486. **4.** City of W N.J., NE of Camden. Pop. 10,246. **5.** City of N central N.C., E of Greensboro. Pop. 37,266. **6.** City of NW Vt., on Lake Champlain NW of Montpelier. Pop 37,712.

Bur·ma (bûr'mə). Republic of SE Asia, on the Bay of Bengal and the Andaman Sea. Cap. Rangoon. Pop. 31,512,000. —**Bur·mese'** (bər-mēz', -mēs'), **Bur'man** (bûr'mən) *adj. & n.*

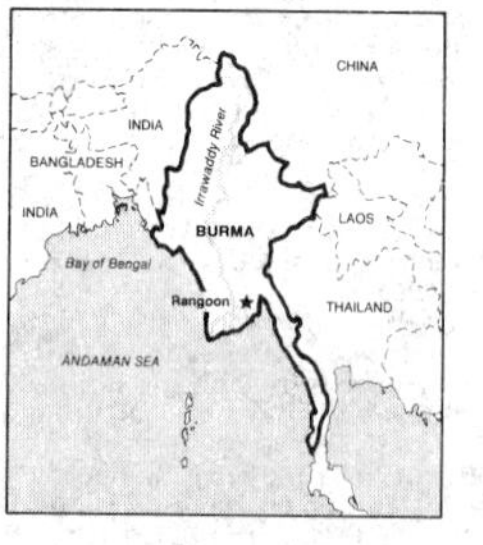

Burma

Bur·na·by (bûr'nə-bē). City of SW B.C., Canada, near Vancouver. Pop. 131,599.

Burn·ley (bûrn'lē). Borough of NW England, N of Manchester. Pop. 92,300.

Burns·ville (bûrnz'vĭl'). City of E Minn., S of Minneapolis. Pop. 35,674.

Bur·rard (bə-rärd'). Inlet of the Strait of Georgia, SW B.C., Canada.

Bur·rill·ville (bûr'əl-vĭl'). Town of NW R.I., NW of Providence. Pop. 13,164.

Bur·sa (bŏŏr-sä', bûr'sə). City of NW Turkey, near the Sea of Marmara. Pop. 466,178.

Bur·ton (bûr'tn). City of central Mich., WSW of Flint. Pop. 29,976.

Burton up·on Trent (ə-pŏn trĕnt', ə-pôn). Borough of W central England, SSW of Derby. Pop. 49,480.

Bu·ru or **Boe·roe** (bōō'rōō). Island of E Indonesia, in the Moluccas W of Ceram.

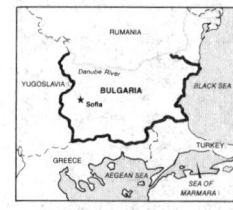

Bu·run·di (bōō-rōōn'dē, -rōōn'-). Republic of E central Africa, NW of Tanzania. Cap. Bujumbura. Pop. 3,864,000. —**Bu·run'di·an** *adj. & n.*

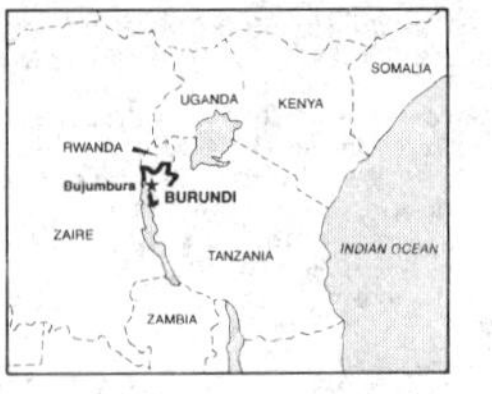

Burundi

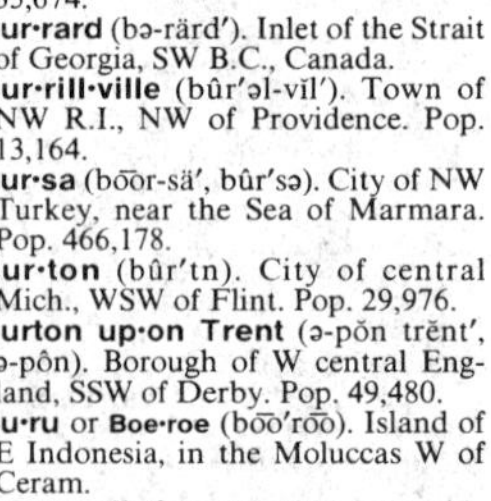

Bulgaria

Bur·y (bĕr'ē). Borough of NE England, part of Greater Manchester. Pop. 180,000.

Bury Saint Ed·munds (sānt ĕd'-məndz). Borough of E central England, ENE of Cambridge. Pop. 26,800.

Bu·sto Ar·si·zio (bōō'stō är-sē'tsyō). City of N Italy, NW of Milan. Pop. 81,139.

Bu·ta·ri·ta·ri (bōō-tä'rē-tä'rē). Atoll of the central Pacific, in Kiribati.

Bute (byōōt). Island of SW Scotland, in the Firth of Clyde.

But·ler (bŭt'lər). City of W Pa., N of Pittsburgh. Pop. 17,026.

Butte (byōōt). City of SW Mont., SSW of Helena. Pop. 37,205.

Bu·tu·an (bōō-tōō'än). City of NE Mindanao, Philippines. Pop. 53,578.

Bu·tung (bōō'tōōng'). Island of central Indonesia, off the SE coast of Sulawesi.

Bu·zău (bōō-zû'ōō). City of SE Rumania, NE of Bucharest. Pop. 102,868.

Buz·zards Bay (bŭz'ərdz). Inlet of the Atlantic in SE Mass.

Byb·los (bĭb'ləs, -lŏs'). Ancient city of Phoenicia, a port NNE of present-day Beirut, Lebanon.

Byd·goszcz (bĭd'gôshch). City of N central Poland, NNE of Poznań. Pop. 343,800.

Bye·lo·rus·sia (byĕl'ō-rŭsh'ə). Variant of **Belorussia**.

Bye·lo·stok (byĭ'lä-stôk'). *Russian.* Bialystok.

Byrd Land (bûrd). Marie Byrd Land.

By·tom (bĕ'tôm', bĭ'-). City of SW Poland, NNW of Katowice. Pop. 231,600.

Byz·an·tine Empire (bĭz'ən-tēn', -tĭn', -tīn', bĭ-zăn'tĭn). E part of the later Roman Empire.

By·zan·ti·um (bĭ-zăn'shē-əm, -tē-əm). Ancient city of Thrace, on the site of present-day Istanbul, Turkey.

C

Ca·ba·na·tuan (kä'bä-nä-twän'). City of central Luzon, Philippines, N of Manila. Metro. area pop. 115,258.

Ca·bin·da (kə-bĭn'də). Territory of Angola, an exclave on the Atlantic between Congo and Zaire.

Ca·bot Strait (kăb'ət). Channel, c. 60 mi (97 km) wide, between SW Newf. and N Cape Breton Is., Canada, connecting the Gulf of St. Lawrence and the Atlantic.

Cá·ce·res (kä'sĕ-rĕs). City of W central Spain, WSW of Madrid. Pop. 64,539.

Cache la Pou·dre (kăsh' lə pōō'dər, -drə). River, c. 125 mi (201 km), of N Colo.

Cad·il·lac (kăd'l-ăk). City of NW Mich., NNE of Grand Rapids. Pop. 10,199.

Cá·diz (kä'dĭz, kə-dĭz', kä'-, kä'thĕs). City of SW Spain, NW of Gibraltar, on the **Gulf of Cádiz**, an inlet of the Atlantic. Pop. 156,328.

Cae·li·an (sē'lē-ən). One of the 7 hills of ancient Rome.

Caen (kän, kăN). City of N France, SW of Le Havre. Pop. 119,474.

Cae·sa·re·a (sē'zə-rē'ə, sĕs'ə-, sĕz'ə-). **1.** Also **Caesarea Pal·e·sti·nae** (păl'-ĭ-stī'nē). Ancient seaport and cap. of Roman Palestine, S of present-day Haifa, Israel. **2.** Also **Caesarea Phil·ip·pi** (fĭl'ə-pī, fĭ-lĭp'ī). Ancient city of N Palestine, near Mt. Hermon in present-day SW Syria. **3.** Also **Caesa·rea Maz·a·ca** (măz'ə-kə). Kayseri.

Ca·glia·ri (käl'yə-rē', kä'lyä-rē'). Cap. of Sardinia, Italy, on the S coast on the **Gulf of Cagliari**, an inlet of the Mediterranean. Pop. 241,472.

Ca·guas (kä'gwäs). City of E central Puerto Rico, S of San Juan. Pop. 87,218.

Ca·ha·ba (kə-hô'bə, -hä'-). River, c. 200 mi (322 km), of central Ala.

Ca·ho·ki·a (kə-hō'kē-ə). Village of SW Ill., near East St. Louis and **Cahokia Mounds**, group of 85 prehistoric Indian earthworks. Pop. 18,904.

Ca·hors (kä-hôr', -ôr'). City of S central France, N of Toulouse. Pop. 20,311.

Cai·cos (kā'kəs). One of the island groups constituting the Turks and Caicos Is., SE of the Bahamas.

Cairn·gorm (kârn'gôrm') also **Cairn·gorms** (-gôrmz'). Range of the Grampians in central Scotland.

Cai·ro. **1.** (kī'rō). Cap. of Egypt, on the Nile in the NE part. Pop. 5,278,000. **2.** (kâ'rō). Town in S Ill., near the confluence of the Mississippi and Ohio rivers. Pop. 5,931. —**Cai·rene'** (-rēn') *adj. & n.*

Ca·ja·mar·ca (kä'hä-mär'kä). City and ancient Incan center of NW Peru, in the Andes. Pop. 37,608.

Cal·a·bar (kăl'ə-bär'). City of SE Nigeria, on the Gulf of Guinea. Pop. 103,000.

Ca·la·bri·a (kə-lā'brē-ə, kä-lä'brē-ä). Region of S Italy, a peninsula forming the toe of the Italian boot.

Ca·lah (kā'lə). Kalakh.

Ca·lais (kă-lā', kăl'ā, kä-lĕ'). City of N France, on the Strait of Dover. Pop. 78,820.

Ca·la·mian (kä'lä-myän'). Islands of the W central Philippines, between Mindoro and Palawan.

Cal·ca·sieu (kăl'kə-shōō'). River of SW La., flowing c. 200 mi (322 km) through **Lake Calcasieu** (c. 15 mi/24 km long) to the Gulf of Mexico.

Cal·cut·ta (kăl-kŭt'ə). City of E India, on the Ganges delta. Metro. area pop. 9,100,000.

Cald·well (kôld'wĕl', -wəl, kōld'-). City of SW Idaho, W of Boise. Pop. 17,699.

Cal·e·don (kăl'ĭ-dən). Town of SE Ont., Canada, NW of Toronto. Pop. 25,209.

Cal·e·do·ni·a (kăl'ĭ-dō'nē-ə, -dōn'-yə). Scotland. —**Cal'e·do'ni·an** *adj. & n.*

Ca·lex·i·co (kə-lĕk'sĭ-kō'). City of S Calif., on the Mexican border. Pop. 14,412.

Cal·ga·ry (kăl'gə-rē). City of S Alta., Canada, S of Edmonton. Pop. 560,618.

Ca·li (kä'lē). City of W Colombia, SW of Bogota. Pop. 1,293,000.

Cal·i·cut (kăl'ĭ-kŭt'). Kozhikode.

Cal·i·for·nia (kăl'ə-fôr'nyə, -nē-ə). **1. Gulf of.** Inlet of the Pacific extending c. 700 mi (1,126 km) between lower California and the NW Mexican mainland. **2.** State of W U.S., on the Pacific. Cap. Sacramento. Pop. 23,668,562. —**Cal'i·for'nian** *adj. & n.*

Cal·la·o (kä-yä'ô). Chief seaport of Peru, on the Pacific near Lima. Pop. 196,919.

Cal·ta·nis·set·ta (kăl'tə-nĭ-sĕt'ə, käl'tä-nēs-sāt'tä). City of central Sicily, Italy, SE of Palermo. Pop. 54,700.

Cal·u·met (kăl'yə-mĕt', -mĭt). Industrial region of NE Ill. and NW Ind., on Lake Michigan SE of Chicago.

Calumet City. City of NE Ill., near Chicago. Pop. 39,673.

Cal·va·ry (kăl'və-rē, kăl'vrē). Hill outside ancient Jerusalem where Jesus was crucified.

Cal·y·don (kăl'ĭ-dŏn', -dən). **1. Gulf of.** Gulf of Patras. **2.** Ancient city of W central Greece, N of the Gulf of Patras.

Cam (kăm). River, c. 40 mi (64 km), of E central England.

Ca·ma·güey (kăm'ə-gwā', kä'-mä-gwā'). City of E central Cuba. Pop. 230,891.

Ca·margue (kä-märg'). Island of SE France, c. 215 sq mi (557 sq km), in the Rhone delta.
Cam·a·ril·lo (kăm'ə-rē'ō). City of S Calif., W of Los Angeles. Pop. 37,732.
Cam·ba·luc (kăm'bə-lŭk'). Khanbalik.
Cam·bay (kăm-bā'), **Gulf of.** Inlet of the Arabian Sea on the NW coast of India.
Cam·ber·well (kăm'bər-wĕl', -wəl). City of S Victoria, Australia, near Melbourne. Pop. 88,700.
Cam·bo·di·a (kăm-bō'dē-ə). Country of SE Asia, between Thailand and Vietnam. Cap. Phnom Penh. Pop. 8,110,000. —**Cam·bo'di·an** *adj. & n.*

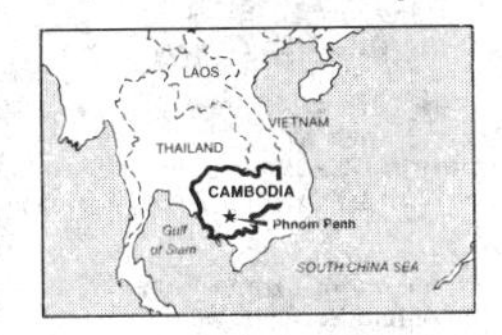

Cambodia

Cam·bri·a (kăm'brē-ə). Wales. —**Cam'bri·an** *adj. & n.*
Cam·bridge (kām'brĭj). **1.** City of SE Ont., Canada, WNW of Hamilton. Pop. 74,435. **2.** City and borough of E central England, NNE of London; site of Cambridge University. Pop. 101,600. **3.** City of E Md., on the Eastern Shore SSE of Baltimore. Pop. 11,703. **4.** City of E Mass., near Boston; site of Harvard University. Pop. 95,322. **5.** City of E Ohio, ENE of Zanesville. Pop. 13,573. —**Can'ta·brig'i·an** *adj. & n.*
Cam·den (kăm'dən). **1.** City of S Ark., SSW of Little Rock. Pop. 15,342. **2.** City of W N.J., opposite Philadelphia, Pa. Pop. 84,910.
Cam·e·roon (kăm'ə-rōōn'). **1.** Volcano, 13,353 ft (4,072.7 m), in W Cameroon. **2.** Also **Came·roun** (käm-rōōn'). Country of W central Africa, E of Nigeria. Cap. Yaoundé. Pop. 7,663,246.

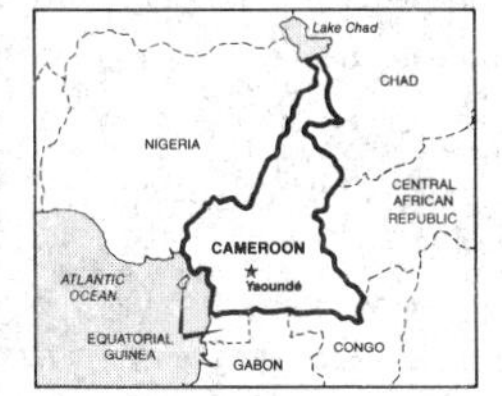

Cameroon

Cam·e·roons (kăm'ə-rōōnz'). Region of W central Africa formerly comprising **British Cameroons** and **French Cameroons** and divided (1960–61) between Cameroon and Nigeria.
Came·roun (käm-rōōn'). Variant of **Cameroon.**
Ca·mo·tes (kä-mô'tĕs). Sea of central Philippines, between Cebu and Leyte.
Cam·pa·gna di Ro·ma (käm-pä'nyä dē rō'mä). Low-lying region surrounding Rome, Italy.
Cam·pa·ni·a (kăm-pā'nē-ə, käm-pä'-nyä). Region of S Italy, on the Tyrrhenian Sea.
Camp·bell (kăm'bəl). **1.** City of W central Calif., near San Jose. Pop. 27,067. **2.** City of NE Ohio, near Youngstown. Pop. 11,619.
Camp·bell·ton (kăm'bəl-tən). City of N N.B., Canada, on the Que. border. Pop. 10,110.
Cam·pe·che (kăm-pē'chē, käm-pĕ'-chĕ). **1. Gulf** or **Bay of.** Part of the Gulf of Mexico W of the Yucatán Peninsula. **2.** City of SE Mexico, on the W coast of the Yucatán Peninsula. Pop. 103,600.
Cam·pi·na Gran·de (käɴ-pē'nə grăɴ'də). City of extreme E Brazil, NW of Recife. Pop. 236,443.
Cam·pi·nas (kăm-pē'nəs, käɴ-). City of SE Brazil, NNW of São Paulo. Pop. 562,400.
Cam·po·bel·lo (kăm'pə-bĕl'ō). Island off SW coast of N.B., Canada.
Cam·po·for·mi·do (käm'pō-fôr'-mē-dō) also **Cam·po For·mi·o** (käm'-pō fôr'myō). Village of NE Italy, SW of Udine; site of French-Austrian treaty signing (1797).
Cam·po Gran·de (käɴ'pōō grăɴ'də). City of S Brazil, NE of the Paraguay border. Pop. 180,361.
Cam·pos (käm'pōōs). City of SE Brazil, NE of Rio de Janeiro. Pop. 352,500.
Cam·ranh or **Cam Ranh Bay** (kăm'-răn', -rän', käm'-). Inlet of the South China Sea in SE Vietnam.
Cam·rose (kăm'rōz'). City of central Alta., Canada, SE of Edmonton. Pop. 11,898.
Ca·na (kā'nə). Village of N Palestine, near Nazareth.
Ca·naan (kā'nən). Ancient region comprising Palestine or the part of it W of the Jordan R.
Can·a·da (kăn'ə-də). Country of N North America. Cap. Ottawa. Pop. 22,992,604. —**Ca·na'di·an** (kə-nā'-dē-ən) *adj. & n.*

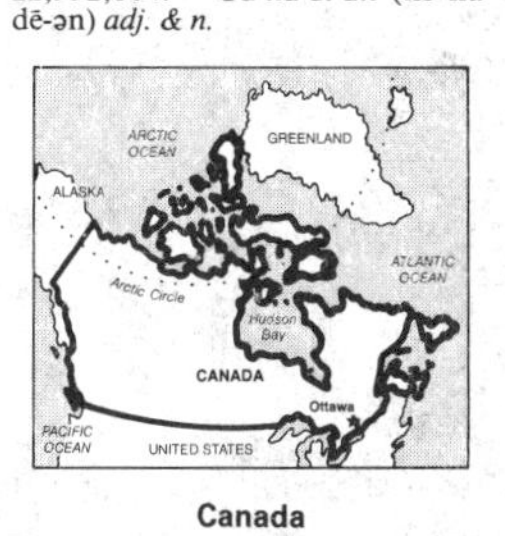

Canada

Canadian. 1. River of S central U.S., flowing 906 mi (1,457.8 km) from NE N.Mex. to the Arkansas R. in E Okla. **2.** Waterfall, c. 160 ft (49 m), forming part of Niagara Falls. **3. Shield.** Laurentian Plateau.
Ca·nal Zone (kə-năl' zōn). Territory across the Isthmus of Panama, formerly administered by the U.S. for the operation of the Panama Canal.
Can·an·dai·gua (kăn'ən-dā'gwə). City of W central N.Y., at the N end of **Canandaigua Lake** (15 mi/24.1 km long), one of the Finger Lakes. Pop. 10,419.
Ca·nar·y (kə-nâr'ē). Spanish islands off NW coast of Africa.
Ca·nav·er·al (kə-năv'ər-əl, -năv'rəl). Cape of E central Atlantic coast of Fla.; site of U.S. Manned Space Flight Center.
Can·ber·ra (kăn'bər-ə, -bĕr'ə). Cap. of Australia, in the SE part. Pop. 221,000.
Can·di·a (kăn'dē-ə). **1. Sea of.** Sea of Crete. **2.** Crete. **3.** City of Crete, Greece, on the island's N coast. Pop. 77,506.
Ca·ney Fork (kā'nē). River, 144 mi (231.7 km), of central Tenn.
Can·i·a·pis·cau (kăn'ē-ə-pĭs'kō, -kou, kăn'yə-). Variant of **Kaniapiscau.**
Can·nae (kăn'ē). Ancient town of SE Italy where Carthaginians under Hannibal defeated the Romans (216 B.C.).
Cannes (kăn, kănz, kän). Resort city of SE France, on the Mediterranean. Pop. 70,527.
Can·nock (kăn'ək). Urban district of E central England, NNW of Birmingham. Pop. 83,600.
Can·on City (kăn'yən). City of S central Colo., WNW of Pueblo. Pop. 13,037.
Can·ons·burg (kăn'ənz-bûrg'). Borough of SW Pa., SW of Pittsburgh. Pop. 10,459.
Ca·no·pus (kə-nō'pəs). Ancient city of N Egypt, E of Alexandria.
Ca·nos·sa (kə-nŏs'ə, kä-nôs'sä). Village of N central Italy, in the Apennines, where Holy Roman Emperor Henry IV submitted to the authority of Pope Gregory VII in 1077.
Can·so (kăn'sō). **1. Strait of.** Channel, 1 mi (1.6 km) wide, between NE N.S. mainland and Cape Breton Is., Canada. **2.** Cape of NE extremity of the N.S. mainland, Canada.
Can·ta·bri·an (kăn-tā'brē-ən). Mountains of N Spain extending c. 300 mi (483 km) along coast of the Bay of Biscay.
Can·ter·bur·y (kăn'tər-bĕr'ē, -brē). **1.** City of SE Australia, near Sydney. Pop. 131,900. **2.** City of SE England, ESE of London. Pop. 117,400.
Can·ton (kăn'tən). **1.** (kăn'tŏn', kăn'tŏn'). Zhu Jiang. **2.** Coral atoll (3.5 sq mi/9.1 sq km) in the central Pacific, largest of the Phoenix Is., controlled jointly by Great Britain and the U.S. **3.** (kăn'tŏn', kăn'tŏn'). Guangzhou, China. **4.** City of W central Ill., WSW of Peoria. Pop 14,626. **5.** Town of E Mass., near Boston. Pop. 18,182. **6.** City of W central Miss., NNE of Jackson. Pop. 11,116. **7.** City of NE Ohio, SSE of Akron. Pop. 94,730.
Can·yon (kăn'yən). City of N Tex., in the Panhandle S of Amarillo. Pop. 10,724.
Can·yon·lands National Park (kăn'yən-lăndz'). Area of SE Utah with deep canyons and erosion-carved land features.
Cap-de-la-Ma·de·leine (kăp'-də-lä-măd'ə-lăn', kăp-də-lä-mäd'-lĕn'). City of S Que., Canada, on the St. Lawrence NE of Montreal. Pop. 33,900.
Cape Bret·on Island (kāp brĕt'n, brĭt'n). Island, 3,970 sq mi (10,282.3 sq km), forming NE part of N.S., Canada.
Cape Cod Bay (kŏd). S part of Massachusetts Bay, W of Cape Cod.
Cape Cor·al (kôr'əl, kŏr'-). City of SW Fla., SW of Fort Myers. Pop. 32, 103.
Cape Fear River (fîr). River of central and SE N.C., flowing 202 mi (325 km) to the Atlantic.
Cape Gi·rar·deau (jə-rär'dō, -rä'-). City of SE Mo., on the Mississippi SSE of St. Louis. Pop. 34,361.
Cape of Good Hope Province (gōōd hōp') also **Cape Province.** Province of S South Africa, on the Atlantic and Indian oceans.
Ca·per·na·um (kə-pûr'nē-əm, -nā-). City of ancient Palestine, on the NW shore of the Sea of Galilee.
Cape Town or **Cape·town** (kāp'-toun'). Legislative cap. of South Africa, on the Atlantic in the extreme SW part. Pop. 697,514.
Cape Verde (vûrd). Island republic in the N Atlantic W of Senegal. Cap. Praia. Pop. 272,071.

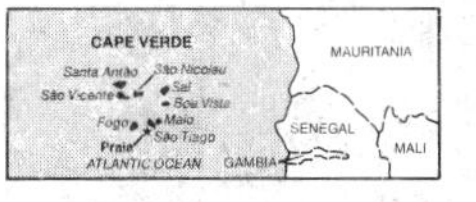

Cape Verde

Cape York Peninsula (yôrk). Peninsula of NE Australia, c. 450 mi (724 km) long, between the S Pacific and Gulf of Carpentaria.
Cap-Ha·ï·tien (kăp-ä-ē-syăɴ') or **Cap Hai·tien** (kăp' hā'shən, kăp'). City of N Haiti, on the Atlantic. Pop. 52,220.
Cap·i·to·line (kăp'ĭ-tə-līn'). One of the 7 hills of ancient Rome.
Cap·i·tol Reef National Park (kăp'-ĭ-tl rēf). Area of S central Utah reserved to protect cliff dwellings and unusual geologic forms.
Cap·pa·do·ci·a (kăp'ə-dō'shə, -shē-ə). Ancient region of Asia Minor in present-day central Turkey.
Ca·pri (kə-prē', kä'prē, kă'-). Island of S Italy, c. 5 sq mi (13 sq km), on S edge of the Bay of Naples.
Cap·u·a (kăp'yōō-ə, kä'pwä). Town of S Italy N of Naples, near site of ancient Roman city of **Capua**, on the Appian Way. Pop. 18,435.
Ca·ra·cas (kə-rä'kəs, -răk'əs). Cap. of Venezuela, in the N part near the Caribbean coast. Pop. 1,662, 627.
Car·bon·dale (kär'bən-dāl'). **1.** City of S Ill., SSE of East St. Louis. Pop. 27,194. **2.** City of NE Pa., NE of Scranton. Pop. 11,255.
Car·cas·sonne (kär-kä-sôn'). City of S France, SE of Toulouse, with intact medieval fortifications. Pop. 42,154.
Car·che·mish (kär'kə-mĭsh', kär-kē'-mĭsh). Ancient Hittite city in present-day S Turkey on the Euphrates.
Cár·de·nas (kär'*th*ĕ-näs'). City of N Cuba, on the Straits of Florida. Pop. 67,400.
Car·diff (kär'dĭf). City of SE Wales, on Bristol Channel. Pop. 282,000.
Car·di·gan Bay (kär'dĭ-gən). Inlet of St. George's Channel in W Wales.
Car·i·a (kâr'ē-ə). Ancient region of SW Asia Minor, with a coastline on the Aegean.
Car·ib·be·an (kăr'ə-bē'ən, kə-rĭb'-ē-ən). Sea of the N Atlantic bounded by the coasts of Central and South America and the West Indies.
Car·i·boo (kăr'ə-bōō'). Mountains of E B.C., Canada, parallel to and W of the Rockies.
Ca·rin·thi·a (kə-rĭn'thē-ə). Region and former duchy of central Europe, in S Austria.
Car·lisle (kär-līl', kär'līl'). **1.** City and borough of NW England, near the Scottish border. Pop. 99,600. **2.** Borough of S Pa., WSW of Harrisburg. Pop. 18,314.
Carls·bad (kärlz'băd'). **1.** Caverns of limestone in **Carlsbad Caverns National Park**, SE N.Mex. **2.** (*also* kärls'bät'). *German.* Karlovy Vary. **3.** City of S Calif., NNW of San Diego. Pop. 35,490. **4.** City of SW N.Mex., on the Pecos R. Pop. 25,496.
Carls·ru·he (kärls'rōō'ə, kärlz'-). Variant of **Karlsruhe.**
Car·mel (kär-mĕl'). **1.** (kär'məl), **Mount.** Ridge of NW Israel extending c. 15 mi (24 km) to the Mediterranean and rising to 1,800 ft (549 m). **2.** Also **Car·mel-by-the-Sea** (-bī-thə-sē'). City of W Calif., near Monterey. Pop. 4,707. **3.** City of central Ind., N of Indianapolis. Pop. 18,272.
Car·ne·gie (kär'nĭ-gē, kär-nĕg'ē). Borough of SW Pa., near Pittsburgh. Pop. 10,099.
Car·nic Alps (kär'nĭk ălps'). Range of the E Alps in S Austria and NE Italy.
Car·ni·o·la (kär'nē-ō'lə, kärn-yō'-). Region of NW Yugoslavia, NE of Istria. —**Car'ni·o'lan** *adj. & n.*
Ca·ro·li·na. 1. (kăr'ə-lī'nə). English colony of E North America, divided in 1729 into **the Car·o·li·nas** (-nəz), North and South Carolina. **2.** (kä'-rô-lē'nä). City of NE Puerto Rico, ESE of San Juan. Pop. 147,100.
Car·o·line (kăr'ə-līn', -lĭn'). Islands of the W Pacific E of the Philippines, part of the U.S. Trust Territory of the Pacific Is.
Car·ol Stream (kăr'əl strēm'). Village of NE Ill., W of Chicago. Pop. 15,472.
Ca·ro·ní (kä-rô-nē'). River of E Venezuela, flowing c. 550 mi (885 km) N to the Orinoco.
Car·pa·thi·an (kär-pā'thē-ən). Mountain system of central Europe in E Czechoslovakia, S Poland, W Ukraine, and N and W Rumania.
Car·pa·thos (kär'pä-thôs', -pə-thŏs'). Variant of **Kárpathos.**
Car·pen·tar·i·a (kär'pĭn-târ'ē-ə), **Gulf of.** Wide inlet of the Arafura Sea in N Australia.
Car·pen·ters·ville (kär'pĭn-tərz-vĭl'). Village of NE Ill., WNW of Chicago. Pop. 23,272.
Car·pin·te·ri·a (kär'pĭn-tə-rē'ə). City of SW Calif., E of Santa Barbara. Pop. 10,835.
Car·ran·tuo·hill (kăr'ən-tōō'əl). Highest mountain of Ireland, 3,414 ft (1,041.3 m), in the SW part in Macgillicuddy's Reeks.
Car·ra·ra (kə-rär'ə, kär-rä'rä). City of N Italy, near the Ligurian Sea. Pop. 70,227.
Car·roll·ton (kăr'əl-tən). **1.** City of W Ga., WSW of Atlanta. Pop. 14,078. **2.** City of N Tex. near Dallas. Pop. 40,591
Car·son (kär'sən). **1.** River of W Nev., flowing c. 125 mi (201 km) NE into **Carson Sink**, an intermittent lake. **2.** City of S Calif., near Los Angeles. Pop. 81,221.
Carson City. Cap. of Nevada, in the

W part near the Calif. border. Pop. 32,022.

Car·stensz (kär'stənz), **Mount.** Djaja Peak.

Car·ta·ge·na (kär'tə-jē'nə, -gā'-, kär'tä-hĕ'nä). **1.** City of NW Colombia, on the Caribbean. Pop. 388,000. **2.** City of SE Spain, on the Mediterranean. Pop. 135,200.

Car·ter·et (kär'tə-rĕt'). Borough of NE N.J., S of Elizabeth. Pop. 20,598.

Car·thage (kär'thĭj). **1.** Ancient city and state on the N coast of Africa, on the Bay of Tunis NE of modern Tunis. **2.** City of SW Mo., NE of Joplin. Pop. 11,104. **—Car'tha·gin'i·an** (kär'thə-jĭn'ē-ən) *adj. & n.*

Car·y (kâr'ē). Town of central N.C., near Raleigh. Pop. 21,612.

Cas·a·blan·ca (kăs'ə-blăng'kə, kä'sə-bläng'kə). City of NW Morocco, on the Atlantic. Pop. 1,371,300.

Cas·a Gran·de (kăs'ə grăn'dē). City of S central Ariz., SSE of Phoenix. Pop. 14,971.

Cas·cade (kăs-kād'). Mountain range of NW U.S., extending from NE Calif. through W Ore. and W Wash.

Cas·co Bay (kăs'kō). Inlet of the Atlantic in SW Me.

Ca·ser·ta (kä-zĕr'tä). City of S Italy, NNE of Naples. Pop. 67,257.

Cash·mere (kăsh'mîr', kăsh-mîr'). Variant of **Kashmir.**

Ca·si·quia·re (kä'sē-kyä'rĕ). River, c. 100 mi (161 km), of S Venezuela, linking the Orinoco and Amazon river systems.

Cas·per (kăs'pər). City of E central Wyo., NW of Cheyenne. Pop. 51,016.

Cas·pi·an Sea (kăs'pē-ən). Salt lake, c. 153,000 sq mi (396,000 sq km), between SE Europe and W Asia.

Cas·sel (kăs'əl, kä'səl). Variant of **Kassel.**

Cas·sel·ber·ry (kăs'əl-bĕr'ē). City of E central Fla., NNE of Orlando. Pop. 15,247.

Cas·tel Gan·dol·fo (käs-tĕl' gän-dôl'fō). Town of central Italy, SE of Rome. Pop. 3,400.

Cas·tel·lam·ma·re di Sta·bia (käs'tĕl-läm-mä'rā dē stä'byä). City of S Italy, on the Bay of Naples. Pop. 74,452.

Cas·tel·lon de la Pla·na (käs'tĕ-lyôn' dĕ lä plä'nä). City of E Spain, on the Mediterranean NNE of Valencia. Pop. 118,648.

Cas·tile (kăs-tēl'). Region and former kingdom of central and N Spain. **—Cas·til'ian** (kă-stĭl'yən, kə-) *adj. & n.*

Cas·ti·lla (käs-tē'lyä). *Spanish.* Castile.

Cas·tle Peak (kăs'əl). Mountain, 14,259 ft (4,349 m), in the Elk Mts. of W central Colo.

Castle Shan·non (shăn'ən). Borough of SW Pa., near Pittsburgh. Pop. 10,164.

Cas·tries (kăs-trē', käs'trĕs', -trĕz', kăs'-). Cap. of St. Lucia in the British West Indies. Pop. 47,600.

Cas·trop-Rau·xel or **Kas·trop-Rau·xel** (käs'trôp-rouk'səl). City of W West Germany, in the Ruhr district SSW of Münster. Pop. 79,264.

Cat·a·li·na (kăt'l-ē'nə). Santa Catalina.

Cat·a·lo·nia (kăt'l-ō'nyə, -nē-ə). Region of NE Spain bordering on France and the Mediterranean. **—Cat'a·lo'nian** *adj. & n.*

Ca·ta·lu·ña (kä'tä-lōō'nyä). *Spanish.* Catalonia.

Ca·ta·mar·ca (kä'tä-mär'kä). City of NW Argentina, NW of Cordoba. Pop. 57,228.

Ca·ta·nia (kə-tăn'ē-ə, -tān'yə, kä-tä'nyä). City of E Sicily, Italy, on the E coast of the Ionian Sea. Pop. 398,426.

Ca·tan·za·ro (kä'tän-dzä'rō). City of S Italy, near the Ionian Sea. Pop. 93,845.

Ca·taw·ba (kə-tô'bə). River, 250 mi (402.3 km), of W N.C. and N S.C.

Ca·thay (kă-thā', kə-). China.

Cath·e·rine (kăth'ə-rĭn, kăth'rĭn), **Mount.** Jebel Katherina.

Cats·kill (kăt'skĭl') also **Cats·kills** (-skĭlz). Mountain range in SE N.Y., rising to 4,204 ft (1,282.2 m).

Cau·ca (kou'kä). River of NW Colombia, flowing c. 600 mi (965 km) N to the Magdalena.

Cau·ca·sus (kô'kə-səs) also **Cau·ca·sia** (kô-kā'zhə, -shə). Mountain range and region of SE European USSR, between the Black and Caspian seas, rising to 18,480 ft (5,636.4 m).

Caucasus In·di·cus (ĭn'dĭ-kəs). Hindu Kush.

Cau·ve·ry (kô'və-rē) also **Ka·ve·ri** (kä'-). River of S India, flowing c. 475 mi (764 km) to the Bay of Bengal.

Ca·vi·te (kä-vē'tĕ, -tə). City of SW Luzon, Philippines, on Manila Bay SW of Manila. Pop. 82,456.

Cawn·pore (kôn'pôr', -pōr'). Kanpur.

Ca·xi·as (kə-shē'əs). **1.** Town of NE Brazil, WNW of Teresina. Pop. 173,082. **2.** Also **Caxias do Sul** (dōō sōōl'). City of S Brazil, N of Pôrto Alegre. Pop. 107,487.

Cay·ce (kā'sē). City of central S.C., near Columbia. Pop. 11,701.

Cay·enne (kī-ĕn', kā-). Cap. of French Guiana, on **Cayenne Is.**, in a river mouth near the Atlantic coast. Pop. 30,461.

Cay·man (kī-măn', kā-măn', kā'mən) also **Cay·mans** (kī-mănz', kā-mănz', kā'mənz). British-administered island group in the Caribbean NW of Jamaica, including **Grand Cayman, Little Cayman,** and **Cayman Brac.** Cap. Georgetown. Pop. 10,652.

Cay·u·ga (kə-yōō'gə, kē-ōō'-, kyōō'-). Lake of W central N.Y., longest (38 mi/61.1 km) of the Finger Lakes.

Ce·bu (sĕ-bōō'). **1.** Island of the central Philippines, one of the Visayans. **2.** City of E coast of Cebu Is. Pop. 413,025.

Ce·dar (sē'dər). River, c. 330 mi (531 km), of SE Minn. and E Iowa.

Cedar City. City of SW Utah, SSW of Salt Lake City. Pop. 10,972.

Cedar Falls. City of NE Iowa, near Waterloo. Pop. 36,322.

Cedar Rapids. City of E central Iowa, WNW of Davenport. Pop. 110,243.

Ce·la·ya (sĕ-lä'yä). City of central Mexico, NW of Mexico City. Pop. 114,365.

Cel·e·bes (sĕl'ə-bēz', sə-lē'bēz', sĕ-lā'bĕs). **1.** Sea of the W Pacific between Sulawesi and S Philippines. **2.** Sulawesi.

Cel·le (tsĕl'ə). City of N West Germany, S of Hamburg. Pop. 74,845.

Cen·ter·ville (sĕn'tər-vĭl'). City of SW Ohio, near Dayton. Pop. 18,886.

Cen·tral Af·ri·can Republic (sĕn'trəl ăf'rĭ-kən). Country of central Africa. Cap. Bangui. Pop. 1,637,000.

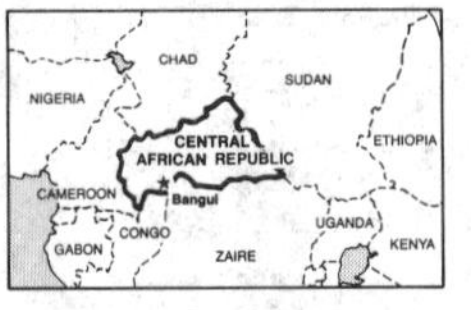

Central African Republic

Central A·mer·i·ca (ə-mĕr'ĭ-kə). Region of S North America from S border of Mexico to N border of Colombia. **—Central A·mer'i·can** *adj. & n.*

Central Falls. City of NE R.I., near Providence. Pop. 16,995.

Cen·tra·lia (sĕn-trāl'yə). **1.** City of S Ill., E of East St. Louis. Pop. 15,126. **2.** City of SW Wash., S of Olympia. Pop. 10,809.

Central Valley. Valley, c. 450 mi (724 km) long, in central Calif.

Cen·tre·ville (sĕn'tər-vĭl'). City of SW Ill., near East St. Louis. Pop. 9,747.

Ceph·a·lo·ni·a (sĕf'ə-lō'nē-ə, -lōn'yə). Largest of the Ionian Is., off the W coast of Greece.

Ce·ram (sā'räm', sē-răm'). **1.** Sea of the W Pacific among the Moluccas of E Indonesia W of New Guinea. **2.** Island of the Moluccas, in E Indonesia.

Cer·es (sîr'ēz). City of central Calif., near Modesto. Pop. 13,281.

Cer·re·do (sĕr-rĕ'*thô*), **Torre de.** Highest peak (8,687 ft/2,649.5 m) of the Cantabrian Mts. in N Spain.

Cer·ri·tos (sə-rē'tōs, -təs). City of S Calif., SE of Los Angeles. Pop. 52,756.

Cer·ro de Pas·co (sĕr'rô dĕ päs'kô, *thĕ*). Mountain, 15,100 ft (4,605.5 m), of central Peru.

Cerro de Pun·ta (pōōn'tä). Highest mountain (4,400 ft/1,342 m) of Puerto Rico, in the Cordillera Central.

Cerro Gor·do (gôr'dô). Mountain pass in S Mexico; site of U.S. victory (1847) in the Mexican War.

Ce·se·na (chā-zē'nä). City of N central Italy, ENE of Florence. Pop. 49,915.

Čes·ké Bu·dě·jo·vi·ce (chĕs'kĕ bōō'dyĕ-yô'vĭ-tsĕ). City of SW Czechoslovakia, on the Vltava. Pop. 89,399.

Čes·ko·slo·ven·sko (chĕs'kô-slô'vĕn-skô). *Czech.* Czechoslovakia.

Ceu·ta (syōō'tə, sā'ōō'tə, sĕ'ōō-tä). Spanish city of NW Africa, on the Strait of Gibraltar. Pop. 65,235.

Cé·vennes (sā-vĕn'). Mountain range of S France, W of the Rhone.

Cey·lon (sĭ-lŏn, sā-). Sri Lanka. **—Cey'lo·nese'** *adj. & n.*

Chad (chăd). **1.** Lake of N central Africa, mainly in Chad. **2.** Country of N central Africa. Cap. Ndjamena. Pop. 4,030,000.

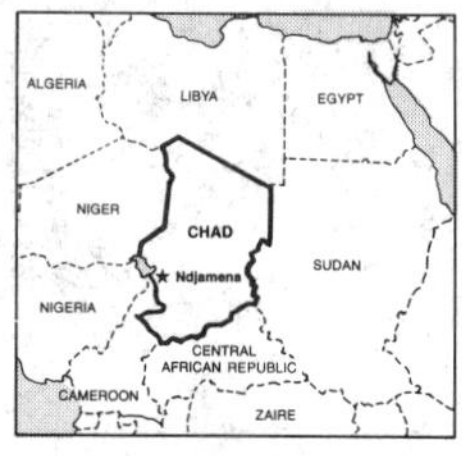

Chad

Chaer·o·ne·a (kĕr'ə-nē'ə, kîr'-). Ancient city of E Greece.

Chal·ce·don (kăl'sĭ-dŏn', kăl-sēd'n). Ancient Greek city of NW Asia Minor, on the Bosporus near present-day Istanbul.

Chal·cid·i·ce (kăl-sĭd'ĭ-sē). Peninsula of NE Greece, projecting into the N Aegean with 3 fingerlike extensions.

Chal·cis (kăl'sĭs). Ancient city of SE Greece, on the W coast of Euboea.

Chal·dae·a also **Chal·de·a** (kăl-dē'ə). Ancient region of S Mesopotamia. **—Chal·dae'an, Chal·de'an** *adj. & n.*

Cha·leur Bay (shə-lōōr', -lûr'). Inlet of the Gulf of St. Lawrence between E Que. and N N.B., Canada.

Cha·lon (shä-lôN') also **Chalon-sur-Saône** (-sür-sōn'). City of E central France, N of Mâcon. Pop. 58,187.

Cha·lôns (shä-lôN') also **Cha·lôns-sur-Marne** (-sür-märn'). City of NE France, on the Marne E of Paris. Pop. 52,275.

Cham·bal (chŭm'bəl). River, c. 550 mi (885 km) of W central India.

Cham·bers·burg (chām'bərz-bûrg'). Borough of S Pa., SW of Harrisburg. Pop. 16,174.

Cham·bé·ry (shäN-bā-rē'). City of SE France, ESE of Lyon. Pop. 54,415.

Cham·be·zi (chăm-bē'zĭ). River, c. 300 mi (483 km), of NE Zambia.

Cham·bly (shăm'blē, shäN-blē'). City of S Que., Canada, on the Richelieu R. E of Montreal. Pop. 12,000.

Cham·bord (shäN-bôr'). Village of N central France, site of Francis I's Renaissance château.

Cha·mi·zal (shăm'ĭ-zăl', chăm'ĭ-săl'). District on N bank of Rio Grande near El Paso, Tex., ceded by U.S. to Mexico in 1963.

Cham·pagne (shăm-pān', shäN-pän'yə). Region and former province of NE France.

Cham·paign (shăm-pān'). City of E central Ill., adjoining Urbana. Pop. 58,133.

Cham·pi·gny (shäN-pē-nyē') also **Cham·pi·gny-sur-Marne** (-sür-märn'). City of N France, near Paris. Pop. 80,291.

Cham·plain (shăm-plān'). Lake of NE N.Y., NW Vt., and S Que., Canada.

Chan·cel·lors·ville (chăn'sə-lərz-vĭl', -slərz-vĭl'). Town of NE Va.; site of Confederate victory (1863).

Chan·chiang also **Chan·kiang** (jĕn'-jyäng'). Zhanjiang.

Chan·di·garh (chŭn'dē-gər). City of N India, N of Delhi; designed by Le Corbusier. Pop. 218,743.

Chan·dler (chănd'lər). City of S central Ariz., SE of Phoenix. Pop. 29,673.

Chang·chow (chăng'jō'). Changzhou.

Chang·chun (chăng'chŭn'). City of NE China, in Manchuria SSW of Harbin. Pop. 1,500,000.

Chang·hua (jăng'hwä). City of W Taiwan, SW of Taipei. Pop. 111,000.

Chang Jiang (chăng' jyăng'). *Chinese.* Yangtze.

Chang·sha (chăng'shä'). City of S China, WSW of Shanghai. Pop. 850,000.

Chang·zhou (chăng'jō). City of E China, on the Grand Canal WNW of Shanghai. Pop. 400,000.

Chan·nel (chăn'əl). Islands of Great Britain in the English Channel off the coast of Normandy, France.

Cha·nute (shə-nōōt'). City of SE Kans., E of Wichita. Pop. 10,506.

Chao Phra·ya (chou prä-yä'). River of Thailand, c. 140 mi (225 km), flowing into the Gulf of Siam.

Cha·pa·la (chä-pä'lä). Lake, 408 sq mi (1,057 sq km), of W central Mexico, SE of Guadalajara.

Chap·el Hill (chăp'əl). Town of N central N.C., WNW of Raleigh. Pop. 32,421.

Cha·pul·te·pec (chə-pŭl'tə-pĕk', chä-pōōl'tē-pĕk'). Rocky hill S of Mexico City, site of a fortress and of major Mexican War battles.

Char·dzhou (chär-jō'). City of SW Central Asian USSR, on the Amu Darya. Pop. 143,000.

Cha·rente (shä-räNt'). River of W France, flowing c. 220 mi (354 km), to the Bay of Biscay.

Cha·ri (shä-rē'). Variant of **Shari.**

Char·i·ton (shăr'ĭ-tn). River, c. 280 mi (451 km), of S Iowa and N Mo.

Char·le·roi (shär-lə-rwä'). City of S Belgium, S of Brussels. Pop. 221,911.

Charles·bourg (chärlz'bûrg', shăl-bōōr'). City of S Que., Canada, near Quebec city. Pop. 70,600.

Charles·ton (chärl'stən). **1.** Mountain, 11,919 ft (3,635.3 m), of SE Nev. **2.** City of E Ill., ESE of Decatur. Pop. 19,355. **3.** City of SE S.C., NE of Savannah. Pop. 69,510. **4.** Cap. of W.Va., in the W central part. Pop. 63,968.

Charles·town (chärlz'toun'). Former city of E Mass., now the oldest part of Boston.

Char·le·ville-Mé·zières (shär-lə-vēl'mē-zē-ĕr'). City of NE France, on the Meuse ENE of Paris. Pop. 60,176.

Char·lotte (shär'lət). City of S N.C., near the S.C. border SSW of Winston-Salem. Pop. 314,447.

Charlotte A·ma·lie (ə-mäl'yə). Cap. of U.S. Virgin Is., on St. Thomas. Pop. 12,220.

Char·lot·ten·burg (shär-lŏt'n-bûrg', -lôt'n-bōōrk'). Former city of Germany, now part of East Berlin.

Char·lottes·ville (shär'ləts-vĭl'). Independent city of central Va., NW of Richmond. Pop. 45,010.

Char·lotte·town (shär'lət-toun'). Cap. of P.E.I., Canada, on the S coast. Pop. 19,133.

Char·tres (shär'trə, shärt). City of N France, SW of Paris. Pop. 38,928.

Châ·teau·guay (shä-tō-gā', shăt'ə-gā'). Town of S Que., Canada, SW of Montreal. Pop. 38,200.

Châ·teau·roux (shä-tō-rōō'). City of central France, SE of Tours. Pop. 53,429.

Châ·teau-Thier·ry (shä-tō-tyĕ-rē'). Town of N France; site of 2nd Battle of the Marne (1918). Pop. 10,858.

Chat·ham (chăt'əm). **1.** Island and island group of New Zealand, in SW Pacific E of South Is. **2.** Town of S Que., Canada, SW of Montreal. Pop. 38,200.

Chat·ta·hoo·chee (chăt'ə-ho͞o'chē). River, 436 mi (701.5 km), of N Ga.
Chat·ta·noo·ga (chăt'ən-o͞o'gə). City of SE Tenn., on the Ga. border SE of Nashville. Pop. 169,565.
Che·bok·sa·ry (chĭ-bŏk-sä'rĭ). City of E central European USSR, on the Volga. Pop. 323,000.
Che·ju (chē'jo͞o'). Island of South Korea, separated from the SW coast by **Cheju Strait**, a 50 mi (80 km) channel linking the Yellow Sea and Korea Strait.
Che·lan (shə-lăn'). Lake of N central Wash., in the Cascade Mts.
Che·liff (shā-lēf'). River, c. 420 mi (676 km), of N Algeria.
Chelms·ford (chĕmz'fərd). **1**. Borough of SE England. Pop. 129,800. **2**. Town of NE Mass., near Lowell. Pop. 31,174.
Chel·sea (chĕl'sē). **1**. District and former borough of Greater London, England. **2**. City of E Mass., near Boston. Pop. 25,431.
Chel·ten·ham (chĕlt'nəm, chĕl'-tən-əm). Borough of W central England. Pop. 85,000.
Che·lya·binsk (chĭ-lyä'bĭnsk). City of W Siberian USSR, S of Sverdlovsk. Pop. 1,042,000.
Che·lyus·kin (chĭ-lyo͞os'kĭn). Cape of N central Siberian USSR; northernmost point of Asia.
Chem·nitz (kĕm'nĭts). Karl-Marx-Stadt.
Che·nab (chĭ-năb', chē-năb'). River, 675 mi (1,086.1 km), of N India and E Pakistan.
Cheng·chow (jŭng'jō'). Zhenzhou.
Cheng·du also **Cheng·tu** (chŭng'-do͞o'). City of central China, WNW of Chongqing. Pop. 1,800,000.
Cher (shĕr). River, c. 220 mi (354 km), of central France.
Cher·bourg (shâr'bo͝org, shĕr-bo͞or'). City of NW France, on the English Channel. Pop. 32,536.
Che·rem·kho·vo (chə-rĕm'KHŏ-vŏ, chĕ'rəm-KHô'vŏ). City of SE Siberian USSR, NW of Irkutsk. Pop. 75,000.
Che·re·po·vets (chĭ-rĭ-pŏ-vyĕts'). City of N central European USSR, N of Moscow. Pop. 274,000.
Cher·i·bon (chĕr'ĭ-bôn'). Tjirebon.
Cher·kas·sy (chər-kä'sĭ). City of S European USSR, on the Dnieper. Pop. 234,000.
Cher·ni·gov (chər-nyē'gəf). City of W central European USSR, NNE of Kiev. Pop. 245,000.
Cher·nov·tsy (chər-nôf'tsĭ). City of SW European USSR, near the Rumanian border. Pop. 221,000.
Cher·o·kee Strip (chĕr'ə-kē strĭp') or **Out·let** (out'lĕt', -lĭt). Plot of land, c. 12,000 sq mi (31,080 sq km), in present-day N Okla., purchased by the U.S. in 1891.
Ches·a·peake (chĕs'ə-pēk'). **1**. **Bay**. Inlet of the Atlantic, in Va. and Md. **2**. Independent city of SE Va., S of Newport News. Pop. 114,226.
Chesh·ire (chĕsh'ər, -ĭr'). Town of S central Conn., W of New Haven. Pop. 21,788.
Ches·ter (chĕs'tər). **1**. Borough of W central England, SSE of Liverpool. Pop. 61,370. **2**. City of SE Pa., on the Delaware R. near Philadelphia. Pop. 45,794.
Ches·ter·field (chĕs'tər-fēld'). **1**. Inlet on NW coast of Hudson Bay, extending E into Keewatin District of N.W.T., Canada. **2**. City of N central England, S of Sheffield. Pop. 96,300.
Chev·i·ot (chĕv'ē-ət, chē'vē-). Hills extending c. 35 mi (56 km) along the English-Scottish border; highest elevation, **The Cheviot** (2,676 ft/816.2 m).
Chev·y Chase (chĕv'ē chās'). Village of W central Md., near Washington, D.C. Pop. 24,000.
Chey·enne (shī-ăn', -ĕn'). **1**. River, c. 290 mi (467 km), of E Wyo. and W S.Dak. **2**. Cap. of Wyo., in the SE part near the Nebr. and Colo. borders. Pop. 47,283.
Chi·ai or **Chia-i** (jē-ī'). City of SW Taiwan, N of Kaohsiung. Pop. 246,513.
Chia·ling (jyä'lĭng'). Jialing.
Chia·mus·su (chyä'mo͞o'so͞o'). *Japanese*. Jiamusi.
Chiang Mai (chyäng' mī') or **Chieng·mai** (chyĕng'mī'). City of NW Thailand, on the Ping R. near the Burmese border. Pop. 93,353.
Chi·an·ti (kē-än'tē, kyän'tē). Range of the Apennines, c. 15 mi (24 km) long, in central Italy.
Chi·ba (chē'bä'). City of E central Honshu, Japan, on the NE shore of Tokyo Bay. Pop. 712,488.
Chi·bou·ga·mau (shə-bo͞o'gə-mə, chē-bo͞o-gä'mou). Town of central Que., Canada, NW of Roberval. Pop. 10,700.
Chi·ca·go (shĭ-kä'gō, -kô'-). City of NE Ill., on Lake Michigan. Pop. 3,005,072.
Chicago Heights. City of NE Ill., S of Chicago. Pop. 37,026.
Chicago Ridge. Village of NE Ill., near Chicago. Pop. 13,473.
Chich·a·gof (chĭch'ə-gôf', -gŏf'). Island of SE Alas., in the N Alexander Archipelago.
Chi·chen It·za (chē-chĕn' ēt-sä', ēt'sə). Ancient Mayan city of central Yucatán, Mexico.
Chich·es·ter (chĭch'ĭ-stər). Borough of S England, near the English Channel E of Southampton. Pop. 20,940.
Chick·a·hom·i·ny (chĭk'ə-hŏm'-ə-nē). River, c. 90 mi (145 km), of E Va.
Chick·a·sa·whay (chĭk'ə-sô'wā). River, c. 210 mi (338 km), of SE Miss.
Chick·a·sha (chĭk'ə-shā'). City of central Okla., SW of Oklahoma City. Pop. 15,828.
Chi·cla·yo (chē-klä'yô). City of NW Peru, near the Pacific coast. Pop. 148,932.
Chi·co (chē'kō). City of N Calif., N of Sacramento. Pop. 26,601.
Chic·o·pee (chĭk'ə-pē). City of SW Mass., near Springfield. Pop. 55,112.
Chi·cou·ti·mi (shĭ-ko͞o'tĭ-mē). **1**. River, c. 100 mi (161 km), of S Que., Canada. **2**. City of S central Que., Canada, on the Saguenay R. N of Quebec city. Pop. 60,400.
Chieng·mai (chyĕng'mī'). Variant of **Chiang Mai**.
Chie·ti (kyā'tē). City of central Italy, near the Adriatic. Pop. 57,140.
Chi·ga·sa·ki (chē'gä-sä'kē). City of E central Honshu, Japan, near Yokohama. Pop. 168,849.
Chi·hua·hua (chē-wä'wä). City of N Mexico. Pop. 369,545.
Chil·e (chĭl'ē, chē'lē). Republic of SW South America, with a long Pacific coastline. Cap. Santiago. Pop. 10,044,940. —**Chil'e·an** *adj. & n.*

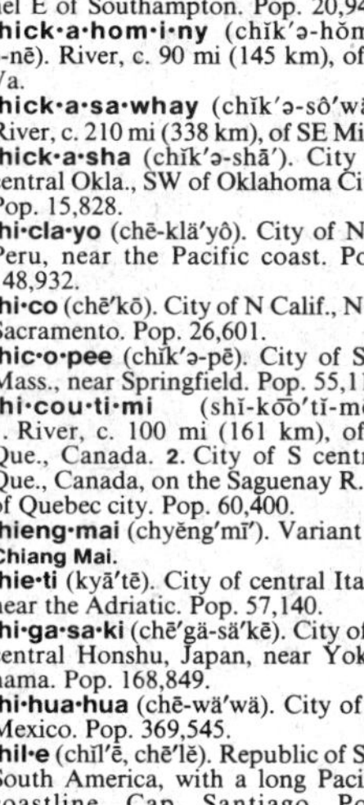

Chile

Chi·lin (jē'lĭn'). Jilin.
Chi·llán (chē-yän'). City of central Chile, ENE of Concepción. Pop. 111,800.
Chil·li·coth·e (chĭl'ĭ-kŏth'ē, -kô'thē). City of S central Ohio, S of Columbus. Pop. 23,420.
Chil·li·wack (chĭl'ĭ-wăk'). City of SW B.C., Canada, on the Fraser R. E of Vancouver. Pop. 28,421.
Chi·lo·é (chĭl'ō-ā', chē'lô-ĕ'). Island off S central Chile.
Chil·pan·cin·go (chĕl-pän-sĕng'gô) or **Chilpancingo de Los Bra·vos** (dĕ lôs brä'vôs). City of S Mexico, SSW of Mexico City. Pop. 56,904.
Chil·tern (chĭl'tərn). Hills of S central England, NE of the upper Thames.
Chi·lung (jē'lo͝ong', kē'-). Keelung.
Chim·bo·ra·zo (chĭm'bə-rä'zō, -rā'-, chĕm'bô-rä'sô). Inactive volcano, 20,561 ft (6,271.1 m), in central Ecuador.
Chim·kent (chĭm-kĕnt'). City of SW Central Asian USSR, N of Tashkent. Pop. 327,000.
Chin (chĭn). Hills of W Burma, rising to 10,018 ft (3,055 m).
Chi·na (chī'nə). **1**. **Sea**. W part of the Pacific, extending along the E coast of Asia from S Japan to the Malay Peninsula and divided by Taiwan into the **East China Sea** and the **South China Sea**. **2**. Also **People's Republic of China**. Country of E Asia. Cap. Beijing. Pop. 930,500,000. **3**. Also **Republic of China**. Taiwan.

China

Chin·chow (jĭn'jō'). Jinzhou.
Chin·co·teague (shĭng'kə-tēg', chĭng'-). Narrow bay in NE Va. and SE Md.
Chin·dwin (chĭn'dwĭn'). River, c. 550 mi (885 km), of NW Burma.
Chin·hae (jĭn'hă'). City of SE South Korea, on Korea Strait. Pop. 108,730.
Chin·ju (jĭn'jo͞o'). City of S South Korea, W of Pusan. Pop. 174,918.
Chin·kiang (jĭn'jyäng', chĭn'kyăng'). Zhenjiang.
Chin·nam·po (chĭn'näm-pō). Nampo.
Chi·no (chē'nō). City of S Calif., E of Los Angeles. Pop. 40,165.
Chiog·gia (kyôd'jä). City of NE Italy, on an island S of Venice. Pop. 38,200.
Chi·os (kī'ŏs, -ōs, kē'-, KHē'ôs). Island of E Greece, in the Aegean off the W coast of Turkey.
Chip·pe·wa (chĭp'ə-wä', -wô', -wā'). River, c. 180 mi (290 km), of NW Wis.
Chippewa Falls. City of W central Wis., near Eau Claire. Pop. 11,845.
Chis·holm Trail (chĭz'əm trāl'). Former cattle trail from San Antonio, Tex., to Abilene, Kans.
Chi·ta (chĭ-tä'). City of SE Siberian USSR, E of Irkutsk. Pop. 308,000.
Chi·tral (chĭ-träl'). River, c. 300 mi (483 km), of N Pakistan and NE Afghanistan.
Chit·ta·gong (chĭt'ə-gŏng'). City of SE Bangladesh, near the Bay of Bengal. Pop. 497,026.
Chka·lov (chkä'lŏf). Orenburg.
Choc·taw·hatch·ee (chŏk'tô-hăch'-ē). River, c. 140 mi (225 km), of S Ala.
Choi·seul (shwä-zœl', -zül). One of the Solomon Is., in the SW Pacific SE of Bougainville Is.
Choi·sy (shwä-zē') or **Choi·sy-le-Roi** (-lə-rwä'). City of N France, SSE of Paris. Pop. 38,705.
Cho·let (shô-lĕ'). City of W France, ESE of Nantes. Pop. 52,976.
Cho·lu·la (chô-lo͞o'lä). Town of E central Mexico; ancient Toltec and Aztec center. Pop. 15,399.
Cho·mo Lha·ri (chō'mō lär'ē). Peak, 23,997 ft (7,319 m), in the SE Himalayas on the Bhutan-China border.
Chong·jin (chœng'jĭn'). City of NE North Korea, on the Sea of Japan. Pop. 306,000.
Chong·ju (chœng'jo͞o'). City of W central South Korea, SSE of Seoul. Pop. 223,016.
Chong·qing (cho͞ong'chyĭng'). City of S central China, on the Yangtze. Pop. 2,900,000.
Chon·ju (chœn'jo͞o'). City of SW South Korea, S of Seoul. Pop. 348,053.
Cho O·yu (chō' ō-yo͞o'). Peak, 26,967 ft (8,225 m), in the central Himalayas on the Nepal-China border.
Chor·zow (hô'zho͞of). City of S Poland, NNW of Katowice. Pop. 149,900.
Cho·sen (chō'sĕn'). Korea.
Cho·shi (chō'shē'). City of E central Honshu, Japan, on the Pacific E of Tokyo. Pop. 90,374.
Cho·ta Nag·pur (chō'tə näg'po͝or). Region of E India, a forested plateau N of the Mahanadi R.
Chou Shan (jō' shän'). Zhoushan.
Christ·church (krīst'chûrch'). **1**. Borough of S central England, on the English Channel. Pop. 38,600. **2**. City of E South Is., New Zealand, near the Pacific coast. Pop. 171,300.
Chris·ti·a·ni·a (krĭs'tē-ăn'ē-ə, -än'-). Oslo.
Chris·tians·burg (krĭs'chənz-bûrg'). Town of SW Va., SW of Roanoke. Pop. 10,345.
Chris·tian·sted (krĭs'chən-stĕd'). Chief city of St. Croix, U.S. Virgin Is., on the N coast. Pop. 3,020.
Christ·mas (krĭs'məs). **1**. Australian-administered island, c. 64 sq mi (166 sq km), in the E Indian Ocean S of W Java. **2**. Largest (c. 222 sq mi/575 sq km) of the Line Is., in the Pacific near the equator and S of Hawaii.
Chu (cho͞o). **1**. Zhu Jiang. **2**. River of S Central Asian USSR, flowing c. 600 mi (965 km) E into Issyk-Kul.
Chu·but (chə-bo͞ot', cho͞o-). River of S Argentina, flowing c. 500 mi (805 km) E to the Atlantic.
Chu·chow (cho͞o'jō'). Zhuzhou.
Chud·sko·ye (cho͞ot'skə-yə). *Russian*. Peipus.
Chu·gach (cho͞o'găch', -găsh'). Range of S Alas. extending from Cook Inlet E to the Canadian border and rising to 13,250 ft (4,041.3 m).
Chuk·chi (cho͝ok'chē). **1**. Sea of the Arctic Ocean between NW Alas. and extreme NE USSR. **2**. Peninsula of extreme NE USSR, across Bering Strait from Alas.
Chu Kiang (cho͞o'jyäng'). Zhu Jiang.
Chu·la Vis·ta (cho͞o'lə vĭs'tə). City of S Calif., near San Diego. Pop. 83,927.
Chu·lym also **Chu·lim** (chə-lĭm', cho͞o-). River of S central Siberian USSR, flowing c. 700 mi (1,126 km) N and W to the Ob.
Chun·chon (cho͞on'chôn'). City of N South Korea, ENE of Seoul. Pop. 140,397.
Chung·king (cho͝ong'kĭng', jo͝ong'-gĭng'). Chongqing.
Chur·chill (chûr'chĭl'). **1**. River of central Sask. and N Man., Canada, flowing c. 1,000 mi (1609 km) NE to Hudson Bay. **2**. River of S Labrador, Canada, flowing 208 mi (334.7 km) over **Churchill Falls** (245 ft/74.7 m high) to Lake Melville.
Chu·so·va·ya (cho͞o-sŏ-vä'yə). River, c. 460 mi (740 km), of E European USSR.
Chu·vash (cho͞o'väsh). Region of W European USSR.
Cic·e·ro (sĭs'ə-rō'). Town of NE Ill., near Chicago. Pop. 61,232.
Cien·fue·gos (syĕn-fwĕ'gôs). City of S central Cuba, on **Cienfuegos Bay**, a narrow-necked inlet of the Caribbean. Pop. 91,800.
Ci·li·cia (sĭ-lĭsh'ə). Ancient country of SE Asia Minor, along the Mediterranean S of the Taurus Mts. —**Ci·li'cian** *adj. & n.*
Cilician Gates (gāts). Gülek Bogaz.
Cim·ar·ron (sĭm'ə-rŏn', -rōn'). River of NE N.Mex., SW Kan., and N Okla., flowing 692 mi (1,113.4 km) E to the Arkansas R.
Cin·cin·na·ti (sĭn'sə-năt'ē, -năt'ə). City of extreme SW Ohio, on the Ohio R. Pop. 385,457.
Cinque Ports (sĭngk' pôrts', pōrts'). Group of seaports of SE England (originally Hastings, Romney, Hythe, Dover, and Sandwich) that formed a maritime and defensive association (11th–19th cent.).
Cin·tra (sĕn'trə). Variant of **Sintra**.
Cir·cas·sia (sər-kăsh'ə, -ē-ə). Region of the USSR, on the NE coast of the Black Sea N of the Caucasus. —**Cir·cas'sian** *adj. & n.*
Cir·cle·ville (sûr'kəl-vĭl'). City of S central Ohio, S of Columbus. Pop. 11,700.
Cis·al·pine Gaul (sĭs-ăl'pīn' gôl',

-pīn′). Part of ancient Gaul S and E of the Alps.

Cis·cau·ca·sia (sĭs′kô-kā′zhə, -shə). Part of the Caucasus region N of the main Caucasus range.

Ci·thae·ron (sĭ-thē′rən). Mountain, 4,622 ft (1,409.7 m), in SE Greece.

Ci·tlal·té·petl (sē′tläl-tā′pĕt-l). Orizaba.

Ciu·dad Bo·lí·var (syōō-*thäth′* bô-lē′-vär). City of E central Venezuela, on the Orinoco. Pop. 134,000.

Ciudad Gua·ya·na (gwä-yä′nä). City of E Venezuela, on the Orinoco. Pop. 168,000.

Ciudad Juá·rez (wär′ĕz). City of N Mexico, on the Rio Grande opposite El Paso, Tex. Pop. 597,096.

Ciudad Tru·jil·lo (trōō-hē′yô). Santo Domingo.

Ciudad Vic·to·ria (vēk-tô′ryä). City of E central Mexico, SSE of Monterrey. Pop. 121,379.

Ci·vi·ta·vec·chia (chē′vē-tä-vĕk′yä). City of W central Italy, on the Tyrrhenian Sea WNW of Rome. Pop. 48,342.

Clac·ton (klăk′tən) also **Clacton-on-Sea** (-ŏn-sē′, -ôn-). Resort town of SE England, on the North Sea. Pop. 39,380.

Clair·ton (klâr′tn). City of SW Pa., SSE of Pittsburgh. Pop. 12,188.

Clare·mont (klâr′mŏnt′). **1.** City of S Calif., near Pomona. Pop. 30,950. **2.** City of SW N.H., near the Vt. border. Pop. 14,557.

Clare·more (klâr′môr′, -mōr′). City of NE Okla., ENE of Tulsa. Pop. 12,085.

Clark Fork (klärk). River, c. 360 mi (579 km), of W Mont. and N Idaho.

Clarks·burg (klärks′bûrg′). City of N W.Va., SSE of Wheeling. Pop. 22,371.

Clarks·dale (klärks′dāl′). City of NW Miss., near the Ark. border. Pop. 21,137.

Clarks·ville (klärks′vĭl′). **1.** Town of S Ind., on the Ohio R. opposite Louisville, Ky. Pop. 15,164. **2.** City of NW Tenn., NW of Nashville. Pop. 54,777.

Claw·son (klô′sən). City of SE Mich., near Detroit. Pop. 15,103.

Clay·ton (klāt′n). City of E Mo., near St. Louis. Pop. 14,219.

Clear·field (klîr′fēld′). City of N Utah, near Ogden. Pop. 17,982.

Clear·wa·ter (klîr′wô′tər, -wŏt′ər). **1.** River, c. 100 mi (161 km), of SW Alta., Canada. **2.** River, c. 130 mi (209 km), of NW Sask. and NE Alta., Canada. **3.** River of N central Idaho, flowing c. 190 mi (306 km) W through the **Clearwater Mts.**, a range of the Rockies. **4.** City of W central Fla., W of Tampa. Pop. 85,450.

Cle·burne (klē′bərn). City of NE Tex., S of Fort Worth. Pop. 19,218.

Cler·mont-Fer·rand (klĕr-môɴ′-fĕ-räɴ′). City of central France, W of Lyon. Pop. 156,900.

Cleve·land (klēv′lənd). **1. Mount.** Highest peak (10,438 ft/3,183.6 m) in Glacier National Park, NW Mont. **2.** City of NW Miss., near the Ark. border. Pop. 14,524. **3.** City of NE Ohio, on Lake Erie. Pop. 573,822. **4.** City of SE Tenn., ENE of Chattanooga. Pop. 26,415. **5.** City of E Tex., NNE of Houston. Pop. 19,218.

Cleveland Heights. City of NE Ohio, near Cleveland. Pop. 56,438.

Cleves (klēvz). City of W West Germany, near the Rhine and the Dutch border. Pop. 44,036.

Cli·chy (klē-shē′). City of N France, near Paris. Pop. 47,764.

Cliff·side Park (klĭf′sīd′). Borough of NE N.J., opposite New York City. Pop. 21,464.

Clif·ton (klĭf′tən). City of NE N.J., near Paterson. Pop. 74,388.

Clinch (klĭnch). River of SW Va. and E Tenn., flowing c. 300 mi (483 km) SW to the Tennessee.

Cling·mans Dome (klĭng′mənz dōm′). Highest (6,642 ft/2,025.8 m) of the Great Smoky Mts., on the N.C.-Tenn. border.

Clin·ton (klĭn′tən). **1.** Town of S Conn., on Long Is. Sound E of New Haven. Pop. 11,195. **2.** City of E central Iowa, NE of Davenport. Pop. 32,828. **3.** Town of E central Mass., NNE of Worcester. Pop. 12,771. **4.** City of W central Miss., WNW of Jackson. Pop. 14,660.

Clip·per·ton (klĭp′ər-tən). French island, c. 2 sq mi (5.2 sq km), in the E Pacific SW of Mexico.

Clo·quet (klō-kā′). City of NE Minn., W of Duluth. Pop. 11,142.

Cloud Peak (kloud). Highest (13,175 ft/4,018.4 m) of the Bighorn Mts., in N Wyo.

Clo·vis (klō′vĭs). **1.** City of S central Calif., near Fresno. Pop. 33,021. **2.** City of E N.Mex., near the Tex. border. Pop. 31,194.

Cluj (klōōzh). City of Rumania, NW of Bucharest. Pop. 273,199.

Clu·ny (klōō′nē, klü-nē′). Town of E central France, NNW of Lyon; center of medieval Cluniac order. Pop. 3,552.

Clyde (klīd). River of SW Scotland, flowing 106 mi (170.6 km) NW to the **Firth of Clyde**, an inlet of the Atlantic.

Clyde·bank (klīd′băngk′). Burgh of W central Scotland, on the Clyde R. Pop. 52,835.

Cni·dus also **Cni·dos** (nī′dəs). Ancient Greek city of SW Asia Minor.

Cnos·sos or **Cnos·sus** (nŏs′əs). Variants of **Knossos.**

Coast (cōst). **1. Mountains.** Range in W B.C., Canada, and SE Alas. extending c. 1,000 mi (1,609 km) parallel to the Pacific coast. **2. Ranges.** Series of ranges of extreme W North America along the Pacific Coast from Lower California to SE Alas.

Coates·ville (kōts′vĭl′). City of SE Pa., W of Philadelphia. Pop. 10,698.

Coats Land (kōts). Region of W Antarctica along the SE shore of the Weddell Sea.

Co·at·za·co·al·cos (kô-ä′tsä-kô-äl′-kôs). City of E Mexico, on the Gulf of Campeche. Pop. 120,059.

Cóbh (kōv). Urban district and resort of S Ireland, on Cork Harbor. Pop. 6,670.

Co·blenz also **Ko·blenz** (kō′blĕnts′). City of W West Germany, at the confluence of the Rhine and Moselle rivers. Pop. 113,795.

Co·bourg (kō′bûrg′). Town of S Ont., Canada, on Lake Ontario ENE of Toronto. Pop. 11,264.

Co·burg (kō′bûrg′, -bərg) **1.** City of SE Australia, near Melbourne. Pop. 57,100. **2.** City of E central West Germany, N of Nuremberg. Pop. 45,906.

Co·cha·bam·ba (kô′chä-bäm′bä). City of E central Bolivia, NNW of Sucre. Pop. 205,002.

Co·chin (kō′chĭn′). **1.** Region and former state of SW India, on the Malabar Coast. **2.** City of SW India, on the Malabar Coast; site of Portuguese settlement (1503). Pop. 439,066.

Cochin Chi·na (chī′nə). Region of S Indochina comprising the S part of present-day Vietnam.

Co·chi·nos Bay (kô-chē′nôs). Bay of Pigs.

Co·co (kô′kô′). River rising in NW Nicaragua and flowing c. 450 mi (724 km) NE on the Nicaragua-Honduras border to the Caribbean.

Co·coa (kō′kō). City of E central Fla., ESE of Orlando.Pop. 16,096.

Cocoa Beach. City of E central Fla., on a barrier beach ESE of Cocoa. Pop. 10,926.

Co·cos (kō′kōs). Island group in the E Indian Ocean SW of Sumatra, administered by Australia.

Cod (kŏd), **Cape.** Peninsula of SE Mass., extending c. 65 mi (105 km) E and N into the Atlantic.

Coeur d'A·lene (kôr də-lān′). City of N Idaho, in the Panhandle E of Spokane, Wash., on **Coeur d'Alene Lake** (c. 60 sq mi/155 sq km). Pop. 20,054.

Cof·fey·ville (kô′fē-vĭl′). City of SE Kans., near the Okla. border. Pop. 15,185.

Co·glians (kōl-yäns′), **Monte.** *Italian.* Kellerwand.

Co·hoes (kə-hōz′). City of E N.Y., on the Hudson R. near Albany. Pop. 18,144.

Coim·ba·tore (koim′bä-tōr′, -tôr′). City of S India, SSW of Bangalore. Pop. 356,368.

Coim·bra (kwēm′brə). City of central Portugal, S of Oporto. Pop. 55,985.

Col·ches·ter (kōl′chĕs′tər, -chĭ-stər). **1.** Borough of SE England, near the North Sea. Pop. 132,800. **2.** Town of NW Vt., near Burlington. Pop. 12,629.

Col·chis (kŏl′kĭs). Ancient region on the Black Sea S of the Caucasus.

Cold Harbor (kōld). Locality in E Va., ENE of Richmond, where Confederates defeated Union forces in 2 battles (1862, 1864).

Cold·wa·ter (kōld′wô′tər, -wŏt′ər). River, 220 mi (354 km), of NW Miss.

Co·li·ma (kô-lē′mä). City of SW Mexico, W of Mexico City. Pop. 72,074.

Col·lege Park (kŏl′ĭj). **1.** City of NW Ga., near Atlanta. Pop. 24,632. **2.** City of central Md., near Washington, D.C. Pop. 23,614.

College Sta·tion (stā′shən). City of E central Tex., NW of Houston. Pop. 37,272.

Col·lings·wood (kŏl′ĭngz-wōōd′). Borough of SW N.J., near Camden. Pop. 15,838.

Col·ling·wood (kŏl′ĭng-wōōd′). Town of S Ont., Canada, at the S end of Georgian Bay. Pop. 11,550.

Col·lins·ville (kŏl′ĭnz-vĭl′). City of SW Ill., near East St. Louis. Pop. 19,613.

Col·mar (kōl′mär, kôl-mär′). City of E France between the Vosges Mts. and the Rhine. Pop. 64,771.

Co·logne (kə-lōn′). City of W West Germany, on the Rhine. Pop. 976,136.

Co·lombes (kô-lôɴb′). City of N France, near Paris. Pop. 83,390.

Co·lom·bi·a (kə-lŭm′bē-ə, kô-lôm′-byä). Country of NW South America with coastlines on the Pacific and the Caribbean. Cap. Bogotá. Pop. 22,551,811. **—Co·lom′bian** *adj. & n.*

Colombia

Co·lom·bo (kō-lŭm′bō). Cap. of Sri Lanka, on the W coast. Metro. area pop. 1,540,000.

Co·lón (kô-lōn′). City of N Panama, at the Caribbean entrance to the Panama Canal. Pop. 73,600.

Co·lo·ni·al Heights (kə-lō′nē-əl). City of SE Va., S of Richmond. Pop. 16,509.

Col·o·ra·do (kŏl′ə-răd′ō, -rä′dō). **1.** River of central Argentina, flowing 530 mi (852.8 km) SE to the Atlantic. **2.** River of the SW U.S., flowing 1,450 mi (2,333 km) SW through the **Colorado Plateau** of W Colo., SE Utah, and W Ariz. to the Gulf of California in NW Mexico. **3.** River of Tex., flowing 894 mi (1,438.5 km) SE to the Gulf of Mexico. **4.** Desert in SE Calif. and NW Mexico. **5.** State of the W central U.S. Cap. Denver. Pop. 2,888,834. **—Col′o·ra′dan** *adj. & n.*

Colorado Springs. City of central Colo., SSE of Denver. Pop. 215,150.

Co·los·sae (kə-lŏs′ē). Ancient city of central Asia Minor. **—Co·los′sian** *adj. & n.*

Col·ton (kōl′tən). City of S Calif., near San Bernardino. Pop. 27,419.

Co·lum·bi·a (kə-lŭm′bē-ə). **1.** River of SE B.C., Canada, and NW U.S., flowing 1,210 mi (1,945 km) S then W along the Wash.-Ore. border to the Pacific. **2. District of.** See **District of Columbia. 3.** Cape on the N coast of Ellesmere Island; northernmost point of Canada. **4.** City of central Mo., NW of Jefferson City. Pop. 62,061. **5.** Borough of SE Pa., near Lancaster. Pop. 10,466. **6.** Cap. of S.C., in the central part. Pop. 99,296. **7.** City of central Tenn., SSW of Nashville. Pop. 25,767.

Columbia Heights. City of E Minn., near Minneapolis. Pop. 20,029.

Co·lum·bus (kə-lŭm′bəs). **1.** City of W Ga., on the Ala. border SSW of Atlanta. Pop. 169,441. **2.** City of S central Ind., SSE of Indianapolis. Pop. 30,292. **3.** City of NE Miss., near the Ala. border. Pop. 27,383. **4.** City of E central Nebr., W of Omaha. Pop. 17,328. **5.** Cap. of Ohio, in the central part. Pop. 564,871.

Col·ville (kŏl′vĭl′, kōl′-). River, c. 320 mi (515 km), of N Alas.

Col·wyn Bay (kŏl′wĭn). Borough of N Wales, on the Irish Sea. Pop. 25,370.

Com·ba·hee (kŭm′bē). River, c. 140 mi (225 km), of S S.C.

Com·mand·er (kə-măn′dər). *English.* Komandorskie.

Com·merce (kŏm′ərs). City of S Calif., near Los Angeles. Pop. 10,509.

Commerce City. City of N central Colo., near Denver. Pop. 16,234.

Com·mon·wealth of Nations (kŏm′ən-wĕlth′) Association consisting of the United Kingdom, its dependencies, and many former British colonies.

Com·mu·nism (kŏm′yə-nĭz′əm), **Mount.** Highest mountain (24,590 ft/7,500 m) in the USSR, in the Pamirs near the Chinese border.

Co·mo (kō′mō). Resort city of N Italy, near the Swiss border at the SW end of **Lake Como** (c. 56 sq mi/145 sq km). Pop. 96,665.

Com·o·rin (kŏm′ər-ĭn). Cape at the southernmost point of India.

Com·o·ro (kŏm′ə-rō′) or **Com·o·ros** (-rōz′). Island group off SE Africa, between Mozambique and Madagascar; an independent nation excluding the French island of Mayotte. Cap. Moroni. Pop. 292,000.

Com·piégne (kôɴ-pyĕn′yə). City of N France, NE of Paris. Pop. 37,669.

Comp·ton (kŏmp′tən). City of S Calif., near Long Beach. Pop. 81,286.

Com·stock Lode (kŏm′stŏk′ lōd). Gold and silver vein discovered in 1859 at Virginia City, W Nev.

Con·a·kry (kŏn′ə-krē). Cap. of Guinea, W Africa, in the SW part on the Atlantic. Metro. area pop. 290,000.

Con·cep·ción (kôn-sĕp′syôn). City of W central Chile, near the Pacific coast SSW of Santiago. Metro. area pop. 395,000.

Concepción del Ur·u·guay (dĕl ōō-rōō-gwī′). City of NE Argentina, on the Uruguay R. N of Buenos Aires. Pop. 38,967.

Con·chos (kôn′chôs). River of NW Mexico, flowing c. 350 mi (563 km) NE to the Rio Grande.

Con·cord (kŏng′kərd). **1.** City of W central Calif., NE of Oakland. Pop. 103,251. **2.** Town of E Mass., WNW of Boston. Pop.16,293. **3.** Cap. of N.H., in the S central part. Pop. 30,400. **4.** (kŏn′kôrd′). City of S central N.C., NE of Charlotte. Pop. 16,942.

Con·cor·dia (kông-kôr′*thy*ä). City of NE Argentina, on the Uruguay R. N of Buenos Aires. Pop. 72,136.

Con·ey Island (kō′nē). Resort district of Brooklyn, New York City, on the Atlantic.

Con·go (kŏng′gō). **1.** River of central Africa, flowing c. 2,900 mi (4,666 km) N, W, and SW through the region of **the Congo** in Zambia and Zaire to the Atlantic. **2.** Republic of W central

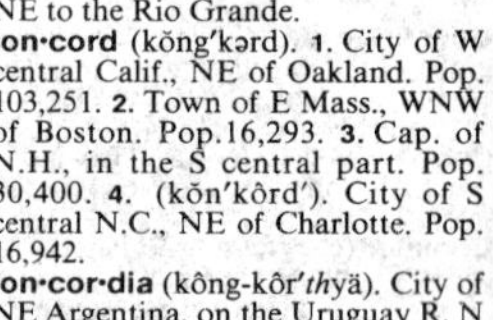

Congo

Africa, W of Zaire. Cap. Brazzaville. Pop. 1,405,000. **3. Democratic Republic of the.** Zaire. —**Con'go·lese'** (-lēz', -lēs') *adj. & n.*

Con·ne·aut (kŏn'ē-ŏt'). City of extreme NE Ohio, on Lake Erie near the Pa. border. Pop. 13,835.

Con·nect·i·cut (kə-nĕt'ĭ-kət). **1.** River of NE U.S., flowing 407 mi (654.9 km) from N N.H. S along the Vt.-N.H. border and through Mass. and Conn. to Long Is. Sound. **2.** State of NE U.S. Cap. Hartford. Pop. 3,107,576.

Con·nells·ville (kŏn'əlz-vĭl'). City of SW Pa., SE of Pittsburgh. Pop. 10,319.

Con·ne·ma·ra (kŏn'ə-mär'ə). Region of W Ireland on the Atlantic coast.

Con·ners·ville (kŏn'ərz-vĭl'). City of E central Ind., E of Indianapolis. Pop. 17,023.

Con·roe (kŏn'rō). City of SE Tex., NNW of Houston. Pop. 18,034.

Con·stance (kŏn'stənts). City of SW West Germany, on the **Lake of Constance** (207 sq mi/ 536.1 sq km), on the borders between SW West Germany, N Switzerland, and W Austria. Pop. 67,948.

Con·stan·ţa (kôn-stän'tsä). City of SE Rumania, on the Black Sea. Pop. 267,612.

Con·stan·tine (kŏn'stən-tēn', kôN-stäN-tēn'). City of NE Algeria, E of Algiers. Pop. 350,183.

Con·stan·ti·no·ple (kŏn'stăn-tə-nō'pəl). Istanbul.

Con·way (kŏn'wā'). **1.** City of central Ark., NNW of Little Rock. Pop. 20,275. **2.** City of E S.C., NE of Charleston. Pop. 10,240.

Cook (kŏŏk). **1. Inlet.** Inlet of the Pacific in S Alas., W of the Kenai Peninsula. **2. Strait.** Channel separating North and South Is., New Zealand. **3. Mount.** Highest mountain, 12,349 ft (3,766.4 m), of New Zealand, on South Is. in the Southern Alps. **4. Mount.** One of the St. Elias Mts., 13,760 ft (4,196.8 m), on the Alas.-Y.T., Canada, border. **5.** Island group of the S Pacific, NE of New Zealand, which holds sovereignty. Pop. 21,227.

Cooke·ville (kŏŏk'vĭl'). City of central Tenn., E of Nashville. Pop. 20,350.

Coo·mas·sie (kōō-mä'sē, -măs'ē). Kumasi.

Coon Rapids (kōōn). City of E Minn., near Minneapolis. Pop. 35,826.

Coo·per City (kōō'pər). City of SE Fla., SW of Fort Lauderdale. Pop. 10,140.

Coo·sa (kōō'sə). River, 286 mi (460.2 km), of NW Ga. and N Ala.

Coos Bay (kōōs). City of SW Ore., SW of Eugene on **Coos Bay**, an inlet of the Pacific. Pop. 14,424.

Co·pán (kō-pän'). Ruined Mayan city in W Honduras.

Co·pen·ha·gen (kō'pən-hā'gən, -hä'-). Cap. of Denmark, in the E part on the E coast of Sjaelland. Metro. area pop. 1,470,000.

Co·pia·pó (kō'pyä-pō'). **1.** Volcano, 19,947 ft (6,083.8 m), in the Andes of N central Chile. **2.** City of N central Chile, W of the volcano. Pop. 51,809.

Cop·per (kŏp'ər). River, c. 300 mi (483 km), of SE Alas.

Cop·per·as Cove (kŏp'ər-əs). City of central Tex., SW of Waco. Pop. 19,469.

Cop·per·mine (kŏp'ər-mīn'). River of N N.W.T., Canada, flowing c. 525 mi (845 km) N to the Arctic Ocean.

Co·quil·hat·ville (kô-kē-yä-vēl'). Mbandaka.

Co·quim·bo (kô-kēm'bô). City of N central Chile, on the Pacific. Pop. 50,405.

Cor·al (kôr'əl, kŏr'-). Sea of the SW Pacific between NE Australia, SE New Guinea, and New Hebrides.

Coral Ga·bles (gā'bəlz). City of SE Fla., near Miami. Pop. 43,241.

Coral Springs. City of SE Fla., near Fort Lauderdale. Pop. 37,349.

Co·ran·tijn (kō'rän-tīn). *Dutch.* Courantyne.

Cor·co·va·do (kôr'kô-vä'dōō). Mountain, 2,310 ft (704.6 m), of SE Brazil, overlooking Rio de Janeiro.

Cor·cy·ra (kôr-sī'rə). Corfu.

Cor·dele (kôr-dēl', kôr'dēl'). City of S central Ga., S of Macon. Pop. 10,914.

Cor·di·lle·ra Cen·tral (kôr'dĭl-yâr'ə sĕn-träl', kôr'*thē*-yĕ'rä). **1.** Central of three ranges of the Andes in W Colombia. **2.** Range of central Dominican Republic. **3.** Range of the Andes in N central Peru. **4.** Range of N Luzon, Philippines. **5.** Range of S central Puerto Rico.

Cordillera de Mé·ri·da (dĕ mĕ'rē-*thä*). Range of W Venezuela.

Cordillera Oc·ci·den·tal (ôk'sē-*thĕn*-täl'). **1.** W range of the Andes in W Colombia. **2.** W range of the Andes in Peru along the Pacific coast.

Cordillera O·rien·tal (ô-ryĕn-täl'). **1.** E range of the Andes in central Bolivia. **2.** E range of the Andes in W Colombia. **3.** E range of the Andes in SE Peru.

Cordillera Re·al (rē-äl'). **1.** Range of the Andes in W Bolivia. **2.** Range of the Andes in Ecuador.

Cor·dil·le·ras (kôr'dĭl-yâr'əz, -dē-yĕ'räs). Entire complex of ranges of W North, Central, and South America from Alas. to Cape Horn.

Cór·do·ba (kôr'dô-bə, -bä). **1.** City of N central Argentina, NW of Buenos Aires. Pop. 985,000. **2.** City of S Spain, on the Guadalquivir R. Pop. 276,255. —**Cor'do·van** *adj. & n.*

Cor·en·tyn (kŏr'ən-tīn'). Variant of **Courantyne.**

Cor·fu (kôr'fōō, -fyōō, kôr-fōō'). **1.** One of the Ionian Is. of Greece, 227 sq mi (587.9 sq km), off the NW mainland coast. **2.** City of NW Greece, on E coast of Corfu. Pop. 28,630.

Cor·inth (kôr'ĭnth, kŏr'-). **1. Gulf of.** Inlet of the Ionian Sea between the Peloponnesus and central Greece. **2.** Isthmus connecting the Peloponnesus to the rest of Greece, crossed by the **Corinth Canal** (4 mi/6.4 km). **3.** Region of ancient Greece including the Isthmus of Corinth and adjacent NE Peloponnesus. **4.** City of Greece in the NE Peloponnesus, on the Gulf of Corinth near site of the ancient city of **Corinth.** Pop. 20,773. **5.** City of NE Miss., near the Tenn. border. Pop. 13,839. —**Co·rin'thi·an** *adj. & n.*

Cork (kôrk). City of S Ireland, a river port near the head of **Cork Harbor,** an inlet of the Atlantic. Pop. 138,267.

Corn Belt (kôrn bĕlt). Agricultural region of the central U.S. centered in Iowa and Ill.

Cor·ner Brook (kôr'nər). City of W central N.F., Canada, WNW of St. John's. Pop. 25,198.

Corn·ing (kôr'nĭng). City of S N.Y., near the Pa. border WNW of Elmira. Pop. 12,953.

Cor·no (kôr'nō), **Mount** or **Monte.** Highest peak (9,560 ft/2,915.8 m) of the Apennines, in central Italy.

Corn·wall (kôrn'wôl'). **1.** Region of extreme SW England. **2.** City of SE Ont., Canada, on the St. Lawrence and the N.Y. border SW of Ottawa. Pop. 46,271.

Corn·wal·lis (kôrn-wŏl'ĭs). Island of N.W.T., Canada, NW of Baffin Island.

Co·ro (kô'rô). City of NW Venezuela, near the Caribbean ENE of Maracaibo. Pop. 68,701.

Cor·o·man·del Coast (kôr'ə-măn'dl). SE coast of India.

Co·ro·na (kə-rō'nə). City of S Calif., near Riverside. Pop. 37,791.

Cor·o·na·do (kôr'ə-nä'dō, kŏr'-). City of S Calif., near San Diego. Pop. 16,859.

Cor·pus Chris·ti (kôr'pəs krĭs'tē). City of S Tex., E of San Antonio on **Corpus Christi Bay,** an arm of the Gulf of Mexico. Pop. 231,999.

Cor·reg·i·dor (kə-rĕg'ĭ-dôr', -dōr', kôr-rĕ'hē-*thôr*'). Island, c. 2 sq mi (5 sq km), of N Philippines, at the entrance to Manila Bay.

Cor·ri·en·tes (kôr'rē-ĕn'tĕs). City of NE Argentina, across the Paraná from Paraguay. Pop. 186,000.

Corse (kôrs). *French.* Corsica.

Cor·si·ca (kôr'sĭ-kə). Island of France, in the Mediterranean N of Sardinia. —**Cor'si·can** *adj. & n.*

Cor·si·ca·na (kôr'sĭ-kăn'ə). City of NE Tex., SSE of Dallas. Pop. 21,712.

Cort·land (kôrt'lənd). City of central N.Y., S of Syracuse. Pop. 20,138.

Co·rum·bá (kô'rōōm-bä'). City of SW Brazil, on the Paraguay R. opposite Bolivia. Pop. 48,607.

Co·ru·ña (kô-rōō'nyä), **La.** See **La Coruña.**

Cor·val·lis (kôr-văl'ĭs). City of W Ore., SSW of Salem. Pop. 40,960.

Cos (kŏs). *Latin.* Kos.

Co·sen·za (kō-zĕn'tsä). City of S Italy, NNE of Reggio di Calabria. Pop. 102,338.

Co·shoc·ton (kō-shŏk'tən). City of central Ohio, ENE of Columbus. Pop. 13,405.

Cos·ta Bra·va (kŏs'tə brä'və, kô'stə, kō'-, kôs'tä brä'vä). NE coast of Spain from Barcelona to the French border.

Cos·ta Me·sa (kŏs'tə mā'sə, kō'stə). City of S Calif., near Santa Ana. Pop. 82,291.

Cos·ta Ri·ca (kŏs'tə rē'kə, kô'stə, kō'-, kôs'tä rē'kä). Country of Central America between Panama and Nicaragua. Cap. San José. Pop. 1,993,800. —**Cos'ta Ri'can** *adj. & n.*

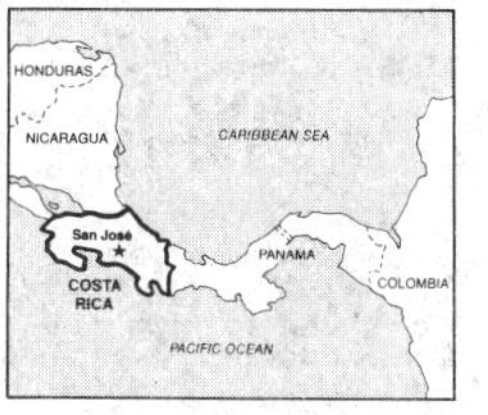

Costa Rica

Côte d'A·zur (kôt dä-zür'). Mediterranean coast of SE France.

Co·ten·tin (kô-täN-tăN'). Peninsula of NW France extending into the English Channel E of the Channel Is.

Côte-Saint-Luc (kōt-sānt-lōōk', -sənt-). City of S Que., Canada, near Montreal. Pop. 26,000.

Co·to·nou (kō'tə-nōō'). City of S Benin, W Africa, on the Gulf of Guinea. Pop. 178,000.

Co·to·pax·i (kō'tə-păk'sē, kô'tô-pä'hē). Active volcano, 19,347 ft (5,900.8 m), in the Andes of central Equador.

Cots·wold (kŏts'wōld', -wəld). Hills of SW England, extending c. 50 mi (80 km) NE from Bristol and rising to c. 1,080 ft (330 m).

Cot·tage Grove (kŏt'ĭj). City of E Minn., near St. Paul. Pop. 18,994.

Cott·bus or **Kott·bus** (kŏt'bəs, kôt'bōōs). City of SE East Germany, near the Polish border. Pop. 107,623.

Cot·ti·an Alps (kŏt'ē-ən ălps'). Alpine range between NW Italy and SE France, rising to 12,602 ft (3,843.6 m).

Cot·ton·wood (kŏt'n-wŏŏd'). River, c. 140 mi (225 km), of SW Minn.

Coun·cil Bluffs (koun'səl blŭfs'). City of SW Iowa, on the Missouri opposite Omaha, Nebr. Pop. 56,449.

Coun·try Club Hills (kŭn'trē klŭb'). City of NE Ill., S of Chicago. Pop. 14,676.

Cour·an·tyne also **Cor·en·tyne** (kôr'ən-tīn'). River, c. 450 mi (725 km), rising in SE Guyana and forming the Guyana-Surinam border in its lower course.

Cour·be·voie (kōōr-bə-vwä'). City of N France, on the Seine near Paris. Pop. 54,448.

Cour·trai (kōōr-trā'). *French.* Kortrijk.

Cov·en·try (kŭv'ĭn-trē). **1.** City of central England, ESE of Birmingham. Pop. 339,300. **2.** Town of W central R.I., SW of Providence. Pop. 27,065.

Co·vi·lhã (kōō-vē-lyäN'). Town of E central Portugal, NE of Lisbon. Pop. 26,530.

Co·vi·na (kō-vē'nə). City of S Calif., E of Los Angeles. Pop. 33,751.

Cov·ing·ton (kŭv'ĭng-tən). **1.** City of N central Ga., ESE of Atlanta. Pop. 10,586. **2.** City of extreme N Ky., on the Ohio opposite Cincinnati. Pop. 49,013. **3.** Independent city of W Va., N of Roanoke. Pop. 9,063.

Cow·ans·ville (kou'ənz-vĭl'). Town of S Que., Canada, SE of Montreal. Pop. 11,900.

Cowes (kouz). Town of N coast of Isle of Wight, S England. Pop. 19,190.

Cow·litz (kou'lĭts). River, c. 130 mi (209 km), of SW Wash.

Crac·ow (krăk'ou, krä'kou, krä'kōōv). *English.* Kraków.

Cra·io·va (krä-yô'vä). City of S Rumania, W of Bucharest. Pop. 230,721.

Cran·brook (krăn'brŏŏk'). City of SE B.C., Canada, near the Alta. and Idaho borders. Pop. 13,510.

Cran·ston (krăn'stən). City of E central R.I., near Providence. Pop. 71,992.

Cra·ter (krā'tər). Lake, c. 20 sq mi (52 sq km) and 1,932 ft (589.3 m) deep, of SW Ore., in a volcanic crater in **Crater Lake National Park.**

Craw·fords·ville (krô'fərdz-vĭl'). City of W central Ind., S of Lafayette. Pop. 13,325.

Cré·cy (krĕs'ē, krā-sē') or **Cré·cy-en-Pon·thieu** (-äN-pôN-tyœ', -tyœ'). Town of N France, NW of Amiens; site of English victory (1346) in the Hundred Years' War.

Cre·mo·na (krĭ-mō'nə, krā-mō'nä). City of N Italy, on the Po SE of Milan. Pop. 82,056.

Crest·wood (krĕst'wŏŏd'). **1.** Village of NE Ill., near Chicago. Pop. 10,712. **2.** City of E Mo., near St. Louis. Pop. 12,815.

Crete (krēt). **1. Sea of.** Part of the S Aegean Sea between Crete and the Cyclades. **2.** Island of SE Greece, in the E Mediterranean. —**Cre'tan** *adj. & n.*

Creve Coeur (krēv' kŏŏr'). City of E Mo., NW of St. Louis. Pop. 12,694.

Crewe (krōō). Borough of W central England, SE of Liverpool. Pop. 50,450.

Cri·me·a (krī-mē'ə, krĭ-). Peninsula of S European USSR, on the Black Sea and Sea of Azov. —**Cri·me'an** *adj.*

Crip·ple Creek (krĭp'əl). Town of central Colo., once a gold-mining center.

Cro·a·tia (krō-ā'shə, -shē-ə). **1.** Region and former kingdom of S Europe, along the NE Adriatic coast. **2.** Region of NW Yugoslavia. —**Cro·a'tian** *adj. & n.*

Croc·o·dile (krŏk'ə-dīl'). Limpopo.

Crom·well (krŏm'wĕl', -wəl). Town of central Conn., S of Hartford. Pop. 10,265.

Cros·by (krôz'bē) or **Great Crosby** (grāt). Borough of NW England, on Liverpool Bay near Liverpool. Pop. 56,750.

Cross (krôs, krŏs). River, c. 300 mi (483 km), of W Cameroon and SE Nigeria.

Cro·to·ne (krō-tō'nā). City of S Italy, on the Ionian Sea NE of Reggio di Calabria; site of ancient city of **Cro·to·na** (krə-tō'nə). Pop. 57,009.

Crow·ley (krou'lē). City of S La., SSW of Baton Rouge. Pop. 16,306.

Crown Point (kroun point'). City of NW Ind., S of Gary. Pop. 16,455.

Crys·tal (krĭs'təl). City of E Minn., near Minneapolis. Pop. 25,543.

Crystal Lake. City of NE Ill., N of Elgin. Pop. 18,590.

Ctes·i·phon (tĕs'ə-fŏn', tĕ'sĭ-). Ancient city of central Iraq, on the Tigris SE of Baghdad.

Cuan·za or **Kwan·za** (kwän'zə). River, c. 600 mi (965 km), of W Angola.

Cu·ba (kyōō'bə, kōō'bä). Island re-

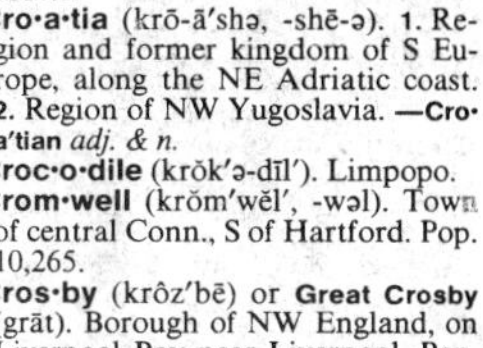

Cuba

public in the Caribbean S of Fla. Cap. Havana. Pop. 8,553,400. —**Cu'ban** *adj. & n.*

Cú·cu·ta (ko͞o'kə-tə, -ko͞o-tä'). City of NE Colombia, near the Venezuelan border. Pop. 355,000.

Cud·a·hy (kŭd'ə-hē). **1.** City of S Calif., SE of Los Angeles. Pop. 17,984. **2.** City of SE Wis., near Milwaukee. Pop. 19,547.

Cuen·ca (kwĕng'kä). City of S central Ecuador, SE of Guayaquil. Pop. 128,788.

Cuer·na·va·ca (kwĕr-nä-vä'kä). City of S central Mexico, in the **Cuernavaca Valley** near Mexico City. Pop. 226,600.

Cu·ia·bá (ko͞o'yə-bä'). City of W central Brazil, W of Brasília. Pop. 83,621.

Cui·to (kwē'tô). River, c. 400 mi (664 km), of SE Angola.

Cu·lia·cán (ko͞o'lyä-kän'). City of W Mexico, on the **Culiacán R.** (c. 175 mi/282 km) WNW of Durango. Pop. 302,200.

Cull·man (kŭl'mən). City of N Ala., N of Birmingham. Pop. 13,084.

Cul·lo·den (kə-lŏd'n, -lōd'n). Moor in N Scotland, E of Inverness; site of defeat of Highland Jacobites by English forces (1746).

Cul·ver City (kŭl'vər). City of S Calif., near Los Angeles. Pop. 38,139.

Cu·mae (kyo͞o'mē). Ancient city and Greek colony of S central Italy, near present-day Naples.

Cu·ma·ná (ko͞o'mä-nä'). City of NE Venezuela, on the Caribbean E of Caracas. Pop. 153,000.

Cum·ber·land (kŭm'bər-lənd). **1.** River of S Ky. and N Tenn., flowing c. 690 mi (1,110 km) W to the Ohio. **2.** Falls, 92 ft (28.1 m) high, on the upper Cumberland in SE Ky. **3. Plateau** or **Mountains.** SW section of the Appalachians, extending along the Va.-Ky. border and into central Tenn. **4. Gap.** Pass, 1,304 ft (397.7 m), through the Cumberland Mts. near junction of Ky., Va., and Tenn. borders. **5.** Town of SE Ont., Canada near Ottawa. Pop. 13,541. **6.** City of NW Md., on the W.Va. border. Pop. 25,933. **7.** Town of NE R.I., near Providence. Pop. 27,069.

Cum·bri·an (kŭm'brē-ən). Mountains of NW England, rising to a height of 3,210 ft (979 m).

Cu·nax·a (kyo͞o-năk'sə). Ancient town of Babylonia, NW of Babylon.

Cu·ne·ne or **Ku·ne·ne** (ko͞o-nā'nə). River, c. 750 mi (1,205 km), of SW Angola, forming the Angola Namibia border in its lower course.

Cu·ne·o (ko͞o'nā-ō). City of NW Italy, W of Genoa. Pop. 55,784.

Cu·per·ti·no (ko͞o'pər-tē'nō). City of W Calif., W of San Jose. Pop. 25,770.

Cu·ra·çao (kyo͞o'rə-sō, ko͞o'rä-sä'ō). Island of the Netherlands Antilles, in the S Caribbean off the NW coast of Venezuela.

Cu·ri·có (ko͞o-rē-kô'). City of central Chile, SSW of Santiago. Pop. 59,621.

Cu·ri·ti·ba (ko͞or'ĭ-tē'bə, ko͞o'rē-). City of SE Brazil, SW of São Paulo. Pop. 905,800.

Cush also **Kush** (kŭsh, ko͝osh). Legendary ancient region of NE Africa, often identified with Ethiopia.

Cutch (kŭch). Variant of **Kutch.**

Cut·tack (kŭ-tăk'). City of E India, SW of Calcutta. Pop. 194,068.

Cux·ha·ven (ko͝oks'hä'fən). City of N West Germany, at the mouth of the Elbe R. Pop. 58,891.

Cuy·a·ho·ga Falls (kī'ə-hō'gə, kə-hō'-, -hô'-, -hä'-). City of NE Ohio, near Akron. Pop. 43,710.

Cu·yu·ni (ko͞o-yo͞o'nē). River, c. 350 mi (563 km), of E Venezuela and NW Guyana.

Cuz·co or **Cus·co** (ko͞o'skō, -skô). City of S Peru, in the Andes ESE of Lima; ancient Inca capital. Pop. 67,658.

Cyc·la·des (sĭk'lə-dēz'). Island of group of SE Greece, in the S Aegean.

Cy·press (sī'prĭs). City of S Calif., near Long Beach. Pop. 40,391.

Cy·prus (sī'prəs). Island republic in the E Mediterranean S of Turkey. Cap. Nicosia. Pop. 639,000. —**Cyp'ri·ot** (sĭp'rē-ət), **Cyp'ri·ote** (-ōt', -ət), **Cyp'ri·an** (-rē-ən) *adj. & n.*

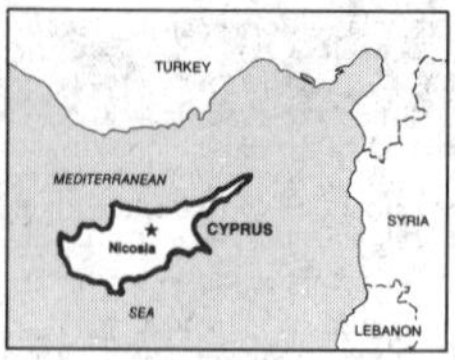

Cyprus

Cyr·e·na·i·ca (sĭr'ə-nā'ĭ-kə, sī'rə-). Ancient region of NE Libya.

Cy·re·ne (sī-rē'nē). Ancient Greek city of Cyrenaica.

Cy·rus (sī'rəs). Kura.

Cy·the·ra (sĭ-thĭr'ə). Island of S Greece, in the Mediterranean S of the Peloponnesus.

Czech·o·slo·va·ki·a (chĕk'ə-slə-vä'kē-ə, -ō-slō-). Country of central Europe. Cap. Prague. Pop. 15,280,148. —**Czech'o·slo'vak, Czech'o·slo·va'ki·an** *adj. & n.*

Czechoslovakia

Czę·stó·cho·wa (chĕɴ'stô-hô'vä). City of S Poland, N of Katowice. Pop. 232,400.

D

Dą·bro·wa Gór·ni·cza (dôm-brô'vä gŏr-nē'chä). City of S Poland, near Katowice. Pop. 137,300.

Dac·ca (dăk'ə). Cap. of Bangladesh, in the E central part. Pop. 1,563,517.

Da·chau (dä'kou, -кнou). City of SE West Germany, near Munich; site of Nazi concentration camp. Pop. 34,162.

Da·ci·a (dā'shē-ə, -shə). Ancient region and Roman province corresponding roughly to modern Rumania. —**Da'ci·an** *adj. & n.*

Da·ho·mey (də-hō'mē, dä-ô-mā'). Benin.

Dai·ren (dī'rĕn'). Lüda.

Da·kar (dä-kär'). Cap. of Senegal, in the W part on Cape Verde. Pop. 798,792.

Da·ko·ta (də-kō'tə). Former U.S. territory divided in 1889 into **the Da·ko·tas** (-təz), North and South Dakota.

Da Lat (dä lät'). City of SE Vietnam, NE of Ho Chi Minh City. Pop. 105,072.

Dal·las (dăl'əs). City of NE Tex., E of Fort Worth. Pop. 904,078.

Dal·ton (dôl'tən). City of NW Ga., SE of Chattanooga, Tenn. Pop. 20,743.

Da·ly City (dā'lē). City of W Calif., near San Francisco. Pop. 78,519.

Da·man·hûr (dä'män-ho͞or'). City of NE Egypt, on the Nile delta NW of Cairo. Pop. 188,927.

Da·mas·cus (də-măs'kəs). Cap. of Syria, in the SW part. Pop. 1,156,000. —**Dam'a·scene'** (dăm'ə-sēn') *adj. & n.*

Dam·a·vand (dăm'ə-vănd', dä'-mä-vänd). Variant of **Demavend.**

Dam·i·et·ta (dăm'ē-ĕt'ə). City of NE Egypt, on the Nile delta NNE of Cairo. Pop. 113,200.

Da·mo·dar (dä'mō-där'). River, c. 370 mi (595 km), of NE India.

Dan (dăn). River, c. 180 mi (290 km), of S Va. and N N.C.

Da Nang (dä' năng'). City of central Vietnam, on the South China Sea. Pop. 492,194.

Dan·bur·y (dăn'bĕr'ē, -bə-rē). City and town of SW Conn., NW of Bridgeport. Pop. 60,470.

Dan·dong (dăn'do͝ong'). City of NE China, on the Yalu R. opposite North Korea. Pop. 300,000.

Da·ni·a (dā'nē-ə). City of SE Fla., near Fort Lauderdale. Pop. 11,811.

Dan·ube (dăn'yo͞ob). River of S central Europe, rising in SW West Germany and flowing c. 1,750 mi (2,816 km) SE through Austria, Hungary, Yugoslavia, and Rumania to the Black Sea. —**Dan·u'bi·an** *adj.*

Dan·vers (dăn'vərz). Town of NE Mass., near Salem. Pop. 24,100.

Dan·ville (dăn'vĭl'). **1.** City of E Ill., ENE of Decatur. Pop. 38,985. **2.** City of central Ky., SSW of Lexington. Pop. 12,942. **3.** Independent city of S Va., near the N.C. border. Pop. 45,642.

Dan·zig (dăn'sĭg, dän'tsĭкн). **1. Gulf of.** Inlet of the S Baltic Sea between N Poland and W European USSR. **2. Free City.** Former state (1919–39) on the Gulf of Danzig surrounding and including Gdańsk. **3.** *German.* Gdańsk.

Dar·by (där'bē). Borough of SE Pa., near Philadelphia. Pop. 11,513.

Dar·da·nelles (där-dn-ĕlz'). Strait, c. 40 mi (65 km) long and 1–4 mi (1.6–6.4 km) wide, connecting the Aegean with the Sea of Marmara.

Dar es Sa·laam (där' ĕs sə-läm'). Cap. of Tanzania, in the E part on the Indian Ocean. Pop. 870,000.

Dar·i·en (dăr'ē-ĕn', dâr'-, dăr'ē-ən, dâr'-). **1.** Town of SW Conn., NW of Stamford. Pop. 18,892. **2.** City of NE Ill., W of Chicago. Pop. 14,968.

Da·ri·én (dâr'ē-ĕn', dä-ryän'). **1. Gulf of.** Bay of the Caribbean between NE Panama and NW Colombia. **2.** Region of E Panama.

Dar·ling (där'lĭng). **1.** River, c. 1,702 mi (2,739 km), of SE Australia. **2.** Range of hills in SW Australia, extending along the coast N and S of Perth.

Dar·ling·ton (där'lĭng-tən). Borough of N England, S of Newcastle-upon-Tyne. Pop. 85,120.

Darm·stadt (därm'stăt, -shtät'). City of central West Germany, near Frankfurt. Pop. 138,661.

Dart·mouth (därt'məth). **1.** City of S N.S., Canada, opposite Halifax. Pop. 65,341. **2.** Town of SE Mass., near New Bedford. Pop. 23,966.

Dar·win (där'wĭn). City of N Australia, on the Timor Sea. Pop. 39,193.

Dasht-e-Ka·vir (däsht'ē-kä-vĭr'). Salt desert of N central Iran.

Da·tong (dä'to͝ong'). City of NE China, W of Beijing. Pop. 350,000.

Dau·gav·pils (dou'gäf-pēls'). City of W European USSR, in Latvia SE of Riga. Pop. 117,000.

Dau·phi·né (dō-fē-nā'). Range of the W Alps in SE France.

Da·vao (dä-vou'). City of SE Mindanao, Philippines, on **Davao Gulf,** an inlet of the Pacific. Pop. 214, 849.

Dav·en·port (dăv'ĭn-pôrt', -pōrt'). City of E Iowa, on the Mississippi opposite Moline and Rock Island, Ill. Pop. 103,264.

Da·vie (dā'vē). Town of SE Fla., SW of Fort Lauderdale. Pop. 20,877.

Da·vis (dā'vĭs). **1.** Strait of the N Atlantic between SE Baffin Is. and SW Greenland. **2.** Mountains of W Tex., SE of El Paso, rising to 8,382 ft (2,556.5 m). **3.** City of N central Calif., W of Sacramento. Pop. 36,640.

Daw·son Creek (dô'sən). City of E B.C., Canada, near the Alta. border NE of Prince George. Pop. 10,528.

Da·xue Shan (dä'sho͞o' shän'). Mountains of S central China, SW of Chengdu.

Day·ton (dāt'n). City of SW Ohio, NNE of Cincinnati. Pop. 203,588.

Day·to·na Beach (dā-tō'nə). City of NE Fla., NNE of Orlando. Pop. 54,176.

Dead Sea (dĕd). Salt lake, c. 390 sq mi (1,010 sq km), between Israel and Jordan; lowest point on earth (surface 1,292 ft/394 m below sea level).

Dear·born (dĭr'bôrn', -bərn). City of SE Mich., W of Detroit. Pop. 90,660.

Dearborn Heights. City of SE Mich., near Detroit. Pop. 67,706.

Death Valley (dĕth). Desert basin, c. 1,500 sq mi (3,885 sq km), of E Calif. and W Nev., containing the lowest point in the Western Hemisphere (280 ft/85.4 m below sea level) and including **Death Valley National Monument.**

De·bre·cen (dĕ'brĕ-tsĕn'). City of E Hungary, E of Budapest. Pop. 195,000.

De·ca·tur (dĭ-kā'tər). **1.** City of N Ala., N of Birmingham. Pop. 42,002. **2.** City of NW Ga., near Atlanta. Pop. 18,404. **3.** City of central Ill., E of Springfield. Pop. 94,081.

Dec·can (dĕk'ən). Plateau of S central India, between the Eastern and Western Ghats.

Ded·ham (dĕd'əm). Town of E Mass., near Boston. Pop. 25,298.

Deer·field (dĭr'fēld'). Village of NE Ill., near Chicago. Pop. 17,430.

Deerfield Beach. City of SE Fla., N of Fort Lauderdale. Pop. 39,193.

Deer Park (dĭr). City of SE Tex., near Houston. Pop. 22,648.

De·fi·ance (dĭ-fī'əns). City of NW Ohio, SW of Toledo. Pop. 16,810.

Deh·ra Dun (dā'rə do͞on'). City of N India, NNE of Delhi. Pop. 166,073.

De Kalb (dĭ kălb'). City of N Ill., SSE of Rockford. Pop. 33,099.

De Land (də lănd'). City of NE Fla., SW of Daytona Beach. Pop. 15,354.

De·la·no (də-lā'nō). City of S central Calif., NNW of Bakersfield. Pop. 16,491.

Del·a·ware (dĕl'ə-wâr'). **1.** River of NE U.S., rising in SE N.Y. and flowing c. 280 mi (451 km) S to **Delaware Bay,** an inlet of the Atlantic between E Del. and SW N.J. **2.** State of NE U.S., on the Atlantic. Cap. Dover. Pop. 595,225. **3.** City of central Ohio, N of Columbus. Pop. 18,780.

Del City (dĕl). City of central Okla., near Oklahoma City. Pop. 28,424.

Delft (dĕlft). City of SW central Netherlands, SE of The Hague. Pop. 83,939.

Del·ga·do (dĕl-gä'dō). Cape on NE coast of Mozambique.

Del·hi (dĕl'ē). **1.** Town of S Ont., Canada, SW of Toronto. Pop. 14,931. **2.** City of N central India, on the Jumna R. Pop. 3,706,558.

Del·mar·va (dĕl-mär'və). Peninsula, c. 180 mi (290 km) long, of NE U.S., between Chesapeake Bay and the Atlantic.

Del·men·horst (dĕl'mən-hôrst'). City of N West Germany, near Bremen. Pop. 72,140.

De·los (dē'lŏs, dĕl'ŏs). Island of SE Greece in the central Cyclades.

Del·phi (dĕl'fī). Ancient town of central Greece, near Mt. Parnassus; seat of an oracle of Apollo.

Del·ray Beach (dĕl'rā). City of SE Fla., N of Boca Raton. Pop. 34,325.

Del Ri·o (dĕl rē'ō). City of SW Tex., on the Rio Grande W of San Antonio. Pop. 30,034.

Dem·a·vend (dĕm'ə-vĕnd') or **Dam·a·vand** (dăm'ə-vănd', dä'mä-vänd). Highest peak (18,934 ft/5,774.9 m) of the Elburz Mts. in N Iran.

Den Hel·der (dən hĕl'dər). City of NW Netherlands, on the North Sea. Pop. 61,761.

Den·i·son (dĕn'ĭ-sən). City of N Tex., near the Okla. border NNE of Dallas. Pop. 23,884.

De·niz·li (dĕ-nēz-lē'). City of SW Turkey, ESE of Izmir. Pop. 134,673.

Den·mark (dĕn'märk'). **1.** Strait, c. 130 mi (209 km) wide, between Greenland and Iceland. **2.** Country of N Europe on Jutland Peninsula and adjacent islands. Cap. Copenhagen. Pop. 5,122,065. —**Dane** (dān) *n.* —**Dan'ish** (dā'nĭsh) *adj. & n.*

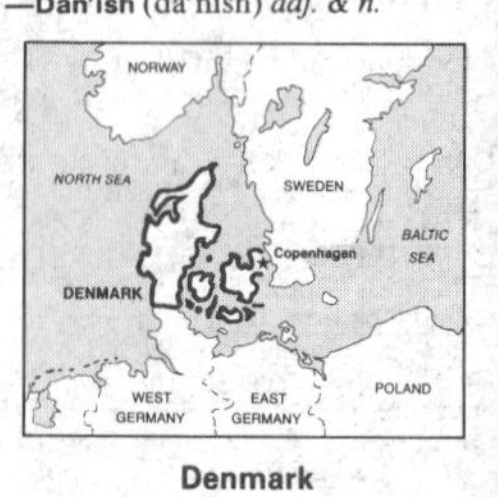

Denmark

Den·nis (dĕn'ĭs). Town of SE Mass., on central Cape Cod. Pop. 12,360.
Den·ton (dĕn'tən). City of NE Tex., NNW of Dallas. Pop. 48,063.
Den·ver (dĕn'vər). Cap. of Colo., in the N central part. Pop. 491,396.
De Pere (də pîr'). City of E Wis., near Green Bay. Pop. 14,892.
De·pew (də-pyōō'). Village of W N.Y., near Buffalo. Pop. 19,819.
Der·by (dûr'bē). **1.** (*also* där'-). City of S central England, NNW of London. Pop. 215,900. **2.** City and town of SW Conn., W of New Haven. Pop. 12,346.
De Rid·der (də rĭd'ər). City of S La., SW of Alexandria. Pop. 11,057.
Der·ry (dĕr'ē). Town of SE N.H., SE of Manchester. Pop. 18,875.
De·se·a·do (dĕ-sĕ-ä'*th*ô). River, c. 380 mi (611 km), of S Argentina.
Des·er·et (dĕz'ə-rĕt'). Area of SW U.S. proposed (1849) by Mormons as a U.S. or an independent state.
Des Moines (də moin'). Cap. of Iowa, in the S central part. Pop. 191,003.
De·sna (dyə-snä'). River, c. 740 mi (1,191 km), of W European USSR.
De So·to (dĭ sō'tō). City of NE Tex., near Dallas. Pop. 15,538.
Des Plaines (dĕs plānz'). **1.** River, c. 110 mi (177 km), of SW Wis. and NE Ill. **2.** City of NE Ill., near Chicago. Pop. 53,568.
Des·sau (dĕs'ou). City of central East Germany, N of Leipzig. Pop. 101,322.
De·troit (dĭ-troit'). City of SE Mich., on the **Detroit R.** (32 mi/51.5 km) opposite Windsor, Ont. Pop. 1,203,-339.
Deur·ne (dûr'nə). City of N Belgium, E of Antwerp. Pop. 78,646.
De·ven·ter (dā'vən-tər). City of E central Netherlands, on the Ijssel R. Pop. 64,561.
Dev·il's Island (dĕv'ĭlz). Island in the Caribbean off French Guiana; formerly a penal colony.
Dev·on (dĕv'ən). Island of NE N.W.T., Canada, between Baffin and Ellesmere Is.
Dezh·nev (dĕzh-nyôf'). Cape of extreme NE Far Eastern USSR, on Bering Strait; easternmost point of Asia.
Dhau·la·gi·ri (dou'lə-gĕr'ē). Peak, 26,810 ft (8,177 m), in the Himalayas of N central Nepal.
Di·a·man·ti·na (dī'ə-mən-tē'nə). River, c. 560 mi (901 km), of E central Australia.
Dia·mond Head (dī'mənd hĕd', dī'-ə-). Promontory, 761 ft (232.1 m) high, on SE coast of Oahu, Hawaii.
Dick·in·son (dĭk'ĭn-sən). City of SW N.Dak., W of Bismarck. Pop. 15,924.
Dien Bien Phu (dyĕn' byĕn' fōō'). Town of NW Vietnam, near the Laos border; site of Vietminh victory over French (1954).
Di·jon (dē-zhôN'). City of E France, SE of Paris. Pop. 151,705.
Di·nar·ic Alps (dĭ-năr'ĭk ălps'). Range of W Yugoslavia, extending c. 400 mi (645 km) along the Adriatic coast.
Di·o·mede (dī'ə-mēd'). Islands in Bering Strait between Alas. and Siberia, comprising **Little Diomede** (U.S.) and **Big Diomede** (USSR).
Dis·mal (dĭz'məl). Swamp of SE Va. and NE N.C.
Dis·trict of Co·lum·bi·a (dĭs'trĭkt'; kə-lŭm'bē-ə). Federal district, 69 sq mi (178.7 sq km), of E U.S., on the Potomac R. between Va. and Md.; coextensive with the city of Washington.
Dix·on (dĭk'sən). City of N Ill., SSW of Rockford. Pop. 15,659.
Di·yar·ba·kir (dē-yär'bä-kîr'). City of SE Turkey, on the Tigris. Pop. 233,289.
Dja·ja Peak (jä'yə). Highest peak of Indonesia, 16,535 ft (5,043.2 m), in central West Irian.
Dja·kar·ta or **Ja·kar·ta** (jə-kär'tə). Cap. of Indonesia, on the Java Sea coast of NW Java. Pop. 6,400,000.
Dji·bou·ti also **Ji·bu·ti** (jĕ-bōō'tē, jə-). **1.** Country of E Africa, on the Gulf of Aden. Pop. 125,000. **2.** Cap. of Djibouti, in the SE part on the Gulf of Aden. Pop. 40,000.

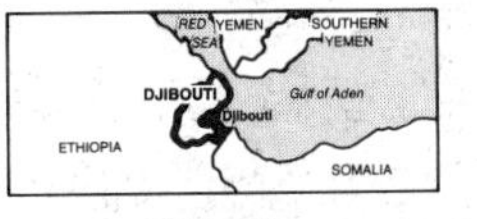

Djibouti

Djok·ja·kar·ta or **Jok·ja·kar·ta** (jŏk'-yə-kär'tə, -jə-) or **Jog·ja·kar·ta** (jŏg'-, jŏk'-). City of Indonesia, in S central Java. Pop. 342,267.
Dne·pro·dzer·zhinsk (dnyĕ'-prə-jər-zhĭnsk'). City of S European USSR, on the Dnieper SW of Kharkov. Pop. 253,000.
Dne·pro·pe·trovsk (dnyĕ'prə-pə-trôfsk'). City of S European USSR, on the Dnieper SSW of Kharkov. Pop. 1,083,000.
Dnie·per (nē'pər, dnyĕ'pĕr). River of W European USSR, rising near Smolensk and flowing c. 1,420 mi (2,285 km) S to the NW Black Sea.
Dnies·ter (nē'stər, dnyĕs'tər). River, c. 850 mi (1,368 km), of SW European USSR.
Dobbs Fer·ry (dŏbz' fer'ē) Village of SE N.Y., on the Hudson near Yonkers. Pop. 10,053.
Do·be·rai (dō'bə-rī'). Peninsula of NW West Irian, New Guinea.
Do·dec·a·nese (dō-dĕk'ə-nēs', -nēz'). Islands of SE Greece, in the Aegean between Turkey and Crete and S of Samos.
Dodge City (dŏj). City of SW Kans., W of Wichita. Pop. 18,001.
Do·do·na (də-dō'nə). Ancient city of NW Greece.
Do·ha (dō'hə, -hä'). Cap. of Qatar, SE Arabia, on the Persian Gulf. Pop. 95,000.
Dol·lard-des-Or·meaux (dô-lär'dā'-zôr-mō'). Town of S Que., Canada, near Montreal. Pop. 39,700.
Do·lo·mites (dō'lə-mīts', dŏl'ə-) or **Do·lo·mite Alps** (-mīt' ălps'). Range of the E Alps in NE Italy.
Dol·ton (dôl'tən, dōl'-). Village of NE Ill., S of Chicago. Pop. 24,766.
Dom·i·ni·ca (dŏm'ə-nē'kə, də-mĭn'-ĭ-kə). Island republic in the E Caribbean, between Guadeloupe and Martinique. Cap. Roseau. Pop. 83,100.
Do·min·i·can Republic (də-mĭn'-ĭ-kən). Republic of the West Indies, on the E part of Hispaniola Is. Cap. Santo Domingo. Pop. 5,660,000.

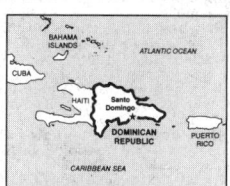

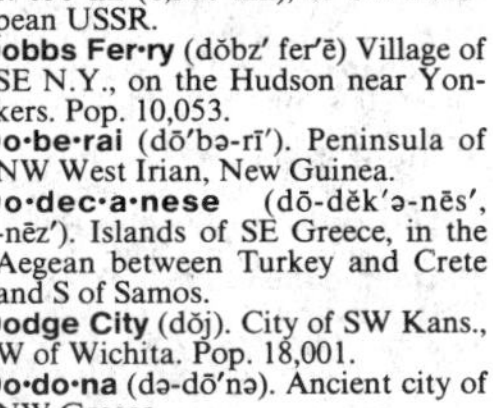

Dominican Republic

Don (dŏn, dôn). River of S European USSR, flowing 1,222 mi (1,966.2 km) into the NE Sea of Azov.
Don·cas·ter (dŏng'kə-stər). Borough of N central England, NE of Sheffield. Pop. 81,530.
Do·nets (dŏ-nĕts'). **1.** River, c. 650 mi (1,046 km), of S European USSR. **2. Basin.** Industrial region of S European USSR, N of the Sea of Azov and W of Donets R.
Door (dōr). Peninsula of E Wis., between Lake Michigan and Green Bay.
Dor·dogne (dôr-dôn'yə). River, c. 305 mi (491 km), of SW France.
Dor·drecht (dôr'drĕkt, -drĕKHt'). City of SW Netherlands, on the Meuse SE of Rotterdam. Pop. 107,453.
Dor·is (dōr'ĭs, dôr'-). Ancient region of central Greece.
Dor·mont (dôr'mŏnt'). Borough of SW Pa., near Pittsburgh. Pop. 11,275.
Dor·set (dôr'sĭt). Cape of SW Baffin Is., E N.W.T., Canada.
Dort (dôrt). Dordrecht.
Dort·mund (dôrt'mənd, -mōōnt'). City of W West Germany, NNE of Cologne. Pop. 609,954.
Dor·val (dôr-văl', -väl'). Town of S Que., Canada, on S shore of Montreal Is. Pop. 19,131.
Do·than (dō'thən). City of SE Ala., near the Fla. border. Pop. 48,750.
Dou·ai (dōō-ā', dwā). Town of N France, NE of Amiens. Pop. 45,239.
Dou·a·la or **Du·a·la** (dōō-ä'lä). City of SW Cameroon, W equatorial Africa, on Bight of Biafra. Pop. 458,246.
Doug·las (dŭg'ləs). **1.** City of SE Ariz., on the Mexican border. Pop. 13,058. **2.** City of S central Ga., SSE of Macon. Pop. 10,980.
Dou·ro (dô'rōō). River, c. 475 mi (764 km), of N Spain and N Portugal.
Do·ver (dō'vər). **1.** Strait, 21 mi (33.8 km) wide, at E end of English Channel between SE England and N France. **2.** Borough of SE England, on the Strait of Dover opposite Calais, France. Pop. 34,160. **3.** Cap. of Del., in the central part. Pop. 23,512. **4.** City of SE N.H., near Portsmouth. Pop. 22,377. **5.** Town of N central N.J., near Morristown. Pop. 14,681. **6.** City of E Ohio, S of Akron. Pop. 11,526.
Dow·ners Grove (dou'nərz). Village of NE Ill., W of Chicago. Pop. 39,274.
Dow·ney (dou'nē). City of S Calif., N of Long Beach. Pop. 82,602.
Downs (dounz). 2 parallel hill ranges of SE England, **The North Downs** and **The South Downs.**
Dra·cut (drā'kət). Town of NE Mass., near Lowell. Pop. 21,249.
Dra·kens·burg (drä'kənz-bûrg'). Range of E South Africa, Lesotho, and Swaziland, rising to 11,425 ft (3,484.6 m).
Drake Passage (drāk). Strait, c. 500 mi (805 km) wide, between Cape Horn and Antarctica.
Dram·men (dräm'ən). City of SE Norway, WSW of Oslo. Pop. 49,700.
Dran·cy (dräN-sē'). City of N central France, near Paris. Pop. 64,430.
Dra·va or **Dra·ve** (drä'və). River, c. 450 mi (725 km), of S Austria and N Yugoslavia.
Dres·den (drĕz'dən, drās'-). City of SE East Germany, on the Elbe ESE of Leipzig. Pop. 514,508.
Drum·mond·ville (drŭm'ənd-vĭl'). City of S Que., Canada, NE of Montreal. Pop. 27,800.
Dry Tor·tu·gas (drī tôr-tōō'gəz). Islands of S Fla., W of Key West; once a pirate base.
Du·a·la (dōō-ä'lä). Variant of **Douala.**
Duar·te (dwär'tē). City of S Calif., ENE of Los Angeles. Pop. 16,766.
Du·bai (dōō-bī'). City and Sheikdom of E United Arab Emirates, E Arabia, on the Persian Gulf. Pop. 60,000.
Du·bawnt (dōō-bônt'). River, 580 mi (993.2 km), of SE N.W.T., Canada, flowing through **Dubawnt Lake** (1,654 sq mi/4,284 sq km).
Dub·lin (dŭb'lĭn). **1.** Cap. of Ireland, in the E central part on the Irish Sea. Pop. 544,586. **2.** Town of W Calif., ESE of Oakland. Pop. 13,641. **3.** City of central Ga., ESE of Macon. Pop. 16,083. **—Dub'lin·er** *n.*
Du·brov·nik (dōō'brôv-nĭk'). City of SW Yugoslavia, on the Adriatic. Pop. 31,106.
Du·buque (də-byōōk'). City of E Iowa, on the Mississippi opposite the Ill.-Wis. border. Pop. 62,321.
Dud·ley (dŭd'lē). Borough of W central England, WNW of Birmingham. Pop. 296,000.
Due·ro (dwĕ'rô). *Spanish.* Douro.
Duis·burg (dūs'bŏrk'). City of W West Germany, at the confluence of the Rhine and Ruhr rivers. Pop. 559,066.
Du·luth (də-lōōth'). City of NE Minn., on Lake Superior opposite Superior, Wis. Pop. 92,811.
Du·mas (dōō'məs). City of N Tex., in the Panhandle N of Amarillo. Pop. 12,194.
Dum·bar·ton (dŭm-bärt'n). Burgh of W Scotland, on the Clyde WNW of Glasgow. Pop. 25,440.
Dum·fries (dŭm-frēs'). Burgh of S Scotland, SSW of Edinburgh. Pop. 29,431.
Du·mont (dōō'mŏnt', dyōō'-). Borough of NE N.J., near Hackensack. Pop. 18,334.
Dum·yat (dōōm-yät'). *Arabic.* Damietta.
Dun·can (dŭng'kən). City of S Okla., SSE of Oklahoma City. Pop. 22,517.
Dun·can·ville (dŭng'kən-vĭl'). City of NE Tex., near Dallas. Pop. 27,781.
Dun·das (dŭn'dəs). Town of S Ont., Canada, near Hamilton. Pop. 19,266.
Dun·dee (dŭn-dē'). City of E central Scotland, on the Firth of Tay. Pop. 190,793.
Dun·e·din (dŭn-ēd'n). **1.** City of SE South Is., New Zealand. Pop. 81,600. **2.** City of W central Fla., N of Clearwater. Pop. 30,203.
Dun·ferm·line (dŭn-fûrm'lĭn). Burgh of E central Scotland, NW of Edinburgh. Pop. 53,418.
Dun·kirk (dŭn'kûrk'). **1.** Also **Dun·kerque** (dœN-kĕrk'). City of N France, on the North Sea. Pop. 83,163. **2.** City of W N.Y., on Lake Erie SW of Buffalo. Pop. 15,310.
Dun Laoghai·re (dŭn lâr'ə). Borough of E central Ireland, on the Irish Sea SE of Dublin. Pop. 54,244.
Dun·more (dŭn'môr', -mōr'). Borough of NE Pa., near Scranton. Pop. 16,781.
Dunn·ville (dŭn'vĭl'). Town of S Ont., Canada, near Lake Erie SSE of Hamilton. Pop. 11,470.
Du·que de Ca·xi·as (dōō'kə də kə-shē'əsh). City of SE Brazil, on Guanabara Bay NNW of Rio de Janeiro. Pop. 639,100.
Du·quesne (dōō-kān'). City of SW Pa., near Pittsburgh. Pop. 10,094.
Du·ran·go (dōō-răng'gō). **1.** (*also* dōō-räng'gô). City of N central Mexico, NNW of Guadalajara. Pop. 218,600. **2.** City of SW Colo., near the N.Mex. border. Pop. 11,426.
Du·rant (də-rănt'). City of S Okla., near the Tex. border SE of Oklahoma City. Pop. 11,972.
Dur·ban (dûr'bən). City of E South Africa, on the Indian Ocean. Pop. 736,852.
Dur·ham (dûr'əm). **1.** City of S Ont., Canada, NW of Toronto. Pop. 272,750. **2.** Borough of NE England, S of Newcastle-upon-Tyne. Pop. 29,490. **3.** Town of SE N.H., NW of Portsmouth. Pop. 10,652. **4.** City of N central N.C., E of Greensboro. Pop. 100,831.
Dur·rës (dōōr'əs). City of W Albania, on the Adriatic. Pop. 61,000.
Du·shan·be (dōō-shăm'bə, -shäm'-). City of SW Central Asian USSR, S of Tashkent. Pop. 501,000.
Düs·sel·dorf (dōōs'əl-dôrf', düs'l-). City of W West Germany, on the Rhine NNW of Cologne. Pop. 594,770.
Dutch East In·dies (dŭch' ēst ĭn'-dēz). Indonesia.
Dutch Gui·a·na (gē-ăn'ə, -ä'nə, gī-). Surinam.
Dutch West In·dies (wĕst ĭn'dēz). Netherlands Antilles.
Dux·bur·y (dŭks'bĕr'ē, -bə-rē). Town of E Mass., SE of Boston. Pop. 11,807.
Dvi·na (dvē-nä'). **1.** Also **Northern Dvina.** River, c. 465 mi (748 km), of N European USSR, flowing into the White Sea. **2.** Also **Western Dvina.** River, c. 635 mi (1,022 km), of W European USSR, flowing to the Gulf of Riga.
Dy·ers·burg (dī'ərz-bûrg'). City of NW Tenn., NNE of Memphis. Pop. 15,856.

E

Ea·gan (ē'gən). City of E Minn., near Minneapolis-St. Paul. Pop. 20,352.
Ea·gle Pass (ē'gəl). City of SW Tex., on the Rio Grande WSW of San Antonio. Pop. 21,407.
Eas·ley (ēz'lē). City of NW S.C., W of Greenville. Pop. 14,264.
East (ēst), **the.** Region of the U.S., E of the Allegheniеs and N of the Mason-Dixon Line.

p pop / r roar / s sauce / sh ship, dish / t tight / th thin, path / *th* this, bathe / ŭ cut / ûr urge / v valve / w with / y yes / z zebra, size / zh vision / ə about, item, edible, gallop, circus / œ *Fr.* feu, *Ger.* schön / ü *Fr.* tu, *Ger.* über / KH *Ger.* ich, *Scot.* loch / N *Fr.* bon.

East An·gli·a (ăng′glē-ə). Anglo-Saxon kingdom of England, in area now occupied by Norfolk and Sussex.
East Ber·lin (bûr-lĭn′). See **Berlin.**
East·bourne (ēst′bôrn′, -bōrn′, -bərn). Borough of in SE England, on the English Channel. Pop. 73,100.
East Cape (kāp). Northeasternmost point of Asia, in Far Eastern USSR on Bering Strait.
East Chi·ca·go (shĭ-kä′gō). City of NW Ind. on Lake Michigan near Chicago, Ill. Pop. 39,786.
East Chi·na Sea (chī′nə). Arm of the Pacific, extending c. 600 mi (965.4 km), between E China and Ryukyu Is.
East Cleve·land (klēv′lənd). City of NE Ohio, near Cleveland. Pop. 36,957.
East De·troit (dĭ-troit′). City of SE Mich., near Detroit. Pop. 38,280.
East·er Island (ē′stər). Chilean island in S Pacific, 2,200 mi (3,450 km) W of the mainland; site of ancient massive sculpted heads.
East·ern Ghats (ē′stərn gôts). Mountain range of S India.
Eastern High·lands (hī′ləndz). Mountain range, extending along entire E coast of Australia.
Eastern Shore (shôr, shōr). Sectors of Md. and Va. lying E of Chesapeake Bay.
East Ger·ma·ny (jûr′mə-nē). See **Germany.**
East Grand Ra·pids (grănd răp′ĭdz). City of SW Mich., near Grand Rapids. Pop. 10,914.
East Green·wich (grĕn′ĭch). Town of central R.I., S of Providence. Pop. 10,211.
East·hamp·ton (ēst-hămp′tən, ēst-hămp′-). Town of W central Mass., near Northhampton. Pop. 15,580.
East Hart·ford (härt′fərd). Town of N central Conn., near Hartford. Pop. 52,563.
East Ha·ven (hā′vən). Town of S Conn., on Long Is. Sound E of New Haven. Pop. 25,028.
East In·dies (ĭn′dēz). **1.** Historically, India. **2.** The Malay Archipelago. **3.** Sometimes, SE Asia.
East·lake (ēst′lāk′). City of NE Ohio, on Lake Erie NE of Cleveland. Pop. 22,104.
East Lan·sing (lăn′sĭng). City of S central Mich., near Lansing. Pop. 48,309.
East Liv·er·pool (lĭv′ər-pōōl′). City of E Ohio, on the W.Va. border S of Youngstown. Pop. 16,687.
East Lon·don (lŭn′dən). City of SE South Africa, on the Indian Ocean. Pop. 119,727.
East Long·mea·dow (lông′mĕd′ō, lŏng′-). Town of SW Mass., near Springfield. Pop. 12,905.
East Lyme (līm). Town of SE Conn., WNW of New London. Pop. 13,780.
East·main (ēst′mān′). River, c. 510 mi (820 km) of central Que., Canada.
East Mo·line (mō-lēn′). City of NW Ill., near Moline. Pop. 20,907.
East·on (ē′stən). **1.** Town of SE Mass., near Brockton. Pop. 16,623. **2.** City of E Pa., N of Philadelphia. Pop. 26,027.
East Or·ange (ôr′ĭnj, ŏr′-). City of NE N.J., near Newark. Pop. 77,025.
East Pe·or·i·a (pē-ôr′ē-ə, -ōr′-). City of N central Ill., opposite Peoria. Pop. 22,385.
East Prov·i·dence (prŏv′ĭ-dəns). City of E R.I., near Providence. Pop. 50,980.
East Prus·sia (prŭsh′ə). Former province of Prussia, divided between Poland and the USSR.
East Ridge (rĭj). City of SE Tenn., near Chattanooga. Pop. 21,236.
East River. Narrow strait connecting Upper New York Bay with Long Is. Sound and separating Manhattan Is. from Long Is.
East Rock·a·way (rŏk′ə-wā′). Village of SE N.Y., on S Long Is. Pop. 10,917.
East Saint Lou·is (sānt lōō′ĭs). City of SW Ill., on the Mississippi opposite St. Louis, Mo. Pop. 55,200.
East Si·ber·i·an Sea (sī-bîr′ē-ən). Arm of the Atlantic, extending from Wrangel Is. to the New Siberian Is.
East York (yôrk′). Borough of metropolitan Toronto, Ont., Can., on Lake Ontario. Pop. 100,858.
Ea·ton·town (ēt′n-toun′). Borough of E central N.J., SE of Red Bank. Pop. 51,509.
Eb·bw Vale (ĕb′ōō vāl). Urban district of SE Wales, NW of Bristol. Pop. 25,670.
Eb·ro (ē′brō, ĕ′brô). River, c. 575 mi (925 km), NE Spain, flowing to the Mediterranean.
Ec·ba·ta·na (ĕk-băt′n-ə). City of ancient Media, on site of present day Hamadan, Iran.
E·corse (ē′kôrs′). City of SE Mich., near Detroit. Pop. 14,447.
Ec·ua·dor (ĕk′wə-dôr′). Republic of NW South America. Cap. Quito. Pop. 7,810,000. **—Ec′ua·dor′i·an** *adj. & n.*

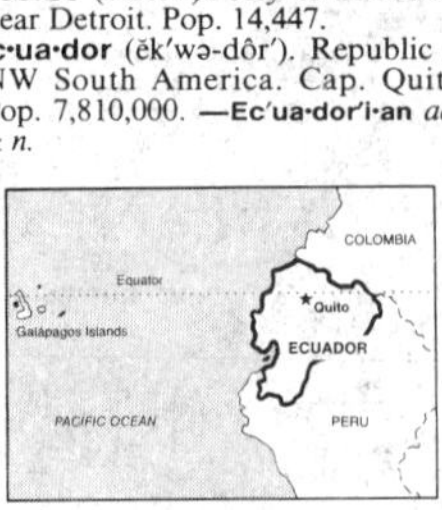

Ecuador

E·dam (ē′dəm, ē′dăm, ā-däm′). Town of N central Netherlands, on the Ijsselmer. Pop. 23,091.
E·de (ā′dā). City of W Nigeria, NNE of Ibadan. Pop. 182,000.
E·den (ēd′n). City of N N.C., near the Va. border. Pop. 15,672.
Eden Prai·rie (prâr′ē). City of E Minn., near Minneapolis. Pop. 16,263.
E·des·sa (ĭ-dĕs′ə). Ancient city of Mesopotamia, on site of present-day Urfa, Turkey.
E·di·na (ĭ-dī′nə). City of E Minn., near Minneapolis. Pop. 46,073.
Ed·in·burg (ĕd′n-bûrg′). City of S Tex., near the Mexican border WNW of Brownsville. Pop. 24,075.
Ed·in·burgh (ĕd′n-bûr′ə). Cap. of Scotland, in the E on the Firth of Forth. Pop. 455,126.
E·dir·ne (ĕ-dîr′nĕ). City of NW Turkey, NW of Istanbul. Pop. 71,927.
E·dis·to (ē′dĭ-stō). River, c. 150 mi (241.4 km), of S S.C.
E·dith Ca·vell (ē′dĭth kăv′əl, kə-vĕl′). Mountain, c. 11,033 ft (336.5 m), in the Rockies of SW Alta, Canada.
Ed·mond (ĕd′mənd). City of central Okla., N of Oklahoma City. Pop. 34,637.
Ed·monds (ĕd′məndz). City of NW Wash., N of Seattle. Pop. 27,526.
Ed·mon·ton (ĕd′mən-tən). Capital of Alta., Canada, in the central part N of Calgary. Pop. 503,773.
Ed·munds·ton (ĕd′mən-stən). City of NW N.B., Canada, at the Me. border. Pop. 12,710.
E·dom (ē′dəm). Ancient country of SW Asia.
Ed·ward (ĕd′wərd). Lake in Great Rift Valley, on the Zaire-Uganda border.
Ed·wards·ville (ĕd′wərdz-vĭl′). City of SW Ill., NNE of East St. Louis. Pop. 12,460.
E·fa·te (ĕ-fä′tē). Island of central Vanuatu, in the New Hebrides.
Ef·fing·ham (ĕf′ĭng-hăm′). City of E central Ill., SE of Decatur. Pop. 11,270.
Eg·a·di (ĕg′ə-dē). Island group in the Mediterranean W of Sicily.
E·ger (ĕ′gĕr). City of NE Hungary, on the **Eger R.** Pop. 60,000.
E·gypt (ē′jĭpt). Republic of NE Africa and SW Asia. Cap. Cairo. Pop. 40,980,000. **—E·gyp′tian** *adj. & n.*
Ei·fel (ī′fəl). Volcanic plateau of West Germany, W of the Rhine R.
Ei·ger (ī′gər). Peak, 13,025 ft (3972.6 m), in the Bernese Alps of W central Switzerland.
Eind·ho·ven (īnt′hō′vən). City of S Netherlands, SE of Rotterdam. Pop. 194,451.
Ei·sen·ach (ī′zə-näKH). City of SW East Germany, W of Erfurt. Pop. 49,850.
El Aai·ún (ĕl ī-yōōn′). Town of NW Morocco, in Western Sahara. Pop. 20,000.
E·lam (ē′ləm). Ancient country of SW Asia, in present-day SW Iran.
El·ba (ĕl′bə). Italian island, 86 sq mi (222.7 sq km), in the Tyrrhenian Sea.
El·be (ĕl′bə, ĕlb). River of Czechoslovakia, East Germany, and West Germany, flowing c. 725 mi (1,165 km) to the North Sea.
El·bert (ĕl′bərt). Highest (14,431 ft/4,401.5 m) of the U.S. Rocky Mts., in central Colo.
El·blag (ĕl′blôNG). City of N Poland, ESE of Gdańsk. Pop. 108,100.
El·brus (ĕl′brōōs′). Highest mountain, 18,481 ft (5,636.7 m), of Europe, in the Caucasus of SE European USSR.
El·burz (ĕl-bŏŏrz′). Mountain range of N Iran, rising to 18,934 ft (5,774.9 km).
El Ca·jon (ĕl kə-hōn′). City of S Calif, near San Diego. Pop. 10,462.
El Cam·po (kăm′pō). City of SE Tex., SW of Houston. Pop. 10,462.
El Cen·tro (sĕn′trō). City of SE Calif., near the Mexican border. Pop. 23,996.
El Cer·ri·to (sə-rē′tō). City of W Calif., near Richmond. Pop. 22,731.
El·che (ĕl′chĕ). City of SE Spain, SW of Alicante. Pop. 136,400.
El Do·ra·do (də-rä′dō, -rā′-). **1.** City of S Ark., near the La. border SSW of Little Rock. Pop. 23,305. **2.** City of SE Kans., ENE of Wichita. Pop. 10,510.
E·lec·tric Peak (ĭ-lĕk′trĭk). Highest peak, 11,155 ft (3,402.3 m), of the Gallatin Range in SW Mont.
El·e·phan·ti·ne (ĕl′ə-făn-tī′nē). Island of SE Egypt, in the Nile.
E·leu·sis (ĭ-lōō′sĭs). Ancient city of Attica, Greece, NW of Athens.
El Fai·yum (ăl fă-yōōm′, fī-, ĕl). Al Fayyam.
El Fer·rol (ĕl′ fĕr-rôl′) or **El Ferrol del Cau·di·llo** (dĕl kou-*th*ē′yō). City of NW Spain, on the Atlantic. Pop. 90,317.
El·gin (ĕl′jĭn). City of NE Ill., NW of Chicago. Pop. 63,798.
El·gon (ĕl′gŏn). Extinct volcano, 14,178 ft (4,324.3 m), on the Kenya-Uganda border.
E·lis (ē′lĭs). Region and city of ancient Greece, in W Peloponnesus.
E·lis·a·beth·ville (ĭ-lĭz′ə-bəth-vĭl′). Lubumbashi.
E·liz·a·beth (ĭ-lĭz′ə-bəth). City of NE N.J., near Newark. Pop. 106,201.
Elizabeth City. City of NE N.C., NW of Raleigh. Pop. 13,784.
E·liz·a·beth·ton (ĭ-lĭz′ə-bəth-tən). City of NE Tenn., NE of Knoxville. Pop. 12,431.
E·liz·a·beth·town (ĭ-lĭz′ə-bəth-toun′). City of central Ky., S of Louisville. Pop 15,380.
Elk (ĕlk). **1.** River, c. 200 mi (320 km), of W Tenn. and Ala. **2.** River, 172 mi (276.7 km), of NW Va. **3.** Range of the Rockies in W central Colo., rising to 14,259 ft (4,349 m).
Elk Grove Village. Village of NE Ill., near Chicago. Pop. 28,907.
Elk·hart (ĕl′kärt). City of N Ind., E of South Bend. Pop. 41,305.
El·len (ĕl′ən). Peak, 11,022 ft (3361.8 m), in S Utah.
El·lens·burg (ĕl′ĭnz-bûrg′). City of central Wash., N of Yakima. Pop. 11,572.
Elles·mere (ĕlz′mîr). Island, 82,119 sq mi (212,688 sq km), of N.W.T., Canada, in the Arctic Ocean; northernmost of the Arctic Archipelago.

Egypt

El·lice (ĕl′ĭs). Group of atolls in the SW Pacific, N of Fiji.
El·li·ott Lake (ĕl′ē-ət, ĕl′yət). Town of SE central Ont., Canada, E of Sault Ste. Marie. Pop. 14,230.
El·lis (ĕl′ĭs). Island of Upper New York Bay, SW of Manhattan.
Ells·worth (ĕlz′wûrth′). **1. Mountains.** Range of Antarctica, S of Ellsworth Land. **2. Land.** High plateau of Antarctica, S of the Antarctic Peninsula.
El Man·su·ra (ĕl′ măn-sōōr′ə). City of N Egypt. Pop. 257,866.
El·mi·ra (ĕl-mī′rə). City of S N.Y., near the Pa. border W of Binghamton. Pop. 12,710.
Elm·hurst (ĕlm′hûrst′). City of NE Ill., near Chicago. Pop. 44,251.
El Mon·te (mŏn′tē). City of S Calif, E of Los Angeles. Pop. 79,494.
Elm·wood Park (ĕlm′wŏŏd′). **1.** Village of NE Ill., near Chicago. Pop. 24,016. **2.** Borough of NE N.J., SE of Paterson. Pop. 18,377.
El O·beid (ĕl′ ō-bād′). Al Ubayyid.
El Pas·o (păs′ō). City of extreme W Tex., on the Rio Grande. Pop. 425,259.
El Re·no (rē′nō). City of central Okla., W of Oklahoma City. Pop. 15,486.
El Sal·va·dor (săl′və-dôr′, säl′-vä-*th*ôr′). Republic of Central America, on the Pacific Ocean. Cap. San Salvador. Pop. 4,360,000. **—El Sal′va·dor′i·an** *adj. & n.*

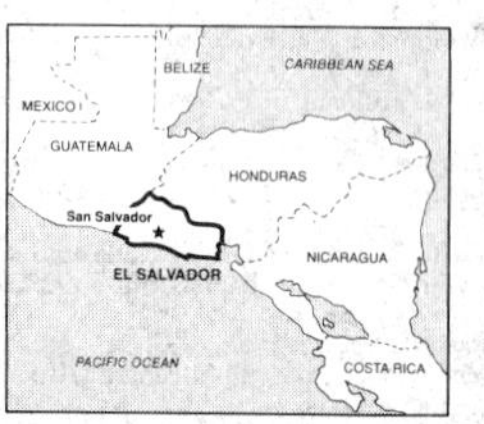

El Salvador

El Se·gun·do (sĭ-gŭn′dō, -gōōn′-). City of S Calif., SW of Los Angeles. Pop. 13,752.
El·si·nore (ĕl′sə-nôr′, -nōr′). Helsingor.
El·wood (ĕl′wŏŏd′). City of E central Ind., NNE of Indianapolis. Pop. 10,867.
E·ly·ri·a (ĭ-lîr′ē-ə) City of N Ohio, WSW of Cleveland. Pop. 57,504.
Em·bar·ras or **Em·bar·ass** (ăm′brô′). River, 185 mi (297.7 km), of E. Ill., flowing to the Wabash R. in SW Ind.
Em·den (ĕm′dən). City of NW West Germany, on the Ems R. Pop. 51,607.
E·mi Kous·si (ā′mē kōō′sē). Highest peak, 11,204 ft (3,417.2 m), of the Tibesti Massif in NW Chad.
Em·maus (ĕ-mā′əs). Borough of E Pa., near Allentown. Pop. 11,001.
Em·men (ĕm′ən). City of NE Netherlands, near the West German border. Metro. area pop. 89,763.
Em·po·ri·a (ĕm-pôr′ē-ə, -pōr′-). City of E central Kans., SSW of Topeka. Pop. 25,287.
Ems (ĕmz, ĕms). River of NW West Germany, flowing c. 208 mi (334.7 km) to the North Sea.
En·der·by Land (ĕn′dər-bē). Region of Antarctica, between Queen Maud Land and Wilkes Land.
En·di·cott (ĕn′dĭ-kət, -kŏt′). Village of S N.Y., near Binghamton. Pop. 14,457.
En·field (ĕn′fēld′). Town of N Conn., on the Mass. border. Pop. 42,695.
En·ga·dine (ĕng′gə-dēn′). Valley of the Inn R. in E Switzerland.
En·ga·ño (ĕng-gä′nyō). Cape of Palau Is., Philippines.
Eng·land (ĭng′glənd). Part of the United Kingdom, the S part of the island of Great Britain. Pop. 46,396,-100. **—Eng′lish** (ĭng′glĭsh) *adj. & n.*
En·gle·wood (ĕng′gəl-wŏŏd′). **1.** City of N central Colo., near Denver. Pop. 30,021. **2.** City of NE N.J., near New York City. Pop. 23,701. **3.** City of W Ohio, near Dayton. Pop. 11,239.

English Channel. Arm of the Atlantic Ocean, c. 350 mi (565 km) long, separating France and Great Britain.
E·nid (ē'nĭd). City of N central Okla., NNW of Oklahoma City. Pop. 50,363.
En·i·we·tok (ĕn'ĭ-wē'tŏk', ĕ-nē'-wĭ-tôk'). Atoll in Marshall Is., W central Pacific; site of U.S. atomic tests.
En·nis (ĕn'ĭs). City of NE Tex., SSE of Dallas. Pop. 12,110.
En·sche·da (ĕn'sKHə-dā'). City of E Netherlands, near the West German border. Pop. 143,042.
En·se·na·da (ĕn'sə-nä'də, än'sä-nä'-dä). City of NW Mexico, on the Pacific. Pop. 77,687.
En·teb·be (ĕn-tĕb'ə). City of S Uganda, on Lake Victoria. Pop. 21,096.
En·ter·prise (ĕn'tər-prīz'). City of SE Ala., NNW of Dothan. Pop. 18,033.
E·nu·gu (ā-nōō'gōō). City of SE Nigeria, E of the Niger R. Pop. 187,000.
Eph·e·sus (ĕf'ĭ-səs). Ancient city of Greek Asia Minor, in W Turkey.
Eph·ra·ta (ĕf'rə-tə). Borough of SE Pa., NE of Lancaster. Pop. 11,095.
Ep·i·dau·rus (ĕp'ĭ-dôr'əs). Ancient city of Greece, on the NE shore of the Peloponnesus.
Ep·som and Ew·ell (ĕp'səm; yōō'əl). Borough of SE England, near London; site of Epsom Downs racetrack. Pop. 70,500.
E·qua·to·ri·al Guin·ea (ē'kwə-tôr'-ē-əl gĭn'ē, -tôr'-, ĕk'wə-). Republic of W central Africa, including islands in the Gulf of Guinea. Cap. Malabo. Pop. 320,000.

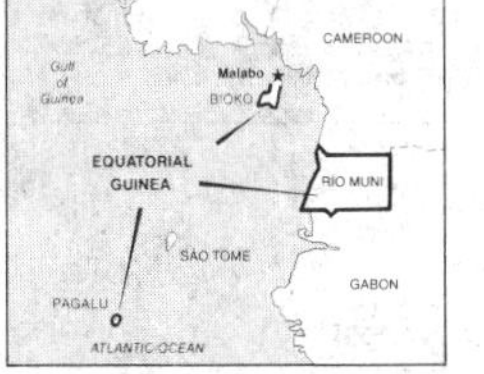

Equatorial Guinea

Er·e·bus (ĕr'ə-bəs). Active volcano, 12,280 ft (3745.4 m), on Ross Is., Antarctica.
E·re·tri·a (ĕ-rē'trē-ə). Ancient city of Greece, on S coast of Euboea.
Er·furt (ĕr'fŏŏrt). City of S central East Germany, WSW of Leipzig. Pop. 209,344.
E·rie (îr'ē). **1.** One of the Great Lakes, between S Ont. and W N.Y., NW Pa., N Ohio, and SE Mich. **2. Canal.** Former artificial waterway extending c. 360 mi (580 km) across central N.Y. from Albany to Buffalo. **3.** City of NW Pa., on Lake Erie SW of Buffalo, N.Y. Pop. 119,123.
Er·i·tre·a (ĕr'ĭ-trē'ə). Region of N Ethiopia. —**Er'i·tre'an** *adj. & n.*
Er·lang·en (ĕr'läng'ən). City of S West Germany, near Nuremberg. Pop. 100,760.
Er·lang·er (ûr'lăng'gər). City of N Ky., near Covington. Pop. 14,433.
Er Rif (ĕr rĭf'). Variant of **Rif.**
Er·y·man·thos or **Er·y·man·thus** (ĕr'-ĭ-măn'thŏs, -thôs, -thōs, -thəs). Mountain range of S Greece, in NW Peloponnesus.
Erz·ge·bir·ge (ĕrts'gə-bîr'gə). Mountain range, extending c. 95 m (155 km) along the border of East Germany and Czechoslavakia.
Er·zu·rum (ĕr'zə-rŏŏm'). City of E Turkey. Pop. 190,121.
Es·bjerg (ĕs'bē-ĕrg, -byĕr). City of SW Denmark, on the North Sea. Pop. 79,310.
Es·cam·bi·a (ĕ-skăm'bē-ə). River, c. 231 mi (371.7 km), of SE Ala. and N Fla.
Es·ca·na·ba (ĕs'kə-nä'bə). City of N Mich., on the Upper Peninsula SSE of Marquette. Pop. 14,355.
Es·con·di·do (ĕs'kən-dē'dō). City of S. Calif, NE of San Diego. Pop. 62,480.
Es·dra·e·lon (ĕs'drā-ē'lŏn, -drə-, ĕz'-). Fertile plain of N Israel, near the Jordan R. valley.
Es·fa·han (ĕs'fə-hän') or **Is·fa·han** (ĭs'-) City of central Iran. Pop. 671,825.
E·sher (ē'shər). Urban district of SE England, near London. Pop. 63,970.
Es·kils·tu·na (ĕs'kĭl-styōō'nä). City of SE Sweden, W of Stockholm. Pop. 90,414.
Es·ki·şe·hir (ĕs'kē-shə-hîr'). City of W central Turkey, W of Ankara. Pop. 309,335.
Es·pi·ri·tu San·to (ĕs-pē'rē-tōō sän'-tō). Island in the S Pacific, largest and westernmost of the New Hebrides.
Es·qui·line (ĕs'kwə-līn', -lĭn). One of the 7 hills of ancient Rome.
Es·sen (ĕs'ən). City of W West Germany, on the Ruhr R. Pop. 652,501.
Es·se·qui·bo (ĕs'ĭ-kwē'bō). River of Guyana, flowing c. 600 mi (965km) to the Atlantic.
Es·sex (ĕs'ĭks).Town of NW Vt., near Burlington. Pop. 14,392.
Ess·ling·en (ĕs'lĭng-ən). City of SW West Germany, on the Neckar. Pop. 91,733.
Es·to·ni·a (ĕ-stō'nē-ə) also **Es·tho·ni·a** (ĕs-thō'-). Region and former country of W European USSR. —**Es·to'ni·an** *adj. & n.*
E·thi·o·pi·a (ē'thē-ō'pē-ə). Country of NE Africa. Cap. Addis Ababa. Pop. 30,400,000. —**E'thi·o'pi·an** *adj. & n.*

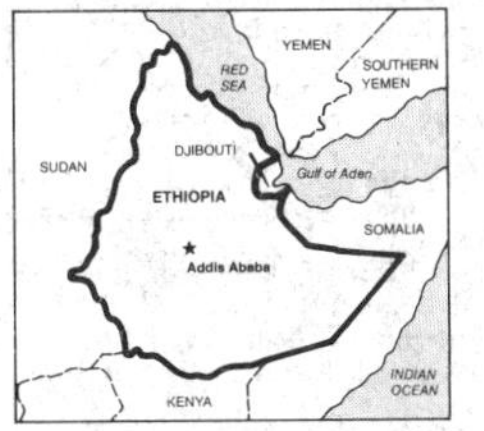

Ethiopia

Et·na (ĕt'nə). Active volcano, 11,122 ft (3,392.2 m), in E Sicily.
E·to·bi·coke (ĭ-tō'bĭ-kō'). SW borough of metropolitan Toronto, Ont., Canada, on Lake Ontario. Pop. 291,102.
E·tru·ri·a (ĭ-trŏŏr'ē-ə). Ancient country of W central Italy, now in Tuscany and parts of Umbria.
Eu·boe·a (yōō-bē'ə). Greek island, 1,467 sq mi (3,800 sq km), in the Aegean.
Eu·clid (yōō'klĭd). City of NE Ohio, near Cleveland. Pop. 59,999.
Eu·fau·la (yə-fô'lə). City of SE Ala., ESE of Montgomery. Pop. 12,097.
Eu·gene (yōō-jēn'). City of W Ore., S of Salem. Pop. 105,624.
Eu·less (yōō'lĭs). City of NE Tex., near Ft. Worth. Pop. 24,002.
Eu·nice (yōō'nĭs). City of S central La., W of Baton Rouge. Pop. 12,479.
Eu·phra·tes (yōō-frā'tēz). River of SW Asia, flowing c. 1,700 mi (2,735 km) from Turkey to the Persian Gulf.
Eur·a·sia (yōō-rā'zhə). Land mass comprising the continents of Europe and Asia. —**Eur·a'sian** *adj. & n.*
Eu·re·ka (yōō-rē'kə). City of NW Calif., S of Crescent City. Pop. 24,153.
Eu·rope (yŏŏr'əp). 6th largest continent, extending W from the Dardanelles, Black Sea, and Ural Mountains. —**Eur'o·pe'an** (yŏŏr'-ə-pē'ən) *adj. & n.*
E·vans (ĕv'ənz). Mountain, 14,260 ft (4,349.3 m), in the Front Range of the Rocky Mts. in N central Colo.
Ev·ans·ton (ĕv'ən-stən). City of NE Ill., N of Chicago. Pop. 73,706.
Ev·ans·ville (ĕv'ənz-vĭl', -vəl). City of SW Ind., on the Ohio R. SSW of Indianapolis. Pop. 130,496.
Ev·er·est (ĕv'ər-ĭst, ĕv'rĭst). Mountain, 29,028 ft (8,853.5 m), of the central Himalayas, on the border of Tibet and Nepal; highest elevation in the world.
Ev·er·ett (ĕv'ər-ĭt, ĕv'rĭt). **1.** City of E Mass., near Boston. Pop. 37,195. **2.** City of NW Wash., N of Seattle. Pop. 54,413.
Ev·er·glades (ĕv'ər-glādz'). Subtropical swamp area of S Fla., including **Everglades National Park.**
Ev·er·green Park (ĕv'ər-grēn'). Village of NE Ill., near Chicago. Pop. 22,260.
Év·reux (ā-vrœ'). Town of N France, WNW of Paris. Pop. 47,412.
Ev·voia (ĕv'yä). *Greek.* Euboea.
E·wab (ē'wôb). Island group of Indonesia, SW of West Irian.
Ex·cel·si·or Springs (ĭk-sĕl'sē-ər). City of W Mo., NE of Kansas City. Pop 10,424.
Ex·e·ter (ĕk'sĭ-tər). **1.** Borough of SW England, on the **Exe R.** (c. 55 mi/90 km) NE of Plymouth. Pop. 95,600. **2.** Town of SE N.H., SW of Portsmouth. Pop. 11,024.
Ex·moor (ĕk'smŏŏr', -smōr'). Moorland plateau of SW England, in Cornwall.
Ex·mouth (ĕk'smouth', -sməth). Urban district of SW England, on the Exe R. Pop. 26,840.
Eyre (âr). **1.** Shallow salt lake of central S Australia. **2.** Peninsula c. 200 mi (322 km) long, in S Australia.

F

Fa·en·za (fä-ĕn'zə, -dzä). City of N central Italy, SE of Bologna. Pop. 40,100.
Faer·oe or **Far·oe** (fâr'ō). Islands of Denmark, in the N Atlantic between Iceland and the Shetlands.
Fa·ga·ras (fə-gə-räsh'). Range of the Transylvanian Alps in S Rumania.
Fa·ial or **Fa·yal** (fə-yäl', fä-). Westernmost island of the Azores, in the N Atlantic.
Fair·banks (fâr'băngks'). City of central Alas., NNE of Anchorage. Pop. 22,645.
Fair·born (fâr'bôrn'). City of SW central Ohio, near Dayton. Pop. 29,702.
Fair·fax (fâr'făks'). Independent city of NE Va., near Washington D.C. Pop. 19,390.
Fair·field (fâr'fēld'). **1.** City of SE Australia, near Sydney. Pop. 120,850. **2.** City of N central Ala., near Birmingham. Pop. 13,040. **3.** City of W Calif., NNE of Oakland. Pop. 58, 099. **4.** Town of SW Conn., on Long Is. Sound. Pop. 54,849. **5.** City of SW Ohio, N of Cincinnati. Pop. 30,777.
Fair·ha·ven (fâr'hā'vən). Town of SE Mass., near New Bedford. Pop. 15,759.
Fair Isle (fâr). Small island at the S tip of the Shetland group.
Fair Lawn (lôn). Borough of NE N.J., near Paterson. Pop. 32,229.
Fair·mont (fâr'mŏnt') **1.** City of S Minn., near the Iowa border SW of Minneapolis. Pop. 11,506. **2.** City of N W.Va., near the border S of Pittsburgh, Pa., Pop. 23,863.
Fair Oaks (ōks). Site, just E of Richmond, Va., of Union victory over the Confederates at the Battle of Seven Pines (1862).
Fair·view (fâr'vyōō'). Borough of NE N.J., near Jersey City. Pop. 10,519.
Fairview Heights. City of SW Ill., ESE of East St. Louis. Pop. 12,414.
Fairview Park. City of NE Ohio, near Cleveland. Pop. 19, 311.
Fair·weath·er (fâr'wĕ*th*'ər). Peak, 15,300 ft (4,666.5 m), on the border between SE Alas. and NW B.C., Canada.
Faiz·a·bad (fī'zə-băd', fī'zä-bäd'). City of N central India, E of Lucknow. Pop. 102,835.
Fa·jar·do (fä-här'*th*ō). Town of NE Puerto Rico. Pop. 26,845.
Fa·ka·ra·va (fä'kə-rä'və). Atoll of the Tuamotu archipelago, French Polynesia, in the S central Pacific.
Fal·kirk (fôl'kûrk'). Burgh of central Scotland, W of Edinburgh. Metro. area pop. 142,058.
Falk·land (fôk'lənd, fôlk'-). Islands of the S Atlantic, E of the Strait of Magellan; claimed by Great Britain and Argentina.
Fall River (fôl). City of SE Mass., on the R.I. border WNW of New Bedford. Pop. 92,574.
Fal·mouth (fôl'məth). Town of SE Mass., on SW Cape Cod. Pop. 23,640.
False Bay (fôls). Inlet of the Atlantic, SW of Cape Town, South Africa.
Fal·ster (făl'stər, fôl'-). Island of SE Denmark, in the Baltic Sea.
Fa·ma·gu·sta (fä'mə-gōō'stə). City of E Cyprus, on the **Bay of Famagusta,** an inlet of the Mediterranean. Pop. 39, 400.
Fan·ning (făn'ĭng). Island of the central Pacific, S of Hawaii, part of Kiribati.
Far·al·lon (făr'ə-lŏn'). Islets in the Pacific, off San Francisco, Calif., W of the Golden Gate.
Far East (făr' ēst'). SE Asia and the Malay archipelago. —**Far' East'ern** *adj. & n.*
Fare·well (fâr-wĕl', fâr'wĕl'). Cape at the S tip of Greenland.
Far·go (făr'gō). City of E N.Dak., E of Bismarck. Pop. 61,308.
Far·i·bault (făr'ə-bō', fâr'-). City of SE Minn., S of Minneapolis. Pop. 16,241.
Far·mers Branch (făr'mərz brănch'). Town of NE Tex., near Dallas. Pop. 24,863.
Far·ming·ton (făr'mĭng-tən). **1.** Town of central Conn., SW of Hartford. Pop. 16,407. **2.** City of SE Mich., near Detroit. Pop. 11,022. **3.** City of NW N.Mex., SSW of Durango, Colo. Pop. 30,729.
Farmington Hills. City of SE Mich., NW of Detroit. Pop. 58,056.
Far·oe (fâr'ō). Variant of **Faeroe.**
Far·rukh·a·bad (fə-rōō'kə-băd', -bäd', -KHä-bäd'). City of N central India, on the Ganges. Pop. 102,768.
Fars (färs, färz) or **Far·si·stan** (făr'-sĭ-stăn', -stän'). Historical region of S Iran, along the Persian Gulf.
Fá·ti·ma (făt'ə-mə, fä'tĭ-mə). Village of W central Portugal, NNE of Lisbon.
Fat·shan (făt'shän'). Foshan.
Fa·yal (fə-yäl', fä-). Variant of **Faial.**
Fay·ette·ville (fā'ĭt-vĭl', -vəl). **1.** City of NW Ark., NNE of Fort Smith. Pop. 36,165. **2.** City of S central N.C., SSW of Raleigh. Pop. 59,507.
Faz·zan (fē-zăn'). Variant of **Fezzan.**
Fear (fîr), **Cape.** Promontory on an island off SE N.C., at the mouth of the Cape Fear R.
Feath·er (fĕ*th*'ər). River of N central Calif., flowing 100 mi (160.9 km) to the Sacramento.
Fed·er·al District (fĕd'ər-əl). **1.** District of E Argentina, site of the capital, Buenos Aires. **2.** District of E central Brazil, site of the capital, Brasília. **3.** District of central Mexico, site of the capital, Mexico City. **4.** District of N Venezuela, site of the capital, Caracas.
Fed·er·at·ed Ma·lay States (fĕd'-ə-rā'tĭd mā'lā, mə-lā'). Former federation of British-protected Malayan states, part of present-day Malaysia.
Fei·ra de San·ta·na (fā'rə də săN-tä'-nə). City of E Brazil, NNW of Salvador. Pop. 127,105.
Feld·berg (fĕlt'bĕrk'). Highest elevation, 4,898 ft (1,493.8 m), in the Black Forest of SW West Germany.
Fen (fŭn). River of N central China, flowing 375 mi (603.4 km) to the Yellow R.
Feng·tien (fŭng'tyĕn'). Shenyang.
Fens (fĕnz), **the.** Lowland district of E England, W and S of the Wash.
Fer·ga·na or **Fer·gha·na** (fĕr-gä'nə, fər-). City of S Central Asian USSR, SW of Andizhan. Pop. 177,000.
Fer·gus Falls (fûr'gəs). City of W Minn., SE of Fargo, N.Dak. Pop. 12,519.
Fer·gu·son (fûr'gə-sən). City of E Mo., near St Louis. Pop. 24,740.
Fer·nan·do de No·ro·nha (fĕr-năN'-dōō də nô-rô'nyə). Island group in the Atlantic off the NE coast of Brazil.
Fer·nan·do Po (fər-năn'dō pō'). Bioko.
Fern·dale (fûrn'dāl'). City of SE

Mich., near Detroit. Pop. 26,227.

Fer·ra·ra (fə-rär′ə, fĕr-rä′rä). City of N Italy, SW of Venice. Pop. 125,200.

Fer·tile Cres·cent (fûr′tl krĕs′ənt). Region of the Middle East, arching across the N part of the Syrian Desert and extending from the Nile to the Tigris and Euphrates.

Fez (fĕz) also **Fès** (fĕs). City of N central Morocco, NE of Casablanca. Pop. 744,900.

Fez·zan or **Faz·zan** (fĕ-zăn′). Region of SW Libya.

Fich·tel·ge·bir·ge (fĭk′təl-gə-bîr′gə, fĭKH′-). Mountain region of E central West Germany, near the East German and Czechoslovak borders.

Fie·so·le (fē-ā′zə-lā′, fyĕ′zō-lā). Resort town of central Italy, near Florence. Pop. 14,760.

Fife (fīf). Region of E Scotland between the Firth of Forth and the Firth of Tay.

Fi·ji (fē′jē). Island country of the SW Pacific, comprising c. 800 islands. Cap. Suva. Pop. 618,979. **—Fi′ji·an** *adj. & n.*

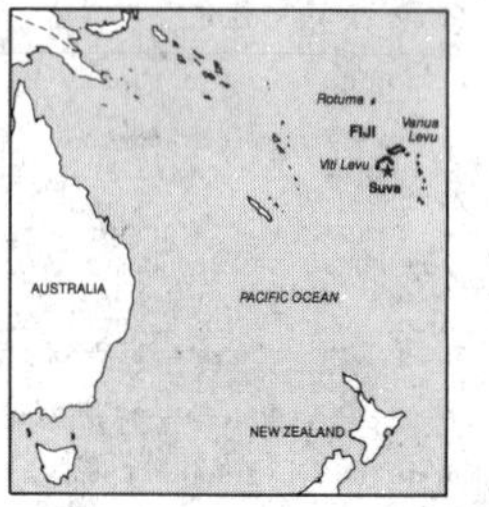

Fiji

Filch·ner Ice Shelf (fĭlk′nər īs′ shĕlf). Ice area of Antarctica, at the W edge of Coats Land and the head of Weddell Sea.

Find·lay (fĭnd′lē). City of NW Ohio, S of Toledo. Pop. 35,594.

Fin·gal's Cave (fĭng′gəlz). Sea cavern of W Scotland, on Staffa Is. in the Inner Hebrides.

Fin·ger Lakes (fĭng′gər). 11 elongated glacial lakes in W central N.Y.

Fin·is·terre (fĭn′ĭ-stâr′, fĕ′nēs-tĕr′rĕ), **Cape.** Rocky promontory of extreme NW Spain, on the Atlantic coast.

Finke (fĭngk). River c. 400 mi (645 km), of central Australia.

Fin·land (fĭn′lənd). **1. Gulf of.** Arm of the Baltic, extending c. 285 mi (460 km) between Finland and the USSR. **2.** Republic of N Europe. Cap. Helsinki. Pop. 4,758,088. **—Finn** (fĭn) *n.* **—Fin′nish** (fĭn′ĭsh) *adj. & n.*

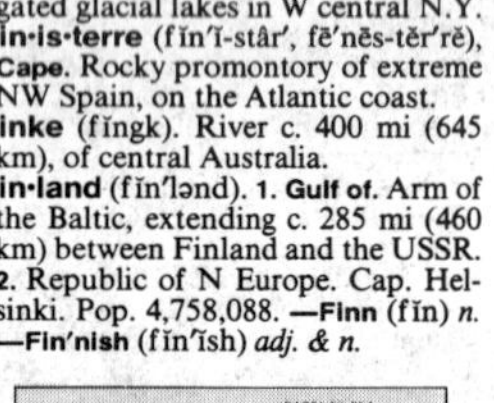

Finland

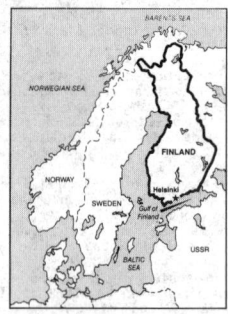

Fin·lay (fĭn′lē). River of N B.C., Canada, flowing c. 250 mi (400 km) to the Peace R.

Fin·ster·aar·horn (fĭn′stər-är′hôrn). Highest peak, 14,032 ft (4,279.8 m), of the Bernese Alps, in S central Switzerland.

Fiord·land (fyôrd′lănd′, fyōrd′-). Mountain area of New Zealand, extending c. 200 mi (321 km) along the SW coast of South Is.

Fire Island (fīr). Barrier island, 32 mi (51.5 km) long, off S shore of Long Is., SE N.Y., including **Fire Island National Seashore.**

Fi·ren·ze (fē-rĕn′dzā). *Italian.* Florence.

Firth (fûrth). See the specific element, e.g., **Firth of Clyde** appears at **Clyde.**

Fish·ers (fĭsh′ərz). Island off the NE tip of Long Is., SE N.Y.

Fitch·burg (fĭch′bûrg′). City of N Mass., N of Worcester. Pop. 39,580.

Fitz·ger·ald (fĭts-jĕr′əld). City of S central Ga., ENE of Albany. Pop. 10,187.

Fi·u·me (fyōō′mā, fe-ōō′-). *Italian.* Rijeka.

Five Forks (fīv′ fôrks′). Crossroads SW of Petersburg in SE Va., where the last important Civil War battle was fought on April 1, 1865.

Flag·staff (flăg′stăf′). City of N central Ariz., NE of Prescott. Pop. 34,641.

Flam·bor·ough Head (flăm′bûr′ə hĕd′, -bə-rə). Promontory on coast of NE England.

Fla·min·i·an Way (flə-mĭn′ē-ən wā′). Ancient Roman road between Rome and the N central Adriatic coast of Italy.

Flan·ders (flăn′dərz). Region of NW Europe, including part of N France and W Belgium and bordered by the North Sea. **—Flem′ing** (flĕm′ĭng) *n.* **—Flem′ish** (-ĭsh) *adj. & n.*

Flat·head (flăt′hĕd′). River, flowing c. 240 mi (385 km) from SE B.C., Canada, to the Clark Fork in NW Mont.

Flat·ter·y (flăt′ə-rē), **Cape.** Headland of NW Wash, at the entrance to Juan de Fuca Strait.

Fleet·wood (flēt′wŏŏd′). Borough of NW England, on Morecambe Bay. Pop. 30,070.

Flens·burg (flĕnz′bûrg, flĕns′bŏŏrk′). City of N West Germany, on **Flensburg Fjord,** an arm of the Baltic at the Danish border. Pop. 88,810.

Fletsch·horn (flĕch′hôrn′). Peak, 13,121 ft (4,001.9 m), in the Lepontine Alps of S Switzerland.

Flin·ders (flĭn′dərz). **1.** Intermittent river of NE Australia, flowing 520 mi (836.7 m) to the Gulf of Carpentaria. **2. Ranges.** Mountain region of S central Australia, extending c. 400 mi (644 km) N from Adelaide.

Flint (flĭnt). **1.** River of SW Ga., flowing 330 mi (530.9 km) to join the Chattahoochee and form the Apalachicola. **2.** City of SE central Mich., NW of Detroit. Pop. 159,611.

Flod·den (flŏd′n). Hill of N England near the Scottish border; site of a battle (1513) in which the English defeated the Scots.

Flor·al Park (flôr′əl, flōr′-). Village of SE N.Y., on W Long Is. near Queens. Pop. 16,805.

Flor·ence (flôr′əns, flōr′-). **1.** City of central Italy, on the Arno R. Pop. 462,690. **2.** City of NW Ala., WNW of Decatur. Pop. 37,029. **3.** City of N central Ky., SW of Cincinnati, Ohio. Pop. 15,586. **4.** City of NE S.C., NE of Columbia. Pop. 30,062. **—Flor′en·tine′** (-ən-tēn′, -tīn′) *adj. & n.*

Flo·res (flôr′əs, -ēz, flōr′-). **1.** Sea of E Indonesia between the Java and Banda seas S of Sulawesi. **2.** (*also* flō′rĭsh). Island of E Indonesia, one of the Lesser Sundas.

Flo·ri·a·nó·po·lis (flôr′ē-ə-nŏp′ə-lĭs, flōr-, flô′ryə-nô′pōō-lēsh′). City of SE Brazil, on an island just off the coast. Pop. 115,665.

Flor·i·da (flôr′ĭ-də, flōr′-). **1. Straits of.** Sea passage between Cuba and the **Florida Keys,** chain of small islands extending SW from Miami to Key West. **2.** Island of SE Solomon Is., SW Pacific. **3.** State of SE U.S. Cap. Tallahassee. Pop. 9,739,992. **—Flo·rid′i·an, Flor′i·dan** *adj. & n.*

Flor·is·sant (flôr′ĭ-sənt, flōr′-). City of E Mo., near St. Louis. Pop. 55,372.

Flush·ing (flŭsh′ĭng). **1.** Vlissingen. **2.** Section of New York City, in N Queens on W Long Is.

Fly (flī). River, c. 650 mi (1,045 km), of Papua New Guinea, in SE New Guinea Is.

Foc·şa·ni (fôk-shän′, -shä′nē). Town of E central Rumania, NW of Brăila. Pop. 62,275.

Fog·gia (fô′jə, -jä). City of S Italy, WNW of Barletta. Pop. 157,727.

Fo·li·gno (fō-lē′nyō). City of central Italy, SE of Perugia. Pop. 46,300.

Folke·stone (fōk′stən, -stōn′). Borough of SE England, on the Strait of Dover WSW of Dover. Pop. 45,610.

Fol·som (fōl′səm). City of central Calif., NE of Sacramento. Pop. 11,003.

Fond du Lac (fŏn′ də lăk′, dyə). City of E Wis., on Lake Winnebago E of Sheboygan. Pop. 35, 863.

Fon·ga·fa·le (fŏn′gə-fä′lē). Cap. of Tuvalu, on Funafuti Is. Pop. 2,200.

Fon·se·ca (fŏn-sĕ′kä), **Gulf of.** Inlet of the Pacific in W Central America, rimmed by El Salvador, Honduras, and Nicaragua.

Fon·taine·bleau (fŏn′tĭn-blō′, fôN-tĕn-blō′). Town of N France, SE of Paris. Pop. 16,778.

Fon·tan·a (fŏn-tăn′ə). City of S Calif., near San Bernardino. Pop. 37,109.

Foo·chow (fōō′jō′, -chou′). Fuzhou.

For·a·ker (fôr′ə-kər, fŏr′-). Peak, 17,280 ft (5,270.4 m), in the Alaska Range of S central Alas.

Forbes (fôrbz). Peak, 11,902 ft (3,630.1 m), in the Rocky Mts., SW Alta., Canada, near the B.C. border.

For·bid·den City (fôr-bĭd′n). Walled area of central Beijing, China, containing palaces of former Chinese rulers.

For·est Grove (fôr′ĭst, fŏr′-). City of NW Ore., W of Portland. Pop. 11,499.

Forest Hill. City of NE Tex., near Fort Worth. Pop. 11,684.

Forest Hills. Section of New York City, in central Queens on W Long Is.

Forest Park. 1. City of NW Ga., near Atlanta. Pop. 18,782. **2.** Village of NE Ill., near Chicago. Pop. 15,177. **3.** City of SW Ohio, near Cincinnati. Pop. 18,675.

For·lì (fôr-lē′). City of N Italy, SE of Bologna. Pop. 92,500.

For·mo·sa (fôr-mō′sə). **1.** Strait of the Pacific between Taiwan and China. **2.** Taiwan.

For·rest City (fôr′ĭst, fŏr′-). City of E Ark., ENE of Little Rock. Pop. 13,756.

For·ta·le·za (fôr-tə-lā′zə, -lĕ′-). City of NE Brazil, on the Atlantic. Pop. 1,255,600.

Fort Ba·yard (fôrt bā′ərd, bī′-, fōrt). Zhanjiang.

Fort Col·lins (kŏl′ĭnz). City of N Colo., NW of Greeley. Pop. 64,632.

Fort-de-France (fôr-də-fräNs′). Cap. of Martinique, French West Indies. Pop. 98,807.

Fort Dodge (dŏj). City of central Iowa, NNW of Des Moines. Pop. 29,423.

Fort E·rie (îr′ē). Town of S Ont., Canada, on the Niagara R. opposite Buffalo, N.Y. Pop. 24,023.

For·tes·cue (fôr′tĭs-kyōō′). River of W Australia, flowing 340 mi (547.1 km) to the Indian Ocean.

Fort George (jôrj). River of W central Que., Canada, flowing 520 mi (336.6 km) to James Bay.

Forth (fôrth, fōrth). River of S central Scotland, flowing c. 60 mi (95 km) to the **Firth of Forth,** an inlet of the North Sea extending c. 55 mi (90 km) into SE Scotland.

Fort-La·my (fôr-lä-mē′). Ndjamena.

Fort Lau·der·dale (lô′dər-dāl′). City of SE Fla., N of Miami Beach. Pop. 153,256.

Fort Lee (lē). Borough of NE N.J., on the Hudson opposite Manhattan. Pop. 32,449.

Fort Mad·i·son (măd′ĭ-sən). City of SE Iowa, SW of Burlington. Pop. 13,520.

Fort Mc·Mur·ray (mĭk-mûr′ē). City of NE Alta., Canada, on the Athabasca R. Pop. 27, 784.

Fort My·ers (mī′ərz). City of SW Fla., N of Naples. Pop. 36,638.

Fort Nel·son (nĕl′sən). River, 260 mi (416.5 km), of NE B.C., Canada.

Fort Payne (pān). City of NE Ala., NE of Gadsden. Pop. 11,485.

Fort Pierce (pîrs). City of E central Fla., NNW of Palm Beach. Pop. 33,802.

Fort Sas·katch·e·wan (săs-kăch′ə-wän′, -wən). Town of central Alta., Canada, NE of Edmonton. Pop. 11,482.

Fort Smith (smĭth). City of NW Ark., WNW of Little Rock. Pop. 71,515.

Fort Thom·as (tŏm′əs). City of N Ky., near Covington. Pop. 16,012.

Fort Wal·ton Beach (wôl′tən). City of NW Fla., E of Pensacola. Pop. 20,829.

Fort Wayne (wān). City of NE Ind., NE of Indianapolis. Pop. 172,196.

Fort Worth (wûrth). City of NE Tex., W of Dallas. Pop. 385,141.

Fo·shan (fō′shän′). City of SE China, near Guangzhou. Pop. 125,000.

Fos·ter City (fô′stər, fŏs′tər). City of W Calif., near San Francisco. Pop. 23,287.

Fos·tor·i·a (fô-stôr′ē-ə, -stōr′-, fŏs-tôr′-, -tōr′-). City of NW Ohio, SSE of Toledo. Pop. 15,743.

Foun·tain Valley (foun′tən). City of S Calif., SE of Los Angeles. Pop. 55,080.

Fou·ta Djal·lon or **Fu·ta Jal·lon** (fōō′-tä jä-lôN′, -lōn′). Mountainous region of NW Guinea, source of the Gambia, Niger, and Senegal rivers.

Fox (fŏks). **1.** River, c. 185 mi (298 km), of SE Wis. and NE Ill. **2.** River of central and E Wis., flowing 176 mi (283.2 km) to Green Bay. **3.** Islands of SW Alas., in the E Aleutians.

Fox·bor·ough or **Fox·bor·o** (fŏks′-bûr′ō). Town of E Mass., W of Brockton. Pop. 14,148.

Foxe Ba·sin (fŏks bā′sĭn). Arm of the Atlantic between Melville Peninsula and Baffin Is. in N.W.T., Canada.

Foyle (foil). River of W Northern Ireland, flowing c. 10 mi (16 km) to **Lough Foyle,** an inlet of the Atlantic.

Fra·ming·ham (frā′mĭng-hăm′). Town of E central Mass., WSW of Boston. Pop. 65,113.

France (frăns). Republic of W Europe. Cap. Paris. Pop. 53,589,000. **—French** (frĕnch) *adj. & n.*

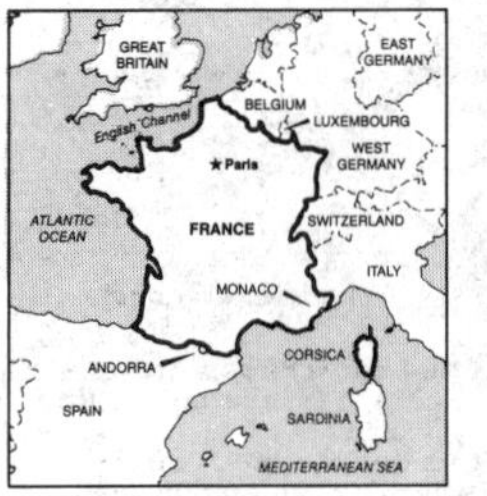

France

Franche-Com·té (fräNsh-côN-tā′). Region and former province of E France.

Fran·co·ni·a (frăng-kō′nē-ə, -nyə, frăn-). Region and former duchy of S West Germany. **—Fran·co′ni·an** *adj. & n.*

Francs (frăngks). Variant of **Franks.**

Frank·en (frăng′kən). *German.* Franconia.

Frank·fort (frăngk′fərt). **1.** City of W central Ind., NNW of Indianapolis. Pop. 15,168. **2.** Cap. of Ky., in the N central part NW of Lexington. Pop. 25,973.

Frank·furt (frănk′fərt, frängk′fŏŏrt′). **1.** Or **Frankfurt am Main** (äm mīn′). City of central West Germany, on the Main R. Metro. area pop. 1,880,000. **2.** Or **Frankfurt an der O·der** (än dĕr ō′dər). City of E East Germany, on the Oder. Pop. 77,175.

Frank·lin (frăngk′lĭn). **1.** Northernmost district of N.W.T., Canada, comprised of the Boothia and Melville peninsulas and the Canadian Arctic Archipelago. **2.** City of S central Ind., SSE of Indianapolis. Pop. 11,563. **3.** Town of SE Mass., near the R.I. border SW of Boston. Pop. 18,217. **4.** City of SW Ohio, NNE of Cincinnati. Pop. 10,711. **5.** City of central Tenn., SSW of Nashville. Pop. 12,407. **6.** City of SE Wis., near Milwaukee. Pop. 16,871.

Franklin D. Roo·se·velt Lake (rō′-

zə-vĕlt′, rōz′vĕlt). Reservoir of NE Wash., formed by Grand Coulee Dam on the Columbia R.

Franklin Park. Village of NE Ill., near Chicago. Pop. 17,507.

Franks or **Francs** (frăngks). Peak, 13,140 ft (4,007.7 m), of the Absaroka Range of the Rocky Mts., in NW Wyo.

Franz Jo·sef Land (frănts′ jō′səf lănd′, fränts yō′zəf länt′). Archipelago in the Arctic Ocean, N of Novaya Zemlya; claimed by the USSR.

Fra·ser (frā′zər). **1.** River of B.C., Canada, flowing c. 850 mi (1,370 km) from the Rocky Mts. near the B.C.-Alta. boundary to the Strait of Georgia at Vancouver. **2.** City of SE Mich., NNE of Detroit. Pop. 14,560.

Fred·er·ick (frĕd′rĭk). City of N Md., W of Baltimore. Pop. 27,557.

Fred·er·icks·burg (frĕd′rĭks-bûrg′). Independent city of NE Va., N of Richmond. Pop. 15,322.

Fred·er·ic·ton (frĕd′rĭk-tən). Cap. of N.B., Canada, in the S central part NW of St. John. Pop. 45,248.

Fred·er·iks·berg (frĕd′rĭks-bûrg′, frĕ′*th*ə-rĕks-bärKH′). City of Denmark, near Copenhagen. Pop. 88,287.

Fre·do·nia (frĭ-dōn′yə). Village of W N.Y., near Lake Erie. Pop. 11,126.

Free·hold (frē′hōld′). Borough of E central N.J., E of Trenton. Pop. 10,020.

Free·port (frē′pôrt′, -pōrt′). **1.** City of NW Bahamas, on Grand Bahama Is. Pop. 15,286. **2.** City of NW Ill., W of Rockford. Pop. 26,406. **3.** Village of SE N.Y., on SW Long Is. Pop. 38,272. **4.** City of SE Tex., on the Gulf of Mexico S of Houston. Pop. 13,444.

Free·town (frē′toun′). Cap. of Sierra Leone, in the W part on the Atlantic. Pop. 274,000.

Frei·berg (frī′bûrg′, -bĕrk′). City of S East Germany, ENE of Karl-Marx-Stadt. Pop. 174,121.

Frei·burg (frī′bo͝ork′). **1.** Or **Freiburg im Breis·gau** (ĭm brīs′gou′). City of SW West Germany, near the Rhine at the edge of the Black Forest. Pop. 174,121. **2.** *German.* Fribourg.

Fre·man·tle (frē-măn′tl). City of SW Australia, on the Indian Ocean near Perth. Pop. 23,500.

Fre·mont (frē′mŏnt′). **1.** City of W Calif., SE of Oakland. Pop. 131,495. **2.** City of E central Nebr., WNW of Omaha. Pop. 23,979. **3.** City of N Ohio, SE of Toledo. Pop. 17,834.

French Broad (frĕnch brôd′). River of W N.C. and E Tenn., flowing 210 mi (337.9 km) to the Holston to form the Tennessee.

French E·qua·to·ri·al Af·ri·ca (ē′-kwə-tôr′ē-əl ăf′rĭ-kə, ĕk′wə-). French federation of W central Africa from 1910 to 1958.

French Gui·a·na (gē-ăn′ə, -ä′nə, gī-ăn′ə). French overseas department of NE South America, on the Atlantic. Cap. Cayenne. Pop. 55,125.

French Mo·roc·co (mə-rŏk′ō). French protectorate over most of present-day Morocco from 1912 to 1956.

French Pol·y·ne·sia (pŏl′ə-nē′zhə, -shə). French overseas territory in the S central Pacific including the Society, Marquesas, Tuamotu, Gambier, and Tubuai Is.

French So·ma·li·land (sō-mä′-lē-lănd′, sə-). Djibouti.

French Su·dan (so͞o-dăn′). Mali.

Fres·no (frĕz′nō). City of S central Calif., SE of San Jose. Pop. 218,202.

Fri·a (frē′ə). Cape of NW Namibia, on the Atlantic.

Fri·bourg (frī′bûrg′, frē-bo͞or′). City of W Switzerland, SW of Bern. Pop. 37,700.

Frid·ley (frĭd′lē). City of E Minn., near Minneapolis. Pop. 30,228.

Fridt·jof Nan·sen Land (frĭt′yôf năn′sən lănd′, năn′sən). Franz Josef Land.

Frie·drichs·ha·fen (frē′drĭKHs-hä′-fən). City of S West Germany, on the Lake of Constance. Pop. 51,541.

Friends·wood (frĕndz′wo͝od′). City of SE Tex., SE of Houston. Pop. 10,719.

Fries·land (frēz′lənd, -lănd′, frēs′-). Region of N Europe, on the North Sea between the Scheldt and Weser rivers.

Fri·o (frē′ō). River of S Tex., flowing 220 mi (354 km) into the Nueces R.

Fri·sian (frĭzh′ən, frē′zhən). Chain of islands in the North Sea off the coasts of the Netherlands, West Germany, and Denmark.

Fri·u·li (frē-o͞o′lē). Region and former duchy of NE Italy, in present-day NE Italy and Slovenia, NW Yugoslavia.

Fri·u·li-Ve·ne·zia Giu·lia (frē-o͞o′-lē-vĕ-nĕt′syä jo͞o′lyä). Region of NE Italy, bounded by Austria in the N and Yugoslavia in the E.

Fro·bish·er Bay (frō′bĭ-shər). Arm of the Atlantic extending c. 150 mi (241 km) into SE Baffin Is., N.W.T., Canada.

Front Range (frŭnt′ rānj′). E range of the Rocky Mts., extending c. 300 mi (482.7 km) in Wyo. and Colo. and rising to 14,274 ft (4,353.6 m).

Front Roy·al (roi′əl). Town of N Va., WNW of Alexandria. Pop. 11,126.

Fro·ward (frō′wərd, -ərd), **Cape.** Southernmost point of mainland South America, in S Chile on the Strait of Magellan.

Frun·ze (fro͞on′zə, -zĕ). City of S Central Asian USSR, on the Chu R. WSW of Alma-Ata. Pop. 543,000.

Fu·chou (fo͞o′jō′, -chou′). Fuzhou.

Fu·chu (fo͞o′cho͞o′). City of E central Honshu, Japan, near Tokyo. Pop. 190,048.

Fuer·te·ven·tu·ra (fwĕr′tē-vĕn-to͞o′-rä). Second-largest (666 sq mi/1,724.9 sq km) of the Canary Is. and closest to the NW coast of Africa.

Fu·jai·rah (fo͞o-jī′rä). Sheikdom of the United Arab Emirates, E Arabia, on the Gulf of Oman. Pop. 760.

Fu·ji (fo͞o′jē). **1.** Or **Fu·ji·ya·ma** (fo͞o′-jē-yä′mä) or **Fu·ji·no·ya·ma** (fo͞o′-jē-nō-yä′mä) or **Fu·ji-san** (fo͞o′jē-sän′). Highest peak (12,388 ft/3,778.3 m) in Japan, in S central Honshu. **2.** City of central Honshu, Japan, at the foot of Mt. Fuji. Pop. 205,752.

Fu·ku·i (fo͞o-ko͞o′ē). City of central Honshu, Japan, NNW of Nagoyo. Pop. 240,264.

Fu·ku·o·ka (fo͞o′ko͞o-ō′kä). City of N Kyushu, Japan, on an inlet of the Sea of Japan. Pop. 1,088,617.

Fu·ku·shi·ma (fo͞o′ko͞o-shē′mä). City of NE Honshu, Japan, N of Yokohama. Pop. 262,847.

Fu·ku·ya·ma (fo͞o′ko͞o-yä′mä). City of W Honshu, Japan, near Kure. Pop. 346,031.

Ful·da (fo͞ol′dä). City of E central West Germany, on the **Fulda R.** (135 mi/217.2 km) near the East German border. Pop. 57,114.

Ful·ler·ton (fo͞ol′ər-tən). City of S Calif., SE of Los Angeles. Pop. 102,034.

Ful·ton (fo͞ol′tən). **1.** City of central Mo., ESE of Columbia. Pop 11,046. **2.** City of N central N.Y., SSE of Oswego. Pop. 13,312.

Fu·na·ba·shi (fo͞o′nä-bä′shē). City of E central Honshu, Japan, on Tokyo Bay. Pop. 479,437.

Fun·chal (fo͞on-shäl′). City of SE Madeira Is., Portugal. Pop. 40,057.

Fun·dy (fŭn′dē), **Bay of.** Inlet of the Atlantic in SE Canada, between N.B. and SW N.S.

Fur·neaux (fûr′nō). Island group off NE Tasmania, Australia, in Bass Strait.

Fürth (fo͞ort, fürt). City of S West Germany, W of Nuremberg. Pop. 98,266.

Fu·san (fo͞o′sän′). *Japanese.* Pusan.

Fu·shun (fo͞o′sho͞on′, -sho͞on′). City of NE China, E of Shenyang. Pop. 1,150,000.

Fu·xin (fo͞o′shĭn′). City of NE China, WNW of Shenyang. Pop. 350,000.

Fu·ta Jal·lon (fo͞o′tä jä-lôN′, -lōn′). Variant of **Fouta Djallon.**

Fu·tu·na (fo͞o-to͞o′nə). Island and island group of the SW Pacific, NE of Fiji; part of the French overseas territory of Wallis and Futuna.

Fu·zhou (fo͞o′jō′). City of SE China, on the Min delta. Pop. 725,000.

Fyn (fün). Island of S central Denmark, W of Sjaelland.

G

Ga·bès (gä′bĕs). City of SE Tunisia, on the **Gulf of Gabès**, an inlet of the Mediterranean. Pop. 40, 585.

Ga·bon (gä-bôN′). Republic of W central Africa. Cap. Libreville. Pop. 550,000.

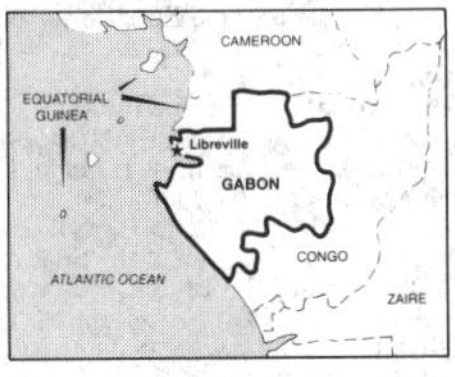

Gabon

Ga·bo·ro·ne (găb′ə-rō′nə, gä′-bə-rōn′). Cap. of Botswana, near the South African border. Pop. 54,000.

Gad·a·ra (găd′ər-ə). Ancient city of Palestine, SE of the Sea of Galilee. **—Gad′a·rene′** (găd′ə-rēn′, găd′ə-rēn′) *adj. & n.*

Ga·des (gā′dēz) or **Ga·dir** (-dîr, -dər). Cádiz.

Gads·den (gădz′dən). **1. Purchase.** Area in extreme S N.Mex. and Ariz., c. 30,000 sq mi (77,700 sq km), purchased (1853) by the U.S. from Mexico. **2.** City of NE Ala., NNW of Anniston. Pop. 47,565.

Ga·e·ta (gä-ā′tä). City of W central Italy, NW of Naples on the **Gulf of Gaeta**, an inlet of the Tyrrhenian Sea. Pop. 24,437.

Gaff·ney (găf′nē). City of NW S.C., near the N.C. border NE of Spartanburg. Pop. 13,453.

Gaf·sa (găf′sə). City of W central Tunisia, W of Sfax. Pop. 42,225.

Ga·han·na (gə-hăn′ə). City of central Ohio, near Columbus. Pop. 18,001.

Gail·lard Cut (gĭl-yärd′, gā′lärd′). Excavation, 8 mi (12.8 km) long, through a hill in the Canal Zone, Panama, occupied by the SE section of the Panama Canal.

Gaines·ville (gānz′vĭl′, -vəl). **1.** City of N Fla., SW of Jacksonville. Pop. 81,371. **2.** City of N central Ga., NE of Atlanta. Pop. 15,280. **3.** Town of NE Tex., NNW of Dallas. Pop. 14,081.

Gaird·ner (gârd′nər). Salt lake of S central Australia, W of Lake Torrens.

Gai·thers·burg (gā′*th*ərz-bûrg′). City of central Md., NNW of Washington, D.C. Pop. 26,424.

Ga·lá·pa·gos (gə-lä′pə-gəs, -lăp′ə-). Island group of Ecuador, in the Pacific c. 650 mi (1,045 km) W of the mainland.

Ga·la·ţi (gä-läts′, -lä′tsē) or **Ga·latz** (gä′läts, gä-läts′). City of E Rumania, on the lower Danube. Pop. 252,884.

Ga·la·tia (gə-lā′shə, -shē-ə). Ancient country of central Asia Minor, in the area around modern Ankara, Turkey. **—Ga·la′tian** *adj. & n.*

Ga·le·ras (gä-lĕ′räs). Volcano, 13,997 ft (4,269.1 m), in the SW Colombian Andes near the Ecuador border.

Gales·burg (gālz′bûrg′). City of NW central Ill., WNW of Peoria. Pop. 35,305.

Ga·li·cia (gə-lĭsh′ə, -ē-ə). **1.** Historical region of SE Poland and W Ukraine. **2.** (*also* gä-lē′syä). Region and ancient kingdom of NW Spain. **—Ga·li′·cian** *adj. & n.*

Gal·i·lee (găl′ə-lē′). **1. Sea of.** Freshwater lake, 64 sq mi (165.8 sq km), bordered by Israel, Syria, and Jordan. **2.** Region of N Israel. **—Gal′i·le′·an** *adj. & n.*

Gal·ion (găl′yən). City of N central Ohio, W of Mansfield. Pop. 12,391.

Ga·li·tsi·ya (gə-lē′tsĭ-yə). *Russian.* Polish Galicia.

Gal·lae·ci·a (gə-lē′shē-ə). Spanish Galicia.

Gal·la·tin (găl′ĭ-tn). **1.** River, c. 120 mi (195 km), of NW Wyo. and SW Mont. **2. Range.** Section of the Rocky Mts. in NW Wyo. and SW Mont., rising to 11,155 ft (3,402.2 m). **3.** City of N Tenn., NE of Nashville. Pop. 17,191.

Galle (gäl). City of S Sri Lanka, on the Indian Ocean. Pop. 79,000.

Gal·li·a (găl′ē-ə, gä′lē-ä). *Latin.* Gaul.

Ga·lli·nas Point (gä-yē′näs). Cape of N central Colombia, northernmost point of South America.

Gal·lip·o·li (gə-lĭp′ə-lē). Peninsula, c. 50 mi (80 km) long, of W Turkey, extending SW between the Aegean and the Dardanelles.

Gal·lo·way (găl′ə-wā′). Region of SW Scotland.

Gal·lup (găl′əp). City of NW N.Mex., near the Ariz. border WNW of Albuquerque. Pop. 18,161.

Gal·ves·ton (găl′vĭ-stən). City of SE Tex., on **Galveston Bay**, an arm of the Gulf of Mexico SE of Houston. Pop. 61,902.

Gal·way (gôl′wā′). **1.** Region of W central Ireland. **2.** City of W central Ireland, on **Galway Bay**, an inlet of the Atlantic. Pop. 36,824.

Gam·bi·a (găm′bē-ə). **1.** River of W Africa, flowing 7,700 mi (1,125 km) from N Guinea through SE Senegal and Gambia to the Atlantic. **2.** Or **The Gambia.** Republic of W Africa, on the Atlantic. Cap. Banjul. Pop. 610,000. **—Gam′bi·an** *adj. & n.*

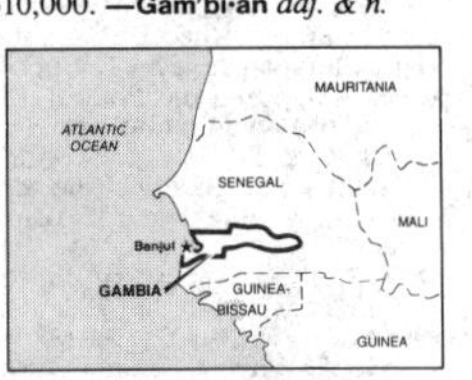

Gambia

Gam·bier (găm′bîr). Islands of the S central Pacific, part of French Polynesia.

Gan (gän). River, c. 550 mi (885 km), of SE China.

Gan·dak (gŭn-dăk′, gŭn′dŭk). River of S Nepal and NE India, flowing 420 mi (675.7 km) to the Ganges.

Gan·der (găn′dər). Town of NE Newf., Canada. Pop. 9,301.

Gan·dzha (gän′jä, -jə). Kirovabad.

Gan·ges (găn′jēz′) or **Gan·ga** (gŭng′-gä). River of N India and Bangladesh, flowing c. 1,560 mi (2,510 km) from the Himalayas to the Bay of Bengal.

Gan·nett Peak (găn′ĭt). Mountain, 13,785 ft (4,231.8 m), of the Wind River Range in central Wyo.

Gao·xiong (gou′shyo͞ong′). Kaohsiung.

Gar·da (gär′də, -dä). Lake, 143 sq mi (370.4 sq km), of N Italy, E of Milan.

Gar·de·na (gär-dē′nə). City of S Calif., near Los Angeles. Pop. 45,165.

Gar·den City (gär′dn). **1.** City of SW Kans., WNW of Dodge City. Pop. 18,256. **2.** City of SE Mich., near Detroit. Pop. 35,640. **3.** Village of SE N.Y., on W Long Is. Pop. 22,927.

Garden Grove. City of S Calif., near Long Beach. Pop. 123,351.

Garden of the Gods (gŏdz). Park, 770 acres (311.9 hectares), of central Colo., noted for rock formations.

Gar·di·ners (gärd′nərz, gär′dn-ərz). Island, c. 3,000 acres (1,215 hectares), of SE N.Y., in **Gardiners Bay** between 2 peninsulas of E Long Is.

Gard·ner (gärd′nər). City of N Mass., near Fitchburg. Pop. 17,900.

Gar·field (gär′fēld′). **1.** Peak, 10,961 ft (3,343.1 m), in the Bitterroot range of the Rocky Mts., in SW Mont. near the Idaho border. **2.** City of NE N.J., near Passaic. Pop. 26,803.

Garfield Heights. City of NE Ohio, near Cleveland. Pop. 33,380.

Ga·ri·glia·no (gä-rē-lyä′nō). River of central Italy, flowing 100 mi (160 km) to the Gulf of Gaeta.

Gar·land (gär′lənd). City of NE Tex., near Dallas. Pop. 138,857.

Gar·misch-Par·ten·kir·chen (gär′-mĭsh-pär′tn-kîr′kən, -KHən). City of S West Germany, SW of Munich. Pop. 27,765.

Gar·mo Peak (gär′mō, gär-mō′). Mt. Communism.

Ga·ronne (gä-rôn'). River of SW France, flowing 402 mi (646.8 km) from the Spanish Pyrenees to the Dordogne to form the Gironde estuary.

Gar·ri·son Reservoir (găr'ĭ-sən). Reservoir, 140 mi (225.2 km) long, of W N.Dak., formed in the Missouri R. by **Garrison Dam.**

Gar·y (găr'ē, gâr'ē). City of NW Ind., on Lake Michigan. Pop. 151,953.

Gas·con·ade (găs'kə-năd'). River, c. 265 mi (426.4 km), of S central Mo.

Gas·co·ny (găs'kə-nē). Region and former province of SW France.

Gash·er·brum (gŭsh'ər-bro͝om'). **1. I.** Peak, 26,470 ft (8,073.3 m), in the Karakoram range of N Kashmir. **2. II.** Peak, 26,630 ft (8,122.1 m), in the Karakoram range NW of Gasherbrum I.

Gas·pé (găs-pā', găs-). **1.** Peninsula of E Que., Canada, between Chaleur Bay and the mouth of the St. Lawrence. **2.** City of E Que., Canada, on **Gaspé Bay** near the E tip of the Gaspé Peninsula. Pop. 16,800.

Ga·stein (gä'stīn'). Valley of central Austria, in the N Hohe Tauern range.

Gas·to·ni·a (găs-tō'nē-ə). City of S N.C., near the S.C. border W of Charlotte. Pop. 47,333.

Gates·head (gātz'hĕd'). Borough of NE England, on the Tyne R. opposite Newcastle-upon-Tyne. Pop. 212,200.

Gates of the Arc·tic National Park (gāts; ärk'tĭk, är'tĭk). Reservation of 7,052,000 acres (2,820,800 hectates) in N central Alas. in the Brooks range.

Gath (găth). Ancient city of Philistia, ENE of Gaza.

Gat·i·neau (găt'n-ō', gä-tē-nō'). **1.** River of SW Que., Canada, flowing c. 240 mi (385 km) to the Ottawa R. **2.** Town of SW Que., Canada, on the Ottawa R. opposite Ottawa. Pop. 77,400.

Ga·tún (gä-to͞on'). Lake of the N Canal Zone, Panama, formed by the **Gatún Dam.**

Gaul (gôl). Ancient name for W Europe S and W of the Rhine, W of the Alps, and N of the Pyrenees, comprising approximately modern France and Belgium.

Ga·var·nie (gä-vär-nē'). Waterfall, 1,385 ft (422.4 m) high, of SW France, in the Pyrenees S of Lourdes and near the **Cirque de Gavarnie,** a natural amphitheater.

Gäv·le (yĕv'lē). City of E Sweden, on the Gulf of Bothnia. Pop. 87,364.

Ga·ya (gī'ə, gə-yä). City of NE India, SSW of Patna. Pop. 179,884.

Ga·za (gä'zə, găz'ə, gā'zə). City of SW Asia, in the **Gaza Strip,** a Mediterranean coastal area (c. 140 sq mi/370 sq km). Pop. 118,272.

Ga·zi·an·tep (gä'zē-än-tĕp'). City of S Asian Turkey, N of Aleppo, Syria. Pop. 371,000.

Gdańsk (gə-dänsk', -dănsk', -dĭɴsk'). City of N Poland, on the Gulf of Danzig near the mouth of the Vistula R. Pop. 449,200.

Gdy·nia (gə-dĭn'ē-ə, -dĭn'yə). City of N Poland, on the Gulf of Danzig NW of Gdańsk. Pop. 232,500.

Ge·ba (gā'bə). Chief river of Guinea-Bissau, flowing 200 mi (321.8 km) to the Atlantic.

Ge·bel Mu·sa (jĕb'əl mo͞o'sə). Mountain group of the S Sinai Peninsula, between Africa and Asia.

Gee·long (jə-lông', -lŏng'). City of SE Australia, SW of Melbourne. Metro. area pop. 141,100.

Ge·la (jĕ'lä). City of S Sicily, Italy, on the Mediterranean. Pop. 75,201.

Ge·li·bo·lu (gĕ'lē-bō-lo͞o'). *Turkish.* Gallipoli.

Gel·sen·kir·chen (gĕl'zən-kîr'kən, -ᴋнən). City of W West Germany, in the Ruhr NE of Essen. Pop. 306,323.

Gen·er·al San Mar·tín (hĕ'nĕ-räl' sän mär-tēn'). City of E Argentina, near Buenos Aires. Pop. 360,573.

Gen·e·see (jĕn'ĭ-sē', jĕn'ĭ-sē'). River of N Pa. and W N.Y., flowing 158 mi (254.2 km) to Lake Ontario.

Ge·ne·va (jə-nē'və). **1. Lake of.** Lake, 224 sq mi (580.2 sq km), on the Swiss-French border between the Alps and the Jura Mts. **2.** City of SW Switzerland, on the Lake of Geneva and bisected by the Rhone. Metro. area pop. 425,000. **3.** City of W central N.Y., on Seneca Lake WSW of Syracuse. Pop. 15,133.

Genk (ᴋнĕnk). City of NE Belgium, ENE of Hasselt. Pop. 61,512.

Gen·ne·vil·liers (zhĕn-vē-lyā'). Town of N central France, on the Seine R. near Paris. Pop. 50,290.

Gen·o·a (jĕn'ō-ə). City of NW Italy, on the Ligurian Sea. Pop. 782,486.

Gen·san (gĕn'sän'). *Japanese.* Wonsan.

Gent (ᴋнent). *Flemish.* Ghent.

Gen·tof·te (gĕn'tŭf'tə). City of E Denmark, on Sjaelland Is. near Copenhagen. Pop. 67,300.

George (jôrj). **1.** Lake of NE Fla., formed by a widening of the St. Johns R. **2.** Glacial lake of NE N.Y., near Lake Champlain. **3.** River of NE Que., Canada, flowing c. 345 mi (555 km) to Ungava Bay.

Georges Bank (jôr'jĭz). Shoal in the Atlantic, E of Cape Cod, Mass.

George·town (jôrj'toun'). **1.** Cap. of the Cayman Is., on Grand Cayman. Pop. 3,975. **2.** Cap. of Guyana, on the Atlantic. Pop. 72,049. **3.** Section of Washington, D.C., in the W. **4.** City of N central Ky., NNW of Lexington. Pop. 10,972. **5.** City of SE S.C., NE of Charleston. Pop. 10,144.

George Town. Penang (sense 2).

Geor·gia (jôr'jə). **1. Strait of.** Channel between mainland B.C. and Vancouver Is., Canada. **2.** Ancient and medieval kingdom coextensive with present-day Georgian SSR. **3.** Region of SE European USSR. **4.** State of SE U.S. Cap. Atlanta. Pop. 5,464,265. **—Geor'gian** *adj. & n.*

Georgian Bay. Extension of Lake Huron in SE Ont., Canada.

Geor·gi·na (jôr-jē'nə). Intermittent river, c. 700 mi (1,125 km), of N central Australia.

Ge·ra (gā'rä). City of S East Germany, ESE of Jena. Pop. 121,980.

Ger·la·chov·ka (gĕr'lä-kôf'kä). Highest peak, 8,737 ft (2,664.8 m), of the Carpathian Mts. in E Czechoslovakia.

Ger·man Dem·o·crat·ic Republic (jûr'mən dĕm'ə-krăt'ĭk). Germany.

German East Af·ri·ca (ēst ăf'rĭ-kə). Former German protectorate in E Africa (1885–1922).

German Fed·er·al Republic (fĕd'ər-əl). Germany.

Ger·ma·ni·a (jər-mā'nē-ə, -nyə). **1.** Ancient region of Europe, N of the Danube and E of the Rhine. **2.** Part of the Roman Empire corresponding to present-day NE France and part of Belgium and the Netherlands.

German New Guin·ea (no͞o' gĭn'ē, nyo͞o'). Former German colony in present-day Papua New Guinea.

Ger·man·town (jûr'mən-toun'). **1.** Residential section of Philadelphia, Pa., site of Revolutionary battle (1777). **2.** Town of extreme SW Tenn., E of Memphis. Pop. 20,459. **3.** Village of SE Wis., near Milwaukee. Pop. 10,729.

Ger·ma·ny (jûr'mə-nē). Former state of N central Europe, bordered on the N by the Baltic and North seas and divided in 1949 into the **German Democratic Republic** (East Germany), cap. East Berlin, pop. 16,715,000; and the **German Federal Republic** (West Germany), cap. Bonn, pop. 61,690,000.

Germany

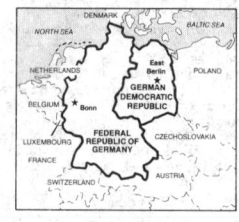

Ger·mis·ton (jûr'mĭ-stən). City of NE South Africa, on the Witwatersrand. Pop. 221,972.

Ge·ro·na (jə-rō'nə, hĕ-rō'nä). City of NE Spain, NE of Barcelona. Pop. 85,522.

Ge·ta·fe (hĕ-tä'fē). Town of central Spain, S of Madrid. Pop. 128,523.

Geth·sem·a·ne (gĕth-sĕm'ə-nē). Garden E of Jerusalem, near the foot of the Mount of Olives.

Get·tys·burg (gĕt'ĭz-bûrg'). Town of S Pa., ESE of Chambersburg; containing **Gettysburg National Military Park,** site of a Union victory in the Civil War (1863), and of Dwight D Eisenhower's farm, a national historic shrine. Pop. 7,194.

Ge·zi·ra (jə-zîr'ə, jĕ-). Region of E central Sudan, between the Blue Nile and White Nile.

Gha·gha·ra (gä'gə-rä'). Gogra.

Gha·na (gä'nə, găn'ə). **1.** Medieval African kingdom in present-day W Mali. **2.** Republic of W Africa, on the Gulf of Guinea. Cap. Accra. Pop. 11,835,000. **—Gha'na·ian, Gha'ni·an** *adj. & n.*

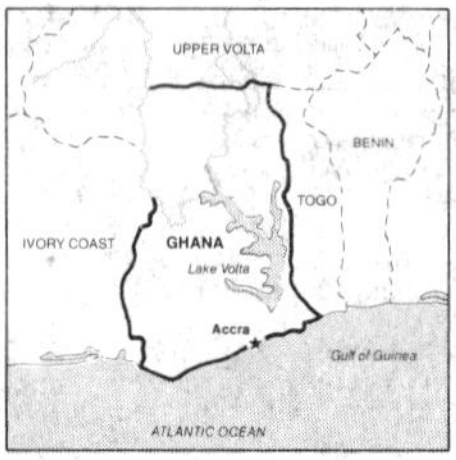

Ghana

Ghats (gôts). Two mountain ranges of S India: the **Eastern Ghats,** extending c. 900 mi (1,450 km) along the Bay of Bengal coast; and the **Western Ghats,** extending c. 1,000 mi (1,600 km) along the Arabian Sea coast.

Gha·zal (gə-zăl', gä-zăl'), **Bahr el.** Bahr el Ghazal.

Ghaz·ni (gäz'nē, gŭz'-). City of E central Afghanistan, SW of Kabul. Pop. 24,000.

Ghaz·ze (gäz'zē). *Arabic.* Gaza.

Ghent (gĕnt). City of W Belgium, NW of Brussels. Pop. 241,695.

Gi·ant's Cause·way (jī'ənts kôz'wā'). Headland on the N coast of Northern Ireland.

Gi·ba·ra Bay (hē-bä'rä). Inlet of the Atlantic on N coast of E Cuba; site of the 1st landing by Columbus in the New World (1492).

Gib·e·on (gĭb'ē-ən). Ancient village of Palestine, near Jerusalem. **—Gib'e·o·nite** *n.*

Gib·ral·tar (jĭ-brôl'tər). British colony, 2.5 sq mi (6.5 sq km), at the NW end of the **Rock of Gibraltar,** a peninsula on the S central coast of Spain in the **Strait of Gibraltar,** connecting the Mediterranean and the Atlantic between Spain and N Africa. Pop. 30,000.

Gib·son (gĭb'sən). Desert of W central Australia, bounded by the Great Sandy Desert on the N and Great Victoria Desert on the S.

Gies·sen (gē'sən). City of central West Germany, N of Frankfurt. Pop. 76,485.

Gi·fu (gē'fo͞o', gē'fo͞o'). City of central Honshu, Japan, NNW of Nagoya. Pop. 410,368.

Gi·jón (hē-hôn'). City of NW central Spain, on the Bay of Biscay. Pop. 256,904.

Gi·la (hē'lə). River of SW N. Mex. and S Ariz., flowing 630 mi (1,013.7 km) to the Colorado.

Gil·bert (gĭl'bərt). Intermittent river of NE Australia, flowing c. 320 mi (515 km) to the Gulf of Carpentaria.

Gilbert and El·lice Islands (ĕl'ĭs). Former British colony, comprised of atolls in the central Pacific; divided into the independent nations of Kiribati and Tuvalu.

Gil·bo·a (gĭl-bō'ə). Hills of NE Israel, at SE edge of the Esdraelon plain.

Gil·e·ad (gĭl'ē-əd, -ăd'). Mountain region of Jordan, E of the Jordan R.

Gil·git (gĭl'gĭt). **1.** Region of Kashmir, in the NW Himalayas; under Pakistani control. **2.** Town in the region, on the **Gilgit R.** (c. 150 mi/241 km), a tributary of the Indus.

Gil·lette (jə-lĕt'). City of NE Wyo., SE of Sheridan. Pop. 12,134.

Gil·ling·ham (jĭl'ĭng-əm). Borough of SE England, N of Maidstone. Pop. 92,800.

Gil·roy (gĭl'roi). City of W Calif., SE of San Jose. Pop. 21,641.

Gin·za (gĭn'zə, -zä'). Shopping and entertainment district of Tokyo, Japan.

Gi·rard (jə-rärd'). City of NE Ohio, near Youngstown. Pop. 12,517.

Gi·rar·dot (hē'rär-thôt'). City of central Colombia, on the Magdalena R. Pop. 61,829.

Gi·re·sun (gē-rĕ-so͞on'). City of NE Turkey, on the Black Sea. Pop. 46,068.

Gir·nar (gîr-när'). Sacred mountain, 3,666 ft (1,118.1 m), of W India.

Gi·ronde (jə-rŏnd', zhə-, zhē-rôɴd'). Estuary, 45 mi (72.4 km), of SW France, formed by the Garonne and Dordogne rivers.

Giur·giu (jo͝or'jo͞o'). City of S Rumania, on the Danube. Pop. 53,072.

Giv·a·ta·yim (gĭv-ä-tä'yĭm). Town of W central Israel, near Tel Aviv-Jaffa. Pop. 49,300.

Gi·za (gē'zə). City of N Egypt, on the Nile near Cairo; site of Great Pyramids. Pop. 1,246,713.

Glace Bay (glās). Town of NW N.S., Canada, on the Atlantic coast of Cape Breton Is. Pop. 10,672.

Gla·cier (glā'shər). Mountain, 10,568 ft (3,223.2 m), of NW central Wash., in the Cascades ENE of Everett.

Glacier Bay National Park. Mountain and glacier area, 3,878,269 acres (1,551,307 hectares) of SE Alas., near Juneau.

Glacier National Park. 1. Reservation, 1,013,100 acres (410,306 hectares) of NW Mont., straddling the Continental Divide. **2.** Reservation in SE B.C., Canada, in the Selkirk Mts.

Glad·beck (glät'bĕk', glăd'-). City of W West Germany, in the Ruhr NNW of Gelsenkirchen. Pop. 80,434.

Glad·stone (glăd'stōn'). City of W Mo., surrounded by Kansas City. Pop. 24,990.

Glå·ma (glô'mä). *Swedish.* Glomma.

Glas·gow (glăs'kō, -gō, glăz'-). **1.** City of SW Scotland, on the Firth of Clyde. Pop. 794,316. **2.** City of S central Ky., E of Bowling Green. Pop. 12,958. **—Glas·we'gian** (-wē'jən) *adj. & n.*

Glass·bor·o (glăs'bûr'ō). Borough of SW N.J., S of Camden. Pop. 14,574.

Glas·ton·bur·y (glăs'tən-bĕr'ē). City of central Conn., SE of Hartford. Pop. 24,327.

Glei·witz (glī'vĭts). *German.* Gliwice.

Glen·coe. 1. (glĕn-kō'). Valley of W Scotland, SE of Loch Leven. **2.** (glĕn'kō). Village of NE Ill., on Lake Michigan near Chicago. Pop. 9,200.

Glen Cove (glĕn cōv'). City of SE N.Y., on NW Long Is. N of Mineola. Pop. 24,618.

Glen·dale (glĕn'dāl'). **1.** City of S central Ariz., near Phoenix. Pop. 96,988. **2.** City of S Calif., near Los Angeles. Pop. 139,060. **3.** City of SE Wis., near Milwaukee. Pop. 13,882.

Glendale Heights. Village of NE Ill., near Chicago. Pop. 23,163.

Glen·do·ra (glĕn-dôr'ə, -dōr'ə). City of S Calif., ENE of Los Angeles. Pop. 38,654.

Glen El·lyn (ĕl'ĭn). Village of NE Ill., near Chicago. Pop. 23,649.

Glen Rock (rŏk). Borough of NE N.J., near Paterson. Pop. 11,497.

Glens Falls. City of E N.Y., on the Hudson NNE of Saratoga Springs. Pop. 15,897.

Glen·view (glĕn'vyo͞o'). Village of NE Ill., near Chicago. Pop. 30,842.

Glen·wood (glĕn'wo͝od'). Village of NE Ill., near Chicago. Pop. 10,538.

Glit·ter·tind·en (glĭt'ər-tĭn'ən). Peak, 8,104 ft (2,471.7 m), of S central Norway.

Gli·wi·ce (glē-vē'tsĕ). City of SW Poland, WNW of Katowice. Pop. 195,300.

Glom·ma (glô'mä). River of Norway,

flowing c. 365 mi (590 km) into the Skagerrak.
Glos·sop (glŏs′əp). Borough of central England, near Manchester. Pop. 24,820.
Glouces·ter (glŏs′tər, glô′stər). **1.** Borough of W central England, on the Severn. Pop. 91,300. **2.** City of NE Mass., on the Atlantic NE of Boston. Pop. 27,768.
Gloucester City. City of SW N.J., near Camden. Pop. 13,121.
Glov·ers·ville (glŭv′ərz-vĭl′). City of E central N.Y., NW of Schenectady. Pop. 17,836.
Gnos·sus (nŏs′əs). Knossos.
Go·a (gō′ə). Former Portuguese colony (1510–1961) of SW India, on the Malabar Coast.
Goa, Da·man, and Di·u (də-män′; dē′yōō). Union territory of W India, on the Arabian Sea, formerly 3 noncontiguous Portuguese colonies.
Goat (gōt). Island of W N.Y., in the Niagara R. dividing Niagara Falls into the American and Canadian falls.
Go·bi (gō′bē). Desert of central Asia, c. 500,000 sq mi (1,295,000 sq km), chiefly in Mongolia.
Go·da·va·ri (gō-dä′və-rē). River of central India, flowing c. 900 mi (1,450 km) from the Western Ghats across the Deccan Plateau to the Bay of Bengal.
Go·des·berg (gō′dĭs-bərg, -dĕs-bĕrk′). Section of Bonn, W West Germany, on the Rhine.
Godt·håb (gôt′hôp′). Cap. of Greenland, on the **Godthåb Fjord** on the SW coast. Pop. 8,545.
God·win Aus·ten (gŏd′wĭn ô′stən, ŏs′tən). 2nd highest mountain in the world, 28,250 ft (8,616.3 m), in the Karakoram range of N Pakistan.
Goffs·town (gôfs′toun, gŏfs′-). Township of S N.H., WNW of Manchester. Pop. 11,315.
Go·ge·bic (gō-gē′bĭk). Mountain range extending 80 mi (128.7 km) from W Upper Peninsula, N Mich., into N Wis.
Gog·ra (gŏg′rə, -rä′). River of central Asia, flowing c. 640 mi (1,030 km) from SW Tibet to the Ganges in E India.
Goi·â·ni·a (goi-ä′nē-ə, -ŭ′nyə). City of S central Brazil, SE of Brasília. Pop. 646,000.
Gök·cha (gœk′chä). *Turkish.* Sevan.
Go·lan Heights (gō′län′ hīts′). Hill region of NE Israel and SW Syria, NE of the Sea of Galilee.
Gol·con·da (gŏl-kŏn′də). Ruined city of SE India.
Gold Coast (gōld). **1.** Section of coastal W Africa along S shore of Ghana. **2.** Former British colony in S part of Gold Coast, now part of Ghana.
Gold·en (gōl′dən). City of N central Colo., W of Denver. Pop. 12,237.
Golden Gate (gāt). Strait in W central Calif. connecting the Pacific and San Francisco Bay.
Golden Horn (hôrn). Inlet of the Bosporus in European Turkey.
Golden Valley. City of E Minn., near Minneapolis. Pop. 22,775.
Golds·bor·o (gōldz′bûr′ō). City of E central N.C., SE of Raleigh. Pop. 31,871.
Gol·go·tha (gŏl′gə-thə). *Hebrew.* Calvary.
Go·mel (gô′mĕl). City of W European USSR, ESE of Bobruisk. Pop. 393,000.
Go·me·ra (gô-mĕ′rä′). Island of the Canary group, in the Atlantic W of Tenerife Is.
Go·mor·ra (gə-môr′ə, -mŏr′ə). Ancient city of Palestine near Sodom.
Go·na·ïves (gô-nä-ēv′). City of W Haiti, on the NE shore of the **Gulf of Gonaïves**, an arm of the Caribbean. Pop. 33,837.
Gon·dar (gŏn′dər, -där). Town of NW Ethiopia, on Lake Tana. Pop. 67,790.
Good Hope (gŏŏd′ hōp′), **Cape of.** Promontory on SW coast of South Africa, S of Cape Town.
Good·win Sands (gŏŏd′wĭn săndz′). Shoals in the Strait of Dover, off the coast of SE England.
Goose Creek (gōōs). City of SE S.C., N of Charleston. Pop. 17,811.
Göp·ping·en (gœp′ĭng-ən). City of S West Germany, ESE of Stuttgart. Pop. 53,034.
Go·rakh·pur (gôr′ək-pŏŏr′, gŏr′-, gō-rək-pŏŏr′). City of N central India, E of Lucknow. Pop. 230,911.
Gor·ham (gôr′əm). Town of SW Me., W of Portland. Pop. 10,101.
Go·ri·zia (gō-rē′tsyä). City of NE Italy, on the Yugoslav border. Pop. 42,580.
Gor·ki or **Gor·ky** also **Gor·kiy** (gôr′kē). City of E European USSR, on the Volga. Pop. 1,358,000.
Gör·litz (gûr′lĭts, gœr′-). City of SE East Germany, E of Dresden. Pop. 81,963.
Gor·lov·ka (gŏr-lôf′kə). City of S European USSR, in the Donets Basin. Pop. 337,000.
Go·ryn (gô′rĭn). River, 410 mi (660 km), of W European USSR.
Gor·zów Wiel·ko·pol·ski (gô′zhōōf vyĕl-kô-pôl′skē). City of W Poland, on the Warta. Pop. 102,500.
Go·shen (gō′shən). City of N Ind., ESE of South Bend. Pop. 19,665.
Gos·lar (gôs′lär). City of E West Germany, at the foot of the Harz Mts. near the border with East Germany. Pop. 52,815.
Gos·port (gŏs′pôrt′, -pōrt′). Borough of S England, W of Portsmouth. Pop. 79,400.
Gö·ta Canal (yœ′tä). Waterway of S Sweden, extending 240 mi (386.2 km) from the Kattegat to the Baltic.
Gö·te·borg (yœ′tə-bôr′ē) or **Goth·en·burg** (gŏth′ən-burg′, gŏt′n-). City of SW Sweden, on the Kattegat. Pop. 434,699.
Go·tha (gō′tä, -thə). City of SW East Germany, W of Erfurt. Pop. 58,369.
Goth·am (gŏth′əm). New York City. —**Goth′am·ite′** *n.*
Got·land (gŏt′lənd, gôt′länd). Region of SE Sweden, in the Baltic, including **Gotland Is.**
Go·to·ret·to (gô′tô-rĕ′tô). Islands of Japan, in the East China Sea off W Kyushu.
Göt·tin·gen (gœt′ĭng-ən). City of E West Germany, ENE of Kassel. Pop. 128,118.
Gott·wald·ov (gôt′väl-dôf′). City of central Czechoslovakia, in Moravia. Pop. 82,926.
Gou·da (gou′də, gōō′-, KHou′də). City of W Netherlands, NE of Rotterdam. Pop. 58,784.
Go·ver·na·dor Va·la·da·res (gōō′-vĕr-nə-dôr′ və-lə-dä′rĭsh). City of SE Brazil, NE of Belo Horizonte. Pop. 125,174.
Gov·er·nors Island (gŭv′ər-nərz). Island of Upper New York Bay, S of Manhattan Is., SE N.Y.
Gow·er (gou′ər). Peninsula of S Wales.
Graf·ton (grăf′tən). Town of S central Mass., near Worcester. Pop. 11,238.
Gra·ham (grā′əm). **1. Land.** Antarctic Peninsula. **2.** Island off NW B.C., Canada, largest of the Queen Charlotte group.
Gra·hams·town (grā′əmz-toun′). City of SE South Africa, ENE of Port Elizabeth. Pop. 41,302.
Gra·ian Alps (grā′ən ălps′, grī′ən). N section of the W Alps, on the border between SE France and NW Italy.
Grain Coast (grān). Historical name of part of the Atlantic coast of W Africa, roughly identical with present-day Liberia.
Gram·pi·ans (grăm′pē-ənz), **the.** Mountain range of central Scotland.
Gra·na·da (grə-nä′də, grä-nä′*th*ä). **1.** Medieval Moorish kingdom of S Spain. **2.** City of SW Nicaragua, at the NW end of Lake Nicaragua. Pop. 56,232. **3.** City of S Spain, SE of Córdoba. Pop. 229,108.
Gran·by (grăn′bē). City of S Que., Canada, ESE of Montreal. Pop. 36,900.
Gran Ca·na·ri·a (grăng′ kä-nä′ryä). *Spanish.* Grand Canary.
Gran Cha·co (grän′ chä′kô). Lowland plain, c. 250,000 sq mi (647,500 sq km), of central South America, divided among Paraguay, Bolivia, and Argentina.
Grand (grănd). **1.** River of S Ont., Canada, flowing c. 165 mi (265 km) to Lake Erie. **2.** River, c. 300 mi (485 km), of SE Iowa and NW Mo. **3.** River of central Mich., flowing 260 mi (418.3 km) to Lake Michigan. **4.** River, 140 mi (225.2 km), of W Mo. **5.** River, 209 mi (336.3 km), of N.Dak. and S.Dak.
Grand At·las (ăt′ləs). Mountains of Morocco, highest section of the Atlas Mts. of NW Africa.
Grand Ba·ha·ma (bə-hä′mə, -hā′-). Island of the Bahama group, in the Atlantic E of West Palm Beach, Fla.
Grand Bal·lon (grän bä-lôN′). Highest mountain, 4,672 ft (1,424.9 m), of the Vosges range in E France.
Grand Banks (băngks). Shoals of the W Atlantic, c. 36,000 sq mi (93,240 sq km), off SE Newf., Canada.
Grand Canal. 1. Longest canal in the world, extending c. 1,000 mi (1,610 km) from Tianjin to Hangzhou. **2.** Principal waterway of Venice, Italy.
Grand Ca·na·ry (kə-nâr′ē). Principal island of the Canary group, in the Atlantic ESE of Tenerife Is.
Grand Can·yon (kăn′yən). **1.** Gorge of the Colorado R. in NW Ariz., 217 mi (349.2 km) long, 4–18 mi (6.4–29 km) wide, and c. 1 mi (1.6 km) deep. **2. National Park.** Area of 1,218,375.2 acres (487,350 hectares) in Ariz., including Grand Canyon and Marble Canyon national monuments. **3. of the Ar·kan·sas** (är′kən-sô′). Royal Gorge. **4. of the Snake** (snāk). Hells Canyon.
Grand Cay·man (kī-män′, kā-măn′, kā′mən). Largest of the Cayman Is., in the Caribbean NW of Jamaica.
Grand Cou·lee (kōō′lē). Gorge, c. 30 mi (48 km) long, of N central Wash., carved by the Columbia R.
Grande Co·more (grăNd kô-môr′). *French.* Great Comoro.
Grande Prai·rie (grănd prâr′ē). City of W Alta., Canada, NW of Edmonton. Pop. 22,718.
Grande-Terre (grăn′târ′, grăNd-tĕr′). Island of E Guadeloupe, in the Leeward Is. of the Caribbean.
Grand Falls. Churchill Falls.
Grand Forks (fôrks). City of E N.Dak., N of Fargo. Pop. 43,765.
Grand Ha·ven (hā′vən). City of SW Mich., on Lake Michigan WNW of Grand Rapids. Pop. 11,763.
Grand Island. City of S Nebr., W of Lincoln. Pop. 33,180.
Grand Junc·tion (jŭngk′shən). City of W Colo., near the Utah border. Pop. 28,144.
Grand Ma·nan (mə-năn′). Island of S N.B., Canada, in the Bay of Fundy.
Grand′Mère (grăN-mĕr′). City of S Que., Canada, NNE of Montreal. Pop. 15,400.
Grand Me·sa (mā′sə). Mountain, c. 10,000 ft (3,050 m), of W Colo.
Grand Prai·rie (prâr′ē). City of NE Tex., near Dallas. Pop. 71,462.
Grand Rap·ids (răp′ĭdz). City of W central Mich., WNW of Lansing. Pop. 181,843.
Grand Te·ton (tē′tŏn′, tēt′n). Highest elevation, 13,766 ft (4,198.6 m), of the Teton Range in **Grand Teton National Park**, NW Wyo.
Grand Trav·erse Bay (trăv′ərs). Arm of Lake Michigan in W central Mich.
Grand Turk (tûrk). Chief island of the Turks and Caicos Is., in the Atlantic SE of the Bahamas.
Grand·view (grănd′vyōō′). City of W Mo., S of Kansas City. Pop. 24,502.
Grand·ville (grănd′vĭl′). City of SW Mich., near Grand Rapids. Pop. 12,412.
Grange·mouth (grānj′məth, -mouth′). Burgh of central Scotland, on the Firth of Forth. Pop. 24,347.
Gran·ite City (grăn′ĭt). City of SW Ill., near East St. Louis. Pop. 36,815.
Granite Peak. Mountain, 12,799 ft (3,903.7 m), of S Mont., NE of Yellowstone National Park.
Gran Pa·ra·di·so (grän′ pä-rä-dē′zō). Highest elevation, 13,324. ft (4,063.8 m), of the Graian Alps in NW Italy.
Gran Sas·so d′I·ta·lia (grän säs′sō dē-tä′lyä). Mountain group of the Apennines in central Italy.
Grants (grănts). City of W N.Mex., W of Albuquerque. Pop. 11,451.
Grants Pass (păs). City of SW Ore., WNW of Medford. Pop. 14,997.
Grape·vine (grāp′vīn′). City of NE Tex., NE of Fort Worth. Pop. 11,801.
Gras·mere (grăs′mîr′). Lake of NW England, in the Lake District.
Grasse (gräs). Town of SE France, W of Nice. Pop. 24,442.
Grau·denz (grou′dĕnts). *German.* Grudziadz.
Graves (gräv′). Region of SW France, in the Garonne valley.
Grays Harbor (grāz). Inlet of the Pacific, W Wash.
Grays Peak. Highest elevation, 14,274 ft (4,353.5 m), of the Front Range in central Colo.
Graz (gräts). City of SE Austria, on the Mur SSW of Vienna. Pop. 250,900.
Great A·ba·co (grāt′ ăb′ə-kō′). Largest island of the Abaco and Cays group in N Bahamas.
Great Ap·pa·la·chi·an Valley (ăp′-ə-lā′chē-ən, -chĭn, -lăch′ĭn). Chain of lowlands of the Appalachian Mts., extending from Canada to Ala.
Great Aus·tra·lian Bight (ô-strāl′-yən bīt′). Bay of the Indian Ocean on the S coast of Australia.
Great Bar·ri·er Reef (băr′ē-ər). Largest coral reef in the world, c. 1,250 mi (2,010 km) long, off the NE coast of Australia.
Great Ba·sin (bā′sĭn). Desert region of W U.S., 210,000 sq mi (543,900 sq km) in area, comprising most of Nev. and parts of Utah, Calif., Idaho, Wyo., and Ore.
Great Bear Lake (bâr). Lake, c. 12,275 sq mi (31,795 sq km), in N central Mackenzie Dist., N.W.T., Canada.
Great Bend (bĕnd). City of central Kans., NW of Wichita. Pop. 16,608.
Great Brit·ain (brĭt′n). **1.** Island off the W coast of Europe, comprising England, Scotland, and Wales. **2.** United Kingdom.
Great Com·o·ro (kŏm′ə-rō′). Largest of the Comoro Is., in the N Mozambique Channel of the Indian Ocean.
Great Di·vid·ing Range (dĭ-vī′dĭng rānj′). Crest line of the Eastern Highlands of Australia.
Great·er An·til·les (grā′tər ăn-tĭl′ēz). Island group of the West Indies, including Cuba, Jamaica, Hispaniola, and Puerto Rico.
Greater Lon·don (lŭn′dən). London, England.
Greater Sun·da (sŭn′də, sōōn′-) also **Sun·das** (-dəz). Islands of Indonesia, including Borneo, Sumatra, Java, and Celebes, in the W part of the Malay Archipelago between the South China Sea and the Indian Ocean.
Great Falls. 1. Waterfall, 35 ft (10.6 m), in the Potomac NW of Washington, D.C., on the Va.-Md. boundary. **2.** City of N central Mont., NNE of Helena. Pop. 56,725.
Great Glen of Scotland (glĕn; skŏt′-lənd). Valley of N Scotland, extending c. 60 mi (96.5 km) from Moray Firth in the NE to Loch Linnhe in the SW.
Great In·di·an Desert (ĭn′dē-ən). Thar.
Great Ka·by·lia (kə-bĭ′lē-ə, -bĭl′ē-ə). Mountainous area of N Algeria, E of Algiers.
Great Kar·roo (kə-rōō′). Karroo.
Great Lakes. Group of 5 freshwater lakes of central North America between the U.S. and Canada, including Lakes Superior, Huron, Erie, Ontario, and Michigan.
Great Na·ma·qua·land (nə-mä′-kwə-lănd′). Region of S Namibia W of the Kalahari Desert.
Great Plains. High grassland region of central North America, extending from the Canadian provinces of Alta., Sask., and Man. S into Tex.
Great Rift Valley (rĭft). Geologic depression of SW Asia and E Africa, extending from the Jordan R. valley to Mozambique.
Great Saint Ber·nard (sānt′ bər-närd′). Alpine pass (8,110 ft/2,473.6 m) on the Italian-Swiss border.

Great Salt Lake (sôlt). Shallow body of salt water, c. 1,000 sq mi (2,590 sq km), of NW Utah, between the Wasatch Mts. on the E and **Great Salt Lake Desert** on the W.

Great Sand Dunes National Monument (sănd′ do͞onz). Reservation containing large, high sand dunes in S Colo., in the Sangre de Cristo Mts.

Great San·dy (săn′dē). Desert of NW Australia, N of Gibson Desert.

Great Slave (slāv). Lake, c. 10,980 sq mi (28,440 sq km), of S N.W.T., Canada; deepest lake (2,015 ft/614.6 m) of North America.

Great Smok·y Mountains (smō′kē). Part of the Appalachian system, on the N.C.-Tenn. border.

Great Vic·to·ri·a (vĭk-tôr′ē-ə; -tōr′-). Desert region of SW Australia.

Great Wall of China (wôl; chī′nə). Fortifications, c. 1,500 mi (2,415 km) long, across N China.

Great Yar·mouth (yär′məth) also **Yarmouth.** Borough of E England, on the North Sea NE of London. Pop. 49,410.

Greece (grēs). Republic of SE Europe, in the S Balkan Peninsula. Cap. Athens. Pop. 8,768,641. **—Gre′cian** (grē′shən) *adj.* **—Greek** (grēk) *adj. & n.*

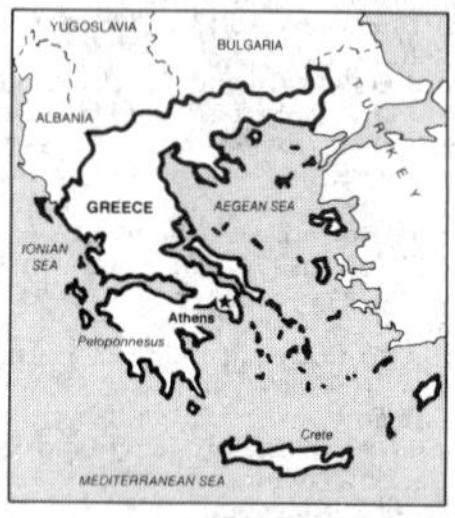

Greece

Gree·ley (grē′lē). City of N Colo., NNE of Denver. Pop. 53,006.

Green (grēn). **1.** River of Ky., flowing 370 mi (595.3 km) to the Ohio R. near Evansville, Ind. **2.** River, flowing 730 mi (1,174.6 km) from W Wyo. through NW Colo. and E Utah to the Colorado R. **3. Mountains.** Range of the Appalachians, extending 250 mi (402.3 km) from S Que., Canada, to W Mass.

Green Bay. City of E Wis., on **Green Bay,** an arm of Lake Michigan N of Milwaukee. Pop. 87,899.

Green·belt (grēn′bĕlt′). City of central Md., near Washington, D.C. Pop. 16,000.

Green·dale (grēn′dāl′). Village of SE Wis., near Milwaukee. Pop. 16,928.

Greene·ville (grēn′vĭl′, -vəl). Town of NE Tenn., ENE of Knoxville. Pop. 14,097.

Green·field (grēn′fēld′). **1.** City of central Ind., E of Indianapolis. Pop. 11,439. **2.** Town of NW Mass., N of Northhampton. Pop. 18,436. **3.** City of SE Wis., near Milwaukee. Pop. 31,467.

Greenfield Park. Town of S Que., Canada, near Montreal. Pop. 18,500.

Green·land (grēn′lənd, -lănd′). **1. Sea.** Section of the S Arctic Ocean, off the E coast of Greenland. **2.** Largest island in the world, c. 840,000 sq mi (2,175,600 sq km), part of Denmark, in the North Atlantic off NE Canada. Cap. Godthåb. Pop. 49,719.

Greenland

Green River. City of SW Wyo., WSW of Rock Springs. Pop. 12,807.

Greens·bor·o (grēnz′bûr′ō). City of N central N.C., E of Winston-Salem. Pop. 155,642.

Greens·burg (grēnz′bûrg′). City of SW Pa., ESE of Pittsburgh. Pop. 17,588.

Green·ville (grēn′vĭl′). **1.** City of W Miss., on the Mississippi N of Vicksburg. Pop. 40,613. **2.** City of E N.C., SE of Rocky Mount. Pop. 35,740. **3.** City of W Ohio, NW of Dayton. Pop. 12,999. **4.** City of NW S.C., NW of Columbia. Pop. 58,242. **5.** City of NE Tex., NE of Dallas. Pop. 22,161.

Green·wich (grĕn′ĭch). **1.** Borough of Greater London, SE England, on the Thames; site of Royal Greenwich Observatory. **2.** Town of SW Conn., on Long Is. Sound near the N.Y. border. Pop. 59,578. **3. Village.** Section of Lower Manhattan, New York City.

Green·wood (grēn′wo͝od′). **1.** City of central Ind., near Indianapolis. Pop. 19,327. **2.** City of W central Miss., E of Greenville. Pop. 20,115. **3.** City of W S.C., WNW of Columbia. Pop. 21,613.

Greer (grîr). City of NW S.C., WNW of Columbia. Pop. 10,525.

Greifs·wald (grīfs′vält′). City of N East Germany, near the North Sea. Pop. 60,636.

Gre·na·da (grə-nā′də). **1.** Island in the Windward Is. of the West Indies, part of the nation of **Grenada,** including the S Grenadines. Cap. St. George's. Pop. 109,609. **2.** City of NW central Miss., NE of Greenville. Pop. 12,641.

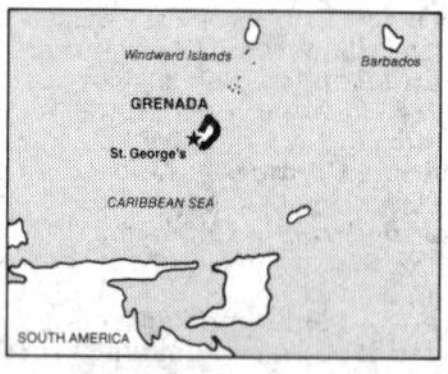

Grenada

Gren·a·dines (grĕn′ə-dēnz′, grĕn′-ə-dēnz′-). Archipelago in the Windward Is. of the E Caribbean, divided between Grenada and the nation of St. Vincent and the Grenadines.

Gre·no·ble (grə-no′bəl, -nôbl′). City of SE France, SSW of Chambéry. Pop. 166,037.

Gresh·am (grĕsh′əm). City of NW Ore., near Portland. Pop. 33,005.

Gret·na (grĕt′nə). City of SE La., on the Mississippi opposite New Orleans. Pop. 20,615.

Gretna Green (grēn). Village of S Scotland, on the English border.

Grey·lock (grā′lŏk′), **Mount.** Highest peak, 3,491 ft (1,064.8 m), in Mass., in the W in the Berkshires.

Grif·fin (grĭf′ĭn). City of W central Ga., SSE of Atlanta. Pop. 20,728.

Grif·fith (grĭf′ĭth). Town of NW Ind., S of Hammond. Pop. 17,026.

Gri·jal·va (grē-häl′vä). River of Central America, flowing c. 400 mi (645 km) from SW Guatemala through SE Mexico to the Gulf of Campeche.

Grims·by (grĭmz′bē). **1.** Borough of E central England, near the mouth of the Humber. Pop. 91,900. **2.** Town of S Ont., Canada, on Lake Ontario ESE of Hamilton. Pop. 15,403.

Grim·sel (grĭm′zəl). Pass, 7,159 ft (2,183.5 m) high, of S Switzerland, between the Rhone and Aare valleys.

Grin·del·wald (grĭn′dəl-vält′). Resort village of central Switzerland, in the Bernese Alps ESE of Interlaken. Pop. 3,511.

Gris-Nez (grē-nā′), **Cape.** Promontory of N France, extending into the Strait of Dover.

Grod·no (grôd′nô). City of W European USSR, on the Neman. Pop. 202,000.

Gro·ning·en (grō′nĭng-ən, ᴋʜrō′). City of NE Netherlands, near the West German border. Pop. 161,322.

Grøn·land (grœn′län′). *Danish.* Greenland.

Groote Ey·landt (gro͞ot′ ī′lənd). Island of N Australia, in the W part of the Gulf of Carpentaria.

Grosse Pointe Farms (grōs′ point färmz′). City of SE Mich., near Detroit. Pop. 10,551.

Grosse Pointe Park. City of SE Mich., near Detroit. Pop. 13,639.

Grosse Pointe Wood. City of SE Mich., near Detroit. Pop. 18,886.

Gros·se·to (grōs-sā′tō). City of central Italy, WNW of Viterbo. Pop. 61,600.

Gross·glock·ner (grōs′gläk′nər). Peak, 12,461 ft (3,800.6 m) high, in S Austria in the Tyrol.

Gros Ventre (grō′ vänt′). River, 100 mi (160.9 km), of W central Wyo.

Grot·on (grŏt′n). Town of SE Conn., on the Thames opposite New London. Pop. 10,086.

Grove City (grōv). City of central Ohio, near Columbus. Pop. 16,793.

Groves (grōvz). City of SE Tex., near Port Arthur and the La. border. Pop. 17,090.

Groz·ny or **Groz·nyy** (grôz′nē). City of SE European USSR, NW of Baku. Pop. 377,000.

Gru·dziadz (gro͞o′jôɴts′). City of N central Poland, NE of Bydgoszcz. Pop. 88,700.

Gua·da·la·ja·ra (gwŏd′l-ə-hä′rə, gwä′*th*ä-lä-hä′rä). **1.** City of SW Mexico, WNW of Mexico City. Pop. 1,813,100. **2.** City of central Spain, NE of Madrid. Pop. 49,130.

Gua·dal·ca·nal (gwŏd′l-kə-năl′). Volcanic island of the W Pacific, largest of the Solomon Is.

Gua·dal·qui·vir (gwä′thäl-kē-vēr′). River of S Spain, flowing c. 350 mi (565 km) to the Gulf of Cádiz.

Gua·da·lupe. **1.** (gwŏd′l-o͞op′, gwŏd′l-o͞o′pē). River, c. 300 mi (485 km), of SE Tex. **2.** (gwŏd′l-o͞op). Mountain range of S N.Mex. and W Tex., rising to **Guadalupe Peak,** 8,751 ft (2,669 m). **3.** (gwä′*th*a-lo͞o′pē). City of NE Mexico, E of Monterrey. Pop. 51,899.

Gua·de·loupe (gwŏd′l-o͞op′). Overseas department of France, in the Leeward Is. of the West Indies. Cap. Basse-Terre. Pop. 324,530.

Gua·dia·na (gwä′dē-änə, -thya′-nä). River of S Spain, flowing 510 mi (820.6 km), partly along the Spanish-Portuguese border, to the Gulf of Cádiz.

Guam (gwäm). Island of the W Pacific, largest (209 sq mi/541.3 sq km) of the Mariana Is.; an unincorporated territory of the U.S. Cap. Agana. Pop. 107,000. **—Gua·ma′ni·an** (gwä-mā′nē-ən) *adj. & n.*

Gua·na·ba·co·a (gwä′nä-bä-kô′ä). City of W Cuba, near Havana. Pop. 69,700.

Gua·na·ba·ra Bay (gwä′nə-bä′rə). Inlet of the Atlantic on the SE coast of Brazil.

Guang·zhou (gwäng′jō). City of S China, on a delta near the South China Sea. Pop. 2,300,000.

Guan·tá·na·mo (gwän-tä′nə-mo′). City of SE Cuba, N of **Guantánamo Bay,** an inlet of the Caribbean. Pop. 155,217.

Gua·po·ré (gwä′po͞o-rĕ′, -pô-). River of central South America, flowing c. 750 mi (1,205 km), partly on the Brazil-Bolivia border, to the Mamoré.

Guá·ri·co (gwä′rē-kō′). River, 300 mi (482.7 km), of W Venezuela.

Gua·te·ma·la (gwä′tə-mä′lə). **1.** Republic of N Central America. Cap. Guatemala. Pop. 7,685,000. **2.** Also **Guatemala City.** Capital of Guatemala, in the S central part. Pop. 793,336. **—Gua′te·ma′lan** *adj. & n.*

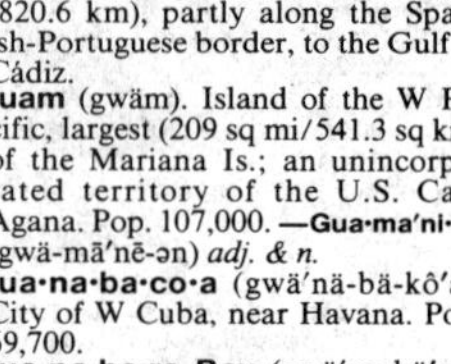

Guatemala

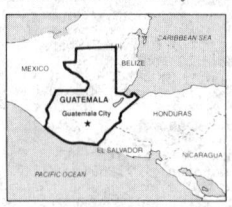

Gua·via·re (gwä-vyä′rĕ). River of central and E Columbia, flowing 650 mi (1,045.8 km) to the Orinoco at the Columbia-Venezuela boundary.

Gua·ya·na (gwä-yä′nä). *Spanish.* Guiana.

Gua·ya·quil (gwä-yä-kēl′). City of W Ecuador, near the mouth of the **Guayas R.,** which drains into the **Gulf of Guayaquil,** an inlet of the Pacific. Pop. 1,022,010.

Guay·mas (gwī′mäs). City of NW Mexico, on the Gulf of California. Pop. 57,492.

Guay·na·bo (gwī-nä′bô). City of NE Puerto Rico, near San Juan. Pop. 65,091.

Guelph (gwĕlf). City of S Ont., Canada, W of Toronto. Pop. 71,408.

Guer·ni·ca (gwâr′nĭk-ə, gĕr-nē′kä). Town of N central Spain, NE of Bilbao. Pop. 11,704.

Guern·sey (gûrn′zē). English island of the SW central English Channel, in the Channel Is.

Gui·an·a (gē-ăn′ə, -ä′nə, gī-ăn′ə). **1.** Region of NE South America, including SE Venezuela, part of N Brazil, and French Guiana, Surinam, and Guyana. **2. Highlands.** Mountainous tableland region of N South America, extending from S and SE Venezuela into Guyana and N Brazil. **—Gui·an′an** *adj. & n.* **—Gui′a·nese′** *adj. & n.*

Gui·enne (gwē-ĕn′, gē-). Region and former province of SW central France.

Guild·ford (gĭl′fərd). Borough of SE England, SW of London. Pop. 58,470.

Guil·ford (gĭl′fərd). Town of S Conn., on Long Is. Sound. Pop. 17,375.

Guilford Court·house (kôrt′hous′, kōrt′-). Locality in N central N.C., near Greensboro; site of American Revolutionary victory (1781).

Gui·lin (gwā′lĭn′). City of SE China, NW of Guangzhou. Pop. 250,000.

Guin·ea (gĭn′ē). **1. Gulf of.** Large open inlet of the Atlantic formed by the great bend in the W central coast of Africa. **2.** Coastal W Africa from Gambia to Angola. **3.** Republic of W central Africa, on the Atlantic. Cap. Conakry. Pop. 5,070,000. **—Guin′e·an** *adj. & n.*

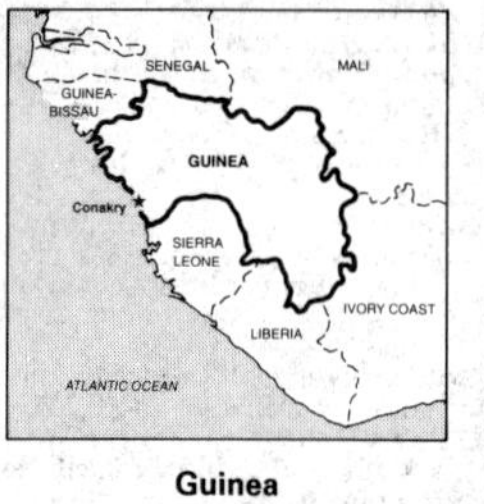

Guinea

Guin·ea-Bis·sau (gĭn′ē-bĭ-sou′). Country of W central Africa, on the Atlantic. Cap. Bissau. Pop. 805,000.

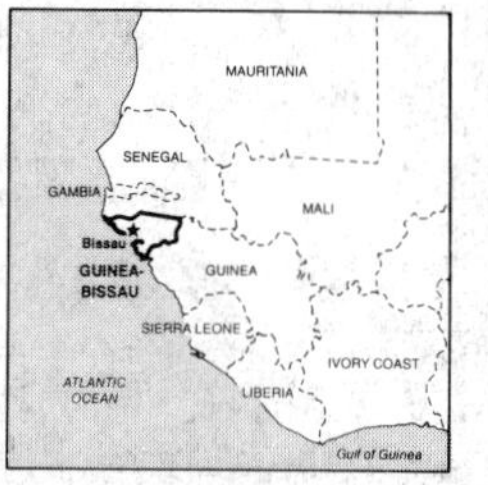

Guinea-Bissau

Gui·yang (gwā′yäng′). City of SW China, ENE of Kunming. Pop. 800,000.

Gu·ja·rat also **Gu·je·rat** (go͝oj′ə-rät′, go͞oj′-) or **Gu·ze·rat** (go͞o-zə-rät′). Region of W India.

Guj·ran·wa·la (go͝oj′rən-wä′lə, go͞oj′-). City of NE Central Pakistan,

N of Lahore. Pop. 323,880.

Gü·lek Bo·gaz (gü-lĕk′ bō-gäz′). Mountain pass of S Turkey, in the Taurus Mts.

Gulf In·tra·coas·tal Waterway (gŭlf ĭn′trə-kō′stəl). Inland waterway of bays, canals, and rivers from NW Fla. to Brownsville, Tex.

Gulf·port (gŭlf′pôrt′, -pōrt′). **1.** City of W Fla., on Tampa Bay near St. Petersburg. Pop. 11,180. **2.** City of SE Miss., on the Intracoastal Waterway W of Biloxi. Pop. 39,676.

Gulf States (stāts). States of the S U.S. with coastlines on the Gulf of Mexico: Fla., Ala., Miss., La., and Tex.

Gulf Stream. Warm ocean current of the N Atlantic, off E North America.

Gum·ti (go͝om′tē). River of N India, flowing c. 500 mi (804.5 km) to the Ganges.

Gunn·bjørn (go͝on′byôrn′). Highest peak, 12,139 ft (3,702.4 m), of Greenland, near the SE coast.

Gun·ni·son (gŭn′ĭ-sən). River, 180 mi (289.6 km), of W central Colo.

Gun·tur (go͝on-to͝or′). City of SE India, NNE of Vijayawada. Pop. 269,991.

Gu·ryev (go͝or′yĭf). City of SW Central Asian USSR, on the Ural R. Pop. 134,000.

Gus·ta·vo A. Ma·de·ro (go͞os-tä′vô ä′ mä-*thĕ*′rô). City of S central Mexico, N of Mexico City. Pop. 1,182,895.

Gü·ters·loh (gü′tərs-lō′). City of W West Germany, SSW of Bielefeld. Pop. 77,792.

Guth·rie (gŭth′rē). City of central Okla., N of Oklahoma City. Pop. 10,312.

Guy·a·na (gī-ăn′ə, -ä′nə). Republic of NE South America, on the Atlantic. Cap. Georgetown. Pop. 921,000. —**Guy′a·nese′** *adj. & n.*

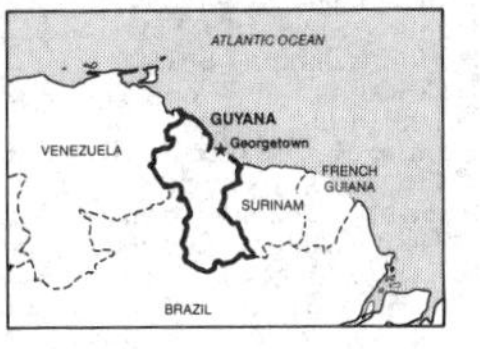

Guyana

Guy·enne (gwē-yĕn′, gē-). Guienne.

Gu·ze·rat (go͞o-zə-rät′). Variant of **Gujarat.**

Gwa·li·or (gwä′lē-ôr′). **1.** Former state of N India. **2.** City of N central India, SSE of Agra. Pop. 384,772.

Győr (dyœr, dyûr). City of NW Hungary, near the Czechoslovak border. Pop. 125,000.

H

Haar·lem (här′ləm). City of W Netherlands, near the North Sea W of Amsterdam. Pop. 158,291.

Haar·lem·mer·meer (här′lə-mər-mâr′). City of W Netherlands, WSW of Amsterdam. Metro. area pop. 77,657.

Ha·chi·no·he (hä′chē-nô′hĕ). City of N Honshu, Japan, on the Pacific. Pop. 238,208.

Hack·en·sack (hăk′ən-săk′). City of NE N.J., near Jersey City. Pop. 36,039.

Ha·da·no (hä-dä′nô). City of E central Honshu, Japan. Pop. 118,528.

Had·don·field (hăd′n-fēld′). Borough of SW N.J., near Camden. Pop. 12,337.

Ha·dri·an's Wall (hā′drē-ənz wôl′). Ancient Roman wall, 73.5 mi (118.3 km) long, in N England.

Hae·ju (hī′jo͞o). City of SW North Korea, on the Yellow Sea S of Pyongyang. Pop. 115,000.

Ha·fun (hä-fo͞on′). Promontory on Indian Ocean coast of NE Somalia; easternmost point of Africa.

Ha·gen (hä′gən). City of W West Germany, NE of Cologne. Pop. 220,676.

Hag·ers·town (hā′gərz-toun′). City of NW Md., WNW of Baltimore. Pop. 34,132.

Hague (hāg), **The.** De facto cap. of the Netherlands, in the W part near the North Sea. Pop. 456,886.

Hai·fa (hī′fə). City of NW Israel, on the Mediterranean. Pop. 229,300.

Hai·kou (hī′kou′, -kō′). City of Hainan Is., S China, on Hainan Strait. Pop. 275,000.

Hai·nan (hī′nän′). **1.** Strait, c. 30 mi (48 km) wide, of S China, between Hainan Is. and the Leizhou peninsula. **2.** Island of S China, in the South China Sea.

Hai·naut (ĕ-nō′). Historical region of SW Belgium and N France.

Haines City (hānz). City of central Fla., SSW of Orlando. Pop. 10,799.

Hai·phong (hī′fŏng′). City of NE Vietnam, on the Red R. delta near the Gulf of Tonkin. Pop. 400,000.

Hai·ti (hā′tē). Country of the West Indies, on W part of the island of Hispaniola. Cap. Port-au-Prince. Pop. 5,040,000. —**Hai′tian** (hā′shən, -tē-ən) *adj. & n.*

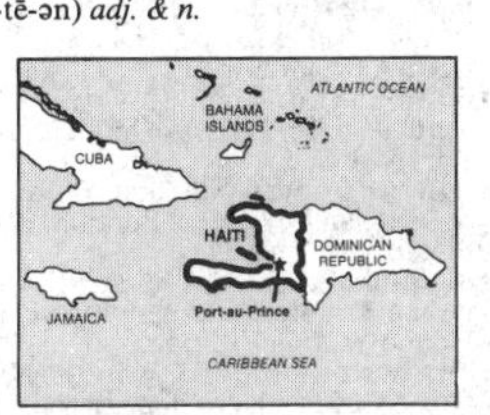

Haiti

Ha·ko·da·te (hä′kô-dä′tĕ). City of SW Hokkaido, Japan, on Tsugaru Strait. Pop. 320,152.

Hal·ber·stadt (häl′bər-shtät′). City of W East Germany, SW of Magdeburg. Pop. 47,919.

Hal·di·mand (hôl′də-mənd). Town of SE Ont., Canada, S of Hamilton. Pop. 16,428.

Ha·le·a·ka·la (hä′lā-ä′kä-lä′). Mountain, 10,025 ft (3,057.6 m), in **Haleakala National Park,** site of world's largest volcanic crater, 2,720 ft (829.6 m) deep, on E Maui, Hawaii.

Hal·fa·ya (häl-fä′yä). Pass through coastal hills in extreme NW Egypt.

Hal·i·car·nas·sus (hăl′ĭ-kär-năs′əs). Ancient Greek city of SW Asia Minor, on the Aegean.

Hal·i·fax (hăl′ə-făks′). **1.** Cap. of N.S., Canada, on the Atlantic in the S central part. Pop. 117,882. **2.** Borough of central England, NE of Manchester. Pop. 88,580.

Hal·lan·dale (hăl′ən-dāl′). City of SE Fla., on the Atlantic S of Fort Lauderdale. Pop. 36,517.

Hal·le (hä′lə). City of S central E Germany, WNW of Leipzig. Pop. 232,543.

Hal·ma·he·ra (häl′mä-hĕ′rä). Island of E Indonesia, largest of the Moluccas, between New Guinea and Sulawesi.

Halm·stad (hälm′städ). City of SW Sweden, on the Kattegat. Pop. 50,400.

Halq al Wa·di (hälk′ äl wä′dē). La Goulette.

Häl·sing·borg (hĕl′sĭng-bôrg′, hĕl′-sĭng-bôr′ē). City of NW Sweden, on the Oresund. Pop. 101,370.

Hal·tem·price (hôl′təm-prīs′). Urban district of NE England, near Hull. Pop. 54,850.

Hal·tom City (hôl′təm). City of NE Tex., near Fort Worth. Pop. 29,014.

Hal·ton Hills (hôl′tən). Town of SE Ont., Canada, near Toronto. Pop. 34,029.

Ha·ma or **Ha·mah** (hä′mä). City of W Syria, on the Orontes R. Pop. 180,000.

Ham·a·dan (hăm′ə-dăn′, -dän′). City of W Iran, WSW of Teheran. Pop. 155,846.

Ha·ma·ma·tsu (hä′mä-mä′tso͞o). City of S central Honshu, Japan, near the Pacific WSW of Tokyo. Pop. 490,827.

Ham·burg (hăm′bûrg′). **1.** (*also* häm′bo͝ork′). City of N West Germany, on the Elbe. Pop. 1,653,043. **2.** Village of W N.Y., S of Buffalo. Pop. 10,582.

Ham·den (hăm′dən). Town of S Conn., N of New Haven. Pop. 51,071.

Ha·meln (hä′məln) or **Ham·e·lin** (hăm′ə-lĭn, hăm′lĭn). City of N West Germany, on the Weser R. SW of Hannover. Pop. 59,005.

Ham·hung (häm′ho͞ong′). City of E central North Korea, near the Sea of Japan coast. Pop. 125,000.

Ham·il·ton (hăm′əl-tən). **1.** Inlet of the N Atlantic in SE Labrador, Newf., Canada. **2.** Churchill R. **3.** Cap. of Bermuda, on Bermuda Is. Pop. 2,060. **4.** City of S Ont., Canada, at W end of Lake Ontario SW of Toronto. Pop. 308,538. **5.** City of N central North Is., New Zealand, SSE of Auckland. Pop. 90,900. **6.** Burgh of S central Scotland, near Glasgow. Pop. 107,490. **7.** City of SW Ohio, N of Cincinnati. Pop. 63,189.

Hamm (häm). City of W West Germany, SSE of Münster. Pop. 171,595.

Ham·mer·fest (häm′ər-fĕst′). Town of N Norway, on an island in the Arctic Ocean; northernmost town of Europe. Pop. 7,457.

Ham·mond (hăm′ənd). **1.** City of NW Ind., adjacent to Gary. Pop. 93,714. **2.** City of SE La., E of Baton Rouge. Pop. 15,043.

Ham·mon·ton (hăm′ən-tən). Town of S N.J., SE of Camden. Pop. 12,298.

Hamp·ton (hămp′tən). **1.** Historic section of London, England; site of Hampton Court Palace. **2.** Town of SE N.H., on the Atlantic SSW of Portsmouth. Pop. 10,493. **3.** Independent city of SE Va., opposite Norfolk, on **Hampton Roads,** outlet of the James and Elizabeth rivers into Chesapeake Bay. Pop. 122,617.

Ham·tramck (hăm-trăm′ĭk). City of SE Mich., surrounded by Detroit. Pop. 21,300.

Han (hän). **1.** River, c. 210 mi (338 km), of S China. **2.** River, c. 700 mi (1,126 km), of central China.

Han·a·han (hăn′ə-hăn′). City of SE S.C., near Charleston. Pop. 13,224.

Ha·nau (hä′nou). City of central West Germany, on the Main R. E of Frankfurt. Pop. 86,144.

Han·dan (hän′dän′). City of E central China, SSW of Beijing. Pop. 480,000.

Han·ford (hăn′fərd). City of S central Calif., SSE of Fresno. Pop. 20,958.

Hang·zhou (häng′jō′) also **Hang·chow** (hăng′chou′, häng′jō′). City of E China, at the head of **Hangzhou Bay,** an inlet of the East China Sea. Pop. 900,000.

Han·ka (hăng′kə, hän′kä). Variant of **Khanka.**

Han·ni·bal (hăn′ə-bəl). City of NE Mo., on the Mississippi NW of St. Louis. Pop. 18,811.

Han·no·ver (hä-nō′vər, -fər) or **Han·o·ver** (hăn′ō′vər). City of N West Germany, SE of Bremen. Pop. 535,854.

Ha·noi (hă-noi′, hă-). Cap. of Vietnam, in the N part on the Red R. Pop. 2,000,000.

Han·o·ver (hăn′ō′vər). **1.** Former kindgom and province of N West Germany. **2.** Variant of **Hannover. 3.** Town of E Mass., SE of Boston. Pop. 11,358. **4.** Borough of NE central Pa., near Wilkes-Barre. Pop. 14,890.

Hanover Park. Village of NE Ill., near Chicago. Pop. 28,850.

Han·tan (hän′dän′). Handan.

Har·a·han (hăr′ə-hăn′). City of SE La., on the Mississippi near New Orleans. Pop. 11,384.

Ha·ran or **Har·ran** (hä-rän′, hā′rən). Ancient city of Mesopotamia, in present-day SE Turkey.

Ha·rar or **Har·rar** (här′ər). City of E central Ethiopia, E of Addis Ababa. Pop. 55,401.

Har·bin (här′bĭn, -bĭn′). City of NE China, in Manchuria. Pop. 2,400,00.

Har·dan·ger·fjord (här-däng′ər-fyōr). Fjord, penetrating 114 mi (183.4 km) from the Atlantic into SW Norway.

Har·dwar (hûr′dwär, hər-dwär′). City of N India, NE of Delhi; a Hindu pilgrimage center. Pop. 77,864.

Har·gei·sa (här-gā′sə) or **Har·ghes·sa** (här-gĕs′ə). City of NW Somalia, E Africa. Pop. 70,000.

Ha·ri Rud (hä′rē ro͞od′, hŭ′rē). River c. 700 mi (1,126 km), of NW Afghanistan, NE Iran, and S Central Asian USSR.

Har·lem (här′ləm). **1.** River channel in New York City, separating the N end of Manhattan Is. from the Bronx. **2.** Section of New York City, in N Manhattan bordering on the Harlem and East rivers.

Har·lin·gen (här′lĭn-jən). City of extreme S Tex., NW of Brownsville. Pop. 43,543.

Har·ney Peak (här′nē). Highest elevation, 7,242 ft (2,208.8 m), of the Black Hills, SW S.Dak.

Har·pers Fer·ry (här′pərz fĕr′ē). Town of extreme E W.Va.; scene of John Brown's rebellion (1859).

Har·per Woods (här′pər). City of SE Mich., near Detroit. Pop. 16,361.

Har·ran (hä-rän′, hā′rən). Variant of **Haran.**

Har·rar (här′ər). Variant of **Harar.**

Har·ris·burg (hăr′ĭs-bûrg′). Cap. of Pa., in the SE part WNW of Philadelphia. Pop. 53,264.

Har·ri·son (hăr′ĭ-sən). **1.** Town of NE N.J., near Newark. Pop. 12,242. **2.** Village of SE N.Y., near Rye. Pop. 23,046.

Har·ri·son·burg (hăr′ĭ-sən-bûrg′). Independent city of N central Va., NNW of Charlottesville. Pop. 19,671.

Har·ro·gate (hăr′ə-gət, -gāt′). Borough of N central England, N of Leeds. Pop. 64,620.

Hart·ford (härt′fərd). Cap. of Conn., in the N central part. Pop. 136,392.

Har·tle·pool (härt′lē-po͞ol′, här′tl-). Borough of NE England, on the North Sea SSE of Newcastle-upon-Tyne. Pop. 95,100.

Har·vard (här′vərd). **1. Mount.** Peak, 14,414 ft (4,396.3 m), in the Sawatch range of W central Colo. **2.** Town of NE Mass., NE of Worcestor. Pop. 12,170.

Har·vey (här′vē). City of NE Ill., near Chicago. Pop. 35,810.

Harz (härts). Mountain range of central Germany, c. 60 mi (100 km) long, extending across the West German-East German border NE of Göttingen.

Has·brouck Heights (hăz′bro͝ok′). Borough of NE N.J., near Hackensack. Pop. 12,166.

Has·selt (häs′əlt). City of NE Belgium, E of Brussels. Metro. area pop. 275,000.

Has·tings (hā′stĭngz). **1.** Borough of SE England, on the Strait of Dover near the site of William the Conqueror's victory over the Saxons (1066). Pop. 74,200. **2.** City of E Minn., SE of St. Paul. Pop. 12,827. **3.** City of S Nebr., S of Grand Island. Pop. 23,045.

Has·tings-on-Hud·son (hā′-stĭngz-ŏn-hŭd′sən). Village of SE N.Y., on the Hudson NNW of Yonkers. Pop. 8,573.

Hatch·ie (hăch′ē). River, c. 180 mi (290 km), of N Miss. and SW Tenn.

Hat·ter·as (hăt′ər-əs). Long barrier island off the E coast of N.C., between Pamlico Sound and the Atlantic, with **Cape Hatteras** projecting from the SE part.

Hat·ties·burg (hăt′ēz-bûrg′). City of SE Miss., SE of Jackson. Pop. 40,829.

Hau·ra·ki Gulf (hou-rä′kē, -răk′ē). Inlet of the S Pacific on the N coast of North Is., New Zealand.

Haute·rive (ōt-rēv′). Town of E Que., Canada, near Baie Comeau. Pop. 14,724.

Ha·van·a (hə-văn′ə). Cap. of Cuba, in the NW part on the Gulf of Mexico. Pop. 1,961,674. —**Ha·van′an** *adj. & n.*

Hav·ant and Wa·ter·loo (hăv′ənt; wô′tər-lo͞o′, wŏt′ər-). Urban district of S England, near the English Channel E of Southhampton. Pop. 116,100.

Ha·vel (hä′fəl). River, c. 215 mi (345 km), of N central East Germany and West Berlin.

Have·lock (hăv′lŏk′). City of E N.C., SE of Raleigh. Pop. 17,718.

Hav·er·hill (hā'vrəl, -vər-əl). City of NE Mass., near Lawrence. Pop. 46,865.
Ha·ví·řov (hä'vîr-zhôf'). Town of N central Czechoslovakia, near Ostrava. Pop. 93,832.
Hav·re (hăv'ər). City of N Mont., NE of Great Falls. Pop. 10,891.
Haw (hô). River, c. 130 mi (209 km), of N central N.C.
Ha·wai·i (hə-wä'ē, -wä'yə). **1.** Largest and southernmost island of the state of Hawaii. **2.** State and island group (**Hawaiian Is.**) of the W U.S., in the central Pacific. Cap. Honolulu. Pop. 965,000. —**Ha·wai'ian** (-wä'yən) *adj. & n.*
Hawaiian Gar·dens (gär'dnz). City of S Calif., SE of Los Angeles. Pop. 10,548.
Hawaii Vol·ca·noes National Park (vŏl-kā'nōz). Park on Hawaii Is., containing 2 active volcanoes.
Ha·wash (hä'wäsh') or **A·wash** (ä'-wäsh'). River, c. 500 mi (805 km), of E Ethiopia.
Hawke Bay (hôk). Inlet of the S Pacific and E central coast of North Is., New Zealand.
Haw·thorne (hô'thôrn'). **1.** City of S Calif., near Los Angeles. Pop. 56,447. **2.** Borough of NE N.J., NNE of Paterson. Pop. 18,200.
Hay (hā). River, c. 530 mi (885 km), of NE B.C., NW Alta., and S N.W.T., Canada, flowing NE to Great Slave Lake.
Hayes (hāz). River, c. 300 mi (483 km), of E Man., Canada, flowing NE to Hudson Bay.
Hays (hāz). City of W central Kans., W of Salina. Pop. 16,301.
Hay·ward (hā'wərd). City of W Calif., SE of Oakland. Pop. 94,167.
Ha·zel Crest (hā'zəl krĕst'). Village of NE Ill., near Chicago. Pop. 13,973.
Hazel Park. City of SE Mich., near Detroit. Pop. 10,914.
Ha·zel·wood (hā'zəl-wŏŏd'). City of E Mo., near St. Louis. Pop. 12,935.
Ha·zle·ton (hā'zəl-tən). City of E central Pa., SSW of Wilkes-Barre. Pop. 27,318.
Heard (hûrd). Australian-claimed island of S Indian Ocean, SSE of Kerguelen Is.
Heart (härt). River, c. 180 mi (290 km), of SW N.Dak.
Heb·ri·des (hĕb'rĭ-dēz'). Islands of W Scotland, in the Atlantic, divided into the **Inner Hebrides**, closer to the Scottish mainland, and the **Outer Hebrides**, to the NW. —**Heb'ri·de'an** *adj. & n.*
He·bron (hē'brən). City of W Jordan, near Jerusalem. Pop. 43,000.
Hec·a·te (hĕk'ə-tē, hĕk'ət). Strait, c. 160 mi (257 km) long and c. 35–80 mi (56–129 km) wide, of W B.C., Canada, separating the Queen Charlotte Is. from coastal islands.
Heer·len (hâr'lən). City of SE Netherlands, near the West German border. Metro. area pop. 267,003.
He·fei (hŭ'fā'). City of E central China, WSW of Nanjing. Pop. 450,000.
He·gang (hŭ'gäng'). City of extreme NE China, in Manchuria near the Soviet border. Pop. 250,000.
Hei·del·berg (hīd'l-bûrg', hī'-dəl-bĕrk'). City of SW West Germany, on the Neckar R. NNW of Stuttgart. Pop. 128,773.
Heil·bronn (hīl'brôn', -brŏn'). City of S West Germany, on the Neckar R. N of Stuttgart. Pop. 111,426.
Hei·long (hā'lŏŏng'). *Chinese.* Amur.
Hek·la (hĕk'lə). Volcano, 4,747 ft (1,447.8 m), of SW Iceland.
Hel·e·na (hĕl'ə-nə). Cap. of Mont., in the W central part. Pop. 23,938.
Hel·go·land (hĕl'gō-lănd', -länt'). Island of N West Germany, one of the N Frisian Is. in **Helgoland Bay**, an inlet of the North Sea SW of Jutland.
Hel·i·con (hĕl'ĭ-kŏn', -kən). Mountain, 5,736 ft (1,749.5 m), of central Greece.
He·li·op·o·lis (hē'lē-ŏp'ə-lĭs). **1.** Ancient city of N Egypt, N of modern Cairo. **2.** Baalbek.
Hel·las (hĕl'əs). *Greek.* Greece.
Hel·les (hĕl'əs), **Cape.** Promontory of NW Turkey, at S end of Gallipoli Peninsula.
Hel·les·pont (hĕl'əs-pŏnt'). Dardanelles.
Hells Canyon (hĕlz). Gorge of the Snake R., on the Idaho-Ore. border.
Hel·mand (hĕl'mənd). River, c. 700 mi (1,125 km), flowing SW across Afghanistan.
Hel·mond (hĕl'mônt'). City of SE Netherlands, ENE of Eindhoven. Pop. 58,490.
Helm·stedt (hĕlm'shtet'). City of E West Germany, at the East German border E of Hannover. Pop. 26,816.
Hel·sing·borg (hĕl'sĭng-bôrg', hĕl'-sĭng-bôr'ē). Hälsingborg.
Hel·sing·ør (hĕl'sĭng-ûr', -œr'). City of E Denmark, on the Oresund. Pop. 56,566.
Hel·sin·ki (hĕl'sĭng'kē, hĕl-sĭng'-). Cap. of Finland, in the S on the Gulf of Finland. Pop. 484,879.
Hel·vel·lyn (hĕl-vĕl'ĭn). Mountain, c. 3,118 ft (951 m), of NW England.
Hel·ve·tia (hĕl-vē'shə, -shē-ə). *Latin.* Switzerland. —**Hel·ve'tian** *adj. & n.*
Hem·el Hemp·stead (hĕm'əl hĕmp'-stĕd', -stĭd). Borough of SE England, NW of London. Pop. 71,150.
Hem·et (hĕm'ĭt). City of S Calif., E of Santa Ana. Pop. 23,211.
Hemp·stead (hĕmp'stĕd', -stĭd). Village of SE N.Y., on W Long Is. S of Mineola. Pop. 40,404.
Hen·der·son (hĕn'dər-sən). **1.** City of NW Ky., on the Ohio R. S of Evansville, Ind. Pop. 24,834. **2.** City of SE Nev., SE of Las Vegas. Pop. 24,363. **3.** City of N N.C., NNE of Raleigh. Pop. 13,522. **4.** City of NE Tex., ESE of Tyler. Pop. 11,473.
Hen·der·son·ville (hĕn'dər-sən-vĭl', -vəl). City of N Tenn., NE of Memphis. Pop. 26,561.
Heng·e·lo (hĕng'ə-lō'). City of E Netherlands, near the West Germany border. Pop. 75,216.
Heng·yang (hŭng'yäng'). City of S central China, SSW of Changsha. Pop. 350,000.
Hen·ley (hĕn'lē) or **Hen·ley-on-Thames** (-ŏn-tĕmz'). Borough of central England, W of London. Pop. 11,860.
Hen·lo·pen (hĕn-lō'pən). Cape of SE Del., at S entrance to Delaware Bay.
Hen·ry (hĕn'rē). Cape of SE Va., at entrance to Chesapeake Bay E of Norfolk.
Her·a·cle·a (hĕr'ə-klē'ə). Ancient Greek city of S Italy, near the Gulf of Taranto.
He·rat (hĕ-rät'). City of NW Afghanistan, on the Hari Rud. Pop. 157,000.
Her·cu·la·ne·um (hûr'kyə-lā'nē-əm). Ancient city of S central Italy, near Naples; destroyed by eruption of Mt. Vesuvius (A.D. 79).
Her·e·ford (hĕr'ə-fərd). **1.** Borough of W central England, SW of Birmingham. Pop. 46,800. **2.** City of NW Tex., in the Panhandle SW of Amarillo. Pop. 15,853.
Her·ford (hĕr'fôrt). City of N central West Germany, WSW of Hannover. Pop. 62,977.
Her·mon (hûr'mən). Highest peak, 9,232 ft (2,815.8 m), of the Anti-Lebanon range, on the Syria-Lebanon border.
Her·mo·sa Beach (hər-mō'sə). City of S Calif., SW of Los Angeles. Pop. 18,070.
Her·mo·sil·lo (ĕr-mô-sē'yô). City of NW Mexico, W of Chihuahua. Pop. 299,700.
Hern·don (hûrn'dən). Town of N Va., WNW of Washington, D.C. Pop. 11,449.
Her·ne (hĕr'nə). City of W West Germany, NE of Essen. Pop. 183,065.
Her·rin (hĕr'ĭn). City of S Ill., SE of East St. Louis. Pop. 10,040.
Her·ten (hĕr'tən). City of W West Germany, N of Essen. Pop. 69,400.
Hert·ford (här'fərd, härt'-). City of SE England, N of London. Pop. 20,760.
Her·ze·go·vi·na (hĕr'tsə-gō-vē'nə, hûr'-). Region of W central Yugoslavia. —**Her'ze·go·vi'ni·an** *adj. & n.*
Hesse (hĕs). Region and former grand duchy of central West Germany. —**Hes'sian** (hĕsh'ən) *adj. & n.*
Hi·a·le·ah (hī'ə-lē'ə). City of SE Fla., near Miami. Pop. 145,254.
Hib·bing (hĭb'ĭng). City of NE Minn., NW of Duluth. Pop. 21,193.
Hi·ber·ni·a (hī-bûr'nē-ə). *Latin.* Ireland. —**Hi·ber'ni·an** *adj. & n.*
Hick·o·ry (hĭk'ə-rē, hĭk'rē). City of W central N.C., NW of Charlotte. Pop. 20,757.
Hickory Hills. City of NE Ill., near Chicago. Pop. 13,778.
Hi·dal·go del Par·ral (ē-*th*äl'gô dĕl pä-räl'). City of N Mexico, S of Chihuahua. Pop. 57,619.
Hi·er·ap·o·lis (hī-ər-ăp'ō-lĭs). Ancient city of NW Asia Minor.
Hier·ro (yĕ'rô). Smallest and westernmost of the Canary Is. of Spain.
Hi·ga·shi-O·sa·ka (hē-gä'shē-ô-sä'-kä). City of W central Honshu, Japan, near Osaka. Pop. 521,635.
High·land (hī'lənd). Town of NW Ind., near Gary. Pop. 22,935.
Highland Park. **1.** City of NE Ill., on Lake Michigan near Chicago. Pop. 30,611. **2.** City of SE Mich., surrounded by Detroit. Pop. 27,909. **3.** Borough of N central N.J., near New Brunswick. Pop. 13,396.
High·lands (hī'ləndz). Mountainous region of N Scotland N of and including the Grampians.
High Point (hī' point'). City on N central N.C., SW of Greensboro. Pop. 64,107.
High Wyc·ombe (wĭk'əm). Borough of S England, WNW of London. Pop. 61,190.
Hil·des·heim (hĭl'dəs-hīm'). City of N central West Germany, SSE of Hannover. Pop. 102,512.
Hills·bor·o (hĭlz'bûr'ō). City of NW Ore., W of Portland. Pop. 27,664.
Hills·bor·ough (hĭlz'bûr'ō). City of W Calif., S of San Francisco. Pop. 10,451.
Hills·dale (hĭlz'dāl'). Borough of NE N.J., near Hackensack. Pop. 10,495.
Hi·lo (hē'lō). City of Hawaii, on E coast of Hawaii Is. Pop. 29,600.
Hil·ver·sum (hĭl'vər-səm). City of central Netherlands, SE of Amsterdam. Pop. 92,964.
Him·a·la·yas (hĭm'ə-lā'əz, hĭ-mäl'-yəz) also **Him·a·la·ya Mountains** (hĭm'ə-lā'ə, hĭ-mäl'yə). Mountain system of S central Asia, extending c. 1,500 mi (2,415 km) through Kashmir, N India, S Tibet, Nepal, Sikkim, and Bhutan. —**Him'a·la'yan** *adj. & n.*
Hi·me·ji (hē'mē-jē', hē-mĕ'jē). City of SW Honshu, Japan, WNW of Kobe. Pop. 446,255.
Hinck·ley (hĭngk'lē). Urban district of central England, E of Birmingham. Pop. 49,310.
Hin·du Kush (hĭn'dōō kŏŏsh'). Mountain range of SW Asia, extending c. 500 mi (805 km) W from N Pakistan to NE Afghanistan.
Hin·du·stan (hĭn'dōō-stăn', -stän', -dōō-). **1.** The Indian subcontinent. **2.** N India.
Hines·ville (hīnz'vĭl', -vəl). City of SE Ga., SW of Savannah. Pop. 11,309.
Hing·ham (hĭng'əm). Town of E Mass., SE of Boston. Pop. 20,339.
Hins·dale (hĭnz'dāl'). Village of NE Ill., near Chicago. Pop. 16,726.
Hip·po (hĭp'ō) also **Hippo Re·gi·us** (rē'jē-əs). Ancient Numidian city of NW Africa, in present-day NE Algeria.
Hi·ra·tsu·ka (hē'rä-tsōō'kä). City of central Honshu, on the Pacific WSW of Yokohama. Pop. 214,299.
Hi·ro·shi·ma (hîr'ə-shē'mə, hĭ-rō'-shĭ-mə). City of SW Honshu, Japan, on the Inland Sea; destroyed by 1st atomic bomb used in warfare (1945). Pop. 899,394.
His·pan·io·la (hĭs'pən-yō'lə). Island of the West Indies E of Cuba, divided between Haiti and the Dominican Republic.
Hi·ta·chi (hē-tä'chē). City of E central Honshu, Japan, on the Pacific NE of Tokyo. Pop. 204,612.
Hitch·in (hĭch'ĭn). Urban district of SE England, NNW of London. Pop. 29,190.
Hi·va O·a also **Hi·va·o·a** (hē'və-ō'ə). Island of the S Pacific, in the SE Marquesas, French Polynesia.
Hi·was·see (hī-wŏs'ē). River, c. 150 mi (241 km), of NE Ga., W N.C., and SE Tenn.
Hjäl·ma·ren (yĕl'mä-rən, -mə-rœn'). Lake, c. 190 sq mi (492 sq km), of S central Sweden.
Hka·ka·bo Ra·zi (kä'kä-bō rä'zē). Highest peak (19,296 ft/5,885.3 m) in Burma, in the extreme N part.
Ho·bart (hō'bərt). **1.** (*also* hō'bärt'). City of SE Tasmania, Australia, on an inlet of the Tasman Sea. Metro. area pop. 170,200. **2.** City of NW Ind., near Gary. Pop. 22,987.
Hobbs (hŏbz). City of SE N.Mex., near the Tex. border SE of Roswell. Pop. 28,794.
Ho·bo·ken (hō'bō'kən). **1.** City of N Belgium, on the Scheldt near Antwerp. Pop. 34,640. **2.** City of NE N.J., opposite Lower Manhattan. Pop. 42,460.
Ho Chi Minh City (hō' chē' mĭn', shē'). City of S Vietnam, near the South China Sea. Pop. 3,500,000.
Ho·dei·da (hō-dā'də, -dī'-). City of W central Yemen, on the Red Sea. Pop. 106,080.
Hód·me·ző·vá·sár·hely (hôd'-mĕ-zœ-vä'shär-hā). City of SE Hungary, near the Tisza R. Pop. 45,100.
Hoek van Hol·land (hŏŏk' vän hô'-länt). *Dutch.* Hook of Holland.
Hof (hōf, hôf). City of E central West Germany, near the East German and Czechoslovak borders. Pop. 53,398.
Ho·fei (hŭ'fā'). Hefei.
Hoff·man Es·tates (hŏf'mən ĭ-stāts'). Village of NE Ill., near Chicago. Pop. 38,258.
Ho·fuf (hōō-fōōf'). City of E Saudi Arabia, E of Riyadh. Pop. 101,271.
Ho·he Tau·ern (hō'ə tou'ərn). Range of the E Alps in S Austria, rising to 12,461 ft (3,800.6 m).
Hoh·hot (hō'hōt'). City of N China, in Inner Mongolia WNW of Beijing. Pop. 450,000.
Hoi·how (hoi'hou'). Haikou.
Ho·kang (hŭ'gäng'). Hegang.
Hok·kai·do (hŏ-kī'dō). 2nd-largest island of Japan, N of Honshu.
Hol·brook (hōl'brŏŏk'). Town of E Mass., near Brockton. Pop. 11,140.
Hol·den (hōl'dən). Town of central Mass., near Worcester. Pop. 13,336.
Hol·guín (ôl-gēn'). City of E Cuba, NNW of Santiago de Cuba. Pop. 129,800.
Hol·land (hŏl'ənd). **1.** The Netherlands. **2.** City of SW Mich., SW of Grand Rapids. Pop. 26,281. —**Hol'land·er** *n.*
Hol·lis·ter (hŏl'ĭ-stər). City of W Calif., SE of San Jose. Pop. 11,488.
Hol·lis·ton (hŏl'ĭ-stən). Town of E central Mass., SW of Boston. Pop. 12,622.
Hol·ly·wood (hŏl'ē-wŏŏd'). **1.** Community of S Calif., part of Los Angeles. **2.** City of SE Fla., on the Atlantic N of Miami Beach. Pop. 117,188.
Ho·lon (hō-lōn'). City of W central Israel, near Tel Aviv-Jaffa. Pop. 128,400.
Hol·stein (hōl'stīn', hôl'shtīn'). Region and former duchy of N West Germany, at the base of the Jutland Peninsula.
Hol·ston (hōl'stən). River, c. 120 mi (193 km), of NE Tenn.
Ho·ly Cross (hō'lē krôs', krŏs'), **Mount of the.** Peak, 13,996 ft (4,268.8 m), in the Sawatch Mts. of W central Colo.
Hol·yoke (hōl'yōk'). City of SW Mass., near Springfield. Pop. 44,678.
Hom·burg (hŏm'bûrg', hôm'bŏŏrk'). City of central West Germany, N of Frankfurt. Pop. 41,581.
Home·stead (hōm'stĕd'). City of SE Fla., SW of Miami. Pop. 20,668.
Home·wood (hōm'wŏŏd'). **1.** City of N central Ala., near Birmingham. Pop. 21,271. **2.** Village of NE Ill., near Chicago. Pop. 19,724.
Homs (hômz, hôms). City of W central Syria, on the Orontes R. Pop. 306,000.
Hon·du·ras (hŏn-dŏŏr'əs, -dyŏŏr'-). **1. Gulf of.** Inlet of the W Caribbean, on the coasts of Belize, Honduras, and Guatemala. **2.** Country of N Central America. Cap. Tegucigalpa. Pop. 3,750,000. —**Hon·du'ran** *adj. & n.*

Hong Kong also **Hong·kong** (hŏng′kŏng′, -kŏng′; hŏng′kŏng′, -kŏng′). British crown colony, 391 sq mi (1,012.7 sq km), on SE coast of China SE of Guangzhou, including **Hong Kong Is.** (32 sq mi/82.9 sq km) and adjacent areas. Cap. Victoria. Pop. 5,265,000.
Hong·shui (ho͝ong′shwā′). River, c. 900 mi (1,448 km), of S China.
Hong·ze (ho͝ong′dzŭ′). Lake, c. 65 mi (105 km) long, of E China N of Nanjing.
Ho·ni·a·ra (hō′nē-är′ə). Cap. of the Solomon Is., on NW coast of Guadalcanal. Pop. 14,942.
Hon·o·lu·lu (hŏn′ə-lo͞o′lo͞o). Cap. of Hawaii, on SE coast of Oahu. Pop. 365,048.
Hon·shu (hŏn′sho͞o). Island of Japan, in the central part between the Sea of Japan and the Pacific.
Hood (ho͝od). **1. Canal.** Narrow arm of W Puget Sound in NW Wash. **2. Mount.** Volcanic peak, 11,235 ft (3,426.7 m), in the Cascade range of NW Ore.
Hoogh·ly (ho͞og′lē). River, c. 160 mi (257 km), of E India, the W branch of the Ganges on its delta.
Hook of Hol·land (ho͝ok; hŏl′ənd). Cape and harbor of SW Netherlands, on the North Sea WNW of Rotterdam.
Hoo·sac (ho͞o′sək). S range of the Green Mts., in NW Mass. and SW Vt.
Hoo·ver (ho͞o′vər). City of N central Ala., near Birmingham. Pop. 15,064.
Ho·pat·cong (hə-păt′kŏng′, -kông′). Borough of N central N.J., on **Lake Hopatcong** (c. 7 mi/11 km long), NNW of Morristown. Pop. 15,531.
Hope (hōp). City of SW Ark., SW of Hot Springs. Pop. 10,331.
Hope·well (hōp′wĕl′). Independent city of E Va., SSE of Richmond. Pop. 23,397.
Hop·kins (hŏp′kĭnz). City of E Minn., near Minneapolis. Pop. 15,336.
Hop·kins·ville (hŏp′kĭnz-vĭl′). City of SW Ky., W of Bowling Green. Pop. 27,318.
Hor·muz also **Hor·moz** (hôr′mŭz′, hôr-mo͞oz′) or **Or·muz** (ôr′-, ôr-). **1.** Strait linking the Persian Gulf with the Gulf of Oman. **2.** Island of S Iran, in the Strait of Hormuz.
Horn (hôrn), **Cape.** Headland of extreme S Chile, in the Tierra del Fuego archipelago; southernmost point of South America.
Hor·nell (hôr-nĕl′). City of SW N.Y., WNW of Elmira. Pop. 10,234.
Hor·sens (hôr′sənz, -səns). City of central Denmark, at the head of **Horsens Fjord**, an inlet of the Kattegat. Pop. 54,533.
Horse·shoe Falls (hôrs′sho͞o′). Canadian Falls.
Hor·sham (hôr′shəm). Urban district of SE England, SSW of London. Pop. 26,770.
Hor·ton (hôr′tn). River, c. 275 mi (442 km), of W N.W.T., Canada.
Hos·pi·ta·let (ŏs′pē-tä-lĕt′). City of NE Spain, SW of Barcelona. Pop. 294,280.
Ho·tan (hō′tän′). Intermittent river of NW China.
Hot Springs (hŏt). City and resort of W central Ark., within **Hot Springs National Park**, WSW of Little Rock. Pop. 35,810.
Hou·ma (hō′mə, ho͞o′-). City of SE La., SW of New Orleans. Pop. 32,602.
Hou·sa·ton·ic (ho͞o′sə-tŏn′ĭk). River, 148 mi (238.1 km), of W Mass. and W Conn.
Hous·ton (hyo͞o′stən). City of SE Tex., NW of Galveston. Pop. 1,594,086.

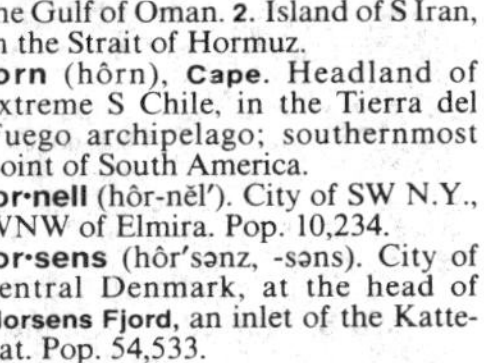

Honduras

Hove (hōv). Borough of SE England, on the English Channel W of Brighton. Pop. 87,800.
How·rah (hou′rä, -rə). City of E India, on the Hooghly R. opposite Calcutta. Pop. 737,877.
Hoy·ers·wer·da (hoi′ərs-vĕr′dä). City of SE East Germany, NNE of Dresden. Pop. 70,133.
Hra·dec Krá·lo·vé (hrä′dĕts krä′lô-vĕ). City of N Czechoslovakia, on the Elbe R. E of Prague. Pop. 93,165.
Hsi·ang (shē-äng′, shyäng). Xiang.
Hsin·chu (shĭn′cho͞o′). City of NW Taiwan, on Formosa Strait SW of Taipei. Pop. 233,459.
Hsin·kao Shan (shĭn′gou′ shän′). Peak, 13,113 ft (3,999.5 m), of E Taiwan, highest elevation on the island.
Huai (hwī). River, c. 680 mi (1,094 km), of E China.
Huai·nan (hwī′nän′). City of E central China, WNW of Nanjing. Pop. 400,000.
Hua·lien (hwä′lyĕn′). City of central Taiwan, on the Pacific. Pop. 101,010.
Hual·la·ga (wä-yä′gä). River, c. 700 mi (1,126 km), of central Peru.
Huan·ca·yo (wäng-kä′yô). City of S central Peru, E of Lima. Pop. 64,777.
Huang (hwäng). Yellow R.
Huang·shi or **Huang·shih** (hwäng′shœ′). City of central China, on the Yangtze SE of Wuhan. Pop. 140,000.
Huas·ca·rán (wäs-kä-rän′). Extinct volcano, 22,205 ft (6,772.5 m), in the Andes of W central Peru.
Hu·bli-Dhar·war (ho͞ob′lē-där′wär′). City of SW India, NW of Bangalore. Pop. 379,166.
Huck·nall (hŭk′nəl). Urban district of central England, NNW of Nottingham. Pop. 27,110.
Hud·ders·field (hŭd′ərz-fēld′). Borough of N central England, NE of Manchester. Pop. 130,060.
Hud·son (hŭd′sən). **1.** Bay of the Atlantic in E central Canada, an inland sea connected to the Atlantic by **Hudson Strait** between S Baffin Is. and N Que. **2.** River, c. 315 mi (505 km), of E N.Y., flowing S to the Atlantic at New York City. **3.** Town of E central Mass., NE of Worcester. Pop. 16,408. **4.** Town of S N.H., near Nashua. Pop. 14,022.
Hue (hwā, hyo͞o-ā′). City of central Vietnam, near the South China Sea. Pop. 199,900.
Huel·va (wĕl′vä). City of SW Spain, on the Gulf of Cádiz. Pop. 125,810.
Hu·ey·town (hyo͞o′ē-toun′). City of N central Ala., near Bessemer. Pop. 13,309.
Hu·he·hot (ho͞o-hā-hōt′). Hohhot.
Hui·la (wē′lä). Volcano, c. 18,700 ft (5,703.5 m), in the Cordillera Central of W Colombia.
Hu·la also **Hu·leh** (ho͞o′lə). Lake of NE Israel, N of the Jordan R.
Hull (hŭl). **1.** City of SW Que., Canada, opposite Ottawa, Ont. Pop. 61,039. **2.** Also **Kings·ton-up·on-Hull** (kĭng′stən-ə-pŏn-hŭl′, -pôn-). Borough of NE England, on the N shore of the Humber. Pop. 275,400.
Hu·lun Nur (ho͞o′lo͞on′ nōr′). Lake of NE China, in W Manchuria near the Soviet border.
Hum·ber (hŭm′bər). Estuary, c. 40 mi (64 km), of the Trent and Ouse rivers in NE England.
Hum·boldt (hŭm′bōlt′). **1.** Ocean current of the S Pacific, flowing N along coasts of N Chile and Peru. **2.** Bay of the Pacific in NW Calif. **3.** River, c. 290 mi (466.6 km), of N Nev. **4.** Glacier in NW Greenland, c. 60 mi (97 km) wide and 300 ft (91.5 m) high. **5.** City of W central Tenn., NNW of Jackson. Pop. 10,209.
Hum·phreys Peak (hŭm′frēz′, hŭm′-). Mountain, 12,633 ft (3,853.1 m), in N Ariz.
Hun·ga·ry (hŭng′gə-rē). Country of central Europe. Cap. Budapest. Pop. 10,945,000. —**Hun·gar′i·an** (hŭng-gâr′ē-ən) *adj. & n.*
Hung·nam (ho͞ong′näm′). City of central North Korea, on the Sea of Japan. Pop. 143,600.
Hung·shui (ho͞ong′shwā′). Hongshui.

Hungary

Hung·tze (ho͞ong′dzŭ′). Hongze.
Hun·ter (hŭn′tər). River, 287 mi (461.8 km), of SE Australia.
Hun·ting·ton (hŭn′tĭng-tən). **1.** City of NE Ind., SW of Fort Wayne. Pop. 16,202. **2.** City of W W.Va., on the Ohio W of Charleston. Pop. 63,684.
Huntington Beach. City of S Calif., SE of Long Beach. Pop. 170,505.
Huntington Park. City of S Calif., near Los Angeles. Pop. 46,223.
Hunts·ville (hŭnts′vĭl′). **1.** Town of SE Ont., Canada, N of Toronto. Pop. 11,031. **2.** City of N central Ala., ENE of Decatur. Pop. 142,513. **3.** City of E central Tex., N of Houston. Pop. 23,936.
Hu·on Gulf (hyo͞o′ŏn). Inlet of the Solomon Sea, on E coast of New Guinea.
Hu·ron (hyo͝or′ən, -ŏn′). **1.** 2nd largest of the Great Lakes, between SE Ont., Canada, and E Mich. **2.** City of E central S.Dak., NW of Sioux Falls. Pop. 13,000.
Hurst (hûrst). City of NE Tex., near Fort Worth. Pop. 31,420.
Hutch·in·son (hŭch′ĭn-sən). City of S central Kans., NW of Wichita. Pop. 40,284.
Huy·ton-with-Ro·by (hīt′n-wĭth-rō′bē). Urban district of NW England, near Liverpool. Pop. 179,700.
Hwang (hwäng). Yellow R.
Hy·atts·ville (hī′əts-vĭl′). City of central Md., near Washington, D.C. Pop. 12,709.
Hyde Park (hīd). **1.** Public park in central Greater London, England. **2.** Village of SE N.Y.; birth and burial place of Franklin D. Roosevelt. Pop. 2,805.
Hy·der·a·bad (hī′dər-ə-băd′, -băd′, hī′drə-). **1.** City of central India, ESE of Bombay. Pop. 1,607,396. **2.** City of S Pakistan, on the Indus. Pop. 600,796.
Hy·ères (ē-âr′, yĕr). **1.** French island group in the Mediterranean off the SE coast of France. **2.** City of SE France, on the Mediterranean. Pop. 29,611.
Hy·met·tus (hī-mĕt′əs). Mountain ridge, c. 3,370 ft (1,028 m), in E central Greece near Athens.
Hyr·ca·ni·a (hər-kā′nē-ə). Province of ancient Persia, on SE shore of the Caspian Sea.

I

Ia·şi (yäsh, yä′shē) also **Jas·sy** (yä′sē). City of NE Rumania, near the Soviet border. Pop. 278,545.
I·ba·dan (ē-bä′dän, -bäd′n). City of SW Nigeria, NNE of Lagos. Pop. 847,000.
I·ba·gué (ē-bä-gĕ′). City of central Colombia, W of Bogotá. Pop. 257,000.
I·be·ri·a (ī-bîr′ē-ə). **1.** The Iberian Peninsula. **2.** Ancient Spain. —**I·be′ri·an** *adj. & n.*
Iberian. Peninsula of SW Europe occupied by Spain and Portugal.
I·bi·cuí (ē-bē-kwē′). River, c. 300 mi (482.7 km), of S Brazil.
I·bi·za (ē-bē′sä) also **I·vi·za** (-vē-). Spanish island of the Balearics, in the W Mediterranean SW of Majorca.
I·ca (ē′kä). City of SW Peru, SSE of Lima. Pop. 73,883.
I·car·i·a (ī-kâr′ē-ə, ī-kâr′-). Variant of **Ikaria.**
Ice·land (īs′lənd). Island republic in the North Atlantic, near the Arctic Circle. Cap. Reykjavík. Pop. 229,000. —**Ice′land·er** *n.* —**Ice·land′ic** *adj.*

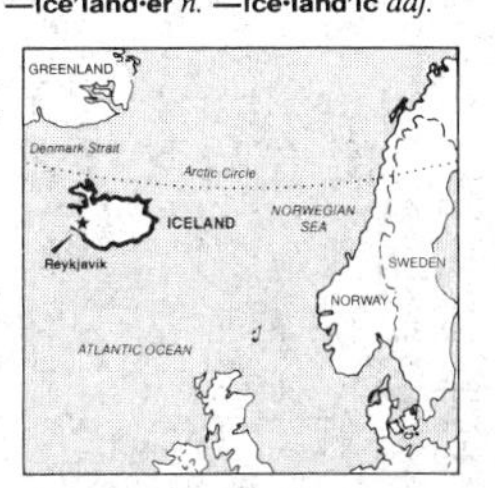

Iceland

I·chi·ha·ra (ē′chē-hä′rä). City of E central Honshu, Japan, on Tokyo Bay opposite Tokyo. Pop. 216,395.
I·chi·no·mi·ya (ē′chē-nô′-mē-yä′). City of central Honshu, Japan, NNW of Nagoya. Pop. 253,138.
I·da (ī′də). **1.** Mountains of NW Turkey, SE of ancient Troy, rising to 5,797 ft (1,768.1 m). **2. Mount.** Highest mountain on Crete (8,058 ft/2,457.7 m), in the central part.
I·da·ho (ī′də-hō′). State of NW U.S. Cap. Boise. Pop. 943,935. —**I′da·ho′an** *adj. & n.*
Idaho Falls. City of SE Idaho, NNE of Pocatello. Pop. 39,590.
Ie·per (yā′pər) also **Y·pres** (ē′prə). City of W Belgium; site of 3 major World War I battles. Pop. 21,000.
I·fe (ē′fē). City of SW Nigeria, E of Ibadan. Pop. 176,000.
I·gua·çú also **I·guas·sú** (ē′gwə-so͞o′). River, c. 380 mi (611 m), of S Brazil, flowing W to the Paraná at the Argentina-Paraguay-Brazil border, just above which it forms **Iguaçú Falls** (2.5 mi/4 km wide).
I·gua·la (ē-gwä′lä). City of S Mexico, SSW of Mexico City. Pop. 45,355.
I·gua·zú (ē′gwä-so͞o′). *Spanish.* Iguaçú.
Ij·mui·den or **IJ·mui·den** (ī-moi′dən). City of W Netherlands, on the North Sea WNW of Amsterdam. Pop. 61,202.
Ijs·sel or **IJs·sel** (ī′səl). River, c. 70 mi (112.6 km), of E Netherlands, flowing out of the Rhine R. N into the Ijsselmeer.
Ijs·sel·meer or **IJs·sel·meer** (ī′səl-mâr′, -mär′). Dike-enclosed lake, 465 sq mi (1,204 sq km), of NW Netherlands.
I·ka·ri·a (ē′kä-rē′ə) also **I·car·i·a** (ī-kâr′ē-ə, ī-kâr′-). Island of SE Greece, in the Aegean W of Samos.
I·ke·da (ē-kĕ′dä). City of S Honshu, Japan, near Osaka. Pop. 101,872.
Ile du Dia·ble (ēl dü dyä′blə). *French.* Devil's Island.
I·le·sha (ē-lā′shä). City of SW Nigeria, E of Ibadan. Pop. 224,000.
I·lhé·us (ē-lyĕ′o͞osh). City of E Brazil, on the Atlantic SSW of Salvador. Pop. 58,529.
I·li (ē′lē′). River, c. 590 mi (949 km), of NW China and SE Central Asian USSR, flowing W and NW into Lake Balkhash.
Il·i·am·na (ĭl′ē-ăm′nə). **1.** Lake, c. 1,000 sq mi (2,590 sq km), of SW Alas. **2.** Volcano, 10,016 ft (3,054.8 m), on N shore of this lake.
I·li·gan (ē-lē′gän). City of W central Mindanao, Philippines, on Mindanao Sea. Metro. area pop. 118,778.
Il·kes·ton (ĭl′kĭ-stən). Borough of central England, NW of Nottingham. Pop. 33,690.
Il·lam·pu (ē-yäm-po͞o′). Peak, 20,873 ft (6,366.3 m), in the Andes of W Bolivia.
Il·li·ma·ni (ē′yē-mä′nē). Mountain, 21,151 ft (6,451.1 m), in the Andes of W Bolivia.
Il·li·nois (ĭl′ə-noi′, -noiz′). **1.** River, 273 mi (439.3 km), of N and W Ill. **2.** Waterway, 336 mi (540.6 km), of N Ill., linking Lake Michigan with the Mississippi and including the Chicago, Des Plaines, and Illinois rivers. **3.** State of N central U.S. Cap. Springfield. Pop. 11,418,461. —**Il′li·nois′an** (-noi′ən, -zən) *adj. & n.*
Il·lyr·i·a (ĭ-lĭr′ē-ə). Ancient region of

the NW Balkan Peninsula, on the Adriatic coast. **—Il·lyr'i·an** *adj.* & *n.*

Il·men (ĭl'mən, ĕl'mĕn). Lake, varying from c. 300 to c. 800 sq mi (780–2,070 sq km), in NW European USSR SSE of Leningrad.

I·lo·i·lo (ē'lô-ē'lô). City of central Philippines, on SE Panay. Pop. 227,027.

I·lo·rin (ē'lôr-ēn', ē-lô'rēn). City of SW Nigeria, NNE of Lagos. Pop. 282,000.

I·ma·ba·ri (ē'mä-bä'rē). City of S Japan, on the Inland Sea coast of N Shikoku. Pop. 123,928.

Im·bros (ĕm'vrôs', -brôs, ĭm'brəs) also **Im·roz** (ĕm-rôz', ĭm-). Island of NW Turkey, in the Aegean off the coast of Gallipoli.

I·mo·la (ē'mō-lä). City of N central Italy, SE of Bologna. Pop. 48,000.

Im·per·ia (ēm-pĕ'ryä). City of NW Italy, on the Ligurian Sea. Pop. 42,159.

Im·pe·ri·al Beach (ĭm-pîr'ē-əl). City of S Calif., on the Mexican border. Pop. 22,689.

Imperial Valley. Region of SE Calif. and NE Lower California, Mexico.

Im·roz (ĕm-rôz', ĭm-). Variant of **Imbros.**

I·na·gua (ē-nä'gwä). Island group of the SE Bahamas, including **Great Inagua** and **Little Inagua.**

I·na·ri (ē'nä-rē). Lake, c. 500 sq mi (1,295 sq km), of N Finland.

In·chon (ĭn'chŏn'). City of NW South Korea, on the Yellow Sea. Pop. 936,497.

In·de·pen·dence (ĭn-dĭ-pĕn'dəns). **1.** City of SE Kans., SE of Wichita. Pop. 10,598. **2.** City of W Mo., E of Kansas City. Pop. 111,806.

In·di·a (ĭn'dē-ə). **1.** Peninsula and subcontinent of S Asia S of the Himalayas, occupied by India, Nepal, Bhutan, Sikkim, Pakistan, and Bangladesh. **2.** Country of S Asia; 2nd most populous in the world. Cap. New Delhi. Pop. 669,860,000. **—In'di·an** *adj.* & *n.*

India

Indian. Ocean, c. 28,350,000 sq mi (73,426,500 sq km), extending from S Asia to Antarctica and from E Africa to SE Australia.

In·di·an·a (ĭn'dē-ăn'ə). **1.** State of N central U.S. Cap. Indianapolis. Pop. 5,490,179. **2.** Borough of W central Pa., ENE of Pittsburgh. Pop. 16,051. **—In'di·an'i·an** *adj.* & *n.*

In·di·an·ap·o·lis (ĭn'dē-ə-năp'ə-lĭs). Cap. of Ind., in the central part. Pop. 700,807.

In·di·a·no·la (ĭn'dē-ə-nō'lə). City of S central Iowa, S of Des Moines. Pop. 10,843.

Indian River. Lagoon extending c. 120 mi (193 km) along E central Fla. coast.

Indian Territory. Former U.S. territory, now part of Okla.

In·dies (ĭn'dēz). **1.** East Indies. **2.** West Indies.

In·di·gir·ka (ĭn'dĭ-gîr'kə). River, c. 1,113 mi (1,791 km), of NE Siberian USSR, flowing N to the E Siberian Sea.

In·di·o (ĭn'dē-ō'). City of SE Calif., E of Santa Ana. Pop. 21,611.

In·do·chi·na (ĭn'dō-chī'nə). **1.** Peninsula of SE Asia, occupied by Vietnam, Laos, Cambodia, Thailand, Burma, and the Malay Peninsula. **2.** Former federation of French colonies and protectorates in SE Asia. **—In'do·chi'nese'** *adj.* & *n.*

In·do·ne·sia (ĭn'də-nē'zhə, -shə, -dō-). Country of SE Asia in the Malay Archipelago, including Sumatra, Java, Sulawesi, the Moluccas, parts of Borneo, New Guinea, and Timor, and many smaller islands. Cap. Djakarta. Pop. 153,510,000. **—In'do·ne'sian** *adj.* & *n.*

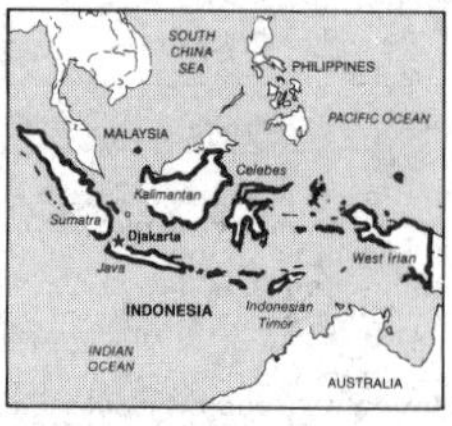

Indonesia

Indonesian Ti·mor (tē'môr', tī-môr'). W part of Timor Is., in the Malay Archipelago.

In·dore (ĭn-dôr', -dōr'). City of W central India, NNE of Bombay. Pop. 543,381.

In·dra·va·ti (ĭn'drə-vä'tē). River, 315 mi (506.8 km), of central India.

In·dus (ĭn'dəs). River of S central Asia, rising in SW Tibet and flowing c. 1,900 mi (3,057 km) NW through Kashmir and SW through Pakistan to the Arabian Sea.

In·gle·wood (ĭng'gəl-wo͝od'). City of S Calif., near Los Angeles. Pop. 94,245.

In·go·da (ĭn-gô'dä). River, 360 mi (579.2 km), of S Siberian USSR.

In·gol·stadt (ĭng'ôl-shtät'). City of S West Germany, on the Danube. Pop. 89,467.

In·gu·lets (ĭn-go͞o'lĕts, ēn-go͞o-lyĕts'). River, c. 340 mi (547 km), of SW European USSR.

Ink·ster (ĭngk'stər). City of SE Mich., near Detroit. Pop. 35,190.

In·land (ĭn'lənd, -lănd'). Sea of the Pacific in S Japan, extending c. 240 mi (386 km) between Honshu, Shikoku, and Kyushu.

Inland Pas·sage (păs'ĭj). Inside Passage.

Inn (ĭn). River of E Switzerland, W Austria, and SE West Germany, flowing c. 320 mi (515 km) to the Danube.

In·ner Heb·ri·des (ĭn'ər hĕb'rĭ-dēz'). See **Hebrides.**

Inner Mon·go·li·a (mŏng-gō'lē-ə, -gōl'yə, mŏn-). Region of NE China.

Inns·bruck (ĭnz'bro͝ok', ĭns'-). City of SW Austria, WSW of Salzburg. Pop. 120,400.

In·side Pas·sage (ĭn'sīd' păs'ĭj). Natural waterway extending c. 950 mi (1,530 km) along coasts of SE Alas. and W B.C., Canada, through the Alexander Archipelago.

In·ter·la·ken (ĭn'tər-lä'kən, ĭn'tər-lä'-kən). Town and resort center of W central Switzerland, SE of Bern. Pop. 4,735.

In·tra·coas·tal Waterway (ĭn'-trə-kō'stəl). System of navigation channels and canals along the U.S. Atlantic and Gulf coasts.

In·ver·car·gill (ĭn'vər-kär'gəl). City of extreme S South Is., New Zealand. Pop. 49,900.

In·ver Grove Heights (ĭn'vər grōv). City of E Minn., near St. Paul. Pop. 17,171.

In·ver·ness (ĭn'vər-nĕs'). Burgh of N Scotland, on the Moray Firth. Pop. 36,595.

Io·án·ni·na (yô-ä'nē-nä'). City of NW Greece, near the Albanian border. Pop. 40,130.

I·o·na (ī-ō'nə). Island of the S Inner Hebrides, NW Scotland.

I·o·ni·a (ī-ō'nē-ə). Ancient region of W Asia Minor, along the Aegean coast. **—I·o'ni·an** *adj.* & *n.*

Ionian. 1. Sea arm of the Mediterranean between W Greece and S Italy and Sicily. **2.** Islands of W Greece in the Ionian Sea.

I·o·wa (ī'ə-wə). **1.** River, c. 329 mi (529.4 km), of N and E Iowa. **2.** State of N central U.S. Cap. Des Moines. Pop. 2,913,387. **—I'o·wan** *adj.* & *n.*

Iowa City. City of E Iowa, SSE of Cedar Rapids. Pop. 50,508.

I·pin (ē'pĭn'). **Yibin.**

I·pho (ē'pō). City of W Malay Peninsula, Malaysia, NNW of Kuala Lumpur. Pop. 247,689.

Ips·wich (ĭp'swĭch'). **1.** City of E Australia, near Brisbane. Pop. 71,200. **2.** Borough of E England, near the North Sea NE of London. Pop. 118,900. **3.** Town of NE Mass., NNE of Salem. Pop. 11,158.

I·qui·que (ē-kē'kĕ). City of NW Chile, on the Pacific. Pop. 63,600.

I·qui·tos (ē-kē'tôs). City of NE Peru, on the Amazon. Pop. 111,327.

I·rá·kli·on (ē-rä'klyôn). *Greek.* Candia (sense 3).

I·ran (ĭ-răn', ĭ-rän', ī-răn'). Country of SW Asia. Cap. Teheran. Pop. 38,940,000. **—I·ra'ni·an** (ĭ-rā'nē-ən, ĭ-rä'-, ī-rä'-) *adj.* & *n.*

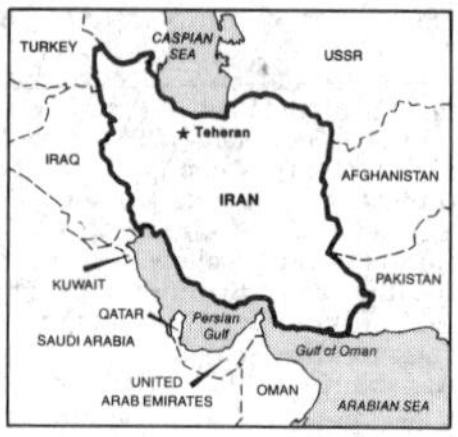

Iran

I·ra·pua·to (ē'rä-pwä'tô). City of central Mexico, E of Guadalajara. Pop. 155,600.

I·raq also **I·rak** (ĭ-răk', ĭ-räk'). Country of SW Asia. Cap. Baghdad. Pop. 13,230,000. **—I·ra'qi** (ĭ-răk'ē, ĭ-räk'ē) *adj.* & *n.*

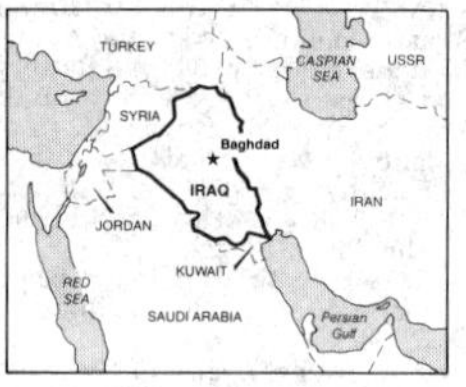

Iraq

I·ra·zú (ē-rä-so͞o'). Volcano, c. 11,260 ft (3,434 m), of central Costa Rica.

Ire·land (īr'lənd). **1.** Island of the British Isles, in the N Atlantic W of Great Britain. **2.** Republic occupying most of Ireland. Cap. Dublin. Pop. 3,455,000. **3.** See **Northern Ireland.** **—I'rish** (ī'rĭsh') *adj.* & *n.*

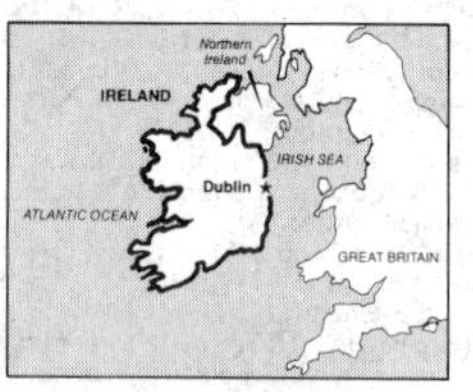

Ireland

Irish. Sea of the N Atlantic between Ireland and Great Britain.

Ir·kutsk (ĭr-ko͞otsk'). City of SE Siberian USSR, near Lake Baikal. Pop. 561,000.

I·ron·de·quoit (ĭ-rŏn'dĭ-kwoit', -kwŏt'). Town of W N.Y., W of Rochester. Pop. 57,648.

I·ron Gate (ī'ərn gāt'). Gorge of the Danube on the Yugoslav-Rumanian border.

I·ron·ton (ī'ərn-tən). City of S Ohio, on the Ohio R. S of Columbus. Pop. 14,290.

Ir·ra·wad·dy (ĭr'ə-wŏd'ē, -wôd'ē). Chief river of Burma, flowing c. 1,000 mi (1,609 km) S to the Andaman Sea.

Ir·tish or **Ir·tysh** (ĭr-tĭsh'). River of NW China and W Siberian USSR, flowing c. 2,650 mi (4,265 km) NW into the Ob.

I·rún (ē-ro͞on'). City of N Spain, near the Bay of Biscay and the French border. Pop. 54,781.

Ir·vine. 1. (ûr'vĭn'). Burgh of SW Scotland, SW of Glasgow. Pop. 57,900. **2.** (ûr'vīn'). City of S Calif., SE of Santa Ana. Pop. 62,134.

Ir·ving (ûr'vĭng). Town of NE Tex., near Dallas. Pop. 109,943.

Ir·ving·ton (ûr'vĭng-tən). Town in NE N.J., near Newark. Pop. 61,493.

Is·a·bel·a (ĭz'ə-bĕl'ə). Largest of the Galápagos Is. of Ecuador.

I·sar (ē'zär). River, c. 160 mi (257 km), of W Austria and SE West Germany.

Is·chia (ĕs'kyä). Island of S Italy, in the Tyrrhenian Sea at the entrance to the Bay of Naples.

I·se (ē'sĕ'). **1.** Bay of the Pacific extending c. 15 mi (24 km) into the S central coast of Honshu, Japan. **2.** City of S Honshu, Japan, on Ise Bay. Pop. 105,624.

I·se·o (ē-zĕ'ō). Lake, 24 sq mi (62 sq km), of N Italy, ENE of Milan.

I·sère (ē-zĕr'). River, c. 180 mi (290 km), of SE France.

I·ser·lohn (ē-zər-lōn'). City of W West Germany, NE of Cologne. Pop. 94,478.

I·se·sa·ki (ē'sĕ-zä'kē). City of central Honshu, Japan. Pop. 104,300.

I·se·yin (ē-sā'yĭn). City of SW Nigeria, NNW of Ibadan. Pop. 115,000.

Is·fa·han (ĭs'fə-hän'). Variant of **Esfahan.**

Ish·i·kar·i Bay (ē'shē-kä'rē). Inlet of the Sea of Japan on W coast of Hokkaido, Japan.

I·shim (ĭ-shĭm', ĭsh-ĕm', ē-shēm'). River, c. 1,130 mi (1,818 km), of W Siberian USSR.

I·shi·no·ma·ki (ē'shē-nô-mä'kē). City of N Honshu, Japan, on the Pacific. Pop. 119,758.

I·sis (ī'sĭs). The upper Thames R., in central England.

Is·kar (ĭs'kär') or **Is·kŭr** (-kər). River, c. 250 mi (402 km), of NW Bulgaria.

Is·ken·de·run (ĭs-kĕn'də-ro͞on', -kĕn'dĕ-ro͞on'). City of S Turkey, on the NE corner of the Mediterranean. Pop. 120,985.

Is·lam·a·bad (ĭs-lä'mə-bäd', ĭz-). Cap. of Pakistan, in the NE part, NE of Rawalpindi. Pop. 77,318.

Ís·land (ēs'länt). *Icelandic.* Iceland.

Is·lay (ī'lā', ī'lə). Island of S Inner Hebrides, W Scotland.

Isle au Haut (ī'lə-hō', -hōt', ē'lə-). Island of S central Me., at entrance to Penobscot Bay.

Isle of (īl). See under final element, e.g., **Isle of Wight** appears at **Wight.**

Isle Roy·ale (roi'əl). Island, c. 210 sq mi (544 sq km), of N Mich., in NW Lake Superior, included with adjacent islands in **Isle Royale National Park.**

I·slip (ī'slĭp). Town of SE N.Y., on Long Is. Pop. 12,100.

Is·ma·i·li·a also **Is·ma·i·li·ya** (ĭs'-mä-ē-lē'ə, -ē'lē-ə, ĭz'-). City of NE Egypt, on the Suez Canal. Pop. 145,478.

Is·par·ta (ĕs-pär'tä, ĭs'pär-tä'). City of W central Turkey, SW of Ankara. Pop. 91,544.

Is·ra·el (ĭz'rē-əl). **1.** Ancient kingdom

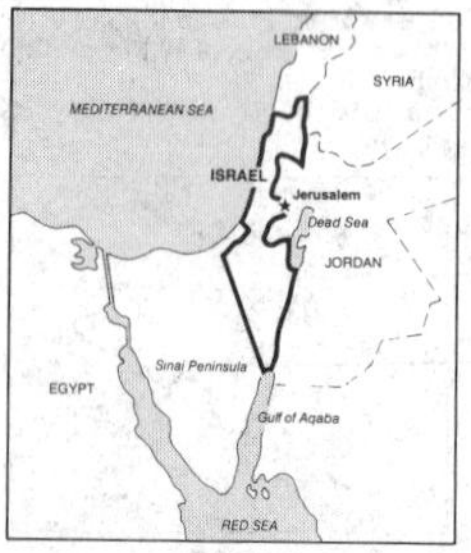

Israel

of N Palestine. **2.** Country of SW Asia, on the E Mediterranean. Cap. Jerusalem. Pop. 3,920,000. **—Is·rae'li** (ĭz-rā'lē) *adj. & n.*

Is·sus (ĭs'əs). Ancient town of SE Asia Minor, near modern Iskenderun, Turkey.

Is·syk-Kul (ĕ'sĭk-kōōl'). Lake, c. 2,395 sq mi (6,203 sq km), of SE Central Asian USSR, in the Tian Shan near the NW Chinese border.

Is·sy-les-Mou·li·neaux (ē-sē'-lā-mōō-lē-nō'). City of N central France, near Paris. Pop. 47,561.

Is·tan·bul (ĭs'tăn-bōōl', -tän-). Largest city of Turkey, in the NW part on the European side of the Bosporus and the Sea of Marmara. Pop. 2,852,-539.

Is·ter (ĭs'tər). Danube.

Is·tri·a (ĭs'trē-ə). Peninsula of NW Yugoslavia, projecting into the N Adriatic. **—Is'tri·an** *adj. & n.*

I·ta·bu·na (ē'tə-bōō'nə). City of E Brazil, SSE of Salvador. Pop. 89,928.

I·ta·lia (ē-tä'lyä). *Italian.* Italy.

It·a·ly (ĭt'l-ē). **1.** Peninsula of S Europe, projecting c. 600 mi (965 km) into the Mediterranean between the Tyrrhenian and Adriatic seas. **2.** Country of S Europe including the peninsula of Italy, Sardinia, and Sicily. Cap. Rome. Pop. 57,230,000. **—I·tal'ian** (ĭ-tăl'yən) *adj. & n.*

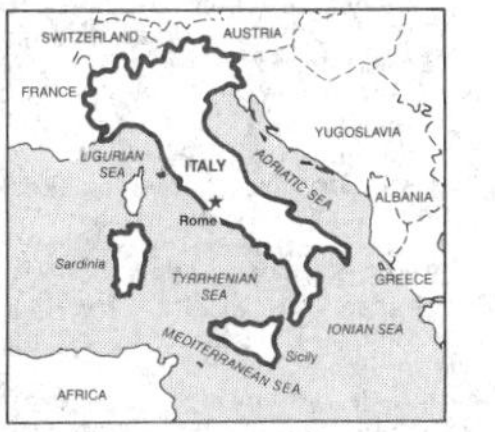

Italy

I·ta·mi (ē-tä'mē). City of S Honshu, Japan, on Osaka Bay near Osaka. Pop. 177,745.

I·ta·pe·cu·ru (ē'tə-pĕ'kōō-rōō'). River, c. 450 mi (724 km), of NE Brazil.

I·tas·ca (ī-tăs'kə). Lake, c. 2 sq mi (5.2 sq km), of NW Minn., at source of the Mississippi R.

I·té·nez (ē-tĕ'nĕs). Guaporé.

Ith·a·ca (ĭth'ə-kə). **1.** Island of W Greece, in the Ionian Is. E of Cephalonia. **2.** City of W central N.Y., on Cayuga Lake SSW of Syracuse. Pop. 28,732. **—Ith'a·can** *adj. & n.*

I·thá·ki (ē-thä'kē). *Greek.* Ithaca.

I·tim·bi·ri (ē'tĭm-bîr'ē). River, c. 350 mi (563 km), of N Zaire.

I·tsu·ku·shi·ma (ē-tsōō'kōō-shē'mä). Island, 12 sq mi (31 sq km), of SW Japan, in the Inland Sea SW of Hiroshima.

It·u·rae·a or **It·u·re·a** (ĭt'yōō-rē'ə, ĭch'ə-rē'ə). Ancient country of NE Palestine. **—It'u·rae'an, It'u·re'an** *adj. & n.*

I·tu·rup (ē'tər-əp). Island of Far Eastern USSR, in the Pacific, largest of the Kuriles.

I·va·no-Fran·kovsk (ĭ-vä'nə-frăng-kôfsk). City of extreme SW European USSR, in the SW Ukraine. Pop. 159,000.

I·va·no·vo (ĭ-vä'nô-vô, ē-vä'nə-və). City of central European USSR, NE of Moscow. Pop. 466,000.

I·vi·za (ē-vē'sä). Variant of **Ibiza.**

I·vo·ry Coast (ī'və-rē, īv'rē). Country of W Africa, on the Gulf of Guinea. Cap. Abidjan. Pop. 8,390,000.

I·vry-sur-Seine (ē-vrē'sür-sĕn'). City of N central France, near Paris. Pop. 62,856.

I·wa·ki (ē-wä'kē). City of NE Honshu, Japan, on the Pacific. Pop. 271,800.

I·wa·ku·ni (ē'wä-kōō'nē). City of SW Honshu, Japan, on the Inland Sea. Pop. 112,200.

I·wo (ē'wō). City of SW Nigeria, near Ibadan. Pop. 214,000.

I·wo Ji·ma (ē'wō jē'mə, -mä). Largest (8 sq mi/21 sq km) of the Volcano Is. of Japan, in the NW Pacific E of Taiwan.

Ix·elles (ēk-sĕl'). City of central Belgium, near Brussels. Pop. 76,545.

Ix·ta·ci·hua·tl also **Iz·tac·ci·hua·tl** (ēs'tä-sē'wät'l). Dormant volcano, 17,342 ft (5,289.3 m), in central Mexico.

I·za·bal (ē-sä-bäl'). Lake, c. 30 mi (48 km) long and 15 mi (24 km) wide, of E Guatemala.

I·zal·co (ē-säl'kô). Active volcano, c. 7,828 ft (2,388 m), of W El Salvador.

I·zhevsk (ē'zhĭfsk, ē-zhĕfsk'). City of E central European USSR, ENE of Kazan. Pop. 562,000.

Iz·ma·il (ez'mä-ēl'). City of SW European USSR, near the Rumanian border. Pop. 84,000.

Iz·mir (ĭz-mîr', ĭz'mîr, ēz-mēr'). City of W Turkey, on the **Gulf of Izmir,** an inlet of the Aegean. Pop. 753,749.

Iz·mit (ĭz-mĭt', ēz-mēt'). City of NW Turkey, on the **Gulf of Izmit,** E extension of the Sea of Marmara. Pop. 191,340.

Iz·nik (ĭz-nĭk', ēz-nēk'). Lake of NW Turkey, E of Sea of Marmara.

Iz·tac·ci·hua·tl (ēs'täk-sē'wät'l). Variant of **Ixtacihuatl.**

I·zu·mi (ē-zōō'mē). City of S Honshu, Japan, near Osaka. Pop. 122,464.

J

Jab·al·pur (jŭb'əl-pōōr', jŭb'əl-pōōr') or **Jub·bul·pore** (jŭb'əl-pōr', jŭb'-əl-pōr'). City of central India, SSE of Delhi. Pop. 426,224.

Jack·son (jăk'sən). **1.** City of S central Mich., W of Detroit. Pop. 39,739. **2.** Cap. of Miss., in the W central part. Pop. 202,895. **3.** City of W Tenn., NE of Memphis. Pop. 49,131.

Jackson Hole (hōl). Valley of NW Wyo., E of the Teton range.

Jack·son·ville (jăk'sən-vĭl'). **1.** City of central Ark., NE of Little Rock. Pop. 27,589. **2.** City of NE Fla., on the St. John R. near the Atlantic and the Ga. border. Pop. 540,898. **3.** City of W central Ill., W of Springfield. Pop. 20,284. **4.** City of E N.C., near the Atlantic NNE of Wilmington. Pop. 17,056. **5.** City of E Tex., SE of Dallas. Pop. 12,264.

Jacksonville Beach. City of NE Fla., on the Atlantic near Jacksonville. Pop. 15,462.

Ja·dot·ville (zhä-dō-vēl'). Likasi.

Ja·én (hä-ĕn'). City of S Spain, NNW of Granada. Pop. 91,158.

Jaf·fa (jăf'ə, yä'fə). Former city of W central Israel, since 1950 a district of Tel Aviv.

Jaff·na (jăf'nə, jäf'-). City of extreme N Sri Lanka, on Palk Strait. Pop. 118,000.

Jai·pur (jī'pōōr'). City of NW India, SW of Delhi. Pop. 615, 258.

Ja·kar·ta (jə-kär'tə). Variant of **Djakarta.**

Ja·la·pa (hä-lä'pä) also **Jalapa En·rí·quez** (ĕn-rē'kĕs). City of E central Mexico, E of Mexico City. Pop. 191,100.

Ja·lu·it (jäl'ōō-ĭt). Atoll in the Marshall Is. of the W Pacific.

Ja·mai·ca (jə-mā'kə). Island republic in the Caribbean S of Cuba. Cap. Kingston. Pop. 2,137,300. **—Ja·mai'can** *adj. & n.*

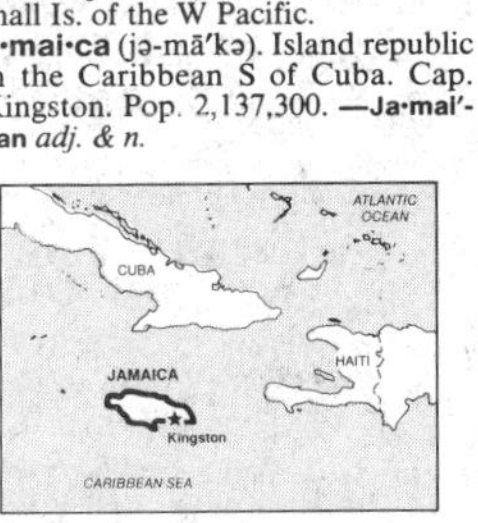

Jamaica

James (jāmz). **1. Bay.** S arm of Hudson Bay in N.W.T., Canada, between NE Ont. and W Que. **2.** River of E N.Dak. and E S.Dak., flowing 710 mi (1,142.4 km) S to the Missouri. **3.** River of Va., flowing 340 mi (547.1 km) E to Chesapeake Bay.

James·town (jāmz'toun'). **1.** Cap. of St. Helena in the S Atlantic. Pop. 1,516. **2.** City of W N.Y., on Chautauqua Lake near the Pa. border. Pop. 35,775. **3.** City of SE N.Dak., E of Bismarck. Pop. 16,280. **4.** Former village of SE Va., first permanent English settlement (1607) in America.

Jam·mu (jŭm'ōō). City of N India, near the Pakistan border S of Srinagar. Pop. 155,338.

Jammu and Kash·mir (kăsh'mîr', kăsh-mîr'). Kashmir.

Jam·na·gar (jäm-nŭg'ər). City of W India, on the Gulf of Kutch. Pop. 199,709.

Jam·shed·pur (jäm'shĕd-pōōr', jäm'shĕd-pōōr'). City of E India, WNW of Calcutta. Pop. 341,576.

Janes·ville (jānz'vĭl'). City of S Wis., N of Beloit. Pop. 51,071.

Jan May·en (yän' mī'ən). Island of Norway, c. 145 sq mi (376 sq km), in the Greenland Sea midway between N Norway and Greenland.

Ja·pan (jə-păn'). **1. Sea of.** Part of the Pacific between Japan and the Asian mainland. **2.** Warm ocean current flowing NE from the Philippine Sea past SE Japan into the N Pacific. **3.** Country of Asia, on an archipelago off the NE coast. Cap. Tokyo. Pop. 117,360,000. **—Jap'a·nese'** (jăp'-ə-nēz', -nēs') *adj. & n.*

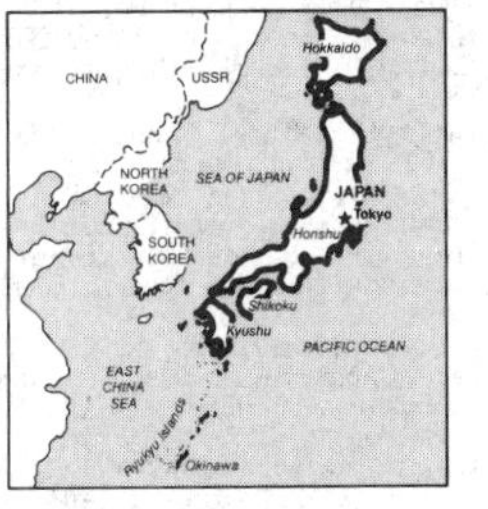

Japan

Ja·pu·rá (zhä-pōō-rä'). River of S Colombia and NW Brazil, flowing c. 1,500 mi (2,414 km) SE to the Amazon.

Jas·per (jăs'pər). City of N central Ala., NW of Birmingham. Pop. 11,894.

Jas·sy (yä'sē). Variant of **Iaşi.**

Ja·va (jä'və, jăv'ə). **1.** Sea of the W Pacific between Java and Borneo. **2.** Island of Indonesia SE of Sumatra.

Ja·va·rí (zhä'vä-rē'). River rising in E Peru and flowing c. 650 mi (1,046 km) along the Peru-Brazil border to the Amazon.

Jean·nette (jə-nĕt'). City of SW Pa., ESE of Pittsburgh. Pop. 13,106.

Jeb·el esh Shar·qi (jĕb'əl ĕsh shĕr'-kə). *Arabic.* Anti-Lebanon.

Jebel Kath·e·ri·na (kăth'ə-rē'nə). Mountain, 8,651 ft (2,638.6 m), of NE Egypt, highest point in Sinai.

Jebel Mu·sa (mōō'sä). Mountain, 2,790 ft (851 m), in N Morocco on the Strait of Gibraltar.

Jebel Toub·kal also **Djeb·el Toub·kal** (jĕb'əl tōōb-käl'). Mountain, 13,671 ft (4,169.7 m), of central Morocco, the highest of the Atlas Mts.

Jed·da (jĕd'ə). Variant of **Jidda.**

Jef·fer·son (jĕf'ər-sən). **1.** River, c. 250 mi (402 km), of SW Mont., a headwater of the Missouri. **2. Mount.** Peak, 10,499 ft (3,202.2 m), in the Cascade range in NW Ore.

Jefferson City. Cap. of Mo., in the central part on the Missouri R. Pop. 33,619.

Jef·fer·son·town (jĕf'ər-sən-toun'). City of N Ky., near Louisville. Pop. 15,795.

Jef·fer·son·ville (jĕf'ər-sən-vĭl'). City of S Ind., on the Ohio opposite Louisville, Ky. Pop. 21,220.

Jeh·lam (jā'ləm). Variant of **Jhelum.**

Je·le·nia Gó·ra (yĕ-lĕ'nyä gōō'rä). City of W Poland, WSW of Poznań. Pop. 86,000.

Je·na (yā'nä). City of S East Germany, SW of Leipzig. Pop. 102,538.

Jen·nings (jĕn'ĭngz). **1.** City of SW La., E of Lake Charles. Pop. 12,401. **2.** City of E Mo., near St. Louis. Pop. 17,026.

Je·qui·tin·hon·ha (zhə-kē'tē-nyō'-nyə). River, c. 500 mi (805 km), of E Brazil.

Je·rez (hĕ-rĕs') also **Jerez de la Fron·te·ra** (dĕ lä frôn-tĕ'rä). City of SW Spain, NW of Cádiz. Pop. 137,700.

Jer·i·cho (jĕr'ĭ-kō'). **1.** Ancient city of Palestine near the NW shore of the Dead Sea. **2.** Town of W Jordan, near site of ancient Jericho. Pop. 6,829.

Jer·sey (jûr'zē). Largest (45 sq mi/116.6 sq km) of the Channel Is. in the English Channel.

Jersey City. City of NE N.J., on the Hudson opposite Lower Manhattan. Pop. 223,532.

Je·ru·sa·lem (jə-rōō'sə-ləm, -zə-). Cap. of Israel, in the E central part. Pop. 398,200.

Jer·vis Bay (jär'vĭs). Inlet of the Tasman Sea on the SE coast of Australia.

Jez·re·el (jĕz'rē-əl, jĕz-rēl'). Plain of N Israel.

Jhang-Ma·ghi·a·na (jŭng'mŭ'gē-ä'-nə). Twin cities of E central Pakistan, WSW of Lahore. Pop. 131,843.

Jhan·si (jän'sē). City of N central India, SSE of Delhi. Pop. 173,292.

Jhe·lum also **Jeh·lam** (jā'ləm). River, c. 480 mi (772 km), of N India and NE Pakistan.

Jia·ling (jyä'lĭng'). River, c. 500 mi (805 km), of central China.

Jia·mu·si (jyä'mōō'sē'). City of NE China, ENE of Harbin. Pop. 300,000.

Jiao·zuo (jyou'dzwō). City of E central China, NNW of Zhengzhou. Pop. 275,000.

Ji·bu·ti (jē-bōō'tē, jĭ-). Variant of **Djibouti.**

Jid·da (jĭd'ə) also **Jed·da** (jĕd'ə). City of W central Saudi Arabia, on the Red Sea. Pop. 561,104.

Ji·lin (jē'lĭn'). City of NE China, E of Changchun. Pop. 775,000.

Ji·long (jē'lōōng'). Keelung.

Ji·nan (jē'nän'). City of E China, on the Yellow R. S of Tianjin. Pop. 1,125,000.

Jing·de·zhen (jyĭng'dŭ'jŭn'). City of SE China, WSW of Shanghai. Pop. 300,000.

Jin·zhou (jyĭn'jō'). City of NE China, ENE of Beijing. Pop. 450,000.

Ji·xi (jē'shē'). City of NE China, near the Soviet border E of Harbin. Pop. 325,000.

João Pes·so·a (zhwouN' pə-sô'ə). City of NE Brazil, near the Atlantic N of Recife. Pop. 197,398.

Jodh·pur (jŏd'pōōr'). City of W India, SW of Delhi. Pop. 317,612.

Jog·ja·kar·ta (jŏg'yə-kär'tə, -jə-, jŏk'-). Variant of **Djokjakarta.**

Jo·han·nes·burg (jō-hăn'ĭs-bûrg', yō-hä'nĭs-). Largest city of South Africa, in the NE part. Pop. 1,432,-643.

John Day (jŏn' dā'). River, 281 mi (452.1 km), of N Ore.

John o'Groat's (ə-grōts'). Point on the NE coast of Scotland, traditionally the N limit of Great Britain.

John·son City (jŏn'sən). **1.** Village of S N.Y., near Binghamton. Pop. 17,126. **2.** City of NE Tenn., ENE of Knoxville. Pop. 39,753.

John·ston (jŏn'stən). Town of N central R.I., near Providence. Pop. 24,907.

Johns·town (jŏnz'toun'). City of SW Pa., E of Pittsburgh. Pop. 35,496.

Jo·hore Bah·ru (jə-hôr' bä'rōō, bə-rōō', -hōr', jō-) also **Jo·hor Ba·ha·ru** (bə-hä'rōō). City of S Malaysia, on S tip of Malay Peninsula opposite Singapore Is. Pop. 136,229.

Join·vi·le or **Join·vil·le** (zhoiN-vē'lē). City of S Brazil, NE of Pôrto Alegre. Pop. 77,760.

Jok·ja·kar·ta (jŏk'yə-kär'tə, -jə-, jŏk'-). Variant of **Djokjakarta.**

Jo·li·et (jō'lē-ĕt', jō'lē-ĕt'). City of NE Ill., SW of Chicago. Pop. 77,956.

Jo·li·ette (zhō'lē-ĕt'). City of S Que., Canada, NNE of Montreal. Pop. 18,118.

Jo·lo (hō'lō, hô-lô'). Island of S Philippines, chief island of the Sulu archipelago.

Jones·bor·o (jōnz'bûr'ō, -bûr'ə). City of NE Ark., NE of Little Rock. Pop. 31,419.

Jön·kö·ping (yœn'chœ'pĭng). City of S Sweden, SW of Stockholm. Pop. 107,652.

Jon·quière (zhôɴ-kyĕr'). City of S Que., Canada, on the Saguenay R. N of Quebec city. Pop. 60,691.

Jop·lin (jŏp'lĭn). City of SW Mo., near the Kans. border WSW of Springfield. Pop. 38,893.

Jop·pa (jŏp'ə). Jaffa.

Jor·dan (jôr'dn). **1.** River of NE Israel and NW Jordan, flowing c. 200 mi (322 km) S through the Sea of Galilee to the Dead Sea. **2.** Country of SW Asia, in NW Arabia. Cap. Amman. Pop. 2,925,000. **—Jor·da'ni·an** (jôr-dā'nē-ən) *adj. & n.*

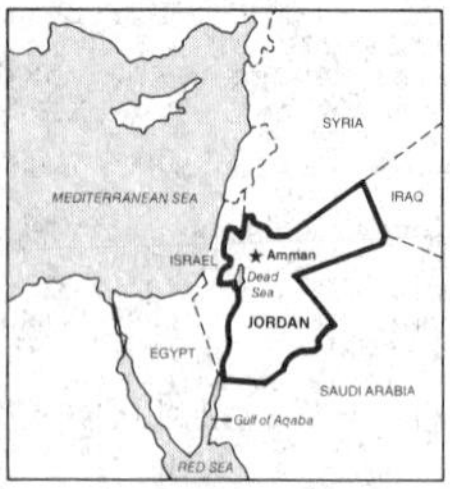

Jordan

Jos (jōs). City of central Nigeria, S of Kano. Pop. 105,000.

Jo·tun·hei·men (yō'to͞on-hā'mən) also **Jo·tun·heim** (-hām'). Range in S central Norway, rising to c. 8,100 ft (2,471 m).

Juan de Fu·ca (hwän' də fo͞o'kə, fyo͞o'-, wän'). Strait, c. 100 mi (161 km) long, between NW Wash. and Vancouver Is., B.C., Canada.

Juan Fer·nán·dez (jo͞o'ən fər-năn'dĕz, hwän' fĕr-nän'dĕs). Island group belonging to Chile, in the SE Pacific W of Chile.

Juá·rez (wär'ĕz, hwä'rĕs). Ciudad Juárez.

Ju·ba (jo͞o'bä). River of S Ethiopia and S Somalia, flowing c. 1,000 mi (1,609 km) S to the Indian Ocean.

Jub·bul·pore (jŭb'əl-pôr', jŭb'əl-pōr'). Variant of **Jabalpur.**

Jú·car (ho͞o'kär). River, c. 300 mi (483 km), of E Spain.

Ju·dah (jo͞o'də). Ancient kingdom of S Palestine.

Ju·de·a also **Ju·dae·a** (jo͞o-dē'ə, -dā'-). Ancient region of S Palestine, comprising present-day S Israel and SW Jordan. **—Ju·de'an, Ju·dae'an** *adj. & n.*

Ju·dith (jo͞o'dĭth). River, 124 mi (199.5 km), of central Mont.

Ju·go·sla·vi·a (yo͞o'gō-slä'vē-ə). Yugoslavia.

Juiz de Fo·ra (zhwēzh' də fô'rə). City of SE Brazil, N of Rio de Janeiro. Pop. 218,832.

Jul·ian Alps (jo͞ol'yən ălps'). Range of the E Alps in NW Yugoslavia and NE Italy.

Jul·lun·dur (jŭl'ən-dər). City of NW India, NNW of Delhi. Pop. 296,106.

Jum·na (jŭm'nə). River of N India, flowing c. 860 mi (1,384 km) SE to the Ganges.

Junc·tion City (jŭngk'shən). City of E central Kans., W of Topeka. Pop. 19,305.

Jun·dia·í (zho͞on'dyə-ē'). City of S Brazil, NW of São Paulo. Pop. 145,785.

Ju·neau (jo͞o'nō'). Cap. of Alas., in the SE Panhandle. Pop. 19,528.

Jung·frau (yo͝ong'frou'). Mountain, c. 13,653 ft (4,164 m), in the Bernese Alps in S central Switzerland.

Ju·ni·at·a (jo͞o'nē-ăt'ə). River, c. 150 mi (241 km), of S central Pa.

Ju·nín (ho͞o-nēn'). **1.** City of E Argentina, W of Buenos Aires. Pop. 59,020. **2.** Town of W central Peru, NE of Lima, where Bolívar and Sucre defeated Spaniards (1824).

Ju·ra (jo͝or'ə, zhü-rä'). Range extending c. 200 mi (322 km) along the French-Swiss border.

Ju·ruá (zho͞o-rwä'). River of E Peru and NW Brazil, flowing c. 1,200 mi (1,931 km) NE to the Amazon.

Ju·rue·na (zho͞o-rwā'nə). River, c. 500 mi (805 km), of W central Brazil.

Jus·tice (jŭs'tĭs). Village of NE Ill., near Chicago. Pop. 10,552.

Jut·land (jŭt'lənd). Peninsula of N Europe, comprising mainland Denmark and N West Germany.

Jyl·land (yül'län). *Danish.* Jutland.

Jy·väs·ky·lä (yü'văs-kü'lä). City of S central Finland, NNE of Helsinki. Pop. 63,599.

K

K2 (kā'to͞o'). Godwin Austen.

Ka·bul (kä'bo͝ol, kə-bo͞ol'). **1.** River, c. 300 mi (483 km), of E Afghanistan and N Pakistan. **2.** Cap. of Afghanistan, in the E part on the Kabul R. Pop. 318,094.

Ka·di·yev·ka or **Ka·di·ev·ka** (kä-dē'yəf-kə). City of S European USSR, in the Ukraine SE of Kharkov. Pop. 137,800.

Ka·do·ma (kä-dô'mä). City of S central Japan, near Osaka. Pop. 142,167.

Ka·du·na (kə-do͞o'nə). City of N Nigeria, NE of Lagos. Pop. 202,000.

Kae·song (kā'sông'). City of S North Korea, near the South Korean border. Pop. 175,000.

Ka·fu·e (kä-fo͞o'ā). River, c. 600 mi (965 km), of central Zambia.

Ka·ge·ra (kä-gā'rä, -gâr'ə). River of E central Africa, chief Nile headwater, flowing c. 250 mi (402 km) along Rwanda-Tanzania border, then E into Lake Victoria.

Ka·go·shi·ma (kä'gô'-shē-mä). City of S Japan, in S Kyushu on **Kagoshima Bay,** an inlet of the East China Sea. Pop. 505,077.

Ka·ho·o·la·we (kä-hō'ō-lä'wē, -vē, kä'ho͞o-lä'-). Island, 45 sq mi (116.6 sq km), of Hawaii, SW of Maui.

Kai·e·teur Falls (kī'ē-to͞or'). Waterfall, 741 ft (226 m) high, in the Potaro R., W central Guyana.

Kai·feng (kī'fŭng'). City of E central China, SSW of Beijing. Pop. 350,000.

Kai·las (kī-läs'). Mountain, 22,022 ft (6,714 m), in the Tibetan Himalayas of SW China.

Kai·lu·a (kī-lo͞o'ä). City of Hawaii, on the E coast of Oahu. Pop. 39,700.

Kair·ouan (kīr-wän', kĕr-wäɴ'). City and Moslem shrine of N Tunisia, S of Tunis. Pop. 54,546.

Kai·sers·lau·tern (kī'zərs-lou'tərn). City of SW West Germany, SW of Frankfurt. Pop. 99,197.

Ka·ki·na·da (kä'kə-nä'də). City of SE India, on the Bay of Bengal NNE of Madras. Pop. 164,200.

Ka·ko·ga·wa (kä-kō'gä-wä). City of S Japan, on S Honshu W of Osaka. Pop. 212,232.

Ka Lae (kä' lä'ā). Southernmost point of Hawaii Is., Hawaii.

Ka·la·ha·ri (kä'lä-hä'rē). Desert of S Botswana and E Namibia.

Ka·lakh (kä'läKH'). Ancient city of Assyria, S of present-day Mosul, Iraq.

Kal·a·ma·zoo (kăl'ə-mə-zo͞o'). City of SW Mich., WSW of Lansing. Pop. 79,722.

Ka·lat also **Khe·lat** (kə-lät'). Region and former state of NW Pakistan.

Kal·gan (käl'gän'). Zhangjiakou.

Kal·goor·lie (kăl-go͝or'lē). Town of SW Australia, ENE of Perth. Pop. 9,064.

Ka·li·ma (kə-lē'mə). City of E Zaire, on Lake Tanganyika. Pop. 62,300.

Ka·li·man·tan (kä'lē-män'tän'). Indonesian part of Borneo.

Ka·li·nin (kä-lē'nĭn). City of central European USSR, NW of Moscow. Pop. 416,000.

Ka·li·nin·grad (kä-lē'nĭn-grăd', kə-lē'nĭn-grät'). City of extreme W European USSR, on the Baltic near the Polish border. Pop. 361,000.

Kal·i·spell (kăl'ĭ-spĕl'). City of NW Mont., near Glacier National Park. Pop. 10,648.

Ka·lisz (kä'lĭsh, -lēsh). City of central Poland, W of Łódź. Pop. 97,700.

Kal·mar (käl'mär, kăl'-). City of SE Sweden, on **Kalmar Sound,** an arm of the Baltic between the Swedish mainland and Öland. Pop. 32,200.

Ka·lu·ga (kä-lo͞o'gə). City of central European USSR, SW of Moscow. Pop. 270,000.

Ka·ma (kä'mə, -mä). River of E European USSR, flowing 1,262 mi (2,030.6 km) into the Volga.

Ka·ma·ku·ra (kä'mä-ko͞o'rä, kä-mä'-ko͞o-rä'). City of central Japan, on the Pacific coast of Honshu S of Yokohama. Pop. 173,331.

Kam·chat·ka (kăm-chăt'kə, -chät'-). Peninsula of Far Eastern USSR, extending c. 750 mi (1,207 km) between the Sea of Okhotsk and the Bering Sea.

Ka·met (kä'mĕt, kŭm'āt'). Mountain, 25,447 ft (7,761.3 m), in the NW Himalayas of N India.

Ka·mi·na (kä-mē'nä). City of S Zaire, ESE of Kinshasa. Pop. 56,300.

Kam·loops (kăm'lo͞ops'). City of S B.C., Canada, NE of Vancouver. Pop. 58,311.

Kam·pa·la (käm-pä'lə). Cap. of Uganda, in the S part on Lake Victoria. Pop. 330,700.

Kam·pu·che·a (kăm'pə-chē'ə, -po͞o-). Cambodia.

Kan (gän). Gan.

Ka·nan·ga (kə-näng'gə). City of S central Zaire, ESE of Kinshasa. Pop. 601,000.

Ka·na·ra (kä'nə-rə). Region of S central India.

Ka·na·ta (kə-nä'tä). City of SE Ont., Canada, near Ottawa. Pop. 18,244.

Ka·na·za·wa (kä'nä-zä'wä, kä-nä'-zä-wä'). City of W central Japan, on the Sea of Japan. Pop. 417,681.

Kan·chen·jun·ga (kŭn'chən-jŭng'gə, -jo͝ong'-, kän'-). Mountain, 28,146 ft (8,584.5 m), in the Himalayas on the Sikkim-Nepal border.

Kan·da·har (kän'də-här', kăn'-, kŭn'-). City of SE Afghanistan, near the Pakistan border. Pop. 243,103.

Kan·dy (kăn'dē). City of central Sri Lanka, ENE of Colombo. Pop. 103,000.

Ka·ne·o·he (kä'nā-ō'hā). City of Hawaii, on E Oahu on **Kaneohe Bay,** an inlet of the Pacific. Pop. 35,600.

Kan·ga·roo (kăng'gə-ro͞o'). Island, 1,680 sq mi (4,351 sq km), off S coast of Australia, SW of Adelaide.

Kan·i·a·pis·cau also **Can·i·a·pis·cau** (kăn'ē-ə-pĭs'kō, -kou, kăn'yə-). River, c. 575 mi (925 km), of N Que., Canada.

Kan·ka·kee (kăng'kə-kē'). **1.** River, 225 mi (362 km), of NW Ind. and NE Ill. **2.** City of NE Ill., on the Kankakee R. SSW of Chicago. Pop. 30,141.

Ka·no (kä'nō). City of N Nigeria, NE of Lagos. Pop. 399,000.

Kan·pur (kän'po͝or). City of N India, on the Ganges SE of Delhi. Pop. 1,154,388.

Kan·sas (kăn'zəs). **1.** River, 169 mi (271.9 km), of NE Kans. **2.** State of the central U.S. Cap. Topeka. Pop. 2,363,208. **—Kan'san** (-zən) *adj. & n.*

Kansas City. 1. City of NE Kans., on the Missouri adjacent to Kansas City, Mo. Pop. 161,087. **2.** City of W Mo., WNW of St. Louis. Pop. 448,159.

Kao·hsiung (gou'shyo͝ong'). City of SW Taiwan, on Formosa Strait. Pop. 1,172,977.

Ka·o·lack (kä'ō-läk, kou'läk). City of W Senegal, W Africa, SSE of Dakar. Pop. 106,899.

Kao·lan (gou'län'). Lanzhou.

Ka·pos·vár (kô'pôsh-vär). City of SW Hungary, SW of Budapest. Pop. 73,000.

Ka·pu·as (kä'po͞o-äs'). River, 710 mi (1,142.4 km), of W Kalimantan, Borneo.

Kap·us·ka·sing (kăp'əs-kā'sĭng). Town of central Ont., Canada, NNE of Sault Ste. Marie. Pop. 11,969.

Ka·ra (kä'rə). Sea of the Arctic Ocean, between Novaya Zemlya and the Siberian mainland.

Ka·ra·chi (kə-rä'chē). City of S Pakistan, on the Arabian Sea. Pop. 3,498,634.

Ka·ra·gan·da (kä'rə-gän-dä'). City of NE Central Asian USSR, NNE of Tashkent. Pop. 577,000.

Ka·ra·ko·ram also **Ka·ra·ko·rum** (kăr'ə-kôr'əm, -kōr'-, kär'-). Range of N Kashmir and SW China.

Ka·ra·ko·rum (kär'ə-kôr'əm, -kōr'-, kär'-). **1.** Variant of **Karakoram. 2.** Ruined ancient Mongol city in central Mongolia.

Ka·ra Kum (kä'rä ko͞om'). Desert of SW Central Asian USSR, between the Caspian Sea and the Amu Darya R.

Kar·ba·la (kär'bə-lə). City of central Iraq, SSW of Baghdad. Pop. 107,500.

Ka·re·li·a (kə-rē'lē-ə, -rēl'yə). Region of NE Europe, mainly in the NW USSR between the Gulf of Finland and the White Sea.

Ka·re·li·an (kə-rē'lē-ən, -rēl'yən). Isthmus in NW European USSR between Lake Ladoga and the Gulf of Finland.

Ka·ri·ba (kə-rē'bə). Lake, c. 165 mi (265.5 km) long, of N Zimbabwe and S Zambia, formed by **Kariba Dam** on the Zambezi R.

Kar·kheh (kär'kĕ, kər-kā'). River, c. 350 mi (563 km), of W Iran and SE Iraq.

Karl-Marx-Stadt (kärl-märk'shtät'). City of S East Germany, SE of Leipzig. Pop. 314,951.

Kar·lo·vy Va·ry (kär'lô-vē vä'rē). City of W Czechoslovakia, WNW of Prague. Pop. 61,212.

Karls·kro·na (kärls-kro͞o'nä). City of SE Sweden, on the Baltic SSW of Stockholm. Pop. 33,400.

Karls·ru·he also **Carls·ru·he** (kärls'-ro͞o'ə, kärlz'-). City of SW West Germany, on the Rhine WNW of Stuttgart. Pop. 271,417.

Karl·stad (kärl'städ'). City of SW Sweden, on Lake Vänern W of Stockholm. Pop. 73,904.

Kar·nak (kär'năk'). Village of E central Egypt, on the Nile on part of site of ancient Thebes.

Kar·ni·sche Al·pen (kär'nĭsh-ə äl'-pən). *German.* Carnic Alps.

Kár·pa·thos also **Car·pa·thos** (kär'-pä-thôs', -pə-thŏs'). Island of SE Greece, in the Dodecanese.

Kar·roo (kə-ro͞o', kă-). Semiarid plateau, c. 100,000 sq mi (259,000 sq km), of W South Africa.

Kars (kärs). City of NE Turkey, near the Soviet border. Pop. 58,651.

Ka·run (kä-ro͞on'). River of W Iran, flowing c. 450 mi (724 km) S into the Shatt-al-Arab.

Kar·vi·ná (kär'vē-nä'). City of N central Czechoslovakia, near the Polish border. Pop. 80,017.

Ka·sai (kä-sī'). River of NE Angola and W Zaire, flowing c. 1,200 mi (1,931 km) into the Congo.

Kash·mir also **Cash·mere** (kăsh'mîr', kăsh-mîr'). Region and former state of N India and NE Pakistan, including in the W part the **Vale of Kashmir,** fertile valley of the Jhelum R.

Kas·kas·ki·a (kəs-kăs'kē-ə). River, c. 300 mi (483 km), of S Ill.

Kas·sa·la (käs'ə-lə). City of NE Sudan, near the Ethiopian border. Pop. 98,751.

Kas·sel also **Cas·sel** (kăs'əl, kä'səl). City of E central West Germany, near the East German border. Pop. 197,667.

Kas·trop-Rau·xel (käs'trôp-rouk'-səl). Variant of **Castrop-Rauxel.**

Ka·su·gai (kä-so͞o'gī). City of central Japan, on Honshu near Nagoya. Pop. 244,114.

Ka·tah·din (kə-täd'n), **Mount.** Mountain 5,267 ft (1,606.4 m), in N central Me.

Ka·tan·ga (kə-täng'gə, -tăng'-). Region of SE Zaire. **—Kat'an·gese'** (kăt'ăng-gēs', -gēz') *adj. & n.*

Ka·thi·a·war (kä'tē-ä-wär', kä'-tē-ə-wär'). Peninsula of W India, projecting into the Arabian Sea between the gulfs of Kutch and Cambay.

Kat·mai (kăt'mī'), **Mount.** Active volcano, c. 6,715 ft (2,048 m), in the Aleutian range of S Alas. at E end of Alaska Peninsula.

Kat·man·du (kăt'măn-do͞o', kăt'-

măn-). Cap. of Nepal, in the central part. Pop. 150,402.
Ka·to·wi·ce (kä'tô-vē'tsĕ). City of S Poland, WNW of Kraków. Pop. 352,300.
Ka·tsi·na (kăt'sĭ-nə, kăt-sē'nə). City of N Nigeria, NW of Kano. Pop. 109,424.
Kat·te·gat (kăt'ĭ-găt'). Strait of the North Sea between SW Sweden and E Jutland, Denmark.
Ka·tun (kä-to͞on'). River, c. 415 mi (668 km), of S Siberian USSR.
Kau·ai (kou'ī', kou-ī'). Island of Hawaii, NW of Oahu.
Kau·kau·na (kô-kô'nə). City of E Wis., near Appleton. Pop. 11,310.
Kau·nas (kou'näs'). City of W European USSR, in central Lithuania. Pop. 377,000.
Ka·vál·la (kə-văl'ə, kä-vä'lä). City of NE Greece, on the Aegean Sea. Pop. 46,234.
Ka·ve·ri (kä'və-rē). Variant of **Cauvery**.
Ka·vir Desert (kä-vîr'). Dasht-e-Kavir.
Ka·wa·go·e (kä-wä'gô-ĕ). City of central Japan, on E central Honshu NW of Tokyo. Pop. 259,317.
Ka·wa·gu·chi (kä-wä'go͞o-chē, kä-wä'go͞o-chē'). City of central Japan, near Tokyo. Pop. 379,357.
Ka·wa·ni·shi (kä-wä'nē-shē). City of S Japan, near Osaka. Pop. 128,861.
Ka·war·tha Lakes (kə-wôr'thə). Group of 14 lakes in SE Ont., Canada, E of Lake Simcoe.
Ka·wa·sa·ki (kä-wä'sä-kē). City of central Japan, on Tokyo Bay near Tokyo. Pop. 1,040,698.
Kay·se·ri (kī'sə-rē', -zə-). City of central Turkey, SE of Ankara. Pop. 273,362.
Ka·zakh (kə-zäk', kä-) or **Ka·zakh·stan** (kə-zäk'stän', -zăk'stăn', kä'-). Region of Central Asian USSR, NE of the Caspian Sea.
Ka·zan (kə-zăn'). **1.** River, c. 455 mi (732 km), of E N.W.T., Canada. **2.** (*also* -zän', kä-zän'). City of E European USSR, on the Volga E of Moscow. Pop. 1,002,000.
Ka·zan·lik (kä-zän-lēk') or **Ka·zan·lŭk** (-lŭk'). City of central Bulgaria, E of Sofia. Pop. 56,483.
Kaz·bek (käz-bĕk'), **Mount.** Extinct volcano, 16,541 ft (5,045 m), of S European USSR, in the central Caucasus.
Kaz·da·gi (käz'dä-gĭ', -dä-ĭ'). *Turkish.* Ida (sense 1).
Kaz·vin (kăz-vēn', käz-). City of NW Iran, WNW of Teheran. Pop. 88,106.
Ke·a·la·ke·ku·a Bay (kā-ä'-lä-kä-ko͞o'ä). Inlet of the Pacific on W coast of Hawaii Is., Hawaii.
Kear·ney (kär'nē). City of S central Nebr., WSW of Grand Island. Pop. 21,158.
Kearns (kûrnz). City of NW Utah, near Salt Lake City. Pop. 17,000.
Kear·ny (kär'nē). Town of NE N.J., E of Newark. Pop. 35,735.
Kecs·ke·mét (kĕch'kĕ-māt'). City of central Hungary, SE of Budapest. Pop. 74,200.
Kee·ling Islands (kē'lĭng). Cocos.
Kee·lung (kē'lo͝ong'). City of N Taiwan, on the East China Sea. Pop. 341,400.
Keene (kēn). City of SW N.H., W of Manchester. Pop. 21,449.
Kee·wa·tin (kē-wāt'n). Administrative district, 228,160 sq mi (590,934.4 sq km), of E N.W.T., Canada.
Ke·fal·li·ni·a (kĕ'fä-lē-nē'ä). *Greek.* Cephalonia.
Kef·la·vík (kyĕb'lə-vēk', kĕf'-). Town of SW Iceland, on the Atlantic WSW of Reykjavík. Pop. 6,539.
Kel·ler·wand (kĕl'ər-vänt). Highest (9,220 ft/2,812.1 m) of the Carnic Alps, on the Austrian-Italian border.
Ke·low·na (kə-lō'nə). City of S B.C., Canada, ENE of Vancouver. Pop. 51,955.
Kel·so (kĕl'sō). City of SW Wash., S of Olympia near the Ore. border. Pop. 11,129.
Ke·me·ro·vo (kĕ'mə-rə-və, -mə-rō'-və, -mə-rə-vō'). City of central Siberian USSR, ENE of Novosibirsk. Pop. 478,000.
Ke·mi·jo·ki (kĕm'ĭ-yô-kĭ). River, c. 345 mi (555 km), of N Finland.
Kemp·ten (kĕmp'tən). City of S West Germany, SW of Munich. Pop. 57,390.
Ke·nai (kē'nī'). Peninsula of S central Alas. between Cook Inlet and the Gulf of Alaska.
Ken·il·worth (kĕn'əl-wûrth'). Town of central England, SE of Birmingham; site of ruined medieval castle. Pop. 19,730.
Ke·ni·tra (kə-nē'trə, kä-nē-trä'). City of N Morocco, NE of Rabat. Pop. 135,960.
Ken·more (kĕn'môr', -mōr'). Village of W N.Y., near Buffalo. Pop. 18,474.
Ken·ne·bec (kĕn'ə-bĕk'). River, 164 mi (263.9 km), of S Me.
Ken·ne·dy (kĕn'ĭ-dē). **1. Mount.** Mountain, 13,095 ft (3,994 m), in the St. Elias range in Y.T., Canada, near the Alas. border. **2. Cape.** Cape Canaveral.
Ken·ner (kĕn'ər). City of SE La., on the Mississippi near New Orleans. Pop. 66,382.
Ken·ne·saw Mountain (kĕn'ĭ-sô'). Lone peak, 1,809 ft (551.7 m), in NW Ga.; site of Civil War battle (1864).
Ken·nett (kĕn'ĭt). City of extreme SE Mo., near the Ark. border. Pop. 10,145.
Ken·ne·wick (kĕn'ə-wĭk'). City of S Wash., on the Columbia WNW of Walla Walla. Pop. 34,397.
Ke·no·ra (kə-nôr'ə, -nōr'ə). Town of W Ont., Canada, at the N end of the Lake of the Woods. Pop. 10,565.
Ke·no·sha (kə-nō'shə). City of extreme SE Wis., on Lake Michigan S of Milwaukee. Pop. 77,685.
Kent (kĕnt). **1.** Region and former kingdom of SE England. **2.** City of NE Ohio, near Akron. Pop. 26,164. **3.** City of W Wash., near Seattle. Pop. 23,152.
Ken·tuck·y (kĭn-tŭk'ē). **1.** River, c. 250 mi (402 km), of N central Ky. **2.** State of E central U.S. Cap. Frankfort. Pop. 3,661,433. **—Ken·tuck'i·an** *adj. & n.*
Kent·wood (kĕnt'wo͝od'). City of W central Mich., near Grand Rapids. Pop. 30,438.
Ken·ya (kĕn'yə, kēn'-). **1. Mount.** Extinct volcano, 17,040 ft (5,197.2 m), in central Kenya. **2.** Country of E central Africa. Cap. Nairobi. Pop. 15,322,000. **—Ken'yan** *adj. & n.*

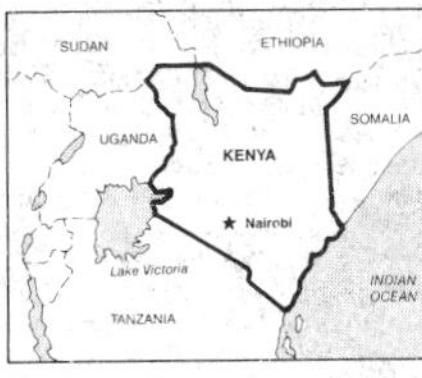

Kenya

Ke·o·kuk (kē'ə-kŭk'). City of extreme SE Iowa, on the Mississippi. Pop. 13,536.
Ke·os (kē'ŏs, kĕ'ôs). Island of Greece, in the NW Cyclades.
Kerch (kĕrch). **1.** Strait connecting the Black Sea and the Sea of Azov in S European USSR. **2.** Peninsula of S European USSR, in the E Crimea between the Black Sea and the Sea of Azov. **3.** City of S European USSR, on Kerch Strait. Pop. 158,000.
Ker·gue·len (kûr'gə-lən). **1.** Island group in the S Indian Ocean, SE of South Africa, administered by France. **2.** Largest island (1,318 sq mi/3,413 sq km) of this group.
Ke·rin·tji or **Ke·rin·chi** (kə-rĭn'chē). Volcano, 12,467 ft (3,802.4 m), in W central Sumatra, Indonesia.
Ker·ky·ra (kĕr'kē-rä, kĕr-kē'rä). *Greek.* Corfu.
Ker·kra·de (kĕr'krä'də). City of SE Netherlands, on the West German border. Pop. 47,001.
Ker·mad·ec (kər-măd'ĕk, -ək). Island group, c. 13 sq mi (33.7 sq km), of the SW Pacific NE of New Zealand, which administers it.
Ker·man (kər-män', kĕr-). City of E central Iran, SE of Teheran. Pop. 140,309.
Ker·man·shah (kĕr-män'shä'). City of W Iran, WSW of Teheran. Pop. 290,861.
Kern (kûrn). River, 155 mi (249.4 km), of S Calif.
Kerr·ville (kûr'vĭl', -vəl). City of SW Tex., NW of San Antonio. Pop. 15,276.
Ker·u·len (kĕr'o͞o-lĕn). River, 785 mi (1,263.1 km), of E Mongolia and NE China.
Ket·ter·ing (kĕt'ər-ĭng). City of SW Ohio, near Dayton. Pop. 61,186.
Ket·tle (kĕt'l). River, c. 160 mi (257 km), of S B.C., Canada, and NE Wash.
Keu·ka (kyo͞o'kə, kā-yo͞o'-). One of the Finger Lakes, c. 18 mi (29 km) long, of W central N.Y.
Kew (kyo͞o). District of W Greater London, England.
Ke·wa·nee (kĭ-wä'nē). City of NW Ill., ESE of Moline. Pop. 14,508.
Ke·wee·naw (kē'wə-nô'). Peninsula of NW Mich., extending c. 60 mi (97 km) NE into Lake Superior W of **Keweenaw Bay.**
Key Lar·go (kē lär'gō). Island off S Fla., largest of the Florida Keys.
Key West (wĕst). City of extreme S Fla., on **Key West Is.**, westernmost of the Florida Keys in the Gulf of Mexico. Pop. 24,292.
Kha·ba·rovsk (kə-bär'əfsk, KHä-bä'-rəfsk). City of SE Far Eastern USSR, on the Amur near the Chinese border. Pop. 538,000.
Khal·ki·dhi·ki (KHäl'kē-*th*ē-kē'). *Greek.* Chalcidice.
Khal·kis (käl-kēs', KHäl-). *Greek.* Chalcis.
Khan·ba·lik (kän'bä-lēk', KHän'-). Ancient city of Mongol China, on site of modern Beijing.
Khan·ka (kăng'kə, hän'kä) also **Han·ka** (hăng'kə, hän'kä). Lake, c. 1,700 sq mi (4,403 sq km), between SE Far Eastern USSR and NE China.
Khar·kov (kär'kôf, -kôv, -kŏf, -kŏv). City of S central European USSR, E of Kiev. Pop. 1,464,000.
Khar·toum also **Khar·tum** (kär-to͞om'). Cap. of Sudan, in the E central part at confluence of the Blue Nile and White Nile. Pop. 333,921.
Khas·ko·vo (KHäs'kə-və, -kô-vô). City of S Bulgaria, ESE of Plovdiv. Pop. 82,636.
Kha·tan·ga (kə-tăng'gə, -täng'-, KHä-tän'gə). River, c. 715 mi (1,150 km), of N central Siberian USSR.
Khe·lat (kə-lät'). Variant of **Kalat.**
Kher·son (hĕr-sôn', KHĕr-). City of SW European USSR, near the Black Sea ENE of Odessa. Pop. 324,000.
Khing·an (shĭng'än). Mountains rising to 5,670 ft (1,729.4 m) in NE China.
Khí·os (KHē'ôs, kī'ŏs). *Greek.* **Chios.**
Khi·va (kē'və, KHē'vä). City of SW Central Asian USSR, on **Khiva oasis** on the Amu Darya, S of the Aral Sea. Pop. 26,000.
Khmel·nit·sky (KHmĭl-nyĕt'skĭ). City of SW European USSR, WSW of Kiev. Pop. 179,000.
Khmer Re·pub·lic (kmĕr rĭ-pŭb'lĭk). Cambodia.
Kho·per (KHō-pyôr'). River, c. 625 mi (1,006 km), of S European USSR.
Khor·ram·shahr also **Khur·ram·shahr** (KHo͝or'räm-shär'). City of SW Iran, near the Persian Gulf. Pop. 146,709.
Kho·tan (kō'tän', KHō-'). Hotan.
Khul·na (ko͝ol'nə). City of SW Bangladesh, near the Ganges delta. Pop. 521,543.
Khu·zi·stan (KHo͞o'zĭ-stän'). Region of SW Iran at the head of the Persian Gulf.
Khy·ber (kī'bər). Pass, c. 3,500 ft (5,632 m), through mountains on the border between W Afghanistan and N Pakistan.
Kia·ling (jyä'lĭng'). Jialing.
Ki·a·mich·i (kī'ə-mĭsh'ē). River, c. 100 mi (161 km), of SE Okla.
Kia·mu·sze (jyä'mo͞o'sŭ'). Jiamusi.
Kick·a·poo (kĭk'ə-po͞o'). River, c. 100 mi (161 km), of SW Wis.
Kid·der·min·ster (kĭd'ər-mĭn'stər). Borough of W central England, WSW of Birmingham. Pop. 49,960.
Kiel (kēl). **1.** Canal, 61 mi (98.1 km) long, of N West Germany, connecting the North Sea and the Baltic. **2.** City of N West Germany, on **Kiel Bay**, an inlet of the Baltic. Pop. 253,967.
Kiel·ce (kyĕlt'sĕ). City of SE Poland, S of Warsaw. Pop. 181,000.
Ki·ev (kē'ĕf, -ĕv, -əf). City of W European USSR, on the Dnieper SW of Moscow. Pop. 2,192,000.
Ki·ga·li (kĭ-gä'lē, kē-). Cap. of Rwanda, in the central part. Pop. 117,700.
Ki·klá·dhes (kē-klä'*th*ĕs). *Greek.* Cyclades.
Ki·lau·e·a (kē'lou-ā'ə). Active volcanic crater on Mauna Loa, Hawaii Is., Hawaii.
Kil·gore (kĭl'gôr', -gōr'). City of E. Tex., E of Tyler. Pop. 10,968.
Kil·i·man·ja·ro (kĭl'ə-mən-jär'ō). Highest mountain in Africa, 19,340 ft (5,898.7 m), in NE Tanzania near the Kenya border.
Kil·leen (kĭ-lēn'). City of central Tex., SW of Waco. Pop. 46,296.
Kil·ling·ly (kĭl'ĭng-lē). Town of NE Conn., on the R.I. border. Pop. 14,519.
Kil·mar·nock (kĭl-mär'nək). Burgh of SW Scotland, SSW of Glasgow. Pop. 50,318.
Kim·ber·ley (kĭm'bər-lē). City of central South Africa, WNW of Bloemfontein. Pop. 105,258.
Kin·a·ba·lu (kĭn'ə-bə-lo͞o'). Highest mountain on Borneo, 13,455 ft (4,103.8 m), in N Sabah, Malaysia.
Ki·nesh·ma (kē'nĭsh-mə). City of central European USSR, NE of Moscow. Pop. 102,000.
King George Mount (kĭng jôrj'). Mountain, 11,226 ft (3,423.9 m), in the Rockies in SE B.C., Canada, near the Alta. border.
King George's Falls (jôr'jĭz). Aughrabies Falls.
Kings (kĭngz). **1.** River, c. 125 mi (201 km), of central Calif., rising in headstreams that flow through the gorges of **Kings Canyon National Park** (719 sq mi/1,862.2 sq km) in the Sierra Nevada. **2. Peak.** Highest (13,528 ft/4,126 m) of the Uinta Mts. in NE Utah.
King's Lynn (kĭngz lĭn'). Borough of E England, near the Wash. Pop. 29,990.
Kings·port (kĭngz'pôrt', -pōrt'). City of NE Tenn., near the Va. border ENE of Knoxville. Pop. 32,027.
King·ston (kĭng'stən). **1.** City of S Ont., Canada, on Lake Ontario near the head of the St. Lawrence. Pop. 60,954. **2.** Cap. of Jamaica, in the SE part on the Caribbean. Pop. 665,050. **3.** City of SE N.Y., on the Hudson SSW of Albany. Pop. 24,481. **4.** Borough of NE central Pa., opposite Wilkes-Barre. Pop. 15,681.
King·ston-up·on-Hull (kĭng'-stən-ə-pŏn-hŭl', -pôn-). Hull.
Kings·town (kĭngz'toun'). Cap. of St. Vincent and the Grenadines in the West Indies, on the SW coast of St. Vincent Is. Pop. 17,258.
Kings·ville (kĭngz'vĭl'). City of S Tex., SW of Corpus Christi. Pop. 28,808.
King·teh·chen (jĭng'dŭ'jŭn'). Jingdezhen.
King Wil·liam (wĭl'yəm). Island of N.W.T., Canada, in the Arctic Ocean SW of Boothia Peninsula.
Kin·sha·sa (kēn-shä'sə, kĭn-). Cap. of Zaire, in the W part on the Congo R. Pop. 2,202,000.
Kin·ston (kĭn'stən). City of E central N.C., SE of Raleigh. Pop. 25,234.
Kin·tyre (kĭn-tīr'). Peninsula of SW Scotland extending c. 40 mi (64 km) between the Atlantic and the Firth of Clyde.
Ki·o·ga or **Ky·o·ga** (kē-ō'gə, kyō'gə). Lake, c. 1,000 sq mi (2,590 sq km), of central Uganda.
Kir·ghiz or **Kir·giz** (kîr-gēz') or **Kir·ghiz·stan** (-gē-stän'). Region of SE Central Asian USSR, bordering on NW China.
Ki·ri·ba·ti (kîr'ĭ-băs', kĭr'ĭ-băs'). Island republic of the W central Pacific, near the equator. Cap. Bairiki. Pop. 56,213.

Ki·rin (kē′rĭn′). Jilin.

Kirk·cal·dy (kûr-kô′dē, -kä′-, -kôl′-). Burgh of E Scotland, on the Firth of Forth. Pop. 50,063.

Kirk·land (kûrk′lənd). City of W central Wash., on Lake Washington near Seattle. Pop. 18,779.

Kirkland Lake. Town of E Ont., Canada, NNE of Sudbury. Pop. 12,460.

Kirk·pat·rick (kûrk-păt′rĭk), **Mount.** Mountain, 14,856 ft (4,531.1 m), of Antarctica, near S edge of Ross Ice Shelf.

Kirks·ville (kûrks′vĭl′). City of N Mo., NW of Hannibal. Pop. 17,167.

Kir·kuk (kĭr-ko͝ok′). City of N Iraq, SE of Mosul. Pop. 207,900.

Kirk·wall (kûrk′wôl′). Burgh of N Scotland, chief town of the Orkney Is. Pop. 4,814.

Kirk·wood (kûrk′wo͝od′). City of E Mo., near St. Louis. Pop. 27,987.

Ki·rov (kē′rəf, -rŏf, -rôf). City of E central European USSR, ENE of Moscow. Pop. 392,000.

Ki·ro·va·bad (kĭ-rō′və-băd′, kē′-rə-vä-bät′). City of S European USSR, SE of Tbilisi. Pop. 237,000.

Ki·ro·vo·grad (kĭ-rō′və-grăd′, kē′-rə-və-grät′). City of SW European USSR, SSE of Kiev. Pop. 242,000.

Kir·yu (kĭr′yo͞o′). City of central Japan, on central Honshu NNW of Tokyo. Pop. 135,055.

Ki·san·ga·ni (kē′săng-gä′nē, kĭ-zăng′gä-nē). City of N Zaire, on the Congo R. Pop. 310,705.

Ki·sa·ra·zu (kē′sä-rä′zo͞o). City of E central Japan, across Tokyo Bay from Tokyo. Pop. 104,516.

Ki·se·levsk (kĭ-sĕ-lyôfsk). City of SW Siberian USSR, ESE of Novosibirsk. Pop. 122,000.

Kish (kĭsh). Ancient city of Mesopotamia, E of present-day Hilla, Iraq.

Ki·shi·nev (kĭsh′ĭ-nĕf′, kē-shĭ-nyôf′). City of SW European USSR, near the Rumanian border. Pop. 519,000.

Ki·shi·wa·da (kē′shē-wä′dä). City of S Japan, near Osaka. Pop. 179,038.

Ki·si (jē′shē′). Jixi.

Kis·ka (kĭs′kə). Island of SW Alas., near W end of the Aleutians.

Kis·lo·vodsk (kēs-lō-vôtsk′). City of S European USSR, in N Caucasus. Pop. 102,000.

Kis·sim·mee (kĭ-sĭm′ē). **1.** River of central Fla., flowing c. 140 mi (225 km) SSE through **Lake Kissimmee** (55 sq mi/142.5 sq km) to Lake Okeechobee. **2.** City of central Fla., S of Orlando. Pop. 15,487.

Kist·na (kĭst′nə). River of S India, flowing c. 800 mi (1,287 km) E to the Bay of Bengal.

Ki·ta·kyu·shu (kē-tä′kyo͞o-sho͞o). City of S Japan, on N coast of Kyushu. Pop. 1,065,084.

Kitch·e·ner (kĭch′ə-nər). City of S Ont., Canada, WSW of Toronto. Pop. 136,091.

Kí·thi·ra (kē′thē-rä). *Greek.* Cythera.

Kit·i·mat (kĭt′ə-măt′). Town of W B.C., Canada, on an inlet of the Pacific E of Prince Rupert. Pop. 11,791.

Kit·ta·tin·ny Mountain (kĭt′ə-tĭn′ē). Ridge of the Appalachians, c. 1,800 ft (549 m), in SE N.Y., NW N.J., and E Pa.

Kit·ter·y (kĭt′ə-rē). Town of extreme SW Me., opposite Portsmouth, N.H. Pop. 7,363.

Kit·ty Hawk (kĭt′ē hôk′). Village of NE N.C., on a sandy peninsula E of Albemarle Sound; site of Wright Brothers' first successful flight (1903).

Ki·twe (kē′twā). City of N central Zambia, near the Zaire border. Pop. 341,000.

Ki·vu (kē′vo͞o). Lake, 1,042 sq mi (2,698.8 sq km), on the Zaire-Rwanda border N of Lake Tanganyika.

Ki·zil·Ir·mak or **Ki·zil Ir·mak** (kĭ-zĭl′-ĭr-mäk′). River of N central Turkey, flowing c. 715 mi (1,150 km) to the Black Sea.

Kjö·len (chœ′lən). Range of NW Sweden and NE Norway.

Klad·no (kläd′nô). City of NW Czechoslovakia, WNW of Prague. Pop. 66,370.

Kla·gen·furt (klä′gən-fo͝ort′). City of S Austria, SW of Graz. Pop. 82,512.

Klai·pe·da (klī′pə-də, -pĕ-dä′). City of W European USSR, in Lithuania on the Baltic. Pop. 178,000.

Klam·ath (klăm′əth). **1.** River flowing c. 263 mi (423 km) from Upper Klamath Lake in SW Ore. through NW Calif. to the Pacific. **2.** Mountains of the Coast Ranges in S Ore. and NW Calif.

Klamath Falls. City of S Ore., near the Calif. border ESE of Medford. Pop. 16,661.

Kle·ve (klā′və). Cleves.

Klon·dike (klŏn′dīk′). River, c. 90 mi (145 km), of E central Y.T., Canada, flowing through **the Klondike** gold-mining region to the Yukon R.

Knife (nīf). River, c. 165 mi (265 km), of W central N.Dak.

Knos·sos also **Cnos·sos** or **Cnos·sus** (nŏs′əs). Ancient city of N Crete, near present-day Candia.

Knox·ville (nŏks′vĭl′, -vəl). City of E Tenn., NE of Chattanooga. Pop. 183,139.

Ko·be (kō′bē, -bä′). City of S Japan, on Osaka Bay in S Honshu. Pop. 1,367,392.

Kø·ben·havn (kœ′bən-houn′). *Danish.* Copenhagen.

Ko·blenz (kō′blĕnts′). Variant of **Coblenz.**

Ko·chi (kô′chē, -chē′). City of S Japan, on the S coast of Shikoku. Pop. 300,830.

Ko·dai·ra (kô-dī′rä). City of central Japan, near Tokyo. Pop. 156,758.

Ko·di·ak (kō′dē-ăk′). Island of S Alas., in the Gulf of Alaska E of Alaska Peninsula.

Ko·fu (kô′fo͞o). City of central Japan, on central Honshu W of Tokyo. Pop. 197,803.

Ko·ga·nei (kô-gä′nā). City of central Japan, near Tokyo. Pop. 103,487.

Ko·kand (kō-kănd′). City of S Central Asian USSR, SE of Tashkent. Pop. 154,000.

Ko·ko·mo (kō′kə-mō′). City of central Ind., N of Indianapolis. Pop. 47,808.

Ko·ko Nor (kō′kō′ nôr′). Qinghai.

Ko·la (kō′lə). Peninsula of NW European USSR, projecting E from Scandinavia between the White Sea and Barents Sea.

Ko·lar Gold Fields (kō-lär′ gōld′ fēldz′). City of S India, SE of Bangalore. Pop. 76,112.

Kol·ding (kôl′dĭng). City of S central Denmark, on the E coast of Jutland. Pop. 55,769.

Kol·ha·pur (kō′lə-po͝or′, kō′lə-po͝or′). City of W India, SSE of Bombay. Pop. 259,050.

Kol·mar (kôl′mär′). *German.* Colmar.

Köln (kœln). *German.* Cologne.

Ko·lom·na (kŏ-lôm′nə). City of central European USSR, SE of Moscow. Pop. 149,000.

Ko·ly·ma (kə-lē′mə, kō-). **1.** River of N Far Eastern USSR, flowing c. 1,335 mi (2,148 km) N to the East Siberian Sea. **2.** Range of N Far Eastern USSR, extending c. 700 mi (1,126 km) E of the Kolyma R.

Ko·ma·ki (kô-mä′kē). City of S Japan, on Honshu near Nagoya. Pop. 101,299.

Ko·man·dor·skie also **Ko·man·dor·skye** (kŏm′ən-dôr′skē). Island group of Far Eastern USSR, in the Bering Sea E of Kamchatka Peninsula.

Ko·ma·ti (kō-mä′tē, kə-). River, c. 500 mi (805 km), of NE South Africa, N Swaziland, and S Mozambique.

Ko·ma·tsu (kô-mä′tso͞o). City of central Japan, on W coast of Honshu SW of Kanazawa. Pop. 103,606.

Ko·mo·do (kə-mō′dō). Island of S central Indonesia, between Sumbawa and Flores Is.

Kom·so·molsk (kŏm′sə-môlsk′). City of S Far Eastern USSR, NNE of Vladivostok. Pop. 269,000.

Ko·na (kō′nə). Region along W coast of Hawaii Is., Hawaii.

Kon·gur (gän′po͝or′), **Mount.** Highest (25,325 ft/7,724.1 m) of the Pamirs, in extreme W China.

Kö·nigs·berg (kā′nĭgz-bûrg′, kœ′-, kœ′nĭkHs-bĕrk′). *German.* Kaliningrad.

Kon·stan·ti·nov·ka (kŏn-stän-tyē′-nəf-kə, -tē′-). City of S European USSR, SSE of Kharkov. Pop. 113,000.

Kon·stanz (kôn′stänts′). *German.* Constance.

Kon·ya also **Kon·ia** (kôn′yä, kôn-yä′). City of SW Turkey, S of Ankara. Pop. 325,850.

Ko·o·lau (kō′ō-lä′o͞o). Range of E Oahu, Hawaii, rising to 3,105 ft (947 m).

Koo·te·nay or **Koo·te·nai** (ko͞ot′n-ā′). River, 407 mi (654.9 km), flowing from SE B.C., Canada, S through NW Mont., NW through N Idaho, and N into B.C., where it widens to form **Kootenay Lake** (64 mi/103 km long) before joining the Columbia.

Ko·peysk (kō-pāsk′, kō-). City of W Siberian USSR, SSE of Sverdlovsk. Pop. 146,000.

Kor·do·fan (kôr′dō-făn′, -fän′). Region of central Sudan.

Ko·re·a (kə-rē′ə, kō-, kô-). **1. Bay.** Inlet of the Yellow Sea between NE China and NW North Korea. **2. Strait.** Channel, c. 110 mi (177 km) wide, between SE South Korea and SW Japan. **3.** Peninsula and former country of E Asia, between the Yellow Sea and the Sea of Japan, divided politically since 1948 between **North Korea** (cap. Pyongyang; pop. 17,072,000) and **South Korea** (cap. Seoul; pop. 37,019,000). —**Ko·re′an** *adj.* & *n.*

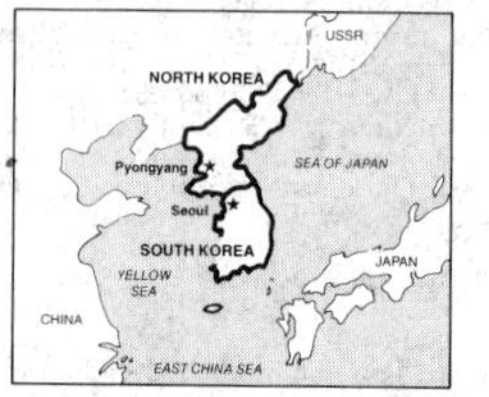

Korea

Kó·rin·thos (kô′rēn-thôs). *Greek.* Corinth.

Ko·ri·ya·ma (kô-rē′yä-mä). City of central Japan, on N Honshu N of Tokyo. Pop. 195,700.

Kö·rös (kœ′rœsh). River, c. 345 mi (555 km), of SE Hungary.

Kort·rijk (kôrt′rīk′). City of W Belgium, W of Brussels. Pop. 75,535.

Kos (kŏs, kôs). Island, 111 sq mi (287.5 sq km), of SE Greece, in the N Dodecanese at the entrance to the **Gulf of Kos,** an inlet of the Aegean on the SW coast of Turkey.

Kos·ci·us·ko (kŏs′ē-ŭs′kō, kŏz′-), **Mount.** Highest mountain (7,316 ft/2,231.4 m) in Australia, in the SE part in the Australian Alps.

Ko·shi·ga·ya (kô-shē′gä-yä). City of central Japan, near Tokyo. Pop. 223,243.

Kosh·tan-Tau (kəsh-tän′tou′, kôsh′-tän-). Mountain, c. 16,880 ft (5,148 m), in the central Caucasus of S European USSR.

Ko·ši·ce (kô′shĭ-tsĕ). City of E Czechoslovakia, near the Hungarian border. Pop. 200,943.

Kos·tro·ma (kəs-trə-mä′, kŏs′-). City of central European USSR, on the Volga NE of Moscow. Pop. 255,000.

Ko·ta (kō′tə). City of NW India, SSW of Delhi. Pop. 212,991.

Ko·ta Kin·a·ba·lu (kō′tə kĭn′-ə-bə-lo͞o′). City of E Malaysia, on NW coast of Sabah on Borneo. Pop. 40,939.

Kott·bus (kŏt′bəs, kôt′bo͝os). Variant of **Cott·bus.**

Kot·ze·bue Sound (kŏt′sĭ-byo͞o′). Inlet of the Chukchi Sea in NW Alas., N of Seward Peninsula.

Kov·no (kôv′nō, -nŏ). *Russian.* Kaunas.

Kov·rov (kŏv-rôf′). City of central European USSR, ENE of Moscow. Pop. 144,000.

Kow·loon (kou′lo͞on′). City of Hong Kong colony, on **Kowloon Peninsula** opposite Hong Kong Is. on the SE coast of China. Pop. 749,600.

Koy·u·kuk (kī′ə-kŭk′). River, c. 500 mi (805 km), of N Alas.

Ko·zhi·kode (kō′zhĭ-kōd′). City of SW India, on the Arabian Sea SW of Bangalore. Pop. 333,979.

Kra (krä). Isthmus, c. 40 mi (64 km) wide, linking Malay Peninsula and the SE Asian mainland.

Kra·ka·to·a (krä′kə-tō′ə, krăk′ə-) also **Kra·ka·tau** (-tou′). Volcanic island of Indonesia between Sumatra and Java.

Kra·ków (krä′ko͞of, krăk′ou, krä′kou, krā′kō). City of S Poland, on the Vistula. Pop. 719,200.

Kra·ma·torsk (krä-mä-tôrsk′). City of S European USSR, SSE of Kharkov. Pop. 180,000.

Kras·no·dar (kräs′nō-där′, krăs′-nə-där′). City of S European USSR, in the N Caucasus near the Black Sea. Pop. 572,000.

Kras·no·yarsk (kräs′nō-yärsk′, krăs′-nə-). City of S central Siberian USSR, on the upper Yenisei. Pop. 807,000.

Kre·feld (krā′fĕld′, -fĕlt′). City of W West Germany, on the Rhine NNW of Cologne. Pop. 223,501.

Kre·men·chug (krĕ′mĕn-cho͞ok′). City of SW European USSR, on the Dnieper SE of Kiev. Pop. 212,000.

Kre·te (krē′tē). *Greek.* Crete.

Krim (krĭm). *Russian.* Crimea.

Krish·na (krĭsh′nə). Kistna.

Kris·tian·sand (krĭs′chən-sănd′, krĭs′tyän-sän′). City of extreme S Norway, on the Skagerrak. Pop. 60,722.

Kri·voi Rog or **Kri·voy Rog** (krĭv′oi rŏg′, rôk′, krē-voi′ rôk′). City of SW European USSR, NE of Odessa. Pop. 657,000.

Kron·shtadt (krŏn′shtät) also **Kron·stadt** (krŏn′-). City and naval base of NW European USSR, on an island in the Gulf of Finland W of Leningrad. Pop. 39,477.

Kru·ger National Park (kro͞o′gər). Wildlife preserve, 8,652 sq mi (22,408.7 sq km), in NE South Africa.

Kru·gers·dorp (kro͞o′gərz-dôrp′, krü′gərs-). City of NE South Africa, WNW of Johannesburg. Pop. 92,725.

Krung Thep (kro͝ong′tăp′). *Thai.* Bangkok.

Krus·né Ho·ry (kro͞osh′nə hô′rĭ, kro͞o′shnyĕ). *Czech.* Erzgebirge.

Kua·la Lum·pur (kwä′lə lo͝om′po͝or′). Cap. of Malaysia, on the SW Malay Peninsula. Pop. 451,728.

Kuang·chow (gwäng′ jō′). Guangzhou.

Ku·ban (ko͞o-băn′, -bän′). River of S European USSR, flowing c. 570 mi (917 km) N and W to the Sea of Azov.

Ku·ching (ko͞o′chĭng). Chief city of Sarawak, Malaysia, in the SW part on the South China Sea. Pop. 63,535.

Kui·by·shev or **Kuy·by·shev** (kwē′-bə-shĕf′, ko͞o′ē-bə-). City of E central European USSR, on the Volga ESE of Moscow. Pop. 1,226,000.

Ku·ma·mo·to (ko͞o-mä′mô-tô). City of S Japan, on W Coast of Kyushu. Pop. 525,613.

Ku·ma·si (ko͞o-mä′sē). City of S central Ghana, NW of Accra. Pop. 345,117.

Ku·na·shir (ko͞o′nə-shĭr′). Southernmost and largest of the Kurile Is. of Far Eastern USSR.

Ku·ne·ne (ko͞o-nā′nə). Variant of **Cunene.**

Kun·gur (ko͞on-go͞or′, ko͞on′go͞or). Kongur.

Kun·lun (ko͞on′lo͞on′). Range of W China extending from the Kashmir border E along N edge of Tibet.

Kun·ming (ko͞on′mĭng′). City of S China, SW of Chongqing. Pop. 1,225,000.

Kun·san (ko͞on′sän′, go͞on′-). City of SW South Korea, on the Yellow Sea S of Seoul. Pop. 167,442.

Kuo·pio (kwô′pyō, ko͞o′ô′pē-ô). City of S central Finland, NNE of Helsinki. Pop. 73,567.

Ku·ra (ko͞o-rä′, ko͞o-). River of NE Turkey and S European USSR, flowing c. 940 mi (1,512 km) NE and SE to the Caspian Sea.

Kurd·i·stan (kûr′dĭ-stăn′, ko͝or′-dĭ-stän′). Highland region of SE Turkey, NE Iraq, and NW Iran.

Ku·re (ko͝o′rĕ′). City of S Japan, in SW Honshu on the Inland Sea. Pop. 234,550.

Kur·gan (ko͝or-găn′). City of W Siberian USSR, ESE of Sverdlovsk. Pop. 316,000.

Ku·rile or **Ku·ril** (ko͝or′ĭl, ko͞o-rēl′). Island chain of extreme E USSR, extending c. 700 mi (1,126 km) in the Pacific between Kamchatka Peninsula and N Hokkaido, Japan. —**Ku·ril′i·an** *adj. & n.*

Kursk (ko͝orsk). City of central European USSR, SSW of Moscow. Pop. 383,000.

Ku·ru·me (ko͞o-ro͞o′mĕ). City of SW Japan, on NW Kyushu SSW of Kitakyushu. Pop. 216,974.

Kush (kŭsh, ko͝osh). Variant of **Cush.**

Ku·shi·ro (ko͞o-shē′rō). City of NE Japan, in SE Hokkaido on the Pacific. Pop. 214,694.

Kus·ko·kwim (kŭs′kə-kwĭm′). River of SW Alas., flowing c. 600 mi (965 km) SW to **Kuskokwim Bay,** an inlet of the Bering Sea.

Ku·sta·nay (ko͞o-stä-nī′). City of W Central Asian USSR, SE of Sverdlovsk. Pop. 169,000.

Ku·ta·i·si (ko͞o-tä-ē′sē). City of S European USSR, WNW of Tbilisi. Pop. 197,000.

Kutch also **Cutch** (kŭch). **1. Gulf of.** Inlet of the Arabian Sea in W India. **2.** See **Rann of Kutch.**

Ku·wait (ko͞o-wāt′, -wīt′). **1.** Country of the NE Arabian Peninsula, at the head of the Persian Gulf. Pop. 1,355,-827. Cap. Kuwait. **2.** Also **Al Kuwait** (äl). Cap. of Kuwait, in the E central part on the Persian Gulf. Pop. 181,774. —**Ku·wait′i** *adj. & n.*

Kuy·by·shev (kwē′bə-shĕf′, ko͞o′-ē-bə-). Variant of **Kuibyshev.**

Kuz·netsk Ba·sin (ko͞oz-nĕtsk′ bä′-sĭn, -nyĕtsk′). Coal-producing region of W Siberian USSR, E of Novosibirsk.

Kwa·ja·lein (kwä′ jə-lən, -lān′). Atoll, 6.5 sq mi (16.8 sq km), in the Marshall Is. of the W Pacific.

Kwan·do (kwän′dō). River, c. 600 mi (965 km), of SE Angola and NE Namibia.

Kwang·chow (gwäng′jō′). Guangzhou.

Kwang·cho·wan (gwäng′jō′wän′). Former coastal territory of SE China on Leizhou Peninsula, leased to France (1898–1946).

Kwang·ju (gwäng′jo͞o′). City of SW South Korea, S of Seoul. Pop. 694,646.

Kwan·tung (gwän′do͝ong′). Former coastal territory of NE China in S Manchuria, leased to Japan (1905–45).

Kwan·za (kwän′zə). Variant of **Cuanza.**

Kwei·lin (gwā′lĭn′). Guilin.

Kwei·sui (gwā′swā′). Hohhot.

Kwei·yang (gwā′yăng′). Guiyang.

Ky·kla·des (kē-klä′*th*ĕs). *Greek.* Cyclades.

Ky·o·ga (kē-ō′gə, kyō′gə). Variant of **Kioga.**

Kyong·song (kyông′sông′). Seoul.

Kyo·to (kē-ō′tō, kyō′tō′). City of S Japan, on S Honshu NE of Osaka. Pop. 1,472,993.

Kyu·shu (kē-o͞o′sho͞o, kyo͞o′sho͞o′). 3rd largest island of SW Japan (13,760 sq mi/35,638 sq km).

Ky·zyl-Kum (kĭ-zĭl′ko͞om′). Desert of S Central Asian USSR, SE of the Aral Sea.

L

Laa·land (lô′län) or **Lol·land** (lŏl′ənd, lô′län). Island of SE Denmark, in the Baltic between Sjaelland and N West Germany.

La Baie (lä bā′). City of S central Que., Canada, on the Saguenay R. near Chicoutimi. Pop. 20,116.

La·be (lä′bĕ). *Czech.* Elbe.

Lab·ra·dor (lăb′rə-dôr′). **1.** Sea of the N Atlantic between NE Canada and SW Greenland. **2.** Ocean current of the NW Atlantic, flowing S from Baffin Bay along the coast of Newf. province. **3.** Peninsula of NE Canada between Hudson Bay and the Atlantic, divided between Que. and Newf. **4.** Mainland territory of Newf., Canada, on NE Labrador Peninsula. —**Lab′ra·dor′e·an, Lab′ra·dor′i·an** *adj. & n.*

La·bu·an (lä′bo͞o-än′, lə-bo͞o′ən). Island of Malaysia, off the W coast of Sabah.

La Ca·na·da-Flint·ridge (lä′kən-yä′-də-flĭnt′rĭj′). Community of SW Calif., near Pasadena. Pop. 20,652.

Lac·ca·dive, Mi·ni·coy, and A·min·di·vi Islands (lăk′ə-dīv′, -dēv′; mĭn′ĭ-koi′; ŭm′ən-dē′vē). Island group in the Arabian Sea, off the SW coast of India.

Lac·e·dae·mon (lăs′ĭ-dē′mən). Sparta. —**Lac′e·dae·mo′ni·an** (-dĭ-mō′nē-ən) *adj. & n.*

La·cey (lā′sē). City of W central Wash., E of Olympia. Pop. 13,940.

La Chaux-de-Fonds (lä shōd-fôɴ′). City of W Switzerland, in the Jura Mts. WNW of Bern. Pop. 38,500.

La·chine (lə-shēn′). City of S Que., Canada, on S Montreal Is. Pop. 41,503.

La·chish (lā′kĭsh). Ancient city of S Palestine, SW of Jerusalem.

Lach·lan (läk′lən). River, c. 922 mi (1,484 km), of SE Australia.

La·chute (lə-sho͞ot′). City of S Que., Canada, W of Montreal. Pop. 11,928.

Lack·a·wan·na (lăk′ə-wŏn′ə). City of W N.Y., near Buffalo. Pop. 22,701.

La·co·ni·a (lə-kō′nē-ə). **1. Gulf of.** Inlet of the Mediterranean on S Coast of Peloponnesus, S Greece. **2.** Ancient region of S Greece on SE Peloponnesus; site of Sparta. **3.** City of central N.H., N of Concord. Pop. 15,575.

La Co·ru·ña (lä′ kô-ro͞o′nyä). City of NW Spain, on the Atlantic. Pop. 228,637.

La Crosse (lə krôs′, krŏs′). City of W Wis., on the Mississippi NW of Madison. Pop. 48,347.

La·dakh (lə-däKH′). Region of N India, in E Kashmir along the Tibetan border.

La·do·ga (lä′dŏ-gä′, -də-gə). Lake, c. 7,000 sq mi (18,130 sq km), of NW European USSR, NE of Leningrad.

La·fay·ette (lăf′ē-ĕt′, lä′fē-). **1.** City of W Calif., near Oakland. Pop. 20,879. **2.** City of W central Ind., on the Wabash R. Pop. 43,011. **3.** City of S central La., WSW of Baton Rouge. Pop. 81,961.

La·gash (lā′găsh). Ancient city of Sumer, S Mesopotamia, in present-day S Iraq.

La·go·a dos Pa·tos (lə-gō′ə do͞osh pä′to͞osh). Tidal lagoon, c. 150 mi (241 km) long, along coast of S Brazil.

La·gos (lā′gŏs, lā′gŏs). Cap. of Nigeria, in the SW on the Gulf of Guinea. Pop. 1,060,800.

La Gou·lette (lä go͞o-lĕt′). City of NE Tunisia, on the Mediterranean near Tunis. Pop. 41,912.

La Grande (lə grănd′). City of NE Ore., SE of Pendleton. Pop. 11,354.

La Grange (lə grānj′). **1.** City of W Ga., near the Ala. border of Columbus. Pop. 24,204. **2.** Village of NE Ill., near Chicago. Pop. 15,681.

La Grange Park. Village of NE Ill., near Chicago. Pop. 13,359.

La Guai·ra (lä gwī′rä). City of N Venezuela, on the Caribbean NW of Caracas. Pop. 20,344.

La·gu·na Beach (lə-go͞o′nə). City of S Calif., SE of Long Beach. Pop. 17,860.

La Ha·bra (lə hä′brə). City of S Calif., near Los Angeles. Pop. 45,232.

La Hague (lə hăg′), **Cape.** Promontory of NW France at the NW tip of the Cotentin Peninsula on the English Channel.

La·hon·tan (lə-hŏn′tən). Extinct Pleistocene lake with remnants surviving in W Nev. and NE Calif.

La·hore (lə-hôr′, -hōr′). City of NE Pakistan, near the Indian border. Pop. 2,022,577.

Lah·ti (lä′tē). City of S central Finland, NNE of Helsinki. Pop. 94,980.

La Jol·la (lə hoi′ə). Pacific beach district of San Diego, Calif.

Lake or **Lake of** (lāk) or **Loch** (lŏk, lôKH). For names of lakes, see the specific element, e.g., for **Lake Erie** see **Erie.**

Lake Charles (chärlz). City of SW La., E of Beaumont, Tex. Pop. 75,051.

Lake District. Scenic area of NW England.

Lake For·est (fôr′ĭst, fŏr′-). City of NE Ill., on Lake Michigan near Chicago. Pop. 15,245.

Lake Hav·a·su City (hăv′ə-so͞o′). City of W central Ariz., on the Calif. border. Pop. 15,737.

Lake Jack·son (jăk′sən). City of SE Tex., SW of Galveston. Pop. 19,102.

Lake·land (lāk′lənd). City of central Fla., ENE of Tampa. Pop. 47,406.

Lake·view (lāk′vyo͞o′). City of S central Mich., near Battle Creek. Pop. 18,000.

Lake·ville (lāk′vĭl′). City of E Minn., S of Minneapolis. Pop. 14,790.

Lake·wood (lāk′wo͝od′). **1.** City of S Calif., near Long Beach. Pop. 74,654. **2.** City of N central Colo., near Denver. Pop. 112,848. **3.** Township of E central N.J., SSE of Freehold. Pop. 25,223. **4.** City of NE Ohio, near Cleveland. Pop. 61,963.

Lake Worth (wûrth). City of SE Fla., on the Atlantic S of West Palm Beach. Pop.27,048.

Lak·shad·weep (lək-shäd′wēp′). Laccadive, Minicoy, and Amindivi Is.

La Lí·ne·a (lä lē′nē-ä). City of SW Spain, on the Mediterranean near Gibraltar. Pop. 57,940.

La Man·cha (lä män′chä). Region of S central Spain.

La Marque (lə märk′). City of SE Tex., near Galveston. Pop. 15,372.

La·me·sa (lə-mē′sə). City of NW Tex., S of Lubbock. Pop. 11,790.

La Me·sa (lə mā′sə). City of S Calif., near San Diego. Pop. 50,342.

La·mi·a (lä-mē′ä). City of E central Greece, NW of Athens. Pop. 37,872.

La Mi·ra·da (lä′ mə-rä′də). City of S Calif., SE of Los Angeles. Pop. 40,986.

La·na·i (lä-nä′ē, lə-nī′). Island of central Hawaii, W of Maui.

Lan·cas·ter (lăng′kăs′tər, -kə-stər, lăn′-). **1.** Sound, c. 50 mi (80 km) wide, between N Baffin Is. and S Devon Is., N.W.T., Canada. **2.** City of NW England, N of Liverpool. Pop. 50,570. **3.** City of S Calif., N of Los Angeles. Pop. 48,027. **4.** Village of W N.Y., near Buffalo. Pop. 13,056. **5.** City of S central Ohio, SE of Columbus. Pop. 34,952. **6.** City of SE Pa., W of Philadelphia. Pop. 54,725. **7.** City of NE Tex., S of Dallas. Pop. 14,807.

Lan·chow (län′jō′). Lanzhou.

Land's End or **Lands End** (lăndz′ ĕnd′). Cape of SW England; westernmost extremity of the country.

Lands·hut (länts′ho͞ot′). City of SE West Germany, on the Isar R. NE of Munich. Pop. 55,538.

Lang·ley (lăng′lē). City of S B.C., Canada, near the Wash. border ESE of Vancouver. Pop. 10,123.

Lans·dale (lănz′dāl′). Borough of SE Pa., N of Philadelphia. Pop. 16,526.

Lans·downe (lănz′doun′). Borough of SE Pa., near Philadelphia. Pop. 11,891.

Lan·sing (lăn′sĭng). **1.** Village of NE Ill., near Chicago and the Ind. border. Pop. 29,039. **2.** Cap. of Mich., in the S central part NW of Detroit. Pop. 130,414.

Lan Tao or **Lan·tao** (län′dou′). Island of Hong Kong, W of Hong Kong Is.

La·nús (lä′no͞os). City of E Argentina, near Buenos Aires. Pop. 449,824.

Lan·zhou (län′jō′). City of central China, on the Yellow R. N of Chengdu. Pop. 950,000.

La·od·i·ce·a (lā-ŏd′ĭ-sē′ə, lā′ə-dĭ-). **1.** Ancient city of W Asia Minor, near present-day Denizli, Turkey. **2.** Latakia.

La·os (lä′ōs, lā′ŏs, lä-ôs′). Country of SE Asia. Cap. Vientiane. Pop. 3,760,-000. —**La·o′tian** (lā-ō′shən) *adj. & n.*

La Pal·ma (lä päl′mä). **1.** Island of Spain, in the NW Canary Is. **2.** City of S Calif., SE of Los Angeles. Pop. 15,663.

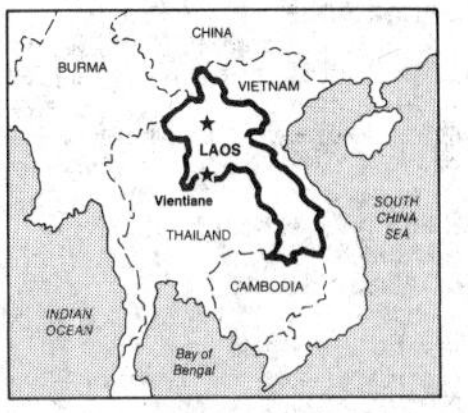

Laos

La Paz (lä päs′, lə päz′). **1.** Administrative cap. of Bolivia, in the W part near Lake Titicaca. Pop. 654,713. **2.** City of NW Mexico, on the Gulf of California. Pop. 46,011.

La Pé·rouse (lä pā-ro͞oz′). Strait of the W Pacific between Sakhalin Is., USSR, and N Hokkaido, Japan.

Lap·land (lăp′lănd′, -lənd). Region of extreme N Europe, including N Norway, N Sweden, N Finland, and Kola Peninsula of NW USSR. —**Lap′land·er** *n.*

La Pla·ta. 1. (lə plä′tə). **Peak.** Mountain, c. 14,336 ft (4,372 m), in the Sawatch range of central Colo. **2.** (lä plä′tä). City of E central Argentina, SE of Buenos Aires. Pop. 435,000.

La Porte (lə pôrt′, pōrt′). **1.** City of NW Ind., WSW of South Bend. Pop. 21,796. **2.** City of SE Tex., on Galveston Bay E of Houston. Pop. 14,062.

Lap·peen·ran·ta (läp′pĕn-rän′tä). City of SE Finland, near the USSR border. Pop. 53,393.

Lap·tev (läp′tĕv, -tĕf, -tyĕf). Sea of the Arctic Ocean, N of E Siberian USSR between the Taimyr Peninsula and New Siberian Is.

La Pu·en·te (lä′ po͞o-ĕn′tē, pwĕn′tē). City of S Calif., near Los Angeles. Pop. 30,882.

L'Aq·ui·la (lä′kwē-lä). City of central Italy, NE of Rome. Pop. 66,644.

Lar·a·mie (lăr′ə-mē). **1.** River, c. 216 mi (348 km), of N Colo. and SE Wyo. **2.** City of SE Wyo., WNW of Cheyenne. Pop. 24,410.

Larch (lärch). River, c. 270 mi (434 km), of N Que., Canada.

La·re·do (lə-rā′dō). City of S Tex., on the Rio Grande SSW of San Antonio. Pop. 91,449.

Lar·go (lär′gō). City of W Fla., NW of St. Petersburg. Pop. 58,977.

La·ri·sa (lä′rē-sä) or **La·ris·sa** (lə-rĭs′-ə). City of E Greece, in Thessaly. Pop. 72,336.

Lark·spur (lärk′spûr′). City of W Calif., near San Francisco. Pop. 11,064.

La Ro·chelle (lä rô-shĕl′). City of W France, on the Bay of Biscay. Pop. 75,367.

La Salle (lə săl′). **1.** City of S Que., Canada, on Montreal Is. and the St. Lawrence. Pop. 76,713. **2.** City of N central Ill., SW of Chicago. Pop. 10,307.

Las·caux (läs-kō′). Cave in SW France containing Paleolithic paintings.

Las Cru·ces (läs kro͞o′sĭs). City of S N.Mex., on the Rio Grande NNE of El Paso, Tex. Pop. 45,086.

La Se·re·na (lä sĕ-rĕ′nä). City of N Chile, near the Pacific N of Valparaiso. Pop. 61,897.

Las Pal·mas (läs päl′mäs). Chief city of the Canary Is. of Spain, on the NE coast of Grand Canary Is. Pop. 357,158.

La Spe·zia (lä spĕ′tsyä). City of NW Italy, on an arm of the Ligurian Sea. Pop. 117,761.

Las·sen Peak (lăs′ən) or **Mount Lassen.** Active volcano, 10,453 ft (3,188.2 m), in the Cascade range in N Calif.

Las Ve·gas (läs vā′gəs). **1.** City of SE Nev., near the Calif. and Ariz. borders. Pop. 164,674. **2.** City of N N.Mex., ESE of Santa Fe. Pop. 14,322.

Lat·a·ki·a (lăt′ə-kē′ə, lä′tä-kē′ä). City of W Syria, on the Mediterranean opposite Cyprus. Pop. 204,000.

La·ti·na (lä-tē′nä). City of W central Italy, SE of Rome. Pop. 83,200.
Lat·in A·mer·i·ca (lăt′n ə-mĕr′ĭ-kə, -ĭn). Countries of the Western Hemisphere S of the U.S. —**Lat′in A·mer′i·can** *n.* —**Lat′in-A·mer′i·can** *adj.*
Latin Quar·ter (kwôr′tər). Section of Paris on the S bank of the Seine.
La·ti·um (lā′shē-əm). Ancient country in W central Italy.
La·trobe (lə-trōb′). Borough of SW Pa., ESE of Pittsburgh. Pop. 10,799.
La Tuque (lə to͝ok′). Town of S Que., Canada, NW of Quebec. Pop. 12,067.
Lat·vi·a (lăt′vē-ə). Region and former country of N Europe on the Baltic. —**Lat′vi·an** *adj.* & *n.*
Lau·der·dale Lakes (lô′dər-dāl′). City of SE Fla., near Fort Lauderdale. Pop. 25,426.
Lau·der·hill (lô′dər-hĭl′). City of SE Fla., near Fort Lauderdale. Pop. 37,271.
Lau·rel (lôr′əl, lŏr′-). **1.** City of central Md., NE of Washington, D.C. Pop. 12,103. **2.** City of SE Miss., NNE of Hattiesburg. Pop. 21,897.
Lau·rens (lôr′ənz, lŏr′-). City of NW S.C., S of Spartanburg. Pop. 10,587.
Lau·ren·tian (lə-rĕn′shən, lôr-ĕn′-). **1.** Or **Lau·ren·tide** (lôr′ən-tīd′, lŏr′-). Mountains of S Que., Canada, N of the St. Lawrence and Ottawa rivers. **2. Plateau** or **Highlands** or **Shield.** Plateau covering E half of Canada.
Lau·rin·burg (lôr′ĭn-bûrg′, lŏr′-). City of S N.C., SW of Fayetteville. Pop. 11,480.
Lau·sanne (lō-zăn′, -zän′). City of W Switzerland, on the N shore of Lake of Geneva. Pop. 128,800.
Lau·zon (lō-zôɴ′). City of S Que., Canada, on the St. Lawrence opposite Quebec city. Pop. 12,663.
La·val. 1. (lə-văl′). City of S Que., Canada, on the Ottawa R. near Montreal. Pop. 246,243. **2.** (lä-väl′). Town of NW France, E of Rennes. Pop. 51,544.
La Verne (lə vûrn′). City of S Calif., E of Los Angeles. Pop. 23,508.
Lawn·dale (lôn′dāl′). City of S Calif., SW of Los Angeles. Pop. 23,460.
Law·rence (lôr′əns, lŏr′-). **1.** City of central Ind., near Indianapolis. Pop. 25,591. **2.** City of NE Kans., on the Kansas R. ESE of Topeka. Pop. 52,738. **3.** City of NE Mass., near the N.H. border NNE of Lowell. Pop. 63,175.
Law·rence·burg (lôr′əns-bûrg′, lŏr′-). City of S Tenn., SSW of Nashville. Pop. 10,175.
Law·ton (lôt′n). City of SW Okla., SW of Oklahoma City. Pop. 80,054.
Lay·san (lī′sän). Island of Hawaii in the Leeward group.
Lay·ton (lāt′n). City of N Utah, S of Ogden. Pop. 22,862.
Leaf (lēf). River, c. 180 mi (290 km), of S central and SE Miss.
League City (lēg). City of SE Tex., SE of Houston. Pop. 16,578.
Lea·ming·ton (lĕ′mĭng-tən). **1.** Also **Leamington Spa** (spä). Borough of central England, near Warwick. Pop. 44,950. **2.** Town of S Ont., Canada, on Lake Erie SW of Windsor. Pop. 11,539.
Leav·en·worth (lĕv′ĭn-wûrth′). City of NE Kans, NW of Kansas City. Pop. 33,656.
Lea·wood (lē′wo͝od′). City of E Kans., near Kansas City. Pop. 13,360.
Leb·a·non (lĕb′ə-nən). **1.** Mountains of Lebanon, extending c. 100 mi (161 km) parallel to the coast and rising to 10,131 ft (3,090 m). **2.** Country of SW Asia, on the Mediterranean N of Israel. Cap. Beirut. Pop. 3,205,000. **3.** City of central Ind., NW of Indianapolis. Pop. 11,456. **4.** City of W N.H., NW of Manchester. Pop. 11,134. **5.** City of W central Ore., E of Corvallis. Pop. 10,413. **6.** City of SE Pa., ENE of Harrisburg. Pop. 25,711. **7.** City of N central Tenn., E of Nashville. Pop. 11,872. —**Leb′a·nese′** (-nēz′, -nēs′) *adj.* & *n.*

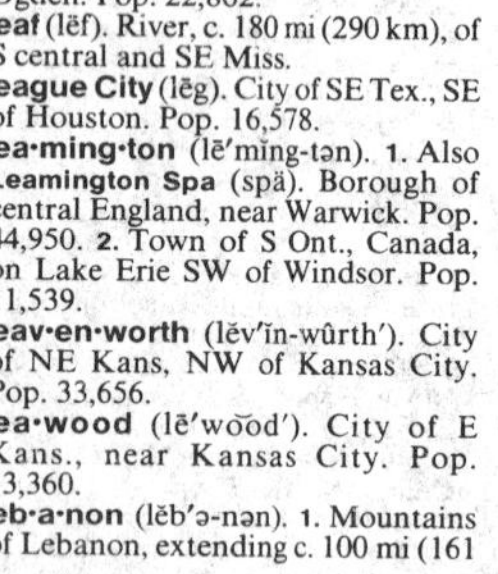

Lebanon

Lec·ce (lĕt′chā). City of extreme SE Italy, E of Taranto. Pop. 90,121.
Lec·co (lĕk′kō). City of N Italy, on Lake Como NNE of Milan. Pop. 52,806.
Lech (lĕkʜ). River, c. 175 mi (280 km), of W Austria and S West Germany.
Le·duc (lĭ-do͞ok′, -dyo͞ok′). Town of central Alta., Canada, S of Edmonton. Pop. 11,603.
Led·yard (lĕd′yərd, lĕj′ərd). Town of SE Conn., NNE of Groton. Pop. 13,735.
Leeds (lēdz). Borough of N central England, NE of Manchester. Pop. 724,300.
Lees·burg (lēz′bûrg′). City of N central Fla., NW of Orlando. Pop. 13,191.
Lee's Sum·mit (lēz sŭm′ĭt). City of W Mo., SE of Kansas City. Pop. 28,741.
Leeu·war·den (lā′wär-dn, -vär-). City of N Netherlands, NE of the Ijsselmeer. Pop. 84,518.
Lee·ward (lē′wərd). **1.** Islands of the West Indies, in the N Lesser Antilles from Virgin Is. SE to Guadeloupe. **2.** Islands of French Polynesia, in the W Society Is. of the S Pacific. **3.** Islands of Hawaii, in the central Pacific WNW of the main islands.
Leg·horn (lĕg′hôrn′). City of NW Italy, on the Ligurian Sea WSW of Florence. Pop. 176,757.
Le·gna·no (lā-nyä′nō). City of NW Italy, near Milan. Pop. 49,600.
Leg·ni·ca (lĕg-nē′tsä). City of SW Poland, W of Wroclaw. Pop. 88,400.
Le Ha·vre (lə hä′vrə, -vər, ä′vrə). City of N France, on the English Channel. Pop. 217,881.
Le·high (lē′hī′). River, c. 103 mi (166 km), of E Pa.
Leices·ter (lĕs′tər). City of central England, ENE of Birmingham. Pop. 276,600.
Lei·den also **Ley·den** (līd′n). City of SW Netherlands, NE of The Hague. Pop. 103,046.
Lein·ster (lĕn′stər, lĭn′-). Historical province of SE Ireland.
Leip·zig (līp′sĭg, -sĭk, -tsĭkʜ). City of S central East Germany, SSW of Berlin. Pop. 563,980.
Leith (lēth). District of Edinburgh, Scotland, on the Firth of Forth.
Lei·zhou (lī′jō′). Peninsula of S China, between the Gulf of Tonkin and the South China Sea.
Lé·man (lē′mən, lə-mäɴ′), **Lake.** Lake of Geneva.
Le Mans (lə mäɴ′). City of NW France, WSW of Paris. Pop. 152,285.
Lem·nos (lĕm′nŏs, -nōs, lĕm′nôs) also **Lim·nos** (lēm′nôs). Island of NE Greece, in the Aegean NW of Lesbos.
Lem·on Grove (lĕm′ən). City of S Calif., near San Diego. Pop. 20,780.
Le·na (lē′nə, lyĕ′-). River of E Siberian USSR, flowing c. 2,670 mi (4,296 m) NE and N to the Laptev Sea.
Le·nex·a (lə-nĕk′sə). City of E Kans., SSW of Kansas City. Pop. 18,639.
Len·in (lĕn′ĭn). Peak, 23,382 ft (7,131.5 m), in the Trans-Alai range of S Central Asian USSR.
Le·nin·a·bad (lĕ′nĭn′ə-băd′, -ä-bät′). City of S Central Asian USSR, on the Syr Darya of Tashkent. Pop. 132,000.
Le·ni·na·kan (lĕ′nĭ-nä-kän′). City of S European USSR, in Armenia near the Turkish border. Pop. 210,000.
Len·in·grad (lĕn′ĭn-grăd′, lĕ-nĭn-grät′). City of NW European USSR, on the Gulf of Finland. Pop. 4,119,000.
Len·insk-Kuz·nets·ki (lĕn′ĭnsk-ko͞oz-nĕts′kĭ). City of S central Siberian USSR, E of Novosibirsk. Pop. 133,000.
Le·noir (lə-nôr′, -nōr′). City of W central N.C., WSW of Winston-Salem. Pop. 13,758.
Lens (läɴs). City of N France, SW of Lille. Pop. 40,199.
Leom·in·ster (lĕm′ĭn-stər). City of N Mass., near Fitchburg. Pop. 34,508.
Le·ón (lĕ-ôn′). **1.** Region and former kingdom of NW Spain. **2.** City of central Mexico, ENE of Guadalajara. Pop. 590,000. **3.** City of W Nicaragua, NW of Lake Managua. Pop. 81,647. **4.** City of NW Spain, at the foot of the Cantabrian Mts. Pop. 122,827.
Le·o·ne (lā-ō′nā), **Monte.** Highest (11,683 ft/3,563.3 m) of the Lepontine Alps, on the Swiss-Italian border.
Le·o·pold II (lē′ə-pōld′). Lake, c. 900 sq mi (2,331 sq km), in W central Zaire.
Le·o·pold·ville (lē′ə-pōld-vĭl′, lā′-, lā-ô-pôld-vēl′). Kinshasa.
Le·pan·to (lĭ-păn′tō, lĕ′pän-tô), **Gulf of.** Gulf of Corinth.
Le·pon·tine Alps (lĭ-pŏn′tīn ălps′). Range of the central Alps in S Switzerland and along the Swiss-Italian border.
Lep·tis Mag·na (lĕp′tĭs măg′nə). Ancient city of Roman Africa, near modern Homs, Libya.
Lé·ri·da (lĕ′rē-*thä*). City of NE Spain, W of Barcelona. Pop. 86,100.
Ler·ma (lĕr′mä). River, c. 350 mi (563 km), of central Mexico.
Ler·wick (lûr′wĭk, lĕr′ĭk). Burgh of N Scotland, on Mainland Is. in the Shetlands. Pop. 6,307.
Les·bos (lĕz′bŏs, -bōs) also **Les·vos** (-vôs). Island of E Greece, in the Aegean near NW coast of Turkey.
Le·so·tho (lə-sō′tō). Kingdom of S Africa, an enclave within E central South Africa. Cap. Maseru. Pop. 1,360,000.
Les·ser An·til·les (lĕs′ər ăn-tĭl′ēz). Island group of the E West Indies, extending in an arc from Curaçao to the Virgin Is.
Lesser Slave Lake (slāv). Lake, 461 sq mi (1,194 sq km), in central Alta., Canada.
Lesser Sun·da (sŭn′də, so͞on′dä) or **Lesser Sun·das** (-dəs, -däz). Island group of S Indonesia from Bali to Timor.
Les·vos (lĕz′vôs). Variant of **Lesbos.**
Letch·worth (lĕch′wûrth′). Urban district of E central England, N of London. Pop. 31,520.
Leth·bridge (lĕth′brĭj). City of S Alta., Canada, SSW of Calgary. Pop. 53,135.
Leu·cas (lo͞o′kəs) or **Lev·kas** (lĕf-käs′). Island of W Greece, in the Ionian Is. N of Cephalonia.
Leuc·tra (lo͞ok′trə). Village of ancient Greece, SW of Thebes; site of Spartan defeat by the Thebans (371 B.C.).
Leu·ven (lœ′vən). *Flemish.* Louvain.
Le·val·lois-Per·ret (lə-väl-wä′pĕ-rĕ′). City of N central France, on the Seine near Paris. Pop. 52,523.
Le·vant (lĭ-vănt′). Countries bordering on the E Mediterranean. —**Le′van·tine′** (-tīn′, -tēn′, -tĭn′) *adj.* & *n.*
Lev·el·land (lĕv′ə-lănd′). City of NW Tex., W of Lubbock. Pop. 13,809.
Le·ven (lē′vən), **Loch. 1.** Arm of Loch Linnhe in W Scotland. **2.** Lake of E Scotland, NNW of Edinburgh.
Le·ver·ku·sen (lā′vər-ko͞o′zən). City of W West Germany, on the Rhine N of Cologne. Pop. 161,453.
Lé·vis (lē′vĭs, lā-vēs′). City of S Que., Canada, on the St. Lawrence opposite Quebec city. Pop. 17,819.
Lev·it·town (lĕv′ĭt-toun′). Urban area of SE N.Y., on W Long Is. Pop. 65,400.
Lev·kas (lĕf-käs′). Variant of **Leucas.**
Lew·es (lo͞o′ĭs). **1.** The upper Yukon R., in S Y.T., Canada, above its junction with the Pelly R. **2.** Borough of SE England, S of London. Pop. 14,170.
Lew·is (lo͞o′ĭs). Range of the Rocky Mts. in NW Mont., rising to 10,448 ft (3,186.6 m).
Lew·is·ton (lo͞o′ĭ-stən). **1.** City of NW Idaho, SSE of Spokane, Wash. Pop. 27,986. **2.** City of SW Me., opposite Auburn. Pop. 40,481.
Lew·is·ville (lo͞o′ĭs-vĭl′, lo͞o′ē-). City of NE Tex., NNW of Dallas. Pop. 24,273.
Lewis with Har·ris (hăr′ĭs). Island of NW Scotland, largest (825 sq mi/2,136.8 sq km) and northernmost of the Outer Hebrides.
Lex·ing·ton (lĕk′sĭng-tən). **1.** City of N central Ky., ESE of Louisville. Pop. 204,165. **2.** Town of E Mass., near Boston; site of 1st Revolutionary War battle (1775). Pop. 29,479. **3.** City of central N.C., S of Winston-Salem. Pop. 15,711.
Ley·den (līd′n). Variant of **Leiden.**
Ley·te (lā′tē, lē′tē). **1.** Gulf of the W Pacific in the Philippines S of Samar and E of Leyte. **2.** Island of the E central Philippines, in the Visayan group N of Mindanao.
Lha·sa (lä′sə, -sä, lăs′ə). City of SW China, traditional cap. of Tibet. Pop. 80,000.
Lho·tse (lō′tsē′). Two peaks of the central Himalayas, 27,923 ft (8,516.5 m) and 27,560 ft (8,405.8 m), on the Nepal-Tibet border.
Lian·yun·gang (lyĕn′yün′gäng′). City of E China, near the Yellow Sea SSW of Qingdao. Pop. 250,000.
Liao (lyou). River of NE China, flowing c. 900 mi (1,448 km) NE and SW to the Gulf of Liaodong.
Liao·dong or **Liao·tung** (lyou′do͝ong′). **1.** N part of the Gulf of Bo Hai in NE China. **2.** Peninsula of NE China projecting SW into the Yellow Sea.
Liao·yang (lyou′yäng′). City of NE China, SSW of Shenyang. Pop. 250,000.
Liao·yu·an or **Liao·yü·an** (lyou′yü′än′). City of NE China S of Changchun. Pop. 250,000.
Li·ard (lē′ərd, lē′ärd, lē-ärd′). River, c. 755 mi (1,215 km), of SE Y.T., N B.C., and SW N.W.T., Canada.
Lib·er·al (lĭb′ər-əl). City of SW Kans., near the Okla. border SW of Dodge City. Pop. 14,911.
Li·be·rec (lĭ′bē-rĕts). City of NW Czechoslovakia, NNE of Prague. Pop. 85,119.
Li·be·ri·a (lī-bîr′ē-ə). Country of W Africa, on the Gulf of Guinea. Cap. Monrovia. Pop. 1,890,000. —**Li·be′ri·an** *adj.* & *n.*

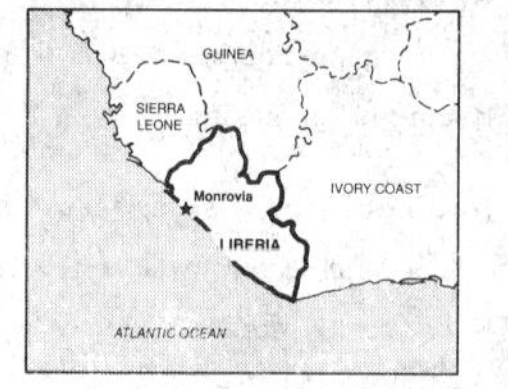

Liberia

Lib·er·ty (lĭb′ər-tē). **1.** Island of SE N.Y., in New York Bay; site of the Statue of Liberty. **2.** City of W Mo., NE of Kansas City. Pop. 16,251.
Lib·er·ty·ville (lĭb′ər-tē-vĭl′). Village of NE Ill., SW of Waukegan. Pop. 16,520.
Li·bre·ville (lē′brə-vēl′). Cap. of Gabon, in the NW on the Gulf of Guinea. Pop. 251,000.
Lib·y·a (lĭb′ē-ə). Country of N Africa, on the Mediterranean W of Egypt. Cap. Tripoli. Pop. 3,030,000. —**Lib′y·an** *adj.* & *n.*

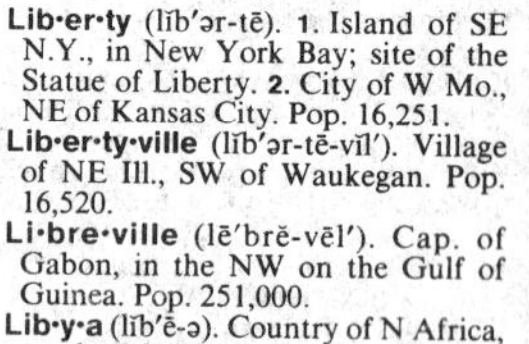

Libya

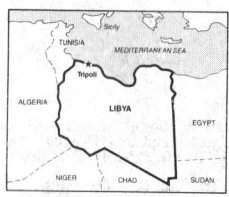

Libyan. Desert of NE Africa, the NE part of the Sahara.
Li·can·cá·bur (lē′kän-kä′bo͝or). Vol-

cano, 19,455 ft (5,993.8 m) of N Chile, near the Bolivian border.

Li·ca·ta (lē-kä'tä). Town of S Sicily, Italy, on the Mediterranean. Pop. 42,250.

Lich·field (lĭch'fēld'). Borough of W central England, NNE of Birmingham. Pop. 23,690.

Lick·ing (lĭk'ĭng). River of NE Ky., flowing c. 320 mi (515 km) NW to the Ohio R. opposite Cincinnati.

Li·di·ce (lĭd'ĭ-sē, lē'dĭ-tsĕ). Village of NW Czechoslovakia; destroyed by German forces (1942).

Li·do (lē'dō). Island in NE Italy separating the lagoon of Venice from the Adriatic.

Liech·ten·stein (lĭk'tən-stīn', lĭKH'-tən-shtīn'). Principality (62 sq mi/161 sq km) in central Europe between Austria and Switzerland. Cap. Vaduz. Pop. 26,000.

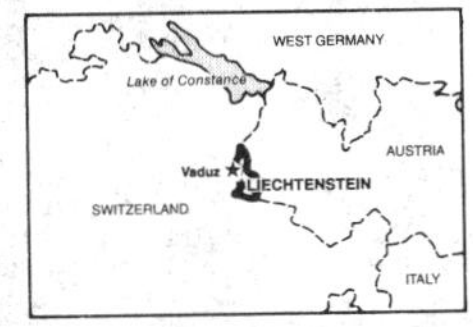

Liechtenstein

Li·ège (lē-āzh', lyĕzh). City of E Belgium, near the Dutch and West German borders. Pop. 220,183.

Lien·yün·kang (lyĕn'yün'gäng'). Lianyungang.

Lie·pa·ya or **Lie·pa·ja** (lyĕ'pä-yä). City of W European USSR, in Latvia on the Baltic. Pop. 108,000.

Liè·vre (lē-ĕv'rə, lyĕv'ər). River, c. 200 mi (322 km), of S Que., Canada.

Lif·fey (lĭf'ē). River of E Ireland, flowing c. 50 mi (80 km) through Dublin to Dublin Bay.

Light·house Point (līt'hous). City of SE Fla., on the Atlantic NE of Pompano Beach. Pop. 11,488.

Li·gu·ri·a (lĭ-gyŏŏr'ē-ə). Region of NW Italy on the **Ligurian Sea**, an arm of the Mediterranean between NW Italy and Corsica. —**Li·gu'ri·an** *adj. & n.*

Li·ka·si (lĭ-kä'sē). City of SE Zaire, NW of Lubumbashi. Pop. 146,394.

Lille also **Lisle** (lēl). City of N France, near the Belgian border. Pop. 172,280.

Li·long·we (lĭ-lông'wā). Cap. of Malawi, in the S central part. Pop. 102,924.

Li·ma. 1. (lē'mə, lē'mä). Cap. of Peru, in the W central part near the Pacific. Metro. area pop. 3,158,417. **2.** (lī'mə). City of NW Ohio, SSW of Toledo. Pop. 47,381.

Li·mas·sol (lĭm'ə-sôl'). City of S Cyprus, on the Mediterranean. Pop. 55,000.

Li·may (lē-mī'). River, c. 250 mi (402 km), of W central Argentina.

Lim·er·ick (lĭm'ər-ĭk, lĭm'rĭk). Borough of SW Ireland, on the Shannon estuary. Pop. 60,665.

Lim·nos (lēm'nôs). Variant of **Lemnos.**

Li·moges (lĭ-mōzh', lē-môzh'). City of W central France, NE of Bordeaux. Pop. 143,689.

Li·món (lē-môn'). City of E Costa Rica, on the Caribbean. Pop. 31,900.

Lim·po·po (lĭm-pō'pō). River of SE Africa, rising near Johannesburg in NE South Africa and flowing c. 1,100 m (1,770 km) in a NE-SE arc to the Indian Ocean in S Mozambique.

Li·na·res (lē-nä'rĕs). City of S Spain, ENE of Córdoba. Pop. 50,520.

Lin·coln (lĭng'kən). **1. Mount.** Peak, 14,284 ft (4,356.6 m), in the Rockies of central Colo. **2.** Borough of E England, NE of Nottingham. Pop. 71,900. **3.** Town of SE Ont., Canada, on Lake Ontario W of Niagara Falls. Pop. 14,296. **4.** City of central Ill., NNE of Springfield. Pop. 16,327. **5.** Cap. of Nebr., in the SE part SW of Omaha. Pop. 171,932. **6.** Town of NE R.I., near Providence. Pop. 16,949.

Lincoln Park. City of SE Mich., near Detroit. Pop. 45,105.

Lin·coln·wood (lĭng'kən-wŏŏd'). Village of NE Ill., near Chicago. Pop. 11,921.

Lin·den (lĭn'dən). City of NE N.J., near Elizabeth. Pop. 37,836.

Lin·den·hurst (lĭn'dən-hûrst'). Village of S N.Y., on S Long Is. near Babylon. Pop. 26,919.

Lin·den·wold (lĭn'dən-wōld'). Borough of SW N.J., SE of Camden. Pop. 18,196.

Lin·des·nes (lĭn'dĭs-nĕs'). Cape of extreme S Norway.

Lind·say (lĭn'zē). Town of S Ont., Canada, NE of Toronto. Pop. 13,755.

Line (līn). Islands of the central Pacific, in Kiribati S of Hawaii and astride the equator.

Lin·ga·yen Gulf (lĭng'gä-yĕn'). Inlet of the South China Sea in W central Luzon, Philippines.

Ling·ga (lĭng'gä). Archipelago of Indonesia off the E central coast of Sumatra.

Lin·guet·ta (lĕng-gwāt'tä). Cape of SW Albania.

Lin·kö·ping (lĭn'chœ'pĭng'). City of S Sweden, SW of Stockholm. Pop. 111,866.

Linn·he (lĭn'ē), **Loch.** Inlet of the Firth of Lorne on W coast of Scotland.

Linz (lĭnts). City of N Austria, on the Danube. Pop. 208,000.

Li·ons (lī'ənz) also **Li·on** (-ən), **Gulf of.** Wide inlet of the Mediterranean on the S coast of France.

Lip·a·ri (lĭp'ə-rē, lē'pä-rē). **1.** Island group of Italy, off the NE coast of Sicily in the Tyrrhenian Sea. **2.** Chief island of this group.

Li·petsk (lē'pĭtsk). City of central European USSR, SSE of Moscow. Pop. 405,000.

Lis·bo·a (lēz-bō'ə). *Portuguese.* Lisbon.

Lis·bon (lĭz'bən). Cap. of Portugal, in the W part on the Tagus R. Pop. 829,900.

Lis·burne (lĭz'bûrn'). Cape on NW coast of Alaska, on the Arctic Ocean SW of Point Barrow.

Li·sieux (lē-zyœ'). Town of N France, S of Le Havre. Pop. 25,521.

Lisle. 1. (lēl). Variant of **Lille. 2.** (līl). Village of NE Ill., W of Chicago. Pop. 13,625.

Lith·u·a·ni·a (lĭth'ōō-ā'nē-ə). Region and former country of N Europe, on the Baltic. —**Lith'u·a'ni·an** *adj. & n.*

Lit·tle A·mer·i·ca (lĭt'l ə-mĕr'ĭ-kə). U.S. base for explorations in W Antarctica, on the Ross Ice Shelf.

Little Big·horn (bĭg'hôrn'). River, c. 90 mi (145 km), of W Wyo. and S Mont.

Little Col·o·ra·do (kŏl'ə-rä'dō, -răd'-ō). River of NE Ariz., flowing c. 315 mi (507 km) NW to the Colorado R.

Little Fork (fôrk). River, c. 132 mi (212 km), of N Minn.

Little Ka·na·wha (kə-nô'wə). River, c. 160 mi (257 km), of N W.Va.

Little Mis·sou·ri (mĭ-zŏŏr'ē, -zŏŏr'ə). **1.** River, c. 145 mi (233 km), of SW Ark. **2.** River of NE Wyo., SE Mont., NW S.Dak., and W N.Dak., flowing c. 560 mi (901 km) NE to the Missouri.

Little Pee Dee (pē' dē'). River, c. 105 mi (169 km), of S central N.C.

Little Rock (rŏk). Cap. of Ark., in the central part. Pop. 153,831.

Little Sioux (sōō). River, c. 221 mi (356 km), of SW Minn. and NW Iowa.

Little Saint Ber·nard (sānt' bər-närd'). Mountain pass through the Savoy Alps between Italy and France, S of Mont Blanc, rising to 7,180 ft (2,190 m).

Little Ten·nes·see (tĕn'ĭ-sē'). River, c. 135 mi (217 km), of NE Ga., SW N.C., and E Tenn.

Lit·tle·ton (lĭt'l-tən). City of N central Colo., near Denver. Pop. 28,349.

Little Wa·bash (wô'băsh'). River, c. 200 mi (322 km), of E Ill.

Liv·er·more (lĭv'ər-môr', -mōr'). City of W Calif., E of San Leandro. Pop. 48,349.

Liv·er·pool (lĭv'ər-pōōl'). Borough of NE England, on the Mersey R. near the Irish Sea. Pop. 520,200.

Liv·ing·stone (lĭv'ĭng-stən). City of S Zambia, on the Zambezi R. and the Zimbabwe border. Pop. 80,000.

Li·vo·ni·a (lĭ-vō'nē-ə, -vōn'yə). **1.** Region of W European USSR comprising S Latvia and N Estonia. **2.** City of SE Mich., near Detroit. Pop. 104,814. —**Li·vo'ni·an** *adj. & n.*

Li·vor·no (lē-vōr'nō). *Italian.* Leghorn.

Liz·ard Point or **Head** (lĭz'ərd). Cape of SW England at S tip of **The Lizard,** peninsula extending S into the English Channel; southernmost point of Great Britain.

Lju·blja·na (lyōō'blyä-nä). City of NW Yugoslavia, on the Sava R. Pop. 173,662.

Llan·dud·no (lăn-dŭd'nō, -dĭd'-). Urban district of NW Wales, on the Irish Sea. Pop. 17,700.

Lla·nel·li or **Lla·nel·ly** (lă-nĕl'ē, hlä-nĕ'hlē). Borough of S Wales, on an inlet of Bristol Channel. Pop. 25,870.

LLoyd·min·ster (loid'mĭn'stər). City on the Alta.-Sask. border, Canada, E of Edmonton. Pop. 10,311.

Llu·llai·lla·co (yōō'yī-yä'kō). Volcano, 22,057 ft (6,727.4 m), in the Andes on the N Chile-Argentina border.

Lo·an·da (lô-än'də). Variant of **Luanda.**

Lo·an·ge (lō-äng'gə). River, c. 425 mi (684 m), of NE Angola and SW Zaire.

Lo·bi·to (lōō-bē'tōō, lō-bē'tō). City of W central Angola, on the Atlantic. Pop. 59,528.

Lo·car·no (lô-kär'nô). Town of S Switzerland, at the N end of Lake Maggiore. Metro. area pop. 41,600.

Loch (lŏk, lôKH). See **Lake.**

Lock·port (lŏk'pôrt', -pōrt'). City of W N.Y., NNE of Buffalo. Pop. 24,844.

Lo·cust Grove (lō'kəst grōv'). Town of SE N.Y., on W Long Is. Pop. 11,648.

Lodge·pole Creek (lŏj'pōl'). River, 212 mi (341.1 km), of SE Wyo., SW Nebr., and NE Colo.

Lo·di (lō'dī'). **1.** (lô'dē). City of N Italy, SE of Milan. Pop. 43,927. **2.** City of central Calif., N of Stockton. Pop. 35,221. **3.** Borough of NE N.J., NE of Passaic. Pop. 23,956.

Łódź (lōōj). City of central Poland, WSW of Warsaw. Pop. 830,800.

Lo·fo·ten (lō'fōōt'n, lōō'fōō-tĕn). Islands off NW coast of Norway, in the Norwegian Sea.

Lo·gan (lō'gən). **1.** Peak, 19,850 ft (6,054.3 m), of the St. Elias range in SW Y.T., Canada, near the Alas. border. **2.** City of N Utah, N of Ogden. Pop. 26,844.

Lo·gans·port (lō'gənz-pôrt', -pōrt'). City of N central Ind., NNW of Kokomo. Pop. 17,899.

Lo·gro·ño (lô-grô'nyä). City of N Spain, on the Ebro R. Pop. 104,928.

Loir (lwär). River, c. 193 mi (311 km), of NW France.

Loire (lwär). Longest river of France, rising in the Cévennes Mts. and flowing c. 630 mi (1,014 km) N and W to the Bay of Biscay.

Lo·ja (lô'hä). City of S Ecuador, SSE of Guayaquil. Pop. 47,268.

Lol·land (lŏl'ənd, lô'län). Variant of **Laaland.**

Lo·ma Lin·da (lō'mə lĭn'də). City of SE Calif., near San Bernardino. Pop. 10,694.

Lo·ma·mi (lō-mä'mē). River of Zaire, flowing c. 900 mi (1,448 km) N to the Congo R.

Lo·mas de Za·mo·ra (lô'mäs dĕ sä-mô'rä). City of E Argentina, S of Buenos Aires. Pop. 410,806.

Lom·bard (lŏm'bärd', lŭm'-). Village of NE Ill., near Chicago. Pop. 37,295.

Lom·bar·dy (lŏm'bər-dē, lŭm'-, lōm-bär'dyä). Region of N Italy. —**Lom'bard** *adj. & n.*

Lom·blen (lŏm-blĕn'). Island of S central Indonesia, in the Lesser Sundas E of Flores Is.

Lom·bok (lŏm-bŏk'). Island of S central Indonesia, in the Lesser Sundas E of Bali.

Lo·mé (lô-mā'). Cap. of Togo, in the S part on the Gulf of Guinea. Pop. 229,400.

Lo·mi·ta (lō-mē'tə). City of S Calif., near Los Angeles. Pop. 17,191.

Lo·mond (lō'mənd), **Loch.** Largest lake in Scotland, 23 mi (37 km) long 1-5 mi (1.6-8 km) wide, in the E central part.

Lom·poc (lŏm'pōk', -pŏk'). City of S Calif., WNW of Santa Barbara. Pop. 26,267.

Lon·don (lŭn'dən). **1.** City of SE Ont., Canada, SW of Toronto. Pop. 256,789. **2.** Cap. of United Kingdom, on the Thames R. in SE England; a metropolitan county consisting of the City of London and 32 surrounding boroughs. Pop. 6,877,100.

Lon·don·der·ry (lŭn'dən-dĕr'ē). **1.** Borough of NW Northern Ireland, WNW of Belfast. Pop. 51,200. **2.** Town of SE N.H., near Manchester. Pop. 13,598.

Long Beach (lông, lŏng). **1.** City of S Calif., SE of Los Angeles. Pop. 361,334. **2.** City of SE N.Y., of S Long Is. Pop. 34,073.

Long Branch (brănch). City of E N.J., on the Atlantic N of Asbury Park. Pop. 29,819.

Long Ea·ton (ēt'n). Urban district of central England, near Nottingham. Pop. 33,560.

Long Island. 1. Sound. Arm of the N Atlantic between Long Is. and Conn. **2.** Island, c. 120 mi (193 km) long, of SE N.Y.

Long·mea·dow (lông'mĕd'ō, lŏng'-). Town of SW Mass., near Springfield. Pop. 16,301.

Long·mont (lông'mŏnt', lŏng'-). City of N Colo., NNE of Boulder. Pop. 42,942.

Longs Peak (lôngz, lŏngz). Peak, 14,255 ft (4,347.8 m), in the Rockies of N. Colo.

Lon·gueil (lông-gāl', lôN-gē-yĕ'). City of S Que., Canada, on the St. Lawrence opposite Montreal. Pop. 122,429.

Long·view (lông'vyōō', lŏng'-). **1.** City of E Tex., W of Shreveport, La. Pop. 62,762. **2.** City of SW Wash., on the Columbia near Kelso. Pop. 31,052.

Long·wood (lông'wŏŏd', lŏng'-). City of E central Fla., N of Orlando. Pop. 10,029.

Look·out (lŏŏk'out'). **1.** Cape of E N.C., SW of Cape Hatteras. **2. Mountain.** Ridge in SE Tenn., site of a Union Civil War victory (1863).

Loop (lōōp), **the.** Central business district of Chicago, Ill.

Lop Nur (lŏp' nōōr') or **Lop Nor** (lôp' nôr'). Marshy depression of NW China.

Lo·rain (lə-rān', lô-). City of N Ohio, on Lake Erie W of Cleveland. Pop. 75,416.

Lor·ca (lôr'kə, -kä). City of SE Spain, W of Cartagena. Pop. 27,400.

Lord Howe (lôrd hou'). Volcanic island of Australia, in the Tasman Sea ENE of Sydney.

Lo·rette·ville (lô-rĕt'vĭl'). City of S Que., Canada, near Quebec city. Pop. 14,767.

Lo·rient (lô-ryäN'). City of NW France, on the Bay of Biscay. Pop. 69,769.

Lorne also **Lorn** (lôrn), **Firth of.** Inlet of the Atlantic on W coast of Scotlant, between Mull Is. and the mainland.

Lor·raine (lō-rān', lô-, lô-rĕn'). Region and former province of NE France.

Los Al·a·mi·tos (lôs ăl'ə-mē'təs, lŏs). City of S Calif., near Long Beach. Pop. 11,529.

Los Al·a·mos (ăl'ə-mōs'). City of N central N.Mex., NW of Santa Fe. Pop. 17,100.

Los Al·tos (ăl'tōs, -təs). City of W Calif., S of Palo Alto. Pop. 25,769.

Los An·ge·les (ăn'jə-ləs, -lēz'). **1.** (*also* äng'hĕ-lĕs'). City of S central Chile, SE of Concepción. Pop. 49,175. **2.** City of S Calif., on the Pacific. Pop. 2,966,763.

Los Ba·nos (bä'nōs, -nəs). City of central Calif., NW of Fresno. Pop. 10,341.

Los Ga·tos (gä'təs). City of W Calif., near San Jose. Pop. 26,593.

Lot (lôt). River, c. 300 mi (483 km), of S France.

Lo·ta (lô'tä). City of S central Chile, on the Pacific SSW of Concepción. Pop. 48,166.

Lough·bor·ough (lŭf'bûr'ə, -bə-rə). Borough of central England, SSW of Nottingham. Pop. 49,010.

Lou·ise (lo͞o-ēz'). Lake of SW Alta., Canada, in the Rocky Mts.

Lou·i·si·ade (lo͞o-ē-zē-äd'). Archipelago of the W Pacific SE of New Guinea; part of Papua New Guinea.

Lou·i·si·an·a (lo͞o-ē'zē-ăn'ə, lo͞o'zē-). **1. Purchase.** Territory of the W U.S. extending from the Mississippi to the Rockies between the Mexican and Canadian borders, purchased (1803) from France. **2.** State of S central U.S. Cap. Baton Rouge. Pop. 4,203,-972.

Lou·is·ville (lo͞o'ē-vĭl', -ə-vəl). City of NW Ky., on the Ohio SW of Cincinnati, Ohio. Pop. 298,451.

Lourdes (lo͝ord, lo͝ordz, lo͝ord). Town of SW France, at the foot of the Pyrenees; site of a Catholic shrine. Pop. 17,870.

Lou·ren·ço Mar·ques (lō-rĕn'sō mär'kĕs, lô-, lô-rĕɴ'so͞o mär'kĕsh). Maputo.

Lou·vain (lo͞o-văɴ'). City of central Belgium, E of Brussels. Pop. 85,632.

Love·land (lŭv'lənd). City of N Colo., S of Fort Collins. Pop. 30,244.

Loves Park (lŭvz). City of N Ill., near Rockford. Pop. 13,192.

Low (lō). Tuamotu.

Low Coun·tries (kŭn'trēz). Belgium, the Netherlands, and Luxembourg.

Low·ell (lō'əl). City of NE Mass., NW of Boston. Pop. 92,418.

Low·er Bur·rell (lō'ər bûr'əl). City of SW Pa., NE of Pittsburgh. Pop. 13,200.

Lower Cal·i·for·nia (kăl'ə-fôr'nyə, -fôr'nē-ə). Peninsula of NW Mexico, extending c. 760 mi (1,223 km) S from the U.S. border.

Lower Klam·ath (klăm'əth). Lake of N Calif., connected with Upper Klamath Lake in S Ore.

Lower Peninsula. Part of Mich. between Lakes Michigan and Huron.

Lowes·toft (lō'stəf, -stôft', -stŏft'). Borough of extreme E England, on the North Sea. Pop. 53,260.

Loy·al·ty (loi'əl-tē). Islands of the SW Pacific, NW of New Caledonia.

Lo·yang (lō'yăng'). Luoyang.

Lu·a·la·ba (lo͞o'ə-lä'bə). River, c. 400 mi (644 km), of E Zaire, a headwater of the Congo.

Lu·an·da (lo͞o-ăn'də) also **Lo·an·da** (lô-ăn'də). Cap. of Angola, in the W part on the Atlantic. Pop. 475,328.

Luang Pra·bang (lwäng' prä-bäng'). City of NW Laos, on the Mekong R. Pop. 43,000.

Lu·ang·wa (lo͞o-äng'wä). River, c. 500 mi (805 km), of E Zambia.

Lu·an·shya (lo͞o-än'shyä). City of N central Zambia, N of Lusaka. Pop. 164,000.

Lub·bock (lŭb'ək). City of NW Tex., S of Amarillo. Pop. 173,979.

Lü·beck (lü'bĕk, lo͞o'-). City of NE West Germany, near the Baltic and the East German border. Pop. 222,120.

Lu·bi·lash (lo͞o-bē'läsh). Upper course of the Sankuru R., flowing 285 mi (459 km) through S Zaire.

Lu·blin (lyo͞o'blĭn, lo͞o'blēn). City of SE Poland, SE of Warsaw. Pop. 63,000.

Lu·bum·ba·shi (lo͞o-bo͞om'bä-shē). City of SE Zaire, near the Zambia border. Pop. 404,000.

Lu·ca·ni·a (lo͞o-kā'nē-ə, -kăn'yə). Peak, 17,147 ft (5,229.8 m), of the St. Elias range in SW Y.T., Canada, near the Alas. border.

Luc·ca (lo͞ok'kä). City of NW Italy, W of Florence. Pop. 91,256.

Lu·cerne (lo͞o-sûrn', lü-sĕrn'). City of central Switzerland, on NW shore of the **Lake of Lucerne** (44 sq mi/114 sq km). Pop. 62,400.

Lu·chow (lo͞o'jō). Hefei.

Luck·now (lŭk'nou). City of N central India, ESE of Delhi. Pop. 749,239.

Lü·da (lü'dä). City of NE China, on Korea Bay at S end of Liaodong Peninsula. Pop. 1,100,000.

Lü·den·scheid (lü'dən-shīt'). City of W West Germany, NW of Cologne. Pop. 74,561.

Lu·dhi·a·na (lo͞o'dē-ä'nä). City of N India, NNW of Delhi. Pop. 397,850.

Lud·low (lŭd'lō). Town of SW Mass., near Springfield. Pop. 18,150.

Lud·wigs·burg (lo͞ot'vĭĸʜs-bûrk'). City of SW West Germany, N of Stuttgart. Pop. 81,049.

Lud·wigs·ha·fen (lo͞ot'vĭĸʜs-hä'fən, lo͞od'-). City of SW West Germany, on the Rhine opposite Mannheim. Pop. 160,479.

Luf·kin (lŭf'kĭn). City of E Tex., NNE of Houston. Pop. 28,562.

Lu·ga·no (lo͞o-gä'nō). Town of S Switzerland, near the Italian border, on the Italian-Swiss **Lake of Lugano** (19 sq mi/49 sq km). Pop. 28,000.

Lu·gansk (lo͞o-gänsk'). Voroshilovgrad.

Lu·go (lo͞o'gô). City of NW Spain, WSW of Oviedo. Pop. 181,556.

Lui·chow (lwā'jō'). Leizhou.

Luik (loik, lo͝ok). *Flemish.* Liège.

Lu·le·å (lo͞o'lĕ-ô'). City of NE Sweden, on the Gulf of Bothnia. Pop. 67,190.

Lu·le·älv (lü'lĕ-ĕlv'). River, c. 275 mi (442 km), of N Sweden.

Lum·ber (lŭm'bər). River, c. 125 mi (201 km), of S central N.C. and NE S.C.

Lum·ber·ton (lŭm'bər-tən). City of S N.C., S of Fayetteville. Pop. 18,340.

Lund (lŭnd). City of S Sweden, NNE of Malmö. Pop. 78,003.

Lun·dy Isle (lŭn'dē). Island off SW coast of England, at the mouth of Bristol Channel.

Lü·ne·burg (lü'nə-bûrk'). City of NE West Germany, SSE of Hamburg. Pop. 62,198.

Lü·nen (lü'nən). City of NW West Germany, ENE of Essen. Pop. 85,685.

Luo·yang (lwō'yăng'). City of E central China, ENE of Xi'an. Pop. 750,000.

Lu·sa·ka (lo͞o-sä'kə). Cap. of Zambia, in the S central part. Pop. 641,000.

Lu·sa·ti·a (lo͞o-sā'shē-ə, -shə). Region of central Europe in SE East Germany and SW Poland. —**Lu·sa'tian** *adj. & n.*

Lü·shun (lü'shŭn'). City of NE China, now part of Lüda.

Lu·si·ta·ni·a (lo͞o'sĭ-tā'nē-ə). Portugal. —**Lu'si·ta'ni·an** *adj. & n.*

Lü·ta (lü'dä'). Lüda.

Lu·ton (lo͞ot'n). Borough of SE England, NNW of London. Pop. 160,300.

Lutsk (lo͞otsk). City of W European USSR, in the W Ukraine NE of Lvov. Pop. 146,000.

Lux·em·bourg (lŭk'səm-bûrg', lük-säɴ-bo͞or') or **Lux·em·burg** (lo͝ok'səm-bo͝ork'). **1.** Country and grand duchy of W Europe, bordering on France, Belgium, and West Germany. Cap. Luxembourg. Pop. 370,000. **2.** Also **Luxembourg City.** Cap. of Luxembourg, in the S part. Pop. 79,300.

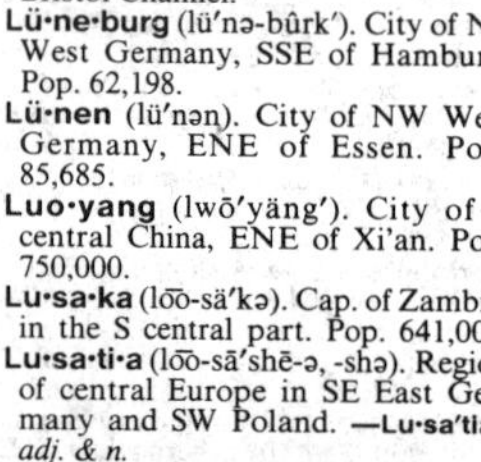

Luxembourg

Lux·or (lŭk'sôr). City of central Egypt, on the Nile on part of the site of ancient Thebes.

Lu·zon (lo͞o-zŏn', -sôn'). Island of the NW Philippines, largest of the archipelago.

Lvov also **L'vov** (lvôf). City of W European USSR, in the W Ukraine near the Polish border. Pop. 676,000.

Lya·khov (lyä'ĸʜəf). Islands of N Siberian USSR, in the S New Siberian group between the Laptev and East Siberian seas.

Lyc·i·a (lĭsh'ē-ə). Ancient country and Roman province of SW Asia Minor on the Aegean. —**Lyc'i·an** *adj. & n.*

Lyd·i·a (lĭd'ē-ə). Ancient country of W central Asia Minor on the Aegean. —**Lyd'i·an** *adj. & n.*

Ly·ell (lī'əl). Peak, 13,095 ft (3,934 m), of the Sierra Nevada in E central Calif.

Lym·ing·ton (lĭm'ĭng-tən). Borough of S England, on the Solent opposite the Isle of Wight. Pop. 36,760.

Lyn·brook (lĭn'bro͝ok'). Village of SE N.Y., on SW Long Is. near Queens. Pop. 20,431.

Lynch·burg (lĭnch'bûrg'). Independent city of SW central Va., ENE of Roanoke. Pop. 66,743.

Lynd·hurst (lĭnd'hûrst'). City of NE Ohio, near Cleveland. Pop. 18,092.

Lynn (lĭn). **1. Canal.** Natural inlet of the Pacific in SE Alas. extending c. 80 mi (129 km) NNW from Juneau. **2.** City of E Mass., near Boston. Pop. 78,471.

Lynn·field (lĭn'fēld'). Town of E Mass., near Lynn. Pop. 11,267.

Lynn·wood (lĭn'wo͝od'). **1.** City of S Calif., near Los Angeles. Pop. 48,548. **2.** City of W central Wash., near Seattle. Pop. 21,937.

Ly·on or **Ly·ons** (lyôɴ). City of E central France, at the confluence of the Rhone and Saône rivers. Pop. 456,716.

Lyth·am Saint Anne's (lĭ*th*'əm sānt ănz'). Borough of NW England, on the Irish Sea N of Liverpool. Pop. 42,120.

M

Maas (mäs). *Dutch.* Meuse.

Maas·tricht (mäs'trĭĸʜt'). City of SE Netherlands, near Belgium. Pop. 110,191.

Ma·cao also **Ma·cau** (mə-kou'). **1.** Peninsula in the South China Sea, W of Hong Kong. **2.** Portuguese overseas province, comprising Macao Peninsula and 2 offshore islands. Cap. Macao (pop. 241,413). Pop. 280,000.

Ma·ca·pá (mə-kə-pä'). City of N Brazil, on the Amazon. Pop. 51,563.

Ma·cas·sar (mə-kăs'ər). Variant of **Makassar.**

Mac·e·do·ni·a (măs'ĭ-dō'nē-ə). **1.** Also **Mac·e·don** (măs'ĭ-dŏn'). Ancient kingdom N of Greece. **2.** Region of SE Europe, including parts of Greece, Bulgaria, and Yugoslavia. **3.** Region of N Greece. —**Mac'e·do'ni·an** *adj. & n.*

Ma·cei·ó (mä'sā-ô'). City of NE Brazil, on the Atlantic. Pop. 242,867.

Mac·gil·li·cud·dy's Reeks (mə-gĭl'ĭ-kŭd'ēz rēks'). Mountain range in SW Ireland, rising to c. 3,000 ft (915 m).

Ma·chi·da (mä-chē'dä). City of E central Honshu, Japan, near Tokyo. Pop. 263,758.

Ma·chu Pic·chu (mä'cho͞o pēk'cho͞o). Ancient Incan fortress city in the Peruvian Alps, NW of Cuzco.

Mac·ken·zie (mə-kĕn'zē). **1.** Range of the N Rocky Mts. in NW Canada. **2.** River of NW Canada, flowing c. 1,120 mi (1,800 km) into Beaufort Sea. **3.** District of N.W.T., Canada.

Mack·i·nac (măk'ĭ-nô'). Island of N Mich. in the **Straits of Mackinac,** connecting Lakes Huron and Michigan.

Ma·comb (mə-kōm'). City of W Ill., WSW of Peoria. Pop. 19,632.

Ma·con (mā'kən). City of central Ga., SE of Atlanta. Pop. 116,860.

Mâ·con (mä-kôɴ'). City of E central France, N of Lyons. Pop. 39,344.

Mac·quar·ie (mə-kwŏr'ē). River, 590 mi (949.3 km), of New South Wales, Australia.

Mac·tan (măk-tăn'). Island of E central Philippines, off the E coast of Cebu Is.

Mad·a·gas·car (măd'ə-găs'kər). Island republic in the Indian Ocean, off the SE coast of Africa. Cap. Antananarivo. Pop. 8,730,000. —**Mad'a·gas'can** *adj. & n.*

Madagascar

Ma·dei·ra (mə-dîr'ə, -dĕr'ə). **1.** River of NW Brazil, flowing c. 900 mi (1,450 km) into the Amazon. **2.** Portuguese archipelago in the N Atlantic W of Morocco. —**Ma·dei'ran** *adj. & n.*

Ma·de·ra (mə-dĕr'ə). City of central Calif., NW of Fresno. Pop. 21,732.

Mad·i·son (măd'ĭ-sən). **1.** River, 183 mi (294.4 km), of NW Mont. **2.** Town of S Conn., on Long Is. Sound. Pop. 14,031. **3.** City of SE Ind., NE of New Albany. Pop. 12,472. **4.** Borough of NE N.J., near Morristown. Pop. 15,357. **5.** Cap. of Wis., in the S central part. Pop. 170,616.

Madison Heights. City of SE Mich., near Detroit. Pop. 35,375.

Mad·i·son·ville (măd'ĭ-sən-vĭl'). City of W Ky., N of Hopkinsville. Pop. 16,979.

Mad·ras (mə-drăs', -dräs'). City of SE India, on the Bay of Bengal. Pop. 2,469,449.

Ma·dre de Di·os (mä'*th*rĕ dĕ dyôs'). River, c. 700 mi (1,125 km), of SE Peru and NW Bolivia.

Ma·drid (mə-drĭd'). Cap. of Spain, on the central plateau. Pop. 3,274,000.

Ma·du·ra (mä-do͝or'ä). Indonesian island, separated from NE Java by **Madura Strait.**

Ma·du·rai (mäd'yo͞o-rī'). City of S India, SW of Madras. Pop. 548,298.

Mae·an·der (mē-ăn'dər). River of W Turkey, the Menderes.

Ma·ga·dan (mä'gə-dăn', -dän'). City of Far Eastern USSR, on the Sea of Okhotsk. Pop. 112,000.

Ma·ga·dha (mä'gə-də). Ancient kingdom of NE India.

Mag·da·le·na (măg'də-lā'nə). River of Colombia, flowing c. 1,000 mi (1,600 km) to the Caribbean.

Mag·de·burg (măg'də-bûrg'). City of W East Germany, SW of Berlin. Pop. 276,089.

Ma·gel·lan (mə-jĕl'ən), **Strait of.** Channel, c. 350 mi (565 km), separating S South America and Tierra del Fuego.

Mag·gio·re (mə-jôr'ē, mäd-jō'rā). Lake of N Italy and S Switzerland.

Ma·ghreb or **Ma·grib** (măg'rəb, mä'grĭb). Region of N Africa, W of Egypt.

Mag·na Grae·ci·a (măg'nə grē'shē-ə, -shə). Ancient Greek colonies of S Italy and Sicily.

Mag·ni·to·gorsk (măg-nē'tō-gôrsk'). City of SW Siberian USSR, in the Ural Mts. Pop. 393,000.

Mag·no·lia (măg-nōl'yə). City of SW Ark., W of El Dorado. Pop. 11,937.

Ma·gog (mā'gŏg). City of S Que., Canada, SW of Sherbrooke. Pop. 13,290.

Ma·hal·la el Ku·bra (mə-hăl'ə ĕl ko͞o'brə). City of Egypt, N of Cairo. Pop. 255,800.

Ma·ha·na·di (mə-hä'nə-dē). River of central India, flowing c. 550 mi (885 km) to the Bay of Bengal.

Ma·hé (mä-hā'). Chief island of the Seychelles, in the Indian Ocean.

Ma·hón (mə-hōn', mä-ôn'). Chief town of Minorca. Pop. 19,279.

Maid·en·head (măd'n-hĕd'). Bor-

ă pat / ā pay / âr care / ä father / b bib / ch church / d deed / ĕ pet / ē be / f fife / g gag / h hat / hw which / ĭ pit / ī pie / îr pier / j judge / k kick / l lid, needle / m mum / n no, sudden / ng thing / ŏ pot / ō toe / ô paw, for / oi noise / ou out / o͝o took / o͞o boot /

ough of S central England, W of London. Pop. 48,210.

Maid·stone (măd′stōn′, -stən). Borough of SE England, ESE of London. Pop. 72,110.

Mai·kop (mī-kôp′). City of S European USSR, SE of Krasnodar. Pop. 127,000.

Main (mīn, mān). River of E West Germany, flowing c. 310 mi (500 km) to the Rhine.

Maine (mān). **1.** (*also* mĕn). Region of NW France, S of Normandy. **2.** State of NE U.S. Cap. Augusta. Pop. 1,124,660.

Main·land (măn′lănd′, -lənd). **1.** Largest of the Orkney Is., N Scotland. **2.** Largest of the Shetland Is., extreme N Scotland.

Main Line (măn′ līn′). Suburbs W of Philadelphia, Pa.

Mainz (mīnts). City of W central West Germany, SW of Frankfort. Pop. 184,030.

Ma·jor·ca (mə-jôr′kə, -yôr′-). Spanish island, largest of the Balearics, in the W Mediterranean. —**Ma·jor′can** *adj. & n.*

Mak·a·lu (mŭk′ə-lo͞o′). Mountain, c. 27,800 ft (8,480 m), in the Himalayas of NE Nepal.

Ma·kas·sar or **Ma·cas·sar** (mə-kăs′-ər). **1.** Strait between Borneo and Celebes. **2.** City of NW Celebes, Indonesia. Pop. 434,766.

Ma·ke·yev·ka (mä-kĕ′yəf-kä′). City of S European USSR, NE of Donetsk. Pop. 437,000.

Ma·khach·ka·la (mə-käch′kə-lä′). City of SE European USSR, on the Caspian Sea. Pop. 231,000.

Ma·kin (mă′kĭn, mä′-). Butaritari.

Mal·a·bar (măl′ə-bär′). Region of SW India, along the Arabian Sea coast.

Mal·a·bo (măl′ə-bō′). Cap. of Equatorial Guinea, on Bioko Is. in the Gulf of Guinea. Pop. 20,000.

Ma·lac·ca (mə-lăk′ə). Strait between Sumatra and the Malay Peninsula, joining the Andaman and S China seas.

Má·la·ga (măl′ə-gə, mä′lä-gä). City of S Spain, NE of Gibraltar. Pop. 408,458.

Mal·a·gas·y Republic (măl′ə-găs′ē). Madagascar.

Ma·lang (mä-läng′). City of E Java, Indonesia. Pop. 341,452.

Ma·lar (mā′lär′) or **Mä·lar·en** (mĕ′-lä-rĕn). Lake of E Sweden, extending W from Stockholm.

Mal·a·spi·na (măl′ə-spē′nə). Glacier in the St. Elias Mts. of SE Alaska.

Ma·la·tya (mä′lä-tyä′). City of E central Turkey, in the Taurus Mts., Pop. 154,056.

Ma·la·wi (mä-lä′wē), Country of SE Africa. Cap. Lilongwe. Pop. 5,975,-000. —**Ma·la′wi·an** *adj. & n.*

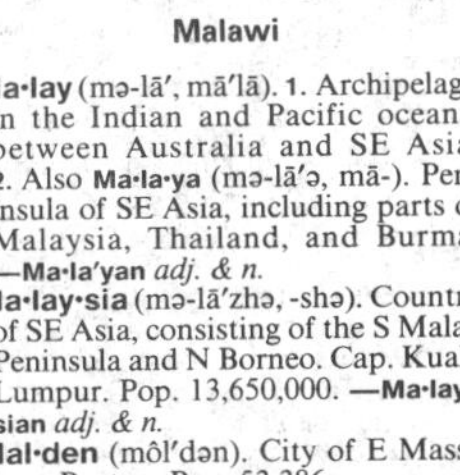

Malawi

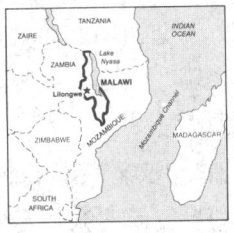

Ma·lay (mə-lā′, mā′lā). **1.** Archipelago in the Indian and Pacific oceans, between Australia and SE Asia. **2.** Also **Ma·la·ya** (mə-lā′ə, mā-). Peninsula of SE Asia, including parts of Malaysia, Thailand, and Burma. —**Ma·la′yan** *adj. & n.*

Ma·lay·sia (mə-lā′zhə, -shə). Country of SE Asia, consisting of the S Malay Peninsula and N Borneo. Cap. Kuala Lumpur. Pop. 13,650,000. —**Ma·lay′sian** *adj. & n.*

Mal·den (môl′dən). City of E Mass., near Boston, Pop. 53,386.

Mal·dives (môl′dīvz, măl′-). Island country in the Indian Ocean SW of Sri Lanka. Cap. Male. Pop. 136,000. —**Mal·div′i·an, Mal·di′van** *adj. & n.*

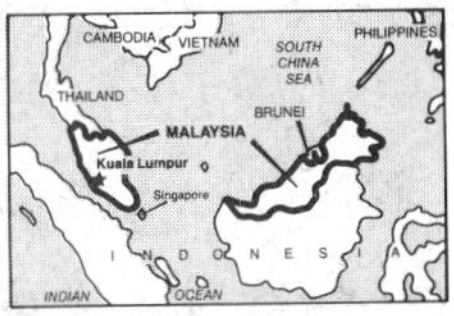

Malaysia

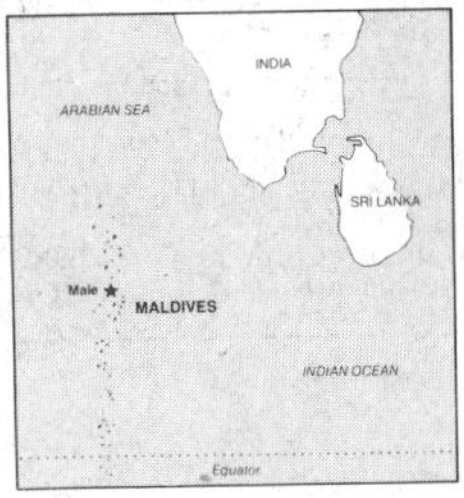

Maldives

Ma·le (mä′lē). Cap. of the Maldives. Pop. 12,000.

Ma·li (mä′lē). Country of W Africa. Cap Bamako. Pop. 6,660,000. —**Ma′li·an** *adj. & n.*

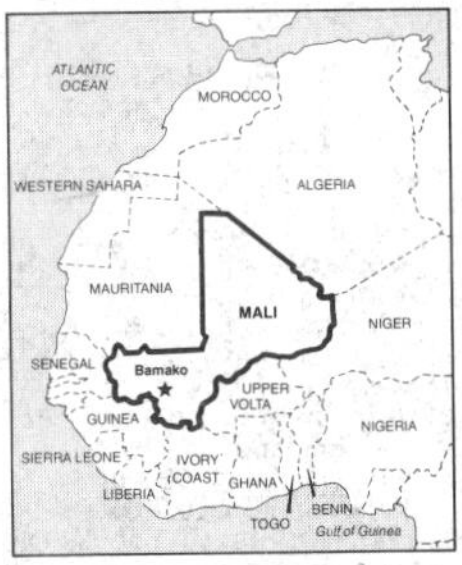

Mali

Mal·lor·ca (mä-yôr′kä, -lyôr′-). *Spanish.* Majorca.

Mal·mö (măl′mō, mäl′mœ). City of S Sweden, opposite Copenhagen. Pop. 243,591.

Mal·ta (môl′tə). Island country in the Mediterranean S of Sicily, coextensive with the **Malta Is.** Cap. Valletta. Pop. 330,000. —**Mal·tese′** (-tēz′, -tēs′) *adj. & n.*

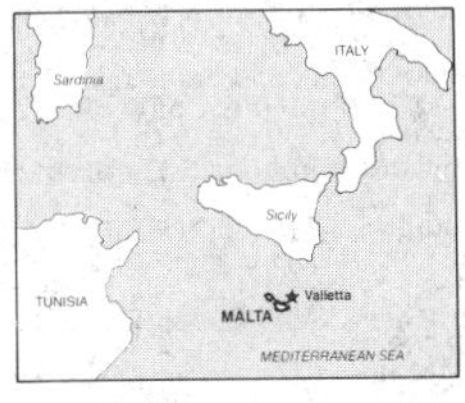

Malta

Mal·vern. **1.** (môl′vərn, mô′-). Hills of W central England, rising to 1,395 ft (425.5 m). **2.** (măl′vərn) City of S central Ark., SW of Little Rock. Pop. 10,147.

Mal·vin·as Islands (măl-vē′nəs). Falkland Is.

Ma·mar·o·neck (mə-măr′ə-nĕk′). Village of SE N.Y., near New York City. Pop. 17,616.

Mam·be·ra·mo (măm′bə-rä′mō). River, c. 500 mi (805 km), of W New Guinea.

Ma·mo·ré (mä-mə-rā′, -mô-). River, c. 600 mi (965 km), of N Bolivia and Brazil.

Man (măn), **Isle of.** British island in the Irish Sea. —**Manx** (măngks) *adj. & n.*

Ma·na·do (mä-nä′dō). Town of NE Celebes, Indonesia. Pop. 169,684.

Ma·na·gua (mä-nä′gwä). **1.** Lake, 390 sq mi (1,014 sq km), of W Nicaragua. **2.** Cap. of Nicaragua, on the lake's S shore. Pop. 375,278.

Ma·nas·sas (mə-năs′əs). Independent city of N Va., near Washington, D.C., site of **Manassas National Battlefield Park,** commemorating the Battles of Bull Run (1861, 1862). Pop. 15,438.

Ma·na·tí (mä-nä-tē′). City of N Puerto Rico, W of San Juan. Pop. 17, 254.

Ma·naus (mə-nous′). City of NW Brazil, on the Rio Negro. Pop. 284,-118.

Man·ches·ter (măn′chĕs′tər). **1.** (*also* -chĭ-stər). Borough of NE England, NE of Liverpool. Pop. 490,000. **2.** Town of central Conn., near Hartford. Pop. 49,761. **3.** City of SE N.H., S of Concord. Pop. 90,936.

Man·chu·kuo (măn′cho͞o′kwō′). Former state of E Asia, in Manchuria and E Inner Mongolia.

Man·chu·ri·a (măn-cho͝or′ē-ə). Region of NE China. —**Man·chu′ri·an** *adj. & n.*

Man·da·lay (măn′də-lā′, măn′də-lā′). City of central Burma, on the Irrawaddy. Pop. 402,000.

Man·dan (măn′dăn). City of S N.Dak., near Bismarck. Pop. 15,513.

Man·ga·lore (măng′gə-lôr′). City of SW India, on the Arabian Sea. Pop. 214,093.

Man·hat·tan (măn-hăt′n). **1.** City of NE Kans., W of Topeka. Pop. 32,644. **2.** Borough of New York City, SE N.Y., mainly on **Manhattan Is.** (22 sq mi/57.2 sq km). Pop. 1,427,533. —**Man·hat′tan·ite′** (-īt′) *n.*

Manhattan Beach. City of S Calif., near Los Angeles. Pop. 31,542.

Ma·nil·a (mə-nĭl′ə). City of SW Luzon, Philippines, on **Manilla Bay,** an inlet of the South China Sea. Pop. 1,438,000.

Man·i·to·ba (măn′ĭ-tō′bə). **1.** Lake, 1,817 sq mi (4,724.2 sq km), of SW Man., Canada. **2.** Province of S central Canada. Cap. Winnipeg. Pop. 1,019,000. —**Man′i·to′ban** *adj. & n.*

Man·i·tou·lin (măn′ĭ-to͞o′lĭn). Island, c. 80 mi (130 km) long, in N Lake Huron.

Man·i·to·woc (măn′ĭ-tə-wŏk′). City of E Wis., on Lake Michigan. Pop. 32,547.

Ma·ni·za·les (mä′nē-sä′lĕs). City of W central Colombia. Pop. 231,066.

Man·ka·to (măn-kā′tō). City of S Minn., SW of Minneapolis. Pop. 28,651.

Man·nar (mə-när′), **Gulf of.** Inlet of the Indian Ocean between S India and Sri Lanka.

Mann·heim (măn′hīm′, män′-). City of central West Germany, on the Rhine. Pop. 320,508.

Man·re·sa (män-rĕ′sä). City of NE Spain, NW of Barcelona. Pop. 57,846.

Mans·field (mănz′fēld′). **1.** Highest peak, 4,393 ft (1,339.9 m), of the Green Mts. of N central Vt. **2.** Borough of central England, N of Nottingham. Pop. 58,450. **3.** Town of NE Conn., N of Willimantic. Pop. 20,634. **4.** Town of SE Mass., SSW of Boston. Pop. 13,453. **5.** City of N central Ohio, WSW of Akron. Pop. 53,927.

Man·te·ca (măn-tē′kə). City of central Calif., E of Oakland. Pop. 24,925.

Man·tu·a (măn′cho͞o-ə, -to͞o-ə, -tyo͞o-ə). City of N Italy, SSW of Verona. Pop. 65,574. —**Man′tu·an** *adj. & n.*

Ma·nus (mä′nəs, -no͞os). Largest of the Admiralty Is., in the SW Pacific.

Man·ville (măn′vĭl′). Borough of N central N.J., near New Brunswick. Pop. 11,278.

Man·za·la (măn-zä′lə), **Lake.** Lagoon of NE Egypt, in the Nile Delta.

Man·za·nil·lo (măn′zə-nē′ō, män′-sä-nē′yô). City of SE Cuba. Pop. 77,880.

Ma·ple Grove (mā′pəl). City of SE Minn., NW of Minneapolis. Pop. 20,525.

Maple Heights. City of NE Ohio, near Cleveland. Pop. 29,735.

Ma·ple·wood (mā′pəl-wo͝od′). **1.** City of SE Minn., near St. Paul. Pop. 26,990. **2.** City of E Mo., near St. Louis. Pop. 10,960.

Ma·pu·to (mä-po͞o′tō). Cap. of Mozambique, on the Indian Ocean. Pop. 383,775.

Ma·quo·ke·ta (mə-kō′kə-tə). River, c. 130 m (210 km), of E Iowa, flowing SE to the Mississippi.

Ma·ra·cai·bo (măr′ə-kī′bō, mä′rä-). City of NW Venezuela, at the outlet of **Lake Maracaibo,** largest lake of South America, S of the Gulf of Venezuela. Pop. 651,574.

Ma·ra·cay (mä-rä-kī′). City of N Venezuela, SW of Caracas. Pop. 255,134.

Mar·ais des Cygnes (mĕr′ē dĭ sēn′, zēn′). River, c. 140 mi (225 km), of E Kans. and W Mo.

Mar·a·jó (mä′rä-zhô′). Island of N Brazil, in the Amazon delta.

Ma·ra·ñón (mä′rä-nyôn′). River flowing c. 1,000 mi (1,610 km) from W central to NE Peru.

Ma·ras (mä-räsh′). City of S central Turkey, in the Taurus Mts. Pop. 128,891.

Mar·a·thon (măr′ə-thŏn′). Plain of ancient Greece, NE of Athens; site of Persian defeat (490 B.C.).

Mar·ble·head (mär′bəl-hĕd′, mär′-bəl-hĕd′). Town of NE Mass., NE of Boston. Pop. 20,126.

Mar·burg (mär′bûrg′, -bo͝ork′). City of central West Germany, N of Frankfurt. Pop. 71,604.

Marche (märsh). Region of central France.

Mar·che (mär′kā) or **the Mar·ches** (-chĭz). Region of E central Italy.

Mar·cy (mär′sē). Mountain, 5,344 ft (1,629.9 m), in the Adirondacks, NE N.Y.

Mar del Pla·ta (mär′ dĕl plä′tä). City of E central Argentina, on the Atlantic. Pop. 302,282.

Ma·ren·go (mə-rĕng′gō, mä-). Village of NW Italy; site (1800) of Napoleon's defeat of the Austrians.

Mar·e·o·tis (măr′ē-ō′tĭs). Lake of N Egypt, in the Nile Delta.

Mar·ga·ri·ta (mär′gä-rē′tä). Island in the Caribbean off Venezuela.

Mar·gate. **1.** (mär′gət, -gāt′). Borough of SE England, NE of Canterbury. Pop. 50,290. **2.** (mär′gāt′). City of SE Fla., NW of Fort Lauderdale. Pop. 36,044.

Mar·i·an·a Islands (mâr′ē-ăn′ə) also **Mar·i·an·as** (-əz). U.S.-administered island group in the W Pacific E of the Philippines.

Ma·ri·a·nao (mär′ē-ə-nou′, mä′-ryä-nä′ô). City of W Cuba, near Havana. Pop. 368,747.

Marianas Trench. Depression (36,198 ft/11,040.4 m) in the floor of the W Pacific SW of Guam.

Ma·ri·as (mə-rī′əs, -əz). River of NW Mont., flowing c. 210 mi (338 km) SE to the Missouri.

Ma·ri·bor (mä′rĭ-bôr). City of NW Yugoslavia, on the Drava. Pop. 97,167.

Ma·rie Byrd Land (mə-rē′ bûrd′) also **Byrd Land.** Region of W Antarctica, E of Amundsen Sea.

Mar·i·et·ta (mâr′ē-ĕt′ə, măr′-). **1.** City of NW Ga., NW of Atlanta. Pop. 30,805. **2.** City of SE Ohio, on the Ohio River. Pop. 16,467.

Ma·ri·na (mə-rē′nə). City of W Calif., near Monterey. Pop. 20,647.

Ma·rin·du·que (mä′rĭn-do͞o′kĕ). Island of the Philippines, S of Luzon.

Mar·i·nette (măr′ə-nĕt′, mĕr′-). City of NE Wis., on Green Bay and the Mich. border. Pop. 11,965.

Mar·i·on (măr′ē-ən, mâr′-). **1.** City of S Ill., W of Harrisburg. Pop. 14,031. **2.** City of E central Ind., NW of Muncie. Pop. 35,874. **3.** City of E central Iowa, near Cedar Rapids. Pop. 19,474. **4.** City of central Ohio, N of Columbus. Pop. 37,040.

Mar·i·time Alps (măr′ĭ-tīm′). Range of the W Alps on the French-Italian border.

Maritime Provinces also **the Mar·i·times** (măr′ĭ-tīmz′). Canadian provinces of N.S., N.B., and P.E.I.

Ma·ri·tsa (mä-rēt′sä). River of W Bulgaria and W Turkey, flowing c.

300 mi (485 km) to the Aegean.
Ma·ri·u·pol (măr'ē-o͞o'pôl). Zhdanov.
Mark·ham (mâr'kəm). **1.** Mountain, 14,272 ft (4,353 m), of Victoria Land, Antarctica. **2.** Village of S Ont., Canada, NNE of Toronto. Pop. 36,684. **3.** City of NE Ill., near Chicago. Pop. 15,172.
Marl (märl). City of W West Germany, in the Ruhr. Pop. 91,779.
Marl·bor·ough or **Marl·bo·ro** (märl'bûr'ō, -bər-ə, môl'-). City of E central Mass., NE of Worcester. Pop. 30,617.
Mar·ma·ra (mär'mər-ə), **Sea of.** Sea of NW Turkey, connected to the Black Sea and the Aegean through the Bosporus and Dardanelles.
Mar·mo·la·da (mär'mō-lä'dä). Mountain, 10,964 ft (3,344 m), in the Dolomites of NE Italy.
Marne (märn). River, c. 325 mi (523 km), of NE France; scene of battles in World Wars I and II.
Ma·ro·ni (mə-rō'nē). River of N South America, flowing c. 450 mi (725 km) along the Surinam-French Guiana border to the Atlantic.
Mar·que·sas Islands (mär-kā'zəs, -zəz, -səz, -səs). Archipelago in the South Pacific, part of French Polynesia.
Mar·quette (mär-kĕt'). City of NW Mich., on Lake Superior. Pop. 23,288.
Mar·ra·kesh or **Mar·ra·kech** (mə-rä'kĕsh, măr'ə-kĕsh'). City of W central Morocco, near the Atlas Mts. Pop. 332,741.
Mar·sa·la (mär-sä'lə). City of W Sicily, on the Mediterranean. Pop. 49,200.
Mar·seilles also **Mar·seille** (mär-sā'). City of SE France, on the Mediterranean. Pop. 908,600.
Mar·shall (mär'shəl). **1.** Islands in the central Pacific, part of U.S. Trust Territory of the Pacific. **2.** City of SW Minn., WSW of New Ulm. Pop. 11,161. **3.** City of N central Mo., E of Kansas City. Pop. 12,781. **4.** City of E Tex., W of Shreveport, La. Pop. 24,921.
Mar·shall·town (mär'shəl-toun'). City of central Iowa, NE of Des Moines. Pop. 26,938.
Marsh·field (märsh'fēld'). **1.** Town of SE Mass., SE of Boston. Pop. 20,916. **2.** City of central Wis., SW of Wausau. Pop. 18,290.
Mar·ston Moor (mär'stən mo͝or'). Site in N England of 1st Civil War battle (1644).
Mar·ta·ban (mär'tə-bän', -bän'), **Gulf of.** Arm of the Andaman Sea off S Burma.
Mar·tha's Vine·yard (mär'thəz vĭn'yərd). Island of SE Mass., off Cape Cod.
Mar·ti·nez (mär-tē'nəs). City of W Calif., NE of Oakland. Pop. 22,582.
Mar·ti·nique (mär'tĭ-nēk', -tn-ēk'). French island and overseas department in the West Indies. Cap. Fort-de-France. Pop. 330,000.
Mar·tins·burg (mär'tnz-bûrg'). City of NE W.Va., in the E Panhandle. Pop. 13,063.
Mar·tins·ville (mär'tnz-vĭl'). **1.** City of central Ind., SW of Indianapolis. Pop. 11,311. **2.** Independent city of S Va., near the N.C. border. Pop. 18,149.
Mar·y·land (mĕr'ə-lənd). State of E U.S. Cap. Annapolis. Pop. 4,216,446. —**Mar'y·land·er** *n.*
Mar·y·ville (mâr'ē-vĭl'). City of E Tenn., S of Knoxville. Pop. 17,480.
Ma·sa·da (mə-sä'də). Ancient mountaintop fortress in SE Israel.
Ma·san (mä'sän'). Port city of SE South Korea. Pop. 154,856.
Mas·ba·te (mäs-bä'tē). Philippine island, in the Visayans S of Luzon.
Mas·ca·rene (măs'kə-rēn'). Islands in the Indian Ocean E of Madagascar.
Mas·er·u (măz'ə-ro͞o'). Cap. of Lesotho, in the W part. Pop. 14,700.
Mash·had (mäsh-häd'). Meshed.
Ma·son City (mā'sən). City of N central Iowa, NW of Waterloo. Pop. 30,144.
Ma·son-Dix·on Line (mā'sən-dĭk'sən). Boundary between Pa. and Md., regarded as division between free and slave states before the Civil War.
Mas·sa (mäs'sä). City of N central Italy, near the Ligurian Sea. Pop. 65,332.
Mas·sa·chu·setts (măs'ə-cho͞o'sĭts). **1. Bay.** Inlet of the Atlantic off E Mass. **2.** State of NE U.S. Cap. Boston. Pop. 5,737,037.
Mas·sa·pe·qua Park (măs-ə-pē'kwə). Village of SE N.Y., on S Long Is. Pop. 19,779.
Mas·se·na (mə-sē'nə). Village of N N.Y., on the St. Lawrence. Pop. 12,851.
Mas·sif Cen·tral (mă-sēf' sĕn-träl', mä-sēf' säN-). Mountainous plateau of S central France.
Mas·si·lon (măs'ə-lŏn'). City of E central Ohio, W of Canton. Pop. 30,557.
Mas·sive (măs'ĭv), **Mount.** Peak, 14,418 ft (4,397.5 m), in the Sawatch Mts. of central Colo.
Ma·su·li·pa·tam (mə-so͞o'lə-pŭt'əm). also **Ma·su·li·pat·nam** (-pŭt'nəm). City of E central India, on the Bay of Bengal. Pop. 112,636.
Ma·su·ri·a (mə-zo͝or'ē-ə, -so͝or'-). Region of NE Poland. —**Ma·su'ri·an** *adj.*
Mat·a·be·le·land (măt'ə-bē'lē-lănd'). Region of SW Zimbabwe.
Ma·ta·di (mə-tä'dē). City of W Zaire, on the Congo R. Pop. 144,000.
Mat·a·gor·da Bay (măt'ə-gôr'də). Inlet of the Gulf of Mexico in SE Tex.
Ma·ta·mo·ros (măt'ə-môr'əs, -môr'-, mä'tä-môr'ôs). City of NE Mexico, on the Rio Grande opposite Brownsville, Tex. Pop. 165,100.
Ma·tane (mə-tăn'). Town of SE Que., Canada, on Gaspé Peninsula. Pop. 12,726.
Ma·tan·zas (mə-tăn'zəs, mä-tän'säs). Port city of W central Cuba. Pop. 85,376.
Mat·a·pan (măt'ə-păn', măt'ə-păn'), **Cape.** S tip of the Greek mainland.
Ma·ta·ró (mä'tä-rō'). City of NE Spain, on the Mediterranean. Pop. 73,129.
Ma·te·ra (mä-tĕr'ä). City of S Italy, in the Apennines. Pop. 48,785.
Ma·thu·ra (mŭt'ə-rə). City of N central India, NW of Agra. Pop. 131,813.
Mat·squi (măt'skwē). Town of SW B.C., Canada, WSW of Chilliwack. Pop. 23,544.
Mat·su (mät'so͞o'). Island in Formosa Strait, E of SE mainland China.
Ma·tsu·do (mä-tso͞o'dô). City of E central Honshu, Japan, near Tokyo. Pop. 358,139.
Ma·tsu·e (mä-tso͞o'ā). Port city of SW Honshu, Japan. Pop. 129,277.
Ma·tsu·mo·to (mä'tso͞o-mô'tô). City of central Honshu, Japan. Pop. 187,225.
Ma·tsu·ya·ma (mä'tso͞o-yä'mä). City of NW Shikoku, Japan, on the Inland Sea. Pop. 374,492.
Mat·tag·a·mi (mə-tăg'ə-mē). River, 275 mi (442.5 km), of E Ont., Canada.
Mat·ta·po·ni (măt'ə-pə-nī'). River, 125 mi (201 km), of E Va.
Mat·ter·horn (măt'ər-hôrn', mä'tər-). Mountain, c. 14,685 ft (4,480 m), in the Pennine Alps on the Italian-Swiss border.
Matte·son (măt'sən). Village of NE Ill., near Chicago. Pop. 10,223.
Mat·toon (mə-to͞on'). City of E central Ill., SE of Decatur. Pop. 19,787.
Ma·tu·rín (mä'to͞o-rēn'). City of NE Venezuela. Pop. 97,257.
Mau·i (mou'ē). Island of Hawaii, NW of Hawaii Is.
Mau·mee (mô-mē', mô'mē). **1.** River of NE Ind. and NW Ohio, flowing c. 130 mi (210 km) into Lake Erie. **2.** City of NW Ohio, near Toledo. Pop. 15,747.
Mau·na Ke·a (mou'nə kā'ə). Dormant volcano, 13,796 ft (4,208 m), in N central Hawaii Is.
Mauna Lo·a (lō'ə). Volcano, 13,680 ft (4,172 m), in S central Hawaii Is.
Mau·re·ta·ni·a (môr'ĭ-tā'nē-ə). Ancient country of N Africa in present-day Morocco and Algeria. —**Mau're·ta'ni·an** *adj. & n.*
Mau·ri·ta·ni·a (môr'ĭ-tā'nē-ə). Islamic republic of NW Africa, on the Atlantic N of Senegal. Cap Nouakchott. Pop. 1,640,000. —**Mau'ri·ta'ni·an** *adj. & n.*

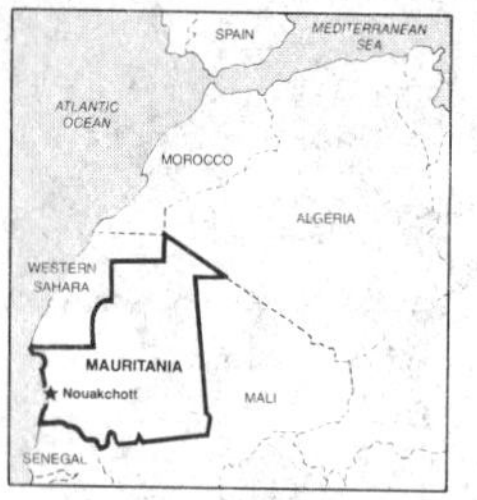

Mauritania

Mau·ri·tius (mô-rĭsh'əs, -ē-əs). Island country in the SW Indian Ocean. Cap. Port Louis. Pop. 920,000. —**Mau·ri'tian** *adj. & n.*

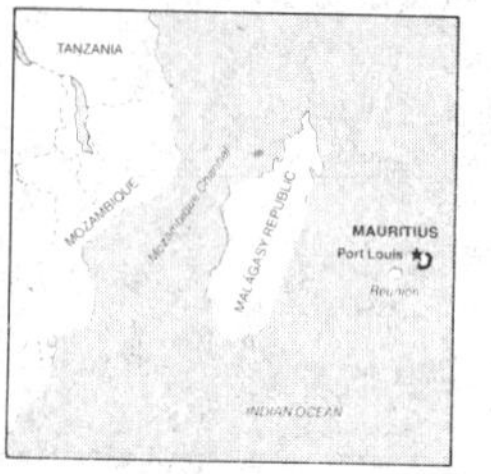

Mauritius

May (mā), **Cape.** Peninsula of S N.J., between the Atlantic and Delaware Bay.
Ma·ya·güez (mī'ə-gwĕz', -gwĕs', mä'yä-gwĕs'). City of W Puerto Rico, WSW of San Juan. Pop. 82,703.
Ma·ya·pán (mä'yä-pän'). Ruined capital of the Maya, in Yucatán, SE Mexico.
May·fair (mā'fâr). District of W London, England.
May·field (mā'fēld'). City of SW Ky., S of Paducah. Pop. 10,705.
Mayfield Heights. City of NE Ohio, near Cleveland. Pop. 21,550.
Ma·yon (mä-yôn'), **Mount.** Volcano, 8,070 ft (2,461 m), in SE Luzon, Philippines.
Ma·yotte (mä-yät', -yôt'). French island of the E Comoros in the Indian Ocean.
May·wood (mā'wo͝od'). **1.** City of S Calif., near Los Angeles. Pop. 21,810. **2.** Village of NE Ill., near Chicago. Pop. 27,998.
Ma·za·tlán (mä'sä-tlän'). City of W Mexico, on the Pacific. Pop. 147,000.
Mba·bane (əm-bä-bän'). Cap. of Swaziland, in the NW part. Pop. 23,000.
Mban·da·ka (əm-bän-dä'kə). City of W Zaire, on the Congo R. Pop. 134,000.
Mbo·mu (əm-bō'mo͞o). Variant of **Bomu.**
Mbu·ji Ma·yi (ĕm-bo͞o'jē mī'yē). City of S central Zaire. Pop. 256,154.
Mc·Al·es·ter (mĭ-kăl'ĭ-stər). City of SE Okla., WSW of Muskogee. Pop. 17,255.
Mc·Al·len (mĭ-kăl'ən). City of S Tex., on the Rio Grande. Pop. 67,042.
Mc·Clure Strait (mĭ-klo͝or'). Arm of the Beaufort Sea, W N.W.T., Canada.
Mc·Comb (mĭ-kōm'). City of SW Miss., ESE of Natchez. Pop. 12,331.
Mc·Hen·ry (mĭk-hĕn'rē, mĭ-kĕn'-). City of NE Ill., W of Waukegan. Pop. 10,908.
Mc·Kees·port (mĭ-kēz'pôrt'). City of SW Pa., near Pittsburgh. Pop. 31,012.
Mc·Kin·ley (mĭ-kĭn'lē), **Mount.** Peak, 20,320 ft (6,198 m), in S central Alas.
Mc·Kin·ney (mĭ-kĭn'ē). City of N Tex., NNE of Dallas. Pop. 16,249.
Mc·Minn·ville (mĭk-mĭn'vĭl'). **1.** City of NW Ore., SW of Portland. Pop. 14,080. **2.** City of central Tenn., NW of Chattanooga. Pop. 10,683.
Mc·Mur·do Sound (mĭk-mûr'dō). Inlet of Antarctica, between Ross Is. and Victoria Land.
Mc·Pher·son (mĭk-fûr'sən). City of central Kans., NNW of Wichita. Pop. 11,753.
Mead (mēd), **Lake.** Reservoir of SE Nev. and NW Ariz., formed by Hoover Dam on the Colorado R.
Mead·ville (mēd'vĭl'). City of NW Pa., S of Erie. Pop. 15,544.
Meaux (mō). City of N France, on the Marne ENE of Paris. Pop. 42,243.
Mec·ca (mĕk'ə). City of W Saudi Arabia; birthplace of Mohammed. Pop. 366,801.
Mech·lin (mĕk'lĭn) also **Me·che·len** (mĕKH'ə-lən). City of N central Belgium. Pop. 77,868.
Meck·len·burg (mĕk'lən-bûrg', -bo͝ork'). Region of N East Germany, on the Baltic.
Me·dan (mē-dän'). City of NE Sumatra, Indonesia. Pop. 635,562.
Me·del·lín (mĕd'l-ēn', mē-*th*ē-yĕn'). City of NW central Colombia, NW of Bogota. Pop. 1,100,082.
Med·field (mĕd'fēld'). Town of E Mass., SW of Boston. Pop. 10,220.
Med·ford (mĕd'fərd). **1.** City of E Mass., near Boston. Pop. 58,076. **2.** City of SW Ore., W of Klamath Falls. Pop. 39,603.
Me·di·a (mē'dē-ə). Ancient country of SW Asia, in NW Iran. —**Me'di·an** *adj. & n.*
Med·i·cine Bow (mĕd'ĭ-sĭn bō'). **1.** River, c. 120 mi (193 km), of S Wyo. **2. Mountains.** Range of E Rockies, in SE Wyo. and N Colo., including **Medicine Bow Peak** (12,013 ft/3,664 m).
Medicine Hat. (hăt). City of SE Alta., Canada, near the Sask. border. Pop. 32,811.
Me·di·na. 1. (mĭ-dē'nə). City of NW Saudi Arabia, N of Mecca. Pop. 198,186. **2.** (-dī'-). City of NE Ohio, WNW of Akron. Pop. 15,268.
Med·i·ter·ra·ne·an (mĕd'ĭ-tə-rā'nē-ən). Sea surrounded by Europe, Asia, Asia Minor, the Near East, and Africa, connecting with the Atlantic through the Strait of Gibraltar.
Mé·doc (mā-dŏk'). Region of SW France.
Mee·rut (mā'rət, mē'-). City of N central India, NE of Delhi. Pop. 271,325.
Meg·a·ra (mĕg'ə-rə). Ancient city of E central Greece, center of **Meg·a·ris** (-rəs), district between the Saronic Gulf and Gulf of Corinth.
Me·gid·do (mĭ-gĭd'ō, -gē'dō). Ancient city of NW Palestine.
Meis·sen (mī'sən). City of SE East Germany, on the Elbe. Pop. 43,561.
Mek·nes (mĕk-nĕs'). City of N Morocco, WSW of Fez. Pop. 248,369.
Me·kong (mā'kông'). River of SE Asia, flowing c. 2,600 mi (4,185 km) from China to the South China Sea through the vast **Mekong Delta** in S Vietnam.
Mel·a·ne·sia (mĕl'ə-nē'zhə, -shə). Island group in the SW Pacific NE of Australia and S of the equator. —**Mel'a·ne'sian** *adj. & n.*
Mel·bourne (mĕl'bərn). **1.** City of SE Australia, SW of Canberra. Metro. area pop. 2,603,000. **2.** City of E central Fla., S of Cocoa Beach. Pop. 45,536.
Me·li·to·pol (mĕl'ĭ-tô'pəl). City of S European USSR, in the Ukraine. Pop. 155,000.
Mel·rose (mĕl'rōz'). City of E Mass., near Boston. Pop. 30,005.
Melrose Park. Village of NE Ill, near Chicago. Pop. 20,735.
Mel·ville (mĕl'vĭl'). **1.** Saltwater lake, c. 1,133 sq mi (2,935 sq km), of SE Labrador, Canada. **2.** Peninsula of E N.W.T., Canada. **3.** Island of N Australia, in the Timor Sea. **4.** Island, c. 16,400 sq mi (42,476 sq km), of N N.W.T., Canada, N of Victoria Is.
Mel·vin·dale (mĕl'vĭn-dāl'). City of SE Mich., near Detroit. Pop. 12,322.
Me·mel (mā'məl). *German.* Klaipeda.
Mem·phis (mĕm'fĭs, mĕmp'-). **1.** Ruined capital of ancient Egypt, on the Nile S of Cairo. **2.** City of SW Tenn., on the Mississippi. Pop. 646,356. —**Mem'phi·an, Mem'phite'** (-fīt') *adj. & n.*
Me·nam (mē-näm'). Chao Phraya.
Me·nash·a (mə-năsh'ə). City of E

Wis., N of Oshkosh. Pop. 14,728.
Men·de·res (mĕn′də-rĕs′). **1.** River of W Turkey, flowing 250 mi (204 km) to the Aegean. **2.** River of NW Turkey, flowing c. 60 mi (97 km) to the Dardanelles.
Men·dip Hills (mĕn′dĭp′). Range in SW England.
Men·do·ci·no (mĕn′də-sē′nō), **Cape.** W extremity of Calif., N of San Francisco.
Men·do·za (mĕn-dō′zə, -dō′sä). City of W Argentina. Pop. 118,568.
Men·lo Park (mĕn′lō). City of W Calif., near Palo Alto. Pop. 25,673.
Me·nom·i·nee (mə-nŏm′ə-nē). **1.** River, 118 mi (190 km), of NW Mich. and NE Wis., flowing through an iron-ore region and into Green Bay. **2.** City of N Mich., on the Wis. border. Pop. 10,099.
Me·nom·o·nee Falls (mə-nŏm′-ə-nē). Village of SE Wis., near Milwaukee. Pop. 27,845.
Me·nom·o·nie (mə-nŏm′ə-nē). City of W Wis., WNW of Eau Claire. Pop. 12,769.
Me·nor·ca (mĕ-nôr′kä). *Spanish.* Minorca.
Men·tor (mĕn′tər). City of NE Ohio, on Lake Erie near Cleveland. Pop. 42,065.
Meq·uon (mĕk′wŏn′). City of SE Wis., N of Milwaukee. Pop. 16,193.
Mer·a·mec (mĕr′ə-măk′). River of E Mo., flowing 207 mi (333 km) to the Mississippi below St. Louis.
Mer·ced (mər-sĕd′). **1.** River, c. 150 mi (240 km), of central Calif. **2.** City of central Calif., NW of Fresno. Pop. 36,499.
Mer·ce·da·rio (mĕr′sĕ-*th*ä′ryō). Mountain, 22,210 ft (6,774 m), of NW Argentina, on the Chilean border.
Mer·ce·des (mĕr-sā′dĕz, mər-sā′dĭs). City of S Tex., WNW of Brownsville. Pop. 11,851.
Mer·cer Island (mûr′sər). City of W central Wash., coextensive with **Mercer Is.**, in Lake Washington near Seattle. Pop. 21,522.
Mer·ci·a (mûr′shē-ə, -shə). Ancient Anglo-Saxon kingdom of central England. **—Mer′ci·an** *adj. & n.*
Mé·ri·da (mĕr′ĭ-də, mĕ′rē-*th*ä′). **1.** City of SE Mexico, in the Yucatán. Pop. 233,900. **2.** City of W Venezuela, SSE of Maracaibo. Pop. 75,634.
Mer·i·den (mĕr′ĭ-dn). City of S central Conn., N of New Haven. Pop. 57,118.
Me·rid·i·an (mə-rĭd′ē-ən). City of E Miss., near the Ala. border. Pop. 46,577.
Mer·o·ë (mĕr′ō-ē′). Ancient Cushite city of N Sudan, on the Nile N of Khartoum.
Mer·ri·am (mĕr′ē-əm). City of E Kans., S of Kansas City. Pop. 10,794.
Mer·rill·ville (mĕr′əl-vĭl′). Town of NW Ind., near Gary. Pop. 27,677.
Mer·ri·mack (mĕr′ə-măk′). **1.** River of S central N.H. and NE Mass., flowing c. 110 mi (175 km) into the Atlantic. **2.** Town of S N.H., S of Manchester. Pop. 15,406.
Mer·ritt (mĕr′ĭt). Island of E Fla., between the mainland and Cape Canaveral.
Mer·sey (mûr′zē). River of NW England, flowing c. 70 mi (113 km) to the Irish Sea at Liverpool.
Mer·sin (mĕr-sēn′). City of S Turkey, on the Mediterranean. Pop. 152,186.
Mer·thyr Tyd·fil (mûr′thər tĭd′vĭl). Borough of S Wales, NW of Cardiff. Pop. 53,680.
Me·sa (mā′sə). City of S central Ariz., near Phoenix. Pop. 152,453.
Me·sa·bi Range (mə-sä′bē). Low hills in NE Minn., with extensive ore deposits.
Mesa Verde National Park (vûrd, vûr′dē). Area of SW Colo., with prehistoric cliff dwellings.
Me·shed (mĕ-shĕd′). City of NE Iran. Pop. 425,000.
Me·so·lón·gi·on (mĕ′sô-lông′gē-ôn). Town of W central Greece, on the Gulf of Patras. Pop. 11,614.
Mes·o·po·ta·mi·a (mĕs′ə-pə-tā′mē-ə). Ancient country of SW Asia, between the Tigris and Euphrates rivers. **—Mes′o·po·ta′mi·an** *adj. & n.*
Mes·quite (mə-skēt′, mĕ-). City of N Tex., near Dallas. Pop. 67,053.
Mes·se·ne (mĭ-sē′nē). Ancient Greek city, in the SW Peloponnesus.
Mes·se·ni·a (mĭ-sē′nē-ə, -nyə). Ancient region of SW Greece, on the Ionian Sea.
Mes·si·na (mĭ-sē′nə, mās-sē′nä). City of NE Sicily, on the **Strait of Messina**, a channel separating Sicily from mainland Italy.
Me·ta (mā′tə, mĕ′tä). River, 685 mi (1,102 km), of NE Colombia, forming part of the border with Venezuela.
Met·a·pon·tum (mĕt′ə-pŏn′təm). Ancient Greek city of SE Italy.
Me·thu·en (mə-thōō′ən, -thyōō′-). Town of NE Mass., on the N.H. border near Lawrence. Pop. 36,701.
Me·tuch·en (mə-tŭch′ən). Borough of NE N.J., near New Brunswick. Pop. 13,762.
Metz (mĕts, mĕs). City of NE France, on the Moselle. Pop. 111,869.
Meuse (myōōz, mœz). River flowing c. 560 mi (901 km) from NE France through S Belgium and SE Netherlands to the North Sea.
Mex·i·cal·i (mĕk′sĭ-kăl′ē, mĕ′hĕ-kä′lĕ). City of NW Mexico, near the Calif. border. Pop. 317,200.
Mex·i·co (mĕk′sĭ-kō′). **1. Gulf of.** Arm of the Atlantic bordering on E Mexico, SE U.S., and Cuba. **2.** Also **Mé·xi·co** (mĕ′hĕ-kô′). Republic of NW Central America. Cap. Mexico City. Pop. 69,381,000. **3.** City of central Mo., NE of Columbia. Pop. 12,276. **—Mex′i·can** *adj. & n.*

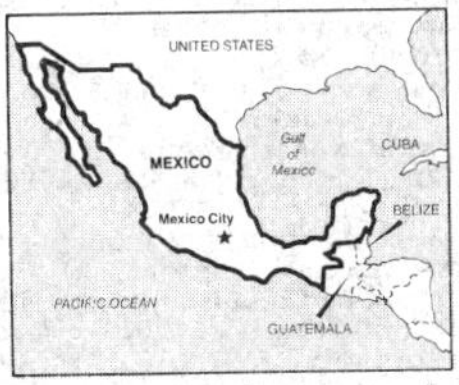

Mexico

Mexico City also **México City.** Cap. of Mexico, at the S end of the central plateau. Pop. 8,591,750.
Mi·am·i (mī-ăm′ē). **1.** Also **Great Miami.** River, c. 160 mi (257 km), of W Ohio, flowing c. 160 mi (257 km) into the Ohio R. **2.** City of SE Fla., on Biscayne Bay S of West Palm Beach. Pop. 346,931. **3.** City of extreme NW Ohio, WSW of Joplin, Mo. Pop. 14,237.
Miami Beach. City of SE Fla., near Miami. Pop. 96,298.
Mi·am·is·burg (mī-ăm′ēz-bûrg′). City of SW Ohio, S of Dayton. Pop. 15,304.
Miami Springs. City of SE Fla., near Miami. Pop. 12,350.
Mich·i·gan (mĭsh′ĭ-gən). **1. Lake.** 3rd largest of the Great Lakes, between Wis. and Mich. **2.** State of N U.S., with an Upper Peninsula bordering on Wis. and Lake Superior. Pop. 9,258,344. Cap. Lansing. **—Mich′i·gan′der** *adj. & n.*
Michigan City. City of NW Ind., on Lake Michigan. Pop. 36,850.
Mi·cro·ne·si·a (mī′krō-nē′zhə, -shə). Islands of the W Pacific, E of the Philippines and N of the equator. **—Mi′cro·ne′sian** *adj. & n.*
Mid·dle At·lan·tic States (mĭd′l ăt-lăn′tĭk). U.S. states of N.Y., Pa., N.J., Del., and Md.
Mid·dle·bor·ough or **Mid·dle·bor·o** (mĭd′l-bûr′ō). Town of SE Mass., N of New Bedford. Pop. 16,404.
Mid·dle·burg Heights (mĭd′l-bûrg′). City of NE Ohio, near Cleveland. Pop. 16,218.
Middle East (ēst). Area of SW Asia and NE Africa. **—Middle East′ern** (ē′stərn) *adj. & n.*
Mid·dles·bor·ough or **Mid·dles·bor·o** (mĭd′lz-bûr′ō). City of SE Ky., on the Va. and Tenn. borders. Pop. 12,251.
Mid·dles·brough (mĭd′lz-brə). Borough of NE England. Pop. 153,900.
Mid·dle·sex (mĭd′l-sĕks′). Borough of NE N.J., NNW of New Brunswick. Pop. 13,480.
Mid·dle·ton (mĭd′l-tən). City of S central Wis., near Madison. Pop. 11,779.
Mid·dle·town (mĭd′l-toun′). **1.** City of central Conn., near Hartford. Pop. 39,040. **2.** City of SE N.Y., WSW of Newburgh. Pop. 21,454. **3.** City of SW Ohio, NNE of Cincinnati. Pop. 43,719. **4.** Borough of SE Pa., near Harrisburg. Pop. 10,122. **5.** Town of SE R.I., near Newport. Pop. 17,216.
Middle West (wĕst). Region of N central U.S., including states in the Upper Mississippi Valley and those bordering on the Great Lakes. **—Middle West′ern** (wĕs′tərn) *adj. & n.* **—Middle West′ern·er** *n.*
Mid·east (mĭd-ēst′). The Middle East. **—Mid·east′ern** *adj.* **—Mid·east′ern·er** *n.*
Mi·di (mē-dē′). The S of France.
Mid·land (mĭd′lənd). **1.** Town of S Ont., Canada, NW of Toronto. Pop. 11,568. **2.** City of central Mich., W of Bay City. Pop. 37,250. **3.** City of W central Tex., WSW of Abilene. Pop. 70,525.
Mid·lands (mĭd′ləndz). The central section of England.
Mid·lo·thi·an (mĭd-lō′thē-ən). **1.** Former county of SE Scotland, surrounding Edinburgh. **2.** Village of NE Ill., near Chicago. Pop. 14,274.
Mid·vale (mĭd′vāl′). City of N Utah, near Salt Lake City. Pop. 10,144.
Mid·way Islands (mĭd′wā′). Coral atoll and U.S. territory in the central Pacific, NW of Honolulu.
Mid·west (mĭd-wĕst′). The Middle West. **—Mid·west′ern** *adj.* **—Mid·west′ern·er** *n.*
Midwest City. City of central Okla., near Oklahoma City. Pop. 49,559.
Mi·lan (mĭ-lăn′, lăn′) also **Mi·lan·o** (mē-lä′nō). City of N Italy. Pop. 1,724,173. **—Mil′a·nese′** (mĭl′ə-nēz′, -nēs′) *adj. & n.*
Mi·le·tus (mī-lē′təs). Ancient Ionian city of W Asia Minor.
Mil·ford (mĭl′fərd). **1.** City of SW Conn., on Long Is. Sound. Pop. 50,898. **2.** City of S Mass., SE of Worcester. Pop. 23,390.
Milk (mĭlk). River, 625 mi (1,006 km), of Alta., Canada., and N Mont.
Mill·brae (mĭl′brā′). City of W Calif., near San Francisco. Pop. 20,058.
Mill·bur·y (mĭl′bûr′ē). Town of S Mass., near Worcester. Pop. 11,808.
Mil·ledge·ville (mĭl′ĭj-vĭl′). City of central Ga., NE of Macon. Pop. 12,176.
Mill·ing·ton (mĭl′ĭng-tən). City of SW Tenn., NE of Memphis. Pop. 20,236.
Mill Valley (mĭl). City of W Calif., near San Francisco. Pop. 12,967.
Mill·ville (mĭl′vĭl′). City of S N.J., W of Atlantic City. Pop. 24,815.
Mi·los (mē′lôs) also **Mi·lo** (mē′lō, mī′). Cyclades island of SE Greece, in the Aegean.
Mil·pi·tas (mĭl′pē′təs). City of W Calif., near San Jose. Pop. 37,820.
Mil·ton (mĭl′tən). **1.** Town of SE Ont., WSW of Toronto. Pop. 10,463. **2.** Town of E Mass., near Boston. Pop. 25,860.
Mil·wau·kee (mĭl-wô′kē). City of SE Wis., on Lake Michigan. Pop. 636,212.
Mil·wau·kie (mĭl-wô′kē). City of NW Ore., near Portland. Pop. 17,931.
Min (mĭn). **1.** River of SE China, flowing c. 350 mi (563 km) to the South China Sea. **2.** River of central China, flowing c. 500 mi (805 km) to the Yangtze.
Minch (mĭnch). Channel, divided into **North Minch** and **Little Minch,** separating NW Scotland from the Outer Hebrides.
Min·da·na·o (mĭn′də-nä′ō, -nou′). Island of S Philippines, NE of Borneo, separated from the Visayan Is. by **Mindanao Sea.**
Min·den (mĭn′dən). **1.** City of N West Germany, on the Weser. Pop. 79,737. **2.** City of NW La., ENE of Shreveport. Pop. 15,074.
Min·do·ro (mĭn-dôr′ō, dōr′ō). Island of W central Philippines, S of Luzon.
Min·e·o·la (mĭn′ē-ō′lə). Village of SE N.Y., on Long Is. Pop. 20,757.
Min·er·al Wells (mĭn′ər-əl, wĕlz′). City of N. Tex., W of Fort Worth. Pop. 14,468.
Mi·nho (mē′nyōō). River, flowing c. 210 (338 km) from NW Spain to the Atlantic.
Min·ne·ap·o·lis (mĭn′ē-ăp′ə-lĭs). City of SE Minn., on the Mississippi adjacent to St. Paul. Pop. 370,951.
Min·ne·so·ta (mĭn′ĭ-sō′tə). **1.** River of S Minn., 332 mi (534 km), flowing to the Mississippi near St. Paul. **2.** State of N U.S., bordering on Ont., Canada, and Lake Superior. Cap. St. Paul. Pop. 4,077,148. **—Min′ne·so′tan** *adj. & n.*
Min·ne·ton·ka (mĭn′ĭ-tŏng′kə). City of SE Minn., near Minneapolis. Pop. 38,683.
Mi·nor·ca (mĭ-nôr′kə). Spanish island in the Balearics of the W Mediterranean. **—Mi·nor′can** *adj. & n.*
Mi·not (mī′nət, -nŏt′). City of N N.Dak., N of Bismarck. Pop. 32,843.
Minsk (mĭnsk). City of W European USSR, SW of Moscow. Pop. 1,215,-000.
Min·ya (mĭn′yə), **Al.** City of N central Egypt. Pop. 122,000.
Minya Kon·ka (kŏng′kə). Peak, 24,900 ft (7,595 km), of central China, in the Himalayas.
Mi·que·lon (mĭk′ə-lŏn′, mĕk-lôɴ′). French island off S Nfld., Canada.
Mir·a·mar (mîr′ə-mär′). City of SE Fla., S of Fort Lauderdale. Pop. 32,813.
Mish·a·wa·ka (mĭsh′ə-wô′kə). City of N. Ind., near South Bend. Pop. 40,224.
Mis·kolc (mĭsh′kōlts). City of NE Hungary, NW of Budapest. Pop. 203,000.
Mis·sion (mĭsh′ən). **1.** Village of SW B.C., Canada, E of Vancouver. Pop. 10,220. **2.** City of S Tex., WNW of Brownsville. Pop. 22,589.
Mis·sion·ar·y Ridge (mĭsh′ə-nĕr′ē). Mountain, in SE Tenn. and NW Ga.; site of Civil War battle (1863).
Mis·sis·sau·ga (mĭs′ə-sô′gə). Town of S Ont., Canada., SW of Toronto. Pop. 156,070.
Mis·sis·sip·pi (mĭs′ĭ-sĭp′ē). **1.** River of central U.S., flowing 2,350 mi (3,780 km) to the Gulf of Mexico. **2. Sound.** Arm of the Gulf of Mexico in S La. and S Ala. **3.** State of S U.S. Cap. Jackson. Pop. 2,520,638. **—Mis′sis·sip′pi·an** *adj. & n.*
Mis·so·lon·ghi (mĭs′ə-lông′gē). Mesolóngion.
Mis·sou·la (mĭ-zōō′lə). City of W Mont., WNW of Helena. Pop. 33,388.
Mis·sou·ri (mĭ-zŏŏr′ē, -zŏŏr′ə). **1.** River of the U.S., rising in W Mont. and flowing c. 2,565 mi (4,127 km) to the Mississippi N of St. Louis, Mo. **2.** State of central U.S. Cap. Jefferson City. Pop. 4,917,444. **—Mis·sou′ri·an** *adj. & n.*
Missouri City. City of SE Tex., SW of Houston. Pop. 24,533.
Mis·tas·si·ni (mĭs′tə-sē′nē). **1.** Lake of central Que., draining into James Bay. **2.** River of central Que., flowing c. 200 mi (321 km) into Lake St. John.
Mis·ti (mēs′tē), **El.** Dormant volcano 19,098 ft (5,825 m), of S Peru, near Arequipa.
Mitch·ell (mĭch′əl). **1. Mount.** Peak, 6,684 ft (2,039 m), of W.N.C., in the Appalachians. **2.** City of SE S.Dak., WNW of Sioux Falls. Pop. 13,916.
Mi·ya·za·ki (mē-yä′zä-kē). City of SE Kyushu, Japan. Pop. 240,000.
Mo·ab (mō′ăb). Ancient kingdom of Jordan, E of the Dead Sea. **—Mo′a·bite′** (mō′ə-bīt′) *adj. & n.*
Mo·ber·ly (mō′bər-lē). City of N central Mo., N of Columbia. Pop. 13,418.
Mo·bile (mō-bēl′). City of SW Ala., on **Mobile Bay,** an inlet of the Gulf of Mexico. Pop. 200,452.
Mo·de·na (mōd′n-ə, mô′dā-nä). City of N Italy, WNW of Bologna. Pop. 178,530.
Mo·des·to (mō-dĕs′tō). City of central Calif., SE of Stockton. Pop. 106,105.
Moe·sia (mē′shə, shē-ə). Ancient region of SE Europe, S of the Danube.

Mog·a·dish·u (mŏg'ə-dĭsh'o͞o, mô'-gä-dē'sho͞o). Cap. of Somalia, on the Indian Ocean. Pop. 230,000.
Mo·gi·lev (mō'gĭ-lĕf', mŏg'ĭ-, mə-gĭ-lyôf'). City of W European USSR, on the Dnieper. Pop. 264,000.
Mo·gol·lon Plateau (mə-gē-ōn', mō'gə-yōn'). Tableland of E central Ariz.
Mo·hács (mō'-häch'). City of S Hungary, on the Danube; site of Ottoman Turk victory (1526) over the Hungarians.
Mo·hawk (mō'hôk'). River of E central N.Y., flowing c. 140 mi (225 km) into the Hudson.
Mo·hen·jo-Da·ro (mō-hĕn'jō-dä'rō). Ruined prehistoric city of Pakistan, in the Indus valley NE of Karachi.
Mo·ja·ve also **Mo·ha·ve** (mō-hä'vē). **1.** River, c. 100 mi (160 km), of S Calif. **2.** Desert, c. 15,000 sq mi (38,850 sq km), of S Calif., SE of the Sierra Nevada.
Mok·po (mŏk'pō', môk'-). City of SW South Korea. Pop. 162,322.
Mol·da·vi·a (mŏl-dā'vē-ə, -vyə). **1.** Historical region of E Rumania. **2.** Region of SW European USSR. —**Mol·da'vi·an** *adj. & n.*
Mo·line (mō-lēn'). City of NW Ill., near Davenport. Pop. 45,709.
Mo·li·se (mô'lē-zā'). Region of S central Italy, on the Adriatic.
Mo·lo·kai (mō'lō-kī', mŏl'ə-). Island of Hawaii, between Oahu and Maui.
Mo·lo·po (mə-lō'pō). Intermittent river of South Africa, flowing c. 600 mi (965 km) W to the Orange.
Mo·luc·cas (mə-lŭk'əz, mō-). Islands of E Indonesia, between Celebes and New Guinea. —**Mo·luc'can** *adj. & n.*
Mom·ba·sa (mŏm-băs'ə, -bä'sä). City of SE Kenya, mainly on **Mombasa Is.**, in the Indian Ocean. Pop. 301,000.
Mon·a·co (mŏn'ə-kō', mə-nä'kō). Principality on the Mediterranean, an enclave in SE France. Cap. Monaco or Monaco-Ville. Pop. 30,000. —**Mon'a·can** *adj. & n.*

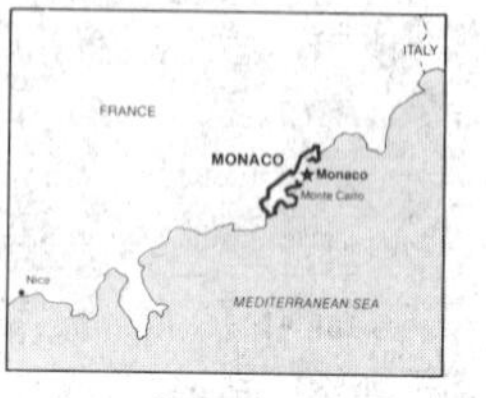

Monaco

Mo·nad·nock (mə-năd'nŏk). Mountain, 3,165 ft (965 m), of SW N.H.
Mo·na Passage (mō'nə). Strait between Puerto Rico and the Dominican Republic, connecting the Atlantic and the Caribbean.
Mön·chen Glad·bach (mœn'KHən glät'bäKH). City of W West Germany, W of Düsseldorf. Pop. 263,356.
Monc·ton (mŭngk'tən). City of SE N.B., Canada, NE of Saint John. Pop. 55,934.
Mo·nes·sen (mə-nĕs'ən). City of SW Pa., S of Pittsburgh. Pop. 11,928.
Mon·go·li·a (mŏng-gō'lē-ə, mŏn-). **1.** Region of E central Asia. **2.** Country of N central Asia, between the USSR and China. Cap. Ulan Bator. Pop. 1,625,000. —**Mon·go'li·an** *adj. & n.*

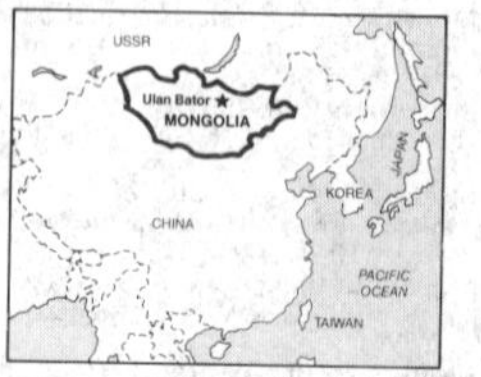

Mongolia

Mon·mouth (mŏn'məth). City of W Ill., WSW of Galesburg. Pop. 10,706.
Mo·non·ga·he·la (mə-nŏn'gə-hē'lə, -nŏng'-). River, 128 mi (206 km), of N W.Va. and SW Pa.
Mon·roe (mən-rō'). **1.** Town of SW Conn., near Bridgeport. Pop. 14,010. **2.** City of N central La., E of Shreveport. Pop. 57,597. **3.** City of SE Mich., SW of Detroit. Pop. 23,531. **4.** City of S N.C., SE of Charlotte. Pop. 12,639. **5.** City of S Wis., SSW of Madison. Pop. 10,027.
Mon·roe·ville (mən-rō'vĭl'). Borough of SW Pa., near Pittsburgh. Pop. 30,977.
Mon·ro·vi·a (mən-rō'vē-ə). **1.** Cap. of Liberia, in the NW part. Pop. 229,300. **2.** City of S Calif., near Los Angeles. Pop. 30,531.
Mons (mōNs). City of SW Belgium, near the French border. Pop. 93,332.
Mon·tan·a (mŏn-tăn'ə). State of the NW U.S. Cap. Helena. Pop. 786,690. —**Mon·tan'an** *adj. & n.*
Mon·tau·ban (môN'-tō-bäN'). City of SW France, N of Toulouse. Pop. 45,895.
Mon·tauk Point (mŏn'tôk'). E extremity of Long Is., in SE N.Y.
Mont Blanc (mônt blängk, môN bläN'). Mountain, 15,771 ft (4,810 m), in the Alps on the French-Italian border.
Mont·clair (mŏnt-klâr'). **1.** City of SE Calif., NE of Pomona. Pop. 22,628. **2.** Town of NE N.J., near Newark. Pop. 38,321.
Mon·te Al·bán (môn'tē äl-bän'). Ruined Zapotec city of SW Mexico.
Mon·te·bel·lo (mŏn'tə-bĕl'ō). City of S Calif., near Los Angeles. Pop. 52,929.
Mon·te Car·lo (mŏn'tē kär'lō). Town of Monaco, on the Riviera. Pop. 9,948.
Mon·te·go Bay (mŏn-tē'gō). Town of NW Jamaica, on the Caribbean. Pop. 43,754.
Mon·te·ne·gro (mŏn'tə-nē'grō). Region of SW Yugoslavia, on the Adriatic.
Mon·te·rey (mŏn'tə-rā'). City of W Calif., S of San Francisco, on **Monterey Bay**, an inlet of the Pacific. Pop. 27,558.
Monterey Park. City of S Calif., near Los Angeles. Pop. 54,338.
Mon·ter·rey (mŏn'tə-rā', môn-tĕ-rā'). City of NE Mexico. Pop. 1,006,200.
Mon·te·vi·de·o (mŏn'tə-vĭ-dā'ō, -vĭd'ē-ō'). Cap. of Uruguay, in the S on the Río de la Plata. Pop. 1,229,700.
Mont·fer·rat (mŏnt-fə-rät', -răt'). Region of NW Italy, S of the Po.
Mont·gom·er·y (mŏnt-gŭm'ə-rē, -gŭm'rē). **1.** Cap. of Ala., in the central part. Pop. 176,860. **2.** City of SW Ohio, near Cincinnati. Pop. 10,088.
Mon·ti·cel·lo (mŏn'tĭ-sĕl'ō). Estate of central Va., home of Thomas Jefferson.
Mont·lu·çon (môN-lü-sôN'). City of central France. Pop. 56,468.
Mont·mag·ny (môN-mä-nyē'). Town of SE Que., Canada, ENE of Quebec city. Pop. 12,432.
Mont·mar·tre (môN-mär'trə). Hill and district of N Paris, France.
Mont·mo·ren·cy Falls (mŏnt'-mə-rĕn'sē). Waterfall, 270 ft (82 m), in S Que., Canada, N of Quebec city, in the **Montmorency River**, flowing 60 mi (97 km) to the St. Lawrence.
Mont·par·nasse (môN-pär-näs'). District of S Paris, France, on the left bank of the Seine.
Mont·pel·ier (mŏnt-pēl'yər). Cap of Vt., in the central part. Pop. 8,241.
Mont·pel·lier (môN-pĕ-lyā'). City of S France, WNW of Marseilles. Pop. 191,354.
Mon·tre·al (mŏn'trē-ôl') or **Mont·ré·al** (môN'rā-äl'). City of S Que., on **Montreal Is.** in the St. Lawrence. Pop. 1,080,546. —**Mon'tre·al'er** *n.*
Montreal North (nôrth) or **Mont·ré·al-Nord** (môN'rā-äl'-nôr). Town of S Que., Canada, near Montreal. Pop. 89,139.
Mon·treuil (môN-trœ'yə). Town of N central France, near Paris. Pop. 96,587.
Mon·treux (môN-trœ'). Resort area of W Switzerland, on Lake Geneva.
Mont Roy·al (môN rwä-yäl'). *French.* Mount Royal.
Mont-Saint-Mi·chel (môN-săN-mē-shĕl'). Small island of NW France, off the coast of Brittany.
Mont·ser·rat (mŏnt'sə-răt'). Island, one of the Leewards, in the British West Indies NW of Guadaloupe.
Mont·ville (mŏnt'vĭl'). Town of SE Conn., near New London. Pop. 16,455.
Mon·za (mŏn'zə, mōn'tsä). City of N Italy, SE of Milan. Pop. 120,574.
Moore (mo͝or, môr). City of central Okla., near Oklahoma City. Pop. 35,063.
Moor·head (mo͝or'hĕd', môr'-). City of NW Minn., near Fargo., N.Dak. Pop. 29,998.
Moose·head (mo͞os'hĕd'). Lake, c. 120 sq mi (311 sq km), of W central Me., N of Augusta.
Moose·jaw (mo͞os'jô). City of central Sask., Canada, W of Regina. Pop. 32,581.
Mo·rad·a·bad (mə-rä'də-bäd'). City of N central India. Pop. 258,590.
Mor·a·ga (mô-rä'gə). City of W Calif., E of Oakland. Pop. 15.014.
Mo·ra·va (mô'rä-vä). **1.** River of N Czechoslovakia, flowing c. 240 mi (386 km) S to the Danube. **2.** River of E Yugoslavia, flowing c. 130 mi (209 km) N to the Danube.
Mo·ra·vi·a (mə-rā'vē-ə, -rä'-, mō-). Region of central Czechoslovakia. —**Mo·ra'vi·an** *adj. & n.*
Moravian Gate (gāt) or **Gap** (găp). Mountain pass of central Europe between the Sudeten and Carpathian Mts.
Mor·ay Firth (mûr'ē). Inlet of the North Sea in NE Scotland.
Mord·vin·i·a (môrd-vĭn'ē-ə) also **Mor·do·vin·i·a** (môr-dō'vĭn-). Region of E European USSR.
Mo·reau (mōr'ō, mô'rō). River of NW S.Dak., flowing 250 mi (402 km) E to the Missouri.
More·cambe and Hey·sham (môr'-kəm; hā'shəm). Borough of NW England, on **Morecambe Bay**, an inlet of the Irish Sea. Pop. 42,010.
Mo·re·lia (mô-rē'lyä). City of SW Mexico, WNW of Mexico City. Pop. 199,100.
More·ton Bay (môr'tn). Inlet of the Pacific in E Australia, the entrance to Brisbane port.
Mor·gan City (môr'gən). City of S La., WSW of New Orleans. Pop. 16,114.
Morgan Hill. City of W Calif., SE of San Jose. Pop. 17,060.
Mor·gan·ton (môr'gən-tən). City of W N.C., ENE of Asheville. Pop. 13,763.
Mor·gan·town (môr'gən-toun'). City of N W.Va., near the Pa. border. Pop. 27,605.
Mo·ri·o·ka (mô'rē-ô'kä). City of N Honshu, Japan. Pop. 220,051.
Mo·roc·co (mə-rŏk'ō). Kingdom of NW Africa, on the Mediterranean and the Atlantic. Cap. Rabat. Pop. 20,050,000. —**Mo·roc'can** *adj. & n.*

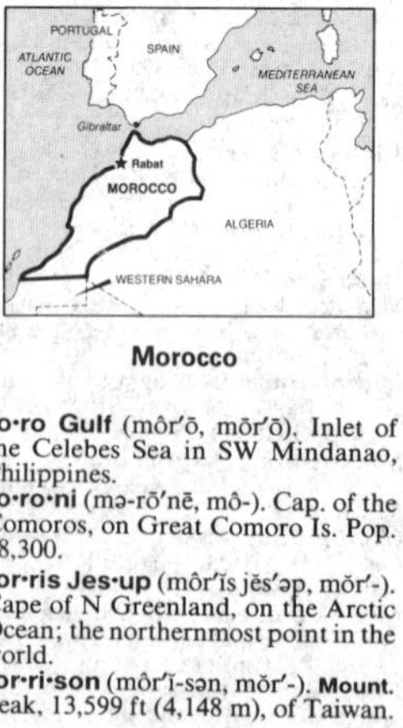

Morocco

Mo·ro Gulf (môr'ō, mōr'ō). Inlet of the Celebes Sea in SW Mindanao, Philippines.
Mo·ro·ni (mə-rō'nē, mô-). Cap. of the Comoros, on Great Comoro Is. Pop. 18,300.
Mor·ris Jes·up (môr'ĭs jĕs'əp, mŏr'-). Cape of N Greenland, on the Arctic Ocean; the northernmost point in the world.
Mor·ri·son (môr'ĭ-sən, mŏr'-). **Mount.** Peak, 13,599 ft (4,148 m), of Taiwan.
Mor·ris·town (môr'ĭs-toun', mŏr'-). **1.** Town of N N.J., WNW of Newark. Pop. 16,614. **2.** City of NE Tenn., ENE of Knoxville. Pop. 19,683.
Mor·ton (môr'tn). Village of central Ill., SE of Peoria. Pop. 14,178.
Morton Grove. Village of NE Ill., near Chicago. Pop. 23,747.
Mos·cow (mŏs'kou, -kō). **1.** Cap. of the USSR, in the W central European part, on the **Moscow R.**, flowing c. 310 mi (499 km) E to the Oka. Pop. 8,011,000. **2.** City of NW Idaho, on the Wash. border. Pop. 16,513.
Mo·selle (mō-zĕl'). River of NE France and W West Germany, flowing 320 mi (515 km) to the Rhine.
Mos·es Lake (mō'zĭz). City of E central Wash., SE of Euphrata. Pop. 10,629.
Mos·kva (mŏsk-vä'). *Russian.* Moscow.
Mos·qui·to Coast (mə-skē'tō). Region of E Nicaragua and NE Honduras.
Moss Point (môs). City of SE Miss., E of Gulfport. Pop. 18,998.
Most (môst). City of NW Czechoslovakia, near the East German border. Pop. 59,909.
Mos·ta·ga·nem (mə-stăg'ə-nĕm', môs-tä-gä-nĕm'). City of NW Algeria, on the Mediterranean. Pop. 101,780.
Mo·sul (mō-so͞ol', mō'so͞ol). City of N Iraq, on the Tigris. Pop. 293,100.
Mo·ta·gua (mô-tä'gwä). River, c. 250 mi (402 km), of S central Guatemala.
Moth·er·well and Wish·aw (mŭth'-ər-wĕl', -wəl; wĭsh'ô). Burgh of S central Scotland, SE of Glasgow. Pop. 74,184.
Moul·mein (mo͞ol-mān', mōl-). City of S Burma, on the Gulf of Martaban. Pop. 173,000.
Moul·trie (mōl'trē). City of SW Ga., SE of Albany. Pop. 15,708.
Mounds View (moundz' vyo͞o'). City of E Minn., near Minneapolis. Pop. 12,593.
Mounds·ville (moundz'vĭl'). City of NW W.Va., in the N Panhandle. Pop. 12,419.
Moun·tain Brook (moun'tən). City of N central Ala., near Birmingham. Pop. 17,400.
Mountain View. City of W Calif., NW of San Jose. Pop. 58,655.
Mount Ath·os (mount ăth'ŏs, ā'thŏs, ā'thôs). See **Athos.**
Mount Clem·ens (klĕm'ənz). City of SE Mich., NNE of Detroit. Pop. 18,806.
Mount Des·ert (dĕz'ərt). Island, c. 100 sq mi (260 sq km), in the Atlantic off the S coast of Me.
Mount·lake Ter·race (mount'lāk' tĕr'əs). City of NW Wash., S of Everett. Pop. 16,534.
Mount Mc·Kin·ley National Park (mĭ-kĭn'lē). Scenic area in the Alaska range, S central Alas.
Mount Pleas·ant (plĕz'ənt). **1.** City of central Mich., WNW of Saginaw. Pop. 23,746. **2.** Town of SE S.C., E of Charleston. Pop. 13,838. **3.** City of E Tex., SW of Texarkana. Pop. 11,003.
Mount Pros·pect (prŏs'pĕkt). Village of NE Ill., near Chicago. Pop. 52,634.
Mount Rai·nier National Park (rā-nîr', rə-). Scenic area in the Cascade range, W central Wash.
Mount Roy·al (roi'əl). Town of S Que., Canada, near Montreal. Pop. 21,561.
Mount Rush·more National Memorial (rŭsh'môr', -mōr'). Mountain in the Black Hills, SW S.Dak., with carved portraits of Washington, Jefferson, Lincoln, and Theodore Roosevelt.
Mount Ver·non (vûr'nən). **1.** Estate of NE Va., on the Potomac near Washington, D.C., home of George Washington. **2.** City of S central Ill., SE of East St. Louis. Pop. 16,995. **3.** City of SE N.Y., near the Bronx. Pop. 66,713. **4.** City of central Ohio, NE of Columbus. Pop. 14,380. **5.** City of NW Wash., SSE of Bellingham. Pop. 13,009.
Mourne (môrn). Mountains of SE Northern Ireland, rising to 2,796 ft (853 m).

Mo·zam·bique (mō′zəm-bēk′, -zăm-, -zäm-). **1.** Arm of the Indian Ocean between Madagascar and Mozambique. **2.** Country of SE Africa. Cap. Maputo. Pop. 10,460,000. **—Mo′zam·bi′can** *adj. & n.*

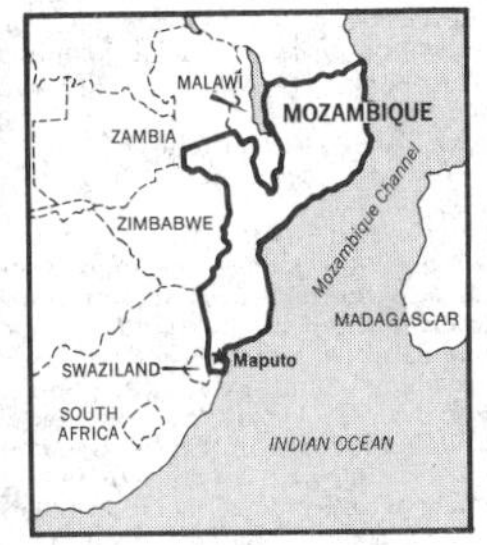

Mozambique

Mu·dan·jiang also **Mu·tan·chiang** (mōō′dän′jyäng′). City of NE China. Pop. 400,000.

Muir Woods National Monument (myŏŏr). Area of W Calif., N of San Francisco, with grove of redwood trees.

Mu·kal·la (mōō-kăl′ə, -käl′ə). Town of Southern Yemen, on the Gulf of Aden. Pop. 65,000.

Muk·den (mŏŏk′dən, -dĕn′, mōōk′-). Shenyang.

Mul·ha·cén (mōō′lä-*th*ĕn′). Mountain, 11,424 ft (3,484 m), of S Spain, in the Sierra Nevada.

Mül·heim (mŏŏl′hīm, myŏŏl′-, mül′-). City of W West Germany, on the Ruhr R. Pop. 190,689.

Mul·house (mü-lōōz′). City of E France, NW of Basel. Pop. 117,013.

Mull (mŭl). Island, one of the Inner Hebrides, of NW Scotland.

Mul·tan (mōōl-tän′). City of E central Pakistan, SW of Lahore. Pop. (metro. area) 542,195.

Mult·no·mah Falls (mŭlt-nō′mə). Waterfall, 620 ft (189 m), in a tributary of the Columbia in NW Ore., E of Portland.

Mün·chen (mün′KHən). *German.* Munich.

Mun·cie (mŭn′sē). City of E Ind., NE of Indianapolis. Pop. 77,216.

Mun·de·lein (mŭn′də-līn′). Village of NE Ill., SW of Waukegan. Pop. 17,053.

Mun·hall (mŭn′hôl′). Borough of SW Pa., near Pittsburgh. Pop. 14,532.

Mu·nich (myōō′nĭk). City of S West Germany, near the Bavarian Alps. Pop. 1,293,590.

Mun·ster (mŭn′stər). **1.** Province and ancient kingdom of SW Ireland. **2.** Town of NW Ind., on the Ill. border. Pop. 20,671.

Mün·ster (mōōn′stər, mŭn′-, mĭn′-, mün′-). City of W West Germany, on the Dortmund-Ems Canal. Pop. 262,567.

Mur (mŏŏr) also **Mu·ra** (mōō′rə). River, c. 300 mi (483 km), of central Austria and NW Yugoslavia.

Mu·rat (mōō-rät′). River of E Turkey, flowing 380 mi (611 km) to the Euphrates.

Mur·chi·son (mûr′chĭ-sən). **1.** Waterfall in the Victoria Nile, NW Uganda, above Lake Albert. **2.** Intermittent river of W Australia, flowing 440 mi (708 km) SW to the Indian Ocean.

Mur·cia (mûr′shə, -shē-ə, mŏŏr′-). **1.** Region and former Moorish kingdom of SE Spain, on the Mediterranean. **2.** City of SE Spain, NNW of Cartagena. Pop. 172,000.

Mu·re·şul (mōō′rĕ-shōōl) also **Mu·res** (-rĕsh′). River, c. 470 mi (756 km), of central Rumania and S Hungary.

Mur·frees·bor·o (mûr′frēz-bûr′ō). City of central Tenn., SW of Nashville. Pop. 32,845.

Mur·gab (mŏŏr-gäb′). River, 530 mi (853 km), of NE Afghanistan and S USSR.

Mur·mansk (mŏŏr-mänsk′, -mănsk′). City of NW European USSR, on a gulf of Barents Sea. Pop. 369,000.

Mu·rom (mōō′rəm). City of W central European USSR, on the Oka. Pop. 111,000.

Mu·ro·ran (mōō-rô′rän). City of SW Hokkaido, Japan. Pop. 158,715.

Mur·ray (mûr′ē, mŭr′ē). **1.** River of Australia, rising in the Australian Alps and flowing 1,609 mi (2,589 km) W to the Indian Ocean S of Adelaide. **2.** City of SW Ky., near the Tenn. border. Pop. 14,248. **3.** City of N Utah, near Salt Lake City. Pop. 25,750.

Mur·rum·bidg·ee (mûr′əm-bĭj′ē). River of SE Australia, flowing c. 1,050 mi (1,689 km) W to the Murray.

Mur·rys·ville (mûr′ēz-vĭl′). Borough of SW Pa., near Pittsburgh. Pop. 16,036.

Mu·sa·shi·no (mōō-sä′shē-nô). City of E central Honshu, Japan, near Tokyo. Pop. 139,204.

Mus·cat (mŭs′kăt′, -kət, mŭs-kăt′). Cap. of Oman, on the Gulf of Oman. Pop. 15,000.

Mus·ca·tine (mŭs′kə-tēn′). City of SE Iowa, WSW of Davenport. Pop. 23,467.

Mus·cle Shoals (mŭs′əl shōlz′). City of NW Ala., on the Tennessee R. Pop. 8,911.

Mus·co·vy (mŭs′kə-vē). **1.** Principality of Moscow (12th–16th cent.). **2.** Russia. **—Mus′co·vite′** *adj. & n.*

Mu·shin (mōō′shĭn′). City of SW Nigeria, near Lagos. Pop. 176,000.

Mu·si (mōō′sē). River, c. 325 mi (523 km), of S Sumatra, Indonesia.

Mus·ke·go (mŭs-kē′gō). City of SE Wis., SW of Milwaukee. Pop. 15,277.

Mus·ke·gon (mŭ-skē′gən). **1.** River of W central Mich., flowing 227 mi (365 km) SW to Lake Michigan. **2.** City of SW Mich., NW of Grand Rapids. Pop. 40,823.

Muskegon Heights. City of SW Mich., near Muskegon. Pop. 14,611.

Mus·king·um (mə-skĭng′əm). River of E Ohio, flowing 111 mi (179 km) SSE to the Ohio.

Mus·ko·gee (mŭs-kō′gē). City of E Okla., SE of Tulsa. Pop. 40,011.

Mus·sel·shell (mŭs′əl-shĕl′). River of central Mont., flowing c. 300 mi (483 km) E and N to the Missouri R.

Mu·tan·chiang (mōō′dän′jyäng′). Mudanjiang.

Mut·tra (mŭ′trə). Mathura.

Muz·tagh (mōōs-tä′). Mountain, 24,757 ft (7,551 m), in W China, near the USSR border.

Mwe·ru (mwā′rōō). Lake, c. 70 mi (113 km) long, in central Africa, on the Zaire-Zambia border.

Myc·a·le (mĭk′ə-lē). Promontory of W Turkey; site of Greek defeat of the Persian fleet (479 B.C.).

My·ce·nae (mī-sē′nē). Ancient Greek city, in the NE Peloponnesus.

Myk·o·nos (mĭk′ə-nŏs′, mē′kô-nôs). Greek island, one of the Cyclades, in the Aegean.

My·ra (mī′rə). Ancient Lycian city of S Asia Minor.

Myr·tle Beach (mûr′tl). City of E S.C., on the Atlantic. Pop. 18,758.

My·si·a (mĭsh′ē-ə). Ancient region of NW Asia Minor. **—My′si·an** *adj. & n.*

My·sore (mī-sôr′, -sōr′). City of S India. Pop. 263,131.

N

Nab·a·tae·a (năb′ə-tē′ə). Ancient kingdom of Arabia, in present-day Jordan. **—Nab·a·tae′an** *adj. & n.*

Na·blus (nä-blōōs′, năb′ləs, nä′bləs). City of W Jordan, N of Jerusalem. Pop. 64,000.

Nack·a (näk′kä). City of E Sweden, on the Baltic near Stockholm. Pop. 56,825.

Nac·og·do·ches (năk′ə-dō′chĭz, -chĭs). City of E Tex., E of Waco. Pop. 27,149.

Na·fud (nä-fōōd′) or **Ne·fud** (nĕ-). Desert area of NW Saudi Arabia.

Na·ga (nä′gə) or **Na·ga·land** (-lănd′). Hill region on the India-Burma border.

Na·go·no (nä-gä′nô). City of central Honshu, Japan, NW of Tokyo. Pop. 244,300.

Na·ga·o·ka (nä′gä-ô′kä, nä-gä′ô-kä′). City of central Honshu, Japan, S of Niigata. Pop. 178,201.

Na·ga·sa·ki (nä′gə-sä′kē, năg′ə-săk′-ē). City of W Kyushu, Japan, on **Nagasaki Bay,** an inlet of the East China Sea. Pop. 447,091.

Na·go·ya (nä-goi′ä, nä′gô-yä′). City of central Honshu, Japan, at the head of Ise Bay. Pop. 2,087,884.

Nag·pur (näg′pŏŏr′, năg-pŏŏr′). City of central India, NE of Bombay. Pop. 866,076.

Nagy·vá·rad (nŏd′yə-vä′rŏd, nŏj′-). *Hungarian.* Oradea.

Na·ha (nä′hä). City of SW Okinawa, Japan, on the East China Sea. Pop. 295,801.

Na·huel Hua·pí (nä-wĕl′ wä-pē′). Lake of SW Argentina, near the Chilean border.

Nai·ro·bi (nī-rō′bē). Cap. of Kenya, in the S central part. Pop. 835,000.

Najd (näjd). Nejd.

Na·khod·ka (nə-KHôt′kə). City of Far Eastern USSR, E of Vladivostok on the Sea of Japan. Pop. 136,000.

Nal·chik (näl′chĭk). City of S European USSR, SE of Rostov. Pop. 211,000.

Na·ma·qua·land (nə-mä′kwə-lănd′) or **Na·ma·land** (nä′mä-lănd′). Region of SW Africa, divided by the Orange R. into **Great Namaqualand** in Namibia and **Little Namaqualand** in South Africa.

Nam·hoi (näm′hoi′). Foshan.

Na·mib (nä′mĭb′, nə-mĭb′). Desert of SW Africa, extending c. 800 mi (1,290 km) along the coast of Namibia.

Na·mib·i·a (nə-mĭb′ē-ə). Territory of SW Africa, currently administered by South Africa. Cap. Windhoek. Pop. 1,035,000. **—Na·mib′i·an** *adj. & n.*

Nam·oi (năm′oi′). River, 526 mi (846.3 km), of SE Australia.

Nam·pa (năm′pə). City of SW Idaho, WSW of Boise. Pop. 25,112.

Nam·po (näm′pō). City of W North Korea, on Korea Bay SW of Pyongyang. Pop. 140,000.

Nam·pu·la (năm-pōō′lə). City of NE Mozambique. Pop. 120,188.

Na·mu Hu (nä′mōō′ hōō′) or **Nam Tso** (näm′ tsô′). Salt lake, 950 sq mi (2,460.5 sq km), of central Tibet, at an altitude of 15,180 ft (4,629.9 m).

Na·mur (nă-mŏŏr′, -mür′). City of S central Belgium, on the Meuse S of Brussels. Pop. 100,712.

Nan (nän). River of W Thailand, flowing 350 mi (543.1 km) to the Ping to form the Chao Phraya.

Na·nai·mo (nə-nī′mō). City of SW B.C., Canada, on Vancouver Is. and the Strait of Georgia. Pop. 40,336.

Nan·chang (nän′chäng′). City of SE China, on the Gan R. Pop. 700,000.

Nan·chong also **Nan·chung** (nän′-chōōng′). City of central China, E of Chengdu. Pop. 225,000.

Nan·cy (năn′sē, näN-sē′). City of NE France, E of Paris. Pop. 107,902.

Nan·da De·vi (nŭn′də dā′vē). Peak, 25,645 ft (7,821.8 m), of N India, in the Himalayas.

Nan·ga Par·bat (nŭng′gə pûr′bət). Peak, 26,660 ft (8,131.3 m), of NW Kashmir, in the Himalayas.

Nan·jing (nän′jĭng′) also **Nan·king** (năn′kĭng′, nän′jĭng′). City of E central China, on the Yangtze NW of Shanghai. Pop. 1,800,000.

Nan Ling (nän′lĭng′). Mountain range of S China, forming a geographic barrier between central and S China.

Nan·ning (nän′nĭng′). City of extreme S China, W of Guangzhou. Pop. 350,000.

Nan·sei Sho·to (nän′sā′ shô′tô′). *Japanese.* Ryukyu Is.

Nan Shan (nän′ shän′). **1.** Mountain range of central China, running NW to SE and rising to c. 20,000 ft (6,100 m). **2.** Nan Ling.

Nan·terre (näN-tĕr′). City of N central France, on the Seine. Pop. 95,032.

Nantes (nänts, näNt). City of W France, on the Loire. Pop. 256,693.

Nan·ti·coke (năn′tĭ-kōk′). **1.** City of SE Ont., Canada, on Lake Erie S of Brantford. Pop. 19,104. **2.** City of NE central Pa., near Wilkes-Barre. Pop. 13,044.

Nan·tong also **Nan·tung** (nän′tōōng′). City of E central China, on the N side of the Yangtze estuary. Pop. 275,000.

Nan·tuck·et (năn-tŭk′ĭt). Island of SE Mass., S of Cape Cod, from which it is separated by **Nantucket Sound,** an arm of the Atlantic.

Nap·a (năp′ə). City of W Calif., N of Oakland. Pop. 50,879.

Na·pa·ta (nə-pā′tə). Ancient city of Nubia, on the Nile.

Na·per·ville (nā′pər-vĭl′). City of NE Ill., near Chicago. Pop. 42,330.

Na·pi·er (nā′pē-ər). City of E central North Is., New Zealand. Pop. 47,900.

Na·ples (nā′pəlz). **1.** City of S central Italy, on the **Bay of Naples,** an arm of the Tyrrhenian Sea. Pop. 1,223,228. **2.** City of SW Fla., on the Gulf of Mexico S of Fort Myers. Pop. 17,581. **—Ne′a·pol′i·tan** (nē′ə-pŏl′ĭ-tən) *adj. & n.*

Na·po (nä′pô). River of N Ecuador and N Peru, flowing 550 mi (884.9 km) to the Amazon.

Na·po·li (nä′pō-lē). *Italian.* Naples.

Na·ra (nä′rä, nä-rä′). City of S Honshu, Japan, near Osaka. Pop. 297,893.

Na·ra·shi·no (nä′rä-shē′nô). City of E central Honshu, Japan, near Tokyo. Pop. 120,257.

Na·ra·yan·ganj (nä-rä′yən-gŭnj). City of E central Bangladesh, SSE of Dacca. Pop. 201,450.

Nar·ba·da (nər-bŭd′ə). River of central India, flowing c. 775 mi (1,245 km) to the Gulf of Cambay.

Nar·bonne (när-bŏn′, -bôn′). City of S France, near the Mediterranean coast. Pop. 39,342.

Na·rev (nä′rəf, nə-ryôf′) or **Na·rew** (nä′rĕf). River, c. 275 mi (445 km), of W European USSR and NE Poland.

Nar·ra·gan·sett (năr′ə-găn′sĭt). Town of S R.I., on **Narragansett Bay,** a deep inlet of the Atlantic, SW of Newport. Pop. 12,088.

Nar·rows (năr′ōz), **The.** Strait of SE N.Y., between Brooklyn and Staten Is., New York City, and connecting Upper and Lower New York bays.

Nar·vik (när′vĭk). City of N Norway, an ice-free port on a fjord opposite Lofoten Is. Pop. 19,202.

Na·ryn (nä-rĭn′). River of S Central Asian USSR, flowing c. 450 mi (725 km) from the Tian Shan to the Syr Darya.

Nash·u·a (năsh′ōō-ə, -ə-wä′). City of S N.H., S of Manchester. Pop. 67,865.

Nash·ville (năsh′vĭl′). Cap. of Tenn., in the central part NW of Chattanooga. Pop. 455,651.

Nass (năs). River of W B.C., Canada, flowing 236 mi (380 km) to the Pacific.

Nas·sau (năs′ô′). **1.** (*also* nä′sou′). Former duchy of central West Germany, N and E of the Main and Rhine rivers. **2.** Cap. of the Bahamas, a port on New Providence. Metro. area pop. 101,503.

Nas·ser (nä′sər, năs′ər). Lake, c. 1,550 sq mi (4,015 sq km), of SE Egypt and N Sudan, formed by the Aswan High Dam on the Nile R.

Na·tal (nə-täl′, -tôl′, -tăl′). City of NE Brazil, on the Atlantic N of Recife. Pop. 343,679.

Na·tash·kwan (nə-tăsh′kwən, -kwŏn′). River of E Canada, flowing 241 mi (387.8 km) from S Labrador across E Que. to the Gulf of St. Lawrence.

Natch·ez (năch′ĭz). City of SW Miss., on the Mississippi SSW of Vicksburg. Pop. 22,015.

Natch·i·toches (năk′ĭ-tŏsh′). City of NW central La., SE of Shreveport. Pop. 16,664.

Na·tick (nā′tĭk). Town of E Mass., WSW of Boston. Pop. 29,461.

Na·tion·al City (năsh′ə-nəl). City of S Calif., near San Diego. Pop. 48,772.

Nau·cra·tis (nô′krə-tĭs). Ancient Egyptian city, on the Nile SE of Alexandria.

Nau·ga·tuck (nô′gə-tŭk′). Town of SW Conn., S of Waterbury. Pop. 26,456.

Na·u·ru (nä-o͞o′ro͞o). Atoll and republic of the central Pacific, just S of the equator and W of Kiribati. Cap. Yaren. Pop. 7,100.

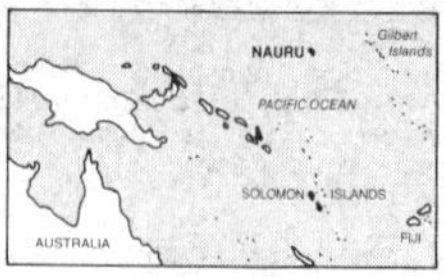

Nauru

Nav·a·jo (năv′ə-hō′, nä′və-). Mountain, 10,416 ft (3,176.8 m), of S Utah.
Na·va·na·gar (nä-və-nŭg′ər). Jamnagar.
Nav·a·ri·no (nä′vä-rē′nô). Chilean island, S of Tierra del Fuego.
Na·varre (nə-vär′). Former kingdom of SW Europe, extending from N Spain into France.
Nav·a·so·ta (năv′ə-sō′tə). River, c. 130 mi (209.2 km), of E central Tex.
Na·vy Island (nā′vē). Island of S Ont., Canada, in the Niagara R. just above Niagara Falls.
Na·wa (nä′wä). Naha.
Nax·os (năk′sŏs, -səs). Largest island, c. 160 sq mi (415 sq km), of the Cyclades, in the Aegean.
Naz·a·reth (năz′ə-rĭth). Town of N Israel, SE of Haifa. Pop. 40,400.
Naze (nāz), **The.** **1.** Headland of SE England, on the North Sea. **2.** Lindesnes.
Ndja·me·na (ən-jä′mə-nə). Cap. of Chad, on the Shari R. Pop. 241,639.
Ndo·la (ən-dō′lə). City of N central Zambia, near Zaire. Pop. 323,000.
Neagh (nā), **Lough.** Lake, 153 sq mi (396.3 sq km), in central Northern Ireland.
Near (nîr). Islands of SW Alas., in the W Aleutians.
Near East (ēst). **1.** Region that includes nations of the E Mediterranean, the Arabian Peninsula, and sometimes NE Africa. **2.** Formerly, the Balkan Peninsula.
Ne·bras·ka (nə-brăs′kə). State of the central U.S., in the Great Plains. Cap. Lincoln. Pop. 1,570,006. —**Ne·bras′kan** *adj. & n.*
Ne·chak·o (nə-chăk′ō). River, 287 mi (461.8 km), of central B.C., Canada.
Nech·es (nĕch′ĭz, nā′chĭz). River of E Tex., flowing 416 mi (669.3 km) to Sabine Lake.
Neck·ar (nĕk′ər, nĕ′kär′). River of SW West Germany, flowing 228 mi (336.9 km) from the Black Forest to the Rhine.
Ne·der·land (nē′dər-lənd). City of SE Tex., near Beaumont and Port Arthur. Pop. 16,855.
Need·ham (nē′dəm). Town of E Mass., near Boston. Pop. 27,901.
Nee·nah (nē′nə). City of E Wis., on Lake Winnebago NNE of Oshkosh. Pop. 23,272.
Ne·fud (nĕ-fo͝od′). Variant of **Nafud.**
Ne·gev (nĕ′gĕv′) or **Ne·geb** (-gĕb′). Desert region, c. 5,140 sq mi (13,315 sq km), of S Israel.
Ne·gro (nĕ′grô), **Río** or **Rio.** **1.** River of Argentina, flowing c. 400 mi (645 km) to the Atlantic. **2.** (*also* -gro͞o). River flowing c. 1,400 mi (2,555 km) from E Colombia to the Amazon near Manaus, Brazil. **3.** River flowing c. 500 mi (805 km) from S Brazil to the Uruguay R. in central Uruguay.
Ne·gros (nā′grōs, nĕ′grôs). Island, 4,905 sq mi (12,704 sq km), of the Philippines, in the Visayan Is. between Panay and Cebu.
Nei·jiang also **Nei·chiang** (nā′jyäng′). City of central China, SE of Chengdu. Pop. 225,000.
Nejd (nĕjd). Plateau region of central Saudi Arabia.
Nel·son (nĕl′sən). **1.** River of Man., Canada, flowing c. 400 mi (645 km) from Lake Winnipeg to Hudson Bay. **2.** Borough of N England, NNE of Burnley. Pop. 31,220. **3.** City of N South Is., New Zealand, at the head of Tasman Bay. Pop. 33,100.
Nem·an (nĕm′ən). River of W European USSR, flowing c. 580 mi (935 km) to the Baltic.
Ne·me·a (nē′mē-ə). Ancient city of Greece, W of Corinth. —**Ne′me·an** *adj. & n.*
Ne·mu·nas (nyĕ′mo͞o-näs′). *Lithuanian.* Neman.
Nen·jiang also **Nen·chiang** (nŭn′-jyäng′). River, 740 mi (1,190.7 km), of NE China.
Ne·o·sho (nē-ō′shō, -shə). River of SE Kans. and NE Okla., flowing c. 460 mi (740 km) to the Arkansas R.
Ne·pal (nə-pôl′, -päl′, -păl′). Kingdom of central Asia, in the Himalayas between India and Tibet. Cap. Katmandu. Pop. 15,155,000. —**Nep′al·ese′** *adj. & n.*

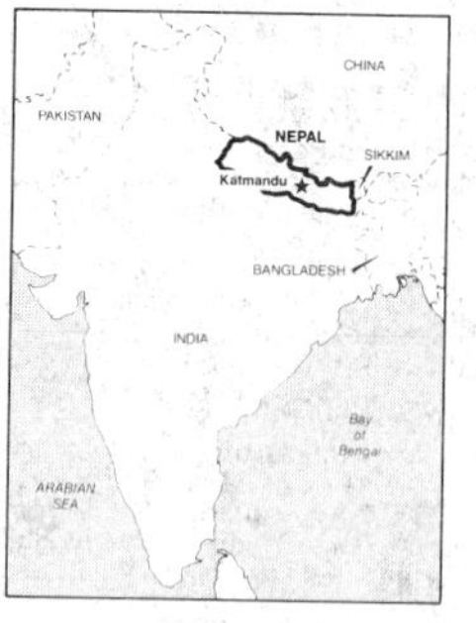

Nepal

Ne·pe·an (nə-pē′ən). City of SE Ont., Canada, E of Kingston. Pop. 82,291.
Ness (nĕs), **Loch.** Lake, 22 mi (35.4 km) long, of N central Scotland.
Ne·tan·ya (nə-tän′yə). City of W central Israel, on the Mediterranean. Pop. 95,900.
Neth·er·lands (nĕ*th*′ər-ləndz). Kingdom of NW Europe, on the North Sea. Constitutional cap. Amsterdam; de facto cap. The Hague. Pop. 14,170,000.

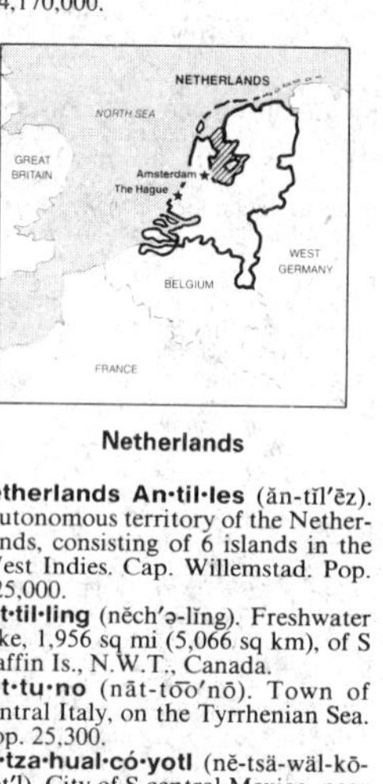

Netherlands

Netherlands An·til·les (ăn-tĭl′ēz). Autonomous territory of the Netherlands, consisting of 6 islands in the West Indies. Cap. Willemstad. Pop. 225,000.
Net·til·ling (nĕch′ə-lĭng). Freshwater lake, 1,956 sq mi (5,066 sq km), of S Baffin Is., N.W.T., Canada.
Net·tu·no (nāt-to͞o′nō). Town of central Italy, on the Tyrrhenian Sea. Pop. 25,300.
Ne·tza·hual·có·yotl (nĕ-tsä-wäl-kō-yōt′l). City of S central Mexico, near Mexico City. Pop. 580,438.
Neu·bran·den·burg (noi-brän′-dən-bo͝ork′). City of N East Germany, S of Greifswald. Pop. 73,258.
Neuil·ly-sur Seine (nœ-yē-sür-sĕn′). City of N central France, near Paris. Pop. 65,983.
Neu·mün·ster (noi-mün′stər). City of N West Germany, SSW of Kiel. Pop. 80,331.
Neun·kir·chen (noin′kîr-KHən). City of W West Germany, NE of Saarbrücken. Pop. 52,216.
Ne·u·quén (nĕ′o͞o-kĕn′). River of W central Argentina, flowing 365 mi (603.3 km) to the Limay to form the Río Negro.
Neuse (no͞os, nyo͞os). River, c. 275 mi (442.5 km), of E N.C.
Neuss (nois). City of W West Germany, near Düsseldorf. Pop. 149,333.
Neus·tri·a (no͞o′strē-ə, nyo͞o′-). W part of the Frankish Merovingian kingdom in the 6th, 7th, and 8th cent., in present-day N France.
Neu·wied (noi′vēt). City of W West Germany, on the Rhine. Pop. 60,461.
Ne·va (nē′və, nyĕ-vä′). River of NW European USSR, flowing 46 mi (74 km) from Lake Ladoga to the Gulf of Finland.
Ne·vad·a (nə-văd′ə, -vä′də). State of the W U.S. Cap. Carson City. Pop. 799,184. —**Ne·vad′an** *aj. & n.*
Ne·vers (nə-vĕr′). City of central France, ESE of Bourges. Pop. 45,480.
Ne·ves (nĕ′vĭsh). Town of SE Brazil, on Guanabara Bay just N of Niterói. Pop. 112,912.
Ne·vis (nē′vĭs). One of the Leeward Is. of the West Indies, in the Caribbean.
New (no͞o, nyo͞o). River of the SE U.S., flowing c. 320 mi (515 km) from the Blue Ridge in NW N.C. to the Kanawha in S central W.Va.
New Al·ba·ny (ôl′bə-nē). City of S Ind., opposite Louisville, Ky. Pop. 37,103.
New Am·ster·dam (ăm′stər-dăm′). Settlement established in 1624 by the Dutch on the S end of Manhattan Is. at the mouth of the Hudson; renamed New York by the British (1664).
New·ark (no͞o′ərk, nyo͞o′-). **1.** City of W Calif., SSE of Oakland. Pop. 32,126. **2.** City of NW Del., WSW of Wilmington. Pop. 25,247. **3.** City of NE N.J., on **Newark Bay,** an inlet of the Atlantic, opposite Jersey City. Pop. 329,248. **4.** Village of W central N.Y., ESE of Rochester. Pop. 10,017. **5.** City of central Ohio, E of Columbus. Pop. 41,200.
New Bed·ford (bĕd′fərd). City of SE Mass., on Buzzards Bay. Pop. 98,478.
New·berg (no͞o′bûrg′, nyo͞o′-). City of NW Ore., SW of Portland. Pop. 10,394.
New Ber·lin (bûr-lĭn′). City of SE Wis., near Milwaukee. Pop. 30,529.
New Bern (bûrn). City of E N.C., SE of Raleigh. Pop. 14,557.
New Braun·fels (broun′fəlz). City of S central Tex., NE of San Antonio. Pop. 22,402.
New Brigh·ton (brīt′n). City of E Minn., near St. Paul. Pop. 23,269.
New Brit·ain (brĭt′n). **1.** Volcanic island, c. 14,600 sq mi (37,815 sq km), of Papua New Guinea, largest of the Bismarck Archipelago. **2.** Town and city of central Conn., SSW of Hartford. Pop. 73,840.
New Bruns·wick (brŭnz′wĭk). **1.** Province of E Canada. Cap. Fredericton. Pop. 677,250. **2.** City of central N.J., SW of Newark. Pop. 41,442.
New·burgh (no͞o′bûrg′, nyo͞o′-). City of SE N.Y., on the Hudson SSW of Poughkeepsie. Pop. 23,438.
New·bur·y·port (no͞o′bə-rē-pôrt′, -pōrt′, nyo͞o′-). City of NE Mass., near the Atlantic ENE of Lawrence. Pop. 15,900.
New Cal·e·do·ni·a (kăl′ĭ-dō′nē-ə, -dōn′yə). French overseas territory in the SW Pacific, including the island of **New Caledonia,** c. 800 mi (1,287.2 km) E of Australia, and several smaller island dependencies. Cap. Nouméa. Pop. 133,233.
New Ca·naan (kā′nən). Town of SW Conn., NNE of Stamford. Pop. 17,931.
New Car·roll·ton (kăr′əl-tən). City of W Md., near Washington, D.C. Pop. 12,632.
New Cas·tile (kăs-tēl′). Region and former kingdom of central Spain.
New·cas·tle (no͞o′kăs′əl, nyo͞o′-). **1.** City of SE Australia, on the Pacific N of Sydney. Pop. 139,400. **2.** Town of S Ont., Canada, on Lake Ontario near Oshawa. Pop. 32,163. **3.** Or **New·cas·tle-un·der-Lyme** (-ŭn′-dər-līm′). Borough of W central England, SSW of Stoke. Pop. 120,700. **4.** Or **New·cas·tle-up·on-Tyne** (-ə-pŏn-tīn′). Borough of NE England, on the Tyne R. opposite Gateshead. Pop. 287,300.
New Cas·tle (kăs′əl). **1.** City of E Ind., S of Muncie. Pop. 20,056. **2.** City of W Pa., NNW of Pittsburgh. Pop. 33,621.
New Del·hi (dĕl′ē). Cap. of India, in the N central part. Pop. 301,801.
New Eng·land (ĭng′glənd). **1.** Mountain range and plateau of SE Australia, part of the Great Dividing Range. **2.** Section of the NE U.S., including Me., N.H., Vt., Mass., Conn., and R.I.
New Fair·field (fâr′fēld′). Town of SW Conn., near the N.Y. border. Pop. 11,260.
New·found·land (no͞o′fən-lənd, -lănd′, nyo͞o′-). Province of E Canada, including the island of **Newfoundland** and nearby islands and the mainland area of Labrador with its adjacent islands. Cap. St. John's. Pop. 557,725. —**New′found·land·er** *n.*
New France (frăns). French colonial territory in North America, including much of SE Canada, the Great Lakes region, and the Mississippi valley.
New Geor·gia (jôr′jə). Chief island of the **New Georgia** group, part of the Solomon Is. in the SW Pacific.
New Glas·gow (glăs′kō, -gō, glăz′-). Town of N N.S., Canada, NE of Halifax. Pop. 10,672.
New Gra·na·da (grə-nä′də). Former Spanish colony of N South America, including present-day Colombia, Ecuador, Panama, and Venezuela.
New Guin·ea (gĭn′ē). **1.** Island, c. 342,000 sq mi (885,780 sq km), in the SW Pacific, N of Australia; the W half is part of Indonesia, and the E is part of Papua New Guinea. **2.** **Trust Territory of.** Former trust territory of Australia, consisting of NE New Guinea, the Bismarck Archipelago, and Bougainville in the Solomons. —**New Guin′e·an** *adj. & n.*
New Hamp·shire (hămp′shər, -shîr′, hăm′-). State of the NE U.S. Cap. Concord. Pop. 920,610. —**New Hamp′shir·ite′** *n.*
New Har·mo·ny (här′mə-nē). Village of SW Ind., on the Wabash; site of utopian community led (1825–28) by Robert Owen.
New Ha·ven (hā′vən). Town and city of S Conn., on Long Is. Sound. Pop. 126,109.
New Heb·ri·des (hĕb′rĭ-dēz′). Island group of the S Pacific, E of Australia, forming the republic of Vanuatu.
New Hope (hōp). City of E Minn., near Minneapolis. Pop. 23,087.
New I·be·ri·a (ī-bîr′ē-ə). City of S La., SW of Baton Rouge. Pop. 32,766.
New·ing·ton (no͞o′ĭng-tən, nyo͞o′-). Town of central Conn., near Hartford. Pop. 28,841.
New Ire·land (īr′lənd). Volcanic island of the SW Pacific, in the Bismarck Archipelago; part of Papua New Guinea.
New Jer·sey (jûr′zē). State of E central U.S., on the Atlantic. Cap. Trenton. Pop. 7,364,158. —**New Jer′sey·ite′** *n.*
New Ken·sing·ton (kĕn′zĭng-tən). City of W central Pa., NW of Pittsburgh. Pop. 17,660.
New Lon·don (lŭn′dən). City of SE Conn., near Long Is. Sound. Pop. 28,842.
New·mar·ket (no͞o′mär′kĭt, nyo͞o′-). Town of S Ont., Canada, N of Toronto. Pop. 26,155.
New Mex·i·co (mĕk′sĭ-ko′). State of SW U.S., on the Mexican border. Cap. Santa Fe. Pop. 1,299,968. —**New Mex′i·can** *adj. & n.*
New Mil·ford (mĭl′fərd). **1.** Town of W Conn., NNE of Danbury. Pop. 19,420. **2.** Borough of NE N.J., near Hackensack. Pop. 16,876.
New·nan (no͞o′nən, nyo͞o′-). City of W Ga., SW of Atlanta. Pop. 11,449.
New Neth·er·land (nĕ*th*′ər-lənd). Dutch colony in North America (1624–64), along the Hudson and lower Delaware rivers.
New Or·leans (ôr′lē-ənz, ôr′lənz, ôr-lēnz′). City of SE La., between the Mississippi and Lake Pontchartrain. Pop. 557,482.
New Phil·a·del·phi·a (fĭl′ə-dĕl′fē-ə). City of NE central Ohio, S of Canton. Pop. 16,883.
New·port (no͞o′pôrt′, -pōrt′, nyo͞o′-).

1. Borough of the Isle of Wight, S England. Pop. 22,430. **2.** City of N Ky., on the Ohio near Covington. Pop. 21,587. **3.** City of SE R.I., on the Atlantic SSE of Providence. Pop. 21,259. **4.** Borough of SE Wales, near the Severn estuary NE of Cardiff. Pop. 132,800.

Newport Beach. City of S Calif., S of Santa Ana. Pop. 63,475.

Newport News (no͞oz, nyo͞oz). Independent city of SE Va., on the James R. and Hampton Roads opposite Norfolk. Pop. 144,903.

New Port Rich·ey (rĭch'ē). City of W Fla., on the Gulf of Mexico NW of Tampa. Pop. 11,196.

New Prov·i·dence (prŏv'ĭ-dəns). **1.** Island of the Bahamas, in the West Indies. **2.** Borough of NE N.J., W of Newark. Pop. 12,426.

New Que·bec (kwĭ-bĕk'). **1.** Region of N Que., Canada, between Hudson Bay and Labrador N of the Eastmain R. **2. Crater.** Meteoric crater, 3 m (4.8 km) in diameter, of N Que., Canada, on the Ungava Peninsula.

New Ro·chelle (rə-shĕl', rō-). City of SE N.Y., on Long Is. Sound E of Mount Vernon. Pop. 70,794.

New Sar·um (săr'əm, sâr'-). Salisbury, England.

New Si·be·ri·an Islands (sī-bîr'ē-ən). Archipelago of N Siberian USSR, in the Arctic Ocean between the Laptev and East Siberian seas.

New Smyr·na Beach (smûr'nə). City of NE Fla., on the Atlantic SSE of Daytona Beach. Pop. 13,557.

New Spain (spān). Spanish viceroyalty (1521–1821), including SW U.S., Mexico, Central America N of Panama, some West Indian islands, and the Philippines.

New Swe·den (swēd'n). Swedish colony (1638–55) in North America, on the Delaware R., including parts of present-day Pa., N.J., and Del.

New·ton (no͞ot'n, nyo͞ot'n). **1.** City of central Iowa, ENE of Des Moines. Pop. 15,292. **2.** City of S central Kans., N of Wichita. Pop. 16,332. **3.** City of E Mass., near Boston. Pop. 83,622.

New·town (no͞o'toun', nyo͞o'-). Town of SW Conn., ENE of Danbury. Pop. 19,107.

New Ulm (ŭlm'). City of S Minn., WNW of Mankato. Pop. 13,755.

New West·min·ster (wĕst-mĭn'stər). City of SW B.C., Canada, on the Fraser R. near Vancouver. Pop. 38,393.

New Wind·sor (wĭn'zər). Windsor, England.

New World (wûrld). The Western Hemisphere.

New York (yôrk). **1. Bay.** Arm of the Atlantic at the mouth of the Hudson R. in SE N.Y. and NE N.J., divided into **Upper New York Bay** and **Lower New York Bay**, connected by the Narrows. **2.** State of NE U.S., one of the Middle Atlantic states. Cap. Albany. Pop. 17,557,288. **3.** Or **New York City.** City of SE N.Y., on New York Bay and the mouth of the Hudson R. Pop. 7,071,030.

New York State Barge Canal. System of inland waterways in N.Y., 525 mi (845 km) long, connecting the Great Lakes with the Hudson R. and Lake Champlain.

New Zea·land (zē'lənd). Island country in the S Pacific, SE of Australia. Cap. Wellington. Pop. 3,125,000. **—New Zea'land·er** *n.*

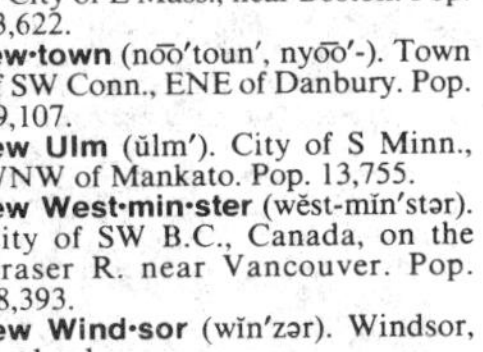

New Zealand

Ne·ya·ga·wa (nĕ'yä-gä'wä). City of SW Honshu, Japan, near Osaka. Pop. 255,864.

Nga·mi (əng-gä'mē), **Lake.** Lake of N Botswana.

Ngau·ru·hoe (əng-gou'rə-hō'ē). Volcano, 7,515 ft (2,292 m) high, of central North Is., New Zealand.

Nha Trang (nyä trăng'). City of S central Vietnam, on the South China Sea. Pop. 216,227.

Ni·ag·a·ra (nī-ăg'rə, -ər-ə). River, flowing 34 mi (54.7 km) from Lake Erie to Lake Ontario, forming part of the boundary between W N.Y. and Ont., Canada.

Niagara Falls. 1. Falls in the Niagara R. between the cities of Niagara Falls, N.Y., and Niagara Falls, Ont., Canada; divided by Goat Is. into the American Falls and the Canadian Falls. **2.** City of S Ont., Canada, on the Niagara R. opposite Niagara Falls, N.Y. Pop. 70,771. **3.** City of W N.Y., on the Niagara R. NNW of Buffalo. Pop. 71,384.

Ni·ag·a·ra-on-the-Lake (nī-ăg'rə-ŏn-thə-lāk', -ər-ə-). Town of S Ont., Canada, on Lake Ontario at the mouth of the Niagara R. Pop. 12,307.

Nia·mey (nyä-mā'). Cap. of Niger, in the SW on the Niger R. Pop. 225,300.

Ni·as (nē'äs'). Volcanic island of Indonesia, in the Indian Ocean off W central Sumatra.

Ni·cae·a (nī-sē'ə). Ancient city of Bithynia, NW Asia Minor. **—Ni·cae'an** *adj.*

Nic·a·ra·gua (nĭk'ə-rä'gwə). **1.** Largest lake, 3,089 sq mi (8,000.5 sq km) of Central America, in SW Nicaragua. **2.** Republic of Central America, on the Caribbean Sea and Pacific Ocean. Cap. Managua. Pop. 2,610,000. **—Ni'ca·ra'guan** *adj. & n.*

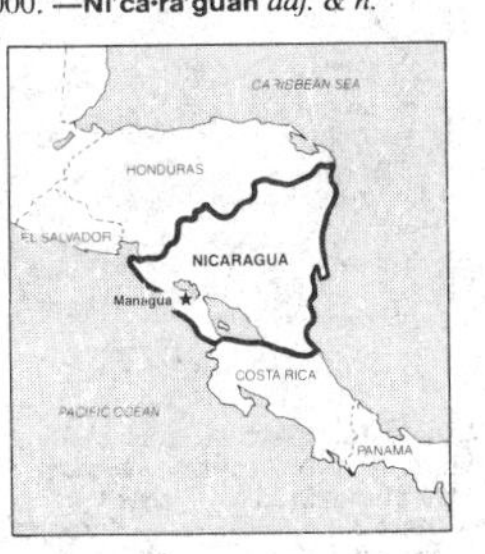

Nicaragua

Nice (nēs). City of SE France, on the Mediterranean. Pop. 344,481.

Nich·o·las·ville (nĭk'ə-ləs-vĭl', -vəl). City of W central Ky., near Lexington. Pop. 10,400.

Nick·el Cen·ter (nĭk'əl sĕn'tər). Town of S central Ont., Canada, WNW of Lake Nipissing. Pop. 12,281.

Nic·o·bar Islands (nĭk'ə-bär'). Indian islands in the Bay of Bengal, NW of Sumatra.

Nic·o·me·di·a (nĭk'ə-mē'dē-ə). Ancient city of NW Asia Minor near the Bosporus in present-day Turkey.

Nic·o·si·a (nĭk'ə-sē'ə). Cap. of Cyprus, in the N central part. Pop. 121,500.

Ni·co·ya (nē-kô'yä), **Gulf of.** Inlet of the Pacific between **Nicoya Peninsula** and the NW mainland of Costa Rica.

Ni·da·ros (nē'dä-rōs'). Trondheim.

Nie·men (nyĕ'mĕn', nē'mən). *Polish.* Neman.

Ni·ger (nī'jər). **1.** River of W Africa, flowing c. 2,600 mi (4,185 km) from Guinea through Mali, Niger, and

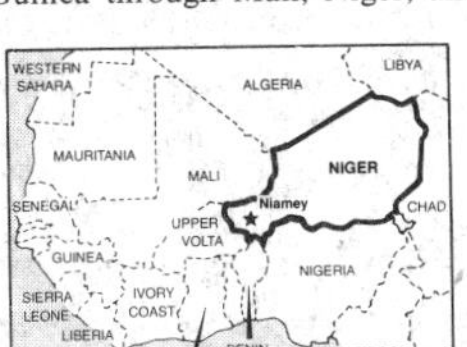

Niger

Nigeria into the Gulf of Guinea. **2.** Republic of W central Africa. Cap. Niamey. Pop. 5,380,000.

Ni·ge·ri·a (nī-jîr'ē-ə). Republic of W Africa, on the Gulf of Guinea. Cap. Lagos. Pop. 78,135,000. **—Ni·ge'ri·an** *adj. & n.*

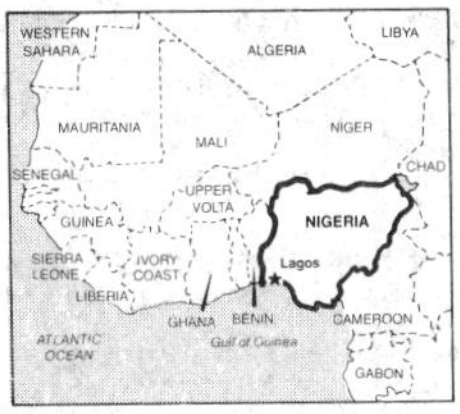

Nigeria

Ni·hon (nē'hŏn', -hôn'). *Japanese.* Japan.

Ni·i·ga·ta (nē'ē-gä'tä). City of N Honshu, Japan, on the Sea of Japan. Pop. 457,783.

Ni·i·ha·ma (nē'ē-hä'mä). City of N Shikoku, Japan. Pop. 133,178.

Ni·i·ha·u (nē'ē-hä'o͞o). Island of Hawaii, W of Kauai Is.

Ni·i·za (nē'ē-zä'). City of E central Honshu, Japan, near Tokyo. Pop. 119,991.

Nij·me·gen (nī'mā'gən) or **Nim·we·gen** (nĭm'vā'gən, -KHən) or **Ni·me·guen** (nī'mā'gən). City of E Netherlands, near the West German border. Pop. 147,614.

Nik·ko (nĕk'kô). Town and pilgrimage center of central Honshu, Japan, N of Tokyo. Pop. 26,279.

Ni·ko·la·yev (nĭ'kō-lä'yəf). Town of S European USSR, in the Ukraine at the mouth of the Bug R. Pop. 449,000.

Ni·ko·pol (nē-kô'pəl, nĭ-). City of S European USSR, in the Ukraine on the Dneiper. Pop. 149,000.

Nile (nīl). Longest river in the world, flowing c. 4,160 mi (6,695 km) through E Africa from its most remote sources in Burundi to a delta on the Mediterranean in NE Egypt.

Niles (nīlz). **1.** Village of NE Ill., near Chicago. Pop. 30,363. **2.** City of SW Mich., N of South Bend, Ind. Pop. 13,115. **3.** City of NE Ohio, near Youngstown. Pop. 23,088.

Ni·me·guen (nī'mā'gən, -KHən). Variant of **Nijmegen.**

Nîmes (nēm). City of SE France, NE of Montpellier. Pop. 127,933.

Nim·rud (nĭm-ro͞od'). Ancient city of Assyria, S of present-day Mosul, Iraq.

Nim·we·gen (nĭm'vā'gən). Variant of **Nijmegen.**

Nin·e·veh (nĭn'ə-və). Ancient cap. of the Assyrian Empire, on the Tigris opposite the site of modern Mosul, Iraq.

Ning·bo also **Ning·po** (nĭng'bō'). City of E China. c. 90 mi (144.8 km) ESE of Hangzhou on Hangzhou Bay. Pop. 300,000.

Ni·o·brar·a (nī'ə-brâr'ə). River, c. 430 mi (690 km), of E Wyo. and NE Nebr.

Niort (nyôr). City of W France, ENE of La Rochelle. Pop. 62,267.

Nip·i·gon (nĭp'ĭ-gŏn'). Lake, c. 1,870 sq mi (4,840 sq km), of central Ont., Canada, N of Lake Superior.

Nip·is·sing (nĭp'ĭ-sĭng). Lake of S Ont., Canada, between the Ottawa R. and Georgian Bay.

Nip·pon (nĭ-pŏn', nĭp'ŏn, nĕp-pôn'). *Japanese.* Japan.

Nip·pur (nĭ-po͝or'). Ancient city of Babylonia, on the Euphrates.

Niš or **Nish** (nĭsh, nēsh). City of E Yugoslavia, near the Bulgarian border. Pop. 127,128.

Ni·shi·no·mi·ya (nē'shē-nô'mē-yä'). City of SW Honshu, Japan, on Osaka Bay. Pop. 410,329.

Ni·te·rói (nē'tə-roi'). City of SE Brazil, on Guanabara Bay opposite Rio de Janeiro. Pop. 376,033.

Ni·tra (nē'trä). City of S central Czechoslovakia, on the **Nitra R.**, a tributary of the Danube. Pop. 72,140.

Ni·u·a·foo (nē-o͞o'ə-fō'). Island of extreme N Tonga, SW central Pacific.

Ni·u·e (nē-o͞o'ā). Island dependency of New Zealand in the S central Pacific E of Tonga.

Ni·ver·nais (nē-vĕr-nĕ'). Region and former province of central France.

Nizh·ni Nov·go·rod (nēzh'nĭ nôv'gə-rət, nĭzh'nē näv'gə-räd'). Gorki.

Nizh·ni Ta·gil (tä-gēl', tə-gĭl'). City of E European USSR, in the E central Urals. Pop. 400,000.

No (nō). Lake of S central Sudan, formed by flood waters of the White Nile.

No·a·tak (nō-ä'täk'). River of NW Alas., flowing c. 400 mi (640 km) to Kotzebue Sound.

No·be·o·ka (nô'bĕ-ô'kä). City of E Kyushu, Japan. Pop. 136,572.

No·bles·ville (nō'bəlz-vĭl'). City of central Ind., N of Indianapolis. Pop. 12,056.

No·gal·es (nə-găl'ĭs, nō-găl'ĭs, -gä'lĭs). **1.** (*also* nô-gä'lĕs). City of NW Mexico, on the Ariz. border contiguous to Nogales, Ariz. Pop. 14,254. **2.** City of S Ariz., on the Mexican border. Pop. 15,683.

No·ginsk (nə-gēnsk'). City of central European USSR, near Moscow. Pop. 120,000.

Nol·i·chuck·y (nŏl'ĭ-chŭk'ē). River, c. 150 mi (240 km), of W N.C. and E Tenn.

Nome (nōm). **1.** Cape on the W Alas. coast, ESE of the city of Nome on Norton Sound. **2.** Westernmost city of the continental U.S., on Seward Peninsula, W Alas. Pop. 2,301.

Non·ni (nŏn'nē', nŭn'-). Nenjiang.

Noot·ka Sound (no͞ot'kə, no͝ot'-). Inlet of the Pacific on the W coast of Vancouver Is., SW B.C., Canada.

Nor·co (nôr'kō). City of S Calif., WSW of Riverside. Pop. 21,126.

Nord·hau·sen (nôrt'hou'zən). City of W East Germany, at the S foot of the Harz Mts. Pop. 46,317.

Nord·kyn (nôr'kün'), **Cape.** Northernmost point of the European mainland, in N Norway E of North Cape.

Nore (nôr, nōr), **the.** Sandbank in the Thames estuary, SE England.

Nor·folk (nôr'fək, -fôk). **1.** Island of the Pacific, a territory of Australia, c. 1,035 mi (1,665 km) NE of Sydney. **2.** City of NE Nebr., NW of Omaha. Pop. 19,449. **3.** Independent city of SE Va., on Hampton Roads SE of Richmond. Pop. 266,979.

Nor·ge (nôr'gə). *Norwegian.* Norway.

Nor·i·cum (nôr'ĭ-kəm, nŏr'-). Province of the Roman Empire, corresponding roughly to modern Austria S of the Danube and W of Vienna.

No·rilsk (nə-rēlsk'). Northernmost city in the USSR, in N Siberia. Pop. 182,000.

Nor·mal (nôr'məl). Town of central Ill., near Bloomington. Pop. 35,672.

Nor·man (nôr'mən). City of central Okla., S of Oklahoma City. Pop. 68,020.

Nor·man·dy (nôr'mən-dē). Region and former province of NW France, on the English Channel. **—Nor'man** *adj. & n.*

Nor·ridge (nôr'ĭj, nŏr'-). Village of NE Ill., near Chicago. Pop. 16,483.

Nor·ris·town (nôr'ĭs-toun', nŏr'-). Borough of SE Pa., NW of Philadelphia. Pop. 34,684.

Norr·kö·ping (nôr'chœ'pĭng). City of SE Sweden, on an inlet of the Baltic. Pop. 119,993.

North (nôrth). **1. Sea.** Arm of the Atlantic NW of central Europe and E of Great Britain. **2. Channel.** Strait, c. 75 mi (120 km) long, between Northern Ireland and Scotland, connecting the Irish Sea and the Atlantic. **3. River.** Part of the Hudson R. estuary separating N.J. and New York City. **4.** Cape on N North Is., New Zealand. **5.** Cape of N Norway, projecting into the Arctic Ocean. **6.** Island, 44,281 sq mi (114,688 sq km), of N New Zealand. **7. the.** U.S. states N of Md. and the Ohio and Missouri rivers.

North Ad·ams (ăd'əmz). City of NW Mass., NNE of Pittsfield. Pop. 18,063.

North A·mer·i·ca (ə-mĕr'ĭ-kə). N

continent of the Western Hemisphere, extending N from the Colombia-Panama border through Central America, the U.S., Canada, and the Arctic Archipelago to the N tip of Greenland. —**North A·mer'i·can** *adj. & n.*

North·amp·ton (nôr-thămp'tən, nôrth-hămp'-). **1.** Borough of central England. Pop. 154,900. **2.** City of W central Mass., N of Springfield. Pop. 29,286.

North An·do·ver (ăn'dō'vər). Town of NE Mass., near Lawrence. Pop. 20,129.

North Ar·ling·ton (är'lĭng-tən). Borough of NE N.J., near Newark. Pop. 16,587.

North At·tle·bor·o (ăt'l-bûr'ō, -bər-ə). Town of SE Mass., NNE of Providence, R.I. Pop. 21,095.

North Au·gus·ta (ô-gŭs'tə). City of SW S.C., near Augusta, Ga. Pop. 13,593.

North Bat·tle·ford (băt'l-fərd). City of W Sask., Canada, on the North Saskatchewan R. NW of Saskatoon. Pop. 13,158.

North Bay. City of SE Ont., Canada, WSW of Sudbury. Pop. 50,203.

North Bell·more (bĕl'môr', -mōr'). Town of SE N.Y., on Long Is. near Hempstead. Pop. 23,600.

North·bor·ough or **North·bor·o** (nôrth'bûr'ō). Town of E central Mass., near Worcester. Pop. 10,568.

North Bran·ford (brăn'fərd). Town of S Conn., E of New Haven. Pop. 11,554.

North·bridge (nôrth'brĭj'). Town of S central Mass., SSE of Worcester. Pop. 12,246.

North·brook (nôrth'brŏŏk'). Village of NE Ill., near Chicago. Pop. 30,735.

North Ca·na·di·an (kə-nā'dē-ən). River of N.Mex. and Okla., flowing 760 mi (1,223 km) to the Canadian R. in E Okla.

North Can·ton (kăn'tən). City of NE central Ohio, near Canton. Pop. 14,228.

North Car·o·li·na (kăr'ə-lī'nə). State of SE U.S., on the Atlantic. Cap. Raleigh. Pop. 5,874,429. —**North Car·o·lin'i·an** (-lĭn'ē-ən) *adj. & n.*

North Charles·ton (chärl'stən). City of SE S.C., near Charleston. Pop. 65,630.

North Chi·ca·go (shĭ-kä'gō, -kô'-). City of NE Ill., on Lake Michigan. Pop. 38,774.

North Col·lege Hill (kŏl'ĭj). City of extreme SW Ohio, near Cincinnati. Pop. 10,990.

North Da·ko·ta (də-kō'tə). State of N central U.S. Cap. Bismarck. Pop. 652,695. —**North Da·ko'tan** *adj. & n.*

North·east (nôrth-ēst'), **the.** Area of the NE U.S. including New England, N.Y., and sometimes Pa. and N.J.

Northeast Pas·sage (păs'ĭj). Water route along the N coast of Europe and Asia, between the Atlantic and Pacific.

North·ern Cook (nôr'*th*ərn kŏŏk'). Islands of the central Pacific N of the Cook Is., under New Zealand administration.

Northern Dvi·na (dvĭ-nä', dvē-). See **Dvina.**

Northern Hem·i·sphere (hĕm'ĭ-sfîr'). The half of the earth N of the equator.

Northern Ire·land (īr'lənd). Component of the United Kingdom, in the NE part of the island of Ireland. Cap. Belfast. Pop. 1,542,200.

Northern Kar·roo (kə-rōō', kă-). Plateau region of E South Africa.

Northern Spor·a·des (spôr'ə-dēz). Islands of E Greece, in the Aegean.

North·field (nôrth'fēld'). City of SE Minn., S of Minneapolis-St. Paul. Pop. 12,562.

North Fork (fôrk). River, c. 100 mi (160 km), of S Mo. and N Ark.

North Fri·sian Islands (frĭzh'ən, frē'zhən). Islands in the North Sea off the West German coast.

North·glenn (nôrth-glĕn'). City of N central Colo., N of Denver. Pop. 29,847.

North Ha·ven (hā'vən). Town of S Conn., NNE of New Haven. Pop. 22,080.

North High·lands (hī'ləndz). Town of N central Calif., near Sacramento. Pop. 36,800.

North Kings·town (kĭngz'stən). Town of S central R.I., on Narragansett Bay SSW of Providence. Pop. 21,938.

North Ko·re·a (kə-rē'ə, kō-, kô-). See **Korea.**

North·lake (nôrth'lāk'). City of NE Ill., near Chicago. Pop. 12,166.

North Las Ve·gas (läs vā'gəs). City of S Nev., near Las Vegas. Pop. 42,739.

North Lau·der·dale (lô'dər-dāl'). City of SE Fla., NW of Fort Lauderdale. Pop. 18,479.

North Lit·tle Rock (lĭt'l rŏk'). City of central Ark., opposite Little Rock. Pop. 64,391.

North Loup (lōōp). River, 212 mi (341.1 km), of N central Nebr.

North Mi·am·i (mī-ăm'ē, -ăm'ə). City of SE Fla., near Miami. Pop. 42,566.

North Miami Beach. City of SE Fla., on the Atlantic. Pop. 36,481.

North Minch (mĭnch). Strait between the mainland of NW Scotland and the Outer Hebrides.

North Olm·sted (ŭm'stĕd', -stĭd). City of NE Ohio, near Cleveland. Pop. 36,486.

North Palm Beach (päm). Village of SE Fla., N of West Palm Beach. Pop. 11,344.

North Plain·field (plān'fēld'). Borough of NE central N.J., WSW of Elizabeth. Pop. 19,108.

North Platte (plăt). **1.** River of W U.S., flowing c. 680 mi (1,095 km) from N Colo. through SE Wyo. and W central Nebr., joining the South Platte in SW Nebr. to form the Platte. **2.** City of W central Nebr., W of Grand Island. Pop. 24,479.

North Pole (pōl). N end of the earth's axis of rotation, a point in the Arctic Ocean.

North·port (nôrth'pôrt', -pōrt'). City of W central Ala., near Tuscaloosa. Pop. 14,332.

North Prov·i·dence (prŏv'ĭ-dəns). Town of NE R.I., NNE of Providence. Pop. 29,188.

North Read·ing (rĕd'ĭng). Town of NE Mass., N of Boston. Pop. 11,455.

North Rich·land Hills (rĭch'lənd). City of NE Tex., near Fort Worth. Pop. 30,592.

North Ridge·ville (rĭj'vĭl'). City of NE Ohio, WSW of Cleveland. Pop. 21,522.

North Roy·al·ton (roi'əl-tən). City of NE Ohio, S of Cleveland. Pop. 17,671.

North Saint Paul (sānt pôl'). City of E Minn., near St. Paul. Pop. 11,921.

North Sas·katch·e·wan (săs-kăch'ə-wän', -wən). River of central Canada, flowing 760 mi (1,222.8 km) from E Alta. to the South Saskatchewan to form the Saskatchewan in central Sask.

North Slope (slōp). Region of N Alas. N of the Brooks range.

North Ton·a·wan·da (tŏn'ə-wŏn'də). City of W N.Y., N of Buffalo. Pop. 35,760.

North·um·ber·land Strait (nôr-thŭm'bər-lənd). Arm of the Gulf of St. Lawrence, separating P.E.I. from N.B. and N.S., Canada.

North·um·bri·a (nôr-thŭm'brē-ə). Anglo-Saxon kingdom of Britain.

North Valley Stream. Town of SE N.Y., on Long Is. Pop. 14,881.

North Van·cou·ver (văn-kōō'vər). City of SW B.C., Canada, on an inlet of the Strait of Georgia opposite Vancouver. Pop. 31,934.

North Vi·et·nam (vē'ĕt-näm', -năm', vē-ĕt'-, vyĕt'-). Former republic of SE Asia (1954–75).

North·west (nôrth'wĕst'), **the. 1.** Formerly, area of the U.S. W of the Mississippi and N of the Missouri R. **2.** U.S. states of Wash., Ore., and Idaho.

North-West Frontier Province. Historical region of NW Pakistan on the Afghanistan border.

Northwest Pas·sage (păs'ĭj). Water route from the Atlantic to the Pacific through the Arctic Archipelago of Canada and N of Canada.

Northwest Ter·ri·to·ries (tĕr'ĭ-tôr'ēz, -tōr'-). Region of NW Canada including the Arctic Archipelago, the islands in Hudson Bay, and the mainland N of the Canadian provinces and between Y.T. and Hudson Bay.

Northwest Ter·ri·to·ry (tĕr'ĭ-tôr'ē, -tōr'ē). Historical U.S. region extending from the Ohio and Mississippi rivers to the Great Lakes.

North York (yôrk). Borough of metropolitan Toronto, S Ont., Canada. Pop. 559,109.

Nor·ton (nôr'tn). **1. Sound.** Inlet of the Bering Sea, W Alas., S of the Seward Peninsula. **2.** Town of SE Mass., NE of Taunton. Pop. 12,690. **3.** City of NE Ohio, near Akron. Pop. 12,242.

Norton Shores. City of W Mich., on Lake Michigan. Pop. 22,025.

Nor·walk (nôr'wôk'). **1.** City of S Calif., NNE of Long Beach. Pop. 85,232. **2.** City of SW Conn., on Long Is. Sound. Pop. 77,767. **3.** City of N Ohio, SSE of Sandusky. Pop. 14,358.

Nor·way (nôr'wā'). Kingdom of N Europe, in the W part of the Scandinavian peninsula. Cap. Oslo. Pop. 4,095,000. —**Nor·we'gian** (nôr-wē'jən) *adj. & n.*

Norway

Norwegian Sea. Section of the Atlantic NW of Norway, between the Greenland and North seas.

Nor·wich. 1. (nŏr'ĭj, -ĭch). Borough of E England, W of Great Yarmouth. Pop. 119,300. **2.** (nôr'wĭch', -ĭch, nŏr'-). City of SE Conn., N of New London. Pop. 38,074.

Nor·wood (nôr'wŏŏd'). **1.** Town of E Mass., SW of Boston. Pop. 29,711. **2.** City of SW Ohio, surrounded by Cincinnati. Pop. 26,342.

No·teć (nô'tĕch). River of NW Poland, flowing c. 270 mi (435 km) to the Warta.

No·to·gae·a or **No·to·ge·a** (nō'tə-jē'ə). Zoogeographic region that includes Australia, New Zealand, and the islands of the SW Pacific.

No·tre Dame Mountains (nō'trə dām', däm', nō'tər). Section of the Appalachians, extending c. 500 mi (800 km) from the Green Mts. of Vt. into the Gaspé Peninsula, Que., Canada.

Not·ta·way (nŏt'ə-wā'). River, c. 140 mi (225 km), of W Que., Canada.

Not·ting·ham (nŏt'ĭng-əm). Borough of central England, N of Leicester. Pop. 278,600.

Not·to·way (nŏt'ə-wā'). River of S Va., flowing 175 mi (281.6 km) to the N.C. border.

Nouak·chott (nwäk-shŏt'). Cap. of Mauritania, in the W part. Pop. 134,986.

Nou·mé·a (nōō-mā'ə). Cap. of New Caledonia, on the island of New Caledonia. Pop. 56,078.

Nova I·gua·çu (nô'və ē'gwə-sōō'). City of SE Brazil, near Rio de Janeiro. Pop. 1,130,300.

No·va·ra (nō-vä'rä). City of N Italy, W of Milan. Pop. 101,947.

No·va Sco·tia (nō'və skō'shə). Province of E Canada. Cap. Halifax. Pop. 828,571. —**No'va Sco'tian** *adj. & n.*

No·va·to (nə-vä'tō). City of W Calif., N of San Rafael. Pop. 43,916.

No·va·ya Zem·lya (nô'və-yə zĕm-lyä'). Archipelago of NW USSR, in the Arctic Ocean between the Barents and Kara seas.

Nov·go·rod (nôv'gə-rŏt'). City of NW European USSR, SSE of Leningrad. Pop. 192,000.

No·vi (nō'vī'). City of SE Mich., NW of Detroit. Pop. 22,525.

No·vi Sad (nô'vē säd'). City of NE Yugoslavia, on the Danube. Pop. 141,712.

No·vo·cher·kassk (nô'və-chər-käsk'). City of SE European USSR, E of Rostov. Pop. 185,000.

No·vo·kuz·netsk (nô'və-kŏŏz-nĕtsk'). City of central Siberian USSR, SSE of Leninsk-Kuznetski. Pop. 545,000.

No·vo·ros·siysk (nô'və-rŏ-sēsk'). City of SE European USSR, on the Black Sea. Pop. 162,000.

No·vo·si·birsk (nô'və-sĭ-bîrsk'). City of S Siberian USSR, on the Ob R. Pop. 1,328,000.

No·wy Sącz (nô'vĭ sônch'). City of SE Poland, SE of Kraków. Pop. 62,600.

Nu (nōō). *Chinese.* Salween.

Nu·bi·a (nōō'bē-ə, nyōō'-). Desert region and ancient kingdom in the Nile valley of S Egypt and N Sudan. —**Nu'bi·an** *adj. & n.*

Nubian Desert. Desert of NE Sudan, extending E of the Nile to the Red Sea.

Nu·e·ces (nōō-ā'sĭs, nyōō-). River of SW Tex., flowing 315 mi (506.8 km) to **Nueces Bay,** an inlet of the Gulf of Mexico near Corpus Christi.

Nue·vo La·re·do (nwĕ'vô lä-rĕ'*th*ô). City of NE Mexico, across the Rio Grande from Laredo, Tex. Pop. 214,200.

Nu·ku·a·lo·fa (nōō'kōō-ə-lô'fə). Cap. of Tonga, in the SW Pacific. Pop. 18,312.

Nu·ku Hi·va (nōō'kōō hē'və). Volcanic island, 127 sq mi (329 sq km), largest of the Marquesas Is. of French Polynesia.

Nu·kus (nōō-kōōs'). City of S Central Asian USSR, on the Amu Darya. Pop. 113,000.

Null·ar·bor Plain (nŭl'ər-bôr', nŭl-är'bər). Region of S central Australia, S of the Great Victoria Desert and N of the Great Australian Bight.

Nu·ma·zu (nōō-mä'zōō). City of S central Honshu, Japan. Pop. 203,699.

Num·foor (nōōm'fôr, -fōr). Island of N West Irian, Indonesia, in the Schouten Is.

Nu·mid·i·a (nōō-mĭd'ē-ə, nyōō-). Ancient country of NW Africa, corresponding roughly to present-day Algeria. —**Nu·mid'i·an** *adj. & n.*

Nun·ea·ton (nŭ-nēt'n). Borough of central England, N of Coventry. Pop. 110,300.

Nu·ni·vak (nōō'nə-văk'). Island off W Alas., in the Bering Sea.

Nu·rem·berg (nŏŏr'əm-bûrg', nyŏŏr'-). City of S West Germany, NNW of Munich. Pop. 484,184.

Nu·ri·stan (nŏŏr'ĭ-stăn'). Region of NE Afghanistan.

Nürn·berg (nürn'bĕrk). **German.** Nuremberg.

Nu·sa Teng·ga·ra (nōō'sə tĕng-gä'rə). Island chain of Indonesia, extending from Bali to Timor.

Nut·ley (nŭt'lē). Town of NE N.J., near Passaic. Pop. 28,998.

Ny·as·a (nī-ăs'ə, nyä'sä). Lake, c. 11,600 sq mi (30,040 sq mi), of SE Africa, between Tanzania, Mozambique, and Malawi.

Ny·as·a·land (nī-ăs'ə-lănd', nyä'-sä-lănd'). Malawi.

Nyir·a·gon·go (nyîr'ə-gông'gō). Volcano of E Zaire, at the N end of Lake Kivu.

Nyí·regy·há·za (nyē'rĕd-yə-hä'zō). City of NE Hungary, N of Debrecen. Pop. 84,600.

O

O·a·hu (ō-ä'hōō). Chief island of Hawaii, between Molokai and Kauai.

Oak Creek (ōk). City of SE Wis., near Milwaukee. Pop. 16,932.
Oak·dale (ōk′dāl′). City of E Minn., near St. Paul. Pop. 12,123.
Oak For·est (fôr′ĭst, fŏr′-). City of NE Ill., near Chicago. Pop. 26,096.
Oak Har·bor (här′bər). City of NW Wash., on Whidbey Is. NW of Everett. Pop. 12,271.
Oak·land (ōk′lənd). **1.** City of W Calif., opposite San Francisco. Pop. 339,288. **2.** Borough of NE N.J., near Paterson. Pop. 13,443.
Oakland Park. City of SE Fla., on the Atlantic coast. Pop. 21,939.
Oak Lawn (lôn). Village of NE Ill., near Chicago. Pop. 60,690.
Oak Park. 1. Village of NE Ill., near Chicago. Pop. 54,887. **2.** City of SE Michigan, near Detroit. Pop. 31,537.
Oak Ridge (rĭj). City of E Tenn., W of Knoxville. Pop. 27,662.
Oak·ville (ōk′vĭl′). Town of S Ont., Canada, on Lake Ontario SW of Toronto. Pop. 70,850.
Oa·xa·ca (wä-hä′kä). City of S central Mexico, S of Orizaba. Pop. 131,200.
Ob (ŏb, ôb, ôp). River, c. 2,300 mi (3,700 km), of W Siberian USSR, flowing to the **Gulf of Ob**, an inlet of the Arctic Ocean.
O·ber·hau·sen (ô′bər-hou′zən). City of W West Germany, in the Ruhr NW of Essen. Pop. 229,613.
O·cal·a (ō-kăl′ə). City of N central Fla., SSE of Gainesville. Pop. 37,170.
O·cean City (ō′shən). City of SE N.J., on the Atlantic SW of Atlantic City. Pop. 13,949.
O·ce·an·i·a (ō′shē-ăn′ē-ə, -ä′nē-ə). Collective name of islands in the S, W, and central Pacific, usually including Australia and New Zealand. **—O′ce·an′i·an** *adj. & n.*
O·cean·side (ō′shən-sīd′). **1.** City of S Calif., NNW of San Diego. Pop. 76,698. **2.** City of SE N.Y., on the S shore of Long Is. Pop. 36,400.
Ocean Springs. City of extreme SE Miss., near Biloxi. Pop. 14,504.
Oc·mul·gee (ōk-mŭl′gē). River, c. 255 mi (410 km), of central Ga.
O·den·se (ō′dən-sə). City of S Denmark, near the **Odense Fjord**, an arm of the Kattegat. Pop. 168,528.
O·der (ō′dər). River of central Europe, flowing c. 562 mi (904.3 km) from N central Czechoslovakia through Poland and East Germany to the Baltic Sea.
O·des·sa (ō-dĕs′ə). **1.** City of SW Tex., WNW of San Angelo. Pop. 90,027. **2.** City of SW European USSR, on **Odessa Bay** of the Black Sea. Pop. 1,057,000.
O'Fal·lon (ō-făl′ən). City of SW Ill., E of East St. Louis. Pop. 10,217.
Of·fen·bach (ôf′ən-bäk′, -bäкн′). City of central West Germany, on the Main R. Pop. 111,310.
O·ga·den (ō-gä′dän′). Region of SE Ethiopia, on the Somalian border.
Og·bo·mo·sho (ŏg′bə-mō′shō, -bō-). City of SW Nigeria, N of Ibadan. Pop. 432,000.
Og·den (ŏg′dən). City of N Utah, N of Salt Lake City. Pop. 64,407.
Og·dens·burg (ŏg′dənz-bûrg′). City of N N.Y., on the St. Lawrence R. Pop. 12,375.
O·gee·chee (ō-gē′chē). River c. 250 mi (402.3 km), of NE Ga.
O·hi·o (ō-hī′ō). **1.** River formed by the confluence of the Allegheny and the Monongahela in W Pa. and flowing 981 mi (1,578.4 km) to the Mississippi in S Ill. **2.** State of N U.S., in the Great Lakes region. Cap. Columbus. Pop. 10,797,419. **—O·hi′o·an** *adj. & n.*
Oil City (oil). City of NW Pa., NNE of Pittsburgh. Pop. 13,881.
Oil Rivers. Large delta region of the Niger R. in S Nigeria.
Oise (wäz). River, 186 mi (299.3 km), of S Belgium and N France.
O·i·ta (ō′ē-tä′, ō-ē′tä). City of NE Japan, on Beppu Bay. Pop. 360,484.
O·jos Del Sa·la·do (ō′hôs dĕl sä-lä′*th*ō). Peak, 22,539 ft (6,875.4 km), in the Andes on the Argentine-Chilean border.
O·ka (ō-kä′). River, c. 925 mi (1,490 km), of central European USSR.
O·ka·nog·an (ō′kə-nŏg′ən). River, c. 300 mi (482.7 km), of S B.C., Canada, and N Wash.
O·ka·van·go (ō′kə-văng′gō). River of W central Africa, flowing c. 1,000 mi (1,610 km) from central Angola to N Botswana.
O·ka·ya·ma (ô-kä′yä-mä). City of SW Japan, on an inlet of the Inland Sea. Pop. 545,737.
O·ka·za·ki (ô-kä′zä-kē). City of central Japan, NE of Okayama. Pop. 262,370.
O·kee·cho·bee (ō′kē-chō′bē). Lake, c. 700 sq mi (1,815 sq km), of SE Fla. N of the Everglades, crossed by the **Okeechobee Waterway**, a man-made and natural water route from the Atlantic to the Gulf of Mexico.
O·ke·fe·no·kee (ō′kə-fə-nō′kē). Large swamp of SE Ga. and N Fla.
O·khotsk (ō-kŏtsk′), **Sea of.** NW arm of the Pacific, W of the Kamchatka Peninsula and Kurile Is.
O·ki·na·wa (ō′kĭ-nou′wə, -nä′wə). **1.** Island group of the central Ryukyu Is., in the W Pacific SW of Japan. **2.** Largest (454 sq mi/1,175.9 sq km) island of the group.
O·kla·ho·ma (ō′klə-hō′mə). State of SW U.S. Cap. Oklahoma City. Pop. 3,025,266. **—O′kla·ho′man** *adj. & n.*
Oklahoma City. Cap. of Oklahoma, in the central part of the state. Pop. 403,213.
Ok·mul·gee (ōk-mŭl′gē). City of E central Okla., near the Arkansas R. Pop. 16,263.
Ö·land (œ′länd′). Narrow island of SE Sweden, in the Baltic Sea.
O·la·the (ō-lā′thə). City of E Kans., SW of Kansas City. Pop. 37,258.
Ol·den·burg (ōl′dən-bûrg′, -bo͝ork′). City of NW West Germany, W of Bremen. Pop. 136,155.
Old·ham (ōl′dəm). Borough of NW England, near Manchester. Pop. 223,500.
Ol·du·vai Gorge (ôl′do͞o-vī′, ōl′də-). Gorge in N Tanzania W of Mt. Kilimanjaro; site of early human remains.
O·le·an (ō′lē-ăn′, ō′lē-ăn′). City of W N.Y., near the Pa. border. Pop. 18,207.
O·lek·ma (ō-lĕk′mə). River, c. 820 mi (1,320 km), of SE Siberian USSR.
O·le·nek (ō′lĭ-nyôk′). River of E Siberian USSR, flowing c. 1,350 mi (2,175 km) to the Laptev Sea.
Ol·i·fants (ŏl′ə-fənts). River, c. 350 mi (563.2 km), of NE South Africa and W Mozambique.
Ol·ives (ŏl′ĭvz), **Mount of,** also **Ol·i·vet** (ŏl′ə-vĕt′). Ridge of hills E of Jerusalem.
O·lo·mouc (ô′lô-mōts′). City of N central Czechoslovakia, on the Morava R. Pop. 102,501.
Olsz·tyn (ôl′shtĭn). City of N Poland, SE of Gdańsk. Pop. 130,400.
Olt (ôlt). River, c. 348 mi (559.9 km), of central Rumania.
O·lym·pi·a (ō-lĭm′pē-ə, ə-lĭm′-). **1.** Plain of NW Peleponnesus, Greece; ancient site of the Olympic Games. **2.** Capital of Wash., on the S end of Puget Sound. Pop. 27,447.
O·lym·pic (ō-lĭm′pĭk). **1.** Mountain range of NW Wash., part of the Coast Ranges. **2.** Peninsula of NW Wash., between the Pacific and Puget Sound. **3. National Park.** Large tract of rugged reserved land on the Olympic Peninsula.
O·lym·pus (ō-lĭm′pəs, ə-lĭm′-). Mountain range of N Greece, near the Aegean coast, rising to 9,570 ft (2,920 m) at **Mount Olympus**, highest point in Greece and mythical home of Greek gods.
Om (ôm). River, c. 450 mi (724 km), of W Siberian USSR.
O·ma·ha (ō′mə-hô′, -hä′). City of E Nebr., on the Missouri R. Pop. 311,681.
O·man (ō-män′, ō′măn). Sultanate of SE Arabian Peninsula, on the **Gulf of Oman**, an arm of the Arabian Sea. Cap. Muscat. Pop. 900,000. **—O·man′i** *adj. & n.*
Om·dur·man (ŏm′do͝or-män′). City of central Sudan, on the White Nile opposite Khartoum. Pop. 299,401.
O·mi·ya (ō-mē′ə). City of Honshu, Japan, near Tokyo. Pop. 354,082.
Om·o·lon (ŏm′ə-lŏn′). River, c. 600 mi (965.4 km), of NE Siberian USSR.
Omsk (ômsk, ŏmsk). City of W Siberian USSR, at confluence of the Irtysh and Om rivers. Pop. 1,028,000.
O·mu·ta (ō′mo͞o-tä′). City of W Kyushu, Japan, NW of Kumamoto. Pop. 163,436.
O·ne·ga (ō-nē′gə, ŏ-nyĕ′gə). Lake, c. 3,800 sq mi (9,840 sq km), of NW European USSR.
O·nei·da (ō-nī′də). **1.** Lake, c. 80 sq mi (210 sq km) of central N.Y., NE of Syracuse. **2.** City of central N.Y., E of Syracuse. Pop. 10,810.
On·e·on·ta (ŏn′ē-ŏn′tə, ō′nē-). City of central N.Y., WSW of Albany. Pop. 14,933.
O·nit·sha (ō-nĭch′ə). City of SE Nigeria, on the Niger R. Pop. 220,000.
On·tar·i·o (ŏn-târ′ē-ō′). **1.** Smallest of the Great Lakes, between SE Ont., Canada, and NW N.Y. **2.** Province of E central Canada. Cap. Toronto. Pop. 8,264,465. **3.** City of S Calif., E of Los Angeles. Pop. 88,280.
O·pa-Lock·a (ō′pə-lŏk′ə). City of SE Fla., near Miami. Pop. 14,460.
O·pe·li·ka (ō′pə-lī′kə). City of E Ala., NW of Phenix City. Pop. 22,087.
Op·e·lou·sas (ŏp′ə-lo͞o′səs). City of S central La., W of Baton Rouge. Pop. 18,903.
O·po·le (ô-pô′lĕ). City of S Poland, on the Oder R. Pop. 114,000.
O·por·to (ō-pôr′tō, -pōr′-). City of NW Portugal, near the mouth of the Douro R. Pop. 335,700.
O·ra·dea (ô-rä′dyä). City of W Rumania, near the Hungarian border. Pop. 178,407.
O·ran (ō-răn′, ō-rän′, ō-räɴ′). City of NW Algeria, on the **Gulf of Oran**, an inlet of the Mediterranean. Pop. 485,139.
Or·ange (ôr′ĭnj, ŏr′-). **1.** River, c. 1,300 mi (2,090 km), of Lesotho, South Africa, and Namibia. **2.** City of S Calif., NNE of Santa Ana. Pop. 91,788. **3.** Town of SW Conn., near New Haven. Pop. 13,237. **4.** City of NE N.J., near Newark. Pop. 31,136. **5.** City of SE Tex., E of Beaumont. Pop. 83,838.
Or·ange·burg (ôr′ĭnj-bûrg′, ŏr′-). City of SE central S.C., SSE of Columbia. Pop. 14,933.
Or·ange·ville (ôr′ĭnj-vĭl′, ŏr′-). Town of S Ont., Canada, WNW of Toronto. Pop. 13,083.
Or·dos (ôr′dŏs). Sandy desert plateau region of Inner Mongolia in N China.
Or·dzho·ni·kid·ze (ôr′jŏn′ĭ-kĭd′zə). City of SE European USSR, on the Terek R. Pop. 283,000.
Ö·re·bro (œ′rə-bro͞o′). City of S central Sweden, W of Lake Hjälmaren. Pop. 116,877.
Or·e·gon (ôr′ĭ-gən, -gŏn′, ŏr′-). **1. Territory.** Historical region of NW North America. **2.** State of NW U.S., in the Pacific Northwest. Cap. Salem. Pop. 2,632,663. **3.** City of NW Ohio, near Toledo. Pop. 18,675. **—Or′e·go′ni·an** (-gō′nē-ən) *adj. & n.*
Oregon City. City of NW Ore. S of Portland. Pop. 14,673.
Oregon Trail (trāl). Historical overland route to the W U.S., from the Missouri R. to the Oregon Territory.
O·re·kho·vo Zu·ye·vo (ō-rĕ′кнə-və zo͞o′yĭ-və). City of W central European USSR, E of Moscow. Pop. 133,000.
O·rel (ō-rĕl′, ô-rĕl′, ŏ-ryôl′). City of central European USSR, on the Oka R. Pop. 309,000.

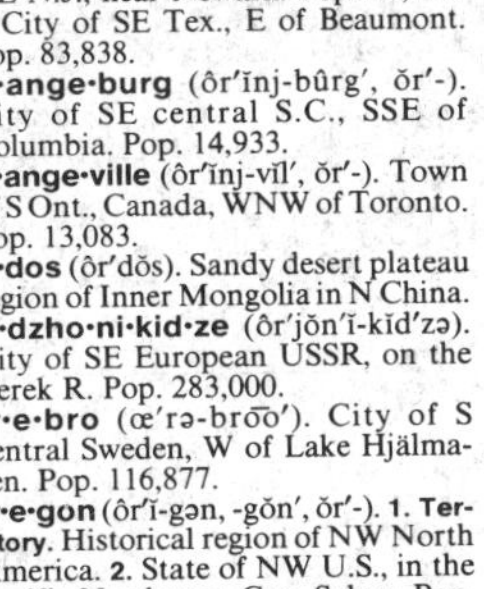

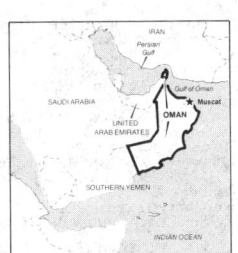

Oman

O·rem (ôr′əm, ŏr′-). City of N central Utah, near Provo. Pop. 52,399.
O·ren·burg (ŏr′ən-bûrg′, ŏ-rĭn-bo͝ork′). City of NW Central Asian USSR, on the Ural R. Pop. 471,000.
O·ren·se (ô-rĕn′sē). City of NW Spain, NW of Madrid. Pop. 77,600.
Ö·re·sund (œ′rə-so͝on′, -sŭn′). Strait between S Sweden and E Denmark, connecting the Baltic Sea with the Kattegat.
O·ril·lia (ô-rĭl′yə). City of S Ont., Canada, N of Toronto. Pop. 23,693.
O·ri·no·co (ôr′ə-nō′kō, ŏr′-). River of Venezuela, flowing c. 1,500 mi (2,415 km), partly along the Columbia-Venezuela border, to the Atlantic.
O·ri·za·ba (ôr′ĭ-zä′bə, ŏr′-, ô′rē-sä′bä). **1.** Volcanic peak, c. 18,701 ft (5,703 m), of E central Mexico, near the city of Orizaba. **2.** City of E central Mexico, W of Veracruz. Pop. 118,400.
Or·khon (ôr′kŏn′). River, c. 300 mi (480 km), of N central Mongolia.
Ork·ney Islands (ôrk′nē) also **Ork·neys** (-nēz). Archipelago of c. 70 islands, in the Atlantic and the North Sea off the NE coast of Scotland.
Or·lan·do (ôr-lăn′dō). City of central Fla., ENE of Tampa. Pop. 128,394.
Or·land Park (ôr′lənd). Village of NE Ill., SW of Chicago. Pop. 23,035.
Or·lé·ans (ôr-lā-äɴ′). City of N central France, on the Loire S of Paris. Pop. 106,246.
Or·ly (ôr′lē, ôr-lē′). City of N central France, a suburb SE of Paris. Pop. 26,109.
Or·mond Beach (ôr′mənd). City of NE Fla., on the Atlantic. Pop. 21,378.
Or·muz (ôr′mŭz′, ôr-mo͞oz′). Variant of **Hormuz**.
O·ro·moc·to (ôr′ə-mŏk′tō, ŏr′-). Town of S central N.B., Canada, on the St. John R. Pop. 10,276.
O·ron·tes (ō-rŏn′tēz). River, c. 250 mi (400 km), flowing through Lebanon, Syria, and S Turkey to the Mediterranean.
Orsk (ôrsk). City of E European USSR, on the Ural R. Pop. 252,000.
Ort·les (ôrt′lās). Range of the Alps in N Italy, rising to **Ortles** peak, 12,792 ft (3,901.6 km).
O·sage (ō′sāj′, ō-sāj′). River c. 360 mi (580 km), of E Kans. and central Mo.
O·sa·ka (ō-sä′kə). City of S Honshu, Japan, on **Osaka Bay**, an inlet of the Pacific. Pop. 2,648,158.
O·sas·co (o͞o-säs′ko͞o). City of SE Brazil, near São Paulo. Pop. 283,303.
Osh·a·wa (ŏsh′ə-wä′, -wə). City of SE Ont., Canada, on Lake Winnebago. Pop. 49,678.
O·shog·bo (ō-shŏb′bō). City of SW Nigeria, NE of Ibadan. Pop. 282,000.
O·si·jek (ô′sē-yĕk). City of N Yugoslavia, on the Drava. Pop. 93,912.
Os·ka·loo·sa (ŏs′kə-lo͞o′sə). City of SE Iowa, SE of Des Moines. Pop. 10,629.
Os·lo (ŏz′lō, ŏs′-). Cap. of Norway, in the SE at the head of the Oslofjord, a deep inlet of the Skagerrak. Pop. 454,819.
Os·na·brück (ŏz′nə-bro͝ok′, ôs′-nä-brük′). City of NW West Germany, NE of Münster. Pop. 158,150.
O·sor·no (ô-sôr′nô). City of S central Chile, S of Concepción. Pop. 71,000.
Os·se·tia (ŏ-sē′shə). Region of the central Caucasus, S European USSR, divided into **North** and **South Ossetia**.
Os·si·ning (ŏs′ə-nĭng′). Village of SE N.Y., on the Hudson R. N of White Plains. Pop. 20,196.
Ost·end (ŏs-tĕnd′, ŏs′tĕnd′). City of NW Belgium, on the North Sea. Pop. 70,125.
Ös·ter·sund (œs′tər-so͞ond′). City of central Sweden, E of Trondheim, Norway. Pop. 41,000.
Os·ti·a (ŏs′tē-ə). Ancient city of E central Italy, at the mouth of the Tiber.
Os·tra·va (ô′strä-vä). City of N central Czechoslovakia, near the Oder R. Pop. 325,473.
Os·we·go (ŏs-wē′gō). City of N central N.Y., on Lake Ontario NW of Syracuse. Pop. 19,793.
Oś·wie·cim (ôsh-vyĕn′tsēm, -chēm). City of SE Poland W of Kraków; site

(as Auschwitz) of Nazi concentration camp. Pop. 44,200.

O·ta·ru (ō'tä-ro͞o', ô-tä'ro͞o). City of SW Hokkaido, Japan, WNW of Sapporo. Pop. 185,737.

O·tsu (ô'tso͞o). City of S Honshu, Japan, near Lake Biwa. Pop. 215,318.

Ot·ta·wa (ŏt'ə-wə, -wä', -wô'). **1.** River, c. 700 mi (1,125 km), of SE Ont. and S Que., Canada, a major tributary of the St. Lawrence. **2.** Cap. of Canada, in SE Ont. at the confluence of the Ottawa R. and Rideau Canal. Pop. 300,678. **3.** City of N central Ill., SW of Aurora. Pop. 18,166. **4.** City of E Kans., SW of Kansas City. Pop. 11,016.

Ot·to·man Em·pire (ŏt'ə-mən ĕm'-pīr). Turkish empire (1299–1919) in SW Asia, NE Africa, and SE Europe.

Ot·tum·wa (ə-tŭm'wə, ō-tŭm'-). City of SE Iowa, SE of Des Moines. Pop. 27,381.

Ouach·i·ta (wŏsh'ĭ-tô'). **1.** River, c. 600 mi (965 km), of SW Ark. and E La. **2.** Low mountain range extending c. 200 mi (320 km) from central Ark. to SE Okla.

Oua·ga·dou·gou (wä'gə-do͞o'go͞o). Capital city of Upper Volta, in the central part of country. Pop. 180,000.

Oudh (oud). Historical region of N central India.

Ouj·da (o͞oj-dä'). City of NE Morocco, near the Algerian border. Pop. 175,532.

Ouse (o͞oz). **1.** Also **Great Ouse** (grāt). River, c. 155 mi (250 km), of S central England. **2.** River, c. 60 mi (100 km), of NE England.

Out·er Mon·go·li·a (out'ər mŏng-gō'lē-ə, -lyə). Mongolia.

Ou·tre·mont (o͞o'trə-mŏnt', o͞o-trə-môN'). City of S Que., Canada, part of Greater Montreal, on Montreal Is. Pop. 27,089.

O·ver·land (ō'vər-lənd). City of E Mo., near St. Louis. Pop. 19,620.

Overland Park. City of E Kans., near Kansas City. Pop. 81,784.

O·vie·do (ō-vyĕ'*thō*). City of NW Spain, near the Cantabrian Mts. Pop. 181,556.

O·wa·ton·na (ō'wə-tŏn'ə). City of SE Minn., S of Minneapolis. Pop. 18,632.

O·wens (ō'wĭnz). River, c. 120 mi (195 km), of SE Calif.

O·wens·bor·o (ō'wĭnz-bûr'ō, -bər-ə'). City of W Ky., on the Ohio R. Pop. 54,450.

O·wen Sound (ō'wĭn). City of SE Ont., Canada, on **Owen Sound,** an inlet of Georgian Bay. Pop. 19,732.

Owen Stan·ley (stăn'lē). Mountain range of SE Papua New Guinea, on New Guinea Is., rising to 13,363 ft (4,075.7 m).

O·wos·so (ə-wŏs'ō, ō-wŏs'ō). City of central Mich., W of Flint. Pop. 16,455.

O·wy·hee (ō-wī'ē, -hē'). River, c. 300 mi (480 km), of SW Idaho, N Nev., and SE Ore.

Ox·ford (ŏks'fərd). **1.** Borough of S central England, on the Thames. Pop. 122,400. **2.** Town of S Mass., SSW of Worcester. Pop. 11,680. **3.** City of N Miss., SSE of Memphis, Tenn. Pop. 9,882. **4.** Village of SW Ohio, NW of Hamilton. Pop. 17,655.

Ox·nard (ŏks'närd'). City of S Calif., WNW of Los Angeles. Pop. 108,195.

O·yo (ō'yō). City of SW Nigeria, SW of Ogbomosho. Pop. 152,000.

O·zark (ō'zärk'). **1. Plateau** also **the O·zarks** (ō'zärks). Upland region of S central U.S., extending from NW Ark. to E Okla. **2.** City of SE Ala., NW of Dothan. Pop. 12,721.

Ozarks, Lake of the. Man-made lake, 93 sq mi (240.9 sq km), of central Mo., formed in the Osage R. by Bagnell Dam.

P

Pa·bia·ni·ce (pä'byä-nē'tsĕ). City of central Poland, SW of Łódź. Pop. 69,800.

Pa·chu·ca (pä-cho͞o'kä) or **Pa·chu·ca de So·to** (dĕ sô'tô). City of central Mexico, NE of Mexico City. Pop. 105,200.

Pa·cif·ic (pə-sĭf'ĭk). Largest and deepest ocean, c. 70,000,000 sq mi (181,300,000 sq km), extending from the W Americas to E Asia and Australia.

Pa·cif·i·ca (pə-sĭf'ĭ-kə). City of W Calif., S of San Francisco. Pop. 36,866.

Pacific Grove. City of W central Calif., near Monterey. Pop. 15,755.

Pacific Islands, Trust Territory of the. U.S.-administered islands of the W Pacific N and NE of New Guinea, including the Carolines, the Marianas (except Guam), and the Marshalls. Pop. 114,773.

Pacific North·west (nôrth-wĕst'). Region of the NW U.S., usually including Wash. and Ore. and sometimes SW B.C., Canada.

Pa·dang (pä-däng', pä'däng'). City of W Sumatra, Indonesia, on the Indian Ocean. Pop. 196,339.

Pa·der·born (pä'dər-bôrn'). City of N central West Germany, NW of Kassel. Pop. 109,218.

Pa·dre (pä'drē, păd'rē). Island, c. 115 mi (185 km) long, paralleling S coast of Tex.

Pad·u·a (păj'o͞o-ə, păd'yo͞o-ə). City of NE Italy, W of Venice. Pop. 242,216.

Pa·du·cah (pə-do͞o'kə, -dyo͞o'-). City of W Ky., on the Ohio R. Pop. 29,315.

Paes·tum (pĕs'təm, pēs'-). Ancient city of SW Italy, on the Gulf of Salerno.

Pa·go Pa·go also **Pa·go·pa·go** (päng'-ō-päng'ō, päng'gō-päng'gō, päng'gō-päng'gō, pä'gō-pä'gō, pä'gō-pä'gō) or **Pan·go Pan·go** (päng'ō päng'ō, päng'-gō päng'gō, päng'gō päng'gō). Cap. of American Samoa, on the S coast of Tutuila Is. Pop. 2,451.

Pa·hang (pə-hăng', -hŭng'). River, c. 285 mi (459 km), of SE Malay Peninsula, Malaysia.

Paines·ville (pānz'vĭl'). City of NE Ohio, NE of Cleveland. Pop. 16,391.

Paint·ed Desert (pān'tĭd). Plateau region of E central Ariz.

Pais·ley (pāz'lē). District of W Scotland, on the Clyde W of Glasgow. Pop. 94,025.

Pak·i·stan (păk'ĭ-stăn', pä'kĭ-stän'). Country of S Asia. Cap. Islamabad. Pop. 88,610,000. **—Pak'i·stan'i** (-stăn'ē, -stä'nē) *adj. & n.*

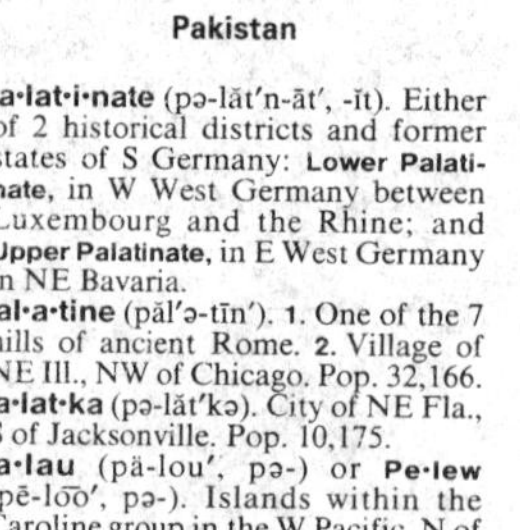

Pakistan

Pa·lat·i·nate (pə-lăt'n-āt', -ĭt). Either of 2 historical districts and former states of S Germany: **Lower Palatinate,** in W West Germany between Luxembourg and the Rhine; and **Upper Palatinate,** in E West Germany in NE Bavaria.

Pal·a·tine (păl'ə-tīn'). **1.** One of the 7 hills of ancient Rome. **2.** Village of NE Ill., NW of Chicago. Pop. 32,166.

Pa·lat·ka (pə-lăt'kə). City of NE Fla., S of Jacksonville. Pop. 10,175.

Pa·lau (pä-lou', pə-) or **Pe·lew** (pē-lo͞o', pə-). Islands within the Caroline group in the W Pacific, N of W New Guinea.

Pa·la·wan (pä-lä'wän). Island, c. 280 mi (451 km) long, of SW Philippines N of Borneo.

Pa·lem·bang (pä'lĕm-bäng'). City of SE Sumatra, Indonesia. Pop. 582,961.

Pa·len·cia (pä-lĕn'syä). City of N central Spain, NNE of Valladolid. Pop. 67,755.

Pa·ler·mo (pə-lûr'mō, -lâr'-, pä-lĕr'-mō). City of NW Sicily, Italy, on the Tyrrhenian Sea. Pop. 693,949.

Pal·es·tine (păl'ĭ-stīn'). **1.** Region of SW Asia between the E Mediterranean shore and the Jordan R. **2.** City of NE central Tex., SE of Dallas. Pop. 15,948. **—Pal'es·tin'i·an** (-stĭn'-ē-ən) *adj. & n.*

Pal·i·sades (păl'ĭ-sādz'). Row of cliffs in NE N.J. along the W bank of the Hudson.

Palisades Park. Borough of NE N.J., near the Hudson opposite Upper Manhattan. Pop. 13,732.

Palk (pôk, pôlk). Strait, 40–85 mi (64–137 km) wide, between India and Sri Lanka.

Pal·ma (päl'mä) also **Pal·ma de Ma·llor·ca** (dĕ mä-lyôr'kä, -yôr'-). City of SW Majorca Is., Spain, on the **Bay of Palma,** an inlet of the Mediterranean. Pop. 287,389.

Palm Bay (päm). City of E Fla., on the Atlantic SE of Orlando. Pop. 18,560.

Palm Beach. City of SE Fla., on the Atlantic E of Lake Okeechobee. Pop. 9,729.

Palm Beach Gar·dens (gâr'dnz). City of SE Fla., near West Palm Beach. Pop. 14,407.

Palm·dale (päm'dāl').City of S Calif., NE of Los Angeles. Pop. 12,277.

Palm Desert. City of SE Calif., E of Los Angeles. Pop. 11,801.

Pal·mer (pä'mər). Town of SW Mass., ENE of Springfield. Pop. 11,389.

Pal·mi·ra (päl-mē'rä). City of W Colombia, WSW of Bogotá. Pop. 168,000.

Palm Springs. City of SE Calif., ESE of Riverside. Pop. 32,271.

Pal·my·ra (păl-mī'rə). Ancient city of central Syria, NE of Damascus.

Pal·o Al·to (păl'ō ăl'tō). City of W Calif., NW of San Jose. Pop. 55,225.

Pal·o·mar (păl'ə-mär'), **Mount.** Peak, 6,126 ft (1,868.4 m), of S Calif., NE of San Diego.

Pa·los Heights (pā'ləs). City of NE Ill., near Chicago. Pop. 11,096.

Pal·os Ver·des Estates (păl'ōs vûr'-dēz, păl'əs). City of S Calif., SSE of Santa Monica. Pop. 14,376.

Pa·louse (pə-lo͞os'). River, c. 140 mi (225 km), of NW Idaho and SE Wash.

Pa·mirs (pä-mîrz', pə-) also **Pa·mir** (-mîr'). Mountain region of S central Asia, in S Central Asian USSR with extensions in N Afghanistan, N Kashmir, and W China.

Pam·li·co Sound (păm'lĭ-kō'). Inlet of the Atlantic, c. 80 mi (129 km) long, between E coast of N.C. and offshore islands.

Pam·pa (păm'pə). City of NW Tex., in the Panhandle NE of Amarillo. Pop. 21,396.

Pam·plo·na (păm-plō'nə, päm-plô'-nä). City of N Spain, SE of San Sebastián. Pop. 175,833.

Pan·a·ma (păn'ə-mä') also **Pan·a·má** (pä'nä-mä'). **1. Gulf of.** Wide inlet of the Pacific on S coast of Panama. **2. Isthmus of.** Isthmus, c. 31 mi (50 km) wide, connecting North and South America and separating the Pacific from the Caribbean Sea. **3.** Ship canal, 51 mi (82.1 km) long, across the Isthmus of Panama in the Canal Zone, connecting the Caribbean Sea with the Pacific. **4. Canal Zone.** See **Canal Zone. 5.** Country of SW Central America. Cap. Panama. Pop. 2,000,000. **6.** Also **Panama City.** Cap. of Panama, in the central part on the Gulf of Panama. Pop. 467,000. **—Pan'a·ma'ni·an** *adj. & n.*

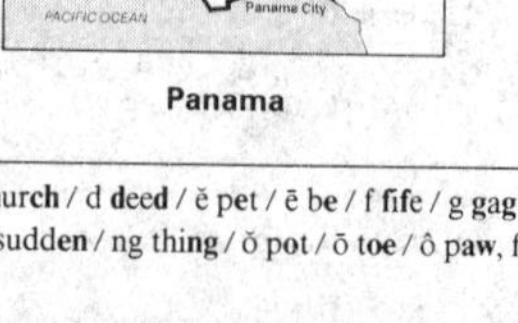

Panama

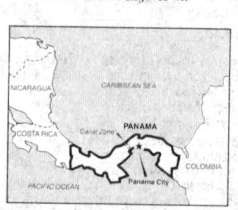

Panama City. 1. Panama (sense 6). **2.** City of NW Fla., ESE of Pensacola. Pop. 33,346.

Pan·a·mint (păn'ə-mĭnt'). Range of SE Calif., near the Nev. border, rising to 11,045 ft (3,368.7 m).

Pa·nay (pä-nī', pə-). Island of the central Philippines, in the Visayan group NW of Negros.

Pan·čev·o (pän'chĕ-vô). City of NE Yugoslavia, near Belgrade. Pop. 54,269.

Pan·go Pan·go (päng'ō päng'ō, päng'gō päng'gō, päng'gō päng'gō). Variant of **Pago Pago.**

Pan·mun·jom (pän'mo͞on'jŏm'). Village of NW South Korea; site of Korean War truce signing (1953).

Pan·no·ni·a (pə-nō'nē-ə). Ancient Roman province of central Europe including present-day W Hungary and N Yugoslavia.

Pá·nu·co (pä'no͞o-kô'). River, c. 315 mi (507 km), of central Mexico.

Pao·ki (bou'jyĕ'). Baoji.

Pao·ting (bou'dĭng'). Baoding.

Pao·tow (bou'tō'). Baotou.

Pa·pal States (pā'pəl). Territories in central Italy ruled by the popes until 1870.

Pap·u·a New Guin·ea (păp'yo͞o-ə no͞o' gĭn'ē, nyo͞o'). Country of the W Pacific, comprising E half of New Guinea, the Bismarck Archipelago, the N Solomons, and adjacent islands. Cap. Port Moresby. Pop. 2,905,000. **—Pap'u·an New Guin'e·an** *n.*

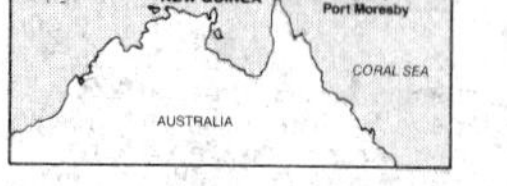

Papua New Guinea

Pa·rá (pə-rä'). River, c. 200 mi (320 km), of N Brazil, the SE distributary of the Amazon.

Par·a·dise (păr'ə-dīs'). City of N central Calif., N of Sacramento. Pop. 22,571.

Paradise Valley. Town of S central Ariz., near Phoenix. Pop. 10,832.

Par·a·gould (păr'ə-go͞old'). City of NE Ark., WNW of Blytheville. Pop. 15,214.

Pa·ra·gua·çu or **Pa·ra·guas·su** (pä'-rə-gwə-so͞o'). River, c. 300 mi (483 km), of E Brazil.

Par·a·guay (păr'ə-gwā', -gwī', pä'-rä-gwī'). **1.** River of W Brazil and Paraguay, flowing c. 1,300 mi (2,092 km) S into the Paraná. **2.** Country of S central South America. Cap. Asunción. Pop. 3,100,000. **—Par'a·guay'an** *adj. & n.*

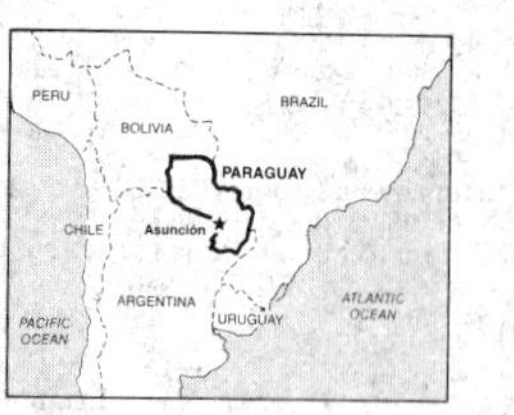

Paraguay

Pa·ra·í·ba (pä'rə-ē'bə) also **Paraíba do Sul** (do͞o so͞ol'). River, c. 650 mi (1,046 km), of SE Brazil.

Par·a·mar·i·bo (păr'ə-măr'ə-bō'). Cap. of Surinam, on the Suriname R. near the Atlantic. Pop. 102,300.

Par·a·mount (păr'ə-mount'). City of S Calif., SE of Los Angeles. Pop. 36,407.

Pa·ram·us (pə-răm'əs). Borough of NE N.J., near Paterson. Pop. 26,474.

Pa·ra·ná (păr'ə-nä', pä'rä-nä'). **1.** River of central South America, rising in E central Brazil and flowing c. 2,040 mi (3,282 km) SW into the

Rio de la Plata in E Argentina. **2.** City of NE Argentina, on the Paraná R. Pop. 127,635.

Pa·ra·na·guá (pä'rə-nə-gwä'). City of SE Brazil, on the Atlantic. Pop. 51,510.

Pa·ra·na·í·ba (pä'rə-nə-ē'bə). River, c. 500 mi (805 km), of S central Brazil.

Par·du·bi·ce (pär'dŏŏ-bĭ'tsĕ). City of N central Czechoslovakia, on the Elbe R. Pop. 93,042.

Par·is (păr'ĭs). **1.** Cap. of France, in the N central part on the Seine. Pop. 2,050,500. **2.** City of NW Tenn., WNW of Nashville. Pop. 10,728. **3.** City of NE Tex., NE of Dallas. Pop. 25,498. —**Pa·ri'sian** (pə-rē'zhən, -rĭzh'ən) *adj. & n.*

Park (pärk). Range of the Rockies in central Colo. and S Wyo., rising to 14,284 ft (4,356.6 m).

Par·kers·burg (pär'kərz-bûrg'). City of NW W.Va., on the Ohio R. N of Charleston. Pop. 39,967.

Park Forest (fôr'ĭst, fŏr'). Village of NE Ill., near Chicago. Pop. 26,222.

Park Ridge (rĭj). City of NE Ill., near Chicago. Pop. 38,704.

Par·ma (pär'mə). **1.** (*also* pär'mä). City of N Italy, SE of Milan. Pop. 176,945. **2.** City of NE Ohio, near Cleveland. Pop. 92,547.

Parma Heights. City of NE Ohio, near Cleveland. Pop. 23,112.

Par·na·í·ba (pär'nə-ē'bə). River, c. 800 mi (1,287 km), of NE Brazil.

Par·nas·sus (pär-năs'əs) also **Par·nas·sós** (-nä-sôs'). Mountain, c. 8,060 ft (2,460 m), of central Greece N of the Gulf of Corinth.

Par·ra·mat·ta (păr'ə-măt'ə). City of SE Australia, near Sydney. Pop. 134,300.

Par·ry (păr'ē). **1.** Channel through the central Arctic Archipelago, N.W.T., Canada, linking Baffin Bay on the E with Beaufort Sea on the W. **2.** Islands of N N.W.T., Canada, in the Arctic Ocean N of Victoria Is.

Par·sons (pär'sənz). City of SE Kans., ESE of Wichita. Pop. 12,898.

Par·thi·a (pär'thē-ə). Ancient country of SW Asia, corresponding to modern NE Iran. —**Par'thi·an** *adj. & n.*

Pas·a·de·na (păs'ə-dē'nə). **1.** City of S Calif., near Los Angeles. Pop. 119,374. **2.** City of S Tex., near Houston. Pop. 112,560.

Pas·ca·gou·la (păs'kə-gōō'lə). City of extreme SE Miss., E of Biloxi. Pop. 29,318.

Pas·co (păs'kō). City of S Wash., on the Columbia near Richland. Pop. 17,944.

Pas·sa·ic (pə-sā'ĭk). City of NE N.J., N of Newark. Pop. 52,463.

Pas·sa·ma·quod·dy Bay (păs'ə-mə-kwŏd'ē). Arm of the Bay of Fundy between S N.B., Canada, and E Me.

Pas·sau (päs'ou). City of SE West Germany, near the Austrian border. Pop. 50,323.

Pas·ta·za (päs-tä'sä). River, c. 400 mi (644 km), of E Ecuador and N Peru.

Pas·to (päs'tô). City of SW Colombia, near the Ecuador border. Pop. 171,000.

Pat·chogue (păch'ŏg', -ôg'). Village of SE N.Y., on S central Long Is. Pop. 11,291.

Pat·er·son (păt'ər-sən). City of NE N.J., N of Newark. Pop. 137,970.

Pat·na (pŭt'nə, păt'-, pŭt'nä'). City of NE India, on the Ganges. Pop. 473,001.

Pa·tos (pä'tōōsh). **Lagoa dos.** See **Lagoa dos Patos.**

Pá·trai (pä'trē). *Greek.* Patras.

Pa·tras (pə-trăs', pă'trəs). City of S Greece, in NW Peloponnesus on the **Gulf of Patras**, an inlet of the Ionian Sea. Pop. 111,607.

Pau (pō). City of SW France, in the foothills of the Pyrenees. Pop. 83,498.

Pa·vi·a (pä-vē'ä). City of NW Italy, S of Milan. Pop. 87,005.

Paw·tuck·et (pô-tŭk'ĭt, pə-). City of NE R.I., on the Mass. border near Providence. Pop. 71,204.

Pay·san·dú (pī'sän-dōō'). City of W Uruguay, on the Uruguay R. Pop. 62,412.

Pea·bod·y (pē'bŏd'ē, -bə-dē). City of NE Mass., near Salem. Pop. 45,976.

Peace (pēs). River, c. 945 mi (1,521 km), of N B.C. and N Alta., Canada.

Pearl (pûrl). **1.** River, 485 mi (780.4 km), of S Miss., forming the Miss.-La. boundary in its lower course. **2.** City of central Miss., near Jackson. Pop. 20,778.

Pearl City. Village of Hawaii, on Pearl Harbor in S Oahu. Pop. 22,200.

Pearl Harbor. Inlet of the Pacific on S coast of Oahu, Hawaii, W of Honolulu.

Pear·land (pâr'lənd, -lănd'). City of SE Tex., near Houston. Pop. 13,248.

Pea·ry Land (pîr'ē). Peninsula of N Greenland, extending into the Arctic Ocean.

Pe·cho·ra (pə-chô'rə). River of NE European USSR, flowing c. 1,120 mi (1,802 m) N into **Pechora Bay**, SE arm of the Barents Sea.

Pe·cos (pā'kəs). **1.** River of E N.Mex. and W Tex., flowing c. 926 mi (1,490 km) SE into the Rio Grande. **2.** City of SW Tex., ESE of El Paso. Pop. 12,855.

Pécs (pāch). City of SW Hungary, near the Yugoslav border. Pop. 170,000.

Pee Dee (pē'dē'). River, c. 233 mi (375 km), of S central N.C. and NE S.C.

Peeks·kill (pēk'skĭl). City of SE N.Y., on the Hudson N of White Plains. Pop. 18,236.

Peel (pēl). River, c. 365 mi (587 km), of N Y.T. and W N.W.T., Canada.

Pe·gu (pĕ-gōō'). City of S Burma, NNE of Rangoon. Pop. 135,000.

Pei (bī). Bai.

Pei·ping (bā'pĭng'). Beijing.

Pei·pus (pī'pəs). Lake, 1,357 sq mi (3,515 sq km), of NW European USSR, SW of Leningrad.

Pe·ka·long·an (pē'kä-lông'gän', -än'). City of N central Java, Indonesia, on the Java Sea. Pop. 111,537.

Pe·kin (pē'kĭn). City of central Ill., S of Peoria. Pop. 33,967.

Pe·king (pē'kĭng', bā'jyĭng'). Beijing.

Pe·la·gi·an (pə-lā'jē-ən, -jən) also **Pe·la·gie** (pä-lä'jä). 3 Italian islands in the Mediterranean between Malta and Tunisia.

Pe·lée (pə-lā'). Volcano, c. 4,800 ft (1,464 m), on N Martinique, French West Indies.

Pe·lew (pē-lōō', pə-). Variant of **Palau.**

Pel·ham (pĕl'əm). Town of SE Ont., Canada, NNW of Welland. Pop. 10,849.

Pel·la (pĕl'ə). Ancient city of Greek Macedonia, NW of modern Salonika.

Pel·ly (pĕl'ē). River, c. 330 mi (531 km), of central Y.T., Canada.

Pel·o·pon·ne·sus (pĕl'ə-pə-nē'səs) also **Pel·o·pon·ne·sos** (-sôs, -sŏs, -sōs) or **Pel·o·pon·nese** (-nēz', -nēs'). Peninsula forming S part of Greece, S of the Gulf of Corinth. —**Pel'o·pon·ne'sian** *adj. & n.*

Pe·lo·tas (pə-lô'təs). City of SE Brazil, on Lagoa dos Patos. Pop. 150,278.

Pem·ba (pĕm'bə). Island of Tanzania, in the Indian Ocean N of Zanzibar.

Pem·broke (pĕm'brŏŏk', -brōk'). **1.** City of SE Ont., Canada, on the Ottawa R. NW of Ottawa. Pop. 14,249. **2.** Town of E Mass., SE of Boston. Pop. 13,487.

Pembroke Pines (pīnz). City of SE Fla., SW of Fort Lauderdale. Pop. 35,776.

Pe·nang (pē-năng', pə-, pē'năng', -näng') or **Pi·nang** (pĭ-năng'). **1.** Island of Malaysia in the N Strait of Malacca off the W coast of the Malay Peninsula. **2.** City of W Malaysia, on Penang Is. Pop. 270,019.

Pen·dle·ton (pĕn'dl-tən). City of NE Ore., SW of Walla Walla, Wash. Pop. 14,521.

Pend O·reille (pŏn'də-rā'). River, c. 100 mi (161 km), rising in **Pend Oreille Lake** (148 sq mi/383.3 sq km), N Idaho, and flowing W, N, and W into the Columbia in S B.C., Canada.

Peng·hu (pŭng'hōō'). *Chinese.* Pescadores.

Peng·pu (pŭng'pōō'). Bengbu.

Pen·ki (bŭn'chē'). Benxi.

Pen·nine (pĕn'īn'). **1. Alps** (ălps). Range of the Alps along the Swiss-Italian border, W of Lake Maggiore, rising to 15,203 ft (4,637 m). **2. Chain** (chān) or **Pen·nines** (-īnz'). Range of hills extending from S Scotland to central England.

Penn·syl·va·ni·a (pĕn'səl-vān'yə, -vā'nē-ə). State of E U.S. Cap. Harrisburg. Pop. 11,866,728. —**Penn'syl·va'ni·an** *adj. & n.*

Pe·nob·scot (pə-nŏb'skŏt', -skət). River of central Me., flowing c. 350 mi (563 km) S into **Penobscot Bay**, an inlet of the Atlantic.

Pen·sa·co·la (pĕn'sə-kō'lə). City of extreme NW Fla., ESE of Mobile, Ala. Pop. 57,619.

Pen·tic·ton (pĕn-tĭk'tən). City of S B.C., Canada, E of Vancouver. Pop. 21,344.

Pent·land Firth (pĕnt'lənd). Channel between NE Scotland and the Orkney Is.

Pen·za (pĕn'zə). City of central European USSR, NNW of Saratov. Pop. 490,000.

Pen·zhi·na (pĕn'zhĭ-nə). **1.** Also **Pen·zhin·ska·ya** (pĕn'zhĭn'skə-yə). Bay of the Sea of Okhotsk, extending c. 185 mi (298 km) into NE Siberia along NW coast of Kamchatka. **2.** River of NE Asian USSR, flowing c. 446 mi (718 km) from the Kolyma Mts. to Penzhina Bay.

Pe·or·i·a (pē-ôr'ē-ə, -ōr'-). **1.** City of S central Ariz., near Phoenix. Pop. 12,251. **2.** City of central Ill., N of Springfield. Pop. 124,160.

Pe·rei·ra (pĕ-rā'rä). City of W central Colombia, W of Bogotá. Pop. 260,000.

Per·ga·mum (pûr'gə-məm) also **Per·ga·mos** (-gə-məs, -mŏs'). Ancient Greek city of W Asia Minor, at site of modern Bergama, W Turkey.

Pér·i·bon·ca (pĕr'ĭ-bŏng'kə). River, c. 280 mi (451 km), of S central Que., Canada.

Perm (pĕrm). City of E European USSR, on the Kama R. Pop. 1,008,000.

Per·nik (pĕr'nĭk). City of W Bulgaria, SW of Sofia. Pop. 91,428.

Per·pi·gnan (pĕr-pē-nyäN'). City of S France, near the Spanish border and the Mediterranean. Pop. 106,426.

Per·rys·burg (pĕr'ēz-bûrg'). City of NW Ohio, near Toledo. Pop. 10,215.

Per·sep·o·lis (pər-sĕp'ə-lĭs). Ruined city of ancient Persia, NE of Shiraz, SW Iran.

Per·sia (pûr'zhə, -shə). Iran. —**Per'sian** *adj. & n.*

Persian Gulf. Arm of the Arabian Sea between Arabia and SW Iran.

Perth (pûrth). **1.** City of SW Australia, near the Indian Ocean. Metro. area pop. 883,600. **2.** Burgh of central Scotland, NNW of Edinburgh. Pop. 44,066.

Perth Am·boy (ăm'boi'). City of E central N.J., on Raritan Bay opposite Staten Is. Pop. 38,951.

Pe·ru (pə-rōō'). **1.** Country of W South America, on the Pacific. Cap. Lima. Pop. 17,995,000. **2.** City of N Ill., opposite La Salle. Pop. 10,886. **3.** City of N Ind., E of Logansport. Pop. 13,764. —**Pe·ru'vi·an** (-vē-ən) *adj. & n.*

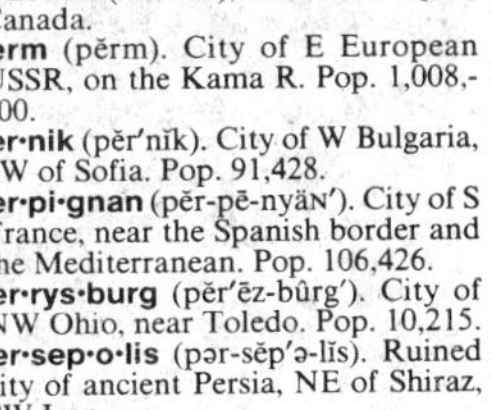

Peru

Pe·ru·gia (pə-rōō'jə, pā-rōō'jä). City of central Italy, overlooking the Tiber N of Rome. Pop. 139,871.

Pe·sa·ro (pā'zä-rō). City of central Italy, on the Adriatic W of Florence. Pop. 90,705.

Pes·ca·do·res (pĕs'kə-dôr'ēz, -ĭs, -dôr'). Islands of Taiwan, in Formosa Strait off W coast of Taiwan.

Pes·ca·ra (pās-kä'rä). City of central Italy, on the Adriatic ENE of Rome. Pop. 137,059.

Pe·sha·war (pə-shä'wər). City of N Pakistan, ESE of Khyber Pass. Pop. 219,562.

Pe·tah Tiq·wa or **Pe·tah Tiq·va** (pĕ-tä' tĕk'və, -vä). City of central Israel, E of Tel Aviv-Jaffa. Pop. 117,000.

Pet·a·lu·ma (pĕt'l-ōō'mə). City of W Calif., NNW of San Rafael. Pop. 33,834.

Pe·ter·bor·ough (pē'tər-bûr'ə, -bər-ə). **1.** City of SE Ont., Canada, NE of Toronto. Pop. 59,683. **2.** Borough of E central England, E of Leicester. Pop. 72,270.

Pe·ters·burg (pē'tərz-bûrg'). Independent city of SE Va., S of Richmond. Pop. 41,055.

Pe·ti·tot (pĕt'ĭ-tō'). River, 295 mi (475 km), of NE B.C. and NW Alta., Canada.

Pe·tra (pē'trə). Ancient city of Edom, in present-day SW Jordan.

Pet·ri·fied Forest National Park (pĕt'rə-fīd'). Section of the Painted Desert in E Ariz. reserved for its petrified trees.

Pet·ro·pav·lovsk (pĕ'trə-päv'ləfsk). **1.** City of N Central Asian USSR, W of Novosibirsk. Pop. 209,000. **2.** Also **Pet·ro·pav·lovsk-Kam·chat·ski** (-kăm-chăt'skē). City of Far Eastern USSR, on the Pacific coast of SE Kamchatka. Pop. 219,000.

Pe·tróp·o·lis (pə-trŏp'ə-lĭs, -trô'pōō-lēsh'). City of SE Brazil, N of Rio de Janeiro. Pop. 116,080.

Pet·ro·za·vodsk (pĕ'trə-zä-vôtsk'). City of NW European USSR, on Lake Onega. Pop. 238,000.

Pforz·heim (pfôrts'hīm, pfōrts'-). City of SW West Germany, WNW of Stuttgart. Pop. 106,677.

Pha·ros (fâr'ŏs'). Peninsula, formerly an island, in Alexandria, N Egypt.

Pharr (fär). City of extreme S Tex., WNW of Brownsville. Pop. 21,381.

Phe·nix City (fē'nĭks). City of E Ala., near Columbus, Ga. Pop. 27,012.

Phil·a·del·phi·a (fĭl'ə-dĕl'fē-ə). City of SE Pa., on the Delaware R. Pop. 1,688,210. —**Phil'a·del'phi·an** *adj. & n.*

Phi·lip·pi (fĭ-lĭp'ī'). Ancient town of N central Macedonia, Greece; site of Antony and Octavian's defeat of Brutus and Cassius (42 B.C.).

Phil·ip·pines (fĭl'ə-pēnz', fĭl'ə-pēnz'). Country of E Asia consisting of the **Philippine Is.**, an archipelago in the W Pacific SE of China. Cap. Manila. Pop. 48,200,000. —**Phil'ip·pine** *adj.*

Philippines

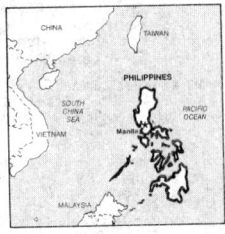

Philippine Sea. Part of the W Pacific E of the Philippines and W of the Marianas.

Phi·lis·ti·a (fĭ-lĭs'tē-ə). Ancient country on SW coast of Palestine.

Phil·lips·burg (fĭl'ĭps-bûrg'). Town of W N.J., on the Delaware R. NE of Bethlehem, Pa. Pop. 16,647.

Phnom Penh (pə-nôm'pĕn', nŏm'pĕn'). Cap. of Cambodia, in the SW part on the Mekong R. Pop. 393,995.

Pho·cae·a (fō-sē'ə). Ancient Ionian Greek city of W Asia Minor, on the Aegean N of modern Izmir, W Turkey.

Pho·cis (fō'sĭs). Region and ancient country of central Greece, N of the Gulf of Corinth.

Phoe·ni·cia (fĭ-nĭsh'ə, -nē'shə). Ancient maritime country of SW Asia consisting of city-states along the E

Mediterranean in present-day Syria and Lebanon. —**Phoe·ni'cian** *adj. & n.*

Phoe·nix (fē'nĭks). **1.** Islands in the central Pacific, N of Samoa. **2.** Cap. of Ariz., in the S central part. Pop. 764,911.

Pia·cen·za (pyä-chĕn'tsä). Town of N Italy, on the Po R. SE of Milan. Pop. 108,888.

Pi·at·ra Ne·amt (pyä'trä nyämts'). City of NE Rumania, E of Cluj. Pop. 83,168.

Pic·a·yune (pĭk'ə-yo͞on'). City of S Miss., near the La. border WNW of Gulfport. Pop. 10,361.

Pick·er·ing (pĭk'ə-rĭng). Town of S Ont., Canada, near Lake Ontario NE of Toronto. Pop. 35,189.

Pi·co Bo·lí·var (pē'kô bô-lē'vär). Highest mountain, 16,411 ft (5,003.4 m), in Venezuela, in the W part S of Lake Maracaibo.

Pico de A·ne·to (dā ä-nā'tō). Highest peak, 11,168 ft (3,406.2 m), of the Pyrenees, in NE Spain near the French border.

Pi·co Ri·ve·ra (pē'kō rə-vîr'ə). City of S Calif., E of Los Angeles. Pop. 53,459.

Pied·mont (pēd'mŏnt'). **1.** Region of NW Italy. **2.** Plateau region of E U.S., extending from N.Y. to Ala. between the Appalachians and the Atlantic coastal plain. **3.** City of W Calif., near Oakland. Pop. 10,498. —**Pied'mon·tese'** *adj. & n.*

Pie·dras Ne·gras (pyĕ'*th*räs nĕ'gräs). City of N Mexico, on the Rio Grande N of Monterrey. Pop. 41,033.

Pierre (pîr). Cap. of S.Dak., in the central part. Pop. 11,973.

Pierre·fonds (pē-ĕr-fôɴ', pyĕr-). City of S Que., Canada, on Montreal Is. W of Montreal. Pop. 35,402.

Pie·ter·mar·itz·burg (pē'tər-măr'ĭts-bûrg'). City of E South Africa, WNW of Durban. Pop. 114,882.

Pigs (pĭgz), **Bay of.** Small inlet of the Caribbean on S coast of W Cuba.

Pikes Peak (pīks). Mountain, 14,110 ft (4,303.6 m), in the Front Range of central Colo.

Pi·ła (pē'lä). City of NW Poland, N of Poznań. Pop. 57,200.

Pil·co·ma·yo (pēl'kô-mä'yô). River of central South America, rising in central Bolivia and flowing c. 1,000 mi (1,609 km) SE along the Argentina-Paraguay border to the Paraguay R.

Pil·sen (pĭl'zən). *German.* Plzeň.

Pi·nang (pĭ-năng'). Variant of **Penang.**

Pi·nar del Rí·o (pē-när' dĕl rē'ô). City of W Cuba, WSW of Havana. Pop. 89,978.

Pin·dus (pĭn'dəs). Mountains of NW Greece, rising to 8,650 ft (2,638.3 m).

Pine Bluff (pīn' blŭf'). City of S central Ark., SSE of Little Rock. Pop. 56,811.

Pi·nel·las Park (pī-nĕl'əs). City of W Fla., near St. Petersburg. Pop. 32,811.

Pines (pīnz), **Isle of.** Island in the Caribbean off SW Cuba.

Pine·ville (pīn'vĭl', -vəl). City of central La., on the Red R. opposite Alexandria. Pop. 12,034.

Ping (pĭng). River, c. 350 mi (563 km), of NW Thailand.

Ping·tung or **Ping·dong** (pĭng'do͝ong'). City of S Taiwan, E of Kaohsiung. Pop. 182,114.

Pi·nole (pə-nōl', pī-). City of W Calif., near Richmond. Pop. 14,253.

Pinsk (pĭnsk, pēnsk). City of W European USSR, WNW of Kiev. Pop. 93,000.

Pio·tr·ków Try·bu·nal·ski (pyô'tər-ko͞of' trē'bo͞o-näl'skē). City of Central Poland, SSE of Łódź. Pop. 70,900.

Piq·ua (pĭk'wā', -wə). City of SW central Ohio, N of Dayton. Pop. 20,480.

Pi·rae·us (pī-rē'əs). City of E central Greece, on the Saronic Gulf near Athens. Pop. 187,362.

Pi·rai·évs (pē'rĕ-ĕfs'). *Greek.* Piraeus.

Pir·ma·sens (pîr'mä-zĕns'). City of SW West Germany, near the French border. Pop. 50,250.

Pir·na (pîr'nä). City of SE East Germany, on the Elbe R. near the Czech border. Pop. 48,233.

Pi·sa (pē'zə, -sä). City of N central Italy, on the Arno R. near the Tyrrhenian Sea. Pop. 103,772. —**Pi'san** *adj. & n.*

Pis·to·ia (pēs-tô'yä). City of N central Italy, NW of Florence. Pop. 84,300.

Pit (pĭt). River, c. 200 mi (322 km), of N Calif.

Pit·cairn (pĭt'kârn'). British-administered island of the S Pacific, ESE of Tahiti.

Pitts·burg (pĭts'bûrg'). **1.** City of W Calif., NE of Oakland. Pop. 33,034. **2.** City of SE Kans., near the Mo. border. Pop. 18,770.

Pitts·burgh (pĭts'bûrg'). City of SW Pa., at the confluence of the Allegheny and Monongahela rivers, forming the Ohio R. Pop. 423,938.

Pitts·field (pĭts'fēld'). City of W Mass., NW of Springfield. Pop. 51,974.

Piu·ra (pyo͞o'rä). City of NW Peru, near the Pacific. Pop. 81,683.

Pla·cen·tia (plə-sĕn'shə). **1.** Bay of the Atlantic in SE Newf., Canada. **2.** City of S Calif., near Santa Ana. Pop. 35,041.

Pla·cid (plăs'ĭd). Lake of NE N.Y., in the Adirondacks.

Plain·field (plān'fēld'). **1.** Town of E Conn., NE of Norwich. Pop. 12,774. **2.** City of NE N.J., SW of Newark. Pop. 45,555.

Plain·view (plān'vyo͞o'). City of NW Tex., S of Amarillo. Pop. 22,187.

Plain·ville (plān'vĭl'). Town of central Conn., SW of Hartford. Pop. 16,401.

Pla·no (plā'nō'). City of NE Tex., near Dallas. Pop. 72,331.

Plan·ta·tion (plăn-tā'shən). City of SE Fla., near Fort Lauderdale. Pop. 48,501.

Plant City (plănt). City of W central Fla., E of Tampa. Pop. 19,270.

Pla·ta (plä'tä), **Río de la.** See **Río de la Plata.**

Pla·tae·a (plə-tē'ə). Ancient city of central Greece, SW of Thebes; site of Greek victory over Persians (479 B.C.).

Platte (plăt). River, c. 310 mi (499 km), of S Nebr.

Platts·burgh (plăts'bûrg'). City of extreme NE N.Y., on Lake Champlain NW of Burlington, Vt. Pop. 21,057.

Plau·en (plou'ən). City of S East Germany, near the NW Erzgebirge. Pop. 79,190.

Pleas·ant Grove (plĕz'ənt). City of N central Utah, near Provo. Pop. 10,669.

Pleasant Hill. City of W Calif., NE of Berkeley. Pop. 25,124.

Pleas·an·ton (plĕz'ən-tən). City of W Calif., SE of Oakland. Pop. 35,160.

Pleas·ant·ville (plĕz'ənt-vĭl'). City of SE N.J., near Atlantic City. Pop. 13,435.

Plev·en (plĕv'ĕn, -ən) or **Plev·na** (-nä, -nə). City of N Bulgaria, NE of Sofia. Pop. 122,916.

Plo·ieş·ti or **Plo·eş·ti** (plô-yĕsht', -yĕsh'tē). City of S central Rumania, N of Bucharest. Pop. 206,138.

Plov·div (plôv'dĭf). City of S Bulgaria, on the Maritsa R. Pop. 342,000.

Plum (plŭm). Borough of SW Pa., near Pittsburgh. Pop. 25,390.

Plym·outh (plĭm'əth). **1.** Borough of SW England, on the English Channel. Pop. 255,500. **2.** Town of W Conn., N of Waterbury. Pop. 10,732. **3.** Town of SE Mass., SE of Boston. Pop. 35,913. **4.** City of SE Minn., near Minneapolis-St. Paul. Pop. 31,615.

Plzeň (pŭl'zĕn'yə). City of W Czechoslovakia, WSW of Prague. Pop. 169,466.

Po (pō). River of N Italy, flowing c. 405 mi (652 km) E to the Adriatic.

Po·be·da Peak (pō-bā'dä). Highest (24,406 ft/7,443.8 m) mountain of the Tian Shan, on the border between S Central Asian USSR and NW China.

Po·ca·tel·lo (pō'kə-tĕl'ō, -tĕl'ə). City of SE Idaho, near the Snake R. Pop. 46,340.

Po·co·no (pō'kə-nō') or **Po·co·nos** (-nōz'). Mountains in NE Pa., rising to c. 1,600 ft (488 m).

Po·dolsk (pə-dôlsk'). City of central European USSR, S of Moscow. Pop. 203,000.

Po Hai (bō'hī'). Bo Hai.

Po·hang (pō'häng'). City of SE South Korea, on an inlet of the Sea of Japan. Pop. 110,000.

Pointe aux Trem·bles (poin'tō-trĕm'bəlz, pwăɴt ō träɴ'blə). City of S Que., Canada, on Montreal Is. N of Montreal. Pop. 35,618.

Pointe Claire (point' klâr'). City of S Que., Canada, on Montreal Is. WSW of Montreal. Pop. 25,917.

Pointe-Noire (pwăɴt-nwär'). City of SW Congo, on the Atlantic. Pop. 135,000.

Point Pleas·ant (point plĕz'ənt). Borough of E N.J., near the Atlantic ESE of Trenton. Pop. 17,747.

Poi·tiers (pwä-tyā'). City of W central France, ESE of Nantes. Pop. 81,313.

Po·land (pō'lənd). Country of central Europe, on the Baltic. Cap. Warsaw. Pop. 35,645,000. —**Po'lish** (pō'lĭsh) *adj. & n.*

Poland

Pol·ta·va (pŏl-tä'və). City of S European USSR, in the Ukraine WSW of Kharkov. Pop. 282,000.

Pol·y·ne·sia (pŏl'ə-nē'zhə, -shə). Scattered islands of the central and S Pacific, roughly between New Zealand, Hawaii, and Easter Is. —**Pol'y·ne'sian** *adj. & n.*

Pom·er·a·ni·a (pŏm'ə-rā'nē-ə, -rān'yə). Historical region of N central Europe along the Baltic in present-day NW Poland and NE East Germany. —**Pom'er·a'ni·an** *adj. & n.*

Po·mo·na (pə-mō'nə). City of S Calif., near Los Angeles. Pop. 92,742.

Pom·pa·no Beach (pŏm'pə-nō'). City of SE Fla., on the Atlantic. Pop. 52,618.

Pom·pe·ii (pŏm-pā', -pā'ē). Ancient city of S Italy, near Naples; destroyed by eruption of Mt. Vesuvius (A.D. 79). —**Pom·pe'ian, Pom·pei'ian** *adj. & n.*

Pomp·ton Lakes (pŏmp'tən). Borough of NE N.J., NW of Paterson. Pop. 10,660.

Pon·ca City (pŏng'kə). City of N Okla., NNE of Oklahoma City. Pop. 26,238.

Pon·ce (pôn'sĕ). City of S Puerto Rico, on the Caribbean. Pop. 161,260.

Pon·di·cher·ry (pŏn'dĭ-chĕr'ē, -shĕr'ē). City of SE India, on the Bay of Bengal SW of Madras. Pop. 90,637.

Pon·ta Del·ga·da (pŏn'tə dĕl-gä'də, pôn'). Chief city of the Azores, on the SW coast of São Miguel Is. Pop. 21,262.

Pont·char·train (pŏn'chər-trān'). Lake, c. 630 sq mi (1,632 sq km), of SE La., N of New Orleans.

Pon·te·ve·dra (pôn'tĕ-vĕ'*th*rä). City of NW Spain, on the Atlantic. Pop. 33,500.

Pon·ti·ac (pŏn'tē-ăk'). **1.** City of N central Ill., NE of Bloomington. Pop. 11,227. **2.** City of SE Mich., NW of Detroit. Pop. 76,715.

Pon·ti·a·nak (pŏn'tē-ä'näk, pôn'-). City of W Borneo, Indonesia, on the Kapuas R. delta. Pop. 217,555.

Pon·tus (pŏn'təs). Ancient country of NE Asia Minor, on the S Black Sea coast.

Pon·ty·pool (pŏn'tə-po͞ol'). Urban district of S Wales, NW of Cardiff. Pop. 90,400.

Poole (po͞ol). Borough of S England, on the English Channel WSW of Southampton. Pop. 115,500.

Poo·na (po͞o'nə). City of W central India, SE of Bombay. Pop. 856,105.

Pop·lar Bluff (pŏp'lər blŭf'). City of SE Mo., near the Ark. border S of St. Louis. Pop. 17,139.

Po·po·ca·té·petl (pō'pə-kăt'ə-pĕt-l, pô'pô-kä-tĕ'pĕt-l). Volcano, 17,887 ft (5,455.5 m), in central Mexico SE of Mexico City.

Por·cu·pine (pôr'kyə-pīn'). River, c. 448 mi (721 km), of N Y.T., Canada, and NE Alas.

Po·ri (pô'rĭ). City of SW Finland, near the Gulf of Bothnia NW of Helsinki. Pop. 79,815.

Por·tage (pôr'tĭj, pōr'-). **1.** City of NW Ind., on Lake Michigan. Pop. 27,409. **2.** City of SW Mich., S of Kalamazoo. Pop. 38,157.

Portage la Prai·rie (lə prâr'ē). City of S Man., Canada, W of Winnipeg. Pop. 12,571.

Port Al·ber·ni (pôrt' ăl-bûr'nē, pōrt'). City of SW B.C., Canada, on S central Vancouver Is. Pop. 19,585.

Port An·ge·les (ăn'jə-lĭs). City of NW Wash., on Juan de Fuca Strait S of Victoria, B.C., Canada. Pop. 17,311.

Port A·pra (ä'prə). Apra Harbor.

Port Ar·thur (är'thər). **1.** Lüshun. **2.** City of extreme SE Tex., near the Gulf of Mexico and the La. border. Pop. 61,195.

Port-au-Prince (pôrt'ō-prĭns', pōrt'-, pôr-tō-prăɴs'). Cap. of Haiti, in the SW part on the Gulf of Gonaïves. Pop. 745,700.

Port Ches·ter (chĕs'tər). Village of SE N.Y., on Long Is. Sound and the Conn. border. Pop. 23,565.

Port Col·borne (kōl'bûrn'). City of S Ont., Canada, on Lake Erie at the S end of the Welland Ship Canal. Pop. 19,449.

Port Co·quit·lam (kō-kwĭt'ləm). City of SW B.C., Canada, on the Fraser R. E of Vancouver. Pop. 23,926.

Port E·liz·a·beth (ĭ-lĭz'ə-bəth). City of SE South Africa, on the Indian Ocean. Pop. 392,231.

Por·ter·ville (pôr'tər-vĭl', pōr'-). City of S central Calif., N of Bakersfield. Pop. 19,707.

Port Har·court (här'kərt, -kôrt', -kōrt'). City of SE Nigeria, in the Niger Delta. Pop. 242,000.

Port Hope (hōp). Town of S Ont., Canada, on Lake Ontario ENE of Toronto. Pop. 10,054.

Port Hue·ne·me (wī-nē'mē). Town of S Calif., near Oxnard. Pop. 17,803.

Port Hu·ron (hyo͝or'ən, -ŏn'). City of SE Mich., on Lake Huron and the St. Clair R. Pop. 33,981.

Port·land (pôrt'lənd, pōrt'-). **1.** City of SW Me., S of Lewiston. Pop. 61,572. **2.** City of NW Ore., near the mouth of the Columbia R. Pop. 366,383. **3.** City of S Tex., near Corpus Christi. Pop. 12,023.

Port La·va·ca (lə-văk'ə). City of SE Tex., on an inlet of the Gulf of Mexico NE of Corpus Christi. Pop. 10,911.

Port Lou·is (lo͞o'ĭs, lo͞o'ē, lo͞o-ē'). Cap. of Mauritius, in the NW on the Indian Ocean. Pop. 142,853.

Port Moo·dy (mo͞o'dē). City of SW B.C., Canada, near Vancouver. Pop. 11,649.

Port Mores·by (môrz'bē, mōrz'-). Cap. of Papua New Guinea, on SE New Guinea Is. Pop. 106,600.

Port Nech·es (nĕch'ĭz). City of extreme SE Tex., near Port Arthur. Pop. 13,944.

Pôr·to (pôr'to͞o). *Portuguese.* Oporto.

Pôrto A·le·gre (ə-lĕ'grə). City of SE Brazil, at N end of Lagoa dos Patos. Pop. 1,183,500.

Port of Spain (spān). Cap. of Trinidad and Tobago, on NW coast of Trinidad. Pop. 42,950.

Por·to-No·vo (pôr'tō-nō'vō, pōr'-). Cap. of Benin, in the SE on an inlet of the Gulf of Guinea. Pop. 104,000.

Port Or·ange (ôr'ĭnj, ŏr'-). City of NE Fla., near Daytona Beach. Pop. 18,756.

Por·to Ri·co (pôr'tə rē'kō, pōr'-). Puerto Rico.

Port Phil·lip Bay (fĭl'əp). Inlet of Bass Strait on SE coast of Australia.

Port Sa·id (sä-ēd'). City of NE Egypt,

ă pat / ā pay / âr care / ä father / b bib / ch church / d deed / ĕ pet / ē be / f fife / g gag / h hat / hw which / ĭ pit / ī pie / îr pier / j judge / k kick / l lid, needle / m mum / n no, sudden / ng thing / ŏ pot / ō toe / ô paw, for / oi noise / ou out / o͝o took / o͞o boot /

at Mediterranean entrance to the Suez Canal. Pop. 271,000.

Port Saint Lu·cie (sānt lo͞o'sē). City of E Fla., near Fort Pierce. Pop. 14,690.

Ports·mouth (pôrt'smәth, pōrt'-). **1.** Borough of S England, on the English Channel opposite the Isle of Wight. Pop. 191,000. **2.** City of SE N.H., opposite Kittery, Me. Pop. 26,254. **3.** City of S Ohio, on the Ohio R. S of Columbus. Pop. 25,943. **4.** City of SE Va., opposite Norfolk. Pop. 104,577.

Port Stan·ley (stăn'lē). See **Stanley**.

Port Su·dan (so͞o-dăn'). City of NE Sudan, on the Red Sea. Pop. 132,631.

Por·tu·gal (pôr'chә-gәl, pōr'-). Country of SW Europe, on the Iberian Peninsula and including Madeira and the Azores. Cap. Lisbon. Pop. 9,980,000. —**Por'tu·gese'** (-gēz', -gēs') *adj. & n.*

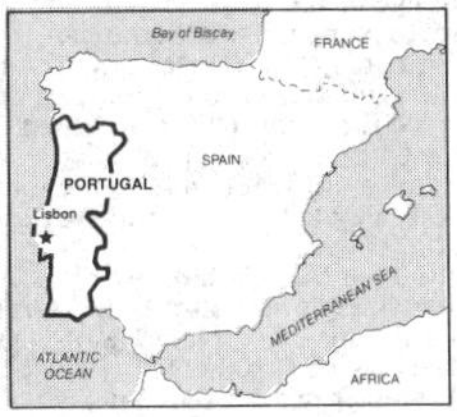

Portugal

Po·sen (pō'zәn). *German.* Poznań.

Po·ta·ro (pō-tä'rō). River, c. 100 mi (160 km), of central Guyana.

Potch·ef·stroom (pŏch'әf-stro͞om', -strōm'). Town of NE South Africa, SW of Johannesburg. Pop. 57,443.

Po·ten·za (pō-tĕn'tsä). City of S Italy, in the Apennines ESE of Naples. Pop. 64,513.

Po·to·mac (pә-tō'mәk). River of E U.S., rising in NE W.Va. and flowing c. 285 mi (459 km) along the Va.-Md border to Chesapeake bay.

Po·to·sí (pô'tô-sē'). City of S central Bolivia, SW of Sucre in the Andes at c. 13,780 ft (4,203 m). Pop. 77,334.

Pots·dam (pŏts'dăm'). **1.** (*also* pôts'däm). City of central East Germany, on the Havel R. near Berlin. Pop. 126,262. **2.** Village of N N.Y., E of Ogdensburg. Pop. 10,635.

Potts·town (pŏts'toun'). Borough of SE Pa., NW of Philadelphia. Pop. 22,729.

Potts·ville (pŏts'vĭl'). City of SE Pa., WNW of Allentown. Pop. 18,195.

Pough·keep·sie (pә-kĭp'sē, pō-). City of SE N.Y., on the Hudson N of New York City. Pop. 29,757.

Pow·der (pou'dәr). **1.** River, c. 150 mi (241 km), of E Ore. **2.** River, c. 486 mi (782 km), of N Wyo. and SE Mont.

Po·yang (pō'yăng'). Lake of E China, SE of Wuhan.

Poz·nań (pôz'nän'yә). City of W central Poland, on the Warta R. Pop. 545,600.

Poz·zuo·li (pōt-tswô'lē). City of S Italy, on the Bay of Naples. Pop. 61,400.

Prague (präg). Cap. of Czechoslovakia, in the W part on the Vltava R. Pop. 1,193,345.

Prai·a (prä'yә). Cap. of Cape Verde Is., on SE coast of São Tiago Is. Pop. 21,494.

Prai·rie Village (prâr'ē). City of E Kans., near Kansas City. Pop. 24,657.

Pra·to (prä'tō). City of central Italy, NW of Florence. Pop. 158,229.

Pratt·ville (prăt'vĭl', -vәl). City of central Ala., NW of Montgomery. Pop. 18,647.

Pres·cott (prĕs'kәt, -kŏt'). City of central Ariz., NNW of Phoenix. Pop. 20,055.

Presque Isle (prĕsk). City of NE Me., near the N.B., Canada, border. Pop. 11,172.

Pres·ton (prĕs'tәn). Borough of NW England, NNE of Liverpool. Pop. 126,200.

Pre·to·ri·a (prĭ-tôr'ē-ә, -tōr'-). Administrative cap. of South Africa, in the NE part NE of Johannesburg. Pop. 545,450.

Prib·i·lof (prĭb'ә-lôf'). Islands of SW Alas., in the Bering Sea.

Prich·ard (prĭch'әrd). City of SW Ala., near Mobile. Pop. 39,541.

Prince Al·bert (prĭns ăl'bәrt). City of central Sask., Canada, on the N Saskatchewan R. Pop. 28,631.

Prince Ed·ward Island (ĕd'wәrd). Island and province of SE Canada, in the S Gulf of St. Lawrence. Cap. Charlottetown. Pop. 118,229.

Prince George (jôrj). City of central B.C., Canada, on the upper Fraser R. Pop. 59,929.

Prince of Wales (wālz). **1.** Island of extreme SE Alas., in the Alexander Archipelago. **2.** Island of N N.W.T., Canada, in the Arctic Ocean NE of Victoria Is.

Prince Ru·pert (ro͞o'pәrt). City of W B.C., Canada, on the Pacific coast near the Alas. border. Pop. 14,754.

Prince·ton (prĭn'stәn). Borough of central N.J., NNE of Trenton. Pop. 12,035.

Prince Wil·liam Sound (wĭl'yәm). Arm of the Gulf of Alaska E of the Kenai Peninsula of S Alas.

Prin·ci·pe (prĭn'sә-pē', -pä', prēɴ'sē-pә). Island, 53 sq mi (137 sq km), in the Gulf of Guinea, W Africa, forming part of the republic of São Tomé and Principe.

Prip·et (prĭp'ĕt', prē'pĕt') or **Pri·pyat** (prē'pyәt). River, c. 440 mi (708 km), of E central European USSR.

Pro·ko·pyevsk (prō-kô'pyәfsk). City of E Siberian USSR, ESE of Novosibirsk. Pop. 266,000.

Pros·pect Heights (prŏs'pĕkt'). City of NE Ill., near Chicago. Pop. 11,808.

Prov·i·dence (prŏv'ĭ-dәns, -dĕns'). Cap. of R.I., in the NE on Narragansett Bay. Pop. 156,804.

Pro·vo (prō'vō). City of N central Utah, SSE of Salt Lake City. Pop. 73,907.

Prud·hoe Bay (pro͞od'hō, prŭd'-). Inlet of the Arctic Ocean on N Alas. coast E of the Colville R. delta.

Prus·sia (prŭsh'ә). Region and former state of N central Europe, including present-day N Germany and N Poland. —**Prus'sian** *adj. & n.*

Pskov (pskôf). City of NW European USSR, SSW of Leningrad. Pop. 177,000.

Pueb·la (pwĕb'lä). City of E central Mexico, ESE of Mexico City. Pop. 678,000.

Pueb·lo (pwĕb'lō). City of S central Colo., SSE of Colorado Springs. Pop. 101,686.

Puer·to Ca·bel·lo (pwĕr'tô kä-bĕ'yô). City of N Venezuela, on the Caribbean W of Caracas. Pop. 72,103.

Puer·to la Cruz (lä kro͞os'). City of N Venezuela, on the Caribbean NE of Barcelona. Pop. 63,276.

Puerto Montt (mônt'). City of S central Chile, on an inlet of the Pacific. Pop. 62,726.

Puerto Ri·co (rē'kō). Island of the West Indies, E of Hispaniola; a self-governing commonwealth of the U.S. Cap. San Juan. Pop. 3,187,570. —**Puerto Ri'can** *adj. & n.*

Pu·get Sound (pyo͞o'jĭt). Inlet of the Pacific, c. 100 mi (160 km) long, in NW Wash.

Pu·la (po͞o'lä). City of NW Yugoslavia, on the Adriatic. Pop. 47,414.

Pu·las·ki (pә-lăs'kē, po͞o-). Town of SW Va., WSW of Roanoke. Pop. 10,106.

Pull·man (po͝ol'mәn). City of SE Wash., near the border W of Moscow, Idaho. Pop. 23,579.

Pun·jab (pŭn-jäb', -jăb', pŭn'jäb', -jăb'). Region of NW India and NW Pakistan. —**Pun·ja'bi** *adj. & n.*

Pun·ta A·re·nas (po͞on'tä ä-rē'näs). City of S Chile, on the Strait of Magellan. Pop. 61,813.

Pu·ra·cé (po͞o-rä-sē'). Volcano, c. 15,420 ft (4,703 m), in the Andes of SW Colombia.

Pur·ga·toire (pûr'gә-twär', pûr'gә-tôr'ē, -tōr'ē). River, c. 186 mi (299 km), of SE Colo.

Pu·rus (po͞o-ro͞os'). River of E central Peru and W Brazil, flowing c. 2,100 mi (3,379 km) NE into the Amazon.

Pu·san (po͞o'sän'). City of extreme SE South Korea, on Korea Strait. Pop. 2,879,570.

Put-in-Bay (po͝ot'ĭn-bā'). Bay of W Lake Erie, where U.S. Navy under Perry defeated a British fleet (1813).

Pu·tu·ma·yo (po͞o'to͞o-mä'yô). River of NW South America, rising in SW Colombia and flowing c. 1,000 mi (1,609 km) along the Colombia-Peru border to the Amazon in NW Brazil.

Puy·al·lup (pyo͞o-ăl'әp, -ä'lәp). City of W central Wash., near Tacoma. Pop. 18,251.

Pyong·yang (pyŭng'yăng', pyông'-yăng'). Cap. of North Korea, in the SW part. Pop. 840,000.

Pyr·e·nees (pîr'ә-nēz'). Mountain range along the French-Spanish border from Bay of Biscay to the Mediterranean, rising to 11,168 ft (3,406.2 m). —**Pyr'e·ne'an** *adj.*

Q

Qa·tar (kä'tär', -tәr). Country of E Arabia, on a peninsula in the Persian Gulf. Cap. Doha. Pop. 160,000.

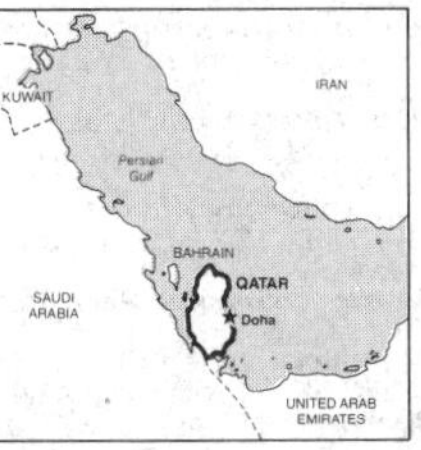

Qatar

Qat·ta·ra Depression (kä-tä'rä). Desert basin of NW Egypt in the Libyan Desert.

Qe·na (kā'nә). City of E central Egypt, on the Nile. Pop. 68,536.

Qing·dao (chyĭng'dou'). City of E China, on the Yellow Sea NNW of Shanghai. Pop. 1,900,000.

Qing·hai (chyĭng'hī'). Salt lake, 1,625 sq mi (4,210 sq km), of N central China.

Qi·qi·har (chē'chē'här'). City of NE China, in Manchuria NW of Harbin. Pop. 1,500,00.

Qom (kōm). Variant of **Qum**.

Qu'Ap·pelle (kwә-pĕl'). River, c. 270 mi (434 km), of S Sask. and SW Man., Canada.

Que·bec (kwĭ-bĕk') or **Qué·bec** (kā-). **1.** Province of E Canada. Cap. Quebec. Pop. 6,234,445. **2.** Cap. of Que., Canada, in the S part on the St. Lawrence R. Pop. 177,082. —**Que·bec'er, Que·beck'er** *n.*

Queens·bor·ough-in-Shep·pey (kwēnz'bûr-ә-ĭn-shĕp'ē). Borough of SE England, on the Isle of Sheppey at the mouth of the Thames. Pop. 31,550.

Queen Char·lotte (kwēn shär'lәt). Islands off W coast of B.C., Canada, separated from Vancouver Is. to the SE by **Queen Charlotte Sound**, an inlet of the Pacific.

Queen E·liz·a·beth (ĭ-lĭz'ә-bәth). Islands of N N.W.T., Canada, in the Arctic Archipelago N of Parry Channel.

Queen Maud Land (môd). Region of Antarctica between the Weddell Sea and Enderby Land.

Queens (kwēnz). Borough of New York City, SE N.Y., on W Long Is. Pop. 1,891,325.

Que·moy (kē-moi', kwē'moi). Island off SE China in Formosa Strait, administered by Taiwan.

Que·ré·ta·ro (kĕ-rĕ'tä-rô'). City of central Mexico, NW of Mexico City. Pop. 176,200.

Quet·ta (kwĕt'ә). City of W central Pakistan. Pop. 137,659.

Que·zal·te·nan·go (kĕ-säl'tĕ-näng'gô). City of SW Guatemala, WNW of Lake Atitlán. Pop. 45,977.

Que·zon City (kā'sōn', -zōn'). City of central Luzon, Philippines, near Manila. Pop. 956,864.

Quil·mes (kēl'mĕs'). City of E Argentina, on the Río de la Plata. Pop. 355,265.

Quim·per (kăɴ-pĕr'). City of NW France, near the Bay of Biscay SSE of Brest. Pop. 55,977.

Quin·cy. **1.** (kwĭn'sē). City of W Ill., on the Mississippi. Pop. 42,352. **2.** (kwĭn'zē). City of E Mass., SE of Boston. Pop. 84,743.

Quir·i·nal (kwĭr'ә-nәl). One of the 7 hills of ancient Rome.

Qui·to (kē'tô). Cap. of Ecuador, in the N central part. Pop. 742,858.

Qum (ko͞om) or **Qom** (kōm). City of W central Iran, SSW of Teheran. Pop. 246,831.

Qum·ran (ko͞om-rän'). Ancient village of Palestine, on the NW shore of the Dead Sea in present-day NW Israel.

Qur·net es Sau·da (ko͞or'nĕt ĕs sä'o͞o-dä). Peak, 10,131 (3,090 m), of the Lebanon Mts. in N Lebanon.

R

Ra·bat (rä-bät'). Cap. of Morocco, in the N part on the Atlantic. Pop. 367,620.

Rab·bah (răb'ә) or **Rab·bath** (răb'-әth). Amman.

Rac·coon (ră-ko͞on'). River, c. 200 mi (322 km), of N Iowa.

Race (rās). Cape at SE end of Newf., Canada, on Avalon Peninsula.

Ra·ci·bórz (rä-chē'bo͞osh). Town of S Poland, on the Oder R. near the Czech border. Pop. 52,900.

Ra·cine (rә-sēn', rā-). City of SE Wis., on Lake Michigan S of Milwaukee. Pop. 85,725.

Rad·ford (răd'fәrd). Independent city of SW Va., WSW of Roanoke. Pop. 13,225.

Ra·dom (rä'dôm). City of SE Poland, S of Warsaw. Pop. 187,600.

Rae·ti·a (rē'shē-ә, -shә). Variant of **Rhaetia**.

Ra·ges (rā'jēz) or **Rha·gae** (-jē). Ancient medieval city of Persia, near present-day Teheran, N Iran.

Ra·gu·sa (rä-go͞o'zä). City of SE Sicily, Italy. Pop. 55,200.

Rah·way (rô'wā'). City of NE N.J., SW of Elizabeth. Pop. 26,723.

Ra·ia·te·a (rä'yä-tā'ä). Volcanic island of the S Pacific, largest of the Leeward group of the Society Is., French Polynesia.

Rai·nier (rā-nîr', rә-), **Mount.** Volcanic peak, 14,408 ft (4,394.4 m), of the Cascade range in W central Wash.

Rain·y (rā'nē). **1.** Lake, c. 345 sq mi (894 sq km), in N Minn. and W Ont., Canada. **2.** River, c. 80 mi (129 km), on the border between N Minn. and SW Ont., Canada.

Rai·pur (rī'po͝or). City of E central India, E of Nagpur. Pop. 174,518.

Rai·sin (rā'zĭn). River, c. 115 mi (185 km), of SE Mich.

Ra·jah·mun·dry (rä'jә-mŭn'drē). City of E central India, on the Godavari R. Pop. 165,912.

Raj·kot (räj'kōt). City of W central India, WSW of Ahmadabad. Pop. 300,612.

Ra·leigh (rô'lē, rä'-). Cap. of N.C., in the E central part. Pop. 149,771.

Ra·lik (rä'lĭk). W chain of the Marshall Is., in the W Pacific.

Ram·a·po (răm'ә-pō'). Range of the Appalachians in S N.Y. and N N.J.

Ra·ma's Bridge (rä'mәz brĭj'). Adam's Bridge.

Ra·mat Gan (rә-mät' gän'). City of W central Israel, near Tel Aviv-Jaffa. Pop. 120,400.

Ram·gan·ga (räm-gŭng'gә). River, c. 350 mi (563 km), of N India.

Ram·sey (răm'zē). **1.** City of E Minn., near Minneapolis. Pop. 10,093.

2. Borough of NE N.J., near the N.Y. border N of Paterson. Pop. 12,899.
Rams·gate (rămz'găt', -gĭt). Borough of SE England, on the Isle of Thanet. Pop. 40,090.
Ran·ca·gua (räng-kä'gwä). City of central Chile, S of Santiago. Pop. 86,404.
Ran·cho Pal·os Ver·des (răn'chō păl'ōs vûr'dēz, păl'əs). City of S Calif., near Long Beach. Pop. 35,227.
Rand (rănd, ränd). Witwatersrand.
Rand·ers (rän'ərs). City of N central Denmark, NNW of Århus. Pop. 62,486.
Ran·dolph (răn'dolf'). Town of E Mass., S of Boston. Pop. 28,218.
Rand·wick (rănd'wĭk). City of SE Australia, near Sydney. Pop. 123,750.
Range·ley Lakes (rānj'lē). Group of lakes in W Me. and N N.H.
Ran·goon (răng-gōōn'). Cap. of Burma, in the S central part on the **Rangoon R.** (c. 185 mi/298 km), E distributary of the Irrawaddy. Pop. 2,276,000.
Ran·noch (răn'ək), **Loch.** Lake, 9.5 mi (15.3 km) long, of central Scotland, in the Grampians.
Rann of Kutch or **Cutch** (rŭn; kŭch). Salt marsh, c. 9,000 sq mi (23,310 sq km), of W India and SE Pakistan between the Gulf of Kutch and the Indus delta.
Ran·toul (răn-tōōl'). Village of E Ill., NNE of Champaign. Pop. 20,161.
Ra·pa (rä'pə). Island of the S Pacific, in S French Polynesia SSE of Tahiti.
Ra·pal·lo (rä-päl'lō). City of NW Italy, on the Ligurian Sea. Pop. 29,809.
Rap·i·dan (răp'ĭ-dăn', răp'ĭ-dăn'). River, c. 90 mi (145 km), of N Va.
Rap·id City (răp'ĭd). City of SW S.Dak., WSW of Pierre. Pop. 46,492.
Rap·pa·han·nock (răp'ə-hăn'ək). River, c. 212 mi (341 km), of NE Va.
Rap·ti (räp'tē). River, c. 400 mi (644 km), of Nepal and N India.
Rar·i·tan Bay (răr'ĭ-tn). W arm of Lower New York Bay off SE N.Y. and NE N.J.
Rar·o·ton·ga (răr'ə-tŏng'gə). Volcanic island of the S Pacific, in the SW Cook Is.
Ras Da·shan (räs dä-shän'). Highest peak, 15,158 ft (4,623.2 m) of Ethiopia, in the N part.
Rasht (răsht) also **Resht** (rĕsht). City of NW Iran, near the Caspian Sea. Pop. 187,203.
Rat (răt). Islands of SW Alas., in the W Aleutians.
Rat·ak (răt'ək). Islands of the W Pacific, E chain of the Marshalls.
Ra·ti·bor (rä'tē-bôr). *German.* Racibórz.
Rat·is·bon (răt'ĭs-bŏn', -ĭz-). Regensburg.
Ra·ton (ră-tōn', -tōōn', rə-). Pass, 7,834 ft (2,389.4 m) high, in the Sangre de Cristo Mts. on the Colo.-N.Mex. border.
Ra·ven·na (rə-vĕn'ə, rä-vĕn'nä). **1.** City of N central Italy, near the Adriatic NE of Florence. Pop. 102,300. **2.** City of NE Ohio, ENE of Akron. Pop. 11,987.
Ra·vi (rä'vē). River, 475 mi (764.3 km), of NW India and NE Pakistan.
Ra·wal·pin·di (rä'wəl-pĭn'dē). City of NE Pakistan, NNW of Lahore. Pop. 372,919.
Raw·lins (rô'lĭnz). City of S Wyo., NE of Laramie. Pop. 11,547.
Ray (rā), **Cape.** Promontory of extreme SW Newf., Canada.
Ray·side-Bal·four (rā'sīd-băl'fôr', -fər). Town of S central Ont., Canada, near Sudbury. Pop. 15,095.
Ray·town (rā'toun'). City of W Mo., near Kansas City. Pop. 31,759.
Read·ing (rĕd'ĭng). **1.** Borough of S central England, W of London. Pop. 138,400. **2.** Town of E Mass., NNW of Boston. Pop. 22,678. **3.** City of SW Ohio, near Cincinnati. Pop. 12,879. **4.** City of SE Pa., NW of Philadelphia. Pop. 78,686.
Re·ci·fe (rĕ-sē'fə). City of NE Brazil, on the Atlantic. Pop. 1,391,800.
Reck·ling·hau·sen (rĕk'lĭng-hou'zən). City of W West Germany, SW of Münster. Pop. 119,472.
Red (rĕd). **1.** Sea, c. 1,450 mi (2,333 km) long, between NE Africa and Arabia. **2.** Lake, 451 sq mi (1,168 sq km), of N Minn. **3.** River of S China and N Vietnam, flowing c. 730 mi (1,175 km) SE into the Gulf of Tonkin. **4.** River of S central U.S., rising in the Tex. Panhandle and flowing 1,018 mi (1,638 km) E and SE along the Tex.-Okla. border and through SW Ark. and N La. into the Mississippi. **5.** River of N central U.S. and S central Canada, flowing c. 310 mi (499 km) N along the Minn.-N.Dak. border into Lake Winnipeg in SE Man., Canada.
Red Bank (băngk). **1.** Borough of E central N.J., SE of Perth Amboy. Pop. 12,031. **2.** City of S Tenn., near Chattanooga. Pop. 13,297.
Red Deer (dîr). **1.** River, c. 385 mi (620 km), of S Alta. and SW Sask., Canada. **2.** City of S central Alta., Canada, on the Red Deer R. Pop. 41,371.
Red·ding (rĕd'ĭng). City of N central Calif., S of Shasta Lake. Pop. 41,995.
Red·ditch (rĕd'ĭch). Urban district of central England, S of Birmingham. Pop. 64,300.
Red·lands (rĕd'ləndz). City of S Calif., near San Bernardino. Pop. 43,619.
Red·mond (rĕd'mənd). City of W central Wash., near Seattle. Pop. 23,318.
Re·don·do Beach (rĭ-dŏn'dō). City of S Calif., S of Los Angeles. Pop. 57,102.
Red Wing (wĭng). City of SE Minn., on the Mississippi SW of St. Paul. Pop. 13,736.
Red·wood City (rĕd'wŏŏd'). City of W Calif., NW of Palo Alto. Pop. 54,965.
Redwood National Park. Reserved area of redwood forests in NW Calif.
Reed·ley (rēd'lē). City of central Calif., SE of Fresno. Pop. 11,071.
Reel·foot (rēl'fŏŏt'). Lake, 20 mi (32 km) long, of NW Tenn.
Re·gens·burg (rā'gəns-bŏŏrk'). City of SW West Germany, on the Danube NNE of Munich. Pop. 132,399.
Reg·gio (rĕd'jō). **1.** Or **Reggio di Ca·la·bri·a** (dē kä-lä'brē-ä) also **Reggio Calabria.** City of extreme S Italy, on the Strait of Messina opposite Sicily. Pop. 181,293. **2.** Or **Reggio nell'E·mi·lia** (nĕl'lā-mē'lyä) also **Reggio E·mi·lia** (ā-mē'lyä). City of N central Italy, WNW of Bologna. Pop. 130,005.
Re·gi·na (rĭ-jī'nə). Cap. of Sask., Canada, in the S part. Pop. 149,593.
Rei·chen·bach (rī'kən-bäk, -KHən-bäKH). Waterfall, 656 ft (201 m), of S central Switzerland.
Reids·ville (rēdz'vĭl', -vəl). City of N N.C., NNE of Greensboro. Pop. 12,492.
Rei·gate (rī'găt', -gĭt). Borough of S England, S of London. Pop. 114,000.
Reims or **Rheims** (rēmz, răNs). City of NE France, ENE of Paris. Pop. 178,381.
Rein·deer (rān'dîr'). Lake, 2,467 sq mi (6,390 sq km), of NE Sask. and NW Man., Canada.
Re·ma·gen (rā'mä'gən). Town of W West Germany, on the Rhine SE of Bonn. Pop. 14,342.
Rem·scheid (rĕm'shīt). City of W West Germany, NE of Cologne. Pop. 129,507.
Rennes (rĕn). City of NW France, in Brittany N of Nantes. Pop. 198,305.
Re·no (rē'nō'). City of W Nev., near the Calif. border. Pop. 100,756.
Rens·se·laer (rĕn'sə-lîr', rĕn'sə-lər). City of E N.Y., on the Hudson opposite Albany. Pop. 9,047.
Ren·ton (rĕn'tən). City of W central Wash., near Seattle. Pop. 30,612.
Re·pen·ti·gny (rĕ-păN-tē-nyē'). Town of S Que., Canada, near Montreal. Pop. 26,698.
Re·pub·li·can (rĭ-pŭb'lĭ-kən). River, c. 420 mi (676 km), of E Colo., S Nebr., and N Kans.
Resht (rĕsht). Variant of **Rasht.**
Re·sis·ten·cia (rĕ'sēs-tĕn'syä). City of NE Argentina, on the Paraná R. Pop. 183,000.
Re·şi·ta (rĕ'shē-tsä). City of W Rumania, in the W Transylvanian Alps. Pop. 90,664.
Re·thondes (rĕ-tôNd'). Village of N France, WNW of Reims; site of World War I armistice signing (1918).
Ré·un·ion (rē-yōōn'yən, rā-ü-nyôn'). Island of France in the W Indian Ocean SW of Mauritius.
Reus (rĕ'ōōs). City of NE Spain, on the Mediterranean. Pop. 84,986.
Reut·ling·en (roit'lĭng'ən). City of SW West Germany, S of Stuttgart. Pop. 94,737.
Re·vere (rĭ-vîr'). City of E Mass., near Boston. Pop. 42,423.
Re·vil·la Gi·ge·do or **Re·vil·la·gi·ge·do** (rĕ-vē'lyä-hē-hā'*th*ō). Islands of Mexico in the Pacific S of Lower California.
Reyes (rāz), **Point.** Cape on N central Calif. coast, WNW of San Francisco.
Rey·kja·vík (rā'kyə-vĕk'). Cap. of Iceland, in the SW part on an inlet of Denmark Strait. Pop. 83,536.
Rey·nolds·burg (rĕn'əldz-bûrg'). City of central Ohio, near Columbus. Pop. 20,661.
Rey·no·sa (rā-nô'sə). City of E Mexico, on the Rio Grande. Pop. 218,700.
Rhae·ti·a also **Rae·ti·a** (rē'shē-ə, -shə). Ancient Roman province including present-day E Switzerland and W Austria. **—Rhae'tian** *adj. & n.*
Rhaetian Alps (ălps). Range of the central Alps in E Switzerland and W Austria.
Rha·gae (ră'jē). Variant of **Rages.**
Rhe·gi·um (rē'jĭ-ŭm). *Latin.* Reggio di Calabria.
Rheims (rēmz, răNs). Variant of **Reims.**
Rhein (rīn). *German.* Rhine.
Rhin (răN). *French.* Rhine.
Rhine (rīn). River of W Europe, rising in E Switzerland and flowing c. 820 mi (1,319 km) N through W West Germany and the Netherlands to the North Sea.
Rhine·land (rīn'lănd', -lənd). Region along the Rhine in West Germany.
Rhode Island (rōd). **1.** Island of R.I., in Narragansett Bay. **2.** State of NE U.S., on the Atlantic. Cap. Providence. Pop. 947,154. **—Rhode Is'land·er** *n.*
Rhodes (rōdz). **1.** Island of SE Greece, in the Aegean off SW Turkey; largest of the Dodecanese. **2.** City of SE Greece on N end of Rhodes Is. Pop. 32,092.
Rho·de·sia (rō-dē'zhə). **1.** Region of S central Africa comprising Zambia and Zimbabwe. **2.** Zimbabwe. **—Rho·de'sian** *adj. & n.*
Rhod·o·pe (rŏd'ə-pē, rō-dō'-). Mountains of S Bulgaria and NE Greece.
Rhon·dda (rŏn'də, rôn'*th*ə). Borough of S Wales, NW of Cardiff. Pop. 81,800.
Rhone or **Rhône** (rōn). River of SW Switzerland and SE France, flowing c. 505 mi (812 km) W and S to the Mediterranean.
Rhyl (rĭl). Urban district of N Wales, on Liverpool Bay. Pop. 22,150.
Ri·al·to (rē-ăl'tō). **1.** Island of Venice, Italy. **2.** City of S Calif., near San Bernardino. Pop. 35,615.
Ri·au (rē'ou). Archipelago of W Indonesia off SE end of the Malay Peninsula.
Ri·a·zan (rē-ä-zän'). Variant of **Ryazan.**
Ri·bei·rão Prê·to (rē'bā-rouN' prĕ'tōō). City of SE Brazil, N of São Paulo. Pop. 190,897.
Rich·ard·son (rĭch'ərd-sən). City of NE Tex., near Dallas. Pop. 72,496.
Ri·che·lieu (rĭsh'ə-lōō', rē-shə-lyœ'). River of S Que., flowing c. 210 mi (338 km) N from Lake Champlain to the St. Lawrence.
Rich·field (rĭch'fēld'). City of E Minn., near Minneapolis. Pop. 37,851.
Rich·land (rĭch'lənd). City of S Wash., on the Columbia ESE of Yakima. Pop. 33,578.
Rich·mond (rĭch'mənd). **1.** City of W Calif., NW of Oakland. Pop. 74,676. **2.** City of E Ind., E of Indianapolis. Pop. 41,349. **3.** City of central Ky., SSE of Lexington. Pop. 21,705. **4.** Borough of New York City, coextensive with Staten Is. Pop. 352,121. **5.** Cap. of Va., in the E central part. Pop. 219,214.
Richmond Heights. 1. City of E Mo., W of St. Louis. Pop. 11,516. **2.** City of NE Ohio, near Cleveland. Pop. 10,095.
Richmond Hill. City of S central Ont., Canada, N of Toronto. Pop. 35,480.
Ri·deau (rĭ-dō'). Canal, 126 mi (202.7 km) long, of S Ont., Canada, connecting the Ottawa R. at Ottawa with Lake Ontario at Kingston.
Ridge·crest (rĭj'krĕst'). City of S central Calif., ENE of Bakersfield. Pop. 15,929.
Ridge·field (rĭj'fēld'). **1.** Town of SW Conn., near the N.Y. border. Pop. 20,120. **2.** Borough of NE N.J., NNE of Jersey City. Pop. 10,294.
Ridgefield Park. Village of NE N.J., near Hackensack. Pop. 12,738.
Ridge·wood (rĭj'wŏŏd'). Village of NE N.J., near Paterson. Pop. 25,208.
Rif also **Riff** (rĭf) or **Er Rif** (ĕr rĭf'). Range of the Atlas Mts. in NE Morocco along the Mediterranean.
Ri·ga (rē'gə). **1. Gulf of.** Inlet of the Baltic off Latvia and Estonia. **2.** City of W European USSR, in Latvia on the Gulf of Riga. Pop. 843,000.
Ri·je·ka (rē-yĕ'kä, rē-ĕk'ə). City of NW Yugoslavia, on the Adriatic. Pop. 132,933.
Rijn (rīn). *Dutch.* Rhine.
Rijs·wijk (rīs'vīk) also **Rys·wick** (rĭz'wĭk). City of W Netherlands, near The Hague. Pop. 52,605.
Ri·mi·ni (rĭm'ə-nē, rē'mē-nē). City of N central Italy, on the Adriatic. Pop. 127,714.
Ri·mous·ki (rĭ-mōō'skē). City of S Que., Canada, on the St. Lawrence NE of Quebec. Pop. 27,897.
Ring·wood (rĭng'wŏŏd'). Borough of NE N.J., near the N.Y. border NNW of Paterson. Pop. 12,625.
Ri·o·bam·ba (rē-ō-bäm'bə). City of central Ecuador, in the Andes S of Quito. Pop. 58,029.
Ri·o Bran·co (rē'ōō brăNg'kōō). River, c. 350 mi (565 km), of NW Brazil.
Rí·o Bra·vo (rē'ô brä'vô). Rio Grande.
Ri·o de Ja·nei·ro (rē'ō dā zhə-nâr'ō, jə-, dē-, rē'ōō də zhə-nā'rōō). City of SE Brazil, on Guanabara Bay. Pop. 5,394,900.
Rí·o de la Pla·ta (rē'ō dĕ lä plä'tä). Estuary of the Paraná and Uruguay rivers on the SE coast of South America, extending c. 225 mi (362 km) between Argentina and Uruguay.
Ri·o de O·ro (rē'ô dĕ ô'rô). S part of Western Sahara, NW Africa.
Rí·o Ga·lle·gos (rē'ô gä-yĕ'gôs). Town of extreme S Argentina, on the Atlantic N of Strait of Magellan. Pop. 271,833.
Ri·o Grande (rē'ō grănd', grăn'dē, grän'dā). River, c. 1,885 mi (3,033 km), of SW U.S., rising in S Colo. and flowing SE to the Gulf of Mexico, forming much of the U.S.-Mexican border.
Ri·o Gran·de (rē'ōō grän'də). **1.** River c. 650 mi (1,046 km), of S Brazil. **2.** City of extreme SE Brazil, at the S entrance of Lagoa dos Patos. Pop. 98,863.
Rí·o Mu·ni (rē'ô mōō'nē). Mainland part of Equatorial Guinea, W Africa.
Rí·o Ne·gro (rē'ōō nā'grōō). **1.** River of E Colombia and NW Brazil, flowing c. 1,400 mi (2,253 km) ESE into the Amazon. **2.** (rē'ô nĕ'grô). River of central Argentina, flowing c. 400 mi (644 km) to the Atlantic. **3.** River of S Brazil and central Uruguay, flowing c. 500 mi (805 km) WSW to the Uruguay R.
Ri·o Roo·se·velt (rē'ōō rō'zə-vĕlt, rōz'vĕlt). River, c. 400 mi (644 km), of W Brazil.
Riv·er·dale (rĭv'ər-dāl'). Village of NE Ill., near Chicago. Pop. 13,233.
Riv·er Edge (rĭv'ər ĕj'). Borough of NE N.J., near Hackensack. Pop. 11,111.
River Forest. Village of NE Ill., near Chicago. Pop. 12,392.
River Grove. Village of NE Ill., near Chicago. Pop. 10,368.
River Rouge (rōōzh). City of SE Mich., near Detroit. Pop. 12,912.

Riv·er·side (rĭv′ər-sīd′). City of S Calif., NE of Santa Ana. Pop. 170,876.
Riv·er·view (rĭv′ər-vyo͞o′). **1.** Town of N.B., Canada, near Moncton. Pop. 14,177. **2.** City of SE Mich., SSW of Detroit. Pop. 14,567.
Riv·i·er·a (rĭv′ē-âr′ə, rē-vyĕ′rä). Coastal resort area of SE France and NW Italy along the Mediterranean.
Riviera Beach. City of SE Fla., on the Atlantic N of West Palm Beach. Pop. 26,596.
Ri·vière-du-Loup (rē-vyâr′do͞o-lo͞o′, -vyĕr′dü-lo͞o). City of E Que., Canada, on the S shore of the St. Lawrence NE of Quebec city. Pop. 13,103.
Ri·yadh (rē-yäd′). Cap. of Saudi Arabia, in the central part. Pop. 666,840.
Ri·za·i·yeh (rĭ-zä′ē′yə). **1.** Urmia. **2.** City of NW Iran, WSW of Tabriz. Pop. 163,991.
Ri·zal (rē-säl′). City of central Luzon, Philippines, on Manila Bay S of Manila. Pop. 286,497.
Road Town (rōd). Cap. of the British Virgin Is., on Tortola Is. Pop. 2,183.
Ro·anne (rô-än′). City of central France, WNW of Lyon. Pop. 55,195.
Ro·a·noke (rō′ə-nōk′). **1.** River, c. 410 mi (660 km), of S Va. and NE N.C. **2.** Island of NE N.C., off the Atlantic coast between Albemarle and Pamlico sounds. **3.** Independent city of SW Va., WSW of Richmond. Pop. 100,427.
Roanoke Rapids. City of NE N.C., near the Va. border NE of Raleigh. Pop. 14,702.
Rob·bins·dale (rŏb′ĭnz-dāl′). City of E Minn., near Minneapolis. Pop. 14,422.
Rob·erts (rŏb′ərts), **Point.** Cape of NW Wash., extending S into the Strait of Georgia from B.C., Canada.
Rob·er·val (rŏb′ər-văl′, rô-bĕr-väl′). City of N Que., Canada, on the W shore of Lake St. John. Pop. 10,500.
Rob·son (rŏb′sən). Mountain, 12,972 ft (3,956.5 m), of E B.C., Canada; highest elevation of the Canadian Rockies.
Robs·town (rŏbz′toun′). City of S Tex., near Corpus Christi. Pop. 12,100.
Ro·ca (rō′kə). Cape of W Portugal, W of Lisbon; W extremity of Europe.
Roch·dale (rŏch′dāl′). Borough of NW England, NNE of Manchester. Pop. 209,000.
Roche·fort (rôsh-fôr′) or **Roche·fort-sur-Mer** (-sür-mĕr′). City of W central France, near the Bay of Biscay NNW of Bordeaux. Pop. 28,155.
Roch·es·ter (rŏch′ĕs′tər, -ĭ-stər). **1.** Borough of SE England, ESE of London. Pop. 56,030. **2.** City of SE Minn., SE of St. Paul. Pop. 57,855. **3.** City of SE N.H., near Dover. Pop. 21,560. **4.** City of W N.Y., ENE of Buffalo. Pop. 241,741.
Rock (rŏk). River, c. 285 mi (459 km), of S Wis. and N Ill.
Rock Creek Butte. Mountain, 9,097 ft (2,774.6 m), of NE Ore., in the Blue Mts.
Rock Falls. City of NW Ill., on the Rock R. opposite Sterling. Pop. 10,624.
Rock·ford (rŏk′fərd). City of N Ill., WNW of Chicago. Pop. 139,712.
Rock·hamp·ton (rŏk-hămp′tən). City of E Australia, near the Pacific NNW of Brisbane. Pop. 53,900.
Rock Hill. City of N S.C., near the border SSW of Charlotte, N.C. Pop. 35,344.
Rock·ies (rŏk′ēz). Rocky Mts.
Rock Island. City of NW Ill., adjacent to Moline. Pop. 47,036.
Rock·land (rŏk′lənd). Town of E Mass., SSE of Boston. Pop. 15,695.
Rock·ledge (rŏk′lĕj′, -lĭj). City of E central Fla., near Cape Canaveral. Pop. 11,877.
Rock Springs. City of SW Wyo., NE of Salt Lake City, Utah. Pop. 19,458.
Rock·ville (rŏk′vĭl′, -vəl). City of central Md., NNW of Washington, D.C. Pop. 43,811.
Rockville Cen·tre (sĕn′tər). Village of SE N.Y., on SW Long Is. Pop. 25,405.
Rock·y (rŏk′ē). Mountain system of N North America, extending from N Mexico to NW Alas.
Rocky Hill. Town of central Conn., near Hartford. Pop. 14,559.
Rocky Mount. City of E central N.C., ENE of Raleigh. Pop. 41,283.
Rocky Mountain National Park. Resort area in the Rockies of N Colo.
Rocky River. City of NE Ohio, near Cleveland. Pop. 21,084.
Ro·dhos (rô′*th*ôs′). *Greek.* Rhodes.
Ro·dri·guez or **Ro·dri·gues** (rō-drē′gəs). One of the Mascarene Is., in the W Indian Ocean E of Mauritius.
Roe·se·la·re (ro͞o-sə-lä′rə). City of W Belgium, WSW of Ghent. Pop. 51,752.
Rog·ers (rŏj′ərz). **1. Mount.** Highest peak of Va., 5,729 ft (1,747.3 m), in the SW part. **2.** City of NW Ark., N of Fayetteville. Pop. 17,351.
Rogue (rōg). River, c. 200 mi (322 km), of SW Ore.
Rohn·ert Park (rō′nərt). City of W Calif., near Santa Rosa. Pop. 22,965.
Rol·la (rŏl′ə). City of central Mo., SE of Jefferson City. Pop. 13,303.
Roll·ing Meadows (rō′lĭng). City of NE Ill., near Chicago. Pop. 20,167.
Ro·ma (rō′mä). *Italian.* Rome.
Ro·ma·gna (rō-män′yə, rō-mä′nyä). Historical region of N central Italy.
Ro·man (rō′män). City of NE Rumania, NNE of Bucharest. Pop. 53,797.
Ro·manche Deep (rō-mänsh′ dēp′). Atlantic ocean depth, c. 25,794 ft (7,864 m), at the equator.
Ro·man Empire (rō′mən). Empire (27 B.C.–A.D. 395) stretching from Britain to North Africa to the Persian Gulf.
Ro·ma·ni·a (rō-mā′nē-ə, -mān′yə). Variant of **Rumania.**
Rom·blon (rŏm-blōn′). **1.** Islands of the central Philippines in the N Visayan Is., in the Sibuyan Sea. **2.** Island of this group, W of Sibuyan Is.
Rome (rōm). **1.** The ancient Roman Empire. **2.** Cap. of Italy, in the W central part on the Tiber R. Pop. 2,911,671. **3.** City of NW Ga., NW of Atlanta. Pop. 29,654. **4.** City of central N.Y., WNW of Utica. Pop. 43,826.
Ro·me·o·ville (rō′mē-ō-vĭl′). Village of NE Ill., N of Joliet. Pop. 15,519.
Rom·u·lus (rŏm′yə-ləs). City of SE Mich., SW of Detroit. Pop. 24,857.
Ron·ces·valles (rŏn′sə-vălz, rôn′sĕz-vä′lyĕs). Pass, 3,468 ft (1,057.7 m) high, through the W Pyrenees.
Ronce·vaux (rôNs-vō′). *French.* Roncesvalles.
Ron·kon·ko·ma (rŏng-kŏng′kə-mə, rŏn-kŏn′-). Town of SE N.Y., on central Long Is. Pop. 20,200.
Ron·ne Ice Shelf (rŏ′nə, rŏn′ə). Area of shelf ice, c. 350 mi (563 km) in diameter, in W Antarctica S of the Weddell Sea.
Roo·de·poort-Ma·rais·burg (ro͞o′də-po͝ort′mə-răz′bûrg′, -mä-rā′bûrk). City of NE South Africa, W of Johannesburg. Pop. 115,366.
Ro·rai·ma (rō-rī′mə). Mountain, 9,094 ft (2,773.7 m), at the junction of the boundaries of Brazil, Guyana, and Venezuela.
Ro·sa (rô′zä, rō′zə), **Monte.** Highest (15,203 ft/4,636.9 m) mountain in the Pennine Alps, on the Swiss-Italian border.
Ro·sa·ri·o (rō-zä′rē-ō, -sä′-, rô-sä′ryô). City of E central Argentina, on the Paraná NW of Buenos Aires. Pop. 810,000.
Rose (rōz). Mountain, 10,778 ft (3,287.3 m), of NW Nev.
Ro·seau (rō-zō′). Cap. of Dominica, in the Windward Is. of the West Indies, on the SW coast. Pop. 10,157.
Rose·burg (rōz′bûrg′). City of SW Ore., SSW of Eugene. Pop. 16,644.
Ro·selle (rō-zĕl′). **1.** Village of NE Ill., WNW of Chicago. Pop. 16,948. **2.** Borough of NE N.J., near Elizabeth. Pop. 20,641.
Roselle Park. Borough of NE N.J., near Elizabeth. Pop. 13,377.
Rose·mead (rōz′mēd′). City of S Calif., near Los Angeles. Pop. 42,604.
Ro·sen·berg (rō′zən-bûrg′). City of SE Tex., SW of Houston. Pop. 17,995.
Ro·set·ta (rō-zĕt′ə). City of N Egypt, on the Nile delta. Pop. 36,711.
Rose·ville (rōz′vĭl′). **1.** City of N central Calif., NE of Sacramento. Pop. 24,347. **2.** City of SE Mich., near Detroit. Pop. 54,311. **3.** City of SE Minn., near St. Paul. Pop. 35,820.
Ros·kil·de (rō′skĭl-do͞o). City of E Denmark, W of Copenhagen. Pop. 48,746.
Ross (rôs, rŏs). **1.** Sea of the Pacific in Antarctica S of New Zealand. **2.** Island of Antarctica in the W Ross Sea. **3. Ice Shelf.** Area of shelf ice, c. 400 mi (644 km) in diameter, in Antarctica S of the Ross Sea.
Ross·bach (rôs′bäKH). Village of S central East Germany, where Frederick II of Prussia defeated the French (1757).
Ros·tock (rŏs′tŏk, rôs′tôk). City of N East Germany, near the Baltic. Pop. 226,667.
Ros·tov (rə-stôf′, rō-) also **Ros·tov-on-Don** (rə-stôf′ŏn-dŏn′, -dôn′). City of S European USSR, on the Don near the Sea of Azov. Pop. 946,000.
Ros·well (rŏz′wĕl′, -wəl). **1.** City of NW Ga., near Atlanta. Pop. 23,337. **2.** City of SE N.Mex., SE of Albuquerque. Pop. 39,676.
Ro·ta (rō′tä). Island of the W Pacific in the S Marianas N of Guam.
Roth·er·ham (rŏ*th*′ər-əm). Borough of N England, near Sheffield. Pop. 248,800.
Ro·to·ru·a (rō′tə-ro͞o′ə). City of central North Is., New Zealand. Pop. 37,700.
Rot·ter·dam (rŏt′ər-dăm′, rôt′ər-däm′). City of SW Netherlands, on the Rhine-Meuse delta SSE of The Hague. Pop. 579,194.
Ro·tu·ma (rō-to͞o′mə). Volcanic island in the SW Pacific N of Fiji.
Rou·baix (ro͞o-bĕ′). City of N France, near Lille. Pop. 109,553.
Rou·en (ro͞o-äN′, -än′). City of N France, on the Seine NW of Paris. Pop. 114,927.
Rou·ma·ni·a (ro͞o-mā′nē-ə, -mān′yə). Variant of **Rumania.**
Round Lake Beach (round). Village of NE Ill., W of Waukegan. Pop. 12,921.
Round Rock (rŏk). City of central Tex., N of Austin. Pop. 11,812.
Rous·sil·lon (ro͞o-sē-yôN′). Region and former province of S France, bordering on Spain and the Mediterranean.
Rou·yn (ro͞o′ĭn, rwăN). City of SW Que., Canada, near the Ont. border. Pop. 17,678.
Rov·no (rôv′nə). City of W European USSR, in the Ukraine NE of Lvov. Pop. 185,000.
Ro·vu·ma (rō-vo͞o′mə). Variant of **Ruvuma.**
Roy (roi). City of N Utah, near Ogden. Pop. 19,694.
Roy·al Gorge (roi′əl). Canyon formed by the Arkansas R. in S central Colo.
Royal Oak (ōk). City of SE Mich., near Detroit. Pop. 70,893.
Royal Tun·bridge Wells (tŭn′brĭj wĕlz′). Borough of SE England, SW of Maidstone. Pop. 44,800.
Ru·an·da (ro͞o-än′də). Variant of **Rwanda.**
Ru·a·pe·hu (ro͞o′ə-pā′ho͞o). Volcanic peak, 9,175 ft (2,798.4 m), in central North Is., New Zealand.
Rub al Kha·li (ro͞ob′ äl KHä′lē, äl kä′lē). Desert in the SE interior of the Arabian Peninsula.
Ru·bi·con (ro͞o′bĭ-kŏn). River, 15 mi (24 km), of N central Italy, flowing NE to the Adriatic.
Ru·dolf (ro͞o′dŏlf′). Lake, c. 2,500 sq mi (6,475 sq km), of NW Kenya.
Ru·eil-Mal·mai·son (rü-ē-yə′-mäl-mā-zôN′). Town of N central France, near Paris. Pop. 62,727.
Ru·fi·ji (ro͞o-fē′jē). River, c. 375 mi (603 km), of central Tanzania.
Ru·fisque (rü-fēsk′). City of W Senegal, on the Atlantic E of Dakar. Pop. 54,000.
Rug·by (rŭg′bē). Borough of central England, ESE of Coventry. Pop. 60,380.
Rü·gen (rü′gən). Island, 358 sq mi (927 sq km), of N East Germany, in the Baltic Sea.
Ruhr (ro͝or). **1.** River of NW West Germany, flowing 145 mi (233.3 km) W to the Rhine. **2.** Industrial region along and N of the Ruhr R.
Ru·ma·ni·a (ro͞o-mā′nē-ə, -mān′yə) also **Ro·ma·ni·a** (rō-) or **Rou·ma·ni·a** (ro͞o-). Country of SE Europe, with a short Black Sea coastline. Cap. Bucharest. Pop. 22,345,000. **—Ru·ma′ni·an** *adj. & n.*

Rumania

Run·ny·mede (rŭn′ĭ-mēd′). Meadow in SE England, on the Thames W of London; site of King John's acceptance of the Magna Carta (1215).
Ru·pert (ro͞o′pərt). River, c. 380 mi (611 km), of W central Que., Canada.
Rus·chuk (ro͞os-cho͝ok′). *Turkish.* Ruse.
Ru·se (ro͞o′sā). City of NE Bulgaria, on the Danube. Pop. 170,594.
Rush·more (rŭsh′môr′, -mōr′). Mountain, 6,200 ft (1,891 m), in the Black Hills of W S.Dak.; a national memorial with massive carved likenesses of Washington, Jefferson, Lincoln, and Theodore Roosevelt.
Rüs·sels·heim (rüs′əls-hīm). City of central West Germany, on the Main R. SW of Frankfurt. Pop. 62,606.
Rus·sia (rŭsh′ə). **1.** Former empire of E Europe and N Asia, superseded by the USSR in 1917. **2.** Union of Soviet Socialist Republics. **3.** Russian Soviet Federated Socialist Republic, in European, Central Asian, Siberian, and Far Eastern USSR, constituting 75 per cent of the nation's total area and extending from the Baltic Sea to the Pacific Ocean. **—Rus′sian** *adj. & n.*
Rus·ta·vi (ro͞o-stä′vē). City of S European USSR, in Georgia SE of Tbilisi. Pop. 132,000.
Rus·ton (rŭs′tən). City of N La., W of Monroe. Pop. 20,585.
Ruth·er·ford (rŭ*th*′ər-fərd, rŭth′-). Borough of NE N.J., near Clifton. Pop. 19,068.
Ru·the·ni·a (ro͞o-thē′nē-ə). Region of W European USSR, in W Ukraine S of the Carpathians. **—Ru·the′ni·an** *adj. & n.*
Rut·land (rŭt′lənd). City of W central Vt., N of Bennington. Pop. 18,436.
Ru·vu·ma (ro͞o-vo͞o′mə) also **Ro·vu·ma** (rō-). River of SE Africa, rising in N Mozambique and flowing c. 450 mi (724 km) E along the Mozambique-Tanzania border to the Indian Ocean.
Ru·wen·zo·ri (ro͞o′wĕn-zōr′ē, -zôr′ē). Mountain range of E central Africa, on the Uganda-Zaire border.
Rwan·da also **Ru·an·da** (ro͞o-än′də). Country of E central Africa, S of Uganda. Cap. Kigali. Pop. 4,780,000. **—Rwan′dan** *adj. & n.*

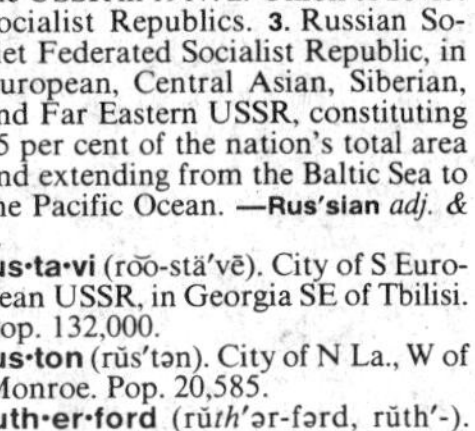

Rwanda

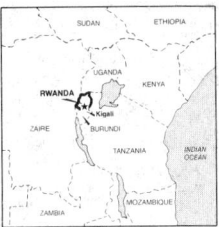

Rya·zan (ryä-zän′) also **Ri·a·zan** (rē-ä-zän′). City of central European

USSR, SE of Moscow. Pop. 462,000.

Ry·binsk (rĭ'bĭnsk). **1.** Reservoir, c. 2,000 sq mi (5,180 sq km), in N central European USSR, on the Volga. **2.** City of N central European USSR, on the Volga NNE of Moscow. Pop. 241,000.

Ryb·nik (rĭb'nĕk). Town of S Poland, WSW of Katowice. Pop. 118,200.

Rye (rī). City of SE N.Y., on Long Is. Sound near New York City. Pop. 15,083.

Rys·wick (rĭz'wĭk). Variant of **Rijswijk**.

Ryu·kyu (ryōō'kyōō, rē-ōō'kyōō). Islands of SW Japan, extending c. 650 mi (1,046 km) between Kyushu, Japan, and Taiwan.

Rze·szów (zhĕ'shōōv). City of SE Poland, E of Kraków. Pop. 116,900.

S

Saa·le (zä'lə). River, c. 265 mi (426 km), of E West Germany and SW East Germany.

Saar (sär, zär). **1.** River, c. 150 mi (241 km), of NE France and W West Germany. **2.** Saarland.

Saar·brück·en (zär-brŏŏk'ən, sär-, zär-brük'-). City of W West Germany, on the Saar R. near the French border. Pop. 194,452.

Saa·re·maa (sär'ə-mä'). Variant of **Sarema**.

Saar·land (zär'lănd', sär'-, zär'länt'). Region of W West Germany in the Saar valley, historically contested with France.

Sa·ba (sä'bä). Island of the N Netherlands Antilles, between St. Martin and St. Eustatius.

Sa·ba·dell (sä'bä-*th*ĕl'). City of NE Spain, NW of Barcelona. Pop. 188,344.

Sa·bah (sä'bä'). Region and state of Malaysia in NE Borneo.

Sa·ba·lan or **Sa·va·lan** (sä'vä-län'). Volcanic cone, 15,784 ft (4,814.1 m), of NW Iran.

Sa·bar·ma·ti (sä'bər-mŭt'ē). River, c. 220 mi (322 km), of W India.

Sa·bi (sä'bē). River, c. 400 mi (644 km), of E Zimbabwe and S Mozambique.

Sa·bine (sə-bēn'). River of E Tex., rising NE of Dallas and flowing c. 575 mi (925 km) E and S to the Gulf of Mexico, in its lower course forming the Tex.-La. border and crossing **Sabine Lake** (c. 17 mi/27.4 km long).

Sa·ble (sā'bəl). **1. Cape.** Promontory of extreme S N.S., Canada. **2. Cape.** Cape of S Fla.; southernmost extremity of the U.S. mainland. **3.** Island off N.S., Canada, ESE of Halifax.

Sab·ra·tha (săb'rə-thə) also **Sab·ra·ta** (-rə-tə). Ancient town of Roman Africa, in modern Libya W of Tripoli.

Sa·co (sô'kō, sä'-, săk'ō). **1.** River, c. 105 mi (169 km), of E N.H. and SW Me. **2.** City of SW Me., SW of Portland. Pop. 12,921.

Sac·ra·men·to (săk'rə-mĕn'tō). **1.** River, c. 380 mi (611 km), of N Calif. **2.** Mountains of S N.Mex. **3.** Cap. of Calif., in the N central part. Pop. 275,741.

Sa·do·va (sä-dō'vä, sä'dô-vä') or **Sa·do·wa** (zä-dō'vä). Village of N Czechoslovakia; site of a Prussian victory (1866) in the Austro-Prussian War.

Sa·fa·qis (sä-fä'kĭs). Sfax.

Sa·fed Koh (sə-fĕd' kō'). Mountain range on the Pakistan-Afghanistan border SE of Kabul, rising to 15,620 ft (4,764.1 km).

Sa·fi (sä'fē, sä'-). City of W Morocco, on the Atlantic WNW of Marrakesh. Pop. 129,113.

Sa·fid Rud (sä-fēd' rōōd') also **Se·fid Rud** (sĕ-). River, c. 450 mi (724 km), of NW Iran.

Sa·ga (sä'gä'). City of W Kyushu, on an inlet of the East China Sea. Pop. 162,038.

Sa·ga·mi Sea (sä-gä'mē). Bay of the W Pacific on the SE coast of Honshu, Japan, SW of Tokyo Bay.

Sa·ga·mi·ha·ra (sä-gä-mē'hä-rä'). City of central Honshu, Japan, near Tokyo. Pop. 439,257.

Sa·gi·naw (săg'ə-nô'). **1.** Bay of Lake Huron extending into E Mich. **2.** City of E central Mich., NNW of Flint. Pop. 77,508.

Sa·gua·ro National Monument (sə-gwär'ō, -wär'ō). Area of saguaro and other desert growth in SE Ariz.

Sag·ue·nay (săg'ə-nā', săg'ə-nā'). River, c. 125 mi (201 km), of S Que., Canada.

Sa·gun·to (sä-gōōn'tô). City of E Spain, NNE of Valencia. Pop. 57,840.

Sa·har·a (sə-hâr'ə, -hä'rə). Vast desert of N Africa, extending from the Atlantic coast to the Nile valley and from the Atlas Mts. S to the Sudan.

Sa·ha·ran·pur (sə-här'ən-pōōr'). City of N central India, NNE of Delhi. Pop. 225,396.

Sai·gon (sī-gŏn'). Ho Chi Minh City.

Sai·maa (sī'mä'). Lake, c. 500 sq mi (1,295 sq km), of SE Finland, largest of the **Saimaa Lakes**, a group of c. 120 connected lakes.

Saint Al·bans (sānt ôl'bənz). **1.** Borough of SE England, near London. Pop. 124,300. **2.** City of W W.Va., W of Charleston. Pop. 12,402.

Saint Al·bert (ăl'bərt). City of central Alta., Canada, NW of Edmonton. Pop. 29,512.

Saint Ann (ăn). City of E Mo., near St. Louis. Pop. 15,523.

Saint Au·gus·tine (ô'gə-stēn'). City of NE Fla., on the Atlantic SSE of Jacksonville. Pop. 11,985.

Saint Aus·tell with Fow·ey (ô'stəl; fō'ē, foi). Borough of SW England, on the English Channel W of Plymouth. Pop. 32,710.

Saint Bar·thol·o·mew (bär-thŏl'ə-myōō') or **Saint-Bar·thél·e·my** (săN-bär-tā-lə-mē'). Island of the French West Indies, NNW of Guadeloupe.

Saint Bru·no de Mon·tar·ville (brōō'nō' də mŏn'tər-vĭl'). Town of S Que., Canada, near Montreal. Pop. 21,272.

Saint Cath·a·rines (kăth'ə-rĭnz', kăth'rĭnz). City of S Ont., Canada, on the Welland Ship Canal. Pop. 123,956.

Saint Charles (chärlz). **1.** City of NE Ill., W of Chicago. Pop. 17,492. **2.** City of E Mo., on the Missouri near St. Louis. Pop. 37,379.

Saint Chris·to·pher (krĭs'tə-fər). Island, 68 sq mi (176 sq km), of the British West Indies WNW of Antigua; part of St. Kitts-Nevis.

Saint Clair (klâr). Lake, c. 490 sq mi (1,269 sq km), between SW Ont., Canada, and SE Mich., connected by the **Saint Clair R.** (40 mi/64.4 km) with Lake Huron.

Saint Clair Shores (klâr). City of SE Mich., near Detroit. Pop. 76,210.

Saint Cloud (kloud). City of central Minn., NW of Minneapolis. Pop. 42,566.

Saint-Cloud (săN-klōō'). Town of N central France, near Paris. Pop. 28,139.

Saint Croix (kroi). **1.** River, c. 164 mi (264 km), of NW Wis. and E Minn. **2.** Largest (81 sq mi/210 sq km) of the U.S. Virgin Is., in the West Indies.

Saint-De·nis (săN-də-nē'). **1.** City of N central France, near Paris. Pop. 96,132. **2.** Cap. of Réunion, on the Indian Ocean. Pop. 103,513.

Sainte Foy (sănt' foi', săNt fwä'). City of S Que., Canada, near Quebec city. Pop. 71,237.

Saint E·li·as (ĭ-lī'əs). **1.** Mountains of the Coast Ranges in SW Y.T., Canada, and E Alas. **2. Mount.** Peak, 18,008 ft (5,492.4 m), in the St. Elias range on the Alas.-Y.T. border.

Sainte Thé·rèse (sānt' tə-rāz', săNt tā-rĕz'). City of S Que., Canada, on the St. Lawrence NW of Montreal. Pop. 17,479.

Saint-É·tienne (săN-tā-tyĕn'). City of SE France, SW of Lyon. Pop. 220,070.

Saint Eu·stache (sănt' ōō-stăsh', săN tœ-stăsh'). Town of S Que., Canada, W of Montreal. Pop. 21,248.

Saint Eu·sta·ti·us (yōō-stā'shəs, -shē-əs). Island of the Netherlands Antilles, in the Leeward Is. NW of St. Christopher.

Saint Fran·cis (frăn'sĭs). **1. Lake.** Expansion of the St. Lawrence R. in SE Ont. and S Que., Canada, SW of Montreal. **2.** River, c. 470 mi (755 km), of SE Mo. and E Ark. **3.** City of SE Wis., near Milwaukee. Pop. 10,066.

Saint Fran·çois (sănt' frän-swä', săN frăN-swä'). River, 165 mi (265.5 km), of S Que., Canada.

Saint Gall (sănt' gôl', săN găl'). Sankt Gallen.

Saint George (jôrj). City of SW Utah, near the Ariz. border. Pop. 11,350.

Saint George's (jôr'jəz). **1. Channel.** Strait, c. 100 mi (161 km) long and 50–95 mi (80–153 km) wide, between W Wales and SE Ireland. **2.** Or **Saint George** (jôrj). Cap. of Grenada, in the West Indies. Pop. 10,000.

Saint-Gilles (săN-zhēl'). City of central Belgium, near Brussels. Pop. 47,932.

Saint Gott·hard (gŏt'ərd). Mountains of the Lepontine Alps in central Switzerland, crossed by **Saint Gotthard Pass** (6,935 ft/2,115.2 m).

Saint He·le·na (hə-lē'nə). Island in the S Atlantic, W of Angola; a British colony. Cap. Jamestown. Pop. 5,147.

Saint Hel·ens (hĕl'ənz) **1. Mount.** Active volcanic peak of the Cascade Range in SW Wash. **2.** Borough of NW England, ENE of Liverpool. Pop. 188,700.

Saint-Hu·bert (sānt'hyōō'bərt). Town of S Que., Canada, near Montreal. Pop. 49,706.

Saint-Hy·a·cinthe (sānt'hī'ə-sĭnth, săN-tyä-săNt'). City of S Que., Canada, ENE of Montreal. Pop. 37,500.

Saint-Jean (săN-zhăN'). City of S Que., Canada, on the Richelieu R. SE of Montreal. Pop. 34,363.

Saint-Jé·rôme (săN-zhā-rōm', sănt'jə-rōm'). City of S Que., Canada, NW of Montreal. Pop. 25,175.

Saint John (jŏn). **1.** Lake, c. 375 sq mi (971 sq km), of S central Que., Canada. **2.** River, c. 418 mi (673 km), of N Me. and W N.B., Canada. **3.** One of the U.S. Virgin Is., in the West Indies E of St. Thomas. **4.** City of S N.B., Canada, at the mouth of the St. John R. on the Bay of Fundy. Pop. 89,956.

Saint Johns (jŏnz). **1.** River, 285 mi (458.6 km), of NE Fla. **2.** Saint-Jean.

Saint John's (jŏnz). **1.** Cap. of Antigua, in the British West Indies, on the N coast. Pop. 21,814. **2.** Cap. of Newf., Canada, on the SE coast of the island. Pop. 86,576.

Saint Jo·seph (jō'zəf, -səf). **1.** River, 210 mi (338 km), of SW Mich. and N Ind. **2.** City of NW Mo., on the Missouri R. NNW of Kansas City. Pop. 76,691.

Saint Kitts (kĭts). St. Christopher.

Saint Kitts-Nev·is (kĭts-nē'vĭs, -nĕv'-ĭs). Island group of the British West Indies, in the Leeward Is. Cap. Basseterre. Pop. 47,457.

Saint Lam·bert (lăm'bərt). City of S Que., Canada, on the St. Lawrence near Montreal. Pop. 20,318.

Saint Lau·rent (săN lô-rän', sănt' lô-rĕnt'). City of S Que., Canada, near Montreal. Pop. 64,404.

Saint Law·rence (lôr'əns, lŏr'-). **1. Gulf of.** Arm of the NW Atlantic off SE Canada, between N.B. and Newf. **2.** River of SE Canada, flowing 744 mi (1,197.1 km) NE from Lake Ontario along the Ont.-N.Y. border and through S Que. to the Gulf of St. Lawrence. **3.** Island off W Alas. S of the Bering Strait.

Saint Lawrence Seaway. **1.** Canal and river route, 182 mi (292.8 km), along the St. Lawrence R. between Lake Ontario and Montreal. **2.** System of rivers, canals, and lakes from the Atlantic through the Great Lakes.

Saint Lé·o·nard (săN lā-ō-när', sănt' lĕn'ərd). City of S Que., Canada, N of Montreal. Pop. 78,452.

Saint Lô (sănt' lō', săN lō'). Town of NW France, W of Caen. Pop. 23,221.

Saint Lou·is (lōō'ĭs, lōō'ē). **1.** (*also* săN lōō-ē', lwē'). Lake, 57 sq mi (148 sq km), of S Que., Canada, SW of Montreal. **2.** River, c. 160 mi (257 km), of NE Minn. **3.** Independent city of E Mo., on the Mississippi just S of the influx of the Missouri R. Pop. 453,085.

Saint-Lou·is (săN-lōō-ē', -lwē'). City of NW Senegal, at the mouth of the Senegal R. Pop. 88,000.

Saint Louis Park. City of E Minn., near Minneapolis. Pop. 42,931.

Saint Lu·cia (lōō'shə, lōō-sē'ə). Island nation of the West Indies, in the Windward Is. S of Martinique. Cap. Castries. Pop. 117,500.

Saint-Ma·lo (săN-mä-lō'). Town of NW France, on the **Gulf of Saint-Malo**, an inlet of the English Channel. Pop. 45,030.

Saint Mar·tin (mär'tn). Island of the West Indies, in the W Leeward Is.; divided between France and the Netherlands.

Saint Mar·ys (mâr'ēz). **1.** River, c. 175 mi (282 km), rising in SE Ga. and flowing on the Ga.-Fla. border to the Atlantic. **2.** River, 63 mi (101.4 km), flowing from Lake Superior to Lake Huron on the Mich.-Ont. border.

Saint Mat·thews (măth'yōōz). City of N Ky., near Louisville. Pop. 13,354.

Saint-Maur-des-Fos·sés (săN-môr-dā-fô-sā'). City of N central France, near Paris. Pop. 80,920.

Saint Mau·rice (sănt' môr'ĭs, mŏr'-, săN mô-rēs'). River, c. 325 mi (525 km), of S Que., Canada.

Saint Mo·ritz (sănt' mə-rĭts', săN mô-rēts'). Resort city of SE Switzerland, on the Inn R. Pop. 7,400.

Saint-Na·zaire (săN-nä-zĕr'). City of W central France, at the mouth of the Loire R. Pop. 69,251.

Saint Paul (pôl). Cap. of Minn., in the E adjacent to Minneapolis. Pop. 270,230.

Saint Paul's Rocks (pôlz). Islets of Brazil, in the Atlantic NE of Natal.

Saint Pe·ter (pē'tər). Lake, 142 sq mi (228 sq km), of S Que., Canada, NE of Montreal.

Saint Pe·ters (pē'tərz). City of E Mo., WNW of St. Louis. Pop. 15,700.

Saint Pe·ters·burg (pē'tərz-bûrg'). **1.** Leningrad. **2.** City of W central Fla., on Tampa Bay. Pop. 236,893.

Saint Pi·erre or **Saint-Pi·erre** (sānt' pîr', pē-âr', săN pyĕr'). **1.** Island of the St. Pierre and Miquelon group, in the N Atlantic S of Newf., Canada. **2.** Cap. of St. Pierre and Miquelon, on St. Pierre Is. Pop. 5,232.

Saint Pierre and Mi·que·lon (mĭk'ə-lŏn', mē-klôN'). French island group, 93 sq mi (241 sq km), in the N Atlantic S of Newf., Canada. Cap. St. Pierre. Pop. 5,840.

Saint-Quen·tin (sănt' kwĕn'tən, săN kăN-tăN'). City of N central France, NNE of Paris. Pop. 67,243.

Saint Si·mons (sī'mənz). Island of SE Ga., in the Atlantic.

Saint Tho·mas (tŏm'əs). **1.** Island of the U.S. Virgin Is., in the West Indies. **2.** City of S Ont., Canada, S of London. Pop. 27,578. **3.** Charlotte Amalie.

Saint-Tro·pez (săN-trô-pā'). Resort town of SE France, on the Mediterranean. Pop. 4,523.

Saint Vin·cent (vĭn'sənt). **1. Cape.** Promontory at SW extremity of Portugal. **2.** Island of St. Vincent and the Grenadines, in the central Windward Is. of the West Indies.

Saint Vincent and the Gren·a·dines (grĕn'ə-dēnz', grĕn'ə-dēnz'). Island nation in the central Windward Is. of the West Indies, comprising St. Vincent Is. and the N. Grenadines. Cap. Kingstown. Pop. 89,129.

Sai·pan (sī-păn', -pän', sī'păn). Island of the W Pacific, in the S Marianas, U.S. Trust Territory of the Pacific Islands. **—Sai'pa·nese'** *adj. & n.*

Sa·is (sā'ĭs). Ancient Egyptian city on the Nile delta.

Sa·ja·ma (sä-hä'mä). Mountain, 21,390 ft (6,524 m), in W Bolivia near the Chilean border.

Sa·kai (sä'kī'). City of S Honshu,

Japan, on Osaka Bay. Pop. 810,120.
Sa·kar·ya (sə-kär'yə). River, c. 490 mi (788 km), of NW Turkey.
Sa·kha·lin (săk'ə-lēn', săk'ə-lēn', sä'KHä-lēn'). Island of SE Far Eastern USSR, in the Sea of Okhotsk N of Hokkaido, Japan.
Sa·ki·shi·ma (sä'kē-shē'mä, sä-kē'-shē-mä'). Islands of Japan in the S Ryuku Is., E of Taiwan.
Sa·kon·net River (sə-kŏn'ĭt). Inlet of the Atlantic extending into SE R.I.
Sal·a·do (sə-lä'dō, sä-lä'*th*ô). **1.** Also **Salado del Nor·te** (dĕl nôr'tē). River of N Argentina, flowing c. 1,250 mi (2,011 km) SE into the Parana. **2.** River of W central Argentina, flowing c. 750 mi (1,207 km) SSE into the Colorado.
Sa·la·jar or **Sa·la·yar** (sə-lä'yär'). Island of central Indonesia, in the Flores Sea off SW Sulawesi.
Sal·a·man·ca (săl'ə-măng'kə, sä'-lä-mäng'kä). **1.** City of central Mexico, NE of Mexico City. Pop. 61,039. **2.** City of W central Spain, WNW of Madrid. Pop. 144,446.
Sal·a·mis (săl'ə-mĭs). **1.** Island of Greece, in the Saronic Gulf E of Athens, near which the Greeks defeated the Persians (480 B.C.). **2.** Ancient city of E Cyprus.
Sal·can·tay (säl'kän-tī'). Highest mountain, 20,500 ft (6,252.5 m), in the Cordillera Oriental, in SE Peru.
Sa·lé (sä-lā') also **Sla** (slä). City of NW Morocco, on the Atlantic near Rabat. Pop. 155,557.
Sa·lem (sā'ləm). **1.** City of SE India, SW of Madras. Pop. 308,716. **2.** City of NE Mass., NE of Boston. Pop. 38,220. **3.** Town of SE N.H., W of Haverhill, Mass. Pop. 24,124. **4.** City of NE Ohio, SW of Youngstown. Pop. 12,869. **5.** Cap. of Ore., in the NW part. Pop. 89,233. **6.** Independent city of SW Va., near Roanoke. Pop. 23,958.
Sa·ler·no (sə-lûr'nō, sä-lĕr'nō). City of S Italy, on the **Gulf of Salerno**, an inlet of the Tyrrhenian Sea. Pop. 161,997.
Sal·ford (sôl'fərd). Borough of NW England, near Manchester. Pop. 252,600.
Sa·li·na (sə-lī'nə). City of central Kans., NNW of Wichita. Pop. 41,843.
Sa·li·nas (sə-lē'nəs). **1.** River, c. 150 mi (241 km), of W central Calif. **2.** City of W Calif., near Monterey. Pop. 80,479.
Salis·bur·y (sôlz'bĕr'ē, -bə-rē). **1.** Borough of S central England, NW of Southampton on SE edge of **Salisbury Plain**, site of Stonehenge. Pop. 35,460. **2.** City of SE Md., on the Eastern Shore S of Dover, Del. Pop. 16,429. **3.** City of W central N.C., SSW of Winston-Salem. Pop. 22,677. **4.** Cap. of Zimbabwe, in the NE part. Pop. 118,500.
Sal·mon (săm'ən). River of central Idaho, rising in the **Salmon River Mts.** (highest elevation, 10,328 ft/3,150 m) and flowing c. 425 mi (684 km) to the Snake R.
Sa·lo·ni·ka (sə-lŏn'ĭ-kə, săl'ə-nē'kə). City of NE Greece, on the **Gulf of Salonika**, an arm of the NW Aegean Sea. Pop. 345,799.
Salt (sôlt). **1.** River, c. 200 mi (322 km), of S Ariz. **2.** River, c. 200 mi (322 km), of NE Mo.
Sal·ta (säl'tä). City of NW Argentina, N of Tucumán. Pop. 254,000.
Sal·ti·llo (säl-tē'yô). City of N Mexico, N of Mexico City. Pop. 245,700.
Salt Lake City. Cap. of Utah, in the N part near Great Salt Lake. Pop. 163,033.
Sal·to (säl'tô). City of NW Uruguay, on the Uruguay R. Pop. 71,881.
Sal·ton Sea (sôl'tən). Lake, 370 sq mi (958.3 sq km), of SE Calif.
Sa·lu·da (sə-lo͞o'də). River, c. 200 mi (322 km), of W S.C.
Sal·va·dor (săl'və-dôr'). **1.** (*also* säl'-vä-*th*ôr'). El Salvador. **2.** (*also* säl'-və-dôr'). City of E Brazil, on the Atlantic. Pop. 1,445,700.
Sal·ween (săl'wēn', săl-wēn'). River of SE Asia, rising in E Tibet and flowing c. 1,750 mi (2,816 km) SE and S through Burma into the Gulf of Martaban.
Salz·burg (sôlz'bûrg', sälz'-, zälts'-bo͝ork'). City of W central Austria, near the West German border WSW of Linz. Pop. 139,000.
Salz·git·ter (zälts'gĭt'ər). City of NE West Germany, SE of Hannover. Pop. 113,427.
Sa·mar (sä'mär). Island of E central Philippines, in the E Visayan group NE of Leyte.
Sa·ma·ra (sə-mär'ə, sä-mä'rə). **1.** River, c. 360 mi (579 km), of SE European USSR. **2.** Kuibyshev.
Sa·mar·i·a (sə-mâr'ē-ə). **1.** Region of ancient Palestine, in present-day NW Jordan. **2.** Ancient N kingdom of Israel. **3.** Ancient city of central Palestine, in present-day NW Jordan. **—Sa·mar'i·tan** (-ĭ-tən) *adj. & n.*
Sam·ar·kand (săm'ər-kănd', sä'-mär-känt'). City of S Central Asian USSR, SW of Tashkent. Pop. 481,000.
Sam·ni·um (săm'nē-əm). Ancient country of central and S Italy. **—Sam'nite** (săm'nīt') *adj. & n.*
Sa·mo·a (sə-mō'ə). Island group of the S Pacific, ENE of Fiji; divided between **American Samoa** and **Western Samoa**. **—Sa·mo'an** *adj. & n.*
Sa·mos (sā'mŏs', săm'ŏs', sä'môs). Island of E Greece, in the Aegean off W coast of Turkey.
Sam·o·thrace (săm'ə-thrās', -ō-thrās'). Island of NE Greece, in the NE Aegean.
Sam·o·thrá·ki (sä'mô-thrä'kē). *Greek.* Samothrace.
Sam·sun (säm-so͞on'). City of N Turkey, on the Black Sea. Pop. 198,266.
San (sän). River, c. 280 mi (451 km), of SE Poland.
San·a or **Sa·n'a** also **Sa·naa** (sä-nä'). Cap. of Yemen, in the central part. Pop. 192,045.
San An·ge·lo (săn ăn'jə-lō'). City of SW Tex., SW of Abilene. Pop. 73,240.
San An·sel·mo (ăn-sĕl'mō). Town of W Calif., near San Francisco. Pop. 11,927.
San An·to·ni·o (ăn-tō'nē-ō'). **1.** River, c. 200 mi (322 km), of S Tex. **2.** Peak, 10,080 ft (3,074.4 m), of the San Gabriel Mts. in S Calif. **3.** City of S central Tex., SSW of Austin. Pop. 785,410.
San Be·ni·to (bə-nē'tō). City of extreme S Tex., near Brownsville. Pop. 17,988.
San Ber·nar·di·no (bûr'nə-dē'nō, -nər-). **1.** Mountains of S Calif., S of the Mojave Desert. **2.** Pass, 6,770 ft (2,063 m), through the Lepontine Alps in SE Switzerland.
San Blas (sän' bläs', sän' bläs'), **Gulf of.** Inlet of the Caribbean off N central Panama.
San Bru·no (bro͞o'nō). City of W Calif., S of San Francisco. Pop. 35,417.
San Car·los (kär'lōs, -ləs). City of W Calif., SE of San Mateo. Pop. 24,710.
San Cle·men·te (klə-mĕn'tē). **1.** Island of S Calif., in SW Santa Barbara Is. S of Santa Catalina. **2.** City of S Calif., SE of Long Beach. Pop. 27,325.
San Cris·tó·bal (săn' krĭs-tō'bəl, sän' krēs-tô'bäl). **1.** Island of Ecuador, in the Galápagos Is. **2.** City of extreme W Venezuela, near the Colombian border. Pop. 249,000.
Sanc·ti-Spí·ri·tus (sängk'tē spē'-rē-to͞os'). City of central Cuba, WNW of Camagüey. Pop. 58,600.
San·da·kan (săn-dä'kən). City of Malaysia on N Borneo, on an inlet of the Sulu Sea. Pop. 42,413.
Sand·hurst (sănd'hûrst'). Village of S central England, SE of Reading; site of the Royal Military Academy.
San·di·a (săn-dē'ə). Peak, 10,676 ft (3,256.2 m), of N central N.Mex., NE of Albuquerque.
San Di·e·go (dē-ā'gō). City of S Calif., on the Pacific near the Mexican border. Pop. 875,504.
San Di·mas (dē'məs). City of S Calif., near Pomona. Pop. 24,014.
San·dring·ham (săn'drĭng-əm). Village of E England, near the Wash; site of a royal estate.
Sand Springs (sănd). City of NE Okla., near Tulsa. Pop. 13,246.
San·dus·ky (sən-dŭs'kē, săn-). **1.** River, c. 150 mi (241 km), of N Ohio. **2.** City of N Ohio, on Lake Erie W of Cleveland. Pop. 31,360.
Sand·wich (sănd'wĭch', săn'-). **1.** Hawaiian Is. **2.** Borough of SE England, N of Dover. Pop. 4,420.
Sand·y City (săn'dē). City of N Utah, near Salt Lake City. Pop. 51,022.
Sandy Hook (ho͝ok). Peninsula of E N.J., at entrance to Lower New York Bay.
San Fer·nan·do. **1.** (sän' fĕr-nän'-dô). City of E Argentina, NW of Buenos Aires. Pop. 119,565. **2.** (săn' fər-năn'dō). City of S Calif., in the **San Fernando Valley**, surrounded by Los Angeles. Pop. 17,731.
San·ford (săn'fərd). **1.** City of central Fla., NNE of Orlando. Pop. 23,176. **2.** City of SW Me., W of Biddeford. Pop. 18,020. **3.** City of central N.C., SW of Raleigh. Pop. 14,773.
San Fran·cis·co (frən-sĭs'kō). **1. Peaks.** Group of 3 peaks in N Ariz., N of Flagstaff, consisting of Mt. Humphreys, Mt. Agassiz, and Mt. Fremont. **2.** City of W Calif., on a peninsula between the Pacific and **San Francisco Bay**, an inlet of the Pacific. Pop. 678,974. **—San Fran·cis'can** (-kən) *n.*
San Ga·bri·el (gā'brē-əl). **1.** Mountains of S Calif., E and NE of Los Angeles, rising to 10,080 ft (3,074.4 m). **2.** City of S Calif., near Los Angeles. Pop. 30,072.
San·ga·mon (săng'gə-mən). River, c. 250 mi (402 km), of central Ill.
San·gay (säng-gī'). Active volcano, 17,454 ft (5,323.5 m), in the Andes of E central Ecuador.
San·ger (săng'ər). City of S central Calif., E of Fresno. Pop. 12,558.
San·gi·he (säng'gē-ä', -gē'ə) also **Sang·i** (säng'gē, säng'ē). **1.** Islands of N central Indonesia, NE of Sulawesi. **2.** Largest (217 sq mi/562 sq km) of the Sangihe Is.
San Gi·mi·gna·no (sän' jē'mē-nyä'-nō). Town of central Italy, NW of Siena. Pop. 2,800.
San·gre de Cris·to (săng'grē dĭ krĭs'tō). Range of the S Rockies extending c. 220 mi (355 km) from S central Colo. into N central N.Mex.
San·i·bel (săn'ə-bəl, -bĕl'). Island of SW Fla., in the Gulf of Mexico SW of Fort Myers.
San I·si·dro (sän' ē-sē'*th*rô). City of E Argentina, near Buenos Aires. Pop. 250,008.
San Ja·cin·to (jə-sĭn'tō). River, c. 130 mi (209 km), of SE Tex.
San Joa·quin (wô-kēn', wä-). River of central Calif., flowing c. 320 mi (515 km), SW and NW through its fertile valley to the Sacramento R.
San Jo·se (hō-zā'). City of W Calif., SE of San Francisco. Pop. 636,550.
San Jo·sé (sän' hô-sĕ', hō-zā'). Cap. of Costa Rica, in the central part. Pop. 239,800.
San Juan (săn' wän', hwän'). **1.** River, c. 360 mi (579 km), of SW Colo., NW N.Mex., and SE Utah. **2.** Range of the Rockies in SW Colo. and N N.Mex. **3.** (*also* sän' hwän'). Hill of E Cuba, near Santiago de Cuba; site of Spanish-American War battle (1898). **4.** Islands of NW Wash., N of Puget Sound. **5.** (*also* sän' hwän'). City of NW Argentina, W of Córdoba. Pop. 115,000. **6.** (*also* sän' hwän'). Cap. of Puerto Rico, in the NE part on the Atlantic. Pop. 422,701.
San Juan Cap·is·tra·no (kăp'ĭ-strä'-nō). City of S Calif., SE of Santa Ana. Pop. 18,959.
Sankt Gal·len (zängt gäl'ən). City of NE Switzerland, E of Zurich. Pop. 73,800.
Sankt Pöl·ten (pœl'tən). City of N central Austria, W of Vienna. Pop. 50,144.
San·ku·ru (säng-ko͞o'ro͞o). River, c. 750 mi (1,207 km), of S and central Zaire.
San Le·an·dro (lē-ăn'drō). City of W Calif., SSE of Oakland. Pop. 63,952.
San Lu·cas (sän lo͞o'kəs, sän' lo͞o'-käs). Cape of W Mexico at the S tip of Lower California.
San Lu·is (lo͞o'ĭs). Valley of N N.Mex. and S Colo. between the San Juan and Sangre de Cristo ranges.
San Luis O·bis·po (ə-bĭs'pō). City of S Calif., NW of Santa Barbara. Pop. 34,252.
San Lu·is Po·to·sí (sän' lo͞o-ēs' pô'tô-sē'). City of central Mexico, NE of León. Pop. 315,200.
San Mar·cos (mär'kəs). **1.** City of S Calif., NNW of San Diego. Pop. 17,479. **2.** City of S central Tex., NE of San Antonio. Pop. 23,420.
San Ma·ri·no (săn' mə-rē'nō). **1.** (*also* sän' mä-rē'nō). Republic, 23 sq mi (60 sq km), within N central Italy, in the Apennines near the Adriatic. Cap. San Marino. Pop. 20,000. **2.** (*also* sän' mä-rē'nō). Cap. of San Marino. Pop. 4,628. **3.** City of S Calif., near Pasadena. Pop. 13,307.

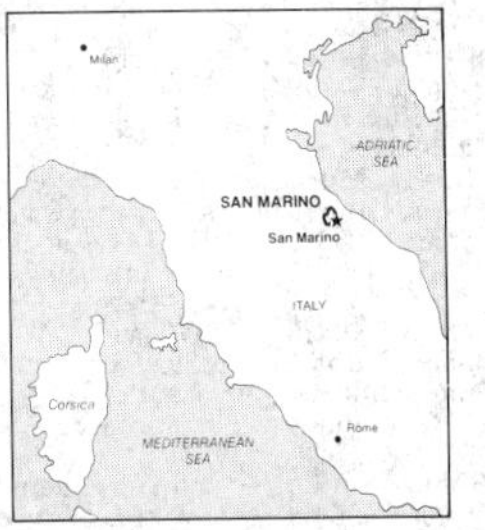

San Marino

San Mar·tín (săn' mär-tēn', săn'). Town of E Argentina, near Buenos Aires. Pop. 24,300.
San Ma·te·o (mə-tā'ō). City of W Calif., SSE of San Francisco. Pop. 77,561.
San Mi·guel (sän' mē-gĕl'). City of E El Salvador. Pop. 72,900.
San Miguel de Tu·cu·mán (dĕ to͞o-ko͞o-män'). Tucumán.
San Ni·co·lás de los Gar·zas (sän' nē-kô-läs' dĕ lôs gär'säs). City of N Mexico, near Monterrey. Pop. 28,803.
San Pab·lo (păb'lō). City of W Calif., NNW of Oakland on **San Pablo Bay**, N arm of San Francisco Bay. Pop. 19,750.
San Pe·dro (pē'drō). Channel between S Calif. mainland and Santa Catalina Is.
San Pe·dro de Ma·co·rís (sän' pĕ'*th*rô dĕ mä-kô-rēs'). City of SE Dominican Republic, on the Caribbean. Pop. 66,022.
San Pe·dro Su·la (sän' pĕ'*th*rô so͞o'-lä). City of NW Honduras. Pop. 172,900.
San Ra·fael (rə-fĕl'). City of W Calif., N of San Francisco. Pop. 44,700.
San Re·mo (săn' rē'mō, rā'-, sän' rā'mō). City of NW Italy, on the Ligurian Sea. Pop. 52,400.
San Sal·va·dor (săn' săl'və-dôr', sän' säl'vä-*th*ôr'). **1.** Island of the central Bahamas. **2.** Cap. of El Salvador, in the W central part. Pop. 397,100.
San Se·bas·tián (săn' sə-băs'chĭn, sän' sĕ-bäs-tyän'). City of N Spain, on the Bay of Biscay near the French border. Pop. 176,023.
San·ta An·a (săn'tə ăn'ə). **1.** (*also* sän'tä ä'nä). City of W El Salvador, NW of San Salvador. Pop. 112,800. **2.** City of S Calif., E of Long Beach. Pop. 203,713.
Santa Bar·ba·ra (bär'bər-ə, bär'brə). **1.** Channel between N Santa Barbara Is. and S Calif. coast. **2.** Islands of Calif., in the Pacific off the S coast. **3.** City of S Calif., on the Pacific WNW of Los Angeles. Pop. 74,542.
Santa Cat·a·li·na (kăt'l-ē'nə). Island of S Calif., in the S Santa Barbara Is.
San·ta Cla·ra (săn'tə klăr'ə, klâr'ə). **1.** (*also* sän'tä klä'rä). City of central Cuba, ESE of Havana. Pop. 152,361. **2.** City of W Calif., near San Jose. Pop. 87,746.
San·ta Cruz (săn'tə kro͞oz'). **1.** (*also* sän'tä kro͞os'). River, c. 250 mi (402 km), of S Argentina. **2.** Islands of the W Pacific in the SE Solomon Is. **3.** Island of S Calif., in the N Santa

Barbara Is. **4.** (*also* sän′tä kro͞os′). City of central Bolivia, NE of Sucre. Pop. 256,946. **5.** City of W Calif., on Monterey Bay SSW of San Jose. Pop. 41,483.

San·ta Cruz de Ten·er·ife (săn′tə kro͞oz′ də tĕn′ə-rĭf′, sän′tä kro͞os′ dĕ te′nē-rē′fĕ). City of the Canary Is., on the NE coast of Tenerife. Pop. 186,949.

San·ta Fe (săn′tə fā′). **1.** (*also* sän′tä fĕ′). City of NE Argentina, on the Salado R. Pop. 282,000. **2.** Cap. of N.Mex., in the N central part. Pop. 48,899.

Santa Fe Springs (fā). City of S Calif., SE of Los Angeles. Pop. 14,559.

Santa Fe Trail. 19th cent. wagon and trade route to the SW U.S., extending from Independence, Mo., to Santa Fe, N.Mex.

San·ta Is·a·bel (săn′tə ĭz′ə-bĕl′, sän′tä ē′sä-bĕl′). **1.** Island of the W Pacific, in E central Solomon Is. **2.** Malabo.

San·ta Ma·ri·a (săn′tə mə-rē′ə). **1.** (*also* sän′tä mä-rē′ä). Active volcano, 12,362 ft (3,770.4 m), of SW Guatemala. **2.** (*also* säN′tə). City of S Brazil, W of Pôrto Alegre. Pop. 183,590. **3.** City of SW Calif., NW of Santa Barbara. Pop. 39,685.

San·ta Mar·ta (sän′tä mär′tä). City of N Colombia, on the Caribbean. Pop. 155,000.

Santa Mon·i·ca (mŏn′ĭ-kə). City of S Calif., on the Pacific W of Los Angeles. Pop. 88,314.

San·tan·der (sän′tän-dĕr′). City of N Spain, on the Bay of Biscay. Pop. 176,363.

Santa Pau·la (pô′lə). City of S Calif., ENE of Ventura. Pop. 20,552.

San·ta·rém (săn′tə-rĕm′, səN-tə-rĕN′). City of N Brazil, on the Amazon. Pop. 163,069.

Santa Ro·sa (rō′zə). **1.** Island of S Calif., in the NW Santa Barbara Is. **2.** Barrier island of NW Fla., extending c. 50 mi (80 km) along the coast of the Gulf of Mexico. **3.** City of W Calif., N of San Francisco. Pop. 83,205.

San·tee (săn-tē′). River, 143 mi (230.1 km), of S.C.

San·ti·a·go (săn′tē-ä′gō, sän-tyä′gô). **1.** Cap. of Chile, in the central part. Metro. area pop. 3,448,700. **2.** Also **Santiago de los Ca·ba·lle·ros** (dĕ′ lôs kä′bä-yĕ′rôs). City of N Dominican Republic, NW of Santo Domingo. Pop. 219,846. **3.** Also **Santiago de Com·pos·te·la** (dă kŏm′pə-stĕl′ə). City of NW Spain, S of La Coruña. Pop. 61,100.

San·ti·a·go de Cu·ba (săn′tē-ä′gō də kyo͞o′bə, sän-tyä′gô dĕ ko͞o′bä). City of SE Cuba, on the Caribbean. Pop. 326,066.

San·tia·go del Es·te·ro (sän-tyä′gô dĕl ĕs-tĕ′rô). City of N central Argentina, N of Córdoba. Pop. 105,127.

San·to An·dré (săN′to͞o äN-drĕ′). City of S Brazil, near São Paulo. Pop. 608,800.

San·to Do·min·go (săn′tō də-mĭng′gō). Cap. of the Dominican Republic, in the S part on the Caribbean. Pop. 979,608.

San·to·rin (săn′tə-rēn′). Island of S Greece, in the S Cyclades.

San·tos (săn′təs, säN′to͞osh). City of SE Brazil, on an offshore island in the Atlantic SE of São Paulo. Pop. 440,700.

São Ber·nar·do do Cam·po (souN bər-när′do͞o do͞o käN′po͞o). City of SE Brazil, near São Paulo. Pop. 267,038.

São Cae·ta·no do Sul (kā-tä′no͞o do͞o so͞ol′). City of SE Brazil, near São Paulo. Pop. 170,675.

São Fran·cis·co (frəN-sĕsh′ko͞o). River of E Brazil, flowing c. 1,800 mi (2,896 km) NNE and E to the Atlantic.

São Gon·ça·lo (go͞oN-sä′lo͞o). City of SE Brazil, on Guanabara Bay opposite Rio de Janeiro. Pop. 633,200.

São João de Me·ri·ti (zhwouN′ də mə-rĕ′tĭ, -rē-tē′). City of SE Brazil, near Rio de Janeiro. Pop. 425,800.

São Jo·sé do Ri·o Prê·to (zho͞o-zĕ′ do͞o rē′o͞o prĕ′to͞o). City of SE Brazil, near São Paulo. Pop. 145,526.

São José dos Cam·pos (do͞osh käN′ po͞osh). City of SE Brazil, NNE of São Paulo. Pop. 190,300.

São Lu·is (lo͞o-ēsh′). City of NE Brazil, on an offshore island in the Atlantic ESE of Belém. Pop. 389,400.

São Ma·nuel (mä-nwĕl′). Teles Pires.

São Mi·guel (mē-gĕl′). Island of the E Azores, largest of the group.

Saône (sōn). River, c. 268 mi (431 km), of E central France.

São Pau·lo (pou′lo͞o). City of SE Brazil, WSW of Rio de Janeiro. Pop. 8,407,500.

São Roque (rô′kĕ). Cape on NE coast of Brazil, N of Natal.

São Tia·go (tyä′go͞o). Island of S Cape Verde, largest of the group.

São To·mé (to͞o-mĕ′). **1.** Island, 319 sq mi (826 sq km), in the Gulf of Guinea on the equator, forming part of the republic of São Tomé and Principe. **2.** Cap. of São Tomé and Principe, on the SE coast of São Tomé Is. Pop. 17,380.

São Tomé and Prin·ci·pe (prĕN′sē-pə). Island republic in the Gulf of Guinea, W Africa. Cap. São Tomé. Pop. 73,631.

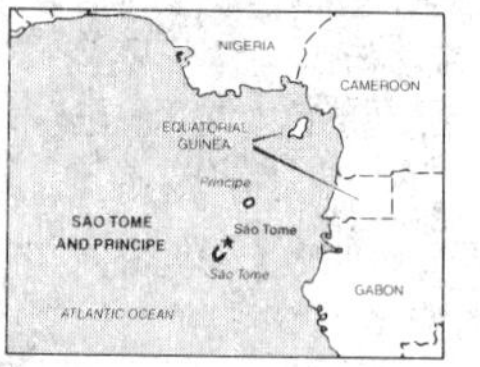

São Tomé and Principe

São Vi·cen·te (vē-săN′tə). City of SE Brazil, on the Atlantic near Santos. Pop. 143,784.

Sap·po·ro (säp-pô′rô). City of SW Hokkaido, Japan, SE of Ishikari Bay. Pop. 1,401,758.

Sa·pul·pa (sə-pŭl′pə). City of NE Okla., SSW of Tulsa. Pop. 15,853.

Saq·qa·ra (sə-kär′ə). Village of N Egypt, near Cairo; site of the oldest pyramid.

Sar·a·gos·sa (săr′ə-gŏs′ə) or **Za·ra·go·za** (sä′rä-gô′sä). City of NE Spain, on the Ebro R. Pop. 563,375.

Sa·ra·je·vo (sä′rä′yĕ-vō, -yĕ-, sâr′ə-yä′-). City of central Yugoslavia, SW of Belgrade. Pop. 244,045.

Sar·a·nac (săr′ə-năk′). Group of 3 lakes of NE N.Y., linked by the **Saranac R.** (c. 100 mi/161 km).

Sa·ransk (sä-ränsk′). City of central European USSR, SSE of Gorki. Pop. 271,000.

Sar·a·so·ta (săr′ə-sō′tə). City of SW Fla., on the Gulf of Mexico S of Tampa Bay. Pop. 48,868.

Sar·a·to·ga (săr′ə-tō′gə). **1.** Lake of E N.Y., SE of Saratoga Springs. **2.** City of W Calif., near San Jose. Pop. 29,261.

Saratoga Springs. City of E N.Y., N of Albany. Pop. 23,906.

Sa·ra·tov (sä-rä′təf). City of S European USSR, on the Volga R. Pop. 864,000.

Sa·ra·wak (sə-rä′wäk). Region and state of Malaysia, on NW Borneo.

Sar·din·i·a (sär-dĭn′ē-ə, -dĭn′yə). Island of Italy, in the Mediterranean S of Corsica. —**Sar·din′i·an** *adj. & n.*

Sar·dis (sär′dĭs). Ancient city of W Asia Minor, NE of modern Izmir, Turkey.

Sa·re·ma or **Saa·re·maa** (sär′ə-mä′). Island of NW European USSR, in the Baltic at the mouth of the Gulf of Riga.

Sar·gas·so Sea (sär-găs′ō). Part of the N Atlantic between the West Indies and the Azores.

Sar·go·dha (sər-gōd′hə). City of NE Pakistan, WNW of Lahore. Pop. 166,391.

Sark (särk). One of the Channel Is., in the English Channel E of Guernsey.

Sar·ma·ti·a (sär-mā′shē-ə, -shə). Ancient region of E Europe between the Vistula and the Volga in present-day E Poland and W European USSR. —**Sar·ma′tian** *adj. & n.*

Sar·ni·a (sär′nē-ə). City of S Ont., Canada, on the St. Clair R. at the S end of Lake Huron. Pop. 50,252.

Sa·ron·ic Gulf (sə-rŏn′ĭk). Arm of the Aegean in S Greece, between Attica and the Peloponnesus E of Corinth.

Sa·ros (sä′rôs). **Gulf of.** Inlet of the NE Aegean off NW Turkey N of Gallipoli.

Sarthe (särt). River, c. 177 mi (285 km), of NW France.

Sa·se·bo (sä-sĕ′bô). City of W Kyushu, Japan, on the East China Sea. Pop. 251,188.

Sas·katch·e·wan (săs-kăch′ə-wän′, -wən). **1.** River, c. 340 mi (550 km), of S central Canada, formed by the confluence of the **North** and **South Saskatchewan** rivers in central Sask. and flowing E to Lake Winnipeg in Man. **2.** Province of S central Canada. Cap. Regina. Pop. 921,323.

Sas·ka·toon (săs′kə-to͞on′). City of central Sask., Canada, NW of Regina. Pop. 133,750.

Sas·sa·ri (säs′sä-rē). City of NW Sardinia, Italy. Pop. 119,597.

Sa·til·la (sə-tĭl′ə). River, c. 220 mi (354 km), of SE Ga.

Sat·pu·ra (săt′po͞o-rə, săt-po͞o′rə). Range of hills in central India, extending c. 600 mi (965 km) along the N edge of the Deccan Plateau.

Sa·tsu·ma (sä′tso͞o-mä′, sä-tso͞o′mä). Peninsula of SW Kyushu, Japan.

Sa·tu-Ma·re (sä′to͞o-mä′rĕ). City of NW Rumania, near the Hungarian border. Pop. 107,852.

Sa·u·di A·ra·bi·a (sä-o͞o′dē ə-rā′bē-ə, sou′dē, sô′-). Kingdom comprising most of the Arabian peninsula. Cap. Riyadh. Pop. 7,012,642. —**Sa·u′di, Sa·u′di A·ra′bi·an** *adj. & n.*

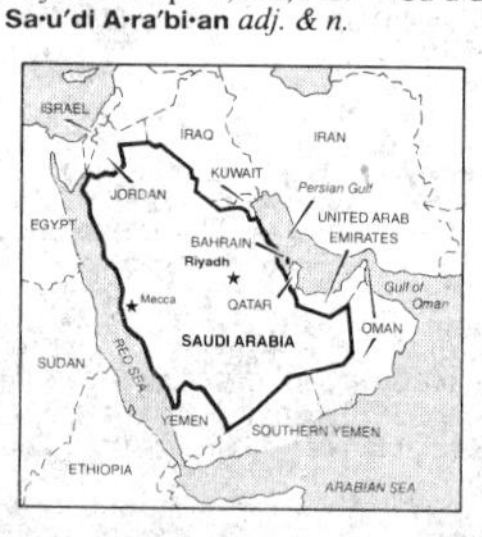

Saudi Arabia

Sau·gus (sô′gəs). Town of NE Mass., near Boston. Pop. 24,746.

Sauk (sôk). Village of NE Ill., near Chicago Heights. Pop. 10,906.

Sault Sainte Ma·rie (so͞o′ sānt′ mə-rē′). **1. Canals.** 3 ship canals, 2 U.S. and 1 Canadian, by-passing the rapids on the St. Marys R. between Lakes Superior and Huron. **2.** City of S Ont., Canada, on the St. Marys R. opposite Sault Ste. Marie, Mich. Pop. 80,548. **3.** City of N Mich., on the St. Marys R. N of Detroit. Pop. 14,448.

Sa·va (sä′vä). River, c. 580 mi (933 km), of N Yugoslavia.

Sa·vai·i or **Sa·vai′i** (sä-vī′ē). Largest (703 sq mi/1,821 sq km) island of Samoa, in Western Samoa.

Sa·va·lan (sä′vä-län′). Variant of **Sabalan.**

Sa·van·nah (sə-văn′ə). **1.** River, c. 314 mi (505 km), forming most of the S.C.-Ga. border. **2.** City of E Ga., near the mouth of the Savannah R. Pop. 141,634.

Sa·vo (sä′vō). Island of the W Pacific, in the SE Solomon Is.

Sa·vo·na (sä-vō′nä). City of NW Italy, on the Ligurian Sea WSW of Genoa. Pop. 78,216.

Sa·voy (sə-voi′). Region and former duchy of SE France, bordering on Switzerland and Italy. —**Sa·voy′ard** (sə-voi′ərd, săv′oi-ärd′) *adj. & n.*

Savoy Alps (ălps). Range of the W Alps in SE France, rising to 15,781 ft (4,813.2 m).

Sa·watch (sə-wŏch). Range of the Rockies in central Colo., rising to 14,431 ft (4,398.6 m).

Saxe (săks). *French.* Saxony.

Sax·on·y (săk′sə-nē). **1.** Former region and duchy of NW Germany. **2.** Former duchy, kingdom, and electorate of central Germany. —**Sax′on** *adj. & n.*

Sa·ya·ma (sä-yä′mä). City of E central Honshu, Japan, near Tokyo. Pop. 121,433.

Sa·yan (sä-yän′). Mountains of S Central Asian and Siberian USSR, W of Lake Baikal.

Say·re·ville (sā′ər-vĭl′, sâr′-). Borough of E central N.J., SSW of Perth Amboy. Pop. 29,969.

Sca·fell Pike (skô′fĕl′ pīk′). Mountain, 3,210 ft (979 m), of the Cumbrians in NW England; highest peak in England.

Sca·man·der (skə-măn′dər). River of NW Turkey, the Menderes.

Scan·di·na·vi·a (skăn′də-nā′vē-ə, -nāv′yə). **1.** Peninsula of N Europe occupied by Norway and Sweden. **2.** Norway, Sweden, and Denmark, and sometimes also Iceland, Finland, and the Faeroe Is. —**Scan′di·na′vi·an** *adj. & n.*

Scap·a Flow (skăp′ə flō′). Anchorage and British naval base in the Orkney Is., N Scotland.

Scar·bor·ough (skär′bûr′ō, -bə-rə). **1.** E borough of metropolitan Toronto, Ont., Canada, on Lake Ontario. Pop. 409,592. **2.** Borough of NE England, on the North Sea N of Hull. Pop. 43,300. **3.** Also **Scar·bor·o.** Town of SW Me., S of Portland. Pop. 11,347.

Scars·dale (skärz′dāl′). City of SE N.Y., near Yonkers. Pop. 17,650.

Schaer·beek (skär′bāk′, sKHär′-). City of central Belgium, near Brussels. Pop. 109,005.

Schaff·hau·sen (shäf′hou′zən). Waterfall, 65 ft (19.8 m) high and 377 ft (115 m) wide, in the Rhine N of Zurich, Switzerland.

Schaum·burg (shäm′bûrg). Village of NE Ill., near Chicago. Pop. 52,319.

Schel·de (skĕl′də, sKHĕl′-). *Flemish & Dutch.* Scheldt.

Scheldt (skĕlt). River of W Europe, rising in N France and flowing c. 270 mi (434 km) NE through W Belgium and SW Netherlands to the North Sea.

Sche·nec·ta·dy (skə-nĕk′tə-dē). City of E N.Y., NW of Albany. Pop. 67,972.

Scher·er·ville (shûr′ər-vĭl′). Town of NE Ind., near Gary. Pop. 13,209.

Schie·dam (skē-däm′, sKHē-). City of SW Netherlands, near Rotterdam. Pop. 74,895.

Schil·ler Park (shĭl′ər). Village of NE Ill., near Chicago. Pop. 11,458.

Schles·wig (shlĕs′wĭg, slĕs′-, shlās′vĭk). **1.** Region and former duchy of N West Germany and S Denmark, in S Jutland. **2.** City of N West Germany, NW of Kiel. Pop. 30,118.

Schou·ten (skout′n, sKHou′tən). Islands of E Indonesia off N coast of West Irian.

Schuyl·kill (sko͞ol′kĭl′, sko͞o′kəl). River, c. 130 mi (209 km), of SE Pa.

Schwa·ben (shvä′bən). *German.* Swabia.

Schwä·bisch Gmünd (shvā′bĭsh gmünt′). City of S West Germany, E of Stuttgart. Pop. 56,621.

Schwein·furt (shvīn′fo͞ort′). City of E central West Germany, on the Main R. E of Frankfurt. Pop. 53,035.

Schwe·rin (shvā-rēn′). City of NW East Germany, SW of Rostock. Pop. 115,950.

Scil·ly (sĭl′ē). Islands of SW England, at the entrance to the English Channel WSW of Land's End.

Sci·o·to (sī-ō′tə). River, 237 mi (381.3 km), of Ohio.

Scit·u·ate (sĭch′ə-wət, -wāt′). Town of E Mass., SE of Boston. Pop. 17,317.

Scone (sko͞on). Village of central Scotland, NE of Perth; coronation site of Scottish kings (1150–1488).

Sco·pus (skō′pəs). Peak, 2,736 ft (834.5 m), in Israeli enclave in NW Jordan NNE of Jerusalem.

Scores·by Sound (skôrz′bē, skōrz′-). Inlet of the Greenland Sea extending c. 200 mi (322 km) into E Greenland.

Sco·tia (skō′shə). Scotland.

Scot·land (skŏt′lənd). Constituent country of the United Kingdom of Great Britain and Northern Ireland, comprising N Great Britain and the Hebrides, Shetland Is., and Orkney Is. Cap. Edinburgh. Pop. 5,167,000. —**Scots** (skŏts) *adj.* —**Scot'tish** (skŏt'ĭsh) *adj. & n.*

Scotts·bluff (skŏts'blŭf'). City of W Nebr., near the Wyo. border. Pop. 14,156.

Scotts·bor·o (skŏts'bûr'ō). City of NE Ala., E of Huntsville. Pop. 14,752.

Scotts·dale (skŏts'dāl'). City of S central Ariz., near Phoenix. Pop. 88,364.

Scran·ton (skrăn'tən). City of NW Pa., NW of Wilkes-Barre. Pop. 88,117.

Scun·thorpe (skŭn'thôrp'). Borough of NE England, SW of Hull. Pop. 67,200.

Scu·ta·ri (sko͞o'tä-rē'). **1.** Lake, c. 25 mi (40 km) long, of S Yugoslavia and NW Albania. **2.** Shkodër.

Scy·ros (sī'rŏs). Variant of **Skyros**.

Scyth·i·a (sĭth'ē-ə). Ancient region of SE Europe and SW Asia, between the mouth of the Danube and the Aral Sea. —**Scyth'i·an** *adj. & n.*

Sea Islands (sē). Chain of islands off the Atlantic coasts of S.C., Ga., and N Fla.

Seal Beach (sēl). City of S Calif., on the Pacific SSE of Los Angeles. Pop. 25,975.

Sear·cy (sûr'sē). City of N central Ark. NE of Little Rock. Pop. 13,645.

Sea·side (sē'sīd'). City of W Calif., on Monterey Bay. Pop. 36,567.

Se·at·tle (sē-ăt'l). City of W central Wash., on Puget Sound and Lake Washington. Pop. 493,846.

Se·ba·go (sə-bā'gō). Lake, c. 12 mi (20 km) long, of SW Me.

Se·bas·to·pol (sə-băs'tə-pōl'). Variant of **Sevastopol**.

Se·cau·cus (sĭ-kô'kəs). Town of NE N.J., near Jersey City. Pop. 13,719.

Se·cun·der·a·bad (sĭ-kŭn'də-rə-băd', -bäd'). City of S central India, near Hyderabad. Pop. 94,416.

Se·da·li·a (sĭ-dāl'yə). City of central Mo., ESE of Kansas City. Pop. 20,927.

Se·dan (sĭ-dăn', sə-däɴ'). Town of NE France, on the Meuse R. Pop. 23,995.

Sedge·moor (sĕj'mo͝or', -môr'). Marshy tract in SW England where the forces of James II defeated the Duke of Monmouth (1685).

See·konk (sē'kŏngk'). Town of SE Mass., on the border near Providence, R.I. Pop. 12,269.

Se·fid Rud (sĕ-fēd' ro͞od'). Variant of **Safid Rud**.

Se·go·vi·a (sĕ-gō'vē-ä, -vyä). **1.** Coco. **2.** City of central Spain, NW of Madrid. Pop. 49,583.

Se·guin (sĭ-gēn'). City of S central Tex., ENE of San Antonio. Pop. 17,854.

Se·gu·ra (sĕ-go͞o'rä). River, c. 200 mi (322 km), of SE Spain.

Seim also **Seym** (sām). River, 460 mi (740 km), of W European USSR.

Seine (sān, sĕn). River of N France, flowing c. 480 mi (772 km) into the **Bay of the Seine**, an inlet of the English Channel.

Sek·on·di-Ta·ko·ra·di (sĕk'ən-dē'-tä-kə-rä'dē). City of SW Ghana, on the Gulf of Guinea. Pop. 160,868.

Se·len·ga (sĕ'lĕng-gä'). River of N Mongolia and S Siberian USSR, flowing c. 750 mi (1,207 km) NE into Lake Baikal.

Se·leu·ci·a (sĭ-lo͞o'shē-ə, -shə). Ancient city of Mesopotamia, on the Tigris below modern Baghdad.

Sel·kirk (sĕl'kûrk'). Range of the Rockies in SE B.C., Canada.

Sel·ma (sĕl'mə). **1.** City of S central Ala., W of Montgomery. Pop. 26,684. **2.** City of central Calif., SE of Fresno. Pop. 10,942.

Se·ma·rang (sə-mär'äng). City of N Java, Indonesia, on the Java Sea. Pop. 646,590.

Sem·i·pa·la·tinsk (sĕ'mĭ-pä-lä'-tĭnsk). City of E Central Asian USSR, on the Irtish R. Pop. 286,000.

Sen·dai (sĕn'dī'). City of NE Honshu, Japan, on the Pacific. Pop. 664,799.

Sen·e·ca (sĕn'ĭ-kə). Largest (67 sq mi/173 sq km) of the Finger Lakes, in W central N.Y.

Sen·e·gal (sĕn'ĭ-gôl'). **1.** River of W Africa, rising in W Mali and flowing c. 1,000 mi (1,609 km) NW and W along the Mauritania-Senegal border to the Atlantic. **2.** Country of W Africa, on the Atlantic. Cap. Dakar. Pop. 5,085,388. —**Sen'e·ga·lese'** (-gô'lēz', -lēs', -gə-) *adj. & n.*

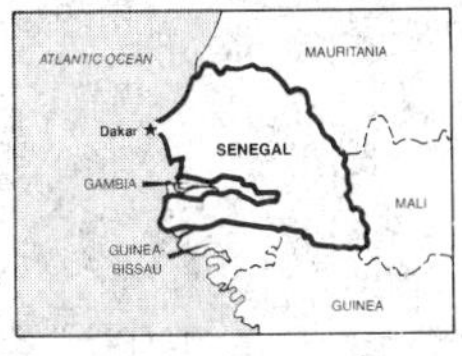

Senegal

Sen·e·gam·bi·a (sĕn'ĭ-găm'bē-ə). Senegal and Gambia.

Sen·lac (sĕn'lăk'). Hill in S England, near Hastings; site of the Battle of Hastings (1066).

Sens (säɴs). Town of N central France, SE of Paris. Pop. 26,463.

Seoul (sōl). Cap. of South Korea, in the NW part. Pop. 8,114,000.

Se·pik (sā'pĭk, sē'pĕk). River, c. 700 mi (1,126 km), of N Papua New Guinea.

Sept-Iles (sĕ-tēl'). City of E Que., Canada, near the mouth of the St. Lawrence R. Pop. 30,617.

Se·quoi·a National Park (sĭ-kwoi'-ə). Area in E central Calif. noted for its sequoia forests and mountain scenery.

Ser·bi·a (sûr'bē-ə). Region and constituent republic of E Yugoslavia. —**Ser'bi·an** *adj. & n.*

Ser·en·get·i (sĕr'ən-gĕt'ē). Plain and wildlife reserve of N Tanzania.

Ser·pu·khov (sĕr-po͞o'kôf, sĕr'-po͞o-KHəf). City of central European USSR, S of Moscow. Pop. 141,000.

Ser·ra da Es·tre·la (sĕr'rə də ĕsh-trĕ'-lə). Range of central Portugal.

Serra do Mar (do͞o mär'). Coastal range of S Brazil.

Serra Pa·ca·rai·ma (pä'kə-rī'mə). *Portuguese.* Sierra Pacaraima.

Serra Pa·ri·ma (pə-rē'mə). *Portuguese.* Sierra Parima.

Ses·tos (sĕs'təs, -tŏs). Ancient town of European Turkey at the narrowest point of the Dardanelles.

Ses·to San Gio·van·ni (sĕs'tō sän' jō-vän'nē). City of N Italy, near Milan. Pop. 98,151.

Sète (sĕt). Town of S France, on the Mediterranean. Pop. 39,258.

Sé·tif (sā-tēf'). City of NE Algeria, ESE of Algiers. Pop. 157,065.

Se·tú·bal (sə-to͞o'bəl, -bäl'). City of S central Portugal, on an inlet of the Atlantic SE of Lisbon. Pop. 50,730.

Se·van (sĕ-vän'). Lake, c. 540 sq mi (1,399 sq km), of S European USSR, in the Caucasus.

Se·vas·to·pol (sə-văs'tə-pōl') also **Se·bas·to·pol** (sə-băs'tə-pōl'). City of SW European USSR, in the Crimea on the Black Sea. Pop. 308,000.

Sev·en Hills (sĕv'ən). City of NE Ohio, near Cleveland. Pop. 13,650.

Sev·ern (sĕv'ərn). **1.** Inlet of W Chesapeake Bay, in central Md. **2.** River of NW Ont., Canada, flowing c. 420 mi (676 km) NE to Hudson Bay. **3.** River of SW Great Britain, rising in W Wales and flowing c. 210 mi (338 km) through W England to the Bristol Channel.

Se·ver·na·ya Zem·lya (sĕv'ər-nə-yä' zĕm'lē-ä'). Archipelago of N Siberian USSR, in the Arctic Ocean N of Taimyr Peninsula.

Se·ver·o·dvinsk (syĭ-vyĭr-ä-dvĭnsk'). City of N European USSR, on the White Sea W of Arkhangelsk. Pop. 203,000.

Se·vier (sə-vîr'). River, c. 280 mi (451 km), of SW Utah.

Se·vil·la (sĕ-vē'lyä). *Spanish.* Seville.

Se·ville (sə-vĭl'). City of SW Spain, on the Guadalquivir R. Pop. 630,329.

Sè·vres (sĕv'rə). City of N central France, on the Seine SW of Paris. Pop. 21,149.

Sew·ard (so͞o'ərd). Peninsula of W Alas., projecting c. 200 mi (322 km) into the Bering Sea just below the Arctic Circle.

Sey·chelles (sā-shĕl', -shĕlz'). Island nation in the W Indian Ocean N of Madagascar. Cap. Victoria. Pop. 52,437.

Sey·han (sā-hän'). River, c. 320 mi (515 km), of S central Turkey.

Seym (sām). Variant of **Seim**.

Sey·mour (sē'môr', -mōr'). **1.** Town of SW Conn., NW of New Haven. Pop. 13,434. **2.** City of SE Ind., S of Columbus. Pop. 15,050.

Sfax (sfäks). City of E Tunisia, on the Gulf of Gabès. Pop. 171,297.

Sha·ba (shä'bə). Region of SE Zaire.

Shah·ja·han·pur (shä'jə-hän'po͝or', -jə-hän'po͝or'). City of N central India, NW of Lucknow. Pop. 135,604.

Shah·pur (shä-po͝or'). Ancient city of SW Iran, W of Shiraz.

Sha·ker Heights (shā'kər). City of NE Ohio, near Cleveland. Pop. 32,487.

Shakh·ty (shäk'tē, shäKH'-). City of S European USSR, NE of Rostov. Pop. 212,000.

Sha·mo·kin (shə-mō'kĭn). City of E central Pa., NNE of Harrisburg. Pop. 10,357.

Shan·dong (shän'do͝ong'). Peninsula of E China, projecting E between the Gulf of Bo Hai and the Yellow Sea.

Shang·hai (shăng-hī', shăng'hī'). City of E China, at the mouth of the Yangtze. Pop. 8,100,000.

Shang·qiu also **Shang·kiu** (shăng'-kyo͞o'). City of E China, ESE of Kaifeng. Pop. 250,000.

Shan·non (shăn'ən). River, c. 240 mi (386 km), of W Ireland.

Shan·tar (shən-tär'). Islands of Far Eastern USSR, in the Sea of Okhotsk NW of Sakhalin.

Shan·tou (shän'tou'). City of SE China, on the South China Sea ENE of Hong Kong. Pop. 325,000.

Shan·tung (shăn'tŭng', shän'do͝ong'). Shandong.

Shao·xing also **Shao·hsing** (shou'-shyĭng'). City of SE China, near the East China Sea SW of Shanghai. Pop. 150,000.

Shao·yang (shou'yăng'). City of S China, SW of Changsha. Pop. 215,000.

Sha·ri (shä'rē) or **Cha·ri** (shä-rē'). River of N central Africa, rising in the Central African Republic and flowing c. 1,400 mi (2,253 km) NW through S Chad to Lake Chad.

Shar·jah (shär-jä'). **1.** Sheikdom of the United Arab Emirates, in E Arabia on the Persian Gulf and the Gulf of Oman. **2.** Chief town of this sheikdom, on the Persian Gulf. Pop. 19,200.

Shark Bay (shärk). Inlet of the Indian Ocean off W central Australia.

Shar·on (shăr'ən). **1.** Town of E Mass., near Brockton. Pop. 13,601. **2.** City of W Pa., on the border NE of Youngstown, Ohio. Pop. 19,057.

Shar·on·ville (shăr'ən-vĭl'). City of SW Ohio, near Cincinnati. Pop. 10,108.

Sharps·burg (shärps'bûrg'). Town of N Maryland; site of Civil War Battle of Antietam (1862).

Shas·ta (shăs'tə), **Mount**. Volcanic peak, 14,162 ft (4,319.4 m), of the Cascade Mts. in N Calif.

Shatt-al-Ar·ab also **Shatt al Ar·ab** (shăt'ăl-ä'răb, -ăr'əb, shät'-). River, c. 120 mi (193 km), of SE Iraq, formed by the confluence of the Tigris and Euphrates rivers.

Shaw·an·gunk (shŏng'gəm, shə-wŏng'gŭngk). Mountains of SE N.Y.

Sha·win·i·gan (shə-wĭn'ĭ-gən). City of S Que., Canada, NW of Trois-Rivières. Pop. 24,921.

Shawinigan-Sud (shə-wĭn'ĭ-gən-so͞od'). Town of S Que., Canada, on the St. Maurice R. near Shawinigan. Pop. 11,155.

Shaw·nee (shô-nē', shô'nē). **1.** City of E Kans., near Kansas City. Pop. 29,653. **2.** City of central Okla., ESE of Oklahoma City. Pop. 26,506.

Shcher·ba·kov (shâr'bə-kôf', shchĕr'-). Rybinsk.

She·be·li (shə-bā'lē). Webbi Shebeli.

She·boy·gan (shə-boi'gən). City of E Wis., on Lake Michigan N of Milwaukee. Pop. 48,085.

Shef·field (shĕf'ēld'). **1.** Borough of N central England, E of Manchester. Pop. 544,200. **2.** City of NW Ala., near Florence. Pop. 11,903.

Sheffield Lake. City of NE Ohio, on Lake Erie W of Cleveland. Pop. 10,484.

Shel·by (shĕl'bē). City of SW N.C., W of Charlotte. Pop. 15,310.

Shel·by·ville (shĕl'bē-vĭl'). **1.** City of central Ind., SE of Indianapolis. Pop. 14,989. **2.** City of central Tenn., SSE of Nashville. Pop. 13,530.

Shel·i·kof (shĕl'ĭ-kôf'). Strait of S Alas., between Alaska Peninsula and Kodiak and Afognak Is.

Shel·ter (shĕl'tər). Island of SE N.Y., between the 2 peninsulas of E Long Is.

Shel·ton (shĕl'tən). City of SW Conn., NNE of Bridgeport. Pop. 31,314.

Shen·an·do·ah (shĕn'ən-dō'ə). **1.** River, c. 150 mi (241 km), of N Va. and NE W.Va. **2. National Park.** Scenic area of N Va. along crest of the Blue Ridge.

Shen·yang (shŭn'yăng'). City of NE China, ENE of Beijing. Pop. 3,300,-000.

Shep·pey (shĕp'ē), **Isle of.** Island, 30 sq mi (80 sq km), of SE England, in the mouth of the Thames.

Sher·brooke (shûr'bro͝ok'). City of S Que., Canada, E of Montreal. Pop. 76,804.

Sher·i·dan (shĕr'ĭ-dən). City of S Wyo., near the Mont. border. Pop. 15,146.

Sher·man (shûr'mən). City of N Tex., near the Okla. border N of Dallas. Pop. 30,413.

's Her·to·gen·bosch (sĕr'tō-gən-bôs', -KHən-). City of S central Netherlands, NNW of Eindhoven. Pop. 87,897.

Sher·wood (shûr'wo͝od'). **1.** Former royal forest of central England. **2.** City of central Ark., near Little Rock. Pop. 10,474.

Shet·land (shĕt'lənd) also **Shet·lands** (-ləndz). Islands of N Scotland, in the Atlantic NE of the Orkney Is.

Shey·enne (shī-ĕn', -ăn'). River, c. 325 mi (523 km), of E N.Dak.

Shi·be·li (shĭ-bā'lē). Webbi Shebeli.

Shi·jia·zhuang also **Shih·kia·chwang** (shœ'jyä'jwäng'). City of NE China, SW of Beijing. Pop. 940,000.

Shi·kar·pur (shĭ-kär'po͝or'). City of S central Pakistan, NNE of Karachi. Pop. 70,924.

Shi·ko·ku (shē'kô-ko͞o', shē-kō'ko͞o). Island of S Japan, between SW Honshu and E Kyushu.

Shil·ka (shĭl'kə). River, c. 345 mi (555 km), of S Far Eastern USSR.

Shil·long (shĭ-lông'). City of NE India, NE of Calcutta. Pop. 87,659.

Shi·loh (shī'lō). **1.** Ancient village of central Palestine, NW of the Dead Sea. **2.** Locality in SW Tenn.; site of Civil War battle (1862).

Shi·mi·zu (shē-mē'zo͞o, shē'mē-zo͞o'). City of E central Honshu, Japan, on Suruga Bay. Pop. 241,578.

Shi·mo·no·se·ki (shĭm'ə-nō-sĕk'ē, shē-mô'nô-sĕ'kē). City of extreme SW Honshu, Japan, on Korea Strait. Pop. 268,964.

Shi·na·no (shĭ-nä'nô). River of central Honshu, Japan, flowing c. 230 mi (371 km) NNE to the Sea of Japan.

Shi·nar (shī'när', -nər). Ancient country on the lower courses of the Tigris and Euphrates.

Shi·raz (shē-räz'). City of SW Iran, SSE of Esfahan. Pop. 416,408.

Shi·re (shē'rā). River, c. 250 mi (402 km), of S Malawi and central Mozambique.

Shi·shal·din (shĭ-shăl'dĭn). Volcano, 9,370 ft (2,857.9 m), of SW Alas. on central Unimak Is.

Shive·ly (shīv'lē). City of N Ky., near Louisville. Pop. 16,819.

Shi·zu·o·ka (shē'zo͞o-ô'kä). City of E central Honshu, Japan, on Suruga Bay. Pop. 458,342.

Shkha·ra (shŭk'hə-rä). Peak, c.

17,064 ft (5,200 m), of the Caucasus in S European USSR.

Shko·dër (shkô′dər). City of NW Albania, on Lake Scutari. Pop. 62,500.

Sho·la·pur (shō′lə-pŏŏr′). City of W central India, ESE of Bombay. Pop. 398,361.

Shore·view (shôr′vyōō′, shōr′-). City of E Minn., near St. Paul. Pop. 17,300.

Shore·wood (shôr′wŏŏd′, shōr′-). Village of SE Wis., near Milwaukee. Pop. 14,327.

Sho·sho·ne (shə-shō′nē). **1.** River, c. 120 mi (193 km), of NW Wyo. **2.** Falls, 212 ft (64.7 m), in the Snake R. of S Idaho.

Shreve·port (shrēv′pôrt′, -pōrt′). City of NW La., near the Tex. border. Pop. 205,815.

Shrews·bur·y (shrōōz′bĕr′ē, -bə-rē). **1.** Borough of W central England, on the Severn WNW of Birmingham. Pop. 56,120. **2.** Town of central Mass., near Worcester. Pop. 22,674.

Shrop·shire (shrŏp′shîr′, -shər). Region and former county of W England, on the Welsh border.

Shu·ma·gin (shōō′mə-gĭn). Islands of SW Alas., off SE coast of the Alaska Peninsula.

Shu·men (shōō′mĕn). City of NE Bulgaria, W of Varna. Pop. 92,157.

Shu·shan (shōō′shăn). Susa.

Si (shyē). Xi.

Si·al·kot (sē-äl′kōt′). City of NE Pakistan, near the Kashmir border N of Lahore. Pop. 183,685.

Si·am (sī-ăm′). **1. Gulf of.** Arm of the South China Sea between the Malay Peninsula and Indochina. **2.** Thailand. **—Si′a·mese′** (sī′ə-mēz′, -mēs′) *adj. & n.*

Si·an (shyē′än′). Xi'an.

Si·ang (shyē-äng′, shyäng). Xiang.

Si·ang·tan (shyē-äng′tän′, shyäng-). Xiangtan.

Šiau·liai (shyou′lyī). City of W European USSR, in Lithuania NNW of Kaunas. Pop. 121,000.

Si·be·ri·a (sī-bîr′ē-ə). Region of Asian USSR, from the Urals to the Pacific. **—Si·be′ri·an** *adj. & n.*

Si·biu (sē-byōō′). City of central Rumania, SSE of Cluj. Pop. 157,519.

Si·bu·yan (sē′bōō-yän′). Sea in central Philippines bordered by S Luzon, Mindoro, and the Visayans.

Si·ci·ly (sĭs′ə-lē). Island of S Italy, W of S end of Italian Peninsula; largest island in the Mediterranean. **—Si·cil′·ian** (sĭ-sĭl′yən, -sĭl′ē-ən) *adj. & n.*

Si·cy·on (sĭsh′ē-ŏn′, sĭs′-). Ancient city of S Greece, in the NE Peloponnesus near the Gulf of Corinth.

Si·di-bel-Ab·bès (sē′dē-bĕl-ə-bĕs′). City of NW Algeria, S of Oran. Pop. 151,148.

Sid·ley (sĭd′lē). Mountain, 13,717 ft (4,183.7 m), in Marie Byrd Land, Antarctica.

Sid·ney (sĭd′nē). City of W central Ohio WNW of Columbus. Pop. 17,657.

Si·don (sīd′n). Ancient city of Phoenicia, on the Mediterranean in present-day SW Lebanon.

Sid·ra (sĭd′rə). **Gulf of.** Inlet of the Mediterranean off N Libya W of Benghazi.

Sie·ben·ge·bir·ge (zē′bən-gə-bîr′-gə). Range of hills in W central West Germany, along the Rhine S of Bonn.

Sie·gen (zē′gən). City of central West Germany, E of Cologne. Pop. 112,740.

Sie·mia·no·wi·ce Śla·skie (shĕ-myä-nô-vē′tsĕ shlôn′skyĕ). City of S Poland near Katowice. Pop. 77,200.

Si·en·a (sē-ĕn′ə, syĕ′nä). City of central Italy, S of Florence. Pop. 63,961. **—Si′e·nese′** (sē′ə-nēz′, -nēs′) *adj. & n.*

Sier·ra de Cór·do·ba (syĕr′rä dĕ kôr′*th*ō-bä). Range extending c. 300 mi (483 km) in central Argentina.

Sier·ra de Gre·dos (syĕr′rä dĕ grĕ′-*th*ôs). Range of W central Spain, W of Madrid.

Sier·ra de Gua·dar·ra·ma (syĕr′rä dĕ gwä-*th*är-rä′mä). Range of central Spain, N of Madrid.

Si·er·ra Le·one (sē-ĕr′ə lē-ōn′, -ōn′ē). Country of W Africa, on the Atlantic coast. Cap. Freetown. Pop. 4,125,000.

Sierra Leone

Si·er·ra Ma·dre (sē-ĕr′ə mä′drā). **1.** (*also* syĕr′rä mä′*th*rē). Mountain system of Mexico, comprising 3 ranges: **a. Sierra Madre del Sur** (dĕl sōōr′), in S Mexico along the Pacific coast. **b. Sierra Madre Oc·ci·den·tal** (ôk′sē-*th*ĕn-täl′), in NW Mexico inland from the Pacific coast. **c. Sierra Madre Or·ien·tal** (ô-ryĕn-täl′), in NE Mexico inland from the Gulf of Mexico coast. **2.** City of S Calif., near Pasedena. Pop. 10,837.

Sier·ra Ma·es·tra (syĕr′rä mä-ĕs′trä). Range of SE Cuba.

Sier·ra Mo·re·na (syĕr′rä mô-rĕ′nä). Range of S Spain, extending c. 375 mi (603 km) E from the Portuguese border.

Si·er·ra Ne·va·da (sē-ĕr′ə nə-vä′də). **1.** (*also* syĕr′rä nĕ-vä′*th*ä). Range of S Spain, along the Mediterranean coast E of Granada, rising to 11,411 ft (3,480.4 m). **2.** Range of E Calif., extending c. 400 mi (644 km) and rising to 14,494 ft (4,420.7 m).

Sier·ra Ne·va·da de Mé·ri·da (syĕr′-rä nĕ-vä′*th*ä dĕ mĕ′rē-*th*ä). Cordillera de Mérida.

Sier·ra Ne·va·da de San·ta Mar·ta (syĕr′rä nĕ-vä′*th*ä dĕ sän′tä mär′tä). Range of N Colombia, along the Caribbean coast, rising to 19,020 ft (5,801.1 m).

Sier·ra Pa·ca·rai·ma (syĕr′rä pä′-kä-rī′mä). Range of SE Venezuela and W Guyana along the Brazilian border.

Sier·ra Pa·ri·ma (syĕr′rä pä-rē′mä). Range of S Venezuela along the Brazilian border SW of Sierra Pacaraima.

Si·er·ra Vis·ta (sē-ĕr′ə vĭs′tə). City of SE Ariz., SE of Tucson. Pop. 25,968.

Sikes·ton (sīk′stən). City of SE Mo., WSW of Cairo, Ill. Pop. 17,431.

Si·kho·te-A·lin (sē′kə-tā′ə-lēn′, sē′-KHô-tĕ-ä-lēn′). Range of extreme SE Far Eastern USSR, extending along the Sea of Japan coast N of Vladivostok.

Sik·kim (sĭk′ĭm). State and former semi-independent protectorate of NE India, in the E Himalayas between Nepal and Bhutan.

Si·le·sia (sī-lē′zhə, -shə, sĭ-). Region of central Europe, chiefly in SW Poland and N Czechoslovakia. **—Si·le′sian** *adj. & n.*

Sil·le·ry (sĭl′ə-rē, sē-yə-rē′). City of S Que., Canada, on the St. Lawrence near Quebec city. Pop. 13,580.

Sil·ver Spring (sĭl′vər). City of central Md., near Washington, D.C. Pop. 84,300.

Sil·vret·ta (sĕl-vrāt′tä). Range of the Alps in E Switzerland and SW Austria, rising to 11,185 ft (3,411.4 m).

Sim·coe (sĭm′kō). **1.** Lake, 539 sq mi (1,396 sq km), of SE Ont., Canada, between Georgian Bay and Lake Ontario. **2.** City of S Ont., Canada, S of Brantford. Pop. 14,149.

Sim·fer·o·pol (sĭm′fə-rō′pəl). City of S European USSR, in the S central Crimea. Pop. 307,000.

Si·mi Valley (sē′mē, sĭm′ē). City of S Calif., near Los Angeles. Pop. 77,500.

Sim·la (sĭm′lə). Town of N India, in the W Himalayas N of Delhi. Pop. 55,368.

Sim·plon (sĭm′plŏn′, säN-plôn′). **1.** Pass, 6590 ft (2,010 m), between the Lepontine and Pennine Alps in S Switzerland near the Italian border. **2.** Tunnel, 12.3 m (19.8 km) long, through Monte Leone on the Italian-Swiss border NE of Simplon Pass.

Simp·son (sĭmp′sən). Desert of central Australia.

Sims·bur·y (sĭmz′bĕr′ē, -bə-rē). Town of N Conn., NW of Hartford. Pop. 21,161.

Si·nai (sī′nī′). **1. Mount.** Mountain, c. 7,500 ft (2,288 m), of NE Egypt on S Sinai Peninsula. **2.** Peninsula of NE Egypt, at N end of the Red Sea.

Sind (sĭnd). Region of S Pakistan along the lower Indus R.

Sin·ga·pore (sĭng′gə-pôr′, -pōr′, sĭng′ə-). **1.** Strait off S end of Malay Peninsula between Singapore Is. and Riau archipelago. **2.** Island, 224 sq mi (580 sq km), off S end of Malay Peninsula. **3.** Country of SE Asia comprising Singapore Is. and adjacent smaller islands. Cap. Singapore. Pop. 2,465,000 **4.** Cap. of Singapore, on Singapore Strait. **—Sin′ga·por′e·an** *adj. & n.*

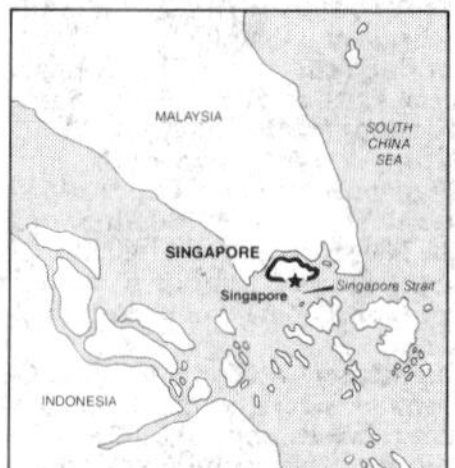

Singapore

Sin·kiang (sĭn′kyăng′, shĭn′jyäng′). Region of NW China.

Si·nop (sə-nôp′). City of N Turkey, on the Black Sea. Pop. 18,381.

Sint-Ni·klaas (sĭnt-nē′kläs). City of N Belgium, near Antwerp. Pop. 68,080.

Sin·tra or **Cin·tra** (sēn′trə). Town of W Portugal, NW of Lisbon. Pop. 7,705.

Sin·ui·ju (shĭn′ē-jōō′). City of W North Korea, on Korea Bay at the mouth of the Yalu R. Pop. 165,000.

Si·on (sē-ôN′). Town of SW Switzerland, on the Rhone R. Pop. 23,400.

Sioux City (sōō). City of W Iowa, on the Missouri near the S. Dak.-Nebr. border. Pop. 82,003.

Sioux Falls. City of SE S.Dak., near the Minn. border. Pop. 81,343.

Sip·par (sĭ-pär′). Ancient city of N Babylonia, on the Euphrates near present-day Baghdad.

Si·ret (sĭ-rĕt′, sē-). River, c. 280 mi (451 km), of NE Rumania.

Si·ros (sī′rŏs′, sē′rôs′). Variant of **Syros.**

Sir Sand·ford (sər săn′fərd), **Mount.** Highest (c. 11,590 ft/3,535 m) of the Selkirk Mts. in SE B.C., Canada.

Sis·ki·you (sĭs′kĭ-yōō′). Range of the Klamath Mts. in N Calif. and SW Ore.

Sit·ka (sĭt′kə). Town of SE Alas., on the W coast of Baranof Is. Pop. 7,803.

Sit·tang (sĭt′tăng′). River of Burma, flowing 350 mi (563 km) S to the Gulf of Martaban.

Sit·ting·bourne and Mil·ton (sĭt′-ĭng-bôrn′, -bōrn′; mĭl′tən). Urban district of SE England, ESE of London. Pop. 32,830.

Sit·twe (sĭ′twā′). City of W Burma, on the Bay of Bengal. Pop. 82,000.

Si·vas (sĭ-väs′, sē-). City of central Turkey, E of Ankara. Pop. 173,881.

Si·vash (sĭ-väsh′). Lagoon, c. 1,000 sq mi (2,590 sq km), of SW European USSR, along the NE coast of the Crimea.

Si·wa (sē′wä). Oasis of NW Egypt, in the Libyan Desert.

Si·wa·lik (sĭ-wä′lĭk). Range of the S Himalaya foothills, extending c. 1,050 mi (1,690 km), from SW Kashmir through N India into S Nepal.

Sjael·land (shĕ′län). Largest island of Denmark, in the E part between the Kattegat and the Baltic.

Ska·gen (skä′gən), **Cape.** The Skaw.

Skag·er·rak also **Skag·er·ak** (skăg′-ə-răk′, skä′gə-räk′). Strait, c. 150 mi (241 km) long and 85 mi (137 km) wide, between Norway and Denmark, linking the North Sea and the Kattegat.

Skag·it (skăj′ĭt). River, c. 150 mi (241 km), of SW B.C., Canada, and NW Wash.

Skag·way (skăg′wā′). Town of SE Alas., at the head of the Lynn Canal NNW of Juneau. Pop. 768.

Skan·e·at·e·les (skăn′ē-ăt′ləs, skĭn′-). One of the Finger Lakes, 14 sq mi (36.3 sq km), in central N.Y.

Skaw (skô), **The.** Cape on N extremity of Jutland, Denmark, extending into the Skagerrak.

Skee·na (skē′nə). River, c. 360 mi (579 km), of W B.C., Canada.

Skel·lef·te (shĕ-lĕf′tə). River, c. 255 mi (410 km), of N Sweden.

Skel·mers·dale and Hol·land (skĕl′mərz-dāl′; hŏl′ənd). Urban district of NW England, NE of Liverpool. Pop. 35,850.

Skid·daw (skĭd′ô). Mountain, 3,054 ft (931.5 m), in NW England.

Ski·en (shē′ən, shā′-). City of SE Norway, SW of Oslo. Pop. 47,450.

Skik·da (skĭk′dä). City of NE Algeria, on the Mediterranean. Pop. 127,968.

Ski·ros (skī′rəs, -rōs′, skē′rôs). Variant of **Skyros.**

Sko·kie (skō′kē). Village of NE Ill., near Chicago. Pop. 60,278.

Skop·lje (skôp′lā′, -yä′, -lyĕ) or **Skop·je** (skôp′yā′, -yĕ). City of SE Yugoslavia, in Macedonia on the Vardar R. Pop. 312,092.

Skunk (skŭngk). River, 264 mi (424.8 km), of central and SE Iowa.

Skye (skī). Island of NW Scotland, in the Inner Hebrides.

Sky·ros also **Ski·ros** (skī′rəs, -rōs′, skē′rôs) or **Scy·ros** (sī′rōs). Island of E Greece, largest of the N Sporades, in the Aegean NE of Euboea.

Sla (slä). Variant of **Salé.**

Slave (slāv). River, c. 310 mi (499 km), of NE Alta and S N.W.T., Canada.

Sla·vo·ni·a (slə-vō′nē-ə). Region of N Yugoslavia between the Drava and Sava rivers. **—Sla·vo′ni·an** *adj. & n.*

Slav·yansk (slä-vyänsk′). City of S European USSR, in the E Ukraine SE of Kharkov. Pop. 141,000.

Sli·dell (slī-dĕl′). City of SE La., NE of New Orleans. Pop. 26,718.

Slide Mountain (slīd). Highest (4,024 ft/1,227.3 m) of the Catskill Mts. in SE N.Y.

Sli·go (slī′gō). City of NW Ireland, on the Atlantic. Pop. 16,836.

Slough (slou). Borough of SE England, near London. Pop. 98,400.

Slo·vak·i·a (slō-vä′kē-ə, -văk′ē-ə). Region of E Czechoslovakia. **—Slo·vak′i·an** *adj. & n.*

Slo·ve·ni·a (slō-vē′nē-ə, -nyə). Region and constituent republic of NW Yugoslavia. **—Slo′vene′, Slo·ve′ni·an** *adj. & n.*

Smith·field (smĭth′fēld′). Town of NE R.I., near Providence. Pop. 16,886.

Smok·y (smō′kē). River, c. 250 mi (402 km), of W central Alta., Canada.

Smoky Hill. River, c. 560 mi (900 km), rising in E Colo. and flowing E across Kans. to the Kansas R.

Smo·lensk (smō-lĕnsk′, smŏ-). City of W central European USSR, on the Dnieper WSW of Moscow. Pop. 305,000.

Smyr·na (smûr′nə). **1.** Izmir. **2.** City of NW Ga., near Atlanta. Pop. 20,312.

Snake (snāk). River of NW U.S., rising in NW Wyo. and flowing 1,038 mi (1,670 km) through S Idaho, along the Ore.-Idaho border, and through SE Wash. into the Columbia.

Snef·fels (snĕf′əlz). Peak, 14,143 ft (4,313.6 m), in the San Juan Mts. of SW Colo.

Sno·qual·mie (snō-kwŏl′mē). **1.** Falls, 270 ft (82.4 m) high, in the **Snoqualmie R.** (45 mi/72 km) of W central Wash. **2.** Pass, 3,004 ft (916.2 m) high, in the Cascade range of W central Wash.

Snow (snō). Mountains of central New Guinea.

Snow·don (snōd′n). Mountain, 3,560 ft (1,085.8 m), of NW Wales.

Snow·y (snō'ē). **1.** River, 278 mi (447 km), of SE Australia. **2.** Range of the Australian Alps, in SE Australia.
Sny·der (snī'dər). City of NW Tex., WNW of Abilene. Pop. 12,705.
So·bat (sō'băt', -bät'). River, c. 205 mi (330 km), of W Ethiopia and SE Sudan.
So·chi (sō'chē, sô'-). City of S European USSR, on the NE shore of the Black Sea. Pop. 291,000.
So·ci·e·ty (sə-sī'ĭ-tē). Islands of French Polynesia, in the S Pacific E of Samoa.
So·co·tra (sə-kō'trə). Island of Southern Yemen, in the Indian Ocean at the mouth of the Gulf of Aden.
Sö·der·täl·je (sœ'dər-tĕl'yē). City of E Sweden, SW of Stockholm. Pop. 79,396.
Sod·om (sŏd'əm). City of ancient Palestine.
So·fi·a (sō'fē-ə, sō-fē'ə). Cap. of Bulgaria, in the W central part. Pop. 1,047, 920.
Sog·na·fjord or **Sog·ne Fjord** (sông'-nə-fyôr). Inlet of the Norwegian Sea, in SW Norway.
So·ho (sō'hō). **1.** District of London, England. **2.** District of New York City, on Manhattan Is.
Sois·sons (swä-sôN'). City of N France, NW of Paris. Pop. 30,009.
So·ka (sô'kä'). City of E central Honshu, Japan, near Tokyo. Pop. 186,759.
So·ko·to (sō'kō-tō', sō-kō'tō). City of NW Nigeria, WNW of Kano. Pop. 104,000.
So·lent (sō'lənt), **The.** Channel, c. 15 mi (24 km) long, between the Isle of Wight and the S English mainland.
So·li·hull (sō'lĭ-hŭl'). Borough of central England, near Birmingham. Pop. 198,300.
So·li·mões (sōō'lē-moiNsh'). The upper Amazon R., from the Río Negro to the Peruvian border.
So·ling·en (zō'lĭng-ən). City of W West Germany, ESE of Düsseldorf. Pop. 166,654.
Sol·na (sôl'nä'). City of E Sweden, near Stockholm. Pop. 51,324.
So·lo (sō'lō). **1.** River, 335 mi (539 km), of Java, Indonesia. **2.** Surakarta.
Sol·o·mon Islands (sŏl'ə-mən) also **Sol·o·mons** (-mənz). **1.** Islands of the W Pacific E of New Guinea, divided between Papua New Guinea and the independent Solomon Is. **2.** Nation comprising the Solomons SE of Bougainville. Cap. Honiara. Pop. 225,000.

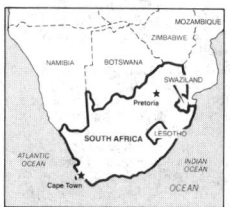

Solomon Islands

So·lon (sō'lən). City of NE Ohio, SE of Cleveland. Pop. 14,341.
So·lo·vets·ki (sə-lä-vyĕt'skē). Islands of N European USSR, in the White Sea.
Sol·way Firth (sŏl'wā'). Arm of the Irish Sea separating NW England from SW Scotland.
So·ma·li·a (sō-mä'lē-ə, -mäl'yə). Country of extreme E Africa, on the Gulf of Aden and the Indian Ocean. Cap. Mogadishu. Pop. 4,535,000. **—So·ma'li·an** *adj.* & *n.*
So·ma·li·land (sō-mä'lē-lănd', sə-). Region of E Africa including Somalia, Djibouti, and parts of E Ethiopia.
Som·er·set (sŭm'ər-sĕt', -sĭt). **1.** Island of N.W.T., Canada, N of the Boothia Peninsula. **2.** City of S central Ky., S of Lexington. Pop. 10,649. **3.** Town of SE Mass., N of Fall River. Pop. 18,813.

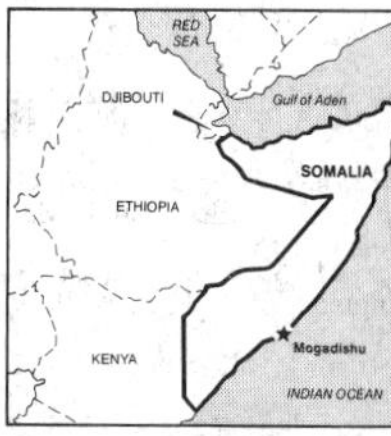

Somalia

Som·ers Point (sŭm'ərz). City of SE N.J., SW of Atlantic City. Pop. 10,330.
Som·ers·worth (sŭm'ərz-wûrth'). City of SE N.H., N of Dover. Pop. 10,350.
Som·er·ville (sŭm'ər-vĭl'). **1.** City of E Mass., near Boston. Pop. 77,372. **2.** Borough of N central N.J., WNW of New Brunswick. Pop. 11,973.
Somme (sôm). River, c. 150 mi (241 km), of N France.
Song·hai also **Song·hay** (sông'hī'). Ancient empire of W Africa.
Song·hua (sōōng'hwä'). River of Manchuria, NE China, rising near the North Korean border and flowing c. 1,150 mi (1,850 km) NW, E, and NE to the Amur.
So·no·ra (sô-nô'rä). River, c. 250 mi (402 km) of NW Mexico.
Soo Canals (sōō). Sault Ste. Marie Canals.
Soo·chow (sōō'jō', -chou'). Suzhou.
So·pot (sô'pôt). City of N Poland, on the Gulf of Danzig near Gdańsk. Pop. 51,800.
Sop·ron (shō'prōn'). City of NW Hungary, near the Austrian border. Pop. 56,000.
So·rel (sə-rĕl', sô-). City of S Que., Canada, at the confluence of the St. Lawrence and Richelieu rivers. Pop. 19,666.
So·ri·a (sô'ryä). Town of N central Spain, W of Saragossa. Pop. 29,315.
So·ro·ca·ba (sôr'ō-kä'bä, sō-rōō-kä'-bə). City of S Brazil, W of São Paulo. Pop. 165,990.
Sor·ren·to (sə-rĕn'tō, sôr-rĕn'tō). Town of S Italy on the **Sorrento Peninsula**, separating the Bay of Naples from the Gulf of Salerno. Pop. 16,868.
So·sno·wiec (sô-snô'vyĕts). City of S Poland, near Katowice. Pop. 241,700.
Sou·fri·ère (sōō'frē-ĕr'). **1.** Volcano, 4,813 ft (1,468 m), on Guadeloupe, French West Indies. **2.** Volcano, 4,048 ft (1,234.6 m), on St. Vincent in St. Vincent and the Grenadines, West Indies.
Sou·ris (sōōr'ĭs). River, c. 450 mi (724 km), of SE Sask., N N.Dak., and SW Man.
Sousse (sōōs) also **Su·sah** (sōō'sə, -zə). City of NE Tunisia, on an inlet of the Mediterranean. Pop. 69,530.
South (south). **1. the.** Region of the SE U.S., S of Pa. and the Ohio R. and E of the Mississippi. **2. Cape.** Ka Lae. **3.** Larger island of New Zealand, SW of North Is.
South Af·ri·ca (ăf'rĭ-kə). Republic of S Africa, on the Atlantic and Indian oceans. Caps. Pretoria and Cape Town. Pop. 29,645,000. **—South Af'ri·can** *adj.* & *n.*

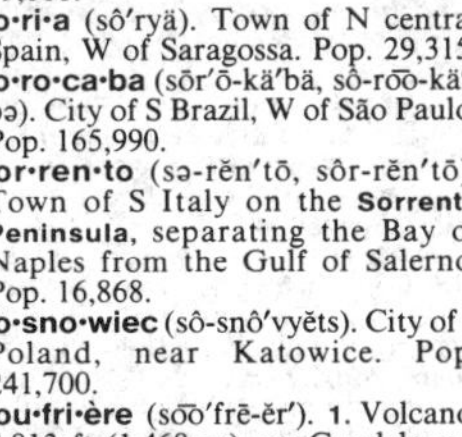

South Africa

South A·mer·i·ca (ə-mĕr'ĭ-kə). Continent of the S Western Hemisphere, SE of North America between the Atlantic and the Pacific. **—South A·mer'i·can** *adj.* & *n.*
South·amp·ton (south-hămp'tən, sou-thămp'-). **1.** Island of N.W.T., Canada, at the entrance to Hudson Bay. **2.** Borough of S central England, on an inlet of the English Channel opposite the Isle of Wight. Pop. 207,800.
South Bend (bĕnd). City of N Ind., near the Mich. border. Pop. 109,727.
South·bridge (south'brĭj'). Town of S Mass., SW of Worcester. Pop. 16,665.
South Bur·ling·ton (bûr'lĭng-tən). City of NW Vt., near Burlington. Pop. 10,679.
South·bur·y (south'bĕr'ē, -bə-rē). Town of SW Conn., SW of Waterbury. Pop. 14,156.
South Car·o·li·na (kăr'ə-lī'nə). State of SE U.S., on the Atlantic. Cap. Columbia. Pop. 3,119,208. **—South Car'o·lin'i·an** (-lĭn'ē-ən) *adj.* & *n.*
South Charles·ton (chärl'stən). City of W W.Va., near Charleston. Pop. 15,968.
South Chi·na Sea (chī'nə). Arm of the W Pacific bounded by SE China, Taiwan, the Philippines, Borneo, and Vietnam.
South Da·ko·ta (də-kō'tə). State of N central U.S. Cap. Pierre. Pop. 690,178. **—South Da·ko'tan** *adj.* & *n.*
South Downs (dounz). Range of hills in SE England.
South El Mon·te (ĕl mŏn'tē). City of S Calif., NNE of Long Beach. Pop. 16,623.
South·end-on-Sea (sou'thĕnd-ŏn-sē', -ôn-). Borough of SE England, at the mouth of the Thames. Pop. 154,700.
South·ern Alps (sŭth'ərn ălps'). Range of W South Is., New Zealand, rising to 12,349 ft (3,766.4 m).
Southern Yem·en (yĕm'ən, yā'mən). See **Yemen.**
South Eu·clid (yōō'klĭd). City of NE Ohio, near Cleveland. Pop. 25,713.
South·field (south'fēld'). City of SE Mich., near Detroit. Pop. 75,568.
South·gate (south'gāt'). City of SE Mich., near Detroit. Pop. 32,058.
South Gate (gāt). City of S Calif., near Los Angeles. Pop. 66,784.
South Geor·gia (jôr'jə). British-administered island of the S Atlantic, E of Cape Horn.
South Hol·land (hŏl'ənd). Village of NE Ill., near Chicago. Pop. 24,977.
South Hous·ton (hyōō'stən). City of SW Tex., near Houston. Pop. 13,293.
South·ing·ton (sŭth'ĭng-tən). Town of central Conn., NE of Waterbury. Pop. 36,879.
South Kings·town (kĭngz'toun'). Town of S R.I., SSW of Providence. Pop. 20,414.
South Ko·re·a (kə-rē'ə, kō-, kô-). See **Korea.**
South Lake Ta·hoe (tä'hō). City of E Calif., on Lake Tahoe near the Nev. border. Pop. 20,681.
South Mi·am·i (mī-ăm'ē, -ăm'ə). City of SE Fla., near Miami. Pop. 10,884.
South Mil·wau·kee (mĭl-wô'kē). City of SE Wis., near Milwaukee. Pop. 21,069.
South Mountain. Ridge of S Pa. and W Md., in the Blue Ridge Mts; site of Civil War battle (1862).
South Na·han·ni (nə-hăn'ē). River, c. 350 mi (563 km), of SW N.W.T., Canada.
South Og·den (ŏg'dən). City of N Utah, near Ogden. Pop. 11,366.
South Or·ange (ôr'ĭnj, ŏr'-). Village of NE N.J., W of Newark. Pop. 16,971.
South Ork·ney (ôrk'nē). British-administered islands in the S Atlantic, SE of Cape Horn.
South Pas·a·de·na (păs'ə-dē'nə). City of S Calif., near Los Angeles. Pop. 22,681.
South Pass. Valley in SW Wyo., at S end of the Wind River Range.
South Plain·field (plān'fēld'). Borough of NE N.J., SW of Elizabeth. Pop. 20,521.
South Platte (plăt). River of central and NE Colo. and W central Nebr., flowing c. 450 mi (724 km) E to the North Platte, forming the Platte.
South Pole (pōl). S end of the earth's axis of rotation, a point in central Antarctica.
South·port (south'pôrt', -pōrt'). Borough of NW England, on Liverpool Bay N of Liverpool. Pop. 86,030.
South Port·land (pôrt'lənd, pōrt'-). City of SW Me., near Portland. Pop. 22,712.
South River. Borough of E central N.J., SW of Perth Amboy. Pop. 14,361.
South Saint Paul (sānt pôl'). City of E Minn., near St. Paul. Pop. 21,235.
South Salt Lake (sôlt). City of N Utah, near Salt Lake City. Pop. 10,561.
South Sand·wich (sănd'wĭch', săn'-). British-administered islands in the S Atlantic ESE of South Georgia Is.
South San Fran·cis·co (săn' frən-sĭs'kō). City of W Calif., on W San Francisco Bay. Pop. 49,393.
South Sas·katch·e·wan (săs-kăch'-ə-wän', -wən). River of Canada, flowing c. 550 mi (890 km) from S Alta. to central Sask. to join the North Saskatchewan and form the Saskatchewan.
South Seas. 1. All seas S of the equator. **2.** The S Pacific.
South Shet·land (shĕt'lənd). Islands in the S Atlantic off the Antarctic Peninsula; claimed by United Kingdom, Argentina, and Chile.
South Shields (shēldz). Borough of NE England, at the mouth of the Tyne R. Pop. 162,600.
South·west (south'wĕst'), **the.** Region of SW U.S., including N.Mex., Ariz., Tex., Calif., Nev., Utah, and Colo.
South-West Af·ri·ca (south'wĕst ăf'rĭ-kə). Namibia.
South Wind·sor (wĭn'zər). Town of N central Conn., NNE of Hartford. Pop. 17,198.
So·vi·et Union (sō'vē-ĕt', sō-vyĕt', sŏv'ē-ĕt). Union of Soviet Socialist Republics.
So·we·to (sə-wĕ'tō). City of NE South Africa, near Johannesburg. Pop. 602,043.
So·ya (sô'yä'). La Pérouse.
Spa (spä). Resort town of E Belgium, in the Ardennes. Pop. 9,766.
Spain (spān). Country of SW Europe, including most of the Iberian Peninsula and the Balearic and Canary Is. Cap. Madrid. Pop. 37,790,000. **—Span'iard** (spăn'yərd) *n.* **—Span'·ish** (spăn'ĭsh) *adj.* & *n.*

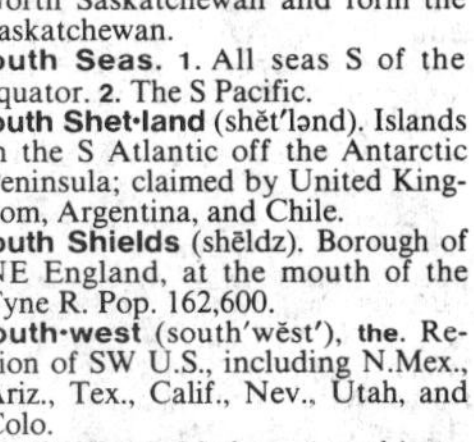

Spain

Spa·la·to (spä'lä-tō). *Italian.* Split.
Span·dau (shpän'dou). District of West Berlin, Germany.
Span·ish (spăn'ĭsh). River, c. 150 mi (240 km), of S Ont., Canada.
Spanish Main (mān). **1.** Coast of N South America in colonial times. **2.** Parts of the Caribbean crossed by Spanish shipping in colonial times.
Spanish Peaks. Two adjacent mountains, 12,683 ft (3,868.3 m) and 13,623 ft (4,155 m), in S Colo.
Spanish Sa·ha·ra (sə-hâr'ə, -hä'rə). Western Sahara.
Spanish Town. Town of SE Jamaica, W of Kingston. Pop. 40,731.
Sparks (spärks). City of W Nev., E of Reno. Pop. 40,780.
Spar·ta (spär'tə). City-state of ancient Greece, in the SE Peloponnesus. **—Spar'tan** *adj.* & *n.*
Spar·tan·burg (spär'tn-bûrg'). City of NW S.C., NW of Columbia. Pop. 43,968.
Speed·way (spēd'wā'). Town of cen-

tral Ind., near Indianapolis. Pop. 12,641.

Spen·cer (spĕn′sər). **1.** City of NW Iowa, on the Little Sioux R. NE of Sioux City. Pop. 11,726. **2.** Town of central Mass., W of Worcester. Pop. 10,774.

Spencer Gulf. Inlet of the Indian Ocean off S central Australia between the Eyre and Yorke peninsulas.

Spey (spā). River, c. 105 mi (169 km), of NE Scotland.

Spey·er (shpī′ər) also **Spires** (spīrz). City of SW West Germany, on the Rhine R. Pop. 43,663.

Spe·zia (spĕ′tsyä). La Spezia.

Spice Islands (spīs). Moluccas.

Spits·ber·gen or **Spitz·ber·gen** (spĭts′bûr′gən). Norwegian archipelago in the Arctic Ocean N of Norway.

Split (splĭt, splēt). City of W Yugoslavia, on the Dalmatian coast of the Adriatic. Pop. 151,875.

Spo·kane (spō-kăn′). City of E Wash., near the Idaho border. Pop. 171,300.

Spo·le·to (spō-lā′tō). City of central Italy, N of Rome. Pop. 32,200.

Spor·a·des (spôr′ə-dēz′). All the islands of Greece in the Aegean excepting the Cyclades.

Spot·syl·va·ni·a (spŏt′səl-vā′nē-ə, -vān′yə). Village of NE Va.; site of a Civil War battle (1864).

Spree (shprā). River, c. 250 mi (402 km), of E East Germany.

Spring·dale (sprĭng′dāl′). **1.** City of NW Ark., near Fayetteville. Pop. 23,185. **2.** City of SW Ohio, near Cincinnati. Pop. 10,111.

Spring·field (sprĭng′fēld′). **1.** Cap. of Ill., in the central part. Pop. 99,637. **2.** City of SW Mass., on the Connecticut R. Pop. 152,319. **3.** City of SW Mo., SE of Kansas City. Pop. 133,116. **4.** Township of NE N.J., W of Newark. Pop. 15,740. **5.** City of W central Ohio, W of Columbus. Pop. 72,563. **6.** City of W central Ore., near Eugene. Pop. 41,621. **7.** City of N Tenn., N of Nashville. Pop. 10,814. **8.** Town of SE Vt., near the N.H. border SE of Rutland. Pop. 10,190.

Springs (sprĭngz). City of NE South Africa, E of Johannesburg. Pop. 142,812.

Spring Valley. Village of SE N.Y., near the N.J. border WNW of White Plains. Pop. 20,537.

Spring·ville (sprĭng′vĭl′). City of N central Utah, near Provo. Pop. 12,101.

Spuy·ten Duy·vil Creek (spīt′n dī′vəl). Tidal channel, now a ship canal, in SE N.Y., separating N Manhattan Is. from the mainland.

Squaw Valley (skwô). Valley of NE Calif. in the Sierra Nevada.

Sri Lan·ka (srē läng′kə). Island nation in the Indian Ocean off the SE coast of India. Cap. Colombo. Pop. 15,470,000. **—Sri Lan′kan** *adj. & n.*

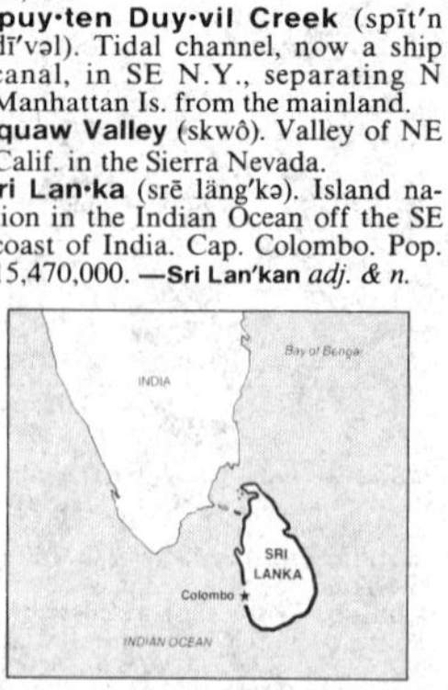

Sri Lanka

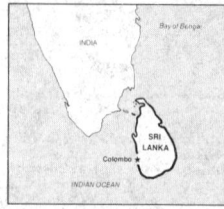

Sri·na·gar (srē-nŭg′ər). City of N India, historic cap. of Kashmir, on the Jhelum R. Pop. 403,413.

St. For entries beginning with **St.**, see **Saint.**

Staf·fa (stăf′ə). Island of W Scotland, in the Inner Hebrides W of Mull.

Staf·ford (stăf′ərd). Borough of W central England, NNW of Birmingham. Pop. 54,860.

Sta·gi·ra (stə-jī′rə) also **Sta·gi·rus** (-rəs). Ancient city of Macedonia, NE Greece; birthplace of Aristotle.

Staines (stānz). Urban district of SE England, on the Thames near London. Pop. 93,500.

Sta·lin·grad (stä′lĭn-grăd′). Volgograd.

Sta·lin Peak (stä′lĭn, stăl′ĭn). Mt. Communism.

Stam·bul also **Stam·boul** (stäm-bo͞ol′, stăm-). The old section of Istanbul.

Stam·ford (stăm′fərd). City of SW Conn., on Long Is. Sound. Pop. 102,453.

Stan·ley (stăn′lē). **1.** Series of falls in the Lualaba R. above Kisangani in N central Zaire. **2. Pool.** Lakelike expansion of the Congo R., c. 320 sq mi (829 sq km), on the Zaire-Congo border at Kinshasa and Brazzaville. **3. Mount.** Peak, 16,795 ft (5,122.5 m), in the Ruwenzori range on the Zaire-Uganda border. **4.** Town of E Falkland Is., on the Atlantic. Pop. 1,081.

Stan·ley·ville (stăn′lē-vĭl′). Kisangani.

Stan·o·voi or **Stan·o·voy** (stăn′ə-voi′, stä′nō-, stän′ə-voi′). Range, c. 450 mi (725 km) long, of SE Far Eastern USSR, N of the Amur R.

Stan·ton (stăn′tən). City of S Calif., NW of Santa Ana. Pop. 21,144.

Sta·ra Za·go·ra (stä′rä zä-gô′rä). City of central Bulgaria, ENE of Plovdiv. Pop. 133,021.

Stark·ville (stärk′vĭl′, -vəl). City of E Miss., W of Columbus. Pop. 15,169.

State Col·lege (stāt kŏl′ĭj). Borough of central Pa., NE of Altoona. Pop. 36,130.

Stat·en (stăt′n). Island in New York Bay, SE N.Y., SW of Manhattan, coextensive with the New York City borough of Richmond.

States·bor·o (stāts′bûr-ō). City of E Ga., WNW of Savannah. Pop. 14,866.

States·ville (stāts′vĭl′, -vəl). City of W central N.C., N of Charlotte. Pop. 18,622.

Staun·ton (stăn′tən). Independent city of W central Va., WNW of Charlottesville. Pop. 21,857.

Sta·vang·er (stä-väng′ər). City of SW Norway, on an inlet of the North Sea. Pop. 90,000.

Stav·ro·pol (stăv-rô′pəl, stäv′rə-). City of S European USSR, SE of Rostov. Pop. 265,000.

Steele (stēl), **Mount.** Mountain, 16,644 ft (5,076.4 m), in the St. Elias range in SW Y.T., Canada.

Steens (stēnz). Mountains of SE Ore.

Stel·vio (stĕl′vyō). Pass, 9,048 ft (2,759.6 m) high, in the central Alps in N Italy near the Swiss and Austrian borders.

Ste·phen·ville (stē′vən-vĭl′, -vəl). **1.** Town of SW Newf., Canada, on the Gulf of St. Lawrence SW of Corner Brook. Pop. 10,284. **2.** City of N central Tex., SW of Fort Worth. Pop. 11,881.

Ster·ling (stûr′lĭng). **1.** City of NE Colo., ENE of Greeley. Pop. 11,385. **2.** City of NW Ill., SW of Rockford. Pop. 16,273.

Sterling Heights. City of SE Mich., near Detroit. Pop. 108,999.

Ster·li·ta·mak (stĕr′lĕ-tä-mäk′). City of E European USSR, E of Kuibyshev. Pop. 224,000.

Stet·tin (shtĕ-tēn′). *German.* Szczecin.

Stet·ti·ner Haff (shtĕ-tē′nər häf′) also **Stet·tin Bay** (shtĕ-tēn′). Lagoon on the Baltic coast between NE East Germany and NW Poland.

Steu·ben·ville (sto͞o′bĭn-vĭl′, styo͞o′-). City of E Ohio, on the Ohio R. near the Pa. border and S of Youngstown. Pop. 26,400.

Ste·ven·age (stē′və-nĭj). Urban district of SE England, N of London. Pop. 73,100.

Ste·vens Point (stē′vĭnz). City of central Wis., S of Wausau. Pop. 22,970.

Stew·art (sto͞o′ərt, styo͞o′-). **1.** River, 331 mi (533 km), of central Y.T., Canada. **2.** Island of S New Zealand, off S coast of South Is.

Sti·kine (stĭ-kēn′). River, 335 mi (539 km), of NW B.C., Canada, and SE Alas.

Still·wa·ter (stĭl′wô′tər, -wŏt′ər). **1.** City of E Minn., ENE of St. Paul. Pop. 12,290. **2.** City of N central Okla., NNE of Oklahoma City. Pop. 38,268.

Stir·ling (stûr′lĭng). Borough of central Scotland, WNW of Edinburgh. Pop. 29,818.

Stock·holm (stŏk′hōlm, -hōm). Cap. of Sweden, in the E part on the Baltic Sea. Pop. 649,384.

Stock·port (stŏk′pôrt′, -pōrt′). City of NW England, near Manchester. Pop. 291,700.

Stock·ton (stŏk′tən). **1.** Stockton-on-Tees. **2.** City of central Calif., on the San Joaquin R. S of Sacramento. Pop. 149,779.

Stock·ton-on-Tees (stŏk′tən-ŏn-tēz′, -ôn-). Borough of NE England, near Middlesbrough. Pop. 171,800.

Stoke-on-Trent (stōk′ŏn-trĕnt′, -ôn-). Borough of W central England, S of Manchester. Pop. 257,200.

Stol·berg (shtôl′bĕrk). City of W West Germany, WSW of Cologne. Pop. 57,552.

Stone·ham (stō′nəm, stōn′hăm′). Town of E Mass., near Boston. Pop. 21,424.

Ston·ey Creek (stō′nē). Town of S Ont., Canada, off Lake Ontario S of Hamilton. Pop. 32,896.

Ston·ing·ton (stō′nĭng-tən). Town of SE Conn., on Long Is. Sound. Pop. 16,220.

Ston·y Point (stō′nē). Village of SE N.Y., on the Hudson; site of Revolutionary War battle (1779). Pop. 8,270.

Stor·fjord (stōr′fyōr). Inlet of the Norwegian Sea, in SW Norway.

Stough·ton (stōt′n). Town of E Mass., near Brockton. Pop. 26,710.

Stour (stour, sto͝or, stōr). River, 40 mi (64.4 km), of SE England, emptying into the North Sea in 2 channels.

Stow (stō). City of NE Ohio, near Akron. Pop. 25,303.

Stral·sund (shträl′zo͝ont). City of N East Germany, on the Baltic opposite Rügen Is. Pop. 73,889.

Stras·bourg (străs′bûrg, sträz′-, sträz′bo͝org, sträz-bo͞or′). City of NE France, near the Rhine R. Pop. 253,384.

Strat·ford (străt′fərd). **1.** City of S Ont., Canada, SW of Toronto. Pop. 26,517. **2.** Stratford-upon-Avon. **3.** Town of SW Conn., NE of Bridgeport. Pop. 50,541.

Strat·ford-up·on-Av·on (străt′fərd-ə-pŏn-ā′vŏn, -vən) or **Strat·ford-on-A·von** (-ŏn-, -ôn-). Borough of central England, SSE of Birmingham. Pop. 20,080.

Stream·wood (strēm′wo͝od′). Village of NE Ill., near Chicago. Pop. 23,456.

Strea·tor (strē′tər). City of N central Ill., NE of Peoria. Pop. 14,769.

Stret·ford (strĕt′fərd). Borough of NW England, near Manchester. Pop. 224,000.

Strí·mon (strē-môn′). *Greek.* Struma.

Strom·bo·li (strŏm′bə-lē, strôm′bō-lē). **1.** Island of S Italy, in the Lipari Is. off NE Sicily. **2.** Volcano, 3,038 ft (926.6 m), on Stromboli Is.

Strongs·ville (strôngz′vĭl′). City of NE Ohio, SSW of Cleveland. Pop. 28,577.

Stru·ma (stro͞o′mä, -mə). River, 216 mi (347.5 km), of W Bulgaria and NE Greece.

Struth·ers (strŭth′ərz). City of NE Ohio, near Youngstown and the Pa. border. Pop. 13,624.

Stry·mon (strī′mən, -män′, strē-môn′). *Greek.* Struma.

Stry·mon·ic Gulf (strī-mŏn′ĭk). Inlet of the Aegean off NE Greece E of Chalcidice.

Stutt·gart (stŭt′gärt′). **1.** City of E central Ark., ESE of Little Rock. Pop. 10,999. **2.** (*also* shto͞ot′gärt). City of SW West Germany, on the Neckar R. Pop. 581,989.

Styr (stĭr, stîr). River, c. 271 mi (436 km), of W European USSR.

Su·bic Bay (so͞o′bĭk). Inlet of the South China Sea off W central Luzon, Philippines, W of Manila Bay.

Su·bo·ti·ca also **Su·bo·ti·tsa** (so͞o′bô′tĭ-tsä). City of NE Yugoslavia, near the Hungarian border. Pop. 88,787.

Sü·chow (shü′jō′). Xuzhou.

Su·cre (so͞o′krĕ). Constitutional cap. of Bolivia, in the central part SE of La Paz. Pop. 62,207.

Su·dan (so͞o-dăn′). **1.** Region of N Africa S of the Sahara and N of the equator. **2.** Country of NE Africa, S of Egypt. Cap. Khartoum. Pop. 18,630,000. **—Su′da·nese′** *adj. & n.*

Sudan

Sud·bur·y (sŭd′bĕr′ē, -bə-rē). **1.** City of central Ont., Canada, N of Georgian Bay. Pop. 92,350. **2.** Town of E Mass., W of Boston. Pop. 14,027.

Su·de·ten (so͞o-dā′tn, zo͞o-). **1.** Sudentenland. **2.** Variant of **Sudetes.**

Su·de·ten·land (so͞o-dāt′n-lănd′, zo͞o-dāt′n-länt′). Region of NW Czechoslovakia along the Polish border.

Su·de·tes (so͞o-dē′tēz, -dā′-) also **Su·de·ten** (so͞o-dāt′n, zo͞o-). Mountains extending c. 185 mi (298 km) along the border between NW Czechoslovakia and SW Poland.

Su·dir·man (so͞o-dîr′mən). Range of New Guinea in central West Irian.

Su·ez (so͞o-ĕz′, so͞o′ĕz). **1. Gulf of.** N arm of the Red Sea off NE Egypt, W of the Sinai Peninsula. **2.** Isthmus of NE Egypt connecting Africa and Asia and traversed by the **Suez Canal** (107 mi/172 km) from the Mediterranean to the Gulf of Suez. **3.** City of NE Egypt, at the head of the Gulf of Suez. Pop. 204,000.

Suf·fern (sŭf′ərn). Village of SE N.Y., on the N.J. border NW of New York City. Pop. 10,794.

Suf·folk (sŭf′ək, -ŏk′). Independent city of SE Va., near Portsmouth. Pop. 47,621.

Sui·sun City (sĭ-so͞on′). City of W central Calif., NNE of Oakland and N of **Suisun Bay,** E arm of San Francisco Bay. Pop. 11,087.

Su·i·ta (so͞o-ē′tə). City of S Honshu, Japan, near Osaka. Pop. 332,413.

Su·kho·na (so͞o-KHô′nə). River, c. 350 mi (563 km), of N European USSR.

Su·khu·mi (so͞o-KHo͞o′mē). City of S European USSR, on the Black Sea. Pop. 116,000.

Suk·kur (sŭk′ər). City of SE Pakistan, on the Indus R. Pop. 158,781.

Su·la·we·si (so͞o′lä-wā′sē). Island of central Indonesia, on the equator E of Borneo.

Sul·phur Springs (sŭl′fər). City of NE Tex., ENE of Dallas. Pop. 12,804.

Su·lu (so͞o′lo͞o). **1.** Sea of the W Pacific between the central Philippines and N Borneo. **2.** Archipelago of the S Philippines SW of Mindanao.

Su·ma·tra (so͞o-mä′trə). Island of W Indonesia, in the Indian Ocean W of Borneo and the Malay Peninsula. **—Su·ma′tran** *adj. & n.*

Sum·ba (so͞om′bä). Island of S central Indonesia, in the Lesser Sundas S of Flores.

Sum·ba·wa (so͞om-bä′wä). Island of S central Indonesia, in the Lesser Sundas W of Flores.

Su·mer (so͞o′mər). Ancient country of Mesopotamia, in present-day S Iraq. **—Su·me′ri·an** *adj. & n.*

Sum·ga·it (so͞om′gä-ēt′). City of S European USSR, on the Caspian Sea. Pop. 196,000.

Sum·mit (sŭm′ĭt). **1.** Village of NE Ill., near Chicago. Pop. 10,110. **2.** City of NE N.J., W of Newark. Pop. 21,071.

Sum·ter (sŭm′tər). City of central N.C., E of Columbia. Pop. 24,890.

Su·my (so͞o′mĭ). City of W European

USSR, in the N Ukraine NW of Kharkov. Pop. 233,000.

Sun (sŭn). River, c. 130 mi (209 km), of NW Mont.

Sun·bur·y (sŭn′bĕr′ē, -bə-rē). City of E central Pa., N of Harrisburg. Pop. 12,292.

Sun·da (sŭn′də, so͞on′-). **1.** Strait between Sumatra and Java. **2.** Also **Sun·das** (-dəz). Islands of the W Malay Archipelago, comprising the **Greater Sundas** (Sumatra, Borneo, Java, and Sulawesi) and the **Lesser Sundas** (from Bali E to Timor).

Sun·der·land (sŭn′dər-lənd). Borough of NE England, near the North Sea ESE of Newcastle-upon-Tyne. Pop. 300,800.

Sunds·vall (sŭnts′väl, so͞onts′-). City of E Sweden, on an inlet of the Gulf of Bothnia. Pop. 52,500.

Sun·ga·ri (so͞ong′gə-rē′). Songhua.

Sun·ny·vale (sŭn′ē-vāl′). City of W Calif., near San Jose. Pop. 106,618.

Sun Prai·rie (prâr′ē). City of S central Wis., NE of Madison. Pop. 12,931.

Sun·rise (sŭn′rīz′). City of SE Fla., near Fort Lauderdale. Pop. 39,681.

Sun Valley. Resort town of S central Idaho, E of Boise. Pop. 545.

Su·pe·ri·or (sə-pîr′ē-ər, so͞o-). **1.** Largest and westernmost of the Great Lakes, 31,820 sq mi (82,414 sq km), between the U.S. and Ont., Canada. **2.** City of NW Wis., on Lake Superior opposite Duluth, Minn. Pop. 29,571.

Su·ra·ba·ya or **Su·ra·ba·ja** (so͞or′ə-bī′ə, -bä′yə). City of NE Java, Indonesia, on the Java Sea. Pop. 1,332,249.

Su·ra·kar·ta (so͞or′ə-kär′tə). City of central Java, Indonesia, on the Solo R. Pop. 414,285.

Su·rat (so͞or′ət, so͞o-rät′, -răt′). City of W central India, on the Gulf of Cambay. Pop. 471,656.

Su·ri·ba·chi (so͞or′ə-bä′chē), **Mount.** Volcanic hill on Iwo Jima in the W Pacific.

Su·ri·nam (so͞or′ə-năm′, so͞or′ə-näm′). **1.** Suriname R. **2.** Also **Su·ri·na·me** (sü-rē-nä′mə). Country of NE South America, on the Atlantic. Cap. Paramaribo. Pop. 425,000. —**Su′ri·nam·ese′** *adj. & n.*

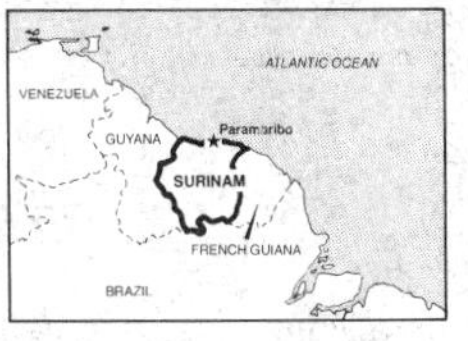

Surinam

Su·ri·na·me (sü-rē-nä′mə). **1.** Also **Su·ri·nam** (so͞or′ə-năm′, so͞or′ə-näm′). River of Surinam, flowing c. 400 mi (644 km) N to the Atlantic. **2.** Surinam.

Sur·rey (sûr′ē, sŭr′ē). Region and former county of SE England, S of London.

Su·ru·ga Bay (so͞o′ro͞o-gä′). Inlet of the Pacific on SE coast of Honshu, Japan, SW of Tokyo.

Su·sa (so͞o′sə, -zə). Ruined city of SW Iran, cap. of ancient Elam.

Su·sah (so͞o′sə, -zə). Variant of **Sousse.**

Sus·que·han·na (sŭs′kwə-hăn′ə). River of NE U.S., rising in central N.Y. and flowing 444 mi (715 km) S through E Pa. and NE Md. to Chesapeake Bay.

Sus·sex (sŭs′ĭks). Region and former county of SE England, on the English Channel S of London.

Suth·er·land (sŭ*th*′ər-lənd). Falls, 1,904 ft (580.7 m) high, on SW South Is., New Zealand.

Sut·lej (sŭt′lĕj). River, c. 900 mi (1,448 km), of SW Tibet, N India, and E Pakistan.

Sut·ton-in-Ash·field (sŭt′n-ĭn-ăsh′fēld′). Urban district of central England, NNW of Nottingham. Pop. 40,330.

Su·va (so͞o′vä). Cap. of Fiji, on the SE coast of Viti Levu. Pop. 63,628.

Su·wal·ki (so͞o-väl′kē). City of NE Poland, N of Bialystok. Pop. 38,500.

Su·wan·nee (sə-wä′nē). River, c. 240 mi (386 km), of SE Ga. and N Fla.

Su·won (so͞o′wän′). City of NW South Korea, S of Seoul. Pop. 266,135.

Su·zhou (so͞o′jō). City of E China, WNW of Shanghai. Pop. 750,000.

Sval·bard (sväl′bär′). Archipelago of Norway comprising Spitsbergen and other islands in the Arctic Ocean N of the Norwegian mainland.

Sverd·lovsk (svĕrd-lôfsk′). City of E European USSR, in the central Urals. Pop. 1,225,000.

Sver·drup (sfĕr′drəp). Islands of N N.W.T., Canada, in the Arctic Ocean W of Ellesmere Is.

Swa·bi·a (swā′bē-ə). Region of SW Germany. —**Swa′bi·an** *adj. & n.*

Swamp·scott (swŏmp′skət, swômp′-). Town of NE Mass., NE of Boston. Pop. 13,837.

Swan (swän). **1.** River, c. 240 mi (386 km), of SW Australia. **2.** River, c. 110 mi (177 km), of E Sask. and W Man., Canada.

Swan·sea (swän′sē). **1.** Town of SE Mass., near Fall River. Pop. 15,461. **2.** Borough of S Wales, on **Swansea Bay,** an inlet of Bristol Channel. Pop. 186,900.

Swa·tow (swä′tou′). Shantou.

Swa·zi·land (swä′zē-lănd′). Country of SE Africa, between South Africa and Mozambique. Cap. Mbabane. Pop. 565,000.

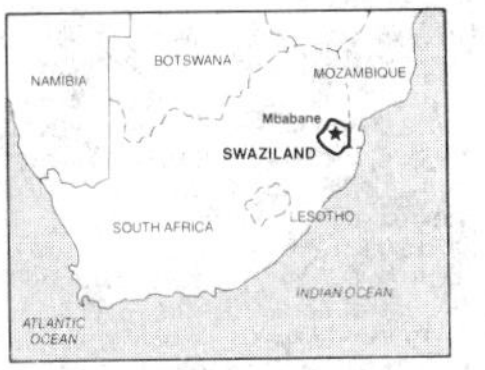

Swaziland

Swe·den (swēd′n). Country of N Europe, on the E Scandinavian peninsula. Cap. Stockholm. Pop. 8,315,010. —**Swede** (swēd) *n.* —**Swed′ish** (swē′dĭsh) *adj. & n.*

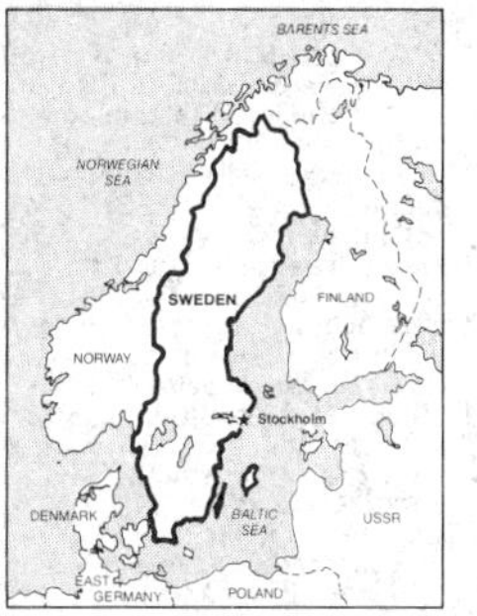

Sweden

Sweet·wa·ter (swēt′wô′tər, -wŏt′ər). City of N central Tex., near Abilene. Pop. 12,242.

Swift Cur·rent (swĭft′ kûr′ənt, kŭr′-). City of SW Sask., Canada, W of Regina. Pop. 14,264.

Swin·don (swĭn′dən). Borough of S central England, ENE of Bristol. Pop. 143,800.

Swit·zer·land (swĭt′sər-lənd). Republic of W central Europe. Cap. Bern. Pop. 6,314,200. —**Swiss** (swĭs) *adj. & n.*

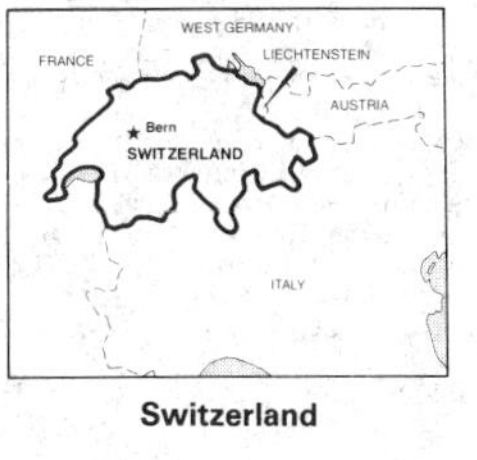

Switzerland

Syb·a·ris (sĭb′ər-ĭs). Ancient Greek city of S Italy, on the Gulf of Taranto.

Syd·ney (sĭd′nē). **1.** City of SE Australia, on an inlet of the Tasman Sea. Metro. area pop. 3,193,300. **2.** City of N.S., Canada, on Cape Breton Is. Pop. 30,645.

Syk·tyv·kar (sĭk-tĭf-kär′). City of NE European USSR, ESE of Arkhangelsk. Pop. 175,000.

Syl·a·cau·ga (sĭl′ə-kô′gə). City of central Ala., E of Birmingham. Pop. 12,708.

Syl·va·ni·a (sĭl-vā′nē-ə, -vān′yə). City of N Ohio, on the Mich. border near Toledo. Pop. 15,527.

Syr·a·cuse (sîr′ə-kyo͞os′, -kyo͞oz′). **1.** City of SE Sicily, Italy, on the Ionian Sea. Pop. 116,755. **2.** City of central N.Y., ESE of Rochester. Pop. 170,105.

Syr Dar·ya (sîr′ där′yə, där-yä′). River of S Central Asian USSR, rising in the Tian Shan and flowing c. 1,380 mi (2,220 km) NW into the Aral Sea.

Sy·ri·a (sîr′ē-ə). Country of SW Asia, on the E Mediterranean coast. Cap. Damascus. Pop. 8,401,100. —**Syr′i·an** *adj. & n.*

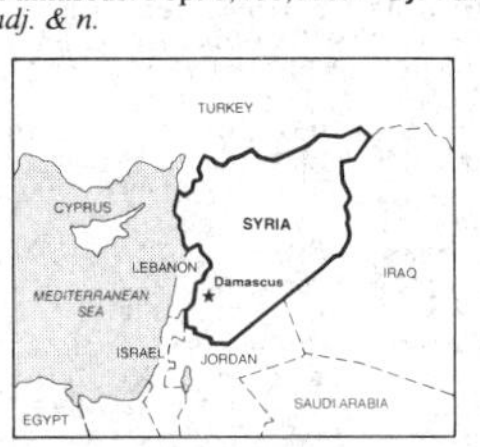

Syria

Syrian. Desert of N Arabian Peninsula, occupying N Saudi Arabia, W Iraq, SE Syria, and E Jordan.

Sy·ros also **Sí·ros** (sī′rŏs′, sē′rôs′). Island of Greece in the N central Cyclades.

Syz·ran (sĭz′răn, sĭz-răn′). City of S central European USSR, on the Volga W of Kuibyshev. Pop. 168,000.

Szcze·cin (shchĕ′tsēn). City of NW Poland, near the mouth of the Oder R. Pop. 388,000.

Sze·ged (sĕ′gĕd). City of S Hungary, on the Tisza R. near the Yugoslavian border. Pop. 175,000.

Szé·kes·fe·hér·vár (sā′kĕsh-fĕ′hăr-vär′). City of central Hungary, on the Danube SSW of Budapest. Pop. 102,000.

Szol·nok (sōl′nōk). City of central Hungary, ESE of Budapest. Pop. 77,000.

Szom·bat·hely (sōm′bôt-hā′). City of W Hungary, near the Austrian border. Pop. 82,000.

T

Ta·al (tä-äl′). **1.** Lake, 94 sq mi (243.5 sq km), of SW Luzon, Philippines, S of Manila. **2.** Island in Lake Taal.

Tab·las (täb′ləs). Island of central Philippines, in the Romblons E of Mindoro.

Ta·ble (tā′bəl). **1. Bay.** Inlet of the Atlantic off SW South Africa; harbor of Cape Town. **2.** Flat-topped mountain, 3,550 ft (1,082.8 m), overlooking Cape Town, SW South Africa.

Ta·briz (tä-brēz′). City of NW Iran, in Azerbaijan E of Lake Urmia. Pop. 598,576.

Ta·bun Bog·do (tä′bo͞on′ bôg′dō). Mountain, 15,266 ft (4,656.1 m), in the Altai Mts. at the junction of the USSR, China, and Mongolia borders.

Ta·chi·ka·wa (tä-chē′kä-wä). City of E central Honshu, Japan, near Tokyo. Pop. 142,793.

Tac·na (täk′nä). Town of S Peru, N of Arica, Chile. Pop. 55,752.

Ta·co·ma (tə-kō′mə). City of W central Wash., on an arm of Puget Sound S of Seattle. Pop. 158,501.

Ta·con·ic (tə-kŏn′ĭk). Range of the Appalachians in SE N.Y. E of the Hudson and in W Mass. and SW Vt.

Ta·dzhik·i·stan (tä-jĭk′ĭ-stăn′, -stän′). Region of S Central Asian USSR, bordering on Afghanistan and China.

Tae·dong (tī-do͝ong′). River, c. 245 mi (394 km), of North Korea.

Tae·gu (tī-go͞o′). City of SE South Korea, NNW of Pusan. Pop. 1,487,098.

Tae·jon (tī-jôn′, -jŏn′). City of SW South Korea, SSE of Seoul. Pop. 508,574.

Ta·fi·lelt (tä-fĭ-lĕlt′) or **Ta·fi·let** (-lĕt′). Oasis, c. 530 sq mi (1,375 sq km), in the Sahara in SE Morocco.

Tag·an·rog (tăg′ən-rŏg′, tä′gän-rôk′). City of S European USSR, on the **Gulf of Taganrog,** an arm of the Sea of Azov. Pop. 278,000.

Ta·gus (tā′gəs). River of the Iberian Peninsula, rising in E central Spain and flowing c. 585 mi (941 km) NW and SW through central Portugal to the Atlantic.

Ta·hi·ti (tə-hē′tē, tä-). Island of the South Pacific, in the Windward group of the Society Is., French Polynesia. —**Ta·hi′tian** *adj. & n.*

Ta·hoe (tä′hō). Lake, 193 sq mi (500 sq km), on the Calif.-Nev. border W of Carson City, Nev.

Ta·hsüeh Shan (tä′swā′ shän′, -shü-ā′). Daxue Shan.

Tai (tī). Lake, c. 1,300 sq mi (3,367 sq km), of E central China, W of Shanghai.

Tai·chung (tī′cho͞ong′, -jo͞ong′). City of W central Taiwan, SW of Taipei. Pop. 585,205.

Tai·myr also **Tai·mir** or **Tay·myr** (tī-mîr′). Peninsula of N central Siberian USSR, extending N between the Laptev and Kara seas.

Tai·nan (tī′nän′). City of SW Taiwan, on the South China Sea. Pop. 572,590.

Tai·na·ron (tĕ′nä-rôn), **Cape.** *Greek.* Cape Matapan.

Tai·pei also **Tai·peh** (tī′pā′, -bā′). Cap. of Taiwan, in the N part. Pop. 2,196,237.

Tai·wan (tī′wän′). Island off the SE coast of China, constituting with the Pescadores and other smaller islands the Republic of China. Cap. Taipei. Pop. 18,055,000. —**Tai′wan·ese′** *adj. & n.*

Tai·yu·an also **Tai·yü·an** (tī′yo͞o-än′, -yü-än′). City of NE China, SW of Beijing. Pop. 1,350,000.

Ta·iz or **Ta′izz** (tä-ĭz′). City of SW Yemen, in the SW. Pop. 81,000.

Tai·zhong (tī′jo͝ong′). Taichung.

Ta·jo (tä′hô). *Spanish.* Tagus.

Ta·ju·mul·co (tä′ho͞o-mo͞ol′kô). Inactive volcano, 13,816 ft (4,213.9 m), in W Guatemala.

Ta·ka·mat·su (tä-kä′mä-tso͞o). City of NE Shikoku, Japan, on the Inland Sea. Pop. 316,662.

Ta·ka·o·ka (tä-kä′ô-kä). City of W central Honshu, Japan, near Toyama Bay. Pop. 174,334.

Ta·ka·ra·zu·ka (tä-kä′rä′zo͞o-kä). City of SW Honshu, Japan, near Osaka and Kobe. Pop. 179,394.

Ta·ka·sa·ki (tä′kä-sä′kē). City of central Honshu, Japan, NW of Tokyo. Pop. 221,432.

Ta·ka·tsu·ki (tä-kä′tso͞o-kē′). City of SW Honshu, Japan, NE of Osaka. Pop. 340,722.

Tak·ka·kaw (tăk′ə-kô′). Falls, 1,650 ft (503.3 m), in SE B.C., Canada.

Ta·kli·ma·kan also **Ta·kla·ma·kan** (tä′klə-mə-kän′). Desert of W China between the Tian Shan and Kunlun Mts.

Ta·ko·ma Park (tə-kō′mə). City of central Md., near Washington, D.C. Pop. 16,231.

Ta·la·ud (tä′lout, -lä′o͞od′) or **Ta·laur** (-lour, -lä′o͝or′). Islands of NE Indonesia, NE of Sulawesi.

Tal·ca (täl′kä). City of central Chile, between Santiago and Concepción. Pop. 115,130.

Tal·ca·hua·no (täl′kä-wä′nô). City of central Chile, on the Pacific near

Concepción. Pop. 183,591.
Tal·la·de·ga (tăl′ə-dē′gə). City of E central Ala., E of Birmingham. Pop. 19,128.
Tal·la·has·see (tăl′ə-hăs′ē). Cap. of Fla., in the Panhandle. Pop. 81,548.
Tal·la·hatch·ie (tăl′ə-hăch′ē). River, c. 230 mi (371 km), of N Miss.
Tal·la·poo·sa (tăl′ə-po͞o′sə). River, 268 mi (431.2 km), of NW Ga. and E Ala.
Tal·linn also **Tal·lin** (tä′lĭn, tăl′ĭn). City of NW European USSR, in Estonia on the Gulf of Finland opposite Helsinki. Pop. 436,000.
Tall·madge (tăl′mĭj). City of NE Ohio, near Akron. Pop. 15,269.
Ta·lu·lah (tə-lo͞o′lə). City of NE La., WNW of Vicksburg, Miss. Pop. 10,392.
Ta·man (tä-män′). Peninsula of S European USSR, projecting W between the Sea of Azov and the Black Sea.
Tam·an·ras·set (tăm′ən-răs′ət). Oasis of S Algeria, in the Sahara.
Tam·a·rac (tăm′ə-răk′). City of SE Fla., NW of Fort Lauderdale. Pop. 29,142.
Ta·ma·tave (tä′mä-täv′). City of NE Madagascar, on the Indian Ocean. Pop. 83,000.
Tam·bo·ra (tăm′bō-rä′, tăm-bôr′ə, -bôr′ə), **Mount.** Volcano, 9,253 ft (2,822.2 m), on Sumbawa Is., S central Indonesia.
Tam·bov (tăm-bôf′). City of central European USSR, SE of Moscow. Pop. 270,000.
Tam·pa (tăm′pə). City of W central Fla., on **Tampa Bay,** an inlet of the Gulf of Mexico. Pop. 271,523.
Tam·pe·re (tăm′pĕ-rĕ). City of SW Finland, NNW of Helsinki. Pop. 165,519.
Tam·pi·co (tăm-pē′kō, tăm-pē′kô). City of E central Mexico, near the Gulf of Mexico NNE of Mexico City. Pop. 240,000.
Tam·ri·da (tăm-rē′də). Chief town of Socotra Is., Southern Yemen.
Tam·worth (tăm′wûrth′). Borough of central England, NE of Birmingham. Pop. 60,300.
Ta·na (tä′nä). **1.** Also **Tsa·na** (tsä′nä). Lake, c. 1,400 sq mi (3,626 sq km), of NW Ethiopia. **2.** River, c. 500 mi (805 km), of Kenya. **3.** River, c. 200 mi (322 km), of NE Norway, forming part of the Norway-Finland border.
Tan·a·na (tăn′ə-nô′). River of Alas., flowing c. 475 mi (764 km) NW to the Yukon R.
Ta·nan·a·rive (tä-nä-nä-rēv′, tə-năn′-ə-). Antananarivo.
Tan·dil (tän-dēl′). City of E Argentina, near Buenos Aires. Pop. 65,876.
Ta·ne·ga·shi·ma (tä-nĕ′gä-shĭ-mä). Island off S Kyushu, Japan.
Tan·ga (tăng′gə). City of NE Tanzania, on the Indian Ocean. Pop. 144,000.
Tan·gan·yi·ka (tăn′gən-yē′kə, tăng′-). **1. Lake.** Lake, c. 12,700 sq mi (32,893 sq km), of E central Africa between Zaire and Tanzania. **2.** Former country of E central Africa that joined with Zanzibar (1964) to form Tanzania. **—Tan′gan·yi′kan** *adj. & n.*
Tan·gier (tăn-jîr′) also **Tan·giers** (-jîrz′). City of N Morocco, on the Strait of Gibraltar. Pop. 187,894.
Tang·shan (däng′shän′). City of NE China, ESE of Beijing. Pop. 650,000.
Ta·nim·bar (tə-nĭm′bär′, tä-). Islands of SE Indonesia, in the S Moluccas.
Ta·nis (tā′nĭs). Ancient city of Egypt, in the E Nile delta.
Tan·jore (tăn-jôr′, -jōr′). Thanjavur.
Tan·ta (tän′tä, -tə). City of N Egypt, in the Nile delta N of Cairo. Pop. 284,636.
Tan·tung (dän′do͝ong′). Dandong.
Tan·za·ni·a (tăn′zə-nē′ə, tăn-ză′-nē-ə). Country of E central Africa, on the Indian Ocean. Cap. Dar es Salaam. Pop. 18,785,000. **—Tan·za′ni·an** *adj. & n.*
Ta·or·mi·na (tä′ôr-mē′nä). Town of E Sicily, Italy, at the foot of Mt. Etna overlooking the Ionian Sea. Pop. 10,104.
Taos (tä′ôs, tous). Resort town of N N.Mex., NNE of Santa Fe. Pop. 3,369.
Ta·pa·chu·la (tä′pä-cho͞o′lä). City of SE Mexico, near the Guatemalan border. Pop. 60,620.

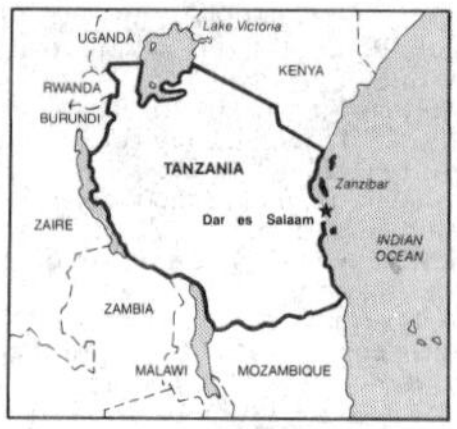

Tanzania

Ta·pa·jós also **Ta·pa·joz** (tä′-pə-zhôsh′). River, c. 600 mi (965 km), of N Brazil.
Tap·pan Zee (tăp′ən zē′). Widening of the Hudson R. in SE N.Y.
Tap·ti (tăp′tē). River, 436 mi (702 km), of W central India.
Ta·qua·ri (tä′kwə-rē′). River, c. 350 mi (563 km), of S central Brazil.
Tar (tär). River, 215 mi (346 km), of NE N.C.
Tar·a (tăr′ə). Village of E Ireland, NW of Dublin; seat of ancient Irish kings.
Ta·ran·to (tä′rän-tō). City of SE Italy, on the **Gulf of Taranto,** an arm of the Ionian Sea. Pop. 247,681.
Ta·ra·wa (tə-rä′wə, tăr′ə-wə, tä′-rä-wä′). Atoll (8 sq mi/21 sq km) of Kiribati, in the N Gilbert Is. of the W Pacific.
Tarbes (tärb). City of SW France, near the Pyrenees WSW of Toulouse. Pop. 54,897.
Ta·ren·tum (tə-rĕn′təm). Taranto.
Ta·rim (dä′rēm′, tä′-). River of NW China, flowing c. 1,300 mi (2,092 km) E to Lop Nur.
Tarn (tärn). River, c. 235 mi (378 km), of S France.
Tar·nów (tär′no͞of′). City of SE Poland, E of Kraków. Pop. 102,800.
Tar·pon Springs (tär′pən). City of W Fla., on the Gulf of Mexico NW of Tampa. Pop. 13,251.
Tar·qui·nia (tär-kwē′nyä). Town of central Italy, WNW of Rome, on site of ancient **Tar·quin·i·i** (-kwĭn′ē-ī).
Tar·ra·go·na (tăr′ə-gō′nə, tär′rä-gô′-nä). City of NE Spain, on the Mediterranean WSW of Barcelona. Pop. 109,969.
Tar·ra·sa (tär-rä′sä). City of NE Spain, NNW of Barcelona. Pop. 160,403.
Tar·ry·town (tăr′ē-toun′). Village of SE N.Y., N of New York City. Pop. 10,648.
Tar·shish (tär′shĭsh). Ancient country on the S coast of Spain.
Tar·sus (tär′səs). City of S Turkey, near the Mediterranean. Pop. 120,271.
Tar·ta·ry (tär′tə-rē) or **Ta·ta·ry** (tä′-). Region of E Europe and Asia controlled by the Tartars in the 13th and 14th cent.
Tar·tu (tär′to͞o). City of NW European USSR, in Estonia SE of Tallinn. Pop. 106,000.
Tash·kent (tăsh-kĕnt′) also **Tash·kend** (-kĕnd′). City of S Central Asian USSR, SW of Lake Balkash. Pop. 1,816,000.
Tas·man (tăz′mən). **1.** Sea of the S Pacific between Australia and New Zealand. **2. Mount.** Mountain, 11,475 ft (3,449.9 m), of the Southern Alps on W central South Is., New Zealand.
Tas·ma·ni·a (tăz-mā′nē-ə). Island state of SE Australia, separated from the mainland by Bass Strait. **—Tas·ma′ni·an** *adj. & n.*
Ta·tar (tä′tər). Strait between Sakhalin and the E Asian mainland.
Ta·ta·ry (tä′tə-rē). Variant of **Tartary.**
Ta·tra (tä′trä, -trə) or **Ta·tras** (-träz, -trəz). Range of the Carpathians along the Czech-Polish border S of Kraków.
Ta·tung (dä′to͝ong′, -do͝ong′). Datong.
Tau·ghan·nock (tə-găn′ək). Falls, 215 ft (65.6 m), of S central N.Y. NW of Ithaca.
Taun·ton (tôn′tən, tän′-, tăn′-). **1.** Borough of SW England, SW of Bristol. Pop. 38,300. **2.** City of SE Mass., N of Fall River. Pop. 45,001.
Tau·nus (tou′nəs, -no͝os). Range of W West Germany, extending NE from the Rhine and N of Mainz.
Tau·po (tou′pō). Lake, 234 sq mi (606 sq km), of central North Is., New Zealand.
Taur·is (tôr′ĭs). Tabriz.
Tau·rus (tôr′əs). Range of S Turkey, extending c. 350 mi (565 km) parallel to the Mediterranean coast.
Tax·co (täs′kô) or **Taxco de A·lar·cón** (dē ä′lär-kôn′). Town of S Mexico, SSW of Mexico City. Pop. 27,089.
Tay (tā). River of central Scotland, rising in the Grampians and flowing c. 118 mi (190 km) E through **Loch Tay** (15 mi/24 km long) to the **Firth of Tay** (25 mi/40.2 km long), an inlet of the North Sea.
Tay·lor (tā′lər). **1.** City of SE Mich., near Dearborn. Pop. 77,568. **2.** City of central Tex., NNE of Austin. Pop. 10,619.
Tay·lor·ville (tā′lər-vĭl′). City of central Ill., SW of Decatur. Pop. 11,386.
Tay·myr (tī-mîr′). Variant of **Taimyr.**
Tbi·li·si (tə-bĭ-lē-sē′, -lē′sē). City of S European USSR, on the Kura R. Pop. 1,080,000.
Tea·neck (tē′nĕk′). Township of NE N.J., ESE of Paterson. Pop. 42,355.
Tea·pot Dome (tē′pŏt dōm′). Former naval oil reserve site in E central Wyo., N of Casper.
Tees (tēz). River, 70 mi (113 km), of NE England.
Te·gu·ci·gal·pa (tə-go͞o′sə-găl′pə, tē-go͞o′sē-gäl′pä). Cap. of Honduras, in the S central part. Pop. 316,800.
Te·hach·a·pi (tə-hăch′ə-pē). Range of S Calif., connecting the Sierra Nevada and the Coast Ranges N of Los Angeles.
Te·he·ran (tĕ′ə-rän′, -răn′, tā′-) or **Teh·ran** (tĕ-rän′). Cap. of Iran, in the N central part. Pop. 4,496,159.
Te·huan·te·pec (tə-wän′tə-pĕk′, tē-wän′tĕ-pĕk′). **1. Isthmus of.** Narrowest part (c. 125 mi/201 km) of S Mexico, between the Gulf of Mexico and the Pacific. **2.** Town of S Mexico, near the **Gulf of Tehuantepec,** a wide inlet of the Pacific. Pop. 16,179.
Te·jo (tĕ′zho͞o). *Portuguese.* Tagus.
Te·jon (tĭ-hōn′). Pass, 4,183 ft (1,275.8 m) high, through the Tehachapi Mts. in SW Calif.
Tel A·viv-Jaf·fa (tĕl′ə-vēv′-jăf′ə, -yä′fə). City of Israel, in the central part on the Mediterranean. Pop. 336,300.
Tel·e·scope Peak (tĕl′ĭ-skōp′). Mountain, c. 11,045 ft (3,368.7 m), in the Panamint Mts. of E Calif.
Te·les Pi·res (tĕ′lĭsh pē′rĭsh). River, c. 600 mi (965 km), of central Brazil.
Te·ma (tē′mə). City of SE Ghana, on the Gulf of Guinea. Pop. 60,767.
Te·meš (tĕ′mĕsh). *Serbian.* Timiş.
Te·mes·vár (tĕ′mesh-vär′). *Hungarian.* Timişoara.
Te·mir·tau (tā′mîr-tou′). City of N Central Asian USSR, NW of Karaganda. Pop. 215,000.
Tem·pe (tĕm′pē′). **1. Vale of.** Valley of N Greece, SE of Mount Olympus. **2.** City of S central Ariz., near Phoenix. Pop. 106,743.
Tem·ple (tĕm′pəl). City of E central Tex., S of Fort Worth. Pop. 42,483.
Temple City. City of S Calif., near Los Angeles. Pop. 28,972.
Temple Ter·race (tĕr′əs). City of W central Fla., near Tampa. Pop. 11,097.
Te·mu·co (tĕ-mo͞o′kô). City of central Chile, S of Concepción. Pop. 138,430.
Ten·a·fly (tĕn′ə-flī′). Borough of NE N.J., near the Hudson R. opposite Yonkers, N.Y. Pop. 13,552.
Ten·er·ife also **Ten·er·iffe** (tĕn′ə-rĭf′, -rēf′, tĕ′nĕ-rē′fĕ). Largest of the Canary Is. of Spain, in the Atlantic.
Ten·gri Khan (tĕng′grē kän′, KHän′, tĕng′rē). Mountain, 22,949 ft (6,999.4 m), in the Tian Shan on the border between S Central Asian USSR and NW China.
Ten·nes·see (tĕn′ĭ-sē′). **1.** River of SE U.S., rising in E Tenn. and flowing c. 652 mi (1,049 km) through N Ala., W Tenn., and W Ky. to the Ohio R. **2.** State of SE U.S. Cap. Nashville. Pop. 4,590,750. **—Ten′nes·se′an** *adj. & n.*
Te·no (tĕ′nô). *Finnish.* Tana R.
Te·noch·ti·tlán (tĕ-nôch′tē-tlän′). Ancient Aztec cap., on the site of present-day Mexico City.
Te·nos (tē′nŏs). Island of Greece, in the N Cyclades SE of Andros.
Ten·sas (tĕn′sô′). River, 250 mi (402 km), of NE La.
Te·o·ti·hua·cán (tĕ′ô-tē′wä-kän′). Ancient city of Mexico, NE of present-day Mexico City.
Te·pic (tĕ-pēk′). City of W Mexico, NW of Guadalajara. Pop. 133,400.
Te·pli·ce (tĕ′plĭ-tsĕ). City of NW Czechoslovakia, in the Erzgebirge near the East German border. Pop. 53,822.
Te·quen·da·ma (tĕ′kĕn-dä′mä). Falls, 482 ft (147 m), in central Colombia.
Ter·cei·ra (tər-sā′rə). Island of Portugal in the central Azores.
Te·rek (tĕ′rĕk). River, c. 370 mi (595 km), of S European USSR.
Te·re·si·na (tĕ′rə-zē′nə). City of NE Brazil, on the Parnaíba R. Pop. 181,071.
Ter·na·te (tər-nä′tā, tĕr-). Island of W Indonesia in the N Moluccas.
Ter·ni (tĕr′nē). City of central Italy, N of Rome. Pop. 113,241.
Ter·no·pol (tər-nō′pəl, tĕr′nə-pôl′). City of W European USSR, in the W Ukraine WSW of Lvov. Pop. 149,000.
Terre·bonne (tĕr-bôn′, -bŭn′). Town of S Que., Canada, N of Montreal. Pop. 11,204.
Ter·re Haute (tĕr′ə hōt′, hŭt′, hôt′). City of W Ind., WSW of Indianapolis. Pop. 61,125.
Ter·rell (tĕr′əl). City of NE Tex., E of Dallas. Pop. 13,225.
Te·ruel (tĕ-rwĕl′). City of E Spain, E of Madrid. Pop. 24,856.
Tes·lin (tĕz′lĭn). Lake, c. 200 sq mi (322 km), of NW B.C. and S Y.T., Canada.
Te·ton (tē′tŏn′, tēt′n). **1.** River, 143 mi (230 km), of NW Mont. **2.** Also **Te·tons** (tē′tŏnz, tēt′nz). Range of the Rockies in NW Wyo. and SE Idaho, S of Yellowstone National Park, rising to 13,747 ft (4,192.8 m).
Te·tuán (tĕ-twän′). City of NE Morocco, on the Mediterranean. Pop. 139,105.
Teu·to·bur·ger Wald (to͞o′tō-bûr′gər wôld, toi′tō-bo͝or′KHər). Range of hills in N central West Germany, between the upper Ems R. and the Weser R.
Te·ve·re (tā′vā-rā). *Italian.* Tiber.
Tewkes·bur·y (to͞oks′bĕr′ē, -bə-rē, tyo͞oks′-). Borough of W central England, on the Severn R.; site of the final defeat (1471) of the Lancastrians in the Wars of the Roses. Pop. 9,210.
Tewks·bur·y (to͞oks′bĕr′ē, -bə-rē, tyo͞oks′-). Town of NE Mass., near Lowell. Pop. 24,635.
Tex·ar·kan·a (tĕk′sär-kăn′ə). **1.** City of SW Ark., on the Tex. border adjacent to Texarkana, Tex. Pop. 21,338. **2.** City of NE Tex. Pop. 31,271.
Tex·as (tĕk′səs). State of S central U.S. Cap. Austin. Pop. 14,228,383. **—Tex′an** *adj. & n.*
Texas City. City of SE Tex., on Galveston Bay. Pop. 41,403.
Tex·el (tĕk′səl, tĕs′əl). Island of NW Netherlands, in the North Sea in the SW Frisian Is.
Tha·ban·tsho·nya·na (tä′bän-chōn-yä′nä). Highest (11,425 ft/3,484.6 m) of the Drakensberg Mts., in Lesotho, S Africa.
Thai·land (tī′lănd′, -lənd). Country of SE Asia, on the Gulf of Siam between Burma and Cambodia. Cap. Bangkok. Pop. 47,845,000. **—Thai** *adj. & n.*
Thames (tĕmz). **1.** River, c. 160 mi (257 km), of SE S Ont., Canada. **2.** River of S England, flowing c. 210 mi (338 km) E to a wide estuary on the North Sea.
Than·et (thăn′ĭt), **Isle of.** Peninsula of SE England, on the North Sea, separated from the mainland by arms of the Stour R.

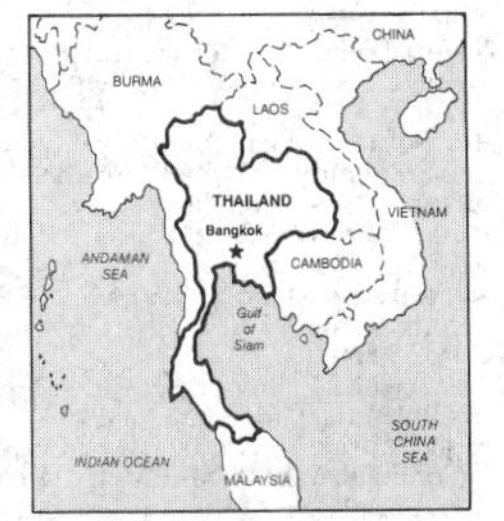

Thailand

Than·ja·vur (tăn′jä-vûr′). City of SE India, on the Cauvery R. delta. Pop. 140,547.
Thap·sus (thăp′səs). Ancient city of N Africa, on the Mediterranean SE of Carthage in present-day Tunisia.
Thar (tär). Desert of NW India and E Pakistan.
Tha·sos (thā′sŏs, thä′sôs). Island of NE Greece, in the N Aegean E of Chalcidice.
Thebes (thēbz). **1.** Also **The·bae** (thē′bē). Ancient cap. of Upper Egypt, on the Nile in present-day central Egypt. **2.** Ancient city of Boeotia, in E central Greece NW of Athens.
The Col·o·ny (*thə* kŏl′ə-nē). City of NE Tex., near Dallas-Fort Worth. Pop. 11,586.
The Dalles (dălz). City of N Ore., on the Columbia E of Portland. Pop. 10,820.
The·lon (thē′lŏn′). River, c. 550 mi (885 km), of S central N.W.T., Canada.
The·ra (thîr′ə). Santorin.
Ther·mop·y·lae (thər-mŏp′ə-lē). Pass of E central Greece, SE of Lamia; site of Spartan stand against Persians (480 B.C.).
Thes·sa·lo·ni·ki (thĕs′ä-lô-nē′kē) or **Thes·sa·lo·ni·ca** (-ə-lō′nī-kə, -lŏn′ĭ-). Salonika.
Thes·sa·ly (thĕs′ə-lē). Region of E central Greece between the Pindus Mts. and the Aegean. —**Thes·sa′lian, Thes′sa·lo′ni·an** *adj. & n.*
Thet·ford Mines (thĕt′fərd mīnz′). City of S Que., Canada, NE of Sherbrooke and S of Quebec city. Pop. 20,784.
The Vil·lage (vĭl′ĭj). City of central Okla., near Oklahoma City. Pop. 11,049.
Thi·bo·daux (tĭb′ō-dō′). City of SE La., WSW of New Orleans. Pop. 15,810.
Thim·bu (thĭm′bo͞o′) also **Thim·phu** (-po͞o′). Cap. of Bhutan, in the W part in the E Himalayas. Pop. 8,982.
Thí·ra (thîr′ə). Santorin.
Tho·hoy·an·dou (tō-hoi′ăn-do͞o′). Cap. of Venda, black enclave in NE South Africa.
Thom·as·ton (tŏm′ə-stən). Town of W central Ga., W of Macon. Pop. 18,200.
Thom·as·ville (tŏm′əs-vĭl′, -vəl). **1.** City of S Ga., NNE of Tallahassee, Fla. Pop. 18,463. **2.** City of central N.C., SE of Winston-Salem. Pop. 14,144.
Thomp·son (tŏm′sən). **1.** River, c. 304 mi (489 km), of S B.C., Canada. **2.** City of N central Man., Canada. Pop. 17,291.
Thorn (tôrn). *German.* Toruń.
Thorn·ton (thôrn′tən). City of N central Colo., N of Denver. Pop. 40,343.
Tho·rold (thôr′əld, thär′-, thûr′-). City of SE Ont., on the Welland Ship Canal SE of St. Catherines. Pop. 15,173.
Thou·sand Islands (thou′zənd). Group of more than 1,500 islands of N N.Y. and SE Ont., Canada, in the St. Lawrence at the outlet of Lake Ontario.
Thousand Oaks (ōks). City of S Calif., W of Los Angeles. Pop. 77,797.
Thrace (thrās). Region and ancient country of SE Balkan Peninsula, N of the Aegean and in ancient times extending as far N as the Danube. —**Thra′cian** *adj. & n.*
Thra·cia (thrā′shə, -shē-ə). Ancient Thrace.
Thu·le (to͞o′lē, thyo͞o′-). Town and U.S. military base of NW Greenland, NW of Cape York. Pop. 357.
Thun (to͞on), **Lake of.** Lake, c. 18 sq mi (47 sq km), in central Switzerland SE of Bern.
Thun·der Bay (thŭn′dər). City of SW Ont., Canada, on **Thunder Bay,** inlet on the NW shore of Lake Superior. Pop. 112,053.
Thu·ner·see (to͞o′nər-zā′). *German.* Thun.
Thu·rin·gi·a (tho͝o-rĭn′jē-ə, -jə). Region of SW East Germany. —**Thu·rin′gi·an** *adj. & n.*
Thur·rock (thûr′ək, thŭr′-). Urban district of SE England, on the Thames E of London. Pop. 127,100.
Thurs·day (thûrz′dē, -dā′). Island of NE Australia, in Torres Strait NW of Cape York.
Thurs·ton (thûr′stən). Island off W Antarctica.
Ti·a·hua·na·co (tē′ə-wə-nä′kō). Site of pre-Incan ruins in W Bolivia, S of Lake Titicaca.
Tian·jin (tyän′jĭn′). City of NE China, near the Gulf of Bo Hai SE of Beijing. Pop. 4,500,000.
Tian Shan (tyän′ shän′). Mountains of central Asia, extending c. 1,500 mi (2,414 km) ENE through S Central Asian USSR and NW China.
Ti·ber (tī′bər). River of central Italy, flowing c. 251 mi (404 km) S and SW through Rome to the Tyrrhenian Sea.
Ti·be·ri·as (tī-bîr′ē-əs). **1. Lake.** Sea of Galilee. **2.** Town of NE Israel, on the Sea of Galilee. Pop. 28,300.
Ti·bes·ti Mas·sif (tĭ-bĕs′tē mă-sēf′). Mountains of N Chad, in the Sahara, rising to 11,204 ft (3,417.2 m).
Ti·bet (tĭ-bĕt′). Region and former semi-independent theocratic state of SW China. —**Ti·bet′an** *adj. & n.*
Ti·bur (tī′bər). Tivoli.
Ti·bu·ron (tē′bo͞o-rôn′). Island of NW Mexico, in the Gulf of California.
Ti·ci·no (tē-chē′nō). River, 154 mi (248 km), of S Switzerland and N Italy.
Ti·con·der·o·ga (tī-kŏn′də-rō′gə, tī′kŏn-). Resort village of NE N.Y., N of Lake George. Pop. 2,938.
Tien Shan (tyĕn′ shän′). Tian Shan.
Tien·tsin (tĭn′tsĭn, tyĕn′-, tyĕn′jĭn′). Tianjin.
Ti·er·ra del Fue·go (tē-ĕr′ə dĕl fo͞o-ā′gō, fyo͞o-, tyĕ′rä dĕl fwĕ′gō). **1.** Archipelago off S South America, separated from the mainland by the Strait of Magellan. **2.** Main island of this archipelago, divided between Chile and Argentina.
Tie·tê (tyə-tā′). River, c. 500 mi (805 km), of S Brazil.
Tif·fin (tĭf′ĭn). City of N central Ohio, SSW of Toledo. Pop. 19,549.
Tif·lis (tĭf′lĭs, tĭf-lēs′). Tbilisi.
Tif·ton (tĭf′tən). City of S central Ga., ESE of Albany. Pop. 13,749.
Ti·gard (tī′gərd). City of NW Ore., near Portland. Pop. 14,286.
Ti·gre (tē′grē). City of E Argentina, near Buenos Aires. Pop. 152,335.
Ti·gris (tī′grĭs). River of SW Asia, rising in E Turkey and flowing c. 1,150 mi (1,850 km) SE through Iraq to the Euphrates R.
Ti·jua·na (tē′ə-wä′nə, tē-wä′-, -hwä′-nä). City of extreme NW Mexico, on the U.S. border. Pop. 535,000.
Ti·kal (tē-käl′). Ruined Mayan city of N Guatemala.
Til·burg (tĭl′bûrg′, -bœrKH′). City of S Netherlands, near the Belgian border. Pop. 151,799.
Til·la·mook Bay (tĭl′ə-mo͝ok′). Inlet of the Pacific off NW Ore.
Ti·ma·ga·mi (tə-mä′gə-mē). Lake, 91 sq mi (236 sq km), of S central Ont., Canada, NE of Sudbury.
Tim·buk·tu also **Tim·buc·too** (tĭm′-bŭk-to͞o′, tĭm-bŭk′to͞o). City of central Mali, near the Niger R. Pop. 11,900.
Tim·gad (tĭm′găd′). Ancient Roman city in NE Algeria.
Ti·miş (tē′mēsh, -mĭsh). River, c. 270 mi (434 km), of W Rumania and N Yugoslavia.
Ti·mi·şoa·ra (tē′mē-shwä′rä). City of W Rumania, near the Yugoslavian border. Pop. 277,779.
Tim·mins (tĭm′ĭnz). City of central Ont., Canada, NE of Sault St. Marie. Pop. 44,251.
Ti·mor (tē′môr, tē-môr′). **1.** Sea of the Indian Ocean between Timor and Australia. **2.** Island of SE Indonesia, easternmost of the Lesser Sundas.
Tim·pa·no·gos (tĭm′pə-nō′gəs), **Mount.** Highest (12,008 ft/3,662.4 m) of the Wasatch Mts., in N central Utah.
Ti·ni·an (tĭn′ē-ăn′, tē-nē-än′). Island of W Pacific in the S Marianas, in the U.S. Trust Territory of the Pacific Is.
Tin·ley Park (tĭn′lē). Village of NE Ill., near Chicago. Pop. 26,171.
Tí·nos (tē′nôs). *Greek.* Tenos.
Tin·tag·el Head (tĭn-tăj′əl hĕd′). Promontory in SW England, in NE Cornwall.
Tip·pe·ca·noe (tĭp′ē-kə-no͞o′). River, c. 170 mi (274 km), of N Ind.
Tip·per·ar·y (tĭp′ə-râr′ē). Region and town of S central Ireland. Pop. 4,929.
Ti·ran (tē-rän′). Strait off the S tip of the Sinai Peninsula, NE Egypt, connecting the Red Sea with the Gulf of Aqaba.
Ti·ra·në also **Ti·ra·na** (tē-rä′nə). Cap. of Albania, in the central part. Pop. 192,300.
Ti·ras·pol (tē-räs′pəl). City of SW European USSR, on the Dniester R. NW of Odessa. Pop. 142,000.
Tîr·gu-Mu·reş (tîr′go͞o-mo͞o′rĕsh′). City of N central Rumania, ESE of Cluj. Pop. 136,679.
Ti·rich Mir (tē′rĭch mîr′). Highest elevation (25,263 ft/7,705.2 m) of the Hindu Kush, in N Pakistan.
Ti·rol (tĭ-rōl′, tī′rōl′, tîr′ōl′, -ōl). Variant of **Tyrol.**
Ti·ruch·chi·rap·pal·li (tĭ-ro͝och′-ĭ-răp′ə-lē, tĭr′o͝o-chĭ-rə-pŭl′ē). City of SE India, on the Cauvery R. Pop. 307,400.
Ti·ryns (tī′rĭnz, tĭr′ĭnz). Ancient city of S Greece, in E Peloponnesus.
Ti·sza (tē′sô) also **Ti·sa** (tē′sä, -sə). River of central Europe, rising in the Carpathians in W Ukraine and flowing c. 600 mi (965 km) W and S across E Hungary and N Yugoslavia to the Danube.
Ti·ti·ca·ca (tē′tē-kä′kä). Largest freshwater lake (c. 3,200 sq mi/8,288 sq km) in South America, in the Andes on the Bolivia-Peru border.
Ti·to·grad (tē′tō-grăd′). City of S Yugoslavia, near the Albanian border. Pop. 54,509.
Ti·tus·ville (tī′təs-vĭl′, -vəl). City of E Fla., E of Orlando. Pop. 31,910.
Tiv·er·ton (tĭv′ər-tən). Town of E R.I., near the Mass. border SE of Providence. Pop. 13,526.
Ti·vo·li (tĭv′ə-lē, tē′vō-lē). City of central Italy, ENE of Rome. Pop. 46,201.
Ti·zi Ou·zou (tē′zē o͞o-zo͞o′). City of N Algeria, E of Algiers. Pop. 108,000.
Tjir·e·bon (chîr′ə-bôn′). City of N Java, Indonesia, on the Java Sea. Pop. 178,529.
Tlal·ne·pan·tla (tläl′nē-pän′tlä). City of S central Mexico, near Mexico City. Pop. 45,575.
Tla·que·pa·que (tlä′kē-pä′kē). City of W central Mexico, near Guadalajara. Pop. 59,760.
Tlem·cen also **Tlem·sen** (tlĕm-sĕn′). City of NW Algeria, near the Moroccan border. Pop. 115,054.
To·ba (tō′bä). Lake, 448 sq mi (1,160 sq km), of N Sumatra, Indonesia.
To·ba·go (tə-bā′gō). Island of Trinidad and Tobago in the SE West Indies, NE of Trinidad.
To·bol (tə-bôl′). River of NE Central Asian USSR, flowing c. 1,050 mi (1,689 km) NE to the Irtish R.
To·bruk (tō′bro͝ok, tō-bro͝ok′). City of NE Libya, on the Mediterranean. Pop. 15,900.
To·can·tins (to͞o-kən-tēNs′). River of central and N Brazil, flowing 1,640 mi (2,639 km) N to the Pará R. SW of Belém.
To·gli·at·ti also **Tol·yat·ti** (tôl-yä′tē). City of E central European USSR, on the Volga NW of Kuibyshev. Pop. 517,000.
To·go (tō′gō). Country of W Africa, on the Gulf of Guinea. Cap. Lomé. Pop. 2,565,000.

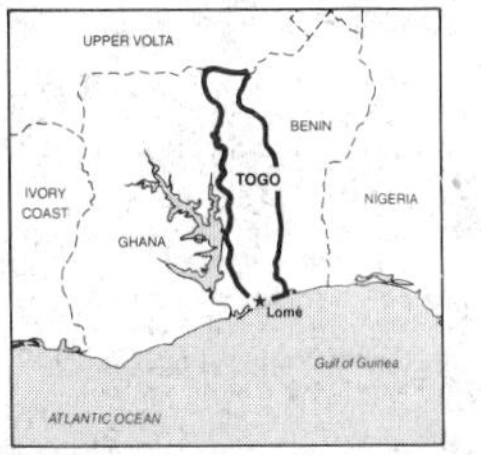

Togo

To·ho·pe·kal·i·ga (tə-hō′pĭ-kăl′ĭ-gə, tə-hŏp′kə-lī′gə). Lake of central Fla., S of Orlando.
To·ka·ra (tō-kä′rä). Islands of Japan in the N Ryukyu group, S of Kyushu.
To·ke·lau (tō′kə-lou′, tô-kĕ-lou′). Islands of New Zealand in the central Pacific N of Samoa.
To·ko·ro·za·wa (tô-kô′rô′zä-wä). City of central Honshu, Japan, near Tokyo. Pop. 236,477.
To·ku·shi·ma (tô-ko͞o′shĭ′mä). City of E Shikoku, Japan, on the Inland Sea. Pop. 249,343.
To·ky·o (tō′kē-ō′). Cap. of Japan, in E central Honshu on **Tokyo Bay,** a 50 mi (80 km) inlet of the Pacific. Pop. 8,349,209.
Tol·bu·khin (tôl-bo͞o′KHĭn). City of NE Bulgaria, N of Varna. Pop. 94,132.
To·le·do (tə-lē′dō). **1.** (*also* tô-lĕ′*th*ô). City of central Spain, near the Tagus R. SSW of Madrid. Pop. 56,414. **2.** City of NW Ohio, on Lake Erie. Pop. 354,635.
To·li·ma (tô-lē′mä). Volcanic mountain, 18,438 ft (5,623.6 m), in W central Colombia.
To·lu·ca (tô-lo͞o′kä). City of S central Mexico, W of Mexico City. Pop. 222,900.
Tol·yat·ti (tôl-yä′tē). Variant of **Togliatti.**
Tom (tŏm, tôm). River, c. 525 mi (845 km), of S Siberian USSR.
To·ma·ko·mai (tô-mä′kô′mī). City of S Hokkaido, Japan, on the Pacific. Pop. 146,088.
To·ma·szów Ma·zo·wiec·ki (tô-mä′shŏof mä-zô-vyĕts′kē). City of E central Poland, SE of Łódź. Pop. 62,800.
Tom·big·bee (tŏm-bĭg′bē). River, c. 400 mi (645 km), of NE Miss. and W Ala.
Tomsk (tŏmsk, tômsk). City of SW Siberian USSR, NE of Novosibirsk. Pop. 431,000.
Ton·a·wan·da (tŏn′ə-wŏn′də). City of W N.Y., near Buffalo. Pop. 18,693.
Ton·bridge (tŭn′brĭj). Urban district of SE England, SE of London. Pop. 31,140.
Ton·ga (tŏng′gə). Island nation of the SW Pacific, E of Fiji. Cap. Nukualofa. Pop. 97,000.
Ton·ga·re·va (tŏng′ə-rē′və, -gə-). Island of the central Pacific in the N Cook Is.
Tong·hua (to͝ong′ hwä′). City of NE China, in Manchuria E of Shenyang. Pop. 175,000.
Tongue (tŭng). River, 246 mi (396 km), of N Wyo. and SE Mont.
Ton·kin (tŏn′kĭn′, tŏng′-). **1. Gulf of.** NW arm of the South China Sea, between N Vietnam and Hainan Is., S China. **2.** Region of N Vietnam.
Ton·le Sap (tŏn′lā′ săp′, säp′). Lake, c. 1,100–3,600 sq mi (2,850–9,325 sq km), of central Cambodia.
Too·el·e (to͞o-ĕl′ē). City of NW Utah, SW of Salt Lake City. Pop. 14,335.
To·pe·ka (tə-pē′kə). Cap. of Kans., in the NE part W of Kansas City. Pop. 115,266.
Tor·bay (tôr′bā′). Borough of SW England, on Lyme Bay. Pop. 108,700.
Tor·cel·lo (tôr-chĕl′lō). Island of NE Italy, in the Lagoon of Venice NE of Venice.
To·ri·no (tō-rē′nō). *Italian.* Turin.
Tor·ne (tôr′nə). River of N Sweden,

rising near the Norwegian border in **Lake Torne** (124 sq mi/321 sq km) and flowing c. 250 mi (402 km) SE to the Gulf of Bothnia, forming the Swedish-Finnish border in its lower course.

Tor·ni·o (tôr′nē-ō). *Finnish.* Torne.

To·ron·to (tə-rŏn′tō). Cap. of Ont., Canada, in the S part on Lake Ontario. Pop. 635,685.

Tor·rance (tôr′əns, tŏr′-). City of S Calif., S of Los Angeles. Pop. 131,497.

Tor·re An·nun·zi·a·ta (tôr′rä ä-nōōn-tsyä′tä). City of S Italy, on the Bay of Naples. Pop. 57,659.

Torre del Gre·co (dĕl grĕ′kō). City of S Italy, on the Bay of Naples. Pop. 101,905.

Tor·rens (tôr′ənz, tŏr′-). Lake, 2,230 sq mi (5,775.7 sq km), of S central Australia.

Tor·re·ón (tôr′rē-ôn′). City of N Mexico, W of Monterrey. Pop. 268,700.

Tor·res (tôr′ĭs, tŏr′-). Strait, c. 95 mi (153 km) wide, between New Guinea and Cape York Peninsula of NE Australia.

Tor·ring·ton (tôr′ĭng-tən, tŏr′-). City of NW Conn., W of Hartford. Pop. 30,987.

Tor·to·la (tôr-tō′lə). Island of the West Indies, in the British Virgin Is.

Tor·tu·ga (tôr-tōō′gə). Island in the West Indies, off N Haiti.

To·ruń (tô′rōōn′yə). City of N central Poland, on the Vistula R. Pop. 170,100.

To·to·wa (tō′tə-wə, -wä′, -wô′). Borough of NE N.J., near Paterson. Pop. 11,448.

Tot·to·ri (tôt-tô′rē). City of SW Honshu, Japan, on the Sea of Japan. Pop. 128,789.

Toub·kal (tōōb-käl′). Jebel Toubkal.

Tou·lon (tōō-lôN′). City of SE France, on the Mediterranean ESE of Marseille. Pop. 181,801.

Tou·louse (tōō-lōōz′). City of S France, on the Garonne SE of Bordeaux. Pop. 373,796.

Tou·raine (tōō-rĕn′). Region and former province of W central France.

Tour·coing (tōōr-kwăN′). City of N France, near Lille and the Belgian border. Pop. 102,239.

Tour·nai also **Tour·nay** (tōōr-nā′, tōōr-). City of SW Belgium, on the Scheldt R. Pop. 46,700.

Tours (tōōr, tōōr). City of W central France, on the Loire. Pop. 140,686.

Towns·ville (tounz′vĭl′, -vəl). City of NE Australia, on the Coral Sea. Pop. 84,900.

Tow·son (tou′sən). City of N Md., near Baltimore. Pop. 83,600.

To·ya·ma (tô-yä′mä). City of W central Honshu, Japan, on **Toyama Bay**, an inlet of the Sea of Japan. Pop. 305,054.

To·yo·ha·shi (tô-yô′hä-shē). City of S central Honshu, Japan, on the Pacific SE of Nagoya. Pop. 304,274.

To·yo·na·ka (tô-yô′nä-kä). City of S Honshu, Japan, near Osaka. Pop. 403,185.

To·yo·ta (toi-ō′tə, tô-yô′tä). City of S central Honshu, Japan, near Nagoya. Pop. 281,609.

Trab·zon (träb-zôn′). **1.** *Turkish.* Trebizond. **2.** City of NE Turkey, on the Black Sea. Pop. 107,412.

Tra·cy (trā′sē). **1.** Town of S Que., Canada, NE of Montreal. Pop. 12,284. **2.** City of W central Calif., SSW of Stockton. Pop. 18,428.

Tra·fal·gar (trə-făl′gər, trä′fäl-gär′). Cape on the SW coast of Spain, NW of the Strait of Gibraltar.

Tra·lee (trə-lē′). Urban district of SW Ireland, at the head of **Tralee Bay**, an inlet of the Atlantic. Pop. 15,011.

Trans A·lai (trăns′ ä-lī′, trănz′). Range of the Pamirs in S Central Asian USSR.

Trans·al·pine Gaul (trăns-ăl′pīn′ gôl′, trănz-). Part of ancient Gaul NW of the Alps, including modern France and Belgium.

Trans·cau·ca·sia (trăns′kô-kā′zhə, -shə, trănz′-). Region of S European USSR, between the Caucasus Mts. and the borders of Turkey and Iran. —**Trans′cau·ca′sian** *adj. & n.*

Trans·kei (trăns-kā′, -kī′). Independent black African homeland in SE South Africa, on the Indian Ocean coast. Cap. Umtata. Pop. 2,500,000. —**Trans·kei′an** *adj. & n.*

Trans·vaal (trăns-väl′, trănz-). Region and province of NE South Africa.

Tran·syl·va·ni·a (trăn′sĭl-vā′nē-ə, -vān′yə). Region of W Rumania. —**Tran′syl·va′ni·an** *adj. & n.*

Transylvanian Alps. S branch of the Carpathian Mts., extending across central Rumania.

Tra·pa·ni (trä′pä-nē). City of NW Sicily, Italy, on the Mediterranean. Pop. 62,400.

Tra·si·me·no (trä′zē-mĕ′nō). Lake, 50 sq mi (130 sq km), in central Italy W of Perugia.

Trav·erse (trăv′ərs). Lake on border between NE S.Dak. and W Minn.

Traverse City. City of N Mich., NNW of Cadillac. Pop. 15,516.

Treb·i·zond (trĕb′ĭ-zŏnd′). Byzantine Greek empire (1204–1461) on the S, E, and N coasts of the Black Sea.

Trent (trĕnt). **1.** River, c. 150 mi (241 km), of SE Ont., Canada. **2.** River, c. 170 mi (275 km), of central England. **3.** Canal system, 240 mi (386.2 km) long, of SE Ont., Canada, connecting Lake Ontario with Georgian Bay. **4.** Also **Tren·to** (trĕn′tō). City of N Italy, NW of Venice. Pop. 99,052.

Tren·ton (trĕn′tən). **1.** Town of SE Ont., Canada, on an inlet of NE Lake Ontario. Pop. 14,848. **2.** City of SE Mich., near Detroit. Pop. 22,762. **3.** Cap. of N.J., in the W central part on the Delaware R. Pop. 92,124.

Trent-Sev·ern (sĕv′ərn). Trent Canal.

Trèves (trĕv). *French.* Trier.

Tre·vi·so (trā-vē′zō). City of NE Italy, N of Venice. Pop. 89,121.

Trier (trîr). City of W West Germany, on the Mosel R. near the Luxembourg border. Pop. 95,736.

Tri·este (trē-ĕst′, trē-ĕs′tä). City of extreme NE Italy, on the **Gulf of Trieste**, an inlet of the Gulf of Venice. Pop. 260,291.

Tri·glav (trē′gläv′). Peak, 9,392 ft (2,862.6 m), in the Julian Alps in NW Yugoslavia.

Tri·ko·ra Peak (trē-kô′rä). Mountain, 15,518 ft (4,733 m), of E West Irian, Indonesia.

Tri·na·cri·a (trī-năk′rē-ə, -nā′krē-ə, trĭ-). Sicily.

Trin·i·dad (trĭn′ĭ-dăd′). Island, 1,864 sq mi (4,828 sq km), of Trinidad and Tobago, in the Atlantic off NE Venezuela. —**Trin′i·dad′i·an** *adj. & n.*

Trinidad and To·ba·go (tə-bā′gō). Country of SE West Indies, consisting of the islands of Trinidad and Tobago. Cap. Port of Spain. Pop. 920,000.

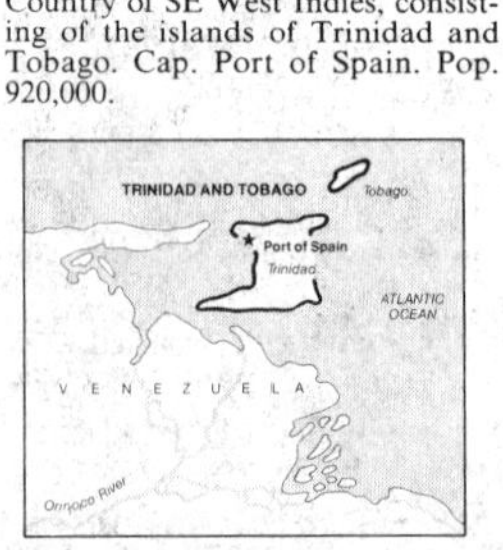

Trinidad and Tobago

Trin·i·ty (trĭn′ĭ-tē). River, c. 360 mi (579 km), of E Tex.

Trip·o·li (trĭp′ə-lē). **1.** City of NW Lebanon, on the Mediterranean. Pop. 175,000. **2.** Cap. of Libya, in the NW on the Mediterranean. Pop. 551,477.

Trip·o·lis (trĭp′ə-lĭs). **1.** Tripolitania. **2.** Tripoli, Lebanon.

Trip·o·li·ta·ni·a (trĭp′ə-lĭ-tā′nē-ə, -nyə). Ancient Phoenician colony in present-day NW Libya.

Tris·tan da Cun·ha (trĭs′tən də kōōn′yə, kōō′nə, trĭs′tăn). **1.** Islands of the S Atlantic, between S Africa and S South America; administered by Great Britain as part of St. Helena. **2.** Chief island of this group.

Tri·van·drum (trĭ-văn′drəm). City of SW India, on the Arabian Sea. Pop. 409,627.

Tro·as (trō′ăs′). Ancient region of NW Asia Minor surrounding Troy.

Tro·bri·and (trō′brē-änd′, -ănd′). Islands of Papua New Guinea, in the Solomon Sea off E New Guinea.

Trois-Ri·vières (trwä-rē-vyĕr′). City of S Que., Canada, at the confluence of the St. Lawrence and St. Maurice rivers. Pop. 52,518.

Trois-Ri·vières-Ouest (trwä-rē-vyĕr-wĕst′). Town of S Que., Canada, near Trois-Rivières. Pop. 10,564.

Troll·hät·tan (trôl′hĕt′än). City of SW Sweden, SW of Lake Vänern. Pop. 49,846.

Trom·be·tas (trôN-bĕ′təsh). River, c. 470 mi (756 km), of N Brazil.

Trom·sø (trŏm′sō′, trōōms′œ). City of N Norway, on an offshore island in the Arctic Ocean. Pop. 45,360.

Trond·heim (trŏn′hăm′, trŏn′-). City of central Norway, on **Trondheim Fjord**, an 80 mi (129 km) inlet of the Norwegian Sea. Pop. 134,683.

Tro·o·dos Mountain (trō′ō-*th*ôs). Highest elevation (6,400 ft/1,952 m) on Cyprus, in the central part.

Trou·ville (trōō-vēl′) or **Trouville-sur-Mer** (-sür-mĕr′). Town of N France, on the English Channel. Pop. 6,618.

Troy (troi). **1.** Ancient city of NW Asia Minor, near the Dardanelles; site of the Trojan War. **2.** City of SE Ala., SE of Montgomery. Pop. 12,587. **3.** City of SE Mich., near Detroit. Pop. 67,102. **4.** City of E N.Y., on the Hudson near Albany. Pop. 56,638. **5.** City of W Ohio, N of Dayton. Pop. 19,086.

Troyes (trwä). City of N France, on the Seine ESE of Paris. Pop. 72,167.

Tru·chas Peaks (trōō′chəs). 3 peaks (highest, 13,110 ft/3,998.6 m) in N N.Mex., N of Santa Fe.

Tru·cial O·man (trōō′shəl ō-män′, ō-măn′). United Arab Emirates.

Truck·ee (trŭk′ē). River, c. 120 mi (193 km), of E Calif. and W Nev.

Tru·ji·llo (trōō-hē′yô). City of NW Peru, NW of Lima. Pop. 127,535.

Trujillo Al·to (äl′tô). Town of NE Puerto Rico, SE of San Juan. Pop. 41,097.

Truk (trŭk, trōōk). Islands of the U.S. Trust Territory of the Pacific Is., in the central Carolines.

Trum·bull (trŭm′bəl). Town of SW Conn., N of Bridgeport. Pop. 32,989.

Tru·ro (trōōr′ō). Town of central N.S., Canada, NNE of Halifax. Pop. 12,840.

Tsa·na (tsä′nä). Variant of **Tana** (sense 1).

Tsang·po (tsäng′pô). The upper Brahmaputra R., in S Tibet, China.

Tsa·ri·tsyn (tsä-rē′tsĭn). Volgograd.

Tse·lin·o·grad (tsĕ′lĭn-nə-grät). City of E Central Asian USSR, WSW of Novosibirsk. Pop. 237,000.

Tsiao·tso (jyou′jō′). Jiaozuo.

Tsi·nan (jē′nän′). Jinan.

Tsing·hai (chĭng′hī′). Qinghai.

Tsing·tao (chĭng′dou′). Qingdao.

Tsi·tsi·har (chē′chē′här′, tsē′tsē′-). Qiqihar.

Tsu (tsōō). City of S Honshu, Japan, on Ise Bay. Pop. 144,587.

Tsu·ga·ru (tsōō-gä′rōō). Strait between Honshu and Hokkaido, N Japan.

Tsun·yi (dzōōn′yē′). Zunyi.

Tsu·shi·ma (tsōō′shĭ-mä′). Islands of SW Japan in Korea Strait, between Kyushu and SE South Korea, separated from Kyushu by **Tsushima Strait**.

Tu·a·mo·tu (tōō′ə-mō′tōō). Archipelago of French Polynesia, in the S Pacific E of Tahiti.

Tü·bing·en (tü′bĭng-ən). City of SW West Germany, on the Neckar SSW of Stuttgart. Pop. 72,167.

Tu·buai (tōō′bōō-ī′, tōōb-wä′ē′). Islands of S French Polynesia, in the S Pacific S of Tahiti.

Tuc·son (tōō′sŏn′). City of SE Ariz., SSE of Phoenix. Pop. 330,537.

Tu·cu·mán (tōō′kōō-män′). City of NW Argentina, NNW of Cordoba. Pop. 375,000.

Tu·ge·la (tōō-gā′lə). River, c. 300 mi (483 km), of E South Africa.

Tu·la (tōō′lə). City of central European USSR, S of Moscow. Pop. 518,000.

Tu·la·gi (tōō-lä′gē). Island of S central Solomon Is., in the W Pacific.

Tu·lare (tōō-lâr′ē, -lâr′). City of S central Calif., SE of Fresno. Pop. 22,475.

Tul·la·ho·ma (tŭl′ə-hō′mə). City of S central Tenn., NW of Chattanooga. Pop. 15,800.

Tul·sa (tŭl′sə). City of NE Okla., NE of Oklahoma City. Pop. 360,919.

Tu·ma·co (tōō-mä′kô). City of SW Colombia, on the Pacific. Metro. area pop. 87,448.

Tu·men (tōō′mŭn′). River of NE North Korea, flowing c. 324 mi (521 km) NE and SE along the Korea-China and Korea-USSR borders to the Sea of Japan.

Tung·hwa (tōōng′hwä′). Tonghua.

Tun·gus·ka (tōōn-gōōs′kä, tōōng-). Any of three rivers of Siberian USSR: **Upper Tunguska**, the lower course of the Angara; **Lower Tunguska**, flowing c. 2,000 mi (3,218 km) N and W to the Yenisei; and **Stony Tunguska**, flowing c. 1,000 mi (1,609 km) WNW to the Yenisei.

Tu·nis (tōō′nĭs, tyōō′-). **1.** Former Barbary state on the N coast of Africa. **2.** Cap. of Tunisia, in the N part on the Mediterranean. Pop. 550,404.

Tu·ni·sia (tōō-nē′zhə, -shə, -nĭzh′ə, -nĭsh′ə, tyōō-). Country of N Africa, on the Mediterranean. Cap. Tunis. Pop. 6,410,000. —**Tu·ni′sian** *adj. & n.*

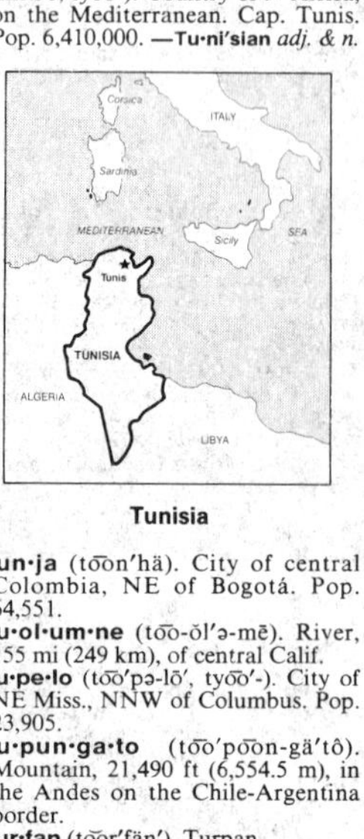

Tunisia

Tun·ja (tōōn′hä). City of central Colombia, NE of Bogotá. Pop. 64,551.

Tu·ol·um·ne (tōō-ŏl′ə-mē). River, 155 mi (249 km), of central Calif.

Tu·pe·lo (tōō′pə-lō′, tyōō′-). City of NE Miss., NNW of Columbus. Pop. 23,905.

Tu·pun·ga·to (tōō′pōōn-gä′tô). Mountain, 21,490 ft (6,554.5 m), in the Andes on the Chile-Argentina border.

Tur·fan (tōōr′fän′). Turpan.

Tu·rin (tōōr′ĭn, tyōō′-, tōōr′ĭn, tyōōr′-). City of NW Italy, on the Po WSW of Milan. Pop. 1,160,686.

Tur·ka·na (tər-kăn′ə), **Lake.** Lake Rudolf.

Tur·key (tûr′kē). Country of SW Asia and SE Europe, between the Mediterranean and Black seas. Cap. Ankara. Pop. 45,955,000. —**Tur′kish** (tûr′kĭsh) *adj. & n.*

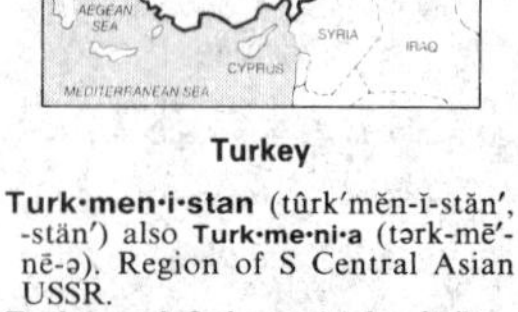

Turkey

Turk·men·i·stan (tûrk′mĕn-ĭ-stăn′, -stän′) also **Turk·me·ni·a** (tərk-mē′nē-ə). Region of S Central Asian USSR.

Turks and Cai·cos (tûrks; kā′kəs, kī′kōs). Island groups of the British West Indies, in the Atlantic SE of the Bahamas; a British colony.

Tur·ku (to͝or'ko͞o'). City of SW Finland, on the Baltic. Pop. 164,586.
Tur·lock (tûr'lŏk'). City of central Calif., SE of Modesto. Pop. 26,291.
Turn·hout (tûrn'hout). City of N Belgium, near the Dutch border. Pop. 37,652.
Tur·pan (to͞or'pän'). Depression (lowest point, 505 ft/154 m below sea level) of NW China, at the E end of the Tian Shan.
Tur·qui·no (to͞or-kē'nô). Peak, 6,560 ft (2,000.8 m), in the Sierra Maestra of SE Cuba.
Tus·ca·loo·sa (tŭs'kə-lo͞o'sə). City of W central Ala., SW of Birmingham. Pop. 75,143.
Tus·ca·ny (tŭs'kə-nē'). Region of NW Italy between the N Apennines and the Ligurian and Tyrrhenian seas. —**Tus'can** *adj. & n.*
Tus·cu·lum (tŭs'kyə-ləm). City of ancient Latium, SE of modern Rome, Italy.
Tus·ke·gee (tŭs-kē'gē). City of E Ala., E of Montgomery. Pop. 12,716.
Tus·tin (tŭs'tĭn). City of S Calif., near Santa Ana. Pop. 32,073.
Tu·tu·i·la (to͞o'to͞o-ē'lä). Largest island of American Samoa, in the S Pacific.
Tu·va·lu (to͞o-väl'o͞o, -vär'-). Island nation of the W Pacific, N of Fiji. Cap. Funafuti. Pop. 7,500.
Tux·pan (to͞os'pän). City of E central Mexico, on the Gulf of Mexico NE of Mexico City. Pop. 33,901.
Tux·tla Gu·tiér·rez (to͞os'tlä go͞o-tyĕr'rĕs). City of SE Mexico, near the Isthmus of Tehuantepec. Pop. 101,700.
Tuz (to͞oz). Shallow salt lake, c. 625 sq mi (1,619 sq km), of central Turkey.
Tuz·la (to͞oz'lä). City of central Yugoslavia, NNE of Sarajevo. Pop. 53,825.
Tweed (twēd). River, 97 mi (156 km), of SE Scotland, forming part of the Scottish-English border.
Twin Cities (twĭn). Minneapolis and St. Paul, Minn.
Twin Falls. City of S central Idaho, in the Snake R. valley. Pop. 26,209.
Two Rivers (to͞o). City of E Wis., on Lake Michigan SE of Green Bay. Pop. 13,354.
Ty·gart (tī'gərt). River, c. 160 mi (257 km), of E and N W.Va.
Ty·ler (tī'lər). City of NE Tex., ESE of Dallas. Pop. 70,508.
Tyn·dall (tĭn'dl). Mountain, 14,025 ft (4,277.6 m), in the Sierra Nevada of S Calif.
Tyne·mouth (tīn'mouth', -məth). Borough of NE England, on the North Sea at the mouth of the **Tyne R.** (80 mi/129 km). Pop. 193,000.
Tyre (tīr). Ancient Phoenician city on the E Mediterranean in present-day S Lebanon.
Ty·ree (tī-rē'), **Mount.** Peak, 16,290 ft (4,968.5 m), of W Antarctica, in the Ellsworth Mts. near the base of the Antarctic Peninsula.
Ty·rol or **Ti·rol** (tĭ-rōl', tī'rôl', tĭr'ōl', -ōl). Region of the E Alps in W Austria and N Italy. —**Tyr'o·lese'** *adj. & n.*
Tyr·rhe·ni·an Sea (tĭ-rē'nē-ən). Part of the Mediterranean between the Italian peninsula and the islands of Corsica, Sardinia, and Sicily.
Tyu·men (tyo͞o-mĕn'). City of SW Siberian USSR, E of Sverdlovsk. Pop. 369,000.
Tze·kung (dzŭ'go͝ong'). Zigong.
Tze·po (dzŭ'pō'). Zibo.

U

Uau·pés (wou-pĕs'). River of NW South America, rising as the **Vaupés** in S central Colombia and flowing c. 500 mi (805 km) ESE through NW Brazil to the Río Negro.
U·ban·gi (yo͞o-băng'gē, o͞o-bäng'-). River of central Africa, flowing c. 700 mi (1,126 km) along the NW border of Zaire to the Congo R.
U·be (o͞o'bĕ'). City of SW Honshu, Japan, on the Inland Sea. Pop. 167,732.
U·ca·ya·li (o͞o'kä-yä'lē). River of E Peru, flowing c. 1,000 mi (1,609 km) N to the Marañón R. to form the Amazon.
Uc·cle (o͞o'klə, ü'klə). City of central Belgium, near Brussels. Pop. 75,861.
U·dai·pur or **U·day·pur** (o͞o-dī'po͝or, o͞o'dī-po͝or'). City of NW India, NE of Ahmadabad. Pop. 161,278.
Ud·de·val·la (o͞od-ə-väl'ä). City of SW Sweden, on an arm of the Skagerrak. Pop. 32,300.
U·di·ne (o͞o'dē-nā). City of NE Italy, NE of Venice. Pop. 102,973.
Ue·le (wē'lā). River, c. 700 mi (1,126 km), of N Zaire.
U·fa (o͞o-fä'). **1.** River, c. 600 mi (965 km), of E European USSR, in the S Urals. **2.** City of E European USSR, in the S Urals at the confluence of the Belaya and Ufa rivers. Pop. 986,000.
U·gan·da (yo͞o-găn'də, o͞o-gän'dä). Country of E central Africa. Cap. Kampala. Pop. 12,115,000. —**U·gan'dan** *adj. & n.*

Uganda

U·ga·rit (o͞o'gə-rēt'). Ancient city of W Syria.
U·in·ta (yo͞o-ĭn'tə). Range of the Rockies extending c. 120 mi (195 km) E from NE Utah to SW Wyo.
U·ji (o͞o'jē'). Town of S Honshu, Japan, near Kyoto. Pop. 150,869.
Uj·jain (o͞o'jīn'). City of central India, E of Ahmadabad. Pop. 203,278.
U·ki·ah (yo͞o-kī'ə). City of NW Calif., NNW of San Francisco. Pop. 12,035.
Uk·kel (ük'əl). *Flemish.* Uccle.
U·kraine (yo͞o-krān', -krīn', yo͞o'krān'). Region of SW European USSR. —**U·krai'ni·an** *adj. & n.*
U·lan Ba·tor (o͞o'län bä'tôr'). Cap. of Mongolia, in the N central part. Pop. 287,000.
U·lan-U·de (o͞o'län o͞o'də). City of S Siberian USSR, near Lake Baikal. Pop. 305,000.
Ulm (o͝olm). City of S West Germany, on the Danube SE of Stuttgart. Pop. 99,560.
U·lu·a (o͞o-lo͞o'ä). River, c. 200 mi (322 km), of W Honduras.
U·lu Dag (o͞o'lo͞o däg'). Mountain, 8,343 ft (2,544.6 m), of NW Turkey, SE of Bursa.
U·lugh Muz·tagh (o͞o'lə məz-tä', -täg'). Highest elevation, 25,340 ft (7,728.7 m), of the Kunlun range in W China.
Ul·ya·novsk (o͞ol-yä'nəfsk). City of E central European USSR, on the Volga NW of Kuibyshev. Pop. 473,000.
U·me (o͞o'mē). River, c. 285 mi (459 km), of N Sweden.
U·me·å (o͞o'mē-ô'). City of NE Sweden, on an inlet of the Gulf of Bothnia. Pop. 52,800.
Umm al Qai·wain (o͝om' äl kī-wīn'). Sheikdom of the United Arab Emirates, in E Arabia on the Persian Gulf. Pop. 2,900.
Um·nak (o͞om'năk'). Island of SW Alas., in the E central Aleutians.
Ump·qua (ŭmp'kwô'). River, c. 200 mi (322 km), of SW Ore.
Um·ta·ta (o͞om-tä'tə). Cap. of the Transkei, in the W central part. Pop. 25,216.
Un·a·las·ka (ŭn'ə-lăs'kə, o͞o'nə-). Island of SW Alas., in the E Aleutians SW of Unimak Is.
Un·com·pah·gre (ŭn'kəm-pä'grē). Peak, 14,306 ft (4,363.3 m), in the San Juan range of the Rockies in SW Colo.
Un·ga·va (ŭng-gä'və, -gä'və, -găv'ə, ŭn-). **1. Bay.** Inlet of Hudson Strait extending c. 200 mi (322 km) into N Que., Canada. **2.** Peninsula of N Que., Canada, between Hudson and Ungava bays.
U·ni·mak (yo͞o'nə-măk'). Island of SW Alas., in the E Aleutians SW of Alaska Peninsula.
Un·ion (yo͞on'yən). **1.** Tokelau. **2.** City of NW S.C., NW of Columbia. Pop. 10,523.
Union City. 1. City of W Calif., SE of Oakland. Pop. 39,406. **2.** City of NE N.J., near Jersey City and the Hudson R. Pop. 55,593. **3.** City of extreme NW Tenn., near the Ky. border NNW of Jackson. Pop. 10,436.
Union of So·vi·et So·cial·ist Re·publics (sō'vē-ĕt' sō'shə-lĭst, -ĭt'). Country of E Europe and N Asia, with coastlines on the Baltic and Black seas and the Arctic and Pacific oceans. Cap. Moscow. Pop. 264,486,000.

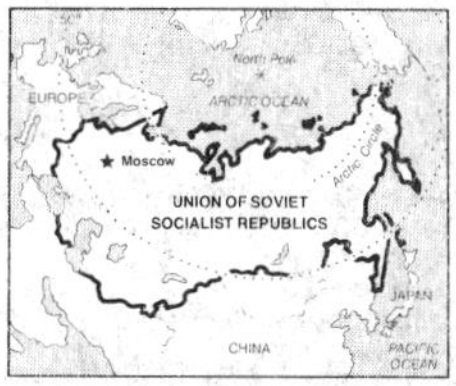

Union of Soviet Socialist Republics

Un·ion·town (yo͞on'yən-toun'). City of SW Pa., near the W.Va. border SSE of Pittsburgh. Pop. 14,510.
U·nit·ed Ar·ab E·mir·ates (yo͞o-nī'tĭd ăr'əb ĭ-mîr'ĭts, -āts', ĕm'ər-ĭts). Country of E Arabia, a federation of 7 sheikdoms on the Persian Gulf and the Gulf of Oman. Cap. Abu Dhabi. Pop. 180,200.

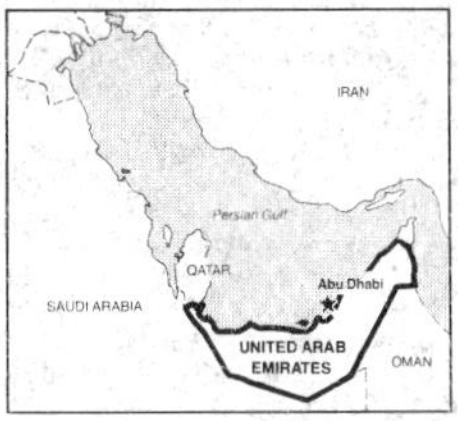

United Arab Emirates

United Arab Republic. 1. Egypt. **2.** Former union of Egypt and Syria (1958–61).
United Kingdom or **United Kingdom of Great Brit·ain and Northern Ire·land** (brĭt'n; īr'lənd). Country of W Europe, comprising England, Scotland, Wales, and Northern Ireland. Cap. London. Pop. 55,880,000.

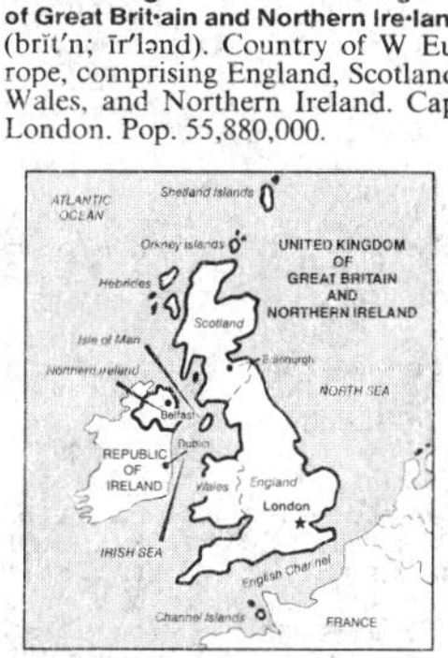

United Kingdom

United States or **United States of A·mer·i·ca** (ə-mĕr'ĭ-kə). Country of central and NW North America, with coastlines on the Atlantic, Pacific, and Arctic oceans. Cap. Washington, D.C. Pop. 226,504,825.
U·ni·ver·sal City (yo͞o'nə-vûr'səl). City of S central Tex., near San Antonio. Pop. 10,720.

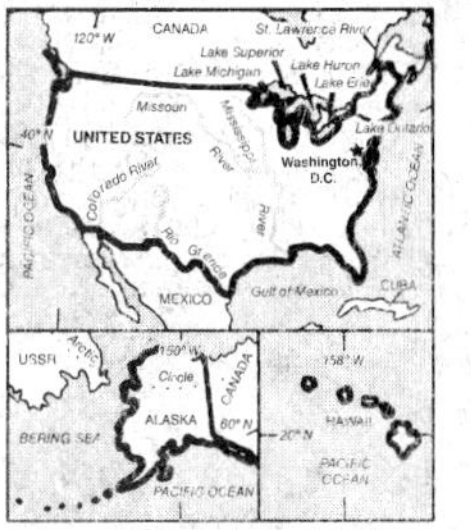

United States of America

U·ni·ver·si·ty City (yo͞o'nə-vûr'sĭ-tē). City of E Mo., near St. Louis. Pop. 42,738.
University Heights. City of NE Ohio, near Cleveland. Pop. 15,401.
University Park. City of NE Tex., near Dallas. Pop. 22,254.
Up·land (ŭp'lənd). City of S Calif., NE of Los Angeles. Pop. 47,647.
U·po·lu (o͞o-pō'lo͞o). Island of Western Samoa, in the S Pacific.
Up·per Ar·ling·ton (ŭp'ər är'lĭng-tən). City of central Ohio, surrounded by Columbus. Pop. 35,648.
Upper Cal·i·for·ni·a (kăl'ĭ-fôr'nē-ə, -fôrn'yə). Spanish possessions along the Pacific coast N of Lower California.
Upper Klam·ath (klăm'əth). Lake of S central Ore.
Upper Peninsula. N part of Mich., separated from the Lower Peninsula by the Straits of Mackinac.
Upper Vol·ta (vŏl'tə, vōl'-, vôl'-). Country of W Africa, S of Mali. Cap. Ouagadougou. Pop. 6,390,000. —**Up·per Vol'tan** *adj. & n.*

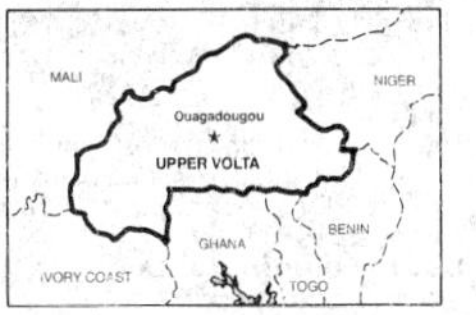

Upper Volta

Upp·sa·la also **Up·sa·la** (ŭp'sə-lä', -sä'lə, o͞op'sä'lä). City of E Sweden, NNW of Stockholm. Pop. 145,032.
Ur (ûr, o͝or). Ancient city of Sumer, S Mesopotamia, on a site in present-day SE Iraq.
U·ral (yo͝or'əl). **1.** River of USSR, rising in the S Urals and flowing 1,574 mi (2,533 km) W and S to the Caspian Sea. **2.** Also **U·rals** (yo͝or'əlz). Range of the USSR forming the traditional boundary between Europe and Asia, extending c. 1,500 mi (2,400 km) from the Arctic Ocean S to Kazakhstan.
U·ralsk (o͞o-rälsk', yo͞o-rälsk'). City of NW Central Asian USSR, on the Ural R. SSE of Kuibyshev. Pop. 170,000.
U·ra·ri·coe·ra or **U·ra·ri·cue·ra** (o͞o-rär'ĭ-kwĕr'ə). River, c. 300 mi (483 km), of NW Brazil.
U·ra·wa (o͞o-rä'wä). City of E central Honshu, Japan, near Tokyo. Pop. 358,180.
Ur·ban·a (ər-băn'ə). **1.** City of E central Ill., adjoining Champaign. Pop. 35,978. **2.** City of W central Ohio, NE of Dayton. Pop. 10,762.
Ur·ban·dale (ûr'bən-dāl'). City of central Iowa, near Des Moines. Pop. 17,869.
Ur·fa (o͝or-fä'). City of SE Turkey, near the Syrian border. Pop. 148,434.
Ur·mi·a (o͝or'mē-ə). Lake, 1,500-2,300 sq mi (3,885-5,957 sq km), of NW Iran, between Tabriz and the Turkish border.
U·rua·pan (o͞o-rwä'pän). City of W central Mexico, W of Mexico City. Pop. 138,300.
U·ru·bam·ba (o͞o'ro͞o-bäm'bä). River, c. 450 mi (724 km), of S Peru.

U·ru·guay (yo͝or'ə-gwī', -gwā', o͞o'-ro͞o-gwī'). **1.** River of SE South America, rising in S Brazil and flowing c. 1,000 mi (1,609 km) W and S on the Brazil-Argentina border and the Argentina-Uruguay border to the Río de la Plata. **2.** Country of SE South America, on the Atlantic and the Río de la Plata. Cap. Montevideo. Pop. 2,763,964. —**U·ru·guay'an** *adj. & n.*

Uruguay

Ü·rüm·qi also **U·rum·chi** (o͞o-ro͞om'-chē). City of NW China, in the Tian Shan. Pop. 400,000.

U·se·dom (o͞o'zə-dôm). Island in the Baltic Sea at the mouth of the Oder, divided between East Germany and Poland.

Ush·ant (ŭsh'ənt). Island of NW France, in the Atlantic off W Brittany.

Us·hua·ia (o͞o-swä'yä). Town of S Argentina, on the S coast of Tierra del Fuego. Pop. 5,373.

Us·ku·dar (o͝os'kə-där', üs-kü-där'). District of Istanbul, Turkey, on the Asian side of the Bosporus.

Us·pa·lla·ta (o͞os'pä-yä'tä). Pass, c. 12,500 ft (3,815 m), through the Andes between Mendoza, Argentina, and Santiago, Chile.

Us·su·ri (o͞o-so͞or'ē). River, c. 365 mi (587 km), of SE Far Eastern USSR, forming part of the USSR-China border.

Ú·stí nad La·bem (o͞os'tē näd lä'-bĕm). City of NW Czechoslovakia, on the Elbe near the East Germany border. Pop. 80,309.

Ust-Ka·me·no·gorsk (o͞ost'-kä-mĕn'ə-gôrsk', -myĭ-nō-gôrsk'). City of E Central Asian USSR, on the Irtish R. S of Novosibirsk. Pop. 280,000.

Ust·yurt (o͞ost'o͞ort'). Desert plateau of Central Asian USSR, between the Caspian and Aral seas.

U·su·ma·cin·ta (o͞o'so͞o-mä-sēn'tä). River, c. 600 mi (965 km), of SE Mexico, forming part of the Guatemala-Mexico border.

U·tah (yo͞o'tô', -tä'). **1.** Lake, c. 145 sq mi (375 sq km), of N central Utah. **2.** State of W U.S. Cap. Salt Lake City. Pop. 1,461,037. —**U'tah·an** *adj. & n.*

U·ti·ca (yo͞o'tĭ-kə). **1.** Ancient city of N Africa, on the Mediterranean NW of Carthage. **2.** City of central N.Y., E of Syracuse. Pop. 75,632.

U·trecht (yo͞o'trĕkt', ü-trĕKHt'). City of central Netherlands, SSE of Amsterdam. Pop. 237,037.

U·tsu·no·mi·ya (o͞o'tso͞o-nô'mē-yä, o͞o-tso͞o'nô-mē'yä). City of central Honshu, Japan, N of Tokyo. Pop. 377,748.

U·val·de (yə-văl'dē). City of SW Tex., WSW of San Antonio. Pop. 14,178.

Ux·bridge (ŭks'brĭj'). Township of central Ont., Canada, N of Toronto. Pop. 10,936.

Ux·mal (o͞osh-mäl'). Ancient ruined Mayan city in Yucatán, SE Mexico.

Uz·bek·i·stan (o͞oz-bĕk'ĭ-stăn', -stän', ŭz-). Region of S Central Asian USSR.

V

Vaal (väl). River of South Africa, flowing c. 750 mi (1,207 km) SW to the Orange R.

Vaa·sa (vä'sä). City of W Finland, on the Gulf of Bothnia. Pop. 58,774.

Vac·a·ville (văk'ə-vĭl'). City of central Calif., WSW of Sacramento. Pop. 43,367.

Va·duz (vä'do͞ots, vä-do͞ots'). Cap. of Liechtenstein, in the W part on the Rhine. Pop. 4,704.

Váh (vä, väKH). River, c. 245 mi (394 km), of E and central Czechoslovakia.

Vai·gach or **Vay·gach** (vī-gäch', vī'-gəch). Island of NE European USSR, in the Kara Sea SE of Novaya Zemlya.

Val-Bé·lair (văl'bā-lâr', văl-bā-lĕr'). Town of S Que., Canada, NW of Quebec city. Pop. 10,716.

Val·dai or **Val·day** (văl-dī'). Hills of NW European USSR, between Leningrad and Moscow.

Val·dez (văl-dēz'). City of S Alas., on an inlet of Prince William Sound. Pop. 3,079.

Val·di·vi·a (väl-dē'vyä). City of S central Chile, near the Pacific. Pop. 106,800.

Val d'Or (văl dôr', väl' dôr', väl dôr'). Town of SW Que., Canada, SE of Rouyn. Pop. 19,915.

Val·dos·ta (văl-dŏs'tə). City of S Ga., ENE of Tallahassee, Fla. Pop. 37,596.

Va·lence (vä-läNs'). City of SE France, on the Rhone S of Lyon. Pop. 68,460.

Va·len·ci·a (və-lĕn'shē-ə, -chə, vä-lĕn'syä). **1.** Region and former kingdom of E Spain, on the Mediterranean S of Catalonia. **2.** City of E Spain, near the **Gulf of Valencia**, a wide inlet of the Mediterranean. Pop. 750,994. **3.** City of N Venezuela, WSW of Caracas on the W shore of **Lake Valencia** (125 sq mi/324 sq km). Pop. 455,000.

Va·len·ci·ennes (və-lĕn'sē-ĕnz', vä-läN-syĕn'). City of N France, near the Belgian border. Pop. 42,473.

Va·len·tia (və-lĕn'shə, -chə). Island off SW Ireland.

Va·let·ta (və-lĕt'ə). Variant of **Valletta**.

Val·la·do·lid (văl'yä-*th*ô-lĕ*th*'). City of N central Spain, NNW of Madrid. Pop. 315,486.

Val·le·jo (və-lā'ō). City of W Calif., on San Pablo Bay N of Oakland. Pop. 80,188.

Val·let·ta also **Va·let·ta** (və-lĕt'ə). Cap. of Malta, on the NE coast. Pop. 14,042.

Val·ley East (văl'ē ēst'). Town of central Ont., Canada, near Sudbury. Pop. 20,606.

Val·ley·field (văl'ē-fēld'). City of S Que., Canada, on the St. Lawrence SW of Montreal. Pop. 29,716.

Valley Forge (fôrj). Village of SE Pa., on the Schuylkill R.; site of Continental Army winter headquarters (1777–78).

Valley Stream. Village of SE N.Y., on SW Long Is. near Queens. Pop. 35,769.

Va·lois (vä-lwä'). Region and former duchy of N France.

Va·lo·na (vä-lō'nä). Variant of **Vlorë**.

Val·pa·rai·so (văl'pə-rā'zō). **1.** (*also* -rī'-). Also **Val·pa·ra·í·so** (väl'pä-rä-ē'-sô). City of central Chile, on the Pacific WNW of Santiago. Pop. 248,200. **2.** City of NW Ind., ESE of Gary. Pop. 22,247.

Van (văn, vän). Lake, 1,419 sq mi (3,675 sq km), of E Turkey.

Van Bu·ren (văn byo͝or'ən). City of NW Ark., opposite Fort Smith. Pop. 11,996.

Van·cou·ver (văn-ko͞o'vər). **1. Mount.** Mountain, 15,700 ft (4,789 m), in the St. Elias range in SW Y.T., Canada, near the Alas. border. **2.** Island, c. 275 mi (442 km) long, of SW Canada, in the Pacific off SW B.C. mainland. **3.** City of SW B.C., Canada, on the Strait of Georgia opposite Vancouver Is. Pop. 410,188. **4.** City of SW Wash., on the Columbia near Portland, Ore. Pop. 42,834.

Van·dal·ia (văn-dāl'yə). City of W central Ohio, N of Dayton. Pop. 13,161.

Van Die·men's Land (dē'mənz). Tasmania.

Vä·nern (vĕ'nərn, vā'-) or **Va·ner** (vĕ'nər). Lake, c. 2,145 sq mi (5,556 sq km), of SW Sweden.

Va·nier (văn'yā'). **1.** City of SE Ont., Canada, on the Ottawa R. Pop. 18,005. **2.** Town of S Que., Canada, adjacent to Quebec city. Pop. 10,683.

Va·nu·a Le·vu (və-no͞o'ə lĕ'vo͞o). Island of Fiji in the S Pacific, NE of Viti Levu.

Va·nu·a·tu (vä'no͞o-ä'to͞o). Island republic of the S Pacific, E of Australia. Cap. Vila. Pop. 112,596.

Van Wert (wûrt). City of W Ohio, near the Ind. border SW of Toledo. Pop. 11,035.

Va·ra·na·si (və-rä'nə-sē). City of N central India, on the Ganges. Pop. 583,856.

Var·dar (vär'där'). River, c. 240 mi (386 km), of S Yugoslavia and NE Greece.

Va·re·se (vä-rā'zā). City of N Italy, NW of Milan. Pop. 91,100.

Var·na (vär'nə, -nä). City of E Bulgaria, on the Black Sea. Pop. 286,382.

Väs·ter·ås (vĕs'tər-ôs'). City of E Sweden, WNW of Stockholm. Pop. 117,257.

Vat·i·can City (văt'ĭ-kən). Independent papal state within Rome, Italy. Pop. 723.

Vat·na·jö·kull (vät'nä-yœ-kül). Glacier, c. 3,150 sq mi (8,160 sq km), in SE Iceland.

Vät·ter (vĕt'ər) or **Vät·tern** (-ərn). Lake, 733 sq mi (1,898.5 sq km), of S central Sweden, SE of Lake Vänern.

Vaughan (vôn, văn). Town of SE Ont., Canada, near Toronto. Pop. 20,131.

Vau·pés (vou-pĕs'). *Spanish.* Uaupés.

Vay·gach (vī-gäch', vī'gəch). Variant of **Vaigach**.

Ve·ga Ba·ja (vĕ'gä bä'hä). Town of N Puerto Rico, WSW of San Juan. Pop. 18,020.

Ve·ii (vē'ī). Ancient city of Etruria, NW of Rome, Italy.

Vej·le (vī'lə). City of central Denmark, in W Jutland on **Vejle Fjord**, narrow inlet of the Kattegat. Pop. 49,471.

Vel·bert (fĕl'bərt). City of W West Germany, in the Ruhr near Essen. Pop. 93,302.

Ve·li·ki·ye Lu·ki (vĕ-lē'kĭ-yĕ lo͞o'kĭ). City of W central European USSR, W of Moscow. Pop. 103,000.

Vel·la La·vel·la (vĕl'ə lə-vĕl'ə, vĕl'ä lä-vĕl'ä). Island of the W Pacific, in the central Solomons.

Vel·lore (və-lôr', -lōr', vĕ-). Town of SE India, W of Madras. Pop. 139,082.

Ven·da (vĕn'də). Independent black African homeland in NE South Africa, near the Zimbabwe border. Cap. Thohoyandou. Pop. 525,000.

Ve·ne·ti·a (və-nē'shē-ə, -shə). **1.** Region of NE Italy and NW Yugoslavia. **2.** Also **Ve·ne·to** (vĕ'nā-tō). Region of N Italy.

Ve·ne·zia (vĕ-nĕ'tsyä). *Italian.* Venice.

Ven·e·zue·la (vĕn'ə-zwā'lə, -zwĕ'-). **1. Gulf of.** Inlet of the Caribbean off NW Venezuela and N Colombia. **2.** Country of N South America, on the Caribbean. Cap. Caracas. Pop. 11,300,000. —**Ven'e·zue'lan** *adj. & n.*

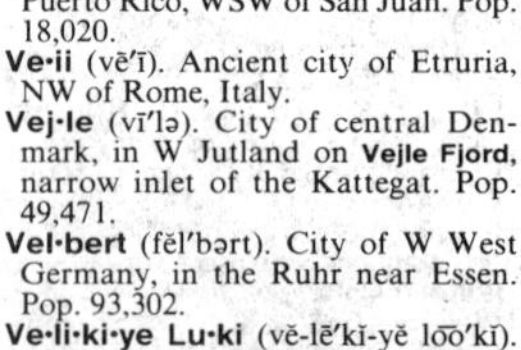

Venezuela

Ven·i·am·i·nof Crater (vĕn-yŏm'-ə-nôf'). Active volcano, 8,225 ft (2,509 m), of SW Alas., on Alaska Peninsula.

Ven·ice (vĕn'ĭs). **1.** City of NE Italy, on islets within a lagoon in the **Gulf of Venice**, a wide inlet of the N Adriatic. Pop. 355,865. **2.** City of SW Fla., S of Sarasota. Pop. 12,153. —**Ve·ne'tian** (və-nē'shən) *adj. & n.*

Ven·lo (vĕn'lō). Town of SE Netherlands, near the West German border. Pop. 62,595.

Ven·ta (vĕn'tə). River, 217 mi (349 km), of NW European USSR in Lithuania and Latvia.

Vent·nor City (vĕnt'nər). City of SE N.J., near Atlantic City. Pop. 11,704.

Ven·tu·ra (vĕn-chŏŏr'ə, -to͞or'ə). City of SW Calif., on the Pacific W of Los Angeles. Pop. 490,500.

Ve·ra·cruz (vĕr'ə-kro͞oz', vĕ'-rä-kro͞os') or **Veracruz Lla·ve** (yä'vĕ). City of E central Mexico, on the Gulf of Mexico E of Puebla. Pop. 295,300.

Ver·cel·li (vĕr-chĕl'lē). City of NW Italy, WSW of Milan. Pop. 54,063.

Ver·de. **1.** (vûr'dē). River, c. 190 mi (306 km), of S Ariz. **2.** (vûrd), **Cape.** Peninsula of W Senegal projecting W into the Atlantic; westernmost point of Africa.

Ver·di·gris (vûr'dĭ-grēs', -grĭs). River, c. 280 mi (451 km), of SE Kans. and NE Okla.

Ver·dun (vər-dŭn', vĕr-dœN'). **1.** City of S Que., Canada, on Montreal Is. near Montreal. Pop. 68,013. **2.** City of NE France, on the Meuse R.; site of prolonged World War I battle (1916). Pop. 23,621.

Ve·ree·ni·ging (fə-rē'nĭ-kĭng, -KHĭng, -gĭng, -rā'-). City of NE South Africa, on the Vaal R. S of Johannesburg. Pop. 172,549.

Ver·kho·yansk (vĭr-KHŏ-yänsk'). Range of E Siberian USSR, parallel to and E of the lower Lena R.

Ver·mil·ion (vər-mĭl'yən). City of N Ohio, on Lake Erie W of Cleveland. Pop. 11,012.

Ver·mont (vər-mŏnt'). State of NE U.S. Cap. Montpelier. Pop. 511,456. —**Ver·mont'er** *n.*

Ver·non (vûr'nən). **1.** City of S B.C., Canada, near the N end of Okanagan Lake. Pop. 17,546. **2.** Town of N Conn., NE of Hartford. Pop. 27,974. **3.** City of N Tex., near the Okla. border. Pop. 12,695.

Ve·ro Beach (vîr'ō). City of E Fla., N of Fort Pierce. Pop. 16,176.

Vé·roi·a (vĕ'rē-ä, -ryä). City of NE Greece, W of Salonika. Pop. 29,528.

Ve·ro·na (və-rō'nə). **1.** City of N Italy, on the Adige R. W of Venice. Pop. 269,763. **2.** Borough of NE N.J., near Passaic. Pop. 14,166.

Ver·sailles (vər-sī', vĕr-). City of N central France, near Paris; site of Louis XIV's palace. Pop. 94,145.

Ves·ta·vi·a Hills (vĕ-stā'vē-ə). City of N central Ala., near Birmingham. Pop. 15,733.

Ves·ter·å·len (vĕs'tə-rô'lən). Archipelago off NW coast of Norway.

Ve·su·vi·us (və-so͞o'vē-əs). Active volcano, 4,190 ft (1,278 m), of Italy, on the E shore of the Bay of Naples.

Vesz·prém (vĕs'prām). City of W Hungary, N of Lake Balaton. Pop. 55,000.

Vet·lu·ga (vĕt-lo͞o'gə). River, 528 mi (850 km), of central European USSR.

Vi·a·reg·gio (vyä-rād'jō). City of NW Italy, on the Tyrrhenian Sea. Pop. 59,600.

Vi·cente Ló·pez (vē-sĕn'tĕ lô'pĕs). City of E central Argentina, near Buenos Aires. Pop. 285,178.

Vi·cen·za (vē-chĕn'tsä). City of NE Italy, ENE of Verona. Pop. 117,571.

Vi·cha·da (vē-chä'*th*ä). River, c. 400 mi (644 km), of E Colombia.

Vi·chu·ga (vĭ-cho͞o'gä). City of central European USSR, on the Volga NNW of Gorki. Pop. 52,000.

Vi·chy (vĭsh'ē, vē-shē'). City and resort of central France; seat of the French government during World War II. Pop. 32,117.

Vicks·burg (vĭks'bûrg'). City of W Miss., on the Mississippi W of Jackson. Pop. 25,434.

Vic·to·ri·a (vĭc-tôr'ē-ə, -tōr'-). **1. Lake.** Also **Victoria Ny·an·za** (nī-ăn'zə, nē-, nyän'zä). Lake, c. 26,830 sq mi (69,490 sq km), of E central Africa, in Uganda, Kenya, and Tanzania; largest lake of Africa. **2.** River, c. 240 mi (386 km), of N Australia. **3.** Falls, c. 420 ft (128 m) high and 1.1 mi (1.7 km) wide, in the Zambesi R. on the Zambia-Zimbabwe border. **4.** Island of N.W.T., Canada, in the Arctic Ocean N of the mainland and S of

Parry Channel. **5. Land.** Region of E Antarctica S of New Zealand, bordering the Ross Sea. **6.** Cap. of B.C., Canada, on SE Vancouver Is. and Juan de Fuca Strait. Pop. 62,551. **7.** Cap. of Hong Kong colony, on NW coast of Hong Kong Is. Pop. 1,026,870. **8.** Cap. of the Seychelles, on NE coast of Mahé Is. Pop. 13,622. **9.** City of SE Tex., SE of San Antonio. Pop. 50,695.

Victoria Nile (nīl). Section of the Nile, c. 260 mi (418 km), between lakes Victoria and Albert in central Uganda.

Victoria Ny·an·za (nī-ăn′zə, nē-, nyän′zä). Lake Victoria.

Vic·to·ri·a·ville (vĭk-tôr′ē-ə-vĭl′, -tōr′-). Town of S Que., Canada, SE of Trois-Rivières. Pop. 21,825.

Vic·tor·ville (vĭk′tər-vĭl′). City of S Calif., N of San Bernardino. Pop. 14,220.

Vi·da·lia (vĭ-dāl′yə). City of SE Ga., W of Savannah. Pop. 10,393.

Vi·din (vē′dĭn). City of extreme NW Bulgaria, on the Danube. Pop. 58,213.

Vi·dor (vī′dər). City of extreme SE Tex., near Beaumont. Pop. 12,117.

Vi·en·na (vē-ĕn′ə). **1.** Cap. of Austria, in the NE part on the Danube. Pop. 1,572,300. **2.** Town of NE Va., W of Washington, D.C. Pop. 15,469. **3.** City of NW W.Va., on the Ohio R. near Parkersburg. Pop. 11,618. —**Vi′en·nese′** (vē′ə-nēz′, -nēs′) *adj. & n.*

Vienne (vyĕn). River, c. 217 mi (349 km), of central France.

Vien·tiane (vyĕn-tyän′). Cap. of Laos, in the N central part on the Mekong R. Pop. 174,229.

Vie·ques (vyĕ′kĕs′). Island, 51 sq mi (132 sq km), off SE Puerto Rico.

Vier·sen (fēr′zən). City of W West Germany, W of Düsseldorf. Pop. 81,419.

Viet·nam (vē-ĕt′näm′, -năm′, vē′ĕt-, vyĕt′-). Country of SE Asia, in E Indochina on the South China Sea. Cap. Hanoi. Pop. 53,550,000. —**Viet′na·mese′** (-nə-mēz′, -mēs′) *adj. & n.*

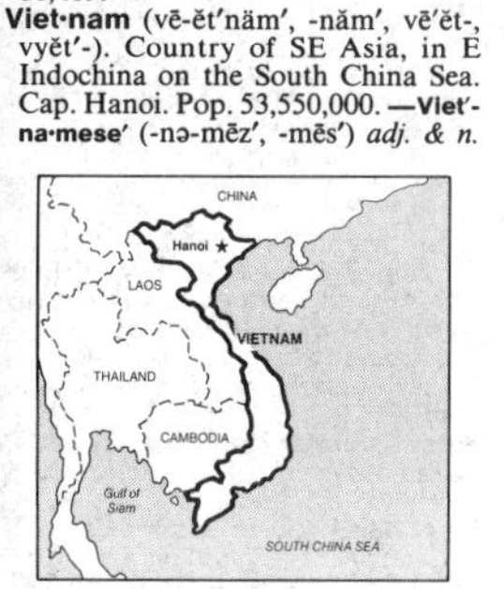

Vietnam

Vi·ge·va·no (vē-jĕ′vä-nō). City of NW Italy, SW of Milan. Pop. 67,034.

Vi·go (vē′gô). City of NW Spain, on the Atlantic. Pop. 260,059.

Vii·pu·ri (vē′pōō-rē′). *Finnish.* Vyborg.

Vi·ja·ya·wa·da also **Vi·ja·ya·va·da** (vĭj′ə-yə-wä′də, -vä′-). City of SE India, near the Kistna R. delta ESE of Hyderabad. Pop. 317,258.

Vi·la (vē′lə). Cap. of Vanuatu, on Efate Is. in the SW Pacific. Pop. 17,400.

Vil·lach (fĭl′äKH). City of S Austria, on the Drava R. Pop. 50,993.

Vi·lla·her·mo·sa (vē′yä-ĕr-mô′sä). City of SE Mexico, E of the Isthmus of Tehuantepec. Pop. 165,500.

Vil·la Park (vĭl′ə). Village of NE Ill., near Chicago. Pop. 23,185.

Vi·lla·vi·cen·ci·o (vē′yä-vē-sĕn′syô). City of central Colombia, SE of Bogotá. Pop. 133,000.

Vil·leur·banne (vēl-ür-bän′). City of SE France, near Lyon. Pop. 116,535.

Vil·ni·us (vĭl′nē-ōōs, -əs) or **Vil·na** (vĭl′nə). City of W European USSR, in SE Lithuania ESE of Kaunas. Pop. 492,000.

Vil·yu·i also **Vil·yuy** (vĭl-yōō′ē). River of E Siberian USSR, flowing c. 1,520 mi (2,446 km) E to the Lena R.

Vim·i·nal (vĭm′ə-nəl). One of the 7 hills of ancient Rome.

Vi·ña del Mar (vē′nyä dĕl mär′). City of central Chile, on the Pacific near Valparaiso. Pop. 262,100.

Vin·cennes. 1. (văN-sĕn′). City of N central France, near Paris. Pop. 44,261. **2.** (vĭn-sĕnz′). City of SW Ind., on the Wabash R. S of Terre Haute. Pop. 20,857.

Vin·dhya (vĭn′dyə). Range of hills in central India, c. 600 mi (965 km) long and rising to c. 3,000 ft (915 m).

Vine·land (vīn′lənd). City of S N.J., SSW of Camden. Pop. 53,753.

Vin·land (vĭn′lənd). Unidentified coastal region of NE North America visited by early Norse voyagers.

Vin·ni·tsa (vĭn′ĭt-sə, vyĕn′nyĭ-tsə). City of SW European USSR, SW of Kiev. Pop. 323,000.

Vin·son Mas·sif (vĭn′sən mă-sēf′, mə-). Peak, 16,860 ft (5,142.3 m), in the Ellsworth Mts. of W Antarctica; highest peak of the continent.

Vir·gin (vûr′jĭn). **1.** River, c. 200 mi (322 km), of SW Utah and SE Nev. **2.** Islands of the West Indies E of Puerto Rico, divided into the **British Virgin Is.** to the NE and the **Virgin Is. of the United States** to the SW.

Vir·gin·ia (vər-jĭn′yə). **1.** State of E U.S., on Chesapeake Bay and the Atlantic. Cap. Richmond. Pop. 5,346,279. **2.** City of NE Minn., NNW of Duluth. Pop. 11,056. —**Vir·gin′ian** *adj. & n.*

Virginia Beach. Independent city of SE Va., on the Atlantic near Norfolk. Pop. 262,199.

Virgin Islands of the United States. SW part of the Virgin Is., 133 sq mi (344 sq km), constituting a U.S. territory. Cap. Charlotte Amalie. Pop. 62,468.

Vi·run·ga (vĭ-rōōng′gä). Range of central Africa in E Zaire, N Rwanda, and SW Uganda.

Vis (vēs). Island of W Yugoslavia, off the Dalmatian coast SSW of Split.

Vi·sa·kha·pat·nam (vĭ-sä′kə-pŭt′-nəm). Vishakhapatnam.

Vi·sa·lia (vĭ-sāl′yə). City of S central Calif., SE of Fresno. Pop. 49,729.

Vi·sa·yan (və-sī′ən, vē-sä′yən) also **Vi·sa·yans** (-ənz, -yənz). Islands of central Philippines, between Luzon and Mindanao.

Vis·by (vĭz′bē, vēs′bü). City of SE Sweden, on W Gotland Is. on the Baltic. Pop. 20,200.

Vis·count Mel·ville (vī′kount mĕl′-vĭl). Sound between Victoria and Melville Is. in N N.W.T., Canada.

Vi·sha·kha·pat·nam (vĭ-shä′kə-pŭt′-nəm). City of E India, on the Bay of Bengal. Pop. 352,504.

Vi·so (vē′zō), **Mount.** Highest of the Cottian Alps, 12,602 ft (3,843.6 m), in NW Italy near the French border.

Vis·ta (vĭs′tə). City of S Calif., N of San Diego. Pop. 35,834.

Vis·tu·la (vĭs′chōō-lə). Longest river of Poland, 678 mi (1,091 km), rising near the Czech border and flowing NE, NW, and N to the Gulf of Danzig.

Vi·tebsk (vē′tĕpsk, vē-tĕpsk′). City of W European USSR, on the Western Dvina R. NE of Minsk. Pop. 303,000.

Vi·ter·bo (vē-tĕr′bō). City of central Italy, NNW of Rome. Pop. 50,000.

Vi·ti Le·vu (vē′tē lĕ′vōō). Largest of the Fiji Is., in the S Pacific.

Vi·tim (vĭ-tēm′). River of SE Siberian USSR, flowing c. 1,140 mi (1,834 km) N to the Lena R.

Vi·to·ri·a (vĭ-tôr′ē-ə, -tōr′-, vē-tô′ryä). City of N central Spain, SSE of Bilbao. Pop. 185,271.

Vi·tó·ri·a (vĭ-tôr′ē-ə, -tōr′-, vē-tô′ryə). City of E Brazil, on the Atlantic NE of Rio de Janeiro. Pop. 163,877.

Vi·try-sur-Seine (vē-trē sür sĕn′). City of N central France, near Paris. Pop. 87,316.

Vit·to·ri·a (vēt-tô′ryä). City of SE Sicily, Italy, W of Ragusa. Pop. 50,739.

Vlaar·ding·en (vlär′dĭng-ən). City of SW Netherlands, near Rotterdam. Pop. 79,531.

Vla·di·mir (vlăd′ə-mîr′, vlä-dē′mîr). City of central European USSR, E of Moscow. Pop. 301,000.

Vlad·i·vos·tok (vlăd′ə-vŏs-tŏk′, -vŏs′-tŏk). City of extreme SE Far Eastern USSR, on the Sea of Japan. Pop. 558,000.

Vlis·sing·en (vlĭs′ĭng-ən). City of SW Netherlands, on the North Sea. Pop. 26,200.

Vlo·rë (vlôr′ə, vlōr′ə) also **Va·lo·na** (vä-lō′nä) or **Vlo·ne** (vlō′nə). City of SW Albania, on **Vlorë Bay,** an inlet of the Adriatic. Pop. 58,400.

Vl·ta·va (vŭl′tä-vä). River, c. 270 mi (434 km), of W Czechoslovakia.

Vo·gel·kop (vō′gəl-kŏp′). Doberai.

Vol·ca·no (vŏl-kā′nō). Islands of Japan in the NW Pacific N of the Marianas.

Vol·ga (vŏl′gə, vôl′-, vōl′-). River of European USSR, rising in the Valdai Hills NW of Moscow and flowing c. 2,300 mi (3,700 km) E and S to the Caspian Sea.

Vol·go·grad (vŏl′gə-grăd′, vôl′-, vōl′-). City of S European USSR, on the Volga. Pop. 939,000.

Vo·log·da (vô′ləg-də). City of NE central European USSR, NNE of Moscow. Pop. 241,000.

Vo·los or **Vó·los** (vô′lôs′). City of E Greece, in Thessaly on the **Gulf of Volos,** an inlet of the Aegean Sea. Pop. 51,290.

Vol·ta (vŏl′tə, vōl′-, vôl′-). River formed in central Ghana by the confluence of the **White Volta** and the **Black Volta,** flowing c. 290 mi (467 km) S through artificial **Lake Volta** (c. 3,275 sq mi/8,482 sq km) to the Gulf of Guinea.

Vol·ta Re·don·da (vôl′tə rə-dôn′də). City of E Brazil, on the Paraíba R. NW of Rio de Janeiro. Pop. 147,261.

Vol·tur·no (vōl-tōōr′nō). River, c. 109 mi (175 km), of S Italy.

Volzh·skiy (vôlzh′skē). City of S European USSR, on the Volga near Volgograd. Pop. 214,000.

Voor·burg (vôr′bərg′, vōr′-, -bûrKH). City of SW Netherlands, near The Hague. Pop. 44,227.

Vor·ku·ta (vər-kōō-tä′). City of extreme NE European USSR, above the Arctic Circle. Pop. 101,000.

Vo·ro·nezh (vŏ-rō′nĭsh). City of central European USSR, on the Don NE of Kharkov. Pop. 796,000.

Vo·ro·shi·lov·grad (vôr′ə-shē′-ləf-grăd′, vŏ-rŏ-shē′ləf-grät′). City of S central European USSR, in the Donets Basin SE of Kharkov. Pop. 469,000.

Vosges (vōzh). Mountains of NE France, extending c. 120 mi (193 km) along the Rhine.

Vra·tsa (vrä′tsä). City of NW Bulgaria, NNE of Sofia. Pop. 64,697.

Vyat·ka (vyät′kə). River, c. 850 mi (1,368 km), of E European USSR.

Vy·borg (vē′bôrg′). City of NW European USSR, NW of Leningrad near the Finnish border. Pop. 77,000.

Vy·cheg·da (vĭ′chĕg-dä). River, 700 mi (1,126 km), of NE European USSR.

W

Waal (väl). S branch of the lower Rhine in S Netherlands.

Wa·bash (wô′băsh′). **1.** River of E central U.S., rising in W Ohio and flowing c. 475 mi (764 km) W and S across Ind. and on the Ind.-Ill. border to the Ohio R. **2.** City of N central Ind., SW of Fort Wayne. Pop. 12,985.

Wa·co (wā′kō). City of E central Tex., S of Dallas-Fort Worth. Pop. 101,261.

Wad·den·zee (väd′n-zā′, vä′dən-). Inlet of the North Sea off N Netherlands, between the Ijsselmeer and the W Frisian Is.

Wad·ding·ton (wŏd′ĭng-tən). **Mount.** Peak, 13,260 ft (4,044.3 m), of the Coast Mts. in SW B.C., Canada.

Wads·worth (wŏdz′wûrth′). City of NE Ohio, W of Akron. Pop. 15,166.

Wa·gram (vä′gräm). Town of NE Austria, near Vienna; site of Napoleon's defeat of the Austrians (1809).

Wa·hi·a·wa (wä′hē-ə-wä′). City of central Oahu, Hawaii. Pop. 17,598.

Wai·a·na·e (wī′ə-nä′ā). Mountains of W Oahu, Hawaii.

Wai·ka·to (wī-kä′tō). Longest river of New Zealand, rising in central North Is. and flowing 270 mi (434 km) NW to the Tasman Sea.

Wai·ki·ki (wī′kĭ-kē′, wī′kē-kē′, wī-kē-kē′). Beach and resort district of Honolulu, Hawaii.

Wai·pa·hu (wī-pä′hōō). City of S Oahu, Hawaii, on the NW shore of Pearl Harbor. Pop. 29,200.

Wa·ka·ya·ma (wä-kä′yä-mä). City of S Honshu, Japan, on the Inland Sea. Pop. 401,462.

Wake (wāk). Island of the W Pacific, between Hawaii and Guam, belonging to the U.S.

Wake·field (wāk′fēld′). Town of E Mass., near Boston. Pop. 24,895.

Wa·la·chi·a (wŏ-lā′kē-ə). Variant of **Wallachia.**

Wał·brzych (väl′bzhĭk). City of SW Poland, SW of Wroclaw. Pop. 132,900.

Wal·che·ren (väl′KHə-rən). Region, formerly an island, of SW Netherlands at the mouth of the Scheldt.

Wal·den (wôl′dən). **1.** Pond of NE Mass., near Concord; site of Henry David Thoreau's cabin. **2.** Town of central Ont., Canada, near Sudbury. Pop. 10,289.

Wald·wick (wôld′wĭk). Borough of NE N.J., NNE of Paterson. Pop. 10,802.

Wales (wālz). Principality of SW Great Britain, W of England; part of the United Kingdom. Pop. 2,774,700. —**Welsh** (wĕlsh) *adj. & n.*

Wal·ker (wô′kər). **1.** Salt lake, c. 105 sq mi (272 sq km), of W Nev., SE of Carson City. **2.** City of W central Mich., near Grand Rapids. Pop. 15,088.

Wal·lace·burg (wŏl′əs-bûrg′). Town of SW Ont., Canada, S of Sarnia. Pop. 11,424.

Wal·la·chi·a also **Wa·la·chi·a** (wŏ-lā′-kē-ə). Region of SE Rumania. —**Wal·la′chi·an** *adj. & n.*

Wal·la Wal·la (wŏl′ə wŏl′ə). City of SE Wash., near the Ore. border SSW of Spokane. Pop. 25,618.

Wal·ling·ford (wŏl′ĭng-fərd). Town of S Conn., NNE of New Haven. Pop. 37,274.

Wal·ling·ton (wŏl′ĭng-tən). Borough of NE N.J., near Passaic. Pop. 10,741.

Wal·lis and Fu·tu·na (wŏl′ĭs; fōō-tōō′nä). 2 island groups of the SW Pacific, W of Samoa and NE of Fiji; a French overseas territory. Pop. 12,000.

Wal·lops (wŏl′əps). Island in the Atlantic off E Va.

Wal·low·a (wä-lou′ə). Mountains of NE Ore.

Wal·nut Creek (wôl′nŭt′, -nət). City of W Calif., NE of Oakland. Pop. 53,643.

Wal·pole (wôl′pōl′, wŏl′-). Town of E Mass., SW of Boston. Pop. 18,859.

Wal·sall (wôl′sôl′, -səl). Borough of W central England, near Birmingham. Pop. 263,400.

Wal·tham (wôl′thăm′). City of E Mass., near Boston. Pop. 58,200.

Wal·ton and Wey·bridge (wôl′tən; wā′brĭj). District of SE England, near London. Pop. 110,000.

Wal·vis Bay (wôl′vĭs). **1.** District of South Africa, c. 374 sq mi (969 sq km), an exclave in W central Namibia on the Atlantic. **2.** City of Walvis Bay district, W central Namibia, on **Walvis Bay,** an inlet of the Atlantic. Pop. 21,725.

Wan·a·que (wŏn′ə-kyōō′). Borough of NE N.J., NNE of Paterson. Pop. 10,025.

Wang·a·nu·i (wŏng′gə-nōō′ē, wŏng′-). City of SW North Is., New Zealand, on Cook Strait. Pop. 37,500.

Wan·tagh (wŏn′tô′). Town of SE N.Y., on the S shore of Long Is. Pop. 22,300.

Wap·si·pin·i·con (wŏp′sĭ-pĭn′ĭ-kən). River, 255 mi (410 km), of SE Minn. and E Iowa.

Wa·ran·gal (wŭ′rəng-gəl, wə-rŭng′-). City of SE India, NE of Hyderabad. Pop. 207,520.

War·bur·ton (wôr′bûrt′n). River of central Australia, flowing 275 mi

p **pop** / r **roar** / s **sauce** / sh **ship, dish** / t **tight** / th **thin, path** / *th* **this, bathe** / ŭ **cut** / ûr **urge** / v **valve** / w **with** / y **yes** / z **zebra, size** / zh **vision** / ə **about, item, edible, gallop, circus** / œ *Fr.* **feu,** *Ger.* **schön** / ü *Fr.* **tu,** *Ger.* **über** / KH *Ger.* **ich,** *Scot.* **loch** / N *Fr.* **bon.**

(442 km) SW of Lake Eyre.
Ware·ham (wâr'hăm', -əm). Town of SE Mass., on Buzzards Bay NE of New Bedford. Pop. 18,457.
War·ner Rob·ins (wôr'nər rŏb'ĭnz). City of central Ga., S of Macon. Pop. 39,839.
War·ren (wôr'ən, wŏr'-). **1.** City of SE Mich., near Detroit. Pop. 161,134. **2.** City of NE Ohio, NW of Youngstown. Pop. 56,629. **3.** Borough of NW Pa., ESE of Erie. Pop. 12,146. **4.** Town of E R.I., NE of Warwick. Pop. 10,640.
War·rens·burg (wôr'ĭnz-bûrg', wŏr'-). City of W central Mo., ESE of Kansas City. Pop. 13,807.
War·rens·ville Heights (wôr'ĭnz-vĭl', wŏr'-). City of NE Ohio, near Cleveland. Pop. 16,565.
War·ring·ton (wôr'ĭng-tən, wŏr'-). Borough of W central England, E of Liverpool. Pop. 168,200.
War·saw (wôr'sô). **1.** Cap. of Poland in the E central part on the Vistula R. Pop. 1,576,600. **2.** City of NE Ind., WNW of Fort Wayne. Pop. 10,647.
War·ta (vär'tä). River, c. 475 mi (764 km), of S and W Poland.
War·wick (wŏr'ĭk, wôr'wĭk). **1.** Borough of central England, SE of Birmingham. Pop. 17,870. **2.** City of E central R.I., on Narragansett Bay S of Providence. Pop. 87,123.
Wa·satch (wô'săch'). Range of the Rockies extending c. 250 mi (402 km) S from SE Idaho to central Utah.
Wash (wŏsh, wôsh), **the.** Inlet of the North Sea off E central England.
Wash·ing·ton (wŏsh'ĭng-tən, wôsh'-). **1.** Lake, c. 20 mi (32 km) long and 4 mi (6 km) wide, in W central Wash., E of Seattle. **2. Mount.** Highest (6,288 ft/1,917.8 m) of the White Mts. in N N.H. **3.** Island of NE Wis., in Lake Michigan off the Door Peninsula. **4.** State of NW U.S., on the Pacific. Cap. Olympia. Pop. 4,130,163. **5.** Cap. of the U.S., coextensive with the District of Columbia. Pop. 637,651. **6.** City of central Ill., E. of Peoria. Pop. 10,364. **7.** City of SW Ind., E of Vincennes. Pop. 11,325. **8.** City of SW central Ohio, SSW of Columbus. Pop. 12,682. **9.** City of SW Pa., SW of Pittsburgh. Pop. 18,363.
Wash·i·ta (wŏsh'ĭ-tô', wôsh'-). River, c. 450 mi (724 km), of NW Tex. and SW Okla.
Wa·tau·ga (wŏ-tô'gə). City of NE Tex., near Fort Worth. Pop. 10,284.
Wat·er·bury (wô'tər-bĕr'ē, -bə-rē, wŏt'ər-). City of W central Conn., NNW of New Haven. Pop. 103,266.
Wa·ter·ford (wô'tər-fərd, wŏt'ər-). **1.** Borough of SE Ireland, SSW of Dublin. Pop. 32,617. **2.** Town of SE Conn., on Long Is. Sound. Pop. 17,843.
Wa·ter·loo (wô'tər-lo͞o', wŏt'ər-, wô'tər-lo͞o', wŏt'ər-). **1.** Town of central Belgium, near Brussels; site Napoleon's final defeat (1815). **2.** City of SE Ont., Canada, near Kitchener. Pop. 50,291. **3.** City of NE Iowa, NW of Cedar Rapids. Pop. 75,985.
Wa·ter·town (wô'tər-toun', wŏt'ər-). **1.** Town of W Conn., near Waterbury. Pop. 19,489. **2.** Town of E Mass., near Boston. Pop. 34,384. **3.** City of N N.Y., N of Syracuse. Pop. 27,861. **4.** City of NE S.Dak., NNW of Sioux Falls. Pop. 15,649. **5.** City of SE Wis., ENE of Madison. Pop. 18,113.
Wa·ter·ville (wô'tər-vĭl', wŏt'ər-). City of S Me., N of Augusta. Pop. 17,779.
Wa·ter·vliet (wô'tər-vlēt', wŏt'ər-). City of E N.Y., on the Hudson near Albany. Pop. 11,354.
Wat·ford (wŏt'fərd). Borough of SE England, near London. Pop. 76,500.
Wat·son·ville (wŏt'sən-vĭl'). City of W Calif., E of Santa Cruz. Pop. 23,543.
Watts (wŏts). District of Los Angeles, Calif.
Wau·ke·gan (wô-kē'gən). City of NE Ill., on Lake Michigan N of Chicago. Pop. 67,653.
Wau·ke·sha (wô'kə-shô'). City of SE Wis., W of Milwaukee. Pop. 50,319.
Wau·sau (wô'sô'). City of N central Wis., WNW of Green Bay. Pop. 32,426.
Wau·wa·to·sa (wô'wə-tō'sə). City of SE Wis., near Milwaukee. Pop. 51,308.
Wax·a·hach·ie (wôk'sə-hăch'ē). City of NE Tex., S of Dallas. Pop. 14,624.
Way·cross (wā'krôs', -krŏs'). City of SE Ga., SW of Savannah. Pop. 19,371.
Way·land (wā'lənd). Town of E Mass., W of Boston. Pop. 12,170.
Wayne (wān). City of SE Mich., WSW of Detroit. Pop. 21,159.
Waynes·bor·o (wānz'bûr'ō, -bər-ə). Independent city of W central Va., W of Charlottesville. Pop. 15,329.
Wa·zir·i·stan (wä-zîr'ĭ-stän', -stăn'). Region of NW Pakistan.
Weath·er·ford (wĕth'ər-fərd). City of NE Tex., W of Fort Worth. Pop. 12,049.
Web·bi She·be·li (wā'bē shĕ-bā'lē) also **We·bi Shi·be·li** (shĭ-bā'lē). River of NE Africa, rising in central Ethiopia and flowing c. 1,200 mi (1,931 km) SE and SW through S Somalia to Indian Ocean coastal swamps.
We·ber (wē'bər). River, c. 125 mi (201 km), of N Utah.
Web·ster (wĕb'stər). Town of S Mass., SSW of Worcester. Pop. 14,480.
Webster Groves. City of E Mo., near St. Louis. Pop. 23,097.
Wed·dell (wĕd'l, wĭ-dĕl'). Sea of the S Atlantic off W Antarctica, E of the Antarctic Peninsula.
Wee·haw·ken (wē-hô'kən, wē'hô-). Township of NE N.J., on the Hudson opposite New York City. Pop. 13,383.
Wei (wā). River of central China, flowing c. 450 mi (724 km) E to the Yellow R.
Wei·fang (wā'făng'). City of E China, at the base of the Shandong Peninsula. Pop. 240,000.
Wei·mar (vī'mär', wī'-). City of SW East Germany, WSW of Leipzig. Pop. 62,803.
Weir·ton (wîr'tn). City of N W.Va., in the Panhandle W of Pittsburgh, Pa. Pop. 24,736.
Weiss·horn (vīs'hôrn). Peak, 14,782 ft (4,508.5 m), of the Pennine Alps in S Switzerland.
Wel·fare (wĕl'fâr'). Island in the East R., off Manhattan Is., SE N.Y.
Wel·land (wĕl'ənd). **1.** Ship canal of SE Ont., Canada, connecting Lake Ontario with Lake Erie and bypassing Niagara Falls. **2.** City of SE Ont., Canada, on the Welland Ship Canal. Pop. 45,261.
Welles·ley (wĕlz'lē). Town of E Mass., WSW of Boston. Pop. 27,209.
Wel·ling·bor·ough (wĕl'ĭng-bûr'ə, -bər-ə). Urban district of central England, ENE of Northampton. Pop. 39,570.
Wel·ling·ton (wĕl'ĭng-tən). Cap. of New Zealand, on an inlet of Cook Strait in extreme S North Is. Pop. 137,600.
Wels (vĕls). City of N Austria, SW of Linz. Pop. 47,279.
Wel·wyn Gar·den City (wĕl'ĭn gär'dn). Urban district of SE England, N of London. Pop. 39,900.
We·natch·ee (wə-năch'ē). City of central Wash., NNE of Yakima. Pop. 17,257.
Wen·zhou also **Wen·chow** (wŭn'jō'). City of E China, near the East China Sea S of Shanghai. Pop. 260,000.
Wer·ra (vĕr'ä). River, 181 mi (291 km), of SW East Germany and central West Germany.
We·sel (vā'zəl). City of W West Germany, on the Rhine NW of Essen. Pop. 56,760.
We·ser (vā'zər). River, c. 300 mi (483 km), of central and N West Germany.
Wes·la·co (wĕs'lə-kō'). City of extreme S Tex., NW of Brownsville. Pop. 19,331.
Wes·sex (wĕs'ĭks). Region and ancient Anglo-Saxon kingdom of S England.
West (wĕst), **the. 1.** Former region of the U.S., W of the Alleghenies. **2.** Region of the U.S., W of the Mississippi.
West Al·lis (ăl'ĭs). City of SE Wis., near Milwaukee. Pop. 63,982.
West Bend (bĕnd). City of SE Wis., NNW of Milwaukee. Pop. 21,484.
West·bor·ough or **West·bor·o** (wĕst'bûr'ō, -bər-ə). Town of E central Mass., near Worcester. Pop. 13,619.
West Bridg·ford (brĭj'fərd). Urban district of N central England, near Nottingham. Pop. 28,340.
West·brook (wĕst'bro͝ok'). City of SW Me., near Portland. Pop. 14,976.
West·bur·y (wĕst'bĕr'ē, -bə-rē). Village of SE N.Y., on W Long Is. near Mineola. Pop. 13,871.
West Cald·well (kôld'wĕl', -wəl). Borough of NE N.J., W of Passaic. Pop. 11,407.
West Car·roll·ton (kăr'əl-tən). City of W central Ohio, near Dayton. Pop. 13,148.
West·ches·ter (wĕst'chĕs'tər). **1.** Village of NE Ill., near Chicago. Pop. 17,730. **2.** Suburban region and county of SE N.Y.
West Ches·ter (chĕs'tər). Borough of SE Pa., W of Philadelphia. Pop. 17,435.
West Chi·ca·go (shĭ-kä'gō, -kô'-). City of NE Ill., near Chicago. Pop. 12,550.
West Co·lum·bi·a (kə-lŭm'bē-ə). City of central S.C., near Columbia. Pop. 10,409.
West Co·vi·na (kō-vē'nə, kə-). City of S Calif., E of Los Angeles. Pop. 80,094.
West Des Moines (də moin'). City of central Iowa, near Des Moines. Pop. 21,894.
Wes·ter·ly (wĕs'tər-lē). Town of extreme SW R.I., on the border E of New London, Conn. Pop. 18,580.
West·ern Dvi·na (wĕs'tərn dvē-nä'). See **Dvina.**
Western Ghats (găts, gôts, gäts). Range of S India, extending c. 800 mi (1,287 km) along the Arabian Sea coast.
Western Islands. Hebrides.
Western Sa·ha·ra (sə-hâr'ə, -hä'rä). Region of NW Africa on the Atlantic coast, partly annexed (1976) and partly occupied (1979) by Morocco.
Western Sa·mo·a (sə-mō'ə). Island nation of the S Pacific, comprising the W half of the Samoa Is. Cap. Apia. Pop. 160,000.

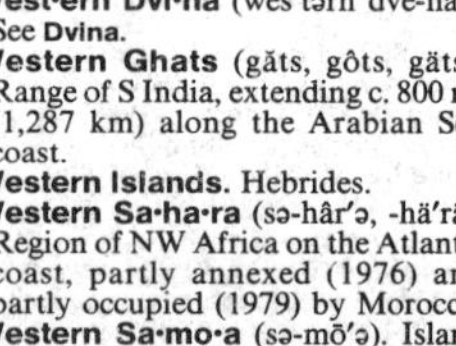

Western Samoa

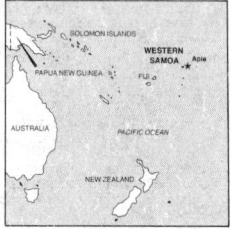

Western Springs. Village of NE Ill., near Chicago. Pop. 12,876.
Wes·ter·ville (wĕs'tər-vĭl'). City of central Ohio, near Columbus. Pop. 23,414.
West Far·go (fär'gō). City of E N.Dak., near Fargo. Pop. 10,099.
West·field (wĕst'fēld'). **1.** City of SW Mass., near Springfield. Pop. 36,465. **2.** Town of NE central N.J., SW of Newark. Pop. 30,447.
West·ford (wĕst'fərd). Town of NE Mass., near Lowell. Pop. 13,434.
West Hart·ford (härt'fərd). Town of central Conn., near Hartford. Pop. 61,301.
West Ha·ven (hā'vən). City of S Conn., near New Haven. Pop. 53,184.
West He·le·na (hĕl'ə-nə). City of E Ark., on the Mississippi R. SSW of Memphis, Tenn. Pop. 11,430.
West In·dies (ĭn'dēz). Islands between SE North America and N South America, separating the Caribbean Sea and the Atlantic, and including the Greater Antilles, the Lesser Antilles, and the Bahamas.
West Indies Associated States. Group of former British colonies in the West Indies, including Antigua, Dominica, St. Kitts-Nevis, St. Lucia, and St. Vincent and the Grenadines.
West I·ri·an (îr'ē-än'). Region and province of Indonesia comprising the W half of New Guinea.
West Jor·dan (jôr'dn). City of N Utah, S of Salt Lake City. Pop. 26,794.
West La·fay·ette (lăf'ē-ĕt', lä'fē-). City of W Ind., on the Wabash R. opposite Lafayette. Pop. 21,247.
West·lake (wĕst'lāk'). City of NE Ohio, near Cleveland. Pop. 19,483.
West·land (wĕst'lənd). City of NE Mich., near Dearborn. Pop. 84,603.
West Linn (lĭn). City of NW Ore., near Oregon City. Pop. 12,956.
West Mem·phis (mĕm'fĭs). City of E Ark., on the Mississippi opposite Memphis, Tenn. Pop. 28,198.
West Mif·flin (mĭf'lĭn). Borough of SW Pa., near Pittsburgh. Pop. 26,279.
West·min·ster (wĕst'mĭn'stər). **1.** City of S Calif., near Long Beach. Pop. 71,133. **2.** City of N central Colo., near Denver. Pop. 50,211.
West Mon·roe (mən-rō'). City of N central La., on the Ouachita R. opposite Monroe. Pop. 14,993.
West·mont (wĕst'mŏnt'). Village of NE Ill., near Chicago. Pop. 16,718.
West·mount (wĕst'mount'). City of S Que., Canada, on Montreal Is. W of Montreal. Pop. 22,153.
West New York (no͞o yôrk', nyo͞o). Town of NE N.J., on the Hudson opposite Manhattan. Pop. 39,194.
Wes·ton (wĕs'tən). Town of E Mass., W of Boston. Pop. 11,169.
Wes·ton-su·per-Mare (wĕs'tən-so͞o'pər-mâr'). Borough of SW England, on the Bristol Channel WSW of Bristol. Pop. 51,960.
West Or·ange (ôr'ĭnj, ŏr'-). Town of NE N.J., near Montclair. Pop. 39,510.
West Palm Beach (päm). City of SE Fla., opposite Palm Beach and N of Fort Lauderdale. Pop. 62,530.
West Pat·er·son (păt'ər-sən). Borough of NE N.J., near Clifton. Pop. 11,293.
West·pha·lia (wĕst-fāl'yə, -fā'lē-ə). Region of W West Germany E of the Rhine and centered in the Ruhr district. **—West·pha'lian** *adj. & n.*
West·port (wĕst'pôrt', -pōrt'). Town of SW Conn., on Long Is. Sound. Pop. 25,290.
West Quod·dy Head (kwŏd'ē hĕd'). Cape of NE Me., S of Eastport at S entrance to Passamaquoddy Bay.
West Saint Paul (sānt pôl'). City of E Minn., near St. Paul. Pop. 18,527.
West Spits·ber·gen (spĭts'bûrg'ən). Largest of the Spitsbergen Is., in the Arctic Ocean N of Norway.
West Spring·field (sprĭng'fēld'). Town of SW Mass., near Springfield. Pop. 27,042.
West U·ni·ver·si·ty Place (yo͞o'nə-vûr'sĭ-tē plās'). City of SE Tex., near Houston. Pop. 12,010.
West Vir·gin·ia (vər-jĭn'yə). State of E central U.S. Cap. Charleston. Pop. 1,949,644. **—West Vir·gin'ian** *adj. & n.*
West War·wick (wôr'ĭk, wôr'wĭk). Town of E central R.I., SSW of Providence. Pop. 27,026.
West·we·go (wĕst-wē'gō). City of SE La., on the Mississippi opposite New Orleans. Pop. 12,663.
West·wood (wĕst'wo͝od'). **1.** Town of E Mass., SW of Boston. Pop. 13,212. **2.** Borough of NE N.J., N of Hackensack. Pop. 10,714.
We·tar (wĕ'tär). Island of SE Indonesia, in the S Moluccas off NE Timor.
Weth·ers·field (wĕth'ərz-fēld'). Town of central Conn., near Hartford. Pop. 26,013.
Wet·ter·horn (vĕt'ər-hôrn'). Peak, c. 12,150 ft (3,706 m), of the Bernese Alps in central Switzerland.
Wey·mouth (wā'məth). Town of E Mass., SSE of Boston. Pop. 55,601.
Weymouth and Port·land (pôrt'lənd, pōrt'-). Borough of S England, on the English Channel WSW of Southampton. Pop. 57,700.
Whales (hwālz, wālz), **Bay of.** Inlet of

the Ross Sea in the Ross Ice Shelf, W Antarctica.

Whea·ton (hwēt'n, wēt'n). **1.** City of NE Ill., near Chicago. Pop. 43,043. **2.** City of central Md., near Washington, D.C. Pop. 73,800.

Wheat Ridge (hwēt' rĭj', wēt'). City of N central Colo., near Denver. Pop. 30,293.

Wheel·er Peak (hwē'lər, wē'-). Mountain, 13,160 ft (4,013.8 m), in N central N.Mex.

Wheel·ing (hwē'lĭng, wē'-). **1.** Village of NE Ill., near Chicago. Pop. 23,266. **2.** City of NW W.Va., in the Panhandle on the Ohio R. Pop. 43,070.

Whid·bey (hwĭd'bē, wĭd'-). Island of NW Wash., in Puget Sound.

Whit·by (hwĭt'bē, wĭt'-). Town of S central Ont., Canada, NE of Toronto. Pop. 32,952.

White (hwīt, wīt). **1.** Sea of NW European USSR, and inlet of the Barents Sea. **2.** River of N Ark. and SW Mo., flowing c. 690 mi (1,110 km) SE to the Mississippi. **3.** River of NW Nebr. and S S.Dak., flowing 325 mi (523 km) E to the Missouri. **4.** River, 160 mi (257 km), of NW Colo. and E Utah. **5.** Mountains of the N Appalachians in N N.H. **6.** Pass, 2,888 ft (880.8 m), through the Coast Mts. between SE Alas. and NW B.C., Canada.

White Bear Lake (bâr). City of E Minn., near St. Paul. Pop. 22,538.

White·fish Bay (hwīt'fĭsh', wīt'-). Village of SE Wis., near Milwaukee. Pop. 14,930.

White·hall (hwīt'hôl', wīt'-). **1.** City of central Ohio, near Columbus. Pop. 21,299. **2.** Borough of SW Pa., near Pittsburgh. Pop. 15,206.

White·ha·ven (hwīt'hā'vən, wīt'-). Borough of NW England, at the entrance to Solway Firth. Pop. 26,260.

White·horse (hwīt'hôrs', wīt'-). Cap. of Y.T., Canada, in the S part of the Yukon R. Pop. 13,311.

White Nile (nīl). Section in the Nile in Sudan from Lake No to Khartoum.

White Plains (plānz). City of SE N.Y., N of New York City. Pop. 46,999.

White Rock (rŏk). City of SE B.C., Canada, on the Strait of Georgia and the U.S. border. Pop. 12,497.

White Sands National Monument (săndz). Area of gypsum sand dunes in S central N.Mex., near site of a bomb and missile testing range.

White Set·tle·ment (sĕt'l-mənt). City of NE Tex., near Fort Worth. Pop. 13,508.

White Vol·ta (vŏl'tə, vōl'-, vôl'-). River of Upper Volta and N Ghana, flowing 550 mi (885 km) S to the Black Volta to form the Volta.

White·wa·ter (hwīt'wô'tər, -wŏt'ər, wīt'-). City of SE Wis., WSW of Milwaukee. Pop. 11,520.

Whit·ney (hwĭt'nē, wĭt'-). **Mount.** 2nd highest peak in the U.S., 14,494 ft (4,420.7 m), in the Sierra Nevada of E central Calif.

Whit·sta·ble (hwĭt'stə-bəl, wĭt'-). Urban district of SE England, on the North Sea E of London. Pop. 26,980.

Whit·ti·er (hwĭt'ē-ər, wĭt'-). City of S Calif., SE of Los Angeles. Pop. 68,872.

Wich·i·ta (wĭch'ĭ-tô'). City of S central Kans., SW of Kansas City. Pop. 279,272.

Wichita Falls. City of N Tex., near the Okla. border NW of Fort Worth. Pop. 94,201.

Wick·liffe (wĭk'lĭf). City of NE Ohio, on Lake Erie NE of Cleveland. Pop. 16,790.

Wick·low (wĭk'lō). Mountains of E Ireland, along the coast S of Dublin.

Wid·nes (wĭd'nĕs', -nĭs). Borough of W central England, ESE of Liverpool. Pop. 120,700.

Wie·ner·wald (vē'nər-vält'). Forested range of NE Austria, just W of Vienna.

Wies·ba·den (vēs'bäd'n). City of central West Germany, on the Rhine W of Frankfurt. Pop. 273,267.

Wig·an (wĭg'ən). Borough of NW England, NE of Liverpool. Pop. 311,200.

Wight (wīt), **Isle of.** Island in the England Channel off S central England.

Wil·bra·ham (wĭl'brə-hăm'). Town of SW Mass., near Springfield. Pop. 12,053.

Wil·helm (vĭl'hĕlm), **Mount.** Highest peak (15,400 ft/4,697 m) of Papua New Guinea, in the Bismarck Mts.

Wil·helms·ha·ven (vĭl'hĕlms-hä'fən). City of NW West Germany, on the North Sea. Pop. 99,426.

Wilkes-Bar·re (wĭlks'băr'ē, -bär'ə). City of NE Pa., NNW of Allentown. Pop. 51,551.

Wilkes Land (wĭlks). Region of E Antarctica S of Australia.

Wil·kins·burg (wĭl'kĭnz-bûrg'). Borough of SW Pa., near Pittsburgh. Pop. 23,669.

Wil·lam·ette (wə-lăm'ĭt). River, 294 mi (473 km), of NW Ore.

Wil·la·pa (wĭl'ə-pô', -pä'). Bay of the Pacific off SW Wash.

Wil·lem·stad (vĭl'əm-stät'). Cap. of the Netherland Antilles, on the S coast of Curaçao. Pop. 50,000.

Wil·liams·burg (wĭl'yəmz-bûrg'). City of SE Va. with restored colonial district, NW of Newport News. Pop. 9,870.

Wil·liam·son (wĭl'yəm-sən), **Mount.** Peak, 14,384 ft (4,387.1 m), in the Sierra Nevada of E central Calif.

Wil·liams·port (wĭl'yəmz-pôrt', -pōrt'). City of central Pa., N of Harrisburg. Pop. 33,401.

Wil·li·man·tic (wĭl'ə-măn'tĭk). City of E Conn., WNW of Windham. Pop. 14,652.

Wil·lis·ton (wĭl'ĭ-stən). City of NW N.Dak., near the Mont. border. Pop. 13,336.

Will·mar (wĭl'mär'). City of SW central Minn., WNW of Minneapolis. Pop. 15,895.

Wil·lough·by (wĭl'ə-bē). City of NE Ohio, on Lake Erie NE of Cleveland. Pop. 19,329.

Wil·lo·wick (wĭl'ə-wĭk'). City of NE Ohio, on Lake Erie near Cleveland. Pop. 17,834.

Wil·mette (wĭl-mĕt'). Village of NE Ill., on Lake Michigan near Chicago. Pop. 28,229.

Wil·ming·ton (wĭl'mĭng-tən). **1.** City of NE Del., SW of Philadelphia, Pa. Pop. 70,195. **2.** Town of E Mass., near Boston. Pop. 17,471. **3.** City of SE N.C., SSE of Raleigh. Pop. 44,000. **4.** City of SW Ohio, SE of Dayton. Pop. 10,431.

Wilms·low (wĭlmz'lō', wĭmz'-). Urban district of NW England, S of Manchester. Pop. 31,250.

Wil·son (wĭl'sən). **1. Mount.** Mountain, 5,710 ft (1,741.6 m), in the San Gabriel range of SW Calif.; site of an observatory. **2.** City of E central N.C., E of Raleigh. Pop. 34,424.

Wil·ton (wĭl'tən). Town of SW Conn., N of Norwalk. Pop. 15,351.

Wilton Man·or (măn'ər). City of SE Fla., near Fort Lauderdale. Pop. 12,742.

Wim·ble·don (wĭm'bəl-dən). District of S Greater London, England.

Win·ches·ter (wĭn'chĕs'tər, -chĭ-stər). **1.** Borough of S central England, WSW of London. Pop. 31,070. **2.** Town of NW Conn., N of Torrington. Pop. 10,841. **3.** City of N central Ky., ESE of Lexington. Pop. 15,216. **4.** Town of E Mass., near Boston. Pop. 20,701. **5.** Independent city of N Va., WNW of Washington, D.C. Pop. 20,217.

Wind (wĭnd). River, c. 120 mi (192 km), of W central Wyo.

Win·der·mere (wĭn'dər-mîr'). Lake, 10.5 mi (17 km) long, of NW England; largest in England.

Wind·ham (wĭn'dəm). **1.** Town of E Conn., NNW of Norwich. Pop. 21,062. **2.** Town of SW Me., near Portland. Pop. 11,282.

Wind·hoek (vĭnt'ho͝ok', -ho͞ok'). Cap. of Namibia, in the central part. Pop. 61,260.

Wind River Range. Range of the Rockies in W Wyo.

Wind·sor (wĭn'zər). **1.** City of S Ont., Canada, on the Detroit R. opposite Detroit, Mich. Pop. 197,235. **2.** Borough of S central England, W of London. Pop. 29,660. **3.** Town of N Conn., near Hartford. Pop. 25,204.

Windsor Locks (lŏks). Town of N Conn., N of Windsor. Pop. 12,190.

Wind·ward (wĭnd'wərd). **1. Passage.** Strait, c. 50 mi (80 km) wide, between Cuba and Haiti. **2.** Islands of the SE West Indies, the S group of the Lesser Antilles, from Martinique S to Grenada. **3.** Islands of the S Pacific, the E group of the Society Is.

Win·field (wĭn'fēld'). City of S Kans., SSE of Wichita. Pop. 10,736.

Win·ne·ba·go (wĭn'ə-bā'gō). Lake, 215 sq mi (557 sq km), of E Wis.

Win·net·ka (wə-nĕt'kə). Village of NE Ill., on Lake Michigan NNW of Evanston. Pop. 12,772.

Win·ni·bi·go·shish (wĭn'ə-bĭ-gō'shĭsh). Lake, 179 sq mi (464 sq km), of N central Minn.

Win·ni·peg (wĭn'ə-pĕg'). **1.** Lake, 9,465 sq mi (24,514 sq km), of S central Man., Canada. **2.** River, c. 200 mi (322 km), of W Ont. and SE Man., Canada. **3.** Cap. of Man., Canada, in the SE part. Pop. 610,000.

Win·ni·pe·go·sis (wĭn'ə-pĭ-gō'sĭs), **Lake.** Lake, 2,086 sq mi (5,403 sq km), of W Man., Canada, W of Lake Winnipeg.

Win·ni·pe·sau·kee (wĭn'ə-pĭ-sô'kē). Lake, 71 sq mi (184 sq km), of E central N.H.

Wi·no·na (wĭ-nō'nə). City of SE Minn., on the Mississippi SE of St. Paul. Pop. 25,075.

Win·ston-Sa·lem (wĭn'stən-sā'ləm). City of N central N.C., NNE of Charlotte. Pop. 131,885.

Win·ter Ha·ven (wĭn'tər hā'vən). City of central Fla., E of Lakeland. Pop. 21,119.

Winter Park. City of central Fla., near Orlando. Pop. 22,314.

Win·ter·thur (vĭn'tər-to͞or'). City of N Switzerland, NE of Zurich. Pop. 86,100.

Win·throp (wĭn'thrəp). Town of E Mass., near Boston. Pop. 19,294.

Win·yah (wĭn'yô'). Bay of the Atlantic off E S.C.

Wis·con·sin (wĭs-kŏn'sĭn). **1.** River of Wis., flowing c. 430 mi (692 km) S and W to the Mississippi. **2.** State of N central U.S. Cap. Madison. Pop. 4,705,335. —**Wis·con'sin·ite'** *n.*

Wisconsin Rapids. City of central Wis., S of Wausau. Pop. 17,995.

Wis·mar (vĭs'mär'). City of NW East Germany, near the Baltic. Pop. 57,055.

With·la·coo·chee (wĭth'lə-ko͞o'chē). **1.** River, c. 160 mi (257 km), of central Fla. **2.** River, c. 115 mi (185 km), of S Ga. and NW Fla.

Wit·ten (vĭt'n). City of W Germany, on the Ruhr R. Pop. 106,185.

Wit·ten·berg (wĭt'n-bûrg', vĭt'n-bĕrk'). City of central East Germany, on the Elbe. Pop. 53,211.

Wit·wa·ters·rand (wĭt-wô'tərz-rănd', -ränd', -wŏt'ərz-). Gold-rich region of NE South Africa, between the Vaal R. and Johannesburg.

Wlo·cla·wek (vlô-tslä'vĕk). City of central Poland, on the Vistula WNW of Warsaw. Pop. 104,400.

Wo·burn (wō'bərn, wo͞o'-). City of E Mass., near Boston. Pop. 36,626.

Wod·zi·slaw Slą·ski (vô-jē'swäf shlôN'skē). City of S Poland, SW of Katowice. Pop. 104,500.

Wo·king (wō'kĭng). Urban district of SE England, SW of London. Pop. 80,500.

Wol·cott (wo͝ol'kət). Town of central Conn., NE of Waterbury. Pop. 13,008.

Wolds (wōldz), **The.** Range of chalk hills along the NE coast of England.

Wolfs·burg (wo͝olfs'bərg, vôlfs'bo͝ork). City of NE West Germany, E of Hannover. Pop. 126,942.

Wol·las·ton (wo͝ol'ə-stən, wŏl'-). Lake, 796 sq mi (2,062 sq km), in NE Sask., Canada.

Wol·lin or **Wo·lin** (vô'lēn). Island of extreme NW Poland, in the Baltic near the mouth of the Oder.

Wol·lon·gong (wo͝ol'ən-găng', -gông). City of SE Australia, on the Tasman Sea SSW of Sydney. Pop. 172,350.

Wol·ver·hamp·ton (wo͝ol'vər-hămp'tən). Borough of W central England, NW of Birmingham. Pop. 258,200.

Won·san (wœn'sän'). City of SE North Korea, on the Sea of Japan. Pop. 215,000.

Wood·bridge (wo͝od'brĭj'). City of NE N.J., SSW of Elizabeth. Pop. 14,200.

Wood Buf·fa·lo National Park (wo͝od' bŭf'ə-lō'). Reserved area of forests and plains in N Alta. and S N.W.T., Canada.

Wood·burn (wo͝od'bərn). City of NW Ore., NE of Salem. Pop. 11,196.

Wood·bur·y (wo͝od'bĕr'ē, -bə-rē). **1.** City of E Minn., near St. Paul. Pop. 10,297. **2.** City of SW N.J., near Camden. Pop. 10,353.

Wood Dale (dāl). City of NE Ill., near Chicago. Pop. 11,251.

Wood·ha·ven (wo͝od'hā'vən). City of SE Mich., near Detroit. Pop. 10,902.

Wood·land (wo͝od'lənd). City of N central Calif., WNW of Sacramento. Pop. 30,235.

Wood·lark (wo͝od'lärk'). Island of Papua New Guinea, in the Solomon Sea off the SE end of New Guinea.

Wood·ridge (wo͝od'rĭj'). Village of NE Ill., near Chicago. Pop. 22,322.

Wood River. City of SW Ill., on the Mississippi near St. Louis, Mo. Pop. 12,449.

Woods (wo͝odz), **Lake of the.** Lake, 1,485 sq mi (3,846 sq km), of SW Ont., Canada, and N central Minn.

Wood·stock (wo͝od'stŏk'). **1.** City of S Ont., on the Thames R. WSW of Toronto. Pop. 26,020. **2.** City of NE Ill., W of Waukegan. Pop. 11,725.

Wood·ward (wo͝od'wərd). City of NW Okla., NW of Oklahoma City. Pop. 13,610.

Wool·wich (wo͝ol'ĭj, -ĭch, -wĭch). Township of S central Ont., Canada, N of Kitchener. Pop. 16,197.

Woon·sock·et (wo͞on-sŏk'ĭt, wo͞on'sŏk'-). City of N R.I., near the Mass. border NNW of Providence. Pop. 45,914.

Woo·ster (wo͝os'tər). City of NE central Ohio, NW of Akron. Pop. 19,289.

Worces·ter (wo͝os'tər). **1.** Borough of W central England, on the Severn SSW of Birmingham. Pop. 75,000. **2.** City of central Mass., W of Boston. Pop. 161,799.

Work·ing·ton (wûr'kĭng-tən). Borough of NW England, on Solway Firth. Pop. 28,260.

Work·sop (wûrk'səp, -sŏp'). Borough of N central England, ESE of Sheffield. Pop. 36,590.

Worms (wûrmz, vôrms). City of S central West Germany, on the Rhine NNW of Mannheim. Pop. 73,505.

Worth (wûrth). Village of NE Ill., near Chicago. Pop. 11,592.

Wor·thing (wûr'*th*ĭng). Borough of SE England, on the English Channel SSW of London. Pop. 90,600.

Wor·thing·ton (wûr'*th*ĭng-tən). **1.** City of SW Minn., near the Iowa border. Pop. 10,243. **2.** City of central Ohio, near Columbus. Pop. 15,016.

Wound·ed Knee (wo͞on'dĭd nē'). Creek of SW S.Dak.; site of last major battle of the Indian Wars (1890).

Wran·gel (răng'gəl). Island of NE Far Eastern USSR, in the Arctic Ocean NW of Bering Strait.

Wran·gell (răng'gəl). **1.** Mountains of S Alas., extending c. 100 mi (161 km) from the Copper R. to the Canadian border. **2. Mount.** Volcano, 14,006 ft (4,272 m), in the Wrangell range of S Alas. **3.** Cape of extreme W Alas., on Attu Is. in the Aleutians. **4.** Island of SE Alas., in the Alexander Archipelago NE of Prince of Wales Is.

Wrath (răth, rôth, räth), **Cape.** Promontory at NW extremity of the Scottish mainland.

Wrex·ham (rĕk'səm). Borough of NE Wales, W of Stoke-on-Trent. Pop. 39,530.

Wro·claw (vrô'tsläf). City of SW Poland, on the Oder R. Pop. 609,100.

Wu (wo͞o). River of central China, flowing c. 500 mi (805 km) E and N to the Yangtze.

Wu·han (wo͞o'hän'). City of E central

China, on the Yangtze. Pop. 3,000,-000.

Wu·hu (wo͞o'ho͞o'). City of E central China, on the Yangtze SSW of Nanjing. Pop. 325,000.

Wup·per·tal (vo͝op'ər-täl'). City of W West Germany, ENE of Düsseldorf. Pop. 394,605.

Würt·tem·berg (wûr'təm-bûrg', vür'-təm-bĕrk'). Region and former kingdom of SW West Germany.

Würz·burg (wûrts'bûrg, vürts'bo͝ork). City of S central West Germany, on the Main R. Pop. 127,370.

Wu·sih or **Wu·xi** (wo͞o'shē'). Changzhou.

Wu·tai Shan (wo͞o'tī' shän'). Range of NE China, extending c. 150 mi (240 km) between Taiyuan and Beijing.

Wy·an·dotte (wī'ən-dŏt'). **1.** Cave in S Ind., W of New Albany. **2.** City of SE Mich., near Detroit. Pop. 34,006.

Wye (wī). River, c. 130 mi (209 km), of E Wales and W England.

Wy·o·ming (wī-ō'mĭng). **1.** State of W U.S. Cap. Cheyenne. Pop. 470,816. **2.** City of W central Mich., near Grand Rapids. Pop. 59,616. **—Wy·o'·ming·ite'** *n.*

X

Xan·thus (zăn'thəs). Ancient city of Lycia, in present-day SW Turkey.

Xen·ia (zēn'yə, zē'nē-ə). City of SW central Ohio, ESE of Dayton. Pop. 24,653.

Xi (shyē). River, c. 300 mi (483 km), of SE China.

Xi'an (shyē'än'). City of central China, SW of Beijing. Pop. 1,900,000.

Xi·ang (shyē'äng'). River, c. 715 mi (1,150 km), of SE China.

Xi·an·tan (shyē-än'tän'). City of S central China, on the Xiang R. SSW of Changsha. Pop. 325,000.

Xin·gu (shĭng-go͞o'). River of central and N Brazil, flowing 1,230 mi (1,979.1 km) to the Amazon.

Xin·xi·ang (shyĭn'shyē-äng'). City of E China, SSE of Taiyuan. Pop. 250,000.

Xu·zhou (shyo͞o'jō'). City of E China, NNW of Nanjing. Pop. 800,000.

Y

Ya·blo·no·vy (yä'blə-nə-vē'). Mountain range in SE Siberian USSR.

Yai·zu (yī'zo͞o'). City of E central Honshu, Japan, near Shizuoka. Pop. 103,544.

Ya·ki·ma (yăk'ə-mə, -mô'). **1.** River, 203 mi (326.6 km), of central and SE Wash. **2.** City of S central Wash., SE of Seattle. Pop. 49,286.

Ya·kut (yä-ko͞ot') also **Ya·kutsk** (yä-ko͞otsk'). Region of NE Siberian USSR.

Ya·kutsk (yä-ko͞otsk'). City of E Siberian USSR, on the Lena R. Pop. 155,000.

Yal·ta (yôl'tə, yäl'-). City of SW European USSR, in S Crimea on the Black Sea. Pop. 81,000.

Ya·lu (yä'lo͞o', -lü'). River, c. 500 mi (805 km), forming part of the North Korea-China border.

Ya·lung (yä'lo͝ong'). River of W China flowing c. 800 mi (1,290 km) to the Yangtze.

Ya·ma·ga·ta (yä'mä-gä'tä). City of N Honshu, Japan, SW of Sendai. Pop. 236,984.

Ya·mal (yə-mäl'). Peninsula of NW Siberian USSR, extending c. 400 mi (643.6 km) between the Kara Sea and the Gulf of Ob.

Ya·ma·to (yä'mä'tô'). City of E central Honshu, Japan, near Tokyo. Pop. 165,858.

Yam·bol (yäm'bôl'). City of SE Bulgaria, E of Stara Zagora. Pop. 81,447.

Yam·pa (yăm'pə). River, c. 250 mi (400 km), of NW Colo.

Ya·na (yä'nə). River, c. 750 mi (1,206.8 km), of central and N Siberian USSR.

Yang·tze (yăng'sē, yăng'dzŭ'). Longest river of China and of Asia, flowing c. 3,450 mi (5,550 km) from Tibet to the East China Sea.

Yang·zhou also **Yang·chou** (yăng'-jō'). City of E central China, on the Grand Canal. Pop. 175,000.

Yank·ton (yăngk'tən). City of SE S.Dak., on the Missouri R. at the Nebr. border. Pop. 12,011.

Yao (you). City of S Honshu, Japan, near Osaka. Pop. 272,706.

Ya·oun·dé (yä-o͞on-dā') or **Yaun·dé** (youn'dā). Cap. of Cameroon, in the central part. Pop. 313,706.

Yap (yăp, yäp). Island group in W Caroline Is. of the W Pacific.

Ya·qui (yä'kē). River, c. 400 mi (643.6 km), of NW Mexico.

Yar·kand (yär-kănd'). River, c. 500 mi (804.5 km), of NW China.

Yar·mouth (yär'məth). **1.** Great Yarmouth. **2.** Town of SE Mass., on central Cape Cod. Pop. 18,449.

Ya·ro·slavl (yə-rō-släv'əl). City of E European USSR, on the upper Volga R. Pop. 603,000.

Yaun·dé (youn'dā). Variant of **Yaoundé**.

Yazd (yäzd). City of central Iran, SE of Esfahan. Pop. 135,978.

Ya·zoo (yă-zo͞o', yăz'o͞o). River, 188 mi (302.5 km), of W Miss.

Yazoo City. City of W central Miss., NNW of Jackson. Pop. 12,426.

Yea·don (yăd'n). Borough of SE Pa., near Philadelphia. Pop. 11,727.

Ye·lets (yĭ-lyĕts'). City of E central USSR, E of Orel. Pop. 112,000.

Yel·low (yĕl'ō). **1. Sea.** Arm of the Pacific, between the Chinese mainland and Korean Peninsula. **2.** River of N China, flowing c. 3,000 mi (4,830 km) to the Gulf of Bo Hai.

Yel·low·knife (yĕl'ō-nīf'). Capital of N.W.T., Canada, on the N shore of Great Slave Lake. Pop. 9,969.

Yel·low·stone (yĕl'ō-stōn'). **1.** River, 671 mi (1,079.6 km) long, of NW Wyo. and Mont. **2. National Park.** Oldest and largest (2,221,773 acres/ 899,818 hectares) of U.S. national parks, mostly in NW Wyo.

Yem·en (yĕm'ən). **1.** Also **North Yemen.** Country of SW Asia, at the SW tip of the Arabian Peninsula. Cap. Sana. Pop. 5,785,000. **2.** Also **Southern Yemen.** Country of SW Asia, at the S edge of the Arabian Peninsula. Cap. Aden. Pop. 1,555,000.

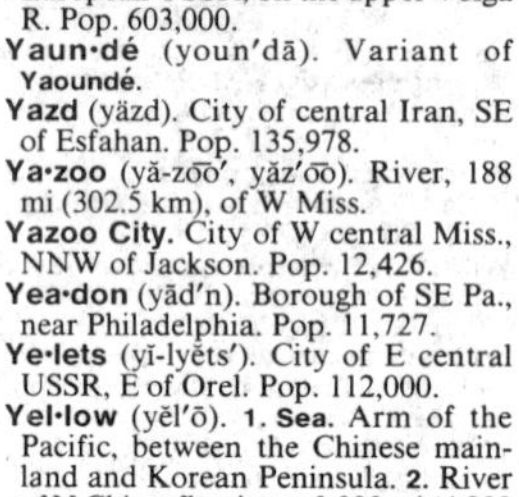

Yemen

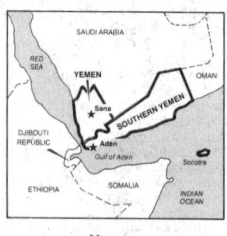

Yen·a·ki·ye·vo (yĕ-nə-kē'yə-və). City of SE European USSR, in the Ukraine near Donetsk. Pop. 115,000.

Ye·ni·sei (yĕn'ĭ-sā'). River of central Siberian USSR, flowing c. 2,500 mi (4,025.6 km) to the Kara Sea.

Yeo·vil (yō'vĭl). Borough of SW England, on the **Yeo R.** S of Bristol. Pop. 26,180.

Ye·re·van (yĕ-rĕ-vän'). City of SE European USSR, S of Tbilisi. Pop. 1,036,000.

Ye·şil Ir·mak (yĕ-shĕl' ĭr-mäk'). River of N Turkey, flowing c. 260 mi (420 km) to the Black Sea.

Yi·bin (yĭ'bĭn'). City of S central China, on the Yangtze WSW of Chongqing. Pop. 250,000.

Yok·kai·chi (yôk-kī'chē). City of W Honshu, Japan, on Ise Bay. Pop. 255,442.

Yo·ko·ha·ma (yō'kə-hä'mə, yô'-kô-hä'mä). City of SE Honshu, Japan, on W shore of Tokyo Bay. Pop. 2,773,322.

Yo·ko·su·ka (yō'kə-so͞o'kə, yô'-kô-so͞o'kə). City of E central Honshu, Japan, near Tokyo. Pop. 421,112.

Yo·na·go (yô-nä'gô). Town of W Honshu, Japan. Pop. 125,291.

Yon·kers (yŏng'kərz). City of SE N.Y., N of New York City. Pop. 195,351.

Yor·ba Lin·da (yôr'bə lĭn'də). City of S Calif., near Anaheim. Pop. 28,254.

York (yôrk). **1. Cape.** Northernmost point of Australia, on Torres Strait at the tip of Cape York Peninsula. **2.** Borough of N England, on the Ouse R. ENE of Leeds. Pop. 100,900. **3.** W borough of metropolitan Toronto, Ont., Canada, on Lake Ontario. Pop. 134,813. **4.** City of S Pa., near the Md. border, SSE of Harrisburg. Pop. 44,619.

Yorke (yôrk). Narrow peninsula of S Australia, bounded by Spencer Gulf.

York·ton (yôrk'tən). City of SE Sask., Canada, NE of Regina. Pop. 14,408.

York·town (yôrk'toun'). Village in SE Va., site of English surrender in Revolutionary War (1781).

Yo·sem·i·te National Park (yō-sĕm'ĭ-tē). Rugged area of E central Calif., including **Yosemite Valley** and **Yosemite Falls** (2,425 ft/ 739.6 m high).

Yosh·kar-O·la (yəsh-kär'ə-lä'). City of E central European USSR, NW of Kazan. Pop. 207,000.

Yo·su (yŭ'so͞o', yō'-). City of S South Korea, on the Korea Strait. Pop. 151,337.

Youngs·town (yŭngz'toun'). City of NE Ohio, near the Pa. border E of Akron. Pop. 115,436.

Y·pres (ē'prə). Variant of **Ieper.**

Yp·si·lan·ti (ĭp'sə-lăn'tē). City of SE Mich., WSW of Detroit. Pop. 24,031.

Yu (yo͞o). River of SE China, flowing c. 400 mi (644 km) E to the Honshui to form the Xi.

Yu·an (yo͞o'än'). *Chinese.* Red R. (sense 3).

Yu·ba City (yo͞o'bə). City of N central Calif., NNW of Sacramento. Pop. 18,736.

Yu·ca·tán (yo͞o'kə-tăn', -kä-tän'). Peninsula, mostly in SE Mexico, separating the Caribbean from the Gulf of Mexico.

Yu·go·sla·vi·a also **Ju·go·sla·vi·a** (yo͞o'gō-slä'vē-ə). Republic of SE Europe, largely in the Balkan Peninsula. Cap. Belgrade. Pop. 21,560,000. **—Yu'go·sla'vi·an** *adj. & n.*

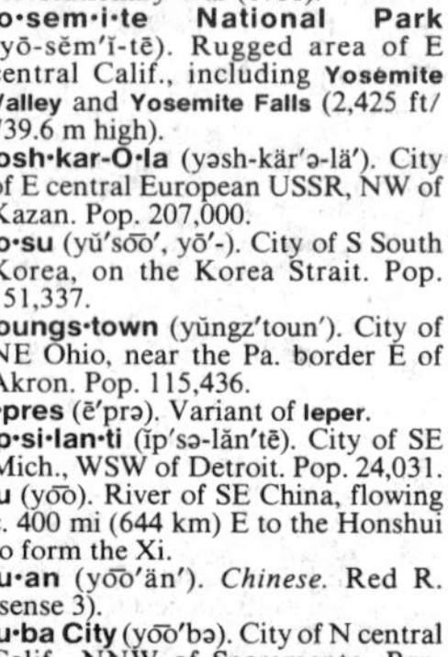

Yugoslavia

Yu·kon (yo͞o'kŏn'). **1.** River flowing c. 2,000 mi (3,220 km) S Y.T., Canada, through Alas. to the Bering Sea. **2.** Territory of NW Canada, E of Alas. Cap. Whitehorse. Pop. 21,836. **3.** City of central Okla., WNW of Oklahoma City. Pop. 17,112.

Yu·ma (yo͞o'mə). City of SW Ariz., on the Calif. border. Pop. 42,433.

Z

Zaan·dam (zän-däm'). City of W Netherlands, near Amsterdam. Pop. 128,809.

Zab (zäb, zăb). **1.** Also **Great Zab.** River, c. 265 mi (426.4 km), of SE Turkey and N Iraq. **2.** Also **Little Zab.** River, c. 250 mi (402.3 km), of NW Iran and N Iraq.

Zab·rze (zäb'zhĕ). City of SW Poland E of Katowice. Pop. 195,000.

Za·ca·te·cas (sä'kä-tĕ'käs). City of N central Mexico, N of Aguascalientes. Pop. 50,251.

Za·dar (zä'där). City of W Yugoslavia, in Croatia on the Dalmatian coast. Pop. 43,187.

Za·gorsk (zä-gôrsk'). City of central European USSR, NE of Moscow. Pop. 108,000.

Za·greb (zä'grĕb). City of NW Yugoslavia, on the Sava R. Pop. 566,084.

Zag·ros (zăg'rəs, -rŏs). Mountain range of W Iran, forming W and S border of the central Iranian plateau.

Zaire (zī'ĭr, zä-ĭr'). Republic of W central Africa, astride the equator. Cap. Kinshasa. Pop. 24,222,000.

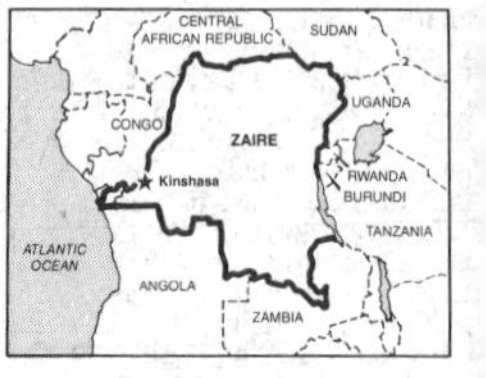

Zaire

Za·ma (zā'mə). Ancient town in present-day N Tunisia; site of decisive defeat of Hannibal by the Romans (202 B.C.).

Zam·be·zi (zăm-bē'zē). River, c. 1,700 mi (2,735 km), of central and S Africa.

Zam·bi·a (zăm'bē-ə, zäm'-). Republic of S central Africa. Cap. Lusaka. Pop. 5,834,000. **—Zam'bi·an** *adj. & n.*

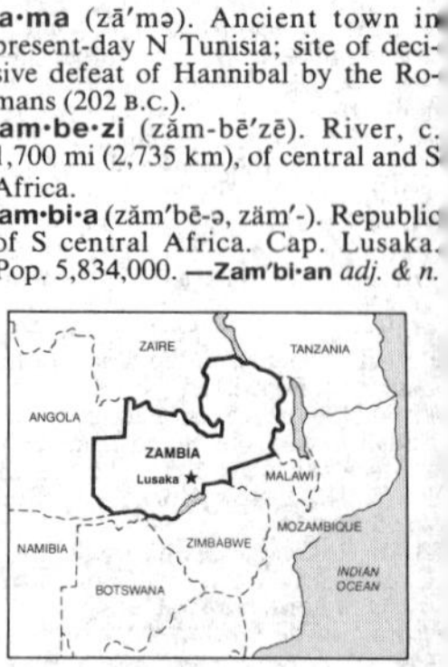

Zambia

Za·mo·ra (sä-mô'rä). City of NW Spain, on the Duero R. Pop. 55,822.

Zanes·ville (zānz'vĭl'). City of E central Ohio, E of Columbus. Pop. 28,655.

Zan·jan (zän-jän'). City of NW Iran, SW of the Caspian Sea. Pop. 99,967.

Zan·zi·bar (zăn'zə-bär'). **1.** Region of E Africa, part of Tanzania. **2.** Island, 641 sq mi (1,660.2 sq km), off the NE coast of Tanzania. **3.** City of Tanzania, on the W coast of Zanzibar Is. Pop. 80,000.

Za·po·ro·zhe (zä'pə-rô'zhyĕ). City of S European USSR, on the Dnieper R. Pop. 799,000.

Za·ra·go·za (sä'rä-gô'sä). Variant of **Saragossa.**

Za·ri·a (zä'rē-ə). City of N Nigeria, NE of Kaduna. Pop. 224,000.

Za·wier·ci (zä-vyĕr'chĕ). City of S Poland, NW of Katowice. Pop. 61,600.

Zea·land (zē'lənd). *English.* Sjælland.

Zeist (zīst). City of central Netherlands, near Utrecht. Pop. 61,532.

Zeitz (tsīts). City of S East Germany, near Leipzig. Pop. 44,135.

Ze·rav·shan (zĕ-räf-shän'). River, c. 460 mi (740 km), of S Central Asian USSR.

Ze·ya (zā'ä, zyā'ə). River of Far Eastern USSR, flowing c. 800 mi (1,290 km) to the Amur.

Zgierz (zgyĕzh). City of E central Poland, near Łódź. Pop. 52,100.

Zhang·jia·kou (jäng'jyä'gō'). City of NE China, near the Great Wall. Pop. 300,000.

Zhan·jiang (jän'jyäng'). City of SE China, SW of Guangzhou. Pop. 200,000.

Zhda·nov (zhdä'nəf). City of S European USSR, on the Sea of Azov. Pop. 507,000.
Zheng·zhou (jŭng'jō'). City of E central China, SSW of Beijing. Pop. 1,100,000.
Zhen·jiang (jŭn'jyäng'). City of E China, on the Grand Canal E of Nanjing. Pop. 100,000.
Zhi·to·mir (zhĭ-tô'mîr). City of SW European USSR, W of Kiev. Pop. 250,000.
Zhou·shan (jō'shän'). Archipelago in the East China Sea, at the entrance to Hangzhou Bay, E China.
Zhu Jiang (jo͞o'jyäng'). River, c. 110 mi (177 km), of SE China, flowing into the South China Sea.
Zhu·zhou (jo͞o'jō'). City of S central China, on the Xiang R. Pop. 250,000.
Zi·bo (dzē'bwō'). City of E China, E of Jinan. Metro. area pop. 900,000.
Zie·lo·no Gó·ra (zhĕ-lô'nä go͞o'rä). City of W Poland, W of Łódź. Pop. 98,000.
Zi·gong (dzē'go͞ong'). City of S central China, W of Chongqing. Pop. 325,000.
Zim·bab·we (zĭm-bä'bwā). Republic of S central Africa. Cap. Salisbury. Pop. 7,130,000. —**Zim·bab'we·an** *adj. & n.*
Zi·on (zī'ən). City of NE Ill., on Lake Michigan. Pop. 17,861.
Zla·to·ust (zlə-tə-o͞ost'). City of E European USSR, in the S Urals. Pop. 199,000.

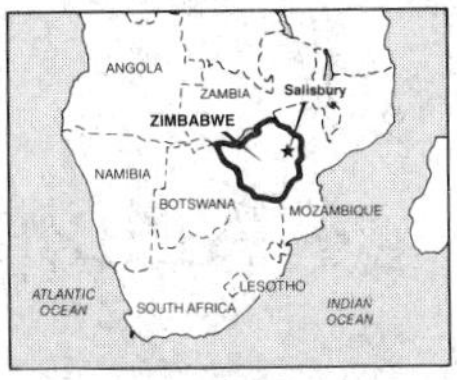

Zimbabwe

Zon·gul·dak (zông'go͝ol-däk'). City of N Turkey, on the Black Sea. Pop. 108,661.
Zug·spit·ze (tso͞ok'shpĭt-sə, zo͞og'-spĭt-). Mountain, 9,271 ft (2,965 m), in the Alps of Bavaria, S West Germany.
Zu·lu·land (zo͞o'lo͞o-lănd'). Historical region of NE South Africa.
Zun·yi (jo͞on'yē'). City of S China, SSE of Chongqing. Pop. 250,000.
Zu·rich (zo͞or'ĭk). City of NE Switzerland, at N tip of **Lake Zurich**. Pop. 374,200.
Zwick·au (tvĭk'ou). City of S East Germany, S of Leipzig. Pop. 123,446.
Zwol·le (zvôl'ə, zwôl'ə). City of N central Netherlands, on the Ijssel R. Pop. 82,190.

Abbreviations

Established or generally preferred forms are given in the following list. The use of small capitals is indicated by a note at the definition.

a 1. Also **a.** are (measurement). 2. *Physics.* atto-.
A 1. Also **a.** or **A.** acre. 2. ammeter. 3. ampere. 4. area.
a. 1. about. 2. acceleration. 3. acreage. 4. acting. 5. adjective. 6. afternoon. 7. Also **A.** amateur. 8. *Lat.* anno (in the year). 9. *Lat.* annus (year). 10. anonymous. 11. Also **A.** answer. 12. *Lat.* ante (before). 13. anterior.
A. 1. academician; academy. 2. alto. 3. America; American.
Å angstrom.
A1C airman, first class.
AA 1. Alcoholics Anonymous. 2. antiaircraft.
A.A. Associate in Arts.
AAA 1. Agricultural Adjustment Administration. 2. American Automobile Association. 3. antiaircraft artillery.
AAAL American Academy of Arts and Letters.
AAAS American Association for the Advancement of Science.
AACS 1. Airways and Air Communications System. 2. Army Airways Communications System.
AAF Army Air Forces.
A and R artists and repertory.
AAPSS American Academy of Political and Social Sciences.
A.A.S. Associate in Applied Sciences.
AAU Amateur Athletic Union.
AAUP American Association of University Professors.
AAUW American Association of University Women.
AB Alberta.
ab. about.
A.B. 1. Or **a.b.** able-bodied seaman. 2. *Lat.* Artium Baccalaureus (Bachelor of Arts).
ABA 1. American Bankers Association. 2. Also **A.B.A.** American Bar Association. 3. American Booksellers Association.
abb. abbess; abbey; abbot.
abbr. or **abbrev.** abbreviation.
ABC 1. Alcoholic Beverage Control. 2. American Broadcasting Company. 3. Australian Broadcasting Company.
ABEND *Computer Sci.* abnormal end of task.
abl. ablative.
ABM antiballistic missile.
abn airborne.
abp. or **Abp.** archbishop.
abr. abridged; abridgment.
ABS American Bible Society.
abs. 1. absence; absent. 2. absolute; absolutely. 3. abstract.
abt. about.
ac 1. acre. 2. air-cooled. 3. Or **AC** alternating current.
Ac *Bible.* Acts.
a.c. 1. Or **a/c** air conditioning. 2. *Lat.* ante cibum (*Med.* before meals).
A.C. 1. air corps. 2. *Lat.* ante Christum (before Christ).
a/c account; account current.
acad. academic; academy.
acct. account; accountant.
ACE American Council on Education.
acet. acetone.
ack. acknowledge; acknowledgment.
ACLU American Civil Liberties Union.
ACP American College of Physicians.
acpt. acceptance.
ACRR American Council on Race Relations.
ACS 1. American Chemical Society. 2. American College of Surgeons.
ACT 1. Action for Children's Television. 2. American College Test.
A.C.T. Australian Capital Territory.
actg. acting.
acv actual cash value.
ACV air-cushion vehicle.
ad. adapter.
AD 1. active duty. 2. air-dried.
A.D. *Lat.* anno Domini (in the year of the Lord). Usually small capitals A.D.
ADA 1. American Dental Association. 2. Americans for Democratic Action.
ADC 1. Also **a.d.c.** aide-de-camp. 2. Aid to Dependent Children. 3. Air Defense Command.
add. addendum.
addn. addition.
addnl. additional.
adf air direction finder.
ad int. *Lat.* ad interim (in the meantime).
adj. 1. adjective. 2. adjunct. 3. adjustment. 4. Also **Adj.** adjutant.
adjt. adjutant.
ad loc. *Lat.* ad locum (to, or at, the place).
adm. administrative; administrator.
Adm. admiral; admiralty.
admin. administration; administrator.
ADP automatic data processing.
adv. 1. adverb; adverbial. 2. *Lat.* adversus (against). 3. advertisement. 4. advisory.
advt. advertisement.
AEA Actors' Equity Association.
AEC Atomic Energy Commission.
AF also **A.F.** 1. air force. 2. audio frequency.
AFAM Ancient Free and Accepted Masons.
AFB air force base.
AFDC Aid to Families with Dependent Children.
Afg. Afghanistan.
AFL 1. Also **A.F. of L.** American Federation of Labor. 2. American Football League.
AFL-CIO also **A.F.L-C.I.O.** American Federation of Labor and Congress of Industrial Organizations.
Afr. Africa; African.
AFT American Federation of Teachers.
aft. afternoon.
AFTRA American Federation of Television and Radio Artists.
A.G. also **AG** 1. adjutant general. 2. attorney general.
agcy. agency.
AGO American Guild of Organists.
agr. agricultural; agriculture.
agric. agriculture; agriculturist.
agt. 1. agent. 2. agreement.
A.h or **a-h** ampere-hour.
A.H. *Lat.* 1. anno Hebraico (in the Hebrew year). 2. anno Hegirae (in the year of the Hegira).
AHA 1. American Historical Association. 2. American Hospital Association.
AHL American Hockey League.
ai airborne intercept.
a.i. *Lat.* ad interim (in the meantime).
AIA American Institute of Architects.
AIChE American Institute of Chemical Engineers.
AK Alaska.
a.k.a. also known as.
AKC American Kennel Club.
AL 1. Alabama. 2. American League. 3. American Legion.
ALA American Library Association.
Ala. Alabama.
A.L.A. Associate in Liberal Arts.
Alas. Alaska.
Alb. Albania; Albanian.
alc. alcohol; alcoholic.
Ald. alderman.
alg. algebra.
Alg. Algeria.
alky. alkalinity.
allo *Mus.* allegro.
a.l.s. or **A.L.S.** autograph letter signed.
alt. 1. alternate. 2. altimeter. 3. altitude.
Alta. Alberta.
am or **AM** amplitude modulation.
Am *Bible.* Amos.
Am. America; American.
A.M. 1. airmail. 2. *Lat.* anno mundi (in the year of the world). Usually small capitals A.M. 3. Also **a.m.** *Lat.* ante meridiem (before noon). Usually small capitals A.M. 4. *Lat.* Artium Magister (Master of Arts).
AMA also **A.M.A.** American Medical Association.
AMC automatic message counting.
Amer. America; American.
Amex American Stock Exchange.
Amn airman.
amp hr. ampere-hour.
AMS Agricultural Marketing Service.
amt. amount.
amu *Physics.* atomic mass unit.
AMVETS American Veterans.
An *Physics.* actinon.
AN also **A.N.** Anglo-Norman.
an. *Lat.* 1. ante (before). 2. anno (in the year).
ANA 1. American Newspaper Association. 2. American Nurses Association. 3. Association of National Advertisers.
anal. 1. analogous; analogy. 2. analysis; analytic.
anat. anatomical; anatomist; anatomy.
anc. ancient.
and. *Mus.* andante.
And. Andorra.
Ang. Angola.
anhydr. anhydrous.
anim. *Mus.* animato.
ann. 1. annals. 2. annual. 3. annuity.
anon. anonymous.
ans. answer.
ANSI American National Standards Institute.
ant. 1. antenna. 2. antiquarian; antiquity. 3. antonym.
Ant. Antarctica.
ANTA American National Theatre and Academy.
anthrop. anthropologic; anthropology.
antiq. 1. antiquarian; antiquary. 2. antiquities. 3. antiquity.
a/o account of.
AOH Ancient Order of Hibernians.
aor. aorist.
AP 1. airplane. 2. air police. 3. American plan. 4. antipersonnel. 5. Or **A.P.** Associated Press.
ap. apothecary.
a.p. 1. additional premium. 2. author's proof.
APA 1. American Philological Association. 2. American Philosophical Association. 3. American Psychiatric Association. 4. American Psychological Association.
APB all points bulletin.
APO or **A.P.O.** Army Post Office.
Apoc. 1. Apocalypse. 2. Apocrypha; Apocryphal.
app. 1. apparatus. 2. appendix. 3. applied. 4. appoint; appointed. 5. apprentice.
appl. applied.
approx. approximate; approximately.
appt. appoint; appointment.
apptd. appointed.
Apr. April.
apt. apartment.
aq. aqueous.
AR 1. Also **A/R** account receivable. 2. Arkansas.
ar. arrival; arrive.
Ar. 1. Arabia; Arabian. 2. Arabic.
A.R. also **AR** 1. Airman Recruit. 2. army regulation.
Arab. 1. Arabia; Arabian. 2. Arabic.
ARC American Red Cross.
arch. 1. archaic; archaism. 2. archery. 3. archipelago. 4. architect; architectural; architecture.
Archbp. archbishop.
archit. architecture.
archt. architect.
arg. argent.
Arg. Argentina; Argentine.
Ariz. Arizona.
Ark. Arkansas.
ARM automated route management.
Arm. Armenia; Armenian.
arr. 1. arranged. 2. arrival; arrive; arrived.
ARS Agricultural Research Service.
art. 1. article. 2. artificial. 3. artillery. 4. artist.
arty. artillery.
ARV *Bible.* American (Standard) Revised Version.
AS 1. Also **A.S.** Anglo-Saxon. 2. antisubmarine.
As. Asia; Asian.
a/s airspeed.
ASA 1. American Society of Appraisers. 2. American Standards Association. 3. American Statistical Association.
ASAP as soon as possible.
asb. asbestos.
ASCAP American Society of Composers, Authors, and Publishers.
ASCE American Society of Civil Engineers.
ASCU Association of State Colleges and Universities.
ASE American Stock Exchange.
asgd. assigned.
asgmt. assignment.
ASL American sign language.
ASME American Society of Mechanical Engineers.
ASPCA American Society for the Prevention of Cruelty to Animals.
assn. association.
assoc. associate; association.
ASSR or **A.S.S.R.** Autonomous Soviet Socialist Republic.
asst. assistant.
asstd. 1. assisted. 2. assorted.
assy. assembly.
Assyr. Assyrian.
ASTM American Society for Testing and Materials.
ASTP Army Specialized Training Program.
astrol. astrologer; astrologic; astrology.
astron. astronomer; astronomical; astronomy.
ASV *Bible.* American Standard Version.
aT *Physics.* attotesla.
At ampere-turn.
AT also **a/t** antitank.
at. 1. airtight. 2. atomic.
athl. athlete; athletic; athletics.
Atl. Atlantic.
atm *Physics.* atmosphere.
atm. or **atmos.** atmosphere; atmospheric.
at. no. also **at no** atomic number.
ATP *Biochem.* adenosine triphosphate.
ATS 1. American Temperance Society. 2. Army Transport Service.
att. 1. attached. 2. attention. 3. attorney.
attn. attention.
attrib. attribute; attributive.
atty. attorney.
Atty. Gen. attorney general.
at wt atomic weight.
a.u. or **A.u.** angstrom unit.
A.U. astronomical unit.
aud. audit; auditor.
aug. augmentative.
Aug. August.
AUS Army of the United States.
Aus. or **Aust.** 1. Australia. 2. Austria.
Austl. Australia; Australian.
auth. 1. authentic. 2. author. 3. authority. 4. authorized.
auto. 1. automatic. 2. automotive.
aux. auxiliary.
AV or **A.V.** 1. audio-visual. 2. *Bible.* Authorized Version.
av. 1. Or **Av.** avenue. 2. average. 3. avoirdupois.
a.v. or **a/v** *Lat.* ad valorem (in proportion to the value).
AVC 1. American Veterans Committee. 2. automatic volume control.
avdp. avoirdupois.
ave. or **Ave.** avenue

avg. average.
avn. aviation.
AW 1. aircraft warning. 2. Articles of War. 3. automatic weapon.
a.w. all water (transportation).
A/W actual weight.
ax. 1. axiom. 2. axis.
AYC American Youth Congress.
AYD American Youth for Democracy.
AYH American Youth Hostels.
AZ Arizona.
az. 1. azimuth. 2. azure.
AZC American Zionist Council.
Azo. Azores.

b *Physics.* barn.
B baryon number.
b. or **B.** 1. base. 2. *Mus.* basso. 3. bay. 4. bolivar. 5. book. 6. born. 7. breadth. 8. brother.
B. 1. bachelor. 2. bacillus. 3. Baumé scale. 4. Bible. 5. British. 6. brotherhood.
Ba *Bible.* Baruch.
Ba. Bahamas.
B.A. 1. *Lat.* Baccalaureus Artium (Bachelor of Arts). 2. British Academy. 3. British Association (for the Advancement of Science).
Bab. Babylonia; Babylonian.
bach. bachelor.
bact. bacteria; bacterial.
bacteriol. bacteriologist; bacteriology.
B.A.E. 1. Bachelor of Aeronautical Engineering. 2. Bachelor of Agricultural Engineering. 3. Bachelor of Architectural Engineering. 4. Bachelor of Art Education. 5. Bachelor of Arts in Education.
B.A.Ed. Bachelor of Arts in Education.
B.Ae.E. Bachelor of Aeronautical Engineering.
bal. balance.
B.A.M. 1. Bachelor of Applied Mathematics. 2. Bachelor of Arts in Music.
B and E breaking and entering.
Bap. or **Bapt.** Baptist.
BAR Browning automatic rifle.
bar. 1. barometer; barometric. 2. barrel.
Barb. Barbados.
B.Arch. Bachelor of Architecture.
Bart. baronet.
B.A.S. or **B.A.Sc.** 1. Bachelor of Agricultural Science. 2. Bachelor of Applied Science.
bat. battalion.
Bav. Bavaria; Bavarian.
bb also **b.b.** ball bearing.
B.B.A. Bachelor of Business Administration.
BBB Better Business Bureau.
BBC British Broadcasting Corporation.
B.B.Ed. Bachelor of Business Education.
bbl or **bbl.** barrel.
B.C. 1. Bachelor of Chemistry. 2. Bachelor of Commerce. 3. before Christ. Usually small capitals B.C. 4. Or **BC** British Columbia.
bcd or **BCD** *Computer Sci.* binary coded decimal.
B.C.E. 1. Bachelor of Chemical Engineering. 2. Bachelor of Civil Engineering. 3. before common era.
BCG bacillus Calmette-Guérin (tuberculosis vaccine).
B.Ch.E. Bachelor of Chemical Engineering.
B.C.L. 1. Bachelor of Canon Law. 2. Bachelor of Civil Law.
B.C.S. 1. Bachelor of Chemical Science. 2. Bachelor of Commercial Science.
BCSE Board of Civil Service Examiners.
BD 1. bank draft. 2. Also **b/d** bills discounted. 3. bomb disposal.
bd. 1. board. 2. bound. 3. bundle.
B.D. Bachelor of Divinity.
b/d 1. barrels per day. 2. brought down.
bd. ft. board foot.
bdl or **bdle.** bundle.
bdrm. bedroom.
bds. bound in boards.
B.D.S. Bachelor of Dental Surgery.
BDSA Business and Defense Services Administration.
BE Board of Education.
B.E. 1. Bachelor of Education. 2. Bachelor of Engineering.
B/E 1. bill of entry. 2. bill of exchange.
Bé Baumé scale.
BEC Bureau of Employees' Compensation.
B.Ed. Bachelor of Education.
BEF British Expeditionary Force.
bef. before.
Bel or **Belg.** Belgian; Belgium.
BEM also **B.E.M.** British Empire Medal.
B.E.M. Bachelor of Engineering of Mines.
B.Eng. Bachelor of Engineering.
B.Eng.Sci. Bachelor of Engineering Science.
bet. between.
BeV *Physics.* billion electron volts.
bf 1. Also **b.f.** or **bf.** boldface. 2. board foot.
b.f. or **B/F** *Accounting.* brought forward.
B.F.A. Bachelor of Fine Arts.
bg. 1. background. 2. bag.
B.G. Brigadier General.
BH bill of health.
bhd. bulkhead.
BHE Bureau of Higher Education.
Bhn. *Metallurgy.* Brinell hardness number.
bhp or **b.hp.** brake horsepower.
BHT butylated hydroxytoluene.
Bhu. Bhutan.
BIA 1. Braille Institute of America. 2. Bureau of Indian Affairs.
Bib. Bible; Biblical.
bibl. or **Bibl.** Biblical.
bibliog. bibliographer; bibliography.
b.i.d. *Lat.* bis in die (*Med.* twice a day).
biog. biographer; biographical; biography.
biol. biological; biologist; biology.
BIS or **B.I.S.** 1. Bank for International Settlements. 2. British Information Service.
B.J. Bachelor of Journalism.
bk. 1. bank. 2. book.
bkg. banking.
bkgd. background.
bklr. *Printing.* black letter.
bkpg. bookkeeping.
bkpt. bankrupt.
bks. 1. barracks. 2. books.
bl. 1. barrel. 2. black. 3. blue.
B.L. 1. Bachelor of Laws. 2. Bachelor of Letters; Bachelor of Literature.
B/L bill of lading.
B.L.A. Bachelor of Liberal Arts.
bld. 1. blood. 2. boldface.
bldg. building.
bldr. builder.
B.Lit. or **B.Litt.** *Lat.* Baccalaureus Litterarum (Bachelor of Literature).
blk. 1. black. 2. block. 3. bulk.
BLS Bureau of Labor Statistics.
B.L.S. Bachelor of Library Science.
blvd. boulevard.
BM basal metabolism.
bm. beam.
b.m. 1. board measure. 2. bowel movement.
B.M. 1. Bachelor of Medicine. 2. Bachelor of Music.
B.M.E. 1. Bachelor of Mechanical Engineering. 2. Bachelor of Mining Engineering. 3. Bachelor of Music Education.
BMOC big man on campus.
BMR basal metabolic rate.
B.M.S. Bachelor of Marine Science.
B.Mus. Bachelor of Music.
bn. or **Bn.** 1. baron. 2. battalion.
B.N.A. British North America.
Bngl. Bangladesh.
B.O.D. biochemical oxygen demand.
Boh. Bohemia; Bohemian.
Bol. Bolivia.
BOQ Bachelor Officers' Quarters.
bor. borough.
bot. 1. botanical; botanist; botany. 2. bottle. 3. bottom.
Bots. Botswana.
boul. boulevard.
bp boiling point.
BP 1. Or **B/P** bills payable. 2. blood pressure. 3. British Pharmacopoeia.
bp. bishop.
B.P. 1. Bachelor of Pharmacy. 2. Bachelor of Philosophy.
bpd barrels per day.
B.Pd. or **B.Pe.** Bachelor of Pedagogy.
B.P.E. Bachelor of Physical Education.
B.Ph. or **B.Phil.** Bachelor of Philosophy.
bpi bits per inch; bytes per inch.
BPOE also **B.P.O.E.** Benevolent and Protective Order of Elks.
br. 1. branch. 2. brief. 3. bronze. 4. brother. 5. brown.
Br. 1. Breton. 2. Britain; British. 3. Brother (religious).
B/R bills receivable.
Braz. Brazil; Brazilian.
B.R.E. Bachelor of Religious Education.
brev. brevet.
Br. Gu. British Guiana.
Br. Hond. British Honduras.
Br. I. British India.
brig. brigade; brigadier.
Brig. Gen. brigadier general.
Brit. Britain; British.
bro. brother.
bros. brothers.
Bru. Brunei.
B.S. 1. Bachelor of Science. 2. balance sheet. 3. bill of sale.
BSA Boy Scouts of America.
B.S.A. Bachelor of Science in Agriculture.
B.S.A.A. Bachelor of Science in Applied Arts.
B.S.Arch. Bachelor of Science in Architecture.
B.Sc. Bachelor of Science.
B.S.Ec. Bachelor of Science in Economics.
B.S.Ed. Bachelor of Science in Education.
B.S.E.E. Bachelor of Science in Electrical Engineering.
B.S.For. Bachelor of Science in Forestry.
B.S.F.S. Bachelor of Science in Foreign Service.
bsh. bushel.
BSI British Standards Institution.
bsk. basket.
B.S.N. Bachelor of Science in Nursing.
Bt. baronet.
B.T. or **B.Th.** Bachelor of Theology.
btry. battery.
Btu British thermal unit.
bu. 1. bureau. 2. Or **bu** bushel.
bul. bulletin.
Bul. or **Bulg.** Bulgaria; Bulgarian.
bull. bulletin.
bur. bureau.
Bur. Burma; Burmese.
bus. business.
B.V. Blessed Virgin.
B.V.M. Blessed Virgin Mary.
bvt. brevet; brevetted.
BW 1. biological warfare. 2. Also **b/w** black and white.
B.W.A. British West Africa.
B.W.I. British West Indies.
bx. box.
b.y. billion years.
BYO bring your own.
BYOB bring your own booze; bring your own bottle.

c 1. *Physics.* candle. 2. carat. 3. centi-. 4. Or **C** *Math.* constant. 5. cubic.
C 1. *Elect.* capacitance. 2. Celsius. 3. centigrade. 4. *Physics.* charge conjugation. 5. coulomb.
c. or **C.** 1. capacity. 2. cape. 3. carton. 4. case. 5. *Baseball.* catcher. 6. cent. 7. centime. 8. century. 9. chapter. 10. church. 11. circa. 12. *Lat.* congius (gallon). 13. consul. 14. copy. 15. copyright. 16. corps.
C. 1. Catholic. 2. Celtic. 3. chancellor. 4. chief. 5. city. 6. companion. 7. Congress. 8. Conservative. 9. court.
ca 1. centare. 2. circa.
CA 1. California. 2. Also **C.A.** chronological age.
C.A. 1. Central America. 2. Or **c.a.** chartered accountant.
c/a current account.
CAA or **C.A.A.** Civil Aeronautics Authority.
CAB Civil Aeronautics Board.
C.A.F. cost and freight.
C.A.G.S. Certificate of Advanced Graduate Studies.
CAI computer-aided instruction.
cal calorie (small).
Cal calorie (large).
cal. 1. calendar. 2. caliber.
Cal. California.
calc. 1. calculation. 2. calculus.
Calif. California.
Cam. Cameroon.
Camb. Cambodia.
can. 1. canceled. 2. canon. 3. canto.
Can. also **Canad.** Canada; Canadian.
canc. canceled; cancellation.
C & W country and western.
Can. Is. Canary Islands.
Cant. Cantonese.
CAP or **C.A.P.** Civil Air Patrol.
cap. 1. capacity. 2. capital (city). 3. capital letter.
caps. 1. capitals (letters). 2. capsule.
Capt. captain.
car. carat.
Card. Cardinal.
CARE Cooperative for American Relief Everywhere.
CAT 1. clear-air turbulence. 2. computerized axial tomography.
cat. catalogue.
cath. 1. cathedral. 2. cathode.
CATV community antenna television.
caus. causative.
cav. 1. cavalier. 2. cavalry. 3. cavity.
CB or **C.B.** citizen's band.
CBC 1. Canadian Broadcasting Corporation. 2. complete blood count.
C.B.D. cash before delivery.
CBI Cumulative Book Index.
CBS Columbia Broadcasting System.
CBW chemical and biological warfare.
cc 1. carbon copy. 2. cubic centimeter.
cc. chapters.
C.C.A. Circuit Court of Appeals.
CCC 1. Civilian Conservation Corps. 2. Commodity Credit Corporation.
CCD Confraternity of Christian Doctrine.
CCF or **C.C.F.** Cooperative Commonwealth Federation of Canada.
cckw. counterclockwise.
CCS combined chiefs of staff.
CCTV closed circuit television.
CCU coronary care unit.
ccw. counterclockwise.
cd *Physics.* candela.
CD 1. Also **C/D** certificate of deposit. 2. Also **C.D.** civil defense. 3. *French.* corps diplomatique (diplomatic corps).
cd. cord.
c.d. cash discount.
CDC Center for Disease Control.
Cdr. commander.
CDT or **C.D.T.** Central Daylight Time.
C.E. 1. chemical engineer. 2. civil engineer. 3. common era.
CED Committee for Economic Development.
CEEB College Entry Examination Board.
CEMF counter-electromotive force.
cen. 1. central. 2. century.
Cen. Afr. Rep. Central African Republic.
cent. 1. centime. 2. central. 3. *Lat.* centum (hundred). 4. century.
CEO also **C.E.O.** chief executive officer.
CERN *French.* Conseil Européen Pour Recherches Nucléaires (European Council for Nuclear Research).
cert. certificate; certification; certified.
certif. certificate.
cet. par. *Lat.* ceteris paribus (other things being equal).
CF cystic fibrosis.
cf. 1. calfskin. 2. *Lat.* confer (compare).
c.f. 1. *Baseball.* center field; center fielder. 2. Or **C.F.** cost and freight.
C/F *Accounting.* carried forward.
CFA also **C.F.A.** chartered financial analyst.
c.f.i. or **C.F.I.** cost, freight, and insurance.
cfm or **c.f.m.** cubic feet per minute.
cfs or **c.f.s.** cubic feet per second.
cg centigram.
c.g. 1. center of gravity. 2. Or **C.G.** consul general.
C.G. 1. coast guard. 2. commanding general.
cgs or **CGS** centimeter-gram-second (system of units).
C.G.T. *French.* Confédération Générale du Travail (General Confederation of Labor).
ch chain (measurement).
ch. 1. Or **Ch.** chaplain. 2. chapter. 3. check. 4. Or **Ch.** chief. 5. child; children. 6. Or **Ch.** church.
Ch. China; Chinese.
c.h. or **C.H.** 1. clearing-house. 2. courthouse. 3. customhouse.
chan. channel.
Chanc. 1. chancellor. 2. chancery.
chap. chapter.
char. charter.
chE. cholinesterase.
Ch.E. chemical engineer.
chem. chemical; chemist; chemistry.
chg. 1. change. 2. charge.
Chin. Chinese.
chl. chloroform.
chm. 1. chairman. 2. *Chess.* checkmate.
Chr *Bible.* Chronicles.
Chr. Christ; Christian.

chron. 1. chronicle. 2. chronological; chronology.
Chron. *Bible.* Chronicles.
chronol. chronological; chronology.
Ci curie.
CI cost and insurance.
CIA Central Intelligence Agency.
CID also **C.I.D.** Criminal Investigation Department (Scotland Yard).
c.i.f. or **C.I.F.** cost, insurance, and freight.
C in C commander in chief.
CIO also **C.I.O.** Congress of Industrial Organizations.
cir or **circ.** circle; circular.
circ. 1. circulation. 2. circumference.
circum. circumference.
cit. 1. citation. 2. cited. 3. citizen.
civ. civil; civilian.
C.J. chief justice.
ck. 1. cask. 2. check. 3. cook.
cl centiliter.
cl. 1. class; classification. 2. clause. 3. clearance. 4. closet. 5. cloth.
c.l. 1. carload. 2. *Sports.* center line. 3. Or **C.L.** civil law. 4. common law.
class. 1. classic; classical. 2. classification; classified; classify.
clk. clerk.
clm. column.
clr. clear.
CLU also **C.L.U.** chartered life underwriter.
cm centimeter.
CM center matched.
c.m. 1. circular mil. 2. center of mass. 3. court-martial.
CMA also **C.M.A.** certified medical assistant.
cmd. command.
cmdg. commanding.
Cmdr. commander.
cml. commercial.
cN centinewton.
C/N credit note.
CNS central nervous system.
Co *Bible.* Corinthians.
CO 1. Colorado. 2. Or **c.o.** commanding officer. 3. Or **C.O.** conscientious objector.
co. 1. company. 2. county.
c.o. 1. *Accounting.* carried over. 2. cash order.
c/o also **c.o.** care of.
COD or **C.O.D.** 1. cash on delivery. 2. collect on delivery.
coef. coefficient.
C. of C. chamber of commerce.
C. of E. Church of England.
C. of S. chief of staff.
cog. cognate.
Col or **Col.** *Bible* Colossians.
col. 1. collect; collected; collector. 2. college; collegiate. 3. colonial; colony. 4. color. 5. column.
Col. 1. Colombia. 2. colonel. 3. Colorado.
COLA cost-of-living adjustment.
coll. 1. collateral. 2. collect; collection; collector. 3. college; collegiate. 4. colloquial; colloquialism.
collat. collateral.
Colo. Colorado.
COM computer-output microfilm; computer-output microfilmer.
com. 1. comedy; comic. 2. comma. 3. commentary. 4. commerce; commercial. 5. Or **Com.** commissioner. 6. Or **Com.** committee. 7. common. 8. commune. 9. communication. 10. community.
Com. 1. commander. 2. commodore. 3. Communist.
comb. 1. combination. 2. combining. 3. combustion.
comd. command.
comdg. commanding.
Comdr. commander.
Comdt. commandant.
coml. commercial.
comm. 1. commerce. 2. commission; commissioner. 3. Also **Comm.** committee. 4. commonwealth. 5. communication.
Como. commodore.
comp. 1. companion. 2. comparative. 3. compensation. 4. compilation; compiled; compiler. 5. complete. 6. compose; composer. 7. composite; composition; compositor. 8. compound. 9. comprehensive. 10. comprising.
compar. comparative.
compd. compound.
compt. compartment.
Comr. commissioner.
con. 1. concerto. 2. *Law.* conclusion. 3. connection. 4. consolidate; consolidated. 5. Or **Con.** consul. 6. continued. 7. *Lat.* conjunx (wife).
Con. Congo.
conc. 1. concentrate. 2. concrete.
cond. 1. condition. 2. conductivity. 3. conductor.
conf. 1. conference. 2. confidential.
confed. confederation.
cong. *Lat.* congius (*Med.* gallon).
Cong. 1. Congregational. 2. Congress; Congressional.
conj. 1. conjugation. 2. conjunction. 3. conjunctive.
Conn. Connecticut.
cons. 1. consigned; consignment. 2. consonant. 3. Or **Cons.** constable. 4. constitution; constitutional. 5. construction.
Cons. consul.
consol. consolidated.
const. 1. Or **Const.** constable. 2. constant. 3. Or **Const.** constitution. 4. construction.
constr. construction.
cont. 1. containing. 2. contents. 3. continent. 4. continue; continued. 5. contract. 6. contraction. 7. control.
contd. continued.
contemp. contemporary.
contr. 1. contract. 2. contraction. 3. contralto. 4. control.
contrib. contribution; contributor.
conv. 1. convention. 2. convertible.
coop. cooperative.
cop. copyright.
Cop. Coptic.
cor. 1. corner. 2. cornet. 3. coroner. 4. corpus. 5. correction. 6. correspondence; correspondent; corresponding.
Cor. *Bible.* Corinthians.
CORE Congress of Racial Equality.
corol. or **coroll.** corollary.
corp. corporation.
corr. 1. correction. 2. correspondence; correspondent.
correl. correlative.
cos cosine.
COS or **C.O.S.** cash on shipment.
cosec cosecant.
cot cotangent.
coth hyperbolic cotangent.
covers versed cosine.
cp *Physics.* candlepower.
cP centipoise.
CP 1. chemically pure. 2. command post. 3. Communist Party.
cp. compare.
C.P. Cape Province.
CPA also **C.P.A.** certified public accountant.
cpd. compound.
CPFF cost plus fixed fee.
CPI consumer price index.
Cpl. corporal.
cpm cycles per minute.
CPO chief petty officer.
CPR cardiopulmonary resuscitation.
cps 1. characters per second. 2. cycles per second.
CPS also **C.P.S.** certified professional secretary.
Cpt. captain.
CPU central processing unit.
CQ call to quarters.
CR *Psychol.* conditioned reflex; conditioned response.
cr. 1. credit; creditor. 2. creek. 3. crescendo. 4. crown.
C.R. Costa Rica.
crit. critic; critical; criticism.
CRT cathode-ray tube.
CS 1. capital stock. 2. chief of staff. 3. Christian Science; Christian Scientist. 4. civil service. 5. conditioned stimulus.
cs. case.
C.S.A. Confederate States of America.
csc cosecant.
CSC civil service commission.
csch hyperbolic cosecant.
CSF cerebrospinal fluid.
csk. 1. cask. 2. countersink.
CSS College Scholarship Service.
CST 1. Or **C.S.T.** Central Standard Time. 2. convulsive shock treatment.
CT 1. Or **C.T.** Central Time. 2. Or **Ct.** Connecticut.
ct. 1. cent. 2. certificate. 3. court.
Ct. count (title).
ctf. certificate.
ctg. or **ctge.** cartage.
ctn cotangent.
ctn. carton.
ctr. 1. center. 2. counter.
cu. or **cu** cubic.
cum. cumulative.
cur. 1. currency. 2. current.
CV cardiovascular.
C.V. Cape Verde.
CVA Columbia Valley Authority.
cvt. convertible.
cw or **CW** continuous wave.
cw. clockwise.
CWO chief warrant officer.
c.w.o. cash with order.
CWS Chemical Warfare Service.
cwt. hundredweight.
CY calendar year.
cyl. cylinder.
CYO Catholic Youth Organization.
CZ or **C.Z.** Canal Zone.
Czech. Czechoslovakia; Czechoslovakian.

d 1. day. 2. deci-. 3. *Physics.* deuteron. 4. dextro-.
d. 1. dam. 2. date. 3. daughter. 4. *Lat.* denarius (penny). 5. Or **D.** deputy. 6. died. 7. Or **D.** dose. 8. Or **D.** drachma.
D 1. Or **D.** democrat; democratic. 2. deutrium.
D. 1. December. 2. department. 3. *Lat.* Deus (God). 4. diopter. 5. Doctor (in academic degrees). 6. *Lat.* Dominus (Lord). 7. Don (title). 8. duchess. 9. duke. 10. Dutch.
da deca-.
DA 1. delayed action. 2. deposit account. 3. Also **D.A.** don't answer.
Da. Danish.
D.A. 1. Also **DA** district attorney. 2. Doctor of Arts.
DAB or **D.A.B.** Dictionary of American Biography.
dag decagram.
DAGC *Electronics.* delayed automatic gain control.
DAH or **D.A.H.** Dictionary of American History.
dam decameter.
Dan. 1. *Bible.* Daniel. 2. Danish.
D & C dilatation and curettage.
DAR 1. damage assessment routine. 2. Daughters of the American Revolution.
das dekastere.
DASD direct access storage device.
dat. dative.
DAV Disabled American Veterans.
dB decibel.
DB or **D.B.** daybook.
d.b.a. doing business as.
D.B.A. Doctor of Business Administration.
D.B.E. Dame Commander of the Order of the British Empire.
d.b.h. diameter at breast height.
D.Bib. Douay Bible.
dbl. double.
dc or **DC** direct current.
DC or **D.C.** District of Columbia.
D.C. 1. *Mus.* da capo. 2. Doctor of Chiropractic.
D.Ch.E. Doctor of Chemical Engineering.
D.C.L. 1. Doctor of Canon Law. 2. Doctor of Civil Law.
DCM also **D.C.M.** Distinguished Conduct Medal.
dd. delivered.
D.D. 1. demand draft. 2. dishonorable discharge. 3. *Lat.* Divinitatis Doctor (Doctor of Divinity).
D.D.S. 1. Doctor of Dental Science. 2. Doctor of Dental Surgery.
DE Delaware.
deb. debenture.
dec. 1. deceased. 2. declaration. 3. declension. 4. declination. 5. decrease.
Dec. December.
decd. deceased.
decl. declension.
D.Ed. Doctor of Education.
def. 1. defective. 2. defendant. 3. defense. 4. deferred. 5. define. 6. definite. 7. definition.
deg or **deg.** degree.
del. 1. delegate; delegation. 2. delete.
Del. Delaware.
dely. delivery.
dem. demurrage.
Dem. Democrat; Democratic.
demon. *Gram.* demonstrative.
Den. Denmark.
denom. denomination.
dent. dental; dentist; dentistry.
dep. 1. depart; departure. 2. department. 3. deponent. 4. deposed. 5. deposit. 6. depot. 7. deputy.
Dep. dependency.
dept. 1. department. 2. deputy.
der. or **deriv.** derivation; derivative.
Des. desert.
det. 1. detach. 2. detachment. 2. detail.
Deut. *Bible.* Deuteronomy.
dev. deviation.
DEW distant early warning.
DF direction finder.
D.F. Defender of the Faith.
D.F.A. Doctor of Fine Arts.
DFC also **D.F.C.** Distinguished Flying Cross.
dft. draft.
dg decigram.
DH designated hitter.
D.H. Doctor of Humanities.
D.H.L. Doctor of Hebrew Letters; Doctor of Hebrew Literature.
dia. diameter.
diag. 1. diagonal. 2. diagram.
dial. 1. dialect; dialectal. 2. dialectic; dialectical. 3. dialogue.
diam diameter.
dict. 1. dictation. 2. dictionary.
diet. dietetics.
dif. or **diff.** difference; different.
dig. digest.
dil. dilute.
dim. 1. dimension. 2. diminished. 3. *Mus.* diminuendo. 4. diminutive.
dimin. 1. *Mus.* diminuendo. 2. diminutive.
din. dinar.
dipl. diplomat; diplomatic.
dir. director.
dis. 1. discount. 2. distance; distant.
disc. discount.
disp. dispensary.
diss. dissertation.
dissd. dissolved.
dist. 1. distance; distant. 2. district.
Dist. Atty. district attorney.
distr. distribution; distributor.
div. 1. divergence. 2. diversion. 3. divided; division. 4. dividend. 5. divorced.
dj dust jacket.
DJ disc jockey.
D.J. 1. district judge. 2. *Lat.* Doctor Juris (Doctor of Law).
DJIA Dow-Jones Industrial Average.
dk. 1. dark. 2. deck. 3. dock.
dkg dekagram.
dkl dekaliter.
dkm dekameter.
dks dekastere.
dl deciliter.
D/L demand loan.
D.Lit. or **D.Litt.** *Lat.* Doctor Litterarum (Doctor of Letters; Doctor of Literature).
DLO dead letter office.
dlr. dealer.
D.L.S. Doctor of Library Science.
dlvy. delivery.
dm decimeter.
DM 1. *Chem.* adamsite. 2. data management. 3. Deutsche mark.
D.M.A. Doctor of Musical Arts.
D.M.D. *Lat.* Dentariae Medicinae Doctor (Doctor of Dental Medicine).
D.M.L. Doctor of Modern Languages.
DMSO dimethylsulfoxide.
DMZ demilitarized zone.
Dn *Bible.* Daniel.
dn. down.
DNB Dictionary of National Biography.
DNC direct numerical control.
do. ditto.
D.O. 1. Doctor of Optometry. 2. Doctor of Osteopathy.
DOA *Med.* dead on arrival.
DOB date of birth.
doc. document.
DOD Department of Defense.
dol. 1. dollar. 2. *Mus.* dolce.
dom. 1. domestic. 2. dominant. 3. dominion.
Dom. Dominican.
D.O.M. *Lat.* Deo Optimo Maximo (to God, the best and the greatest).
Dom. Rep. Dominican Republic.
DOS disk operating system.
doz. dozen.
DP 1. data processing. 2. dew point. 3. Also **D.P.** displaced person. 4. *Baseball.* double play.
DPH Department of Public Health.
D.Ph. or **D.Phil.** Doctor of Philosophy.
dpt. 1. department. 2. deponent.
DPT diptheria, pertussis, tetanus (vaccine).
DPW Department of Public Works.
dr dram.
DR dead reckoning.
dr. 1. debit. 2. debtor.
Dr. 1. doctor. 2. drive (in street names).
dram. dramatic; dramatist.
dr ap apothecaries' dram.
dr avdp avoirdupois dram.
dr t troy dram.
ds decistere.
DS data set.
d.s. 1. Or **D.S.** *Mus.* dal segno. 2. *Com-*

merce. days after sight. **3.** document signed.
DSC also **D.S.C.** Distinguished Service Cross.
DSM also **D.S.M.** Distinguished Service Medal.
DSO or **D.S.O.** Distinguished Service Order.
d.s.p. *Lat.* decessit sine prole (died without issue).
DST or **D.S.T.** daylight-saving time.
Dt *Bible.* Deuteronomy.
DT or **D.T.** daylight time.
d.t. double time.
D.T. Doctor of Theology.
D.T.'s delirium tremens.
Du. **1.** duke (title). **2.** Dutch.
dup. duplicate.
D.V. **1.** *Lat.* Deo volente (God willing). **2.** *Bible.* Douay Version.
D.V.M. Doctor of Veterinary Medicine.
DW **1.** dead weight. **2.** distilled water.
D/W dock warrant.
DWI driving while intoxicated.
dwt. pennyweight.
dy. **1.** delivery. **2.** duty.
dyn *Physics.* dyne.
dz. dozen.

e **1.** electron. **2.** Or **e.** *Baseball.* error.
E **1.** Earth. **2.** Also **E.** or **e** or **e.** east. **3.** Or **E.** English. **4.** excellent.
e. or **E.** engineer; engineering.
E. earl.
ea. each.
EbN east by north.
EbS east by south.
Ec. Ecuador.
E.C. Established Church.
eccl. or **eccles.** ecclesiastic; ecclesiastical.
Eccles. *Bible.* Ecclesiastes.
ECCS emergency core cooling system.
ECG electrocardiogram.
ECL emitter-coupled logic.
ECM European Common Market.
ecol. ecological; ecology.
econ. economics; economist; economy.
ed. **1.** edition; editor. **2.** education.
E.D. election district.
edit. edition; editor.
Ed.M. *Lat.* Educationis Magister (Master of Education).
EDP electronic data processing.
EDT or **E.D.T.** Eastern Daylight Time.
educ. education; educational.
e.e. errors excepted.
E.E. electrical engineer; electrical engineering.
EEC European Economic Community.
EEG electroencephalogram; electroencephalograph.
EENT or **E.E.N.T.** eye, ear, nose, and throat.
EEO equal employment opportunity.
eff. efficiency.
EFTS electronic funds transfer system.
Eg. Egypt; Egyptian.
e.g. *Lat.* exempli gratia (for example).
EGD electrogasdynamics.
EHF extremely high frequency.
EHV extra high voltage.
E.I. East Indian; East Indies.
EKG electrocardiogram; electrocardiograph.
el. elevation.
elec. electric; electrical; electrician; electricity.
elem. elementary.
elev. elevation.
ELF extremely low frequency.
EM **1.** electromagnetic. **2.** enlisted man.
E.M. Engineer of Mines.
emf or **EMF** electromotive force.
EMT **1.** electrical-metallic tubing. **2.** emergency medical technician. **3.** end of magnetic tape.
emu electromagnetic unit.
enc. or **encl.** enclosed; enclosure.
ency. or **encyc.** or **encycl.** encyclopedia.
ENE east-northeast.
eng. **1.** engine. **2.** engineer; engineering.
Eng. England; English.
engin. engineering.
engr. **1.** engineer. **2.** engraved; engraver; engraving.
enl. **1.** enlarged. **2.** enlisted.
Ens. ensign.
entom. entomologic; entomology.
e.o. *Lat.* ex officio (by virtue of office).
e.o.m. end of month.
Ep *Bible.* Ephesians.
EP **1.** extended play. **2.** European plan.
Eph. *Bible.* Ephesians.
Epis. **1.** Episcopal; Episcopalian. **2.** Epistle.
Episc. Episcopal; Episcopalian.
Epist. Epistle.
eq. **1.** equal. **2.** equation. **3.** equivalent.
E.Q. educational quotient.
Equat. Gui. Equatorial Guinea.
equip. equipment.
equiv. equivalency; equivalent.
ER emergency room.
ERA **1.** *Baseball.* earned run average. **2.** Equal Rights Amendment.
ERIC Educational Resources Information Center.
ESE east-southeast.
Esk. Eskimo.
ESL English as a second language.
ESOP employee stock ownership plan.
ESP extrasensory perception.
esp. especially.
Esq. Esquire (title).
ESR electron spin resonance.
Est *Bible.* Esther.
EST or **E.S.T.** Eastern Standard Time.
est. **1.** established. **2.** *Law.* estate. **3.** estimate.
esu electrostatic unit.
ET **1.** Or **E.T.** Eastern Time. **2.** elapsed time.
ETA or **e.t.a.** estimated time of arrival.
et al. *Lat.* et alii (and others).
etc. *Lat.* et cetera (and so forth).
ETD or **e.t.d.** estimated time of departure.
Eth. Ethiopia.
ETV educational television.
etym. or **etymol.** etymological; etymology.
Eur. Europe; European.
EURATOM European Atomic Energy Community.
eV electron volt.
EVA extravehicular activity.
evan. or **evang.** evangelical; evangelist.
evg. evening.
EW enlisted woman.
Ex or **Ex.** *Bible.* Exodus.
ex. **1.** examination. **2.** example. **3.** except; excepted; exception. **4.** exchange. **5.** executive. **6.** express. **7.** extra.
exam. examination.
exc. **1.** excellent. **2.** except; exception.
Exc. Excellency.
exch. **1.** exchange. **2.** Or **Exch.** exchequer.
excl. **1.** exclamation. **2.** exclusive.
exec. **1.** executive. **2.** executor.
Exod. *Bible.* Exodus.
exp *Math.* exponential.
exp. **1.** expenses. **2.** experiment; experimental. **3.** expiration; expired. **4.** export; exporter. **5.** express.
expt. experiment.
exptl. experimental.
exr. executor.
exrx. executrix.
ext. **1.** extension. **2.** external; externally. **3.** extinct. **4.** extra. **5.** extract.
Ezek. or **Ezk** *Bible.* Ezekiel.
Ezr *Bible.* Ezra.

f **1.** *Physics.* femto-. **2.** focal length. **3.** Or **F.** *Mus.* forte. **4.** function.
F **1.** Fahrenheit. **2.** farad. **3.** Or **F.** fellow (of a university or other institution).
f. **1.** farthing. **2.** Or **F** also **f.** or **F.** female. **3.** Or **F.** *Gram.* feminine. **4.** Or **F.** *Metallurgy.* fine. **5.** Or **F.** folio. **6.** following. **7.** *Sports.* foul. **8.** franc.
F. **1.** February. **2.** French. **3.** Friday.
f/ relative aperture of a lens.
FA **1.** field artillery. **2.** Or **F.A.** fine art. **3.** football association.
f.a. fire alarm.
FAA Federal Aviation Administration.
f.a.a. or **F.A.A.** free of all average.
fac. **1.** facsimile. **2.** faculty.
FACP or **F.A.C.P.** Fellow of the American College of Physicians.
FACS or **F.A.C.S.** Fellow of the American College of Surgeons.
FAD flavin adenine dinucleotide.
Fahr. Fahrenheit.
FAIA or **F.A.I.A.** Fellow of the American Institute of Architects.
Falk. Is. Falkland Islands.
FAM Free and Accepted Masons.
fam. **1.** familiar. **2.** family.
FAO Food and Agriculture Organization.
FAQ fair average quality.
Far. Faraday.
FAS Foreign Agricultural Service.
f.a.s. also **F.A.S.** free alongside ship.
fasc. fascicle.
fath or **fath.** fathom.
fb also **f.b.** fullback.
F.B. **1.** foreign body. **2.** freight bill.
FBA or **F.B.A.** Fellow of the British Academy.
FBI also **F.B.I.** Federal Bureau of Investigation.
fc foot-candle.
f.c. *Printing.* **1.** follow copy. **2.** font change.
FCA Farm Credit Administration.
fcap. or **fcp.** foolscap.
FCC Federal Communications Commission.
FCS or **F.C.S.** Fellow of the Chemical Society.
fcy. fancy.
FD **1.** fatal dose. **2.** fire department. **3.** focal distance.
fd. fjord.
F.D. *Lat.* Fidei Defensor (Defender of the Faith).
FDA Food and Drug Administration.
FDIC Federal Deposit Insurance Corporation.
Feb. February.
fec. *Lat.* fecit (he, or she, made or did it).
fed. federal; federated; federation.
fem. female; feminine.
FEP front end processor.
FEPC Fair Employment Practices Commission.
FET field effect transistor.
feud. feudal; feudalism.
ff *Mus.* fortissimo.
ff. **1.** folios. **2.** following.
FFA Future Farmers of America.
FFV Order of the First Families of Virginia.
FG fine grain.
f.g. *Sports.* field goal; field goals.
FHA Federal Housing Administration.
FHLBB Federal Home Loan Bank Board.
fhp or **f.hp.** friction horsepower.
FICA Federal Insurance Contributions Act.
fict. **1.** fiction. **2.** fictitious.
fid. fidelity.
FIFO *Accounting.* first in, first out.
fig. **1.** figurative; figuratively. **2.** figure.
fin. **1.** finance; financial. **2.** finish.
Fin. Finland; Finnish.
fl fluid.
fL foot-lambert.
FL **1.** Florida. **2.** focal length. **3.** foreign languages.
fl. **1.** floor. **2.** florin. **3.** *Lat.* floruit (flourished). **4.** fluid. **5.** flute.
Fla. Florida.
fld. field.
fl dr fluid dram.
Flor. Florida.
fl oz fluid ounce.
FM **1.** field manual. **2.** Or **F.M.** field marshal. **3.** Or **fm** frequency modulation.
fm. **1.** fathom. **2.** from.
FMB Federal Maritime Board.
FMCS Federal Mediation and Conciliation Service.
FMN flavin mononucleotide.
fn. footnote.
FNMA Federal National Mortgage Association.
FO **1.** Or **F.O.** field officer. **2.** field order. **3.** finance officer. **4.** Or **F/O** flight officer. **5.** Or **F.O.** Foreign Office.
f.o.b. also **F.O.B.** free on board.
FOBS fractional orbital bombardment system.
FOE Fraternal Order of Eagles.
fol. **1.** folio. **2.** following.
for. **1.** foreign. **2.** forest; forestry.
fort. fortification.
fp freezing point.
fp. foolscap.
f.p.a. or **F.P.A.** free of particular average.
FPC **1.** Federal Power Commission. **2.** fish protein concentrate. **3.** Friends Peace Committee.
fpm or **f.p.m.** feet per minute.
FPO fleet post office.
fps or **f.p.s.** **1.** feet per second. **2.** frames per second.
fr. **1.** franc. **2.** from.
Fr. **1.** father (clergyman). **2.** France; French. **3.** frater. **4.** Frau. **5.** friar. **6.** Friday.
f.r. *Lat.* folio recto (right-hand page).
FRB Federal Reserve Board.
FRCP or **F.R.C.P.** Fellow of the Royal College of Physicians.
FRCS or **F.R.C.S.** Fellow of the Royal College of Surgeons.
freq. **1.** frequency. **2.** frequentative. **3.** frequently.
F.R.G. Federal Republic of Germany.
FRGS or **F.R.G.S.** Fellow of the Royal Geographical Society.
Fr. Gu. French Guiana.
Fri. Friday.
Fris. Frisian.
Frl. Fräulein.
front. frontispiece.
FRS **1.** Federal Reserve System. **2.** Or **F.R.S.** Fellow of the Royal Society.
Frs. Frisian.
frt. freight.
FS **1.** Foreign Service. **2.** Forest Service.
FSA Federal Security Agency.
FSH follicle-stimulating hormone.
FSLIC Federal Savings and Loan Insurance Corporation.
ft foot.
ft. fort; fortification.
FTA Future Teachers of America.
FTC Federal Trade Commission.
ft-c foot-candle.
fth. fathom.
ft-lb foot-pound.
fur. furlong.
furn. furnished.
fut. *Gram.* future.
f.v. *Lat.* folio verso (on the back of the page).
FWA Federal Works Agency.
FWD front-wheel drive.
fwd. *Sports.* forward.
FX foreign exchange.
FY fiscal year.
FYI for your information.
FZS or **F.Z.S.** Fellow of the Zoological Society.

g **1.** acceleration of gravity. **2.** gram.
G **1.** *Physics.* gauss. **2.** giga-. **3.** Or **G.** good. **4.** *Physics.* gravitation constant.
g. **1.** gender. **2.** genitive. **3.** Or **G.** gourde. **4.** Or **G.** guilder. **5.** Or **G.** guinea (money). **6.** Or **G.** gulf.
ga gauge.
Ga *Bible.* Galatians.
GA **1.** general agent. **2.** Also **G.A.** general assembly. **3.** Or **Ga.** Georgia.
G.A. general average.
gal. gallon.
Gal. *Bible.* Galatians.
galv. galvanized.
Gam. Gambia.
GAO General Accounting Office.
GAPA ground-to-air pilotless aircraft.
GAR or **G.A.R.** Grand Army of the Republic.
GATT General Agreement on Tariffs and Trade.
GAW guaranteed annual wage.
gaz. gazette; gazetteer.
G.B. Great Britain.
GBF Great Books Foundation.
GC gigacycle.
GCA ground control approach.
G.C.B. Knight of the Grand Cross, Order of the Bath.
gcd or **g.c.d.** greatest common divisor.
gcf or **g.c.f.** greatest common factor.
GCI ground control intercept.
GCM Good Conduct Medal.
GCT or **G.c.t.** Greenwich civil time.
gd. good.
G.D. grand duchy.
gde. gourde.
G.D.R. German Democratic Republic.
gds. goods.
GED general educational development.
GEM ground-effect machine.
gen. **1.** gender. **2.** general; generally. **3.** generator. **4.** generic. **5.** genitive. **6.** genus.
Gen. **1.** general (military rank). **2.** *Bible.* Genesis.
genit. genitive.
genl. general.
geog. geographer; geographic; geography.
geol. geologic; geologist; geology.
geom. geometric; geometry.
ger. gerund.
Ger. German; Germany.
GeV *Physics.* Giga-electron volts.

GFE government-furnished equipment.
GFWC General Federation of Women's Clubs.
GHQ general headquarters.
gi gill (liquid measure).
GI 1. gastrointestinal. **2.** general issue. **3.** Also **G.I.** Government Issue.
Gib. Gibraltar.
GIGO *Computer Sci.* garbage in, garbage out.
Gk. Greek.
gl. gloss.
gld. guilder.
gloss. glossary.
gm gram.
GM or **G.M. 1.** general manager. **2.** grand master.
GMAT 1. Graduate Management Admissions Test. **2.** Or **G.m.a.t.** Greenwich mean astronomical time.
GMT or **G.m.t.** Greenwich mean time.
GMW gram-molecular weight.
Gn *Bible.* Genesis.
GNP gross national product.
GO general order.
GOP or **G.O.P.** Grand Old Party (Republican).
Goth. Gothic.
gov. 1. government. **2.** Or **Gov.** governor.
Gov. Gen. governor general.
govt. government.
G.P. or **GP** general practitioner.
GPA grade-point average.
g.p.d. gallons per day.
g.p.m. gallons per minute.
GPO 1. general post office. **2.** Government Printing Office.
g.p.s. gallons per second.
GPU or **G.P.U.** *Russian.* Gosudarstvennoye Politicheskoye Upravlenie (Government Political Administration).
GQ general quarters.
gr. 1. grade. **2.** grain. **3.** gross. **4.** group.
Gr. Greece; Greek.
grad. graduate; graduated.
gram. grammar.
GRAS generally recognized as safe.
Grc. Greece.
Grnld. Greenland.
gro. gross.
gr. wt. gross weight.
GS 1. general staff. **2.** ground speed.
GSA General Services Administration.
GSC general staff corps.
GSO general staff officer.
GST or **G.s.t.** Greenwich sidereal time.
GSUSA Girl Scouts of the United States of America.
gt. 1. gilt. **2.** great. **3.** *Med.* gutta.
Gt. Brit. Great Britain.
G.T.C. good till canceled.
gtd. guaranteed.
GTS gas turbine ship.
gtt. *Med.* guttae.
GU 1. genitourinary. **2.** Guam.
Guad. Guadaloupe.
guar. guaranteed.
Guat. Guatemala.
Guin. Guinea.
Guy. Guyana.
gym. gymnasium; gymnastics.
gyn. gynecological; gynecologist; gynecology.

h 1. hecto-. **2.** Or **h.** hit. **3.** hour. **4.** *Physics.* Planck's constant.
H 1. *Physics.* Hamiltonian. **2.** henry. **3.** humidity.
h. 1. Or **H.** harbor. **2.** Or **H.** hard; hardness. **3.** Or **H.** height. **4.** Or **H.** high. **5.** Or **H.** *Mus.* horn. **6.** hundred. **7.** Or **H.** husband.
ha 1. hectare. **2.** hour angle.
h.a. *Lat.* hoc anno (this year).
Hab or **Hab.** *Bible.* Habakkuk.
hab. corp. habeas corpus.
Hag. *Bible.* Haggai.
Hai. Haiti.
hb or **hb.** halfback.
Hb hemoglobin.
H.B.M. Her, or His, Britannic Majesty.
H.C. 1. Holy Communion. **2.** House of Commons.
hcf or **h.c.f.** highest common factor.
HD heavy-duty.
hd. head.
hdbk. handbook.
hdkf. handkerchief.
hdqrs. headquarters.
hdwe. hardware.
HE high explosive.
H.E. 1. His Eminence. **2.** Her, or His, Excellency.
Heb or **Heb.** *Bible.* Hebrews.
Heb. Hebrew.
her. heraldry.
herp. herpetology.
HEW Department of Health, Education, and Welfare.
hex. hexagon; hexagonal.
hf high frequency.
HF height finding.
hf. half.
hfs hyperfine structure.
hg 1. hectogram. **2.** heliogram.
Hg *Bible.* Haggai.
HG also **H.G.** High German.
hgb. hemoglobin.
HGH human growth hormone.
hgt. height.
hgwy. highway.
H.H. 1. Her, or His, Highness. **2.** His Holiness.
hhd hogshead.
HH.D. *Lat.* Humanitatum Doctor (Doctor of Humanities).
HHFA Housing and Home Finance Agency.
HI Hawaii.
H.I. Hawaiian Islands.
HIA Horological Institute of America.
HIAA Health Insurance Association of America.
HID headache, insomnia, depression (syndrome).
HIF Health Information Foundation.
H.I.H. Her, or His, Imperial Highness.
HII Health Insurance Institute.
H.I.M. Her, or His, Imperial Majesty.
hist. historian; historical; history.
hl hectoliter.
H.L. House of Lords.
hld. hold.
HLF Heart and Lung Foundation.
hlt. halt.
hm hectometer.
H.M. Her, or His, Majesty.
HMAS or **H.M.A.S.** Her, or His, Majesty's Australian Ship.
HMC or **H.M.C.** Her, or His, Majesty's Customs.
HMCS or **H.M.C.S.** Her, or His, Majesty's Canadian Ship.
HMF or **H.M.F.** Her, or His, Majesty's Forces.
HMO 1. health maintenance organization. **2.** heart minute output.
HMS or **H.M.S.** Her, or His, Majesty's Ship.
Ho *Bible.* Hosea.
ho. house.
Hon. 1. Honorable (title). **2.** Or **hon.** honorary.
Hond. Honduras.
HOP high oxygen pressure.
HOPE Health Opportunity for People Everywhere.
hor. horizontal.
hort. horticultural; horticulture.
Hos. *Bible.* Hosea.
hosp. hospital.
hp horsepower.
HP high pressure.
HPF highest possible frequency.
HQ or **h.q.** headquarters.
hr hour.
Hr. Herr.
h.r. home run.
H.R. 1. home rule. **2.** House of Representatives.
H.R.E. Holy Roman Emperor; Holy Roman Empire.
H. Rept. House report.
H. Res. House resolution.
H.R.H. Her, or His, Royal Highness.
hrs hours.
HS or **H.S.** high school.
HSAA Health Sciences Advisory Award.
HSGT high-speed ground transit.
H.S.H. Her, or His, Serene Highness.
HST 1. Or **H.S.T.** Hawaiian Standard Time. **2.** hypersonic transport.
ht height.
HT 1. Or **H.T.** Hawaiian Time. **2.** halftime. **3.** halftone. **4.** hydrotherapy.
Hts. Heights.
HUD or **H.U.D.** Housing and Urban Development.
Hun. or **Hung.** Hungarian; Hungary.
HV 1. high velocity. **2.** high-voltage.
hvy. heavy.
HW 1. high water. **2.** hot water.
HWM high-water mark.
hwy. highway.
hy. henry.
hyp. 1. hypotenuse. **2.** hypothesis.
hypoth. hypothesis.
Hz hertz.

i 1. Or **i** *Elect.* current. **2.** *Math.* imaginary unit. **3.** interest. **4.** intransitive. **5.** Or **i.** island; isle.
I isospin.
IA or **Ia.** Iowa.
i.a. *Lat.* in absentia (in absence).
IAA indoleacetic acid.
IAAF International Amateur Athletic Federation.
IADB Inter-American Defense Board.
IAEA International Atomic Energy Agency.
IAP international airport.
IARU International Amateur Radio Union.
IAS indicated air speed.
IAU 1. International Association of Universities. **2.** International Astronomical Union.
ib. or **ibid.** *Lat.* ibidem (in the same place).
ICA International Cooperation Administration.
ICAO International Civil Aviation Organization.
ICBM intercontinental ballistic missile.
ICC 1. Indian Claims Commission. **2.** Interstate Commerce Commission.
ICE internal-combustion engine.
Ice. or **Icel.** Iceland; Icelandic.
ICFTU International Confederation of Free Trade Unions.
ICR Institute for Cancer Research.
ICU intensive care unit.
ID 1. Or **Id.** Idaho. **2.** Also **I.D.** identification. **3.** Intelligence Department. **4.** intradermal.
id. *Lat.* idem (the same).
i.d. inside diameter.
IDDD international direct distance dialing.
IDP 1. inosine diphosphate. **2.** integrated data processing. **3.** international driving permit.
IE industrial engineer; industrial engineering.
i.e. *Lat.* id est (that is).
IEEE Institute of Electrical and Electronic Engineers.
IF or **i.f.** intermediate frequency.
IFC International Finance Corporation.
IFF identification, friend or foe.
IFO identified flying object.
Ig immunoglobulin.
IG or **I.G.** inspector general.
ign. ignition.
IGY International Geophysical Year.
ihp or **i.hp.** indicated horsepower.
IL Illinois.
ILA International Longshoremen's Association.
ILGWU or **I.L.G.W.U.** International Ladies' Garment Workers' Union.
ill. illustrated; illustration; illustrator.
Ill. Illinois.
illus. illustrated; illustration; illustrator.
ILO International Labor Organization.
ILP or **I.L.P.** Independent Labour Party.
ILS instrument landing system.
IM intramuscular.
IMF International Monetary Fund.
imit. imitate; imitation.
immun. immunity; immunization.
immunol. immunology.
imp. 1. imperative. **2.** imperfect. **3.** imperial. **4.** import; imported; importer. **5.** important. **6.** imprimatur.
in or **in.** inch.
IN Indiana.
inbd. inboard.
inc. 1. income. **2.** incomplete. **3.** Also **Inc.** incorporated. **4.** increase.
incl. including; inclusive.
incog. incognito.
incr. 1. increase. **2.** incremental.
ind. 1. independence; independent. **2.** index. **3.** indigo. **4.** industrial; industry.
Ind. 1. India. **2.** Indian. **3.** Indiana. **4.** Indies.
Ind. E. industrial engineer.
indef. indefinite.
indic. 1. *Gram.* indicative. **2.** indicator.
indn. indication.
Indon. Indonesia; Indonesian.
indus. industrial; industry.
inf. 1. Or **Inf.** infantry. **2.** inferior. **3.** infinitive. **4.** influence. **5.** information.
infin. infinitive.
infl. influence; influenced.
INH isoniazid.
inj. injection.
INP International News Photo.
inq. inquiry.
I.N.R.I. *Lat.* Iesus Nazarenus Rex Iudaeorum (Jesus of Nazareth, King of the Jews).
INS International News Service.
ins. 1. inspector. **2.** insulated; insulation. **3.** insurance.
insp. inspected; inspector.
inst. 1. instant. **2.** Or **Inst.** institute; institution. **3.** instrument.
instr. 1. instruction; instructor. **2.** instrument.
int. 1. interest. **2.** interior. **3.** internal. **4.** international. **5.** interval.
inter. intermediate.
interj. interjection.
interp. interpreter.
interrog. interrogative.
intl. international.
intr. intransitive.
intro. introduction; introductory.
inv. 1. invented; invention; inventor. **2.** invoice.
I/O input/output.
Ion. Ionic.
IOOF Independent Order of Odd Fellows.
IPA 1. International Phonetic Alphabet. **2.** International Phonetic Association. **3.** isopropyl alcohol.
ips or **i.p.s.** inches per second.
IQ or **I.Q.** intelligence quotient.
i.q. *Lat.* idem quod (the same as).
IR 1. information retrieval. **2.** infrared.
Ir. Irish.
IRA 1. Individual Retirement Account. **2.** Also **I.R.A.** Irish Republican Army.
IRBM Intermediate Range Ballistic Missile.
Ire. Ireland.
irid. iridescent.
IRO International Refugee Organization.
irreg. irregular; irregularly.
IRS Internal Revenue Service.
Is *Bible.* Isaiah.
is. or **Is.** island.
Isa. *Bible.* Isaiah.
ISBN International Standard Book Number.
isl. island.
Isr. Israel; Israeli.
IST insulin shock therapy.
isth. isthmus.
ISV International Scientific Vocabulary.
It. Italian; Italy.
ITA Initial Teaching Alphabet.
ital. italic.
Ital. Italian; Italy.
ITO International Trade Organization.
ITU 1. International Telecommunication Union. **2.** International Typographical Union.
IU international unit.
IUD intrauterine device.
IV intravenous; intravenously.
IW 1. index word. **2.** isotopic weight.
i.w. inside width.
IWW also **I.W.W.** Industrial Workers of the World.

J 1. current density. **2.** joule.
J. 1. journal. **2.** judge. **3.** justice.
JA 1. joint account. **2.** Also **J.A.** judge advocate.
JAG also **J.A.G.** Judge Advocate General.
Jam. Jamaica.
Jan. January.
Jap. Japan; Japanese.
Jav. Javanese.
Jb *Bible.* Job.
J.C.D. *Lat.* Juris Canonici Doctor (Doctor of Canon Law).
JCL *Computer Sci.* job control language.
JCS or **J.C.S.** Joint Chiefs of Staff.
jct. junction.
JD 1. Justice Department. **2.** Also **J.D.** juvenile delinquent.
J.D. *Lat.* Jurum Doctor (Doctor of Laws).
Jdt *Bible.* Judith.
Jer. *Bible.* Jeremiah.
JFET junction field effect transistor.
JFK John Fitzgerald Kennedy International Airport.
jg junior grade.
Jg *Bible.* Judges.
JIT job instruction training.
JJ 1. judges. **2.** justices.
Jl *Bible.* Joel.

Jm *Bible.* James.
Jn *Bible.* John.
jnr. junior.
Jon or **Jon.** *Bible.* Jonah.
Jos *Bible.* Joshua.
Josh. *Bible.* Joshua.
jour. 1. journal; journalist. 2. journeyman.
JP or **J.P.** justice of the peace.
Jr *Bible.* Jeremiah.
jr. or **Jr.** junior.
JRC Junior Red Cross.
J.S.D. *Lat.* Juris Scientiae Doctor (Doctor of Juristic Science).
jt. joint.
Judg. *Bible.* Judges.
jun. or **Jun.** junior.
junc. junction.
JV junior varsity.
jwlr. jeweler.

k 1. karat. 2. kilo-.
K 1. kaon. 2. kelvin (temperature unit). 3. Kelvin (temperature scale). 4. kindergarten. 5. *Chess.* king. 6. *Bible.* Kings.
k. or **K.** 1. king. 2. knight. 3. kopeck. 4. koruna. 5. krona. 6. krone.
ka cathode.
KB *Chess.* king's bishop.
kc kilocycle.
K.C. 1. King's Counsel. 2. Also **KC** Knights of Columbus.
kcal kilocalorie.
kcs or **kc/s** kilocycles per second.
KD 1. kiln-dried. 2. knocked down.
Ken. Kentucky.
keV kiloelectron volt.
kg kilogram.
kg. keg.
K.G. Knight of the Order of the Garter.
KGB or **K.G.B.** *Russian.* Komitět Gosudarstvěnnoi Bezopasnost'i (Commission of State Security).
KKK or **K.K.K.** Ku Klux Klan.
km kilometer.
kmph kilometers per hour.
kmps kilometers per second.
kn. 1. knot. 2. krona. 3. krone.
Knt knight.
K of C Knights of Columbus.
Kor. Korea; Korean.
KP 1. *Chess.* king's pawn. 2. kitchen police.
K.P. Knights of Pythias.
KR *Chess.* king's rook.
kr. 1. krona. 2. krone.
KS Kansas.
Kt *Chess.* knight.
kt. karat.
Kuw. Kuwait.
kW kilowatt.
kWh kilowatt-hour.
KY or **Ky.** Kentucky.

l liter.
L 1. lambert. 2. Also **L.** large.
l. 1. Also **L.** lake. 2. land. 3. late. 4. left. 5. length. 6. line. 7. lira.
L. 1. Latin. 2. licentiate (in titles). 3. Linnaean. 4. lodge (society).
LA or **La.** Louisiana.
L.A. 1. Legislative Assembly. 2. local agent. 3. Also **LA** Los Angeles.
lab. laboratory.
Lab. Labrador.
lam. laminated.
Lam. *Bible.* Lamentations.
lang. language.
lat. latitude.
Lat. 1. Latin. 2. Latvia; Latvian.
lav. lavatory.
LB Labrador.
lb. *Lat.* libra (pound).
lc also **l.c.** lower case.
LC 1. landing craft. 2. Or **L.C.** Library of Congress.
L/C letter of credit.
lcd or **l.c.d.** lowest common denominator.
LCL less-than-carload lot.
lcm or **l.c.m.** least common multiple.
LCM landing craft, mechanized.
L.Cpl. lance corporal.
LCS landing craft, support.
LCT 1. landing craft, tank. 2. local civil time.
ld. 1. *Printing.* lead. 2. load.
Ld. 1. limited. 2. lord (title).
LD 1. learning disability; learning-disabled. 2. lethal dose.
LDC less-developed country.
ldg. landing.
lea. 1. league. 2. leather.
Leb. Lebanese; Lebanon.
lect. lecture.
lectr. lecturer.
leg. 1. legal. 2. legate. 3. *Mus.* legato. 4. legislation; legislative; legislature.
legis. legislation; legislative; legislature.
Leso. Lesotho.
Lev. *Bible.* Leviticus.
lex. lexicon.
lf 1. Also **l.f.** or **lf.** lightface. 2. low frequency.
LG also **L.G.** Low German.
lg. or **lge.** large.
l.h. also **LH** left hand.
li link (unit of measurement).
L.I. Long Island.
lib. 1. liberal. 2. librarian; library.
Lib. 1. Liberal. 2. Liberia; Liberian.
Liech. Liechtenstein.
lieut. lieutenant.
LIFO *Accounting.* last in, first out.
lim. limit.
lin. 1. lineal. 2. linear.
ling. linguistics.
liq. 1. liquid. 2. liquor.
lit. 1. liter. 2. literal; literally. 3. literary 4. literature.
Lit.B. or **Litt.B.** *Lat.* Litterarum Baccalaureus (Bachelor of Letters; Bachelor of Literature).
Lit.D. or **Litt.D.** *Lat.* Litterarum Doctor (Doctor of Letters; Doctor of Literature).
lith. lithograph; lithographic; lithography.
Lith. Lithuania; Lithuanian.
litho. or **lithog.** lithograph; lithographic; lithography.
Lk *Bible.* Luke.
ll or **ll.** lines.
LL.B. *Lat.* Legum Baccalaureus (Bachelor of Laws).
LL.D. *Lat.* Legum Doctor (Doctor of Laws).
LL.M. *Lat.* Legum Magister (Master of Laws).
lm lumen.
Lm *Bible.* Lamentations.
LM lunar module.
LMT local mean time.
ln Napierian logarithm.
LNG liquefied natural gas.
loc. cit. *Lat.* loco citato (in the place cited).
long. longitude.
LOOM Loyal Order of Moose.
loq. *Lat.* loquitur (speaks).
LPG liquefied petroleum gas.
LPM or **lpm** lines per minute.
LPN or **L.P.N.** licensed practical nurse.
L.S. *Lat.* locus sigilli (the place of the seal).
LSAT Law School Admissions Test.
LSD 1. least significant digit. 2. lysergic acid diethylamid.
LSS lifesaving service.
lt. light.
Lt. lieutenant.
l.t. or **LT** local time.
Lt. Col. lieutenant colonel.
Lt. Comdr. lieutenant commander.
ltd. or **Ltd.** limited.
Lt. Gen. lieutenant general.
Lt. Gov. lieutenant governor.
Luth. Lutheran.
Lux. Luxembourg.
Lv *Bible.* Leviticus.
lv. 1. leave. 2. livre.
LW low water.
LWM low-water mark.
LWV League of Women Voters.
lx lux.
LXX Septuagint.
lyr. lyric.

m 1. Or **M** *Printing.* a. em. b. pica em. 2. *Physics.* mass. 3. meter (measure). 4. milli-. 5. Or **M** *Physics.* modulus.
M 1. *Bible.* Maccabees. 2. *Physics.* Mach number. 3. mega-. 4. *Chem.* metal. 5. *Logic.* middle term of a syllogism. 6. *Chem.* molar. 7. *Physics.* moment. 8. *Physics.* mutual inductance.
m. 1. manual. 2. married. 3. Or **M.** male. 4. Or **M.** masculine. 5. Or **M.** medium. 6. Or **M.** meridian. 7. Or **M.** *Lat.* merides (noon). 8. mile. 9. month. 10. morning.
M. 1. majesty. 2. mark (currency). 3. master (in titles). 4. medieval. 5. member (in titles). 6. mill (currency). 7. minim (liquid measure). 8. Monday. 9. Monsieur.
mA milliampere.
MA 1. Maritime Administration. 2. Massachusetts. 3. Also **M.A.** mental age. 4. Also **M.A.** military academy.
M.A. *Lat.* Magister Artium (Master of Arts).
M.A.B.E. Master of Agricultural Business and Economics.
Maced. Macedonia; Macedonian.
mach. machine; machinery; machinist.
Mad. or **Madag.** Madagascar.
M.A.E. 1. Master of Aeronautical Engineering. 2. Master of Art Education. 3. Master of Arts in Education.
M.A.Ed. Master of Arts in Education.
mag. 1. magazine. 2. magnetism. 3. magneto. 4. magnitude.
M.Agr. Master of Agriculture.
Maj. major.
Maj. Gen. major general.
Mal. 1. *Bible.* Malachi. 2. Malay; Malayan.
Mala. Malaysia.
M.A.L.S. Master of Arts in Library Science.
man. manual.
Man. Manitoba.
manuf. or **manufac.** manufacture.
MAO monoamine oxidase.
MAP modified American plan.
mar. 1. maritime. 2. married.
Mar. March.
March. marchioness.
marg. margin.
Mart. Martinique.
masc. masculine.
MASH Mobile Army Surgical Hospital.
Mass. Massachusetts.
mat. matinee.
M.A.T. Master of Arts in Teaching.
math. mathematical; mathematician; mathematics.
Matt. *Bible.* Matthew.
max. maximum.
mb millibar.
MB Manitoba.
M.B.A. Master of Business Administration.
mc millicurie.
Mc megacycle.
MC 1. Marine Corps. 2. Medical Corps. 3. Or **M.C.** Member of Congress.
M.C. or **m.c.** master of ceremonies.
MCAT Medical College Admissions Test.
mcf thousand cubic feet.
M.C.L. Master of Civil Law.
MD 1. Or **Md.** Maryland. 2. medical department. 3. muscular dystrophy.
M.D. *Lat.* Medicinae Doctor (Doctor of Medicine).
m/d months after date.
Mdm. Madam.
M.D.S. Master of Dental Surgery.
mdse. merchandise.
ME 1. Or **Me.** Maine. 2. Also **M.E.** Middle English.
M.E. 1. mechanical engineer; mechanical engineering. 2. medical examiner. 3. military engineer. 4. mining engineer.
meas. measurable; measure.
mech. 1. mechanical; mechanics. 2. mechanism.
med. 1. medical; medicine. 2. medieval. 3. medium.
M.Ed. Master of Education.
Medit. Mediterranean.
Med. Lat. Medieval Latin.
mem. 1. member. 2. memoir. 3. memorandum. 4. memorial.
mep or **m.e.p.** mean effective pressure.
mer. meridian.
messrs. messieurs.
met. 1. metaphor. 2. metaphysics. 3. meteorological; meteorology. 4. metropolitan.
metal. or **metall.** metallurgic; metallurgy.
metaph. 1. metaphor; metaphoric. 2. metaphysics.
meteor. or **meteorol.** meteorological; meteorology.
METO Middle East Treaty Organization.
mev or **Mev** million electron volts.
Mex. Mexican; Mexico.
mf medium frequency.
mF millifarad.
m.f. *Mus.* mezzo-forte.
M.F.A. Master of Fine Arts.
mfd. manufactured.
mfg. manufacture; manufactured; manufacturing.
MFN most-favored nation.
mfr. manufacture; manufacturer.
mg milligram.
M.G. Major General.
Mgr. 1. Or **mgr.** manager. 2. Monseigneur; Monsignor.
mgt. management.
mH millihenry.
MH 1. Medal of Honor. 2. mental health.
MHD magnetohydrodynamic.
M.H.L. Master of Hebrew Literature.
MHW mean high water.
MHz megahertz.
Mi *Bible.* Micah.
MI 1. Michigan. 2. military intelligence.
mi. 1. mile. 2. mill (monetary unit).
MIA missing in action.
Mic. *Bible.* Micah.
Mich. Michigan.
mid. middle.
mil. military; militia.
min. 1. mineralogical; mineralogy. 2. minimum. 3. mining. 4. minor. 5. Or **min** minute.
Minn. Minnesota.
misc. miscellaneous.
Miss. Mississippi.
Mk *Bible.* Mark.
mk. 1. mark. 2. markka.
mks meter-kilogram-second (system of units).
mksA meter-kilogram-second-ampere (system of units).
mkt. market.
mktg. marketing.
ml milliliter.
Ml *Bible.* Malachi.
ML also **M.L.** Medieval Latin.
MLA or **M.L.A.** Modern Language Association.
MLD minimum lethal dose.
Mlle. Mademoiselle.
Mlles. Mesdemoiselles.
M.L.S. Master of Library Science.
MLW mean low water.
mm millimeter.
MM. Messieurs.
m.m. *Lat.* mutatis mutandis (with the necessary changes having been made).
Mme. Madame.
Mmes. Mesdames.
mmf or **m.m.f.** magnetomotive force.
MMPI Minnesota Multiphasic Personality Inventory.
MN 1. magnetic north. 2. Minnesota.
mngr. manager.
MO or **Mo.** Missouri.
mo. month.
m.o. or **M.O.** 1. mail order. 2. medical officer. 3. modus operandi. 4. Also **MO** money order.
mod *Math.* modulus.
mod. 1. moderate. 2. *Mus.* moderato. 3. modern.
modif. modification.
MOL Manned Orbital Laboratory.
mol. molecular; molecule.
mol wt molecular weight.
m.o.m. middle of month.
mon. 1. monastery. 2. monetary.
Mon. Monday.
Mong. Mongolia; Mongolian.
Mont. Montana.
MOR middle-of-the-road.
mor. morocco (leather).
Mor. Moroccan; Morocco.
morph. morphological; morphology.
mos. months.
Moz. Mozambique.
mp or **m.p.** 1. melting point. 2. *Mus.* mezzo-piano.
MP or **M.P.** 1. military police; military policeman. 2. mounted police.
M.P. Member of Parliament.
M.P.A. 1. Master of Public Administration. 2. Master of Public Accounting.
M.Pd. Master of Pedagogy.
M.P.E. Master of Physical Education.
mpg or **m.p.g.** miles per gallon.
mph or **m.p.h.** miles per hour.
M.P.H. Master of Public Health.
Mr. Mister.
mRNA messenger RNA.
ms millisecond.
MS 1. Mississippi. 2. multiple sclerosis.
ms. or **MS.** or **ms** manuscript.
M.S. or **M.Sc.** *Lat.* Magister Scientiae (Master of Science).
msec millisecond.
MSG monosodium glutamate.
msg. message.
Msgr. Monseigneur; Monsignor.
M.Sgt. master sergeant.
MSH melanocyte-stimulating hormone.
M.S. in L.S. Master of Science in Library Science.
m.s.l. or **M.S.L.** mean sea level.
mss. or **MSS.** or **mss** manuscripts.

MST or **M.S.T.** Mountain Standard Time.
M.S.W. 1. Master of Social Welfare. 2. Master of Social Work.
Mt *Bible.* Matthew.
MT 1. Montana. 2. Or **M.T.** Mountain Time.
mt. or **Mt.** mount; mountain.
m.t. or **M.T.** metric ton.
mtg. 1. meeting. 2. mortgage.
mtge. mortgage.
mtn. mountain.
mts. or **Mts.** mountains.
mun. or **munic.** municipal; municipality.
mus. 1. museum. 2. music; musical; musician.
Mus.B. *Lat.* Musicae Baccalaureus (Bachelor of Music).
Mus.D. or **Mus.Dr.** *Lat.* Musicae Doctor (Doctor of Music).
Mus. M. *Lat.* Magister Musicae (Master of Music).
mV millivolt.
MV 1. mean variation. 2. megavolt. 3. motor vessel.
MVA Missouri Valley Authority.
MVD *Russian.* Ministeyrstvo Vnutreynnikh Deyl (Ministry of Internal Affairs).
MVP most valuable player.
mW milliwatt.
MW megawatt.
Mx *Physics.* maxwell.
mxd. mixed.
m.y. million years.
myc. or **mycol.** mycological; mycology.
myth. or **mythol.** mythological; mythology.

n 1. Or **N** *Printing.* en. 2. nano-. 3. neutron. 4. Also **N** or **n-** *Chem.* normal. 5. *Math.* Symbol for an indefinite number.
N 1. Avogadro number. 2. *Chess.* knight. 3. newton. 4. Also **N.** or **n** or **n.** north; northern.
n. 1. *Lat.* natus (born). 2. *Commerce.* net. 3. Or **N.** noon. 4. note. 5. noun. 6. number.
N. 1. Norse. 2. November.
Na *Bible.* Nahum.
N.A. 1. Narcotics Anonymous. 2. National Academician; National Academy. 3. North America. 4. not applicable. 5. not available.
N.A.A. 1. National Aeronautic Association. 2. National Automobile Association.
NAACP or **N.A.A.C.P.** National Association for the Advancement of Colored People.
NAB New American Bible.
NACU National Association of Colleges and Universities.
NAD nicotinamide-adenine dinucleotide.
NADP nicotinamide-adenine dinucleotide phosphate.
Nah. *Bible.* Nahum.
NAIA National Association of Intercollegiate Athletes.
NAM or **N.A.M.** National Association of Manufacturers.
NAMH National Association for Mental Health.
NAPA National Association of Performing Artists.
NASA National Aeronautics and Space Administration.
NASCAR National Association of Stock Car Auto Racing.
NASD National Association of Securities Dealers.
nat. 1. national. 2. native. 3. natural.
NATE National Association of Teachers of English.
natl. national.
NATO North Atlantic Treaty Organization.
NATS Naval Air Transport Service.
naut. nautical.
nav. 1. naval. 2. navigable. 3. navigation.
Nb *Bible.* Numbers.
NB 1. narrow band. 2. Or **N.B.** New Brunswick.
n.b. or **N.B.** nota bene.
NBA also **N.B.A.** 1. National Basketball Association. 2. National Boxing Association. 3. narrow-band allocation.
NBC National Broadcasting Corporation.
NbE north by east.
NBS National Bureau of Standards.
NbW north by west.
NC 1. no charge. 2. Or **N.C.** North Carolina. 3. numerical control. 4. Nurse Corps.
NCAA or **N.C.A.A.** National Collegiate Athletic Association.
N.Cal. New Caledonia.
NCC National Council of Churches.
NCO or **N.C.O.** noncommissioned officer.
NCTE National Council of Teachers of English.
NCTM National Council of Teachers of Mathematics.
ND or **N.D.** North Dakota.
n.d. or **N.D.** no date.
N.Dak. North Dakota.
NDEA National Defense Education Act.
Ne *Bible.* Nehemiah.
NE 1. Nebraska. 2. Or **N.E.** New England. 3. northeast. 4. not equal to.
NEA National Education Association.
NEB New English Bible.
NEbE northeast by east.
NEbN northeast by north.
Nebr. Nebraska.
NED or **N.E.D.** New English Dictionary (Oxford).
neg. negative.
Neh. *Bible.* Nehemiah.
Nep. Nepal.
NEP or **N.E.P.** New Economic Policy.
n.e.s. not elsewhere specified.
NET National Educational Television.
Neth. Netherlands.
neur. or **neurol.** neurological; neurology.
neut. 1. neuter. 2. neutral.
Nev. Nevada.
Newf. Newfoundland.
New Hebr. New Hebrides.
New M. New Mexico.
New Test. New Testament.
NF 1. Also **N.F.** National Formulary. 2. neurofibromatosis. 3. Newfoundland.
n/f no funds.
NFC National Football Conference.
NFL National Football League.
Nfld. Newfoundland.
NG also **N.G.** 1. National Guard. 2. no good.
NGr or **NGr.** New Greek.
NH or **N.H.** New Hampshire.
N.Heb. New Hebrides.
NHI National Health Insurance.
NHL National Hockey League.
Nic. Nicaragua.
Nig. Nigeria.
NIH National Institutes of Health.
N.Ire. Northern Ireland.
NIT 1. National Intelligence Test. 2. National Invitational Tournament.
NJ or **N.J.** New Jersey.
NKVD or **N.K.V.D.** *Russian.* Narodny Kommissariat Vnutrennikh Del (People's Commissariat for Internal Affairs).
NL 1. National League. 2. Also **n.l.** new line. 3. Also **N.L.** New Latin.
n.l. *Lat.* non licet (not permitted).
N.L. *Lat.* non liquet (not clear).
NLF National Liberation Front.
NLRB also **N.L.R.B.** National Labor Relations Board.
nm 1. Or **n.m.** nautical mile. 2. nuclear magneton.
NM or **N.M.** New Mexico.
N.Mex. New Mexico.
NNE north-northeast.
NNW north-northwest.
no. or **No.** 1. north; northern. 2. number.
n.o.p. not otherwise provided (for).
Nor. 1. Norman. 2. north. 3. Norway; Norwegian.
norm. normal.
Norm. Norman.
Norw. Norway; Norwegian.
nos. or **Nos.** numbers.
n.o.s. not otherwise specified.
Nov. November.
NOW 1. National Organization for Women. 2. negotiable order of withdrawal.
NP neuropsychiatric; neuropsychiatry.
N.P. notary public.
NPN nonprotein nitrogen.
n.p.t. normal pressure and temperature.
NRA also **N.R.A.** 1. National Recovery Administration. 2. National Rifle Association. 3. Naval Reserve Association.
NRC 1. National Research Council. 2. Nuclear Regulatory Commission.
ns or **nsec** nanosecond.
NS 1. Or **N.S.** Nova Scotia. 2. nuclear ship.
n.s. 1. new series. 2. not specified.
N.S. New Style.
n/s not sufficient.
NSC National Security Council.
NSE National Stock Exchange.
NSF National Science Foundation.
n.s.f. or **N.S.F.** not sufficient funds.
N.S.P.C.A. National Society for the Prevention of Cruelty to Animals.
N.S.W. New South Wales.
NT 1. Also **N.T.** New Testament. 2. Northwest Territories.
n.t.p. or **N.T.P.** normal temperature and pressure.
nt. wt. net weight.
num. 1. number. 2. numeral.
Num. *Bible.* Numbers.
numis. or **numism.** numismatic; numismatics.
NV Nevada.
NW northwest.
NWbN northwest by north.
NWbW northwest by west.
n.wt. net weight.
N.W.T. Northwest Territories.
NY or **N.Y.** New York.
NYC or **N.Y.C.** New York City.
NYP not yet published.
NYSE New York Stock Exchange.
N.Z. New Zealand.

O 1. Or **O.** ocean. 2. Or **O.** order.
o. 1. *Lat.* octarius (pint). 2. Or **O.** octavo.
O. 1. October. 2. Ohio.
o/a on or about.
OAPC Office of Alien Property Custodian.
OAS Organization of American States.
Ob *Bible.* Obadiah.
ob. 1. *Lat.* obiit (he, or she, died). 2. *Lat.* obiter (incidentally). 3. oboe. 4. obstetric.
Obad. *Bible.* Obadiah.
O.B.E. 1. Officer of the Order of the British Empire. 2. Also **OBE** Order of the British Empire.
obj. 1. *Gram.* object; objective. 2. objection.
obl. 1. oblique. 2. oblong.
obs. 1. obscure. 2. observation. 3. Or **Obs.** observatory. 4. obsolete. 5. obstetric; obstetrician; obstetrics.
obstet. obstetric; obstetrics.
obv. obverse.
OC also **O.C.** Office of Censorship.
oc. or **Oc.** ocean.
o.c. *Lat.* opere citato (in the work cited).
O.C. 1. Officer Commanding. 2. Old Catholic.
o/c overcharge.
OCAS Organization of Central American States.
occ. 1. occident; occidental. 2. occupation.
occas. occasional; occasionally.
OCD Office of Civil Defense.
OCS Officer Candidate School.
oct. octavo.
Oct. October.
o.d. 1. *Lat.* oculus dexter (right eye). 2. olive drab. 3. on demand. 4. outside diameter.
O.D. 1. Doctor of Optometry. 2. officer of the day. 3. Also **o/d** overdraft. 4. overdrawn.
Oe oersted.
OE also **O.E.** Old English.
OECD Organization for Economic Cooperation and Development.
OED also **O.E.D.** Oxford English Dictionary.
OEO Office of Economic Opportunity.
off. office; officer; official.
O.F.M. Order of Friars Minor.
O.F.S. Orange Free State.
OG or **O.G.** 1. officer of the guard. 2. original gum.
OGPU or **O.G.P.U.** *Russian.* Ob'edinyonnoye Gosudarstvennoye Politicheskoye Upravlenie (Unified Government Political Administration).
OH Ohio.
OHMS or **O.H.M.S.** On Her, or His, Majesty's Service.
OIT Office of International Trade.
OK Oklahoma.
Okla. Oklahoma.
Om. Oman.
OM. ostmark.
O.M. Order of Merit.
OMB Office of Management and Budget.
ON 1. Also **O.N.** Old Norse. 2. Ontario.
ONI Office of Naval Intelligence.
ONR Office of Naval Research.
Ont. Ontario.
O.O.D. officer of the deck.
op or **OP** or **op.** or **o.p.** out of print.
op. 1. Also **Op.** operation. 2. opposite. 3. Also **Op.** opus.
O.P. Order of Preachers.
op. cit. *Lat.* opere citato (in the work cited).
OPEC Organization of Petroleum Exporting Countries.
opp. opposite.
opt. 1. optative. 2. optical; optician; optics. 3. optimum. 4. optional.
OR or **Or.** Oregon.
o.r. owner's risk.
O.R. or **OR** operating room.
orch. orchestra.
ord. 1. order. 2. ordinal. 3. ordinance. 4. ordnance.
ordn. ordnance.
Ore. Oregon.
org. 1. organic. 2. organization; organized.
orig. original; originally.
ornith. ornithologic; ornithology.
orth. orthopedic; orthopedics.
o.s. 1. *Lat.* oculus sinister (left eye). 2. old series. 3. Or **o/s** out of stock.
O.S. 1. Old Style. 2. ordinary seaman.
OSA or **O.S.A.** Order of St. Augustine.
OSB or **O.S.B.** Order of St. Benedict.
OSF or **O.S.F.** Order of St. Francis.
OSU or **O.S.U.** Order of St. Ursula.
OT also **O.T.** Old Testament.
o.t. or **O.T.** 1. occupational therapy. 2. overtime.
OTB off-track betting.
OTC also **O.T.C.** 1. Officer in Tactical Command. 2. Officers' Training Corps.
otol. otology.
OTS also **O.T.S.** Officers' Training School.
OWI Office of War Information.
Ox. or **Oxf.** Oxford.
Oxon. *Lat.* Oxoniensis (of Oxford).
oz also **oz.** ounce.
oz ap apothecaries' ounce.
oz av or **oz avdp** avoirdupois ounce.
oz t troy ounce.

p 1. momentum. 2. *Physics.* pico-. 3. Or **p.** *Mus.* piano (a direction). 4. Symbol for proton.
P 1. parental generation. 2. *Physics.* parity. 3. *Chess.* pawn. 4. petite. 5. *Bible.* Peter. 6. *Physics.* pressure.
p. 1. page. 2. part. 3. participle. 4. past. 5. penny. 6. per. 7. peseta. 8. peso. 9. pint. 10. pipe. 11. pole. 12. population. 13. Or **P.** president. 14. Or **P.** prince. 15. purl.
P. priest.
PA 1. Or **Pa.** Pennsylvania. 2. public-address system.
p.a. *Lat.* per annum (by the year).
P.A. 1. Or **P/A** power of attorney. 2. press agent. 3. prosecuting attorney.
Pac. or **Pacif.** Pacific.
Pak. Pakistan.
Pal. Palestine.
pam. pamphlet.
Pan. Panama.
P and L profit and loss.
par. 1. paragraph. 2. parallel. 3. parenthesis. 4. parish.
Par. or **Para.** Paraguay.
paren. parenthesis.
parl. parliamentary.
Parl. Parliament.
part. 1. participle. 2. particular.
pass. 1. passage. 2. passenger. 3. passive.
pat. patent.
patd. patented.
path. or **pathol.** pathological; pathology.
PAU or **P.A.U.** Pan American Union.
PAYE or **P.A.Y.E.** 1. pay as you earn. 2. pay as you enter.
payt. payment.
P.B. 1. passbook. 2. prayer book.
PBI protein-bound iodine.
PBS Public Broadcasting System.
PBX also **P.B.X.** private branch (telephone) exchange.
p.c. 1. *Lat.* post cibum (after meals). 2. per cent. 3. Also **p/c** or **P/C** petty cash. 4. post card.
P.C. 1. Past Commander. 2. Police

Constable. 3. Post Commander. 4. Privy Council.
p/c or **P/C** prices current.
PCB polychlorinated biphenyl.
PCP phencyclidine.
pct. per cent.
pd. paid.
p.d. or **P.D.** per diem.
P.D. 1. Police Department. 2. postal district. 3. potential difference.
Pd.B. *Lat.* Pedagogiae Baccalaureus (Bachelor of Pedagogy).
Pd.D. *Lat.* Pedagogiae Doctor (Doctor of Pedagogy).
Pd.M. *Lat.* Pedagogiae Magister (Master of Pedagogy).
PDT or **P.D.T.** Pacific Daylight Time.
pe also **p.e.** printer's error.
PE Prince Edward Island.
P.E. 1. physical education. 2. *Statistics.* probable error. 3. professional engineer.
P.E.I. Prince Edward Island.
pen. or **Pen.** peninsula.
P.E.N. International Association of Poets, Playwrights, Editors, Essayists, and Novelists.
Penn. or **Penna.** Pennsylvania.
per. 1. period. 2. person.
perf. 1. perfect. 2. perforated.
perm. permanent.
perp. perpendicular.
pers. 1. person. 2. personal.
Pers. Persia; Persian.
pert. pertaining.
pet. petroleum.
Pet. *Bible.* Peter.
petr. petrology.
petrog. petrography.
petrol. petrology.
pf. 1. pfennig. 2. preferred.
Pfc or **Pfc.** private first class.
pfd. preferred.
pfg. pfennig.
pg. page.
Pg. Portugal; Portuguese.
P.G. 1. paying guest. 2. postgraduate.
PGA Professional Golfers' Association.
Ph *Bible.* Philippians.
PH also **P.H.** 1. Public Health. 2. Purple Heart.
ph. phase.
PHA Public Housing Administration.
phar. or **Phar.** pharmaceutical; pharmacist; pharmacopoeia; pharmacy.
Phar.B. *Lat.* Pharmaciae Baccalaureus (Bachelor of Pharmacy).
Phar.D. *Lat.* Pharmaciae Doctor (Doctor of Pharmacy).
pharm. or **Pharm.** pharmaceutical; pharmacist; pharmacopoeia; pharmacy.
Phar.M. *Lat.* Pharmaciae Magister (Master of Pharmacy).
Ph.B. *Lat.* Philosophiae Baccalaureus (Bachelor of Philosophy).
Ph.C. Pharmaceutical Chemist.
Ph.D. *Lat.* Philosophiae Doctor (Doctor of Philosophy).
Ph.G. graduate in pharmacy.
phil. philosopher; philosophical; philosophy.
Phil. 1. *Bible.* Philippians. 2. Philippines.
Philem. *Bible.* Philemon.
Phil. I. or **Phil. Is.** Philippine Islands.
philol. philology.
philos. philosopher; philosophical; philosophy.
Phm *Bible.* Philemon.
Ph.M. *Lat.* Philosophiae Magister (Master of Philosophy).
phon. 1. phonetic; phonetics. 2. phonology.
photog. photography.
photom. photometry.
phr. phrase.
phren. phrenology.
PHS Public Health Service.
phys. 1. physical. 2. physician. 3. physicist; physics. 4. physiological; physiology.
physiol. physiological; physiology.
P.I. Philippine Islands.
pinx. *Lat.* pinxit (he, or she, painted this).
PK psychokinesis.
pk. 1. pack. 2. park. 3. peak. 4. Or **pk** peck.
pkg. or **pkge.** package.
pkt. packet.
PKU phenylketonuria.
pl. 1. Or **Pl.** place. 2. plate. 3. plural.
plat. 1. plateau. 2. platform. 3. platoon.
plf. plaintiff.
pln. plain.
PLO Palestine Liberation Organization.
plu. plural.
pm also **p-m** phase modulation.
PM or **P.M.** 1. past master. 2. police magistrate. 3. postmaster. 4. provost marshal.
pm. premium.
p.m. also **P.M.** post mortem.
P.M. 1. Also **p.m.** post meridiem. Usually small capitals P.M. 2. Prime Minister.
P.M.G. postmaster general.
pmk. postmark.
pmt. payment.
p.n. or **P/N** promissory note.
pneum. pneumatic; pneumatics.
p.n.g. persona non grata.
po or **p.o.** *Baseball.* putout.
PO or **P.O.** 1. Personnel Officer. 2. Also **p.o.** petty officer. 3. postal order. 4. Also **p.o.** post office.
POE or **P.O.E.** port of entry.
poet. poetic; poetical; poetry.
pol. political; politician; politics.
Pol. Poland; Polish.
polit. political; politics.
pop. 1. popular. 2. population.
Port. Portugal; Portuguese.
pos. 1. position. 2. positive.
poss. 1. possession. 2. possessive. 3. possible; possibly.
pot. potential.
POW or **P.O.W.** prisoner of war.
pp or **pp.** *Mus.* pianissimo.
pp. 1. pages. 2. past participle.
p.p. or **P.P.** 1. parcel post. 2. parish priest. 3. past participle. 4. postpaid.
ppd. 1. postpaid. 2. prepaid.
pph. pamphlet.
P.P.S. also **p.p.s.** *Lat.* post postscriptum (additional postscript).
ppt. precipitate.
pptn. precipitation.
p.q. previous question.
P.Q. or **PQ** Province of Quebec.
Pr *Bible.* Proverbs.
PR or **P.R.** 1. public relations. 2. Puerto Rico.
pr. 1. pair. 2. present. 3. price. 4. printing. 5. pronoun.
Pr. 1. priest. 2. prince. 3. Provençal.
P.R. proportional representation.
prec. preceding.
pred. predicate.
pref. 1. preface; prefatory. 2. preference; preferred. 3. prefix.
prem. premium.
prep. 1. preparation; preparatory; prepare. 2. preposition.
prepd. prepared.
prepn. preparation.
pres. 1. present. 2. president.
Pres. President.
Presb. or **Presby.** Presbyterian.
pret. preterit.
PRF 1. pulse recurrence frequency. 2. pulse repetition frequency.
prf. proof.
prim. 1. primary. 2. primitive.
prin. 1. principal. 2. principle.
print. printing.
priv. 1. private. 2. privative.
p.r.n. *Lat.* pro re nata (*Med.* as the situation demands).
PRO also **P.R.O.** public relations officer.
pro. professional.
prob. 1. probable; probably. 2. problem.
proc. 1. proceedings. 2. process.
prod. 1. produce. 2. produced. 3. product; production.
prof. 1. professional. 2. Also **Prof.** professor.
prom. promontory.
pron. 1. pronominal; pronoun. 2. pronounced; pronunciation.
prop. 1. proper; properly. 2. property. 3. proposition. 4. proprietary; proprietor.
propr. proprietor.
pros. prosody.
Pros. Atty. prosecuting attorney.
Prot. Protestant.
protec. protectorate.
prov. 1. province; provincial. 2. provisional. 3. provost.
Prov. 1. Provençal. 2. *Bible.* Proverbs.
prox. proximo.
Ps or **Ps.** *Bible.* Psalm; Psalms.
p.s. passenger steamer.
P.S. 1. permanent secretary. 2. Police Sergeant. 3. Also **p.s.** postscript. 4. public school.
PSAT Preliminary Scholastic Aptitude Test.
psec picosecond.
pseud. pseudonym.
psf or **p.s.f.** pounds per square foot.
psi or **p.s.i.** pounds per square inch.
PST or **P.S.T.** Pacific Standard Time.
psych. or **psychol.** psychological; psychologist; psychology.
pt. 1. part. 2. payment. 3. pint. 4. point. 5. port. 6. preterit.
p.t. *Lat.* pro tempore (temporarily).
P.T. 1. Also **PT** Pacific Time. 2. physical therapy. 3. physical training. 4. postal telegraph.
pta. peseta.
PTA or **P.T.A.** Parent-Teacher Association.
ptg. printing.
p.t.o. or **PTO** please turn over.
PTV 1. public television. 2. pay television.
pty. proprietary.
pub. 1. public. 2. publication. 3. published; publisher.
publ. 1. publication. 2. published; publisher.
PV polyvinyl.
PVC polyvinyl chloride.
pvt. or **Pvt.** private.
PWA also **P.W.A.** Public Works Administration.
pwr. power.
pwt. pennyweight.
pxt. *Lat.* pinxit (he, or she, painted this).
pyro. pyrotechnics.

Q 1. *Chess.* queen. 2. quetzal.
q. 1. quart. 2. quarter. 3. quarterly. 4. Also **Q.** quarto. 5. query. 6. question. 7. quintal. 8. quire.
qb quarterback.
QB *Chess.* queen's bishop.
Q.B. Queen's Bench.
QC quartermaster corps.
Q.C. Queen's Counsel.
Q.E.D. *Lat.* quod erat demonstrandum (which was to be demonstrated).
Q.E.F. *Lat.* quod erat faciendum (which was to be done).
QF quick-firing.
q.i.d. *Lat.* quater in die (*Med.* four times a day).
QKt *Chess.* queen's knight.
ql. quintal.
Qld. Queensland.
qlty. quality.
QM quartermaster.
Q.M. *Lat.* quaque mane (every morning).
QMC quartermaster corps.
QMG Quartermaster General.
qn. question.
Qo *Bible.* Ecclesiastes.
QP *Chess.* queen's pawn.
q.p. or **q.pl.** *Lat.* quantum placet (as much as you please).
qq. questions.
qq.v. *Lat.* quae vide (which [things] see).
QR *Chess.* queen's rook.
qr. 1. quarter. 2. quarterly. 3. quire.
q.s. *Lat.* quantum sufficit (as much as suffices).
QSO *Astron.* quasi-stellar object.
QSRS *Astron.* quasi-stellar radio source.
qt or **qt.** quart.
qt. quantity.
qto. quarto.
qty. quantity.
qu. 1. queen. 2. query. 3. question.
quad. 1. quadrangle. 2. quadrant.
qual. qualitative.
quant. quantitative.
quar. 1. quarter. 2. quarterly.
Que. Quebec.
ques. question.
quot. quotation.
q.v. *Lat.* quod vide (which see).

r 1. Or **R** radius. 2. Or **R** *Elect.* resistance. 3. Or **r.** *Sports.* run.
R 1. *Chem.* gas constant. 2. *Chem.* radical. 3. Or **R.** Réaumur (scale). 4. *Eccles.* response. 5. roentgen (unit of radiation). 6. *Chess.* rook.
r. 1. Or **R.** railroad; railway. 2. range. 3. rare. 4. retired. 5. Or **R.** right. 6. Or **R.** river. 7. Or **R.** road. 8. rod (unit of length). 9. rouble. 10. *Card Games.* rubber. 11. Or **R.** rupee.
R. 1. rabbi. 2. rector. 3. regius. 4. Republican. 5. royal.
Ra. Range.
R.A. 1. rear admiral. 2. Or **RA** Regular Army. 3. *Astron.* right ascension. 4. Royal Academy; Royal Academician.
rad. 1. radical. 2. radio. 3. radius. 4. radix.
RAF also **R.A.F.** Royal Air Force.
RAM also **R.A.M.** Royal Academy of Music.
R & B rhythm and blues.
R & D research and development.
R and R rest and recreation.
RBC or **rbc** red blood cell; red blood (cell) count.
RBE *Physics.* relative biological effectiveness.
rbi also **r.b.i.** run batted in.
RC 1. Red Cross. 2. Roman Catholic.
RCAF also **R.C.A.F.** Royal Canadian Air Force.
R.C.Ch. Roman Catholic Church.
RCMP also **R.C.M.P.** Royal Canadian Mounted Police.
R.C.P. Royal College of Physicians.
rcpt. receipt.
R.C.S. Royal College of Surgeons.
rct. recruit.
rd rod (unit of length).
RD rural delivery.
rd. 1. Or **Rd.** road. 2. round.
RDA recommended daily allowance.
RDF radio direction finder.
Re. rupee.
R.E. or **RE** real estate.
rec. 1. receipt. 2. record; recording. 3. recreation.
recd. or **rec'd.** received.
recip. reciprocal; reciprocity.
rect. 1. receipt. 2. rectangle; rectangular. 3. rectified. 4. rector; rectory.
red. reduced; reduction.
ref. 1. referee. 2. reference. 3. referred. 4. refining. 5. reformation; reformed. 6. refunding.
refl. 1. reflection; reflective. 2. reflex; reflexive.
reg. 1. regent. 2. regiment. 3. region. 4. register; registered. 5. registrar. 6. registry. 7. regular; regularly. 8. regulation. 9. regulator.
regd. registered.
regt. regiment.
Regt. regent.
rel. 1. relating. 2. relative. 3. released. 4. religion; religious.
rem. remittance.
rep. 1. repair. 2. repetition. 3. report. 4. reporter. 5. Or **Rep.** representative. 6. reprint. 7. Or **Rep.** republic.
Rep. Republican.
r.e.p. roentgen equivalent, physical.
repl. replace; replacement.
repr. representing.
rept. report.
Repub. 1. republic. 2. Republican.
req. 1. require; required. 2. requisition.
reqd. required.
RES reticuloendothelial system.
res. 1. research. 2. reserve. 3. residence; resident; resides. 4. resolution.
Res. 1. Reservation. 2. Reservoir.
resp. 1. respective; respectively. 2. respiration.
ret. 1. retain. 2. retired. 3. return.
rev. 1. revenue. 2. reverse; reversed. 3. review; reviewed. 4. revise; revision. 5. Or **Rev.** revolution.
Rev. 1. *Bible.* Revelation. 2. reverend (title).
Rev. Ver. *Bible.* Revised Version.
RF radio frequency.
rf. 1. reef. 2. refund.
r.f. right field; right fielder.
RFD also **R.F.D.** rural free delivery.
r.h. 1. relative humidity. 2. Also **RH** right hand.
rhbdr. rhombohedron.
rheo. rheostat.
rhet. rhetoric.
rhomb. rhombic.
rhp or **r.hp.** rated horsepower.
RI or **R.I.** Rhode Island.
R.I.P. *Lat.* requiescat in pace (may he, or she, rest in peace).
rit. *Mus.* ritardando.
riv. river.
RJ road junction.
Rm *Bible.* Romans.
RM also **Rm.** reichsmark.
rm. 1. ream. 2. room.
rms root mean square.
RMS 1. Railway Mail Service. 2. Also **R.M.S.** Royal Mail Service. 3. Also **R.M.S.** Royal Mail Steamship.
RN or **R.N.** 1. registered nurse. 2. Royal Navy.
RNA ribonucleic acid.
rnd. round.
RNR or **R.N.R.** Royal Naval Reserve.
ro. rood (measure).
rom also **rom.** roman (type).
ROM *Computer Sci.* read-only memory.
Rom. 1. Roman. 2. Romance (lan-

guage). 3. Romania; Romanian. 4. *Bible.* Romans.
rot. rotating; rotation.
ROTC Reserve Officers' Training Corps.
rpm or **r.p.m.** revolutions per minute.
R.P.O. Railway Post Office.
rps or **r.p.s.** revolutions per second.
rpt. 1. repeat. 2. report.
R.Q. respiratory quotient.
RR also **R.R.** 1. railroad. 2. rural route.
R.R. Right Reverend.
RRB Railroad Retirement Board.
rRNA ribosomal RNA.
RS 1. recording secretary. 2. right side. 3. Also **R.S.** Royal Society.
RSFSR or **R.S.F.S.R.** Russian Soviet Federated Socialist Republic.
RSV or **R.S.V.** *Bible.* Revised Standard Version.
R.S.V.P. or **r.s.v.p.** *French.* répondez s'il vous plaît (please reply).
Rt *Bible.* Ruth.
RT 1. radio telephone. 2. room temperature.
rt. right.
rte. route.
Rt. Hon. Right Honorable.
Rt. Rev. Right Reverend.
Rus. or **Russ.** Russia; Russian.
Rv *Bible.* Revelations.
RV or **R.V.** *Bible.* Revised Version.
Rw. Rwanda.
R.W. 1. Right Worshipful. 2. Right Worthy.
rwy. or **ry.** railway.

s 1. second (unit of time). 2. second of arc. 3. siemens. 4. stere.
S 1. *Bible.* Samuel. 2. seaman. 3. Also **S.** or **s** or **s.** south; southern. 4. *Physics.* strangeness.
s. 1. Or **S.** school. 2. Or **S.** sea. 3. see. 4. semi-. 5. shilling. 6. singular. 7. sire. 8. sister. 9. small. 10. Or **S.** society. 11. solo. 12. son. 13. Or **S.** soprano. 14. sou. 15. stock. 16. substantive. 17. surplus.
S. 1. Sabbath. 2. saint. 3. Saturday. 4. Saxon. 5. September. 6. *Med.* signature. 7. signor; signore. 8. Sunday.
SA Salvation Army.
s.a. *Lat.* sine anno (without date).
S.A. 1. South Africa. 2. South America.
Sab. Sabbath.
SAC Strategic Air Command.
SACEUR Supreme Allied Commander, Europe.
S.Afr. South Africa.
Sal. El Salvador.
SALT Strategic Arms Limitations Talks.
SAM surface-to-air-missile.
Sam. *Bible.* Samuel.
s. ap. apothecaries' scruple.
SAR Sons of the American Revolution.
SASE self-addressed stamped envelope.
Sask. Saskatchewan.
SAT A trademark for Scholastic Aptitude Test.
sat. saturate; saturation.
Sat. Saturday.
Sau. Ar. Saudi Arabia.
S.Austl. South Australia.
Sax. Saxon; Saxony.
SB simultaneous broadcast.
sb. substantive.
S.B. *Lat.* Scientiae Baccalaureus (Bachelor of Science).
SBA Small Business Administration.
SbE south by east.
SBN Standard Book Number.
SbW south by west.
SC 1. Security Council. 2. Or **S.C.** South Carolina.
sc. 1. scale. 2. scene. 3. *Lat.* scilicet (namely). 4. scruple (weight). 5. *Lat.* sculpsit (he, or she, sculptured [it]). 5. science.
Sc. Scotch; Scottish.
s.c. also **sc** small capitals.
S.C. Supreme Court.
Scand. Scandinavia; Scandinavian.
SCAP Supreme Commander for the Allied Powers.
SCC storage connecting circuit.
sch. school.
sci. science; scientific.
SCLC Southern Christian Leadership Conference.
Scot. Scotch; Scotland; Scottish.
scr. scruple (unit of weight).
Script. Scriptural; Scriptures.
sct. scout.
sctd. scattered.
sculp. 1. Or **sculpt.** *Lat.* sculpsit (he, or she, sculptured [it]). 2. sculptor; sculptress; sculpture.
SD 1. sight draft. 2. Or **S.D.** South Dakota. 3. special delivery. 4. standard deviation.
sd. sound.
s.d. *Lat.* sine die (indefinitely).
S.Dak. South Dakota.
SDS Students for a Democratic Society.
SE 1. southeast; southeastern. 2. standard English. 3. stock exchange.
SEATO Southeast Asia Treaty Organization.
SEbE southeast by east.
SEbS southeast by south.
sec 1. secant. 2. second. 3. secondary.
SEC Securities and Exchange Commission.
sec. 1. secretary. 2. sector. 3. *Lat.* secundum (according to).
sect. section.
secy. secretary.
sed. sediment.
sel. select; selected.
SEM scanning electron microscope.
sem. seminary.
Sem. Semitic.
sen. or **Sen.** 1. senate; senator. 2. senior.
sep. separate; separation.
Sep. September.
sepd. separated.
Sept. September.
seq. 1. sequel. 2. *Lat.* sequens (the following).
seqq. *Lat.* sequentia (the following [things]).
ser. 1. serial. 2. series. 3. sermon.
Serb. Serbia; Serbian.
serv. 1. servant. 2. service.
sess. session.
SF science fiction.
sf. *Mus.* sforzando.
Sfc. sergeant first class.
sfz. *Mus.* sforzando.
sg specific gravity.
Sg *Bible.* Song of Songs.
SG surgeon general.
S.G. or **SG** solicitor general.
sgd. signed.
Sgt. sergeant.
Sgt. Maj. sergeant major.
sh. 1. share. 2. sheet.
Shak. Shakespeare.
SHAPE Supreme Headquarters Allied Powers, Europe.
shf or **SHF** superhigh frequency.
shp or **s.hp.** shaft horsepower.
shpt. shipment.
shr. share.
Si *Bible.* Sirach (Ecclesiasticus).
SI *French.* Système Internationale d'Unités (International System of Units).
Sib. Siberia; Siberian.
Sic. Sicilian; Sicily.
SIDS sudden infant death syndrome.
sig. 1. signal. 2. signature. 3. Or **Sig.** signor; signore.
sing. singular.
S.J. Society of Jesus.
S.J.D. *Lat.* Scientiae Juridicae Doctor (Doctor of Juridicial Science).
SK Saskatchewan.
sk. sack.
Skr. or **Skt.** Sanskrit.
SL 1. sea level 2. south latitude.
sl. slightly.
S.L. Sierra Leone.
s.l.a.n. *Lat.* sine loco, anno, vel nomine (without place, year, or name).
Slav. Slavic.
sld. 1. sailed. 2. sealed. 3. sold.
SLIP symmetric list processor.
SLV standard launch vehicle.
SM 1. sergeant major. 2. Or **S.M.** soldier's medal.
sm. small.
S.M. Scientiae Major (Master of Science).
S.M.Sgt. Senior Master Sergeant.
s.n. *Lat.* sine nomine (without name).
SNCC Student Nonviolent Coordinating Committee.
SNG synthetic natural gas.
so. or **So.** south; southern.
s.o. 1. seller's option. 2. strikeout.
SOB *Slang.* son of a bitch.
soc. 1. social. 2. socialist. 3. society.
SOF sound on film.
sol. 1. solicitor. 2. soluble. 3. solution.
Sol. Is. Solomon Islands.
soln. solution.
Som. Somalia.
SOP standard operating procedure.
sop. soprano.
soph. sophomore.
sou. or **Sou.** south; southern.
sov. sovereign (coin).
Sov. Un. Soviet Union.
SP 1. self-propelled. 2. shore patrol; shore police.
sp. 1. special. 2. specialist. 3. species. 4. specific. 5. spelling.
Sp. Spain; Spanish.
s.p. *Lat.* sine prole (without issue).
Span. Spanish.
SPCA Society for the Prevention of Cruelty to Animals.
SPCC Society for the Prevention of Cruelty to Children.
spec. 1. special. 2. specification. 3. speculation.
specif. specifically.
sp gr specific gravity.
sp ht specific heat.
spp. species (plural).
SPQR small profits, quick returns.
S.P.Q.R. *Lat.* Senatus Populusque Romanus (the Senate and the People of Rome).
SPR Society for Psychical Research.
spr. spring.
s.p.s. *Lat.* sine prole supersite (without surviving issue).
spt. seaport.
sq. 1. squadron. 2. square.
sr steradian.
Sr. 1. Or **sr.** senior. 2. señor. 3. sister (religious).
Sra. señora.
SRO standing room only.
Srta. señorita.
ss. *Lat.* 1. Or **ss** scilicet (namely). 2. semis (one half).
S.S. 1. Or **SS** steamship. 2. Sunday school. 3. sworn statement.
s/s same size.
SSA Social Security Administration.
SSE south-southeast.
S.Sgt. staff sergeant.
SSI Supplemental Security Income.
ssp. subspecies.
SSR or **S.S.R.** Soviet Socialist Republic.
SSRC Social Science Research Council.
SSS Selective Service System.
SST supersonic transport.
SSW south-southwest.
ST standard time.
st. 1. stanza. 2. start. 3. state. 4. Or **St.** statute. 5. stet. 6. stitch. 7. stone. 8. Or **St.** strait. 9. Or **St.** street. 10. strophe.
St. saint.
s.t. short ton.
sta. 1. station. 2. stationary.
stat. 1. *Lat.* statim (immediately). 2. stationary. 3. statistics. 4. statuary. 5. statute.
stbd. starboard.
std. standard.
Ste. *French.* sainte (feminine form of saint).
steno or **stenog.** also **sten.** stenographer; stenography.
ster. sterling.
St. Ex. stock exchange.
stg. sterling.
stge. storage.
stip. 1. stipend. 2. stipulation.
stk. stock.
S.T.M. *Lat.* Sacrae Theologiae Magister (Master of Sacred Theology).
STOL short takeoff and landing.
STP standard temperature and pressure.
STR synchronous transmitter receiver.
str. 1. steamer. 2. Or **Str.** strait. 3. stringed.
stud. student.
sub. 1. subaltern. 2. substitute. 3. suburb; suburban.
subj. 1. subject. 2. subjective. 3. subjunctive.
subs. subscription.
subst. 1. substantive. 2. substitute.
Sud. Sudan.
suf. or **suff.** 1. sufficient. 2. suffix.
Sun. Sunday.
sup. 1. superior. 2. *Gram.* superlative. 3. *Gram.* supine. 4. supplement. 5. supply. 6. *Lat.* supra (above).
super. 1. superintendent. 2. superior.
supp. or **suppl.** supplement; supplementary.
supr. supreme.
supt. or **Supt.** superintendent.
supvr. supervisor.
sur. 1. surface. 2. surplus.
Sur. Surinam.
surg. surgeon; surgery; surgical.
surr. surrender.
s.v. 1. Also **SV** sailing vessel. 2. *Lat.* sub verbo; sub voce ([look] under the word).
svgs. savings.
sw short wave.
SW southwest.
sw. switch.
Sw. Sweden; Swedish.
Swaz. Swaziland.
swbd or **swbd.** switchboard.
SWbS southwest by south.
SWbW southwest by west.
Swe. or **Swed.** Sweden; Swedish.
Switz. Switzerland.
swp. swamp.
sym. 1. symbol. 2. symmetric. 3. symphony.
syn. synonymous; synonym; synonymy.
synd. syndicate.
Syr. 1. Syria; Syrian. 2. Syriac.

t 1. ton. 2. troy (system of weights).
T 1. surface tension. 2. temperature. 3. *Physics.* tera-. 4. tesla. 5. *Math.* time reversal.
t. 1. *Commerce.* tare. 2. teaspoons; teaspoonful. 3. tempo. 4. *Lat.* tempore (in the time of). 5. Or **T.** *Mus.* tenor. 6. *Gram.* tense. 7. terminal. 8. Or **T.** territory. 9. Or **T.** time. 10. Or **T.** town; township. 11. transit. 12. *Gram.* transitive.
T. 1. tablespoon; tablespoonful. 2. Testament. 3. Tuesday.
TA teaching assistant.
tab. table.
TAC Tactical Air Command.
TAG the Adjutant General.
tan tangent.
Tan. Tanzania.
TAS 1. telephone answering system. 2. true airspeed.
Tas. or **Tasm.** Tasmania; Tasmanian.
TAT Thematic Apperception Test.
Tb *Bible.* Tobit.
TB also **T.B.** tuberculosis.
t.b. 1. trial balance. 2. Also **T.B.** tubercle bacillus.
tbs. or **tbsp.** tablespoon; tablespoonful.
tchr. teacher.
TD 1. Also **td** touchdown. 2. Also **T.D.** treasury department.
TDN also **T.D.N.** total digestible nutrients.
tech. technical.
technol. technological; technology.
TEFL teaching English as a foreign language.
t.e.g. top edges gilt.
tel. 1. telegram. 2. telegraph; telegraphic. 3. telephone.
teleg. 1. telegram. 2. telegraph; telegraphic; telegraphy.
temp. 1. temperance. 2. temperature. 3. template. 4. temporary. 5. *Lat.* tempore (in the time of).
ten. 1. tenor. 2. *Mus.* tenuto.
Tenn. Tennessee.
ter. 1. terrace. 2. territorial; territory.
term. 1. terminal. 2. termination.
terr. 1. terrace. 2. territorial; territory.
TESL teaching English as a second language.
TESOL teachers of English to speakers of other languages.
test. 1. testator. 2. testatrix. 3. testimony.
Test. Testament.
Teut. Teuton; Teutonic.
Tex. Texas.
T.F. Territorial Force.
tfr. transfer.
t.g. type genus.
TGIF thank God it's Friday.
Th *Bible.* Thessalonians.
Th. Thursday.
Thai. Thailand.
Th.B. *Lat.* Theologiae Baccalaureus (Bachelor of Theology).
THC tetrahydrocannibol.
Th.D. *Lat.* Theologiae Doctor (Doctor of Theology).
theat. theater.
theol. theologian; theological; theology.
therap. therapeutic; therapeutics.
Thess. *Bible.* Thessalonians.
Th.M. *Lat.* Theologiae Magister (Master of Theology).
thp or **t.hp.** thrust horsepower.
Thurs. also **Thur.** Thursday.
THz terahertz.
t.i.d. *Lat.* ter in die (*Med.* three times a day).
Tim. *Bible.* Timothy.
tit. title.

tk. truck.
TKO technical knockout.
tkt. ticket.
t.l. or **t/l** total loss.
TLC tender loving care.
t.l.o. total loss only.
tlr. tailor.
Tm *Bible.* Timothy.
TM trademark.
t.m. true mean.
TMV tobacco mosaic virus.
TN Tennessee.
tn. 1. ton. 2. town. 3. train.
tng. training.
tnpk. turnpike.
TNT trinitrotoluene.
t.o. turnover.
topog. topographic; topography.
tp. township.
t.p. title page.
tpk. turnpike.
TR or **T-R** transmit-receive.
tr. 1. *Gram.* transitive. 2. translated; translation; translator. 3. transpose; transposition. 4. treasurer. 5. *Law.* trust; trustee.
trans. 1. transaction. 2. *Gram.* transitive. 3. translated; translation; translator. 4. transportation. 5. transpose; transposition. 6. transverse.
transl. translated; translation.
transp. transportation.
trav. traveler; travels.
treas. treasurer; treasury.
trib. tributary.
trig. also **trigon.** trigonometric; trigonometry.
tripl. triplicate.
trit. triturate.
tRNA transfer RNA.
trop. tropic; tropical.
trp. troop.
T.S. also **t.s.** *Physics.* tensile strength.
T.Sgt. Technical Sergeant.
TSH thyroid-stimulating hormone.
tsp. teaspoon; teaspoonful.
Tt *Bible.* Titus.
TT 1. telegraphic transfer. 2. teletypewriter. 3. transit time. 4. tuberculin tested.
Tu. Tuesday.
T.U. trade union.
T.U.C. Trades Union Congress.
Tues. Tuesday.
Tun. Tunisia; Tunisian.
Tur. or **Turk.** Turkey; Turkish.
TVA Tennessee Valley Authority.
twp. township.
TX Texas.
typ. typographer; typographical; typography.
typo. or **typog.** typographer; typographical; typography.
typw. typewriter; typewritten.

U *Math.* union.
u. 1. Or **U.** uncle. 2. unit. 3. Or **U.** upper.
U. university.
U.A.E. United Arab Emirates.
U.A.R. United Arab Republic.
UAW or **U.A.W.** 1. United Automobile, Aerospace, and Agricultural Implement Workers. 2. United Automobile Workers.
u.c. also **UC** upper case.
UCMJ Uniform Code of Military Justice.
UCS universal character set.
UDC universal decimal classification.
Ug. Uganda.
UGT urgent (telegram).
uhf or **UHF** ultrahigh frequency.
U.K. United Kingdom.
ult. 1. ultimate; ultimately. 2. ultimo.
UMT Universal Military Training.
UMTS Universal Military Training Service.
UMW United Mine Workers.
UN or **U.N.** United Nations.
unan. unanimous.
unb. or **unbd.** unbound.
UNESCO United Nations Educational, Scientific, and Cultural Organization.
UNICEF United Nations International Children's Emergency Fund.
Unit. Unitarian; Unitarianism.
univ. 1. universal. 2. Or **Univ.** university.
Univ. Universalist.
unm. unmarried.
unp. unpaged.
UNRRA United Nations Relief and Rehabilitation Administration.
UNRWA United Nations Relief and Works Agency.
up. upper.
UPI or **U.P.I.** United Press International.
UPU Universal Postal Union.
Ur. Uruguay.
URA Urban Renewal Administration.
US or **U.S.** United States.
u.s. *Lat.* 1. ubi supra (where [mentioned] above). 2. ut supra (as above).
U.S. 1. Uncle Sam. 2. Uniform System (of lens aperture).
USA or **U.S.A.** 1. United States Army. 2. United States of America.
USAF also **U.S.A.F.** United States Air Force.
USAFI or **U.S.A.F.I.** United States Armed Forces Institute.
USAR United States Army Reserve.
USAREUR United States Army, Europe.
U.S.C. United States Code.
U.S.C.A. United States Code Annotated.
USCG also **U.S.C.G.** United States Coast Guard.
USDA United States Department of Agriculture.
USES United States Employment Service.
USIA United States Information Agency.
U.S.M. United States Mail.
USMC also **U.S.M.C.** United States Marine Corps.
USN also **U.S.N.** United States Navy.
USNA also **U.S.N.A.** United States Naval Academy.
USNR United States Naval Reserve.
USO or **U.S.O.** United Service Organizations.
U.S.P. United States Pharmacopoeia.
U.S.P.O. also **USPO** United States Post Office.
U.S.S. 1. United States Senate. 2. Also **USS** United States Ship.
USSR or **U.S.S.R.** Union of Soviet Socialist Republics.
usu. usually.
usw. *German.* und so weiter (and so forth).
UT Utah.
ut dict. *Lat.* ut dictum (*Med.* as directed).
UV ultraviolet.
UW underwriter.
ux. *Lat.* uxor (wife).
UXB unexploded bomb.

V 1. *Physics.* velocity. 2. victory. 3. *Elect.* volt. 4. volume.
v. 1. verb. 2. verse. 3. version. 4. verso. 5. versus. 6. Or **V.** very (in titles). 7. Or **V.** vice (in titles). 8. vide. 9. Or **V.** village. 10. violin. 11. vocative. 12. voice. 13. volume (book). 14. vowel.
V. 1. venerable (in titles). 2. viscount; viscountess.
VA or **Va.** Virginia.
V.A. 1. Also **VA** Veterans' Administration. 2. vicar apostolic. 3. vice admiral.
VAB voice answer back.
vac. vacuum.
V.Adm. vice admiral.
val. 1. valley. 2. valuation; value.
VAR visual-aural range.
var. 1. variable. 2. variant. 3. variation. 4. variety. 5. various.
VAT value-added tax.
Vat. Vatican.
vb. verb; verbal.
VC also **V.C.** Vietcong.
V.C. 1. vice chairman. 2. vice chancellor. 3. vice consul. 4. Victoria Cross.
VD also **V.D.** venereal disease.
v.d. 1. vapor density. 2. various dates.
VDT visual display terminal.
vel. 1. vellum. 2. velocity.
Ven. venerable.
Venez. Venezuela.
ver. 1. verse. 2. version.
vers versed sine.
vert. vertical.
vet. 1. veteran. 2. veterinarian; veterinary.
veter. veterinary.
V.F. 1. vicar forane. 2. Also **VF** video frequency. 3. Also **VF** visual field.
VFD volunteer fire department.
VFR visual flight rules.
VFW also **V.F.W.** Veterans of Foreign Wars.
V.G. vicar general.
vhf or **VHF** very high frequency.
VI or **V.I.** Virgin Islands.
v.i. *Lat.* vide infra (see below).
V.I. volume indicator.
vic. 1. vicar. 2. vicinity.
Viet. Vietnam; Vietnamese.
vil. village.
VIN vehicle identification number.
Vir. Is. Virgin Islands.
vis. 1. visibility. 2. visual.
Vis. or **Visct.** viscount; viscountess.
VISTA Volunteers in Service to America.
viz. *Lat.* videlicet (namely).
vlf or **VLF** very low frequency.
V.M.D. *Lat.* Veterinariae Medicinae Doctor (Doctor of Veterinary Medicine).
VO verbal order.
vo. verso.
voc. vocative.
vocab. vocabulary.
vol. 1. volcano. 2. volume. 3. volunteer.
vou. voucher.
VP 1. variable pitch. 2. verb phrase. 3. Or **V.P.** vice president.
vs. versus.
v.s. *Lat.* vide supra (see above).
V.S. veterinary surgeon.
vss. 1. verses. 2. versions.
V/STOL vertical short takeoff and landing.
VT 1. vacuum tube. 2. variable time. 3. Vermont.
VTOL vertical takeoff and landing.
VTR videotape recorder.
VU volume unit.
Vul. Vulgate.
vulg. vulgar.
Vulg. Vulgate.
vv. verses.
v.v. vice versa.

w or **W** *Physics.* work.
W 1. *Elect.* watt. 2. Also **W.** or **w** or **w.** west; western.
w. 1. week. 2. weight. 3. wide. 4. width. 5. wife. 6. with.
W. 1. Wednesday. 2. Welsh.
WA 1. Washington. 2. with average.
W.A. Western Australia.
WAAC Women's Army Auxiliary Corps.
WAAF Women's Auxiliary Air Force.
WAC Women's Army Corps.
WAF Women in the Air Force.
war. warrant.
Wash. Washington.
WATS Wide-Area Telephone Service.
WAVES Women Accepted for Volunteer Emergency Service (U.S. Navy).
Wb *Physics.* weber.
w.b. 1. water ballast. 2. Also **W.B.** waybill. 3. westbound.
W.B. Weather Bureau.
WBC or **wbc** white blood cell; white blood (cell) count.
WbN west by north.
WbS west by south.
w.c. 1. water closet. 2. without charge.
WCTU or **W.C.T.U.** Women's Christian Temperance Union.
WD or **W.D.** War Department.
wd. 1. wood. 2. word.
Wed. Wednesday.
wf or **w.f.** wrong font.
WFTU World Federation of Trade Unions.
w.g. wire gauge.
WH watt-hour.
wh. white.
whf. wharf.
WHO World Health Organization.
W-hr watt-hour.
whs. warehouse.
whsle. wholesale.
WI Wisconsin.
w.i. when issued (financial stock).
W.I. West Indian; West Indies.
WIA wounded in action.
wk. 1. weak. 2. week. 3. work.
wkly. weekly.
WL or **w.l.** 1. water line. 2. wavelength.
wmk. watermark.
WNW west-northwest.
WO or **W.O.** warrant officer.
w/o without.
w.o.c. without compensation.
WP 1. weather permitting. 2. word processing; word processor. 3. Or **w/p** without prejudice.
WPA Work Projects Administration.
wpm or **w.p.m.** words per minute.
wpn. weapon.
WR or **W.r.** Wassermann reaction.
WRAC or **W.R.A.C.** Women's Royal Army Corps.
WRAF or **W.R.A.F.** Women's Royal Air Force.
Ws *Bible.* Wisdom.
WS working storage.
WSA War Shipping Administration.
WSW west-southwest.
wt. weight.
WV or **W.Va.** West Virginia.
WVS Women's Volunteer Service.
WW I or **W.W.I** World War I.
WW II or **W.W.II** World War II.
WY or **Wyo.** Wyoming.

x 1. *Math.* abscissa. 2. *Printing.* broken type. 3. by. 4. Or **X** power of magnification. 5. Or **X** *Math.* a. Unknown number. b. algebraic variable.
X 1. Christ; Christian. 2. extra. 3. *Elect.* reactance. 4. times (multiplied by). 5. Used to indicate location, as on a map. 6. Also **x** unknown.
x. ex.
XD or **x-div.** ex dividend.
XI or **x-int.** ex interest.
XL 1. extra large. 2. extra long.
Xn Christian.
Xnty Christianity.

y *Math.* ordinate.
Y 1. *Elect.* admittance. 2. *Physics.* hypercharge. 3. yen (currency). 4. a. YMCA b. YMHA. c. YWCA. d. YWHA. 5. yeoman.
y. year.
yd yard (measurement).
yel. yellow.
Yem. Yemen.
yeo. yeoman; yeomanry.
YMCA or **Y.M.C.A.** Young Men's Christian Association.
YMHA or **Y.M.H.A.** Young Men's Hebrew Association.
YOB year of birth.
yr. 1. year. 2. younger. 3. your.
YT or **Y.T.** Yukon Territory.
Yug. or **Yugo.** Yugoslavia; Yugoslavian.
YWCA or **Y.W.C.A.** Young Women's Christian Association.
YWHA or **Y.W.H.A.** Young Women's Hebrew Association.

Z 1. atomic number. 2. *Elect.* impedance.
z. 1. zero. 2. zone.
z.B. *German.* zum Beispiel (for example).
Zc *Bible.* Zechariah.
Zech. *Bible.* Zechariah.
Zeph. *Bible.* Zephaniah.
Zl zloty.
zool. zoological; zoology.
Zp *Bible.* Zephaniah.
ZPG zero population growth.

FOUR-YEAR COLLEGES AND UNIVERSITIES

We acknowledge Time Share Corporation, Hanover, New Hampshire 03755, as the primary source of information in this section.

Abilene Christian University Abilene, TX 79691; private; 4,000
Abilene Christian University—Dallas Garland, TX 75041; private; 550
Adams State College Alamosa, CO 81102; public; 2,000
Adelphi University Garden City, NY 11530; private; 5,500
Adrian College Adrian, MI 49221; private; 1,100
Aero-Space Institute Chicago, IL 60610; private; 125
Agnes Scott College Decatur, GA 30030; private; 550
Alabama A and M University Normal, Al 35762; public; 3,500
Alabama State University Montgomery, AL 36195; public; 3,700
Alaska Bible College Glennallen, AK 99588; private; 40
Alaska Pacific University Anchorage, AK 99504; private; 130
Albany College of Pharmacy Albany, NY 12208; private; 580
Albany State College Albany, GA 31705; public; 1,600
Albertus Magnus College New Haven, CT 06511; private; 580
Albion College Albion, MI 49224; private; 1,900
Albright College Reading, PA 19603; private; 1,400
Alcorn State University Lorman, MS 39096; public; 2,800
Alderson Broaddus College Philippi, WV 26416; private; 820
Alfred University Alfred, NY 14802; private; 2,400
Allegheny College Meadville, PA 16335; private; 1,900
Allegheny Wesleyan College Salem, PH 44460; private; 80
Allentown College of St. Francis De Sales Center Valley, PA 18034; private; 900
Allen University Columbia, SC 29204; private; 460
Alliance College Cambridge Springs, PA 16403; private; 250
Alma College Alma, MI 48801; private; 1,200
Alvernia College Reading, PA 19607; private; 700
Alverno College Milwaukee, WI 53215; private; 1,400
Ambassador College Pasadena, CA 91123; private; 500
American Baptist College Nashville, TN 37207; private; 160
American College in Paris 75007 Paris, France; private; 550
American College of Puerto Rico Bayamon PR 00619; private; 2,400
American College of Switzerland 1854 Leysin, Switzerland; private; 220
American Conservatory of Music Chicago, IL 60603; private; 320
American International College Springfield, MA 01109; private; 1,500
American Technological University Killeen, TX 76541; private; 400
American University Washington D.C. 20016; private; 4,500
American University in Cairo New York, NY 10017; private; 100
American University of Beirut Beirut, Lebanon; private; 4,900
Amherst College Amherst, MA 01102; private; 1,500
Anderson College Anderson, IN 46011; private; 1,800
Andrews University Berrien Springs, MI 49104; private; 2,100
Angelo State University San Angelo, TX 76909; public; 5,400
Anna Maria College Paxton, MA 01612; private; 550
Antillian College Mayaguez, PR 00708; private; 760
Antioch College—Yellow Springs Yellow Springs, OH 45387; private; 850
Antioch—Native American Educational Services Chicago, IL 60640; private; 50
Antioch University—Philadelphia Philadelphia, PA 19108; private; 390
Antioch University—West San Francisco, CA 94108; private; 700
Appalachian Bible College Bradley, WV 25818; private; 240
Appalachian State University Boone, NC 28608; public; 8,700
Aquinas College Grand Rapids, MI 49506; private; 2,200
Arizona College of the Bible Phoenix, AZ 85021; private; 140
Arizona State University Tempe, AZ 85281; public, 27,700
Arkansas Baptist College Little Rock, AR 72202; private; 580
Arkansas College Batesville, AR 72501; private; 540
Arkansas State University State University, AR 72467; public; 7,000
Arkansas Tech University Russelville, AR 72801; public; 3,000
Arlington Baptist College Arlington, TX 76012; private; 500
Armstrong College Berkeley, CA 94704; private; 250
Armstrong State College Savannah, GA 31406; public; 2,900
Art Center College of Design Pasadena, CA 91103; private; 1000
Asbury College Wilmore, KY 40390; private; 1,200
Ashland College Ashland, OH 44805; private; 1,400
Assumption College Worcester, MA 01609; private; 1,500
Athens State College Athens, AL 35611; public; 1200
Atlanta Christian College East Point, GA 30344; private; 220
Atlanta College of Art Atlanta, GA 30309; private; 240
Atlantic Christian College Wilson, NC 27893; private; 1,600
Atlantic Union College South Lancaster, MA 01561; private; 700
Auburn University Auburn University, AL 36849; public; 16,800
Auburn University—Montgomery Montgomery, AL 36117; public; 4,400
Augsburg College Minneapolis, MN 55454; private; 1,600
Augusta College Augusta, GA 30910; public; 3,500
Augustana College Rock Island, IL 61201; private; 2,400
Augustana College Sioux Falls, SD 47197; private; 2,100
Aurora College Aurora, IL 60507; private; 1200
Austin College Sherman, TX 75090; private; 1,200
Austin Peay State University Clarksville, TN 37040; public; 4,400
Averett College Danville, VA 24541; private; 1,000
Avila College Kansas City, MO 64145; private; 1,900
Azusa Pacific College Azusa, CA 91702; private; 1200

Babson College Wellesley, MA 02157; private; 1,300
Baker University Baldwin City, KS 66006; private; 860
Baldwin-Wallace College Berea, OH 44017; private; 2,000
Ball State University Muncie, IN 47306; public; 16,000
Baltimore Hebrew College Baltimore, MD 21215; private; 90
Baptist Bible College Springfield, MO 65803; private; 1,800
Baptist Bible College of Denver Broomsfield, CO 80020; private; 110
Baptist Bible College of Pennsylvania Clarks Summit, PA 18411; private; 780
Baptist Christian College Shreveport, LA 71108; private; 300
Baptist College at Charleston Charleston, SC 29411; private; 2,300
Barat College Lake Forest, IL 60045; private; 750
Barber-Scotia College Concord, NC 28025; private; 400
Bard College Annandale-on-Hudson, NY 12504; private; 700
Barnard College of Columbia University New York, NY 10027; private; 2,500
Barrington College Barrington, RI 02806; private; 520
Barry College Miami Shores, FL 33161; private; 1,700
Bartlesville Wesleyan College Bartlesville, OK 74003; private; 740
Bates College Lewiston, ME 04240; private; 1,500
Bayamon Central University Bayamon, PR 00619; public; 2,000
Baylor College of Medicine Houston, TX 77025; private; 30
Baylor University Waco, TX 76706; private; 8,900
Beacon College Washington, DC 20009; private; 60
Beaver College Glenside, PA 19038; private; 1,100
Belhaven College Jackson, MS 39202; private; 890
Bellarmine College Louisville, KY 40205; private; 2,100
Belleview College Westminster, CO 80030; private; 25
Bellevue College Bellevue, NE 68005; private; 2,400
Belmont Abbey College Belmont, NC 28012; private; 800
Belmont College Nashville, TN 37203; private; 1,700
Beloit College Beloit, WI 53511; private; 1,000
Bemidji State University Bemidji, MN 56601; public; 4,200
Benedict College Columbia, SC 29204; private; 1,400
Benedictine College Atchison, KS 66002; private; 1,100
Benjamin Franklin University Washington, DC 20036; private; 400
Bennett College Greensboro, NC 27420; private; 600
Bennington College Bennington, VT 05201; private; 600
Bentley College Waltham, MA 02154; private; 3,600
Berea College Berea, KY 40404; private; 1,500
Berklee College of Music Boston, MA 02215; private; 2,600
Berkshire Christian College Lenox, MA 01240; private; 150
Berry College Mount Berry, GA 30149; private; 1,500
Bethany Bible College Santa Cruz, CA 95,066; private; 600
Bethany College Lindsborg, KS 67456; private; 900
Bethany College Bethany, WV 26032; private; 900
Bethany Nazarene College Bethany, OK 73008; private; 1,300
Bethel College Mishawaka, IN 46544; private; 500
Bethel College North Newton, KS 67114; private; 760
Bethel College St. Paul, MN 55112; private; 2,000
Bethel College McKenzie, TN 38201; private; 400
Bethune-Cookman College Daytona Beach, FL 32015; private; 1,800
Beulah Heights Bible College Atlanta, GA 30316; private; 100
Big Sky Bible College Lewiston, MT 59457; private; 160
Biola College La Mirada, CA 90639; private; 2,400
Birmingham-Southern College Birmingham, AL 35204; private; 1,400
Biscayne College Miami, FL 33054; private; 3,400
Bishop College Dallas, TX 75241; private; 1,000
Blackburn College Carlinville, IL 62626; private; 500
Black Hills State College Spearfish, SD 57783; public; 2,200
Bloomfield College Bloomfield, NJ 07003; private; 730
Bloomsburg State College Bloomsburg, PA 17815; public; 5,900
Bluefield College Bluefield, VA 24605; private; 430
Bluefield State College Bluefield, WV 24701; public; 2,300
Blue Mountain College Blue Mountain, MS 38610; private; 370
Bluffton College Bluffton, OH 45817; private; 670
Bob Jones University Greenville, SC 29614; private; 4,700
Boise State University Boise, ID 83725; public; 9,800
Boricua College New York, NY 10025; private; 900
Borromeo College of Ohio Wickliffe, OH 44092; private; 110
Boston College Chestnut Hill, MA 02167; private; 10,300
Boston Conservatory of Music Boston, MA 02115; private; 520
Boston State College Boston, MA 02115; public; 8,500
Boston University Boston, MA 02215; private; 13,300
Bowdoin College Brunswick, ME 04011; private; 1,400
Bowie State College Bowie, MD 20715; public; 2,100
Bowling Green State University Bowling Green, OH 43403; public; 15,600
Bradford College Bradford, MA 01830; private; 380
Bradley University Peoria, IL 61625; private; 4,600
Brandeis University Waltham, MA 02254; private; 2,800
Brenau College Gainesville, GA 30501; private; 700
Brescia College Owensboro, KY 42301; private; 870
Briar Cliff College Sioux City, IA 51104; private; 1,300
Bridgeport Engineering Institute Bridgeport, CT 06606; private; 760
Bridgewater College Bridgewater, VA 22812; private; 950
Bridgewater State College Bridgewater; MA 02324; public; 4,400
Brigham Young University Provo, UT 84602; private; 24,100
Brigham Young University—Hawaii Laie, Oahu, HI 96762; private; 1,800
Bristol College Bristol, TN 37620; private; 230
Brooks Institute Santa Barbara, CA 93108; private; 790
Brown University Providence, RI 02912; private; 5,200
Bryan College Dayton, TN 37321; private; 600
Bryant College Smithfield, RI 02917; private; 2,800
Bryn Mawr College Bryn Mawr, PA 19010; private; 1,100
Bucknell University Lewisburg, PA 17837; private; 3,100
Buena Vista College Storm Lake, IA 50588; private; 950
Burlington College Burlington, VT 05401; private; 140
Butler University Indianapolis, IN 46208; private; 2,700

Cabrini College Radnor, PA 19087; private; 800
Caldwell College Caldwell, NJ 07006; private; 710

California Baptist College Riverside, CA 92504; private; 730
California Christian College Fresno, CA 93703; private; 40
California College of Arts and Crafts Oakland, CA 94618; private; 950
California College of Commerce Long Beach, CA 90813; private; 150
California Institute of Technology Pasadena, CA 91125; private; 840
California Institute of the Arts Valencia, CA 91355; private; 580
California Lutheran College Thousand Oaks, CA 91360; private; 1,400
California Maritime Academy Vallejo, CA 94590; private; 500
California State College California, PA 15419; public; 3,800
California State College—Bakersfield Bakersfield, CA 93309; public; 2,200
California State College—San Bernadino San Bernadino, CA 92407; public; 3,200
California State College—Stanislaus Turlock, CA 95380; public; 2,800
California State Polytechnic University—Pomona Pomona, CA 91768; public; 14,400
California State Polytechnic University—San Luis Obispo San Luis Obispo, CA 93407; public; 15,000
California State University—Chico Chico, CA 95929; public; 11,400
California State University—Dominquez Hills Carson, CA 90747; public; 7,000
California State University—Fresno Fresno, CA 93740; public; 12,600
California State University—Fullerton Fullerton, CA 92634; public; 18,100
California State University—Hayward Hayward, CA 94542; public; 7,900
California State University—Long Beach Long Beach, CA 90840; public; 24,100
California State University—Los Angeles Los Angeles, CA 90032; public; 15,500
California State University—Northridge Northridge, CA 91330; public; 21,800
California State University—Sacramento Sacramento, CA 95819; public; 15,600
Calument College Whiting, IN 46394; private; 1,400
Calvary Bible College Kansas City, MO 64147; private; 440
Calvin College Grand Rapids, MI 49506; private; 4,000
Cameron University Lawton, OK 73505; private; 4,900
Campbellsville College Campbellsville, KY 42718; private; 700
Campbell University Buies Creek, NC 27506; private; 2,000
Canisius College Buffalo, NY 14208; private; 2,400
Capital University Columbus, OH 43209; private; 1,600
Capitol Institute of Technology Kensington, MD 20795; private; 800
Cardinal Glennon College St. Louis, MO 63119; private; 80
Cardinal Newman College St. Louis, MO 63121; private; 100
Cardinal Stritch College Milwaukee, WI 53217; private; 740
Caribbean University College Bayamon, PR 00618; private; 1,900
Carleton College Northfield, MN 55057; private; 1,700
Carlow College Pittsburgh; PA 15213; private; 980
Carnegie-Mellon University Pittsburgh, PA 15213; private; 3,900
Carroll College Helena, MT 59601; private; 1,300
Carroll College Waukesha, WI 53186; private; 1,200
Carson-Newman College Jefferson City, TN 37760; private; 1,700
Carthage College Kenosha, WI 53140; private; 1,300
Carver Bible Institute and College Atlanta, GA 30313; private; 70
Case Western Reserve University Cleveland, OH 44106; private; 3,200
Castleton State College Castleton, VT; public, 1,700
Catawba College Salisbury, NC 28,144; private; 1,000
Cathedral College of the Immaculate Conception Douglaston, NY 11362; private; 120
Catholic University of America Washington, DC 20064; private; 2,800
Catholic University of Puerto Rico Ponce, PR 00731; private; 2,100
Cedar Crest College Allentown, PA 18104; private; 860
Cedarville College Cedarville, OH 45314; private; 1,600
Centenary College Hackettstown, NJ 07840; private; 700
Centenary College of Louisiana Shreveport, LA 71104; private; 900
Center for Creative Studies—College of Art and Design Detroit, MI 48202; private; 1,100
Center for Early Education Los Angeles, CA 90048; private; 20
Central Baptist College Conway, AR 72032; private; 200
Central Bible College Springfield, MO 65802; private; 1,100
Central Christian College of the Bible Moberly, MO 65270; private; 120
Central College Pella, IA 50219; private; 1,500
Central Connecticut State College New Britain, CT 06050; public; 10,000
Central Methodist College Fayette, MO 65248; private; 650
Central Michigan University Mount Pleasant, MI 48858; public; 15,000
Central Missouri State University Warrensburg, MO 64093; public; 8,700
Central New England College of Technology Worcester, MA 01610; private; 480
Central State University Wilberforce, OH 45384; public; 2,500
Central State University Edmond, OK 73034; public; 9,000
Central Washington University Ellensburg, WA 98926; public; 5,900
Central Wesleyan College Central, SC 29630; private; 410
Centre College of Kentucky Danville, KY 40422; private; 750
Chadron State College Chadron, NE 69357; public; 1,500
Chaminade University of Honolulu Honolulu, HI 96816; private; 2,200
Chapman College Orange, CA 92666; private; 1,200
Chatham College Pittsburgh, PA 15232; private; 600
Chestnut Hill College Philadelphia, PA 19118; private; 650
Cheyney State College Cheyney, PA 19319; public; 2,600
Chicago State University Chicago, IL 60628; public; 5,100
Christ College Irvine Irvine, CA 92715; private; 170
Christian Brothers College Memphis, TN 38104; private; 1,400
Christian Heritage College El Cajon, CA 92021; private; 400
Christopher Newport College Newport News, VA 23606; public; 4,000
Cincinnati Bible College Cincinnati, OH 45204; private; 600
Circleville Bible College Circleville, OH 43113; private; 250
City College Seattle, WA 98104; public; 2,500
Claflin College Orangeburg, SC 29115; private; 900
Claremont Men's College Claremont, CA 91711; public; 800
Clarion State College Clarion, PA 16214; public; 4,600
Clark College Atlanta, GA 30314; private; 2,000
Clarke College Dubuque, IA 52001; private; 770
Clarkson College Potsdam, NY 13676; private; 3,400
Clark University Worcester, MA 01610; private; 2,000
Clearwater Christian College Clearwater, FL 33519; private; 200
Cleary College Ypsilanti, MI 48197; private; 700
Clemson University Clemson, SC 29631; public; 9,500
Cleveland College of Jewish Studies Beachwood, OH 44122; private; 150
Cleveland Institute of Art Cleveland, OH 44106; private; 530
Cleveland Institute of Music Cleveland, OH 44106; private; 190
Cleveland State University Cleveland, OH 44115; public; 14,300
Coe College Cedar Rapids, IA 51402; private; 1,400
Cogswell College San Francisco, CA 94108; private; 450
Coker College Hartsville, SC 29550; private; 330
Colby College Waterville, ME 04901; private; 1,700
Colby-Sawyer College New London, NH 03257; private; 700
Colegio Cesar Chavez Mount Angel, OR 97362; private; 100
Coleman College La Mesa, CA 92041; private; 700
Colgate University Hamilton, NY 13346; private; 2,600
College for Human Services New York, NY 10016; private; 400
College Misericordia Dallas, PA 18612; private; 1,100
College of Charleston Charleston, SC 29401; public; 4,700
College of Great Falls Great Falls, MT 59405; private; 1,200
College of Idaho Caldwell, ID 83605; private; 550
College of Insurance New York, NY 10038; private; 1,900
College of Mount St. Joseph on the Ohio Mount St. Joseph, OH 45051; private; 1,700
College of Mount St. Vincent New York, NY 10471; private; 1,300
College of New Rochelle—School of Arts and Sciences New Rochelle, NY 10801; private; 4,400
College of Notre Dame Belmont, CA 94002; private; 950
College of Notre Dame of Maryland Baltimore, MD 21210; private; 540
College of Our Lady of the Elms Chicopee, MA 01013; private; 500
College of Santa Fe Santa Fe, NM 87501; private; 1,200
College of St. Benedict St. Joseph, MN 56374; private; 1,700
College of St. Catherine St. Paul, MN 55105; private; 2,400
College of St. Elizabeth Convent Station, NJ 07961; private; 850
College of St. Francis Joliet, IL 60435; private; 800
College of St. Joseph the Provider Rutland, VT 05701; private; 350
College of St. Mary Omaha, NE 68124; private; 600
College of St. Rose Albany, NY 12203; private; 2,000
College of St. Scholastica Duluth, MN 55811; private; 1,100
College of St. Teresa Winona, MN 55897; private; 650
College of St. Thomas St. Paul, MN 55105; private; 3,400
College of the Academy of the New Church Bryn Athyn, PA 19009; private; 150
College of the Atlantic Bar Harbor, ME 04609; private; 180
College of the Holy Cross Worcester, MA 01610; private; 2,500
College of the Ozarks Clarksville, AR 72830; private; 720
College of the Palm Beaches West Palm Beach, FL 33402; private; 250
College of the Southwest Hobbs, NM 88240; private; 220
College of the Virgin Islands St. Thomas, VI 00801; public; 2,000
College of William and Mary Williamsburg, VA 23185; public; 4,600
College of Wooster Wooster, OH 44691; private; 1,800
Colorado College Colorado Springs, CO 80903; private; 1900
Colorado School of Mines Golden, CO 80401; public; 2,300
Colorado State University Fort Collins, CO 80523; public; 15,200
Colorado Technical College Colorado Springs, CO 80907; private; 590
Colorado Women's College Denver, CO 80220; private; 500
Columbia Bible College Columbia, SC 29230; private; 590
Columbia Christian College Portland, OR 97200; private; 310
Columbia College Los Angeles, CA 90038; private; 320
Columbia College Chicago, IL 60605; private; 4,000
Columbia College Columbia, MO 65216; private; 820
Columbia College Columbia, SC 29203; private; 1,000
Columbia Union College Takoma Park, MD 20012; private; 900
Columbia University—Columbia College New York, NY 10027; private; 2,800
Columbus College Columbus, GA 31993; public; 4,000
Columbus College of Art and Design Columbus, OH 43215; private; 1,000
Combs College of Music Philadelphia, PA 19119; private; 230
Conception Seminary College Conception, MO 64433; private; 90
Concord College Athens, WV 24712; public; 2,200
Concordia College River Forest, IL 60,305; private; 1,100
Concordia College Ann Arbor, MI 48105; private; 550
Concordia College Moorhead, MN 56560; private; 2,600
Concordia College St. Paul, MN 55104; private; 700
Concordia College Bronxville, NY 10708; private; 500
Concordia College Portland, OR 97211; private; 330
Concordia College Milwaukee, WI 53208; private; 520
Concordia Teachers College Seward, NE 68434; private; 1,100
Connecticut College New London, CT 06320; private; 1,800
Conservatory of Music of Puerto Rico Hato Rey, PR 00918; private; 270
Converse College Spartanburg, SC 29301; private; 740
Cooper Union New York, NY 10003; private; 900
Coppin State College Baltimore, MD 21216; public; 2,600
Corcoran School of Art Washington, DC 20006; private; 250
Cornell College Mount Vernon, IA 52314; private; 950
Cornell University Ithaca, NY 14850; private; 12,100
Cornish Institute of Allied Arts Seattle, WA 98102; private; 450
Corpus Christi State University Corpus Christi, TX 78412; public; 3,000
Covenant College Lookout Mountain, TN 37350; private; 540
Creighton University Omaha, NE 68178; private; 3,700
Culver-Stockton College Canton, MO 63435; private; 580
Cumberland College Williamsburg, KY 40769; private; 2,100
CUNY—Bernard Baruch College New York, NY 10010; public; 12,500
CUNY—Brooklyn College Brooklyn, NY 11210; public; 19,000
CUNY—City College New York, NY 10031; public; 10,600
CUNY—College of Staten Island Staten Island, NY 10301; public; 10,000
CUNY—Hunter College New York, NY 10021; public; 14,000
CUNY—John Jay College of Criminal Justice New York, NY 10019; public; 5,500
CUNY—Lehman College Bronx, NY 10468; public; 8,500
CUNY—Medgar Evers College Brooklyn, NY 11225; public; 1,080
CUNY—Queens College Flushing, NY 11367; public; 17,500
CUNY—York College Jamaica, NY 11432; public; 3,600
Curry College Milton, MA 02186; private; 1,400
Curtis Institute of Music Philadelphia, PA 19103; private; 160

Daemen College Amherst, NY 14226; private; 1,300
Dakota State College Madison, SD 57042; public; 1,000
Dakota Wesleyan University Mitchell, SD 57301; private; 520
Dallas Baptist College Dallas, TX 75211; private; 1,300
Dallas Bible College Dallas, TX 75228; private; 240
Dallas Christian College Dallas, TX 75234; private; 150
Dana College Blair, NE 68008; private; 540

Daniel Webster College Nashua, NH 03063; private; 500
Dartmouth College Hanover, NH 03755; private; 4,000
David Lipscomb College Nashville, TN 37203; private; 2,300
Davidson College Davidson, NC 28036; private; 1,400
Davis and Elkins College Elkins, WV 26241; private; 990
Defiance College Defiance, OH 43512; private; 800
Delaware State College Dover, DE 19901; public; 2,100
Delaware Valley College of Science and Agriculture Doylestown, PA 18901; private; 1,400
De Lourdes College Des Plaines, IL 60016; private; 275
Delta State University Cleveland, MS 38733; public; 3,200
Denison University Granville, OH 43023; private; 2,100
Denver Baptist Bible College Broomville, CO 80020; private; 250
DePaul University Chicago, IL 60604; private; 8,500
DePauw University Greencastle, IN 46135; private; 2,400
Deree College Athens, Greece; private; 1,300
Detroit College of Business Dearborn, MI 48126; private; 2,400
Devry Institute of Technology Phoenix, AZ 85016; private; 3,200
DeVry Institute of Technology Chicago, IL 60618; private; 3,800
Dickinson College Carlisle, PA 17013; private; 1,700
Dickinson State College Dickinson, ND 58601; public; 1,200
Dillard College New Orleans, LA 70122; private; 1,200
Divine Word College Epworth, IA 52045; private; 90
Doane College Crete, NE 68333; private; 660
Dominican College of Blauvelt Orangeburg, NY 10962; private; 1,400
Dominican College of San Rafael San Rafael, CA 94901; private; 500
Dominican School of Philosophy and Theology Berkeley, CA 95709; private; 20
Don Bosco College Newton, NJ 07860; private; 90
Dordt College Sioux Center, IA 11769; private; 1,200
Dowling College Oakdale, NY 11769; private; 1,900
Drake University Des Moines, IA 50311; private; 4,900
Drew University—College of Liberal Arts Madison, NJ 07940; private; 1,600
Drexel University Philadelphia, PA 19104; private; 7,000
Dr. Martin Luther College New Ulm, MN 56073; private; 780
Drury College Springfield, MO 65802; private; 1,100
Duke University Durham, NC 27706; private; 5,700
Duquesne University Pittsburgh, PA 15219; private; 4,600
Dyke College Cleveland, OH 44114; private; 1,600
D'Youville College Buffalo, NY 14201; private; 1,500

Earlham College Richmond, IN 47374; private; 1,100
East Carolina University Greenville, NC 27834; public; 11,000
East Central Oklahoma State University Ada, OK 74820; public; 4,000
Eastern College St. Davids, PA 19087; private; 710
Eastern Connecticut State College Willimantic, CT 06226; public; 2,200
Eastern Illinois University Charleston, IL 61920; public; 9,000
Eastern Kentucky University Richmond, KY 40475; public; 11,500
Eastern Mennonite College Harrisonburg, VA 22801; private; 1,100
Eastern Michigan University Ypsilanti, MI 48197; public; 13,600
Eastern Montana College Billings, MT 59101; public; 3,600
Eastern Nazarene College Quincy, MA 02170; private; 770
Eastern New Mexico University Portales, NM 88130; public; 3,800
Eastern Oregon State College La Grande, OR 97850; public; 1,700
Eastern Washington University Cheney, WA 99004; public; 6,500
East Stroudsburg State College East Stroudsburg, PA 18301; public; 3,600
East Tennessee State University Johnson City, TN 37614; public; 7,900
East Texas Baptist College Marshall, TX 75670; private; 920
East Texas State University Commerce, TX 75428; public; 5,300
Eckerd College St. Petersburg, FL 33733; private; 1,100
Edgecliff College Cincinnati, OH 45206; private; 900
Edgewood College Madison, WI 53711; private; 700
Edinboro State College Edinboro, PA 16412; public; 4,900
Edward Waters College Jacksonville, FL 32209; private; 740
Eisenhower College of Rochester Institute of Technology Seneca Falls, NY 13148; private; 600
Elizabeth City State University Elizabeth City, NC 27909; public; 1,700
Elizabethtown College Elizabethtown, PA 17022; private; 1,500
Elmhurst College Elmhurst, IL 60126; private; 1,700
Elmira College Elmira, NY 14901; private; 1,000
Elon College Elon College, NC 27244; private; 2,600
Embry-Riddle Aeronautical University Prescott, AZ 86301; private; 6,200
Emerson College Boston, MA 02116; private; 1,600
Emmanuel College Boston, MA 02115; private; 1,000
Emmanuel College School of Christian Ministries Franklin Springs, GA 30639; private; 150
Emory and Henry College Emory, VA 24327; private; 850
Emory University Atlanta, GA 30322; private; 3,000
Emporia State University Emporia, KS 66801; public; 4,500
Erskine College Due West, SC 29639; private; 650
Eugene Bible College Eugene, OR 97405; private; 110
Eureka College Eureka, IL 61530; private; 480
Evangel College Springfield, MO 65802; private; 1,900
Evergreen State College Olympia, WA 98505; public; 2,800

Fairfield University Fairfield, CT 06430; private; 2,900
Fairleigh Dickinson University—Madison Madison, NJ 07940; private; 3,400
Fairleigh Dickinson University—Rutherford Rutherford, NJ 07666; private; 2,600
Fairleigh Dickinson University—Teaneck Teaneck, NJ 07666; private; 5,500
Fairmont State College Fairmont, WV 26554; public; 5,200
Faith Baptist Bible College Ankeny, IA 50021; private; 440
Fayettville State University Fayetteville, NC 28303; public; 2,300
Felician College Lodi, NJ 07644; private; 760
Ferris State College Big Rapids, MI 49307; public; 11,000
Ferrum College Ferrum, VA 24088; private; 1,500
Findlay College Findlay, OH 45840; private; 1,100
Finlay Engineering College Kansas City, MO 64114; private; 500
Fisk University Nashville, TN 37203; private; 1,000
Fitchburg State College Fitchburg, MA 01420; public; 5,700
Flagler College St. Augustine, FL 32084; private; 800
Flaming Rainbow University Stilwell, OK 74960; private; 330
Florida A and M University Tallahassee, FL 32307; public; 5,500
Florida Atlantic University Boca Raton, FL 33431; public; 5,200
Florida Beacon College Largo, FL 33541; private; 50
Florida Institute of Technology Melbourne, FL 32901; private; 3,700
Florida Institute of Technology—School of Applied Technology Jensen Beach, FL 33457; private; 900
Florida International University Miami, FL 33199; public; 10,800
Florida Memorial College Miami, FL 33054; private; 870
Florida Southern College Lakeland, FL 33802; private; 1,700
Florida State University Tallahassee, FL 32306; public; 17,000
Fontbonne College St. Louis, MO 63105; private; 810
Fordham University—Lincoln Center New York, NY 10023; private; 3,800
Fordham University—Rose Hill Bronx, NY 10458; private; 4,200
Fort Hays State University Hays, KS 67601; public; 4,200
Fort Lauderdale College Fort Lauderdale, FL 33301; private; 930
Fort Lewis College Durango, CO 81301; public; 3,200
Fort Valley State College Fort Valley, GA 31030; public; 1,900
Fort Wayne Bible College Fort Wayne, IN 46807; private; 480
Fort Wright College Spokane, WA 99204; private; 450
Framingham State College Framingham, MA 01701; public; 3,100
Francis Marion College Florence, SC 29501; public; 2,600
Franklin and Marshall College Lancaster, PA 17604; private; 2,100
Franklin College Franklin, IN 46131; private; 630
Franklin Pierce College Rindge, NH 03461; private; 990
Franklin University Columbus, OH 43215; private; 4,600
Freed-Hardeman College Henderson, TN 37205; private; 1,500
Free Will Baptist Bible College Nashville, TN 37205; private; 530
Fresno Pacific College Fresno, CA 93702; private; 500
Friends Bible College Haviland, KS 67059; private; 170
Friendship College Rock Hill, SC 29730; private; 350
Friends University Wichita, KS 67213; private; 940
Friends World College Huntington, NY 11743; private; 160
Frostburg State College Frostburg, MD 21532; public 3,200
Furman University Greenville, SC 29163; private; 2,400

Gannon University Erie, PA 16541; private; 2,600
Gardner-Webb College Boiling Springs, NC 28017; private; 1,400
Gately Christian University Guntersville, AL 35976; private; 130
General Motors Institute Flint, MI 48502; private; 2,300
Geneva College Beaver Falls, PA 15010; private; 1,400
George Fox College Newberg, OR 97132; private; 750
George Mason University Fairfax, VA 22030; public; 9,600
Georgetown College Georgetown, KY 40324; private; 1,100
Georgetown University Washington, DC 20057; private; 5,500
George Washington University Washington, DC 20052; private; 6,100
George Williams College Downers Grove, IL 60515; private; 580
Georgia College Milledgeville, GA 31601; public; 2,800
Georgia Institute of Technology Atlanta, GA 30332; public; 9,300
Georgian Court College Lakewood, NJ 08701; private; 800
Georgia Southern College Statesboro, GA 30458; public; 5,500
Georgia Southwestern College Americus, GA 31709; public; 1,800
Georgia State University Atlanta, GA 30303; public; 13,400
Gettysburg College Gettysburg, PA 17325; private; 1,900
Glassboro State College Glassboro, NJ 08028; public; 6,400
Glenville State College Glenville, WV 26531; public; 1,600
Goddard College Plainfield, VT 05667; private; 300
God's Bible School and College Cincinnati, OH 45210; private; 250
Golden Gate University San Francisco, CA 94105; private; 2,800
Goldey Beacom College Wilmington, DE 19808; private; 1,500
Gonzaga University Spokane, WA 99258; private; 2,000
Gordon College Wenham, MA 01984; private; 1,000
Goshen College Goshen, IN 46526; private; 1,300
Goucher College Towson, MD 21204; private; 950
Governors State University Park Forest South, IL 60466; public; 1,700
Grace Bible College Grand Rapids, MI 49509; private; 200
Grace College Winona Lake, IN 46590; private; 900
Grace College of the Bible Omaha, NE 68108; private; 460
Graceland College Lamoni, IA 50140; private; 1,300
Grambling State University Grambling, LA 71245; public; 3,600
Grand Canyon College Phoenix, AZ 85017; private; 1,200
Grand Rapids Baptist College Grand Rapids, MI 49505; private; 980
Grand Valley State Colleges Allendale, MI 49401; public; 6,200
Grand View College Des Moines, IA 50316; private; 1,200
Gratz College Philadelphia, PA 19141; private; 140
Great Lakes Bible College Lansing, MI 48901; private; 210
Green Mountain College Poultney, VT 05764; private; 500
Greensboro College Greensboro, NC 27420; private; 680
Greenville College Greenville, IL 62246; private; 860
Grinnell College Grinnell, IA 50112; private; 1,200
Grove City College Grove City, PA 16127; public; 2,200
Guilford College Greensboro, NC 27410; private; 1,200
Gulf Coast Bible College Houston, TX 77008; private; 350
Gustavus Adolphus College St. Peter, MN 56082; private; 2,400
Gwynedd-Mercy College Gwynedd Valley, PA 19437; private; 1,900

Hahnemann College of Allied Health Professions Philadelphia, PA 19102; private; 730
Hamilton College Clinton, NY 13323; private; 1,600
Hamline University St. Paul, MN 55104; private; 1,200
Hampden-Sydney College Hampden-Sydney, VA 23943; private; 730
Hampshire College Amherst, MA 01002; private; 1,200
Hampton Institute Hampton, VA 23668; private; 3,200
Hannibal-LeGrange College Hannibal, MO 63401; private; 430
Hanover College Hanover, IN 47243; private; 1,000
Harding University Searcy, AR 72143; private; 3,000
Hardin-Simmons University Abilene, TX 79601; private; 2,000
Harris Stowe State College St. Louis, MO 63103; private; 1,200
Hartwick College Oneonta, NY 13820; private; 1,400
Harvard and Radcliffe Colleges Cambridge, MA 02138; private; 6,600
Harvey Mudd College Claremont, CA 91711; private; 480
Hastings College Hastings, NE 68901; private; 780
Haverford College Haverford, PA 19041; private; 1,000

Hawaii Loa College Kaneohe, HI 96744; private; 340
Hawaii Pacific College Honolulu, HI 96744; private; 2,000
Heald Engineering College San Francisco, CA 94109; private; 1,500
Hebrew College Brookline, MA 02146; private; 130
Hebrew Theological College Skokie, IL 60076; private; 200
Hebrew Union College Los Angeles, CA 90007; private; 40
Hebrew Union College New York, NY 10023; private; 150
Heidelberg College Tiffin, OH 44883; private; 760
Hellenic College Brookline, MA 02146; private; 120
Henderson State University Arkadelphia, AR 71923; public; 3.000
Hendrix College Conway, AR 72023; private; 1,000
High Point College High Point, NC 27262; private; 1,400
Hillsdale College Hillsdale, MI 49242; private; 1,000
Hillsdale Free Will Baptist College Moore, OK 73153; private; 160
Hiram College Hiram, OH 44234; private; 1,100
Hobart College Geneva, NY 14456; private; 1,000
Hofstra University Hempstead, NY 11550; private; 10,500
Hollins College Hollins College, VA 24020; private; 850
Holy Apostles College Cromwell, CT 06416; private; 100
Holy Family College Fremont, CA 94538; private; 450
Holy Family College Philadelphia, PA 19114; private; 1,200
Holy Names College Oakland, CA 94619; private; 550
Holy Redeemer College Waterford, WI 53185; private; 50
Holy Trinity Orthodox Seminary Jordanville, NY 13361; private; 40
Hong Kong Baptist College Kowloon, Hong Kong; private; 3,300
Hood College Frederick, MD 21701; private; 1,100
Hope College Holland, MI 49423; private; 2,400
Houghton College Houghton, NY 14744; private; 1,200
Houston Baptist University Houston, TX 77074; private; 2,000
Howard Payne University Brownwood, TX 76801; private; 1,200
Howard University Washington, DC 20059; private, 7,400
Humboldt State University Arcata, CA 95521; public; 6,700
Huntingdon College Montgomery, AL 36106; private; 650
Huntington College Huntington, IN 46750; private; 510
Huron College Huron, SD 57350; private; 350
Husson College Bangor, ME 04401; private; 1,200
Huston-Tillotson College Austin, TX 78702; private; 710

Idaho State University Pocatello, ID 83209; public; 5,400
Illinois Benedictine College Lisle, IL 60532; private; 1,800
Illinois College Jacksonville, IL 62650; private; 800
Illinois Institute of Technology Chicago, IL 60616; private; 4,300
Illinois State University Normal, IL 61761; public; 17,600
Illinois Wesleyan University Bloomington, IL 61701; private; 1,700
Immaculata College Immaculata, PA 19345; private; 1,400
Immanuel Lutheran College Eau Claire, WI 54701; private; 60
Incarnate Word College San Antonio, TX 78209; private; 1,300
Indiana Central University Indianapolis, IN 46227; private; 2,900
Indiana Institute of Technology Fort Wayne, IN 46803; private; 600
Indiana State University—Evansville Evansville, IN 47712; public; 3,300
Indiana State University—Terre Haute Terre Haute, IN 47809; public; 10,200
Indiana University—Bloomington Bloomington, IN 47405; public; 24,000
Indiana University—Kokomo Kokomo, IN 46901; public; 2,400
Indiana University—Northwest Gary, IN 46408; private; 4,500
Indiana University of Pennsylvania Indiana, PA 15705; public; 11,100
Indiana University—Purdue University at Fort Wayne Fort Wayne, IN 46805; public; 8,900
Indiana University—Purdue University at Indianapolis Indianapolis, IN 46202; public; 14,800
Indiana University—South Bend South Bend, IN 46615; public; 6,200
Indiana University—Southeast New Albany, IN 47150; public; 3,900
Inter-American University of Puerto Rico—Arecibo Branch Arecibo, PR 00612; private; 13,300
Inter-American University of Puerto Rico—Metropolitan Campus Hato Rey, PR 00919; private; 2,000
Inter-American University—San German Regional College San German, PR 00753; private; 11,000
Intermountain Bible College Grand Junction, CO 81501; private; 90
International Bible College Florence, AL 35630; private; 300
International College Honolulu, HI 96809; private; 150
International Institute of the Americas of World University Hato Rey, PR 00917; private; 4,000
Iona College New Rochelle, NY 10801; private; 3,600
Iowa State University Ames, IA 50011; public; 20,800
Iowa Wesleyan College Mt. Pleasant, IA 52641; private; 730
Ithaca College Ithaca, NY 14850; private; 4,600

Jackson State University Jackson, MS 39217; public; 7,700
Jacksonville State University Jacksonville, AL 36265; public; 6,000
Jacksonville University Jacksonville, FL 32211; private; 2,200
James Madison University Harrisonburg, VA 22801; public; 7,600
Jamestown College Jamestown, ND 58401; private; 560
Jarvis Christian College Hawkins, TX 75765; private; 650
Jersey City State College Jersey City, NJ 07305; public; 7,700
Jewish Theological Seminary of America New York, NY 10027; private; 160
John Brown University Siloam Springs, AR 72761; private; 800
John Carroll University University Heights, OH 44118; private; 3,300
John F. Kennedy University—Evenings Orinda, CA 94563; private; 200
Johns Hopkins University Baltimore, MD 21218; private; 2,200
Johnson and Wales College Providence, RI 02903; private; 5,500
Johnson Bible College Knoxville, TN 37920; private; 400
Johnson C. Smith University Charlotte, NC 28216; private; 1,400
Johnson State College Johnson, VT 05656; public; 810
Jones College Orlando, FL 32803; private; 1,300
Jones College—Jacksonville Jacksonville, FL 32211; private; 1,200
Jordan College Cedar Springs, MI 49319; private; 810
Judson College Marion, AL 36756; private; 460
Judson College Elgin, IL 60120; private; 500
Juilliard School New York, NY 10023; private; 660
Juniata College Huntingdon, PA 16652; private; 1,300

Kalamazoo College Kalamazoo, MI 49007; private 1,500
Kansas City Art Institute Kansas City, MO 64111; private; 590
Kansas City College and Bible School Overland Park, KS 66204; private; 100
Kansas Newman College Wichita, KS 67213; private; 660
Kansas State University Manhattan, KS 66506; public; 17,000
Kansas Wesleyan Salina, KS 67401; private; 500
Kean College of New Jersey Union, NJ 07083; private 12,000
Kearney State College Kearney, NE 68847; public; 5,800
Keene State College Keene, NH 03431; public; 2,600
Kendall College Evanston, IL 60201; private; 400
Kendall School of Design Grand Rapids, MI 49503; private; 480
Kennesaw College Marietta, GA 30061; public; 3,900
Kent State University Kent, OH 44242; public; 15,000
Kentucky Christian College Grayson, KY 41143; private; 500
Kentucky State University Frankfort, KY 40601; public; 2,600
Kentucky Wesleyan College Owensboro, KY 42301; private; 970
Kenyon College Gambler, OH 43022; private; 1,500
Keuka College Keuka Park, NY 14478; private; 550
King College Bristol, TN 37620; private; 380
King's College Wilkes Barre, PA 18711; private; 2,200
Knox College Galesburg, IL 61401; private; 1,000
Knoxville College Knoxville, TN 37921; private; 700
Kutztown State College Kutztown, PA 19530; public; 5,000

Lafayette College Easton, PA 18042; private; 2,100
La Grange College La Grange, GA 30240; private; 900
Lake Erie College Painesville, OH 44077; private; 1,100
Lake Forest College Lake Forest, IL 60045; private; 1,100
Lakeland College Sheboygan, WI 53081; private; 930
Lake Superior State College Sault Ste. Marie, MI 49783; public; 2,500
Lamar University Beaumont, TX 77710; public; 13,000
Lambuth College Jackson, TN 38301; private; 750
Lancaster Bible College Lancaster, PA 17601; private; 450
Lander College Greenwood, SC 29646; private; 1,800
Lane College Jackson, TN 38301; private; 700
Langston University Langston, OK 73050; private; 1,100
Laredo State University Laredo, TX 78040; public; 440
La Roche College Pittsburgh, PA 15237; private; 1,300
La Salle College Philadelphia, PA 19141; private; 6,400
Lawrence Institute of Technology Southfield, MI 48075; private; 5,200
Lawrence University Appleton, WI 54911; private; 1,200
Lebanon Valley College Annville, PA 17003; private; 950
Lee College Cleveland, TN 37311; private; 1,300
Lehigh University Bethlehem, PA 18015; private; 4,200
Le Moyne College Syracuse, NY 13224; private; 1,800
Le Moyne-Owen College Memphis, TN 38126; private; 1,000
Lenoir-Rhyne College Hickory, NC 28601; private; 1,300
Lesley College Cambridge, MA 02238; private; 830
LeTourneau College (Le Tourneau Christian College) Longview, TX 75602; private; 1,100
Lewis and Clark College Portland, OR 97219; private; 1,900
Lewis-Clark State College Lewiston, ID 83501; public; 2,400
Lewis University Romeoville, IL 60441; private; 2,500
Lexington Baptist College Lexington, KY 40502; private; 90
Liberty Baptist College Lynchburg, VA 24506; private; 3,200
L.I.F.E. Bible College Los Angeles, CA 90026; private; 470
Limestone College Gaffney, SC 29340; private; 1,500
Lincoln Christian College Lincoln, IL 62656; private; 500
Lincoln Memorial University Harrogate, TN 37752; private; 1,000
Lincoln University San Francisco, CA 94118; private; 1,100
Lincoln University Jefferson City, MO 65101; public; 2,500
Lincoln University Lincoln University, PA 19352; public; 1,400
Lindenwood Colleges St. Charles, MO 63301; private; 1,500
Linfield College McMinnville, OR 97128; private; 1,200
Livingstone College Salisbury, NC 28144; private; 700
Livingston University Livingston, AL 35470; public; 920
Lock Haven State College Lock Haven, PA 17745; public; 2,500
Loma Linda University Loma Linda, CA 92350; private; 3,100
Loma Linda University—La Sierra Riverside, CA 92515; private; 2,300
Long Island University—Brooklyn Brooklyn, NY 11201; private; 7,600
Long Island University—College of Pharmacy/Health Sciences Brooklyn, NY 11201; private; 1,200
Long Island University—C.W. Post College Greenvale, NY 11548; private; 13,000
Long Island University—Southampton College Southampton, NY 11968; private; 1,300
Longwood College Farmsville, VA 23901; private; 2,400
Loras College Dubuque, IA 52001; private; 1,900
Loretto Heights College Denver, CO 80236; private; 930.
Los Angeles Baptist College Newhall, CA 91322; private; 360
Louisiana College Pineville, LA 71360; private; 1,300
Louisiana State University—A and M College Baton Rouge, LA 70803; public; 21,500
Louisiana State University—Shreveport Shreveport, LA 71115; public 3,400
Louisiana Tech University Ruston, LA 71272; public; 9,100
Louisville School of Art Louisville, KY 40204; private; 150
Loyola College Baltimore, MD 21210; private; 2,300
Loyola Marymount University Los Angeles, CA 90045; private; 3,500
Loyola University New Orleans, LA 70118; private; 3,000
Loyola University of Chicago Chicago, IL 60611; private; 8,800
Lubbock Christian College Lubbock TX 79407; private; 1,300
Lutheran Bible Institute Issaquah, WA 98027; private; 190
Luther College Decorah, IA 52101; private; 2,100
Lycoming College Williamsport, PA 17701; private; 1,100
Lynchburg College Lynchburg, VA 24501; private; 1,900
Lyndon State College Lyndonville, VT 05851; private; 1,100

Macalester College St. Paul, MN 55105; private; 1,700
MacMurray College Jacksonville, IL 62650; private; 750
Madonna College Livonia, MI 48150; private; 3,200
Maharishi International University Fairfield, IA 52556; private; 740
Maine Maritime Academy Castine, ME 04421; public; 650
Malone College Canton, OH 44709; private; 780
Manchester College North Manchester, IN 46962; private; 1,200
Manhattan Christian College

Manhattan, KS 66502; private; 330
Manhattan College Riverdale, NY 10471; private; 4,500
Manhattan School of Music New York, NY 10027; private; 440
Manhattanville College Purchase, NY 10577; private; 950
Mankato State University Mankato, MN 56001; public; 9,900
Mannes College of Music New York, NY 10021; private; 200
Mansfield State College Mansfield, PA 16933; public; 2,500
Marian College Indianapolis, IN 46222; private; 900
Marian College Fond Du Lac, WI 54935; private; 500
Marietta College Marietta, OH 45750; private; 1,400
Marion College Marion, IN 46952; private; 1,100
Marist College Poughkeepsie, NY 12601; private; 1,800
Marlboro College Marlboro, VT 05344; private; 240
Marquette University Milwaukee, WI 53233; private; 8,900
Marshall University Huntington, WV 25705; public; 9,400
Mars Hill College Mars Hill, NC 28754; private; 1,500
Mary Baldwin College Staunton, VA 24401; private; 830
Mary College Bismarck ND 58501; private; 1,000
Marycrest College Davenport, IA 52804; private; 800
Marygrove College Detroit, MI 48221; private; 900
Maryland Institute, College of Art Baltimore, MD 21217; private; 750
Marylhurst College for Lifelong Learning Marylhurst, OR 97036; private; 800
Marymount College Tarrytown, NY 10591; private; 1,300
Marymount College of Kansas Salina, KS 67401; private; 850
Marymount College of Virginia Arlington, VA 22207; private; 1,100
Marymount Manhattan College New York, NY 10021; private; 2,300
Maryville College Maryville, TN 37801; private; 650
Maryville College—St. Louis St. Louis, MO 63141; private; 1,300
Mary Washington College Fredericksburg, VA 22401; public; 2,500
Marywood College Scranton, PA 18509; private; 2,200
Massachusetts College of Art Boston, MA 02215; public; 1,000
Massachusetts College of Pharmacy and Allied Health Sciences Boston, MA 02115; private; 1,100
Massachusetts College of Pharmacy and Allied Health Sciences—Hampden Springfield, MA 01119; private; 100
Massachusetts Institute of Technology Cambridge, MA 02139; private; 4,500
Massachusetts Maritime Academy Buzzards Bay, MA 02532; public; 850
Mayville State College Mayville, ND 58257; public; 650
McKendree College Lebanon, IL 62258; private; 815
McMurry College Abilene, TX 79697; private; 1,500
McNeese State University Lake Charles, LA 70609; public; 4,700
McPherson College McPherson, KS 67460; private; 500
Medaille College Buffalo, NY 14214; private; 670
Medical College of Georgia Augusta, GA 30912; public; 810
Memphis Academy of Arts Memphis, TN 38112; private; 220
Memphis State University Memphis, TN 38152; public; 14,300
Menlo College Menlo Park, CA 94025; private; 310
Mercer University Macon, GA 31207; private; 2,100
Mercer University—Atlanta Atlanta, GA 30341; private; 1,300
Mercer University School of Pharmacy Atlanta, GA 30312; private; 330
Mercy College Dobbs Ferry, NY 10522; private; 10,000
Mercy College of Detroit Detroit, MI 48219; private; 2,500
Mercyhurst College Erie, PA 16546; private; 1,400
Meredith College Raleigh, NC 27611; private; 1,400
Merrimack College North Andover, MA 01845; private; 3,500
Mesa College Grand Junction, CO 81501; public; 2,800
Messiah College Grantham, PA 17027; private; 1,300
Methodist College Fayetteville, NC 28301; private; 790
Metropolitan State College Denver, CO 80204; public; 15,500
Metropolitan State University St. Paul, MN 55101; public; 2,000
Miami Christian College Miami, FL 33167; private; 200
Miami University Oxford, OH 45056; public; 14,000
Michigan State University East Lansing, MI 48824; public; 36,600
Michigan Technological University Houghton, MI 49931; public; 7,600
Mid-America Nazarene College Olathe, KS 66061; private; 1,400
Middlebury College Middlebury, VT 05753; private; 1,900
Middle Tennessee State University Murfreesboro, TN 37132; public; 9,600
Midland Lutheran College Fremont, NE 68025; private; 830
Mid-South Bible College Memphis, TN 38112; private; 140
Midwest Christian College Oklahoma City, OK 73111; private; 120
Midwest College of Engineering Lombard, IL 60148; private; 250
Midwestern State University Wichita Falls, TX 76308; public; 4,000
Miles College Birmingham, AL 35208; private; 1,100
Millersville State College Millersville, PA 17551; public; 5,700
Milligan College Milligan College, TN 37682; private; 750
Millikin University Decatur, IL 62522; private; 1,500
Millsaps College Jackson, MS 39210; private; 1,000
Mills College Oakland, CA 94613; private; 800
Milton College Milton, WI 53563; private; 300
Milwaukee Institute of Art and Design Milwaukee, WI 53211; private; 250
Milwaukee School of Engineering Milwaukee, WI 53201; private; 1,500
Minneapolis College of Art and Design Minneapolis, MN 55404; private; 680
Minnesota Bible College Rochester, MN 55901; private; 120
Minot State College Minot, ND 58701; public; 2,500
Mississippi College Clinton, MS 39058; private; 1,800
Mississippi Industrial College Holly Springs, MS 38635; private; 250
Mississippi State University Mississippi State, MS 39762; public; 8,900
Mississippi University for Women Columbus, MS 39701; public; 2,000
Mississippi Valley State University Itta Bena, MS 38941; public; 2,900
Missouri Baptist College St. Louis, MO 63141; private; 480
Missouri Institute of Technology Kansas City, MO 64114; private; 1,500
Missouri Southern State College Joplin, MO 64801; public; 4,000
Missouri Valley College Marshall, MO 65340; private; 500
Missouri Western State College St. Joseph, MO 64507; public; 4,000
Mobile College Mobile, AL 36613; private; 1,100
Molloy College Rockville Centre, NY 11570; private; 1,500
Monmouth College Monmouth, IL 61462; private; 700
Monmouth College West Long Branch, NJ 07764; private; 3,000
Montana College of Mineral Science and Technology Butte, MT 59701; public; 1,600
Montana State University Bozeman, MT 59717; public; 9,700
Montclair State College Upper Montclair, NJ 07043; public; 10,000
Monterey Institute of International Studies Monterey, CA 93940; private; 90
Moody Bible Institute Chicago, IL 60610; private; 1,300
Moore College of Art Philadelphia, PA 19103; private; 700
Moorhead State University Moorhead, MN 56560; public; 7,300
Moravian College Bethlehem, PA 18018; private; 1,300
Morehead State University Morehead, KY 40351; private; 5,300
Morehouse College Atlanta, GA 30314; private; 1,900
Morgan State University Baltimore, MD 21239; public; 4,000
Morningside College Sioux City, IA 51106; private; 1,400
Morris Brown College Atlanta, GA 30314; private; 1,800
Morris College Sumter, SC 29150; private; 730
Morrison Institute of Technology Morrison, IL 61270; private; 300
Mount Angel Seminary St. Benedict, OR 97373; private; 10
Mount Holyoke College South Hadley, MA 01075; private; 1,900
Mount Marty College Yankton, SD 57078; private; 600
Mount Mary College Milwaukee, WI 53222; private, 1,100
Mount Mercy College Cedar Rapids, IA 52402; private; 1,000
Mount Saint Mary College Newburgh, NY 12550; private; 1,100
Mount Saint Mary's College Emmitsburg, MD 21727; private; 1,400
Mount Senario College Ladysmith, WI 54848; private; 470
Mount St. Clare College Clinton, IA 52732; private; 400
Mount St. Mary's College Los Angeles, CA 90049; private; 1,000
Mount Union College Alliance, OH 44601; private; 1,100
Mount Vernon Bible College Mount Vernon, OH 43050; private; 100
Mount Vernon College Washington, DC 20007; private; 480
Mount Vernon Nazarene College Mount Vernon, OH 43050; private; 1,000
Muhlenberg College Allentown, PA 18104; private; 1,500
Multnomah School of the Bible Portland, OR 97220; private; 600
Mundelein College Chicago, IL 60660; private; 1,500
Murray State University Murray, KY 42071; public; 6,500
Museum Art School Portland, OR 97205; private; 150
Music and Arts Institute of San Francisco San Francisco, CA 94115; private; 100
Muskingum College New Concord, OH 43762; private; 1,000

Naropa Institute Boulder, CO 80302; private; 800
Nasson College Springvale, ME 04083; private; 530
Nathaniel Hawthorne College Antrim, NH 03440; private; 550
National American Educational Service(s) Chicago, IL 60640
National College of Business Rapid City, SD 57709; private; 1,200
National College of Business—Albuquerque Albuquerque, NM 87108; private; 150
National College of Chiropractic Lombard, IL 60148; private; 400
National College of Education Evanston, IL 60201; private; 700
National College of Education—Urbana Chicago, IL 60601; private; 480
National University San Diego, CA 92108; public; 3,500
Nazareth College Nazareth, MI 49074; private; 600
Nazareth College of Rochester Rochester, NY 14610; private; 1,900
Nebraska Christian College Norfolk, NE 68701; private; 210
Nebraska Wesleyan University Lincoln, NE 68504; private; 1,100
Neumann College Aston, PA 19014; private; 770
Newberry College Newberry, SC 29108; private; 820
New College of California San Francisco, CA 94110; private; 250
New College of the University of South Florida Sarasota, FL 33580; public; 500
New England Baptist Bible College Portland, ME 04101; private; 30
New England College Arundel, Sussex BN18 ODA, England; private; 230
New England College Henniker, NH 03242; private; 1,400
New England Conservatory of Music Boston, MA 02115; private; 480
New Hampshire College Manchester, NH 03104; private; 4,100
New Jersey Institute of Technology Newark, NJ 07102; public; 4,700
New Mexico Highlands University Las Vegas, NM 87701; public; 1,800
New Mexico Institute of Mining and Technology Socorro, NM 87801; public; 1,000
New Mexico State University Las Cruces, NM 88003; public; 12,300
Newport College—Salve Regina Newport, RI 02840; private; 1,260
New School of Music Philadelphia, PA 19103; private; 85
New School of Social Research New York, NY 10011; private; 20,300
New York Institute of Technology Old Westbury, NY 11568; private; 9,500
New York Institute of Technology—Metropolitan Center New York, NY 10023; private; 2,600
New York School of Interior Design New York, NY 10022; private; 1,000
New York University New York, NY 10012; private; 12,700
Niagara University Niagara University, NY 14109; private; 3,000
Nicholls State University Thibodaux, LA 70310; public; 5,800
Nichols College Dudley, MA 01570; private; 900
Norfolk State University Norfolk, VA 23504; public; 7,200
North Adams State College North Adams, MA 01247; public; 2,200
North Carolina Agricultural and Technical State University Greensboro, NC 27411; public; 4,900
North Carolina Central University Durham, NC 27707; public; 4,000
North Carolina School of the Arts Winston-Salem, NC 27107; public; 460
North Carolina State University—Raleigh Raleigh, NC 27650; public; 15,000
North Carolina Wesleyan College Rocky Mount, NC 27801; private; 870
North Central Bible College Minneapolis, MN 55404; private; 700
North Central College Naperville, IL 60566; private; 1,200
North Dakota State University Fargo, ND 58105; public; 8,200
Northeastern Bible College Essex Fells, NJ 07021; private; 330
Northeastern Illinois University Chicago, IL 60625; public; 8,000
Northeastern Oklahoma State University Tahlequah, OK 74464; public; 5,500
Northeastern University Boston, MA 02115; private; 17,800
Northeast Louisiana University Monroe, LA 71209; public; 8,900
Northeast Missouri State University Kirksville, MO 63501; public; 6,500
Northern Arizona University Flagstaff, AZ 86011; public; 11,000
Northern Illinois University De Kalb, IL 60115; public; 18,100
Northern Kentucky University Highland Heights, KY 41076; public; 7,200
Northern Michigan University Marquette, MI 49855; public; 8,300
Northern Montana College Havre, MT 59501; public; 1,400
Northern State College Aberdeen, SD 57401; public; 2,400
North Georgia College Dahlonega, GA 30533; public; 1,700
Northland College Ashland, WI 54806; private; 630
North Park College Chicago, IL 60625; private; 1,300
Northrop University Inglewood, CA 90306; private; 1,400
North Texas State University Denton, TX 76203; public; 70
Northwest Bible College Minot,

ND 58701; private; 250
Northwest Christian College Eugene, OR 97401; private; 300
Northwest College Kirkland, WA 98033; private; 800
Northwestern College Orange City, IA 51041; private; 960
Northwestern College Roseville, MN 55113; private; 800
Northwestern Oklahoma State University Alva, OK 73717; public; 1,800
Northwestern State University Natchitoches, LA 71457; public; 6,000
Northwestern University Evanston, IL 60201; private; 6,800
Northwest Missouri State University Maryville, MO 64468; public; 4,900
Northwest Nazarene College Nampa, ID 83651; private; 1,300
Northwood Institute Midland, MI 48640; private; 1,800
Norwich University Northfield, VT 05663; private; 1,600
Notre Dame College Manchester, NH 03104; private; 700
Notre Dame College Cleveland, OH 44121; private; 610
Nova University Fort Lauderdale, FL 33314; private; 1,100
Nyack College Nyack, NY 10960; private; 580

Oakland City College Oakland City, IN 47660; private; 610
Oakland University Rochester, MI 48063; public; 12,000
Oakwood College Huntsville, AL 35806; private; 1,300
Oberlin College Oberlin, OH 44074; private; 2,700
Oblate College Washington, DC 20017; private; 40
Occidental College Los Angeles, CA 90041; private; 1,700
Oglethorpe University Atlanta, GA 30319; private; 1,200
Ohio Dominican College Columbus, OH 43219; private; 940
Ohio Institute of Technology Columbus, OH 43209; private; 3,800
Ohio Northern University Ada, OH 45810; private; 2,200
Ohio State University Columbus, OH 43210; public; 41,800
Ohio State University—Lima Lima, OH 45804; public; 920
Ohio State University—Mansfield Mansfield, OH 44906; public; 1,100
Ohio University Athens, OH 45701; public; 12,200
Ohio University—Lancaster Lancaster, OH 43130; public; 1,600
Ohio Wesleyan University Delaware, OH 43015; private; 2,300
Oklahoma Baptist University Shawnee, OK 74801; private; 1,500
Oklahoma Christian College Oklahoma City, OK 73111; private; 1,700
Oklahoma City University Oklahoma City, OK 73106; private; 1,600
Oklahoma Southwestern College Oklahoma City, OK 73127; private; 4,400
Oklahoma State University Stillwater, OK 74078; public; 19,000
Old Dominion University Norfolk, VA 23508; public; 10,100
Olivet College Olivet, MI 49076; private; 650
Olivet Nazarene College Kankakee, IL 60901; private; 2,000
O'Moore School of Interior Architecture and Design Franklin, TN 37604; private; 120
Open Bible College Des Moines, IA 50321; private; 120
Oral Roberts University Tulsa, OK 74171; private; 3,500
Oregon College of Education Monmouth, OR 97361; public; 3,200
Oregon Institute of Technology Klamath Falls, OR 97601; public; 2,700
Oregon State University Corvallis, OR 97331; public; 14,700
Otis Art Institute of Parsons School of Design Los Angeles, CA 90057; private; 310
Ottawa University Ottawa, KS 66067; private; 500
Otterbein College Westerville, OH 43081; private; 1,700
Ouachita Baptist University Arkadelphia, AR 71923; private; 1,700
Our Lady of Holy Cross College New Orleans, LA 70114; private; 780
Our Lady of the Lake—University of San Antonio San Antonio, TX 78285; private; 1,200
Ozark Bible College Joplin, MO 64801; private; 800

Pace University New York, NY 10038; private; 10,200
Pace University—College of White Plains White Plains, NY 10603; private; 1,300
Pace University—Pleasantville/Briarcliff Pleasantville, NY 10570; private; 4,400
Pacific Christian College Fullerton, CA 92631; private; 540
Pacific Lutheran University Tacoma, WA 98447; private; 2,900
Pacific Oaks College Pasadena, CA 91103; private; 6
Pacific States University Los Angeles, CA 90006; private; 600
Pacific Union College Angwin, CA 94508; private; 2,100
Pacific University Forest Grove, OR 97116; private; 1,100
Paine College Augusta, GA 30910; private; 750
Palm Beach Atlantic College West Palm Beach, FL 33401; private; 600
Panama Canal College APO Miami, FL 34002; public; 1,700
Pan American University Edinburg, TX 78539; public; 8,400
Panhandle State University Goodwell, OK 73939; public; 1,200
Park College Kansas City, MO 64152; private; 470
Parks College of Aeronautical Technology of St. Louis University Cahokia, IL 62206; private; 1,100
Parsons School of Design New York, NY 10011; private; 1,500
Patten Bible College Oakland, CA 94601; private; 200
Paul Quinn College Waco, TX 76704; private; 440
Peabody Conservatory of Music Baltimore, MD 21202; private; 290
Pembroke State University Pembroke, NC 28372; public; 2,300
Pennsylvania State University University Park, PA 16802; public; 27,700
Pennsylvania State University—Behrend Erie, PA 16563; public; 1,800
Pennsylvania State University—Capitol Middletown, PA 17057; public; 1,600
Pepperdine University Los Angeles, CA 90044; private; 2,800
Pepperdine University—Seaver College Malibu, CA 90265; private; 2,300
Peru State College Peru, NE 68421; public; 900
Pfeiffer College Misenheimer, NC 28109; private; 840
Philadelphia College of Art Philadelphia, PA 19102; private; 1,200
Philadelphia College of Bible Langhorne, PA 19047; private; 500
Philadelphia College of Pharmacy and Science Philadelphia, PA 19104; private; 1,000
Philadelphia College of the Performing Arts Philadelphia, PA 19102; private; 360
Philadelphia College of Textiles and Science Philadelphia, PA 19144; private; 1,600
Philander Smith College Little Rock, AR 72203; private; 940
Phillipe University Enid, OK 73701; private; 1,300
Piedmont Bible College Winston-Salem, NC 27101; private; 460
Piedmont College Demorest, GA 30535; private; 490
Pikeville College Pikeville, KY 41501; private; 620
Pillsbury Baptist Bible College Owatonna, MN 55060; private; 700
Pine Manor College Chestnut Hill, MA 02167; private; 540
Pittsburg State University Pittsburg, KS 66762; public; 3,800
Pitzer College Claremont, CA 91711; private; 750
Platte Valley Bible College Scotts Bluff, NE 69361; private; 50
Plymouth State College Plymouth, NH 03264; public; 3,400
Point Loma College San Diego, CA 92106; private; 1,800
Point Park College Pittsburgh, PA; private; 2,200
Polytechnic Institute of New York Brooklyn, NY 11201; private; 2,200
Pomona College Claremont, CA 91711; private; 1,300
Pontifical College Josephinum Columbus, OH 43085; private; 90
Portland School of Art Portland, ME 04101; private; 250
Portland State University Portland, OR 97207; public; 12,000
Post College Waterbury, CT 06708; private; 1,400
Prairie View A and M University Prairie View, TX 77445; public; 4,700
Pratt Institute Brooklyn, NY 11205; private; 3,400
Presbyterian College Clinton, SC 29325; private; 950
Princeton University Princeton, NJ 08544; private; 4,500
Principia College Elsah, IL 62028; private; 850
Providence College Providence, RI 02918; private; 3,500
Puget Sound College of the Bible Edmonds, WA 98020; private; 200
Purdue University West Lafayette, IN 47907; public; 27,100
Purdue University—Calumet Hammond, IN 46323; public; 5,800
Purdue University—North Central Westville, IN 46391; public; 2,200

Queens College Charlotte, NC 28274; private; 650
Quincy College Quincy, IL 62301; private; 1,800
Quinnipiac College Hamden, CT 06518; private; 2,400

Rabbinical College of America Morristown, NJ 07960; private; 230
Rabbinical Seminary of America Forest Hills, NY 11375; private; 160
Radford University Radford, VA 24142; private; 5,000
Ramapo College of New Jersey Mahwah, NJ 07430; private; 4,600
Randolph-Macon College Ashland, VA 23005; private; 950
Randolph-Macon Woman's College Lynchburg, VA 24503; private; 750
Reed College Portland, OR 97202; private; 1100
Reformed Bible College Grand Rapids, MI 49506; private; 230
Regis College Denver, CO 80221; private; 1,300
Regis College Weston, MA 02193; private; 1,100
Rensselaer Polytechnic Institute Troy, NY 12181; private; 4,200
Rhode Island College Providence, RI 02908; public; 6,100
Rhode Island School of Design Providence, RI 02903; private; 1,400
Rice University Houston, TX 77001; private; 2,400
Richmond College London W8 5PN England; private; 500
Rider College Lawrenceville, NJ 08648; private; 4,600
Ringling School of Art Sarasota, FL 33580; private; 480
Rio Grande College/Community College Rio Grande, OH 45674; private; 1,300
Ripon College Ripon, WI 54971; private; 950
Rivier College Nashua, NH 03060; private; 650
Roanoke Bible College Elizabeth City, NC 27909; private; 170
Roanoke College Salem, VA 24153; private; 1,300
Robert Morris College Coraopolis, PA 15108; private; 4,700
Roberts Wesleyan College Rochester, NY 14624; private; 620
Rochester Institute of Technology Rochester, NY 14623; private; 8,600
Rockford College Rockford, IL 61101; private; 1,200
Rockhurst College Kansas City, MO 64110; private; 1,400
Rockmont College Denver, CO 80226; private; 330
Rocky Mountain College Billings, MT 59102; private; 440
Roger Williams College Bristol, RI 02809; private; 2,500
Roger Williams College—Providence Providence, RI 02809; private; 2,200
Rollins College Winter Park, FL 32789; private; 1,400
Roosevelt University Chicago, IL 60605; private; 4,300
Rosary College River Forest, IL 60305; private; 920
Rose-Hulman Institute of Technology Terre Haute, IN 47803; private; 1,200
Rosemont College Rosemont, PA 19010; private; 600
Rush University—Colleges of Nursing and Health Sciences Chicago, IL 60612; private; 280
Russell Sage College Troy, NY 12180; private; 1,400
Rust College Holly Springs, MS 38635; private; 750
Rutgers University—Camden College of Arts and Sciences Camden, NJ 08102; public; 3,000
Rutgers University—College of Engineering New Brunswick, NJ 08903; public; 2,500
Rutgers University—College of Nursing—Newark Newark, NJ 07102; public; 590
Rutgers University—College of Pharmacy New Brunswick, NJ 08903; public; 690
Rutgers University—Cook College New Brunswick, NJ 08903; public; 2,800
Rutgers University—Douglass College New Brunswick, NJ 08903; public; 3,700
Rutgers University—Livingston College New Brunswick, NJ 08903; public; 3,400
Rutgers University—Mason Gross School of the Arts New Brunswick, NJ 08903; public; 200
Rutgers University—Newark College of Arts and Sciences Newark, NJ 07102; public; 3,900
Rutgers University—Rutgers College New Brunswick, NJ 08903; public; 8,200
Rutgers University—University College New Brunswick, NJ 08903; public; 3,400

Sacred Heart College Belmont, NC 28012; private; 500
Sacred Heart Seminary Detroit, MI 48206; private; 164
Sacred Heart University Bridgeport, CT 06606; private; 2,200
Saginaw Valley State College University Center, MI 48710; public; 3,700
Salem College Winston-Salem, NC 27108; public; 650
Salem College Salem, WV 26426; private; 1,300
Salem State College Salem, MA 01970; public; 7,700
Salisbury State College Salisbury, MD 21801; public; 3,300
Samford University Birmingham, AL 35229; private; 3,000
Sam Houston State University Huntsville, TX 77340; public; 9,100
San Diego State University Calexico, CA 92231; public; 260
San Diego State University San Diego, CA 92182; public; 25,300
San Francisco Art Institute San Francisco, CA 94133; private; 790
San Francisco Conservatory of Music San Francisco,CA 94122; private; 180
San Francisco State University San Francisco, CA 94132; public; 18,000
Sangamon State University Springfield, IL 62708; public; 1,800
San Jose Bible College San Jose, CA 95108; private; 300
San Jose State University San Jose, CA 95192; public; 20,400
Sarah Lawrence College Bronxville, NY 10708; private; 850
Savannah State College Savannah, GA 31404; public; 2,300
Schiller International University 6900 Heidelberg, West Germany; private; 480

School for International Training Brattleboro, VT 05301; private; 160
School of the Art Institute of Chicago Chicago, IL 60603; private; 1,600
School of the Museum of Fine Arts Affiliated with Tufts University; Boston, MA 02115; private; 830
School of the Ozarks Point Lookout, MO 65726; private; 1,200
School of Visual Arts New York, NY 10010; private; 4,000
Scripps College Claremont, CA 91711; private; 570
Seattle Pacific University Seattle, WA 98119; private; 2,400
Seattle University Seattle, WA 98122; private; 2,500
Selma University Selma, AL 36701; private; 20
Seminary of St. Pius X Erlanger, KY 41018; private; 100
Seton Hall University South Orange, NJ 07079; private; 6,800
Seton Hill College Greensburg, PA 15601; private; 900
Shaw College at Detroit Detroit, MI 48202; private; 630
Shaw University Raleigh, NC 27611; private; 1,600
Sheldon Jackson College Sitka, AK 99835; private; 130
Shenandoah College and Conservatory of Music Winchester, VA 22601; private; 950
Shepherd College Shepherdstown, WV 25443; public; 3,000
Sherwood Music School Chicago, IL 60605; private; 50
Shimer College Waukegan, IL 60085; private; 100
Shippensburg State College Shippensburg, PA 17257; public; 4,900
Shorter College Rome, GA 30161; private; 850
Siena College Loudonville, NY 12211; private; 2,400
Siena Heights College Adrian, MI 49221; private; 1,400
Sierra Nevada College Incline Village, NV 89450; private; 180
Silver Lake College Manitowoc, WI 54220; private; 350
Simmons College Boston, MA 02115; private; 1,800
Simmons University Bible College Louisville, KY 40210; private; 130
Simon's Rock Early College of Bard College Great Barrington, MA 01230; private; 280
Simpson College San Francisco, CA 94134; private; 230
Simpson College Indianola, IA 50125; private; 850
Sinte Gleska College Rosebud, SD 57570; private; 350
Sioux Falls College Sioux Falls, SD 57101; private; 850
Skidmore College Saratoga Springs, NY 12866; private; 2,100
Slippery Rock State College Slippery Rock, PA 16057; public; 4,600
Smith College Northampton, MA 01063; private; 2,700
Sonoma State University Rohnert Park, CA 94928; public; 4,100
South Carolina State College Orangeburg, SC 29117; public; 3,500
South Dakota School of Mines and Technology Rapid City, SD 57701; public; 1,900
South Dakota State University Brookings, SD 57007; public; 6,300
Southeastern Baptist College Laurel, MS 39440; private; 180
Southeastern Bible College Birmingham, AL 35256; private; 250
Southeastern College Lakeland, FL 33801; private; 1,200
Southeastern Louisiana University Hammond, LA 70402; public; 7,700
Southeastern Massachusetts University North Dartmouth, MA 02747; public; 5,000
Southeastern Oklahoma State University Durant, OK 74701; public; 4,300
Southeastern University Washington, DC 20024; private; 1,100
Southeast Missouri State University Cape Girardeau, MO 63701; public; 8,400
Southern Arkansas University Magnolia, AR 71753; public; 1,900
Southern Bible College Houston, TX 77015; private; 140
Southern California College Costa Mesa, CA 92626; private; 710
Southern California Institute of Architecture Santa Monica, CA 90404; private; 250
Southern Connecticut State College New Haven, CT 06515; public; 6,600
Southern Illinois University Edwardsville, IL 62026; public; 7,800
Southern Illinois University—Carbondale Carbondale, IL 62901; public; 19,300
Southern Methodist College Orangeburg, SC 29115; private; 70
Southern Methodist University Dallas, TX 75275; private; 5,900
Southern Missionary College Collegedale, TN 37315; private; 2,100
Southern Oregon State College Ashland, OR 97520; public; 4,000
Southern Technical Institute Marietta, GA 30060; public; 2,600
Southern University—Baton Rouge Baton Rouge, LA 70813; public; 9,000
Southern University—New Orleans New Orleans, LA 70126; public, 2,700
Southern Utah State College Cedar City, UT 84720; public; 2,100
Southern Vermont College Bennington, VT 05201; public; 650
Southwest Baptist College Bolivar, MO 65613; private; 1,500
Southwestern Adventist College Keene, TX 76059; private; 700
Southwestern Assemblies of God College Waxahachie, TX 75165; private; 700
Southwestern Baptist College Phoenix, AZ 85032; private; 190
Southwestern College Winfield, KS 67156; private; 650
Southwestern—Memphis Memphis, TN 38112; private; 1,100
Southwestern Oklahoma State University Weatherford, OK 73096; public; 4,400
Southwestern University Georgetown, TX 78626; private; 1,000
Southwest Missouri State University Springfield, MO 65802; public; 14,000
Southwest State University Marshall, MN 56258; public; 2,100
Southwest Texas State University San Marcos, TX 78666; public; 13,500
Spalding College Louisville, KY 40203; private; 840
Spelman College Atlanta, GA 30314; private; 1,400
Spertus College of Judaica Chicago, IL 60605; private; 470
Spring Arbor College Spring Arbor, MI 49283; private; 840
Springfield College Springfield, MA 01109; private; 2,100
Spring Garden College Chestnut Hill, PA 19118; private; 1,100
Spring Hill College Mobile, AL 36608; private; 900
St. Alphonsus College Suffield, CT 06078; private; 60
St. Ambrose College Davenport, IA 52803; private; 2,000
St. Andrew's Presbyterian College Laurinburg, NC 28352; private; 750
Stanford University Stanford, CA 94305; private; 6,600
St. Anselm College Manchester, NH 03102; private; 1,900
St. Augustine's College Raleigh, NC 27611; private; 1,800
St. Basil's College Stamford, CT 06902; private; 20
St. Bonaventure University St. Bonaventure, NY 14778; private; 2,300
St. Cloud State University St. Cloud, MN 56301; public; 10,700
St. Edward's University Austin, TX 78704; private; 2,300
Steed College Johnson City, TN 37601; private; 600
Stephen F. Austin State University Nacagdoches, TX 75962; public; 9,800
Stephens College Columbia, MO 65215; private; 1,300
Sterling College Sterling, KS 67579; private; 490
Stetson University Deland, FL 32720; private; 2,000
Stevens Institute of Technology Hoboken, NJ 07030; private; 1,600
St. Francis College Fort Wayne, IN 46808; private; 800
St. Francis College Brooklyn, NY 11201; private; 2,900
St. Francis College Loretto, PA 15940; private; 1,200
St. Hyacinth College and Seminary Granby, MA 01033; private; 50
Stillman College Tuscaloosa, AL 35401; private; 700
St. John Fisher College Rochester, NY 14618; private; 2,900
St. John's College Annapolis, MD 21404; private; 380
St. John's College Santa Fe, NM 87501; private; 300
St. John's Seminary College of Liberal Arts Brighton, MA 02135; private; 85
St. John's University Collegeville, MN 56321; private; 2,000
St. John's University Jamaica/Queens/Staten Island Jamaica, NY 11439; private; 12,400
St. John Vianney College Seminary Miami, FL 33165; private; 60
St. Joseph College West Hartford, CT 06117; private; 800
St. Joseph's College Rensselaer, IN 47978; private; 1,000
St. Joseph's College North Windham, ME 04062; private; 500
St. Joseph's College Brooklyn, NY 11205; private; 2,300
St. Joseph's College—Suffolk Patchogue, NY 11772; private; 1,000
St. Joseph Seminary College St. Benedict, IA 70457; private; 110
St. Joseph's University Philadelphia, PA 19131; private; 2,300
St. Lawrence University Canton, NY 13617; private; 2,300
St. Leo College St. Leo, FL 33574; private; 1,200
St. Louis Christian College Florissant, MO 63033; private; 200
St. Louis College of Pharmacy St. Louis, MO 63110; private; 680
St. Louis Conservatory of Music St. Louis, MO 63130; private; 110
St. Louis University St. Louis, MO 63103; private; 7,200
St. Martin's College Lacey, WA 98503; private; 780
St. Mary College Leavenworth, KS 66048; private; 860
St. Mary of the Plains College Dodge City, KS 67801; private; 650
St. Mary-of-the-Woods College St. Mary-of-the-Woods, IN 47876; private; 710
St. Mary's College Notre Dame, IN 46556; private; 1,820
St. Mary's College Orchard Lake, MI 48033; private; 250
St. Mary's College Winona, MN 55987; private; 1,300
St. Mary's College of California Moraga, CA 94575; private; 2,000
St. Mary's College of Maryland St. Mary's City, MD 20686; public; 1,300
St. Mary's Dominican College New Orleans, LA 70114; private; 900
St. Mary's Seminary and College Baltimore, MD 21210; private; 70
St. Mary's University of San Antonio San Antonio, TX 78284; private; 2,200
St. Meinrad College St. Meinrad, IN 47577; private; 210
St. Michael's College Winooski, VT 05405; private; 1,600
St. Norbert College De Pere, WI 54115; private; 1,600
Stockton State College Pomona, NJ 08240; public; 4,800
St. Olaf College Northfield, MN 55057; private; 3,100
Stonehill College North Easton, MA 02356; private; 1,700
St. Patrick's College Mountain View, CA 94042; private; 100
St. Paul Bible College Bible College, MN 55375; private; 660
St. Paul's College Lawrenceville, VA 23868; private; 690
St. Peter's College Jersey City, NJ 07306; private; 2,500
Strayer College Washington, DC 20005; private; 1,700
St. Thomas Aquinas College Sparkill, NY 10968; private; 1,500
St. Vincent College Latrobe, PA 15650; private; 880
St. Xavier College Chicago, IL 60655; private; 2,200
Suffolk University Boston, MA 02114; private; 2,800
Sul Ross State University Alpine, TX 79830; public; 1,600
Sul Ross State University—Uvalde Study Center Uvalde, TX 78801; public, 300
SUNY—Albany Albany, NY 12222; public; 11,000
SUNY—Binghamton Binghamton, NY 13901; public; 8,600
SUNY—Buffalo Buffalo, NY 14214; public; 17,000
SUNY—College at Brockport Brockport, NY 14420; public; 7,400
SUNY—College at Buffalo Buffalo, NY 14222; public; 10,100
SUNY—College at Cortland Cortland, NY 13045; public; 5,500
SUNY—College at Fredonia Fredonia, NY 14063; public; 4,800
SUNY—College at Geneseo Geneseo, NY 14454; public; 4,480
SUNY—College at New Paltz New Paltz, NY 12561; public; 5,400
SUNY—College at Old Westbury Old Westbury, NY 11568; public; 3,200
SUNY—College at Oneonta Oneonta, NY 13820; public; 5,800
SUNY—College at Oswego Oswego, NY 13126; public; 6,600
SUNY—College at Plattsburgh Plattsburgh, NY 12901; public; 5,900
SUNY—College at Potsdam Potsdam, NY 13676; public; 4,100
SUNY—College at Purchase Purchase, NY 10577; public; 2,400
SUNY—College of Agriculture and Life Sciences at Cornell Ithaca, NY 14853; public; 3,000
SUNY—College of Ceramics at Alfred Alfred, NY 14802; public; 640
SUNY—College of Environmental Science and Forestry Syracuse, NY 13210; public; 1,400
SUNY—College of Human Ecology at Cornell Ithaca, NY 14853; public; 1,200
SUNY—College of Technology Utica, NY 13502; public; 2,900
SUNY—Empire State College Saratoga Springs, NY 12866; public; 3,500
SUNY—Fashion Institute of Technology New York, NY 10001; public; 10,000
SUNY—Maritime College Bronx, NY 10465; public; 900
SUNY—School of Industrial and Labor Relations at Cornell Ithaca, NY 14853; public; 620
SUNY—Stony Brook Stony Brook, NY 11794; public; 9,500
SUNY—Upstate Medical Center Syracuse, NY 13210; public; 260
Susquehanna University Selinsgrove, PA 17870; private; 1,500
Swain School of Design New Bedford, MA 02740; private; 200
Swarthmore College Swarthmore, PA 19081; private; 1,300
Sweet Briar College Sweet Briar, VA 24595; private; 670
Syracuse University Syracuse, NY 13210; private; 11,000

Tabor College Hillsboro, KS 67063; private; 480
Talladega College Talladega, AL 35160; private; 790
Tampa College Medical Education Center Tampa, FL 33609; private; 480
Tarkio College Tarkio, MO 64491; private; 580
Tarleton State University Stephenville, TX 76402; public; 3,600
Taylor University Upland, IN 46989; private; 1,600
Temple University Philadelphia, PA 19122; public; 17,000
Tennessee State University Nashville, TN 37203; public; 5,700
Tennessee Technological University Cookeville, TN 38501; public; 7,200
Tennessee Temple University Chattanooga, TN 37404; private; 4,000
Tennessee Wesleyan College Athens, TN 37303; private; 530
Texas A and I University—Kingsville Kingsville, TX 78363; public; 4,400
Texas A and M University College Station, TX 77843; public; 28,000
Texas A and M University at Gal-

veston Galveston, TX 77553; public; 600
Texas Christian University Forth Worth, TX 76129; private; 5,300
Texas College Tyler, TX 78155; private; 500
Texas Lutheran College Seguin, TX 78155; private; 1,000
Texas Southern University Houston, TX 77004; public; 7,300
Texas Tech University Lubbock, TX 79409; public; 23,000
Texas Wesleyan College Forth Worth, TX 76105; private; 1,700
Texas Woman's University Denton, TX 76204; public; 4,400
The American University Washington, DC 20016; private; 5,000
The Citadel Charleston, SC 29409; public; 2,000
The Kings College Briarcliff Manor, NY 10510; private; 850
Thiel College Greenville, PA 16125; private; 950
Thomas A. Edison College Trenton, NJ 08625; private; 360
Thomas Aquinas College Santa Paula, CA 93060; private; 120
Thomas College Waterville, ME 04901; private; 500
Thomas Jefferson University College of Allied Health Sciences; Philadelphia, PA 19107; private; 620
Thomas More College Fort Mitchell, KY 41017; private; 1,300
Tiffin University Tiffin, OH 44883; private; 450
Tift College Forsyth, GA 31029; private; 430
Toccoa Falls College Toccoa Falls, GA 30598; private; 620
Tougaloo College Tougaloo, MS 39174; private; 890
Touro College New York, NY 10036; private; 2,000
Towson State University Towson, MD 21204; public; 13,800
Transylvania University Lexington, KY 40508; private; 810
Trenton State College Trenton, NJ 08625; public; 8,600
Trevecca Nazarene College Nashville, TN 37210; private; 1,000
Trinity Bible Institute Ellendale, ND 58436; private; 380
Trinity Christian College Palos Heights, IL 60463; private; 410
Trinity College Hartford, CT 06106; private; 1,700
Trinity College Washington, DC 20017; private; 800
Trinity College Dunedin, FL 33528; private; 120
Trinity College Deerfield, IL 60015; private; 700
Trinity College Burlington, VT 05401; private; 780
Trinity University San Antonio, TX 78284; private; 3,300
Tri-State University Angola, IN 46703; private; 1,300
Troy State University Troy, AL 36082; public; 5,700
Troy State University—Dothan/Ft. Rucker Dothan, AL 36301; public; 900
Troy State University—Montgomery Montgomery, AL 36104; public; 1,900
Tufts University Medford, MA 02155; private; 4,500
Tulane University New Orleans, LA 70118; private; 5000
Tusculum College Greeneville, TN 37743; private; 400
Tuskegee Institute Tuskegee, AL 36088; private; 3,500

Union College Barbourville, KY 40906; private; 550
Union College Lincoln, NE 68506; private; 900
Union College Schenectady, NY 12308; private; 2,000
Union for Experimenting Colleges and University Cincinnati, OH 45202; private; 200
Union University Jackson, TN 38301; private; 1,300
United States Air Force Academy USAF Academy, CO 80840; public; 4,500
United States Coast Guard Academy New London, CT 06320; public; 900
United States International University San Diego, CA 92131; private; 1,100
United States Merchant Marine Academy Kings Point, NY 11024; public; 1,100
United States Military Academy West Point, NY 10996; public; 4,400
United States Naval Academy Annapolis, MD 21402; public; 4,500
United Wesleyan College Allentown, PA 18103; private; 240
Unity College Unity, ME 04988; private; 350
Universidad Politecnica de Puerto Rico Hato Rey, PR 00918; public; 410
University of Akron Akron, OH 44325; public; 20,100
University of Alabama University, AL 35486; public; 14,100
University of Alabama—Birmingham Birmingham, AL 35294; public; 10,100
University of Alabama—Huntsville Huntsville, AL 35807; public; 5,000
University of Alaska—Anchorage Anchorage, AK 99504; public; 4,000
University of Alaska—Fairbanks Fairbanks, AK 99701; public; 3,400
University of Alaska—Juneau Juneau, AK 99803; public; 2,000
University of Albuquerque Albuquerque, NM 87140; private; 2,100
University of Arizona Tucson, AZ 85721; public; 26,600
University of Arkansas Fayetteville, AR 72701; public; 12,900
University of Arkansas—Little Rock Little Rock, AR 72204; public; 9,000
University of Arkansas—Monticello Monticello, AR 71655; public; 2,000
University of Arkansas—Pine Bluff Pine Bluff, AR 71601; public; 3,100
University of Baltimore Baltimore, MD 21201; public; 3,000
University of Bridgeport Bridgeport, CT 06602; private; 4,900
University of California—Berkeley Berkeley, CA 94720; public; 20,100
University of California—Davis Davis, CA 95616; public; 13,700
University of California—Irvine Irvine, CA 92717; public; 7,700
University of California—Los Angeles Los Angeles, CA 90024; public; 20,900
University of California—Riverside Riverside, CA 92521; public; 3,300
University of California—San Diego La Jolla, CA 92093; public; 9,100
University of California—Santa Barbara Santa Barbara, CA 93106; public; 12,600
University of California—Santa Cruz Santa Cruz, CA 95064; public; 6,000
University of Central Arkansas Conway, AR 72032; public; 5,100
University of Central Florida Orlando, FL 32816; public; 12,800
University of Charleston Charleston, WV 25304; private; 1,900
University of Chicago—The College Chicago, IL 60637; private; 2,700
University of Cincinnati Cincinnati, OH 45221; public; 33,300
University of Colorado Boulder, CO 80309; public; 17,800
University of Colorado—Colorado Springs Colorado Springs, CO 80907; public; 3,500
University of Colorado—Denver Denver, CO 80202; public; 5,700
University of Connecticut Storrs, CT 06268; public; 15,100
University of Dallas Irving, TX 75061; private; 1,100
University of Dayton Dayton, OH 45469; private; 7,000
University of Delaware Newark, DE; private; 13,700
University of Denver Denver, CO ; private; 4,900
University of Detroit Detroit, MI 48221; private; 3,700
University of Dubuque Dubuque, IA 52001; private; 1,100
University of Evansville Evansville, IN 47702; private; 5,200
University of Florida Gainesville, FL 32611; public; 24,300
University of Georgia Athens, GA 30602; public; 17,000
University of Guam Mangilao, GU 96913; public; 2,200
University of Hartford West Hartford, CT 06117; private; 7,100
University of Hawaii—College of Arts and Sciences Hilo, HI 96720; public; 1,620
University of Hawaii—Manoa Honolulu, HI 96822; public; 14,700
University of Hawaii—West Oahu College Aiea, HI 96701; public; 300
University of Health Sciences—Chicago Medical School North Chicago, IL 60062; private; 470
University of Houston Houston, TX 77004; public; 24,300
University of Houston—Clear Lake City Houston, TX 77058; public; 2,700
University of Houston—Downtown Houston, TX 77002; public; 800
University of Houston—Victoria Victoria, TX 77901; public; 800
University of Idaho Moscow, ID 83843; public; 7,300
University of Illinois—Chicago Circle Chicago, IL 60680; public; 17,500
University of Illinois—Medical Center Chicago, IL 60612; public; 1,700
University of Illinois—Urbana/Champaign Urbana, IL 61801; public; 26,500
University of Iowa Iowa City, IA 52242; public; 17,200
University of Judaism Los Angeles, CA 90024; private; 100
University of Kansas Lawrence, KS 66045; public; 18,300
University of Kansas—College of Health Sciences and Hospital Kansas City, KS 66103; public; 520
University of Kentucky Lexington, KY 40506; public; 18,300
University of La Verne La Verne, CA 91750; private; 1,200
University of Louisville Louisville, KY 40208; public; 15,100
University of Lowell Lowell, MA 01854; public; 7,600
University of Maine—Augusta Augusta, ME 04330; public; 3,400
University of Maine—Farmington Farmington, ME 04938; public; 2,000
University of Maine—Fort Kent Fort Kent, ME 04743; public; 620
University of Maine—Machias Machias, ME 04654; public; 650
University of Maine—Orono Orono, ME 04473; public; 10,000
University of Maine—Presque Isle Presque Isle, ME 04769; public; 1,400
University of Mary Hardin—Baylor Belton, TX 76513; private; 1,100
University of Maryland—Baltimore County Baltimore, MD 21228; public; 5,500
University of Maryland—College Park College Park, MD 20742; public; 30,300
University of Maryland—Eastern Shore Princess Anne, MD 21853; public; 1,100
University of Maryland—University College College Park, MD 20742; public; 10,700
University of Massachusetts—Amherst Amherst, MA 01003; public; 19,000
University of Massachusetts—Boston Boston, MA 02125; public; 8,300
University of Miami Coral Gables, FL 33124; private; 10,200
University of Michigan—Ann Arbor Ann Arbor, MI 48109; public; 22,500
University of Michigan—Dearborn Dearborn, MI 48128; public; 6,000
University of Michigan—Flint Flint, MI 48503; public; 4,300
University of Minnesota—Duluth Duluth, MN 55182; public; 7,100
University of Minnesota—Morris Morris, MN 56267; public; 1,700
University of Minnesota—Twin Cities Minneapolis, MN 55455; public; 39,900
University of Mississippi University, MS 38677; public; 7,900
University of Mississippi Medical Center Jackson, MS 39216; public; 500
University of Missouri—Columbia Columbia, MO 65201; public; 24,000
University of Missouri—Kansas City Kansas City, MO 64110; public; 6,600
University of Missouri—Rolla Rolla, MO 65401; public; 5,800
University of Missouri—St. Louis St. Louis, MO 63121; public; 9,600
University of Montana Missoula, MT 59812; public; 7,400
University of Montevallo Montevallo, AL 35115; public; 2,300
University of Nebraska—Lincoln Lincoln, NE 68508; public; 17,700
University of Nebraska—Omaha Omaha, NE 68182; public; 13,200
University of Nevada—Las Vegas Las Vegas, NV 89154; public; 6,700
University of Nevada—Reno Reno, NV 89557; public; 7,200
University of New England—St. Francis College Biddeford, ME 04005; private; 400
University of New Hampshire Durham, NH 03824; public; 9,500
University of New Haven West Haven, CT 06516; private; 5,400
University of New Mexico Albuquerque, NM 87131; public; 18,300
University of New Orleans New Orleans, LA 70122; public; 12,700
University of North Alabama Florence, AL 35632; public; 4,700
University of North Carolina—Asheville Asheville, NC 28814; public; 2,100
University of North Carolina—Chapel Hill Chapel Hill, NC 27514; public; 14,900
University of North Carolina—Charlotte Charlotte, NC 28223; public; 8,100
University of North Carolina—Greensboro Greensboro, NC 27412; public; 7,400
University of North Carolina—Wilmington Wilmington, NC 28403; public; 4,600
University of North Dakota Grand Forks, ND 58202; public; 9,700
University of Northern Colorado Greeley, CO 80639; public; 9,200
University of Northern Iowa Cedar Falls, IA 50613; public; 11,000
University of North Florida Jacksonville, FL 32216; public; 3,700
University of Notre Dame Notre Dame, IN 46556; private; 7,100
University of Oklahoma—Health Oklahoma City, OK 73190; public; 1,000
University of Oklahoma—Norman Norman, OK 73019; public; 17,000
University of Oregon Eugene, OR 97403; public; 13,000
University of Oregon—Health Portland, OR 97201; public; 2,000
University of Pennsylvania Philadelphia, PA 19104; private; 8,500
University of Phoenix Phoenix, AZ 85004; private; 800
University of Pittsburgh Pittsburgh, PA 15620; private; 18,961
University of Pittsburgh—Bradford Bradford, PA 16701; private; 800
University of Pittsburgh—Greensburg Greensburg, PA 15601; private; 1,100
University of Pittsburgh—Johnstown Johnstown, PA 15904; private; 3,000
University of Portland Portland, OR 97203; private; 2,200
University of Puerto Rico Cayey, PR 00633; public; 2,600
University of Puerto Rico—Humacao University College Humacao, PR 00661; public; 3,300
University of Puerto Rico—Mayaguez Mayaguez, PR 00708; public; 9,000
University of Puerto Rico—Medical Science San Juan, PR 00936; public; 1,200
University of Puerto Rico—Rio Piedras Rio Piedras, PR 00931; public; 20,400
University of Puget Sound Tacoma, WA 98416; private; 2,800
University of Redlands Redlands, CA 92373; private; 1,200
University of Rhode Island Kingston, RI 02881; public; 9,000

University of Richmond Richmond, VA 23173; private; 2,600
University of Rochester Rochester, NY 14627; private; 4,500
University of San Diego San Diego, CA 92110; private; 2,900
University of San Francisco San Francisco, CA 94117; private; 3,500
University of Santa Clara Santa Clara, CA 95053; private; 3,500
University of Sarasota Sarasota, FL 33577; private; 400
University of Science and Arts of Oklahoma Chickasha, OK 73018; public; 1,400
University of Scranton Scranton, PA 18510; private; 2,800
University of South Alabama Mobile, AL 36688; public; 6,600
University of South Carolina Columbia, SC 29208; public; 19,000
University of South Carolina—Aiken Aiken, SC 29801; public; 1,700
University of South Carolina—Coastal Carolina Conway, SC 29526; public; 1,900
University of South Carolina—Spartanburg Spartanburg, SC 29303; public; 2,700
University of South Dakota Vermillion, SD 57069; public; 4,600
University of South Dakota at Springfield Springfield, SD 57062; public; 850
University of Southern California Los Angeles, CA 90007; private; 15,300
University of Southern Colorado Pueblo, CO 81001; public; 4,000
University of Southern Maine Gorham, ME 04038; public; 7,600
University of Southern Mississippi Hattiesburg, MS 39401; public; 8,700
University of South Florida Tampa, FL 33620; public; 18,100
University of Southwestern Louisiana Lafayette, LA 70504; public; 12,400
University of Steubenville Steubenville, OH 43952; private; 950
University of St. Thomas Houston, TX 77006
University of Tampa Tampa, FL 33606; private; 1,700
University of Tennessee—Center for the Health Sciences Memphis, TN 38163; public; 660
University of Tennessee—Chattanooga Chattanooga, TN 37401; public; 6,200
University of Tennessee—Knoxville Knoxville, TN 37916; public; 23,200
University of Tennessee—Martin Martin, TN 38238; public; 5,400
University of Texas—Arlington Arlington, TX 76019; public; 17,400
University of Texas—Austin Austin, TX 78712; public; 36,600
University of Texas—Dallas Richardson, TX 75080; public; 3,300
University of Texas—El Paso El Paso, TX 79968; public; 13,900
University of Texas—Health Science Center—San Antonio San Antonio, TX 78284; public; 600
University of Texas Medical Branch—Galveston Galveston, TX 77550; public; 580
University of Texas—Permian Basin Odessa, TX 79762; public; 850
University of Texas—San Antonio San Antonio, TX 78285; public; 7,700
University of Texas—Tyler Tyler, TX 75701; public; 1,200
University of the Americas Puebla, Mexico; private; 3,100
University of the District of Columbia Washington, DC 20004; public; 14,000
University of the Pacific Stockton, CA 95211; private; 3,600
University of the Sacred Heart Santurce, PR 00924; private; 6,200
University of the South Sewanee, TN 37375; private; 1,000
University of the State of New York—R.E.D. Albany, NY 12230; public; 21,000
University of Toledo Toledo, OH 43606; public; 13,300
University of Tulsa Tulsa, OK 74104; private; 4,500
University of Utah Salt Lake City, UT 84112; public; 17,500
University of Vermont Burlington, VT 05405; public; 7,400
University of Virginia Charlottesville, VA 22903; public; 16,400
University of Virginia—Clinch Wise, VA 24293; Public; 1,000
University of Warwick Coventry CV4 7AL, England; private; 4,400
University of Washington Seattle, WA 98105; public; 26,400
University of West Florida Pensacola, FL 32504; public; 4,400
University of West Los Angeles Culver City, CA 90230; private; 200
University of Wisconsin—Eau Claire Eau Claire, WI 54701; public; 10,000
University of Wisconsin—Green Bay Green Bay, WI 54302; public; 3,900
University of Wisconsin—La Crosse La Crosse, WI 54601; public; 8,300
University of Wisconsin—Madison Madison, WI 53706; public; 41,300
University of Wisconsin—Milwaukee Milwaukee, WI 53201; public; 20,600
University of Wisconsin—Oshkosh Oshkosh, WI 54901; public; 12,500
University of Wisconsin—Parkside Kenosha, WI 53141; public; 5,200
University of Wisconsin—Platteville Platteville, WI 53818; public; 5,000
University of Wisconsin—River Falls River Falls, WI 54022; public; 5,000
University of Wisconsin—Stevens Point Stevens Point, WI 54481; public; 8,600
University of Wisconsin—Stout Menomonie, WI 54751; public; 6,500
University of Wisconsin—Superior Superior, WI 54880; public; 1,800
University of Wisconsin—Whitewater Whitewater, WI 53190; public; 12,500
University of Wyoming Laramie, WY 82071; public; 7,300
Upper Iowa University Fayette, IA 52142; private; 430
Upsala College East Orange, NJ 07019; private; 1,200
Urbana College Urbana, OH 43078; private; 800
Ursinus College Collegeville, PA 19426; private; 1,100
Ursuline College Pepper Pike, OH 44124; private; 840
Utah State University Logan, UT 84322; public; 8,500
Utica College of Syracuse University Utica, NY 13421; private; 1,500

Valdosta State College Valdosta, GA 31601; public; 3,900
Valley City State College Valley City, ND 58072; public; 1,100
Valley Forge Christian College Phoenixville, PA 19460; private; 500
Valparaiso Technical Institute Valparaiso, IN 46383; private; 200
Valparaiso University Valparaiso, IN 46383; private; 3,800
Vanderbilt University Nashville, TN 37212; private; 5,500
Vandercook College of Music Chicago, IL 60616; private; 90
Vassar College Poughkeepsie, NY 12601; private; 2,400
Vennard College University Park, IA 52595; private; 200
Vermont College of Norwich University Montpelier, VT 05602; private; 450
Villa Maria College Erie, PA 16505; private; 700
Villanova University Villanova, PA 19085; private; 6,000
Virginia Commonwealth University Richmond, VA 23284; private; 14,300
Virginia Intermont College Bristol, VA 24201; private; 700
Virginia Military Institute Lexington, VA 24450; public; 1,300
Virginia Polytechnic Institute and State University Blacksburg, VA 24061; public; 17,900
Virginia State University Petersburg, VA 23803; public; 3,900
Virginia Union University Richmond, VA 23220; private; 1,100
Virginia Wesleyan College Norfolk, VA 23502; private; 850
Viterbo College La Crosse, WI 54601; private; 1,000
Voorhees College Denmark, SC 29042; private; 610

Wabash College Crawfordsville, IN 47933; private; 800
Wadhams Hall Seminary College Ogdensburg, NY 13669; private; 60
Wagner College Staten Island, NY 10301; private; 2,000
Wake Forest University Winston-Salem, NC 27109; private; 3,200
Walla Walla College College Place, WA 99324; private; 1,900
Walsh College Canton, OH 44720; private; 800
Walsh College of Accountancy and Business Administration Troy, MI 48084; private; 1,300
Warner Pacific College Portland, OR 97215; private; 500
Warner Southern College Lake Wales, FL 33853; private; 300
Warren Wilson College Swannanoa, NC 28778; private; 500
Wartburg College Waverly, IA 50677; private; 1,100
Washburn University of Topeka Topeka, KS 66621; private
Washington and Jefferson College Washington, PA 15301; private; 1,100
Washington and Lee University Lexington, VA 24450; private; 1,400
Washington Bible College Lanham, MD 20801; private; 500
Washington College Chestertown, MD 21620; private; 750
Washington International College Washington, DC 20006; private; 370
Washington State University Pullman, WA 99164; public; 14,700
Washington University St. Louis, MO 63130; private; 4,500
Wayland Baptist College Plainview, TX 79072; private; 1,400
Waynesburg College Waynesburg, PA 15370; private; 870
Wayne State College Wayne, NE 68787; public; 2,100
Wayne State University Detroit, MI 48202; public; 23,200
Webber College Babson Park, FL 33827; private; 180
Webb Institute of Naval Architecture Glen Cove NY 11542; private; 80
Weber State College Ogden, UT 84408; public;
Webster College St. Louis, MO 63119; private; 1,100
Wellesley College Wellesley, MA 02181; private; 2,200
Wells College Aurora, NY 13026; private; 500
Wentworth Institute of Technology Boston, MA 02115; private; 3,000
Wesleyan College Macon, GA 31297; private; 2,500
Wesleyan University Middletown, CT 06457; private; 2,500
Wesley College Dover, DE 19901; private; 1,000
Wesley College Florence, MS 39073; private; 90
Westbrook College Portland, ME 04103; private; 900
West Chester State College West Chester, PA 19380; public; 6,000
West Coast Bible College Fresno, CA 93710; private; 210
West Coast University—Evenings Los Angeles, CA 90020; private; 350
West Coast University—Orange County—Evenings Orange, CA 92668; private; 250
Western Apostolic Bible College Stockton, CA 95205; private; 100
Western Baptist College Salem, OR 97302; private; 400
Western Bible College Morrison, CO 80465; private; 210
Western Carolina University Cullowhee, NC 28723; public; 5,400
Western Connecticut State College Danbury, CT 06810; public; 5,600
Western Illinois University Macomb, IL 61455; public; 11,300
Western International University Phoenix, AZ 85021; private; 350
Western Kentucky University Bowling Green, KY 42101; public; 10,500
Western Maryland College Westminster, MD 21157; private; 1,300
Western Michigan University Kalamazoo, MI 49008; public; 17,300
Western Montana College Dillon, MT 59725; public; 770
Western New England College Springfield, MA 01119; private; 2,800
Western New Mexico University Silver City, NM 88061; public; 1,500
Western State College of Colorado Gunnison, CO 81230; public; 3,300
Western States College of Engineering Inglewood, CA 90301; private; 100
Western Washington University Bellingham, WA 98225; public; 8,600
Westfield State College Westfield, MA 01085; public; 3,000
West Georgia College Carrollton, GA 30118; public; 4,100
West Liberty State College West Liberty, WV 26074; public; 2,700
Westmar College Le Mars, IA 51031; private; 650
Westminster Choir College Princeton, NJ 08540; private; 380
Westminster College Salt Lake City, UT 84105; private; 1,100
Westminster College Fulton, MO 65251; private; 680
Westminster College New Wilmington, PA 16142; private; 1,600
Westmont College Santa Barbara, CA 93108; private; 1,100
West Texas State University Canyon, TX 79016; public; 5,300
West Virginia Institute of Technology Montgomery, WV 25136; public; 3,300
West Virginia State College Charleston, WV 25312; public; 4,400
West Virginia University Morgantown, WV 26506; public; 14,500
West Virginia Wesleyan College Buckhannon, WV 26201; private; 1,800
Wheaton College Wheaton, IL 60187; private; 2,000
Wheaton College Norton, MA 02766; private; 1,200
Wheeling College Wheeling, WV 26003; private; 850
Wheelock College Boston, MA 02215; private; 590
Whitman College Walla Walla, WA 99362; private; 1,100
Whittier College Whittier, CA 90608; private; 1,200
Whitworth Bible College Brookhaven, MS 39601; private; 40
Whitworth College Spokane, WA 99251; private; 1,300
Wichita State University Wichita, KS 67204; public; 13,500
Widener College Chester, PA 10913; private; 1,900
Wilberforce University Wilberforce, OH 45384; private; 1,100
Wiley College Marshall, TX 75670; private; 670
Wilkes College Wilkes-Barre, PA 18766; private; 2,100
Willamette University Salem, OR 97301; private; 1,300
William Carey College Hattiesburg, MS 39401; private; 1,400
William Jewell College Liberty, MO 64068; private; 1,700
William Paterson College Wayne, NJ 07470; public; 10,300
William Penn College Oskaloosa, IA 52577; private; 600
Williams College Williamstown, MA 01267; private; 1,900
William Smith College Geneva, NY 14456; private; 750
William Tyndale College Farmington Hills, MI 48018; private; 360
William Woods College Fulton, MO 65251; private; 1,000
Wilmington College New Castle, DE 19720; private; 950
Wilmington College of Ohio Wilmington, OH 45177; private; 780
Wilson College Chambersburg, PA 17201; private; 200
Wingate College Wingate, NC 28174; private; 1,500
Winona State University Winona, MN 55987; public; 4,500

Winston-Salem Bible College Winston-Salem, NC 27102; private; 50

Winston-Salem State University Winston-Salem, NC 27102; public; 2,100

Winthrop College Rock Hill, SC 29733; public; 4,000

Wisconsin Conservatory of Music Milwaukee, WI 53202; private; 180

Wittenberg University Springfield, OH 45501; private; 2,300

Wofford College Spartanburg, SC 29301; private; 1,000

Woodbury University Los Angeles, CA 90017; private; 1,400

Worcester Polytechnic Institute Worcester, MA 01503; private; 2,400

Worcester State College Worcester, MA 01602; public; 3,100

World College West San Anselmo, CA; private; 70

Wright State University Dayton, OH 45435; public; 11,700

Xavier University Cincinnati, OH 45207; private; 3,100

Xavier University of Louisiana New Orleans, LA 70125; private; 1,900

Yale University New Haven, CT 06520; private; 5,100

Yankton College Yankton, SD 57078; private; 280

Yeshiva College—Main Center New York, NY 10033; private; 2,400

Yeshiva University of Los Angeles Los Angeles, CA 90035; private; 60

York College of Pennsylvania York, PA 17405; private; 3,700

Youngstown State University Youngstown, OH 44555; public; 14,300

TWO-YEAR COLLEGES AND UNIVERSITIES

Abraham Baldwin Agricultural College Tifton, GA 31794; public; 2,500
Academy of Aeronautics Flushing, NY 11371; private; 2,000
Adams State College Alamosa, CO 81102; public; 2,000
Adelphi University Garden City, NY 11530; private; 5,500
Adirondack Community College Glens Falls, NY 12801; public; 2,700
Aiken Technical College Aiken, SC 29801; public; 1,100
Aims Community College Greeley, CO 80631; public; 4,800
Alabama Aviation and Technical College Ozark, AL 36360; public; 720
Alabama Christian College Montgomery, AL 36193; private; 1,600
Alabama Lutheran Academy and College Selma, AL 36701; private; 230
Alabama State University Montgomery, AL 36101; public; 4,800
Alabama Technical College Gadsden, AL 35903; public; 960
Albany Business College Albany, NY 12210; private; 750
Albany Junior College Albany GA 31707; private; 1860
Alderson Broaddus College Philippi, WV 26416; private; 820
Alexander City State Junior College Alexander City, AL 35010; public; 1,200
Alice Lloyd College Pippa Passes, KY 41844; private; 400
Allan Hancock College Santa Maria, CA 93454; public; 9,000
Allegany Community College Cumberland, MD 21502; public; 1,800
Allen County Community Junior College Iola, KS 66749; public; 950
Allentown Business School Allentown, PA 18101; private; 350
Alliance College Cambridge Springs, PA 16403; private; 250
Alpena Community College Alpena, MI 49707; public; 2,000
Alvernia College Reading, PA 19607; private; 700
Alverno College Milwaukee, WI 53215; private; 1,400
Alvin Community College Alvin, TX 77511; public; 3,100
Amarillo College Amarillo, TX 79178; public; 5,200
American Academy of Art Chicago, IL 60604; private; 980
American Academy of Dramatic Arts New York, NY 10016; private; 450
American Academy of Dramatic Arts-West Pasadena, CA 91104; private; 260
American College in Paris 75007 Paris, France; private; 550
American College of Puerto Rico Bayamon, PR 00619; private; 1,800
American College of Switzerland Les Avants/Montreux, Switzerland 1833; private; 240
American Institute of Business Des Moines, IA 50321; private; 900
American River College—Placerville Placerville, CA 95667; public; 2,800
American River College—Sacramento Sacramento, CA 95841; public; 21,400
American Samoa Community College Pago Pago, American Samoa 96799; public; 1,200
Anchorage Community College Anchorage, AK 99504; public; 9,100
Ancilla College Donaldson, IN 46513; private; 300
Anderson College Anderson, SC 29621; private; 1,200
Andover College Portland, ME 04101; private; 580
Andrew College Cuthbert, GA 31740; private; 350
Angelina College Lufkin, TX 75901; private; 2,100
Anne Arundel Community College Arnold, MD 21012; public; 7,400
Anoka-Ramsey Community College Coon Rapids, MN 55433; public; 4,300
Anson Technical Institute Ansonville, NC 28007; public; 500
Antelope Valley College Lancaster, CA 93534; public; 7,000
Aquinas Junior College Milton, MA 02186; private; 365
Aquinas Junior College Newton, MA 02158; private; 500
Aquinas Junior College Nashville, TN 37205; private; 390
Arapahoe Community College Littleton, CO 80120; public; 6,200
Arizona Western College Yuma, AZ 85364; public; 4,000
Arkansas State University—Beebe Beebe, AR 72012; public; 780
Armstrong College Berkeley, CA 94704; private; 250
Armstrong State College Savannah, GA 31406; public; 3,400
Art Institute of Atlanta Atlanta, GA 30326; private; 650
Asheboro College Asheboro, NC 27203; private; 180
Asheville-Buncombe Technical College Asheville, NC 28801; public; 1,800
Ashland College Ashland, OH 44805; private; 1,600
Ashland Community College Ashland, KY 41101; public; 1,400
Asnuntuck Community College Enfield, CT 06082; public; 1,600
Assumption College for Sisters Mendham, NJ 07945; private; 30
Atlanta Junior College Atlanta, GA 30310; private; 1,400
Atlantic Community College Mays Landing, NJ 08330; public; 3,900
Augusta College Augusta, GA 30910; public; 3,500
Austin Community College Austin, MN 55912; public; 890
Austin Community College Austin, TX 78768; public; 12,000
Averett College Danville, VA 24541; private; 1000

Bacone College Muskogee, OK 74401; private 500
Bainbridge Junior College Bainbridge, GA 31717; private; 600
Baker Junior College Flint, MI 48507; private; 1,600
Bakersfield College Bakersfield, CA 93305; public; 13,600
Bangor Community College Bangor, ME 04401; public; 750
Barstow College Barstow, CA 92311; public; 1,500
Bartlesville Wesleyan College Bartlesville, OK 74003; private; 700
Barton County Community College Great Bend, KS 67530; public; 2,500
Bassist College Portland, OR 97205; private; 180
Bauder Fashion College Miami, FL 33131; private; 620
Bayamon Central University Bayamon, PR 00619; public; 3000
Bay de Noc Community College Escanaba, MI 49829; public; 1,500
Bay Path Junior College Longmeadow, MA 01106; private; 700
Bay State Junior College of Business Boston, MA 02116; private; 930
Beal College Bangor, ME 04401; private; 590
Beaufort County Community College Beaufort, SC 29902; public; 1,100
Beaufort Technical College Beaufort, SC 29902; public; 1,600
Becker Junior College—Leicester Leicester, MA 01524; private; 510
Becker Junior College—Worcester Worcester, MA 01609; private; 680
Beckley College Beckley, WV 25801; private; 1,300
Bee County College Beeville, TX 78102; public; 2,000
Beirut University College Beirut, Lebanon; public; 390
Bellarmine College Louisville, KY 40205; private; 2,000
Belleville Area College Belleville, IL 62221; public; 12,500
Bellevue Community College Bellevue, WA 98007; public; 10,500
Belmont College Nashville, TN 37203; private; 1,700
Belmont Technical College St. Clairsville, OH 43950; private; 1,200
Bemidji State University Bemidji, MN 56601; public; 4,200
Bergen Community College Paramus, NJ 07652; public; 11,000
Berkeley School Little Falls, NJ 07424; public; 540
Berkeley School—Long Island Hicksville, NY 11801; public; 300
Berkeley School—New York New York, NY 10074; public; 400
Berkeley School—Westchester White Plains, NY 10604; public; 730
Berkshire Community College Pittsfield, MA 01201; public; 3,000
Bessemer State Technical College Bessemer, AL 35021; public; 2,100
Bethany Lutheran College Mankato, MN 56001; private; 280
Bethel College Mishawaka, IN 46544; private; 500
Big Bend Community College Moses Lake, WA 98837; public; 2,600
Bismarck Junior College Bismarck, ND 58501; public; 2,300
Black Hawk College—East Kewanee, IL 61443; public; 1,100
Black Hawk College—Quad-Cities Moline, IL 61265; public; 6,400
Blackhawk Technical Institute Janesville, WI 53545; public; 2,000
Black Hills State College Spearfish, SD 57783; public; 2,200
Bladen Technical College Dublin, NC 28332; public; 500
Blanton's Junior College Asheville, NC 28801; private; 380
Blinn College Brenham, TX 77833; public; 2,500
Bliss College Columbus, OH 43214; private; 450
Bluefield College Bluefield, VA 24605; private; 430
Bluefield State College Bluefield, WV 24701; public; 2,700
Blue Hills Technical Institute Canton, MA 02021; private; 510
Blue Mountain Community College Pendleton, OR 97801; public; 2,500
Blue Ridge Community College Weyers Cave, VA 24486; public; 2,300
Blue Ridge Technical College Flat Rock, NC 28731; public; 950
Boise State University Boise, ID 83725; public; 9,600
Booker T. Washington Business College Birmingham, AL 35203; private; 330
Boricua College New York, NY 10025; private; 870
Bossier Parish Community College Bossier City, LA 71111; public; 1,400
Bowling Green State University—Firelands Huron, OH 44839; public; 1,100
Bradford College Bradford, MA 01830; private; 380
Brainerd Community College Brainerd, MN 56401; public; 620
Brandywine College Wilmington, DE 19803; private; 870
Branson Art Training Center New York, NY 10010; private; 100
Brazosport College Lake Jackson, TX 77566; public; 3,700
Brescia College Owensboro, KY 42301; private; 870
Brevard College Brevard, NC 28712; private; 750
Brevard Community College Cocoa, FL 32922; public; 9,200
Brewer State Junior College Fayette, AL 35555; public; 550
Brewton-Parker College Mount Vernon, GA 30445; private; 900
Briarwood College Southington, CT 06489; private; 350
Bristol College Bristol, TN 37620; private; 250
Bristol Community College Fall River, MA 02720; public; 2,400
Brookdale Community College Lincroft, NJ 07738; public; 1,500
Brookhaven College Farmers Branch, TX 75234; private; 6,300
Brooks College Long Beach, CA 90804; private; 950
Broome Community College Binghamton, NY 13902; public; 6,800
Broward Community College Fort Lauderdale, FL 33301; public; 24,500
Brunswick Junior College Brunswick, GA 31520; public; 1,200
Bryant College Smithfield, RI 02917; private; 2,800
Bryant-Stratton Business Institute Buffalo, NY 14202; private; 460
Bryant-Stratton Business Institute Clarence, NY 14031; private; 400
Bryant-Stratton Business Institute Rochester, NY 14604; private; 3,400
Bucks County Community College Newtown, PA 18940; public; 9,000
Bunker Hill Community College Boston, MA 02129; public; 6,100
Burlington College Burlington, VT 05401; private; 120
Burlington County College Pemberton, NJ 08068; public; 7,000
Butler County Community College El Dorado, KS 67042; public; 2,200
Butler County Community College Butler, PA 16001; public; 2,350
Butler University Indianapolis, IN 46208; private; 2,100
Butte Community College Oroville, CA 95965; public; 10,000

Cabrillo College Aptos, CA 95003; private; 9,400
C.A. Fredd State Technical College Tuscaloosa, AL 35401; 380
Caguas City College Caguas, PR 00625; public; 850
Caldwell Community College and Technical Institute Lenoir, NC 28645; public; 2,000
Calhoun State Community College Decatur, AL 35602; public; 5,200
Calumet College Whiting, IN 46394; private; 1,400
Camden County College Blackwood, NJ 08012; public; 8,400
Canada College Redwood City, CA 94061; public; 9,000
Cape Cod Community College Barnstable, MA 02668; public; 1,800
Cape Fear Technical Institute Wilmington, NC 28401; public; 1,900
Capital City Business College Little Rock, AR 72204; private; 570
Capitol Institute of Technology Kensington, MD 20795; private; 800

Cardinal Stritch College Milwaukee, WI 53217; private; 740

Caribbean University College Bayamon, PR 00619; private; 1,600

Carl Albert Junior College Poteau, OK 74953; public; 1,600

Carl Sandburg College Galesburg, IL 61401; public; 3,500

Carroll College Helena, MT 59625; private; 1,400

Carteret Technical College Morehead City, NC 28557; public; 990

Casco Bay College Portland, ME 04101; private; 270

Casper College Casper, WY 82601; public; 1,600

Castle Junior College Windham, NH 03087; private; 120

Castleton State College Castleton, VT 05735; public; 1,300

Catawba Valley Technical College Hickory, NC 28601; public; 2,300

Catonsville Community College Catonsville, MD 21228; public; 11,900

Cayuga County Community College Auburn, NY 13021; public; 2,800

Cazenovia College Cazenovia, NY 13035; private; 540

Cecil Community College North East, MD 21901; public; 1,200

Cecils Junior College Asheville, NC 28806; private; 250

Cedar Valley College Lancaster, TX 75134; private; 1,800

Centenary College Hackettstown, NJ 07840; private; 700

Center for Degree Studies Scranton, PA 18515; private; 6,000

Center for Early Education Los Angeles, CA 90048; private; 20

Central Arizona College Coolidge, AZ 85228; public; 6,900

Central Carolina Technical College Sanford, NC 27330; public; 2,100

Central City Business Institute Syracuse, NY 13203; private; 1,000

Central College McPherson, KS 67460; private; 280

Central Florida Community College Ocala, FL 32670; public; 2,800

Centralia Community College Centralia, WA 98531; public; 5,300

Central Maine Vocational-Technical Institute Auburn, ME 04210; public; 380

Central New England College of Technology Worcester, MA 01610; private; 660

Central Ohio Technical College Newark, OH 43055; public; 1,200

Central Oregon Community College Bend, OR 97701; public; 7,000

Central Pennsylvania Business School Summerdale, PA 17093; private; 800

Central Piedmont Community College Charlotte, NC 28204; public; 24,600

Central Technical Community College Hastings, NE 68901; public; 1,620

Central Texas College Killeen, TX 76541; public; 5,000

Central Virginia Community College Lynchburg, VA 24502; public; 4,000

Central Wyoming College Riverton, WY 82501; public; 700

Central YMCA Community College Chicago, IL 60606; private; 5,000

Cerritos College Norwalk, CA 90650; public; 21,000

Cerro Coso Community College Ridgecrest, CA 93555; public; 4,000

Chabot College Hayward, CA 94545; public; 18,900

Chadron State College Chadron, NE 69337; public; 1,900

Chaffey College Alta Loma, CA 91701; public; 12,000

Chamberlayne Junior College Boston, MA. 02116; private; 950

Chaminade University of Honolulu Honolulu, HI 96816; private; 2,200

Champlain College Burlington, VT 05402; private; 1,900

Charles County Community College La Plata, MD 20646; private; 3,800

Charles S. Mott Community College Flint, MI 48503; public; 9,000

Chatfield College St. Martin, OH 45118; private; 200

Chattahoochee Valley Community College Phenix City, AL 36867; public; 2,400

Chattanooga State Technical Community College Chattanooga, TN 37406; public; 4,900

Chauncey Sparks State Technical College Eufaula, AL 36027; public; 480

Chemeketa Community College Salem, OR 97309; public; 43,000

Chesapeake College Wye Mills, MD 21679; public; 3,200

Chesterfield-Marlboro Technical College Cheraw, SC 29520; public; 610

Chicago City College—Daley Chicago, IL 60652; public; 5,400

Chicago City College—Kennedy/King Chicago, IL 60621; public; 9,200

Chicago City College—Loop Chicago, IL 60601; public; 7,500

Chicago City College—Malcolm X Chicago, IL 60612; public; 4,800

Chicago City College—Truman Chicago, IL 60640; public; 6,000

Chicago City College—Wilbur Wright Chicago, IL 60634; public; 6,700

Chicago City-wide College Chicago, IL 60601; public; 13,000

Chipola Junior College Marianna, FL 32446; public; 1,100

Chowan College Murfreesboro, NC 27855; private; 1,100

Christ College—Irvine Irvine, CA 92715; private; 220

Cincinnati Bible College Cincinnati, OH 45204; private; 600

Cincinnati Technical College Cincinnati, OH 45223; public, 3,800

Cisco Junior College Cisco, TX 76437; public; 1,500

Citrus College Azusa, CA 91702; public; 9,000

City College of San Francisco San Francisco, CA 94112; public; 29,500

Clackamas Community College Oregon City, OR 97045; public; 6,200

Claremore Junior College Claremore, OK 74017; public; 1,900

Clarendon College Clarendon, TX 79226; public; 950

Clarion State College—Venango Oil City, PA 16301; public; 450

Clark College Indianapolis, IN 46202; public; 700

Clark College Vancouver, WA 98663; public; 5,300

Clark County Community College North Las Vegas, NV 89030; public; 10,800

Clarke College Newton, MS 39345; private; 170

Clark Technical College Springfield, OH 45501; public; 2,700

Clatsop Community College Astoria, OR 97103; public; 3,000

Clayton Junior College Morrow, GA 30260; public; 3,000

Cleary College Ypsilanti, MI 48197; public; 700

Cleveland State Community College Cleveland, TN 37311; public; 3,500

Cleveland Technical College Shelby, NC 28150; public; 1,200

Clinton Community College Clinton, IA 52732; public; 900

Clinton Community College Plattsburg, NY 12901; public; 1,300

Clinton Junior College Rock Hill, SC 29730; public; 130

Cloud County Community College Concordia, KS 66901; public; 2,300

Coahoma Junior College Clarksdale, MS 38614; public; 1,400

Coastal Carolina Community College Jacksonville, NC 28540; public; 2,400

Coastline Community College Fountain Valley, CA 92708; public; 28,000

Cochise College Douglas, AZ 85607; public; 4,200

Coffeyville Community College Coffeyville, KS 67337; public; 1,000

Colby Community College Colby, KS 67701; public; 2,100

Colby-Sawyer College New London, NH 03257; private; 700

Coleman College San Diego, CA 92110; private; 800

College Misercordia Dallas, PA 18612; private; 1,120

College of Alameda Alameda, CA 94501; public; 7,500

College of Boca Raton Boca Raton, FL 33431; private; 550

College of Du Page Glen Ellyn, IL 60137; public; 26,300

College of Eastern Utah Price, UT 84501; public; 1,100

College of Ganado Ganado, AZ 86505; private; 450

College of Insurance New York, NY 10038; private; 1,900

College of Lake County Grayslake, IL 60030; public; 11,200

College of Marin Kentfield, CA 94904; public; 6,900

College of Notre Dame Belmont, CA 94002; private; 950

College of San Mateo San Mateo, CA 94402; public; 15,000

College of Southern Idaho Twin Falls, ID 83301; public; 3,200

College of St. Joseph the Provider Rutland, VT 05701; private; 290

College of St. Mary Omaha, NE 68124; private; 750

College of the Academy of the New Church Bryn Athyn, PA 19009; private; 130

College of the Albemarle Elizabeth City, NC 27909; public; 1,200

College of the Canyons Valencia, CA 91355; public; 3,700

College of the Desert Palm Desert, CA 92260; public; 11,000

College of the Mainland Texas City, TX 77590; public; 2,500

College of the Redwoods Eureka, CA 95501; public; 9,500

College of the Sequoias Visalia, CA 93277; public; 7,600

College of the Siskiyous Weed, CA 96094; public; 2,500

College of the Virgin Islands St. Thomas, VI 00801; public; 1,500

Colorado Mountain College—East Leadville, CO 80461; public; 800

Colorado Mountain College—West Glenwood Springs, CO 81601; public; 740

Colorado Northwestern Community College Rangely, CO 81648; public; 1,500

Columbia Basin College Tri-Cities, WA 99302; public; 2,000

Columbia Christian College Portland, OR 97220; private; 310

Columbia College Columbia, CA 95310; private; 3,750

Columbia College Columbia, MO 65216; private; 850

Columbia College-Hollywood Hollywood, CA 90038; private; 300

Columbia—Greene Community College Hudson, NY 12534; public; 1,300

Columbia Junior College of Business Columbia, SC 29201; private; 880

Columbia State Community College Columbia, TN 38401; public; 1,900

Columbia Union College Takoma Park, MD 20012; private; 870

Columbus College Columbus, GA 31907; public; 4,000

Columbus International College Seville-13, Spain; private; 180

Columbus Technical Institute Columbus, OH 43216; public; 7,500

Community College of Allegheny County—Allegheny Pittsburgh, PA 15212; public; 6,800

Community College of Allegheny County—North Pittsburgh, PA 15237; public; 3,000

Community College of Allegheny County—South West Mifflin, PA 15122; public; 3,000

Community College of Baltimore Baltimore, MD 21202; public; 7,800

Community College of Beaver County Monaca, PA 15021; public; 2,200

Community College of Denver—Auraria Denver, CO 80204; public; 4,000

Community College of Denver—North Campus Westminster, CO 80030; public; 5,200

Community College of Denver—Red Rocks Golden, CO 80401; public; 5,400

Community College of Philadelphia Philadelphia, PA 19107; public; 11,800

Community College of Rhode Island—Flanagan Lincoln, RI 02865; public; 3,100

Community College of Rhode Island—Knight Warwick, RI 02866; public; 4,600

Community College of the Air Force Montgomery, AL 36112; public; 127,000

Community College of the Finger Lakes Canandaigua, NY 14424; public; 2,900

Community College of Vermont Montpelier, VT 05602; public; 2,200

Compton Community College Compton, CA 90221; public; 6,000

Concordia College Ann Arbor, MI 48105; private; 550

Concordia College Bronxville, NY 10708; private; 400

Concordia College Portland, OR 97211; private; 330

Concordia College Milwaukee, WI 53208; private; 520

Concordia Lutheran College Austin, TX 78705; private; 360

Connors State College Warner, OK 74469; public; 1,300

Contra Costa College San Pablo, CA 94806; public; 9,028

Cooke County College Gainesville, TX 76240; public; 1,500

Copiah-Lincoln Junior College Wesson, MS 39191; public; 1,500

Corning Community College Corning, NY 14830; public; 2,800

Cosumnes River College Sacramento, CA 95823; public; 6,000

Cottey College Nevada, MO 64772; private; 350

County College of Morris Randolph, NJ 07869; public; 10,700

Cowley County Community College Arkansas City, KS 67005; public; 1,800

Crafton Hills College Yucaipa, CA 92399; public; 3,600

Crandall College Macon, GA 31201; private; 350

Craven Community College New Bern, NC 28560; public; 1,400

Crosier Seminary Junior College Onamia, MN 56359; private; 30

Crowder College Neosho, MO 64850; public; 1,200

Crowley's Ridge College Paragould, AR 72450; private; 60

Cuesta College San Luis Obispo, CA 93406; public; 6,000

Culinary Institute of America Hyde Park, NY 12538; private; 1,700

Culver-Stockton College Canton, MO 63435; private; 530

Cumberland College of Tennessee Lebanon, TN 37087; private; 500

Cumberland County College Vineland, NJ 08360; public; 2,500

CUNY—Borough of Manhattan Community College New York, NY 10019; public; 8,700

CUNY—Bronx Community College Bronx, NY 10453; public; 7,600

CUNY—Hostos Community College Bronx, NY 10451; public; 3,000

CUNY—John Jay College of Criminal Justice New York, NY 10019; public; 5,500

CUNY—Kingborough Community College Manhattan Beach, Brooklyn, NY 11235; public; 10,000

CUNY—LaGuardia Community College Long Island City, NY 11101; public; 6,500

CUNY—Medgar Evers College Brooklyn, NY 11225; public; 3,000

CUNY—New York City Technical College Brooklyn, NY 11201; public; 14,000

CUNY—Queensborough Community College Bayside, NY 11364; public; 1,800

Cuyahoga Community College—Eastern Warrensville Township, OH 44122; public; 4,700

Cuyahoga Community College—Metropolitan Cleveland, OH 44115; public; 10,000

Cuyahoga Community College—Western Parma, OH 44130; public; 12,500

Cypress College Cypress, CA 90630; public; 12,500

Dabney S. Lancaster Community College Clifton Forge, VA 24422; public; 1,100

Dakota State College Madison, SD 57042; public; 900

Dakota Wesleyan University

Mitchell, SD 57301; private; 510
Dalton Junior College Dalton, GA 30720; private; 1,400
Daniel Webster College Nashua, NH 03063; private; 500
Danville Area Community College Danville, IL 61832; public; 1,300
Danville Community College Danville, VA 24541; public; 2,700
Davenport College Grand Rapids, MI 49503; private; 3,000
Davidson County Community College Lexington, NC 27292; public; 2,000
Davis Junior College Toledo, OH 43604; private; 250
Dawson Community College Glendive, MT 59330; public; 350
Daytona Beach Community College Daytona Beach, FL 32015; public; 4,500
Dean Junior College Franklin, MA 02038; private; 1,900
De Anza College Cupertino, CA 95014; 29,000
Dekalb Community College Clarkston, GA 30021; public; 13,900
Delaware County Community College Media, PA 19063; public; 6,000
Delaware Technical and Community College—Southern Georgetown, DE 19947; public; 2,900
Delaware Technical and Community College—Stanton Newark, DE 19702; public; 2,400
Delaware Technical and Community College—Terry Dover, DE 19901; public; 1,200
Delaware Technical and Community College—Wilmington Wilmington, DE 19801; public; 1,540
Delgado College—City Park New Orleans, LA 70119; public; 9,000
Del Mar College Corpus Christi, TX 78404; public; 8,300
Delta College University Center, MI 48710; public; 9,500
Denmark Technical College Denmark, SC 29042; public; 670
Des Moines Area Community College—Ankeny Ankeny, IA 50021; public; 5,700
Des Moines Area Community College—Boone Boone, IA 50036; public; 650
Detroit College of Business Dearborn, MI 48126; private; 2,400
DeVry Institute of Technology Phoenix, AZ 85016; private; 3,200
DeVry Institute of Technology Atlanta, GA 30341; private; 1,700
DeVry Institute of Technology Chicago, IL 60618; private; 3,800
Diablo Valley College Pleasant Hill, CA 94523; public; 13,500
District One Technical Institute Eau Claire, WI 54701; public; 3,000
Dixie College Saint George, UT 84770; public; 1,600
Dodge City Community College Dodge City, KS 67801; public; 1,200
Dominican College Orangeburg, NY 10962; private; 1,300
Don Bosco Technical Institute Rosemead, CA 91770; private; 340
Donnelly College Kansas City, KS 66102; private; 930
Douglas MacArthur State Technical College Opp, AL 36467; public; 500
D-Q University Davis, CA 95616; private; 140
Draughon's Junior College Savannah, GA 31406; private; 750
Draughon's Junior College Memphis, TN 38116; private; 900
Draughon's Junior College of Business—Knoxville Branch Knoxville, TN 37919; private; 590
Draughon's Junior College of Business—Nashville Branch Nashville, TN 37203; private; 450
Dundalk Community College Baltimore, MD 21222; public; 2,300
Durham Technical Institute Durham, NC 27703; public; 2,600
Dutchess Community College Poughkeepsie, NY 12601; public; 6,700
Dyersburg State Community College Dyersburg, TN 38024; public; 1,100
Dyke College Cleveland, OH 44114; private; 1,400

East Arkansas Community College Forrest City, AR 72335; public; 850
East Central Junior College Decatur, MS 39327; public; 2,100
East Central Junior College Union, MO 63084; public; 790
Eastern Arizona College Thatcher, AZ 85552; public; 3,700
Eastern Connecticut State College Willimantic, CT 06226; public; 2,300
Eastern Maine Vocational Technical Institute Bangor, ME 04401; public; 600
Eastern Mennonite College Harrisonburg, VA 22801; private; 960
Eastern New Mexico University—Clovis Clovis, NM 88101; public; 880
Eastern New Mexico University—Roswell Roswell, NM 88201; public; 1,200
Eastern Oklahoma State College Wilburton, OK 74578; public; 2,400
Eastern Shore Community College Melfa, VA 23410; public; 500
Eastern Wyoming College Torrington, WY 82240; public; 810
Eastfield College Mesquite, TX 75150; public; 8,200
East Los Angeles College Monterey Park, CA 91754; public; 16,500
East Mississippi Junior College Scooba, MS 39358; public; 330
Edgecombe Technical Institute Tarboro, NC 27886; public; 1,000
Edgewood College Madison, WI 53711; private; 700
Edinboro State College Edinboro, PA 16412; public; 4,900
Edison Community College Fort Myers, FL 33907; public; 5,500
Edison State Community College Piqua, OH 45356; public 2,000
Edmonds Community College Lynnwood, WA 98036; public; 8,000
Edmondson Junior College Chattanooga, TN 37411; private; 420
Edward Williams College Hackensack, NJ 07601; private; 600
El Camino College Via Torrance, CA 90506; public; 30,500
El Centro College of the Dallas County Community College District Dallas, TX 75202; public; 6,400
Electronic Data Processing College of Puerto Rico Hato Rey, PR 00918; public; 1,800
Elgin Community College Elgin, IL 60120; public; 5,500
Elizabeth Seton College Yonkers, NY 10701; private; 1,200
Elizabethtown College Elizabethtown, PA 17022; private; 1,500
Elizabethtown Community College Elizabethtown, KY 42701; public; 1,800
Elkhart Institute of Technology Elkhart, IN 46514; private; 450
Ellsworth Community College Iowa Falls, IA 50126; public; 990
Elmira College Elmira, NY 14901; private; 1,100
El Paso Community College El Paso, TX 79998; public; 13,000
El Reno Junior College El Reno, OK 73036; public; 1,400
Emanuel County Junior College Swainsboro, GA 30401; private; 440
Embry-Riddle Aeronautical University Prescott, AZ 83602; private; 830
Emmanuel College Franklin Springs, GA 30639; private; 500
Emmanuel College Boston, MA 02115; private; 380
Emporia State University Emporia, KS 66801; public; 4,500
Endicott College Beverly, MA 01915; private; 810
Enterprise State Junior College Enterprise, AL 36330; public; 1,900
Erie Community College-North Buffalo, NY 14221; public; 780
Essex Agricultural and Technical Institute Hathorne, MA 01937; public; 700
Essex Community College Baltimore, MD 21237; public; 9,600
Essex County College Newark, NJ 07102; public; 6,300
Everett Community College Everett, WA 98201; public; 9,000
Evergreen Valley College San Jose, CA 95135; public; 9,200

Fairmont State College Fairmont, WV 26554; public; 5,200
Fashion and Art Institute of Dallas Dallas, TX 75220; private; 200
Fashion Institute of Design and Merchandising Los Angeles, CA 90014; private; 2,500
Faulkner State Junior College Bay Minette, AL 36507; public; 1,700
Fayetteville Technical Institute Fayetteville, NC 28303; public; 5,300
Feather River College Quincy, CA 95971; private; 870
Felician College Chicago, IL 60659; private; 410
Felician College Lodi, NJ 07644; private; 760
Fergus Falls Community College Fergus Falls, MN 56537; public; 500
Ferrum College Ferrum, VA 24088; private; 1,500
Findlay College Findlay, OH 45840; private; 1,100
Fisher Junior College Boston, MA 02116; private; 560
Five Towns College Merrick, NY 11566; private; 400
Flathead Valley Community College Kalispell, MT 59901; public; 1,500
Florence-Darlington Technical College Florence, SC 29501; public; 2,200
Florida Beacon College Largo, FL 33541; private; 50
Florida College Temple Terrace, FL 33617; private; 500
Florida Institute of Technology Melbourne, FL 32901; private; 3,700
Florida Institute of Technology School of Applied Technology Jensen Beach, FL 33457; private; 900
Florida Junior College—Jacksonville Jacksonville, FL 32202; public; 14,100
Florida Keys Community College Key West, FL 33040; public; 2,200
Floyd Junior College Rome, GA 30161; public; 1,400
Foothill College Los Altos, CA 94022; public; 14,000
Forsyth School for Dental Hygienists Boston, MA 02115; private; 200
Forsyth Technical Institute Winston-Salem, NC 27103; public; 2,700
Fort Hays State University Hays, KS 67601; public; 4,200
Fort Lewis College Durango, CO 81301; public; 3,300
Fort Scott Community Junior College Fort Scott, KS 66701; public; 1,100
Fort Steilacoom Community College Tacoma, WA 98499; public; 10,300
Fort Wayne Bible College Fort Wayne, IN 46807; private; 480
Fox Valley Technical Institute Appleton, WI 54911; 7,000
Franklin College Switzerland New York, NY 10021; private; 160
Franklin Institute of Boston Boston, MA 02116; private; 550
Franklin University Columbus, OH 43215; private; 4,600
Frank Phillips College Borger, TX 79007; public; 820
Frederick Community College Frederick, MD 21701; public; 2,100
Freed-Hardeman College Henderson, TN 38340; private; 1,500
Freeman Junior College Freeman, SD 57029; private; 80
Fresno City College Fresno, CA 93741; public; 15,400
Friendship College Rock Hill, SC 29730; private; 400
Fullerton College Fullerton, CA 92634; public; 19,100
Fulton-Montgomery Community College Johnstown, NY 12095; public; 1,600

Gadsden State Junior College Gadsden, AL 35903; public; 3,700
Gainesville Junior College Gainesville, GA 30501; private; 1,600
Galveston College Galveston, TX 77550; public; 1,300
Garden City Community College Garden City, KS 67846; public; 1,500
Garland County Community College Hot Springs, AR 71901; public; 1,500
Garrett Community College McHenry, MD 21541; public; 650
Gaston College Dallas, NC 28034; private; 2,800
Gateway Technical Institute—Elkhorn Elkhorn, WI 53121; public; 100
Gateway Technical Institute—Kenosha Kenosha, WI 53140; public; 7,200
Gateway Technical Institute—Racine Racine, WI 53403; public; 5,300
Gavilan Community College Gilroy, CA 95020; public; 3,200
Genesee Community College Batavia, NY 14020; public; 2,300
Geneva College Beaver Falls, PA 15010; private; 1,400
George Corley Wallace State Community College Selma, AL 36701; public; 2,000
George C. Wallace State Community College Dothan, AL 36301; public; 3,000
George C. Wallace State Community College Hanceville, AL 35077; public; 1,700
Georgia Military College Milledgeville, GA 31061; public; 450
Georgia State University Atlanta, GA 30303; public; 13,400
Germanna Community College Locust Grove, VA 22508; public; 1,200
Glendale Community College Glendale, AZ 85302; public; 1,400
Glendale Community College Glendale, CA 91208; public; 10,000
Glen Oaks Community College Centreville, MI 49032; public; 1,200
Glenville State College Glenville, WV 26351; public; 1,900
Gloucester County College Sewell, NJ 08080; public; 3,100
Gogebic Community College Ironwood, MI 49938; public; 1,500
Golden Valley Lutheran College Minneapolis, MN 55422; private; 590
Golden West College Huntington Beach, CA 92647; public; 22,100
Goldey Beacom College Wilmington, DE 19808; private; 1,040
Gordon Junior College Barnesville, GA 30204; public; 1,500
Grand Rapids Junior College Grand Rapids, MI 49503; public; 12,000
Grand Rapids School of the Bible and Music Grand Rapids, MI 49506; private; 550
Grand View College Des Moines, IA 50316; private; 1,300
Grays Harbor College Aberdeen, WA 98520; public; 3,100
Grayson County College Denison, TX 75020; public; 3,600
Greater Hartford Community College Hartford, CT 06105; public; 2,800
Greater New Haven State Technical College North Haven, CT 06473; public; 600
Greenfield Community College Greenfield Community College Greenfield, MA 01301; public; 2,400
Green Mountain College Poultney, VT 05764; private; 500
Green River Community College Auburn, WA 98002; public; 8,000
Greenville Technical College Greenville, SC 29606; public; 12,000
Grossmont College El Cajon, CA 92020; public; 15,900
Guilford Technical Institute Jamestown, NC 27282; public; 4,200
Gulf Coast Community College Panama City, FL 32401; public; 4,300
Gwynedd-Mercy College Gwynedd Valley, PA 19437; private; 1,900

Hagerstown Junior College Hagerstown, MD 21740; private; 2,200
Halifax Community College Weldon, NC 27890; public; 980
Hannibal-LaGrange College Hannibal, MO 63401; private; 450
Harcum Junior College Bryn Mawr, PA 19010; private; 800
Hardbarger Junior College of Business Raleigh, NC 27602; public; 1,200
Harford Community College Bel Air, MD 21014; public; 4,200
Harper Councill Trenholm State Technical College Montgomery, AL 36108; public; 1,100

Harriman College Harriman, NY 10926; private; 400
Harrington Institute of Interior Design Chicago, IL 60605; private; 500
Harrisburg Area Community College Harrisburg, PA 17110; public; 5,500
Harry M. Ayers State Technical College Anniston, AL 36202; public; 680
Hartford College for Women Hartford, CT 06105; private; 230
Hartford State Technical College Hartford, CT 06106; public; 1,800
Hartnell College Salinas, CA 93901; public; 8,000
Haskell Indian Junior College Lawrence, KS 66044; public; 1,100
Hawaii Pacific College Honolulu, HI 96813; public; 1,600
Hawkeye Institute of Technology Waterloo, IA 50704; public; 2,000
Haywood Technical College Clyde, NC 28721; public; 890
Hazard Community College Hazard, KY 41701; public; 300
Henderson Community College Henderson, KY 42420; public; 840
Henderson County Junior College Athens, TX 75751; public; 2,700
Henry Ford Community College Dearborn, MI 48128; public; 16,500
Herkimer County Community College Herkimer, NY 13350; public; 2,200
Hesser College Manchester, NH 03101; public; 1,300
Hesston College Hesston, KS 67062; private; 680
Hibbing Community College Hibbing, MN 55746; public; 800
Highland Community College Freeport, IL 61032; public; 2,000
Highland Community College Highland, KS 66035; public; 650
Highland Park Community College Highland Park, MI 48203; public; 2,700
Highline Community College Midway, WA 98031; public; 10,000
Hilbert College Hamburg, NY 14075; private; 600
Hill Junior College Hillsboro, TX 76645; public; 1,100
Hillsborough Community College Tampa, FL 33622; public; 11,000
Hillsdale Free Will Baptist College Moore, OK 73153; private; 160
Hinds Junior College Raymond, MS 39154; public; 6,800
Hiwassee College Madisonville, TN 37354; private; 580
Hobson State Technical College Thomasville, AL 36784; public; 360
Hocking Technical College Nelsonville, OH 45764; public; 2,600
Holmes Junior College Goodman, MS 39079; private; 750
Holy Cross Junior College Notre Dame, IN 46556; private; 290
Holyoke Community College Holyoke, MA 01040; public; 4,900
Honolulu Community College Honolulu, HI 96817; public; 4,500
Hopkinsville Community College Hopkinsville, KY 42240; public; 1,000
Horry-Georgetown Technical College Conway, SC 29526; public; 550
Houghton College—Buffalo West Seneca, NY 14224; private; 120
Housatonic Community College Bridgeport, CT 06608; public; 2,800
Houston Community College Houston, TX 77007; public; 26,800
Howard College Big Spring, TX 79720; public; 1,200
Howard Community College Columbia, MD 21044; public; 3,100
Hudson County Community College Commission Jersey City, NJ 07306; public; 2,800
Hudson Valley Community College Troy, NY 12180; public; 6,500
Humacao University College Humacao, PR 00661; public; 3,200
Humphreys College Stockton, CA 95207; private; 280
Husson College Bangor, ME 04401; private; 1,200
Hutchinson Community College Hutchinson, KS 67501; public; 2,600

Illinois Central College East Peoria, IL 61635; public; 14,500
Illinois Eastern Community College—Frontier Fairfield, IL 62837; public; 3,400
Illinois Eastern Community College—Lincoln Trail Robinson, IL 62454; public; 1,600
Illinois Eastern Community College—Olney Central Olney, IL 62450; public; 2,300
Illinois Eastern Community College—Wabash Valley Mount Carmel, IL 62863; public; 3,000
Illinois Valley Community College Oglesbly, IL 61348; public; 4,200
Immanuel Lutheran College Eau Claire, WI 54701; private; 60
Imperial Valley College Imperial, CA 92251; public; 6,000
Independence Community College Independence, KS 67301; public; 1,100
Indiana Business College Indianapolis, IN 46204; private; 300
Indiana Central University Indianapolis, IN 46227; private; 2,900
Indiana University—East Richmond, IN 47374; public; 1,500
Indiana University—Kokomo Kokomo, IN 46901; public; 2,700
Indiana University of Pennsylvania—Armstrong County Kittanning, PA 16201; public; 440
Indiana University of Pennsylvania—Punxsutawney Punxsutawney, PA 15767; public; 270
Indiana University—Purdue University at Fort Wayne Fort Wayne, IN 46805; public; 7,900
Indiana University—Purdue University at Indianapolis Indianapolis, IN 46202; public; 14,500
Indiana University—Southeast New Albany, IN 47150; public; 3,900
Indiana Vocational Technical College—Columbus Columbus, IN 47201; public; 790
Indiana Vocational Technical College—Eastcentral Muncie, IN 47302; public; 2,200
Indiana Vocational Technical College—Fort Wayne Fort Wayne, IN 46805; public; 3,500
Indiana Vocational Technical College—Indianapolis Indianapolis, IN 46202; public; 4,500
Indiana Vocational Technical College—Kokomo Kokomo, IN 46901; public; 1,800
Indiana Vocational Technical College—Lafayette Lafayette, IN 47904; public; 1,100
Indiana Vocational Technical College—Northcentral South Bend, IN 46619; public; 2,100
Indiana Vocational Technical College—Northwest Gary, IN 46409; public; 2,700
Indiana Vocational Technical College—Southcentral Sellersburg, IN 47172; public; 1,200
Indiana Vocational Technical College—Southeast Madison, IN 47250; public; 400
Indiana Vocational Technical College—Southwest Evansville, IN 47710; public; 1,500
Indiana Vocational Technical College—Terre Haute Terre Haute, IN 47802; public; 1,500
Indiana Vocational Technical College—Whitewater Richmond, IN 47374; public; 920
Indian Hills Community Center—Centerville Centerville, IA 52544; public; 300
Indian Hills Community College—Airport Ottumwa, IA 52501; public; 1,400
Indian Hills Community College—Ottumwa Heights Ottumwa, IA 52501; public; 350
Indian River Community College Fort Pierce, FL 33450; public; 6,500
Indian Valley Colleges Novato, CA 94947; public; 3,600
Institute of American Indian Arts Santa Fe, NM 87501; public; 200
Institute of Design and Construction Brooklyn, NY 11201; public; 280
Instituto Tecnico Comercial Junior College Rio Piedras, PR 00926; private; 1,300
Inter-American University Aquadilla Regional College Aquadilla, PR 00603; public; 1,700
Inter-American University Arecibo Regional College Arecibo, PR 00612; public; 1,200
Inter-American University Barranquitas Regional College Barranquitas, PR 00615; public; 1,200
Inter-American University Fajardo Regional College Fajardo, PR 00648; public; 1,200
Inter-American University Guayama Regional College Guayama, PR 00654; public; 1,000
Inter-American University Metropolitan Campus Hato Rey, PR 00919; public; 10,900
Inter-American University Ponce Regional College Ponce, PR 00731; public; 1,800
Interboro Institute New York, NY 10003; private; 540
International Bible College Florence, AL 35630; private; 150
International Business College Fort Wayne, IN 46804; private; 480
International Fine Arts College Miami, FL 33132; private; 260
Inver Hills Community College Inver Grove Heights, MN 55075; public; 4,000
Iowa Central Community College Fort Dodge, IA 50533; public; 2,900
Iowa Lakes Community College—Estherville Estherville, IA 51334; public; 1,700
Iowa Lakes Community College—South Emmetsburg, IA 50536; public; 670
Iowa Western Community College Council Bluffs, IA 51501; public; 2,700
Iowa Western Community College—Clarinda Clarinda, IA 51632; public; 300
Isothermal Community College Spindale, NC 28139; public; 70
Itasca Community College Grand Rapids, MN 55744; public; 500
Itawamba Junior College Fulton, MS 38843; public; 1,500

Jackson Community College Jackson, MI 49201; public; 11,500
Jackson State Community College Jackson, TN 38301; public; 2,700
Jacksonville College Jacksonville, TX 75766; private; 300
James H. Faulkner State Junior College Bay Minette, AL 36507; public; 1,424
James Sprunt Technical College Kenansville, NC 28349; public; 700
Jamestown Business College Jamestown, NY 14701; private; 280
Jamestown Community College Jamestown, NY 14701; public; 3,900
Jefferson College Hillsboro, MO 63050; public; 2,400
Jefferson Community College Louisville, KY 40201; public; 1,800
Jefferson Community College Watertown, NY 13601; public; 5,000
Jefferson Davis State Junior College Brewton, AL 36426; public; 850
Jefferson State Junior College Birmingham, AL 35215; public; 7,000
Jefferson Technical College Steubenville, OH 43952; public; 1,500
J.F. Drake State Technical College Huntsville, AL 35811; public; 900
John A. Gupton College Nashville, TN 37203; private; 40
John A. Logan College Carterville, IL 62918; public; 2,100
John Brown University Siloam Springs, AR 72761; private; 800
John M. Patterson State Technical College Montgomery, AL 36116; public; 850
Johnson and Wales College Providence, RI 02903; private; 5,500
Johnson County Community College Overland Park, KS 66210; public; 6,400
Johnson School of Technology Scranton, PA 18508; private; 560
Johnson State College Johnson, VT 05656; public; 890
Johnston Technical Institute Smithfield, NC 27577; public; 1,500
John Tyler Community College Chester, VA 23831; public; 4,300
John Wood Community College Overland Park, KS 66210; public; 4,100
Joliet Junior College Joliet, IL 60436; public; 10,690
Jones County Junior College Ellisville, MS 39437; public; 2,400
J. Sargeant Reynolds Community College Richmond, VA 23241; public; 9,900
Judson Baptist College The Dalles, OR 97058; private; 300
Junior College of Albany Albany, NY 12208; private; 960

Kalamazoo Valley Community College Kalamazoo, MI 49009; public; 7,200
Kankakee Community College Kankakee, IL 60901; public; 2,600
Kansas City Kansas Community College Kansas City, KS 66112; public; 3,400
Kansas State University Manhattan, KS 66506; public; 17,000
Kansas Technical Institute Salina, KS 67401; public; 20
Kapiolani Community College Honolulu, HI 96814; public; 4,500
Kaskaskia College Centralia, IL 62801; public; 3,000
Katharine Gibbs School New York, NY 10017; private; 770
Katharine Gibbs School—Huntington Melville, NY 11742; private; 330
Kauai Community College Lihue, Kauai, HI 96766; public; 1,100
Kellogg Community College Battle Creek, MI 49016; public; 4,600
Kemper Military School and College Boonville, MO 65233; private; 70
Kendall College Evanston, IL 60201; private; 400
Kendall School of Design Grand Rapids, MI 49503; private; 500
Kennesaw College Marietta, GA 30061; public; 3,900
Kent State University—Ashtabula Ashtabula, OH 44004; public; 1,100
Kent State University—East Liverpool East Liverpool, OH 43920; public; 630
Kent State University—Geauga Burton, OH 44021; public; 350
Kent State University—Salem Regional Salem, OH 44460; public; 540
Kent State University—Stark Regional Canton, OH 44720; public; 2,000
Kent State University—Trumbull Warren, OH 44483; public; 1,600
Kent State University—Tuscarawas New Philadelphia, OH 44663; public; 880
Kentucky Junior College of Business Lexington, KY 40508; private; 550
Kentucky Wesleyan College Owensboro, KY 42301; private; 970
Ketchikan Community College Ketchikan, AK 99901; public; 1,000
Kettering College of Medical Arts Kettering, OH 45429; private; 430
Keystone Junior College La Plume, PA 18440; private; 800
Kilgore College Kilgore, TX 75662; public; 4,100
Kirkwood Community College Cedar Rapids, IA 52406; public; 5,200
Kirtland Community College Roscommon, MI 48653; public; 1,800
Kishwaukee College Malta, IL 60150; public; 4,000

LaBette Community Junior College Parsons, KS 67351; public; 1,900
Laboratory Institute of Merchandising New York, NY 10022; private; 280
Laboure Junior College Boston, MA 02124; private; 450
Lackawanna Junior College Scranton, PA 18503; private; 1,000
Lake City Community College Lake City, FL 32055; public; 3,000
Lakeland College of Business and Fashion Lakeland, FL 33802; private; 290
Lakeland Community College Mentor, OH 44060; public; 7,600
Lake Land College Mattoon, IL 61938; public; 3,900

Lake Michigan College Benton Harbor, MI 49022; public; 3,500
Lake Region Junior College Devils Lake, ND 58301; public; 550
Lakeshore Technical Institute Cleveland, WI 53015; public; 2,400
Lake-Sumter Community College Leesburg, FL 32748; public; 2,000
Lake Superior State College Sault Ste. Marie, MI 49783; public; 2,500
Lake Tahoe Community College South Lake Tahoe, CA 95702; public; 1,300
Lakewood Community College White Bear Lake, MN 55110; public; 3,800
Lamar Community College Lamar, CO 81052; public; 500
Lamar University—College of Technical Arts Beaumont, TX 77710; public; 11,300
Lander College Greenwood, SC 29646; public; 1,800
Lane Community College Eugene, OR 97405; public; 8,500
Laney College Oakland, CA 94607; public; 13,000
Lansing Community College Lansing, MI 48912; public; 20,000
Laramie County Community College Cheyenne, WY 82001; public; 2,500
Laredo Junior College Laredo, TX 78040; public; 3,400
Lasell Junior College Newton, MA 02166; private; 670
Lassen College Susanville, CA 96130; public; 3,000
Latter-Day Saints Business College Salt Lake City, UT 84111; private; 1,000
Lawrence Institute of Technology Southfield, MI 48075; private; 5,300
Lawson State Community College Birmingham, AL 35221; public; 2,000
Lebanon College Lebanon, NH 03766; private; 70
Lee College Baytown, TX 77520; public; 5,000
Lees Junior College Jackson, KY 41339; private; 300
Lees-McRae College Banner Elk, NC 28604; private; 740
Leeward Community College Pearl City, HI 96782; public; 5,500
Lehigh County Community College Schnecksville, PA 18078; public; 3,500
Lenoir Community College Kinston, NC 28501; public; 1,800
Lewis and Clark Community College Godfrey, IL 62035; public; 5,700
Lewis College of Business Detroit, MI 48235; private; 500
Lewis University Romeoville, IL 60441; private; 2,500
Lexington Technical Institute Lexington, KY 40506; public; 2,100
Lima Technical College Lima, OH 45804; public; 1,900
Lincoln College Lincoln, IL 62656; private; 490
Lincoln Land Community College Springfield, IL 62708; public; 6,500
Lindsey Wilson College Columbia, KY 42728; private; 410
Linn-Benton Community College Albany, OR 97321; public; 8,000
Livingston University Livingston, AL 35470; public; 950
Lockyear College Evansville, IN 47706; private; 1,000
Loma Linda University—La Sierra Riverside, CA 92515; private; 2,300
Lomax-Hannon Junior College Greenville, AL 36037; private; 150
Long Beach City College Long Beach, CA 90808; public; 30,200
Long Island College Hospital School of Nursing Brooklyn, NY 11201; private; 90
Longview Community College Lee's Summit, MO 64063; public; 4,000
Lon Morris College Jacksonville, TX 75766; private; 380
Lorain County Community College Elyria, OH 44035; public; 6,200
Lord Fairfax Community College Middletown, VA 22645; public; 2,000
Los Angeles Baptist College Newhall, CA 91322; private; 360
Los Angeles City College Los Angeles, CA 90029; public, 21,200
Los Angeles Harbor College Wilmington, CA 90744; public; 11,500
Los Angeles Mission College San Fernando, CA 91343; private; 4,000
Los Angeles Pierce College Woodland Hills, CA 91371; public; 23,100
Los Angeles Southwest College Los Angeles, CA 90047; public; 7,000
Los Angeles Trade-Technical College Los Angeles, CA 90015; public; 18,000
Los Angeles Valley College Van Nuys, CA 91401; public; 23,000
Los Medanos College Pittsburg, CA 94565; private; 5,600
Louisburg College Louisburg, NC 27549; private; 750
Louisiana State University—Alexandria Alexandria, LA 71301; public; 1,400
Louisiana State University—Eunice Eunice, LA 70535; public; 1,400
Lourdes College Sylvania, OH 43560; private; 600
Lower Columbia College Longview, WA 98632; public; 5,500
Loyola University New Orleans, LA 70118; private; 3,000
Lurleen B. Wallace State Junior College Andalusia, AL 36420; public; 900
Luzerne County Community College Nanticoke, PA 18634; public; 3,400

MacCormac Junior College Chicago, IL 60604; private; 520
Macomb County Community College—Center Mt. Clemens, MI 48044; public; 28,400
Macomb County Community College—South Warren, MI 48093; public; 21,500
Macon Junior College Macon, GA 31297; public; 2,500
Madison Area Technical College Madison, WI 53703; public; 10,000
Madison Business College Madison, WI 53703; private; 300
Madisonville Community College Madisonville, KY 42431; public; 840
Madonna College Livonia, MI 48150; private; 3,200
Mallinckrodt College Wilmette, IL 60091; private; 270
Malone College Canton, OH 44709; private; 780
Manatee Junior College Bradenton, FL 33507; public; 5,000
Manchester Community College Manchester, CT 06040; public; 4,700
Mankato State University Mankato, MN 56001; public; 9,900
Manor Junior College Jenkintown, PA 19046; private; 390
Mansfield State College Mansfield, PA 16933; public; 2,500
Maple Woods Community College Kansas City, MO 64156; public; 2,200
Maria College Albany, NY 12208; private; 550
Marian College Indianapolis, IN 46222; private; 880
Maria Regina College Syracuse, NY 13208; private; 430
Maricopa Technical Community College Phoenix, AZ 85004; public; 3,200
Marion Military Institute Marion, AL 36756; private; 240
Marion Technical College Marion, OH 43302; public; 1,200
Marshalltown Community College Marshalltown, IA 50158; public; 1,400
Marshall University Huntington, WV 25701; public; 9,400
Martin College Pulaski, TN 38478; private; 300
Martin Community College Williamston, NC 27892; public; 760
Marygrove College Detroit, MI 48221; private; 890
Mary Holmes College West Point, MS 39773; private; 400
Maryland College of Art and Design Silver Spring, MD 20902; private; 260
Marymount College of Virginia Arlington, VA 22207; private; 1,100
Marymount Palos Verdes College Rancho Palos Verdes, CA 90274; private; 380
Maryville College—St. Louis St. Louis, MO 63141; private; 1,300
Massachusetts Bay Community College Wellesley Hills, MA 02181; public; 3,200
Massasoit Community College Brockton, MA 02402; public; 6,500
Mater Dei College Ogdensburg, NY 13669; private; 320
Mattatuck Community College Waterbury, CT 06708; public; 3,300
Maui Community College Kahului, Maui, HI 96732; public; 1,800
Mayland Technical Institute Spruce Pine, NC 28777; private; 500
Maysville Community College Maysville, KY 41056; public; 510
Mayville State College Mayville, ND 58257; public; 650
McCook Community College McCook, NE 69001; public; 630
McDowell Technical College Marion, NC 28752; public; 550
McHenry County College Crystal Lake, IL 60014; public; 4,300
McIntosh College Dover, NH 03820; private; 240
McKenzie College Chattanooga, TN 37401; private; 500
McLennan Community College Waco, TX 76708; public; 4,100
Meharry Medical College Nashville, TN 37208; private
Mendocino College Ukiah, CA 95482; public; 4,400
Menlo College Menlo Park, CA 94025; private; 380
Merced College Merced, CA 95340; public; 8,000
Mercer County Community College Trenton, NJ 08690; public; 7,700
Mercy College Dobbs Ferry, NY 10522; private; 10,000
Mercy College of Detroit Detroit, MI 48219; private; 2,500
Meridian Junior College Meridian, MS 39301; public; 2,700
Merritt College Oakland, CA 94619; public; 10,500
Mesabi Community College Virginia, MN 55792; public; 950
Mesa College Grand Junction, CO 81501; public; 3,900
Mesa Community College Mesa, AZ 85202; public; 13,500
Metropolitan Technical Community College Omaha, NE 68103; public; 6,400
Miami-Dade Community College Miami, FL 33176; public; 960
Miami-Jacobs Junior College of Business Dayton, OH 45401; private; 750
Miami University—Hamilton Hamilton, OH 45011; public; 1,600
Miami University—Middletown Middletown, OH 45042; public; 1,800
Michigan Christian College Rochester, MI 48063; private; 350
Michigan Technological University Houghton, MI 49931; public; 7,600
Middle Georgia College Cochran, GA 31014; public; 1,500
Middlesex Community College Middletown, CT 06457; public; 1,400
Middlesex Community College Bedford, MA 01730; public; 2,500
Middlesex County College Edison, NJ 08817; public; 11,000
Midland College Midland, TX 79701; public; 2,800
Midland Lutheran College Fremont, NE 68025; private; 860
Midlands Technical College Columbia, SC 29205; public; 5,900
Mid Michigan Community College Harrison, MI 48625; public; 10,500
Mid-Plains Community College North Platte, NE 69101; public; 1,700
Midstate College Peoria, IL 61602; private; 330
Mid-State Technical Institute—Marshfield Marshfield, WI 54449; public; 250
Mid-State Technical Institute—Wisconsin Rapids Wisconsin Rapids, WI 54494; public; 1,100
Midway College Midway, KY 40347; public; 350
Miles Community College Miles City, MT 59301; public; 900
Milwaukee Area Technical College Milwaukee, WI 53203; public; 66,400
Milwaukee School of Engineering Milwaukee, WI 53201; private; 1,500
Milwaukee Stratton College Milwaukee, WI 53202; private; 480
Mineral Area College Flat River, MO 63601; public; 1,400
Ministerial Institute and College West Point, MS 39773; private; 390
Minneapolis Community College Minneapolis, MN 55403; public; 3,000
Minnesota Bible College Rochester, MN 55901; private; 120
MiraCosta College Oceanside, CA 92054; public; 9,000
Mission College Santa Clara, CA 95054; public; 9,100
Mississippi County Community College Blytheville, AR 72315; public; 1,300
Mississipppi Delta Junior College Moorhead, MS 38761; public; 2,600
Mississippi Gulf Coast Junior College—Jackson Gautier, MS 39553; public; 2,400
Mississippi Gulf Coast Junior College—Jefferson Davis Gulfport, MS 39501; public; 1,800
Mississippi Gulf Coast Junior College—Perkinston Perkinston, MS 39573; public; 910
Missouri Institute of Technology Kansas City, MO 64114; public; 1,900
Missouri Southern State College Joplin, MO 64801; public; 3,800
Missouri Valley College Marshall, MO 65340; private; 500
Missouri Western State College St. Joseph, MO 64507; public; 4,100
Mitchell College New London, CT 06320; private; 750
Mitchell Community College Statesville, NC 28677; public; 2,000
Moberly Junior College Moberly, MO 65270; public; 1,000
Modesto Junior College Modesto, CA 95350; public; 13,500
Mohave Community College—Kingman Kingman, AZ 86401; public; 3,400
Mohawk Valley Community College Utica, NY 13501; public; 4,700
Mohegan Community College Norwich, CT 06360; public; 1,900
Molloy College Rockville Centre, NY 11570; private; 1,500
Monmouth College West Long Beach, NJ 07764; private; 3,000
Monroe Business Institute Bronx, NY 10468; private; 1,100
Monroe Community College Rochester, NY 14623; public; 1,100
Monroe County Community College Monroe, MI 48161; public; 2,200
Montcalm Community College Sidney, MI 48885; public; 1,600
Monterey Peninsula College Monterey, CA 93940; public; 8,500
Montgomery College—Germantown Germantown, MD 20767; public; 1,600
Montgomery College—Rockville Rockville, MD 20850; public; 11,200
Montgomery College—Takoma Park Takoma Park, MD 20012; public; 2,900
Montgomery County Community College Blue Bell, PA 19422; public; 7,500
Montgomery Technical Institute Troy, NC 27371; private; 450
Montreat-Anderson College Montreat, NC 28757; private; 410
Moorpark College Moorpark, CA 93021; public; 9,200
Moraine Park Technical Institute—Fond Du Lac Fond Du Lac, WI 54935; public; 1,500
Moraine Park Technical Institute—West Bend West Bend, WI 53095; public; 3,500
Moraine Valley Community College Palos Hills, IL 60465; public; 10,900
Morgan Community College Fort Morgan, CO 80701; public; 850
Morris Junior College of Business Melbourne, FL 32935; private; 200
Morrison Institute of Technology Morrison, IL 61270; public; 300
Morristown College Morristown, TN 37814; private; 120
Morton College Cicero, IL 60650; public; 4,200
Motlow State Community College

Tullahoma, TN 37388; public; 1,600

Mountain Empire Community College Big Stone Gap, VA 24219; public; 2,400

Mountain View College Dallas, TX 75211; private; 6,500

Mount Aloysius Junior College Cresson, PA 16630; private; 520

Mount Hood Community College Gresham, OR 97030; public; 11,000

Mount Ida Junior College Newton Centre, MA 02159; private; 810

Mount Marty College Yankton, SD 57078; private; 600

Mount Olive College Mount Olive, NC 28365; private; 410

Mount Sacred Heart College Hamden, CT 06514; private; 20

Mount San Antonio College Walnut, CA 91789; public; 21,300

Mount San Jacinto College San Jacinto, CA 92383; public; 3,500

Mount Senario College Ladysmith, WI 54848; private; 370

Mount St. Clare College Clinton, IA 52732; private; 400

Mount Vernon College Washington, DC 20007; private; 490

Mount Wachusett Community College Gardner, MA 01440; public; 3,500

Murray State College Tishomingo, OK 73460; public; 1,500

Muscatine Community College Muscatine, IA 52761; public; 1,000

Muskegon Business College Muskegon, MI 49442; private; 1,100

Muskegon Community College Muskegon, MI 49442; public; 5,300

Muskingum Area Technical College Zanesville, OH 43701; private; 1,300

Napa College Napa, CA 94558; public; 6,300

Nash Technical Institute Rocky Mount, NC 27801; public; 1,200

Nashville State Technical Institute Nashville, TN 37209; public; 5,300

Nassau Community College Garden City, NY 11530; public; 20,600

Nasson College Springvale, ME 04083; private; 600

Natchez Junior College Natchez, MS 39120; private; 50

Nathaniel Hawthorne College Antrim, NH 03440; private; 550

National Business College Roanoke, VA 24009; private; 620

National College—Albuquerque Albuquerque, NM 87110; private; 150

National College of Business Rapid City, SD 57709; private; 1,100

Navajo Community College Tsaile, AZ 86556; private; 2,000

Navarro College Corsicana, TX 75110; public; 2,000

Nazarene Bible College Colorado Springs, CO 80935; private; 590

Nebraska Wesleyan University Lincoln, NE 68504; private; 1,200

Nebraska Western College Scottsbluff, NE 69361; public; 1,400

Neosho County Community Junior College Chanute, KS 66720; public; 870

Newbury College—Boston Campus Boston, MA 02115; private; 1,000

Newbury Junior College—Holliston Holliston, MA 01746; private; 1,100

New England Culinary Institute Montpelier, VT 05602; private; 6

New England Institute of Applied Arts and Sciences for Funeral Service Education Boston, MA 02215; private; 150

New England Institute of Technology Providence, RI 20907; private; 900

New Hampshire College Manchester, NH 03104; private; 4,100

New Hampshire Technical Institute Concord, NH 03301; public; 2,000

New Hampshire Vocational Technical College Berlin, NH 03570; public; 350

New Hampshire Vocational Technical College Laconia, NH 03246; public; 250

New Hampshire Vocational Technical College Manchester, NH 03102; public; 200

New Hampshire Vocational Technical College Nashua, NH 03060; public; 370

New Hampshire Vocational Technical College Portsmouth, NH 03801; public; 920

New Mexico Junior College Hobbs, NM 88240; public; 1,400

New Mexico Military Institute Roswell, NM 88201; public; 700

New Mexico State University—Alamogordo Alamogordo, NM 88310; public; 1,300

New Mexico State University—Carlsbad Carlsbad, NM 88220; public; 600

New Mexico State University—Grants Grants, NM 87020; public; 670

New Mexico State University—Las Cruces Las Cruces, NM 88003; public; 12,300

New Mexico State University—San Juan Framington, NM 87401; public; 1,500

New River Community College Dublin, VA 24084; public; 3,300

New York Institute of Technology—New York New York, NY 10023; private; 2,600

Niagara County Community College Sanborn, NY 14132; public; 4,100

Nicolet College and Technical Institute Rhinelander, WI 54501; public; 3,500

Normandale Community College Bloomington, MN 55431; public; 5,000

Northampton County Area Community College Bethlehem, PA 18017; public; 3,800

North Arkansas Community College Harrison, AR 72601; public; 880

North Central Michigan College Petoskey, MI 49770; public; 2,000

North Central Technical College Mansfield, OH 44901; public; 1,800

North Central Technical Institute Wausau, WI 54401; public; 2,700

North Country Community College Saranac Lake, NY 12983; public; 1,400

North Dakota State School of Science Wahpeton, ND 58075; public; 3,400

North Dakota State University—Bottineau Branch and Institute of Forestry Bottineau, ND 58318; public; 400

Northeast Alabama State Junior College Rainsville, AL 35986; public; 1,000

Northeastern Christian Junior College Villanova, PA 19085; private; 200

Northeastern Junior College Sterling, CO 80751; public; 2,700

Northeastern Oklahoma Agricultural and Mechanical College Miami, OK 74354; public; 2,800

Northeast Iowa Technical Institute Calmar, IA 52132; public; 1,400

Northeast Louisiana University Monroe, LA 71209; public; 8,900

Northeast Mississippi Junior College Booneville, MS 38829; public; 3,300

Northeast Technical Community College Norfolk, NE 68701; public; 1,500

Northeast Wisconsin Technical Institute Green Bay, WI 54303; public; 2,900

Northern Essex Community College Haverhill, MA 01830; public; 7,000

Northern Kentucky University Highland Heights, KY 41076; public; 7,600

Northern Michigan University Marquette, MI 49855; public; 8,300

Northern Montana College Havre, MT 59501; public; 1,400

Northern Nevada Community College Elko, NV 89801; public; 1,500

Northern New Mexico Community College Espanola, NM 87532

Northern Oklahoma College Tonkawa, OK 74653; public; 1,500

Northern State College Aberdeen, SD 57401; public; 2,450

Northern Virginia Community College Annandale, VA 22003; public; 33,900

North Florida Junior College Madison, FL 32340; public; 960

North Greenville College Tigerville, SC 29688; private; 640

North Harris County College Houston, TX 77073; public; 7,500

North Hennepin State Community College Brooklyn Park, MN 55445; public; 4,400

North Idaho College Coeur D'Alene, ID 83814; public; 2,500

North Iowa Area Community College Mason City, IA 50401; public; 1,700

Northlake College Irving, TX 75062; public; 4,000

Northland Community College Thief River Falls, MN 56701; public; 580

Northland Pioneer College Holbrook, AZ 86025; public; 6,000

North Seattle Community College Seattle, WA 98103; public; 9,600

North Shore Community College Beverly, MA 01915; public; 5,100

Northwest Alabama State Junior College Phil Campbell, AL 35581; public; 1,100

Northwest Bible College Minot, ND 58701; private; 250

Northwest Community College Powell, WY 82435; public; 1,600

Northwestern Connecticut Community College Winsted, CT 06098; public; 2,500

Northwestern Michigan College Traverse City, MI 49684; public; 3,400

Northwest Iowa Technical College Sheldon, IA 51201; public; 600

Northwest Mississippi Junior College Senatobia, MS 38668; public; 3,100

Northwest Nazarene College Nampa, ID 83651; private; 1,400

Northwest Technical College Archbold, OH 43502; public; 840

Northwood Institute West Baden, IN 47469; private; 130

Northwood Institute—Texas Cedar Hill, TX 75104; private; 400

Norwalk Community College Norwalk, CT 06854; public; 3,200

Norwalk State Technical College Norwalk, CT 06611; public; 1,000

Notre Dame College Manchester, NH 03104; private; 400

Nyack College Nyack, NY 10960; private; 560

Oakland City College Oakland City, IN 47660; private; 500

Oakland Community College Bloomfield Hills, MI 48013; public; 22,800

Oakton Community College Des Plaines, IL 60016; public; 7,000

Odessa College Odessa, TX 79762; public; 4,300

Oglala Sioux Community College Pine Ridge, SD; public; 500

Ohio Institute of Technology Columbus, OH 43209; private; 3,800

Ohio State University Agricultural Technical Institute Wooster, OH 44691; public; 770

Ohio State University—Mansfield Mansfield, OH 44906; public; 1,100

Ohio State University—Marion Marion, OH 43302; public; 820

Ohio State University—Newark Newark, OH 43055; public; 1,100

Ohio University Athens, OH 45701; public; 12,200

Ohio University—Belmont County St. Clairsville, OH 43950; public; 940

Ohio University—Chillicothe Chillicothe, OH 45601; public; 1,300

Ohio University—Ironton Ironton, OH 45638; public; 1,100

Ohio University—Lancaster Lancaster, OH 43140; public; 1,600

Ohio University—Zanesville Zanesville, OH 43701; public; 880

Ohio Valley College Parkersburg, WV 26101; private; 280

Okaloosa-Walton Junior College Niceville, FL 32578; public; 9,000

Oklahoma Baptist University Shawnee, OK 74801; private; 1,500

Oklahoma School of Business Tulsa, OK 74135; private; 350

Oklahoma State University Technical Institute Oklahoma City, OK 73107; public; 3,000

Olean Business Institute Olean, NY 14760; private; 180

Olive-Harvey City College of Chicago Chicago, IL 60628; public; 4,500

Olympia Technical Community College Olympia, WA 98502; public; 3,900

Olympic College Bremerton, WA 98310; public; 8,500

O'Moore School of Interior Architecture and Design Franklin, TN 37604; private; 90

Onondaga Community College Syracuse, NY 13215; public; 5,800

Open Bible College Des Moines, IA 50321; private; 120

Orangeburg-Calhoun Technical College Orangeburg, SC 29115; public; 2,500

Orange Coast College Costa Mesa, CA 92626; public; 30,000

Orange County Community College Middletown, NY 10940; public; 5,100

Oregon Institute of Technology Klamath Falls, OR 97601; public; 2,700

Oscar Rose Junior College Midwest City, OK 73110; public; 9,000

Otis Art Institute of Parsons School of Design Los Angeles, CA 90057; private; 130

Our Lady of Holy Cross College New Orleans, LA 70119; private; 800

Owensboro Business College Owensboro, KY 42301; public; 350

Owens Technical College Toledo, OH 43699; public; 3,500

Oxnard College Oxnard, CA 93033; public; 6,500

Pace University-Pleasantville/Briarcliff Pleasantville, NY 10570; private; 4,400

Pacific Christian College Fullerton, CA 92631; private; 540

Paducah Community College Paducah, KY 42001; public; 1,900

Palm Beach Atlantic College West Palm Beach, FL 33401; private; 600

Palm Beach Junior College Lake Worth, FL 33461; public; 10,000

Palomar College San Marcos, CA 92069; public; 16,500

Palo Verde College Blythe, CA 92225; public; 660

Pamlico Technical Institute Grantsboro, NC 28529; public; 180

Panama Canal College Dodds, Panama, APO Miami, FL 34002; public; 1,600

Pan American University Edinburg, TX 78539; public; 8,200

Panola Junior College Carthage, TX 75633; public; 1,000

Paris Junior College Paris, TX 75460; public; 2,000

Parkersburg Community College Parkersburg, WV 26101; public; 3,100

Parkland College Champaign, IL 61820; public; 8,000

Parsons School of Design New York, NY 10011; private; 1,400

Pasadena City College Pasadena, CA 91106; public; 20,000

Pasco-Hernando Community College Dade City, FL 33525; public; 3,200

Passaic County College Paterson, NJ 07509; public; 3,100

Patrick Henry Community College Martinsville, VA 24112; public; 1,600

Patrick Henry State Junior College Monroeville, AL 36460; public; 780

Paul D. Camp Community College Franklin, VA 23851; public; 1,200

Paul Smiths College Paul Smiths, NY 12970; private; 1,200

Peace College Raleigh, NC 27604; private; 500

Pearl River Junior College Poplarville, MS 39470; public; 2,200

Peirce Junior College Philadelphia, PA 19102; private; 1,700

Peninsula College Port Angeles, WA 98362; public; 3,700

Pennco Tech Bristol, PA 19007; private; 680

Pennsylvania State University—Allentown Fogelsville, PA 18051; public; 410

Pennsylvania State University—Altoona Altoona, PA 16603; public; 2,200

Pennsylvania State University—Beaver Monaca, PA 15061; public; 1,100

Pennsylvania State University—Behrend Erie, PA 16510; public; 1,800

Pennsylvania State University—Berks Reading, PA 19608; public; 1,000

Pennsylvania State University—Delaware County Media, PA 19063; public; 1,200

Pennsylvania State University—DuBois DuBois, PA 15801; public; 780

Pennsylvania State University—Fayette Uniontown, PA 15401; public; 1,000

Pennsylvania State University—Hazleton Hazleton, PA 18201; public; 1,300

Pennsylvania State University—McKeesport McKeesport, PA 15132; public; 1,400

Pennsylvania State University—Mont Alto Mont Alto, PA 17237; public; 960

Pennsylvania State University—New Kensington New Kensington, PA 15068; public; 1,200

Pennsylvania State University—Ogontz Abington, PA 19001; public; 1,800

Pennsylvania State University—Schuylkill Schuylkill Haven, PA 17972; public; 850

Pennsylvania State University—Shenango Valley Sharon, PA 16146; public; 900

Pennsylvania State University—Wilkes-Barre Wilkes-Barre, PA 18708; public; 600

Pennsylvania State University—Worthington Scranton Dunmore, PA 18512; public; 1,500

Pennsylvania State University—York York, PA 17403; public; 1,000

Penn Valley Community College Kansas City, MO 64111; public; 5,200

Pensacola Junior College Pensacola, FL 32504; public; 17,000

Peru State College Peru, NE 68421; public; 900

Philadelphia College of the Performing Arts Philadelphia, PA 19102; private; 360

Phillips College Augusta, GA 30902; private; 440

Phillips College Columbus, GA 31901; private; 600

Phillips College Gulfport, MS 39501; private; 720

Phillips College of New Orleans Metairie, LA 70002; private; 350

Phillips County Community College Helena, AR 72342; public; 1,500

Phillips University Enid, OK 73701; private; 1,300

Phoenix College Phoenix, AZ 85013; public; 14,000

Piedmont Technical College Roxboro, NC 27573; public; 840

Piedmont Technical College Greenwood, SC 29646; public; 1,800

Piedmont Virginia Community College Charlottesville, VA 22901; public; 3,800

Pikes Peak Community College Colorado Springs, CO 80916; public; 5,900

Pikeville College Pikeville, KY 41501; private; 620

Pillsbury Baptist Bible College Owatonna, MN 55060; private; 700

Pima Community College Tucson, AZ 85709; public; 20,000

Pinebrook Junior College Coopersburg, PA 18036; private; 140

Pine Manor College Chestnut Hill, MA 02167; private; 540

Pioneer Community College Kansas City, MO 64111; public; 800

Pitt Community College Greenville, NC 27834; public; 2,400

Platte Technical Community College Columbus, NE 68601; public; 930

Plymouth State College Plymouth, NH 03264; public; 3,400

Point Park College Pittsburgh, PA 15222; private; 2,200

Polk Community College Winter Haven, FL 33880; public; 5,000

Porterville College Porterville, CA 93257; public; 2,300

Portland Community College Portland, OR 97219; public; 30,000

Post College Waterbury, CT 06708; private; 1,400

Potomac State College Keyser, WV 26726; public; 1,100

Powelson Business Institute Syracuse, NY 13202; private; 480

Prairie State College Chicago Heights, IL 60411; public; 6,600

Pratt Community College Pratt, KS 67124; public; 2,000

Pratt Phoenix School New York, NY 10016; private; 150

Prentiss Normal and Industrial Institute Prentiss, MS 39474; private; 200

Presentation College Aberdeen, SD 57401; private; 300

Prestonburg Community College Largo, MD 20870; public; 720

Pueblo Vocational Community College Pueblo, CO 81004; public; 1,000

Puerto Rico Junior College Rio Piedra, PR 00928; public; 7,100

Purdue University West Lafayette, IN 47907; public; 27,100

Purdue University—Calumet Hammond, IN 46323; public; 5,800

Purdue University—North Central Westville, IN 46391; public; 2,100

Quincy Junior College Quincy, MA 02169; public; 4,000

Quinegaug Valley Community College Danielson, CT 06329; public; 940

Quinnipiac College Hamden, CT 06518; private; 2,400

Quinsigamond Community College Worcester, MA 01606; public; 2,100

Rainy River Community College International Falls, MN 56649; public; 520

Ramirez College of Business and Technology Santurce, PR 00910; private; 720

Randolph Technical College Asheboro, NC 27203; public; 1,000

Ranger Junior College Ranger, TX 76470; public; 800

Rappahanock Community College Glenns, VA 23149; public; 1,300

Reading Area Community College Reading, PA 19602; public; 1,400

Reinhardt College Waleska, GA 30183; private; 550

Rend Lake College Ina, IL 62846; public; 3,500

Reno Business College Reno, NV 89502; private; 150

Rice College North Charleston, SC 29406; public; 500

Richard Bland College Petersburg, VA 23803; public; 1,200

Richland College Dallas, TX 75243; public; 11,000

Richland Community College Decatur, IL 62526; public; 5,000

Richmond College London W8 5PN, England; private; 500

Richmond Technical Institute Hamlet, NC 28345; public; 1,000

Rio Grande Community College Rio Grande, OH 45674; private; 1,250

Rio Hondo College Whittier, CA 90608; public; 1,200

Riverside City College Riverside, CA 92506; public; 14,300

Rivier College Nashua, NH 03060; private; 1,100

Roanoke-Chowan Technical College Ahoskie, NC 27910; public; 560

Robert Morris College—Carthage Carthage, IL 62321; private; 1,200

Robeson Technical College Lumberton, NC 28358; public; 1,500

Rochester Business Institute Rochester, NY 14604; private; 210

Rochester Community College Rochester, MN 55901; public; 3,100

Rockingham Community College Wentworth, NC 27375; public; 1,700

Rockmont College Denver, CO 80226; private; 330

Rock Valley College Rockford, IL 61101; public; 7,600

Rogue Community College Grants Pass, OR 97526; public; 3,200

Rowan Technical Institute Salisbury, NC 28144; public; 1,900

Roxbury Community College Roxbury, MA 02119; public; 700

Rutledge College Spartanburg, SC 29303; private; 700

Sacramento City College Sacramento, CA 95822; public; 13,800

Sacred Heart University Bridgeport, CT 06606; private; 2,200

Saddleback College Mission Viejo, CA 92691; private; 25,000

Salem College Salem, WV 26426; private; 1,400

Salem College at Clarksburg Clarksburg, WV 26301; private; 550

Salish-Kootenai Community College Pablo, MT 59855; public; 400

Sampson Technical Institute Clinton, NC 28328; public; 950

San Antonio College San Antonio, TX 78284; public; 21,500

San Bernardino Valley College San Bernardino, CA 92403; public; 15,000

Sandhills Community College Carthage, NC 28327; public; 1,800

San Diego Evening College San Diego, CA 92108; public; 20,000

San Diego Mesa College San Diego, CA 92111; public; 23,400

San Diego Miramar College San Diego, CA 92126; public; 4,000

San Francisco College of Mortuary Science San Francisco, CA 94109; private; 70

San Jacinto College—Central Pasadena, TX 77505; public; 18,500

San Jacinto College—North Houston, TX 77049; public; 3,000

San Joaquin Delta College Stockton, CA 95207; public; 20,900

San Jose City College San Jose, CA 95128; public; 14,300

Santa Ana College Santa Ana, CA 92706; public; 18,800

Santa Barbara City College Santa Barbara, CA 93105; public; 10,000

Santa Fe Community College Gainesville, FL 32601; public; 7,800

Santa Monica College Santa Monica, CA 90405; public; 18,500

Santa Rosa Junior College Santa Rosa, CA 95401; public; 23,000

Sauk Valley College Dixon,IL 61021; public; 4,700

Sayre Junior College Sayre, OK 73662; public; 380

Schenectady County Community College Schenectady, NY 12305; public; 2,800

Schiller International University 6900 Heidelberg, West Germany; private; 480

Schoolcraft College Livonia, MI 48152; public; 8,200

Schreiner College Kerrville, TX 78028; private; 480

Scott Community College Bettendorf, IA 52722; public; 2,400

Scott Community College—Palmer Campus Bettendorf, IA 52722; public; 2,400

Scottsdale Community College Scottsdale, AZ 85253; public; 6,800

S.D. Bishop State Junior College Mobile, AL 36603; public; 1,400

Seattle Central Community College Seattle, WA 98122; public; 10,000

Selma University Selma, AL 36701; private; 630

Seminole Community College Sanford, FL 32771; public; 4,700

Seminole Junior College Seminole, OK 74868; public; 1,600

Seward County Community College Liberal, KS 67901; public; 600

Shasta College Redding, CA 96001; public; 13,500

Shawnee College Ullin, IL 62992; private; 2,200

Shawnee State Community College Portsmouth, OH 45662; public; 1,900

Shelby State Community College Memphis, TN 38104; public; 5,600

Sheldon Jackson College Sitka, AK 99835; private; 250

Shelton State Community College Tuscaloosa, AL 35401; public; 3,000

Shenandoah College and Conservatory of Music Winchester, VA 22601; private; 950

Shepherd College Shepherdstown, WV 25443; public; 3,000

Sheridan College Sheridan, WY 82801; public; 1,100

Shoreline Community College Seattle, WA 98133; public; 8,000

Shorter College North Little Rock, AR 72114; private; 200

Sierra College Rocklin, CA 95677; public; 9,400

Silver Lake College Manitowoc, WI 54220; private; 350

Simon's Rock Early College of Bard College Great Barrington, MA 01230; private; 300

Sinclair Community College Dayton, OH 45402; public; 17,100

Sinte Gleska College Rosebud, SD 57570; private; 350

Sioux Empire College Hawarden, IA 51023; private; 350

Skagit Valley College Mt. Vernon, WA 98273; public; 6,500

Skyline College San Bruno, CA 94066; public; 7,900

Snead State Junior College Boaz, AL 35957; public; 1,000

Snow College Ephraim, UT 84627; public; 1,200

Solano Community College Suisun City, CA 94585; public; 9,000

Somerset Community College Somerset, KY 42501; public; 1,100

Somerset County College Somerville, NJ 08876; public; 4,200

South Central Community College New Haven, CT 06511; public; 2,000

Southeast Community College Cumberland, KY 40823; public; 580

Southeast Community College—Fairbury Fairbury, NE 68352; public; 470

Southeast Community College—Lincoln Lincoln, NE 68520; public; 2,600

Southeast Community College—Milford Milford, NE 68405; public; 900

Southeastern Baptist Theological Seminary Wake Forest, NC 27587; private; 1,000

Southeastern Community College Whiteville, NC 28472; public; 2,100

Southeastern Community College—North West Burlington, IA 52655; public; 1,800

Southeastern Community College—South Keokuk, IA 52632; public; 400

Southeastern Illinois College Harrisburg, IL 62946; public; 2,800

Southeastern Louisiana University Hammond, LA 70401; public; 7,700

Southeastern University Washington, DC 20024; private; 1,100

Southern Arkansas University—El Dorado El Dorado, AR 71730; public; 540

Southern Arkansas University—Technical Branch Camden, AR 71701; public; 630

Southern Baptist College Walnut Ridge, AR 72476; private; 380

Southern Illinois University—Carbondale School of Technical Careers Carbondale, IL 62901; public; 19,300

Southern Institute Birmingham, AL 35255; private; 300

Southern Junior College of Business Birmingham, AL 35203; private; 1,200

Southern Maine Vocational Technical Institute South Portland, ME 04106; public; 1,200

Southern Ohio College Cincinnati, OH 45237; public; 3,300

Southern Oregon State College Ashland, OR 97520; public; 4,700

Southern Seminary Junior College Buena Vista, VA 24416; private; 300

Southern State Community College Hillsboro, OH 45133; public; 1,500

Southern Technical Institute Marietta, GA 30060; private; 2,600

Southern Union State Junior College Wadley, AL 36276; public; 1,400

Southern University—New Orleans New Orleans, LA 70126; private; 3,500

Southern University—Shreveport—Bossier City Shreveport, LA 71107; private; 710

Southern Vermont College Ben-

nington, VT 05201; private; 600
Southern Vocational College Tuskegee, AL 36083; public; 460
Southern West Virginia Community College Williamson, WV 25661; public; 3,100
Southern West Virginia Community College—Logan Logan, WV 25601; public; 1,900
South Florida Junior College Avon Park, FL 33825; public; 1,000
South Georgia College Douglas, GA 31533; public; 1,200
South Oklahoma City Junior College Oklahoma City, OK 73159; public; 7,300
South Plains College Levelland, TX 79336; public; 2,800
South Seattle Community College Seattle, WA 98106; public; 8,000
Southside Virginia Community College Alberta, VA 23821; public; 1,900
Southwest Baptist College Bolivar, MO 65613; private; 1,500
Southwestern Christian College Terrell, TX 75160; private; 280
Southwestern College Chula Vista, CA 92010; public; 13,200
Southwestern Community College Creston, IA 50801; public; 540
Southwestern Junior College Waxahachi, TX 75165; private; 550
Southwestern Michigan College Dowagiac, MI 49047; public; 2,500
Southwestern Oregon Community College Coos Bay, OR 97420; public; 5,600
Southwestern Technical Institute Sylva, NC 28779; public; 1,700
Southwest Mississippi Junior College Summit, MS 39666; public; 1,100
Southwest State Technical College Mobile, AL 36690; public; 1,000
Southwest Texas Junior College Uvalde, TX 78801; public; 2,200
Southwest Virginia Community College Richlands, VA 24641; public; 3,500
Southwest Wisconsin Vocational Technical Institute Fennimore, WI 53809; public; 750
Spartanburg Methodist College Spartanburg, SC 29301; private; 1,000
Spartanburg Technical College Spartanburg, SC 29303; public; 3,200
Spartan School of Aeronautics Tulsa, OK 74151; private; 1,800
Spokane Community College Spokane, WA 99207; public; 7,400
Spokane Falls Community College Spokane, WA 99204; public; 5,000
Spoon River College Canton, IL 61520; public; 1,600
Springfield College in Illinois Springfield, IL 62702; private; 480
Springfield Technical Community College Springfield, MA 01105; public; 3,300
Spring Garden College Chestnut Hill, PA 19118; private; 1,100
Standing Rock Community College Fort Yates, ND 58538; public; 210
Stanly Technical College Albermarle, NC 28001; private; 950
St. Anselm College Manchester, NH 03102; private; 1,600
Stark Technical College Canton, OH 44720; public; 2,700
State Community College of East St. Louis East St. Louis, IL 62201; public; 1,700
State Fair Community College Sedalia, MO 65301; public; 1,500
State Technical Institute—Knoxville Knoxville, TN 37919; public; 2,200
State Technical Institute—Memphis Memphis, TN 38134; public; 5,800
St. Bernard Parish Community College Chalmette, LA 70043; public; 520
St. Catharine College St. Catharine, KY 40061; private; 240
St. Clair County Community College Port Huron, MI 48060; public; 3,300
Steed College Johnson City, TN 37601; private; 600
Stevens Henager College Ogden, UT 84401; private; 600
St. Francis College Fort Wayne, IN 46808; private; 800
St. Gregory's College Shawnee, OK 74801; private; 340
St. John's College Winfield, KS 67156; private; 270
St. John's River Community College Palatka, FL 32077; public; 1,600
St. John's River Community College—Florida School of the Arts Palatka, FL 32077; public; 110
St. John's University Jamaica, NY 11439; private; 12,400
St. John Vianney College Seminary Miami, FL 33165; private; 60
St. Louis Community College—Florissant Valley St. Louis, MO 63135; public; 11,600
St. Louis Community College—Forest Park St. Louis, MO 63110; public; 7,500
St. Louis Community College—Meramec Kirkwood, MO 63122; public; 11,100
St. Mary's College Orchard Lake, MI 48033; private;250
St. Mary's College Raleigh, NC 27611; private; 320
St. Mary's College of O'Fallon O'Fallon, MO 63366; private; 560
St. Mary's Junior College Minneapolis,MN 55454; private; 750
St. Paul's College Concordia, MO 64020; private; 130
St. Petersburg Junior College St. Petersburg, FL 33733; public; 15,000
St. Peter's College Jersey City, NJ 07306; private; 2,300
St. Phillips's College San Antonio, TX 78203; public; 7,100
Strayer College Washington, DC 20005; private; 1,700
Sue Bennett College London, KY 40741; private; 280
Suffolk County Community College Selden, NY 11784; public; 20,000
Sullivan County Community College Loch Sheldrake, NY 12759; public; 1,700
Sullivan Junior College of Business Louisville, KY 40205; private; 1,300
Sumter Area Technical College Sumter, SC 29150; public; 1,600
SUNY—Agri and Tech College—Alfred Alfred, NY 14802; public; 4,100
SUNY—Agri and Tech College—Canton Canton, NY 13617; public; 2,600
SUNY—Agri and Tech College—Cobleskill Cobleskill, NY 12043; public; 2,700
SUNY—Agri and Tech College—Delhi Delhi, NY 13753; public; 2,700
SUNY—Agri and Tech College—Farmingdale Farmingdale, NY 11735; public; 13,500
SUNY—Agri and Tech College—Morrisville Morrisville, NY 13408; public; 3,200
SUNY—Fashion Institute of Technology New York, NY 10001; public; 3,500
SUNY—Rockland Community College Suffern, NY 10901; public; 7,500
SUNY—Upstate Medical Center Syracuse, NY 13210; public; 260
Suomi College Hancock, MI 49930; private; 550
Surry Community College Dobson, NC 27017; public; 1,900

Tacoma Community College Tacoma, WA 98465; public; 6,300
Taft College Taft, CA 93268; public; 1,300
Tallahassee Community College Tallahassee, FL 32304; public; 3,900
Tarrant County Junior College District Fort Worth, TX 76102; public; 20,800
Taylor Business Institute New York, NY 10119; private; 1,200
Taylor University Upland, IN 46989; private, 1,600
Technical Career Institutes New York, NY 10001; private; 1,800
Technical College of Alamance Haw River, NC 27258; public; 1,800
Temple Junior College Temple, TX 76501; public; 2,400
Temple University Philadelphia, PA 19122; public; 18,000
Temple University—Ambler Ambler, PA 19002; public; 5,800
Tennessee Valley Center—Tuscumbia Tuscumbia, AL 35674; public; 360
Terra Technical College Fremont, OH 43420; public; 2,200
Texarkana Community College Texarkana, TX 75501; public; 4,300
Texas Southmost College Brownsville, TX 78520; public; 4,200
Texas State Technical Institute—Amarillo Amarillo, TX 79111; public; 730
Texas State Technical Institute—Harlingen Harlingen, TX 78550; public; 2,500
Texas State Technical Institute—Waco Waco, TX 76705; public; 4,500
Thaddeus Stevens State School of Technology Lancaster, PA 17602; public; 410
Thames Valley State Technical College Norwich, CT 06360; public; 1,700
Thomas A. Edison State College Trenton, NJ 08625; private; 4,000
Thomas College Waterville, ME 04901; private; 500
Thomas County Community College Thomasville, GA 31792; private; 350
Thomas More College Fort Mitchell, KY 41017; private; 1,300
Thomas Nelson Community College Hampton, VA 23670; public; 6,000
Thornton Community College South Holland, IL 60473; public; 10,000
Three Rivers Community College Poplar Bluff, MO 63901; public; 1,700
Tidewater Community College—Chesapeake Chesapeake, VA 23320; public; 2,000
Tidewater Community College—Frederick Portsmouth, VA 23703; public; 4,500
Tidewater Community College—Virginia Beach Virginia Beach, VA 23456; public; 8,500
Tiffin University Tiffin, OH 44883; private; 450
Tobe-Coburn School for Fashion Careers New York, NY 10021; private; 220
Toccoa Falls College Toccoa Falls, GA 30598; private; 620
Tomlinson College Cleveland, TN 37311; private; 270
Tompkins Cortland Community College Dryden, NY 13053; public; 3,200
Treasure Valley Community College Ontario, OR 97914; public; 1,400
Trenton Junior College Trenton, MO 64683; public; 610
Trevecca Nazarene College Nashville, TN 37210; private; 1,000
Tri-County Community College Murphy, NC 28906; public; 650
Tri-County Technical College Pendleton, SC 29670; public; 2,400
Trident Technical College—North North Charleston, SC 29405; public; 5,500
Trident Technical College—Palmer Charleston, SC 29411; public; 5,400
Trinidad State Junior College Trinidad, CO 81081; public; 1,200
Trinity Bible Institute Ellendale, ND 58436; private; 380
Triton College River Grove, IL 60171; public; 22,000
Trocaire College Buffalo, NY 14220; private; 780
Truckee Meadows Community College—Reno/Sparks Campus Sparks, NV 89431; public; 7,300
Truett-McConnell College Cleveland, GA 30528; private; 670
Tulsa Junior College Tulsa, OK 74119; public; 11,000
Tunxis Community College Farmington, CT 06032; public; 2,600
Tyler Junior College Tyler, TX 75711; public; 8,000

Ulster County Community College Stone Ridge, NY 12484; public; 3,000
Umpqua Community College Roseburg, OR 97470; public; 5,200
Union College Cranford, NJ 07016; private; 420
Union County Technical Institute Scotch Plains, NJ 07076; public; 2,700
United Wesleyan College Allentown, PA 18103; private; 240
Unity College Unity, ME 04988; private; 350
University of Akron—Community and Technical College Akron, OH 44325; public; 4,700
University of Alaska—Juneau Juneau, AK 99803; public; 2,200
University of Alaska—Kenai Peninsula Community College Soldotna, AK 99669; public; 1,200
University of Alaska—Kodiak Community College Kodiak, AK 99615; public; 1,000
University of Alaska—Kuskokwim Community College Bethel, AK 99559; public; 1,000
University of Alaska—Matanuska/Susitna Community College Palmer, AK 99645; public; 660
University of Alaska—Northwest Community College Nome, AK 99762; public; 350
University of Alaska—Sitka Community College Sitka, AK 99835; public; 750
University of Albuquerque Albuquerque, NM 87140; private; 2,000
University of Arkansas—Little Rock Little Rock, AR 72204; public; 9,000
University of Charleston Charleston, WV 25304; private; 2,000
University of Cincinnati Cincinnati, OH 45221; public; 33,300
University of Cincinnati—Raymond Walters College Cincinnati, OH 45236; public; 3,000
University of Delaware Newark, DE 19711; private; 13,700
University of Evansville Evansville, IN 47702; private; 5,200
University of Evansville—British Campus: Harlaxton College Grantham, Lincolnshire, England; private; 160
University of Guam Mangilao, Guam 96913; public; 2,200
University of Hartford West Hartford, CT 06117; private; 7,100
University of Hawaii at Hilo—Hawaii Community College Hilo, HI 96720; public; 1,700
University of Hawaii—Windward Community College Kaneohe, HI 96744; public; 1,400
University of La Verne La Verne, CA 91750; private; 1,200
University of Maine—Augusta Augusta, ME 04330; public; 3,400
University of Maine—Farmington Farmington, ME 04938; public; 2,000
University of Maine—Fort Kent Fort Kent, ME 04743; public; 620
University of Maine—Orono Orono, ME 04473; public; 10,300
University of Massachusetts—Stockbridge School of Agriculture Amherst, MA 01003; public; 500
University of Minnesota Technical College—Crookston Crookston, MN 56716; public; 1,200
University of Minnesota Technical College—Waseca Waseca, MN 56093; public; 1,100
University of Nebraska—Omaha Omaha, NE 68182; public; 13,200
University of New Hampshire—Merrimack Valley Manchester, NH 03102; public; 1,600
University of New Hampshire—Thompson School of Applied Science Durham, NH 03824; public; 480
University of New Mexico—Gallup Gallup, NM 87301; public; 1,200
University of North Dakota—Williston Williston, ND 58801; public; 550
University of Pittsburgh—Bradford Bradford, PA 16701; private; 800
University of Pittsburgh—Titusville Titusville, PA 16354; private; 600
University of Puerto Rico—Rio Piedras Rio Piedras, PR 00931; public; 20,400
University of South Carolina Columbia, SC 29208; public; 18,600

University of South Carolina—Aiken Aiken, SC 29801; public; 1,200
University of South Carolina—Beaufort Beaufort, SC 29902; public; 500
University of South Carolina—Lancaster Lancaster, SC 29720; public; 750
University of South Carolina—Salkehatchie Allendale, SC 29810; public; 500
University of South Carolina—Sumter Sumter, SC 29150; public; 1,200
University of South Carolina—Union Union, SC 29379; public; 290
University of South Dakota—Springfield Springfield, SD 57062; public; 850
University of Southern Maine Gorham, ME 04038; public; 6,600
University of Steubenville Steubenville, OH 43952; private; 950
University of the District of Columbia Washington, DC 20004; public; 14,000
University of the Sacred Heart Santurce, PR 00924; private; 6,000
University of Toledo Toledo, OH 43606; public; 4,100
University of Wisconsin Center—Baraboo/Sauk Baraboo, WI 53913; public; 450
University of Wisconsin Center—Barron County Rice Lake, WI 54868; public; 380
University of Wisconsin Center—Fond Du Lac Fond Du Lac, WI 54935; public; 560
University of Wisconsin Center—Fox Valley Menasha, WI 54952; public; 1,100
University of Wisconsin—Green Bay Green Bay, WI 54302; public; 3,900
University of Wisconsin Center—Manitowoc County Manitowoc, WI 54220; public; 390
University of Wisconsin Center—Marathon County Wausau, WI 54401; public; 1,100
University of Wisconsin—Marinette Center Marinette, WI 54143; public; 390
University of Wisconsin—Marshfield/Wood Marshfield, WI 54449; public; 710
University of Wisconsin Center—Richland Richland Center, WI 53581; public; 290
University of Wisconsin Center—Rock County Janesville, WI 53545; public; 810
University of Wisconsin Center—Sheboygan County Sheboygan, WI 53081; public; 670
University of Wisconsin Center—Washington County West Bend, WI 53095; public; 620
University of Wisconsin Center—Waukesha Waukesha, WI 53186; public; 1,900
University of Wisconsin—Stevens Point Stevens Point, WI 54481; public; 8,600
Ursuline College Pepper Pike, OH 44124; private; 1,100
Utah Technical College—Provo Provo, UT 84601; public; 4,000
Utah Technical College—Salt Lake Salt Lake City, UT 84107; public; 7,000
Utica Junior College Utica MS 39175; public; 920
Utica School of Commerce Utica, NY 13501; private; 280

Valley City State College Valley City, ND 58072; public; 1,200
Valley Forge Military Junior College Wayne, PA 19087; private; 130
Valparaiso Technical Institute Valparaiso, IN 46383; private; 200
Vance-Granville Community College Henderson, NC 27536; public; 1,100
Vennard College University Park, IA 52595; private; 200
Ventura College Ventura, CA 93003; public; 13,000
Vermilion Community College Ely, MN 55731; public; 460
Vermont College of Norwich University—Two Year Division Montpelier, VT 05602; private; 450
Vermont Technical College Randolph Center, VT 05061; public; 650
Victoria College Victoria, TX 77901; public; 2,500
Villa Julie College Stevenson, MD 21153; private; 810
Villa Maria College of Buffalo Buffalo, NY 14225; private; 840
Virginia Highlands Community College Abingdon, VA 24210; public; 1,500
Virginia Intermont College Bristol, VA 24201; private; 700
Virginia Western Community College Roanoke, VA 24015; public; 5,600
Vista College Berkeley, CA 94704; private; 10,800
Volunteer State Community College Gallatin, TN 37066; public; 4,200

Wake Technical College Raleigh, NC 27603; public; 1,800
Walker State Technical College Sumitron, AL 35148; public; 800
Walla Walla Community College Walla Walla, WA 99362; public; 5,400
Walsh College Canton, OH 44720; private; 850
Walters State Community College Morristown, TN 37814; public; 3,900
Washburn University—Topeka Topeka, KS 66621; public; 5,200
Washington Technical College Marietta, OH 45750; public; 920
Washtenaw Community College Ann Arbor, MI 48106; public; 8,500
Watterson College Louisville, KY 40218; private; 1,000
Waubonsee Community College Sugar Grove, IL 60554; public; 6,100
Waukesha County Technical Institute Pewaukee, WI 53072; public; 3,900
Waycross Junior College Waycross, GA 31501; public; 430
Wayne Community College Goldsboro, NC 27530; public; 2,400
Wayne County Community College Detroit, MI 48201; public; 20,000
Wayne General and Technical College Orrville, OH 44667; private; 790
Waynesburg College Waynesburg, PA 15370; private; 870
Weatherford College Weatherford,TX 76086; public; 1,900
Weber State College Ogden, UT 84408; public; 10,000
Wenatchee Valley College Wenatchee, WA 98801; public; 4,200
Wentworth Institute of Technology Boston, MA 02115; private; 3,000
Wentworth Military Academy Lexington, MO 64067; private; 310
Westbrook College Portland, ME 04103; private; 900
Westchester Business Institute White Plains, NY 10606; private; 520
Westchester Community College Valhalla, NY 10595; public; 8,200
Western Baptist College Salem, OR 97302; private; 400
Western Montana College Dillion, MT 59725; public; 770
Western Nevada Community College Carson City, NV 89701; public; 3,200
Western New Mexico University Silver City, NM 88061; public; 1,800
Western Oklahoma State College Altus, OK 73521; public; 1,900
Western Piedmont Community College Morganton, NC 28655; public; 1,500
Western Texas College Snyder, TX 79549; public; 1,200
Western Wisconsin Technical Institute LaCrosse, WI 54601; public; 3,200
Western Wyoming Community College Rock Springs, WY 82901; public; 3,500
Westmoreland County Community College Youngwood, PA 15697; public; 2,800
West Shore Community College Scottsville, MI 49454; public; 1,000
West Valley Community College Saratoga, CA 95070; public; 16,000
West Virginia Institute of Technology Montgomery, WV 25136; public; 3,300
West Virginia Northern Community College Wheeling, WV 26003; public; 3,900
West Virginia State College Institute, WV 25112; public; 4,400
West Virginia Wesleyan College Buckhannon, WV 26201; private; 1,800
Wharton County Junior College Wharton, TX 77488; public; 2,100
Whatcom Community College Bellingham, WA 98225; public; 2,500
White Pines College Chester, NH 03036; private; 150
Wilkes Community College Wilkesboro, NC 28659; public; 2,000
Williamsburg Technical Education Center Kingstree, SC 29556; public; 540
Williamsport Area Community College Williamsport, PA 17701; public; 3,100
Willmar Community College Willmar; MN 56201; public; 870
Wilmington College New Castle, DE 19720; private; 950
Wilson College Chambersburg, PA 17201; private; 240
Wilson County Technical Institute Wilson, NC 27893; public; 1,200
Wingate College Wingate, NC 28174; private; 1,400
Winsalm College Winston-Salem, NC 27101; private; 330
Winston-Salem Bible College Winston-Salem, NC 27102; private; 120
Wisconsin Indianhead Technical Institute—Ashland Ashland, WI 54871; public; 350
Wisconsin Indianhead Technical Institute—New Richmond New Richmond, WI 54806; public; 500
Wisconsin Indianhead Technical Institute—Superior Superior, WI 54880; public; 700
Wisconsin Lutheran College Milwaukee, WI 53226; private; 100
Wood School New York, NY 10017; private; 500
Wooster Business College Wooster, OH 44691; private; 110
Worcester Junior College Worcester, MA 01610; private; 960
Worthington Community College Worthington, MN 56187; public; 750
Wor-Wic Tech Community College Salisbury, MD 21801; public; 1,000
Wright State University—Western Ohio Celina, OH 45822; public; 880
Wytheville Community College Wytheville, VA 24382; public; 2,300

Yakima Valley Community College Yakima, WA 98907; public; 6,500
Yankton College Yankton, SD 57078; private; 280
Yavapai College Prescott, AZ 86301; public; 4,900
York College York, NE 68467; private; 360
York Technical College Rock Hill, SC 29730; private; 1,800
Youngstown State University Youngstown, OH 44555; public; 5,100

Picture Credits

The following list of credits includes the names of organizations and individuals who helped secure illustrations for the Dictionary. The editors wish to thank all of them—as well as others not specifically mentioned—for their assistance. The credits are arranged alphabetically by entry word, which is printed in boldface type. In those cases where two or more illustrations are credited to the same entry word, dashes are used to separate them sequentially from top to bottom.

The abbreviations EPA, MFA, and SDZ stand for, respectively, Editorial Photocolor Archives, Inc., the Museum of Fine Arts, Boston, and the Zoological Society of San Diego.

In the Biographical Credits the abbreviations BA, LC, and NPG stand for, respectively, Bettmann Archive, Library of Congress, and National Portrait Gallery (Smithsonian Institution).

aardvark Photo Researchers; **abacus** Allen Smith—Laurel Cook; **abbey** British Tourist Authority; **Aberdeen Angus** Photo Researchers; **abstractionism** Picture Cube; **Abyssinian cat** Photo Researchers; **acanthus** Allen Moore; **acacia** Laurel Cook; **accordion** M. Hohner, Inc.; **ace** U.S. Playing Card Co.; **achene** Laurel Cook; **Achilles** MFA; **acorn** Laurel Cook; **acrobatics** Ringling Brothers and Barnum & Bailey Circus; **acropolis** Greek National Tourist Office; **acupuncture** Picture Cube; **addax, adder**[2] SDZ; **adenoid** Neil Hardy; **adjacent angle** Carl Bass; **adobe** Albuquerque Convention and Visitors Bureau; **Adonis** EPA; **adz** Jean Erdoes; **Aegisthus, Aeolian harp** MFA; **Aeolus** EPA; **aerialist** Frank Siteman; **aerosol bomb** Laurel Cook; **Afghan** Frank Siteman; **Afghan hound** Evelyn Shafer; **African violet, agaric, agave** Laurel Cook; **Agnus Dei** EPA; **agouti** SDZ; **aigrette** Bettmann Archive; **ailanthus** Laurel Cook; **aileron** Frank Siteman; **Airedale** Evelyn Shafer; **Ajax** MFA; **albatross** Photo Researchers; **alfalfa, alimentary canal** Laurel Cook; **allegory** New York State Historical Assoc.; **almond** Laurel Cook; **alpaca** SDZ; **alpenhorn, alpenstock** Bettmann Archive; **alpine** Picture Cube; **alsike clover** Laurel Cook; **alter** George Robinson; **alternate** Ethel Hausman; **alternate angle** Carl Bass; **althorn** American Music Conference; **amaryllis** Burpee Seeds; **Amazon** MFA; **Amish** Pennsylvania Dutch Visitors Bureau; **amoeba** Grant Heilman; **amphitheater** Greek National Tourist Office; **amphora, amulet** MFA; **anchor** Lester D. Olin, Mystic Seaport; **andiron** MFA; **Andromeda** George Lindbloom; **aneurysm** Laurel Cook; **angel** MFA; **angelfish** Marineland of Florida; **angle**[2] Carl Bass; **Angora goat** USDA; **annual ring** Cal Sacks—USDA; **annunciation** The Metropolitan Museum of Art; **anole** Grant Heilman; **anopheles** USDA; **ansate cross** EPA; **anteater** SDZ; **antelope** Photo Researchers; **anthemion** EPA; **anther** Grant Heilman; **anthurium** Laurel Cook; **anticline** from *Principles of Geology*, 2nd edition, by James Gilluly, A.C. Waters, and A.O. Woodford, W.H. Freeman and Co., copyright 151; **Anubis** EPA; **anvil** "Steelways," published by The American Iron and Steel Institute; **aorta** Neil Hardy; **aoudad, ape** SDZ; **aphid** USDA; **Aphrodite** MFA; **Apollo, apostle** EPA; **apparatus** Jean Claude Le Jeune, Stock, Boston; **appliqué** Shelburne Museum; **apricot, apse** Laurel Cook; **Aquarius** George Lindbloom; **aqueduct** French Government Tourist Office; **Aquila** George Lindbloom; **Arabian** Grant Heilman; **arch**[1] French Government Tourist Office; **archaic smile** EPA; **architrave** Laurel Cook; **argali** Matthew Kalmenoff; **Argus** MFA; **Aries** George Lindbloom; **armadillo** Interior: Sport Fisheries and Wildlife; **armillary sphere** EPA; **armoire, armor** MFA; **arrowhead** Frank Siteman—Ethel Hausman; **artesian well** Laurel Cook; **artichoke** Photo Researchers; **art nouveau** William Doyle Galleries; **arum** Ethel Hausman; **ash**[2] Matthew Kalmenoff; **aspidistra** Laurel Cook; **ass**[1] SDZ; **aster** Laurel Cook; **astrolabe** EPA; **astronaut** NASA; **asymptote** Carl Bass; **Atalanta** E.J. Poynter; **Athena, Atlas** EPA; **atoll** from *Principles of Geology*, 3rd edition, by James Gilluly, A.C. Waters, and A.O. Woodford, W.H. Freeman and Co., copyright 1968; **atomic bomb** U.S. Air Force; **atomizer** Frank Siteman; **atrium** Isabella Stewart Gardner Museum; **auger** Stanley Tool Co.; **auk** Photo Researchers; **Auriga** George Lindbloom; **autograph** courtesy of Charles Hamilton, Autographs; **Autoharp** Advertisers Photographying Co.; **avocado** Laurel Cook; **avocet** Interior; Sport Fisheries and Wildlife; **awl, ax** Stanley Tool Co.; **azalea** Laurel Cook.

baboon SDZ; **Bacchus** EPA; **bachelor's-button** Laurel Cook; **backgammon** Prints Division, New York Public Library; **backhand** Peter Southwick, Stock, Boston; **backpack** George Bellerose, Stock, Boston; **bagpipe** British Tourist Authority; **bagworm** Photo Researchers; **balalaika** The Metropolitan Museum of Art; **balance** Frank Siteman; **balance beam** Cary Wolinsky, Stock, Boston; **bald cypress, bale** USDA; **balloon** Albuquerque Convention and Visitors Bureau; **Baltimore oriole** Photo Researchers; **banana** Laurel Cook; **bandoleer** U.S. Navy; **baneberry** Laurel Cook; **banjo** Allen Smith; **banyan** Photo Researchers; **baobab** Picture Cube; **Barbary ape** SDZ; **bargello** Laurel Cook; **bark**[3], **barkentine** *Sailing and Small Craft Down the Ages*, copyright 1940 by the U.S. Naval Institute, Annapolis, Maryland; **barn** Grant Heilman; **barnacle** Allen Moore: **barometer** Frank Siteman—MFA; **bartizan** EPA; **bascule** British Tourist Authority; **basenji** Evelyn Shafer; **basket** MFA; **bass**[1] Interior: Sport Fisheries and Wildlife; **basset hound** Evelyn Shafer; **bassoon** Ron Schick; **bat**[2] Matthew Kalmenoff; **bathyscaph** U.S. Navy; **batter**[2] Boston Red Sox; **battlement** British Tourist Authority; **bayonet** Library of Congress; **bay window** Jeffrey Dunn; **beagle** Evelyn Shafer; **beaker** Frank Siteman; **bear**[2] USDA; **bearskin** British Tourist Authority; **beaver** USDA; **Bedlington terrier** Evelyn Shafer; **beef** Jean Erdoes; **beetle**[1] USDA; **begonia** Laurel Cook; **belfry** Jeffrey Dunn; **bell** Philadelphia Convention and Visitors Bureau; **belladonna** Laurel Cook; **bellows** Ronald Bowen; **bench mark** Allen Moore; **benzene ring** John Keaveny; **beret** U.S. Navy; **Bessemer converter** John Keaveny—American Iron and Steel Institute; **betel palm** Laurel Cook; **bevel gear** Carl Bass; **bicycle** AMF Inc.; **Big Dipper** George Lindbloom; **bighorn** Photo Researchers; **billiards** Frank Siteman; **billy goat** SDZ; **binnacle** Mystic Seaport; **binoculars** Frank Siteman; **bipinnate** Laurel Cook; **biplane** Smithsonian Institution; **bird-of-paradise flower** Laurel Cook; **bison** SDZ; **bit**[2] Stanley Tool Co.; **bittern**[1] Photo Researchers; **bittersweet, blackberry, black-eyed Susan** Laurel Cook; **black widow** Photo Researchers; **blast furnace** U.S. Steel Corp.; **blastoff** NASA; **bleeding-heart** Laurel Cook; **blesbok** Photo Researchers; **blimp**[1] Goodyear Tire and Rubber Co.; **blinder** Frank Siteman; **blister beetle** Photo Researchers; **block** Ronald Bowen; **blockhouse** John Keaveny; **bloodhound** Evelyn Shafer; **bloodroot** "Common Poisonous Plants," by John M. Kingsbury, Cornell Extension Bulletin 538; **bloomer**[2] Bettmann Archive; **blowtorch** Frank Siteman; **blueberry** Laurel Cook; **blue jay, boa constrictor** Photo Researchers; **boar** USDA; **boatbill** Photo Researchers; **bobcat** USDA; **bobolink** Photo Researchers; **bobwhite** Jackson Abbott; **bog** Ocean Spray Cranberries, Inc.; **bola** *Centaurs of Many Lands*, by Edward L. Tinker, Humanities Research Center, University of Texas, drawing by Albert Guiraldez; **boll weevil** USDA; **bolt**[1] Russell, Burdsall, and Kalmenoff; **bomb** Laurel Cook; **bomber** U.S. Air Force; **boneset** Matthew Kalmenoff; **bongo**[2] Frank Siteman; **bonnet** Smithsonian Institution; **bonsai** Frank Siteman; **boomerang** Jeffrey Dunn; **boot**[1] Frank Siteman; **Boötes** George Lindbloom; **borzoi, Boston terrier** Evelyn Shafer; **bottle-nosed dolphin** Photo Researchers; **bouncing Bet** "Common Poisonous Plants," by John M. Kingsbury, Cornell Extension Bulletin 538; **bow**[3] AMF Inc.; **bowline** from *The Ashley Book of Knots*, by Clifford W. Ashley, copyright 1944, reprinted by permission of Doubleday & Co., Inc.; **boxer**[2] Evelyn Shafer; **box kite** *Buch des Fluges*, Hermann Hoernes, Wien. G. Szelinski, 1911–12; **boysenberry** Laurel Cook; **brace** Stanley Tool Co.; **bracket fungus** Photo Researchers; **Braille** The Urban Studio; **brain** Neil Hardy; **brand** Bill Browning, Montana Chamber of Commerce; **Brazil nut, breadfruit** Laurel Cook; **breaker**[1] Frank Siteman; **bridge** Vermont Development Agency; **bridle** Picture Cube; **brig**[1], **brigantine** *Sailing and Small Craft Down the Ages*, copyright 1940 by the U.S. Naval Institute, Annapolis, Maryland; **Brittany spaniel** Evelyn Shafer; **brocade** MFA; **bronchus** Neil Hardy; **brontosaur** Matthew Kalmenoff; **brooch** EPA; **Brussels sprout** Laurel Cook; **bubble chamber** University of California Lawrence Radiation Laboratory, Berkeley; **buck**[1] SDZ; **Buddha** MFA; **budgerigar** Photo Researchers; **buffalo** USDA; **bulldog** Evelyn Shafer; **bulldozer** International Harvester; **bullfrog** SDZ; **bullmastiff** Evelyn Shafer; **bullroarer** Charles C. Colley, Arizona Historical Society; **bull terrier** Evelyn Shafer; **bumblebee** USDA; **buoy** U.S. Coast Guard; **Bunsen burner** Jeffrey Dunn; **burnoose** Picture Cube; **bust**[1] MFA; **buttercup** Laurel Cook; **butterfly** Jeffrey Dunn; **butterfly fish** NOAA; **buttonhole stitch** Singer Co.; **Byzantine** Frank Siteman.

cabin Allen Moore; **cable car** Albuquerque Convention and Visitors Bureau; **cable stitch** Paul Light/Light Wave; **cacomistle** Photo Researchers; **cactus** USDA; **caduceus** Frank Siteman; **Cairn terrier** Evelyn Shafer; **calceolaria** Laurel Cook; **calculator** Hewlett-Packard; **California poppy** Laurel Cook; **calliper** Frank Siteman; **cells** Laurel Cook; **calumet** Museum of the American Indian, Heye Foundation; **cam** Frank Siteman; **camel** Picture Cube; **camellia** Laurel Cook; **cameo** MFA; **campanile** EPA; **camper** Winnebago Industries, Inc.; **canal** Frank Siteman; **canary** Photo Researchers; **cancer** George Lindbloom; **candelabrum** Frank Siteman; **candlestick** MFA; **Canis Major, Canis Minor** Georg Lindbloom; **cannon** Picture Cube; **canopy** The Metropolitan Museum of Art; **cantaloupe** Laurel Cook; **canvasback** Interior: Sport Fisheries and Wildlife; **canyon** Allen Moore; **cap** Jon Chase; **caparison** The Metropolitan Museum of Art; **cape**[1] Ben Kahn Furs Corp.; **capital**[2] MFA; **capitol** Library of Congress; **Capricorn** George Lindbloom; **capstan** Mystic Seaport; **carbine** Frank Siteman; **carburetor** Richard Glassman; **cardioid** Carl Bass; **caribou** Steve McCutcheon, Alaska Pictorial Services; **caricature** Bettmann Archive—Culver Pictures, Inc.; **carillon** Allen Moore; **carob** Mathew Kalmenoff; **carpus** W. Carter; **carrot** Laurel Cook; **cart** The Staten Island Historical Society; **cartwheel** Allen Smith; **casaba** Laurel Cook; **cascade** Allen Moore; **casement** *Stagecraft and Scene Design*, by H.P. Philippi, Houghton Mifflin Co.; **cashew** Laurel Cook; **Cashmere goat** Photo Researchers; **cassava** Laurel Cook; **Cassiopeia** George Lindbloom; **caster** MFA; **castle** Burton Holmes Collection, EKM-Nepenthe; **catafalque** John F. Kennedy Library; **catalpa** Photo Researchers; **catapult** Cal Sacks; **catbird** Grant Heilman; **catcher** Picture Cube; **catfish** Interior: Sport Fisheries and Wildlife; **cathode-ray tube** Jean Erdoes; **catwalk** Jeffrey Dunn; **cauliflower** Laurel Cook; **C clef** Franco Colombo Publications, New York; **cedar, celery** Laurel Cook; **cell** Neil Hardy; **cello** Ron Schick; **Celtic cross, cenotaph** Allen Moore; **centaur** The Metropolitan Museum of Art; **Centaurus** George Lindbloom; **century plant** Laurel Cook; **Cepheus** George Lindbloom; **Cerberus** MFA; **cerebellum, cerebral cortex** Laurel Cook; **cestus**[2] Culver Pictures, Inc.; **Cetus** George Lindbloom; **chafing dish** MFA; **chalice** MFA; **chambered nautilus** Jeffrey Dunn; **chameleon** Photo Researchers; **chandelier** Allen Moore; **chariot** The Metropolitan Museum of Art; **charm** MFA; **chase**[2] Frank Siteman; **checkers** Picture Cube; **cheetah** *Drawing at the Zoo*, by Raymond Sheppard, Studio Publications, 1949; **chef** Jon Chase; **cherry** Laurel Cook; **cherub** Frank Siteman; **chestnut** Laurel Cook; **chevron** Jeffrey Dunn; **chick** Ralston Purina; **chickpea, chicory** Laurel Cook; **chiffonier** Sotheby Parke Bernet; **chihuahua** Evelyn Shafer; **chimera** EPA; **chimney sweep** Picture Cube; **chimpanzee, chinchilla** SDZ; **chipmunk** U.S. Forest Service; **chisel** Stanley Tool Co.; **choir** Ellis Herwig, Stock, Boston; **chokecherry** Laurel Cook; **chopsticks** Allen Smith; **chorus** Martha Swope; **chow**[1] Evelyn Shafer; **Christmas cactus** Laurel Cook; **Christmas rose** "Common Poisonous Plants," by John Kingsbury, Cornell Extension Bulletin 538; **chromosome** Grant Heilman; **chrysalis** Matthew Kalmenoff; **chuck**[2] Frank Siteman; **chukar** Photo Researchers; **church** Samuel Chamberlain; **churn** Donald F. Eaton, Old Sturbridge Village; **ciborium** MFA; **cicada** Photo Researchers; **circle** Carl Bass; **circus** Ringling Brothers and Barnum & Bailey Circus; **cirrocumulus, cirrus** Grant Heilman; **cithara, cittern** The Metropolitan Museum of Art; **cityscape** Port Authority of NY and NJ: **civet** Matthew Kalmenoff; **clam**[1] NOAA; **clamp** Stanley Tool Co.; **clapboard** Frank Siteman; **clarinet** Ron Schick; **clavicle** Laurel Cook; **claw hammer, cleaver** Stanley Tool Co.; **clematis** Laurel Cook; **cliff** British Tourist Authority; **cliff dweller** Allen Moore; **climbing iron** reprinted from *Dictionary of Americanisms on Historical Principles*, by Mitford M. Mathews, by permission of The University of Chicago Press; **climbing perch** Matthew Kalmenoff; **clip** James Scherer; **clipper** Mystic Seaport; **clitellum** Photo Researchers; **clock**[1] MFA; **cloister** The Metropolitan Museum of Art; **clove**[1] Laurel Cook; **cloverleaf** Allen Moore; **clown** Ringling Brothers and Barnum & Bailey Circus; **Clumber spaniel** Evelyn Shafer; **Clydesdale** Anheuser Busch, Inc.; **coat of arms** MFA; **coaxial cable** Laurel Cook; **cobra** SDZ; **Cochin China** Matthew Kalmenoff; **cockade** Frank Siteman; **cocker spaniel** Evelyn Shafer; **cockpit** Frank Siteman; **cockroach** Grant Heilman; **coconut** Laurel Cook; **codpiece** EPA; **coffee** Laurel Cook; **cogwheel, colander** Frank Siteman; **coleus** Laurel Cook; **coliseum** EPA; **college** Bradford F. Herzog, Wellesley College; **collie** Evelyn Shafer; **colt** Frank Siteman; **columbine** Laurel Cook; **column** Allen Moore; **combine** International Harvester, Inc.; **comet** Yerkes Observatory Photograph; **commode** MFA; **compact**[1] Allen Moore; **compass** Allen Smith; **compass card** E. S. McNally and Co.; **complementary angles** Laurel Cook; **component** Carl Bass; **composite** Matthew Kalmenoff; **compote** Jeffrey Dunn; **compound eye** Grant Heilman; **compound leaf** Laurel Cook; **computer** Digital Equipment Corp.; **concave** Carl Bass; **concertina** Allen Moore; **conch, concrete** Frank Siteman; **condensation** Allen Moore; **condor** U.S. Department of the Interior; **conductor** courtesy of the Chicago Symphony Orchestra; **cone** Carl Bass—Allen Moore; **Conestoga wagon** reprinted from *Dictionary of Americanisms on Historical Principles*, by Mitford M. Mathews, by permission of The University of Chicago Press; **confluence** Peter Vandermark; **conger** Matthew Kalmenoff; **conic section** Laurel Cook; **conning tower** Allen Moore; **conservatory** Lord & Burnham; **console table** EPA—Sotheby Parke Bernet; **constable** British Tourist Authority; **contact lens** Bausch & Lomb; **container** Allen Moore; **contortionist** Circus World Museum, Baraboo, WI; **contour map** U.S. Geological Survey; **control tower** Allen Smith; **convertible** General Motors; **convex** Carl Bass; **conveyer** National Coffee Association of the USA; **coot** SDZ; **coping saw** Stanley Tool Co.; **copperhead** SDZ; **coral** Frank Siteman; **coral snake** SDZ; **corbie-step** Princeton University Library; **cordate** Laurel Cook; **Corinthian** Allen Moore—after Nicholson; **corn[1]**, **cornflower** Laurel Cook; **cornice** Allen Moore; **cornucopia** Frank Siteman; **coronation** UPI, Inc.; **coronet** EPA; **cortege** John F. Kennedy Library; **corvette** Culver Pictures, Inc.; **costume** Allen Smith; **cotter pin** John Keaveny; **cotyledon** Matthew Kalmenoff; **coupler** Allen Moore; **courthouse** Jeffrey Dunn; **courtyard, coveralls** Allen Moore; **covered bridge** Vermont Development Agency; **covered wagon** Library of Congress; **cowbane** Matthew Kalmenoff; **cowbird** Grant Heilman; **cowboy** *The Charles M. Russell Book*, by Harold McCracken; **cowry** Jeffrey Dunn; **coxswain** Allen Moore; **coyote** SDZ; **crab[1]** Matthew Kalmenoff; **cradle** MFA; **crampon** Allen Moore; **cranberry** Laurel Cook; **crane** SDZ—Bucyrus-Erie Co.; **crater** NASA; **cravat, crazy quilt** Allen Moore; **creamer** MFA; **crèche** Allen Moore; **creel** L. L. Bean, Inc.; **crenate, crescent** Laurel Cook; **crest** Allen Moore; **crewel** Allen Smith; **cricket[1]** Grant Heilman; **cricket[2]** UPI, Inc.; **crochet** Frank Siteman; **crocodile** SDZ; **crocus** Laurel Cook; **croft, crop** Allen Moore; **crosier** MFA; **crosstree** Mystic Seaport; **cross vault** Sturgis, *Dictionary of Architecture*; **crossword puzzle** Allen Smith; **crow[1]** Grant Heilman; **crowbar** Stanley Tool Co.; **crown** British Tourist Authority; **crow's-nest** Jeffrey Dunn; **crucible** Frank Siteman; **cruet** Anchor Hocking Corp.; **Crux** George Lindbloom; **crystal** Waterford Glass Inc.; **crystal ball** Allen Moore; **cube** Carl Bass; **cubism** MFA; **cuckoo** Grant Heilman; **cuckoo clock** Allen Moore; **cuckoopint** Matthew Kalmenoff; **culottes** Allen Moore; **cultivator** Grant Heilman; **cumin** American Spice Trade Association; **cummerbund** Allen Moore; **cumulonimbus** Grant Heilman; **cuneate** Laurel Cook; **cuneiform** Frank Siteman; **Cupid** The Metropolitan Museum of Art; **cupola** Library of Congress; **curette** Allen Moore; **curfew** Jackson M. Abbott; **current** Laurel Cook; **cusk, custard apple** Matthew Kalmenoff; **customhouse** Library of Congress; **cutlass** Bettman Archive; **cutter** Mystic Seaport; **cuttlefish** Matthew Kalmenoff; **cyclamen** Laurel Cook; **cycloid** Carl Bass; **cyclotron** John Keaveny; **Cygnus** George Lindbloom; **cylinder** Carl Bass; **cymbal** Ron Schick; **cypress** Laurel Cook; **cypress vine** Matthew Kalmenoff.

dachshund Evelyn Shafer; **daffodil** Laurel Cook; **dagger** The Metropolitan Museum of Art; **daguerreotype** Allen Moore, courtesy of Henry Deeks; **daisy** Laurel Cook; **Dalmatian** Evelyn Schafer; **dam[1]** Idaho Department of Commerce and Development; **damascene** Reed and Barton; **dandelion** Laurel Cook; **Dandie Dinmont** Evelyn Shafer; **Daphne** EPA; **daredevil** UPI, Inc.; **dart** Frank Siteman; **dashiki** Picture Cube; **date line** Francis & Shaw, Inc.; **date palm, davit, dayflower, day lily** Laurel Cook; **deadeye** Mystic Seaport; **death mask** The Metropolitan Museum of Art; **decanter** Waterford Glass, Inc.; **decoy** L.L. Bean, Inc. **decurrent** Matthew Kalmenoff; **decussate** Laurel Cook; **deer** Interior: Sport Fisheries and Wildlife; **deerhound** Evelyn Shafer; **deer mouse** Grant Heilman; **delft** MFA; **demijohn** Jeffrey Dunn; **dentate** Laurel Cook; **DNA** Grant Heilman; **depot** Union Pacific Railroad; **derby** Library of Congress; **derrick** Standard Oil Co.—Mobil Oil Corp.; **derringer** Frank Siteman; **dervish** *Ridpath's Universal History*, by John Clark Ridpath, Merrill and Baker, NY, copyright 1899; **desert[1]** Frank Siteman; **desk** MFA; **desman** Matthew Kalmenoff; **deuce[1]** U.S. Playing Card; **Devl** EPA; **dewlap** Grant Heilman; **dhow** Mystic Seaport; **diamond** U.S. Playing Card; **diamondback** SDZ; **Diana** The Metropolitan Museum of Art; **diatom** Grant Heilman; **dice** Frank Siteman; **dickcissel** Photo Researchers; **die[2]** Reed and Barton; **diesel engine** Daimler-Benz Aktiengesellschaft; **diffusion** Grant Heilman; **digestive system** Neil Hardy; **digital** Timex; **digitate** Laurel Cook; **dihedral angle** Carl Bass; **dilapidate** Allen Moore; **dimorphism** Matthew Kalmenoff; **dinghy** Peter Vandermark; **diode** Allen Moore; **Dionysus** MFA; **diorama** Museum of Science, Boston; **dipper** Jeffrey Dunn; **diptych** The Metropolitan Museum of Art; **dirndl** Allen Moore; **discus** Barbara Alper, Stock, Boston; **dish** MFA; **disposal** In-sink-erator, Racine, WI; **dissected** Ethel Hausman; **distaff** Shelburne Museum; **distort** Jon Chase; **diver** AMF, Inc.; **DNA** Grant Heilman; **Doberman pinscher** Evelyn Shafer; **dodecagon, dodecahedron, dogwood** Laurel Cook; **dolly** Allen Moore; **dolly** Jeffrey Dunn; **dolphin** Marineland of Florida; **dome** Frank Siteman; **domino[2]** Picture Cube; **donkey** Grant Heilman; **Doric** Allen Moore; **Doric order** After Nicholson; **dormer** Frank Siteman; **dory[1]** Mystic Seaport; **double bass** Ron Schick; **double-decker** Frank Siteman; **dracaena** Laurel Cook; **Draco** George Lindbloom; **dragon** Prints Division, NYPL; **dragonet** Matthew Kalmenoff; **dragonfly** Photo Researchers; **drawbridge** Elizabeth Hamlin, Stock, Boston; **drawknife** Jeffrey Dunn; **dreadnought** Naval Photographic Center; **dredge[1]** Frank Siteman; **dribble** Boston Celtics; **driftwood** George Bellerose, Stock, Boston; **drill[1]** Mobil Oil Corp.; **drogue parachute** NASA; **dromedary** SDZ; **drum** Ron Schick; **drum major** Owen Franken, Stock, Boston; **drum majorette** University of Texas; **dry cell** Cal Sacks; **dry dock** Allen Moore; **duck[1]** Allen Smith; **duel** Library of Congress; **dugong** Matthew Kalmenoff; **dulcimer** Picture Cube; **dune** Frank Siteman; **dust** Library of Congress; **dustpan** Frank Siteman; **Dutchman's-breeches** Laurel Cook.

eagle SDZ; **ear[1]** Neil Hardy; **earphone** Allen Smith; **earthquake** Library of Congress; **earthworm** Photo Researchers; **easel** Sotheby Park Bernet; **eaves** *The Gingerbread Age*, by John Maass, Rinehart & Co., Inc., copyright 1957; **echidna** SDZ; **echinus** Laurel Cook; **echo** EPA; **eclipse** NASA; **edelweiss** Laurel Cook; **edh** Alice Koeth; **eel** *Ichthyology*, by Lagler, Bardach, and Miller, John Wiley & Sons, copyright 1962; **egg[1]** Photo Researchers; **egg-and-dart** EPA; **egret, eider, eland** SDZ; **elderberry** Laurel Cook; **Electra** MFA; **electric furnace** U.S. Steel Corp.; **electric guitar** Allen Moore; **electroencephalogram** Medcraft Electronic Corp.; **electromagnet** Peter Vandermark; **elephant** SDZ; **elevated railway** Allen Moore; **elk** USDA; **ellipse, ellipsoid** Carl Bass; **elm** Laurel Cook; **elytron** Matthew Kalmenoff; **emarginate** Laurel Cook; **embankment** Allen Moore; **embroidery** MFA; **embryo** Grant Heilman; **endive, endocarp** Laurel Cook; **endocrine gland** Neil Hardy; **English horn** Walter Silver; **engraving** MFA; **ensiform** Laurel Cook; **ensign** Allen Moore; **entablature** Walter Silver; **entrechat** *The Classic Ballet*, by Muriel Stuart, Knopf, copyright 1952; **entwine** Frank Siteman; **Eos** MFA; **epaulet** Photographie Bulloz; **epergne** MFA; **epicycloid** Carl Bass; **equinox** The American Museum of Natural History; **Erlenmeyer flask** Jeffrey Dunn; **ermine** Photo Researchers—Colonial Williamsburg; **Eros** MFA; **erosion** USDA; **escalator** Frank Siteman; **escritoire** MFA; **escutcheon** Allen Moore; **esophagus** Neil Hardy; **esplanade** Jeffrey Dunn; **étagère** MFA; **Eton collar** Bettmann Archive; **eucalyptus** Laurel Cook—Photo Researchers; **Europa** EPA; **everglade** Photo Researchers; **ewer** MFA; **excavation, excavator** Frank Siteman; **experiment** Jeffrey Dunn; **exterior angle** Carl Bass; **extinguisher** Allen Smith; **eye** Neil Hardy; **eyelet** Frank Siteman.

façade Greater San Antonio Chamber of Commerce; **face angle** Laurel Cook; **factory** Allen Moore; **faience** EPA; **fairy shrimp** Photo Researchers; **falcon** Allen Moore; **fallow deer** Photo Researchers; **fan[1]** MFA; **fang** SDZ; **fanlight** Jeffrey Dunn; **fan palm** Laurel Cook; **fantail** Photo Researchers; **farm** USDA; **farrier** Allen Moore; **farthingale** MFA; **fatigue** Allen Moore; **faucet** "Handbook of Building Terms and Definitions," by Herbert Waugh and Nelson Burbank, Simmons-Boardman Publishing Corp.—Allen Moore; **fawn[2]** SDZ; **feather** Laurel Cook; **feather star** Matthew Kalmenoff; **featherstitch** *The Basic Stitches of Embroidery*, by N. Victoria Wade, Victoria and Albert Museum; **fedora** Allen Moore; **feedbag** Frank Siteman; **felucca** Burton Holmes Collection, EKM-Nepenthe; **femur** Laurel Cook; **fencing** Bruce Repko; **fender** Jeffrey Dunn; **ferret[1]** Interior: Sport Fisheries and Wildlife; **Ferris wheel** Eli Bridge Co.; **ferrotype, ferrule** Allen Moore; **ferryboat** Frank Siteman; **feverfew** Matthew Kalmenoff; **fez** Jeffrey Dunn; **fibula** Laurel Cook; **fichu** *What People Wore*, by Douglas Gorsline, copyright 1951, 1952 by David Gorsline, reprinted by permission of Viking Press; **fiddle** Frank Siteman; **fiddlehead** Laurel Cook; **fiddler crab** Photo Researchers; **fife** Peter Southwick, Stock, Boston; **fig** Laurel Cook; **figurehead** Jeff Albertson, Stock, Boston; **figure skating** Picture Cube; **figurine** MFA; **filament** Grant Heilman; **file[2]** Cal Sacks; **filefish** Photo Researchers; **filigree** Frank Siteman; **fimbriate** Matthew Kalmenoff; **fin[1]** Frank Siteman; **finial** Allen Moore; **firefighter** Jon Chase; **fire irons** Jeffrey Dunn; **fire tower** Allen Moore; **firing line** U.S. Navy; **fish** Francis & Shaw, Inc.; **fisher** SDZ; **fjord** Burton Holmes Collection, EKM-Nepenthe; **flag[1]** Frank Siteman; **flamingo** Photo Researchers; **flask** Jeffrey Dunn—Allen Moore; **flatboat** Library of Congress; **flea** USDA; **flèche** Frank Siteman; **fleur-de-lis** Jeffrey Dunn; **flicker[1]** Photo Researchers; **flight deck** Allen Moore; **flintlock** The Metropolitan Museum of Art; **flock[1]** USDA; **flounder[2]** NOAA; **flower, fluke[2]** Matthew Kalmenoff; **flute** Ron Schick; **flying buttress** Bibliothèque Nationale; **flying squirrel** Grant Heilman—Photo Researchers; **fob[1]** Allen Moore; **folium** Carl Bass; **follicle** Grant Heilman; **font[1]** MFA; **football** Dennis Desprois; **footbridge** Allen Moore; **forceps** *Stedman's Medical Dictionary*, 21st Edition, copyright 1966, The William's and Wilkins Co.; **forehand** Christopher Morrow, Stock, Boston; **foreshorten** EPA; **forge[1]** Donald F. Eaton, Old Sturbridge Village; **forget-me-not** Laurel Cook; **fork lift** Allen Moore; **fort** Library of Congress; **fossil** The American Museum of Natural History; **foundation** Frank Siteman; **fountain** The White House; **fountain pen** Parker Pen Co.; **four-poster** Jeffrey Dunn; **foxglove** Laurel Cook; **fox terrier** Evelyn Shafer; **framework** Allen Smith; **francolin** Photo Researchers; **freesia** Laurel Cook; **French horn** Ron Schick; **fret[3]** Allen Moore; **frieze[1]** Picture Cube; **frigate** Mary Anne Stets, Mystic Seaport; **frigate bird** Grant Heilman; **fringe** Allen Moore; **frock coat** *What People Wore*, by Douglas Gorsline, copyright 1951, 1952 by David Gorsline, reprinted by permission of Viking Press; **frontal bone, frustum, fuchsia** Laurel Cook; **fulcrum** Frances Davies; **funnel** Jeffrey Dunn; **furrow** Allen Moore; **fur seal** Photo Researchers; **fuse[2]** Bussmann Mfg. Div., McGraw-Edison Co.—Jeffrey Dunn.

gable The House of the Seven Gables, Salem, Mass.; **gaff** Laurel Cook; **gaiter** Allen Moore; **galaxy** Hale Observatories; **gallbladder** Laurel Cook; **galleon** Walter Silver; **gambrel roof** Grant Heilman; **gangplank** Frank Siteman; **Ganymede** MFA; **gar[1]** Matthew Kalmenoff; **gardenia** Laurel Cook; **gargoyle, garland, garter** Frank Siteman; **gas mask** Allen Smith; **gastropod** Grant Heilman; **gateway** Allen Moore; **gauntlet[1]** The Metropolitan Museum of Art; **gavel[1]** Jeffrey Dunn; **gazelle** SDZ; **gear** Picture Cube; **gecko** Grant Heilman; **Gemini** George Lindbloom; **generator** Ellis Herwig, Stock, Boston—*The Way Things Work*, Simon & Schuster, copyright 1967; **Geneva cross** Laurel Cook; **geode** Frank Siteman; **geodesic dome** Allen Moore; **geranium** Laurel Cook; **gerbil** Photo Researchers; **German shepherd** Evelyn Shafer; **gerrymander** Library of Congress; **geyser** National Park Service; **ghost town** Bill Browning, Montana Chamber of Commerce; **gibbon, Gila monster** SDZ; **gill[1]** Neil Hardy; **ginseng** Laurel Cook; **giraffe** SDZ; **girandole** Bettmann Archive; **girder** Frank Siteman; **glacier** Alaska Division of Tourism, Alaska Historical Library; **gladiolus** Laurel Cook; **glass blowing** EKM-Nepenthe; **glissade** *The Classic Ballet*, by Muriel Stuart, Knopf, copyright 1952; **globe** Jeffrey Dunn; **glockenspiel** American Music Conference; **glove** courtesy of Spaulding; **gloxinia** Laurel Cook; **glyph** Paul Light/Light Wave; **gnarled** Allen Moore; **gnu** SDZ; **goat** USDA; **goatee** Frank Siteman; **goblet** John van Schalkwyk, Shreve, Crump and Low, Inc.; **golden eagle** Interior: Sport Fisheries and Wildlife; **goldenrod** Laurel Cook; **goldfinch** Grant Heilman; **gondola** J. Goerg—Italian Government Travel Office; **gong** Allen Moore; **goose[1]** USDA; **gooseberry** Laurel Cook; **gopher** Matthew Kalmenoff; **Gorgon** MFA; **gorilla** SDZ; **Gothic, gourd** Frank Siteman; **Graces** MFA; **grackle** Grant Heilman; **graft[1]**, **grain elevator** Frank Siteman; **grampus** Matthew Kalmenoff; **grandfather clock** MFA; **grand piano** Steinway & Sons; **grape, grapefruit** Laurel Cook; **grappling iron** Jeffrey Dunn; **grater** Frank Siteman; **gravestone** Allen Smith; **grayling** Matthew Kalmenoff; **great horned owl** Grant Heilman; **great seal** Frank Siteman; **greenhouse** Lord & Burnham; **grenade** Jeffrey Dunn; **greyhound** Evelyn Shafer; **griffin** The Metropolitan Museum of Art; **grille** Frank Siteman; **gristmill** Allen Moore; **groin** The Metropolitan Museum of Art; **grouse[1]**, **grove** USDA; **guava** Laurel Cook; **Guernsey** The American Guernsey Cattle Club; **guitar** Allen Moore; **gypsy moth** Grant Heilman.

hacksaw Stanley Tool Co.; **haik** Cal Sacks; **halibut** NOAA; **halo** MFA; **halter[1]** Ralston Purina Co.; **hammer** Stanley Tool Co.; **hammerhead** Matthew Kalmenoff; **hammock[1]** Frank Siteman; **hamper[2]** Steele Canvas Basket Co., Inc.; **hamster** USDA; **handbill** International Harvester; **handcart, handcuff, handlebar mustache** Frank Siteman; **hand organ** Bettmann Archive; **handstand** Ron Schick; **hang glider** Jon Chase; **hansom** Shelburne Museum; **hare** USDA; **harmonica** M. Hohner; **harp** courtesy of Lyon & Healy Harps; **harpsichord** MFA; **harrow[1]** International Harvester; **hartebeest** Photo Researchers; **harvest** USDA; **hastate** Laurel Cook; **hatchet** Stanley Tool Co.; **hawk[1]** Allen Moore; **hawksbill** Photo Researchers; **hawthorn** Laurel Cook; **haystack** Frank Siteman; **hazel, heart** Laurel Cook; **hearth** The Society for the Preservation of New England Antiquities; **heather** Laurel Cook; **heath hen** Matthew Kalmenoff; **Hebe, hector** MFA; **Heimlich maneuver** Laurel Cook; **helicon** *The History of Musical Instruments*, by Curt Sachs, copyright 1940 by W.W. Norton, renewed 1968 by Irene Sachs; **helicopter** U.S. Army; **helix** Carl Bass; **hellebore** Laurel Cook; **helmet** Elizabeth Hamlin, Stock, Boston; **helmsman** Mystic Seaport; **hemlock, hemp, henna, hepatica** Laurel Cook; **Hepplewhite** MFA; **Hercules** MFA—George Lindbloom; **hermaphrodite brig** *Sailing and Small Craft Down the Ages*, copyright 1940 by the U.S. Naval Institute, Annapolis; **Hermes** MFA; **hermit crab** Matthew Kalmenoff; **heron** Interior: Sport Fisheries and Wildlife; **heterocercal** Matthew Kalmenoff; **hexagram** Carl Bass; **hibachi** Jeffrey Dunn; **hibiscus, hickory** Laurel Cook; **hieroglyphic** MFA; **highboy** Sotheby Parke Bernet; **high jump** Frank Siteman; **high relief, hilt** MFA; **hippopotamus** SDZ; **hobnail** John Keaveny; **hockey** Harvard Sports News Bureau; **hogfish** Matthew Kalmenoff; **hoist** Frank Siteman; **holly, hollyhock** Laurel Cook; **holster** Allen Smith; **homocercal** Matthew Kalmenoff; **honeycomb** Grant Heilman; **honeysuckle** Laurel Cook; **hookah** Frank Siteman; **hoop skirt** Bettmann Archive; **hop[2]** Matthew Kalmenoff; **horn** art by Enid Kotschning from "Horns and Antlers" by Walter Modell, copyright April, 1969, by Scientific American, Inc., all rights reserved; **horned toad** USDA; **hornet** Grant Heilman; **horse** Frank Siteman—Francis & Shaw, Inc.; **horse chestnut** Laurel Cook; **horseshoe crab** Photo Researchers; **hourglass** Allen Moore; **howdah** Frank Siteman; **howitzer** U.S. Navy; **hull** Allen Moore; **hummingbird** Grant Heilman; **hurdle** Picture Cube; **hurdy-gurdy** MFA; **hyacinth** Laurel Cook; **Hydra** Grant Heilman; **hydrangea** Laurel Cook; **hydrant** Allen Moore; **hydrofoil** Boeing Marine Systems; **hyena** SDZ; **hyperbola, hyperbolic paraboloid, hyperboloid** Carl Bass; **hypodermic needle** Frank Siteman.

ibex SDZ; **icebreaker** U.S. Coast Guard; **ice pick** Frank Siteman; **ice-skate** Mike Mazzaschi, Stock, Boston; **ichneumon, ichneumon fly, ichthyosaur** Matthew Kalmenoff; **ideogram** Ta-tsun Chen; **idol** MFA; **igloo** Alaska Division of Tourism, Alaska Historical Library; **ignition** *Harper Encyclopedia of Science*, ed. by James R. Newman, Harper & Row, 1967; **illuminate** Empire State Building Co.; **illumination** MFA; **illusion** Carl Bass; **imbricate** Roche; **immigrant** Library of Congress; **impatiens** Laurel Cook; **imperial[2]** Bettmann Archive; **impost[2]** The Metropolitan Museum of Art; **inauguration** UPI, Inc.; **Incan** EKM-Nepenthe; **incandescent lamp** General Electric; **incubator** Joseph Marchetti; **Indian corn** Frank Siteman; **Indian paintbrush** Laurel Cook; **Indian tobacco** Matthew Kalmenoff; **indigo** Laurel Cook; **infanta** EPA/Alinari-Scala; **ingot** American Iron & Steel Institute; **inkstand** MFA; **inlay** The Metropolitan Museum of Art; **inscription** Allen Moore; **insect** Matthew Kalmenoff; **insignia** Frank Siteman; **instrument, instrument panel** Allen Smith; **insulation, insulator** Frank Siteman; **intaglio** MFA; **interior angle** Cal Sacks; **interlace, interlock** Allen Moore; **intertwine** New-York Historical Society; **involucel** Matthew Kalmenoff; **io moth** Photo Researchers; **Ionic** Allen Moore; **iris** Laurel Cook; **Irish setter, Irish terrier, Irish wolfhound** Evelyn Shafer; **ironwork** Frank Siteman; **ironworks** American Iron & Steel Institute; **Isis** MFA; **ivory** Allen Smith; **ivory-billed woodpecker** Photo Researchers, **ivy** Laurel Cook.

jabot Frank Siteman; **jack** Allen Moore; **jackal** SDZ; **jackhammer** Jon Chase; **jack-in-the-pulpit** Laurel Cook; **jaguar** SDZ; **jalousie** Allen Moore; **Japanese beetle** Photo Researchers; **jasmine** Laurel Cook; **jay[2]** Photo Researchers; **jellyfish** Grant Heilman; **jerkin** Jeffrey Dunn; **jet[2]** Gates Learjet; **jet engine** Pratt and Whitney; **jetty[1]** Jeffrey Dunn; **jewelweed** Ethel Hausman; **jew's-harp** Allen Moore; **jigsaw** Jeffrey Dunn; **jimsonweed** Laurel Cook; **jockey** Suffolk Downs; **joist** Laurel Cook; **joker** U.S. Playing Card Co.; **jonquil** Laurel Cook;

Joshua tree, judo Frank Siteman; **juggler** *Circus*, Bertha B. Burlieth, Putnam, copyright 1930; **juke box** Jeffrey Dunn; **junk**[2] Mystic Seaport; **Jupiter** NASA; **jute** Laurel Cook.

kabuki EPA/Sotheby Parke Bernet; **kangaroo, kangaroo rat** SDZ; **kapok** Laurel Cook; **karate** Picture Cube; **kayak** Great Canadian; **kazoo** Frank Siteman; **keel**[1] Mystic Seaport; **keg** Anheuser Busch, Inc.; **kepi** Frank Siteman; **kerf** Weyerhaeuser; **Kerry blue terrier** Evelyn Shafer; **key**[1] Pencil Points, December 1939; **keystone** Peter Vandermark; **killdeer** Photo Researchers; **kiln** Frank Siteman; **kilt** Allen Moore; **kimono** Allen Smith; **king** U.S. Playing Card Co.; **King Charles spaniel** Evelyn Shafer; **kingfisher** Photo Researchers; **kiosk** Picture Cube; **Klein bottle** Laurel Cook; **klieg light** UPI, Inc.; **Knickerbocker** Allen Moore; **knocker** Allen Smith; **knot**[1] Frank Siteman; **knurl** Allen Moore; **koala** SDZ; **Komodo dragon** Photo Researchers; **kraken** Bettmann Archive; **Krishna**[1] EPA; **Ku Klux Klan** Wide World Photos; **kumquat** Laurel Cook.

Labrador retriever Evelyn Shafer; **lace** Allen Smith; **lacewing** Photo Researchers; **lacrosse** Morse Photography courtesy of Harvard University; **ladder** Fire Dept., Washington, D.C.; **ladle** MFA; **lady's-slipper** Laurel Cook; **lamb** Allen Moore—Cal Sacks; **lamp** Frank Siteman; **lamprey** Photo Researchers—Matthew Kalmenoff; **lanceolate** Laurel Cook; **landing strip** Frank Siteman; **lap joint** Jeffrey Dunn; **larch** Laurel Cook; **large intestine** Neil Hardy; **lariat** Montana Chamber of Commerce; **larva** Grant Heilman; **laser** Daphne Prout; **Last Supper** EPA; **lattice** Allen Smith; **laurel, lavender** Laurel Cook; **lawn mower** Frank Siteman; **lazy tongs** Laurel Cook; **leaf spring** *Van Nostrand's Scientific Encyclopedia*, 3rd ed., D. Van Nostrand Co., copyright 1938, 1947, 1958; **leek** Laurel Cook; **leg-of-mutton** Bettmann Archive; **lei**[1] Hawaii Visitors Bureau; **lemon** Laurel Cook; **lemur** SDZ; **lens** Frank Siteman; **Leo** George Lindbloom; **leopard** SDZ; **leotard** Danskin, Inc.; **lettuce** Laurel Cook; **levee**[1], **level** Frank Siteman; **lever** Frances Davies; **Lhasa apso** Evelyn Shafer; **Libra** George Lindbloom; **lichen** Frank Siteman; **lifeboat** Cunard Line Ltd.; **life jacket, life preserver** Frank Siteman; **lighthouse, light meter** Allen Moore; **lightning rod** Electra Protection Co.—Allen Smith; **light pen** Allen Moore; **lilac, lily, lily of the valley** Laurel Cook; **lily pad** Frank Siteman; **lime**[1] Laurel Cook; **line of force** *The Physics of Electricity and Magnetism*, by Scott, John Wiley and Sons; **link**[1] Acco-American Chain Division; **Linotype** Frank Siteman; **lion** Grant Heilman; **litchi** Laurel Cook; **litter** Allen Moore; **Little Dipper** George Lindbloom; **live oak** Laurel Cook; **liver**[1] Neil Hardy; **llama** SDZ; **lobster, lobster pot** Frank Siteman; **locket** Allen Moore; **locomotive** Frank Siteman; **locust** Grant Heilman—Laurel Cook; **loganberry** Laurel Cook; **longbow** Mansell Collection; **loom**[2] Frank Siteman; **loosestrife, loquat** Laurel Cook; **lorgnette** Bettmann Archive; **lotus** Laurel Cook; **loupe** Frank Siteman; **louver** Allen Moore; **love-in-a-mist** Laurel Cook; **love seat** Sotheby Parke Bernet; **low relief** The Metropolitan Museum of Art; **lug**[1] Allen Moore; **luge** Lake Placid Chamber of Commerce; **lungfish** Matthew Kalmenoff; **lupine**[1] Laurel Cook; **lure** Frank Siteman; **lute**[1] MFA; **Lyra** George Lindbloom; **lyre** MFA.

macaw Photo Researchers; **macramé** Walter Silver; **Madonna** EPA; **maenad** MFA; **Magen David** Argenziano Associates; **magician** Peter Menzel, Stock, Boston; **magnet** Grant Heilman; **magnifying glass** Peter Vandermark; **magnolia** Laurel Cook; **malamute** Evelyn Shafer; **mallard** Frank Siteman; **mandala** *The Theory and Practice of Mandala*, by Giuseppe Tucci, Rider & Co., London, 1961; **mandible** Laurel Cook; **mandolin** MFA; **mandrake** Laurel Cook; **mane** Peter Vandermark; **mangle**[2] Walter Silver; **mangrove** Laurel Cook; **mansard, mantel** Jeffrey Dunn; **manticore** *The Book of Beasts*, by T.H. White, Jonathan Cape Ltd.; **manual alphabet** Gallaudet College, Washington, D.C.; **Manx cat** Photo Researchers; **maple** Laurel Cook; **maraca** Frank Siteman; **marathon** Jeffrey Dunn; **marigold** Laurel Cook; **marionette** Peter Vandermark; **marmoset** SDZ; **marquetry** Peter Vandermark; **Mars** NASA—MFA; **mascot** Allen Moore; **mask** MFA; **mastoid process** Neil Hardy; **matador** Burton Holmes Collection, EKM-Nepenthe; **matzo** Jeffrey Dunn; **mausoleum** *Handbook of Greek and Roman Architecture*, 2nd ed., by Donald Struan Robertson, Cambridge University Press, 1954; **maxilla, May apple** Laurel Cook; **Maypole** Bettmann Archive; **maze** Carl Bass; **meander** Peter Vandermark; **medal, Medal of Honor** U.S. Air Force; **Medea** MFA; **medicine man** The American Museum of Natural History; **medlar** Laurel Cook; **Medusa** Picture Cube; **meerschaum** Frank Siteman; **megaphone** Peter Vandermark; **melon** Laurel Cook; **melting point** Dick Morrill, Inc.; **memorial** Allen Moore; **Menelaus** MFA; **Menorah** Consulate General of Israel; **Mercator projection** Laurel Cook; **Mercury** Paul Laccavole; **merganser** Interior: Sport Fisheries and Wildlife; **metacarpus** Kip Carter; **metacenter** Laurel Cook; **metamorphosis** Photo Researchers; **metope** Mary Evans Picture Library, London; **micrometer, microphone** Peter Vandermark; **microscope** Bausch & Lomb; **midget, migrant** Library of Congress; **milestone** Walter Silver; **milkweed** Laurel Cook; **mill**[1] American Iron and Steel Institute; **mimosa** Laurel Cook; **miner** Jon Chase; **miniature, Minotaur** The Metropolitan Museum of Art; **minuteman** U.S. Treasury Dept.; **mirror** MFA; **missel thrush** Photo Researchers; **mission** George Robinson; **mistletoe** Laurel Cook; **miter** MFA; **miter joint** Ed McLaughlin; **mitt** Spaulding; **Möbius strip** Peter Vandermark; **moccasin** Allen Smith; **modular, moiré** Frank Siteman; **mold**[1] MFA—Allen Moore; **mold**[2] Phoebe McGuire; **monarch** Photo Researchers; **monkey** SDZ; **monkey wrench** Peter Vandermark; **monocle** Nicholas Sapieha, Stock, Boston; **monstrance** Peter Vandermark; **montage** Frank Siteman; **monument** Allen Smith; **Morgan** American Morgan Horse Association, Inc.; **morion**[1] The Metropolitan Museum of Art; **morning-glory** Laurel Cook; **morris** Picture Cube; **mortar** MFA—U.S. Army; **mortarboard** Frank Siteman; **mortise** Allen Moore; **mosaic** Worcester Art Museum; **mosquito** Grant Heilman; **mountain ash** Ethel Hausman; **mountain laurel** Laurel Cook; **mousetrap** Walter Silver; **mouth** Neil Hardy; **mule**[1] USDA; **multifoil** Allen Moore; **mural** J. Berndt, Stock, Boston; **Murphy bed** Bettman Archive; **Muse** EPA; **mushroom** Laurel Cook; **muskrat** USDA; **mustard** Laurel Cook; **mute** Peter Vandermark; **muzzle** Evelyn Shafer; **myna** Photo Researchers; **myrtle** Laurel Cook.

nail © The Hearst Corporation, reprinted from *Popular Mechanics*; **narcissus** Laurel Cook—EPA; **narwhal** Photo Researchers; **nasal, nasturtium** Laurel Cook; **nautch** *Word Costumes*, by Angela Bradshaw, Adam and Charles Black, London, 1952; **nautilus** Jeffrey Dunn; **nave**[1] Allen Moore; **neckerchief** Boy Scouts of America; **needlepoint** Allen Moore; **Neptune** The Metropolitan Museum of Art; **nest** Photo Researchers; **netsuke** EPA/Sotheby Parke Bernet; **newel post** Allen Moore; **Newfoundland** Evelyn Shafer; **newt** Photo Researchers; **niche** Allen Moore; **nightingale** Photo Researchers; **Nike** MFA; **nipper** Peter Vandermark; **No**[1] EPA/Sotheby Parke Bernet; **nomograph** Carl Bass; **noose** Phoebe McGuire; **Norfolk Island pine** Laurel Cook; **normal distribution** Carl Bass; **nose** Neil Hardy; **note** Cal Sacks; **nuclear reactor** U.S. Atomic Energy Commission; **nucleus** Neil Hardy; **nut** Cal Sacks; **nutcracker** Peter Vandermark; **nutmeg** Laurel Cook.

oarfish Matthew Kalmenoff; **obelisk** Allen Moore; **obi** Allen Smith; **oboe** Ron Schick; **observatory** Hale Observatories; **obtuse angle** Carl Bass; **ocelot** SDZ; **octagon, octahedron** Carl Bass; **octopus** Grant Heilman; **odalisque** The Metropolitan Museum of Art; **Odysseus, Oedipus** MFA; **oil well** Library of Congress; **okapi** SDZ; **okra** Laurel Cook; **Old English sheepdog** Evelyn Shafer; **oleander, olive** Laurel Cook; **Olympic games** UPI, Inc.; **onion** Laurel Cook; **opah** Matthew Kalmenoff; **open-hearth** Cal Sacks; **opera glasses** MFA; **opera hat** George Eastman House Collection; **Ophiuchus** George Lindbloom; **opossum** SDZ; **optic nerve, orange** Laurel Cook; **orangutan** SDZ; **orbit, orchid** Laurel Cook; **Orestes** MFA; **organ grinder** Bettmann Archive; **organ-pipe cactus** USDA; **Oriental rug** Sotheby Park Bernet; **origami** Frank Siteman; **Orion** George Lindbloom; **orthogonal projection** Carl Bass; **oryx** Photo Researchers; **osculation** Laurel Cook; **Osiris** The Metropolitan Museum of Art; **osprey, ostrich** Photo Researchers; **otter** SDZ; **outboard motor** Allen Smith; **oval** Frank Siteman; **ovate** *Pacific Coast Trees*, by Lloyd Lyman, University of California Press; **overpass** Allen Smith; **ovum** Neil Hardy; **ox** Donald F. Eaton, Old Sturbridge Village; **oyster, oystercatcher** Photo Researchers.

pachysandra Laurel Cook; **pad**[1] Boston Bruins; **paddy wagon, padlock** Frank Siteman; **pagoda** EKM-Nepenthe; **painter**[1] Jon Chase; **painter**[2] Jeffrey Dunn; **paisley** Allen Moore; **palanquin** Burton Holmes Collection, EKM-Nepenthe; **palette** Allen Moore; **pallet**[1] Peter Vandermark; **Pan** MFA; **pancreas** Neil Hardy; **panda** National Zoological Park; **panicle** Laurel Cook; **pannier** George Bellerose, Stock, Boston; **pansy, papaw** Laurel Cook; **papaya** U.S. Forest Service—Laurel Cook; **papoose** The Museum of the American Indian, Heye Foundation; **parabola, paraboloid** Carl Bass; **parachute** NASA; **parallel bars** Peter Vandermark; **parapet** Cal Sacks; **parasol** Burton Holmes Collection, EKM-Nepenthe; **parietal bone** Laurel Cook; **Paris** The Metropolitan Museum of Art; **parquetry** Peter Vandermark; **parrot** USDA; **parsnip** Laurel Cook; **partridge** Photo Researchers; **passionflower** Laurel Cook; **patchwork** Peter Vandermark; **patella** Laurel Cook; **pawl** Allen Moore—Diamond Studios; **pawnshop** Jeffrey Dunn; **pea, peach**[1] Laurel Cook; **peacock** Grant Heilman; **peanut, pear** Laurel Cook; **peavey** Allen Moore; **pecan** Laurel Cook; **peccary** SDZ; **pectoral muscle** Neil Hardy; **pedestal** Allen Smith; **peen** Stanley Tool Co.; **Pegasus** George Lindbloom—MFA; **Pekingese** Evelyn Shafer; **pelican** Frank Siteman; **pelvis** Neil Hardy; **pendant** Allen Moore; **pendulum** Cal Sacks; **pennant** Jeffrey Dunn; **penny** Allen Smith; **pentacle** Carl Bass; **peony, pepper** Laurel Cook; **pepper mill** Allen Smith; **perambulator** Frank Siteman; **percussion instrument** Jeffrey Dunn; **peregrine falcon** Allen Moore; **perfoliate** Laurel Cook; **pergola** Allen Moore; **periscope** Cal Sacks; **periwinkle**[2] Laurel Cook; **Persephone** MFA; **Perseus** George Lindbloom; **Persian cat** Photo Researchers; **persimmon** Laurel Cook; **perspective** Isabella Stewart Gardner Museum—Cal Sacks; **pestle** Jeffrey Dunn; **petunia** Laurel Cook; **pewter** MFA; **phalanx** B. Carter; **Pharaoh** MFA; **pheasant** Grant Heilman; **philodendron, phlox** Laurel Cook; **photoelectric cell** Cal Sacks; **phylactery** Religious News Services; **piano**[1] Steinway & Sons; **picket fence** Peter Vandermark; **pier** Port Authority of New York & New Jersey; **pietà** MFA; **pilaster** Allen Moore; **pilgrim** Library of Congress; **piling** Frank Siteman; **pillory** Bettmann Archive; **pimpernel** Laurel Cook; **pincers** Cal Sacks—Frank Siteman; **pineapple, pink**[1] Laurel Cook; **pinking shears** Jeffrey Dunn; **pintail** Photo Researchers; **pipeline** Peter Vandermark; **piranha** Photo Researchers; **Pisces** George Lindbloom; **pitcher**[2] MFA; **pitcher plant** Laurel Cook; **pitchfork** Cal Sacks; **pitch pipe** Jeffrey Dunn; **pith helmet, place kick** Frank Siteman; **plaid** Allen Moore; **planarian** Phoebe McGuire; **plane**[2] Stanley Tool Co.; **plane tree** *Pacific Coast Trees*, by Howard E. McMinn and Evelyn Maino, University of California Press, 1963; **plantain**[1], **plantain**[2] Laurel Cook; **platen, platform** Allen Moore; **platypus** Matthew Kalmenoff; **player piano** Jeffrey Dunn; **pleat** Allen Moore; **pliers** Stanley Tool Co.; **plinth, plow** Allen Moore; **plum**[1] Laurel Cook; **plumb** Peter Vandermark; **plunger** Allen Moore; **Plymouth Rock** USDA; **pocketknife** Allen Smith; **pogo stick** Peter Vandermark; **poinsettia** Laurel Cook; **poison hemlock** "Common Poisonous Plants," by J.M. Kingsbury, Cornell Extension Bulletin 538; **poison ivy, poison oak** Laurel Cook; **poker**[1] Allen Moore; **polar bear** SDZ; **polar coordinate** Carl Bass; **pole vault** Pamela Schuyler, Stock, Boston; **polo** © Walter Chandoha; **pomander** Allen Moore; **pomegranate** Laurel Cook; **pommel** Allen Moore; **poncho** Picture Cube; **pony express** Bettmann Archive; **poodle** Evelyn Shafer; **poppy** Laurel Cook; **porcelain** MFA; **porcupine** SDZ; **pork** Cal Sacks; **porringer** MFA; **porthole** Peter Vandermark; **Portuguese man-of-war** Grant Heilman; **portulaca** Laurel Cook; **Poseidon** MFA; **poster**[1] Circus World Museum, Baraboo, WI; **postimpressionism** MFA; **potato** Laurel Cook; **potbelly stove** Bettmann Archive; **potter**[1] Old Sturbridge Village; **potter's wheel** Frank Siteman; **power plant** Jeffrey Dunn; **prairie dog** SDZ; **pre-Columbian** MFA; **pressure suit** NASA; **pricket** MFA; **prickly pear** Frank Siteman; **prie-dieu** MFA; **primitive** MFA; **primrose** Laurel Cook; **printed circuit, printing press** Allen Moore; **prism** Cal Sacks; **probe** NASA; **produce** Frank Siteman; **profile** MFA; **prohibition** Library of Congress; **Prometheus** MFA; **pronghorn** Photo Researchers; **prop root** Laurel Cook; **prospector** Library of Congress; **Proteus** Bettmann Archive; **protozoan** Grant Heilman; **protractor** Keuffel & Esser Co.; **psyche** EPA; **Ptolemaic system** Phoebe McGuire; **puffball** Photo Researchers; **puffin** Picture Cube; **pug**[1] Evelyn Shafer; **pulley** Picture Cube; **pulmonary** Laurel Cook; **pump**[1] Christopher Morrow, Stock, Boston; **punt**[1] Mystic Seaport; **puppet** Allen Smith; **Purple Heart** U.S. Air Force; **pushup** Ron Schick; **pussy willow** Laurel Cook; **puttee** Bettmann Archive; **pyramid** Frank Siteman.

quadrangle *Words: The New Dictionary*, Grosset & Dunlap, 1947; **quahog** Peter Vandermark; **quarrel**[2] Phoebe McGuire; **quarry**[2] Allen Moore; **quarter-deck** *The Ship*, by Bjorn Landstrom, illustrations copyright 1961 by Bjorn Landstrom, reprinted by permission of Doubleday & Co., Inc.; **quarter horse** Grant Heilman; **quartz** Peter Vandermark; **quatrefoil** Allen Moore; **Queen Anne's lace, queen post** Laurel Cook; **quill** Matthew Kalmenoff; **quillwort** Laurel Cook; **quilt** Allen Moore; **quiver** George Bellerose, Stock, Boston.

rabbit Picture Cube; **race** Suffolk Downs; **rack**[1] Cal Sacks; **radial symmetry** Allen Moore; **radiometer** Peter Vandermark; **radish** Laurel Cook; **radius** Neil Hardy; **raft**[1] Library of Congress; **ragweed** Laurel Cook; **rampant, ramrod** Allen Moore; **rapier** Bettmann Archive; **rasp** Frank Siteman; **raspberry** Laurel Cook; **ratchet** Diamond Studios; **rattle**[1] MFA; **rattlesnake** Grant Heilman; **rattlesnake flag** Frank Siteman; **raven**[1] Photo Researchers; **ray**[2] New England Aquarium; **realism** The Metropolitan Museum of Art; **reamer** Allen Moore; **reaper** International Harvester; **rebus** collection of Mr. & Mrs. Sherman Post Haight; **recorder** Ron Schick; **red clover, Red Cross, red mulberry** Laurel Cook; **reel**[1] Frank Siteman; **re-entrant angle** Carl Bass; **referee, reflection** Allen Moore; **regalia** UPI, Inc.; **regiment** Library of Congress; **register** NCR Corp.; **relief** EKM-Nepenthe; **reliquary** The Metropolitan Museum of Art; **remora** Matthew Kalmenoff; **reniform** Phoebe McGuire; **reptile** Photo Researchers; **reredos** Art and Architecture Division, NYPL; **reseda** Laurel Cook; **resistor** Frank Siteman; **respirator** Walter Silver; **retable** MFA; **retort**[2] Laurel Cook; **retriever** Evelyn Shafer; **revetment** Allen Moore; **Revolutionary War** Marblehead Chamber of Commerce; **revolver** Smith and Wesson; **rhesus monkey** Grant Heilman; **rhinoceros** Grant Heilman; **Rhodesian ridgeback** Evelyn Shafer; **rhododendron, rhubarb** Laurel Cook; **rib** Neil Hardy; **ridgepole** *Words: The New Dictionary*, Grosset & Dunlap, 1947; **rifle**[1] U.S. Navy; **rigging** Mystic Seaport; **ring**[1] Allen Smith; **ring-necked pheasant** Ralston Purina; **rink** Allen Moore; **ripsaw** Peter Vandermark; **roadrunner** Matthew Kalmenoff; **robin** Photo Researchers; **robot** 20th-Century Fox Film Corp.; **rockaway** Shelburne Museum; **rocking chair** MFA; **rodeo** Jon Chase; **roller coaster** Magic Mountain; **roller-skate** Allen Moore; **rolling mill** *McGraw-Hill Encyclopedia of Science and Technology*, copyright 1966, used by permission of McGraw-Hill Book Co.; **rorqual** Matthew Kalmenoff; **Rorschach test** Jeffrey Dunn; **rose**[1] Laurel Cook; **rose window** Frank Siteman; **rotisserie** Allen Moore; **Round Table** Bettmann Archive; **rowan, rubber plant** Laurel Cook; **rubbing** Walter Silver, courtesy of Nancy Woolley; **ruby-throated hummingbird** Jackson Abbott; **rug** The Metropolitan Museum of Art; **rumble seat** Allen Moore; **runabout** Bettmann Archive; **runcinate** Ethel Hausman; **rune**[1] Alice Koeth; **rung**[1] Peter Vandermark; **running board** William Litant, Museum of Transportation, Boston.

sabot Bettmann Archive; **sacrum** Laurel Cook; **saddle** Allen Smith; **safety net** Circus World Museum, Baraboo, WI; **Sagittarius** George Lindbloom; **saguaro** Grant Heilman; **Saint Bernard** Evelyn Shafer; **salamander** Photo Researchers; **salmon** NOAA; **saltbox** Laurel Cook; **saluki** Evelyn Shafer; **salute** Allen Moore; **salver** EPA/Sotheby Parke Bernet; **samara** Laurel Cook; **samovar** Murray Belsky; **sampan** Rick Smolar, Stock, Boston; **sampler** MFA; **sand** Donald Dietz, Stock, Boston; **sandal**[1], **sand dollar** Allen Moore; **sandwich man** Culver Pictures, Inc.; **sansevieria** Laurel Cook; **sap** Vermont Development Agency; **sapsucker** Photo Researchers; **sarcophagus** MFA—The Metropolitan Museum of Art; **sari** Frank Siteman; **sassafras** Laurel Cook; **Saturn** NASA; **satyr** MFA; **savin** Laurel Cook; **saw**[1] Stanley Tool Co.; **saxophone** Ron Schick; **scaffold** Vanguard Mfg., Inc.; **scale**[3] Frank Siteman; **scallop** Frank Siteman—MFA; **scalpel** Allen Moore; **scapula** Laurel Cook; **scarab** The Metropolitan Museum of Art; **Scaramouch** Bibliothèque Nationale; **scepter** Bettmann Archive; **schnauzer** Evelyn Shafer; **schooner** Mystic Seaport; **scissortail** Interior: Sport Fisheries and Wildlife; **sconce**[2] MFA; **scoop, score** Allen Moore; **scorpion** Grant Heilman; **Scorpius** George Lindbloom; **Scottish deerhound, Scottish terrier** Evelyn Shafer; **scrape** Stanley Tool Co.; **screech owl** Grant Heilman; **screwdriver** Stanley Tool Co.; **scrimshaw** Nantucket Historical Association; **scuba** NEA; **sculptress** Frank Siteman; **scuttle**[2] Allen Moore; **scythe** Frank Siteman; **sea anemone** Grant Heilman; **sea cucumber** NOAA; **sea gull** Allen Moore; **sea horse** Grant Heilman; **sea lion** Nat Fair; **sea otter** Matthew Kalmenoff; **seat belt** Davis Aircraft Products Co., Inc.; **sea urchin** Grant Heilman; **secretary** MFA; **secund** Ethel Hausman; **sedan** Walter Silver; **sedilia** *A History of Architecture*, 17th ed., by Banister Fletcher, Athlone Press, University of London; **seesaw** Frank Siteman; **seismograph, seismometer** Seismographic Stations, University of California, Berkeley; **self-heal** Ethel Hausman; **semaphore** Allen

Moore; **semipalmate** Matthew Kalmenoff; **Seneca snakeroot, senna** Laurel Cook; **sentry box** Frank Siteman; **sepal** Laurel Cook; **sequoia** U.S. Forest Service; **serpent** MFA; **serrate, sessile** Matthew Kalmenoff; **settee, Sèvres** MFA; **sewing machine** Frank Siteman; **sexpartite** *A History of Architecture*, 17th ed., by Banister Fletcher, Athlone Press, University of London; **sextant** Frank Siteman; **shagbark** Grant Heilman; **shallot, shamrock** Laurel Cook; **sharple** Mystic Seaport; **shawl** Murray Belsky; **shear** Allen Moore; **shed**[2] Frank Siteman; **shell** Frank Siteman—U.S. Navy; **shepherd's-purse** Library of the New York Botanical Gardens; **Sheraton** MFA; **Shetland pony** © Walter Chandoha; **shillelagh** Allen Moore; **shinleaf** Matthew Kalmenoff; **Shiva** EPA; **shoemaker** Allen Moore; **shofar** EPA/Sotheby Parke Bernet; **shooting star** Laurel Cook; **shore**[1] Cape Cod Chamber of Commerce; **shoreline** Allen Moore; **shorthorn** USDA; **shovel** Allen Moore; **shutter** Frank Siteman; **Siamese cat** Allen Smith; **sickle** Frank Siteman; **sidecar** Allen Moore; **side-wheeler** Mystic Seaport; **sieve** Frank Siteman; **sight** Naval Photographic Center; **signal, silhouette** Allen Moore; **silo** Bill Browning, Montana Chamber of Commerce; **silverfish** Photo Researchers; **sine curve** Carl Bass; **siphon** Laurel Cook; **sitar, skateboard, skeleton, skewer, skid** Allen Moore; **skimmer, skink** Grant Heilman; **skull** Frank Siteman; **skunk** SDZ; **skyline, skyscraper** Port Authority of New York & New Jersey; **sled** Princeton University Library; **sledge** Steve McCutcheon, Alaska Pictorial Service; **sledgehammer** Stanley Tool Co.; **sleigh** George M. Cushing; **slide** Allen Moore; **slippery elm** Laurel Cook; **sloop** Mystic Seaport; **slot machine** Frank Siteman; **sluice** Idaho Power Co.; **smallclothes** Bettmann Archive; **small intestine** Neil Hardy; **smartweed** Library of the New York Botanical Gardens; **smocking** Allen Moore; **snail** Grant Heilman; **snakeroot** "Common Poisonous Plants," by John Kingsbury, Cornell Extension Bulletin 538; **snapdragon** Laurel Cook; **snapping turtle** Photo Researchers; **snout** Ralston Purina; **snow leopard** SDZ; **snowmobile** Frank Siteman; **snuffer**[2] Peter Vandermark; **soccer** Harvard University; **soda fountain** Allen Smith; **sofa** Allen Moore; **solar panel** Picture Cube; **Solomon's seal** Matthew Kalmenoff; **sorrel** Laurel Cook; **soursop** Matthew Kalmenoff; **sousaphone** Bettmann Archive; **soybean** Laurel Cook; **space shuttle, space walk** NASA; **spade**[2] U.S. Playing Card Co.; **spadix** Matthew Kalmenoff; **spanker** Mystic Seaport; **spark plug** Peter Vandermark; **sparrow hawk** Grant Heilman; **spat**[3] Allen Moore; **spathe** Matthew Kalmenoff; **spear** Frank Siteman; **spearmint** Laurel Cook; **sperm whale** Matthew Kalmenoff; **sphenoid bone** Laurel Cook; **sphinx** Frank Siteman; **sphygmomanometer** Allen Moore; **spider** Grant Heilman; **spider monkey** Photo Researchers; **spigot** Walter Silver; **spine** Neil Hardy; **spinnaker** Mystic Seaport; **spinning wheel** Donald F. Eaton, Old Sturbridge Village; **spiny lobster** Matthew Kalmenoff; **spiral** Allen Moore; **splat**[1] MFA; **splay** Art & Architecture Division, NYPL; **spleen** Laurel Cook; **spline** Cal Sacks; **spoke**[1] Peter Vandermark; **sponge** Marineland of Florida—NOAA; **spoonbill** Grant Heilman; **sporran** Allen Moore; **spreader** Mystic Seaport; **springer spaniel** Evelyn Shafer; **sprinkler** USDA; **sprit** Mystic Seaport; **sprocket** Peter Vandermark; **squash**[1] Laurel Cook; **squid** NOAA; **squirrel** Allen Moore; **stag** Interior: Sport Fisheries and Wildlife; **stalactite** Grant Heilman; **stamen** Matthew Kalmenoff; **star anise, star apple** Laurel Cook; **starfish** NOAA; **stargazer** Matthew Kalmenoff; **statuary** Frank Siteman; **statue** MFA; **steam engine** *McGraw-Hill Encyclopedia of Science and Technology*, copyright 1960, used by permission of McGraw-Hill Book Co.; **steeple** Newport County Chamber of Commerce, Newport, RI; **steeplechase** Allen Moore; **stein** Peter Vandermark; **stepladder** Frank Siteman; **stern**[2] The Science Museum, London; **stethoscope** Armed Forces Institute of Pathology; **Stetson** Standard Oil Co. (NJ); **Stilson** Peter Vandermark; **stilt** Ringling Brothers and Barnum & Bailey Circus; **stirrup** Allen Moore; **stole**[1] EPA; **stomach** Neil Hardy; **stonemason** Allen Moore; **stopwatch** Peter Vandermark; **stork** Photo Researchers; **stove**[1] Allen Moore; **straight razor** Peter Vandermark; **straining beam** Laurel Cook; **stratocumulus** Grant Heilman; **strawberry** Laurel Cook; **streetcar** Allen Moore; **string bean** Laurel Cook; **strop** Peter Vandermark; **strut** EPA; **style** Matthew Kalmenoff; **submarine** U.S. Navy; **subway** Allen Moore; **suction** NEA; **suffragette** Library of Congress; **sugar beet, sumac** Laurel Cook; **sunburst** Peter Vandermark; **sun dial** Allen Moore; **sun disk** Laurel Cook; **sunfish** Interior: Sport Fisheries and Wildlife; **sunflower** Laurel Cook; **supreme court** U.S. Supreme Court; **surfboard** Frank Siteman; **suspender** Allen Smith; **suspension bridge** Elizabeth Hamlin, Stock, Boston; **swan** USDA; **swastika** *Lore and Lure of Outer Space*, by Ernst and Johanna Lehner, Tudor, copyright 1964—Frank Siteman; **sweet pea, sweetsop, sweet William** Laurel Cook; **swing** Allen Moore; **sword** Bettmann Archive; **synagogue** Arnold Jarmak, Chelsea Press Inc.

tabernacle Allen Moore; **tachina fly** Photo Researchers; **tadpole, takahe** Matthew Kalmenoff; **talapoin** Photo Researchers; **talaria** MFA; **talisman** Walter Silver; **tamarin** SDZ; **tamarind** Laurel Cook; **tambourine** Walter Silver; **tam-o'-shanter** Allen Moore; **tangent** Carl Bass; **tangram** *Tangrams: Picture-making Puzzle Game*, by Peter Van Note, Charles E. Tuttle Co., copyright 1966; **tank** U.S. Navy; **tankard** MFA; **tansy** Laurel Cook; **tarot** Walter Silver; **tartan**[1], **tassel** Allen Moore; **Taurus** George Lindbloom; **teapot** MFA; **telescope** Allen Moore; **temple**[1] EKM-Nepenthe; **tenrec** Photo Researchers; **tentacle** New England Aquarium; **tepee** Library of Congress; **tetrahedron** Carl Bass; **thatch** Frank Siteman; **thermometer** Walter Silver; **Theseus, Thetis** MFA; **thimble** Walter Silver; **thistle** Laurel Cook; **thorn** Alice Koeth; **three-decker** Picture Cube; **thresh** Princeton University Library, Sinclair Hamilton Collection; **throne** Bettmann Archive; **thunderbird** Tourism Collection, Alaska Historical Library; **tiara** EPA—Bettmann Archive; **tibia** Laurel Cook; **tide**[1] NFB Phototheque; **Tiffany glass** William Doyle Galleries, Inc.; **tiger lily** Laurel Cook; **tile** Allen Moore; **tiller**[2] Mystic Seaport; **time clock** Walter Silver; **timothy** Laurel Cook; **tippet** MFA; **toad** Frank Siteman; **toby** Walter Silver; **toga** MFA; **toggle bolt** Walter Silver; **tomahawk** Museum of the American Indian, Heye Foundation; **tomato** Laurel Cook; **tom-tom** Walter Silver; **tongs** MFA; **tooth** Neil Hardy; **tooth shell** Matthew Kalmenoff; **top hat** Frank Siteman; **topiary** Allen Moore; **torah** Jewish Theological Seminary of America; **torii** Burton Holmes Collection/EKM-Nepenthe; **totem pole** Tourism Collection, Alaska Historical Library; **totipalmate** Matthew Kalmenoff; **toucan** Photo Researchers; **tower** Frank Siteman; **tracery** Walter Silver; **track and field** Frank Siteman—Picture Cube; **tractor** International Harvester; **traffic light** Walter Silver; **tragopan, trailing arbutus** Matthew Kalmenoff; **train** Union Pacific Railroad Photo; **trampoline** Jon Chase; **transept** Laurel Cook; **transit** Frank Siteman; **transom** Walter Silver; **trapeze** Frank Siteman; **treadmill** Walter Silver; **treasury note** Chase Manhattan Bank Photo; **trefoil** Allen Moore; **trellis** Walter Silver; **trestle** Frank Siteman; **triangle** Carl Bass—Ron Schick; **triceratops** Matthew Kalmenoff; **tricorn** Frank Siteman; **tricycle** Allen Moore; **triplane** Culver Pictures; **tripod** Allen Moore; **triptych** MFA; **triton**[1] MFA; **trivet** MFA; **Trojan horse** Bettmann Archive; **trolley** Allen Moore; **trombone** Ron Schick; **trophy** Owen Franken, Stock, Boston; **trough** USDA; **trowel** Allen Moore; **trumpet** Ron Schick; **trunk** Allen Moore; **truss bridge, try square** Walter Silver; **T-square** Allen Moore; **tuba** Ron Schick; **tulip** Laurel Cook; **tuning fork** Kitching Scientific; **tureen** MFA; **Turk's-head** *The Ashley Book of Knots*, copyright 1944 by Clifford W. Ashley, reprinted by permission of Doubleday & Co., Inc.; **turnip** Laurel Cook; **turnpike** Allen Smith; **turtle**[1] Photo Researchers; **tutu** Bettmann Archive; **tweezers** Walter Silver; **twinflower, twin-leaf** Laurel Cook; **tympanum** Frank Siteman; **type** Herb Randle; **typewriter** SCM Corp.; **tyrannosaur** Matthew Kalmenoff.

U-bolt Chicago Hardware & Fixture Co.; **ukulele** Jeffrey Dunn; **ulna** Neil Hardy; **umbra, umbrella tree** Laurel Cook; **Uncle Sam** Bettmann Archive; **underpass** Frank Siteman; **unicorn** The Metropolitan Museum of Art; **unicycle** Frank Siteman; **union jack, universal joint** Laurel Cook; **upholstery** Allen Moore; **uproot** Frank Siteman; **Uranus** NASA; **urn** MFA; **utensil** Allen Moore.

vaccination Frank Siteman; **valance** Jeffrey Dunn; **valentine** Bettmann Archive; **valerian** Laurel Cook; **valve** Jeffrey Dunn; **vampire** Matthew Kalmenoff; **vase** Waterford Glass Inc.; **vat** Allen Moore; **vault**[1], **veil, vender** Frank Siteman; **Venetian blind** Allen Moore; **Venus** EPA; **Venus's-flytrap** Laurel Cook; **vermiform appendix** Neil Hardy; **vernier caliper** Frank Siteman; **vest** L.L. Bean; **viaduct** French Government Tourist Office; **vibraphone** Jeffrey Dunn; **viburnum** Laurel Cook; **video terminal** Digital Equipment Corp.; **viking** Library of Congress; **violet** Laurel Cook; **violin** Ron Schick; **virginal** MFA; **Virginia creeper** Laurel Cook; **Virgo** George Lindbloom; **visor** MFA; **volcanic** Frank Siteman; **volcano** UPI, Inc.; **votary** MFA; **voting machine** Jeffrey Dunn; **vulture** Grant Heilman.

wader, waffle iron Allen Moore; **wahoo**[1] Laurel Cook; **walkie-talkie** Allen Moore; **walking stick** Photo Researchers; **wallaby** SDZ; **walnut, wandering jew** Laurel Cook; **warming pan** MFA; **washboard** Allen Moore; **wasp** USDA; **wasp waist** Culver Pictures; **watch** Walter Silver; **water buffalo** SDZ; **waterfall** National Park Service; **water hyacinth, water lily, watermelon** Laurel Cook; **water ouzel** Photo Researchers; **water wheel** Allen Moore; **wattle** Picture Cube; **waveform** Carl Bass; **weasel** SDZ; **weather vane** Frank Siteman; **weave** Cal Sacks; **Wedgwood** MFA; **weeping willow** Laurel Cook; **weevil** USDA; **weld**[1] Jon Chase; **well**[1] Cal Sacks; **Welsh corgi, Welsh terrier** Evelyn Shafer; **whale**[1] Marineland of Florida; **whaleboat** Mystic Seaport; **wharf** Allen Moore; **wheat** Laurel Cook; **Wheatstone bridge** Carl Bass; **wheel bug** Matthew Kalmenoff; **wheelbarrow** Allan Moore; **wheelchair** Jeffrey Dunn; **whelk**[1] Grant Heilman; **wherry** Mystic Seaport; **whetstone** Jeffrey Dunn; **whip** from *The Charles M. Russell Book*, by Harold McCracken; **whippet** Evelyn Shafer; **whippoorwill** Photo Researchers; **whirligig** Allen Moore; **whisker** Marineland of Florida; **whistle** Allen Moore; **white oak, white pine** Laurel Cook; **whooping crane** Interior: Sport Fisheries and Wildlife; **whorl** Roche; **wicker** Allan Moore; **widow's walk** Allen Moore; **wig** The British Tourist Authority; **wigwam** Museum of the American Indian, Heye Foundation; **wild ginger, willow** Laurel Cook; **wimple** Bettmann Archive; **winch** Allen Moore; **windlass** Mystic Seaport; **windmill** Culver Pictures—Frank Siteman; **wind rose** *McGraw-Hill Encyclopedia of Science and Technology*, copyright 1960, used by permission of McGraw-Hill Book Co.; **Windsor chair** EPA/Sotheby Parke Bernet; **wine cellar, wineskin** Allen Moore; **wing chair** MFA; **wintergreen, wisteria** Laurel Cook; **witchcraft** Library of Congress; **witch hazel** Laurel Cook; **wolf, wolverine** SDZ; **wooden Indian** Allen Moore; **wood sorrel** Laurel Cook; **woofer** Jeffrey Dunn; **woolly bear** Photo Researchers; **Worcester** The Metropolitan Museum of Art; **word processing** WANG Laboratories; **workbench** Allen Moore; **worm gear** Jeffrey Dunn; **wrecker** Allen Moore; **wrench** Stanley Tool Co.; **wrestling** Allen Moore.

x-ray Armed Forces Institute of Pathology; **xylophone** Ron Schick; **yam** Laurel Cook; **yarmulke** Walter Silver; **yarrow** Laurel Cook; **yeast** *Botany*, 3rd ed., by Carl L. Wilson and Walter E. Loomis, copyright 1952, 1957, 1962 by Holt, Rinehart and Winston, Inc.; **yew** Laurel Cook; **yogh** Alice Koeth; **yoke** Moorhouse Collection, University of Oregon Library; **Yorkshire terrier** Evelyn Shafer; **yucca** Laurel Cook; **zebra** SDZ; **zebu** Matthew Kalmenoff; **zeppelin** Bettmann Archive; **Zeus** The Metropolitan Museum of Art; **zinnia** Laurel Cook; **zither** MFA; **zodiac** zodiac design adapted from zodiac drawn by Hans Holbein and Albrecht Dürer, reproduced with permission from *Shakespeare's Globe Playhouse* by Irwin Smith, copyright 1956 Charles Scribner's Sons; **zone, zucchini** Laurel Cook; **zygodactyl** *A New Dictionary of Birds*, ed. by A.L. Thomson, McGraw-Hill Book Co. and The British Ornithologists' Union, 1964; **zygomatic** Laurel Cook.

BIOGRAPHICAL CREDITS

Hank Aaron LC; **Bella Abzug** copyright Christopher Brown/Picture Group; **Abigail Adams, John Adams,** LC; **Louisa May Alcott** NPG; **Muhammad Ali, Marian Anderson** BA; **Edmund Andros** LC; **Susan B. Anthony** NPG; **Louis Armstrong** BA; **Chester A. Arthur, Stephen Austin** LC; **Johann Sebastian Bach, Robert Baden-Powell** BA; **Phineas T. Barnum, Clara Barton** LC; **Jack Benny** copyright Mickey Pfleger/Picture Group; **Sarah Bernhardt** BA; **Leonard Bernstein** copyright Michael Grecco/Picture Group; **Mary McLeod Bethune** NPG; **Black Hawk** LC; **Alice Stone Blackwell** NPG; **John Wilkes Booth** LC; **Johannes Brahms, Charlotte Brontë, Robert Browning** BA; **James Buchanan** LC; **Luther Burbank** NPG; **Aaron Burr** LC; **Richard E. Byrd** NPG; **Sebastian Cabot, Jimmy Carter, Jacques Cartier** LC; **Enrico Caruso** BA; **George Washington Carver, Mary Cassatt** NPG; **Fidel Castro** United Nations; **Carrie Chapman Catt** NPG; **Charlie Chaplin** Keystone View Co.; **Cesar Chávez** copyright Mickey Pfleger/Picture Group; **Shirley Chisholm** copyright Shepard Sherbell/Picture Group; **Winston Churchill** NPG; **Grover Cleveland** LC; **William Cody** NPG; **Christopher Columbus, Calvin Coolidge, Davy Crockett** LC; **Oliver Cromwell, Marie Curie** BA; **George Armstrong Custer** LC; **Clarence Darrow** BA; **Moshe Dayan** Picture Cube; **Eugene V. Debs** BA; **Baron De La Warr** LC; **Charles Dickens, Emily Dickinson, Walt Disney, Benjamin Disraeli** BA; **Stephen A. Douglas** LC; **W.E.B. Du Bois** NPG; **Amelia Earhart** LC; **Edward VIII, Albert Einstein** BA; **Dwight D. Eisenhower** LC; **Elizabeth II** Lou Jones; **John Endecott** LC; **Douglas Fairbanks** EKM-Nepenthe; **David G. Farragut, Millard Fillmore, Gerald R. Ford** LC; **Stephen Foster** NPG; **Benjamin Franklin** LC; **Mohandas Gandhi** BA; **James A. Garfield, George III, Geronimo, Elbridge Gerry** LC; **Emma Goldman, Goya** BA; **Ulysses S. Grant** LC; **Ella Grasso** Governor's Office, Connecticut; **D.W. Griffith** BA; **Johann Gutenberg** Culver Pictures; **Woody Guthrie** BA; **Alexander Hamilton, Warren G. Harding, Benjamin Harrison, William Henry Harrison, Nathaniel Hawthorne, Rutherford B. Hayes** LC; **Jascha Heifetz, Ernest Hemingway, Henry VIII, Adolf Hitler** BA; **Herbert Hoover, Henry Hudson** LC; **Langston Hughes** NPG; **Aldous Huxley, Isabella I** BA; **Andrew Jackson** LC; **Mick Jagger** copyright Michael Gordon/Picture Group; **Thomas Jefferson** U.S. Bureau of Printing and Engraving; **Andrew Johnson, Lyndon B. Johnson** LC; **Joseph** NPG; **Helen Keller** BA; **John F. Kennedy** LC; **Nikita Khrushchev** United Nations; **Martin Luther King, Jr.** NAACP; **Marquis de Lafayette** BA; **Antoine Lavoisier** The Metropolitan Museum of Art; **Huddie Ledbetter** NPG; **Robert E. Lee** LC; **John Lennon** copyright Richard DiLello/Picture Group; **Leonardo da Vinci** BA; **Liliuokalani** Brown Brothers; **Abraham Lincoln** U.S. Bureau of Printing and Engraving; **Henry Wadsworth Longfellow** NPG; **Mary Lyon** Mount Holyoke College; **Douglas MacArthur, Dolley Madison** LC; **James Madison** U.S. Bureau of Printing and Engraving; **Horace Mann, Guglielmo Marconi** BA; **John Marshall, Maximilian, William McKinley** LC; **Golda Meir** The Picture Cube; **H.L. Mencken** NPG; **Klemens von Metternich** LC; **Edna St. Vincent Millay** NPG; **Claude Monet** BA; **James Monroe** U.S. Bureau of Printing and Engraving; **Bernard Law Montgomery** Wide World; **Samuel F.B. Morse** LC; **Grandma Moses, Benito Mussolini, Napoleon I** BA; **Nefertiti** EPA-Alinari-Scala; **Horatio Nelson, Isaac Newton** BA; **Richard M. Nixon** LC; **Alfred Nobel, Eugene O'Neill, Jesse Owens, Thomas Paine, George Patton, Anna Pavlova** BA; **I.M. Pei** copyright Jerry Berndt/Picture Group; **Frances Perkins** NPG; **Pablo Picasso, Mary Pickford** EKM-Nepenthe; **Franklin Pierce, Charles Cotesworth Pinckney, Pocahontas, Edgar Allan Poe, James K. Polk** LC; **Joseph Pulitzer, Sergei Rachmaninoff** BA; **Walter Raleigh** LC; **Grigori Rasputin** BA; **Ronald Reagan** The White House; **Rembrandt** BA; **Paul Revere** LC; **Paul Robeson** NPG; **Jackie Robinson** LC; **Norman Rockwell** Norman Rockwell copyright 1960 *Saturday Evening Post*; **Theodore Roosevelt, Eleanor Roosevelt, Franklin D. Roosevelt, Babe Ruth** LC; **Carl Sandburg** NPG; **Margaret Sanger** BA; **Antonio López de Santa Anna** LC; **Franz Schubert** BA; **Dred Scott, Sequoya** LC; **Elizabeth Seton** NPG; **William Shakespeare** BA; **William T. Sherman, Sitting Bull, Margaret Chase Smith** LC; **Benjamin Spock** copyright Christopher Brown/Picture Group; **Joseph Stalin** U.S. Army; **Elizabeth Cady Stanton** LC; **Gloria Steinem** copyright Christopher Brown/Picture Group; **Jeb Stuart, Peter Stuyvesant** LC; **Jonathan Swift** BA; **William Howard Taft, Zachary Taylor** LC; **Teresa** copyright John Foraste—Brown University/Picture Group; **Lev Tolstoy, Arturo Toscanini, Leon Trotsky** BA; **Harry S Truman** LC; **Harriet Tubman** BA; **Tutankhamen** The Metropolitan Museum of Art; **John Tyler** LC; **Martin Van Buren** LC; **Vincent van Gogh** BA; **Giovanni da Verrazano** LC; **Victoria** BA; **Barbara Walters** copyright Stephen J. Sherman/Picture Group; **George Washington, Daniel Webster** LC; **Orson Welles** Frank Siteman; **Mae West** EKM-Nepenthe; **Edith Wharton** BA; **Walt Whitman** LC; **Oscar Wilde** BA; **Woodrow Wilson** LC; **Frank Lloyd Wright, Andrew Wyeth, Émile Zola** BA.

INDEX